GB Rail T

Monday 14 May 20

Britain's national railway network and ... operated by the Train Companies included in this Timetable, who wor... network offering a range of travel opportunities. Details and identificati...

This Timetable contains rail service... ail and shipping connections with Ireland, the Isle of Man, the Isle of Wight and the Channel Islands. Network Rail operates ...ged stations however the remainder are operated on their behalf by the Train Operating Companies. Details are shown in the Station Index. The Timetable Network Map shows the number of the individual table for each route.

Contents

YOUR FEEDBACK IS VALUABLE TO US

If you have any comments on the content of this book or feedback on how you feel it could be improved then please contact the Publications Manager by writing to;

Victoria Fox
Network Rail
Floor 4
Station House
Elder Gate
Milton Keynes
Buckinghamshire, MK9 1BB

Or e-mail: Victoria.Fox@NetworkRail.Co.Uk

Services on Public Holidays

An amended service will operate on many parts of the rail network during Public Holidays and you are strongly advised to confirm your journey details if travelling around a holiday period. For more information visit www.nationalrail.co.uk/holidays

Engineering Work

It is sometimes necessary to carry out essential Engineering Work which means that services may be changed, particularly late at night or at weekends to allow this work to be carried out. Engineering Work is usually planned many weeks in advance and details of changes to train times can be obtained from the National Rail Enquiries website – www.nationalrail.co.uk/engineering

National Rail Conditions of Carriage

Details of the conditions against which all National Rail tickets are issued, including the conditions which apply to the carriage of luggage and cycles can be obtained from the National Rail Enquiries website – www.nationalrail.co.uk/nrcc

What's New?

Welcome to the National Rail Timetable valid from Monday 14 May 2012 to Saturday 08 Dec 2012.

Arriva Trains Wales

01.50 (Sun) Fishguard Harbour to Cardiff Central.

Will now call at Whitland, Carmarthen, Llanelli then will run non-stop to Cardiff Central. Customers for Swansea are to change at Carmarthen and connect into 02.50 (Bus) from Carmarthen running non-stop to Swansea

05.13 (SX) Machynlleth to Pwllheli

Will now call additionally at Criccieth

Dovey Jn

This has now become a "Request Stop" station. Therefore customers wishing to board a service must make a clear handsignal to attracted the drivers attention, or inform the conductor to allow the train to stop to allow them to alight.

East Midlands Trains

On weekdays the 0610 St Pancras to Sheffield service will start at 0545 and run earlier throughout. The 0637 St Pancras to Sheffield service will call additionally at Wellingborough.

The following additional weekday services will run:

0656 Ambergate to Derby

1544 Lincoln to Newark North Gate

The following services will be extended:

1723 Lincoln to Grimsby will start at Newark North Gate at 1645

1825 Leicester to Nottingham will be extended to Lincoln

The 0645 Nottingham to Skegness weekday service will depart earlier at 0641 to provide a connection to the East Coast train services at Grantham

On Sundays, the following services will be amended to run throughout the year:

1725 Lincoln to Newark North Gate

1756 Newark to Lincoln

Greater Anglia

The former National Express East Anglia franchise is now operated by Abellio under the name 'Greater Anglia'. As usual, the summer Saturday timetable on the Norwich to Great Yarmouth line will be enhanced, including the through trains to and from London. The hourly summer Sunday timetable on the Sheringham branch will continue later this year, running until the end of September before reverting to the winter two-hourly pattern. There will be a special service in operation for the Olympic and Paralympic period with some longer trains and additional late-night services.

ScotRail

ScotRail's timetable will run for one year, from 11 December 2011 – 8 December 2012.
Additional services will include; two in each direction between Glasgow/Edinburgh – Inverness (on Sundays as well as every weekday); up to three services between Glasgow – Dundee; three more trains, each way, between Girvan – Ayr; and one peak Elgin – Inverness morning service. There will also be up to five more calls in each direction at Broughty Ferry.

Southern

Following infrastructure upgrades to enable longer trains to run, some trains will be extended up to 10 cars on the Sydenham to London Bridge route and extended up to 12 cars on the East Grinstead to London Bridge and Victoria route. Associated with this there are some minor changes to peak train services in the Metro area and on the Mainline.

Southeastern

As a result of the completion of the Thameslink Upgrade works at London Blackfriars Station, Southeastern services that currently operate between Victoria and Sevenoaks and Orpington via Catford will run between London Blackfriars and Sevenoaks via Catford. This applies in the late evening Mondays to Fridays and all day Saturday and Sunday.

How to use this Timetable

Some tables are self-contained (such as Table 1 London–Shoeburyness) showing every train running between any two stations on the route. Train journey lengths vary from the under ¾ mile Stourbridge Town to Stourbridge Junction shuttle to the 773 mile Aberdeen to Penzance service. To show details of longer-distance services in a single table, short-distance services are omitted, these appearing in separate 'composite' tables.

WHICH TABLE?

General Layout of the Timetable

There are several ways of finding the correct table(s) for a journey. Tables start with the north bank of the Thames and radiate anti-clockwise around London as far as the south bank (Table 212, London-Faversham-Margate) with non-London tables (like the Cardiff Valleys) placed close to the appropriate London route. Internal Scottish routes follow from Table 216. Tables numbered 400-406 cover domestic Sleeper services. Once familiar with to this geographic layout, required tables can usually be found with relative ease, but there are more precise methods:

Using the Index

Look up your destination. If it appears in up to five tables, those tables are listed (for example Hilsea appears in Tables 156, 157, 158, 165 and 188). If it appears in six or more then there may be sub-divisions. If your destination is sub-divided in this way and your origin is NOT shown (for example Shipley is not shown under Lancaster) then look up the origin instead as it probably has fewer tables. Alongside the station name is shown a two character code indicating which operator is responsible for operating the facilities at that station (see also Train Operator pages).

Using the Timetable Network Map

If your journey is more complicated and involves several changes between tables, the Timetable Network Map will be very useful. For example, to plan a journey from North Berwick to Pontypridd one would not expect to find both in the same table. The map makes it clear that one has to change at Edinburgh and Cardiff and, as there is no through service between North Berwick and Pontypridd, allows one to look up possible routes, for example, via Crewe and Shrewsbury (Tables 65 and 131), Crewe and Birmingham (Tables 57 and 65) or York and Birmingham (Tables 51 and 57).

Using Route/Network Diagrams

For many tables a Route or Network Diagram is also provided. Route Diagrams are generally used for longer distance tables (for example Table 26) and show the route and stations served in diagrammatic form as well as the principal connecting links. Network Diagrams (for example Tables 152–154) are generally used where there is a dense network of shorter distance routes and show *all* stations and routes in the area concerned in diagrammatic form.

Using the Table

Having found the table you require make sure you look at the correct set of pages: Mondays to Fridays, Mondays to Saturdays, Saturdays, Sundays plus any relevant dates. Look for the station from which you will leave, read across until you find a suitable train, then read down to see when you will arrive at your destination.

↪ indicates the train is continued **in** a later column.

↩ indicates the train is continued **from** an earlier column.

Bold times denote through trains whilst light, *italic*, times are connections (Please read carefully the section on the "Connections" page). Check if there is a column-heading and if there is, refer to the foot of the table for an explanation.

Because of the large number of services that 'cross' Midnight, a Railway Timetable needs to be precise in the meaning of 'a day'. Trains starting their journeys before Midnight are shown towards the end of a table – but if you are looking for the 'last' train do not stop there, as there may be later ones at the start of the table!

A train crossing Midnight will be shown in full at the END of a table and any column heading denoting the day of the week applies to the day the train STARTS. For example a 2350 train headed 'SO' (see the general notes on inside front cover) commences 2350 Saturday and runs into Sunday. The train will also be shown at the front of the Sunday table with the times prior to Midnight shown with note 'p', e.g. 23p50, to indicate that they refer to the previous night.

Do not worry about the ambiguity as to which day Midnight itself belongs, for, to avoid this problem, all times skip from 2359 to 0001 and neither 0000 nor 2400 is ever used!

A two character code is shown at the head of each train column indicating which operator is providing the train service (see also Train Operator pages).

How to use this Timetable (continued)

Mileages between stations served (but not those shown for connecting purposes) are shown on the first page of each Timetable

Unique Timetable Number (as shown on the Insert Map and in the Index to Stations)

Indicates the Operating Company of the train concerned

Indicates the days of the week (and in some cases dates) on which the Timetable operates

Stations served

Catering Information

Table 97

Colne, Burnley, Accrington and Blackburn—Preston—Blackpool

Mondays to Saturdays

Principal stations on the route are shown in **bold**

Miles	Miles		NT	NT	NT	NT	NT		NT	NT	NT	NT	NT	NT	NT	NT
																SO
			◇	◇						◇	◇			◇	◇	◇
							J									K
			⊼	⊼						⊼	⊼			⊼	⊼	
0	—	**Colne** d	......	......	09 25	......	......	......	......	......	......	10 16	......	......	......	......
2	—	Nelson d	.	.	09 31	.	.	.	.	.	.	10 22	.	.	.	.
3½	—	Briefield d	......	......	09 34	......	......	......	......	......	......	10 25	......	......	......	......
5½	—	**Burnley Central** 98 d	.	.	09 39	.	.	.	.	.	.	10 30	.	.	.	.
6	—	Burnley Barracks 98 d	......	......	......	......	......	......	......	......	......	10 32	......	......	......	......
—	—	Leeds 39 d	08 18	.	.	.	.	.	.	09 18	.	.	.	10 18	.	.
—	—	Burnley Manchester Road 39 d	09 21	......	......	......	......	......	......	10 21	......	......	......	11 21	......	......
7	—	Rose Grove d	.	.	09 44	.	.	.	.	.	10 36	.	.	.	.	.
8½	—	Hapton d	......	......	......	......	......	......	......	......	......	10 39	......	......	......	......
10	—	Huncoat d	.	.	.	.	.	.	.	.	.	10 42	.	.	.	.
11½	—	Accrington d	09 31	......	09 51	......	......	......	......	10 31	......	10 46	......	11 31	......	......
12½	—	Church & Oswaldtwistle d	.	.	09 54	.	.	.	.	.	.	10 49	.	.	.	.
14½	—	Rishton d	......	......	09 58	......	......	......	......	......	......	10 52	......	......	......	......
18	—	**Blackburn** a	09 39	......	10 03	......	......	......	......	10 39	......	10 57	.	11 39	.	.
—	—	Manchester Victoria 94 a	*10 39*	......	*11 06*	......	......	......	......	......	......	*12 06*	......	......	......	......
—	—	Clitheroe 94 d	.	.	.	.	.	.	.	*09 58*	.	.	.	*10 58*	.	.
—	—	**Blackburn** d	09 39	......	10 03	......	......	......	......	10 39	......	10 59	......	11 39	......	......
19½	—	Mill Hill (Lancashire) d	.	.	10 06	.	.	.	.	.	.	11 02	.	.	.	.
20	—	Cherry Tree d	......	......	10 08	......	......	......	......	......	......	11 04	......	......	......	......
21	—	Pleasington d	.	.	.	.	.	.	.	.	.	11 06	.	.	.	.
26	—	Bamber Bridge d	......	......	10 16	......	......	......	......	......	......	11 13	......	......	......	......
27½	—	Lostock Hall d	.	.	10 19	.	.	.	.	.	.	11 15	.	.	.	.
30	—	**Preston 10** a	09 56	......	10 26	......	......	......	......	10 56	......	11 24	......	11 56	......	......
—	—	London Euston 65 a	*12c 55*	.	.	.	.	.	.	*14c 75*	.	.	.	*14g 49*	.	.
—	—	London Euston 65 d	......	......	......	......	......	......	*07f 40*	......	......	*08f 40*	......	......	......	......
—	0	**Preston 10** d	09 58	10 02	10 27	10 32	10 38	.	10 50	10 58	11 02	11 26	11 45	11 58	12 02	12 21
35½	5½	Salwick d	......	......	......	......	~	......	......	......	......	......	......	......	......	~
37½	7½	Kirkham & Wesham d	.	.	10 36	.	~	.	10 59	.	.	11 35	11 54	.	.	~
41	—	Moss Side d	......	......	......	......	~	......	......	......	......	11 40	......	......	......	~
43½	—	Lytham d	.	.	10 44	.	~	.	.	.	.	11 44	.	.	.	~
44½	—	Ansdell & Fairhaven d	......	......	10 47	......	~	......	......	......	......	11 47	......	......	......	~
46½	—	St Annes-on-the-Sea d	.	.	10 51	.	~	.	.	.	.	11 51	.	.	.	~
48½	—	Squires Gate d	......	......	10 54	......	~	......	......	......	......	11 54	......	......	......	~
49½	—	Blackpool Pleasure Beach d	.	.	10 57	.	~	.	.	.	.	11 57	.	.	.	~
50	—	**Blackpool South** a	......	......	11 02	......	~	......	......	......	......	12 02	......	......	......	~
—	14½	Poulton-le-Fylde d	10 14	10 18	.	.	~	.	11 07	11 14	11 18	.	12 02	12 14	12 18	~
—	16½	Layton d	......	......	......	......	~	......	11 10	......	......	......	12 06	......	......	~
—	17½	Blackpool North a	10 24	10 28	.	10 57	11 04	.	11 18	11 24	11 28	.	12 13	12 24	12 28	12 50

For general notes see front of timetable

J Mondays to Fridays until 1 November and from 31 March, also Saturdays until 2 November and from 1 March
K Until 2 November
c Saturdays arr. 10 minutes later
f Saturdays dep. 10 minutes earlier
g Saturdays arr. 1500

Train runs on **S**aturdays **O**nly (see also page called 'References and Symbols used in this Timetable')

Seat Reservations symbols

For non-connecting stations only - indicates that additional services between these stations are included on other Timetables (see also below 'Route Diagrams')

Train time in *italics* indicate connecting times. The letter **'a'** alongside a connecting station indicates the arrival time at that station. Conversely, the letter **'d'** indicates the departure time

Indicates the minimum interchange time (in minutes) that should be allowed when connecting between trains. Where no figure is shown, a minimum of 5 minutes should be allowed

Intra-time letter indicating note at foot of page

For connecting stations only - indicates the Timetables on which the full service to and from the connecting station can be found (see also below under Route Diagrams)

A wavy line indicates that the train does not run on all dates included in the Timetable. In all such cases an additional headnote (in this case **'J'**) will be used to provide full details

Train times indicate that the train stops at the station concerned. Arrival times are denoted by **'a'** against the station name and departure times by **'d'**. Where there is no time shown against a station then the train concerned does not serve that station

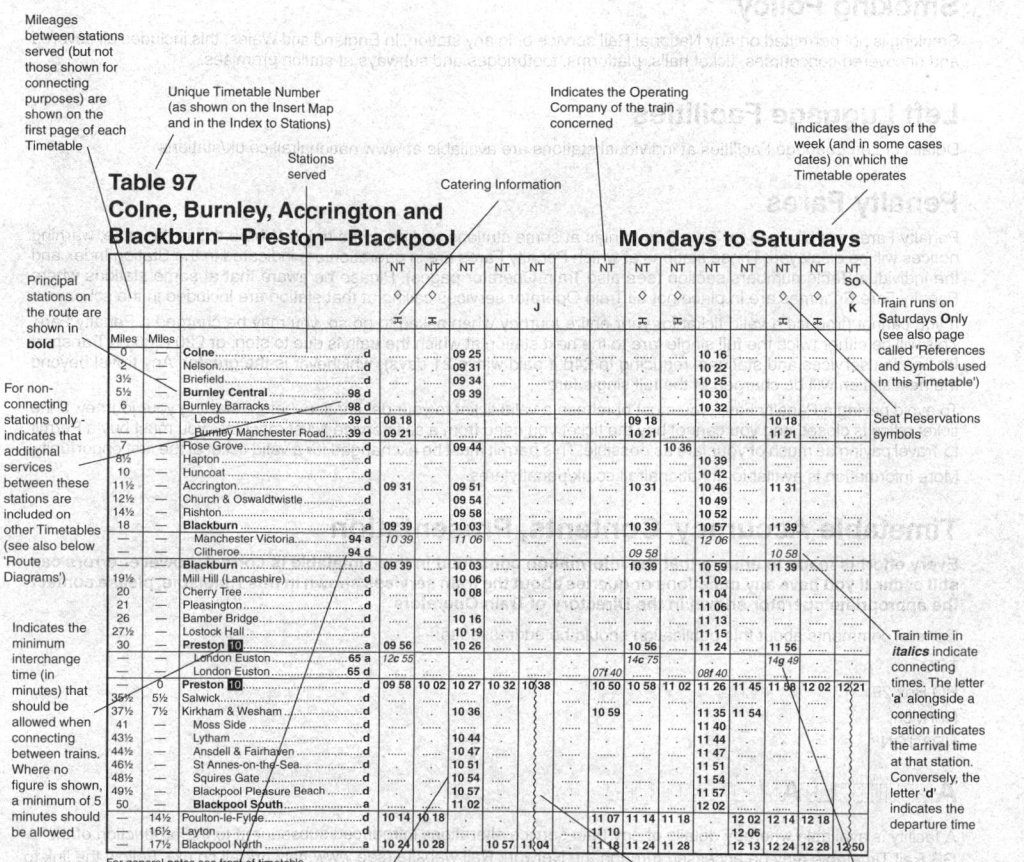

Route/Network Diagrams (see previous page): For many tables a Route/Network Diagram is also provided to show the routes and stations served in diagrammatic form. Where this is the case, a reference to the Route/Network Diagram will be provided at the top of each page of the Timetable concerned. Timetable numbers for connecting or alternative services will not be included within the Table itself; instead this will be indicated on the accompanying Route/Network Diagram

General Information

Smoking Policy

Smoking is not permitted on any National Rail service or in any station. In England and Wales, this includes all covered and uncovered concourses, ticket halls, platforms, footbridges and subways at station premises.

Left Luggage Facilities

Details of Left Luggage Facilities at individual stations are available at www.nationalrail.co.uk/stations

Penalty Fares

Penalty Fares are charged by Train Companies at some stations and on some trains. Where this is the case, warning notices will be displayed. Those stations at which Penalty Fares are in operation are indicated in the Station Index and the individual Table numbers section (see also Train Operator pages). Please be aware that at some stations where Penalty Fare Schemes are in place not all Train Operator services calling at that station are included in the scheme.

If you cannot produce a valid ticket for your entire journey when asked to do so, you may be charged a Penalty Fare. This will be either twice the full single fare to the next station at which the train is due to stop, or £20 (£80 on Transport for London services and stations, reducing to £40 if paid within 21 days), whichever is the greater. Any travel beyond the next station will be charged at the full single fare.

To avoid paying a Penalty Fare, you must purchase a valid ticket to your destination, before starting your journey. If the ticket office is closed and you cannot buy the ticket you need from a self service ticket machine, you must buy a Permit to Travel paying as much of your fare as possible. This permit must be exchanged for a valid ticket at the first opportunity.

More information is available at nationalrail.co.uk/penaltyfares.

Timetable Accuracy, Contents, Presentation

Every effort is made to ensure that the information contained in this Timetable is correct, however errors can still occur. If you have any questions or queries about the train services shown in this Timetable, please contact the appropriate operator shown in the Directory of Train Operators.

General comments about this publication should be addressed to:–

TSO,
PO Box 29,
Norwich,
NR3 1GN

A□□□□□□□□□□A□ □□□□ □□□□

A facility is available whereby details of any train service alterations introduced subsequent to the production of the GB Rail Timetable may be accessed through the Network Rail website (see www.networkrail.co.uk). Follow the link to the "Timetables" on the home page. For up to date timetables, incorporating any changes to services please select the 'Route index / Timetable links' document link. From time to time, further alterations may apply at short notice and details of these may be found at http://www.nationalrail.co.uk/service_disruptions/currentAndFuture.html.

Other National Rail Timetables

Regional and route specific Timetables are available from individual train companies. Please contact the relevant train company to request the latest version of the Timetable you require.

National Rail Enquiries offers an online 'Pocket Timetable' service which gives you the flexibility to create a customised Timetable based around your origin and destination, your own time requirements and the days of the week that you intend to travel. Visit www.nationalrail.co.uk/pockettimetables for more details.

Connections

Bold type times in vertical columns in the timetable show direct trains. In a few cases, where one train overtakes another, the times appear in more than one column and arrow symbols indicate where the train continues in the Timetable.

Many more journey opportunities are possible by changing trains. To help plan such journeys, times in light italic type are shown in some of the Timetables for departures (if the time is earlier than the bold type times for the station below in the column at which you should change trains) or arrivals (if they are later than the bold type times for the station above in the column at which you should change trains).

Where light type italic times are not shown you may have to refer to other tables in the book to work out your connecting services. In order to find the right table to reference, first look at the Route/Network Diagram that covers the table you are working from. This will show the principal connecting links and their table references, which may include the destination you are searching for. If your journey is not covered, follow the advice given on 'How to use this Timetable' under the headings 'Using the Timetable Network Map' and 'Using the Index'.

Connections between trains cannot be guaranteed. The nature of the integrated operation of railway passenger services means that to delay one train to await customers from a late running train arriving at a station may cause significant disruption to many other customers when they make connections at other stations along the route. Every endeavour is made to minimise the total disruption and particular attention is given to services operating infrequently and the last train services each day.

The aim of all Train Operating Companies is to run punctually; inevitably some disruption occurs from time to time. When planning a journey you may wish to consider the effects which any disruption could have and to allow some contingency margin when planning connections.

Minimum Interchange Times at Stations

Unless a connection is shown by times printed in light type, you should generally allow a minimum of five minutes between arrival and departure.

The exceptions to this rule are indicated by minimum interchange times (e.g. **15**) alongside the station name in the tables. In certain cases the minimum interchange time is different according to the Train Operators involved.

These are detailed below:-

STATION AND 'STANDARD' MINIMUM CONNECTIONAL ALLOWANCE (Minutes)		***EXCEPTIONS Showing the Train Operator(s) and minimum connectional allowance applicable***		**STATION AND 'STANDARD' MINIMUM CONNECTIONAL ALLOWANCE (Minutes)**		***EXCEPTIONS Showing the Train Operator(s) and minimum connectional allowance applicable***		**STATION AND 'STANDARD' MINIMUM CONNECTIONAL ALLOWANCE (Minutes)**		***EXCEPTIONS Showing the Train Operator(s) and minimum connectional allowance applicable***	
Barnham	5	*SN*	2	Guildford	5	*GW*	4	Redhill	5	*SN*	3
Bournemouth	5	*SW*	3	Leatherhead	5	*SN*	3	St. Denys	5	*SW*	3
Brighton	10	*SN*	4	London Blackfriars	3	SE	5	Southampton Central	5	*SN, SW*	4
Cardiff Central	7	*AW*	3*	London Victoria	15	*SE, SN*	10	Tulse Hill	3	FC	4
Clapham Junction	10	*SN*	5	Luton	10	*FC*	4	Wimbledon	6	*SN, FC*	5
Gatwick Airport	10	*SN*	5	Luton Airport Parkway	7	*FC*	4				

Example

At Barnham a different minimum connectional allowance applies for Train Operator SN. This means that if your journey involves changing between two trains *both of which* are operated by SN, you need only allow 2 minutes. If, however, one or both trains are provided by any other Operator then the minimum of 5 minutes (as shown after the station name) applies.

* Applicable to Valley Lines services only (table 130).

Train Information

National Rail Enquiries

Timetable and Fares are available 24 hours a day at www.nationalrail.co.uk or, if you are on the move, at mobile.nationalrail.co.uk

National Rail Enquiries provides up-to-the-minute advice on all aspects of journey planning, fares and buying tickets, live train running updates and other useful information.

08457 48 49 50 **24 Hours Daily**

(calls may be recorded for training purposes)

0845 60 40 500 **Welsh Language**

0845 60 50 600 **Textphone – 0600 - 2100 Daily**

TrainTracker

For live train times for today and train Timetables for the next three months call TrainTracker™ on:

0871 200 49 50

Average calls to TrainTracker cost 10p a minute from a BT Landline. Charges from other operators may vary. Calls may be recorded for training purposes.

TrainTracker Text

For live departure and arrival times direct to your mobile text station name to TrainTracker™ Text on:

8 49 50

TrainTracker texts cost 25p for each successful response (plus usual text costs)

Train company numbers for disabled passengers requiring assistance:–

Company	Telephone	Textphone
Arriva Trains Wales	08453 003 005	0845 605 0600
c2c	01702 357640	08457 125 988
Chiltern Railways	08456 005 165	08457 078051
CrossCountry	0844 811 0125	0844 811 0126
East Coast	08457 225 225	18001 08457 225 225
East Midlands Trains	08457 125 678	18001 08457 125 678
Eurostar	08432 186 186	Not available
First Capital Connect	0800 058 2844	0800 975 1052
First Great Western	0800 197 1329/0845 600 5604	0800 294 9209
First Hull Trains	08450 710 222	08456 786 967
First TransPennine Express	0800 107 2149	0800 107 2061
Gatwick Express	0800 138 1016	0800 138 1018
Grand Central	0844 811 0072	0845 305 6815
Greater Anglia	0800 028 28 78	0845 606 7245
Heathrow Connect	0845 678 6975	0800 294 9209
Heathrow Express	0845 600 1515	Not available
Island Line	0800 528 2100	0800 692 0792
London Midland	0800 0924260	0844 811 0134
London Overground	0845 601 4867	020 3031 9331
Merseyrail	0151 702 2071	0870 0552 681
Northern	0808 1561606	08456 045 608
ScotRail	0800 912 2 901	18001 0800 912 2 901
South West Trains	0800 52 82 100	0800 692 0792
Southeastern	0800 783 4524	0800 783 4548
Southern	0800 138 1016	0800 138 1018
Virgin Trains	08457 443366	08457 443367

Train Information (continued)

London Travel Information

0843 222 1234	24 hours (Daily)	www.tfl.gov.uk

Services to Europe on Eurostar via the Channel Tunnel

08432 186 186	0800-1900 (Daily) 0900-1700 (S+S)	www.eurostar.com

Ireland

NI Railways 028 90 66 6630	0700-2000 (M-F) 0800-1800 (S+S)	www.translink.co.uk
Iarnrod Eireann (IE) (Irish Rail)	00 353 183 66 222	www.irishrail.ie

Transport Direct

Plan journeys by car, bus, train, tube, coach, plane at www.transportdirect.info. Transport Direct is the first door-to-door on-line journey planner for Great Britain.

It's free to use; simply enter your departure point, destination and time of travel and Transport Direct will offer a number of options by different modes of transport - both public and private. Journey plans are presented as step-by-step instructions supported by detailed maps including bus stops and other points of interest to travellers. Tickets for rail and coach journeys can be booked via retail web sites without the need to re-enter journey details. Transport Direct includes live travel news for rail and car users. The car journey planner gives route information that takes account of historical traffic level data, offering the user the choice to travel at a different time, or choose public transport. When travelling by public transport, users can adjust their expected walking speed to plan rail, coach and bus connections more efficiently. You can also access Transport Direct via mobile phone and PDA to find out when your next train is due or to check road conditions.

Bus Information in Great Britain

For details of buses within Greater London ring the Transport for London line: 0843 222 1234 (24-hours).

Bus information for the rest of Great Britain is available nationally from 'Traveline' which is run by local authorities and bus operators. There are regional call centres all of which share the same telephone number and any centre will switch calls pertaining to another part of the country through to the relevant centre. Alternatively codes for reaching the appropriate centre direct can be obtained from www.traveline.info/powercodes.html

The number is 0871 200 22 33 (calls from landlines cost 10p per minute) and centres are open at least between the hours of 0800 and 2000 daily (except Christmas Day and Boxing Day). Website: www.traveline.info

PlusBus

PlusBus is an easy-to-use add-on to your train ticket which gives unlimited bus travel on most bus services around the whole urban area of your origin or destination town or city. ***PlusBus*** is available to many towns and cities across Great Britain with season tickets also available for most ***PlusBus*** destinations. For more information visit www.plusbus.info

Traintaxi

Taxi symbols on the Station index pages

Where appears against any station that has sub-entries, there will be a taxi rank outside the station from which taxis should usually be available. This also applies to Basingstoke, Bournemouth, Chelmsford, Cheltenham, Colchester, Lincoln, Middlesbrough, Milton Keynes, Northampton, Sunderland and Swindon.

Where appears against any other station, there will be a taxi rank or a cab office within 100 metres of the station. However, you are advised to check availability before travelling, and to pre-book if necessary. Indication of a rank or office is no guarantee of cabs being available.

Visit **www.traintaxi.co.uk** for information on cab firms serving **all** train, tram, metro and underground stations in Great Britain, and all bus and ferry destinations listed in this *GB Rail Timetable*.

Rail Travel for Disabled Passengers

All train operators are able to carry disabled passengers and can provide additional assistance for boarding and alighting and information during train journeys.

If using a wheelchair, it is recommended that passengers book assistance in advance as space on trains for wheelchair users is limited.

National Rail produce a booklet called 'Rail Travel Made Easy' which details the provisions Train Companies make for disabled people. The booklet is available from major stations or can be obtained by writing to: Rail Travel Made Easy, PO Box 11631, Laurencekirk AB30 9AA. Alternatively, you can download a copy by visiting www.nationalrail.co.uk/passenger_services/disabled_passengers/

You can also see what facilities and services are available at stations throughout the UK, including stop-free routes by visiting www.nationalrail.co.uk

Seat Reservations, Luggage, Cycles and Animals

Seat Reservations

You can reserve seats on any train marked Ⓡ, 🅁, ◇ or ✗ at the top of the column in the timetable pages. Further detailed information is shown in the Directory of Train Operators.

Reservations can normally be made from about 12 weeks in advance of the day of travel, up to about 2 hours before the train departs from its start point, or, for early morning trains, up to 1600 hours the previous evening.

Where and How to Reserve

You can reserve either by visiting a station identified in the Index pages by ◇, or a rail appointed travel agent or by calling one of the telephone booking facilities listed on each Train Operator's page. Telephone reservations are only available when made in conjunction with purchasing a ticket. When reserving you will need to tell your station or agent:

1. Starting and finishing point of your journey.
2. Date of travel (Take care if your departure is soon after Midnight – see "How to use this Timetable").
3. Departure time of train.
4. Number of seats required.
5. You may be able to specify other preferences such as facing or back to direction of travel*, window seat, seat in Restaurant Car where available, seats round a table or airline style with fold down table where available.

   *Customers should note that some trains reverse their direction of travel during the journey.
6. First Class or Standard Accommodation (if you do not specify class of travel it will be assumed that you require Standard Accommodation).

Names on Seats

Your name can be included in your seat reservation label or on the electronic display above your seat, if you wish, when travelling First Class on some East Coast, East Midlands Trains and Greater Anglia services or First and Standard Class on CrossCountry, First Great Western, First TransPennine Express, ScotRail and Virgin Trains services.

Connecting Reservations

If your journey involves changing between trains on which seats are reservable (including journeys crossing London or other major cities), through reservations on both services are available.

Children

Seats may be reserved for children, however, for a child under 5 years of age a seat may be reserved only if an appropriate child rail ticket is held.

Reservations Recommended

Trains shown 🅁 at the head of a column in the Timetable pages are expected to be very busy. Seat Reservations are therefore recommended for a comfortable journey and will consequently be provided free of charge to holders of valid travel tickets.

Seat Reservations, Luggage, Cycles and Animals (continued)

Reservations Compulsory

On trains shown Ⓡ at the head of a column, Seat Reservations are compulsory and are available free of charge. Passengers may not be able to board the train if they do not have a reservation.

Trains For Weekends Away

Most long distance services after 1400 on Fridays and on Saturday mornings, also trains arriving in London on Sunday evenings and Monday mornings can be extremely busy. Customers are advised to reserve seats in advance if planning to travel at these times.

Travelling at Peak Holiday Periods

Trains are usually extremely busy immediately before and after Bank Holidays and in some cases access to trains is only by reservation and/or boarding pass. Customers are advised to reserve seats as early as possible.

Cycles by Train

You can take your cycle on many National Rail services, however reservations may be required and restrictions may apply for peak services. Folded cycles can be carried on most train services. More information is shown in the Directory of Train Operators, the National Rail 'Cycling by Train' leaflet and online at www.nationalrail.co.uk/cycling. Cycle storage is also available at many stations.

Weekend First

Weekend First is available on many CrossCountry, East Coast*, East Midlands Trains, First Great Western*, First TransPennine Express*, Grand Central*, Greater Anglia, ScotRail*, South West Trains* and Virgin Trains services on Saturdays, Sundays and Bank Holidays. If you hold a ticket for travel in Standard Class, you may be able to upgrade to the added comfort of First Class Accommodation on payment of an additional fare. On some services a 'Weekend First' ticket allows you to upgrade to First Class at weekends and Bank Holidays. Holders of Annual Gold Cards may also be able to upgrade on off-peak services for a small amount. Costs vary depending on the journey you are making.

*may only be purchased on trains at time of travel

More information can be found at www.nationalrail.co.uk/firstclass

Customers' Luggage and Animals

Customers may take up to 3 items of personal luggage free of charge; this includes 2 large items (such as suitcases or rucksacks) and 1 item of smaller hand luggage (such as a briefcase). Folded prams, non-folding prams and carrycots are also able to be carried. Full details of the free allowances are available at stations. Excess luggage and certain more bulky items (such as skis) may be carried, subject to available space, at an extra charge. On Gatwick Express services, bulky items such as skis are conveyed free in the luggage van. There is plenty of space on board for other luggage.

Passengers may take dogs, cats and other small animals (maximum two per passenger), free of charge and subject to certain conditions, provided they do not endanger or inconvenience other passengers or staff.

ScotRail allows dogs to accompany able-bodied passengers in Sleeper Services subject to a charge for cleaning of the compartment. The booking must be First Class, Standard Class with two people travelling together, or a Solo supplement is payable for exclusive use of a twin-berth cabin. First Great Western do **not** allow animals (except Guide Dogs) to travel in Sleeper Accommodation. There is no charge for Guide Dogs.

More information can be found at www.nationalrail.co.uk/luggageandanimals

Directory of Train Operators

The following pages contain details of the Train Operating Companies who operate trains included in this Timetable and indicate the services they provide.

Each operator is identified by a two character code listed below. The codes are displayed in the index alongside the station name indicating which operator is responsible for operating the facilities at that station. The code is also shown at the head of each train column in the timetable pages indicating which operator is providing the train service.

17 stations are the operating responsibility of Network Rail and are shown in the index by the code NR and information about Network Rail is shown at the end of the Train Operating Company pages.

Page No	Train Company Name	Code
13	Arriva Trains Wales	AW
14	c2c	CC
15	CrossCountry	XC
16	Chiltern Railways	CH
17	Devon & Cornwall Railway	DC
18	East Coast	GR
19	East Midlands Trains	EM
20	First Capital Connect	FC
21	First Great Western	GW
22	First Hull Trains	HT
23	First TransPennine Express	TP
24	Gatwick Express	GX
25	Grand Central	GC
26	Greater Anglia	LE
27	Heathrow Connect	HC
28	Heathrow Express	HX
29	Island Line	IL
30	London Midland	LM
31	London Overground	LO
32	Merseyrail	ME
33	North Yorkshire Moors Railway	NY
34	Northern	NT
35	ScotRail	SR
36	South West Trains	SW
37	Southeastern	SE
38	Southern	SN
39	Virgin Trains	VT
40	West Coast Railway Co.	WR

Arriva Trains Wales

AW

ADDRESS

St Mary's House
47 Penarth Road
Cardiff CF10 5DJ
Telephone: 0845 6061 660
Website: www.arrivatrainswales.co.uk
Email: customer.relations@arrivatrainswales.co.uk

MANAGING DIRECTOR

Tim Bell

RESERVATIONS AND TICKETS BY TELEPHONE AND ONLINE

Tickets may be booked in advance and seats reserved, by telephone, from the following numbers (0800–2000 daily):

0870 9000 773 for Great Britain, tickets and reservations. 0870 9000 767 for Group and 0845 300 3005 for Disabled travel arrangements. Textphone 0845 758 5469 Please allow 5 days for delivery.

RESERVATION DETAILS

All seat reservations are free to ticket holders.

CATERING ON TRAINS

At-seat catering service of cold snacks, sandwiches and hot and cold drinks on all services marked 🛒, for all or part of the journey.

Complimentary meal service for first class and a counter service of hot and cold snacks for standard class on trains with ☒.

Train catering on Arriva Trains Wales services is provided by:

At Seat Catering (2003) Ltd
St Mary's House
47 Penarth Road
Cardiff
CF10 5DJ

CYCLES

See Cycling by Train leaflet, a guide to Arriva Trains Wales services for full details.

LOST PROPERTY

Contact Arriva Trains Wales Customer Relations on 0845 6061 660.

TRAIN SERVICE UPDATE

Please consult our website at www.arrivatrainswales.co.uk for real time service updates.

PENALTY FARES

Penalty Fares are not in force on Arriva Trains Wales services. Customers are reminded that they must have a valid ticket when boarding at a staffed station, if not it will be necessary to charge you the full single/return fare for the journey.

DISABLED PEOPLE'S PROTECTION POLICY

Address as above.

CODE OF PRACTICE FOR COMMENTS, COMPLAINTS AND SUGGESTIONS

Address as above.

ALCOHOL POLICY

Arriva Trains Wales have prohibited the consumption of alcohol on all services and stations between Caerphilly - Rhymney, and Pontypridd - Treherbert/Merthr Tydfil/Aberdare

c2c

CC

A member of the National Express Group plc

ADDRESS	2nd Floor Cutlers Court 115 Houndsditch London EC3A 7BR Telephone: 0845 601 4873 Website: www.c2c-online.co.uk
MANAGING DIRECTOR	Julian Drury
RESERVATIONS AND TICKETS BY TELEPHONE AND ONLINE	Online through c2c-online.co.uk or Tel: 08457 44 44 22 open Monday to Saturday 08.00 - 20.00; Sunday 10.00 - 20.00 **c2c Group Travel:** Call our Ticket sales hotline on 08457 44 44 22 selecting 'Group Travel' to find out more. **c2c Assisted Travel:** Tel: 01702 357 640 open 05.30 - 22.00 Monday to Friday; Saturday 06.00 - 21.00; Sunday 07.00 - 17.00
RESERVATION DETAILS	Reservations are not available.
CATERING ON TRAINS	Not available.
CYCLES	• Cycles are not permitted on weekday services arriving in London Fenchurch Street between 07.15 and 09.45, or leaving London Fenchurch Street between 16.30 and 18.42. • If you plan to travel with 3 or more cyclists please contact the cycle helpline on 01702 357640 where we can advise you further. • Tandems and tricycles are not permitted. • During engineering work, cycles cannot be accommodated on c2c replacement bus services. • Motorcycles cannot be carried on any service. • Cycles are carried at owners risk (see National Rail Conditions of Carriage) or for further information visit www.nationalrail.co.uk. • Cycles must be carried in the designated area on the train and must not obstruct doors and aisles. • Reservations are not required. • Please do not lock your cycle to any part of the train. You are also reminded not to leave your cycle unattended at any time during your journey. You can view which stations have cycle bays by visiting c2c-online.co.uk
LOST PROPERTY	c2c Rail Ltd, Westcliff Station, Station Road, Westcliff-on-Sea, SS0 7SB Telephone: 01702 357 699
TRAIN SERVICE UPDATE	Real time up to date train running information is available on the c2c website www.c2c-online.co.uk, the National Rail Enquiries website at nationalrail.co.uk or on BBC Ceefax page 433.
PENALTY FARES	If you travel without a valid ticket you may be charged a penalty fare of £20 or twice the full single fare, whichever is the greater.
DISABLED PEOPLE'S PROTECTION POLICY	Available from:- Customer Relations c2c Rail Ltd, FREEPOST ADM3968, Southend, SS1 1ZS Telephone: 0845 601 4873 Open Monday to Friday 08.00 - 18.00 Textphone: 0845 606 7245 Available Monday to Friday 08.30 - 17.00
CODE OF PRACTICE FOR COMMENTS, COMPLAINTS AND SUGGESTIONS	Available from Customer Relations at the above address

XC **CrossCountry** XC

CrossCountry

ADDRESS

CrossCountry
5th Floor, Cannon House,
18 Priory Queensway, Birmingham B4 6BS
Telephone: 08447 369 123
Textphone: 0121 200 6420
Fax: 0121 200 6005
Website: www.crosscountrytrains.co.uk
Email: customer.relations@crosscountrytrains.co.uk

MANAGING DIRECTOR

Andy Cooper

RESERVATIONS AND TICKETS BY TELEPHONE AND ONLINE

On-line at crosscountrytrains.co.uk is the easiest way to purchase your tickets.

If you prefer, you can also make telephone bookings on 0844 811 0124 between 0800 and 2200 daily. Parties of 10 or more should contact Group Travel on 0871 244 2388 between 0800 and 1800 weekdays

RESERVATION DETAILS

You are strongly advised to make a seat reservation in advance; especially when travelling on trains shown with the ▣ symbol in timetables. Seat reservations are free of charge.

CATERING ON TRAINS

Catering is available on most CrossCountry trains.

In First Class, on weekdays between 0630 and 1830 customers can enjoy complimentary light refreshments including hot and soft drinks, served at seat. In Standard Class we offer a range of quality snacks, sandwiches and hot drinks plus soft and alcoholic beverages between 0600 and 2000. For more information on the Nottingham - Cardiff and Birmingham - Stansted Airport routes please refer to our timetables.

CYCLES

We do not charge to carry your cycle. However, as space is very limited you will need to reserve in advance on nearly all our services. Please enquire before travelling. We are unable to accept powered cycles, tricycles, tandems or trailers on any of our services.

LOST PROPERTY

Contact Customer Relations on 08447 369 123 between 0800 and 2000 Monday to Saturday; or email lost.property@crosscountrytrains.co.uk

TRAIN SERVICE UPDATE

Details of major disruption to services and weekend engineering work are summarised on BBC Ceefax and BBCi on digital TV. Live travel updates are available on-line at crosscountrytrains.co.uk and details of all service disruptions can be found at nationalrail.co.uk/disruption/

PENALTY FARES

A Penalty Fares scheme is not currently in operation on CrossCountry trains. Visit crosscountrytrains.co.uk for the most up to date information. Should you board one of our trains without a valid ticket you will be charged the full Single or Return fare for your journey unless the ticket office is closed and a self-service ticket machine is not available.

DISABLED PEOPLE'S PROTECTION POLICY

We provide a Journey Care service for the disabled, elderly and infirm. By phoning our team on 0844 811 0125, textphone 0844 811 0126, beforehand we will, where possible, arrange help for your journey. Our Disabled People's Protection Policy is available on-line at crosscountrytrains.co.uk

CODE OF PRACTICE FOR COMMENTS, COMPLAINTS AND SUGGESTIONS

Copies of our Complaints Handling Procedure and Passenger's Charter are available on-line at crosscountrytrains.co.uk

Chiltern Railways

ADDRESS

Customer Services
Banbury ICC
Merton Street
Banbury
Oxfordshire OX16 4RN
Telephone: 08456 005 165 (Mondays to Fridays 0830-1730)
Fax: 01926 729 914
Website: www.chilternrailways.co.uk

MANAGING DIRECTOR

Rob Brighouse

RESERVATIONS AND TICKETS BY TELEPHONE AND ONLINE

Telephone 08456 005 165 (0700-2000, 7 days a week)

RESERVATION DETAILS

Reservations can be made for travel in the Business Zone of our Mainline Silver trains. Reservations are not available on any other services.

CATERING ON TRAINS

Our Mainline Silver trains offer an on-board kitchen serving drinks and freshly cooked bacon-rolls and pastries on morning trains, Mondays to Fridays. An at-seat catering service is available on Mondays to Fridays on most other Mainline trains arriving in London before 1345 and leaving London between 0700 and 1445. If your train does not offer catering do not forget that our main stations offer excellent catering facilities. For more details check our website. Please allow enough time to purchase your refreshments before boarding your train.

CYCLES

Subject to space being available, and at the discretion of our staff, you can take your bike (except tandems) on any Chiltern Railways train on Saturdays, Sundays or Public Holidays. On Mondays to Fridays you can also use most of our trains. The only exceptions are our busiest peak hour services. For the safety and comfort of all our passengers bikes are not allowed at any point during the journey on any train:

- Arriving London Marylebone or Birmingham Moor Street from 0745 to 1000
- Leaving London Marylebone or Birmingham Moor Street from 1630 to 1930

On our Mainline Silver trains you must put your bike in the special storage area at one end of the train. We are sorry, but bikes cannot be taken on rail replacement buses at any time. There are no restrictions on folding bikes at any time, provided they are fully folded. For information about cycle storage facilities at our stations see our website. Cycles can be hired from just outside London Marylebone station. For information visit www.tfl.gov.uk/barclayscyclehire.

LOST PROPERTY

If we find any item of lost property, we will always do our best to contact the owner if they can be identified. Items can be collected from London Marylebone up to 3 months after they have been handed in - we charge a collection fee to cover our administration costs.

If you lose something on one of our trains or stations you can report it by:

* Using the online form on our website

* Using a Lost Property Form available at any Chiltern Railways ticket office, and returning it to a member of Chiltern Railways Staff.

* By phone, fax or post using the contact details below:

Phone: 08456 005 165
Fax: 020 7333 3002
Write to: Chiltern Railways Lost Property
Marylebone Station
London NW1 6JJ.

Lost Property Office Operating Hours: Mondays to Fridays 1200 to 2000. Please allow up to 2 weeks for processing lost items. If you do not hear from us in that period, you should assume the item has not been found.

TRAIN SERVICE UPDATE

Visit our website www.chilternrailways.co.uk for current train running information and details of changes to train times because of engineering work or other special events.

PENALTY FARES

If you do not have a valid rail ticket for the journey you are making, you will have to pay a Penalty Fare of £20 or twice the single fare, whichever is the greater, for the journey you are making on Chiltern Railways services. For full details write to the above address, or see our website.

DISABLED PEOPLE'S PROTECTION POLICY

Copies of the Disabled People's Protection Policy can be obtained from the above address, or from our website.

CODE OF PRACTICE FOR COMMENTS, COMPLAINTS AND SUGGESTIONS

If you have any comments, complaints or suggestions regarding Chiltern Railways services, please write to the address shown above or telephone 08456 005 165 (0830-1730 Mondays to Fridays), Fax 01926 729 914. Alternatively you can use the 'Contact Us' option on our website.

Devon & Cornwall Railway

ADDRESS

MANAGING DIRECTOR

RESERVATIONS AND TICKETS BY TELEPHONE AND ONLINE

RESERVATION DETAILS

CATERING ON TRAINS

CYCLES

LOST PROPERTY

TRAIN SERVICE UPDATE

PENALTY FARES

DISABLED PEOPLE'S PROTECTION POLICY

CODE OF PRACTICE FOR COMMENTS, COMPLAINTS AND SUGGESTIONS

New operator due to commence operation during this Timetable – for full details see National Rail website nearer the time

East Coast

ADDRESS	Freepost RSRJ-LJCX-GHST Plymouth PL4 6AB Telephone: 08457 225 333 Open 0700-2200 Monday to Sunday Fax: 0191 227 5986 Website: www.eastcoast.co.uk Email: customers@eastcoast.co.uk	
MANAGING DIRECTOR	Karen Boswell	
RESERVATIONS AND TICKETS BY TELEPHONE AND ONLINE	Internet	Purchase tickets via the internet 24 hours a day at www.eastcoast.co.uk
	Self service ticket machines are available at all East Coast stations. Purchase tickets for today or collect pre-booked tickets.	
	Travel enquiries and Telesales 08457 225 225 Open 0800-2000 Monday-Saturday, 1000-2000 Sunday	
	Group Travel	Open 0800-2000 Monday-Friday
	Discounts may be available for groups of 10 or more people.	
	Assisted Travel	Open 0800-2000 Monday-Saturday, 1000-2000 Sunday
	Web support	0800-2000 Monday to Saturday, 1000-2000 Sunday
	The minimum transaction is £10. Please allow 7 days from the time of booking for tickets to reach you through the post.	
RESERVATION DETAILS	Seat Reservations can usually be made on any East Coast train up to ten weeks in advance. They are available to any ticket holder upon request, and are compulsory with some ticket types. Only one reservation can be made per single journey.	
CATERING ON TRAINS	Passengers travelling in First Class will receive complimentary food and drink on board. For shorter journeys, you will be offered non-alcoholic drinks and snacks, while on longer trips you can look forward to something a little more substantial. Passengers in Standard Class can enjoy a wide range of refreshments from our caféBAR. An at-seat trolley service will also be available on selected services.	
CYCLES	Bicycles are welcome on East Coast trains. A reservation must be made and bookings are subject to space being available. Reservations can be made by calling 08457 225 225 or at any East Coast ticket office.	
LOST PROPERTY	If you lose something on a East Coast train or at a station please speak to a member of staff or contact us on 08457 225 333. Please note that charges are normally made for returning items of lost property and that we are unable to forward items of lost property on train services.	
TRAIN SERVICE UPDATE	Visit www.eastcoast.co.uk or call National Rail Enquiries on 08457 48 49 50 (calls may be recorded for training purposes).	
PENALTY FARES	East Coast does not operate a Penalty Fares scheme. However, you should always purchase a ticket valid for travel before you board any East Coast service as only full fare tickets are sold on our trains. The only exception being Disabled Railcard holders who will be sold appropriate discounted tickets on-board.	
DISABLED PEOPLE'S PROTECTION POLICY	A copy of our DPPP can be obtained free of charge from the address at the top of this page. Our Assisted Travel Team can help you plan your journey and organise tickets, assistance and Seat Reservations. To ensure the best possible levels of assistance we recommend that you contact us no later than 1800 the day before you intend to travel. Telephone 08457 225 225 or textphone 18001 08457 225 225* (open 0800-2000 Monday-Saturday, 1000-2000 Sunday). * Please note that this number should only be used to contact the Assisted Travel Team. For all other enquiries please telephone 08457 225 225.	
CODE OF PRACTICE FOR COMMENTS, COMPLAINTS AND SUGGESTIONS	Our Passenger's Charter is available from all East Coast stations or from our website www.eastcoast.co.uk. All correspondence should be sent using the address at the top of this page.	

EM **East Midlands Trains** EM

ADDRESS	East Midlands Trains Prospect Place Millennium Way Pride Park Derby DE24 8HG Telephone: 08457 125 678 Website: www.eastmidlandstrains.co.uk Email: getintouch@eastmidlandstrains.co.uk
MANAGING DIRECTOR	David Horne
RESERVATIONS AND TICKETS BY TELEPHONE AND ONLINE	Buy your tickets online at eastmidlandstrains.co.uk. You can buy tickets for all rail journeys (within Great Britain) with us. Alternatively call 08457 125 678 between 0800-2000 (7 days a week).
RESERVATION DETAILS	Seat Reservations on East Midlands Trains services are free. Just book in advance when you buy your ticket. We advise that you always make a reservation, as seats cannot be guaranteed without one. On our Local Services reservations are available on the Liverpool to Norwich services.
CATERING ON TRAINS	On our East Midlands London Services (to/from St Pancras International), we offer a range of delicious food options, plus snacks and hot and cold drinks. A trolley service is available on selected East Midlands Local Services (denoted by a symbol within the Timetable).
CYCLES	Two bicycles per train are accepted for free on all East Midlands Trains services; however reservations must be made in advance on reservable Services subject to availability.
LOST PROPERTY	Please allow a minimum of 24 hours for the items to be received at a lost property office. If your item is located you may be charged for the return of it and will be advised of this cost. To enquire about lost property, please call our Lost Property office, ideally between the hours of 1000 and 1600 Monday to Saturday on 0844 546 0037.
TRAIN SERVICE UPDATE	Details of services and real time running information, including travel alerts by email are available through our website. Visit www.eastmidlandstrains.co.uk. Alternatively, call National Rail Enquiries on 08457 48 49 50 (calls may be recorded for training purposes).
PENALTY FARES	You should always buy a ticket in advance of boarding your train. Penalty Fares may be in operation on your service.
DISABLED PEOPLE'S PROTECTION POLICY	We aim to make travelling with us accessible to all our customers. If you require assistance in travelling, have special needs or mobility problems please call our team on 08457 125 678 option 3 to arrange help for your journey. A text direct service is also available on 18001 08457 125 678 (for people with hearing problems).
CODE OF PRACTICE FOR COMMENTS, COMPLAINTS AND SUGGESTIONS	Our Customer Relations team is available to receive your comments, complaints or suggestions. Please write to Customer Relations at the above address, or email getintouch@eastmidlandstrains.co.uk or call us on 08457 125 678 (option 5, 3 and 2)

First Capital Connect

A member of the First Rail Division

ADDRESS

Freepost, RRBR-REEJ-KTKY
First Capital Connect
Customer Relations Department
PO Box 443
Plymouth PL4 6WP
Telephone: 0845 026 4700 (open 7 days a week 0700-2200 with the exception of Christmas Day)
Fax: 0845 676 9904
Website: www.firstcapitalconnect.co.uk
Email: customer.relations.fcc@firstgroup.com

MANAGING DIRECTOR

Neal Lawson

RESERVATIONS AND TICKETS BY TELEPHONE AND ONLINE

First Capital Connect does not offer telesales, however tickets can be booked at www.firstcapitalconnect.co.uk

RESERVATION DETAILS

Reservations are not available.

CATERING ON TRAINS

None.

CYCLES

We welcome passengers with bicycles on services where they can be safely accommodated. Folding bicycles can be carried at any time. However we are unable to carry non-folding bicycles:

- At any time between Drayton Park and Moorgate.
- On Great Northern route trains south of Stevenage and Hertford North timed to arrive in London between 0700 and 0930 or depart from London between 1600 and 1900 Monday to Friday. (Restrictions do not apply on Saturdays, Sundays and Public Holidays.)
- On Great Northern route trains between Cambridge and Ely that are timed to arrive at or depart from Cambridge between 0745 and 0845 with the exception of the 0715 and 0745 departures from London King's Cross Monday to Friday. (Restrictions do not apply on Saturdays, Sundays and Public Holidays)
- On the Great Northern route between Royston and Cambridge on the 0706 train from London King's Cross which departs Royston at 0806 and is due to arrive at Cambridge at 0829.
- On Thameslink route trains travelling towards London that are timed to arrive at or pass through any central London station between 0700 and 1000, or travelling away from London and timed to depart from or pass through any central London station between 1600 and 1900 Monday to Friday. (Restrictions do not apply on Saturdays, Sundays and Public Holidays.)
- On replacement bus services unless otherwise stated in associated publicity.
- On any train where your bicycle may cause an obstruction to other customers (i.e. where a number of people are standing) or when a member of staff asks you to remove your bicycle.
- On many London Underground lines – see tfl.gov.uk for details.

LOST PROPERTY

In order to trace lost property please contact our Customer Relations department on 0845 026 4700, between 0700 - 2200 Monday to Sunday.

TRAIN SERVICE UPDATE

For current train information call National Rail enquiries on 08457 48 49 50 (calls may be recorded for training purposes) or check our website at: www.firstcapitalconnect.co.uk/live-info

PENALTY FARES

First Capital Connect operates a Penalty Fares System. If you do not have a valid ticket or permit to travel, you will be liable to pay a penalty fare. This is £20 or twice the appropriate single fare to the next station stop, whichever is greater. This does not apply for travel from Crews Hill. If you do not buy a ticket, you could also be prosecuted and this can lead to a Criminal Conviction.

DISABLED PEOPLE'S PROTECTION POLICY

Our Disabled People's Protection Policy is available from Customer Relations, and is also available on our website and available at all staffed stations. First Capital Connect operates a dedicated telephone and textphone service for disabled or mobility impaired customers, the contact details are: Telephone: 0800 058 2844, 0800 975 1052

These are available 0700 - 2200, every day, with the exception of Christmas Day.

CODE OF PRACTICE FOR COMMENTS, COMPLAINTS AND SUGGESTIONS

Our Passenger's Charter details our code of practice and is available from all staffed stations and from our Customer Relations Department. The Customer Relations Department will be happy to assist with any comments, complaints or suggestions and can be contacted using the contact details above.

First Great Western

A member of the First Rail Division

ADDRESS

Milford House
1 Milford Street
Swindon SN1 1HL
Telephone: 01793 499400
Fax: 01793 499460
Website: www.firstgreatwestern.co.uk. On our website you can create and print your own personalised timetables, download complete timetable booklets, find departure and arrival times for specific journeys, buy tickets, obtain live timetable updates specific to individual stations, check any late alterations to our services, view promotions and contact us with your comments.

MANAGING DIRECTOR

Mark Hopwood

RESERVATIONS AND TICKETS BY TELEPHONE AND ONLINE

Tickets may be booked in advance using credit and debit cards and seats reserved by ringing **08457 000 125** (open 0700-2200 daily). Allow at least 5 working days for postal delivery. A next day delivery can be arranged at £5 per transaction. Arrangements can be made for tickets to be collected from Fast Ticket machines (the credit or debit card used for purchase will be needed at many stations). For Group Travel call **08457 000 125**.

RESERVATION DETAILS

A seat reservation, free of charge, can be made at the time of purchasing your ticket. Additional reservations, including those made by season ticket holders, are subject to a £5 fee.

CATERING ON TRAINS

Most First Great Western high speed services offer an Express Café service with freshly brewed coffee, hot baguettes and paninis and a wide range of drinks and snacks.

A Travelling Chef is available on many weekday services, preparing meals and snacks to order for both First and Standard Class customers. On a small number of weekday services, a Pullman restaurant provides à la carte dining to First and Standard Class customers, subject to availability.

First Class customers also enjoy additional complimentary services:

- An at-seat trolley service offering light refreshments (available on most Monday to Friday services between 0700-1900), including hot and cold drinks and light snacks appropriate to the time of day. The trolley also offers a range of items for sale from our Express Café.
- At the weekend and on weekdays after 1900, complimentary refreshments are available from the Express Cafe on production of valid travel tickets.

CYCLES

First Great Western welcomes customers with bicycles on services where they can be safely accommodated. However it is not possible to carry bicycles on some services, particularly during peak periods. For full details of when bicycles cannot be carried or when reservations are required please visit our website or pick up a leaflet at any of our staffed stations.

LOST PROPERTY

Customers who have left property on First Great Western services should contact our Customer Services team on **08457 000 125**.

TRAIN SERVICE UPDATE

For current train information including details of engineering work please visit our website: www.firstgreatwestern.co.uk

PENALTY FARES

These operate on most of our services. A penalty fare of £20 or twice the appropriate single fare to the next station stop (whichever is the greater) will be charged to anybody who is unable to produce a valid ticket or other authority when required to do so. For further information, pick up a leaflet about Penalty Fares from any staffed station.

DISABLED PEOPLE'S PROTECTION POLICY

Available from Customer Services Team
First Great Western
PO Box 313
Plymouth PL4 6YD
Tel: 08457 000 125
Email: fgwfeedback@firstgroup.com
Opening hours 0700-2200 daily

Customers requiring assistance should contact 0800 197 1329 (18001 0800 197 1329 textphone service), if possible giving 24 hours notice of travel plans.

CODE OF PRACTICE FOR COMMENTS, COMPLAINTS AND SUGGESTIONS

Your views leaflets and copies of the Passenger's Charter are available to download from our website www.firstgreatwestern.co.uk, at all staffed First Great Western stations or alternatively from the Customer Services Team at the address above.

First Hull Trains

ADDRESS	First Hull Trains Customer Services Freepost RLYY-XSTG-YXCK 4th Floor Europa House 184 Ferensway Hull HU1 3UT Telephone: 08456 76 99 05 Website: www.hulltrains.co.uk Email: customer.services@hulltrains.co.uk
MANAGING DIRECTOR	Cath Bellamy
RESERVATIONS AND TICKETS BY TELEPHONE AND ONLINE	First Hull Trains tickets can be booked in advance and seats reserved by ringing 08450 710 222 (0700 to 2200 Monday to Friday and 0800 to 1900 Saturday and Sunday). Please allow five working days for delivery. Tickets on departure are available.
RESERVATION DETAILS	Seat Reservations are free for First and Standard Class ticket holders. Season Ticket holders may reserve seats at a cost of £2 for First Class and £1 for Standard Class.
CATERING ON TRAINS	First Hull Trains provides a buffet on all services, and a comprehensive catering package for First Class passengers. Catering is subject to availability and may be limited when services are disrupted by engineering works or Bank Holidays.
CYCLES	Cycles and tandems are carried free of charge, however, a reservation is compulsory. Please telephone 08450 710 222
LOST PROPERTY	Please contact Customer Services.
TRAIN SERVICE UPDATE	Available at www.hulltrains.co.uk, or by telephone on 08450 710222.
PENALTY FARES	Penalty Fares are not in force on any Hull Trains Service
DISABLED PEOPLE'S PROTECTION POLICY	Available at: www.hulltrains.co.uk. Alternatively, a copy can be requested from Customer Services.
CODE OF PRACTICE FOR COMMENTS, COMPLAINTS AND SUGGESTIONS	First Hull Trains' Passenger's Charter is available at www.hulltrains.co.uk. Alternatively, any comments, complaints or suggestions can be sent to Customer Services

First TransPennine Express

A joint venture between First and Keolis

ADDRESS	7th Floor Bridgewater House 60 Whitworth Street Manchester M1 6LT Telephone: 08700 005151 Website: www.tpexpress.co.uk
MANAGING DIRECTOR	Nick Donovan
RESERVATIONS AND TICKETS BY TELEPHONE AND ONLINE	Reservations and tickets are available at www.tpexpress.co.uk and from all local staffed stations.
RESERVATION DETAILS	Seat Reservations are available at staffed stations. Seat Reservations for travel on First TransPennine Express services can be booked up until the day before travel. There is no charge for making a Seat Reservation if you have a rail ticket, or buy one at the same time.
CATERING ON TRAINS	Catering trolley services are available between 0700 and 1900 Monday to Friday on First TransPennine Express trains between Manchester Piccadilly and York, Manchester Piccadilly and Doncaster and Manchester Piccadilly and Preston. In addition to the above, all services between Manchester Airport, Manchester Piccadilly, Carlisle, Glasgow Central and Edinburgh convey a trolley service for the whole journey. This facility is also provided at weekends.
CYCLES	Customers may take their bicycle with them on First TransPennine Express trains at no extra cost. As space is limited to two bicycles per train, reservations for cycle space should be made at least 24 hours before the journey.
LOST PROPERTY	Customers who have left their property on First TransPennine Express trains or stations should contact 0845 600 1672.
TRAIN SERVICE UPDATE	For current train information call National Rail Enquiries on 0845 48 49 50 (calls may be recorded for monitoring purposes) or check our website at: www.tpexpress.co.uk/travelupdates
PENALTY FARES	Penalty Fares are not applicable on First TransPennine Express services. Customers are reminded that they must have a valid ticket when they travel. If not it will be necessary to charge the full Open Single or Return Fare for the journey.
DISABLED PEOPLE'S PROTECTION POLICY	Available online at www.tpexpress.co.uk and also from: Customer Relations First TransPennine Express ADMAIL 3878 Freepost Manchester M1 9YB Customers who have special needs and require customer assistance should contact us on 0800 107 2149. A textphone service is available on 0800 107 2061.
CODE OF PRACTICE FOR COMMENTS, COMPLAINTS AND SUGGESTIONS	Feedback leaflets and copies of the Passenger's Charter are available from all stations served by First TransPennine Express services or alternatively contact: Customer Relations, First TransPennine Express, ADMAIL 3878, Freepost, Manchester M1 9YB. Telephone: 0845 600 1671 Email: tpecustomer.relations@firstgroup.com

Gatwick Express

GX

ADDRESS	Southern Customer Services PO Box 3021 Bristol BS2 2BS Telephone: 0845 850 1530 Fax: 020 8929 8687 (Overseas: +44 208 9298687) Website: www.gatwickexpress.com Email: comments@southernrailway.com
MANAGING DIRECTOR	Chris Burchell
RESERVATIONS AND TICKETS BY TELEPHONE AND ONLINE	Reservations are not necessary on Gatwick Express services. For information and telesales please call 0845 850 1530. Tickets can also be purchased through our website at www.gatwickexpress.com
RESERVATION DETAILS	Reservations are not available.
CATERING ON TRAINS	An at-seat trolley service of drinks and light refreshments is available throughout the day.
CYCLES	Cycles and other bulky items such as skis are conveyed free in the luggage van of the Gatwick Expresss trains that do not run to/from Brighton. On the following trains, cycles are not permitted unless they are standard size folding cycles provided they are folded, Brighton depart 0632, 0640, 0656, 0715, 0730, 0744, Gatwick Airport depart 0705, 0720, 0735, 0750, 0805, 0820, London Victoria depart 1730, 1745, 1800, 1815, 1830, 1845.
LOST PROPERTY	Please call our Lost Property Office on 0845 850 15 30, select option 2.
TRAIN SERVICE UPDATE	Journey time is 30 minutes (35 minutes on Sundays). First Class and Express Class accommodation is available. From London Victoria at 0330, 0430, 0500 then every 15 minutes (15, 30, 45, 00 minutes past each hour) until 0001, 0030. From Gatwick Airport at 0435, 0520, 0550 then every 15 minutes (05, 20, 35, 50 minutes past each hour) until 0050, 0135. For current train information call 0845 850 15 30, select option 2.
PENALTY FARES	Penalty Fares will be applied for passengers without the correct ticket between Brighton and Gatwick Airport. The only passengers permitted to buy a ticket on the train are those travelling between Gatwick Airport and London Victoria in either direction.
DISABLED PEOPLE'S PROTECTION POLICY	Customers requiring assistance can book this prior to travel. Arrangements can be made by calling 0845 138 1016, textphone available 0800 138 1018. It is advisable to give 24 hours notice of travel plans, although customers will be given assistance if they arrive at the stations without notice but please allow a little extra time.
CODE OF PRACTICE FOR COMMENTS, COMPLAINTS AND SUGGESTIONS	Initially comments or issues requiring immediate attention should be addressed to any member of Gatwick Express staff on the train or platforms. Additionally Customer Comments forms and our Passenger's Charter are available at Gatwick Express ticket offices. Alternatively you may write to the address above.

Grand Central

GC

ADDRESS

Grand Central Railway Company Ltd
River House
17 Museum Street
York YO1 7DJ
Telephone: 0845 603 4852
Fax: 01904 466066
Website: www.grandcentralrail.com
Email: customer.services@grandcentralrail.com

MANAGING DIRECTOR

Tom Clift

RESERVATIONS AND TICKETS BY TELEPHONE AND ONLINE

Reservations are strongly advised on Friday afternoons, at weekends and Bank Holidays. Tickets and seat Reservations are available in advance on our website www.grandcentralrail.com or over the phone by calling 0844 811 0071 (Mon - Fri 9 - 5pm) You can book tickets for all rail journeys in the UK with us. Tickets booked in advance can be sent by post (allow 5 working days), collected from self service ticket machines at certain stations or sent electronically by text message or email to print at home.
Tickets can also be purchased from the staff on the train without paying a penalty for last-minute travel.
For group bookings, business travel and Carnet tickets please call 0845 603 4852

RESERVATION DETAILS

Complimentary Seat Reservations are available; these must be booked at least 24 hours in advance. To guarantee a seat we advise that you always make a reservation. Reservations are strongly advised on Friday afternoons, at weekends and Bank Holidays.

CATERING ON TRAINS

A buffet service is available on all services. In First class customers enjoy complimentary light refreshments including hot and cold drinks, served at-seat. Daily and weekend newspapers are provided. In Standard class a buffet is available offering a selection of fair trade and locally sourced products, including hot, soft and alcoholic drinks, sandwiches, crisps and a large selection of other sweet and savoury snacks.

CYCLES

Normal sized cycles are conveyed free of charge subject to room being available, cycle reservations can be made by calling 0845 603 4852 or at any station ticket office. Cycle reservations are not normally required, but if a group of cyclists are travelling, you should call 0845 603 4852 to reserve cycle space.
During engineering work cycles cannot be accommodated on replacement bus services.

LOST PROPERTY

For trains travelling towards Sunderland or Bradford, please contact Northern Rail's Lost Property office on 0845 00 00 125. For trains travelling towards London, please contact King's Cross Lost Property Office on 0207 837 4334.

TRAIN SERVICE UPDATE

For live travel updates contact National Rail Enquiries on 08457 48 49 50, visit www.nationalrail.co.uk or call Train Tracker on 0871 200 4950. You can also text your station to 8 49 50 for live departures.

Details of weekend engineering work will be available on our website www.grandcentralrail.com or by calling 0845 603 4852.

DISABLED PEOPLE'S PROTECTION POLICY

Assisted travel can be booked by calling 0844 811 0072 (0800-2200 7 days a week) or using our text phone service on 0845 305 6815 please call at least 48 hours in advance. Our full Disabled People's Protection Policy is available on our website, by calling 0845 603 4852 or by writing to us at the address above. Copies are also available at staffed stations on our route.

CODE OF PRACTICE FOR COMMENTS, COMPLAINTS AND SUGGESTIONS

Copies of our Complaint Handling Guide, Passenger's Charter and comments forms are available from the above address or on our website. Customer Services can be contacted on 0845 603 4852. Copies of comments forms are available at staffed stations on our route and from any member of Grand Central staff.

Greater Anglia

ADDRESS

Contact Centre
Greater Anglia
Norwich Railway Station
Station Approach
Norwich NR1 1EF
Telephone: 0845 600 7245
Fax: 01603 214567
Website: www.greateranglia.com
Email: contactcentre@greateranglia.co.uk

MANAGING DIRECTOR

Ruud Haket

RESERVATIONS AND TICKETS BY TELEPHONE AND ONLINE

Tickets may be booked in advance by telephoning 0845 600 7245 between 0800 and 2200 (Mondays to Fridays) and 0900 and 1800 (weekends and Bank Holidays). For Business Travel, please telephone 0845 850 9080

RESERVATION DETAILS

Greater Anglia offers Seat Reservations on services between London Liverpool Street and Norwich at a charge of £2.50 per seat (£1 for season ticket holders).

CATERING ON TRAINS

Hot and cold drinks, sandwiches and light snacks are generally available on main line services between Norwich and London Liverpool Street and on Stansted Express services. Complimentary light refreshments will be available to First Class customers on these services.

CYCLES

Accompanied bicycles are conveyed free of charge on most GA services, but are not permitted on Stansted Express services at any time or on weekday peak services to and from London. A similar restriction also applies at Cambridge. On main line and rural services, the number of bicycles per train is limited, so a free reservation is recommended. For further details, please call Greater Anglia customer services on 0845 600 7245.

LOST PROPERTY

If you have lost an item of property on one of our trains or stations, please contact Greater Anglia customer services on 0845 600 7245 or email us at lostproperty@greateranglia.co.uk

TRAIN SERVICE UPDATE

For current train service information, please contact GA customer services on 0845 600 7245 or call our recorded information line on 020 7247 5488.

PENALTY FARES

Greater Anglia operates a Penalty Fares System on most of its network, except on designated 'paytrain' routes and from certain specified stations without ticket issuing facilities. Stations within the Penalty Fares area are identified by warning notices at each entrance. When travelling from these stations, you must have a valid ticket for your journey. For journeys where Oyster Pay as you Go (PAYG) is accepted, you must hold a valid Oyster card which has been touched in at the start of your journey. Oyster PAYG is not valid for travel outside the area where PAYG is accepted. If you cannot present a valid ticket for the journey you are making, you may be liable for a Penalty Fare (minimum £20).

DISABLED PEOPLE'S PROTECTION POLICY

Available from: Contact Centre, Greater Anglia, Norwich Station, Station Approach, Norwich NR1 1EF.

Customers who require assistance are recommended to book at least 24 hours in advance on 0800 028 2878 or Textphone 0845 606 7245.

CODE OF PRACTICE FOR COMMENTS, COMPLAINTS AND SUGGESTIONS

Available from: Contact Centre, Greater Anglia, Norwich Station, Station Approach, Norwich NR1 1EF.

The Greater Anglia Passenger's Charter is also available from the same address.

Heathrow Connect

HC

A joint venture between First Rail Division and BAA (Heathrow Express)

ADDRESS	Freepost RLRZ-TZXE-BYKY Heathrow Connect 6th Floor, 50 Eastbourne Terrace London W2 6LX Telephone: 0845 678 6975 Fax: 020 8750 6615 Website: www.heathrowconnect.com Email: web_customer_correspondence@baa.com
MANAGING DIRECTORS	*Heathrow Connect is a joint venture between First Great Western and BAA (Heathrow Express).* Mark Hopwood (First Great Western) Keith Greenfield (Heathrow Express)
RESERVATIONS AND TICKETS BY TELEPHONE AND ONLINE	Reservations are not necessary. Tickets can be booked by telephone on 0845 700 0125. Open 0700-2200 (0800-1900 Saturdays and Sundays). Allow 3 working days for delivery. A next day delivery can be arranged at £5 per transaction. Tickets may also be purchased through our website www.heathrowconnect.com
RESERVATION DETAILS	Reservations are not available.
CATERING ON TRAINS	Catering on trains is not available.
CYCLES	Cycles are carried free of charge, but are not allowed on trains timed to arrive at London Paddington between 0745-0945, or depart London Paddington between 1630-1830 Mondays to Fridays. In the interest of safety and customer comfort, we reserve the right to limit the number of cycles at other times.
LOST PROPERTY	Property lost at Paddington Station is collected by Network Rail, who can be contacted on 020 7313 1514. For items lost at Heathrow Airport call 020 8745 7727. For items lost on Heathrow Express trains, please ask our Customer Service Representatives, or alternatively email Heathrow Airport Lost Property at lrh.lostproperty@bagport.co.uk
TRAIN SERVICE UPDATE	For current train information call 0845 678 6975. Website: www.heathrowconnect.com
PENALTY FARES	Penalty Fares apply at stations between Hayes & Harlington and Paddington (incl). Customers are liable to a Penalty Fare of £20 to the next station stop.
DISABLED PEOPLE'S PROTECTION POLICY	This is available from Customer Relations at the above address and telephone number.
CODE OF PRACTICE FOR COMMENTS, COMPLAINTS AND SUGGESTIONS	It is our aim to try and resolve any issues or grievances on the spot. All our Customer Services Representative have a supply of comment forms and our Customer Care Line on 0845 604 15 15 can deal with any issues over the telephone or submit any comments to web_customer_correspondance@baa.com. If you wish to write with a suggestion or complain, please write to Customer Relations at the address at the top of this page, or through our website www.heathrowexpress.com

Heathrow Express

HX

ADDRESS	Heathrow Express Customer Relations FREEPOST London W2 6LG Telephone: 0845 604 1515 (call centre) Fax: 020 8750 6615 Website: www.heathrowexpress.com Email: web_customer_correspondence@baa.com
MANAGING DIRECTOR	Keith Greenfield
RESERVATIONS AND TICKETS BY TELEPHONE AND ONLINE	Reservations are not necessary on Heathrow Express services. Tickets may be purchased online and from www.heathrowexpress.com as well as our ticket offices at Heathrow Airport, Paddington station and other appointed outlets. For details call our Customer Services team on 0845 600 1515 (24 hour service - local rate call) or visit www.heathrowexpress.com
RESERVATION DETAILS	Reservations are not available.
CATERING ON TRAINS	As the overall journey time is only 15 minutes, or 21 minutes to Terminal 5, there is currently no catering on Heathrow Express services.
CYCLES	Limited accommodation is available for cycles on Heathrow Express services, for passengers flying with their cycles from the airport. Heathrow Express reserve the right to limit the number of cycles conveyed on each train to no more than three at busy times. Cyclists not travelling onwards by air may use the service to and from Heathrow Terminals, subject to space being available for airline passengers.
LOST PROPERTY	Property lost at Paddington station is collected by Network Rail, who can be contacted on 020 7313 1514. For items lost at Heathrow Airport call 020 8745 7727. For items lost on Heathrow Express trains, please ask our Customer Service Representatives, or alternatively write to: Excess Baggage Co., Heathrow Airport, Middlesex UB3 5AP or email to heathrow.lostproperty@excess-baggage.com
TRAIN SERVICE UPDATE	For current information on train services please contact our customer care line on 0845 604 15 15, or through our website www.heathrowexpress.com
PENALTY FARES	Penalty Fares do not apply on Heathrow Express services, therefore customers may join the train without having first purchased a ticket or authority to travel. Customer Service Representatives on every train will accept cash, debit and credit cards, for ticket purchase. Please note however for tickets purchased on board there is a £5.00 premium to pay. Only full fare tickets are available to purchase on board the train. (However Disabled Railcard is accepted on board).
DISABLED PEOPLE'S PROTECTION POLICY	Heathrow Express trains have been specially designed with the needs of the disabled in mind. Platforms at all our stations give level access into the trains and there is space for wheelchairs on all trains. For further information on facilities for the disabled, call the Customer Care Line on 0845 604 15 15, or write to the Managing Director at the address at the top of this page.
CODE OF PRACTICE FOR COMMENTS, COMPLAINTS AND SUGGESTIONS	It is our aim to try and resolve any issues or grievances on the spot. All our Customer Service Representatives have a supply of comment forms and our Customer Care Line on 0845 604 15 15 can deal with any issues over the telephone or submit any comments at web_customer_correspondence@baa.com. If you wish to write with a suggestion or complaint, please write to the Managing Director at the address at the top of this page, or through our website www.heathrowexpress.com

Island Line Trains

IL

ADDRESS	Friars Bridge Court 41–45 Blackfriars Road London SE1 8NZ Telephone: 08700 005151 Fax: 020 7620 5177 Website: www.southwesttrains.co.uk Email: customerrelations@swtrains.co.uk
MANAGING DIRECTOR	Tim Shoveller
RESERVATIONS AND TICKETS BY TELEPHONE AND ONLINE	Reservations are not required on Island Line Trains services. Group travel information can be obtained by calling 023 8072 8162.
RESERVATION DETAILS	Reservations are not available.
CATERING ON TRAINS	There are no catering facilities on trains.
CYCLES	A maximum of 4 cycles may be carried in the Shanklin end of all trains at no extra charge. For the safety and comfort of our passengers, the guard may refuse to carry any further cycles on the train.
LOST PROPERTY	All items of lost property are retained at Ryde Esplanade Ticket Office. If you have lost an item please telephone the Ticket Office on 01983 562492 (0900-1700 Daily). A charge may be applicable on collection.
TRAIN SERVICE UPDATE	For current train information, please call our helpline on 0845 6000 650 or visit www.islandlinetrains.co.uk
PENALTY FARES	Penalty Fares are not in force on any Island Line Trains services.
DISABLED PEOPLE'S PROTECTION POLICY	Island Line Trains is committed to making travel easier for customers with disabilities including wheelchair users. For travel on the mainland, please call our Assisted Travel line on 0800 5282 100 (textphone 0800 692 0792), giving 24 hours notice before travelling. Please note that scooters cannot be conveyed on any Island Line Trains Service. For journeys wholly within Island Line Trains, please telephone 01983 812591 giving 24 hours notice if assistance is required.
CODE OF PRACTICE FOR COMMENTS, COMPLAINTS AND SUGGESTIONS	Feedback leaflets are available at Ryde Esplanade or Shanklin Ticket Offices. Copies of Island Line Trains' and South West Trains' Passenger's Charters are available from any staffed station or by writing to: Customer Service Centre South West Trains Overline House Southampton SO15 1GW Telephone 0845 6000 650 Fax 023 8072 8187 Email: customerrelations@swtrains.co.uk The Passenger's Charter is also featured on the website www.islandlinetrains.co.uk and www.southwesttrains.co.uk

London Midland

ADDRESS	PO Box 4323 Birmingham B2 4JB Telephone: 0844 811 0133 Website: www.londonmidland.com Email: comments@londonmidland.com
MANAGING DIRECTOR	Patrick Verwer
RESERVATIONS AND TICKETS BY TELEPHONE AND ONLINE	Tickets can be booked in advance on-line at www.londonmidland.com or by ringing 0844 811 0133, 0800-2000 Monday to Sunday, please allow 5 days for delivery.
RESERVATION DETAILS	Seat reservations are not available. Group travel enquiries and bookings can be made on 0844 811 0133.
CATERING ON TRAINS	Catering is not available.
CYCLES	Cycles are carried free of charge on most off-peak services, however, advance reservations are required for our Birmingham–Liverpool, Birmingham-London and Crewe–London services. Cycles cannot be conveyed on trains arriving into London Euston between 0700 and 0959 and departing London Euston between 1600 and 1859 on Mondays to Fridays (excluding Bank Holidays). Folding cycles, completely folded down, are regarded as accompanied luggage and carried free.
LOST PROPERTY	Enquiries can be made at your nearest staffed station or by ringing Customer Relations on 0844 811 0133.
TRAIN SERVICE UPDATE	Available from National Rail Enquiries on 08457 48 49 50 (calls may be recorded for training purposes).
PENALTY FARES	A Penalty Fares System is in place across most of the London Midland network. If you board a service from a staffed station without a valid ticket or permit to travel, you will be liable to a £20 penalty fare or twice the standard single fare to the next station whichever is the greater. You can only purchase a ticket on-train when travelling from an unstaffed station. Details of the scheme are available at www.londonmidland.com or by writing to Customer Relations at the address below.
DISABLED PEOPLE'S PROTECTION POLICY	Available from Customer Relations London Midland PO Box 4323 Birmingham B2 4JB Telephone: 0844 811 0133
CODE OF PRACTICE FOR COMMENTS, COMPLAINTS AND SUGGESTIONS	Available from Customer Relations at the above address.

London Overground

LO

Operated by London Overground Rail Operations Ltd. (LOROL)
on behalf of Rail for London Ltd., a subsidiary of TfL

ADDRESS

125 Finchley Road
London NW3 6HY
Telephone: 0845 601 4867
Textphone 020 3031 9331
Website: www.tfl.gov.uk/overground
Email: overgroundinfo@tfl.gov.uk

MANAGING DIRECTOR

Steve Murphy

RESERVATIONS AND TICKETS BY TELEPHONE AND ONLINE

Tickets may be booked in advance and seats reserved on many long distance national rail services from most London Overground ticket offices. Oyster tickets may be purchased online from https://oyster.tfl.gov.uk

RESERVATION DETAILS

Reservations are not available.

CATERING ON TRAINS

Catering is not provided on London Overground services.

CYCLES

London Overground allows folding bicycles free of charge on all trains at all times, provided it is safe to do so. Non-folding bicycles are also accepted free of charge but due to space constraints they are not permitted on the following routes between the times shown:

- Willesden Junction (High Level) and Gospel Oak in both directions Mondays to Fridays (except Public Holidays) 0700-1000 and 1600-1900
- Gospel Oak and Blackhorse Road in both directions Mondays to Fridays (except Public Holidays) 0700-1000 and 1600-1900
- Watford Junction and Euston Mondays to Fridays (except Public Holidays) on services timed to arrive at Euston 0700-1000 or depart from Euston 1600-1900
- Highbury & Islington and New Cross/Crystal Palace/West Croydon in both directions Mondays to Fridays (except Public Holidays) 0700-1000 and 1600-1900.

Only one bicycle is allowed per customer within a limit of one bicycle per vestibule area. Tandems and three-wheeled vehicles cannot be accomodated on any London Overground train. Only folding bicycles can be carried on buses that replace trains due to engineering work.

LOST PROPERTY

Please contact the TfL Lost Property Office at Baker Street on 0845 330 9882 or our Customer Services Team on 0845 601 4867.

TRAIN SERVICE UPDATE

Information about London Overground services and fares can be obtained by telephoning either:

- London Travel Information on 0843 222 1234
- National Rail Enquiries 08457 48 49 50 (calls may be recorded for training purposes). (Textphone 08456 050 600, 0800-2000 daily)

A wide range of information about London Overground is also available from our website: www.tfl.gov.uk/overground

PENALTY FARES

London Overground operates a Penalty Fares Scheme. If you cannot produce, on request, a valid ticket for your entire journey or, when using Oyster to pay as you go, your Oyster card containing a record of the start of your Pay as you go journey, you will be liable to pay a Penalty Fare.

DISABLED PEOPLE'S PROTECTION POLICY

This can be obtained at any London Overground station or from our Customer Services Team at the above address.

CODE OF PRACTICE FOR COMMENTS, COMPLAINTS AND SUGGESTIONS

For a copy of the London Overground Customer Charter leaflet please ask at any London Overground station or contact our Customer Services Team at the above address.

Merseyrail

A Serco/Abellio company

ADDRESS	Rail House Lord Nelson Street Liverpool L1 1JF Telephone: 0151 702 2071 Website: www.merseyrail.org
MANAGING DIRECTOR	Maarten Spaargaren
RESERVATIONS AND TICKETS BY TELEPHONE AND ONLINE	Tickets may be booked in advance and seats reserved from most Merseyrail stations for National Rail Services.
RESERVATION DETAILS	Reservations are not available.
CATERING ON TRAINS	Catering is not available.
CYCLES	Cycles carried free of charge at any time, subject to sufficient space being available.
LOST PROPERTY	Please contact:- Lost Property Office James Street Station James Street Liverpool L2 7PQ Phone: 0151 702 2951
TRAIN SERVICE UPDATE	For current train information please call 08457 48 49 50 (calls may be recorded for training purposes).
PENALTY FARES	Please refer to notices displayed at stations for details of the Penalty Fare Scheme in operation.
DISABLED PEOPLE'S PROTECTION POLICY	Available from:– Customer Relations Merseyrail Rail House Lord Nelson Street Liverpool L1 1JF Phone : 0151 702 2071 (Textphone 0870 0552 681) Fax : 0151 702 2413 or email: comment@merseyrail.org
CODE OF PRACTICE FOR COMMENTS, COMPLAINTS AND SUGGESTIONS	Available from above address

North Yorkshire Moors Railway

NY

(Operators of steam and heritage services between
Whitby, Grosmont, Goathland and Pickering)

ADDRESS	Pickering Station Pickering North Yorkshire YO18 7AJ Telephone: 01751-472508 (Customer Services and Information) Fax: 01751-476048 Website: www.nymr.co.uk Email: info@nymr.co.uk
GENERAL MANAGER	Philip Benham
RESERVATIONS AND TICKETS BY TELEPHONE AND ONLINE	Telephone: 01751-472508 Hours of operation: 31 March to 4 November and other operating dates: 0930-1630 (Monday - Friday), 1000-1430 (Saturday and Sunday); All other times: 1000-1430 (Monday - Friday). At least 7 days should be allowed for receipt of tickets purchased by telephone. National Rail tickets can be booked in advance from our office in Whitby – telephone 01947 605872.
RESERVATION DETAILS	Reservations are not available on normal services. They can be made for groups of 20 or more passengers and are required on North Yorkshire Moors Railways dining train services (between Pickering and Grosmont).
CATERING ON TRAINS	An at-seat trolley service of drinks and snacks is provided on most trains.
CYCLES	Cycles and dogs are carried for a charge of £2 (subject to space being available).
LOST PROPERTY	Enquiries about lost property should be made to Pickering Station at the above, or by telephone 01751-472508.
TRAIN SERVICE UPDATE	Updated train service information on all North Yorkshire Moors Railway is available on the website (see address above). A 'talking timetable' is also available giving current details of all North Yorkshire Moors Railway services by telephoning 01751-473535.
PENALTY FARES	Penalty Fares are not in force on any North Yorkshire Moors Railway service.
DISABLED PEOPLE'S PROTECTION POLICY	Available from the address above, or Pickering and Grosmont Stations.
CODE OF PRACTICE FOR COMMENTS, COMPLAINTS AND SUGGESTIONS	North Yorkshire Moors Railway welcomes comments from passengers. Comments/suggestion cards are available from stations and on-board staff, or alternatively please write to the General Manager. Details of the company's policy are available from the above address, or Pickering and Grosmont Stations.

Northern

NT

A joint venture between Serco and Abellio

ADDRESS	Northern Rail Ltd Northern House 9 Rougier Street York YO1 6HZ Telephone: 08700 005151 Website: www.northernrail.org
MANAGING DIRECTOR	Ian Bevan
RESERVATIONS AND TICKETS BY TELEPHONE AND ONLINE	Reservations and tickets are available from all local staffed stations.
RESERVATION DETAILS	Tickets can be purchased in advance on-line at www.northernrail.org. Reservations and tickets are also available from all local staffed stations. For groups of 10 or more travelling on the Leeds-Settle-Carlisle line telephone 0800 9800 766, between 0900 and 1700 on Mondays to Fridays to make a booking. All accommodation on Northern trains is Standard Class.
CATERING ON TRAINS	On most Leeds-Settle-Carlisle services, food and drink can be purchased from the trolley which will pass through the train.
CYCLES	Up to two cycles can be carried on each service. This is subject to space being available, however, and cannot be booked in advance. For further details telephone 0845 000 0125.
LOST PROPERTY	Call 0845 000 0125, contact your nearest staffed station or write to Northern at the address below.
TRAIN SERVICE UPDATE	Information about Northern services and fares can be obtained by telephoning: **08457 48 49 50** (calls may be recorded for training purposes) or access the website on www.nationalrail.co.uk For more information on our services, please visit our website on www.northernrail.org The latest information on train running is available by phoning TrainTracker™ from National Rail Enquiries on 0871 200 4915 or by texting TrainTracker™. Text to 84950.
PENALTY FARES	Penalty Fares are not in force on any Northern service.
DISABLED PERSON'S PROTECTION POLICY	If you would like a copy of Northern's Policy or wish to arrange assistance for your journey, please phone: 0808 1561606. (Textphone 0845 604 5608) or by writing to Customer Relations, Northern, FREEPOST (RLSL-ABEC-BGUU), Leeds LS1 4DY or email: assistance@northernrail.org
CODE OF PRACTICE FOR COMMENTS, COMPLAINTS AND SUGGESTIONS	Please contact our Customer Helpline on 0845 000 0125, a textphone is available on 0845 604 5608. Alternatively you can write to us at: Customer Relations, Northern, FREEPOST (RLSL-ABEC-BGUU), Leeds LS1 4DY. If you would like a copy of the Northern Passenger's Charter, or Northern's Guide for Customers with Disabilities please contact our Customer Relations team.

ScotRail

A member of the First Rail Division

ADDRESS

1st Floor
Atrium Court
50 Waterloo Street
Glasgow G2 6HQ
Telephone: 08700 00 51 51
Fax: 0141 335 4592
Website: www.scotrail.co.uk
Email: scotrailcustomer.relations@firstgroup.com

MANAGING DIRECTOR

Steve Montgomery

RESERVATIONS AND TICKETS BY TELEPHONE AND ONLINE

Tickets may be purchased in advance and Sleepers or seats reserved, by telephone, using a debit/credit card from the following number: 08457 550033 (opening hours 0700-2200)

Please allow 5 days for tickets by post, tickets on departure arrangements available at selected stations. Tickets can also be purchased through the website - www.scotrail.co.uk

ScotRail customers can buy selected Caledonian Sleeper tickets online - and have the ticket confirmation sent to their mobile phone. Passengers simply turn up for their train, show the text message to train staff and hop on board. A confirmatory email is sent as a back-up. This free SMS service is only available for 'Bargain Berth' tickets on the Caledonian Sleeper, which connects Scottish cities to Central London. Tickets can be booked up to 12 weeks in advance of travel - and right up until Midday on the day of travel, subject to availability. The berths start from just £19, one way.

RESERVATION DETAILS

Seat Reservations are free and can be made from 12 weeks in advance up to approximately two hours prior to the departure of the train.

CATERING ON TRAINS

A Lounge Car is provided on all Caledonian Sleeper services offering a wide range of drinks, snacks and hot meals. A trolley service is available on many longer-distance daytime services as indicated in the timetable.

CYCLES

Cycles are carried free on all ScotRail services subject to availability. Reservations are required on Caledonian Sleeper services and on longer distance routes. Tandems, tricycles, cycle trailers, motorcycles, mopeds or motorised cycles are not carried on any ScotRail service.

LOST PROPERTY

Please phone 0141 335 3276 (0700-1900 Mon-Sat)

TRAIN SERVICE UPDATE

Register with JourneyAlert on our website: www.scotrail.co.uk/disruption

Alternatively, download our mobile app by texting ScotRail to 86688.

PENALTY FARES

Penalty Fares are not in force on any ScotRail services.

DISABLED PEOPLE'S PROTECTION POLICY

Available from ScotRail Customer, PO Box 7031, Fort William PH33 6WW. Tel: 0800 912 2 901 or 18001 0800 912 2 901 Fax: 0141 335 4611

Travel arrangements may be made for disabled people by calling 0800 912 2 901*. A light travel scooter, length 104cm, width 56cm with a turning radius of 99cm and combined weight of 300kg can be conveyed. Details of station facilities and information on accessibility are available at www.nationalrail.co.uk or www.scotrail.co.uk.

*For assisted travel, an advance notice is appreciated.

CODE OF PRACTICE FOR COMMENTS, COMPLAINTS AND SUGGESTIONS

ScotRail welcomes comments on the services we provide. A leaflet is available at all staffed ScotRail stations and also from the Customer Relations Manager at the address above. Tel: 0845 601 5929. Feedback can also be provided via our website. Click on the Contact Us link on our homepage.

South West Trains

SW

ADDRESS

Friars Bridge Court
41–45 Blackfriars Road
London SE1 8NZ
Telephone: 08700 005151 Fax: 020 7620 5177
Website: www.southwesttrains.co.uk
Email: customerrelations@swtrains.co.uk

MANAGING DIRECTOR

Tim Shoveller

RESERVATIONS AND TICKETS BY TELEPHONE AND ONLINE

Tickets may be booked in advance by telephone, on the following number: 0845 6000 650.

Tickets may also be purchased via the South West Trains website (see above). When ordering, please allow 5 working days for ticket delivery.

RESERVATION DETAILS

Reservations are not available.

CATERING ON TRAINS

Catering on South West Trains is provided on those services marked with the symbol for all or part of the journey. Catering may be provided from a buffet area, at seat trolley service or a combination of both according to the route and time of day. Comments on the service should be sent to the Customer Service Centre at the address below.

CYCLES

A limited number of cycles can be carried on most of our services except during the Monday to Friday peak periods. Restrictions apply on certain routes into and out of London Waterloo between 0715 and 1000 and between 1645 and 1900. At all times some services require advance reservations, as space is limited.

To obtain full details of South West Trains Cycling Policy and full details of routes and times when cycles are not carried visit www.southwesttrains.co.uk, pick up a leaflet from stations served by South West Trains or contact our Customer Service Centre at the address shown.

Cycles that can be folded to a size which allows them to be carried safely in the luggage racks on our services may be carried folded at all times.

For reasons of safety and comfort of our passengers, if the available identified cycle spaces on the train are already taken, the guard has the right to refuse to carry any further cycles on that train.

LOST PROPERTY

A lost property helpline is available between 0730-1900 Mondays to Fridays by calling 020 7401 7861

TRAIN SERVICE UPDATE

For current train information, please call our helpline on 0845 6000 650 or visit www.southwesttrains.co.uk

PENALTY FARES

South West Trains has a duty to its fare paying passengers to ensure no-one travels for free. To this end South West Trains operates a Penalty Fares Scheme across its network, with the only exceptions being Dean, Mottisfont & Dunbridge and Romsey.

Passengers travelling to and from stations within the penalty fares area without a valid ticket may be liable to a penalty of £20 or twice the single fare to the next station at which their train stops (whichever is the greater).

DISABLED PEOPLE'S PROTECTION POLICY

For a copy of this publication, please contact the Customer Service Centre at the address below.

Assistance for mobility impaired passengers can be arranged by telephoning 0800 5282 100 between 0600 - 2200 daily. Please give at least 24 hours notice.

A textphone facility is available on 0800 6920 792 (calls are charged at local rates).

CODE OF PRACTICE FOR COMMENTS, COMPLAINTS AND SUGGESTIONS

Copies of South West Trains Passenger's Charter are available from any staffed station or by writing to:
Customer Service Centre, South West Trains, Overline House, Blechynden Terrace, Southampton SO15 1GW
Telephone 0845 6000 650. Fax 023 8072 8187
Email: customerrelations@swtrains.co.uk
The Passenger's Charter is also available on our website www.southwesttrains.co.uk

Southeastern

SE

ADDRESS

Southeastern Customer Services
PO Box 63428
London SE1P 5FD
Telephone: 0845 000 2222
Assisted Travel: 0800 783 4524 (Textphone 0800 783 4548)
Fax: 0845 678 6976
Textphone: 0800 783 4548

Website: southeasternrailway.co.uk

Southeastern Customer Services is staffed 24 hours a day, seven days a week (closed Christmas Day). Comments and complaints are dealt with here by post, fax, and website as well as on the telephone.

MANAGING DIRECTOR

Charles Horton

RESERVATIONS AND TICKETS BY TELEPHONE AND ONLINE

Group travel (parties of 10 persons or more) on Southeastern services must be booked at least seven days in advance so that space can be allocated. To order, go to southeasternrailway.co.uk, select tickets, then group, then complete the online form.

Customers can buy or renew their Season Tickets for one month or longer online at southeasternrailway.co.uk or by completing the Season Ticket application form at their local ticket office.

RESERVATIONS

Reservations are not available. Reservations are only needed on Southeastern services for Group Travel and mobility impaired customers who require assistance.

CATERING ON TRAINS

Catering is available on some services.

CYCLES

Cycles are not permitted on peak time services, which are those timed to arrive in London terminals between 0700 and 0959, and those timed to leave between 1600 and 1859. Folding cycles are permitted provided they are folded.

LOST PROPERTY

Customers who have lost property on a train or at a station should contact Southeastern Customer Services on 0845 000 2222.

TRAIN SERVICE UPDATE

For current train running information contact Southeastern Customer Services on 0845 000 2222.

Information is also available from national and local radio station travel updates on Ceefax page 433, and from our website: southeasternrailway.co.uk, select journey.

PENALTY FARES

Southeastern operate a Penalty Fares Scheme on all routes. You must buy a valid ticket (or permit to travel) for your journey before boarding a train. If you do not have a valid ticket or permit to travel, you may have to pay a Penalty Fare of £20.00 or twice the single fare, whichever is the greater. Please pick up a Penalty Fare leaflet from a staffed station for your information.

DISABLED PEOPLE'S PROTECTION POLICY

Copies of 'Making Rail Accessible' are available from any Southeastern sales point and Southeastern Customer Services.

If you have any special needs and would like help with planning your journey anywhere in Great Britain please call 0800 783 4524 or use the Textphone 0800 783 4548 - open 24 hours a day.

The Southeastern Assisted Travel team will offer advice and make any special arrangements you need. If at least 24 hours' notice can be given, this will be very much appreciated.

CODE OF PRACTICE FOR COMMENTS, COMPLAINTS AND SUGGESTIONS

Southeastern Passengers' Charter leaflets are available at any Southeastern sales point or Southeastern Customer Services at the address shown above.

Southern

ADDRESS

Southern Customer Services
PO Box 3021
Bristol BS2 2BS
Telephone: 08451 27 29 20 (Customer Services)
Fax: 08451 27 29 30 (Customer Services)
Website: www.southernrailway.com
Email: comments@southernrailway.com

MANAGING DIRECTOR

Chris Burchell

RESERVATIONS AND TICKETS BY TELEPHONE AND ONLINE

Discounted Advance Tickets are available from the Southern website.

RESERVATION DETAILS

Reservations are only required for Advance tickets. These reservations authorise the holder to travel on the specified train but do not identify individual seats.

CATERING ON TRAINS

A light refreshment of food and drinks is available on trains marked with ☕ in the timetable.

CYCLES

Standard size folding cycles are welcome on all Southern trains (as long as they are folded) at any time. During peak periods, for non-folding cycles different restrictions apply at each station so please check with the station or our website before travelling.

LOST PROPERTY

Please call Southern Customer Services on 08451 27 29 20.

TRAIN SERVICE UPDATE

For current train information call Customer Services on 08451 27 29 20 or check our website at www.southernrailway.com

PENALTY FARES

Southern operate a Penalty Fares Scheme on all routes. You must buy a valid ticket (or permit to travel) for your journey before boarding a train. If you do not have a valid ticket or permit to travel, you may have to pay a Penalty Fare of £20.00 or twice the single fare, whichever is the greater. Please pick up a Penalty Fare leaflet from a staffed station for your information.

DISABLED PEOPLE'S PROTECTION POLICY

Available from Southern Customer Services at
PO Box 3021
Bristol BS2 2BS.

To get advice about accessible travel or to book assistance please call 0800 136 1016; Minicom/textphone – 0800 138 1018, Fax – 0800 138 1017

CODE OF PRACTICE FOR COMMENTS, COMPLAINTS AND SUGGESTIONS

Write to Southern Customer Services at the above address.

Copies of Southern Passenger's charter are available from any staffed station. You can also obtain a copy by contacting Customer Services or from Southern's website.

Virgin Trains

VT

The trading name of West Coast Trains Ltd

ADDRESS	Virgin Trains 85 Smallbrook Queensway Birmingham B5 4HA Telephone: 0845 000 8000 Textphone: 0121 654 7528 Website: www.virgintrains.com Email: customer.relations@virgintrains.co.uk
CHIEF EXECUTIVE	Tony Collins
MANAGING DIRECTOR	Chris Gibb
RESERVATIONS AND TICKETS BY TELEPHONE AND ONLINE	Buy tickets for Virgin Trains and any other train company in Great Britain on the internet at www.virgintrains.com or by calling 0871 977 4222 (calls to this number cost 10p a minute from a BT landline; calls from other operators may vary and cost more) - between 0800 and 2200 7 days a week. If you have a disability or have specific needs and wish to arrange assistance on your journey call the Virgin Trains JourneyCare service on 08457 44 33 66 (Textphone 08457 44 33 67) between 0800 and 2200 every day except Christmas Day or Boxing Day.
RESERVATION DETAILS	You are strongly advised to make a Seat Reservation in advance. Reservations can be made for the Quiet Zone carriage, where customers should refrain from using mobile phones or creating unnecessary noise. On routes to and from London, Standard Class Quiet Zone is in coach A and in coach H for First Class. On other routes, Quiet Zone is located in Standard Class, coach F. Seat reservations are free of charge.
CATERING ON TRAINS	In First Class on a Pendolino from Monday to Friday customers can enjoy a selection of snacks throughout the day, including a cooked breakfast on many morning peak services. In addition, Fairtrade tea, Fairtrade coffee, soft drinks and alcoholic drinks (alcohol is not offered with breakfast services) are served at seat throughout the day. A complimentary newspaper is also available. In First Class on Super Voyager from Monday to Friday customers can enjoy complimentary light refreshments, including Fairtrade tea, Fairtrade coffee, soft drinks and a newspaper with an at-seat service available, on most services. In Standard, we have a wide range of snacks and sandwiches, Fairtrade teas, fresh ground Fairtrade coffee, soft and alcoholic drinks and a selection of non-food items available at our onboard shop. The shop is generally open throughout. Pendolinos offer an at-seat trolley service to standard customers on Mondays to Fridays. For more information about our onboard service pick up a copy of Travelling with Virgin Trains.
CYCLES	Subject to availability of space cycles can be carried on all trains. Most trains can carry 3 cycles, and on journeys to and from London Euston, Pendolinos can carry tandems (however, tandems are not carried on Voyager services). An advance reservation is required for all journeys.
LOST PROPERTY	Call Customer Relations on 0845 000 8000 – 0830 to 1800 Mondays to Fridays, 0900 to 1600 Saturdays, answerphone available at all other times.
TRAIN SERVICE UPDATE	Details of any disruption to services or weekend engineering work are summarised on BBC Ceefax and on BBCi on digital TV. Details of Engineering work can also be found at www.virgintrains.com.
PENALTY FARES	Penalty Fares are not applicable on any Virgin Trains service.
DISABLED PEOPLE'S PROTECTION POLICY	Our Customer Relations Manager (at the address above) will be pleased to supply a free copy of the Disabled People's Protection Policy. It can also be downloaded at www.virgintrains.com. For information on station accessibility and to arrange special help please contact Virgin Trains JourneyCare (details above).
CODE OF PRACTICE FOR COMMENTS, COMPLAINTS AND SUGGESTIONS	We want you to tell us what you think of our service, good or bad. A copy of our Code of Practice for handling comments, complaints and suggestions together with Virgin Trains Passenger's Charter is available free on request from our Customer Relations Manager at the above address.

West Coast Railway Company

(Operators of the 'Jacobite' and 'Cambrian' Steam Services)

ADDRESS	Jesson Way Carnforth Lancashire LA5 9UR Telephone: 01524 737751/737753 Fax: 01524 735518 Website: www.westcoastrailways.co.uk Email: jacobite@wcrc.co.uk
GENERAL MANAGER	Mrs Pat Marshall
COMMERCIAL MANAGER	James Shuttleworth
RESERVATIONS AND TICKETS BY TELEPHONE AND ONLINE	Advance bookings are recommended and can be made on line, at www.westcoastrailways.co.uk, by post (enclose SAE) to the Carnforth Office (address above) or by telephone, on 01524 737751/737753, during normal office hours. Credit cards accepted. Tickets can also be purchased from the WCR Guard/Train Manager, on the train, on the day of travel (subject to availablility).
RESERVATION DETAILS	Phone 01524 737751/737753
CATERING ON TRAINS	A buffet service, serving hot and cold drinks and cold snacks, is available on all trains.
CYCLES	Cycles carried free of charge, subject to space.
LOST PROPERTY	Telephone: 01524 737751/737753
PENALTY FARES	Penalty Fares are not in force on any West Coast Railway Company service.
TRAIN SERVICE UPDATE	For current train information please phone 08457 48 49 50 (calls may be recorded for training purposes).
DISABLED PEOPLE'S PROTECTION POLICY	Available from the above address.
CODE OF PRACTICE FOR COMMENTS, COMPLAINTS AND SUGGESTIONS	West Coast Railway Company welcomes comments on services provided. Write to Carnforth office (address above).

Network Rail

ADDRESS	King's Place York Way London N1 9AG Telephone: 020 7557 8000 Fax: 020 7557 9000 Website: www.networkrail.co.uk
CHIEF EXECUTIVE	David Higgins

Network Rail is responsible for operating 17 managed stations, indicated in the index by the code **NR**. Details of facilities provided, including the Disabled Peoples Protection Policy, are obtainable from the Network Rail Station Manager at the following station addresses:–

London Bridge	Network Rail Offices, Platform 14, London Bridge Station, Station Approach, London SE1 9SP
London Cannon Street	Cannon Street Station, Cannon Street, London EC4N 6AP
London Charing Cross	Network Rail Offices, Charing Cross Station, The Strand, London WC2 5HS
London Euston	Room 430, Stephenson Room, East Colonnade, Euston, London NW1 2RT
London Fenchurch Street	Network Rail Office, Fenchurch Place, London EC3M 4AJ
London King's Cross	Room 304, West Side Offices, King's Cross Station, London N1 9AP
London Liverpool Street	Network Rail Station Reception, Platform 10, Liverpool Street Station, London EC2M 7PY
London Paddington	Room B115, Tournament House, Paddington Station, London W2 1FT
London Victoria	3rd Floor, Kent Side Offices, Victoria Station, London SW1V 1JU
London Waterloo	CP2-4-G General Offices, Waterloo Station, London SE1 8SW
Birmingham New Street	Reception, Network Rail Offices, Station Forecourt, Birmingham New Street Station, Birmingham B2 4ND
Edinburgh	Room 255, North Block, Waverley Station, Edinburgh EH1 1BB
Glasgow Central	Glasgow Central Station, Gordon Street, Glasgow G1 3SL
Leeds	Room 405, Administration Block, Leeds City Station, Leeds LS1 4DY
Manchester Piccadilly	9th Floor, Piccadilly Tower, Piccadilly Station, Manchester M60 7RA
Liverpool Lime Street	Station Manager, The Barrier Line Building, Liverpool Lime Street Station, Liverpool L1 1JF
London St Pancras International	Station Reception, St Pancras International Station, Pancras Road, London NW1 2QP

Staffed Left Luggage facilities, offering maximum security, are available at all Network Rail Stations.

If you wish to raise any issue concerning the rail infrastructure or the 17 managed stations operated by Network Rail (excluding matters concerning the running of trains or ticket purchase) please call the national 24 hour Helpline:- **08457 11 41 41**

Other Addresses

Department for Transport

Great Minster House, 33 Horseferry Road, London SW1P 4DR

Telephone: 0300 330 3000

Email: rail@dft.gsi.gov.uk

Office of Rail Regulation

One Kemble Street, London WC2B 4AN

Telephone: 020 7282 2000

Fax: 020 7282 2040

Chair of the Board: Anna Walker
Chief Executive: Richard Price

The main areas of the Regulator's statutory functions are:

- the issue, modification and enforcement of licences to operate trains, networks, stations and light maintenance depots;
- the approval of agreements for access by operators of railway assets to track, stations and light maintenance depots;
- the enforcement of domestic competition law; and consumer protection including a duty under the Railways Act 1993 in relation to the protection of the interests of users of railway services, including the disabled.

Publications are available from:

Sue MacSwan, The Library, ORR, 1 Waterhouse Square, 138–142 Holborn, London EC1N 2TQ

Telephone: 020 7282 2001

Email: rail.library@orr.gsi.gov.uk

Association of Train Operating Companies (ATOC)

3rd Floor, 40 Bernard Street, London WC1N 1BY

Telephone: 020 7841 8000

Chief Executive: Michael Roberts

ATOC represents the interests of most of the national and international passenger Train Operating Companies whose services are shown in this timetable. It manages a range of network services, products and responsibilities on behalf of these train operators including:

- the National Rail Conditions of Carriage (the passenger's contract with the train operators)
- the National Rail Enquiries Service
- the licensing of rail appointed travel agents
- National Railcards, the London Travelcard and Network Railcard.

London Underground Limited

Head Office

55 Broadway, London SW1H 0BD

Telephone: 020 7222 5600

Responsible for the operation of stations indicated in the Stations Index by the code **LT**

How to Cross London

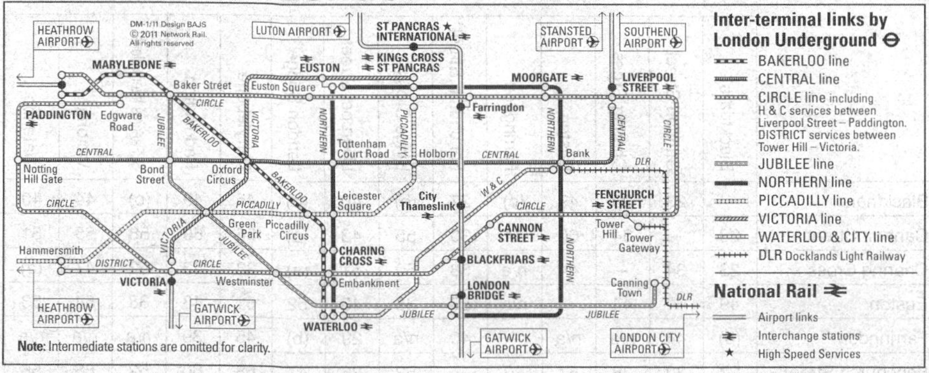

Introduction

The time taken to travel between London's stations will vary from journey to journey dependent on distance, mode of transport, time of day and the need to change en route. The quickest way to cross London is usually by the Underground network with frequent services operating between the following hours*:

- 0530 to 0015 on Monday to Friday
- 0630 to 0115 on Saturday
- 0700 to 0001 on Sunday

(* Times shown are approximate)

Buses also link many of London's main terminal stations including an extensive network of Night Bus services.

Ticket & Fares

Rail tickets for journeys routed via London are valid for transfer by London Underground or First Capital Connect services between London terminal stations, and other designated interchange stations* appropriate to the route of the through journey being made, at no extra cost. For example a Brighton to Leeds ticket is valid on London Underground services from Victoria to Kings Cross (Victoria Line), or alternatively on First Capital Connect services to St Pancras International. A Chelmsford to Southampton ticket is valid on London Underground services to Waterloo via either Liverpool Street (Circle Line) or Stratford (Jubilee Line).

(*NB. check on which cross London routes your ticket is valid before you travel. A break of journey is permitted at an intermediate Underground station, but a further ticket must be purchased in order to continue the journey)

London's Fare Zones – National Rail, Underground and Docklands Light Railway (DLR) stations within the Greater London area are in one of nine Fare Zones. Single and return tickets are available for through journeys to and from all Underground and DLR stations with prices determined by the number of zones crossed or travelled through.

A range of day and longer period Travelcards are also available and provide unlimited travel on National Rail, London Underground, London Overground, Docklands Light Railway and Tramlink services within the Fare Zones for which they are valid. All Travelcards, irrespective of the zones for which they are issued, can also be used on any London bus displaying this sign ⊖.

For information on ticket prices and availability contact your local staffed station, call National Rail Enquiries anytime on **08457 48 49 50*** (Textphone **0845 60 50 600**), or visit www.nationalrail.co.uk. * Calls may be recorded for training purposes.

More detailed information about London's Underground and Bus services, also Docklands Light Railway and London Tramlink is available anytime from London Travel Information on **0843 222 1234** (textphone **020 7918 3015**) or visit **www.tfl.gov.uk**.

First Capital Connect and Southeastern

First Capital Connect operates fast, direct services from Bedford, Luton and St Albans via Central London to East Croydon, Gatwick Airport and Brighton and stopping trains between Luton, St Albans, North London, the City, Streatham, Wimbledon and Sutton. There are nine Central London First Capital Connect stations with Underground connections. First Capital Connect connects with East Midlands Trains at Luton, Luton Airport Parkway, London St Pancras and Bedford – see Tables 52 and 53.

Southeastern, in partnership with First Capital Connect also operate trains between Kentish Town, the City and Sevenoaks and at peak times between Bedford, Luton, the City and various destinations in Kent.

London Overground

Direct trains run between:

- Richmond and Stratford
- Clapham Junction and Willesden Jn / Stratford
- Watford Junction and Euston
- Gospel Oak and Barking
- Highbury & Islington and New Cross / Crystal Palace / West Croydon

Southern Services

Direct trains are provided between East Croydon, South London, Clapham Junction and stations to Watford Junction and Milton Keynes Central. These trains also stop at Imperial Wharf, West Brompton, Kensington (Olympia) and Shepherd's Bush. See table 176.

These trains provide connections to most of the Southern network at Clapham Junction.

Passengers requiring step free interchange for Southern main line trains to Gatwick Airport and the Sussex Coast should change at East Croydon, and step free interchange for Southern Metro trains is usually available at Balham.

Interchange for the West Midlands and North West is available at either Watford Junction or Milton Keynes.

Cross London Transfer Times (in minutes)

	Blackfriars	Cannon Street	Charing Cross	Euston	Farringdon	Fenchurch Street*	Kings Cross	Liverpool Street	London Bridge	Marylebone	Paddington	St Pancras International †	Victoria	Waterloo
Blackfriars	–	23	23	49	(b)	27	(b)	40	(b)	45	49	(b)	44	40
Cannon Street	23	–	34	60	44	30	55	43	(a)	56	60	58	55	51
Charing Cross	23	34	–	44	n/a	38	50	51	(a)	38	43	52	47	(a)
Euston	49	60	44	–	n/a	57	35	43	52	51	43	38	54	53
Farringdon	(b)	44	n/a	n/a	–	40	n/a	29	(b)	45	39	n/a	n/a	n/a
Fenchurch Street*	27	30	38	57	40	–	52	26	47	68	60	52	68	56
Kings Cross	(b)	55	50	35	n/a	52	–	41	50	50	45	30	56	55
Liverpool Street	40	43	51	43	29	26	41	–	49	56	55	41	126	62
London Bridge	(b)	(a)	(a)	52	(b)	47	50	49	–	58	62	60	n/a	(a)
Marylebone	45	56	38	51	45	68	50	56	58	–	32	53	58	47
Paddington	49	60	43	43	39	60	45	55	62	32	–	45	62	51
St Pancras International †	(b)	58	52	38	(b)	52	30	41	60	53	45	–	56	61
Victoria	44	55	47	54	n/a	68	56	126	n/a	58	62	56	–	124
Waterloo	40	51	(a)	53	n/a	56	55	62	(a)	47	51	61	124	–

All times are based on use of London Underground services and are shown as a guide only – extra time should be allowed during the early morning/late evening and on Sundays.

* Tower Hill Underground Station

† An additional 35 minutes should be allowed for Eurostar Connections

(a) Direct train services available (operated by Southeastern)

(b) Direct train services available (operated by First Capital Connect)

n/a Transfer not likely to be required as part of a through rail journey

Some other useful transfers

If your journey requires a transfer between any of the following pairs of stations, you should allow a margin of at least the number of minutes shown when planning connections. All transfers are assumed to be by foot unless otherwise stated.

Ash Vale – North Camp	19
Bicester North – Town	30
Burnley Central – Manchester Rd	25
Burscough Bridge – Junction	20
Canterbury East – West	25
Catford – Bridge	10
Clock House – Kent House	15
Dorchester South – West	15
Dorking – Dorking Deepdene	9
East Croydon – West Croydon	25
Edenbridge – Edenbridge Town	20
Enfield Chase – Town	29
Falkirk High – Grahamston	44
Farnborough Main – North	24
Forest Gate – Wanstead Park	13
Gainsborough Central – Lea Rd	33
Hackney Central – Downs	14
Harringay – Green Lanes	14
Heath High Level – Low Level	10
Hertford North – East	34
Maidstone Barracks – East	16
New Mills Central – Newtown	25
Penge East – West	19
Purley Oaks – Sanderstead	10
Seven Sisters – South Tottenham	14
Southend Central – Victoria	17
Upper Warlingham – Whyteleafe	10
Walthamstow Central – Queen's Rd	14
West Hampstead – Thameslink	11
Windsor & Eton Central – Riverside	14
Yeovil Junction – Yeovil Pen Mill	15*

* This is a bus service which runs every 30 mins between 0700 and 1900 Mondays to Saturdays.

Airport Links

Aberdeen Airport

Aberdeen Airport is close to Dyce station, from where trains operate to Aberdeen, Elgin and Inverness. There are also some direct trains to Glasgow and Edinburgh. A shuttle bus runs between Dyce station and the airport, connecting with most trains during the day.

For full bus timetable information, call **0871 200 22 33**, or visit **www.travelinescotland.com**

Birmingham International Airport

Birmingham Airport is alongside Birmingham International station. The free Air-Rail Link transit system operates to the passenger terminals about every 2 minutes with a journey time of less than 2 minutes. Birmingham International station is served by direct trains from London Euston and Manchester Piccadilly. In addition a frequent service operates between Birmingham New Street and Birmingham International providing connections at Birmingham New Street to and from all parts of the country. (See Tables 65, 66, 68, 71, 74 and 116). Regular buses operated by National Express West Midlands (966) also run from Solihull station (see Tables 71 and 115) and through fares are available by purchasing a PlusBus ticket. The journey time is approximately 20 minutes and through ticketing is available. Solihull is served by Chiltern Railways services from London Marylebone, Gerrards Cross, Beaconsfield, High Wycombe, Princes Risborough, Haddenham & Thame Parkway, Bicester North, Banbury, Leamington Spa and Warwick and by London Midland local services.

Bournemouth (Hurn) International Airport

Bournemouth (Hurn) International Airport now has an hourly bus service to and from Bournemouth station. See www.bournemouth-airport-shuttle.co.uk or phone 01202 557007 for details.

Bristol International Airport

The Bristol Airport Flyer is the only express link between Bristol Temple Meads station, Bristol Bus Station, Clifton and Bristol Airport. The journey time to the city centre is approximately 30 minutes with services operating (every 10 minutes at Peak times) daily between 0230 and 0045.

Cardiff International Airport

The airport is served by a free bus link from Rhoose Cardiff International Rail Station to/from the airport operated by New Adventure Travel. Full details of the timetable and further information can be obtained from Traveline on **0871 200 22 33** or visit **www.traveline.info.**

Bus Service X91 also operates from Cardiff Central Bus Station (Stand F1) directly to the airport. Journey time is approximately 30 minutes and through ticketing is available from any rail station. The airport is also served by bus X5 which is operated by Watts Coaches on a Sunday with a two hourly frequency.

Coventry Airport

Coventry Airport is accessible from Coventry rail station by a scheduled bus service (No. 539). A combined discounted bus and rail ticket can be purchased for travel to the airport. For bus times call **0871 200 22 33** or visit **www.traveline.info.**

Durham Tees Valley Airport

Durham Tees Valley Airport is located 7 miles east of Darlington Rail station. For information about Durham Tees Valley Airport visit www.durhamteesvalleyairport.com.

From Darlington - Arriva service 12 operates half-hourly throughout the day Mondays to Saturdays and hourly early mornings, evenings and Sundays, from Parkgate outside Darlington Station direct to the airport site. Journey time is approximately 25 minutes.

Please note that when the service is operating two buses an hour that one bus an hour serves the airport terminal directly whilst the other terminates at the hotel on the airport site. The hotel is a 10-minute walk from the terminal building.

For more information please telephone Traveline on **0871 200 22 33** or visit **www.traveline.info**

East Midlands Airport

The most convenient way to get to East Midlands Airport is via East Midlands Parkway Station, served by East Midlands Trains.

A taxi transfer service operates between East Midlands Parkway and the Airport. To guarantee a great price, book your taxi in advance at www.eastmidlandstrains.co.uk/taxi and fill out a booking form. Please ensure that you book at least 12 hours or more in advance of the taxi being required.

Edinburgh Airport

There are two ways to get to Edinburgh Airport by rail and bus:

- If you are travelling from Fife, Dundee and other areas north, you should catch a train to Inverkeithing – from here a frequent bus service operates to Edinburgh Airport
- If you are travelling from other parts of Scotland, including the Glasgow area, you should catch a train to Haymarket or Edinburgh Waverley – a frequent bus service operates to Edinburgh Airport from both these stations

For full bus timetable information, call **0871 200 22 33**, or visit **www.travelinescotland.com**

Exeter International Airport

Stagecoach operates an hourly daytime service (Service Number 56) from Exeter St. Davids station forecourt direct to Exeter Airport. For more information call Traveline on **0871 200 22 33** or visit **www.traveline.info.**

Airport Links (continued)

Glasgow Airport

There are three ways to get to Glasgow Airport by rail and bus:

- If you are travelling from Ayrshire or Inverclyde, you should catch a train to Paisley Gilmour Street – a frequent bus service operates from here to Glasgow Airport
- If you are travelling from north west Glasgow, Milngavie, Dumbarton, Helensburgh and the West Highlands, you should catch a train to Partick – from here a frequent bus service operates to Glasgow Airport
- If you are travelling from other parts of Scotland, including Edinburgh and the central belt, you should catch a train to Glasgow Central or Glasgow Queen Street – a frequent bus service operates to Glasgow Airport from both these stations

For full bus timetable information, call **0871 200 22 33**, or visit **www.travelinescotland.com**

Leeds Bradford International Airport

Leeds Bradford International Airport is located to the north of the cities of Bradford and Leeds, to the south of Harrogate and to the west of York. For more information on Leeds Bradford International Airport visit **www.leedsbradfordairport.co.uk**

From Leeds - Centrebus Airport Direct 757, operates half hourly throughout the day Mondays to Saturdays (hourly early mornings, evenings and Sundays) every day from Stand S7 from outside Leeds Rail Station (Leeds Station Interchange). The journey time is approximately 40 minutes. Through ticketing is available.

From Bradford - a half hourly combined service, provided by Centrebus Airport Direct services 737 and 747, operates throughout the day from Bradford Interchange rail station. Airport Direct 747 also operates close to Bradford Forster Square rail station (hourly). The journey time from Bradford is approximately 40 minutes. Through ticketing is available with a PlusBus ticket.

From Harrogate - Airport Direct 737, operates hourly, every day from Harrogate Bus Station to the airport. The journey time from Harrogate is approximately 35 minutes.

From York - There is no bus service between York and the airport. If you are travelling from the North East, please travel via Leeds, purchasing a combined rail and bus travel ticket.

Centrebus Airport Direct services 737, 747 and 757 run alongside other local bus services which link to Leeds Bradford International Airport.

For more information please telephone Traveline on **0871 200 22 33** or visit **www.traveline.info**

Liverpool John Lennon Airport

Regular bus services operate between Liverpool John Lennon Airport and the Liverpool South Parkway station; journey time is 10 minutes. Liverpool South Parkway is served by direct services from North, South and East Liverpool, Leeds, York, Sheffield, Nottingham, Manchester, Warrington, Southport, Crewe, Stafford, Wolverhampton and Birmingham.

The airport is located to the south of the city centre. A direct bus service operates between Lime Street, Moorfields and James Street stations to the airport seven days a week. Buses run every 30 minutes between 0600 & 0100 hours from the Liverpool City Centre Stations to the Airport, and between 0515 and 0015 from the Airport to the Liverpool City Centre Stations. Journey time is approximately 45 minutes.

For further information please contact **0871 200 22 33**, or visit **www.traveline.info**.

London City Airport

London City Airport is located in London's Docklands, to the east of the capital. There are no National Rail services direct to the airport.

Access to the airport is available via the Docklands Light Railway to and from London City Airport Station which is located next to the terminal building. Between Central London and the airport, passengers can travel on the London Underground Jubilee Line and change at Canning Town for the Docklands Light Railway. Connections between National Rail and the Docklands Light Railway are available at Greenwich, Lewisham, Limehouse, Stratford and Woolwich Arsenal.

For further information on London City Airport telephone **020 7646 0088** or visit **www.londoncityairport.com**.

London Gatwick Airport

Gatwick has its own railway station underneath the South Terminal. Access to the North Terminal is via a free transit.

Airport to/from London

Gatwick Express operate a dedicated non-stop service every 15 minutes throughout most of the day between London Victoria and Gatwick Airport (See Table 186).

Southern provides frequent trains throughout the day and hourly throughout the night between London Victoria and Gatwick Airport (See Table 186).

First Capital Connect operate direct services throughout the day between London St Pancras International, Farringdon, City Thameslink, London Blackfriars, London Bridge and Gatwick Airport (generally every 15 mins, See Table 52), a reduced frequency operates throughout the night. The most convenient connection option is Victoria. Overnight and at weekends it may be necessary to use London bus or Tube services to travel to/from stations north of London Bridge. Your rail ticket will be valid.

Airport to/from Reading

First Great Western operate a direct rail service between Reading and Gatwick – (See Table 148). Customers using this route should allow at least 7 minutes at Reading to make a connection.

Other direct services to/from Airport

Southern also operates direct services to/from Hastings, Southampton, Portsmouth and intermediate stations on the South Coast (See Tables 186, 187, 188, 189) Clapham Jn and East Croydon (SeeTable 186).

First Great Western operate services from Wokingham, North Camp and Guildford (See Table 148).

Airport Links (continued)

First Capital Connect provide regular direct services from Gatwick Airport to St. Albans, Luton, Bedford, East Croydon, Haywards Heath and Brighton (See Table 52). At Luton Airport Parkway, Luton and Bedford, they also offer convenient connections with East Midlands Trains to Leicester, Derby, Nottingham and Sheffield (See Table 53).

London Heathrow Airport

Airport to/from Central London

Heathrow Express operates a direct high-speed rail service from the Airport to London Paddington. Stations are located in all Heathrow terminals - Heathrow Central (Terminals 1, 2 & 3), Terminal 4 and Terminal 5. Journey time is 15 minutes between Paddington and Terminals 1, 2 and 3, with a further 6 minutes to Terminal 5. Trains run every 15 minutes. A free transfer service operates to Terminal 4 from Heathrow Central, departing every 15 minutes and arriving in 4 minutes.

- 0510 to 2325 from Paddington
- 0507 to 2342 from Heathrow Terminal 5 (0503 to 2348 on Sundays)
- 0512 to 2348 from Heathrow Terminal 1, 2 and 3 (0508 to 2353 on Sundays)

For further details see Table 118.

Through tickets can be purchased from any National Rail or London Underground Station to the airport via Heathrow Express.

For further information visit **www.heathrowexpress.com**.

Heathrow Connect operates a local rail service every 30 minutes between Heathrow Central and London Paddington, calling at Hayes & Harlington, Southall, Hanwell, West Ealing and Ealing Broadway. For details see Table 117.

Through tickets are available from most stations.

The London Underground Piccadilly Line connects central London with all five terminals (Terminal 1/2/3, Terminal 4 and Terminal 5).

Through single and return tickets can be issued to customers travelling via a Rail terminus in Zone 1. Sample journey time from Piccadilly Circus to the Airport is approximately one hour.

Airport to/from Reading

RailAir coaches leave from Reading railway station every 20 minutes during the daytime on Mondays to Fridays (every 30 minutes early weekday mornings and evenings, on weekends and public holidays). The luxury, air-conditioned coaches run non-stop to Terminals 1, 2 and 3 in 40-50 minutes. On the return journey from Heathrow Airport they only pick up passengers at Heathrow Central Bus Station (stands one and two) and not the terminals. Customers travelling to/from Terminal 4 should use Heathrow Connect from Terminal 1.

Follow the RailAir signs from your platform at Reading station. You can buy your ticket in the RailAir lounge, or combined rail and coach tickets are also available from many stations. You should allow 15 minutes at Reading to transfer between train and coach.

For further information telephone **0118 957 9425** or visit **www.RailAir.com.**

Airport to/from Woking

Coaches leave at half-hourly intervals throughout most of the day to/from Terminal 5 and Heathrow Central Bus Station (for Terminals 1, 2 and 3) (see Table 158A).

Customers travelling to Heathrow should exit on platform 5 and the coach leaves from outside the station.

On arrival at Woking customers should allow at least 10 minutes to transfer to your train after the arrival of the coach at the station. Combined rail and coach tickets are available from most National Rail stations and from the Railair sales points at the airport. Tickets may also be booked at **www.nationalexpress.com** or by calling **08717 818 181**. For through trains and coach times, telephone **08457 48 49 50.** (calls may be recorded for training purposes)

Airport to/from Feltham

London Buses operates frequent bus services from Feltham Station to Heathrow Airport. Route 285 operates to Hatton Cross and Heathrow Central Bus Station for Terminals 1, 2 and 3. Buses operate every 10 minutes during the day, 15 minutes in the evenings and on Sundays and 30 minutes throughout the night.

Route 490 operates to Hatton Cross and Terminals 4 and 5. Buses operate every 12 minutes during the day, 20 minutes in the evenings and on Sundays.

Customers should allow 10 minutes at Feltham to transfer between train and bus from the station forecourt adjoining platform 1.

Other direct services to/from Airport

A coach service, Green Line 724, runs throughout the day between Heathrow, West Drayton, Uxbridge, Rickmansworth, Watford, St. Albans, Hatfield, Welwyn Garden City, Hertford and Harlow. Tickets can only be purchased on the coach. A frequent bus service (route 140) runs 24 hours between Hayes & Harlington and Heathrow Airport (Central Bus Station).

For further information telephone **0870 608 7261** (Green Line Travel Information)

London Luton Airport

A frequent dedicated shuttle bus links Luton Airport with Luton Airport Parkway station – journey time 5 minutes. Luton Airport Parkway is served by frequent First Capital Connect services direct to Bedford, Central London, South London, Gatwick Airport and Brighton – see Table 52 for details. East Midlands Trains services link Luton Airport Parkway with St Pancras International and Leicester, Derby, Nottingham and Sheffield – see Table 53 for details.

In addition a coach link operates between the Airport, Luton railway station and town centre and Milton Keynes Central railway station and town centre (see Table 65B for details).

Airport Links (continued)

London Stansted Airport

Stansted Airport has its own railway station right in the heart of the airport terminal building.

The Stansted Express is a dedicated rail service operating between London Liverpool Street and Stansted Airport station (See Table 22). Trains run every 15 minutes throughout the day, seven days per week.

CrossCountry operates an hourly express service seven days a week between Birmingham and Stansted Airport calling at Leicester, Peterborough and Cambridge – see Table 49 – offering connections with services to Yorkshire and the North East. Customers should be advised to arrive at the airport 1 hour 45 minutes prior to their latest check-in time.

London Southend Airport

Southend Airport is served by its own brand new station adjacent to the airport, operated by Stobart Group. The station is served by trains on the London Liverpool Street to Southend Victoria line, generally every 20 minutes (every 10 minutes at peak times). Journey times to and from London are 52-54 minutes off-peak (55-56 minutes at peak times) and 62 minutes on Sundays.

Manchester Airport

The airport railway station is right in the heart of the airport complex, linked by covered travellators. The station is served by up to 8 trains per hour from Manchester Piccadilly and direct services operate between Middlesbrough, Newcastle, York, Leeds, Huddersfield, Cleethorpes, Doncaster, Sheffield, Edinburgh, Glasgow, Carlisle, Barrow-in-Furness, Windermere, Lancaster, Preston, Liverpool and the Airport. Additional regular services operate during the day, to/from many stations which can be found under the entry for Manchester Airport in the index in this timetable.

Newcastle Airport

Tyne & Wear Metro trains operate every 12 - 15 minutes most of the day between Newcastle Central Station and Newcastle Airport providing links with Northern, East Coast, First TransPennine Express and CrossCountry services. The journey time is about 25 minutes.

Tyne & Wear Metro services also run to Sunderland Rail station, a journey time of about an hour providing connections with Northern and Grand Central services.

Through ticketing is available to Newcastle Airport via the Tyne & Wear Metro.

For information please telephone Traveline on **0871 200 22 33** or visit **www.traveline.info**

Prestwick International Airport

Prestwick International Airport has its own rail station, served by fast and frequent trains from Glasgow, Paisley, Ayr and intermediate stations.

See Table 221 for details.

Robin Hood Airport

Doncaster Airport or Doncaster Sheffield

Robin Hood Airport is situated 7 miles south of Doncaster. For more information on Robin Hood Airport visit **www.robinhoodairport.com**

From Doncaster - First service 91 runs half hourly throughout the day Mondays to Saturdays, hourly early mornings, evenings and Sundays from Doncaster Frenchgate Interchange, which is adjacent to Doncaster Rail station, direct to the airport. Journey time is approximately 25 minutes.

Through ticketing is available to Robin Hood Airport via service 91.

Service 91 runs alongside other local bus services which link to Robin Hood Airport, including service X19 from Barnsley.

For more information please telephone Traveline on **0871 200 22 33** or visit **www.traveline.info**

Southampton Airport

Southampton Airport (Parkway) station is adjacent to Southampton Airport.

South West Trains operate up to 3 trains per hour between London Waterloo, Winchester and Southampton Airport (Parkway) with up to 2 direct services to Bournemouth, Poole, Wareham and Weymouth and most intermediate stations (See Table 158).

CrossCountry services link Southampton Airport Parkway with Bournemouth, Reading, Oxford, Newcastle and Manchester (see Table 51).

On Saturdays Southern operate trains every two hours between Brighton, Worthing, Chichester, Havant, Cosham, Fareham and Southampton Airport, at other times use Southern's regular trains to Southampton Central and connecting train to Southampton Airport.

Station index and table numbers

10 Connection time
Ⓟ Station Car Park
🚲 Bicycle storage facility
◇ Seat reservations can be made at this station
⚠ Penalty Fare Schemes in operation on some or all services from this station
🚕 Taxi rank or cab office at station, or signposted and within 100 metres
ⓤ Unstaffed station
[ ] Station Operator Code

A

Abbey Wood [SE] Ⓟ 🚲 ◇ ⚠ 🚕 200
Aber [AW] Ⓟ 130
Abercynon [AW] ⓤ 130
Aberdare [AW] **3** Ⓟ ◇ 130
Aberdeen [SR] Ⓟ 🚲 ◇ 🚕
- Birmingham 51, 65
- Blackpool 65
- Bournemouth 51
- Bristol 51
- Cambridge 26
- Cardiff 51
- Carlisle 65
- Crewe 65, *Sleepers* 402
- Darlington 26
- Derby 51
- Doncaster 26
- Dundee 229
- Dyce 240
- Edinburgh 229
- Elgin 240
- Exeter 51
- Glasgow 229
- Grantham 26
- Inverkeithing 229
- Inverness 240
- Inverurie 240
- Kirkcaldy 229
- Kyle of Lochalsh 239
- Leeds 26
- Liverpool 65
- London 26, *Sleepers* 402
- Manchester 65
- Newcastle 26
- Newport (South Wales) 51
- Norwich 26
- Oxenholme Lake District 65
- Oxford 51
- Paignton 51
- Penzance 51
- Perth 229
- Peterborough 26
- Plymouth 51
- Preston 65, *Sleepers* 402
- Reading 51
- Sheffield 26
- Southampton 51
- Stirling 229
- Thurso 239
- Torquay 51
- Watford 65
- Wick 239
- York 26

Aberdour [SR] Ⓟ 🚲 242
Aberdovey [AW] 🚲 ⓤ 75
Abererch [AW] ⓤ 75
Abergavenny [AW] Ⓟ 🚲 ◇ 🚕 131
Abergele & Pensarn [AW] Ⓟ ⓤ 81
Aberystwyth [AW] Ⓟ ◇ 🚕 75
Accrington [NT] Ⓟ ◇ 🚕 41, 97
Achanalt [SR] Ⓟ 🚲 ⓤ 239
Achnasheen [SR] Ⓟ 🚲 ⓤ 239
Achnashellach [SR] Ⓟ 🚲 ⓤ 239
Acklington [NT] Ⓟ 🚲 ⓤ 48
Acle [LE] Ⓟ 🚲 ⓤ 15
Acocks Green [LM] Ⓟ ⚠ 71
Acton Bridge [LM] Ⓟ ⓤ 91
Acton Central [LO] 🚲 ⚠ 59
Acton Main Line [GW] ⚠ 117
Acton, South [LO] (see South Acton)
Adderley Park [LM] ◇ ⚠ 68
Addiewell [SR] Ⓟ 🚲 ⓤ 225
Addlestone [SW] ⚠ 🚕 149
Adisham [SE] Ⓟ ⚠ ⓤ 212
Adlington (Cheshire) [NT] Ⓟ ⓤ 84
Adlington (Lancashire) [NT] Ⓟ 82
Adwick [NT] Ⓟ 🚲 ⓤ 29, 31
Agbrigg [NT] (See Sandal & Agbrigg)
Aigburth [ME] Ⓟ ⚠ 103
Ainsdale [ME] Ⓟ ⚠ 103
Aintree [ME] Ⓟ ⚠ 103
Airbles [SR] Ⓟ 🚲 ⓤ 226
Airdrie [SR] Ⓟ 🚲 ◇ 🚕 226
Albany Park [SE] ◇ ⚠ 200
Albrighton [LM] Ⓟ ⓤ 74
Alderley Edge [NT] Ⓟ 🚲 84
Aldermaston [GW] Ⓟ ⓤ 116
Aldershot [SW] Ⓟ 🚲 ◇ ⚠ 🚕 149, 155
Aldrington [SN] ⚠ ⓤ 188
Alexandra Palace [FC] 🚲 ⚠ 🚕 24
Alexandra Parade [SR] 🚲 ⓤ 226
Alexandria [SR] Ⓟ 🚲 226
Alfreton [EM] Ⓟ ◇ ⚠ 🚕 34, 49, 53
Allens West [NT] 🚲 ⓤ 44
Alloa [SR] Ⓟ 🚲 ⓤ 230
Alness [SR] Ⓟ 🚲 ⓤ 239
Alnmouth for Alnwick [NT] Ⓟ 🚲 ◇ 26, 48, 51
Alresford [LE] 🚲 ⚠ 11
Alsager [EM] ⓤ 50, 67
Althorne [LE] Ⓟ 🚲 ⓤ 5
Althorpe [NT] ⓤ 29
Altnabreac [SR] 🚲 ⓤ 239
Alton [SW] Ⓟ 🚲 ◇ ⚠ 🚕 155
Altrincham [NT] Ⓟ 🚲 ◇ 🚕 88
Alvechurch [LM] Ⓟ ⚠ ⓤ 69
Ambergate [EM] Ⓟ ⓤ 56
Amberley [SN] 🚲 ⚠ ⓤ 188
Amersham [LT] Ⓟ 🚲 ⚠ 🚕 114
Ammanford [AW] ⓤ 129
Ancaster [EM] Ⓟ ⓤ 19
Anderston [SR] 🚲 226
Andover [SW] Ⓟ 🚲 ⚠ ◇ 🚕 160
Anerley [LO] 🚲 ⚠ 178
Angel Road [LE] ⚠ ⓤ 22
Angmering [SN] **3** Ⓟ 🚲 ◇ ⚠ 🚕 188
Annan [SR] Ⓟ 🚲 ⓤ 216
Anniesland [SR] 🚲 🚕 226, 232
Ansdell & Fairhaven [NT] ⓤ 97
Appleby [NT] Ⓟ ◇ 36
Appledore (Kent) [SN] ⓤ 189
Appleford [GW] ⓤ 116
Appley Bridge [NT] Ⓟ ⓤ 82
Apsley [LM] Ⓟ 66
Arbroath [SR] Ⓟ 🚲 ◇ 🚕 26, 51, 229, *Sleepers* 402
Ardgay [SR] Ⓟ 🚲 ⓤ 239
Ardlui [SR] 🚲 ⓤ 227, *Sleepers* 404
Ardrossan Harbour [SR] Ⓟ 🚲 ⓤ 221, *Ship* 221A
Ardrossan South Beach [SR] Ⓟ 🚲 221
Ardrossan Town [SR] 🚲 ⓤ 221
Ardwick [NT] ⓤ 78, 79
Argyle Street [SR] 226
Arisaig [SR] Ⓟ 🚲 ⓤ 227
Arlesey [FC] Ⓟ 🚲 ⚠ 25
Armadale [SR] Ⓟ 🚲 ⓤ 226
Armadale (Skye) *Ship* 227A
Armathwaite [NT] Ⓟ ⓤ 36
Arnside [TP] ⓤ 82
Arram [NT] ⓤ 43
Arrochar & Tarbet [SR] Ⓟ 🚲 ⓤ 227, *Sleepers* 404
Arundel [SN] Ⓟ 🚲 ◇ ⚠ 🚕 188
Ascot [SW] **3** Ⓟ 🚲 ◇ ⚠ 🚕 149
Ascott-under-Wychwood [GW] ⓤ 126
Ash [SW] Ⓟ 🚲 ◇ ⚠ 148, 149
Ash Vale [SW] 🚲 ◇ ⚠ 149, 155
Ashburys [NT] ⓤ 78, 79
Ashchurch for Tewkesbury [GW] Ⓟ 🚲 ⓤ 57
Ashfield [SR] 🚲 ⓤ 232
Ashford International [SE] Ⓟ 🚲 ◇ ⚠ 🚕 189, 194, 196, 207
Ashford (Surrey) [SW] Ⓟ 🚲 ◇ ⚠ 149
Ashley [NT] Ⓟ ⓤ 88
Ashtead [SN] Ⓟ 🚲 ◇ ⚠ 152, 182
Ashton-under-Lyne [NT] Ⓟ 🚲 39
Ashurst [SN] Ⓟ ⚠ ⓤ 184
Ashurst New Forest [SW] Ⓟ 🚲 ⚠ ⓤ 158
Ashwell & Morden [FC] Ⓟ 🚲 ⚠ 25
Askam [NT] Ⓟ ⓤ 100
Aslockton [EM] Ⓟ ⓤ 19
Aspatria [NT] Ⓟ ⓤ 100
Aspley Guise [LM] ⓤ 64
Aston [LM] ⚠ 69, 70
Atherstone [LM] Ⓟ ⓤ 67
Atherton [NT] Ⓟ 🚲 82
Attadale [SR] 🚲 ⓤ 239
Attenborough [EM] ⚠ ⓤ 56, 57

Station index and table numbers

■10 Connection time
Ⓟ Station Car Park
🚲 Bicycle storage facility
◇ Seat reservations can be made at this station
⚠ Penalty Fare Schemes in operation on some or all services from this station
🚕 Taxi rank or cab office at station, or signposted and within 100 metres
Ⓤ Unstaffed station
[ ] Station Operator Code

Attleborough [LE] Ⓟ Ⓤ 17
Auchinleck [SR] Ⓟ 🚲 Ⓤ 216
Audley End [LE] Ⓟ 🚲 ⚠ 🚕 22, 49
Aughton Park [ME] ⚠ 103
Aviemore [SR] Ⓟ 🚲 ◇ 🚕 229, *Sleepers* 403
Avoncliff [GW] Ⓤ 123
Avonmouth [GW] ■2 Ⓟ 🚲 Ⓤ 133
Axminster [SW] Ⓟ 🚲 ◇ 🚕 160
Aylesbury [CH] Ⓟ 🚲 ◇ ⚠ 🚕 114, 115
Aylesbury Vale Parkway [CH] Ⓟ 🚲 ◇ ⚠ 114
Aylesford [SE] ⚠ Ⓤ 208
Aylesham [SE] Ⓟ ◇ ⚠ 212
Ayr [SR] Ⓟ 🚲 ◇ 🚕 218, 221,221B

B

Bache [ME] Ⓤ 106
Backwell [GW] (see Nailsea)
Baglan [AW] Ⓟ 🚲 Ⓤ 128
Bagshot [SW] Ⓟ 🚲 ◇ ⚠ 149
Baildon [NT] Ⓟ Ⓤ 38
Baillieston [SR] 🚲 Ⓤ 220
Balcombe [SN] ◇ ⚠ 52, 186
Baldock [FC] Ⓟ ⚠ 25
Balham [SN] ■4 ◇ ⚠ 🚕 176, 177, 178, 182
Balloch [SR] 🚲 🚕 226
Balmossie [SR] 🚲 Ⓤ 229
Bamber Bridge [NT] Ⓟ Ⓤ 97
Bamford [NT] Ⓟ Ⓤ 78
Banavie [SR] Ⓟ 🚲 Ⓤ 227
Banbury [CH] Ⓟ 🚲 ◇ ⚠ 🚕 51, 71, 75, 115, 116
Bangor (Gwynedd) [AW] Ⓟ ◇ 🚕 65, 81, 131
Bank Hall [ME] ⚠ 103
Banstead [SN] ⚠ Ⓤ 182
Barassie [SR] Ⓟ 🚲 Ⓤ 221
Bardon Mill [NT] Ⓟ Ⓤ 48
Bare Lane [NT] Ⓟ Ⓤ 36, 98
Bargeddie [SR] Ⓟ 🚲 Ⓤ 220
Bargoed [AW] 🚕 130
Barking [CC] ◇ ⚠ 🚕 1, 62
Barlaston Orchard Place *Bus* 67
Barming [SE] Ⓟ ◇ ⚠ 196
Barmouth [AW] 🚲 75
Barnehurst [SE] ■4 Ⓟ ◇ ⚠ 🚕 200
Barnes [SW] 🚲 ◇ ⚠ 149
Barnes Bridge [SW] 🚲 ◇ ⚠ Ⓤ 149
Barnetby [TP] Ⓟ Ⓤ 27, 29, 30
Barnham [SN] Ⓟ 🚲 ◇ ⚠ 🚕 123, 188
Barnhill [SR] 🚲 Ⓤ 226
Barnsbury [LO] (see Caledonian Road)
Barnsley [NT] Ⓟ 🚲 ◇ 🚕 30, 34
Barnstaple [GW] Ⓟ 🚲 ◇ 🚕 136
Barnt Green [LM] Ⓟ ⚠ Ⓤ 69, 71
Barrhead [SR] Ⓟ 🚲 🚕 222
Barrhill [SR] Ⓟ 🚲 218
Barrow Haven [NT] Ⓤ 29
Barrow-in-Furness [TP] Ⓟ ◇ 🚕 65, 82, 100
Barrow Upon Soar [EM] ⚠ Ⓤ 53
Barry [AW] ■3 Ⓟ ◇ 🚕 130
Barry Docks [AW] Ⓤ 130
Barry Island [AW] Ⓤ 130
Barry Links [SR] 🚲 Ⓤ 229
Barton-on-Humber [NT] Ⓟ Ⓤ 29
Basildon [CC] 🚲 ◇ ⚠ 🚕 1
Basingstoke [SW] Ⓟ 🚲 ◇ ⚠ 🚕
- Aberdeen 51
- Bath 160
- Birmingham 51
- Bournemouth 158
- Bristol 160
- Brockenhurst 158
- Clapham Junction 155
- Coventry 51
- Crewe 51
- Derby 51
- Dorchester 158
- Dundee 51
- Eastleigh 158
- Edinburgh 51
- Exeter 160
- Fareham 158
- Farnborough 158
- Glasgow 51
- Leeds 51
- London 155
- Lymington 158
- Manchester 51
- Newcastle 51
- Oxford 51
- Poole 158
- Portsmouth 158
- Preston 51
- Reading 122
- Salisbury 160
- Sheffield 51
- Southampton 158
- Southampton Airport 158
- Stoke-on-Trent 51
- Surbiton 155
- Weymouth 158
- Weybridge 155
- Wimbledon 155
- Winchester 158
- Woking 155
- Wolverhampton 51
- Yeovil 160
- York 51

Bat & Ball [SE] Ⓟ ⚠ Ⓤ 52, 195
Bath Spa [GW] ■7 Ⓟ 🚲 ◇ ⚠ 🚕 123, 125, 132, 135, 160
Bathgate [SR] Ⓟ 🚲 ◇ 🚕 226
Batley [NT] Ⓟ 🚲 Ⓤ 39
Battersby [NT] Ⓤ 45
Battersea Park [SN] ■4 ◇ ⚠ 177, 178
Battle [SE] Ⓟ ◇ ⚠ 🚕 206
Battlesbridge [LE] Ⓟ 🚲 Ⓤ 5
Bayford [FC] Ⓟ ⚠ Ⓤ 24
Beaconsfield [CH] Ⓟ 🚲 ◇ ⚠ 🚕 115
Bearley [LM] Ⓟ ⚠ Ⓤ 115
Bearsden [SR] Ⓟ 🚲 🚕 226
Bearsted [SE] Ⓟ 🚲 ◇ ⚠ 196
Beasdale [SR] 🚲 Ⓤ 227
Beaulieu Road [SW] 🚲 ⚠ Ⓤ 158
Beauly [SR] Ⓟ 🚲 Ⓤ 239
Bebington [ME] Ⓟ ⚠ 🚕 106
Beccles [LE] Ⓟ 🚲 Ⓤ 13
Beckenham Hill [SE] 🚲 ◇ ⚠ 52, 195
Beckenham Junction [SE] ■4 Ⓟ 🚲 ◇ ⚠ 🚕 177, 195
Bedford [FC] ■7 Ⓟ 🚲 ◇ ⚠ 🚕
- Barnsley 53
- Bletchley 64
- Brighton 52, 186
- Chesterfield 53
- Derby 53
- Doncaster 53
- East Croydon 52
- Gatwick Airport 52, 186
- Haywards Heath 52, 186
- Herne Hill 52
- Hove 186
- Kettering 53
- Leeds 53
- Leicester 53
- London 52
- Luton 52
- Luton Airport Parkway 52
- Meadowhall 53
- Nottingham 53
- Redhill 52, 186
- St Albans 52
- Sheffield 53
- Sutton (Surrey) 52
- Wakefield 53
- Wellingborough 53
- Wimbledon 52
- York 53

Bedford St Johns [LM] Ⓤ 64
Bedhampton [SW] 🚲 ◇ ⚠ 156, 157, 188
Bedminster [GW] Ⓤ 134
Bedworth [LM] Ⓟ Ⓤ 67
Bedwyn [GW] Ⓟ 🚲 Ⓤ 116
Beeston [EM] Ⓟ 🚲 ◇ ⚠ 53, 56, 57
Bekesbourne [SE] Ⓟ ⚠ Ⓤ 212
Belfast
- Port of *Ship* (via Ayr/Cairnryan) 221B

Belle Vue [NT] Ⓤ 78

Station index and table numbers

[10] Connection time
Ⓟ Station Car Park
🚲 Bicycle storage facility
◇ Seat reservations can be made at this station
⚠ Penalty Fare Schemes in operation on some or all services from this station
🚕 Taxi rank or cab office at station, or signposted and within 100 metres
Ⓤ Unstaffed station
[ ] Station Operator Code

Bellgrove [SR] 🚲 Ⓤ 226
Bellingham [SE] 🚲 ◇ ⚠ 52, 195
Bellshill [SR] Ⓟ 🚲 225, 226
Belmont [SN] ⚠ Ⓤ 182
Belper [EM] ⚠ Ⓤ 56
Beltring [SE] ⚠ Ⓤ 208
Belvedere [SE] ◇ ⚠ 200
Bempton [NT] Ⓤ 43
Ben Rhydding [NT] Ⓟ Ⓤ 38
Benfleet [CC] Ⓟ 🚲 ◇ ⚠ 🚕 1
Bentham [NT] Ⓟ Ⓤ 36
Bentley [SW] Ⓟ 🚲 ◇ ⚠ 155
Bentley (S. Yorks.) [NT] Ⓟ 🚲 Ⓤ 29, 31
Bere Alston [GW] Ⓟ Ⓤ 139
Bere Ferrers [GW] Ⓟ 🚲 Ⓤ 139
Berkhamsted [LM] Ⓟ 🚲 ◇ ⚠ 🚕 66, 176
Berkswell [LM] Ⓟ 🚲 ⚠ 68
Berney Arms [LE] 🚲 Ⓤ 15
Berry Brow [NT] Ⓤ 34
Berrylands [SW] Ⓟ 🚲 ◇ ⚠ 152
Berwick [SN] Ⓟ 🚲 ◇ ⚠ 189
Berwick-upon-Tweed [GR] Ⓟ 🚲 ◇ 🚕 26, 26K, 51
Bescar Lane [NT] Ⓤ 82
Bescot Stadium [LM] Ⓟ ◇ ⚠ 70
Betchworth [GW] Ⓤ 148
Bethnal Green [LE] 🚲 ⚠ Ⓤ 20, 21, 22
Betws-y-Coed [AW] Ⓤ 102
Beverley [NT] Ⓟ ◇ 🚕 43
Bexhill [SN] [4] ◇ ⚠ 🚕 189
Bexley [SE] Ⓟ ◇ ⚠ 🚕 200
Bexleyheath [SE] Ⓟ 🚲 ◇ ⚠ 🚕 200
Bicester North [CH] [3] Ⓟ 🚲 ◇ ⚠ 🚕 115
Bicester Town [CH] Ⓟ 🚲 Ⓤ 116
Bickley [SE] [4] Ⓟ ◇ ⚠ 52, 195
Bidston [ME] Ⓟ ⚠ 101, 106
Biggleswade [FC] Ⓟ 🚲 ⚠ 25
Bilbrook [LM] Ⓤ 74
Billericay [LE] Ⓟ 🚲 ⚠ 🚕 5
Billingham [NT] 🚲 🚕 Ⓤ 44
Billingshurst [SN] Ⓟ 🚲 ◇ ⚠ 🚕 188
Bingham [EM] Ⓟ Ⓤ 19
Bingley [NT] Ⓟ 🚲 ◇ 36
Birchgrove [AW] Ⓤ 130
Birchington-on-Sea [SE] Ⓟ 🚲 ◇ ⚠ 🚕 194, 212
Birchwood [TP] Ⓟ 🚲 🚕 39, 89
Birkbeck [SN] ⚠ Ⓤ 177
Birkdale [ME] Ⓟ ⚠ 103
Birkenhead Central [ME] ⚠ 106
Birkenhead North [ME] ⚠ 106
Birkenhead Park [ME] ⚠ 106
Birmingham International [VT] (for National Exhibition Centre and Airport) Ⓟ 🚲 ◇ ⚠ 🚕
Aberdeen 65
Aberystwyth 75
Banbury 71
Bangor (Gwynedd) 65, 81
Basingstoke 51
Birmingham 68
Blackpool 65
Bournemouth 51
Carlisle 65
Chester 65, 75, 81
Clapham Junction 66
Coventry 68
Crewe 65, 81
Derby 51
Dundee 65
East Croydon 66
Edinburgh 51, 65
Glasgow 51, 65
Holyhead 65, 75, 81
Inverness 65
Leamington Spa 71
Leeds 51
Liverpool 65
London 66, 116
Manchester 65
Manchester Airport 65
Milton Keynes Central 66
Newcastle 51
Northampton 66
Nottingham 51
Oxenholme Lake District 65
Oxford 51
Preston 65
Pwllheli 75
Reading 51
Rugby 66
Sheffield 51
Shrewsbury 75
Southampton 51
Stafford 68
Stoke-on-Trent 65
Watford 66
Wolverhampton 68
Wrexham 75
York 51
Birmingham
Moor Street [CH] ◇ ⚠ 🚕
New Street [NR] [12] 🚲 ◇ ⚠ 🚕
Snow Hill [LM] Ⓟ ◇ ⚠
Aberdeen 51, 65
Aberystwyth 75
Banbury 71
Bangor (Gwynedd) 65, 81
Barmouth 75
Barrow-in-Furness 65
Basingstoke 51
Birmingham International 68
Blackpool 65
Bournemouth 51
Bristol 57
Bromsgrove 71
Burton-on-Trent 57
Cambridge 49
Cardiff 57
Carlisle 65
Cheltenham Spa 57
Chester 75, 81
Clapham Junction 66
Coventry 68
Crewe 65
Darlington 51
Derby 57
Douglas (IOM) 98A
Dundee 51, 65
East Croydon 66
Edinburgh 51, 65
Ely 49
Exeter 51
Glasgow 51, 65
Gloucester 57
Hereford 71
Holyhead 65, 81
Inverness 65
Kidderminster 71
Leamington Spa 71
Leeds 51
Leicester 57
Lichfield 69
Liverpool 65, 91
Llandudno 81
London 66, 115, 116
Longbridge 69
Manchester 65, 84
Manchester Airport 65, 84
Milton Keynes Central 66
Newcastle 51
Newport (South Wales) 57
Northampton 66
Norwich 49
Nottingham 57
Nuneaton 57
Oxenholme Lake District 65
Oxford 116
Paignton 135
Penzance 135
Peterborough 49
Plymouth 135
Preston 65
Reading 116
Redditch 69
Rugby 66
Rugeley 70
Sheffield 51
Shrewsbury 74
Solihull 71
Southampton 51
Stafford 68
Stansted Airport 49
Stockport 65
Stoke-on-Trent 65
Stourbridge 71
Stratford-upon-Avon 71
Telford 74
Torquay 135
Walsall 70
Warrington 65
Warwick 71
Watford 66
Wigan 65
Wolverhampton 68
Worcester 71
Wrexham 75

[10] Connection time
Ⓟ Station Car Park
🚲 Bicycle storage facility
◇ Seat reservations can be made at this station
⚠ Penalty Fare Schemes in operation on some or all services from this station
🚕 Taxi rank or cab office at station, or signposted and within 100 metres
Ⓤ Unstaffed station
[ ] Station Operator Code

Station index and table numbers

York 51
Birnam [SR] (see Dunkeld)
Bishop Auckland [NT] Ⓟ 🚕 Ⓤ 44
Bishopbriggs [SR] 🚲 228, 230
Bishops Lydeard Hithermead *Bus* 135E
Bishops Stortford [LE] Ⓟ 🚲 ◇ ⚠ 🚕 22
Bishopstone [SN] Ⓤ 189
Bishopton [SR] Ⓟ 🚲 219
Bitterne [SW] Ⓟ 🚲 ⚠ Ⓤ 165
Blackburn [NT] Ⓟ ◇ 🚕 41, 94, 97
Blackfriars [FC] (see London)
Blackheath [SE] [4] ◇ ⚠ 🚕 200
Blackhorse Road [LT] ⚠ 62
Blackpool
North [NT] Ⓟ ◇ 🚕
Pleasure Beach [NT] Ⓤ
South [NT] 🚕 Ⓤ
Birmingham 65
Birmingham International 65
Blackburn 97
Bolton 82
Bradford 41
Burnley 97
Colne 97
Coventry 65
Crewe 65
Lancaster 65
Leeds 41
Liverpool 65, 90
London 65
Manchester 82
Manchester Airport 82
Milton Keynes Central 65
Preston 97
Rugby 65
St Helens 90
Stafford 65
Stockport 82
Warrington 65
Watford 65
Wigan 65
Wolverhampton 65
York 41
Blackridge [SR] Ⓟ 🚲 Ⓤ 226
Blackrod [NT] Ⓤ 82
Blackwater [GW] Ⓟ Ⓤ 148
Blaenau Ffestiniog [AW] Ⓤ 102
Blair Atholl [SR] Ⓟ 🚲 229, *Sleepers* 403
Blairhill [SR] Ⓟ 🚲 🚕 226
Blake Street [LM] Ⓟ ⚠ 69
Blakedown [LM] Ⓟ ⚠ Ⓤ 71
Blantyre [SR] Ⓟ 🚲 226
Blaydon [NT] Ⓤ 48
Bleasby [EM] Ⓤ 27
Bledlow, Village Hall *Bus* 115A
Bletchley [LM] Ⓟ 🚲 ◇ ⚠ 🚕 64, 66, 176
Bloxwich [LM] ⚠ Ⓤ 70
Bloxwich North [LM] ⚠ Ⓤ 70
Bluewater [SE] (see Greenhithe for Bluewater)
Blundellsands & Crosby [ME] Ⓟ ⚠ 103
Blythe Bridge [EM] Ⓟ Ⓤ 50
Bodmin Mount Folly *Bus* 135C
Bodmin Parkway [GW] Ⓟ 🚲 ◇ 🚕 51, 135, *Bus* 135C, *Sleepers* 406
Bodorgan [AW] Ⓟ Ⓤ 81
Bognor Regis [SN] Ⓟ 🚲 ◇ ⚠ 🚕 188
Bogston [SR] 🚲 Ⓤ 219
Bolton [NT] 🚲 ◇ 🚕 65, 82, 94
Bolton-upon-Dearne [NT] Ⓟ Ⓤ 31
Bookham [SW] Ⓟ 🚲 ◇ ⚠ 🚕 152, 182
Bootle [NT] Ⓤ 100
Bootle New Strand [ME] ⚠ 🚕 103
Bootle Oriel Road [ME] Ⓟ ⚠ 103
Bordesley [LM] ⚠ Ⓤ 71
Borehamwood [FC] (see Elstree)
Borough Green & Wrotham [SE] Ⓟ ◇ ⚠ 🚕 196
Borth [AW] Ⓟ Ⓤ 75
Bosham [SN] 🚲 ⚠ 188
Boston [EM] Ⓟ 🚲 ◇ 🚕 19
Botley [SW] Ⓟ 🚲 ⚠ Ⓤ 158
Bottesford [EM] Ⓟ Ⓤ 19
Bourne End [GW] [3] Ⓟ 🚲 ⚠ 120
Bournemouth [SW] Ⓟ 🚲 ◇ ⚠ 🚕 51, 158
Bournville [LM] ⚠ 69
Bow Brickhill [LM] Ⓤ 64
Bowes Park [FC] ⚠ 24
Bowling [SR] Ⓟ 🚲 Ⓤ 226
Box Hill & Westhumble [SN] Ⓟ ⚠ Ⓤ 152, 182
Bracknell [SW] Ⓟ 🚲 ◇ ⚠ 🚕 149
Bradford
Forster Square [NT] Ⓟ 🚲 ◇ 🚕
Interchange [NT] 🚲 ◇ 🚕
Blackpool 41
Blackburn 41
Brighouse 41
Cambridge 26
Carlisle 36
Grantham 26
Halifax 41
Huddersfield 41
Ilkley 38
Lancaster 36
Leeds 37
London 26
Manchester 41
Morecambe 36
Newark 26
Norwich 26
Peterborough 26
Preston 41
Retford 26
Rochdale 41
Selby 40
Settle 36
Shipley 37
Skipton 36
York 40
Bradford-on-Avon [GW] Ⓟ 🚲 ◇ 🚕 123, 160
Brading [IL] Ⓟ Ⓤ 167
Braintree [LE] Ⓟ 🚲 ⚠ 🚕 11
Braintree Freeport [LE] 🚲 ⚠ Ⓤ 11
Bramhall [NT] 84
Bramley (Hants) [GW] ⚠ 122
Bramley [NT] Ⓟ Ⓤ 37, 41
Brampton (Cumbria) [NT] Ⓟ Ⓤ 48
Brampton (Suffolk) [LE] Ⓤ 13
Branchton [SR] Ⓟ 🚲 Ⓤ 219
Brandon [LE] Ⓟ Ⓤ 17
Branksome [SW] Ⓟ 🚲 ◇ ⚠ 158
Braystones [NT] Ⓤ 100
Bredbury [NT] Ⓟ 🚲 78
Breich [SR] 🚲 Ⓤ 225
Brentford [SW] Ⓟ 🚲 ◇ 🚕 149
Brentwood [LE] Ⓟ 🚲 ⚠ 🚕 5
Bricket Wood [LM] Ⓤ 61
Bridge of Allan [SR] Ⓟ 🚲 Ⓤ 229,230
Bridge of Orchy [SR] Ⓟ 🚲 Ⓤ 227, *Sleepers* 404
Bridgend [AW] Ⓟ 🚲 ◇ 🚕 125, 128, 130
Bridgeton [SR] 🚲 🚕 226
Bridgwater [GW] Ⓟ ◇ 134, 135
Bridlington [NT] Ⓟ 🚲 ◇ 🚕 43
Brierfield [NT] Ⓟ Ⓤ 97
Brigg [NT] Ⓟ Ⓤ 30
Brighouse [NT] Ⓟ Ⓤ 26, 32, 41
Brighton [SN] [10] Ⓟ 🚲 ◇ ⚠ 🚕
Ashford International 189
Bath Spa 123
Bedford 52
Bognor Regis 188
Bristol 123
Cardiff 123
Chichester 188
Eastbourne 189
East Croydon 176, 186
Elstree & Borehamwood 52
Gatwick Airport 186
Hastings 189
Haywards Heath 186
Hove 188
Isle of Wight 167
Kensington (Olympia) 176
Lewes 189
Littlehampton 188
London 186
Luton 52
Luton Airport Parkway 52
Mill Hill Broadway 52
Milton Keynes Central 176
Portsmouth 188

Station index and table numbers

[10] Connection time
Ⓟ Station Car Park
🚲 Bicycle storage facility
◇ Seat reservations can be made at this station
⚠ Penalty Fare Schemes in operation on some or all services from this station
🚕 Taxi rank or cab office at station, or signposted and within 100 metres
Ⓤ Unstaffed station
[ ] Station Operator Code

Radlett 52
Redhill 186
St Albans 52
Salisbury 123
Seaford 189
Southampton Central 188
Watford Junction 176
West Hampstead Thameslink 52
Worthing 188
Brimsdown [LE] ⚠ 22
Brinnington [NT] 78
Bristol International Airport *Bus* 🚕 125B
Bristol
Parkway [GW] [7] Ⓟ 🚲 ◇ ⚠ 🚕
Temple Meads [GW] [10] Ⓟ 🚲 ◇ ⚠ 🚕
Aberdeen 51
Bath Spa 132
Birmingham 57
Brighton 123
Bristol International Airport *Bus* 125B
Cardiff 132
Carlisle 51
Cheltenham Spa 57
Crewe 51
Darlington 51
Derby 57
Dundee 51
Edinburgh 51
Exeter 135
Glasgow 51
Gloucester 134
Leeds 51
London 125, 160
Manchester 51
Newcastle 51
Newport (South Wales) 132
Nottingham 57
Paignton 135
Penzance 135
Plymouth 135
Portsmouth 123
Preston 51
Reading 125
Salisbury 123
Severn Beach 133
Sheffield 51
Slough 125
Southampton Central 123
Stoke-on-Trent 51
Swindon 125
Taunton 134
Temple Meads/Parkway 134
Torquay 135
Westbury 123
Weston-super-Mare 134
Weymouth 123
Wolverhampton 51
Worcester 57
York 51
Brithdir [AW] Ⓤ 130
British Steel Redcar [NT] Ⓤ 44
Briton Ferry [AW] Ⓟ Ⓤ 128
Brixton [SE] ◇ ⚠ 195
Broad Green [NT] 90
Broadbottom [NT] Ⓟ 79
Broadstairs [SE] Ⓟ 🚲 ◇ 🚕 194, 207, 212
Brockenhurst [SW] [3] Ⓟ 🚲 ◇ ⚠ 🚕 51, 158
Brockholes [NT] Ⓤ 34
Brockley [LO] 🚲 ⚠ 178
Brodick *Ship* 221A
Bromborough [ME] Ⓟ 🚲 ⚠ 106
Bromborough Rake [ME] ⚠ 106
Bromley Cross [NT] Ⓟ 🚲 94
Bromley North [SE] Ⓟ ◇ ⚠ 🚕 204
Bromley South [SE] [4] ◇ ⚠ 🚕 52, 195, 196, 212
Bromsgrove [LM] Ⓟ Ⓤ 69, 71
Brondesbury [LO] 🚲 ⚠ 59
Brondesbury Park [LO] 🚲 ⚠ 59
Brookmans Park [FC] Ⓟ 🚲 ⚠ 24
Brookwood [SW] [3] Ⓟ 🚲 ◇ ⚠ 🚕 155
Broome [AW] Ⓤ 129
Broomfleet [NT] Ⓟ Ⓤ 29
Brora [SR] Ⓟ 🚲 Ⓤ 239
Brough [TP] Ⓟ 🚲 ◇ 🚕 29, 39
Broughty Ferry [SR] 🚲 Ⓤ 229
Broxbourne [LE] [3] Ⓟ 🚲 ⚠ 🚕 22
Bruce Grove [LE] ⚠ 21
Brundall [LE] Ⓟ 🚲 15
Brundall Gardens [LE] 🚲 Ⓤ 15
Brunstane [SR] 🚲 Ⓤ 242
Brunswick [ME] Ⓟ 🚲 103
Bruton [GW] Ⓟ Ⓤ 123
Bryn [NT] Ⓤ 90
Buckenham [LE] 🚲 Ⓤ 15
Buckingham (Tesco) *Bus* 65A
Buckley [AW] Ⓟ Ⓤ 101
Bucknell [AW] Ⓤ 129
Buckshaw Parkway [NT] Ⓟ 82
Bude Strand *Bus* 135D
Bugle [GW] 🚲 Ⓤ 142
Builth Road [AW] Ⓤ 129
Bulwell [EM] Ⓟ Ⓤ 55
Bures [LE] 🚲 Ⓤ 10
Burgess Hill [SN] [4] Ⓟ 🚲 ◇ ⚠ 🚕 52, 186, 188
Burley Park [NT] Ⓟ Ⓤ 35
Burley-in-Wharfedale [NT] Ⓟ 🚲 Ⓤ 38
Burnage [NT] 85
Burneside [TP] Ⓤ 83
Burnham [GW] Ⓟ 🚲 ⚠ 🚕 117
Burnham-on-Crouch [LE] Ⓟ 🚲 5
Burnham-on-Sea [GW] (see Highbridge)
Burnley Barracks [NT] Ⓤ 97
Burnley Central [NT] Ⓟ ◇ 97
Burnley Manchester Road [NT] Ⓟ Ⓤ 41, 97
Burnside [SR] 🚲 223
Burntisland [SR] Ⓟ 🚲 242
Burry Port [AW] (see Pembrey)
Burscough Bridge [NT] Ⓟ 82
Burscough Junction [NT] Ⓟ Ⓤ 99
Bursledon [SW] Ⓟ 🚲 ⚠ Ⓤ 165
Burton Joyce [EM] Ⓤ 27
Burton-on-Trent [EM] Ⓟ ◇ 🚕 51, 57
Bury St Edmunds [LE] Ⓟ 🚲 ◇ 🚕 14
Busby [SR] Ⓟ 🚲 Ⓤ 222
Bushey [LO] Ⓟ 🚲 ⚠ 🚕 60, 66
Bush Hill Park [LE] Ⓟ ⚠ 🚕 21
Butlers Lane [LM] ⚠ 69
Buxted [SN] Ⓟ 🚲 ⚠ 184
Buxton [NT] Ⓟ ◇ 82, 86
Byfleet & New Haw [SW] 🚲 ◇ ⚠ 🚕 149, 155
Bynea [AW] Ⓤ 129

C

Cadoxton [AW] Ⓟ ◇ 130
Caerau Park *Bus* 128A
Caerau (Square) *Bus* 128A
Caergwrle [AW] Ⓤ 101
Caerphilly [AW] [3] Ⓟ 🚲 ◇ 🚕 130
Caersws [AW] Ⓟ Ⓤ 75
Cairnryan (Loch Ryan Port) *Ship* 221B
Caldercruix [SR] Ⓟ 🚲 Ⓤ 226
Caldicot [AW] Ⓤ 132
Caledonian Rd & Barnsbury [LO] ⚠ 59
Calstock [GW] Ⓟ 🚲 Ⓤ 139
Cam & Dursley [GW] Ⓟ 🚲 Ⓤ 134
Camberley [SW] Ⓟ 🚲 ◇ ⚠ 🚕 149
Camborne [GW] Ⓟ 🚲 ◇ 🚕 51, 135, *Sleepers* 406
Cambridge [LE] Ⓟ 🚲 ◇ ⚠ 🚕
Birmingham 49
Bishops Stortford 22
Broxbourne 22
Doncaster 26
Edinburgh 26
Ely 17
Finsbury Park 25
Grantham 26
Harlow 22
Harwich International 14
Hitchin 25
Ipswich 14
Kings Lynn 17
Leeds 26
Leicester 49

Station index and table numbers

- **10** Connection time
- ℗ Station Car Park
- 🚲 Bicycle storage facility
- ◇ Seat reservations can be made at this station
- ⚠ Penalty Fare Schemes in operation on some or all services from this station
- 🚕 Taxi rank or cab office at station, or signposted and within 100 metres
- ⓤ Unstaffed station
- [ ] Station Operator Code

Liverpool 49
London
ings Cross 17, 25
iverpool St. 17, 22
Manchester 49
Newark 26
Newcastle 26
Norwich 17
Nottingham 49
Peterborough 17
Retford 26
Royston 25
Sheffield 49
Stansted Airport 22
Stevenage 25
Stockport 49
Tottenham Hale 22
Welwyn Garden City 25
York 26
Cambridge Heath [LE] ⚠ ⓤ 21
Cambuslang [SR] 🚲 🚕 225, 226
Camden Road [LO] 🚲 ⚠ 59
Camelon [SR] ℗ 🚲 ⓤ 224, 230
Canada Water [LT] 178
Canley [LM] ℗ 🚲 ⚠ 68
Canna *Ship* 227A
Cannock [LM] ℗ ⚠ ⓤ 70
Cannon Street [NR] (see London)
Canonbury [LO] ⚠ 59,178
Canterbury East [SE] **4** ℗ 🚲 ◇ ⚠ 🚕 212
Canterbury West [SE] **4** ℗ 🚲 ◇ ⚠ 🚕 194, 207
Cantley [LE] ℗ 🚲 ⓤ 15
Capenhurst [ME] ℗ ⓤ 106
Carbis Bay [GW] ℗ ⓤ 144
Cardenden [SR] ℗ 🚲 ⓤ 242
Cardiff
Bay [AW] ⓤ
Central [AW] **7** ℗ 🚲 ◇ 🚕
Queen Street [AW] **3** ◇
Aberdeen 51
Aberystwyth 75
Bangor (Gwynedd) 81, 131
Barry Island 130
Bath Spa 132
Birmingham 57
Bridgend 128, 130
Brighton 123
Bristol 132
Cardiff International Airport *Bus* 125C (also see Rhoose)
Cheltenham Spa 57
Chester 75, 81, 131
Coryton 130
Crewe 131
Darlington 51
Derby 57
Dundee 51
Durham 51
Ebbw Vale Parkway 127
Edinburgh 51
Exeter 135
Fishguard Harbour 128
Gloucester 132
Hereford 131
Holyhead 81, 131
Leeds 51
Llandudno Junction 81, 131
London 125
Maesteg 128
Manchester 131
Merthyr Tydfil 130
Milford Haven 128
Newcastle 51
Newport (South Wales) 132
Nottingham 57
Paignton 135
Penzance 135
Plymouth 135
Pontypridd 130
Portsmouth 123
Reading 125
Rhoose 130
Rhymney 130
Rosslare Harbour 128
Sheffield 51
Shrewsbury 131
Slough 125
Southampton Central 123
Swansea 128
Swindon 125
Taunton 132, 134
Torquay 135
Treherbert 130
Weymouth 123
Worcester 57
Wrexham 75
York 51
Cardiff International Airport *Bus* 🚕 125C
Cardiff International Airport [AW] (see Rhoose)
Cardonald [SR] 🚲 219
Cardross [SR] ℗ 🚲 226
Carfin [SR] ℗ 🚲 ⓤ 225
Cark [NT] ℗ ⓤ 82
Carlisle [VT] **8** ℗ 🚲 ◇ 🚕
Aberdeen 65
Barrow-in-Furness 100
Birmingham 65
Blackpool 36, 65
Bolton 65
Bournemouth 51
Bradford 36
Bristol 51
Coventry 65
Crewe 65
Dumfries 216
Dundee 65
Exeter 51
Edinburgh 65
Glasgow 65, 216
Haymarket 65
Hexham 48
Inverness 65
Kilmarnock 216
Lancaster 65
Leeds 36
Liverpool 65
London 65, *Sleepers* 400, 401
Manchester 65
Manchester Airport 65
Milton Keynes Central 65
Motherwell 65
Newcastle 48
Oxenholme Lake District 65
Oxford 51
Penzance 51
Perth 65
Plymouth 51
Preston 65
Reading 51
Rugby 65
Settle 36
Skipton 36
Southampton 51
Stafford 65
Warrington 65
Watford 65, *Sleepers* 400, 401
Whitehaven 100
Wigan 65
Wolverhampton 65
Workington 100
Carlton [EM] ℗ ⓤ 27
Carluke [SR] ℗ 🚲 226
Carmarthen [AW] ℗ 🚲 ◇ ⚠ 🚕 128
Carmyle [SR] 🚲 ⓤ 220
Carnforth [TP] ℗ ⓤ 36, 82
Carnoustie [SR] ℗ 🚲 🚕 ⓤ 229, *Sleepers* 402
Carntyne [SR] 🚲 ⓤ 226
Carpenders Park [LO] 🚲 ⚠ 🚕 60
Carrbridge [SR] ℗ 🚲 ⓤ 229
Carshalton [SN] ℗ ◇ ⚠ 52, 179, 182
Carshalton Beeches [SN] ◇ ⚠ 182
Carstairs [SR] 🚲 65, 225, *Sleepers* 401
Cartsdyke [SR] 🚲 219
Castle Bar Park [GW] 117
Castle Cary [GW] ℗ ◇ 🚕 123, 135
Castlebay *Ship* 227C
Castleford [NT] ℗ 🚕 ⓤ 32, 34
Castleton (Greater Manchester) **[NT]** ℗ ⓤ 41
Castleton Moor [NT] ℗ ⓤ 45
Caterham [SN] 🚲 ◇ ⚠ 🚕 181
Catford [SE] 🚲 ◇ ⚠ 52, 195
Catford Bridge [SE] 🚲 ◇ ⚠ 203
Cathays [AW] ⓤ 130
Cathcart [SR] 🚲 223
Cattal [NT] 🚲 ⓤ 35
Catterick Camp Centre *Bus* 26H
Catterick Garrison Kemmel *Bus* 26H
Catterick Garrison Tesco *Bus* 26H

Station index and table numbers

[10] Connection time
Ⓟ Station Car Park
🚲 Bicycle storage facility
◇ Seat reservations can be made at this station
⚠ Penalty Fare Schemes in operation on some or all services from this station
🚕 Taxi rank or cab office at station, or signposted and within 100 metres
Ⓤ Unstaffed station
[ ] Station Operator Code

Causeland [GW] Ⓤ 140
Cefn-y-Bedd [AW] Ⓟ 101
Chadwell Heath [LE] 🚲 ⚠ 5
Chafford Hundred [CC] Ⓟ 🚲 ◇ ⚠ 1
Chalfont & Latimer [LT] Ⓟ 🚲 ⚠ 🚕 114
Chalkwell [CC] 🚲 ◇ ⚠ 🚕 1
Chandlers Ford [SW] Ⓟ 🚲 ◇ ⚠ 158
Chapel-en-le-Frith [NT] Ⓟ Ⓤ 86
Chapelton [GW] Ⓟ Ⓤ 136
Chapeltown [NT] Ⓤ 34
Chappel & Wakes Colne [LE] 🚲 Ⓤ 10
Charing [SE] Ⓟ ◇ ⚠ 196
Charing Cross (Glasgow) **[SR]** 🚲 226
Charing Cross [NR] (see London)
Charlbury [GW] Ⓟ 🚲 126
Charlton [SE] [4] ◇ ⚠ 200
Chartham [SE] ⚠ Ⓤ 207
Chassen Road [NT] 89
Chatelherault [SR] 🚲 Ⓤ 226
Chatham [SE] [4] Ⓟ ◇ ⚠ 🚕 194, 200, 212
Chathill [NT] Ⓟ Ⓤ 48
Cheadle Hulme [NT] Ⓟ 🚲 84
Cheam [SN] Ⓟ 🚲 ◇ ⚠ 🚕 182
Cheddington [LM] Ⓟ 66
Chelford [NT] Ⓟ 🚲 Ⓤ 84
Chelmsford [LE] [3] Ⓟ 🚲 ◇ ⚠ 🚕 11
Chelsfield [SE] [3] Ⓟ ◇ ⚠ 🚕 204
Cheltenham Spa [GW] Ⓟ 🚲 ◇ 🚕 51, 57, 125
Chepstow [AW] Ⓟ 132
Cherry Tree [NT] Ⓟ Ⓤ 97
Chertsey [SW] Ⓟ 🚲 ◇ ⚠ 🚕 149
Cheshunt [LE] Ⓟ 🚲 ⚠ 🚕 21, 22
Chessington North [SW] Ⓟ 🚲 ◇ ⚠ 🚕 152
Chessington South [SW] Ⓟ 🚲 ◇ ⚠ 152
Chester [AW] Ⓟ ◇ 🚕
Altrincham 88
Bangor (Gwynedd) 81
Birmingham 75, 81
Cardiff 75, 81, 131
Crewe 81
Hereford 131
Holyhead 81
Liverpool 106
Llandudno 81
Llandudno Junction 81
London 65
Manchester 81, 88
Newport (South Wales) 131
Northwich 88
Rhyl 81
Runcorn East 81
Shrewsbury 75, 131
Stafford 65
Stockport 88
Warrington 81
Wolverhampton 65, 75
Wrexham 75
Chester Road [LM] Ⓟ ⚠ 69
Chesterfield [EM] Ⓟ 🚲 ◇ ⚠ 🚕 34, 49, 51, 53
Chester-le-Street [NT] Ⓟ 🚲 ◇ 🚕 Ⓤ 26, 39, 44, 51
Chestfield & Swalecliffe [SE] ◇ ⚠ 212
Chetnole [GW] Ⓤ 123
Chichester [SN] [4] Ⓟ 🚲 ◇ ⚠ 🚕 123, 165, 188
Chilham [SE] Ⓟ ⚠ Ⓤ 207
Chilworth [GW] Ⓤ 148
Chingford [LE] Ⓟ 🚲 ⚠ 🚕 20
Chinley [NT] Ⓟ Ⓤ 78
Chinnor, Estover Way *Bus* 115A
Chinnor, Lower Road *Bus* 115A
Chinnor, The Red Lion *Bus* 115A
Chinnor, The Wheatsheaf *Bus* 115A
Chippenham [GW] Ⓟ 🚲 ◇ ⚠ 🚕 123, 125
Chipping Norton West Street *Bus* 126A
Chipstead [SN] Ⓟ ⚠ 181
Chirk [AW] Ⓟ Ⓤ 75
Chislehurst [SE] Ⓟ ◇ ⚠ 🚕 204
Chiswick [SW] Ⓟ 🚲 Ⓤ 149
Cholsey [GW] Ⓟ 🚲 116
Chorley [NT] Ⓟ ◇ 82
Chorleywood [LT] Ⓟ 🚲 ⚠ 🚕 114
Christchurch [SW] Ⓟ 🚲 ◇ ⚠ 🚕 158
Christs Hospital [SN] Ⓟ 🚲 ◇ ⚠ 188
Church Fenton [NT] Ⓟ 🚲 Ⓤ 33, 40
Church & Oswaldtwistle [NT] Ⓤ 97
Church Stretton [AW] Ⓟ Ⓤ 129, 131
Cilmeri [AW] Ⓤ 129
City Thameslink [FC] (see London)
Clacton-on-Sea [LE] Ⓟ 🚲 ◇ ⚠ 🚕 11
Clandon [SW] Ⓟ 🚲 ◇ ⚠ 152
Clapham High Street [SN] 🚲 ⚠ Ⓤ 178
Clapham Junction [SW] [10] ◇ ⚠
Alton 155
Andover 160
Ascot 149
Basingstoke 155, 158
Bexhill 189
Birmingham 66
Birmingham International 66
Bognor Regis 188
Bournemouth 158
Brighton 186
Bristol 160
Chertsey 149
Chessington 152
Chichester 188
Coventry 66
Crystal Palace 177, 178
Dorking 152, 182
Eastbourne 189
East Croydon 175, 176
East Grinstead 184
Effingham Junction 152
Epsom 152, 182
Epsom Downs 182
Exeter 160
Gatwick Airport 186
Guildford 152, 156
Hampton Court 152
Hastings 189
Haywards Heath 186
Horsham 186
Hounslow 149
Hove 186
Kensington (Olympia) 66, 176, 186
Kingston 149, 152
Lewes 189
London
ictoria 175, 177
aterloo 149, 152
Milton Keynes Central 66, 176
Northampton 66
Oxted 184
Portsmouth 156, 158, 188
Purley 175
Reading 149
Redhill 186
Rugby 66
Salisbury 160
Shepperton 152
Southampton 158, 188
Staines 149
Surbiton 152
Sutton (Surrey) 182
Tattenham Corner 181
Twickenham 149
Uckfield 184
Watford Junction 66, 176, 186
West Croydon 177
Weybridge 155
Willesden Junction 176, 186
Wimbledon 152
Windsor 149
Woking 155
Worthing 188
Yeovil Junction 160
Clapham (Nth Yorkshire) [NT] Ⓟ Ⓤ 36
Clapton [LE] ⚠ 20, 22
Clarbeston Road [AW] Ⓤ 128
Clarkston [SR] 🚲 222
Claverdon [LM] ⚠ Ⓤ 115
Claygate [SW] Ⓟ 🚲 ◇ ⚠ 🚕 152
Cleethorpes [TP] Ⓟ 🚲 ◇ 🚕 27, 29, 30
Cleland [SR] Ⓟ 🚲 Ⓤ 225

Station index and table numbers

- [10] Connection time
- Ⓟ Station Car Park
- 🚲 Bicycle storage facility
- ◇ Seat reservations can be made at this station
- ⚠ Penalty Fare Schemes in operation on some or all services from this station
- 🚕 Taxi rank or cab office at station, or signposted and within 100 metres
- Ⓤ Unstaffed station
- [ ] Station Operator Code

Clifton [NT] Ⓤ 82
Clifton Down [GW] Ⓟ Ⓤ 133
Clitheroe [NT] Ⓟ 94
Clock House [SE] 🚲 ◇ ⚠ 🚕 203
Clunderwen [AW] Ⓟ Ⓤ 128
Clydebank [SR] 🚲 🚕 226
Coatbridge Central [SR] Ⓟ 🚲 🚕 Ⓤ 224, 226
Coatbridge Sunnyside [SR] Ⓟ 🚲 226
Coatdyke [SR] Ⓟ 🚲 Ⓤ 226
Cobham & Stoke d'Abernon [SW] Ⓟ 🚲 ◇ ⚠ 🚕 152
Codsall [LM] Ⓟ Ⓤ 74
Cogan [AW] Ⓟ Ⓤ 130
Colchester [LE] [4] Ⓟ 🚲 ◇ ⚠ 🚕 10, 11, 14
Colchester Town [LE] Ⓟ 🚲 ⚠ 11
Coleshill Parkway [LM] Ⓟ 🚲 ◇ 🚕 49, 57
Coll *Ship* 227B
Collingham [EM] Ⓤ 27
Collington [SN] ⚠ Ⓤ 189
Colne [NT] Ⓟ Ⓤ 97
Colonsay *Ship* 227B
Colwall [LM] Ⓟ ⚠ Ⓤ 71, 126
Colwyn Bay [AW] Ⓟ ◇ 🚕 81
Combe [GW] Ⓤ 126
Commondale [NT] Ⓤ 45
Congleton [NT] Ⓟ ◇ 51, 65, 84
Conisbrough [NT] Ⓟ Ⓤ 29
Connel Ferry [SR] Ⓟ 🚲 Ⓤ 227
Cononley [NT] Ⓟ Ⓤ 36
Conway Park [ME] 106
Conwy [AW] Ⓤ 81
Cooden Beach [SN] Ⓟ 🚲 ◇ ⚠ 189
Cookham [GW] Ⓟ 120
Cooksbridge [SN] Ⓟ ⚠ Ⓤ 189
Coombe Junction Halt [GW] Ⓤ 140
Copplestone [GW] Ⓟ Ⓤ 136
Corbridge [NT] Ⓟ Ⓤ 48
Corby [EM] ⚠ 53
Corby George Street *Bus* 26B
Corkerhill [SR] 🚲 Ⓤ 217
Corkickle [NT] Ⓤ 100
Corpach [SR] Ⓟ 🚲 Ⓤ 227
Corrour [SR] 🚲 Ⓤ 227, *Sleepers* 404
Coryton [AW] Ⓤ 130
Coseley [LM] Ⓟ ⚠ 68
Cosford [LM] Ⓟ Ⓤ 74, 75
Cosham [SW] Ⓟ 🚲 ◇ ⚠ 🚕 123, 158, 165, 188
Cottingham [NT] Ⓟ 🚕 Ⓤ 43
Cottingley [NT] Ⓤ 39
Coulsdon South [SN] Ⓟ ⚠ 🚕 186
Coulsdon Town [SN] Ⓟ ◇ 181
Coventry [VT] Ⓟ 🚲 ◇ ⚠ 🚕
Aberdeen 65
Barrow-in-Furness 65
Banbury 71
Basingstoke 51
Birmingham 68
Birmingham International 68
Blackpool 65
Bournemouth 51
Brighton 66
Carlisle 65
Clapham Junction 66
Crewe 65
Derby 51
Dundee 65
East Croydon 66
Edinburgh 51, 65
Gatwick Airport 66
Glasgow 51, 65
Holyhead 65
Inverness 65
Leamington Spa 71
Leeds 51
Liverpool 65
London 66
Manchester 65
Manchester Airport 65
Milton Keynes Central 66
Newcastle 51
Northampton 66
Nuneaton 67
Oxenholme Lake District 65
Oxford 51
Preston 65
Reading 51
Rugby 66
Sheffield 51
Southampton 51
Stafford 67, 68
Stoke-on-Trent 65
Watford 66
Wolverhampton 68
York 51
Cowden [SN] Ⓟ ⚠ Ⓤ 184
Cowdenbeath [SR] 🚲 ◇ 242
Cradley Heath [LM] Ⓟ 🚲 ◇ ⚠ 71, 115
Craigendoran [SR] Ⓟ 🚲 Ⓤ 226
Craignure *Ship* 227B
Cramlington [NT] Ⓟ 🚲 Ⓤ 48
Craven Arms [AW] Ⓟ Ⓤ 129, 131
Crawley [SN] Ⓟ 🚲 ◇ ⚠ 🚕 186, 188
Crayford [SE] Ⓟ ◇ ⚠ 200
Crediton [GW] Ⓟ 🚲 Ⓤ 136
Cressing [LE] 🚲 ⚠ Ⓤ 11
Cressington [ME] Ⓟ ⚠ 103
Creswell [EM] Ⓤ 55
Crewe [VT] [10] Ⓟ 🚲 ◇ 🚕
Aberdeen 65, *Sleepers* 402
Bangor (Gwynedd) 81
Barrow-in-Furness 65
Birmingham 65
Birmingham International 65
Blackpool 65
Bournemouth 51
Bristol 51
Cardiff 131
Carlisle 65
Cheltenham Spa 51
Chester 81
Coventry 65, 67
Derby 50
Douglas (IOM) 98A
Dundee 65, *Sleepers* 402
Edinburgh 65
Exeter 51
Fort William *Sleepers* 404
Glasgow 65
Hartford 91
Hereford 131
Holyhead 81
Inverkeithing *Sleepers* 402
Inverness 65, *Sleepers* 403
Kirkcaldy *Sleepers* 402
Lancaster 65
Liverpool 91
Liverpool South Parkway 91
Llandudno 81
London 65, 67
Manchester 84
Manchester Airport 84
Milton Keynes Central 65, 67
Newport (South Wales) 131
Northampton 67
Oxenholme Lake District 65
Oxford 51
Paignton 51
Penzance 51
Perth 65, *Sleepers* 403
Plymouth 51
Preston 65
Reading 51
Rugby 65, 67
Runcorn 91
Shrewsbury 131
Southampton 51
Stafford 65, 67
Stirling *Sleepers* 403
Stockport 84
Stoke-on-Trent 50
Torquay 51
Watford 65
Wilmslow 84
Wolverhampton 65
Crewkerne [SW] Ⓟ 🚲 ◇ ⚠ 160
Crews Hill [FC] ⚠ Ⓤ 24
Crianlarich [SR] Ⓟ 🚲 Ⓤ 227, *Sleepers* 404
Criccieth [AW] Ⓟ 🚲 Ⓤ 75
Cricklewood [FC] 🚲 ◇ ⚠ 52
Croftfoot [SR] 🚲 223
Crofton Park [SE] ◇ ⚠ 52, 195
Cromer [LE] Ⓟ 🚲 Ⓤ 16
Cromford [EM] Ⓟ Ⓤ 54, 56
Crompton [NT] (see Shaw)
Crookston [SR] 🚲 Ⓤ 217
Crosby [ME] (see Blundellsands)
Crossflatts [NT] Ⓟ 🚲 Ⓤ 36
Cross Gates [NT] Ⓟ 40

Station index and table numbers

■10 Connection time
Ⓟ Station Car Park
🚲 Bicycle storage facility
◇ Seat reservations can be made at this station
⚠ Penalty Fare Schemes in operation on some or all services from this station
🚕 Taxi rank or cab office at station, or signposted and within 100 metres
Ⓤ Unstaffed station
[ ] Station Operator Code

Cross Keys [AW] Ⓤ 127
Crosshill [SR] 223
Crossmyloof [SR] 🚲 Ⓤ 222
Croston [NT] Ⓟ Ⓤ 99
Crouch Hill [LO] ⚠ 62
Crowborough [SN] Ⓟ 🚲 ◇ ⚠ 184
Crowhurst [SE] Ⓟ ⚠ 206
Crowle [NT] Ⓤ 29
Crowthorne [GW] Ⓟ 🚲 148
Croy [SR] ■3 Ⓟ 🚲 228, 230
Croydon
see East Croydon
see South Croydon
see West Croydon
Crystal Palace [LO] ■4 Ⓟ ⚠ 🚕 177, 178
Cuddington [NT] Ⓟ Ⓤ 88
Cuffley [FC] Ⓟ 🚲 ⚠ 🚕 24
Culham [GW] Ⓟ 🚲 Ⓤ 116
Culrain [SR] 🚲 Ⓤ 239
Cumbernauld [SR] Ⓟ 🚲 🚕 224
Cupar [SR] Ⓟ 🚲 ◇ 51, 229
Curriehill [SR] Ⓟ 🚲 Ⓤ 225
Cuxton [SE] Ⓟ ⚠ Ⓤ 208
Cwmbach [AW] Ⓟ Ⓤ 130
Cwmbran [AW] Ⓟ 🚲 ◇ 🚕 131
Cynghordy [AW] Ⓤ 129

D

Dagenham Dock [CC] Ⓟ 🚲 ◇ ⚠ 1
Daisy Hill [NT] Ⓟ 🚲 82
Dalgety Bay [SR] Ⓟ 🚲 🚕 Ⓤ 242
Dalmally [SR] Ⓟ 🚲 Ⓤ 227
Dalmarnock [SR] 226
Dalmeny [SR] Ⓟ 🚲 242
Dalmuir [SR] Ⓟ 🚲 226, 227, *Sleepers* 404
Dalreoch [SR] Ⓟ 🚲 226
Dalry [SR] Ⓟ 🚲 Ⓤ 221
Dalston [NT] Ⓟ Ⓤ 100
Dalston Junction [LO] 🚲 ⚠ 178
Dalston Kingsland [LO] ⚠ 59
Dalton [NT] Ⓟ Ⓤ 82
Dalwhinnie [SR] Ⓟ 🚲 Ⓤ 229, *Sleepers* 403
Danby [NT] Ⓟ Ⓤ 45
Danescourt [AW] Ⓤ 130
Danzey [LM] Ⓟ ⚠ Ⓤ 71
Darlington [GR] ■7 Ⓟ 🚲 ◇ 🚕
Aberdeen 26
Birmingham 51
Bishop Auckland 44
Bournemouth 51
Bristol 51
Cambridge 26
Cardiff 51
Catterick Garrison *Bus* 26H
Derby 51
Doncaster 26
Durham 26
Dundee 26
Edinburgh 26
Exeter 51
Glasgow 26
Grantham 26
Huddersfield 39
Leeds 26
Liverpool 39
London 26
Manchester 39
Manchester Airport 39
Middlesbrough 44
Newark 26
Newcastle 26
Newport (South Wales) 51
Norwich 26
Northallerton 26
Oxford 51
Paignton 51
Penzance 51
Peterborough 26
Plymouth 51
Reading 51
Redcar 44
Retford 26
Richmond *Bus* 26H
Saltburn 44
Sheffield 26
Southampton 51
Stansted Airport 26
Sunderland 26, 44
Torquay 51
Whitby 45
York 26
Darnall [NT] Ⓤ 30
Darnley [SR] (see Priesthill)
Darsham [LE] Ⓟ 🚲 Ⓤ 13
Dartford [SE] ■4 Ⓟ ◇ ⚠ 🚕 200, 212
Darton [NT] Ⓟ Ⓤ 34
Darwen [NT] Ⓤ 94
Datchet [SW] 🚲 ◇ ⚠ 149
Davenport [NT] Ⓟ 86
Dawlish [GW] Ⓟ ◇ 🚕 51, 135
Dawlish Warren [GW] Ⓟ 🚲 Ⓤ 135
Deal [SE] Ⓟ 🚲 ◇ ⚠ 🚕 194, 207
Dean [GW] 🚲 Ⓤ 158
Deansgate [NT] 82, 84, 85, 86, 89
Deganwy [AW] Ⓤ 81, 102
Deighton [NT] Ⓤ 39
Delamere [NT] Ⓟ Ⓤ 88
Denby Dale [NT] Ⓟ Ⓤ 34
Denham [CH] Ⓟ 🚲 ◇ ⚠ 🚕 115
Denham Golf Club [CH] ⚠ Ⓤ 115
Denmark Hill [SE] ■4 ◇ ⚠ 52, 178, 195, 200
Dent [NT] Ⓟ Ⓤ 36
Denton [NT] Ⓤ 78
Deptford [SE] ◇ ⚠ 200
Derby [EM] ■6 Ⓟ 🚲 ◇ ⚠ 🚕
Barnsley 53
Bedford 53
Belper 53, 56
Birmingham 57
Birmingham International 51
Bournemouth 51
Bristol 57
Burton-on-Trent 57
Cardiff 57
Chesterfield 53
Coventry 51
Crewe 50
Doncaster 53
Edinburgh 51
Exeter 51
Gloucester 57
Kettering 53
Leeds 53
Leicester 53
London 53
Long Eaton 56
Loughborough 53
Luton 53
Market Harborough 53
Matlock 56
Meadowhall 53
Newcastle 51
Newport (South Wales) 57
Nottingham 56
Oxford 51
Paignton 51
Penzance 51
Plymouth 51
Reading 51
Sheffield 53
Southampton 51
Stoke-on-Trent 50
Wakefield 53
Wellingborough 53
York 53
Derby Road [LE] 🚲 Ⓤ 13
Dereham 🚕 *Bus* 26A
Devonport [GW] Ⓟ 🚲 Ⓤ 135, 139
Dewsbury [TP] Ⓟ 🚲 ◇ 🚕 39, 41
Didcot Parkway [GW] Ⓟ 🚲 ◇ ⚠ 🚕 116, 125
Digby & Sowton [GW] Ⓟ Ⓤ 136
Dilton Marsh [GW] Ⓤ 123
Dinas Powys [AW] Ⓤ 130
Dinas Rhondda [AW] Ⓟ Ⓤ 130
Dingle Road [AW] Ⓤ 130
Dingwall [SR] Ⓟ 🚲 ◇ 🚕 239
Dinsdale [NT] Ⓤ 44
Dinting [NT] ■3 Ⓟ 🚲 79
Disley [NT] Ⓟ 86
Diss [LE] Ⓟ 🚲 ◇ 🚕 11
Dockyard [GW] Ⓤ 135, 139
Dodworth [NT] Ⓟ Ⓤ 34
Dolau [AW] 🚲 Ⓤ 129
Doleham [SN] Ⓤ 189
Dolgarrog [AW] Ⓤ 102
Dolwyddelan [AW] Ⓟ Ⓤ 102

Station index and table numbers

10 Connection time
Ⓟ Station Car Park
🚲 Bicycle storage facility
◇ Seat reservations can be made at this station
⚠ Penalty Fare Schemes in operation on some or all services from this station
🚕 Taxi rank or cab office at station, or signposted and within 100 metres
⊛ Unstaffed station
[ ] Station Operator Code

Doncaster [GR] 7 Ⓟ 🚲 ◇ 🚕
- Aberdeen 26
- Bedford 53
- Birmingham 51
- Bournemouth 51
- Bristol 51
- Cambridge 26
- Cleethorpes 29
- Darlington 26
- Derby 53
- Dundee 26
- Durham 26
- Edinburgh 26
- Exeter 51
- Gainsborough 18
- Glasgow 26
- Goole 29
- Grantham 26
- Grimsby 29
- Hull 29
- Leeds 31
- Leicester 53
- Lincoln 18
- London 26
- Luton 53
- Manchester 29
- Manchester Airport 29
- Middlesbrough 26
- Newark 26
- Newcastle 26
- Norwich 26
- Nottingham 53
- Oxford 51
- Paignton 51
- Penzance 51
- Peterborough 18, 26
- Plymouth 51
- Reading 51
- Retford 26
- Robin Hood Airport *Bus* 26F
- Rotherham 29
- Scunthorpe 29
- Selby 29
- Sheffield 29
- Sleaford 18
- Southampton 51
- Spalding 18
- Stansted Airport 26
- Stevenage 26
- Stockport 29
- Sunderland 26
- Torquay 51
- Wakefield 31
- York 26

Doncaster Interchange *Bus* 🚕 26F
Dorchester South [SW] Ⓟ 🚲 ◇ ⚠ 🚕 158
Dorchester West [GW] ⊛ 123, 158
Dore & Totley [NT] Ⓟ ⊛ 78
Dorking [SN] 4 Ⓟ 🚲 ◇ ⚠ 🚕 152, 182
Dorking Deepdene [GW] ⊛ 148
Dorking West [GW] ⊛ 148
Dormans [SN] ◇ ⚠ 184
Dorridge [LM] Ⓟ 🚲 ◇ ⚠ 71, 115
Douglas (IOM) *Ship* 98A
Dove Holes [NT] Ⓟ ⊛ 86
Dovercourt [LE] Ⓟ 🚲 11
Dover Priory [SE] 4 Ⓟ 🚲 ◇ ⚠ 🚕 194, 207, 212
Dovey Junction [AW] 4 ⊛ 75
Downham Market [FC] Ⓟ 🚲 ⚠ 🚕 17
Drayton Green [GW] ⊛ 117
Drayton Park [FC] 🚲 ⚠ 24
Drem [SR] Ⓟ 🚲 ⊛ 238
Driffield [NT] Ⓟ 🚲 🚕 43
Drigg [NT] ⊛ 100
Droitwich Spa [LM] Ⓟ ◇ ⚠ 71
Dronfield [NT] Ⓟ ⊛ 34
Drumchapel [SR] Ⓟ 🚲 🚕 226
Drumfrochar [SR] 🚲 ⊛ 219
Drumgelloch [SR] Ⓟ 🚲 ⊛ 226
Drumry [SR] Ⓟ 🚲 226
Dublin Ferryport *Ship* 81A
Duddeston [LM] ⚠ 69, 70
Dudley Port [LM] Ⓟ ⚠ 68
Duffield [EM] Ⓟ ⚠ ⊛ 56
Duirinish [SR] Ⓟ 🚲 ⊛ 239
Duke Street [SR] 🚲 ⊛ 226
Dullingham [LE] Ⓟ 🚲 ⊛ 14
Dumbarton Central [SR] 🚲 ◇ 🚕 226, 227
Dumbarton East [SR] 🚲 ⊛ 226
Dumbreck [SR] 🚲 ⊛ 217
Dumfries [SR] Ⓟ 🚲 ◇ 🚕 216
Dumpton Park [SE] ⚠ ⊛ 212
Dun Laoghaire *Ship* 81A
Dunbar [GR] Ⓟ 🚲 ◇ 26, 51, 238
Dunblane [SR] Ⓟ 🚲 ◇ 229, 230, *Sleepers* 403
Duncraig [SR] 🚲 ⊛ 239
Dundee [SR] Ⓟ 🚲 ◇ 🚕 26, 51, 65, 229, *Sleepers* 402
Dunfermline Queen Margaret [SR] Ⓟ 🚲 ⊛ 242
Dunfermline Town [SR] Ⓟ 🚲 ◇ 🚕 242
Dunkeld & Birnam [SR] Ⓟ 🚲 ⊛ 229, *Sleepers* 403
Dunlop [SR] 🚲 ⊛ 222
Dunoon *Ship* 219A
Dunrobin Castle [SR] ⊛ *Summer only* 239
Duns *Bus* 26K
Dunstable *Bus* 52A
Dunster Steep *Bus* 135E
Dunston [NT] ⊛ 48
Dunton Green [SE] Ⓟ ⚠ ⊛ 204
Durham [GR] Ⓟ 🚲 ◇ 🚕 26, 39, 44, 51
Durrington-on-Sea [SN] 🚲 ⚠ 188
Dursley [GW] (see Cam & Dursley)
Dyce [SR] Ⓟ 🚲 🚕 ⊛ 229, 240
Dyffryn Ardudwy [AW] ⊛ 75

E

Eaglescliffe [NT] Ⓟ 🚲 🚕 ⊛ 26, 44
Ealing Broadway [GW] 3 ◇ ⚠ 🚕 116, 117
Earlestown [NT] 8 81, 90
Earley [SW] Ⓟ 🚲 ⚠ 149
Earlsfield [SW] 🚲 ◇ ⚠ 152, 155
Earlston *Bus* 26K
Earlswood (Surrey) [SN] 🚲 ◇ ⚠ 186
Earlswood (West Midlands) [LM] Ⓟ ⚠ ⊛ 71
East Croydon [SN] 🚲 ◇ ⚠ 🚕
- Bedford 52
- Bexhill 189
- Birmingham 66
- Birmingham International 66
- Bognor Regis 188
- Brighton 186
- Caterham 181
- Chichester 188
- Clapham Junction 175, 176
- Coventry 66
- Eastbourne 189
- East Grinstead 184
- Gatwick Airport 186
- Hastings 189
- Haywards Heath 186
- Horsham 186
- Hove 186
- Kensington (Olympia) 66, 176, 186
- Lewes 189
- Littlehampton 188
- London 175
- Luton 52
- Luton Airport Parkway 52
- Milton Keynes Central 66, 176
- Northampton 66
- Norwood Junction 177, 178
- Oxted 184
- Portsmouth 188
- Purley 175
- Redhill 186
- Rugby 66
- St Albans 52
- St Pancras International 52
- Seaford 189
- Southampton Central 188
- Tattenham Corner 181
- Tonbridge 186
- Uckfield 184
- Watford Junction 66, 176, 186
- West Hampstead Thameslink 52
- Wolverhampton 66
- Worthing 188

East Didsbury [NT] Ⓟ 85
East Dulwich [SN] ⚠ 177, 179
East Farleigh [SE] Ⓟ ⚠ ⊛ 208
East Garforth [NT] ⊛ 40

Station index and table numbers

[10] Connection time
Ⓟ Station Car Park
🚲 Bicycle storage facility
◇ Seat reservations can be made at this station
⚠ Penalty Fare Schemes in operation on some or all services from this station
🚕 Taxi rank or cab office at station, or signposted and within 100 metres
Ⓤ Unstaffed station
[ ] Station Operator Code

East Grinstead [SN] Ⓟ 🚲 ◇ ⚠ 🚕 184
East Kilbride [SR] Ⓟ 🚲 ◇ 🚕 222
East Malling [SE] ⚠ Ⓤ 196
East Midlands Parkway [EM] ⚠ 53
East Tilbury [CC] ◇ ⚠ 1
East Worthing [SN] ⚠ Ⓤ 188
Eastbourne [SN] [4] Ⓟ 🚲 ◇ ⚠ 🚕 189
Eastbrook [AW] Ⓟ Ⓤ 130
Easterhouse [SR] Ⓟ 🚲 226
Eastham Rake [ME] Ⓟ 🚲 ⚠ 106
Eastleigh [SW] [3] Ⓟ 🚲 ◇ ⚠ 🚕 158, 188
Eastrington [NT] Ⓤ 29
Ebbsfleet International [SE] ◇ ⚠ 🚕 194, 200, 207, 208, 212
Ebbw Vale Parkway [AW] Ⓟ Ⓤ 127
Eccles [NT] Ⓟ 90
Eccles Road [LE] Ⓟ Ⓤ 17
Eccleston Park [NT] 90
Edale [NT] Ⓟ Ⓤ 78
Eden Camp *Bus* 26G
Eden Park [SE] ◇ ⚠ 203
Eden Project *Bus* 135B
Edenbridge [SN] Ⓟ ⚠ Ⓤ 186
Edenbridge Town [SN] Ⓟ 🚲 ◇ ⚠ 🚕 184
Edge Hill [NT] Ⓟ 89, 90, 91
Edinburgh [NR] [10] Ⓟ 🚲 ◇ 🚕
Aberdeen 229
Airdrie 226
Bathgate 226
Birmingham New Street 51, 65
Birmingham International 51, 65
Blackpool 65
Bournemouth 51
Bristol 51
Cambridge 26
Cardiff 51
Carlisle 65
Carstairs 225
Cowdenbeath 242
Crewe 65
Croy 228
Dalmuir 226
Darlington 26
Derby 51
Doncaster 26
Dunbar 238
Dunblane 230
Dundee 229
Dunfermline 242
Dyce 229
Edinburgh Park 226, 230
Exeter 51
Falkirk 228, 230
Fort William 227
Glasgow 225, 226, 228
Glenrothes with Thornton 242
Grantham 26
Helensburgh 226
Inverkeithing 242
Inverness 229
Inverurie 229
Kirkcaldy 242
Lancaster 65
Larbert 230
Leeds 26
Linlithgow 230
Liverpool 65
Livingston 225, 226
London 26, *Sleepers* 400
Mallaig 227
Manchester 65
Manchester Airport 65
Markinch 229
Milngavie 226
Motherwell 225
Newcastle 26
Newcraighall 242
Newport (South Wales) 51
North Berwick 238
Oban 227
Oxenholme Lake District 65
Oxford 51
Paignton 51
Penzance 51
Perth 229
Peterborough 26
Plymouth 51
Polmont 230
Preston 65
Reading 51
Sheffield 26
Shotts 225
Southampton 51
Stafford 65
Stirling 230
Thurso 239
Torquay 51
Warrington 65
Watford 65, *Sleepers* 400
West Calder 225
Western Isles *Ship* 239B
Wigan 65
York 26
Edinburgh Park [SR] 🚲 Ⓤ 226, 230
Edmonton Green [LE] ⚠ 21
Effingham Junction [SW] [6] Ⓟ 🚲 ◇ ⚠ 152, 182
Eggesford [GW] Ⓟ Ⓤ 136
Egham [SW] Ⓟ 🚲 ◇ ⚠ 🚕 149
Egton [NT] Ⓤ 45
Eigg *Ship* 227A
Elephant & Castle [FC] 🚲 ◇ ⚠
Ashford 196
Bromley South 195
Canterbury 212
Catford 195
Chatham 212
Dover 212
East Croydon 177
Faversham 212
London 52, 177
Luton 52
Maidstone 196
Margate 212
Ramsgate 212
Rochester 212
St Albans 52
St Pancras International 52, 177
Sevenoaks 195
Streatham 177
Sutton (Surrey) 179
Swanley 195
Wimbledon 179
Elgin [SR] Ⓟ 🚲 ◇ 🚕 240
Ellesmere Port [ME] 🚕 106, 109
Elmers End [SE] [4] Ⓟ 🚲 ◇ ⚠ 203
Elmstead Woods [SE] Ⓟ ◇ ⚠ 🚕 204
Elmswell [LE] 🚲 Ⓤ 14
Elsecar [NT] Ⓤ 34
Elsenham [LE] 🚲 ⚠ 22
Elstree & Borehamwood [FC] Ⓟ 🚲 ◇ ⚠ 🚕 52
Eltham [SE] Ⓟ 🚲 ◇ ⚠ 🚕 200
Elton (Ches.) **[NT]** (see Ince & Elton)
Elton & Orston [EM] Ⓟ Ⓤ 19
Ely [LE] [4] Ⓟ 🚲 ◇ ⚠ 🚕 14, 17, 49
Emerson Park [LE] 🚲 ⚠ Ⓤ 4
Emsworth [SN] Ⓟ 🚲 ◇ ⚠ 188
Enfield Chase [FC] Ⓟ 🚲 ⚠ 24
Enfield Lock [LE] 🚲 ⚠ 22
Enfield Town [LE] ⚠ 🚕 21
Entwistle [NT] Ⓤ 94
Epsom [SN] [3] 🚲 ◇ ⚠ 🚕 152, 182
Epsom Downs [SN] ⚠ Ⓤ 182
Erdington [LM] ⚠ 69
Eridge [SN] 🚲 ◇ ⚠ 184
Erith [SE] ◇ ⚠ 🚕 200
Esher [SW] Ⓟ 🚲 ◇ ⚠ 🚕 155
Eskdale [NT] (see Ravenglass)
Essex Road [FC] 🚲 ⚠ 24
Etchingham [SE] Ⓟ 🚲 ◇ ⚠ 206
Eton (see Windsor)
Euston [NR] (see London)
Euxton Balshaw Lane [NT] Ⓟ Ⓤ 90
Evesham [GW] Ⓟ 🚲 🚕 126
Ewell East [SN] Ⓟ 🚲 ◇ ⚠ 182
Ewell West [SW] Ⓟ 🚲 ◇ ⚠ 152
Exeter
Central [GW] Ⓟ 🚲 ◇
St Davids [GW] [6] Ⓟ 🚲 ◇ ⚠ 🚕
St Thomas [GW] Ⓤ
Aberdeen 51
Andover 160
Barnstaple 136
Basingstoke 160
Birmingham 51
Bristol 135
Bude Strand *Bus* 135D
Cardiff 135
Carlisle 51

Station index and table numbers

■10 Connection time
Ⓟ Station Car Park
🚲 Bicycle storage facility
◇ Seat reservations can be made at this station
⚠ Penalty Fare Schemes in operation on some or all services from this station
🚕 Taxi rank or cab office at station, or signposted and within 100 metres
Ⓤ Unstaffed station
[ ] Station Operator Code

Clapham Junction 160
Crewe 51
Derby 51
Dundee 51
Edinburgh 51
Exmouth 136
Glasgow 51
Holsworthy *Bus* 135D
Leeds 51
London 135, 160, *Sleepers* 406
Manchester 51
Newcastle 51
Newport (South Wales) 135
Newquay 135
Newton Abbot 135
Nottingham 51
Okehampton *Summer only* 136
Okehampton West Street *Bus* 135D
Paignton 135
Penzance 135
Plymouth 135
Preston 51
Reading 135, *Sleepers* 406
Salisbury 160
Sheffield 51
Taunton 135
Torquay 135
Truro 135
Weston-super-Mare 135
Wolverhampton 51
York 51
Exhibition Centre [SR] 🚲 226
Exmouth [GW] Ⓟ 🚲 ◇ 135, 136
Exton [GW] Ⓟ 🚲 Ⓤ 136
Eynsford [SE] Ⓟ ◇ ⚠ 52, 195

F

Fairbourne [AW] Ⓟ Ⓤ 75
Fairfield [NT] Ⓤ 78
Fairhaven [NT] (see Ansdell)
Fairlie [SR] Ⓟ 🚲 Ⓤ 221
Fairwater [AW] Ⓤ 130
Falconwood [SE] ◇ ⚠ 🚕 200
Falkirk Grahamston [SR] Ⓟ 🚲 ◇ 🚕 224, 230, *Sleepers* 403
Falkirk High [SR] Ⓟ 🚲 ◇ 🚕 228
Falls of Cruachan [SR] Ⓤ *Summer only* 227
Falmer [SN] Ⓟ 🚲 ⚠ 189
Falmouth Docks [GW] Ⓟ Ⓤ 143
Falmouth Town [GW] Ⓤ 143
Fambridge [LE] (North Fambridge)
Fareham [SW] Ⓟ 🚲 ◇ ⚠ 🚕 123, 158, 165, 188
Farnborough (Main) [SW] Ⓟ 🚲 ◇ ⚠ 🚕 155,158
Farnborough North [GW] Ⓟ Ⓤ 148
Farncombe [SW] Ⓟ 🚲 ◇ ⚠ 156
Farnham [SW] Ⓟ 🚲 ◇ ⚠ 🚕 155
Farningham Road [SE] Ⓟ ◇ ⚠ 212
Farnworth [NT] 82
Farringdon [LT] (see London)
Fauldhouse [SR] Ⓟ 🚲 Ⓤ 225
Faversham [SE] ■2 Ⓟ 🚲 ◇ ⚠ 🚕 194, 212
Faygate [SN] ⚠ Ⓤ 186
Fazakerley [ME] ⚠ 103
Fearn [SR] Ⓟ 🚲 Ⓤ 239
Featherstone [NT] Ⓤ 32
Felixstowe [LE] 🚲 🚕 Ⓤ 13
Feltham [SW] Ⓟ 🚲 ◇ ⚠ 149
Fenchurch Street [NR] (see London)
Feniton [SW] Ⓟ 🚲 ◇ ⚠ 160
Fenny Stratford [LM] Ⓤ 64
Fernhill [AW] Ⓤ 130
Ferriby [NT] Ⓟ 🚲 Ⓤ 29
Ferryside [AW] Ⓤ 128
Ffairfach [AW] Ⓤ 129
Filey [NT] Ⓟ 🚕 Ⓤ 43
Filton Abbey Wood [GW] Ⓟ 🚲 123, 132, 134, 135
Finchley Road & Frognal [LO] ⚠ 59
Finsbury Park [FC] ⚠ 🚕 24, 25
Finstock [GW] Ⓤ 126
Fishbourne (Sussex) [SN] ⚠ Ⓤ 188
Fishersgate [SN] ⚠ Ⓤ 188
Fishguard & Goodwick [AW] Ⓤ 128
Fishguard Harbour [AW] Ⓤ 128
Fiskerton [EM] Ⓟ Ⓤ 27
Fitzwilliam [NT] Ⓟ Ⓤ 31
Five Ways [LM] ⚠ 69
Flamingo Land *Bus* 26G
Fleet [SW] Ⓟ 🚲 ◇ ⚠ 🚕 155, 158
Flimby [NT] Ⓤ 100
Flint [AW] Ⓟ ◇ 81
Flitwick [FC] Ⓟ 🚲 ◇ ⚠ 🚕 52
Flixton [NT] 🚲 89
Flowery Field [NT] Ⓤ 79
Folkestone Central [SE] Ⓟ 🚲 ◇ ⚠ 🚕 194, 207
Folkestone West [SE] Ⓟ ◇ ⚠ 194, 207
Ford [SN] ■4 🚲 ◇ ⚠ 188
Forest Gate [LE] 🚲 ⚠ 5
Forest Hill [LO] ■4 Ⓟ 🚲 ◇ ⚠ 🚕 178
Formby [ME] Ⓟ 🚲 ⚠ 103
Forres [SR] Ⓟ 🚲 ◇ 🚕 240
Forsinard [SR] Ⓟ 🚲 Ⓤ 239
Fort Matilda [SR] Ⓟ 🚲 Ⓤ 219
Fort William [SR] Ⓟ 🚲 ◇ 🚕 227, *Ship* 227A, *Sleepers* 404
Four Oaks [LM] Ⓟ ⚠ 69
Foxfield [NT] Ⓤ 100
Foxton [FC] ⚠ Ⓤ 25
Frant [SE] Ⓟ ◇ ⚠ 206
Fratton [SW] Ⓟ 🚲 ◇ ⚠ 🚕 123, 156, 157, 158, 165, 188
Freshfield [ME] Ⓟ 🚲 ⚠ 103
Freshford [GW] Ⓟ Ⓤ 123
Frimley [SW] Ⓟ 🚲 ◇ ⚠ 149
Frinton-on-Sea [LE] Ⓟ 🚲 ⚠ 11
Frizinghall [NT] Ⓟ Ⓤ 36, 37, 38
Frodsham [AW] Ⓟ Ⓤ 81
Frognal [LO] (see Finchley Road)
Frome [GW] Ⓟ 🚲 🚕 123
Fulwell [SW] 🚲 ◇ ⚠ 149, 152
Furness Vale [NT] Ⓤ 86
Furze Platt [GW] 120

G

Gainsborough Central [NT] Ⓟ Ⓤ 30
Gainsborough Lea Road [EM] Ⓟ 🚲 Ⓤ 18, 30
Galton Bridge (Smethwick) [LM] (see Smethwick Galton Bridge)
Garelochhead [SR] Ⓟ 🚲 Ⓤ 227, *Sleepers* 404
Garforth [NT] Ⓟ 🚲 39, 40
Gargrave [NT] Ⓤ 36
Garrowhill [SR] 🚲 226
Garscadden [SR] 🚲 226
Garsdale [NT] Ⓟ Ⓤ 36
Garston (Hertfordshire) [LM] Ⓤ 61
Garswood [NT] Ⓟ 90
Gartcosh [SR] Ⓟ 🚲 Ⓤ 224
Garth (Powys) [AW] Ⓤ 129
Garth (Mid Glamorgan) [AW] Ⓤ 128
Garve [SR] Ⓟ 🚲 Ⓤ 239
Gateshead [NT] (see Metrocentre)
Gathurst [NT] Ⓟ 🚲 Ⓤ 82
Gatley [NT] Ⓟ 85
Gatwick Airport [NR] ■10 ◇ ⚠ 🚕
Bedford 52
Bognor Regis 188
Brighton 186
Chichester 188
City Thameslink 52, 186
Clapham Junction 176, 186
Eastbourne 189
East Croydon 176, 186
Elstree & Borehamwood 52
Guildford 148
Hastings 189
Haywards Heath 186
Hove 186
Kensington (Olympia) 176
Lewes 189
London 186
Luton 52, 186
Luton Airport Parkway 52
Mill Hill Broadway 52

Station index and table numbers

[10] Connection time
Ⓟ Station Car Park
🚲 Bicycle storage facility
◇ Seat reservations can be made at this station
⚠ Penalty Fare Schemes in operation on some or all services from this station
🚕 Taxi rank or cab office at station, or signposted and within 100 metres
Ⓤ Unstaffed station
[ ] Station Operator Code

■10 Connection time
Ⓟ Station Car Park
🚲 Bicycle storage facility
◇ Seat reservations can be made at this station
⚠ Penalty Fare Schemes in operation on some or all services from this station
🚕 Taxi rank or cab office at station, or signposted and within 100 metres
⊛ Unstaffed station
[ ] Station Operator Code

Station index and table numbers

Grantham [GR] ■7 Ⓟ 🚲 ◇ 🚕 19, 26, 49
Grateley [SW] Ⓟ 🚲 ⚠ ⊛ 160
Gravelly Hill [LM] ⚠ 69
Gravesend [SE] ■4 Ⓟ ◇ ⚠ 🚕 194, 200, 208, 212
Grays [CC] Ⓟ 🚲 ◇ ⚠ 🚕 1
Great Ayton [NT] Ⓟ 🚲 ⊛ 45
Great Bentley [LE] 🚲 ⚠ 11
Great Chesterford [LE] ⚠ 22
Great Coates [NT] ⊛ 29
Great Malvern [LM] Ⓟ ◇ ⚠ 🚕 71, 126
Great Missenden [CH] Ⓟ 🚲 ◇ ⚠ 🚕 114
Great Yarmouth [LE] Ⓟ 🚲 ◇ 🚕 15
Green Lane [ME] ⚠ 106
Green Road [NT] Ⓟ ⊛ 100
Greenbank [NT] Ⓟ ⊛ 88
Greenfaulds [SR] Ⓟ 🚲 ⊛ 224
Greenfield [NT] 🚲 39
Greenford [LT] Ⓟ ⚠ 🚕 117
Greenhithe for Bluewater [SE] ◇ ⚠ 200, 212
Greenock Central [SR] Ⓟ 🚲 219
Greenock West [SR] 🚕 219
Greenwich [SE] ■4 ◇ ⚠ 200
Gretna Green [SR] Ⓟ 🚲 ⊛ 216
Grimsby Docks [NT] ⊛ 29
Grimsby Town [TP] Ⓟ 🚲 ◇ 🚕 26, 27, 29, 30
Grindleford [NT] ⊛ 78
Grosmont [NT] [NY] Ⓟ ⊛ 45
Grove Park [SE] ■4 ◇ ⚠ 🚕 204
Guide Bridge [NT] Ⓟ 78, 79
Guildford [SW] Ⓟ 🚲 ◇ ⚠ 🚕
  Ascot 149
  Birmingham 51
  Clapham Junction 152, 155, 156
  Gatwick Airport 148
  London 152, 155, 156
  Portsmouth 156
  Reading 148
  Surbiton 152
  West Croydon 182
Guiseley [NT] Ⓟ 🚲 ◇ 38
Gunnersbury [LT] 59
Gunnislake [GW] Ⓟ 🚲 ⊛ 139
Gunton [LE] Ⓟ 🚲 ⊛ 16
Gwersyllt [AW] Ⓟ ⊛ 101
Gypsy Lane [NT] 🚲 ⊛ 45

H

Habrough [NT] Ⓟ ⊛ 27, 29, 30
Hackbridge [SN] Ⓟ ◇ ⚠ 52, 179, 182
Hackney Central [LO] 🚲 ⚠ 🚕 59
Hackney Downs [LE] 🚲 ⚠ 20, 21, 22
Hackney Wick [LO] 🚲 ⚠ 59
Haddenham & Thame Parkway [CH] Ⓟ 🚲 ◇ ⚠ 🚕 115
Haddiscoe [LE] Ⓟ 🚲 ⊛ 15
Hadfield [NT] Ⓟ 🚲 79
Hadley Wood [FC] ⚠ 24
Hag Fold [NT] 82
Haggerston [LO] 🚲 ⚠ 178
Hagley [LM] Ⓟ ⚠ 71
Hairmyres [SR] Ⓟ 🚲 ⊛ 222
Hale [NT] Ⓟ 88
Halesworth [LE] Ⓟ 🚲 ⊛ 13
Halewood [NT] 89
Halifax [NT] Ⓟ 🚲 ◇ 🚕 26, 32, 41
Hall Green [LM] Ⓟ ⚠ 71
Hall I' Th' Wood [NT] ⊛ 94
Hall Road [ME] 🚲 ⚠ 103
Halling [SE] ⚠ ⊛ 208
Haltwhistle [NT] Ⓟ 🚲 ⊛ 48
Ham Street [SN] Ⓟ ◇ ⚠ 189
Hamble [SW] 🚲 ⚠ ⊛ 165
Hamilton Central [SR] Ⓟ 🚲 ◇ 🚕 226
Hamilton Square [ME] ◇ ⚠ 🚕 106
Hamilton West [SR] Ⓟ 🚲 🚕 226
Hammerton [NT] Ⓟ ⊛ 35
Hampden Park [SN] ■4 ◇ ⚠ 189
Hampstead Heath [LO] 🚲 ⚠ 59
Hampstead (South) [LO] (see South Hampstead)
Hampstead (West) (see West Hampstead) (see West Hampstead Thameslink)
Hampton [SW] 🚲 ⚠ 152
Hampton-in-Arden [LM] Ⓟ ⚠ 68
Hampton Court [SW] Ⓟ 🚲 ◇ ⚠ 152
Hampton Wick [SW] 🚲 ⚠ 149, 152
Hamstead [LM] ⚠ 70
Hamworthy [SW] 🚲 ◇ ⚠ 158
Hanborough [GW] Ⓟ 🚲 ⊛ 126
Handforth [NT] 🚲 84
Hanley Bus Station *Bus* 67
Hanwell [GW] 🚲 ⚠ 117
Hapton [NT] ⊛ 97
Harlech [AW] Ⓟ 🚲 ⊛ 75
Harlesden [LT] 60
Harling Road [LE] Ⓟ 🚲 ⊛ 17
Harlington (Beds.) **[FC]** Ⓟ 🚲 ◇ ⚠ 🚕 52
Harlington (Middx.) **[GW]** (see Hayes & Harlington)
Harlow Mill [LE] Ⓟ 🚲 ⚠ 22
Harlow Town [LE] Ⓟ 🚲 ◇ ⚠ 🚕 22
Harold Wood [LE] Ⓟ 🚲 ⚠ 🚕 5
Harpenden [FC] Ⓟ 🚲 ◇ ⚠ 🚕 52
Harrietsham [SE] Ⓟ ◇ ⚠ 196
Harringay [FC] ⚠ 24
Harringay Green Lanes [LO] 🚲 ⚠ 62
Harrington [NT] Ⓟ ⊛ 100
Harrogate [NT] Ⓟ 🚲 ◇ 🚕 26, 35
Harrow & Wealdstone [LT] Ⓟ ⚠ 🚕 60, 66, 176, 177
Harrow Road [CH] (see Sudbury & Harrow Road)
Harrow Sudbury Hill [CH] (see Sudbury Hill Harrow)
Harrow-on-the-Hill [LT] ■3 Ⓟ 🚲 ⚠ 🚕 114
Hartford [LM] Ⓟ ◇ 65, 91
Hartlebury [LM] Ⓟ ⚠ ⊛ 71
Hartlepool [NT] Ⓟ 🚲 ◇ 🚕 26, 44
Hartwood [SR] Ⓟ 🚲 ⊛ 225
Harwich International [LE] 🚲 ◇ 11, 14
Harwich Town [LE] 🚲 ⊛ 11
Haslemere [SW] ■4 Ⓟ 🚲 ◇ ⚠ 🚕 156
Hassocks [SN] ■4 Ⓟ 🚲 ◇ ⚠ 🚕 52, 186
Hastings [SE] ■4 Ⓟ ◇ ⚠ 🚕 189, 206
Hatch End [LO] Ⓟ 🚲 ⚠ 🚕 60
Hatfield [FC] Ⓟ 🚲 ⚠ 🚕 24, 25
Hatfield & Stainforth [NT] Ⓟ 🚕 ⊛ 29
Hatfield Peverel [LE] Ⓟ 🚲 ⚠ 11
Hathersage [NT] Ⓟ ⊛ 78
Hattersley [NT] ⊛ 79
Hatton (Derbyshire) **[EM]** (see Tutbury & Hatton)
Hatton (Warwickshire) **[CH]** Ⓟ ⚠ ⊛ 71, 115
Havant [SW] Ⓟ 🚲 ◇ ⚠ 🚕 123, 156, 157, 165, 188
Havenhouse [EM] ⊛ 19
Haverfordwest [AW] Ⓟ ◇ 🚕 128
Hawarden [AW] Ⓟ ⊛ 101
Hawarden Bridge [AW] ⊛ 101
Hawkhead [SR] 🚲 ⊛ 217
Haydon Bridge [NT] Ⓟ 🚲 ⊛ 48
Haydons Road [FC] Ⓟ ⚠ 52, 179
Hayes & Harlington [GW] ■3 Ⓟ 🚲 ◇ ⚠ 🚕 117
Hayes (Kent) [SE] Ⓟ 🚲 ◇ ⚠ 🚕 203
Hayle [GW] Ⓟ ⊛ 51, 135, *Sleepers* 406
Haymarket (Edinburgh) **[SR]** Ⓟ 🚲 ◇ 🚕
  Aberdeen 229
  Bathgate 226
  Birmingham 51, 65
  Birmingham International 51, 65
  Blackpool 65
  Bournemouth 51
  Bristol 51
  Cambridge 26
  Carlisle 65
  Carstairs 225

Station index and table numbers

■10 Connection time
Ⓟ Station Car Park
🚲 Bicycle storage facility
◇ Seat reservations can be made at this station
⚠ Penalty Fare Schemes in operation on some or all services from this station
🚕 Taxi rank or cab office at station, or signposted and within 100 metres
ⓤ Unstaffed station
[ ] Station Operator Code

[10] Connection time
℗ Station Car Park
🚲 Bicycle storage facility
◇ Seat reservations can be made at this station
⚠ Penalty Fare Schemes in operation on some or all services from this station
🚕 Taxi rank or cab office at station, or signposted and within 100 metres
Ⓤ Unstaffed station
[ ] Station Operator Code

Station index and table numbers

Hull 39
Leeds 39
Liverpool 39
London 26
Manchester 39
Manchester Airport 39
Meadowhall 34
Middlesbrough 39
Newcastle 39
Peterborough 26
Scarborough 39
Selby 39, 41
Sheffield 34
Wakefield 39
York 39
Hull [TP] ℗ 🚲 ◇ 🚕
Aberdeen 26
Beverley 43
Bridlington 43
Cambridge 26
Darlington 26
Doncaster 29
Durham 26
Edinburgh 26
Filey 43
Glasgow 26
Goole 29
Grantham 26
Huddersfield 39
Leeds 39
Liverpool 39
London 26, 29
Manchester 29, 39
Manchester Airport 29, 39
Newark 26
Newcastle 26
Norwich 26
Peterborough 26
Retford 26
Scarborough 43
Selby 29
Sheffield 29
Stockport 29
York 33
Hull Paragon Interchange 🚕 *Bus* 29
Humphrey Park [NT] Ⓤ 89
Huncoat [NT] Ⓤ 97
Hungerford [GW] ℗ 🚲 🚕 Ⓤ 116, 135
Hunmanby [NT] Ⓤ 43
Hunstanton Bus Station *Bus* 17A
Hunts Cross [ME] ⚠ 89, 103
Huntingdon [FC] ℗ 🚲 ◇ ⚠ 🚕 25
Huntly [SR] ℗ 🚲 ◇ 240
Hurst Green [SN] **[3]** ℗ 🚲 ◇ ⚠ 184
Hutton Cranswick [NT] ℗ Ⓤ 43
Huyton [NT] ℗ 90
Hyde [NT] (see Newton for Hyde)
Hyde Central [NT] ℗ Ⓤ 78
Hyde North [NT] ℗ Ⓤ 78
Hykeham [EM] ℗ Ⓤ 27
Hyndland [SR] 🚲 226
Hythe (Essex) **[LE]** 🚲 ⚠ Ⓤ 11

I

IBM [SR] 🚲 Ⓤ 219
Ifield [SN] 🚲 ◇ ⚠ 186
Ilford [LE] **[2]** 🚲 ◇ ⚠ 5
Ilkley [NT] ℗ 🚲 ◇ 38
Imperial Wharf [LO] 🚲 ⚠ 66, 176, 177
Ince [NT] Ⓤ 82
Ince & Elton [NT] ℗ Ⓤ 109
Ingatestone [LE] ℗ 🚲 ⚠ 11
Insch [SR] ℗ 🚲 Ⓤ 240
Invergordon [SR] ℗ 🚲 Ⓤ 239
Invergowrie [SR] 🚲 Ⓤ 229
Inverkeithing [SR] ℗ 🚲 ◇ 🚕
Aberdeen 229
Birmingham 51
Bournemouth 51
Bristol 51
Carlisle 51
Crewe *Sleepers* 402
Derby 51
Dundee 229
Edinburgh 242
Inverness 229
London 26, *Sleepers* 402
Newcastle 26
Oxford 51
Penzance 51
Perth 229
Plymouth 51
Preston 51, *Sleepers* 402
Reading 51
Sheffield 51
Southampton 51
York 26
Inverkip [SR] ℗ 🚲 Ⓤ 219
Inverness [SR] ℗ 🚲 ◇ 🚕
Aberdeen 240
Birmingham 65
Cambridge 26
Carlisle 65
Crewe 65, *Sleepers* 403
Dingwall 239
Edinburgh 229
Elgin 240
Glasgow 229
Inverkeithing 229
Kingussie 229
Kirkcaldy 229
Kyle of Lochalsh 239
Leeds 26
Liverpool 65
London 26, 65, *Sleepers* 403
Manchester 65
Newcastle 26
Norwich 26
Orkney Isles *Ship* 239A
Perth 229
Preston 65, *Sleepers* 403
Stirling 229
Thurso 239
Western Isles *Ship* 239B
Wick 239
York 26
Inverness Bus Station 🚕 *Bus* 239B
Invershin [SR] ℗ 🚲 Ⓤ 239
Inverurie [SR] ℗ 🚲 ◇ 🚕 229, 240
Ipswich [LE] ℗ 🚲 ◇ 🚕 11, 13, 14, 17
Irlam [NT] ℗ Ⓤ 89
Irvine [SR] ℗ 🚲 🚕 221
Isle of Man *Ship* 98A
Isle of Wight [IL] 158, 167
Isleworth [SW] ℗ 🚲 ⚠ 🚕 Ⓤ 149
Islington (see Highbury & Islington)
Islip [CH] ℗ 🚲 Ⓤ 116
Iver [GW] 🚲 ⚠ 117
Ivybridge [GW] ℗ 🚲 Ⓤ 135

J

James Street [ME] (see Liverpool)
Jewellery Quarter [LM] ⚠ 71
Johnston [AW] Ⓤ 128
Johnstone [SR] ℗ 🚲 🚕 221
Jordanhill [SR] 🚲 Ⓤ 226

K

Kearsley [NT] Ⓤ 82
Kearsney [SE] ℗ ⚠ 212
Keighley [NT] ℗ 🚲 ◇ 🚕 26, 36
Keith [SR] ℗ 🚲 ◇ 240
Kelvedon [LE] ℗ 🚲 ⚠ 11
Kelvindale [SR] ℗ 🚲 Ⓤ 232
Kemble [GW] ℗ ◇ 🚕 125
Kempston Hardwick [LM] Ⓤ 64
Kempton Park [SW] ⚠ 152
Kemsing [SE] ℗ ⚠ Ⓤ 196
Kemsley [SE] ⚠ Ⓤ 212
Kendal [TP] ℗ 🚕 Ⓤ 83
Kenley [SN] ℗ ◇ ⚠ 181
Kennett [LE] ℗ 🚲 Ⓤ 14
Kennishead [SR] 🚲 Ⓤ 222
Kensal Green [LT] 60
Kensal Rise [LO] 🚲 ⚠ 59
Kensington (Olympia) [LO] ℗ 🚲 ◇ ⚠ 66, 176, 177
Kent House [SE] **[4]** 🚲 ◇ ⚠ 195
Kentish Town [LT] ⚠ 🚕 52, 195
Kentish Town West [LO] 🚲 ⚠ 59
Kenton [LT] 60
Kenton (South) [LT] (see South Kenton)

Station index and table numbers

■10 Connection time
Ⓟ Station Car Park
🚲 Bicycle storage facility
◇ Seat reservations can be made at this station
⚠ Penalty Fare Schemes in operation on some or all services from this station
🚕 Taxi rank or cab office at station, or signposted and within 100 metres
Ⓤ Unstaffed station
[ ] Station Operator Code

Kents Bank [NT] Ⓤ 82
Kettering [EM] ■4 Ⓟ 🚲 ◇ ⚠ 🚕 53
Kettering Library *Bus* 26B
Kew Bridge [SW] 🚲 Ⓤ 149
Kew Gardens [LT] 59
Keyham [GW] Ⓤ 135, 139
Keynsham [GW] Ⓟ 🚲 123, 132
Kidbrooke [SE] Ⓟ 🚲 ◇ ⚠ 200
Kidderminster [LM] Ⓟ ◇ ⚠ 🚕 71, 115
Kidsgrove [EM] Ⓟ ◇ 50, 67, 84
Kidwelly [AW] Ⓤ 128
Kilburn High Road [LO] ⚠ 60
Kilcreggan *Ship* 219A
Kildale [NT] Ⓟ Ⓤ 45
Kildonan [SR] Ⓟ 🚲 Ⓤ 239
Kilgetty [AW] Ⓤ 128
Kilmarnock [SR] ■3 Ⓟ 🚲 ◇ 🚕 216, 218, 222
Kilmaurs [SR] Ⓟ 🚲 Ⓤ 222
Kilpatrick [SR] Ⓟ 🚲 Ⓤ 226
Kilwinning [SR] Ⓟ 🚲 🚕 218, 221
Kinbrace [SR] Ⓟ 🚲 Ⓤ 239
Kingham [GW] Ⓟ 🚲 126, *Bus* 126A
Kinghorn [SR] 🚲 242
Kings Cross [NR] (see London)
Kings Langley [LM] Ⓟ 🚲 🚕 66
Kings Lynn [FC] Ⓟ 🚲 ◇ 🚕 17, *Bus* 17A
Kings Lynn Bus Station 🚕 *Bus* 26A
Kings Norton [LM] Ⓟ ◇ ⚠ 69
Kings Nympton [GW] Ⓟ Ⓤ 136
Kings Park [SR] 🚲 223
Kings Sutton [CH] ⚠ Ⓤ 115, 116
Kingsknowe [SR] Ⓟ Ⓤ 225
Kingston [SW] ◇ ⚠ 🚕 149, 152
Kingswood [SN] Ⓟ ◇ ⚠ 181
Kingussie [SR] Ⓟ 🚲 229, *Sleepers* 403
Kintbury [GW] Ⓟ 🚲 Ⓤ 116
Kirby Cross [LE] 🚲 ⚠ Ⓤ 11
Kirkby [ME] Ⓟ ⚠ 🚕 82, 103
Kirkby in Ashfield [EM] Ⓟ Ⓤ 55
Kirkby-in-Furness [NT] Ⓤ 100
Kirkby Stephen [NT] Ⓟ Ⓤ 36
Kirkcaldy [SR] Ⓟ 🚲 ◇ 🚕
  Aberdeen 229
  Birmingham 51
  Bournemouth 51
  Bristol 51
  Carlisle 51
  Crewe *Sleepers* 402
  Derby 51
  Dundee 229
  Edinburgh 242
  Inverness 229
  London 26, *Sleepers* 402
  Newcastle 26
  Oxford 51
  Penzance 51
  Perth 229
  Plymouth 51
  Preston 51, *Sleepers* 402
  Reading 51
  Sheffield 51
  Southampton 51
  York 26
Kirkconnel [SR] Ⓟ 🚲 Ⓤ 216
Kirkdale [ME] ⚠ 103
Kirkham & Wesham [NT] Ⓟ ◇ 82, 97
Kirk Sandall [NT] Ⓟ Ⓤ 29
Kirkhill [SR] Ⓟ 🚲 Ⓤ 223
Kirknewton [SR] Ⓟ 🚲 Ⓤ 225
Kirkoswald [NT] (see Lazonby)
Kirkwood [SR] Ⓤ 220
Kirton Lindsey [NT] Ⓟ Ⓤ 30
Kiveton Bridge [NT] Ⓤ 30
Kiveton Park [NT] Ⓟ 🚲 Ⓤ 30
Knaresborough [NT] Ⓟ Ⓤ 35
Knebworth [FC] Ⓟ 🚲 ⚠ 24, 25
Knighton [AW] Ⓤ 129
Knockholt [SE] Ⓟ ◇ ⚠ 204
Knottingley [NT] Ⓟ Ⓤ 32
Knucklas [AW] Ⓤ 129
Knutsford [NT] Ⓟ 88
Kyle of Lochalsh [SR] Ⓟ 🚲 ◇ 239, *Ship* 239B

L

Ladybank [SR] Ⓟ 🚲 51, 229
Ladywell [SE] 🚲 ◇ ⚠ 203
Laindon [CC] Ⓟ 🚲 ◇ ⚠ 🚕 1
Lairg [SR] Ⓟ 🚲 Ⓤ 239
Lake [IL] (IOW) Ⓤ 167
Lake District [VT] (see Oxenholme)
Lakenheath [LE] Ⓤ 17
Lamphey [AW] Ⓤ 128
Lanark [SR] Ⓟ 🚲 🚕 226
Lancaster [VT] ■6 Ⓟ 🚲 ◇ 🚕
  Aberdeen 65
  Barrow-in-Furness 82
  Birmingham 65
  Blackpool 65
  Bolton 82
  Bournemouth 51
  Bradford 36
  Bristol 51
  Carlisle 65
  Chorley 82
  Crewe 65
  Douglas (IOM) 98A
  Edinburgh 65
  Exeter 51
  Glasgow 65
  Heysham Port 98
  Leeds 36
  Liverpool 65
  London 65
  Manchester 82
  Manchester Airport 82
  Millom 100
  Milton Keynes Central 65
  Morecambe 98
  Oxenholme Lake District 65
  Oxford 51
  Paignton 51
  Penzance 51
  Plymouth 51
  Preston 65
  Reading 51
  Skipton 36
  Southampton 51
  Stafford 65
  Torquay 51
  Warrington 65
  Whitehaven 100
  Wigan 65
  Windermere 65
  Workington 100
Lancing [SN] Ⓟ 🚲 ◇ ⚠ 🚕 188
Landywood [LM] Ⓟ ⚠ Ⓤ 70
Langbank [SR] Ⓟ 🚲 Ⓤ 219
Langho [NT] Ⓟ Ⓤ 94
Langley [GW] Ⓟ 🚲 ⚠ 🚕 117
Langley Green [LM] Ⓟ ⚠ 71
Langley Mill [EM] Ⓟ Ⓤ 34, 49, 53
Langside [SR] 🚲 Ⓤ 223
Langwathby [NT] Ⓤ 36
Langwith - Whaley Thorns [EM] Ⓤ 55
Lapford [GW] Ⓤ 136
Lapworth [CH] Ⓟ ⚠ Ⓤ 71, 115
Larbert [SR] Ⓟ 🚲 ◇ 🚕 229, 230
Largs [SR] Ⓟ 🚲 🚕 221
Larkhall [SR] 🚲 Ⓤ 226
Latimer [LT] (see Chalfont & Latimer)
Latchmere [SN] 177
Laurencekirk [SR] Ⓟ 🚲 Ⓤ 229
Lawrence Hill [GW] Ⓤ 133, 134
Layton [NT] Ⓟ Ⓤ 82, 97
Lazonby & Kirkoswald [NT] Ⓤ 36
Lea Green [NT] Ⓟ 🚲 90
Lea Hall [LM] Ⓟ ⚠ 68
Leagrave [FC] Ⓟ 🚲 ◇ ⚠ 🚕 52
Lealholm [NT] Ⓤ 45
Leamington Spa [CH] ■8 Ⓟ 🚲 ◇ ⚠ 🚕 51, 71, 75, 115, 116
Leasowe [ME] Ⓟ ⚠ 106
Leatherhead [SN] Ⓟ 🚲 ◇ ⚠ 🚕 152, 182
Ledbury [LM] Ⓟ ⚠ Ⓤ 71, 126
Lee [SE] Ⓟ ◇ ⚠ 200
Leeds [NR] ■10 Ⓟ 🚲 ◇ 🚕
  Barnsley 34
  Bedford 53
  Birmingham 51
  Birmingham International 51
  Blackburn 41
  Blackpool 41
  Bournemouth 51
  Bradford 37

■10 Connection time
Ⓟ Station Car Park
🚲 Bicycle storage facility
◇ Seat reservations can be made at this station
⚠ Penalty Fare Schemes in operation on some or all services from this station
🚕 Taxi rank or cab office at station, or signposted and within 100 metres
Ⓤ Unstaffed station
[ ] Station Operator Code

Station index and table numbers

Station index and table numbers

[10] Connection time
Ⓟ Station Car Park
🚲 Bicycle storage facility
◇ Seat reservations can be made at this station
⚠ Penalty Fare Schemes in operation on some or all services from this station
🚕 Taxi rank or cab office at station, or signposted and within 100 metres
Ⓤ Unstaffed station
[ ] Station Operator Code

Wolverhampton 65
York 39
Liverpool Landing Stage *Ship* 98A
Liverpool South Parkway [ME] [7] Ⓟ 🚲 ⚠ 🚕 39,49, 65, 89, 91, 103
Liverpool Street [NR] (see London)
Livingston North [SR] Ⓟ 🚲 Ⓤ 226
Livingston South [SR] Ⓟ 🚲 Ⓤ 225
Llanaber [AW] Ⓤ 75
Llanbedr [AW] Ⓤ 75
Llanbister Road [AW] Ⓤ 129
Llanbradach [AW] Ⓟ Ⓤ 130
Llandaf [AW] Ⓟ 130
Llandanwg [AW] Ⓤ 75
Llandecwyn [AW] Ⓤ 75
Llandeilo [AW] Ⓟ Ⓤ 129
Llandovery [AW] Ⓟ Ⓤ 129
Llandrindod [AW] Ⓟ ◇ 129
Llandudno [AW] ◇ 🚕 81, 102
Llandudno Junction [AW] Ⓟ ◇ 🚕 65, 81, 102, 131
Llandybie [AW] Ⓟ Ⓤ 129
Llanelli [AW] ◇ 128, 129
Llanfairfechan [AW] Ⓟ Ⓤ 81
Llanfairpwll [AW] Ⓟ Ⓤ 81
Llangadog [AW] Ⓤ 129
Llangammarch [AW] Ⓤ 129
Llangennech [AW] Ⓤ 129
Llangynllo [AW] Ⓤ 129
Llanharan [AW] Ⓟ Ⓤ 128
Llanhilleth [AW] Ⓟ Ⓤ 127
Llanishen [AW] Ⓟ Ⓤ 130
Llanrwst [AW] Ⓤ 102
Llansamlet [AW] Ⓟ Ⓤ 128
Llantwit Major [AW] Ⓟ 🚲 Ⓤ 130
Llanwrda [AW] Ⓤ 129
Llanwrtyd [AW] Ⓟ Ⓤ 129
Llwyngwril [AW] Ⓤ 75
Llwynypia [AW] Ⓟ Ⓤ 130
Loch Awe [SR] Ⓟ 🚲 Ⓤ 227
Loch Eil Outward Bound [SR] 🚲 Ⓤ 227
Lochailort [SR] Ⓟ 🚲 Ⓤ 227
Lochboisdale *Ship* 227C
Locheilside [SR] Ⓟ 🚲 Ⓤ 227
Lochgelly [SR] Ⓟ 🚲 Ⓤ 242
Lochluichart [SR] Ⓟ Ⓤ 239
Lochmaddy *Ship* 239B
Lochwinnoch [SR] Ⓟ 🚲 Ⓤ 221
Lockerbie [SR] Ⓟ 🚲 ◇ 🚕 51, 65
Lockwood [NT] Ⓟ Ⓤ 34
London
Blackfriars [FC] [3] ◇ ⚠ 🚕
Cannon Street [NR] [4] ◇ ⚠ 🚕
Charing Cross [NR] [4] ◇ ⚠ 🚕
City Thameslink [FC] [3] ◇ ⚠ 🚕
Euston [NR] [15] Ⓟ 🚲 ◇ ⚠ 🚕
Farringdon [LT] [3] ⚠
Fenchurch Street [NR] [7] ◇ ⚠ 🚕
Kings Cross [NR] [15] Ⓟ 🚲 ◇ ⚠ 🚕
Liverpool Street [NR] [15] 🚲 ◇ ⚠ 🚕
London Bridge [NR] [4] 🚲 ◇ ⚠ 🚕
Marylebone [CH] [10] 🚲 ◇ ⚠ 🚕
Moorgate [LT] ⚠
Paddington [NR] [15] Ⓟ 🚲 ◇ ⚠ 🚕
St Pancras International [NR] [15] Ⓟ ◇ ⚠ 🚕
Victoria [NR] [15] Ⓟ 🚲 ◇ ⚠ 🚕
Waterloo [NR] [15] Ⓟ 🚲 ◇ ⚠ 🚕
Waterloo East [SE] [4] ⚠
Aberdeen 26, *Sleepers* 402
Aldershot 149, 155
Alexandra Palace 24
Alnmouth 26
Alton 155
Amersham 114
Arbroath 26, *Sleepers* 402
Ascot 149
Ashford International 196, 207
Aviemore *Sleepers* 403
Aylesbury 114, 115
Balham 177, 178
Banbury 115, 116
Bangor (Gwynedd) 65
Barking 1
Barnsley 53
Barrow-in-Furness 65
Basingstoke 155, 158
Bath Spa 125, 160
Beckenham Junction 177, 195
Bedford 52
Belper 53
Berwick-upon-Tweed 26
Bexhill 189
Bicester 115, 116
Birmingham 66, 115, 116
Birmingham International 66
Bishops Stortford 22
Blackburn 97
Blackpool 65
Bletchley 66
Bodmin Parkway 135, *Sleepers* 406
Bognor Regis 188
Bourne End 120
Bournemouth 158
Bradford 26
Braintree 11
Brighton 186
Bristol 125, 160
Bromley North 204
Bromley South 195
Broxbourne 22
Camborne 135, *Sleepers* 406
Cambridge 22, 25
Canterbury 207, 212
Cardiff 125
Carlisle 65, *Sleepers* 400, 401
Carstairs 65, *Sleepers* 401
Carmarthen 128
Caterham 181
Chatham 200, 212
Chelmsford 11
Cheltenham Spa 125
Chertsey 149
Chessington 152
Chester 65
Chesterfield 53
Chichester 188
Chingford 20
Clacton-on-Sea 11
Clapton 20, 22
Cleethorpes 29
Colchester 11
Coventry 66
Crewe 65
Cromer 16
Crystal Palace 177, 178
Darlington 26
Dartford 200
Derby 53
Didcot 116
Doncaster 26, 53
Dorking 152, 182
Douglas (IOM) 98A
Dover 207, 212
Dundee 26, *Sleepers* 402
Durham 26
Eaglescliffe 26
Eastbourne 189
East Croydon 175
East Grinstead 184
Edinburgh 26, *Sleepers* 400
Effingham Junction 152
Ely 17
Enfield Town 21
Epsom 152, 182
Epsom Downs 182
Exeter 135, 160, *Sleepers* 406
Fareham 158, 188
Felixstowe 13
Finsbury Park 24, 25
Folkestone 207
Fort William *Sleepers* 404
Gatwick Airport 186
Gillingham (Kent) 200, 212
Glasgow 26, 65, *Sleepers* 401
Gloucester 125
Grantham 26
Gravesend 200
Grays 1
Great Yarmouth 15
Greenford 117
Grove Park 204
Guildford 152, 155, 156
Halifax 26
Hampton Court 152

Station index and table numbers

- ■10 Connection time
- ℗ Station Car Park
- Bicycle storage facility
- ◇ Seat reservations can be made at this station
- Penalty Fare Schemes in operation on some or all services from this station
- Taxi rank or cab office at station, or signposted and within 100 metres
- Unstaffed station
- [ ] Station Operator Code

Station index and table numbers

[10]	Connection time
℗	Station Car Park
🚲	Bicycle storage facility
◇	Seat reservations can be made at this station
⚠	Penalty Fare Schemes in operation on some or all services from this station
🚕	Taxi rank or cab office at station, or signposted and within 100 metres
🚹	Unstaffed station
[ ]	Station Operator Code

Worthing 188
Wrexham 65, 75
Yarmouth (IOW) 158
York 26, 53
London Bridge [NR] (see London)
London Fields [LE] ⚠ 🚹 21
London Gatwick Airport [NR] (see Gatwick Airport)
London Heathrow Airport [HX] (see Heathrow Airport)
London Luton Airport (see also Luton Airport Parkway) 🚕 *Bus* 65B
London Southend Airport [LE] 5
London Road (Brighton) [SN] ◇ ⚠ 189
London Road (Guildford) [SW] ℗ 🚲 ◇ ⚠ 🚕 152
London Stansted Airport [LE] (see Stansted Airport)
Long Buckby [LM] ℗ 68
Long Eaton [EM] ℗ 🚲 ◇ ⚠ 53, 56, 57
Long Preston [NT] ℗ 🚹 36
Longbeck [NT] 🚲 🚹 44
Longbridge [LM] ◇ ⚠ 69
Longcross [SW] ⚠ 🚹 149
Longfield [SE] ℗ ◇ ⚠ 🚕 212
Longniddry [SR] ℗ 🚲 🚹 238
Longport [EM] ℗ 🚹 50, 84
Longton [EM] ℗ 🚹 50
Looe [GW] ℗ 🚲 🚹 140
Lostock [NT] ℗ 82
Lostock Gralam [NT] ℗ 🚹 88
Lostock Hall [NT] ℗ 🚹 97
Lostwithiel [GW] ℗ 🚹 51,135, *Sleepers* 406
Loughborough [EM] ℗ 🚲 ◇ ⚠ 🚕 53
Loughborough Junction [FC] 🚲 ◇ ⚠ 52, 177, 179, 195
Lowdham [EM] ℗ 🚹 27
Lower Sydenham [SE] 🚲 ◇ ⚠ 203
Lowestoft [LE] ℗ 🚲 ◇ 🚕 13, 15
Ludlow [AW] ℗ ◇ 131
Luton [FC] [10] ℗ 🚲 ◇ ⚠ 🚕 52, *Bus* 52A, 53, *Bus* 65B
Luton Airport (see London Luton Airport)
Luton Airport Parkway [FC] [7] ℗ 🚲 ◇ ⚠ 🚕 52, 53, 177, 179, 186
Luxulyan [GW] ℗ 🚹 142
Lydney [AW] ℗ 🚹 132
Lye [LM] ℗ ⚠ 71
Lymington Pier [SW] 🚲 ⚠ 🚹 158
Lymington Town [SW] ℗ 🚲 ◇ ⚠ 158
Lympstone Commando [GW] 🚹 136
Lympstone Village [GW] ℗ 🚲 🚹 136
Lytham [NT] 🚹 97

M

Macclesfield [VT] ℗ 🚲 ◇ 🚕 51, 65, 84
Machynlleth [AW] [4] ℗ ◇ 75
Maesteg [AW] ℗ 🚹 128, *Bus* 128A
Maesteg (Ewenny Road) [AW] 🚹 128
Maghull [ME] ℗ 🚲 ⚠ 🚕 103
Maidenhead [GW] [3] ℗ 🚲 ◇ ⚠ 🚕 116, 117, 120
Maiden Newton [GW] ℗ 🚹 123
Maidstone Barracks [SE] ⚠ 🚹 208
Maidstone East [SE] [4] ℗ ◇ ⚠ 🚕 196
Maidstone West [SE] [4] ℗ ◇ ⚠ 🚕 194, 200, 207, 208
Malden Manor [SW] ℗ 🚲 ◇ ⚠ 152
Mallaig [SR] 🚲 ◇ 227, *Ship* 227A
Malton [TP] ℗ 🚲 ◇ 🚕 39
Malvern Link [LM] ℗ ◇ ⚠ 71, 126
Manchester
Oxford Road [NT] ◇ 🚕
Piccadilly [NR] [10] ℗ 🚲 ◇ 🚕
Victoria [NT] ◇ 🚕
Aberdeen 65
Altrincham 88
Bangor (Gwynedd) 81
Barrow-in-Furness 82
Birmingham 65
Birmingham International 65
Blackpool 82
Bolton 82
Bournemouth 51
Bradford 41
Bristol 51
Burnley 97
Buxton 86
Cambridge 49
Cardiff 131
Carlisle 65
Carmarthen 128
Cheadle Hulme 84
Chester 81, 88
Chinley 78
Cleethorpes 29
Clitheroe 94
Coventry 65
Crewe 84
Darlington 39
Doncaster 29
Douglas (IOM) 98A
Dundee 65
Durham 39
Edinburgh 65
Exeter 51
Glasgow 65
Glossop 79
Grimsby 29
Guide Bridge 78
Hadfield 79
Heysham Port 98A
Holyhead 81
Huddersfield 39
Hull 29, 39
Inverness 65
Kirkby 82
Lancaster 82
Leeds 39, 41
Liverpool 89, 90
Liverpool South Parkway 89
Llandudno 81
London 65
Macclesfield 84
Manchester Airport 85
Marple 78
Middlesbrough 39
Milford Haven 128
Milton Keynes Central 65
Motherwell 65
Newcastle 39
New Mills 78, 86
Newport (South Wales) 131
Northwich 88
Nottingham 49
Oxenholme Lake District 65
Oxford 51
Paignton 51
Penzance 51
Peterborough 49
Plymouth 51
Preston 82
Reading 51
Rhyl 81
Rochdale 41
Rose Hill Marple 78
Rugby 65
St Helens 90
Salford 82
Scarborough 39
Sheffield 78
Shrewsbury 131
Southampton 51
Southport 82
Stafford 84
Stalybridge 39
Stansted Airport 49
Stockport 84
Stoke-on-Trent 84
Swansea 131
Tenby 128
Torquay 51
Wakefield 39
Warrington 89, 90
Watford 65
Wigan 82
Wilmslow 84
Windermere 82

Station index and table numbers

- **10** Connection time
- Ⓟ Station Car Park
- 🚲 Bicycle storage facility
- ◇ Seat reservations can be made at this station
- ⚠ Penalty Fare Schemes in operation on some or all services from this station
- 🚕 Taxi rank or cab office at station, or signposted and within 100 metres
- Ⓤ Unstaffed station
- [ ] Station Operator Code

Wolverhampton 65
York 39
Manchester Airport [TP] ◇
Bangor (Gwynedd) 81
Barrow-in-Furness 82
Birmingham 65
Birmingham International 65
Blackburn 94
Blackpool 82
Bolton 82
Carlisle 65
Coventry 65
Crewe 84
Darlington 39
Doncaster 29
Durham 39
Edinburgh 65
Glasgow 65
Huddersfield 39
Hull 29, 39
Holyhead 81
Lancaster 82
Leeds 39
Liverpool 89
London 65
Manchester 85
Middlesbrough 39
Motherwell 65
Newcastle 39
Oxenholme Lake District 82
Penrith North Lakes 65
Preston 82
St Helens 90
Salford 82
Scarborough 39
Sheffield 78
Southport 82
Stafford 65, 84
Wakefield 39
Warrington 89
Watford 65
Wigan 82
Wilmslow 84
Windermere 82
Wolverhampton 65
York 39
Manea [LE] Ⓤ 14, 17
Manningtree [LE] **2** Ⓟ 🚲 ⚠ 🚕 11, 14
Manor Park [LE] 🚲 ⚠ 5
Manor Road [ME] 🚲 ⚠ 106
Manorbier [AW] Ⓤ 128
Manors [NT] Ⓤ 48
Mansfield [EM] Ⓟ 🚲 🚕 55
Mansfield Woodhouse [EM] Ⓟ Ⓤ 55
March [LE] Ⓟ ◇ 🚕 14, 17, 49
Marden [SE] Ⓟ ◇ ⚠ 207
Margate [SE] **4** Ⓟ 🚲 ◇ ⚠ 🚕 194, 207, 212
Market Harborough [EM] Ⓟ 🚲 ◇ ⚠ 🚕 53
Market Rasen [EM] Ⓟ 🚲 Ⓤ 27
Markinch [SR] Ⓟ 🚲 🚕 51, 229
Marks Tey [LE] **2** Ⓟ 🚲 ⚠ 10, 11
Marlow [GW] 🚲 Ⓤ 120
Marple [NT] Ⓟ 🚲 78
Marsden [NT] Ⓟ Ⓤ 39
Marske [NT] 🚲 Ⓤ 44
Marston Green [LM] Ⓟ ◇ ⚠ 68
Martin Mill [SE] Ⓟ ⚠ 207
Martins Heron [SW] Ⓟ 🚲 ◇ ⚠ 149
Marton [NT] Ⓟ 🚲 Ⓤ 45
Maryhill [SR] 🚲 Ⓤ 232
Maryland [LE] 🚲 ⚠ 🚕 5
Marylebone [CH] (see London)
Maryport [NT] Ⓟ Ⓤ 100
Matlock [EM] Ⓟ Ⓤ 56
Matlock Bath [EM] Ⓟ Ⓤ 56
Mauldeth Road [NT] 85
Maxwell Park [SR] 🚲 Ⓤ 223
Maybole [SR] Ⓟ 🚲 Ⓤ 218
Maze Hill [SE] ◇ ⚠ 200
Meadowhall [NT] Ⓟ 🚲 ◇
Barnsley 34
Castleford 34
Cleethorpes 29
Doncaster 29
Gainsborough 30
Grimsby 29
Huddersfield 34
Hull 29
Leeds 31
Lincoln 30
Manchester 29
Manchester Airport 29
Penistone 34
Pontefract 33
Retford 30
Rotherham 29
Scunthorpe 29
Sheffield 29
Wakefield 31
Worksop 30
York 29, 33
Meldreth [FC] Ⓟ 🚲 ⚠ 25
Melksham [GW] Ⓟ Ⓤ 123
Melrose *Bus* 26K
Melton [LE] Ⓟ 🚲 🚕 Ⓤ 13
Melton Mowbray [EM] Ⓟ 🚲 ◇ 🚕 49, 53
Menheniot [GW] Ⓟ Ⓤ 135
Menston [NT] Ⓟ 🚲 ◇ 38
Meols [ME] Ⓟ 🚲 ⚠ 🚕 106
Meols Cop [NT] Ⓤ 82
Meopham [SE] Ⓟ ◇ ⚠ 🚕 212
Merryton [SR] 🚲 Ⓤ 226
Merstham [SN] Ⓟ 🚲 ◇ ⚠ 🚕 186
Merthyr Tydfil [AW] Ⓟ ◇ 130
Merthyr Vale [AW] Ⓤ 130
Metheringham [EM] Ⓟ 🚲 Ⓤ 18
Metrocentre [NT] Ⓤ 44, 48
Mexborough [NT] Ⓟ 🚲 ◇ 29
Micheldever [SW] Ⓟ 🚲 ◇ ⚠ 158
Micklefield [NT] Ⓟ 🚲 Ⓤ 40
Middlesbrough [TP] Ⓟ 🚲 ◇ 🚕 26, 39, 44, 45
Middlewood [NT] Ⓤ 86
Midgham [GW] Ⓟ Ⓤ 116
Milford Haven [AW] Ⓟ 🚕 Ⓤ 128
Milford (Surrey) [SW] Ⓟ 🚲 ⚠ 156
Millbrook (Bedfordshire) [LM] Ⓤ 64
Millbrook (Hants.) [SW] 🚲 ⚠ Ⓤ 158
Mill Hill Broadway [FC] Ⓟ 🚲 ◇ ⚠ 52
Mill Hill (Lancashire) [NT] Ⓤ 97
Milliken Park [SR] 🚲 Ⓤ 221
Millom [NT] Ⓟ Ⓤ 100
Mills Hill [NT] Ⓟ Ⓤ 41
Milngavie [SR] Ⓟ 🚲 226
Milton Keynes Central [LM] Ⓟ 🚲 ◇ ⚠ 🚕
Birmingham International 66
Birmingham New Street 66
Blackpool 65
Bletchley 66
Brighton 66
Coventry 66, 67
Crewe 65, 67
Edinburgh 65
Gatwick Airport 66
Glasgow 65
Lancaster 65
Liverpool 65
London 67
Manchester 65
Northampton 66, 67
Oxenholme Lake District 65
Preston 65
Rugby 66, 67
Stafford 65, 67
Stockport 65
Stoke-on-Trent 65, 67
Tring 66
Warrington 65
Watford Junction 66, 176, 177
Wembley Central 66, 176, 177
Wigan 65
Wolverhampton 66
Minehead Bancks Street *Bus* 135E
Minehead Butlins *Bus* 135E
Minehead Parade *Bus* 135E
Minffordd [AW] Ⓤ 75
Minster [SE] **4** Ⓟ ⚠ Ⓤ 207
Mirfield [NT] Ⓟ 🚲 Ⓤ 39, 41
Mistley [LE] 🚲 Ⓤ 11
Mitcham Eastfields [SN] ◇ ⚠ 52, 179, 182
Mitcham Junction [SN] Ⓟ 🚲 ◇ ⚠ 52, 179, 182

Station index and table numbers

■10 Connection time
Ⓟ Station Car Park
🚲 Bicycle storage facility
◇ Seat reservations can be made at this station
⚠ Penalty Fare Schemes in operation on some or all services from this station
🚕 Taxi rank or cab office at station, or signposted and within 100 metres
Ⓤ Unstaffed station
[ ] Station Operator Code

Mobberley [NT] Ⓤ 88
Monifieth [SR] 🚲 Ⓤ 229
Monks Risborough [CH] ⚠ Ⓤ 115
Montpelier [GW] 🚲 Ⓤ 133
Montrose [SR] Ⓟ 🚲 ◇ 🚕 26, 51, 229, *Sleepers* 402
Moorfields [ME] (see Liverpool)
Moorgate [LT] ⚠ 24
Moorside [NT] 82
Moorthorpe [NT] Ⓟ Ⓤ 31, 33
Morar [SR] Ⓟ 🚲 Ⓤ 227
Morchard Road [GW] Ⓟ Ⓤ 136
Morden (Herts) **[FC]** (see Ashwell & Morden)
Morden South [FC] ⚠ Ⓤ 52, 179
Morecambe [NT] Ⓟ 🚲 ◇ 36, 98, 98A
Moreton (Dorset) [SW] Ⓟ 🚲 Ⓤ 158
Moreton (Merseyside) [ME] 🚲 ⚠ 🚕 106
Moreton-in-Marsh [GW] Ⓟ 🚲 ◇ 126
Morfa Mawddach [AW] Ⓤ 75
Morley [NT] Ⓟ Ⓤ 39
Morpeth [NT] Ⓟ 🚲 ◇ 🚕 26, 48, 51
Mortimer [GW] Ⓟ 122
Mortlake [SW] Ⓟ 🚲 ◇ ⚠ 149
Moses Gate [NT] Ⓤ 82
Moss Side [NT] Ⓤ 97
Mossley (Greater Manchester) [NT] Ⓟ 🚲 39
Mossley Hill [NT] Ⓟ 89, 91
Mosspark [SR] 🚲 Ⓤ 217
Moston [NT] Ⓤ 41
Motherwell [SR] Ⓟ 🚲 ◇ 🚕
Birmingham 51, 65
Bournemouth 51
Bristol 51
Crewe 65
Cumbernauld 224
Darlington 26
Doncaster 26
Edinburgh 225
Exeter 51
Glasgow 225, 226
Liverpool 65
London 26, 65, *Sleepers* 401
Manchester 65
Manchester Airport 65
Newcastle 26
Oxenholme Lake District 65
Oxford 51
Paignton 51
Penzance 51
Peterborough 26
Plymouth 51
Reading 51
Southampton 51
Torquay 51
Watford 65, *Sleepers* 401
York 26
Motspur Park [SW] ◇ ⚠ 152
Mottingham [SE] Ⓟ ◇ ⚠ 200
Mottisfont & Dunbridge [GW] Ⓤ 158
Mouldsworth [NT] Ⓟ Ⓤ 88
Moulsecoomb [SN] ◇ ⚠ 189
Mount Florida [SR] 🚲 223
Mount Vernon [SR] 🚲 Ⓤ 220
Mountain Ash [AW] Ⓟ Ⓤ 130
Muck *Ship* 227A
Muir of Ord [SR] Ⓟ 🚲 Ⓤ 239
Muirend [SR] 🚲 223
Musselburgh [SR] Ⓟ 🚲 Ⓤ 238
Mytholmroyd [NT] Ⓤ 41

N

Nafferton [NT] Ⓤ 43
Nailsea & Backwell [GW] Ⓟ 🚲 134
Nairn [SR] Ⓟ 🚲 ◇ 🚕 240
Nantwich [AW] Ⓤ 131
Narberth [AW] Ⓤ 128
Narborough [EM] Ⓟ 57
National Exhibition Centre [VT] (see Birmingham International)
Navigation Road [NT] Ⓤ 88
Neath [AW] Ⓟ 🚲 ◇ 🚕 125, 128
Needham Market [LE] Ⓤ 11, 14
Neilston [SR] Ⓟ 🚲 🚕 223
Nelson [NT] Ⓟ 97
Neston [AW] Ⓟ Ⓤ 101
Netherfield [EM] Ⓤ 19
Nethertown [NT] Ⓟ Ⓤ 100
Netley [SW] Ⓟ 🚲 ◇ 165
New Barnet [FC] Ⓟ 🚲 ⚠ 24
New Beckenham [SE] ■4 Ⓟ 🚲 ◇ ⚠ 203
New Brighton [ME] ⚠ 106
New Clee [NT] Ⓤ 29
New Cross [SE] ■4 🚲 ◇ ⚠ 178, 199, 200, 203, 204
New Cross Gate [LO] ■4 🚲 ⚠ 175, 178, 181, 182, 186
New Cumnock [SR] Ⓟ 🚲 Ⓤ 216
New Eltham [SE] Ⓟ ◇ ⚠ 200
New Haw [SW] (see Byfleet & New Haw)
New Holland [NT] 🚲 Ⓤ 29
New Hythe [SE] ⚠ Ⓤ 208
New Inn [AW] (see Pontypool and New Inn)
New Lane [NT] Ⓤ 82
New Malden [SW] ■6 Ⓟ 🚲 ◇ ⚠ 🚕 152
New Mills Central [NT] 78
New Mills Newtown [NT] Ⓟ 🚲 86
New Milton [SW] Ⓟ 🚲 ◇ ⚠ 🚕 158
New Pudsey [NT] Ⓟ 🚲 ◇ 37, 41
New Southgate [FC] Ⓟ ⚠ 24
Newark Castle [EM] Ⓟ 🚲 Ⓤ 27
Newark North Gate [GR] ■7 Ⓟ 🚲 ◇ 🚕 26, 27
Newbridge [AW] Ⓟ Ⓤ 127
Newbury [GW] Ⓟ 🚲 ◇ 🚕 116, 135
Newbury Racecourse [GW] Ⓤ 116
Newcastle [GR] ■8 Ⓟ 🚲 ◇ 🚕
Aberdeen 26
Alnmouth 26
Arbroath 26
Berwick-upon-Tweed 26
Birmingham 51
Birmingham International 51
Bournemouth 51
Bradford 39
Bristol 51
Cambridge 26
Cardiff 51
Carlisle 48
Chathill 48
Darlington 26
Derby 51
Doncaster 26
Dundee 26
Edinburgh 26
Exeter 51
Glasgow 26, 216
Grantham 26
Haltwhistle 48
Hartlepool 44
Hexham 48
Huddersfield 39
Hull 26
Leeds 26
Liverpool 39
London 26
Manchester 39
Manchester Airport 39
MetroCentre 48
Middlesbrough 44
Morpeth 48
Newark 26
Newport (South Wales) 51
Northallerton 26
Norwich 26
Oxford 51
Paignton 51
Penzance 51
Peterborough 26
Plymouth 51
Preston 39
Reading 51
Retford 26
Sheffield 26
Southampton 51
Stansted Airport 26
Stockton 44
Sunderland 44
Torquay 51
Whitby 45
York 26
Newcraighall [SR] Ⓟ 🚲 Ⓤ 242
Newhaven Harbour [SN] ◇ Ⓤ 189

10 Connection time
Ⓟ Station Car Park
🚲 Bicycle storage facility
◇ Seat reservations can be made at this station
⚠ Penalty Fare Schemes in operation on some or all services from this station
🚕 Taxi rank or cab office at station, or signposted and within 100 metres
Ⓤ Unstaffed station
[ ] Station Operator Code

Station index and table numbers

Station index and table numbers

[10] Connection time
Ⓟ Station Car Park
🚲 Bicycle storage facility
◇ Seat reservations can be made at this station
⚠ Penalty Fare Schemes in operation on some or all services from this station
🚕 Taxi rank or cab office at station, or signposted and within 100 metres
Ⓤ Unstaffed station
[ ] Station Operator Code

Wellingborough 53
Worksop 55
York 53
Nuneaton [LM] Ⓟ ◇ 🚕 49, 57, 65, 66, 67
Nunhead [SE] [4] ◇ ⚠ 52, 195, 200
Nunthorpe [NT] Ⓟ 🚲 Ⓤ 45
Nutbourne [SN] ⚠ Ⓤ 188
Nutfield [SN] ⚠ Ⓤ 186

O

Oakengates [LM] Ⓟ Ⓤ 74
Oakham [EM] Ⓟ ◇ 🚕 49, 53
Oakleigh Park [FC] ⚠ 🚕 24
Oban [SR] Ⓟ 🚲 ◇ 🚕 227, *Ship* 227B, 227C
Ockendon [CC] Ⓟ 🚲 ◇ ⚠ 🚕 1
Ockley [SN] Ⓟ ⚠ Ⓤ 182
Okehampton 136
Okehampton West Street *Bus* 135D
Old Hill [LM] Ⓟ ⚠ 71
Old Roan [ME] ⚠ 103
Old Street [LT] ⚠ 24
Oldfield Park [GW] 🚲 123, 132
Olton [LM] Ⓟ ⚠ 71
Ore [SN] Ⓤ 189, 206
Ormskirk [ME] Ⓟ 🚲 ◇ ⚠ 🚕 99, 103
Orpington [SE] [4] Ⓟ ◇ ⚠ 🚕 195, 199, 204, 206, 207
Orrell [NT] Ⓤ 82
Orrell Park [ME] ⚠ 103
Orston [EM] (see Elton & Orston)
Oswaldtwistle [NT] (see Church & Oswaldtwistle)
Otford [SE] [4] Ⓟ ◇ ⚠ 52, 195, 196
Oulton Broad North [LE] Ⓟ 🚲 Ⓤ 15
Oulton Broad South [LE] Ⓟ 🚲 Ⓤ 13
Oundle (Market Place) *Bus* 26B
Outwood [NT] Ⓟ 🚲 Ⓤ 31
Overpool [ME] Ⓤ 106
Overton [SW] Ⓟ 🚲 ◇ ⚠ 160
Oxenholme Lake District [VT] Ⓟ 🚲 ◇ 🚕 51, 65, 82, 83
Oxford [GW] Ⓟ 🚲 ◇ 🚕 51, 116,*Bus* 126
Oxshott [SW] Ⓟ 🚲 ◇ ⚠ 🚕 152
Oxted [SN] [3] Ⓟ 🚲 ◇ ⚠ 🚕 184

P

Paddington [NR] (see London)
Paddock Wood [SE] [4] Ⓟ 🚲 ◇ ⚠ 🚕 207, 208
Padgate [NT] Ⓟ Ⓤ 89
Padstow Old Rly Station *Bus* 135C
Paignton [GW] Ⓟ 🚲 ◇ 🚕 51, 135
Paisley Canal [SR] 🚲 Ⓤ 217
Paisley Gilmour Street [SR] Ⓟ 🚲 ◇ 🚕
Ayr 221
Ardrossan 221
Belfast *Ship* 221B
Clyde Coast *Ship* 219A, 219B, 221A
Glasgow 219, 221
Gourock 219
Largs 221
Stranraer 218
Wemyss Bay 219
Paisley St James [SR] 🚲 Ⓤ 219
Palmers Green [FC] Ⓟ ⚠ 24
Pangbourne [GW] Ⓟ 🚲 116
Pannal [NT] Ⓟ 🚲 Ⓤ 35
Pantyffynnon [AW] Ⓤ 129
Par [GW] Ⓟ ◇ 51, 135, 142, *Sleepers* 406
Parbold [NT] 82
Park Street [LM] Ⓤ 61
Parkhouse [SR] (see Possilpark & Parkhouse)
Parkstone (Dorset) [SW] Ⓟ 🚲 ◇ 158
Parson Street [GW] Ⓤ 134
Partick [SR] 🚲 226
Parton [NT] Ⓟ Ⓤ 100
Patchway [GW] Ⓟ Ⓤ 132
Patricroft [NT] Ⓤ 90
Patterton [SR] Ⓟ 🚲 Ⓤ 223
Peartree [EM] Ⓤ 50
Peckham Rye [SN] [4] 🚲 ◇ ⚠ 52, 177, 178, 179, 195, 200
Pegswood [NT] Ⓤ 48
Pemberton [NT] Ⓤ 82
Pembrey & Burry Port [AW] Ⓟ Ⓤ 128
Pembroke [AW] Ⓟ Ⓤ 128
Pembroke Dock [AW] Ⓟ Ⓤ 128
Penally [AW] Ⓤ 128
Penarth [AW] Ⓟ ◇ 🚕 130
Pencoed [AW] Ⓤ 128
Pengam [AW] Ⓟ Ⓤ 130
Penge East [SE] Ⓟ 🚲 ◇ ⚠ 195
Penge West [LO] 🚲 ⚠ 178
Penhelig [AW] Ⓤ 75
Penistone [NT] Ⓟ 🚲 Ⓤ 34
Penketh [NT] (see Sankey for Penketh)
Penkridge [LM] Ⓟ Ⓤ 65, 68
Penmaenmawr [AW] Ⓤ 81
Penmere [GW] Ⓟ 🚲 Ⓤ 143
Penrhiwceiber [AW] Ⓤ 130
Penrhyndeudraeth [AW] Ⓟ 🚲 Ⓤ 75
Penrith North Lakes [VT] Ⓟ 🚲 ◇ 🚕 51, 65, *Bus* 65F
Penryn [GW] 🚲 Ⓤ 143
Pensarn (Gwynedd) **[AW]** Ⓤ 75
Penshurst [SN] ⚠ Ⓤ 186
Pentre-bach [AW] Ⓤ 130
Pen-y-bont [AW] Ⓟ Ⓤ 129
Penychain [AW] Ⓤ 75
Penyffordd [AW] Ⓟ Ⓤ 101
Penzance [GW] Ⓟ 🚲 ◇ 🚕 51, 135, 144, *Sleepers* 406
Perranwell [GW] Ⓟ 🚲 Ⓤ 143
Perry Barr [LM] ◇ ⚠ 70
Pershore [GW] Ⓟ 🚲 Ⓤ 126
Perth [SR] Ⓟ 🚲 ◇ 🚕 26, 65, 229, *Sleepers* 403
Peterborough [GR] [8] Ⓟ 🚲 ◇ ⚠ 🚕
Aberdeen 26
Birmingham 49
Bradford 26
Cambridge 17
Corby George Street *Bus* 26B
Darlington 26
Dereham *Bus* 26A
Doncaster 26
Dundee 26
Edinburgh 26
Ely 17
Grantham 26
Grimsby 26
Hitchin 25
Hull 26
Huntingdon 25
Ipswich 17
Kettering Library *Bus* 26B
Kings Lynn *Bus* 26A
Leeds 26
Leicester 49
Lincoln 18, 26
Liverpool 49
London 14, 25
Manchester 49
March 17
Newark 26
Newcastle 26
Norwich 17
Nottingham 49
Nuneaton 49
Oundle (Market Place) *Bus* 26B
Retford 26
Sheffield 49
Spalding 18
Stansted Airport 49
Stevenage 25
Stockport 49
Swaffham *Bus* 26A
Wakefield 26
York 26
Petersfield [SW] Ⓟ 🚲 ◇ ⚠ 🚕 156
Petts Wood [SE] [4] Ⓟ ◇ ⚠ 🚕 195, 199, 204
Pevensey & Westham [SN] Ⓟ 🚲 ⚠ 189
Pevensey Bay [SN] Ⓤ 189
Pewsey [GW] Ⓟ 🚲 ◇ ⚠ 135
Pickering [NY] Ⓟ 🚲 45

■10 Connection time
Ⓟ Station Car Park
🚲 Bicycle storage facility
◇ Seat reservations can be made at this station
⚠ Penalty Fare Schemes in operation on some or all services from this station
🚕 Taxi rank or cab office at station, or signposted and within 100 metres
Ⓤ Unstaffed station
[ ] Station Operator Code

Station index and table numbers

Pickering Eastgate *Bus* 26G
Pilning [GW] Ⓟ Ⓤ 132
Pinhoe [SW] ⚠ Ⓤ 160
Pitlochry [SR] Ⓟ 🚲 🚕 229, *Sleepers* 403
Pitsea [CC] Ⓟ 🚲 ◇ ⚠ 🚕 1
Pleasington [NT] Ⓟ Ⓤ 97
Pleasure Beach [NT] (see Blackpool)
Plockton [SR] Ⓟ 🚲 Ⓤ 239
Pluckley [SE] Ⓟ 🚲 ◇ ⚠ 207
Plumley [NT] Ⓟ Ⓤ 88
Plumpton [SN] Ⓟ ◇ ⚠ 189
Plumstead [SE] ◇ ⚠ 200
Plymouth [GW] Ⓟ 🚲 ◇ ⚠ 🚕
Aberdeen 51
Birmingham 51, 135
Bristol 135
Cardiff 135
Carlisle 51
Crewe 51
Derby 51
Dundee 51
Edinburgh 51
Exeter 135
Glasgow 51
Gunnislake 139
Leeds 51
London 135, *Sleepers* 406
Manchester 51
Newcastle 51
Newton Abbot 135
Nottingham 51
Paignton 135
Penzance 135
Preston 51
Reading 135, *Sleepers* 406
Sheffield 51
Taunton 135
Torquay 135
Wolverhampton 51
York 51
Pokesdown [SW] 🚲 ◇ ⚠ 158
Polegate [SN] Ⓟ 🚲 ◇ ⚠ 🚕 189
Polesworth [LM] Ⓟ Ⓤ 67
Pollokshaws East [SR] 🚲 Ⓤ 223
Pollokshaws West [SR] 🚲 Ⓤ 222
Pollokshields East [SR] 🚲 223
Pollokshields West [SR] 🚲 Ⓤ 223
Polmont [SR] ■3 Ⓟ 🚲 ◇ 🚕 228, 230
Polsloe Bridge [GW] Ⓤ 136
Ponders End [LE] ⚠ 22
Pontarddulais [AW] Ⓟ Ⓤ 129
Pontefract Baghill [NT] Ⓟ Ⓤ 33
Pontefract Monkhill [NT] Ⓟ Ⓤ 26, 31, 32
Pontefract Tanshelf [NT] Ⓟ Ⓤ 32
Pontlottyn [AW] Ⓟ Ⓤ 130
Pont-y-Pant [AW] Ⓤ 102
Pontyclun [AW] Ⓟ Ⓤ 128
Pontypool & New Inn [AW] Ⓟ Ⓤ 131
Pontypridd [AW] ■3 🚲 ◇ 🚕 130
Poole [SW] ■4 Ⓟ 🚲 ◇ ⚠ 🚕 158
Poppleton [NT] Ⓟ 🚲 Ⓤ 35
Portchester [SW] 🚲 ⚠ 158, 165, 188
Port Glasgow [SR] 🚲 🚕 219
Porth [AW] Ⓟ ◇ 130
Porthmadog [AW] Ⓤ 75
Portlethen [SR] Ⓟ 🚲 Ⓤ 229
Portslade [SN] Ⓟ 🚲 ◇ ⚠ 188
Portsmouth Arms [GW] Ⓟ Ⓤ 136
Portsmouth
Harbour [SW] 🚲 ◇ ⚠ 🚕
& Southsea [SW] Ⓟ 🚲 ◇ ⚠ 🚕
Bognor Regis 188
Brighton 188
Bristol 123
Cardiff 123
Chichester 188
Crawley 188
East Croydon 188
Exeter 160
Fareham 165
Gatwick Airport 188
Guildford 156
Haslemere 156
Havant 157
Horsham 188
Littlehampton 188
London 156, 158, 188
Reading
ia Eastleigh 158
ia Guildford 156
Redhill 188
Ryde 167
Salisbury 123
Sandown 167
Shanklin 167
Southampton Central 165
Winchester 158
Worthing 188
Port Sunlight [ME] 🚲 ⚠ 106
Port Talbot Parkway [AW] Ⓟ 🚲 ◇ 🚕 125, 128
Possilpark & Parkhouse [SR] 🚲 Ⓤ 232
Potters Bar [FC] Ⓟ ◇ ⚠ 🚕 24, 25
Poulton-le-Fylde [NT] Ⓟ ◇ 🚕 41, 82, 97
Poynton [NT] Ⓟ 84
Prees [AW] Ⓤ 131
Prescot [NT] Ⓟ 90
Prestatyn [AW] ◇ 🚕 Ⓤ 81
Prestbury [NT] Ⓟ Ⓤ 84
Preston [VT] ■8 Ⓟ 🚲 ◇ 🚕
Aberdeen 65, *Sleepers* 402
Barrow-in-Furness 82
Birmingham 65
Birmingham International 65
Blackburn 97
Blackpool 97
Bolton 82
Bournemouth 51
Bradford 41
Bristol 51
Burnley 97
Carlisle 65
Chorley 82
Clitheroe 94, 97
Colne 97
Coventry 65
Crewe 65
Douglas (IOM) 98A
Dundee 65, *Sleepers* 402
Edinburgh 65
Exeter 51
Fort William *Sleepers* 404
Glasgow 65
Inverkeithing *Sleepers* 402
Inverness 65, *Sleepers* 403
Kirkcaldy *Sleepers* 402
Lancaster 65
Leeds 41
Liverpool 90
London 65
Manchester 82
Manchester Airport 82
Milton Keynes Central 65
Ormskirk 99
Oxenholme Lake District 65
Oxford 51
Paignton 51
Penzance 51
Perth 65, *Sleepers* 403
Plymouth 51
Reading 51
Rugby 65
Southampton 51
Stafford 65
Stirling *Sleepers* 403
Stockport 82
Torquay 51
Warrington 65
Watford 65
Wigan 65
Windermere 65
Wolverhampton 65
York 41
Preston Park [SN] ◇ ⚠ 52, 186, 188
Preston (Fishergate) *Bus* 65E
Prestonpans [SR] Ⓟ 🚲 Ⓤ 238
Prestwick International Airport 🚕 Ⓤ 218, 221
Prestwick Town [SR] Ⓟ 🚲 🚕 218, 221
Priesthill & Darnley [SR] 🚲 Ⓤ 222
Princes Risborough [CH] ■2 Ⓟ 🚲 ◇ ⚠ 🚕 115, 115A
Prittlewell [LE] Ⓟ 🚲 ⚠ 5
Prudhoe [NT] Ⓟ 🚲 Ⓤ 48
Pulborough [SN] Ⓟ 🚲 ◇ ⚠ 🚕 188
Purfleet [CC] Ⓟ 🚲 ◇ ⚠ 1

Station index and table numbers

■10 Connection time
Ⓟ Station Car Park
🚲 Bicycle storage facility
◇ Seat reservations can be made at this station
⚠ Penalty Fare Schemes in operation on some or all services from this station
🚕 Taxi rank or cab office at station, or signposted and within 100 metres
Ⓤ Unstaffed station
[ ] Station Operator Code

Purley [SN] ■4 Ⓟ ◇ ⚠ 🚕 175, 181, 186
Purley Oaks [SN] Ⓟ ⚠ 175, 181
Putney [SW] 🚲 ◇ ⚠ 149
Pwllheli [AW] 🚲 🚕 75
Pyle [AW] Ⓟ 🚲 Ⓤ 128

Q

Quakers Yard [AW] Ⓤ 130
Queenborough [SE] Ⓟ ◇ ⚠ 212
Queens Park (Glasgow) **[SR]** 🚲 223
Queen s Park (London) **[LT]** 60
Queens Road, Peckham [SN] 🚲 ◇ ⚠ 177, 178, 179
Queen s Road, Walthamstow [LO] (see Walthamstow Queen s Road)
Queenstown Road (Battersea) [SW] ⚠ Ⓤ 149
Quintrell Downs [GW] Ⓤ 142

R

Radcliffe (Notts.) **[EM]** Ⓟ Ⓤ 19
Radlett [FC] Ⓟ 🚲 ◇ ⚠ 🚕 52
Radley [GW] Ⓟ Ⓤ 116
Radyr [AW] ■3 Ⓟ 🚲 ◇ 130
Rainford [NT] Ⓟ Ⓤ 82
Rainham (Essex) **[CC]** Ⓟ 🚲 ◇ ⚠ 1
Rainham (Kent) [SE] Ⓟ ◇ ⚠ 🚕 194, 212
Rainhill [NT] 90
Ramsgate [SE] ■4 Ⓟ 🚲 ◇ ⚠ 🚕 194, 207, 212
Ramsgreave & Wilpshire [NT] Ⓟ Ⓤ 94
Rannoch [SR] Ⓟ 🚲 Ⓤ 227, *Sleepers* 404
Rauceby [EM] Ⓤ 19
Ravenglass for Eskdale [NT] Ⓤ 100
Ravensbourne [SE] ◇ ⚠ 52, 195
Ravensthorpe [NT] Ⓤ 39
Rawcliffe [NT] Ⓤ 32
Rayleigh [LE] Ⓟ 🚲 ⚠ 🚕 5
Raynes Park [SW] ■6 🚲 ◇ ⚠ 🚕 152
Reading [GW] ■7 Ⓟ 🚲 ◇ ⚠ 🚕
Aberdeen 51
Ascot 149
Banbury 116
Basingstoke 122
Bath Spa 125
Birmingham 116
Bodmin Parkway 135, *Sleepers* 406
Bournemouth 158
Bristol 125
Camborne 135, *Sleepers* 406
Cardiff 125
Carlisle 51
Cheltenham Spa 125
Clapham Junction 149
Coventry 51
Crewe 51
Derby 51
Didcot 116
Dundee 51
Edinburgh 51
Exeter 135, *Sleepers* 406
Gatwick Airport 148
Glasgow 51
Gloucester 125
Guildford 148
Hayle 135, *Sleepers* 406
Heathrow Airport *Bus* 125A
Henley-on-Thames 121
Hereford 126
Leamington Spa 116
Leeds 51
Liskeard 135, *Sleepers* 406
London 116, 117, 149
Lostwithiel 135, *Sleepers* 406
Manchester 51
Milford Haven 128
Moreton-in-Marsh 126
Newbury 116
Newcastle 51
Newport (South Wales) 125
Newton Abbot 135, *Sleepers* 406
Oxford 116
Paignton 135
Par 135, *Sleepers* 406
Penzance 135, *Sleepers* 406
Plymouth 135, *Sleepers* 406
Poole 158
Portsmouth
ia Basingstoke 158
ia Guildford 156
Preston 51
Redhill 148
Redruth 135, *Sleepers* 406
Rosslare Harbour 128
Sheffield 51
Slough 117
Southampton 158
St Austell 135, *Sleepers* 406
St Erth 135, *Sleepers* 406
Staines 149
Swansea 125
Swindon 125
Taunton 135
Torquay 135
Truro 135, *Sleepers* 406
Weston-super-Mare 125
Weymouth 158
Winchester 158
Wolverhampton 51
Worcester 126
York 51
Reading West [GW] ■3 116, 122
Rectory Road [LE] ⚠ 21
Redbridge [SW] Ⓟ ⚠ Ⓤ 158
Redcar British Steel [NT] Ⓤ 44
Redcar Central [NT] Ⓟ 🚲 ◇ 🚕 44
Redcar East [NT] 🚲 Ⓤ 44
Reddish North [NT] Ⓟ 🚲 78
Reddish South [NT] Ⓤ 78
Redditch [LM] Ⓟ ◇ ⚠ 69
Redhill [SN] Ⓟ 🚲 ◇ ⚠ 🚕 148, 186, 188
Redland [GW] 🚲 Ⓤ 133
Redruth [GW] Ⓟ 🚲 ◇ 🚕 51, 135, *Sleepers* 406
Reedham (Norfolk) [LE] Ⓟ 🚲 Ⓤ 15
Reedham (Surrey) **[SN]** ⚠ 181
Reigate [SN] Ⓟ 🚲 ◇ ⚠ 148, 186
Renton [SR] 🚲 Ⓤ 226
Retford [GR] ■10 Ⓟ 🚲 ◇ 🚕 26, 30
Rhiwbina [AW] Ⓤ 130
Rhoose Cardiff Int. Airport [AW] Ⓟ 🚲 Ⓤ 130
Rhosneigr [AW] Ⓤ 81
Rhyl [AW] ◇ 🚕 81
Rhymney [AW] ■3 Ⓟ 🚕 Ⓤ 130
Ribblehead [NT] Ⓟ Ⓤ 36
Rice Lane [ME] ⚠ 103
Richmond (Greater London) **[SW]** Ⓟ 🚲 ◇ ⚠ 🚕 59, 149
Richmond (Market) 🚕 *Bus* 26H
Rickmansworth [LT] Ⓟ 🚲 ⚠ 114
Riddlesdown [SN] 🚲 ◇ ⚠ 184
Ridgmont [LM] Ⓤ 64
Riding Mill [NT] Ⓟ 🚲 Ⓤ 48
Risca & Pontymister [AW] Ⓟ Ⓤ 127
Rishton [NT] Ⓟ 🚲 Ⓤ 97
Robin Hood Airport 🚕 *Bus* 26F
Robertsbridge [SE] Ⓟ ◇ ⚠ 206
Roby [NT] 90
Rochdale [NT] Ⓟ ◇ 🚕 41, 82
Roche [GW] Ⓤ 142
Rochester [SE] ■4 Ⓟ ◇ ⚠ 🚕 194, 200, 212
Rochford [LE] Ⓟ 🚲 ⚠ 🚕 5
Rock Ferry [ME] Ⓟ 🚲 ◇ ⚠ 🚕 106
Rogart [SR] Ⓟ 🚲 Ⓤ 239
Rogerstone [AW] Ⓟ Ⓤ 127
Rolleston [EM] Ⓤ 27
Roman Bridge [AW] Ⓤ 102
Romford [LE] 🚲 ◇ ⚠ 🚕 4, 5, 11
Romiley [NT] Ⓟ 🚲 78
Romsey [GW] Ⓟ 🚲 123, 158
Roose [NT] Ⓟ Ⓤ 82
Rose Grove [NT] Ⓤ 97
Rose Hill Marple [NT] Ⓟ 🚲 ◇ 78
Rosslare Harbour *Ship* 128
Rosyth [SR] Ⓟ Ⓤ 242
Rotherham Central [NT] Ⓟ ◇ 🚕 29, 31, 33

[10] Connection time
Ⓟ Station Car Park
🚲 Bicycle storage facility
◇ Seat reservations can be made at this station
⚠ Penalty Fare Schemes in operation on some or all services from this station
🚕 Taxi rank or cab office at station, or signposted and within 100 metres
Ⓤ Unstaffed station
[ ] Station Operator Code

Station index and table numbers

Rotherhithe [LO] 🚲 ⚠ 178
Rothesay *Ship* 219B
Roughton Road [LE] 🚲 Ⓤ 16
Rowlands Castle [SW] Ⓟ 🚲 ◇ ⚠ 156
Rowley Regis [LM] Ⓟ ◇ ⚠ 71, 115
Roy Bridge [SR] 🚲 Ⓤ 227, *Sleepers* 404
Roydon [LE] Ⓟ ⚠ 22
Royston [FC] Ⓟ 🚲 ◇ ⚠ 🚕 25
Ruabon [AW] Ⓟ Ⓤ 75
Rufford [NT] Ⓟ Ⓤ 99
Rugby [VT] Ⓟ 🚲 ◇ 🚕 65, 66, 67, 68
Rugeley Town [LM] Ⓟ Ⓤ 70
Rugeley Trent Valley [LM] Ⓤ 67, 70
Ruislip [CH] (see South and West Ruislip)
Rum *Ship* 227A
Runcorn [VT] Ⓟ 🚲 ◇ 🚕 65, 91
Runcorn East [AW] Ⓟ 81
Ruskington [EM] Ⓟ 🚲 Ⓤ 18
Ruswarp [NT] Ⓤ 45
Rutherglen [SR] 🚲 226
Ryde Esplanade [IL] ◇ 🚕 167
Ryde Pier Head [IL] Ⓟ 🚲 ◇ 167
Ryde St. Johns Road [IL] Ⓟ 🚲 Ⓤ 167
Ryder Brow [NT] Ⓤ 78
Rye [SN] Ⓟ ⚠ 🚕 189
Rye House [LE] ⚠ 22

S

St Albans [FC] Ⓟ 🚲 ◇ ⚠ 🚕 52, 186
St Albans Abbey [LM] Ⓟ Ⓤ 61
St Andrews Bus Station *Bus* 229, 229A
St Andrews Road [GW] Ⓟ 🚲 Ⓤ 133
St Annes-on-the-Sea [NT] Ⓟ ◇ 🚕 97
St Austell [GW] Ⓟ 🚲 ◇ 🚕 51, 135, *Bus* 135B, *Sleepers* 406
St Bees [NT] Ⓟ Ⓤ 100
St Budeaux Ferry Road [GW] Ⓤ 135, 139
St Budeaux Victoria Road [GW] Ⓤ 139
St Columb Road [GW] Ⓟ Ⓤ 142
St Denys [SW] Ⓟ 🚲 ◇ ⚠ 158, 165
St Erth [GW] Ⓟ ◇ 51, 135, 144, *Sleepers* 406
St Germans [GW] Ⓤ 135
St Helens Central [NT] Ⓟ ◇ 🚕 90
St Helens Junction [NT] Ⓟ 90
St Helier (Surrey) **[FC]** 🚲 ⚠ Ⓤ 52, 179
St Ives [GW] Ⓟ Ⓤ 144
St James' Park [GW] Ⓤ 136
St James Street [LE] 🚲 ⚠ 20
St Johns [SE] ◇ ⚠ 199, 200, 203, 204
St Keyne Wishing Well Halt [GW] Ⓤ 140
St Leonards Warrior Square [SE] [4] Ⓟ ◇ ⚠ 🚕 189, 206
St Margarets (Herts.) [LE] Ⓟ ⚠ 🚕 22
St Margarets (Greater London) **[SW]** 🚲 ◇ ⚠ 🚕 149
St Mary Cray [SE] Ⓟ ◇ ⚠ 52, 195, 196, 212
St Michaels [ME] Ⓟ ⚠ 103
St Neots [FC] Ⓟ 🚲 ⚠ 🚕 25
St Pancras International (see London)
Salford Central [NT] 82, 94
Salford Crescent [NT] 82, 94
Salfords [SN] ◇ ⚠ 186
Salhouse [LE] Ⓟ 🚲 Ⓤ 16
Salisbury [SW] Ⓟ 🚲 ◇ ⚠ 🚕 123, 158, 160
Saltaire [NT] Ⓤ 36
Saltash [GW] Ⓟ 🚲 Ⓤ 135
Saltburn [NT] Ⓤ 44
Saltcoats [SR] Ⓟ 🚲 🚕 221
Saltmarshe [NT] Ⓟ Ⓤ 29
Salwick [NT] Ⓤ 97
Sampford Courtenay Ⓤ 136
Sandal & Agbrigg [NT] Ⓟ 🚲 Ⓤ 31
Sandbach [NT] Ⓟ 🚲 84
Sanderstead [SN] Ⓟ ◇ ⚠ 🚕 184
Sandhills [ME] ⚠ 103
Sandhurst [GW] Ⓤ 148
Sandling [SE] Ⓟ ◇ ⚠ 207
Sandown [IL] Ⓟ 🚲 Ⓤ 167
Sandplace [GW] Ⓤ 140
Sandringham Norwich Gates *Bus* 17A
Sandringham Visitor Centre *Bus* 17A
Sandwell & Dudley [LM] Ⓟ 🚲 ◇ ⚠ 🚕 66, 68, 74
Sandwich [SE] Ⓟ ◇ ⚠ 194, 207
Sandy [FC] Ⓟ 🚲 ⚠ 25
Sankey for Penketh [NT] Ⓟ 89
Sanquhar [SR] Ⓟ 🚲 Ⓤ 216
Sarn [AW] Ⓟ Ⓤ 128
Saundersfoot [AW] Ⓤ 128
Saunderton [CH] Ⓟ 🚲 ⚠ Ⓤ 115
Sawbridgeworth [LE] Ⓟ ⚠ 22
Saxilby [EM] Ⓟ 🚲 Ⓤ 18, 30
Saxmundham [LE] Ⓟ 🚲 Ⓤ 13
Scarborough [TP] Ⓟ 🚲 ◇ 🚕 26, 39, 43
Scotscalder [SR] Ⓟ 🚲 Ⓤ 239
Scotstounhill [SR] Ⓟ 🚲 226
Scrabster *Ship* 239A
Scunthorpe [TP] Ⓟ ◇ 🚕 29
Sea Mills [GW] 🚲 Ⓤ 133
Seaford [SN] Ⓟ 🚲 ◇ ⚠ 🚕 189
Seaforth & Litherland [ME] ⚠ 🚕 103
Seaham [NT] Ⓟ Ⓤ 44
Seamer [TP] Ⓟ Ⓤ 39, 43
Seascale [NT] Ⓟ Ⓤ 100
Seaton Carew [NT] Ⓟ 🚲 Ⓤ 44
Seer Green [CH] Ⓟ 🚲 ⚠ 115
Selby [TP] Ⓟ 🚲 ◇ 🚕 26, 29, 39, 40, 41
Selhurst [SN] [4] 🚲 ◇ ⚠ 176, 177
Selkirk *Bus* 65G
Sellafield [NT] Ⓟ Ⓤ 100
Selling [SE] Ⓟ ⚠ Ⓤ 212
Selly Oak [LM] Ⓟ 🚲 ◇ ⚠ 69
Settle [NT] Ⓟ ◇ 36
Seven Kings [LE] 🚲 ⚠ 5
Seven Sisters [LE] ⚠ 21, 22
Sevenoaks [SE] [4] Ⓟ ◇ ⚠ 🚕 52, 195, 204, 206, 207
Severn Beach [GW] 🚲 Ⓤ 133
Severn Tunnel Junction [AW] Ⓟ 🚲 ◇ 123, 132
Shadwell [LO] ⚠ 178
Shalford [GW] Ⓟ Ⓤ 148
Shanklin [IL] Ⓟ 🚲 ◇ 🚕 167
Shawford [SW] Ⓟ 🚲 Ⓤ 158
Shawlands [SR] 🚲 Ⓤ 223
Sheerness-on-Sea [SE] 🚲 ◇ ⚠ 🚕 212
Sheffield [EM] [7] Ⓟ 🚲 ◇ ⚠ 🚕
Barnsley 34
Birmingham 51
Bournemouth 51
Bristol 51
Cambridge 49
Cardiff 51
Chesterfield 53
Cleethorpes 29
Darlington 26
Derby 53
Doncaster 29
Edinburgh 26
Exeter 51
Glasgow 26
Goole 29
Grimsby 29
Huddersfield 34
Hull 29
Leeds 31
Leicester 53
Lincoln 30
Liverpool 89
London 53
Luton 53
Manchester 78
Manchester Airport 78
Meadowhall 29, 35
Newcastle 26

Station index and table numbers

■10 Connection time
Ⓟ Station Car Park
🚲 Bicycle storage facility
◇ Seat reservations can be made at this station
⚠ Penalty Fare Schemes in operation on some or all services from this station
🚕 Taxi rank or cab office at station, or signposted and within 100 metres
Ⓤ Unstaffed station
[ ] Station Operator Code

New Mills 78
Newport (South Wales) 51
Norwich 49
Nottingham 53
Oxford 51
Paignton 51
Penistone 34
Penzance 51
Peterborough 49
Plymouth 51
Reading 51
Retford 30
Rotherham 29
Scunthorpe 29
Southampton 51
Stockport 78
Torquay 51
Wakefield 31
Warrington 89
York 29
Shelford [LE] ⚠ 22
Shenfield [LE] ■3 Ⓟ 🚲 ◇ ⚠ 🚕 5, 11
Shenstone [LM] Ⓟ ⚠ 69
Shepherd s Bush [LO] ⚠ 66, 176, 177
Shepherds Well [SE] Ⓟ ⚠ 212
Shepley [NT] Ⓤ 34
Shepperton [SW] Ⓟ 🚲 ◇ ⚠ 🚕 152
Shepreth [FC] Ⓟ 🚲 ⚠ Ⓤ 25
Sherborne [SW] Ⓟ 🚲 ◇ ⚠ 🚕 160
Sherburn-in-Elmet [NT] Ⓤ 33
Sheringham [LE] Ⓟ 🚲 Ⓤ 16
Shettleston [SR] Ⓟ 🚲 🚕 226
Shieldmuir [SR] 🚲 Ⓤ 226
Shifnal [LM] Ⓟ Ⓤ 74
Shildon [NT] Ⓤ 44
Shiplake [GW] Ⓟ Ⓤ 121
Shipley [NT] Ⓟ 🚲 ◇ 26, 36, 37, 38
Shippea Hill [LE] Ⓟ Ⓤ 17
Shipton [GW] Ⓤ 126
Shirebrook [EM] Ⓤ 55
Shirehampton [GW] Ⓟ 🚲 Ⓤ 133
Shireoaks [NT] Ⓤ 30
Shirley [LM] Ⓟ 🚲 ◇ ⚠ 71
Shoeburyness [CC] Ⓟ 🚲 ◇ ⚠ 🚕 1
Sholing [SW] 🚲 ⚠ Ⓤ 165
Shoreditch High Street [LO] 🚲 ⚠ 178
Shoreham (Kent) [SE] Ⓟ ⚠ Ⓤ 52, 195
Shoreham-by-Sea (Sussex) **[SN]** Ⓟ 🚲 ◇ ⚠ 🚕 188
Shortlands [SE] ■4 Ⓟ 🚲 ◇ ⚠ 52, 195
Shotton [AW] Ⓟ 🚕 81
Shotton High Level [AW] Ⓟ 🚕 101
Shotts [SR] Ⓟ 🚲 225
Shrewsbury [AW] Ⓟ ◇ 🚕
Aberystwyth 75
Bangor (Gwynedd) 131
Barmouth 75
Birmingham 74
Cardiff 131
Chester 75, 131
Crewe 131
Hereford 131
Holyhead 131
Llandudno Junction 131
Llandrindod 129
Llanelli 129
Machynlleth 75
Manchester 131
Newport (South Wales) 131
Pwllheli 75
Swansea 129
Telford Central 74
Whitchurch (Salop) 131
Wrexham 75
Wolverhampton 74
Sidcup [SE] ■4 Ⓟ ◇ ⚠ 🚕 200
Sileby [EM] ⚠ Ⓤ 53
Silecroft [NT] Ⓤ 100
Silsden [NT] (see Steeton & Silsden)
Silkstone Common [NT] Ⓟ Ⓤ 34
Silverdale [NT] Ⓤ 82
Silver Street [LE] ⚠ 21
Singer [SR] 🚲 🚕 226
Sittingbourne [SE] ■4 Ⓟ ◇ ⚠ 🚕 194, 212
Skegness [EM] 🚲 ◇ 🚕 19
Skewen [AW] Ⓟ Ⓤ 128
Skipton [NT] Ⓟ 🚲 ◇ 🚕 26, 36
Slade Green [SE] ■4 Ⓟ ◇ ⚠ 200
Slaithwaite [NT] Ⓟ Ⓤ 39
Slateford [SR] 🚲 Ⓤ 225
Sleaford [EM] Ⓟ 🚲 ◇ 🚕 18, 19
Sleights [NT] Ⓟ Ⓤ 45
Slough [GW] ■3 Ⓟ 🚲 ◇ ⚠ 🚕 116, 117, 119, 125, 135
Small Heath [LM] ⚠ 71
Smallbrook Junction [IL] Ⓤ 167
Smethwick Galton Bridge [LM] ■7 ◇ ⚠ 68, 71, 74, 75
Smethwick Rolfe Street [LM] ⚠ 68
Smithy Bridge [NT] Ⓟ Ⓤ 41
Snaith [NT] Ⓟ Ⓤ 32
Snodland [SE] Ⓟ ⚠ 🚕 Ⓤ 208
Snowdown [SE] ⚠ Ⓤ 212
Sole Street [SE] Ⓟ ◇ ⚠ 212
Solihull [LM] Ⓟ 🚲 ◇ ⚠ 71, 115
Somerleyton [LE] Ⓟ 🚲 Ⓤ 15
South Acton [LO] 🚲 ⚠ 59
South Bank [NT] 🚲 Ⓤ 44
South Bermondsey [SN] ◇ ⚠ 177, 178, 179
South Croydon [SN] ■4 Ⓟ ◇ ⚠ 175, 176, 181, 184
South Elmsall [NT] Ⓟ 🚲 Ⓤ 31
South Greenford [GW] Ⓤ 117
South Gyle [SR] Ⓟ 🚲 Ⓤ 242
South Hampstead [LO] ⚠ 60
South Kenton [LT] 60
South Merton [FC] ⚠ Ⓤ 52, 179
South Milford [NT] Ⓟ Ⓤ 39, 40
South Ruislip [CH] Ⓟ 🚲 ⚠ 🚕 115
South Tottenham [LO] ⚠ 62
South Wigston [EM] Ⓤ 57
South Woodham Ferrers [LE] Ⓟ 🚲 🚕 5
Southall [GW] ⚠ 117
Southampton Airport Parkway [SW] Ⓟ 🚲 ◇ ⚠ 🚕 51, 158, 188
Southampton Central [SW] Ⓟ 🚲 ◇ ⚠ 🚕
Aberdeen 51
Basingstoke 158
Bath Spa 123
Birmingham 51
Bognor Regis 188
Bournemouth 158
Brighton 188
Bristol 123
Brockenhurst 158
Cardiff 123
Carlisle 51
Chichester 188
Clapham Junction 158, 188
Crawley 188
Crewe 51
Derby 51
Dorchester 158
Dundee 51
East Croydon 188
Eastleigh 158
Edinburgh 51
Exeter 160
Fareham 165, 188
Gatwick Airport 188
Glasgow 51
Havant 165, 188
Horsham 188
Leeds 51
Littlehampton 188
London 158, 188
Lymington Pier 158
Manchester 51
Newcastle 51
Newport (South Wales) 123
Oxford 51
Poole 158
Portsmouth 165
Preston 51
Reading 158
Redhill 188
Romsey 123
Ryde 167
Salisbury 123
Shanklin 167
Sheffield 51
Swindon 123
Westbury (Wilts.) 123
Weymouth 158
Winchester 158

■10 Connection time
Ⓟ Station Car Park
🚲 Bicycle storage facility
◇ Seat reservations can be made at this station
⚠ Penalty Fare Schemes in operation on some or all services from this station
🚕 Taxi rank or cab office at station, or signposted and within 100 metres
Ⓤ Unstaffed station
[ ] Station Operator Code

Station index and table numbers

Woking 158
Wolverhampton 51
Worthing 188
Yarmouth (IOW) 158
Yeovil 160
York 51
Southbourne [SN] ◇ ⚠ 188
Southbury [LE] ⚠ 21
Southease [SN] Ⓤ 189
Southend Airport [LE] ⚠ 🚕 5
Southend Central [CC] Ⓟ 🚲 ◇ ⚠ 🚕 1
Southend East [CC] Ⓟ 🚲 ◇ ⚠ 1
Southend Victoria [LE] 🚲 ◇ ⚠ 🚕 5
Southminster [LE] Ⓟ 🚲 Ⓤ 5
Southport [ME] 🚲 ◇ ⚠ 🚕 82, 103
Southsea [SW] (see Portsmouth & Southsea)
Southwick [SN] 🚲 ◇ ⚠ 188
Sowerby Bridge [NT] Ⓟ 🚲 Ⓤ 41
Sowton [GW] (see Digby & Sowton)
Spalding [EM] Ⓟ 🚲 🚕 18
Spean Bridge [SR] Ⓟ 🚲 Ⓤ 227, *Sleepers* 404
Spital [ME] 🚲 ⚠ 106
Spondon [EM] ⚠ Ⓤ 56
Spooner Row [LE] Ⓤ 17
Spring Road [LM] ⚠ 71
Springburn [SR] 🚲 224, 226
Springfield [SR] 🚲 Ⓤ 229
Squires Gate [NT] Ⓤ 97
Stafford [VT] Ⓟ 🚲 ◇ 🚕
Bangor (Gwynedd) 65
Birmingham 68
Blackpool 65
Bournemouth 51
Bristol 51
Carlisle 65
Chester 65
Coventry 67, 68
Crewe 65
Edinburgh 65
Exeter 51
Glasgow 65
Holyhead 65
Lichfield 67
Liverpool 65
London 65
Manchester 84
Manchester Airport 84
Nuneaton 67
Oxenholme Lake District 65
Oxford 51
Paignton 51
Penzance 51
Plymouth 51
Preston 65
Reading 51
Rugby 65
Southampton 51
Stockport 84
Stoke-on-Trent 65, 68A
Tamworth 67
Torquay 51
Watford 65
Wolverhampton 68
Staines [SW] Ⓟ 🚲 ◇ ⚠ 🚕 149
Stainforth [NT] (see Hatfield & Stainforth)
Stallingborough [NT] Ⓤ 29
Stalybridge [TP] Ⓟ 🚲 ◇ 39
Stamford [EM] Ⓟ ◇ 49
Stamford Hill [LE] ⚠ 21
Stanford-le-Hope [CC] Ⓟ 🚲 ◇ ⚠ 1
Stanlow & Thornton [NT] Ⓤ 109
Stansted Airport [LE] 🚲 ◇ ⚠ 🚕 17, 22, 26, 49
Stansted Mountfitchet [LE] Ⓟ 🚲 ⚠ 🚕 22
Staplehurst [SE] Ⓟ 🚲 ◇ ⚠ 🚕 207
Stapleton Road [GW] 🚲 Ⓤ 133, 134
Starbeck [NT] 🚲 Ⓤ 35
Starcross [GW] 🚲 Ⓤ 135
Staveley [TP] Ⓤ 83
Stechford [LM] ⚠ 68
Steeton & Silsden [NT] Ⓟ 🚲 Ⓤ 36
Stepps [SR] Ⓟ 🚲 Ⓤ 224
Stevenage [FC] ■4 Ⓟ 🚲 ◇ ⚠ 🚕 24, 25, 26
Stevenston [SR] 🚲 Ⓤ 221
Stewartby [LM] Ⓤ 64
Stewarton [SR] Ⓟ 🚲 Ⓤ 222
Stirling [SR] Ⓟ 🚲 ◇ 🚕 26, 229, 230, *Sleepers* 403
Stockport [VT] Ⓟ 🚲 ◇ 🚕
Altrincham 88
Birmingham 65
Birmingham International 65
Blackpool 82
Bolton 82
Bournemouth 51
Bristol 51
Buxton 86
Cambridge 49
Cardiff 131
Chester 88
Coventry 65
Crewe 84
Doncaster 29
Ely 49
Exeter 51
Hazel Grove 86
Hull 29
Liverpool 89
London 65
Macclesfield 84
Manchester 84
Newport (South Wales) 131
Northwich 88
Norwich 49
Nottingham 49
Oxford 51
Paignton 51
Penzance 51
Peterborough 49
Plymouth 51
Preston 82
Reading 51
Rugby 65
Salford Crescent 82
Sheffield 78
Southampton 51
Stafford 84
Stoke-on-Trent 84
Torquay 51
Watford 65
Wigan 82
Wolverhampton 65
Stocksfield [NT] Ⓟ 🚲 Ⓤ 48
Stocksmoor [NT] Ⓟ 🚲 Ⓤ 34
Stockton [NT] 🚲 🚕 Ⓤ 44
Stoke d'Abernon [SW] (see Cobham)
Stoke Mandeville [CH] Ⓟ 🚲 ⚠ 114
Stoke Newington [LE] ⚠ 21
Stoke-on-Trent [VT] Ⓟ 🚲 ◇ 🚕 50, 51, 65, 67, 84
Stone [LM] 67
Stone Crown Street *Bus* 67
Stone Granville Square *Bus* 67
Stone Crossing [SE] ◇ ⚠ 200
Stonebridge Park [LT] 60
Stonegate [SE] Ⓟ 🚲 ◇ ⚠ 206
Stonehaven [SR] Ⓟ 🚲 ◇ 26, 51, 229, *Sleepers* 402
Stonehouse [GW] Ⓟ 125
Stoneleigh [SW] 🚲 ◇ ⚠ 152
Stornoway *Ship* 239B
Stourbridge Junction [LM] ■2 Ⓟ ◇ ⚠ 71, 72, 115
Stourbridge Town [LM] ⚠ 72
Stowmarket [LE] Ⓟ 🚲 ◇ 🚕 11, 14
Stranraer [SR] 🚲 ◇ 218
Stratford (London) **[LE]** ■7 ⚠ 🚕
Barking 1
Basildon 1
Bishops Stortford 22
Braintree 11
Broxbourne 22
Bury St. Edmunds 14
Cambridge 14
Chelmsford 11
Cheshunt 22
Clacton-on-Sea 11
Colchester 11
Ely 14
Gospel Oak 59, 176
Hackney 59
Harlow 22
Harwich 11
Hertford East 22
Highbury & Islington 59, 176
Ilford 5
Ipswich 11
London 5
Manningtree 11

Station index and table numbers

[10] Connection time
Ⓟ Station Car Park
🚲 Bicycle storage facility
◇ Seat reservations can be made at this station
⚠ Penalty Fare Schemes in operation on some or all services from this station
🚕 Taxi rank or cab office at station, or signposted and within 100 metres
Ⓤ Unstaffed station
[ ] Station Operator Code

Norwich 11
Peterborough 14
Richmond 59
Romford 5
Shenfield 5
Shoeburyness 1
Southend 1, 5
Southminster 5
Stansted Airport 22
Stowmarket 11
Tottenham Hale 22
Upminster 1
Walton-on-the-Naze 11
West Hampstead 59, 176
Wickford 5
Willesden Junction 59
Witham 11
Stratford International [SE] ⚠ 194, 200, 207, 208, 212
Stratford-upon-Avon [LM] Ⓟ 🚲 ◇ ⚠ 🚕 71, 115
Strathcarron [SR] Ⓟ 🚲 Ⓤ 239
Strawberry Hill [SW] 🚲 ◇ ⚠ 149, 152
Streatham [SN] [4] ◇ ⚠ 52, 177, 179
Streatham Common [SN] [4] Ⓟ 🚲 ◇ ⚠ 176, 177
Streatham Hill [SN] ◇ ⚠ 🚕 177, 178
Streatley [GW] (see Goring & Streatley)
Streethouse [NT] Ⓟ Ⓤ 32
Strines [NT] Ⓟ Ⓤ 78
Stromeferry [SR] Ⓟ 🚲 Ⓤ 239
Stromness 🚕 *Ship* 239A
Strood [SE] [4] Ⓟ 🚲 ◇ ⚠ 🚕 194, 200, 208, 212
Stroud [GW] Ⓟ 🚲 ◇ 🚕 125
Sturry [SE] ⚠ 207
Styal [NT] Ⓟ Ⓤ 84
Sudbury (Suffolk) **[LE]** 🚲 Ⓤ 10
Sudbury & Harrow Road [CH] ⚠ Ⓤ 115
Sudbury Hill Harrow [CH] ⚠ Ⓤ 115
Sugar Loaf [AW] Ⓤ 129
Summerston [SR] Ⓤ 232
Sunbury [SW] Ⓟ 🚲 ◇ ⚠ 152
Sunderland [NT] ◇ 🚕 26, 44, 48
Sundridge Park [SE] Ⓟ ◇ ⚠ 204
Sunningdale [SW] Ⓟ 🚲 ◇ ⚠ 🚕 149
Sunnymeads [SW] ⚠ Ⓤ 149
Surbiton [SW] [6] Ⓟ 🚲 ◇ ⚠ 🚕 152, 155
Surrey Quays [LO] 🚲 ⚠ 178
Sutton Coldfield [LM] Ⓟ 🚲 ◇ ⚠ 69
Sutton Common [FC] ⚠ Ⓤ 52, 179
Sutton Parkway [EM] Ⓟ Ⓤ 55
Sutton (Surrey) [SN] [4] Ⓟ 🚲 ◇ ⚠ 🚕 52, 179, 182
Swaffham *Bus* 26A
Swale [SE] ⚠ Ⓤ 212
Swalecliffe [SE] (see Chestfield & Swalecliffe)
Swanley [SE] [4] Ⓟ ◇ ⚠ 🚕 52, 195, 196, 212
Swanscombe [SE] ◇ ⚠ 200
Swansea [AW] Ⓟ 🚲 ◇ 🚕
Bristol 128
Cardiff 128
Camarthen 128
Crewe 131
Derby 57
Fishguard Harbour 128
Gloucester 57
Hereford 131
Llandrindod 129
London 125, 128
Manchester 128, 131
Pembroke Dock 128
Portsmouth 128
Reading 125, 128
Rosslare Harbour 128
Shrewsbury 129
Slough 125
Tenby 128
Swanwick [SW] Ⓟ 🚲 ◇ ⚠ 🚕 165, 188
Sway [SW] Ⓟ 🚲 ◇ ⚠ 158
Swaythling [SW] Ⓟ 🚲 ◇ ⚠ 158
Swinderby [EM] Ⓤ 27
Swindon [GW] Ⓟ 🚲 ◇ ⚠ 🚕 123, 125
Swineshead [EM] Ⓤ 19
Swinton (Gtr. Manchester) **[NT]** 82
Swinton (S. Yorks.) [NT] Ⓟ 🚲 ◇ 29, 31, 33
Sydenham [LO] ◇ 🚲 ⚠ 🚕 178
Sydenham Hill [SE] Ⓟ ⚠ 195
Syon Lane [SW] 🚲 ⚠ Ⓤ 149
Syston [EM] Ⓟ ⚠ Ⓤ 53

T

Tackley [GW] Ⓤ 116
Tadworth [SN] ◇ ⚠ 181
Taffs Well [AW] [3] Ⓟ Ⓤ 130
Tain [SR] Ⓟ Ⓤ 239
Talsarnau [AW] Ⓤ 75
Talybont [AW] Ⓤ 75
Tal-y-Cafn [AW] Ⓤ 102
Tame Bridge Parkway [LM] Ⓟ 🚲 ◇ ⚠ 70, 75
Tamworth [LM] Ⓟ ◇ 🚕 51, 57, 65, 67
Taplow [GW] Ⓟ 🚲 ⚠ 🚕 117
Tarbert *Ship* 239B
Tattenham Corner [SN] Ⓟ ◇ ⚠ 181
Taunton [GW] Ⓟ 🚲 ◇ ⚠ 🚕 51, 134, 135, *Bus* 135E
Taynuilt [SR] Ⓟ 🚲 Ⓤ 227
Teddington [SW] 🚲 ◇ ⚠ 149, 152
Tees-side Airport [NT] Ⓤ 44
Teignmouth [GW] Ⓟ 🚲 ◇ 🚕 51, 135
Telford Central [LM] Ⓟ ◇ 🚕 74, 75
Templecombe [SW] Ⓟ 🚲 ◇ ⚠ 160
Tenby [AW] Ⓟ Ⓤ 128
Tewkesbury [GW] (see Ashchurch)
Teynham [SE] Ⓟ ◇ ⚠ 212
Thame [CH] (see Haddenham & Thame Parkway)
Thames Ditton [SW] 🚲 ⚠ 152
Thatcham [GW] Ⓟ 🚲 116, 135
Thatto Heath [NT] Ⓟ 90
The Hawthorns [LM] Ⓟ ⚠ 71
The Lakes (Warwickshire) **[LM]** ⚠ Ⓤ 71
Theale [GW] Ⓟ 🚲 116, 135
Theobalds Grove [LE] ⚠ 21
Thetford [LE] Ⓟ ◇ 🚕 17, 49
Thirsk [TP] Ⓟ ◇ 26, 39
Thornaby [TP] Ⓟ 🚲 ◇ 🚕 39, 44
Thorne North [NT] Ⓟ 🚲 29
Thorne South [NT] Ⓟ Ⓤ 29
Thornford [GW] Ⓤ 123
Thornhill [AW] (see Lisvane)
Thornliebank [SR] 🚲 Ⓤ 222
Thornton (Ches.) **[NT]** (see Stanlow & Thornton)
Thornton (Fife) **[SR]** (see Glenrothes With Thornton)
Thornton Abbey [NT] Ⓤ 29
Thorntonhall [SR] 🚲 Ⓤ 222
Thornton Heath [SN] 🚲 ◇ ⚠ 🚕 176, 177
Thorpe Bay [CC] Ⓟ 🚲 ◇ ⚠ 🚕 1
Thorpe Culvert [EM] Ⓟ Ⓤ 19
Thorpe-le-Soken [LE] [1] Ⓟ 🚲 ⚠ 11
Three Bridges [SN] [4] Ⓟ 🚲 ◇ ⚠ 🚕 52, 186, 188
Three Oaks [SN] Ⓤ 189
Thurgarton [EM] Ⓤ 27
Thurnscoe [NT] Ⓟ Ⓤ 31
Thurso [SR] Ⓟ 🚲 ◇ 🚕 239, *Ship* 239A
Thurston [LE] Ⓟ 🚲 Ⓤ 14
Tilbury Riverside [CC] Ⓤ *Bus* 1A
Tilbury Town [CC] [3] 🚲 ◇ ⚠ 1, *Bus* 1A
Tile Hill [LM] Ⓟ ⚠ 68
Tilehurst [GW] Ⓟ 🚲 116
Tipton [LM] Ⓟ ⚠ 68
Tiree *Ship* 227B
Tir-phil [AW] Ⓟ Ⓤ 130
Tisbury [SW] Ⓟ 🚲 ◇ ⚠ 160
Tiverton Parkway [GW] Ⓟ 🚲 ◇ ⚠ 🚕 51, 135
Todmorden [NT] Ⓟ 🚲 🚕 41

Station index and table numbers

[10] Connection time
Ⓟ Station Car Park
🚲 Bicycle storage facility
◇ Seat reservations can be made at this station
⚠ Penalty Fare Schemes in operation on some or all services from this station
🚕 Taxi rank or cab office at station, or signposted and within 100 metres
Ⓤ Unstaffed station
[ ] Station Operator Code

Tolworth [SW] Ⓟ 🚲 ◇ ⚠ 🚕 152
Tonbridge [SE] [4] Ⓟ 🚲 ◇ ⚠ 🚕 186, 204, 206, 207, 208
Ton Pentre [AW] Ⓤ 130
Tondu [AW] Ⓟ Ⓤ 128
Tonfanau [AW] Ⓤ 75
Tonypandy [AW] Ⓤ 130
Tooting [FC] ◇ ⚠ 52, 179
Topsham [GW] Ⓟ 🚲 Ⓤ 136
Torquay [GW] Ⓟ 🚲 ◇ 🚕 51, 135
Torre [GW] Ⓟ Ⓤ 135
Totley [NT] (see Dore & Totley)
Totnes [GW] Ⓟ 🚲 ◇ ⚠ 🚕 51, 135, *Sleepers* 406
Tottenham Hale [LE] ⚠ 🚕 22
Tottenham South [LO] (see South Tottenham)
Totton [SW] Ⓟ 🚲 ◇ ⚠ 158
Town Green [ME] Ⓟ ⚠ 103
Trafford Park [NT] 🚕 Ⓤ 89
Treforest [AW] Ⓟ ◇ 130
Treforest Estate [AW] Ⓤ 130
Trehafod [AW] Ⓟ Ⓤ 130
Treherbert [AW] Ⓤ 130
Treorchy [AW] Ⓟ Ⓤ 130
Trimley [LE] Ⓟ 🚲 Ⓤ 13
Tring [LM] Ⓟ 🚲 ⚠ 🚕 66, 176
Troed-y-rhiw [AW] Ⓤ 130
Troon [SR] Ⓟ 🚲 🚕 218, 221
Trowbridge [GW] Ⓟ 🚲 ◇ 🚕 123, 160
Truro [GW] Ⓟ 🚲 ◇ 🚕 51, 135, 143, *Sleepers* 406
Tulloch [SR] Ⓟ 🚲 Ⓤ 227, *Sleepers* 404
Tulse Hill [SN] [3] ◇ ⚠ 52, 177, 179, 182
Tunbridge Wells [SE] [4] Ⓟ 🚲 ◇ ⚠ 🚕 206
Turkey Street [LE] ⚠ 21
Tutbury & Hatton [EM] Ⓤ 50
Twickenham [SW] Ⓟ 🚲 ◇ ⚠ 149
Twyford [GW] [3] Ⓟ 🚲 ⚠ 🚕 116, 117, 121
Ty Croes [AW] Ⓤ 81
Ty Glas [AW] Ⓤ 130
Tygwyn [AW] Ⓟ Ⓤ 75
Tyndrum Lower [SR] Ⓟ 🚲 Ⓤ 227
Tyndrum Upper [SR] (see Upper Tyndrum)
Tyseley [LM] ⚠ 71
Tywyn [AW] 🚲 Ⓤ 75

U

Uckfield [SN] Ⓟ 🚲 ◇ ⚠ 184
Uddingston [SR] Ⓟ 🚲 🚕 225, 226
Uig *Ship* 239B
Ulceby [NT] Ⓤ 29
Ullapool *Ship* 239B
Ulleskelf [NT] Ⓤ 33, 40
Ulverston [TP] ◇ 82
Umberleigh [GW] Ⓟ Ⓤ 136
University [LM] ◇ ⚠ 69, 71
Uphall [SR] Ⓟ 🚲 Ⓤ 226
Upholland [NT] Ⓤ 82
Upminster [CC] Ⓟ 🚲 ◇ ⚠ 🚕 1, 4
Upper Halliford [SW] ◇ ⚠ 152
Upper Holloway [LO] ⚠ 62
Upper Tyndrum [SR] Ⓟ 🚲 Ⓤ 227, *Sleepers* 404
Upper Warlingham [SN] Ⓟ 🚲 ◇ ⚠ 🚕 184
Upton [AW] Ⓤ 101
Upwey [SW] Ⓟ 🚲 ⚠ Ⓤ 123, 158
Urmston [NT] Ⓟ 🚲 Ⓤ 89
Uttoxeter [EM] Ⓟ Ⓤ 50

V

Valley [AW] Ⓟ Ⓤ 81
Vauxhall (London) **[SW]** ◇ ⚠ 149, 152, 155
Victoria [NR] (see London)
Virginia Water [SW] Ⓟ 🚲 ◇ ⚠ 🚕 149

W

Waddon [SN] ◇ ⚠ 182
Wadebridge Bus Station *Bus* 135C
Wadhurst [SE] Ⓟ ◇ ⚠ 206
Wainfleet [EM] Ⓟ 🚲 Ⓤ 19
Wakefield
  Kirkgate [NT] [4] Ⓟ 🚲 Ⓤ
  Westgate [GR] [7] Ⓟ 🚲 ◇ 🚕
 Barnsley 34
 Bedford 53
 Birmingham 51
 Bournemouth 51
 Bristol 51
 Cambridge 26
 Derby 53
 Doncaster 31
 Exeter 51
 Huddersfield 39
 Knottingley 32
 Leeds 31
 Leicester 53
 Liverpool 39
 London 26, 53
 Luton 53
 Manchester 39
 Manchester Airport 39
 Meadowhall 31
 Newquay 51
 Norwich 26
 Nottingham 53
 Paignton 51
 Penzance 51
 Plymouth 51
 Pontefract 32
 Sheffield 31
 Southampton 51
 Torquay 51
Wakes Colne [LE] (see Chappel & Wakes Colne)
Walkden [NT] 82
Wallasey Grove Road [ME] Ⓟ ⚠ 106
Wallasey Village [ME] ⚠ 106
Wallington [SN] Ⓟ ◇ ⚠ 🚕 182
Wallyford [SR] Ⓟ 🚲 Ⓤ 238
Walmer [SE] Ⓟ ◇ ⚠ 🚕 207
Walsall [LM] ◇ ⚠ 70
Walsden [NT] Ⓤ 41
Waltham Cross [LE] Ⓟ ⚠ 🚕 22
Walthamstow Central [LE] Ⓟ 🚲 ⚠ 🚕 20
Walthamstow Queen s Road [LO] 🚲 ⚠ 62
Walton (Merseyside) [ME] ⚠ 103
Walton-on-the-Naze [LE] 🚲 ⚠ 11
Walton-on-Thames [SW] Ⓟ 🚲 ◇ ⚠ 🚕 155
Wanborough [SW] ⚠ Ⓤ 148, 149
Wandsworth Common [SN] Ⓟ 🚲 ◇ ⚠ 🚕 176, 177, 178
Wandsworth Road [SN] ⚠ Ⓤ 176, 178
Wandsworth Town [SW] 🚲 ◇ ⚠ 149
Wanstead Park [LO] 🚲 ⚠ 62
Wapping [LO] 🚲 ⚠ 178
Warblington [SN] ⚠ Ⓤ 188
Ware [LE] Ⓟ 🚲 ⚠ 🚕 22
Wareham [SW] Ⓟ 🚲 ◇ ⚠ 🚕 158
Wargrave [GW] Ⓟ 🚲 Ⓤ 121
Warminster [GW] Ⓟ 🚲 ◇ 🚕 123, 160
Warnham [SN] ⚠ Ⓤ 182
Warrington
  Bank Quay [VT] Ⓟ ◇ 🚕
  Central [TP] Ⓟ 🚲 ◇ 🚕
 Aberdeen 65
 Bangor (Gwynedd) 81
 Birmingham 65
 Bournemouth 51
 Bristol 51
 Cambridge 49
 Carlisle 65
 Chester 81
 Crewe 65
 Dundee 65
 Edinburgh 65
 Ellesmere Port 109

Station index and table numbers

[10] Connection time
Ⓟ Station Car Park
🚲 Bicycle storage facility
◇ Seat reservations can be made at this station
⚠ Penalty Fare Schemes in operation on some or all services from this station
🚕 Taxi rank or cab office at station, or signposted and within 100 metres
Ⓤ Unstaffed station
[ ] Station Operator Code

■10 Connection time
℗ Station Car Park
🚲 Bicycle storage facility
◇ Seat reservations can be made at this station
⚠ Penalty Fare Schemes in operation on some or all services from this station
🚕 Taxi rank or cab office at station, or signposted and within 100 metres
⊛ Unstaffed station
[ ] Station Operator Code

Station index and table numbers

Whatstandwell [EM] ℗ ⊛ 56
Whifflet [SR] ℗ 🚕 ⊛ 220, 224, 226
Whimple [SW] ℗ 🚲 ⚠ ⊛ 160
Whinhill [SR] 🚲 ⊛ 219
Whiston [NT] ℗ 90
Whitby [NT] ℗ ◇ 🚕 45
Whitby Bus Station 🚕 *Bus* 26G
Whitchurch (Cardiff) [AW] ⊛ 130
Whitchurch (Hants.) [SW] ℗ 🚲 ◇ ⚠ 160
Whitchurch (Shrops) [AW] ℗ ⊛ 131
White Hart Lane [LE] ⚠ 21
White Notley [LE] 🚲 ⚠ ⊛ 11
Whitechapel [LT] 178
Whitecraigs [SR] ℗ 🚲 223
Whitehaven [NT] ℗ ◇ 100
Whitland [AW] ℗ ⊛ 128
Whitley Bridge [NT] ℗ ⊛ 32
Whitlock's End [LM] ⚠ ⊛ 71
Whitstable [SE] ℗ ◇ ⚠ 🚕 194, 212
Whittlesea [LE] ℗ ⊛ 14, 17
Whittlesford Parkway [LE] ℗ 🚲 ⚠ 22
Whitton [SW] 🚲 ◇ ⚠ 149
Whitwell [EM] ⊛ 55
Whyteleafe [SN] ℗ 🚲 ◇ ⚠ 181
Whyteleafe South [SN] ℗ 🚲 ◇ ⚠ 181
Wick [SR] ℗ 🚲 ◇ 🚕 239
Wickford [LE] ■2 ℗ 🚲 ⚠ 🚕 5
Wickham Market [LE] ℗ 🚲 ⊛ 13
Widdrington [NT] ℗ 🚲 ⊛ 48
Widnes [NT] ℗ 🚕 49, 89
Widney Manor [LM] ℗ ⚠ 71
Wigan
North Western [VT] ℗ ◇ 🚕
Wallgate [NT] 🚲 🚕
Barrow-in-Furness 65
Birmingham 65
Blackpool 90
Bolton 82
Bournemouth 51
Bristol 51
Carlisle 65
Crewe 65
Edinburgh 65
Exeter 51
Glasgow 65
Kirkby 82
Lancaster 65
Liverpool 82, 90
London 65
Manchester 82
Milton Keynes Central 65
Manchester Airport 82
Paignton 51
Penzance 51
Plymouth 51
Preston 65
Oxenholme Lake District 65
Oxford 51
Reading 51
St Helens 90
Southampton 51
Southport 82
Stafford 65
Stockport 82
Torquay 51
Warrington 65
Wolverhampton 65
Windermere 65
Wigton [NT] ℗ 🚕 ⊛ 100
Wildmill [AW] ⊛ 128
Willesden Junction [LO] 🚲 ⚠ 59, 60, 176
Williamwood [SR] 🚲 223
Willington [EM] ⊛ 57
Wilmcote [LM] ⚠ ⊛ 71, 115
Wilmslow [NT] ℗ 🚲 ◇ 🚕 51, 65, 84, 85, 131
Wilnecote [LM] ⊛ 57
Wilpshire [NT] (see Ramsgreave and Wilpshire)
Wimbledon [SW] ■6 ℗ 🚲 ◇ ⚠ 🚕 52, 152, 155, 179, 182
Wimbledon Chase [FC] ⚠ ⊛ 52, 179
Winchelsea [SN] ⊛ 189
Winchester [SW] ℗ 🚲 ◇ ⚠ 🚕 51, 158
Winchfield [SW] ℗ 🚲 ◇ ⚠ 155
Winchmore Hill [FC] ⚠ 24
Windermere [TP] ℗ ◇ 🚕 65, 82, 83
Windsor & Eton Central [GW] ⚠ 🚕 119
Windsor & Eton Riverside [SW] ℗ 🚲 ◇ ⚠ 🚕 149
Winnersh [SW] 🚲 ◇ ⚠ 149
Winnersh Triangle [SW] ◇ ⚠ 149
Winsford [LM] ℗ ◇ 91
Wisbech *Bus* 🚕 26A
Wishaw [SR] ℗ 🚲 226
Witham [LE] ■2 ℗ 🚲 ◇ ⚠ 🚕 11
Witley [SW] ℗ 🚲 ⚠ 156
Witton [LM] ⚠ 70
Wivelsfield [SN] ■4 🚲 ◇ ⚠ 52, 186, 189
Wivenhoe [LE] ■3 ℗ 🚲 ⚠ 🚕 11
Woburn Sands [LM] ⊛ 64
Woking [SW] ℗ 🚲 ◇ ⚠ 🚕
Aldershot 155
Basingstoke 155
Bournemouth 158
Bristol 160
Exeter 160
Fareham 158
Guildford 156
Heathrow Airport *Bus* 158A
London 149, 155, 156
Portsmouth 156
Salisbury 160
Southampton 158
Surbiton 155
Weymouth 158
Wokingham [SW] ℗ 🚲 ◇ ⚠ 🚕 148, 149
Woldingham [SN] ℗ 🚲 ◇ ⚠ 184
Wolverhampton [VT] ■7 ℗ 🚲 ◇ ⚠ 🚕
Bangor (Gwynedd) 65
Birmingham 68
Birmingham International 68
Bournemouth 51
Bristol 51
Carlisle 65
Chester 65, 75
Coventry 68
Crewe 65
Edinburgh 65
Exeter 51
Glasgow 65
Holyhead 65
Liverpool 65
London 66
Macclesfield 84
Manchester 65
Manchester Airport 65
Oxenholme Lake District 65
Oxford 51
Paignton 51
Penzance 51
Plymouth 51
Preston 65
Reading 51
Rugby 66
Shrewsbury 74
Southampton 51
Stafford 68
Stockport 65
Stoke-on-Trent 65
Torquay 51
Walsall 70
Watford 66
Wrexham 75
Wolverton [LM] ℗ 🚲 66
Wombwell [NT] ℗ ⊛ 34
Wood End [LM] ⚠ ⊛ 71
Wood Street [LE] ⚠ 20
Woodbridge [LE] ℗ 🚲 🚕 ⊛ 13
Woodgrange Park [LO] 🚲 ⚠ 62
Woodhall [SR] 🚲 219
Woodham Ferrers [LE] (South Woodham Ferrers)
Woodhouse [NT] ℗ ⊛ 30
Woodlesford [NT] ℗ 🚲 ⊛ 32, 34
Woodley [NT] ℗ ⊛ 78
Woodmansterne [SN] ⚠ 181
Woodsmoor [NT] 86
Wool [SW] ℗ 🚲 ◇ ⚠ 🚕 158
Woolston [SW] ℗ 🚲 ◇ ⚠ 165
Woolwich Arsenal [SE] ■4 ℗ ◇ ⚠ 🚕 200
Woolwich Dockyard [SE] ◇ ⚠ 200
Wootton Wawen [LM] ⚠ ⊛ 71

Station index and table numbers

[10] Connection time
Ⓟ Station Car Park
🚲 Bicycle storage facility
◇ Seat reservations can be made at this station
⚠ Penalty Fare Schemes in operation on some or all services from this station
🚕 Taxi rank or cab office at station, or signposted and within 100 metres
ⓤ Unstaffed station
[ ] Station Operator Code

Worcester Foregate Street [LM] [7] ◇ ⚠ 🚕 71, 126
Worcester Shrub Hill [LM] [7] Ⓟ ◇ ⚠ 🚕 57, 71, 125, 126
Worcester Park [SW] Ⓟ 🚲 ◇ ⚠ 🚕 152
Workington [NT] Ⓟ ◇ 100
Workington (Bus Station) *Bus* 65F
Worksop [NT] Ⓟ ◇ 30, 55
Worle [GW] Ⓟ 🚲 ⓤ 134
Worplesdon [SW] Ⓟ 🚲 ◇ ⚠ 155, 156
Worstead [LE] Ⓟ 🚲 ⓤ 16
Worthing [SN] [4] Ⓟ 🚲 ◇ ⚠ 🚕 123, 188
Wrabness [LE] Ⓟ 🚲 ⓤ 11
Wraysbury [SW] Ⓟ ⚠ ⓤ 149
Wrenbury [AW] Ⓟ ⓤ 131
Wressle [NT] ⓤ 29
Wrexham Central [AW] ⓤ 101
Wrexham General [AW] Ⓟ ◇ 🚕 65, 75, 101
Wrotham [SE] (see Borough Green & Wrotham)
Wroxham [LE] (see Hoveton & Wroxham)
Wye [SE] Ⓟ ◇ ⚠ 207
Wylam [NT] Ⓟ 🚲 ⓤ 48
Wylde Green [LM] Ⓟ ⚠ 69
Wymondham [LE] Ⓟ 🚕 17
Wythall [LM] ⚠ 71

Y

Yalding [SE] Ⓟ ⚠ ⓤ 208
Yardley Wood [LM] Ⓟ ⚠ 71
Yarm [TP] Ⓟ ⓤ 39
Yarmouth (IOW) *Ship* 🚕 158
Yate [GW] Ⓟ 🚲 134
Yatton [GW] Ⓟ 🚲 134
Yeoford [GW] ⓤ 136
Yeovil Bus Station *Bus* [SW] Ⓟ 🚲 *A,
Yeovil Junction [SW] Ⓟ 🚲 ◇ ⚠ 🚕 123A,160
Yeovil Pen Mill [GW] Ⓟ ◇ 123, 123A
Yetminster [GW] Ⓟ ⓤ 123
Ynyswen [AW] ⓤ 130
Yoker [SR] 🚲 ⓤ 226
York [GR] [8] Ⓟ 🚲 ◇ 🚕
Aberdeen 26
Bedford 53
Birmingham 51
Birmingham International 51
Blackpool 41
Bournemouth 51
Bradford 40
Bristol 51
Cambridge 26
Cardiff 51
Darlington 26
Derby 53
Doncaster 26
Dundee 26
Eden Camp *Bus* 26G
Edinburgh 26
Exeter 51
Flamingo Land *Bus* 26G
Glasgow 26
Grantham 26
Halifax 41
Harrogate 35
Hartlepool 26
Huddersfield 39
Hull 33
Knaresborough 35
Leeds 35, 40
Leicester 53
Liverpool 39
London 26
Luton 53
Manchester 39
Manchester Airport 39
Middlesbrough 26
Newark 26
Newcastle 26
Newport (South Wales) 51
Newton Abbot 51
Norwich 26
Nottingham 53
Oxford 51
Paignton 51
Penzance 51
Peterborough 26
Pickering Eastgate *Bus* 26G
Plymouth 51
Preston 41
Reading 51
Retford 26
Scarborough 39
Selby 33
Sheffield 29
Stansted Airport 26
Southampton 51
Sunderland 26
Torquay 51
Whitby *Bus* 26G
Yorton [AW] Ⓟ ⓤ 131
Ystrad Mynach [AW] [3] Ⓟ ◇ 130
Ystrad Rhondda [AW] Ⓟ ⓤ 130

Network Diagram for Tables 1, 4

DM-1/06
Design BAJS

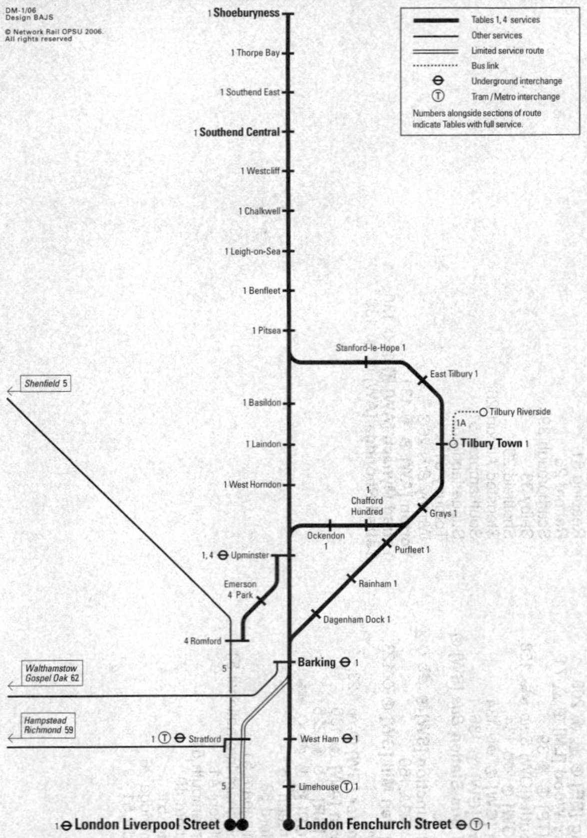

until 26 July

London - Southend Central and Shoeburyness

Network Diagram - see first page of Table I

Miles	Miles	Miles				CC MO A	CC MX	CC MX	CC MO A	CC MX	CC MX	CC MO A	CC MX	CC MX		CC MX	CC MX	CC MO A	CC MX	CC MX	CC MX	CC MX	CC MO	CC MX		CC MX
0	0	—	**London Fenchurch St** [7]	⊖	d	22p50	22p50	23p00			23p05	23p10	23p10			23p20	23p35	23p40	23p40	23p50	00 01		00 10	00 15		00 25
1¾	1¾	—	Limehouse		d	22p54	22p54				23p09	23p14	23p14			23p24	23p39	23p44	23p44	23p54			00 14	00 19		00 29
4¾	4¾	—	West Ham	⊖	d	22p59	22p59	23p08			23p14	23p19	23p19			23p29	23p44	23p49	23p49	23p59	00 09		00 19	00 24		00 34
—	—	—	**London Liverpool St** [15]	⊖	d																					
—	—	—	Stratford [7]	⊖	d																					
7½	7½	—	Barking	⊖	d	23p04	23p05	23p14			23p20	23p24	23p25			23p35	23p50	23p54	23p55	00 05	00 15		00 24	00 30		00 40
15¼	—	0	Upminster	⊖	d	23p12	23p14	23p23				23p32	23p34			23p44		00 02	00 04	00 14	00 24		00 32			00 49
—	—	3	Ockendon		d	23p18	23p19									23p49				00 19						
—	—	5	Chafford Hundred		d	23p21	23p23									23p53				00 23						
19¼	—	—	West Horndon		d							23p37	23p39					00 07	00 09				00 37			00 54
22¾	—	—	Laindon		d			23p31				23p42	23p44					00 12	00 16		00 32		00 42			00 59
24½	—	—	Basildon		d			23p34				23p45	23p47					00 15	00 19		00 35		00 45			01 02
—	10½	—	Dagenham Dock		d						23p25						23p55							00 35		
—	12¾	—	Rainham		d						23p29						23p59							00 39		
—	16	—	Purfleet		d						23p34						00 04							00 44		
—	19¾	7½	Grays		d	23p25	23p27				23p42					23p57	00a10			00 27				00a50		
—	21½	—	**Tilbury Town** [3]		d	23p28	23p30				23p45					00 01				00 30						
—	25¼	—	East Tilbury		d	23p34	23p36				23p51					00 06				00 36						
—	27¼	—	Stanford-le-Hope		d	23p37	23p40				23p55			←		00 10				00 40						
26½	32¼	—	Pitsea		d	23p45	23p48		←	←	00 06	23p49	23p52	00 06		00 18		00 19	00 22	00 48		←	00 49			01 06
29¼	35	—	Benfleet		d	23p49	23p52	23p41	23p49	23p52	→	23p52	23p56	00 10		00 22		00 22	00 26	00 52	00 42	00 52	00 52			01 10
32½	38¼	—	Leigh-on-Sea		d	→	→	23p45	23p53	23p56		23p57	23p59	00 15		00 27		00 27	00 31	→	00 46	00 56	00 57			01 14
34	39¾	—	Chalkwell		d			23p48	23p56	23p59		23p59	00 03	00 18		00 30		00 29	00 34		00 49	00 59	00 59			01 17
34¾	40½	—	Westcliff		d			23p51	23p58	00 02		00 02	00 06	00 20		00 32		00 32	00 36		00 52	01 02	01 02			01 20
35¾	41½	—	**Southend Central**		a			23p54	00 01	00 05		00 05	00 09	00 23		00 35		00 35	00 39		00 55	01 05	01 05			01 23
—	—	—			d			23p54	00 01	00 05		00 06	00 09	00 23		00 35		00 36	00 40		00 55	01 05	01 06			01 23
36½	42¼	—	Southend East		d			23p56	00 03	00 07		00 08	00 11	00 26		00 38		00 38	00 42		00 57	01 07	01 08			01 25
38	43¾	—	Thorpe Bay		d			23p59	00 06	00 11		00 10	00 15	00 29		00 41		00 40	00 46		01 01	01 11	01 11			01 29
39½	45¼	—	**Shoeburyness**		a			00 06	00 13	00 17		00 18	00 21	00 36		00 48		00 48	00 52		01 07	01 17	01 18			01 35

			CC	CC	CC	CC	CC	CC	CC	CC		CC	CC	CC	CC	CC	CC	CC	CC	CC		CC	CC	CC	CC	CC
London Fenchurch St [7]	⊖	d		05 10		05 40				06 10		06 20	06 40		06 44	06 48	07 00	07 09	07 13	07 15		07 30	07 40	07 43	07 48	07 50
Limehouse		d		05 14		05 44				06 14		06 24	06 44		06 48	06 52		07 13					07 44			07 54
West Ham	⊖	d		05 19		05 49				06 19		06 29	06 49		06 53	06 57	07 08	07 18		07 23		07 38	07 49	07 53		07 59
London Liverpool St [15]	⊖	d																								
Stratford [7]	⊖	d																								
Barking	⊖	d		05 25	05 39	05 55	05 45	06 05		06 25		06 35	06 55	06 50	07 00	07 03	07 14	07 25	07 26	07 29		07 44	07 55	07 58		08 05
Upminster	⊖	d	05 28	05 34	05 48	06 04			06 31	06 34			07 04		07 10		07 23	07 34		07 38		07 53	08 04		08 09	08 15
Ockendon		d	05 33		05 56				06 36						07 15					07 45					08 16	
Chafford Hundred		d	05 37		06 00				06 40						07 19					07 49					08 20	
West Horndon		d		05 39		06 09				06 39			07 09					07 39					08 09			08 20
Laindon		d		05 44		06 14				06 45			07 14					07 44					08 14			08a26
Basildon		d		05 47		06 17				06 48			07 17				07 33	07 47				08 03	08 17			
Dagenham Dock		d					05 50	06 10				06 40		06 55		07 08			07 31					08 03		
Rainham		d					05 54	06 14				06 44		06 59		07 12			07 35					08 07		
Purfleet		d					05 59	06 19				06 49		07 04		07 17			07 40					08 13		
Grays		d	05a41		06a05		06 05	06 25	06a44			06 55		07 10	07a23	07 25			07 46	07 54				08 18	08 25	
Tilbury Town [3]		d					06 08	06 28				06 58		07 13		07 28				07 58				08 22		
East Tilbury		d					06 14	06 34				07 04		07 19		07 34				08 04				08 28		
Stanford-le-Hope		d					06 18	06 38				07 08		07 23		07 38			07 56	08 08				08 32	08 35	
Pitsea		d		05 51		06 21	06 26	06a46		06 51		07 18	07 22	07a31		07a46		07 51	08a03	08a15			08 21	08 41	08a44	
Benfleet		d		05 55		06 25	06 31			06 55		07 22	07 26				07 39	07 55				08 09	08 25	→		
Leigh-on-Sea		d		06 00		06 30	06 35			07 00		07 27	07 30				07 44	07 59				08 14	08 30			
Chalkwell		d		06 03		06 33	06 38			07 03		07 30	07 33				07 47	08 02				08 17	08 33			
Westcliff		d		06 05		06 35	06 41			07 05		07 32	07 36				07 49	08 05				08 19	08 35			
Southend Central		a		06 08		06 38	06 43			07 08		07 35	07 38				07 52	08 07				08 22	08 38			
		d		06 08		06 38	06 43			07 08		07 35	07 38				07 52	08 07				08 22	08 38			
Southend East		d		06 10		06 40	06 45			07 10		07 37	07 40				07 54	08 09				08 24	08 40			
Thorpe Bay		d		06 14		06 44	06 49			07 14		07 40	07 44				07 58	08 13				08 28	08 44			
Shoeburyness		a		06 18		06 48	06 53			07 20		07 45	07 48				08 02	08 17				08 32	08 48			

			CC	CC	CC	CC		CC	CC	CC	CC	CC	CC	CC	CC	CC		CC	CC	CC	CC	CC	CC	CC	CC	CC
London Fenchurch St [7]	⊖	d	08 00		08 03	08 09		08 14	08 20	08 30		08 40	08 50	08 54	09 00			09 10	09 16	09 20	09 30		09 35	09 40		09 50
Limehouse		d			08 07	08 13			08 24			08 44	08 54					09 14	09 20	09 24			09 39	09 44		09 54
West Ham	⊖	d	08 08		08 12	08 18		08 23	08 29	08 38		08 49	08 59		09 08			09 19	09 25	09 29	09 38		09 44	09 49		09 59
London Liverpool St [15]	⊖	d																								
Stratford [7]	⊖	d																								
Barking	⊖	d	08 14		08 18	08 24		08 30	08 37	08 45		08 55	09 07	09 09	09 16			09 25	09 31	09 35	09 44		09 50	09 55		10 05
Upminster	⊖	d	08 23			08 33		08 41		08 54		09 04		09 18	09 25			09 34		09 45	09 53			10 04		10 14
Ockendon		d						08 46						09 23						09 50						10 19
Chafford Hundred		d						08 50						09 27						09 54						10 23
West Horndon		d				08 38						09 09						09 39						10 09		
Laindon		d	08 31			08 44				09 03		09 14			09 34			09 44			10 01			10 14		
Basildon		d	08 34			08 47				09 06		09 17			09 37			09 47			10 04			10 17		
Dagenham Dock		d			08 23				08 42				09 12						09 36				09 55			
Rainham		d			08 27				08 46				09 16						09 40				09 59			
Purfleet		d			08 33				08 51				09 21						09 45				10 04			
Grays		d			08 38			08a54	08 57				09 27	09a31					09 51	09 58			10a10			10 27
Tilbury Town [3]		d			08 42				09 00				09 30						09 54	10 02						10 30
East Tilbury		d			08 48				09 06				09 36						10 00	10 08						10 36
Stanford-le-Hope		d		←	08 52				09 10		←		09 40						10 04	10 12					←	10 40
Pitsea		d	08 38	08 41	08a59	08 51			09 18	09 09	09 18	09 21	09 48			←		09 51	10 12	10 25		←		10 21	10 25	10 48
Benfleet		d	08 42	08 45		08 55			→	09 13	09 22	09 26	09 52		09 43	09 52		09 55	10 16	→	10 11	10 16		10 25	10 29	10 52
Leigh-on-Sea		d	08 46	08 50		08 59				09 18	09 27	09 30	→		09 48	09 57		10 00	→		10 15	10 20		10 30	10 34	→
Chalkwell		d	08 49	08 53		09 02				09 21	09 30	09 33			09 51	10 00		10 03			10 18	10 23		10 33	10 37	
Westcliff		d	08 52	08 55		09 05				09 23	09 32	09 36			09 53	10 02		10 05			10 21	10 26		10 35	10 39	
Southend Central		a	08 54	08 58		09 08				09 26	09 35	09 38			09 56	10 05		10 08			10 23	10 29		10 38	10 42	
		d	08 55			09 08				09 26		09 38			09 56			10 08			10 23			10 38		
Southend East		d	08 57			09 10				09 28		09 40			09 58			10 10			10 25			10 40		
Thorpe Bay		d	09 00			09 14				09 32		09 44			10 02			10 14			10 29			10 44		
Shoeburyness		a	09 05			09 18				09 36		09 48			10 06			10 18			10 33			10 48		

A from 21 May until 23 July

Table I

Mondays to Fridays

until 26 July

London - Southend Central and Shoeburyness

Network Diagram - see first page of Table I

		CC	CC	CC	CC	CC	CC	CC	CC	CC	CC	CC	CC	CC	CC	CC	CC	CC	CC	CC	CC	CC
London Fenchurch St 7 ⊖	d	10 00		10 05	10 10	10 20	10 30		10 35	10 40	10 50	11 00		11 05	11 10	11 20	11 30		11 35	11 40	11 50	12 00
Limehouse	d			10 09	10 14	10 24			10 39	10 44	10 54			11 09	11 14	11 24			11 39	11 44	11 54	
West Ham ⊖	d	10 08		10 14	10 19	10 29	10 38		10 44	10 49	10 59	11 08		11 14	11 19	11 29	11 38		11 44	11 49	11 59	12 08
London Liverpool St 15 ⊖	d																					
Stratford 7 ⊖	d																					
Barking ⊖	d	10 14		10 20	10 25	10 35	10 44		10 50	10 55	11 05	11 14		11 20	11 25	11 35	11 44		11 50	11 55	12 05	12 14
Upminster ⊖	d	10 23			10 34	10 44	10 53			11 04	11 14	11 23			11 34	11 44	11 53			12 04	12 14	12 23
Ockendon	d					10 49					11 19					11 49					12 19	
Chafford Hundred	d					10 53					11 23					11 53					12 23	
West Horndon	d				10 39					11 09					11 39					12 09		
Laindon	d	10 31			10 44		11 01			11 14		11 31			11 44		12 01			12 14		12 31
Basildon	d	10 34			10 47		11 04			11 17		11 34			11 47		12 04			12 17		12 34
Dagenham Dock	d			10 25					10 55					11 25					11 55			
Rainham	d			10 29					10 59					11 29					11 59			
Purfleet	d			10 34					11 04					11 34					12 04			
Grays	d			10a40		10 57			11a10		11 27			11a40		11 57			12a10		12 27	
Tilbury Town 3	d					11 00					11 30					12 00					12 30	
East Tilbury	d					11 06					11 36					12 06					12 36	
Stanford-le-Hope	d					11 10					11 40					12 10					12 40	
Pitsea	d		←		10 51	11 18		←		11 21	11 48		←		11 51	12 18		←		12 21	12 48	
Benfleet	d	10 41	10 52		10 55	11 22	11 11	11 22		11 25	11 52	11 41	11 52		11 55	12 22	12 11	12 22		12 25	12 52	12 41
Leigh-on-Sea	d	10 45	10 56		11 00	→	11 15	11 26		11 30	→	11 45	11 57		12 00	→	12 15	12 26		12 30	→	12 45
Chalkwell	d	10 48	10 59		11 03		11 18	11 29		11 33		11 48	12 00		12 03		12 18	12 29		12 33		12 48
Westcliff	d	10 51	11 02		11 05		11 21	11 32		11 35		11 51	12 02		12 05		12 21	12 32		12 35		12 51
Southend Central	a	10 53	11 05		11 08		11 23	11 35		11 38		11 53	12 05		12 08		12 23	12 35		12 38		12 53
	d	10 53			11 08		11 23			11 38		11 53			12 08		12 23			12 38		12 53
Southend East	d	10 55			11 10		11 25			11 40		11 55			12 10		12 25			12 40		12 55
Thorpe Bay	d	10 59			11 14		11 29			11 44		11 59			12 14		12 29			12 44		12 59
Shoeburyness	a	11 03			11 18		11 33			11 48		12 03			12 18		12 33			12 48		13 03

		CC	CC	CC	CC	CC	CC	CC	CC	CC	CC	CC	CC	CC	CC	CC	CC	CC	CC	CC	CC	CC	CC
London Fenchurch St 7 ⊖	d		12 05	12 10	12 20	12 30		12 35	12 40	12 50	13 00		13 05	13 10	13 20	13 30		13 35	13 40	13 50	14 00		14 05
Limehouse	d		12 09	12 14	12 24			12 39	12 44	12 54			13 09	13 14	13 24			13 39	13 44	13 54			14 09
West Ham ⊖	d		12 14	12 19	12 29	12 38		12 44	12 49	12 59	13 08		13 14	13 19	13 29	13 38		13 44	13 49	13 59	14 08		14 14
London Liverpool St 15 ⊖	d																						
Stratford 7 ⊖	d																						
Barking ⊖	d		12 20	12 25	12 35	12 44		12 50	12 55	13 05	13 14		13 20	13 25	13 35	13 44		13 50	13 55	14 05	14 14		14 20
Upminster ⊖	d			12 34	12 44	12 53			13 04	13 14	13 23			13 34	13 44	13 53			14 04	14 14	14 23		
Ockendon	d				12 49					13 19					13 49					14 19			
Chafford Hundred	d				12 53					13 23					13 53					14 23			
West Horndon	d			12 39					13 09					13 39					14 09				
Laindon	d			12 44		13 01			13 14		13 31			13 44		14 01			14 14		14 31		
Basildon	d			12 47		13 04			13 17		13 34			13 47		14 04			14 17		14 34		
Dagenham Dock	d		12 25					12 55					13 25					13 55					14 25
Rainham	d		12 29					12 59					13 29					13 59					14 29
Purfleet	d		12 34					13 04					13 34					14 04					14 34
Grays	d		12a40		12 57			13a10		13 27			13a40		13 57			14a10		14 27			14a40
Tilbury Town 3	d				13 00					13 30					14 00					14 30			
East Tilbury	d				13 06					13 36					14 06					14 36			
Stanford-le-Hope	d				13 10					13 40					14 10					14 40			
Pitsea	d	←		12 51	13 18		←		13 21	13 48		←		13 51	14 18		←		14 21	14 48		←	
Benfleet	d	12 52		12 55	13 22	13 11	13 22		13 25	13 52	13 41	13 52		13 55	14 22	14 11	14 22		14 25	14 52	14 41	14 52	
Leigh-on-Sea	d	12 57		13 00	→	13 15	13 27		13 30	→	13 45	13 57		14 00	→	14 15	14 26		14 30	→	14 45	14 56	
Chalkwell	d	13 00		13 03		13 18	13 30		13 33		13 48	14 00		14 03		14 18	14 29		14 33		14 48	14 59	
Westcliff	d	13 02		13 05		13 21	13 32		13 35		13 51	14 02		14 05		14 21	14 32		14 35		14 51	15 02	
Southend Central	a	13 05		13 08		13 23	13 35		13 38		13 53	14 05		14 08		14 23	14 35		14 38		14 53	15 05	
	d			13 08		13 23			13 38		13 53			14 08		14 23			14 38		14 53		
Southend East	d			13 10		13 25			13 40		13 55			14 10		14 25			14 40		14 55		
Thorpe Bay	d			13 14		13 29			13 44		13 59			14 14		14 29			14 44		14 59		
Shoeburyness	a			13 18		13 33			13 48		14 03			14 18		14 33			14 48		15 03		

		CC	CC	CC	CC	CC	CC	CC	CC	CC	CC	CC	CC	CC	CC	CC	CC	CC	CC	CC	CC	CC
London Fenchurch St 7 ⊖	d	14 10	14 20	14 30		14 35	14 40	14 50	15 00		15 05	15 10	15 20	15 25	15 30	15 35	15 40		15 50	15 55	16 00	16 10
Limehouse	d	14 14	14 24			14 39	14 44	14 54			15 09	15 14	15 24			15 39	15 44		15 54	15 59		16 14
West Ham ⊖	d	14 19	14 29	14 38		14 44	14 49	14 59	15 08		15 14	15 19	15 29	15 33	15 38	15 44	15 49		15 59	16 04	16 08	16 19
London Liverpool St 15 ⊖	d																					
Stratford 7 ⊖	d																					
Barking ⊖	d	14 25	14 35	14 44		14 50	14 55	15 05	15 14		15 20	15 25	15 35	15 39	15 44	15 50	15 54		16 05	16 10	16 14	16 25
Upminster ⊖	d	14 34	14 44	14 53			15 04	15 14	15 23			15 34	15 44	15 48	15 53		16 02		16 14		16 23	16 34
Ockendon	d		14 49					15 19					15 49						16 19			
Chafford Hundred	d		14 53					15 23					15 53						16 23			
West Horndon	d	14 39					15 09					15 39					16 07					16 39
Laindon	d	14 44		15 01			15 14		15 31			15 44		15 56	16 01		16 12					16 44
Basildon	d	14 47		15 04			15 17		15 34			15 47		15 59	16 04		16 15				16 33	16 47
Dagenham Dock	d					14 55					15 25					15 55				16 15		
Rainham	d					14 59					15 29					15 59				16 19		
Purfleet	d					15 04					15 34					16 04				16 25		
Grays	d		14 57			15a10		15 27			15a40		15 57			16a10			16 27	16a33		
Tilbury Town 3	d		15 00					15 30					16 00						16 30			
East Tilbury	d		15 06					15 36					16 06						16 36			
Stanford-le-Hope	d		15 10					15 40					16 10					←	16 40			
Pitsea	d	14 51	15 18		←		15 21	15 48		←		15 51	16 22	16 03			16 19	16 22	16a48			16 51
Benfleet	d	14 55	15 22	15 11	15 22		15 25	15 52	15 41	15 52		15 55	→	16 07	16 11		16 22	16 26			16 40	16 55
Leigh-on-Sea	d	15 00	→	15 15	15 26		15 30	→	15 45	15 56		16 00		16a12	16 15		16 27	16 30			16 45	17 00
Chalkwell	d	15 03		15 18	15 29		15 33		15 48	15 59		16 03			16 18		16 29	16 33			16 48	17 03
Westcliff	d	15 05		15 21	15 32		15 35		15 51	16 02		16 05			16 21		16 32	16 36			16 50	17 05
Southend Central	a	15 08		15 23	15 35		15 38		15 53	16 05		16 08			16 23		16 34	16 41			16 53	17 08
	d	15 08		15 23			15 38		15 53			16 08			16 23		16 35				16 53	17 08
Southend East	d	15 10		15 25			15 40		15 55			16 10			16 25		16 37				16 55	17 10
Thorpe Bay	d	15 14		15 29			15 44		15 59			16 14			16 29		16 39				16 59	17 14
Shoeburyness	a	15 18		15 33			15 48		16 03			16 20			16 33		16 44				17 05	17 20

Table I

Mondays to Fridays

until 26 July

London - Southend Central and Shoeburyness

Network Diagram - see first page of Table I

		CC	CC	CC	CC	CC	CC	CC	CC	CC	CC	CC	CC	CC	CC	CC	CC	CC	CC	CC	CC	CC	CC
London Fenchurch St 7 ⊖	d	16 13	16 20	16 28	16 30	16 34	16 37	16 45	16 48	16 55	17 00	17 02	17 05	17 07	17 10	17 15	17 18	17 20	17 23	17 26	17 30	17 32	17 35
Limehouse	d	16 17	16 24		16 34	16 38	16 41	16 49	16 52	16 59			17 09	17 12	17 15	17 19		17 24	17 28	17 30			17 39
West Ham ⊖	d	16 22	16 29	16 36	16 39	16 43	16 46		16 57	17 04				17 17	17 20		17 26	17 29	17 33	17 35		17 40	17 44
London Liverpool St 15 ⊖	d																						
Stratford 7 ⊖	d																						
Barking ⊖	d	16 28	16 35		16 45	16 49	16 52	16 59	17 03	17 10		17 15	17 19	17 22	17 26			17 35	17 39	17 42		17 46	17 50
Upminster ⊖	d		16 45		16 55		17 02	17 07	17 13			17 24		17 31		17 36	17 40		17 47			17 56	
Ockendon	d		16 50				17 08					17 29										18 02	
Chafford Hundred	d		16 54				17 12					17 34										18 06	
West Horndon	d				17 00				17 18					17 36					17 52				
Laindon	d			16 56	17a08			17 16	17a26				17 35	17a43				17 51	17a59				18 07
Basildon	d			16 59				17 19					17 39				17 50	17 55					18 10
Dagenham Dock	d	16 33				16 54				17 15					17 31					17 47			
Rainham	d	16 37				16 58				17 19					17 35					17 51			
Purfleet	d	16 43				17 04				17 25					17 40					17 56			
Grays	d	16 49	16 59			17 10	17a18			17 31		17a40			17 46					18 02		18a13	
Tilbury Town 3	d	16 52	17 02			17 13				17 34					17 50					18 06			
East Tilbury	d	16 58	17 08			17 19				17 40					17 56					18 12			
Stanford-le-Hope	d	17 02	17a15			17 23				17 44					18 00					18 16			
Pitsea	d	17a12				17a33		17 23		17a54			17 42		18a09		17 54	17 58		18a25			18 14
Benfleet	d			17 06				17 27			17 33		17 46			17 52	17 58	18 03			18 08		18 18
Leigh-on-Sea	d			17 11				17 32			17 38		17 51			17 56	18 02	18 07			18 12		18 23
Chalkwell	d			17 14				17 34			17 41		17 53			17 59	18 05	18 10			18 15		18 26
Westcliff	d			17 16				17 37			17 43		17 56			18 02	18 08	18 13			18 18		18 28
Southend Central	a			17 19				17 39			17 46		17 58			18 04	18 13	18 15			18 20		18 31
	d			17 19				17 39			17 46		17 58			18 04		18 15			18 20		18 31
Southend East	d			17 21				17 41			17 48		18 00			18 06		18 17			18 22		18 33
Thorpe Bay	d			17 24				17 44			17 50		18 03			18 10		18 21			18 26		18 36
Shoeburyness	a			17 31				17 51			17 57		18 11			18 16		18 28			18 32		18 43

		CC	CC	CC	CC	CC	CC	CC	CC	CC	CC	CC	CC	CC	CC	CC	CC	CC	CC	CC	CC	CC	CC
London Fenchurch St 7 ⊖	d	17 37	17 41	17 45	17 47	17 51	17 53	17 56	18 00	18 02	18 06	18 09			18 12	18 21			18 23	18 27		18 31	18 35
Limehouse	d	17 42	17 45	17 49	17 52		17 57	18 00		18 06	18 10	18 13			18 16				18 27	18 31		18 35	18 39
West Ham ⊖	d	17 47	17 50		17 57	17 59		18 05	18 08	18 11		18 18			18 21				18 32	18 36		18 40	
London Liverpool St 15 ⊖	d																						
Stratford 7 ⊖	d																						
Barking ⊖	d	17 53	17 56					18 08	18 11	18 17	18 20	18 24			18 28					18 42		18 46	18 49
Upminster ⊖	d	18 03			18 10	18 14				18 27		18 34							18 46	18 51			18 58
Ockendon	d				18 15					18 33									18 51				19 06
Chafford Hundred	d				18 20					18 38									18 55				19 11
West Horndon	d	18 08					18 21					18 39								18 56			
Laindon	d	18a15					18 27				18 37	18 43				18 47				19 01			
Basildon	d					18 24	18 31		18 35		18 41	18 47				18 51				19 04			
Dagenham Dock	d		18 01					18 16							18 33							18 51	
Rainham	d		18 05					18 20							18 37							18 55	
Purfleet	d		18 11					18 25							18 42							19 01	
Grays	d		18 17		18a26			18 31		18 42					18 48				19 00			19 07	19a17
Tilbury Town 3	d		18 20					18 35		18 46					18 52				19 03			19 10	
East Tilbury	d		18 26					18 41		18 52					18 58				19 09			19 16	
Stanford-le-Hope	d		18 30					18 45		18 56			←	←	19 02				19 13		←	19 20	
Pitsea	d		18a40			18 28	18 34	18 57	18 38	19 03	18 44	18 50	18 57	19 03	19a11		←	←	19 21	19 08	19 21	19a30	
Benfleet	d			18 24		18 32	18 39	→	18 43	→	18 49	18 54	19 03	19 07		18 58	19 03	19 07	→	19 12	19 25		
Leigh-on-Sea	d			18 28		18 37	18 43		18 47		18 53	18 59	→	→		19 03	19 07	19a14		19 16	→		
Chalkwell	d			18 31		18 40	18 46		18 50		18 56	19 01				19 06	19 10			19 19			
Westcliff	d			18 34		18 42	18 49		18 53		18 59	19 04				19 08	19 13			19 21			
Southend Central	a			18 36		18 45	18 51		18 55		19 01	19 09				19 11	19 15			19 24			
	d			18 36		18 45	18 51		18 55		19 01					19 11	19 15			19 24			
Southend East	d			18 38		18 47	18 53		18 57		19 03					19 13	19 17			19 26			
Thorpe Bay	d			18 42		18 50	18 57		19 01		19 07					19 16	19 21			19 28			
Shoeburyness	a			18 48		18 58	19 03		19 07		19 13					19 23	19 28			19 35			

		CC	CC	CC	CC	CC	CC	CC	CC	CC	CC	CC	CC	CC	CC	CC	CC	CC	CC	CC	CC	CC
London Fenchurch St 7 ⊖	d	18 42		18 46	18 51	19 00	19 02	19 05		19 08	19 11	19 20	19 30		19 32	19 35	19 40	19 50	20 00		20 05	20 10
Limehouse	d			18 51	18 55			19 09		19 12	19 15	19 24			19 36	19 39	19 44	19 54			20 09	20 14
West Ham ⊖	d	18 50		18 56	19 00		19 10			19 17	19 20	19 29			19 41	19 44	19 49	19 59	20 08		20 14	20 19
London Liverpool St 15 ⊖	d																					
Stratford 7 ⊖	d																					
Barking ⊖	d			19 01	19 06		19 16	19 19		19 23	19 26	19 35			19 47	19 50	19 55	20 05	20 14		20 20	20 25
Upminster ⊖	d			19 10			19 26	19 30			19 35	19 44	19 50		19 56		20 04	20 14	20 23			20 34
Ockendon	d						19 33					19 49						20 19				
Chafford Hundred	d						19 39					19 53						20 23				
West Horndon	d			19 15							19 40				20 01		20 09					20 39
Laindon	d			19 20		19 26					19 45				20a07		20 14		20 31			20 44
Basildon	d	19 12		19 23				19 40			19 48		20 00				20 17		20 34			20 47
Dagenham Dock	d				19 11					19 28						19 55					20 25	
Rainham	d				19 15					19 32						19 59					20 29	
Purfleet	d				19 21					19 37						20 04					20 34	
Grays	d				19 27		19 46			19a43		19 57				20a10		20 27			20a40	
Tilbury Town 3	d				19 30		19 50					20 00						20 30				
East Tilbury	d				19 36		19 56					20 06						20 36				
Stanford-le-Hope	d				19 40		20 00		←			20 10						20 40				
Pitsea	d		←	19 26	19 48		20a07	19 44	19 48		19 52	20 18		←			20 21	20 48		←		20 51
Benfleet	d	19 19	19 25	19 30	→	19 33		19 48	19 52		19 56	20 22	20 06	20 22			20 26	20 52	20 41	20 52		20 55
Leigh-on-Sea	d	19 24	19a32	19 35		19 38		19 52	19 56		20 00	→	20 11	20 27			20 30	→	20 45	20 56		21 00
Chalkwell	d	19 27		19 37		19 41		19 55	19 59		20 03		20 14	20 30			20 33		20 48	20 59		21 03
Westcliff	d	19 29		19 40		19 43		19 58	20 02		20 06		20 16	20 32			20 36		20 51	21 02		21 05
Southend Central	a	19 32		19 42		19 46		20 00	20 07		20 08		20 19	20 35			20 38		20 53	21 05		21 08
	d	19 32		19 42		19 46		20 00			20 08		20 19				20 38		20 53			21 08
Southend East	d	19 34		19 44		19 48		20 02			20 10		20 21				20 40		20 55			21 10
Thorpe Bay	d	19 37		19 47		19 50		20 06			20 14		20 25				20 44		20 59			21 14
Shoeburyness	a	19 44		19 53		19 57		20 10			20 18		20 29				20 48		21 03			21 18

Table I

London - Southend Central and Shoeburyness

Mondays to Fridays

until 26 July

Network Diagram - see first page of Table I

		CC	CC	CC	CC	CC	CC		CC	CC	CC	CC	CC	CC	CC	CC	CC		CC	CC	CC	CC	CC	CC	CC
London Fenchurch St 7 ⊖	d	20 20	20 30			20 40	20 50		21 00		21 05	21 10	21 20	21 30			21 40		21 50	22 00		22 05	22 10	22 20	22 35
Limehouse	d	20 24	20 34			20 44	20 54				21 09	21 14	21 24	21 34			21 44		21 54			22 09	22 14	22 24	22 39
West Ham ⊖	d	20 29	20 39			20 49	20 59		21 08		21 14	21 19	21 29	21 39			21 49		21 59	22 08		22 14	22 19	22 29	22 44
London Liverpool St 15 ⊖	d				20 35											21 35									
Stratford 7 ⊖	d				20 43											21 43									
Barking ⊖	d	20 35	20 45		20 50	20 55	21 05		21 14		21 20	21 25	21 35	21 45		21 50	21 55		22 05	22 14		22 20	22 25	22 35	22 50
Upminster ⊖	d	20 44	20 54			21 04	21 14		21 23			21 34	21 44	21 54			22 04		22 14	22 23			22 34	22 44	
Ockendon	d	20 49					21 19						21 49						22 19					22 49	
Chafford Hundred	d	20 53					21 23						21 53						22 23					22 53	
West Horndon	d					21 09						21 39					22 09						22 39		
Laindon	d		21 02			21 14			21 31			21 44		22 02			22 14			22 31			22 44		
Basildon	d		21 05			21 17			21 34			21 47		22 05			22 17			22 34			22 47		
Dagenham Dock	d				20 55						21 25					21 55						22 25			22 55
Rainham	d				20 59						21 29					21 59						22 29			22 59
Purfleet	d				21 04						21 34					22 04						22 34			23 04
Grays	d	20 57			21a12		21 27				21a40		21 57			22a12			22 27			22a40		22 57	23a10
Tilbury Town 3	d	21 00					21 30						22 00						22 30					23 00	
East Tilbury	d	21 06					21 36						22 06						22 36					23 06	
Stanford-le-Hope	d	21 10					21 40						22 10						22 40					23 10	
Pitsea	d	21 18		←		21 21	21 48			←		21 51	22 18		←		22 21		22 48		←		22 51	23 18	
Benfleet	d	21 22	21 12	21 22		21 25	21 52		21 41	21 52		21 55	22 22	22 12	22 22		22 25		22 52	22 41	22 52		22 55	23 22	
Leigh-on-Sea	d	→	21 16	21 26		21 30	→		21 45	21 56		22 00	→	22 16	22 26		22 30		→	22 45	22 56		23 00	23 26	
Chalkwell	d		21 19	21 29		21 33			21 48	21 59		22 03		22 19	22 29		22 33			22 48	22 59		23 03	23 29	
Westcliff	d		21 22	21 32		21 35			21 51	22 02		22 05		22 22	22 32		22 35			22 51	23 02		23 06	23 32	
Southend Central	a		21 24	21 35		21 38			21 53	22 05		22 08		22 24	22 35		22 38			22 53	23 05		23 08	23 35	
	d		21 24			21 38			21 53			22 08		22 24			22 38			22 53	23 05		23 08	23 35	
Southend East	d		21 26			21 40			21 55			22 10		22 26			22 40			22 55	23 07		23 10	23 37	
Thorpe Bay	d		21 30			21 44			21 59			22 14		22 30			22 44			22 59	23 10		23 14	23 41	
Shoeburyness	a		21 34			21 48			22 03			22 18		22 34			22 48			23 03	23 15		23 18	23 47	

		CC	CC		CC	CC	CC	CC	CC	CC	CC	CC	CC
London Fenchurch St 7 ⊖	d	22 40	22 50		23 00		23 05	23 10		23 20	23 35	23 40	23 50
Limehouse	d	22 44	22 54				23 09	23 14		23 24	23 39	23 44	23 54
West Ham ⊖	d	22 49	22 59		23 08		23 14	23 19		23 29	23 44	23 49	23 59
London Liverpool St 15 ⊖	d												
Stratford 7 ⊖	d												
Barking ⊖	d	22 55	23 05		23 14		23 20	23 25		23 35	23 50	23 55	00 05
Upminster ⊖	d	23 04	23 14		23 23			23 34		23 44		00 04	00 14
Ockendon	d		23 19							23 49			00 19
Chafford Hundred	d		23 23							23 53			00 23
West Horndon	d	23 09						23 39				00 09	
Laindon	d	23 14			23 31			23 44				00 16	
Basildon	d	23 17			23 34			23 47				00 19	
Dagenham Dock	d						23 25				23 55		
Rainham	d						23 29				23 59		
Purfleet	d						23 34				00 04		
Grays	d		23 27				23 42			23 57	00a10		00 27
Tilbury Town 3	d		23 30				23 45			00 01			00 30
East Tilbury	d		23 36				23 51			00 06			00 36
Stanford-le-Hope	d		23 40				23 55		←	00 10			00 40
Pitsea	d	23 22	23 48			←	00 06	23 52	00 06	00 18		00 22	00 48
Benfleet	d	23 26	23 52		23 41	23 52	→	23 56	00 10	00 22		00 26	00 52
Leigh-on-Sea	d	23 30	→		23 45	23 56		23 59	00 15	00 27		00 31	00 56
Chalkwell	d	23 33			23 48	23 59		00 03	00 18	00 30		00 34	00 59
Westcliff	d	23 36			23 51	00 02		00 06	00 20	00 32		00 36	01 02
Southend Central	a	23 39			23 54	00 05		00 09	00 23	00 35		00 39	01 05
	d	23 39			23 54	00 05		00 09	00 23	00 35		00 40	01 05
Southend East	d	23 41			23 56	00 07		00 11	00 26	00 38		00 42	01 07
Thorpe Bay	d	23 45			23 59	00 11		00 15	00 29	00 41		00 46	01 11
Shoeburyness	a	23 51			00 06	00 17		00 21	00 36	00 48		00 52	01 17

Table I

London - Southend Central and Shoeburyness

Mondays to Fridays

27 July to 10 August

Network Diagram - see first page of Table I

		CC	CC	CC	CC	CC	CC	CC	CC	CC		CC	CC	CC	CC	CC	CC	CC	CC	CC		CC	CC	CC	CC
		MO		MX		MX	MO		MX			MX	MO		MX		MX		MX			MX	MO		MX
			A	B	A	B		A	B	A		B		A	B	A	B	A	B	A		B		A	B
London Fenchurch St 7 ⊖	d	22p50	22p50	22p50	23p00	23p00				23p05		23p05	23p10	23p10	23p10			23p20	23p20	23p35		23p37	23p40	23p40	23p40
Limehouse	d	22p54	22p54	22p54						23p09		23p09	23p14	23p14	23p14			23p24	23p24	23p39		23p41	23p44	23p44	23p44
West Ham ⊖	d	23p01	22p59	23p01	23p08	23p10				23p14		23p15	23p21	23p19	23p21			23p29	23p31	23p44		23p47	23p51	23p49	23p51
London Liverpool St 15 ⊖	d																								
Stratford 7 ⊖	d																								
Barking ⊖	d	23p06	23p05	23p06	23p14	23p15				23p20		23p21	23p26	23p25	23p26			23p35	23p36	23p50		23p53	23p56	23p55	23p57
Upminster ⊖	d	23p14	23p14	23p15	23p23	23p24							23p35	23p34	23p35			23p44	23p45				00 05	00 04	00 06
Ockendon	d	23p19	23p19	23p20														23p49	23p50						
Chafford Hundred	d	23p23	23p23	23p24														23p53	23p54						
West Horndon	d												23p40	23p39	23p40								00 10	00 09	00 11
Laindon	d				23p31	23p33							23p44	23p44	23p46								00 14	00 16	00 17
Basildon	d				23p34	23p36							23p47	23p47	23p49								00 17	00 19	00 20
Dagenham Dock	d									23p25		23p26								23p55		23p58			
Rainham	d									23p29		23p30								23p59		00 02			
Purfleet	d									23p34		23p35								00 04		00 07			
Grays	d	23p27	23p27	23p28						23p42		23p43						23p57	23p58	00a10		00a13			
Tilbury Town 3	d	23p30	23p30	23p32						23p45		23p46						00 01	00 02						
East Tilbury	d	23p35	23p36	23p38						23p51		23p52						00 06	00 07						
Stanford-le-Hope	d	23p39	23p40	23p42						23p55		23p56				←	←	00 10	00 11						
Pitsea	d	23p47	23p48	23p49			←	←	←	00 06		00 07	23p51	23p52	23p53	00 06	00 07	00 18	00 20				00 21	00 22	00 24
Benfleet	d	23p50	23p52	23p53	23p41	23p42	23p50	23p52	23p53	→		→	23p55	23p56	23p57	00 10	00 11	00 22	00 24				00 25	00 26	00 28
Leigh-on-Sea	d	→	→	→	23p45	23p47	23p55	23p56	23p58				23p59	23p59	00 02	00 15	00 16	00 27	00 28				00 29	00 31	00 32
Chalkwell	d				23p48	23p50	23p57	23p59	00 01				00 02	00 03	00 05	00 18	00 19	00 30	00 31				00 32	00 34	00 35
Westcliff	d				23p51	23p52	23p59	00 02	00 03				00 04	00 06	00 07	00 20	00 21	00 32	00 34				00 34	00 36	00 38
Southend Central	a				23p54	23p55	00 03	00 05	00 06				00 08	00 09	00 10	00 23	00 24	00 35	00 37				00 38	00 39	00 41
	d				23p54	23p55	00 03	00 05	00 06				00 08	00 09	00 10	00 23	00 24	00 35	00 37				00 38	00 40	00 41
Southend East	d				23p56	23p58	00 05	00 07	00 09				00 11	00 11	00 13	00 26	00 27	00 38	00 39				00 41	00 42	00 44
Thorpe Bay	d				23p59	00 01	00 07	00 11	00 12				00 12	00 15	00 16	00 29	00 30	00 41	00 43				00 42	00 46	00 47
Shoeburyness	a				00 06	00 08	00 15	00 17	00 19				00 21	00 21	00 23	00 36	00 37	00 48	00 49				00 51	00 52	00 54

		CC	CC	CC	CC	CC		CC	CC	CC	CC	CC	CC	CC	CC	CC		CC	CC	CC	CC	CC	CC	CC	CC
									MO					MO											
		A	B	A	B	A		B		A	B	A	B		B										
London Fenchurch St 7 ⊖	d	23p50	23p50	00 01	00 01				00 10	00 15	00 18	00 25	00 30	00 50	00 50			05 10		05 40				06 10	06 20
Limehouse	d	23p54	23p54						00 14	00 19	00 22	00 29	00 34	00 54	00 54			05 14		05 44				06 14	06 24
West Ham ⊖	d	23p59	00 01	00 09	00 11				00 21	00 24	00 28	00 34	00 41	01 01	01 01			05 19		05 49				06 19	06 29
London Liverpool St 15 ⊖	d																								
Stratford 7 ⊖	d																								
Barking ⊖	d	00 05	00 07	00 15	00 17				00 26	00 30	00 34	00 40	00 47	01 06	01 06			05 25	05 39	05 55	05 45	06 05		06 25	06 35
Upminster ⊖	d	00 14	00 16	00 24	00 26				00 35			00 49	00 56	01 15	01 15	05 28		05 34	05 48	06 04			06 31	06 34	
Ockendon	d	00 19	00 21													05 33			05 56				06 36		
Chafford Hundred	d	00 23	00 25													05 37			06 00				06 40		
West Horndon	d								00 40			00 54	01 01	01 20	01 20			05 39		06 09				06 39	
Laindon	d			00 32	00 35				00 44			00 59	01 07	01 24	01 26			05 44		06 14				06 45	
Basildon	d			00 35	00 38				00 47			01 02	01 10	01 27	01 29			05 47		06 17				06 48	
Dagenham Dock	d									00 35	00 39										05 50	06 10			06 40
Rainham	d									00 39	00 43										05 54	06 14			06 44
Purfleet	d									00 44	00 48										05 59	06 19			06 49
Grays	d	00 27	00 29							00a50	00a54					05a41			06a05		06 05	06 25	06a44		06 55
Tilbury Town 3	d	00 30	00 33																		06 08	06 28			06 58
East Tilbury	d	00 36	00 39																		06 14	06 34			07 04
Stanford-le-Hope	d	00 40	00 43																		06 18	06 38			07 08
Pitsea	d	00 48	00 50			←		←	00 51			01 06	01 13	01 31	01 32			05 51		06 21	06 26	06a46		06 51	07 18
Benfleet	d	00 52	00 54	00 42	00 44	00 52		00 54	00 55			01 10	01 17	01 35	01 36			05 55		06 25	06 31			06 55	07 22
Leigh-on-Sea	d	→	→	00 46	00 49	00 56		00 59	00 59			01 14	01 22	01 39	01 41			06 00		06 30	06 35			07 00	07 27
Chalkwell	d			00 49	00 52	00 59		01 02	01 02			01 17	01 25	01 42	01 44			06 03		06 33	06 38			07 03	07 30
Westcliff	d			00 52	00 54	01 02		01 04	01 04			01 20	01 27	01 44	01 46			06 05		06 35	06 41			07 05	07 32
Southend Central	a			00 55	00 57	01 05		01 07	01 07			01 23	01 30	01 48	01 49			06 08		06 38	06 43			07 08	07 35
	d			00 55	00 57	01 05		01 07	01 07			01 23	01 30	01 48	01 49			06 08		06 38	06 43			07 08	07 35
Southend East	d			00 57	01 00	01 07		01 10	01 10			01 25	01 33	01 51	01 52			06 10		06 40	06 45			07 10	07 37
Thorpe Bay	d			01 01	01 03	01 11		01 13	01 11			01 29	01 36	01 53	01 55			06 14		06 44	06 49			07 14	07 40
Shoeburyness	a			01 07	01 10	01 17		01 20	01 21			01 35	01 43	02 01	02 02			06 18		06 48	06 53			07 20	07 45

A 27 July

B from 31 July until 10 August

Table I

Mondays to Fridays

27 July to 10 August

London - Southend Central and Shoeburyness

Network Diagram - see first page of Table I

	CC		CC	CC	CC	CC	CC	CC	CC	CC	CC		CC	CC	CC	CC	CC	CC	CC	CC	CC		CC	CC
London Fenchurch St [7] ⊖ d	06 40			06 44	06 48	07 00	07 09	07 13	07 15	07 30	07 40		07 43	07 48	07 50	08 00		08 03	08 09	08 14	08 20		08 30	
Limehouse d	06 44			06 48	06 52		07 13				07 44				07 54			08 07	08 13		08 24			
West Ham ⊖ d	06 49			06 53	06 57	07 08	07 18		07 23	07 38	07 49		07 53		07 59	08 08		08 12	08 18	08 23	08 29		08 38	
London Liverpool St [15] ⊖ d																								
Stratford [7] ⊖ d																								
Barking ⊖ d	06 55		06 50	07 00	07 03	07 14	07 25	07 26	07 29	07 44	07 55		07 58		08 05	08 14		08 18	08 24	08 30	08 37		08 45	
Upminster ⊖ d	07 04			07 10		07 23	07 34		07 38	07 53	08 04			08 09	08 15	08 23			08 33	08 41			08 54	
Ockendon d				07 15					07 45					08 16						08 46				
Chafford Hundred d				07 19					07 49					08 20						08 50				
West Horndon d	07 09						07 39				08 09				08 20				08 38					
Laindon d	07 14						07 44				08 14				08a26	08 31			08 44				09 03	
Basildon d	07 17					07 33	07 47			08 03	08 17					08 34			08 47				09 06	
Dagenham Dock d			06 55		07 08			07 31					08 03					08 23			08 42			
Rainham d			06 59		07 12			07 35					08 07					08 27			08 46			
Purfleet d			07 04		07 17			07 40					08 13					08 33			08 51			
Grays d			07 10	07a23	07 25			07 46	07 54				08 18	08 25				08 38		08a54	08 57			
Tilbury Town [3] d			07 13		07 28				07 58				08 22					08 42			09 00			
East Tilbury d			07 19		07 34				08 04				08 28					08 48			09 06			
Stanford-le-Hope d			07 23		07 38			07 56	08 08				08 32	08 35			←	08 52			09 10			←
Pitsea d	07 22		07a31		07a46		07 51	08a03	08a15		08 21		08 41	08a44		08 38	08 41	08a59	08 51		09 18		09 09	09 18
Benfleet d	07 26					07 39	07 55			08 09	08 25		→			08 42	08 45		08 55		→		09 13	09 22
Leigh-on-Sea d	07 30					07 44	07 59			08 14	08 30					08 46	08 50		08 59				09 18	09 27
Chalkwell d	07 33					07 47	08 02			08 17	08 33					08 49	08 53		09 02				09 21	09 30
Westcliff d	07 36					07 49	08 05			08 19	08 35					08 52	08 55		09 05				09 23	09 32
Southend Central a	07 38					07 52	08 07			08 22	08 38					08 54	08 58		09 08				09 26	09 35
d	07 38					07 52	08 07			08 22	08 38					08 55			09 08				09 26	
Southend East d	07 40					07 54	08 09			08 24	08 40					08 57			09 10				09 28	
Thorpe Bay d	07 44					07 58	08 13			08 28	08 44					09 00			09 14				09 32	
Shoeburyness a	07 48					08 02	08 17			08 32	08 48					09 05			09 18				09 36	

	CC	CC	CC	CC	CC	CC	CC		CC	CC	CC	CC	CC	CC	CC	CC	CC		CC	CC	CC	CC	CC	CC
London Fenchurch St [7] ⊖ d	08 40	08 50	08 54	09 00		09 10	09 16		09 20	09 30		09 35	09 40		09 50	10 00			10 05	10 10	10 20	10 30		10 35
Limehouse d	08 44	08 54				09 14	09 20		09 24			09 39	09 44		09 54				10 09	10 14	10 24			10 39
West Ham ⊖ d	08 49	08 59		09 08		09 19	09 25		09 29	09 38		09 44	09 49		09 59	10 08			10 14	10 19	10 29	10 38		10 44
London Liverpool St [15] ⊖ d																								
Stratford [7] ⊖ d																								
Barking ⊖ d	08 55	09 07	09 09	09 16		09 25	09 31		09 35	09 44		09 50	09 55		10 05	10 14			10 20	10 25	10 35	10 44		10 50
Upminster ⊖ d	09 04		09 18	09 25		09 34			09 45	09 53			10 04		10 14	10 23				10 34	10 44	10 53		
Ockendon d			09 23						09 50						10 19						10 49			
Chafford Hundred d			09 27						09 54						10 23						10 53			
West Horndon d	09 09					09 39							10 09							10 39				
Laindon d	09 14			09 34		09 44				10 01			10 14			10 31				10 44		11 01		
Basildon d	09 17			09 37		09 47				10 04			10 17			10 34				10 47		11 04		
Dagenham Dock d		09 12					09 36					09 55							10 25					10 55
Rainham d		09 16					09 40					09 59							10 29					10 59
Purfleet d		09 21					09 45					10 04							10 34					11 04
Grays d		09 27	09a31				09 51		09 58			10a10			10 27				10a40		10 57			11a10
Tilbury Town [3] d		09 30					09 54		10 02						10 30						11 00			
East Tilbury d		09 36					10 00		10 08						10 36						11 06			
Stanford-le-Hope d		09 40					10 04		10 12					←	10 40						11 10			
Pitsea d	09 21	09 48			←	09 51	10 12		10 25		←		10 21	10 25	10 48		←			10 51	11 18		←	
Benfleet d	09 26	09 52		09 43	09 52	09 55	10 16		→	10 11	10 16		10 25	10 29	10 52	10 41	10 52			10 55	11 22	11 11	11 22	
Leigh-on-Sea d	09 30	→		09 48	09 57	10 00	→			10 15	10 20		10 30	10 34	→	10 45	10 56			11 00	→	11 15	11 26	
Chalkwell d	09 33			09 51	10 00	10 03				10 18	10 23		10 33	10 37		10 48	10 59			11 03		11 18	11 29	
Westcliff d	09 36			09 53	10 02	10 05				10 21	10 26		10 35	10 39		10 51	11 02			11 05		11 21	11 32	
Southend Central a	09 38			09 56	10 05	10 08				10 23	10 29		10 38	10 42		10 53	11 05			11 08		11 23	11 35	
d	09 38			09 56		10 08				10 23			10 38			10 53				11 08		11 23		
Southend East d	09 40			09 58		10 10				10 25			10 40			10 55				11 10		11 25		
Thorpe Bay d	09 44			10 02		10 14				10 29			10 44			10 59				11 14		11 29		
Shoeburyness a	09 48			10 06		10 18				10 33			10 48			11 03				11 18		11 33		

	CC	CC	CC		CC	CC	CC	CC	CC	CC	CC	CC	CC		CC	CC	CC	CC	CC	CC	CC	CC	CC	
London Fenchurch St [7] ⊖ d	10 40	10 50	11 00			11 05	11 10	11 20	11 30		11 35	11 40	11 50		12 00		12 05	12 10	12 20	12 30		12 35	12 40	
Limehouse d	10 44	10 54				11 09	11 14	11 24			11 39	11 44	11 54				12 09	12 14	12 24			12 39	12 44	
West Ham ⊖ d	10 49	10 59	11 08			11 14	11 19	11 29	11 38		11 44	11 49	11 59		12 08		12 14	12 19	12 29	12 38		12 44	12 49	
London Liverpool St [15] ⊖ d																								
Stratford [7] ⊖ d																								
Barking ⊖ d	10 55	11 05	11 14			11 20	11 25	11 35	11 44		11 50	11 55	12 05		12 14		12 20	12 25	12 35	12 44		12 50	12 55	
Upminster ⊖ d	11 04	11 14	11 23				11 34	11 44	11 53			12 04	12 14		12 23			12 34	12 44	12 53			13 04	
Ockendon d		11 19						11 49					12 19						12 49					
Chafford Hundred d		11 23						11 53					12 23						12 53					
West Horndon d	11 09						11 39					12 09						12 39					13 09	
Laindon d	11 14		11 31				11 44		12 01			12 14			12 31			12 44		13 01			13 14	
Basildon d	11 17		11 34				11 47		12 04			12 17			12 34			12 47		13 04			13 17	
Dagenham Dock d						11 25					11 55						12 25					12 55		
Rainham d						11 29					11 59						12 29					12 59		
Purfleet d						11 34					12 04						12 34					13 04		
Grays d		11 27				11a40		11 57			12a10		12 27				12a40		12 57			13a10		
Tilbury Town [3] d		11 30						12 00					12 30						13 00					
East Tilbury d		11 36						12 06					12 36						13 06					
Stanford-le-Hope d		11 40						12 10					12 40						13 10					
Pitsea d	11 21	11 48			←		11 51	12 18		←		12 21	12 48			←		12 51	13 18		←		13 21	
Benfleet d	11 25	11 52	11 41		11 52		11 55	12 22	12 11	12 22		12 25	12 52		12 41	12 52		12 55	13 22	13 11	13 22		13 25	
Leigh-on-Sea d	11 30	→	11 45		11 57		12 00	→	12 15	12 26		12 30	→		12 45	12 57		13 00	→	13 15	13 27		13 30	
Chalkwell d	11 33		11 48		12 00		12 03		12 18	12 29		12 33			12 48	13 00		13 03		13 18	13 30		13 33	
Westcliff d	11 35		11 51		12 02		12 05		12 21	12 32		12 35			12 51	13 02		13 05		13 21	13 32		13 35	
Southend Central a	11 38		11 53		12 05		12 08		12 23	12 35		12 38			12 53	13 05		13 08		13 23	13 35		13 38	
d	11 38		11 53				12 08		12 23			12 38			12 53			13 08		13 23			13 38	
Southend East d	11 40		11 55				12 10		12 25			12 40			12 55			13 10		13 25			13 40	
Thorpe Bay d	11 44		11 59				12 14		12 29			12 44			12 59			13 14		13 29			13 44	
Shoeburyness a	11 48		12 03				12 18		12 33			12 48			13 03			13 18		13 33			13 48	

Table I

Mondays to Fridays

27 July to 10 August

London - Southend Central and Shoeburyness

Network Diagram - see first page of Table I

	CC	CC	CC	CC	CC	CC	CC	CC	CC		CC	CC	CC	CC	CC	CC	CC	CC	CC		CC	CC	CC	CC
London Fenchurch St [7] ⊖ d	12 50	13 00		13 05	13 10	13 20	13 30		13 35		13 40	13 50	14 00		14 05	14 10	14 20	14 30			14 35	14 40	14 50	15 00
Limehouse d	12 54			13 09	13 14	13 24			13 39		13 44	13 54			14 09	14 14	14 24				14 39	14 44	14 54	
West Ham ⊖ d	12 59	13 08		13 14	13 19	13 29	13 38		13 44		13 49	13 59	14 08		14 14	14 19	14 29	14 38			14 44	14 49	14 59	15 08
London Liverpool St [15] ⊖ d																								
Stratford [7] ⊖ d																								
Barking ⊖ d	13 05	13 14		13 20	13 25	13 35	13 44		13 50		13 55	14 05	14 14		14 20	14 25	14 35	14 44			14 50	14 55	15 05	15 14
Upminster ⊖ d	13 14	13 23			13 34	13 44	13 53				14 04	14 14	14 23			14 34	14 44	14 53				15 04	15 14	15 23
Ockendon d	13 19					13 49						14 19					14 49						15 19	
Chafford Hundred d	13 23					13 53						14 23					14 53						15 23	
West Horndon d					13 39						14 09					14 39						15 09		
Laindon d		13 31			13 44		14 01				14 14		14 31			14 44		15 01				15 14		15 31
Basildon d		13 34			13 47		14 04				14 17		14 34			14 47		15 04				15 17		15 34
Dagenham Dock d				13 25					13 55						14 25						14 55			
Rainham d				13 29					13 59						14 29						14 59			
Purfleet d				13 34					14 04						14 34						15 04			
Grays d	13 27			13a40		13 57			14a10			14 27			14a40		14 57				15a10		15 27	
Tilbury Town [3] d	13 30					14 00						14 30					15 00						15 30	
East Tilbury d	13 36					14 06						14 36					15 06						15 36	
Stanford-le-Hope d	13 40					14 10						14 40					15 10						15 40	
Pitsea d	13 48		←		13 51	14 18		←			14 21	14 48		←		14 51	15 18		←			15 21	15 48	
Benfleet d	13 52	13 41	13 52		13 55	14 22	14 11	14 22			14 25	14 52	14 41	14 52		14 55	15 22	15 11	15 22			15 25	15 52	15 41
Leigh-on-Sea d	→	13 45	13 57		14 00	→	14 15	14 26			14 30	→	14 45	14 56		15 00	→	15 15	15 26			15 30	→	15 45
Chalkwell d		13 48	14 00		14 03		14 18	14 29			14 33		14 48	14 59		15 03		15 18	15 29			15 33		15 48
Westcliff d		13 51	14 02		14 05		14 21	14 32			14 35		14 51	15 02		15 05		15 21	15 32			15 35		15 51
Southend Central a		13 53	14 05		14 08		14 23	14 35			14 38		14 53	15 05		15 08		15 23	15 35			15 38		15 53
d		13 53			14 08		14 23				14 38		14 53			15 08		15 23				15 38		15 53
Southend East d		13 55			14 10		14 25				14 40		14 55			15 10		15 25				15 40		15 55
Thorpe Bay d		13 59			14 14		14 29				14 44		14 59			15 14		15 29				15 44		15 59
Shoeburyness a		14 03			14 18		14 33				14 48		15 03			15 18		15 33				15 48		16 03

	CC	CC	CC	CC	CC		CC	CC	CC	CC	CC	CC	CC	CC	CC		CC	CC	CC	CC	CC	CC	CC	CC
London Fenchurch St [7] ⊖ d		15 05	15 10	15 20	15 25		15 30	15 35	15 40		15 50	15 55	16 00	16 10	16 13		16 20	16 28	16 30	16 34	16 37	16 45	16 48	16 55
Limehouse d		15 09	15 14	15 24				15 39	15 44		15 54	15 59		16 14	16 17		16 24		16 34	16 38	16 41	16 49	16 52	16 59
West Ham ⊖ d		15 14	15 19	15 29	15 33		15 38	15 44	15 49		15 59	16 04	16 08	16 19	16 22		16 29	16 36	16 39	16 43	16 46		16 57	17 04
London Liverpool St [15] ⊖ d																								
Stratford [7] ⊖ d																								
Barking ⊖ d		15 20	15 25	15 35	15 39		15 44	15 50	15 54		16 05	16 10	16 14	16 25	16 28		16 35		16 45	16 49	16 52	16 59	17 03	17 10
Upminster ⊖ d			15 34	15 44	15 48		15 53		16 02		16 14		16 23	16 34			16 45		16 55		17 02	17 07	17 13	
Ockendon d				15 49							16 19						16 50				17 08			
Chafford Hundred d				15 53							16 23						16 54				17 12			
West Horndon d			15 39						16 07					16 39					17 00				17 18	
Laindon d			15 44		15 56		16 01		16 12					16 44				16 56	17a08			17 16	17a26	
Basildon d			15 47		15 59		16 04		16 15				16 33	16 47				16 59				17 19		
Dagenham Dock d		15 25						15 55				16 15			16 33					16 54				17 15
Rainham d		15 29						15 59				16 19			16 37					16 58				17 19
Purfleet d		15 34						16 04				16 25			16 43					17 04				17 25
Grays d		15a40		15 57				16a10			16 27	16a33			16 49		16 59			17 10	17a18			17 31
Tilbury Town [3] d				16 00							16 30				16 52		17 02			17 13				17 34
East Tilbury d				16 06							16 36				16 58		17 08			17 19				17 40
Stanford-le-Hope d				16 10						←	16 40				17 02		17a15			17 23				17 44
Pitsea d	←		15 51	16 22	16 03				16 19	16 22	16a48			16 51	17a12					17a33		17 23		17a54
Benfleet d	15 52		15 55	→	16 07		16 11		16 22	16 26			16 40	16 55				17 06				17 27		
Leigh-on-Sea d	15 56		16 00		16a12		16 15		16 27	16 30			16 45	17 00				17 11				17 32		
Chalkwell d	15 59		16 03				16 18		16 29	16 33			16 48	17 03				17 14				17 34		
Westcliff d	16 02		16 05				16 21		16 32	16 36			16 50	17 05				17 16				17 37		
Southend Central a	16 05		16 08				16 23		16 34	16 41			16 53	17 08				17 19				17 39		
d			16 08				16 23		16 35				16 53	17 08				17 19				17 39		
Southend East d			16 10				16 25		16 37				16 55	17 10				17 21				17 41		
Thorpe Bay d			16 14				16 29		16 39				16 59	17 14				17 24				17 44		
Shoeburyness a			16 20				16 33		16 44				17 05	17 20				17 31				17 51		

	CC		CC	CC	CC	CC	CC	CC	CC	CC	CC		CC	CC	CC	CC	CC	CC	CC	CC	CC		CC	CC
London Fenchurch St [7] ⊖ d	17 00		17 02	17 05	17 07	17 10	17 15	17 18	17 20	17 23	17 26		17 30	17 32	17 35	17 37	17 41	17 45	17 47	17 51	17 53		17 56	18 00
Limehouse d				17 09	17 12	17 15	17 19		17 24	17 28	17 30				17 39	17 42	17 45	17 49	17 52		17 57		18 00	
West Ham ⊖ d					17 17	17 20		17 26	17 29	17 33	17 35			17 40	17 44	17 47	17 50		17 57	17 59			18 05	18 08
London Liverpool St [15] ⊖ d																								
Stratford [7] ⊖ d																								
Barking ⊖ d			17 15	17 19	17 22	17 26			17 35	17 39	17 42			17 46	17 50	17 53	17 56				18 08		18 11	
Upminster ⊖ d			17 24		17 31		17 36	17 40		17 47				17 56		18 03			18 10	18 14				
Ockendon d			17 29											18 02					18 15					
Chafford Hundred d			17 34											18 06					18 20					
West Horndon d					17 36					17 52						18 08					18 21			
Laindon d				17 35	17a43				17 51	17a59					18 07	18a15					18 27			
Basildon d				17 39				17 50	17 55						18 10					18 24	18 31			18 35
Dagenham Dock d						17 31					17 47						18 01						18 16	
Rainham d						17 35					17 51						18 05						18 20	
Purfleet d						17 40					17 56						18 11						18 25	
Grays d			17a40			17 46					18 02			18a13			18 17		18a26				18 31	
Tilbury Town [3] d						17 50					18 06						18 20						18 35	
East Tilbury d						17 56					18 12						18 26						18 41	
Stanford-le-Hope d						18 00					18 16						18 30						18 45	
Pitsea d				17 42		18a09		17 54	17 58		18a25				18 14		18a40			18 28	18 34		18 57	18 38
Benfleet d	17 33			17 46			17 52	17 58	18 03				18 08		18 18			18 24		18 32	18 39		→	18 43
Leigh-on-Sea d	17 38			17 51			17 56	18 02	18 07				18 12		18 23			18 28		18 37	18 43			18 47
Chalkwell d	17 41			17 53			17 59	18 05	18 10				18 15		18 26			18 31		18 40	18 46			18 50
Westcliff d	17 43			17 56			18 02	18 08	18 13				18 18		18 28			18 34		18 42	18 49			18 53
Southend Central a	17 46			17 58			18 04	18 13	18 15				18 20		18 31			18 36		18 45	18 51			18 55
d	17 46			17 58			18 04		18 15				18 20		18 31			18 36		18 45	18 51			18 55
Southend East d	17 48			18 00			18 06		18 17				18 22		18 33			18 38		18 47	18 53			18 57
Thorpe Bay d	17 50			18 03			18 10		18 21				18 26		18 36			18 42		18 50	18 57			19 01
Shoeburyness a	17 57			18 11			18 16		18 28				18 32		18 43			18 48		18 58	19 03			19 07

Table 1

London - Southend Central and Shoeburyness

Mondays to Fridays

27 July to 10 August

Network Diagram - see first page of Table 1

		CC	CC	CC	CC	CC	CC	CC		CC	CC	CC	CC	CC	CC	CC	CC	CC		CC	CC	CC	CC	CC	CC
London Fenchurch St 7 ⊖	d	18 02	18 06	18 09			18 12	18 21				18 23	18 27		18 31	18 35	18 42			18 46	18 51	19 00	19 02	19 05	
Limehouse	d	18 06	18 10	18 13			18 16					18 27	18 31		18 35	18 39				18 51	18 55			19 09	
West Ham ⊖	d	18 11		18 18			18 21					18 32	18 36		18 40		18 50			18 56	19 00		19 10		
London Liverpool St 15 ⊖	d																								
Stratford 7 ⊖	d																								
Barking ⊖	d	18 17	18 20	18 24			18 28						18 42		18 46	18 49				19 01	19 06		19 16	19 19	
Upminster ⊖	d	18 27		18 34								18 46	18 51			18 58				19 10			19 26	19 30	
Ockendon	d	18 33										18 51				19 06							19 33		
Chafford Hundred	d	18 38										18 55				19 11							19 39		
West Horndon	d			18 39									18 56							19 15					
Laindon	d		18 37	18 43				18 47					19 01							19 20		19 26			
Basildon	d		18 41	18 47				18 51					19 04				19 12			19 23				19 40	
Dagenham Dock	d						18 33								18 51						19 11				
Rainham	d						18 37								18 55						19 15				
Purfleet	d						18 42								19 01						19 21				
Grays	d	18 42					18 48					19 00			19 07	19a17					19 27		19 46		
Tilbury Town 3	d	18 46					18 52					19 03			19 10						19 30		19 50		
East Tilbury	d	18 52					18 58					19 09			19 16						19 36		19 56		
Stanford-le-Hope	d	18 56			←	←	19 02					19 13		←	19 20						19 40		20 00		←
Pitsea	d	19 03	18 44	18 50	18 57	19 03	19a11			←	←	19 21	19 08	19 21	19a30			←		19 26	19 48		20a07	19 44	19 48
Benfleet	d	→	18 49	18 54	19 03	19 07		18 58		19 03	19 07	→	19 12	19 25			19 19	19 25		19 30	→	19 33		19 48	19 52
Leigh-on-Sea	d		18 53	18 59	→	→		19 03		19 07	19a14		19 16	→			19 24	19a32		19 35		19 38		19 52	19 56
Chalkwell	d		18 56	19 01				19 06		19 10			19 19				19 27			19 37		19 41		19 55	19 59
Westcliff	d		18 59	19 04				19 08		19 13			19 21				19 29			19 40		19 43		19 58	20 02
Southend Central	a		19 01	19 09				19 11		19 15			19 24				19 32			19 42		19 46		20 00	20 07
	d		19 01					19 11		19 15			19 24				19 32			19 42		19 46		20 00	
Southend East	d		19 03					19 13		19 17			19 26				19 34			19 44		19 48		20 02	
Thorpe Bay	d		19 07					19 16		19 21			19 28				19 37			19 47		19 50		20 06	
Shoeburyness	a		19 13					19 23		19 28			19 35				19 44			19 53		19 57		20 10	

		CC	CC	CC		CC	CC	CC	CC	CC	CC	CC	CC	CC		CC	CC	CC	CC	CC	CC	CC	CC	CC	
London Fenchurch St 7 ⊖	d	19 08	19 11	19 20		19 30		19 32	19 35	19 40	19 50	20 00		20 05		20 10	20 20	20 30		20 35	20 40	20 50	21 00		
Limehouse	d	19 12	19 15	19 24				19 36	19 39	19 44	19 54			20 09		20 14	20 24	20 34		20 39	20 44	20 54			
West Ham ⊖	d	19 17	19 20	19 29				19 41	19 44	19 49	19 59	20 08		20 14		20 19	20 29	20 39		20 44	20 49	20 59	21 08		
London Liverpool St 15 ⊖	d																								
Stratford 7 ⊖	d																								
Barking ⊖	d	19 23	19 26	19 35				19 47	19 50	19 55	20 05	20 14		20 20		20 25	20 35	20 45		20 50	20 55	21 05	21 14		
Upminster ⊖	d		19 35	19 44		19 50		19 56		20 04	20 14	20 23				20 34	20 44	20 54			21 04	21 14	21 23		
Ockendon	d			19 49							20 19						20 49					21 19			
Chafford Hundred	d			19 53							20 23						20 53					21 23			
West Horndon	d		19 40					20 01		20 09						20 39					21 09				
Laindon	d		19 45					20a07		20 14		20 31				20 44		21 02			21 14		21 31		
Basildon	d		19 48			20 00				20 17		20 34				20 47		21 05			21 17		21 34		
Dagenham Dock	d	19 28							19 55					20 25						20 55					
Rainham	d	19 32							19 59					20 29						20 59					
Purfleet	d	19 37							20 04					20 34						21 04					
Grays	d	19a43		19 57					20a10		20 27			20a40			20 57			21a10		21 27			
Tilbury Town 3	d			20 00							20 30						21 00					21 30			
East Tilbury	d			20 06							20 36						21 06					21 36			
Stanford-le-Hope	d			20 10							20 40						21 10					21 40			
Pitsea	d		19 52	20 18			←			20 21	20 48		←			20 51	21 18		←		21 21	21 48		←	
Benfleet	d		19 56	20 22		20 06	20 22			20 26	20 52	20 41	20 52			20 55	21 22	21 12	21 22		21 25	21 52	21 41	21 52	
Leigh-on-Sea	d		20 00	→		20 11	20 27			20 30	→	20 45	20 56			21 00	→	21 16	21 26		21 30	→	21 45	21 56	
Chalkwell	d		20 03			20 14	20 30			20 33		20 48	20 59			21 03		21 19	21 29		21 33		21 48	21 59	
Westcliff	d		20 06			20 16	20 32			20 36		20 51	21 02			21 05		21 22	21 32		21 35		21 51	22 02	
Southend Central	a		20 08			20 19	20 35			20 38		20 53	21 05			21 08		21 24	21 35		21 38		21 53	22 05	
	d		20 08			20 19				20 38		20 53				21 08		21 24			21 38		21 53		
Southend East	d		20 10			20 21				20 40		20 55				21 10		21 26			21 40		21 55		
Thorpe Bay	d		20 14			20 25				20 44		20 59				21 14		21 30			21 44		21 59		
Shoeburyness	a		20 18			20 29				20 48		21 03				21 18		21 34			21 48		22 03		

		CC	CC	CC	CC	CC	CC	CC	CC	CC		CC	CC	CC	CC	CC	CC	CC	CC	CC		CC	CC	CC	CC
London Fenchurch St 7 ⊖	d	21 05	21 10	21 20	21 30		21 35	21 40	21 50	22 00			22 05	22 11	22 20	22 35	22 40	22 50	23 00			23 05	23 10		23 20
Limehouse	d	21 09	21 14	21 24	21 34		21 39	21 44	21 54				22 09	22 15	22 24	22 39	22 44	22 54				23 09	23 14		23 24
West Ham ⊖	d	21 14	21 19	21 29	21 39		21 44	21 49	21 59	22 10			22 15	22 22	22 31	22 45	22 51	23 01	23 10			23 15	23 21		23 31
London Liverpool St 15 ⊖	d																								
Stratford 7 ⊖	d																								
Barking ⊖	d	21 20	21 25	21 35	21 45		21 50	21 55	22 05	22 15			22 21	22 27	22 36	22 51	22 56	23 06	23 15			23 21	23 26		23 36
Upminster ⊖	d		21 34	21 44	21 54			22 04	22 14	22 24				22 36	22 45		23 05	23 15	23 24				23 35		23 45
Ockendon	d			21 49					22 19						22 50			23 20							23 50
Chafford Hundred	d			21 53					22 23						22 54			23 24							23 54
West Horndon	d		21 39					22 09						22 41			23 10						23 40		
Laindon	d		21 44		22 02			22 14		22 33				22 47			23 16		23 33				23 46		
Basildon	d		21 47		22 05			22 17		22 36				22 50			23 19		23 36				23 49		
Dagenham Dock	d	21 25					21 55						22 26			22 56						23 26			
Rainham	d	21 29					21 59						22 30			23 00						23 30			
Purfleet	d	21 34					22 04						22 35			23 05						23 35			
Grays	d	21a40		21 57			22a10		22 27				22a41		22 58	23a11		23 28				23 43			23 58
Tilbury Town 3	d			22 00					22 30						23 02			23 32				23 46			00 02
East Tilbury	d			22 06					22 36						23 08			23 38				23 52			00 07
Stanford-le-Hope	d			22 10					22 40						23 12			23 42				23 56		←	00 11
Pitsea	d		21 51	22 18		←		22 21	22 48			←		22 53	23 19		23 23	23 49		←		00 07	23 53	00 07	00 20
Benfleet	d		21 55	22 22	22 12	22 22		22 25	22 52	22 42		22 52		22 57	23 23		23 27	23 53	23 42	23 53		→	23 57	00 11	00 24
Leigh-on-Sea	d		22 00	→	22 16	22 26		22 30	→	22 47		22 56		23 02	23 28		23 32	→	23 47	23 58			00 02	00 16	00 28
Chalkwell	d		22 03		22 19	22 29		22 33		22 50		22 59		23 05	23 31		23 35		23 50	00 01			00 05	00 19	00 31
Westcliff	d		22 05		22 22	22 32		22 35		22 52		23 02		23 07	23 33		23 37		23 52	00 03			00 07	00 21	00 34
Southend Central	a		22 08		22 24	22 35		22 38		22 55		23 05		23 10	23 36		23 40		23 55	00 06			00 10	00 24	00 37
	d		22 08		22 24			22 38		22 55		23 05		23 10	23 36		23 40		23 55	00 06			00 10	00 24	00 37
Southend East	d		22 10		22 26			22 40		22 57		23 07		23 12	23 39		23 43		23 58	00 09			00 13	00 27	00 39
Thorpe Bay	d		22 14		22 30			22 44		23 00		23 10		23 15	23 42		23 46		00 01	00 12			00 16	00 30	00 43
Shoeburyness	a		22 18		22 34			22 48		23 05		23 15		23 22	23 49		23 53		00 08	00 19			00 23	00 37	00 49

Table 1

London - Southend Central and Shoeburyness

Mondays to Fridays

27 July to 10 August

Network Diagram - see first page of Table 1

		CC	CC	CC
London Fenchurch St 7 ⊖	d	23 37	23 40	23 50
Limehouse	d	23 41	23 44	23 54
West Ham ⊖	d	23 47	23 51	00 01
London Liverpool St 15 ⊖	d			
Stratford 7 ⊖	d			
Barking ⊖	d	23 53	23 57	00 07
Upminster ⊖	d		00 06	00 16
Ockendon	d			00 21
Chafford Hundred	d			00 25
West Horndon	d		00 11	
Laindon	d		00 17	
Basildon	d		00 20	
Dagenham Dock	d	23 58		
Rainham	d	00 02		
Purfleet	d	00 07		
Grays	d	00a13		00 29
Tilbury Town 3	d			00 33
East Tilbury	d			00 39
Stanford-le-Hope	d			00 43
Pitsea	d		00 24	00 50
Benfleet	d		00 28	00 54
Leigh-on-Sea	d		00 32	00 59
Chalkwell	d		00 35	01 02
Westcliff	d		00 38	01 04
Southend Central	a		00 41	01 07
	d		00 41	01 07
Southend East	d		00 44	01 10
Thorpe Bay	d		00 47	01 13
Shoeburyness	a		00 54	01 20

Mondays to Fridays

13 August to 28 August

		CC A	CC B	CC MX	CC MX	CC A	CC B	CC MX	CC MX	CC A		CC B	CC MX	CC MX	CC MX	CC MX	CC A	CC B	CC MX	CC MX		CC MX	CC MX	CC A	CC B
London Fenchurch St 7 ⊖	d	22p50	22p50	22p50	23p00				23p05	23p10		23p10	23p10		23p20	23p35	23p40	23p40	23p40	23p50		00 01		00 10	00 10
Limehouse	d	22p54	22p54	22p54					23p09	23p14		23p14	23p14		23p24	23p39	23p44	23p44	23p44	23p54				00 14	00 14
West Ham ⊖	d	22p59	23p01	22p59	23p08				23p14	23p19		23p21	23p19		23p29	23p44	23p49	23p51	23p49	23p59		00 09		00 19	00 21
London Liverpool St 15 ⊖	d																								
Stratford 7 ⊖	d																								
Barking ⊖	d	23p04	23p06	23p05	23p14				23p20	23p24		23p26	23p25		23p35	23p50	23p54	23p56	23p55	00 05		00 15		00 24	00 26
Upminster ⊖	d	23p12	23p14	23p14	23p23					23p32		23p35	23p34		23p44		00 02	00 05	00 04	00 14		00 24		00 32	00 35
Ockendon	d	23p18	23p19	23p19											23p49					00 19					
Chafford Hundred	d	23p21	23p23	23p23											23p53					00 23					
West Horndon	d									23p37		23p40	23p39				00 07	00 10	00 09					00 37	00 40
Laindon	d				23p31					23p42		23p44	23p44				00 12	00 14	00 16			00 32		00 42	00 44
Basildon	d				23p34					23p45		23p47	23p47				00 15	00 17	00 19			00 35		00 45	00 47
Dagenham Dock	d								23p25							23p55									
Rainham	d								23p29							23p59									
Purfleet	d								23p34							00 04									
Grays	d	23p25	23p27	23p27					23p42						23p57	00a10				00 27					
Tilbury Town 3	d	23p28	23p30	23p30					23p45						00 01					00 30					
East Tilbury	d	23p34	23p35	23p36					23p51						00 06					00 36					
Stanford-le-Hope	d	23p37	23p39	23p40					23p55					←	00 10					00 40					
Pitsea	d	23p45	23p47	23p48		←	←	←	00 06	23p49		23p51	23p52	00 06	00 18		00 19	00 21	00 22	00 48			←	00 49	00 51
Benfleet	d	23p49	23p50	23p52	23p41	23p49	23p50	23p52	→	23p52		23p55	23p56	00 10	00 22		00 22	00 25	00 26	00 52		00 42	00 52	00 52	00 55
Leigh-on-Sea	d	→	→	→	23p45	23p53	23p55	23p56		23p57		23p59	23p59	00 15	00 27		00 27	00 29	00 31	→		00 46	00 56	00 57	00 59
Chalkwell	d				23p48	23p56	23p57	23p59		23p59		00 02	00 03	00 18	00 30		00 29	00 32	00 34			00 49	00 59	00 59	01 02
Westcliff	d				23p51	23p58	23p59	00 02		00 02		00 04	00 06	00 20	00 32		00 32	00 34	00 36			00 52	01 02	01 02	01 04
Southend Central	a				23p54	00 01	00 03	00 05		00 05		00 08	00 09	00 23	00 35		00 35	00 38	00 39			00 55	01 05	01 05	01 07
	d				23p54	00 01	00 03	00 05		00 06		00 08	00 09	00 23	00 35		00 36	00 38	00 40			00 55	01 05	01 06	01 07
Southend East	d				23p56	00 03	00 05	00 07		00 08		00 11	00 11	00 26	00 38		00 38	00 41	00 42			00 57	01 07	01 08	01 10
Thorpe Bay	d				23p59	00 06	00 07	00 11		00 10		00 12	00 15	00 29	00 41		00 40	00 42	00 46			01 01	01 11	01 11	01 11
Shoeburyness	a				00 06	00 13	00 15	00 17		00 18		00 21	00 21	00 36	00 48		00 48	00 51	00 52			01 07	01 17	01 18	01 21

A 20 August, 27 August

B 13 August

London - Southend Central and Shoeburyness

Mondays to Fridays

13 August to 28 August

Network Diagram - see first page of Table I

		CC MX	CC MX	CC A	CC	CC		CC	CC	CC	CC	CC	CC	CC	CC	CC		CC	CC	CC	CC	CC	CC	CC	CC
London Fenchurch St 7 ⊖	d	00 15	00 25	00 50		05 10			05 40				06 10	06 20	06 40			06 44	06 48	07 00	07 09	07 13	07 15	07 30	07 40
Limehouse	d	00 19	00 29	00 54		05 14			05 44				06 14	06 24	06 44			06 48	06 52		07 13				07 44
West Ham ⊖	d	00 24	00 34	01 01		05 19			05 49				06 19	06 29	06 49			06 53	06 57	07 08	07 18		07 23	07 38	07 49
London Liverpool St 15 ⊖	d																								
Stratford 7 ⊖	d																								
Barking ⊖	d	00 30	00 40	01 06		05 25		05 39	05 55	05 45	06 05		06 25	06 35	06 55	06 50		07 00	07 03	07 14	07 25	07 26	07 29	07 44	07 55
Upminster ⊖	d		00 49	01 15	05 28	05 34		05 48	06 04			06 31	06 34		07 04			07 10		07 23	07 34		07 38	07 53	08 04
Ockendon	d				05 33			05 56				06 36						07 15					07 45		
Chafford Hundred	d				05 37			06 00				06 40						07 19					07 49		
West Horndon	d		00 54	01 20		05 39			06 09				06 39		07 09						07 39				08 09
Laindon	d		00 59	01 24		05 44			06 14				06 45		07 14						07 44				08 14
Basildon	d		01 02	01 27		05 47			06 17				06 48		07 17					07 33	07 47			08 03	08 17
Dagenham Dock	d	00 35								05 50	06 10			06 40		06 55			07 08			07 31			
Rainham	d	00 39								05 54	06 14			06 44		06 59			07 12			07 35			
Purfleet	d	00 44								05 59	06 19			06 49		07 04			07 17			07 40			
Grays	d	00a50			05a41			06a05		06 05	06 25	06a44		06 55		07 10		07a23	07 25			07 46	07 54		
Tilbury Town 3	d									06 08	06 28			06 58		07 13			07 28				07 58		
East Tilbury	d									06 14	06 34			07 04		07 19			07 34				08 04		
Stanford-le-Hope	d									06 18	06 38			07 08		07 23			07 38			07 56	08 08		
Pitsea	d		01 06	01 31		05 51			06 21	06 26	06a46		06 51	07 18	07 22	07a31			07a46		07 51	08a03	08a15		08 21
Benfleet	d		01 10	01 35		05 55			06 25	06 31			06 55	07 22	07 26					07 39	07 55			08 09	08 25
Leigh-on-Sea	d		01 14	01 39		06 00			06 30	06 35			07 00	07 27	07 30					07 44	07 59			08 14	08 30
Chalkwell	d		01 17	01 42		06 03			06 33	06 38			07 03	07 30	07 33					07 47	08 02			08 17	08 33
Westcliff	d		01 20	01 44		06 05			06 35	06 41			07 05	07 32	07 36					07 49	08 05			08 19	08 35
Southend Central	a		01 23	01 48		06 08			06 38	06 43			07 08	07 35	07 38					07 52	08 07			08 22	08 38
	d		01 23	01 48		06 08			06 38	06 43			07 08	07 35	07 38					07 52	08 07			08 22	08 38
Southend East	d		01 25	01 51		06 10			06 40	06 45			07 10	07 37	07 40					07 54	08 09			08 24	08 40
Thorpe Bay	d		01 29	01 53		06 14			06 44	06 49			07 14	07 40	07 44					07 58	08 13			08 28	08 44
Shoeburyness	a		01 35	02 01		06 18			06 48	06 53			07 20	07 45	07 48					08 02	08 17			08 32	08 48

		CC		CC	CC	CC	CC	CC	CC	CC	CC	CC		CC	CC	CC	CC	CC	CC	CC	CC	CC		CC	CC
London Fenchurch St 7 ⊖	d	07 43		07 48	07 50	08 00		08 03	08 09	08 14	08 20	08 30			08 40	08 50	08 54	09 00		09 10	09 16	09 20		09 30	
Limehouse	d				07 54			08 07	08 13		08 24				08 44	08 54				09 14	09 20	09 24			
West Ham ⊖	d	07 53			07 59	08 08		08 12	08 18	08 23	08 29	08 38			08 49	08 59		09 08		09 19	09 25	09 29		09 38	
London Liverpool St 15 ⊖	d																								
Stratford 7 ⊖	d																								
Barking ⊖	d	07 58			08 05	08 14		08 18	08 24	08 30	08 37	08 45			08 55	09 07	09 09	09 16		09 25	09 31	09 35		09 44	
Upminster ⊖	d			08 09	08 15	08 23			08 33	08 41		08 54			09 04		09 18	09 25		09 34		09 45		09 53	
Ockendon	d			08 16						08 46							09 23					09 50			
Chafford Hundred	d			08 20						08 50							09 27					09 54			
West Horndon	d				08 20				08 38						09 09					09 39					
Laindon	d				08a26	08 31			08 44			09 03			09 14			09 34		09 44				10 01	
Basildon	d					08 34			08 47			09 06			09 17			09 37		09 47				10 04	
Dagenham Dock	d	08 03						08 23			08 42					09 12					09 36				
Rainham	d	08 07						08 27			08 46					09 16					09 40				
Purfleet	d	08 13						08 33			08 51					09 21					09 45				
Grays	d	08 18		08 25				08 38		08a54	08 57					09 27	09a31				09 51	09 58			
Tilbury Town 3	d	08 22						08 42			09 00					09 30					09 54	10 02			
East Tilbury	d	08 28						08 48			09 06					09 36					10 00	10 08			
Stanford-le-Hope	d	08 32		08 35			←	08 52			09 10			←		09 40					10 04	10 12			
Pitsea	d	08 41		08a44		08 38	08 41	08a59	08 51		09 18	09 09		09 18	09 21	09 48			←	09 51	10 12	10 25			←
Benfleet	d	→				08 42	08 45		08 55		→	09 13		09 22	09 26	09 52		09 43	09 52	09 55	10 16	→		10 11	10 16
Leigh-on-Sea	d					08 46	08 50		08 59			09 18		09 27	09 30	→		09 48	09 57	10 00	→			10 15	10 20
Chalkwell	d					08 49	08 53		09 02			09 21		09 30	09 33			09 51	10 00	10 03				10 18	10 23
Westcliff	d					08 52	08 55		09 05			09 23		09 32	09 36			09 53	10 02	10 05				10 21	10 26
Southend Central	a					08 54	08 58		09 08			09 26		09 35	09 38			09 56	10 05	10 08				10 23	10 29
	d					08 55			09 08			09 26			09 38			09 56		10 08				10 23	
Southend East	d					08 57			09 10			09 28			09 40			09 58		10 10				10 25	
Thorpe Bay	d					09 00			09 14			09 32			09 44			10 02		10 14				10 29	
Shoeburyness	a					09 05			09 18			09 36			09 48			10 06		10 18				10 33	

		CC	CC	CC	CC	CC	CC	CC		CC	CC	CC	CC	CC	CC	CC	CC	CC		CC	CC	CC	CC	CC	CC
London Fenchurch St 7 ⊖	d	09 35	09 40		09 50	10 00		10 05		10 10	10 20	10 30		10 35	10 40	10 50	11 00			11 05	11 10	11 20	11 30		11 35
Limehouse	d	09 39	09 44		09 54			10 09		10 14	10 24			10 39	10 44	10 54				11 09	11 14	11 24			11 39
West Ham ⊖	d	09 44	09 49		09 59	10 08		10 14		10 19	10 29	10 38		10 44	10 49	10 59	11 08			11 14	11 19	11 29	11 38		11 44
London Liverpool St 15 ⊖	d																								
Stratford 7 ⊖	d																								
Barking ⊖	d	09 50	09 55		10 05	10 14		10 20		10 25	10 35	10 44		10 50	10 55	11 05	11 14			11 20	11 25	11 35	11 44		11 50
Upminster ⊖	d		10 04		10 14	10 23				10 34	10 44	10 53			11 04	11 14	11 23				11 34	11 44	11 53		
Ockendon	d				10 19						10 49					11 19						11 49			
Chafford Hundred	d				10 23						10 53					11 23						11 53			
West Horndon	d		10 09							10 39					11 09						11 39				
Laindon	d		10 14			10 31				10 44		11 01			11 14		11 31				11 44		12 01		
Basildon	d		10 17			10 34				10 47		11 04			11 17		11 34				11 47		12 04		
Dagenham Dock	d	09 55						10 25						10 55						11 25					11 55
Rainham	d	09 59						10 29						10 59						11 29					11 59
Purfleet	d	10 04						10 34						11 04						11 34					12 04
Grays	d	10a10			10 27			10a40			10 57			11a10		11 27				11a40		11 57			12a10
Tilbury Town 3	d				10 30						11 00					11 30						12 00			
East Tilbury	d				10 36						11 06					11 36						12 06			
Stanford-le-Hope	d			←	10 40						11 10					11 40						12 10			
Pitsea	d		10 21	10 25	10 48		←			10 51	11 18		←		11 21	11 48		←			11 51	12 18		←	
Benfleet	d		10 25	10 29	10 52	10 41	10 52			10 55	11 22	11 11	11 22		11 25	11 52	11 41	11 52			11 55	12 22	12 11	12 22	
Leigh-on-Sea	d		10 30	10 34	→	10 45	10 56			11 00	→	11 15	11 26		11 30	→	11 45	11 57			12 00	→	12 15	12 26	
Chalkwell	d		10 33	10 37		10 48	10 59			11 03		11 18	11 29		11 33		11 48	12 00			12 03		12 18	12 29	
Westcliff	d		10 35	10 39		10 51	11 02			11 05		11 21	11 32		11 35		11 51	12 02			12 05		12 21	12 32	
Southend Central	a		10 38	10 42		10 53	11 05			11 08		11 23	11 35		11 38		11 53	12 05			12 08		12 23	12 35	
	d		10 38			10 53				11 08		11 23			11 38		11 53				12 08		12 23		
Southend East	d		10 40			10 55				11 10		11 25			11 40		11 55				12 10		12 25		
Thorpe Bay	d		10 44			10 59				11 14		11 29			11 44		11 59				12 14		12 29		
Shoeburyness	a		10 48			11 03				11 18		11 33			11 48		12 03				12 18		12 33		

A 13 August

Table I

London - Southend Central and Shoeburyness

Mondays to Fridays

13 August to 28 August

Network Diagram - see first page of Table I

		CC	CC	CC		CC	CC	CC	CC	CC	CC	CC	CC	CC		CC	CC	CC	CC	CC	CC	CC	CC	CC
London Fenchurch St 7 ⊖	d	11 40	11 50	12 00			12 05	12 10	12 20	12 30		12 35	12 40	12 50		13 00		13 05	13 10	13 20	13 30		13 35	13 40
Limehouse	d	11 44	11 54				12 09	12 14	12 24			12 39	12 44	12 54				13 09	13 14	13 24			13 39	13 44
West Ham ⊖	d	11 49	11 59	12 08			12 14	12 19	12 29	12 38		12 44	12 49	12 59		13 08		13 14	13 19	13 29	13 38		13 44	13 49
London Liverpool St 15 ⊖	d																							
Stratford 7 ⊖	d																							
Barking ⊖	d	11 55	12 05	12 14			12 20	12 25	12 35	12 44		12 50	12 55	13 05		13 14		13 20	13 25	13 35	13 44		13 50	13 55
Upminster ⊖	d	12 04	12 14	12 23				12 34	12 44	12 53			13 04	13 14		13 23			13 34	13 44	13 53			14 04
Ockendon	d		12 19						12 49					13 19						13 49				
Chafford Hundred	d		12 23						12 53					13 23						13 53				
West Horndon	d	12 09						12 39					13 09						13 39					14 09
Laindon	d	12 14		12 31				12 44		13 01			13 14			13 31			13 44		14 01			14 14
Basildon	d	12 17		12 34				12 47		13 04			13 17			13 34			13 47		14 04			14 17
Dagenham Dock	d						12 25					12 55						13 25					13 55	
Rainham	d						12 29					12 59						13 29					13 59	
Purfleet	d						12 34					13 04						13 34					14 04	
Grays	d		12 27				12a40		12 57			13a10		13 27				13a40		13 57			14a10	
Tilbury Town 3	d		12 30						13 00					13 30						14 00				
East Tilbury	d		12 36						13 06					13 36						14 06				
Stanford-le-Hope	d		12 40						13 10					13 40						14 10				
Pitsea	d	12 21	12 48			←		12 51	13 18		←		13 21	13 48			←		13 51	14 18		←		14 21
Benfleet	d	12 25	12 52	12 41		12 52		12 55	13 22	13 11	13 22		13 25	13 52		13 41	13 52		13 55	14 22	14 11	14 22		14 25
Leigh-on-Sea	d	12 30	→	12 45		12 57		13 00	→	13 15	13 27		13 30	→		13 45	13 57		14 00	→	14 15	14 26		14 30
Chalkwell	d	12 33		12 48		13 00		13 03		13 18	13 30		13 33			13 48	14 00		14 03		14 18	14 29		14 33
Westcliff	d	12 35		12 51		13 02		13 05		13 21	13 32		13 35			13 51	14 02		14 05		14 21	14 32		14 35
Southend Central	a	12 38		12 53		13 05		13 08		13 23	13 35		13 38			13 53	14 05		14 08		14 23	14 35		14 38
	d	12 38		12 53				13 08		13 23			13 38			13 53			14 08		14 23			14 38
Southend East	d	12 40		12 55				13 10		13 25			13 40			13 55			14 10		14 25			14 40
Thorpe Bay	d	12 44		12 59				13 14		13 29			13 44			13 59			14 14		14 29			14 44
Shoeburyness	a	12 48		13 03				13 18		13 33			13 48			14 03			14 18		14 33			14 48

		CC	CC	CC	CC	CC	CC	CC	CC	CC		CC	CC	CC	CC	CC	CC	CC	CC	CC		CC	CC	CC	CC
London Fenchurch St 7 ⊖	d	13 50	14 00		14 05	14 10	14 20	14 30		14 35		14 40	14 50	15 00		15 05	15 10	15 20	15 25	15 30		15 35	15 40		15 50
Limehouse	d	13 54			14 09	14 14	14 24			14 39		14 44	14 54			15 09	15 14	15 24				15 39	15 44		15 54
West Ham ⊖	d	13 59	14 08		14 14	14 19	14 29	14 38		14 44		14 49	14 59	15 08		15 14	15 19	15 29	15 33	15 38		15 44	15 49		15 59
London Liverpool St 15 ⊖	d																								
Stratford 7 ⊖	d																								
Barking ⊖	d	14 05	14 14		14 20	14 25	14 35	14 44		14 50		14 55	15 05	15 14		15 20	15 25	15 35	15 39	15 44		15 50	15 54		16 05
Upminster ⊖	d	14 14	14 23			14 34	14 44	14 53				15 04	15 14	15 23			15 34	15 44	15 48	15 53			16 02		16 14
Ockendon	d	14 19					14 49						15 19					15 49							16 19
Chafford Hundred	d	14 23					14 53						15 23					15 53							16 23
West Horndon	d					14 39						15 09					15 39						16 07		
Laindon	d		14 31			14 44		15 01				15 14		15 31			15 44		15 56	16 01			16 12		
Basildon	d		14 34			14 47		15 04				15 17		15 34			15 47		15 59	16 04			16 15		
Dagenham Dock	d				14 25					14 55						15 25						15 55			
Rainham	d				14 29					14 59						15 29						15 59			
Purfleet	d				14 34					15 04						15 34						16 04			
Grays	d	14 27			14a40		14 57			15a10			15 27			15a40		15 57				16a10			16 27
Tilbury Town 3	d	14 30					15 00						15 30					16 00							16 30
East Tilbury	d	14 36					15 06						15 36					16 06							16 36
Stanford-le-Hope	d	14 40					15 10						15 40					16 10						←	16 40
Pitsea	d	14 48		←		14 51	15 18		←			15 21	15 48		←		15 51	16 22	16 03				16 19	16 22	16a48
Benfleet	d	14 52	14 41	14 52		14 55	15 22	15 11	15 22			15 25	15 52	15 41	15 52		15 55	→	16 07	16 11			16 22	16 26	
Leigh-on-Sea	d	→	14 45	14 56		15 00	→	15 15	15 26			15 30	→	15 45	15 56		16 00		16a12	16 15			16 27	16 30	
Chalkwell	d		14 48	14 59		15 03		15 18	15 29			15 33		15 48	15 59		16 03			16 18			16 29	16 33	
Westcliff	d		14 51	15 02		15 05		15 21	15 32			15 35		15 51	16 02		16 05			16 21			16 32	16 36	
Southend Central	a		14 53	15 05		15 08		15 23	15 35			15 38		15 53	16 05		16 08			16 23			16 34	16 41	
	d		14 53			15 08		15 23				15 38		15 53			16 08			16 23			16 35		
Southend East	d		14 55			15 10		15 25				15 40		15 55			16 10			16 25			16 37		
Thorpe Bay	d		14 59			15 14		15 29				15 44		15 59			16 14			16 29			16 39		
Shoeburyness	a		15 03			15 18		15 33				15 48		16 03			16 20			16 33			16 44		

		CC	CC	CC	CC	CC		CC	CC	CC	CC	CC	CC	CC	CC	CC		CC	CC	CC	CC	CC	CC	CC	CC
London Fenchurch St 7 ⊖	d	15 55	16 00	16 10	16 13	16 20		16 28	16 30	16 34	16 37	16 45	16 48	16 55	17 00	17 02		17 05	17 07	17 10	17 15	17 18	17 20	17 23	17 26
Limehouse	d	15 59		16 14	16 17	16 24			16 34	16 38	16 41	16 49	16 52	16 59				17 09	17 12	17 15	17 19		17 24	17 28	17 30
West Ham ⊖	d	16 04	16 08	16 19	16 22	16 29		16 36	16 39	16 43	16 46		16 57	17 04					17 17	17 20		17 26	17 29	17 33	17 35
London Liverpool St 15 ⊖	d																								
Stratford 7 ⊖	d																								
Barking ⊖	d	16 10	16 14	16 25	16 28	16 35			16 45	16 49	16 52	16 59	17 03	17 10		17 15		17 19	17 22	17 26			17 35	17 39	17 42
Upminster ⊖	d		16 23	16 34		16 45			16 55		17 02	17 07	17 13			17 24			17 31		17 36	17 40		17 47	
Ockendon	d					16 50					17 08					17 29									
Chafford Hundred	d					16 54					17 12					17 34									
West Horndon	d			16 39					17 00				17 18						17 36					17 52	
Laindon	d			16 44				16 56	17a08			17 16	17a26					17 35	17a43				17 51	17a59	
Basildon	d		16 33	16 47				16 59				17 19						17 39				17 50	17 55		
Dagenham Dock	d	16 15			16 33					16 54				17 15						17 31					17 47
Rainham	d	16 19			16 37					16 58				17 19						17 35					17 51
Purfleet	d	16 25			16 43					17 04				17 25						17 40					17 56
Grays	d	16a33			16 49	16 59				17 10	17a18			17 31		17a40				17 46					18 02
Tilbury Town 3	d				16 52	17 02				17 13				17 34						17 50					18 06
East Tilbury	d				16 58	17 08				17 19				17 40						17 56					18 12
Stanford-le-Hope	d				17 02	17a15				17 23				17 44						18 00					18 16
Pitsea	d			16 51	17a12					17a33		17 23		17a54				17 42		18a09		17 54	17 58		18a25
Benfleet	d		16 40	16 55				17 06				17 27			17 33			17 46			17 52	17 58	18 03		
Leigh-on-Sea	d		16 45	17 00				17 11				17 32			17 38			17 51			17 56	18 02	18 07		
Chalkwell	d		16 48	17 03				17 14				17 34			17 41			17 53			17 59	18 05	18 10		
Westcliff	d		16 50	17 05				17 16				17 37			17 43			17 56			18 02	18 08	18 13		
Southend Central	a		16 53	17 08				17 19				17 39			17 46			17 58			18 04	18 13	18 15		
	d		16 53	17 08				17 19				17 39			17 46			17 58			18 04		18 15		
Southend East	d		16 55	17 10				17 21				17 41			17 48			18 00			18 06		18 17		
Thorpe Bay	d		16 59	17 14				17 24				17 44			17 50			18 03			18 10		18 21		
Shoeburyness	a		17 05	17 20				17 31				17 51			17 57			18 11			18 16		18 28		

Table 1

London - Southend Central and Shoeburyness

Mondays to Fridays

13 August to 28 August

Network Diagram - see first page of Table 1

		CC		CC	CC	CC	CC	CC	CC	CC	CC	CC		CC	CC	CC	CC	CC	CC	CC	CC	CC		CC	CC
London Fenchurch St ⊖	d	17 30		17 32	17 35	17 37	17 41	17 45	17 47	17 51	17 53	17 56		18 00	18 02	18 06	18 09			18 12	18 21				18 23
Limehouse	d				17 39	17 42	17 45	17 49	17 52		17 57	18 00			18 06	18 10	18 13			18 16					18 27
West Ham ⊖	d			17 40	17 44	17 47	17 50		17 57	17 59		18 05		18 08	18 11		18 18			18 21					18 32
London Liverpool St ⊖	d																								
Stratford ⊖	d																								
Barking ⊖	d			17 46	17 50	17 53	17 56				18 08	18 11			18 17	18 20	18 24			18 28					
Upminster ⊖	d			17 56		18 03			18 10	18 14					18 27		18 34								18 46
Ockendon	d			18 02					18 15						18 33										18 51
Chafford Hundred	d			18 06					18 20						18 38										18 55
West Horndon	d					18 08					18 21						18 39								
Laindon	d				18 07	18a15					18 27					18 37	18 43				18 47				
Basildon	d				18 10					18 24	18 31			18 35		18 41	18 47				18 51				
Dagenham Dock	d						18 01					18 16								18 33					
Rainham	d						18 05					18 20								18 37					
Purfleet	d						18 11					18 25								18 42					
Grays	d			18a13			18 17		18a26			18 31			18 42					18 48					19 00
Tilbury Town	d						18 20					18 35			18 46					18 52					19 03
East Tilbury	d						18 26					18 41			18 52					18 58					19 09
Stanford-le-Hope	d						18 30					18 45			18 56			←	←	19 02					19 13
Pitsea	d				18 14		18a40			18 28	18 34	18 57		18 38	19 03	18 44	18 50	18 57	19 03	19a11		←		←	19 21
Benfleet	d	18 08			18 18			18 24		18 32	18 39	→		18 43	→	18 49	18 54	19 03	19 07		18 58	19 03		19 07	→
Leigh-on-Sea	d	18 12			18 23			18 28		18 37	18 43			18 47		18 53	18 59	→	→		19 03	19 07		19a14	
Chalkwell	d	18 15			18 26			18 31		18 40	18 46			18 50		18 56	19 01				19 06	19 10			
Westcliff	d	18 18			18 28			18 34		18 42	18 49			18 53		18 59	19 04				19 08	19 13			
Southend Central	a	18 20			18 31			18 36		18 45	18 51			18 55		19 01	19 09				19 11	19 15			
	d	18 20			18 31			18 36		18 45	18 51			18 55		19 01					19 11	19 15			
Southend East	d	18 22			18 33			18 38		18 47	18 53			18 57		19 03					19 13	19 17			
Thorpe Bay	d	18 26			18 36			18 42		18 50	18 57			19 01		19 07					19 16	19 21			
Shoeburyness	a	18 32			18 43			18 48		18 58	19 03			19 07		19 13					19 23	19 28			

		CC	CC	CC	CC	CC	CC	CC		CC	CC	CC	CC	CC	CC	CC	CC	CC		CC	CC	CC	CC	CC	CC
London Fenchurch St ⊖	d	18 27		18 31	18 35	18 42		18 46		18 51	19 00	19 02	19 05		19 08	19 11	19 20	19 30			19 32	19 35	19 40	19 50	20 00
Limehouse	d	18 31		18 35	18 39			18 51		18 55			19 09		19 12	19 15	19 24				19 36	19 39	19 44	19 54	
West Ham ⊖	d	18 36		18 40		18 50		18 56		19 00		19 10			19 17	19 20	19 29				19 41	19 44	19 49	19 59	20 08
London Liverpool St ⊖	d																								
Stratford ⊖	d																								
Barking ⊖	d	18 42		18 46	18 49			19 01		19 06		19 16	19 19		19 23	19 26	19 35				19 47	19 50	19 55	20 05	20 14
Upminster ⊖	d	18 51			18 58			19 10				19 26	19 30			19 35	19 44	19 50			19 56		20 04	20 14	20 23
Ockendon	d				19 06							19 33					19 49							20 19	
Chafford Hundred	d				19 11							19 39					19 53							20 23	
West Horndon	d	18 56						19 15								19 40					20 01		20 09		
Laindon	d	19 01						19 20			19 26					19 45					20a07		20 14		20 31
Basildon	d	19 04				19 12		19 23					19 40			19 48		20 00					20 17		20 34
Dagenham Dock	d			18 51						19 11					19 28							19 55			
Rainham	d			18 55						19 15					19 32							19 59			
Purfleet	d			19 01						19 21					19 37							20 04			
Grays	d			19 07	19a17					19 27		19 46			19a43		19 57					20a10		20 27	
Tilbury Town	d			19 10						19 30		19 50					20 00							20 30	
East Tilbury	d			19 16						19 36		19 56					20 06							20 36	
Stanford-le-Hope	d		←	19 20						19 40		20 00		←			20 10							20 40	
Pitsea	d	19 08	19 21	19a30			←	19 26		19 48		20a07	19 44	19 48		19 52	20 18			←			20 21	20 48	
Benfleet	d	19 12	19 25			19 19	19 25	19 30		→	19 33		19 48	19 52		19 56	20 22	20 06		20 22			20 26	20 52	20 41
Leigh-on-Sea	d	19 16	→			19 24	19a32	19 35			19 38		19 52	19 56		20 00	→	20 11		20 27			20 30	→	20 45
Chalkwell	d	19 19				19 27		19 37			19 41		19 55	19 59		20 03		20 14		20 30			20 33		20 48
Westcliff	d	19 21				19 29		19 40			19 43		19 58	20 02		20 06		20 16		20 32			20 36		20 51
Southend Central	a	19 24				19 32		19 42			19 46		20 00	20 07		20 08		20 19		20 35			20 38		20 53
	d	19 24				19 32		19 42			19 46		20 00			20 08		20 19					20 38		20 53
Southend East	d	19 26				19 34		19 44			19 48		20 02			20 10		20 21					20 40		20 55
Thorpe Bay	d	19 28				19 37		19 47			19 50		20 06			20 14		20 25					20 44		20 59
Shoeburyness	a	19 35				19 44		19 53			19 57		20 10			20 18		20 29					20 48		21 03

		CC	CC	CC		CC	CC	CC	CC	CC	CC	CC	CC	CC		CC	CC	CC	CC	CC	CC	CC	CC	CC	
London Fenchurch St ⊖	d		20 05	20 10		20 20	20 30			20 40	20 50	21 00		21 05		21 10	21 20	21 30			21 40	21 50	22 00		
Limehouse	d		20 09	20 14		20 24	20 34			20 44	20 54			21 09		21 14	21 24	21 34			21 44	21 54			
West Ham ⊖	d		20 14	20 19		20 29	20 39			20 49	20 59	21 08		21 14		21 19	21 29	21 39			21 49	21 59	22 08		
London Liverpool St ⊖	d								20 35											21 35					
Stratford ⊖	d								20 43											21 43					
Barking ⊖	d		20 20	20 25		20 35	20 45		20 50	20 55	21 05	21 14		21 20		21 25	21 35	21 45		21 50	21 55	22 05	22 14		
Upminster ⊖	d			20 34		20 44	20 54			21 04	21 14	21 23				21 34	21 44	21 54			22 04	22 14	22 23		
Ockendon	d					20 49					21 19						21 49					22 19			
Chafford Hundred	d					20 53					21 23						21 53					22 23			
West Horndon	d			20 39						21 09						21 39					22 09				
Laindon	d			20 44			21 02			21 14		21 31				21 44		22 02			22 14		22 31		
Basildon	d			20 47			21 05			21 17		21 34				21 47		22 05			22 17		22 34		
Dagenham Dock	d		20 25						20 55					21 25						21 55					
Rainham	d		20 29						20 59					21 29						21 59					
Purfleet	d		20 34						21 04					21 34						22 04					
Grays	d		20a40			20 57			21a12		21 27			21a40			21 57			22a12		22 27			
Tilbury Town	d					21 00					21 30						22 00					22 30			
East Tilbury	d					21 06					21 36						22 06					22 36			
Stanford-le-Hope	d					21 10					21 40						22 10					22 40			
Pitsea	d	←		20 51		21 18		←		21 21	21 48		←			21 51	22 18		←		22 21	22 48		←	
Benfleet	d	20 52		20 55		21 22	21 12	21 22		21 25	21 52	21 41	21 52			21 55	22 22	22 12	22 22		22 25	22 52	22 41	22 52	
Leigh-on-Sea	d	20 56		21 00		→	21 16	21 26		21 30	→	21 45	21 56			22 00	→	22 16	22 26		22 30	→	22 45	22 56	
Chalkwell	d	20 59		21 03			21 19	21 29		21 33		21 48	21 59			22 03		22 19	22 29		22 33		22 48	22 59	
Westcliff	d	21 02		21 05			21 22	21 32		21 35		21 51	22 02			22 05		22 22	22 32		22 35		22 51	23 02	
Southend Central	a	21 05		21 08			21 24	21 35		21 38		21 53	22 05			22 08		22 24	22 35		22 38		22 53	23 05	
	d			21 08			21 24			21 38		21 53				22 08		22 24			22 38		22 53	23 05	
Southend East	d			21 10			21 26			21 40		21 55				22 10		22 26			22 40		22 55	23 07	
Thorpe Bay	d			21 14			21 30			21 44		21 59				22 14		22 30			22 44		22 59	23 10	
Shoeburyness	a			21 18			21 34			21 48		22 03				22 18		22 34			22 48		23 03	23 15	

Table 1

London - Southend Central and Shoeburyness

Mondays to Fridays

13 August to 28 August

Network Diagram - see first page of Table 1

		CC	CC	CC	CC	CC	CC	CC	CC	CC		CC	CC	CC	CC	CC	CC
London Fenchurch St ⊖	d	22 05	22 10	22 20	22 35	22 40	22 50	23 00		23 05		23 10		23 20	23 35	23 40	23 50
Limehouse	d	22 09	22 14	22 24	22 39	22 44	22 54			23 09		23 14		23 24	23 39	23 44	23 54
West Ham ⊖	d	22 14	22 19	22 29	22 44	22 49	22 59	23 08		23 14		23 19		23 29	23 44	23 49	23 59
London Liverpool St ⊖	d																
Stratford ⊖	d																
Barking ⊖	d	22 20	22 25	22 35	22 50	22 55	23 05	23 14		23 20		23 25		23 35	23 50	23 55	00 05
Upminster ⊖	d		22 34	22 44		23 04	23 14	23 23				23 34		23 44		00 04	00 14
Ockendon	d			22 49			23 19							23 49			00 19
Chafford Hundred	d			22 53			23 23							23 53			00 23
West Horndon	d		22 39			23 09						23 39				00 09	
Laindon	d		22 44			23 14		23 31				23 44				00 16	
Basildon	d		22 47			23 17		23 34				23 47				00 19	
Dagenham Dock	d	22 25			22 55					23 25					23 55		
Rainham	d	22 29			22 59					23 29					23 59		
Purfleet	d	22 34			23 04					23 34					00 04		
Grays	d	22a40		22 57	23a10		23 27			23 42				23 57	00a10		00 27
Tilbury Town	d			23 00			23 30			23 45				00 01			00 30
East Tilbury	d			23 06			23 36			23 51				00 06			00 36
Stanford-le-Hope	d			23 10			23 40			23 55			←	00 10			00 40
Pitsea	d		22 51	23 18		23 22	23 48		←	00 06		23 52	00 06	00 18		00 22	00 48
Benfleet	d		22 55	23 22		23 26	23 52	23 41	23 52	→		23 56	00 10	00 22		00 26	00 52
Leigh-on-Sea	d		23 00	23 26		23 30	→	23 45	23 56			23 59	00 15	00 27		00 31	00 56
Chalkwell	d		23 03	23 29		23 33		23 48	23 59			00 03	00 18	00 30		00 34	00 59
Westcliff	d		23 06	23 32		23 36		23 51	00 02			00 06	00 20	00 32		00 36	01 02
Southend Central	a		23 08	23 35		23 39		23 54	00 05			00 09	00 23	00 35		00 39	01 05
	d		23 08	23 35		23 39		23 54	00 05			00 09	00 23	00 35		00 40	01 05
Southend East	d		23 10	23 37		23 41		23 56	00 07			00 11	00 26	00 38		00 42	01 07
Thorpe Bay	d		23 14	23 41		23 45		23 59	00 11			00 15	00 29	00 41		00 46	01 11
Shoeburyness	a		23 18	23 47		23 51		00 06	00 17			00 21	00 36	00 48		00 52	01 17

Mondays to Fridays

29 August to 7 September

		CC A	CC B	CC C	CC B	CC C	CC A	CC B	CC C	CC B		CC C	CC A	CC B	CC C	CC B	CC C	CC B	CC C	CC B		CC C	CC A	CC B	CC C
London Fenchurch St ⊖	d	22p50	22p50	22p50	23p00	23p00				23p05		23p05	23p10	23p10	23p10			23p20	23p20	23p35		23p37	23p40	23p40	23p40
Limehouse	d	22p54	22p54	22p54						23p09		23p09	23p14	23p14	23p14			23p24	23p24	23p39		23p41	23p44	23p44	23p44
West Ham ⊖	d	23p01	22p59	23p01	23p08	23p10				23p14		23p15	23p21	23p19	23p21			23p29	23p31	23p44		23p47	23p51	23p49	23p51
London Liverpool St ⊖	d																								
Stratford ⊖	d																								
Barking ⊖	d	23p06	23p05	23p06	23p14	23p15				23p20		23p21	23p26	23p25	23p26			23p35	23p36	23p50		23p53	23p56	23p55	23p57
Upminster ⊖	d	23p14	23p14	23p15	23p23	23p24							23p35	23p34	23p35			23p44	23p45				00 05	00 04	00 06
Ockendon	d	23p19	23p19	23p20														23p49	23p50						
Chafford Hundred	d	23p23	23p23	23p24														23p53	23p54						
West Horndon	d												23p40	23p39	23p40								00 10	00 09	00 11
Laindon	d				23p31	23p33							23p44	23p44	23p46								00 14	00 16	00 17
Basildon	d				23p34	23p36							23p47	23p47	23p49								00 17	00 19	00 20
Dagenham Dock	d									23p25		23p26								23p55		23p58			
Rainham	d									23p29		23p30								23p59		00 02			
Purfleet	d									23p34		23p35								00 04		00 07			
Grays	d	23p27	23p27	23p28						23p42		23p43						23p57	23p58	00a10		00a13			
Tilbury Town	d	23p30	23p30	23p32						23p45		23p46						00 01	00 02						
East Tilbury	d	23p35	23p36	23p38						23p51		23p52						00 06	00 07						
Stanford-le-Hope	d	23p39	23p40	23p42						23p55		23p56				←	←	00 10	00 11						
Pitsea	d	23p47	23p48	23p49			←	←	←	00 06		00 07	23p51	23p52	23p53	00 06	00 07	00 18	00 20				00 21	00 22	00 24
Benfleet	d	23p50	23p52	23p53	23p41	23p42	23p50	23p52	23p53	→		→	23p55	23p56	23p57	00 10	00 11	00 22	00 24				00 25	00 26	00 28
Leigh-on-Sea	d	→	→	→	23p45	23p47	23p55	23p56	23p58				23p59	23p59	00 02	00 15	00 16	00 27	00 28				00 29	00 31	00 32
Chalkwell	d				23p48	23p50	23p57	23p59	00 01				00 02	00 03	00 05	00 18	00 19	00 30	00 31				00 32	00 34	00 35
Westcliff	d				23p51	23p52	23p59	00 02	00 03				00 04	00 06	00 07	00 20	00 21	00 32	00 34				00 34	00 36	00 38
Southend Central	a				23p54	23p55	00 03	00 05	00 06				00 08	00 09	00 10	00 23	00 24	00 35	00 37				00 38	00 39	00 41
	d				23p54	23p55	00 03	00 05	00 06				00 08	00 09	00 10	00 23	00 24	00 35	00 37				00 38	00 40	00 41
Southend East	d				23p56	23p58	00 05	00 07	00 09				00 11	00 11	00 13	00 26	00 27	00 38	00 39				00 41	00 42	00 44
Thorpe Bay	d				23p59	00 01	00 07	00 11	00 12				00 12	00 15	00 16	00 29	00 30	00 41	00 43				00 42	00 46	00 47
Shoeburyness	a				00 06	00 08	00 15	00 17	00 19				00 21	00 21	00 23	00 36	00 37	00 48	00 49				00 51	00 52	00 54

A 3 September **B** 29 August **C** not 29 August, 3 September

London - Southend Central and Shoeburyness

Network Diagram - see first page of Table I

		CC A	CC B	CC A	CC B	CC A		CC B	CC C	CC A	CC B	CC A	CC B	CC C	CC B	CC		CC	CC	CC	CC	CC	CC	CC	CC
London Fenchurch St	⊖ d	23p50	23p50	00 01	00 01				00 10	00 15	00 18	00 25	00 30	00 50	00 50			05 10		05 40				06 10	06 20
Limehouse	d	23p54	23p54						00 14	00 19	00 22	00 29	00 34	00 54	00 54			05 14		05 44				06 14	06 24
West Ham	⊖ d	23p59	00 01	00 09	00 11				00 21	00 24	00 28	00 34	00 41	01 01	01 01			05 19		05 49				06 19	06 29
London Liverpool St	⊖ d																								
Stratford	⊖ d																								
Barking	⊖ d	00 05	00 07	00 15	00 17				00 26	00 30	00 34	00 40	00 47	01 06	01 06			05 25	05 39	05 55	05 45	06 05		06 25	06 35
Upminster	⊖ d	00 14	00 16	00 24	00 26				00 35			00 49	00 56	01 15	01 15	05 28		05 34	05 48	06 04			06 31	06 34	
Ockendon	d	00 19	00 21													05 33			05 56				06 36		
Chafford Hundred	d	00 23	00 25													05 37			06 00				06 40		
West Horndon	d								00 40			00 54	01 01	01 20	01 20			05 39		06 09				06 39	
Laindon	d			00 32	00 35				00 44			00 59	01 07	01 24	01 26			05 44		06 14				06 45	
Basildon	d			00 35	00 38				00 47			01 02	01 10	01 27	01 29			05 47		06 17				06 48	
Dagenham Dock	d									00 35	00 39										05 50	06 10			06 40
Rainham	d									00 39	00 43										05 54	06 14			06 44
Purfleet	d									00 44	00 48										05 59	06 19			06 49
Grays	d	00 27	00 29							00a50	00a54					05a41			06a05		06 05	06 25	06a44		06 55
Tilbury Town	d	00 30	00 33																		06 08	06 28			06 58
East Tilbury	d	00 36	00 39																		06 14	06 34			07 04
Stanford-le-Hope	d	00 40	00 43																		06 18	06 38			07 08
Pitsea	d	00 48	00 50			←		←	00 51			01 06	01 13	01 31	01 32			05 51		06 21	06 26	06a46		06 51	07 18
Benfleet	d	00 52	00 54	00 42	00 44	00 52		00 54	00 55			01 10	01 17	01 35	01 36			05 55		06 25	06 31			06 55	07 22
Leigh-on-Sea	d	→	→	00 46	00 49	00 56		00 59	00 59			01 14	01 22	01 39	01 41			06 00		06 30	06 35			07 00	07 27
Chalkwell	d			00 49	00 52	00 59		01 02	01 02			01 17	01 25	01 42	01 44			06 03		06 33	06 38			07 03	07 30
Westcliff	d			00 52	00 54	01 02		01 04	01 04			01 20	01 27	01 44	01 46			06 05		06 35	06 41			07 05	07 32
Southend Central	a			00 55	00 57	01 05		01 07	01 07			01 23	01 30	01 48	01 49			06 08		06 38	06 43			07 08	07 35
	d			00 55	00 57	01 05		01 07	01 07			01 23	01 30	01 48	01 49			06 08		06 38	06 43			07 08	07 35
Southend East	d			00 57	01 00	01 07		01 10	01 10			01 25	01 33	01 51	01 52			06 10		06 40	06 45			07 10	07 37
Thorpe Bay	d			01 01	01 03	01 11		01 13	01 11			01 29	01 36	01 53	01 55			06 14		06 44	06 49			07 14	07 40
Shoeburyness	a			01 07	01 10	01 17		01 20	01 21			01 35	01 43	02 01	02 02			06 18		06 48	06 53			07 20	07 45

		CC		CC	CC	CC	CC	CC	CC	CC	CC	CC		CC	CC	CC	CC	CC	CC	CC	CC	CC		CC	CC
London Fenchurch St	⊖ d	06 40			06 44	06 48	07 00	07 09	07 13	07 15	07 30	07 40		07 43	07 48	07 50	08 00		08 03	08 09	08 14	08 20		08 30	
Limehouse	d	06 44			06 48	06 52		07 13				07 44				07 54			08 07	08 13		08 24			
West Ham	⊖ d	06 49			06 53	06 57	07 08	07 18		07 23	07 38	07 49		07 53		07 59	08 08		08 12	08 18	08 23	08 29		08 38	
London Liverpool St	⊖ d																								
Stratford	⊖ d																								
Barking	⊖ d	06 55		06 50	07 00	07 03	07 14	07 25	07 26	07 29	07 44	07 55		07 58		08 05	08 14		08 18	08 24	08 30	08 37		08 45	
Upminster	⊖ d	07 04			07 10		07 23	07 34		07 38	07 53	08 04			08 09	08 15	08 23			08 33	08 41			08 54	
Ockendon	d				07 15					07 45					08 16						08 46				
Chafford Hundred	d				07 19					07 49					08 20						08 50				
West Horndon	d	07 09						07 39				08 09				08 20				08 38					
Laindon	d	07 14						07 44				08 14				08a26	08 31			08 44				09 03	
Basildon	d	07 17					07 33	07 47			08 03	08 17					08 34			08 47				09 06	
Dagenham Dock	d			06 55		07 08			07 31					08 03					08 23			08 42			
Rainham	d			06 59		07 12			07 35					08 07					08 27			08 46			
Purfleet	d			07 04		07 17			07 40					08 13					08 33			08 51			
Grays	d			07 10	07a23	07 25			07 46	07 54				08 18	08 25				08 38		08a54	08 57			
Tilbury Town	d			07 13		07 28				07 58				08 22					08 42			09 00			
East Tilbury	d			07 19		07 34				08 04				08 28					08 48			09 06			
Stanford-le-Hope	d			07 23		07 38			07 56	08 08				08 32	08 35			←	08 52			09 10			←
Pitsea	d	07 22		07a31		07a46		07 51	08a03	08a15		08 21		08 41	08a44		08 38	08 41	08a59	08 51		09 18		09 09	09 18
Benfleet	d	07 26					07 39	07 55			08 09	08 25		→			08 42	08 45		08 55		→		09 13	09 22
Leigh-on-Sea	d	07 30					07 44	07 59			08 14	08 30					08 46	08 50		08 59				09 18	09 27
Chalkwell	d	07 33					07 47	08 02			08 17	08 33					08 49	08 53		09 02				09 21	09 30
Westcliff	d	07 36					07 49	08 05			08 19	08 35					08 52	08 55		09 05				09 23	09 32
Southend Central	a	07 38					07 52	08 07			08 22	08 38					08 54	08 58		09 08				09 26	09 35
	d	07 38					07 52	08 07			08 22	08 38					08 55			09 08				09 26	
Southend East	d	07 40					07 54	08 09			08 24	08 40					08 57			09 10				09 28	
Thorpe Bay	d	07 44					07 58	08 13			08 28	08 44					09 00			09 14				09 32	
Shoeburyness	a	07 48					08 02	08 17			08 32	08 48					09 05			09 18				09 36	

		CC	CC	CC	CC	CC	CC	CC		CC	CC	CC	CC	CC	CC	CC	CC	CC		CC	CC	CC	CC	CC	CC
London Fenchurch St	⊖ d	08 40	08 50	08 54	09 00		09 10	09 16		09 20	09 30		09 35	09 40		09 50	10 00			10 05	10 10	10 20	10 30		10 35
Limehouse	d	08 44	08 54				09 14	09 20		09 24			09 39	09 44		09 54				10 09	10 14	10 24			10 39
West Ham	⊖ d	08 49	08 59		09 08		09 19	09 25		09 29	09 38		09 44	09 49		09 59	10 08			10 14	10 19	10 29	10 38		10 44
London Liverpool St	⊖ d																								
Stratford	⊖ d																								
Barking	⊖ d	08 55	09 07	09 09	09 16		09 25	09 31		09 35	09 44		09 50	09 55		10 05	10 14			10 20	10 25	10 35	10 44		10 50
Upminster	⊖ d	09 04		09 18	09 25		09 34			09 45	09 53			10 04		10 14	10 23				10 34	10 44	10 53		
Ockendon	d			09 23						09 50						10 19						10 49			
Chafford Hundred	d			09 27						09 54						10 23						10 53			
West Horndon	d	09 09					09 39							10 09							10 39				
Laindon	d	09 14			09 34		09 44				10 01			10 14			10 31				10 44		11 01		
Basildon	d	09 17			09 37		09 47				10 04			10 17			10 34				10 47		11 04		
Dagenham Dock	d		09 12					09 36					09 55							10 25					10 55
Rainham	d		09 16					09 40					09 59							10 29					10 59
Purfleet	d		09 21					09 45					10 04							10 34					11 04
Grays	d		09 27	09a31				09 51		09 58			10a10			10 27				10a40		10 57			11a10
Tilbury Town	d		09 30					09 54		10 02						10 30						11 00			
East Tilbury	d		09 36					10 00		10 08						10 36						11 06			
Stanford-le-Hope	d		09 40					10 04		10 12					←	10 40						11 10			
Pitsea	d	09 21	09 48			←	09 51	10 12		10 25		←		10 21	10 25	10 48		←			10 51	11 18		←	
Benfleet	d	09 26	09 52		09 43	09 52	09 55	10 16		→	10 11	10 16		10 25	10 29	10 52	10 41	10 52			10 55	11 22	11 11	11 22	
Leigh-on-Sea	d	09 30	→		09 48	09 57	10 00	→			10 15	10 20		10 30	10 34	→	10 45	10 56			11 00	→	11 15	11 26	
Chalkwell	d	09 33			09 51	10 00	10 03				10 18	10 23		10 33	10 37		10 48	10 59			11 03		11 18	11 29	
Westcliff	d	09 36			09 53	10 02	10 05				10 21	10 26		10 35	10 39		10 51	11 02			11 05		11 21	11 32	
Southend Central	a	09 38			09 56	10 05	10 08				10 23	10 29		10 38	10 42		10 53	11 05			11 08		11 23	11 35	
	d	09 38			09 56		10 08				10 23			10 38			10 53				11 08		11 23		
Southend East	d	09 40			09 58		10 10				10 25			10 40			10 55				11 10		11 25		
Thorpe Bay	d	09 44			10 02		10 14				10 29			10 44			10 59				11 14		11 29		
Shoeburyness	a	09 48			10 06		10 18				10 33			10 48			11 03				11 18		11 33		

A 29 August B not 29 August, 3 September C 3 September

London - Southend Central and Shoeburyness

Network Diagram - see first page of Table I

		CC	CC	CC		CC	CC	CC	CC	CC	CC	CC	CC	CC		CC	CC	CC	CC	CC	CC	CC	CC	CC	
London Fenchurch St	⊖ d	10 40	10 50	11 00			11 05	11 10	11 20	11 30		11 35	11 40	11 50		12 00		12 05	12 10	12 20	12 30		12 35	12 40	
Limehouse	d	10 44	10 54				11 09	11 14	11 24			11 39	11 44	11 54				12 09	12 14	12 24			12 39	12 44	
West Ham	⊖ d	10 49	10 59	11 08			11 14	11 19	11 29	11 38		11 44	11 49	11 59		12 08		12 14	12 19	12 29	12 38		12 44	12 49	
London Liverpool St	⊖ d																								
Stratford	⊖ d																								
Barking	⊖ d	10 55	11 05	11 14			11 20	11 25	11 35	11 44		11 50	11 55	12 05		12 14		12 20	12 25	12 35	12 44		12 50	12 55	
Upminster	⊖ d	11 04	11 14	11 23				11 34	11 44	11 53			12 04	12 14		12 23			12 34	12 44	12 53			13 04	
Ockendon	d		11 19						11 49					12 19						12 49					
Chafford Hundred	d		11 23						11 53					12 23						12 53					
West Horndon	d	11 09						11 39					12 09						12 39					13 09	
Laindon	d	11 14		11 31				11 44		12 01			12 14			12 31			12 44		13 01			13 14	
Basildon	d	11 17		11 34				11 47		12 04			12 17			12 34			12 47		13 04			13 17	
Dagenham Dock	d						11 25					11 55						12 25					12 55		
Rainham	d						11 29					11 59						12 29					12 59		
Purfleet	d						11 34					12 04						12 34					13 04		
Grays	d		11 27				11a40		11 57			12a10		12 27				12a40		12 57			13a10		
Tilbury Town	d		11 30						12 00					12 30						13 00					
East Tilbury	d		11 36						12 06					12 36						13 06					
Stanford-le-Hope	d		11 40						12 10					12 40						13 10					
Pitsea	d	11 21	11 48			←		11 51	12 18		←		12 21	12 48			←		12 51	13 18		←		13 21	
Benfleet	d	11 25	11 52	11 41		11 52		11 55	12 22	12 11	12 22		12 25	12 52		12 41	12 52		12 55	13 22	13 11	13 22		13 25	
Leigh-on-Sea	d	11 30	→	11 45		11 57		12 00	→	12 15	12 26		12 30	→		12 45	12 57		13 00	→	13 15	13 27		13 30	
Chalkwell	d	11 33		11 48		12 00		12 03		12 18	12 29		12 33			12 48	13 00		13 03		13 18	13 30		13 33	
Westcliff	d	11 35		11 51		12 02		12 05		12 21	12 32		12 35			12 51	13 02		13 05		13 21	13 32		13 35	
Southend Central	a	11 38		11 53		12 05		12 08		12 23	12 35		12 38			12 53	13 05		13 08		13 23	13 35		13 38	
	d	11 38		11 53				12 08		12 23			12 38			12 53			13 08		13 23			13 38	
Southend East	d	11 40		11 55				12 10		12 25			12 40			12 55			13 10		13 25			13 40	
Thorpe Bay	d	11 44		11 59				12 14		12 29			12 44			12 59			13 14		13 29			13 44	
Shoeburyness	a	11 48		12 03				12 18		12 33			12 48			13 03			13 18		13 33			13 48	

		CC	CC	CC	CC	CC	CC	CC	CC	CC		CC	CC	CC	CC	CC	CC	CC	CC	CC		CC	CC	CC	CC
London Fenchurch St	⊖ d	12 50	13 00		13 05	13 10	13 20	13 30		13 35		13 40	13 50	14 00		14 05	14 10	14 20	14 30			14 35	14 40	14 50	15 00
Limehouse	d	12 54			13 09	13 14	13 24			13 39		13 44	13 54			14 09	14 14	14 24				14 39	14 44	14 54	
West Ham	⊖ d	12 59	13 08		13 14	13 19	13 29	13 38		13 44		13 49	13 59	14 08		14 14	14 19	14 29	14 38			14 44	14 49	14 59	15 08
London Liverpool St	⊖ d																								
Stratford	⊖ d																								
Barking	⊖ d	13 05	13 14		13 20	13 25	13 35	13 44		13 50		13 55	14 05	14 14		14 20	14 25	14 35	14 44			14 50	14 55	15 05	15 14
Upminster	⊖ d	13 14	13 23			13 34	13 44	13 53				14 04	14 14	14 23			14 34	14 44	14 53				15 04	15 14	15 23
Ockendon	d	13 19					13 49						14 19					14 49						15 19	
Chafford Hundred	d	13 23					13 53						14 23					14 53						15 23	
West Horndon	d					13 39						14 09					14 39						15 09		
Laindon	d		13 31			13 44		14 01				14 14		14 31			14 44		15 01				15 14		15 31
Basildon	d		13 34			13 47		14 04				14 17		14 34			14 47		15 04				15 17		15 34
Dagenham Dock	d				13 25					13 55						14 25						14 55			
Rainham	d				13 29					13 59						14 29						14 59			
Purfleet	d				13 34					14 04						14 34						15 04			
Grays	d	13 27			13a40		13 57			14a10			14 27			14a40		14 57				15a10		15 27	
Tilbury Town	d	13 30					14 00						14 30					15 00						15 30	
East Tilbury	d	13 36					14 06						14 36					15 06						15 36	
Stanford-le-Hope	d	13 40					14 10						14 40					15 10						15 40	
Pitsea	d	13 48		←		13 51	14 18		←			14 21	14 48		←		14 51	15 18		←			15 21	15 48	
Benfleet	d	13 52	13 41	13 52		13 55	14 22	14 11	14 22			14 25	14 52	14 41	14 52		14 55	15 22	15 11	15 22			15 25	15 52	15 41
Leigh-on-Sea	d	→	13 45	13 57		14 00	→	14 15	14 26			14 30	→	14 45	14 56		15 00	→	15 15	15 26			15 30	→	15 45
Chalkwell	d		13 48	14 00		14 03		14 18	14 29			14 33		14 48	14 59		15 03		15 18	15 29			15 33		15 48
Westcliff	d		13 51	14 02		14 05		14 21	14 32			14 35		14 51	15 02		15 05		15 21	15 32			15 35		15 51
Southend Central	a		13 53	14 05		14 08		14 23	14 35			14 38		14 53	15 05		15 08		15 23	15 35			15 38		15 53
	d		13 53			14 08		14 23				14 38		14 53			15 08		15 23				15 38		15 53
Southend East	d		13 55			14 10		14 25				14 40		14 55			15 10		15 25				15 40		15 55
Thorpe Bay	d		13 59			14 14		14 29				14 44		14 59			15 14		15 29				15 44		15 59
Shoeburyness	a		14 03			14 18		14 33				14 48		15 03			15 18		15 33				15 48		16 03

		CC	CC	CC	CC	CC		CC	CC	CC	CC	CC	CC	CC	CC	CC		CC	CC	CC	CC	CC	CC	CC	CC
London Fenchurch St	⊖ d		15 05	15 10	15 20	15 25		15 30	15 35	15 40		15 50	15 55	16 00	16 10	16 13		16 20	16 28	16 30	16 34	16 37	16 45	16 48	16 55
Limehouse	d		15 09	15 14	15 24				15 39	15 44		15 54	15 59		16 14	16 17		16 24		16 34	16 38	16 41	16 49	16 52	16 59
West Ham	⊖ d		15 14	15 19	15 29	15 33		15 38	15 44	15 49		15 59	16 04	16 08	16 19	16 22		16 29	16 36	16 39	16 43	16 46		16 57	17 04
London Liverpool St	⊖ d																								
Stratford	⊖ d																								
Barking	⊖ d		15 20	15 25	15 35	15 39		15 44	15 50	15 54		16 05	16 10	16 14	16 25	16 28		16 35		16 45	16 49	16 52	16 59	17 03	17 10
Upminster	⊖ d			15 34	15 44	15 48		15 53		16 02		16 14		16 23	16 34			16 45		16 55		17 02	17 07	17 13	
Ockendon	d				15 49							16 19						16 50				17 08			
Chafford Hundred	d				15 53							16 23						16 54				17 12			
West Horndon	d			15 39						16 07					16 39					17 00				17 18	
Laindon	d			15 44		15 56		16 01		16 12					16 44				16 56	17a08			17 16	17a26	
Basildon	d			15 47		15 59		16 04		16 15				16 33	16 47				16 59				17 19		
Dagenham Dock	d		15 25						15 55				16 15			16 33					16 54				17 15
Rainham	d		15 29						15 59				16 19			16 37					16 58				17 19
Purfleet	d		15 34						16 04				16 25			16 43					17 04				17 25
Grays	d		15a40		15 57				16a10			16 27	16a33			16 49		16 59			17 10	17a18			17 31
Tilbury Town	d				16 00							16 30				16 52		17 02			17 13				17 34
East Tilbury	d				16 06							16 36				16 58		17 08			17 19				17 40
Stanford-le-Hope	d				16 10						←	16 40				17 02		17a15			17 23				17 44
Pitsea	d	←		15 51	16 22	16 03				16 19	16 22	16a48			16 51	17a12					17a33		17 23		17a54
Benfleet	d	15 52		15 55	→	16 07		16 11		16 22	16 26			16 40	16 55				17 06				17 27		
Leigh-on-Sea	d	15 56		16 00		16a12		16 15		16 27	16 30			16 45	17 00				17 11				17 32		
Chalkwell	d	15 59		16 03				16 18		16 29	16 33			16 48	17 03				17 14				17 34		
Westcliff	d	16 02		16 05				16 21		16 32	16 36			16 50	17 05				17 16				17 37		
Southend Central	a	16 05		16 08				16 23		16 34	16 41			16 53	17 08				17 19				17 39		
	d			16 08				16 23		16 35				16 53	17 08				17 19				17 39		
Southend East	d			16 10				16 25		16 37				16 55	17 10				17 21				17 41		
Thorpe Bay	d			16 14				16 29		16 39				16 59	17 14				17 24				17 44		
Shoeburyness	a			16 20				16 33		16 44				17 05	17 20				17 31				17 51		

29 August to 7 September

London - Southend Central and Shoeburyness

Network Diagram - see first page of Table I

		CC		CC	CC	CC	CC	CC	CC	CC	CC	CC		CC	CC	CC	CC	CC	CC	CC	CC	CC		CC	CC
London Fenchurch St ⊖	d	17 00		17 02	17 05	17 07	17 10	17 15	17 18	17 20	17 23	17 26		17 30	17 32	17 35	17 37	17 41	17 45	17 47	17 51	17 53		17 56	18 00
Limehouse	d				17 09	17 12	17 15	17 19		17 24	17 28	17 30				17 39	17 42	17 45	17 49	17 52		17 57		18 00	
West Ham ⊖	d					17 17	17 20		17 26	17 29	17 33	17 35			17 40	17 44	17 47	17 50		17 57	17 59			18 05	18 08
London Liverpool St ⊖	d																								
Stratford ⊖	d																								
Barking ⊖	d			17 15	17 19	17 22	17 26			17 35	17 39	17 42			17 46	17 50	17 53	17 56				18 08		18 11	
Upminster ⊖	d			17 24		17 31		17 36	17 40		17 47				17 56		18 03			18 10	18 14				
Ockendon	d			17 29											18 02					18 15					
Chafford Hundred	d			17 34											18 06					18 20					
West Horndon	d					17 36					17 52						18 08					18 21			
Laindon	d				17 35	17a43				17 51	17a59					18 07	18a15					18 27			
Basildon	d				17 39				17 50	17 55						18 10					18 24	18 31			18 35
Dagenham Dock	d						17 31					17 47						18 01						18 16	
Rainham	d						17 35					17 51						18 05						18 20	
Purfleet	d						17 40					17 56						18 11						18 25	
Grays	d			17a40			17 46					18 02			18a13			18 17		18a26				18 31	
Tilbury Town	d						17 50					18 06						18 20						18 35	
East Tilbury	d						17 56					18 12						18 26						18 41	
Stanford-le-Hope	d						18 00					18 16						18 30						18 45	
Pitsea	d				17 42		18a09		17 54	17 58		18a25				18 14		18a40			18 28	18 34		18 57	18 38
Benfleet	d	17 33			17 46			17 52	17 58	18 03				18 08		18 18			18 24		18 32	18 39		→	18 43
Leigh-on-Sea	d	17 38			17 51			17 56	18 02	18 07				18 12		18 23			18 28		18 37	18 43			18 47
Chalkwell	d	17 41			17 53			17 59	18 05	18 10				18 15		18 26			18 31		18 40	18 46			18 50
Westcliff	d	17 43			17 56			18 02	18 08	18 13				18 18		18 28			18 34		18 42	18 49			18 53
Southend Central	a	17 46			17 58			18 04	18 13	18 15				18 20		18 31			18 36		18 45	18 51			18 55
	d	17 46			17 58			18 04		18 15				18 20		18 31			18 36		18 45	18 51			18 55
Southend East	d	17 48			18 00			18 06		18 17				18 22		18 33			18 38		18 47	18 53			18 57
Thorpe Bay	d	17 50			18 03			18 10		18 21				18 26		18 36			18 42		18 50	18 57			19 01
Shoeburyness	a	17 57			18 11			18 16		18 28				18 32		18 43			18 48		18 58	19 03			19 07

		CC	CC	CC	CC	CC	CC	CC		CC	CC	CC	CC	CC	CC	CC	CC	CC		CC	CC	CC	CC	CC	CC
London Fenchurch St ⊖	d	18 02	18 06	18 09			18 12	18 21				18 23	18 27		18 31	18 35	18 42			18 46	18 51	19 00	19 02	19 05	
Limehouse	d	18 06	18 10	18 13			18 16					18 27	18 31		18 35	18 39				18 51	18 55			19 09	
West Ham ⊖	d	18 11		18 18			18 21					18 32	18 36		18 40		18 50			18 56	19 00		19 10		
London Liverpool St ⊖	d																								
Stratford ⊖	d																								
Barking ⊖	d	18 17	18 20	18 24			18 28						18 42		18 46	18 49				19 01	19 06		19 16	19 19	
Upminster ⊖	d	18 27		18 34								18 46	18 51			18 58				19 10			19 26	19 30	
Ockendon	d	18 33										18 51				19 06							19 33		
Chafford Hundred	d	18 38										18 55				19 11							19 39		
West Horndon	d			18 39									18 56							19 15					
Laindon	d		18 37	18 43				18 47					19 01							19 20		19 26			
Basildon	d		18 41	18 47				18 51					19 04				19 12			19 23				19 40	
Dagenham Dock	d						18 33								18 51						19 11				
Rainham	d						18 37								18 55						19 15				
Purfleet	d						18 42								19 01						19 21				
Grays	d	18 42					18 48					19 00			19 07	19a17					19 27		19 46		
Tilbury Town	d	18 46					18 52					19 03			19 10						19 30		19 50		
East Tilbury	d	18 52					18 58					19 09			19 16						19 36		19 56		
Stanford-le-Hope	d	18 56			←	←	19 02					19 13		←	19 20						19 40		20 00		←
Pitsea	d	19 03	18 44	18 50	18 57	19 03	19a11			←	←	19 21	19 08	19 21	19a30			←		19 26	19 48		20a07	19 44	19 48
Benfleet	d	→	18 49	18 54	19 03	19 07		18 58		19 03	19 07	→	19 12	19 25			19 19	19 25		19 30	→	19 33		19 48	19 52
Leigh-on-Sea	d		18 53	18 59	→	→		19 03		19 07	19a14		19 16	→			19 24	19a32		19 35		19 38		19 52	19 56
Chalkwell	d		18 56	19 01				19 06		19 10			19 19				19 27			19 37		19 41		19 55	19 59
Westcliff	d		18 59	19 04				19 08		19 13			19 21				19 29			19 40		19 43		19 58	20 02
Southend Central	a		19 01	19 09				19 11		19 15			19 24				19 32			19 42		19 46		20 00	20 07
	d		19 01					19 11		19 15			19 24				19 32			19 42		19 46		20 00	
Southend East	d		19 03					19 13		19 17			19 26				19 34			19 44		19 48		20 02	
Thorpe Bay	d		19 07					19 16		19 21			19 28				19 37			19 47		19 50		20 06	
Shoeburyness	a		19 13					19 23		19 28			19 35				19 44			19 53		19 57		20 10	

		CC	CC	CC		CC	CC	CC	CC	CC	CC	CC	CC	CC		CC	CC	CC	CC	CC	CC	CC	CC	CC	
London Fenchurch St ⊖	d	19 08	19 11	19 20		19 30		19 32	19 35	19 40	19 50	20 00		20 05		20 10	20 20	20 30		20 35	20 40	20 50	21 00		
Limehouse	d	19 12	19 15	19 24				19 36	19 39	19 44	19 54			20 09		20 14	20 24	20 34		20 39	20 44	20 54			
West Ham ⊖	d	19 17	19 20	19 29				19 41	19 44	19 49	19 59	20 08		20 14		20 19	20 29	20 39		20 44	20 49	20 59	21 08		
London Liverpool St ⊖	d																								
Stratford ⊖	d																								
Barking ⊖	d	19 23	19 26	19 35				19 47	19 50	19 55	20 05	20 14		20 20		20 25	20 35	20 45		20 50	20 55	21 05	21 14		
Upminster ⊖	d		19 35	19 44		19 50		19 56		20 04	20 14	20 23				20 34	20 44	20 54			21 04	21 14	21 23		
Ockendon	d			19 49							20 19						20 49					21 19			
Chafford Hundred	d			19 53							20 23						20 53					21 23			
West Horndon	d		19 40					20 01		20 09						20 39					21 09				
Laindon	d		19 45					20a07		20 14		20 31				20 44		21 02			21 14		21 31		
Basildon	d		19 48			20 00				20 17		20 34				20 47		21 05			21 17		21 34		
Dagenham Dock	d	19 28							19 55					20 25						20 55					
Rainham	d	19 32							19 59					20 29						20 59					
Purfleet	d	19 37							20 04					20 34						21 04					
Grays	d	19a43		19 57					20a10		20 27			20a40			20 57			21a10		21 27			
Tilbury Town	d			20 00							20 30						21 00					21 30			
East Tilbury	d			20 06							20 36						21 06					21 36			
Stanford-le-Hope	d			20 10							20 40						21 10					21 40			
Pitsea	d		19 52	20 18			←			20 21	20 48		←			20 51	21 18		←		21 21	21 48		←	
Benfleet	d		19 56	20 22		20 06	20 22			20 26	20 52	20 41	20 52			20 55	21 22	21 12	21 22		21 25	21 52	21 41	21 52	
Leigh-on-Sea	d		20 00	→		20 11	20 27			20 30	→	20 45	20 56			21 00	→	21 16	21 26		21 30	→	21 45	21 56	
Chalkwell	d		20 03			20 14	20 30			20 33		20 48	20 59			21 03		21 19	21 29		21 33		21 48	21 59	
Westcliff	d		20 06			20 16	20 32			20 36		20 51	21 02			21 05		21 22	21 32		21 35		21 51	22 02	
Southend Central	a		20 08			20 19	20 35			20 38		20 53	21 05			21 08		21 24	21 35		21 38		21 53	22 05	
	d		20 08			20 19				20 38		20 53				21 08		21 24			21 38		21 53		
Southend East	d		20 10			20 21				20 40		20 55				21 10		21 26			21 40		21 55		
Thorpe Bay	d		20 14			20 25				20 44		20 59				21 14		21 30			21 44		21 59		
Shoeburyness	a		20 18			20 29				20 48		21 03				21 18		21 34			21 48		22 03		

29 August to 7 September

London - Southend Central and Shoeburyness

Network Diagram - see first page of Table I

		CC	CC	CC	CC	CC	CC	CC	CC	CC		CC	CC	CC	CC	CC	CC	CC	CC	CC		CC	CC	CC	CC
London Fenchurch St ⊖	d	21 05	21 10	21 20	21 30		21 35	21 40	21 50	22 00			22 05	22 11	22 20	22 35	22 40	22 50	23 00			23 05	23 10		23 20
Limehouse	d	21 09	21 14	21 24	21 34		21 39	21 44	21 54				22 09	22 15	22 24	22 39	22 44	22 54				23 09	23 14		23 24
West Ham ⊖	d	21 14	21 19	21 29	21 39		21 44	21 49	21 59	22 10			22 15	22 22	22 31	22 45	22 51	23 01	23 10			23 15	23 21		23 31
London Liverpool St ⊖	d																								
Stratford ⊖	d																								
Barking ⊖	d	21 20	21 25	21 35	21 45		21 50	21 55	22 05	22 15			22 21	22 27	22 36	22 51	22 56	23 06	23 15			23 21	23 26		23 36
Upminster ⊖	d		21 34	21 44	21 54			22 04	22 14	22 24				22 36	22 45		23 05	23 15	23 24				23 35		23 45
Ockendon	d			21 49					22 19						22 50			23 20							23 50
Chafford Hundred	d			21 53					22 23						22 54			23 24							23 54
West Horndon	d		21 39					22 09						22 41			23 10						23 40		
Laindon	d		21 44		22 02			22 14		22 33				22 47			23 16		23 33				23 46		
Basildon	d		21 47		22 05			22 17		22 36				22 50			23 19		23 36				23 49		
Dagenham Dock	d	21 25					21 55						22 26			22 56						23 26			
Rainham	d	21 29					21 59						22 30			23 00						23 30			
Purfleet	d	21 34					22 04						22 35			23 05						23 35			
Grays	d	21a40		21 57			22a10		22 27				22a41		22 58	23a11		23 28				23 43			23 58
Tilbury Town	d			22 00					22 30						23 02			23 32				23 46			00 02
East Tilbury	d			22 06					22 36						23 08			23 38				23 52			00 07
Stanford-le-Hope	d			22 10					22 40						23 12			23 42				23 56		←	00 11
Pitsea	d		21 51	22 18		←		22 21	22 48			←		22 53	23 19		23 23	23 49		←		00 07	23 53	00 07	00 20
Benfleet	d		21 55	22 22	22 12	22 22		22 25	22 52	22 42		22 52		22 57	23 23		23 27	23 53	23 42	23 53		→	23 57	00 11	00 24
Leigh-on-Sea	d		22 00	→	22 16	22 26		22 30	→	22 47		22 56		23 02	23 28		23 32	→	23 47	23 58			00 02	00 16	00 28
Chalkwell	d		22 03		22 19	22 29		22 33		22 50		22 59		23 05	23 31		23 35		23 50	00 01			00 05	00 19	00 31
Westcliff	d		22 05		22 22	22 32		22 35		22 52		23 02		23 07	23 33		23 37		23 52	00 03			00 07	00 21	00 34
Southend Central	a		22 08		22 24	22 35		22 38		22 55		23 05		23 10	23 36		23 40		23 55	00 06			00 10	00 24	00 37
	d		22 08		22 24			22 38		22 55		23 05		23 10	23 36		23 40		23 55	00 06			00 10	00 24	00 37
Southend East	d		22 10		22 26			22 40		22 57		23 07		23 12	23 39		23 43		23 58	00 09			00 13	00 27	00 39
Thorpe Bay	d		22 14		22 30			22 44		23 00		23 10		23 15	23 42		23 46		00 01	00 12			00 16	00 30	00 43
Shoeburyness	a		22 18		22 34			22 48		23 05		23 15		23 22	23 49		23 53		00 08	00 19			00 23	00 37	00 49

		CC	CC	CC
London Fenchurch St ⊖	d	23 37	23 40	23 50
Limehouse	d	23 41	23 44	23 54
West Ham ⊖	d	23 47	23 51	00 01
London Liverpool St ⊖	d			
Stratford ⊖	d			
Barking ⊖	d	23 53	23 57	00 07
Upminster ⊖	d		00 06	00 16
Ockendon	d			00 21
Chafford Hundred	d			00 25
West Horndon	d		00 11	
Laindon	d		00 17	
Basildon	d		00 20	
Dagenham Dock	d	23 58		
Rainham	d	00 02		
Purfleet	d	00 07		
Grays	d	00a13		00 29
Tilbury Town	d			00 33
East Tilbury	d			00 39
Stanford-le-Hope	d			00 43
Pitsea	d		00 24	00 50
Benfleet	d		00 28	00 54
Leigh-on-Sea	d		00 32	00 59
Chalkwell	d		00 35	01 02
Westcliff	d		00 38	01 04
Southend Central	a		00 41	01 07
	d		00 41	01 07
Southend East	d		00 44	01 10
Thorpe Bay	d		00 47	01 13
Shoeburyness	a		00 54	01 20

London - Southend Central and Shoeburyness

Network Diagram - see first page of Table 1

		CC	CC	CC	CC	CC	CC	CC	CC	CC		CC	CC	CC	CC	CC	CC	CC	CC	CC		CC	CC	CC	CC
		MO		MX	MX	MO		MX	MX	MO			MX	MX	MX	MX	MO		MX	MX		MX	MX	MO	
		A	B			A	B			A		B					A	B						A	B
London Fenchurch St ⊖	d	22p50	22p50	22p50	23p00				23p05	23p10		23p10	23p10		23p20	23p35	23p40	23p40	23p40	23p50		00 01		00 10	00 10
Limehouse	d	22p54	22p54	22p54					23p09	23p14		23p14	23p14		23p24	23p39	23p44	23p44	23p44	23p54				00 14	00 14
West Ham ⊖	d	22p59	23p01	22p59	23p08				23p14	23p19		23p21	23p19		23p29	23p44	23p49	23p51	23p49	23p59		00 09		00 19	00 21
London Liverpool St ⊖	d																								
Stratford ⊖	d																								
Barking ⊖	d	23p04	23p06	23p05	23p14				23p20	23p24		23p26	23p25		23p35	23p50	23p54	23p56	23p55	00 05		00 15		00 24	00 26
Upminster ⊖	d	23p12	23p14	23p14	23p23					23p32		23p35	23p34		23p44		00 02	00 05	00 04	00 14		00 24		00 32	00 35
Ockendon	d	23p18	23p19	23p19											23p49					00 19					
Chafford Hundred	d	23p21	23p23	23p23											23p53					00 23					
West Horndon	d									23p37		23p40	23p39				00 07	00 10	00 09					00 37	00 40
Laindon	d				23p31					23p42		23p44	23p44				00 12	00 14	00 16			00 32		00 42	00 44
Basildon	d				23p34					23p45		23p47	23p47				00 15	00 17	00 19			00 35		00 45	00 47
Dagenham Dock	d								23p25							23p55									
Rainham	d								23p29							23p59									
Purfleet	d								23p34							00 04									
Grays	d	23p25	23p27	23p27					23p42						23p57	00a10				00 27					
Tilbury Town	d	23p28	23p30	23p30					23p45						00 01					00 30					
East Tilbury	d	23p34	23p35	23p36					23p51						00 06					00 36					
Stanford-le-Hope	d	23p37	23p39	23p40					23p55					←	00 10					00 40					
Pitsea	d	23p45	23p47	23p48		←	←	←	00 06	23p49		23p51	23p52	00 06	00 18		00 19	00 21	00 22	00 48			←	00 49	00 51
Benfleet	d	23p49	23p50	23p52	23p41	23p49	23p50	23p52	→	23p52		23p55	23p56	00 10	00 22		00 22	00 25	00 26	00 52		00 42	00 52	00 52	00 55
Leigh-on-Sea	d	→	→	→	23p45	23p53	23p55	23p56		23p57		23p59	23p59	00 15	00 27		00 27	00 29	00 31	→		00 46	00 56	00 57	00 59
Chalkwell	d				23p48	23p56	23p57	23p59		23p59		00 02	00 03	00 18	00 30		00 29	00 32	00 34			00 49	00 59	00 59	01 02
Westcliff	d				23p51	23p58	23p59	00 02		00 02		00 04	00 06	00 20	00 32		00 32	00 34	00 36			00 52	01 02	01 02	01 04
Southend Central	a				23p54	00 01	00 03	00 05		00 05		00 08	00 09	00 23	00 35		00 35	00 38	00 39			00 55	01 05	01 05	01 07
	d				23p54	00 01	00 03	00 05		00 06		00 08	00 09	00 23	00 35		00 36	00 38	00 40			00 55	01 05	01 06	01 07
Southend East	d				23p56	00 03	00 05	00 07		00 08		00 11	00 11	00 26	00 38		00 38	00 41	00 42			00 57	01 07	01 08	01 10
Thorpe Bay	d				23p59	00 06	00 07	00 11		00 10		00 12	00 15	00 29	00 41		00 40	00 42	00 46			01 01	01 11	01 11	01 11
Shoeburyness	a				00 06	00 13	00 15	00 17		00 18		00 21	00 21	00 36	00 48		00 48	00 51	00 52			01 07	01 17	01 18	01 21

		CC	CC	CC	CC	CC		CC	CC	CC	CC	CC	CC	CC	CC	CC		CC	CC	CC	CC	CC	CC	CC	CC
		MX	MX																						
				B																					
London Fenchurch St ⊖	d	00 15	00 25	00 50		05 10			05 40				06 10	06 20	06 40			06 44	06 48	07 00	07 09	07 13	07 15	07 30	07 40
Limehouse	d	00 19	00 29	00 54		05 14			05 44				06 14	06 24	06 44			06 48	06 52		07 13				07 44
West Ham ⊖	d	00 24	00 34	01 01		05 19			05 49				06 19	06 29	06 49			06 53	06 57	07 08	07 18		07 23	07 38	07 49
London Liverpool St ⊖	d																								
Stratford ⊖	d																								
Barking ⊖	d	00 30	00 40	01 06		05 25		05 39	05 55	05 45	06 05		06 25	06 35	06 55	06 50		07 00	07 03	07 14	07 25	07 26	07 29	07 44	07 55
Upminster ⊖	d		00 49	01 15	05 28	05 34		05 48	06 04			06 31	06 34		07 04			07 10		07 23	07 34		07 38	07 53	08 04
Ockendon	d				05 33			05 56				06 36						07 15					07 45		
Chafford Hundred	d				05 37			06 00				06 40						07 19					07 49		
West Horndon	d		00 54	01 20		05 39			06 09				06 39		07 09						07 39				08 09
Laindon	d		00 59	01 24		05 44			06 14				06 45		07 14						07 44				08 14
Basildon	d		01 02	01 27		05 47			06 17				06 48		07 17					07 33	07 47			08 03	08 17
Dagenham Dock	d	00 35								05 50	06 10			06 40		06 55			07 08			07 31			
Rainham	d	00 39								05 54	06 14			06 44		06 59			07 12			07 35			
Purfleet	d	00 44								05 59	06 19			06 49		07 04			07 17			07 40			
Grays	d	00a50			05a41			06a05		06 05	06 25	06a44		06 55		07 10		07a23	07 25			07 46	07 54		
Tilbury Town	d									06 08	06 28			06 58		07 13			07 28				07 58		
East Tilbury	d									06 14	06 34			07 04		07 19			07 34				08 04		
Stanford-le-Hope	d									06 18	06 38			07 08		07 23			07 38			07 56	08 08		
Pitsea	d		01 06	01 31		05 51			06 21	06 26	06a46		06 51	07 18	07 22	07a31			07a46		07 51	08a03	08a15		08 21
Benfleet	d		01 10	01 35		05 55			06 25	06 31			06 55	07 22	07 26					07 39	07 55			08 09	08 25
Leigh-on-Sea	d		01 14	01 39		06 00			06 30	06 35			07 00	07 27	07 30					07 44	07 59			08 14	08 30
Chalkwell	d		01 17	01 42		06 03			06 33	06 38			07 03	07 30	07 33					07 47	08 02			08 17	08 33
Westcliff	d		01 20	01 44		06 05			06 35	06 41			07 05	07 32	07 36					07 49	08 05			08 19	08 35
Southend Central	a		01 23	01 48		06 08			06 38	06 43			07 08	07 35	07 38					07 52	08 07			08 22	08 38
	d		01 23	01 48		06 08			06 38	06 43			07 08	07 35	07 38					07 52	08 07			08 22	08 38
Southend East	d		01 25	01 51		06 10			06 40	06 45			07 10	07 37	07 40					07 54	08 09			08 24	08 40
Thorpe Bay	d		01 29	01 53		06 14			06 44	06 49			07 14	07 40	07 44					07 58	08 13			08 28	08 44
Shoeburyness	a		01 35	02 01		06 18			06 48	06 53			07 20	07 45	07 48					08 02	08 17			08 32	08 48

A from 17 September

B 10 September

London - Southend Central and Shoeburyness

Network Diagram - see first page of Table 1

		CC		CC	CC	CC	CC	CC	CC	CC	CC	CC		CC	CC	CC	CC	CC	CC	CC	CC	CC		CC	CC
London Fenchurch St ⊖	d	07 43		07 48	07 50	08 00		08 03	08 09	08 14	08 20	08 30			08 40	08 50	08 54	09 00		09 10	09 16	09 20		09 30	
Limehouse	d				07 54			08 07	08 13		08 24				08 44	08 54				09 14	09 20	09 24			
West Ham ⊖	d	07 53			07 59	08 08		08 12	08 18	08 23	08 29	08 38			08 49	08 59		09 08		09 19	09 25	09 29		09 38	
London Liverpool St ⊖	d																								
Stratford ⊖	d																								
Barking ⊖	d	07 58			08 05	08 14		08 18	08 24	08 30	08 37	08 45			08 55	09 07	09 09	09 16		09 25	09 31	09 35		09 44	
Upminster ⊖	d			08 09	08 15	08 23			08 33	08 41		08 54			09 04		09 18	09 25		09 34		09 45		09 53	
Ockendon	d			08 16						08 46							09 23					09 50			
Chafford Hundred	d			08 20						08 50							09 27					09 54			
West Horndon	d				08 20				08 38						09 09					09 39					
Laindon	d				08a26	08 31			08 44			09 03			09 14			09 34		09 44				10 01	
Basildon	d					08 34			08 47			09 06			09 17			09 37		09 47				10 04	
Dagenham Dock	d	08 03						08 23			08 42					09 12					09 36				
Rainham	d	08 07						08 27			08 46					09 16					09 40				
Purfleet	d	08 13						08 33			08 51					09 21					09 45				
Grays	d	08 18		08 25				08 38		08a54	08 57					09 27	09a31				09 51	09 58			
Tilbury Town	d	08 22						08 42			09 00					09 30					09 54	10 02			
East Tilbury	d	08 28						08 48			09 06					09 36					10 00	10 08			
Stanford-le-Hope	d	08 32		08 35			←	08 52			09 10			←		09 40					10 04	10 12			
Pitsea	d	08 41		08a44		08 38	08 41	08a59	08 51		09 18	09 09		09 18	09 21	09 48			←	09 51	10 12	10 25			←
Benfleet	d	→				08 42	08 45		08 55		→	09 13		09 22	09 26	09 52		09 43	09 52	09 55	10 16	→		10 11	10 16
Leigh-on-Sea	d					08 46	08 50		08 59			09 18		09 27	09 30	→		09 48	09 57	10 00	→			10 15	10 20
Chalkwell	d					08 49	08 53		09 02			09 21		09 30	09 33			09 51	10 00	10 03				10 18	10 23
Westcliff	d					08 52	08 55		09 05			09 23		09 32	09 36			09 53	10 02	10 05				10 21	10 26
Southend Central	a					08 54	08 58		09 08			09 26		09 35	09 38			09 56	10 05	10 08				10 23	10 29
	d					*08 55*			*09 08*			*09 26*			*09 38*			*09 56*		*10 08*				*10 23*	
Southend East	d					*08 57*			*09 10*			*09 28*			*09 40*			*09 58*		*10 10*				*10 25*	
Thorpe Bay	d					*09 00*			*09 14*			*09 32*			*09 44*			*10 02*		*10 14*				*10 29*	
Shoeburyness	a					09 05			09 18			09 36			09 48			10 06		10 18				10 33	

		CC	CC	CC	CC	CC	CC	CC		CC	CC	CC	CC	CC	CC	CC	CC	CC		CC	CC	CC	CC	CC	CC
London Fenchurch St ⊖	d	09 35	09 40		09 50	10 00		10 05		10 10	10 20	10 30		10 35	10 40	10 50	11 00			11 05	11 10	11 20	11 30		11 35
Limehouse	d	09 39	09 44		09 54			10 09		10 14	10 24			10 39	10 44	10 54				11 09	11 14	11 24			11 39
West Ham ⊖	d	09 44	09 49		09 59	10 08		10 14		10 19	10 29	10 38		10 44	10 49	10 59	11 08			11 14	11 19	11 29	11 38		11 44
London Liverpool St ⊖	d																								
Stratford ⊖	d																								
Barking ⊖	d	09 50	09 55		10 05	10 14		10 20		10 25	10 35	10 44		10 50	10 55	11 05	11 14			11 20	11 25	11 35	11 44		11 50
Upminster ⊖	d		10 04		10 14	10 23				10 34	10 44	10 53			11 04	11 14	11 23				11 34	11 44	11 53		
Ockendon	d				10 19						10 49					11 19						11 49			
Chafford Hundred	d				10 23						10 53					11 23						11 53			
West Horndon	d		10 09							10 39					11 09						11 39				
Laindon	d		10 14			10 31				10 44		11 01			11 14		11 31				11 44		12 01		
Basildon	d		10 17			10 34				10 47		11 04			11 17		11 34				11 47		12 04		
Dagenham Dock	d	09 55						10 25						10 55						11 25					11 55
Rainham	d	09 59						10 29						10 59						11 29					11 59
Purfleet	d	10 04						10 34						11 04						11 34					12 04
Grays	d	10a10			10 27			10a40			10 57			11a10		11 27				11a40		11 57			12a10
Tilbury Town	d				10 30						11 00					11 30						12 00			
East Tilbury	d				10 36						11 06					11 36						12 06			
Stanford-le-Hope	d			←	10 40						11 10					11 40						12 10			
Pitsea	d		10 21	10 25	10 48		←			10 51	11 18		←		11 21	11 48		←			11 51	12 18		←	
Benfleet	d		10 25	10 29	10 52	10 41	10 52			10 55	11 22	11 11	11 22		11 25	11 52	11 41	11 52			11 55	12 22	12 11	12 22	
Leigh-on-Sea	d		10 30	10 34	→	10 45	10 56			11 00	→	11 15	11 26		11 30	→	11 45	11 57			12 00	→	12 15	12 26	
Chalkwell	d		10 33	10 37		10 48	10 59			11 03		11 18	11 29		11 33		11 48	12 00			12 03		12 18	12 29	
Westcliff	d		10 35	10 39		10 51	11 02			11 05		11 21	11 32		11 35		11 51	12 02			12 05		12 21	12 32	
Southend Central	a		10 38	10 42		10 53	11 05			11 08		11 23	11 35		11 38		11 53	12 05			12 08		12 23	12 35	
	d		10 38			10 53				11 08		11 23			11 38		11 53				12 08		12 23		
Southend East	d		10 40			10 55				11 10		11 25			11 40		11 55				12 10		12 25		
Thorpe Bay	d		10 44			10 59				11 14		11 29			11 44		11 59				12 14		12 29		
Shoeburyness	a		10 48			11 03				11 18		11 33			11 48		12 03				12 18		12 33		

		CC	CC	CC		CC	CC	CC	CC	CC	CC	CC	CC	CC		CC	CC	CC	CC	CC	CC	CC	CC	CC	
London Fenchurch St ⊖	d	11 40	11 50	12 00			12 05	12 10	12 20	12 30		12 35	12 40	12 50		13 00		13 05	13 10	13 20	13 30		13 35	13 40	
Limehouse	d	11 44	11 54				12 09	12 14	12 24			12 39	12 44	12 54				13 09	13 14	13 24			13 39	13 44	
West Ham ⊖	d	11 49	11 59	12 08			12 14	12 19	12 29	12 38		12 44	12 49	12 59		13 08		13 14	13 19	13 29	13 38		13 44	13 49	
London Liverpool St ⊖	d																								
Stratford ⊖	d																								
Barking ⊖	d	11 55	12 05	12 14			12 20	12 25	12 35	12 44		12 50	12 55	13 05		13 14		13 20	13 25	13 35	13 44		13 50	13 55	
Upminster ⊖	d	12 04	12 14	12 23				12 34	12 44	12 53			13 04	13 14		13 23			13 34	13 44	13 53			14 04	
Ockendon	d		12 19						12 49					13 19						13 49					
Chafford Hundred	d		12 23						12 53					13 23						13 53					
West Horndon	d	12 09						12 39					13 09						13 39					14 09	
Laindon	d	12 14		12 31				12 44		13 01			13 14			13 31			13 44		14 01			14 14	
Basildon	d	12 17		12 34				12 47		13 04			13 17			13 34			13 47		14 04			14 17	
Dagenham Dock	d						12 25					12 55						13 25					13 55		
Rainham	d						12 29					12 59						13 29					13 59		
Purfleet	d						12 34					13 04						13 34					14 04		
Grays	d		12 27				12a40		12 57			13a10		13 27				13a40		13 57			14a10		
Tilbury Town	d		12 30						13 00					13 30						14 00					
East Tilbury	d		12 36						13 06					13 36						14 06					
Stanford-le-Hope	d		12 40						13 10					13 40						14 10					
Pitsea	d	12 21	12 48			←		12 51	13 18		←		13 21	13 48			←		13 51	14 18		←		14 21	
Benfleet	d	12 25	12 52	12 41		12 52		12 55	13 22	13 11	13 22		13 25	13 52		13 41	13 52		13 55	14 22	14 11	14 22		14 25	
Leigh-on-Sea	d	12 30	→	12 45		12 57		13 00	→	13 15	13 27		13 30	→		13 45	13 57		14 00	→	14 15	14 26		14 30	
Chalkwell	d	12 33		12 48		13 00		13 03		13 18	13 30		13 33			13 48	14 00		14 03		14 18	14 29		14 33	
Westcliff	d	12 35		12 51		13 02		13 05		13 21	13 32		13 35			13 51	14 02		14 05		14 21	14 32		14 35	
Southend Central	a	12 38		12 53		13 05		13 08		13 23	13 35		13 38			13 53	14 05		14 08		14 23	14 35		14 38	
	d	12 38		12 53				13 08		13 23			13 38			13 53			14 08		14 23			14 38	
Southend East	d	12 40		12 55				13 10		13 25			13 40			13 55			14 10		14 25			14 40	
Thorpe Bay	d	12 44		12 59				13 14		13 29			13 44			13 59			14 14		14 29			14 44	
Shoeburyness	a	12 48		13 03				13 18		13 33			13 48			14 03			14 18		14 33			14 48	

Table 1

London - Southend Central and Shoeburyness

Mondays to Fridays

from 10 September

Network Diagram - see first page of Table 1

	CC	CC	CC	CC	CC	CC	CC	CC	CC		CC	CC	CC	CC	CC	CC	CC	CC	CC		CC	CC	CC	CC
London Fenchurch St 7 ⊖ d	13 50	14 00		14 05	14 10	14 20	14 30		14 35		14 40	14 50	15 00		15 05	15 10	15 20	15 25	15 30		15 35	15 40		15 50
Limehouse d	13 54			14 09	14 14	14 24			14 39		14 44	14 54			15 09	15 14	15 24				15 39	15 44		15 54
West Ham ⊖ d	13 59	14 08		14 14	14 19	14 29	14 38		14 44		14 49	14 59	15 08		15 14	15 19	15 29	15 33	15 38		15 44	15 49		15 59
London Liverpool St 15 ⊖ d																								
Stratford 7 ⊖ d																								
Barking ⊖ d	14 05	14 14		14 20	14 25	14 35	14 44		14 50		14 55	15 05	15 14		15 20	15 25	15 35	15 39	15 44		15 50	15 54		16 05
Upminster ⊖ d	14 14	14 23			14 34	14 44	14 53				15 04	15 14	15 23			15 34	15 44	15 48	15 53			16 02		16 14
Ockendon d	14 19					14 49						15 19					15 49							16 19
Chafford Hundred d	14 23					14 53						15 23					15 53							16 23
West Horndon d					14 39						15 09					15 39						16 07		
Laindon d		14 31			14 44		15 01				15 14		15 31			15 44		15 56	16 01			16 12		
Basildon d		14 34			14 47		15 04				15 17		15 34			15 47		15 59	16 04			16 15		
Dagenham Dock d				14 25					14 55						15 25						15 55			
Rainham d				14 29					14 59						15 29						15 59			
Purfleet d				14 34					15 04						15 34						16 04			
Grays d	14 27			14a40		14 57			15a10			15 27			15a40		15 57				16a10			16 27
Tilbury Town 3 d	14 30					15 00						15 30					16 00							16 30
East Tilbury d	14 36					15 06						15 36					16 06							16 36
Stanford-le-Hope d	14 40					15 10						15 40					16 10						←	16 40
Pitsea d	14 48		←		14 51	15 18		←			15 21	15 48		←		15 51	16 22	16 03				16 19	16 22	16a48
Benfleet d	14 52	14 41	14 52		14 55	15 22	15 11	15 22			15 25	15 52	15 41	15 52		15 55	→	16 07	16 11			16 22	16 26	
Leigh-on-Sea d	→	14 45	14 56		15 00	→	15 15	15 26			15 30	→	15 45	15 56		16 00		16a12	16 15			16 27	16 30	
Chalkwell d		14 48	14 59		15 03		15 18	15 29			15 33		15 48	15 59		16 03			16 18			16 29	16 33	
Westcliff d		14 51	15 02		15 05		15 21	15 32			15 35		15 51	16 02		16 05			16 21			16 32	16 36	
Southend Central a		14 53	15 05		15 08		15 23	15 35			15 38		15 53	16 05		16 08			16 23			16 34	16 41	
d		14 53			15 08		15 23				15 38		15 53			16 08			16 23			16 35		
Southend East d		14 55			15 10		15 25				15 40		15 55			16 10			16 25			16 37		
Thorpe Bay d		14 59			15 14		15 29				15 44		15 59			16 14			16 29			16 39		
Shoeburyness a		15 03			15 18		15 33				15 48		16 03			16 20			16 33			16 44		

	CC	CC	CC	CC	CC		CC	CC	CC	CC	CC	CC	CC	CC	CC		CC	CC	CC	CC	CC	CC	CC	CC
London Fenchurch St 7 ⊖ d	15 55	16 00	16 10	16 13	16 20		16 28	16 30	16 34	16 37	16 45	16 48	16 55	17 00	17 02		17 05	17 07	17 10	17 15	17 18	17 20	17 23	17 26
Limehouse d	15 59		16 14	16 17	16 24			16 34	16 38	16 41	16 49	16 52	16 59				17 09	17 12	17 15	17 19		17 24	17 28	17 30
West Ham ⊖ d	16 04	16 08	16 19	16 22	16 29		16 36	16 39	16 43	16 46		16 57	17 04					17 17	17 20		17 26	17 29	17 33	17 35
London Liverpool St 15 ⊖ d																								
Stratford 7 ⊖ d																								
Barking ⊖ d	16 10	16 14	16 25	16 28	16 35			16 45	16 49	16 52	16 59	17 03	17 10		17 15		17 19	17 22	17 26			17 35	17 39	17 42
Upminster ⊖ d		16 23	16 34		16 45			16 55		17 02	17 07	17 13			17 24			17 31		17 36	17 40		17 47	
Ockendon d					16 50					17 08					17 29									
Chafford Hundred d					16 54					17 12					17 34									
West Horndon d			16 39					17 00				17 18						17 36					17 52	
Laindon d			16 44				16 56	17a08			17 16	17a26					17 35	17a43				17 51	17a59	
Basildon d		16 33	16 47				16 59				17 19						17 39				17 50	17 55		
Dagenham Dock d	16 15			16 33					16 54				17 15						17 31					17 47
Rainham d	16 19			16 37					16 58				17 19						17 35					17 51
Purfleet d	16 25			16 43					17 04				17 25						17 40					17 56
Grays d	16a33			16 49	16 59				17 10	17a18			17 31		17a40				17 46					18 02
Tilbury Town 3 d				16 52	17 02				17 13				17 34						17 50					18 06
East Tilbury d				16 58	17 08				17 19				17 40						17 56					18 12
Stanford-le-Hope d				17 02	17a15				17 23				17 44						18 00					18 16
Pitsea d			16 51	17a12					17a33		17 23		17a54				17 42		18a09		17 54	17 58		18a25
Benfleet d		16 40	16 55				17 06				17 27			17 33			17 46			17 52	17 58	18 03		
Leigh-on-Sea d		16 45	17 00				17 11				17 32			17 38			17 51			17 56	18 02	18 07		
Chalkwell d		16 48	17 03				17 14				17 34			17 41			17 53			17 59	18 05	18 10		
Westcliff d		16 50	17 05				17 16				17 37			17 43			17 56			18 02	18 08	18 13		
Southend Central a		16 53	17 08				17 19				17 39			17 46			17 58			18 04	18 13	18 15		
d		16 53	17 08				17 19				17 39			17 46			17 58			18 04		18 15		
Southend East d		16 55	17 10				17 21				17 41			17 48			18 00			18 06		18 17		
Thorpe Bay d		16 59	17 14				17 24				17 44			17 50			18 03			18 10		18 21		
Shoeburyness a		17 05	17 20				17 31				17 51			17 57			18 11			18 16		18 28		

	CC		CC	CC	CC	CC	CC	CC	CC	CC	CC		CC	CC	CC	CC	CC	CC	CC	CC	CC		CC	CC
London Fenchurch St 7 ⊖ d	17 30		17 32	17 35	17 37	17 41	17 45	17 47	17 51	17 53	17 56		18 00	18 02	18 06	18 09			18 12	18 21				18 23
Limehouse d				17 39	17 42	17 45	17 49	17 52		17 57	18 00			18 06	18 10	18 13			18 16					18 27
West Ham ⊖ d			17 40	17 44	17 47	17 50		17 57	17 59		18 05		18 08	18 11		18 18			18 21					18 32
London Liverpool St 15 ⊖ d																								
Stratford 7 ⊖ d																								
Barking ⊖ d			17 46	17 50	17 53	17 56				18 08	18 11			18 17	18 20	18 24			18 28					
Upminster ⊖ d			17 56		18 03			18 10	18 14					18 27		18 34								18 46
Ockendon d			18 02					18 15						18 33										18 51
Chafford Hundred d			18 06					18 20						18 38										18 55
West Horndon d					18 08					18 21						18 39								
Laindon d				18 07	18a15					18 27					18 37	18 43				18 47				
Basildon d				18 10					18 24	18 31			18 35		18 41	18 47				18 51				
Dagenham Dock d						18 01					18 16								18 33					
Rainham d						18 05					18 20								18 37					
Purfleet d						18 11					18 25								18 42					
Grays d			18a13			18 17		18a26			18 31			18 42					18 48					19 00
Tilbury Town 3 d						18 20					18 35			18 46					18 52					19 03
East Tilbury d						18 26					18 41			18 52					18 58					19 09
Stanford-le-Hope d						18 30					18 45			18 56			←	←	19 02					19 13
Pitsea d				18 14		18a40			18 28	18 34	18 57		18 38	19 03	18 44	18 50	18 57	19 03	19a11		←		←	19 21
Benfleet d	18 08			18 18			18 24		18 32	18 39	→		18 43	→	18 49	18 54	19 03	19 07		18 58	19 03		19 07	→
Leigh-on-Sea d	18 12			18 23			18 28		18 37	18 43			18 47		18 53	18 59	→	→		19 03	19 07		19a14	
Chalkwell d	18 15			18 26			18 31		18 40	18 46			18 50		18 56	19 01				19 06	19 10			
Westcliff d	18 18			18 28			18 34		18 42	18 49			18 53		18 59	19 04				19 08	19 13			
Southend Central a	18 20			18 31			18 36		18 45	18 51			18 55		19 01	19 09				19 11	19 15			
d	18 20			18 31			18 36		18 45	18 51			18 55		19 01					19 11	19 15			
Southend East d	18 22			18 33			18 38		18 47	18 53			18 57		19 03					19 13	19 17			
Thorpe Bay d	18 26			18 36			18 42		18 50	18 57			19 01		19 07					19 16	19 21			
Shoeburyness a	18 32			18 43			18 48		18 58	19 03			19 07		19 13					19 23	19 28			

Table 1

London - Southend Central and Shoeburyness

Mondays to Fridays

from 10 September

Network Diagram - see first page of Table 1

	CC	CC	CC	CC	CC	CC	CC		CC	CC	CC	CC	CC	CC	CC	CC	CC		CC	CC	CC	CC	CC	CC
London Fenchurch St 7 ⊖ d	18 27		18 31	18 35	18 42		18 46		18 51	19 00	19 02	19 05		19 08	19 11	19 20	19 30			19 32	19 35	19 40	19 50	20 00
Limehouse d	18 31		18 35	18 39			18 51		18 55			19 09		19 12	19 15	19 24				19 36	19 39	19 44	19 54	
West Ham ⊖ d	18 36		18 40		18 50		18 56		19 00		19 10			19 17	19 20	19 29				19 41	19 44	19 49	19 59	20 08
London Liverpool St 15 ⊖ d																								
Stratford 7 ⊖ d																								
Barking ⊖ d	18 42		18 46	18 49			19 01		19 06		19 16	19 19		19 23	19 26	19 35				19 47	19 50	19 55	20 05	20 14
Upminster ⊖ d	18 51			18 58			19 10				19 26	19 30			19 35	19 44	19 50			19 56		20 04	20 14	20 23
Ockendon d				19 06							19 33					19 49							20 19	
Chafford Hundred d				19 11							19 39					19 53							20 23	
West Horndon d	18 56						19 15								19 40					20 01		20 09		
Laindon d	19 01						19 20			19 26					19 45					20a07		20 14		20 31
Basildon d	19 04				19 12		19 23					19 40			19 48		20 00					20 17		20 34
Dagenham Dock d			18 51						19 11					19 28							19 55			
Rainham d			18 55						19 15					19 32							19 59			
Purfleet d			19 01						19 21					19 37							20 04			
Grays d			19 07	19a17					19 27		19 46			19a43		19 57					20a10		20 27	
Tilbury Town 3 d			19 10						19 30		19 50					20 00							20 30	
East Tilbury d			19 16						19 36		19 56					20 06							20 36	
Stanford-le-Hope d		←	19 20						19 40		20 00		←			20 10							20 40	
Pitsea d	19 08	19 21	19a30			←	19 26		19 48		20a07	19 44	19 48		19 52	20 18			←			20 21	20 48	
Benfleet d	19 12	19 25			19 19	19 25	19 30		→	19 33		19 48	19 52		19 56	20 22	20 06		20 22			20 26	20 52	20 41
Leigh-on-Sea d	19 16	→			19 24	19a32	19 35			19 38		19 52	19 56		20 00	→	20 11		20 27			20 30	→	20 45
Chalkwell d	19 19				19 27		19 37			19 41		19 55	19 59		20 03		20 14		20 30			20 33		20 48
Westcliff d	19 21				19 29		19 40			19 43		19 58	20 02		20 06		20 16		20 32			20 36		20 51
Southend Central a	19 24				19 32		19 42			19 46		20 00	20 07		20 08		20 19		20 35			20 38		20 53
d	19 24				19 32		19 42			19 46		20 00			20 08		20 19					20 38		20 53
Southend East d	19 26				19 34		19 44			19 48		20 02			20 10		20 21					20 40		20 55
Thorpe Bay d	19 28				19 37		19 47			19 50		20 06			20 14		20 25					20 44		20 59
Shoeburyness a	19 35				19 44		19 53			19 57		20 10			20 18		20 29					20 48		21 03

	CC	CC	CC		CC	CC	CC	CC	CC	CC	CC	CC	CC		CC	CC	CC	CC	CC	CC	CC	CC	CC	
London Fenchurch St 7 ⊖ d		20 05	20 10		20 20	20 30			20 40	20 50	21 00		21 05		21 10	21 20	21 30			21 40	21 50	22 00		
Limehouse d		20 09	20 14		20 24	20 34			20 44	20 54			21 09		21 14	21 24	21 34			21 44	21 54			
West Ham ⊖ d		20 14	20 19		20 29	20 39			20 49	20 59	21 08		21 14		21 19	21 29	21 39			21 49	21 59	22 08		
London Liverpool St 15 ⊖ d								20 35											21 35					
Stratford 7 ⊖ d								20 43											21 43					
Barking ⊖ d		20 20	20 25		20 35	20 45		20 50	20 55	21 05	21 14		21 20		21 25	21 35	21 45		21 50	21 55	22 05	22 14		
Upminster ⊖ d			20 34		20 44	20 54			21 04	21 14	21 23				21 34	21 44	21 54			22 04	22 14	22 23		
Ockendon d					20 49					21 19						21 49					22 19			
Chafford Hundred d					20 53					21 23						21 53					22 23			
West Horndon d			20 39						21 09						21 39					22 09				
Laindon d			20 44			21 02			21 14		21 31				21 44		22 02			22 14		22 31		
Basildon d			20 47			21 05			21 17		21 34				21 47		22 05			22 17		22 34		
Dagenham Dock d		20 25						20 55					21 25						21 55					
Rainham d		20 29						20 59					21 29						21 59					
Purfleet d		20 34						21 04					21 34						22 04					
Grays d		20a40			20 57			21a12		21 27			21a40			21 57			22a12		22 27			
Tilbury Town 3 d					21 00					21 30						22 00					22 30			
East Tilbury d					21 06					21 36						22 06					22 36			
Stanford-le-Hope d					21 10					21 40						22 10					22 40			
Pitsea d	←		20 51		21 18		←		21 21	21 48		←			21 51	22 18		←		22 21	22 48		←	
Benfleet d	20 52		20 55		21 22	21 12	21 22		21 25	21 52	21 41	21 52			21 55	22 22	22 12	22 22		22 25	22 52	22 41	22 52	
Leigh-on-Sea d	20 56		21 00		→	21 16	21 26		21 30	→	21 45	21 56			22 00	→	22 16	22 26		22 30	→	22 45	22 56	
Chalkwell d	20 59		21 03			21 19	21 29		21 33		21 48	21 59			22 03		22 19	22 29		22 33		22 48	22 59	
Westcliff d	21 02		21 05			21 22	21 32		21 35		21 51	22 02			22 05		22 22	22 32		22 35		22 51	23 02	
Southend Central a	21 05		21 08			21 24	21 35		21 38		21 53	22 05			22 08		22 24	22 35		22 38		22 53	23 05	
d			21 08			21 24			21 38		21 53				22 08		22 24			22 38		22 53	23 05	
Southend East d			21 10			21 26			21 40		21 55				22 10		22 26			22 40		22 55	23 07	
Thorpe Bay d			21 14			21 30			21 44		21 59				22 14		22 30			22 44		22 59	23 10	
Shoeburyness a			21 18			21 34			21 48		22 03				22 18		22 34			22 48		23 03	23 15	

	CC	CC	CC	CC	CC	CC	CC	CC	CC		CC	CC	CC	CC	CC	CC
London Fenchurch St 7 ⊖ d	22 05	22 10	22 20	22 35	22 40	22 50	23 00		23 05		23 10		23 20	23 35	23 40	23 50
Limehouse d	22 09	22 14	22 24	22 39	22 44	22 54			23 09		23 14		23 24	23 39	23 44	23 54
West Ham ⊖ d	22 14	22 19	22 29	22 44	22 49	22 59	23 08		23 14		23 19		23 29	23 44	23 49	23 59
London Liverpool St 15 ⊖ d																
Stratford 7 ⊖ d																
Barking ⊖ d	22 20	22 25	22 35	22 50	22 55	23 05	23 14		23 20		23 25		23 35	23 50	23 55	00 05
Upminster ⊖ d		22 34	22 44		23 04	23 14	23 23				23 34		23 44		00 04	00 14
Ockendon d			22 49			23 19							23 49			00 19
Chafford Hundred d			22 53			23 23							23 53			00 23
West Horndon d		22 39			23 09						23 39				00 09	
Laindon d		22 44			23 14		23 31				23 44				00 16	
Basildon d		22 47			23 17		23 34				23 47				00 19	
Dagenham Dock d	22 25			22 55					23 25					23 55		
Rainham d	22 29			22 59					23 29					23 59		
Purfleet d	22 34			23 04					23 34					00 04		
Grays d	22a40		22 57	23a10		23 27			23 42				23 57	00a10		00 27
Tilbury Town 3 d			23 00			23 30			23 45				00 01			00 30
East Tilbury d			23 06			23 36			23 51				00 06			00 36
Stanford-le-Hope d			23 10			23 40			23 55			←	00 10			00 40
Pitsea d		22 51	23 18		23 22	23 48		←	00 06		23 52	00 06	00 18		00 22	00 48
Benfleet d		22 55	23 22		23 26	23 52	23 41	23 52	→		23 56	00 10	00 22		00 26	00 52
Leigh-on-Sea d		23 00	23 26		23 30	→	23 45	23 56			23 59	00 15	00 27		00 31	00 56
Chalkwell d		23 03	23 29		23 33		23 48	23 59			00 03	00 18	00 30		00 34	00 59
Westcliff d		23 06	23 32		23 36		23 51	00 02			00 06	00 20	00 32		00 36	01 02
Southend Central a		23 08	23 35		23 39		23 54	00 05			00 09	00 23	00 35		00 39	01 05
d		23 08	23 35		23 39		23 54	00 05			00 09	00 23	00 35		00 40	01 05
Southend East d		23 10	23 37		23 41		23 56	00 07			00 11	00 26	00 38		00 42	01 07
Thorpe Bay d		23 14	23 41		23 45		23 59	00 11			00 15	00 29	00 41		00 46	01 11
Shoeburyness a		23 18	23 47		23 51		00 06	00 17			00 21	00 36	00 48		00 52	01 17

London - Southend Central and Shoeburyness

Saturdays until 21 July

Network Diagram - see first page of Table 1

		CC	CC	CC	CC	CC	CC	CC	CC	CC	CC	CC	CC	CC	CC	CC	CC	CC	CC	CC	CC	CC	CC
London Fenchurch St	⊖ d	22p50	23p00		23p05	23p10		23p20	23p35	23p40	23p50	00 01		00 15	00 25			05 10	05 35	05 50	06 05	06 10	06 20
Limehouse	d	22p54			23p09	23p14		23p24	23p39	23p44	23p54			00 19	00 29			05 14	05 39	05 54	06 09	06 14	06 24
West Ham	⊖ d	22p59	23p08		23p14	23p19		23p29	23p44	23p49	23p59	00 09		00 24	00 34			05 19	05 44	05 59	06 14	06 19	06 29
London Liverpool St	⊖ d																						
Stratford	⊖ d																						
Barking	⊖ d	23p05	23p14		23p20	23p25		23p35	23p50	23p55	00 05	00 15		00 30	00 40			05 24	05 49	06 04	06 19	06 24	06 34
Upminster	⊖ d	23p14	23p23			23p34		23p44		00 04	00 14	00 24			00 49	05 05	05 27	05 32		06 12		06 32	06 42
Ockendon	d	23p19						23p49			00 19					05a12	05 32			06 18			06 48
Chafford Hundred	d	23p23						23p53			00 23						05 36			06 21			06 51
West Horndon	d					23p39				00 09					00 54			05 37				06 37	
Laindon	d		23p31			23p44				00 16		00 32			00 59			05 42				06 42	
Basildon	d		23p34			23p47				00 19		00 35			01 02			05 45				06 45	
Dagenham Dock	d				23p25				23p55					00 35					05 54		06 24		
Rainham	d				23p29				23p59					00 39					05 57		06 27		
Purfleet	d				23p34				00 04					00 44					06 03		06 33		
Grays	d	23p27			23p42			23p57	00a10		00 27			00a50			05a42		06a12	06 25	06a42		06 55
Tilbury Town	d	23p30			23p45			00 01			00 30									06 28			06 58
East Tilbury	d	23p36			23p51			00 06			00 36									06 34			07 04
Stanford-le-Hope	d	23p40			23p55		←	00 10			00 40									06 37			07 07
Pitsea	d	23p48		←	00 06	23p52	00 06	00 18		00 22	00 48		←		01 06			05 50		06 45		06 49	07 15
Benfleet	d	23p52	23p41	23p52	→	23p56	00 10	00 22		00 26	00 52	00 42	00 52		01 10			05 54		06 49		06 52	07 19
Leigh-on-Sea	d	→	23p45	23p56		23p59	00 15	00 27		00 31	→	00 46	00 56		01 14			05 58		06 53		06 57	07 23
Chalkwell	d		23p48	23p59		00 03	00 18	00 30		00 34		00 49	00 59		01 17			06 01		06 56		06 59	07 26
Westcliff	d		23p51	00 02		00 06	00 20	00 32		00 36		00 52	01 02		01 20			06 03		06 58		07 02	07 28
Southend Central	a		23p54	00 05		00 09	00 23	00 35		00 39		00 55	01 05		01 23			06 06		07 04		07 05	07 34
	d		23p54	00 05		00 09	00 23	00 35		00 40		00 55	01 05		01 23			06 07				07 06	
Southend East	d		23p56	00 07		00 11	00 26	00 38		00 42		00 57	01 07		01 25			06 09				07 08	
Thorpe Bay	d		23p59	00 11		00 15	00 29	00 41		00 46		01 01	01 11		01 29			06 12				07 10	
Shoeburyness	a		00 06	00 17		00 21	00 36	00 48		00 52		01 07	01 17		01 35			06 19				07 18	

		CC	CC	CC	CC	CC	CC	CC	CC	CC	CC	CC	CC	CC	CC	CC	CC	CC	CC	CC	CC	CC
London Fenchurch St	⊖ d	06 35	06 40	06 50	07 05	07 10	07 20	07 35	07 40	07 50	08 05	08 10	08 20	08 35	08 40	08 50	09 00		09 05	09 10	09 20	09 30
Limehouse	d	06 39	06 44	06 54	07 09	07 14	07 24	07 39	07 44	07 54	08 09	08 14	08 24	08 39	08 44	08 54			09 09	09 14	09 24	
West Ham	⊖ d	06 44	06 49	06 59	07 14	07 19	07 29	07 44	07 49	07 59	08 14	08 19	08 29	08 44	08 49	08 59	09 08		09 14	09 19	09 29	09 38
London Liverpool St	⊖ d																					
Stratford	⊖ d																					
Barking	⊖ d	06 49	06 54	07 04	07 19	07 24	07 34	07 49	07 54	08 04	08 19	08 24	08 34	08 49	08 54	09 04	09 13		09 19	09 24	09 34	09 43
Upminster	⊖ d		07 02	07 12		07 32	07 42		08 02	08 12		08 32	08 42		09 02	09 12	09 21			09 32	09 42	09 51
Ockendon	d			07 18			07 48			08 18			08 48			09 18					09 48	
Chafford Hundred	d			07 21			07 51			08 21			08 51			09 21					09 51	
West Horndon	d		07 07			07 37			08 07			08 37			09 07					09 37		
Laindon	d		07 12			07 42			08 12			08 42			09 12		09 29			09 42		09 59
Basildon	d		07 15			07 45			08 15			08 45			09 15		09 32			09 45		10 02
Dagenham Dock	d	06 54			07 24			07 54			08 24			08 54					09 24			
Rainham	d	06 57			07 27			07 57			08 27			08 57					09 27			
Purfleet	d	07 03			07 33			08 03			08 33			09 03					09 33			
Grays	d	07a12		07 25	07a42		07 55	08a12		08 25	08a42		08 55	09a12		09 25			09a42		09 55	
Tilbury Town	d			07 28			07 58			08 28			08 58			09 28					09 58	
East Tilbury	d			07 34			08 04			08 34			09 04			09 34					10 04	
Stanford-le-Hope	d			07 37			08 07			08 37			09 07			09 37					10 07	
Pitsea	d		07 19	07 45		07 49	08 15		08 19	08 45		08 49	09 15		09 19	09 45		←		09 49	10 15	
Benfleet	d		07 22	07 49		07 52	08 19		08 22	08 49		08 52	09 19		09 22	09 49	09 38	09 49		09 52	10 19	10 08
Leigh-on-Sea	d		07 27	07 53		07 57	08 23		08 27	08 53		08 57	09 23		09 27	→	09 42	09 53		09 57	→	10 12
Chalkwell	d		07 29	07 56		07 59	08 26		08 29	08 56		08 59	09 26		09 29		09 45	09 56		09 59		10 15
Westcliff	d		07 32	07 58		08 02	08 28		08 32	08 58		09 02	09 28		09 32		09 47	09 58		10 02		10 17
Southend Central	a		07 35	08 04		08 05	08 34		08 35	09 04		09 05	09 34		09 35		09 50	10 04		10 05		10 20
	d		07 36			08 06			08 36			09 06			09 36		09 50			10 06		10 20
Southend East	d		07 38			08 08			08 38			09 08			09 38		09 52			10 08		10 22
Thorpe Bay	d		07 40			08 10			08 40			09 10			09 40		09 55			10 10		10 25
Shoeburyness	a		07 48			08 18			08 48			09 18			09 48		10 02			10 18		10 32

		CC		CC	CC	CC	CC	CC	CC	CC	CC	CC	CC	CC	CC	CC	CC	CC	CC	CC	CC	CC
London Fenchurch St	⊖ d		and at the same minutes past each hour until		19 35	19 40	19 50	20 00		20 05	20 10	20 20	20 35	20 40	20 50	21 00		21 05	21 10	21 20	21 35	21 40
Limehouse	d				19 39	19 44	19 54			20 09	20 14	20 24	20 39	20 44	20 54			21 09	21 14	21 24	21 39	21 44
West Ham	⊖ d				19 44	19 49	19 59	20 08		20 14	20 19	20 29	20 44	20 49	20 59	21 08		21 14	21 19	21 29	21 44	21 49
London Liverpool St	⊖ d																					
Stratford	⊖ d																					
Barking	⊖ d				19 49	19 54	20 04	20 13		20 19	20 24	20 34	20 49	20 54	21 04	21 13		21 19	21 24	21 34	21 49	21 54
Upminster	⊖ d					20 02	20 12	20 21			20 32	20 42		21 02	21 12	21 21			21 32	21 42		22 02
Ockendon	d						20 18					20 48			21 18					21 48		
Chafford Hundred	d						20 21					20 51			21 21					21 51		
West Horndon	d					20 07					20 37			21 07					21 37			22 07
Laindon	d					20 12		20 29			20 42			21 12		21 29			21 42			22 12
Basildon	d					20 15		20 32			20 45			21 15		21 32			21 45			22 15
Dagenham Dock	d				19 54					20 24			20 54					21 24			21 54	
Rainham	d				19 57					20 27			20 57					21 27			21 57	
Purfleet	d				20 03					20 33			21 03					21 33			22 03	
Grays	d				20a12		20 25			20a42		20 55	21a12		21 25			21a42		21 55	22a12	
Tilbury Town	d						20 28					20 58			21 28					21 58		
East Tilbury	d						20 34					21 04			21 34					22 04		
Stanford-le-Hope	d						20 37					21 07			21 37					22 07		
Pitsea	d	←		←		20 19	20 45		←		20 49	21 15		21 19	21 45		←		21 49	22 15		22 19
Benfleet	d	10 19		20 19		20 22	20 49	20 38	20 49		20 52	21 19		21 22	21 49	21 38	21 49		21 52	22 19		22 22
Leigh-on-Sea	d	10 23		20 23		20 27	→	20 42	20 53		20 57	21 23		21 27	→	21 42	21 53		21 57	22 23		22 27
Chalkwell	d	10 26		20 26		20 29		20 45	20 56		20 59	21 26		21 29		21 45	21 56		21 59	22 26		22 29
Westcliff	d	10 28		20 28		20 32		20 47	20 58		21 02	21 28		21 32		21 47	21 58		22 02	22 28		22 32
Southend Central	a	10 34		20 34		20 35		20 50	21 04		21 05	21 34		21 35		21 50	22 04		22 05	22 34		22 35
	d					20 36		20 50			21 06			21 36		21 50			22 06			22 36
Southend East	d					20 38		20 52			21 08			21 38		21 52			22 08			22 38
Thorpe Bay	d					20 40		20 55			21 10			21 40		21 55			22 10			22 40
Shoeburyness	a					20 48		21 02			21 18			21 48		22 02			22 18			22 48

London - Southend Central and Shoeburyness

Saturdays until 21 July

Network Diagram - see first page of Table 1

		CC	CC	CC	CC	CC	CC	CC	CC	CC	CC	CC	CC	CC	CC	CC	CC	CC
London Fenchurch St	⊖ d	21 50	22 00		22 05	22 10	22 20	22 35	22 40	22 50	23 05	23 10		23 20	23 35	23 40		23 50
Limehouse	d	21 54			22 09	22 14	22 24	22 39	22 44	22 54	23 09	23 14		23 24	23 39	23 44		23 54
West Ham	⊖ d	21 59	22 08		22 14	22 19	22 29	22 44	22 49	22 59	23 14	23 19		23 29	23 44	23 49		23 59
London Liverpool St	⊖ d																	
Stratford	⊖ d																	
Barking	⊖ d	22 04	22 13		22 19	22 24	22 34	22 49	22 54	23 04	23 19	23 24		23 34	23 49	23 54		00 04
Upminster	⊖ d	22 12	22 21			22 32	22 42		23 02	23 12		23 32		23 42		00 02		00 12
Ockendon	d	22 18					22 48			23 18				23 48				00 18
Chafford Hundred	d	22 21					22 51			23 21				23 51				00 21
West Horndon	d					22 37			23 07			23 37				00 07		
Laindon	d		22 29			22 42			23 12			23 42				00 12		
Basildon	d		22 32			22 45			23 15			23 45				00 15		
Dagenham Dock	d				22 24			22 54			23 24				23 54			
Rainham	d				22 27			22 57			23 27				23 57			
Purfleet	d				22 33			23 03			23 33				00 03			
Grays	d	22 25			22a42		22 55	23a12		23 25	23 38			23 55	00 08			00 25
Tilbury Town	d	22 28					22 58			23 28	23 41			23 58	00 11			00 28
East Tilbury	d	22 34					23 04			23 34	23 47			00 04	00 17			00 34
Stanford-le-Hope	d	22 37					23 07			23 37	23 50		←	00 07	00 20		←	00 37
Pitsea	d	22 45		←		22 49	23 15		23 19	23 45	23 58	23 49	23 58	00 15	00 28	00 19	00 28	00 45
Benfleet	d	22 49	22 38	22 49		22 52	23 19		23 22	23 49	→	23 52	00 01	00 19	→	00 22	00 31	00 49
Leigh-on-Sea	d	→	22 42	22 53		22 57	23 23		23 27	23 53		23 57	00 06	00 23		00 27	00 36	00 53
Chalkwell	d		22 45	22 56		22 59	23 26		23 29	23 56		23 59	00 08	00 26		00 29	00 38	00 56
Westcliff	d		22 47	22 58		23 02	23 28		23 32	23 58		00 02	00 11	00 28		00 32	00 41	00 58
Southend Central	a		22 50	23 04		23 05	23 31		23 35	00 01		00 05	00 14	00 31		00 35	00 44	01 01
	d		22 50			23 06	23 31		23 36	00 01		00 06	00 14	00 31		00 36	00 44	01 01
Southend East	d		22 52			23 08	23 34		23 38	00 04		00 08	00 16	00 34		00 38	00 46	01 04
Thorpe Bay	d		22 55			23 10	23 36		23 41	00 06		00 11	00 19	00 36		00 41	00 49	01 06
Shoeburyness	a		23 02			23 18	23 43		23 48	00 13		00 18	00 26	00 43		00 48	00 56	01 13

Saturdays 28 July to 11 August

		CC	CC	CC	CC	CC	CC	CC	CC	CC	CC	CC	CC	CC	CC	CC	CC	CC	CC	CC	CC	CC	CC
London Fenchurch St	⊖ d	22p50	23p00		23p05	23p10		23p20	23p37	23p40	23p50	00 01		00 18	00 30	00 50			05 10	05 35	05 50	06 05	06 10
Limehouse	d	22p54			23p09	23p14		23p24	23p41	23p44	23p54			00 22	00 34	00 54			05 14	05 39	05 54	06 09	06 14
West Ham	⊖ d	23p01	23p10		23p15	23p21		23p31	23p47	23p51	00 01	00 11		00 28	00 41	01 01			05 19	05 44	05 59	06 14	06 19
London Liverpool St	⊖ d																						
Stratford	⊖ d																						
Barking	⊖ d	23p06	23p15		23p21	23p26		23p36	23p53	23p57	00 07	00 17		00 34	00 47	01 06			05 24	05 49	06 04	06 19	06 24
Upminster	⊖ d	23p15	23p24			23p35		23p45		00 06	00 16	00 26			00 56	01 15	05 05	05 27	05 32		06 12		06 32
Ockendon	d	23p20						23p50			00 21						05a12	05 32			06 18		
Chafford Hundred	d	23p24						23p54			00 25							05 36			06 21		
West Horndon	d					23p40				00 11					01 01	01 20			05 37				06 37
Laindon	d		23p33			23p46				00 17		00 35			01 07	01 26			05 42				06 42
Basildon	d		23p36			23p49				00 20		00 38			01 10	01 29			05 45				06 45
Dagenham Dock	d				23p26				23p58					00 39						05 54		06 24	
Rainham	d				23p30				00 02					00 43						05 57		06 27	
Purfleet	d				23p35				00 07					00 48						06 03		06 33	
Grays	d	23p28			23p43			23p58	00a13		00 29			00a54				05a42		06a12	06 25	06a42	
Tilbury Town	d	23p32			23p46			00 02			00 33										06 28		
East Tilbury	d	23p38			23p52			00 07			00 39										06 34		
Stanford-le-Hope	d	23p42			23p56		←	00 11			00 43										06 37		
Pitsea	d	23p49		←	00 07	23p53	00 07	00 20		00 24	00 50		←		01 13	01 32			05 50		06 45		06 49
Benfleet	d	23p53	23p42	23p53	→	23p57	00 11	00 24		00 28	00 54	00 44	00 54		01 17	01 36			05 54		06 49		06 52
Leigh-on-Sea	d	→	23p47	23p58		00 02	00 16	00 28		00 32	→	00 49	00 59		01 22	01 41			05 58		06 53		06 57
Chalkwell	d		23p50	00 01		00 05	00 19	00 31		00 35		00 52	01 02		01 25	01 44			06 01		06 56		06 59
Westcliff	d		23p52	00 03		00 07	00 21	00 34		00 38		00 54	01 04		01 27	01 46			06 03		06 58		07 02
Southend Central	a		23p55	00 06		00 10	00 24	00 37		00 41		00 57	01 07		01 30	01 49			06 06		07 04		07 05
	d		23p55	00 06		00 10	00 24	00 37		00 41		00 57	01 07		01 30	01 49			06 07				07 06
Southend East	d		23p58	00 09		00 13	00 27	00 39		00 44		01 00	01 10		01 33	01 52			06 09				07 08
Thorpe Bay	d		00 01	00 12		00 16	00 30	00 43		00 47		01 03	01 13		01 36	01 55			06 12				07 10
Shoeburyness	a		00 08	00 19		00 23	00 37	00 49		00 54		01 10	01 20		01 43	02 02			06 19				07 18

28 July to 11 August

London - Southend Central and Shoeburyness

Network Diagram - see first page of Table I

		CC	CC	CC	CC	CC	CC	CC	CC A	CC	CC	CC A	CC	CC A	CC	CC	CC A	CC	CC A	CC	CC	CC A	CC
London Fenchurch St ⊖	d	06 20	06 35	06 40	06 50	07 05	07 10	07 20	07 30	07 35	07 40	07 45	07 50	08 00	08 05	08 10	08 15	08 20	08 30	08 35	08 40	08 45	08 50
Limehouse	d	06 24	06 39	06 44	06 54	07 09	07 14	07 24		07 39	07 44		07 54		08 09	08 14		08 24		08 39	08 44		08 54
West Ham ⊖	d	06 29	06 44	06 49	06 59	07 14	07 19	07 29	07 41	07 44	07 49	07 56	07 59	08 11	08 14	08 19	08 26	08 29	08 41	08 44	08 49	08 56	08 59
London Liverpool St ⊖	d																						
Stratford ⊖	d																						
Barking ⊖	d	06 34	06 49	06 54	07 04	07 19	07 24	07 34		07 49	07 54		08 04		08 19	08 24		08 34		08 49	08 54		09 04
Upminster ⊖	d	06 42		07 02	07 12		07 32	07 42			08 02		08 12			08 32		08 42			09 02		09 12
Ockendon	d	06 48			07 18			07 48					08 18					08 48					09 18
Chafford Hundred	d	06 51			07 21			07 51					08 21					08 51					09 21
West Horndon	d			07 07			07 37				08 07					08 37					09 07		
Laindon	d			07 12			07 42				08 12					08 42					09 12		
Basildon	d			07 15			07 45				08 15					08 45					09 15		
Dagenham Dock	d		06 54			07 24				07 54					08 24					08 54			
Rainham	d		06 57			07 27				07 57					08 27					08 57			
Purfleet	d		07 03			07 33				08 03					08 33					09 03			
Grays	d	06 55	07a12		07 25	07a42		07 55		08a12			08 25		08a42			08 55		09a12			09 25
Tilbury Town	d	06 58			07 28			07 58					08 28					08 58					09 28
East Tilbury	d	07 04			07 34			08 04					08 34					09 04					09 34
Stanford-le-Hope	d	07 07			07 37			08 07					08 37					09 07					09 37
Pitsea	d	07 15		07 19	07 45		07 49	08 15			08 19		08 45			08 49		09 15			09 19		09 45
Benfleet	d	07 19		07 22	07 49		07 52	08 19			08 22		08 49			08 52		09 19			09 22		09 49
Leigh-on-Sea	d	07 23		07 27	07 53		07 57	08 23	08a11		08 27	08a32	08 53	08a42		08 57	09a03	09 23	09a13		09 27	09a32	→
Chalkwell	d	07 26		07 29	07 56		07 59	08 26			08 29		08 56			08 59		09 26			09 29		
Westcliff	d	07 28		07 32	07 58		08 02	08 28			08 32		08 58			09 02		09 28			09 32		
Southend Central	a	07 34		07 35	08 04		08 05	08 34			08 35		09 04			09 05		09 34			09 35		
	d			07 36			08 06				08 36					09 06					09 36		
Southend East	d			07 38			08 08				08 38					09 08					09 38		
Thorpe Bay	d			07 40			08 10				08 40					09 10					09 40		
Shoeburyness	a			07 48			08 18				08 48					09 18					09 48		

		CC A	CC	CC	CC	CC	CC A	CC	CC	CC	CC	CC	CC	CC	CC	CC	CC		CC	CC	CC
London Fenchurch St ⊖	d	08 55	09 00		09 05	09 10	09 15	09 20	09 30		09 35	09 40	09 50	10 00		10 05	10 10	and at the same minutes past each hour until	20 10	20 20	20 35
Limehouse	d				09 09	09 14		09 24			09 39	09 44	09 54			10 09	10 14		20 14	20 24	20 39
West Ham ⊖	d	09 06	09 08		09 14	09 19	09 26	09 29	09 38		09 44	09 49	09 59	10 08		10 14	10 19		20 19	20 29	20 44
London Liverpool St ⊖	d																				
Stratford ⊖	d																				
Barking ⊖	d		09 13		09 19	09 24		09 34	09 43		09 49	09 54	10 04	10 13		10 19	10 24		20 24	20 34	20 49
Upminster ⊖	d		09 21			09 32		09 42	09 51			10 02	10 12	10 21			10 32		20 32	20 42	
Ockendon	d							09 48					10 18							20 48	
Chafford Hundred	d							09 51					10 21							20 51	
West Horndon	d					09 37						10 07					10 37		20 37		
Laindon	d		09 29			09 42			09 59			10 12		10 29			10 42		20 42		
Basildon	d		09 32			09 45			10 02			10 15		10 32			10 45		20 45		
Dagenham Dock	d				09 24						09 54					10 24					20 54
Rainham	d				09 27						09 57					10 27					20 57
Purfleet	d				09 33						10 03					10 33					21 03
Grays	d				09a42			09 55			10a12		10 25			10a42				20 55	21a12
Tilbury Town	d							09 58					10 28							20 58	
East Tilbury	d							10 04					10 34							21 04	
Stanford-le-Hope	d							10 07					10 37							21 07	
Pitsea	d			←		09 49		10 15		←		10 19	10 45		←		10 49		20 49	21 15	
Benfleet	d		09 38	09 49		09 52		10 19	10 08	10 19		10 22	10 49	10 38	10 49		10 52		20 52	21 19	
Leigh-on-Sea	d	09a38	09 42	09 53		09 57	10a02	→	10 12	10 23		10 27	→	10 42	10 53		10 57		20 57	21 23	
Chalkwell	d		09 45	09 56		09 59			10 15	10 26		10 29		10 45	10 56		10 59		20 59	21 26	
Westcliff	d		09 47	09 58		10 02			10 17	10 28		10 32		10 47	10 58		11 02		21 02	21 28	
Southend Central	a		09 50	10 04		10 05			10 20	10 34		10 35		10 50	11 04		11 05		21 05	21 34	
	d		09 50			10 06			10 20			10 36		10 50			11 06		21 06		
Southend East	d		09 52			10 08			10 22			10 38		10 52			11 08		21 08		
Thorpe Bay	d		09 55			10 10			10 25			10 40		10 55			11 10		21 10		
Shoeburyness	a		10 02			10 18			10 32			10 48		11 02			11 18		21 18		

A not from 28 July until 4 August

28 July to 11 August

London - Southend Central and Shoeburyness

Network Diagram - see first page of Table I

		CC	CC	CC	CC	CC	CC	CC	CC	CC	CC	CC	CC	CC	CC	CC	CC	CC	CC	CC	CC	CC	CC
London Fenchurch St ⊖	d	20 40	20 50	21 00		21 05	21 10	21 20	21 35	21 40	21 50	22 00		22 05	22 10	22 20	22 35	22 40	22 50	23 05	23 10		23 20
Limehouse	d	20 44	20 54			21 09	21 14	21 24	21 39	21 44	21 54			22 09	22 14	22 24	22 39	22 44	22 54	23 09	23 14		23 24
West Ham ⊖	d	20 49	20 59	21 08		21 14	21 19	21 29	21 44	21 49	21 59	22 10		22 15	22 21	22 31	22 45	22 51	23 01	23 16	23 21		23 31
London Liverpool St ⊖	d																						
Stratford ⊖	d																						
Barking ⊖	d	20 54	21 04	21 13		21 19	21 24	21 34	21 49	21 54	22 04	22 15		22 20	22 26	22 36	22 50	22 56	23 06	23 21	23 26		23 36
Upminster ⊖	d	21 02	21 12	21 21			21 32	21 42		22 02	22 12	22 24			22 35	22 45		23 05	23 15		23 35		23 45
Ockendon	d		21 18					21 48			22 18					22 50			23 20				23 50
Chafford Hundred	d		21 21					21 51			22 21					22 54			23 24				23 54
West Horndon	d	21 07					21 37			22 07					22 40			23 10			23 40		
Laindon	d	21 12		21 29			21 42			22 12		22 32			22 44			23 14			23 44		
Basildon	d	21 15		21 32			21 45			22 15		22 35			22 47			23 17			23 47		
Dagenham Dock	d					21 24			21 54					22 25			22 55			23 25			
Rainham	d					21 27			21 57					22 28			22 58			23 29			
Purfleet	d					21 33			22 03					22 34			23 04			23 34			
Grays	d		21 25			21a42		21 55	22a12		22 25			22a42		22 58	23a12		23 28	23 40			23 58
Tilbury Town	d		21 28					21 58			22 28					23 01			23 31	23 43			00 01
East Tilbury	d		21 34					22 04			22 34					23 06			23 36	23 48			00 06
Stanford-le-Hope	d		21 37					22 07			22 37					23 10			23 40	23 52		←	00 10
Pitsea	d	21 19	21 45		←		21 49	22 15		22 19	22 45		←		22 51	23 18		23 21	23 48	23 59	23 51	23 59	00 18
Benfleet	d	21 22	21 49	21 38	21 49		21 52	22 19		22 22	22 49	22 40	22 49		22 55	23 21		23 25	23 51	→	23 55	00 03	00 21
Leigh-on-Sea	d	21 27	→	21 42	21 53		21 57	22 23		22 27	→	22 45	22 53		22 59	23 26		23 29	23 56		23 59	00 07	00 26
Chalkwell	d	21 29		21 45	21 56		21 59	22 26		22 29		22 47	22 56		23 02	23 28		23 32	23 58		00 02	00 10	00 28
Westcliff	d	21 32		21 47	21 58		22 02	22 28		22 32		22 50	22 58		23 04	23 31		23 34	00 01		00 04	00 12	00 31
Southend Central	a	21 35		21 50	22 04		22 05	22 34		22 35		22 52	23 04		23 08	23 34		23 38	00 04		00 08	00 15	00 34
	d	21 36		21 50			22 06			22 36		22 53			23 08	23 34		23 38	00 04		00 08	00 15	00 34
Southend East	d	21 38		21 52			22 08			22 38		22 55			23 10	23 36		23 41	00 06		00 11	00 18	00 36
Thorpe Bay	d	21 40		21 55			22 10			22 40		22 57			23 13	23 39		23 43	00 09		00 13	00 20	00 39
Shoeburyness	a	21 48		22 02			22 18			22 48		23 05			23 20	23 45		23 51	00 15		00 21	00 28	00 45

		CC	CC	CC	CC
London Fenchurch St ⊖	d	23 35	23 40		23 50
Limehouse	d	23 39	23 44		23 54
West Ham ⊖	d	23 46	23 52		00 01
London Liverpool St ⊖	d				
Stratford ⊖	d				
Barking ⊖	d	23 51	23 58		00 07
Upminster ⊖	d		00 06		00 15
Ockendon	d				00 21
Chafford Hundred	d				00 24
West Horndon	d		00 11		
Laindon	d		00 16		
Basildon	d		00 19		
Dagenham Dock	d	23 55			
Rainham	d	23 59			
Purfleet	d	00 04			
Grays	d	00 10			00 28
Tilbury Town	d	00 13			00 31
East Tilbury	d	00 18			00 37
Stanford-le-Hope	d	00 22		←	00 40
Pitsea	d	00 29	00 23	00 29	00 48
Benfleet	d	→	00 26	00 33	00 52
Leigh-on-Sea	d		00 31	00 37	00 56
Chalkwell	d		00 33	00 40	00 59
Westcliff	d		00 36	00 42	01 01
Southend Central	a		00 38	00 45	01 04
	d		00 39	00 45	01 04
Southend East	d		00 41	00 48	01 07
Thorpe Bay	d		00 44	00 50	01 09
Shoeburyness	a		00 51	00 58	01 17

18 August to 25 August

		CC	CC	CC	CC	CC	CC	CC	CC	CC	CC	CC	CC	CC	CC	CC	CC	CC	CC	CC	CC	CC	CC
London Fenchurch St ⊖	d	22p50	23p00		23p05	23p10		23p20	23p35	23p40	23p50	00 01		00 15	00 25			05 10	05 35	05 50	06 05	06 10	06 20
Limehouse	d	22p54			23p09	23p14		23p24	23p39	23p44	23p54			00 19	00 29			05 14	05 39	05 54	06 09	06 14	06 24
West Ham ⊖	d	22p59	23p08		23p14	23p19		23p29	23p44	23p49	23p59	00 11		00 24	00 34			05 19	05 44	05 59	06 14	06 19	06 29
London Liverpool St ⊖	d																						
Stratford ⊖	d																						
Barking ⊖	d	23p05	23p14		23p20	23p25		23p35	23p50	23p55	00 05	00 17		00 30	00 40			05 24	05 49	06 04	06 19	06 24	06 34
Upminster ⊖	d	23p14	23p23			23p34		23p44		00 04	00 14	00 26			00 49	05 05	05 27	05 32		06 12		06 32	06 42
Ockendon	d	23p19						23p49			00 19					05a12	05 32			06 18			06 48
Chafford Hundred	d	23p23						23p53			00 23						05 36			06 21			06 51
West Horndon	d					23p39				00 09					00 54			05 37				06 37	
Laindon	d		23p31			23p44				00 16		00 35			00 59			05 42				06 42	
Basildon	d		23p34			23p47				00 19		00 38			01 02			05 45				06 45	
Dagenham Dock	d				23p25				23p55					00 35					05 54		06 24		
Rainham	d				23p29				23p59					00 39					05 57		06 27		
Purfleet	d				23p34				00 04					00 44					06 03		06 33		
Grays	d	23p27			23p42			23p57	00a10		00 27			00a50			05a42		06a12	06 25	06a42		06 55
Tilbury Town	d	23p30			23p45			00 01			00 30									06 28			06 58
East Tilbury	d	23p36			23p51			00 06			00 36									06 34			07 04
Stanford-le-Hope	d	23p40			23p55		←	00 10			00 40									06 37			07 07
Pitsea	d	23p48		←	00 06	23p52	00 06	00 18		00 22	00 48		←		01 06			05 50		06 45		06 49	07 15
Benfleet	d	23p52	23p41	23p52	→	23p56	00 10	00 22		00 26	00 52	00 44	00 52		01 10			05 54		06 49		06 52	07 19
Leigh-on-Sea	d	→	23p45	23p56		23p59	00 15	00 27		00 31	→	00 49	00 56		01 14			05 58		06 53		06 57	07 23
Chalkwell	d		23p48	23p59		00 03	00 18	00 30		00 34		00 52	00 59		01 17			06 01		06 56		06 59	07 26
Westcliff	d		23p51	00 02		00 06	00 20	00 32		00 36		00 54	01 02		01 20			06 03		06 58		07 02	07 28
Southend Central	a		23p54	00 05		00 09	00 23	00 35		00 39		00 57	01 05		01 23			06 06		07 04		07 05	07 34
	d		23p54	00 05		00 09	00 23	00 35		00 40		00 57	01 05		01 23			06 07				07 06	
Southend East	d		23p56	00 07		00 11	00 26	00 38		00 42		01 00	01 07		01 25			06 09				07 08	
Thorpe Bay	d		23p59	00 11		00 15	00 29	00 41		00 46		01 03	01 11		01 29			06 12				07 10	
Shoeburyness	a		00 06	00 17		00 21	00 36	00 48		00 52		01 10	01 17		01 35			06 19				07 18	

Table 1

Saturdays

18 August to 25 August

London - Southend Central and Shoeburyness

Network Diagram - see first page of Table 1

		CC	CC	CC	CC	CC	CC	CC	CC	CC	CC	CC	CC	CC	CC	CC	CC	CC	CC	CC	CC	CC
London Fenchurch St [7] ⊖	d	06 35	06 40	06 50	07 05	07 10	07 20	07 35	07 40	07 50	08 05	08 10	08 20	08 35	08 40	08 50	09 00		09 05	09 10	09 20	09 30
Limehouse	d	06 39	06 44	06 54	07 09	07 14	07 24	07 39	07 44	07 54	08 09	08 14	08 24	08 39	08 44	08 54			09 09	09 14	09 24	
West Ham ⊖	d	06 44	06 49	06 59	07 14	07 19	07 29	07 44	07 49	07 59	08 14	08 19	08 29	08 44	08 49	08 59	09 08		09 14	09 19	09 29	09 38
London Liverpool St [15] ⊖	d																					
Stratford [7] ⊖	d																					
Barking ⊖	d	06 49	06 54	07 04	07 19	07 24	07 34	07 49	07 54	08 04	08 19	08 24	08 34	08 49	08 54	09 04	09 13		09 19	09 24	09 34	09 43
Upminster ⊖	d		07 02	07 12		07 32	07 42		08 02	08 12		08 32	08 42		09 02	09 12	09 21			09 32	09 42	09 51
Ockendon	d			07 18			07 48			08 18			08 48			09 18					09 48	
Chafford Hundred	d			07 21			07 51			08 21			08 51			09 21					09 51	
West Horndon	d		07 07			07 37			08 07			08 37			09 07					09 37		
Laindon	d		07 12			07 42			08 12			08 42			09 12		09 29			09 42		09 59
Basildon	d		07 15			07 45			08 15			08 45			09 15		09 32			09 45		10 02
Dagenham Dock	d	06 54			07 24			07 54			08 24			08 54					09 24			
Rainham	d	06 57			07 27			07 57			08 27			08 57					09 27			
Purfleet	d	07 03			07 33			08 03			08 33			09 03					09 33			
Grays	d	07a12		07 25	07a42		07 55	08a12		08 25	08a42		08 55	09a12		09 25			09a42		09 55	
Tilbury Town [3]	d			07 28			07 58			08 28			08 58			09 28					09 58	
East Tilbury	d			07 34			08 04			08 34			09 04			09 34					10 04	
Stanford-le-Hope	d			07 37			08 07			08 37			09 07			09 37					10 07	
Pitsea	d		07 19	07 45		07 49	08 15		08 19	08 45		08 49	09 15		09 19	09 45		←		09 49	10 15	
Benfleet	d		07 22	07 49		07 52	08 19		08 22	08 49		08 52	09 19		09 22	09 49	09 38	09 49		09 52	10 19	10 08
Leigh-on-Sea	d		07 27	07 53		07 57	08 23		08 27	08 53		08 57	09 23		09 27	→	09 42	09 53		09 57	→	10 12
Chalkwell	d		07 29	07 56		07 59	08 26		08 29	08 56		08 59	09 26		09 29		09 45	09 56		09 59		10 15
Westcliff	d		07 32	07 58		08 02	08 28		08 32	08 58		09 02	09 28		09 32		09 47	09 58		10 02		10 17
Southend Central	a		07 35	08 04		08 05	08 34		08 35	09 04		09 05	09 34		09 35		09 50	10 04		10 05		10 20
	d		07 36			08 06			08 36			09 06			09 36		09 50			10 06		10 20
Southend East	d		07 38			08 08			08 38			09 08			09 38		09 52			10 08		10 22
Thorpe Bay	d		07 40			08 10			08 40			09 10			09 40		09 55			10 10		10 25
Shoeburyness	a		07 48			08 18			08 48			09 18			09 48		10 02			10 18		10 32

		CC		CC	CC	CC	CC	CC	CC	CC	CC	CC	CC	CC	CC	CC	CC	CC	CC	CC	CC	CC
London Fenchurch St [7] ⊖	d				19 35	19 40	19 50	20 00		20 05	20 10	20 20	20 35	20 40	20 50	21 00		21 05	21 10	21 20	21 35	21 40
Limehouse	d				19 39	19 44	19 54			20 09	20 14	20 24	20 39	20 44	20 54			21 09	21 14	21 24	21 39	21 44
West Ham ⊖	d				19 44	19 49	19 59	20 08		20 14	20 19	20 29	20 44	20 49	20 59	21 08		21 14	21 19	21 29	21 44	21 49
London Liverpool St [15] ⊖	d																					
Stratford [7] ⊖	d																					
Barking ⊖	d				19 49	19 54	20 04	20 13		20 19	20 24	20 34	20 49	20 54	21 04	21 13		21 19	21 24	21 34	21 49	21 54
Upminster ⊖	d					20 02	20 12	20 21			20 32	20 42		21 02	21 12	21 21			21 32	21 42		22 02
Ockendon	d						20 18					20 48			21 18					21 48		
Chafford Hundred	d						20 21					20 51			21 21					21 51		
West Horndon	d					20 07					20 37			21 07					21 37			22 07
Laindon	d		and at the same minutes past each hour until			20 12		20 29			20 42			21 12		21 29			21 42			22 12
Basildon	d					20 15		20 32			20 45			21 15		21 32			21 45			22 15
Dagenham Dock	d				19 54					20 24			20 54					21 24			21 54	
Rainham	d				19 57					20 27			20 57					21 27			21 57	
Purfleet	d				20 03					20 33			21 03					21 33			22 03	
Grays	d				20a12		20 25			20a42		20 55	21a12		21 25			21a42		21 55	22a12	
Tilbury Town [3]	d						20 28					20 58			21 28					21 58		
East Tilbury	d						20 34					21 04			21 34					22 04		
Stanford-le-Hope	d						20 37					21 07			21 37					22 07		
Pitsea	d	←		←		20 19	20 45		←		20 49	21 15		21 19	21 45		←		21 49	22 15		22 19
Benfleet	d	10 19		20 19		20 22	20 49	20 38	20 49		20 52	21 19		21 22	21 49	21 38	21 49		21 52	22 19		22 22
Leigh-on-Sea	d	10 23		20 23		20 27	→	20 42	20 53		20 57	21 23		21 27	→	21 42	21 53		21 57	22 23		22 27
Chalkwell	d	10 26		20 26		20 29		20 45	20 56		20 59	21 26		21 29		21 45	21 56		21 59	22 26		22 29
Westcliff	d	10 28		20 28		20 32		20 47	20 58		21 02	21 28		21 32		21 47	21 58		22 02	22 28		22 32
Southend Central	a	10 34		20 34		20 35		20 50	21 04		21 05	21 34		21 35		21 50	22 04		22 05	22 34		22 35
	d					20 36		20 50			21 06			21 36		21 50			22 06			22 36
Southend East	d					20 38		20 52			21 08			21 38		21 52			22 08			22 38
Thorpe Bay	d					20 40		20 55			21 10			21 40		21 55			22 10			22 40
Shoeburyness	a					20 48		21 02			21 18			21 48		22 02			22 18			22 48

		CC	CC	CC	CC	CC	CC	CC	CC	CC	CC	CC	CC	CC	CC	CC	CC	CC
London Fenchurch St [7] ⊖	d	21 50	22 00		22 05	22 10	22 20	22 35	22 40	22 50	23 05	23 10		23 20	23 35	23 40		23 50
Limehouse	d	21 54			22 09	22 14	22 24	22 39	22 44	22 54	23 09	23 14		23 24	23 39	23 44		23 54
West Ham ⊖	d	21 59	22 08		22 14	22 19	22 29	22 44	22 49	22 59	23 14	23 19		23 29	23 44	23 49		23 59
London Liverpool St [15] ⊖	d																	
Stratford [7] ⊖	d																	
Barking ⊖	d	22 04	22 13		22 19	22 24	22 34	22 49	22 54	23 04	23 19	23 24		23 34	23 49	23 54		00 04
Upminster ⊖	d	22 12	22 21			22 32	22 42		23 02	23 12		23 32		23 42		00 02		00 12
Ockendon	d	22 18					22 48			23 18				23 48				00 18
Chafford Hundred	d	22 21					22 51			23 21				23 51				00 21
West Horndon	d					22 37			23 07			23 37				00 07		
Laindon	d		22 29			22 42			23 12			23 42				00 12		
Basildon	d		22 32			22 45			23 15			23 45				00 15		
Dagenham Dock	d				22 24			22 54			23 24				23 54			
Rainham	d				22 27			22 57			23 27				23 57			
Purfleet	d				22 33			23 03			23 33				00 03			
Grays	d	22 25			22a42		22 55	23a12		23 25	23 38			23 55	00 08			00 25
Tilbury Town [3]	d	22 28					22 58			23 28	23 41			23 58	00 11			00 28
East Tilbury	d	22 34					23 04			23 34	23 47			00 04	00 17			00 34
Stanford-le-Hope	d	22 37					23 07			23 37	23 50		←	00 07	00 20		←	00 37
Pitsea	d	22 45		←		22 49	23 15		23 19	23 45	23 58	23 49	23 58	00 15	00 28	00 19	00 28	00 45
Benfleet	d	22 49	22 38	22 49		22 52	23 19		23 22	23 49	→	23 52	00 01	00 19	→	00 22	00 31	00 49
Leigh-on-Sea	d	→	22 42	22 53		22 57	23 23		23 27	23 53		23 57	00 06	00 23		00 27	00 36	00 53
Chalkwell	d		22 45	22 56		22 59	23 26		23 29	23 56		23 59	00 08	00 26		00 29	00 38	00 56
Westcliff	d		22 47	22 58		23 02	23 28		23 32	23 58		00 02	00 11	00 28		00 32	00 41	00 58
Southend Central	a		22 50	23 04		23 05	23 31		23 35	00 01		00 05	00 14	00 31		00 35	00 44	01 01
	d		22 50			23 06	23 31		23 36	00 01		00 06	00 14	00 31		00 36	00 44	01 01
Southend East	d		22 52			23 08	23 34		23 38	00 04		00 08	00 16	00 34		00 38	00 46	01 04
Thorpe Bay	d		22 55			23 10	23 36		23 41	00 06		00 11	00 19	00 36		00 41	00 49	01 06
Shoeburyness	a		23 02			23 18	23 43		23 48	00 13		00 18	00 26	00 43		00 48	00 56	01 13

Table 1

Saturdays

1 September to 8 September

London - Southend Central and Shoeburyness

Network Diagram - see first page of Table 1

		CC	CC	CC	CC	CC	CC	CC	CC	CC	CC	CC	CC	CC	CC	CC	CC	CC	CC	CC	CC	CC	CC
London Fenchurch St [7] ⊖	d	22p50	23p00		23p05	23p10		23p20	23p37	23p40	23p50	00 01		00 18	00 30	00 50			05 10	05 35	05 50	06 05	06 10
Limehouse	d	22p54			23p09	23p14		23p24	23p41	23p44	23p54			00 22	00 34	00 54			05 14	05 39	05 54	06 09	06 14
West Ham ⊖	d	23p01	23p10		23p15	23p21		23p31	23p47	23p51	00 01	00 11		00 28	00 41	01 01			05 19	05 44	05 59	06 14	06 19
London Liverpool St [15] ⊖	d																						
Stratford [7] ⊖	d																						
Barking ⊖	d	23p06	23p15		23p21	23p26		23p36	23p53	23p57	00 07	00 17		00 34	00 47	01 06			05 24	05 49	06 04	06 19	06 24
Upminster ⊖	d	23p15	23p24			23p35		23p45		00 06	00 16	00 26			00 56	01 15	05 05	05 27	05 32		06 12		06 32
Ockendon	d	23p20						23p50			00 21						05a12	05 32			06 18		
Chafford Hundred	d	23p24						23p54			00 25							05 36			06 21		
West Horndon	d					23p40				00 11					01 01	01 20			05 37				06 37
Laindon	d		23p33			23p46				00 17		00 35			01 07	01 26			05 42				06 42
Basildon	d		23p36			23p49				00 20		00 38			01 10	01 29			05 45				06 45
Dagenham Dock	d				23p26				23p58					00 39						05 54		06 24	
Rainham	d				23p30				00 02					00 43						05 57		06 27	
Purfleet	d				23p35				00 07					00 48						06 03		06 33	
Grays	d	23p28			23p43			23p58	00a13		00 29			00a54				05a42		06a12	06 25	06a42	
Tilbury Town [3]	d	23p32			23p46			00 02			00 33										06 28		
East Tilbury	d	23p38			23p52			00 07			00 39										06 34		
Stanford-le-Hope	d	23p42			23p56		←	00 11			00 43										06 37		
Pitsea	d	23p49		←	00 07	23p53	00 07	00 20		00 24	00 50		←		01 13	01 32			05 50		06 45		06 49
Benfleet	d	23p53	23p42	23p53	→	23p57	00 11	00 24		00 28	00 54	00 44	00 54		01 17	01 36			05 54		06 49		06 52
Leigh-on-Sea	d	→	23p47	23p58		00 02	00 16	00 28		00 32	→	00 49	00 59		01 22	01 41			05 58		06 53		06 57
Chalkwell	d		23p50	00 01		00 05	00 19	00 31		00 35		00 52	01 02		01 25	01 44			06 01		06 56		06 59
Westcliff	d		23p52	00 03		00 07	00 21	00 34		00 38		00 54	01 04		01 27	01 46			06 03		06 58		07 02
Southend Central	a		23p55	00 06		00 10	00 24	00 37		00 41		00 57	01 07		01 30	01 49			06 06		07 04		07 05
	d		23p55	00 06		00 10	00 24	00 37		00 41		00 57	01 07		01 30	01 49			06 07				07 06
Southend East	d		23p58	00 09		00 13	00 27	00 39		00 44		01 00	01 10		01 33	01 52			06 09				07 08
Thorpe Bay	d		00 01	00 12		00 16	00 30	00 43		00 47		01 03	01 13		01 36	01 55			06 12				07 10
Shoeburyness	a		00 08	00 19		00 23	00 37	00 49		00 54		01 10	01 20		01 43	02 02			06 19				07 18

		CC	CC	CC	CC	CC	CC	CC	CC	CC	CC	CC	CC	CC	CC	CC	CC	CC	CC	CC	CC	CC	CC
London Fenchurch St [7] ⊖	d	06 20	06 35	06 40	06 50	07 05	07 10	07 20	07 35	07 40	07 50	08 05	08 10	08 20	08 35	08 40	08 50	09 00		09 05	09 10	09 20	09 30
Limehouse	d	06 24	06 39	06 44	06 54	07 09	07 14	07 24	07 39	07 44	07 54	08 09	08 14	08 24	08 39	08 44	08 54			09 09	09 14	09 24	
West Ham ⊖	d	06 29	06 44	06 49	06 59	07 14	07 19	07 29	07 44	07 49	07 59	08 14	08 19	08 29	08 44	08 49	08 59	09 08		09 14	09 19	09 29	09 38
London Liverpool St [15] ⊖	d																						
Stratford [7] ⊖	d																						
Barking ⊖	d	06 34	06 49	06 54	07 04	07 19	07 24	07 34	07 49	07 54	08 04	08 19	08 24	08 34	08 49	08 54	09 04	09 13		09 19	09 24	09 34	09 43
Upminster ⊖	d	06 42		07 02	07 12		07 32	07 42		08 02	08 12		08 32	08 42		09 02	09 12	09 21			09 32	09 42	09 51
Ockendon	d	06 48			07 18			07 48			08 18			08 48			09 18					09 48	
Chafford Hundred	d	06 51			07 21			07 51			08 21			08 51			09 21					09 51	
West Horndon	d			07 07			07 37			08 07			08 37			09 07					09 37		
Laindon	d			07 12			07 42			08 12			08 42			09 12		09 29			09 42		09 59
Basildon	d			07 15			07 45			08 15			08 45			09 15		09 32			09 45		10 02
Dagenham Dock	d		06 54			07 24			07 54			08 24			08 54					09 24			
Rainham	d		06 57			07 27			07 57			08 27			08 57					09 27			
Purfleet	d		07 03			07 33			08 03			08 33			09 03					09 33			
Grays	d	06 55	07a12		07 25	07a42		07 55	08a12		08 25	08a42		08 55	09a12		09 25			09a42		09 55	
Tilbury Town [3]	d	06 58			07 28			07 58			08 28			08 58			09 28					09 58	
East Tilbury	d	07 04			07 34			08 04			08 34			09 04			09 34					10 04	
Stanford-le-Hope	d	07 07			07 37			08 07			08 37			09 07			09 37					10 07	
Pitsea	d	07 15		07 19	07 45		07 49	08 15		08 19	08 45		08 49	09 15		09 19	09 45		←		09 49	10 15	
Benfleet	d	07 19		07 22	07 49		07 52	08 19		08 22	08 49		08 52	09 19		09 22	09 49	09 38	09 49		09 52	10 19	10 08
Leigh-on-Sea	d	07 23		07 27	07 53		07 57	08 23		08 27	08 53		08 57	09 23		09 27	→	09 42	09 53		09 57	→	10 12
Chalkwell	d	07 26		07 29	07 56		07 59	08 26		08 29	08 56		08 59	09 26		09 29		09 45	09 56		09 59		10 15
Westcliff	d	07 28		07 32	07 58		08 02	08 28		08 32	08 58		09 02	09 28		09 32		09 47	09 58		10 02		10 17
Southend Central	a	07 34		07 35	08 04		08 05	08 34		08 35	09 04		09 05	09 34		09 35		09 50	10 04		10 05		10 20
	d			07 36			08 06			08 36			09 06			09 36		09 50			10 06		10 20
Southend East	d			07 38			08 08			08 38			09 08			09 38		09 52			10 08		10 22
Thorpe Bay	d			07 40			08 10			08 40			09 10			09 40		09 55			10 10		10 25
Shoeburyness	a			07 48			08 18			08 48			09 18			09 48		10 02			10 18		10 32

		CC		CC	CC	CC	CC	CC	CC	CC	CC	CC	CC	CC	CC	CC	CC	CC	CC	CC	CC	CC
London Fenchurch St [7] ⊖	d				19 35	19 40	19 50	20 00		20 05	20 10	20 20	20 35	20 40	20 50	21 00		21 05	21 10	21 20	21 35	21 40
Limehouse	d				19 39	19 44	19 54			20 09	20 14	20 24	20 39	20 44	20 54			21 09	21 14	21 24	21 39	21 44
West Ham ⊖	d				19 44	19 49	19 59	20 08		20 14	20 19	20 29	20 44	20 49	20 59	21 08		21 14	21 19	21 29	21 44	21 49
London Liverpool St [15] ⊖	d																					
Stratford [7] ⊖	d																					
Barking ⊖	d				19 49	19 54	20 04	20 13		20 19	20 24	20 34	20 49	20 54	21 04	21 13		21 19	21 24	21 34	21 49	21 54
Upminster ⊖	d					20 02	20 12	20 21			20 32	20 42		21 02	21 12	21 21			21 32	21 42		22 02
Ockendon	d						20 18					20 48			21 18					21 48		
Chafford Hundred	d						20 21					20 51			21 21					21 51		
West Horndon	d					20 07					20 37			21 07					21 37			22 07
Laindon	d		and at the same minutes past each hour until			20 12		20 29			20 42			21 12		21 29			21 42			22 12
Basildon	d					20 15		20 32			20 45			21 15		21 32			21 45			22 15
Dagenham Dock	d				19 54					20 24			20 54					21 24			21 54	
Rainham	d				19 57					20 27			20 57					21 27			21 57	
Purfleet	d				20 03					20 33			21 03					21 33			22 03	
Grays	d				20a12		20 25			20a42		20 55	21a12		21 25			21a42		21 55	22a12	
Tilbury Town [3]	d						20 28					20 58			21 28					21 58		
East Tilbury	d						20 34					21 04			21 34					22 04		
Stanford-le-Hope	d						20 37					21 07			21 37					22 07		
Pitsea	d	←		←		20 19	20 45		←		20 49	21 15		21 19	21 45		←		21 49	22 15		22 19
Benfleet	d	10 19		20 19		20 22	20 49	20 38	20 49		20 52	21 19		21 22	21 49	21 38	21 49		21 52	22 19		22 22
Leigh-on-Sea	d	10 23		20 23		20 27	→	20 42	20 53		20 57	21 23		21 27	→	21 42	21 53		21 57	22 23		22 27
Chalkwell	d	10 26		20 26		20 29		20 45	20 56		20 59	21 26		21 29		21 45	21 56		21 59	22 26		22 29
Westcliff	d	10 28		20 28		20 32		20 47	20 58		21 02	21 28		21 32		21 47	21 58		22 02	22 28		22 32
Southend Central	a	10 34		20 34		20 35		20 50	21 04		21 05	21 34		21 35		21 50	22 04		22 05	22 34		22 35
	d					20 36		20 50			21 06			21 36		21 50			22 06			22 36
Southend East	d					20 38		20 52			21 08			21 38		21 52			22 08			22 38
Thorpe Bay	d					20 40		20 55			21 10			21 40		21 55			22 10			22 40
Shoeburyness	a					20 48		21 02			21 18			21 48		22 02			22 18			22 48

Table 1

London - Southend Central and Shoeburyness

Saturdays 1 September to 8 September

Network Diagram - see first page of Table 1

	CC	CC	CC	CC	CC	CC	CC	CC	CC	CC	CC	CC	CC	CC	CC	CC	CC
London Fenchurch St ⊖ d	21 50	22 00		22 05	22 10	22 20	22 35	22 40	22 50	23 05	23 10		23 20	23 35	23 40		23 50
Limehouse d	21 54			22 09	22 14	22 24	22 39	22 44	22 54	23 09	23 14		23 24	23 39	23 44		23 54
West Ham ⊖ d	21 59	22 10		22 15	22 21	22 31	22 45	22 51	23 01	23 16	23 21		23 31	23 46	23 52		00 01
London Liverpool St ⊖ d																	
Stratford ⊖ d																	
Barking ⊖ d	22 04	22 15		22 20	22 26	22 36	22 50	22 56	23 06	23 21	23 26		23 36	23 51	23 58		00 07
Upminster ⊖ d	22 12	22 24			22 35	22 45		23 05	23 15		23 35		23 45		00 06		00 15
Ockendon d	22 18					22 50			23 20				23 50				00 21
Chafford Hundred d	22 21					22 54			23 24				23 54				00 24
West Horndon d					22 40			23 10			23 40				00 11		
Laindon d		22 32			22 44			23 14			23 44				00 16		
Basildon d		22 35			22 47			23 17			23 47				00 19		
Dagenham Dock d				22 25			22 55			23 25				23 55			
Rainham d				22 28			22 58			23 29				23 59			
Purfleet d				22 34			23 04			23 34				00 04			
Grays d	22 25			22a42		22 58	23a12		23 28	23 40			23 58	00 10			00 28
Tilbury Town d	22 28					23 01			23 31	23 43			00 01	00 13			00 31
East Tilbury d	22 34					23 06			23 36	23 48			00 06	00 18			00 37
Stanford-le-Hope d	22 37					23 10			23 40	23 52		←	00 10	00 22		←	00 40
Pitsea d	22 45		←		22 51	23 18		23 21	23 48	23 59	23 51	23 59	00 18	00 29	00 23	00 29	00 48
Benfleet d	22 49	22 40	22 49		22 55	23 21		23 25	23 51	→	23 55	00 03	00 21	→	00 26	00 33	00 52
Leigh-on-Sea d	→	22 45	22 53		22 59	23 26		23 29	23 56		23 59	00 07	00 26		00 31	00 37	00 56
Chalkwell d		22 47	22 56		23 02	23 28		23 32	23 58		00 02	00 10	00 28		00 33	00 40	00 59
Westcliff d		22 50	22 58		23 04	23 31		23 34	00 01		00 04	00 12	00 31		00 36	00 42	01 01
Southend Central a		22 52	23 04		23 08	23 34		23 38	00 04		00 08	00 15	00 34		00 38	00 45	01 04
d		22 53			23 08	23 34		23 38	00 04		00 08	00 15	00 34		00 39	00 45	01 04
Southend East d		22 55			23 10	23 36		23 41	00 06		00 11	00 18	00 36		00 41	00 48	01 07
Thorpe Bay d		22 57			23 13	23 39		23 43	00 09		00 13	00 20	00 39		00 44	00 50	01 09
Shoeburyness a		23 05			23 20	23 45		23 51	00 15		00 21	00 28	00 45		00 51	00 58	01 17

Saturdays from 15 September

	CC	CC	CC	CC	CC	CC	CC	CC	CC	CC	CC	CC	CC	CC	CC	CC	CC	CC	CC	CC	CC	CC
London Fenchurch St ⊖ d	22p50	23p00		23p05	23p10		23p20	23p35	23p40	23p50	00 01		00 15	00 25			05 10	05 35	05 50	06 05	06 10	06 20
Limehouse d	22p54			23p09	23p14		23p24	23p39	23p44	23p54			00 19	00 29			05 14	05 39	05 54	06 09	06 14	06 24
West Ham ⊖ d	22p59	23p08		23p14	23p19		23p29	23p44	23p49	23p59	00 09		00 24	00 34			05 19	05 44	05 59	06 14	06 19	06 29
London Liverpool St ⊖ d																						
Stratford ⊖ d																						
Barking ⊖ d	23p05	23p14		23p20	23p25		23p35	23p50	23p55	00 05	00 15		00 30	00 40			05 24	05 49	06 04	06 19	06 24	06 34
Upminster ⊖ d	23p14	23p23			23p34		23p44		00 04	00 14	00 24			00 49	05 05	05 27	05 32		06 12		06 32	06 42
Ockendon d	23p19						23p49			00 19					05a12	05 32			06 18			06 48
Chafford Hundred d	23p23						23p53			00 23						05 36			06 21			06 51
West Horndon d					23p39				00 09					00 54			05 37				06 37	
Laindon d		23p31			23p44				00 16		00 32			00 59			05 42				06 42	
Basildon d		23p34			23p47				00 19		00 35			01 02			05 45				06 45	
Dagenham Dock d				23p25				23p55					00 35					05 54		06 24		
Rainham d				23p29				23p59					00 39					05 57		06 27		
Purfleet d				23p34				00 04					00 44					06 03		06 33		
Grays d	23p27			23p42			23p57	00a10		00 27			00a50			05a42		06a12	06 25	06a42		06 55
Tilbury Town d	23p30			23p45			00 01			00 30									06 28			06 58
East Tilbury d	23p36			23p51			00 06			00 36									06 34			07 04
Stanford-le-Hope d	23p40			23p55		←	00 10			00 40									06 37			07 07
Pitsea d	23p48		←	00 06	23p52	00 06	00 18		00 22	00 48		←		01 06			05 50		06 45		06 49	07 15
Benfleet d	23p52	23p41	23p52	→	23p56	00 10	00 22		00 26	00 52	00 42	00 52		01 10			05 54		06 49		06 52	07 19
Leigh-on-Sea d	→	23p45	23p56		23p59	00 15	00 27		00 31	→	00 46	00 56		01 14			05 58		06 53		06 57	07 23
Chalkwell d		23p48	23p59		00 03	00 18	00 30		00 34		00 49	00 59		01 17			06 01		06 56		06 59	07 26
Westcliff d		23p51	00 02		00 06	00 20	00 32		00 36		00 52	01 02		01 20			06 03		06 58		07 02	07 28
Southend Central a		23p54	00 05		00 09	00 23	00 35		00 39		00 55	01 05		01 23			06 06		07 04		07 05	07 34
d		23p54	00 05		00 09	00 23	00 35		00 40		00 55	01 05		01 23			06 07				07 06	
Southend East d		23p56	00 07		00 11	00 26	00 38		00 42		00 57	01 07		01 25			06 09				07 08	
Thorpe Bay d		23p59	00 11		00 15	00 29	00 41		00 46		01 01	01 11		01 29			06 12				07 10	
Shoeburyness a		00 06	00 17		00 21	00 36	00 48		00 52		01 07	01 17		01 35			06 19				07 18	

	CC	CC	CC	CC	CC	CC	CC	CC	CC	CC	CC	CC	CC	CC	CC	CC	CC	CC	CC	CC	CC
London Fenchurch St ⊖ d	06 35	06 40	06 50	07 05	07 10	07 20	07 35	07 40	07 50	08 05	08 10	08 20	08 35	08 40	08 50	09 00		09 05	09 10	09 20	09 30
Limehouse d	06 39	06 44	06 54	07 09	07 14	07 24	07 39	07 44	07 54	08 09	08 14	08 24	08 39	08 44	08 54			09 09	09 14	09 24	
West Ham ⊖ d	06 44	06 49	06 59	07 14	07 19	07 29	07 44	07 49	07 59	08 14	08 19	08 29	08 44	08 49	08 59	09 08		09 14	09 19	09 29	09 38
London Liverpool St ⊖ d																					
Stratford ⊖ d																					
Barking ⊖ d	06 49	06 54	07 04	07 19	07 24	07 34	07 49	07 54	08 04	08 19	08 24	08 34	08 49	08 54	09 04	09 13		09 19	09 24	09 34	09 43
Upminster ⊖ d		07 02	07 12		07 32	07 42		08 02	08 12		08 32	08 42		09 02	09 12	09 21			09 32	09 42	09 51
Ockendon d			07 18			07 48			08 18			08 48			09 18					09 48	
Chafford Hundred d			07 21			07 51			08 21			08 51			09 21					09 51	
West Horndon d		07 07			07 37			08 07			08 37			09 07					09 37		
Laindon d		07 12			07 42			08 12			08 42			09 12		09 29			09 42		09 59
Basildon d		07 15			07 45			08 15			08 45			09 15		09 32			09 45		10 02
Dagenham Dock d	06 54			07 24			07 54			08 24			08 54					09 24			
Rainham d	06 57			07 27			07 57			08 27			08 57					09 27			
Purfleet d	07 03			07 33			08 03			08 33			09 03					09 33			
Grays d	07a12		07 25	07a42		07 55	08a12		08 25	08a42		08 55	09a12		09 25			09a42		09 55	
Tilbury Town d			07 28			07 58			08 28			08 58			09 28					09 58	
East Tilbury d			07 34			08 04			08 34			09 04			09 34					10 04	
Stanford-le-Hope d			07 37			08 07			08 37			09 07			09 37					10 07	
Pitsea d		07 19	07 45		07 49	08 15		08 19	08 45		08 49	09 15		09 19	09 45		←		09 49	10 15	
Benfleet d		07 22	07 49		07 52	08 19		08 22	08 49		08 52	09 19		09 22	09 49	09 38	09 49		09 52	10 19	10 08
Leigh-on-Sea d		07 27	07 53		07 57	08 23		08 27	08 53		08 57	09 23		09 27	→	09 42	09 53		09 57	→	10 12
Chalkwell d		07 29	07 56		07 59	08 26		08 29	08 56		08 59	09 26		09 29		09 45	09 56		09 59		10 15
Westcliff d		07 32	07 58		08 02	08 28		08 32	08 58		09 02	09 28		09 32		09 47	09 58		10 02		10 17
Southend Central a		07 35	08 04		08 05	08 34		08 35	09 04		09 05	09 34		09 35		09 50	10 04		10 05		10 20
d		07 36			08 06			08 36			09 06			09 36		09 50			10 06		10 20
Southend East d		07 38			08 08			08 38			09 08			09 38		09 52			10 08		10 22
Thorpe Bay d		07 40			08 10			08 40			09 10			09 40		09 55			10 10		10 25
Shoeburyness a		07 48			08 18			08 48			09 18			09 48		10 02			10 18		10 32

Table 1

London - Southend Central and Shoeburyness

Saturdays from 15 September

Network Diagram - see first page of Table 1

	CC		CC	CC	CC	CC	CC	CC	CC	CC	CC	CC	CC	CC	CC	CC	CC	CC	CC	CC	CC
London Fenchurch St ⊖ d				19 35	19 40	19 50	20 00		20 05	20 10	20 20	20 35	20 40	20 50	21 00		21 05	21 10	21 20	21 35	21 40
Limehouse d				19 39	19 44	19 54			20 09	20 14	20 24	20 39	20 44	20 54			21 09	21 14	21 24	21 39	21 44
West Ham ⊖ d				19 44	19 49	19 59	20 08		20 14	20 19	20 29	20 44	20 49	20 59	21 08		21 14	21 19	21 29	21 44	21 49
London Liverpool St ⊖ d																					
Stratford ⊖ d																					
Barking ⊖ d				19 49	19 54	20 04	20 13		20 19	20 24	20 34	20 49	20 54	21 04	21 13		21 19	21 24	21 34	21 49	21 54
Upminster ⊖ d					20 02	20 12	20 21			20 32	20 42		21 02	21 12	21 21			21 32	21 42		22 02
Ockendon d						20 18					20 48			21 18					21 48		
Chafford Hundred d						20 21					20 51			21 21					21 51		
West Horndon d					20 07					20 37			21 07					21 37			22 07
Laindon d		and at the same minutes past each hour until			20 12		20 29			20 42			21 12		21 29			21 42			22 12
Basildon d					20 15		20 32			20 45			21 15		21 32			21 45			22 15
Dagenham Dock d				19 54					20 24			20 54					21 24			21 54	
Rainham d				19 57					20 27			20 57					21 27			21 57	
Purfleet d				20 03					20 33			21 03					21 33			22 03	
Grays d				20a12		20 25			20a42		20 55	21a12		21 25			21a42		21 55	22a12	
Tilbury Town d						20 28					20 58			21 28					21 58		
East Tilbury d						20 34					21 04			21 34					22 04		
Stanford-le-Hope d						20 37					21 07			21 37					22 07		
Pitsea d	←		←		20 19	20 45		←		20 49	21 15		21 19	21 45		←		21 49	22 15		22 19
Benfleet d	10 19		20 19		20 22	20 49	20 38	20 49		20 52	21 19		21 22	21 49	21 38	21 49		21 52	22 19		22 22
Leigh-on-Sea d	10 23		20 23		20 27	→	20 42	20 53		20 57	21 23		21 27	→	21 42	21 53		21 57	22 23		22 27
Chalkwell d	10 26		20 26		20 29		20 45	20 56		20 59	21 26		21 29		21 45	21 56		21 59	22 26		22 29
Westcliff d	10 28		20 28		20 32		20 47	20 58		21 02	21 28		21 32		21 47	21 58		22 02	22 28		22 32
Southend Central a	10 34		20 34		20 35		20 50	21 04		21 05	21 34		21 35		21 50	22 04		22 05	22 34		22 35
d					20 36		20 50			21 06			21 36		21 50			22 06			22 36
Southend East d					20 38		20 52			21 08			21 38		21 52			22 08			22 38
Thorpe Bay d					20 40		20 55			21 10			21 40		21 55			22 10			22 40
Shoeburyness a					20 48		21 02			21 18			21 48		22 02			22 18			22 48

	CC	CC	CC	CC	CC	CC	CC	CC	CC	CC	CC	CC	CC	CC	CC	CC	CC
London Fenchurch St ⊖ d	21 50	22 00		22 05	22 10	22 20	22 35	22 40	22 50	23 05	23 10		23 20	23 35	23 40		23 50
Limehouse d	21 54			22 09	22 14	22 24	22 39	22 44	22 54	23 09	23 14		23 24	23 39	23 44		23 54
West Ham ⊖ d	21 59	22 08		22 14	22 19	22 29	22 44	22 49	22 59	23 14	23 19		23 29	23 44	23 49		23 59
London Liverpool St ⊖ d																	
Stratford ⊖ d																	
Barking ⊖ d	22 04	22 13		22 19	22 24	22 34	22 49	22 54	23 04	23 19	23 24		23 34	23 49	23 54		00 04
Upminster ⊖ d	22 12	22 21			22 32	22 42		23 02	23 12		23 32		23 42		00 02		00 12
Ockendon d	22 18					22 48			23 18				23 48				00 18
Chafford Hundred d	22 21					22 51			23 21				23 51				00 21
West Horndon d					22 37			23 07			23 37				00 07		
Laindon d		22 29			22 42			23 12			23 42				00 12		
Basildon d		22 32			22 45			23 15			23 45				00 15		
Dagenham Dock d				22 24			22 54			23 24				23 54			
Rainham d				22 27			22 57			23 27				23 57			
Purfleet d				22 33			23 03			23 33				00 03			
Grays d	22 25			22a42		22 55	23a12		23 25	23 38			23 55	00 08			00 25
Tilbury Town d	22 28					22 58			23 28	23 41			23 58	00 11			00 28
East Tilbury d	22 34					23 04			23 34	23 47			00 04	00 17			00 34
Stanford-le-Hope d	22 37					23 07			23 37	23 50		←	00 07	00 20		←	00 37
Pitsea d	22 45		←		22 49	23 15		23 19	23 45	23 58	23 49	23 58	00 15	00 28	00 19	00 28	00 45
Benfleet d	22 49	22 38	22 49		22 52	23 19		23 22	23 49	→	23 52	00 01	00 19	→	00 22	00 31	00 49
Leigh-on-Sea d	→	22 42	22 53		22 57	23 23		23 27	23 53		23 57	00 06	00 23		00 27	00 36	00 53
Chalkwell d		22 45	22 56		22 59	23 26		23 29	23 56		23 59	00 08	00 26		00 29	00 38	00 56
Westcliff d		22 47	22 58		23 02	23 28		23 32	23 58		00 02	00 11	00 28		00 32	00 41	00 58
Southend Central a		22 50	23 04		23 05	23 31		23 35	00 01		00 05	00 14	00 31		00 35	00 44	01 01
d		22 50			23 06	23 31		23 36	00 01		00 06	00 14	00 31		00 36	00 44	01 01
Southend East d		22 52			23 08	23 34		23 38	00 04		00 08	00 16	00 34		00 38	00 46	01 04
Thorpe Bay d		22 55			23 10	23 36		23 41	00 06		00 11	00 19	00 36		00 41	00 49	01 06
Shoeburyness a		23 02			23 18	23 43		23 48	00 13		00 18	00 26	00 43		00 48	00 56	01 13

Sundays until 22 July

	CC	CC	CC	CC	CC	CC	CC	CC	CC	CC	CC	CC	CC	CC	CC	CC	CC	CC	CC	CC	CC	CC
London Fenchurch St ⊖ d	22p50	23p05	23p10		23p20	23p35	23p40		23p50	00 10	00 40	06 40		07 10	07 40	07 50	08 10			08 40	08 50	09 10
Limehouse d	22p54	23p09	23p14		23p24	23p39	23p44		23p54	00 14	00 44	06 44		07 14	07 44	07 54	08 14			08 44	08 54	09 14
West Ham ⊖ d	22p59	23p14	23p19		23p29	23p44	23p49		23p59	00 19	00 49	06 49		07 19	07 49	07 59	08 19			08 49	08 59	09 19
London Liverpool St ⊖ d																						
Stratford ⊖ d																						
Barking ⊖ d	23p04	23p19	23p24		23p34	23p49	23p54		00 04	00 24	00 54	06 54	07 04	07 24	07 54	08 04	08 24	08 29	08 34	08 54	09 04	09 24
Upminster ⊖ d	23p12		23p32		23p42		00 02		00 12	00 32	01 02	07 02	07 12	07 32	08 02	08 12	08 32		08 42	09 02	09 12	09 32
Ockendon d	23p18				23p48				00 18				07 18			08 18			08 48		09 18	
Chafford Hundred d	23p21				23p51				00 21				07 21			08 21			08 51		09 21	
West Horndon d			23p37				00 07			00 37	01 07	07 07		07 37	08 07		08 37			09 07		09 37
Laindon d			23p42				00 12			00 42	01 12	07 12		07 42	08 12		08 42			09 12		09 42
Basildon d			23p45				00 15			00 45	01 15	07 15		07 45	08 15		08 45			09 15		09 45
Dagenham Dock d		23p24				23p54												08 33				
Rainham d		23p27				23p57												08 37				
Purfleet d		23p33				00 03												08 42				
Grays d	23p25	23p38			23p55	00 08			00 25				07 25			08 25		08a50	08 55		09 25	
Tilbury Town d	23p28	23p41			23p58	00 11			00 28				07 28			08 28			08 58		09 28	
East Tilbury d	23p34	23p47			00 04	00 17			00 34				07 34			08 34			09 04		09 34	
Stanford-le-Hope d	23p37	23p50		←	00 07	00 20		←	00 37				07 37			08 37			09 07		09 37	
Pitsea d	23p45	23p58	23p49	23p58	00 15	00 28	00 19	00 28	00 45	00 49	01 19	07 19	07 45	07 49	08 19	08 45	08 49		09 15	09 19	09 45	09 49
Benfleet d	23p49	→	23p52	00 01	00 19	→	00 22	00 31	00 49	00 52	01 22	07 22	07 49	07 52	08 22	08 49	08 52		09 19	09 22	09 49	09 52
Leigh-on-Sea d	23p53		23p57	00 06	00 23		00 27	00 36	00 53	00 57	01 27	07 27	07 53	07 57	08 27	08 53	08 57		09 23	09 27	09 53	09 57
Chalkwell d	23p56		23p59	00 08	00 26		00 29	00 38	00 56	00 59	01 29	07 29	07 56	07 59	08 29	08 56	08 59		09 26	09 29	09 56	09 59
Westcliff d	23p58		00 02	00 11	00 28		00 32	00 41	00 58	01 02	01 32	07 32	07 58	08 02	08 32	08 58	09 02		09 28	09 32	09 58	10 02
Southend Central a	00 01		00 05	00 14	00 31		00 35	00 44	01 01	01 05	01 35	07 34	08 04	08 05	08 34	09 04	09 05		09 34	09 35	10 04	10 05
d	00 01		00 06	00 14	00 31		00 36	00 44	01 01	01 06	01 36	07 36		08 06	08 36		09 06			09 36		10 06
Southend East d	00 04		00 08	00 16	00 34		00 38	00 46	01 04	01 08	01 38	07 38		08 08	08 38		09 08			09 38		10 08
Thorpe Bay d	00 06		00 11	00 19	00 36		00 41	00 49	01 06	01 11	01 41	07 40		08 10	08 40		09 10			09 40		10 10
Shoeburyness a	00 13		00 18	00 26	00 43		00 48	00 56	01 13	01 18	01 48	07 48		08 18	08 48		09 18			09 48		10 18

London - Southend Central and Shoeburyness

Sundays until 22 July

Network Diagram - see first page of Table I

		CC	CC	CC	CC	CC		CC	CC		CC	CC	CC	CC	CC		CC A	CC B	CC	CC	CC	CC	CC	CC
London Fenchurch St 7 ⊖	d			09 40	09 50	10 10			10 20		19 20	19 40	19 50	20 10			20 20	20 20	20 40	20 50	21 10		21 20	21 40
Limehouse	d			09 44	09 54	10 14			10 24		19 24	19 44	19 54	20 14			20 24	20 24	20 44	20 54	21 14		21 24	21 44
West Ham ⊖	d			09 49	09 59	10 19			10 29		19 29	19 49	19 59	20 19			20 29	20 29	20 49	20 59	21 19		21 29	21 49
London Liverpool St 15 ⊖	d																							
Stratford 7 ⊖	d																							
Barking ⊖	d	09 29	09 34	09 54	10 04	10 24		10 29	10 34		19 34	19 54	20 04	20 24	20 29		20 34	20 34	20 54	21 04	21 24	21 29	21 34	21 54
Upminster ⊖	d		09 42	10 02	10 12	10 32			10 42		19 42	20 02	20 12	20 32			20 42	20 42	21 02	21 12	21 32		21 42	22 02
Ockendon	d		09 48		10 18				10 48		19 48		20 18				20 48	20 48		21 18			21 48	
Chafford Hundred	d		09 51		10 21				10 51		19 51		20 21				20 51	20a55		21 21			21 51	
West Horndon	d			10 07		10 37						20 07		20 37					21 07		21 37			22 07
Laindon	d			10 12		10 42				and at the same minutes past each hour until		20 12		20 42					21 12		21 42			22 12
Basildon	d			10 15		10 45						20 15		20 45					21 15		21 45			22 15
Dagenham Dock	d	09 33						10 33							20 33							21 33		
Rainham	d	09 37						10 37							20 37							21 37		
Purfleet	d	09 42						10 42							20 42							21 42		
Grays	d	09a50	09 55		10 25			10a50	10 55		19 55		20 25		20a50		20 55			21 25		21a50	21 55	
Tilbury Town 3	d		09 58		10 28				10 58		19 58		20 28				20 58			21 28			21 58	
East Tilbury	d		10 04		10 34				11 04		20 04		20 34				21 04			21 34			22 04	
Stanford-le-Hope	d		10 07		10 37				11 07		20 07		20 37				21 07			21 37			22 07	
Pitsea	d		10 15	10 19	10 45	10 49			11 15		20 15	20 19	20 45	20 49			21 15		21 19	21 45	21 49		22 15	22 19
Benfleet	d		10 19	10 22	10 49	10 52			11 19		20 19	20 22	20 49	20 52			21 19		21 22	21 49	21 52		22 19	22 22
Leigh-on-Sea	d		10 23	10 27	10 53	10 57			11 23		20 23	20 27	20 53	20 57			21 23		21 27	21 53	21 57		22 23	22 27
Chalkwell	d		10 26	10 29	10 56	10 59			11 26		20 26	20 29	20 56	20 59			21 26		21 29	21 56	21 59		22 26	22 29
Westcliff	d		10 28	10 32	10 58	11 02			11 28		20 28	20 32	20 58	21 02			21 28		21 32	21 58	22 02		22 28	22 32
Southend Central	a		10 34	10 35	11 04	11 05			11 34		20 34	20 35	21 04	21 05			21 32		21 35	22 04	22 05		22 31	22 35
	d			10 36		11 06						20 36		21 06			21 32		21 36		22 06		22 31	22 36
Southend East	d			10 38		11 08						20 38		21 08			21 34		21 38		22 08		22 33	22 38
Thorpe Bay	d			10 40		11 10						20 40		21 10			21 36		21 40		22 10		22 36	22 40
Shoeburyness	a			10 48		11 18						20 48		21 18			21 44		21 48		22 18		22 43	22 48

		CC		CC	CC	CC	CC	CC
London Fenchurch St 7 ⊖	d	21 50		22 10	22 40	22 50	23 10	23 40
Limehouse	d	21 54		22 14	22 44	22 54	23 14	23 44
West Ham ⊖	d	21 59		22 19	22 49	22 59	23 19	23 49
London Liverpool St 15 ⊖	d							
Stratford 7 ⊖	d							
Barking ⊖	d	22 04		22 24	22 54	23 04	23 24	23 54
Upminster ⊖	d	22 12		22 32	23 02	23 12	23 32	00 02
Ockendon	d	22 18				23 18		
Chafford Hundred	d	22 21				23 21		
West Horndon	d			22 37	23 07		23 37	00 07
Laindon	d			22 42	23 12		23 42	00 12
Basildon	d			22 45	23 15		23 45	00 15
Dagenham Dock	d							
Rainham	d							
Purfleet	d							
Grays	d	22 25				23 25		
Tilbury Town 3	d	22 28				23 28		
East Tilbury	d	22 34				23 34		
Stanford-le-Hope	d	22 37				23 37		
Pitsea	d	22 45		22 49	23 19	23 45	23 49	00 19
Benfleet	d	22 49		22 52	23 22	23 49	23 52	00 22
Leigh-on-Sea	d	22 53		22 57	23 27	23 53	23 57	00 27
Chalkwell	d	22 56		22 59	23 29	23 56	23 59	00 29
Westcliff	d	22 58		23 02	23 32	23 58	00 02	00 32
Southend Central	a	23 01		23 05	23 35	00 01	00 05	00 35
	d	23 01		23 06	23 36	00 01	00 06	00 36
Southend East	d	23 03		23 08	23 38	00 03	00 08	00 38
Thorpe Bay	d	23 06		23 10	23 40	00 06	00 10	00 40
Shoeburyness	a	23 13		23 18	23 48	00 13	00 18	00 48

A from 3 June until 22 July, not 8 July

B 8 July

London - Southend Central and Shoeburyness

Sundays 29 July to 12 August

Network Diagram - see first page of Table I

		CC	CC	CC	CC	CC	CC	CC	CC	CC		CC	CC	CC	CC	CC	CC	CC A	CC	CC A		CC	CC A	CC A	CC
London Fenchurch St 7 ⊖	d	22p50	23p05	23p10		23p20	23p35	23p40		23p50		00 10	00 40	00 50	06 40		07 10	07 30	07 40	07 45		07 50	07 58	08 05	08 10
Limehouse	d	22p54	23p09	23p14		23p24	23p39	23p44		23p54		00 14	00 44	00 54	06 44		07 14		07 44			07 54			08 14
West Ham ⊖	d	23p01	23p16	23p21		23p31	23p46	23p52		00 01		00 21	00 51	01 01	06 49		07 19	07 41	07 49	07 56		07 59	08 09	08 16	08 19
London Liverpool St 15 ⊖	d																								
Stratford 7 ⊖	d																								
Barking ⊖	d	23p06	23p21	23p26		23p36	23p51	23p58		00 07		00 26	00 56	01 06	06 54	07 04	07 24		07 54			08 04			08 24
Upminster ⊖	d	23p15		23p35		23p45		00 06		00 15		00 35	01 05	01 15	07 02	07 12	07 32		08 02			08 12			08 32
Ockendon	d	23p20				23p50				00 21						07 18						08 18			
Chafford Hundred	d	23p24				23p54				00 24						07 21						08 21			
West Horndon	d			23p40				00 11				00 40	01 10	01 20	07 07		07 37		08 07						08 37
Laindon	d			23p44				00 16				00 44	01 14	01 24	07 12		07 42		08 12						08 42
Basildon	d			23p47				00 19				00 47	01 17	01 27	07 15		07 45		08 15						08 45
Dagenham Dock	d		23p25				23p55																		
Rainham	d		23p29				23p59																		
Purfleet	d		23p34				00 04																		
Grays	d	23p28	23p40			23p58	00 10			00 28						07 25						08 25			
Tilbury Town 3	d	23p31	23p43			00 01	00 13			00 31						07 28						08 28			
East Tilbury	d	23p36	23p48			00 06	00 18			00 37						07 34						08 34			
Stanford-le-Hope	d	23p40	23p52		←	00 10	00 22		←	00 40						07 37						08 37			
Pitsea	d	23p48	23p59	23p51	23p59	00 18	00 29	00 23	00 29	00 48		00 51	01 21	01 31	07 19	07 45	07 49		08 19			08 45			08 49
Benfleet	d	23p51	→	23p55	00 03	00 21	→	00 26	00 33	00 52		00 55	01 25	01 35	07 22	07 49	07 52		08 22			08 49			08 52
Leigh-on-Sea	d	23p56		23p59	00 07	00 26		00 31	00 37	00 56		00 59	01 29	01 39	07 27	07 53	07 57	08a11	08 27	08a33		08 53	08a40	08a50	08 57
Chalkwell	d	23p58		00 02	00 10	00 28		00 33	00 40	00 59		01 02	01 32	01 42	07 29	07 56	07 59		08 29			08 56			08 59
Westcliff	d	00 01		00 04	00 12	00 31		00 36	00 42	01 01		01 04	01 34	01 44	07 32	07 58	08 02		08 32			08 58			09 02
Southend Central	a	00 04		00 08	00 15	00 34		00 38	00 45	01 04		01 08	01 38	01 48	07 34	08 04	08 05		08 34			09 04			09 05
	d	00 04		00 08	00 15	00 34		00 39	00 45	01 04		01 08	01 38	01 48	07 36		08 06		08 36						09 06
Southend East	d	00 06		00 11	00 18	00 36		00 41	00 48	01 07		01 11	01 41	01 51	07 38		08 08		08 38						09 08
Thorpe Bay	d	00 09		00 13	00 20	00 39		00 44	00 50	01 09		01 13	01 43	01 53	07 40		08 10		08 40						09 10
Shoeburyness	a	00 15		00 21	00 28	00 45		00 51	00 58	01 17		01 21	01 51	02 01	07 48		08 18		08 48						09 18

		CC A	CC	CC A	CC A	CC		CC	CC A	CC	CC A	CC A	CC	CC A	CC A	CC		CC	CC	CC	CC	CC	CC	
London Fenchurch St 7 ⊖	d	08 22		08 30	08 36			08 40	08 46	08 50	08 58	09 06	09 10	09 13	09 28				09 40	09 50	10 10		10 20	
Limehouse	d							08 44		08 54			09 14						09 44	09 54	10 14		10 24	
West Ham ⊖	d	08 33		08 41	08 47			08 49	08 57	08 59	09 09	09 17	09 19	09 24	09 39				09 49	09 59	10 19		10 29	
London Liverpool St 15 ⊖	d																							
Stratford 7 ⊖	d																							
Barking ⊖	d		08 29			08 34		08 54		09 04			09 24			09 29		09 34	09 54	10 04	10 24	10 29	10 34	
Upminster ⊖	d					08 42		09 02		09 12			09 32					09 42	10 02	10 12	10 32		10 42	
Ockendon	d					08 48				09 18								09 48		10 18			10 48	
Chafford Hundred	d					08 51				09 21								09 51		10 21			10 51	
West Horndon	d							09 07					09 37						10 07		10 37			
Laindon	d							09 12					09 42						10 12		10 42			and at the same minutes past each hour until
Basildon	d							09 15					09 45						10 15		10 45			
Dagenham Dock	d		08 33													09 33						10 33		
Rainham	d		08 37													09 37						10 37		
Purfleet	d		08 42													09 42						10 42		
Grays	d		08a50			08 55				09 25						09a50		09 55		10 25		10a50	10 55	
Tilbury Town 3	d					08 58				09 28								09 58		10 28			10 58	
East Tilbury	d					09 04				09 34								10 04		10 34			11 04	
Stanford-le-Hope	d					09 07				09 37								10 07		10 37			11 07	
Pitsea	d					09 15		09 19		09 45			09 49					10 15	10 19	10 45	10 49		11 15	
Benfleet	d					09 19		09 22		09 49			09 52					10 19	10 22	10 49	10 52		11 19	
Leigh-on-Sea	d	09a05		09a11	09a17	09 23		09 27	09a33	09 53	09a39	09a50	09 57	10a03	10a09			10 23	10 27	10 53	10 57		11 23	
Chalkwell	d					09 26		09 29		09 56			09 59					10 26	10 29	10 56	10 59		11 26	
Westcliff	d					09 28		09 32		09 58			10 02					10 28	10 32	10 58	11 02		11 28	
Southend Central	a					09 34		09 35		10 04			10 05					10 34	10 35	11 04	11 05		11 34	
	d							09 36					10 06						10 36		11 06			
Southend East	d							09 38					10 08						10 38		11 08			
Thorpe Bay	d							09 40					10 10						10 40		11 10			
Shoeburyness	a							09 48					10 18						10 48		11 18			

		CC		CC	CC	CC	CC	CC	CC	CC	CC	CC		CC	CC	CC	CC	CC	CC	CC	CC
London Fenchurch St 7 ⊖	d	19 20		19 40	19 50	20 10		20 20	20 40	20 50	21 10			21 20	21 40	21 50	22 10	22 40	22 50	23 10	23 40
Limehouse	d	19 24		19 44	19 54	20 14		20 24	20 44	20 54	21 14			21 24	21 44	21 54	22 14	22 44	22 54	23 14	23 44
West Ham ⊖	d	19 29		19 49	19 59	20 19		20 29	20 49	20 59	21 19			21 29	21 49	21 59	22 21	22 51	23 01	23 21	23 51
London Liverpool St 15 ⊖	d																				
Stratford 7 ⊖	d																				
Barking ⊖	d	19 34		19 54	20 04	20 24	20 29	20 34	20 54	21 04	21 24	21 29		21 34	21 54	22 04	22 26	22 56	23 06	23 26	23 56
Upminster ⊖	d	19 42		20 02	20 12	20 32		20 42	21 02	21 12	21 32			21 42	22 02	22 12	22 35	23 05	23 14	23 35	00 05
Ockendon	d	19 48			20 18			20 48		21 18				21 48		22 18			23 19		
Chafford Hundred	d	19 51			20 21			20 51		21 21				21 51		22 21			23 23		
West Horndon	d			20 07		20 37			21 07		21 37				22 07		22 40	23 10		23 40	00 10
Laindon	d			20 12		20 42			21 12		21 42				22 12		22 44	23 14		23 44	00 14
Basildon	d			20 15		20 45			21 15		21 45				22 15		22 47	23 17		23 47	00 17
Dagenham Dock	d						20 33					21 33									
Rainham	d						20 37					21 37									
Purfleet	d						20 42					21 42									
Grays	d	19 55			20 25		20a50	20 55		21 25		21a50		21 55		22 25			23 27		
Tilbury Town 3	d	19 58			20 28			20 58		21 28				21 58		22 28			23 30		
East Tilbury	d	20 04			20 34			21 04		21 34				22 04		22 34			23 35		
Stanford-le-Hope	d	20 07			20 37			21 07		21 37				22 07		22 37			23 39		
Pitsea	d	20 15		20 19	20 45	20 49		21 15	21 19	21 45	21 49			22 15	22 19	22 45	22 51	23 21	23 47	23 51	00 21
Benfleet	d	20 19		20 22	20 49	20 52		21 19	21 22	21 49	21 52			22 19	22 22	22 49	22 55	23 25	23 50	23 55	00 25
Leigh-on-Sea	d	20 23		20 27	20 53	20 57		21 23	21 27	21 53	21 57			22 23	22 27	22 53	22 59	23 29	23 55	23 59	00 29
Chalkwell	d	20 26		20 29	20 56	20 59		21 26	21 29	21 56	21 59			22 26	22 29	22 56	23 02	23 32	23 57	00 02	00 32
Westcliff	d	20 28		20 32	20 58	21 02		21 28	21 32	21 58	22 02			22 28	22 32	22 58	23 04	23 34	23 59	00 04	00 34
Southend Central	a	20 34		20 35	21 04	21 05		21 32	21 35	22 04	22 05			22 31	22 35	23 01	23 08	23 38	00 03	00 08	00 38
	d			20 36		21 06		21 32	21 36		22 06			22 31	22 36	23 01	23 08	23 38	00 03	00 08	00 38
Southend East	d			20 38		21 08		21 34	21 38		22 08			22 33	22 38	23 03	23 11	23 41	00 05	00 11	00 41
Thorpe Bay	d			20 40		21 10		21 36	21 40		22 10			22 36	22 40	23 06	23 12	23 42	00 07	00 12	00 42
Shoeburyness	a			20 48		21 18		21 44	21 48		22 18			22 43	22 48	23 13	23 21	23 51	00 15	00 21	00 51

A not from 29 July until 5 August

Table 1

Sundays

19 August to 26 August

London - Southend Central and Shoeburyness

Network Diagram - see first page of Table 1

		CC	CC	CC	CC	CC	CC	CC	CC	CC	CC	CC	CC	CC	CC	CC	CC	CC	CC	CC	CC	CC	CC
London Fenchurch St 7 ⊖	d	22p50	23p05	23p10		23p20	23p35	23p40		23p50	00 10	00 40	06 40		07 10	07 40	07 50	08 10			08 40	08 50	09 10
Limehouse	d	22p54	23p09	23p14		23p24	23p39	23p44		23p54	00 14	00 44	06 44		07 14	07 44	07 54	08 14			08 44	08 54	09 14
West Ham ⊖	d	22p59	23p14	23p19		23p29	23p44	23p49		23p59	00 19	00 49	06 49		07 19	07 49	07 59	08 19			08 49	08 59	09 19
London Liverpool St 15 ⊖	d																						
Stratford 7 ⊖	d																						
Barking ⊖	d	23p04	23p19	23p24		23p34	23p49	23p54		00 04	00 24	00 54	06 54	07 04	07 24	07 54	08 04	08 24	08 29	08 34	08 54	09 04	09 24
Upminster ⊖	d	23p12		23p32		23p42		00 02		00 12	00 32	01 02	07 02	07 12	07 32	08 02	08 12	08 32		08 42	09 02	09 12	09 32
Ockendon	d	23p18				23p48				00 18				07 18			08 18			08 48		09 18	
Chafford Hundred	d	23p21				23p51				00 21				07 21			08 21			08 51		09 21	
West Horndon	d			23p37				00 07			00 37	01 07	07 07		07 37	08 07		08 37			09 07		09 37
Laindon	d			23p42				00 12			00 42	01 12	07 12		07 42	08 12		08 42			09 12		09 42
Basildon	d			23p45				00 15			00 45	01 15	07 15		07 45	08 15		08 45			09 15		09 45
Dagenham Dock	d		23p24				23p54												08 33				
Rainham	d		23p27				23p57												08 37				
Purfleet	d		23p33				00 03												08 42				
Grays	d	23p25	23p38			23p55	00 08			00 25				07 25			08 25		08a50	08 55		09 25	
Tilbury Town 3	d	23p28	23p41			23p58	00 11			00 28				07 28			08 28			08 58		09 28	
East Tilbury	d	23p34	23p47			00 04	00 17			00 34				07 34			08 34			09 04		09 34	
Stanford-le-Hope	d	23p37	23p50		←	00 07	00 20		←	00 37				07 37			08 37			09 07		09 37	
Pitsea	d	23p45	23p58	23p49	23p58	00 15	00 28	00 19	00 28	00 45	00 49	01 19	07 19	07 45	07 49	08 19	08 45	08 49		09 15	09 19	09 45	09 49
Benfleet	d	23p49	→	23p52	00 01	00 19	→	00 22	00 31	00 49	00 52	01 22	07 22	07 49	07 52	08 22	08 49	08 52		09 19	09 22	09 49	09 52
Leigh-on-Sea	d	23p53		23p57	00 06	00 23		00 27	00 36	00 53	00 57	01 27	07 27	07 53	07 57	08 27	08 53	08 57		09 23	09 27	09 53	09 57
Chalkwell	d	23p56		23p59	00 08	00 26		00 29	00 38	00 56	00 59	01 29	07 29	07 56	07 59	08 29	08 56	08 59		09 26	09 29	09 56	09 59
Westcliff	d	23p58		00 02	00 11	00 28		00 32	00 41	00 58	01 02	01 32	07 32	07 58	08 02	08 32	08 58	09 02		09 28	09 32	09 58	10 02
Southend Central	a	00 01		00 05	00 14	00 31		00 35	00 44	01 01	01 05	01 35	07 34	08 04	08 05	08 34	09 04	09 05		09 34	09 35	10 04	10 05
	d	00 01		00 06	00 14	00 31		00 36	00 44	01 01	01 06	01 36	07 36		08 06	08 36		09 06			09 36		10 06
Southend East	d	00 04		00 08	00 16	00 34		00 38	00 46	01 04	01 08	01 38	07 38		08 08	08 38		09 08			09 38		10 08
Thorpe Bay	d	00 06		00 11	00 19	00 36		00 41	00 49	01 06	01 11	01 41	07 40		08 10	08 40		09 10			09 40		10 10
Shoeburyness	a	00 13		00 18	00 26	00 43		00 48	00 56	01 13	01 18	01 48	07 48		08 18	08 48		09 18			09 48		10 18

		CC	CC	CC	CC	CC	CC	CC	and at the same minutes past each hour until	CC	CC	CC	CC	CC	CC	CC	CC	CC	CC	CC	CC	CC
London Fenchurch St 7 ⊖	d			09 40	09 50	10 10		10 20		19 20	19 40	19 50	20 10		20 20	20 40	20 50	21 10		21 20	21 40	21 50
Limehouse	d			09 44	09 54	10 14		10 24		19 24	19 44	19 54	20 14		20 24	20 44	20 54	21 14		21 24	21 44	21 54
West Ham ⊖	d			09 49	09 59	10 19		10 29		19 29	19 49	19 59	20 19		20 29	20 49	20 59	21 19		21 29	21 49	21 59
London Liverpool St 15 ⊖	d																					
Stratford 7 ⊖	d																					
Barking ⊖	d	09 29	09 34	09 54	10 04	10 24	10 29	10 34		19 34	19 54	20 04	20 24	20 29	20 34	20 54	21 04	21 24	21 29	21 34	21 54	22 04
Upminster ⊖	d		09 42	10 02	10 12	10 32		10 42		19 42	20 02	20 12	20 32		20 42	21 02	21 12	21 32		21 42	22 02	22 12
Ockendon	d		09 48		10 18			10 48		19 48		20 18			20 48		21 18			21 48		22 18
Chafford Hundred	d		09 51		10 21			10 51		19 51		20 21			20 51		21 21			21 51		22 21
West Horndon	d			10 07		10 37					20 07		20 37			21 07		21 37			22 07	
Laindon	d			10 12		10 42					20 12		20 42			21 12		21 42			22 12	
Basildon	d			10 15		10 45					20 15		20 45			21 15		21 45			22 15	
Dagenham Dock	d	09 33					10 33							20 33					21 33			
Rainham	d	09 37					10 37							20 37					21 37			
Purfleet	d	09 42					10 42							20 42					21 42			
Grays	d	09a50	09 55		10 25		10a50	10 55		19 55		20 25		20a50	20 55		21 25		21a50	21 55		22 25
Tilbury Town 3	d		09 58		10 28			10 58		19 58		20 28			20 58		21 28			21 58		22 28
East Tilbury	d		10 04		10 34			11 04		20 04		20 34			21 04		21 34			22 04		22 34
Stanford-le-Hope	d		10 07		10 37			11 07		20 07		20 37			21 07		21 37			22 07		22 37
Pitsea	d		10 15	10 19	10 45	10 49		11 15		20 15	20 19	20 45	20 49		21 15	21 19	21 45	21 49		22 15	22 19	22 45
Benfleet	d		10 19	10 22	10 49	10 52		11 19		20 19	20 22	20 49	20 52		21 19	21 22	21 49	21 52		22 19	22 22	22 49
Leigh-on-Sea	d		10 23	10 27	10 53	10 57		11 23		20 23	20 27	20 53	20 57		21 23	21 27	21 53	21 57		22 23	22 27	22 53
Chalkwell	d		10 26	10 29	10 56	10 59		11 26		20 26	20 29	20 56	20 59		21 26	21 29	21 56	21 59		22 26	22 29	22 56
Westcliff	d		10 28	10 32	10 58	11 02		11 28		20 28	20 32	20 58	21 02		21 28	21 32	21 58	22 02		22 28	22 32	22 58
Southend Central	a		10 34	10 35	11 04	11 05		11 34		20 34	20 35	21 04	21 05		21 32	21 35	22 04	22 05		22 31	22 35	23 01
	d			10 36		11 06					20 36		21 06		21 32	21 36		22 06		22 31	22 36	23 01
Southend East	d			10 38		11 08					20 38		21 08		21 34	21 38		22 08		22 33	22 38	23 03
Thorpe Bay	d			10 40		11 10					20 40		21 10		21 36	21 40		22 10		22 36	22 40	23 06
Shoeburyness	a			10 48		11 18					20 48		21 18		21 44	21 48		22 18		22 43	22 48	23 13

		CC	CC	CC	CC	CC
London Fenchurch St 7 ⊖	d	22 10	22 40	22 50	23 10	23 40
Limehouse	d	22 14	22 44	22 54	23 14	23 44
West Ham ⊖	d	22 19	22 49	22 59	23 19	23 49
London Liverpool St 15 ⊖	d					
Stratford 7 ⊖	d					
Barking ⊖	d	22 24	22 54	23 04	23 24	23 54
Upminster ⊖	d	22 32	23 02	23 12	23 32	00 02
Ockendon	d			23 18		
Chafford Hundred	d			23 21		
West Horndon	d	22 37	23 07		23 37	00 07
Laindon	d	22 42	23 12		23 42	00 12
Basildon	d	22 45	23 15		23 45	00 15
Dagenham Dock	d					
Rainham	d					
Purfleet	d					
Grays	d			23 25		
Tilbury Town 3	d			23 28		
East Tilbury	d			23 34		
Stanford-le-Hope	d			23 37		
Pitsea	d	22 49	23 19	23 45	23 49	00 19
Benfleet	d	22 52	23 22	23 49	23 52	00 22
Leigh-on-Sea	d	22 57	23 27	23 53	23 57	00 27
Chalkwell	d	22 59	23 29	23 56	23 59	00 29
Westcliff	d	23 02	23 32	23 58	00 02	00 32
Southend Central	a	23 05	23 35	00 01	00 05	00 35
	d	23 06	23 36	00 01	00 06	00 36
Southend East	d	23 08	23 38	00 03	00 08	00 38
Thorpe Bay	d	23 10	23 40	00 06	00 10	00 40
Shoeburyness	a	23 18	23 48	00 13	00 18	00 48

Table 1

Sundays

2 September to 9 September

London - Southend Central and Shoeburyness

Network Diagram - see first page of Table 1

		CC	CC	CC	CC	CC	CC	CC	CC	CC	CC	CC	CC	CC	CC	CC	CC	CC	CC	CC	CC	CC	CC
London Fenchurch St 7 ⊖	d	22p50	23p05	23p10		23p20	23p35	23p40		23p50	00 10	00 40	00 50	06 40		07 10	07 40	07 50	08 10			08 40	08 50
Limehouse	d	22p54	23p09	23p14		23p24	23p39	23p44		23p54	00 14	00 44	00 54	06 44		07 14	07 44	07 54	08 14			08 44	08 54
West Ham ⊖	d	23p01	23p16	23p21		23p31	23p46	23p52		00 01	00 21	00 51	01 01	06 49		07 19	07 49	07 59	08 19			08 49	08 59
London Liverpool St 15 ⊖	d																						
Stratford 7 ⊖	d																						
Barking ⊖	d	23p06	23p21	23p26		23p36	23p51	23p58		00 07	00 26	00 56	01 06	06 54	07 04	07 24	07 54	08 04	08 24	08 29	08 34	08 54	09 04
Upminster ⊖	d	23p15		23p35		23p45		00 06		00 15	00 35	01 05	01 15	07 02	07 12	07 32	08 02	08 12	08 32		08 42	09 02	09 12
Ockendon	d	23p20				23p50				00 21					07 18			08 18			08 48		09 18
Chafford Hundred	d	23p24				23p54				00 24					07 21			08 21			08 51		09 21
West Horndon	d			23p40				00 11			00 40	01 10	01 20	07 07		07 37	08 07		08 37			09 07	
Laindon	d			23p44				00 16			00 44	01 14	01 24	07 12		07 42	08 12		08 42			09 12	
Basildon	d			23p47				00 19			00 47	01 17	01 27	07 15		07 45	08 15		08 45			09 15	
Dagenham Dock	d		23p25				23p55													08 33			
Rainham	d		23p29				23p59													08 37			
Purfleet	d		23p34				00 04													08 42			
Grays	d	23p28	23p40			23p58	00 10			00 28					07 25			08 25		08a50	08 55		09 25
Tilbury Town 3	d	23p31	23p43			00 01	00 13			00 31					07 28			08 28			08 58		09 28
East Tilbury	d	23p36	23p48			00 06	00 18			00 37					07 34			08 34			09 04		09 34
Stanford-le-Hope	d	23p40	23p52		←	00 10	00 22		←	00 40					07 37			08 37			09 07		09 37
Pitsea	d	23p48	23p59	23p51	23p59	00 18	00 29	00 23	00 29	00 48	00 51	01 21	01 31	07 19	07 45	07 49	08 19	08 45	08 49		09 15	09 19	09 45
Benfleet	d	23p51	→	23p55	00 03	00 21	→	00 26	00 33	00 52	00 55	01 25	01 35	07 22	07 49	07 52	08 22	08 49	08 52		09 19	09 22	09 49
Leigh-on-Sea	d	23p56		23p59	00 07	00 26		00 31	00 37	00 56	00 59	01 29	01 39	07 27	07 53	07 57	08 27	08 53	08 57		09 23	09 27	09 53
Chalkwell	d	23p58		00 02	00 10	00 28		00 33	00 40	00 59	01 02	01 32	01 42	07 29	07 56	07 59	08 29	08 56	08 59		09 26	09 29	09 56
Westcliff	d	00 01		00 04	00 12	00 31		00 36	00 42	01 01	01 04	01 34	01 44	07 32	07 58	08 02	08 32	08 58	09 02		09 28	09 32	09 58
Southend Central	a	00 04		00 08	00 15	00 34		00 38	00 45	01 04	01 08	01 38	01 48	07 34	08 04	08 05	08 34	09 04	09 05		09 34	09 35	10 04
	d	00 04		00 08	00 15	00 34		00 39	00 45	01 04	01 08	01 38	01 48	07 36		08 06	08 36		09 06			09 36	
Southend East	d	00 06		00 11	00 18	00 36		00 41	00 48	01 07	01 11	01 41	01 51	07 38		08 08	08 38		09 08			09 38	
Thorpe Bay	d	00 09		00 13	00 20	00 39		00 44	00 50	01 09	01 13	01 43	01 53	07 40		08 10	08 40		09 10			09 40	
Shoeburyness	a	00 15		00 21	00 28	00 45		00 51	00 58	01 17	01 21	01 51	02 01	07 48		08 18	08 48		09 18			09 48	

		CC	CC	CC	CC	CC	CC	CC	CC	and at the same minutes past each hour until	CC	CC	CC	CC	CC	CC	CC	CC	CC	CC	CC	CC
London Fenchurch St 7 ⊖	d	09 10			09 40	09 50	10 10		10 20		19 20	19 40	19 50	20 10		20 20	20 40	20 50	21 10		21 20	21 40
Limehouse	d	09 14			09 44	09 54	10 14		10 24		19 24	19 44	19 54	20 14		20 24	20 44	20 54	21 14		21 24	21 44
West Ham ⊖	d	09 19			09 49	09 59	10 19		10 29		19 29	19 49	19 59	20 19		20 29	20 49	20 59	21 19		21 29	21 49
London Liverpool St 15 ⊖	d																					
Stratford 7 ⊖	d																					
Barking ⊖	d	09 24	09 29	09 34	09 54	10 04	10 24	10 29	10 34		19 34	19 54	20 04	20 24	20 29	20 34	20 54	21 04	21 24	21 29	21 34	21 54
Upminster ⊖	d	09 32		09 42	10 02	10 12	10 32		10 42		19 42	20 02	20 12	20 32		20 42	21 02	21 12	21 32		21 42	22 02
Ockendon	d			09 48		10 18			10 48		19 48		20 18			20 48		21 18			21 48	
Chafford Hundred	d			09 51		10 21			10 51		19 51		20 21			20 51		21 21			21 51	
West Horndon	d	09 37			10 07		10 37					20 07		20 37			21 07		21 37			22 07
Laindon	d	09 42			10 12		10 42					20 12		20 42			21 12		21 42			22 12
Basildon	d	09 45			10 15		10 45					20 15		20 45			21 15		21 45			22 15
Dagenham Dock	d		09 33					10 33							20 33					21 33		
Rainham	d		09 37					10 37							20 37					21 37		
Purfleet	d		09 42					10 42							20 42					21 42		
Grays	d		09a50	09 55		10 25		10a50	10 55		19 55		20 25		20a50	20 55		21 25		21a50	21 55	
Tilbury Town 3	d			09 58		10 28			10 58		19 58		20 28			20 58		21 28			21 58	
East Tilbury	d			10 04		10 34			11 04		20 04		20 34			21 04		21 34			22 04	
Stanford-le-Hope	d			10 07		10 37			11 07		20 07		20 37			21 07		21 37			22 07	
Pitsea	d	09 49		10 15	10 19	10 45	10 49		11 15		20 15	20 19	20 45	20 49		21 15	21 19	21 45	21 49		22 15	22 19
Benfleet	d	09 52		10 19	10 22	10 49	10 52		11 19		20 19	20 22	20 49	20 52		21 19	21 22	21 49	21 52		22 19	22 22
Leigh-on-Sea	d	09 57		10 23	10 27	10 53	10 57		11 23		20 23	20 27	20 53	20 57		21 23	21 27	21 53	21 57		22 23	22 27
Chalkwell	d	09 59		10 26	10 29	10 56	10 59		11 26		20 26	20 29	20 56	20 59		21 26	21 29	21 56	21 59		22 26	22 29
Westcliff	d	10 02		10 28	10 32	10 58	11 02		11 28		20 28	20 32	20 58	21 02		21 28	21 32	21 58	22 02		22 28	22 32
Southend Central	a	10 05		10 34	10 35	11 04	11 05		11 34		20 34	20 35	21 04	21 05		21 32	21 35	22 04	22 05		22 31	22 35
	d	10 06			10 36		11 06					20 36		21 06		21 32	21 36		22 06		22 31	22 36
Southend East	d	10 08			10 38		11 08					20 38		21 08		21 34	21 38		22 08		22 33	22 38
Thorpe Bay	d	10 10			10 40		11 10					20 40		21 10		21 36	21 40		22 10		22 36	22 40
Shoeburyness	a	10 18			10 48		11 18					20 48		21 18		21 44	21 48		22 18		22 43	22 48

		CC	CC	CC	CC	CC	CC
London Fenchurch St 7 ⊖	d	21 50	22 10	22 40	22 50	23 10	23 40
Limehouse	d	21 54	22 14	22 44	22 54	23 14	23 44
West Ham ⊖	d	21 59	22 21	22 51	23 01	23 21	23 51
London Liverpool St 15 ⊖	d						
Stratford 7 ⊖	d						
Barking ⊖	d	22 04	22 26	22 56	23 06	23 26	23 56
Upminster ⊖	d	22 12	22 35	23 05	23 14	23 35	00 05
Ockendon	d	22 18			23 19		
Chafford Hundred	d	22 21			23 23		
West Horndon	d		22 40	23 10		23 40	00 10
Laindon	d		22 44	23 14		23 44	00 14
Basildon	d		22 47	23 17		23 47	00 17
Dagenham Dock	d						
Rainham	d						
Purfleet	d						
Grays	d	22 25			23 27		
Tilbury Town 3	d	22 28			23 30		
East Tilbury	d	22 34			23 35		
Stanford-le-Hope	d	22 37			23 39		
Pitsea	d	22 45	22 51	23 21	23 47	23 51	00 21
Benfleet	d	22 49	22 55	23 25	23 50	23 55	00 25
Leigh-on-Sea	d	22 53	22 59	23 29	23 55	23 59	00 29
Chalkwell	d	22 56	23 02	23 32	23 57	00 02	00 32
Westcliff	d	22 58	23 04	23 34	23 59	00 04	00 34
Southend Central	a	23 01	23 08	23 38	00 03	00 08	00 38
	d	23 01	23 08	23 38	00 03	00 08	00 38
Southend East	d	23 03	23 11	23 41	00 05	00 11	00 41
Thorpe Bay	d	23 06	23 12	23 42	00 07	00 12	00 42
Shoeburyness	a	23 13	23 21	23 51	00 15	00 21	00 51

Table 1

London - Southend Central and Shoeburyness

Sundays from 16 September

Network Diagram - see first page of Table 1

		CC	CC	CC	CC	CC	CC	CC	CC	CC	CC	CC	CC	CC	CC	CC	CC	CC	CC	CC	CC	CC	CC
London Fenchurch St [7] ⊖	d	22p50	23p05	23p10		23p20	23p35	23p40		23p50	00 10	00 40	06 40		07 10	07 40	07 50	08 10			08 40	08 50	09 10
Limehouse	d	22p54	23p09	23p14		23p24	23p39	23p44		23p54	00 14	00 44	06 44		07 14	07 44	07 54	08 14			08 44	08 54	09 14
West Ham ⊖	d	22p59	23p14	23p19		23p29	23p44	23p49		23p59	00 19	00 49	06 49		07 19	07 49	07 59	08 19			08 49	08 59	09 19
London Liverpool St [15] ⊖	d																						
Stratford [7] ⊖	d																						
Barking ⊖	d	23p04	23p19	23p24		23p34	23p49	23p54		00 04	00 24	00 54	06 54	07 04	07 24	07 54	08 04	08 24	08 29	08 34	08 54	09 04	09 24
Upminster ⊖	d	23p12		23p32		23p42		00 02		00 12	00 32	01 02	07 02	07 12	07 32	08 02	08 12	08 32		08 42	09 02	09 12	09 32
Ockendon	d	23p18				23p48				00 18				07 18			08 18			08 48		09 18	
Chafford Hundred	d	23p21				23p51				00 21				07 21			08 21			08 51		09 21	
West Horndon	d			23p37				00 07			00 37	01 07	07 07		07 37	08 07		08 37			09 07		09 37
Laindon	d			23p42				00 12			00 42	01 12	07 12		07 42	08 12		08 42			09 12		09 42
Basildon	d			23p45				00 15			00 45	01 15	07 15		07 45	08 15		08 45			09 15		09 45
Dagenham Dock	d		23p24				23p54												08 33				
Rainham	d		23p27				23p57												08 37				
Purfleet	d		23p33				00 03												08 42				
Grays	d	23p25	23p38			23p55	00 08			00 25				07 25			08 25		08a50	08 55		09 25	
Tilbury Town [3]	d	23p28	23p41			23p58	00 11			00 28				07 28			08 28			08 58		09 28	
East Tilbury	d	23p34	23p47			00 04	00 17			00 34				07 34			08 34			09 04		09 34	
Stanford-le-Hope	d	23p37	23p50		←	00 07	00 20		←	00 37				07 37			08 37			09 07		09 37	
Pitsea	d	23p45	23p58	23p49	23p58	00 15	00 28	00 19	00 28	00 45	00 49	01 19	07 19	07 45	07 49	08 19	08 45	08 49		09 15	09 19	09 45	09 49
Benfleet	d	23p49	→	23p52	00 01	00 19	→	00 22	00 31	00 49	00 52	01 22	07 22	07 49	07 52	08 22	08 49	08 52		09 19	09 22	09 49	09 52
Leigh-on-Sea	d	23p53		23p57	00 06	00 23		00 27	00 36	00 53	00 57	01 27	07 27	07 53	07 57	08 27	08 53	08 57		09 23	09 27	09 53	09 57
Chalkwell	d	23p56		23p59	00 08	00 26		00 29	00 38	00 56	00 59	01 29	07 29	07 56	07 59	08 29	08 56	08 59		09 26	09 29	09 56	09 59
Westcliff	d	23p58		00 02	00 11	00 28		00 32	00 41	00 58	01 02	01 32	07 32	07 58	08 02	08 32	08 58	09 02		09 28	09 32	09 58	10 02
Southend Central	a	00 01		00 05	00 14	00 31		00 35	00 44	01 01	01 05	01 35	07 34	08 04	08 05	08 34	09 04	09 05		09 34	09 35	10 04	10 05
	d	00 01		00 06	00 14	00 31		00 36	00 44	01 01	01 06	01 36	07 36		08 06	08 36		09 06			09 36		10 06
Southend East	d	00 04		00 08	00 16	00 34		00 38	00 46	01 04	01 08	01 38	07 38		08 08	08 38		09 08			09 38		10 08
Thorpe Bay	d	00 06		00 11	00 19	00 36		00 41	00 49	01 06	01 11	01 41	07 40		08 10	08 40		09 10			09 40		10 10
Shoeburyness	a	00 13		00 18	00 26	00 43		00 48	00 56	01 13	01 18	01 48	07 48		08 18	08 48		09 18			09 48		10 18

		CC	CC	CC	CC	CC	CC	CC		CC	CC	CC	CC	CC	CC	CC	CC	CC	CC	CC	CC	CC
London Fenchurch St [7] ⊖	d			09 40	09 50	10 10		10 20		19 20	19 40	19 50	20 10		20 20	20 40	20 50	21 10		21 20	21 40	21 50
Limehouse	d			09 44	09 54	10 14		10 24		19 24	19 44	19 54	20 14		20 24	20 44	20 54	21 14		21 24	21 44	21 54
West Ham ⊖	d			09 49	09 59	10 19		10 29		19 29	19 49	19 59	20 19		20 29	20 49	20 59	21 19		21 29	21 49	21 59
London Liverpool St [15] ⊖	d																					
Stratford [7] ⊖	d																					
Barking ⊖	d	09 29	09 34	09 54	10 04	10 24	10 29	10 34		19 34	19 54	20 04	20 24	20 29	20 34	20 54	21 04	21 24	21 29	21 34	21 54	22 04
Upminster ⊖	d		09 42	10 02	10 12	10 32		10 42		19 42	20 02	20 12	20 32		20 42	21 02	21 12	21 32		21 42	22 02	22 12
Ockendon	d		09 48		10 18			10 48		19 48		20 18			20 48		21 18			21 48		22 18
Chafford Hundred	d		09 51		10 21			10 51		19 51		20 21			20 51		21 21			21 51		22 21
West Horndon	d			10 07		10 37			and at		20 07		20 37			21 07		21 37			22 07	
Laindon	d			10 12		10 42			the same		20 12		20 42			21 12		21 42			22 12	
Basildon	d			10 15		10 45			minutes		20 15		20 45			21 15		21 45			22 15	
Dagenham Dock	d	09 33					10 33		past					20 33					21 33			
Rainham	d	09 37					10 37		each					20 37					21 37			
Purfleet	d	09 42					10 42		hour until					20 42					21 42			
Grays	d	09a50	09 55		10 25		10a50	10 55		19 55		20 25		20a50	20 55		21 25		21a50	21 55		22 25
Tilbury Town [3]	d		09 58		10 28			10 58		19 58		20 28			20 58		21 28			21 58		22 28
East Tilbury	d		10 04		10 34			11 04		20 04		20 34			21 04		21 34			22 04		22 34
Stanford-le-Hope	d		10 07		10 37			11 07		20 07		20 37			21 07		21 37			22 07		22 37
Pitsea	d		10 15	10 19	10 45	10 49		11 15		20 15	20 19	20 45	20 49		21 15	21 19	21 45	21 49		22 15	22 19	22 45
Benfleet	d		10 19	10 22	10 49	10 52		11 19		20 19	20 22	20 49	20 52		21 19	21 22	21 49	21 52		22 19	22 22	22 49
Leigh-on-Sea	d		10 23	10 27	10 53	10 57		11 23		20 23	20 27	20 53	20 57		21 23	21 27	21 53	21 57		22 23	22 27	22 53
Chalkwell	d		10 26	10 29	10 56	10 59		11 26		20 26	20 29	20 56	20 59		21 26	21 29	21 56	21 59		22 26	22 29	22 56
Westcliff	d		10 28	10 32	10 58	11 02		11 28		20 28	20 32	20 58	21 02		21 28	21 32	21 58	22 02		22 28	22 32	22 58
Southend Central	a		10 34	10 35	11 04	11 05		11 34		20 34	20 35	21 04	21 05		21 32	21 35	22 04	22 05		22 31	22 35	23 01
	d			10 36		11 06					20 36		21 06		21 32	21 36		22 06		22 31	22 36	23 01
Southend East	d			10 38		11 08					20 38		21 08		21 34	21 38		22 08		22 33	22 38	23 03
Thorpe Bay	d			10 40		11 10					20 40		21 10		21 36	21 40		22 10		22 36	22 40	23 06
Shoeburyness	a			10 48		11 18					20 48		21 18		21 44	21 48		22 18		22 43	22 48	23 13

		CC	CC	CC	CC	CC
London Fenchurch St [7] ⊖	d	22 10	22 40	22 50	23 10	23 40
Limehouse	d	22 14	22 44	22 54	23 14	23 44
West Ham ⊖	d	22 19	22 49	22 59	23 19	23 49
London Liverpool St [15] ⊖	d					
Stratford [7] ⊖	d					
Barking ⊖	d	22 24	22 54	23 04	23 24	23 54
Upminster ⊖	d	22 32	23 02	23 12	23 32	00 02
Ockendon	d			23 18		
Chafford Hundred	d			23 21		
West Horndon	d	22 37	23 07		23 37	00 07
Laindon	d	22 42	23 12		23 42	00 12
Basildon	d	22 45	23 15		23 45	00 15
Dagenham Dock	d					
Rainham	d					
Purfleet	d					
Grays	d			23 25		
Tilbury Town [3]	d			23 28		
East Tilbury	d			23 34		
Stanford-le-Hope	d			23 37		
Pitsea	d	22 49	23 19	23 45	23 49	00 19
Benfleet	d	22 52	23 22	23 49	23 52	00 22
Leigh-on-Sea	d	22 57	23 27	23 53	23 57	00 27
Chalkwell	d	22 59	23 29	23 56	23 59	00 29
Westcliff	d	23 02	23 32	23 58	00 02	00 32
Southend Central	a	23 05	23 35	00 01	00 05	00 35
	d	23 06	23 36	00 01	00 06	00 36
Southend East	d	23 08	23 38	00 03	00 08	00 38
Thorpe Bay	d	23 10	23 40	00 06	00 10	00 40
Shoeburyness	a	23 18	23 48	00 13	00 18	00 48

Table 1

Shoeburyness and Southend Central - London

Mondays to Fridays until 26 July

Network Diagram - see first page of Table 1

Miles	Miles	Miles			CC MX	CC MX	CC MX	CC	CC	CC	CC	CC	CC	CC	CC	CC	CC	CC	CC	CC	CC	CC	CC
0	0	—	**Shoeburyness**	d			23p05		04 20		04 40	05 00		05 13	05 23			05 27		05 45			05 56
1½	1½	—	Thorpe Bay	d			23p09		04 24		04 44	05 04		05 17	05 27			05 31		05 49		05 56	06 00
3	3	—	Southend East	d			23p12		04 27		04 47	05 07		05 20	05 30			05 34		05 52		05 59	06 03
3¾	3¾	—	**Southend Central**	a			23p14		04 29		04 49	05 09		05 22	05 32			05 36		05 54		06 01	06 05
—	—	—		d	22p50		23p15		04 29		04 50	05 09		05 23	05 32			05 36	05 47	05 54		06 02	06 06
4¾	4¾	—	Westcliff	d	22p53		23p17		04 31		04 52	05 11		05 25	05 34			05 38	05 49	05 56		06 04	06 08
5½	5½	—	Chalkwell	d	22p55		23p19		04 34		04 54	05 14		05 27	05 37			05 41	05 51	05 59		06 06	06 10
7	7	—	Leigh-on-Sea	d	22p58		23p22		04 37		04 57	05 17		05 30	05 40			05 44	05 54	06 02		06 09	06 13
10¼	10¼	—	Benfleet	d	23p03		23p27		04 41		05 02	05 21		05 35	05 44			05 48	05 59	06 07		06 14	06 18
13	13	—	Pitsea	d	23p07		23p32		04 45		05 06	05 25		05 39	05 48			05 52	06 04	06 11		06 24	
—	18	—	Stanford-le-Hope	d	23p14			04 29			05 13			05 46				05 59	06 11			06 31	
—	20	—	East Tilbury	d	23p18			04 33			05 17			05 50				06 03	06 15			06 35	
—	23¾	—	**Tilbury Town** [3]	d	23p24			04 39			05 23			05 56				06 09	06 21			06 41	
—	25½	0	Grays	d	23p27	23p33		04 42		05 09	05 26		05 48	06 00			06 11	06 13	06 25		06 29	06 45	
—	29¼	—	Purfleet	d		23p38					05 32			06 05				06 19			06 34	06 51	
—	32½	—	Rainham	d		23p43					05 37			06 10				06 24			06 40	06 56	
—	34¾	—	Dagenham Dock	d		23p47					05 40			06 14				06 27			06 43	07 00	
15	—	—	Basildon	d			23p36		04 49			05 29			05 52					06 15			06 25
16¾	—	—	Laindon	d			23p39		04 52			05 32			05 55					06 18			06 29
20¼	—	—	West Horndon	d			23p44		04 57			05 37			06 00					06 23			
—	—	2½	Chafford Hundred	d	23p31			04 46		05 13			05 52				06 15		06 30				
—	—	4½	Ockendon	d	23p35			04 50		05 17			05 56				06 19		06 37				
24¼	—	7½	Upminster ⊖	d	23p42		23p50	04 57	05 03	05a22		05 43	06 01		06 06	←	06a25		06 44	06 29			06 38
32	37¾	—	Barking ⊖	d	23p50	23p55	23p58	05 06	05 11		05 46	05 51	06 10	06 20	06 15	06 20		06 33	→	06 38	06 50	07 06	
—	—	—	Stratford [7] ⊖	a		00 09		05 13						→								→	
—	—	—	**London Liverpool St** [15] ⊖	a		00 20		05 27															
35	40¾	—	West Ham ⊖	d	23p56		00 04		05 17		05 52	05 57	06 15		06 21	06 26		06 39		06 44	06 55		
37¾	43½	—	Limehouse	d	00 01		00 09		05 22		05 57	06 02	06 20		06 26	06 31		06 44		06 49	07 00		06 55
39½	45¼	—	**London Fenchurch St** [7] ⊖	a	00 05		00 13		05 28		06 03	06 08	06 27		06 30	06 37		06 50		06 53	→		07 01

		CC	CC	CC	CC	CC	CC	CC	CC	CC	CC	CC	CC	CC	CC	CC	CC	CC	CC	CC	CC	CC	CC
Shoeburyness	d			06 04			06 13		06 17		06 28			06 33	06 46							06 51	
Thorpe Bay	d			06 08		06 13	06 17		06 21		06 32			06 37	06 50							06 55	
Southend East	d			06 11		06 16	06 20		06 24		06 35			06 40	06 53							06 58	
Southend Central	a			06 13		06 18	06 22		06 26		06 37			06 42	06 55							07 00	
	d			06 13		06 18	06 23		06 26		06 38			06 42	06 55							07 00	
Westcliff	d			06 15		06 20	06 25		06 28		06 40			06 44	06 57							07 02	
Chalkwell	d			06 18		06 23	06 27		06 31		06 42			06 47	07 00							07 05	
Leigh-on-Sea	d			06 21		06 26	06 30		06 34		06 45			06 50	07 03							07 08	
Benfleet	d			06 26		06 31	06 35		06 39		06 50			06 55	07 08							07 13	
Pitsea	d			06 30		06 39			06 43				06 52	06 59				07 00			07 16	07 17	
Stanford-le-Hope	d					06 46							06 59					07 07			07 23		
East Tilbury	d					06 50							07 03					07 11			07 27		
Tilbury Town [3]	d					06 56							07 09					07 18			07 33		
Grays	d				06 50	07 00							07 13					07 22	07 30		07 37		
Purfleet	d					07 05							07 18						07 35				
Rainham	d					07 11							07 24						07 41				
Dagenham Dock	d					07 14							07 27						07 44				
Basildon	d			06 34			06 42		06 47		06 57			07 03	07 15							07 21	
Laindon	d			06 37					06 50					07 07			07 20			07 37		07 25	
West Horndon	d			06 42					06 55					07 12			07 25			07 42			
Chafford Hundred	d				06 54													07 26			07 41		
Ockendon	d		←		06 58					←								07 30			07 46		
Upminster ⊖	d		06 44	06 48	07 05			←	07 01	07 05	07 10	←		07 18		←	07 30	07 37		07 47	07 54		←
Barking ⊖	d			06 57	→	07 21	07 01	07 06	07 10	07 14		07 21	07 34	07 27		07 34	07 39	07 46	07 51	07 56		07 42	07 46
Stratford [7] ⊖	a					→							→					→	→	→			
London Liverpool St [15] ⊖	a																						
West Ham ⊖	d	←	06 58	07 03			07 07	07 12	07 16	07 20	07 23	07 26				07 39	07 44					07 47	07 52
Limehouse	d	07 00	07 03					07 17	07 21	07 25		07 32		07 36		07 44	07 49					07 52	
London Fenchurch St [7] ⊖	a	07 07	07 09	07 13			07 17	07 23	07 27	07 31	07 34	07 38		07 42	07 45	07 51	07 56				08 17	07 59	08 02

		CC	CC	CC	CC	CC	CC	CC	CC	CC	CC	CC	CC	CC	CC	CC	CC	CC	CC	CC	CC	CC	CC
Shoeburyness	d		07 03				07 17					07 22		07 34							07 49		
Thorpe Bay	d		07 07			07 12	07 21					07 26		07 38					07 42		07 53		
Southend East	d		07 10			07 15	07 24					07 29		07 41					07 45		07 56		
Southend Central	a		07 12			07 17	07 26					07 31		07 43					07 47		07 58		
	d	07 08	07 13			07 18	07 27					07 32		07 43					07 48		07 59		
Westcliff	d	07 10	07 15			07 20	07 29					07 34		07 45					07 50		08 01		
Chalkwell	d	07 12	07 17			07 22	07 31					07 36		07 48					07 52		08 03		
Leigh-on-Sea	d	07 16	07 20			07 25	07 34					07 39		07 51					07 55		08 06		
Benfleet	d	07 20	07 25			07 30	07 39					07 44		07 56					08 00		08 11		
Pitsea	d	07 25				07 34					07 41	07 48					07 48	07 52	08 04				
Stanford-le-Hope	d	07 32								07 42	07 48						07 55	08 00					08 11
East Tilbury	d	07 36									07 52							08 04					08 15
Tilbury Town [3]	d	07 42									07 58							08 10					08 21
Grays	d	07 46								07 52	08 02						08 06	08 14					08 25
Purfleet	d	07 51									08 07							08 19					
Rainham	d	07 57									08 13							08 25					
Dagenham Dock	d	08 00									08 16							08 28					
Basildon	d		07 32			07 39						07 53							08 09				
Laindon	d					07 42			07 50			07 56				08 07			08 12			08 22	
West Horndon	d								07 55							08 12						08 27	
Chafford Hundred	d									07 57							08 10						08 29
Ockendon	d									08 01							08 17						08 33
Upminster ⊖	d			←	←			←	08 02	08 09			←	08 13	←	08 17	08 24			←	08 28	08 32	08 40
Barking ⊖	d	08 07		07 51	07 56	07 59		08 07	08 10	08 18	08 23	08 13	08 18		08 23	08 26		08 35	08 29	08 35		08 42	08 50
Stratford [7] ⊖	a	→								→	→							→					→
London Liverpool St [15] ⊖	a																						
West Ham ⊖	d			07 57	08 01			08 12	08 16			08 19	08 23		08 28	08 32	08 38		08 35			08 47	
Limehouse	d		07 59	08 02	08 06	08 08	08 13	08 17	08 21			08 24		08 30	08 33	08 37			08 40	08 45	08 48	08 52	
London Fenchurch St [7] ⊖	a		08 05	08 08	08 12	08 15	08 19	08 24	08 27			08 31	08 34	08 37	08 40	08 43	08 48		08 46	08 51	08 55	08 58	

Table I

Mondays to Fridays

until 26 July

Shoeburyness and Southend Central - London

Network Diagram - see first page of Table I

		CC	CC	CC	CC	CC	CC	CC	CC	CC	CC	CC	CC	CC	CC	CC	CC	CC	CC	CC	CC	CC
Shoeburyness	d		07 54		08 05					08 11		08 25					08 40					09 05
Thorpe Bay	d		07 58		08 09					08 15		08 29					08 44					09 09
Southend East	d		08 01		08 12					08 18		08 32					08 47					09 12
Southend Central	a		08 03		08 14					08 20		08 34					08 49					09 14
	d		08 03		08 15					08 20		08 34					08 50			09 06		09 15
Westcliff	d		08 05		08 17					08 22		08 36					08 52			09 08		09 17
Chalkwell	d		08 08		08 19					08 25		08 39					08 54			09 10		09 19
Leigh-on-Sea	d		08 11		08 22					08 28		08 42					08 57			09 13		09 22
Benfleet	d		08 16		08 27					08 33		08 47					09 02			09 18		09 27
Pitsea	d	08 12	08 20						08 35	08 37		08 51				08 54	09 06				09 08	09 32
Stanford-le-Hope	d	08 19						08 33	08 42							09 01					09 16	
East Tilbury	d	08 23						08 37	08 46							09 05					09 20	
Tilbury Town [3]	d	08 29						08 43	08 52							09 11					09 26	
Grays	d	08 33						08 47	08 56					09 03		09 15					09 29	
Purfleet	d	08 39						08 52						09 08		09 20						
Rainham	d	08 44						08 58						09 13		09 26						
Dagenham Dock	d	08 48						09 01						09 17		09 29						
Basildon	d		08 24							08 41		08 55					09 11			09 25		09 36
Laindon	d		08 28				08 38			08 45					09 04		09 14		09 17	09 28		09 39
West Horndon	d						08 43								09 10				09 22			09 44
Chafford Hundred	d								09 01												09 34	
Ockendon	d								09 05				←								09 38	
Upminster ⊖	d			←		←	08 49		09 12	08 54	←	09 06	09 12		09 16			←	09 28	09 38	09 45	09 50
Barking ⊖	d	08 54	08 45	08 50		08 54	08 58	09 08	→	09 03	09 08		09 21	09 23	09 25	09 35	09 30	09 35	09 37	09 46	09 53	09 58
Stratford [7] ⊖	a	→						→								→						
London Liverpool St [15] ⊖	a																					
West Ham ⊖	d		08 51	08 55		09 00	09 04			09 09			09 26	09 29	09 31				09 43	09 52	09 59	10 04
Limehouse	d		08 56			09 05	09 09			09 14	09 17	09 23	09 31	09 34	09 36			09 44	09 48	09 57	10 04	10 09
London Fenchurch St [7] ⊖	a		09 02	09 06	09 08	09 11	09 15			09 20	09 23	09 29	09 38	09 40	09 43		09 45	09 51	09 54	10 03	10 08	10 13

		CC	CC	CC	CC	CC	CC	CC	CC	CC	and at the same minutes past each hour until	CC	CC	CC	CC	CC	CC	CC	CC	CC	CC	CC
Shoeburyness	d			09 20		09 35			09 50				15 05			15 20		15 35			15 50	
Thorpe Bay	d			09 24		09 39			09 54				15 09			15 24		15 39			15 54	
Southend East	d			09 27		09 42			09 57				15 12			15 27		15 42			15 57	
Southend Central	a			09 29		09 44			09 59				15 14			15 29		15 44			15 59	
	d		09 20	09 30		09 45		09 50	10 00				15 15		15 20	15 30		15 45		15 48	16 00	
Westcliff	d		09 23	09 32		09 47		09 53	10 02				15 17		15 23	15 32		15 47		15 50	16 02	
Chalkwell	d		09 25	09 34		09 49		09 55	10 04				15 19		15 25	15 34		15 49		15 53	16 04	
Leigh-on-Sea	d		09 28	09 37		09 52		09 58	10 07				15 22		15 28	15 37		15 52		15 56	16 07	
Benfleet	d		09 33	09 42		09 57		10 03	10 12				15 27		15 33	15 42		15 57		16 00	16 12	
Pitsea	d		09 37			10 02		10 07					15 32		15 37			16 02		16 04		
Stanford-le-Hope	d		09 44					10 14							15 44					16 11		
East Tilbury	d		09 48					10 18							15 48					16 15		
Tilbury Town [3]	d		09 54					10 24							15 54					16 21		
Grays	d	09 46	09 57				10 16	10 27						15 46	15 57				16 16	16 26		
Purfleet	d	09 51					10 21							15 51					16 21			
Rainham	d	09 56					10 26							15 56					16 26			
Dagenham Dock	d	10 00					10 30							16 00					16 30			
Basildon	d			09 49		10 06			10 19				15 36			15 49		16 06			16 19	
Laindon	d			09 52		10 09			10 22				15 39			15 52		16 09			16 22	
West Horndon	d					10 14							15 44					16 14				
Chafford Hundred	d		10 01					10 31							16 01					16 30		
Ockendon	d		10 05		←			10 35		←		←			16 05		←			16 34		←
Upminster ⊖	d		10 12	10 02	10 12	10 20		10 42	10 32	10 42		15 42	15 50		16 12	16 02	16 12	16 20		16 41	16 30	16 41
Barking ⊖	d	10 06	→	10 10	10 20	10 28	10 36	→	10 40	10 50		15 50	15 58	16 06	→	16 10	16 20	16 28	16 36	→	16 38	16 49
Stratford [7] ⊖	a																					
London Liverpool St [15] ⊖	a																					
West Ham ⊖	d	10 11		10 16	10 26	10 34	10 41		10 46	10 56		15 56	16 04	16 11		16 17	16 26	16 34			16 44	
Limehouse	d	10 16			10 31	10 39	10 46			11 01		16 01	16 09	16 16			16 31	16 39				
London Fenchurch St [7] ⊖	a	10 21		10 24	10 35	10 43	10 51		10 54	11 05		16 05	16 13	16 21		16 26	16 36	16 43	16 48		16 52	17 03

		CC	CC	CC	CC	CC	CC	CC	CC	CC	CC	CC	CC	CC	CC	CC	CC	CC	CC	CC	CC	CC
Shoeburyness	d	16 05				16 15			16 28					16 50		16 56						17 10
Thorpe Bay	d	16 09				16 19			16 32					16 54		17 00						17 14
Southend East	d	16 12				16 22			16 35					16 57		17 03						17 17
Southend Central	a	16 14				16 24			16 37					16 59		17 05						17 19
	d	16 15			16 19	16 25	16 31		16 38				16 53	17 00		17 06						17 19
Westcliff	d	16 17			16 21	16 27	16 33		16 40				16 55	17 02		17 08						17 21
Chalkwell	d	16 19			16 23	16 29	16 35		16 42				16 58	17 04		17 10						17 24
Leigh-on-Sea	d	16 22			16 26	16 32	16 38		16 45				17 01	17 07		17 13						17 27
Benfleet	d	16 27			16 31	16 37	16 43		16 50				17 05	17 12		17 18						17 32
Pitsea	d	16 31			16 35		16 47		16 54			16 57	17 09	17 16		17 22					17 28	17 36
Stanford-le-Hope	d				16 42							17 04						17 19			17 35	
East Tilbury	d				16 46							17 08						17 23			17 39	
Tilbury Town [3]	d				16 52							17 14						17 29			17 46	
Grays	d		16 39	16 52	16 57							17 18			17 22			17 32	17 46		17 51	
Purfleet	d		16 44	16 57											17 27			17 38	17 51			
Rainham	d		16 49	17 02											17 32			17 43	17 56			
Dagenham Dock	d		16 53	17 06											17 36			17 46	18 00			
Basildon	d	16 35				16 43	16 51		16 58				17 13	17 20		17 26						17 40
Laindon	d	16 38							17 01		17 13		17 17							17 49		17 44
West Horndon	d	16 43							17 06				17 22							17 54		
Chafford Hundred	d				17 01							17 23									17 55	
Ockendon	d				17 08					←		17 32					←				18 01	
Upminster ⊖	d	16 48			17 15	16 54		←	17 11	17 15	17 23	17 39	17 28	17 31			17 39			18 00	18 08	
Barking ⊖	d	16 57	17 00	17 16	→	17 03	17 09	17 16	17 20	17 25	17 32	→	17 36	17 40	17 42	17 44	17 47	17 52	18 06	18 08	18 16	
Stratford [7] ⊖	a			→																		
London Liverpool St [15] ⊖	a																					
West Ham ⊖	d	17 02				17 09		17 22		17 31						17 49		17 58	18 11	18 14		
Limehouse	d	17 08	17 10			17 14			17 29		17 42							18 03		18 19		
London Fenchurch St [7] ⊖	a	17 12	17 15			17 18	17 24	17 30	17 33	17 39	17 46		17 49	17 52	17 54	17 58	18 00	18 08	18 20	18 23	18 29	18 11

Table I

Mondays to Fridays

until 26 July

Shoeburyness and Southend Central - London

Network Diagram - see first page of Table I

		CC	CC	CC	CC	CC	CC	CC	CC	CC	CC	CC	CC	CC	CC	CC	CC	CC	CC	CC	CC	CC	CC
Shoeburyness	d			17 30		17 46			18 05			18 20			18 35			18 50			19 05		
Thorpe Bay	d			17 34		17 50			18 09			18 24			18 39			18 54			19 09		
Southend East	d			17 37		17 53			18 12			18 27			18 42			18 57			19 12		
Southend Central	a			17 39		17 55			18 14			18 29			18 44			18 59			19 15		
	d			17 40		17 56			18 15		18 20	18 30			18 45		18 48	19 00			19 15		19 20
Westcliff	d			17 42		17 58			18 17		18 23	18 32			18 47		18 51	19 02			19 17		19 23
Chalkwell	d			17 44		18 00			18 19		18 25	18 34			18 49		18 53	19 04			19 19		19 25
Leigh-on-Sea	d			17 47		18 03			18 22		18 28	18 37			18 52		18 56	19 07			19 22		19 28
Benfleet	d			17 52		18 08			18 27		18 33	18 42			18 57		19 01	19 12			19 27		19 33
Pitsea	d		17 45	17 56	18 01	18 12		18 14	18 32		18 37				19 02		19 05				19 32		19 37
Stanford-le-Hope	d		17 52		18 08			18 21			18 44						19 12						19 44
East Tilbury	d		17 56		18 12			18 25			18 48						19 16						19 48
Tilbury Town [3]	d		18 02		18 18			18 31			18 54						19 22						19 54
Grays	d		18 06		18 22			18 35		18 54	18 57					19 22	19 25					19 48	19 57
Purfleet	d		18 11					18 40		18 59						19 27						19 53	
Rainham	d		18 16					18 45		19 04						19 32						19 58	
Dagenham Dock	d		18 20					18 49		19 08						19 36						20 02	
Basildon	d			18 00		18 16			18 36			18 49			19 06			19 19			19 36		
Laindon	d	18 06		18 03		18 19			18 39			18 52			19 09			19 22			19 39		
West Horndon	d	18 11				18 24			18 44						19 14						19 44		
Chafford Hundred	d				18 27						19 02						19 29						20 01
Ockendon	d				18 33		←				19 07			←			19 34			←			20 05
Upminster ⊖	d	18 17			18 39	18 31	18 39		18 50		19 13	19 02	←	19 13	19 20		19 40	19 32	←	19 40	19 50		20 12
Barking ⊖	d	18 25	18 27		→	18 39		18 55	18 58	19 14	→	19 10	19 14	19 22	19 28	19 42	→	19 40	19 42	19 50	19 58	20 12	→
Stratford [7] ⊖	a									→						→						→	
London Liverpool St [15] ⊖	a																						
West Ham ⊖	d	18 30	18 33	18 26		18 45		19 00	19 04			19 16	19 20	19 27	19 34			19 46	19 48	19 56	20 04		
Limehouse	d	18 35	18 38			18 50		19 05	19 09					19 32	19 39				19 53	20 01	20 09		
London Fenchurch St [7] ⊖	a	18 39	18 42	18 34		18 54	18 59	19 10	19 13			19 24	19 28	19 37	19 43			19 54	19 58	20 05	20 13		

		CC	CC	CC	CC	CC	CC	CC	CC	CC	CC	CC	CC	CC	CC	CC	CC	CC	CC	CC	CC	CC	CC
Shoeburyness	d	19 20			19 35			19 50			20 05			20 20			20 35			21 05			21 20	
Thorpe Bay	d	19 24			19 39			19 54			20 09			20 24			20 39			21 09			21 24	
Southend East	d	19 27			19 42			19 57			20 12			20 27			20 42			21 12			21 27	
Southend Central	a	19 29			19 44			19 59			20 14			20 29			20 44			21 14			21 29	
	d	19 30			19 45		19 50	20 00			20 15		20 20	20 30			20 45		20 50	21 15		21 20	21 30	
Westcliff	d	19 32			19 47		19 53	20 02			20 17		20 23	20 32			20 47		20 53	21 17		21 23	21 32	
Chalkwell	d	19 34			19 49		19 55	20 04			20 19		20 25	20 34			20 49		20 55	21 19		21 25	21 34	
Leigh-on-Sea	d	19 37			19 52		19 58	20 07			20 22		20 28	20 37			20 52		20 58	21 22		21 28	21 37	
Benfleet	d	19 42			19 57		20 03	20 12			20 27		20 33	20 42			20 57		21 03	21 27		21 33	21 42	
Pitsea	d				20 02		20 07				20 32		20 37				21 02		21 07	21 32		21 37		
Stanford-le-Hope	d						20 14						20 44						21 14			21 44		
East Tilbury	d						20 18						20 48						21 18			21 48		
Tilbury Town [3]	d						20 24						20 54						21 24			21 54		
Grays	d					20 16	20 27					20 46	20 57					21 16	21 27		21 46	21 57		
Purfleet	d					20 21						20 51						21 21			21 51			
Rainham	d					20 26						20 56						21 26			21 56			
Dagenham Dock	d					20 30						21 00						21 30			22 00			
Basildon	d	19 49			20 06			20 19			20 36			20 49			21 06			21 36			21 49	
Laindon	d	19 52			20 09			20 22			20 39			20 52			21 09			21 39			21 52	
West Horndon	d				20 14						20 44						21 14			21 44				
Chafford Hundred	d						20 31						21 01						21 31			22 01		
Ockendon	d			←			20 35		←				21 05		←				21 35			22 05		←
Upminster ⊖	d	20 02	←	20 12	20 20		20 42	20 32	20 42		20 50		21 12	21 02	21 12	21 20			21 42	21 50		22 12	22 02	22 12
Barking ⊖	d	20 10	20 12	20 20	20 28	20 36	→	20 40	20 50	20 51	20 58	21 06	→	21 10	21 20	21 28	21 36		21 50	21 58	22 06	→	22 10	22 20
Stratford [7] ⊖	a		20 21							21 00		21 15												
London Liverpool St [15] ⊖	a		20 33							21 12		21 26												
West Ham ⊖	d	20 16		20 26	20 34	20 41		20 46	20 56		21 04			21 16	21 26	21 34	21 41	21 56	22 04	22 11		22 16	22 26	
Limehouse	d			20 31	20 39	20 46			21 01		21 09				21 31	21 39	21 46	22 01	22 09	22 16			22 31	
London Fenchurch St [7] ⊖	a	20 25		20 35	20 43	20 51		20 54	21 05		21 13			21 24	21 35	21 43	21 52	22 05	22 13	22 21		22 24	22 35	

		CC	CC	CC	CC	CC	CC	CC	CC	CC	CC
Shoeburyness	d	21 35			22 05			22 35			23 05
Thorpe Bay	d	21 39			22 09			22 39			23 09
Southend East	d	21 42			22 12			22 42			23 12
Southend Central	a	21 45			22 14			22 44			23 14
	d	21 45		21 50	22 15		22 20	22 45	22 50		23 15
Westcliff	d	21 47		21 53	22 17		22 23	22 47	22 53		23 17
Chalkwell	d	21 49		21 55	22 19		22 25	22 49	22 55		23 19
Leigh-on-Sea	d	21 52		21 58	22 22		22 28	22 52	22 58		23 22
Benfleet	d	21 57		22 03	22 27		22 33	22 57	23 03		23 27
Pitsea	d	22 02		22 07	22 32		22 37	23 02	23 07		23 32
Stanford-le-Hope	d			22 14			22 44		23 14		
East Tilbury	d			22 18			22 48		23 18		
Tilbury Town [3]	d			22 24			22 54		23 24		
Grays	d		22 16	22 27		22 46	22 57		23 27	23 33	
Purfleet	d		22 21			22 51				23 38	
Rainham	d		22 26			22 56				23 43	
Dagenham Dock	d		22 30			23 00				23 47	
Basildon	d	22 06			22 36			23 06			23 36
Laindon	d	22 09			22 39			23 09			23 39
West Horndon	d	22 14			22 44			23 14			23 44
Chafford Hundred	d			22 31			23 01		23 31		
Ockendon	d			22 35			23 05		23 35		
Upminster ⊖	d	22 20		22 42	22 50		23 12	23 20	23 42		23 50
Barking ⊖	d	22 28	22 36	22 50	22 58	23 06	23 20	23 28	23 50	23 55	23 58
Stratford [7] ⊖	a									00 09	
London Liverpool St [15] ⊖	a									00 20	
West Ham ⊖	d	22 34	22 41	22 56	23 04	23 11	23 26	23 34	23 56		00 04
Limehouse	d	22 39	22 46	23 01	23 09	23 16	23 31	23 39	00 01		00 09
London Fenchurch St [7] ⊖	a	22 43	22 52	23 05	23 13	23 21	23 35	23 43	00 05		00 13

Shoeburyness and Southend Central - London

Network Diagram - see first page of Table 1

		CC	CC	CC	CC	CC	CC	CC	CC	CC		CC	CC	CC	CC	CC	CC	CC	CC	CC		CC	CC	CC	CC
		A	B	A	B	A	B	B																	
Shoeburyness	d					23p05		23p05		04 20			04 40	05 00		05 13	05 23			05 27			05 45		
Thorpe Bay	d					23p09		23p09		04 24			04 44	05 04		05 17	05 27			05 31			05 49		05 56
Southend East	d					23p12		23p12		04 27			04 47	05 07		05 20	05 30			05 34			05 52		05 59
Southend Central	a					23p14		23p14		04 29			04 49	05 09		05 22	05 32			05 36			05 54		06 01
	d	22p50	22p50			23p15		23p15		04 29			04 50	05 09		05 23	05 32			05 36		05 47	05 54		06 02
Westcliff	d	22p53	22p53			23p17		23p17		04 31			04 52	05 11		05 25	05 34			05 38		05 49	05 56		06 04
Chalkwell	d	22p55	22p55			23p19		23p19		04 34			04 54	05 14		05 27	05 37			05 41		05 51	05 59		06 06
Leigh-on-Sea	d	22p58	22p58			23p22		23p22		04 37			04 57	05 17		05 30	05 40			05 44		05 54	06 02		06 09
Benfleet	d	23p03	23p03			23p27		23p27		04 41			05 02	05 21		05 35	05 44			05 48		05 59	06 07		06 14
Pitsea	d	23p07	23p07			23p32		23p32		04 45			05 06	05 25		05 39	05 48			05 52		06 04	06 11		06 24
Stanford-le-Hope	d	23p14	23p14						04 29				05 13			05 46				05 59		06 11			06 31
East Tilbury	d	23p18	23p18						04 33				05 17			05 50				06 03		06 15			06 35
Tilbury Town 3	d	23p24	23p24						04 39				05 23			05 56				06 09		06 21			06 41
Grays	d	23p27	23p27	23p33	23p33				04 42			05 09	05 26		05 48	06 00			06 11	06 13		06 25		06 29	06 45
Purfleet	d			23p38	23p38								05 32			06 05				06 19				06 34	06 51
Rainham	d			23p43	23p43								05 37			06 10				06 24				06 40	06 56
Dagenham Dock	d			23p47	23p47								05 40			06 14				06 27				06 43	07 00
Basildon	d					23p36		23p36		04 49				05 29			05 52						06 15		
Laindon	d					23p39		23p39		04 52				05 32			05 55						06 18		
West Horndon	d					23p44		23p44		04 57				05 37			06 00						06 23		
Chafford Hundred	d	23p31	23p31						04 46			05 13			05 52				06 15			06 30			
Ockendon	d	23p35	23p35						04 50			05 17			05 56				06 19			06 37			
Upminster	⊖ d	23p42	23p42			23p50		23p50	04 57	05 03		05a22		05 43	06 01		06 06	←	06a25			06 44	06 29		
Barking	⊖ d	23p50	23p51	23p55	23p55	23p58		00 02	05 06	05 11			05 46	05 51	06 10	06 20	06 15	06 20		06 33		→	06 38	06 50	07 06
Stratford 7	⊖ a			00 09					05 13							↪									↪
London Liverpool St 15	⊖ a			00 20					05 27																
West Ham	⊖ d	23p56	00 01		00 06	00 04	←	00 12		05 17			05 52	05 57	06 15		06 21	06 26		06 39			06 44	06 55	
Limehouse	d	00 01	00 06		00 11	00 09	00 11	00 17		05 22			05 57	06 02	06 20		06 26	06 31		06 44			06 49	07 00	
London Fenchurch St 7	⊖ a	00 05	00 11		→	00 13	00 18	00 24		05 28			06 03	06 08	06 27		06 30	06 37		06 50			06 53	→	

		CC	CC	CC	CC	CC		CC	CC	CC	CC	CC	CC	CC	CC	CC		CC	CC	CC	CC	CC	CC	CC	CC
Shoeburyness	d	05 56			06 04				06 13		06 17		06 28			06 33		06 46							06 51
Thorpe Bay	d	06 00			06 08			06 13	06 17		06 21		06 32			06 37		06 50							06 55
Southend East	d	06 03			06 11			06 16	06 20		06 24		06 35			06 40		06 53							06 58
Southend Central	a	06 05			06 13			06 18	06 22		06 26		06 37			06 42		06 55							07 00
	d	06 06			06 13			06 18	06 23		06 26		06 38			06 42		06 55							07 00
Westcliff	d	06 08			06 15			06 20	06 25		06 28		06 40			06 44		06 57							07 02
Chalkwell	d	06 10			06 18			06 23	06 27		06 31		06 42			06 47		07 00							07 05
Leigh-on-Sea	d	06 13			06 21			06 26	06 30		06 34		06 45			06 50		07 03							07 08
Benfleet	d	06 18			06 26			06 31	06 35		06 39		06 50			06 55		07 08							07 13
Pitsea	d				06 30			06 39			06 43				06 52	06 59					07 00			07 16	07 17
Stanford-le-Hope	d							06 46							06 59						07 07			07 23	
East Tilbury	d							06 50							07 03						07 11			07 27	
Tilbury Town 3	d							06 56							07 09						07 18			07 33	
Grays	d					06 50		07 00							07 13						07 22	07 30		07 37	
Purfleet	d							07 05							07 18							07 35			
Rainham	d							07 11							07 24							07 41			
Dagenham Dock	d							07 14							07 27							07 44			
Basildon	d	06 25			06 34				06 42		06 47		06 57			07 03		07 15							07 21
Laindon	d	06 29			06 37						06 50					07 07				07 20			07 37		07 25
West Horndon	d				06 42						06 55					07 12				07 25			07 42		
Chafford Hundred	d					06 54															07 26			07 41	
Ockendon	d			←		06 58						←									07 30			07 46	
Upminster	⊖ d	06 38		06 44	06 48	07 05				←	07 01	07 05	07 10	←		07 18			←	07 30	07 37		07 47	07 54	
Barking	⊖ d				06 57	→		07 21	07 01	07 06	07 10	07 14		07 21	07 34	07 27			07 34	07 39	07 46	07 51	07 56		07 42
Stratford 7	⊖ a							↪							↪						↪	↪	↪		
London Liverpool St 15	⊖ a																								
West Ham	⊖ d		←	06 58	07 03				07 07	07 12	07 16	07 20	07 23	07 26					07 39	07 44					07 47
Limehouse	d	06 55	07 00	07 03						07 17	07 21	07 25		07 32		07 36			07 44	07 49					07 52
London Fenchurch St 7	⊖ a	07 01	07 07	07 09	07 13				07 17	07 23	07 27	07 31	07 34	07 38		07 42		07 45	07 51	07 56				08 17	07 59

		CC		CC	CC	CC	CC	CC	CC	CC	CC	CC		CC	CC	CC	CC	CC	CC	CC	CC	CC		CC	CC
Shoeburyness	d				07 03				07 17						07 22		07 34								07 49
Thorpe Bay	d				07 07			07 12	07 21						07 26		07 38					07 42			07 53
Southend East	d				07 10			07 15	07 24						07 29		07 41					07 45			07 56
Southend Central	a				07 12			07 17	07 26						07 31		07 43					07 47			07 58
	d			07 08	07 13			07 18	07 27						07 32		07 43					07 48			07 59
Westcliff	d			07 10	07 15			07 20	07 29						07 34		07 45					07 50			08 01
Chalkwell	d			07 12	07 17			07 22	07 31						07 36		07 48					07 52			08 03
Leigh-on-Sea	d			07 16	07 20			07 25	07 34						07 39		07 51					07 55			08 06
Benfleet	d			07 20	07 25			07 30	07 39						07 44		07 56					08 00			08 11
Pitsea	d			07 25				07 34						07 41	07 48					07 48	07 52	08 04			
Stanford-le-Hope	d			07 32								07 42		07 48						07 55	08 00				
East Tilbury	d			07 36										07 52							08 04				
Tilbury Town 3	d			07 42										07 58							08 10				
Grays	d			07 46								07 52		08 02						08 06	08 14				
Purfleet	d			07 51										08 07							08 19				
Rainham	d			07 57										08 13							08 25				
Dagenham Dock	d			08 00										08 16							08 28				
Basildon	d				07 32			07 39							07 53							08 09			
Laindon	d							07 42			07 50				07 56				08 07			08 12			
West Horndon	d										07 55								08 12						
Chafford Hundred	d											07 57								08 10					
Ockendon	d											08 01								08 17					
Upminster	⊖ d	←				←	←			←	08 02	08 09				←	08 13	←	08 17	08 24				←	08 28
Barking	⊖ d	07 46		08 07		07 51	07 56	07 59		08 07	08 10	08 18		08 23	08 13	08 18		08 23	08 26		08 35	08 29		08 35	
Stratford 7	⊖ a			↪								↪		↪							↪				
London Liverpool St 15	⊖ a																								
West Ham	⊖ d	07 52				07 57	08 01			08 12	08 16				08 19	08 23		08 28	08 32	08 38		08 35			
Limehouse	d				07 59	08 02	08 06	08 08	08 13	08 17	08 21				08 24		08 30	08 33	08 37			08 40		08 45	08 48
London Fenchurch St 7	⊖ a	08 02			08 05	08 08	08 12	08 15	08 19	08 24	08 27				08 31	08 34	08 37	08 40	08 43	08 48		08 46		08 51	08 55

A 27 July

B MX from 31 July until 10 August

		CC	CC	CC	CC	CC	CC	CC		CC	CC	CC	CC	CC	CC	CC	CC	CC		CC	CC	CC	CC	CC	CC
Shoeburyness	d				07 54		08 05						08 11		08 25						08 40				
Thorpe Bay	d				07 58		08 09						08 15		08 29						08 44				
Southend East	d				08 01		08 12						08 18		08 32						08 47				
Southend Central	a				08 03		08 14						08 20		08 34						08 49				
	d				08 03		08 15						08 20		08 34						08 50			09 06	
Westcliff	d				08 05		08 17						08 22		08 36						08 52			09 08	
Chalkwell	d				08 08		08 19						08 25		08 39						08 54			09 10	
Leigh-on-Sea	d				08 11		08 22						08 28		08 42						08 57			09 13	
Benfleet	d				08 16		08 27						08 33		08 47						09 02			09 18	
Pitsea	d			08 12	08 20							08 35	08 37		08 51					08 54	09 06				09 08
Stanford-le-Hope	d		08 11	08 19							08 33	08 42								09 01					09 16
East Tilbury	d		08 15	08 23							08 37	08 46								09 05					09 20
Tilbury Town 3	d		08 21	08 29							08 43	08 52								09 11					09 26
Grays	d		08 25	08 33							08 47	08 56					09 03			09 15					09 29
Purfleet	d			08 39							08 52						09 08			09 20					
Rainham	d			08 44							08 58						09 13			09 26					
Dagenham Dock	d			08 48							09 01						09 17			09 29					
Basildon	d				08 24								08 41		08 55						09 11			09 25	
Laindon	d	08 22			08 28					08 38			08 45					09 04			09 14		09 17	09 28	
West Horndon	d	08 27								08 43								09 10					09 22		
Chafford Hundred	d		08 29									09 01													09 34
Ockendon	d		08 33									09 05				←									09 38
Upminster	⊖ d	08 32	08 40			←		←		08 49		09 12	08 54	←	09 06	09 12		09 16				←	09 28	09 38	09 45
Barking	⊖ d	08 42	08 50	08 54	08 45	08 50		08 54		08 58	09 08	→	09 03	09 08		09 21	09 23	09 25		09 35	09 30	09 35	09 37	09 46	09 53
Stratford 7	⊖ a		↪	↪							↪									↪					
London Liverpool St 15	⊖ a																								
West Ham	⊖ d	08 47			08 51	08 55		09 00		09 04			09 09			09 26	09 29	09 31					09 43	09 52	09 59
Limehouse	d	08 52			08 56			09 05		09 09			09 14	09 17	09 23	09 31	09 34	09 36				09 44	09 48	09 57	10 04
London Fenchurch St 7	⊖ a	08 58			09 02	09 06	09 08	09 11		09 15			09 20	09 23	09 29	09 38	09 40	09 43			09 45	09 51	09 54	10 03	10 08

		CC	CC	CC		CC	CC	CC	CC	CC	CC	CC		CC		CC	CC	CC	CC	CC	CC	CC	CC	CC
Shoeburyness	d	09 05				09 20		09 35			09 50		and at the same minutes past each hour until			15 05			15 20		15 35			15 50
Thorpe Bay	d	09 09				09 24		09 39			09 54					15 09			15 24		15 39			15 54
Southend East	d	09 12				09 27		09 42			09 57					15 12			15 27		15 42			15 57
Southend Central	a	09 14				09 29		09 44			09 59					15 14			15 29		15 44			15 59
	d	09 15		09 20		09 30		09 45		09 50	10 00					15 15		15 20	15 30		15 45		15 48	16 00
Westcliff	d	09 17		09 23		09 32		09 47		09 53	10 02					15 17		15 23	15 32		15 47		15 50	16 02
Chalkwell	d	09 19		09 25		09 34		09 49		09 55	10 04					15 19		15 25	15 34		15 49		15 53	16 04
Leigh-on-Sea	d	09 22		09 28		09 37		09 52		09 58	10 07					15 22		15 28	15 37		15 52		15 56	16 07
Benfleet	d	09 27		09 33		09 42		09 57		10 03	10 12					15 27		15 33	15 42		15 57		16 00	16 12
Pitsea	d	09 32		09 37				10 02		10 07						15 32		15 37			16 02		16 04	
Stanford-le-Hope	d			09 44						10 14								15 44					16 11	
East Tilbury	d			09 48						10 18								15 48					16 15	
Tilbury Town 3	d			09 54						10 24								15 54					16 21	
Grays	d		09 46	09 57					10 16	10 27							15 46	15 57				16 16	16 26	
Purfleet	d		09 51						10 21								15 51					16 21		
Rainham	d		09 56						10 26								15 56					16 26		
Dagenham Dock	d		10 00						10 30								16 00					16 30		
Basildon	d	09 36				09 49		10 06			10 19					15 36			15 49		16 06			16 19
Laindon	d	09 39				09 52		10 09			10 22					15 39			15 52		16 09			16 22
West Horndon	d	09 44						10 14								15 44					16 14			
Chafford Hundred	d			10 01						10 31								16 01					16 30	
Ockendon	d			10 05			←			10 35		←		←				16 05		←			16 34	
Upminster	⊖ d	09 50		10 12		10 02	10 12	10 20		10 42	10 32	10 42		15 42		15 50		16 12	16 02	16 12	16 20		16 41	16 30
Barking	⊖ d	09 58	10 06	→		10 10	10 20	10 28	10 36	→	10 40	10 50		15 50		15 58	16 06	→	16 10	16 20	16 28	16 36	→	16 38
Stratford 7	⊖ a																							
London Liverpool St 15	⊖ a																							
West Ham	⊖ d	10 04	10 11			10 16	10 26	10 34	10 41		10 46	10 56		15 56		16 04	16 11		16 17	16 26	16 34			16 44
Limehouse	d	10 09	10 16				10 31	10 39	10 46			11 01		16 01		16 09	16 16			16 31	16 39			
London Fenchurch St 7	⊖ a	10 13	10 21			10 24	10 35	10 43	10 51		10 54	11 05		16 05		16 13	16 21		16 26	16 36	16 43	16 48		16 52

			CC	CC	CC	CC	CC	CC	CC	CC	CC		CC	CC	CC	CC	CC	CC	CC	CC	CC		CC	CC	CC
Shoeburyness	d			16 05				16 15			16 28						16 50		16 56						
Thorpe Bay	d			16 09				16 19			16 32						16 54		17 00						
Southend East	d			16 12				16 22			16 35						16 57		17 03						
Southend Central	a			16 14				16 24			16 37						16 59		17 05						
	d			16 15			16 19	16 25	16 31		16 38					16 53	17 00		17 06						
Westcliff	d			16 17			16 21	16 27	16 33		16 40					16 55	17 02		17 08						
Chalkwell	d			16 19			16 23	16 29	16 35		16 42					16 58	17 04		17 10						
Leigh-on-Sea	d			16 22			16 26	16 32	16 38		16 45					17 01	17 07		17 13						
Benfleet	d			16 27			16 31	16 37	16 43		16 50					17 05	17 12		17 18						
Pitsea	d			16 31			16 35		16 47		16 54				16 57	17 09	17 16		17 22						17 28
Stanford-le-Hope	d						16 42								17 04						17 19				17 35
East Tilbury	d						16 46								17 08						17 23				17 39
Tilbury Town 3	d						16 52								17 14						17 29				17 46
Grays	d				16 39	16 52	16 57								17 18			17 22			17 32		17 46		17 51
Purfleet	d				16 44	16 57												17 27			17 38		17 51		
Rainham	d				16 49	17 02												17 32			17 43		17 56		
Dagenham Dock	d				16 53	17 06												17 36			17 46		18 00		
Basildon	d			16 35				16 43	16 51		16 58					17 13	17 20		17 26						
Laindon	d			16 38							17 01			17 13		17 17								17 49	
West Horndon	d			16 43							17 06					17 22								17 54	
Chafford Hundred	d						17 01								17 23										17 55
Ockendon	d		←				17 08						←		17 32					←					18 01
Upminster	⊖ d		16 41	16 48			17 15	16 54		←	17 11		17 15	17 23	17 39	17 28	17 31			17 39				18 00	18 08
Barking	⊖ d		16 49	16 57	17 00	17 16	→	17 03	17 09	17 16	17 20		17 25	17 32	→	17 36	17 40	17 42	17 44	17 47	17 52		18 06	18 08	18 16
Stratford 7	⊖ a					↪																			
London Liverpool St 15	⊖ a																								
West Ham	⊖ d			17 02				17 09		17 22			17 31						17 49		17 58		18 11	18 14	
Limehouse	d			17 08	17 10			17 14			17 29			17 42							18 03			18 19	
London Fenchurch St 7	⊖ a		17 03	17 12	17 15			17 18	17 24	17 30	17 33		17 39	17 46		17 49	17 52	17 54	17 58	18 00	18 08		18 20	18 23	18 29

Table 1

Mondays to Fridays

27 July to 10 August

Shoeburyness and Southend Central - London

Network Diagram - see first page of Table 1

		CC	CC	CC	CC	CC	CC		CC	CC	CC	CC	CC	CC	CC	CC	CC		CC	CC	CC	CC	CC	CC	CC
Shoeburyness	d	17 10			17 30		17 46				18 05			18 20			18 35				18 51			19 05	
Thorpe Bay	d	17 14			17 34		17 50				18 09			18 24			18 39				18 55			19 09	
Southend East	d	17 17			17 37		17 53				18 12			18 27			18 42				18 58			19 12	
Southend Central	a	17 19			17 39		17 55				18 14			18 29			18 44				19 00			19 15	
	d	17 19			17 40		17 56				18 15		18 20	18 30			18 45			18 49	19 01			19 15	
Westcliff	d	17 21			17 42		17 58				18 17		18 23	18 32			18 47			18 51	19 03			19 17	
Chalkwell	d	17 24			17 44		18 00				18 19		18 25	18 34			18 49			18 53	19 05			19 19	
Leigh-on-Sea	d	17 27			17 47		18 03				18 22		18 28	18 37			18 52			18 56	19 08			19 22	
Benfleet	d	17 32			17 52		18 08				18 27		18 33	18 42			18 57			19 01	19 13			19 27	
Pitsea	d	17 36		17 45	17 56	18 01	18 12			18 14	18 32		18 37				19 02			19 05				19 32	
Stanford-le-Hope	d			17 52		18 08				18 21			18 44							19 12					
East Tilbury	d			17 56		18 12				18 25			18 48							19 16					
Tilbury Town ■	d			18 02		18 18				18 31			18 54							19 22					
Grays	d			18 06		18 22				18 35		18 54	18 57						19 22	19 25					19 48
Purfleet	d			18 11						18 40		18 59							19 27						19 53
Rainham	d			18 16						18 45		19 04							19 32						19 58
Dagenham Dock	d			18 20						18 49		19 08							19 36						20 02
Basildon	d	17 40			18 00		18 16				18 36			18 49			19 06				19 19			19 36	
Laindon	d	17 44	18 06		18 03		18 19				18 39			18 52			19 09				19 22			19 39	
West Horndon	d		18 11				18 24				18 44						19 14							19 44	
Chafford Hundred	d					18 27							19 02							19 29					
Ockendon	d					18 33			←				19 07			←				19 34			←		
Upminster ⊖	d		18 17			18 39	18 31		18 39		18 50		19 13	19 02	←	19 13	19 20			19 40	19 32	←	19 40	19 50	
Barking ⊖	d		18 25	18 27		→	18 39			18 55	18 58	19 14	→	19 10	19 14	19 22	19 28		19 42	→	19 40	19 42	19 50	19 58	20 13
Stratford ■ ⊖	a											→							→						→
London Liverpool St ■ ⊖	a																								
West Ham ⊖	d		18 30	18 33	18 26		18 45			19 00	19 04			19 16	19 20	19 27	19 34				19 46	19 48	19 56	20 04	
Limehouse	d		18 35	18 38			18 50			19 05	19 09					19 32	19 39					19 53	20 01	20 09	
London Fenchurch St ■ ⊖	a	18 11	18 39	18 42	18 34		18 54		18 59	19 10	19 13			19 24	19 28	19 37	19 43				19 54	19 58	20 05	20 13	

		CC	CC		CC	CC	CC	CC	CC	CC	CC	CC	CC		CC	CC	CC	CC	CC	CC	CC	CC	CC		CC
Shoeburyness	d		19 20				19 35			19 50		20 05				20 20		20 35			21 05				21 20
Thorpe Bay	d		19 24				19 39			19 54		20 09				20 24		20 39			21 09				21 24
Southend East	d		19 27				19 42			19 57		20 12				20 27		20 42			21 12				21 27
Southend Central	a		19 29				19 44			19 59		20 14				20 29		20 44			21 14				21 29
	d	19 20	19 30				19 45		19 50	20 00		20 15			20 20	20 30		20 45		20 50	21 15		21 20		21 30
Westcliff	d	19 23	19 32				19 47		19 53	20 02		20 17			20 23	20 32		20 47		20 53	21 17		21 23		21 32
Chalkwell	d	19 25	19 34				19 49		19 55	20 04		20 19			20 25	20 34		20 49		20 55	21 19		21 25		21 34
Leigh-on-Sea	d	19 28	19 37				19 52		19 58	20 07		20 22			20 28	20 37		20 52		20 58	21 22		21 28		21 37
Benfleet	d	19 33	19 42				19 57		20 03	20 12		20 27			20 33	20 42		20 57		21 03	21 27		21 33		21 42
Pitsea	d	19 37					20 02		20 07			20 32			20 37			21 02		21 07	21 32		21 37		
Stanford-le-Hope	d	19 44							20 14						20 44					21 14			21 44		
East Tilbury	d	19 48							20 18						20 48					21 18			21 48		
Tilbury Town ■	d	19 54							20 24						20 54					21 24			21 54		
Grays	d	19 57						20 16	20 27				20 46		20 57				21 16	21 27		21 46	21 57		
Purfleet	d							20 21					20 51						21 21			21 51			
Rainham	d							20 26					20 56						21 26			21 56			
Dagenham Dock	d							20 30					21 00						21 30			22 00			
Basildon	d		19 49				20 06			20 19		20 36				20 49		21 06			21 36				21 49
Laindon	d		19 52				20 09			20 22		20 39				20 52		21 09			21 39				21 52
West Horndon	d						20 14					20 44						21 14			21 44				
Chafford Hundred	d	20 01							20 31						21 01					21 31			22 01		
Ockendon	d	20 05				←			20 35		←				21 05		←			21 35			22 05		
Upminster ⊖	d	20 12	20 02		←	20 12	20 20		20 42	20 32	20 42	20 50			21 12	21 02	21 12	21 20		21 42	21 50		22 12		22 02
Barking ⊖	d	→	20 10		20 13	20 20	20 28	20 36	→	20 40	20 50	20 58	21 06		→	21 10	21 20	21 28	21 36	21 50	21 58	22 06	→		22 11
Stratford ■ ⊖	a																								
London Liverpool St ■ ⊖	a																								
West Ham ⊖	d		20 16		20 18	20 26	20 34	20 41		20 46	20 56	21 04	21 11			21 16	21 26	21 34	21 41	21 56	22 04	22 14			22 19
Limehouse	d				20 23	20 31	20 39	20 46			21 01	21 09	21 16				21 31	21 39	21 46	22 01	22 09	22 19			22 24
London Fenchurch St ■ ⊖	a		20 25		20 28	20 35	20 43	20 51		20 54	21 05	21 13	21 21			21 24	21 35	21 43	21 51	22 05	22 13	22 26			22 31

		CC	CC	CC	CC	CC	CC	CC	CC		CC	CC	CC
Shoeburyness	d		21 35			22 05			22 35				23 05
Thorpe Bay	d		21 39			22 09			22 39				23 09
Southend East	d		21 42			22 12			22 42				23 12
Southend Central	a		21 45			22 14			22 44				23 14
	d		21 45		21 50	22 15		22 20	22 45		22 50		23 15
Westcliff	d		21 47		21 53	22 17		22 23	22 47		22 53		23 17
Chalkwell	d		21 49		21 55	22 19		22 25	22 49		22 55		23 19
Leigh-on-Sea	d		21 52		21 58	22 22		22 28	22 52		22 58		23 22
Benfleet	d		21 57		22 03	22 27		22 33	22 57		23 03		23 27
Pitsea	d		22 02		22 07	22 32		22 37	23 02		23 07		23 32
Stanford-le-Hope	d				22 14			22 44			23 14		
East Tilbury	d				22 18			22 48			23 18		
Tilbury Town ■	d				22 24			22 54			23 24		
Grays	d			22 16	22 27		22 48	22 57			23 27	23 33	
Purfleet	d			22 21			22 53					23 38	
Rainham	d			22 26			22 58					23 43	
Dagenham Dock	d			22 30			23 02					23 47	
Basildon	d		22 06			22 36			23 06				23 36
Laindon	d		22 09			22 39			23 09				23 39
West Horndon	d		22 14			22 44			23 14				23 44
Chafford Hundred	d				22 31			23 01			23 31		
Ockendon	d	←			22 35			23 05			23 35		
Upminster ⊖	d	22 12	22 20		22 42	22 50		23 12	23 20		23 42		23 50
Barking ⊖	d	22 20	22 28	22 37	22 51	23 00	23 10	23 21	23 29		23 51	23 55	00 02
Stratford ■ ⊖	a												
London Liverpool St ■ ⊖	a												
West Ham ⊖	d	22 28	22 36	22 45	23 00	23 10	23 20	23 30	23 40		00 01	00 06	00 12
Limehouse	d	22 34	22 42	22 50	23 05	23 15	23 25	23 35	23 45		00 06	00 11	00 17
London Fenchurch St ■ ⊖	a	22 40	22 48	22 58	23 12	23 22	23 32	23 42	23 52		00 11	00 18	00 24

Table 1

Mondays to Fridays

13 August to 28 August

Shoeburyness and Southend Central - London

Network Diagram - see first page of Table 1

		CC	CC	CC	CC	CC	CC	CC	CC	CC		CC	CC	CC	CC	CC	CC	CC	CC	CC		CC	CC	CC	CC
		MX	MX	MX																					
Shoeburyness	d			23p05		04 20		04 40	05 00			05 13	05 23			05 27		05 45				05 56			06 04
Thorpe Bay	d			23p09		04 24		04 44	05 04			05 17	05 27			05 31		05 49		05 56		06 00			06 08
Southend East	d			23p12		04 27		04 47	05 07			05 20	05 30			05 34		05 52		05 59		06 03			06 11
Southend Central	a			23p14		04 29		04 49	05 09			05 22	05 32			05 36		05 54		06 01		06 05			06 13
	d	22p50		23p15		04 29		04 50	05 09			05 23	05 32			05 36	05 47	05 54		06 02		06 06			06 13
Westcliff	d	22p53		23p17		04 31		04 52	05 11			05 25	05 34			05 38	05 49	05 56		06 04		06 08			06 15
Chalkwell	d	22p55		23p19		04 34		04 54	05 14			05 27	05 37			05 41	05 51	05 59		06 06		06 10			06 18
Leigh-on-Sea	d	22p58		23p22		04 37		04 57	05 17			05 30	05 40			05 44	05 54	06 02		06 09		06 13			06 21
Benfleet	d	23p03		23p27		04 41		05 02	05 21			05 35	05 44			05 48	05 59	06 07		06 14		06 18			06 26
Pitsea	d	23p07		23p32		04 45		05 06	05 25			05 39	05 48			05 52	06 04	06 11		06 24					06 30
Stanford-le-Hope	d	23p14			04 29			05 13				05 46				05 59	06 11			06 31					
East Tilbury	d	23p18			04 33			05 17				05 50				06 03	06 15			06 35					
Tilbury Town ■	d	23p24			04 39			05 23				05 56				06 09	06 21			06 41					
Grays	d	23p27	23p33		04 42		05 09	05 26		05 48		06 00			06 11	06 13	06 25		06 29	06 45					
Purfleet	d		23p38					05 32				06 05				06 19			06 34	06 51					
Rainham	d		23p43					05 37				06 10				06 24			06 40	06 56					
Dagenham Dock	d		23p47					05 40				06 14				06 27			06 43	07 00					
Basildon	d			23p36		04 49			05 29				05 52					06 15				06 25			06 34
Laindon	d			23p39		04 52			05 32				05 55					06 18				06 29			06 37
West Horndon	d			23p44		04 57			05 37				06 00					06 23							06 42
Chafford Hundred	d	23p31			04 46		05 13			05 52					06 15		06 30								
Ockendon	d	23p35			04 50		05 17			05 56					06 19		06 37							←	
Upminster ⊖	d	23p42		23p50	04 57	05 03	05a22		05 43	06 01			06 06	←	06a25		06 44	06 29				06 38		06 44	06 48
Barking ⊖	d	23p50	23p55	23p58	05 06	05 11		05 46	05 51	06 10		06 20	06 15	06 20		06 33	→	06 38	06 50	07 06					06 57
Stratford ■ ⊖	a		00 09		05 13							→								→					
London Liverpool St ■ ⊖	a		00 20		05 27																				
West Ham ⊖	d	23p56		00 04		05 17		05 52	05 57	06 15			06 21	06 26		06 39		06 44	06 55				←	06 58	07 03
Limehouse	d	00 01		00 09		05 22		05 57	06 02	06 20			06 26	06 31		06 44		06 49	07 00			06 55	07 00	07 03	
London Fenchurch St ■ ⊖	a	00 05		00 13		05 28		06 03	06 08	06 27			06 30	06 37		06 50		06 53	→			07 01	07 07	07 09	07 13

		CC	CC	CC	CC	CC		CC	CC	CC	CC	CC	CC	CC	CC	CC		CC	CC	CC	CC	CC	CC	CC	CC
Shoeburyness	d			06 13		06 17			06 28			06 33	06 46								06 51			07 03	
Thorpe Bay	d		06 13	06 17		06 21			06 32			06 37	06 50								06 55			07 07	
Southend East	d		06 16	06 20		06 24			06 35			06 40	06 53								06 58			07 10	
Southend Central	a		06 18	06 22		06 26			06 37			06 42	06 55								07 00			07 12	
	d		06 18	06 23		06 26			06 38			06 42	06 55								07 00		07 08	07 13	
Westcliff	d		06 20	06 25		06 28			06 40			06 44	06 57								07 02		07 10	07 15	
Chalkwell	d		06 23	06 27		06 31			06 42			06 47	07 00								07 05		07 12	07 17	
Leigh-on-Sea	d		06 26	06 30		06 34			06 45			06 50	07 03								07 08		07 16	07 20	
Benfleet	d		06 31	06 35		06 39			06 50			06 55	07 08								07 13		07 20	07 25	
Pitsea	d		06 39			06 43					06 52	06 59				07 00				07 16	07 17		07 25		
Stanford-le-Hope	d		06 46								06 59					07 07				07 23			07 32		
East Tilbury	d		06 50								07 03					07 11				07 27			07 36		
Tilbury Town ■	d		06 56								07 09					07 18				07 33			07 42		
Grays	d	06 50	07 00								07 13					07 22		07 30		07 37			07 46		
Purfleet	d		07 05								07 18							07 35					07 51		
Rainham	d		07 11								07 24							07 41					07 57		
Dagenham Dock	d		07 14								07 27							07 44					08 00		
Basildon	d			06 42		06 47			06 57			07 03	07 15								07 21			07 32	
Laindon	d					06 50						07 07			07 20				07 37		07 25				
West Horndon	d					06 55						07 12			07 25				07 42						
Chafford Hundred	d	06 54														07 26				07 41					
Ockendon	d	06 58						←								07 30				07 46					
Upminster ⊖	d	07 05			←	07 01		07 05	07 10	←		07 18		←	07 30	07 37			07 47	07 54		←			←
Barking ⊖	d	→	07 21	07 01	07 06	07 10		07 14		07 21	07 34	07 27		07 34	07 39	07 46		07 51	07 56		07 42	07 46	08 07		07 51
Stratford ■ ⊖	a		→								→					→		→	→				→		
London Liverpool St ■ ⊖	a																								
West Ham ⊖	d			07 07	07 12	07 16		07 20	07 23	07 26				07 39	07 44						07 47	07 52			07 57
Limehouse	d				07 17	07 21		07 25		07 32		07 36		07 44	07 49						07 52			07 59	08 02
London Fenchurch St ■ ⊖	a			07 17	07 23	07 27		07 31	07 34	07 38		07 42	07 45	07 51	07 56					08 17	07 59	08 02		08 05	08 08

		CC		CC	CC	CC	CC	CC	CC	CC	CC	CC		CC	CC	CC	CC	CC	CC	CC	CC	CC		CC	CC
Shoeburyness	d				07 17					07 22		07 34								07 49					07 54
Thorpe Bay	d			07 12	07 21					07 26		07 38						07 42		07 53					07 58
Southend East	d			07 15	07 24					07 29		07 41						07 45		07 56					08 01
Southend Central	a			07 17	07 26					07 31		07 43						07 47		07 58					08 03
	d			07 18	07 27					07 32		07 43						07 48		07 59					08 03
Westcliff	d			07 20	07 29					07 34		07 45						07 50		08 01					08 05
Chalkwell	d			07 22	07 31					07 36		07 48						07 52		08 03					08 08
Leigh-on-Sea	d			07 25	07 34					07 39		07 51						07 55		08 06					08 11
Benfleet	d			07 30	07 39					07 44		07 56						08 00		08 11					08 16
Pitsea	d			07 34					07 41	07 48						07 48	07 52	08 04						08 12	08 20
Stanford-le-Hope	d							07 42	07 48							07 55	08 00					08 11		08 19	
East Tilbury	d								07 52								08 04					08 15		08 23	
Tilbury Town ■	d								07 58								08 10					08 21		08 29	
Grays	d							07 52	08 02							08 06	08 14					08 25		08 33	
Purfleet	d								08 07								08 19							08 39	
Rainham	d								08 13								08 25							08 44	
Dagenham Dock	d								08 16								08 28							08 48	
Basildon	d			07 39						07 53								08 09							08 24
Laindon	d			07 42			07 50			07 56					08 07			08 12			08 22				08 28
West Horndon	d						07 55								08 12						08 27				
Chafford Hundred	d							07 57								08 10						08 29			
Ockendon	d							08 01								08 17						08 33			
Upminster ⊖	d	←				←	08 02	08 09			←	08 13		←	08 17	08 24			←	08 28	08 32	08 40			
Barking ⊖	d	07 56		07 59		08 07	08 10	08 18	08 23	08 13	08 18			08 23	08 26		08 35	08 29	08 35		08 42	08 50		08 54	08 45
Stratford ■ ⊖	a							→	→								→					→		→	
London Liverpool St ■ ⊖	a																								
West Ham ⊖	d	08 01				08 12	08 16			08 19	08 23			08 28	08 32	08 38		08 35			08 47				08 51
Limehouse	d	08 06		08 08	08 13	08 17	08 21			08 24		08 30		08 33	08 37			08 40	08 45	08 48	08 52				08 56
London Fenchurch St ■ ⊖	a	08 12		08 15	08 19	08 24	08 27			08 31	08 34	08 37		08 40	08 43	08 48		08 46	08 51	08 55	08 58				09 02

Shoeburyness and Southend Central - London

Network Diagram - see first page of Table I

		CC	CC	CC	CC	CC	CC	CC		CC	CC	CC	CC	CC	CC	CC	CC	CC		CC	CC	CC	CC	CC	CC
Shoeburyness	d		08 05					08 11			08 25					08 40						09 05			09 20
Thorpe Bay	d		08 09					08 15			08 29					08 44						09 09			09 24
Southend East	d		08 12					08 18			08 32					08 47						09 12			09 27
Southend Central	a		08 14					08 20			08 34					08 49						09 14			09 29
	d		08 15					08 20			08 34					08 50				09 06		09 15		09 20	09 30
Westcliff	d		08 17					08 22			08 36					08 52				09 08		09 17		09 23	09 32
Chalkwell	d		08 19					08 25			08 39					08 54				09 10		09 19		09 25	09 34
Leigh-on-Sea	d		08 22					08 28			08 42					08 57				09 13		09 22		09 28	09 37
Benfleet	d		08 27					08 33			08 47					09 02				09 18		09 27		09 33	09 42
Pitsea	d						08 35	08 37			08 51				08 54	09 06					09 08	09 32		09 37	
Stanford-le-Hope	d					08 33	08 42								09 01						09 16			09 44	
East Tilbury	d					08 37	08 46								09 05						09 20			09 48	
Tilbury Town 3	d					08 43	08 52								09 11						09 26			09 54	
Grays	d					08 47	08 56						09 03		09 15						09 29		09 46	09 57	
Purfleet	d					08 52							09 08		09 20								09 51		
Rainham	d					08 58							09 13		09 26								09 56		
Dagenham Dock	d					09 01							09 17		09 29								10 00		
Basildon	d							08 41			08 55					09 11				09 25		09 36			09 49
Laindon	d				08 38			08 45						09 04		09 14		09 17		09 28		09 39			09 52
West Horndon	d				08 43									09 10				09 22				09 44			
Chafford Hundred	d						09 01														09 34			10 01	
Ockendon	d						09 05					←									09 38			10 05	
Upminster ⊖	d	←		←	08 49		09 12	08 54		←	09 06	09 12		09 16			←	09 28		09 38	09 45	09 50		10 12	10 02
Barking ⊖	d	08 50		08 54	08 58	09 08	→	09 03		09 08		09 21	09 23	09 25	09 35	09 30	09 35	09 37		09 46	09 53	09 58	10 06	→	10 10
Stratford 7 ⊖	a					→									→										
London Liverpool St 15 ⊖	a																								
West Ham ⊖	d	08 55		09 00	09 04			09 09				09 26	09 29	09 31				09 43		09 52	09 59	10 04	10 11		10 16
Limehouse	d			09 05	09 09			09 14		09 17	09 23	09 31	09 34	09 36			09 44	09 48		09 57	10 04	10 09	10 16		
London Fenchurch St 7 ⊖	a	09 06	09 08	09 11	09 15			09 20		09 23	09 29	09 38	09 40	09 43		09 45	09 51	09 54		10 03	10 08	10 13	10 21		10 24

		CC	CC	CC		CC	CC	CC		CC	CC	CC	CC		CC	CC	CC	CC	CC	CC	CC	CC	CC	
Shoeburyness	d		09 35				09 50		and at the same minutes past each hour until		15 05				15 20		15 35			15 50		16 05		
Thorpe Bay	d		09 39				09 54				15 09				15 24		15 39			15 54		16 09		
Southend East	d		09 42				09 57				15 12				15 27		15 42			15 57		16 12		
Southend Central	a		09 44				09 59				15 14				15 29		15 44			15 59		16 14		
	d		09 45			09 50	10 00				15 15		15 20		15 30		15 45		15 48	16 00		16 15		
Westcliff	d		09 47			09 53	10 02				15 17		15 23		15 32		15 47		15 50	16 02		16 17		
Chalkwell	d		09 49			09 55	10 04				15 19		15 25		15 34		15 49		15 53	16 04		16 19		
Leigh-on-Sea	d		09 52			09 58	10 07				15 22		15 28		15 37		15 52		15 56	16 07		16 22		
Benfleet	d		09 57			10 03	10 12				15 27		15 33		15 42		15 57		16 00	16 12		16 27		
Pitsea	d		10 02			10 07					15 32		15 37				16 02		16 04			16 31		
Stanford-le-Hope	d					10 14							15 44						16 11					
East Tilbury	d					10 18							15 48						16 15					
Tilbury Town 3	d					10 24							15 54						16 21					
Grays	d			10 16		10 27						15 46	15 57					16 16	16 26				16 39	
Purfleet	d			10 21								15 51						16 21					16 44	
Rainham	d			10 26								15 56						16 26					16 49	
Dagenham Dock	d			10 30								16 00						16 30					16 53	
Basildon	d		10 06				10 19				15 36				15 49		16 06			16 19		16 35		
Laindon	d		10 09				10 22				15 39				15 52		16 09			16 22		16 38		
West Horndon	d		10 14								15 44						16 14					16 43		
Chafford Hundred	d					10 31							16 01						16 30					
Ockendon	d	←				10 35		←		←			16 05			←			16 34		←			
Upminster ⊖	d	10 12	10 20			10 42	10 32	10 42		15 42	15 50		16 12		16 02	16 12	16 20		16 41	16 30	16 41	16 48		
Barking ⊖	d	10 20	10 28	10 36		→	10 40	10 50		15 50	15 58	16 06	→		16 10	16 20	16 28	16 36	→	16 38	16 49	16 57	17 00	
Stratford 7 ⊖	a																							
London Liverpool St 15 ⊖	a																							
West Ham ⊖	d	10 26	10 34	10 41			10 46	10 56		15 56	16 04	16 11			16 17	16 26	16 34			16 44		17 02		
Limehouse	d	10 31	10 39	10 46				11 01		16 01	16 09	16 16				16 31	16 39					17 08	17 10	
London Fenchurch St 7 ⊖	a	10 35	10 43	10 51			10 54	11 05		16 05	16 13	16 21			16 26	16 36	16 43	16 48		16 52	17 03	17 12	17 15	

		CC	CC	CC	CC	CC	CC	CC	CC	CC		CC	CC	CC	CC	CC	CC	CC	CC	CC		CC	CC	CC	CC
Shoeburyness	d			16 15			16 28						16 50		16 56							17 10			17 30
Thorpe Bay	d			16 19			16 32						16 54		17 00							17 14			17 34
Southend East	d			16 22			16 35						16 57		17 03							17 17			17 37
Southend Central	a			16 24			16 37						16 59		17 05							17 19			17 39
	d		16 19	16 25	16 31		16 38					16 53	17 00		17 06							17 19			17 40
Westcliff	d		16 21	16 27	16 33		16 40					16 55	17 02		17 08							17 21			17 42
Chalkwell	d		16 23	16 29	16 35		16 42					16 58	17 04		17 10							17 24			17 44
Leigh-on-Sea	d		16 26	16 32	16 38		16 45					17 01	17 07		17 13							17 27			17 47
Benfleet	d		16 31	16 37	16 43		16 50					17 05	17 12		17 18							17 32			17 52
Pitsea	d		16 35		16 47		16 54			16 57		17 09	17 16		17 22					17 28		17 36		17 45	17 56
Stanford-le-Hope	d		16 42							17 04							17 19			17 35				17 52	
East Tilbury	d		16 46							17 08							17 23			17 39				17 56	
Tilbury Town 3	d		16 52							17 14							17 29			17 46				18 02	
Grays	d	16 52	16 57							17 18				17 22			17 32	17 46		17 51				18 06	
Purfleet	d	16 57												17 27			17 38	17 51						18 11	
Rainham	d	17 02												17 32			17 43	17 56						18 16	
Dagenham Dock	d	17 06												17 36			17 46	18 00						18 20	
Basildon	d			16 43	16 51		16 58					17 13	17 20		17 26							17 40			18 00
Laindon	d						17 01		17 13			17 17							17 49			17 44	18 06		18 03
West Horndon	d						17 06					17 22							17 54				18 11		
Chafford Hundred	d		17 01							17 23										17 55					
Ockendon	d		17 08					←		17 32						←				18 01					
Upminster ⊖	d		17 15	16 54		←	17 11	17 15	17 23	17 39		17 28	17 31			17 39			18 00	18 08			18 17		
Barking ⊖	d	17 16	→	17 03	17 09	17 16	17 20	17 25	17 32	→		17 36	17 40	17 42	17 44	17 47	17 52	18 06	18 08	18 16			18 25	18 27	
Stratford 7 ⊖	a	→																							
London Liverpool St 15 ⊖	a																								
West Ham ⊖	d			17 09		17 22		17 31							17 49		17 58	18 11	18 14				18 30	18 33	18 26
Limehouse	d			17 14			17 29		17 42								18 03		18 19				18 35	18 38	
London Fenchurch St 7 ⊖	a			17 18	17 24	17 30	17 33	17 39	17 46			17 49	17 52	17 54	17 58	18 00	18 08	18 20	18 23	18 29		18 11	18 39	18 42	18 34

Table I

Mondays to Fridays

13 August to 28 August

Shoeburyness and Southend Central - London

Network Diagram - see first page of Table I

		CC	CC	CC	CC	CC		CC	CC	CC	CC	CC	CC	CC	CC	CC		CC	CC	CC	CC	CC	CC	CC	CC
Shoeburyness	d		17 46			18 05				18 20			18 35			18 50				19 05			19 20		
Thorpe Bay	d		17 50			18 09				18 24			18 39			18 54				19 09			19 24		
Southend East	d		17 53			18 12				18 27			18 42			18 57				19 12			19 27		
Southend Central	a		17 55			18 14				18 29			18 44			18 59				19 15			19 29		
	d		17 56			18 15			18 20	18 30			18 45		18 48	19 00				19 15		19 20	19 30		
Westcliff	d		17 58			18 17			18 23	18 32			18 47		18 51	19 02				19 17		19 23	19 32		
Chalkwell	d		18 00			18 19			18 25	18 34			18 49		18 53	19 04				19 19		19 25	19 34		
Leigh-on-Sea	d		18 03			18 22			18 28	18 37			18 52		18 56	19 07				19 22		19 28	19 37		
Benfleet	d		18 08			18 27			18 33	18 42			18 57		19 01	19 12				19 27		19 33	19 42		
Pitsea	d	18 01	18 12		18 14	18 32			18 37				19 02		19 05					19 32		19 37			
Stanford-le-Hope	d	18 08			18 21				18 44						19 12							19 44			
East Tilbury	d	18 12			18 25				18 48						19 16							19 48			
Tilbury Town 3	d	18 18			18 31				18 54						19 22							19 54			
Grays	d	18 22			18 35			18 54	18 57					19 22	19 25						19 48	19 57			
Purfleet	d				18 40			18 59						19 27							19 53				
Rainham	d				18 45			19 04						19 32							19 58				
Dagenham Dock	d				18 49			19 08						19 36							20 02				
Basildon	d		18 16			18 36				18 49			19 06			19 19				19 36			19 49		
Laindon	d		18 19			18 39				18 52			19 09			19 22				19 39			19 52		
West Horndon	d		18 24			18 44							19 14							19 44					
Chafford Hundred	d	18 27							19 02						19 29							20 01			
Ockendon	d	18 33		←					19 07			←			19 34				←			20 05			←
Upminster ⊖	d	18 39	18 31	18 39		18 50			19 13	19 02	←	19 13	19 20		19 40	19 32		←	19 40	19 50		20 12	20 02	←	20 12
Barking ⊖	d	→	18 39		18 55	18 58		19 14	→	19 10	19 14	19 22	19 28	19 42	→	19 40		19 42	19 50	19 58	20 12	→	20 10	20 12	20 20
Stratford 7 ⊖	a							→						→							→			20 21	
London Liverpool St 15 ⊖	a																							20 33	
West Ham ⊖	d		18 45		19 00	19 04				19 16	19 20	19 27	19 34			19 46		19 48	19 56	20 04			20 16		20 26
Limehouse	d		18 50		19 05	19 09						19 32	19 39					19 53	20 01	20 09					20 31
London Fenchurch St 7 ⊖	a		18 54	18 59	19 10	19 13				19 24	19 28	19 37	19 43			19 54		19 58	20 05	20 13			20 25		20 35

		CC		CC	CC	CC	CC	CC	CC	CC	CC	CC		CC	CC	CC	CC	CC	CC	CC	CC	CC		CC	CC
Shoeburyness	d	19 35				19 50			20 05			20 20			20 35			21 05			21 20			21 35	
Thorpe Bay	d	19 39				19 54			20 09			20 24			20 39			21 09			21 24			21 39	
Southend East	d	19 42				19 57			20 12			20 27			20 42			21 12			21 27			21 42	
Southend Central	a	19 44				19 59			20 14			20 29			20 44			21 14			21 29			21 45	
	d	19 45			19 50	20 00			20 15		20 20	20 30			20 45		20 50	21 15		21 20	21 30			21 45	
Westcliff	d	19 47			19 53	20 02			20 17		20 23	20 32			20 47		20 53	21 17		21 23	21 32			21 47	
Chalkwell	d	19 49			19 55	20 04			20 19		20 25	20 34			20 49		20 55	21 19		21 25	21 34			21 49	
Leigh-on-Sea	d	19 52			19 58	20 07			20 22		20 28	20 37			20 52		20 58	21 22		21 28	21 37			21 52	
Benfleet	d	19 57			20 03	20 12			20 27		20 33	20 42			20 57		21 03	21 27		21 33	21 42			21 57	
Pitsea	d	20 02			20 07				20 32		20 37				21 02		21 07	21 32		21 37				22 02	
Stanford-le-Hope	d				20 14						20 44						21 14			21 44					
East Tilbury	d				20 18						20 48						21 18			21 48					
Tilbury Town 3	d				20 24						20 54						21 24			21 54					
Grays	d			20 16	20 27					20 46	20 57					21 16	21 27		21 46	21 57					22 16
Purfleet	d			20 21						20 51						21 21			21 51						22 21
Rainham	d			20 26						20 56						21 26			21 56						22 26
Dagenham Dock	d			20 30						21 00						21 30			22 00						22 30
Basildon	d	20 06				20 19			20 36			20 49			21 06			21 36			21 49			22 06	
Laindon	d	20 09				20 22			20 39			20 52			21 09			21 39			21 52			22 09	
West Horndon	d	20 14							20 44						21 14			21 44						22 14	
Chafford Hundred	d				20 31						21 01						21 31			22 01					
Ockendon	d				20 35		←				21 05			←			21 35			22 05		←			
Upminster ⊖	d	20 20			20 42	20 32	20 42		20 50		21 12	21 02		21 12	21 20		21 42	21 50		22 12	22 02	22 12		22 20	
Barking ⊖	d	20 28		20 36	→	20 40	20 50	20 51	20 58	21 06	→	21 10		21 20	21 28	21 36	21 50	21 58	22 06	→	22 10	22 20		22 28	22 36
Stratford 7 ⊖	a							21 00		21 15															
London Liverpool St 15 ⊖	a							21 12		21 26															
West Ham ⊖	d	20 34		20 41		20 46	20 56		21 04			21 16		21 26	21 34	21 41	21 56	22 04	22 11		22 16	22 26		22 34	22 41
Limehouse	d	20 39		20 46			21 01		21 09					21 31	21 39	21 46	22 01	22 09	22 16			22 31		22 39	22 46
London Fenchurch St 7 ⊖	a	20 43		20 51		20 54	21 05		21 13			21 24		21 35	21 43	21 52	22 05	22 13	22 21		22 24	22 35		22 43	22 52

		CC	CC	CC	CC	CC	CC	CC		CC
Shoeburyness	d		22 05			22 35				23 05
Thorpe Bay	d		22 09			22 39				23 09
Southend East	d		22 12			22 42				23 12
Southend Central	a		22 14			22 44				23 14
	d	21 50	22 15		22 20	22 45	22 50			23 15
Westcliff	d	21 53	22 17		22 23	22 47	22 53			23 17
Chalkwell	d	21 55	22 19		22 25	22 49	22 55			23 19
Leigh-on-Sea	d	21 58	22 22		22 28	22 52	22 58			23 22
Benfleet	d	22 03	22 27		22 33	22 57	23 03			23 27
Pitsea	d	22 07	22 32		22 37	23 02	23 07			23 32
Stanford-le-Hope	d	22 14			22 44		23 14			
East Tilbury	d	22 18			22 48		23 18			
Tilbury Town 3	d	22 24			22 54		23 24			
Grays	d	22 27		22 46	22 57		23 27	23 33		
Purfleet	d			22 51				23 38		
Rainham	d			22 56				23 43		
Dagenham Dock	d			23 00				23 47		
Basildon	d		22 36			23 06				23 36
Laindon	d		22 39			23 09				23 39
West Horndon	d		22 44			23 14				23 44
Chafford Hundred	d	22 31			23 01		23 31			
Ockendon	d	22 35			23 05		23 35			
Upminster ⊖	d	22 42	22 50		23 12	23 20	23 42			23 50
Barking ⊖	d	22 50	22 58	23 06	23 20	23 28	23 50	23 55		23 58
Stratford 7 ⊖	a							00 09		
London Liverpool St 15 ⊖	a							00 20		
West Ham ⊖	d	22 56	23 04	23 11	23 26	23 34	23 56			00 04
Limehouse	d	23 01	23 09	23 16	23 31	23 39	00 01			00 09
London Fenchurch St 7 ⊖	a	23 05	23 13	23 21	23 35	23 43	00 05			00 13

Table I

Mondays to Fridays

29 August to 7 September

Shoeburyness and Southend Central - London

Network Diagram - see first page of Table I

		CC A	CC B	CC A	CC B	CC A	CC B	CC B	CC	CC		CC	CC	CC	CC	CC	CC	CC	CC	CC		CC	CC	CC	CC
Shoeburyness	d					23p05		23p05		04 20			04 40	05 00		05 13	05 23			05 27			05 45		
Thorpe Bay	d					23p09		23p09		04 24			04 44	05 04		05 17	05 27			05 31			05 49		05 56
Southend East	d					23p12		23p12		04 27			04 47	05 07		05 20	05 30			05 34			05 52		05 59
Southend Central	a					23p14		23p14		04 29			04 49	05 09		05 22	05 32			05 36			05 54		06 01
	d	22p50	22p50			23p15		23p15		04 29			04 50	05 09		05 23	05 32			05 36		05 47	05 54		06 02
Westcliff	d	22p53	22p53			23p17		23p17		04 31			04 52	05 11		05 25	05 34			05 38		05 49	05 56		06 04
Chalkwell	d	22p55	22p55			23p19		23p19		04 34			04 54	05 14		05 27	05 37			05 41		05 51	05 59		06 06
Leigh-on-Sea	d	22p58	22p58			23p22		23p22		04 37			04 57	05 17		05 30	05 40			05 44		05 54	06 02		06 09
Benfleet	d	23p03	23p03			23p27		23p27		04 41			05 02	05 21		05 35	05 44			05 48		05 59	06 07		06 14
Pitsea	d	23p07	23p07			23p32		23p32		04 45			05 06	05 25		05 39	05 48			05 52		06 04	06 11		06 24
Stanford-le-Hope	d	23p14	23p14						04 29				05 13			05 46				05 59		06 11			06 31
East Tilbury	d	23p18	23p18						04 33				05 17			05 50				06 03		06 15			06 35
Tilbury Town 3	d	23p24	23p24						04 39				05 23			05 56				06 09		06 21			06 41
Grays	d	23p27	23p27	23p33	23p33				04 42			05 09	05 26		05 48	06 00			06 11	06 13		06 25		06 29	06 45
Purfleet	d			23p38	23p38								05 32			06 05				06 19				06 34	06 51
Rainham	d			23p43	23p43								05 37			06 10				06 24				06 40	06 56
Dagenham Dock	d			23p47	23p47								05 40			06 14				06 27				06 43	07 00
Basildon	d					23p36		23p36		04 49				05 29			05 52						06 15		
Laindon	d					23p39		23p39		04 52				05 32			05 55						06 18		
West Horndon	d					23p44		23p44		04 57				05 37			06 00						06 23		
Chafford Hundred	d	23p31	23p31						04 46			05 13			05 52				06 15			06 30			
Ockendon	d	23p35	23p35						04 50			05 17			05 56				06 19			06 37			
Upminster	⊖ d	23p42	23p42			23p50		23p50	04 57	05 03		05a22		05 43	06 01		06 06	←	06a25			06 44	06 29		
Barking	⊖ d	23p50	23p51	23p55	23p55	23p58		00 02	05 06	05 11			05 46	05 51	06 10	06 20	06 15	06 20		06 33		→	06 38	06 50	07 06
Stratford 7	⊖ a			00 09					05 13							→									→
London Liverpool St 15	⊖ a			00 20					05 27																
West Ham	⊖ d	23p56	00 01		00 06	00 04	←	00 12		05 17			05 52	05 57	06 15		06 21	06 26		06 39			06 44	06 55	
Limehouse	d	00 01	00 06		00 11	00 09	00 11	00 17		05 22			05 57	06 02	06 20		06 26	06 31		06 44			06 49	07 00	
London Fenchurch St 7	⊖ a	00 05	00 11		→	00 13	00 18	00 24		05 28			06 03	06 08	06 27		06 30	06 37		06 50			06 53	→	

		CC	CC	CC	CC	CC		CC	CC	CC	CC	CC	CC	CC	CC	CC		CC	CC	CC	CC	CC	CC	CC	CC
Shoeburyness	d	05 56			06 04				06 13		06 17		06 28			06 33		06 46							06 51
Thorpe Bay	d	06 00			06 08			06 13	06 17		06 21		06 32			06 37		06 50							06 55
Southend East	d	06 03			06 11			06 16	06 20		06 24		06 35			06 40		06 53							06 58
Southend Central	a	06 05			06 13			06 18	06 22		06 26		06 37			06 42		06 55							07 00
	d	06 06			06 13			06 18	06 23		06 26		06 38			06 42		06 55							07 00
Westcliff	d	06 08			06 15			06 20	06 25		06 28		06 40			06 44		06 57							07 02
Chalkwell	d	06 10			06 18			06 23	06 27		06 31		06 42			06 47		07 00							07 05
Leigh-on-Sea	d	06 13			06 21			06 26	06 30		06 34		06 45			06 50		07 03							07 08
Benfleet	d	06 18			06 26			06 31	06 35		06 39		06 50			06 55		07 08							07 13
Pitsea	d				06 30			06 39			06 43				06 52	06 59					07 00			07 16	07 17
Stanford-le-Hope	d							06 46							06 59						07 07			07 23	
East Tilbury	d							06 50							07 03						07 11			07 27	
Tilbury Town 3	d							06 56							07 09						07 18			07 33	
Grays	d					06 50		07 00							07 13						07 22	07 30		07 37	
Purfleet	d							07 05							07 18							07 35			
Rainham	d							07 11							07 24							07 41			
Dagenham Dock	d							07 14							07 27							07 44			
Basildon	d	06 25			06 34				06 42		06 47		06 57			07 03		07 15							07 21
Laindon	d	06 29			06 37						06 50					07 07				07 20			07 37		07 25
West Horndon	d				06 42						06 55					07 12				07 25			07 42		
Chafford Hundred	d					06 54															07 26			07 41	
Ockendon	d			←		06 58						←									07 30			07 46	
Upminster	⊖ d	06 38		06 44	06 48	07 05				←	07 01	07 05	07 10	←		07 18			←	07 30	07 37		07 47	07 54	
Barking	⊖ d				06 57	→		07 21	07 01	07 06	07 10	07 14		07 21	07 34	07 27			07 34	07 39	07 46	07 51	07 56		07 42
Stratford 7	⊖ a							→							→						→	→	→		
London Liverpool St 15	⊖ a																								
West Ham	⊖ d		←	06 58	07 03				07 07	07 12	07 16	07 20	07 23	07 26					07 39	07 44					07 47
Limehouse	d	06 55	07 00	07 03						07 17	07 21	07 25		07 32		07 36			07 44	07 49					07 52
London Fenchurch St 7	⊖ a	07 01	07 07	07 09	07 13				07 17	07 23	07 27	07 31	07 34	07 38		07 42		07 45	07 51	07 56				08 17	07 59

		CC		CC	CC	CC	CC	CC	CC	CC	CC	CC		CC	CC	CC	CC	CC	CC	CC	CC	CC		CC	CC
Shoeburyness	d				07 03				07 17						07 22		07 34								07 49
Thorpe Bay	d				07 07			07 12	07 21						07 26		07 38					07 42			07 53
Southend East	d				07 10			07 15	07 24						07 29		07 41					07 45			07 56
Southend Central	a				07 12			07 17	07 26						07 31		07 43					07 47			07 58
	d			07 08	07 13			07 18	07 27						07 32		07 43					07 48			07 59
Westcliff	d			07 10	07 15			07 20	07 29						07 34		07 45					07 50			08 01
Chalkwell	d			07 12	07 17			07 22	07 31						07 36		07 48					07 52			08 03
Leigh-on-Sea	d			07 16	07 20			07 25	07 34						07 39		07 51					07 55			08 06
Benfleet	d			07 20	07 25			07 30	07 39						07 44		07 56					08 00			08 11
Pitsea	d			07 25				07 34						07 41	07 48					07 48	07 52	08 04			
Stanford-le-Hope	d			07 32								07 42		07 48						07 55	08 00				
East Tilbury	d			07 36										07 52							08 04				
Tilbury Town 3	d			07 42										07 58							08 10				
Grays	d			07 46								07 52		08 02						08 06	08 14				
Purfleet	d			07 51										08 07							08 19				
Rainham	d			07 57										08 13							08 25				
Dagenham Dock	d			08 00										08 16							08 28				
Basildon	d				07 32			07 39							07 53							08 09			
Laindon	d							07 42			07 50				07 56				08 07			08 12			
West Horndon	d										07 55								08 12						
Chafford Hundred	d											07 57								08 10					
Ockendon	d											08 01								08 17					
Upminster	⊖ d	←				←	←			←	08 02	08 09				←	08 13	←	08 17	08 24				←	08 28
Barking	⊖ d	07 46		08 07		07 51	07 56	07 59		08 07	08 10	08 18		08 23	08 13	08 18		08 23	08 26		08 35	08 29		08 35	
Stratford 7	⊖ a			→								→		→							→				
London Liverpool St 15	⊖ a																								
West Ham	⊖ d	07 52				07 57	08 01			08 12	08 16				08 19	08 23		08 28	08 32	08 38		08 35			
Limehouse	d				07 59	08 02	08 06	08 08	08 13	08 17	08 21				08 24		08 30	08 33	08 37			08 40		08 45	08 48
London Fenchurch St 7	⊖ a	08 02			08 05	08 08	08 12	08 15	08 19	08 24	08 27				08 31	08 34	08 37	08 40	08 43	08 48		08 46		08 51	08 55

A 29 August

B not 29 August, 3 September

Table I

Mondays to Fridays

29 August to 7 September

Shoeburyness and Southend Central - London

Network Diagram - see first page of Table I

		CC	CC	CC	CC	CC	CC	CC		CC	CC	CC	CC	CC	CC	CC	CC	CC		CC	CC	CC	CC	CC	CC
Shoeburyness	d				07 54		08 05						08 11		08 25						08 40				
Thorpe Bay	d				07 58		08 09						08 15		08 29						08 44				
Southend East	d				08 01		08 12						08 18		08 32						08 47				
Southend Central	a				08 03		08 14						08 20		08 34						08 49				
	d				08 03		08 15						08 20		08 34						08 50			09 06	
Westcliff	d				08 05		08 17						08 22		08 36						08 52			09 08	
Chalkwell	d				08 08		08 19						08 25		08 39						08 54			09 10	
Leigh-on-Sea	d				08 11		08 22						08 28		08 42						08 57			09 13	
Benfleet	d				08 16		08 27						08 33		08 47						09 02			09 18	
Pitsea	d			08 12	08 20							08 35	08 37		08 51					08 54	09 06				09 08
Stanford-le-Hope	d		08 11	08 19							08 33	08 42								09 01					09 16
East Tilbury	d		08 15	08 23							08 37	08 46								09 05					09 20
Tilbury Town 3	d		08 21	08 29							08 43	08 52								09 11					09 26
Grays	d		08 25	08 33							08 47	08 56					09 03			09 15					09 29
Purfleet	d			08 39							08 52						09 08			09 20					
Rainham	d			08 44							08 58						09 13			09 26					
Dagenham Dock	d			08 48							09 01						09 17			09 29					
Basildon	d				08 24								08 41		08 55						09 11			09 25	
Laindon	d	08 22			08 28					08 38			08 45					09 04			09 14		09 17	09 28	
West Horndon	d	08 27								08 43								09 10					09 22		
Chafford Hundred	d		08 29									09 01													09 34
Ockendon	d		08 33									09 05				←									09 38
Upminster	⊖ d	08 32	08 40			←		←		08 49		09 12	08 54	←	09 06	09 12		09 16				←	09 28	09 38	09 45
Barking	⊖ d	08 42	08 50	08 54	08 45	08 50		08 54		08 58	09 08	→	09 03	09 08		09 21	09 23	09 25		09 35	09 30	09 35	09 37	09 46	09 53
Stratford 7	⊖ a		→	→							→									→					
London Liverpool St 15	⊖ a																								
West Ham	⊖ d	08 47			08 51	08 55		09 00		09 04			09 09			09 26	09 29	09 31					09 43	09 52	09 59
Limehouse	d	08 52			08 56			09 05		09 09			09 14	09 17	09 23	09 31	09 34	09 36				09 44	09 48	09 57	10 04
London Fenchurch St 7	⊖ a	08 58			09 02	09 06	09 08	09 11		09 15			09 20	09 23	09 29	09 38	09 40	09 43			09 45	09 51	09 54	10 03	10 08

		CC	CC	CC		CC	CC	CC	CC	CC	CC	CC	and at the same minutes past each hour until	CC		CC	CC	CC	CC	CC	CC	CC	CC	CC
Shoeburyness	d	09 05				09 20		09 35			09 50					15 05			15 20		15 35			15 50
Thorpe Bay	d	09 09				09 24		09 39			09 54					15 09			15 24		15 39			15 54
Southend East	d	09 12				09 27		09 42			09 57					15 12			15 27		15 42			15 57
Southend Central	a	09 14				09 29		09 44			09 59					15 14			15 29		15 44			15 59
	d	09 15		09 20		09 30		09 45		09 50	10 00					15 15		15 20	15 30		15 45		15 48	16 00
Westcliff	d	09 17		09 23		09 32		09 47		09 53	10 02					15 17		15 23	15 32		15 47		15 50	16 02
Chalkwell	d	09 19		09 25		09 34		09 49		09 55	10 04					15 19		15 25	15 34		15 49		15 53	16 04
Leigh-on-Sea	d	09 22		09 28		09 37		09 52		09 58	10 07					15 22		15 28	15 37		15 52		15 56	16 07
Benfleet	d	09 27		09 33		09 42		09 57		10 03	10 12					15 27		15 33	15 42		15 57		16 00	16 12
Pitsea	d	09 32		09 37				10 02		10 07						15 32		15 37			16 02		16 04	
Stanford-le-Hope	d			09 44						10 14								15 44					16 11	
East Tilbury	d			09 48						10 18								15 48					16 15	
Tilbury Town 3	d			09 54						10 24								15 54					16 21	
Grays	d		09 46	09 57					10 16	10 27							15 46	15 57				16 16	16 26	
Purfleet	d		09 51						10 21								15 51					16 21		
Rainham	d		09 56						10 26								15 56					16 26		
Dagenham Dock	d		10 00						10 30								16 00					16 30		
Basildon	d	09 36				09 49		10 06			10 19					15 36			15 49		16 06			16 19
Laindon	d	09 39				09 52		10 09			10 22					15 39			15 52		16 09			16 22
West Horndon	d	09 44						10 14								15 44					16 14			
Chafford Hundred	d			10 01						10 31								16 01					16 30	
Ockendon	d			10 05			←			10 35		←		←				16 05		←			16 34	
Upminster	⊖ d	09 50		10 12		10 02	10 12	10 20		10 42	10 32	10 42		15 42		15 50		16 12	16 02	16 12	16 20		16 41	16 30
Barking	⊖ d	09 58	10 06	→		10 10	10 20	10 28	10 36	→	10 40	10 50		15 50		15 58	16 06	→	16 10	16 20	16 28	16 36	→	16 38
Stratford 7	⊖ a																							
London Liverpool St 15	⊖ a																							
West Ham	⊖ d	10 04	10 11			10 16	10 26	10 34	10 41		10 46	10 56		15 56		16 04	16 11		16 17	16 26	16 34			16 44
Limehouse	d	10 09	10 16				10 31	10 39	10 46			11 01		16 01		16 09	16 16			16 31	16 39			
London Fenchurch St 7	⊖ a	10 13	10 21			10 24	10 35	10 43	10 51		10 54	11 05		16 05		16 13	16 21		16 26	16 36	16 43	16 48		16 52

			CC	CC	CC	CC	CC	CC	CC	CC	CC		CC	CC	CC	CC	CC	CC	CC	CC	CC		CC	CC	CC
Shoeburyness	d			16 05				16 15			16 28						16 50		16 56						
Thorpe Bay	d			16 09				16 19			16 32						16 54		17 00						
Southend East	d			16 12				16 22			16 35						16 57		17 03						
Southend Central	a			16 14				16 24			16 37						16 59		17 05						
	d			16 15			16 19	16 25	16 31		16 38					16 53	17 00		17 06						
Westcliff	d			16 17			16 21	16 27	16 33		16 40					16 55	17 02		17 08						
Chalkwell	d			16 19			16 23	16 29	16 35		16 42					16 58	17 04		17 10						
Leigh-on-Sea	d			16 22			16 26	16 32	16 38		16 45					17 01	17 07		17 13						
Benfleet	d			16 27			16 31	16 37	16 43		16 50					17 05	17 12		17 18						
Pitsea	d			16 31			16 35		16 47		16 54				16 57	17 09	17 16		17 22						17 28
Stanford-le-Hope	d						16 42								17 04						17 19				17 35
East Tilbury	d						16 46								17 08						17 23				17 39
Tilbury Town 3	d						16 52								17 14						17 29				17 46
Grays	d				16 39	16 52	16 57								17 18			17 22			17 32		17 46		17 51
Purfleet	d				16 44	16 57												17 27			17 38		17 51		
Rainham	d				16 49	17 02												17 32			17 43		17 56		
Dagenham Dock	d				16 53	17 06												17 36			17 46		18 00		
Basildon	d			16 35				16 43	16 51		16 58					17 13	17 20		17 26						
Laindon	d			16 38							17 01			17 13		17 17								17 49	
West Horndon	d			16 43							17 06					17 22								17 54	
Chafford Hundred	d						17 01								17 23										17 55
Ockendon	d		←				17 08						←		17 32					←					18 01
Upminster	⊖ d		16 41	16 48			17 15	16 54		←	17 11		17 15	17 23	17 39	17 28	17 31			17 39				18 00	18 08
Barking	⊖ d		16 49	16 57	17 00	17 16	→	17 03	17 09	17 16	17 20		17 25	17 32	→	17 36	17 40	17 42	17 44	17 47	17 52		18 06	18 08	18 16
Stratford 7	⊖ a					→																			
London Liverpool St 15	⊖ a																								
West Ham	⊖ d			17 02				17 09		17 22			17 31						17 49		17 58		18 11	18 14	
Limehouse	d			17 08	17 10			17 14			17 29			17 42							18 03			18 19	
London Fenchurch St 7	⊖ a		17 03	17 12	17 15			17 18	17 24	17 30	17 33		17 39	17 46		17 49	17 52	17 54	17 58	18 00	18 08		18 20	18 23	18 29

Table I

Shoeburyness and Southend Central - London

Mondays to Fridays

29 August to 7 September

Network Diagram - see first page of Table I

		CC	CC	CC	CC	CC	CC		CC	CC	CC	CC	CC	CC	CC	CC	CC		CC	CC	CC	CC	CC	CC	CC
Shoeburyness	d	17 10			17 30		17 46				18 05			18 20			18 35				18 51			19 05	
Thorpe Bay	d	17 14			17 34		17 50				18 09			18 24			18 39				18 55			19 09	
Southend East	d	17 17			17 37		17 53				18 12			18 27			18 42				18 58			19 12	
Southend Central	a	17 19			17 39		17 55				18 14			18 29			18 44				19 00			19 15	
	d	17 19			17 40		17 56				18 15		18 20	18 30			18 45			18 49	19 01			19 15	
Westcliff	d	17 21			17 42		17 58				18 17		18 23	18 32			18 47			18 51	19 03			19 17	
Chalkwell	d	17 24			17 44		18 00				18 19		18 25	18 34			18 49			18 53	19 05			19 19	
Leigh-on-Sea	d	17 27			17 47		18 03				18 22		18 28	18 37			18 52			18 56	19 08			19 22	
Benfleet	d	17 32			17 52		18 08				18 27		18 33	18 42			18 57			19 01	19 13			19 27	
Pitsea	d	17 36		17 45	17 56	18 01	18 12			18 14	18 32		18 37				19 02			19 05				19 32	
Stanford-le-Hope	d			17 52		18 08				18 21			18 44							19 12					
East Tilbury	d			17 56		18 12				18 25			18 48							19 16					
Tilbury Town 3	d			18 02		18 18				18 31			18 54							19 22					
Grays	d			18 06		18 22				18 35		18 54	18 57						19 22	19 25					19 48
Purfleet	d			18 11						18 40		18 59							19 27						19 53
Rainham	d			18 16						18 45		19 04							19 32						19 58
Dagenham Dock	d			18 20						18 49		19 08							19 36						20 02
Basildon	d	17 40			18 00		18 16				18 36			18 49			19 06				19 19			19 36	
Laindon	d	17 44	18 06		18 03		18 19				18 39			18 52			19 09				19 22			19 39	
West Horndon	d		18 11				18 24				18 44						19 14							19 44	
Chafford Hundred	d					18 27							19 02							19 29					
Ockendon	d					18 33			←				19 07			←				19 34			←		
Upminster ⊖	d		18 17			18 39	18 31		18 39		18 50		19 13	19 02	←	19 13	19 20			19 40	19 32	←	19 40	19 50	
Barking ⊖	d		18 25	18 27		→	18 39			18 55	18 58	19 14	→	19 10	19 14	19 22	19 28		19 42	→	19 40	19 42	19 50	19 58	20 13
Stratford 7 ⊖	a											→							→						→
London Liverpool St 15 ⊖	a																								
West Ham ⊖	d		18 30	18 33	18 26		18 45			19 00	19 04			19 16	19 20	19 27	19 34				19 46	19 48	19 56	20 04	
Limehouse	d		18 35	18 38			18 50			19 05	19 09					19 32	19 39					19 53	20 01	20 09	
London Fenchurch St 7 ⊖	a	18 11	18 39	18 42	18 34		18 54		18 59	19 10	19 13			19 24	19 28	19 37	19 43				19 54	19 58	20 05	20 13	

		CC	CC		CC	CC	CC	CC	CC	CC	CC	CC	CC		CC	CC	CC	CC	CC	CC	CC	CC	CC		CC
Shoeburyness	d		19 20				19 35			19 50		20 05				20 20		20 35			21 05				21 20
Thorpe Bay	d		19 24				19 39			19 54		20 09				20 24		20 39			21 09				21 24
Southend East	d		19 27				19 42			19 57		20 12				20 27		20 42			21 12				21 27
Southend Central	a		19 29				19 44			19 59		20 14				20 29		20 44			21 14				21 29
	d	19 20	19 30				19 45		19 50	20 00		20 15			20 20	20 30		20 45		20 50	21 15		21 20		21 30
Westcliff	d	19 23	19 32				19 47		19 53	20 02		20 17			20 23	20 32		20 47		20 53	21 17		21 23		21 32
Chalkwell	d	19 25	19 34				19 49		19 55	20 04		20 19			20 25	20 34		20 49		20 55	21 19		21 25		21 34
Leigh-on-Sea	d	19 28	19 37				19 52		19 58	20 07		20 22			20 28	20 37		20 52		20 58	21 22		21 28		21 37
Benfleet	d	19 33	19 42				19 57		20 03	20 12		20 27			20 33	20 42		20 57		21 03	21 27		21 33		21 42
Pitsea	d	19 37					20 02		20 07			20 32			20 37			21 02		21 07	21 32		21 37		
Stanford-le-Hope	d	19 44							20 14						20 44					21 14			21 44		
East Tilbury	d	19 48							20 18						20 48					21 18			21 48		
Tilbury Town 3	d	19 54							20 24						20 54					21 24			21 54		
Grays	d	19 57						20 16	20 27				20 46		20 57				21 16	21 27		21 46	21 57		
Purfleet	d							20 21					20 51						21 21			21 51			
Rainham	d							20 26					20 56						21 26			21 56			
Dagenham Dock	d							20 30					21 00						21 30			22 00			
Basildon	d		19 49				20 06			20 19		20 36				20 49		21 06			21 36				21 49
Laindon	d		19 52				20 09			20 22		20 39				20 52		21 09			21 39				21 52
West Horndon	d						20 14					20 44						21 14			21 44				
Chafford Hundred	d	20 01							20 31						21 01					21 31			22 01		
Ockendon	d	20 05				←			20 35		←				21 05		←			21 35			22 05		
Upminster ⊖	d	20 12	20 02		←	20 12	20 20		20 42	20 32	20 42	20 50			21 12	21 02	21 12	21 20		21 42	21 50		22 12		22 02
Barking ⊖	d	→	20 10		20 13	20 20	20 28	20 36	→	20 40	20 50	20 58	21 06		→	21 10	21 20	21 28	21 36	21 50	21 58	22 06	→		22 11
Stratford 7 ⊖	a																								
London Liverpool St 15 ⊖	a																								
West Ham ⊖	d		20 16		20 18	20 26	20 34	20 41		20 46	20 56	21 04	21 11			21 16	21 26	21 34	21 41	21 56	22 04	22 14			22 19
Limehouse	d				20 23	20 31	20 39	20 46			21 01	21 09	21 16				21 31	21 39	21 46	22 01	22 09	22 19			22 24
London Fenchurch St 7 ⊖	a		20 25		20 28	20 35	20 43	20 51		20 54	21 05	21 13	21 21			21 24	21 35	21 43	21 51	22 05	22 13	22 26			22 31

		CC	CC	CC	CC	CC	CC	CC	CC		CC	CC	CC
Shoeburyness	d		21 35			22 05			22 35				23 05
Thorpe Bay	d		21 39			22 09			22 39				23 09
Southend East	d		21 42			22 12			22 42				23 12
Southend Central	a		21 45			22 14			22 44				23 14
	d		21 45		21 50	22 15		22 20	22 45		22 50		23 15
Westcliff	d		21 47		21 53	22 17		22 23	22 47		22 53		23 17
Chalkwell	d		21 49		21 55	22 19		22 25	22 49		22 55		23 19
Leigh-on-Sea	d		21 52		21 58	22 22		22 28	22 52		22 58		23 22
Benfleet	d		21 57		22 03	22 27		22 33	22 57		23 03		23 27
Pitsea	d		22 02		22 07	22 32		22 37	23 02		23 07		23 32
Stanford-le-Hope	d				22 14			22 44			23 14		
East Tilbury	d				22 18			22 48			23 18		
Tilbury Town 3	d				22 24			22 54			23 24		
Grays	d			22 16	22 27		22 48	22 57			23 27	23 33	
Purfleet	d			22 21			22 53					23 38	
Rainham	d			22 26			22 58					23 43	
Dagenham Dock	d			22 30			23 02					23 47	
Basildon	d		22 06			22 36			23 06				23 36
Laindon	d		22 09			22 39			23 09				23 39
West Horndon	d		22 14			22 44			23 14				23 44
Chafford Hundred	d				22 31			23 01			23 31		
Ockendon	d	←			22 35			23 05			23 35		
Upminster ⊖	d	22 12	22 20		22 42	22 50		23 12	23 20		23 42		23 50
Barking ⊖	d	22 20	22 28	22 37	22 51	23 00	23 10	23 21	23 29		23 51	23 55	00 02
Stratford 7 ⊖	a												
London Liverpool St 15 ⊖	a												
West Ham ⊖	d	22 28	22 36	22 45	23 00	23 10	23 20	23 30	23 40		00 01	00 06	00 12
Limehouse	d	22 34	22 42	22 50	23 05	23 15	23 25	23 35	23 45		00 06	00 11	00 17
London Fenchurch St 7 ⊖	a	22 40	22 48	22 58	23 12	23 22	23 32	23 42	23 52		00 11	00 18	00 24

Table I

Shoeburyness and Southend Central - London

Mondays to Fridays

from 10 September

Network Diagram - see first page of Table I

		CC MX	CC MX	CC MX	CC	CC	CC	CC	CC	CC		CC	CC	CC	CC	CC	CC	CC	CC	CC		CC	CC	CC	CC
Shoeburyness	d			23p05		04 20		04 40	05 00			05 13	05 23			05 27		05 45				05 56			06 04
Thorpe Bay	d			23p09		04 24		04 44	05 04			05 17	05 27			05 31		05 49		05 56		06 00			06 08
Southend East	d			23p12		04 27		04 47	05 07			05 20	05 30			05 34		05 52		05 59		06 03			06 11
Southend Central	a			23p14		04 29		04 49	05 09			05 22	05 32			05 36		05 54		06 01		06 05			06 13
	d	22p50		23p15		04 29		04 50	05 09			05 23	05 32			05 36	05 47	05 54		06 02		06 06			06 13
Westcliff	d	22p53		23p17		04 31		04 52	05 11			05 25	05 34			05 38	05 49	05 56		06 04		06 08			06 15
Chalkwell	d	22p55		23p19		04 34		04 54	05 14			05 27	05 37			05 41	05 51	05 59		06 06		06 10			06 18
Leigh-on-Sea	d	22p58		23p22		04 37		04 57	05 17			05 30	05 40			05 44	05 54	06 02		06 09		06 13			06 21
Benfleet	d	23p03		23p27		04 41		05 02	05 21			05 35	05 44			05 48	05 59	06 07		06 14		06 18			06 26
Pitsea	d	23p07		23p32		04 45		05 06	05 25			05 39	05 48			05 52	06 04	06 11		06 24					06 30
Stanford-le-Hope	d	23p14			04 29			05 13				05 46				05 59	06 11			06 31					
East Tilbury	d	23p18			04 33			05 17				05 50				06 03	06 15			06 35					
Tilbury Town 3	d	23p24			04 39			05 23				05 56				06 09	06 21			06 41					
Grays	d	23p27	23p33		04 42		05 09	05 26		05 48		06 00			06 11	06 13	06 25		06 29	06 45					
Purfleet	d		23p38					05 32				06 05				06 19			06 34	06 51					
Rainham	d		23p43					05 37				06 10				06 24			06 40	06 56					
Dagenham Dock	d		23p47					05 40				06 14				06 27			06 43	07 00					
Basildon	d			23p36		04 49			05 29				05 52					06 15				06 25			06 34
Laindon	d			23p39		04 52			05 32				05 55					06 18				06 29			06 37
West Horndon	d			23p44		04 57			05 37				06 00					06 23							06 42
Chafford Hundred	d	23p31			04 46		05 13			05 52					06 15		06 30								
Ockendon	d	23p35			04 50		05 17			05 56					06 19		06 37							←	
Upminster ⊖	d	23p42		23p50	04 57	05 03	05a22		05 43	06 01			06 06	←	06a25		06 44	06 29				06 38		06 44	06 48
Barking ⊖	d	23p50	23p55	23p58	05 06	05 11		05 46	05 51	06 10		06 20	06 15	06 20		06 33	→	06 38	06 50	07 06					06 57
Stratford 7 ⊖	a		00 09		05 13							→								→					
London Liverpool St 15 ⊖	a		00 20		05 27																				
West Ham ⊖	d	23p56		00 04		05 17		05 52	05 57	06 15			06 21	06 26		06 39		06 44	06 55				←	06 58	07 03
Limehouse	d	00 01		00 09		05 22		05 57	06 02	06 20			06 26	06 31		06 44		06 49	07 00			06 55	07 00	07 03	
London Fenchurch St 7 ⊖	a	00 05		00 13		05 28		06 03	06 08	06 27			06 30	06 37		06 50		06 53	→			07 01	07 07	07 09	07 13

		CC	CC	CC	CC	CC		CC	CC	CC	CC	CC	CC	CC	CC	CC		CC	CC	CC	CC	CC	CC	CC	CC
Shoeburyness	d			06 13		06 17			06 28			06 33	06 46								06 51			07 03	
Thorpe Bay	d		06 13	06 17		06 21			06 32			06 37	06 50								06 55			07 07	
Southend East	d		06 16	06 20		06 24			06 35			06 40	06 53								06 58			07 10	
Southend Central	a		06 18	06 22		06 26			06 37			06 42	06 55								07 00			07 12	
	d		06 18	06 23		06 26			06 38			06 42	06 55								07 00		07 08	07 13	
Westcliff	d		06 20	06 25		06 28			06 40			06 44	06 57								07 02		07 10	07 15	
Chalkwell	d		06 23	06 27		06 31			06 42			06 47	07 00								07 05		07 12	07 17	
Leigh-on-Sea	d		06 26	06 30		06 34			06 45			06 50	07 03								07 08		07 16	07 20	
Benfleet	d		06 31	06 35		06 39			06 50			06 55	07 08								07 13		07 20	07 25	
Pitsea	d		06 39			06 43					06 52	06 59				07 00				07 16	07 17		07 25		
Stanford-le-Hope	d		06 46								06 59					07 07				07 23			07 32		
East Tilbury	d		06 50								07 03					07 11				07 27			07 36		
Tilbury Town 3	d		06 56								07 09					07 18				07 33			07 42		
Grays	d	06 50	07 00								07 13					07 22		07 30		07 37			07 46		
Purfleet	d		07 05								07 18							07 35					07 51		
Rainham	d		07 11								07 24							07 41					07 57		
Dagenham Dock	d		07 14								07 27							07 44					08 00		
Basildon	d			06 42		06 47			06 57			07 03	07 15								07 21			07 32	
Laindon	d					06 50						07 07			07 20				07 37		07 25				
West Horndon	d					06 55						07 12			07 25				07 42						
Chafford Hundred	d	06 54														07 26				07 41					
Ockendon	d	06 58						←								07 30				07 46					
Upminster ⊖	d	07 05			←	07 01		07 05	07 10	←		07 18		←	07 30	07 37			07 47	07 54		←			←
Barking ⊖	d	→	07 21	07 01	07 06	07 10		07 14		07 21	07 34	07 27		07 34	07 39	07 46		07 51	07 56		07 42	07 46	08 07		07 51
Stratford 7 ⊖	a		→								→					→		→	→				→		
London Liverpool St 15 ⊖	a																								
West Ham ⊖	d			07 07	07 12	07 16		07 20	07 23	07 26				07 39	07 44						07 47	07 52			07 57
Limehouse	d				07 17	07 21		07 25		07 32		07 36		07 44	07 49						07 52			07 59	08 02
London Fenchurch St 7 ⊖	a			07 17	07 23	07 27		07 31	07 34	07 38		07 42	07 45	07 51	07 56					08 17	07 59	08 02		08 05	08 08

		CC		CC	CC	CC	CC	CC	CC	CC	CC	CC		CC	CC	CC	CC	CC	CC	CC	CC	CC		CC	CC
Shoeburyness	d				07 17					07 22		07 34								07 49					07 54
Thorpe Bay	d			07 12	07 21					07 26		07 38						07 42		07 53					07 58
Southend East	d			07 15	07 24					07 29		07 41						07 45		07 56					08 01
Southend Central	a			07 17	07 26					07 31		07 43						07 47		07 58					08 03
	d			07 18	07 27					07 32		07 43						07 48		07 59					08 03
Westcliff	d			07 20	07 29					07 34		07 45						07 50		08 01					08 05
Chalkwell	d			07 22	07 31					07 36		07 48						07 52		08 03					08 08
Leigh-on-Sea	d			07 25	07 34					07 39		07 51						07 55		08 06					08 11
Benfleet	d			07 30	07 39					07 44		07 56						08 00		08 11					08 16
Pitsea	d			07 34					07 41	07 48						07 48	07 52	08 04						08 12	08 20
Stanford-le-Hope	d							07 42	07 48							07 55	08 00					08 11		08 19	
East Tilbury	d								07 52								08 04					08 15		08 23	
Tilbury Town 3	d								07 58								08 10					08 21		08 29	
Grays	d							07 52	08 02							08 06	08 14					08 25		08 33	
Purfleet	d								08 07								08 19							08 39	
Rainham	d								08 13								08 25							08 44	
Dagenham Dock	d								08 16								08 28							08 48	
Basildon	d			07 39						07 53								08 09							08 24
Laindon	d			07 42			07 50			07 56					08 07			08 12			08 22				08 28
West Horndon	d						07 55								08 12						08 27				
Chafford Hundred	d							07 57								08 10						08 29			
Ockendon	d							08 01								08 17						08 33			
Upminster ⊖	d	←				←	08 02	08 09			←	08 13		←	08 17	08 24			←	08 28	08 32	08 40			
Barking ⊖	d	07 56		07 59		08 07	08 10	08 18	08 23	08 13	08 18			08 23	08 26		08 35	08 29	08 35		08 42	08 50		08 54	08 45
Stratford 7 ⊖	a							→	→								→					→		→	
London Liverpool St 15 ⊖	a																								
West Ham ⊖	d	08 01				08 12	08 16			08 19	08 23			08 28	08 32	08 38		08 35			08 47				08 51
Limehouse	d	08 06		08 08	08 13	08 17	08 21			08 24		08 30		08 33	08 37			08 40	08 45	08 48	08 52				08 56
London Fenchurch St 7 ⊖	a	08 12		08 15	08 19	08 24	08 27			08 31	08 34	08 37		08 40	08 43	08 48		08 46	08 51	08 55	08 58				09 02

Shoeburyness and Southend Central - London

Network Diagram - see first page of Table I

		CC	CC	CC	CC	CC	CC	CC		CC	CC	CC	CC	CC	CC	CC	CC	CC		CC	CC	CC	CC	CC	CC
Shoeburyness	d		08 05					08 11			08 25					08 40						09 05			09 20
Thorpe Bay	d		08 09					08 15			08 29					08 44						09 09			09 24
Southend East	d		08 12					08 18			08 32					08 47						09 12			09 27
Southend Central	a		08 14					08 20			08 34					08 49						09 14			09 29
	d		08 15					08 20			08 34					08 50				09 06		09 15		09 20	09 30
Westcliff	d		08 17					08 22			08 36					08 52				09 08		09 17		09 23	09 32
Chalkwell	d		08 19					08 25			08 39					08 54				09 10		09 19		09 25	09 34
Leigh-on-Sea	d		08 22					08 28			08 42					08 57				09 13		09 22		09 28	09 37
Benfleet	d		08 27					08 33			08 47					09 02				09 18		09 27		09 33	09 42
Pitsea	d						08 35	08 37			08 51				08 54	09 06					09 08	09 32		09 37	
Stanford-le-Hope	d					08 33	08 42								09 01						09 16			09 44	
East Tilbury	d					08 37	08 46								09 05						09 20			09 48	
Tilbury Town [3]	d					08 43	08 52								09 11						09 26			09 54	
Grays	d					08 47	08 56						09 03		09 15						09 29		09 46	09 57	
Purfleet	d					08 52							09 08		09 20								09 51		
Rainham	d					08 58							09 13		09 26								09 56		
Dagenham Dock	d					09 01							09 17		09 29								10 00		
Basildon	d							08 41			08 55					09 11				09 25		09 36			09 49
Laindon	d				08 38			08 45						09 04		09 14		09 17		09 28		09 39			09 52
West Horndon	d				08 43									09 10				09 22				09 44			
Chafford Hundred	d						09 01														09 34			10 01	
Ockendon	d						09 05					←									09 38			10 05	
Upminster ⊖	d	←		←	08 49		09 12	08 54		←	09 06	09 12		09 16			←	09 28		09 38	09 45	09 50		10 12	10 02
Barking ⊖	d	08 50		08 54	08 58	09 08	→	09 03		09 08		09 21	09 23	09 25	09 35	09 30	09 35	09 37		09 46	09 53	09 58	10 06	→	10 10
Stratford [7] ⊖	a					→									→										
London Liverpool St [15] ⊖	a																								
West Ham ⊖	d	08 55		09 00	09 04			09 09				09 26	09 29	09 31				09 43		09 52	09 59	10 04	10 11		10 16
Limehouse	d			09 05	09 09			09 14		09 17	09 23	09 31	09 34	09 36			09 44	09 48		09 57	10 04	10 09	10 16		
London Fenchurch St [7] ⊖	a	09 06	09 08	09 11	09 15			09 20		09 23	09 29	09 38	09 40	09 43		09 45	09 51	09 54		10 03	10 08	10 13	10 21		10 24

		CC	CC	CC		CC	CC	CC			CC	CC	CC	CC		CC	CC	CC	CC	CC	CC	CC	CC	CC	
Shoeburyness	d		09 35				09 50					15 05				15 20		15 35			15 50		16 05		
Thorpe Bay	d		09 39				09 54					15 09				15 24		15 39			15 54		16 09		
Southend East	d		09 42				09 57					15 12				15 27		15 42			15 57		16 12		
Southend Central	a		09 44				09 59					15 14				15 29		15 44			15 59		16 14		
	d		09 45			09 50	10 00					15 15		15 20		15 30		15 45		15 48	16 00		16 15		
Westcliff	d		09 47			09 53	10 02					15 17		15 23		15 32		15 47		15 50	16 02		16 17		
Chalkwell	d		09 49			09 55	10 04					15 19		15 25		15 34		15 49		15 53	16 04		16 19		
Leigh-on-Sea	d		09 52			09 58	10 07					15 22		15 28		15 37		15 52		15 56	16 07		16 22		
Benfleet	d		09 57			10 03	10 12					15 27		15 33		15 42		15 57		16 00	16 12		16 27		
Pitsea	d		10 02			10 07						15 32		15 37				16 02		16 04			16 31		
Stanford-le-Hope	d					10 14			and at					15 44						16 11					
East Tilbury	d					10 18			the same					15 48						16 15					
Tilbury Town [3]	d					10 24			minutes					15 54						16 21					
Grays	d			10 16		10 27			past				15 46	15 57					16 16	16 26				16 39	
Purfleet	d			10 21					each				15 51						16 21					16 44	
Rainham	d			10 26					hour until				15 56						16 26					16 49	
Dagenham Dock	d			10 30									16 00						16 30					16 53	
Basildon	d		10 06				10 19					15 36				15 49		16 06			16 19		16 35		
Laindon	d		10 09				10 22					15 39				15 52		16 09			16 22		16 38		
West Horndon	d		10 14									15 44						16 14					16 43		
Chafford Hundred	d					10 31								16 01						16 30					
Ockendon	d	←				10 35		←			←			16 05			←			16 34		←			
Upminster ⊖	d	10 12	10 20			10 42	10 32	10 42			15 42	15 50		16 12		16 02	16 12	16 20		16 41	16 30	16 41	16 48		
Barking ⊖	d	10 20	10 28	10 36		→	10 40	10 50			15 50	15 58	16 06	→		16 10	16 20	16 28	16 36	→	16 38	16 49	16 57	17 00	
Stratford [7] ⊖	a																								
London Liverpool St [15] ⊖	a																								
West Ham ⊖	d	10 26	10 34	10 41			10 46	10 56			15 56	16 04	16 11			16 17	16 26	16 34			16 44		17 02		
Limehouse	d	10 31	10 39	10 46				11 01			16 01	16 09	16 16				16 31	16 39					17 08	17 10	
London Fenchurch St [7] ⊖	a	10 35	10 43	10 51			10 54	11 05			16 05	16 13	16 21			16 26	16 36	16 43	16 48		16 52	17 03	17 12	17 15	

		CC	CC	CC	CC	CC	CC	CC	CC	CC		CC	CC	CC	CC	CC	CC	CC	CC	CC		CC	CC	CC	CC
Shoeburyness	d			16 15			16 28						16 50		16 56							17 10			17 30
Thorpe Bay	d			16 19			16 32						16 54		17 00							17 14			17 34
Southend East	d			16 22			16 35						16 57		17 03							17 17			17 37
Southend Central	a			16 24			16 37						16 59		17 05							17 19			17 39
	d		16 19	16 25	16 31		16 38					16 53	17 00		17 06							17 19			17 40
Westcliff	d		16 21	16 27	16 33		16 40					16 55	17 02		17 08							17 21			17 42
Chalkwell	d		16 23	16 29	16 35		16 42					16 58	17 04		17 10							17 24			17 44
Leigh-on-Sea	d		16 26	16 32	16 38		16 45					17 01	17 07		17 13							17 27			17 47
Benfleet	d		16 31	16 37	16 43		16 50					17 05	17 12		17 18							17 32			17 52
Pitsea	d		16 35		16 47		16 54			16 57		17 09	17 16		17 22					17 28		17 36		17 45	17 56
Stanford-le-Hope	d		16 42							17 04							17 19			17 35				17 52	
East Tilbury	d		16 46							17 08							17 23			17 39				17 56	
Tilbury Town [3]	d		16 52							17 14							17 29			17 46				18 02	
Grays	d	16 52	16 57							17 18				17 22			17 32	17 46		17 51				18 06	
Purfleet	d	16 57												17 27			17 38	17 51						18 11	
Rainham	d	17 02												17 32			17 43	17 56						18 16	
Dagenham Dock	d	17 06												17 36			17 46	18 00						18 20	
Basildon	d			16 43	16 51		16 58					17 13	17 20		17 26							17 40			18 00
Laindon	d						17 01		17 13			17 17							17 49			17 44	18 06		18 03
West Horndon	d						17 06					17 22							17 54				18 11		
Chafford Hundred	d		17 01							17 23										17 55					
Ockendon	d		17 08					←		17 32						←				18 01					
Upminster ⊖	d		17 15	16 54		←	17 11	17 15	17 23	17 39		17 28	17 31			17 39			18 00	18 08			18 17		
Barking ⊖	d	17 16	→	17 03	17 09	17 16	17 20	17 25	17 32	→		17 36	17 40	17 42	17 44	17 47	17 52	18 06	18 08	18 16			18 25	18 27	
Stratford [7] ⊖	a	→																							
London Liverpool St [15] ⊖	a																								
West Ham ⊖	d			17 09		17 22		17 31							17 49		17 58	18 11	18 14				18 30	18 33	18 26
Limehouse	d			17 14			17 29		17 42								18 03		18 19				18 35	18 38	
London Fenchurch St [7] ⊖	a			17 18	17 24	17 30	17 33	17 39	17 46			17 49	17 52	17 54	17 58	18 00	18 08	18 20	18 23	18 29		18 11	18 39	18 42	18 34

Shoeburyness and Southend Central - London

Network Diagram - see first page of Table I

		CC	CC	CC	CC	CC		CC	CC	CC	CC	CC	CC	CC	CC	CC		CC	CC	CC	CC	CC	CC	CC	CC
Shoeburyness	d		17 46			18 05				18 20			18 35			18 50				19 05			19 20		
Thorpe Bay	d		17 50			18 09				18 24			18 39			18 54				19 09			19 24		
Southend East	d		17 53			18 12				18 27			18 42			18 57				19 12			19 27		
Southend Central	a		17 55			18 14				18 29			18 44			18 59				19 15			19 29		
	d		17 56			18 15			18 20	18 30			18 45		18 48	19 00				19 15		19 20	19 30		
Westcliff	d		17 58			18 17			18 23	18 32			18 47		18 51	19 02				19 17		19 23	19 32		
Chalkwell	d		18 00			18 19			18 25	18 34			18 49		18 53	19 04				19 19		19 25	19 34		
Leigh-on-Sea	d		18 03			18 22			18 28	18 37			18 52		18 56	19 07				19 22		19 28	19 37		
Benfleet	d		18 08			18 27			18 33	18 42			18 57		19 01	19 12				19 27		19 33	19 42		
Pitsea	d	18 01	18 12		18 14	18 32			18 37				19 02		19 05					19 32		19 37			
Stanford-le-Hope	d	18 08			18 21				18 44						19 12							19 44			
East Tilbury	d	18 12			18 25				18 48						19 16							19 48			
Tilbury Town [3]	d	18 18			18 31				18 54						19 22							19 54			
Grays	d	18 22			18 35			18 54	18 57					19 22	19 25						19 48	19 57			
Purfleet	d				18 40			18 59						19 27							19 53				
Rainham	d				18 45			19 04						19 32							19 58				
Dagenham Dock	d				18 49			19 08						19 36							20 02				
Basildon	d		18 16			18 36				18 49			19 06			19 19				19 36			19 49		
Laindon	d		18 19			18 39				18 52			19 09			19 22				19 39			19 52		
West Horndon	d		18 24			18 44							19 14							19 44					
Chafford Hundred	d	18 27							19 02						19 29							20 01			
Ockendon	d	18 33		←					19 07			←			19 34				←			20 05			←
Upminster ⊖	d	18 39	18 31	18 39		18 50			19 13	19 02	←	19 13	19 20		19 40	19 32		←	19 40	19 50		20 12	20 02	←	20 12
Barking ⊖	d	→	18 39		18 55	18 58		19 14	→	19 10	19 14	19 22	19 28	19 42	→	19 40		19 42	19 50	19 58	20 12	→	20 10	20 12	20 20
Stratford [7] ⊖	a							→						→							→			20 21	
London Liverpool St [15] ⊖	a																							20 33	
West Ham ⊖	d		18 45		19 00	19 04				19 16	19 20	19 27	19 34			19 46		19 48	19 56	20 04			20 16		20 26
Limehouse	d		18 50		19 05	19 09						19 32	19 39					19 53	20 01	20 09					20 31
London Fenchurch St [7] ⊖	a		18 54	18 59	19 10	19 13				19 24	19 28	19 37	19 43			19 54		19 58	20 05	20 13			20 25		20 35

		CC		CC	CC	CC	CC	CC	CC	CC	CC	CC		CC	CC	CC	CC	CC	CC	CC	CC	CC		CC	CC
Shoeburyness	d	19 35				19 50			20 05			20 20			20 35			21 05			21 20			21 35	
Thorpe Bay	d	19 39				19 54			20 09			20 24			20 39			21 09			21 24			21 39	
Southend East	d	19 42				19 57			20 12			20 27			20 42			21 12			21 27			21 42	
Southend Central	a	19 44				19 59			20 14			20 29			20 44			21 14			21 29			21 45	
	d	19 45			19 50	20 00			20 15		20 20	20 30			20 45		20 50	21 15		21 20	21 30			21 45	
Westcliff	d	19 47			19 53	20 02			20 17		20 23	20 32			20 47		20 53	21 17		21 23	21 32			21 47	
Chalkwell	d	19 49			19 55	20 04			20 19		20 25	20 34			20 49		20 55	21 19		21 25	21 34			21 49	
Leigh-on-Sea	d	19 52			19 58	20 07			20 22		20 28	20 37			20 52		20 58	21 22		21 28	21 37			21 52	
Benfleet	d	19 57			20 03	20 12			20 27		20 33	20 42			20 57		21 03	21 27		21 33	21 42			21 57	
Pitsea	d	20 02			20 07				20 32		20 37				21 02		21 07	21 32		21 37				22 02	
Stanford-le-Hope	d				20 14						20 44						21 14			21 44					
East Tilbury	d				20 18						20 48						21 18			21 48					
Tilbury Town [3]	d				20 24						20 54						21 24			21 54					
Grays	d			20 16	20 27					20 46	20 57					21 16	21 27		21 46	21 57					22 16
Purfleet	d			20 21						20 51						21 21			21 51						22 21
Rainham	d			20 26						20 56						21 26			21 56						22 26
Dagenham Dock	d			20 30						21 00						21 30			22 00						22 30
Basildon	d	20 06				20 19			20 36			20 49			21 06			21 36			21 49			22 06	
Laindon	d	20 09				20 22			20 39			20 52			21 09			21 39			21 52			22 09	
West Horndon	d	20 14							20 44						21 14			21 44						22 14	
Chafford Hundred	d				20 31						21 01						21 31			22 01					
Ockendon	d				20 35		←				21 05			←			21 35			22 05		←			
Upminster ⊖	d	20 20			20 42	20 32	20 42		20 50		21 12	21 02		21 12	21 20		21 42	21 50		22 12	22 02	22 12		22 20	
Barking ⊖	d	20 28		20 36	→	20 40	20 50	20 51	20 58	21 06	→	21 10		21 20	21 28	21 36	21 50	21 58	22 06	→	22 10	22 20		22 28	22 36
Stratford [7] ⊖	a							21 00		21 15															
London Liverpool St [15] ⊖	a							21 12		21 26															
West Ham ⊖	d	20 34		20 41		20 46	20 56		21 04			21 16		21 26	21 34	21 41	21 56	22 04	22 11		22 16	22 26		22 34	22 41
Limehouse	d	20 39		20 46			21 01		21 09					21 31	21 39	21 46	22 01	22 09	22 16			22 31		22 39	22 46
London Fenchurch St [7] ⊖	a	20 43		20 51		20 54	21 05		21 13			21 24		21 35	21 43	21 52	22 05	22 13	22 21		22 24	22 35		22 43	22 52

		CC	CC	CC	CC	CC	CC	CC		CC
Shoeburyness	d		22 05			22 35				23 05
Thorpe Bay	d		22 09			22 39				23 09
Southend East	d		22 12			22 42				23 12
Southend Central	a		22 14			22 44				23 14
	d	21 50	22 15		22 20	22 45	22 50			23 15
Westcliff	d	21 53	22 17		22 23	22 47	22 53			23 17
Chalkwell	d	21 55	22 19		22 25	22 49	22 55			23 19
Leigh-on-Sea	d	21 58	22 22		22 28	22 52	22 58			23 22
Benfleet	d	22 03	22 27		22 33	22 57	23 03			23 27
Pitsea	d	22 07	22 32		22 37	23 02	23 07			23 32
Stanford-le-Hope	d	22 14			22 44		23 14			
East Tilbury	d	22 18			22 48		23 18			
Tilbury Town [3]	d	22 24			22 54		23 24			
Grays	d	22 27		22 46	22 57		23 27	23 33		
Purfleet	d			22 51				23 38		
Rainham	d			22 56				23 43		
Dagenham Dock	d			23 00				23 47		
Basildon	d		22 36			23 06				23 36
Laindon	d		22 39			23 09				23 39
West Horndon	d		22 44			23 14				23 44
Chafford Hundred	d	22 31			23 01		23 31			
Ockendon	d	22 35			23 05		23 35			
Upminster ⊖	d	22 42	22 50		23 12	23 20	23 42			23 50
Barking ⊖	d	22 50	22 58	23 06	23 20	23 28	23 50	23 55		23 58
Stratford [7] ⊖	a							00 09		
London Liverpool St [15] ⊖	a							00 20		
West Ham ⊖	d	22 56	23 04	23 11	23 26	23 34	23 56			00 04
Limehouse	d	23 01	23 09	23 16	23 31	23 39	00 01			00 09
London Fenchurch St [7] ⊖	a	23 05	23 13	23 21	23 35	23 43	00 05			00 13

Shoeburyness and Southend Central - London

Network Diagram - see first page of Table I

		CC	CC	CC	CC	CC	CC	CC	CC	CC		CC	CC	CC	CC	CC	CC	CC	CC	CC		CC	CC	CC	CC
Shoeburyness	d			23p05		04 20		05 05				05 35			06 05			06 35				07 05			07 35
Thorpe Bay	d			23p09		04 23		05 08				05 38			06 08			06 38				07 08			07 38
Southend East	d			23p12		04 26		05 11				05 41			06 11			06 41				07 11			07 41
Southend Central	a			23p14		04 28		05 13				05 43			06 13			06 43				07 13			07 43
	d	22p50		23p15		04 29		05 14		05 20		05 44		05 50	06 14		06 20	06 44		06 50		07 14		07 20	07 44
Westcliff	d	22p53		23p17		04 31		05 16		05 23		05 46		05 53	06 16		06 23	06 46		06 53		07 16		07 23	07 46
Chalkwell	d	22p55		23p19		04 33		05 18		05 25		05 48		05 55	06 18		06 25	06 48		06 55		07 18		07 25	07 48
Leigh-on-Sea	d	22p58		23p22		04 36		05 21		05 28		05 51		05 58	06 21		06 28	06 51		06 58		07 21		07 28	07 51
Benfleet	d	23p03		23p27		04 40		05 25		05 32		05 55		06 02	06 25		06 32	06 55		07 02		07 25		07 32	07 55
Pitsea	d	23p07		23p32		04 44		05 29		05 36		05 59		06 06	06 29		06 36	06 59		07 06		07 29		07 36	07 59
Stanford-le-Hope	d	23p14			04 29					05 42				06 12			06 42			07 12				07 42	
East Tilbury	d	23p18			04 32					05 45				06 15			06 45			07 15				07 45	
Tilbury Town 3	d	23p24			04 38					05 51				06 21			06 51			07 21				07 51	
Grays	d	23p27	23p33		04 41				05 48	05 54			06 18	06 24		06 48	06 54		07 18	07 24			07 48	07 54	
Purfleet	d		23p38						05 53				06 23			06 53			07 23				07 53		
Rainham	d		23p43						05 58				06 28			06 58			07 28				07 58		
Dagenham Dock	d		23p47						06 02				06 32			07 02			07 32				08 02		
Basildon	d			23p36		04 47		05 32				06 02			06 32			07 02				07 32			08 02
Laindon	d			23p39		04 50		05 35				06 05			06 35			07 05				07 35			08 05
West Horndon	d			23p44		04 55		05 40				06 10			06 40			07 10				07 40			08 10
Chafford Hundred	d	23p31			04 45					05 59				06 29			06 59			07 29				07 59	
Ockendon	d	23p35			04 49		05 16			06 02				06 32			07 02			07 32				08 02	
Upminster	⊖ d	23p42		23p50	04a57	05 02	05a23	05 46		06 09		06 16		06 39	06 46		07 09	07 16		07 39		07 46		08 09	08 16
Barking	⊖ d	23p50	23p55	23p58		05 10		05 54	06 08	06 17		06 24	06 38	06 47	06 54	07 08	07 17	07 24	07 38	07 47		07 54	08 08	08 17	08 24
Stratford 7	⊖ a		00 09																						
London Liverpool St 15	⊖ a		00 20																						
West Ham	⊖ d	23p56		00 04		05 16		06 00	06 14	06 23		06 30	06 44	06 53	07 00	07 14	07 23	07 30	07 44	07 53		08 00	08 14	08 23	08 30
Limehouse	d	00 01		00 09		05 21		06 05	06 19	06 28		06 35	06 49	06 58	07 05	07 19	07 28	07 35	07 49	07 58		08 05	08 19	08 28	08 35
London Fenchurch St 7	⊖ a	00 05		00 13		05 27		06 12	06 26	06 34		06 42	06 56	07 04	07 12	07 26	07 34	07 42	07 56	08 04		08 12	08 26	08 34	08 42

		CC	CC	CC	CC	CC		CC	CC	CC	CC	CC	CC	CC	CC	CC		CC	CC	CC	CC	CC	CC	CC	CC
Shoeburyness	d			07 50				08 05			08 20			08 35				08 50			09 05			09 20	
Thorpe Bay	d			07 53				08 08			08 23			08 38				08 53			09 08			09 23	
Southend East	d			07 56				08 11			08 26			08 41				08 56			09 11			09 26	
Southend Central	a			07 58				08 13			08 28			08 43				08 58			09 13			09 28	
	d		07 50	07 59				08 14		08 20	08 29			08 44		08 50		08 59			09 14		09 20	09 29	
Westcliff	d		07 53	08 01				08 16		08 23	08 31			08 46		08 53		09 01			09 16		09 23	09 31	
Chalkwell	d		07 55	08 03				08 18		08 25	08 33			08 48		08 55		09 03			09 18		09 25	09 33	
Leigh-on-Sea	d		07 58	08 06				08 21		08 28	08 36			08 51		08 58		09 06			09 21		09 28	09 36	
Benfleet	d		08 02	08 10				08 25		08 32	08 40			08 55		09 02		09 10			09 25		09 32	09 40	
Pitsea	d		08 06					08 29		08 36				08 59		09 06					09 29		09 36		
Stanford-le-Hope	d		08 12							08 42						09 12							09 42		
East Tilbury	d		08 15							08 45						09 15							09 45		
Tilbury Town 3	d		08 21							08 51						09 21							09 51		
Grays	d	08 18	08 24						08 48	08 54					09 18	09 24						09 48	09 54		
Purfleet	d	08 23							08 53						09 23							09 53			
Rainham	d	08 28							08 58						09 28							09 58			
Dagenham Dock	d	08 32							09 02						09 32							10 02			
Basildon	d			08 16				08 32			08 46			09 02				09 16			09 32			09 46	
Laindon	d			08 19				08 35			08 49			09 05				09 19			09 35			09 49	
West Horndon	d							08 40						09 10							09 40				
Chafford Hundred	d		08 29							08 59						09 29							09 59		
Ockendon	d		08 32			←				09 02			←			09 32				←			10 02		
Upminster	⊖ d		08 39	08 28	←	08 39		08 46		09 09	08 58	←	09 09	09 16		09 39		09 28	←	09 39	09 46		10 09	09 58	←
Barking	⊖ d	08 38	→	08 36	08 38	08 47		08 54	09 08	→	09 06	09 08	09 17	09 24	09 38	→		09 36	09 38	09 47	09 54	10 08	→	10 06	10 08
Stratford 7	⊖ a	→							→						→							→			
London Liverpool St 15	⊖ a																								
West Ham	⊖ d			08 42	08 44	08 53		09 00			09 12	09 14	09 23	09 30				09 42	09 44	09 53	10 00			10 12	10 14
Limehouse	d				08 49	08 58		09 05				09 19	09 28	09 35					09 49	09 58	10 05				10 19
London Fenchurch St 7	⊖ a			08 53	08 56	09 04		09 12			09 23	09 26	09 34	09 42				09 53	09 56	10 04	10 12			10 23	10 26

		CC		CC	CC	CC	CC	CC	CC	CC	CC	CC		CC	CC	CC	CC	CC	CC	CC	CC	CC		CC	CC
Shoeburyness	d			09 35			09 50			10 05				10 20			10 35			10 50				11 05	
Thorpe Bay	d			09 38			09 53			10 08				10 23			10 38			10 53				11 08	
Southend East	d			09 41			09 56			10 11				10 26			10 41			10 56				11 11	
Southend Central	a			09 43			09 58			10 13				10 28			10 43			10 58				11 13	
	d			09 44		09 50	09 59			10 14		10 20		10 29			10 44		10 50	10 59				11 14	
Westcliff	d			09 46		09 53	10 01			10 16		10 23		10 31			10 46		10 53	11 01				11 16	
Chalkwell	d			09 48		09 55	10 03			10 18		10 25		10 33			10 48		10 55	11 03				11 18	
Leigh-on-Sea	d			09 51		09 58	10 06			10 21		10 28		10 36			10 51		10 58	11 06				11 21	
Benfleet	d			09 55		10 02	10 10			10 25		10 32		10 40			10 55		11 02	11 10				11 25	
Pitsea	d			09 59		10 06				10 29		10 36					10 59		11 06					11 29	
Stanford-le-Hope	d					10 12						10 42							11 12						
East Tilbury	d					10 15						10 45							11 15						
Tilbury Town 3	d					10 21						10 51							11 21						
Grays	d				10 18	10 24					10 48	10 54						11 18	11 24						11 48
Purfleet	d				10 23						10 53							11 23							11 53
Rainham	d				10 28						10 58							11 28							11 58
Dagenham Dock	d				10 32						11 02							11 32							12 02
Basildon	d			10 02			10 16			10 32				10 46			11 02			11 16				11 32	
Laindon	d			10 05			10 19			10 35				10 49			11 05			11 19				11 35	
West Horndon	d			10 10						10 40							11 10							11 40	
Chafford Hundred	d					10 29						10 59							11 29						
Ockendon	d	←				10 32			←			11 02				←			11 32			←			
Upminster	⊖ d	10 09		10 16		10 39	10 28	←	10 39	10 46		11 09		10 58	←	11 09	11 16		11 39	11 28	←	11 39		11 46	
Barking	⊖ d	10 17		10 24	10 38	→	10 36	10 38	10 47	10 54	11 08	→		11 06	11 08	11 17	11 24	11 38	→	11 36	11 38	11 47		11 54	12 08
Stratford 7	⊖ a				→						→							→							→
London Liverpool St 15	⊖ a																								
West Ham	⊖ d	10 23		10 30			10 42	10 44	10 53	11 00				11 12	11 14	11 23	11 30			11 42	11 44	11 53		12 00	
Limehouse	d	10 28		10 35				10 49	10 58	11 05					11 19	11 28	11 35				11 49	11 58		12 05	
London Fenchurch St 7	⊖ a	10 34		10 42			10 53	10 56	11 04	11 12				11 23	11 26	11 34	11 42			11 53	11 56	12 04		12 12	

Table I

Saturdays
until 21 July

Shoeburyness and Southend Central - London

Network Diagram - see first page of Table I

		CC	CC	CC	CC	CC	CC	CC		CC	CC	CC	CC	CC	CC	CC	CC	CC		CC	CC	CC	CC	CC	CC
Shoeburyness	d		11 20			11 35				11 50			12 05			12 20				12 35			12 50		
Thorpe Bay	d		11 23			11 38				11 53			12 08			12 23				12 38			12 53		
Southend East	d		11 26			11 41				11 56			12 11			12 26				12 41			12 56		
Southend Central	a		11 28			11 43				11 58			12 13			12 28				12 43			12 58		
	d	11 20	11 29			11 44		11 50		11 59			12 14		12 20	12 29				12 44		12 50	12 59		
Westcliff	d	11 23	11 31			11 46		11 53		12 01			12 16		12 23	12 31				12 46		12 53	13 01		
Chalkwell	d	11 25	11 33			11 48		11 55		12 03			12 18		12 25	12 33				12 48		12 55	13 03		
Leigh-on-Sea	d	11 28	11 36			11 51		11 58		12 06			12 21		12 28	12 36				12 51		12 58	13 06		
Benfleet	d	11 32	11 40			11 55		12 02		12 10			12 25		12 32	12 40				12 55		13 02	13 10		
Pitsea	d	11 36				11 59		12 06					12 29		12 36					12 59		13 06			
Stanford-le-Hope	d	11 42						12 12							12 42							13 12			
East Tilbury	d	11 45						12 15							12 45							13 15			
Tilbury Town 3	d	11 51						12 21							12 51							13 21			
Grays	d	11 54					12 18	12 24						12 48	12 54						13 18	13 24			
Purfleet	d						12 23							12 53							13 23				
Rainham	d						12 28							12 58							13 28				
Dagenham Dock	d						12 32							13 02							13 32				
Basildon	d		11 46			12 02				12 16			12 32			12 46				13 02			13 16		
Laindon	d		11 49			12 05				12 19			12 35			12 49				13 05			13 19		
West Horndon	d					12 10							12 40							13 10					
Chafford Hundred	d	11 59						12 29							12 59							13 29			
Ockendon	d	12 01			←			12 32				←			13 02			←				13 32			←
Upminster	⊖ d	12 09	11 58	←	12 09	12 16		12 39		12 28	←	12 39	12 46		13 09	12 58	←	13 09		13 16		13 39	13 28	←	13 39
Barking	⊖ d	→	12 06	12 08	12 17	12 24	12 38	→		12 36	12 38	12 47	12 54	13 08	→	13 06	13 08	13 17		13 24	13 38	→	13 36	13 38	13 47
Stratford 7	⊖ a						→							→							→				
London Liverpool St 15	⊖ a																								
West Ham	⊖ d		12 12	12 14	12 23	12 30				12 42	12 44	12 53	13 00			13 12	13 14	13 23		13 30			13 42	13 44	13 53
Limehouse	d			12 19	12 28	12 35					12 49	12 58	13 05				13 19	13 28		13 35				13 49	13 58
London Fenchurch St 7	⊖ a		12 23	12 26	12 34	12 42				12 53	12 56	13 04	13 12			13 23	13 26	13 34		13 42			13 53	13 56	14 04

		CC	CC	CC		CC	CC	CC	CC	CC	CC	CC	CC	CC		CC	CC	CC	CC	CC	CC	CC	CC	CC	
Shoeburyness	d	13 05				13 20			13 35			13 50				14 05			14 20			14 35			
Thorpe Bay	d	13 08				13 23			13 38			13 53				14 08			14 23			14 38			
Southend East	d	13 11				13 26			13 41			13 56				14 11			14 26			14 41			
Southend Central	a	13 13				13 28			13 43			13 58				14 13			14 28			14 43			
	d	13 14		13 20		13 29			13 44		13 50	13 59				14 14		14 20	14 29			14 44		14 50	
Westcliff	d	13 16		13 23		13 31			13 46		13 53	14 01				14 16		14 23	14 31			14 46		14 53	
Chalkwell	d	13 18		13 25		13 33			13 48		13 55	14 03				14 18		14 25	14 33			14 48		14 55	
Leigh-on-Sea	d	13 21		13 28		13 36			13 51		13 58	14 06				14 21		14 28	14 36			14 51		14 58	
Benfleet	d	13 25		13 32		13 40			13 55		14 02	14 10				14 25		14 32	14 40			14 55		15 02	
Pitsea	d	13 29		13 36					13 59		14 06					14 29		14 36				14 59		15 06	
Stanford-le-Hope	d			13 42							14 12							14 42						15 12	
East Tilbury	d			13 45							14 15							14 45						15 15	
Tilbury Town 3	d			13 51							14 21							14 51						15 21	
Grays	d		13 48	13 54						14 18	14 24						14 48	14 54					15 18	15 24	
Purfleet	d		13 53							14 23							14 53						15 23		
Rainham	d		13 58							14 28							14 58						15 28		
Dagenham Dock	d		14 02							14 32							15 02						15 32		
Basildon	d	13 32				13 46			14 02			14 16				14 32			14 46			15 02			
Laindon	d	13 35				13 49			14 05			14 19				14 35			14 49			15 05			
West Horndon	d	13 40							14 10							14 40						15 10			
Chafford Hundred	d			13 59							14 29							14 59						15 29	
Ockendon	d			14 02				←			14 32			←				15 02			←			15 32	
Upminster	⊖ d	13 46		14 09		13 58	←	14 09	14 16		14 39	14 28	←	14 39		14 46		15 09	14 58	←	15 09	15 16		15 39	
Barking	⊖ d	13 54	14 08	→		14 06	14 08	14 17	14 24	14 38	→	14 36	14 38	14 47		14 54	15 08	→	15 06	15 08	15 17	15 24	15 38	→	
Stratford 7	⊖ a		→							→							→						→		
London Liverpool St 15	⊖ a																								
West Ham	⊖ d	14 00				14 12	14 14	14 23	14 30			14 42	14 44	14 53		15 00			15 12	15 14	15 23	15 30			
Limehouse	d	14 05					14 19	14 28	14 35				14 49	14 58		15 05				15 19	15 28	15 35			
London Fenchurch St 7	⊖ a	14 12				14 23	14 26	14 34	14 42			14 53	14 56	15 04		15 12			15 23	15 26	15 34	15 42			

		CC	CC	CC	CC	CC	CC	CC	CC	CC		CC	CC	CC	CC	CC	CC	CC	CC	CC		CC	CC	CC	CC
Shoeburyness	d	14 50			15 05			15 20				15 35			15 50			16 05				16 20			16 35
Thorpe Bay	d	14 53			15 08			15 23				15 38			15 53			16 08				16 23			16 38
Southend East	d	14 56			15 11			15 26				15 41			15 56			16 11				16 26			16 41
Southend Central	a	14 58			15 13			15 28				15 43			15 58			16 13				16 28			16 43
	d	14 59			15 14		15 20	15 29				15 44		15 50	15 59			16 14		16 20		16 29			16 44
Westcliff	d	15 01			15 16		15 23	15 31				15 46		15 53	16 01			16 16		16 23		16 31			16 46
Chalkwell	d	15 03			15 18		15 25	15 33				15 48		15 55	16 03			16 18		16 25		16 33			16 48
Leigh-on-Sea	d	15 06			15 21		15 28	15 36				15 51		15 58	16 06			16 21		16 28		16 36			16 51
Benfleet	d	15 10			15 25		15 32	15 40				15 55		16 02	16 10			16 25		16 32		16 40			16 55
Pitsea	d				15 29		15 36					15 59		16 06				16 29		16 36					16 59
Stanford-le-Hope	d						15 42							16 12						16 42					
East Tilbury	d						15 45							16 15						16 45					
Tilbury Town 3	d						15 51							16 21						16 51					
Grays	d					15 48	15 54						16 18	16 24					16 48	16 54					
Purfleet	d					15 53							16 23						16 53						
Rainham	d					15 58							16 28						16 58						
Dagenham Dock	d					16 02							16 32						17 02						
Basildon	d	15 16			15 32			15 46				16 02			16 16			16 32				16 46			17 02
Laindon	d	15 19			15 35			15 49				16 05			16 19			16 35				16 49			17 05
West Horndon	d				15 40							16 10						16 40							17 10
Chafford Hundred	d						15 59							16 29						16 59					
Ockendon	d			←			16 02			←				16 32			←			17 02				←	
Upminster	⊖ d	15 28	←	15 39	15 46		16 09	15 58	←	16 09		16 16		16 39	16 28	←	16 39	16 46		17 09		16 58	←	17 09	17 16
Barking	⊖ d	15 36	15 38	15 47	15 54	16 08	→	16 06	16 08	16 17		16 24	16 38	→	16 36	16 38	16 47	16 54	17 08	→		17 06	17 08	17 17	17 24
Stratford 7	⊖ a					→							→						→						
London Liverpool St 15	⊖ a																								
West Ham	⊖ d	15 42	15 44	15 53	16 00			16 12	16 14	16 23		16 30			16 42	16 44	16 53	17 00				17 12	17 14	17 23	17 30
Limehouse	d		15 49	15 58	16 05				16 19	16 28		16 35				16 49	16 58	17 05					17 19	17 28	17 35
London Fenchurch St 7	⊖ a	15 53	15 56	16 04	16 12			16 23	16 26	16 34		16 42			16 53	16 56	17 04	17 12				17 23	17 26	17 34	17 42

Saturdays

until 21 July

Shoeburyness and Southend Central - London

Network Diagram - see first page of Table 1

		CC	CC	CC	CC	CC		CC	CC	CC	CC	CC	CC	CC	CC	CC		CC	CC	CC	CC	CC	CC	CC	CC
Shoeburyness	d			16 50				17 05			17 20			17 35				17 50			18 05			18 20	
Thorpe Bay	d			16 53				17 08			17 23			17 38				17 53			18 08			18 23	
Southend East	d			16 56				17 11			17 26			17 41				17 56			18 11			18 26	
Southend Central	a			16 58				17 13			17 28			17 43				17 58			18 13			18 28	
	d		16 50	16 59				17 14		17 20	17 29			17 44		17 50		17 59			18 14		18 20	18 29	
Westcliff	d		16 53	17 01				17 16		17 23	17 31			17 46		17 53		18 01			18 16		18 23	18 31	
Chalkwell	d		16 55	17 03				17 18		17 25	17 33			17 48		17 55		18 03			18 18		18 25	18 33	
Leigh-on-Sea	d		16 58	17 06				17 21		17 28	17 36			17 51		17 58		18 06			18 21		18 28	18 36	
Benfleet	d		17 02	17 10				17 25		17 32	17 40			17 55		18 02		18 10			18 25		18 32	18 40	
Pitsea	d		17 06					17 29		17 36				17 59		18 06					18 29		18 36		
Stanford-le-Hope	d		17 12							17 42						18 12							18 42		
East Tilbury	d		17 15							17 45						18 15							18 45		
Tilbury Town 3	d		17 21							17 51						18 21							18 51		
Grays	d	17 18	17 24						17 48	17 54					18 18	18 24						18 48	18 54		
Purfleet	d	17 23							17 53						18 23							18 53			
Rainham	d	17 28							17 58						18 28							18 58			
Dagenham Dock	d	17 32							18 02						18 32							19 02			
Basildon	d			17 16				17 32			17 46			18 02				18 16			18 32			18 46	
Laindon	d			17 19				17 35			17 49			18 05				18 19			18 35			18 49	
West Horndon	d							17 40						18 10							18 40				
Chafford Hundred	d		17 29							17 59						18 29							18 59		
Ockendon	d		17 32			←				18 02			←			18 32				←			19 02		
Upminster ⊖	d		17 39	17 28	←	17 39		17 46		18 09	17 58	←	18 09	18 16		18 39		18 28	←	18 39	18 46		19 09	18 58	←
Barking ⊖	d	17 38	→	17 36	17 38	17 47		17 54	18 08	→	18 06	18 08	18 17	18 24	18 38	→		18 36	18 38	18 47	18 54	19 08	→	19 06	19 08
Stratford 7 ⊖	a	→							→						→							→			
London Liverpool St 15 ⊖	a																								
West Ham ⊖	d			17 42	17 44	17 53		18 00			18 12	18 14	18 23	18 30				18 42	18 44	18 53	19 00			19 12	19 14
Limehouse	d				17 49	17 58		18 05				18 19	18 28	18 35					18 49	18 58	19 05				19 19
London Fenchurch St 7 ⊖	a			17 53	17 56	18 04		18 12			18 23	18 26	18 34	18 42				18 53	18 56	19 04	19 12			19 23	19 26

		CC		CC	CC	CC	CC	CC	CC	CC	CC	CC		CC	CC	CC	CC	CC	CC	CC	CC	CC		CC	CC
Shoeburyness	d			18 35			18 50			19 05				19 20			19 35			19 50				20 05	
Thorpe Bay	d			18 38			18 53			19 08				19 23			19 38			19 53				20 08	
Southend East	d			18 41			18 56			19 11				19 26			19 41			19 56				20 11	
Southend Central	a			18 43			18 58			19 13				19 28			19 43			19 58				20 13	
	d			18 44		18 50	18 59			19 14		19 20		19 29			19 44		19 50	19 59				20 14	
Westcliff	d			18 46		18 53	19 01			19 16		19 23		19 31			19 46		19 53	20 01				20 16	
Chalkwell	d			18 48		18 55	19 03			19 18		19 25		19 33			19 48		19 55	20 03				20 18	
Leigh-on-Sea	d			18 51		18 58	19 06			19 21		19 28		19 36			19 51		19 58	20 06				20 21	
Benfleet	d			18 55		19 02	19 10			19 25		19 32		19 40			19 55		20 02	20 10				20 25	
Pitsea	d			18 59		19 06				19 29		19 36					19 59		20 06					20 29	
Stanford-le-Hope	d					19 12						19 42							20 12						
East Tilbury	d					19 15						19 45							20 15						
Tilbury Town 3	d					19 21						19 51							20 21						
Grays	d				19 18	19 24					19 48	19 54						20 18	20 24						20 48
Purfleet	d				19 23						19 53							20 23							20 53
Rainham	d				19 28						19 58							20 28							20 58
Dagenham Dock	d				19 32						20 02							20 32							21 02
Basildon	d			19 02			19 16			19 32				19 46			20 02			20 16				20 32	
Laindon	d			19 05			19 19			19 35				19 49			20 05			20 19				20 35	
West Horndon	d			19 10						19 40							20 10							20 40	
Chafford Hundred	d					19 29						19 59							20 29						
Ockendon	d	←				19 32			←			20 02				←			20 32			←			
Upminster ⊖	d	19 09		19 16		19 39	19 28	←	19 39	19 46		20 09		19 58	←	20 09	20 16		20 39	20 28	←	20 39		20 46	
Barking ⊖	d	19 17		19 24	19 38	→	19 36	19 38	19 47	19 54	20 08	→		20 06	20 08	20 17	20 24	20 38	→	20 36	20 38	20 47		20 54	21 08
Stratford 7 ⊖	a				→						→							→							
London Liverpool St 15 ⊖	a																								
West Ham ⊖	d	19 23		19 30			19 42	19 44	19 53	20 00				20 12	20 14	20 23	20 30			20 42	20 44	20 53		21 00	21 14
Limehouse	d	19 28		19 35				19 49	19 58	20 05					20 19	20 28	20 35				20 49	20 58		21 05	21 19
London Fenchurch St 7 ⊖	a	19 34		19 42			19 53	19 56	20 04	20 12				20 23	20 26	20 34	20 42			20 53	20 56	21 04		21 12	21 26

		CC	CC	CC	CC	CC	CC	CC		CC	CC	CC	CC	CC	CC	CC	CC	CC		CC	CC	CC	CC	CC	
Shoeburyness	d		20 35			20 50				21 05			21 35			22 05				22 35			23 05		
Thorpe Bay	d		20 38			20 53				21 08			21 38			22 08				22 38			23 08		
Southend East	d		20 41			20 56				21 11			21 41			22 11				22 41			23 11		
Southend Central	a		20 43			20 58				21 13			21 43			22 13				22 43			23 13		
	d	20 20	20 44		20 50	20 59				21 14		21 20	21 44		21 50	22 14		22 20		22 44		22 50	23 14	23 20	
Westcliff	d	20 23	20 46		20 53	21 01				21 16		21 23	21 46		21 53	22 16		22 23		22 46		22 53	23 16	23 23	
Chalkwell	d	20 25	20 48		20 55	21 03				21 18		21 25	21 48		21 55	22 18		22 25		22 48		22 55	23 18	23 25	
Leigh-on-Sea	d	20 28	20 51		20 58	21 06				21 21		21 28	21 51		21 58	22 21		22 28		22 51		22 58	23 21	23 28	
Benfleet	d	20 32	20 55		21 02	21 10				21 25		21 32	21 55		22 02	22 25		22 32		22 55		23 02	23 25	23 32	
Pitsea	d	20 36	20 59		21 06					21 29		21 36	21 59		22 06	22 29		22 36		22 59		23 06	23 29	23 36	
Stanford-le-Hope	d	20 42			21 12							21 42			22 12			22 42				23 12		23 42	
East Tilbury	d	20 45			21 15							21 45			22 15			22 45				23 15		23 45	
Tilbury Town 3	d	20 51			21 21							21 51			22 21			22 51				23 21		23 51	
Grays	d	20 54		21 18	21 24						21 48	21 54		22 18	22 24		22 48	22 54			23 18	23 24		23 54	
Purfleet	d			21 23							21 53			22 23			22 53				23 23				
Rainham	d			21 28							21 58			22 28			22 58				23 28				
Dagenham Dock	d			21 32							22 02			22 32			23 02				23 32				
Basildon	d		21 02			21 16				21 32			22 02			22 32				23 02			23 32		
Laindon	d		21 05			21 19				21 35			22 05			22 35				23 05			23 35		
West Horndon	d		21 10							21 40			22 10			22 40				23 10			23 40		
Chafford Hundred	d	20 59			21 29							21 59			22 29			22 59				23 29		23 59	
Ockendon	d	21 02			21 32			←				22 02			22 32			23 02				23 32		00 02	
Upminster ⊖	d	21 09	21 16		21 39	21 28	←	21 39		21 46		22 09	22 16		22 39	22 46		23 09		23 16		23 39	23 46	00 08	
Barking ⊖	d	21 17	21 24	21 38	→	21 36	21 38	21 47		21 54	22 08	22 17	22 24	22 38	22 47	22 54	23 08	23 17		23 24	23a39	23 47	23 55	00a18	
Stratford 7 ⊖	a			→																					
London Liverpool St 15 ⊖	a																								
West Ham ⊖	d	21 23	21 30			21 42	21 44	21 53		22 00	22 14	22 23	22 30	22 44	22 53	23 00	23 14	23 23		23 30		23 53	00 01		
Limehouse	d	21 28	21 35				21 49	21 58		22 05	22 19	22 28	22 35	22 49	22 58	23 05	23 19	23 28		23 35		23 58	00 06		
London Fenchurch St 7 ⊖	a	21 34	21 42			21 53	21 56	22 04		22 12	22 26	22 34	22 42	22 56	23 04	23 12	23 26	23 34		23 42		00 04	00 12		

Saturdays

28 July to 11 August

Shoeburyness and Southend Central - London

Network Diagram - see first page of Table 1

		CC	CC	CC	CC	CC	CC	CC	CC	CC		CC	CC	CC	CC	CC	CC	CC	CC	CC		CC	CC	CC	CC
Shoeburyness	d			23p05		04 20		05 05				05 35			06 05			06 35				07 05			07 35
Thorpe Bay	d			23p09		04 23		05 08				05 38			06 08			06 38				07 08			07 38
Southend East	d			23p12		04 26		05 11				05 41			06 11			06 41				07 11			07 41
Southend Central	a			23p14		04 28		05 13				05 43			06 13			06 43				07 13			07 43
	d	22p50		23p15		04 29		05 14		05 20		05 44		05 50	06 14		06 20	06 44		06 50		07 14		07 20	07 44
Westcliff	d	22p53		23p17		04 31		05 16		05 23		05 46		05 53	06 16		06 23	06 46		06 53		07 16		07 23	07 46
Chalkwell	d	22p55		23p19		04 33		05 18		05 25		05 48		05 55	06 18		06 25	06 48		06 55		07 18		07 25	07 48
Leigh-on-Sea	d	22p58		23p22		04 36		05 21		05 28		05 51		05 58	06 21		06 28	06 51		06 58		07 21		07 28	07 51
Benfleet	d	23p03		23p27		04 40		05 25		05 32		05 55		06 02	06 25		06 32	06 55		07 02		07 25		07 32	07 55
Pitsea	d	23p07		23p32		04 44		05 29		05 36		05 59		06 06	06 29		06 36	06 59		07 06		07 29		07 36	07 59
Stanford-le-Hope	d	23p14			04 29					05 42				06 12			06 42			07 12				07 42	
East Tilbury	d	23p18			04 32					05 45				06 15			06 45			07 15				07 45	
Tilbury Town 3	d	23p24			04 38					05 51				06 21			06 51			07 21				07 51	
Grays	d	23p27	23p33		04 41				05 48	05 54			06 18	06 24		06 48	06 54		07 18	07 24			07 48	07 54	
Purfleet	d		23p38						05 53				06 23			06 53			07 23				07 53		
Rainham	d		23p43						05 58				06 28			06 58			07 28				07 58		
Dagenham Dock	d		23p47						06 02				06 32			07 02			07 32				08 02		
Basildon	d			23p36		04 47		05 32				06 02			06 32			07 02				07 32			08 02
Laindon	d			23p39		04 50		05 35				06 05			06 35			07 05				07 35			08 05
West Horndon	d			23p44		04 55		05 40				06 10			06 40			07 10				07 40			08 10
Chafford Hundred	d	23p31			04 45					05 59				06 29			06 59			07 29				07 59	
Ockendon	d	23p35			04 49		05 16			06 02				06 32			07 02			07 32				08 02	
Upminster ⊖	d	23p42		23p50	04a57	05 02	05a23	05 46		06 09		06 16		06 39	06 46		07 09	07 16		07 39		07 46		08 09	08 16
Barking ⊖	d	23p51	23p55	00 02		05 10		05 54	06 08	06 17		06 24	06 38	06 47	06 54	07 08	07 17	07 24	07 38	07 47		07 54	08 08	08 17	08 24
Stratford 7 ⊖	a																								
London Liverpool St 15 ⊖	a																								
West Ham ⊖	d	00 01	00 06	00 12		05 16		06 00	06 14	06 23		06 30	06 44	06 53	07 00	07 14	07 23	07 30	07 44	07 53		08 00	08 14	08 23	08 30
Limehouse	d	00 06	00 11	00 17		05 21		06 05	06 19	06 28		06 35	06 49	06 58	07 05	07 19	07 28	07 35	07 49	07 58		08 05	08 19	08 28	08 35
London Fenchurch St 7 ⊖	a	00 11	00 18	00 24		05 27		06 12	06 26	06 34		06 42	06 56	07 04	07 12	07 26	07 34	07 42	07 56	08 04		08 12	08 26	08 34	08 42

		CC A	CC B	CC	CC	CC A		CC B	CC	CC	CC	CC	CC	CC	CC	CC		CC	CC	CC	CC	CC	CC	CC	CC
Shoeburyness	d				07 50					08 05			08 20			08 35				08 50			09 05		
Thorpe Bay	d				07 53					08 08			08 23			08 38				08 53			09 08		
Southend East	d				07 56					08 11			08 26			08 41				08 56			09 11		
Southend Central	a				07 58					08 13			08 28			08 43				08 58			09 13		
	d			07 50	07 59					08 14		08 20	08 29			08 44			08 50	08 59			09 14		09 20
Westcliff	d			07 53	08 01					08 16		08 23	08 31			08 46			08 53	09 01			09 16		09 23
Chalkwell	d			07 55	08 03					08 18		08 25	08 33			08 48			08 55	09 03			09 18		09 25
Leigh-on-Sea	d			07 58	08 06					08 21		08 28	08 36			08 51			08 58	09 06			09 21		09 28
Benfleet	d			08 02	08 10					08 25		08 32	08 40			08 55			09 02	09 10			09 25		09 32
Pitsea	d			08 06						08 29		08 36				08 59			09 06				09 29		09 36
Stanford-le-Hope	d			08 12								08 42							09 12						09 42
East Tilbury	d			08 15								08 45							09 15						09 45
Tilbury Town 3	d			08 21								08 51							09 21						09 51
Grays	d	08 18	08 18	08 24							08 48	08 54						09 18	09 24					09 48	09 54
Purfleet	d	08 23	08 23								08 53							09 23						09 53	
Rainham	d	08 28	08 28								08 58							09 28						09 58	
Dagenham Dock	d	08 32	08 32								09 02							09 32						10 02	
Basildon	d				08 16					08 32			08 46			09 02				09 16			09 32		
Laindon	d				08 19					08 35			08 49			09 05				09 19			09 35		
West Horndon	d									08 40						09 10							09 40		
Chafford Hundred	d			08 29								08 59							09 29						09 59
Ockendon	d			08 32					←			09 02			←				09 32			←			10 02
Upminster ⊖	d			08 39	08 28	←		←	08 39	08 46		09 09	08 58	←	09 09	09 16			09 39	09 28	←	09 39	09 46		10 09
Barking ⊖	d	08 38	08 38	→	08 36	08 38		08 38	08 47	08 54	09 08	→	09 06	09 08	09 17	09 24		09 38	→	09 36	09 38	09 47	09 54	10 08	→
Stratford 7 ⊖	a	→	→								→							→						→	
London Liverpool St 15 ⊖	a																								
West Ham ⊖	d				08 42	08 44		08 44	08 53	09 00			09 12	09 14	09 23	09 30				09 42	09 44	09 53	10 00		
Limehouse	d					08 49		08 49	08 58	09 05				09 19	09 28	09 35					09 49	09 58	10 05		
London Fenchurch St 7 ⊖	a				08 53	08 56		09 00	09 04	09 12			09 23	09 26	09 34	09 42				09 53	09 56	10 04	10 12		

		CC		CC	CC	CC	CC	CC	CC	CC	CC	CC		CC	CC	CC	CC	CC	CC	CC	CC	CC		CC	CC
Shoeburyness	d	09 20				09 35			09 50			10 05				10 20			10 35			10 50			
Thorpe Bay	d	09 23				09 38			09 53			10 08				10 23			10 38			10 53			
Southend East	d	09 26				09 41			09 56			10 11				10 26			10 41			10 56			
Southend Central	a	09 28				09 43			09 58			10 13				10 28			10 43			10 58			
	d	09 29				09 44		09 50	09 59			10 14			10 20	10 29			10 44		10 50	10 59			
Westcliff	d	09 31				09 46		09 53	10 01			10 16			10 23	10 31			10 46		10 53	11 01			
Chalkwell	d	09 33				09 48		09 55	10 03			10 18			10 25	10 33			10 48		10 55	11 03			
Leigh-on-Sea	d	09 36				09 51		09 58	10 06			10 21			10 28	10 36			10 51		10 58	11 06			
Benfleet	d	09 40				09 55		10 02	10 10			10 25			10 32	10 40			10 55		11 02	11 10			
Pitsea	d					09 59		10 06				10 29			10 36				10 59		11 06				
Stanford-le-Hope	d							10 12							10 42						11 12				
East Tilbury	d							10 15							10 45						11 15				
Tilbury Town 3	d							10 21							10 51						11 21				
Grays	d						10 18	10 24						10 48	10 54					11 18	11 24				
Purfleet	d						10 23							10 53						11 23					
Rainham	d						10 28							10 58						11 28					
Dagenham Dock	d						10 32							11 02						11 32					
Basildon	d	09 46				10 02			10 16			10 32				10 46			11 02			11 16			
Laindon	d	09 49				10 05			10 19			10 35				10 49			11 05			11 19			
West Horndon	d					10 10						10 40							11 10						
Chafford Hundred	d							10 29							10 59						11 29				
Ockendon	d				←			10 32			←				11 02			←			11 32				←
Upminster ⊖	d	09 58		←	10 09	10 16		10 39	10 28	←	10 39	10 46			11 09	10 58	←	11 09	11 16		11 39	11 28		←	11 39
Barking ⊖	d	10 06		10 08	10 17	10 24	10 38	→	10 36	10 38	10 47	10 54		11 08	→	11 06	11 08	11 17	11 24	11 38	→	11 36		11 38	11 47
Stratford 7 ⊖	a						→							→						→					
London Liverpool St 15 ⊖	a																								
West Ham ⊖	d	10 12		10 14	10 23	10 30			10 42	10 44	10 53	11 00				11 12	11 14	11 23	11 30			11 42		11 44	11 53
Limehouse	d			10 19	10 28	10 35				10 49	10 58	11 05					11 19	11 28	11 35					11 49	11 58
London Fenchurch St 7 ⊖	a	10 23		10 26	10 34	10 42			10 53	10 56	11 04	11 12				11 23	11 26	11 34	11 42			11 53		11 56	12 04

A not 11 August

B not from 28 July until 4 August

Table I

Saturdays

28 July to 11 August

Shoeburyness and Southend Central - London

Network Diagram - see first page of Table I

		CC	CC	CC	CC	CC	CC	CC		CC	CC	CC	CC	CC	CC	CC	CC	CC		CC	CC	CC	CC	CC	CC
Shoeburyness	d	11 05			11 20			11 35				11 50			12 05			12 20				12 35			12 50
Thorpe Bay	d	11 08			11 23			11 38				11 53			12 08			12 23				12 38			12 53
Southend East	d	11 11			11 26			11 41				11 56			12 11			12 26				12 41			12 56
Southend Central	a	11 13			11 28			11 43				11 58			12 13			12 28				12 43			12 58
	d	11 14		11 20	11 29			11 44			11 50	11 59			12 14		12 20	12 29				12 44		12 50	12 59
Westcliff	d	11 16		11 23	11 31			11 46			11 53	12 01			12 16		12 23	12 31				12 46		12 53	13 01
Chalkwell	d	11 18		11 25	11 33			11 48			11 55	12 03			12 18		12 25	12 33				12 48		12 55	13 03
Leigh-on-Sea	d	11 21		11 28	11 36			11 51			11 58	12 06			12 21		12 28	12 36				12 51		12 58	13 06
Benfleet	d	11 25		11 32	11 40			11 55			12 02	12 10			12 25		12 32	12 40				12 55		13 02	13 10
Pitsea	d	11 29		11 36				11 59			12 06				12 29		12 36					12 59		13 06	
Stanford-le-Hope	d			11 42							12 12						12 42							13 12	
East Tilbury	d			11 45							12 15						12 45							13 15	
Tilbury Town 3	d			11 51							12 21						12 51							13 21	
Grays	d		11 48	11 54						12 18	12 24					12 48	12 54					13 18	13 24	
Purfleet	d		11 53							12 23						12 53						13 23		
Rainham	d		11 58							12 28						12 58						13 28		
Dagenham Dock	d		12 02							12 32						13 02						13 32		
Basildon	d	11 32			11 46			12 02				12 16			12 32			12 46				13 02			13 16
Laindon	d	11 35			11 49			12 05				12 19			12 35			12 49				13 05			13 19
West Horndon	d	11 40						12 10							12 40							13 10			
Chafford Hundred	d			11 59							12 29						12 59							13 29	
Ockendon	d			12 01			←				12 32			←			13 02				←			13 32	
Upminster ⊖	d	11 46		12 09	11 58	←	12 09	12 16			12 39	12 28	←	12 39	12 46		13 09	12 58		←	13 09	13 16		13 39	13 28
Barking ⊖	d	11 54	12 08	→	12 06	12 08	12 17	12 24		12 38	→	12 36	12 38	12 47	12 54	13 08	→	13 06		13 08	13 17	13 24	13 38	→	13 36
Stratford 7 ⊖	a		→							→						→						→		
London Liverpool St 15 ⊖	a																								
West Ham ⊖	d	12 00			12 12	12 14	12 23	12 30				12 42	12 44	12 53	13 00			13 12		13 14	13 23	13 30			13 42
Limehouse	d	12 05				12 19	12 28	12 35					12 49	12 58	13 05					13 19	13 28	13 35			
London Fenchurch St 7 ⊖	a	12 12			12 23	12 26	12 34	12 42				12 53	12 56	13 04	13 12			13 23		13 26	13 34	13 42			13 53

		CC	CC	CC		CC	CC	CC	CC	CC	CC	CC	CC	CC		CC	CC	CC	CC	CC	CC	CC	CC	CC	
																					A			A	
Shoeburyness	d			13 05				13 20			13 35			13 50				14 05				14 20			
Thorpe Bay	d			13 08				13 23			13 38			13 53				14 08				14 23			
Southend East	d			13 11				13 26			13 41			13 56				14 11				14 26			
Southend Central	a			13 13				13 28			13 43			13 58				14 13				14 28			
	d			13 14			13 20	13 29			13 44		13 50	13 59				14 14		14 20		14 29			
Westcliff	d			13 16			13 23	13 31			13 46		13 53	14 01				14 16		14 23		14 31			
Chalkwell	d			13 18			13 25	13 33			13 48		13 55	14 03				14 18		14 25		14 33			
Leigh-on-Sea	d			13 21			13 28	13 36			13 51		13 58	14 06				14 21		14 28	14 32	14 36		14 45	
Benfleet	d			13 25			13 32	13 40			13 55		14 02	14 10				14 25		14 32		14 40			
Pitsea	d			13 29			13 36				13 59		14 06					14 29		14 36					
Stanford-le-Hope	d						13 42						14 12							14 42					
East Tilbury	d						13 45						14 15							14 45					
Tilbury Town 3	d						13 51						14 21							14 51					
Grays	d					13 48	13 54					14 18	14 24						14 48	14 54					
Purfleet	d					13 53						14 23							14 53						
Rainham	d					13 58						14 28							14 58						
Dagenham Dock	d					14 02						14 32							15 02						
Basildon	d			13 32				13 46			14 02			14 16				14 32				14 46			
Laindon	d			13 35				13 49			14 05			14 19				14 35				14 49			
West Horndon	d			13 40							14 10							14 40							
Chafford Hundred	d						13 59						14 29							14 59					
Ockendon	d		←				14 02			←			14 32				←			15 02					
Upminster ⊖	d	←	13 39	13 46			14 09	13 58	←	14 09	14 16		14 39	14 28		←	14 39	14 46		15 09		14 58	←		
Barking ⊖	d	13 38	13 47	13 54		14 08	→	14 06	14 08	14 17	14 24	14 38	→	14 36		14 38	14 47	14 54	15 08	→		15 06	15 08		
Stratford 7 ⊖	a					→						→							→						
London Liverpool St 15 ⊖	a																								
West Ham ⊖	d	13 44	13 53	14 00				14 12	14 14	14 23	14 30			14 42		14 44	14 53	15 00			15 04	15 12	15 14	15 19	
Limehouse	d	13 49	13 58	14 05					14 19	14 28	14 35					14 49	14 58	15 05					15 19		
London Fenchurch St 7 ⊖	a	13 56	14 04	14 12				14 23	14 26	14 34	14 42			14 53		14 56	15 04	15 12			15 16	15 23	15 26	15 30	

A not from 28 July until 4 August

Table I

Saturdays

28 July to 11 August

Shoeburyness and Southend Central - London

Network Diagram - see first page of Table I

		CC	CC	CC	CC	CC	CC	CC	CC	CC		CC	CC	CC	CC	CC	CC	CC	CC	CC		CC	CC	CC	CC
						A			A						A			A						A	
Shoeburyness	d		14 35				14 50					15 05				15 20				15 35					15 50
Thorpe Bay	d		14 38				14 53					15 08				15 23				15 38					15 53
Southend East	d		14 41				14 56					15 11				15 26				15 41					15 56
Southend Central	a		14 43				14 58					15 13				15 28				15 43					15 58
	d		14 44		14 50		14 59					15 14		15 20		15 29				15 44			15 50		15 59
Westcliff	d		14 46		14 53		15 01					15 16		15 23		15 31				15 46			15 53		16 01
Chalkwell	d		14 48		14 55		15 03					15 18		15 25		15 33				15 48			15 55		16 03
Leigh-on-Sea	d		14 51		14 58	15 02	15 06		15 15			15 21		15 28	15 31	15 36		15 47		15 51			15 58	16 02	16 06
Benfleet	d		14 55		15 02		15 10					15 25		15 32		15 40				15 55			16 02		16 10
Pitsea	d		14 59		15 06							15 29		15 36						15 59			16 06		
Stanford-le-Hope	d				15 12									15 42									16 12		
East Tilbury	d				15 15									15 45									16 15		
Tilbury Town 3	d				15 21									15 51									16 21		
Grays	d			15 18	15 24								15 48	15 54								16 18	16 24		
Purfleet	d			15 23									15 53									16 23			
Rainham	d			15 28									15 58									16 28			
Dagenham Dock	d			15 32									16 02									16 32			
Basildon	d		15 02				15 16					15 32				15 46				16 02					16 16
Laindon	d		15 05				15 19					15 35				15 49				16 05					16 19
West Horndon	d		15 10									15 40								16 10					
Chafford Hundred	d				15 29									15 59									16 29		
Ockendon	d	←			15 32					←				16 02					←				16 32		
Upminster ⊖	d	15 09	15 16		15 39		15 28	←		15 39		15 46		16 09		15 58	←		16 09	16 16			16 39		16 28
Barking ⊖	d	15 17	15 24	15 38	→		15 36	15 38		15 47		15 54	16 08	→		16 06	16 08		16 17	16 24		16 38	→		16 36
Stratford 7 ⊖	a			→									→									→			
London Liverpool St 15 ⊖	a																								
West Ham ⊖	d	15 23	15 30			15 35	15 42	15 44	15 49	15 53		16 00			16 05	16 12	16 14	16 19	16 23	16 30				16 35	16 42
Limehouse	d	15 28	15 35					15 49		15 58		16 05					16 19		16 28	16 35					
London Fenchurch St 7 ⊖	a	15 34	15 42			15 46	15 53	15 56	16 00	16 04		16 12			16 16	16 23	16 26	16 30	16 34	16 42				16 46	16 53

		CC	CC	CC	CC	CC		CC	CC	CC	CC	CC	CC	CC	CC	CC		CC	CC	CC	CC	CC	CC	CC	CC
			A																						
Shoeburyness	d				16 05				16 20			16 35			16 50				17 05			17 20			17 35
Thorpe Bay	d				16 08				16 23			16 38			16 53				17 08			17 23			17 38
Southend East	d				16 11				16 26			16 41			16 56				17 11			17 26			17 41
Southend Central	a				16 13				16 28			16 43			16 58				17 13			17 28			17 43
	d				16 14			16 20	16 29			16 44		16 50	16 59				17 14		17 20	17 29			17 44
Westcliff	d				16 16			16 23	16 31			16 46		16 53	17 01				17 16		17 23	17 31			17 46
Chalkwell	d				16 18			16 25	16 33			16 48		16 55	17 03				17 18		17 25	17 33			17 48
Leigh-on-Sea	d		16 15		16 21			16 28	16 36			16 51		16 58	17 06				17 21		17 28	17 36			17 51
Benfleet	d				16 25			16 32	16 40			16 55		17 02	17 10				17 25		17 32	17 40			17 55
Pitsea	d				16 29			16 36				16 59		17 06					17 29		17 36				17 59
Stanford-le-Hope	d							16 42						17 12							17 42				
East Tilbury	d							16 45						17 15							17 45				
Tilbury Town 3	d							16 51						17 21							17 51				
Grays	d					16 48		16 54					17 18	17 24						17 48	17 54				
Purfleet	d					16 53							17 23							17 53					
Rainham	d					16 58							17 28							17 58					
Dagenham Dock	d					17 02							17 32							18 02					
Basildon	d				16 32				16 46			17 02			17 16				17 32			17 46			18 02
Laindon	d				16 35				16 49			17 05			17 19				17 35			17 49			18 05
West Horndon	d				16 40							17 10							17 40						18 10
Chafford Hundred	d							16 59						17 29							17 59				
Ockendon	d			←				17 02			←			17 32				←			18 02			←	
Upminster ⊖	d	←		16 39	16 46			17 09	16 58	←	17 09	17 16		17 39	17 28	←		17 39	17 46		18 09	17 58	←	18 09	18 16
Barking ⊖	d	16 38		16 47	16 54	17 08		→	17 06	17 08	17 17	17 24	17 38	→	17 36	17 38		17 47	17 54	18 08	→	18 06	18 08	18 17	18 24
Stratford 7 ⊖	a					→							→							→					
London Liverpool St 15 ⊖	a																								
West Ham ⊖	d	16 44	16 49	16 53	17 00				17 12	17 14	17 23	17 30			17 42	17 44		17 53	18 00			18 12	18 14	18 23	18 30
Limehouse	d	16 49		16 58	17 05					17 19	17 28	17 35				17 49		17 58	18 05				18 19	18 28	18 35
London Fenchurch St 7 ⊖	a	16 56	17 00	17 04	17 12				17 23	17 26	17 34	17 42			17 53	17 56		18 04	18 12			18 23	18 26	18 34	18 42

A not from 28 July until 4 August

Table 1

Saturdays

28 July to 11 August

Shoeburyness and Southend Central - London

Network Diagram - see first page of Table 1

		CC		CC	CC	CC	CC	CC	CC	CC	CC	CC		CC	CC	CC	CC	CC	CC	CC	CC	CC		CC	CC
Shoeburyness	d				17 50			18 05			18 20				18 35			18 50			19 05				19 20
Thorpe Bay	d				17 53			18 08			18 23				18 38			18 53			19 08				19 23
Southend East	d				17 56			18 11			18 26				18 41			18 56			19 11				19 26
Southend Central	a				17 58			18 13			18 28				18 43			18 58			19 13				19 28
	d			17 50	17 59			18 14		18 20	18 29				18 44		18 50	18 59			19 14			19 20	19 29
Westcliff	d			17 53	18 01			18 16		18 23	18 31				18 46		18 53	19 01			19 16			19 23	19 31
Chalkwell	d			17 55	18 03			18 18		18 25	18 33				18 48		18 55	19 03			19 18			19 25	19 33
Leigh-on-Sea	d			17 58	18 06			18 21		18 28	18 36				18 51		18 58	19 06			19 21			19 28	19 36
Benfleet	d			18 02	18 10			18 25		18 32	18 40				18 55		19 02	19 10			19 25			19 32	19 40
Pitsea	d			18 06				18 29		18 36					18 59		19 06				19 29			19 36	
Stanford-le-Hope	d			18 12						18 42							19 12							19 42	
East Tilbury	d			18 15						18 45							19 15							19 45	
Tilbury Town 3	d			18 21						18 51							19 21							19 51	
Grays	d	18 18		18 24					18 48	18 54						19 18	19 24					19 48		19 54	
Purfleet	d	18 23							18 53							19 23						19 53			
Rainham	d	18 28							18 58							19 28						19 58			
Dagenham Dock	d	18 32							19 02							19 32						20 02			
Basildon	d				18 16			18 32			18 46				19 02			19 16			19 32				19 46
Laindon	d				18 19			18 35			18 49				19 05			19 19			19 35				19 49
West Horndon	d							18 40							19 10						19 40				
Chafford Hundred	d			18 29						18 59							19 29							19 59	
Ockendon	d			18 32			←			19 02				←			19 32			←				20 02	
Upminster ⊖	d			18 39	18 28	←	18 39	18 46		19 09	18 58	←		19 09	19 16		19 39	19 28	←	19 39	19 46			20 09	19 58
Barking ⊖	d	18 38		→	18 36	18 38	18 47	18 54	19 08	→	19 06	19 08		19 17	19 24	19 38	→	19 36	19 38	19 47	19 54	20 08		→	20 06
Stratford 7 ⊖	a	→							→							→						→			
London Liverpool St 15 ⊖	a																								
West Ham ⊖	d				18 42	18 44	18 53	19 00			19 12	19 14		19 23	19 30			19 42	19 44	19 53	20 00				20 12
Limehouse	d					18 49	18 58	19 05				19 19		19 28	19 35				19 49	19 58	20 05				
London Fenchurch St 7 ⊖	a				18 53	18 56	19 04	19 12			19 23	19 26		19 34	19 42			19 53	19 56	20 04	20 12				20 23

		CC	CC	CC	CC	CC	CC	CC		CC	CC	CC	CC	CC	CC	CC	CC	CC		CC	CC	CC	CC	CC	CC
Shoeburyness	d			19 35			19 50				20 05			20 35			20 50				21 05			21 35	
Thorpe Bay	d			19 38			19 53				20 08			20 38			20 53				21 08			21 38	
Southend East	d			19 41			19 56				20 11			20 41			20 56				21 11			21 41	
Southend Central	a			19 43			19 58				20 13			20 43			20 58				21 13			21 43	
	d			19 44		19 50	19 59				20 14		20 20	20 44		20 50	20 59				21 14		21 20	21 44	
Westcliff	d			19 46		19 53	20 01				20 16		20 23	20 46		20 53	21 01				21 16		21 23	21 46	
Chalkwell	d			19 48		19 55	20 03				20 18		20 25	20 48		20 55	21 03				21 18		21 25	21 48	
Leigh-on-Sea	d			19 51		19 58	20 06				20 21		20 28	20 51		20 58	21 06				21 21		21 28	21 51	
Benfleet	d			19 55		20 02	20 10				20 25		20 32	20 55		21 02	21 10				21 25		21 32	21 55	
Pitsea	d			19 59		20 06					20 29		20 36	20 59		21 06					21 29		21 36	21 59	
Stanford-le-Hope	d					20 12							20 42			21 12							21 42		
East Tilbury	d					20 15							20 45			21 15							21 45		
Tilbury Town 3	d					20 21							20 51			21 21							21 51		
Grays	d				20 18	20 24						20 48	20 54		21 18	21 24						21 48	21 54		22 18
Purfleet	d				20 23							20 53			21 23							21 53			22 23
Rainham	d				20 28							20 58			21 28							21 58			22 28
Dagenham Dock	d				20 32							21 02			21 32							22 02			22 32
Basildon	d			20 02			20 16				20 32			21 02			21 16				21 32			22 02	
Laindon	d			20 05			20 19				20 35			21 05			21 19				21 35			22 05	
West Horndon	d			20 10							20 40			21 10							21 40			22 10	
Chafford Hundred	d					20 29							20 59			21 29							21 59		
Ockendon	d		←			20 32				←			21 02			21 32				←			22 02		
Upminster ⊖	d	←	20 09	20 16		20 39	20 28	←		20 39	20 46		21 09	21 16		21 39	21 28	←		21 39	21 46		22 09	22 16	
Barking ⊖	d	20 08	20 17	20 24	20 38	→	20 36	20 38		20 47	20 54	21 08	21 17	21 24	21 38	→	21 36	21 38		21 47	21 54	22 08	22 17	22 24	22 38
Stratford 7 ⊖	a				→										→										
London Liverpool St 15 ⊖	a																								
West Ham ⊖	d	20 14	20 23	20 30			20 42	20 44		20 53	21 00	21 14	21 23	21 30			21 42	21 44		21 53	22 03	22 17	22 25	22 32	22 47
Limehouse	d	20 19	20 28	20 35				20 49		20 58	21 05	21 19	21 28	21 35				21 49		21 58	22 08	22 22	22 31	22 38	22 52
London Fenchurch St 7 ⊖	a	20 26	20 34	20 42			20 53	20 56		21 04	21 12	21 26	21 34	21 42			21 53	21 56		22 04	22 15	22 29	22 37	22 44	22 59

		CC	CC	CC		CC	CC	CC	CC	CC	CC
Shoeburyness	d		22 05				22 35			23 05	
Thorpe Bay	d		22 08				22 38			23 08	
Southend East	d		22 11				22 41			23 11	
Southend Central	a		22 13				22 43			23 13	
	d	21 50	22 14			22 20	22 44		22 50	23 14	23 20
Westcliff	d	21 53	22 16			22 23	22 46		22 53	23 16	23 23
Chalkwell	d	21 55	22 18			22 25	22 48		22 55	23 18	23 25
Leigh-on-Sea	d	21 58	22 21			22 28	22 51		22 58	23 21	23 28
Benfleet	d	22 02	22 25			22 32	22 55		23 02	23 25	23 32
Pitsea	d	22 06	22 29			22 36	22 59		23 06	23 29	23 36
Stanford-le-Hope	d	22 12				22 42			23 12		23 42
East Tilbury	d	22 15				22 45			23 15		23 45
Tilbury Town 3	d	22 21				22 51			23 21		23 51
Grays	d	22 24		22 48		22 54		23 18	23 24		23 54
Purfleet	d			22 53				23 23			
Rainham	d			22 58				23 28			
Dagenham Dock	d			23 02				23 32			
Basildon	d		22 32				23 02			23 32	
Laindon	d		22 35				23 05			23 35	
West Horndon	d		22 40				23 10			23 40	
Chafford Hundred	d	22 29				23 02			23 32		00 02
Ockendon	d	22 32				23 05			23 35		00 05
Upminster ⊖	d	22 39	22 46			23 12	23 16		23 42	23 46	00 11
Barking ⊖	d	22 47	22 54	23 08		23 20	23 24	23 39	23 50	23 55	00 20
Stratford 7 ⊖	a										
London Liverpool St 15 ⊖	a										
West Ham ⊖	d	22 55	23 03	23 18		23 28	23 33	23 48	23 58	00 03	00 30
Limehouse	d	23 01	23 08	23 23		23 34	23 38	23 53	00 03	00 09	00 35
London Fenchurch St 7 ⊖	a	23 07	23 15	23 30		23 40	23 45	23 59	00 09	00 15	00 42

Table 1

Saturdays

18 August to 25 August

Shoeburyness and Southend Central - London

Network Diagram - see first page of Table 1

		CC	CC	CC	CC	CC	CC	CC	CC	CC		CC	CC	CC	CC	CC	CC	CC	CC	CC		CC	CC	CC	CC
Shoeburyness	d			23p05		04 20		05 05				05 35			06 05			06 35				07 05			07 35
Thorpe Bay	d			23p09		04 23		05 08				05 38			06 08			06 38				07 08			07 38
Southend East	d			23p12		04 26		05 11				05 41			06 11			06 41				07 11			07 41
Southend Central	a			23p14		04 28		05 13				05 43			06 13			06 43				07 13			07 43
	d	22p50		23p15		04 29		05 14		05 20		05 44		05 50	06 14		06 20	06 44		06 50		07 14		07 20	07 44
Westcliff	d	22p53		23p17		04 31		05 16		05 23		05 46		05 53	06 16		06 23	06 46		06 53		07 16		07 23	07 46
Chalkwell	d	22p55		23p19		04 33		05 18		05 25		05 48		05 55	06 18		06 25	06 48		06 55		07 18		07 25	07 48
Leigh-on-Sea	d	22p58		23p22		04 36		05 21		05 28		05 51		05 58	06 21		06 28	06 51		06 58		07 21		07 28	07 51
Benfleet	d	23p03		23p27		04 40		05 25		05 32		05 55		06 02	06 25		06 32	06 55		07 02		07 25		07 32	07 55
Pitsea	d	23p07		23p32		04 44		05 29		05 36		05 59		06 06	06 29		06 36	06 59		07 06		07 29		07 36	07 59
Stanford-le-Hope	d	23p14			04 29					05 42				06 12			06 42			07 12				07 42	
East Tilbury	d	23p18			04 32					05 45				06 15			06 45			07 15				07 45	
Tilbury Town 3	d	23p24			04 38					05 51				06 21			06 51			07 21				07 51	
Grays	d	23p27	23p33		04 41				05 48	05 54			06 18	06 24		06 48	06 54		07 18	07 24			07 48	07 54	
Purfleet	d		23p38						05 53				06 23			06 53			07 23				07 53		
Rainham	d		23p43						05 58				06 28			06 58			07 28				07 58		
Dagenham Dock	d		23p47						06 02				06 32			07 02			07 32				08 02		
Basildon	d			23p36		04 47		05 32				06 02			06 32			07 02				07 32			08 02
Laindon	d			23p39		04 50		05 35				06 05			06 35			07 05				07 35			08 05
West Horndon	d			23p44		04 55		05 40				06 10			06 40			07 10				07 40			08 10
Chafford Hundred	d	23p31			04 45					05 59				06 29			06 59			07 29				07 59	
Ockendon	d	23p35			04 49		05 16			06 02				06 32			07 02			07 32				08 02	
Upminster ⊖	d	23p42		23p50	04a57	05 02	05a23	05 46		06 09		06 16		06 39	06 46		07 09	07 16		07 39		07 46		08 09	08 16
Barking ⊖	d	23p50	23p55	23p58		05 10		05 54	06 08	06 17		06 24	06 38	06 47	06 54	07 08	07 17	07 24	07 38	07 47		07 54	08 08	08 17	08 24
Stratford 7 ⊖	a		00 09																						
London Liverpool St 15 ⊖	a		00 20																						
West Ham ⊖	d	23p56		00 04		05 16		06 00	06 14	06 23		06 30	06 44	06 53	07 00	07 14	07 23	07 30	07 44	07 53		08 00	08 14	08 23	08 30
Limehouse	d	00 01		00 09		05 21		06 05	06 19	06 28		06 35	06 49	06 58	07 05	07 19	07 28	07 35	07 49	07 58		08 05	08 19	08 28	08 35
London Fenchurch St 7 ⊖	a	00 05		00 13		05 27		06 12	06 26	06 34		06 42	06 56	07 04	07 12	07 26	07 34	07 42	07 56	08 04		08 12	08 26	08 34	08 42

		CC	CC	CC	CC	CC		CC	CC	CC	CC	CC	CC	CC	CC	CC		CC	CC	CC	CC	CC	CC	CC	CC
Shoeburyness	d			07 50				08 05			08 20			08 35				08 50			09 05			09 20	
Thorpe Bay	d			07 53				08 08			08 23			08 38				08 53			09 08			09 23	
Southend East	d			07 56				08 11			08 26			08 41				08 56			09 11			09 26	
Southend Central	a			07 58				08 13			08 28			08 43				08 58			09 13			09 28	
	d		07 50	07 59				08 14		08 20	08 29			08 44		08 50		08 59			09 14		09 20	09 29	
Westcliff	d		07 53	08 01				08 16		08 23	08 31			08 46		08 53		09 01			09 16		09 23	09 31	
Chalkwell	d		07 55	08 03				08 18		08 25	08 33			08 48		08 55		09 03			09 18		09 25	09 33	
Leigh-on-Sea	d		07 58	08 06				08 21		08 28	08 36			08 51		08 58		09 06			09 21		09 28	09 36	
Benfleet	d		08 02	08 10				08 25		08 32	08 40			08 55		09 02		09 10			09 25		09 32	09 40	
Pitsea	d		08 06					08 29		08 36				08 59		09 06					09 29		09 36		
Stanford-le-Hope	d		08 12							08 42						09 12							09 42		
East Tilbury	d		08 15							08 45						09 15							09 45		
Tilbury Town 3	d		08 21							08 51						09 21							09 51		
Grays	d	08 18	08 24						08 48	08 54					09 18	09 24						09 48	09 54		
Purfleet	d	08 23							08 53						09 23							09 53			
Rainham	d	08 28							08 58						09 28							09 58			
Dagenham Dock	d	08 32							09 02						09 32							10 02			
Basildon	d			08 16				08 32			08 46			09 02				09 16			09 32			09 46	
Laindon	d			08 19				08 35			08 49			09 05				09 19			09 35			09 49	
West Horndon	d							08 40						09 10							09 40				
Chafford Hundred	d		08 29							08 59						09 29							09 59		
Ockendon	d		08 32			←				09 02			←			09 32				←			10 02		
Upminster ⊖	d		08 39	08 28	←	08 39		08 46		09 09	08 58	←	09 09	09 16		09 39		09 28	←	09 39	09 46		10 09	09 58	←
Barking ⊖	d	08 38	→	08 36	08 38	08 47		08 54	09 08	→	09 06	09 08	09 17	09 24	09 38	→		09 36	09 38	09 47	09 54	10 08	→	10 06	10 08
Stratford 7 ⊖	a	→							→						→							→			
London Liverpool St 15 ⊖	a																								
West Ham ⊖	d			08 42	08 44	08 53		09 00			09 12	09 14	09 23	09 30				09 42	09 44	09 53	10 00			10 12	10 14
Limehouse	d				08 49	08 58		09 05				09 19	09 28	09 35					09 49	09 58	10 05				10 19
London Fenchurch St 7 ⊖	a			08 53	08 56	09 04		09 12			09 23	09 26	09 34	09 42				09 53	09 56	10 04	10 12			10 23	10 26

		CC		CC	CC	CC	CC	CC	CC	CC	CC	CC		CC	CC	CC	CC	CC	CC	CC	CC	CC		CC	CC
Shoeburyness	d			09 35			09 50			10 05				10 20			10 35			10 50				11 05	
Thorpe Bay	d			09 38			09 53			10 08				10 23			10 38			10 53				11 08	
Southend East	d			09 41			09 56			10 11				10 26			10 41			10 56				11 11	
Southend Central	a			09 43			09 58			10 13				10 28			10 43			10 58				11 13	
	d			09 44		09 50	09 59			10 14		10 20		10 29			10 44		10 50	10 59				11 14	
Westcliff	d			09 46		09 53	10 01			10 16		10 23		10 31			10 46		10 53	11 01				11 16	
Chalkwell	d			09 48		09 55	10 03			10 18		10 25		10 33			10 48		10 55	11 03				11 18	
Leigh-on-Sea	d			09 51		09 58	10 06			10 21		10 28		10 36			10 51		10 58	11 06				11 21	
Benfleet	d			09 55		10 02	10 10			10 25		10 32		10 40			10 55		11 02	11 10				11 25	
Pitsea	d			09 59		10 06				10 29		10 36					10 59		11 06					11 29	
Stanford-le-Hope	d					10 12						10 42							11 12						
East Tilbury	d					10 15						10 45							11 15						
Tilbury Town 3	d					10 21						10 51							11 21						
Grays	d				10 18	10 24					10 48	10 54						11 18	11 24						11 48
Purfleet	d				10 23						10 53							11 23							11 53
Rainham	d				10 28						10 58							11 28							11 58
Dagenham Dock	d				10 32						11 02							11 32							12 02
Basildon	d			10 02			10 16			10 32				10 46			11 02			11 16				11 32	
Laindon	d			10 05			10 19			10 35				10 49			11 05			11 19				11 35	
West Horndon	d			10 10						10 40							11 10							11 40	
Chafford Hundred	d					10 29						10 59							11 29						
Ockendon	d	←				10 32			←			11 02				←			11 32			←			
Upminster ⊖	d	10 09		10 16		10 39	10 28	←	10 39	10 46		11 09		10 58	←	11 09	11 16		11 39	11 28	←	11 39		11 46	
Barking ⊖	d	10 17		10 24	10 38	→	10 36	10 38	10 47	10 54	11 08	→		11 06	11 08	11 17	11 24	11 38	→	11 36	11 38	11 47		11 54	12 08
Stratford 7 ⊖	a				→						→							→							→
London Liverpool St 15 ⊖	a																								
West Ham ⊖	d	10 23		10 30			10 42	10 44	10 53	11 00				11 12	11 14	11 23	11 30			11 42	11 44	11 53		12 00	
Limehouse	d	10 28		10 35				10 49	10 58	11 05					11 19	11 28	11 35				11 49	11 58		12 05	
London Fenchurch St 7 ⊖	a	10 34		10 42			10 53	10 56	11 04	11 12				11 23	11 26	11 34	11 42			11 53	11 56	12 04		12 12	

18 August to 25 August

Shoeburyness and Southend Central - London

Network Diagram - see first page of Table 1

		CC	CC	CC	CC	CC	CC	CC		CC	CC	CC	CC	CC	CC	CC	CC	CC		CC	CC	CC	CC	CC	CC
Shoeburyness	d		11 20			11 35				11 50			12 05			12 20				12 35			12 50		
Thorpe Bay	d		11 23			11 38				11 53			12 08			12 23				12 38			12 53		
Southend East	d		11 26			11 41				11 56			12 11			12 26				12 41			12 56		
Southend Central	a		11 28			11 43				11 58			12 13			12 28				12 43			12 58		
	d	11 20	11 29			11 44		11 50		11 59			12 14		12 20	12 29				12 44		12 50	12 59		
Westcliff	d	11 23	11 31			11 46		11 53		12 01			12 16		12 23	12 31				12 46		12 53	13 01		
Chalkwell	d	11 25	11 33			11 48		11 55		12 03			12 18		12 25	12 33				12 48		12 55	13 03		
Leigh-on-Sea	d	11 28	11 36			11 51		11 58		12 06			12 21		12 28	12 36				12 51		12 58	13 06		
Benfleet	d	11 32	11 40			11 55		12 02		12 10			12 25		12 32	12 40				12 55		13 02	13 10		
Pitsea	d	11 36				11 59		12 06					12 29		12 36					12 59		13 06			
Stanford-le-Hope	d	11 42						12 12							12 42							13 12			
East Tilbury	d	11 45						12 15							12 45							13 15			
Tilbury Town	d	11 51						12 21							12 51							13 21			
Grays	d	11 54					12 18	12 24						12 48	12 54						13 18	13 24			
Purfleet	d						12 23							12 53							13 23				
Rainham	d						12 28							12 58							13 28				
Dagenham Dock	d						12 32							13 02							13 32				
Basildon	d		11 46			12 02				12 16			12 32			12 46				13 02			13 16		
Laindon	d		11 49			12 05				12 19			12 35			12 49				13 05			13 19		
West Horndon	d					12 10							12 40							13 10					
Chafford Hundred	d	11 59						12 29							12 59							13 29			
Ockendon	d	12 01			←			12 32				←			13 02			←				13 32			←
Upminster	⊖ d	12 09	11 58	←	12 09	12 16		12 39		12 28	←	12 39	12 46		13 09	12 58	←	13 09		13 16		13 39	13 28	←	13 39
Barking	⊖ d	→	12 06	12 08	12 17	12 24	12 38	→		12 36	12 38	12 47	12 54	13 08	→	13 06	13 08	13 17		13 24	13 38	→	13 36	13 38	13 47
Stratford 7	⊖ a						→							→							→				
London Liverpool St 15	⊖ a																								
West Ham	⊖ d		12 12	12 14	12 23	12 30				12 42	12 44	12 53	13 00			13 12	13 14	13 23		13 30			13 42	13 44	13 53
Limehouse	d			12 19	12 28	12 35					12 49	12 58	13 05				13 19	13 28		13 35				13 49	13 58
London Fenchurch St 7	⊖ a		12 23	12 26	12 34	12 42				12 53	12 56	13 04	13 12			13 23	13 26	13 34		13 42			13 53	13 56	14 04

		CC	CC	CC		CC	CC	CC	CC	CC	CC	CC	CC	CC		CC	CC	CC	CC	CC	CC	CC	CC	CC	
Shoeburyness	d	13 05				13 20			13 35			13 50				14 05			14 20			14 35			
Thorpe Bay	d	13 08				13 23			13 38			13 53				14 08			14 23			14 38			
Southend East	d	13 11				13 26			13 41			13 56				14 11			14 26			14 41			
Southend Central	a	13 13				13 28			13 43			13 58				14 13			14 28			14 43			
	d	13 14		13 20		13 29			13 44		13 50	13 59				14 14		14 20	14 29			14 44		14 50	
Westcliff	d	13 16		13 23		13 31			13 46		13 53	14 01				14 16		14 23	14 31			14 46		14 53	
Chalkwell	d	13 18		13 25		13 33			13 48		13 55	14 03				14 18		14 25	14 33			14 48		14 55	
Leigh-on-Sea	d	13 21		13 28		13 36			13 51		13 58	14 06				14 21		14 28	14 36			14 51		14 58	
Benfleet	d	13 25		13 32		13 40			13 55		14 02	14 10				14 25		14 32	14 40			14 55		15 02	
Pitsea	d	13 29		13 36					13 59		14 06					14 29		14 36				14 59		15 06	
Stanford-le-Hope	d			13 42							14 12							14 42						15 12	
East Tilbury	d			13 45							14 15							14 45						15 15	
Tilbury Town	d			13 51							14 21							14 51						15 21	
Grays	d		13 48	13 54						14 18	14 24						14 48	14 54					15 18	15 24	
Purfleet	d		13 53							14 23							14 53						15 23		
Rainham	d		13 58							14 28							14 58						15 28		
Dagenham Dock	d		14 02							14 32							15 02						15 32		
Basildon	d	13 32				13 46			14 02			14 16				14 32			14 46			15 02			
Laindon	d	13 35				13 49			14 05			14 19				14 35			14 49			15 05			
West Horndon	d	13 40							14 10							14 40						15 10			
Chafford Hundred	d			13 59							14 29							14 59						15 29	
Ockendon	d			14 02				←			14 32			←				15 02			←			15 32	
Upminster	⊖ d	13 46		14 09		13 58	←	14 09	14 16		14 39	14 28	←	14 39		14 46		15 09	14 58	←	15 09	15 16		15 39	
Barking	⊖ d	13 54	14 08	→		14 06	14 08	14 17	14 24	14 38	→	14 36	14 38	14 47		14 54	15 08	→	15 06	15 08	15 17	15 24	15 38	→	
Stratford 7	⊖ a		→							→							→						→		
London Liverpool St 15	⊖ a																								
West Ham	⊖ d	14 00				14 12	14 14	14 23	14 30			14 42	14 44	14 53		15 00			15 12	15 14	15 23	15 30			
Limehouse	d	14 05					14 19	14 28	14 35				14 49	14 58		15 05				15 19	15 28	15 35			
London Fenchurch St 7	⊖ a	14 12				14 23	14 26	14 34	14 42			14 53	14 56	15 04		15 12			15 23	15 26	15 34	15 42			

		CC	CC	CC	CC	CC	CC	CC	CC	CC		CC	CC	CC	CC	CC	CC	CC	CC	CC		CC	CC	CC	CC
Shoeburyness	d	14 50			15 05			15 20				15 35			15 50			16 05				16 20			16 35
Thorpe Bay	d	14 53			15 08			15 23				15 38			15 53			16 08				16 23			16 38
Southend East	d	14 56			15 11			15 26				15 41			15 56			16 11				16 26			16 41
Southend Central	a	14 58			15 13			15 28				15 43			15 58			16 13				16 28			16 43
	d	14 59			15 14		15 20	15 29				15 44		15 50	15 59			16 14		16 20		16 29			16 44
Westcliff	d	15 01			15 16		15 23	15 31				15 46		15 53	16 01			16 16		16 23		16 31			16 46
Chalkwell	d	15 03			15 18		15 25	15 33				15 48		15 55	16 03			16 18		16 25		16 33			16 48
Leigh-on-Sea	d	15 06			15 21		15 28	15 36				15 51		15 58	16 06			16 21		16 28		16 36			16 51
Benfleet	d	15 10			15 25		15 32	15 40				15 55		16 02	16 10			16 25		16 32		16 40			16 55
Pitsea	d				15 29		15 36					15 59		16 06				16 29		16 36					16 59
Stanford-le-Hope	d						15 42							16 12						16 42					
East Tilbury	d						15 45							16 15						16 45					
Tilbury Town	d						15 51							16 21						16 51					
Grays	d					15 48	15 54						16 18	16 24					16 48	16 54					
Purfleet	d					15 53							16 23						16 53						
Rainham	d					15 58							16 28						16 58						
Dagenham Dock	d					16 02							16 32						17 02						
Basildon	d	15 16			15 32			15 46				16 02			16 16			16 32				16 46			17 02
Laindon	d	15 19			15 35			15 49				16 05			16 19			16 35				16 49			17 05
West Horndon	d				15 40							16 10						16 40							17 10
Chafford Hundred	d						15 59							16 29						16 59					
Ockendon	d			←			16 02			←				16 32			←			17 02				←	
Upminster	⊖ d	15 28	←	15 39	15 46		16 09	15 58	←	16 09		16 16		16 39	16 28	←	16 39	16 46		17 09		16 58	←	17 09	17 16
Barking	⊖ d	15 36	15 38	15 47	15 54	16 08	→	16 06	16 08	16 17		16 24	16 38	→	16 36	16 38	16 47	16 54	17 08	→		17 06	17 08	17 17	17 24
Stratford 7	⊖ a					→							→						→						
London Liverpool St 15	⊖ a																								
West Ham	⊖ d	15 42	15 44	15 53	16 00			16 12	16 14	16 23		16 30			16 42	16 44	16 53	17 00				17 12	17 14	17 23	17 30
Limehouse	d		15 49	15 58	16 05				16 19	16 28		16 35				16 49	16 58	17 05					17 19	17 28	17 35
London Fenchurch St 7	⊖ a	15 53	15 56	16 04	16 12			16 23	16 26	16 34		16 42			16 53	16 56	17 04	17 12				17 23	17 26	17 34	17 42

18 August to 25 August

Shoeburyness and Southend Central - London

Network Diagram - see first page of Table 1

		CC	CC	CC	CC	CC		CC	CC	CC	CC	CC	CC	CC	CC	CC		CC	CC	CC	CC	CC	CC	CC	CC
Shoeburyness	d			16 50				17 05			17 20			17 35				17 50			18 05			18 20	
Thorpe Bay	d			16 53				17 08			17 23			17 38				17 53			18 08			18 23	
Southend East	d			16 56				17 11			17 26			17 41				17 56			18 11			18 26	
Southend Central	a			16 58				17 13			17 28			17 43				17 58			18 13			18 28	
	d		16 50	16 59				17 14		17 20	17 29			17 44		17 50		17 59			18 14		18 20	18 29	
Westcliff	d		16 53	17 01				17 16		17 23	17 31			17 46		17 53		18 01			18 16		18 23	18 31	
Chalkwell	d		16 55	17 03				17 18		17 25	17 33			17 48		17 55		18 03			18 18		18 25	18 33	
Leigh-on-Sea	d		16 58	17 06				17 21		17 28	17 36			17 51		17 58		18 06			18 21		18 28	18 36	
Benfleet	d		17 02	17 10				17 25		17 32	17 40			17 55		18 02		18 10			18 25		18 32	18 40	
Pitsea	d		17 06					17 29		17 36				17 59		18 06					18 29		18 36		
Stanford-le-Hope	d		17 12							17 42						18 12							18 42		
East Tilbury	d		17 15							17 45						18 15							18 45		
Tilbury Town	d		17 21							17 51						18 21							18 51		
Grays	d	17 18	17 24						17 48	17 54					18 18	18 24						18 48	18 54		
Purfleet	d	17 23							17 53						18 23							18 53			
Rainham	d	17 28							17 58						18 28							18 58			
Dagenham Dock	d	17 32							18 02						18 32							19 02			
Basildon	d			17 16				17 32			17 46			18 02				18 16			18 32			18 46	
Laindon	d			17 19				17 35			17 49			18 05				18 19			18 35			18 49	
West Horndon	d							17 40						18 10							18 40				
Chafford Hundred	d		17 29							17 59						18 29							18 59		
Ockendon	d		17 32			←				18 02			←			18 32				←			19 02		
Upminster	⊖ d		17 39	17 28	←	17 39		17 46		18 09	17 58	←	18 09	18 16		18 39		18 28	←	18 39	18 46		19 09	18 58	←
Barking	⊖ d	17 38	→	17 36	17 38	17 47		17 54	18 08	→	18 06	18 08	18 17	18 24	18 38	→		18 36	18 38	18 47	18 54	19 08	→	19 06	19 08
Stratford 7	⊖ a	→							→						→							→			
London Liverpool St 15	⊖ a																								
West Ham	⊖ d			17 42	17 44	17 53		18 00			18 12	18 14	18 23	18 30				18 42	18 44	18 53	19 00			19 12	19 14
Limehouse	d				17 49	17 58		18 05				18 19	18 28	18 35					18 49	18 58	19 05				19 19
London Fenchurch St 7	⊖ a			17 53	17 56	18 04		18 12			18 23	18 26	18 34	18 42				18 53	18 56	19 04	19 12			19 23	19 26

		CC		CC	CC	CC	CC	CC	CC	CC	CC	CC		CC	CC	CC	CC	CC	CC	CC	CC	CC		CC	CC
Shoeburyness	d			18 35			18 50			19 05				19 20			19 35			19 50				20 05	
Thorpe Bay	d			18 38			18 53			19 08				19 23			19 38			19 53				20 08	
Southend East	d			18 41			18 56			19 11				19 26			19 41			19 56				20 11	
Southend Central	a			18 43			18 58			19 13				19 28			19 43			19 58				20 13	
	d			18 44		18 50	18 59			19 14		19 20		19 29			19 44		19 50	19 59				20 14	
Westcliff	d			18 46		18 53	19 01			19 16		19 23		19 31			19 46		19 53	20 01				20 16	
Chalkwell	d			18 48		18 55	19 03			19 18		19 25		19 33			19 48		19 55	20 03				20 18	
Leigh-on-Sea	d			18 51		18 58	19 06			19 21		19 28		19 36			19 51		19 58	20 06				20 21	
Benfleet	d			18 55		19 02	19 10			19 25		19 32		19 40			19 55		20 02	20 10				20 25	
Pitsea	d			18 59		19 06				19 29		19 36					19 59		20 06					20 29	
Stanford-le-Hope	d					19 12						19 42							20 12						
East Tilbury	d					19 15						19 45							20 15						
Tilbury Town	d					19 21						19 51							20 21						
Grays	d				19 18	19 24					19 48	19 54						20 18	20 24						20 48
Purfleet	d				19 23						19 53							20 23							20 53
Rainham	d				19 28						19 58							20 28							20 58
Dagenham Dock	d				19 32						20 02							20 32							21 02
Basildon	d			19 02			19 16			19 32				19 46			20 02			20 16				20 32	
Laindon	d			19 05			19 19			19 35				19 49			20 05			20 19				20 35	
West Horndon	d			19 10						19 40							20 10							20 40	
Chafford Hundred	d					19 29						19 59							20 29						
Ockendon	d	←				19 32			←			20 02				←			20 32			←			
Upminster	⊖ d	19 09		19 16		19 39	19 28	←	19 39	19 46		20 09		19 58	←	20 09	20 16		20 39	20 28	←	20 39		20 46	
Barking	⊖ d	19 17		19 24	19 38	→	19 36	19 38	19 47	19 54	20 08	→		20 06	20 08	20 17	20 24	20 38	→	20 36	20 38	20 47		20 54	21 08
Stratford 7	⊖ a				→						→							→							
London Liverpool St 15	⊖ a																								
West Ham	⊖ d	19 23		19 30			19 42	19 44	19 53	20 00				20 12	20 14	20 23	20 30			20 42	20 44	20 53		21 00	21 14
Limehouse	d	19 28		19 35				19 49	19 58	20 05					20 19	20 28	20 35				20 49	20 58		21 05	21 19
London Fenchurch St 7	⊖ a	19 34		19 42			19 53	19 56	20 04	20 12				20 23	20 26	20 34	20 42			20 53	20 56	21 04		21 12	21 26

		CC	CC	CC	CC	CC	CC	CC		CC	CC	CC	CC	CC	CC	CC	CC	CC		CC	CC	CC	CC	CC	
Shoeburyness	d		20 35			20 50				21 05			21 35			22 05				22 35			23 05		
Thorpe Bay	d		20 38			20 53				21 08			21 38			22 08				22 38			23 08		
Southend East	d		20 41			20 56				21 11			21 41			22 11				22 41			23 11		
Southend Central	a		20 43			20 58				21 13			21 43			22 13				22 43			23 13		
	d	20 20	20 44		20 50	20 59				21 14		21 20	21 44		21 50	22 14		22 20		22 44		22 50	23 14	23 20	
Westcliff	d	20 23	20 46		20 53	21 01				21 16		21 23	21 46		21 53	22 16		22 23		22 46		22 53	23 16	23 23	
Chalkwell	d	20 25	20 48		20 55	21 03				21 18		21 25	21 48		21 55	22 18		22 25		22 48		22 55	23 18	23 25	
Leigh-on-Sea	d	20 28	20 51		20 58	21 06				21 21		21 28	21 51		21 58	22 21		22 28		22 51		22 58	23 21	23 28	
Benfleet	d	20 32	20 55		21 02	21 10				21 25		21 32	21 55		22 02	22 25		22 32		22 55		23 02	23 25	23 32	
Pitsea	d	20 36	20 59		21 06					21 29		21 36	21 59		22 06	22 29		22 36		22 59		23 06	23 29	23 36	
Stanford-le-Hope	d	20 42			21 12							21 42			22 12			22 42				23 12		23 42	
East Tilbury	d	20 45			21 15							21 45			22 15			22 45				23 15		23 45	
Tilbury Town	d	20 51			21 21							21 51			22 21			22 51				23 21		23 51	
Grays	d	20 54		21 18	21 24						21 48	21 54		22 18	22 24		22 48	22 54			23 18	23 24		23 54	
Purfleet	d			21 23							21 53			22 23			22 53				23 23				
Rainham	d			21 28							21 58			22 28			22 58				23 28				
Dagenham Dock	d			21 32							22 02			22 32			23 02				23 32				
Basildon	d		21 02			21 16				21 32			22 02			22 32				23 02			23 32		
Laindon	d		21 05			21 19				21 35			22 05			22 35				23 05			23 35		
West Horndon	d		21 10							21 40			22 10			22 40				23 10			23 40		
Chafford Hundred	d	20 59			21 29							21 59			22 29			22 59				23 29		23 59	
Ockendon	d	21 02			21 32			←				22 02			22 32			23 02				23 32		00 02	
Upminster	⊖ d	21 09	21 16		21 39	21 28	←	21 39		21 46		22 09	22 16		22 39	22 46		23 09		23 16		23 39	23 46	00 08	
Barking	⊖ d	21 17	21 24	21 38	→	21 36	21 38	21 47		21 54	22 08	22 17	22 24	22 38	22 47	22 54	23 08	23 17		23 24	23a39	23 47	23 55	00a18	
Stratford 7	⊖ a			→																					
London Liverpool St 15	⊖ a																								
West Ham	⊖ d	21 23	21 30			21 42	21 44	21 53		22 00	22 14	22 23	22 30	22 44	22 53	23 00	23 14	23 23		23 30		23 53	00 01		
Limehouse	d	21 28	21 35				21 49	21 58		22 05	22 19	22 28	22 35	22 49	22 58	23 05	23 19	23 28		23 35		23 58	00 06		
London Fenchurch St 7	⊖ a	21 34	21 42			21 53	21 56	22 04		22 12	22 26	22 34	22 42	22 56	23 04	23 12	23 26	23 34		23 42		00 04	00 12		

Table 1

Saturdays

1 September to 8 September

Shoeburyness and Southend Central - London

Network Diagram - see first page of Table 1

		CC	CC	CC	CC	CC	CC	CC	CC	CC		CC	CC	CC	CC	CC	CC	CC	CC	CC		CC	CC	CC	CC
Shoeburyness	d			23p05		04 20		05 05				05 35			06 05			06 35				07 05			07 35
Thorpe Bay	d			23p09		04 23		05 08				05 38			06 08			06 38				07 08			07 38
Southend East	d			23p12		04 26		05 11				05 41			06 11			06 41				07 11			07 41
Southend Central	a			23p14		04 28		05 13				05 43			06 13			06 43				07 13			07 43
	d	22p50		23p15		04 29		05 14		05 20		05 44		05 50	06 14		06 20	06 44		06 50		07 14		07 20	07 44
Westcliff	d	22p53		23p17		04 31		05 16		05 23		05 46		05 53	06 16		06 23	06 46		06 53		07 16		07 23	07 46
Chalkwell	d	22p55		23p19		04 33		05 18		05 25		05 48		05 55	06 18		06 25	06 48		06 55		07 18		07 25	07 48
Leigh-on-Sea	d	22p58		23p22		04 36		05 21		05 28		05 51		05 58	06 21		06 28	06 51		06 58		07 21		07 28	07 51
Benfleet	d	23p03		23p27		04 40		05 25		05 32		05 55		06 02	06 25		06 32	06 55		07 02		07 25		07 32	07 55
Pitsea	d	23p07		23p32		04 44		05 29		05 36		05 59		06 06	06 29		06 36	06 59		07 06		07 29		07 36	07 59
Stanford-le-Hope	d	23p14			04 29					05 42				06 12			06 42			07 12				07 42	
East Tilbury	d	23p18			04 32					05 45				06 15			06 45			07 15				07 45	
Tilbury Town 3	d	23p24			04 38					05 51				06 21			06 51			07 21				07 51	
Grays	d	23p27	23p33		04 41				05 48	05 54			06 18	06 24		06 48	06 54		07 18	07 24			07 48	07 54	
Purfleet	d		23p38						05 53				06 23			06 53			07 23				07 53		
Rainham	d		23p43						05 58				06 28			06 58			07 28				07 58		
Dagenham Dock	d		23p47						06 02				06 32			07 02			07 32				08 02		
Basildon	d			23p36		04 47		05 32				06 02			06 32			07 02				07 32			08 02
Laindon	d			23p39		04 50		05 35				06 05			06 35			07 05				07 35			08 05
West Horndon	d			23p44		04 55		05 40				06 10			06 40			07 10				07 40			08 10
Chafford Hundred	d	23p31			04 45					05 59				06 29			06 59			07 29				07 59	
Ockendon	d	23p35			04 49		05 16			06 02				06 32			07 02			07 32				08 02	
Upminster ⊖	d	23p42		23p50	04a57	05 02	05a23	05 46		06 09		06 16		06 39	06 46		07 09	07 16		07 39		07 46		08 09	08 16
Barking ⊖	d	23p51	23p55	00 02		05 10		05 54	06 08	06 17		06 24	06 38	06 47	06 54	07 08	07 17	07 24	07 38	07 47		07 54	08 08	08 17	08 24
Stratford 7 ⊖	a																								
London Liverpool St 15 ⊖	a																								
West Ham ⊖	d	00 01	00 06	00 12		05 16		06 00	06 14	06 23		06 30	06 44	06 53	07 00	07 14	07 23	07 30	07 44	07 53		08 00	08 14	08 23	08 30
Limehouse	d	00 06	00 11	00 17		05 21		06 05	06 19	06 28		06 35	06 49	06 58	07 05	07 19	07 28	07 35	07 49	07 58		08 05	08 19	08 28	08 35
London Fenchurch St 7 ⊖	a	00 11	00 18	00 24		05 27		06 12	06 26	06 34		06 42	06 56	07 04	07 12	07 26	07 34	07 42	07 56	08 04		08 12	08 26	08 34	08 42

		CC	CC	CC	CC	CC		CC	CC	CC	CC	CC	CC	CC	CC	CC		CC	CC	CC	CC	CC	CC	CC	CC
Shoeburyness	d			07 50				08 05			08 20			08 35				08 50			09 05			09 20	
Thorpe Bay	d			07 53				08 08			08 23			08 38				08 53			09 08			09 23	
Southend East	d			07 56				08 11			08 26			08 41				08 56			09 11			09 26	
Southend Central	a			07 58				08 13			08 28			08 43				08 58			09 13			09 28	
	d		07 50	07 59				08 14		08 20	08 29			08 44		08 50		08 59			09 14		09 20	09 29	
Westcliff	d		07 53	08 01				08 16		08 23	08 31			08 46		08 53		09 01			09 16		09 23	09 31	
Chalkwell	d		07 55	08 03				08 18		08 25	08 33			08 48		08 55		09 03			09 18		09 25	09 33	
Leigh-on-Sea	d		07 58	08 06				08 21		08 28	08 36			08 51		08 58		09 06			09 21		09 28	09 36	
Benfleet	d		08 02	08 10				08 25		08 32	08 40			08 55		09 02		09 10			09 25		09 32	09 40	
Pitsea	d		08 06					08 29		08 36				08 59		09 06					09 29		09 36		
Stanford-le-Hope	d		08 12							08 42						09 12							09 42		
East Tilbury	d		08 15							08 45						09 15							09 45		
Tilbury Town 3	d		08 21							08 51						09 21							09 51		
Grays	d	08 18	08 24						08 48	08 54					09 18	09 24						09 48	09 54		
Purfleet	d	08 23							08 53						09 23							09 53			
Rainham	d	08 28							08 58						09 28							09 58			
Dagenham Dock	d	08 32							09 02						09 32							10 02			
Basildon	d			08 16				08 32			08 46			09 02				09 16			09 32			09 46	
Laindon	d			08 19				08 35			08 49			09 05				09 19			09 35			09 49	
West Horndon	d							08 40						09 10							09 40				
Chafford Hundred	d		08 29							08 59						09 29							09 59		
Ockendon	d		08 32			←				09 02			←			09 32				←			10 02		
Upminster ⊖	d		08 39	08 28	←	08 39		08 46		09 09	08 58	←	09 09	09 16		09 39		09 28	←	09 39	09 46		10 09	09 58	←
Barking ⊖	d	08 38	→	08 36	08 38	08 47		08 54	09 08	→	09 06	09 08	09 17	09 24	09 38	→		09 36	09 38	09 47	09 54	10 08	→	10 06	10 08
Stratford 7 ⊖	a	→							→						→							→			
London Liverpool St 15 ⊖	a																								
West Ham ⊖	d			08 42	08 44	08 53		09 00			09 12	09 14	09 23	09 30				09 42	09 44	09 53	10 00			10 12	10 14
Limehouse	d				08 49	08 58		09 05				09 19	09 28	09 35					09 49	09 58	10 05				10 19
London Fenchurch St 7 ⊖	a			08 53	08 56	09 04		09 12			09 23	09 26	09 34	09 42				09 53	09 56	10 04	10 12			10 23	10 26

		CC		CC	CC	CC	CC	CC	CC	CC	CC	CC		CC	CC	CC	CC	CC	CC	CC	CC	CC		CC	CC
Shoeburyness	d			09 35			09 50			10 05				10 20			10 35			10 50				11 05	
Thorpe Bay	d			09 38			09 53			10 08				10 23			10 38			10 53				11 08	
Southend East	d			09 41			09 56			10 11				10 26			10 41			10 56				11 11	
Southend Central	a			09 43			09 58			10 13				10 28			10 43			10 58				11 13	
	d			09 44		09 50	09 59			10 14		10 20		10 29			10 44		10 50	10 59				11 14	
Westcliff	d			09 46		09 53	10 01			10 16		10 23		10 31			10 46		10 53	11 01				11 16	
Chalkwell	d			09 48		09 55	10 03			10 18		10 25		10 33			10 48		10 55	11 03				11 18	
Leigh-on-Sea	d			09 51		09 58	10 06			10 21		10 28		10 36			10 51		10 58	11 06				11 21	
Benfleet	d			09 55		10 02	10 10			10 25		10 32		10 40			10 55		11 02	11 10				11 25	
Pitsea	d			09 59		10 06				10 29		10 36					10 59		11 06					11 29	
Stanford-le-Hope	d					10 12						10 42							11 12						
East Tilbury	d					10 15						10 45							11 15						
Tilbury Town 3	d					10 21						10 51							11 21						
Grays	d				10 18	10 24					10 48	10 54						11 18	11 24						11 48
Purfleet	d				10 23						10 53							11 23							11 53
Rainham	d				10 28						10 58							11 28							11 58
Dagenham Dock	d				10 32						11 02							11 32							12 02
Basildon	d			10 02			10 16			10 32				10 46			11 02			11 16				11 32	
Laindon	d			10 05			10 19			10 35				10 49			11 05			11 19				11 35	
West Horndon	d			10 10						10 40							11 10							11 40	
Chafford Hundred	d					10 29						10 59							11 29						
Ockendon	d	←				10 32			←			11 02				←			11 32			←			
Upminster ⊖	d	10 09		10 16		10 39	10 28	←	10 39	10 46		11 09		10 58	←	11 09	11 16		11 39	11 28	←	11 39		11 46	
Barking ⊖	d	10 17		10 24	10 38	→	10 36	10 38	10 47	10 54	11 08	→		11 06	11 08	11 17	11 24	11 38	→	11 36	11 38	11 47		11 54	12 08
Stratford 7 ⊖	a				→						→							→							→
London Liverpool St 15 ⊖	a																								
West Ham ⊖	d	10 23		10 30			10 42	10 44	10 53	11 00				11 12	11 14	11 23	11 30			11 42	11 44	11 53		12 00	
Limehouse	d	10 28		10 35				10 49	10 58	11 05					11 19	11 28	11 35				11 49	11 58		12 05	
London Fenchurch St 7 ⊖	a	10 34		10 42			10 53	10 56	11 04	11 12				11 23	11 26	11 34	11 42			11 53	11 56	12 04		12 12	

Table 1

Saturdays

1 September to 8 September

Shoeburyness and Southend Central - London

Network Diagram - see first page of Table 1

		CC	CC	CC	CC	CC	CC	CC		CC	CC	CC	CC	CC	CC	CC	CC	CC		CC	CC	CC	CC	CC	CC
Shoeburyness	d		11 20			11 35				11 50			12 05			12 20				12 35			12 50		
Thorpe Bay	d		11 23			11 38				11 53			12 08			12 23				12 38			12 53		
Southend East	d		11 26			11 41				11 56			12 11			12 26				12 41			12 56		
Southend Central	a		11 28			11 43				11 58			12 13			12 28				12 43			12 58		
	d	11 20	11 29			11 44		11 50		11 59			12 14		12 20	12 29				12 44		12 50	12 59		
Westcliff	d	11 23	11 31			11 46		11 53		12 01			12 16		12 23	12 31				12 46		12 53	13 01		
Chalkwell	d	11 25	11 33			11 48		11 55		12 03			12 18		12 25	12 33				12 48		12 55	13 03		
Leigh-on-Sea	d	11 28	11 36			11 51		11 58		12 06			12 21		12 28	12 36				12 51		12 58	13 06		
Benfleet	d	11 32	11 40			11 55		12 02		12 10			12 25		12 32	12 40				12 55		13 02	13 10		
Pitsea	d	11 36				11 59		12 06					12 29		12 36					12 59		13 06			
Stanford-le-Hope	d	11 42						12 12							12 42							13 12			
East Tilbury	d	11 45						12 15							12 45							13 15			
Tilbury Town 3	d	11 51						12 21							12 51							13 21			
Grays	d	11 54					12 18	12 24						12 48	12 54						13 18	13 24			
Purfleet	d						12 23							12 53							13 23				
Rainham	d						12 28							12 58							13 28				
Dagenham Dock	d						12 32							13 02							13 32				
Basildon	d		11 46			12 02				12 16			12 32			12 46				13 02			13 16		
Laindon	d		11 49			12 05				12 19			12 35			12 49				13 05			13 19		
West Horndon	d					12 10							12 40							13 10					
Chafford Hundred	d	11 59						12 29							12 59							13 29			
Ockendon	d	12 01			←			12 32				←			13 02			←				13 32			←
Upminster ⊖	d	12 09	11 58	←	12 09	12 16		12 39		12 28	←	12 39	12 46		13 09	12 58	←	13 09		13 16		13 39	13 28	←	13 39
Barking ⊖	d	→	12 06	12 08	12 17	12 24	12 38	→		12 36	12 38	12 47	12 54	13 08	→	13 06	13 08	13 17		13 24	13 38	→	13 36	13 38	13 47
Stratford 7 ⊖	a						→							→							→				
London Liverpool St 15 ⊖	a																								
West Ham ⊖	d		12 12	12 14	12 23	12 30				12 42	12 44	12 53	13 00			13 12	13 14	13 23		13 30			13 42	13 44	13 53
Limehouse	d			12 19	12 28	12 35					12 49	12 58	13 05				13 19	13 28		13 35				13 49	13 58
London Fenchurch St 7 ⊖	a		12 23	12 26	12 34	12 42				12 53	12 56	13 04	13 12			13 23	13 26	13 34		13 42			13 53	13 56	14 04

		CC	CC	CC		CC	CC	CC	CC	CC	CC	CC	CC	CC		CC	CC	CC	CC	CC	CC	CC	CC	CC	
Shoeburyness	d	13 05				13 20			13 35			13 50				14 05			14 20			14 35			
Thorpe Bay	d	13 08				13 23			13 38			13 53				14 08			14 23			14 38			
Southend East	d	13 11				13 26			13 41			13 56				14 11			14 26			14 41			
Southend Central	a	13 13				13 28			13 43			13 58				14 13			14 28			14 43			
	d	13 14		13 20		13 29			13 44		13 50	13 59				14 14		14 20	14 29			14 44		14 50	
Westcliff	d	13 16		13 23		13 31			13 46		13 53	14 01				14 16		14 23	14 31			14 46		14 53	
Chalkwell	d	13 18		13 25		13 33			13 48		13 55	14 03				14 18		14 25	14 33			14 48		14 55	
Leigh-on-Sea	d	13 21		13 28		13 36			13 51		13 58	14 06				14 21		14 28	14 36			14 51		14 58	
Benfleet	d	13 25		13 32		13 40			13 55		14 02	14 10				14 25		14 32	14 40			14 55		15 02	
Pitsea	d	13 29		13 36					13 59		14 06					14 29		14 36				14 59		15 06	
Stanford-le-Hope	d			13 42							14 12							14 42						15 12	
East Tilbury	d			13 45							14 15							14 45						15 15	
Tilbury Town 3	d			13 51							14 21							14 51						15 21	
Grays	d		13 48	13 54						14 18	14 24						14 48	14 54					15 18	15 24	
Purfleet	d		13 53							14 23							14 53						15 23		
Rainham	d		13 58							14 28							14 58						15 28		
Dagenham Dock	d		14 02							14 32							15 02						15 32		
Basildon	d	13 32				13 46			14 02			14 16				14 32			14 46			15 02			
Laindon	d	13 35				13 49			14 05			14 19				14 35			14 49			15 05			
West Horndon	d	13 40							14 10							14 40						15 10			
Chafford Hundred	d			13 59							14 29							14 59						15 29	
Ockendon	d			14 02				←			14 32			←				15 02			←			15 32	
Upminster ⊖	d	13 46		14 09		13 58	←	14 09	14 16		14 39	14 28	←	14 39		14 46		15 09	14 58	←	15 09	15 16		15 39	
Barking ⊖	d	13 54	14 08	→		14 06	14 08	14 17	14 24	14 38	→	14 36	14 38	14 47		14 54	15 08	→	15 06	15 08	15 17	15 24	15 38	→	
Stratford 7 ⊖	a		→							→							→						→		
London Liverpool St 15 ⊖	a																								
West Ham ⊖	d	14 00				14 12	14 14	14 23	14 30			14 42	14 44	14 53		15 00			15 12	15 14	15 23	15 30			
Limehouse	d	14 05					14 19	14 28	14 35				14 49	14 58		15 05				15 19	15 28	15 35			
London Fenchurch St 7 ⊖	a	14 12				14 23	14 26	14 34	14 42			14 53	14 56	15 04		15 12			15 23	15 26	15 34	15 42			

		CC	CC	CC	CC	CC	CC	CC	CC	CC		CC	CC	CC	CC	CC	CC	CC	CC	CC		CC	CC	CC	CC
Shoeburyness	d	14 50			15 05			15 20				15 35			15 50			16 05				16 20			16 35
Thorpe Bay	d	14 53			15 08			15 23				15 38			15 53			16 08				16 23			16 38
Southend East	d	14 56			15 11			15 26				15 41			15 56			16 11				16 26			16 41
Southend Central	a	14 58			15 13			15 28				15 43			15 58			16 13				16 28			16 43
	d	14 59			15 14		15 20	15 29				15 44		15 50	15 59			16 14		16 20		16 29			16 44
Westcliff	d	15 01			15 16		15 23	15 31				15 46		15 53	16 01			16 16		16 23		16 31			16 46
Chalkwell	d	15 03			15 18		15 25	15 33				15 48		15 55	16 03			16 18		16 25		16 33			16 48
Leigh-on-Sea	d	15 06			15 21		15 28	15 36				15 51		15 58	16 06			16 21		16 28		16 36			16 51
Benfleet	d	15 10			15 25		15 32	15 40				15 55		16 02	16 10			16 25		16 32		16 40			16 55
Pitsea	d				15 29		15 36					15 59		16 06				16 29		16 36					16 59
Stanford-le-Hope	d						15 42							16 12						16 42					
East Tilbury	d						15 45							16 15						16 45					
Tilbury Town 3	d						15 51							16 21						16 51					
Grays	d					15 48	15 54						16 18	16 24					16 48	16 54					
Purfleet	d					15 53							16 23						16 53						
Rainham	d					15 58							16 28						16 58						
Dagenham Dock	d					16 02							16 32						17 02						
Basildon	d	15 16			15 32			15 46				16 02			16 16			16 32				16 46			17 02
Laindon	d	15 19			15 35			15 49				16 05			16 19			16 35				16 49			17 05
West Horndon	d				15 40							16 10						16 40							17 10
Chafford Hundred	d						15 59							16 29						16 59					
Ockendon	d			←			16 02			←				16 32			←			17 02				←	
Upminster ⊖	d	15 28	←	15 39	15 46		16 09	15 58	←	16 09		16 16		16 39	16 28	←	16 39	16 46		17 09		16 58	←	17 09	17 16
Barking ⊖	d	15 36	15 38	15 47	15 54	16 08	→	16 06	16 08	16 17		16 24	16 38	→	16 36	16 38	16 47	16 54	17 08	→		17 06	17 08	17 17	17 24
Stratford 7 ⊖	a					→							→						→						
London Liverpool St 15 ⊖	a																								
West Ham ⊖	d	15 42	15 44	15 53	16 00			16 12	16 14	16 23		16 30			16 42	16 44	16 53	17 00				17 12	17 14	17 23	17 30
Limehouse	d		15 49	15 58	16 05				16 19	16 28		16 35				16 49	16 58	17 05					17 19	17 28	17 35
London Fenchurch St 7 ⊖	a	15 53	15 56	16 04	16 12			16 23	16 26	16 34		16 42			16 53	16 56	17 04	17 12				17 23	17 26	17 34	17 42

1 September to 8 September

Shoeburyness and Southend Central - London

Network Diagram - see first page of Table I

	CC	CC	CC	CC	CC		CC	CC	CC	CC	CC	CC	CC	CC	CC		CC	CC	CC	CC	CC	CC	CC	CC
Shoeburyness d			16 50				17 05			17 20			17 35				17 50			18 05			18 20	
Thorpe Bay d			16 53				17 08			17 23			17 38				17 53			18 08			18 23	
Southend East d			16 56				17 11			17 26			17 41				17 56			18 11			18 26	
Southend Central a			16 58				17 13			17 28			17 43				17 58			18 13			18 28	
d		16 50	16 59				17 14		17 20	17 29			17 44		17 50		17 59			18 14		18 20	18 29	
Westcliff d		16 53	17 01				17 16		17 23	17 31			17 46		17 53		18 01			18 16		18 23	18 31	
Chalkwell d		16 55	17 03				17 18		17 25	17 33			17 48		17 55		18 03			18 18		18 25	18 33	
Leigh-on-Sea d		16 58	17 06				17 21		17 28	17 36			17 51		17 58		18 06			18 21		18 28	18 36	
Benfleet d		17 02	17 10				17 25		17 32	17 40			17 55		18 02		18 10			18 25		18 32	18 40	
Pitsea d		17 06					17 29		17 36				17 59		18 06					18 29		18 36		
Stanford-le-Hope d		17 12							17 42						18 12							18 42		
East Tilbury d		17 15							17 45						18 15							18 45		
Tilbury Town 8 d		17 21							17 51						18 21							18 51		
Grays d	17 18	17 24						17 48	17 54					18 18	18 24						18 48	18 54		
Purfleet d	17 23							17 53						18 23							18 53			
Rainham d	17 28							17 58						18 28							18 58			
Dagenham Dock d	17 32							18 02						18 32							19 02			
Basildon d			17 16				17 32			17 46			18 02				18 16			18 32			18 46	
Laindon d			17 19				17 35			17 49			18 05				18 19			18 35			18 49	
West Horndon d							17 40						18 10							18 40				
Chafford Hundred d		17 29							17 59						18 29							18 59		
Ockendon d		17 32			←				18 02			←			18 32				←			19 02		
Upminster ⊖ d		17 39	17 28	←	17 39		17 46		18 09	17 58	←	18 09	18 16		18 39		18 28	←	18 39	18 46		19 09	18 58	←
Barking ⊖ d	17 38	→	17 36	17 38	17 47		17 54	18 08	→	18 06	18 08	18 17	18 24	18 38	→		18 36	18 38	18 47	18 54	19 08	→	19 06	19 08
Stratford 7 ⊖ a	→							→						→							→			
London Liverpool St 15 ⊖ a																								
West Ham ⊖ d			17 42	17 44	17 53		18 00			18 12	18 14	18 23	18 30				18 42	18 44	18 53	19 00			19 12	19 14
Limehouse d				17 49	17 58		18 05				18 19	18 28	18 35					18 49	18 58	19 05				19 19
London Fenchurch St 7 ⊖ a			17 53	17 56	18 04		18 12			18 23	18 26	18 34	18 42				18 53	18 56	19 04	19 12			19 23	19 26

	CC		CC	CC	CC	CC	CC	CC	CC	CC	CC		CC	CC	CC	CC	CC	CC	CC	CC	CC		CC	CC
Shoeburyness d			18 35			18 50			19 05				19 20			19 35			19 50				20 05	
Thorpe Bay d			18 38			18 53			19 08				19 23			19 38			19 53				20 08	
Southend East d			18 41			18 56			19 11				19 26			19 41			19 56				20 11	
Southend Central a			18 43			18 58			19 13				19 28			19 43			19 58				20 13	
d			18 44		18 50	18 59			19 14		19 20		19 29			19 44		19 50	19 59				20 14	
Westcliff d			18 46		18 53	19 01			19 16		19 23		19 31			19 46		19 53	20 01				20 16	
Chalkwell d			18 48		18 55	19 03			19 18		19 25		19 33			19 48		19 55	20 03				20 18	
Leigh-on-Sea d			18 51		18 58	19 06			19 21		19 28		19 36			19 51		19 58	20 06				20 21	
Benfleet d			18 55		19 02	19 10			19 25		19 32		19 40			19 55		20 02	20 10				20 25	
Pitsea d			18 59		19 06				19 29		19 36					19 59		20 06					20 29	
Stanford-le-Hope d					19 12						19 42							20 12						
East Tilbury d					19 15						19 45							20 15						
Tilbury Town 8 d					19 21						19 51							20 21						
Grays d				19 18	19 24					19 48	19 54						20 18	20 24						20 48
Purfleet d				19 23						19 53							20 23							20 53
Rainham d				19 28						19 58							20 28							20 58
Dagenham Dock d				19 32						20 02							20 32							21 02
Basildon d			19 02			19 16			19 32				19 46			20 02			20 16				20 32	
Laindon d			19 05			19 19			19 35				19 49			20 05			20 19				20 35	
West Horndon d			19 10						19 40							20 10							20 40	
Chafford Hundred d					19 29						19 59							20 29						
Ockendon d	←				19 32			←			20 02				←			20 32			←			
Upminster ⊖ d	19 09		19 16		19 39	19 28	←	19 39	19 46		20 09		19 58	←	20 09	20 16		20 39	20 28	←	20 39		20 46	
Barking ⊖ d	19 17		19 24	19 38	→	19 36	19 38	19 47	19 54	20 08	→		20 06	20 08	20 17	20 24	20 38	→	20 36	20 38	20 47		20 54	21 08
Stratford 7 ⊖ a				→						→							→							
London Liverpool St 15 ⊖ a																								
West Ham ⊖ d	19 23		19 30			19 42	19 44	19 53	20 00				20 12	20 14	20 23	20 30			20 42	20 44	20 53		21 00	21 14
Limehouse d	19 28		19 35				19 49	19 58	20 05					20 19	20 28	20 35				20 49	20 58		21 05	21 19
London Fenchurch St 7 ⊖ a	19 34		19 42			19 53	19 56	20 04	20 12				20 23	20 26	20 34	20 42			20 53	20 56	21 04		21 12	21 26

	CC	CC	CC	CC	CC	CC	CC		CC	CC	CC	CC	CC	CC	CC	CC	CC		CC	CC	CC	CC	CC	
Shoeburyness d		20 35			20 50				21 05			21 35			22 05				22 35			23 05		
Thorpe Bay d		20 38			20 53				21 08			21 38			22 08				22 38			23 08		
Southend East d		20 41			20 56				21 11			21 41			22 11				22 41			23 11		
Southend Central a		20 43			20 58				21 13			21 43			22 13				22 43			23 13		
d	20 20	20 44		20 50	20 59				21 14		21 20	21 44		21 50	22 14		22 20		22 44		22 50	23 14	23 20	
Westcliff d	20 23	20 46		20 53	21 01				21 16		21 23	21 46		21 53	22 16		22 23		22 46		22 53	23 16	23 23	
Chalkwell d	20 25	20 48		20 55	21 03				21 18		21 25	21 48		21 55	22 18		22 25		22 48		22 55	23 18	23 25	
Leigh-on-Sea d	20 28	20 51		20 58	21 06				21 21		21 28	21 51		21 58	22 21		22 28		22 51		22 58	23 21	23 28	
Benfleet d	20 32	20 55		21 02	21 10				21 25		21 32	21 55		22 02	22 25		22 32		22 55		23 02	23 25	23 32	
Pitsea d	20 36	20 59		21 06					21 29		21 36	21 59		22 06	22 29		22 36		22 59		23 06	23 29	23 36	
Stanford-le-Hope d	20 42			21 12							21 42			22 12			22 42				23 12		23 42	
East Tilbury d	20 45			21 15							21 45			22 15			22 45				23 15		23 45	
Tilbury Town 8 d	20 51			21 21							21 51			22 21			22 51				23 21		23 51	
Grays d	20 54		21 18	21 24						21 48	21 54		22 18	22 24		22 48	22 54			23 18	23 24		23 54	
Purfleet d			21 23							21 53			22 23			22 53				23 23				
Rainham d			21 28							21 58			22 28			22 58				23 28				
Dagenham Dock d			21 32							22 02			22 32			23 02				23 32				
Basildon d		21 02			21 16				21 32			22 02			22 32				23 02			23 32		
Laindon d		21 05			21 19				21 35			22 05			22 35				23 05			23 35		
West Horndon d		21 10							21 40			22 10			22 40				23 10			23 40		
Chafford Hundred d	20 59			21 29							21 59			22 29			23 02				23 32		00 02	
Ockendon d	21 02			21 32			←				22 02			22 32			23 05				23 35		00 05	
Upminster ⊖ d	21 09	21 16		21 39	21 28	←	21 39		21 46		22 09	22 16		22 39	22 46		23 12		23 16		23 42	23 46	00 11	
Barking ⊖ d	21 17	21 24	21 38	→	21 36	21 38	21 47		21 54	22 08	22 17	22 24	22 38	22 47	22 54	23 08	23 20		23 24	23 39	23 50	23 55	00 20	
Stratford 7 ⊖ a			→																					
London Liverpool St 15 ⊖ a																								
West Ham ⊖ d	21 23	21 30			21 42	21 44	21 53		22 03	22 17	22 25	22 32	22 47	22 55	23 03	23 18	23 28		23 33	23 48	23 58	00 03	00 30	
Limehouse d	21 28	21 35				21 49	21 58		22 08	22 22	22 31	22 38	22 52	23 01	23 08	23 23	23 34		23 38	23 53	00 03	00 09	00 35	
London Fenchurch St 7 ⊖ a	21 34	21 42			21 53	21 56	22 04		22 15	22 29	22 37	22 44	22 59	23 07	23 15	23 30	23 40		23 45	23 59	00 09	00 15	00 42	

from 15 September

Shoeburyness and Southend Central - London

Network Diagram - see first page of Table I

	CC	CC	CC	CC	CC	CC	CC	CC	CC		CC	CC	CC	CC	CC	CC	CC	CC	CC		CC	CC	CC	CC
Shoeburyness d			23p05		04 20		05 05				05 35			06 05			06 35				07 05			07 35
Thorpe Bay d			23p09		04 23		05 08				05 38			06 08			06 38				07 08			07 38
Southend East d			23p12		04 26		05 11				05 41			06 11			06 41				07 11			07 41
Southend Central a			23p14		04 28		05 13				05 43			06 13			06 43				07 13			07 43
d	22p50		23p15		04 29		05 14		05 20		05 44		05 50	06 14		06 20	06 44		06 50		07 14		07 20	07 44
Westcliff d	22p53		23p17		04 31		05 16		05 23		05 46		05 53	06 16		06 23	06 46		06 53		07 16		07 23	07 46
Chalkwell d	22p55		23p19		04 33		05 18		05 25		05 48		05 55	06 18		06 25	06 48		06 55		07 18		07 25	07 48
Leigh-on-Sea d	22p58		23p22		04 36		05 21		05 28		05 51		05 58	06 21		06 28	06 51		06 58		07 21		07 28	07 51
Benfleet d	23p03		23p27		04 40		05 25		05 32		05 55		06 02	06 25		06 32	06 55		07 02		07 25		07 32	07 55
Pitsea d	23p07		23p32		04 44		05 29		05 36		05 59		06 06	06 29		06 36	06 59		07 06		07 29		07 36	07 59
Stanford-le-Hope d	23p14			04 29					05 42				06 12			06 42			07 12				07 42	
East Tilbury d	23p18			04 32					05 45				06 15			06 45			07 15				07 45	
Tilbury Town 8 d	23p24			04 38					05 51				06 21			06 51			07 21				07 51	
Grays d	23p27	23p33		04 41				05 48	05 54			06 18	06 24		06 48	06 54		07 18	07 24			07 48	07 54	
Purfleet d		23p38						05 53				06 23			06 53			07 23				07 53		
Rainham d		23p43						05 58				06 28			06 58			07 28				07 58		
Dagenham Dock d		23p47						06 02				06 32			07 02			07 32				08 02		
Basildon d			23p36		04 47		05 32				06 02			06 32			07 02				07 32			08 02
Laindon d			23p39		04 50		05 35				06 05			06 35			07 05				07 35			08 05
West Horndon d			23p44		04 55		05 40				06 10			06 40			07 10				07 40			08 10
Chafford Hundred d	23p31			04 45					05 59				06 29			06 59			07 29				07 59	
Ockendon d	23p35			04 49		05 16			06 02				06 32			07 02			07 32				08 02	
Upminster ⊖ d	23p42		23p50	04a57	05 02	05a23	05 46		06 09		06 16		06 39	06 46		07 09	07 16		07 39		07 46		08 09	08 16
Barking ⊖ d	23p50	23p55	23p58		05 10		05 54	06 08	06 17		06 24	06 38	06 47	06 54	07 08	07 17	07 24	07 38	07 47		07 54	08 08	08 17	08 24
Stratford 7 ⊖ a		00 09																						
London Liverpool St 15 ⊖ a		00 20																						
West Ham ⊖ d	23p56		00 04		05 16		06 00	06 14	06 23		06 30	06 44	06 53	07 00	07 14	07 23	07 30	07 44	07 53		08 00	08 14	08 23	08 30
Limehouse d	00 01		00 09		05 21		06 05	06 19	06 28		06 35	06 49	06 58	07 05	07 19	07 28	07 35	07 49	07 58		08 05	08 19	08 28	08 35
London Fenchurch St 7 ⊖ a	00 05		00 13		05 27		06 12	06 26	06 34		06 42	06 56	07 04	07 12	07 26	07 34	07 42	07 56	08 04		08 12	08 26	08 34	08 42

	CC	CC	CC	CC	CC		CC	CC	CC	CC	CC	CC	CC	CC	CC		CC	CC	CC	CC	CC	CC	CC	CC
Shoeburyness d			07 50				08 05			08 20			08 35				08 50			09 05			09 20	
Thorpe Bay d			07 53				08 08			08 23			08 38				08 53			09 08			09 23	
Southend East d			07 56				08 11			08 26			08 41				08 56			09 11			09 26	
Southend Central a			07 58				08 13			08 28			08 43				08 58			09 13			09 28	
d		07 50	07 59				08 14		08 20	08 29			08 44		08 50		08 59			09 14		09 20	09 29	
Westcliff d		07 53	08 01				08 16		08 23	08 31			08 46		08 53		09 01			09 16		09 23	09 31	
Chalkwell d		07 55	08 03				08 18		08 25	08 33			08 48		08 55		09 03			09 18		09 25	09 33	
Leigh-on-Sea d		07 58	08 06				08 21		08 28	08 36			08 51		08 58		09 06			09 21		09 28	09 36	
Benfleet d		08 02	08 10				08 25		08 32	08 40			08 55		09 02		09 10			09 25		09 32	09 40	
Pitsea d		08 06					08 29		08 36				08 59		09 06					09 29		09 36		
Stanford-le-Hope d		08 12							08 42						09 12							09 42		
East Tilbury d		08 15							08 45						09 15							09 45		
Tilbury Town 8 d		08 21							08 51						09 21							09 51		
Grays d	08 18	08 24						08 48	08 54					09 18	09 24						09 48	09 54		
Purfleet d	08 23							08 53						09 23							09 53			
Rainham d	08 28							08 58						09 28							09 58			
Dagenham Dock d	08 32							09 02						09 32							10 02			
Basildon d			08 16				08 32			08 46			09 02				09 16			09 32			09 46	
Laindon d			08 19				08 35			08 49			09 05				09 19			09 35			09 49	
West Horndon d							08 40						09 10							09 40				
Chafford Hundred d		08 29							08 59						09 29							09 59		
Ockendon d		08 32			←				09 02			←			09 32				←			10 02		
Upminster ⊖ d		08 39	08 28	←	08 39		08 46		09 09	08 58	←	09 09	09 16		09 39		09 28	←	09 39	09 46		10 09	09 58	←
Barking ⊖ d	08 38	→	08 36	08 38	08 47		08 54	09 08	→	09 06	09 08	09 17	09 24	09 38	→		09 36	09 38	09 47	09 54	10 08	→	10 06	10 08
Stratford 7 ⊖ a	→							→						→							→			
London Liverpool St 15 ⊖ a																								
West Ham ⊖ d			08 42	08 44	08 53		09 00			09 12	09 14	09 23	09 30				09 42	09 44	09 53	10 00			10 12	10 14
Limehouse d				08 49	08 58		09 05				09 19	09 28	09 35					09 49	09 58	10 05				10 19
London Fenchurch St 7 ⊖ a			08 53	08 56	09 04		09 12			09 23	09 26	09 34	09 42				09 53	09 56	10 04	10 12			10 23	10 26

	CC		CC	CC	CC	CC	CC	CC	CC	CC	CC		CC	CC	CC	CC	CC	CC	CC	CC	CC		CC	CC
Shoeburyness d			09 35			09 50			10 05				10 20			10 35			10 50				11 05	
Thorpe Bay d			09 38			09 53			10 08				10 23			10 38			10 53				11 08	
Southend East d			09 41			09 56			10 11				10 26			10 41			10 56				11 11	
Southend Central a			09 43			09 58			10 13				10 28			10 43			10 58				11 13	
d			09 44		09 50	09 59			10 14		10 20		10 29			10 44		10 50	10 59				11 14	
Westcliff d			09 46		09 53	10 01			10 16		10 23		10 31			10 46		10 53	11 01				11 16	
Chalkwell d			09 48		09 55	10 03			10 18		10 25		10 33			10 48		10 55	11 03				11 18	
Leigh-on-Sea d			09 51		09 58	10 06			10 21		10 28		10 36			10 51		10 58	11 06				11 21	
Benfleet d			09 55		10 02	10 10			10 25		10 32		10 40			10 55		11 02	11 10				11 25	
Pitsea d			09 59		10 06				10 29		10 36					10 59		11 06					11 29	
Stanford-le-Hope d					10 12						10 42							11 12						
East Tilbury d					10 15						10 45							11 15						
Tilbury Town 8 d					10 21						10 51							11 21						
Grays d				10 18	10 24					10 48	10 54						11 18	11 24						11 48
Purfleet d				10 23						10 53							11 23							11 53
Rainham d				10 28						10 58							11 28							11 58
Dagenham Dock d				10 32						11 02							11 32							12 02
Basildon d			10 02			10 16			10 32				10 46			11 02			11 16				11 32	
Laindon d			10 05			10 19			10 35				10 49			11 05			11 19				11 35	
West Horndon d			10 10						10 40							11 10							11 40	
Chafford Hundred d					10 29						10 59							11 29						
Ockendon d	←				10 32			←			11 02				←			11 32			←			
Upminster ⊖ d	10 09		10 16		10 39	10 28	←	10 39	10 46		11 09		10 58	←	11 09	11 16		11 39	11 28	←	11 39		11 46	
Barking ⊖ d	10 17		10 24	10 38	→	10 36	10 38	10 47	10 54	11 08	→		11 06	11 08	11 17	11 24	11 38	→	11 36	11 38	11 47		11 54	12 08
Stratford 7 ⊖ a				→						→							→							→
London Liverpool St 15 ⊖ a																								
West Ham ⊖ d	10 23		10 30			10 42	10 44	10 53	11 00				11 12	11 14	11 23	11 30			11 42	11 44	11 53		12 00	
Limehouse d	10 28		10 35				10 49	10 58	11 05					11 19	11 28	11 35				11 49	11 58		12 05	
London Fenchurch St 7 ⊖ a	10 34		10 42			10 53	10 56	11 04	11 12				11 23	11 26	11 34	11 42			11 53	11 56	12 04		12 12	

Shoeburyness and Southend Central - London

Network Diagram - see first page of Table 1

		CC	CC	CC	CC	CC	CC	CC		CC	CC	CC	CC	CC	CC	CC	CC	CC		CC	CC	CC	CC	CC	CC
Shoeburyness	d		11 20			11 35				11 50			12 05			12 20				12 35			12 50		
Thorpe Bay	d		11 23			11 38				11 53			12 08			12 23				12 38			12 53		
Southend East	d		11 26			11 41				11 56			12 11			12 26				12 41			12 56		
Southend Central	a		11 28			11 43				11 58			12 13			12 28				12 43			12 58		
	d	11 20	11 29			11 44		11 50		11 59			12 14		12 20	12 29				12 44		12 50	12 59		
Westcliff	d	11 23	11 31			11 46		11 53		12 01			12 16		12 23	12 31				12 46		12 53	13 01		
Chalkwell	d	11 25	11 33			11 48		11 55		12 03			12 18		12 25	12 33				12 48		12 55	13 03		
Leigh-on-Sea	d	11 28	11 36			11 51		11 58		12 06			12 21		12 28	12 36				12 51		12 58	13 06		
Benfleet	d	11 32	11 40			11 55		12 02		12 10			12 25		12 32	12 40				12 55		13 02	13 10		
Pitsea	d	11 36				11 59		12 06					12 29		12 36					12 59		13 06			
Stanford-le-Hope	d	11 42						12 12							12 42							13 12			
East Tilbury	d	11 45						12 15							12 45							13 15			
Tilbury Town	d	11 51						12 21							12 51							13 21			
Grays	d	11 54					12 18	12 24						12 48	12 54						13 18	13 24			
Purfleet	d						12 23							12 53							13 23				
Rainham	d						12 28							12 58							13 28				
Dagenham Dock	d						12 32							13 02							13 32				
Basildon	d		11 46			12 02				12 16			12 32			12 46				13 02			13 16		
Laindon	d		11 49			12 05				12 19			12 35			12 49				13 05			13 19		
West Horndon	d					12 10							12 40							13 10					
Chafford Hundred	d	11 59						12 29							12 59							13 29			
Ockendon	d	12 01			←			12 32				←			13 02			←				13 32			←
Upminster ⊖	d	12 09	11 58	←	12 09	12 16		12 39		12 28	←	12 39	12 46		13 09	12 58	←	13 09		13 16		13 39	13 28	←	13 39
Barking ⊖	d	→	12 06	12 08	12 17	12 24	12 38	→		12 36	12 38	12 47	12 54	13 08	→	13 06	13 08	13 17		13 24	13 38	→	13 36	13 38	13 47
Stratford ⊖	a						→							→							→				
London Liverpool St ⊖	a																								
West Ham ⊖	d		12 12	12 14	12 23	12 30				12 42	12 44	12 53	13 00			13 12	13 14	13 23		13 30			13 42	13 44	13 53
Limehouse	d			12 19	12 28	12 35					12 49	12 58	13 05				13 19	13 28		13 35				13 49	13 58
London Fenchurch St ⊖	a		12 23	12 26	12 34	12 42				12 53	12 56	13 04	13 12			13 23	13 26	13 34		13 42			13 53	13 56	14 04

		CC	CC	CC		CC	CC	CC	CC	CC	CC	CC	CC	CC		CC	CC	CC	CC	CC	CC	CC	CC	CC	
Shoeburyness	d	13 05				13 20			13 35			13 50				14 05			14 20			14 35			
Thorpe Bay	d	13 08				13 23			13 38			13 53				14 08			14 23			14 38			
Southend East	d	13 11				13 26			13 41			13 56				14 11			14 26			14 41			
Southend Central	a	13 13				13 28			13 43			13 58				14 13			14 28			14 43			
	d	13 14		13 20		13 29			13 44		13 50	13 59				14 14		14 20	14 29			14 44		14 50	
Westcliff	d	13 16		13 23		13 31			13 46		13 53	14 01				14 16		14 23	14 31			14 46		14 53	
Chalkwell	d	13 18		13 25		13 33			13 48		13 55	14 03				14 18		14 25	14 33			14 48		14 55	
Leigh-on-Sea	d	13 21		13 28		13 36			13 51		13 58	14 06				14 21		14 28	14 36			14 51		14 58	
Benfleet	d	13 25		13 32		13 40			13 55		14 02	14 10				14 25		14 32	14 40			14 55		15 02	
Pitsea	d	13 29		13 36					13 59		14 06					14 29		14 36				14 59		15 06	
Stanford-le-Hope	d			13 42							14 12							14 42						15 12	
East Tilbury	d			13 45							14 15							14 45						15 15	
Tilbury Town	d			13 51							14 21							14 51						15 21	
Grays	d		13 48	13 54						14 18	14 24						14 48	14 54					15 18	15 24	
Purfleet	d		13 53							14 23							14 53						15 23		
Rainham	d		13 58							14 28							14 58						15 28		
Dagenham Dock	d		14 02							14 32							15 02						15 32		
Basildon	d	13 32				13 46			14 02			14 16				14 32			14 46			15 02			
Laindon	d	13 35				13 49			14 05			14 19				14 35			14 49			15 05			
West Horndon	d	13 40							14 10							14 40						15 10			
Chafford Hundred	d			13 59							14 29							14 59						15 29	
Ockendon	d			14 02				←			14 32			←				15 02			←			15 32	
Upminster ⊖	d	13 46		14 09		13 58	←	14 09	14 16		14 39	14 28	←	14 39		14 46		15 09	14 58	←	15 09	15 16		15 39	
Barking ⊖	d	13 54	14 08	→		14 06	14 08	14 17	14 24	14 38	→	14 36	14 38	14 47		14 54	15 08	→	15 06	15 08	15 17	15 24	15 38	→	
Stratford ⊖	a		→							→							→						→		
London Liverpool St ⊖	a																								
West Ham ⊖	d	14 00				14 12	14 14	14 23	14 30			14 42	14 44	14 53		15 00			15 12	15 14	15 23	15 30			
Limehouse	d	14 05					14 19	14 28	14 35				14 49	14 58		15 05				15 19	15 28	15 35			
London Fenchurch St ⊖	a	14 12				14 23	14 26	14 34	14 42			14 53	14 56	15 04		15 12			15 23	15 26	15 34	15 42			

		CC	CC	CC	CC	CC	CC	CC	CC	CC		CC	CC	CC	CC	CC	CC	CC	CC	CC		CC	CC	CC	CC
Shoeburyness	d	14 50			15 05			15 20				15 35			15 50			16 05				16 20			16 35
Thorpe Bay	d	14 53			15 08			15 23				15 38			15 53			16 08				16 23			16 38
Southend East	d	14 56			15 11			15 26				15 41			15 56			16 11				16 26			16 41
Southend Central	a	14 58			15 13			15 28				15 43			15 58			16 13				16 28			16 43
	d	14 59			15 14		15 20	15 29				15 44		15 50	15 59			16 14		16 20		16 29			16 44
Westcliff	d	15 01			15 16		15 23	15 31				15 46		15 53	16 01			16 16		16 23		16 31			16 46
Chalkwell	d	15 03			15 18		15 25	15 33				15 48		15 55	16 03			16 18		16 25		16 33			16 48
Leigh-on-Sea	d	15 06			15 21		15 28	15 36				15 51		15 58	16 06			16 21		16 28		16 36			16 51
Benfleet	d	15 10			15 25		15 32	15 40				15 55		16 02	16 10			16 25		16 32		16 40			16 55
Pitsea	d				15 29		15 36					15 59		16 06				16 29		16 36					16 59
Stanford-le-Hope	d						15 42							16 12						16 42					
East Tilbury	d						15 45							16 15						16 45					
Tilbury Town	d						15 51							16 21						16 51					
Grays	d					15 48	15 54						16 18	16 24					16 48	16 54					
Purfleet	d					15 53							16 23						16 53						
Rainham	d					15 58							16 28						16 58						
Dagenham Dock	d					16 02							16 32						17 02						
Basildon	d	15 16			15 32			15 46				16 02			16 16			16 32				16 46			17 02
Laindon	d	15 19			15 35			15 49				16 05			16 19			16 35				16 49			17 05
West Horndon	d				15 40							16 10						16 40							17 10
Chafford Hundred	d						15 59							16 29						16 59					
Ockendon	d			←			16 02			←				16 32			←			17 02				←	
Upminster ⊖	d	15 28	←	15 39	15 46		16 09	15 58	←	16 09		16 16		16 39	16 28	←	16 39	16 46		17 09		16 58	←	17 09	17 16
Barking ⊖	d	15 36	15 38	15 47	15 54	16 08	→	16 06	16 08	16 17		16 24	16 38	→	16 36	16 38	16 47	16 54	17 08	→		17 06	17 08	17 17	17 24
Stratford ⊖	a					→							→						→						
London Liverpool St ⊖	a																								
West Ham ⊖	d	15 42	15 44	15 53	16 00			16 12	16 14	16 23		16 30			16 42	16 44	16 53	17 00				17 12	17 14	17 23	17 30
Limehouse	d		15 49	15 58	16 05				16 19	16 28		16 35				16 49	16 58	17 05					17 19	17 28	17 35
London Fenchurch St ⊖	a	15 53	15 56	16 04	16 12			16 23	16 26	16 34		16 42			16 53	16 56	17 04	17 12				17 23	17 26	17 34	17 42

Table 1 — Saturdays from 15 September

Shoeburyness and Southend Central - London

Network Diagram - see first page of Table 1

		CC	CC	CC	CC	CC		CC	CC	CC	CC	CC	CC	CC	CC	CC		CC	CC	CC	CC	CC	CC	CC	CC
Shoeburyness	d			16 50				17 05			17 20			17 35				17 50			18 05			18 20	
Thorpe Bay	d			16 53				17 08			17 23			17 38				17 53			18 08			18 23	
Southend East	d			16 56				17 11			17 26			17 41				17 56			18 11			18 26	
Southend Central	a			16 58				17 13			17 28			17 43				17 58			18 13			18 28	
	d		16 50	16 59				17 14		17 20	17 29			17 44		17 50		17 59			18 14		18 20	18 29	
Westcliff	d		16 53	17 01				17 16		17 23	17 31			17 46		17 53		18 01			18 16		18 23	18 31	
Chalkwell	d		16 55	17 03				17 18		17 25	17 33			17 48		17 55		18 03			18 18		18 25	18 33	
Leigh-on-Sea	d		16 58	17 06				17 21		17 28	17 36			17 51		17 58		18 06			18 21		18 28	18 36	
Benfleet	d		17 02	17 10				17 25		17 32	17 40			17 55		18 02		18 10			18 25		18 32	18 40	
Pitsea	d		17 06					17 29		17 36				17 59		18 06					18 29		18 36		
Stanford-le-Hope	d		17 12							17 42						18 12							18 42		
East Tilbury	d		17 15							17 45						18 15							18 45		
Tilbury Town	d		17 21							17 51						18 21							18 51		
Grays	d	17 18	17 24						17 48	17 54					18 18	18 24						18 48	18 54		
Purfleet	d	17 23							17 53						18 23							18 53			
Rainham	d	17 28							17 58						18 28							18 58			
Dagenham Dock	d	17 32							18 02						18 32							19 02			
Basildon	d			17 16				17 32			17 46			18 02				18 16			18 32			18 46	
Laindon	d			17 19				17 35			17 49			18 05				18 19			18 35			18 49	
West Horndon	d							17 40						18 10							18 40				
Chafford Hundred	d		17 29							17 59						18 29							18 59		
Ockendon	d		17 32			←				18 02			←			18 32				←			19 02		
Upminster ⊖	d		17 39	17 28	←	17 39		17 46		18 09	17 58	←	18 09	18 16		18 39		18 28	←	18 39	18 46		19 09	18 58	←
Barking ⊖	d	17 38	→	17 36	17 38	17 47		17 54	18 08	→	18 06	18 08	18 17	18 24	18 38	→		18 36	18 38	18 47	18 54	19 08	→	19 06	19 08
Stratford ⊖	a	→							→						→							→			
London Liverpool St ⊖	a																								
West Ham ⊖	d			17 42	17 44	17 53		18 00			18 12	18 14	18 23	18 30				18 42	18 44	18 53	19 00			19 12	19 14
Limehouse	d				17 49	17 58		18 05				18 19	18 28	18 35					18 49	18 58	19 05				19 19
London Fenchurch St ⊖	a			17 53	17 56	18 04		18 12			18 23	18 26	18 34	18 42				18 53	18 56	19 04	19 12			19 23	19 26

		CC		CC	CC	CC	CC	CC	CC	CC	CC	CC		CC	CC	CC	CC	CC	CC	CC	CC	CC		CC	CC
Shoeburyness	d			18 35			18 50			19 05				19 20			19 35			19 50				20 05	
Thorpe Bay	d			18 38			18 53			19 08				19 23			19 38			19 53				20 08	
Southend East	d			18 41			18 56			19 11				19 26			19 41			19 56				20 11	
Southend Central	a			18 43			18 58			19 13				19 28			19 43			19 58				20 13	
	d			18 44		18 50	18 59			19 14		19 20		19 29			19 44		19 50	19 59				20 14	
Westcliff	d			18 46		18 53	19 01			19 16		19 23		19 31			19 46		19 53	20 01				20 16	
Chalkwell	d			18 48		18 55	19 03			19 18		19 25		19 33			19 48		19 55	20 03				20 18	
Leigh-on-Sea	d			18 51		18 58	19 06			19 21		19 28		19 36			19 51		19 58	20 06				20 21	
Benfleet	d			18 55		19 02	19 10			19 25		19 32		19 40			19 55		20 02	20 10				20 25	
Pitsea	d			18 59		19 06				19 29		19 36					19 59		20 06					20 29	
Stanford-le-Hope	d					19 12						19 42							20 12						
East Tilbury	d					19 15						19 45							20 15						
Tilbury Town	d					19 21						19 51							20 21						
Grays	d				19 18	19 24					19 48	19 54						20 18	20 24						20 48
Purfleet	d				19 23						19 53							20 23							20 53
Rainham	d				19 28						19 58							20 28							20 58
Dagenham Dock	d				19 32						20 02							20 32							21 02
Basildon	d			19 02			19 16			19 32				19 46			20 02			20 16				20 32	
Laindon	d			19 05			19 19			19 35				19 49			20 05			20 19				20 35	
West Horndon	d			19 10						19 40							20 10							20 40	
Chafford Hundred	d					19 29						19 59							20 29						
Ockendon	d	←				19 32			←			20 02				←			20 32			←			
Upminster ⊖	d	19 09		19 16		19 39	19 28	←	19 39	19 46		20 09		19 58	←	20 09	20 16		20 39	20 28	←	20 39		20 46	
Barking ⊖	d	19 17		19 24	19 38	→	19 36	19 38	19 47	19 54	20 08	→		20 06	20 08	20 17	20 24	20 38	→	20 36	20 38	20 47		20 54	21 08
Stratford ⊖	a				→						→							→							
London Liverpool St ⊖	a																								
West Ham ⊖	d	19 23		19 30			19 42	19 44	19 53	20 00				20 12	20 14	20 23	20 30			20 42	20 44	20 53		21 00	21 14
Limehouse	d	19 28		19 35				19 49	19 58	20 05					20 19	20 28	20 35				20 49	20 58		21 05	21 19
London Fenchurch St ⊖	a	19 34		19 42			19 53	19 56	20 04	20 12				20 23	20 26	20 34	20 42			20 53	20 56	21 04		21 12	21 26

		CC	CC	CC	CC	CC	CC	CC		CC	CC	CC	CC	CC	CC	CC	CC	CC		CC	CC	CC	CC	CC	
Shoeburyness	d		20 35			20 50				21 05			21 35			22 05				22 35			23 05		
Thorpe Bay	d		20 38			20 53				21 08			21 38			22 08				22 38			23 08		
Southend East	d		20 41			20 56				21 11			21 41			22 11				22 41			23 11		
Southend Central	a		20 43			20 58				21 13			21 43			22 13				22 43			23 13		
	d	20 20	20 44		20 50	20 59				21 14		21 20	21 44		21 50	22 14		22 20		22 44		22 50	23 14	23 20	
Westcliff	d	20 23	20 46		20 53	21 01				21 16		21 23	21 46		21 53	22 16		22 23		22 46		22 53	23 16	23 23	
Chalkwell	d	20 25	20 48		20 55	21 03				21 18		21 25	21 48		21 55	22 18		22 25		22 48		22 55	23 18	23 25	
Leigh-on-Sea	d	20 28	20 51		20 58	21 06				21 21		21 28	21 51		21 58	22 21		22 28		22 51		22 58	23 21	23 28	
Benfleet	d	20 32	20 55		21 02	21 10				21 25		21 32	21 55		22 02	22 25		22 32		22 55		23 02	23 25	23 32	
Pitsea	d	20 36	20 59		21 06					21 29		21 36	21 59		22 06	22 29		22 36		22 59		23 06	23 29	23 36	
Stanford-le-Hope	d	20 42			21 12							21 42			22 12			22 42				23 12		23 42	
East Tilbury	d	20 45			21 15							21 45			22 15			22 45				23 15		23 45	
Tilbury Town	d	20 51			21 21							21 51			22 21			22 51				23 21		23 51	
Grays	d	20 54		21 18	21 24						21 48	21 54		22 18	22 24		22 48	22 54			23 18	23 24		23 54	
Purfleet	d			21 23							21 53			22 23			22 53				23 23				
Rainham	d			21 28							21 58			22 28			22 58				23 28				
Dagenham Dock	d			21 32							22 02			22 32			23 02				23 32				
Basildon	d		21 02			21 16				21 32			22 02			22 32				23 02			23 32		
Laindon	d		21 05			21 19				21 35			22 05			22 35				23 05			23 35		
West Horndon	d		21 10							21 40			22 10			22 40				23 10			23 40		
Chafford Hundred	d	20 59			21 29							21 59			22 29			22 59				23 29		23 59	
Ockendon	d	21 02			21 32			←				22 02			22 32			23 02				23 32		00 02	
Upminster ⊖	d	21 09	21 16		21 39	21 28	←	21 39		21 46		22 09	22 16		22 39	22 46		23 09		23 16		23 39	23 46	00 08	
Barking ⊖	d	21 17	21 24	21 38	→	21 36	21 38	21 47		21 54	22 08	22 17	22 24	22 38	22 47	22 54	23 08	23 17		23 24	23a39	23 47	23 55	00a18	
Stratford ⊖	a			→																					
London Liverpool St ⊖	a																								
West Ham ⊖	d	21 23	21 30			21 42	21 44	21 53		22 00	22 14	22 23	22 30	22 44	22 53	23 00	23 14	23 23		23 30		23 53	00 01		
Limehouse	d	21 28	21 35				21 49	21 58		22 05	22 19	22 28	22 35	22 49	22 58	23 05	23 19	23 28		23 35		23 58	00 06		
London Fenchurch St ⊖	a	21 34	21 42			21 53	21 56	22 04		22 12	22 26	22 34	22 42	22 56	23 04	23 12	23 26	23 34		23 42		00 04	00 12		

Shoeburyness and Southend Central - London

Sundays

until 22 July

Network Diagram - see first page of Table 1

		CC	CC	CC	CC	CC	CC	CC	CC	CC		CC	CC	CC	CC	CC	CC		CC		CC	CC	CC	CC
Shoeburyness	d		23p05		05 35	06 05	06 11	06 35	07 05	07 11		07 35	08 05			08 35					21 05			21 35
Thorpe Bay	d		23p08		05 38	06 08	06 14	06 38	07 08	07 14		07 38	08 08			08 38					21 08			21 38
Southend East	d		23p11		05 41	06 11	06 17	06 41	07 11	07 17		07 41	08 11			08 41					21 11			21 41
Southend Central	a		23p13		05 43	06 13	06 19	06 43	07 13	07 19		07 43	08 13			08 43					21 13			21 43
	d	22p50	23p14	23p20	05 44	06 14	06 20	06 44	07 14	07 20		07 44	08 14	08 20		08 44	08 50		20 50		21 14	21 20		21 44
Westcliff	d	22p53	23p16	23p23	05 46	06 16	06 23	06 46	07 16	07 23		07 46	08 16	08 23		08 46	08 53		20 53		21 16	21 23		21 46
Chalkwell	d	22p55	23p18	23p25	05 48	06 18	06 25	06 48	07 18	07 25		07 48	08 18	08 25		08 48	08 55		20 55		21 18	21 25		21 48
Leigh-on-Sea	d	22p58	23p21	23p28	05 51	06 21	06 28	06 51	07 21	07 28		07 51	08 21	08 28		08 51	08 58		20 58		21 21	21 28		21 51
Benfleet	d	23p02	23p25	23p32	05 55	06 25	06 32	06 55	07 25	07 32		07 55	08 25	08 32		08 55	09 02		21 02		21 25	21 32		21 55
Pitsea	d	23p06	23p29	23p36	05 59	06 29	06 36	06 59	07 29	07 36		07 59	08 29	08 36		08 59	09 06		21 06		21 29	21 36		21 59
Stanford-le-Hope	d	23p12		23p42			06 42			07 42				08 42			09 12	and at the same minutes past each hour until	21 12			21 42		
East Tilbury	d	23p15		23p45			06 45			07 45				08 45			09 15		21 15			21 45		
Tilbury Town 3	d	23p21		23p51			06 51			07 51				08 51			09 21		21 21			21 51		
Grays	d	23p24		23p54			06 54			07 54				08 54	08 59		09 24		21 24			21 54	21 59	
Purfleet	d														09 04								22 04	
Rainham	d														09 09								22 09	
Dagenham Dock	d														09 13								22 13	
Basildon	d		23p32		06 02	06 32		07 02	07 32			08 02	08 32			09 02					21 32			22 02
Laindon	d		23p35		06 05	06 35		07 05	07 35			08 05	08 35			09 05					21 35			22 05
West Horndon	d		23p40		06 10	06 40		07 10	07 40			08 10	08 40			09 10					21 40			22 10
Chafford Hundred	d	23p29		23p59			06 59			07 59				08 59			09 29		21 29			21 59		
Ockendon	d	23p32		00 02			07 02			08 02				09 02			09 32		21 32			22 02		
Upminster ⊖	d	23p39	23p46	00 08	06 16	06 46	07 09	07 16	07 46	08 09		08 16	08 46	09 09		09 16	09 39		21 39		21 46	22 09		22 16
Barking ⊖	d	23p47	23p55	00a18	06 25	06 55	07 17	07 25	07 55	08 17		08 25	08 55	09 17	09a20	09 25	09 47		21 47		21 55	22 17	22a20	22 25
Stratford 7 ⊖	a																							
London Liverpool St 15 ⊖	a																							
West Ham ⊖	d	23p53	00 01		06 31	07 01	07 23	07 31	08 01	08 23		08 31	09 01	09 23		09 31	09 53		21 53		22 01	22 23		22 31
Limehouse	d	23p58	00 06		06 36	07 06	07 28	07 36	08 06	08 28		08 36	09 06	09 28		09 36	09 58		21 58		22 06	22 28		22 36
London Fenchurch St 7 ⊖	a	00 04	00 12		06 42	07 12	07 34	07 42	08 12	08 34		08 42	09 12	09 34		09 42	10 04		22 04		22 12	22 34		22 42

		CC	CC	CC
Shoeburyness	d	22 05		22 35
Thorpe Bay	d	22 08		22 38
Southend East	d	22 11		22 41
Southend Central	a	22 13		22 43
	d	22 14	22 20	22 44
Westcliff	d	22 16	22 23	22 46
Chalkwell	d	22 18	22 25	22 48
Leigh-on-Sea	d	22 21	22 28	22 51
Benfleet	d	22 25	22 32	22 55
Pitsea	d	22 29	22 36	22 59
Stanford-le-Hope	d		22 42	
East Tilbury	d		22 45	
Tilbury Town 3	d		22 51	
Grays	d		22 54	
Purfleet	d			
Rainham	d			
Dagenham Dock	d			
Basildon	d	22 32		23 02
Laindon	d	22 35		23 05
West Horndon	d	22 40		23 10
Chafford Hundred	d		22 59	
Ockendon	d		23 02	
Upminster ⊖	d	22 46	23 09	23 16
Barking ⊖	d	22 55	23 17	23 25
Stratford 7 ⊖	a			
London Liverpool St 15 ⊖	a			
West Ham ⊖	d	23 01	23 23	23 31
Limehouse	d	23 06	23 28	23 36
London Fenchurch St 7 ⊖	a	23 12	23 34	23 42

Shoeburyness and Southend Central - London

Sundays

29 July to 12 August

Network Diagram - see first page of Table 1

		CC	CC	CC	CC	CC	CC	CC	CC	CC		CC	CC	CC	CC	CC	CC		CC		CC	CC A	CC A	CC
Shoeburyness	d		23p05		05 35	06 05	06 11	06 35	07 05	07 11		07 35	08 05			08 35					14 05			
Thorpe Bay	d		23p08		05 38	06 08	06 14	06 38	07 08	07 14		07 38	08 08			08 38					14 08			
Southend East	d		23p11		05 41	06 11	06 17	06 41	07 11	07 17		07 41	08 11			08 41					14 11			
Southend Central	a		23p13		05 43	06 13	06 19	06 43	07 13	07 19		07 43	08 13			08 43					14 13			
	d	22p50	23p14	23p20	05 44	06 14	06 20	06 44	07 14	07 20		07 44	08 14	08 20		08 44	08 50		13 50		14 14			14 20
Westcliff	d	22p53	23p16	23p23	05 46	06 16	06 23	06 46	07 16	07 23		07 46	08 16	08 23		08 46	08 53		13 53		14 16			14 23
Chalkwell	d	22p55	23p18	23p25	05 48	06 18	06 25	06 48	07 18	07 25		07 48	08 18	08 25		08 48	08 55		13 55		14 18			14 25
Leigh-on-Sea	d	22p58	23p21	23p28	05 51	06 21	06 28	06 51	07 21	07 28		07 51	08 21	08 28		08 51	08 58		13 58		14 21	14 35	14 45	14 28
Benfleet	d	23p02	23p25	23p32	05 55	06 25	06 32	06 55	07 25	07 32		07 55	08 25	08 32		08 55	09 02		14 02		14 25			14 32
Pitsea	d	23p06	23p29	23p36	05 59	06 29	06 36	06 59	07 29	07 36		07 59	08 29	08 36		08 59	09 06		14 06		14 29			14 36
Stanford-le-Hope	d	23p12		23p42			06 42			07 42				08 42			09 12	and at the same minutes past each hour until	14 12					14 42
East Tilbury	d	23p15		23p45			06 45			07 45				08 45			09 15		14 15					14 45
Tilbury Town 3	d	23p21		23p51			06 51			07 51				08 51			09 21		14 21					14 51
Grays	d	23p24		23p54			06 54			07 54				08 54	08 59		09 24		14 24					14 54
Purfleet	d														09 04									
Rainham	d														09 09									
Dagenham Dock	d														09 13									
Basildon	d		23p32		06 02	06 32		07 02	07 32			08 02	08 32			09 02					14 32			
Laindon	d		23p35		06 05	06 35		07 05	07 35			08 05	08 35			09 05					14 35			
West Horndon	d		23p40		06 10	06 40		07 10	07 40			08 10	08 40			09 10					14 40			
Chafford Hundred	d	23p32		00 02			06 59			07 59				08 59			09 29		14 29					14 59
Ockendon	d	23p35		00 05			07 02			08 02				09 02			09 32		14 32					15 02
Upminster ⊖	d	23p42	23p46	00 11	06 16	06 46	07 09	07 16	07 46	08 09		08 16	08 46	09 09		09 16	09 39		14 39		14 46			15 09
Barking ⊖	d	23p50	23p55	00 20	06 25	06 55	07 17	07 25	07 55	08 17		08 25	08 55	09 17	09a20	09 25	09 47		14 47		14 55			15 17
Stratford 7 ⊖	a																							
London Liverpool St 15 ⊖	a																							
West Ham ⊖	d	23p58	00 03	00 30	06 31	07 01	07 23	07 31	08 01	08 23		08 31	09 01	09 23		09 31	09 53		14 53		15 01	15 08	15 15	15 23
Limehouse	d	00 03	00 09	00 35	06 36	07 06	07 28	07 36	08 06	08 28		08 36	09 06	09 28		09 36	09 58		14 58		15 06			15 28
London Fenchurch St 7 ⊖	a	00 09	00 15	00 42	06 42	07 12	07 34	07 42	08 12	08 34		08 42	09 12	09 34		09 42	10 04		15 04		15 12	15 19	15 27	15 34

		CC	CC	CC A	CC A	CC A		CC	CC	CC A	CC A	CC A	CC	CC	CC	CC A		CC A	CC A	CC	CC	CC A	CC	CC	CC
Shoeburyness	d		14 35						15 05						15 35						16 05				16 35
Thorpe Bay	d		14 38						15 08						15 38						16 08				16 38
Southend East	d		14 41						15 11						15 41						16 11				16 41
Southend Central	a		14 43						15 13						15 43						16 13				16 43
	d		14 44					14 50	15 14				15 20		15 44					15 50	16 14		16 20		16 44
Westcliff	d		14 46					14 53	15 16				15 23		15 46					15 53	16 16		16 23		16 46
Chalkwell	d		14 48					14 55	15 18				15 25		15 48					15 55	16 18		16 25		16 48
Leigh-on-Sea	d		14 51	15 01	15 07	15 18		14 58	15 21	15 25	15 36	15 48	15 28		15 51	15 55		16 05	16 15	15 58	16 21	16 32	16 28		16 51
Benfleet	d		14 55					15 02	15 25				15 32		15 55					16 02	16 25		16 32		16 55
Pitsea	d		14 59					15 06	15 29				15 36		15 59					16 06	16 29		16 36		16 59
Stanford-le-Hope	d							15 12					15 42							16 12			16 42		
East Tilbury	d							15 15					15 45							16 15			16 45		
Tilbury Town 3	d							15 21					15 51							16 21			16 51		
Grays	d	14 59						15 24					15 54	15 59						16 24			16 54	16 59	
Purfleet	d	15 04												16 04										17 04	
Rainham	d	15 09												16 09										17 09	
Dagenham Dock	d	15 13												16 13										17 13	
Basildon	d		15 02						15 32						16 02						16 32				17 02
Laindon	d		15 05						15 35						16 05						16 35				17 05
West Horndon	d		15 10						15 40						16 10						16 40				17 10
Chafford Hundred	d							15 29					15 59							16 29			16 59		
Ockendon	d							15 32					16 02							16 32			17 02		
Upminster ⊖	d		15 16					15 39	15 46				16 09		16 16					16 39	16 46		17 09		17 16
Barking ⊖	d	15a20	15 25					15 47	15 55				16 17	16a20	16 25					16 47	16 55		17 17	17a20	17 25
Stratford 7 ⊖	a																								
London Liverpool St 15 ⊖	a																								
West Ham ⊖	d		15 31	15 36	15 40	15 49		15 53	16 01	16 05	16 11	16 19	16 23		16 31	16 35		16 38	16 46	16 53	17 01	17 07	17 23		17 31
Limehouse	d		15 36					15 58	16 06				16 28		16 36					16 58	17 06		17 28		17 36
London Fenchurch St 7 ⊖	a		15 42	15 47	15 51	16 00		16 04	16 12	16 16	16 22	16 30	16 34		16 42	16 46		16 49	17 00	17 04	17 12	17 18	17 34		17 42

		CC		CC		CC	CC	CC	CC	CC	CC		CC	CC	CC	CC	CC	CC
Shoeburyness	d			17 05		20 05			20 35		21 05				21 35	22 05		22 35
Thorpe Bay	d			17 08		20 08			20 38		21 08				21 38	22 08		22 38
Southend East	d			17 11		20 11			20 41		21 11				21 41	22 11		22 41
Southend Central	a			17 13		20 13			20 43		21 13				21 43	22 13		22 43
	d	16 50		17 14		20 14	20 20		20 44	20 50	21 14		21 20		21 44	22 14	22 20	22 44
Westcliff	d	16 53		17 16		20 16	20 23		20 46	20 53	21 16		21 23		21 46	22 16	22 23	22 46
Chalkwell	d	16 55		17 18		20 18	20 25		20 48	20 55	21 18		21 25		21 48	22 18	22 25	22 48
Leigh-on-Sea	d	16 58		17 21		20 21	20 28		20 51	20 58	21 21		21 28		21 51	22 21	22 28	22 51
Benfleet	d	17 02		17 25		20 25	20 32		20 55	21 02	21 25		21 32		21 55	22 25	22 32	22 55
Pitsea	d	17 06		17 29		20 29	20 36		20 59	21 06	21 29		21 36		21 59	22 29	22 36	22 59
Stanford-le-Hope	d	17 12			and at the same minutes past each hour until		20 42			21 12			21 42				22 42	
East Tilbury	d	17 15					20 45			21 15			21 45				22 45	
Tilbury Town 3	d	17 21					20 51			21 21			21 51				22 51	
Grays	d	17 24					20 54	20 59		21 24			21 54	21 59			22 54	
Purfleet	d							21 04						22 04				
Rainham	d							21 09						22 09				
Dagenham Dock	d							21 13						22 13				
Basildon	d			17 32		20 32			21 02		21 32				22 02	22 32		23 02
Laindon	d			17 35		20 35			21 05		21 35				22 05	22 35		23 05
West Horndon	d			17 40		20 40			21 10		21 40				22 10	22 40		23 10
Chafford Hundred	d	17 29					20 59			21 29			21 59				22 59	
Ockendon	d	17 32					21 02			21 32			22 02				23 02	
Upminster ⊖	d	17 39		17 46		20 46	21 09		21 16	21 39	21 46		22 09		22 16	22 46	23 09	23 17
Barking ⊖	d	17 47		17 55		20 55	21 17	21a20	21 25	21 47	21 55		22 17	22a20	22 25	22 55	23 17	23 26
Stratford 7 ⊖	a																	
London Liverpool St 15 ⊖	a																	
West Ham ⊖	d	17 53		18 01		21 01	21 23		21 31	21 53	22 02		22 24		22 32	23 02	23 25	23 35
Limehouse	d	17 58		18 06		21 06	21 28		21 36	21 58	22 08		22 30		22 38	23 08	23 30	23 40
London Fenchurch St 7 ⊖	a	18 04		18 12		21 12	21 34		21 42	22 04	22 14		22 36		22 44	23 14	23 37	23 48

A not from 29 July until 5 August

Table 1

Shoeburyness and Southend Central - London

Sundays

19 August to 26 August

Network Diagram - see first page of Table 1

		CC	CC	CC	CC	CC	CC	CC	CC	CC		CC	CC	CC	CC	CC	CC		CC		CC	CC	CC	CC
Shoeburyness	d		23p05		05 35	06 05	06 11	06 35	07 05	07 11		07 35	08 05			08 35					21 05			21 35
Thorpe Bay	d		23p08		05 38	06 08	06 14	06 38	07 08	07 14		07 38	08 08			08 38					21 08			21 38
Southend East	d		23p11		05 41	06 11	06 17	06 41	07 11	07 17		07 41	08 11			08 41					21 11			21 41
Southend Central	a		23p13		05 43	06 13	06 19	06 43	07 13	07 19		07 43	08 13			08 43					21 13			21 43
	d	22p50	23p14	23p20	05 44	06 14	06 20	06 44	07 14	07 20		07 44	08 14	08 20		08 44	08 50		20 50		21 14	21 20		21 44
Westcliff	d	22p53	23p16	23p23	05 46	06 16	06 23	06 46	07 16	07 23		07 46	08 16	08 23		08 46	08 53		20 53		21 16	21 23		21 46
Chalkwell	d	22p55	23p18	23p25	05 48	06 18	06 25	06 48	07 18	07 25		07 48	08 18	08 25		08 48	08 55		20 55		21 18	21 25		21 48
Leigh-on-Sea	d	22p58	23p21	23p28	05 51	06 21	06 28	06 51	07 21	07 28		07 51	08 21	08 28		08 51	08 58		20 58		21 21	21 28		21 51
Benfleet	d	23p02	23p25	23p32	05 55	06 25	06 32	06 55	07 25	07 32		07 55	08 25	08 32		08 55	09 02		21 02		21 25	21 32		21 55
Pitsea	d	23p06	23p29	23p36	05 59	06 29	06 36	06 59	07 29	07 36		07 59	08 29	08 36		08 59	09 06		21 06		21 29	21 36		21 59
Stanford-le-Hope	d	23p12		23p42			06 42			07 42				08 42			09 12	and at the same minutes past each hour until	21 12			21 42		
East Tilbury	d	23p15		23p45			06 45			07 45				08 45			09 15		21 15			21 45		
Tilbury Town [3]	d	23p21		23p51			06 51			07 51				08 51			09 21		21 21			21 51		
Grays	d	23p24		23p54			06 54			07 54				08 54	08 59		09 24		21 24			21 54	21 59	
Purfleet	d														09 04								22 04	
Rainham	d														09 09								22 09	
Dagenham Dock	d														09 13								22 13	
Basildon	d		23p32		06 02	06 32		07 02	07 32			08 02	08 32			09 02					21 32			22 02
Laindon	d		23p35		06 05	06 35		07 05	07 35			08 05	08 35			09 05					21 35			22 05
West Horndon	d		23p40		06 10	06 40		07 10	07 40			08 10	08 40			09 10					21 40			22 10
Chafford Hundred	d	23p29		23p59			06 59			07 59				08 59			09 29		21 29			21 59		
Ockendon	d	23p32		00 02			07 02			08 02				09 02			09 32		21 32			22 02		
Upminster ⊖	d	23p39	23p46	00 08	06 16	06 46	07 09	07 16	07 46	08 09		08 16	08 46	09 09		09 16	09 39		21 39		21 46	22 09		22 16
Barking ⊖	d	23p47	23p55	00a18	06 25	06 55	07 17	07 25	07 55	08 17		08 25	08 55	09 17	09a20	09 25	09 47		21 47		21 55	22 17	22a20	22 25
Stratford [7] ⊖	a																							
London Liverpool St [15] ⊖	a																							
West Ham ⊖	d	23p53	00 01		06 31	07 01	07 23	07 31	08 01	08 23		08 31	09 01	09 23		09 31	09 53		21 53		22 01	22 23		22 31
Limehouse	d	23p58	00 06		06 36	07 06	07 28	07 36	08 06	08 28		08 36	09 06	09 28		09 36	09 58		21 58		22 06	22 28		22 36
London Fenchurch St [7] ⊖	a	00 04	00 12		06 42	07 12	07 34	07 42	08 12	08 34		08 42	09 12	09 34		09 42	10 04		22 04		22 12	22 34		22 42

		CC	CC	CC
Shoeburyness	d	22 05		22 35
Thorpe Bay	d	22 08		22 38
Southend East	d	22 11		22 41
Southend Central	a	22 13		22 43
	d	22 14	22 20	22 44
Westcliff	d	22 16	22 23	22 46
Chalkwell	d	22 18	22 25	22 48
Leigh-on-Sea	d	22 21	22 28	22 51
Benfleet	d	22 25	22 32	22 55
Pitsea	d	22 29	22 36	22 59
Stanford-le-Hope	d		22 42	
East Tilbury	d		22 45	
Tilbury Town [3]	d		22 51	
Grays	d		22 54	
Purfleet	d			
Rainham	d			
Dagenham Dock	d			
Basildon	d	22 32		23 02
Laindon	d	22 35		23 05
West Horndon	d	22 40		23 10
Chafford Hundred	d		22 59	
Ockendon	d		23 02	
Upminster ⊖	d	22 46	23 09	23 16
Barking ⊖	d	22 55	23 17	23 25
Stratford [7] ⊖	a			
London Liverpool St [15] ⊖	a			
West Ham ⊖	d	23 01	23 23	23 31
Limehouse	d	23 06	23 28	23 36
London Fenchurch St [7] ⊖	a	23 12	23 34	23 42

Sundays

2 September to 9 September

		CC	CC	CC	CC	CC	CC	CC	CC	CC		CC	CC	CC	CC	CC	CC		CC		CC	CC	CC	CC
Shoeburyness	d		23p05		05 35	06 05	06 11	06 35	07 05	07 11		07 35	08 05			08 35					21 05			21 35
Thorpe Bay	d		23p08		05 38	06 08	06 14	06 38	07 08	07 14		07 38	08 08			08 38					21 08			21 38
Southend East	d		23p11		05 41	06 11	06 17	06 41	07 11	07 17		07 41	08 11			08 41					21 11			21 41
Southend Central	a		23p13		05 43	06 13	06 19	06 43	07 13	07 19		07 43	08 13			08 43					21 13			21 43
	d	22p50	23p14	23p20	05 44	06 14	06 20	06 44	07 14	07 20		07 44	08 14	08 20		08 44	08 50		20 50		21 14	21 20		21 44
Westcliff	d	22p53	23p16	23p23	05 46	06 16	06 23	06 46	07 16	07 23		07 46	08 16	08 23		08 46	08 53		20 53		21 16	21 23		21 46
Chalkwell	d	22p55	23p18	23p25	05 48	06 18	06 25	06 48	07 18	07 25		07 48	08 18	08 25		08 48	08 55		20 55		21 18	21 25		21 48
Leigh-on-Sea	d	22p58	23p21	23p28	05 51	06 21	06 28	06 51	07 21	07 28		07 51	08 21	08 28		08 51	08 58		20 58		21 21	21 28		21 51
Benfleet	d	23p02	23p25	23p32	05 55	06 25	06 32	06 55	07 25	07 32		07 55	08 25	08 32		08 55	09 02		21 02		21 25	21 32		21 55
Pitsea	d	23p06	23p29	23p36	05 59	06 29	06 36	06 59	07 29	07 36		07 59	08 29	08 36		08 59	09 06		21 06		21 29	21 36		21 59
Stanford-le-Hope	d	23p12		23p42			06 42			07 42				08 42			09 12	and at the same minutes past each hour until	21 12			21 42		
East Tilbury	d	23p15		23p45			06 45			07 45				08 45			09 15		21 15			21 45		
Tilbury Town [3]	d	23p21		23p51			06 51			07 51				08 51			09 21		21 21			21 51		
Grays	d	23p24		23p54			06 54			07 54				08 54	08 59		09 24		21 24			21 54	21 59	
Purfleet	d														09 04								22 04	
Rainham	d														09 09								22 09	
Dagenham Dock	d														09 13								22 13	
Basildon	d		23p32		06 02	06 32		07 02	07 32			08 02	08 32			09 02					21 32			22 02
Laindon	d		23p35		06 05	06 35		07 05	07 35			08 05	08 35			09 05					21 35			22 05
West Horndon	d		23p40		06 10	06 40		07 10	07 40			08 10	08 40			09 10					21 40			22 10
Chafford Hundred	d	23p32		00 02			06 59			07 59				08 59			09 29		21 29			21 59		
Ockendon	d	23p35		00 05			07 02			08 02				09 02			09 32		21 32			22 02		
Upminster ⊖	d	23p42	23p46	00 11	06 16	06 46	07 09	07 16	07 46	08 09		08 16	08 46	09 09		09 16	09 39		21 39		21 46	22 09		22 16
Barking ⊖	d	23p50	23p55	00 20	06 25	06 55	07 17	07 25	07 55	08 17		08 25	08 55	09 17	09a20	09 25	09 47		21 47		21 55	22 17	22a20	22 25
Stratford [7] ⊖	a																							
London Liverpool St [15] ⊖	a																							
West Ham ⊖	d	23p58	00 03	00 30	06 31	07 01	07 23	07 31	08 01	08 23		08 31	09 01	09 23		09 31	09 53		21 53		22 02	22 24		22 32
Limehouse	d	00 03	00 09	00 35	06 36	07 06	07 28	07 36	08 06	08 28		08 36	09 06	09 28		09 36	09 58		21 58		22 08	22 30		22 38
London Fenchurch St [7] ⊖	a	00 09	00 15	00 42	06 42	07 12	07 34	07 42	08 12	08 34		08 42	09 12	09 34		09 42	10 04		22 04		22 14	22 36		22 44

Table 1

Shoeburyness and Southend Central - London

Sundays

2 September to 9 September

Network Diagram - see first page of Table 1

		CC	CC	CC
Shoeburyness	d	22 05		22 35
Thorpe Bay	d	22 08		22 38
Southend East	d	22 11		22 41
Southend Central	a	22 13		22 43
	d	22 14	22 20	22 44
Westcliff	d	22 16	22 23	22 46
Chalkwell	d	22 18	22 25	22 48
Leigh-on-Sea	d	22 21	22 28	22 51
Benfleet	d	22 25	22 32	22 55
Pitsea	d	22 29	22 36	22 59
Stanford-le-Hope	d		22 42	
East Tilbury	d		22 45	
Tilbury Town [3]	d		22 51	
Grays	d		22 54	
Purfleet	d			
Rainham	d			
Dagenham Dock	d			
Basildon	d	22 32		23 02
Laindon	d	22 35		23 05
West Horndon	d	22 40		23 10
Chafford Hundred	d		22 59	
Ockendon	d		23 02	
Upminster ⊖	d	22 46	23 09	23 17
Barking ⊖	d	22 55	23 17	23 26
Stratford [7] ⊖	a			
London Liverpool St [15] ⊖	a			
West Ham ⊖	d	23 02	23 25	23 35
Limehouse	d	23 08	23 30	23 40
London Fenchurch St [7] ⊖	a	23 14	23 37	23 48

Sundays

from 16 September

		CC	CC	CC	CC	CC	CC	CC	CC	CC		CC	CC	CC	CC	CC	CC		CC		CC	CC	CC	CC
Shoeburyness	d		23p05		05 35	06 05	06 11	06 35	07 05	07 11		07 35	08 05			08 35					21 05			21 35
Thorpe Bay	d		23p08		05 38	06 08	06 14	06 38	07 08	07 14		07 38	08 08			08 38					21 08			21 38
Southend East	d		23p11		05 41	06 11	06 17	06 41	07 11	07 17		07 41	08 11			08 41					21 11			21 41
Southend Central	a		23p13		05 43	06 13	06 19	06 43	07 13	07 19		07 43	08 13			08 43					21 13			21 43
	d	22p50	23p14	23p20	05 44	06 14	06 20	06 44	07 14	07 20		07 44	08 14	08 20		08 44	08 50		20 50		21 14	21 20		21 44
Westcliff	d	22p53	23p16	23p23	05 46	06 16	06 23	06 46	07 16	07 23		07 46	08 16	08 23		08 46	08 53		20 53		21 16	21 23		21 46
Chalkwell	d	22p55	23p18	23p25	05 48	06 18	06 25	06 48	07 18	07 25		07 48	08 18	08 25		08 48	08 55		20 55		21 18	21 25		21 48
Leigh-on-Sea	d	22p58	23p21	23p28	05 51	06 21	06 28	06 51	07 21	07 28		07 51	08 21	08 28		08 51	08 58		20 58		21 21	21 28		21 51
Benfleet	d	23p02	23p25	23p32	05 55	06 25	06 32	06 55	07 25	07 32		07 55	08 25	08 32		08 55	09 02		21 02		21 25	21 32		21 55
Pitsea	d	23p06	23p29	23p36	05 59	06 29	06 36	06 59	07 29	07 36		07 59	08 29	08 36		08 59	09 06		21 06		21 29	21 36		21 59
Stanford-le-Hope	d	23p12		23p42			06 42			07 42				08 42			09 12	and at the same minutes past each hour until	21 12			21 42		
East Tilbury	d	23p15		23p45			06 45			07 45				08 45			09 15		21 15			21 45		
Tilbury Town [3]	d	23p21		23p51			06 51			07 51				08 51			09 21		21 21			21 51		
Grays	d	23p24		23p54			06 54			07 54				08 54	08 59		09 24		21 24			21 54	21 59	
Purfleet	d														09 04								22 04	
Rainham	d														09 09								22 09	
Dagenham Dock	d														09 13								22 13	
Basildon	d		23p32		06 02	06 32		07 02	07 32			08 02	08 32			09 02					21 32			22 02
Laindon	d		23p35		06 05	06 35		07 05	07 35			08 05	08 35			09 05					21 35			22 05
West Horndon	d		23p40		06 10	06 40		07 10	07 40			08 10	08 40			09 10					21 40			22 10
Chafford Hundred	d	23p29		23p59			06 59			07 59				08 59			09 29		21 29			21 59		
Ockendon	d	23p32		00 02			07 02			08 02				09 02			09 32		21 32			22 02		
Upminster ⊖	d	23p39	23p46	00 08	06 16	06 46	07 09	07 16	07 46	08 09		08 16	08 46	09 09		09 16	09 39		21 39		21 46	22 09		22 16
Barking ⊖	d	23p47	23p55	00a18	06 25	06 55	07 17	07 25	07 55	08 17		08 25	08 55	09 17	09a20	09 25	09 47		21 47		21 55	22 17	22a20	22 25
Stratford [7] ⊖	a																							
London Liverpool St [15] ⊖	a																							
West Ham ⊖	d	23p53	00 01		06 31	07 01	07 23	07 31	08 01	08 23		08 31	09 01	09 23		09 31	09 53		21 53		22 01	22 23		22 31
Limehouse	d	23p58	00 06		06 36	07 06	07 28	07 36	08 06	08 28		08 36	09 06	09 28		09 36	09 58		21 58		22 06	22 28		22 36
London Fenchurch St [7] ⊖	a	00 04	00 12		06 42	07 12	07 34	07 42	08 12	08 34		08 42	09 12	09 34		09 42	10 04		22 04		22 12	22 34		22 42

		CC	CC	CC
Shoeburyness	d	22 05		22 35
Thorpe Bay	d	22 08		22 38
Southend East	d	22 11		22 41
Southend Central	a	22 13		22 43
	d	22 14	22 20	22 44
Westcliff	d	22 16	22 23	22 46
Chalkwell	d	22 18	22 25	22 48
Leigh-on-Sea	d	22 21	22 28	22 51
Benfleet	d	22 25	22 32	22 55
Pitsea	d	22 29	22 36	22 59
Stanford-le-Hope	d		22 42	
East Tilbury	d		22 45	
Tilbury Town [3]	d		22 51	
Grays	d		22 54	
Purfleet	d			
Rainham	d			
Dagenham Dock	d			
Basildon	d	22 32		23 02
Laindon	d	22 35		23 05
West Horndon	d	22 40		23 10
Chafford Hundred	d		22 59	
Ockendon	d		23 02	
Upminster ⊖	d	22 46	23 09	23 16
Barking ⊖	d	22 55	23 17	23 25
Stratford [7] ⊖	a			
London Liverpool St [15] ⊖	a			
West Ham ⊖	d	23 01	23 23	23 31
Limehouse	d	23 06	23 28	23 36
London Fenchurch St [7] ⊖	a	23 12	23 34	23 42

Table 1A

Mondays to Fridays

Tilbury Town - Tilbury Riverside

Bus Service

Network Diagram - see first page of Table 1

		CC	CC	CC	CC	CC	CC	CC	CC	CC		CC	CC	CC	CC	CC	CC	CC	CC	CC		CC	CC	CC	CC
Tilbury Town 3	d	05 40	06 18	06 50	07 18	07 45	08 13	08 38	09 03	09 33	...	10 03	10 33	11 03	11 33	12 03	12 33	13 03	13 33	14 03	...	14 33	15 03	15 33	16 03
Tilbury Riverside	a	05 47	06 25	06 57	07 25	07 52	08 20	08 45	09 10	09 40		10 10	10 40	11 10	11 40	12 10	12 40	13 10	13 40	14 10		14 40	15 10	15 40	16 10

		CC	CC	CC	CC	CC		CC
Tilbury Town 3	d	16 33	17 03	17 33	18 00	18 30	...	19 00
Tilbury Riverside	a	16 40	17 10	17 40	18 07	18 37		19 07

Saturdays

		CC	CC	CC	CC	CC	CC	CC	CC	CC		CC	CC	CC	CC	CC	CC	CC	CC	CC		CC	CC	CC	CC
Tilbury Town 3	d	05 40	06 15	07 01	07 31	08 01	08 31	09 01	09 31	10 01	...	10 31	11 01	11 31	12 01	12 31	13 01	13 31	14 01	14 31	...	15 01	15 31	16 01	16 31
Tilbury Riverside	a	05 47	06 22	07 08	07 38	08 08	08 38	09 08	09 38	10 08		10 38	11 08	11 38	12 08	12 38	13 08	13 38	14 08	14 38		15 08	15 38	16 08	16 38

		CC	CC	CC	CC	CC
Tilbury Town 3	d	17 01	17 31	18 01	18 31	19 01
Tilbury Riverside	a	17 08	17 38	18 08	18 38	19 08

No Sunday Service

Table 1A

Mondays to Fridays

Tilbury Riverside - Tilbury Town

Bus Service

Network Diagram - see first page of Table 1

		CC	CC	CC	CC	CC	CC	CC	CC	CC		CC	CC	CC	CC	CC	CC	CC	CC	CC		CC	CC	CC	CC
Tilbury Riverside	d	05 50	06 30	07 00	07 30	07 55	08 23	08 50	09 12	09 42	...	10 12	10 42	11 12	11 42	12 12	12 42	13 12	13 42	14 12	...	14 42	15 12	15 42	16 12
Tilbury Town 3	a	05 57	06 37	07 07	07 37	08 02	08 30	08 57	09 19	09 49		10 19	10 49	11 19	11 49	12 19	12 49	13 19	13 49	14 19		14 49	15 19	15 49	16 19

		CC	CC	CC	CC	CC		CC
Tilbury Riverside	d	16 40	17 15	17 45	18 15	18 40	...	19 10
Tilbury Town 3	a	16 47	17 22	17 52	18 22	18 47		19 17

Saturdays

		CC	CC	CC	CC	CC	CC	CC	CC	CC		CC	CC	CC	CC	CC	CC	CC	CC	CC		CC	CC	CC	CC
Tilbury Riverside	d	05 50	06 30	07 10	07 50	08 09	08 39	09 09	09 39	10 09	...	10 39	11 09	11 39	12 09	12 39	13 09	13 39	14 09	14 39	...	15 09	15 39	16 09	16 39
Tilbury Town 3	a	05 57	06 37	07 17	07 57	08 16	08 46	09 16	09 46	10 16		10 46	11 16	11 46	12 16	12 46	13 16	13 46	14 16	14 46		15 16	15 46	16 16	16 46

		CC	CC	CC	CC	CC
Tilbury Riverside	d	17 09	17 39	18 09	18 39	19 09
Tilbury Town 3	a	17 16	17 46	18 16	18 46	19 16

No Sunday Service

Table 4

Mondays to Fridays

Romford - Upminster

Network Diagram - see first page of Table 1

Miles			LE	LE	LE	LE	LE	LE	LE		LE
0	Romford	d	06 12	06 42	07 06	07 30	07 54	08 18	08 42	and every 30 minutes until	19 42
2	Emerson Park	d	06 16	06 46	07 10	07 34	07 58	08 22	08 46		19 46
3½	Upminster ⊖	a	06 20	06 50	07 14	07 38	08 02	08 26	08 50		19 50

Saturdays

		LE		LE
Romford	d	06 12	and every 30 minutes until	19 42
Emerson Park	d	06 16		19 46
Upminster ⊖	a	06 20		19 50

No Sunday Service

Table 4

Mondays to Fridays

Upminster - Romford

Network Diagram - see first page of Table 1

Miles			LE	LE	LE	LE	LE	LE	LE		LE
0	Upminster ⊖	d	*06 24*	*06 54*	*07 18*	*07 42*	*08 06*	*08 30*	*08 54*	*and every 30 minutes* until	*19 54*
1½	Emerson Park	d	06 28	06 58	07 22	07 46	08 10	08 34	08 58		19 58
3½	Romford	a	06 32	07 02	07 26	07 50	08 14	08 38	09 02		20 02

Saturdays

		LE		LE
Upminster ⊖	d	06 24	and every 30 minutes until	19 54
Emerson Park	d	06 28		19 58
Romford	a	06 32		20 02

No Sunday Service

Network Diagram for Tables 5, 10, 11

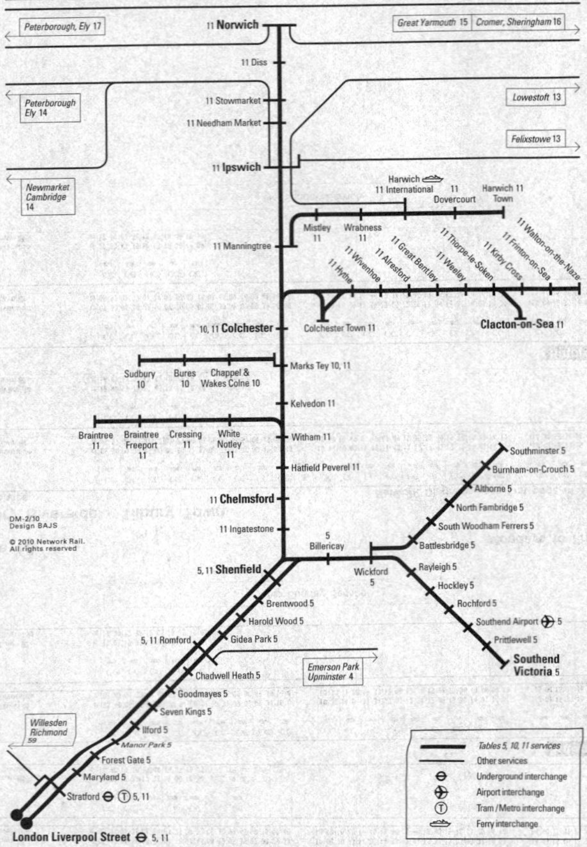

DM-2/30
Design BAJS

London - Shenfield, Southminster and Southend Victoria

Network Diagram - see first Page of Table 5

Miles	Miles			LE	LE	LE	LE	LE	LE	LE	LE	LE		LE	LE	LE	LE	LE	LE	LE	LE	LE		LE	LE
						MO				MO	MX			MO								MO			MO
				■1	■1	■1		◇■1	■1			■1		■1	■1	■1	■1					■1			
				A	B	C	A	B ⛴	B	C		A		C	A	B	B	A	B	A	B			B	
0	—	**London Liverpool Street** [15] ⊖	d	23p15		23p15	23p20	23p30		23p35	23p35	23p45		23p45	23p48	23p50		23p50	23p55	00 01	00 01	00 02		←	00 05
4	—	Stratford [7] ⊖	d	23p22		23p22	23p27	23b39		23p42	23p42	23p52		23p52	23p55	23p57		23p57	00 02	00 08	00 10	00 09		00 10	00 12
4½	—	Maryland	d				23p29			23p43	23p44							23p59	00 04	00 10	→			00 12	00 13
5¼	—	Forest Gate	d				23p31			23p45	23p46							00 01	00 06	00 12				00 14	00 15
6¼	—	Manor Park	d				23p33			23p47	23p48							00 03	00 08	00 14				00 16	00 17
7¼	—	Ilford [2]	d				23p36			23p50	23p51							00 06	00 11	00 17				00 19	00 20
8½	—	Seven Kings	d				23p38			23p53	23p53							00 08	00 13	00 19				00 21	00 23
9¼	—	Goodmayes	d				23p40			23p55	23p55							00 10	00 15	00 21				00 23	00 25
10	—	Chadwell Heath	d				23p42			23p57	23p57							00 12	00 17	00 23				00 25	00 27
12½	—	Romford	d			23p33	23p46			23p59	00 02			00 03				00 16	00 21	00 27				00 29	00 30
13½	—	Gidea Park [2]	d			23p37	23p50			00 04	00 05			00 07				00 20	00 25	00a31				00a32	00a36
15	—	Harold Wood	d			23p40	23p53			00 07	00 08			00 10				00 23	00 28						
18¼	—	Brentwood	d			23p44	23p57			00 11	00 12			00 14				00 27	00 32						
—	—	**Shenfield** [3]	a	23p38		23p50	00 03	00 02		00 18	00 18	00 08		00 20	00 10	00 20		00 33	00 38			00 30			
20¼	—	**Shenfield** [3]	d	23p39	23p43	23p50			00 05			00 09		00 20			00 23								
24¼	—	Billericay	d	23p45	23p49	23p56			00 11			00 15		00 26			00 29								
29	0	**Wickford** [2]	d	23p51	23p55	00 01			00 17			00 21		00 31			00 35								
—	2½	Battlesbridge	d																						
—	5	South Woodham Ferrers	d																						
—	8¼	North Fambridge	d																						
—	11¼	Althorne	d																						
—	14¼	Burnham-on-Crouch	d																						
—	16½	**Southminster**	a																						
33	—	Rayleigh	d	23p56	00 01	00 06			00 22			00 26		00 36			00 40								
36	—	Hockley	d	00 01	00 05	00 11			00 27			00 31		00 41			00 45								
38¾	—	Rochford	d	00 04	00 08	00 14			00 30			00 34		00 44			00 48								
39¾	—	Southend Airport ✈	d	00 07	00 11	00 17			00 33			00 37		00 47			00 51								
41	—	Prittlewell	d	00 10	00 14				00 36			00 40					00 54								
41½	—	**Southend Victoria**	a	00 18	00 18	00 27			00 40			00 48		00 57			00 58								

		LE	LE	LE	LE	LE	LE	LE		LE	LE	LE	LE	LE	LE	LE	LE	LE		LE	LE	LE	LE	LE	LE
			MO				MX	MX		MO	MO	MX	MX												
		■1	■1	■1	■1	■1					■1	■1	■1		■1	■1	■1				■1	■1		■1	■1
		A		A	B	B																			
London Liverpool Street [15] ⊖	d	00 15	00 15	00 18	00 18		00 20	00 32		00 35	00 45	00 46	00 50	00 55		05 23		05 28		05 37	05 52	05 55	06 00	06 02	
Stratford [7] ⊖	d	00 22	00 22	00 25	00 25		00 27	00 39		00 42	00 52	00 53	00 57	01 02		05 30		05 35		05 44	06a01	06 02	06 07	06 09	
Maryland	d						00 29	00 41		00 43				01 04						05 46			06 09		
Forest Gate	d						00 31	00 43		00 45				01 06						05 48			06 11		
Manor Park	d						00 33	00 45		00 47				01 08						05 50			06 13		
Ilford [2]	d						00 36	00 48		00 50				01 11				05 40		05 53			06 16		
Seven Kings	d						00 38	00 50		00 53				01 13				05 42		05 55			06 18		
Goodmayes	d						00 40	00 52		00 55				01 15						05 57			06 20		
Chadwell Heath	d						00 42	00 54		00 57				01 17						05 59			06 22		
Romford	d	00 32	00 33		00 37		00 46	00 58		01 00	01 03		01 08	01 21		05 38		05 48		06 03			06 26		
Gidea Park [2]	d		00 37				00 50	01a02		01a06	01 07	01 07		01 25				05 51		06 07			06 30		
Harold Wood	d		00 40				00 53				01 10			01 28				05 54		06 10			06 33		
Brentwood	d		00 44				00 57				01 14			01 32				05 59		06 14			06 37		
Shenfield [3]	a	00 44	00 50	00 47	00 50		01 03				01 20	01 17	01 20	01 38		05 47		06 04		06 20		06 18	06 43	06 24	
Shenfield [3]	d	00 45	00 50			00 53					01 20		01 20				05 56	06 04				06 19			06 33
Billericay	d	00 51	00 56			00 59					01 26		01 26				06 02	06 10				06 25			06 39
Wickford [2]	d	00 56	01 01			01 04					01 31		01 31		05 16		06 09	06 16				06 31			06 46
Battlesbridge	d														05 20		06 13								06 50
South Woodham Ferrers	d														05 24		06 17								06 54
North Fambridge	d														05 41		06 24								07 03
Althorne	d														05 46		06 29								07 08
Burnham-on-Crouch	d														05 51		06 34								07 13
Southminster	a														05 57		06 40								07 19
Rayleigh	d	01 01	01 06			01 09					01 36		01 36					06 21				06 36			
Hockley	d	01 06	01 11			01 14					01 41		01 41					06 26				06 41			
Rochford	d	01 09	01 14			01 17					01 44		01 44					06 29				06 44			
Southend Airport ✈	d	01 12	01 17			01 20					01 47		01 47					06 32				06 47			
Prittlewell	d	01 15				01 23							01 50					06 35				06 50			
Southend Victoria	a	01 23	01 27			01 27					01 57		01 58					06 39				06 55			

A FO until 15 June, MX from 22 June until 26 July
B TWThO until 21 June
C from 21 May until 23 July
b Previous night, stops to pick up only

Table 5

Mondays to Fridays

until 26 July

London - Shenfield, Southminster and Southend Victoria

Network Diagram - see first Page of Table 5

Station		LE	LE ■	LE ■	LE	LE	LE ■	LE ■	LE	LE ■	LE	LE ■	LE	LE ■	LE ■	LE	LE ■	LE ■	LE ■	LE	LE
London Liverpool Street 15 ⊖	d	06 10	06 12	06 15	06 20	06 30	06 35	06 38	06 40	06 48	06 50	06 55	07 00	07 02	07 08	07 10		07 13	07 18	07 20	07 30
Stratford 7 ⊖	d	06 17	06 19	06 22	06 27	06 37	06 42	06 45	06 47	06 55	06 57	07 02	07 07	07 09	07 15	07 17		07 20	07 25	07 27	07 37
Maryland	d	06 19			06 29	06 39			06 49		06 59		07 09			07 19				07 29	07 39
Forest Gate	d	06 21			06 31	06 41			06 51		07 01		07 11			07 21				07 31	07 41
Manor Park	d	06 23			06 33	06 43			06 53		07 03		07 13			07 23				07 33	07 43
Ilford 2	d	06 26			06 36	06 46			06 56		07 06		07 16			07 26				07 36	07 46
Seven Kings	d	06 28			06 38	06 48			06 58		07 08		07 18			07 28				07 38	07 48
Goodmayes	d	06 30			06 40	06 50			07 00		07 10		07 20			07 30				07 40	07 50
Chadwell Heath	d	06 32			06 42	06 52			07 02		07 12		07 22			07 32				07 42	07 52
Romford	d	06 36			06 46	06 56			07 06		07 16		07 26			07 36		07 28		07 46	07 56
Gidea Park 2	d	06 40			06 50	07 00			07 10		07 20		07 30			07 40				07 50	08 00
Harold Wood	d	06 43			06 53	07 03			07 13		07 23		07 33			07 43				07 53	08 03
Brentwood	d	06 47			06 57	07 07			07 17		07 27		07 37			07 47				07 57	08 07
Shenfield 3	a	06 53	06 35	06 38	07 03	07 13	06 58	07 00	07 23	07 11	07 33	07 18	07 43	07 24	07 30	07 53		07 38	07 40	08 03	08 13
Shenfield 3	d			06 39			06 59					07 19						07 39			
Billericay	d			06 45			07 05					07 25						07 45			
Wickford 2	d			06 51			07 11					07 31					07 36	07 51			
Battlesbridge	d																07 40				
South Woodham Ferrers	d																07 44				
North Fambridge	d																07 53				
Althorne	d																07 58				
Burnham-on-Crouch	d																08 03				
Southminster	a																08 09				
Rayleigh	d			06 56			07 16					07 36						07 56			
Hockley	d			07 01			07 21					07 41						08 01			
Rochford	d			07 04			07 24					07 44						08 04			
Southend Airport ✈	d			07 07			07 27					07 47						08 07			
Prittlewell	d			07 10			07 30					07 50						08 10			
Southend Victoria	a			07 14			07 34					07 54						08 14			

Station		LE ■	LE ■	LE	LE ■	LE	LE ■	LE ■	LE	LE ■	LE ■	LE	LE ■	LE ■	LE	LE	LE ■	LE ■	LE ■	LE	LE ■	LE	LE ■
London Liverpool Street 15 ⊖	d	07 33	07 36	07 40	07 46	07 50		07 57	08 00	08 00	08 06	08 10	08 13	08 17	08 20	08 30		08 32	08 36	08 40	08 48	08 50	08 55
Stratford 7 ⊖	d	07 42	07 45	07 47	07 54	07 57		08 05	08 07	08 08	08 14	08 17	08 21	08 25	08 27	08 37		08 42	08 45	08 47	08 55	08 57	09 02
Maryland	d			07 49		07 59			08 09			08 19			08 29	08 39				08 49		08 59	
Forest Gate	d			07 51		08 01			08 11			08 21			08 31	08 41				08 51		09 01	
Manor Park	d			07 53		08 03			08 13			08 23			08 33	08 43				08 53		09 03	
Ilford 2	d			07 56		08 06			08 16			08 26			08 36	08 46				08 56		09 06	
Seven Kings	d			07 58		08 08			08 18			08 28			08 38	08 48				08 58		09 08	
Goodmayes	d			08 00		08 10			08 20			08 30			08 40	08 50				09 00		09 10	
Chadwell Heath	d			08 02		08 12			08 22			08 32			08 42	08 52				09 02		09 12	
Romford	d			08 06		08 16			08 26			08 36			08 46	08 56				09 06		09 16	
Gidea Park 2	d			08 10		08 20			08 30			08 40			08 50	09 00				09 10		09 20	
Harold Wood	d			08 13		08 23			08 33			08 43			08 53	09 03				09 13		09 23	
Brentwood	d			08 17		08 27			08 37			08 47			08 57	09 07				09 17		09 27	
Shenfield 3	a	07 59	08 01	08 25	08 10	08 35		08 22	08 43	08 25	08 30	08 53	08 38	08 41	09 03	09 13		08 59	09 01	09 23	09 11	09 33	09 18
Shenfield 3	d	07 59						08 22					08 39					08 59					09 19
Billericay	d	08 05						08 28					08 45					09 05					09 25
Wickford 2	d	08 11					08 16	08 34					08 51				08 56	09 11					09 31
Battlesbridge	d						08 20										09 00						
South Woodham Ferrers	d						08 24										09 04						
North Fambridge	d						08 31										09 11						
Althorne	d						08 36										09 16						
Burnham-on-Crouch	d						08 41										09 21						
Southminster	a						08 47										09 27						
Rayleigh	d	08 16						08 39					08 56					09 16					09 36
Hockley	d	08 21						08 44					09 01					09 21					09 41
Rochford	d	08 24						08 47					09 04					09 24					09 44
Southend Airport ✈	d	08 27						08 50					09 07					09 27					09 47
Prittlewell	d	08 30						08 53					09 10					09 30					09 50
Southend Victoria	a	08 34						08 57					09 14					09 34					09 54

Table 5

Mondays to Fridays

until 26 July

London - Shenfield, Southminster and Southend Victoria

Network Diagram - see first Page of Table 5

Station		LE	LE ■	LE	LE ■	LE ■	LE ■	LE	LE	LE ■	LE ■	LE	LE ■	LE	LE ■	LE ■	LE	LE ■	LE	LE ■	LE ■	LE	LE
London Liverpool Street 15 ⊖	d	09 00	09 02	09 10		09 13	09 18	09 20	09 30	09 34	09 38	09 40	09 48	09 50		09 55	10 00	10 02	10 10	10 13	10 18	10 20	10 30
Stratford 7 ⊖	d	09 07	09 09	09 17		09 21	09 25	09 27	09 37	09 42	09 45	09 47	09 55	09 57		10 02	10 07	10 09	10 17	10 20	10 25	10 27	10 37
Maryland	d	09 09		09 19				09 29	09 39			09 49		09 59			10 09		10 19			10 29	10 39
Forest Gate	d	09 11		09 21				09 31	09 41			09 51		10 01			10 11		10 21			10 31	10 41
Manor Park	d	09 13		09 23				09 33	09 43			09 53		10 03			10 13		10 23			10 33	10 43
Ilford 2	d	09 16		09 26				09 36	09 46			09 56		10 06			10 16		10 26			10 36	10 46
Seven Kings	d	09 18		09 28				09 38	09 48			09 58		10 08			10 18		10 28			10 38	10 48
Goodmayes	d	09 20		09 30				09 40	09 50			10 00		10 10			10 20		10 30			10 40	10 50
Chadwell Heath	d	09 22		09 32				09 42	09 52			10 02		10 12			10 22		10 32			10 42	10 52
Romford	d	09 26		09 36				09 46	09 56		09 53	10 06		10 16			10 26		10 36	10 28		10 46	10 56
Gidea Park 2	d	09 30		09 40				09 50	10 00			10 10		10 20			10 30		10 40			10 50	11 00
Harold Wood	d	09 33		09 43				09 53	10 03			10 13		10 23			10 33		10 43			10 53	11 03
Brentwood	d	09 37		09 47				09 57	10 07			10 17		10 27			10 37		10 47			10 57	11 07
Shenfield 3	a	09 43	09 24	09 53		09 38	09 40	10 03	10 13	09 58	10 02	10 23	10 11	10 33		10 18	10 43	10 24	10 53	10 38	10 40	11 03	11 13
Shenfield 3	d					09 39				09 59						10 19				10 39			
Billericay	d					09 45				10 05						10 25				10 45			
Wickford 2	d				09 36	09 51				10 11					10 16	10 31				10 51			
Battlesbridge	d				09 40										10 20								
South Woodham Ferrers	d				09 44										10 24								
North Fambridge	d				09 51										10 31								
Althorne	d				09 56										10 36								
Burnham-on-Crouch	d				10 01										10 41								
Southminster	a				10 07										10 47								
Rayleigh	d					09 56				10 16						10 36				10 56			
Hockley	d					10 01				10 21						10 41				11 01			
Rochford	d					10 04				10 24						10 44				11 04			
Southend Airport ✈	d					10 07				10 27						10 47				11 07			
Prittlewell	d					10 10				10 30						10 50				11 10			
Southend Victoria	a					10 14				10 34						10 54				11 14			

Station		LE ■	LE ■	LE ■	LE	LE ■	LE	LE ■	LE	LE ■	LE	LE ■	LE ■	LE ■	LE	LE	LE ■	LE ■	LE	LE ■	LE	LE ■
London Liverpool Street 15 ⊖	d		10 35	10 38	10 40	10 48	10 50	10 55	11 00	11 02	11 10		11 13	11 18	11 20	11 30	11 35	11 38	11 40	11 48	11 50	
Stratford 7 ⊖	d		10 42	10 45	10 47	10 55	10 57	11 02	11 07	11 09	11 17		11 20	11 25	11 27	11 37	11 42	11 45	11 47	11 55	11 57	
Maryland	d				10 49		10 59		11 09		11 19				11 29	11 39			11 49		11 59	
Forest Gate	d				10 51		11 01		11 11		11 21				11 31	11 41			11 51		12 01	
Manor Park	d				10 53		11 03		11 13		11 23				11 33	11 43			11 53		12 03	
Ilford 2	d				10 56		11 06		11 16		11 26				11 36	11 46			11 56		12 06	
Seven Kings	d				10 58		11 08		11 18		11 28				11 38	11 48			11 58		12 08	
Goodmayes	d				11 00		11 10		11 20		11 30				11 40	11 50			12 00		12 10	
Chadwell Heath	d				11 02		11 12		11 22		11 32				11 42	11 52			12 02		12 12	
Romford	d			10 53	11 06		11 16		11 26		11 36		11 28		11 46	11 56		11 53	12 06		12 16	
Gidea Park 2	d				11 10		11 20		11 30		11 40				11 50	12 00			12 10		12 20	
Harold Wood	d				11 13		11 23		11 33		11 43				11 53	12 03			12 13		12 23	
Brentwood	d				11 17		11 27		11 37		11 47				11 57	12 07			12 17		12 27	
Shenfield 3	a		10 58	11 02	11 23	11 11	11 33	11 18	11 43	11 24	11 53		11 38	11 40	12 03	12 13	11 58	12 02	12 23	12 11	12 33	
Shenfield 3	d		10 59					11 19					11 39				11 59					
Billericay	d		11 05					11 25					11 45				12 05					
Wickford 2	d	10 56	11 11					11 31				11 36	11 51				12 11					12 16
Battlesbridge	d	11 00										11 40										12 20
South Woodham Ferrers	d	11 04										11 44										12 24
North Fambridge	d	11 11										11 51										12 31
Althorne	d	11 16										11 56										12 36
Burnham-on-Crouch	d	11 21										12 01										12 41
Southminster	a	11 27										12 07										12 47
Rayleigh	d		11 16					11 36					11 56				12 16					
Hockley	d		11 21					11 41					12 01				12 21					
Rochford	d		11 24					11 44					12 04				12 24					
Southend Airport ✈	d		11 27					11 47					12 07				12 27					
Prittlewell	d		11 30					11 50					12 10				12 30					
Southend Victoria	a		11 34					11 54					12 14				12 34					

London - Shenfield, Southminster and Southend Victoria

Network Diagram - see first Page of Table 5

		LE ■	LE	LE ■	LE	LE ■	LE ■	LE		LE	LE ■	LE ■	LE ■	LE	LE ■	LE	LE ■	LE		LE ■	LE	LE ■	LE ■	LE ■	LE
London Liverpool Street ⊖	d	11 55	12 00	12 02	12 10	12 13	12 18	12 20		12 30		12 35	12 38	12 40	12 48	12 50	12 55	13 00		13 02	13 10		13 13	13 18	13 20
Stratford ■ ⊖	d	12 02	12 07	12 09	12 17	12 20	12 25	12 27		12 37		12 42	12 45	12 47	12 55	12 57	13 02	13 07		13 09	13 17		13 20	13 25	13 27
Maryland	d		12 09		12 19			12 29		12 39				12 49		12 59		13 09			13 19				13 29
Forest Gate	d		12 11		12 21			12 31		12 41				12 51		13 01		13 11			13 21				13 31
Manor Park	d		12 13		12 23			12 33		12 43				12 53		13 03		13 13			13 23				13 33
Ilford ■	d		12 16		12 26			12 36		12 46				12 56		13 06		13 16			13 26				13 36
Seven Kings	d		12 18		12 28			12 38		12 48				12 58		13 08		13 18			13 28				13 38
Goodmayes	d		12 20		12 30			12 40		12 50				13 00		13 10		13 20			13 30				13 40
Chadwell Heath	d		12 22		12 32			12 42		12 52				13 02		13 12		13 22			13 32				13 42
Romford	d		12 26		12 36	12 28		12 46		12 56			12 53	13 06		13 16		13 26			13 36		13 28		13 46
Gidea Park ■	d		12 30		12 40			12 50		13 00				13 10		13 20		13 30			13 40				13 50
Harold Wood	d		12 33		12 43			12 53		13 03				13 13		13 23		13 33			13 43				13 53
Brentwood	d		12 37		12 47			12 57		13 07				13 17		13 27		13 37			13 47				13 57
Shenfield ■	a	12 18	12 43	12 24	12 53	12 38	12 40	13 03		13 13		12 58	13 02	13 23	13 11	13 33	13 18	13 43		13 24	13 53		13 38	13 40	14 03
Shenfield ■	d	12 19				12 39						12 59					13 19						13 39		
Billericay	d	12 25				12 45						13 05					13 25						13 45		
Wickford ■	d	12 31				12 51					12 56	13 11					13 31					13 36	13 51		
Battlesbridge	d										13 00											13 40			
South Woodham Ferrers	d										13 04											13 44			
North Fambridge	d										13 11											13 51			
Althorne	d										13 16											13 56			
Burnham-on-Crouch	d										13 21											14 01			
Southminster	a										13 27											14 07			
Rayleigh	d	12 36				12 56						13 16					13 36						13 56		
Hockley	d	12 41				13 01						13 21					13 41						14 01		
Rochford	d	12 44				13 04						13 24					13 44						14 04		
Southend Airport ✈	d	12 47				13 07						13 27					13 47						14 07		
Prittlewell	d	12 50				13 10						13 30					13 50						14 10		
Southend Victoria	a	12 54				13 14						13 34					13 54						14 14		

		LE	LE ■	LE ■		LE	LE ■	LE	LE ■	LE ■	LE	LE ■	LE	LE ■		LE ■	LE	LE	LE ■	LE ■	LE ■	LE	LE ■	LE	
London Liverpool Street ⊖	d	13 30	13 35	13 38		13 40	13 48	13 50		13 55	14 00	14 02	14 10	14 13		14 18	14 20	14 30		14 35	14 38	14 40	14 48	14 50	
Stratford ■ ⊖	d	13 37	13 42	13 45		13 47	13 55	13 57		14 02	14 07	14 09	14 17	14 20		14 25	14 27	14 37		14 42	14 45	14 47	14 55	14 57	
Maryland	d	13 39				13 49		13 59			14 09		14 19				14 29	14 39				14 49		14 59	
Forest Gate	d	13 41				13 51		14 01			14 11		14 21				14 31	14 41				14 51		15 01	
Manor Park	d	13 43				13 53		14 03			14 13		14 23				14 33	14 43				14 53		15 03	
Ilford ■	d	13 46				13 56		14 06			14 16		14 26				14 36	14 46				14 56		15 06	
Seven Kings	d	13 48				13 58		14 08			14 18		14 28				14 38	14 48				14 58		15 08	
Goodmayes	d	13 50				14 00		14 10			14 20		14 30				14 40	14 50				15 00		15 10	
Chadwell Heath	d	13 52				14 02		14 12			14 22		14 32				14 42	14 52				15 02		15 12	
Romford	d	13 56		13 53		14 06		14 16			14 26		14 36	14 28			14 46	14 56			14 53	15 06		15 16	
Gidea Park ■	d	14 00				14 10		14 20			14 30		14 40				14 50	15 00				15 10		15 20	
Harold Wood	d	14 03				14 13		14 23			14 33		14 43				14 53	15 03				15 13		15 23	
Brentwood	d	14 07				14 17		14 27			14 37		14 47				14 57	15 07				15 17		15 27	
Shenfield ■	a	14 13	13 58	14 02		14 23	14 11	14 33		14 18	14 43	14 24	14 53	14 38		14 40	15 03	15 13		14 58	15 02	15 23	15 11	15 33	
Shenfield ■	d		13 59							14 19				14 39						14 59					
Billericay	d		14 05							14 25				14 45						15 05					
Wickford ■	d		14 11						14 16	14 31				14 51					14 56	15 11					
Battlesbridge	d								14 20										15 00						
South Woodham Ferrers	d								14 24										15 04						
North Fambridge	d								14 31										15 11						
Althorne	d								14 36										15 16						
Burnham-on-Crouch	d								14 41										15 21						
Southminster	a								14 47										15 27						
Rayleigh	d		14 16							14 36				14 56						15 16					
Hockley	d		14 21							14 41				15 01						15 21					
Rochford	d		14 24							14 44				15 04						15 24					
Southend Airport ✈	d		14 27							14 47				15 07						15 27					
Prittlewell	d		14 30							14 50				15 10						15 31					
Southend Victoria	a		14 34							14 54				15 14						15 34					

London - Shenfield, Southminster and Southend Victoria

Network Diagram - see first Page of Table 5

		LE ■	LE	LE ■	LE	LE ■	LE ■	LE ■	LE	LE		LE ■	LE ■	LE	LE ■	LE	LE ■	LE ■	LE	LE ■		LE	LE ■	LE ■	LE ■
London Liverpool Street ⊖	d	14 55	15 00	15 02	15 10		15 13	15 18	15 20	15 30		15 35	15 38	15 40	15 48	15 50		15 55	16 00	16 02		16 10	16 10	16 14	16 17
Stratford ■ ⊖	d	15 02	15 07	15 09	15 17		15 20	15 25	15 27	15 37		15 42	15 45	15 47	15 55	15 57		16 02	16 07	16 09		16 17	16 18	16 22	16 25
Maryland	d		15 09		15 19				15 29	15 39				15 49		15 59			16 09			16 19			
Forest Gate	d		15 11		15 21				15 31	15 41				15 51		16 01			16 11			16 21			
Manor Park	d		15 13		15 23				15 33	15 43				15 53		16 03			16 13			16 23			
Ilford ■	d		15 16		15 26				15 36	15 46				15 56		16 06			16 16			16 26			
Seven Kings	d		15 18		15 28				15 38	15 48				15 58		16 08			16 18			16 28			
Goodmayes	d		15 20		15 30				15 40	15 50				16 00		16 10			16 20			16 30			
Chadwell Heath	d		15 22		15 32				15 42	15 52				16 02		16 12			16 22			16 32			
Romford	d		15 26		15 36		15 28		15 46	15 56			15 53	16 06		16 16			16 26			16 36			
Gidea Park ■	d		15 30		15 40				15 50	16 00				16 10		16 20			16 30			16 40			
Harold Wood	d		15 33		15 43				15 53	16 03				16 13		16 23			16 33			16 43			
Brentwood	d		15 37		15 47				15 57	16 07				16 17		16 27			16 37			16 47			
Shenfield ■	a	15 18	15 43	15 24	15 53		15 38	15 40	16 03	16 13		15 58	16 02	16 23	16 11	16 33		16 18	16 43	16 24		16 53	16 34	16 38	16 41
Shenfield ■	d	15 19					15 39					15 59						16 19					16 34		
Billericay	d	15 25					15 45					16 05						16 25					16 41		
Wickford ■	d	15 31				15 36	15 51					16 11					16 14	16 31					16 48		
Battlesbridge	d					15 40											16 18								
South Woodham Ferrers	d					15 44											16 22								
North Fambridge	d					15 51											16 29								
Althorne	d					15 56											16 34								
Burnham-on-Crouch	d					16 01											16 39								
Southminster	a					16 07											16 45								
Rayleigh	d	15 36					15 56					16 16						16 36					16 53		
Hockley	d	15 41					16 01					16 21						16 41					16 57		
Rochford	d	15 44					16 04					16 24						16 44					17 01		
Southend Airport ✈	d	15 47					16 07					16 27						16 47					17 03		
Prittlewell	d	15 50					16 10					16 30						16 50					17 06		
Southend Victoria	a	15 54					16 14					16 34						16 54					17 15		

		LE	LE ■	LE	LE ■	LE ■		LE	LE	LE ■	LE ■	LE ■	LE	LE ■	LE	LE ■		LE	LE	LE ◇■	LE ■	LE	LE ■	LE	LE ■
London Liverpool Street ⊖	d	16 20	16 24	16 28	16 32	16 34		16 36	16 40		16 40	16 44	16 47	16 47	16 50	16 54		16 57	17 00	17 02	17 04	17 07	17 08	17 10	17 12
Stratford ■ ⊖	d	16 27	16 32	16 35		16 42		16 43	16 47		16 48	16a52	16 54	16 55	16 57	17 02		17 04	17 07	17 10	17 13	17 14	17a16	17 17	17a20
Maryland	d	16 29		16 37					16 49						16 59				17 09					17 19	
Forest Gate	d	16 31		16 39					16 51						17 01				17 11					17 21	
Manor Park	d	16 33		16 41					16 53						17 03				17 13					17 23	
Ilford ■	d	16 36		16 44				16 50	16 56				17 00		17 06			17 10	17 16			17 20		17 26	
Seven Kings	d	16 38		16 47				16 52					17 02					17 12				17 22			
Goodmayes	d	16 40		16 49				16 54					17 04					17 14				17 24			
Chadwell Heath	d	16 42		16 51				16 56	17 00				17 06		17 10			17 16	17 20			17 26		17 30	
Romford	d	16 46		16 55				17 00	17 04				17 10		17 14			17 20	17 24			17 30		17 34	
Gidea Park ■	d	16 50		17a00				17 04	17a10				17 14		17a20			17 24	17a30			17 34		17a40	
Harold Wood	d	16 53						17 07					17 17					17 27				17 37			
Brentwood	d	16 57						17 11					17 21					17 31				17 41			
Shenfield ■	a	17 03	16 49		16 54	16 58		17 19			17 04		17 29	17 11		17 19		17 39			17 30	17 49			
Shenfield ■	d		16 49								17 04					17 19					17 30				
Billericay	d		16 56								17 11					17 26					17 37				
Wickford ■	d		17 03							17 06	17 18					17 33					17 44				
Battlesbridge	d									17 10															
South Woodham Ferrers	d									17 14															
North Fambridge	d									17 21															
Althorne	d									17 26															
Burnham-on-Crouch	d									17 31															
Southminster	a									17 37															
Rayleigh	d		17 08								17 23					17 38					17 49				
Hockley	d		17 12								17 27					17 42					17 53				
Rochford	d		17 16								17 31					17 46					17 57				
Southend Airport ✈	d		17 18								17 33					17 48					17 59				
Prittlewell	d		17 21								17 36					17 51					18 02				
Southend Victoria	a		17 27								17 42					17 57					18 08				

London - Shenfield, Southminster and Southend Victoria

Network Diagram - see first Page of Table 5

		LE 1	LE	LE 1	LE	LE 1 A	LE 1 A	LE 1	LE	LE	LE 1	LE 1	LE	LE 1	LE	LE 1 A	LE	LE 1	LE	LE	LE	LE 1
London Liverpool Street 15 ⊖	d	17 15	17 17	17 18	17 20	17 20	17 22	17 25	17 27	17 30	17 32	17 34	17 36	17 38	17 39	17 40	17 42	17 45	17 46	17 49	17 52	17 52
Stratford 7 ⊖	d	17 23	17 24	17a26	17 27	17 29	17 31	17 34	17 34	17 37	17a40	17 43	17 43	17a47	17 46	17 49	17 49	17 53	17 53	17 56	17 59	18a01
Maryland	d				17 29					17 39			17 45						17 55			
Forest Gate	d				17 31					17 41							17 52				18 02	
Manor Park	d				17 33					17 43					17 50					18 00		
Ilford 2	d		17 30		17 36				17 40	17 46			17 50		17 53		17 56		18 00	18 03	18 06	
Seven Kings	d		17 32						17 42				17 52		17 56		17 59		18 02	18 06	18 09	
Goodmayes	d		17 34						17 44				17 54		17 58		18 01		18 04	18 08	18 11	
Chadwell Heath	d		17 36		17 40				17 46	17 50			17 56		18 00		18 03		18 06	18 10	18 13	
Romford	d		17 40		17 44				17 50	17 54			18 00		18 04		18 07		18 10	18 14	18 17	
Gidea Park 2	d		17 44		17a50				17 54	18a00			18 04		18a09		18a12		18 14	18 18	18a22	
Harold Wood	d		17 47						17 57				18 07						18 17	18 21		
Brentwood	d		17 51						18 01				18 11						18 21	18 25		
Shenfield 3	a	17 39	17 59			17 45		17 51	18 09			17 59	18 19			18 05		18 09	18 29	18 33		
Shenfield 3	d	17 39						17 52				17 59						18 09		18 36		
Billericay	d	17 46						17 58				18 06						18 16		→		
Wickford 2	d	17 53					18 00	18 05				18 13						18 23				
Battlesbridge	d						18 04															
South Woodham Ferrers	d						18 08															
North Fambridge	d						18 14															
Althorne	d						18 19															
Burnham-on-Crouch	d						18 24															
Southminster	a						18 32															
Rayleigh	d	17 58						18 10				18 18						18 28				
Hockley	d	18 02						18 15				18 22						18 32				
Rochford	d	18 06						18 18				18 26						18 36				
Southend Airport ✈	d	18 08						18 21				18 28						18 38				
Prittlewell	d	18 11						18 24				18 31						18 41				
Southend Victoria	a	18 17						18 30				18 37						18 47				

		LE 1	LE	LE 1	LE	LE 1	LE	LE 1	LE 1	LE	LE	LE	LE 1	LE 1	LE	LE 1	LE	LE 1	LE 1	LE	LE	LE 1	LE 1
London Liverpool Street 15 ⊖	d	17 54	17 56	17 58	17 59	18 00	18 02	18 02	18 05		18 07	18 10	18 12	18 14	18 17	18 18	18 20	18 20	18 25	18 27	18 30	18 32	18 35
Stratford 7 ⊖	d	18 03	18 03	18a06	18 06	18 09	18 09	18 11	18 14		18 14	18 17	18a21	18 23	18 24	18a27	18 27	18 29	18 33	18 34	18 37	18a40	18 43
Maryland	d		18 05									18 19					18 29				18 39		
Forest Gate	d						18 12					18 21					18 31				18 41		
Manor Park	d				18 10							18 23					18 33				18 43		
Ilford 2	d		18 10		18 13		18 16				18 20	18 26			18 30		18 36			18 40	18 46		
Seven Kings	d		18 12		18 16		18 19				18 22				18 32					18 42			
Goodmayes	d		18 14		18 18		18 21				18 24				18 34					18 44			
Chadwell Heath	d		18 16		18 20		18 23				18 26	18 30			18 36		18 40			18 46	18 50		
Romford	d		18 20		18 24		18 27				18 30	18 34			18 40		18 44			18 50	18 54		
Gidea Park 2	d		18 24		18a29		18a32				18 34	18a40			18 44		18a50			18 54	19a00		
Harold Wood	d		18 27								18 37				18 47					18 57			
Brentwood	d		18 31							←	18 41				18 51					19 01			
Shenfield 3	a	18 19	18 39			18 25			18 31	18 33	18 49			18 40	18 59			18 45	18 50	19 09			18 59
Shenfield 3	d	18 19							18 31	18 36				18 41					18 50				18 59
Billericay	d	18 26							18 38	18 42				18 47					18 57				19 06
Wickford 2	d	18 33						18 41	18 45	18 49				18 54					19 04				19 13
Battlesbridge	d							18 45															
South Woodham Ferrers	d							18 49															
North Fambridge	d							18 55															
Althorne	d							19 00															
Burnham-on-Crouch	d							19 05															
Southminster	a							19 13															
Rayleigh	d	18 38							18 50	18 54				18 59					19 09				19 18
Hockley	d	18 42							18 55	18 59				19 04					19 13				19 22
Rochford	d	18 46							18 58	19 02				19 07					19 17				19 26
Southend Airport ✈	d	18 48							19 01	19 05				19 10					19 19				19 28
Prittlewell	d	18 51							19 04	19 08				19 13					19 22				19 31
Southend Victoria	a	18 58							19 10	19 14				19 19					19 28				19 37

A The Stratford call is subjtect to introduction during the currency of the timetable.

London - Shenfield, Southminster and Southend Victoria

Network Diagram - see first Page of Table 5

		LE	LE 1	LE	LE 1	LE 1	LE	LE 1	LE	LE 1	LE	LE	LE 1	LE 1	LE	LE 1	LE 1	LE	LE	LE 1	LE 1	LE 1
London Liverpool Street 15 ⊖	d	18 37	18 38	18 40	18 41	18 45	18 47	18 48	18 50	18 55	18 57	19 00	19 02	19 08	19 10	19 15	19 18	19 20	19 30	19 32	19 35	19 38
Stratford 7 ⊖	d	18 44	18 46	18 47	18 49	18 53	18 54	18a56	18 57	19 03	19 04	19 07	19 09	19a15	19 17	19 22	19 25	19 27	19 37	19a39	19 42	19 45
Maryland	d			18 49					18 59			19 09			19 19			19 29	19 39			
Forest Gate	d			18 51					19 01			19 11			19 21			19 31	19 41			
Manor Park	d			18 53					19 03			19 13			19 23			19 33	19 43			
Ilford 2	d	18 50		18 56			19 00		19 06		19 10	19 16			19 26			19 36	19 46			
Seven Kings	d	18 52					19 02				19 12	19 18			19 28			19 38	19 48			
Goodmayes	d	18 54					19 04				19 14	19 20			19 30			19 40	19 50			
Chadwell Heath	d	18 56		19 00			19 06		19 10		19 16	19 22			19 32			19 42	19 52			
Romford	d	19 00		19 04			19 10		19 14		19 20	19 26			19 36			19 46	19 56			
Gidea Park 2	d	19 04		19 08			19 14		19a20		19 24	19 30			19 40			19 50	20 00			
Harold Wood	d	19 07		19 11			19 17				19 27	19 33			19 43			19 53	20 03			
Brentwood	d	19 11		19 15			19 21				19 31	19 37			19 47			19 57	20 07			
Shenfield 3	a	19 19	19 02	19 23		19 10	19 29			19 20	19 39	19 43	19 24		19 53	19 38	19 40	20 03	20 13		19 58	20 00
Shenfield 3	d					19 10				19 20						19 39					19 59	
Billericay	d					19 17				19 27						19 45					20 05	
Wickford 2	d				19 19	19 24				19 34						19 51					20 11	
Battlesbridge	d				19 23																	
South Woodham Ferrers	d				19 27																	
North Fambridge	d				19 34																	
Althorne	d				19 39																	
Burnham-on-Crouch	d				19 44																	
Southminster	a				19 52																	
Rayleigh	d					19 29				19 39						19 56					20 16	
Hockley	d					19 33				19 43						20 01					20 21	
Rochford	d					19 37				19 47						20 04					20 24	
Southend Airport ✈	d					19 39				19 49						20 07					20 27	
Prittlewell	d					19 42				19 52						20 10					20 30	
Southend Victoria	a					19 47				19 58						20 14					20 34	

		LE	LE 1	LE	LE 1	LE 1	LE	LE 1	LE	LE 1	LE 1	LE	LE	LE 1	LE 1	CC	LE 1	LE	LE 1	LE	LE 1	LE	LE 1
London Liverpool Street 15 ⊖	d	19 40	19 48	19 50		19 55	20 00	20 02	20 10	20 13	20 18	20 20	20 30		20 35	20 35	20 38	20 40	20 48	20 50	20 55	21 00	21 02
Stratford 7 ⊖	d	19 47	19 55	19 57		20 02	20 07	20 09	20 17	20 20	20 25	20 27	20 37		20 42	20a43	20 45	20 47	20 55	20 57	21 02	21 07	21 09
Maryland	d	19 49		19 59			20 09		20 19			20 29	20 39					20 49		20 59		21 09	
Forest Gate	d	19 51		20 01			20 11		20 21			20 31	20 41					20 51		21 01		21 11	
Manor Park	d	19 53		20 03			20 13		20 23			20 33	20 43					20 53		21 03		21 13	
Ilford 2	d	19 56		20 06			20 16		20 26			20 36	20 46					20 56		21 06		21 16	
Seven Kings	d	19 58		20 08			20 18		20 28			20 38	20 48					20 58		21 08		21 18	
Goodmayes	d	20 00		20 10			20 20		20 30			20 40	20 50					21 00		21 10		21 20	
Chadwell Heath	d	20 02		20 12			20 22		20 32			20 42	20 52					21 02		21 12		21 22	
Romford	d	20 06		20 16			20 26		20 36	20 28		20 46	20 56				20 53	21 06		21 16		21 26	
Gidea Park 2	d	20 10		20 20			20 30		20 40			20 50	21 00					21 10		21 20		21 30	
Harold Wood	d	20 13		20 23			20 33		20 43			20 53	21 03					21 13		21 23		21 33	
Brentwood	d	20 17		20 27			20 37		20 47			20 57	21 07					21 17		21 27		21 37	
Shenfield 3	a	20 23	20 11	20 33		20 18	20 43	20 24	20 53	20 38	20 40	21 03	21 13		20 58		21 02	21 23	21 11	21 33	21 18	21 43	21 24
Shenfield 3	d					20 19				20 39					20 59						21 19		
Billericay	d					20 25				20 45					21 05						21 25		
Wickford 2	d				20 16	20 31				20 51				20 56	21 11						21 31		
Battlesbridge	d				20 20									21 00									
South Woodham Ferrers	d				20 24									21 04									
North Fambridge	d				20 31									21 11									
Althorne	d				20 36									21 16									
Burnham-on-Crouch	d				20 41									21 21									
Southminster	a				20 47									21 27									
Rayleigh	d					20 36				20 56					21 16						21 36		
Hockley	d					20 41				21 01					21 21						21 41		
Rochford	d					20 44				21 04					21 24						21 44		
Southend Airport ✈	d					20 47				21 07					21 27						21 47		
Prittlewell	d					20 50				21 10					21 30						21 50		
Southend Victoria	a					20 54				21 14					21 34						21 54		

Table 5

Mondays to Fridays

until 26 July

London - Shenfield, Southminster and Southend Victoria

Network Diagram - see first Page of Table 5

		LE	LE ■1	LE ■1	LE ■1	LE	LE	LE ■1	CC	LE ■1	LE	LE ■1	LE	LE ■1	LE ■1	LE ■1	LE	LE ■1 A ThFO	LE ■1	LE	LE ■1 A	LE ■1 B MT WO	LE
London Liverpool Street [15] ⊖	d	21 10		21 13	21 18	21 20	21 30	21 35	21 35	21 38	21 40	21 48	21 50		21 55	22 02	22 05	22 13	22 18	22 20		22 25	22 35
Stratford [7] ⊖	d	21 17		21 20	21 25	21 27	21 37	21 42	21a43	21 45	21 47	21 55	21 57		22 02	22 09	22 12	22 20	22 25	22 27		22 32	22 42
Maryland	d	21 19				21 29	21 39				21 49		21 59				22 14			22 29			22 44
Forest Gate	d	21 21				21 31	21 41				21 51		22 01				22 16			22 31			22 46
Manor Park	d	21 23				21 33	21 43				21 53		22 03				22 18			22 33			22 48
Ilford [2]	d	21 26				21 36	21 46				21 56		22 06				22 21			22 36			22 51
Seven Kings	d	21 28				21 38	21 48				21 58		22 08				22 23			22 38			22 53
Goodmayes	d	21 30				21 40	21 50				22 00		22 10				22 25			22 40			22 55
Chadwell Heath	d	21 32				21 42	21 52				22 02		22 12				22 27			22 42			22 57
Romford	d	21 36		21 28		21 46	21 56			21 53	22 06		22 16				22 31	22 28		22 46			23 01
Gidea Park [2]	d	21 40				21 50	22 00				22 10		22 20				22 35			22 50			23 05
Harold Wood	d	21 43				21 53	22 03				22 13		22 23				22 38			22 53			23 08
Brentwood	d	21 47				21 57	22 07				22 17		22 27				22 42			22 57			23 12
Shenfield [3]	a	21 53		21 38	21 40	22 03	22 13	21 58		22 02	22 23	22 11	22 33		22 18	22 24	22 48	22 38	22 40	23 03		22 48	23 18
Shenfield [3]	d			21 39				21 59							22 19			22 39				22 49	
Billericay	d			21 45				22 05							22 25			22 45				22 55	
Wickford [2]	d		21 36	21 51				22 11						22 16	22 31			22 51			22 56	23 01	
Battlesbridge	d		21 40											22 20							23 00		
South Woodham Ferrers	d		21 44											22 24							23 04		
North Fambridge	d		21 51											22 31							23 11		
Althorne	d		21 56											22 36							23 16		
Burnham-on-Crouch	d		22 01											22 41							23 21		
Southminster	a		22 07											22 47							23 27		
Rayleigh	d			21 56				22 16							22 36			22 56				23 06	
Hockley	d			22 01				22 21							22 41			23 01				23 11	
Rochford	d			22 04				22 24							22 44			23 04				23 14	
Southend Airport ✈	d			22 07				22 27							22 47			23 07				23 17	
Prittlewell	d			22 10				22 30							22 50			23 10				23 20	
Southend Victoria	a			22 14				22 34							22 54			23 14				23 24	

		LE ■1 A	LE ■1 B MT WO	LE ■1 A	LE ■1 B MT WO	LE ■1 B MT WO	LE A	LE B MT WO	LE ■1 A	LE A	LE ■1 B MT WO	LE ■1 A	LE B MT WO	LE ■1 A	LE ■1 B MT WO	LE A	LE ◇■1 B MT WO	LE	LE ■1 A	LE ■1 A	LE ■1 B MT WO	LE A	LE A
London Liverpool Street [15] ⊖	d	22 38		22 45	22 50		22 50	22 55	23 02	23 05	23 10	23 15	23 15	23 18		23 20	23 30	23 35	23 45	23 48	23 50	23 50	23 55
Stratford [7] ⊖	d	22 45		22 52	22 57		22 57	23 02	23 09	23 12	23 17	23 22	23 22	23 25		23 27	23u39	23 42	23 52	23 55	23 57	23 57	00 02
Maryland	d						22 59	23 04		23 14			23 24			23 29		23 44				23 59	00 04
Forest Gate	d						23 01	23 06		23 16			23 26			23 31		23 46				00 01	00 06
Manor Park	d						23 03	23 08		23 18			23 28			23 33		23 48				00 03	00 08
Ilford [2]	d						23 06	23 11		23 21			23 31			23 36		23 51				00 06	00 11
Seven Kings	d						23 08	23 13		23 23			23 33			23 38		23 53				00 08	00 13
Goodmayes	d						23 10	23 15		23 25			23 35			23 40		23 55				00 10	00 15
Chadwell Heath	d						23 12	23 17		23 27			23 37			23 42		23 57				00 12	00 17
Romford	d						23 16	23 21		23 31			23 41			23 46		00 02				00 16	00 21
Gidea Park [2]	d						23 20	23 25		23 35			23 45			23 50		00 05				00 20	00 25
Harold Wood	d						23 23	23 28		23 38			23 48			23 53		00 08				00 23	00 28
Brentwood	d						23 27	23 32		23 42			23 52			23 57		00 12				00 27	00 32
Shenfield [3]	a	23 00		23 08	23 20		23 33	23 38	23 24	23 48	23 40	23 38	23 58	23 40		00 03	00 02	00 18	00 08	00 10	00 20	00 33	00 38
Shenfield [3]	d			23 09		23 23						23 39			23 43				00 09				
Billericay	d			23 15		23 29						23 45			23 49				00 15				
Wickford [2]	d		23 06	23 21		23 35						23 51			23 55				00 21				
Battlesbridge	d		23 10																				
South Woodham Ferrers	d		23 14																				
North Fambridge	d		23 21																				
Althorne	d		23 26																				
Burnham-on-Crouch	d		23 31																				
Southminster	a		23 37																				
Rayleigh	d			23 26		23 40						23 56			00 01				00 26				
Hockley	d			23 31		23 45						00 01			00 05				00 31				
Rochford	d			23 34		23 48						00 04			00 08				00 34				
Southend Airport ✈	d			23 37		23 51						00 07			00 11				00 37				
Prittlewell	d			23 40		23 54						00 10			00 14				00 40				
Southend Victoria	a			23 48		23 58						00 18			00 18				00 48				

A until 15 June, from 21 June until 26 July **B** until 20 June

Table 5

Mondays to Fridays

27 July to 10 August

London - Shenfield, Southminster and Southend Victoria

Network Diagram - see first Page of Table 5

		LE MO ■1	LE MO ■1	LE ■1 B MX	LE ■1 C	LE C	LE B MX	LE MO	LE ■1 B MX	LE MO ■1	LE B MX	LE MO	LE C	LE B MX	LE MO	LE MO ■1	LE ■1 B MX	LE MO ■1	LE B MX	LE MO	LE ■1 C	LE B MX	LE MO	LE MO ■1
London Liverpool Street [15] ⊖	d	23p10		23p10	23p15	23p20	23p22	23p22	23p25	23p25	23p32	23p32	23p35	←	←	23p35	23p40	23p40	23p42	23p42	23p45	←	←	23p45
Stratford [7] ⊖	d	23p22		23p22	23p22	23p27	23p33	23p33	23p37	23p37	23p43	23p43	23p42	23p43	23p43	23p45	23p52	23p52	23p53	23p53	23p52	23p53	23p53	23p54
Maryland	d					23p29					→	→	23p44						→	→				
Forest Gate	d					23p31	23p36	23p36					23p46	23p46	23p46							23p56	23p56	
Manor Park	d					23p33	23p38	23p38					23p48	23p48	23p48							23p58	23p58	
Ilford [2]	d					23p36	23p41	23p41					23p51	23p51	23p51							00 01	00 01	
Seven Kings	d					23p38	23p43	23p43					23p53	23p53	23p53							00 03	00 03	
Goodmayes	d					23p40	23p45	23p45					23p55	23p55	23p55							00 05	00 05	
Chadwell Heath	d					23p42	23p47	23p47					23p57	23p57	23p57							00 07	00 07	
Romford	d					23p46	23p51	23p51					00 02	00 02	00 02							00 12	00 11	
Gidea Park [2]	d					23p50	23p55	23p55					00 05	00 05	00 05							00 15	00 15	
Harold Wood	d					23p53	23p58	23p58					00 08	00 08	00 08							00 18	00 18	
Brentwood	d					23p57	00 02	00 02					00 12	00 12	00 12							00 22	00 22	
Shenfield [3]	a	23p37		23p38	23p38	00 03	00 08	00 09	23p53	23p52			00 18	00 18	00 19	00 01	00 08	00 09			00 08	00 28	00 29	00 10
Shenfield [3]	d	23p38		23p39	23p39				23p54	23p54							00 09	00 09			00 09			
Billericay	d	23p45		23p45	23p45				23p59	23p59							00 15	00 15			00 15			
Wickford [2]	d	23p51	23p56	23p51	23p51				00 06	00 06							00 21	00 21			00 21			
Battlesbridge	d		00 01																					
South Woodham Ferrers	d		00 04																					
North Fambridge	d		00 11																					
Althorne	d		00 16																					
Burnham-on-Crouch	d		00 21																					
Southminster	a		00 27																					
Rayleigh	d	23p56		23p56	23p56				00 11	00 11							00 26	00 26			00 26			
Hockley	d	00 01		00 01	00 01				00 16	00 16							00 31	00 31			00 31			
Rochford	d	00 04		00 04	00 04				00 19	00 19							00 34	00 34			00 34			
Southend Airport ✈	d	00 07		00 07	00 07				00 22	00 22							00 37	00 37			00 37			
Prittlewell	d	00 10		00 10	00 10				00 25	00 25							00 40	00 40			00 40			
Southend Victoria	a	00 14		00 14	00 18				00 29	00 29							00 44	00 44			00 48			

B from 31 July until 10 August **C** 27 July

Table 5

Mondays to Fridays
27 July to 10 August

London - Shenfield, Southminster and Southend Victoria

Network Diagram - see first Page of Table 5

		LE 1 A	LE 1 B	LE B	LE MX A	LE MO		LE MX 1 A	LE MO 1	LE B	LE MO	LE MX A	LE MO 1	LE C	LE 1 C	LE 1 B		LE C	LE 1 C	LE 1 C	LE 1 B	LE 1 C	LE 1 C	LE B	LE C
London Liverpool Street 15 ⊖	d	23p45	23p48	23p50	23p52	23p52		23p55	23p55	00 01	00 02	00 02	00 02	00 12	00 12	00 15		←	←	00 15	00 18	←	00 18	00 20	00 22
Stratford 7 ⊖	d	23p54	23p55	23p57	00 03	00 03		00 07	00 07	00 08	00 13	00 13	00a11	00 23	00 24	00 22		00 23	00 24	00 27	00 25	00 27	00a27	00 27	00 33
Maryland	d			23p59						00 10				→	→					→				00 29	
Forest Gate	d			00 01	00 06	00 06				00 12	00 16	00 16						00 26						00 31	00 36
Manor Park	d			00 03	00 08	00 08				00 14	00 18	00 18						00 28						00 33	00 38
Ilford 2	d			00 06	00 11	00 11				00 17	00 21	00 21						00 31						00 36	00 41
Seven Kings	d			00 08	00 13	00 13				00 19	00 23	00 23						00 33						00 38	00 43
Goodmayes	d			00 10	00 15	00 15				00 21	00 25	00 25						00 35						00 40	00 45
Chadwell Heath	d			00 12	00 17	00 17				00 23	00 27	00 27						00 37						00 42	00 47
Romford	d			00 16	00 21	00 21				00 27	00 31	00 31				00 32		00 41						00 46	00 51
Gidea Park 2	d			00 20	00 25	00 25				00a31	00 35	00 35						00 45						00 50	00 55
Harold Wood	d			00 23	00 28	00 28					00 38	00 38						00 48						00 53	00 58
Brentwood	d			00 27	00 32	00 32					00 42	00 42						00 52						00 57	01 02
Shenfield 3	a	00 11	00 10	00 33	00 38	00 39		00 23	00 22		00 48	00 49				00 44		00 58	00 40		00 47	00 45		01 03	01 08
Shenfield 3	d							00 24	00 24							00 45						00 46			
Billericay	d							00 30	00 30							00 51						00 52			
Wickford 2	d							00 36	00 36							00 56						00 58			
Battlesbridge	d																								
South Woodham Ferrers	d																								
North Fambridge	d																								
Althorne	d																								
Burnham-on-Crouch	d																								
Southminster	a																								
Rayleigh	d							00 41	00 41							01 01						01 03			
Hockley	d							00 46	00 46							01 06						01 08			
Rochford	d							00 49	00 49							01 09						01 11			
Southend Airport ✈	d							00 52	00 52							01 12						01 14			
Prittlewell	d							00 55	00 55							01 15						01 17			
Southend Victoria	a							00 59	00 59							01 23						01 21			

		LE B		LE C	LE 1 C	LE C	LE 1 B	LE 1 C	LE 1 B	LE 1 C	LE C	LE B		LE C	LE C	LE 1 C	LE C	LE C	LE C	LE C	LE C	LE C		LE C	LE 1
London Liverpool Street 15 ⊖	d	00 32		00 32	00 40	00 42	00 46	00 46	00 50	←	00 52	00 55		←	01 02	01 10	01 12	01 22	01 32	01 42	01 52	02 02		02 12	
Stratford 7 ⊖	d	00 39		00 43	00 52	00 53	00 53	01 00	00 57	01 00	01 03	01 02		01 03	01 13	01 22	01 23	01 33	01 43	01 53	02 03	02 13		02 23	
Maryland	d	00 41						→			→	01 04													
Forest Gate	d	00 43		00 46		00 56						01 06		01 06	01 16		01 26	01 36	01 46	01 56	02 06	02 16		02 26	
Manor Park	d	00 45		00 48		00 58						01 08		01 08	01 18		01 28	01 38	01 48	01 58	02 08	02 18		02 28	
Ilford 2	d	00 48		00 51		01 01						01 11		01 11	01 21		01 31	01 41	01 51	02 01	02 11	02 21		02 31	
Seven Kings	d	00 50		00 53		01 03						01 13		01 13	01 23		01 33	01 43	01 53	02 03	02 13	02 23		02 33	
Goodmayes	d	00 52		00 55		01 05						01 15		01 15	01 25		01 35	01 45	01 55	02 05	02 15	02 25		02 35	
Chadwell Heath	d	00 54		00 57		01 07						01 17		01 17	01 27		01 37	01 47	01 57	02 07	02 17	02 27		02 37	
Romford	d	00 58		01 01		01 11			01 08			01 21		01 21	01 31		01 41	01 51	02 01	02 11	02 21	02 31		02 41	
Gidea Park 2	d	01a02		01 05		01 15	01 07					01 25		01 25	01 35		01 45	01 55	02a05	02 15	02a25	02 35		02a45	
Harold Wood	d			01 08		01 18						01 28		01 28	01 38		01 48	01 58		02 18		02 38			
Brentwood	d			01 12		01 22						01 32		01 32	01 42		01 52	02 02		02 22		02 42			
Shenfield 3	a			01 18	01 07	01 28	01 17		01 20	01 17		01 38		01 38	01 48	01 37	01 58	02 08		02 28		02 48			
Shenfield 3	d				01 09				01 20							01 39									
Billericay	d				01 15				01 26							01 45									
Wickford 2	d				01 21				01 31							01 51									05 16
Battlesbridge	d																								05 20
South Woodham Ferrers	d																								05 24
North Fambridge	d																								05 41
Althorne	d																								05 46
Burnham-on-Crouch	d																								05 51
Southminster	a																								05 57
Rayleigh	d				01 26				01 36							01 56									
Hockley	d				01 31				01 41							02 01									
Rochford	d				01 34				01 44							02 04									
Southend Airport ✈	d				01 37				01 47							02 07									
Prittlewell	d				01 40				01 50							02 10									
Southend Victoria	a				01 44				01 58							02 14									

A from 31 July until 10 August
B 27 July
C not 27 July

Table 5

Mondays to Fridays
27 July to 10 August

London - Shenfield, Southminster and Southend Victoria

Network Diagram - see first Page of Table 5

		LE 1	LE 1	LE	LE	LE 1	LE 1	LE		LE 1	LE 1	LE	LE 1	LE 1	LE	LE	LE 1	LE 1		LE	LE 1	LE	LE 1	LE	
London Liverpool Street 15 ⊖	d	05 23		05 28	05 37	05 52	05 55	06 00		06 02		06 10	06 12	06 15	06 20	06 30	06 35	06 38		06 40	06 48	06 50	06 55	07 00	
Stratford 7 ⊖	d	05 30		05 35	05 45	06a01	06 02	06 08		06 09		06 18	06 19	06 22	06 28	06 38	06 42	06 45		06 48	06 55	06 58	07 02	07 08	
Maryland	d																								
Forest Gate	d				05 48			06 11				06 21			06 31	06 41				06 51		07 01		07 11	
Manor Park	d				05 50			06 13				06 23			06 33	06 43				06 53		07 03		07 13	
Ilford 2	d			05 40	05 53			06 16				06 26			06 36	06 46				06 56		07 06		07 16	
Seven Kings	d			05 42	05 55			06 18				06 28			06 38	06 48				06 58		07 08		07 18	
Goodmayes	d				05 57			06 20				06 30			06 40	06 50				07 00		07 10		07 20	
Chadwell Heath	d				05 59			06 22				06 32			06 42	06 52				07 02		07 12		07 22	
Romford	d	05 38		05 48	06 03			06 26				06 36			06 46	06 56				07 06		07 16		07 26	
Gidea Park 2	d			05 51	06 07			06 30				06 40			06 50	07 00				07 10		07 20		07 30	
Harold Wood	d			05 54	06 10			06 33				06 43			06 53	07 03				07 13		07 23		07 33	
Brentwood	d			05 59	06 14			06 37				06 47			06 57	07 07				07 17		07 27		07 37	
Shenfield 3	a	05 47		06 04	06 20		06 18	06 43		06 24		06 53	06 35	06 38	07 03	07 13	06 58	07 00		07 23	07 11	07 33	07 18	07 43	
Shenfield 3	d		05 56	06 04			06 19				06 33			06 39			06 59						07 19		
Billericay	d		06 02	06 10			06 25				06 39			06 45			07 05						07 25		
Wickford 2	d		06 09	06 16			06 31				06 46			06 51			07 11						07 31		
Battlesbridge	d		06 13								06 50														
South Woodham Ferrers	d		06 17								06 54														
North Fambridge	d		06 24								07 03														
Althorne	d		06 29								07 08														
Burnham-on-Crouch	d		06 34								07 13														
Southminster	a		06 40								07 19														
Rayleigh	d			06 21			06 36							06 56			07 16						07 36		
Hockley	d			06 26			06 41							07 01			07 21						07 41		
Rochford	d			06 29			06 44							07 04			07 24						07 44		
Southend Airport ✈	d			06 32			06 47							07 07			07 27						07 47		
Prittlewell	d			06 35			06 50							07 10			07 30						07 50		
Southend Victoria	a			06 39			06 55							07 14			07 34						07 54		

		LE 1	LE 1	LE		LE 1	LE 1	LE 1	LE	LE	LE 1	LE 1	LE	LE 1		LE	LE 1	LE 1	LE 1	LE	LE 1	LE	LE	LE 1	
London Liverpool Street 15 ⊖	d	07 02	07 08	07 10			07 13	07 18	07 20	07 30	07 33	07 36	07 40	07 46		07 50		07 57	08 00	08 00	08 06	08 07	08 10	08 13	
Stratford 7 ⊖	d	07 09	07 15	07 18			07 20	07 25	07 28	07 38	07 42	07 45	07 48	07 54		07 58		08 05	08 08	08 08	08 14	08 14	08 18	08 21	
Maryland	d																								
Forest Gate	d			07 21					07 31	07 41			07 51			08 01				08 11			08 21		
Manor Park	d			07 23					07 33	07 43			07 53			08 03				08 13			08 23		
Ilford 2	d			07 26					07 36	07 46			07 56			08 06				08 16		08 21	08 26		
Seven Kings	d			07 28					07 38	07 48			07 58			08 08				08 18			08 28		
Goodmayes	d			07 30					07 40	07 50			08 00			08 10				08 20			08 30		
Chadwell Heath	d			07 32					07 42	07 52			08 02			08 12				08 22			08 32		
Romford	d			07 36			07 28		07 46	07 56			08 06			08 16				08 26		08 29	08 36		
Gidea Park 2	d			07 40					07 50	08 00			08 10			08 20				08 30		08a35	08 40		
Harold Wood	d			07 43					07 53	08 03			08 13			08 23				08 33			08 43		
Brentwood	d			07 47					07 57	08 07			08 17			08 27				08 37			08 47		
Shenfield 3	a	07 24	07 30	07 53			07 38	07 40	08 03	08 13	07 59	08 01	08 25	08 10		08 35		08 22	08 25	08 43	08 30		08 53	08 38	
Shenfield 3	d						07 39				07 59							08 22						08 39	
Billericay	d						07 45				08 05							08 28						08 45	
Wickford 2	d					07 36	07 51				08 11						08 16	08 34						08 51	
Battlesbridge	d					07 40											08 20								
South Woodham Ferrers	d					07 44											08 24								
North Fambridge	d					07 53											08 31								
Althorne	d					07 58											08 36								
Burnham-on-Crouch	d					08 03											08 41								
Southminster	a					08 09											08 47								
Rayleigh	d						07 56				08 16							08 39						08 56	
Hockley	d						08 01				08 21							08 44						09 01	
Rochford	d						08 04				08 24							08 47						09 04	
Southend Airport ✈	d						08 07				08 27							08 50						09 07	
Prittlewell	d						08 10				08 30							08 53						09 10	
Southend Victoria	a						08 16				08 34							08 57						09 14	

Table 5

Mondays to Fridays

27 July to 10 August

London - Shenfield, Southminster and Southend Victoria

Network Diagram - see first Page of Table 5

Station		LE	LE 1	LE	LE	LE	LE 1	LE 1	LE 1	LE		LE	LE 1	LE	LE	LE 1	LE	LE	LE 1	LE		LE	LE 1	LE 1	LE
London Liverpool Street 15 ⊖	d	08 17	08 17	08 20	08 27	08 30		08 32	08 36	08 40		08 43	08 48	08 50	08 52	08 55	08 55	09 00	09 02	09 05		09 10		09 13	09 15
Stratford 7 ⊖	d	08 24	08 25	08 28	08 34	08 38		08 42	08 45	08 48		08 52	08 55	08 58	09 01	09 02	09 04	09 07	09 09	09 12		09 17		09 21	09 24
Maryland	d																								
Forest Gate	d			08 31		08 41				08 51				09 01				09 11				09 21			
Manor Park	d			08 33		08 43				08 53				09 03				09 13				09 23			
Ilford 2	d	08a31		08 36	08a41	08 46				08 56		08 59		09 06	09 09		09a11	09 16		09 21		09 26			09 31
Seven Kings	d			08 38		08 48				08 58				09 08				09 18				09 28			
Goodmayes	d			08 40		08 50				09 00				09 10				09 20				09 30			
Chadwell Heath	d			08 42		08 52				09 02				09 12				09 22				09 32			
Romford	d			08 46		08 56				09 06		09 09		09 16	09 19			09 26		09 29		09 36			09 39
Gidea Park 2	d			08 50		09 00				09 10		09a15		09 20	09a25			09 30		09a35		09 40			09a45
Harold Wood	d			08 53		09 03				09 13				09 23				09 33				09 43			
Brentwood	d			08 57		09 07				09 17				09 27				09 37				09 47			
Shenfield 3	a		08 41	09 03		09 13		08 59	09 01	09 23			09 11	09 33		09 18		09 43	09 24			09 53		09 38	
Shenfield 3	d							08 59								09 19								09 39	
Billericay	d							09 05								09 25								09 45	
Wickford 2	d						08 56	09 11								09 31							09 36	09 51	
Battlesbridge	d						09 00																09 40		
South Woodham Ferrers	d						09 04																09 44		
North Fambridge	d						09 11																09 51		
Althorne	d						09 16																09 56		
Burnham-on-Crouch	d						09 21																10 01		
Southminster	a						09 27																10 07		
Rayleigh	d							09 16								09 36								09 56	
Hockley	d							09 21								09 41								10 01	
Rochford	d							09 24								09 44								10 04	
Southend Airport ✈	d							09 27								09 47								10 07	
Prittlewell	d							09 30								09 50								10 10	
Southend Victoria	a							09 34								09 54								10 14	

Station		LE 1	LE	LE	LE	LE		LE 1	LE 1	LE	LE 1	LE	LE 1	LE 1	LE	LE 1		LE	LE 1	LE 1	LE	LE	LE 1	LE 1	LE 1
London Liverpool Street 15 ⊖	d	09 18	09 20	09 24	09 30	09 33		09 34	09 38	09 40	09 48	09 50		09 55	10 00	10 02		10 10	10 13	10 18	10 20	10 30		10 35	10 38
Stratford 7 ⊖	d	09 25	09 28	09 32	09 37	09 40		09 42	09 45	09 48	09 55	09 58		10 02	10 08	10 09		10 18	10 20	10 25	10 28	10 38		10 42	10 45
Maryland	d																								
Forest Gate	d		09 31		09 41					09 51		10 01			10 11			10 21			10 31	10 41			
Manor Park	d		09 33		09 43					09 53		10 03			10 13			10 23			10 33	10 43			
Ilford 2	d		09 36	09 39	09 46	09 51				09 56		10 06			10 16			10 26			10 36	10 46			
Seven Kings	d		09 38		09 48					09 58		10 08			10 18			10 28			10 38	10 48			
Goodmayes	d		09 40		09 50					10 00		10 10			10 20			10 30			10 40	10 50			
Chadwell Heath	d		09 42		09 52					10 02		10 12			10 22			10 32			10 42	10 52			
Romford	d		09 46	09 49	09 56	09 59			09 53	10 06		10 16			10 26			10 36	10 28		10 46	10 56			10 53
Gidea Park 2	d		09 50	09a55	10 00	10a05				10 10		10 20			10 30			10 40			10 50	11 00			
Harold Wood	d		09 53		10 03					10 13		10 23			10 33			10 43			10 53	11 03			
Brentwood	d		09 57		10 07					10 17		10 27			10 37			10 47			10 57	11 07			
Shenfield 3	a	09 40	10 03		10 13			09 58	10 02	10 23	10 11	10 33		10 18	10 43	10 24		10 53	10 38	10 40	11 03	11 13		10 58	11 02
Shenfield 3	d							09 59						10 19					10 39					10 59	
Billericay	d							10 05						10 25					10 45					11 05	
Wickford 2	d							10 11					10 16	10 31					10 51				10 56	11 11	
Battlesbridge	d												10 20										11 00		
South Woodham Ferrers	d												10 24										11 04		
North Fambridge	d												10 31										11 11		
Althorne	d												10 36										11 16		
Burnham-on-Crouch	d												10 41										11 21		
Southminster	a												10 47										11 27		
Rayleigh	d							10 16						10 36					10 56					11 16	
Hockley	d							10 21						10 41					11 01					11 21	
Rochford	d							10 24						10 44					11 04					11 24	
Southend Airport ✈	d							10 27						10 47					11 07					11 27	
Prittlewell	d							10 30						10 50					11 10					11 30	
Southend Victoria	a							10 34						10 54					11 14					11 34	

Table 5

Mondays to Fridays

27 July to 10 August

London - Shenfield, Southminster and Southend Victoria

Network Diagram - see first Page of Table 5

Station		LE		LE 1	LE	LE 1	LE	LE 1	LE	LE 1	LE 1	LE 1		LE	LE	LE 1	LE 1	LE	LE 1	LE	LE 1	LE 1		LE	LE 1
London Liverpool Street 15 ⊖	d	10 40		10 48	10 50	10 55	11 00	11 02	11 10		11 13	11 18		11 20	11 30	11 35	11 38	11 40	11 48	11 50		11 55		12 00	12 02
Stratford 7 ⊖	d	10 48		10 55	10 58	11 02	11 08	11 09	11 18		11 20	11 25		11 28	11 38	11 42	11 45	11 48	11 55	11 58		12 02		12 08	12 09
Maryland	d																								
Forest Gate	d	10 51			11 01		11 11		11 21					11 31	11 41			11 51		12 01				12 11	
Manor Park	d	10 53			11 03		11 13		11 23					11 33	11 43			11 53		12 03				12 13	
Ilford 2	d	10 56			11 06		11 16		11 26					11 36	11 46			11 56		12 06				12 16	
Seven Kings	d	10 58			11 08		11 18		11 28					11 38	11 48			11 58		12 08				12 18	
Goodmayes	d	11 00			11 10		11 20		11 30					11 40	11 50			12 00		12 10				12 20	
Chadwell Heath	d	11 02			11 12		11 22		11 32					11 42	11 52			12 02		12 12				12 22	
Romford	d	11 06			11 16		11 26		11 36		11 28			11 46	11 56		11 53	12 06		12 16				12 26	
Gidea Park 2	d	11 10			11 20		11 30		11 40					11 50	12 00			12 10		12 20				12 30	
Harold Wood	d	11 13			11 23		11 33		11 43					11 53	12 03			12 13		12 23				12 33	
Brentwood	d	11 17			11 27		11 37		11 47					11 57	12 07			12 17		12 27				12 37	
Shenfield 3	a	11 23		11 11	11 33	11 18	11 43	11 24	11 53		11 38	11 40		12 03	12 13	11 58	12 02	12 23	12 11	12 33		12 18		12 43	12 24
Shenfield 3	d					11 19					11 39					11 59						12 19			
Billericay	d					11 25					11 45					12 05						12 25			
Wickford 2	d					11 31				11 36	11 51					12 11					12 16	12 31			
Battlesbridge	d									11 40											12 20				
South Woodham Ferrers	d									11 44											12 24				
North Fambridge	d									11 51											12 31				
Althorne	d									11 56											12 36				
Burnham-on-Crouch	d									12 01											12 41				
Southminster	a									12 07											12 47				
Rayleigh	d					11 36					11 56					12 16						12 36			
Hockley	d					11 41					12 01					12 21						12 41			
Rochford	d					11 44					12 04					12 24						12 44			
Southend Airport ✈	d					11 47					12 07					12 27						12 47			
Prittlewell	d					11 50					12 10					12 30						12 50			
Southend Victoria	a					11 54					12 14					12 34						12 54			

Station		LE	LE 1	LE 1	LE	LE	LE 1	LE 1		LE 1	LE	LE 1	LE	LE 1	LE	LE 1	LE	LE 1		LE 1	LE 1	LE	LE	LE 1	LE 1
London Liverpool Street 15 ⊖	d	12 10	12 13	12 18	12 20	12 30		12 35		12 38	12 40	12 48	12 50	12 55	13 00	13 02	13 10			13 13	13 18	13 20	13 30	13 35	13 38
Stratford 7 ⊖	d	12 18	12 20	12 25	12 28	12 38		12 42		12 45	12 48	12 55	12 58	13 02	13 08	13 09	13 18			13 20	13 25	13 28	13 38	13 42	13 45
Maryland	d																								
Forest Gate	d	12 21			12 31	12 41					12 51		13 01		13 11		13 21					13 31	13 41		
Manor Park	d	12 23			12 33	12 43					12 53		13 03		13 13		13 23					13 33	13 43		
Ilford 2	d	12 26			12 36	12 46					12 56		13 06		13 16		13 26					13 36	13 46		
Seven Kings	d	12 28			12 38	12 48					12 58		13 08		13 18		13 28					13 38	13 48		
Goodmayes	d	12 30			12 40	12 50					13 00		13 10		13 20		13 30					13 40	13 50		
Chadwell Heath	d	12 32			12 42	12 52					13 02		13 12		13 22		13 32					13 42	13 52		
Romford	d	12 36	12 28		12 46	12 56				12 53	13 06		13 16		13 26		13 36			13 28		13 46	13 56		13 53
Gidea Park 2	d	12 40			12 50	13 00					13 10		13 20		13 30		13 40					13 50	14 00		
Harold Wood	d	12 43			12 53	13 03					13 13		13 23		13 33		13 43					13 53	14 03		
Brentwood	d	12 47			12 57	13 07					13 17		13 27		13 37		13 47					13 57	14 07		
Shenfield 3	a	12 53	12 38	12 40	13 03	13 13		12 58		13 02	13 23	13 11	13 33	13 18	13 43	13 24	13 53			13 38	13 40	14 03	14 13	13 58	14 02
Shenfield 3	d		12 39					12 59						13 19						13 39				13 59	
Billericay	d		12 45					13 05						13 25						13 45				14 05	
Wickford 2	d		12 51				12 56	13 11						13 31				13 36		13 51				14 11	
Battlesbridge	d						13 00											13 40							
South Woodham Ferrers	d						13 04											13 44							
North Fambridge	d						13 11											13 51							
Althorne	d						13 16											13 56							
Burnham-on-Crouch	d						13 21											14 01							
Southminster	a						13 27											14 07							
Rayleigh	d		12 56					13 16						13 36						13 56				14 16	
Hockley	d		13 01					13 21						13 41						14 01				14 21	
Rochford	d		13 04					13 24						13 44						14 04				14 24	
Southend Airport ✈	d		13 07					13 27						13 47						14 07				14 27	
Prittlewell	d		13 10					13 30						13 50						14 10				14 30	
Southend Victoria	a		13 14					13 34						13 54						14 14				14 34	

Table 5

Mondays to Fridays

27 July to 10 August

London - Shenfield, Southminster and Southend Victoria

Network Diagram - see first Page of Table 5

		LE	LE [1]	LE		LE [1]	LE [1]	LE	LE [1]	LE	LE [1]	LE [1]	LE	LE		LE [1]	LE [1]	LE [1]	LE	LE [1]	LE	LE [1]	LE	LE [1]	
London Liverpool Street [15] ⊖	d	13 40	13 48	13 50			13 55	14 00	14 02	14 10	14 13	14 18	14 20	14 30			14 35	14 38	14 40	14 48	14 50	14 55	15 00	15 02	
Stratford [7] ⊖	d	13 48	13 55	13 58			14 02	14 08	14 09	14 18	14 20	14 25	14 28	14 38			14 42	14 45	14 48	14 55	14 58	15 02	15 08	15 09	
Maryland	d																								
Forest Gate	d	13 51		14 01				14 11		14 21			14 31	14 41					14 51		15 01		15 11		
Manor Park	d	13 53		14 03				14 13		14 23			14 33	14 43					14 53		15 03		15 13		
Ilford [2]	d	13 56		14 06				14 16		14 26			14 36	14 46					14 56		15 06		15 16		
Seven Kings	d	13 58		14 08				14 18		14 28			14 38	14 48					14 58		15 08		15 18		
Goodmayes	d	14 00		14 10				14 20		14 30			14 40	14 50					15 00		15 10		15 20		
Chadwell Heath	d	14 02		14 12				14 22		14 32			14 42	14 52					15 02		15 12		15 22		
Romford	d	14 06		14 16				14 26		14 36	14 28		14 46	14 56				14 53	15 06		15 16		15 26		
Gidea Park [2]	d	14 10		14 20				14 30		14 40			14 50	15 00					15 10		15 20		15 30		
Harold Wood	d	14 13		14 23				14 33		14 43			14 53	15 03					15 13		15 23		15 33		
Brentwood	d	14 17		14 27				14 37		14 47			14 57	15 07					15 17		15 27		15 37		
Shenfield [3]	a	14 23	14 11	14 33			14 18	14 43	14 24	14 53	14 38	14 40	15 03	15 13			14 58	15 02	15 23	15 11	15 33	15 18	15 43	15 24	
Shenfield [3]	d						14 19				14 39						14 59					15 19			
Billericay	d						14 25				14 45						15 05					15 25			
Wickford [2]	d					14 16	14 31				14 51					14 56	15 11					15 31			
Battlesbridge	d					14 20										15 00									
South Woodham Ferrers	d					14 24										15 04									
North Fambridge	d					14 31										15 11									
Althorne	d					14 36										15 16									
Burnham-on-Crouch	d					14 41										15 21									
Southminster	a					14 47										15 27									
Rayleigh	d						14 36				14 56						15 16					15 36			
Hockley	d						14 41				15 01						15 21					15 41			
Rochford	d						14 44				15 04						15 24					15 44			
Southend Airport ✈	d						14 47				15 07						15 27					15 47			
Prittlewell	d						14 50				15 10						15 31					15 50			
Southend Victoria	a						14 54				15 14						15 34					15 54			

		LE	LE [1]	LE [1]	LE [1]	LE	LE	LE [1]	LE [1]	LE		LE [1]	LE	LE [1]	LE [1]	LE	LE [1]	LE [1]	LE	LE [1]		LE [1]	LE	LE [1]	LE
London Liverpool Street [15] ⊖	d	15 10		15 13	15 18	15 20	15 30	15 35	15 38	15 40		15 48	15 50		15 55	16 00	16 02	16 10	16 10	16 14		16 17	16 20	16 24	16 28
Stratford [7] ⊖	d	15 18		15 20	15 25	15 28	15 38	15 42	15 45	15 48		15 55	15 58		16 02	16 08	16 09	16 18	16 18	16 22		16 25	16 28	16 32	16 36
Maryland	d																								
Forest Gate	d	15 21				15 31	15 41			15 51			16 01			16 11			16 21				16 31		16 39
Manor Park	d	15 23				15 33	15 43			15 53			16 03			16 13			16 23				16 33		16 41
Ilford [2]	d	15 26				15 36	15 46			15 56			16 06			16 16			16 26				16 36		16 44
Seven Kings	d	15 28				15 38	15 48			15 58			16 08			16 18			16 28				16 38		16 47
Goodmayes	d	15 30				15 40	15 50			16 00			16 10			16 20			16 30				16 40		16 49
Chadwell Heath	d	15 32				15 42	15 52			16 02			16 12			16 22			16 32				16 42		16 51
Romford	d	15 36		15 28		15 46	15 56		15 53	16 06			16 16			16 26			16 36				16 46		16 55
Gidea Park [2]	d	15 40				15 50	16 00			16 10			16 20			16 30			16 40				16 50		17a00
Harold Wood	d	15 43				15 53	16 03			16 13			16 23			16 33			16 43				16 53		
Brentwood	d	15 47				15 57	16 07			16 17			16 27			16 37			16 47				16 57		
Shenfield [3]	a	15 53		15 38	15 40	16 03	16 13	15 58	16 02	16 23		16 11	16 33		16 18	16 43	16 24	16 34	16 53	16 38		16 41	17 03	16 49	
Shenfield [3]	d			15 39				15 59							16 19			16 34						16 49	
Billericay	d			15 45				16 05							16 25			16 41						16 56	
Wickford [2]	d		15 36	15 51				16 11						16 14	16 31			16 48						17 03	
Battlesbridge	d		15 40											16 18											
South Woodham Ferrers	d		15 44											16 22											
North Fambridge	d		15 51											16 29											
Althorne	d		15 56											16 34											
Burnham-on-Crouch	d		16 01											16 39											
Southminster	a		16 07											16 45											
Rayleigh	d			15 56				16 16							16 36			16 53						17 08	
Hockley	d			16 01				16 21							16 41			16 57						17 12	
Rochford	d			16 04				16 24							16 44			17 01						17 16	
Southend Airport ✈	d			16 07				16 27							16 47			17 03						17 18	
Prittlewell	d			16 10				16 30							16 50			17 06						17 21	
Southend Victoria	a			16 14				16 34							16 54			17 15						17 27	

Table 5

Mondays to Fridays

27 July to 10 August

London - Shenfield, Southminster and Southend Victoria

Network Diagram - see first Page of Table 5

		LE [1]	LE [1]	LE	LE	LE [1]		LE [1]	LE [1]	LE	LE [1]	LE	LE [1]	LE	LE	LE ◇[1]		LE [1]	LE	LE [1]	LE	LE [1]	LE [1]	LE	LE [1]
London Liverpool Street [15] ⊖	d	16 32	16 34	16 36	16 40			16 40	16 44	16 47	16 47	16 50	16 54	16 57	17 00	17 02		17 04	17 07	17 08	17 10	17 12	17 15	17 17	17 18
Stratford [7] ⊖	d		16 42	16 43	16 48			16 48	16a52	16 54	16 55	16 58	17 02	17 04	17 08	17 10		17 13	17 14	17a16	17 18	17a20	17 23	17 24	17a26
Maryland	d																								
Forest Gate	d				16 51							17 01			17 11						17 21				
Manor Park	d				16 53							17 03			17 13						17 23				
Ilford [2]	d			16 50	16 56					17 00		17 06		17 10	17 16				17 20		17 26			17 30	
Seven Kings	d			16 52						17 02				17 12					17 22					17 32	
Goodmayes	d			16 54						17 04				17 14					17 24					17 34	
Chadwell Heath	d			16 56	17 00					17 06		17 10		17 16	17 20				17 26		17 30			17 36	
Romford	d			17 00	17 04					17 10		17 14		17 20	17 24				17 30		17 34			17 40	
Gidea Park [2]	d			17 04	17a10					17 14		17a20		17 24	17a30				17 34		17a40			17 44	
Harold Wood	d			17 07						17 17				17 27					17 37					17 47	
Brentwood	d			17 11						17 21				17 31					17 41					17 51	
Shenfield [3]	a	16 54	16 58	17 19				17 04		17 29	17 11		17 19	17 39				17 30	17 49				17 39	17 59	
Shenfield [3]	d							17 04					17 19					17 30					17 39		
Billericay	d							17 11					17 26					17 37					17 46		
Wickford [2]	d					17 06		17 18					17 33					17 44					17 53		
Battlesbridge	d					17 10																			
South Woodham Ferrers	d					17 14																			
North Fambridge	d					17 21																			
Althorne	d					17 26																			
Burnham-on-Crouch	d					17 31																			
Southminster	a					17 37																			
Rayleigh	d							17 23					17 38					17 49					17 58		
Hockley	d							17 27					17 42					17 53					18 02		
Rochford	d							17 31					17 46					17 57					18 06		
Southend Airport ✈	d							17 33					17 48					17 59					18 08		
Prittlewell	d							17 36					17 51					18 02					18 11		
Southend Victoria	a							17 42					17 57					18 08					18 17		

		LE		LE [1] A	LE [1] A	LE [1]	LE	LE	LE [1]	LE [1]	LE	LE [1]		LE	LE [1] A	LE	LE [1]	LE	LE	LE	LE [1]	LE [1]		LE	LE [1]
London Liverpool Street [15] ⊖	d	17 20		17 20	17 22	17 25	17 27	17 30	17 32	17 34	17 36	17 38		17 39	17 40	17 42	17 45	17 46	17 49	17 52	17 52	17 54		17 56	17 58
Stratford [7] ⊖	d	17 28		17 29	17 31	17 34	17 34	17 38	17a40	17 43	17 43	17a47		17 46	17 49	17 49	17 53	17 53	17 56	17 59	18a01	18 03		18 03	18a06
Maryland	d																								
Forest Gate	d	17 31						17 41								17 52				18 02					
Manor Park	d	17 33						17 43						17 50					18 00						
Ilford [2]	d	17 36					17 40	17 46			17 50			17 53		17 56		18 00	18 03	18 06				18 10	
Seven Kings	d						17 42				17 52			17 56		17 59		18 02	18 06	18 09				18 12	
Goodmayes	d						17 44				17 54			17 58		18 01		18 04	18 08	18 11				18 14	
Chadwell Heath	d	17 40					17 46	17 50			17 56			18 00		18 03		18 06	18 10	18 13				18 16	
Romford	d	17 44					17 50	17 54			18 00			18 04		18 07		18 10	18 14	18 17				18 20	
Gidea Park [2]	d	17a50					17 54	18a00			18 04			18a09		18a12		18 14	18 18	18a22				18 24	
Harold Wood	d						17 57				18 07							18 17	18 21					18 27	
Brentwood	d						18 01				18 11							18 21	18 25					18 31	
Shenfield [3]	a			17 45		17 51	18 09			17 59	18 19				18 05		18 09	18 29	18 33			18 19		18 39	
Shenfield [3]	d					17 52				17 59							18 09		18 36			18 19			
Billericay	d					17 58				18 06							18 16		→			18 26			
Wickford [2]	d				18 00	18 05				18 13							18 23					18 33			
Battlesbridge	d				18 04																				
South Woodham Ferrers	d				18 08																				
North Fambridge	d				18 14																				
Althorne	d				18 19																				
Burnham-on-Crouch	d				18 24																				
Southminster	a				18 32																				
Rayleigh	d					18 10				18 18							18 28					18 38			
Hockley	d					18 15				18 22							18 32					18 42			
Rochford	d					18 18				18 26							18 36					18 46			
Southend Airport ✈	d					18 21				18 28							18 38					18 48			
Prittlewell	d					18 24				18 31							18 41					18 51			
Southend Victoria	a					18 30				18 37							18 47					18 58			

A The Stratford call is subjtect to introduction during the currency of the timetable.

27 July to 10 August

London - Shenfield, Southminster and Southend Victoria

Network Diagram - see first Page of Table 5

		LE	LE ■	LE	LE ■	LE ■	LE	LE		LE	LE ■	LE ■	LE	LE ■	LE	LE ■	LE ■	LE		LE	LE ■	LE ■	LE	LE ■	LE
London Liverpool Street ⊖	d	17 59	18 00	18 02	18 02	18 05		18 07		18 10	18 12	18 14	18 17	18 18	18 20	18 20	18 25	18 27		18 30	18 32	18 35	18 37	18 38	18 40
Stratford ⊖	d	18 06	18 09	18 09	18 11	18 14		18 14		18 18	18a21	18 23	18 24	18a27	18 28	18 29	18 33	18 34		18 38	18a40	18 43	18 44	18 46	18 48
Maryland	d																								
Forest Gate	d			18 12						18 21					18 31					18 41					18 51
Manor Park	d	18 10								18 23					18 33					18 43					18 53
Ilford	d	18 13		18 16				18 20		18 26			18 30		18 36			18 40		18 46			18 50		18 56
Seven Kings	d	18 16		18 19				18 22					18 32					18 42					18 52		
Goodmayes	d	18 18		18 21				18 24					18 34					18 44					18 54		
Chadwell Heath	d	18 20		18 23				18 26		18 30			18 36		18 40			18 46		18 50			18 56		19 00
Romford	d	18 24		18 27				18 30		18 34			18 40		18 44			18 50		18 54			19 00		19 04
Gidea Park	d	18a29		18a32				18 34		18a40			18 44		18a50			18 54		19a00			19 04		19 08
Harold Wood	d							18 37					18 47					18 57					19 07		19 11
Brentwood	d						←	18 41					18 51					19 01					19 11		19 15
Shenfield	a		18 25			18 31	18 33	18 49				18 40	18 59			18 45	18 50	19 09				18 59	19 19	19 02	19 23
Shenfield	d					18 31	18 36					18 41					18 50					18 59			
Billericay	d					18 38	18 42					18 47					18 57					19 06			
Wickford	d				18 41	18 45	18 49					18 54					19 04					19 13			
Battlesbridge	d				18 45																				
South Woodham Ferrers	d				18 49																				
North Fambridge	d				18 55																				
Althorne	d				19 00																				
Burnham-on-Crouch	d				19 05																				
Southminster	a				19 13																				
Rayleigh	d					18 50	18 54					18 59					19 09					19 18			
Hockley	d					18 55	18 59					19 04					19 13					19 22			
Rochford	d					18 58	19 02					19 07					19 17					19 26			
Southend Airport ✈	d					19 01	19 05					19 10					19 19					19 28			
Prittlewell	d					19 04	19 08					19 13					19 22					19 31			
Southend Victoria	a					19 10	19 14					19 19					19 28					19 37			

		LE ■	LE ■	LE		LE ■	LE	LE ■	LE	LE	LE ■	LE ■	LE	LE ■		LE	LE ■	LE	LE	LE ■	LE ■	LE ■	LE	LE ■	LE
London Liverpool Street ⊖	d	18 41	18 45	18 47		18 48	18 50	18 55	18 57	19 00	19 02	19 08	19 10	19 15		19 17	19 18	19 20	19 30	19 32	19 35	19 38	19 40	19 48	19 50
Stratford ⊖	d	18 49	18 53	18 54		18a56	18 58	19 03	19 04	19 08	19 09	19a15	19 18	19 22		19 24	19 25	19 28	19 38	19a39	19 42	19 45	19 48	19 55	19 58
Maryland	d																								
Forest Gate	d						19 01			19 11			19 21					19 31	19 41				19 51		20 01
Manor Park	d						19 03			19 13			19 23					19 33	19 43				19 53		20 03
Ilford	d			19 00			19 06		19 10	19 16			19 26			19 30		19 36	19 46				19 56		20 06
Seven Kings	d			19 02					19 12	19 18			19 28			19 32		19 38	19 48				19 58		20 08
Goodmayes	d			19 04					19 14	19 20			19 30			19 34		19 40	19 50				20 00		20 10
Chadwell Heath	d			19 06			19 10		19 16	19 22			19 32			19 36		19 42	19 52				20 02		20 12
Romford	d			19 10			19 14		19 20	19 26			19 36			19 40		19 46	19 56				20 06		20 16
Gidea Park	d			19 14			19a20		19 24	19 30			19 40			19a44		19 50	20 00				20 10		20 20
Harold Wood	d			19 17					19 27	19 33			19 43					19 53	20 03				20 13		20 23
Brentwood	d			19 21					19 31	19 37			19 47					19 57	20 07				20 17		20 27
Shenfield	a		19 10	19 29				19 20	19 39	19 43	19 24		19 53	19 38			19 40	20 03	20 13		19 58	20 00	20 23	20 11	20 33
Shenfield	d		19 10					19 20						19 39							19 59				
Billericay	d		19 17					19 27						19 45							20 05				
Wickford	d	19 19	19 24					19 34						19 51							20 11				
Battlesbridge	d	19 23																							
South Woodham Ferrers	d	19 27																							
North Fambridge	d	19 34																							
Althorne	d	19 39																							
Burnham-on-Crouch	d	19 44																							
Southminster	a	19 52																							
Rayleigh	d		19 29					19 39						19 56							20 16				
Hockley	d		19 33					19 43						20 01							20 21				
Rochford	d		19 37					19 47						20 04							20 24				
Southend Airport ✈	d		19 39					19 49						20 07							20 27				
Prittlewell	d		19 42					19 52						20 10							20 30				
Southend Victoria	a		19 47					19 58						20 14							20 34				

27 July to 10 August

London - Shenfield, Southminster and Southend Victoria

Network Diagram - see first Page of Table 5

		LE ■	LE ■	LE	LE ■	LE	LE ■	LE ■	LE	LE		LE ■	LE ■	LE ■	LE	LE ■	LE	LE ■	LE	LE ■		LE	LE ■	LE ■	LE ■
London Liverpool Street ⊖	d		19 55	20 00	20 02	20 10	20 13	20 18	20 20	20 30			20 35	20 38	20 40	20 48	20 50	20 55	21 00	21 02		21 10		21 13	21 18
Stratford ⊖	d		20 02	20 08	20 09	20 18	20 20	20 25	20 28	20 38			20 42	20 45	20 48	20 55	20 58	21 02	21 08	21 09		21 18		21 20	21 25
Maryland	d																								
Forest Gate	d			20 11		20 21			20 31	20 41					20 51		21 01		21 11			21 21			
Manor Park	d			20 13		20 23			20 33	20 43					20 53		21 03		21 13			21 23			
Ilford	d			20 16		20 26			20 36	20 46					20 56		21 06		21 16			21 26			
Seven Kings	d			20 18		20 28			20 38	20 48					20 58		21 08		21 18			21 28			
Goodmayes	d			20 20		20 30			20 40	20 50					21 00		21 10		21 20			21 30			
Chadwell Heath	d			20 22		20 32			20 42	20 52					21 02		21 12		21 22			21 32			
Romford	d			20 26		20 36	20 28		20 46	20 56					21 06		21 16		21 26			21 36			
Gidea Park	d			20 30		20 40			20 50	21 00					21 10		21 20		21 30			21 40			
Harold Wood	d			20 33		20 43			20 53	21 03					21 13		21 23		21 33			21 43			
Brentwood	d			20 37		20 47			20 57	21 07					21 17		21 27		21 37			21 47			
Shenfield	a		20 18	20 43	20 24	20 53	20 38	20 40	21 03	21 13			20 58	21 00	21 23	21 11	21 33	21 18	21 43	21 24		21 53		21 38	21 40
Shenfield	d		20 19				20 39						20 59					21 19						21 39	
Billericay	d		20 25				20 45						21 05					21 25						21 45	
Wickford	d	20 16	20 31				20 51					20 56	21 11					21 31					21 36	21 51	
Battlesbridge	d	20 20										21 00											21 40		
South Woodham Ferrers	d	20 24										21 04											21 44		
North Fambridge	d	20 31										21 11											21 51		
Althorne	d	20 36										21 16											21 56		
Burnham-on-Crouch	d	20 41										21 21											22 01		
Southminster	a	20 47										21 27											22 07		
Rayleigh	d		20 36				20 56						21 16					21 36						21 56	
Hockley	d		20 41				21 01						21 21					21 41						22 01	
Rochford	d		20 44				21 04						21 24					21 44						22 04	
Southend Airport ✈	d		20 47				21 07						21 27					21 47						22 07	
Prittlewell	d		20 50				21 10						21 30					21 50						22 10	
Southend Victoria	a		20 54				21 14						21 34					21 54						22 14	

		LE	LE	LE ■	LE ■	LE		LE ■	LE ■	LE	LE ■	LE ■	LE ■	LE ■	LE	LE ■		LE ■	LE ■	LE	LE ■	LE ■	LE ■	LE	LE ■
London Liverpool Street ⊖	d	21 20	21 30	21 35	21 38	21 40		21 42	21 48	21 50		21 50	21 56	22 02	22 02	22 10		22 12	22 15	22 17	22 22		22 25	22 32	22 35
Stratford ⊖	d	21 28	21 38	21 42	21 45	21 48		21a51	21 55	21 58		22 02	22a04	22 10	22 13	22 22		22a21	22 24	22 28	22a31		22 37	22 43	22 44
Maryland	d																								
Forest Gate	d	21 31	21 41			21 51				22 01					22 16					22 31				22 46	
Manor Park	d	21 33	21 43			21 53				22 03					22 18					22 33				22 48	
Ilford	d	21 36	21 46			21 56				22 06					22 21					22 36				22 51	
Seven Kings	d	21 38	21 48			21 58				22 08					22 23					22 38				22 53	
Goodmayes	d	21 40	21 50			22 00				22 10					22 25					22 40				22 55	
Chadwell Heath	d	21 42	21 52			22 02				22 12					22 27					22 42				22 57	
Romford	d	21 46	21 56			22 06				22 16					22 31					22 46				23 01	
Gidea Park	d	21 50	22 00			22 10				22 20					22 35					22 50				23 05	
Harold Wood	d	21 53	22 03			22 13				22 23					22 38					22 53				23 08	
Brentwood	d	21 57	22 07			22 17				22 27					22 42					22 57				23 12	
Shenfield	a	22 03	22 13	21 58	22 00	22 23			22 11	22 33		22 18		22 26	22 48	22 38			22 40	23 03			22 53	23 18	23 00
Shenfield	d			21 59								22 19				22 39							22 54		
Billericay	d			22 05								22 25				22 45							23 00		
Wickford	d			22 11							22 16	22 31				22 51						22 56	23 06		
Battlesbridge	d										22 20											23 00			
South Woodham Ferrers	d										22 24											23 04			
North Fambridge	d										22 31											23 11			
Althorne	d										22 36											23 16			
Burnham-on-Crouch	d										22 41											23 21			
Southminster	a										22 47											23 27			
Rayleigh	d			22 16								22 36				22 56							23 11		
Hockley	d			22 21								22 41				23 01							23 16		
Rochford	d			22 24								22 44				23 04							23 19		
Southend Airport ✈	d			22 27								22 47				23 07							23 22		
Prittlewell	d			22 30								22 50				23 10							23 25		
Southend Victoria	a			22 34								22 54				23 14							23 29		

Table 5

London - Shenfield, Southminster and Southend Victoria

Mondays to Fridays

27 July to 10 August

Network Diagram - see first Page of Table 5

		LE 1	LE 1	LE	LE 1	LE	LE 1	LE 1	LE	LE 1	LE 1	LE 1	LE 1	LE	LE 1	LE	LE 1	LE 1	LE	LE 1	LE 1 A	LE	LE 1
London Liverpool Street 15 ⊖	d	22 40	22 42	22 42	22 45	22 52	22 52	22 55	23 02	23 07	23 10	23 12		23 12	23 15	23 22	23 22	23 25	23 32	23 35	23 40	23 42	23 42
Stratford 7 ⊖	d	22 52	22a51	22 53	22 54	23 03	23a01	23 07	23 13	23 17	23 22	23a21		23 23	23 25	23 33	23a31	23 37	23 43	23 45	23 52	23 53	23a52
Maryland	d																						
Forest Gate	d			22 56		23 06			23 16					23 26		23 36			23 46			23 56	
Manor Park	d			22 58		23 08			23 18					23 28		23 38			23 48			23 58	
Ilford 2	d			23 01		23 11			23 21					23 31		23 41			23 51			00 01	
Seven Kings	d			23 03		23 13			23 23					23 33		23 43			23 53			00 03	
Goodmayes	d			23 05		23 15			23 25					23 35		23 45			23 55			00 05	
Chadwell Heath	d			23 07		23 17			23 27					23 37		23 47			23 57			00 07	
Romford	d			23 11		23 21			23 31					23 41		23 51			00 02			00 12	
Gidea Park 2	d			23 15		23 25			23 35					23 45		23 55			00 05			00 15	
Harold Wood	d			23 18		23 28			23 38					23 48		23 58			00 08			00 18	
Brentwood	d			23 22		23 32			23 42					23 52		00 02			00 12			00 22	
Shenfield 3	a	23 08		23 28	23 11	23 38		23 23	23 48	23 33	23 38			23 58	23 43	00 08		23 53	00 18	23 59	00 08	00 28	
Shenfield 3	d	23 09						23 24			23 39							23 54			00 09		
Billericay	d	23 15						23 30			23 45							23 59			00 15		
Wickford 2	d	23 21						23 36			23 51		23p56					00 06			00 21		
Battlesbridge	d												00 01										
South Woodham Ferrers	d												00 04										
North Fambridge	d												00 11										
Althorne	d												00 16										
Burnham-on-Crouch	d												00 21										
Southminster	a												00 27										
Rayleigh	d	23 26						23 41			23 56							00 11			00 26		
Hockley	d	23 31						23 46			00 01							00 16			00 31		
Rochford	d	23 34						23 49			00 04							00 19			00 34		
Southend Airport ✈	d	23 37						23 52			00 07							00 22			00 37		
Prittlewell	d	23 40						23 55			00 10							00 25			00 40		
Southend Victoria	a	23 44						23 59			00 14							00 29			00 44		

		LE 1	LE	LE 1
London Liverpool Street 15 ⊖	d	23 45	23 52	23 55
Stratford 7 ⊖	d	23 54	00 03	00 07
Maryland	d			
Forest Gate	d		00 06	
Manor Park	d		00 08	
Ilford 2	d		00 11	
Seven Kings	d		00 13	
Goodmayes	d		00 15	
Chadwell Heath	d		00 17	
Romford	d		00 21	
Gidea Park 2	d		00 25	
Harold Wood	d		00 28	
Brentwood	d		00 32	
Shenfield 3	a	00 11	00 38	00 23
Shenfield 3	d			00 24
Billericay	d			00 30
Wickford 2	d			00 36
Battlesbridge	d			
South Woodham Ferrers	d			
North Fambridge	d			
Althorne	d			
Burnham-on-Crouch	d			
Southminster	a			
Rayleigh	d			00 41
Hockley	d			00 46
Rochford	d			00 49
Southend Airport ✈	d			00 52
Prittlewell	d			00 55
Southend Victoria	a			00 59

A not 27 July

Table 5

London - Shenfield, Southminster and Southend Victoria

Mondays to Fridays

13 August to 28 August

Network Diagram - see first Page of Table 5

		LE 1 A	LE 1 A	LE MX 1	LE 1 B	LE MX	LE A	LE 1 A	LE A	LE B	LE MX	LE A	LE 1 A	LE 1 A	LE A	LE MX 1	LE 1 B	LE A	LE 1 A	LE MX 1	LE MX	LE A	LE 1 A	LE MX
London Liverpool Street 15 ⊖	d	23p10		23p15	23p15	23p20	23p22	23p25	23p32	23p35	23p35	←	23p35	23p40	23p42	23p45	23p45	←	23p45	23p48	23p50	23p52	23p55	00 01
Stratford 7 ⊖	d	23p22		23p22	23p22	23p27	23p33	23p37	23p43	23p42	23p42	23p43	23p45	23p52	23p53	23p52	23p52	23p53	23p54	23p55	23p57	00 03	00 07	00 08
Maryland	d					23p29			→	23p43	23p44				→						23p59			00 10
Forest Gate	d					23p31	23p36			23p45	23p46	23p46						23p56			00 01	00 06		00 12
Manor Park	d					23p33	23p38			23p47	23p48	23p48						23p58			00 03	00 08		00 14
Ilford 2	d					23p36	23p41			23p50	23p51	23p51						00 01			00 06	00 11		00 17
Seven Kings	d					23p38	23p43			23p53	23p53	23p53						00 03			00 08	00 13		00 19
Goodmayes	d					23p40	23p45			23p55	23p55	23p55						00 05			00 10	00 15		00 21
Chadwell Heath	d					23p42	23p47			23p57	23p57	23p57						00 07			00 12	00 17		00 23
Romford	d				23p33	23p46	23p51			23p59	00 02	00 02					00 03	00 11			00 16	00 21		00 27
Gidea Park 2	d				23p37	23p50	23p55			00 04	00 05	00 05					00 07	00 15			00 20	00 25		00a31
Harold Wood	d				23p40	23p53	23p58			00 07	00 08	00 08					00 10	00 18			00 23	00 28		
Brentwood	d				23p44	23p57	00 02			00 11	00 12	00 12					00 14	00 22			00 27	00 32		
Shenfield 3	a	23p37		23p38	23p50	00 03	00 09	23p52		00 18	00 18	00 19	00 01	00 09		00 08	00 20	00 29	00 10	00 10	00 33	00 39	00 22	
Shenfield 3	d	23p38		23p39	23p50			23p54						00 09		00 09	00 20						00 24	
Billericay	d	23p45		23p45	23p56			23p59						00 15		00 15	00 26						00 30	
Wickford 2	d	23p51	23p56	23p51	00 01			00 06						00 21		00 21	00 31						00 36	
Battlesbridge	d		00 01																					
South Woodham Ferrers	d		00 04																					
North Fambridge	d		00 11																					
Althorne	d		00 16																					
Burnham-on-Crouch	d		00 21																					
Southminster	a		00 27																					
Rayleigh	d	23p56		23p56	00 06			00 11						00 26		00 26	00 36						00 41	
Hockley	d	00 01		00 01	00 11			00 16						00 31		00 31	00 41						00 46	
Rochford	d	00 04		00 04	00 14			00 19						00 34		00 34	00 44						00 49	
Southend Airport ✈	d	00 07		00 07	00 17			00 22						00 37		00 37	00 47						00 52	
Prittlewell	d	00 10		00 10				00 25						00 40		00 40							00 55	
Southend Victoria	a	00 14		00 18	00 27			00 29						00 44		00 48	00 57						00 59	

		LE 1 B	LE 1 A	LE A	LE B	LE A	LE A	LE 1 A	LE MX 1	LE 1 A	LE 1 B	LE A	LE 1 A	LE MX 1	LE 1 A	LE 1 B	LE 1 A	LE MX	LE A	LE MX	LE A	LE B	LE A
London Liverpool Street 15 ⊖	d	00 02	00 02	00 02	00 05	←	00 12	00 12	00 15	00 15	00 15	←	←	00 18	←		00 18	00 20	00 22	00 32	00 32	00 35	←
Stratford 7 ⊖	d	00 09	00a11	00 13	00 12	00 13	00 23	00 24	00 22	00 27	00 22	00 23	00 24	00 25	00 27		00a27	00 27	00 33	00 39	00 43	00 42	00 43
Maryland	d			→	00 13		→	→		→								00 29		00 41	→	00 43	
Forest Gate	d				00 15	00 16						00 26						00 31	00 36	00 43		00 45	00 46
Manor Park	d				00 17	00 18						00 28						00 33	00 38	00 45		00 47	00 48
Ilford 2	d				00 20	00 21						00 31						00 36	00 41	00 48		00 50	00 51
Seven Kings	d				00 23	00 23						00 33						00 38	00 43	00 50		00 53	00 53
Goodmayes	d				00 25	00 25						00 35						00 40	00 45	00 52		00 55	00 55
Chadwell Heath	d				00 27	00 27						00 37						00 42	00 47	00 54		00 57	00 57
Romford	d				00 30	00 31			00 32		00 33	00 41						00 46	00 51	00 58		01 00	01 01
Gidea Park 2	d				00a36	00 35					00 37	00 45						00 50	00 55	01a02		01a06	01 05
Harold Wood	d					00 38					00 40	00 48						00 53	00 58				01 08
Brentwood	d					00 42					00 44	00 52				←		00 57	01 02				01 12
Shenfield 3	a	00 30				00 48			00 44		00 50	00 58	00 40	00 47	00 45	00 50		01 03	01 08				01 18
Shenfield 3	d								00 45		00 50				00 46	00 50							
Billericay	d								00 51		→				00 52	00 56							
Wickford 2	d								00 56						00 58	01 01							
Battlesbridge	d																						
South Woodham Ferrers	d																						
North Fambridge	d																						
Althorne	d																						
Burnham-on-Crouch	d																						
Southminster	a																						
Rayleigh	d								01 01						01 03	01 06							
Hockley	d								01 06						01 08	01 11							
Rochford	d								01 09						01 11	01 14							
Southend Airport ✈	d								01 12						01 14	01 17							
Prittlewell	d								01 15						01 17								
Southend Victoria	a								01 23						01 21	01 27							

A 13 August

B 20 August, 27 August

London - Shenfield, Southminster and Southend Victoria

Network Diagram - see first Page of Table 5

	LE ■ A	LE A	LE ■ B	LE MX ■	LE A	LE ■ A	LE MX ■	LE ■ A	LE A	LE C	LE A	LE A	LE ■ A	LE A	LE A	LE A	LE A	LE A	LE A	LE A	LE ■
London Liverpool Street ⊖ d	00 40	00 42	00 45	00 46	←	00 46	00 50	←	00 52	00 55	←	01 02	01 10	01 12	01 22	01 32	01 42	01 52	02 02	02 12	
Stratford ⊖ d	00 52	00 53	00 52	00 53	00 53	01 00	00 57	01 00	01 03	01 02	01 03	01 13	01 22	01 23	01 33	01 43	01 53	02 03	02 13	02 23	
Maryland d		→				→			→	01 04											
Forest Gate d					00 56					01 06	01 06	01 16		01 26	01 36	01 46	01 56	02 06	02 16	02 26	
Manor Park d					00 58					01 08	01 08	01 18		01 28	01 38	01 48	01 58	02 08	02 18	02 28	
Ilford d					01 01					01 11	01 11	01 21		01 31	01 41	01 51	02 01	02 11	02 21	02 31	
Seven Kings d					01 03					01 13	01 13	01 23		01 33	01 43	01 53	02 03	02 13	02 23	02 33	
Goodmayes d					01 05					01 15	01 15	01 25		01 35	01 45	01 55	02 05	02 15	02 25	02 35	
Chadwell Heath d					01 07					01 17	01 17	01 27		01 37	01 47	01 57	02 07	02 17	02 27	02 37	
Romford d			01 03		01 11		01 08			01 21	01 21	01 31		01 41	01 51	02 01	02 11	02 21	02 31	02 41	
Gidea Park d			01 07	01 07	01 15					01 25	01 25	01 35		01 45	01 55	02a05	02 15	02a25	02 35	02a45	
Harold Wood d			01 10		01 18					01 28	01 28	01 38		01 48	01 58		02 18		02 38		
Brentwood d			01 14		01 22					01 32	01 32	01 42		01 52	02 02		02 22		02 42		
Shenfield a	01 07		01 20	01 17	01 28		01 20	01 17		01 38	01 38	01 48	01 37	01 58	02 08		02 28		02 48		
Shenfield d	01 09		01 20				01 20						01 39								
Billericay d	01 15		01 26				01 26						01 45								
Wickford d	01 21		01 31				01 31						01 51								05 16
Battlesbridge d																					05 20
South Woodham Ferrers d																					05 24
North Fambridge d																					05 41
Althorne d																					05 46
Burnham-on-Crouch d																					05 51
Southminster a																					05 57
Rayleigh d	01 26		01 36				01 36						01 56								
Hockley d	01 31		01 41				01 41						02 01								
Rochford d	01 34		01 44				01 44						02 04								
Southend Airport ✈ d	01 37		01 47				01 47						02 07								
Prittlewell d	01 40						01 50						02 10								
Southend Victoria a	01 44		01 57				01 58						02 14								

	LE ■	LE ■	LE	LE	LE ■	LE ■	LE	LE ■	LE ■	LE	LE ■	LE ■	LE	LE	LE ■	LE ■	LE	LE ■	LE	LE ■	LE
London Liverpool Street ⊖ d	05 23		05 28	05 37	05 52	05 55	06 00	06 02		06 10	06 12	06 15	06 20	06 30	06 35	06 38	06 40	06 48	06 50	06 55	07 00
Stratford ⊖ d	05 30		05 35	05 44	06a01	06 02	06 07	06 09		06 17	06 19	06 22	06 27	06 37	06 42	06 45	06 47	06 55	06 57	07 02	07 07
Maryland d				05 46			06 09			06 19			06 29	06 39			06 49		06 59		07 09
Forest Gate d				05 48			06 11			06 21			06 31	06 41			06 51		07 01		07 11
Manor Park d				05 50			06 13			06 23			06 33	06 43			06 53		07 03		07 13
Ilford d			05 40	05 53			06 16			06 26			06 36	06 46			06 56		07 06		07 16
Seven Kings d			05 42	05 55			06 18			06 28			06 38	06 48			06 58		07 08		07 18
Goodmayes d				05 57			06 20			06 30			06 40	06 50			07 00		07 10		07 20
Chadwell Heath d				05 59			06 22			06 32			06 42	06 52			07 02		07 12		07 22
Romford d	05 38		05 48	06 03			06 26			06 36			06 46	06 56			07 06		07 16		07 26
Gidea Park d			05 51	06 07			06 30			06 40			06 50	07 00			07 10		07 20		07 30
Harold Wood d			05 54	06 10			06 33			06 43			06 53	07 03			07 13		07 23		07 33
Brentwood d			05 59	06 14			06 37			06 47			06 57	07 07			07 17		07 27		07 37
Shenfield a	05 47		06 04	06 20		06 18	06 43	06 24		06 53	06 35	06 38	07 03	07 13	06 58	07 00	07 23	07 11	07 33	07 18	07 43
Shenfield d		05 56	06 04			06 19			06 33			06 39			06 59					07 19	
Billericay d		06 02	06 10			06 25			06 39			06 45			07 05					07 25	
Wickford d		06 09	06 16			06 31			06 46			06 51			07 11					07 31	
Battlesbridge d		06 13							06 50												
South Woodham Ferrers d		06 17							06 54												
North Fambridge d		06 24							07 03												
Althorne d		06 29							07 08												
Burnham-on-Crouch d		06 34							07 13												
Southminster a		06 40							07 19												
Rayleigh d			06 21			06 36						06 56			07 16					07 36	
Hockley d			06 26			06 41						07 01			07 21					07 41	
Rochford d			06 29			06 44						07 04			07 24					07 44	
Southend Airport ✈ d			06 32			06 47						07 07			07 27					07 47	
Prittlewell d			06 35			06 50						07 10			07 30					07 50	
Southend Victoria a			06 39			06 55						07 14			07 34					07 54	

A 13 August
B 20 August, 27 August
C not 13 August

Table 5

Mondays to Fridays

13 August to 28 August

London - Shenfield, Southminster and Southend Victoria

Network Diagram - see first Page of Table 5

	LE ■	LE ■	LE	LE ■	LE ■	LE ■	LE	LE	LE ■	LE ■	LE	LE ■	LE	LE ■	LE ■	LE	LE ■	LE ■	LE	LE ■	LE ■
London Liverpool Street ⊖ d	07 02	07 08	07 10		07 13	07 18	07 20	07 30	07 33	07 36	07 40	07 46	07 50		07 57	08 00	08 00	08 06	08 10	08 13	08 17
Stratford ⊖ d	07 09	07 15	07 17		07 20	07 25	07 27	07 37	07 42	07 45	07 47	07 54	07 57		08 05	08 07	08 08	08 14	08 17	08 21	08 25
Maryland d			07 19				07 29	07 39			07 49		07 59			08 09			08 19		
Forest Gate d			07 21				07 31	07 41			07 51		08 01			08 11			08 21		
Manor Park d			07 23				07 33	07 43			07 53		08 03			08 13			08 23		
Ilford d			07 26				07 36	07 46			07 56		08 06			08 16			08 26		
Seven Kings d			07 28				07 38	07 48			07 58		08 08			08 18			08 28		
Goodmayes d			07 30				07 40	07 50			08 00		08 10			08 20			08 30		
Chadwell Heath d			07 32				07 42	07 52			08 02		08 12			08 22			08 32		
Romford d			07 36		07 28		07 46	07 56			08 06		08 16			08 26			08 36		
Gidea Park d			07 40				07 50	08 00			08 10		08 20			08 30			08 40		
Harold Wood d			07 43				07 53	08 03			08 13		08 23			08 33			08 43		
Brentwood d			07 47				07 57	08 07			08 17		08 27			08 37			08 47		
Shenfield a	07 24	07 30	07 53		07 38	07 40	08 03	08 13	07 59	08 01	08 25	08 10	08 35		08 22	08 43	08 25	08 30	08 53	08 38	08 41
Shenfield d					07 39				07 59						08 22					08 39	
Billericay d					07 45				08 05						08 28					08 45	
Wickford d				07 36	07 51				08 11					08 16	08 34					08 51	
Battlesbridge d				07 40										08 20							
South Woodham Ferrers d				07 44										08 24							
North Fambridge d				07 53										08 31							
Althorne d				07 58										08 36							
Burnham-on-Crouch d				08 03										08 41							
Southminster a				08 09										08 47							
Rayleigh d					07 56				08 16						08 39					08 56	
Hockley d					08 01				08 21						08 44					09 01	
Rochford d					08 04				08 24						08 47					09 04	
Southend Airport ✈ d					08 07				08 27						08 50					09 07	
Prittlewell d					08 10				08 30						08 53					09 10	
Southend Victoria a					08 16				08 34						08 57					09 14	

	LE	LE	LE ■	LE ■	LE ■	LE	LE ■	LE	LE ■	LE	LE ■	LE	LE ■	LE ■	LE ■	LE	LE	LE ■	LE ■	LE	LE ■	LE
London Liverpool Street ⊖ d	08 20	08 30		08 32	08 36	08 40	08 48	08 50	08 55	09 00	09 02	09 10		09 13	09 18	09 20	09 30	09 34	09 38	09 40	09 48	09 50
Stratford ⊖ d	08 27	08 37		08 42	08 45	08 47	08 55	08 57	09 02	09 07	09 09	09 17		09 21	09 25	09 27	09 37	09 42	09 45	09 47	09 55	09 57
Maryland d	08 29	08 39				08 49		08 59		09 09		09 19				09 29	09 39			09 49		09 59
Forest Gate d	08 31	08 41				08 51		09 01		09 11		09 21				09 31	09 41			09 51		10 01
Manor Park d	08 33	08 43				08 53		09 03		09 13		09 23				09 33	09 43			09 53		10 03
Ilford d	08 36	08 46				08 56		09 06		09 16		09 26				09 36	09 46			09 56		10 06
Seven Kings d	08 38	08 48				08 58		09 08		09 18		09 28				09 38	09 48			09 58		10 08
Goodmayes d	08 40	08 50				09 00		09 10		09 20		09 30				09 40	09 50			10 00		10 10
Chadwell Heath d	08 42	08 52				09 02		09 12		09 22		09 32				09 42	09 52			10 02		10 12
Romford d	08 46	08 56				09 06		09 16		09 26		09 36				09 46	09 56		09 53	10 06		10 16
Gidea Park d	08 50	09 00				09 10		09 20		09 30		09 40				09 50	10 00			10 10		10 20
Harold Wood d	08 53	09 03				09 13		09 23		09 33		09 43				09 53	10 03			10 13		10 23
Brentwood d	08 57	09 07				09 17		09 27		09 37		09 47				09 57	10 07			10 17		10 27
Shenfield a	09 03	09 13		08 59	09 01	09 23	09 11	09 33	09 18	09 43	09 24	09 53		09 38	09 40	10 03	10 13	09 58	10 02	10 23	10 11	10 33
Shenfield d				08 59					09 19					09 39				09 59				
Billericay d				09 05					09 25					09 45				10 05				
Wickford d			08 56	09 11					09 31				09 36	09 51				10 11				
Battlesbridge d			09 00										09 40									
South Woodham Ferrers d			09 04										09 44									
North Fambridge d			09 11										09 51									
Althorne d			09 16										09 56									
Burnham-on-Crouch d			09 21										10 01									
Southminster a			09 27										10 07									
Rayleigh d				09 16					09 36					09 56				10 16				
Hockley d				09 21					09 41					10 01				10 21				
Rochford d				09 24					09 44					10 04				10 24				
Southend Airport ✈ d				09 27					09 47					10 07				10 27				
Prittlewell d				09 30					09 50					10 10				10 30				
Southend Victoria a				09 34					09 54					10 14				10 34				

Table 5

Mondays to Fridays

13 August to 28 August

London - Shenfield, Southminster and Southend Victoria

Network Diagram - see first Page of Table 5

	LE 1	LE 1	LE	LE 1	LE		LE 1	LE 1	LE	LE	LE 1	LE 1	LE 1	LE	LE 1		LE	LE 1	LE	LE 1	LE	LE 1	LE 1	LE 1
London Liverpool Street 15 ⊖ d		09 55	10 00	10 02	10 10		10 13	10 18	10 20	10 30		10 35	10 38	10 40	10 48		10 50	10 55	11 00	11 02	11 10		11 13	11 18
Stratford 7 ⊖ d		10 02	10 07	10 09	10 17		10 20	10 25	10 27	10 37		10 42	10 45	10 47	10 55		10 57	11 02	11 07	11 09	11 17		11 20	11 25
Maryland d			10 09		10 19				10 29	10 39				10 49			10 59		11 09		11 19			
Forest Gate d			10 11		10 21				10 31	10 41				10 51			11 01		11 11		11 21			
Manor Park d			10 13		10 23				10 33	10 43				10 53			11 03		11 13		11 23			
Ilford 2 d			10 16		10 26				10 36	10 46				10 56			11 06		11 16		11 26			
Seven Kings d			10 18		10 28				10 38	10 48				10 58			11 08		11 18		11 28			
Goodmayes d			10 20		10 30				10 40	10 50				11 00			11 10		11 20		11 30			
Chadwell Heath d			10 22		10 32				10 42	10 52				11 02			11 12		11 22		11 32			
Romford d			10 26		10 36		10 28		10 46	10 56			10 53	11 06			11 16		11 26		11 36		11 28	
Gidea Park 2 d			10 30		10 40				10 50	11 00				11 10			11 20		11 30		11 40			
Harold Wood d			10 33		10 43				10 53	11 03				11 13			11 23		11 33		11 43			
Brentwood d			10 37		10 47				10 57	11 07				11 17			11 27		11 37		11 47			
Shenfield 3 a		10 18	10 43	10 24	10 53		10 38	10 40	11 03	11 13		10 58	11 02	11 23	11 11		11 33	11 18	11 43	11 24	11 53		11 38	11 40
Shenfield 3 d		10 19					10 39					10 59						11 19					11 39	
Billericay d		10 25					10 45					11 05						11 25					11 45	
Wickford 2 d	10 16	10 31					10 51				10 56	11 11						11 31				11 36	11 51	
Battlesbridge d	10 20										11 00											11 40		
South Woodham Ferrers d	10 24										11 04											11 44		
North Fambridge d	10 31										11 11											11 51		
Althorne d	10 36										11 16											11 56		
Burnham-on-Crouch d	10 41										11 21											12 01		
Southminster a	10 47										11 27											12 07		
Rayleigh d		10 36					10 56					11 16						11 36					11 56	
Hockley d		10 41					11 01					11 21						11 41					12 01	
Rochford d		10 44					11 04					11 24						11 44					12 04	
Southend Airport ✈ d		10 47					11 07					11 27						11 47					12 07	
Prittlewell d		10 50					11 10					11 30						11 50					12 10	
Southend Victoria a		10 54					11 14					11 34						11 54					12 14	

	LE		LE	LE 1	LE 1	LE	LE 1	LE	LE 1	LE 1	LE		LE 1	LE	LE 1	LE 1	LE	LE	LE 1	LE 1	LE 1		LE	LE 1
London Liverpool Street 15 ⊖ d	11 20		11 30	11 35	11 38	11 40	11 48	11 50		11 55	12 00		12 02	12 10	12 13	12 18	12 20	12 30		12 35	12 38		12 40	12 48
Stratford 7 ⊖ d	11 27		11 37	11 42	11 45	11 47	11 55	11 57		12 02	12 07		12 09	12 17	12 20	12 25	12 27	12 37		12 42	12 45		12 47	12 55
Maryland d	11 29		11 39			11 49		11 59			12 09			12 19			12 29	12 39					12 49	
Forest Gate d	11 31		11 41			11 51		12 01			12 11			12 21			12 31	12 41					12 51	
Manor Park d	11 33		11 43			11 53		12 03			12 13			12 23			12 33	12 43					12 53	
Ilford 2 d	11 36		11 46			11 56		12 06			12 16			12 26			12 36	12 46					12 56	
Seven Kings d	11 38		11 48			11 58		12 08			12 18			12 28			12 38	12 48					12 58	
Goodmayes d	11 40		11 50			12 00		12 10			12 20			12 30			12 40	12 50					13 00	
Chadwell Heath d	11 42		11 52			12 02		12 12			12 22			12 32			12 42	12 52					13 02	
Romford d	11 46		11 56		11 53	12 06		12 16			12 26			12 36	12 28		12 46	12 56			12 53		13 06	
Gidea Park 2 d	11 50		12 00			12 10		12 20			12 30			12 40			12 50	13 00					13 10	
Harold Wood d	11 53		12 03			12 13		12 23			12 33			12 43			12 53	13 03					13 13	
Brentwood d	11 57		12 07			12 17		12 27			12 37			12 47			12 57	13 07					13 17	
Shenfield 3 a	12 03		12 13	11 58	12 02	12 23	12 11	12 33		12 18	12 43		12 24	12 53	12 38	12 40	13 03	13 13		12 58	13 02		13 23	13 11
Shenfield 3 d				11 59						12 19					12 39					12 59				
Billericay d				12 05						12 25					12 45					13 05				
Wickford 2 d				12 11					12 16	12 31					12 51				12 56	13 11				
Battlesbridge d									12 20										13 00					
South Woodham Ferrers d									12 24										13 04					
North Fambridge d									12 31										13 11					
Althorne d									12 36										13 16					
Burnham-on-Crouch d									12 41										13 21					
Southminster a									12 47										13 27					
Rayleigh d				12 16						12 36					12 56					13 16				
Hockley d				12 21						12 41					13 01					13 21				
Rochford d				12 24						12 44					13 04					13 24				
Southend Airport ✈ d				12 27						12 47					13 07					13 27				
Prittlewell d				12 30						12 50					13 10					13 30				
Southend Victoria a				12 34						12 54					13 14					13 34				

Table 5

Mondays to Fridays

13 August to 28 August

London - Shenfield, Southminster and Southend Victoria

Network Diagram - see first Page of Table 5

	LE	LE 1	LE	LE 1	LE	LE 1	LE 1		LE 1	LE	LE	LE 1	LE 1	LE	LE 1	LE	LE 1		LE 1	LE	LE 1	LE	LE 1	LE 1
London Liverpool Street 15 ⊖ d	12 50	12 55	13 00	13 02	13 10		13 13		13 18	13 20	13 30	13 35	13 38	13 40	13 48	13 50			13 55	14 00	14 02	14 10	14 13	14 18
Stratford 7 ⊖ d	12 57	13 02	13 07	13 09	13 17		13 20		13 25	13 27	13 37	13 42	13 45	13 47	13 55	13 57			14 02	14 07	14 09	14 17	14 20	14 25
Maryland d	12 59		13 09		13 19					13 29	13 39			13 49		13 59				14 09		14 19		
Forest Gate d	13 01		13 11		13 21					13 31	13 41			13 51		14 01				14 11		14 21		
Manor Park d	13 03		13 13		13 23					13 33	13 43			13 53		14 03				14 13		14 23		
Ilford 2 d	13 06		13 16		13 26					13 36	13 46			13 56		14 06				14 16		14 26		
Seven Kings d	13 08		13 18		13 28					13 38	13 48			13 58		14 08				14 18		14 28		
Goodmayes d	13 10		13 20		13 30					13 40	13 50			14 00		14 10				14 20		14 30		
Chadwell Heath d	13 12		13 22		13 32					13 42	13 52			14 02		14 12				14 22		14 32		
Romford d	13 16		13 26		13 36		13 28			13 46	13 56		13 53	14 06		14 16				14 26		14 36	14 28	
Gidea Park 2 d	13 20		13 30		13 40					13 50	14 00			14 10		14 20				14 30		14 40		
Harold Wood d	13 23		13 33		13 43					13 53	14 03			14 13		14 23				14 33		14 43		
Brentwood d	13 27		13 37		13 47					13 57	14 07			14 17		14 27				14 37		14 47		
Shenfield 3 a	13 33	13 18	13 43	13 24	13 53		13 38		13 40	14 03	14 13	13 58	14 02	14 23	14 11	14 33			14 18	14 43	14 24	14 53	14 38	14 40
Shenfield 3 d		13 19					13 39					13 59							14 19				14 39	
Billericay d		13 25					13 45					14 05							14 25				14 45	
Wickford 2 d		13 31				13 36	13 51					14 11					14 16		14 31				14 51	
Battlesbridge d						13 40											14 20							
South Woodham Ferrers d						13 44											14 24							
North Fambridge d						13 51											14 31							
Althorne d						13 56											14 36							
Burnham-on-Crouch d						14 01											14 41							
Southminster a						14 07											14 47							
Rayleigh d		13 36					13 56					14 16							14 36				14 56	
Hockley d		13 41					14 01					14 21							14 41				15 01	
Rochford d		13 44					14 04					14 24							14 44				15 04	
Southend Airport ✈ d		13 47					14 07					14 27							14 47				15 07	
Prittlewell d		13 50					14 10					14 30							14 50				15 10	
Southend Victoria a		13 54					14 14					14 34							14 54				15 14	

	LE	LE	LE 1		LE 1	LE 1	LE	LE 1	LE	LE 1	LE	LE 1	LE		LE 1	LE 1	LE 1	LE	LE	LE 1	LE 1	LE	LE 1	
London Liverpool Street 15 ⊖ d	14 20	14 30			14 35	14 38	14 40	14 48	14 50	14 55	15 00	15 02	15 10			15 13	15 18	15 20	15 30	15 35	15 38	15 40	15 48	
Stratford 7 ⊖ d	14 27	14 37			14 42	14 45	14 47	14 55	14 57	15 02	15 07	15 09	15 17			15 20	15 25	15 27	15 37	15 42	15 45	15 47	15 55	
Maryland d	14 29	14 39					14 49		14 59		15 09		15 19					15 29	15 39			15 49		
Forest Gate d	14 31	14 41					14 51		15 01		15 11		15 21					15 31	15 41			15 51		
Manor Park d	14 33	14 43					14 53		15 03		15 13		15 23					15 33	15 43			15 53		
Ilford 2 d	14 36	14 46					14 56		15 06		15 16		15 26					15 36	15 46			15 56		
Seven Kings d	14 38	14 48					14 58		15 08		15 18		15 28					15 38	15 48			15 58		
Goodmayes d	14 40	14 50					15 00		15 10		15 20		15 30					15 40	15 50			16 00		
Chadwell Heath d	14 42	14 52					15 02		15 12		15 22		15 32					15 42	15 52			16 02		
Romford d	14 46	14 56				14 53	15 06		15 16		15 26		15 36			15 28		15 46	15 56		15 53	16 06		
Gidea Park 2 d	14 50	15 00					15 10		15 20		15 30		15 40					15 50	16 00			16 10		
Harold Wood d	14 53	15 03					15 13		15 23		15 33		15 43					15 53	16 03			16 13		
Brentwood d	14 57	15 07					15 17		15 27		15 37		15 47					15 57	16 07			16 17		
Shenfield 3 a	15 03	15 13			14 58	15 02	15 23	15 11	15 33	15 18	15 43	15 24	15 53			15 38	15 40	16 03	16 13	15 58	16 02	16 23	16 11	
Shenfield 3 d					14 59					15 19						15 39				15 59				
Billericay d					15 05					15 25						15 45				16 05				
Wickford 2 d			14 56		15 11					15 31					15 36	15 51				16 11				
Battlesbridge d			15 00												15 40									
South Woodham Ferrers d			15 04												15 44									
North Fambridge d			15 11												15 51									
Althorne d			15 16												15 56									
Burnham-on-Crouch d			15 21												16 01									
Southminster a			15 27												16 07									
Rayleigh d					15 16					15 36						15 56				16 16				
Hockley d					15 21					15 41						16 01				16 21				
Rochford d					15 24					15 44						16 04				16 24				
Southend Airport ✈ d					15 27					15 47						16 07				16 27				
Prittlewell d					15 31					15 50						16 10				16 30				
Southend Victoria a					15 34					15 54						16 14				16 34				

Table 5

Mondays to Fridays

13 August to 28 August

London - Shenfield, Southminster and Southend Victoria

Network Diagram - see first Page of Table 5

		LE	LE 1	LE 1	LE	LE 1	LE	LE 1	LE 1	LE 1		LE	LE 1	LE	LE 1	LE 1	LE	LE	LE 1	LE 1		LE 1	LE	LE 1	LE
London Liverpool Street 15 ⊖	d	15 50		15 55	16 00	16 02	16 10	16 10	16 14	16 17		16 20	16 24	16 28	16 32	16 34	16 36	16 40		16 40		16 44	16 47	16 47	16 50
Stratford 7 ⊖	d	15 57		16 02	16 07	16 09	16 17	16 18	16 22	16 25		16 27	16 32	16 35		16 42	16 43	16 47		16 48		16a52	16 54	16 55	16 57
Maryland	d	15 59			16 09		16 19					16 29		16 37				16 49							16 59
Forest Gate	d	16 01			16 11		16 21					16 31		16 39				16 51							17 01
Manor Park	d	16 03			16 13		16 23					16 33		16 41				16 53							17 03
Ilford 2	d	16 06			16 16		16 26					16 36		16 44			16 50	16 56					17 00		17 06
Seven Kings	d	16 08			16 18		16 28					16 38		16 47			16 52						17 02		
Goodmayes	d	16 10			16 20		16 30					16 40		16 49			16 54						17 04		
Chadwell Heath	d	16 12			16 22		16 32					16 42		16 51			16 56	17 00					17 06		17 10
Romford	d	16 16			16 26		16 36					16 46		16 55			17 00	17 04					17 10		17 14
Gidea Park 2	d	16 20			16 30		16 40					16 50		17a00			17 04	17a10					17 14		17a20
Harold Wood	d	16 23			16 33		16 43					16 53					17 07						17 17		
Brentwood	d	16 27			16 37		16 47					16 57					17 11						17 21		
Shenfield 3	a	16 33		16 18	16 43	16 24	16 53	16 34	16 38	16 41		17 03	16 49		16 54	16 58	17 19			17 04			17 29	17 11	
Shenfield 3	d			16 19				16 34					16 49							17 04					
Billericay	d			16 25				16 41					16 56							17 11					
Wickford 3	d		16 14	16 31				16 48					17 03						17 06	17 18					
Battlesbridge	d		16 18																17 10						
South Woodham Ferrers	d		16 22																17 14						
North Fambridge	d		16 29																17 21						
Althorne	d		16 34																17 26						
Burnham-on-Crouch	d		16 39																17 31						
Southminster	a		16 45																17 37						
Rayleigh	d			16 36				16 53					17 08							17 23					
Hockley	d			16 41				16 57					17 12							17 27					
Rochford	d			16 44				17 01					17 16							17 31					
Southend Airport ✈	d			16 47				17 03					17 18							17 33					
Prittlewell	d			16 50				17 06					17 21							17 36					
Southend Victoria	a			16 54				17 15					17 27							17 42					

		LE 1	LE	LE	LE ◇1	LE 1		LE	LE 1	LE	LE 1	LE 1	LE	LE 1	LE	LE 1		LE 1	LE 1	LE	LE	LE 1	LE 1	LE	LE 1
																A		A							
London Liverpool Street 15 ⊖	d	16 54	16 57	17 00	17 02	17 04		17 07	17 08	17 10	17 12	17 15	17 17	17 18	17 20	17 20		17 22	17 25	17 27	17 30	17 32	17 34	17 36	17 38
Stratford 7 ⊖	d	17 02	17 04	17 07	17 10	17 13		17 14	17a16	17 17	17a20	17 23	17 24	17a26	17 27	17 29		17 31	17 34	17 34	17 37	17a40	17 43	17 43	17a47
Maryland	d			17 09						17 19					17 29						17 39			17 45	
Forest Gate	d			17 11						17 21					17 31						17 41				
Manor Park	d			17 13						17 23					17 33						17 43				
Ilford 2	d		17 10	17 16				17 20		17 26			17 30		17 36					17 40	17 46			17 50	
Seven Kings	d		17 12					17 22					17 32							17 42				17 52	
Goodmayes	d		17 14					17 24					17 34							17 44				17 54	
Chadwell Heath	d		17 16	17 20				17 26		17 30			17 36		17 40					17 46	17 50			17 56	
Romford	d		17 20	17 24				17 30		17 34			17 40		17 44					17 50	17 54			18 00	
Gidea Park 2	d		17 24	17a30				17 34		17a40			17 44		17a50					17 54	18a00			18 04	
Harold Wood	d		17 27					17 37					17 47							17 57				18 07	
Brentwood	d		17 31					17 41					17 51							18 01				18 11	
Shenfield 3	a	17 19	17 39			17 30		17 49				17 39	17 59			17 45			17 51	18 09			17 59	18 19	
Shenfield 3	d	17 19				17 30						17 39							17 52				17 59		
Billericay	d	17 26				17 37						17 46							17 58				18 06		
Wickford 3	d	17 33				17 44						17 53						18 00	18 05				18 13		
Battlesbridge	d																	18 04							
South Woodham Ferrers	d																	18 08							
North Fambridge	d																	18 14							
Althorne	d																	18 19							
Burnham-on-Crouch	d																	18 24							
Southminster	a																	18 32							
Rayleigh	d	17 38				17 49						17 58							18 10				18 18		
Hockley	d	17 42				17 53						18 02							18 15				18 22		
Rochford	d	17 46				17 57						18 06							18 18				18 26		
Southend Airport ✈	d	17 48				17 59						18 08							18 21				18 28		
Prittlewell	d	17 51				18 02						18 11							18 24				18 31		
Southend Victoria	a	17 57				18 08						18 17							18 30				18 37		

A The Stratford call is subjtect to introduction during the currency of the timetable.

Table 5

Mondays to Fridays

13 August to 28 August

London - Shenfield, Southminster and Southend Victoria

Network Diagram - see first Page of Table 5

		LE		LE 1	LE	LE 1	LE	LE	LE	LE 1	LE 1	LE		LE 1	LE	LE 1	LE	LE 1	LE 1	LE	LE	LE		LE 1	LE 1
				A																					
London Liverpool Street 15 ⊖	d	17 39		17 40	17 42	17 45	17 46	17 49	17 52	17 52	17 54	17 56		17 58	17 59	18 00	18 02	18 02	18 05		18 07	18 10		18 12	18 14
Stratford 7 ⊖	d	17 46		17 49	17 49	17 53	17 53	17 56	17 59	18a01	18 03	18 03		18a06	18 06	18 09	18 09	18 11	18 14		18 14	18 17		18a21	18 23
Maryland	d						17 55					18 05										18 19			
Forest Gate	d				17 52				18 02								18 12					18 21			
Manor Park	d	17 50						18 00							18 10							18 23			
Ilford 2	d	17 53			17 56		18 00	18 03	18 06			18 10			18 13		18 16				18 20	18 26			
Seven Kings	d	17 56			17 59		18 02	18 06	18 09			18 12			18 16		18 19				18 22				
Goodmayes	d	17 58			18 01		18 04	18 08	18 11			18 14			18 18		18 21				18 24				
Chadwell Heath	d	18 00			18 03		18 06	18 10	18 13			18 16			18 20		18 23				18 26	18 30			
Romford	d	18 04			18 07		18 10	18 14	18 17			18 20			18 24		18 27				18 30	18 34			
Gidea Park 2	d	18a09			18a12		18 14	18 18	18a22			18 24			18a29		18a32				18 34	18a40			
Harold Wood	d						18 17	18 21				18 27									18 37				
Brentwood	d						18 21	18 25				18 31								←	18 41				
Shenfield 3	a			18 05		18 09	18 29	18 33			18 19	18 39				18 25			18 31	18 33	18 49				18 40
Shenfield 3	d					18 09		18 36			18 19								18 31	18 36					18 41
Billericay	d					18 16		→			18 26								18 38	18 42					18 47
Wickford 3	d					18 23					18 33							18 41	18 45	18 49					18 54
Battlesbridge	d																	18 45							
South Woodham Ferrers	d																	18 49							
North Fambridge	d																	18 55							
Althorne	d																	19 00							
Burnham-on-Crouch	d																	19 05							
Southminster	a																	19 13							
Rayleigh	d					18 28					18 38								18 50	18 54					18 59
Hockley	d					18 32					18 42								18 55	18 59					19 04
Rochford	d					18 36					18 46								18 58	19 02					19 07
Southend Airport ✈	d					18 38					18 48								19 01	19 05					19 10
Prittlewell	d					18 41					18 51								19 04	19 08					19 13
Southend Victoria	a					18 47					18 58								19 10	19 14					19 19

		LE	LE 1	LE	LE 1	LE 1	LE	LE		LE 1	LE 1	LE	LE 1	LE	LE 1	LE 1	LE	LE 1		LE	LE 1	LE	LE	LE 1	LE 1
London Liverpool Street 15 ⊖	d	18 17	18 18	18 20	18 20	18 25	18 27	18 30		18 32	18 35	18 37	18 38	18 40	18 41	18 45	18 47	18 48		18 50	18 55	18 57	19 00	19 02	19 08
Stratford 7 ⊖	d	18 24	18a27	18 27	18 29	18 33	18 34	18 37		18a40	18 43	18 44	18 46	18 47	18 49	18 53	18 54	18a56		18 57	19 03	19 04	19 07	19 09	19a15
Maryland	d			18 29				18 39						18 49						18 59			19 09		
Forest Gate	d			18 31				18 41						18 51						19 01			19 11		
Manor Park	d			18 33				18 43						18 53						19 03			19 13		
Ilford 2	d	18 30		18 36			18 40	18 46				18 50		18 56			19 00			19 06		19 10	19 16		
Seven Kings	d	18 32					18 42					18 52					19 02					19 12	19 18		
Goodmayes	d	18 34					18 44					18 54					19 04					19 14	19 20		
Chadwell Heath	d	18 36		18 40			18 46	18 50				18 56		19 00			19 06			19 10		19 16	19 22		
Romford	d	18 40		18 44			18 50	18 54				19 00		19 04			19 10			19 14		19 20	19 26		
Gidea Park 2	d	18 44		18a50			18 54	19a00				19 04		19 08			19 14			19a20		19 24	19 30		
Harold Wood	d	18 47					18 57					19 07		19 11			19 17					19 27	19 33		
Brentwood	d	18 51					19 01					19 11		19 15			19 21					19 31	19 37		
Shenfield 3	a	18 59			18 45	18 50	19 09				18 59	19 19	19 02	19 23		19 10	19 29				19 20	19 39	19 43	19 24	
Shenfield 3	d					18 50					18 59					19 10					19 20				
Billericay	d					18 57					19 06					19 17					19 27				
Wickford 3	d					19 04					19 13				19 19	19 24					19 34				
Battlesbridge	d														19 23										
South Woodham Ferrers	d														19 27										
North Fambridge	d														19 34										
Althorne	d														19 39										
Burnham-on-Crouch	d														19 44										
Southminster	a														19 52										
Rayleigh	d					19 09					19 18					19 29					19 39				
Hockley	d					19 13					19 22					19 33					19 43				
Rochford	d					19 17					19 26					19 37					19 47				
Southend Airport ✈	d					19 19					19 28					19 39					19 49				
Prittlewell	d					19 22					19 31					19 42					19 52				
Southend Victoria	a					19 28					19 37					19 47					19 58				

A The Stratford call is subjtect to introduction during the currency of the timetable.

London - Shenfield, Southminster and Southend Victoria

Mondays to Fridays
13 August to 28 August

Network Diagram - see first Page of Table 5

Station		LE	LE ■	LE ■		LE	LE	LE ■	LE ■	LE ■	LE	LE ■	LE	LE ■		LE ■	LE	LE ■	LE	LE ■	LE ■	LE	LE	LE ■	
London Liverpool Street ⊖	d	19 10	19 15	19 18		19 20	19 30	19 32	19 35	19 38	19 40	19 48	19 50			19 55	20 00	20 02	20 10	20 13	20 18	20 20	20 30		
Stratford ⊖	d	19 17	19 22	19 25		19 27	19 37	19a39	19 42	19 45	19 47	19 55	19 57			20 02	20 07	20 09	20 17	20 20	20 25	20 27	20 37		
Maryland	d	19 19				19 29	19 39				19 49		19 59				20 09		20 19			20 29	20 39		
Forest Gate	d	19 21				19 31	19 41				19 51		20 01				20 11		20 21			20 31	20 41		
Manor Park	d	19 23				19 33	19 43				19 53		20 03				20 13		20 23			20 33	20 43		
Ilford	d	19 26				19 36	19 46				19 56		20 06				20 16		20 26			20 36	20 46		
Seven Kings	d	19 28				19 38	19 48				19 58		20 08				20 18		20 28			20 38	20 48		
Goodmayes	d	19 30				19 40	19 50				20 00		20 10				20 20		20 30			20 40	20 50		
Chadwell Heath	d	19 32				19 42	19 52				20 02		20 12				20 22		20 32			20 42	20 52		
Romford	d	19 36				19 46	19 56				20 06		20 16				20 26		20 36	20 28		20 46	20 56		
Gidea Park	d	19 40				19 50	20 00				20 10		20 20				20 30		20 40			20 50	21 00		
Harold Wood	d	19 43				19 53	20 03				20 13		20 23				20 33		20 43			20 53	21 03		
Brentwood	d	19 47				19 57	20 07				20 17		20 27				20 37		20 47			20 57	21 07		
Shenfield	a	19 53	19 38	19 40		20 03	20 13		19 58	20 00	20 23	20 11	20 33			20 18	20 43	20 24	20 53	20 38	20 40	21 03	21 13		
Shenfield	d		19 39						19 59							20 19				20 39					
Billericay	d		19 45						20 05							20 25				20 45					
Wickford	d		19 51						20 11					20 16		20 31				20 51				20 56	
Battlesbridge	d													20 20										21 00	
South Woodham Ferrers	d													20 24										21 04	
North Fambridge	d													20 31										21 11	
Althorne	d													20 36										21 16	
Burnham-on-Crouch	d													20 41										21 21	
Southminster	a													20 47										21 27	
Rayleigh	d		19 56						20 16							20 36				20 56					
Hockley	d		20 01						20 21							20 41				21 01					
Rochford	d		20 04						20 24							20 44				21 04					
Southend Airport ✈	d		20 07						20 27							20 47				21 07					
Prittlewell	d		20 10						20 30							20 50				21 10					
Southend Victoria	a		20 14						20 34							20 54				21 14					

Station		LE ■	CC	LE ■	LE	LE ■	LE	LE ■	LE	LE ■		LE	LE ■	LE ■	LE ■	LE	LE	LE ■	CC	LE ■		LE	LE ■	LE	LE ■
London Liverpool Street ⊖	d	20 35	20 35	20 38	20 40	20 48	20 50	20 55	21 00	21 02		21 10		21 13	21 18	21 20	21 30	21 35	21 35	21 38		21 40	21 48	21 50	
Stratford ⊖	d	20 42	20a43	20 45	20 47	20 55	20 57	21 02	21 07	21 09		21 17		21 20	21 25	21 27	21 37	21 42	21a43	21 45		21 47	21 55	21 57	
Maryland	d				20 49		20 59		21 09			21 19				21 29	21 39					21 49		21 59	
Forest Gate	d				20 51		21 01		21 11			21 21				21 31	21 41					21 51		22 01	
Manor Park	d				20 53		21 03		21 13			21 23				21 33	21 43					21 53		22 03	
Ilford	d				20 56		21 06		21 16			21 26				21 36	21 46					21 56		22 06	
Seven Kings	d				20 58		21 08		21 18			21 28				21 38	21 48					21 58		22 08	
Goodmayes	d				21 00		21 10		21 20			21 30				21 40	21 50					22 00		22 10	
Chadwell Heath	d				21 02		21 12		21 22			21 32				21 42	21 52					22 02		22 12	
Romford	d			20 53	21 06		21 16		21 26			21 36		21 28		21 46	21 56			21 53		22 06		22 16	
Gidea Park	d				21 10		21 20		21 30			21 40				21 50	22 00					22 10		22 20	
Harold Wood	d				21 13		21 23		21 33			21 43				21 53	22 03					22 13		22 23	
Brentwood	d				21 17		21 27		21 37			21 47				21 57	22 07					22 17		22 27	
Shenfield	a	20 58		21 02	21 23	21 11	21 33	21 18	21 43	21 24		21 53		21 38	21 40	22 03	22 13	21 58		22 02		22 23	22 11	22 33	
Shenfield	d	20 59						21 19						21 39				21 59							
Billericay	d	21 05						21 25						21 45				22 05							
Wickford	d	21 11						21 31					21 36	21 51				22 11							22 16
Battlesbridge	d												21 40												22 20
South Woodham Ferrers	d												21 44												22 24
North Fambridge	d												21 51												22 31
Althorne	d												21 56												22 36
Burnham-on-Crouch	d												22 01												22 41
Southminster	a												22 07												22 47
Rayleigh	d	21 16						21 36						21 56				22 16							
Hockley	d	21 21						21 41						22 01				22 21							
Rochford	d	21 24						21 44						22 04				22 24							
Southend Airport ✈	d	21 27						21 47						22 07				22 27							
Prittlewell	d	21 30						21 50						22 10				22 30							
Southend Victoria	a	21 34						21 54						22 14				22 34							

London - Shenfield, Southminster and Southend Victoria

Mondays to Fridays
13 August to 28 August

Network Diagram - see first Page of Table 5

Station		LE ■	LE ■	LE	LE ■	LE ■		LE	LE	LE ■	LE ■	LE ■	LE	LE ■	LE	LE ■		LE ■	LE	LE	LE ■	LE ■	LE		
London Liverpool Street ⊖	d	21 55	22 02	22 05	22 13	22 18		22 20	22 35	22 38		22 45	22 50	23 02	23 05	23 15		23 18	23 20	23 35	23 45	23 48	23 50		
Stratford ⊖	d	22 02	22 09	22 12	22 20	22 25		22 27	22 42	22 45		22 52	22 57	23 09	23 12	23 22		23 25	23 27	23 42	23 52	23 55	23 57		
Maryland	d			22 14				22 29	22 44				22 59		23 14				23 29	23 44			23 59		
Forest Gate	d			22 16				22 31	22 46				23 01		23 16				23 31	23 46			00 01		
Manor Park	d			22 18				22 33	22 48				23 03		23 18				23 33	23 48			00 03		
Ilford	d			22 21				22 36	22 51				23 06		23 21				23 36	23 51			00 06		
Seven Kings	d			22 23				22 38	22 53				23 08		23 23				23 38	23 53			00 08		
Goodmayes	d			22 25				22 40	22 55				23 10		23 25				23 40	23 55			00 10		
Chadwell Heath	d			22 27				22 42	22 57				23 12		23 27				23 42	23 57			00 12		
Romford	d			22 31	22 28			22 46	23 01				23 16		23 31				23 46	00 02			00 16		
Gidea Park	d			22 35				22 50	23 05				23 20		23 35				23 50	00 05			00 20		
Harold Wood	d			22 38				22 53	23 08				23 23		23 38				23 53	00 08			00 23		
Brentwood	d			22 42				22 57	23 12				23 27		23 42				23 57	00 12			00 27		
Shenfield	a	22 18	22 24	22 48	22 38	22 40		23 03	23 18	23 00		23 08	23 33	23 24	23 48	23 38		23 40	00 03	00 18	00 08	00 10	00 33		
Shenfield	d	22 19			22 39							23 09				23 39					00 09				
Billericay	d	22 25			22 45							23 15				23 45					00 15				
Wickford	d	22 31			22 51						22 56	23 21				23 51					00 21				
Battlesbridge	d										23 00														
South Woodham Ferrers	d										23 04														
North Fambridge	d										23 11														
Althorne	d										23 16														
Burnham-on-Crouch	d										23 21														
Southminster	a										23 27														
Rayleigh	d	22 36			22 56							23 26				23 56					00 26				
Hockley	d	22 41			23 01							23 31				00 01					00 31				
Rochford	d	22 44			23 04							23 34				00 04					00 34				
Southend Airport ✈	d	22 47			23 07							23 37				00 07					00 37				
Prittlewell	d	22 50			23 10							23 40				00 10					00 40				
Southend Victoria	a	22 54			23 14							23 48				00 18					00 48				

Mondays to Fridays
29 August to 7 September

Station		LE ■ A	LE ■ B	LE ■ C	LE C	LE B	LE A	LE ■ B	LE ■ A	LE B		LE A	LE C	LE ■ A	LE ■ B	LE ■ A	LE B	LE A	LE ■ C	LE ■ A		LE ■ B	LE ■ C	LE C	LE B
London Liverpool Street ⊖	d	23p10	23p10	23p15	23p20	23p22	23p22	23p25	23p25	23p32		23p32	23p35	23p35	23p40	23p40	23p42	23p42	23p45	23p45		23p45	23p48	23p50	23p52
Stratford ⊖	d	23p22	23p22	23p22	23p27	23p32	23p32	23p37	23p37	23p42		23p42	23p42	23p45	23p52	23p52	23p52	23p52	23p52	23p54		23p54	23p55	23p57	00 02
Maryland	d				23p29	23p34	23p34			23p44		23p44	23p44				23p54	23p54						23p59	00 04
Forest Gate	d				23p31	23p36	23p36			23p46		23p46	23p46				23p56	23p56						00 01	00 06
Manor Park	d				23p33	23p38	23p38			23p48		23p48	23p48				23p58	23p58						00 03	00 08
Ilford	d				23p36	23p41	23p41			23p51		23p51	23p51				00 01	00 01						00 06	00 11
Seven Kings	d				23p38	23p43	23p43			23p53		23p53	23p53				00 03	00 03						00 08	00 13
Goodmayes	d				23p40	23p45	23p45			23p55		23p55	23p55				00 05	00 05						00 10	00 15
Chadwell Heath	d				23p42	23p47	23p47			23p57		23p57	23p57				00 07	00 07						00 12	00 17
Romford	d				23p46	23p51	23p51			00 02		00 02	00 02				00 12	00 11						00 16	00 21
Gidea Park	d				23p50	23p55	23p55			00 05		00 05	00 05				00 15	00 15						00 20	00 25
Harold Wood	d				23p53	23p58	23p58			00 08		00 08	00 08				00 18	00 18						00 23	00 28
Brentwood	d				23p57	00 02	00 02			00 12		00 12	00 12				00 22	00 22						00 27	00 32
Shenfield	a	23p37	23p38	23p38	00 03	00 08	00 09	23p53	23p52	00 18		00 19	00 18	00 01	00 08	00 09	00 28	00 29	00 08	00 10		00 11	00 10	00 33	00 38
Shenfield	d	23p38	23p39	23p39				23p54	23p54						00 09	00 09			00 09						
Billericay	d	23p45	23p45	23p45				23p59	23p59						00 15	00 15			00 15						
Wickford	d	23p51	23p51	23p51				00 06	00 06						00 21	00 21			00 21						
Battlesbridge	d																								
South Woodham Ferrers	d																								
North Fambridge	d																								
Althorne	d																								
Burnham-on-Crouch	d																								
Southminster	a																								
Rayleigh	d	23p56	23p56	23p56				00 11	00 11						00 26	00 26			00 26						
Hockley	d	00 01	00 01	00 01				00 16	00 16						00 31	00 31			00 31						
Rochford	d	00 04	00 04	00 04				00 19	00 19						00 34	00 34			00 34						
Southend Airport ✈	d	00 07	00 07	00 07				00 22	00 22						00 37	00 37			00 37						
Prittlewell	d	00 10	00 10	00 10				00 25	00 25						00 40	00 40			00 40						
Southend Victoria	a	00 14	00 14	00 18				00 29	00 29						00 44	00 44			00 48						

A 3 September

B not 29 August, 3 September

C 29 August

29 August to 7 September

London - Shenfield, Southminster and Southend Victoria

Network Diagram - see first Page of Table 5

		LE A	LE ■ B	LE ■ A	LE C	LE A	LE B	LE ■ A	LE D	LE ■ D	LE ■ C	LE ■ D	LE ■ D	LE ■ C	LE ■ D	LE ■ D	LE C	LE D	LE C	LE D	LE ■ D	LE D	LE ■ C
London Liverpool Street ■ ⊖	d	23p52	23p55	23p55	00 01	00 02	00 02	00 02	00 12	00 12	00 15	←	00 15	00 18	←	00 18	00 20	00 22	00 32	00 32	00 40	00 42	00 46
Stratford ■ ⊖	d	00 02	00 07	00 07	00 08	00 12	00 12	00a11	00 22	00 24	00 22	00 24	00 27	00 25	00 27	00a27	00 27	00 32	00 39	00 42	00 52	00 52	00 53
Maryland	d	00 04			00 10	00 14	00 14		00 24	→			→				00 29	00 34	00 41	00 44		00 54	
Forest Gate	d	00 06			00 12	00 16	00 16		00 26								00 31	00 36	00 43	00 46		00 56	
Manor Park	d	00 08			00 14	00 18	00 18		00 28								00 33	00 38	00 45	00 48		00 58	
Ilford ■	d	00 11			00 17	00 21	00 21		00 31								00 36	00 41	00 48	00 51		01 01	
Seven Kings	d	00 13			00 19	00 23	00 23		00 33								00 38	00 43	00 50	00 53		01 03	
Goodmayes	d	00 15			00 21	00 25	00 25		00 35								00 40	00 45	00 52	00 55		01 05	
Chadwell Heath	d	00 17			00 23	00 27	00 27		00 37								00 42	00 47	00 54	00 57		01 07	
Romford	d	00 21			00 27	00 31	00 31		00 41		00 32						00 46	00 51	00 58	01 01		01 11	
Gidea Park ■	d	00 25			00a31	00 35	00 35		00 45								00 50	00 55	01a02	01 05		01 15	01 07
Harold Wood	d	00 28				00 38	00 38		00 48								00 53	00 58		01 08		01 18	
Brentwood	d	00 32				00 42	00 42		00 52								00 57	01 02		01 12		01 22	
Shenfield ■	a	00 39	00 23	00 22		00 48	00 49		00 58		00 44	00 40		00 47	00 45		01 03	01 08		01 18	01 07	01 28	01 17
Shenfield ■	d		00 24	00 24							00 45				00 46						01 09		
Billericay	d		00 30	00 30							00 51				00 52						01 15		
Wickford ■	d		00 36	00 36							00 56				00 58						01 21		
Battlesbridge	d																						
South Woodham Ferrers	d																						
North Fambridge	d																						
Althorne	d																						
Burnham-on-Crouch	d																						
Southminster	a																						
Rayleigh	d		00 41	00 41							01 01				01 03						01 26		
Hockley	d		00 46	00 46							01 06				01 08						01 31		
Rochford	d		00 49	00 49							01 09				01 11						01 34		
Southend Airport ✈	d		00 52	00 52							01 12				01 14						01 37		
Prittlewell	d		00 55	00 55							01 15				01 17						01 40		
Southend Victoria	a		00 59	00 59							01 23				01 21						01 44		

		LE ■ D	LE ■ C	LE ■ D	LE D	LE C	LE D	LE ■ D	LE D	LE D	LE D	LE D	LE D	LE D	LE D	LE ■	LE ■	LE ■	LE	LE	LE ■	LE ■
London Liverpool Street ■ ⊖	d	00 46	00 50	←	00 52	00 55	01 02	01 10	01 12	01 22	01 32	01 42	01 52	02 02	02 12		05 23		05 28	05 37	05 52	05 55
Stratford ■ ⊖	d	01 00	00 57	01 00	01 02	01 02	01 12	01 22	01 22	01 32	01 42	01 52	02 02	02 12	02 22		05 30		05 35	05 44	06a01	06 02
Maryland	d	→			01 04	01 04	01 14		01 24	01 34	01 44	01 54	02 04	02 14	02 24					05 46		
Forest Gate	d				01 06	01 06	01 16		01 26	01 36	01 46	01 56	02 06	02 16	02 26					05 48		
Manor Park	d				01 08	01 08	01 18		01 28	01 38	01 48	01 58	02 08	02 18	02 28					05 50		
Ilford ■	d				01 11	01 11	01 21		01 31	01 41	01 51	02 01	02 11	02 21	02 31				05 40	05 53		
Seven Kings	d				01 13	01 13	01 23		01 33	01 43	01 53	02 03	02 13	02 23	02 33				05 42	05 55		
Goodmayes	d				01 15	01 15	01 25		01 35	01 45	01 55	02 05	02 15	02 25	02 35					05 57		
Chadwell Heath	d				01 17	01 17	01 27		01 37	01 47	01 57	02 07	02 17	02 27	02 37					05 59		
Romford	d		01 08		01 21	01 21	01 31		01 41	01 51	02 01	02 11	02 21	02 31	02 41		05 38		05 48	06 03		
Gidea Park ■	d				01 25	01 25	01 35		01 45	01 55	02a05	02 15	02a25	02 35	02a45				05 51	06 07		
Harold Wood	d				01 28	01 28	01 38		01 48	01 58		02 18		02 38					05 54	06 10		
Brentwood	d				01 32	01 32	01 42		01 52	02 02		02 22		02 42					05 59	06 14		
Shenfield ■	a		01 20	01 17	01 38	01 38	01 48	01 37	01 58	02 08		02 28		02 48			05 47		06 04	06 20		06 18
Shenfield ■	d		01 20					01 39										05 56	06 04			06 19
Billericay	d		01 26					01 45										06 02	06 10			06 25
Wickford ■	d		01 31					01 51								05 16		06 09	06 16			06 31
Battlesbridge	d															05 20		06 13				
South Woodham Ferrers	d															05 24		06 17				
North Fambridge	d															05 41		06 24				
Althorne	d															05 46		06 29				
Burnham-on-Crouch	d															05 51		06 34				
Southminster	a															05 57		06 40				
Rayleigh	d		01 36					01 56											06 21			06 36
Hockley	d		01 41					02 01											06 26			06 41
Rochford	d		01 44					02 04											06 29			06 44
Southend Airport ✈	d		01 47					02 07											06 32			06 47
Prittlewell	d		01 50					02 10											06 35			06 50
Southend Victoria	a		01 58					02 14											06 39			06 55

A 3 September
B not 29 August, 3 September
C 29 August
D not 29 August

29 August to 7 September

London - Shenfield, Southminster and Southend Victoria

Network Diagram - see first Page of Table 5

		LE	LE ■	LE ■	LE	LE ■	LE ■	LE	LE	LE ■	LE ■	LE	LE ■	LE	LE ■	LE	LE ◇■	LE ■	LE ■	LE	LE ■	LE ■	LE ■
London Liverpool Street ■ ⊖	d	06 00	06 02		06 10	06 12	06 15	06 20	06 30	06 35	06 38	06 40	06 48	06 50	06 55	07 00	07 00	07 02	07 08	07 10		07 13	07 18
Stratford ■ ⊖	d	06 07	06 09		06 17	06 19	06 22	06 27	06 37	06 42	06 45	06 47	06 55	06 57	07 02	07 07		07 09	07 15	07 17		07 20	07 25
Maryland	d	06 09			06 19			06 29	06 39			06 49		06 59		07 09				07 19			
Forest Gate	d	06 11			06 21			06 31	06 41			06 51		07 01		07 11				07 21			
Manor Park	d	06 13			06 23			06 33	06 43			06 53		07 03		07 13				07 23			
Ilford ■	d	06 16			06 26			06 36	06 46			06 56		07 06		07 16				07 26			
Seven Kings	d	06 18			06 28			06 38	06 48			06 58		07 08		07 18				07 28			
Goodmayes	d	06 20			06 30			06 40	06 50			07 00		07 10		07 20				07 30			
Chadwell Heath	d	06 22			06 32			06 42	06 52			07 02		07 12		07 22				07 32			
Romford	d	06 26			06 36			06 46	06 56			07 06		07 16		07 26				07 36		07 28	
Gidea Park ■	d	06 30			06 40			06 50	07 00			07 10		07 20		07 30				07 40			
Harold Wood	d	06 33			06 43			06 53	07 03			07 13		07 23		07 33				07 43			
Brentwood	d	06 37			06 47			06 57	07 07			07 17		07 27		07 37				07 47			
Shenfield ■	a	06 43	06 24		06 53	06 35	06 38	07 03	07 13	06 58	07 00	07 23	07 11	07 33	07 18	07 43		07 24	07 30	07 53		07 38	07 40
Shenfield ■	d			06 33			06 39			06 59					07 19							07 39	
Billericay	d			06 39			06 45			07 05					07 25							07 45	
Wickford ■	d			06 46			06 51			07 11					07 31						07 36	07 51	
Battlesbridge	d			06 50																	07 40		
South Woodham Ferrers	d			06 54																	07 44		
North Fambridge	d			07 03																	07 53		
Althorne	d			07 08																	07 58		
Burnham-on-Crouch	d			07 13																	08 03		
Southminster	a			07 19																	08 09		
Rayleigh	d						06 56			07 16					07 36							07 56	
Hockley	d						07 01			07 21					07 41							08 01	
Rochford	d						07 04			07 24					07 44							08 04	
Southend Airport ✈	d						07 07			07 27					07 47							08 07	
Prittlewell	d						07 10			07 30					07 50							08 10	
Southend Victoria	a						07 14			07 34					07 54							08 16	

		LE	LE	LE ■	LE ■	LE	LE ■	LE	LE ■	LE ■	LE	LE ■	LE ■	LE	LE	LE ■	LE	LE ■	LE	LE	LE	LE ■
London Liverpool Street ■ ⊖	d	07 20	07 30	07 33	07 36	07 40	07 46	07 50		07 57	08 00	08 00	08 06	08 07	08 10	08 13	08 17	08 17	08 20	08 27	08 30	
Stratford ■ ⊖	d	07 27	07 37	07 42	07 45	07 47	07 54	07 57		08 04	08 07	08 08	08 14	08 14	08 17	08 21	08 24	08 25	08 27	08 34	08 37	
Maryland	d	07 29	07 39			07 49		07 59			08 09				08 19				08 29		08 39	
Forest Gate	d	07 31	07 41			07 51		08 01			08 11				08 21				08 31		08 41	
Manor Park	d	07 33	07 43			07 53		08 03			08 13				08 23				08 33		08 43	
Ilford ■	d	07 36	07 46			07 56		08 06			08 16			08 21	08 26		08a31		08 36	08a41	08 46	
Seven Kings	d	07 38	07 48			07 58		08 08			08 18				08 28				08 38		08 48	
Goodmayes	d	07 40	07 50			08 00		08 10			08 20				08 30				08 40		08 50	
Chadwell Heath	d	07 42	07 52			08 02		08 12			08 22				08 32				08 42		08 52	
Romford	d	07 46	07 56			08 06		08 16			08 26			08 29	08 36				08 46		08 56	
Gidea Park ■	d	07 50	08 00			08 10		08 20			08 30			08a35	08 40				08 50		09 00	
Harold Wood	d	07 53	08 03			08 13		08 23			08 33				08 43				08 53		09 03	
Brentwood	d	07 57	08 07			08 17		08 27			08 37				08 47				08 57		09 07	
Shenfield ■	a	08 03	08 13	07 59	08 01	08 25	08 10	08 35		08 21	08 43	08 25	08 30		08 53	08 38		08 41	09 03		09 13	
Shenfield ■	d			07 59						08 21						08 39						
Billericay	d			08 05						08 27						08 45						
Wickford ■	d			08 11					08 16	08 33						08 51						08 56
Battlesbridge	d								08 20													09 00
South Woodham Ferrers	d								08 24													09 04
North Fambridge	d								08 31													09 11
Althorne	d								08 36													09 16
Burnham-on-Crouch	d								08 41													09 21
Southminster	a								08 47													09 27
Rayleigh	d			08 16						08 38						08 56						
Hockley	d			08 21						08 43						09 01						
Rochford	d			08 24						08 46						09 04						
Southend Airport ✈	d			08 27						08 49						09 07						
Prittlewell	d			08 30						08 52						09 10						
Southend Victoria	a			08 34						08 56						09 14						

Table 5

Mondays to Fridays

29 August to 7 September

London - Shenfield, Southminster and Southend Victoria

Network Diagram - see first Page of Table 5

		LE 1	LE 1	LE	LE	LE 1	LE	LE	LE 1	LE		LE	LE 1	LE	LE	LE 1	LE 1	LE	LE 1	LE		LE	LE	LE	LE 1
London Liverpool Street [15] ⊖	d	08 32	08 36	08 40	08 43	08 48	08 50	08 52	08 55	08 55		09 00	09 02	09 05	09 10		09 13	09 15	09 18	09 20		09 24	09 30	09 33	09 34
Stratford [7] ⊖	d	08 42	08 45	08 47	08 52	08 55	08 57	09 01	09 02	09 04		09 07	09 09	09 12	09 17		09 21	09 24	09 25	09 27		09 32	09 37	09 40	09 42
Maryland	d			08 49			08 59					09 09			09 19					09 29			09 39		
Forest Gate	d			08 51			09 01					09 11			09 21					09 31			09 41		
Manor Park	d			08 53			09 03					09 13			09 23					09 33			09 43		
Ilford [2]	d			08 56	08 59		09 06	09 09		09a11		09 16		09 21	09 26			09 31		09 36		09 39	09 46	09 51	
Seven Kings	d			08 58			09 08					09 18			09 28					09 38			09 48		
Goodmayes	d			09 00			09 10					09 20			09 30					09 40			09 50		
Chadwell Heath	d			09 02			09 12					09 22			09 32					09 42			09 52		
Romford	d			09 06	09 09		09 16	09 19				09 26		09 29	09 36			09 39		09 46		09 49	09 56	09 59	
Gidea Park [2]	d			09 10	09a15		09 20	09a25				09 30		09a35	09 40			09a45		09 50		09a55	10 00	10a05	
Harold Wood	d			09 13			09 23					09 33			09 43					09 53			10 03		
Brentwood	d			09 17			09 27					09 37			09 47					09 57			10 07		
Shenfield [3]	a	08 59	09 01	09 23		09 11	09 33		09 18			09 43	09 24		09 53		09 38		09 40	10 03			10 13		09 58
Shenfield [3]	d	08 59							09 19								09 39								09 59
Billericay	d	09 05							09 25								09 45								10 05
Wickford [2]	d	09 11							09 31							09 36	09 51								10 11
Battlesbridge	d															09 40									
South Woodham Ferrers	d															09 44									
North Fambridge	d															09 51									
Althorne	d															09 56									
Burnham-on-Crouch	d															10 01									
Southminster	a															10 07									
Rayleigh	d	09 16							09 36								09 56								10 16
Hockley	d	09 21							09 41								10 01								10 21
Rochford	d	09 24							09 44								10 04								10 24
Southend Airport ✈	d	09 27							09 47								10 07								10 27
Prittlewell	d	09 30							09 50								10 10								10 30
Southend Victoria	a	09 34							09 54								10 14								10 34

		LE 1	LE	LE 1	LE	LE 1		LE 1	LE	LE 1	LE	LE 1	LE 1	LE	LE	LE 1		LE 1	LE 1	LE	LE 1	LE	LE 1	LE	LE 1
London Liverpool Street [15] ⊖	d	09 38	09 40	09 48	09 50			09 55	10 00	10 02	10 10	10 13	10 18	10 20	10 30			10 35	10 38	10 40	10 48	10 50	10 55	11 00	11 02
Stratford [7] ⊖	d	09 45	09 47	09 55	09 57			10 02	10 07	10 09	10 17	10 20	10 25	10 27	10 37			10 42	10 45	10 47	10 55	10 57	11 02	11 07	11 09
Maryland	d		09 49		09 59				10 09		10 19			10 29	10 39					10 49		10 59		11 09	
Forest Gate	d		09 51		10 01				10 11		10 21			10 31	10 41					10 51		11 01		11 11	
Manor Park	d		09 53		10 03				10 13		10 23			10 33	10 43					10 53		11 03		11 13	
Ilford [2]	d		09 56		10 06				10 16		10 26			10 36	10 46					10 56		11 06		11 16	
Seven Kings	d		09 58		10 08				10 18		10 28			10 38	10 48					10 58		11 08		11 18	
Goodmayes	d		10 00		10 10				10 20		10 30			10 40	10 50					11 00		11 10		11 20	
Chadwell Heath	d		10 02		10 12				10 22		10 32			10 42	10 52					11 02		11 12		11 22	
Romford	d	09 53	10 06		10 16				10 26		10 36	10 28		10 46	10 56				10 53	11 06		11 16		11 26	
Gidea Park [2]	d		10 10		10 20				10 30		10 40			10 50	11 00					11 10		11 20		11 30	
Harold Wood	d		10 13		10 23				10 33		10 43			10 53	11 03					11 13		11 23		11 33	
Brentwood	d		10 17		10 27				10 37		10 47			10 57	11 07					11 17		11 27		11 37	
Shenfield [3]	a	10 02	10 23	10 11	10 33			10 18	10 43	10 24	10 53	10 38	10 40	11 03	11 13			10 58	11 02	11 23	11 11	11 33	11 18	11 43	11 24
Shenfield [3]	d							10 19				10 39						10 59					11 19		
Billericay	d							10 25				10 45						11 05					11 25		
Wickford [2]	d					10 16		10 31				10 51				10 56		11 11					11 31		
Battlesbridge	d					10 20										11 00									
South Woodham Ferrers	d					10 24										11 04									
North Fambridge	d					10 31										11 11									
Althorne	d					10 36										11 16									
Burnham-on-Crouch	d					10 41										11 21									
Southminster	a					10 47										11 27									
Rayleigh	d							10 36				10 56						11 16					11 36		
Hockley	d							10 41				11 01						11 21					11 41		
Rochford	d							10 44				11 04						11 24					11 44		
Southend Airport ✈	d							10 47				11 07						11 27					11 47		
Prittlewell	d							10 50				11 10						11 30					11 50		
Southend Victoria	a							10 54				11 14						11 34					11 54		

Table 5

Mondays to Fridays

29 August to 7 September

London - Shenfield, Southminster and Southend Victoria

Network Diagram - see first Page of Table 5

		LE		LE 1	LE 1	LE 1	LE	LE	LE 1	LE 1	LE	LE 1		LE	LE 1	LE 1	LE	LE 1	LE	LE 1	LE 1	LE		LE	LE 1
London Liverpool Street [15] ⊖	d	11 10			11 13	11 18	11 20	11 30	11 35	11 38	11 40	11 48		11 50		11 55	12 00	12 02	12 10	12 13	12 18	12 20		12 30	
Stratford [7] ⊖	d	11 17			11 20	11 25	11 27	11 37	11 42	11 45	11 47	11 55		11 57		12 02	12 07	12 09	12 17	12 20	12 25	12 27		12 37	
Maryland	d	11 19					11 29	11 39			11 49			11 59			12 09		12 19			12 29		12 39	
Forest Gate	d	11 21					11 31	11 41			11 51			12 01			12 11		12 21			12 31		12 41	
Manor Park	d	11 23					11 33	11 43			11 53			12 03			12 13		12 23			12 33		12 43	
Ilford [2]	d	11 26					11 36	11 46			11 56			12 06			12 16		12 26			12 36		12 46	
Seven Kings	d	11 28					11 38	11 48			11 58			12 08			12 18		12 28			12 38		12 48	
Goodmayes	d	11 30					11 40	11 50			12 00			12 10			12 20		12 30			12 40		12 50	
Chadwell Heath	d	11 32					11 42	11 52			12 02			12 12			12 22		12 32			12 42		12 52	
Romford	d	11 36			11 28		11 46	11 56		11 53	12 06			12 16			12 26		12 36	12 28		12 46		12 56	
Gidea Park [2]	d	11 40					11 50	12 00			12 10			12 20			12 30		12 40			12 50		13 00	
Harold Wood	d	11 43					11 53	12 03			12 13			12 23			12 33		12 43			12 53		13 03	
Brentwood	d	11 47					11 57	12 07			12 17			12 27			12 37		12 47			12 57		13 07	
Shenfield [3]	a	11 53			11 38	11 40	12 03	12 13	11 58	12 02	12 23	12 11		12 33		12 18	12 43	12 24	12 53	12 38	12 40	13 03		13 13	
Shenfield [3]	d				11 39				11 59							12 19				12 39					
Billericay	d				11 45				12 05							12 25				12 45					
Wickford [2]	d			11 36	11 51				12 11						12 16	12 31				12 51					12 56
Battlesbridge	d			11 40											12 20										13 00
South Woodham Ferrers	d			11 44											12 24										13 04
North Fambridge	d			11 51											12 31										13 11
Althorne	d			11 56											12 36										13 16
Burnham-on-Crouch	d			12 01											12 41										13 21
Southminster	a			12 07											12 47										13 27
Rayleigh	d				11 56				12 16							12 36				12 56					
Hockley	d				12 01				12 21							12 41				13 01					
Rochford	d				12 04				12 24							12 44				13 04					
Southend Airport ✈	d				12 07				12 27							12 47				13 07					
Prittlewell	d				12 10				12 30							12 50				13 10					
Southend Victoria	a				12 14				12 34							12 54				13 14					

		LE 1	LE 1	LE	LE 1	LE	LE 1	LE		LE 1	LE	LE 1	LE 1	LE 1	LE	LE	LE 1	LE 1		LE	LE 1	LE	LE 1	LE 1	LE
London Liverpool Street [15] ⊖	d	12 35	12 38	12 40	12 48	12 50	12 55	13 00		13 02	13 10		13 13	13 18	13 20	13 30	13 35	13 38		13 40	13 48	13 50		13 55	14 00
Stratford [7] ⊖	d	12 42	12 45	12 47	12 55	12 57	13 02	13 07		13 09	13 17		13 20	13 25	13 27	13 37	13 42	13 45		13 47	13 55	13 57		14 02	14 07
Maryland	d			12 49		12 59		13 09			13 19				13 29	13 39				13 49		13 59			14 09
Forest Gate	d			12 51		13 01		13 11			13 21				13 31	13 41				13 51		14 01			14 11
Manor Park	d			12 53		13 03		13 13			13 23				13 33	13 43				13 53		14 03			14 13
Ilford [2]	d			12 56		13 06		13 16			13 26				13 36	13 46				13 56		14 06			14 16
Seven Kings	d			12 58		13 08		13 18			13 28				13 38	13 48				13 58		14 08			14 18
Goodmayes	d			13 00		13 10		13 20			13 30				13 40	13 50				14 00		14 10			14 20
Chadwell Heath	d			13 02		13 12		13 22			13 32				13 42	13 52				14 02		14 12			14 22
Romford	d		12 53	13 06		13 16		13 26			13 36		13 28		13 46	13 56		13 53		14 06		14 16			14 26
Gidea Park [2]	d			13 10		13 20		13 30			13 40				13 50	14 00				14 10		14 20			14 30
Harold Wood	d			13 13		13 23		13 33			13 43				13 53	14 03				14 13		14 23			14 33
Brentwood	d			13 17		13 27		13 37			13 47				13 57	14 07				14 17		14 27			14 37
Shenfield [3]	a	12 58	13 02	13 23	13 11	13 33	13 18	13 43		13 24	13 53		13 38	13 40	14 03	14 13	13 58	14 02		14 23	14 11	14 33		14 18	14 43
Shenfield [3]	d	12 59					13 19						13 39				13 59							14 19	
Billericay	d	13 05					13 25						13 45				14 05							14 25	
Wickford [2]	d	13 11					13 31					13 36	13 51				14 11						14 16	14 31	
Battlesbridge	d											13 40											14 20		
South Woodham Ferrers	d											13 44											14 24		
North Fambridge	d											13 51											14 31		
Althorne	d											13 56											14 36		
Burnham-on-Crouch	d											14 01											14 41		
Southminster	a											14 07											14 47		
Rayleigh	d	13 16					13 36						13 56				14 16							14 36	
Hockley	d	13 21					13 41						14 01				14 21							14 41	
Rochford	d	13 24					13 44						14 04				14 24							14 44	
Southend Airport ✈	d	13 27					13 47						14 07				14 27							14 47	
Prittlewell	d	13 30					13 50						14 10				14 30							14 50	
Southend Victoria	a	13 34					13 54						14 14				14 34							14 54	

Table 5

Mondays to Fridays

29 August to 7 September

London - Shenfield, Southminster and Southend Victoria

Network Diagram - see first Page of Table 5

		LE [1]	LE	LE [1]	LE [1]	LE	LE	LE [1]	LE [1]	LE [1]	LE	LE [1]	LE	LE [1]	LE	LE [1]	LE	LE [1]	LE [1]	LE [1]	LE	LE
London Liverpool Street [15] ⊖	d	14 02	14 10	14 13	14 18	14 20	14 30		14 35	14 38	14 40	14 48	14 50	14 55	15 00	15 02	15 10		15 13	15 18	15 20	15 30
Stratford [7] ⊖	d	14 09	14 17	14 20	14 25	14 27	14 37		14 42	14 45	14 47	14 55	14 57	15 02	15 07	15 09	15 17		15 20	15 25	15 27	15 37
Maryland	d		14 19			14 29	14 39				14 49		14 59		15 09		15 19				15 29	15 39
Forest Gate	d		14 21			14 31	14 41				14 51		15 01		15 11		15 21				15 31	15 41
Manor Park	d		14 23			14 33	14 43				14 53		15 03		15 13		15 23				15 33	15 43
Ilford [2]	d		14 26			14 36	14 46				14 56		15 06		15 16		15 26				15 36	15 46
Seven Kings	d		14 28			14 38	14 48				14 58		15 08		15 18		15 28				15 38	15 48
Goodmayes	d		14 30			14 40	14 50				15 00		15 10		15 20		15 30				15 40	15 50
Chadwell Heath	d		14 32			14 42	14 52				15 02		15 12		15 22		15 32				15 42	15 52
Romford	d		14 36	14 28		14 46	14 56			14 53	15 06		15 16		15 26		15 36		15 28		15 46	15 56
Gidea Park [2]	d		14 40			14 50	15 00				15 10		15 20		15 30		15 40				15 50	16 00
Harold Wood	d		14 43			14 53	15 03				15 13		15 23		15 33		15 43				15 53	16 03
Brentwood	d		14 47			14 57	15 07				15 17		15 27		15 37		15 47				15 57	16 07
Shenfield [3]	a	14 24	14 53	14 38	14 40	15 03	15 13		14 58	15 02	15 23	15 11	15 33	15 18	15 43	15 24	15 53		15 38	15 40	16 03	16 13
Shenfield [3]	d			14 39					14 59					15 19					15 39			
Billericay	d			14 45					15 05					15 25					15 45			
Wickford [2]	d			14 51				14 56	15 11					15 31				15 36	15 51			
Battlesbridge	d							15 00										15 40				
South Woodham Ferrers	d							15 04										15 44				
North Fambridge	d							15 11										15 51				
Althorne	d							15 16										15 56				
Burnham-on-Crouch	d							15 21										16 01				
Southminster	a							15 27										16 07				
Rayleigh	d			14 56					15 16					15 36					15 56			
Hockley	d			15 01					15 21					15 41					16 01			
Rochford	d			15 04					15 24					15 44					16 04			
Southend Airport ✈	d			15 07					15 27					15 47					16 07			
Prittlewell	d			15 10					15 31					15 50					16 10			
Southend Victoria	a			15 14					15 34					15 54					16 14			

		LE [1]	LE [1]	LE	LE [1]	LE	LE [1]	LE [1]	LE	LE [1]	LE	LE [1]	LE [1]	LE [1]	LE	LE [1]	LE	LE [1]	LE [1]	LE	LE	LE [1]	LE [1]
London Liverpool Street [15] ⊖	d	15 35	15 38	15 40	15 48	15 50		15 55	16 00	16 02	16 10	16 10	16 14	16 17	16 20	16 24	16 28	16 32	16 34	16 36	16 40		16 40
Stratford [7] ⊖	d	15 42	15 45	15 47	15 55	15 57		16 02	16 07	16 09	16 17	16 18	16 22	16 25	16 27	16 32	16 35		16 42	16 43	16 47		16 48
Maryland	d			15 49		15 59			16 09		16 19				16 29		16 37				16 49		
Forest Gate	d			15 51		16 01			16 11		16 21				16 31		16 39				16 51		
Manor Park	d			15 53		16 03			16 13		16 23				16 33		16 41				16 53		
Ilford [2]	d			15 56		16 06			16 16		16 26				16 36		16 44			16 50	16 56		
Seven Kings	d			15 58		16 08			16 18		16 28				16 38		16 47			16 52			
Goodmayes	d			16 00		16 10			16 20		16 30				16 40		16 49			16 54			
Chadwell Heath	d			16 02		16 12			16 22		16 32				16 42		16 51			16 56	17 00		
Romford	d		15 53	16 06		16 16			16 26		16 36				16 46		16 55			17 00	17 04		
Gidea Park [2]	d			16 10		16 20			16 30		16 40				16 50		17a00			17 04	17a10		
Harold Wood	d			16 13		16 23			16 33		16 43				16 53					17 07			
Brentwood	d			16 17		16 27			16 37		16 47				16 57					17 11			
Shenfield [3]	a	15 58	16 02	16 23	16 11	16 33		16 18	16 43	16 24	16 53	16 34	16 38	16 41	17 03	16 49		16 54	16 58	17 25			17 04
Shenfield [3]	d	15 59						16 19				16 34				16 49							17 04
Billericay	d	16 05						16 25				16 41				16 56							17 11
Wickford [2]	d	16 11					16 14	16 31				16 48				17 03						17 06	17 18
Battlesbridge	d						16 18															17 10	
South Woodham Ferrers	d						16 22															17 14	
North Fambridge	d						16 29															17 21	
Althorne	d						16 34															17 26	
Burnham-on-Crouch	d						16 39															17 31	
Southminster	a						16 45															17 37	
Rayleigh	d	16 16						16 36				16 53				17 08							17 23
Hockley	d	16 21						16 41				16 57				17 12							17 27
Rochford	d	16 24						16 44				17 01				17 16							17 31
Southend Airport ✈	d	16 27						16 47				17 03				17 18							17 33
Prittlewell	d	16 30						16 50				17 06				17 21							17 36
Southend Victoria	a	16 34						16 54				17 15				17 27							17 42

Table 5

Mondays to Fridays

29 August to 7 September

London - Shenfield, Southminster and Southend Victoria

Network Diagram - see first Page of Table 5

		LE [1]	LE	LE [1]	LE	LE [1]	LE	LE	LE ◇[1]	LE [1]	LE	LE [1]	LE	LE [1]	LE [1]	LE	LE [1]	LE	LE [1]	LE [1]	LE [1]	LE	LE
London Liverpool Street [15] ⊖	d	16 44	16 47	16 47	16 50	16 54	16 57	17 00	17 02	17 04	17 07	17 08	17 10	17 12	17 15	17 17	17 18	17 20	17 20	17 22	17 25	17 27	17 30
Stratford [7] ⊖	d	16a52	16 54	16 55	16 57	17 02	17 04	17 07	17 10	17 13	17 14	17a16	17 17	17a20	17 23	17 24	17a26	17 27	17 29	17 31	17 34	17 34	17 37
Maryland	d				16 59			17 09					17 19					17 29					17 39
Forest Gate	d				17 01			17 11					17 21					17 31					17 41
Manor Park	d				17 03			17 13					17 23					17 33					17 43
Ilford [2]	d		17 00		17 06		17 10	17 16			17 20		17 26			17 30		17 36				17 40	17 46
Seven Kings	d		17 02				17 12				17 22					17 32						17 42	
Goodmayes	d		17 04				17 14				17 24					17 34						17 44	
Chadwell Heath	d		17 06		17 10		17 16	17 20			17 26		17 30			17 36		17 40				17 46	17 50
Romford	d		17 10		17 14		17 20	17 24			17 30		17 34			17 40		17 44				17 50	17 54
Gidea Park [2]	d		17 14		17a20		17 24	17a30			17 34		17a40			17 44		17a50				17 54	18a00
Harold Wood	d		17 17				17 27				17 37					17 47						17 57	
Brentwood	d		17 21				17 31				17 41					17 51						18 01	
Shenfield [3]	a		17 29	17 11		17 19	17 39			17 30	17 49				17 39	17 59			17 45		17 51	18 09	
Shenfield [3]	d					17 19				17 30					17 39						17 52		
Billericay	d					17 26				17 37					17 46						17 58		
Wickford [2]	d					17 33				17 44					17 53					18 00	18 05		
Battlesbridge	d																			18 04			
South Woodham Ferrers	d																			18 08			
North Fambridge	d																			18 14			
Althorne	d																			18 19			
Burnham-on-Crouch	d																			18 24			
Southminster	a																			18 32			
Rayleigh	d					17 38				17 49					17 58						18 10		
Hockley	d					17 42				17 53					18 02						18 15		
Rochford	d					17 46				17 57					18 06						18 18		
Southend Airport ✈	d					17 48				17 59					18 08						18 21		
Prittlewell	d					17 51				18 02					18 11						18 24		
Southend Victoria	a					17 57				18 08					18 17						18 30		

		LE [1]	LE [1]	LE	LE [1]	LE	LE [1] A	LE	LE [1]	LE	LE	LE	LE [1]	LE [1]	LE	LE [1]	LE	LE [1]	LE	LE [1]	LE [1]	LE
London Liverpool Street [15] ⊖	d	17 32	17 34	17 36	17 38	17 39	17 40	17 42	17 45	17 46	17 49	17 52	17 52	17 54	17 56	17 58	17 59	18 00	18 02	18 02	18 05	
Stratford [7] ⊖	d	17a40	17 43	17 43	17a47	17 46	17 49	17 49	17 53	17 53	17 56	17 59	18a01	18 03	18 03	18a06	18 06	18 09	18 09	18 11	18 14	
Maryland	d			17 45						17 55					18 05							
Forest Gate	d							17 52				18 02							18 12			
Manor Park	d					17 50					18 00						18 10					
Ilford [2]	d			17 50		17 53		17 56		18 00	18 03	18 06			18 10		18 13		18 16			
Seven Kings	d			17 52		17 56		17 59		18 02	18 06	18 09			18 12		18 16		18 19			
Goodmayes	d			17 54		17 58		18 01		18 04	18 08	18 11			18 14		18 18		18 21			
Chadwell Heath	d			17 56		18 00		18 03		18 06	18 10	18 13			18 16		18 20		18 23			
Romford	d			18 00		18 04		18 07		18 10	18 14	18 17			18 20		18 24		18 27			
Gidea Park [2]	d			18 04		18a09		18a12		18 14	18 18	18a22			18 24		18a29		18a32			
Harold Wood	d			18 07						18 17	18 21				18 27							
Brentwood	d			18 11						18 21	18 25				18 31							←
Shenfield [3]	a		17 59	18 19			18 05		18 09	18 29	18 33			18 19	18 39			18 25			18 31	18 33
Shenfield [3]	d		17 59						18 09		18 36			18 19							18 31	18 36
Billericay	d		18 06						18 16		→			18 26							18 38	18 42
Wickford [2]	d		18 13						18 23					18 33						18 41	18 45	18 49
Battlesbridge	d																			18 45		
South Woodham Ferrers	d																			18 49		
North Fambridge	d																			18 55		
Althorne	d																			19 00		
Burnham-on-Crouch	d																			19 05		
Southminster	a																			19 13		
Rayleigh	d		18 18						18 28					18 38							18 50	18 54
Hockley	d		18 22						18 32					18 42							18 55	18 59
Rochford	d		18 26						18 36					18 46							18 58	19 02
Southend Airport ✈	d		18 28						18 38					18 48							19 01	19 05
Prittlewell	d		18 31						18 41					18 51							19 04	19 08
Southend Victoria	a		18 37						18 47					18 58							19 10	19 14

A The Stratford call is subjtect to introduction during the currency of the timetable.

London - Shenfield, Southminster and Southend Victoria

Network Diagram - see first Page of Table 5

		LE	LE	LE ■	LE ■	LE	LE ■	LE		LE ■	LE ■	LE	LE	LE ■	LE ■	LE	LE ■	LE		LE ■	LE ■	LE	LE ■	LE	LE ■
London Liverpool Street ■ ⊖	d	18 07	18 10	18 12	18 14	18 17	18 18	18 20		18 20	18 25	18 27	18 30	18 32	18 35	18 37	18 38	18 40		18 41	18 45	18 47	18 48	18 50	18 55
Stratford ■ ⊖	d	18 14	18 17	18a21	18 23	18 24	18a27	18 27		18 29	18 33	18 34	18 37	18a40	18 43	18 44	18 46	18 47		18 49	18 53	18 54	18a56	18 57	19 03
Maryland	d		18 19					18 29					18 39					18 49						18 59	
Forest Gate	d		18 21					18 31					18 41					18 51						19 01	
Manor Park	d		18 23					18 33					18 43					18 53						19 03	
Ilford ■	d	18 20	18 26			18 30		18 36				18 40	18 46			18 50		18 56				19 00		19 06	
Seven Kings	d	18 22				18 32						18 42				18 52						19 02			
Goodmayes	d	18 24				18 34						18 44				18 54						19 04			
Chadwell Heath	d	18 26	18 30			18 36		18 40				18 46	18 50			18 56		19 00				19 06		19 10	
Romford	d	18 30	18 34			18 40		18 44				18 50	18 54			19 00		19 04				19 10		19 14	
Gidea Park ■	d	18 34	18a40			18 44		18a50				18 54	19a00			19 04		19 08				19 14		19a20	
Harold Wood	d	18 37				18 47						18 57				19 07		19 11				19 17			
Brentwood	d	18 41				18 51						19 01				19 11		19 15				19 21			
Shenfield ■	a	18 49			18 40	18 59				18 45	18 50	19 09			18 59	19 19	19 02	19 23			19 10	19 29			19 20
Shenfield ■	d				18 41						18 50				18 59						19 10				19 20
Billericay	d				18 47						18 57				19 06						19 17				19 27
Wickford ■	d				18 54						19 04				19 13					19 19	19 24				19 34
Battlesbridge	d																			19 23					
South Woodham Ferrers	d																			19 27					
North Fambridge	d																			19 34					
Althorne	d																			19 39					
Burnham-on-Crouch	d																			19 44					
Southminster	a																			19 52					
Rayleigh	d				18 59						19 09				19 18						19 29				19 39
Hockley	d				19 04						19 13				19 22						19 33				19 43
Rochford	d				19 07						19 17				19 26						19 37				19 47
Southend Airport ✈	d				19 10						19 19				19 28						19 39				19 49
Prittlewell	d				19 13						19 22				19 31						19 42				19 52
Southend Victoria	a				19 19						19 28				19 37						19 47				19 58

		LE	LE	LE ■		LE ■	LE	LE ■	LE	LE ■	LE	LE	LE ■	LE ■	LE ■		LE	LE ■	LE	LE ■	LE ■	LE	LE ■	LE	LE ■
London Liverpool Street ■ ⊖	d	18 57	19 00	19 02		19 08	19 10	19 15	19 17	19 18	19 20	19 30	19 32	19 35	19 38		19 40	19 48	19 50		19 55	20 00	20 02	20 10	20 13
Stratford ■ ⊖	d	19 04	19 07	19 09		19a15	19 17	19 22	19 24	19 25	19 27	19 37	19a39	19 42	19 45		19 47	19 55	19 57		20 02	20 07	20 09	20 17	20 20
Maryland	d		19 09				19 19				19 29	19 39					19 49		19 59			20 09		20 19	
Forest Gate	d		19 11				19 21				19 31	19 41					19 51		20 01			20 11		20 21	
Manor Park	d		19 13				19 23				19 33	19 43					19 53		20 03			20 13		20 23	
Ilford ■	d	19 10	19 16				19 26		19 30		19 36	19 46					19 56		20 06			20 16		20 26	
Seven Kings	d	19 12	19 18				19 28		19 32		19 38	19 48					19 58		20 08			20 18		20 28	
Goodmayes	d	19 14	19 20				19 30		19 34		19 40	19 50					20 00		20 10			20 20		20 30	
Chadwell Heath	d	19 16	19 22				19 32		19 36		19 42	19 52					20 02		20 12			20 22		20 32	
Romford	d	19 20	19 26				19 36		19 40		19 46	19 56					20 06		20 16			20 26		20 36	20 28
Gidea Park ■	d	19 24	19 30				19 40		19a44		19 50	20 00					20 10		20 20			20 30		20 40	
Harold Wood	d	19 27	19 33				19 43				19 53	20 03					20 13		20 23			20 33		20 43	
Brentwood	d	19 31	19 37				19 47				19 57	20 07					20 17		20 27			20 37		20 47	
Shenfield ■	a	19 39	19 43	19 24			19 53	19 38		19 40	20 03	20 13		19 58	20 00		20 23	20 11	20 33		20 18	20 43	20 24	20 53	20 38
Shenfield ■	d							19 39						19 59							20 19				20 39
Billericay	d							19 45						20 05							20 25				20 45
Wickford ■	d							19 51						20 11						20 16	20 31				20 51
Battlesbridge	d																			20 20					
South Woodham Ferrers	d																			20 24					
North Fambridge	d																			20 31					
Althorne	d																			20 36					
Burnham-on-Crouch	d																			20 41					
Southminster	a																			20 47					
Rayleigh	d							19 56						20 16							20 36				20 56
Hockley	d							20 01						20 21							20 41				21 01
Rochford	d							20 04						20 24							20 44				21 04
Southend Airport ✈	d							20 07						20 27							20 47				21 07
Prittlewell	d							20 10						20 30							20 50				21 10
Southend Victoria	a							20 14						20 34							20 54				21 14

London - Shenfield, Southminster and Southend Victoria

Network Diagram - see first Page of Table 5

		LE ■	LE	LE	LE ■	LE ■	LE ■	LE	LE ■	LE		LE ■	LE	LE ■	LE	LE ■	LE ■	LE ■	LE	LE		LE ■	LE ■	LE	LE ■
London Liverpool Street ■ ⊖	d	20 18	20 20	20 30		20 35	20 38	20 40	20 48	20 50		20 55	21 00	21 02	21 10		21 13	21 18	21 20	21 30		21 35	21 38	21 40	21 42
Stratford ■ ⊖	d	20 25	20 27	20 37		20 42	20 45	20 47	20 55	20 57		21 02	21 07	21 09	21 17		21 20	21 25	21 27	21 37		21 42	21 45	21 47	21a51
Maryland	d		20 29	20 39				20 49		20 59			21 09		21 19				21 29	21 39				21 49	
Forest Gate	d		20 31	20 41				20 51		21 01			21 11		21 21				21 31	21 41				21 51	
Manor Park	d		20 33	20 43				20 53		21 03			21 13		21 23				21 33	21 43				21 53	
Ilford ■	d		20 36	20 46				20 56		21 06			21 16		21 26				21 36	21 46				21 56	
Seven Kings	d		20 38	20 48				20 58		21 08			21 18		21 28				21 38	21 48				21 58	
Goodmayes	d		20 40	20 50				21 00		21 10			21 20		21 30				21 40	21 50				22 00	
Chadwell Heath	d		20 42	20 52				21 02		21 12			21 22		21 32				21 42	21 52				22 02	
Romford	d		20 46	20 56				21 06		21 16			21 26		21 36				21 46	21 56				22 06	
Gidea Park ■	d		20 50	21 00				21 10		21 20			21 30		21 40				21 50	22 00				22 10	
Harold Wood	d		20 53	21 03				21 13		21 23			21 33		21 43				21 53	22 03				22 13	
Brentwood	d		20 57	21 07				21 17		21 27			21 37		21 47				21 57	22 07				22 17	
Shenfield ■	a	20 40	21 03	21 13		20 58	21 00	21 23	21 11	21 33		21 18	21 43	21 24	21 53		21 38	21 40	22 03	22 13		21 58	22 00	22 23	
Shenfield ■	d					20 59						21 19					21 39					21 59			
Billericay	d					21 05						21 25					21 45					22 05			
Wickford ■	d				20 56	21 11						21 31				21 36	21 51					22 11			
Battlesbridge	d				21 00											21 40									
South Woodham Ferrers	d				21 04											21 44									
North Fambridge	d				21 11											21 51									
Althorne	d				21 16											21 56									
Burnham-on-Crouch	d				21 21											22 01									
Southminster	a				21 27											22 07									
Rayleigh	d					21 16						21 36					21 56					22 16			
Hockley	d					21 21						21 41					22 01					22 21			
Rochford	d					21 24						21 44					22 04					22 24			
Southend Airport ✈	d					21 27						21 47					22 07					22 27			
Prittlewell	d					21 30						21 50					22 10					22 30			
Southend Victoria	a					21 34						21 54					22 14					22 34			

		LE ■	LE	LE ■	LE ■	LE ■		LE	LE ■	LE ■	LE ■	LE	LE ■	LE ■	LE ■	LE		LE ■	LE ■	LE ■	LE	LE ■	LE	LE ■	LE ■
London Liverpool Street ■ ⊖	d	21 48	21 50		21 50	22 02		22 02	22 10	22 12	22 15	22 17	22 22		22 25	22 32		22 35	22 40	22 42	22 42	22 45	22 52	22 52	22 55
Stratford ■ ⊖	d	21 55	21 57		22 02	22 10		22 12	22 22	22a21	22 24	22 27	22a31		22 37	22 42		22 44	22 52	22a51	22 52	22 54	23 02	23a01	23 07
Maryland	d		21 59					22 14				22 29				22 44					22 54		23 04		
Forest Gate	d		22 01					22 16				22 31				22 46					22 56		23 06		
Manor Park	d		22 03					22 18				22 33				22 48					22 58		23 08		
Ilford ■	d		22 06					22 21				22 36				22 51					23 01		23 11		
Seven Kings	d		22 08					22 23				22 38				22 53					23 03		23 13		
Goodmayes	d		22 10					22 25				22 40				22 55					23 05		23 15		
Chadwell Heath	d		22 12					22 27				22 42				22 57					23 07		23 17		
Romford	d		22 16					22 31				22 46				23 01					23 11		23 21		
Gidea Park ■	d		22 20					22 35				22 50				23 05					23 15		23 25		
Harold Wood	d		22 23					22 38				22 53				23 08					23 18		23 28		
Brentwood	d		22 27					22 42				22 57				23 12					23 22		23 32		
Shenfield ■	a	22 11	22 33		22 18	22 26		22 48	22 38		22 40	23 03			22 53	23 18		23 00	23 08		23 28	23 11	23 38		23 23
Shenfield ■	d				22 19				22 39						22 54				23 09						23 24
Billericay	d				22 25				22 45						23 00				23 15						23 30
Wickford ■	d			22 16	22 31				22 51					22 56	23 06				23 21						23 36
Battlesbridge	d			22 20										23 00											
South Woodham Ferrers	d			22 24										23 04											
North Fambridge	d			22 31										23 11											
Althorne	d			22 36										23 16											
Burnham-on-Crouch	d			22 41										23 21											
Southminster	a			22 47										23 27											
Rayleigh	d				22 36				22 56						23 11				23 26						23 41
Hockley	d				22 41				23 01						23 16				23 31						23 46
Rochford	d				22 44				23 04						23 19				23 34						23 49
Southend Airport ✈	d				22 47				23 07						23 22				23 37						23 52
Prittlewell	d				22 50				23 10						23 25				23 40						23 55
Southend Victoria	a				22 54				23 14						23 29				23 44						23 59

Mondays to Fridays

29 August to 7 September

London - Shenfield, Southminster and Southend Victoria

Network Diagram - see first Page of Table 5

		LE	LE 1	LE 1	LE 1	LE 1	LE	LE 1	LE	LE 1	LE 1	LE	LE 1	LE 1	LE	LE 1	LE 1	LE	LE 1
London Liverpool Street 15 ⊖	d	23 02	23 07	23 10	23 12		23 12	23 15	23 22	23 22	23 25	23 32	23 35	23 40	23 42	23 42	23 45	23 52	23 55
Stratford 7 ⊖	d	23 12	23 17	23 22	23a21		23 22	23 25	23 32	23a31	23 37	23 42	23 45	23 52	23 52	23a52	23 54	00 02	00 07
Maryland	d	23 14					23 24		23 34			23 44			23 54			00 04	
Forest Gate	d	23 16					23 26		23 36			23 46			23 56			00 06	
Manor Park	d	23 18					23 28		23 38			23 48			23 58			00 08	
Ilford 2	d	23 21					23 31		23 41			23 51			00 01			00 11	
Seven Kings	d	23 23					23 33		23 43			23 53			00 03			00 13	
Goodmayes	d	23 25					23 35		23 45			23 55			00 05			00 15	
Chadwell Heath	d	23 27					23 37		23 47			23 57			00 07			00 17	
Romford	d	23 31					23 41		23 51			00 02			00 12			00 21	
Gidea Park 2	d	23 35					23 45		23 55			00 05			00 15			00 25	
Harold Wood	d	23 38					23 48		23 58			00 08			00 18			00 28	
Brentwood	d	23 42					23 52		00 02			00 12			00 22			00 32	
Shenfield 3	a	23 48	23 33	23 38			23 58	23 43	00 08		23 53	00 18	23 59	00 08	00 28		00 11	00 38	00 23
Shenfield 3	d			23 39							23 54			00 09					00 24
Billericay	d			23 45							23 59			00 15					00 30
Wickford 2	d			23 51		23p56					00 06			00 21					00 36
Battlesbridge	d					00 01													
South Woodham Ferrers	d					00 04													
North Fambridge	d					00 11													
Althorne	d					00 16													
Burnham-on-Crouch	d					00 21													
Southminster	a					00 27													
Rayleigh	d			23 56							00 11			00 26					00 41
Hockley	d			00 01							00 16			00 31					00 46
Rochford	d			00 04							00 19			00 34					00 49
Southend Airport ✈	d			00 07							00 22			00 37					00 52
Prittlewell	d			00 10							00 25			00 40					00 55
Southend Victoria	a			00 14							00 29			00 44					00 59

Mondays to Fridays

from 10 September

		LE 1 A	LE 1 A	LE FO 1 B	LE 1 C	LE 1 D MO	LE FO B	LE A	LE 1 A	LE ◇1 C	LE A	LE D MO	LE MX	LE 1 A	LE 1 C	LE 1 A	LE A	LE FO 1 B	LE A	LE 1 D MO	LE 1 A	LE FO 1 B	LE 1 C	LE 1 C
London Liverpool Street 15 ⊖	d	23p10		23p15		23p15	23p20	23p22	23p25	23p30	23p32	23p35	23p35	23p35		23p40	23p42	23p45		23p45	23p45	23p48	23p50	
Stratford 7 ⊖	d	23p22		23p22		23p22	23p27	23p32	23p37	23b39	23p42	23p42	23p42	23p45		23p52	23p52	23p52		23p52	23p54	23p55	23p57	
Maryland	d						23p29	23p34			23p44	23p43	23p44				23p54							
Forest Gate	d						23p31	23p36			23p46	23p45	23p46				23p56							
Manor Park	d						23p33	23p38			23p48	23p47	23p48				23p58							
Ilford 2	d						23p36	23p41			23p51	23p50	23p51				00 01							
Seven Kings	d						23p38	23p43			23p53	23p53	23p53				00 03							
Goodmayes	d						23p40	23p45			23p55	23p55	23p55				00 05							
Chadwell Heath	d						23p42	23p47			23p57	23p57	23p57				00 07							
Romford	d					23p33	23p46	23p51			00 02	23p59	00 02				00 11			00 03				
Gidea Park 2	d					23p37	23p50	23p55			00 05	00 04	00 05				00 15			00 07				
Harold Wood	d					23p40	23p53	23p58			00 08	00 07	00 08				00 18		←	00 10				
Brentwood	d					23p44	23p57	00 02			00 12	00 11	00 12				00 22		00 12	00 14				
Shenfield 3	a	23p37		23p38		23p50	00 03	00 09	23p52	00 02	→	00 18	00 18	00 01		00 09	→	00 08	00 19	00 20	00 10	00 10	00 20	
Shenfield 3	d	23p38		23p39	23p43	23p50			23p54						00 05	00 09		00 09		00 20				00 23
Billericay	d	23p45		23p45	23p49	23p56			23p59						00 11	00 15		00 15		00 26				00 29
Wickford 2	d	23p51	23p56	23p51	23p55	00 01			00 06						00 17	00 21		00 21		00 31				00 35
Battlesbridge	d		00 01																					
South Woodham Ferrers	d		00 04																					
North Fambridge	d		00 11																					
Althorne	d		00 16																					
Burnham-on-Crouch	d		00 21																					
Southminster	a		00 27																					
Rayleigh	d	23p56		23p56	00 01	00 06			00 11						00 22	00 26		00 26		00 36				00 40
Hockley	d	00 01		00 01	00 05	00 11			00 16						00 27	00 31		00 31		00 41				00 45
Rochford	d	00 04		00 04	00 08	00 14			00 19						00 30	00 34		00 34		00 44				00 48
Southend Airport ✈	d	00 07		00 07	00 11	00 17			00 22						00 33	00 37		00 37		00 47				00 51
Prittlewell	d	00 10		00 10	00 14				00 25						00 36	00 40		00 40						00 54
Southend Victoria	a	00 14		00 18	00 18	00 27			00 29						00 40	00 44		00 48		00 57				00 58

A 10 September
B also from 11 September until 13 September
C TWThO from 18 September
D from 17 September
b Previous night, stops to pick up only

Mondays to Fridays

from 10 September

London - Shenfield, Southminster and Southend Victoria

Network Diagram - see first Page of Table 5

		LE A	LE FO B	LE A	LE C	LE 1 A	LE FO B	LE C	LE MO 1 D	LE C	LE A	LE 1 A	LE MO D	LE A	LE 1 A	LE FO 1 B	LE 1 A	LE MO 1 D	LE 1 A	LE FO 1 B	LE 1 C	LE 1 A	LE MO 1 D
London Liverpool Street 15 ⊖	d		23p50	23p52	23p55	23p55	00 01	00 01	00 02	←	00 02	00 02	00 05	00 12	00 12	00 15	00 15	00 15	←	00 18	00 18	←	
Stratford 7 ⊖	d		23p57	00 02	00 02	00 07	00 08	00 10	00 09	00 10	00 12	00a11	00 12	00 22	00 24	00 22	00 27	00 22	00 24	00 25	00 25	00 27	
Maryland	d		23p59	00 04	00 04		00 10	→		00 12	00 14		00 13	00 24	→		→						
Forest Gate	d		00 01	00 06	00 06		00 12			00 14	00 16		00 15	00 26									
Manor Park	d		00 03	00 08	00 08		00 14			00 16	00 18		00 17	00 28									
Ilford 2	d		00 06	00 11	00 11		00 17			00 19	00 21		00 20	00 31									
Seven Kings	d		00 08	00 13	00 13		00 19			00 21	00 23		00 23	00 33									
Goodmayes	d		00 10	00 15	00 15		00 21			00 23	00 25		00 25	00 35									
Chadwell Heath	d		00 12	00 17	00 17		00 23			00 25	00 27		00 27	00 37									
Romford	d		00 16	00 21	00 21		00 27			00 29	00 31		00 30	00 41		00 32		00 33			00 37		
Gidea Park 2	d		00 20	00 25	00 25		00a31			00a32	00 35		00a36	00 45				00 37					
Harold Wood	d	←	00 23	00 28	00 28						00 38			00 48				00 40					
Brentwood	d	00 22	00 27	00 32	00 32						00 42			00 52				00 44					←
Shenfield 3	a	00 29	00 33	00 39	00 38	00 22			00 30		00 48			→		00 44		00 50	00 40	00 47	00 50	00 45	00 50
Shenfield 3	d					00 24										00 45		00 50				00 46	00 50
Billericay	d					00 30										00 51		→				00 52	00 56
Wickford 2	d					00 36										00 56						00 58	01 01
Battlesbridge	d																						
South Woodham Ferrers	d																						
North Fambridge	d																						
Althorne	d																						
Burnham-on-Crouch	d																						
Southminster	a																						
Rayleigh	d					00 41										01 01						01 03	01 06
Hockley	d					00 46										01 06						01 08	01 11
Rochford	d					00 49										01 09						01 11	01 14
Southend Airport ✈	d					00 52										01 12						01 14	01 17
Prittlewell	d					00 55										01 15						01 17	
Southend Victoria	a					00 59										01 23						01 21	01 27

		LE 1 A	LE 1 C	LE A	LE MX	LE A	LE MX	LE A	LE MO D	LE 1 A	LE A	LE MO 1 D	LE MX 1	LE 1 A	LE MX 1	LE 1 A	LE A	LE A	LE E	LE A	LE 1 A	LE A
London Liverpool Street 15 ⊖	d	00 18			00 20	00 22	00 32	00 32	00 35	00 40	00 42	00 45	00 46	00 46	00 50	←		00 52	00 55	01 02	01 10	01 12
Stratford 7 ⊖	d	00a27			00 27	00 32	00 39	00 42	00 42	00 52	00 52	00 52	00 53	01 00	00 57	01 00		01 02	01 02	01 12	01 22	01 22
Maryland	d				00 29	00 34	00 41	00 44	00 43		00 54			→				01 04	01 04	01 14		01 24
Forest Gate	d				00 31	00 36	00 43	00 46	00 45		00 56							01 06	01 06	01 16		01 26
Manor Park	d				00 33	00 38	00 45	00 48	00 47		00 58							01 08	01 08	01 18		01 28
Ilford 2	d				00 36	00 41	00 48	00 51	00 50		01 01							01 11	01 11	01 21		01 31
Seven Kings	d				00 38	00 43	00 50	00 53	00 53		01 03							01 13	01 13	01 23		01 33
Goodmayes	d				00 40	00 45	00 52	00 55	00 55		01 05							01 15	01 15	01 25		01 35
Chadwell Heath	d				00 42	00 47	00 54	00 57	00 57		01 07							01 17	01 17	01 27		01 37
Romford	d				00 46	00 51	00 58	01 01	01 00		01 11	01 03			01 08			01 21	01 21	01 31		01 41
Gidea Park 2	d				00 50	00 55	01a02	01 05	01a06		01 15	01 07	01 07					01 25	01 25	01 35		01 45
Harold Wood	d			←	00 53	00 58		01 08			01 18	01 10					←	01 28	01 28	01 38		01 48
Brentwood	d			00 52	00 57	01 02		01 12			01 22	01 14					01 22	01 32	01 32	01 42		01 52
Shenfield 3	a			00 58	01 03	01 08		01 18		01 07	→	01 20	01 17		01 20	01 17	01 28	01 38	01 38	01 48	01 37	01 58
Shenfield 3	d		00 53							01 09		01 20			01 20						01 39	
Billericay	d		00 59							01 15		01 26			01 26						01 45	
Wickford 2	d		01 04							01 21		01 31			01 31						01 51	
Battlesbridge	d																					
South Woodham Ferrers	d																					
North Fambridge	d																					
Althorne	d																					
Burnham-on-Crouch	d																					
Southminster	a																					
Rayleigh	d		01 09							01 26		01 36			01 36						01 56	
Hockley	d		01 14							01 31		01 41			01 41						02 01	
Rochford	d		01 17							01 34		01 44			01 44						02 04	
Southend Airport ✈	d		01 20							01 37		01 47			01 47						02 07	
Prittlewell	d		01 23							01 40					01 50						02 10	
Southend Victoria	a		01 27							01 44		01 57			01 58						02 14	

A 10 September
B also from 11 September until 13 September
C TWThO from 18 September
D from 17 September
E not 10 September

Table 5

Mondays to Fridays
from 10 September

London - Shenfield, Southminster and Southend Victoria

Network Diagram - see first Page of Table 5

		LE A	LE A	LE A	LE A	LE A	LE A	LE [1]		LE [1]	LE [1]	LE	LE	LE [1]	LE [1]	LE	LE [1]	LE [1]		LE	LE [1]	LE [1]	LE	LE	LE [1]
London Liverpool Street [15] ⊖	d	01 22	01 32	01 42	01 52	02 02	02 12			05 23		05 28	05 37	05 52	05 55	06 00	06 02			06 10	06 12	06 15	06 20	06 30	06 35
Stratford [7] ⊖	d	01 32	01 42	01 52	02 02	02 12	02 22			05 30		05 35	05 44	06a01	06 02	06 07	06 09			06 17	06 19	06 22	06 27	06 37	06 42
Maryland	d	01 34	01 44	01 54	02 04	02 14	02 24						05 46			06 09				06 19			06 29	06 39	
Forest Gate	d	01 36	01 46	01 56	02 06	02 16	02 26						05 48			06 11				06 21			06 31	06 41	
Manor Park	d	01 38	01 48	01 58	02 08	02 18	02 28						05 50			06 13				06 23			06 33	06 43	
Ilford [2]	d	01 41	01 51	02 01	02 11	02 21	02 31					05 40	05 53			06 16				06 26			06 36	06 46	
Seven Kings	d	01 43	01 53	02 03	02 13	02 23	02 33					05 42	05 55			06 18				06 28			06 38	06 48	
Goodmayes	d	01 45	01 55	02 05	02 15	02 25	02 35						05 57			06 20				06 30			06 40	06 50	
Chadwell Heath	d	01 47	01 57	02 07	02 17	02 27	02 37						05 59			06 22				06 32			06 42	06 52	
Romford	d	01 51	02 01	02 11	02 21	02 31	02 41			05 38		05 48	06 03			06 26				06 36			06 46	06 56	
Gidea Park [2]	d	01 55	02a05	02 15	02a25	02 35	02a45					05 51	06 07			06 30				06 40			06 50	07 00	
Harold Wood	d	01 58		02 18		02 38						05 54	06 10			06 33				06 43			06 53	07 03	
Brentwood	d	02 02		02 22		02 42						05 59	06 14			06 37				06 47			06 57	07 07	
Shenfield [3]	a	02 08		02 28		02 48				05 47		06 04	06 20		06 18	06 43	06 24			06 53	06 35	06 38	07 03	07 13	06 58
Shenfield [3]	d										05 56	06 04			06 19			06 33				06 39			06 59
Billericay	d										06 02	06 10			06 25			06 39				06 45			07 05
Wickford [2]	d							05 16			06 09	06 16			06 31			06 46				06 51			07 11
Battlesbridge	d							05 20			06 13							06 50							
South Woodham Ferrers	d							05 24			06 17							06 54							
North Fambridge	d							05 41			06 24							07 03							
Althorne	d							05 46			06 29							07 08							
Burnham-on-Crouch	d							05 51			06 34							07 13							
Southminster	a							05 57			06 40							07 19							
Rayleigh	d											06 21			06 36							06 56			07 16
Hockley	d											06 26			06 41							07 01			07 21
Rochford	d											06 29			06 44							07 04			07 24
Southend Airport ✈	d											06 32			06 47							07 07			07 27
Prittlewell	d											06 35			06 50							07 10			07 30
Southend Victoria	a											06 39			06 55							07 14			07 34

		LE [1]	LE	LE [1]		LE	LE [1]	LE	LE ◇[1]	LE [1]	LE [1]	LE	LE [1]	LE [1]		LE [1]	LE	LE	LE [1]	LE [1]	LE	LE [1]	LE	LE [1]	
London Liverpool Street [15] ⊖	d	06 38	06 40	06 48		06 50	06 55	07 00	07 00	07 02	07 08	07 10		07 13		07 18	07 20	07 30	07 33	07 36	07 40	07 46	07 50		
Stratford [7] ⊖	d	06 45	06 47	06 55		06 57	07 02	07 07		07 09	07 15	07 17		07 20		07 25	07 27	07 37	07 42	07 45	07 47	07 54	07 57		
Maryland	d		06 49			06 59		07 09				07 19					07 29	07 39			07 49		07 59		
Forest Gate	d		06 51			07 01		07 11				07 21					07 31	07 41			07 51		08 01		
Manor Park	d		06 53			07 03		07 13				07 23					07 33	07 43			07 53		08 03		
Ilford [2]	d		06 56			07 06		07 16				07 26					07 36	07 46			07 56		08 06		
Seven Kings	d		06 58			07 08		07 18				07 28					07 38	07 48			07 58		08 08		
Goodmayes	d		07 00			07 10		07 20				07 30					07 40	07 50			08 00		08 10		
Chadwell Heath	d		07 02			07 12		07 22				07 32					07 42	07 52			08 02		08 12		
Romford	d		07 06			07 16		07 26				07 36		07 28			07 46	07 56			08 06		08 16		
Gidea Park [2]	d		07 10			07 20		07 30				07 40					07 50	08 00			08 10		08 20		
Harold Wood	d		07 13			07 23		07 33				07 43					07 53	08 03			08 13		08 23		
Brentwood	d		07 17			07 27		07 37				07 47					07 57	08 07			08 17		08 27		
Shenfield [3]	a	07 00	07 23	07 11		07 33	07 18	07 43		07 24	07 30	07 53		07 38		07 40	08 03	08 13	07 59	08 01	08 25	08 10	08 35		
Shenfield [3]	d						07 19							07 39					07 59						
Billericay	d						07 25							07 45					08 05						
Wickford [2]	d						07 31						07 36	07 51					08 11					08 16	
Battlesbridge	d												07 40											08 20	
South Woodham Ferrers	d												07 44											08 24	
North Fambridge	d												07 53											08 31	
Althorne	d												07 58											08 36	
Burnham-on-Crouch	d												08 03											08 41	
Southminster	a												08 09											08 47	
Rayleigh	d						07 36							07 56					08 16						
Hockley	d						07 41							08 01					08 21						
Rochford	d						07 44							08 04					08 24						
Southend Airport ✈	d						07 47							08 07					08 27						
Prittlewell	d						07 50							08 10					08 30						
Southend Victoria	a						07 54							08 16					08 34						

A 10 September

Table 5

Mondays to Fridays
from 10 September

London - Shenfield, Southminster and Southend Victoria

Network Diagram - see first Page of Table 5

		LE [1]	LE	LE [1]	LE [1]	LE	LE [1]	LE [1]	LE	LE		LE [1]	LE [1]	LE [1]	LE	LE [1]	LE	LE [1]	LE	LE [1]		LE	LE [1]	LE [1]	LE [1]
London Liverpool Street [15] ⊖	d	07 57	08 00	08 00	08 06	08 10	08 13	08 17	08 20	08 30			08 32	08 36	08 40	08 48	08 50	08 55	09 00	09 02		09 10		09 13	09 18
Stratford [7] ⊖	d	08 05	08 07	08 08	08 14	08 17	08 21	08 25	08 27	08 37			08 42	08 45	08 47	08 55	08 57	09 02	09 07	09 09		09 17		09 21	09 25
Maryland	d		08 09			08 19			08 29	08 39					08 49		08 59		09 09			09 19			
Forest Gate	d		08 11			08 21			08 31	08 41					08 51		09 01		09 11			09 21			
Manor Park	d		08 13			08 23			08 33	08 43					08 53		09 03		09 13			09 23			
Ilford [2]	d		08 16			08 26			08 36	08 46					08 56		09 06		09 16			09 26			
Seven Kings	d		08 18			08 28			08 38	08 48					08 58		09 08		09 18			09 28			
Goodmayes	d		08 20			08 30			08 40	08 50					09 00		09 10		09 20			09 30			
Chadwell Heath	d		08 22			08 32			08 42	08 52					09 02		09 12		09 22			09 32			
Romford	d		08 26			08 36			08 46	08 56					09 06		09 16		09 26			09 36			
Gidea Park [2]	d		08 30			08 40			08 50	09 00					09 10		09 20		09 30			09 40			
Harold Wood	d		08 33			08 43			08 53	09 03					09 13		09 23		09 33			09 43			
Brentwood	d		08 37			08 47			08 57	09 07					09 17		09 27		09 37			09 47			
Shenfield [3]	a	08 22	08 43	08 25	08 30	08 53	08 38	08 41	09 03	09 13			08 59	09 01	09 23	09 11	09 33	09 18	09 43	09 24		09 53		09 38	09 40
Shenfield [3]	d	08 22					08 39						08 59					09 19						09 39	
Billericay	d	08 28					08 45						09 05					09 25						09 45	
Wickford [2]	d	08 34					08 51					08 56	09 11					09 31					09 36	09 51	
Battlesbridge	d											09 00											09 40		
South Woodham Ferrers	d											09 04											09 44		
North Fambridge	d											09 11											09 51		
Althorne	d											09 16											09 56		
Burnham-on-Crouch	d											09 21											10 01		
Southminster	a											09 27											10 07		
Rayleigh	d	08 39					08 56						09 16					09 36						09 56	
Hockley	d	08 44					09 01						09 21					09 41						10 01	
Rochford	d	08 47					09 04						09 24					09 44						10 04	
Southend Airport ✈	d	08 50					09 07						09 27					09 47						10 07	
Prittlewell	d	08 53					09 10						09 30					09 50						10 10	
Southend Victoria	a	08 57					09 14						09 34					09 54						10 14	

		LE	LE	LE [1]	LE [1]	LE		LE [1]	LE	LE [1]	LE [1]	LE	LE [1]	LE	LE [1]	LE [1]		LE	LE	LE [1]	LE [1]	LE [1]	LE	LE [1]	LE
London Liverpool Street [15] ⊖	d	09 20	09 30	09 34	09 38	09 40		09 48	09 50		09 55	10 00	10 02	10 10	10 13	10 18		10 20	10 30		10 35	10 38	10 40	10 48	10 50
Stratford [7] ⊖	d	09 27	09 37	09 42	09 45	09 47		09 55	09 57		10 02	10 07	10 09	10 17	10 20	10 25		10 27	10 37		10 42	10 45	10 47	10 55	10 57
Maryland	d	09 29	09 39			09 49			09 59			10 09		10 19				10 29	10 39				10 49		10 59
Forest Gate	d	09 31	09 41			09 51			10 01			10 11		10 21				10 31	10 41				10 51		11 01
Manor Park	d	09 33	09 43			09 53			10 03			10 13		10 23				10 33	10 43				10 53		11 03
Ilford [2]	d	09 36	09 46			09 56			10 06			10 16		10 26				10 36	10 46				10 56		11 06
Seven Kings	d	09 38	09 48			09 58			10 08			10 18		10 28				10 38	10 48				10 58		11 08
Goodmayes	d	09 40	09 50			10 00			10 10			10 20		10 30				10 40	10 50				11 00		11 10
Chadwell Heath	d	09 42	09 52			10 02			10 12			10 22		10 32				10 42	10 52				11 02		11 12
Romford	d	09 46	09 56		09 53	10 06			10 16			10 26		10 36	10 28			10 46	10 56			10 53	11 06		11 16
Gidea Park [2]	d	09 50	10 00			10 10			10 20			10 30		10 40				10 50	11 00				11 10		11 20
Harold Wood	d	09 53	10 03			10 13			10 23			10 33		10 43				10 53	11 03				11 13		11 23
Brentwood	d	09 57	10 07			10 17			10 27			10 37		10 47				10 57	11 07				11 17		11 27
Shenfield [3]	a	10 03	10 13	09 58	10 02	10 23		10 11	10 33		10 18	10 43	10 24	10 53	10 38	10 40		11 03	11 13		10 58	11 02	11 23	11 11	11 33
Shenfield [3]	d			09 59							10 19				10 39						10 59				
Billericay	d			10 05							10 25				10 45						11 05				
Wickford [2]	d			10 11						10 16	10 31				10 51					10 56	11 11				
Battlesbridge	d									10 20										11 00					
South Woodham Ferrers	d									10 24										11 04					
North Fambridge	d									10 31										11 11					
Althorne	d									10 36										11 16					
Burnham-on-Crouch	d									10 41										11 21					
Southminster	a									10 47										11 27					
Rayleigh	d			10 16							10 36				10 56						11 16				
Hockley	d			10 21							10 41				11 01						11 21				
Rochford	d			10 24							10 44				11 04						11 24				
Southend Airport ✈	d			10 27							10 47				11 07						11 27				
Prittlewell	d			10 30							10 50				11 10						11 30				
Southend Victoria	a			10 34							10 54				11 14						11 34				

London - Shenfield, Southminster and Southend Victoria

Network Diagram - see first Page of Table 5

		LE ■		LE	LE ■	LE	LE ■	LE ■	LE ■	LE	LE	LE ■		LE ■	LE	LE ■	LE	LE ■	LE ■	LE	LE ■	LE		LE ■	LE ■
London Liverpool Street ■ ⊖	d	10 55		11 00	11 02	11 10		11 13	11 18	11 20	11 30	11 35		11 38	11 40	11 48	11 50		11 55	12 00	12 02	12 10		12 13	12 18
Stratford ■ ⊖	d	11 02		11 07	11 09	11 17		11 20	11 25	11 27	11 37	11 42		11 45	11 47	11 55	11 57		12 02	12 07	12 09	12 17		12 20	12 25
Maryland	d			11 09		11 19				11 29	11 39				11 49		11 59			12 09		12 19			
Forest Gate	d			11 11		11 21				11 31	11 41				11 51		12 01			12 11		12 21			
Manor Park	d			11 13		11 23				11 33	11 43				11 53		12 03			12 13		12 23			
Ilford ■	d			11 16		11 26				11 36	11 46				11 56		12 06			12 16		12 26			
Seven Kings	d			11 18		11 28				11 38	11 48				11 58		12 08			12 18		12 28			
Goodmayes	d			11 20		11 30				11 40	11 50				12 00		12 10			12 20		12 30			
Chadwell Heath	d			11 22		11 32				11 42	11 52				12 02		12 12			12 22		12 32			
Romford	d			11 26		11 36		11 28		11 46	11 56			11 53	12 06		12 16			12 26		12 36		12 28	
Gidea Park ■	d			11 30		11 40				11 50	12 00				12 10		12 20			12 30		12 40			
Harold Wood	d			11 33		11 43				11 53	12 03				12 13		12 23			12 33		12 43			
Brentwood	d			11 37		11 47				11 57	12 07				12 17		12 27			12 37		12 47			
Shenfield ■	a	11 18		11 43	11 24	11 53		11 38	11 40	12 03	12 13	11 58		12 02	12 23	12 11	12 33		12 18	12 43	12 24	12 53		12 38	12 40
Shenfield ■	d	11 19						11 39				11 59							12 19					12 39	
Billericay	d	11 25						11 45				12 05							12 25					12 45	
Wickford ■	d	11 31					11 36	11 51				12 11					12 16	12 31						12 51	
Battlesbridge	d						11 40											12 20							
South Woodham Ferrers	d						11 44											12 24							
North Fambridge	d						11 51											12 31							
Althorne	d						11 56											12 36							
Burnham-on-Crouch	d						12 01											12 41							
Southminster	a						12 07											12 47							
Rayleigh	d	11 36						11 56				12 16							12 36					12 56	
Hockley	d	11 41						12 01				12 21							12 41					13 01	
Rochford	d	11 44						12 04				12 24							12 44					13 04	
Southend Airport ✈	d	11 47						12 07				12 27							12 47					13 07	
Prittlewell	d	11 50						12 10				12 30							12 50					13 10	
Southend Victoria	a	11 54						12 14				12 34							12 54					13 14	

		LE	LE	LE ■	LE ■	LE ■	LE	LE ■		LE	LE ■	LE	LE ■	LE	LE ■	LE ■	LE ■	LE		LE	LE ■	LE ■	LE	LE ■	LE
London Liverpool Street ■ ⊖	d	12 20	12 30		12 35	12 38	12 40	12 48		12 50	12 55	13 00	13 02	13 10		13 13	13 18	13 20		13 30	13 35	13 38	13 40	13 48	13 50
Stratford ■ ⊖	d	12 27	12 37		12 42	12 45	12 47	12 55		12 57	13 02	13 07	13 09	13 17		13 20	13 25	13 27		13 37	13 42	13 45	13 47	13 55	13 57
Maryland	d	12 29	12 39				12 49			12 59		13 09		13 19				13 29		13 39			13 49		13 59
Forest Gate	d	12 31	12 41				12 51			13 01		13 11		13 21				13 31		13 41			13 51		14 01
Manor Park	d	12 33	12 43				12 53			13 03		13 13		13 23				13 33		13 43			13 53		14 03
Ilford ■	d	12 36	12 46				12 56			13 06		13 16		13 26				13 36		13 46			13 56		14 06
Seven Kings	d	12 38	12 48				12 58			13 08		13 18		13 28				13 38		13 48			13 58		14 08
Goodmayes	d	12 40	12 50				13 00			13 10		13 20		13 30				13 40		13 50			14 00		14 10
Chadwell Heath	d	12 42	12 52				13 02			13 12		13 22		13 32				13 42		13 52			14 02		14 12
Romford	d	12 46	12 56			12 53	13 06			13 16		13 26		13 36		13 28		13 46		13 56		13 53	14 06		14 16
Gidea Park ■	d	12 50	13 00				13 10			13 20		13 30		13 40				13 50		14 00			14 10		14 20
Harold Wood	d	12 53	13 03				13 13			13 23		13 33		13 43				13 53		14 03			14 13		14 23
Brentwood	d	12 57	13 07				13 17			13 27		13 37		13 47				13 57		14 07			14 17		14 27
Shenfield ■	a	13 03	13 13		12 58	13 02	13 23	13 11		13 33	13 18	13 43	13 24	13 53		13 38	13 40	14 03		14 13	13 58	14 02	14 23	14 11	14 33
Shenfield ■	d				12 59						13 19					13 39					13 59				
Billericay	d				13 05						13 25					13 45					14 05				
Wickford ■	d			12 56	13 11						13 31				13 36	13 51					14 11				
Battlesbridge	d			13 00											13 40										
South Woodham Ferrers	d			13 04											13 44										
North Fambridge	d			13 11											13 51										
Althorne	d			13 16											13 56										
Burnham-on-Crouch	d			13 21											14 01										
Southminster	a			13 27											14 07										
Rayleigh	d				13 16						13 36					13 56					14 16				
Hockley	d				13 21						13 41					14 01					14 21				
Rochford	d				13 24						13 44					14 04					14 24				
Southend Airport ✈	d				13 27						13 47					14 07					14 27				
Prittlewell	d				13 30						13 50					14 10					14 30				
Southend Victoria	a				13 34						13 54					14 14					14 34				

London - Shenfield, Southminster and Southend Victoria

Network Diagram - see first Page of Table 5

		LE ■	LE ■	LE		LE ■	LE	LE ■	LE ■	LE	LE	LE ■	LE ■	LE ■		LE	LE ■	LE	LE ■	LE	LE ■	LE	LE ■	LE ■	
London Liverpool Street ■ ⊖	d		13 55	14 00		14 02	14 10	14 13	14 18	14 20	14 30		14 35	14 38		14 40	14 48	14 50	14 55	15 00	15 02	15 10		15 13	
Stratford ■ ⊖	d		14 02	14 07		14 09	14 17	14 20	14 25	14 27	14 37		14 42	14 45		14 47	14 55	14 57	15 02	15 07	15 09	15 17		15 20	
Maryland	d			14 09			14 19			14 29	14 39					14 49		14 59		15 09		15 19			
Forest Gate	d			14 11			14 21			14 31	14 41					14 51		15 01		15 11		15 21			
Manor Park	d			14 13			14 23			14 33	14 43					14 53		15 03		15 13		15 23			
Ilford ■	d			14 16			14 26			14 36	14 46					14 56		15 06		15 16		15 26			
Seven Kings	d			14 18			14 28			14 38	14 48					14 58		15 08		15 18		15 28			
Goodmayes	d			14 20			14 30			14 40	14 50					15 00		15 10		15 20		15 30			
Chadwell Heath	d			14 22			14 32			14 42	14 52					15 02		15 12		15 22		15 32			
Romford	d			14 26			14 36	14 28		14 46	14 56			14 53		15 06		15 16		15 26		15 36		15 28	
Gidea Park ■	d			14 30			14 40			14 50	15 00					15 10		15 20		15 30		15 40			
Harold Wood	d			14 33			14 43			14 53	15 03					15 13		15 23		15 33		15 43			
Brentwood	d			14 37			14 47			14 57	15 07					15 17		15 27		15 37		15 47			
Shenfield ■	a		14 18	14 43		14 24	14 53	14 38	14 40	15 03	15 13		14 58	15 02		15 23	15 11	15 33	15 18	15 43	15 24	15 53		15 38	
Shenfield ■	d		14 19					14 39					14 59						15 19					15 39	
Billericay	d		14 25					14 45					15 05						15 25					15 45	
Wickford ■	d	14 16	14 31					14 51				14 56	15 11						15 31				15 36	15 51	
Battlesbridge	d	14 20										15 00											15 40		
South Woodham Ferrers	d	14 24										15 04											15 44		
North Fambridge	d	14 31										15 11											15 51		
Althorne	d	14 36										15 16											15 56		
Burnham-on-Crouch	d	14 41										15 21											16 01		
Southminster	a	14 47										15 27											16 07		
Rayleigh	d		14 36					14 56					15 16						15 36					15 56	
Hockley	d		14 41					15 01					15 21						15 41					16 01	
Rochford	d		14 44					15 04					15 24						15 44					16 04	
Southend Airport ✈	d		14 47					15 07					15 27						15 47					16 07	
Prittlewell	d		14 50					15 10					15 31						15 50					16 10	
Southend Victoria	a		14 54					15 14					15 34						15 54					16 14	

		LE ■	LE	LE	LE ■	LE ■	LE	LE ■	LE	LE ■		LE ■	LE	LE ■	LE	LE ■	LE ■	LE ■	LE	LE ■		LE	LE ■	LE ■	LE
London Liverpool Street ■ ⊖	d	15 18	15 20	15 30	15 35	15 38	15 40	15 48	15 50			15 55	16 00	16 02	16 10	16 10	16 14	16 17	16 20	16 24		16 28	16 32	16 34	16 36
Stratford ■ ⊖	d	15 25	15 27	15 37	15 42	15 45	15 47	15 55	15 57			16 02	16 07	16 09	16 17	16 18	16 22	16 25	16 27	16 32		16 35		16 42	16 43
Maryland	d		15 29	15 39			15 49		15 59				16 09		16 19				16 29			16 37			
Forest Gate	d		15 31	15 41			15 51		16 01				16 11		16 21				16 31			16 39			
Manor Park	d		15 33	15 43			15 53		16 03				16 13		16 23				16 33			16 41			
Ilford ■	d		15 36	15 46			15 56		16 06				16 16		16 26				16 36			16 44			16 50
Seven Kings	d		15 38	15 48			15 58		16 08				16 18		16 28				16 38			16 47			16 52
Goodmayes	d		15 40	15 50			16 00		16 10				16 20		16 30				16 40			16 49			16 54
Chadwell Heath	d		15 42	15 52			16 02		16 12				16 22		16 32				16 42			16 51			16 56
Romford	d		15 46	15 56		15 53	16 06		16 16				16 26		16 36				16 46			16 55			17 00
Gidea Park ■	d		15 50	16 00			16 10		16 20				16 30		16 40				16 50			17a00			17 04
Harold Wood	d		15 53	16 03			16 13		16 23				16 33		16 43				16 53						17 07
Brentwood	d		15 57	16 07			16 17		16 27				16 37		16 47				16 57						17 11
Shenfield ■	a	15 40	16 03	16 13	15 58	16 02	16 23	16 11	16 33			16 18	16 43	16 24	16 53	16 34	16 38	16 41	17 03	16 49			16 54	16 58	17 19
Shenfield ■	d				15 59							16 19				16 34				16 49					
Billericay	d				16 05							16 25				16 41				16 56					
Wickford ■	d				16 11					16 14		16 31				16 48				17 03					
Battlesbridge	d									16 18															
South Woodham Ferrers	d									16 22															
North Fambridge	d									16 29															
Althorne	d									16 34															
Burnham-on-Crouch	d									16 39															
Southminster	a									16 45															
Rayleigh	d				16 16							16 36				16 53				17 08					
Hockley	d				16 21							16 41				16 57				17 12					
Rochford	d				16 24							16 44				17 01				17 16					
Southend Airport ✈	d				16 27							16 47				17 03				17 18					
Prittlewell	d				16 30							16 50				17 06				17 21					
Southend Victoria	a				16 34							16 54				17 15				17 27					

Table 5

Mondays to Fridays
from 10 September

London - Shenfield, Southminster and Southend Victoria

Network Diagram - see first Page of Table 5

		LE	LE 1	LE 1	LE 1	LE	LE 1	LE	LE 1	LE	LE	LE ◇1	LE 1	LE	LE 1	LE	LE 1	LE 1	LE	LE 1	LE	LE 1 A	LE 1 A
London Liverpool Street 15 ⊖	d	16 40		16 40	16 44	16 47	16 47	16 50	16 54	16 57	17 00	17 02	17 04	17 07	17 08	17 10	17 12	17 15	17 17	17 18	17 20	17 20	17 22
Stratford 7 ⊖	d	16 47		16 48	16a52	16 54	16 55	16 57	17 02	17 04	17 07	17 10	17 13	17 14	17a16	17 17	17a20	17 23	17 24	17a26	17 27	17 29	17 31
Maryland	d	16 49						16 59			17 09					17 19					17 29		
Forest Gate	d	16 51						17 01			17 11					17 21					17 31		
Manor Park	d	16 53						17 03			17 13					17 23					17 33		
Ilford 2	d	16 56				17 00		17 06		17 10	17 16			17 20		17 26			17 30		17 36		
Seven Kings	d					17 02				17 12				17 22					17 32				
Goodmayes	d					17 04				17 14				17 24					17 34				
Chadwell Heath	d	17 00				17 06		17 10		17 16	17 20			17 26		17 30			17 36		17 40		
Romford	d	17 04				17 10		17 14		17 20	17 24			17 30		17 34			17 40		17 44		
Gidea Park 2	d	17a10				17 14		17a20		17 24	17a30			17 34		17a40			17 44		17a50		
Harold Wood	d					17 17				17 27				17 37					17 47				
Brentwood	d					17 21				17 31				17 41					17 51				
Shenfield 3	a			17 04		17 29	17 11		17 19	17 39			17 30	17 49				17 39	17 59			17 45	
Shenfield 3	d			17 04					17 19				17 30					17 39					
Billericay	d			17 11					17 26				17 37					17 46					
Wickford 2	d		17 06	17 18					17 33				17 44					17 53					18 00
Battlesbridge	d		17 10																				18 04
South Woodham Ferrers	d		17 14																				18 08
North Fambridge	d		17 21																				18 14
Althorne	d		17 26																				18 19
Burnham-on-Crouch	d		17 31																				18 24
Southminster	a		17 37																				18 32
Rayleigh	d			17 23					17 38				17 49					17 58					
Hockley	d			17 27					17 42				17 53					18 02					
Rochford	d			17 31					17 46				17 57					18 06					
Southend Airport ✈	d			17 33					17 48				17 59					18 08					
Prittlewell	d			17 36					17 51				18 02					18 11					
Southend Victoria	a			17 42					17 57				18 08					18 17					

		LE 1	LE	LE	LE 1	LE 1	LE	LE 1	LE	LE 1 A	LE	LE 1	LE	LE	LE	LE 1	LE 1	LE	LE 1	LE	LE 1	LE
London Liverpool Street 15 ⊖	d	17 25	17 27	17 30	17 32	17 34	17 36	17 38	17 39	17 40	17 42	17 45	17 46	17 49	17 52	17 52	17 54	17 56	17 58	17 59	18 00	18 02
Stratford 7 ⊖	d	17 34	17 34	17 37	17a40	17 43	17 43	17a47	17 46	17 49	17 49	17 53	17 53	17 56	17 59	18a01	18 03	18 03	18a06	18 06	18 09	18 09
Maryland	d			17 39			17 45						17 55					18 05				
Forest Gate	d			17 41							17 52				18 02							18 12
Manor Park	d			17 43					17 50					18 00						18 10		
Ilford 2	d		17 40	17 46			17 50		17 53		17 56		18 00	18 03	18 06			18 10		18 13		18 16
Seven Kings	d		17 42				17 52		17 56		17 59		18 02	18 06	18 09			18 12		18 16		18 19
Goodmayes	d		17 44				17 54		17 58		18 01		18 04	18 08	18 11			18 14		18 18		18 21
Chadwell Heath	d		17 46	17 50			17 56		18 00		18 03		18 06	18 10	18 13			18 16		18 20		18 23
Romford	d		17 50	17 54			18 00		18 04		18 07		18 10	18 14	18 17			18 20		18 24		18 27
Gidea Park 2	d		17 54	18a00			18 04		18a09		18a12		18 14	18 18	18a22			18 24		18a29		18a32
Harold Wood	d		17 57				18 07						18 17	18 21				18 27				
Brentwood	d		18 01				18 11						18 21	18 25				18 31				
Shenfield 3	a	17 51	18 09			17 59	18 19			18 05		18 09	18 29	18 33			18 19	18 39			18 25	
Shenfield 3	d	17 52				17 59						18 09		18 36			18 19					
Billericay	d	17 58				18 06						18 16		→			18 26					
Wickford 2	d	18 05				18 13						18 23					18 33					
Battlesbridge	d																					
South Woodham Ferrers	d																					
North Fambridge	d																					
Althorne	d																					
Burnham-on-Crouch	d																					
Southminster	a																					
Rayleigh	d	18 10				18 18						18 28					18 38					
Hockley	d	18 15				18 22						18 32					18 42					
Rochford	d	18 18				18 26						18 36					18 46					
Southend Airport ✈	d	18 21				18 28						18 38					18 48					
Prittlewell	d	18 24				18 31						18 41					18 51					
Southend Victoria	a	18 30				18 37						18 47					18 58					

A The Stratford call is subjtect to introduction during the currency of the timetable.

Table 5

Mondays to Fridays
from 10 September

London - Shenfield, Southminster and Southend Victoria

Network Diagram - see first Page of Table 5

		LE 1	LE 1	LE	LE	LE	LE 1	LE 1	LE	LE 1	LE	LE 1	LE 1	LE	LE	LE 1	LE 1	LE	LE 1	LE	LE 1	LE 1	LE
London Liverpool Street 15 ⊖	d	18 02	18 05		18 07	18 10	18 12	18 14	18 17	18 18	18 20	18 20	18 25	18 27	18 30	18 32	18 35	18 37	18 38	18 40	18 41	18 45	18 47
Stratford 7 ⊖	d	18 11	18 14		18 14	18 17	18a21	18 23	18 24	18a27	18 27	18 29	18 33	18 34	18 37	18a40	18 43	18 44	18 46	18 47	18 49	18 53	18 54
Maryland	d					18 19					18 29				18 39					18 49			
Forest Gate	d					18 21					18 31				18 41					18 51			
Manor Park	d					18 23					18 33				18 43					18 53			
Ilford 2	d				18 20	18 26			18 30		18 36			18 40	18 46			18 50		18 56			19 00
Seven Kings	d				18 22				18 32					18 42				18 52					19 02
Goodmayes	d				18 24				18 34					18 44				18 54					19 04
Chadwell Heath	d				18 26	18 30			18 36		18 40			18 46	18 50			18 56		19 00			19 06
Romford	d				18 30	18 34			18 40		18 44			18 50	18 54			19 00		19 04			19 10
Gidea Park 2	d				18 34	18a40			18 44		18a50			18 54	19a00			19 04		19 08			19 14
Harold Wood	d				18 37				18 47					18 57				19 07		19 11			19 17
Brentwood	d			←	18 41				18 51					19 01				19 11		19 15			19 21
Shenfield 3	a		18 31	18 33	18 49			18 40	18 59			18 45	18 50	19 09			18 59	19 19	19 02	19 23		19 10	19 29
Shenfield 3	d		18 31	18 36				18 41					18 50				18 59					19 10	
Billericay	d		18 38	18 42				18 47					18 57				19 06					19 17	
Wickford 2	d	18 41	18 45	18 49				18 54					19 04				19 13				19 19	19 24	
Battlesbridge	d	18 45																			19 23		
South Woodham Ferrers	d	18 49																			19 27		
North Fambridge	d	18 55																			19 34		
Althorne	d	19 00																			19 39		
Burnham-on-Crouch	d	19 05																			19 44		
Southminster	a	19 13																			19 52		
Rayleigh	d		18 50	18 54				18 59					19 09				19 18					19 29	
Hockley	d		18 55	18 59				19 04					19 13				19 22					19 33	
Rochford	d		18 58	19 02				19 07					19 17				19 26					19 37	
Southend Airport ✈	d		19 01	19 05				19 10					19 19				19 28					19 39	
Prittlewell	d		19 04	19 08				19 13					19 22				19 31					19 42	
Southend Victoria	a		19 10	19 14				19 19					19 28				19 37					19 47	

		LE 1	LE	LE 1	LE	LE	LE 1	LE 1	LE	LE 1	LE 1	LE	LE	LE 1	LE 1	LE 1	LE	LE 1	LE	LE 1	LE 1	LE
London Liverpool Street 15 ⊖	d	18 48	18 50	18 55	18 57	19 00	19 02	19 08	19 10	19 15	19 18	19 20	19 30	19 32	19 35	19 38	19 40	19 48	19 50		19 55	20 00
Stratford 7 ⊖	d	18a56	18 57	19 03	19 04	19 07	19 09	19a15	19 17	19 22	19 25	19 27	19 37	19a39	19 42	19 45	19 47	19 55	19 57		20 02	20 07
Maryland	d		18 59			19 09			19 19			19 29	19 39				19 49		19 59			20 09
Forest Gate	d		19 01			19 11			19 21			19 31	19 41				19 51		20 01			20 11
Manor Park	d		19 03			19 13			19 23			19 33	19 43				19 53		20 03			20 13
Ilford 2	d		19 06		19 10	19 16			19 26			19 36	19 46				19 56		20 06			20 16
Seven Kings	d				19 12	19 18			19 28			19 38	19 48				19 58		20 08			20 18
Goodmayes	d				19 14	19 20			19 30			19 40	19 50				20 00		20 10			20 20
Chadwell Heath	d		19 10		19 16	19 22			19 32			19 42	19 52				20 02		20 12			20 22
Romford	d		19 14		19 20	19 26			19 36			19 46	19 56				20 06		20 16			20 26
Gidea Park 2	d		19a20		19 24	19 30			19 40			19 50	20 00				20 10		20 20			20 30
Harold Wood	d				19 27	19 33			19 43			19 53	20 03				20 13		20 23			20 33
Brentwood	d				19 31	19 37			19 47			19 57	20 07				20 17		20 27			20 37
Shenfield 3	a			19 20	19 39	19 43	19 24		19 53	19 38	19 40	20 03	20 13		19 58	20 00	20 23	20 11	20 33		20 18	20 43
Shenfield 3	d			19 20						19 39					19 59						20 19	
Billericay	d			19 27						19 45					20 05						20 25	
Wickford 2	d			19 34						19 51					20 11					20 16	20 31	
Battlesbridge	d																			20 20		
South Woodham Ferrers	d																			20 24		
North Fambridge	d																			20 31		
Althorne	d																			20 36		
Burnham-on-Crouch	d																			20 41		
Southminster	a																			20 47		
Rayleigh	d			19 39						19 56					20 16						20 36	
Hockley	d			19 43						20 01					20 21						20 41	
Rochford	d			19 47						20 04					20 24						20 44	
Southend Airport ✈	d			19 49						20 07					20 27						20 47	
Prittlewell	d			19 52						20 10					20 30						20 50	
Southend Victoria	a			19 58						20 14					20 34						20 54	

London - Shenfield, Southminster and Southend Victoria

Network Diagram - see first Page of Table 5

		LE ■	LE	LE ■	LE ■	LE	LE	LE ■	LE ■	CC	LE ■	LE	LE ■	LE	LE ■	LE	LE ■	LE	LE ■	LE ■	LE ■	LE	LE
London Liverpool Street 15 ⊖	d	20 02	20 10	20 13	20 18	20 20	20 30		20 35	20 35	20 38	20 40	20 48	20 50	20 55	21 00	21 02	21 10		21 13	21 18	21 20	21 30
Stratford 7 ⊖	d	20 09	20 17	20 20	20 25	20 27	20 37		20 42	20a43	20 45	20 47	20 55	20 57	21 02	21 07	21 09	21 17		21 20	21 25	21 27	21 37
Maryland	d		20 19			20 29	20 39					20 49		20 59		21 09		21 19				21 29	21 39
Forest Gate	d		20 21			20 31	20 41					20 51		21 01		21 11		21 21				21 31	21 41
Manor Park	d		20 23			20 33	20 43					20 53		21 03		21 13		21 23				21 33	21 43
Ilford 2	d		20 26			20 36	20 46					20 56		21 06		21 16		21 26				21 36	21 46
Seven Kings	d		20 28			20 38	20 48					20 58		21 08		21 18		21 28				21 38	21 48
Goodmayes	d		20 30			20 40	20 50					21 00		21 10		21 20		21 30				21 40	21 50
Chadwell Heath	d		20 32			20 42	20 52					21 02		21 12		21 22		21 32				21 42	21 52
Romford	d		20 36	20 28		20 46	20 56				20 53	21 06		21 16		21 26		21 36		21 28		21 46	21 56
Gidea Park 2	d		20 40			20 50	21 00					21 10		21 20		21 30		21 40				21 50	22 00
Harold Wood	d		20 43			20 53	21 03					21 13		21 23		21 33		21 43				21 53	22 03
Brentwood	d		20 47			20 57	21 07					21 17		21 27		21 37		21 47				21 57	22 07
Shenfield 3	a	20 24	20 53	20 38	20 40	21 03	21 13		20 58		21 02	21 23	21 11	21 33	21 18	21 43	21 24	21 53		21 38	21 40	22 03	22 13
Shenfield 3	d			20 39					20 59						21 19					21 39			
Billericay	d			20 45					21 05						21 25					21 45			
Wickford 2	d			20 51				20 56	21 11						21 31				21 36	21 51			
Battlesbridge	d							21 00											21 40				
South Woodham Ferrers	d							21 04											21 44				
North Fambridge	d							21 11											21 51				
Althorne	d							21 16											21 56				
Burnham-on-Crouch	d							21 21											22 01				
Southminster	a							21 27											22 07				
Rayleigh	d			20 56					21 16						21 36					21 56			
Hockley	d			21 01					21 21						21 41					22 01			
Rochford	d			21 04					21 24						21 44					22 04			
Southend Airport ✈	d			21 07					21 27						21 47					22 07			
Prittlewell	d			21 10					21 30						21 50					22 10			
Southend Victoria	a			21 14					21 34						21 54					22 14			

		LE ■	CC	LE ■	LE	LE ■	LE	LE ■	LE ■	LE ■	LE	LE ■ A	LE ■	LE	LE ■ A	LE ■ B	LE	LE ■ A	LE ■ B	LE ■ A	LE ■ B	LE ■ B	LE A
London Liverpool Street 15 ⊖	d	21 35	21 35	21 38	21 40	21 48	21 50		21 55	22 02	22 05	22 13	22 18	22 20		22 25	22 35	22 38		22 45	22 50		22 50
Stratford 7 ⊖	d	21 42	21a43	21 45	21 47	21 55	21 57		22 02	22 09	22 12	22 20	22 25	22 27		22 32	22 42	22 45		22 52	22 57		22 57
Maryland	d				21 49		21 59				22 14			22 29			22 44						22 59
Forest Gate	d				21 51		22 01				22 16			22 31			22 46						23 01
Manor Park	d				21 53		22 03				22 18			22 33			22 48						23 03
Ilford 2	d				21 56		22 06				22 21			22 36			22 51						23 06
Seven Kings	d				21 58		22 08				22 23			22 38			22 53						23 08
Goodmayes	d				22 00		22 10				22 25			22 40			22 55						23 10
Chadwell Heath	d				22 02		22 12				22 27			22 42			22 57						23 12
Romford	d			21 53	22 06		22 16				22 31	22 28		22 46			23 01						23 16
Gidea Park 2	d				22 10		22 20				22 35			22 50			23 05						23 20
Harold Wood	d				22 13		22 23				22 38			22 53			23 08						23 23
Brentwood	d				22 17		22 27				22 42			22 57			23 12						23 27
Shenfield 3	a	21 58		22 02	22 23	22 11	22 33		22 18	22 24	22 48	22 38	22 40	23 03		22 48	23 18	23 00		23 08	23 20		23 33
Shenfield 3	d	21 59							22 19			22 39				22 49				23 09		23 23	
Billericay	d	22 05							22 25			22 45				22 55				23 15		23 29	
Wickford 2	d	22 11						22 16	22 31			22 51			22 56	23 01			23 06	23 21		23 35	
Battlesbridge	d							22 20							23 00				23 10				
South Woodham Ferrers	d							22 24							23 04				23 14				
North Fambridge	d							22 31							23 11				23 21				
Althorne	d							22 36							23 16				23 26				
Burnham-on-Crouch	d							22 41							23 21				23 31				
Southminster	a							22 47							23 27				23 37				
Rayleigh	d	22 16							22 36			22 56				23 06				23 26		23 40	
Hockley	d	22 21							22 41			23 01				23 11				23 31		23 45	
Rochford	d	22 24							22 44			23 04				23 14				23 34		23 48	
Southend Airport ✈	d	22 27							22 47			23 07				23 17				23 37		23 51	
Prittlewell	d	22 30							22 50			23 10				23 20				23 40		23 54	
Southend Victoria	a	22 34							22 54			23 14				23 24				23 48		23 58	

A ThFO, also from 10 September until 12 September

B MTWO from 17 September

London - Shenfield, Southminster and Southend Victoria

Network Diagram - see first Page of Table 5

		LE A	LE ■ B	LE B	LE ■ A	LE ■ B	LE A	LE ■ B	LE ■ A	LE B	LE ◇■ A	LE	LE ■ B	LE ■ B	LE ■ A	LE B	LE A
London Liverpool Street 15 ⊖	d	22 55	23 02	23 05	23 10	23 15	23 15	23 18		23 20	23 30	23 35	23 45	23 48	23 50	23 50	23 55
Stratford 7 ⊖	d	23 02	23 09	23 12	23 17	23 22	23 22	23 25		23 27	23u39	23 42	23 52	23 55	23 57	23 57	00 02
Maryland	d	23 04		23 14			23 24			23 29		23 44				23 59	00 04
Forest Gate	d	23 06		23 16			23 26			23 31		23 46				00 01	00 06
Manor Park	d	23 08		23 18			23 28			23 33		23 48				00 03	00 08
Ilford 2	d	23 11		23 21			23 31			23 36		23 51				00 06	00 11
Seven Kings	d	23 13		23 23			23 33			23 38		23 53				00 08	00 13
Goodmayes	d	23 15		23 25			23 35			23 40		23 55				00 10	00 15
Chadwell Heath	d	23 17		23 27			23 37			23 42		23 57				00 12	00 17
Romford	d	23 21		23 31			23 41			23 46		00 02				00 16	00 21
Gidea Park 2	d	23 25		23 35			23 45			23 50		00 05				00 20	00 25
Harold Wood	d	23 28		23 38			23 48			23 53		00 08				00 23	00 28
Brentwood	d	23 32		23 42			23 52			23 57		00 12				00 27	00 32
Shenfield 3	a	23 38	23 24	23 48	23 40	23 38	23 58	23 40		00 03	00 02	00 18	00 08	00 10	00 20	00 33	00 38
Shenfield 3	d					23 39			23 43				00 09				
Billericay	d					23 45			23 49				00 15				
Wickford 2	d					23 51			23 55				00 21				
Battlesbridge	d																
South Woodham Ferrers	d																
North Fambridge	d																
Althorne	d																
Burnham-on-Crouch	d																
Southminster	a																
Rayleigh	d					23 56			00 01				00 26				
Hockley	d					00 01			00 05				00 31				
Rochford	d					00 04			00 08				00 34				
Southend Airport ✈	d					00 07			00 11				00 37				
Prittlewell	d					00 10			00 14				00 40				
Southend Victoria	a					00 18			00 18				00 48				

Saturdays
until 21 July

		LE ■	LE	LE	LE ■	LE ■	LE	LE	LE ■	LE ■	LE	LE	LE ■	LE ■	LE	LE ■	LE ■	LE ■	LE ■	LE ■	LE	LE ■	LE ■
London Liverpool Street 15 ⊖	d	23p15	23p20	23p35	23p45	23p48	23p50	00 01	00 15	00 18	00 20	00 32	00 46	00 50	00 55	05 21			05 28	05 34	05 40	05 51	06 02
Stratford 7 ⊖	d	23p22	23p27	23p42	23p52	23p55	23p57	00 08	00 22	00 25	00 27	00 39	00 53	00 57	01 02	05a30			05 35	05 41	05 47	06a00	06 09
Maryland	d		23p29	23p44			23p59	00 10			00 29	00 41			01 04						05 49		
Forest Gate	d		23p31	23p46			00 01	00 12			00 31	00 43			01 06						05 51		
Manor Park	d		23p33	23p48			00 03	00 14			00 33	00 45			01 08						05 53		
Ilford 2	d		23p36	23p51			00 06	00 17			00 36	00 48			01 11				05 40		05 56		
Seven Kings	d		23p38	23p53			00 08	00 19			00 38	00 50			01 13				05 42		05 58		
Goodmayes	d		23p40	23p55			00 10	00 21			00 40	00 52			01 15						06 00		
Chadwell Heath	d		23p42	23p57			00 12	00 23			00 42	00 54			01 17						06 02		
Romford	d		23p46	00 02			00 16	00 27	00 32		00 46	00 58		01 08	01 21				05 48	05 49	06 06		
Gidea Park 2	d		23p50	00 05			00 20	00a31			00 50	01a02	01 07		01 25				05 51		06 10		
Harold Wood	d		23p53	00 08			00 23				00 53				01 28				05 54		06 13		
Brentwood	d		23p57	00 12			00 27				00 57				01 32				05 59		06 17		
Shenfield 3	a	23p38	00 03	00 18	00 08	00 10	00 33		00 44	00 47	01 03		01 17	01 20	01 38				06 04	05 58	06 23		06 24
Shenfield 3	d	23p39			00 09				00 45					01 20					06 04				
Billericay	d	23p45			00 15				00 51					01 26					06 10				
Wickford 2	d	23p51			00 21				00 56					01 31			05 36	06 12	06 16				
Battlesbridge	d																05 40	06 16					
South Woodham Ferrers	d																05 44	06 20					
North Fambridge	d																05 51	06 31					
Althorne	d																05 56	06 36					
Burnham-on-Crouch	d																06 01	06 41					
Southminster	a																06 07	06 47					
Rayleigh	d	23p56			00 26				01 01					01 36					06 22				
Hockley	d	00 01			00 31				01 06					01 41					06 26				
Rochford	d	00 04			00 34				01 09					01 44					06 30				
Southend Airport ✈	d	00 07			00 37				01 12					01 47					06 32				
Prittlewell	d	00 10			00 40				01 15					01 50					06 35				
Southend Victoria	a	00 18			00 48				01 23					01 58					06 39				

A MTWO from 17 September

B ThFO, also from 10 September until 12 September

Table 5

Saturdays until 21 July

London - Shenfield, Southminster and Southend Victoria

Network Diagram - see first Page of Table 5

		LE 1	LE 1	LE	LE	LE 1	LE 1	LE 1	LE	LE 1	LE	LE 1	LE	LE 1	LE	LE 1	LE 1	LE 1	LE	LE	LE 1	LE 1	LE
London Liverpool Street 15 ⊖	d	12 13	12 18	12 20	12 30		12 35	12 38	12 40	12 48	12 50	12 55	13 00	13 02	13 10		13 13	13 18	13 20	13 30	13 35	13 38	13 40
Stratford 7 ⊖	d	12 20	12 25	12 27	12 37		12 42	12 45	12 47	12 55	12 57	13 02	13 07	13 09	13 17		13 20	13 25	13 27	13 37	13 42	13 45	13 47
Maryland	d			12 29	12 39				12 49		12 59		13 09		13 19				13 29	13 39			13 49
Forest Gate	d			12 31	12 41				12 51		13 01		13 11		13 21				13 31	13 41			13 51
Manor Park	d			12 33	12 43				12 53		13 03		13 13		13 23				13 33	13 43			13 53
Ilford 2	d			12 36	12 46				12 56		13 06		13 16		13 26				13 36	13 46			13 56
Seven Kings	d			12 38	12 48				12 58		13 08		13 18		13 28				13 38	13 48			13 58
Goodmayes	d			12 40	12 50				13 00		13 10		13 20		13 30				13 40	13 50			14 00
Chadwell Heath	d			12 42	12 52				13 02		13 12		13 22		13 32				13 42	13 52			14 02
Romford	d	12 28		12 46	12 56			12 53	13 06		13 16		13 26		13 36		13 28		13 46	13 56		13 53	14 06
Gidea Park 2	d			12 50	13 00				13 10		13 20		13 30		13 40				13 50	14 00			14 10
Harold Wood	d			12 53	13 03				13 13		13 23		13 33		13 43				13 53	14 03			14 13
Brentwood	d			12 57	13 07				13 17		13 27		13 37		13 47				13 57	14 07			14 17
Shenfield 3	a	12 38	12 40	13 03	13 13		12 58	13 02	13 23	13 11	13 33	13 18	13 43	13 24	13 53		13 38	13 40	14 03	14 13	13 58	14 02	14 23
Shenfield 3	d	12 39					12 59					13 19					13 39				13 59		
Billericay	d	12 45					13 05					13 25					13 45				14 05		
Wickford 2	d	12 51				12 56	13 11					13 31				13 36	13 51				14 11		
Battlesbridge	d					13 00										13 40							
South Woodham Ferrers	d					13 04										13 44							
North Fambridge	d					13 11										13 51							
Althorne	d					13 16										13 56							
Burnham-on-Crouch	d					13 21										14 01							
Southminster	a					13 27										14 07							
Rayleigh	d	12 56					13 16					13 36					13 56				14 16		
Hockley	d	13 01					13 21					13 41					14 01				14 21		
Rochford	d	13 04					13 24					13 44					14 04				14 24		
Southend Airport ✈	d	13 07					13 27					13 47					14 07				14 27		
Prittlewell	d	13 10					13 30					13 50					14 10				14 30		
Southend Victoria	a	13 14					13 34					13 54					14 14				14 34		

		LE 1	LE	LE 1	LE 1	LE	LE 1	LE	LE 1	LE 1	LE	LE	LE 1	LE 1	LE 1	LE	LE 1	LE	LE 1	LE	LE 1	LE	LE 1
London Liverpool Street 15 ⊖	d	13 48	13 50		13 55	14 00	14 02	14 10	14 13	14 18	14 20	14 30		14 35	14 38	14 40	14 48	14 50	14 55	15 00	15 02	15 10	
Stratford 7 ⊖	d	13 55	13 57		14 02	14 07	14 09	14 17	14 20	14 25	14 27	14 37		14 42	14 45	14 47	14 55	14 57	15 02	15 07	15 09	15 17	
Maryland	d		13 59			14 09		14 19			14 29	14 39				14 49		14 59		15 09		15 19	
Forest Gate	d		14 01			14 11		14 21			14 31	14 41				14 51		15 01		15 11		15 21	
Manor Park	d		14 03			14 13		14 23			14 33	14 43				14 53		15 03		15 13		15 23	
Ilford 2	d		14 06			14 16		14 26			14 36	14 46				14 56		15 06		15 16		15 26	
Seven Kings	d		14 08			14 18		14 28			14 38	14 48				14 58		15 08		15 18		15 28	
Goodmayes	d		14 10			14 20		14 30			14 40	14 50				15 00		15 10		15 20		15 30	
Chadwell Heath	d		14 12			14 22		14 32			14 42	14 52				15 02		15 12		15 22		15 32	
Romford	d		14 16			14 26		14 36	14 28		14 46	14 56			14 53	15 06		15 16		15 26		15 36	
Gidea Park 2	d		14 20			14 30		14 40			14 50	15 00				15 10		15 20		15 30		15 40	
Harold Wood	d		14 23			14 33		14 43			14 53	15 03				15 13		15 23		15 33		15 43	
Brentwood	d		14 27			14 37		14 47			14 57	15 07				15 17		15 27		15 37		15 47	
Shenfield 3	a	14 11	14 33		14 18	14 43	14 24	14 53	14 38	14 40	15 03	15 13		14 58	15 02	15 23	15 11	15 33	15 18	15 43	15 24	15 53	
Shenfield 3	d				14 19				14 39					14 59					15 19				
Billericay	d				14 25				14 45					15 05					15 25				
Wickford 2	d			14 16	14 31				14 51				14 56	15 11					15 31				15 36
Battlesbridge	d			14 20									15 00										15 40
South Woodham Ferrers	d			14 24									15 04										15 44
North Fambridge	d			14 31									15 11										15 51
Althorne	d			14 36									15 16										15 56
Burnham-on-Crouch	d			14 41									15 21										16 01
Southminster	a			14 47									15 27										16 07
Rayleigh	d				14 36				14 56					15 16					15 36				
Hockley	d				14 41				15 01					15 21					15 41				
Rochford	d				14 44				15 04					15 24					15 44				
Southend Airport ✈	d				14 47				15 07					15 27					15 47				
Prittlewell	d				14 50				15 10					15 30					15 50				
Southend Victoria	a				14 54				15 14					15 34					15 54				

Table 5

Saturdays until 21 July

London - Shenfield, Southminster and Southend Victoria

Network Diagram - see first Page of Table 5

		LE 1	LE 1	LE	LE	LE 1	LE 1	LE	LE 1	LE	LE 1	LE 1	LE	LE 1	LE	LE 1	LE 1	LE	LE	LE 1	LE 1	LE 1
London Liverpool Street 15 ⊖	d	15 13	15 18	15 20	15 30	15 35	15 38	15 40	15 48	15 50		15 55	16 00	16 02	16 10	16 13	16 18	16 20	16 30		16 35	16 38
Stratford 7 ⊖	d	15 20	15 25	15 27	15 37	15 42	15 45	15 47	15 55	15 57		16 02	16 07	16 09	16 17	16 20	16 25	16 27	16 37		16 42	16 45
Maryland	d			15 29	15 39			15 49		15 59			16 09		16 19			16 29	16 39			
Forest Gate	d			15 31	15 41			15 51		16 01			16 11		16 21			16 31	16 41			
Manor Park	d			15 33	15 43			15 53		16 03			16 13		16 23			16 33	16 43			
Ilford 2	d			15 36	15 46			15 56		16 06			16 16		16 26			16 36	16 46			
Seven Kings	d			15 38	15 48			15 58		16 08			16 18		16 28			16 38	16 48			
Goodmayes	d			15 40	15 50			16 00		16 10			16 20		16 30			16 40	16 50			
Chadwell Heath	d			15 42	15 52			16 02		16 12			16 22		16 32			16 42	16 52			
Romford	d	15 28		15 46	15 56		15 53	16 06		16 16			16 26		16 36	16 28		16 46	16 56			16 53
Gidea Park 2	d			15 50	16 00			16 10		16 20			16 30		16 40			16 50	17 00			
Harold Wood	d			15 53	16 03			16 13		16 23			16 33		16 43			16 53	17 03			
Brentwood	d			15 57	16 07			16 17		16 27			16 37		16 47			16 57	17 07			
Shenfield 3	a	15 38	15 40	16 03	16 13	15 58	16 02	16 23	16 11	16 33		16 18	16 43	16 24	16 53	16 38	16 40	17 03	17 13		16 58	17 02
Shenfield 3	d	15 39				15 59						16 19				16 39					16 59	
Billericay	d	15 45				16 05						16 25				16 45					17 05	
Wickford 2	d	15 51				16 11					16 16	16 31				16 51				16 56	17 11	
Battlesbridge	d										16 20									17 00		
South Woodham Ferrers	d										16 24									17 04		
North Fambridge	d										16 31									17 11		
Althorne	d										16 36									17 16		
Burnham-on-Crouch	d										16 41									17 21		
Southminster	a										16 47									17 27		
Rayleigh	d	15 56				16 16						16 36				16 56					17 16	
Hockley	d	16 01				16 21						16 41				17 01					17 21	
Rochford	d	16 04				16 24						16 44				17 04					17 24	
Southend Airport ✈	d	16 07				16 27						16 47				17 07					17 27	
Prittlewell	d	16 10				16 30						16 50				17 10					17 30	
Southend Victoria	a	16 14				16 34						16 54				17 14					17 34	

		LE	LE 1	LE	LE 1	LE	LE 1	LE	LE 1	LE 1	LE 1	LE	LE	LE 1	LE 1	LE	LE 1	LE	LE 1	LE 1	LE	LE 1	LE
London Liverpool Street 15 ⊖	d	16 40	16 48	16 50	16 55	17 00	17 02	17 10		17 13	17 18	17 20	17 30	17 35	17 38	17 40	17 48	17 50		17 55	18 00	18 02	18 10
Stratford 7 ⊖	d	16 47	16 55	16 57	17 02	17 07	17 09	17 17		17 20	17 25	17 27	17 37	17 42	17 45	17 47	17 55	17 57		18 02	18 07	18 09	18 17
Maryland	d	16 49		16 59		17 09		17 19				17 29	17 39			17 49		17 59			18 09		18 19
Forest Gate	d	16 51		17 01		17 11		17 21				17 31	17 41			17 51		18 01			18 11		18 21
Manor Park	d	16 53		17 03		17 13		17 23				17 33	17 43			17 53		18 03			18 13		18 23
Ilford 2	d	16 56		17 06		17 16		17 26				17 36	17 46			17 56		18 06			18 16		18 26
Seven Kings	d	16 58		17 08		17 18		17 28				17 38	17 48			17 58		18 08			18 18		18 28
Goodmayes	d	17 00		17 10		17 20		17 30				17 40	17 50			18 00		18 10			18 20		18 30
Chadwell Heath	d	17 02		17 12		17 22		17 32				17 42	17 52			18 02		18 12			18 22		18 32
Romford	d	17 06		17 16		17 26		17 36		17 28		17 46	17 56		17 53	18 06		18 16			18 26		18 36
Gidea Park 2	d	17 10		17 20		17 30		17 40				17 50	18 00			18 10		18 20			18 30		18 40
Harold Wood	d	17 13		17 23		17 33		17 43				17 53	18 03			18 13		18 23			18 33		18 43
Brentwood	d	17 17		17 27		17 37		17 47				17 57	18 07			18 17		18 27			18 37		18 47
Shenfield 3	a	17 23	17 11	17 33	17 18	17 43	17 24	17 53		17 38	17 40	18 03	18 13	17 58	18 02	18 23	18 11	18 33		18 18	18 43	18 24	18 53
Shenfield 3	d				17 19					17 39				17 59						18 19			
Billericay	d				17 25					17 45				18 05						18 25			
Wickford 2	d				17 31				17 36	17 51				18 11					18 16	18 31			
Battlesbridge	d								17 40										18 20				
South Woodham Ferrers	d								17 44										18 24				
North Fambridge	d								17 51										18 31				
Althorne	d								17 56										18 36				
Burnham-on-Crouch	d								18 01										18 41				
Southminster	a								18 07										18 47				
Rayleigh	d				17 36					17 56				18 16						18 36			
Hockley	d				17 41					18 01				18 21						18 41			
Rochford	d				17 44					18 04				18 24						18 44			
Southend Airport ✈	d				17 47					18 07				18 27						18 47			
Prittlewell	d				17 50					18 10				18 30						18 50			
Southend Victoria	a				17 54					18 14				18 34						18 54			

London - Shenfield, Southminster and Southend Victoria

Network Diagram - see first Page of Table 5

		LE ■	LE	LE ■	LE ■	LE ■		LE ■	LE ■	LE	LE ■	LE ■	LE	LE ■	LE	LE ■		LE ■	LE ■	LE	LE	LE ■	LE ■	LE	LE ■
London Liverpool Street ■ ⊖	d	06 05	06 10	06 18	06 21			06 35	06 38	06 40	06 48	06 55	07 00	07 02	07 10			07 13	07 18	07 20	07 30	07 35	07 38	07 40	07 48
Stratford ■ ⊖	d	06 12	06 17	06 25	06a30			06 42	06 45	06 47	06 55	07 02	07 07	07 09	07 17			07 20	07 25	07 27	07 37	07 42	07 45	07 47	07 55
Maryland	d		06 19							06 49			07 09		07 19					07 29	07 39			07 49	
Forest Gate	d		06 21							06 51			07 11		07 21					07 31	07 41			07 51	
Manor Park	d		06 23							06 53			07 13		07 23					07 33	07 43			07 53	
Ilford ■	d		06 26							06 56			07 16		07 26					07 36	07 46			07 56	
Seven Kings	d		06 28							06 58			07 18		07 28					07 38	07 48			07 58	
Goodmayes	d		06 30							07 00			07 20		07 30					07 40	07 50			08 00	
Chadwell Heath	d		06 32							07 02			07 22		07 32					07 42	07 52			08 02	
Romford	d		06 36						06 53	07 06			07 26		07 36			07 28		07 46	07 56		07 53	08 06	
Gidea Park ■	d		06 40							07 10			07 30		07 40					07 50	08 00			08 10	
Harold Wood	d		06 43							07 13			07 33		07 43					07 53	08 03			08 13	
Brentwood	d		06 47							07 17			07 37		07 47					07 57	08 07			08 17	
Shenfield ■	a	06 30	06 53	06 40				06 58	07 02	07 23	07 11	07 18	07 43	07 24	07 53			07 38	07 40	08 03	08 13	07 58	08 02	08 23	08 11
Shenfield ■	d	06 30						06 59				07 19						07 39				07 59			
Billericay	d	06 36						07 05				07 25						07 45				08 05			
Wickford ■	d	06 43				06 56		07 11				07 31				07 36		07 51				08 11			
Battlesbridge	d					07 00										07 40									
South Woodham Ferrers	d					07 04										07 44									
North Fambridge	d					07 11										07 51									
Althorne	d					07 16										07 56									
Burnham-on-Crouch	d					07 21										08 01									
Southminster	a					07 27										08 07									
Rayleigh	d	06 48						07 16				07 36						07 56				08 16			
Hockley	d	06 53						07 21				07 41						08 01				08 21			
Rochford	d	06 56						07 24				07 44						08 04				08 24			
Southend Airport ✈	d	06 59						07 27				07 47						08 07				08 27			
Prittlewell	d	07 02						07 30				07 50						08 10				08 30			
Southend Victoria	a	07 05						07 34				07 54						08 14				08 34			

		LE		LE ■	LE ■	LE	LE ■	LE	LE ■	LE ■	LE	LE		LE ■	LE ■	LE ■	LE	LE ■	LE	LE ■	LE	LE ■		LE	LE ■
London Liverpool Street ■ ⊖	d	07 50			07 55	08 00	08 02	08 10	08 13	08 18	08 20	08 30			08 35	08 38	08 40	08 48	08 50	08 55	09 00	09 02		09 10	
Stratford ■ ⊖	d	07 57			08 02	08 07	08 09	08 17	08 20	08 25	08 27	08 37			08 42	08 45	08 47	08 55	08 57	09 02	09 07	09 09		09 17	
Maryland	d	07 59				08 09		08 19			08 29	08 39					08 49		08 59		09 09			09 19	
Forest Gate	d	08 01				08 11		08 21			08 31	08 41					08 51		09 01		09 11			09 21	
Manor Park	d	08 03				08 13		08 23			08 33	08 43					08 53		09 03		09 13			09 23	
Ilford ■	d	08 06				08 16		08 26			08 36	08 46					08 56		09 06		09 16			09 26	
Seven Kings	d	08 08				08 18		08 28			08 38	08 48					08 58		09 08		09 18			09 28	
Goodmayes	d	08 10				08 20		08 30			08 40	08 50					09 00		09 10		09 20			09 30	
Chadwell Heath	d	08 12				08 22		08 32			08 42	08 52					09 02		09 12		09 22			09 32	
Romford	d	08 16				08 26		08 36	08 28		08 46	08 56				08 53	09 06		09 16		09 26			09 36	
Gidea Park ■	d	08 20				08 30		08 40			08 50	09 00					09 10		09 20		09 30			09 40	
Harold Wood	d	08 23				08 33		08 43			08 53	09 03					09 13		09 23		09 33			09 43	
Brentwood	d	08 27				08 37		08 47			08 57	09 07					09 17		09 27		09 37			09 47	
Shenfield ■	a	08 33			08 18	08 43	08 24	08 53	08 38	08 40	09 03	09 13			08 58	09 02	09 23	09 11	09 33	09 18	09 43	09 24		09 53	
Shenfield ■	d				08 19				08 39						08 59					09 19					
Billericay	d				08 25				08 45						09 05					09 25					
Wickford ■	d			08 16	08 31				08 51					08 56	09 11					09 31					09 36
Battlesbridge	d			08 20										09 00											09 40
South Woodham Ferrers	d			08 24										09 04											09 44
North Fambridge	d			08 31										09 11											09 51
Althorne	d			08 36										09 16											09 56
Burnham-on-Crouch	d			08 41										09 21											10 01
Southminster	a			08 47										09 27											10 07
Rayleigh	d				08 36				08 56						09 16					09 36					
Hockley	d				08 41				09 01						09 21					09 41					
Rochford	d				08 44				09 04						09 24					09 44					
Southend Airport ✈	d				08 47				09 07						09 27					09 47					
Prittlewell	d				08 50				09 10						09 30					09 50					
Southend Victoria	a				08 54				09 14						09 34					09 54					

London - Shenfield, Southminster and Southend Victoria

Network Diagram - see first Page of Table 5

		LE ■	LE ■	LE	LE	LE ■	LE ■	LE		LE ■	LE	LE ■	LE ■	LE	LE ■	LE	LE ■	LE ■		LE	LE	LE ■	LE ■	LE ■	LE
London Liverpool Street ■ ⊖	d	09 13	09 18	09 20	09 30	09 35	09 38	09 40		09 48	09 50		09 55	10 00	10 02	10 10	10 13	10 18		10 20	10 30		10 35	10 38	10 40
Stratford ■ ⊖	d	09 20	09 25	09 27	09 37	09 42	09 45	09 47		09 55	09 57		10 02	10 07	10 09	10 17	10 20	10 25		10 27	10 37		10 42	10 45	10 47
Maryland	d			09 29	09 39			09 49			09 59			10 09		10 19				10 29	10 39				10 49
Forest Gate	d			09 31	09 41			09 51			10 01			10 11		10 21				10 31	10 41				10 51
Manor Park	d			09 33	09 43			09 53			10 03			10 13		10 23				10 33	10 43				10 53
Ilford ■	d			09 36	09 46			09 56			10 06			10 16		10 26				10 36	10 46				10 56
Seven Kings	d			09 38	09 48			09 58			10 08			10 18		10 28				10 38	10 48				10 58
Goodmayes	d			09 40	09 50			10 00			10 10			10 20		10 30				10 40	10 50				11 00
Chadwell Heath	d			09 42	09 52			10 02			10 12			10 22		10 32				10 42	10 52				11 02
Romford	d	09 28		09 46	09 56		09 53	10 06			10 16			10 26		10 36	10 28			10 46	10 56			10 53	11 06
Gidea Park ■	d			09 50	10 00			10 10			10 20			10 30		10 40				10 50	11 00				11 10
Harold Wood	d			09 53	10 03			10 13			10 23			10 33		10 43				10 53	11 03				11 13
Brentwood	d			09 57	10 07			10 17			10 27			10 37		10 47				10 57	11 07				11 17
Shenfield ■	a	09 38	09 40	10 03	10 13	09 58	10 02	10 23		10 11	10 33		10 18	10 43	10 24	10 53	10 38	10 40		11 03	11 13		10 58	11 02	11 23
Shenfield ■	d	09 39				09 59							10 19				10 39						10 59		
Billericay	d	09 45				10 05							10 25				10 45						11 05		
Wickford ■	d	09 51				10 11						10 16	10 31				10 51					10 56	11 11		
Battlesbridge	d											10 20										11 00			
South Woodham Ferrers	d											10 24										11 04			
North Fambridge	d											10 31										11 11			
Althorne	d											10 36										11 16			
Burnham-on-Crouch	d											10 41										11 21			
Southminster	a											10 47										11 27			
Rayleigh	d	09 56				10 16							10 36				10 56						11 16		
Hockley	d	10 01				10 21							10 41				11 01						11 21		
Rochford	d	10 04				10 24							10 44				11 04						11 24		
Southend Airport ✈	d	10 07				10 27							10 47				11 07						11 27		
Prittlewell	d	10 10				10 30							10 50				11 10						11 30		
Southend Victoria	a	10 14				10 34							10 54				11 14						11 34		

		LE ■	LE	LE ■		LE	LE ■	LE	LE ■	LE ■	LE ■	LE	LE	LE ■		LE ■	LE	LE ■	LE	LE ■	LE ■	LE	LE ■	LE
London Liverpool Street ■ ⊖	d	10 48	10 50	10 55		11 00	11 02	11 10		11 13	11 18	11 20	11 30	11 35		11 38	11 40	11 48	11 50		11 55	12 00	12 02	12 10
Stratford ■ ⊖	d	10 55	10 57	11 02		11 07	11 09	11 17		11 20	11 25	11 27	11 37	11 42		11 45	11 47	11 55	11 57		12 02	12 07	12 09	12 17
Maryland	d		10 59			11 09		11 19				11 29	11 39				11 49		11 59			12 09		12 19
Forest Gate	d		11 01			11 11		11 21				11 31	11 41				11 51		12 01			12 11		12 21
Manor Park	d		11 03			11 13		11 23				11 33	11 43				11 53		12 03			12 13		12 23
Ilford ■	d		11 06			11 16		11 26				11 36	11 46				11 56		12 06			12 16		12 26
Seven Kings	d		11 08			11 18		11 28				11 38	11 48				11 58		12 08			12 18		12 28
Goodmayes	d		11 10			11 20		11 30				11 40	11 50				12 00		12 10			12 20		12 30
Chadwell Heath	d		11 12			11 22		11 32				11 42	11 52				12 02		12 12			12 22		12 32
Romford	d		11 16			11 26		11 36		11 28		11 46	11 56			11 53	12 06		12 16			12 26		12 36
Gidea Park ■	d		11 20			11 30		11 40				11 50	12 00				12 10		12 20			12 30		12 40
Harold Wood	d		11 23			11 33		11 43				11 53	12 03				12 13		12 23			12 33		12 43
Brentwood	d		11 27			11 37		11 47				11 57	12 07				12 17		12 27			12 37		12 47
Shenfield ■	a	11 11	11 33	11 18		11 43	11 24	11 53		11 38	11 40	12 03	12 13	11 58		12 02	12 23	12 11	12 33		12 18	12 43	12 24	12 53
Shenfield ■	d			11 19						11 39				11 59							12 19			
Billericay	d			11 25						11 45				12 05							12 25			
Wickford ■	d			11 31					11 36	11 51				12 11						12 16	12 31			
Battlesbridge	d								11 40											12 20				
South Woodham Ferrers	d								11 44											12 24				
North Fambridge	d								11 51											12 31				
Althorne	d								11 56											12 36				
Burnham-on-Crouch	d								12 01											12 41				
Southminster	a								12 07											12 47				
Rayleigh	d			11 36						11 56				12 16							12 36			
Hockley	d			11 41						12 01				12 21							12 41			
Rochford	d			11 44						12 04				12 24							12 44			
Southend Airport ✈	d			11 47						12 07				12 27							12 47			
Prittlewell	d			11 50						12 10				12 30							12 50			
Southend Victoria	a			11 54						12 14				12 34							12 54			

Saturdays
until 21 July

London - Shenfield, Southminster and Southend Victoria

Network Diagram - see first Page of Table 5

		LE 1	LE 1	LE	LE	LE 1	LE 1	LE 1	LE	LE 1	LE	LE 1	LE	LE 1	LE	LE 1	LE 1	LE 1	LE	LE	LE 1	LE 1
London Liverpool Street 15 ⊖	d	18 13	18 18	18 20	18 30		18 35	18 38	18 40	18 48	18 50	18 55	19 00	19 02	19 10		19 13	19 18	19 20	19 30	19 32	19 35
Stratford 7 ⊖	d	18 20	18 25	18 27	18 37		18 42	18 45	18 47	18 55	18 57	19 02	19 07	19 09	19 17		19 20	19 25	19 27	19 37	19 39	19 43
Maryland	d			18 29	18 39				18 49		18 59		19 09		19 19				19 29	19 39		
Forest Gate	d			18 31	18 41				18 51		19 01		19 11		19 21				19 31	19 41		
Manor Park	d			18 33	18 43				18 53		19 03		19 13		19 23				19 33	19 43		
Ilford 2	d			18 36	18 46				18 56		19 06		19 16		19 26				19 36	19 46		
Seven Kings	d			18 38	18 48				18 58		19 08		19 18		19 28				19 38	19 48		
Goodmayes	d			18 40	18 50				19 00		19 10		19 20		19 30				19 40	19 50		
Chadwell Heath	d			18 42	18 52				19 02		19 12		19 22		19 32				19 42	19 52		
Romford	d	18 28		18 46	18 56			18 53	19 06		19 16		19 26		19 36		19 28		19 46	19 56		
Gidea Park 2	d			18 50	19 00				19 10		19 20		19 30		19 40				19 50	20 00		
Harold Wood	d			18 53	19 03				19 13		19 23		19 33		19 43				19 53	20 03		
Brentwood	d			18 57	19 07				19 17		19 27		19 37		19 47				19 57	20 07		
Shenfield 3	a	18 38	18 40	19 03	19 13		18 58	19 02	19 23	19 11	19 33	19 18	19 43	19 24	19 53		19 38	19 40	20 03	20 13	19 56	19 59
Shenfield 3	d	18 39					18 59					19 19					19 39					20 00
Billericay	d	18 45					19 05					19 25					19 45					20 06
Wickford 2	d	18 51				18 56	19 11					19 31				19 36	19 51					20 12
Battlesbridge	d					19 00										19 40						
South Woodham Ferrers	d					19 04										19 44						
North Fambridge	d					19 11										19 51						
Althorne	d					19 16										19 56						
Burnham-on-Crouch	d					19 21										20 01						
Southminster	a					19 27										20 07						
Rayleigh	d	18 56					19 16					19 36					19 56					20 17
Hockley	d	19 01					19 21					19 41					20 01					20 22
Rochford	d	19 04					19 24					19 44					20 04					20 25
Southend Airport ✈	d	19 07					19 27					19 47					20 07					20 28
Prittlewell	d	19 10					19 30					19 50					20 10					20 31
Southend Victoria	a	19 14					19 34					19 54					20 14					20 35

		LE 1	LE	LE 1	LE	LE 1	LE 1	LE	LE 1	LE	LE 1	LE 1	LE	LE	LE 1	LE 1	LE 1	LE	LE 1	LE	LE 1	LE 1	LE
London Liverpool Street 15 ⊖	d	19 38	19 40	19 48	19 50		19 55	20 00	20 02	20 10	20 13	20 18	20 20	20 30		20 35	20 38	20 40	20 48	20 50	20 55	21 02	21 05
Stratford 7 ⊖	d	19 46	19 47	19 55	19 57		20 02	20 07	20 09	20 17	20 20	20 25	20 27	20 37		20 42	20 45	20 47	20 55	20 57	21 02	21 09	21 12
Maryland	d		19 49		19 59			20 09		20 19			20 29	20 39				20 49		20 59			21 14
Forest Gate	d		19 51		20 01			20 11		20 21			20 31	20 41				20 51		21 01			21 16
Manor Park	d		19 53		20 03			20 13		20 23			20 33	20 43				20 53		21 03			21 18
Ilford 2	d		19 56		20 06			20 16		20 26			20 36	20 46				20 56		21 06			21 21
Seven Kings	d		19 58		20 08			20 18		20 28			20 38	20 48				20 58		21 08			21 23
Goodmayes	d		20 00		20 10			20 20		20 30			20 40	20 50				21 00		21 10			21 25
Chadwell Heath	d		20 02		20 12			20 22		20 32			20 42	20 52				21 02		21 12			21 27
Romford	d	19 54	20 06		20 16			20 26		20 36	20 28		20 46	20 56			20 53	21 06		21 16			21 31
Gidea Park 2	d		20 10		20 20			20 30		20 40			20 50	21 00				21 10		21 20			21 35
Harold Wood	d		20 13		20 23			20 33		20 43			20 53	21 03				21 13		21 23			21 38
Brentwood	d		20 17		20 27			20 37		20 47			20 57	21 07				21 17		21 27			21 42
Shenfield 3	a	20 03	20 23	20 11	20 33		20 18	20 43	20 24	20 53	20 38	20 40	21 03	21 13		20 58	21 02	21 23	21 11	21 33	21 18	21 24	21 48
Shenfield 3	d						20 19				20 39					20 59					21 19		
Billericay	d						20 25				20 45					21 05					21 25		
Wickford 2	d					20 16	20 31				20 51				20 56	21 11					21 31		
Battlesbridge	d					20 20									21 00								
South Woodham Ferrers	d					20 24									21 04								
North Fambridge	d					20 31									21 11								
Althorne	d					20 36									21 16								
Burnham-on-Crouch	d					20 41									21 21								
Southminster	a					20 47									21 27								
Rayleigh	d						20 36				20 56					21 16					21 36		
Hockley	d						20 41				21 01					21 21					21 41		
Rochford	d						20 44				21 04					21 24					21 44		
Southend Airport ✈	d						20 47				21 07					21 27					21 47		
Prittlewell	d						20 50				21 10					21 30					21 50		
Southend Victoria	a						20 54				21 14					21 34					21 54		

Table 5

Saturdays
until 21 July

London - Shenfield, Southminster and Southend Victoria

Network Diagram - see first Page of Table 5

		LE 1	LE 1	LE 1	LE	LE 1	LE	LE 1	LE 1	LE	LE 1	LE 1	LE 1	LE	LE 1	LE 1	LE	LE	LE 1	LE 1	LE 1	LE	LE 1
London Liverpool Street 15 ⊖	d		21 13	21 18	21 20	21 35	21 35	21 38	21 48	21 50		21 55	22 02	22 05	22 13	22 18	22 20	22 35	22 38		22 45	22 50	23 02
Stratford 7 ⊖	d		21 20	21 25	21 27	21 42	21 42	21 45	21 55	21 57		22 02	22 09	22 12	22 20	22 25	22 27	22 42	22 45		22 52	22 57	23 09
Maryland	d				21 29		21 44			21 59				22 14			22 29	22 44				22 59	
Forest Gate	d				21 31		21 46			22 01				22 16			22 31	22 46				23 01	
Manor Park	d				21 33		21 48			22 03				22 18			22 33	22 48				23 03	
Ilford 2	d				21 36		21 51			22 06				22 21			22 36	22 51				23 06	
Seven Kings	d				21 38		21 53			22 08				22 23			22 38	22 53				23 08	
Goodmayes	d				21 40		21 55			22 10				22 25			22 40	22 55				23 10	
Chadwell Heath	d				21 42		21 57			22 12				22 27			22 42	22 57				23 12	
Romford	d		21 28		21 46		22 01	21 53		22 16				22 31	22 28		22 46	23 01	22 53			23 16	
Gidea Park 2	d				21 50		22 05			22 20				22 35			22 50	23 05				23 20	
Harold Wood	d				21 53		22 08			22 23				22 38			22 53	23 08				23 23	
Brentwood	d				21 57		22 12			22 27				22 42			22 57	23 12				23 27	
Shenfield 3	a		21 38	21 40	22 03	21 57	22 18	22 02	22 11	22 33		22 18	22 24	22 48	22 38	22 40	23 03	23 18	23 02		23 08	23 33	23 24
Shenfield 3	d		21 39			21 59						22 19			22 39						23 09		
Billericay	d		21 45			22 05						22 25			22 45						23 15		
Wickford 2	d	21 36	21 51			22 11					22 16	22 31			22 51					22 56	23 21		
Battlesbridge	d	21 40									22 20									23 00			
South Woodham Ferrers	d	21 44									22 24									23 04			
North Fambridge	d	21 51									22 31									23 11			
Althorne	d	21 56									22 36									23 16			
Burnham-on-Crouch	d	22 01									22 41									23 21			
Southminster	a	22 07									22 47									23 27			
Rayleigh	d		21 56			22 16						22 36			22 56						23 26		
Hockley	d		22 01			22 21						22 41			23 01						23 31		
Rochford	d		22 04			22 24						22 44			23 04						23 34		
Southend Airport ✈	d		22 07			22 27						22 47			23 07						23 37		
Prittlewell	d		22 10			22 30						22 50			23 10						23 40		
Southend Victoria	a		22 14			22 34						22 54			23 14						23 48		

		LE	LE 1	LE 1	LE	LE	LE 1	LE 1	LE
London Liverpool Street 15 ⊖	d	23 05	23 15	23 18	23 20	23 35	23 45	23 48	23 50
Stratford 7 ⊖	d	23 12	23 22	23 25	23 27	23 42	23 52	23 55	23 57
Maryland	d	23 14			23 29	23 44			23 59
Forest Gate	d	23 16			23 31	23 46			00 01
Manor Park	d	23 18			23 33	23 48			00 03
Ilford 2	d	23 21			23 36	23 51			00 06
Seven Kings	d	23 23			23 38	23 53			00 08
Goodmayes	d	23 25			23 40	23 55			00 10
Chadwell Heath	d	23 27			23 42	23 57			00 12
Romford	d	23 31			23 46	00 02			00 16
Gidea Park 2	d	23 35			23 50	00 05			00 20
Harold Wood	d	23 38			23 53	00 08			00 23
Brentwood	d	23 42			23 57	00 12			00 27
Shenfield 3	a	23 48	23 38	23 40	00 03	00 18	00 08	00 10	00 33
Shenfield 3	d		23 39				00 09		
Billericay	d		23 45				00 15		
Wickford 2	d		23 51				00 21		
Battlesbridge	d								
South Woodham Ferrers	d								
North Fambridge	d								
Althorne	d								
Burnham-on-Crouch	d								
Southminster	a								
Rayleigh	d		23 56				00 26		
Hockley	d		00 01				00 31		
Rochford	d		00 04				00 34		
Southend Airport ✈	d		00 07				00 37		
Prittlewell	d		00 10				00 40		
Southend Victoria	a		00 18				00 48		

Table 5

Saturdays
28 July to 11 August

London - Shenfield, Southminster and Southend Victoria

Network Diagram - see first Page of Table 5

		LE 1	LE 1	LE	LE 1	LE	LE 1	LE	LE 1	LE	LE 1	LE	LE	LE 1	LE 1	LE 1	LE	LE	LE 1	LE 1	LE	LE 1	LE 1	LE	LE
							A												B				B		
London Liverpool Street 15 ⊖	d	23p10		23p22	23p25	23p32	23p40	23p42	23p45	23p52	23p55	00 02	00 12	00 12	00 15	00 18	00 22	00 32	00 33	00 40	00 42	00 46	00 48	00 52	01 02
Stratford 7 ⊖	d	23p22		23p33	23p37	23p43	23p52	23p53	23p54	00 03	00 07	00 13	00 23	00 24	00 27	00a27	00 33	00 43	00 42	00 52	00 53	01 00	00a57	01 03	01 13
Maryland	d																								
Forest Gate	d			23p36		23p46		23p56		00 06		00 16	00 26				00 36	00 46			00 56			01 06	01 16
Manor Park	d			23p38		23p48		23p58		00 08		00 18	00 28				00 38	00 48			00 58			01 08	01 18
Ilford 2	d			23p41		23p51		00 01		00 11		00 21	00 31				00 41	00 51			01 01			01 11	01 21
Seven Kings	d			23p43		23p53		00 03		00 13		00 23	00 33				00 43	00 53			01 03			01 13	01 23
Goodmayes	d			23p45		23p55		00 05		00 15		00 25	00 35				00 45	00 55			01 05			01 15	01 25
Chadwell Heath	d			23p47		23p57		00 07		00 17		00 27	00 37				00 47	00 57			01 07			01 17	01 27
Romford	d			23p51		00 02		00 12		00 21		00 31	00 41				00 51	01 01			01 11			01 21	01 31
Gidea Park 2	d			23p55		00 05		00 15		00 25		00 35	00 45				00 55	01 05			01 15			01 25	01 35
Harold Wood	d			23p58		00 08		00 18		00 28		00 38	00 48				00 58	01 08			01 18			01 28	01 38
Brentwood	d			00 02		00 12		00 22		00 32		00 42	00 52				01 02	01 12			01 22			01 32	01 42
Shenfield 3	a	23p38		00 08	23p53	00 18	00 08	00 28	00 11	00 38	00 23	00 49	00 58	00 40	00 45		01 08	01 18		01 07	01 28	01 17		01 38	01 48
Shenfield 3	d	23p39			23p54		00 09				00 24				00 46					01 09					
Billericay	d	23p45			23p59		00 15				00 30				00 52					01 15					
Wickford 2	d	23p51	23p56		00 06		00 21				00 36				00 58					01 21					
Battlesbridge	d		00 01																						
South Woodham Ferrers	d		00 04																						
North Fambridge	d		00 11																						
Althorne	d		00 16																						
Burnham-on-Crouch	d		00 21																						
Southminster	a		00 27																						
Rayleigh	d	23p56			00 11		00 26				00 41				01 03					01 26					
Hockley	d	00 01			00 16		00 31				00 46				01 08					01 31					
Rochford	d	00 04			00 19		00 34				00 49				01 11					01 34					
Southend Airport ✈	d	00 07			00 22		00 37				00 52				01 14					01 37					
Prittlewell	d	00 10			00 25		00 40				00 55				01 17					01 40					
Southend Victoria	a	00 14			00 29		00 44				00 59				01 21					01 44					

		LE 1	LE 1	LE 1	LE	LE 1	LE	LE	LE 1	LE	LE	LE	LE	LE 1	LE 1	LE 1	LE 1	LE 1	LE	LE 1	LE 1	LE	LE	LE 1	LE 1
		B		B		B			B																
London Liverpool Street 15 ⊖	d	01 03	01 10	01 12	01 12	01 18	01 22	01 32	01 40	01 42	01 52	02 02	02 12	05 21			05 28	05 34	05 40	05 51	06 02	06 05	06 10	06 18	06 21
Stratford 7 ⊖	d	01a12	01 22	01 25	01 23	01a27	01 33	01 43	01 52	01 53	02 03	02 13	02 23	05a30			05 35	05 41	05 48	06a00	06 09	06 12	06 18	06 25	06a30
Maryland	d																								
Forest Gate	d				01 26		01 36	01 46		01 56	02 06	02 16	02 26						05 51				06 21		
Manor Park	d				01 28		01 38	01 48		01 58	02 08	02 18	02 28						05 53				06 23		
Ilford 2	d				01 31		01 41	01 51		02 01	02 11	02 21	02 31				05 40		05 56				06 26		
Seven Kings	d				01 33		01 43	01 53		02 03	02 13	02 23	02 33				05 42		05 58				06 28		
Goodmayes	d				01 35		01 45	01 55		02 05	02 15	02 25	02 35						06 00				06 30		
Chadwell Heath	d				01 37		01 47	01 57		02 07	02 17	02 27	02 37						06 02				06 32		
Romford	d				01 41		01 51	02 01		02 11	02 21	02 31	02 41				05 48	05 49	06 06				06 36		
Gidea Park 2	d				01 45		01 55	02a05		02 15	02a25	02 35	02a45				05 51		06 10				06 40		
Harold Wood	d				01 48		01 58			02 18		02 38					05 54		06 13				06 43		
Brentwood	d				01 52		02 02			02 22		02 42					05 59		06 17				06 47		
Shenfield 3	a		01 37	01 40	01 58		02 08		02 07	02 28		02 48					06 04	05 58	06 23		06 24	06 30	06 53	06 40	
Shenfield 3	d		01 39						02 09								06 04					06 30			
Billericay	d		01 45						02 15								06 10					06 36			
Wickford 2	d		01 51						02 21						05 36	06 12	06 16					06 43			
Battlesbridge	d														05 40	06 16									
South Woodham Ferrers	d														05 44	06 20									
North Fambridge	d														05 51	06 31									
Althorne	d														05 56	06 36									
Burnham-on-Crouch	d														06 01	06 41									
Southminster	a														06 07	06 47									
Rayleigh	d		01 56						02 26								06 22					06 48			
Hockley	d		02 01						02 31								06 26					06 53			
Rochford	d		02 04						02 34								06 30					06 56			
Southend Airport ✈	d		02 07						02 37								06 32					06 59			
Prittlewell	d		02 10						02 40								06 35					07 02			
Southend Victoria	a		02 14						02 44								06 39					07 05			

A not 28 July

B 28 July only

Table 5

Saturdays
28 July to 11 August

London - Shenfield, Southminster and Southend Victoria

Network Diagram - see first Page of Table 5

		LE 1	LE 1	LE 1	LE	LE 1	LE 1	LE	LE 1	LE	LE 1	LE		LE 1	LE		LE	LE 1	LE 1	LE	LE 1	LE	LE 1	LE 1	LE
London Liverpool Street 15 ⊖	d		06 35	06 38	06 40	06 48	06 55	07 00	07 02	07 10		07 13		07 18	07 20		07 30	07 35	07 38	07 40	07 48	07 50		07 55	08 00
Stratford 7 ⊖	d		06 42	06 45	06 48	06 55	07 02	07 08	07 09	07 18		07 20		07 25	07 28		07 38	07 42	07 45	07 48	07 55	07 58		08 02	08 08
Maryland	d																								
Forest Gate	d				06 51			07 11		07 21					07 31		07 41			07 51		08 01			08 11
Manor Park	d				06 53			07 13		07 23					07 33		07 43			07 53		08 03			08 13
Ilford 2	d				06 56			07 16		07 26					07 36		07 46			07 56		08 06			08 16
Seven Kings	d				06 58			07 18		07 28					07 38		07 48			07 58		08 08			08 18
Goodmayes	d				07 00			07 20		07 30					07 40		07 50			08 00		08 10			08 20
Chadwell Heath	d				07 02			07 22		07 32					07 42		07 52			08 02		08 12			08 22
Romford	d			06 53	07 06			07 26		07 36		07 28			07 46		07 56		07 53	08 06		08 16			08 26
Gidea Park 2	d				07 10			07 30		07 40					07 50		08 00			08 10		08 20			08 30
Harold Wood	d				07 13			07 33		07 43					07 53		08 03			08 13		08 23			08 33
Brentwood	d				07 17			07 37		07 47					07 57		08 07			08 17		08 27			08 37
Shenfield 3	a		06 58	07 02	07 23	07 11	07 18	07 43	07 24	07 53		07 39		07 40	08 03		08 13	07 58	08 02	08 23	08 11	08 33		08 18	08 43
Shenfield 3	d		06 59				07 19					07 39						07 59						08 19	
Billericay	d		07 05				07 25					07 45						08 05						08 25	
Wickford 2	d	06 56	07 11				07 31				07 36	07 51						08 11					08 16	08 31	
Battlesbridge	d	07 00									07 40												08 20		
South Woodham Ferrers	d	07 04									07 44												08 24		
North Fambridge	d	07 11									07 51												08 31		
Althorne	d	07 16									07 56												08 36		
Burnham-on-Crouch	d	07 21									08 01												08 41		
Southminster	a	07 27									08 07												08 47		
Rayleigh	d		07 16				07 36					07 57						08 16						08 36	
Hockley	d		07 21				07 41					08 01						08 21						08 41	
Rochford	d		07 24				07 44					08 05						08 24						08 44	
Southend Airport ✈	d		07 27				07 47					08 07						08 27						08 47	
Prittlewell	d		07 30				07 50					08 10						08 30						08 50	
Southend Victoria	a		07 34				07 54					08 14						08 34						08 54	

		LE 1	LE	LE 1	LE 1	LE	LE	LE 1	LE 1	LE 1	LE	LE 1	LE	LE 1	LE	LE 1	LE	LE 1	LE 1	LE 1	LE	LE	LE 1	LE 1	LE
London Liverpool Street 15 ⊖	d	08 02	08 10	08 13	08 18	08 20	08 30		08 35	08 38	08 40	08 48	08 50	08 55	09 00	09 02	09 10		09 13	09 18	09 20	09 30	09 35	09 38	09 40
Stratford 7 ⊖	d	08 09	08 18	08 20	08 25	08 28	08 38		08 42	08 45	08 48	08 55	08 58	09 02	09 08	09 09	09 18		09 20	09 25	09 28	09 38	09 42	09 45	09 48
Maryland	d																								
Forest Gate	d		08 21			08 31	08 41				08 51		09 01		09 11		09 21				09 31	09 41			09 51
Manor Park	d		08 23			08 33	08 43				08 53		09 03		09 13		09 23				09 33	09 43			09 53
Ilford 2	d		08 26			08 36	08 46				08 56		09 06		09 16		09 26				09 36	09 46			09 56
Seven Kings	d		08 28			08 38	08 48				08 58		09 08		09 18		09 28				09 38	09 48			09 58
Goodmayes	d		08 30			08 40	08 50				09 00		09 10		09 20		09 30				09 40	09 50			10 00
Chadwell Heath	d		08 32			08 42	08 52				09 02		09 12		09 22		09 32				09 42	09 52			10 02
Romford	d		08 36	08 28		08 46	08 56			08 53	09 06		09 16		09 26		09 36		09 28		09 46	09 56		09 53	10 06
Gidea Park 2	d		08 40			08 50	09 00				09 10		09 20		09 30		09 40				09 50	10 00			10 10
Harold Wood	d		08 43			08 53	09 03				09 13		09 23		09 33		09 43				09 53	10 03			10 13
Brentwood	d		08 47			08 57	09 07				09 17		09 27		09 37		09 47				09 57	10 07			10 17
Shenfield 3	a	08 24	08 53	08 38	08 40	09 03	09 13		08 58	09 02	09 23	09 11	09 33	09 18	09 43	09 24	09 53		09 38	09 40	10 03	10 13	09 58	10 02	10 23
Shenfield 3	d			08 39					08 59					09 19					09 39				09 59		
Billericay	d			08 45					09 05					09 25					09 45				10 05		
Wickford 2	d			08 51				08 56	09 11					09 31				09 36	09 51				10 11		
Battlesbridge	d							09 00										09 40							
South Woodham Ferrers	d							09 04										09 44							
North Fambridge	d							09 11										09 51							
Althorne	d							09 16										09 56							
Burnham-on-Crouch	d							09 21										10 01							
Southminster	a							09 27										10 07							
Rayleigh	d			08 56					09 16					09 36					09 56				10 16		
Hockley	d			09 01					09 21					09 41					10 01				10 21		
Rochford	d			09 04					09 24					09 44					10 04				10 24		
Southend Airport ✈	d			09 07					09 27					09 47					10 07				10 27		
Prittlewell	d			09 10					09 30					09 50					10 10				10 30		
Southend Victoria	a			09 14					09 34					09 54					10 14				10 34		

Saturdays
28 July to 11 August

London - Shenfield, Southminster and Southend Victoria

Network Diagram - see first Page of Table 5

		LE 1	LE	LE 1	LE 1	LE	LE 1	LE	LE 1	LE 1	LE	LE	LE 1	LE 1	LE 1	LE	LE 1	LE	LE 1	LE	LE 1	LE
London Liverpool Street 15 ⊖	d	09 48	09 50		09 55	10 00	10 02	10 10	10 13	10 18	10 20	10 30		10 35	10 38	10 40	10 48	10 50	10 55	11 00	11 02	11 10
Stratford 7 ⊖	d	09 55	09 58		10 02	10 08	10 09	10 18	10 20	10 25	10 28	10 38		10 42	10 45	10 48	10 55	10 58	11 02	11 08	11 09	11 18
Maryland	d																					
Forest Gate	d		10 01			10 11		10 21			10 31	10 41				10 51		11 01		11 11		11 21
Manor Park	d		10 03			10 13		10 23			10 33	10 43				10 53		11 03		11 13		11 23
Ilford 2	d		10 06			10 16		10 26			10 36	10 46				10 56		11 06		11 16		11 26
Seven Kings	d		10 08			10 18		10 28			10 38	10 48				10 58		11 08		11 18		11 28
Goodmayes	d		10 10			10 20		10 30			10 40	10 50				11 00		11 10		11 20		11 30
Chadwell Heath	d		10 12			10 22		10 32			10 42	10 52				11 02		11 12		11 22		11 32
Romford	d		10 16			10 26		10 36	10 28		10 46	10 56				11 06		11 16		11 26		11 36
Gidea Park 2	d		10 20			10 30		10 40			10 50	11 00				11 10		11 20		11 30		11 40
Harold Wood	d		10 23			10 33		10 43			10 53	11 03				11 13		11 23		11 33		11 43
Brentwood	d		10 27			10 37		10 47			10 57	11 07				11 17		11 27		11 37		11 47
Shenfield 3	a	10 11	10 33		10 18	10 43	10 24	10 53	10 38	10 40	11 03	11 13		10 58	11 00	11 23	11 11	11 33	11 18	11 43	11 24	11 53
Shenfield 3	d				10 19				10 39					10 59					11 19			
Billericay	d				10 25				10 45					11 05					11 25			
Wickford 2	d			10 16	10 31				10 51				10 56	11 11					11 31			
Battlesbridge	d			10 20									11 00									
South Woodham Ferrers	d			10 24									11 04									
North Fambridge	d			10 31									11 11									
Althorne	d			10 36									11 16									
Burnham-on-Crouch	d			10 41									11 21									
Southminster	a			10 47									11 27									
Rayleigh	d				10 36				10 56					11 16					11 36			
Hockley	d				10 41				11 01					11 21					11 41			
Rochford	d				10 44				11 04					11 24					11 44			
Southend Airport ✈	d				10 47				11 07					11 27					11 47			
Prittlewell	d				10 50				11 10					11 30					11 50			
Southend Victoria	a				10 54				11 14					11 34					11 54			

		LE 1	LE 1	LE 1	LE	LE	LE 1	LE 1	LE	LE 1	LE	LE 1	LE 1	LE	LE 1	LE	LE 1	LE 1	LE	LE	LE 1	LE 1	LE
London Liverpool Street 15 ⊖	d		11 13	11 18	11 20	11 30	11 35	11 38	11 40	11 48	11 50		11 55	12 00	12 02	12 10	12 13	12 18	12 20	12 30		12 35	12 40
Stratford 7 ⊖	d		11 20	11 25	11 28	11 38	11 42	11 45	11 48	11 55	11 58		12 02	12 08	12 09	12 18	12 20	12 25	12 28	12 38		12 42	12 48
Maryland	d																						
Forest Gate	d				11 31	11 41			11 51		12 01			12 11		12 21			12 31	12 41			12 51
Manor Park	d				11 33	11 43			11 53		12 03			12 13		12 23			12 33	12 43			12 53
Ilford 2	d				11 36	11 46			11 56		12 06			12 16		12 26			12 36	12 46			12 56
Seven Kings	d				11 38	11 48			11 58		12 08			12 18		12 28			12 38	12 48			12 58
Goodmayes	d				11 40	11 50			12 00		12 10			12 20		12 30			12 40	12 50			13 00
Chadwell Heath	d				11 42	11 52			12 02		12 12			12 22		12 32			12 42	12 52			13 02
Romford	d		11 28		11 46	11 56		11 53	12 06		12 16			12 26		12 36	12 28		12 46	12 56			13 06
Gidea Park 2	d				11 50	12 00			12 10		12 20			12 30		12 40			12 50	13 00			13 10
Harold Wood	d				11 53	12 03			12 13		12 23			12 33		12 43			12 53	13 03			13 13
Brentwood	d				11 57	12 07			12 17		12 27			12 37		12 47			12 57	13 07			13 17
Shenfield 3	a		11 38	11 40	12 03	12 13	11 58	12 02	12 23	12 11	12 33		12 18	12 43	12 24	12 53	12 38	12 40	13 03	13 13		12 58	13 23
Shenfield 3	d		11 39				11 59						12 19				12 39					12 59	
Billericay	d		11 45				12 05						12 25				12 45					13 05	
Wickford 2	d	11 36	11 51				12 11					12 16	12 31				12 51				12 56	13 11	
Battlesbridge	d	11 40										12 20									13 00		
South Woodham Ferrers	d	11 44										12 24									13 04		
North Fambridge	d	11 51										12 31									13 11		
Althorne	d	11 56										12 36									13 16		
Burnham-on-Crouch	d	12 01										12 41									13 21		
Southminster	a	12 07										12 47									13 27		
Rayleigh	d		11 56				12 16						12 36				12 56					13 16	
Hockley	d		12 01				12 21						12 41				13 01					13 21	
Rochford	d		12 04				12 24						12 44				13 04					13 24	
Southend Airport ✈	d		12 07				12 27						12 47				13 07					13 27	
Prittlewell	d		12 10				12 30						12 50				13 10					13 30	
Southend Victoria	a		12 14				12 34						12 54				13 14					13 34	

Table 5

Saturdays
28 July to 11 August

London - Shenfield, Southminster and Southend Victoria

Network Diagram - see first Page of Table 5

		LE 1	LE	LE 1	LE	LE 1	LE	LE 1	LE 1	LE 1	LE	LE	LE 1	LE 1	LE	LE 1	LE	LE 1	LE 1	LE	LE 1	LE	LE 1
London Liverpool Street 15 ⊖	d	12 48	12 50	12 55	13 00	13 02	13 10		13 13	13 18	13 20	13 30	13 35	13 38	13 40	13 48	13 50		13 55	14 00	14 02	14 10	14 13
Stratford 7 ⊖	d	12 55	12 58	13 02	13 08	13 09	13 18		13 20	13 25	13 28	13 38	13 42	13 45	13 48	13 55	13 58		14 02	14 08	14 09	14 18	14 20
Maryland	d																						
Forest Gate	d		13 01		13 11		13 21				13 31	13 41			13 51		14 01			14 11		14 21	
Manor Park	d		13 03		13 13		13 23				13 33	13 43			13 53		14 03			14 13		14 23	
Ilford 2	d		13 06		13 16		13 26				13 36	13 46			13 56		14 06			14 16		14 26	
Seven Kings	d		13 08		13 18		13 28				13 38	13 48			13 58		14 08			14 18		14 28	
Goodmayes	d		13 10		13 20		13 30				13 40	13 50			14 00		14 10			14 20		14 30	
Chadwell Heath	d		13 12		13 22		13 32				13 42	13 52			14 02		14 12			14 22		14 32	
Romford	d		13 16		13 26		13 36		13 28		13 46	13 56		13 53	14 06		14 16			14 26		14 36	14 28
Gidea Park 2	d		13 20		13 30		13 40				13 50	14 00			14 10		14 20			14 30		14 40	
Harold Wood	d		13 23		13 33		13 43				13 53	14 03			14 13		14 23			14 33		14 43	
Brentwood	d		13 27		13 37		13 47				13 57	14 07			14 17		14 27			14 37		14 47	
Shenfield 3	a	13 11	13 33	13 18	13 43	13 24	13 53		13 38	13 40	14 03	14 13	13 58	14 02	14 23	14 11	14 33		14 18	14 43	14 24	14 53	14 38
Shenfield 3	d			13 19					13 39				13 59						14 19				14 39
Billericay	d			13 25					13 45				14 05						14 25				14 45
Wickford 2	d			13 31				13 36	13 51				14 11					14 16	14 31				14 51
Battlesbridge	d							13 40										14 20					
South Woodham Ferrers	d							13 44										14 24					
North Fambridge	d							13 51										14 31					
Althorne	d							13 56										14 36					
Burnham-on-Crouch	d							14 01										14 41					
Southminster	a							14 07										14 47					
Rayleigh	d			13 36					13 56				14 16						14 36				14 56
Hockley	d			13 41					14 01				14 21						14 41				15 01
Rochford	d			13 44					14 04				14 24						14 44				15 04
Southend Airport ✈	d			13 47					14 07				14 27						14 47				15 07
Prittlewell	d			13 50					14 10				14 30						14 50				15 10
Southend Victoria	a			13 54					14 14				14 34						14 54				15 14

		LE 1	LE	LE	LE 1	LE 1	LE	LE 1	LE	LE 1	LE	LE 1	LE	LE 1	LE 1	LE 1	LE	LE	LE 1	LE 1	LE	LE 1
London Liverpool Street 15 ⊖	d	14 18	14 20	14 30		14 35	14 40	14 48	14 50	14 55	15 00	15 02	15 10		15 13	15 18	15 20	15 30	15 35	15 38	15 40	15 48
Stratford 7 ⊖	d	14 25	14 28	14 38		14 42	14 48	14 55	14 58	15 02	15 08	15 09	15 18		15 20	15 25	15 28	15 38	15 42	15 45	15 48	15 55
Maryland	d																					
Forest Gate	d		14 31	14 41			14 51		15 01		15 11		15 21				15 31	15 41			15 51	
Manor Park	d		14 33	14 43			14 53		15 03		15 13		15 23				15 33	15 43			15 53	
Ilford 2	d		14 36	14 46			14 56		15 06		15 16		15 26				15 36	15 46			15 56	
Seven Kings	d		14 38	14 48			14 58		15 08		15 18		15 28				15 38	15 48			15 58	
Goodmayes	d		14 40	14 50			15 00		15 10		15 20		15 30				15 40	15 50			16 00	
Chadwell Heath	d		14 42	14 52			15 02		15 12		15 22		15 32				15 42	15 52			16 02	
Romford	d		14 46	14 56			15 06		15 16		15 26		15 36		15 28		15 46	15 56		15 53	16 06	
Gidea Park 2	d		14 50	15 00			15 10		15 20		15 30		15 40				15 50	16 00			16 10	
Harold Wood	d		14 53	15 03			15 13		15 23		15 33		15 43				15 53	16 03			16 13	
Brentwood	d		14 57	15 07			15 17		15 27		15 37		15 47				15 57	16 07			16 17	
Shenfield 3	a	14 40	15 03	15 13		14 58	15 23	15 11	15 33	15 18	15 43	15 24	15 53		15 38	15 40	16 03	16 13	15 58	16 02	16 23	16 11
Shenfield 3	d					14 59				15 19					15 39				15 59			
Billericay	d					15 05				15 25					15 45				16 05			
Wickford 2	d				14 56	15 11				15 31				15 36	15 51				16 11			
Battlesbridge	d				15 00									15 40								
South Woodham Ferrers	d				15 04									15 44								
North Fambridge	d				15 11									15 51								
Althorne	d				15 16									15 56								
Burnham-on-Crouch	d				15 21									16 01								
Southminster	a				15 27									16 07								
Rayleigh	d					15 16				15 36					15 56				16 16			
Hockley	d					15 21				15 41					16 01				16 21			
Rochford	d					15 24				15 44					16 04				16 24			
Southend Airport ✈	d					15 27				15 47					16 07				16 27			
Prittlewell	d					15 30				15 50					16 10				16 30			
Southend Victoria	a					15 34				15 54					16 14				16 34			

London - Shenfield, Southminster and Southend Victoria

Network Diagram - see first Page of Table 5

		LE	LE ■	LE ■	LE	LE ■	LE	LE ■		LE ■	LE	LE	LE ■	LE ■	LE	LE ■	LE	LE ■		LE	LE ■	LE	LE ■	LE ■	LE ■
London Liverpool Street [15] ⊖	d	15 50		15 55	16 00	16 02	16 10	16 13		16 18	16 20	16 30		16 35	16 40	16 48	16 50	16 55		17 00	17 02	17 10		17 13	17 18
Stratford [7] ⊖	d	15 58		16 02	16 08	16 09	16 18	16 20		16 25	16 28	16 38		16 42	16 48	16 55	16 58	17 02		17 08	17 09	17 18		17 20	17 25
Maryland	d																								
Forest Gate	d	16 01			16 11		16 21				16 31	16 41			16 51		17 01			17 11		17 21			
Manor Park	d	16 03			16 13		16 23				16 33	16 43			16 53		17 03			17 13		17 23			
Ilford [2]	d	16 06			16 16		16 26				16 36	16 46			16 56		17 06			17 16		17 26			
Seven Kings	d	16 08			16 18		16 28				16 38	16 48			16 58		17 08			17 18		17 28			
Goodmayes	d	16 10			16 20		16 30				16 40	16 50			17 00		17 10			17 20		17 30			
Chadwell Heath	d	16 12			16 22		16 32				16 42	16 52			17 02		17 12			17 22		17 32			
Romford	d	16 16			16 26		16 36	16 28			16 46	16 56			17 06		17 16			17 26		17 36		17 28	
Gidea Park [2]	d	16 20			16 30		16 40				16 50	17 00			17 10		17 20			17 30		17 40			
Harold Wood	d	16 23			16 33		16 43				16 53	17 03			17 13		17 23			17 33		17 43			
Brentwood	d	16 27			16 37		16 47				16 57	17 07			17 17		17 27			17 37		17 47			
Shenfield [3]	a	16 33		16 18	16 43	16 24	16 53	16 38		16 40	17 03	17 13		16 58	17 23	17 11	17 33	17 18		17 43	17 24	17 53		17 38	17 40
Shenfield [3]	d			16 19				16 39						16 59				17 19						17 39	
Billericay	d			16 25				16 45						17 05				17 25						17 45	
Wickford [2]	d		16 16	16 31				16 51					16 56	17 11				17 31					17 36	17 51	
Battlesbridge	d		16 20										17 00										17 40		
South Woodham Ferrers	d		16 24										17 04										17 44		
North Fambridge	d		16 31										17 11										17 51		
Althorne	d		16 36										17 16										17 56		
Burnham-on-Crouch	d		16 41										17 21										18 01		
Southminster	a		16 47										17 27										18 07		
Rayleigh	d			16 36				16 56						17 16				17 36						17 56	
Hockley	d			16 41				17 01						17 21				17 41						18 01	
Rochford	d			16 44				17 04						17 24				17 44						18 04	
Southend Airport ✈	d			16 47				17 07						17 27				17 47						18 07	
Prittlewell	d			16 50				17 10						17 30				17 50						18 10	
Southend Victoria	a			16 54				17 14						17 34				17 54						18 14	

		LE	LE	LE ■		LE ■	LE	LE ■	LE	LE ■	LE ■	LE	LE ■	LE		LE ■	LE ■	LE	LE	LE ■	LE ■	LE	LE ■	LE	
London Liverpool Street [15] ⊖	d	17 20	17 30	17 35		17 38	17 40	17 48	17 50		17 55	18 00	18 02	18 10		18 13	18 18	18 20	18 30		18 35	18 40	18 48	18 50	
Stratford [7] ⊖	d	17 28	17 38	17 42		17 45	17 48	17 55	17 58		18 02	18 08	18 09	18 18		18 20	18 25	18 28	18 38		18 42	18 48	18 55	18 58	
Maryland	d																								
Forest Gate	d	17 31	17 41				17 51		18 01			18 11		18 21				18 31	18 41			18 51		19 01	
Manor Park	d	17 33	17 43				17 53		18 03			18 13		18 23				18 33	18 43			18 53		19 03	
Ilford [2]	d	17 36	17 46				17 56		18 06			18 16		18 26				18 36	18 46			18 56		19 06	
Seven Kings	d	17 38	17 48				17 58		18 08			18 18		18 28				18 38	18 48			18 58		19 08	
Goodmayes	d	17 40	17 50				18 00		18 10			18 20		18 30				18 40	18 50			19 00		19 10	
Chadwell Heath	d	17 42	17 52				18 02		18 12			18 22		18 32				18 42	18 52			19 02		19 12	
Romford	d	17 46	17 56			17 53	18 06		18 16			18 26		18 36		18 28		18 46	18 56			19 06		19 16	
Gidea Park [2]	d	17 50	18 00				18 10		18 20			18 30		18 40				18 50	19 00			19 10		19 20	
Harold Wood	d	17 53	18 03				18 13		18 23			18 33		18 43				18 53	19 03			19 13		19 23	
Brentwood	d	17 57	18 07				18 17		18 27			18 37		18 47				18 57	19 07			19 17		19 27	
Shenfield [3]	a	18 03	18 13	17 58		18 02	18 23	18 11	18 33		18 18	18 43	18 24	18 53		18 38	18 40	19 03	19 13		18 58	19 23	19 11	19 33	
Shenfield [3]	d			17 59							18 19					18 39					18 59				
Billericay	d			18 05							18 25					18 45					19 05				
Wickford [2]	d			18 11						18 16	18 31					18 51				18 56	19 11				
Battlesbridge	d									18 20										19 00					
South Woodham Ferrers	d									18 24										19 04					
North Fambridge	d									18 31										19 11					
Althorne	d									18 36										19 16					
Burnham-on-Crouch	d									18 41										19 21					
Southminster	a									18 47										19 27					
Rayleigh	d			18 16							18 36					18 56					19 16				
Hockley	d			18 21							18 41					19 01					19 21				
Rochford	d			18 24							18 44					19 04					19 24				
Southend Airport ✈	d			18 27							18 47					19 07					19 27				
Prittlewell	d			18 30							18 50					19 10					19 30				
Southend Victoria	a			18 34							18 54					19 14					19 34				

London - Shenfield, Southminster and Southend Victoria

Network Diagram - see first Page of Table 5

		LE ■	LE	LE ■	LE	LE ■	LE ■	LE ■	LE	LE		LE ■	LE ■	LE	LE ■	LE	LE ■	LE ■	LE	LE ■		LE	LE ■	LE ■	LE
London Liverpool Street [15] ⊖	d	18 55	19 00	19 02	19 10		19 13	19 18	19 20	19 30		19 35	19 38	19 40	19 48	19 50		19 55	20 00	20 02		20 10	20 13	20 18	20 20
Stratford [7] ⊖	d	19 02	19 08	19 09	19 18		19 20	19 25	19 28	19 38		19 43	19 46	19 48	19 55	19 58		20 02	20 08	20 09		20 18	20 20	20 25	20 28
Maryland	d																								
Forest Gate	d		19 11		19 21				19 31	19 41				19 51		20 01			20 11			20 21			20 31
Manor Park	d		19 13		19 23				19 33	19 43				19 53		20 03			20 13			20 23			20 33
Ilford [2]	d		19 16		19 26				19 36	19 46				19 56		20 06			20 16			20 26			20 36
Seven Kings	d		19 18		19 28				19 38	19 48				19 58		20 08			20 18			20 28			20 38
Goodmayes	d		19 20		19 30				19 40	19 50				20 00		20 10			20 20			20 30			20 40
Chadwell Heath	d		19 22		19 32				19 42	19 52				20 02		20 12			20 22			20 32			20 42
Romford	d		19 26		19 36		19 28		19 46	19 56			19 54	20 06		20 16			20 26			20 36	20 28		20 46
Gidea Park [2]	d		19 30		19 40				19 50	20 00				20 10		20 20			20 30			20 40			20 50
Harold Wood	d		19 33		19 43				19 53	20 03				20 13		20 23			20 33			20 43			20 53
Brentwood	d		19 37		19 47				19 57	20 07				20 17		20 27			20 37			20 47			20 57
Shenfield [3]	a	19 18	19 43	19 24	19 53		19 38	19 40	20 03	20 13		19 59	20 03	20 23	20 11	20 33		20 18	20 43	20 24		20 53	20 38	20 40	21 03
Shenfield [3]	d	19 19					19 39					20 00						20 19					20 39		
Billericay	d	19 25					19 45					20 06						20 25					20 45		
Wickford [2]	d	19 31				19 36	19 51					20 12					20 16	20 31					20 51		
Battlesbridge	d					19 40											20 20								
South Woodham Ferrers	d					19 44											20 24								
North Fambridge	d					19 51											20 31								
Althorne	d					19 56											20 36								
Burnham-on-Crouch	d					20 01											20 41								
Southminster	a					20 07											20 47								
Rayleigh	d	19 36					19 56					20 17						20 36					20 56		
Hockley	d	19 41					20 01					20 22						20 41					21 01		
Rochford	d	19 44					20 04					20 25						20 44					21 04		
Southend Airport ✈	d	19 47					20 07					20 28						20 47					21 07		
Prittlewell	d	19 50					20 10					20 31						20 50					21 10		
Southend Victoria	a	19 54					20 14					20 35						20 54					21 14		

		LE	LE ■	LE ■	LE ■	LE		LE ■	LE	LE ■	LE ■	LE	LE ■	LE ■	LE ■	LE		LE ■	LE	LE ■	LE ■	LE ■	LE	LE ■	LE ■
London Liverpool Street [15] ⊖	d	20 30		20 35	20 38	20 40		20 48	20 50	20 55	21 02	21 05		21 13	21 18	21 20		21 35	21 35	21 38	21 42	21 48	21 50		21 50
Stratford [7] ⊖	d	20 38		20 42	20 45	20 48		20 55	20 58	21 02	21 09	21 13		21 20	21 25	21 28		21 42	21 43	21 45	21a51	21 55	21 58		22 02
Maryland	d																								
Forest Gate	d	20 41				20 51			21 01			21 16				21 31			21 46				22 01		
Manor Park	d	20 43				20 53			21 03			21 18				21 33			21 48				22 03		
Ilford [2]	d	20 46				20 56			21 06			21 21				21 36			21 51				22 06		
Seven Kings	d	20 48				20 58			21 08			21 23				21 38			21 53				22 08		
Goodmayes	d	20 50				21 00			21 10			21 25				21 40			21 55				22 10		
Chadwell Heath	d	20 52				21 02			21 12			21 27				21 42			21 57				22 12		
Romford	d	20 56			20 53	21 06			21 16			21 31		21 28		21 46			22 01	21 53			22 16		
Gidea Park [2]	d	21 00				21 10			21 20			21 35				21 50			22 05				22 20		
Harold Wood	d	21 03				21 13			21 23			21 38				21 53			22 08				22 23		
Brentwood	d	21 07				21 17			21 27			21 42				21 57			22 12				22 27		
Shenfield [3]	a	21 13		20 58	21 02	21 23		21 11	21 33	21 18	21 24	21 48		21 38	21 40	22 03		21 57	22 18	22 02		22 11	22 33		22 18
Shenfield [3]	d			20 59						21 19				21 39				21 59							22 19
Billericay	d			21 05						21 25				21 45				22 05							22 25
Wickford [2]	d		20 56	21 11						21 31			21 36	21 51				22 11						22 16	22 31
Battlesbridge	d		21 00										21 40											22 20	
South Woodham Ferrers	d		21 04										21 44											22 24	
North Fambridge	d		21 11										21 51											22 31	
Althorne	d		21 16										21 56											22 36	
Burnham-on-Crouch	d		21 21										22 01											22 41	
Southminster	a		21 27										22 07											22 47	
Rayleigh	d			21 16						21 36				21 56				22 16							22 36
Hockley	d			21 21						21 41				22 01				22 21							22 41
Rochford	d			21 24						21 44				22 04				22 24							22 44
Southend Airport ✈	d			21 27						21 47				22 07				22 27							22 47
Prittlewell	d			21 30						21 50				22 10				22 30							22 50
Southend Victoria	a			21 34						21 54				22 14				22 34							22 54

Table 5

Saturdays
28 July to 11 August

London - Shenfield, Southminster and Southend Victoria

Network Diagram - see first Page of Table 5

		LE 1	LE 1	LE	LE 1	LE 1	LE 1	LE	LE 1	LE 1	LE 1	LE	LE 1	LE 1	LE 1	LE	LE 1	LE	LE 1	LE 1	LE	LE 1
London Liverpool Street 15 ⊖	d	21 56	22 02	22 02	22 10	22 12	22 15	22 17	22 22		22 25	22 32	22 35	22 40	22 42	22 42	22 45	22 52	22 52	22 55	23 02	23 07
Stratford 7 ⊖	d	22a04	22 10	22 13	22 22	22a21	22 24	22 28	22a31		22 37	22 43	22 44	22 52	22a51	22 53	22 54	23 03	23a01	23 07	23 13	23 17
Maryland	d																					
Forest Gate	d			22 16				22 31				22 46				22 56		23 06			23 16	
Manor Park	d			22 18				22 33				22 48				22 58		23 08			23 18	
Ilford 2	d			22 21				22 36				22 51				23 01		23 11			23 21	
Seven Kings	d			22 23				22 38				22 53				23 03		23 13			23 23	
Goodmayes	d			22 25				22 40				22 55				23 05		23 15			23 25	
Chadwell Heath	d			22 27				22 42				22 57				23 07		23 17			23 27	
Romford	d			22 31				22 46				23 01				23 11		23 21			23 31	
Gidea Park 2	d			22 35				22 50				23 05				23 15		23 25			23 35	
Harold Wood	d			22 38				22 53				23 08				23 18		23 28			23 38	
Brentwood	d			22 42				22 57				23 12				23 22		23 32			23 42	
Shenfield 3	a		22 26	22 48	22 38		22 40	23 03			22 53	23 18	23 00	23 08		23 28	23 11	23 38		23 23	23 48	23 33
Shenfield 3	d				22 39						22 54			23 09						23 24		
Billericay	d				22 45						23 00			23 15						23 30		
Wickford 2	d				22 51					22 56	23 06			23 21						23 36		
Battlesbridge	d									23 00												
South Woodham Ferrers	d									23 04												
North Fambridge	d									23 11												
Althorne	d									23 16												
Burnham-on-Crouch	d									23 21												
Southminster	a									23 27												
Rayleigh	d				22 56						23 11			23 26						23 41		
Hockley	d				23 01						23 16			23 31						23 46		
Rochford	d				23 04						23 19			23 34						23 49		
Southend Airport ✈	d				23 07						23 22			23 37						23 52		
Prittlewell	d				23 10						23 25			23 40						23 55		
Southend Victoria	a				23 14						23 29			23 44						23 59		

		LE 1	LE 1	LE 1	LE	LE 1	LE	LE 1	LE	LE 1	LE 1	LE	LE 1	LE 1	LE	LE 1
London Liverpool Street 15 ⊖	d	23 10	23 12		23 12	23 15	23 22	23 25	23 32	23 35	23 40	23 42	23 42	23 45	23 52	23 55
Stratford 7 ⊖	d	23 22	23a21		23 23	23 25	23 33	23 37	23 43	23 45	23 52	23 53	23a51	23 54	00 03	00 07
Maryland	d															
Forest Gate	d				23 26		23 36		23 46			23 56			00 06	
Manor Park	d				23 28		23 38		23 48			23 58			00 08	
Ilford 2	d				23 31		23 41		23 51			00 01			00 11	
Seven Kings	d				23 33		23 43		23 53			00 03			00 13	
Goodmayes	d				23 35		23 45		23 55			00 05			00 15	
Chadwell Heath	d				23 37		23 47		23 57			00 07			00 17	
Romford	d				23 41		23 51		00 02			00 12			00 21	
Gidea Park 2	d				23 45		23 55		00 05			00 15			00 25	
Harold Wood	d				23 48		23 58		00 08			00 18			00 28	
Brentwood	d				23 52		00 02		00 12			00 22			00 32	
Shenfield 3	a	23 38			23 58	23 43	00 08	23 53	00 18	00 01	00 08	00 28		00 11	00 38	00 23
Shenfield 3	d	23 39						23 54			00 09					00 24
Billericay	d	23 45						23 59			00 15					00 30
Wickford 2	d	23 51		23 56				00 06			00 21					00 36
Battlesbridge	d			00 01												
South Woodham Ferrers	d			00 04												
North Fambridge	d			00 11												
Althorne	d			00 16												
Burnham-on-Crouch	d			00 21												
Southminster	a			00 27												
Rayleigh	d	23 56						00 11			00 26					00 41
Hockley	d	00 01						00 16			00 31					00 46
Rochford	d	00 04						00 19			00 34					00 49
Southend Airport ✈	d	00 07						00 22			00 37					00 52
Prittlewell	d	00 10						00 25			00 40					00 55
Southend Victoria	a	00 14						00 29			00 44					00 59

Table 5

Saturdays
18 August to 25 August

London - Shenfield, Southminster and Southend Victoria

Network Diagram - see first Page of Table 5

		LE 1	LE	LE	LE 1	LE 1	LE	LE	LE 1	LE 1	LE	LE	LE 1	LE 1	LE	LE 1	LE 1	LE 1	LE 1	LE 1	LE	LE 1	LE 1
London Liverpool Street 15 ⊖	d	23p15	23p20	23p35	23p45	23p48	23p50	00 01	00 15	00 18	00 20	00 32	00 46	00 50	00 55	05 21			05 28	05 34	05 40	05 51	06 02
Stratford 7 ⊖	d	23p22	23p27	23p42	23p52	23p55	23p57	00 08	00 22	00 25	00 27	00 39	00 53	00 57	01 02	05a30			05 35	05 41	05 47	06a00	06 09
Maryland	d		23p29	23p44			23p59	00 10			00 29	00 41			01 04						05 49		
Forest Gate	d		23p31	23p46			00 01	00 12			00 31	00 43			01 06						05 51		
Manor Park	d		23p33	23p48			00 03	00 14			00 33	00 45			01 08						05 53		
Ilford 2	d		23p36	23p51			00 06	00 17			00 36	00 48			01 11				05 40		05 56		
Seven Kings	d		23p38	23p53			00 08	00 19			00 38	00 50			01 13				05 42		05 58		
Goodmayes	d		23p40	23p55			00 10	00 21			00 40	00 52			01 15						06 00		
Chadwell Heath	d		23p42	23p57			00 12	00 23			00 42	00 54			01 17						06 02		
Romford	d		23p46	00 02			00 16	00 27	00 32		00 46	00 58		01 08	01 21				05 48	05 49	06 06		
Gidea Park 2	d		23p50	00 05			00 20	00a31			00 50	01a02	01 07		01 25				05 51		06 10		
Harold Wood	d		23p53	00 08			00 23				00 53				01 28				05 54		06 13		
Brentwood	d		23p57	00 12			00 27				00 57				01 32				05 59		06 17		
Shenfield 3	a	23p38	00 03	00 18	00 08	00 10	00 33		00 44	00 47	01 03		01 17	01 20	01 38				06 04	05 58	06 23		06 24
Shenfield 3	d	23p39			00 09				00 45					01 20					06 04				
Billericay	d	23p45			00 15				00 51					01 26					06 10				
Wickford 2	d	23p51			00 21				00 56					01 31			05 36	06 12	06 16				
Battlesbridge	d																05 40	06 16					
South Woodham Ferrers	d																05 44	06 20					
North Fambridge	d																05 51	06 31					
Althorne	d																05 56	06 36					
Burnham-on-Crouch	d																06 01	06 41					
Southminster	a																06 07	06 47					
Rayleigh	d	23p56			00 26				01 01					01 36					06 22				
Hockley	d	00 01			00 31				01 06					01 41					06 26				
Rochford	d	00 04			00 34				01 09					01 44					06 30				
Southend Airport ✈	d	00 07			00 37				01 12					01 47					06 32				
Prittlewell	d	00 10			00 40				01 15					01 50					06 35				
Southend Victoria	a	00 18			00 48				01 23					01 58					06 39				

		LE 1	LE	LE 1	LE 1	LE 1	LE 1	LE 1	LE	LE 1	LE 1	LE	LE 1	LE	LE 1	LE 1	LE 1	LE	LE	LE 1	LE 1	LE	LE 1
London Liverpool Street 15 ⊖	d	06 05	06 10	06 18	06 21		06 35	06 38	06 40	06 48	06 55	07 00	07 02	07 10		07 13	07 18	07 20	07 30	07 35	07 38	07 40	07 48
Stratford 7 ⊖	d	06 12	06 17	06 25	06a30		06 42	06 45	06 47	06 55	07 02	07 07	07 09	07 17		07 20	07 25	07 27	07 37	07 42	07 45	07 47	07 55
Maryland	d		06 19						06 49			07 09		07 19				07 29	07 39			07 49	
Forest Gate	d		06 21						06 51			07 11		07 21				07 31	07 41			07 51	
Manor Park	d		06 23						06 53			07 13		07 23				07 33	07 43			07 53	
Ilford 2	d		06 26						06 56			07 16		07 26				07 36	07 46			07 56	
Seven Kings	d		06 28						06 58			07 18		07 28				07 38	07 48			07 58	
Goodmayes	d		06 30						07 00			07 20		07 30				07 40	07 50			08 00	
Chadwell Heath	d		06 32						07 02			07 22		07 32				07 42	07 52			08 02	
Romford	d		06 36					06 53	07 06			07 26		07 36		07 28		07 46	07 56		07 53	08 06	
Gidea Park 2	d		06 40						07 10			07 30		07 40				07 50	08 00			08 10	
Harold Wood	d		06 43						07 13			07 33		07 43				07 53	08 03			08 13	
Brentwood	d		06 47						07 17			07 37		07 47				07 57	08 07			08 17	
Shenfield 3	a	06 30	06 53	06 40			06 58	07 02	07 23	07 11	07 18	07 43	07 24	07 53		07 38	07 40	08 03	08 13	07 58	08 02	08 23	08 11
Shenfield 3	d	06 30					06 59				07 19					07 39				07 59			
Billericay	d	06 36					07 05				07 25					07 45				08 05			
Wickford 2	d	06 43				06 56	07 11				07 31				07 36	07 51				08 11			
Battlesbridge	d					07 00									07 40								
South Woodham Ferrers	d					07 04									07 44								
North Fambridge	d					07 11									07 51								
Althorne	d					07 16									07 56								
Burnham-on-Crouch	d					07 21									08 01								
Southminster	a					07 27									08 07								
Rayleigh	d	06 48					07 16				07 36					07 56				08 16			
Hockley	d	06 53					07 21				07 41					08 01				08 21			
Rochford	d	06 56					07 24				07 44					08 04				08 24			
Southend Airport ✈	d	06 59					07 27				07 47					08 07				08 27			
Prittlewell	d	07 02					07 30				07 50					08 10				08 30			
Southend Victoria	a	07 05					07 34				07 54					08 14				08 34			

Table 5

Saturdays

18 August to 25 August

London - Shenfield, Southminster and Southend Victoria

Network Diagram - see first Page of Table 5

		LE		LE [1]	LE [1]	LE	LE [1]	LE	LE [1]	LE [1]	LE	LE		LE [1]	LE [1]	LE [1]	LE	LE [1]	LE	LE [1]	LE	LE [1]		LE	LE [1]
London Liverpool Street 15 ⊖	d	07 50			07 55	08 00	08 02	08 10	08 13	08 18	08 20	08 30			08 35	08 38	08 40	08 48	08 50	08 55	09 00	09 02		09 10	
Stratford 7 ⊖	d	07 57			08 02	08 07	08 09	08 17	08 20	08 25	08 27	08 37			08 42	08 45	08 47	08 55	08 57	09 02	09 07	09 09		09 17	
Maryland	d	07 59				08 09		08 19			08 29	08 39					08 49		08 59		09 09			09 19	
Forest Gate	d	08 01				08 11		08 21			08 31	08 41					08 51		09 01		09 11			09 21	
Manor Park	d	08 03				08 13		08 23			08 33	08 43					08 53		09 03		09 13			09 23	
Ilford 2	d	08 06				08 16		08 26			08 36	08 46					08 56		09 06		09 16			09 26	
Seven Kings	d	08 08				08 18		08 28			08 38	08 48					08 58		09 08		09 18			09 28	
Goodmayes	d	08 10				08 20		08 30			08 40	08 50					09 00		09 10		09 20			09 30	
Chadwell Heath	d	08 12				08 22		08 32			08 42	08 52					09 02		09 12		09 22			09 32	
Romford	d	08 16				08 26		08 36	08 28		08 46	08 56				08 53	09 06		09 16		09 26			09 36	
Gidea Park 2	d	08 20				08 30		08 40			08 50	09 00					09 10		09 20		09 30			09 40	
Harold Wood	d	08 23				08 33		08 43			08 53	09 03					09 13		09 23		09 33			09 43	
Brentwood	d	08 27				08 37		08 47			08 57	09 07					09 17		09 27		09 37			09 47	
Shenfield 3	a	08 33			08 18	08 43	08 24	08 53	08 38	08 40	09 03	09 13			08 58	09 02	09 23	09 11	09 33	09 18	09 43	09 24		09 53	
Shenfield 3	d				08 19				08 39						08 59					09 19					
Billericay	d				08 25				08 45						09 05					09 25					
Wickford 2	d			08 16	08 31				08 51					08 56	09 11					09 31					09 36
Battlesbridge	d			08 20										09 00											09 40
South Woodham Ferrers	d			08 24										09 04											09 44
North Fambridge	d			08 31										09 11											09 51
Althorne	d			08 36										09 16											09 56
Burnham-on-Crouch	d			08 41										09 21											10 01
Southminster	a			08 47										09 27											10 07
Rayleigh	d				08 36				08 56						09 16					09 36					
Hockley	d				08 41				09 01						09 21					09 41					
Rochford	d				08 44				09 04						09 24					09 44					
Southend Airport ✈	d				08 47				09 07						09 27					09 47					
Prittlewell	d				08 50				09 10						09 30					09 50					
Southend Victoria	a				08 54				09 14						09 34					09 54					

		LE [1]	LE [1]	LE	LE	LE [1]	LE [1]	LE		LE [1]	LE	LE [1]	LE [1]	LE	LE [1]	LE	LE [1]	LE [1]		LE	LE	LE [1]	LE [1]	LE [1]	LE
London Liverpool Street 15 ⊖	d	09 13	09 18	09 20	09 30	09 35	09 38	09 40		09 48	09 50		09 55	10 00	10 02	10 10	10 13	10 18		10 20	10 30		10 35	10 38	10 40
Stratford 7 ⊖	d	09 20	09 25	09 27	09 37	09 42	09 45	09 47		09 55	09 57		10 02	10 07	10 09	10 17	10 20	10 25		10 27	10 37		10 42	10 45	10 47
Maryland	d			09 29	09 39			09 49			09 59			10 09		10 19				10 29	10 39				10 49
Forest Gate	d			09 31	09 41			09 51			10 01			10 11		10 21				10 31	10 41				10 51
Manor Park	d			09 33	09 43			09 53			10 03			10 13		10 23				10 33	10 43				10 53
Ilford 2	d			09 36	09 46			09 56			10 06			10 16		10 26				10 36	10 46				10 56
Seven Kings	d			09 38	09 48			09 58			10 08			10 18		10 28				10 38	10 48				10 58
Goodmayes	d			09 40	09 50			10 00			10 10			10 20		10 30				10 40	10 50				11 00
Chadwell Heath	d			09 42	09 52			10 02			10 12			10 22		10 32				10 42	10 52				11 02
Romford	d	09 28		09 46	09 56		09 53	10 06			10 16			10 26		10 36	10 28			10 46	10 56			10 53	11 06
Gidea Park 2	d			09 50	10 00			10 10			10 20			10 30		10 40				10 50	11 00				11 10
Harold Wood	d			09 53	10 03			10 13			10 23			10 33		10 43				10 53	11 03				11 13
Brentwood	d			09 57	10 07			10 17			10 27			10 37		10 47				10 57	11 07				11 17
Shenfield 3	a	09 38	09 40	10 03	10 13	09 58	10 02	10 23		10 11	10 33		10 18	10 43	10 24	10 53	10 38	10 40		11 03	11 13		10 58	11 02	11 23
Shenfield 3	d	09 39				09 59							10 19				10 39						10 59		
Billericay	d	09 45				10 05							10 25				10 45						11 05		
Wickford 2	d	09 51				10 11						10 16	10 31				10 51					10 56	11 11		
Battlesbridge	d											10 20										11 00			
South Woodham Ferrers	d											10 24										11 04			
North Fambridge	d											10 31										11 11			
Althorne	d											10 36										11 16			
Burnham-on-Crouch	d											10 41										11 21			
Southminster	a											10 47										11 27			
Rayleigh	d	09 56				10 16							10 36				10 56						11 16		
Hockley	d	10 01				10 21							10 41				11 01						11 21		
Rochford	d	10 04				10 24							10 44				11 04						11 24		
Southend Airport ✈	d	10 07				10 27							10 47				11 07						11 27		
Prittlewell	d	10 10				10 30							10 50				11 10						11 30		
Southend Victoria	a	10 14				10 34							10 54				11 14						11 34		

Table 5

Saturdays

18 August to 25 August

London - Shenfield, Southminster and Southend Victoria

Network Diagram - see first Page of Table 5

		LE [1]	LE	LE [1]		LE	LE [1]	LE	LE [1]	LE [1]	LE [1]	LE	LE	LE [1]		LE [1]	LE	LE [1]	LE	LE [1]	LE [1]	LE	LE [1]	LE	
London Liverpool Street 15 ⊖	d	10 48	10 50	10 55		11 00	11 02	11 10		11 13	11 18	11 20	11 30	11 35		11 38	11 40	11 48	11 50		11 55	12 00	12 02	12 10	
Stratford 7 ⊖	d	10 55	10 57	11 02		11 07	11 09	11 17		11 20	11 25	11 27	11 37	11 42		11 45	11 47	11 55	11 57		12 02	12 07	12 09	12 17	
Maryland	d		10 59			11 09		11 19				11 29	11 39				11 49		11 59			12 09		12 19	
Forest Gate	d		11 01			11 11		11 21				11 31	11 41				11 51		12 01			12 11		12 21	
Manor Park	d		11 03			11 13		11 23				11 33	11 43				11 53		12 03			12 13		12 23	
Ilford 2	d		11 06			11 16		11 26				11 36	11 46				11 56		12 06			12 16		12 26	
Seven Kings	d		11 08			11 18		11 28				11 38	11 48				11 58		12 08			12 18		12 28	
Goodmayes	d		11 10			11 20		11 30				11 40	11 50				12 00		12 10			12 20		12 30	
Chadwell Heath	d		11 12			11 22		11 32				11 42	11 52				12 02		12 12			12 22		12 32	
Romford	d		11 16			11 26		11 36		11 28		11 46	11 56			11 53	12 06		12 16			12 26		12 36	
Gidea Park 2	d		11 20			11 30		11 40				11 50	12 00				12 10		12 20			12 30		12 40	
Harold Wood	d		11 23			11 33		11 43				11 53	12 03				12 13		12 23			12 33		12 43	
Brentwood	d		11 27			11 37		11 47				11 57	12 07				12 17		12 27			12 37		12 47	
Shenfield 3	a	11 11	11 33	11 18		11 43	11 24	11 53		11 38	11 40	12 03	12 13	11 58		12 02	12 23	12 11	12 33		12 18	12 43	12 24	12 53	
Shenfield 3	d			11 19						11 39				11 59							12 19				
Billericay	d			11 25						11 45				12 05							12 25				
Wickford 2	d			11 31					11 36	11 51				12 11						12 16	12 31				
Battlesbridge	d								11 40											12 20					
South Woodham Ferrers	d								11 44											12 24					
North Fambridge	d								11 51											12 31					
Althorne	d								11 56											12 36					
Burnham-on-Crouch	d								12 01											12 41					
Southminster	a								12 07											12 47					
Rayleigh	d			11 36						11 56				12 16							12 36				
Hockley	d			11 41						12 01				12 21							12 41				
Rochford	d			11 44						12 04				12 24							12 44				
Southend Airport ✈	d			11 47						12 07				12 27							12 47				
Prittlewell	d			11 50						12 10				12 30							12 50				
Southend Victoria	a			11 54						12 14				12 34							12 54				

		LE [1]	LE [1]	LE	LE	LE [1]	LE [1]	LE [1]	LE	LE [1]		LE	LE [1]	LE	LE [1]	LE	LE [1]	LE [1]	LE [1]	LE		LE	LE [1]	LE [1]	LE
London Liverpool Street 15 ⊖	d	12 13	12 18	12 20	12 30		12 35	12 38	12 40	12 48		12 50	12 55	13 00	13 02	13 10		13 13	13 18	13 20		13 30	13 35	13 38	13 40
Stratford 7 ⊖	d	12 20	12 25	12 27	12 37		12 42	12 45	12 47	12 55		12 57	13 02	13 07	13 09	13 17		13 20	13 25	13 27		13 37	13 42	13 45	13 47
Maryland	d			12 29	12 39				12 49			12 59		13 09		13 19				13 29		13 39			13 49
Forest Gate	d			12 31	12 41				12 51			13 01		13 11		13 21				13 31		13 41			13 51
Manor Park	d			12 33	12 43				12 53			13 03		13 13		13 23				13 33		13 43			13 53
Ilford 2	d			12 36	12 46				12 56			13 06		13 16		13 26				13 36		13 46			13 56
Seven Kings	d			12 38	12 48				12 58			13 08		13 18		13 28				13 38		13 48			13 58
Goodmayes	d			12 40	12 50				13 00			13 10		13 20		13 30				13 40		13 50			14 00
Chadwell Heath	d			12 42	12 52				13 02			13 12		13 22		13 32				13 42		13 52			14 02
Romford	d	12 28		12 46	12 56			12 53	13 06			13 16		13 26		13 36		13 28		13 46		13 56		13 53	14 06
Gidea Park 2	d			12 50	13 00				13 10			13 20		13 30		13 40				13 50		14 00			14 10
Harold Wood	d			12 53	13 03				13 13			13 23		13 33		13 43				13 53		14 03			14 13
Brentwood	d			12 57	13 07				13 17			13 27		13 37		13 47				13 57		14 07			14 17
Shenfield 3	a	12 38	12 40	13 03	13 13		12 58	13 02	13 23	13 11		13 33	13 18	13 43	13 24	13 53		13 38	13 40	14 03		14 13	13 58	14 02	14 23
Shenfield 3	d	12 39					12 59						13 19					13 39					13 59		
Billericay	d	12 45					13 05						13 25					13 45					14 05		
Wickford 2	d	12 51				12 56	13 11						13 31				13 36	13 51					14 11		
Battlesbridge	d					13 00											13 40								
South Woodham Ferrers	d					13 04											13 44								
North Fambridge	d					13 11											13 51								
Althorne	d					13 16											13 56								
Burnham-on-Crouch	d					13 21											14 01								
Southminster	a					13 27											14 07								
Rayleigh	d	12 56					13 16						13 36					13 56					14 16		
Hockley	d	13 01					13 21						13 41					14 01					14 21		
Rochford	d	13 04					13 24						13 44					14 04					14 24		
Southend Airport ✈	d	13 07					13 27						13 47					14 07					14 27		
Prittlewell	d	13 10					13 30						13 50					14 10					14 30		
Southend Victoria	a	13 14					13 34						13 54					14 14					14 34		

London - Shenfield, Southminster and Southend Victoria

Network Diagram - see first Page of Table 5

		LE 1	LE	LE 1	LE 1	LE		LE 1	LE	LE 1	LE 1	LE	LE	LE 1	LE 1	LE 1		LE	LE 1	LE	LE 1	LE	LE 1	LE	LE 1
London Liverpool Street 15 ⊖	d	13 48	13 50		13 55	14 00		14 02	14 10	14 13	14 18	14 20	14 30		14 35	14 38		14 40	14 48	14 50	14 55	15 00	15 02	15 10	
Stratford 7 ⊖	d	13 55	13 57		14 02	14 07		14 09	14 17	14 20	14 25	14 27	14 37		14 42	14 45		14 47	14 55	14 57	15 02	15 07	15 09	15 17	
Maryland	d		13 59			14 09			14 19			14 29	14 39					14 49		14 59		15 09		15 19	
Forest Gate	d		14 01			14 11			14 21			14 31	14 41					14 51		15 01		15 11		15 21	
Manor Park	d		14 03			14 13			14 23			14 33	14 43					14 53		15 03		15 13		15 23	
Ilford 2	d		14 06			14 16			14 26			14 36	14 46					14 56		15 06		15 16		15 26	
Seven Kings	d		14 08			14 18			14 28			14 38	14 48					14 58		15 08		15 18		15 28	
Goodmayes	d		14 10			14 20			14 30			14 40	14 50					15 00		15 10		15 20		15 30	
Chadwell Heath	d		14 12			14 22			14 32			14 42	14 52					15 02		15 12		15 22		15 32	
Romford	d		14 16			14 26			14 36	14 28		14 46	14 56			14 53		15 06		15 16		15 26		15 36	
Gidea Park 2	d		14 20			14 30			14 40			14 50	15 00					15 10		15 20		15 30		15 40	
Harold Wood	d		14 23			14 33			14 43			14 53	15 03					15 13		15 23		15 33		15 43	
Brentwood	d		14 27			14 37			14 47			14 57	15 07					15 17		15 27		15 37		15 47	
Shenfield 3	a	14 11	14 33		14 18	14 43		14 24	14 53	14 38	14 40	15 03	15 13		14 58	15 02		15 23	15 11	15 33	15 18	15 43	15 24	15 53	
Shenfield 3	d				14 19					14 39					14 59						15 19				
Billericay	d				14 25					14 45					15 05						15 25				
Wickford 2	d			14 16	14 31					14 51				14 56	15 11						15 31				15 36
Battlesbridge	d			14 20										15 00											15 40
South Woodham Ferrers	d			14 24										15 04											15 44
North Fambridge	d			14 31										15 11											15 51
Althorne	d			14 36										15 16											15 56
Burnham-on-Crouch	d			14 41										15 21											16 01
Southminster	a			14 47										15 27											16 07
Rayleigh	d				14 36					14 56					15 16						15 36				
Hockley	d				14 41					15 01					15 21						15 41				
Rochford	d				14 44					15 04					15 24						15 44				
Southend Airport ✈	d				14 47					15 07					15 27						15 47				
Prittlewell	d				14 50					15 10					15 30						15 50				
Southend Victoria	a				14 54					15 14					15 34						15 54				

		LE 1		LE 1	LE	LE	LE 1	LE 1	LE	LE 1	LE	LE 1		LE 1	LE	LE 1	LE	LE 1	LE 1	LE	LE	LE 1		LE 1	LE 1
London Liverpool Street 15 ⊖	d	15 13		15 18	15 20	15 30	15 35	15 38	15 40	15 48	15 50			15 55	16 00	16 02	16 10	16 13	16 18	16 20	16 30			16 35	16 38
Stratford 7 ⊖	d	15 20		15 25	15 27	15 37	15 42	15 45	15 47	15 55	15 57			16 02	16 07	16 09	16 17	16 20	16 25	16 27	16 37			16 42	16 45
Maryland	d				15 29	15 39			15 49		15 59				16 09		16 19			16 29	16 39				
Forest Gate	d				15 31	15 41			15 51		16 01				16 11		16 21			16 31	16 41				
Manor Park	d				15 33	15 43			15 53		16 03				16 13		16 23			16 33	16 43				
Ilford 2	d				15 36	15 46			15 56		16 06				16 16		16 26			16 36	16 46				
Seven Kings	d				15 38	15 48			15 58		16 08				16 18		16 28			16 38	16 48				
Goodmayes	d				15 40	15 50			16 00		16 10				16 20		16 30			16 40	16 50				
Chadwell Heath	d				15 42	15 52			16 02		16 12				16 22		16 32			16 42	16 52				
Romford	d	15 28			15 46	15 56		15 53	16 06		16 16				16 26		16 36	16 28		16 46	16 56				16 53
Gidea Park 2	d				15 50	16 00			16 10		16 20				16 30		16 40			16 50	17 00				
Harold Wood	d				15 53	16 03			16 13		16 23				16 33		16 43			16 53	17 03				
Brentwood	d				15 57	16 07			16 17		16 27				16 37		16 47			16 57	17 07				
Shenfield 3	a	15 38		15 40	16 03	16 13	15 58	16 02	16 23	16 11	16 33			16 18	16 43	16 24	16 53	16 38	16 40	17 03	17 13			16 58	17 02
Shenfield 3	d	15 39					15 59							16 19				16 39						16 59	
Billericay	d	15 45					16 05							16 25				16 45						17 05	
Wickford 2	d	15 51					16 11					16 16		16 31				16 51				16 56		17 11	
Battlesbridge	d											16 20										17 00			
South Woodham Ferrers	d											16 24										17 04			
North Fambridge	d											16 31										17 11			
Althorne	d											16 36										17 16			
Burnham-on-Crouch	d											16 41										17 21			
Southminster	a											16 47										17 27			
Rayleigh	d	15 56					16 16							16 36				16 56						17 16	
Hockley	d	16 01					16 21							16 41				17 01						17 21	
Rochford	d	16 04					16 24							16 44				17 04						17 24	
Southend Airport ✈	d	16 07					16 27							16 47				17 07						17 27	
Prittlewell	d	16 10					16 30							16 50				17 10						17 30	
Southend Victoria	a	16 14					16 34							16 54				17 14						17 34	

London - Shenfield, Southminster and Southend Victoria

Network Diagram - see first Page of Table 5

		LE	LE 1	LE	LE 1	LE	LE 1	LE		LE 1	LE 1	LE 1	LE	LE	LE 1	LE 1	LE	LE 1		LE	LE 1	LE 1	LE	LE 1	LE
London Liverpool Street 15 ⊖	d	16 40	16 48	16 50	16 55	17 00	17 02	17 10			17 13	17 18	17 20	17 30	17 35	17 38	17 40	17 48		17 50		17 55	18 00	18 02	18 10
Stratford 7 ⊖	d	16 47	16 55	16 57	17 02	17 07	17 09	17 17			17 20	17 25	17 27	17 37	17 42	17 45	17 47	17 55		17 57		18 02	18 07	18 09	18 17
Maryland	d	16 49		16 59		17 09		17 19					17 29	17 39			17 49			17 59			18 09		18 19
Forest Gate	d	16 51		17 01		17 11		17 21					17 31	17 41			17 51			18 01			18 11		18 21
Manor Park	d	16 53		17 03		17 13		17 23					17 33	17 43			17 53			18 03			18 13		18 23
Ilford 2	d	16 56		17 06		17 16		17 26					17 36	17 46			17 56			18 06			18 16		18 26
Seven Kings	d	16 58		17 08		17 18		17 28					17 38	17 48			17 58			18 08			18 18		18 28
Goodmayes	d	17 00		17 10		17 20		17 30					17 40	17 50			18 00			18 10			18 20		18 30
Chadwell Heath	d	17 02		17 12		17 22		17 32					17 42	17 52			18 02			18 12			18 22		18 32
Romford	d	17 06		17 16		17 26		17 36			17 28		17 46	17 56		17 53	18 06			18 16			18 26		18 36
Gidea Park 2	d	17 10		17 20		17 30		17 40					17 50	18 00			18 10			18 20			18 30		18 40
Harold Wood	d	17 13		17 23		17 33		17 43					17 53	18 03			18 13			18 23			18 33		18 43
Brentwood	d	17 17		17 27		17 37		17 47					17 57	18 07			18 17			18 27			18 37		18 47
Shenfield 3	a	17 23	17 11	17 33	17 18	17 43	17 24	17 53			17 38	17 40	18 03	18 13	17 58	18 02	18 23	18 11		18 33		18 18	18 43	18 24	18 53
Shenfield 3	d				17 19						17 39				17 59							18 19			
Billericay	d				17 25						17 45				18 05							18 25			
Wickford 2	d				17 31					17 36	17 51				18 11						18 16	18 31			
Battlesbridge	d									17 40											18 20				
South Woodham Ferrers	d									17 44											18 24				
North Fambridge	d									17 51											18 31				
Althorne	d									17 56											18 36				
Burnham-on-Crouch	d									18 01											18 41				
Southminster	a									18 07											18 47				
Rayleigh	d				17 36						17 56				18 16							18 36			
Hockley	d				17 41						18 01				18 21							18 41			
Rochford	d				17 44						18 04				18 24							18 44			
Southend Airport ✈	d				17 47						18 07				18 27							18 47			
Prittlewell	d				17 50						18 10				18 30							18 50			
Southend Victoria	a				17 54						18 14				18 34							18 54			

		LE 1	LE 1	LE		LE	LE 1	LE 1	LE 1	LE	LE 1	LE	LE 1	LE		LE 1	LE	LE 1	LE 1	LE 1	LE	LE	LE 1	LE 1	
London Liverpool Street 15 ⊖	d	18 13	18 18	18 20		18 30		18 35	18 38	18 40	18 48	18 50	18 55	19 00		19 02	19 10		19 13	19 18	19 20	19 30	19 32	19 35	
Stratford 7 ⊖	d	18 20	18 25	18 27		18 37		18 42	18 45	18 47	18 55	18 57	19 02	19 07		19 09	19 17		19 20	19 25	19 27	19 37	19 39	19 43	
Maryland	d			18 29		18 39				18 49		18 59		19 09			19 19				19 29	19 39			
Forest Gate	d			18 31		18 41				18 51		19 01		19 11			19 21				19 31	19 41			
Manor Park	d			18 33		18 43				18 53		19 03		19 13			19 23				19 33	19 43			
Ilford 2	d			18 36		18 46				18 56		19 06		19 16			19 26				19 36	19 46			
Seven Kings	d			18 38		18 48				18 58		19 08		19 18			19 28				19 38	19 48			
Goodmayes	d			18 40		18 50				19 00		19 10		19 20			19 30				19 40	19 50			
Chadwell Heath	d			18 42		18 52				19 02		19 12		19 22			19 32				19 42	19 52			
Romford	d	18 28		18 46		18 56			18 53	19 06		19 16		19 26			19 36		19 28		19 46	19 56			
Gidea Park 2	d			18 50		19 00				19 10		19 20		19 30			19 40				19 50	20 00			
Harold Wood	d			18 53		19 03				19 13		19 23		19 33			19 43				19 53	20 03			
Brentwood	d			18 57		19 07				19 17		19 27		19 37			19 47				19 57	20 07			
Shenfield 3	a	18 38	18 40	19 03		19 13		18 58	19 02	19 23	19 11	19 33	19 18	19 43		19 24	19 53		19 38	19 40	20 03	20 13	19 56	19 59	
Shenfield 3	d	18 39						18 59					19 19						19 39					20 00	
Billericay	d	18 45						19 05					19 25						19 45					20 06	
Wickford 2	d	18 51					18 56	19 11					19 31					19 36	19 51					20 12	
Battlesbridge	d						19 00											19 40							
South Woodham Ferrers	d						19 04											19 44							
North Fambridge	d						19 11											19 51							
Althorne	d						19 16											19 56							
Burnham-on-Crouch	d						19 21											20 01							
Southminster	a						19 27											20 07							
Rayleigh	d	18 56						19 16					19 36						19 56					20 17	
Hockley	d	19 01						19 21					19 41						20 01					20 22	
Rochford	d	19 04						19 24					19 44						20 04					20 25	
Southend Airport ✈	d	19 07						19 27					19 47						20 07					20 28	
Prittlewell	d	19 10						19 30					19 50						20 10					20 31	
Southend Victoria	a	19 14						19 34					19 54						20 14					20 35	

Table 5

Saturdays

18 August to 25 August

London - Shenfield, Southminster and Southend Victoria

Network Diagram - see first Page of Table 5

		LE 1	LE	LE 1	LE	LE 1	LE 1	LE	LE 1	LE		LE 1	LE 1	LE	LE	LE 1	LE 1	LE 1	LE	LE 1		LE	LE 1	LE 1	LE
London Liverpool Street 15 ⊖	d	19 38	19 40	19 48	19 50		19 55	20 00	20 02	20 10		20 13	20 18	20 20	20 30		20 35	20 38	20 40	20 48		20 50	20 55	21 02	21 05
Stratford 7 ⊖	d	19 46	19 47	19 55	19 57		20 02	20 07	20 09	20 17		20 20	20 25	20 27	20 37		20 42	20 45	20 47	20 55		20 57	21 02	21 09	21 12
Maryland	d		19 49		19 59			20 09		20 19				20 29	20 39				20 49			20 59			21 14
Forest Gate	d		19 51		20 01			20 11		20 21				20 31	20 41				20 51			21 01			21 16
Manor Park	d		19 53		20 03			20 13		20 23				20 33	20 43				20 53			21 03			21 18
Ilford 2	d		19 56		20 06			20 16		20 26				20 36	20 46				20 56			21 06			21 21
Seven Kings	d		19 58		20 08			20 18		20 28				20 38	20 48				20 58			21 08			21 23
Goodmayes	d		20 00		20 10			20 20		20 30				20 40	20 50				21 00			21 10			21 25
Chadwell Heath	d		20 02		20 12			20 22		20 32				20 42	20 52				21 02			21 12			21 27
Romford	d	19 54	20 06		20 16			20 26		20 36		20 28		20 46	20 56			20 53	21 06			21 16			21 31
Gidea Park 2	d		20 10		20 20			20 30		20 40				20 50	21 00				21 10			21 20			21 35
Harold Wood	d		20 13		20 23			20 33		20 43				20 53	21 03				21 13			21 23			21 38
Brentwood	d		20 17		20 27			20 37		20 47				20 57	21 07				21 17			21 27			21 42
Shenfield 3	a	20 03	20 23	20 11	20 33		20 18	20 43	20 24	20 53		20 38	20 40	21 03	21 13		20 58	21 02	21 23	21 11		21 33	21 18	21 24	21 48
Shenfield 3	d						20 19					20 39					20 59						21 19		
Billericay	d						20 25					20 45					21 05						21 25		
Wickford 2	d					20 16	20 31					20 51				20 56	21 11						21 31		
Battlesbridge	d					20 20										21 00									
South Woodham Ferrers	d					20 24										21 04									
North Fambridge	d					20 31										21 11									
Althorne	d					20 36										21 16									
Burnham-on-Crouch	d					20 41										21 21									
Southminster	a					20 47										21 27									
Rayleigh	d						20 36					20 56					21 16						21 36		
Hockley	d						20 41					21 01					21 21						21 41		
Rochford	d						20 44					21 04					21 24						21 44		
Southend Airport ✈	d						20 47					21 07					21 27						21 47		
Prittlewell	d						20 50					21 10					21 30						21 50		
Southend Victoria	a						20 54					21 14					21 34						21 54		

		LE 1	LE 1	LE 1	LE	LE 1		LE	LE 1	LE 1	LE	LE 1	LE 1	LE 1	LE	LE 1		LE 1	LE	LE	LE 1	LE 1	LE 1	LE	LE 1
London Liverpool Street 15 ⊖	d		21 13	21 18	21 20	21 35		21 35	21 38	21 48	21 50		21 55	22 02	22 05	22 13		22 18	22 20	22 35	22 38		22 45	22 50	23 02
Stratford 7 ⊖	d		21 20	21 25	21 27	21 42		21 42	21 45	21 55	21 57		22 02	22 09	22 12	22 20		22 25	22 27	22 42	22 45		22 52	22 57	23 09
Maryland	d				21 29			21 44			21 59				22 14				22 29	22 44				22 59	
Forest Gate	d				21 31			21 46			22 01				22 16				22 31	22 46				23 01	
Manor Park	d				21 33			21 48			22 03				22 18				22 33	22 48				23 03	
Ilford 2	d				21 36			21 51			22 06				22 21				22 36	22 51				23 06	
Seven Kings	d				21 38			21 53			22 08				22 23				22 38	22 53				23 08	
Goodmayes	d				21 40			21 55			22 10				22 25				22 40	22 55				23 10	
Chadwell Heath	d				21 42			21 57			22 12				22 27				22 42	22 57				23 12	
Romford	d		21 28		21 46			22 01	21 53		22 16				22 31	22 28			22 46	23 01	22 53			23 16	
Gidea Park 2	d				21 50			22 05			22 20				22 35				22 50	23 05				23 20	
Harold Wood	d				21 53			22 08			22 23				22 38				22 53	23 08				23 23	
Brentwood	d				21 57			22 12			22 27				22 42				22 57	23 12				23 27	
Shenfield 3	a		21 38	21 40	22 03	21 57		22 18	22 02	22 11	22 33		22 18	22 24	22 48	22 38		22 40	23 03	23 18	23 02		23 08	23 33	23 24
Shenfield 3	d		21 39			21 59							22 19			22 39							23 09		
Billericay	d		21 45			22 05							22 25			22 45							23 15		
Wickford 2	d	21 36	21 51			22 11						22 16	22 31			22 51						22 56	23 21		
Battlesbridge	d	21 40										22 20										23 00			
South Woodham Ferrers	d	21 44										22 24										23 04			
North Fambridge	d	21 51										22 31										23 11			
Althorne	d	21 56										22 36										23 16			
Burnham-on-Crouch	d	22 01										22 41										23 21			
Southminster	a	22 07										22 47										23 27			
Rayleigh	d		21 56			22 16							22 36			22 56							23 26		
Hockley	d		22 01			22 21							22 41			23 01							23 31		
Rochford	d		22 04			22 24							22 44			23 04							23 34		
Southend Airport ✈	d		22 07			22 27							22 47			23 07							23 37		
Prittlewell	d		22 10			22 30							22 50			23 10							23 40		
Southend Victoria	a		22 14			22 34							22 54			23 14							23 48		

Table 5

Saturdays

18 August to 25 August

London - Shenfield, Southminster and Southend Victoria

Network Diagram - see first Page of Table 5

		LE		LE 1	LE 1	LE	LE	LE 1	LE 1	LE
London Liverpool Street 15 ⊖	d	23 05		23 15	23 18	23 20	23 35	23 45	23 48	23 50
Stratford 7 ⊖	d	23 12		23 22	23 25	23 27	23 42	23 52	23 55	23 57
Maryland	d	23 14				23 29	23 44			23 59
Forest Gate	d	23 16				23 31	23 46			00 01
Manor Park	d	23 18				23 33	23 48			00 03
Ilford 2	d	23 21				23 36	23 51			00 06
Seven Kings	d	23 23				23 38	23 53			00 08
Goodmayes	d	23 25				23 40	23 55			00 10
Chadwell Heath	d	23 27				23 42	23 57			00 12
Romford	d	23 31				23 46	00 02			00 16
Gidea Park 2	d	23 35				23 50	00 05			00 20
Harold Wood	d	23 38				23 53	00 08			00 23
Brentwood	d	23 42				23 57	00 12			00 27
Shenfield 3	a	23 48		23 38	23 40	00 03	00 18	00 08	00 10	00 33
Shenfield 3	d			23 39				00 09		
Billericay	d			23 45				00 15		
Wickford 2	d			23 51				00 21		
Battlesbridge	d									
South Woodham Ferrers	d									
North Fambridge	d									
Althorne	d									
Burnham-on-Crouch	d									
Southminster	a									
Rayleigh	d			23 56				00 26		
Hockley	d			00 01				00 31		
Rochford	d			00 04				00 34		
Southend Airport ✈	d			00 07				00 37		
Prittlewell	d			00 10				00 40		
Southend Victoria	a			00 18				00 48		

Saturdays

1 September to 8 September

		LE 1	LE	LE 1	LE	LE 1	LE	LE 1	LE	LE 1		LE	LE	LE 1	LE 1	LE 1	LE	LE	LE 1	LE		LE 1	LE	LE	LE 1
London Liverpool Street 15 ⊖	d	23p10	23p22	23p25	23p32	23p40	23p42	23p45	23p52	23p55		00 02	00 12	00 12	00 15	00 18	00 22	00 32	00 40	00 42		00 46	00 52	01 02	01 10
Stratford 7 ⊖	d	23p22	23p32	23p37	23p42	23p52	23p52	23p54	00 02	00 07		00 12	00 22	00 24	00 27	00a27	00 32	00 42	00 52	00 52		01 00	01 02	01 12	01 22
Maryland	d		23p34		23p44		23p54		00 04			00 14	00 24				00 34	00 44		00 54			01 04	01 14	
Forest Gate	d		23p36		23p46		23p56		00 06			00 16	00 26				00 36	00 46		00 56			01 06	01 16	
Manor Park	d		23p38		23p48		23p58		00 08			00 18	00 28				00 38	00 48		00 58			01 08	01 18	
Ilford 2	d		23p41		23p51		00 01		00 11			00 21	00 31				00 41	00 51		01 01			01 11	01 21	
Seven Kings	d		23p43		23p53		00 03		00 13			00 23	00 33				00 43	00 53		01 03			01 13	01 23	
Goodmayes	d		23p45		23p55		00 05		00 15			00 25	00 35				00 45	00 55		01 05			01 15	01 25	
Chadwell Heath	d		23p47		23p57		00 07		00 17			00 27	00 37				00 47	00 57		01 07			01 17	01 27	
Romford	d		23p51		00 02		00 12		00 21			00 31	00 41				00 51	01 01		01 11			01 21	01 31	
Gidea Park 2	d		23p55		00 05		00 15		00 25			00 35	00 45				00 55	01 05		01 15			01 25	01 35	
Harold Wood	d		23p58		00 08		00 18		00 28			00 38	00 48				00 58	01 08		01 18			01 28	01 38	
Brentwood	d		00 02		00 12		00 22		00 32			00 42	00 52				01 02	01 12		01 22			01 32	01 42	
Shenfield 3	a	23p38	00 08	23p53	00 18	00 08	00 28	00 11	00 38	00 23		00 49	00 58	00 40	00 45		01 08	01 18	01 07	01 28		01 17	01 38	01 48	01 37
Shenfield 3	d	23p39		23p54		00 09				00 24					00 46				01 09						01 39
Billericay	d	23p45		23p59		00 15				00 30					00 52				01 15						01 45
Wickford 2	d	23p51		00 06		00 21				00 36					00 58				01 21						01 51
Battlesbridge	d																								
South Woodham Ferrers	d																								
North Fambridge	d																								
Althorne	d																								
Burnham-on-Crouch	d																								
Southminster	a																								
Rayleigh	d	23p56		00 11		00 26				00 41					01 03				01 26						01 56
Hockley	d	00 01		00 16		00 31				00 46					01 08				01 31						02 01
Rochford	d	00 04		00 19		00 34				00 49					01 11				01 34						02 04
Southend Airport ✈	d	00 07		00 22		00 37				00 52					01 14				01 37						02 07
Prittlewell	d	00 10		00 25		00 40				00 55					01 17				01 40						02 10
Southend Victoria	a	00 14		00 29		00 44				00 59					01 21				01 44						02 14

London - Shenfield, Southminster and Southend Victoria

Network Diagram - see first Page of Table 5

		LE	LE	LE	LE	LE		LE	LE	LE	LE	LE	LE	LE	LE	LE		LE	LE	LE	LE	LE	LE	LE	LE
										1	1	1	1	1		1		1			1	1	1	1	1
London Liverpool Street 15 ⊖	d	01 12	01 22	01 32	01 42	01 52		02 02	02 12	05 21			05 28	05 34	05 40	05 51		06 02	06 05	06 10	06 18	06 21		06 35	06 38
Stratford 7 ⊖	d	01 22	01 32	01 42	01 52	02 02		02 12	02 22	05a30			05 35	05 41	05 47	06a00		06 09	06 12	06 17	06 25	06a30		06 42	06 45
Maryland	d	01 24	01 34	01 44	01 54	02 04		02 14	02 24						05 49					06 19					
Forest Gate	d	01 26	01 36	01 46	01 56	02 06		02 16	02 26						05 51					06 21					
Manor Park	d	01 28	01 38	01 48	01 58	02 08		02 18	02 28						05 53					06 23					
Ilford 2	d	01 31	01 41	01 51	02 01	02 11		02 21	02 31				05 40		05 56					06 26					
Seven Kings	d	01 33	01 43	01 53	02 03	02 13		02 23	02 33				05 42		05 58					06 28					
Goodmayes	d	01 35	01 45	01 55	02 05	02 15		02 25	02 35						06 00					06 30					
Chadwell Heath	d	01 37	01 47	01 57	02 07	02 17		02 27	02 37						06 02					06 32					
Romford	d	01 41	01 51	02 01	02 11	02 21		02 31	02 41				05 48	05 49	06 06					06 36					06 53
Gidea Park 2	d	01 45	01 55	02a05	02 15	02a25		02 35	02a45				05 51		06 10					06 40					
Harold Wood	d	01 48	01 58		02 18			02 38					05 54		06 13					06 43					
Brentwood	d	01 52	02 02		02 22			02 42					05 59		06 17					06 47					
Shenfield 3	a	01 58	02 08		02 28			02 48					06 04	05 58	06 23			06 24	06 30	06 53	06 40			06 58	07 02
Shenfield 3	d												06 04						06 30					06 59	
Billericay	d												06 10						06 36					07 05	
Wickford 2	d										05 36	06 12	06 16						06 43				06 56	07 11	
Battlesbridge	d										05 40	06 16											07 00		
South Woodham Ferrers	d										05 44	06 20											07 04		
North Fambridge	d										05 51	06 31											07 11		
Althorne	d										05 56	06 36											07 16		
Burnham-on-Crouch	d										06 01	06 41											07 21		
Southminster	a										06 07	06 47											07 27		
Rayleigh	d												06 22						06 48					07 16	
Hockley	d												06 26						06 53					07 21	
Rochford	d												06 30						06 56					07 24	
Southend Airport ✈	d												06 32						06 59					07 27	
Prittlewell	d												06 35						07 02					07 30	
Southend Victoria	a												06 39						07 05					07 34	

		LE		LE	LE	LE	LE	LE	LE	LE	LE	LE		LE	LE	LE	LE	LE	LE	LE	LE	LE		LE	LE
				1	1		1		1		1				1	1		1		1	1			1	
London Liverpool Street 15 ⊖	d	06 40		06 48	06 55	07 00	07 02	07 10		07 13	07 18	07 20		07 30	07 35	07 38	07 40	07 48	07 50		07 55	08 00		08 02	08 10
Stratford 7 ⊖	d	06 47		06 55	07 02	07 07	07 09	07 17		07 20	07 25	07 27		07 37	07 42	07 45	07 47	07 55	07 57		08 02	08 07		08 09	08 17
Maryland	d	06 49				07 09		07 19				07 29		07 39			07 49		07 59			08 09			08 19
Forest Gate	d	06 51				07 11		07 21				07 31		07 41			07 51		08 01			08 11			08 21
Manor Park	d	06 53				07 13		07 23				07 33		07 43			07 53		08 03			08 13			08 23
Ilford 2	d	06 56				07 16		07 26				07 36		07 46			07 56		08 06			08 16			08 26
Seven Kings	d	06 58				07 18		07 28				07 38		07 48			07 58		08 08			08 18			08 28
Goodmayes	d	07 00				07 20		07 30				07 40		07 50			08 00		08 10			08 20			08 30
Chadwell Heath	d	07 02				07 22		07 32				07 42		07 52			08 02		08 12			08 22			08 32
Romford	d	07 06				07 26		07 36		07 28		07 46		07 56		07 53	08 06		08 16			08 26			08 36
Gidea Park 2	d	07 10				07 30		07 40				07 50		08 00			08 10		08 20			08 30			08 40
Harold Wood	d	07 13				07 33		07 43				07 53		08 03			08 13		08 23			08 33			08 43
Brentwood	d	07 17				07 37		07 47				07 57		08 07			08 17		08 27			08 37			08 47
Shenfield 3	a	07 23		07 11	07 18	07 43	07 24	07 53		07 39	07 40	08 03		08 13	07 58	08 02	08 23	08 11	08 33		08 18	08 43		08 24	08 53
Shenfield 3	d				07 19					07 39					07 59						08 19				
Billericay	d				07 25					07 45					08 05						08 25				
Wickford 2	d				07 31				07 36	07 51					08 11					08 16	08 31				
Battlesbridge	d								07 40											08 20					
South Woodham Ferrers	d								07 44											08 24					
North Fambridge	d								07 51											08 31					
Althorne	d								07 56											08 36					
Burnham-on-Crouch	d								08 01											08 41					
Southminster	a								08 07											08 47					
Rayleigh	d				07 36					07 57					08 16						08 36				
Hockley	d				07 41					08 01					08 21						08 41				
Rochford	d				07 44					08 05					08 24						08 44				
Southend Airport ✈	d				07 47					08 07					08 27						08 47				
Prittlewell	d				07 50					08 10					08 30						08 50				
Southend Victoria	a				07 54					08 14					08 34						08 54				

London - Shenfield, Southminster and Southend Victoria

Network Diagram - see first Page of Table 5

		LE	LE	LE	LE	LE	LE	LE		LE	LE	LE	LE	LE	LE	LE	LE	LE		LE	LE	LE	LE	LE	LE
		1	1			1	1	1			1		1		1		1	1		1			1	1	
London Liverpool Street 15 ⊖	d	08 13	08 18	08 20	08 30		08 35	08 38		08 40	08 48	08 50	08 55	09 00	09 02	09 10		09 13		09 18	09 20	09 30	09 35	09 38	09 40
Stratford 7 ⊖	d	08 20	08 25	08 27	08 37		08 42	08 45		08 47	08 55	08 57	09 02	09 07	09 09	09 17		09 20		09 25	09 27	09 37	09 42	09 45	09 47
Maryland	d			08 29	08 39					08 49		08 59		09 09		09 19					09 29	09 39			09 49
Forest Gate	d			08 31	08 41					08 51		09 01		09 11		09 21					09 31	09 41			09 51
Manor Park	d			08 33	08 43					08 53		09 03		09 13		09 23					09 33	09 43			09 53
Ilford 2	d			08 36	08 46					08 56		09 06		09 16		09 26					09 36	09 46			09 56
Seven Kings	d			08 38	08 48					08 58		09 08		09 18		09 28					09 38	09 48			09 58
Goodmayes	d			08 40	08 50					09 00		09 10		09 20		09 30					09 40	09 50			10 00
Chadwell Heath	d			08 42	08 52					09 02		09 12		09 22		09 32					09 42	09 52			10 02
Romford	d	08 28		08 46	08 56			08 53		09 06		09 16		09 26		09 36		09 28			09 46	09 56		09 53	10 06
Gidea Park 2	d			08 50	09 00					09 10		09 20		09 30		09 40					09 50	10 00			10 10
Harold Wood	d			08 53	09 03					09 13		09 23		09 33		09 43					09 53	10 03			10 13
Brentwood	d			08 57	09 07					09 17		09 27		09 37		09 47					09 57	10 07			10 17
Shenfield 3	a	08 38	08 40	09 03	09 13		08 58	09 02		09 23	09 11	09 33	09 18	09 43	09 24	09 53		09 38		09 40	10 03	10 13	09 58	10 02	10 23
Shenfield 3	d	08 39					08 59						09 19					09 39					09 59		
Billericay	d	08 45					09 05						09 25					09 45					10 05		
Wickford 2	d	08 51				08 56	09 11						09 31				09 36	09 51					10 11		
Battlesbridge	d					09 00											09 40								
South Woodham Ferrers	d					09 04											09 44								
North Fambridge	d					09 11											09 51								
Althorne	d					09 16											09 56								
Burnham-on-Crouch	d					09 21											10 01								
Southminster	a					09 27											10 07								
Rayleigh	d	08 56					09 16						09 36					09 56					10 16		
Hockley	d	09 01					09 21						09 41					10 01					10 21		
Rochford	d	09 04					09 24						09 44					10 04					10 24		
Southend Airport ✈	d	09 07					09 27						09 47					10 07					10 27		
Prittlewell	d	09 10					09 30						09 50					10 10					10 30		
Southend Victoria	a	09 14					09 34						09 54					10 14					10 34		

		LE	LE	LE		LE	LE	LE	LE	LE	LE	LE	LE	LE		LE	LE	LE	LE	LE	LE	LE	LE	LE	
		1		1		1		1		1	1			1		1	1		1		1		1		
London Liverpool Street 15 ⊖	d	09 48	09 50			09 55	10 00	10 02	10 10	10 13	10 18	10 20	10 30			10 35	10 38	10 40	10 48	10 50	10 55	11 00	11 02	11 10	
Stratford 7 ⊖	d	09 55	09 57			10 02	10 07	10 09	10 17	10 20	10 25	10 27	10 37			10 42	10 45	10 47	10 55	10 57	11 02	11 07	11 09	11 17	
Maryland	d		09 59				10 09		10 19			10 29	10 39					10 49		10 59		11 09		11 19	
Forest Gate	d		10 01				10 11		10 21			10 31	10 41					10 51		11 01		11 11		11 21	
Manor Park	d		10 03				10 13		10 23			10 33	10 43					10 53		11 03		11 13		11 23	
Ilford 2	d		10 06				10 16		10 26			10 36	10 46					10 56		11 06		11 16		11 26	
Seven Kings	d		10 08				10 18		10 28			10 38	10 48					10 58		11 08		11 18		11 28	
Goodmayes	d		10 10				10 20		10 30			10 40	10 50					11 00		11 10		11 20		11 30	
Chadwell Heath	d		10 12				10 22		10 32			10 42	10 52					11 02		11 12		11 22		11 32	
Romford	d		10 16				10 26		10 36	10 28		10 46	10 56					11 06		11 16		11 26		11 36	
Gidea Park 2	d		10 20				10 30		10 40			10 50	11 00					11 10		11 20		11 30		11 40	
Harold Wood	d		10 23				10 33		10 43			10 53	11 03					11 13		11 23		11 33		11 43	
Brentwood	d		10 27				10 37		10 47			10 57	11 07					11 17		11 27		11 37		11 47	
Shenfield 3	a	10 11	10 33			10 18	10 43	10 24	10 53	10 38	10 40	11 03	11 13			10 58	11 00	11 23	11 11	11 33	11 18	11 43	11 24	11 53	
Shenfield 3	d					10 19				10 39						10 59					11 19				
Billericay	d					10 25				10 45						11 05					11 25				
Wickford 2	d			10 16		10 31				10 51				10 56		11 11					11 31				
Battlesbridge	d			10 20										11 00											
South Woodham Ferrers	d			10 24										11 04											
North Fambridge	d			10 31										11 11											
Althorne	d			10 36										11 16											
Burnham-on-Crouch	d			10 41										11 21											
Southminster	a			10 47										11 27											
Rayleigh	d					10 36				10 56						11 16					11 36				
Hockley	d					10 41				11 01						11 21					11 41				
Rochford	d					10 44				11 04						11 24					11 44				
Southend Airport ✈	d					10 47				11 07						11 27					11 47				
Prittlewell	d					10 50				11 10						11 30					11 50				
Southend Victoria	a					10 54				11 14						11 34					11 54				

Table 5

Saturdays

1 September to 8 September

London - Shenfield, Southminster and Southend Victoria

Network Diagram - see first Page of Table 5

		LE 1	LE 1	LE 1	LE	LE	LE 1	LE 1	LE	LE 1		LE	LE 1	LE 1	LE	LE 1	LE	LE 1	LE 1	LE		LE	LE 1	LE 1	LE
London Liverpool Street 15 ⊖	d		11 13	11 18	11 20	11 30	11 35	11 38	11 40	11 48		11 50		11 55	12 00	12 02	12 10	12 13	12 18	12 20		12 30		12 35	12 40
Stratford 7 ⊖	d		11 20	11 25	11 27	11 37	11 42	11 45	11 47	11 55		11 57		12 02	12 07	12 09	12 17	12 20	12 25	12 27		12 37		12 42	12 47
Maryland	d				11 29	11 39			11 49			11 59			12 09		12 19			12 29		12 39			12 49
Forest Gate	d				11 31	11 41			11 51			12 01			12 11		12 21			12 31		12 41			12 51
Manor Park	d				11 33	11 43			11 53			12 03			12 13		12 23			12 33		12 43			12 53
Ilford 2	d				11 36	11 46			11 56			12 06			12 16		12 26			12 36		12 46			12 56
Seven Kings	d				11 38	11 48			11 58			12 08			12 18		12 28			12 38		12 48			12 58
Goodmayes	d				11 40	11 50			12 00			12 10			12 20		12 30			12 40		12 50			13 00
Chadwell Heath	d				11 42	11 52			12 02			12 12			12 22		12 32			12 42		12 52			13 02
Romford	d		11 28		11 46	11 56		11 53	12 06			12 16			12 26		12 36	12 28		12 46		12 56			13 06
Gidea Park 2	d				11 50	12 00			12 10			12 20			12 30		12 40			12 50		13 00			13 10
Harold Wood	d				11 53	12 03			12 13			12 23			12 33		12 43			12 53		13 03			13 13
Brentwood	d				11 57	12 07			12 17			12 27			12 37		12 47			12 57		13 07			13 17
Shenfield 3	a		11 38	11 40	12 03	12 13	11 58	12 02	12 23	12 11		12 33		12 18	12 43	12 24	12 53	12 38	12 40	13 03		13 13		12 58	13 23
Shenfield 3	d		11 39				11 59							12 19				12 39						12 59	
Billericay	d		11 45				12 05							12 25				12 45						13 05	
Wickford 2	d	11 36	11 51				12 11						12 16	12 31				12 51					12 56	13 11	
Battlesbridge	d	11 40											12 20										13 00		
South Woodham Ferrers	d	11 44											12 24										13 04		
North Fambridge	d	11 51											12 31										13 11		
Althorne	d	11 56											12 36										13 16		
Burnham-on-Crouch	d	12 01											12 41										13 21		
Southminster	a	12 07											12 47										13 27		
Rayleigh	d		11 56				12 16							12 36				12 56						13 16	
Hockley	d		12 01				12 21							12 41				13 01						13 21	
Rochford	d		12 04				12 24							12 44				13 04						13 24	
Southend Airport ✈	d		12 07				12 27							12 47				13 07						13 27	
Prittlewell	d		12 10				12 30							12 50				13 10						13 30	
Southend Victoria	a		12 14				12 34							12 54				13 14						13 34	

		LE 1	LE	LE 1	LE	LE 1		LE	LE 1	LE 1	LE 1	LE	LE	LE 1	LE 1	LE		LE 1	LE	LE 1	LE 1	LE	LE 1	LE	LE 1
London Liverpool Street 15 ⊖	d	12 48	12 50	12 55	13 00	13 02		13 10		13 13	13 18	13 20	13 30	13 35	13 38	13 40		13 48	13 50		13 55	14 00	14 02	14 10	14 13
Stratford 7 ⊖	d	12 55	12 57	13 02	13 07	13 09		13 17		13 20	13 25	13 27	13 37	13 42	13 45	13 47		13 55	13 57		14 02	14 07	14 09	14 17	14 20
Maryland	d		12 59		13 09			13 19				13 29	13 39			13 49			13 59			14 09		14 19	
Forest Gate	d		13 01		13 11			13 21				13 31	13 41			13 51			14 01			14 11		14 21	
Manor Park	d		13 03		13 13			13 23				13 33	13 43			13 53			14 03			14 13		14 23	
Ilford 2	d		13 06		13 16			13 26				13 36	13 46			13 56			14 06			14 16		14 26	
Seven Kings	d		13 08		13 18			13 28				13 38	13 48			13 58			14 08			14 18		14 28	
Goodmayes	d		13 10		13 20			13 30				13 40	13 50			14 00			14 10			14 20		14 30	
Chadwell Heath	d		13 12		13 22			13 32				13 42	13 52			14 02			14 12			14 22		14 32	
Romford	d		13 16		13 26			13 36		13 28		13 46	13 56		13 53	14 06			14 16			14 26		14 36	14 28
Gidea Park 2	d		13 20		13 30			13 40				13 50	14 00			14 10			14 20			14 30		14 40	
Harold Wood	d		13 23		13 33			13 43				13 53	14 03			14 13			14 23			14 33		14 43	
Brentwood	d		13 27		13 37			13 47				13 57	14 07			14 17			14 27			14 37		14 47	
Shenfield 3	a	13 11	13 33	13 18	13 43	13 24		13 53		13 38	13 40	14 03	14 13	13 58	14 02	14 23		14 11	14 33		14 18	14 43	14 24	14 53	14 38
Shenfield 3	d			13 19						13 39				13 59							14 19				14 39
Billericay	d			13 25						13 45				14 05							14 25				14 45
Wickford 2	d			13 31					13 36	13 51				14 11						14 16	14 31				14 51
Battlesbridge	d								13 40											14 20					
South Woodham Ferrers	d								13 44											14 24					
North Fambridge	d								13 51											14 31					
Althorne	d								13 56											14 36					
Burnham-on-Crouch	d								14 01											14 41					
Southminster	a								14 07											14 47					
Rayleigh	d			13 36						13 56				14 16							14 36				14 56
Hockley	d			13 41						14 01				14 21							14 41				15 01
Rochford	d			13 44						14 04				14 24							14 44				15 04
Southend Airport ✈	d			13 47						14 07				14 27							14 47				15 07
Prittlewell	d			13 50						14 10				14 30							14 50				15 10
Southend Victoria	a			13 54						14 14				14 34							14 54				15 14

Table 5

Saturdays

1 September to 8 September

London - Shenfield, Southminster and Southend Victoria

Network Diagram - see first Page of Table 5

		LE 1		LE	LE	LE 1	LE 1	LE	LE 1	LE	LE 1	LE		LE 1	LE	LE 1	LE 1	LE 1	LE	LE	LE 1	LE 1		LE	LE 1
London Liverpool Street 15 ⊖	d	14 18		14 20	14 30		14 35	14 40	14 48	14 50	14 55	15 00		15 02	15 10		15 13	15 18	15 20	15 30	15 35	15 38		15 40	15 48
Stratford 7 ⊖	d	14 25		14 27	14 37		14 42	14 47	14 55	14 57	15 02	15 07		15 09	15 17		15 20	15 25	15 27	15 37	15 42	15 45		15 47	15 55
Maryland	d			14 29	14 39			14 49		14 59		15 09			15 19				15 29	15 39				15 49	
Forest Gate	d			14 31	14 41			14 51		15 01		15 11			15 21				15 31	15 41				15 51	
Manor Park	d			14 33	14 43			14 53		15 03		15 13			15 23				15 33	15 43				15 53	
Ilford 2	d			14 36	14 46			14 56		15 06		15 16			15 26				15 36	15 46				15 56	
Seven Kings	d			14 38	14 48			14 58		15 08		15 18			15 28				15 38	15 48				15 58	
Goodmayes	d			14 40	14 50			15 00		15 10		15 20			15 30				15 40	15 50				16 00	
Chadwell Heath	d			14 42	14 52			15 02		15 12		15 22			15 32				15 42	15 52				16 02	
Romford	d			14 46	14 56			15 06		15 16		15 26			15 36		15 28		15 46	15 56		15 53		16 06	
Gidea Park 2	d			14 50	15 00			15 10		15 20		15 30			15 40				15 50	16 00				16 10	
Harold Wood	d			14 53	15 03			15 13		15 23		15 33			15 43				15 53	16 03				16 13	
Brentwood	d			14 57	15 07			15 17		15 27		15 37			15 47				15 57	16 07				16 17	
Shenfield 3	a	14 40		15 03	15 13		14 58	15 23	15 11	15 33	15 18	15 43		15 24	15 53		15 38	15 40	16 03	16 13	15 58	16 02		16 23	16 11
Shenfield 3	d						14 59				15 19						15 39				15 59				
Billericay	d						15 05				15 25						15 45				16 05				
Wickford 2	d					14 56	15 11				15 31					15 36	15 51				16 11				
Battlesbridge	d					15 00										15 40									
South Woodham Ferrers	d					15 04										15 44									
North Fambridge	d					15 11										15 51									
Althorne	d					15 16										15 56									
Burnham-on-Crouch	d					15 21										16 01									
Southminster	a					15 27										16 07									
Rayleigh	d						15 16				15 36						15 56				16 16				
Hockley	d						15 21				15 41						16 01				16 21				
Rochford	d						15 24				15 44						16 04				16 24				
Southend Airport ✈	d						15 27				15 47						16 07				16 27				
Prittlewell	d						15 30				15 50						16 10				16 30				
Southend Victoria	a						15 34				15 54						16 14				16 34				

		LE	LE 1	LE 1	LE	LE 1	LE	LE 1		LE 1	LE	LE	LE 1	LE 1	LE	LE 1	LE	LE 1		LE	LE 1	LE	LE 1	LE 1	LE 1
London Liverpool Street 15 ⊖	d	15 50		15 55	16 00	16 02	16 10	16 13		16 18	16 20	16 30		16 35	16 40	16 48	16 50	16 55		17 00	17 02	17 10		17 13	17 18
Stratford 7 ⊖	d	15 57		16 02	16 07	16 09	16 17	16 20		16 25	16 27	16 37		16 42	16 47	16 55	16 57	17 02		17 07	17 09	17 17		17 20	17 25
Maryland	d	15 59			16 09		16 19				16 29	16 39			16 49		16 59			17 09		17 19			
Forest Gate	d	16 01			16 11		16 21				16 31	16 41			16 51		17 01			17 11		17 21			
Manor Park	d	16 03			16 13		16 23				16 33	16 43			16 53		17 03			17 13		17 23			
Ilford 2	d	16 06			16 16		16 26				16 36	16 46			16 56		17 06			17 16		17 26			
Seven Kings	d	16 08			16 18		16 28				16 38	16 48			16 58		17 08			17 18		17 28			
Goodmayes	d	16 10			16 20		16 30				16 40	16 50			17 00		17 10			17 20		17 30			
Chadwell Heath	d	16 12			16 22		16 32				16 42	16 52			17 02		17 12			17 22		17 32			
Romford	d	16 16			16 26		16 36	16 28			16 46	16 56			17 06		17 16			17 26		17 36		17 28	
Gidea Park 2	d	16 20			16 30		16 40				16 50	17 00			17 10		17 20			17 30		17 40			
Harold Wood	d	16 23			16 33		16 43				16 53	17 03			17 13		17 23			17 33		17 43			
Brentwood	d	16 27			16 37		16 47				16 57	17 07			17 17		17 27			17 37		17 47			
Shenfield 3	a	16 33		16 18	16 43	16 24	16 53	16 38		16 40	17 03	17 13		16 58	17 23	17 11	17 33	17 18		17 43	17 24	17 53		17 38	17 40
Shenfield 3	d			16 19				16 39						16 59				17 19						17 39	
Billericay	d			16 25				16 45						17 05				17 25						17 45	
Wickford 2	d		16 16	16 31				16 51					16 56	17 11				17 31					17 36	17 51	
Battlesbridge	d		16 20										17 00										17 40		
South Woodham Ferrers	d		16 24										17 04										17 44		
North Fambridge	d		16 31										17 11										17 51		
Althorne	d		16 36										17 16										17 56		
Burnham-on-Crouch	d		16 41										17 21										18 01		
Southminster	a		16 47										17 27										18 07		
Rayleigh	d			16 36				16 56						17 16				17 36						17 56	
Hockley	d			16 41				17 01						17 21				17 41						18 01	
Rochford	d			16 44				17 04						17 24				17 44						18 04	
Southend Airport ✈	d			16 47				17 07						17 27				17 47						18 07	
Prittlewell	d			16 50				17 10						17 30				17 50						18 10	
Southend Victoria	a			16 54				17 14						17 34				17 54						18 14	

Saturdays

1 September to 8 September

London - Shenfield, Southminster and Southend Victoria

Network Diagram - see first Page of Table 5

		LE	LE	LE 1	LE 1	LE	LE 1	LE	LE 1	LE 1	LE	LE 1	LE	LE 1	LE 1	LE	LE	LE 1	LE 1	LE	LE 1	LE
London Liverpool Street 15 ⊖	d	17 20	17 30	17 35	17 38	17 40	17 48	17 50		17 55	18 00	18 02	18 10	18 13	18 18	18 20	18 30		18 35	18 40	18 48	18 50
Stratford 7 ⊖	d	17 27	17 37	17 42	17 45	17 47	17 55	17 57		18 02	18 07	18 09	18 17	18 20	18 25	18 27	18 37		18 42	18 47	18 55	18 57
Maryland	d	17 29	17 39			17 49		17 59			18 09		18 19			18 29	18 39			18 49		18 59
Forest Gate	d	17 31	17 41			17 51		18 01			18 11		18 21			18 31	18 41			18 51		19 01
Manor Park	d	17 33	17 43			17 53		18 03			18 13		18 23			18 33	18 43			18 53		19 03
Ilford 2	d	17 36	17 46			17 56		18 06			18 16		18 26			18 36	18 46			18 56		19 06
Seven Kings	d	17 38	17 48			17 58		18 08			18 18		18 28			18 38	18 48			18 58		19 08
Goodmayes	d	17 40	17 50			18 00		18 10			18 20		18 30			18 40	18 50			19 00		19 10
Chadwell Heath	d	17 42	17 52			18 02		18 12			18 22		18 32			18 42	18 52			19 02		19 12
Romford	d	17 46	17 56		17 53	18 06		18 16			18 26		18 36	18 28		18 46	18 56			19 06		19 16
Gidea Park 2	d	17 50	18 00			18 10		18 20			18 30		18 40			18 50	19 00			19 10		19 20
Harold Wood	d	17 53	18 03			18 13		18 23			18 33		18 43			18 53	19 03			19 13		19 23
Brentwood	d	17 57	18 07			18 17		18 27			18 37		18 47			18 57	19 07			19 17		19 27
Shenfield 3	a	18 03	18 13	17 58	18 02	18 23	18 11	18 33		18 18	18 43	18 24	18 53	18 38	18 40	19 03	19 13		18 58	19 23	19 11	19 33
Shenfield 3	d			17 59						18 19				18 39					18 59			
Billericay	d			18 05						18 25				18 45					19 05			
Wickford 2	d			18 11					18 16	18 31				18 51				18 56	19 11			
Battlesbridge	d								18 20									19 00				
South Woodham Ferrers	d								18 24									19 04				
North Fambridge	d								18 31									19 11				
Althorne	d								18 36									19 16				
Burnham-on-Crouch	d								18 41									19 21				
Southminster	a								18 47									19 27				
Rayleigh	d			18 16						18 36				18 56					19 16			
Hockley	d			18 21						18 41				19 01					19 21			
Rochford	d			18 24						18 44				19 04					19 24			
Southend Airport ✈	d			18 27						18 47				19 07					19 27			
Prittlewell	d			18 30						18 50				19 10					19 30			
Southend Victoria	a			18 34						18 54				19 14					19 34			

		LE 1	LE	LE 1	LE	LE 1	LE 1	LE 1	LE	LE	LE 1	LE 1	LE 1	LE	LE 1	LE	LE 1	LE 1	LE	LE 1	LE	LE 1	LE 1
London Liverpool Street 15 ⊖	d	18 55	19 00	19 02	19 10		19 13	19 18	19 20	19 30	19 32	19 35	19 38	19 40	19 48	19 50		19 55	20 00	20 02	20 10	20 13	20 18
Stratford 7 ⊖	d	19 02	19 07	19 09	19 17		19 20	19 25	19 27	19 37	19 39	19 43	19 46	19 47	19 55	19 57		20 02	20 07	20 09	20 17	20 20	20 25
Maryland	d		19 09		19 19				19 29	19 39				19 49		19 59			20 09		20 19		
Forest Gate	d		19 11		19 21				19 31	19 41				19 51		20 01			20 11		20 21		
Manor Park	d		19 13		19 23				19 33	19 43				19 53		20 03			20 13		20 23		
Ilford 2	d		19 16		19 26				19 36	19 46				19 56		20 06			20 16		20 26		
Seven Kings	d		19 18		19 28				19 38	19 48				19 58		20 08			20 18		20 28		
Goodmayes	d		19 20		19 30				19 40	19 50				20 00		20 10			20 20		20 30		
Chadwell Heath	d		19 22		19 32				19 42	19 52				20 02		20 12			20 22		20 32		
Romford	d		19 26		19 36		19 28		19 46	19 56			19 54	20 06		20 16			20 26		20 36	20 28	
Gidea Park 2	d		19 30		19 40				19 50	20 00				20 10		20 20			20 30		20 40		
Harold Wood	d		19 33		19 43				19 53	20 03				20 13		20 23			20 33		20 43		
Brentwood	d		19 37		19 47				19 57	20 07				20 17		20 27			20 37		20 47		
Shenfield 3	a	19 18	19 43	19 24	19 53		19 38	19 40	20 03	20 13	19 56	19 59	20 03	20 23	20 11	20 33		20 18	20 43	20 24	20 53	20 38	20 40
Shenfield 3	d	19 19					19 39					20 00						20 19				20 39	
Billericay	d	19 25					19 45					20 06						20 25				20 45	
Wickford 2	d	19 31				19 36	19 51					20 12					20 16	20 31				20 51	
Battlesbridge	d					19 40											20 20						
South Woodham Ferrers	d					19 44											20 24						
North Fambridge	d					19 51											20 31						
Althorne	d					19 56											20 36						
Burnham-on-Crouch	d					20 01											20 41						
Southminster	a					20 07											20 47						
Rayleigh	d	19 36					19 56					20 17						20 36				20 56	
Hockley	d	19 41					20 01					20 22						20 41				21 01	
Rochford	d	19 44					20 04					20 25						20 44				21 04	
Southend Airport ✈	d	19 47					20 07					20 28						20 47				21 07	
Prittlewell	d	19 50					20 10					20 31						20 50				21 10	
Southend Victoria	a	19 54					20 14					20 35						20 54				21 14	

Saturdays

1 September to 8 September

London - Shenfield, Southminster and Southend Victoria

Network Diagram - see first Page of Table 5

		LE	LE	LE 1	LE 1	LE 1	LE	LE 1	LE	LE 1	LE 1	LE	LE 1	LE 1	LE 1	LE	LE 1	LE	LE 1	LE 1	LE 1	LE	LE 1
London Liverpool Street 15 ⊖	d	20 20	20 30		20 35	20 38	20 40	20 48	20 50	20 55	21 02	21 05		21 13	21 18	21 20	21 35	21 35	21 38	21 42	21 48	21 50	
Stratford 7 ⊖	d	20 27	20 37		20 42	20 45	20 47	20 55	20 57	21 02	21 09	21 12		21 20	21 25	21 27	21 42	21 42	21 45	21a51	21 55	21 57	
Maryland	d	20 29	20 39				20 49		20 59			21 14				21 29		21 44				21 59	
Forest Gate	d	20 31	20 41				20 51		21 01			21 16				21 31		21 46				22 01	
Manor Park	d	20 33	20 43				20 53		21 03			21 18				21 33		21 48				22 03	
Ilford 2	d	20 36	20 46				20 56		21 06			21 21				21 36		21 51				22 06	
Seven Kings	d	20 38	20 48				20 58		21 08			21 23				21 38		21 53				22 08	
Goodmayes	d	20 40	20 50				21 00		21 10			21 25				21 40		21 55				22 10	
Chadwell Heath	d	20 42	20 52				21 02		21 12			21 27				21 42		21 57				22 12	
Romford	d	20 46	20 56			20 53	21 06		21 16			21 31		21 28		21 46		22 01	21 53			22 16	
Gidea Park 2	d	20 50	21 00				21 10		21 20			21 35				21 50		22 05				22 20	
Harold Wood	d	20 53	21 03				21 13		21 23			21 38				21 53		22 08				22 23	
Brentwood	d	20 57	21 07				21 17		21 27			21 42				21 57		22 12				22 27	
Shenfield 3	a	21 03	21 13		20 58	21 02	21 23	21 11	21 33	21 18	21 24	21 48		21 38	21 40	22 03	21 57	22 18	22 02		22 11	22 33	
Shenfield 3	d				20 59					21 19				21 39			21 59						
Billericay	d				21 05					21 25				21 45			22 05						
Wickford 2	d			20 56	21 11					21 31			21 36	21 51			22 11						22 16
Battlesbridge	d			21 00									21 40										22 20
South Woodham Ferrers	d			21 04									21 44										22 24
North Fambridge	d			21 11									21 51										22 31
Althorne	d			21 16									21 56										22 36
Burnham-on-Crouch	d			21 21									22 01										22 41
Southminster	a			21 27									22 07										22 47
Rayleigh	d				21 16					21 36				21 56			22 16						
Hockley	d				21 21					21 41				22 01			22 21						
Rochford	d				21 24					21 44				22 04			22 24						
Southend Airport ✈	d				21 27					21 47				22 07			22 27						
Prittlewell	d				21 30					21 50				22 10			22 30						
Southend Victoria	a				21 34					21 54				22 14			22 34						

		LE 1	LE 1	LE	LE 1	LE 1	LE 1	LE	LE 1	LE 1	LE 1	LE	LE 1	LE 1	LE 1	LE	LE 1	LE	LE 1	LE 1	LE	LE 1
London Liverpool Street 15 ⊖	d	21 50	22 02	22 02	22 10	22 12	22 15	22 17	22 22		22 25	22 32	22 35	22 40	22 42	22 42	22 45	22 52	22 52	22 55	23 02	23 07
Stratford 7 ⊖	d	22 02	22 09	22 12	22 22	22a21	22 24	22 27	22a31		22 37	22 42	22 44	22 52	22a51	22 52	22 54	23 02	23a01	23 07	23 12	23 17
Maryland	d			22 14				22 29				22 44				22 54		23 04			23 14	
Forest Gate	d			22 16				22 31				22 46				22 56		23 06			23 16	
Manor Park	d			22 18				22 33				22 48				22 58		23 08			23 18	
Ilford 2	d			22 21				22 36				22 51				23 01		23 11			23 21	
Seven Kings	d			22 23				22 38				22 53				23 03		23 13			23 23	
Goodmayes	d			22 25				22 40				22 55				23 05		23 15			23 25	
Chadwell Heath	d			22 27				22 42				22 57				23 07		23 17			23 27	
Romford	d			22 31				22 46				23 01				23 11		23 21			23 31	
Gidea Park 2	d			22 35				22 50				23 05				23 15		23 25			23 35	
Harold Wood	d			22 38				22 53				23 08				23 18		23 28			23 38	
Brentwood	d			22 42				22 57				23 12				23 22		23 32			23 42	
Shenfield 3	a	22 18	22 24	22 48	22 38		22 40	23 03			22 53	23 18	23 00	23 08		23 28	23 11	23 38		23 23	23 48	23 33
Shenfield 3	d	22 19			22 39						22 54			23 09						23 24		
Billericay	d	22 25			22 45						23 00			23 15						23 30		
Wickford 2	d	22 31			22 51					22 56	23 06			23 21						23 36		
Battlesbridge	d									23 00												
South Woodham Ferrers	d									23 04												
North Fambridge	d									23 11												
Althorne	d									23 16												
Burnham-on-Crouch	d									23 21												
Southminster	a									23 27												
Rayleigh	d	22 36			22 56						23 11			23 26						23 41		
Hockley	d	22 41			23 01						23 16			23 31						23 46		
Rochford	d	22 44			23 04						23 19			23 34						23 49		
Southend Airport ✈	d	22 47			23 07						23 22			23 37						23 52		
Prittlewell	d	22 50			23 10						23 25			23 40						23 55		
Southend Victoria	a	22 54			23 14						23 29			23 44						23 59		

Table 5

Saturdays
1 September to 8 September

London - Shenfield, Southminster and Southend Victoria

Network Diagram - see first Page of Table 5

		LE ■	LE ■	LE ■	LE	LE ■	LE	LE ■	LE		LE ■	LE ■	LE	LE ■	LE ■	LE	LE ■
London Liverpool Street 15 ⊖	d	23 10	23 12		23 12	23 15	23 22	23 25	23 32		23 35	23 40	23 42	23 42	23 45	23 52	23 55
Stratford 7 ⊖	d	23 22	23a21		23 22	23 25	23 32	23 37	23 42		23 45	23 52	23 52	23a51	23 54	00 02	00 07
Maryland	d				23 24		23 34		23 44				23 54			00 04	
Forest Gate	d				23 26		23 36		23 46				23 56			00 06	
Manor Park	d				23 28		23 38		23 48				23 58			00 08	
Ilford 2	d				23 31		23 41		23 51				00 01			00 11	
Seven Kings	d				23 33		23 43		23 53				00 03			00 13	
Goodmayes	d				23 35		23 45		23 55				00 05			00 15	
Chadwell Heath	d				23 37		23 47		23 57				00 07			00 17	
Romford	d				23 41		23 51		00 02				00 12			00 21	
Gidea Park 2	d				23 45		23 55		00 05				00 15			00 25	
Harold Wood	d				23 48		23 58		00 08				00 18			00 28	
Brentwood	d				23 52		00 02		00 12				00 22			00 32	
Shenfield 3	a	23 38			23 58	23 43	00 08	23 53	00 18		00 01	00 08	00 28		00 11	00 38	00 23
Shenfield 3	d	23 39						23 54				00 09					00 24
Billericay	d	23 45						23 59				00 15					00 30
Wickford 2	d	23 51		23 56				00 06				00 21					00 36
Battlesbridge	d			00 01													
South Woodham Ferrers	d			00 04													
North Fambridge	d			00 11													
Althorne	d			00 16													
Burnham-on-Crouch	d			00 21													
Southminster	a			00 27													
Rayleigh	d	23 56						00 11				00 26					00 41
Hockley	d	00 01						00 16				00 31					00 46
Rochford	d	00 04						00 19				00 34					00 49
Southend Airport ✈	d	00 07						00 22				00 37					00 52
Prittlewell	d	00 10						00 25				00 40					00 55
Southend Victoria	a	00 14						00 29				00 44					00 59

Saturdays
from 15 September

		LE ■	LE	LE	LE ■	LE ■	LE	LE	LE ■	LE ■		LE	LE	LE ■	LE ■	LE	LE ■	LE ■	LE ■	LE ■		LE ■	LE	LE ■	LE ■
London Liverpool Street 15 ⊖	d	23p15	23p20	23p35	23p45	23p48	23p50	00 01	00 15	00 18		00 20	00 32	00 46	00 50	00 55	05 21			05 28		05 34	05 40	05 51	06 02
Stratford 7 ⊖	d	23p22	23p27	23p42	23p52	23p55	23p57	00 08	00 22	00 25		00 27	00 39	00 53	00 57	01 02	05a30			05 35		05 41	05 47	06a00	06 09
Maryland	d		23p29	23p44			23p59	00 10				00 29	00 41			01 04							05 49		
Forest Gate	d		23p31	23p46			00 01	00 12				00 31	00 43			01 06							05 51		
Manor Park	d		23p33	23p48			00 03	00 14				00 33	00 45			01 08							05 53		
Ilford 2	d		23p36	23p51			00 06	00 17				00 36	00 48			01 11				05 40			05 56		
Seven Kings	d		23p38	23p53			00 08	00 19				00 38	00 50			01 13				05 42			05 58		
Goodmayes	d		23p40	23p55			00 10	00 21				00 40	00 52			01 15							06 00		
Chadwell Heath	d		23p42	23p57			00 12	00 23				00 42	00 54			01 17							06 02		
Romford	d		23p46	00 02			00 16	00 27	00 32			00 46	00 58		01 08	01 21				05 48		05 49	06 06		
Gidea Park 2	d		23p50	00 05			00 20	00a31				00 50	01a02	01 07		01 25				05 51			06 10		
Harold Wood	d		23p53	00 08			00 23					00 53				01 28				05 54			06 13		
Brentwood	d		23p57	00 12			00 27					00 57				01 32				05 59			06 17		
Shenfield 3	a	23p38	00 03	00 18	00 08	00 10	00 33		00 44	00 47		01 03		01 17	01 20	01 38				06 04		05 58	06 23		06 24
Shenfield 3	d	23p39			00 09				00 45						01 20					06 04					
Billericay	d	23p45			00 15				00 51						01 26					06 10					
Wickford 2	d	23p51			00 21				00 56						01 31			05 36	06 12	06 16					
Battlesbridge	d																	05 40	06 16						
South Woodham Ferrers	d																	05 44	06 20						
North Fambridge	d																	05 51	06 31						
Althorne	d																	05 56	06 36						
Burnham-on-Crouch	d																	06 01	06 41						
Southminster	a																	06 07	06 47						
Rayleigh	d	23p56			00 26				01 01						01 36					06 22					
Hockley	d	00 01			00 31				01 06						01 41					06 26					
Rochford	d	00 04			00 34				01 09						01 44					06 30					
Southend Airport ✈	d	00 07			00 37				01 12						01 47					06 32					
Prittlewell	d	00 10			00 40				01 15						01 50					06 35					
Southend Victoria	a	00 18			00 48				01 23						01 58					06 39					

Table 5

Saturdays
from 15 September

London - Shenfield, Southminster and Southend Victoria

Network Diagram - see first Page of Table 5

		LE ■	LE	LE ■	LE ■	LE ■		LE ■	LE ■	LE	LE ■	LE ■	LE	LE ■	LE	LE ■		LE ■	LE ■	LE	LE	LE ■	LE ■	LE	LE ■
London Liverpool Street 15 ⊖	d	06 05	06 10	06 18	06 21			06 35	06 38	06 40	06 48	06 55	07 00	07 02	07 10			07 13	07 18	07 20	07 30	07 35	07 38	07 40	07 48
Stratford 7 ⊖	d	06 12	06 17	06 25	06a30			06 42	06 45	06 47	06 55	07 02	07 07	07 09	07 17			07 20	07 25	07 27	07 37	07 42	07 45	07 47	07 55
Maryland	d		06 19							06 49			07 09		07 19					07 29	07 39			07 49	
Forest Gate	d		06 21							06 51			07 11		07 21					07 31	07 41			07 51	
Manor Park	d		06 23							06 53			07 13		07 23					07 33	07 43			07 53	
Ilford 2	d		06 26							06 56			07 16		07 26					07 36	07 46			07 56	
Seven Kings	d		06 28							06 58			07 18		07 28					07 38	07 48			07 58	
Goodmayes	d		06 30							07 00			07 20		07 30					07 40	07 50			08 00	
Chadwell Heath	d		06 32							07 02			07 22		07 32					07 42	07 52			08 02	
Romford	d		06 36						06 53	07 06			07 26		07 36			07 28		07 46	07 56		07 53	08 06	
Gidea Park 2	d		06 40							07 10			07 30		07 40					07 50	08 00			08 10	
Harold Wood	d		06 43							07 13			07 33		07 43					07 53	08 03			08 13	
Brentwood	d		06 47							07 17			07 37		07 47					07 57	08 07			08 17	
Shenfield 3	a	06 30	06 53	06 40				06 58	07 02	07 23	07 11	07 18	07 43	07 24	07 53			07 38	07 40	08 03	08 13	07 58	08 02	08 23	08 11
Shenfield 3	d	06 30						06 59				07 19						07 39				07 59			
Billericay	d	06 36						07 05				07 25						07 45				08 05			
Wickford 2	d	06 43				06 56		07 11				07 31				07 36		07 51				08 11			
Battlesbridge	d					07 00										07 40									
South Woodham Ferrers	d					07 04										07 44									
North Fambridge	d					07 11										07 51									
Althorne	d					07 16										07 56									
Burnham-on-Crouch	d					07 21										08 01									
Southminster	a					07 27										08 07									
Rayleigh	d	06 48						07 16				07 36						07 56				08 16			
Hockley	d	06 53						07 21				07 41						08 01				08 21			
Rochford	d	06 56						07 24				07 44						08 04				08 24			
Southend Airport ✈	d	06 59						07 27				07 47						08 07				08 27			
Prittlewell	d	07 02						07 30				07 50						08 10				08 30			
Southend Victoria	a	07 05						07 34				07 54						08 14				08 34			

		LE		LE ■	LE ■	LE	LE ■	LE	LE ■	LE ■	LE	LE		LE ■	LE ■	LE ■	LE	LE ■	LE	LE ■	LE	LE ■		LE	LE ■
London Liverpool Street 15 ⊖	d	07 50			07 55	08 00	08 02	08 10	08 13	08 18	08 20	08 30			08 35	08 38	08 40	08 48	08 50	08 55	09 00	09 02		09 10	
Stratford 7 ⊖	d	07 57			08 02	08 07	08 09	08 17	08 20	08 25	08 27	08 37			08 42	08 45	08 47	08 55	08 57	09 02	09 07	09 09		09 17	
Maryland	d	07 59				08 09		08 19			08 29	08 39					08 49		08 59		09 09			09 19	
Forest Gate	d	08 01				08 11		08 21			08 31	08 41					08 51		09 01		09 11			09 21	
Manor Park	d	08 03				08 13		08 23			08 33	08 43					08 53		09 03		09 13			09 23	
Ilford 2	d	08 06				08 16		08 26			08 36	08 46					08 56		09 06		09 16			09 26	
Seven Kings	d	08 08				08 18		08 28			08 38	08 48					08 58		09 08		09 18			09 28	
Goodmayes	d	08 10				08 20		08 30			08 40	08 50					09 00		09 10		09 20			09 30	
Chadwell Heath	d	08 12				08 22		08 32			08 42	08 52					09 02		09 12		09 22			09 32	
Romford	d	08 16				08 26		08 36	08 28		08 46	08 56				08 53	09 06		09 16		09 26			09 36	
Gidea Park 2	d	08 20				08 30		08 40			08 50	09 00					09 10		09 20		09 30			09 40	
Harold Wood	d	08 23				08 33		08 43			08 53	09 03					09 13		09 23		09 33			09 43	
Brentwood	d	08 27				08 37		08 47			08 57	09 07					09 17		09 27		09 37			09 47	
Shenfield 3	a	08 33			08 18	08 43	08 24	08 53	08 38	08 40	09 03	09 13			08 58	09 02	09 23	09 11	09 33	09 18	09 43	09 24		09 53	
Shenfield 3	d				08 19				08 39						08 59					09 19					
Billericay	d				08 25				08 45						09 05					09 25					
Wickford 2	d			08 16	08 31				08 51					08 56	09 11					09 31					09 36
Battlesbridge	d			08 20										09 00											09 40
South Woodham Ferrers	d			08 24										09 04											09 44
North Fambridge	d			08 31										09 11											09 51
Althorne	d			08 36										09 16											09 56
Burnham-on-Crouch	d			08 41										09 21											10 01
Southminster	a			08 47										09 27											10 07
Rayleigh	d				08 36				08 56						09 16					09 36					
Hockley	d				08 41				09 01						09 21					09 41					
Rochford	d				08 44				09 04						09 24					09 44					
Southend Airport ✈	d				08 47				09 07						09 27					09 47					
Prittlewell	d				08 50				09 10						09 30					09 50					
Southend Victoria	a				08 54				09 14						09 34					09 54					

London - Shenfield, Southminster and Southend Victoria

Network Diagram - see first Page of Table 5

		LE 1	LE 1	LE	LE	LE 1	LE 1	LE		LE 1	LE	LE 1	LE 1	LE	LE 1	LE	LE 1	LE 1		LE	LE	LE 1	LE 1	LE 1	LE
London Liverpool Street [15] ⊖	d	09 13	09 18	09 20	09 30	09 35	09 38	09 40		09 48	09 50		09 55	10 00	10 02	10 10	10 13	10 18		10 20	10 30		10 35	10 38	10 40
Stratford [7] ⊖	d	09 20	09 25	09 27	09 37	09 42	09 45	09 47		09 55	09 57		10 02	10 07	10 09	10 17	10 20	10 25		10 27	10 37		10 42	10 45	10 47
Maryland	d			09 29	09 39			09 49			09 59			10 09		10 19				10 29	10 39				10 49
Forest Gate	d			09 31	09 41			09 51			10 01			10 11		10 21				10 31	10 41				10 51
Manor Park	d			09 33	09 43			09 53			10 03			10 13		10 23				10 33	10 43				10 53
Ilford [2]	d			09 36	09 46			09 56			10 06			10 16		10 26				10 36	10 46				10 56
Seven Kings	d			09 38	09 48			09 58			10 08			10 18		10 28				10 38	10 48				10 58
Goodmayes	d			09 40	09 50			10 00			10 10			10 20		10 30				10 40	10 50				11 00
Chadwell Heath	d			09 42	09 52			10 02			10 12			10 22		10 32				10 42	10 52				11 02
Romford	d	09 28		09 46	09 56		09 53	10 06			10 16			10 26		10 36	10 28			10 46	10 56			10 53	11 06
Gidea Park [2]	d			09 50	10 00			10 10			10 20			10 30		10 40				10 50	11 00				11 10
Harold Wood	d			09 53	10 03			10 13			10 23			10 33		10 43				10 53	11 03				11 13
Brentwood	d			09 57	10 07			10 17			10 27			10 37		10 47				10 57	11 07				11 17
Shenfield [3]	a	09 38	09 40	10 03	10 13	09 58	10 02	10 23		10 11	10 33		10 18	10 43	10 24	10 53	10 38	10 40		11 03	11 13		10 58	11 02	11 23
Shenfield [3]	d	09 39				09 59							10 19				10 39						10 59		
Billericay	d	09 45				10 05							10 25				10 45						11 05		
Wickford [2]	d	09 51				10 11						10 16	10 31				10 51					10 56	11 11		
Battlesbridge	d											10 20										11 00			
South Woodham Ferrers	d											10 24										11 04			
North Fambridge	d											10 31										11 11			
Althorne	d											10 36										11 16			
Burnham-on-Crouch	d											10 41										11 21			
Southminster	a											10 47										11 27			
Rayleigh	d	09 56				10 16							10 36				10 56						11 16		
Hockley	d	10 01				10 21							10 41				11 01						11 21		
Rochford	d	10 04				10 24							10 44				11 04						11 24		
Southend Airport ✈	d	10 07				10 27							10 47				11 07						11 27		
Prittlewell	d	10 10				10 30							10 50				11 10						11 30		
Southend Victoria	a	10 14				10 34							10 54				11 14						11 34		

		LE 1	LE	LE 1		LE	LE 1	LE	LE 1	LE 1	LE 1	LE	LE	LE 1		LE 1	LE	LE 1	LE	LE 1	LE 1	LE	LE 1	LE	
London Liverpool Street [15] ⊖	d	10 48	10 50	10 55		11 00	11 02	11 10		11 13	11 18	11 20	11 30	11 35		11 38	11 40	11 48	11 50		11 55	12 00	12 02	12 10	
Stratford [7] ⊖	d	10 55	10 57	11 02		11 07	11 09	11 17		11 20	11 25	11 27	11 37	11 42		11 45	11 47	11 55	11 57		12 02	12 07	12 09	12 17	
Maryland	d		10 59			11 09		11 19				11 29	11 39				11 49		11 59			12 09		12 19	
Forest Gate	d		11 01			11 11		11 21				11 31	11 41				11 51		12 01			12 11		12 21	
Manor Park	d		11 03			11 13		11 23				11 33	11 43				11 53		12 03			12 13		12 23	
Ilford [2]	d		11 06			11 16		11 26				11 36	11 46				11 56		12 06			12 16		12 26	
Seven Kings	d		11 08			11 18		11 28				11 38	11 48				11 58		12 08			12 18		12 28	
Goodmayes	d		11 10			11 20		11 30				11 40	11 50				12 00		12 10			12 20		12 30	
Chadwell Heath	d		11 12			11 22		11 32				11 42	11 52				12 02		12 12			12 22		12 32	
Romford	d		11 16			11 26		11 36		11 28		11 46	11 56			11 53	12 06		12 16			12 26		12 36	
Gidea Park [2]	d		11 20			11 30		11 40				11 50	12 00				12 10		12 20			12 30		12 40	
Harold Wood	d		11 23			11 33		11 43				11 53	12 03				12 13		12 23			12 33		12 43	
Brentwood	d		11 27			11 37		11 47				11 57	12 07				12 17		12 27			12 37		12 47	
Shenfield [3]	a	11 11	11 33	11 18		11 43	11 24	11 53		11 38	11 40	12 03	12 13	11 58		12 02	12 23	12 11	12 33		12 18	12 43	12 24	12 53	
Shenfield [3]	d			11 19						11 39				11 59							12 19				
Billericay	d			11 25						11 45				12 05							12 25				
Wickford [2]	d			11 31					11 36	11 51				12 11						12 16	12 31				
Battlesbridge	d								11 40											12 20					
South Woodham Ferrers	d								11 44											12 24					
North Fambridge	d								11 51											12 31					
Althorne	d								11 56											12 36					
Burnham-on-Crouch	d								12 01											12 41					
Southminster	a								12 07											12 47					
Rayleigh	d			11 36						11 56				12 16							12 36				
Hockley	d			11 41						12 01				12 21							12 41				
Rochford	d			11 44						12 04				12 24							12 44				
Southend Airport ✈	d			11 47						12 07				12 27							12 47				
Prittlewell	d			11 50						12 10				12 30							12 50				
Southend Victoria	a			11 54						12 14				12 34							12 54				

Table 5

Saturdays
from 15 September

London - Shenfield, Southminster and Southend Victoria

Network Diagram - see first Page of Table 5

		LE 1	LE 1	LE	LE	LE 1	LE 1	LE 1	LE	LE 1		LE	LE 1	LE	LE 1	LE	LE 1	LE 1	LE 1	LE		LE	LE 1	LE 1	LE
London Liverpool Street [15] ⊖	d	12 13	12 18	12 20	12 30		12 35	12 38	12 40	12 48		12 50	12 55	13 00	13 02	13 10		13 13	13 18	13 20		13 30	13 35	13 38	13 40
Stratford [7] ⊖	d	12 20	12 25	12 27	12 37		12 42	12 45	12 47	12 55		12 57	13 02	13 07	13 09	13 17		13 20	13 25	13 27		13 37	13 42	13 45	13 47
Maryland	d			12 29	12 39				12 49			12 59		13 09		13 19				13 29		13 39			13 49
Forest Gate	d			12 31	12 41				12 51			13 01		13 11		13 21				13 31		13 41			13 51
Manor Park	d			12 33	12 43				12 53			13 03		13 13		13 23				13 33		13 43			13 53
Ilford [2]	d			12 36	12 46				12 56			13 06		13 16		13 26				13 36		13 46			13 56
Seven Kings	d			12 38	12 48				12 58			13 08		13 18		13 28				13 38		13 48			13 58
Goodmayes	d			12 40	12 50				13 00			13 10		13 20		13 30				13 40		13 50			14 00
Chadwell Heath	d			12 42	12 52				13 02			13 12		13 22		13 32				13 42		13 52			14 02
Romford	d	12 28		12 46	12 56			12 53	13 06			13 16		13 26		13 36		13 28		13 46		13 56		13 53	14 06
Gidea Park [2]	d			12 50	13 00				13 10			13 20		13 30		13 40				13 50		14 00			14 10
Harold Wood	d			12 53	13 03				13 13			13 23		13 33		13 43				13 53		14 03			14 13
Brentwood	d			12 57	13 07				13 17			13 27		13 37		13 47				13 57		14 07			14 17
Shenfield [3]	a	12 38	12 40	13 03	13 13		12 58	13 02	13 23	13 11		13 33	13 18	13 43	13 24	13 53		13 38	13 40	14 03		14 13	13 58	14 02	14 23
Shenfield [3]	d	12 39					12 59						13 19					13 39					13 59		
Billericay	d	12 45					13 05						13 25					13 45					14 05		
Wickford [2]	d	12 51				12 56	13 11						13 31				13 36	13 51					14 11		
Battlesbridge	d					13 00											13 40								
South Woodham Ferrers	d					13 04											13 44								
North Fambridge	d					13 11											13 51								
Althorne	d					13 16											13 56								
Burnham-on-Crouch	d					13 21											14 01								
Southminster	a					13 27											14 07								
Rayleigh	d	12 56					13 16						13 36					13 56					14 16		
Hockley	d	13 01					13 21						13 41					14 01					14 21		
Rochford	d	13 04					13 24						13 44					14 04					14 24		
Southend Airport ✈	d	13 07					13 27						13 47					14 07					14 27		
Prittlewell	d	13 10					13 30						13 50					14 10					14 30		
Southend Victoria	a	13 14					13 34						13 54					14 14					14 34		

		LE 1	LE	LE 1	LE 1	LE		LE 1	LE	LE 1	LE 1	LE	LE	LE 1	LE 1	LE 1		LE	LE 1	LE	LE 1	LE	LE 1	LE	LE 1
London Liverpool Street [15] ⊖	d	13 48	13 50		13 55	14 00		14 02	14 10	14 13	14 18	14 20	14 30		14 35	14 38		14 40	14 48	14 50	14 55	15 00	15 02	15 10	
Stratford [7] ⊖	d	13 55	13 57		14 02	14 07		14 09	14 17	14 20	14 25	14 27	14 37		14 42	14 45		14 47	14 55	14 57	15 02	15 07	15 09	15 17	
Maryland	d		13 59			14 09			14 19			14 29	14 39					14 49		14 59		15 09		15 19	
Forest Gate	d		14 01			14 11			14 21			14 31	14 41					14 51		15 01		15 11		15 21	
Manor Park	d		14 03			14 13			14 23			14 33	14 43					14 53		15 03		15 13		15 23	
Ilford [2]	d		14 06			14 16			14 26			14 36	14 46					14 56		15 06		15 16		15 26	
Seven Kings	d		14 08			14 18			14 28			14 38	14 48					14 58		15 08		15 18		15 28	
Goodmayes	d		14 10			14 20			14 30			14 40	14 50					15 00		15 10		15 20		15 30	
Chadwell Heath	d		14 12			14 22			14 32			14 42	14 52					15 02		15 12		15 22		15 32	
Romford	d		14 16			14 26			14 36	14 28		14 46	14 56			14 53		15 06		15 16		15 26		15 36	
Gidea Park [2]	d		14 20			14 30			14 40			14 50	15 00					15 10		15 20		15 30		15 40	
Harold Wood	d		14 23			14 33			14 43			14 53	15 03					15 13		15 23		15 33		15 43	
Brentwood	d		14 27			14 37			14 47			14 57	15 07					15 17		15 27		15 37		15 47	
Shenfield [3]	a	14 11	14 33		14 18	14 43		14 24	14 53	14 38	14 40	15 03	15 13		14 58	15 02		15 23	15 11	15 33	15 18	15 43	15 24	15 53	
Shenfield [3]	d				14 19					14 39					14 59						15 19				
Billericay	d				14 25					14 45					15 05						15 25				
Wickford [2]	d			14 16	14 31					14 51				14 56	15 11						15 31				15 36
Battlesbridge	d			14 20										15 00											15 40
South Woodham Ferrers	d			14 24										15 04											15 44
North Fambridge	d			14 31										15 11											15 51
Althorne	d			14 36										15 16											15 56
Burnham-on-Crouch	d			14 41										15 21											16 01
Southminster	a			14 47										15 27											16 07
Rayleigh	d				14 36					14 56					15 16						15 36				
Hockley	d				14 41					15 01					15 21						15 41				
Rochford	d				14 44					15 04					15 24						15 44				
Southend Airport ✈	d				14 47					15 07					15 27						15 47				
Prittlewell	d				14 50					15 10					15 30						15 50				
Southend Victoria	a				14 54					15 14					15 34						15 54				

Table 5

Saturdays

from 15 September

London - Shenfield, Southminster and Southend Victoria

Network Diagram - see first Page of Table 5

		LE [1]		LE [1]	LE	LE	LE [1]	LE [1]	LE	LE [1]	LE	LE [1]		LE [1]	LE	LE [1]	LE	LE [1]	LE [1]	LE	LE	LE [1]		LE [1]	LE [1]
London Liverpool Street [15] ⊖	d	15 13		15 18	15 20	15 30	15 35	15 38	15 40	15 48	15 50			15 55	16 00	16 02	16 10	16 13	16 18	16 20	16 30			16 35	16 38
Stratford [7] ⊖	d	15 20		15 25	15 27	15 37	15 42	15 45	15 47	15 55	15 57			16 02	16 07	16 09	16 17	16 20	16 25	16 27	16 37			16 42	16 45
Maryland	d				15 29	15 39			15 49		15 59				16 09		16 19			16 29	16 39				
Forest Gate	d				15 31	15 41			15 51		16 01				16 11		16 21			16 31	16 41				
Manor Park	d				15 33	15 43			15 53		16 03				16 13		16 23			16 33	16 43				
Ilford [2]	d				15 36	15 46			15 56		16 06				16 16		16 26			16 36	16 46				
Seven Kings	d				15 38	15 48			15 58		16 08				16 18		16 28			16 38	16 48				
Goodmayes	d				15 40	15 50			16 00		16 10				16 20		16 30			16 40	16 50				
Chadwell Heath	d				15 42	15 52			16 02		16 12				16 22		16 32			16 42	16 52				
Romford	d	15 28			15 46	15 56		15 53	16 06		16 16				16 26		16 36	16 28		16 46	16 56				16 53
Gidea Park [2]	d				15 50	16 00			16 10		16 20				16 30		16 40			16 50	17 00				
Harold Wood	d				15 53	16 03			16 13		16 23				16 33		16 43			16 53	17 03				
Brentwood	d				15 57	16 07			16 17		16 27				16 37		16 47			16 57	17 07				
Shenfield [3]	a	15 38		15 40	16 03	16 13	15 58	16 02	16 23	16 11	16 33			16 18	16 43	16 24	16 53	16 38	16 40	17 03	17 13			16 58	17 02
Shenfield [3]	d	15 39					15 59							16 19				16 39						16 59	
Billericay	d	15 45					16 05							16 25				16 45						17 05	
Wickford [2]	d	15 51					16 11					16 16		16 31				16 51				16 56		17 11	
Battlesbridge	d											16 20										17 00			
South Woodham Ferrers	d											16 24										17 04			
North Fambridge	d											16 31										17 11			
Althorne	d											16 36										17 16			
Burnham-on-Crouch	d											16 41										17 21			
Southminster	a											16 47										17 27			
Rayleigh	d	15 56					16 16							16 36				16 56						17 16	
Hockley	d	16 01					16 21							16 41				17 01						17 21	
Rochford	d	16 04					16 24							16 44				17 04						17 24	
Southend Airport ✈	d	16 07					16 27							16 47				17 07						17 27	
Prittlewell	d	16 10					16 30							16 50				17 10						17 30	
Southend Victoria	a	16 14					16 34							16 54				17 14						17 34	

		LE	LE [1]	LE	LE [1]	LE	LE [1]	LE		LE [1]	LE [1]	LE [1]	LE	LE	LE [1]	LE [1]	LE	LE [1]		LE	LE [1]	LE [1]	LE	LE [1]	LE
London Liverpool Street [15] ⊖	d	16 40	16 48	16 50	16 55	17 00	17 02	17 10			17 13	17 18	17 20	17 30	17 35	17 38	17 40	17 48		17 50		17 55	18 00	18 02	18 10
Stratford [7] ⊖	d	16 47	16 55	16 57	17 02	17 07	17 09	17 17			17 20	17 25	17 27	17 37	17 42	17 45	17 47	17 55		17 57		18 02	18 07	18 09	18 17
Maryland	d	16 49		16 59		17 09		17 19					17 29	17 39			17 49			17 59			18 09		18 19
Forest Gate	d	16 51		17 01		17 11		17 21					17 31	17 41			17 51			18 01			18 11		18 21
Manor Park	d	16 53		17 03		17 13		17 23					17 33	17 43			17 53			18 03			18 13		18 23
Ilford [2]	d	16 56		17 06		17 16		17 26					17 36	17 46			17 56			18 06			18 16		18 26
Seven Kings	d	16 58		17 08		17 18		17 28					17 38	17 48			17 58			18 08			18 18		18 28
Goodmayes	d	17 00		17 10		17 20		17 30					17 40	17 50			18 00			18 10			18 20		18 30
Chadwell Heath	d	17 02		17 12		17 22		17 32					17 42	17 52			18 02			18 12			18 22		18 32
Romford	d	17 06		17 16		17 26		17 36			17 28		17 46	17 56		17 53	18 06			18 16			18 26		18 36
Gidea Park [2]	d	17 10		17 20		17 30		17 40					17 50	18 00			18 10			18 20			18 30		18 40
Harold Wood	d	17 13		17 23		17 33		17 43					17 53	18 03			18 13			18 23			18 33		18 43
Brentwood	d	17 17		17 27		17 37		17 47					17 57	18 07			18 17			18 27			18 37		18 47
Shenfield [3]	a	17 23	17 11	17 33	17 18	17 43	17 24	17 53			17 38	17 40	18 03	18 13	17 58	18 02	18 23	18 11		18 33		18 18	18 43	18 24	18 53
Shenfield [3]	d				17 19						17 39				17 59							18 19			
Billericay	d				17 25						17 45				18 05							18 25			
Wickford [2]	d				17 31					17 36	17 51				18 11						18 16	18 31			
Battlesbridge	d									17 40											18 20				
South Woodham Ferrers	d									17 44											18 24				
North Fambridge	d									17 51											18 31				
Althorne	d									17 56											18 36				
Burnham-on-Crouch	d									18 01											18 41				
Southminster	a									18 07											18 47				
Rayleigh	d				17 36						17 56				18 16							18 36			
Hockley	d				17 41						18 01				18 21							18 41			
Rochford	d				17 44						18 04				18 24							18 44			
Southend Airport ✈	d				17 47						18 07				18 27							18 47			
Prittlewell	d				17 50						18 10				18 30							18 50			
Southend Victoria	a				17 54						18 14				18 34							18 54			

Table 5

Saturdays

from 15 September

London - Shenfield, Southminster and Southend Victoria

Network Diagram - see first Page of Table 5

		LE [1]	LE [1]	LE		LE	LE [1]	LE [1]	LE [1]	LE	LE [1]	LE	LE [1]	LE		LE [1]	LE	LE [1]	LE [1]	LE [1]	LE	LE	LE [1]	LE [1]	
London Liverpool Street [15] ⊖	d	18 13	18 18	18 20		18 30		18 35	18 38	18 40	18 48	18 50	18 55	19 00		19 02	19 10		19 13	19 18	19 20	19 30	19 32	19 35	
Stratford [7] ⊖	d	18 20	18 25	18 27		18 37		18 42	18 45	18 47	18 55	18 57	19 02	19 07		19 09	19 17		19 20	19 25	19 27	19 37	19 39	19 43	
Maryland	d			18 29		18 39				18 49		18 59		19 09			19 19				19 29	19 39			
Forest Gate	d			18 31		18 41				18 51		19 01		19 11			19 21				19 31	19 41			
Manor Park	d			18 33		18 43				18 53		19 03		19 13			19 23				19 33	19 43			
Ilford [2]	d			18 36		18 46				18 56		19 06		19 16			19 26				19 36	19 46			
Seven Kings	d			18 38		18 48				18 58		19 08		19 18			19 28				19 38	19 48			
Goodmayes	d			18 40		18 50				19 00		19 10		19 20			19 30				19 40	19 50			
Chadwell Heath	d			18 42		18 52				19 02		19 12		19 22			19 32				19 42	19 52			
Romford	d	18 28		18 46		18 56			18 53	19 06		19 16		19 26			19 36		19 28		19 46	19 56			
Gidea Park [2]	d			18 50		19 00				19 10		19 20		19 30			19 40				19 50	20 00			
Harold Wood	d			18 53		19 03				19 13		19 23		19 33			19 43				19 53	20 03			
Brentwood	d			18 57		19 07				19 17		19 27		19 37			19 47				19 57	20 07			
Shenfield [3]	a	18 38	18 40	19 03		19 13		18 58	19 02	19 23	19 11	19 33	19 18	19 43		19 24	19 53		19 38	19 40	20 03	20 13	19 56	19 59	
Shenfield [3]	d	18 39						18 59					19 19						19 39					20 00	
Billericay	d	18 45						19 05					19 25						19 45					20 06	
Wickford [2]	d	18 51					18 56	19 11					19 31					19 36	19 51					20 12	
Battlesbridge	d						19 00											19 40							
South Woodham Ferrers	d						19 04											19 44							
North Fambridge	d						19 11											19 51							
Althorne	d						19 16											19 56							
Burnham-on-Crouch	d						19 21											20 01							
Southminster	a						19 27											20 07							
Rayleigh	d	18 56						19 16					19 36						19 56					20 17	
Hockley	d	19 01						19 21					19 41						20 01					20 22	
Rochford	d	19 04						19 24					19 44						20 04					20 25	
Southend Airport ✈	d	19 07						19 27					19 47						20 07					20 28	
Prittlewell	d	19 10						19 30					19 50						20 10					20 31	
Southend Victoria	a	19 14						19 34					19 54						20 14					20 35	

		LE [1]	LE	LE [1]	LE	LE [1]	LE [1]	LE	LE [1]	LE		LE [1]	LE [1]	LE	LE	LE [1]	LE [1]	LE [1]	LE	LE [1]		LE	LE [1]	LE [1]	LE
London Liverpool Street [15] ⊖	d	19 38	19 40	19 48	19 50		19 55	20 00	20 02	20 10		20 13	20 18	20 20	20 30		20 35	20 38	20 40	20 48		20 50	20 55	21 02	21 05
Stratford [7] ⊖	d	19 46	19 47	19 55	19 57		20 02	20 07	20 09	20 17		20 20	20 25	20 27	20 37		20 42	20 45	20 47	20 55		20 57	21 02	21 09	21 12
Maryland	d		19 49		19 59			20 09		20 19				20 29	20 39				20 49			20 59			21 14
Forest Gate	d		19 51		20 01			20 11		20 21				20 31	20 41				20 51			21 01			21 16
Manor Park	d		19 53		20 03			20 13		20 23				20 33	20 43				20 53			21 03			21 18
Ilford [2]	d		19 56		20 06			20 16		20 26				20 36	20 46				20 56			21 06			21 21
Seven Kings	d		19 58		20 08			20 18		20 28				20 38	20 48				20 58			21 08			21 23
Goodmayes	d		20 00		20 10			20 20		20 30				20 40	20 50				21 00			21 10			21 25
Chadwell Heath	d		20 02		20 12			20 22		20 32				20 42	20 52				21 02			21 12			21 27
Romford	d	19 54	20 06		20 16			20 26		20 36		20 28		20 46	20 56			20 53	21 06			21 16			21 31
Gidea Park [2]	d		20 10		20 20			20 30		20 40				20 50	21 00				21 10			21 20			21 35
Harold Wood	d		20 13		20 23			20 33		20 43				20 53	21 03				21 13			21 23			21 38
Brentwood	d		20 17		20 27			20 37		20 47				20 57	21 07				21 17			21 27			21 42
Shenfield [3]	a	20 03	20 23	20 11	20 33		20 18	20 43	20 24	20 53		20 38	20 40	21 03	21 13		20 58	21 02	21 23	21 11		21 33	21 18	21 24	21 48
Shenfield [3]	d						20 19					20 39					20 59						21 19		
Billericay	d						20 25					20 45					21 05						21 25		
Wickford [2]	d					20 16	20 31					20 51				20 56	21 11						21 31		
Battlesbridge	d					20 20										21 00									
South Woodham Ferrers	d					20 24										21 04									
North Fambridge	d					20 31										21 11									
Althorne	d					20 36										21 16									
Burnham-on-Crouch	d					20 41										21 21									
Southminster	a					20 47										21 27									
Rayleigh	d						20 36					20 56					21 16						21 36		
Hockley	d						20 41					21 01					21 21						21 41		
Rochford	d						20 44					21 04					21 24						21 44		
Southend Airport ✈	d						20 47					21 07					21 27						21 47		
Prittlewell	d						20 50					21 10					21 30						21 50		
Southend Victoria	a						20 54					21 14					21 34						21 54		

Table 5

Saturdays
from 15 September

London - Shenfield, Southminster and Southend Victoria

Network Diagram - see first Page of Table 5

		LE	LE	LE	LE	LE		LE	LE	LE	LE	LE	LE	LE	LE	LE		LE	LE	LE	LE	LE	LE	LE	LE
		1	1	1		1			1	1		1	1	1		1		1			1	1	1		1
London Liverpool Street 15 ⊖	d		21 13	21 18	21 20	21 35		21 35	21 38	21 48	21 50		21 55	22 02	22 05	22 13		22 18	22 20	22 35	22 38		22 45	22 50	23 02
Stratford 7 ⊖	d		21 20	21 25	21 27	21 42		21 42	21 45	21 55	21 57		22 02	22 09	22 12	22 20		22 25	22 27	22 42	22 45		22 52	22 57	23 09
Maryland	d				21 29			21 44			21 59				22 14				22 29	22 44				22 59	
Forest Gate	d				21 31			21 46			22 01				22 16				22 31	22 46				23 01	
Manor Park	d				21 33			21 48			22 03				22 18				22 33	22 48				23 03	
Ilford 2	d				21 36			21 51			22 06				22 21				22 36	22 51				23 06	
Seven Kings	d				21 38			21 53			22 08				22 23				22 38	22 53				23 08	
Goodmayes	d				21 40			21 55			22 10				22 25				22 40	22 55				23 10	
Chadwell Heath	d				21 42			21 57			22 12				22 27				22 42	22 57				23 12	
Romford	d		21 28		21 46			22 01	21 53		22 16				22 31	22 28			22 46	23 01	22 53			23 16	
Gidea Park 2	d				21 50			22 05			22 20				22 35				22 50	23 05				23 20	
Harold Wood	d				21 53			22 08			22 23				22 38				22 53	23 08				23 23	
Brentwood	d				21 57			22 12			22 27				22 42				22 57	23 12				23 27	
Shenfield 3	a		21 38	21 40	22 03	21 57		22 18	22 02	22 11	22 33		22 18	22 24	22 48	22 38		22 40	23 03	23 18	23 02		23 08	23 33	23 24
Shenfield 3	d		21 39			21 59							22 19			22 39							23 09		
Billericay	d		21 45			22 05							22 25			22 45							23 15		
Wickford 2	d	21 36	21 51			22 11						22 16	22 31			22 51						22 56	23 21		
Battlesbridge	d	21 40										22 20										23 00			
South Woodham Ferrers	d	21 44										22 24										23 04			
North Fambridge	d	21 51										22 31										23 11			
Althorne	d	21 56										22 36										23 16			
Burnham-on-Crouch	d	22 01										22 41										23 21			
Southminster	a	22 07										22 47										23 27			
Rayleigh	d		21 56			22 16							22 36			22 56							23 26		
Hockley	d		22 01			22 21							22 41			23 01							23 31		
Rochford	d		22 04			22 24							22 44			23 04							23 34		
Southend Airport ✈	d		22 07			22 27							22 47			23 07							23 37		
Prittlewell	d		22 10			22 30							22 50			23 10							23 40		
Southend Victoria	a		22 14			22 34							22 54			23 14							23 48		

		LE		LE	LE	LE	LE	LE	LE	LE
				1	1			1	1	
London Liverpool Street 15 ⊖	d	23 05		23 15	23 18	23 20	23 35	23 45	23 48	23 50
Stratford 7 ⊖	d	23 12		23 22	23 25	23 27	23 42	23 52	23 55	23 57
Maryland	d	23 14				23 29	23 44			23 59
Forest Gate	d	23 16				23 31	23 46			00 01
Manor Park	d	23 18				23 33	23 48			00 03
Ilford 2	d	23 21				23 36	23 51			00 06
Seven Kings	d	23 23				23 38	23 53			00 08
Goodmayes	d	23 25				23 40	23 55			00 10
Chadwell Heath	d	23 27				23 42	23 57			00 12
Romford	d	23 31				23 46	00 02			00 16
Gidea Park 2	d	23 35				23 50	00 05			00 20
Harold Wood	d	23 38				23 53	00 08			00 23
Brentwood	d	23 42				23 57	00 12			00 27
Shenfield 3	a	23 48		23 38	23 40	00 03	00 18	00 08	00 10	00 33
Shenfield 3	d			23 39				00 09		
Billericay	d			23 45				00 15		
Wickford 2	d			23 51				00 21		
Battlesbridge	d									
South Woodham Ferrers	d									
North Fambridge	d									
Althorne	d									
Burnham-on-Crouch	d									
Southminster	a									
Rayleigh	d			23 56				00 26		
Hockley	d			00 01				00 31		
Rochford	d			00 04				00 34		
Southend Airport ✈	d			00 07				00 37		
Prittlewell	d			00 10				00 40		
Southend Victoria	a			00 18				00 48		

Table 5

Sundays
until 22 July

London - Shenfield, Southminster and Southend Victoria

Network Diagram - see first Page of Table 5

		LE	LE	LE	LE	LE	LE	LE	LE	LE		LE	LE	LE	LE	LE	LE	LE	LE	LE		LE	LE	LE	LE
		1			1	1			1	1				1			1			1		1			1
																A		B	A	A		B	B	A	
																		Bus					Bus		
London Liverpool Street 15 ⊖	d	23p15	23p20	23p35	23p45	23p48	23p50	00 01	00 15	00 18		00 20	00 32	00 50	00 55	06 35		06 35	07 05	07 15				07 35	
Stratford 7 ⊖	d	23p22	23p27	23p42	23p52	23p55	23p57	00 08	00 22	00 25		00 27	00 39	00 57	01 02	06 42		06 55	07 12	07 22				07 42	
Maryland	d		23p29	23p44			23p59	00 10				00 29	00 41		01 04	06 43			07 13					07 43	
Forest Gate	d		23p31	23p46			00 01	00 12				00 31	00 43		01 06	06 45			07 15					07 45	
Manor Park	d		23p33	23p48			00 03	00 14				00 33	00 45		01 08	06 47			07 17					07 47	
Ilford 2	d		23p36	23p51			00 06	00 17				00 36	00 48		01 11	06 50		07 10	07 20					07 50	
Seven Kings	d		23p38	23p53			00 08	00 19				00 38	00 50		01 13	06 53			07 23					07 53	
Goodmayes	d		23p40	23p55			00 10	00 21				00 40	00 52		01 15	06 55			07 25					07 55	
Chadwell Heath	d		23p42	23p57			00 12	00 23				00 42	00 54		01 17	06 57			07 27					07 57	
Romford	d		23p46	00 02			00 16	00 27	00 32			00 46	00 58	01 08	01 21	07 00		07 30	07 30	07 33				08 00	
Gidea Park 2	d		23p50	00 05			00 20	00a31				00 50	01a02		01 25	07 04		07 37	07 34	07 37				08 04	
Harold Wood	d		23p53	00 08			00 23					00 53			01 28	07 07		07 44	07 37	07 40			←	08 07	
Brentwood	d		23p57	00 12			00 27					00 57			01 32	07 11		07 59	07 41	07 44			07 59	08 11	
Shenfield 3	a	23p38	00 03	00 18	00 08	00 10	00 33		00 44	00 47		01 03		01 20	01 38	07 18		→	07 48	07 50			08 09	08 18	
Shenfield 3	d	23p39			00 09				00 45					01 20						07 50		07 50			
Billericay	d	23p45			00 15				00 51					01 26						07 56		07 56			
Wickford 2	d	23p51			00 21				00 56					01 31			07 30			08 01		08 01			08 05
Battlesbridge	d																07 34								08 09
South Woodham Ferrers	d																07 38								08 13
North Fambridge	d																07 44								08 20
Althorne	d																07 49								08 25
Burnham-on-Crouch	d																07 54								08 30
Southminster	a																08 00								08 36
Rayleigh	d	23p56			00 26				01 01					01 36						08 06		08 06			
Hockley	d	00 01			00 31				01 06					01 41						08 11		08 11			
Rochford	d	00 04			00 34				01 09					01 44						08 14		08 14			
Southend Airport ✈	d	00 07			00 37				01 12					01 47						08 17		08 17			
Prittlewell	d	00 10			00 40				01 15					01 50											
Southend Victoria	a	00 18			00 48				01 23					01 58						08 25		08 25			

		LE	LE	LE	LE	LE		LE	LE	LE	LE	LE	LE	LE	LE	LE		LE	LE	LE	LE	LE	LE
		1	1	1	1			1	◇1	1		1	1		1			1		1		1	1
		A	B		A				B	A				A									
London Liverpool Street 15 ⊖	d	07 45		07 55	08 02	08 05		08 15	08 30	08 32	08 35		08 45	08 47	09 02	09 05		09 15	09 17	09 32	09 35		09 45
Stratford 7 ⊖	d	07 52		08 02	08 09	08 12		08 22		08 39	08 42		08 52	08 54	09 09	09 12		09 22	09 24	09 39	09 42		09 52
Maryland	d					08 13					08 43					09 13					09 43		
Forest Gate	d					08 15					08 45			08 57		09 15			09 27		09 45		
Manor Park	d					08 17					08 47			08 59		09 17			09 29		09 47		
Ilford 2	d					08 20					08 50			09 02		09 20			09 32		09 50		
Seven Kings	d					08 23					08 53			09 04		09 23			09 34		09 53		
Goodmayes	d					08 25					08 55			09 06		09 25			09 36		09 55		
Chadwell Heath	d					08 27					08 57			09 08		09 27			09 38		09 57		
Romford	d	08 03				08 30		08 33			09 00		09 03	09 12		09 30		09 33	09 42		10 00		10 03
Gidea Park 2	d	08 07				08 34		08 37			09 04		09 07	09a17		09 34		09 37	09a47		10 04		10 07
Harold Wood	d	08 10				08 37		08 40			09 07		09 10			09 37		09 40			10 07		10 10
Brentwood	d	08 14				08 41		08 44			09 11		09 14			09 41		09 44			10 11		10 14
Shenfield 3	a	08 20		08 24	08 30	08 48		08 50	08 57	09 00	09 18		09 20		09 30	09 48		09 50		10 00	10 18		10 20
Shenfield 3	d	08 20	08 20					08 50					09 20					09 50					10 20
Billericay	d	08 26	08 26					08 56					09 26					09 56					10 26
Wickford 2	d	08 31	08 31					09 01				09 05	09 31					10 01				10 05	10 31
Battlesbridge	d											09 09										10 09	
South Woodham Ferrers	d											09 13										10 13	
North Fambridge	d											09 20										10 20	
Althorne	d											09 25										10 25	
Burnham-on-Crouch	d											09 30										10 30	
Southminster	a											09 36										10 36	
Rayleigh	d	08 36	08 36					09 06					09 36					10 06					10 36
Hockley	d	08 41	08 41					09 11					09 41					10 11					10 41
Rochford	d	08 44	08 44					09 14					09 44					10 14					10 44
Southend Airport ✈	d	08 47	08 47					09 17					09 47					10 17					10 47
Prittlewell	d																						
Southend Victoria	a	08 55	08 55					09 25					09 55					10 25					10 55

A from 1 July until 22 July

B until 24 June

Table 5

Sundays
until 22 July

London - Shenfield, Southminster and Southend Victoria

Network Diagram - see first Page of Table 5

		LE		LE	LE 1	LE	LE 1	LE	LE 1	LE	LE 1	LE 1	LE	LE 1	LE	LE 1	LE	LE 1	LE	LE 1	LE 1	LE
London Liverpool Street 15 ⊖	d	09 47		19 47	20 02	20 05	20 15	20 17	20 32	20 35		20 45	20 47	21 02	21 05	21 15	21 17	21 32	21 35		21 45	21 47
Stratford 7 ⊖	d	09 54		19 54	20 09	20 12	20 22	20 24	20 39	20 42		20 52	20 54	21 09	21 12	21 22	21 24	21 39	21 42		21 52	21 54
Maryland	d					20 13				20 43					21 13				21 43			
Forest Gate	d	09 57		19 57		20 15		20 27		20 45			20 57		21 15		21 27		21 45			21 57
Manor Park	d	09 59		19 59		20 17		20 29		20 47			20 59		21 17		21 29		21 47			21 59
Ilford 2	d	10 02		20 02		20 20		20 32		20 50			21 02		21 20		21 32		21 50			22 02
Seven Kings	d	10 04		20 04		20 23		20 34		20 53			21 04		21 23		21 34		21 53			22 04
Goodmayes	d	10 06		20 06		20 25		20 36		20 55			21 06		21 25		21 36		21 55			22 06
Chadwell Heath	d	10 08		20 08		20 27		20 38		20 57			21 08		21 27		21 38		21 57			22 08
Romford	d	10 12		20 12		20 30	20 33	20 42		21 00		21 03	21 12		21 30	21 33	21 42		22 00		22 03	22 12
Gidea Park 2	d	10a17	and at the same minutes past each hour until	20a17		20 34	20 37	20a47		21 04		21 07	21a15		21 34	21 37	21a47		22 04		22 07	22a17
Harold Wood	d					20 37	20 40			21 07		21 10			21 37	21 40			22 07		22 10	
Brentwood	d					20 41	20 44			21 11		21 14			21 41	21 44			22 11		22 14	
Shenfield 3	a				20 30	20 48	20 50		21 00	21 18		21 20		21 30	21 48	21 50		22 00	22 18		22 20	
Shenfield 3	d						20 50					21 20				21 50					22 20	
Billericay	d						20 56					21 26				21 56					22 26	
Wickford 2	d						21 01				21 05	21 31				22 01				22 05	22 31	
Battlesbridge	d										21 09									22 09		
South Woodham Ferrers	d										21 13									22 13		
North Fambridge	d										21 20									22 20		
Althorne	d										21 25									22 25		
Burnham-on-Crouch	d										21 30									22 30		
Southminster	a										21 36									22 36		
Rayleigh	d						21 06					21 36				22 06					22 36	
Hockley	d						21 11					21 41				22 11					22 41	
Rochford	d						21 14					21 44				22 14					22 44	
Southend Airport ✈	d						21 17					21 47				22 17					22 47	
Prittlewell	d																					
Southend Victoria	a						21 25					21 55				22 25					22 55	

		LE 1	LE	LE 1	LE	LE 1	LE	LE 1	LE 1	LE	LE 1	LE 1	LE	LE 1
London Liverpool Street 15 ⊖	d	22 02	22 05	22 15	22 17	22 32	22 35	22 45	23 02	23 05	23 15	23 32	23 35	23 45
Stratford 7 ⊖	d	22 09	22 12	22 22	22 24	22 39	22 42	22 52	23 09	23 12	23 22	23 39	23 42	23 52
Maryland	d		22 13				22 43			23 13			23 43	
Forest Gate	d		22 15		22 27		22 45			23 15			23 45	
Manor Park	d		22 17		22 29		22 47			23 17			23 47	
Ilford 2	d		22 20		22 32		22 50			23 20			23 50	
Seven Kings	d		22 23		22 34		22 53			23 23			23 53	
Goodmayes	d		22 25		22 36		22 55			23 25			23 55	
Chadwell Heath	d		22 27		22 38		22 57			23 27			23 57	
Romford	d		22 30	22 33	22 42		23 00	23 03		23 30	23 33		23 59	00 03
Gidea Park 2	d		22 34	22 37	22a47		23 04	23 07		23 34	23 37		00 04	00 07
Harold Wood	d		22 37	22 40			23 07	23 10		23 37	23 40		00 07	00 10
Brentwood	d		22 41	22 44			23 11	23 14		23 41	23 44		00 11	00 14
Shenfield 3	a	22 30	22 48	22 50		23 00	23 18	23 20	23 30	23 48	23 50	23 59	00 18	00 20
Shenfield 3	d			22 50				23 20			23 50			00 20
Billericay	d			22 56				23 26			23 56			00 26
Wickford 2	d			23 01				23 31			00 01			00 31
Battlesbridge	d													
South Woodham Ferrers	d													
North Fambridge	d													
Althorne	d													
Burnham-on-Crouch	d													
Southminster	a													
Rayleigh	d			23 06				23 36			00 06			00 36
Hockley	d			23 11				23 41			00 11			00 41
Rochford	d			23 14				23 44			00 14			00 44
Southend Airport ✈	d			23 17				23 47			00 17			00 47
Prittlewell	d													
Southend Victoria	a			23 27				23 57			00 27			00 57

Table 5

Sundays
29 July to 12 August

London - Shenfield, Southminster and Southend Victoria

Network Diagram - see first Page of Table 5

		LE 1	LE	LE 1	LE 1	LE	LE 1	LE 1	LE	LE 1	LE	LE 1	LE	LE	LE 1	LE 1	LE 1	LE	LE	LE 1	LE	LE 1	LE	LE
London Liverpool Street 15 ⊖	d	23p10	23p22		23p25	23p32	23p35	23p40	23p42	23p45	23p52	23p55	00 02	00 12	00 12	00 15	00 18	00 22	00 32	00 40	00 42	00 46	00 52	01 02
Stratford 7 ⊖	d	23p22	23p33		23p37	23p43	23p45	23p52	23p53	23p54	00 03	00 07	00 13	00 23	00 24	00 27	00a27	00 33	00 43	00 52	00 53	01 00	01 03	01 13
Maryland	d																							
Forest Gate	d		23p36			23p46			23p56		00 06		00 16	00 26				00 36	00 46		00 56		01 06	01 16
Manor Park	d		23p38			23p48			23p58		00 08		00 18	00 28				00 38	00 48		00 58		01 08	01 18
Ilford 2	d		23p41			23p51			00 01		00 11		00 21	00 31				00 41	00 51		01 01		01 11	01 21
Seven Kings	d		23p43			23p53			00 03		00 13		00 23	00 33				00 43	00 53		01 03		01 13	01 23
Goodmayes	d		23p45			23p55			00 05		00 15		00 25	00 35				00 45	00 55		01 05		01 15	01 25
Chadwell Heath	d		23p47			23p57			00 07		00 17		00 27	00 37				00 47	00 57		01 07		01 17	01 27
Romford	d		23p51			00 02			00 12		00 21		00 31	00 41				00 51	01 01		01 11		01 21	01 31
Gidea Park 2	d		23p55			00 05			00 15		00 25		00 35	00 45				00 55	01 05		01 15		01 25	01 35
Harold Wood	d		23p58			00 08			00 18		00 28		00 38	00 48				00 58	01 08		01 18		01 28	01 38
Brentwood	d		00 02			00 12			00 22		00 32		00 42	00 52				01 02	01 12		01 22		01 32	01 42
Shenfield 3	a	23p38	00 08		23p53	00 18	00 01	00 08	00 28	00 11	00 38	00 23	00 48	00 58	00 40	00 45		01 08	01 18	01 07	01 28	01 17	01 38	01 48
Shenfield 3	d	23p39			23p54			00 09				00 24				00 46				01 09				
Billericay	d	23p45			23p59			00 15				00 30				00 52				01 15				
Wickford 2	d	23p51		23p56	00 06			00 21				00 36				00 58				01 21				
Battlesbridge	d			00 01																				
South Woodham Ferrers	d			00 04																				
North Fambridge	d			00 11																				
Althorne	d			00 16																				
Burnham-on-Crouch	d			00 21																				
Southminster	a			00 27																				
Rayleigh	d	23p56			00 11			00 26				00 41				01 03				01 26				
Hockley	d	00 01			00 16			00 31				00 46				01 08				01 31				
Rochford	d	00 04			00 19			00 34				00 49				01 11				01 34				
Southend Airport ✈	d	00 07			00 22			00 37				00 52				01 14				01 37				
Prittlewell	d	00 10			00 25			00 40				00 55				01 17				01 40				
Southend Victoria	a	00 14			00 29			00 44				00 59				01 21				01 44				

		LE 1	LE	LE	LE	LE	LE	LE	LE	LE	LE	LE	LE 1	LE 1	LE	LE 1	LE	LE 1	LE	LE 1	LE 1	LE 1	LE 1
London Liverpool Street 15 ⊖	d	01 10	01 12	01 22	01 32	01 42	01 52	02 02	02 12	06 05	06 35	07 05		07 15	07 20	07 35	07 35	07 38	07 50		07 55	07 55	08 02
Stratford 7 ⊖	d	01 22	01 23	01 33	01 43	01 53	02 03	02 13	02 23	06 13	06 43	07 13		07 22	07 28	07 42	07 43	07 47	07 58		08 02	08 02	08 09
Maryland	d																						
Forest Gate	d		01 26	01 36	01 46	01 56	02 06	02 16	02 26	06 16	06 46	07 16			07 31		07 46		08 01				
Manor Park	d		01 28	01 38	01 48	01 58	02 08	02 18	02 28	06 18	06 48	07 18			07 33		07 48		08 03				
Ilford 2	d		01 31	01 41	01 51	02 01	02 11	02 21	02 31	06 21	06 51	07 21			07 36		07 51		08 06				
Seven Kings	d		01 33	01 43	01 53	02 03	02 13	02 23	02 33	06 23	06 53	07 23			07 38		07 53		08 08				
Goodmayes	d		01 35	01 45	01 55	02 05	02 15	02 25	02 35	06 25	06 55	07 25			07 40		07 55		08 10				
Chadwell Heath	d		01 37	01 47	01 57	02 07	02 17	02 27	02 37	06 27	06 57	07 27			07 42		07 57		08 12				
Romford	d		01 41	01 51	02 01	02 11	02 21	02 31	02 41	06 31	07 01	07 31			07 46		08 01		08 16				
Gidea Park 2	d		01 45	01 55	02a05	02 15	02a25	02 35	02a45	06 35	07 05	07 35			07 50		08 05		08 20				
Harold Wood	d		01 48	01 58		02 18		02 38		06 38	07 08	07 38			07 53		08 08		08 23				
Brentwood	d		01 52	02 02		02 22		02 42		06 42	07 12	07 42			07 57		08 12		08 27				
Shenfield 3	a	01 37	01 58	02 08		02 28		02 48		06 49	07 19	07 49		07 38	08 04	07 58	08 20	08 02	08 34		08 18	08 21	08 24
Shenfield 3	d	01 39												07 39		07 59					08 19		
Billericay	d	01 45												07 45		08 05					08 25		
Wickford 2	d	01 51											07 30	07 51		08 11				08 16	08 31		
Battlesbridge	d												07 34							08 20			
South Woodham Ferrers	d												07 38							08 24			
North Fambridge	d												07 44							08 31			
Althorne	d												07 49							08 36			
Burnham-on-Crouch	d												07 54							08 41			
Southminster	a												08 00							08 47			
Rayleigh	d	01 56												07 56		08 16					08 36		
Hockley	d	02 01												08 01		08 21					08 41		
Rochford	d	02 04												08 04		08 24					08 44		
Southend Airport ✈	d	02 07												08 07		08 27					08 47		
Prittlewell	d	02 10												08 10		08 30					08 50		
Southend Victoria	a	02 14												08 14		08 34					08 54		

Table 5

Sundays

29 July to 12 August

London - Shenfield, Southminster and Southend Victoria

Network Diagram - see first Page of Table 5

		LE		LE 1	LE 1	LE	LE 1	LE	LE 1	LE	LE 1	LE 1		LE 1		LE 1	LE	LE 1	LE 1	LE	LE 1	LE	LE 1	LE
London Liverpool Street 15 ⊖	d	08 05		08 15	08 18	08 20	08 35	08 35	08 38	08 50		08 55		18 55		19 02	19 05	19 15	19 18	19 20	19 35	19 35	19 38	19 50
Stratford 7 ⊖	d	08 13		08 22	08 25	08 28	08 42	08 43	08 47	08 58		09 02		19 02		19 09	19 13	19 22	19 25	19 28	19 43	19 43	19 47	19 58
Maryland	d																							
Forest Gate	d	08 16				08 31		08 46		09 01							19 16			19 31		19 46		20 01
Manor Park	d	08 18				08 33		08 48		09 03							19 18			19 33		19 48		20 03
Ilford 2	d	08 21				08 36		08 51		09 06							19 21			19 36		19 51		20 06
Seven Kings	d	08 23				08 38		08 53		09 08							19 23			19 38		19 53		20 08
Goodmayes	d	08 25				08 40		08 55		09 10							19 25			19 40		19 55		20 10
Chadwell Heath	d	08 27				08 42		08 57		09 12							19 27			19 42		19 57		20 12
Romford	d	08 31				08 46		09 01		09 16							19 31			19 46		20 01		20 16
Gidea Park 2	d	08 35				08 50		09 05		09 20			and at				19 35			19 50		20 05		20 20
Harold Wood	d	08 38				08 53		09 08		09 23			the same				19 38			19 53		20 08		20 23
Brentwood	d	08 42				08 57		09 12		09 27			minutes				19 42			19 57		20 12		20 27
Shenfield 3	a	08 49		08 38	08 40	09 04	08 58	09 20	09 02	09 34		09 18	past	19 18		19 24	19 49	19 38	19 40	20 04	19 59	20 20	20 02	20 34
Shenfield 3	d			08 39			08 59					09 19	each	19 19				19 39			20 00			
Billericay	d			08 45			09 05					09 25	hour until	19 25				19 45			20 06			
Wickford 2	d			08 51			09 11				09 16	09 31		19 31				19 51			20 12			
Battlesbridge	d										09 20													
South Woodham Ferrers	d										09 24													
North Fambridge	d										09 31													
Althorne	d										09 36													
Burnham-on-Crouch	d										09 41													
Southminster	a										09 47													
Rayleigh	d			08 56			09 16					09 36		19 36				19 56			20 17			
Hockley	d			09 01			09 21					09 41		19 41				20 01			20 22			
Rochford	d			09 04			09 24					09 44		19 44				20 04			20 25			
Southend Airport ✈	d			09 07			09 27					09 47		19 47				20 07			20 28			
Prittlewell	d			09 10			09 30					09 50		19 50				20 10			20 31			
Southend Victoria	a			09 14			09 34					09 54		19 54				20 14			20 35			

			LE 1	LE 1	LE 1	LE	LE 1	LE 1	LE	LE 1	LE		LE 1	LE	LE 1	LE 1	LE 1	LE	LE 1	LE 1	LE		LE 1	LE	LE 1
London Liverpool Street 15 ⊖	d			19 55	20 02	20 05	20 15	20 18	20 20	20 35	20 35		20 38	20 50		20 55	21 02	21 05	21 15	21 18	21 20		21 35	21 35	21 38
Stratford 7 ⊖	d			20 02	20 09	20 13	20 22	20 25	20 28	20 42	20 43		20 47	20 58		21 02	21 09	21 13	21 22	21 25	21 28		21 42	21 43	21 47
Maryland	d																								
Forest Gate	d					20 16			20 31		20 46			21 01				21 16			21 31			21 46	
Manor Park	d					20 18			20 33		20 48			21 03				21 18			21 33			21 48	
Ilford 2	d					20 21			20 36		20 51			21 06				21 21			21 36			21 51	
Seven Kings	d					20 23			20 38		20 53			21 08				21 23			21 38			21 53	
Goodmayes	d					20 25			20 40		20 55			21 10				21 25			21 40			21 55	
Chadwell Heath	d					20 27			20 42		20 57			21 12				21 27			21 42			21 57	
Romford	d					20 31			20 46		21 01			21 16				21 31			21 46			22 01	
Gidea Park 2	d					20 35			20 50		21 05			21 20				21 35			21 50			22 05	
Harold Wood	d					20 38			20 53		21 08			21 23				21 38			21 53			22 08	
Brentwood	d					20 42			20 57		21 12			21 27				21 42			21 57			22 12	
Shenfield 3	a			20 18	20 24	20 49	20 38	20 40	21 04	20 58	21 20		21 02	21 34		21 18	21 24	21 49	21 38	21 40	22 04		21 58	22 20	22 02
Shenfield 3	d			20 19			20 39			20 59						21 19			21 39				21 59		
Billericay	d			20 25			20 45			21 05						21 25			21 45				22 05		
Wickford 2	d		20 16	20 31			20 51			21 11					21 16	21 31			21 51				22 11		
Battlesbridge	d		20 20												21 20										
South Woodham Ferrers	d		20 24												21 24										
North Fambridge	d		20 31												21 31										
Althorne	d		20 36												21 36										
Burnham-on-Crouch	d		20 41												21 41										
Southminster	a		20 47												21 47										
Rayleigh	d			20 36			20 56			21 16						21 36			21 56				22 16		
Hockley	d			20 41			21 01			21 21						21 41			22 01				22 21		
Rochford	d			20 44			21 04			21 24						21 44			22 04				22 24		
Southend Airport ✈	d			20 47			21 07			21 27						21 47			22 07				22 27		
Prittlewell	d			20 50			21 10			21 30						21 50			22 10				22 30		
Southend Victoria	a			20 54			21 14			21 34						21 54			22 14				22 34		

Table 5

Sundays

29 July to 12 August

London - Shenfield, Southminster and Southend Victoria

Network Diagram - see first Page of Table 5

		LE	LE 1	LE 1	LE 1	LE 1	LE		LE 1	LE 1	LE	LE 1	LE 1	LE	LE 1	LE 1	LE	LE 1	LE	LE 1	LE	LE 1	LE 1	LE	LE 1
London Liverpool Street 15 ⊖	d	21 50		21 50	21 56	22 02	22 02		22 10	22 15	22 17		22 25	22 32	22 35	22 40	22 42	22 45	22 52	22 55	23 02	23 07	23 10	23 12	
Stratford 7 ⊖	d	21 58		22 02	22a04	22 10	22 13		22 22	22 24	22 28		22 37	22 43	22 44	22 52	22 53	22 54	23 03	23 07	23 13	23 17	23 22	23 23	
Maryland	d																								
Forest Gate	d	22 01					22 16				22 31			22 46			22 56		23 06		23 16			23 26	
Manor Park	d	22 03					22 18				22 33			22 48			22 58		23 08		23 18			23 28	
Ilford 2	d	22 06					22 21				22 36			22 51			23 01		23 11		23 21			23 31	
Seven Kings	d	22 08					22 23				22 38			22 53			23 03		23 13		23 23			23 33	
Goodmayes	d	22 10					22 25				22 40			22 55			23 05		23 15		23 25			23 35	
Chadwell Heath	d	22 12					22 27				22 42			22 57			23 07		23 17		23 27			23 37	
Romford	d	22 16					22 31				22 46			23 01			23 11		23 21		23 31			23 41	
Gidea Park 2	d	22 20					22 35				22 50			23 05			23 15		23 25		23 35			23 45	
Harold Wood	d	22 23					22 38				22 53			23 08			23 18		23 28		23 38			23 48	
Brentwood	d	22 27					22 42				22 57			23 12			23 22		23 32		23 42			23 52	
Shenfield 3	a	22 34		22 18		22 26	22 49		22 38	22 40	23 04		22 53	23 19	23 00	23 08	23 29	23 10	23 39	23 23	23 49	23 33	23 37	23 59	
Shenfield 3	d			22 19					22 39				22 54			23 09				23 24			23 38		
Billericay	d			22 25					22 45				23 00			23 15				23 30			23 45		
Wickford 2	d		22 16	22 31					22 51			22 56	23 06			23 21				23 36			23 51		23 56
Battlesbridge	d		22 20									23 00													00 01
South Woodham Ferrers	d		22 24									23 04													00 04
North Fambridge	d		22 31									23 11													00 11
Althorne	d		22 36									23 16													00 16
Burnham-on-Crouch	d		22 41									23 21													00 21
Southminster	a		22 47									23 27													00 27
Rayleigh	d			22 36					22 56				23 11			23 26				23 41			23 56		
Hockley	d			22 41					23 01				23 16			23 31				23 46			00 01		
Rochford	d			22 44					23 04				23 19			23 34				23 49			00 04		
Southend Airport ✈	d			22 47					23 07				23 22			23 37				23 52			00 07		
Prittlewell	d			22 50					23 10				23 25			23 40				23 55			00 10		
Southend Victoria	a			22 54					23 14				23 29			23 44				23 59			00 14		

		LE 1	LE		LE 1	LE	LE 1	LE 1	LE	LE 1	LE	LE 1
London Liverpool Street 15 ⊖	d	23 15	23 22		23 25	23 32	23 35	23 40	23 42	23 45	23 52	23 55
Stratford 7 ⊖	d	23 25	23 33		23 37	23 43	23 45	23 52	23 53	23 54	00 03	00 07
Maryland	d											
Forest Gate	d		23 36			23 46			23 56		00 06	
Manor Park	d		23 38			23 48			23 58		00 08	
Ilford 2	d		23 41			23 51			00 01		00 11	
Seven Kings	d		23 43			23 53			00 03		00 13	
Goodmayes	d		23 45			23 55			00 05		00 15	
Chadwell Heath	d		23 47			23 57			00 07		00 17	
Romford	d		23 51			00 02			00 11		00 21	
Gidea Park 2	d		23 55			00 05			00 15		00 25	
Harold Wood	d		23 58			00 08			00 18		00 28	
Brentwood	d		00 02			00 12			00 22		00 32	
Shenfield 3	a	23 41	00 09		23 52	00 19	00 01	00 09	00 29	00 10	00 39	00 22
Shenfield 3	d				23 54			00 09				00 24
Billericay	d				23 59			00 15				00 30
Wickford 2	d				00 06			00 21				00 36
Battlesbridge	d											
South Woodham Ferrers	d											
North Fambridge	d											
Althorne	d											
Burnham-on-Crouch	d											
Southminster	a											
Rayleigh	d				00 11			00 26				00 41
Hockley	d				00 16			00 31				00 46
Rochford	d				00 19			00 34				00 49
Southend Airport ✈	d				00 22			00 37				00 52
Prittlewell	d				00 25			00 40				00 55
Southend Victoria	a				00 29			00 44				00 59

Table 5

Sundays
19 August to 26 August

London - Shenfield, Southminster and Southend Victoria

Network Diagram - see first Page of Table 5

		LE 1	LE	LE	LE 1	LE 1	LE	LE	LE 1	LE 1	LE	LE	LE 1	LE	LE	LE	LE 1	LE 1	LE	LE 1	LE 1	LE 1	LE 1
London Liverpool Street 15 ⊖	d	23p15	23p20	23p35	23p45	23p48	23p50	00 01	00 15	00 18	00 20	00 32	00 50	00 55	06 35	07 05		07 15	07 35		07 45	07 55	08 02
Stratford 7 ⊖	d	23p22	23p27	23p42	23p52	23p55	23p57	00 08	00 22	00 25	00 27	00 39	00 57	01 02	06 42	07 12		07 22	07 42		07 52	08 02	08 09
Maryland	d		23p29	23p44			23p59	00 10			00 29	00 41		01 04	06 43	07 13			07 43				
Forest Gate	d		23p31	23p46			00 01	00 12			00 31	00 43		01 06	06 45	07 15			07 45				
Manor Park	d		23p33	23p48			00 03	00 14			00 33	00 45		01 08	06 47	07 17			07 47				
Ilford 2	d		23p36	23p51			00 06	00 17			00 36	00 48		01 11	06 50	07 20			07 50				
Seven Kings	d		23p38	23p53			00 08	00 19			00 38	00 50		01 13	06 53	07 23			07 53				
Goodmayes	d		23p40	23p55			00 10	00 21			00 40	00 52		01 15	06 55	07 25			07 55				
Chadwell Heath	d		23p42	23p57			00 12	00 23			00 42	00 54		01 17	06 57	07 27			07 57				
Romford	d		23p46	00 02			00 16	00 27	00 32		00 46	00 58	01 08	01 21	07 00	07 30		07 33	08 00		08 03		
Gidea Park 2	d		23p50	00 05			00 20	00a31			00 50	01a02		01 25	07 04	07 34		07 37	08 04		08 07		
Harold Wood	d		23p53	00 08			00 23				00 53			01 28	07 07	07 37		07 40	08 07		08 10		
Brentwood	d		23p57	00 12			00 27				00 57			01 32	07 11	07 41		07 44	08 11		08 14		
Shenfield 3	a	23p38	00 03	00 18	00 08	00 10	00 33		00 44	00 47	01 03		01 20	01 38	07 18	07 48		07 50	08 18		08 20	08 24	08 30
Shenfield 3	d	23p39			00 09				00 45				01 20					07 50			08 20		
Billericay	d	23p45			00 15				00 51				01 26					07 56			08 26		
Wickford 2	d	23p51			00 21				00 56				01 31				07 30	08 01		08 05	08 31		
Battlesbridge	d																07 34			08 09			
South Woodham Ferrers	d																07 38			08 13			
North Fambridge	d																07 44			08 20			
Althorne	d																07 49			08 25			
Burnham-on-Crouch	d																07 54			08 30			
Southminster	a																08 00			08 36			
Rayleigh	d	23p56			00 26				01 01				01 36					08 06			08 36		
Hockley	d	00 01			00 31				01 06				01 41					08 11			08 41		
Rochford	d	00 04			00 34				01 09				01 44					08 14			08 44		
Southend Airport ✈	d	00 07			00 37				01 12				01 47					08 17			08 47		
Prittlewell	d	00 10			00 40				01 15				01 50										
Southend Victoria	a	00 18			00 48				01 23				01 58					08 25			08 55		

		LE	LE 1	LE 1	LE	LE 1	LE 1	LE	LE 1	LE	LE 1	LE		LE	LE 1	LE	LE 1	LE 1	LE	LE 1	LE	LE 1
London Liverpool Street 15 ⊖	d	08 05	08 15	08 32	08 35		08 45	08 47	09 02	09 05	09 15	09 17		21 17	21 32	21 35		21 45	21 47	22 02	22 05	22 15
Stratford 7 ⊖	d	08 12	08 22	08 39	08 42		08 52	08 54	09 09	09 12	09 22	09 24		21 24	21 39	21 42		21 52	21 54	22 09	22 12	22 22
Maryland	d	08 13			08 43					09 13						21 43					22 13	
Forest Gate	d	08 15			08 45			08 57		09 15		09 27		21 27		21 45			21 57		22 15	
Manor Park	d	08 17			08 47			08 59		09 17		09 29		21 29		21 47			21 59		22 17	
Ilford 2	d	08 20			08 50			09 02		09 20		09 32		21 32		21 50			22 02		22 20	
Seven Kings	d	08 23			08 53			09 04		09 23		09 34		21 34		21 53			22 04		22 23	
Goodmayes	d	08 25			08 55			09 06		09 25		09 36		21 36		21 55			22 06		22 25	
Chadwell Heath	d	08 27			08 57			09 08		09 27		09 38		21 38		21 57			22 08		22 27	
Romford	d	08 30	08 33		09 00		09 03	09 12		09 30	09 33	09 42		21 42		22 00		22 03	22 12		22 30	22 33
Gidea Park 2	d	08 34	08 37		09 04		09 07	09a17		09 34	09 37	09a47	and at the same minutes past each hour until	21a47		22 04		22 07	22a17		22 34	22 37
Harold Wood	d	08 37	08 40		09 07		09 10			09 37	09 40					22 07		22 10			22 37	22 40
Brentwood	d	08 41	08 44		09 11		09 14			09 41	09 44					22 11		22 14			22 41	22 44
Shenfield 3	a	08 48	08 50	09 00	09 18		09 20		09 30	09 48	09 50				22 00	22 18		22 20		22 30	22 48	22 50
Shenfield 3	d		08 50				09 20				09 50							22 20				22 50
Billericay	d		08 56				09 26				09 56							22 26				22 56
Wickford 2	d		09 01			09 05	09 31				10 01						22 05	22 31				23 01
Battlesbridge	d					09 09											22 09					
South Woodham Ferrers	d					09 13											22 13					
North Fambridge	d					09 20											22 20					
Althorne	d					09 25											22 25					
Burnham-on-Crouch	d					09 30											22 30					
Southminster	a					09 36											22 36					
Rayleigh	d		09 06				09 36				10 06							22 36				23 06
Hockley	d		09 11				09 41				10 11							22 41				23 11
Rochford	d		09 14				09 44				10 14							22 44				23 14
Southend Airport ✈	d		09 17				09 47				10 17							22 47				23 17
Prittlewell	d																					
Southend Victoria	a		09 25				09 55				10 25							22 55				23 27

Table 5

Sundays
19 August to 26 August

London - Shenfield, Southminster and Southend Victoria

Network Diagram - see first Page of Table 5

		LE	LE 1	LE	LE 1	LE 1	LE	LE 1	LE 1	LE	LE 1
London Liverpool Street 15 ⊖	d	22 17	22 32	22 35	22 45	23 02	23 05	23 15	23 32	23 35	23 45
Stratford 7 ⊖	d	22 24	22 39	22 42	22 52	23 09	23 12	23 22	23 39	23 42	23 52
Maryland	d			22 43			23 13			23 43	
Forest Gate	d	22 27		22 45			23 15			23 45	
Manor Park	d	22 29		22 47			23 17			23 47	
Ilford 2	d	22 32		22 50			23 20			23 50	
Seven Kings	d	22 34		22 53			23 23			23 53	
Goodmayes	d	22 36		22 55			23 25			23 55	
Chadwell Heath	d	22 38		22 57			23 27			23 57	
Romford	d	22 42		23 00	23 03		23 30	23 33		23 59	00 03
Gidea Park 2	d	22a47		23 04	23 07		23 34	23 37		00 04	00 07
Harold Wood	d			23 07	23 10		23 37	23 40		00 07	00 10
Brentwood	d			23 11	23 14		23 41	23 44		00 11	00 14
Shenfield 3	a		23 00	23 18	23 20	23 30	23 48	23 50	23 59	00 18	00 20
Shenfield 3	d				23 20			23 50			00 20
Billericay	d				23 26			23 56			00 26
Wickford 2	d				23 31			00 01			00 31
Battlesbridge	d										
South Woodham Ferrers	d										
North Fambridge	d										
Althorne	d										
Burnham-on-Crouch	d										
Southminster	a										
Rayleigh	d				23 36			00 06			00 36
Hockley	d				23 41			00 11			00 41
Rochford	d				23 44			00 14			00 44
Southend Airport ✈	d				23 47			00 17			00 47
Prittlewell	d										
Southend Victoria	a				23 57			00 27			00 57

Sundays
2 September to 9 September

		LE 1	LE 1	LE	LE 1	LE	LE 1	LE 1	LE	LE 1	LE	LE 1	LE	LE	LE 1	LE 1	LE 1	LE	LE	LE 1	LE	LE 1	LE	LE
London Liverpool Street 15 ⊖	d	23p10		23p22	23p25	23p32	23p35	23p40	23p42	23p45	23p52	23p55	00 02	00 12	00 12	00 15	00 18	00 22	00 32	00 40	00 42	00 46	00 52	01 02
Stratford 7 ⊖	d	23p22		23p32	23p37	23p42	23p45	23p52	23p52	23p54	00 02	00 07	00 12	00 22	00 24	00 27	00a27	00 32	00 42	00 52	00 52	01 00	01 02	01 12
Maryland	d			23p34		23p44			23p54		00 04		00 14	00 24				00 34	00 44		00 54		01 04	01 14
Forest Gate	d			23p36		23p46			23p56		00 06		00 16	00 26				00 36	00 46		00 56		01 06	01 16
Manor Park	d			23p38		23p48			23p58		00 08		00 18	00 28				00 38	00 48		00 58		01 08	01 18
Ilford 2	d			23p41		23p51			00 01		00 11		00 21	00 31				00 41	00 51		01 01		01 11	01 21
Seven Kings	d			23p43		23p53			00 03		00 13		00 23	00 33				00 43	00 53		01 03		01 13	01 23
Goodmayes	d			23p45		23p55			00 05		00 15		00 25	00 35				00 45	00 55		01 05		01 15	01 25
Chadwell Heath	d			23p47		23p57			00 07		00 17		00 27	00 37				00 47	00 57		01 07		01 17	01 27
Romford	d			23p51		00 02			00 12		00 21		00 31	00 41				00 51	01 01		01 11		01 21	01 31
Gidea Park 2	d			23p55		00 05			00 15		00 25		00 35	00 45				00 55	01 05		01 15		01 25	01 35
Harold Wood	d			23p58		00 08			00 18		00 28		00 38	00 48				00 58	01 08		01 18		01 28	01 38
Brentwood	d			00 02		00 12			00 22		00 32		00 42	00 52				01 02	01 12		01 22		01 32	01 42
Shenfield 3	a	23p38		00 08	23p53	00 18	00 01	00 08	00 28	00 11	00 38	00 23	00 48	00 58	00 40	00 45		01 08	01 18	01 07	01 28	01 17	01 38	01 48
Shenfield 3	d	23p39			23p54			00 09				00 24				00 46				01 09				
Billericay	d	23p45			23p59			00 15				00 30				00 52				01 15				
Wickford 2	d	23p51	23p56		00 06			00 21				00 36				00 58				01 21				
Battlesbridge	d		00 01																					
South Woodham Ferrers	d		00 04																					
North Fambridge	d		00 11																					
Althorne	d		00 16																					
Burnham-on-Crouch	d		00 21																					
Southminster	a		00 27																					
Rayleigh	d	23p56			00 11			00 26				00 41				01 03				01 26				
Hockley	d	00 01			00 16			00 31				00 46				01 08				01 31				
Rochford	d	00 04			00 19			00 34				00 49				01 11				01 34				
Southend Airport ✈	d	00 07			00 22			00 37				00 52				01 14				01 37				
Prittlewell	d	00 10			00 25			00 40				00 55				01 17				01 40				
Southend Victoria	a	00 14			00 29			00 44				00 59				01 21				01 44				

London - Shenfield, Southminster and Southend Victoria

Network Diagram - see first Page of Table 5

		LE 1	LE	LE	LE	LE	LE	LE	LE	LE	LE	LE	LE 1	LE 1	LE	LE 1	LE	LE 1	LE	LE 1	LE 1	LE 1	LE 1
London Liverpool Street ⊖	d	01 10	01 12	01 22	01 32	01 42	01 52	02 02	02 12	06 05	06 35	07 05		07 15	07 20	07 35	07 35	07 38	07 50		07 55	07 55	08 02
Stratford ⊖	d	01 22	01 22	01 32	01 42	01 52	02 02	02 12	02 22	06 12	06 42	07 12		07 22	07 27	07 42	07 42	07 47	07 57		08 02	08 02	08 09
Maryland	d		01 24	01 34	01 44	01 54	02 04	02 14	02 24	06 14	06 44	07 14			07 29		07 44		07 59				
Forest Gate	d		01 26	01 36	01 46	01 56	02 06	02 16	02 26	06 16	06 46	07 16			07 31		07 46		08 01				
Manor Park	d		01 28	01 38	01 48	01 58	02 08	02 18	02 28	06 18	06 48	07 18			07 33		07 48		08 03				
Ilford	d		01 31	01 41	01 51	02 01	02 11	02 21	02 31	06 21	06 51	07 21			07 36		07 51		08 06				
Seven Kings	d		01 33	01 43	01 53	02 03	02 13	02 23	02 33	06 23	06 53	07 23			07 38		07 53		08 08				
Goodmayes	d		01 35	01 45	01 55	02 05	02 15	02 25	02 35	06 25	06 55	07 25			07 40		07 55		08 10				
Chadwell Heath	d		01 37	01 47	01 57	02 07	02 17	02 27	02 37	06 27	06 57	07 27			07 42		07 57		08 12				
Romford	d		01 41	01 51	02 01	02 11	02 21	02 31	02 41	06 31	07 01	07 31			07 46		08 01		08 16				
Gidea Park	d		01 45	01 55	02a05	02 15	02a25	02 35	02a45	06 35	07 05	07 35			07 50		08 05		08 20				
Harold Wood	d		01 48	01 58		02 18		02 38		06 38	07 08	07 38			07 53		08 08		08 23				
Brentwood	d		01 52	02 02		02 22		02 42		06 42	07 12	07 42			07 57		08 12		08 27				
Shenfield	a	01 37	01 58	02 08		02 28		02 48		06 49	07 19	07 49		07 38	08 04	07 58	08 20	08 02	08 34		08 18	08 21	08 24
Shenfield	d	01 39												07 39		07 59					08 19		
Billericay	d	01 45												07 45		08 05					08 25		
Wickford	d	01 51											07 30	07 51		08 11				08 16	08 31		
Battlesbridge	d												07 34							08 20			
South Woodham Ferrers	d												07 38							08 24			
North Fambridge	d												07 44							08 31			
Althorne	d												07 49							08 36			
Burnham-on-Crouch	d												07 54							08 41			
Southminster	a												08 00							08 47			
Rayleigh	d	01 56												07 56		08 16					08 36		
Hockley	d	02 01												08 01		08 21					08 41		
Rochford	d	02 04												08 04		08 24					08 44		
Southend Airport ✈	d	02 07												08 07		08 27					08 47		
Prittlewell	d	02 10												08 10		08 30					08 50		
Southend Victoria	a	02 14												08 14		08 34					08 54		

		LE	LE 1	LE 1	LE	LE 1	LE	LE 1	LE	LE 1	LE 1	and at the same minutes past each hour until	LE 1	LE 1	LE	LE 1	LE 1	LE	LE 1	LE 1	LE	LE 1
London Liverpool Street ⊖	d	08 05	08 15	08 18	08 20	08 35	08 35	08 38	08 50		08 55		18 55	19 02	19 05	19 15	19 18	19 20	19 32	19 35	19 35	19 38
Stratford ⊖	d	08 12	08 22	08 25	08 27	08 42	08 42	08 47	08 57		09 02		19 02	19 09	19 12	19 22	19 25	19 27	19 41	19 43	19 42	19 47
Maryland	d	08 14			08 29		08 44		08 59						19 14			19 29			19 44	
Forest Gate	d	08 16			08 31		08 46		09 01						19 16			19 31			19 46	
Manor Park	d	08 18			08 33		08 48		09 03						19 18			19 33			19 48	
Ilford	d	08 21			08 36		08 51		09 06						19 21			19 36			19 51	
Seven Kings	d	08 23			08 38		08 53		09 08						19 23			19 38			19 53	
Goodmayes	d	08 25			08 40		08 55		09 10						19 25			19 40			19 55	
Chadwell Heath	d	08 27			08 42		08 57		09 12						19 27			19 42			19 57	
Romford	d	08 31			08 46		09 01		09 16						19 31			19 46			20 01	
Gidea Park	d	08 35			08 50		09 05		09 20						19 35			19 50			20 05	
Harold Wood	d	08 38			08 53		09 08		09 23						19 38			19 53			20 08	
Brentwood	d	08 42			08 57		09 12		09 27						19 42			19 57			20 12	
Shenfield	a	08 49	08 38	08 40	09 04	08 58	09 20	09 02	09 34		09 18		19 18	19 24	19 49	19 38	19 40	20 04	19 56	19 59	20 20	20 02
Shenfield	d		08 39			08 59					09 19		19 19			19 39				20 00		
Billericay	d		08 45			09 05					09 25		19 25			19 45				20 06		
Wickford	d		08 51			09 11				09 16	09 31		19 31			19 51				20 12		
Battlesbridge	d									09 20												
South Woodham Ferrers	d									09 24												
North Fambridge	d									09 31												
Althorne	d									09 36												
Burnham-on-Crouch	d									09 41												
Southminster	a									09 47												
Rayleigh	d		08 56			09 16					09 36		19 36			19 56				20 17		
Hockley	d		09 01			09 21					09 41		19 41			20 01				20 22		
Rochford	d		09 04			09 24					09 44		19 44			20 04				20 25		
Southend Airport ✈	d		09 07			09 27					09 47		19 47			20 07				20 28		
Prittlewell	d		09 10			09 30					09 50		19 50			20 10				20 31		
Southend Victoria	a		09 14			09 34					09 54		19 54			20 14				20 35		

Table 5

Sundays

2 September to 9 September

London - Shenfield, Southminster and Southend Victoria

Network Diagram - see first Page of Table 5

		LE	LE 1	LE 1	LE 1	LE	LE 1	LE 1	LE	LE 1	LE	LE 1	LE	LE 1	LE 1	LE 1	LE	LE 1	LE 1	LE	LE 1	LE
London Liverpool Street ⊖	d	19 50		19 55	20 02	20 05	20 15	20 18	20 20	20 35	20 35	20 38	20 50		20 55	21 02	21 05	21 15	21 18	21 20	21 35	21 35
Stratford ⊖	d	19 57		20 02	20 09	20 12	20 22	20 25	20 27	20 42	20 42	20 47	20 57		21 02	21 09	21 12	21 22	21 25	21 27	21 42	21 42
Maryland	d	19 59				20 14			20 29		20 44		20 59				21 14			21 29		21 44
Forest Gate	d	20 01				20 16			20 31		20 46		21 01				21 16			21 31		21 46
Manor Park	d	20 03				20 18			20 33		20 48		21 03				21 18			21 33		21 48
Ilford	d	20 06				20 21			20 36		20 51		21 06				21 21			21 36		21 51
Seven Kings	d	20 08				20 23			20 38		20 53		21 08				21 23			21 38		21 53
Goodmayes	d	20 10				20 25			20 40		20 55		21 10				21 25			21 40		21 55
Chadwell Heath	d	20 12				20 27			20 42		20 57		21 12				21 27			21 42		21 57
Romford	d	20 16				20 31			20 46		21 01		21 16				21 31			21 46		22 01
Gidea Park	d	20 20				20 35			20 50		21 05		21 20				21 35			21 50		22 05
Harold Wood	d	20 23				20 38			20 53		21 08		21 23				21 38			21 53		22 08
Brentwood	d	20 27				20 42			20 57		21 12		21 27				21 42			21 57		22 12
Shenfield	a	20 34		20 18	20 24	20 49	20 38	20 40	21 04	20 58	21 20	21 02	21 34		21 18	21 24	21 49	21 38	21 40	22 04	21 58	22 20
Shenfield	d			20 19			20 39			20 59					21 19			21 39			21 59	
Billericay	d			20 25			20 45			21 05					21 25			21 45			22 05	
Wickford	d		20 16	20 31			20 51			21 11				21 16	21 31			21 51			22 11	
Battlesbridge	d		20 20											21 20								
South Woodham Ferrers	d		20 24											21 24								
North Fambridge	d		20 31											21 31								
Althorne	d		20 36											21 36								
Burnham-on-Crouch	d		20 41											21 41								
Southminster	a		20 47											21 47								
Rayleigh	d			20 36			20 56			21 16					21 36			21 56			22 16	
Hockley	d			20 41			21 01			21 21					21 41			22 01			22 21	
Rochford	d			20 44			21 04			21 24					21 44			22 04			22 24	
Southend Airport ✈	d			20 47			21 07			21 27					21 47			22 07			22 27	
Prittlewell	d			20 50			21 10			21 30					21 50			22 10			22 30	
Southend Victoria	a			20 54			21 14			21 34					21 54			22 14			22 34	

		LE 1	LE	LE 1	LE 1	LE 1	LE	LE 1	LE 1	LE	LE 1	LE 1	LE	LE 1	LE 1	LE	LE 1	LE	LE 1	LE	LE 1	LE 1	LE
London Liverpool Street ⊖	d	21 38	21 50		21 50	22 02	22 02	22 10	22 15	22 17		22 25	22 32	22 35	22 40	22 42	22 45	22 52	22 55	23 02	23 07	23 10	23 12
Stratford ⊖	d	21 47	21 57		22 02	22 09	22 12	22 22	22 24	22 27		22 37	22 42	22 44	22 52	22 52	22 54	23 02	23 07	23 12	23 17	23 22	23 22
Maryland	d		21 59				22 14			22 29			22 44			22 54		23 04		23 14			23 24
Forest Gate	d		22 01				22 16			22 31			22 46			22 56		23 06		23 16			23 26
Manor Park	d		22 03				22 18			22 33			22 48			22 58		23 08		23 18			23 28
Ilford	d		22 06				22 21			22 36			22 51			23 01		23 11		23 21			23 31
Seven Kings	d		22 08				22 23			22 38			22 53			23 03		23 13		23 23			23 33
Goodmayes	d		22 10				22 25			22 40			22 55			23 05		23 15		23 25			23 35
Chadwell Heath	d		22 12				22 27			22 42			22 57			23 07		23 17		23 27			23 37
Romford	d		22 16				22 31			22 46			23 01			23 11		23 21		23 31			23 41
Gidea Park	d		22 20				22 35			22 50			23 05			23 15		23 25		23 35			23 45
Harold Wood	d		22 23				22 38			22 53			23 08			23 18		23 28		23 38			23 48
Brentwood	d		22 27				22 42			22 57			23 12			23 22		23 32		23 42			23 52
Shenfield	a	22 02	22 34		22 18	22 24	22 49	22 38	22 40	23 04		22 53	23 19	23 00	23 08	23 29	23 10	23 39	23 23	23 49	23 33	23 37	23 59
Shenfield	d				22 19			22 39				22 54			23 09				23 24			23 38	
Billericay	d				22 25			22 45				23 00			23 15				23 30			23 45	
Wickford	d			22 16	22 31			22 51			22 56	23 06			23 21				23 36			23 51	
Battlesbridge	d			22 20							23 00												
South Woodham Ferrers	d			22 24							23 04												
North Fambridge	d			22 31							23 11												
Althorne	d			22 36							23 16												
Burnham-on-Crouch	d			22 41							23 21												
Southminster	a			22 47							23 27												
Rayleigh	d				22 36			22 56				23 11			23 26				23 41			23 56	
Hockley	d				22 41			23 01				23 16			23 31				23 46			00 01	
Rochford	d				22 44			23 04				23 19			23 34				23 49			00 04	
Southend Airport ✈	d				22 47			23 07				23 22			23 37				23 52			00 07	
Prittlewell	d				22 50			23 10				23 25			23 40				23 55			00 10	
Southend Victoria	a				22 54			23 14				23 29			23 44				23 59			00 14	

Table 5

Sundays

2 September to 9 September

London - Shenfield, Southminster and Southend Victoria

Network Diagram - see first Page of Table 5

		LE [1]	LE [1]	LE	LE [1]	LE	LE [1]	LE [1]	LE	LE [1]	LE	LE [1]
London Liverpool Street [15] ⊖	d		23 15	23 22	23 25	23 32	23 35	23 40	23 42	23 45	23 52	23 55
Stratford [7] ⊖	d		23 25	23 32	23 37	23 42	23 45	23 52	23 52	23 54	00 02	00 07
Maryland	d			23 34		23 44			23 54		00 04	
Forest Gate	d			23 36		23 46			23 56		00 06	
Manor Park	d			23 38		23 48			23 58		00 08	
Ilford [2]	d			23 41		23 51			00 01		00 11	
Seven Kings	d			23 43		23 53			00 03		00 13	
Goodmayes	d			23 45		23 55			00 05		00 15	
Chadwell Heath	d			23 47		23 57			00 07		00 17	
Romford	d			23 51		00 02			00 11		00 21	
Gidea Park [2]	d			23 55		00 05			00 15		00 25	
Harold Wood	d			23 58		00 08			00 18		00 28	
Brentwood	d			00 02		00 12			00 22		00 32	
Shenfield [3]	a		23 41	00 09	23 52	00 19	00 01	00 09	00 29	00 10	00 39	00 22
Shenfield [3]	d				23 54			00 09				00 24
Billericay	d				23 59			00 15				00 30
Wickford [2]	d	23 56			00 06			00 21				00 36
Battlesbridge	d	00 01										
South Woodham Ferrers	d	00 04										
North Fambridge	d	00 11										
Althorne	d	00 16										
Burnham-on-Crouch	d	00 21										
Southminster	a	00 27										
Rayleigh	d				00 11			00 26				00 41
Hockley	d				00 16			00 31				00 46
Rochford	d				00 19			00 34				00 49
Southend Airport ✈	d				00 22			00 37				00 52
Prittlewell	d				00 25			00 40				00 55
Southend Victoria	a				00 29			00 44				00 59

Sundays

from 16 September

		LE [1]	LE	LE	LE [1]	LE [1]	LE	LE	LE [1]	LE [1]	LE	LE	LE [1]	LE	LE [1]	LE [1]	LE 🚌	LE [1]	LE [1]	LE [1]	LE	LE [1]	LE ◇[1]
London Liverpool Street [15] ⊖	d	23p15	23p20	23p35	23p45	23p48	23p50	00 01	00 15	00 18	00 20	00 32	00 50	00 55			06 35			07 55	08 05	08 15	08 30
Stratford [7] ⊖	d	23p22	23p27	23p42	23p52	23p55	23p57	00 08	00 22	00 25	00 27	00 39	00 57	01 02			06 55			08 02	08 12	08 22	
Maryland	d		23p29	23p44			23p59	00 10			00 29	00 41		01 04							08 13		
Forest Gate	d		23p31	23p46			00 01	00 12			00 31	00 43		01 06							08 15		
Manor Park	d		23p33	23p48			00 03	00 14			00 33	00 45		01 08							08 17		
Ilford [2]	d		23p36	23p51			00 06	00 17			00 36	00 48		01 11			07 10				08 20		
Seven Kings	d		23p38	23p53			00 08	00 19			00 38	00 50		01 13							08 23		
Goodmayes	d		23p40	23p55			00 10	00 21			00 40	00 52		01 15							08 25		
Chadwell Heath	d		23p42	23p57			00 12	00 23			00 42	00 54		01 17							08 27		
Romford	d		23p46	00 02			00 16	00 27	00 32		00 46	00 58	01 08	01 21			07 30				08 30	08 33	
Gidea Park [2]	d		23p50	00 05			00 20	00a31			00 50	01a02		01 25			07 37				08 34	08 37	
Harold Wood	d		23p53	00 08			00 23				00 53			01 28			07 44				08 37	08 40	
Brentwood	d		23p57	00 12			00 27				00 57			01 32			07 59				08 41	08 44	
Shenfield [3]	a	23p38	00 03	00 18	00 08	00 10	00 33		00 44	00 47	01 03		01 20	01 38			08 09			08 24	08 48	08 50	08 57
Shenfield [3]	d	23p39			00 09				00 45				01 20			07 50			08 20			08 50	
Billericay	d	23p45			00 15				00 51				01 26			07 56			08 26			08 56	
Wickford [2]	d	23p51			00 21				00 56				01 31		07 30	08 01		08 05	08 31			09 01	
Battlesbridge	d														07 34			08 09					
South Woodham Ferrers	d														07 38			08 13					
North Fambridge	d														07 44			08 20					
Althorne	d														07 49			08 25					
Burnham-on-Crouch	d														07 54			08 30					
Southminster	a														08 00			08 36					
Rayleigh	d	23p56			00 26				01 01				01 36			08 06			08 36			09 06	
Hockley	d	00 01			00 31				01 06				01 41			08 11			08 41			09 11	
Rochford	d	00 04			00 34				01 09				01 44			08 14			08 44			09 14	
Southend Airport ✈	d	00 07			00 37				01 12				01 47			08 17			08 47			09 17	
Prittlewell	d	00 10			00 40				01 15				01 50										
Southend Victoria	a	00 18			00 48				01 23				01 58			08 25			08 55			09 25	

Table 5

Sundays

from 16 September

London - Shenfield, Southminster and Southend Victoria

Network Diagram - see first Page of Table 5

		LE	LE [1]	LE [1]	LE [1]	LE	LE [1]	LE	LE [1]	LE	LE [1]	LE [1]	LE		LE	LE [1]	LE	LE [1]	LE	LE [1]	LE	LE [1]
London Liverpool Street [15] ⊖	d	08 35		08 45	09 02	09 05	09 15	09 17	09 32	09 35		09 45	09 47		21 47	22 02	22 05	22 15	22 17	22 32	22 35	22 45
Stratford [7] ⊖	d	08 42		08 52	09 09	09 12	09 22	09 24	09 39	09 42		09 52	09 54		21 54	22 09	22 12	22 22	22 24	22 39	22 42	22 52
Maryland	d	08 43				09 13				09 43							22 13				22 43	
Forest Gate	d	08 45				09 15		09 27		09 45			09 57		21 57		22 15		22 27		22 45	
Manor Park	d	08 47				09 17		09 29		09 47			09 59		21 59		22 17		22 29		22 47	
Ilford [2]	d	08 50				09 20		09 32		09 50			10 02		22 02		22 20		22 32		22 50	
Seven Kings	d	08 53				09 23		09 34		09 53			10 04		22 04		22 23		22 34		22 53	
Goodmayes	d	08 55				09 25		09 36		09 55			10 06		22 06		22 25		22 36		22 55	
Chadwell Heath	d	08 57				09 27		09 38		09 57			10 08		22 08		22 27		22 38		22 57	
Romford	d	09 00		09 03		09 30	09 33	09 42		10 00		10 03	10 12	and at the same minutes past each hour until	22 12		22 30	22 33	22 42		23 00	23 03
Gidea Park [2]	d	09 04		09 07		09 34	09 37	09a47		10 04		10 07	10a17		22a17		22 34	22 37	22a47		23 04	23 07
Harold Wood	d	09 07		09 10		09 37	09 40			10 07		10 10					22 37	22 40			23 07	23 10
Brentwood	d	09 11		09 14		09 41	09 44			10 11		10 14					22 41	22 44			23 11	23 14
Shenfield [3]	a	09 18		09 20	09 30	09 48	09 50		10 00	10 18		10 20				22 30	22 48	22 50		23 00	23 18	23 20
Shenfield [3]	d			09 20			09 50					10 20						22 50				23 20
Billericay	d			09 26			09 56					10 26						22 56				23 26
Wickford [2]	d		09 05	09 31			10 01				10 05	10 31						23 01				23 31
Battlesbridge	d		09 09								10 09											
South Woodham Ferrers	d		09 13								10 13											
North Fambridge	d		09 20								10 20											
Althorne	d		09 25								10 25											
Burnham-on-Crouch	d		09 30								10 30											
Southminster	a		09 36								10 36											
Rayleigh	d			09 36			10 06					10 36						23 06				23 36
Hockley	d			09 41			10 11					10 41						23 11				23 41
Rochford	d			09 44			10 14					10 44						23 14				23 44
Southend Airport ✈	d			09 47			10 17					10 47						23 17				23 47
Prittlewell	d																					
Southend Victoria	a			09 55			10 25					10 55						23 27				23 57

		LE [1]	LE	LE [1]	LE [1]	LE	LE [1]
London Liverpool Street [15] ⊖	d	23 02	23 05	23 15	23 32	23 35	23 45
Stratford [7] ⊖	d	23 09	23 12	23 22	23 39	23 42	23 52
Maryland	d		23 13			23 43	
Forest Gate	d		23 15			23 45	
Manor Park	d		23 17			23 47	
Ilford [2]	d		23 20			23 50	
Seven Kings	d		23 23			23 53	
Goodmayes	d		23 25			23 55	
Chadwell Heath	d		23 27			23 57	
Romford	d		23 30	23 33		23 59	00 03
Gidea Park [2]	d		23 34	23 37		00 04	00 07
Harold Wood	d		23 37	23 40		00 07	00 10
Brentwood	d		23 41	23 44		00 11	00 14
Shenfield [3]	a	23 30	23 48	23 50	23 59	00 18	00 20
Shenfield [3]	d			23 50			00 20
Billericay	d			23 56			00 26
Wickford [2]	d			00 01			00 31
Battlesbridge	d						
South Woodham Ferrers	d						
North Fambridge	d						
Althorne	d						
Burnham-on-Crouch	d						
Southminster	a						
Rayleigh	d			00 06			00 36
Hockley	d			00 11			00 41
Rochford	d			00 14			00 44
Southend Airport ✈	d			00 17			00 47
Prittlewell	d						
Southend Victoria	a			00 27			00 57

Southend Victoria, Southminster and Shenfield - London

Network Diagram - see first Page of Table 5

Miles	Miles			LE MX ◇1 A	LE FO ◇1 B	LE C	LE FO D	LE ◇1 C	LE FO 1 D	LE MO ◇1 E	CC MX	LE MO E	LE FO D	LE 1 C	LE C	LE	CC	LE	LE	LE 1	LE	LE	LE 1
0	—	**Southend Victoria**	d													04 00			04 30				05 00
0½	—	Prittlewell	d													04 02			04 32				05 02
1¾	—	Southend Airport ✈	d													04 05			04 35				05 05
2¾	—	Rochford	d													04 08			04 38				05 08
5½	—	Hockley	d													04 12			04 42				05 11
8¼	—	Rayleigh	d													04 16			04 46				05 16
—	0	**Southminster**	d						22p56					23p06									
—	2¼	Burnham-on-Crouch	d						23p00					23p10									
—	5¼	Althorne	d						23p05					23p15									
—	8¼	North Fambridge	d						23p11					23p21									
—	11½	South Woodham Ferrers	d						23p16					23p26									
—	14	Battlesbridge	d						23p20					23p30									
12½	16½	**Wickford** 2	d						23p26					23p36		04 21			04 51				05 21
17¼	—	Billericay	d						23p32					23p42		04 28			04 58				05 27
—	—	**Shenfield** 3	a						23p39					23p49		04 39			05 09				05 35
21¼	—	**Shenfield** 3	d			23p27	23p29	23p38	23p39			23p43	23p44	23p52	23p54	04 39			05 09	05 24		05 29	05 35
23¼	—	Brentwood	d			23p30	23p32					23p46	23p47		23p57	04 42			05 12			05 32	
26½	—	Harold Wood	d			23p35	23p37					23p51	23p52		00 02	04 47			05 17			05 37	
28	—	Gidea Park 2	d			23p39	23p41					23p55	23p56		00 06	04 51			05 21	05 31		05 41	
29	—	Romford	d			23p41	23p43		23p47			23p57	23p58	00 03	00 08	04 53			05 23			05 43	
31½	—	Chadwell Heath	d			23p45	23p47					00 01	00 02		00 12	04 57			05 27			05 47	
32¼	—	Goodmayes	d			23p47	23p49					00 03	00 04		00 14	04 59			05 29			05 49	
33	—	Seven Kings	d			23p49	23p51					00 05	00 06		00 16	05 01			05 31	05 36		05 51	
34¼	—	Ilford 2	d			23p52	23p54					00 08	00 09		00 19	05 04		05 09	05 34		05 39	05 54	
35¼	—	Manor Park	d			23p55	23p57					00 10	00 12		00 22			05 11			05 41	05 57	
36¼	—	Forest Gate	d			23p57	23p59					00 12	00 14		00 24			05 14			05 44	05 59	
37	—	Maryland	d			23p59	00 01					00 14	00 16		00 26			05 16			05 46	06 01	
37½	—	Stratford 7 ⊖	d	23b52	23b52	00 02	00 04	00s04	23p56	23b57	00 09	00 16	00 19	00 13	00 29	05 10	05 14	05 18	05 40	05 42	05 48	06 04	05 49
41½	—	**London Liverpool Street** 15 ⊖	a	00 02	00 02	00 11	00 12	00 14	00 05	00 08	00 20	00 26	00 27	00 22	00 38	05 18	05 27	05 26	05 48	05 55	05 56	06 12	05 58

		LE	LE 1	LE 1	LE 1	LE	LE	LE	LE 1	LE	LE 1	LE ◇1	LE	LE 1	LE 1	LE	LE	LE 1	LE 1	LE 1	LE
Southend Victoria	d			05 20					05 40					06 00				06 11			
Prittlewell	d			05 22					05 42					06 02				06 13			
Southend Airport ✈	d			05 25					05 45					06 05				06 16			
Rochford	d			05 28					05 48					06 08				06 19			
Hockley	d			05 31					05 51					06 11				06 22			
Rayleigh	d			05 36					05 56					06 16				06 27			
Southminster	d				05 26															06 09	
Burnham-on-Crouch	d				05 30															06 13	
Althorne	d				05 35															06 18	
North Fambridge	d				05 41															06 24	
South Woodham Ferrers	d				05 46															06 30	
Battlesbridge	d				05 50															06 34	
Wickford 2	d			05 41	05a56				06 01					06 21				06 32		06 40	
Billericay	d			05 47					06 07					06 27				06 39		06 46	
Shenfield 3	a			05 55					06 15					06 35				06 45		06 52	
Shenfield 3	d	05 44	05 53	05 55			06 04	06 14	06 15	06 24	06 25		06 34	06 35	06 41		06 44	06 45	06 50	06 53	
Brentwood	d	05 47					06 07	06 17		06 27			06 37				06 47				
Harold Wood	d	05 52					06 12	06 22		06 32			06 42				06 52				
Gidea Park 2	d	05 56				06 06	06 16	06 26		06 36			06 45			06 49	06 55				06 59
Romford	d	05 58				06 08	06 18	06 28		06 38			06 48			06 51	06 58				07 01
Chadwell Heath	d	06 02				06 12	06 22	06 32		06 42			06 52			06 55	07 02				07 05
Goodmayes	d	06 04				06 14	06 24	06 34		06 44						06 57					07 07
Seven Kings	d	06 06				06 16	06 26	06 36		06 46						06 59					07 09
Ilford 2	d	06 09				06 19	06 29	06 39		06 49			06 57			07 02	07 07				07 12
Manor Park	d	06 12				06 22	06 32	06 42		06 52						07 05					07 15
Forest Gate	d	06 14				06 24	06 34	06 44		06 54						07 07					07 17
Maryland	d	06 16				06 26	06 36	06 46		06 56						07 09					07 19
Stratford 7 ⊖	d	06 19	06 07	06 10		06 29	06 39	06 49	06 29	06 59	06 39		07 03	06 49	06s57	07 12	07 15	07s02	07s06	07s09	07 22
London Liverpool Street 15 ⊖	a	06 27	06 16	06 19		06 37	06 47	06 57	06 40	07 07	06 48	06 54	07 13	06 58	07 09	07 22	07 25	07 13	07 18	07 21	07 32

A from 26 June until 26 July
B until 22 June
C TWThO until 21 June
D until 15 June, MX from 22 June until 26 July
E from 21 May until 23 July
b Previous night, stops to set down only

Southend Victoria, Southminster and Shenfield - London

Network Diagram - see first Page of Table 5

		LE	LE	LE	LE	LE 1	LE 1	LE	LE	LE 1	LE 1	LE 1	LE	LE	LE 1	LE 1	LE	LE	LE 1	LE 1
Southend Victoria	d		06 26				06 40				06 50					07 03				
Prittlewell	d		06 28				06 42				06 52					07 05				
Southend Airport ✈	d		06 31				06 45				06 55					07 08				
Rochford	d		06 34				06 48				06 58					07 11				
Hockley	d		06 38				06 51				07 01					07 14				
Rayleigh	d		06 42				06 56				07 06					07 19				
Southminster	d														06 48					
Burnham-on-Crouch	d														06 52					
Althorne	d														06 57					
North Fambridge	d														07 04					
South Woodham Ferrers	d														07 10					
Battlesbridge	d														07 14					
Wickford 2	d		06 47				07 01				07 11				07 19	07 24				
Billericay	d		06 54				07 08				07 18				07 26	07 31				
Shenfield 3	a		07 01				07 14				07 24				07 32					
Shenfield 3	d	06 54	07 01		07 04	07 08	07 14		07 14	07 19	07 24			07 24	07 32			07 34	07 38	07 41
Brentwood	d	06 57			07 07				07 17					07 27				07 37		
Harold Wood	d	07 02			07 12				07 22					07 32				07 42		
Gidea Park 2	d	07 05		07 09	07 15			07 19	07 25				07 29	07 35			07 39	07 45		
Romford	d	07 08		07 11	07 18			07 21	07 28				07 31	07 38			07 41	07 48		
Chadwell Heath	d	07 12		07 15	07 22			07 25	07 32				07 35	07 42			07 45	07 52		
Goodmayes	d			07 17				07 27	07 34				07 37	07 44			07 47	07 54		
Seven Kings	d			07 19				07 29	07 36				07 39	07 46			07 49	07 56		
Ilford 2	d	07 17		07 22	07 27			07 32	07 39				07 42	07 49			07 52	07 59		
Manor Park	d			07 25				07 35					07 45				07 55			
Forest Gate	d			07 27				07 37					07 47				07 57			
Maryland	d			07 29				07 39					07 49				07 59			
Stratford 7 ⊖	d	07 25	07s19	07 32	07 35	07s23	07s31	07 42	07 45	07s35	07s41	07 44	07 52	07 55	07 50	07s52	08 02	08 05	07s55	07s58
London Liverpool Street 15 ⊖	a	07 35	07 30	07 42	07 45	07 35	07 42	07 52	07 55	07 46	07 52	07 56	08 02	08 05	08 01	08 03	08 12	08 15	08 07	08 09

		LE	LE	LE 1	LE 1	LE	LE	LE	LE	LE 1	LE	LE 1	LE 1	LE 1	LE 1	LE	LE	LE	LE 1	LE 1
Southend Victoria	d			07 13					07 18	07 23				07 32					07 42	
Prittlewell	d			07 15					07 20	07 25				07 34					07 44	
Southend Airport ✈	d			07 18					07 23	07 28				07 37					07 47	
Rochford	d			07 21					07 26	07 31				07 40					07 50	
Hockley	d			07 24					07 30	07 34				07 43					07 53	
Rayleigh	d			07 29					07 34	07 39				07 48					07 58	
Southminster	d																			07 37
Burnham-on-Crouch	d																			07 41
Althorne	d																			07 46
North Fambridge	d																			07 52
South Woodham Ferrers	d																			07 59
Battlesbridge	d																			
Wickford 2	d			07 34					07 39	07 44				07 53					08 03	08 07
Billericay	d			07 41					07 46	07 51				08 00					08 10	08 14
Shenfield 3	a			07 47					07 53	07 57				08 06					08 16	
Shenfield 3	d		07 44	07 47	07 50		07 50		07 54	07 57	08 00	08 01		08 06	08 09			08 10	08 16	
Brentwood	d		07 47				07 53		07 57		08 03							08 13		
Harold Wood	d		07 52				07 58		08 02		08 08							08 18		
Gidea Park 2	d	07 49	07 55			07 59	08 02	08 05	08 09		08 12					08 15	08 19	08 22		
Romford	d	07 51	07 58			08 01	08 04	08 07	08 11		08 14					08 17	08 21	08 24		
Chadwell Heath	d	07 55	08 02			08 05	08 08	08 11	08 15		08 18					08 21	08 25	08 28		
Goodmayes	d	07 57	08 04			08 07	08 10	08 13	08 17		08 20					08 23	08 27	08 30		
Seven Kings	d	07 59	08 06			08 09	08 12	08 15	08 19		08 22					08 25	08 29	08 32		
Ilford 2	d	08 02	08 09			08 12	08 15	08 18	08 22		08 25					08 28	08 32	08 35		
Manor Park	d	08 05						08 21								08 31				
Forest Gate	d	08 07						08 23								08 33				
Maryland	d	08 09						08 25								08 35				
Stratford 7 ⊖	d	08 12	08 15	08s04	08s07	08 18	08 21	08 28	08 31	08s15	08 34	08s18		08s23	08s25	08 38	08 41	08 44	08s33	08s35
London Liverpool Street 15 ⊖	a	08 22	08 25	08 15	08 19	08 28	08 31	08 38	08 41	08 26	08 43	08 30	08 32	08 36	08 38	08 48	08 51	08 53	08 46	08 48

Southend Victoria, Southminster and Shenfield - London

Network Diagram - see first Page of Table 5

		LE	LE	LE	LE	LE		LE	LE			LE	LE	LE	LE	LE		LE	LE	LE	LE	LE	LE	LE	LE
		■				■		■	■						■	■					■	■		■	■
Southend Victoria	d							07 52							08 03						08 12				
Prittlewell	d							07 54							08 05						08 14				
Southend Airport	d							07 57							08 08						08 17				
Rochford	d							08 00							08 11						08 20				
Hockley	d							08 03							08 14						08 23				
Rayleigh	d							08 08							08 19						08 28				
Southminster	d																								08 16
Burnham-on-Crouch	d																								08 20
Althorne	d																								08 25
North Fambridge	d																								08 31
South Woodham Ferrers	d																								08 37
Battlesbridge	d																								08 41
Wickford 2	d							08 13							08 24						08 33				08 46
Billericay	d							08 20							08 31						08 40				08 53
Shenfield 3	a							08 26							08 37						08 46				08 59
Shenfield 3	d	08 21			08 22	08 24		08 26	08 29					08 32	08 37	08 42				08 44	08 46	08 51	08 54	08 55	08 59
Brentwood	d				08 25									08 35						08 47			08 57		
Harold Wood	d				08 30									08 40						08 52			09 02		
Gidea Park 2	d			08 29	08 34								08 41	08 44					08 51	08 56			09 06		
Romford	d			08 31	08 36								08 43	08 46					08 53	08 58	08 55		09 08		
Chadwell Heath	d			08 35	08 40								08 47	08 50					08 57	09 02			09 12		
Goodmayes	d			08 37	08 42								08 49	08 52					08 59	09 04			09 14		
Seven Kings	d			08 39	08 44								08 51	08 54					09 01	09 06			09 16		
Ilford 2	d		08 38	08 42	08 47							08 50	08 54	08 57				09 00	09 04	09 09			09 19		
Manor Park	d		08 41									08 53						09 03		09 12			09 22		
Forest Gate	d		08 43									08 55						09 05		09 14			09 24		
Maryland	d		08 45									08 57						09 07		09 16			09 26		
Stratford 7 ⊖	d	08s38	08 48	08 51	08 54	08s41		08s43	08s45			09 00	09 03	09 06	08s56	08s59		09 10	09 13	09 19	09s05	09s08	09 29		09s16
London Liverpool Street 15 ⊖	a	08 50	08 58	09 01	09 03	08 54		08 56	08 58			09 10	09 13	09 14	09 08	09 11		09 20	09 23	09 27	09 16	09 19	09 37	09 21	09 29

		LE				LE	LE	LE	LE	LE	LE	LE		LE	LE	LE	LE	LE	LE	LE	LE	LE		LE	LE
		■						■		■	■	■			■		■	■			■	■		■	
Southend Victoria	d	08 30									08 52						09 10				09 30				
Prittlewell	d	08 32									08 54						09 12				09 32				
Southend Airport	d	08 35									08 57						09 15				09 35				
Rochford	d	08 38									09 00						09 18				09 38				
Hockley	d	08 41									09 03						09 21				09 41				
Rayleigh	d	08 46									09 08						09 26				09 46				
Southminster	d											08 56										09 36			
Burnham-on-Crouch	d											09 00										09 40			
Althorne	d											09 05										09 45			
North Fambridge	d											09 11										09 51			
South Woodham Ferrers	d											09 16										09 56			
Battlesbridge	d											09 20										10 00			
Wickford 2	d	08 51									09 13	09a26					09 31				09 51	10a06			
Billericay	d	08 58									09 20						09 37				09 57				
Shenfield 3	a	09 04									09 27						09 45				10 05				
Shenfield 3	d	09 04				09 04	09 14	09 21	09 24	09 25	09 27			09 34	09 38	09 44	09 45	09 51	09 54	10 04	10 05			10 08	10 14
Brentwood	d					09 07	09 17		09 27					09 37		09 47			09 57	10 07					10 17
Harold Wood	d					09 12	09 22		09 32					09 42		09 52			10 02	10 12					10 22
Gidea Park 2	d					09 16	09 26		09 36					09 46		09 56			10 06	10 16					10 26
Romford	d					09 18	09 28		09 38					09 48		09 58	09 53		10 08	10 18					10 28
Chadwell Heath	d					09 22	09 32		09 42					09 52		10 02			10 12	10 22					10 32
Goodmayes	d					09 24	09 34		09 44					09 54		10 04			10 14	10 24					10 34
Seven Kings	d					09 26	09 36		09 46					09 56		10 06			10 16	10 26					10 36
Ilford 2	d					09 29	09 39		09 49					09 59		10 09			10 19	10 29					10 39
Manor Park	d					09 32	09 42		09 52					10 02		10 12			10 22	10 32					10 42
Forest Gate	d					09 34	09 44		09 54					10 04		10 14			10 24	10 34					10 44
Maryland	d					09 36	09 46		09 56					10 06		10 16			10 26	10 36					10 46
Stratford 7 ⊖	d	09s22				09 39	09 49	09s37	09 59	09s41	09s43			10 09	09 52	10 19	10 01	10 05	10 29	10 39	10 19			10 22	10 49
London Liverpool Street 15 ⊖	a	09 33				09 47	09 58	09 49	10 07	09 53	09 55			10 17	10 01	10 27	10 10	10 14	10 37	10 47	10 28			10 31	10 57

Southend Victoria, Southminster and Shenfield - London

Network Diagram - see first Page of Table 5

		LE	LE	LE		LE	LE	LE		LE	LE	LE	LE	LE	LE	LE	LE	LE		LE	LE	LE		LE	LE
		■		■			■			■	■	■			■	■		■			■	■			■
Southend Victoria	d			09 50						10 10					10 30						10 50				
Prittlewell	d			09 52						10 12					10 32						10 52				
Southend Airport	d			09 55						10 15					10 35						10 55				
Rochford	d			09 58						10 18					10 38						10 58				
Hockley	d			10 01						10 21					10 41						11 01				
Rayleigh	d			10 06						10 26					10 46						11 06				
Southminster	d										10 16											10 56			
Burnham-on-Crouch	d										10 20											11 00			
Althorne	d										10 25											11 05			
North Fambridge	d										10 31											11 11			
South Woodham Ferrers	d										10 36											11 16			
Battlesbridge	d										10 40											11 20			
Wickford 2	d			10 11						10 31	10a46				10 51						11 11	11a26			
Billericay	d			10 17						10 37					10 57						11 17				
Shenfield 3	a			10 25						10 45					11 05						11 25				
Shenfield 3	d	10 18	10 24	10 25		10 34	10 38	10 44		10 45		10 51	10 54	11 04	11 05	11 08	11 14	11 20		11 24	11 25			11 34	11 38
Brentwood	d		10 27			10 37		10 47					10 57	11 07			11 17			11 27				11 37	
Harold Wood	d		10 32			10 42		10 52					11 02	11 12			11 22			11 32				11 42	
Gidea Park 2	d		10 36			10 46		10 56					11 06	11 16			11 26			11 36				11 46	
Romford	d	10 26	10 38			10 48		10 58		10 53			11 08	11 18			11 28	11 28		11 38				11 48	
Chadwell Heath	d		10 42			10 52		11 02					11 12	11 22			11 32			11 42				11 52	
Goodmayes	d		10 44			10 54		11 04					11 14	11 24			11 34			11 44				11 54	
Seven Kings	d		10 46			10 56		11 06					11 16	11 26			11 36			11 46				11 56	
Ilford 2	d		10 49			10 59		11 09					11 19	11 29			11 39			11 49				11 59	
Manor Park	d		10 52			11 02		11 12					11 22	11 32			11 42			11 52				12 02	
Forest Gate	d		10 54			11 04		11 14					11 24	11 34			11 44			11 54				12 04	
Maryland	d		10 56			11 06		11 16					11 26	11 36			11 46			11 56				12 06	
Stratford 7 ⊖	d	10 34	10 59	10 39		11 09	10 52	11 19		11 01		11 05	11 29	11 39	11 19	11 22	11 49	11 36		11 59	11 39			12 09	11 52
London Liverpool Street 15 ⊖	a	10 43	11 07	10 48		11 17	11 01	11 27		11 10		11 14	11 37	11 47	11 28	11 31	11 57	11 45		12 07	11 48			12 17	12 01

		LE	LE	LE		LE	LE	LE	LE	LE	LE	LE	LE	LE			LE	LE	LE	LE	LE	LE	LE	LE	
			■	■				■	■	■		■		■				■		■	■	■			
Southend Victoria	d		11 10					11 30						11 50						12 10					
Prittlewell	d		11 12					11 32						11 52						12 12					
Southend Airport	d		11 15					11 35						11 55						12 15					
Rochford	d		11 18					11 38						11 58						12 18					
Hockley	d		11 21					11 41						12 01						12 21					
Rayleigh	d		11 26					11 46						12 06						12 26					
Southminster	d								11 36												12 16				
Burnham-on-Crouch	d								11 40												12 20				
Althorne	d								11 45												12 25				
North Fambridge	d								11 51												12 31				
South Woodham Ferrers	d								11 56												12 36				
Battlesbridge	d								12 00												12 40				
Wickford 2	d		11 31					11 51	12a06					12 11						12 31	12a46				
Billericay	d		11 37					11 57						12 17						12 37					
Shenfield 3	a		11 45					12 05						12 25						12 45					
Shenfield 3	d	11 44	11 45	11 51		11 54	12 04	12 05		12 08	12 14	12 20	12 24	12 25			12 34	12 38	12 44	12 45		12 51	12 54	13 04	
Brentwood	d	11 47				11 57	12 07				12 17		12 27				12 37		12 47				12 57	13 07	
Harold Wood	d	11 52				12 02	12 12				12 22		12 32				12 42		12 52				13 02	13 12	
Gidea Park 2	d	11 56				12 06	12 16				12 26		12 36				12 46		12 56				13 06	13 16	
Romford	d	11 58	11 53			12 08	12 18				12 28	12 28	12 38				12 48		12 58	12 53			13 08	13 18	
Chadwell Heath	d	12 02				12 12	12 22				12 32		12 42				12 52		13 02				13 12	13 22	
Goodmayes	d	12 04				12 14	12 24				12 34		12 44				12 54		13 04				13 14	13 24	
Seven Kings	d	12 06				12 16	12 26				12 36		12 46				12 56		13 06				13 16	13 26	
Ilford 2	d	12 09				12 19	12 29				12 39		12 49				12 59		13 09				13 19	13 29	
Manor Park	d	12 12				12 22	12 32				12 42		12 52				13 02		13 12				13 22	13 32	
Forest Gate	d	12 14				12 24	12 34				12 44		12 54				13 04		13 14				13 24	13 34	
Maryland	d	12 16				12 26	12 36				12 46		12 56				13 06		13 16				13 26	13 36	
Stratford 7 ⊖	d	12 19	12 01	12 05		12 29	12 39	12 19		12 22	12 49	12 36	12 59	12 39			13 09	12 52	13 19	13 01		13 05	13 29	13 39	
London Liverpool Street 15 ⊖	a	12 27	12 10	12 14		12 37	12 47	12 28		12 31	12 57	12 45	13 07	12 48			13 17	13 01	13 27	13 10		13 14	13 37	13 47	

until 26 July

Southend Victoria, Southminster and Shenfield - London

Network Diagram - see first Page of Table 5

		LE 1	LE 1	LE	LE 1	LE	LE 1	LE 1		LE		LE 1	LE	LE 1	LE 1	LE	LE	LE 1	LE 1	LE 1		LE	LE 1	LE	LE 1
Southend Victoria	d	12 30					12 50							13 10				13 30							13 50
Prittlewell	d	12 32					12 52							13 12				13 32							13 52
Southend Airport ✈	d	12 35					12 55							13 15				13 35							13 55
Rochford	d	12 38					12 58							13 18				13 38							13 58
Hockley	d	12 41					13 01							13 21				13 41							14 01
Rayleigh	d	12 46					13 06							13 26				13 46							14 06
Southminster	d							12 56											13 36						
Burnham-on-Crouch	d							13 00											13 40						
Althorne	d							13 05											13 45						
North Fambridge	d							13 11											13 51						
South Woodham Ferrers	d							13 16											13 56						
Battlesbridge	d							13 20											14 00						
Wickford 2	d	12 51					13 11	13a26						13 31				13 51	14a06						14 11
Billericay	d	12 57					13 17							13 37				13 57							14 17
Shenfield 3	a	13 05					13 25							13 45				14 05							14 25
Shenfield 3	d	13 05	13 08	13 14	13 20	13 24	13 25			13 34		13 38	13 44	13 45	13 51	13 54	14 04	14 05		14 08		14 14	14 20	14 24	14 25
Brentwood	d			13 17		13 27				13 37			13 47			13 57	14 07					14 17		14 27	
Harold Wood	d			13 22		13 32				13 42			13 52			14 02	14 12					14 22		14 32	
Gidea Park 2	d			13 26		13 36				13 46			13 56			14 06	14 16					14 26		14 36	
Romford	d			13 28	13 28	13 38				13 48			13 58	13 53		14 08	14 18					14 28	14 28	14 38	
Chadwell Heath	d			13 32		13 42				13 52			14 02			14 12	14 22					14 32		14 42	
Goodmayes	d			13 34		13 44				13 54			14 04			14 14	14 24					14 34		14 44	
Seven Kings	d			13 36		13 46				13 56			14 06			14 16	14 26					14 36		14 46	
Ilford 2	d			13 39		13 49				13 59			14 09			14 19	14 29					14 39		14 49	
Manor Park	d			13 42		13 52				14 02			14 12			14 22	14 32					14 42		14 52	
Forest Gate	d			13 44		13 54				14 04			14 14			14 24	14 34					14 44		14 54	
Maryland	d			13 46		13 56				14 06			14 16			14 26	14 36					14 46		14 56	
Stratford 7 ⊖	d	13 19	13 22	13 49	13 36	13 59	13 39			14 09		13 52	14 19	14 01	14 05	14 29	14 39	14 19		14 22		14 49	14 36	14 59	14 39
London Liverpool Street 15 ⊖	a	13 28	13 31	13 57	13 45	14 07	13 48			14 17		14 01	14 27	14 10	14 14	14 37	14 47	14 28		14 31		14 57	14 45	15 07	14 48

			LE	LE 1	LE	LE 1		LE 1	LE 1	LE	LE	LE 1	LE 1	LE	LE 1	LE		LE 1	LE 1		LE	LE 1	LE	LE 1	LE 1
Southend Victoria	d					14 10						14 30						14 50						15 10	
Prittlewell	d					14 12						14 32						14 52						15 12	
Southend Airport ✈	d					14 15						14 35						14 55						15 15	
Rochford	d					14 18						14 38						14 58						15 18	
Hockley	d					14 21						14 41						15 01						15 21	
Rayleigh	d					14 26						14 46						15 06						15 26	
Southminster	d							14 16											14 56						
Burnham-on-Crouch	d							14 20											15 00						
Althorne	d							14 25											15 05						
North Fambridge	d							14 31											15 11						
South Woodham Ferrers	d							14 36											15 16						
Battlesbridge	d							14 40											15 20						
Wickford 2	d					14 31		14a46				14 51						15 11	15a26					15 31	
Billericay	d					14 37						14 57						15 17						15 37	
Shenfield 3	a					14 45						15 05						15 25						15 45	
Shenfield 3	d		14 34	14 38	14 44	14 45			14 51	14 54	15 04	15 05	15 08	15 14	15 20	15 24		15 25			15 34	15 38	15 44	15 45	15 51
Brentwood	d		14 37		14 47					14 57	15 07			15 17		15 27					15 37		15 47		
Harold Wood	d		14 42		14 52					15 02	15 12			15 22		15 32					15 42		15 52		
Gidea Park 2	d		14 46		14 56					15 06	15 16			15 26		15 36					15 46		15 56		
Romford	d		14 48		14 58	14 53				15 08	15 18			15 28	15 28	15 38					15 48		15 58	15 53	
Chadwell Heath	d		14 52		15 02					15 12	15 22			15 32		15 42					15 52		16 02		
Goodmayes	d		14 54		15 04					15 14	15 24			15 34		15 44					15 54		16 04		
Seven Kings	d		14 56		15 06					15 16	15 26			15 36		15 46					15 56		16 06		
Ilford 2	d		14 59		15 09					15 19	15 29			15 39		15 49					15 59		16 09		
Manor Park	d		15 02		15 12					15 22	15 32			15 42		15 52					16 02		16 12		
Forest Gate	d		15 04		15 14					15 24	15 34			15 44		15 54					16 04		16 14		
Maryland	d		15 06		15 16					15 26	15 36			15 46		15 56					16 06		16 16		
Stratford 7 ⊖	d		15 09	14 52	15 19	15 01			15 05	15 29	15 39	15 19	15 22	15 49	15 36	15 59		15 39			16 09	15 52	16 19	16 01	16 05
London Liverpool Street 15 ⊖	a		15 17	15 01	15 27	15 10			15 15	15 37	15 47	15 28	15 33	15 57	15 45	16 07		15 48			16 17	16 01	16 27	16 11	16 14

until 26 July

Southend Victoria, Southminster and Shenfield - London

Network Diagram - see first Page of Table 5

		LE		LE	LE 1	LE 1	LE 1	LE	LE 1	LE	LE 1			LE	LE 1	LE	LE 1	LE 1	LE 1	LE	LE	LE 1		LE 1	LE
Southend Victoria	d				15 30						15 50						16 10					16 30			
Prittlewell	d				15 32						15 52						16 12					16 32			
Southend Airport ✈	d				15 35						15 55						16 15					16 35			
Rochford	d				15 38						15 58						16 18					16 38			
Hockley	d				15 41						16 01						16 21					16 41			
Rayleigh	d				15 46						16 06						16 26					16 46			
Southminster	d					15 36												16 14							
Burnham-on-Crouch	d					15 40												16 18							
Althorne	d					15 45												16 23							
North Fambridge	d					15 51												16 29							
South Woodham Ferrers	d					15 56												16 34							
Battlesbridge	d					16 00												16 38							
Wickford 2	d				15 51	16a06					16 11						16 31	16a44				16 51			
Billericay	d				15 57						16 17						16 37					16 57			
Shenfield 3	a				16 05						16 25						16 45					17 05			
Shenfield 3	d	15 54		16 04	16 05		16 08	16 14	16 20	16 24	16 25			16 34	16 38	16 44	16 45		16 51	16 54	17 04	17 05		17 08	17 14
Brentwood	d	15 57		16 07				16 17		16 27				16 37		16 47				16 57	17 07				17 17
Harold Wood	d	16 02		16 12				16 22		16 32				16 42		16 52				17 02	17 12				17 22
Gidea Park 2	d	16 06		16 16				16 26		16 35				16 46		16 56				17 06	17 16				17 26
Romford	d	16 08		16 18				16 28		16 38				16 48		16 58				17 08	17 18				17 28
Chadwell Heath	d	16 12		16 22				16 32		16 42				16 52		17 02				17 12	17 22				17 32
Goodmayes	d	16 14		16 24				16 34		16 44				16 54		17 04				17 14	17 24				17 34
Seven Kings	d	16 16		16 26				16 36		16 46				16 56		17 06				17 16	17 26				17 36
Ilford 2	d	16 19		16 29				16 39		16 49				16 59		17 09				17 19	17 29				17 39
Manor Park	d	16 22		16 32				16 42		16 52				17 02		17 12				17 22	17 32				
Forest Gate	d	16 24		16 34				16 44		16 54				17 04		17 14				17 24	17 34				
Maryland	d	16 26		16 36				16 46		16 56				17 06		17 16				17 26	17 36				
Stratford 7 ⊖	d	16 29		16 39	16 19		16 22	16 49	16 34	16 59	16 39			17 09	16 52	17 19	16 59		17 05	17 29	17 39	17 19		17 22	17 45
London Liverpool Street 15 ⊖	a	16 37		16 47	16 28		16 31	16 57	16 44	17 07	16 48			17 17	17 03	17 27	17 13		17 16	17 37	17 47	17 29		17 34	17 53

		LE 1	LE	LE	LE 1	LE 1	LE ◇1	LE		LE	LE 1	LE	LE	LE 1	LE 1	LE 1	LE	LE		LE 1	LE	LE	LE 1	LE 1	LE
Southend Victoria	d				16 50									17 10						17 25				17 35	
Prittlewell	d				16 52									17 12						17 27				17 37	
Southend Airport ✈	d				16 55									17 15						17 30				17 40	
Rochford	d				16 58									17 18						17 33				17 43	
Hockley	d				17 01									17 21						17 36				17 46	
Rayleigh	d				17 06									17 26						17 41				17 51	
Southminster	d														17 06										
Burnham-on-Crouch	d														17 10										
Althorne	d														17 15										
North Fambridge	d														17 21										
South Woodham Ferrers	d														17 26										
Battlesbridge	d														17 30										
Wickford 2	d				17 11									17 31	17 37					17 46				17 56	
Billericay	d				17 17									17 37						17 52				18 02	
Shenfield 3	a				17 25									17 45	17 48					18 00				18 10	
Shenfield 3	d	17 22		17 24	17 25	17 28				17 34	17 38		17 44	17 45	17 49	17 51		17 54		18 00		18 04	18 08	18 10	
Brentwood	d			17 27						17 37			17 47					17 57				18 07			
Harold Wood	d			17 32						17 42			17 52					18 02				18 12			
Gidea Park 2	d		17 32	17 36				17 42		17 46		17 52	17 56				18 02	18 06			18 12	18 16			18 22
Romford	d		17 34	17 38				17 44		17 48		17 54	17 58				18 04	18 08			18 14	18 18			18 24
Chadwell Heath	d			17 42						17 52			18 02					18 12				18 22			
Goodmayes	d			17 44						17 54			18 04					18 14				18 24			
Seven Kings	d			17 46						17 56			18 06					18 16				18 26			
Ilford 2	d		17 42	17 49				17 52		17 59		18 02	18 09				18 12	18 19			18 22	18 29			18 32
Manor Park	d		17 45					17 55				18 05					18 15				18 25				18 35
Forest Gate	d		17 47					17 57				18 07					18 17				18 27				18 37
Maryland	d		17 49					17 59				18 09					18 19				18 29				18 39
Stratford 7 ⊖	d	17 36	17 52	17 55	17 39	17 42		18 02		18 05	17 52	18 12	18 15	17 59	18 08	18 06	18 22	18 25		18 14	18 32	18 35	18 22	18 25	18 42
London Liverpool Street 15 ⊖	a	17 46	18 00	18 03	17 49	17 53	17 58	18 10		18 13	18 01	18 20	18 23	18 11	18 17	18 15	18 30	18 33		18 24	18 40	18 43	18 31	18 35	18 50

Southend Victoria, Southminster and Shenfield - London

Network Diagram - see first Page of Table 5

		LE	LE ■	LE	LE	LE ■	LE ■	LE	LE ■	LE ■	LE ■	LE	LE ■	LE	LE ■	LE	LE ■	LE ■	LE ■	LE	LE ■
Southend Victoria	d					17 50				18 05					18 20		18 30				
Prittlewell	d					17 52				18 07					18 22		18 32				
Southend Airport ✈	d					17 55				18 10					18 25		18 35				
Rochford	d					17 58				18 13					18 28		18 38				
Hockley	d					18 01				18 16					18 31		18 41				
Rayleigh	d					18 06				18 21					18 36		18 46				
Southminster	d										17 56										
Burnham-on-Crouch	d										18 00										
Althorne	d										18 05										
North Fambridge	d										18 14										
South Woodham Ferrers	d										18 19										
Battlesbridge	d										18 23										
Wickford 2	d					18 11				18 26	18a29				18 41		18 51				
Billericay	d					18 17				18 32					18 47		18 57				
Shenfield 3	a					18 25				18 40					18 55		19 05				
Shenfield 3	d	18 14	18 20		18 24	18 25	18 27	18 34	18 38	18 40		18 44	18 51	18 54	18 57	19 04	19 05	19 08	19 13	19 14	19 20
Brentwood	d	18 17			18 27			18 37				18 47		18 57		19 07				19 17	
Harold Wood	d	18 22			18 32			18 42				18 52		19 02		19 12				19 22	
Gidea Park 2	d	18 26		18 32	18 36			18 46				18 56		19 06		19 16				19 26	
Romford	d	18 28	18 28	18 34	18 38			18 48				18 58		19 08		19 18				19 28	19 28
Chadwell Heath	d	18 32			18 42			18 52				19 02		19 12		19 22				19 32	
Goodmayes	d	18 34			18 44			18 54				19 04		19 14		19 24				19 34	
Seven Kings	d	18 36			18 46			18 56				19 06		19 16		19 26				19 36	
Ilford 2	d	18 39		18 42	18 49			18 59				19 09		19 19		19 29				19 39	
Manor Park	d			18 45	18 52			19 02				19 12		19 22		19 32				19 42	
Forest Gate	d			18 47	18 54			19 04				19 14		19 24		19 34				19 44	
Maryland	d			18 49	18 56			19 06				19 16		19 26		19 36				19 46	
Stratford 7 ⊖	d	18 45	18 36	18 52	18 59	18 39	18 42	19 09	18 52	18 55		19 19	19 05	19 29	19 11	19 39	19 19	19 22	19 27	19 49	19 36
London Liverpool Street 15 ⊖	a	18 53	18 45	19 00	19 07	18 48	18 51	19 17	19 01	19 04		19 27	19 14	19 37	19 20	19 47	19 28	19 31	19 36	19 57	19 45

		LE	LE ■	LE ■	LE	LE ■	LE	LE ■	LE ■	LE ■	LE	LE	LE ■	LE ■	CC	LE ■	LE	LE ■	LE	LE ■	LE
Southend Victoria	d		18 50					19 10					19 30							19 50	
Prittlewell	d		18 52					19 12					19 32							19 52	
Southend Airport ✈	d		18 55					19 15					19 35							19 55	
Rochford	d		18 58					19 18					19 38							19 58	
Hockley	d		19 01					19 21					19 41							20 01	
Rayleigh	d		19 06					19 26					19 46							20 06	
Southminster	d			18 36										19 19							
Burnham-on-Crouch	d			18 40										19 23							
Althorne	d			18 45										19 28							
North Fambridge	d			19 01										19 34							
South Woodham Ferrers	d			19 06										19 39							
Battlesbridge	d			19 10										19 43							
Wickford 2	d		19 11	19 17				19 31					19 51	19 55						20 11	
Billericay	d		19 17	19 23				19 37					19 57							20 17	
Shenfield 3	a		19 25	19 33				19 45					20 05	20 08						20 25	
Shenfield 3	d	19 24	19 25		19 34	19 38	19 44	19 45	19 51		19 54	20 04	20 05			20 08	20 14	20 20	20 24	20 25	20 34
Brentwood	d	19 27			19 37		19 47				19 57	20 07					20 17		20 27		20 37
Harold Wood	d	19 32			19 42		19 52				20 02	20 12					20 22		20 32		20 42
Gidea Park 2	d	19 36			19 46		19 56				20 06	20 16					20 26		20 36		20 46
Romford	d	19 38			19 48		19 58	19 53			20 08	20 18					20 28	20 28	20 38		20 48
Chadwell Heath	d	19 42			19 52		20 02				20 12	20 22					20 32		20 42		20 52
Goodmayes	d	19 44			19 54		20 04				20 14	20 24					20 34		20 44		20 54
Seven Kings	d	19 46			19 56		20 06				20 16	20 26					20 36		20 46		20 56
Ilford 2	d	19 49			19 59		20 09				20 19	20 29					20 39		20 49		20 59
Manor Park	d	19 52			20 02		20 12				20 22	20 32					20 42		20 52		21 02
Forest Gate	d	19 54			20 04		20 14				20 24	20 34					20 44		20 54		21 04
Maryland	d	19 56			20 06		20 16				20 26	20 36					20 46		20 56		21 06
Stratford 7 ⊖	d	19 59	19 39		20 09	19 52	20 19	20 01	20 05	20 14	20 29	20 39	20 19		20 21	20 22	20 49	20 36	20 59	20 39	21 09
London Liverpool Street 15 ⊖	a	20 07	19 48		20 17	20 01	20 27	20 10	20 14	20 23	20 37	20 47	20 28		20 33	20 31	20 57	20 45	21 07	20 48	21 17

Southend Victoria, Southminster and Shenfield - London

Network Diagram - see first Page of Table 5

		LE ■	CC	LE	LE ■	LE ■	LE ■	LE ■	CC	LE	LE	LE ■	LE ■	LE	LE	LE ■	LE ■	LE ■	LE	LE ■	LE	LE ■
Southend Victoria	d				20 10							20 30				20 50						21 10
Prittlewell	d				20 12							20 32				20 52						21 12
Southend Airport ✈	d				20 15							20 35				20 55						21 15
Rochford	d				20 18							20 38				20 58						21 18
Hockley	d				20 21							20 41				21 01						21 21
Rayleigh	d				20 26							20 46				21 06						21 26
Southminster	d					20 16											20 56					
Burnham-on-Crouch	d					20 20											21 00					
Althorne	d					20 25											21 05					
North Fambridge	d					20 31											21 11					
South Woodham Ferrers	d					20 36											21 16					
Battlesbridge	d					20 40											21 20					
Wickford 2	d				20 31	20a46						20 51				21 11	21a26					21 31
Billericay	d				20 37							20 57				21 17						21 37
Shenfield 3	a				20 45							21 05				21 25						21 45
Shenfield 3	d	20 38		20 44	20 45		20 47	20 53		20 54	21 04	21 05	21 08	21 14	21 24	21 25		21 27	21 34	21 38	21 44	21 45
Brentwood	d			20 47						20 57	21 07			21 17	21 27				21 37		21 47	
Harold Wood	d			20 52						21 02	21 12			21 22	21 32				21 42		21 52	
Gidea Park 2	d			20 56						21 06	21 16			21 26	21 36				21 46		21 56	
Romford	d			20 58	20 53					21 08	21 18			21 28	21 38				21 48		21 58	21 53
Chadwell Heath	d			21 02						21 12	21 22			21 32	21 42				21 52		22 02	
Goodmayes	d			21 04						21 14	21 24			21 34	21 44				21 54		22 04	
Seven Kings	d			21 06						21 16	21 26			21 36	21 46				21 56		22 06	
Ilford 2	d			21 09						21 19	21 29			21 39	21 49				21 59		22 09	
Manor Park	d			21 12						21 22	21 32			21 42	21 52				22 02		22 12	
Forest Gate	d			21 14						21 24	21 34			21 44	21 54				22 04		22 14	
Maryland	d			21 16						21 26	21 36			21 46	21 56				22 06		22 16	
Stratford 7 ⊖	d	20 52	21 00	21 19	21 01			21 07	21 15	21 29	21 39	21 19	21 22	21 49	21 59	21 39		21 42	22 09	21 52	22 19	22 01
London Liverpool Street 15 ⊖	a	21 01	21 12	21 27	21 10		21 12	21 16	21 26	21 37	21 47	21 28	21 31	21 57	22 07	21 48		21 51	22 17	22 01	22 27	22 10

		LE ■	LE	LE ■	LE ■	LE ■	LE ■	LE	LE ■	LE ◇■	LE	LE	LE ■	LE ■	LE ■	LE ■	LE ■	LE	LE ■	LE ■	LE ■
				A	B					B 🚌	B	A	A	B		B	A	B	B		A
Southend Victoria	d			21 30	21 30								22 00	22 00							
Prittlewell	d			21 32	21 32								22 02	22 02							
Southend Airport ✈	d			21 35	21 35								22 05	22 05							
Rochford	d			21 38	21 38								22 08	22 08							
Hockley	d			21 41	21 41								22 11	22 11							
Rayleigh	d			21 46	21 46								22 16	22 16							
Southminster	d					21 36									22 16						
Burnham-on-Crouch	d					21 40									22 20						
Althorne	d					21 45									22 25						
North Fambridge	d					21 51									22 31						
South Woodham Ferrers	d					21 56									22 36						
Battlesbridge	d					22 00									22 40						
Wickford 2	d			21 51	21 51	22a07							22 21	22 21	22a46						
Billericay	d			21 57	21 57								22 27	22 27							
Shenfield 3	a			22 05	22 05								22 35	22 35							
Shenfield 3	d	21 51	21 59		22 05		22 08	22 14	22 20		22 29	22 34		22 35		22 38	22 38	22 44	22 51		22 51
Brentwood	d		22 02					22 17			22 32	22 37						22 47			
Harold Wood	d		22 07					22 22			22 37	22 42						22 52			
Gidea Park 2	d		22 11					22 26			22 41	22 46						22 56			
Romford	d		22 13					22 28	22 28		22 43	22 48						22 58			
Chadwell Heath	d		22 17					22 32			22 47	22 52						23 02			
Goodmayes	d		22 19					22 34			22 49	22 54						23 04			
Seven Kings	d		22 21					22 36			22 51	22 56						23 06			
Ilford 2	d		22 24					22 39			22 54	22 59						23 09			
Manor Park	d		22 27					22 42			22 57	23 02						23 12			
Forest Gate	d		22 29					22 44			22 59	23 04						23 14			
Maryland	d		22 31					22 46			23 01	23 06						23 16			
Stratford 7 ⊖	d	22 05	22 34		22 19		22 22	22 49	22 36		23 04	23 09		22 49		22 52	22 54	23 19	23 05	23 06	23 11
London Liverpool Street 15 ⊖	a	22 14	22 42		22 28		22 31	22 57	22 45	22 55	23 12	23 18		22 58		23 01	23 03	23 27	23 15	23 15	23 20

A MTWO until 20 June

B ThFO until 15 June, from 21 June until 26 July

until 26 July

Southend Victoria, Southminster and Shenfield - London

Network Diagram - see first Page of Table 5

	LE	LE	LE	LE	LE	LE	LE	LE	LE	LE	LE	LE	LE	LE	LE	LE	LE	LE
			■	■	■	■		■	■			■	■	◇■	■		■	
	A	B	A	B	B	A	B	B	A	A	B	A	B	A	B	B	A	A
Southend Victoria d			22 30	22 30								23 00	23 00					
Prittlewell d			22 32	22 32								23 02	23 02					
Southend Airport ✈ d			22 35	22 35								23 05	23 05					
Rochford d			22 38	22 38								23 08	23 08					
Hockley d			22 41	22 41								23 11	23 11					
Rayleigh d			22 46	22 46								23 16	23 16					
Southminster d															22 56		23 06	
Burnham-on-Crouch d															23 00		23 10	
Althorne d															23 05		23 15	
North Fambridge d															23 11		23 21	
South Woodham Ferrers d															23 16		23 26	
Battlesbridge d															23 20		23 30	
Wickford 2 d			22 51	22 51								23 21	23 21		23 26		23 36	
Billericay d			22 57	22 57								23 27	23 27		23 32		23 42	
Shenfield 3 a			23 05	23 05								23 35	23 35		23 39		23 49	
Shenfield 3 d	22 54	22 59		23 05	23 08	23 08	23 14	23 20	23 20	23 27	23 29		23 35	23 38	23 39	23 44	23 52	23 54
Brentwood d	22 57	23 02					23 17			23 30	23 32					23 47		23 57
Harold Wood d	23 02	23 07					23 22			23 35	23 37					23 52		00 02
Gidea Park 2 d	23 06	23 11					23 26			23 39	23 41					23 56		00 06
Romford d	23 08	23 13				23 19	23 28	23 28	23 31	23 41	23 43				23 47	23 58	00 03	00 08
Chadwell Heath d	23 12	23 17					23 32			23 45	23 47					00 02		00 12
Goodmayes d	23 14	23 19					23 34			23 47	23 49					00 04		00 14
Seven Kings d	23 16	23 21					23 36			23 49	23 51					00 06		00 16
Ilford 2 d	23 19	23 24					23 39			23 52	23 54					00 09		00 19
Manor Park d	23 22	23 27					23 42			23 55	23 57					00 12		00 22
Forest Gate d	23 24	23 29					23 44			23 57	23 59					00 14		00 24
Maryland d	23 26	23 31					23 46			23 59	00 01					00 16		00 26
Stratford 7 ⊖ d	23 29	23 34		23 19	23 22	23 31	23 49	23 36	23 41	00 02	00 04		23 49	00s04	23 56	00 19	00 13	00 29
London Liverpool Street 15 ⊖ a	23 38	23 42		23 28	23 31	23 40	23 57	23 45	23 50	00 11	00 12		23 58	00 14	00 05	00 27	00 22	00 38

Mondays to Fridays

27 July to 10 August

	LE	LE MO	LE	LE	LE	LE	LE	LE	LE	CC	LE	LE	LE	LE	LE	LE	LE	LE	LE	LE	LE
	◇■	■				■			■		■										
	C		D	E	C	C	C	E	E	C	E	E	E	E	E	E	E	E	E	E	
Southend Victoria d									23p10												04 00
Prittlewell d									23p12												04 02
Southend Airport ✈ d									23p15												04 05
Rochford d									23p18												04 08
Hockley d									23p21												04 12
Rayleigh d									23p26												04 16
Southminster d						22p56															
Burnham-on-Crouch d						23p00															
Althorne d						23p05															
North Fambridge d						23p11															
South Woodham Ferrers d						23p16															
Battlesbridge d						23p20															
Wickford 2 d						23p26			23p31												04 21
Billericay d						23p32			23p37												04 28
Shenfield 3 a						23p39			23p45												04 39
Shenfield 3 d				23p29	23p29	23p39	23p44	23p44	23p45				23p59	00 14		00 29	00 44				04 39
Brentwood d				23p32	23p32		23p47	23p47					00 02	00 17		00 32	00 47				04 42
Harold Wood d				23p37	23p37		23p52	23p52					00 07	00 22		00 37	00 52				04 47
Gidea Park 2 d				23p41	23p41		23p56	23p56					00 11	00 26		00 41	00 56				04 51
Romford d				23p43	23p43	23p47	23p58	23p58					00 13	00 28		00 43	00 58				04 53
Chadwell Heath d				23p47	23p47		00 02	00 02					00 17	00 32		00 47	01 02				04 57
Goodmayes d				23p49	23p49		00 04	00 04					00 19	00 34		00 49	01 04				04 59
Seven Kings d				23p51	23p51		00 06	00 06					00 21	00 36		00 51	01 06				05 01
Ilford 2 d				23p54	23p54		00 09	00 09					00 24	00 39		00 54	01 09				05 04
Manor Park d				23p57	23p57		00 12	00 12					00 27	00 42		00 57	01 12				
Forest Gate d				23p59	23p59		00 14	00 14					00 29	00 44		00 59	01 14				
Maryland d					00 01		00 16														
Stratford 7 ⊖ d	23b52	23p54	23p54	00 04	00 04	23p56	00 19	00 20	00 08	00 09	00 12	00 30	00 40	00 50	01 00	01 10	01 20	01 30	01 40	01 50	05 10
London Liverpool Street 15 ⊖ a	00 02	00 02	00 02	00 12	00 12	00 05	00 27	00 28	00 16	00 20	00 20	00 38	00 48	00 58	01 08	01 18	01 28	01 38	01 48	01 58	05 18

A MTWO until 20 June
B ThFO until 15 June, from 21 June until 26 July
C 27 July
D MX from 31 July until 10 August
E not 27 July
b Previous night, stops to set down only

27 July to 10 August

Southend Victoria, Southminster and Shenfield - London

Network Diagram - see first Page of Table 5

	CC	LE	LE	LE	LE	LE	LE	LE	LE	LE	LE	LE	LE	LE	LE	LE	LE	LE	LE	LE
				■			■		■	■	■				■		■		■	■
Southend Victoria d			04 30				05 00			05 20					05 40				06 00	
Prittlewell d			04 32				05 02			05 22					05 42				06 02	
Southend Airport ✈ d			04 35				05 05			05 25					05 45				06 05	
Rochford d			04 38				05 08			05 28					05 48				06 08	
Hockley d			04 42				05 11			05 31					05 51				06 11	
Rayleigh d			04 46				05 16			05 36					05 56				06 16	
Southminster d											05 26									
Burnham-on-Crouch d											05 30									
Althorne d											05 35									
North Fambridge d											05 41									
South Woodham Ferrers d											05 46									
Battlesbridge d											05 50									
Wickford 2 d			04 51				05 21			05 41	05a56				06 01				06 21	
Billericay d			04 58				05 27			05 47					06 07				06 27	
Shenfield 3 a			05 09				05 35			05 55					06 15				06 35	
Shenfield 3 d			05 09	05 24		05 29	05 35	05 44	05 53	05 55			06 04	06 14	06 15	06 24	06 25	06 34	06 35	06 41
Brentwood d			05 12			05 32		05 47					06 07	06 17		06 27		06 37		
Harold Wood d			05 17			05 37		05 52					06 12	06 22		06 32		06 42		
Gidea Park 2 d			05 21	05 31		05 41		05 56				06 06	06 16	06 26		06 36		06 45		
Romford d			05 23			05 43		05 58				06 08	06 18	06 28		06 38		06 48		
Chadwell Heath d			05 27			05 47		06 02				06 12	06 22	06 32		06 42		06 52		
Goodmayes d			05 29			05 49		06 04				06 14	06 24	06 34		06 44				
Seven Kings d			05 31	05 36		05 51		06 06				06 16	06 26	06 36		06 46				
Ilford 2 d		05 09	05 34		05 39	05 54		06 09				06 19	06 29	06 39		06 49		06 57		
Manor Park d		05 11			05 41	05 57		06 12				06 22	06 32	06 42		06 52				
Forest Gate d		05 14			05 44	05 59		06 14				06 24	06 34	06 44		06 54				
Maryland d																				
Stratford 7 ⊖ d	05 14	05 18	05 40	05 42	05 48	06 04	05 49	06 19	06 07	06 10		06 29	06 39	06 49	06 29	06 59	06 39	07 03	06 49	06s57
London Liverpool Street 15 ⊖ a	05 27	05 26	05 48	05 55	05 56	06 12	05 58	06 27	06 16	06 19		06 37	06 47	06 57	06 40	07 07	06 48	07 13	06 58	07 09

	LE	LE	LE	LE	LE	LE	LE	LE	LE	LE	LE	LE	LE	LE	LE	LE	LE	LE	LE
			■	■	■						■	■	■			■	■	■	
Southend Victoria d			06 11					06 26					06 40				06 50		
Prittlewell d			06 13					06 28					06 42				06 52		
Southend Airport ✈ d			06 16					06 31					06 45				06 55		
Rochford d			06 19					06 34					06 48				06 58		
Hockley d			06 22					06 38					06 51				07 01		
Rayleigh d			06 27					06 42					06 56				07 06		
Southminster d					06 09														
Burnham-on-Crouch d					06 13														
Althorne d					06 18														
North Fambridge d					06 24														
South Woodham Ferrers d					06 30														
Battlesbridge d					06 34														
Wickford 2 d			06 32		06 40			06 47					07 01				07 11		
Billericay d			06 39		06 46			06 54					07 08				07 18		
Shenfield 3 a			06 45		06 52			07 01					07 14				07 24		
Shenfield 3 d		06 44	06 45	06 50	06 53		06 54	07 01		07 04	07 08		07 14		07 14	07 19	07 24		
Brentwood d		06 47					06 57			07 07					07 17				
Harold Wood d		06 52					07 02			07 12					07 22				
Gidea Park 2 d	06 49	06 55				06 59	07 05		07 09	07 15				07 19	07 25				07 29
Romford d	06 51	06 58				07 01	07 08		07 11	07 18				07 21	07 28				07 31
Chadwell Heath d	06 55	07 02				07 05	07 12		07 15	07 22				07 25	07 32				07 35
Goodmayes d	06 57					07 07			07 17					07 27	07 34				07 37
Seven Kings d	06 59					07 09			07 19					07 29	07 36				07 39
Ilford 2 d	07 02	07 07				07 12	07 17		07 22	07 27				07 32	07 39				07 42
Manor Park d	07 05					07 15			07 25					07 35					07 45
Forest Gate d	07 07					07 17			07 27					07 37					07 47
Maryland d																			
Stratford 7 ⊖ d	07 12	07 15	07s02	07s06	07s09	07 22	07 25	07s19	07 32	07 35	07s23		07s31	07 42	07 45	07s35	07s41	07 44	07 52
London Liverpool Street 15 ⊖ a	07 22	07 25	07 13	07 18	07 21	07 32	07 35	07 30	07 42	07 45	07 35	07 38	07 42	07 52	07 55	07 46	07 52	07 56	08 02

Table 5

Mondays to Fridays

27 July to 10 August

Southend Victoria, Southminster and Shenfield - London

Network Diagram - see first Page of Table 5

		LE	LE ■	LE ■	LE	LE	LE ■	LE ■			LE	LE	LE ■	LE ■		LE	LE	LE		LE	LE ■	LE	LE ■		LE ■
Southend Victoria	d			07 03									07 13							07 18	07 23				07 32
Prittlewell	d			07 05									07 15							07 20	07 25				07 34
Southend Airport ✈	d			07 08									07 18							07 23	07 28				07 37
Rochford	d			07 11									07 21							07 26	07 31				07 40
Hockley	d			07 14									07 24							07 30	07 34				07 43
Rayleigh	d			07 19									07 29							07 34	07 39				07 48
Southminster	d		06 48																						
Burnham-on-Crouch	d		06 52																						
Althorne	d		06 57																						
North Fambridge	d		07 04																						
South Woodham Ferrers	d		07 10																						
Battlesbridge	d		07 14																						
Wickford 2	d		07 19	07 24									07 34							07 39	07 44				07 53
Billericay	d		07 26	07 31									07 41							07 46	07 51				08 00
Shenfield 3	a		07 32										07 47							07 53	07 57				08 06
Shenfield 3	d	07 24	07 32			07 34	07 38	07 41				07 44	07 47	07 50			07 50			07 54	07 57	08 00	08 01		08 06
Brentwood	d	07 27				07 37						07 47					07 53			07 57		08 03			
Harold Wood	d	07 32				07 42						07 52					07 58			08 02		08 08			
Gidea Park 2	d	07 35			07 39	07 45					07 49	07 55				07 59	08 02	08 05		08 09		08 12			
Romford	d	07 38			07 41	07 48					07 51	07 58				08 01	08 04	08 07		08 11		08 14			
Chadwell Heath	d	07 42			07 45	07 52					07 55	08 02				08 05	08 08	08 11		08 15		08 18			
Goodmayes	d	07 44			07 47	07 54					07 57	08 04				08 07	08 10	08 13		08 17		08 20			
Seven Kings	d	07 46			07 49	07 56					07 59	08 06				08 09	08 12	08 15		08 19		08 22			
Ilford 2	d	07 49			07 52	07 59					08 02	08 09				08 12	08 15	08 18		08 22		08 25			
Manor Park	d				07 55						08 05							08 21							
Forest Gate	d				07 57						08 07							08 23							
Maryland	d																								
Stratford 7 ⊖	d	07 55	07 50	07s52	08 02	08 05	07s55	07s58			08 12	08 15	08s04	08s07		08 18	08 21	08 28		08 31	08s15	08 34	08s18		08s23
London Liverpool Street 15 ⊖	a	08 05	08 01	08 03	08 12	08 15	08 07	08 09			08 22	08 25	08 15	08 19		08 28	08 31	08 38		08 41	08 26	08 43	08 30		08 36

		LE ■		LE		LE	LE	LE ■	LE ■	LE ■	LE	LE	LE	LE ■		LE ■	LE ■			LE	LE	LE	LE ■	LE ■	
Southend Victoria	d							07 42								07 52							08 03		
Prittlewell	d							07 44								07 54							08 05		
Southend Airport ✈	d							07 47								07 57							08 08		
Rochford	d							07 50								08 00							08 11		
Hockley	d							07 53								08 03							08 14		
Rayleigh	d							07 58								08 08							08 19		
Southminster	d								07 37																
Burnham-on-Crouch	d								07 41																
Althorne	d								07 46																
North Fambridge	d								07 52																
South Woodham Ferrers	d								07 59																
Battlesbridge	d																								
Wickford 2	d							08 03	08 07							08 13							08 24		
Billericay	d							08 10	08 14							08 20							08 31		
Shenfield 3	a							08 16								08 26							08 37		
Shenfield 3	d	08 09					08 10	08 16		08 21			08 22	08 24		08 26	08 29					08 32	08 37	08 42	
Brentwood	d						08 13						08 25									08 35			
Harold Wood	d						08 18						08 30									08 40			
Gidea Park 2	d			08 15		08 19	08 22					08 29	08 34								08 41	08 44			
Romford	d			08 17		08 21	08 24					08 31	08 36								08 43	08 46			
Chadwell Heath	d			08 21		08 25	08 28					08 35	08 40								08 47	08 50			
Goodmayes	d			08 23		08 27	08 30					08 37	08 42								08 49	08 52			
Seven Kings	d			08 25		08 29	08 32					08 39	08 44								08 51	08 54			
Ilford 2	d			08 28		08 32	08 35				08 38	08 42	08 47							08 50	08 54	08 57			
Manor Park	d			08 31							08 41									08 53					
Forest Gate	d			08 33							08 43									08 55					
Maryland	d																								
Stratford 7 ⊖	d	08s25		08 38		08 41	08 44	08s33	08s35	08s38	08 48	08 51	08 54	08s41		08s43	08s45			09 00	09 03	09 06	08s56	08s59	
London Liverpool Street 15 ⊖	a	08 38		08 48		08 51	08 53	08 46	08 48	08 50	08 58	09 01	09 03	08 54		08 56	08 58			09 10	09 13	09 14	09 08	09 11	

Table 5

Mondays to Fridays

27 July to 10 August

Southend Victoria, Southminster and Shenfield - London

Network Diagram - see first Page of Table 5

		LE	LE	LE	LE ■	LE ■	LE	LE ■		LE ■		LE ■	LE ■	LE ◇■	LE	LE	LE ■	LE	LE ■	LE ■		LE ■	LE	LE ■	LE
Southend Victoria	d				08 12							08 30								08 52					
Prittlewell	d				08 14							08 32								08 54					
Southend Airport ✈	d				08 17							08 35								08 57					
Rochford	d				08 20							08 38								09 00					
Hockley	d				08 23							08 41								09 03					
Rayleigh	d				08 28							08 46								09 08					
Southminster	d									08 16												08 56			
Burnham-on-Crouch	d									08 20												09 00			
Althorne	d									08 25												09 05			
North Fambridge	d									08 31												09 11			
South Woodham Ferrers	d									08 37												09 16			
Battlesbridge	d									08 41												09 20			
Wickford 2	d				08 33					08 46		08 51								09 13		09a26			
Billericay	d				08 40					08 53		08 58								09 20					
Shenfield 3	a				08 46					08 59		09 04								09 27					
Shenfield 3	d			08 44	08 46	08 51	08 54	08 55		08 59		09 04			09 04	09 14	09 21	09 24	09 25	09 27			09 34	09 38	09 44
Brentwood	d			08 47			08 57								09 07	09 17		09 27					09 37		09 47
Harold Wood	d			08 52			09 02								09 12	09 22		09 32					09 42		09 52
Gidea Park 2	d		08 51	08 56			09 06								09 16	09 26		09 36					09 46		09 56
Romford	d		08 53	08 58	08 55		09 08								09 18	09 28		09 38					09 48		09 58
Chadwell Heath	d		08 57	09 02			09 12								09 22	09 32		09 42					09 52		10 02
Goodmayes	d		08 59	09 04			09 14								09 24	09 34		09 44					09 54		10 04
Seven Kings	d		09 01	09 06			09 16								09 26	09 36		09 46					09 56		10 06
Ilford 2	d	09 00	09 04	09 09			09 19								09 29	09 39		09 49					09 59		10 09
Manor Park	d	09 03		09 12			09 22								09 32	09 42		09 52					10 02		10 12
Forest Gate	d	09 05		09 14			09 24								09 34	09 44		09 54					10 04		10 14
Maryland	d																								
Stratford 7 ⊖	d	09 10	09 13	09 19	09s05	09s08	09 29			09s17		09s22			09 39	09 49	09s37	09 59	09s41	09s44			10 09	09 52	10 19
London Liverpool Street 15 ⊖	a	09 20	09 23	09 27	09 16	09 19	09 37	09 21		09 29		09 33	09 36	09 40	09 47	09 58	09 49	10 07	09 53	09 55			10 17	10 01	10 27

		LE ■	LE ■	LE	LE	LE ■		LE ■	LE ■	LE	LE ■	LE	LE ■	LE ■	LE	LE ■		LE	LE ■	LE ■	LE ■	LE	LE	LE ■	LE ■
Southend Victoria	d	09 10				09 30							09 50						10 10					10 30	
Prittlewell	d	09 12				09 32							09 52						10 12					10 32	
Southend Airport ✈	d	09 15				09 35							09 55						10 15					10 35	
Rochford	d	09 18				09 38							09 58						10 18					10 38	
Hockley	d	09 21				09 41							10 01						10 21					10 41	
Rayleigh	d	09 26				09 46							10 06						10 26					10 46	
Southminster	d							09 36												10 16					
Burnham-on-Crouch	d							09 40												10 20					
Althorne	d							09 45												10 25					
North Fambridge	d							09 51												10 31					
South Woodham Ferrers	d							09 56												10 36					
Battlesbridge	d							10 00												10 40					
Wickford 2	d	09 31				09 51		10a06					10 11						10 31	10a46				10 51	
Billericay	d	09 37				09 57							10 17						10 37					10 57	
Shenfield 3	a	09 45				10 05							10 25						10 45					11 05	
Shenfield 3	d	09 45	09 51	09 54	10 04	10 05			10 08	10 14	10 18	10 24	10 25		10 34	10 38		10 44	10 45		10 51	10 54	11 04	11 05	11 08
Brentwood	d			09 57	10 07					10 17		10 27			10 37			10 47				10 57	11 07		
Harold Wood	d			10 02	10 12					10 22		10 32			10 42			10 52				11 02	11 12		
Gidea Park 2	d			10 06	10 16					10 26		10 36			10 46			10 56				11 06	11 16		
Romford	d	09 53		10 08	10 18					10 28	10 26	10 38			10 48			10 58	10 53			11 08	11 18		
Chadwell Heath	d			10 12	10 22					10 32		10 42			10 52			11 02				11 12	11 22		
Goodmayes	d			10 14	10 24					10 34		10 44			10 54			11 04				11 14	11 24		
Seven Kings	d			10 16	10 26					10 36		10 46			10 56			11 06				11 16	11 26		
Ilford 2	d			10 19	10 29					10 39		10 49			10 59			11 09				11 19	11 29		
Manor Park	d			10 22	10 32					10 42		10 52			11 02			11 12				11 22	11 32		
Forest Gate	d			10 24	10 34					10 44		10 54			11 04			11 14				11 24	11 34		
Maryland	d																								
Stratford 7 ⊖	d	10 01	10 05	10 29	10 39	10 19			10 22	10 49	10 34	10 59	10 39		11 09	10 52		11 19	11 01		11 05	11 29	11 39	11 19	11 22
London Liverpool Street 15 ⊖	a	10 10	10 14	10 37	10 47	10 28			10 31	10 57	10 43	11 07	10 48	10 55	11 17	11 01		11 27	11 10		11 14	11 37	11 47	11 29	11 31

A The East Anglian

Southend Victoria, Southminster and Shenfield - London

Network Diagram - see first Page of Table 5

		LE		LE [1]	LE	LE [1]	LE [1]		LE	LE [1]	LE	LE [1]		LE [1]	LE	LE	LE [1]	LE [1]	LE [1]	LE	LE [1]	LE		LE [1]	
Southend Victoria	d					10 50						11 10					11 30							11 50	
Prittlewell	d					10 52						11 12					11 32							11 52	
Southend Airport ✈	d					10 55						11 15					11 35							11 55	
Rochford	d					10 58						11 18					11 38							11 58	
Hockley	d					11 01						11 21					11 41							12 01	
Rayleigh	d					11 06						11 26					11 46							12 06	
Southminster	d						10 56											11 36							
Burnham-on-Crouch	d						11 00											11 40							
Althorne	d						11 05											11 45							
North Fambridge	d						11 11											11 51							
South Woodham Ferrers	d						11 16											11 56							
Battlesbridge	d						11 20											12 00							
Wickford [2]	d					11 11	11a26					11 31					11 51	12a06						12 11	
Billericay	d					11 17						11 37					11 57							12 17	
Shenfield [3]	a					11 25						11 45					12 05							12 25	
Shenfield [3]	d	11 14		11 20	11 24	11 25			11 34	11 38	11 44	11 45		11 51	11 54	12 04	12 05		12 08	12 14	12 20	12 24		12 25	
Brentwood	d	11 17			11 27				11 37		11 47				11 57	12 07				12 17		12 27			
Harold Wood	d	11 22			11 32				11 42		11 52				12 02	12 12				12 22		12 32			
Gidea Park [2]	d	11 26			11 36				11 46		11 56				12 06	12 16				12 26		12 36			
Romford	d	11 28		11 28	11 38				11 48		11 58	11 53			12 08	12 18				12 28	12 28	12 38			
Chadwell Heath	d	11 32			11 42				11 52		12 02				12 12	12 22				12 32		12 42			
Goodmayes	d	11 34			11 44				11 54		12 04				12 14	12 24				12 34		12 44			
Seven Kings	d	11 36			11 46				11 56		12 06				12 16	12 26				12 36		12 46			
Ilford [2]	d	11 39			11 49				11 59		12 09				12 19	12 29				12 39		12 49			
Manor Park	d	11 42			11 52				12 02		12 12				12 22	12 32				12 42		12 52			
Forest Gate	d	11 44			11 54				12 04		12 14				12 24	12 34				12 44		12 54			
Maryland	d																								
Stratford [7] ⊖	d	11 49		11 36	11 59	11 39			12 09	11 52	12 19	12 01		12 05	12 29	12 39	12 19		12 22	12 49	12 36	12 59		12 39	
London Liverpool Street [15] ⊖	a	11 57		11 45	12 07	11 48			12 17	12 01	12 27	12 10		12 14	12 37	12 47	12 29		12 31	12 57	12 45	13 07		12 48	

		LE	LE [1]	LE	LE [1]	LE [1]	LE [1]	LE		LE	LE [1]	LE [1]	LE	LE [1]	LE	LE [1]	LE [1]			LE	LE [1]	LE	LE [1]	LE [1]	LE
Southend Victoria	d				12 10						12 30					12 50							13 10		
Prittlewell	d				12 12						12 32					12 52							13 12		
Southend Airport ✈	d				12 15						12 35					12 55							13 15		
Rochford	d				12 18						12 38					12 58							13 18		
Hockley	d				12 21						12 41					13 01							13 21		
Rayleigh	d				12 26						12 46					13 06							13 26		
Southminster	d					12 16											12 56								
Burnham-on-Crouch	d					12 20											13 00								
Althorne	d					12 25											13 05								
North Fambridge	d					12 31											13 11								
South Woodham Ferrers	d					12 36											13 16								
Battlesbridge	d					12 40											13 20								
Wickford [2]	d				12 31	12a46					12 51					13 11	13a26						13 31		
Billericay	d				12 37						12 57					13 17							13 37		
Shenfield [3]	a				12 45						13 05					13 25							13 45		
Shenfield [3]	d	12 34	12 38	12 44	12 45		12 51	12 54		13 04	13 05	13 08	13 14	13 20	13 24	13 25				13 34	13 38	13 44	13 45	13 51	13 54
Brentwood	d	12 37		12 47				12 57		13 07			13 17		13 27					13 37		13 47			13 57
Harold Wood	d	12 42		12 52				13 02		13 12			13 22		13 32					13 42		13 52			14 02
Gidea Park [2]	d	12 46		12 56				13 06		13 16			13 26		13 36					13 46		13 56			14 06
Romford	d	12 48		12 58	12 53			13 08		13 18			13 28	13 28	13 38					13 48		13 58	13 53		14 08
Chadwell Heath	d	12 52		13 02				13 12		13 22			13 32		13 42					13 52		14 02			14 12
Goodmayes	d	12 54		13 04				13 14		13 24			13 34		13 44					13 54		14 04			14 14
Seven Kings	d	12 56		13 06				13 16		13 26			13 36		13 46					13 56		14 06			14 16
Ilford [2]	d	12 59		13 09				13 19		13 29			13 39		13 49					13 59		14 09			14 19
Manor Park	d	13 02		13 12				13 22		13 32			13 42		13 52					14 02		14 12			14 22
Forest Gate	d	13 04		13 14				13 24		13 34			13 44		13 54					14 04		14 14			14 24
Maryland	d																								
Stratford [7] ⊖	d	13 09	12 52	13 19	13 01		13 05	13 29		13 39	13 19	13 22	13 49	13 36	13 59	13 39				14 09	13 52	14 19	14 01	14 05	14 29
London Liverpool Street [15] ⊖	a	13 17	13 01	13 27	13 10		13 14	13 37		13 47	13 28	13 31	13 57	13 45	14 07	13 48				14 17	14 01	14 27	14 10	14 14	14 37

Southend Victoria, Southminster and Shenfield - London

Network Diagram - see first Page of Table 5

		LE	LE [1]	LE [1]		LE [1]	LE	LE [1]	LE	LE [1]	LE ◇[1] 🚌	LE	LE [1]	LE		LE [1]	LE [1]	LE [1]	LE	LE	LE [1]	LE [1]	LE	LE [1]	
Southend Victoria	d		13 30							13 50						14 10					14 30				
Prittlewell	d		13 32							13 52						14 12					14 32				
Southend Airport ✈	d		13 35							13 55						14 15					14 35				
Rochford	d		13 38							13 58						14 18					14 38				
Hockley	d		13 41							14 01						14 21					14 41				
Rayleigh	d		13 46							14 06						14 26					14 46				
Southminster	d			13 36													14 16								
Burnham-on-Crouch	d			13 40													14 20								
Althorne	d			13 45													14 25								
North Fambridge	d			13 51													14 31								
South Woodham Ferrers	d			13 56													14 36								
Battlesbridge	d			14 00													14 40								
Wickford [2]	d		13 51	14a06						14 11						14 31	14a46				14 51				
Billericay	d		13 57							14 17						14 37					14 57				
Shenfield [3]	a		14 05							14 25						14 45					15 05				
Shenfield [3]	d	14 04	14 05			14 08	14 14	14 20	14 24	14 25		14 34	14 38	14 44		14 45		14 51	14 54	15 04	15 05	15 08	15 14	15 20	
Brentwood	d	14 07					14 17		14 27			14 37		14 47					14 57	15 07			15 17		
Harold Wood	d	14 12					14 22		14 32			14 42		14 52					15 02	15 12			15 22		
Gidea Park [2]	d	14 16					14 26		14 36			14 46		14 56					15 06	15 16			15 26		
Romford	d	14 18					14 28	14 28	14 38			14 48		14 58					15 08	15 18			15 28	15 28	
Chadwell Heath	d	14 22					14 32		14 42			14 52		15 02					15 12	15 22			15 32		
Goodmayes	d	14 24					14 34		14 44			14 54		15 04					15 14	15 24			15 34		
Seven Kings	d	14 26					14 36		14 46			14 56		15 06					15 16	15 26			15 36		
Ilford [2]	d	14 29					14 39		14 49			14 59		15 09					15 19	15 29			15 39		
Manor Park	d	14 32					14 42		14 52			15 02		15 12					15 22	15 32			15 42		
Forest Gate	d	14 34					14 44		14 54			15 04		15 14					15 24	15 34			15 44		
Maryland	d																								
Stratford [7] ⊖	d	14 39	14 19			14 22	14 49	14 36	14 59	14 39		15 09	14 52	15 19		14 59		15 05	15 29	15 39	15 19	15 22	15 49	15 36	
London Liverpool Street [15] ⊖	a	14 47	14 28			14 31	14 57	14 45	15 07	14 48	14 55	15 17	15 01	15 27		15 08		15 15	15 37	15 47	15 28	15 33	15 57	15 45	

		LE	LE [1]	LE [1]		LE	LE [1]	LE	LE [1]	LE		LE [1]	LE	LE	LE [1]	LE [1]	LE [1]	LE	LE	LE		LE [1]	LE	LE [1]	
Southend Victoria	d		14 50						15 10						15 30									15 50	
Prittlewell	d		14 52						15 12						15 32									15 52	
Southend Airport ✈	d		14 55						15 15						15 35									15 55	
Rochford	d		14 58						15 18						15 38									15 58	
Hockley	d		15 01						15 21						15 41									16 01	
Rayleigh	d		15 06						15 26						15 46									16 06	
Southminster	d			14 56												15 36									
Burnham-on-Crouch	d			15 00												15 40									
Althorne	d			15 05												15 45									
North Fambridge	d			15 11												15 51									
South Woodham Ferrers	d			15 16												15 56									
Battlesbridge	d			15 20												16 00									
Wickford [2]	d		15 11	15a26					15 31						15 51	16a06								16 11	
Billericay	d		15 17						15 37						15 57									16 17	
Shenfield [3]	a		15 25						15 45						16 05									16 25	
Shenfield [3]	d	15 24	15 25			15 34	15 38	15 44	15 45			15 51	15 54	16 04	16 05		16 08			16 14		16 20	16 24	16 25	
Brentwood	d	15 27				15 37		15 47					15 57	16 07						16 17			16 27		
Harold Wood	d	15 32				15 42		15 52					16 02	16 12						16 22			16 32		
Gidea Park [2]	d	15 36				15 46		15 56					16 06	16 16						16 26			16 36		
Romford	d	15 38				15 48		15 58	15 53				16 08	16 18						16 28			16 38		
Chadwell Heath	d	15 42				15 52		16 02					16 12	16 22						16 32			16 42		
Goodmayes	d	15 44				15 54		16 04					16 14	16 24						16 34			16 44		
Seven Kings	d	15 46				15 56		16 06					16 16	16 26						16 36			16 46		
Ilford [2]	d	15 49				15 59		16 09					16 19	16 29						16 39			16 49		
Manor Park	d	15 52				16 02		16 12					16 22	16 32						16 42			16 52		
Forest Gate	d	15 54				16 04		16 14					16 24	16 34						16 44			16 54		
Maryland	d																								
Stratford [7] ⊖	d	15 59	15 39			16 09	15 52	16 19	16 01	16 03		16 05	16 29	16 39	16 19		16 22	16 23	16 34	16 48		16 34	16 58	16 39	
London Liverpool Street [15] ⊖	a	16 07	15 48			16 17	16 01	16 27	16 11	16 13		16 14	16 37	16 47	16 28		16 31	16 31	16 42	16 57		16 44	17 07	16 48	

27 July to 10 August

Southend Victoria, Southminster and Shenfield - London

Network Diagram - see first Page of Table 5

		LE	LE	LE [1]	LE	LE [1]		LE [1]	LE	LE [1]	LE	LE	LE	LE [1]	LE [1]	LE		LE	LE	LE [1]	LE	LE	LE [1]	LE	LE [1]
Southend Victoria	d					16 10								16 30									16 50		
Prittlewell	d					16 12								16 32									16 52		
Southend Airport ✈	d					16 15								16 35									16 55		
Rochford	d					16 18								16 38									16 58		
Hockley	d					16 21								16 41									17 01		
Rayleigh	d					16 26								16 46									17 06		
Southminster	d							16 14																	
Burnham-on-Crouch	d							16 18																	
Althorne	d							16 23																	
North Fambridge	d							16 29																	
South Woodham Ferrers	d							16 34																	
Battlesbridge	d							16 38																	
Wickford [2]	d					16 31		16a44						16 51									17 11		
Billericay	d					16 37								16 57									17 17		
Shenfield [3]	a					16 45								17 05									17 25		
Shenfield [3]	d		16 34	16 38	16 44	16 45				16 51		16 54	17 04	17 05	17 08				17 14	17 22		17 24	17 25		17 28
Brentwood	d		16 37		16 47							16 57	17 07						17 17			17 27			
Harold Wood	d		16 42		16 52							17 02	17 12						17 22			17 32			
Gidea Park [2]	d		16 46		16 56							17 06	17 16						17 26		17 32	17 36			
Romford	d		16 48		16 58							17 08	17 18						17 28		17 34	17 38			
Chadwell Heath	d		16 52		17 02							17 12	17 22						17 32			17 42			
Goodmayes	d		16 54		17 04							17 14	17 24						17 34			17 44			
Seven Kings	d		16 56		17 06							17 16	17 26						17 36			17 46			
Ilford [2]	d		16 59		17 09							17 19	17 29						17 39		17 42	17 49			
Manor Park	d		17 02		17 12							17 22	17 32								17 45				
Forest Gate	d		17 04		17 14							17 24	17 34								17 47				
Maryland	d																								
Stratford [7] ⊖	d	16 51	17 08	16 52	17 19	16 59			17 01	17 05	17 11	17 29	17 38	17 19	17 22	17 24		17 34	17 45	17 36	17 52	17 55	17 39	17 41	17 42
London Liverpool Street [15] ⊖	a	16 59	17 17	17 03	17 27	17 13			17 09	17 16	17 20	17 37	17 47	17 29	17 34	17 32		17 42	17 53	17 46	18 00	18 03	17 49	17 49	17 53

				LE	LE	LE [1]	LE	LE	LE [1]	LE [1]	LE [1]	LE		LE	LE [1]	LE	LE	LE [1]	LE [1]	LE	LE	LE [1]		LE	LE
Southend Victoria	d								17 10						17 25				17 35						
Prittlewell	d								17 12						17 27				17 37						
Southend Airport ✈	d								17 15						17 30				17 40						
Rochford	d								17 18						17 33				17 43						
Hockley	d								17 21						17 36				17 46						
Rayleigh	d								17 26						17 41				17 51						
Southminster	d									17 06															
Burnham-on-Crouch	d									17 10															
Althorne	d									17 15															
North Fambridge	d									17 21															
South Woodham Ferrers	d									17 26															
Battlesbridge	d									17 30															
Wickford [2]	d								17 31	17 37					17 46				17 56						
Billericay	d								17 37						17 52				18 02						
Shenfield [3]	a								17 45	17 48					18 00				18 10						
Shenfield [3]	d				17 34	17 38		17 44	17 45	17 49	17 51			17 54	18 00		18 04	18 08	18 10		18 14	18 20			18 24
Brentwood	d				17 37			17 47						17 57			18 07				18 17				18 27
Harold Wood	d				17 42			17 52						18 02			18 12				18 22				18 32
Gidea Park [2]	d			17 42	17 46		17 52	17 56				18 02		18 06		18 12	18 16			18 22	18 26			18 32	18 36
Romford	d			17 44	17 48		17 54	17 58				18 04		18 08		18 14	18 18			18 24	18 28	18 28		18 34	18 38
Chadwell Heath	d				17 52			18 02						18 12			18 22				18 32				18 42
Goodmayes	d				17 54			18 04						18 14			18 24				18 34				18 44
Seven Kings	d				17 56			18 06						18 16			18 26				18 36				18 46
Ilford [2]	d			17 52	17 59		18 02	18 09				18 12		18 19		18 22	18 29			18 32	18 39			18 42	18 49
Manor Park	d			17 55			18 05					18 15				18 25				18 35				18 45	18 52
Forest Gate	d			17 57			18 07					18 17				18 27				18 37				18 47	18 54
Maryland	d																								
Stratford [7] ⊖	d			18 02	18 05	17 52	18 12	18 15	17 59	18 08	18 06	18 22		18 25	18 14	18 32	18 35	18 22	18 25	18 42	18 45	18 36		18 52	18 59
London Liverpool Street [15] ⊖	a			18 10	18 13	18 01	18 20	18 23	18 11	18 17	18 15	18 30		18 33	18 24	18 40	18 43	18 31	18 35	18 50	18 53	18 45		19 00	19 07

Table 5

Mondays to Fridays

27 July to 10 August

Southend Victoria, Southminster and Shenfield - London

Network Diagram - see first Page of Table 5

		LE [1]	LE [1]		LE	LE [1]	LE [1]	LE [1]		LE	LE [1]	LE	LE [1]	LE	LE [1]	LE [1]	LE [1]	LE		LE [1]	LE	LE [1]	LE [1]		LE
Southend Victoria	d	17 50					18 05						18 20		18 30							18 50			
Prittlewell	d	17 52					18 07						18 22		18 32							18 52			
Southend Airport ✈	d	17 55					18 10						18 25		18 35							18 55			
Rochford	d	17 58					18 13						18 28		18 38							18 58			
Hockley	d	18 01					18 16						18 31		18 41							19 01			
Rayleigh	d	18 06					18 21						18 36		18 46							19 06			
Southminster	d							17 56															18 36		
Burnham-on-Crouch	d							18 00															18 40		
Althorne	d							18 05															18 45		
North Fambridge	d							18 14															19 01		
South Woodham Ferrers	d							18 19															19 06		
Battlesbridge	d							18 23															19 10		
Wickford [2]	d	18 11					18 26	18a29					18 41		18 51							19 11	19 17		
Billericay	d	18 17					18 32						18 47		18 57							19 17	19 23		
Shenfield [3]	a	18 25					18 40						18 55		19 05							19 25	19 33		
Shenfield [3]	d	18 25	18 27		18 34	18 38	18 40			18 44	18 51	18 54	18 57	19 04	19 05	19 08	19 13	19 14		19 20	19 24	19 25			19 34
Brentwood	d				18 37					18 47		18 57		19 07				19 17			19 27				19 37
Harold Wood	d				18 42					18 52		19 02		19 12				19 22			19 32				19 42
Gidea Park [2]	d				18 46					18 56		19 06		19 16				19 26			19 36				19 46
Romford	d				18 48					18 58		19 08		19 18				19 28		19 28	19 38				19 48
Chadwell Heath	d				18 52					19 02		19 12		19 22				19 32			19 42				19 52
Goodmayes	d				18 54					19 04		19 14		19 24				19 34			19 44				19 54
Seven Kings	d				18 56					19 06		19 16		19 26				19 36			19 46				19 56
Ilford [2]	d				18 59					19 09		19 19		19 29				19 39			19 49				19 59
Manor Park	d				19 02					19 12		19 22		19 32				19 42			19 52				20 02
Forest Gate	d				19 04					19 14		19 24		19 34				19 44			19 54				20 04
Maryland	d																								
Stratford [7] ⊖	d	18 39	18 42		19 09	18 52	18 55			19 19	19 05	19 29	19 11	19 39	19 19	19 22	19 27	19 49		19 36	19 59	19 39			20 09
London Liverpool Street [15] ⊖	a	18 48	18 51		19 17	19 01	19 04			19 27	19 14	19 37	19 20	19 47	19 28	19 31	19 36	19 57		19 45	20 07	19 48			20 17

		LE [1]	LE	LE [1]		LE [1]	LE [1]	LE	LE	LE [1]	LE [1]	LE [1]	LE	LE [1]		LE	LE [1]		LE	LE [1]	LE	LE [1]	LE [1]	LE [1]	
Southend Victoria	d			19 10						19 30							19 50					20 10			
Prittlewell	d			19 12						19 32							19 52					20 12			
Southend Airport ✈	d			19 15						19 35							19 55					20 15			
Rochford	d			19 18						19 38							19 58					20 18			
Hockley	d			19 21						19 41							20 01					20 21			
Rayleigh	d			19 26						19 46							20 06					20 26			
Southminster	d										19 19												20 16		
Burnham-on-Crouch	d										19 23												20 20		
Althorne	d										19 28												20 25		
North Fambridge	d										19 34												20 31		
South Woodham Ferrers	d										19 39												20 36		
Battlesbridge	d										19 43												20 40		
Wickford [2]	d			19 31						19 51	19 55						20 11					20 31	20a46		
Billericay	d			19 37						19 57							20 17					20 37			
Shenfield [3]	a			19 45						20 05	20 08						20 25					20 45			
Shenfield [3]	d	19 38	19 44	19 45		19 51		19 54	20 04	20 05		20 08	20 14	20 20		20 24	20 25		20 34	20 38	20 44	20 45		20 47	
Brentwood	d		19 47					19 57	20 07				20 17			20 27			20 37		20 47				
Harold Wood	d		19 52					20 02	20 12				20 22			20 32			20 42		20 52				
Gidea Park [2]	d		19 56					20 06	20 16				20 26			20 36			20 46		20 56				
Romford	d		19 58	19 53				20 08	20 18				20 28	20 28		20 38			20 48		20 58	20 53			
Chadwell Heath	d		20 02					20 12	20 22				20 32			20 42			20 52		21 02				
Goodmayes	d		20 04					20 14	20 24				20 34			20 44			20 54		21 04				
Seven Kings	d		20 06					20 16	20 26				20 36			20 46			20 56		21 06				
Ilford [2]	d		20 09					20 19	20 29				20 39			20 49			20 59		21 09				
Manor Park	d		20 12					20 22	20 32				20 42			20 52			21 02		21 12				
Forest Gate	d		20 14					20 24	20 34				20 44			20 54			21 04		21 14				
Maryland	d																								
Stratford [7] ⊖	d	19 52	20 19	20 01		20 05	20 14	20 29	20 39	20 19		20 22	20 49	20 36		20 59	20 39		21 09	20 52	21 19	21 01			
London Liverpool Street [15] ⊖	a	20 01	20 27	20 10		20 14	20 23	20 37	20 47	20 28		20 31	20 57	20 45		21 07	20 48		21 17	21 01	21 27	21 10		21 12	

Table 5

Mondays to Fridays

27 July to 10 August

Southend Victoria, Southminster and Shenfield - London

Network Diagram - see first Page of Table 5

		LE 1	LE	LE	LE 1	LE 1	LE	LE	LE 1	LE 1		LE 1		LE	LE 1	LE	LE 1	LE 1	LE	LE 1		LE 1	LE 1	LE	LE 1
Southend Victoria	d				20 30				20 50								21 10			21 30					
Prittlewell	d				20 32				20 52								21 12			21 32					
Southend Airport ✈	d				20 35				20 55								21 15			21 35					
Rochford	d				20 38				20 58								21 18			21 38					
Hockley	d				20 41				21 01								21 21			21 41					
Rayleigh	d				20 46				21 06								21 26			21 46					
Southminster	d									20 56												21 36			
Burnham-on-Crouch	d									21 00												21 40			
Althorne	d									21 05												21 45			
North Fambridge	d									21 11												21 51			
South Woodham Ferrers	d									21 16												21 56			
Battlesbridge	d									21 20												22 00			
Wickford 2	d				20 51				21 11	21a26							21 31			21 51		22a07			
Billericay	d				20 57				21 17								21 37			21 57					
Shenfield 3	a				21 05				21 25								21 45			22 05					
Shenfield 3	d	20 53	20 54	21 04	21 05	21 08	21 14	21 24	21 25			21 27		21 34	21 38	21 44	21 45	21 51	21 59	22 05			22 08	22 14	22 20
Brentwood	d		20 57	21 07			21 17	21 27						21 37		21 47			22 02					22 17	
Harold Wood	d		21 02	21 12			21 22	21 32						21 42		21 52			22 07					22 22	
Gidea Park 2	d		21 06	21 16			21 26	21 36						21 46		21 56			22 11					22 26	
Romford	d		21 08	21 18			21 28	21 38						21 48		21 58			22 13					22 28	
Chadwell Heath	d		21 12	21 22			21 32	21 42						21 52		22 02			22 17					22 32	
Goodmayes	d		21 14	21 24			21 34	21 44						21 54		22 04			22 19					22 34	
Seven Kings	d		21 16	21 26			21 36	21 46						21 56		22 06			22 21					22 36	
Ilford 2	d		21 19	21 29			21 39	21 49						21 59		22 09			22 24					22 41	
Manor Park	d		21 22	21 32			21 42	21 52						22 02		22 12			22 27					22 44	
Forest Gate	d		21 24	21 34			21 44	21 54						22 04		22 14			22 29					22 46	
Maryland	d																								
Stratford 7 ⊖	d	21 07	21 29	21 39	21 19	21 22	21 49	21 59	21 39			21 42		22 09	21 52	22 19	22 05	22 13	22 34	22 24			22 28	22 52	22 40
London Liverpool Street 15 ⊖	a	21 16	21 37	21 47	21 28	21 31	21 57	22 07	21 48			21 51		22 20	22 01	22 27	22 13	22 21	22 42	22 32			22 36	23 00	22 48

		LE	LE	LE	LE 1	LE		LE 1	LE 1	LE 1	LE	LE 1	LE 1	LE	LE	LE 1		LE 1	LE 1	LE	LE	LE	LE 1	LE	
Southend Victoria	d	21 50						22 10				22 30						22 50					23 10		
Prittlewell	d	21 52						22 12				22 32						22 52					23 12		
Southend Airport ✈	d	21 55						22 15				22 35						22 55					23 15		
Rochford	d	21 58						22 18				22 38						22 58					23 18		
Hockley	d	22 01						22 21				22 41						23 01					23 21		
Rayleigh	d	22 06						22 26				22 46						23 06					23 26		
Southminster	d								22 16										22 56						
Burnham-on-Crouch	d								22 20										23 00						
Althorne	d								22 25										23 05						
North Fambridge	d								22 31										23 11						
South Woodham Ferrers	d								22 36										23 16						
Battlesbridge	d								22 40										23 20						
Wickford 2	d	22 11						22 31	22a46			22 51						23 11	23a26				23 31		
Billericay	d	22 17						22 37				22 57						23 17					23 37		
Shenfield 3	a	22 25						22 45				23 05						23 25					23 45		
Shenfield 3	d	22 25		22 29	22 38	22 44		22 45		22 51	22 59	23 05	23 08		23 14	23 20		23 25			23 29	23 44	23 45	23 59	
Brentwood	d			22 32		22 47					23 02				23 17						23 32	23 47		00 02	
Harold Wood	d			22 37		22 52					23 07				23 22						23 37	23 52		00 07	
Gidea Park 2	d			22 41		22 56					23 11				23 26						23 41	23 56		00 11	
Romford	d			22 43		22 58					23 13				23 28						23 43	23 58		00 13	
Chadwell Heath	d			22 47		23 02					23 17				23 32						23 47	00 02		00 17	
Goodmayes	d			22 49		23 04					23 19				23 34						23 49	00 04		00 19	
Seven Kings	d			22 51		23 06					23 21				23 36						23 51	00 06		00 21	
Ilford 2	d			22 54		23 09					23 24				23 39						23 54	00 09		00 24	
Manor Park	d			22 57		23 12					23 27				23 42						23 57	00 12		00 27	
Forest Gate	d			22 59		23 14					23 29				23 45						23 59	00 14		00 29	
Maryland	d																								
Stratford 7 ⊖	d	22 44	22 48	23 04	22 58	23 19		23 08		23 12	23 36	23 24	23 28	23 32	23 50	23 40		23 44		23 54	00 04	00 20	00 08	00 40	
London Liverpool Street 15 ⊖	a	22 52	22 58	23 12	23 06	23 27		23 16		23 20	23 44	23 32	23 36	23 40	23 58	23 48		23 52		00 02	00 12	00 28	00 16	00 48	

Table 5

Mondays to Fridays

13 August to 28 August

Southend Victoria, Southminster and Shenfield - London

Network Diagram - see first Page of Table 5

		LE MX	LE A				LE MX 1	LE ◇1 B	LE B	LE MX		LE A	LE 1 A	CC MX	LE 1 A	LE A	LE A	LE A	LE A	LE A		LE A	LE A	LE A	LE A
Southend Victoria	d												23p10												
Prittlewell	d												23p12												
Southend Airport ✈	d												23p15												
Rochford	d												23p18												
Hockley	d												23p21												
Rayleigh	d												23p26												
Southminster	d						22p56																		
Burnham-on-Crouch	d						23p00																		
Althorne	d						23p05																		
North Fambridge	d						23p11																		
South Woodham Ferrers	d						23p16																		
Battlesbridge	d						23p20																		
Wickford 2	d						23p26						23p31												
Billericay	d						23p32						23p37												
Shenfield 3	a						23p39						23p45												
Shenfield 3	d	23p29	23p29				23p39		23p43	23p44		23p44	23p45				23p59	00 14		00 29		00 44			
Brentwood	d	23p32	23p32						23p46	23p47		23p47					00 02	00 17		00 32		00 47			
Harold Wood	d	23p37	23p37						23p51	23p52		23p52					00 07	00 22		00 37		00 52			
Gidea Park 2	d	23p41	23p41						23p55	23p56		23p56					00 11	00 26		00 41		00 56			
Romford	d	23p43	23p43				23p47		23p57	23p58		23p58					00 13	00 28		00 43		00 58			
Chadwell Heath	d	23p47	23p47						00 01	00 02		00 02					00 17	00 32		00 47		01 02			
Goodmayes	d	23p49	23p49						00 03	00 04		00 04					00 19	00 34		00 49		01 04			
Seven Kings	d	23p51	23p51						00 05	00 06		00 06					00 21	00 36		00 51		01 06			
Ilford 2	d	23p54	23p54						00 08	00 09		00 09					00 24	00 39		00 54		01 09			
Manor Park	d	23p57	23p57						00 10	00 12		00 12					00 27	00 42		00 57		01 12			
Forest Gate	d	23p59	23p59						00 12	00 14		00 14					00 29	00 44		00 59		01 14			
Maryland	d	00 01							00 14	00 16															
Stratford 7 ⊖	d	00 04	00 04				23p56	23b57	00 16	00 19		00 20	00 08	00 09	00 12	00 30	00 40	00 50	01 00	01 10		01 20	01 30	01 40	01 50
London Liverpool Street 15 ⊖	a	00 12	00 12				00 05	00 08	00 26	00 27		00 28	00 16	00 20	00 20	00 38	00 48	00 58	01 08	01 18		01 28	01 38	01 48	01 58

		LE	CC	LE	LE	LE 1		LE	LE	LE 1	LE	LE 1	LE 1	LE 1		LE		LE	LE	LE 1	LE	LE 1		LE	LE 1
Southend Victoria	d	04 00			04 30					05 00			05 20							05 40					06 00
Prittlewell	d	04 02			04 32					05 02			05 22							05 42					06 02
Southend Airport ✈	d	04 05			04 35					05 05			05 25							05 45					06 05
Rochford	d	04 08			04 38					05 08			05 28							05 48					06 08
Hockley	d	04 12			04 42					05 11			05 31							05 51					06 11
Rayleigh	d	04 16			04 46					05 16			05 36							05 56					06 16
Southminster	d													05 26											
Burnham-on-Crouch	d													05 30											
Althorne	d													05 35											
North Fambridge	d													05 41											
South Woodham Ferrers	d													05 46											
Battlesbridge	d													05 50											
Wickford 2	d	04 21			04 51					05 21			05 41	05a56						06 01					06 21
Billericay	d	04 28			04 58					05 27			05 47							06 07					06 27
Shenfield 3	a	04 39			05 09					05 35			05 55							06 15					06 35
Shenfield 3	d	04 39			05 09	05 24			05 29	05 35	05 44	05 53	05 55					06 04	06 14	06 15	06 24	06 25		06 34	06 35
Brentwood	d	04 42			05 12				05 32		05 47							06 07	06 17		06 27			06 37	
Harold Wood	d	04 47			05 17				05 37		05 52							06 12	06 22		06 32			06 42	
Gidea Park 2	d	04 51			05 21	05 31			05 41		05 56					06 06		06 16	06 26		06 36			06 45	
Romford	d	04 53			05 23				05 43		05 58					06 08		06 18	06 28		06 38			06 48	
Chadwell Heath	d	04 57			05 27				05 47		06 02					06 12		06 22	06 32		06 42			06 52	
Goodmayes	d	04 59			05 29				05 49		06 04					06 14		06 24	06 34		06 44				
Seven Kings	d	05 01			05 31	05 36			05 51		06 06					06 16		06 26	06 36		06 46				
Ilford 2	d	05 04		05 09	05 34			05 39	05 54		06 09					06 19		06 29	06 39		06 49			06 57	
Manor Park	d			05 11				05 41	05 57		06 12					06 22		06 32	06 42		06 52				
Forest Gate	d			05 14				05 44	05 59		06 14					06 24		06 34	06 44		06 54				
Maryland	d			05 16				05 46	06 01		06 16					06 26		06 36	06 46		06 56				
Stratford 7 ⊖	d	05 10	05 14	05 18	05 40	05 42		05 48	06 04	05 49	06 19	06 07	06 10			06 29		06 39	06 49	06 29	06 59	06 39		07 03	06 49
London Liverpool Street 15 ⊖	a	05 18	05 27	05 26	05 48	05 55		05 56	06 12	05 58	06 27	06 16	06 19			06 37		06 47	06 57	06 40	07 07	06 48		07 13	06 58

A 13 August

B 20 August, 27 August

b Previous night, stops to set down only

13 August to 28 August

Southend Victoria, Southminster and Shenfield - London

Network Diagram - see first Page of Table 5

	LE	LE	LE	LE	LE	LE	LE	LE	LE	LE	LE	LE	LE	LE	LE	LE	LE
	1			1	1	1						1	1			1	1
Southend Victoria d				06 11					06 26				06 40				06 50
Prittlewell d				06 13					06 28				06 42				06 52
Southend Airport ✈ d				06 16					06 31				06 45				06 55
Rochford d				06 19					06 34				06 48				06 58
Hockley d				06 22					06 38				06 51				07 01
Rayleigh d				06 27					06 42				06 56				07 06
Southminster d						06 09											
Burnham-on-Crouch d						06 13											
Althorne d						06 18											
North Fambridge d						06 24											
South Woodham Ferrers d						06 30											
Battlesbridge d						06 34											
Wickford 2 d				06 32		06 40			06 47				07 01				07 11
Billericay d				06 39		06 46			06 54				07 08				07 18
Shenfield 3 a				06 45		06 52			07 01				07 14				07 24
Shenfield 3 d	06 41		06 44	06 45	06 50	06 53		06 54	07 01		07 04	07 08	07 14		07 14	07 19	07 24
Brentwood d			06 47					06 57			07 07				07 17		
Harold Wood d			06 52					07 02			07 12				07 22		
Gidea Park 2 d		06 49	06 55				06 59	07 05		07 09	07 15			07 19	07 25		
Romford d		06 51	06 58				07 01	07 08		07 11	07 18			07 21	07 28		
Chadwell Heath d		06 55	07 02				07 05	07 12		07 15	07 22			07 25	07 32		
Goodmayes d		06 57					07 07			07 17				07 27	07 34		
Seven Kings d		06 59					07 09			07 19				07 29	07 36		
Ilford 2 d		07 02	07 07				07 12	07 17		07 22	07 27			07 32	07 39		
Manor Park d		07 05					07 15			07 25				07 35			
Forest Gate d		07 07					07 17			07 27				07 37			
Maryland d		07 09					07 19			07 29				07 39			
Stratford 7 ⊖ d	06s57	07 12	07 15	07s02	07s06	07s09	07 22	07 25	07s19	07 32	07 35	07s23	07s31	07 42	07 45	07s35	07s41
London Liverpool Street 15 ⊖ a	07 09	07 22	07 25	07 13	07 18	07 21	07 32	07 35	07 30	07 42	07 45	07 35	07 42	07 52	07 55	07 46	07 52

	LE	LE	LE	LE	LE	LE	LE	LE	LE	LE	LE	LE	LE	LE	LE	LE	LE	LE	LE
			1	1			1	1			1	1					1		1
Southend Victoria d				07 03							07 13					07 18	07 23		
Prittlewell d				07 05							07 15					07 20	07 25		
Southend Airport ✈ d				07 08							07 18					07 23	07 28		
Rochford d				07 11							07 21					07 26	07 31		
Hockley d				07 14							07 24					07 30	07 34		
Rayleigh d				07 19							07 29					07 34	07 39		
Southminster d			06 48																
Burnham-on-Crouch d			06 52																
Althorne d			06 57																
North Fambridge d			07 04																
South Woodham Ferrers d			07 10																
Battlesbridge d			07 14																
Wickford 2 d			07 19	07 24							07 34					07 39	07 44		
Billericay d			07 26	07 31							07 41					07 46	07 51		
Shenfield 3 a			07 32								07 47					07 53	07 57		
Shenfield 3 d		07 24	07 32			07 34	07 38	07 41		07 44	07 47	07 50		07 50		07 54	07 57	08 00	08 01
Brentwood d		07 27				07 37				07 47				07 53		07 57		08 03	
Harold Wood d		07 32				07 42				07 52				07 58		08 02		08 08	
Gidea Park 2 d	07 29	07 35			07 39	07 45			07 49	07 55			07 59	08 02	08 05	08 09		08 12	
Romford d	07 31	07 38			07 41	07 48			07 51	07 58			08 01	08 04	08 07	08 11		08 14	
Chadwell Heath d	07 35	07 42			07 45	07 52			07 55	08 02			08 05	08 08	08 11	08 15		08 18	
Goodmayes d	07 37	07 44			07 47	07 54			07 57	08 04			08 07	08 10	08 13	08 17		08 20	
Seven Kings d	07 39	07 46			07 49	07 56			07 59	08 06			08 09	08 12	08 15	08 19		08 22	
Ilford 2 d	07 42	07 49			07 52	07 59			08 02	08 09			08 12	08 15	08 18	08 22		08 25	
Manor Park d	07 45				07 55				08 05						08 21				
Forest Gate d	07 47				07 57				08 07						08 23				
Maryland d	07 49				07 59				08 09						08 25				
Stratford 7 ⊖ d	07 52	07 55	07 50	07s52	08 02	08 05	07s55	07s58	08 12	08 15	08s04	08s07	08 18	08 21	08 28	08 31	08s15	08 34	08s18
London Liverpool Street 15 ⊖ a	08 02	08 05	08 01	08 03	08 12	08 15	08 07	08 09	08 22	08 25	08 15	08 19	08 28	08 31	08 38	08 41	08 26	08 43	08 30

13 August to 28 August

Southend Victoria, Southminster and Shenfield - London

Network Diagram - see first Page of Table 5

	LE	LE	LE	LE	LE	LE	LE	LE	LE	LE	LE	LE	LE	LE	LE	LE	LE	LE
	1	1				1	1	1				1	1	1				1
Southend Victoria d	07 32					07 42							07 52					08 03
Prittlewell d	07 34					07 44							07 54					08 05
Southend Airport ✈ d	07 37					07 47							07 57					08 08
Rochford d	07 40					07 50							08 00					08 11
Hockley d	07 43					07 53							08 03					08 14
Rayleigh d	07 48					07 58							08 08					08 19
Southminster d							07 37											
Burnham-on-Crouch d							07 41											
Althorne d							07 46											
North Fambridge d							07 52											
South Woodham Ferrers d							07 59											
Battlesbridge d																		
Wickford 2 d	07 53					08 03	08 07						08 13					08 24
Billericay d	08 00					08 10	08 14						08 20					08 31
Shenfield 3 a	08 06					08 16							08 26					08 37
Shenfield 3 d	08 06	08 09			08 10	08 16		08 21			08 22	08 24	08 26	08 29			08 32	08 37
Brentwood d					08 13						08 25						08 35	
Harold Wood d					08 18						08 30						08 40	
Gidea Park 2 d			08 15	08 19	08 22					08 29	08 34					08 41	08 44	
Romford d			08 17	08 21	08 24					08 31	08 36					08 43	08 46	
Chadwell Heath d			08 21	08 25	08 28					08 35	08 40					08 47	08 50	
Goodmayes d			08 23	08 27	08 30					08 37	08 42					08 49	08 52	
Seven Kings d			08 25	08 29	08 32					08 39	08 44					08 51	08 54	
Ilford 2 d			08 28	08 32	08 35				08 38	08 42	08 47				08 50	08 54	08 57	
Manor Park d			08 31						08 41						08 53			
Forest Gate d			08 33						08 43						08 55			
Maryland d			08 35						08 45						08 57			
Stratford 7 ⊖ d	08s23	08s25	08 38	08 41	08 44	08s33	08s35	08s38	08 48	08 51	08 54	08s41	08s43	08s45	09 00	09 03	09 06	08s56
London Liverpool Street 15 ⊖ a	08 36	08 38	08 48	08 51	08 53	08 46	08 48	08 50	08 58	09 01	09 03	08 54	08 56	08 58	09 10	09 13	09 14	09 08

	LE	LE	LE	LE	LE	LE	LE	LE	LE	LE	LE	LE	LE	LE	LE	LE	LE	LE	LE	LE
	1				1	1		1	1	1			1		1	1	1		1	
Southend Victoria d					08 12					08 30						08 52				
Prittlewell d					08 14					08 32						08 54				
Southend Airport ✈ d					08 17					08 35						08 57				
Rochford d					08 20					08 38						09 00				
Hockley d					08 23					08 41						09 03				
Rayleigh d					08 28					08 46						09 08				
Southminster d									08 16								08 56			
Burnham-on-Crouch d									08 20								09 00			
Althorne d									08 25								09 05			
North Fambridge d									08 31								09 11			
South Woodham Ferrers d									08 37								09 16			
Battlesbridge d									08 41								09 20			
Wickford 2 d					08 33				08 46	08 51						09 13	09a26			
Billericay d					08 40				08 53	08 58						09 20				
Shenfield 3 a					08 46				08 59	09 04						09 27				
Shenfield 3 d	08 42			08 44	08 46	08 51	08 54	08 55	08 59	09 04	09 04	09 14	09 21	09 24	09 25	09 27		09 34	09 38	09 44
Brentwood d				08 47			08 57				09 07	09 17		09 27				09 37		09 47
Harold Wood d				08 52			09 02				09 12	09 22		09 32				09 42		09 52
Gidea Park 2 d			08 51	08 56			09 06				09 16	09 26		09 36				09 46		09 56
Romford d			08 53	08 58	08 55		09 08				09 18	09 28		09 38				09 48		09 58
Chadwell Heath d			08 57	09 02			09 12				09 22	09 32		09 42				09 52		10 02
Goodmayes d			08 59	09 04			09 14				09 24	09 34		09 44				09 54		10 04
Seven Kings d			09 01	09 06			09 16				09 26	09 36		09 46				09 56		10 06
Ilford 2 d		09 00	09 04	09 09			09 19				09 29	09 39		09 49				09 59		10 09
Manor Park d		09 03		09 12			09 22				09 32	09 42		09 52				10 02		10 12
Forest Gate d		09 05		09 14			09 24				09 34	09 44		09 54				10 04		10 14
Maryland d		09 07		09 16			09 26				09 36	09 46		09 56				10 06		10 16
Stratford 7 ⊖ d	08s59	09 10	09 13	09 19	09s05	09s08	09 29		09s16	09s22	09 39	09 49	09s37	09 59	09s41	09s43		10 09	09 52	10 19
London Liverpool Street 15 ⊖ a	09 11	09 20	09 23	09 27	09 16	09 19	09 37	09 21	09 29	09 33	09 47	09 58	09 49	10 07	09 53	09 55		10 17	10 01	10 27

13 August to 28 August

Southend Victoria, Southminster and Shenfield - London

Network Diagram - see first Page of Table 5

	LE ■	LE ■	LE	LE	LE ■		LE ■	LE ■	LE	LE ■	LE	LE ■
Southend Victoria d	09 10				09 30							09 50
Prittlewell d	09 12				09 32							09 52
Southend Airport ✈ d	09 15				09 35							09 55
Rochford d	09 18				09 38							09 58
Hockley d	09 21				09 41							10 01
Rayleigh d	09 26				09 46							10 06
Southminster d							09 36					
Burnham-on-Crouch d							09 40					
Althorne d							09 45					
North Fambridge d							09 51					
South Woodham Ferrers d							09 56					
Battlesbridge d							10 00					
Wickford ■ d	09 31				09 51		10a06					10 11
Billericay d	09 37				09 57							10 17
Shenfield ■ a	09 45				10 05							10 25
Shenfield ■ d	09 45	09 51	09 54	10 04	10 05			10 08	10 14	10 18	10 24	10 25
Brentwood d			09 57	10 07					10 17		10 27	
Harold Wood d			10 02	10 12					10 22		10 32	
Gidea Park ■ d			10 06	10 16					10 26		10 36	
Romford d	09 53		10 08	10 18					10 28	10 26	10 38	
Chadwell Heath d			10 12	10 22					10 32		10 42	
Goodmayes d			10 14	10 24					10 34		10 44	
Seven Kings d			10 16	10 26					10 36		10 46	
Ilford ■ d			10 19	10 29					10 39		10 49	
Manor Park d			10 22	10 32					10 42		10 52	
Forest Gate d			10 24	10 34					10 44		10 54	
Maryland d			10 26	10 36					10 46		10 56	
Stratford ■ ⊖ d	10 01	10 05	10 29	10 39	10 19			10 22	10 49	10 34	10 59	10 39
London Liverpool Street 15 ⊖ a	10 10	10 14	10 37	10 47	10 28			10 31	10 57	10 43	11 07	10 48

	LE ■ ⊡	LE	LE ■		LE	LE ■	LE ■	LE ■	LE	LE	LE ■	LE ■
Southend Victoria d						10 10					10 30	
Prittlewell d						10 12					10 32	
Southend Airport ✈ d						10 15					10 35	
Rochford d						10 18					10 38	
Hockley d						10 21					10 41	
Rayleigh d						10 26					10 46	
Southminster d							10 16					
Burnham-on-Crouch d							10 20					
Althorne d							10 25					
North Fambridge d							10 31					
South Woodham Ferrers d							10 36					
Battlesbridge d							10 40					
Wickford ■ d						10 31	10a46				10 51	
Billericay d						10 37					10 57	
Shenfield ■ a						10 45					11 05	
Shenfield ■ d		10 34	10 38		10 44	10 45		10 51	10 54	11 04	11 05	11 08
Brentwood d		10 37			10 47				10 57	11 07		
Harold Wood d		10 42			10 52				11 02	11 12		
Gidea Park ■ d		10 46			10 56				11 06	11 16		
Romford d		10 48			10 58	10 53			11 08	11 18		
Chadwell Heath d		10 52			11 02				11 12	11 22		
Goodmayes d		10 54			11 04				11 14	11 24		
Seven Kings d		10 56			11 06				11 16	11 26		
Ilford ■ d		10 59			11 09				11 19	11 29		
Manor Park d		11 02			11 12				11 22	11 32		
Forest Gate d		11 04			11 14				11 24	11 34		
Maryland d		11 06			11 16				11 26	11 36		
Stratford ■ ⊖ d		11 09	10 52		11 19	11 01		11 05	11 29	11 39	11 19	11 22
London Liverpool Street 15 ⊖ a	10 55	11 17	11 01		11 27	11 10		11 14	11 37	11 47	11 28	11 31

	LE		LE ■	LE	LE ■	LE ■		LE	LE ■	LE	LE ■	
Southend Victoria d					10 50						11 10	
Prittlewell d					10 52						11 12	
Southend Airport ✈ d					10 55						11 15	
Rochford d					10 58						11 18	
Hockley d					11 01						11 21	
Rayleigh d					11 06						11 26	
Southminster d						10 56						
Burnham-on-Crouch d						11 00						
Althorne d						11 05						
North Fambridge d						11 11						
South Woodham Ferrers d						11 16						
Battlesbridge d						11 20						
Wickford ■ d					11 11	11a26					11 31	
Billericay d					11 17						11 37	
Shenfield ■ a					11 25						11 45	
Shenfield ■ d	11 14		11 20	11 24	11 25			11 34	11 38	11 44	11 45	
Brentwood d	11 17			11 27				11 37		11 47		
Harold Wood d	11 22			11 32				11 42		11 52		
Gidea Park ■ d	11 26			11 36				11 46		11 56		
Romford d	11 28		11 28	11 38				11 48		11 58	11 53	
Chadwell Heath d	11 32			11 42				11 52		12 02		
Goodmayes d	11 34			11 44				11 54		12 04		
Seven Kings d	11 36			11 46				11 56		12 06		
Ilford ■ d	11 39			11 49				11 59		12 09		
Manor Park d	11 42			11 52				12 02		12 12		
Forest Gate d	11 44			11 54				12 04		12 14		
Maryland d	11 46			11 56				12 06		12 16		
Stratford ■ ⊖ d	11 49		11 36	11 59	11 39			12 09	11 52	12 19	12 01	
London Liverpool Street 15 ⊖ a	11 57		11 45	12 07	11 48			12 17	12 01	12 27	12 10	

	LE ■	LE	LE	LE ■	LE ■	LE ■	LE	LE ■	LE		LE ■	
Southend Victoria d				11 30							11 50	
Prittlewell d				11 32							11 52	
Southend Airport ✈ d				11 35							11 55	
Rochford d				11 38							11 58	
Hockley d				11 41							12 01	
Rayleigh d				11 46							12 06	
Southminster d					11 36							
Burnham-on-Crouch d					11 40							
Althorne d					11 45							
North Fambridge d					11 51							
South Woodham Ferrers d					11 56							
Battlesbridge d					12 00							
Wickford ■ d				11 51	12a06						12 11	
Billericay d				11 57							12 17	
Shenfield ■ a				12 05							12 25	
Shenfield ■ d	11 51	11 54	12 04	12 05		12 08	12 14	12 20	12 24		12 25	
Brentwood d		11 57	12 07				12 17		12 27			
Harold Wood d		12 02	12 12				12 22		12 32			
Gidea Park ■ d		12 06	12 16				12 26		12 36			
Romford d		12 08	12 18				12 28	12 28	12 38			
Chadwell Heath d		12 12	12 22				12 32		12 42			
Goodmayes d		12 14	12 24				12 34		12 44			
Seven Kings d		12 16	12 26				12 36		12 46			
Ilford ■ d		12 19	12 29				12 39		12 49			
Manor Park d		12 22	12 32				12 42		12 52			
Forest Gate d		12 24	12 34				12 44		12 54			
Maryland d		12 26	12 36				12 46		12 56			
Stratford ■ ⊖ d	12 05	12 29	12 39	12 19		12 22	12 49	12 36	12 59		12 39	
London Liverpool Street 15 ⊖ a	12 14	12 37	12 47	12 28		12 31	12 57	12 45	13 07		12 48	

13 August to 28 August

Southend Victoria, Southminster and Shenfield - London

Network Diagram - see first Page of Table 5

	LE	LE ■	LE	LE ■	LE ■	LE ■	LE		LE	LE ■	LE ■	LE
Southend Victoria d				12 10						12 30		
Prittlewell d				12 12						12 32		
Southend Airport ✈ d				12 15						12 35		
Rochford d				12 18						12 38		
Hockley d				12 21						12 41		
Rayleigh d				12 26						12 46		
Southminster d					12 16							
Burnham-on-Crouch d					12 20							
Althorne d					12 25							
North Fambridge d					12 31							
South Woodham Ferrers d					12 36							
Battlesbridge d					12 40							
Wickford ■ d				12 31	12a46					12 51		
Billericay d				12 37						12 57		
Shenfield ■ a				12 45						13 05		
Shenfield ■ d	12 34	12 38	12 44	12 45		12 51	12 54		13 04	13 05	13 08	13 14
Brentwood d	12 37		12 47				12 57		13 07			13 17
Harold Wood d	12 42		12 52				13 02		13 12			13 22
Gidea Park ■ d	12 46		12 56				13 06		13 16			13 26
Romford d	12 48		12 58	12 53			13 08		13 18			13 28
Chadwell Heath d	12 52		13 02				13 12		13 22			13 32
Goodmayes d	12 54		13 04				13 14		13 24			13 34
Seven Kings d	12 56		13 06				13 16		13 26			13 36
Ilford ■ d	12 59		13 09				13 19		13 29			13 39
Manor Park d	13 02		13 12				13 22		13 32			13 42
Forest Gate d	13 04		13 14				13 24		13 34			13 44
Maryland d	13 06		13 16				13 26		13 36			13 46
Stratford ■ ⊖ d	13 09	12 52	13 19	13 01		13 05	13 29		13 39	13 19	13 22	13 49
London Liverpool Street 15 ⊖ a	13 17	13 01	13 27	13 10		13 14	13 37		13 47	13 28	13 31	13 57

	LE ■	LE	LE ■	LE ■			LE	LE ■	LE	LE ■	LE ■	LE
Southend Victoria d			12 50							13 10		
Prittlewell d			12 52							13 12		
Southend Airport ✈ d			12 55							13 15		
Rochford d			12 58							13 18		
Hockley d			13 01							13 21		
Rayleigh d			13 06							13 26		
Southminster d				12 56								
Burnham-on-Crouch d				13 00								
Althorne d				13 05								
North Fambridge d				13 11								
South Woodham Ferrers d				13 16								
Battlesbridge d				13 20								
Wickford ■ d			13 11	13a26						13 31		
Billericay d			13 17							13 37		
Shenfield ■ a			13 25							13 45		
Shenfield ■ d	13 20	13 24	13 25				13 34	13 38	13 44	13 45	13 51	13 54
Brentwood d		13 27					13 37		13 47			13 57
Harold Wood d		13 32					13 42		13 52			14 02
Gidea Park ■ d		13 36					13 46		13 56			14 06
Romford d	13 28	13 38					13 48		13 58	13 53		14 08
Chadwell Heath d		13 42					13 52		14 02			14 12
Goodmayes d		13 44					13 54		14 04			14 14
Seven Kings d		13 46					13 56		14 06			14 16
Ilford ■ d		13 49					13 59		14 09			14 19
Manor Park d		13 52					14 02		14 12			14 22
Forest Gate d		13 54					14 04		14 14			14 24
Maryland d		13 56					14 06		14 16			14 26
Stratford ■ ⊖ d	13 36	13 59	13 39				14 09	13 52	14 19	14 01	14 05	14 29
London Liverpool Street 15 ⊖ a	13 45	14 07	13 48				14 17	14 01	14 27	14 10	14 14	14 37

	LE	LE ■	LE ■		LE ■	LE	LE ■	LE	LE ■	LE ◇■ ⊡	LE	LE ■
Southend Victoria d		13 30							13 50			
Prittlewell d		13 32							13 52			
Southend Airport ✈ d		13 35							13 55			
Rochford d		13 38							13 58			
Hockley d		13 41							14 01			
Rayleigh d		13 46							14 06			
Southminster d			13 36									
Burnham-on-Crouch d			13 40									
Althorne d			13 45									
North Fambridge d			13 51									
South Woodham Ferrers d			13 56									
Battlesbridge d			14 00									
Wickford ■ d		13 51	14a06						14 11			
Billericay d		13 57							14 17			
Shenfield ■ a		14 05							14 25			
Shenfield ■ d	14 04	14 05			14 08	14 14	14 20	14 24	14 25		14 34	14 38
Brentwood d	14 07					14 17		14 27			14 37	
Harold Wood d	14 12					14 22		14 32			14 42	
Gidea Park ■ d	14 16					14 26		14 36			14 46	
Romford d	14 18					14 28	14 28	14 38			14 48	
Chadwell Heath d	14 22					14 32		14 42			14 52	
Goodmayes d	14 24					14 34		14 44			14 54	
Seven Kings d	14 26					14 36		14 46			14 56	
Ilford ■ d	14 29					14 39		14 49			14 59	
Manor Park d	14 32					14 42		14 52			15 02	
Forest Gate d	14 34					14 44		14 54			15 04	
Maryland d	14 36					14 46		14 56			15 06	
Stratford ■ ⊖ d	14 39	14 19			14 22	14 49	14 36	14 59	14 39		15 09	14 52
London Liverpool Street 15 ⊖ a	14 47	14 28			14 31	14 57	14 45	15 07	14 48	14 55	15 17	15 01

	LE		LE ■	LE ■	LE ■	LE	LE	LE ■	LE ■	LE	LE ■	
Southend Victoria d			14 10					14 30				
Prittlewell d			14 12					14 32				
Southend Airport ✈ d			14 15					14 35				
Rochford d			14 18					14 38				
Hockley d			14 21					14 41				
Rayleigh d			14 26					14 46				
Southminster d				14 16								
Burnham-on-Crouch d				14 20								
Althorne d				14 25								
North Fambridge d				14 31								
South Woodham Ferrers d				14 36								
Battlesbridge d				14 40								
Wickford ■ d			14 31	14a46				14 51				
Billericay d			14 37					14 57				
Shenfield ■ a			14 45					15 05				
Shenfield ■ d	14 44		14 45		14 51	14 54	15 04	15 05	15 08	15 14	15 20	
Brentwood d	14 47					14 57	15 07			15 17		
Harold Wood d	14 52					15 02	15 12			15 22		
Gidea Park ■ d	14 56					15 06	15 16			15 26		
Romford d	14 58		14 53			15 08	15 18			15 28	15 28	
Chadwell Heath d	15 02					15 12	15 22			15 32		
Goodmayes d	15 04					15 14	15 24			15 34		
Seven Kings d	15 06					15 16	15 26			15 36		
Ilford ■ d	15 09					15 19	15 29			15 39		
Manor Park d	15 12					15 22	15 32			15 42		
Forest Gate d	15 14					15 24	15 34			15 44		
Maryland d	15 16					15 26	15 36			15 46		
Stratford ■ ⊖ d	15 19		15 01		15 05	15 29	15 39	15 19	15 22	15 49	15 36	
London Liverpool Street 15 ⊖ a	15 27		15 10		15 15	15 37	15 47	15 28	15 33	15 57	15 45	

Table 5

Mondays to Fridays

13 August to 28 August

Southend Victoria, Southminster and Shenfield - London

Network Diagram - see first Page of Table 5

		LE	LE 1	LE 1		LE	LE 1	LE	LE 1	LE 1		LE	LE	LE 1	LE 1	LE 1	LE	LE 1	LE	LE 1			LE	LE 1	LE
Southend Victoria	d		14 50						15 10					15 30						15 50					
Prittlewell	d		14 52						15 12					15 32						15 52					
Southend Airport ✈	d		14 55						15 15					15 35						15 55					
Rochford	d		14 58						15 18					15 38						15 58					
Hockley	d		15 01						15 21					15 41						16 01					
Rayleigh	d		15 06						15 26					15 46						16 06					
Southminster	d			14 56											15 36										
Burnham-on-Crouch	d			15 00											15 40										
Althorne	d			15 05											15 45										
North Fambridge	d			15 11											15 51										
South Woodham Ferrers	d			15 16											15 56										
Battlesbridge	d			15 20											16 00										
Wickford 2	d		15 11	15a26					15 31					15 51	16a06					16 11					
Billericay	d		15 17						15 37					15 57						16 17					
Shenfield 3	a		15 25						15 45					16 05						16 25					
Shenfield 3	d	15 24	15 25			15 34	15 38	15 44	15 45	15 51		15 54	16 04	16 05		16 08	16 14	16 20	16 24	16 25			16 34	16 38	16 44
Brentwood	d	15 27				15 37		15 47				15 57	16 07				16 17		16 27				16 37		16 47
Harold Wood	d	15 32				15 42		15 52				16 02	16 12				16 22		16 32				16 42		16 52
Gidea Park 2	d	15 36				15 46		15 56				16 06	16 16				16 26		16 35				16 46		16 56
Romford	d	15 38				15 48		15 58	15 53			16 08	16 18				16 28		16 38				16 48		16 58
Chadwell Heath	d	15 42				15 52		16 02				16 12	16 22				16 32		16 42				16 52		17 02
Goodmayes	d	15 44				15 54		16 04				16 14	16 24				16 34		16 44				16 54		17 04
Seven Kings	d	15 46				15 56		16 06				16 16	16 26				16 36		16 46				16 56		17 06
Ilford 2	d	15 49				15 59		16 09				16 19	16 29				16 39		16 49				16 59		17 09
Manor Park	d	15 52				16 02		16 12				16 22	16 32				16 42		16 52				17 02		17 12
Forest Gate	d	15 54				16 04		16 14				16 24	16 34				16 44		16 54				17 04		17 14
Maryland	d	15 56				16 06		16 16				16 26	16 36				16 46		16 56				17 06		17 16
Stratford 7 ⊖	d	15 59	15 39			16 09	15 52	16 19	16 01	16 05		16 29	16 39	16 19		16 22	16 49	16 34	16 59	16 39			17 09	16 52	17 19
London Liverpool Street 15 ⊖	a	16 07	15 48			16 17	16 01	16 27	16 11	16 14		16 37	16 47	16 28		16 31	16 57	16 44	17 07	16 48			17 17	17 03	17 27

		LE 1	LE 1	LE 1	LE	LE		LE 1	LE 1	LE	LE 1	LE	LE	LE 1	LE 1			LE	LE	LE 1	LE	LE	LE 1	LE 1	LE 1
Southend Victoria	d	16 10						16 30						16 50									17 10		
Prittlewell	d	16 12						16 32						16 52									17 12		
Southend Airport ✈	d	16 15						16 35						16 55									17 15		
Rochford	d	16 18						16 38						16 58									17 18		
Hockley	d	16 21						16 41						17 01									17 21		
Rayleigh	d	16 26						16 46						17 06									17 26		
Southminster	d		16 14																					17 06	
Burnham-on-Crouch	d		16 18																					17 10	
Althorne	d		16 23																					17 15	
North Fambridge	d		16 29																					17 21	
South Woodham Ferrers	d		16 34																					17 26	
Battlesbridge	d		16 38																					17 30	
Wickford 2	d	16 31	16a44					16 51						17 11									17 31	17 37	
Billericay	d	16 37						16 57						17 17									17 37		
Shenfield 3	a	16 45						17 05						17 25									17 45	17 48	
Shenfield 3	d	16 45		16 51	16 54	17 04		17 05	17 08	17 14	17 22		17 24	17 25	17 28				17 34	17 38		17 44	17 45	17 49	17 51
Brentwood	d				16 57	17 07				17 17			17 27						17 37			17 47			
Harold Wood	d				17 02	17 12				17 22			17 32						17 42			17 52			
Gidea Park 2	d				17 06	17 16				17 26		17 32	17 36					17 42	17 46		17 52	17 56			
Romford	d				17 08	17 18				17 28		17 34	17 38					17 44	17 48		17 54	17 58			
Chadwell Heath	d				17 12	17 22				17 32			17 42						17 52			18 02			
Goodmayes	d				17 14	17 24				17 34			17 44						17 54			18 04			
Seven Kings	d				17 16	17 26				17 36			17 46						17 56			18 06			
Ilford 2	d				17 19	17 29				17 39		17 42	17 49					17 52	17 59		18 02	18 09			
Manor Park	d				17 22	17 32						17 45						17 55			18 05				
Forest Gate	d				17 24	17 34						17 47						17 57			18 07				
Maryland	d				17 26	17 36						17 49						17 59			18 09				
Stratford 7 ⊖	d	16 59		17 05	17 29	17 39		17 19	17 22	17 45	17 36	17 52	17 55	17 39	17 42			18 02	18 05	17 52	18 12	18 15	17 59	18 08	18 06
London Liverpool Street 15 ⊖	a	17 13		17 16	17 37	17 47		17 29	17 34	17 53	17 46	18 00	18 03	17 49	17 53			18 10	18 13	18 01	18 20	18 23	18 11	18 17	18 15

Table 5

Mondays to Fridays

13 August to 28 August

Southend Victoria, Southminster and Shenfield - London

Network Diagram - see first Page of Table 5

		LE		LE	LE 1	LE	LE	LE 1	LE 1	LE	LE	LE 1		LE	LE	LE 1	LE 1		LE	LE 1	LE 1	LE 1		LE	LE 1
Southend Victoria	d				17 25				17 35							17 50					18 05				
Prittlewell	d				17 27				17 37							17 52					18 07				
Southend Airport ✈	d				17 30				17 40							17 55					18 10				
Rochford	d				17 33				17 43							17 58					18 13				
Hockley	d				17 36				17 46							18 01					18 16				
Rayleigh	d				17 41				17 51							18 06					18 21				
Southminster	d																					17 56			
Burnham-on-Crouch	d																					18 00			
Althorne	d																					18 05			
North Fambridge	d																					18 14			
South Woodham Ferrers	d																					18 19			
Battlesbridge	d																					18 23			
Wickford 2	d				17 46				17 56							18 11					18 26	18a29			
Billericay	d				17 52				18 02							18 17					18 32				
Shenfield 3	a				18 00				18 10							18 25					18 40				
Shenfield 3	d			17 54	18 00		18 04	18 08	18 10		18 14	18 20			18 24	18 25	18 27		18 34	18 38	18 40			18 44	18 51
Brentwood	d			17 57			18 07				18 17				18 27				18 37					18 47	
Harold Wood	d			18 02			18 12				18 22				18 32				18 42					18 52	
Gidea Park 2	d	18 02		18 06		18 12	18 16			18 22	18 26			18 32	18 36				18 46					18 56	
Romford	d	18 04		18 08		18 14	18 18			18 24	18 28	18 28		18 34	18 38				18 48					18 58	
Chadwell Heath	d			18 12			18 22				18 32				18 42				18 52					19 02	
Goodmayes	d			18 14			18 24				18 34				18 44				18 54					19 04	
Seven Kings	d			18 16			18 26				18 36				18 46				18 56					19 06	
Ilford 2	d	18 12		18 19		18 22	18 29			18 32	18 39			18 42	18 49				18 59					19 09	
Manor Park	d	18 15				18 25				18 35				18 45	18 52				19 02					19 12	
Forest Gate	d	18 17				18 27				18 37				18 47	18 54				19 04					19 14	
Maryland	d	18 19				18 29				18 39				18 49	18 56				19 06					19 16	
Stratford 7 ⊖	d	18 22		18 25	18 14	18 32	18 35	18 22	18 25	18 42	18 45	18 36		18 52	18 59	18 39	18 42		19 09	18 52	18 55			19 19	19 05
London Liverpool Street 15 ⊖	a	18 30		18 33	18 24	18 40	18 43	18 31	18 35	18 50	18 53	18 45		19 00	19 07	18 48	18 51		19 17	19 01	19 04			19 27	19 14

		LE	LE 1	LE	LE 1	LE 1	LE 1	LE		LE 1	LE	LE 1	LE 1		LE	LE 1	LE	LE 1		LE 1	LE 1	LE	LE	LE 1	LE 1
Southend Victoria	d		18 20		18 30							18 50						19 10						19 30	
Prittlewell	d		18 22		18 32							18 52						19 12						19 32	
Southend Airport ✈	d		18 25		18 35							18 55						19 15						19 35	
Rochford	d		18 28		18 38							18 58						19 18						19 38	
Hockley	d		18 31		18 41							19 01						19 21						19 41	
Rayleigh	d		18 36		18 46							19 06						19 26						19 46	
Southminster	d												18 36												19 19
Burnham-on-Crouch	d												18 40												19 23
Althorne	d												18 45												19 28
North Fambridge	d												19 01												19 34
South Woodham Ferrers	d												19 06												19 39
Battlesbridge	d												19 10												19 43
Wickford 2	d		18 41		18 51							19 11	19 17					19 31						19 51	19 55
Billericay	d		18 47		18 57							19 17	19 23					19 37						19 57	
Shenfield 3	a		18 55		19 05							19 25	19 33					19 45						20 05	20 08
Shenfield 3	d	18 54	18 57	19 04	19 05	19 08	19 13	19 14		19 19	19 24	19 25			19 34	19 38	19 44	19 45		19 51		19 54	20 04	20 05	
Brentwood	d	18 57		19 07				19 17			19 27				19 37		19 47					19 57	20 07		
Harold Wood	d	19 02		19 12				19 22			19 32				19 42		19 52					20 02	20 12		
Gidea Park 2	d	19 06		19 16				19 26			19 36				19 46		19 56					20 06	20 16		
Romford	d	19 08		19 18				19 28		19 27	19 38				19 48		19 58	19 53				20 08	20 18		
Chadwell Heath	d	19 12		19 22				19 32			19 42				19 52		20 02					20 12	20 22		
Goodmayes	d	19 14		19 24				19 34			19 44				19 54		20 04					20 14	20 24		
Seven Kings	d	19 16		19 26				19 36			19 46				19 56		20 06					20 16	20 26		
Ilford 2	d	19 19		19 29				19 39			19 49				19 59		20 09					20 19	20 29		
Manor Park	d	19 22		19 32				19 42			19 52				20 02		20 12					20 22	20 32		
Forest Gate	d	19 24		19 34				19 44			19 54				20 04		20 14					20 24	20 34		
Maryland	d	19 26		19 36				19 46			19 56				20 06		20 16					20 26	20 36		
Stratford 7 ⊖	d	19 29	19 11	19 39	19 19	19 22	19 27	19 49		19 36	19 59	19 39			20 09	19 52	20 19	20 01		20 05	20 14	20 29	20 39	20 19	
London Liverpool Street 15 ⊖	a	19 37	19 20	19 47	19 28	19 31	19 36	19 57		19 45	20 07	19 48			20 17	20 01	20 27	20 10		20 14	20 23	20 37	20 47	20 28	

Southend Victoria, Southminster and Shenfield - London

Network Diagram - see first Page of Table 5

		CC	LE 1	LE		LE 1	LE	LE 1	LE ◇1	LE	LE 1	CC	LE	LE 1		LE 1	LE 1	LE 1	CC	LE	LE	LE 1	LE 1	LE	
Southend Victoria	d							19 50						20 10								20 30			
Prittlewell	d							19 52						20 12								20 32			
Southend Airport ✈	d							19 55						20 15								20 35			
Rochford	d							19 58						20 18								20 38			
Hockley	d							20 01						20 21								20 41			
Rayleigh	d							20 06						20 26								20 46			
Southminster	d															20 16									
Burnham-on-Crouch	d															20 20									
Althorne	d															20 25									
North Fambridge	d															20 31									
South Woodham Ferrers	d															20 36									
Battlesbridge	d															20 40									
Wickford 2	d							20 11						20 31		20a46						20 51			
Billericay	d							20 17						20 37								20 57			
Shenfield 3	a							20 25						20 45								21 05			
Shenfield 3	d		20 08	20 14		20 20	20 24	20 25		20 34	20 38		20 44	20 45			20 47	20 53		20 54	21 04	21 05	21 08	21 14	
Brentwood	d			20 17			20 27			20 37			20 47							20 57	21 07			21 17	
Harold Wood	d			20 22			20 32			20 42			20 52							21 02	21 12			21 22	
Gidea Park 2	d			20 26			20 36			20 46			20 56							21 06	21 16			21 26	
Romford	d			20 28		20 28	20 38			20 48			20 58	20 53						21 08	21 18			21 28	
Chadwell Heath	d			20 32			20 42			20 52			21 02							21 12	21 22			21 32	
Goodmayes	d			20 34			20 44			20 54			21 04							21 14	21 24			21 34	
Seven Kings	d			20 36			20 46			20 56			21 06							21 16	21 26			21 36	
Ilford 2	d			20 39			20 49			20 59			21 09							21 19	21 29			21 39	
Manor Park	d			20 42			20 52			21 02			21 12							21 22	21 32			21 42	
Forest Gate	d			20 44			20 54			21 04			21 14							21 24	21 34			21 44	
Maryland	d			20 46			20 56			21 06			21 16							21 26	21 36			21 46	
Stratford 7 ⊖	d	20 21	20 22	20 49		20 36	20 59	20 39		21 09	20 52	21 00	21 19	21 01				21 07	21 15	21 29	21 39	21 19	21 22	21 49	
London Liverpool Street 15 ⊖	a	20 33	20 31	20 57		20 45	21 07	20 48	20 55	21 17	21 01	21 12	21 27	21 10			21 12	21 16	21 26	21 37	21 47	21 28	21 31	21 57	

		LE	LE 1	LE 1	LE 1		LE	LE 1	LE	LE 1		LE 1	LE	LE 1	LE 1	LE 1	LE	LE 1	LE ◇1	LE		LE 1	LE 1	LE 1	LE
Southend Victoria	d		20 50							21 10				21 30								22 00			
Prittlewell	d		20 52							21 12				21 32								22 02			
Southend Airport ✈	d		20 55							21 15				21 35								22 05			
Rochford	d		20 58							21 18				21 38								22 08			
Hockley	d		21 01							21 21				21 41								22 11			
Rayleigh	d		21 06							21 26				21 46								22 16			
Southminster	d			20 56											21 36								22 16		
Burnham-on-Crouch	d			21 00											21 40								22 20		
Althorne	d			21 05											21 45								22 25		
North Fambridge	d			21 11											21 51								22 31		
South Woodham Ferrers	d			21 16											21 56								22 36		
Battlesbridge	d			21 20											22 00								22 40		
Wickford 2	d		21 11	21a26						21 31				21 51	22a07							22 21	22a46		
Billericay	d		21 17							21 37				21 57								22 27			
Shenfield 3	a		21 25							21 45				22 05								22 35			
Shenfield 3	d	21 24	21 25		21 27		21 34	21 38	21 44	21 45		21 51	21 59	22 05		22 08	22 14	22 20		22 29		22 35		22 38	22 44
Brentwood	d	21 27					21 37		21 47				22 02				22 17			22 32					22 47
Harold Wood	d	21 32					21 42		21 52				22 07				22 22			22 37					22 52
Gidea Park 2	d	21 36					21 46		21 56				22 11				22 26			22 41					22 56
Romford	d	21 38					21 48		21 58	21 53			22 13				22 28	22 28		22 43					22 58
Chadwell Heath	d	21 42					21 52		22 02				22 17				22 32			22 47					23 02
Goodmayes	d	21 44					21 54		22 04				22 19				22 34			22 49					23 04
Seven Kings	d	21 46					21 56		22 06				22 21				22 36			22 51					23 06
Ilford 2	d	21 49					21 59		22 09				22 24				22 39			22 54					23 09
Manor Park	d	21 52					22 02		22 12				22 27				22 42			22 57					23 12
Forest Gate	d	21 54					22 04		22 14				22 29				22 44			22 59					23 14
Maryland	d	21 56					22 06		22 16				22 31				22 46			23 01					23 16
Stratford 7 ⊖	d	21 59	21 39		21 42		22 09	21 52	22 19	22 01		22 05	22 34	22 19		22 22	22 49	22 36		23 04		22 49		22 52	23 19
London Liverpool Street 15 ⊖	a	22 07	21 48		21 51		22 17	22 01	22 27	22 10		22 14	22 42	22 28		22 31	22 57	22 45	22 55	23 12		22 58		23 01	23 27

Southend Victoria, Southminster and Shenfield - London

Network Diagram - see first Page of Table 5

		LE 1	LE 1	LE	LE 1	LE 1		LE	LE 1	LE	LE 1	LE 1	LE
Southend Victoria	d				22 30						23 00		
Prittlewell	d				22 32						23 02		
Southend Airport ✈	d				22 35						23 05		
Rochford	d				22 38						23 08		
Hockley	d				22 41						23 11		
Rayleigh	d				22 46						23 16		
Southminster	d											22 56	
Burnham-on-Crouch	d											23 00	
Althorne	d											23 05	
North Fambridge	d											23 11	
South Woodham Ferrers	d											23 16	
Battlesbridge	d											23 20	
Wickford 2	d				22 51						23 21	23 26	
Billericay	d				22 57						23 27	23 32	
Shenfield 3	a				23 05						23 35	23 39	
Shenfield 3	d	22 51		22 59	23 05	23 08		23 14	23 20	23 29	23 35	23 39	23 44
Brentwood	d			23 02				23 17		23 32			23 47
Harold Wood	d			23 07				23 22		23 37			23 52
Gidea Park 2	d			23 11				23 26		23 41			23 56
Romford	d			23 13				23 28	23 28	23 43		23 47	23 58
Chadwell Heath	d			23 17				23 32		23 47			00 02
Goodmayes	d			23 19				23 34		23 49			00 04
Seven Kings	d			23 21				23 36		23 51			00 06
Ilford 2	d			23 24				23 39		23 54			00 09
Manor Park	d			23 27				23 42		23 57			00 12
Forest Gate	d			23 29				23 44		23 59			00 14
Maryland	d			23 31				23 46		00 01			00 16
Stratford 7 ⊖	d	23 05	23 06	23 34	23 19	23 22		23 49	23 36	00 04	23 49	23 56	00 19
London Liverpool Street 15 ⊖	a	23 15	23 15	23 42	23 28	23 31		23 57	23 45	00 12	23 58	00 05	00 27

Mondays to Fridays

29 August to 7 September

		LE ◇1	LE 1	LE		LE	LE 1	LE	LE	LE 1		CC	LE 1	LE	LE	LE	LE	LE	LE	LE		LE	LE	LE	CC
		A	B	C			A	A	D	D		A	D	D	D	D	D	D	D	D		D	D		
Southend Victoria	d									23p10														04 00	
Prittlewell	d									23p12														04 02	
Southend Airport ✈	d									23p15														04 05	
Rochford	d									23p18														04 08	
Hockley	d									23p21														04 12	
Rayleigh	d									23p26														04 16	
Southminster	d						22p56																		
Burnham-on-Crouch	d						23p00																		
Althorne	d						23p05																		
North Fambridge	d						23p11																		
South Woodham Ferrers	d						23p16																		
Battlesbridge	d						23p20																		
Wickford 2	d						23p26			23p31														04 21	
Billericay	d						23p32			23p37														04 28	
Shenfield 3	a						23p39			23p45														04 39	
Shenfield 3	d					23p29	23p39	23p44	23p44	23p45					23p59	00 14		00 29	00 44					04 39	
Brentwood	d					23p32		23p47	23p47						00 02	00 17		00 32	00 47					04 42	
Harold Wood	d					23p37		23p52	23p52						00 07	00 22		00 37	00 52					04 47	
Gidea Park 2	d					23p41		23p56	23p56						00 11	00 26		00 41	00 56					04 51	
Romford	d					23p43	23p47	23p58	23p58						00 13	00 28		00 43	00 58					04 53	
Chadwell Heath	d					23p47		00 02	00 02						00 17	00 32		00 47	01 02					04 57	
Goodmayes	d					23p49		00 04	00 04						00 19	00 34		00 49	01 04					04 59	
Seven Kings	d					23p51		00 06	00 06						00 21	00 36		00 51	01 06					05 01	
Ilford 2	d					23p54		00 09	00 09						00 24	00 39		00 54	01 09					05 04	
Manor Park	d					23p57		00 12	00 12						00 27	00 42		00 57	01 12						
Forest Gate	d					23p59		00 14	00 14						00 29	00 44		00 59	01 14						
Maryland	d					00 01		00 16	00 16																
Stratford 7 ⊖	d	23b52	23p54	23p54		00 04	23p56	00 19	00 20	00 08		00 09	00 12	00 30	00 40	00 50	01 00	01 10	01 20	01 30		01 40	01 50	05 10	05 14
London Liverpool Street 15 ⊖	a	00 02	00 02	00 02		00 12	00 05	00 27	00 28	00 16		00 20	00 20	00 38	00 48	00 58	01 08	01 18	01 28	01 38		01 48	01 58	05 18	05 27

A 29 August
B 3 September
C not 29 August, 3 September
D not 29 August
b Previous night, stops to set down only

Southend Victoria, Southminster and Shenfield - London

Network Diagram - see first Page of Table 5

	LE	LE	LE 1	LE	LE	LE 1	LE	LE 1	LE 1	LE 1	LE	LE	LE	LE 1	LE	LE 1	LE	LE 1	LE 1	LE
Southend Victoria d		04 30				05 00			05 20					05 40				06 00		
Prittlewell d		04 32				05 02			05 22					05 42				06 02		
Southend Airport ✈ d		04 35				05 05			05 25					05 45				06 05		
Rochford d		04 38				05 08			05 28					05 48				06 08		
Hockley d		04 42				05 11			05 31					05 51				06 11		
Rayleigh d		04 46				05 16			05 36					05 56				06 16		
Southminster d										05 26										
Burnham-on-Crouch d										05 30										
Althorne d										05 35										
North Fambridge d										05 41										
South Woodham Ferrers d										05 46										
Battlesbridge d										05 50										
Wickford d		04 51				05 21			05 41	05a56				06 01				06 21		
Billericay d		04 58				05 27			05 47					06 07				06 27		
Shenfield a		05 09				05 35			05 55					06 15				06 35		
Shenfield d		05 09	05 24		05 29	05 35	05 44	05 53	05 55			06 04	06 14	06 15	06 24	06 25	06 34	06 35	06 41	
Brentwood d		05 12			05 32		05 47					06 07	06 17		06 27		06 37			
Harold Wood d		05 17			05 37		05 52					06 12	06 22		06 32		06 42			
Gidea Park d		05 21	05 31		05 41		05 56				06 06	06 16	06 26		06 36		06 45			06 49
Romford d		05 23			05 43		05 58				06 08	06 18	06 28		06 38		06 48			06 51
Chadwell Heath d		05 27			05 47		06 02				06 12	06 22	06 32		06 42		06 52			06 55
Goodmayes d		05 29			05 49		06 04				06 14	06 24	06 34		06 44					06 57
Seven Kings d		05 31	05 36		05 51		06 06				06 16	06 26	06 36		06 46					06 59
Ilford d	05 09	05 34		05 39	05 54		06 09				06 19	06 29	06 39		06 49		06 57			07 02
Manor Park d	05 11			05 41	05 57		06 12				06 22	06 32	06 42		06 52					07 05
Forest Gate d	05 14			05 44	05 59		06 14				06 24	06 34	06 44		06 54					07 07
Maryland d	05 16			05 46	06 01		06 16				06 26	06 36	06 46		06 56					07 09
Stratford ⊖ d	05 18	05 40	05 42	05 48	06 04	05 49	06 19	06 07	06 10		06 29	06 39	06 49	06 29	06 59	06 39	07 03	06 49	06s57	07 12
London Liverpool Street 15 ⊖ a	05 26	05 48	05 55	05 56	06 12	05 58	06 27	06 16	06 19		06 37	06 47	06 57	06 40	07 07	06 48	07 13	06 58	07 09	07 22

	LE	LE 1	LE 1	LE 1	LE	LE	LE	LE	LE	LE 1	LE 1	LE	LE	LE 1	LE 1	LE 1	LE	LE
Southend Victoria d		06 11					06 26				06 40				06 50			
Prittlewell d		06 13					06 28				06 42				06 52			
Southend Airport ✈ d		06 16					06 31				06 45				06 55			
Rochford d		06 19					06 34				06 48				06 58			
Hockley d		06 22					06 38				06 51				07 01			
Rayleigh d		06 27					06 42				06 56				07 06			
Southminster d				06 09														
Burnham-on-Crouch d				06 13														
Althorne d				06 18														
North Fambridge d				06 24														
South Woodham Ferrers d				06 30														
Battlesbridge d				06 34														
Wickford d		06 32		06 40			06 47				07 01				07 11			
Billericay d		06 39		06 46			06 54				07 08				07 18			
Shenfield a		06 45		06 52			07 01				07 14				07 24			
Shenfield d	06 44	06 45	06 50	06 53		06 54	07 01		07 04	07 08	07 14		07 14	07 19	07 24			07 24
Brentwood d	06 47					06 57			07 07				07 17					07 27
Harold Wood d	06 52					07 02			07 12				07 22					07 32
Gidea Park d	06 55				06 59	07 05		07 09	07 15			07 19	07 25				07 29	07 35
Romford d	06 58				07 01	07 08		07 11	07 18			07 21	07 28				07 31	07 38
Chadwell Heath d	07 02				07 05	07 12		07 15	07 22			07 25	07 32				07 35	07 42
Goodmayes d					07 07			07 17				07 27	07 34				07 37	07 44
Seven Kings d					07 09			07 19				07 29	07 36				07 39	07 46
Ilford d	07 07				07 12	07 17		07 22	07 27			07 32	07 39				07 42	07 49
Manor Park d					07 15			07 25				07 35					07 45	
Forest Gate d					07 17			07 27				07 37					07 47	
Maryland d					07 19			07 29				07 39					07 49	
Stratford ⊖ d	07 15	07s02	07s06	07s09	07 22	07 25	07s19	07 32	07 35	07s23	07s31	07 42	07 45	07s35	07s41	07 44	07 52	07 55
London Liverpool Street 15 ⊖ a	07 25	07 13	07 18	07 21	07 32	07 35	07 30	07 42	07 45	07 35	07 42	07 52	07 55	07 46	07 52	07 56	08 02	08 05

Southend Victoria, Southminster and Shenfield - London

Network Diagram - see first Page of Table 5

	LE 1	LE 1	LE	LE	LE 1	LE 1	LE	LE	LE 1	LE 1	LE	LE	LE	LE	LE 1	LE	LE 1	LE 1	LE 1
Southend Victoria d		07 03							07 13					07 18	07 23			07 32	
Prittlewell d		07 05							07 15					07 20	07 25			07 34	
Southend Airport ✈ d		07 08							07 18					07 23	07 28			07 37	
Rochford d		07 11							07 21					07 26	07 31			07 40	
Hockley d		07 14							07 24					07 30	07 34			07 43	
Rayleigh d		07 19							07 29					07 34	07 39			07 48	
Southminster d	06 48																		
Burnham-on-Crouch d	06 52																		
Althorne d	06 57																		
North Fambridge d	07 04																		
South Woodham Ferrers d	07 10																		
Battlesbridge d	07 14																		
Wickford d	07 19	07 24							07 34					07 39	07 44			07 53	
Billericay d	07 26	07 31							07 41					07 46	07 51			08 00	
Shenfield a	07 32								07 47					07 53	07 57			08 06	
Shenfield d	07 32			07 34	07 38	07 41		07 44	07 47	07 50		07 50		07 54	07 57	08 00	08 01	08 06	08 09
Brentwood d				07 37				07 47				07 53		07 57		08 03			
Harold Wood d				07 42				07 52				07 58		08 02		08 08			
Gidea Park d			07 39	07 45			07 49	07 55			07 59	08 02	08 05	08 09		08 12			
Romford d			07 41	07 48			07 51	07 58			08 01	08 04	08 07	08 11		08 14			
Chadwell Heath d			07 45	07 52			07 55	08 02			08 05	08 08	08 11	08 15		08 18			
Goodmayes d			07 47	07 54			07 57	08 04			08 07	08 10	08 13	08 17		08 20			
Seven Kings d			07 49	07 56			07 59	08 06			08 09	08 12	08 15	08 19		08 22			
Ilford d			07 52	07 59			08 02	08 09			08 12	08 15	08 18	08 22		08 25			
Manor Park d			07 55				08 05						08 21						
Forest Gate d			07 57				08 07						08 23						
Maryland d			07 59				08 09						08 25						
Stratford ⊖ d	07 50	07s52	08 02	08 05	07s55	07s58	08 12	08 15	08s04	08s07	08 18	08 21	08 28	08 31	08s15	08 34	08s18	08s23	08s25
London Liverpool Street 15 ⊖ a	08 01	08 03	08 12	08 15	08 07	08 09	08 22	08 25	08 15	08 19	08 28	08 31	08 38	08 41	08 26	08 43	08 30	08 36	08 38

	LE	LE	LE	LE 1	LE 1	LE 1	LE	LE	LE	LE 1	LE 1	LE 1	LE	LE	LE	LE 1	LE 1	LE
Southend Victoria d				07 42							07 52					08 03		
Prittlewell d				07 44							07 54					08 05		
Southend Airport ✈ d				07 47							07 57					08 08		
Rochford d				07 50							08 00					08 11		
Hockley d				07 53							08 03					08 14		
Rayleigh d				07 58							08 08					08 19		
Southminster d					07 37													
Burnham-on-Crouch d					07 41													
Althorne d					07 46													
North Fambridge d					07 52													
South Woodham Ferrers d					07 59													
Battlesbridge d																		
Wickford d				08 03	08 07						08 13					08 24		
Billericay d				08 10	08 14						08 20					08 31		
Shenfield a				08 16							08 26					08 37		
Shenfield d			08 10	08 16		08 21			08 22	08 24	08 26	08 29			08 32	08 37	08 42	
Brentwood d			08 13						08 25						08 35			
Harold Wood d			08 18						08 30						08 40			
Gidea Park d	08 15	08 19	08 22					08 29	08 34					08 41	08 44			
Romford d	08 17	08 21	08 24					08 31	08 36					08 43	08 46			
Chadwell Heath d	08 21	08 25	08 28					08 35	08 40					08 47	08 50			
Goodmayes d	08 23	08 27	08 30					08 37	08 42					08 49	08 52			
Seven Kings d	08 25	08 29	08 32					08 39	08 44					08 51	08 54			
Ilford d	08 28	08 32	08 35				08 38	08 42	08 47				08 50	08 54	08 57			09 00
Manor Park d	08 31						08 41						08 53					09 03
Forest Gate d	08 33						08 43						08 55					09 05
Maryland d	08 35						08 45						08 57					09 07
Stratford ⊖ d	08 38	08 41	08 44	08s33	08s35	08s38	08 48	08 51	08 54	08s41	08s43	08s45	09 00	09 03	09 06	08s56	08s59	09 10
London Liverpool Street 15 ⊖ a	08 48	08 51	08 53	08 46	08 48	08 50	08 58	09 01	09 03	08 54	08 56	08 58	09 10	09 13	09 14	09 08	09 11	09 20

Southend Victoria, Southminster and Shenfield - London

Network Diagram - see first Page of Table 5

		LE	LE	LE	LE	LE	LE		LE	LE				LE	LE	LE	LE	LE	LE	LE		LE	LE	LE	LE
				■	■		■		■	■						■		■	■	■			■		■
Southend Victoria	d			08 12						08 30									08 52						09 10
Prittlewell	d			08 14						08 32									08 54						09 12
Southend Airport ✈	d			08 17						08 35									08 57						09 15
Rochford	d			08 20						08 38									09 00						09 18
Hockley	d			08 23						08 41									09 03						09 21
Rayleigh	d			08 28						08 46									09 08						09 26
Southminster	d								08 16											08 56					
Burnham-on-Crouch	d								08 20											09 00					
Althorne	d								08 25											09 05					
North Fambridge	d								08 31											09 11					
South Woodham Ferrers	d								08 37											09 16					
Battlesbridge	d								08 41											09 20					
Wickford 2	d			08 33					08 46	08 51									09 13	09a26					09 31
Billericay	d			08 40					08 53	08 58									09 20						09 37
Shenfield 3	a			08 46					08 59	09 04									09 27						09 45
Shenfield 3	d		08 44	08 46	08 51	08 54	08 55		08 59	09 04				09 04	09 14	09 21	09 24	09 25	09 27			09 34	09 38	09 44	09 45
Brentwood	d		08 47			08 57								09 07	09 17		09 27					09 37		09 47	
Harold Wood	d		08 52			09 02								09 12	09 22		09 32					09 42		09 52	
Gidea Park 2	d	08 51	08 56			09 06								09 16	09 26		09 36					09 46		09 56	
Romford	d	08 53	08 58	08 55		09 08								09 18	09 28		09 38					09 48		09 58	09 53
Chadwell Heath	d	08 57	09 02			09 12								09 22	09 32		09 42					09 52		10 02	
Goodmayes	d	08 59	09 04			09 14								09 24	09 34		09 44					09 54		10 04	
Seven Kings	d	09 01	09 06			09 16								09 26	09 36		09 46					09 56		10 06	
Ilford 2	d	09 04	09 09			09 19								09 29	09 39		09 49					09 59		10 09	
Manor Park	d		09 12			09 22								09 32	09 42		09 52					10 02		10 12	
Forest Gate	d		09 14			09 24								09 34	09 44		09 54					10 04		10 14	
Maryland	d		09 16			09 26								09 36	09 46		09 56					10 06		10 16	
Stratford 7 ⊖	d	09 13	09 19	09s05	09s08	09 29			09s17	09s22				09 39	09 49	09s37	09 59	09s41	09s44			10 09	09 52	10 19	10 01
London Liverpool Street 15 ⊖	a	09 23	09 27	09 16	09 19	09 37	09 21		09 29	09 33				09 47	09 58	09 49	10 07	09 53	09 55			10 17	10 01	10 27	10 10

		LE	LE	LE	LE	LE		LE	LE	LE	LE	LE	LE	LE	LE	LE		LE	LE	LE	LE	LE	LE	LE	LE
		■			■	■		■		■		■	■ ■ ☕		■			■	■	■			■	■	
Southend Victoria	d				09 30							09 50						10 10					10 30		
Prittlewell	d				09 32							09 52						10 12					10 32		
Southend Airport ✈	d				09 35							09 55						10 15					10 35		
Rochford	d				09 38							09 58						10 18					10 38		
Hockley	d				09 41							10 01						10 21					10 41		
Rayleigh	d				09 46							10 06						10 26					10 46		
Southminster	d					09 36													10 16						
Burnham-on-Crouch	d					09 40													10 20						
Althorne	d					09 45													10 25						
North Fambridge	d					09 51													10 31						
South Woodham Ferrers	d					09 56													10 36						
Battlesbridge	d					10 00													10 40						
Wickford 2	d				09 51	10a06						10 11						10 31	10a46				10 51		
Billericay	d				09 57							10 17						10 37					10 57		
Shenfield 3	a				10 05							10 25						10 45					11 05		
Shenfield 3	d	09 51	09 54	10 04	10 05			10 08	10 14	10 18	10 24	10 25		10 34	10 38	10 44		10 45		10 51	10 54	11 04	11 05	11 08	11 14
Brentwood	d		09 57	10 07					10 17		10 27			10 37		10 47					10 57	11 07			11 17
Harold Wood	d		10 02	10 12					10 22		10 32			10 42		10 52					11 02	11 12			11 22
Gidea Park 2	d		10 06	10 16					10 26		10 36			10 46		10 56					11 06	11 16			11 26
Romford	d		10 08	10 18					10 28	10 26	10 38			10 48		10 58		10 53			11 08	11 18			11 28
Chadwell Heath	d		10 12	10 22					10 32		10 42			10 52		11 02					11 12	11 22			11 32
Goodmayes	d		10 14	10 24					10 34		10 44			10 54		11 04					11 14	11 24			11 34
Seven Kings	d		10 16	10 26					10 36		10 46			10 56		11 06					11 16	11 26			11 36
Ilford 2	d		10 19	10 29					10 39		10 49			10 59		11 09					11 19	11 29			11 39
Manor Park	d		10 22	10 32					10 42		10 52			11 02		11 12					11 22	11 32			11 42
Forest Gate	d		10 24	10 34					10 44		10 54			11 04		11 14					11 24	11 34			11 44
Maryland	d		10 26	10 36					10 46		10 56			11 06		11 16					11 26	11 36			11 46
Stratford 7 ⊖	d	10 05	10 29	10 39	10 19			10 22	10 49	10 34	10 59	10 39		11 09	10 52	11 19		11 01		11 05	11 29	11 39	11 19	11 22	11 49
London Liverpool Street 15 ⊖	a	10 14	10 37	10 47	10 28			10 31	10 57	10 43	11 07	10 48	10 55	11 17	11 01	11 27		11 10		11 14	11 37	11 47	11 29	11 31	11 57

A The East Anglian

Southend Victoria, Southminster and Shenfield - London

Network Diagram - see first Page of Table 5

		LE		LE	LE	LE		LE	LE	LE	LE	LE		LE	LE	LE	LE	LE	LE	LE	LE	LE			LE
		■			■	■			■		■	■				■	■	■		■		■			
Southend Victoria	d				10 50						11 10					11 30						11 50			
Prittlewell	d				10 52						11 12					11 32						11 52			
Southend Airport ✈	d				10 55						11 15					11 35						11 55			
Rochford	d				10 58						11 18					11 38						11 58			
Hockley	d				11 01						11 21					11 41						12 01			
Rayleigh	d				11 06						11 26					11 46						12 06			
Southminster	d					10 56											11 36								
Burnham-on-Crouch	d					11 00											11 40								
Althorne	d					11 05											11 45								
North Fambridge	d					11 11											11 51								
South Woodham Ferrers	d					11 16											11 56								
Battlesbridge	d					11 20											12 00								
Wickford 2	d				11 11	11a26					11 31					11 51	12a06					12 11			
Billericay	d				11 17						11 37					11 57						12 17			
Shenfield 3	a				11 25						11 45					12 05						12 25			
Shenfield 3	d	11 20		11 24	11 25			11 34	11 38	11 44	11 45	11 51		11 54	12 04	12 05		12 08	12 14	12 20	12 24	12 25			12 34
Brentwood	d			11 27				11 37		11 47				11 57	12 07				12 17		12 27				12 37
Harold Wood	d			11 32				11 42		11 52				12 02	12 12				12 22		12 32				12 42
Gidea Park 2	d			11 36				11 46		11 56				12 06	12 16				12 26		12 36				12 46
Romford	d	11 28		11 38				11 48		11 58	11 53			12 08	12 18				12 28	12 28	12 38				12 48
Chadwell Heath	d			11 42				11 52		12 02				12 12	12 22				12 32		12 42				12 52
Goodmayes	d			11 44				11 54		12 04				12 14	12 24				12 34		12 44				12 54
Seven Kings	d			11 46				11 56		12 06				12 16	12 26				12 36		12 46				12 56
Ilford 2	d			11 49				11 59		12 09				12 19	12 29				12 39		12 49				12 59
Manor Park	d			11 52				12 02		12 12				12 22	12 32				12 42		12 52				13 02
Forest Gate	d			11 54				12 04		12 14				12 24	12 34				12 44		12 54				13 04
Maryland	d			11 56				12 06		12 16				12 26	12 36				12 46		12 56				13 06
Stratford 7 ⊖	d	11 36		11 59	11 39			12 09	11 52	12 19	12 01	12 05		12 29	12 39	12 19		12 22	12 49	12 36	12 59	12 39			13 09
London Liverpool Street 15 ⊖	a	11 45		12 07	11 48			12 17	12 01	12 27	12 10	12 14		12 37	12 47	12 29		12 31	12 57	12 45	13 07	12 48			13 17

		LE	LE	LE	LE	LE	LE	LE		LE	LE	LE	LE	LE	LE	LE		LE		LE	LE	LE	LE	LE	LE
		■		■	■	■				■	■		■		■	■				■		■	■		
Southend Victoria	d			12 10						12 30					12 50							13 10			
Prittlewell	d			12 12						12 32					12 52							13 12			
Southend Airport ✈	d			12 15						12 35					12 55							13 15			
Rochford	d			12 18						12 38					12 58							13 18			
Hockley	d			12 21						12 41					13 01							13 21			
Rayleigh	d			12 26						12 46					13 06							13 26			
Southminster	d				12 16											12 56									
Burnham-on-Crouch	d				12 20											13 00									
Althorne	d				12 25											13 05									
North Fambridge	d				12 31											13 11									
South Woodham Ferrers	d				12 36											13 16									
Battlesbridge	d				12 40											13 20									
Wickford 2	d			12 31	12a46					12 51					13 11	13a26						13 31			
Billericay	d			12 37						12 57					13 17							13 37			
Shenfield 3	a			12 45						13 05					13 25							13 45			
Shenfield 3	d	12 38	12 44	12 45		12 51	12 54	13 04		13 05	13 08	13 14	13 20	13 24	13 25			13 34		13 38	13 44	13 45	13 51	13 54	14 04
Brentwood	d		12 47				12 57	13 07				13 17		13 27				13 37			13 47			13 57	14 07
Harold Wood	d		12 52				13 02	13 12				13 22		13 32				13 42			13 52			14 02	14 12
Gidea Park 2	d		12 56				13 06	13 16				13 26		13 36				13 46			13 56			14 06	14 16
Romford	d		12 58	12 53			13 08	13 18				13 28	13 28	13 38				13 48			13 58	13 53		14 08	14 18
Chadwell Heath	d		13 02				13 12	13 22				13 32		13 42				13 52			14 02			14 12	14 22
Goodmayes	d		13 04				13 14	13 24				13 34		13 44				13 54			14 04			14 14	14 24
Seven Kings	d		13 06				13 16	13 26				13 36		13 46				13 56			14 06			14 16	14 26
Ilford 2	d		13 09				13 19	13 29				13 39		13 49				13 59			14 09			14 19	14 29
Manor Park	d		13 12				13 22	13 32				13 42		13 52				14 02			14 12			14 22	14 32
Forest Gate	d		13 14				13 24	13 34				13 44		13 54				14 04			14 14			14 24	14 34
Maryland	d		13 16				13 26	13 36				13 46		13 56				14 06			14 16			14 26	14 36
Stratford 7 ⊖	d	12 52	13 19	13 01		13 05	13 29	13 39		13 19	13 22	13 49	13 36	13 59	13 39			14 09		13 52	14 19	14 01	14 05	14 29	14 39
London Liverpool Street 15 ⊖	a	13 01	13 27	13 10		13 14	13 37	13 47		13 28	13 31	13 57	13 45	14 07	13 48			14 17		14 01	14 27	14 10	14 14	14 37	14 47

Southend Victoria, Southminster and Shenfield - London

Network Diagram - see first Page of Table 5

		LE ■	LE ■	LE ■	LE	LE ■	LE	LE ■	LE ◇■	LE	LE ■	LE	LE ■	LE ■	LE ■	LE	LE	LE ■	LE ■	LE	LE ■	LE
Southend Victoria	d	13 30						13 50					14 10					14 30				
Prittlewell	d	13 32						13 52					14 12					14 32				
Southend Airport ✈	d	13 35						13 55					14 15					14 35				
Rochford	d	13 38						13 58					14 18					14 38				
Hockley	d	13 41						14 01					14 21					14 41				
Rayleigh	d	13 46						14 06					14 26					14 46				
Southminster	d		13 36											14 16								
Burnham-on-Crouch	d		13 40											14 20								
Althorne	d		13 45											14 25								
North Fambridge	d		13 51											14 31								
South Woodham Ferrers	d		13 56											14 36								
Battlesbridge	d		14 00											14 40								
Wickford ■	d	13 51	14a06					14 11					14 31	14a46				14 51				
Billericay	d	13 57						14 17					14 37					14 57				
Shenfield ■	a	14 05						14 25					14 45					15 05				
Shenfield ■	d	14 05		14 08	14 14	14 20	14 24	14 25		14 34	14 38	14 44	14 45		14 51	14 54	15 04	15 05	15 08	15 14	15 20	15 24
Brentwood	d				14 17		14 27			14 37		14 47				14 57	15 07			15 17		15 27
Harold Wood	d				14 22		14 32			14 42		14 52				15 02	15 12			15 22		15 32
Gidea Park ■	d				14 26		14 36			14 46		14 56				15 06	15 16			15 26		15 36
Romford	d				14 28	14 28	14 38			14 48		14 58				15 08	15 18			15 28	15 28	15 38
Chadwell Heath	d				14 32		14 42			14 52		15 02				15 12	15 22			15 32		15 42
Goodmayes	d				14 34		14 44			14 54		15 04				15 14	15 24			15 34		15 44
Seven Kings	d				14 36		14 46			14 56		15 06				15 16	15 26			15 36		15 46
Ilford ■	d				14 39		14 49			14 59		15 09				15 19	15 29			15 39		15 49
Manor Park	d				14 42		14 52			15 02		15 12				15 22	15 32			15 42		15 52
Forest Gate	d				14 44		14 54			15 04		15 14				15 24	15 34			15 44		15 54
Maryland	d				14 46		14 56			15 06		15 16				15 26	15 36			15 46		15 56
Stratford ■ ⊖	d	14 19		14 22	14 49	14 36	14 59	14 39		15 09	14 52	15 19	14 59		15 05	15 29	15 39	15 19	15 22	15 49	15 36	15 59
London Liverpool Street ■ ⊖	a	14 28		14 31	14 57	14 45	15 07	14 48	14 55	15 17	15 01	15 27	15 08		15 15	15 37	15 47	15 28	15 33	15 57	15 45	16 07

		LE ■	LE ■	LE	LE ■	LE	LE ■	LE	LE ■	LE	LE	LE ■	LE ■	LE ■	LE	LE	LE	LE ■	LE	LE ■	LE
Southend Victoria	d	14 50					15 10					15 30								15 50	
Prittlewell	d	14 52					15 12					15 32								15 52	
Southend Airport ✈	d	14 55					15 15					15 35								15 55	
Rochford	d	14 58					15 18					15 38								15 58	
Hockley	d	15 01					15 21					15 41								16 01	
Rayleigh	d	15 06					15 26					15 46								16 06	
Southminster	d		14 56										15 36								
Burnham-on-Crouch	d		15 00										15 40								
Althorne	d		15 05										15 45								
North Fambridge	d		15 11										15 51								
South Woodham Ferrers	d		15 16										15 56								
Battlesbridge	d		15 20										16 00								
Wickford ■	d	15 11	15a26				15 31					15 51	16a06							16 11	
Billericay	d	15 17					15 37					15 57								16 17	
Shenfield ■	a	15 25					15 45					16 05								16 25	
Shenfield ■	d	15 25		15 34	15 38	15 44	15 45		15 51	15 54	16 04	16 05		16 08			16 14	16 20	16 24	16 25	
Brentwood	d			15 37		15 47				15 57	16 07						16 17		16 27		
Harold Wood	d			15 42		15 52				16 02	16 12						16 22		16 32		
Gidea Park ■	d			15 46		15 56				16 06	16 16						16 26		16 36		
Romford	d			15 48		15 58	15 53			16 08	16 18						16 28		16 38		
Chadwell Heath	d			15 52		16 02				16 12	16 22						16 32		16 42		
Goodmayes	d			15 54		16 04				16 14	16 24						16 34		16 44		
Seven Kings	d			15 56		16 06				16 16	16 26						16 36		16 46		
Ilford ■	d			15 59		16 09				16 19	16 29						16 39		16 49		
Manor Park	d			16 02		16 12				16 22	16 32						16 42		16 52		
Forest Gate	d			16 04		16 14				16 24	16 34						16 44		16 54		
Maryland	d			16 06		16 16				16 26	16 36						16 46		16 56		
Stratford ■ ⊖	d	15 39		16 09	15 52	16 19	16 01	16 03	16 05	16 29	16 39	16 19		16 22	16 23	16 34	16 49	16 34	16 59	16 39	16 52
London Liverpool Street ■ ⊖	a	15 48		16 17	16 01	16 27	16 11	16 13	16 14	16 37	16 47	16 28		16 31	16 31	16 42	16 58	16 44	17 08	16 48	17 00

Southend Victoria, Southminster and Shenfield - London

Network Diagram - see first Page of Table 5

		LE	LE ■	LE	LE ■	LE ■	LE	LE ■	LE	LE	LE	LE ■	LE ■	LE	LE	LE	LE ■	LE	LE	LE ■	LE	LE ■
Southend Victoria	d				16 10							16 30								16 50		
Prittlewell	d				16 12							16 32								16 52		
Southend Airport ✈	d				16 15							16 35								16 55		
Rochford	d				16 18							16 38								16 58		
Hockley	d				16 21							16 41								17 01		
Rayleigh	d				16 26							16 46								17 06		
Southminster	d					16 14																
Burnham-on-Crouch	d					16 18																
Althorne	d					16 23																
North Fambridge	d					16 29																
South Woodham Ferrers	d					16 34																
Battlesbridge	d					16 38																
Wickford ■	d				16 31	16a44						16 51								17 11		
Billericay	d				16 37							16 57								17 17		
Shenfield ■	a				16 45							17 05								17 25		
Shenfield ■	d	16 34	16 38	16 44	16 45			16 51		16 54	17 04	17 05	17 08			17 14	17 22		17 24	17 25		17 28
Brentwood	d	16 37		16 47						16 57	17 07					17 17			17 27			
Harold Wood	d	16 42		16 52						17 02	17 12					17 22			17 32			
Gidea Park ■	d	16 46		16 56						17 06	17 16					17 26		17 32	17 36			
Romford	d	16 48		16 58						17 08	17 18					17 28		17 34	17 38			
Chadwell Heath	d	16 52		17 02						17 12	17 22					17 32			17 42			
Goodmayes	d	16 54		17 04						17 14	17 24					17 34			17 44			
Seven Kings	d	16 56		17 06						17 16	17 26					17 36			17 46			
Ilford ■	d	16 59		17 09						17 19	17 29					17 39		17 42	17 49			
Manor Park	d	17 02		17 12						17 22	17 32							17 45				
Forest Gate	d	17 04		17 14						17 24	17 34							17 47				
Maryland	d	17 06		17 16						17 26	17 36							17 49				
Stratford ■ ⊖	d	17 09	16 52	17 19	16 59		17 02	17 05	17 12	17 29	17 39	17 19	17 22	17 24	17 34	17 45	17 36	17 52	17 55	17 39	17 42	17 42
London Liverpool Street ■ ⊖	a	17 18	17 03	17 27	17 13		17 10	17 16	17 20	17 37	17 48	17 29	17 34	17 32	17 42	17 53	17 46	18 00	18 03	17 49	17 50	17 53

		LE	LE	LE ■	LE	LE	LE ■	LE ■	LE ■	LE	LE	LE ■	LE	LE	LE ■	LE ■	LE	LE	LE ■	LE	LE	LE ■
Southend Victoria	d						17 10					17 25				17 35						17 50
Prittlewell	d						17 12					17 27				17 37						17 52
Southend Airport ✈	d						17 15					17 30				17 40						17 55
Rochford	d						17 18					17 33				17 43						17 58
Hockley	d						17 21					17 36				17 46						18 01
Rayleigh	d						17 26					17 41				17 51						18 06
Southminster	d							17 06														
Burnham-on-Crouch	d							17 10														
Althorne	d							17 15														
North Fambridge	d							17 21														
South Woodham Ferrers	d							17 26														
Battlesbridge	d							17 30														
Wickford ■	d						17 31	17 37				17 46				17 56						18 11
Billericay	d						17 37					17 52				18 02						18 17
Shenfield ■	a						17 45	17 48				18 00				18 10						18 25
Shenfield ■	d		17 34	17 38		17 44	17 45	17 49	17 51		17 54	18 00		18 04	18 08	18 10		18 14	18 20		18 24	18 25
Brentwood	d		17 37			17 47					17 57			18 07				18 17			18 27	
Harold Wood	d		17 42			17 52					18 02			18 12				18 22			18 32	
Gidea Park ■	d	17 42	17 46		17 52	17 56				18 02	18 06		18 12	18 16			18 22	18 26		18 32	18 36	
Romford	d	17 44	17 48		17 54	17 58				18 04	18 08		18 14	18 18			18 24	18 28	18 28	18 34	18 38	
Chadwell Heath	d		17 52			18 02					18 12			18 22				18 32			18 42	
Goodmayes	d		17 54			18 04					18 14			18 24				18 34			18 44	
Seven Kings	d		17 56			18 06					18 16			18 26				18 36			18 46	
Ilford ■	d	17 52	17 59		18 02	18 09				18 12	18 19		18 22	18 29			18 32	18 39		18 42	18 49	
Manor Park	d	17 55			18 05					18 15			18 25				18 35			18 45	18 52	
Forest Gate	d	17 57			18 07					18 17			18 27				18 37			18 47	18 54	
Maryland	d	17 59			18 09					18 19			18 29				18 39			18 49	18 56	
Stratford ■ ⊖	d	18 02	18 05	17 52	18 12	18 15	17 59	18 08	18 06	18 22	18 25	18 14	18 32	18 35	18 22	18 25	18 42	18 45	18 36	18 52	18 59	18 39
London Liverpool Street ■ ⊖	a	18 10	18 13	18 01	18 20	18 23	18 11	18 17	18 15	18 30	18 33	18 24	18 40	18 43	18 31	18 35	18 50	18 53	18 45	19 00	19 07	18 48

Southend Victoria, Southminster and Shenfield - London

29 August to 7 September

Network Diagram - see first Page of Table 5

	LE 1		LE	LE 1	LE 1	LE 1	LE		LE 1	LE	LE 1	LE	LE 1	LE 1	LE 1	LE	LE 1		LE	LE 1	LE 1		LE	LE 1
Southend Victoria d					18 05						18 20		18 30							18 50				
Prittlewell d					18 07						18 22		18 32							18 52				
Southend Airport ✈ d					18 10						18 25		18 35							18 55				
Rochford d					18 13						18 28		18 38							18 58				
Hockley d					18 16						18 31		18 41							19 01				
Rayleigh d					18 21						18 36		18 46							19 06				
Southminster d						17 56															18 36			
Burnham-on-Crouch d						18 00															18 40			
Althorne d						18 05															18 45			
North Fambridge d						18 14															19 01			
South Woodham Ferrers d						18 19															19 06			
Battlesbridge d						18 23															19 10			
Wickford 2 d					18 26	18a29					18 41		18 51							19 11	19 17			
Billericay d					18 32						18 47		18 57							19 17	19 23			
Shenfield 3 a					18 40						18 55		19 05							19 25	19 33			
Shenfield 3 d	18 27		18 34	18 38	18 40		18 44		18 51	18 54	18 57	19 04	19 05	19 08	19 13	19 14	19 20		19 24	19 25			19 34	19 38
Brentwood d			18 37				18 47			18 57		19 07				19 17			19 27				19 37	
Harold Wood d			18 42				18 52			19 02		19 12				19 22			19 32				19 42	
Gidea Park 2 d			18 46				18 56			19 06		19 16				19 26			19 36				19 46	
Romford d			18 48				18 58			19 08		19 18				19 28	19 28		19 38				19 48	
Chadwell Heath d			18 52				19 02			19 12		19 22				19 32			19 42				19 52	
Goodmayes d			18 54				19 04			19 14		19 24				19 34			19 44				19 54	
Seven Kings d			18 56				19 06			19 16		19 26				19 36			19 46				19 56	
Ilford 2 d			18 59				19 09			19 19		19 29				19 39			19 49				19 59	
Manor Park d			19 02				19 12			19 22		19 32				19 42			19 52				20 02	
Forest Gate d			19 04				19 14			19 24		19 34				19 44			19 54				20 04	
Maryland d			19 06				19 16			19 26		19 36				19 46			19 56				20 06	
Stratford 7 ⊖ d	18 42		19 09	18 52	18 55		19 19		19 05	19 29	19 11	19 39	19 19	19 22	19 27	19 49	19 36		19 59	19 39			20 09	19 52
London Liverpool Street 15 ⊖ a	18 51		19 17	19 01	19 04		19 27		19 14	19 37	19 20	19 47	19 28	19 31	19 36	19 57	19 45		20 07	19 48			20 17	20 01

	LE	LE 1	LE 1		LE 1	LE	LE	LE 1	LE 1	LE 1	LE	LE 1	LE		LE 1		LE	LE 1	LE	LE 1	LE 1	LE 1	LE 1	
Southend Victoria d		19 10						19 30							19 50					20 10				
Prittlewell d		19 12						19 32							19 52					20 12				
Southend Airport ✈ d		19 15						19 35							19 55					20 15				
Rochford d		19 18						19 38							19 58					20 18				
Hockley d		19 21						19 41							20 01					20 21				
Rayleigh d		19 26						19 46							20 06					20 26				
Southminster d									19 19												20 16			
Burnham-on-Crouch d									19 23												20 20			
Althorne d									19 28												20 25			
North Fambridge d									19 34												20 31			
South Woodham Ferrers d									19 39												20 36			
Battlesbridge d									19 43												20 40			
Wickford 2 d		19 31						19 51	19 55						20 11					20 31	20a46			
Billericay d		19 37						19 57							20 17					20 37				
Shenfield 3 a		19 45						20 05	20 08						20 25					20 45				
Shenfield 3 d	19 44	19 45	19 51			19 54	20 04	20 05		20 08	20 14	20 20	20 24		20 25		20 34	20 38	20 44	20 45		20 47	20 53	
Brentwood d	19 47					19 57	20 07				20 17		20 27				20 37		20 47					
Harold Wood d	19 52					20 02	20 12				20 22		20 32				20 42		20 52					
Gidea Park 2 d	19 56					20 06	20 16				20 26		20 36				20 46		20 56					
Romford d	19 58	19 53				20 08	20 18				20 28	20 28	20 38				20 48		20 58	20 53				
Chadwell Heath d	20 02					20 12	20 22				20 32		20 42				20 52		21 02					
Goodmayes d	20 04					20 14	20 24				20 34		20 44				20 54		21 04					
Seven Kings d	20 06					20 16	20 26				20 36		20 46				20 56		21 06					
Ilford 2 d	20 09					20 19	20 29				20 39		20 49				20 59		21 09					
Manor Park d	20 12					20 22	20 32				20 42		20 52				21 02		21 12					
Forest Gate d	20 14					20 24	20 34				20 44		20 54				21 04		21 14					
Maryland d	20 16					20 26	20 36				20 46		20 56				21 06		21 16					
Stratford 7 ⊖ d	20 19	20 01	20 05		20 14	20 29	20 39	20 19		20 22	20 49	20 36	20 59		20 39		21 09	20 52	21 19	21 01			21 07	
London Liverpool Street 15 ⊖ a	20 27	20 10	20 14		20 23	20 37	20 47	20 28		20 31	20 57	20 45	21 07		20 48		21 17	21 01	21 27	21 10		21 12	21 16	

Table 5

Mondays to Fridays

Southend Victoria, Southminster and Shenfield - London

29 August to 7 September

Network Diagram - see first Page of Table 5

	LE	LE	LE 1	LE 1	LE	LE	LE 1	LE 1	LE 1			LE	LE 1	LE	LE 1	LE 1	LE	LE 1	LE 1		LE 1	LE	LE 1	LE
Southend Victoria d			20 30				20 50								21 10			21 30						21 50
Prittlewell d			20 32				20 52								21 12			21 32						21 52
Southend Airport ✈ d			20 35				20 55								21 15			21 35						21 55
Rochford d			20 38				20 58								21 18			21 38						21 58
Hockley d			20 41				21 01								21 21			21 41						22 01
Rayleigh d			20 46				21 06								21 26			21 46						22 06
Southminster d								20 56											21 36					
Burnham-on-Crouch d								21 00											21 40					
Althorne d								21 05											21 45					
North Fambridge d								21 11											21 51					
South Woodham Ferrers d								21 16											21 56					
Battlesbridge d								21 20											22 00					
Wickford 2 d			20 51				21 11	21a26							21 31			21 51	22a07					22 11
Billericay d			20 57				21 17								21 37			21 57						22 17
Shenfield 3 a			21 05				21 25								21 45			22 05						22 25
Shenfield 3 d	20 54	21 04	21 05	21 08	21 14	21 24	21 25		21 27			21 34	21 38	21 44	21 45	21 51	21 59	22 05			22 08	22 14	22 20	22 25
Brentwood d	20 57	21 07			21 17	21 27						21 37		21 47			22 02					22 17		
Harold Wood d	21 02	21 12			21 22	21 32						21 42		21 52			22 07					22 22		
Gidea Park 2 d	21 06	21 16			21 26	21 36						21 46		21 56			22 11					22 26		
Romford d	21 08	21 18			21 28	21 38						21 48		21 58			22 13					22 28		
Chadwell Heath d	21 12	21 22			21 32	21 42						21 52		22 02			22 17					22 32		
Goodmayes d	21 14	21 24			21 34	21 44						21 54		22 04			22 19					22 34		
Seven Kings d	21 16	21 26			21 36	21 46						21 56		22 06			22 21					22 36		
Ilford 2 d	21 19	21 29			21 39	21 49						21 59		22 09			22 24					22 41		
Manor Park d	21 22	21 32			21 42	21 52						22 02		22 12			22 27					22 44		
Forest Gate d	21 24	21 34			21 44	21 54						22 04		22 14			22 29					22 46		
Maryland d	21 26	21 36			21 46	21 56						22 06		22 16			22 31					22 48		
Stratford 7 ⊖ d	21 29	21 39	21 19	21 22	21 49	21 59	21 39		21 42			22 09	21 52	22 19	22 05	22 13	22 34	22 24			22 28	22 52	22 40	22 44
London Liverpool Street 15 ⊖ a	21 37	21 47	21 28	21 31	21 57	22 07	21 48		21 51			22 20	22 01	22 27	22 13	22 21	22 42	22 32			22 36	23 00	22 48	22 52

	LE	LE	LE 1	LE	LE 1		LE 1	LE 1	LE	LE 1	LE 1	LE	LE	LE 1	LE 1		LE 1	LE	LE	LE	LE 1	LE		
Southend Victoria d					22 10					22 30					22 50						23 10			
Prittlewell d					22 12					22 32					22 52						23 12			
Southend Airport ✈ d					22 15					22 35					22 55						23 15			
Rochford d					22 18					22 38					22 58						23 18			
Hockley d					22 21					22 41					23 01						23 21			
Rayleigh d					22 26					22 46					23 06						23 26			
Southminster d							22 16										22 56							
Burnham-on-Crouch d							22 20										23 00							
Althorne d							22 25										23 05							
North Fambridge d							22 31										23 11							
South Woodham Ferrers d							22 36										23 16							
Battlesbridge d							22 40										23 20							
Wickford 2 d					22 31		22a46			22 51					23 11		23a26				23 31			
Billericay d					22 37					22 57					23 17						23 37			
Shenfield 3 a					22 45					23 05					23 25						23 45			
Shenfield 3 d		22 29	22 38	22 44	22 45			22 51	22 59	23 05	23 08		23 14	23 20	23 25				23 29	23 44	23 45	23 59		
Brentwood d		22 32		22 47					23 02				23 17						23 32	23 47		00 02		
Harold Wood d		22 37		22 52					23 07				23 22						23 37	23 52		00 07		
Gidea Park 2 d		22 41		22 56					23 11				23 26						23 41	23 56		00 11		
Romford d		22 43		22 58					23 13				23 28						23 43	23 58		00 13		
Chadwell Heath d		22 47		23 02					23 17				23 32						23 47	00 02		00 17		
Goodmayes d		22 49		23 04					23 19				23 34						23 49	00 04		00 19		
Seven Kings d		22 51		23 06					23 21				23 36						23 51	00 06		00 21		
Ilford 2 d		22 54		23 09					23 24				23 39						23 54	00 09		00 24		
Manor Park d		22 57		23 12					23 27				23 42						23 57	00 12		00 27		
Forest Gate d		22 59		23 14					23 29				23 45						23 59	00 14		00 29		
Maryland d		23 01		23 16					23 31				23 47						00 01	00 16				
Stratford 7 ⊖ d	22 48	23 04	22 58	23 19	23 08			23 12	23 36	23 24	23 28	23 32	23 50	23 40	23 44			23 54	00 04	00 20	00 08	00 40		
London Liverpool Street 15 ⊖ a	22 58	23 12	23 06	23 27	23 16			23 20	23 44	23 32	23 36	23 40	23 58	23 48	23 52			00 02	00 12	00 28	00 16	00 48		

Southend Victoria, Southminster and Shenfield - London

Network Diagram - see first Page of Table 5

	LE	LE	LE		LE	LE	LE	LE	LE		LE	LE	LE	LE	CC	LE	LE	LE	LE		LE	LE	LE	LE
						FO		FO				FO			MX									
	◇1	◇1	1				◇1	1	◇1					1		1	1							
	A	B	C		D	E	D	F	G		G	F	C	C		C	D	D	C		C	C	C	C
Southend Victoria d														23p10										
Prittlewell d														23p12										
Southend Airport ✈ d														23p15										
Rochford d														23p18										
Hockley d														23p21										
Rayleigh d														23p26										
Southminster d								22p56									23p06							
Burnham-on-Crouch d								23p00									23p10							
Althorne d								23p05									23p15							
North Fambridge d								23p11									23p21							
South Woodham Ferrers d								23p16									23p26							
Battlesbridge d								23p20									23p30							
Wickford 2 d								23p26						23p31			23p36							
Billericay d								23p32						23p37			23p42							
Shenfield 3 a								23p39						23p45			23p49							
Shenfield 3 d					23p27	23p29	23p38	23p39			23p43	23p44	23p44	23p45			23p52	23p54			23p59	00 14		00 29
Brentwood d					23p30	23p32					23p46	23p47	23p47					23p57			00 02	00 17		00 32
Harold Wood d					23p35	23p37					23p51	23p52	23p52					00 02			00 07	00 22		00 37
Gidea Park 2 d					23p39	23p41					23p55	23p56	23p56					00 06			00 11	00 26		00 41
Romford d					23p41	23p43		23p47			23p57	23p58	23p58				00 03	00 08			00 13	00 28		00 43
Chadwell Heath d					23p45	23p47					00 01	00 02	00 02					00 12			00 17	00 32		00 47
Goodmayes d					23p47	23p49					00 03	00 04	00 04					00 14			00 19	00 34		00 49
Seven Kings d					23p49	23p51					00 05	00 06	00 06					00 16			00 21	00 36		00 51
Ilford 2 d					23p52	23p54					00 08	00 09	00 09					00 19			00 24	00 39		00 54
Manor Park d					23p55	23p57					00 10	00 12	00 12					00 22			00 27	00 42		00 57
Forest Gate d					23p57	23p59					00 12	00 14	00 14					00 24			00 29	00 44		00 59
Maryland d					23p59	00 01					00 14	00 16	00 16					00 26						
Stratford 7 ⊖ d	23b52	23b52	23p54		00 02	00 04	00s04	23p56	23b57		00 16	00 19	00 20	00 08	00 09	00 12	00 13	00 29	00 30		00 40	00 50	01 00	01 10
London Liverpool Street 15 ⊖ a	00 02	00 02	00 02		00 11	00 12	00 14	00 05	00 08		00 26	00 27	00 28	00 16	00 20	00 20	00 22	00 38	00 38		00 48	00 58	01 08	01 18

	LE	LE	LE	LE	LE		CC	LE	LE	LE	LE	LE	LE	LE	LE		LE	LE		LE	LE	LE	LE	LE
										1			1		1		1	1					1	
	C	C	C	C																				
Southend Victoria d					04 00				04 30				05 00				05 20						05 40	
Prittlewell d					04 02				04 32				05 02				05 22						05 42	
Southend Airport ✈ d					04 05				04 35				05 05				05 25						05 45	
Rochford d					04 08				04 38				05 08				05 28						05 48	
Hockley d					04 12				04 42				05 11				05 31						05 51	
Rayleigh d					04 16				04 46				05 16				05 36						05 56	
Southminster d																		05 26						
Burnham-on-Crouch d																		05 30						
Althorne d																		05 35						
North Fambridge d																		05 41						
South Woodham Ferrers d																		05 46						
Battlesbridge d																		05 50						
Wickford 2 d					04 21				04 51				05 21				05 41	05a56					06 01	
Billericay d					04 28				04 58				05 27				05 47						06 07	
Shenfield 3 a					04 39				05 09				05 35				05 55						06 15	
Shenfield 3 d	00 44				04 39				05 09	05 24		05 29	05 35	05 44	05 53		05 55				06 04	06 14	06 15	06 24
Brentwood d	00 47				04 42				05 12			05 32		05 47							06 07	06 17		06 27
Harold Wood d	00 52				04 47				05 17			05 37		05 52							06 12	06 22		06 32
Gidea Park 2 d	00 56				04 51				05 21	05 31		05 41		05 56						06 06	06 16	06 26		06 36
Romford d	00 58				04 53				05 23			05 43		05 58						06 08	06 18	06 28		06 38
Chadwell Heath d	01 02				04 57				05 27			05 47		06 02						06 12	06 22	06 32		06 42
Goodmayes d	01 04				04 59				05 29			05 49		06 04						06 14	06 24	06 34		06 44
Seven Kings d	01 06				05 01				05 31	05 36		05 51		06 06						06 16	06 26	06 36		06 46
Ilford 2 d	01 09				05 04			05 09	05 34		05 39	05 54		06 09						06 19	06 29	06 39		06 49
Manor Park d	01 12							05 11			05 41	05 57		06 12						06 22	06 32	06 42		06 52
Forest Gate d	01 14							05 14			05 44	05 59		06 14						06 24	06 34	06 44		06 54
Maryland d								05 16			05 46	06 01		06 16						06 26	06 36	06 46		06 56
Stratford 7 ⊖ d	01 20	01 30	01 40	01 50	05 10		05 14	05 18	05 40	05 42	05 48	06 04	05 49	06 19	06 07		06 10			06 29	06 39	06 49	06 29	06 59
London Liverpool Street 15 ⊖ a	01 28	01 38	01 48	01 58	05 18		05 27	05 26	05 48	05 55	05 56	06 12	05 58	06 27	06 16		06 19			06 37	06 47	06 57	06 40	07 07

A from 11 September until 14 September
B FO from 21 September
C 10 September
D TWThO from 18 September
E also from 10 September until 13 September
F also from 11 September until 13 September
G MO from 17 September
b Previous night, stops to set down only

Table 5

Mondays to Fridays
from 10 September

Southend Victoria, Southminster and Shenfield - London

Network Diagram - see first Page of Table 5

	LE			LE	LE	LE	LE	LE	LE	LE	LE			LE	LE	LE	LE	LE	LE		LE		LE	LE
	1				1	1			1	1	1								1		1			
Southend Victoria d					06 00				06 11							06 26					06 40			
Prittlewell d					06 02				06 13							06 28					06 42			
Southend Airport ✈ d					06 05				06 16							06 31					06 45			
Rochford d					06 08				06 19							06 34					06 48			
Hockley d					06 11				06 22							06 38					06 51			
Rayleigh d					06 16				06 27							06 42					06 56			
Southminster d											06 09													
Burnham-on-Crouch d											06 13													
Althorne d											06 18													
North Fambridge d											06 24													
South Woodham Ferrers d											06 30													
Battlesbridge d											06 34													
Wickford 2 d					06 21				06 32		06 40					06 47					07 01			
Billericay d					06 27				06 39		06 46					06 54					07 08			
Shenfield 3 a					06 35				06 45		06 52					07 01					07 14			
Shenfield 3 d	06 25			06 34	06 35	06 41		06 44	06 45	06 50	06 53				06 54	07 01		07 04	07 08		07 14			07 14
Brentwood d				06 37				06 47							06 57			07 07						07 17
Harold Wood d				06 42				06 52							07 02			07 12						07 22
Gidea Park 2 d				06 45			06 49	06 55						06 59	07 05		07 09	07 15					07 19	07 25
Romford d				06 48			06 51	06 58						07 01	07 08		07 11	07 18					07 21	07 28
Chadwell Heath d				06 52			06 55	07 02						07 05	07 12		07 15	07 22					07 25	07 32
Goodmayes d							06 57							07 07			07 17						07 27	07 34
Seven Kings d							06 59							07 09			07 19						07 29	07 36
Ilford 2 d				06 57			07 02	07 07						07 12	07 17		07 22	07 27					07 32	07 39
Manor Park d							07 05							07 15			07 25						07 35	
Forest Gate d							07 07							07 17			07 27						07 37	
Maryland d							07 09							07 19			07 29						07 39	
Stratford 7 ⊖ d	06 39			07 03	06 49	06s57	07 12	07 15	07s02	07s06	07s09			07 22	07 25	07s19	07 32	07 35	07s23		07s31		07 42	07 45
London Liverpool Street 15 ⊖ a	06 48			07 13	06 58	07 09	07 22	07 25	07 13	07 18	07 21			07 32	07 35	07 30	07 42	07 45	07 35		07 42		07 52	07 55

	LE		LE	LE	LE	LE	LE		LE	LE	LE	LE	LE		LE	LE	LE		LE		LE	LE	LE	LE
	1		1	1			1		1			1	1				1		1					
Southend Victoria d			06 50						07 03								07 13							07 18
Prittlewell d			06 52						07 05								07 15							07 20
Southend Airport ✈ d			06 55						07 08								07 18							07 23
Rochford d			06 58						07 11								07 21							07 26
Hockley d			07 01						07 14								07 24							07 30
Rayleigh d			07 06						07 19								07 29							07 34
Southminster d							06 48																	
Burnham-on-Crouch d							06 52																	
Althorne d							06 57																	
North Fambridge d							07 04																	
South Woodham Ferrers d							07 10																	
Battlesbridge d							07 14																	
Wickford 2 d			07 11				07 19		07 24								07 34							07 39
Billericay d			07 18				07 26		07 31								07 41							07 46
Shenfield 3 a			07 24				07 32										07 47							07 53
Shenfield 3 d	07 19		07 24			07 24	07 32				07 34	07 38	07 41			07 44	07 47		07 50			07 50		07 54
Brentwood d						07 27					07 37					07 47						07 53		07 57
Harold Wood d						07 32					07 42					07 52						07 58		08 02
Gidea Park 2 d					07 29	07 35				07 39	07 45				07 49	07 55					07 59	08 02	08 05	08 09
Romford d					07 31	07 38				07 41	07 48				07 51	07 58					08 01	08 04	08 07	08 11
Chadwell Heath d					07 35	07 42				07 45	07 52				07 55	08 02					08 05	08 08	08 11	08 15
Goodmayes d					07 37	07 44				07 47	07 54				07 57	08 04					08 07	08 10	08 13	08 17
Seven Kings d					07 39	07 46				07 49	07 56				07 59	08 06					08 09	08 12	08 15	08 19
Ilford 2 d					07 42	07 49				07 52	07 59				08 02	08 09					08 12	08 15	08 18	08 22
Manor Park d					07 45					07 55					08 05								08 21	
Forest Gate d					07 47					07 57					08 07								08 23	
Maryland d					07 49					07 59					08 09								08 25	
Stratford 7 ⊖ d	07s35		07s41	07 44	07 52	07 55	07 50		07s52	08 02	08 05	07s55	07s58		08 12	08 15	08s04		08s07		08 18	08 21	08 28	08 31
London Liverpool Street 15 ⊖ a	07 46		07 52	07 56	08 02	08 05	08 01		08 03	08 12	08 15	08 07	08 09		08 22	08 25	08 15		08 19		08 28	08 31	08 38	08 41

Southend Victoria, Southminster and Shenfield - London

Network Diagram - see first Page of Table 5

		LE ■	LE	LE ■			LE ■	LE ■		LE	LE	LE	LE ■	LE ■		LE ■	LE	LE	LE	LE ■	LE ■	LE ■			
Southend Victoria	d	07 23					07 32						07 42								07 52				
Prittlewell	d	07 25					07 34						07 44								07 54				
Southend Airport ✈	d	07 28					07 37						07 47								07 57				
Rochford	d	07 31					07 40						07 50								08 00				
Hockley	d	07 34					07 43						07 53								08 03				
Rayleigh	d	07 39					07 48						07 58								08 08				
Southminster	d													07 37											
Burnham-on-Crouch	d													07 41											
Althorne	d													07 46											
North Fambridge	d													07 52											
South Woodham Ferrers	d													07 59											
Battlesbridge	d																								
Wickford 2	d	07 44					07 53						08 03	08 07							08 13				
Billericay	d	07 51					08 00						08 10	08 14							08 20				
Shenfield 3	a	07 57					08 06						08 16								08 26				
Shenfield 3	d	07 57	08 00	08 01			08 06	08 09				08 10	08 16			08 21			08 22	08 24	08 26	08 29			
Brentwood	d		08 03									08 13							08 25						
Harold Wood	d		08 08									08 18							08 30						
Gidea Park 2	d		08 12							08 15	08 19	08 22						08 29	08 34						
Romford	d		08 14							08 17	08 21	08 24						08 31	08 36						
Chadwell Heath	d		08 18							08 21	08 25	08 28						08 35	08 40						
Goodmayes	d		08 20							08 23	08 27	08 30						08 37	08 42						
Seven Kings	d		08 22							08 25	08 29	08 32						08 39	08 44						
Ilford 2	d		08 25							08 28	08 32	08 35					08 38	08 42	08 47						
Manor Park	d									08 31							08 41								
Forest Gate	d									08 33							08 43								
Maryland	d									08 35							08 45								
Stratford 7 ⊖	d	08s15	08 34	08s18			08s23	08s25		08 38	08 41	08 44	08s33	08s35		08s38	08 48	08 51	08 54	08s41	08s43	08s45			
London Liverpool Street 15 ⊖	a	08 26	08 43	08 30			08 36	08 38		08 48	08 51	08 53	08 46	08 48		08 50	08 58	09 01	09 03	08 54	08 56	08 58			

		LE	LE	LE	LE ■	LE ■	LE	LE	LE	LE ■		LE ■	LE	LE ■	LE ■	LE ■			LE	LE		LE ■	LE	LE ■	LE ■
Southend Victoria	d				08 03					08 12						08 30									08 52
Prittlewell	d				08 05					08 14						08 32									08 54
Southend Airport ✈	d				08 08					08 17						08 35									08 57
Rochford	d				08 11					08 20						08 38									09 00
Hockley	d				08 14					08 23						08 41									09 03
Rayleigh	d				08 19					08 28						08 46									09 08
Southminster	d														08 16										
Burnham-on-Crouch	d														08 20										
Althorne	d														08 25										
North Fambridge	d														08 31										
South Woodham Ferrers	d														08 37										
Battlesbridge	d														08 41										
Wickford 2	d				08 24					08 33					08 46	08 51									09 13
Billericay	d				08 31					08 40					08 53	08 58									09 20
Shenfield 3	a				08 37					08 46					08 59	09 04									09 27
Shenfield 3	d			08 32	08 37	08 42			08 44	08 46		08 51	08 54	08 55	08 59	09 04			09 04	09 14		09 21	09 24	09 25	09 27
Brentwood	d			08 35					08 47				08 57						09 07	09 17			09 27		
Harold Wood	d			08 40					08 52				09 02						09 12	09 22			09 32		
Gidea Park 2	d		08 41	08 44				08 51	08 56				09 06						09 16	09 26			09 36		
Romford	d		08 43	08 46				08 53	08 58	08 55			09 08						09 18	09 28			09 38		
Chadwell Heath	d		08 47	08 50				08 57	09 02				09 12						09 22	09 32			09 42		
Goodmayes	d		08 49	08 52				08 59	09 04				09 14						09 24	09 34			09 44		
Seven Kings	d		08 51	08 54				09 01	09 06				09 16						09 26	09 36			09 46		
Ilford 2	d	08 50	08 54	08 57			09 00	09 04	09 09				09 19						09 29	09 39			09 49		
Manor Park	d	08 53					09 03		09 12				09 22						09 32	09 42			09 52		
Forest Gate	d	08 55					09 05		09 14				09 24						09 34	09 44			09 54		
Maryland	d	08 57					09 07		09 16				09 26						09 36	09 46			09 56		
Stratford 7 ⊖	d	09 00	09 03	09 06	08s56	08s59	09 10	09 13	09 19	09s05		09s08	09 29		09s16	09s22			09 39	09 49		09s37	09 59	09s41	09s43
London Liverpool Street 15 ⊖	a	09 10	09 13	09 14	09 08	09 11	09 20	09 23	09 27	09 16		09 19	09 37	09 21	09 29	09 33			09 47	09 58		09 49	10 07	09 53	09 55

Southend Victoria, Southminster and Shenfield - London

Network Diagram - see first Page of Table 5

		LE ■	LE	LE ■	LE	LE ■		LE ■	LE	LE	LE ■	LE ■	LE ■	LE	LE ■	LE		LE ■		LE	LE ■	LE	LE ■	LE ■	LE ■
Southend Victoria	d					09 10					09 30							09 50					10 10		
Prittlewell	d					09 12					09 32							09 52					10 12		
Southend Airport ✈	d					09 15					09 35							09 55					10 15		
Rochford	d					09 18					09 38							09 58					10 18		
Hockley	d					09 21					09 41							10 01					10 21		
Rayleigh	d					09 26					09 46							10 06					10 26		
Southminster	d	08 56										09 36												10 16	
Burnham-on-Crouch	d	09 00										09 40												10 20	
Althorne	d	09 05										09 45												10 25	
North Fambridge	d	09 11										09 51												10 31	
South Woodham Ferrers	d	09 16										09 56												10 36	
Battlesbridge	d	09 20										10 00												10 40	
Wickford 2	d	09a26				09 31					09 51	10a06						10 11					10 31	10a46	
Billericay	d					09 37					09 57							10 17					10 37		
Shenfield 3	a					09 45					10 05							10 25					10 45		
Shenfield 3	d		09 34	09 38	09 44	09 45		09 51	09 54	10 04	10 05		10 08	10 14	10 18	10 24		10 25		10 34	10 38	10 44	10 45		10 51
Brentwood	d		09 37		09 47				09 57	10 07				10 17		10 27				10 37		10 47			
Harold Wood	d		09 42		09 52				10 02	10 12				10 22		10 32				10 42		10 52			
Gidea Park 2	d		09 46		09 56				10 06	10 16				10 26		10 36				10 46		10 56			
Romford	d		09 48		09 58	09 53			10 08	10 18				10 28	10 26	10 38				10 48		10 58	10 53		
Chadwell Heath	d		09 52		10 02				10 12	10 22				10 32		10 42				10 52		11 02			
Goodmayes	d		09 54		10 04				10 14	10 24				10 34		10 44				10 54		11 04			
Seven Kings	d		09 56		10 06				10 16	10 26				10 36		10 46				10 56		11 06			
Ilford 2	d		09 59		10 09				10 19	10 29				10 39		10 49				10 59		11 09			
Manor Park	d		10 02		10 12				10 22	10 32				10 42		10 52				11 02		11 12			
Forest Gate	d		10 04		10 14				10 24	10 34				10 44		10 54				11 04		11 14			
Maryland	d		10 06		10 16				10 26	10 36				10 46		10 56				11 06		11 16			
Stratford 7 ⊖	d		10 09	09 52	10 19	10 01		10 05	10 29	10 39	10 19		10 22	10 49	10 34	10 59		10 39		11 09	10 52	11 19	11 01		11 05
London Liverpool Street 15 ⊖	a		10 17	10 01	10 27	10 10		10 14	10 37	10 47	10 28		10 31	10 57	10 43	11 07		10 48		11 17	11 01	11 27	11 10		11 14

		LE		LE	LE ■	LE ■	LE	LE ■	LE	LE ■	LE ■			LE	LE ■	LE	LE ■	LE ■	LE	LE	LE ■	LE ■		LE ■	LE
Southend Victoria	d				10 30					10 50							11 10				11 30				
Prittlewell	d				10 32					10 52							11 12				11 32				
Southend Airport ✈	d				10 35					10 55							11 15				11 35				
Rochford	d				10 38					10 58							11 18				11 38				
Hockley	d				10 41					11 01							11 21				11 41				
Rayleigh	d				10 46					11 06							11 26				11 46				
Southminster	d										10 56											11 36			
Burnham-on-Crouch	d										11 00											11 40			
Althorne	d										11 05											11 45			
North Fambridge	d										11 11											11 51			
South Woodham Ferrers	d										11 16											11 56			
Battlesbridge	d										11 20											12 00			
Wickford 2	d				10 51					11 11	11a26						11 31				11 51	12a06			
Billericay	d				10 57					11 17							11 37				11 57				
Shenfield 3	a				11 05					11 25							11 45				12 05				
Shenfield 3	d	10 54		11 04	11 05	11 08	11 14	11 20	11 24	11 25				11 34	11 38	11 44	11 45	11 51	11 54	12 04	12 05			12 08	12 14
Brentwood	d	10 57		11 07			11 17		11 27					11 37		11 47			11 57	12 07					12 17
Harold Wood	d	11 02		11 12			11 22		11 32					11 42		11 52			12 02	12 12					12 22
Gidea Park 2	d	11 06		11 16			11 26		11 36					11 46		11 56			12 06	12 16					12 26
Romford	d	11 08		11 18			11 28	11 28	11 38					11 48		11 58	11 53		12 08	12 18					12 28
Chadwell Heath	d	11 12		11 22			11 32		11 42					11 52		12 02			12 12	12 22					12 32
Goodmayes	d	11 14		11 24			11 34		11 44					11 54		12 04			12 14	12 24					12 34
Seven Kings	d	11 16		11 26			11 36		11 46					11 56		12 06			12 16	12 26					12 36
Ilford 2	d	11 19		11 29			11 39		11 49					11 59		12 09			12 19	12 29					12 39
Manor Park	d	11 22		11 32			11 42		11 52					12 02		12 12			12 22	12 32					12 42
Forest Gate	d	11 24		11 34			11 44		11 54					12 04		12 14			12 24	12 34					12 44
Maryland	d	11 26		11 36			11 46		11 56					12 06		12 16			12 26	12 36					12 46
Stratford 7 ⊖	d	11 29		11 39	11 19	11 22	11 49	11 36	11 59	11 39				12 09	11 52	12 19	12 01	12 05	12 29	12 39	12 19			12 22	12 49
London Liverpool Street 15 ⊖	a	11 37		11 47	11 28	11 31	11 57	11 45	12 07	11 48				12 17	12 01	12 27	12 10	12 14	12 37	12 47	12 28			12 31	12 57

Southend Victoria, Southminster and Shenfield - London

Network Diagram - see first Page of Table 5

		LE 1	LE	LE 1	LE	LE 1	LE	LE 1	LE 1	LE 1	LE	LE	LE 1	LE 1	LE	LE 1	LE	LE 1	LE 1	LE	LE 1
Southend Victoria	d			11 50				12 10					12 30					12 50			
Prittlewell	d			11 52				12 12					12 32					12 52			
Southend Airport ✈	d			11 55				12 15					12 35					12 55			
Rochford	d			11 58				12 18					12 38					12 58			
Hockley	d			12 01				12 21					12 41					13 01			
Rayleigh	d			12 06				12 26					12 46					13 06			
Southminster	d								12 16										12 56		
Burnham-on-Crouch	d								12 20										13 00		
Althorne	d								12 25										13 05		
North Fambridge	d								12 31										13 11		
South Woodham Ferrers	d								12 36										13 16		
Battlesbridge	d								12 40										13 20		
Wickford 2	d			12 11				12 31	12a46				12 51					13 11	13a26		
Billericay	d			12 17				12 37					12 57					13 17			
Shenfield 3	a			12 25				12 45					13 05					13 25			
Shenfield 3	d	12 20	12 24	12 25	12 34	12 38	12 44	12 45		12 51	12 54	13 04	13 05	13 08	13 14	13 20	13 24	13 25		13 34	13 38
Brentwood	d		12 27		12 37		12 47				12 57	13 07			13 17		13 27			13 37	
Harold Wood	d		12 32		12 42		12 52				13 02	13 12			13 22		13 32			13 42	
Gidea Park 2	d		12 36		12 46		12 56				13 06	13 16			13 26		13 36			13 46	
Romford	d	12 28	12 38		12 48		12 58	12 53			13 08	13 18			13 28	13 28	13 38			13 48	
Chadwell Heath	d		12 42		12 52		13 02				13 12	13 22			13 32		13 42			13 52	
Goodmayes	d		12 44		12 54		13 04				13 14	13 24			13 34		13 44			13 54	
Seven Kings	d		12 46		12 56		13 06				13 16	13 26			13 36		13 46			13 56	
Ilford 2	d		12 49		12 59		13 09				13 19	13 29			13 39		13 49			13 59	
Manor Park	d		12 52		13 02		13 12				13 22	13 32			13 42		13 52			14 02	
Forest Gate	d		12 54		13 04		13 14				13 24	13 34			13 44		13 54			14 04	
Maryland	d		12 56		13 06		13 16				13 26	13 36			13 46		13 56			14 06	
Stratford 7 ⊖	d	12 36	12 59	12 39	13 09	12 52	13 19	13 01		13 05	13 29	13 39	13 19	13 22	13 49	13 36	13 59	13 39		14 09	13 52
London Liverpool Street 15 ⊖	a	12 45	13 07	12 48	13 17	13 01	13 27	13 10		13 14	13 37	13 47	13 28	13 31	13 57	13 45	14 07	13 48		14 17	14 01

		LE	LE 1	LE 1	LE	LE	LE 1	LE 1	LE 1	LE	LE 1	LE	LE 1	LE	LE 1	LE	LE 1	LE 1	LE 1	LE	LE
Southend Victoria	d		13 10				13 30						13 50				14 10				
Prittlewell	d		13 12				13 32						13 52				14 12				
Southend Airport ✈	d		13 15				13 35						13 55				14 15				
Rochford	d		13 18				13 38						13 58				14 18				
Hockley	d		13 21				13 41						14 01				14 21				
Rayleigh	d		13 26				13 46						14 06				14 26				
Southminster	d							13 36										14 16			
Burnham-on-Crouch	d							13 40										14 20			
Althorne	d							13 45										14 25			
North Fambridge	d							13 51										14 31			
South Woodham Ferrers	d							13 56										14 36			
Battlesbridge	d							14 00										14 40			
Wickford 2	d		13 31				13 51	14a06					14 11				14 31	14a46			
Billericay	d		13 37				13 57						14 17				14 37				
Shenfield 3	a		13 45				14 05						14 25				14 45				
Shenfield 3	d	13 44	13 45	13 51	13 54	14 04	14 05		14 08	14 14	14 20	14 24	14 25	14 34	14 38	14 44	14 45		14 51	14 54	15 04
Brentwood	d	13 47			13 57	14 07				14 17		14 27		14 37		14 47				14 57	15 07
Harold Wood	d	13 52			14 02	14 12				14 22		14 32		14 42		14 52				15 02	15 12
Gidea Park 2	d	13 56			14 06	14 16				14 26		14 36		14 46		14 56				15 06	15 16
Romford	d	13 58	13 53		14 08	14 18				14 28	14 28	14 38		14 48		14 58	14 53			15 08	15 18
Chadwell Heath	d	14 02			14 12	14 22				14 32		14 42		14 52		15 02				15 12	15 22
Goodmayes	d	14 04			14 14	14 24				14 34		14 44		14 54		15 04				15 14	15 24
Seven Kings	d	14 06			14 16	14 26				14 36		14 46		14 56		15 06				15 16	15 26
Ilford 2	d	14 09			14 19	14 29				14 39		14 49		14 59		15 09				15 19	15 29
Manor Park	d	14 12			14 22	14 32				14 42		14 52		15 02		15 12				15 22	15 32
Forest Gate	d	14 14			14 24	14 34				14 44		14 54		15 04		15 14				15 24	15 34
Maryland	d	14 16			14 26	14 36				14 46		14 56		15 06		15 16				15 26	15 36
Stratford 7 ⊖	d	14 19	14 01	14 05	14 29	14 39	14 19		14 22	14 49	14 36	14 59	14 39	15 09	14 52	15 19	15 01		15 05	15 29	15 39
London Liverpool Street 15 ⊖	a	14 27	14 10	14 14	14 37	14 47	14 28		14 31	14 57	14 45	15 07	14 48	15 17	15 01	15 27	15 10		15 15	15 37	15 47

Southend Victoria, Southminster and Shenfield - London

Network Diagram - see first Page of Table 5

		LE 1	LE 1	LE	LE 1	LE	LE 1	LE 1	LE	LE 1	LE	LE 1	LE 1	LE	LE	LE 1	LE 1	LE 1	LE	LE 1	LE	LE 1
Southend Victoria	d	14 30					14 50					15 10				15 30						15 50
Prittlewell	d	14 32					14 52					15 12				15 32						15 52
Southend Airport ✈	d	14 35					14 55					15 15				15 35						15 55
Rochford	d	14 38					14 58					15 18				15 38						15 58
Hockley	d	14 41					15 01					15 21				15 41						16 01
Rayleigh	d	14 46					15 06					15 26				15 46						16 06
Southminster	d							14 56									15 36					
Burnham-on-Crouch	d							15 00									15 40					
Althorne	d							15 05									15 45					
North Fambridge	d							15 11									15 51					
South Woodham Ferrers	d							15 16									15 56					
Battlesbridge	d							15 20									16 00					
Wickford 2	d	14 51					15 11	15a26				15 31				15 51	16a06					16 11
Billericay	d	14 57					15 17					15 37				15 57						16 17
Shenfield 3	a	15 05					15 25					15 45				16 05						16 25
Shenfield 3	d	15 05	15 08	15 14	15 20	15 24	15 25		15 34	15 38	15 44	15 45	15 51	15 54	16 04	16 05		16 08	16 14	16 20	16 24	16 25
Brentwood	d			15 17		15 27			15 37		15 47			15 57	16 07				16 17		16 27	
Harold Wood	d			15 22		15 32			15 42		15 52			16 02	16 12				16 22		16 32	
Gidea Park 2	d			15 26		15 36			15 46		15 56			16 06	16 16				16 26		16 35	
Romford	d			15 28	15 28	15 38			15 48		15 58	15 53		16 08	16 18				16 28		16 38	
Chadwell Heath	d			15 32		15 42			15 52		16 02			16 12	16 22				16 32		16 42	
Goodmayes	d			15 34		15 44			15 54		16 04			16 14	16 24				16 34		16 44	
Seven Kings	d			15 36		15 46			15 56		16 06			16 16	16 26				16 36		16 46	
Ilford 2	d			15 39		15 49			15 59		16 09			16 19	16 29				16 39		16 49	
Manor Park	d			15 42		15 52			16 02		16 12			16 22	16 32				16 42		16 52	
Forest Gate	d			15 44		15 54			16 04		16 14			16 24	16 34				16 44		16 54	
Maryland	d			15 46		15 56			16 06		16 16			16 26	16 36				16 46		16 56	
Stratford 7 ⊖	d	15 19	15 22	15 49	15 36	15 59	15 39		16 09	15 52	16 19	16 01	16 05	16 29	16 39	16 19		16 22	16 49	16 34	16 59	16 39
London Liverpool Street 15 ⊖	a	15 28	15 33	15 57	15 45	16 07	15 48		16 17	16 01	16 27	16 11	16 14	16 37	16 47	16 28		16 31	16 57	16 44	17 07	16 48

		LE	LE 1	LE	LE 1	LE 1	LE 1	LE	LE	LE 1	LE 1	LE	LE 1	LE	LE	LE 1	LE 1	LE	LE	LE 1	LE
Southend Victoria	d				16 10					16 30						16 50					
Prittlewell	d				16 12					16 32						16 52					
Southend Airport ✈	d				16 15					16 35						16 55					
Rochford	d				16 18					16 38						16 58					
Hockley	d				16 21					16 41						17 01					
Rayleigh	d				16 26					16 46						17 06					
Southminster	d					16 14															
Burnham-on-Crouch	d					16 18															
Althorne	d					16 23															
North Fambridge	d					16 29															
South Woodham Ferrers	d					16 34															
Battlesbridge	d					16 38															
Wickford 2	d				16 31	16a44				16 51						17 11					
Billericay	d				16 37					16 57						17 17					
Shenfield 3	a				16 45					17 05						17 25					
Shenfield 3	d	16 34	16 38	16 44	16 45		16 51	16 54	17 04	17 05	17 08	17 14	17 22		17 24	17 25	17 28		17 34	17 38	
Brentwood	d	16 37		16 47				16 57	17 07			17 17			17 27				17 37		
Harold Wood	d	16 42		16 52				17 02	17 12			17 22			17 32				17 42		
Gidea Park 2	d	16 46		16 56				17 06	17 16			17 26		17 32	17 36			17 42	17 46		17 52
Romford	d	16 48		16 58				17 08	17 18			17 28		17 34	17 38			17 44	17 48		17 54
Chadwell Heath	d	16 52		17 02				17 12	17 22			17 32			17 42				17 52		
Goodmayes	d	16 54		17 04				17 14	17 24			17 34			17 44				17 54		
Seven Kings	d	16 56		17 06				17 16	17 26			17 36			17 46				17 56		
Ilford 2	d	16 59		17 09				17 19	17 29			17 39		17 42	17 49			17 52	17 59		18 02
Manor Park	d	17 02		17 12				17 22	17 32					17 45				17 55			18 05
Forest Gate	d	17 04		17 14				17 24	17 34					17 47				17 57			18 07
Maryland	d	17 06		17 16				17 26	17 36					17 49				17 59			18 09
Stratford 7 ⊖	d	17 09	16 52	17 19	16 59		17 05	17 29	17 39	17 19	17 22	17 45	17 36	17 52	17 55	17 39	17 42	18 02	18 05	17 52	18 12
London Liverpool Street 15 ⊖	a	17 17	17 03	17 27	17 13		17 16	17 37	17 47	17 29	17 34	17 53	17 46	18 00	18 03	17 49	17 53	18 10	18 13	18 01	18 20

from 10 September

Southend Victoria, Southminster and Shenfield - London

Network Diagram - see first Page of Table 5

		LE	LE 1	LE 1	LE 1	LE	LE	LE 1	LE	LE	LE 1	LE 1	LE	LE	LE 1	LE	LE	LE 1	LE 1	LE	LE 1
Southend Victoria	d		17 10					17 25				17 35						17 50			
Prittlewell	d		17 12					17 27				17 37						17 52			
Southend Airport ✈	d		17 15					17 30				17 40						17 55			
Rochford	d		17 18					17 33				17 43						17 58			
Hockley	d		17 21					17 36				17 46						18 01			
Rayleigh	d		17 26					17 41				17 51						18 06			
Southminster	d			17 06																	
Burnham-on-Crouch	d			17 10																	
Althorne	d			17 15																	
North Fambridge	d			17 21																	
South Woodham Ferrers	d			17 26																	
Battlesbridge	d			17 30																	
Wickford 2	d		17 31	17 37				17 46				17 56						18 11			
Billericay	d		17 37					17 52				18 02						18 17			
Shenfield 3	a		17 45	17 48				18 00				18 10						18 25			
Shenfield 3	d	17 44	17 45	17 49	17 51		17 54	18 00		18 04	18 08	18 10		18 14	18 20		18 24	18 25	18 27	18 34	18 38
Brentwood	d	17 47					17 57			18 07				18 17			18 27			18 37	
Harold Wood	d	17 52					18 02			18 12				18 22			18 32			18 42	
Gidea Park 2	d	17 56				18 02	18 06		18 12	18 16			18 22	18 26		18 32	18 36			18 46	
Romford	d	17 58				18 04	18 08		18 14	18 18			18 24	18 28	18 28	18 34	18 38			18 48	
Chadwell Heath	d	18 02					18 12			18 22				18 32			18 42			19 52	
Goodmayes	d	18 04					18 14			18 24				18 34			18 44			18 54	
Seven Kings	d	18 06					18 16			18 26				18 36			18 46			18 56	
Ilford 2	d	18 09				18 12	18 19		18 22	18 29			18 32	18 39		18 42	18 49			18 59	
Manor Park	d					18 15			18 25				18 35			18 45	18 52			19 02	
Forest Gate	d					18 17			18 27				18 37			18 47	18 54			19 04	
Maryland	d					18 19			18 29				18 39			18 49	18 56			19 06	
Stratford 7 ⊖	d	18 15	17 59	18 08	18 06	18 22	18 25	18 14	18 32	18 35	18 22	18 25	18 42	18 45	18 36	18 52	18 59	18 39	18 42	19 09	18 52
London Liverpool Street 15 ⊖	a	18 23	18 11	18 17	18 15	18 30	18 33	18 24	18 40	18 43	18 31	18 35	18 50	18 53	18 45	19 00	19 07	18 48	18 51	19 17	19 01

		LE 1	LE 1	LE	LE 1	LE	LE 1	LE	LE 1	LE 1	LE 1	LE	LE 1	LE	LE 1	LE 1	LE	LE 1	LE	LE 1	LE 1	LE 1
Southend Victoria	d	18 05					18 20		18 30						18 50					19 10		
Prittlewell	d	18 07					18 22		18 32						18 52					19 12		
Southend Airport ✈	d	18 10					18 25		18 35						18 55					19 15		
Rochford	d	18 13					18 28		18 38						18 58					19 18		
Hockley	d	18 16					18 31		18 41						19 01					19 21		
Rayleigh	d	18 21					18 36		18 46						19 06					19 26		
Southminster	d		17 56													18 36						
Burnham-on-Crouch	d		18 00													18 40						
Althorne	d		18 05													18 45						
North Fambridge	d		18 14													19 01						
South Woodham Ferrers	d		18 19													19 06						
Battlesbridge	d		18 23													19 10						
Wickford 2	d	18 26	18a29				18 41		18 51						19 11	19 17				19 31		
Billericay	d	18 32					18 47		18 57						19 17	19 23				19 37		
Shenfield 3	a	18 40					18 55		19 05						19 25	19 33				19 45		
Shenfield 3	d	18 40		18 44	18 51	18 54	18 57	19 04	19 05	19 08	19 13	19 14	19 20	19 24	19 25		19 34	19 38	19 44	19 45	19 51	
Brentwood	d			18 47		18 57		19 07				19 17		19 27			19 37		19 47			
Harold Wood	d			18 52		19 02		19 12				19 22		19 32			19 42		19 52			
Gidea Park 2	d			18 56		19 06		19 16				19 26		19 36			19 46		19 56			
Romford	d			18 58		19 08		19 18				19 28	19 28	19 38			19 48		19 58	19 53		
Chadwell Heath	d			19 02		19 12		19 22				19 32		19 42			19 52		20 02			
Goodmayes	d			19 04		19 14		19 24				19 34		19 44			19 54		20 04			
Seven Kings	d			19 06		19 16		19 26				19 36		19 46			19 56		20 06			
Ilford 2	d			19 09		19 19		19 29				19 39		19 49			19 59		20 09			
Manor Park	d			19 12		19 22		19 32				19 42		19 52			20 02		20 12			
Forest Gate	d			19 14		19 24		19 34				19 44		19 54			20 04		20 14			
Maryland	d			19 16		19 26		19 36				19 46		19 56			20 06		20 16			
Stratford 7 ⊖	d	18 55		19 19	19 05	19 29	19 11	19 39	19 19	19 22	19 27	19 49	19 36	19 59	19 39		20 09	19 52	20 19	20 01	20 05	20 14
London Liverpool Street 15 ⊖	a	19 04		19 27	19 14	19 37	19 20	19 47	19 28	19 31	19 36	19 57	19 45	20 07	19 48		20 17	20 01	20 27	20 10	20 14	20 23

from 10 September

Southend Victoria, Southminster and Shenfield - London

Network Diagram - see first Page of Table 5

		LE	LE	LE 1	LE 1	CC	LE 1	LE	LE 1	LE	LE 1	LE	LE 1	CC	LE	LE 1	LE 1	LE 1	LE 1	CC	LE
Southend Victoria	d			19 30							19 50					20 10					
Prittlewell	d			19 32							19 52					20 12					
Southend Airport ✈	d			19 35							19 55					20 15					
Rochford	d			19 38							19 58					20 18					
Hockley	d			19 41							20 01					20 21					
Rayleigh	d			19 46							20 06					20 26					
Southminster	d				19 19												20 16				
Burnham-on-Crouch	d				19 23												20 20				
Althorne	d				19 28												20 25				
North Fambridge	d				19 34												20 31				
South Woodham Ferrers	d				19 39												20 36				
Battlesbridge	d				19 43												20 40				
Wickford 2	d			19 51	19 55						20 11					20 31	20a46				
Billericay	d			19 57							20 17					20 37					
Shenfield 3	a			20 05	20 08						20 25					20 45					
Shenfield 3	d	19 54	20 04	20 05			20 08	20 14	20 20	20 24	20 25	20 34	20 38		20 44	20 45		20 47	20 53		20 54
Brentwood	d	19 57	20 07					20 17		20 27		20 37			20 47						20 57
Harold Wood	d	20 02	20 12					20 22		20 32		20 42			20 52						21 02
Gidea Park 2	d	20 06	20 16					20 26		20 36		20 46			20 56						21 06
Romford	d	20 08	20 18					20 28	20 28	20 38		20 48			20 58	20 53					21 08
Chadwell Heath	d	20 12	20 22					20 32		20 42		20 52			21 02						21 12
Goodmayes	d	20 14	20 24					20 34		20 44		20 54			21 04						21 14
Seven Kings	d	20 16	20 26					20 36		20 46		20 56			21 06						21 16
Ilford 2	d	20 19	20 29					20 39		20 49		20 59			21 09						21 19
Manor Park	d	20 22	20 32					20 42		20 52		21 02			21 12						21 22
Forest Gate	d	20 24	20 34					20 44		20 54		21 04			21 14						21 24
Maryland	d	20 26	20 36					20 46		20 56		21 06			21 16						21 26
Stratford 7 ⊖	d	20 29	20 39	20 19		20 21	20 22	20 49	20 36	20 59	20 39	21 09	20 52	21 00	21 19	21 01			21 07	21 15	21 29
London Liverpool Street 15 ⊖	a	20 37	20 47	20 28		20 33	20 31	20 57	20 45	21 07	20 48	21 17	21 01	21 12	21 27	21 10		21 12	21 16	21 26	21 37

		LE	LE 1	LE 1	LE	LE	LE 1	LE 1	LE 1	LE	LE 1	LE	LE 1	LE 1	LE	LE 1 A	LE 1 B	LE 1	LE 1	LE	LE 1
Southend Victoria	d		20 30				20 50						21 10			21 30	21 30				
Prittlewell	d		20 32				20 52						21 12			21 32	21 32				
Southend Airport ✈	d		20 35				20 55						21 15			21 35	21 35				
Rochford	d		20 38				20 58						21 18			21 38	21 38				
Hockley	d		20 41				21 01						21 21			21 41	21 41				
Rayleigh	d		20 46				21 06						21 26			21 46	21 46				
Southminster	d							20 56										21 36			
Burnham-on-Crouch	d							21 00										21 40			
Althorne	d							21 05										21 45			
North Fambridge	d							21 11										21 51			
South Woodham Ferrers	d							21 16										21 56			
Battlesbridge	d							21 20										22 00			
Wickford 2	d		20 51				21 11	21a26					21 31			21 51	21 51	22a07			
Billericay	d		20 57				21 17						21 37			21 57	21 57				
Shenfield 3	a		21 05				21 25						21 45			22 05	22 05				
Shenfield 3	d	21 04	21 05	21 08	21 14	21 24	21 25		21 27	21 34	21 38	21 44	21 45	21 51	21 59		22 05		22 08	22 14	22 20
Brentwood	d	21 07			21 17	21 27				21 37		21 47			22 02					22 17	
Harold Wood	d	21 12			21 22	21 32				21 42		21 52			22 07					22 22	
Gidea Park 2	d	21 16			21 26	21 36				21 46		21 56			22 11					22 26	
Romford	d	21 18			21 28	21 38				21 48		21 58	21 53		22 13					22 28	22 28
Chadwell Heath	d	21 22			21 32	21 42				21 52		22 02			22 17					22 32	
Goodmayes	d	21 24			21 34	21 44				21 54		22 04			22 19					22 34	
Seven Kings	d	21 26			21 36	21 46				21 56		22 06			22 21					22 36	
Ilford 2	d	21 29			21 39	21 49				21 59		22 09			22 24					22 39	
Manor Park	d	21 32			21 42	21 52				22 02		22 12			22 27					22 42	
Forest Gate	d	21 34			21 44	21 54				22 04		22 14			22 29					22 44	
Maryland	d	21 36			21 46	21 56				22 06		22 16			22 31					22 46	
Stratford 7 ⊖	d	21 39	21 19	21 22	21 49	21 59	21 39		21 42	22 09	21 52	22 19	22 01	22 05	22 34		22 19		22 22	22 49	22 36
London Liverpool Street 15 ⊖	a	21 47	21 28	21 31	21 57	22 07	21 48		21 51	22 17	22 01	22 27	22 10	22 14	22 42		22 28		22 31	22 57	22 45

A MTWO from 17 September

B ThFO, also from 10 September until 12 September

Mondays to Fridays
from 10 September

Southend Victoria, Southminster and Shenfield - London

Network Diagram - see first Page of Table 5

		LE A	LE B	LE ■ B	LE ■ A	LE ■	LE ■ A	LE ■ B	LE A	LE ■ A	LE ■	LE ■ B	LE B	LE A	LE ■ B	LE ■ A	LE ■ A	LE ■ B	LE A	LE ■ A	LE ■ B	LE B
Southend Victoria	d			22 00	22 00										22 30	22 30						
Prittlewell	d			22 02	22 02										22 32	22 32						
Southend Airport ✈	d			22 05	22 05										22 35	22 35						
Rochford	d			22 08	22 08										22 38	22 38						
Hockley	d			22 11	22 11										22 41	22 41						
Rayleigh	d			22 16	22 16										22 46	22 46						
Southminster	d					22 16																
Burnham-on-Crouch	d					22 20																
Althorne	d					22 25																
North Fambridge	d					22 31																
South Woodham Ferrers	d					22 36																
Battlesbridge	d					22 40																
Wickford 2	d			22 21	22 21	22a46									22 51	22 51						
Billericay	d			22 27	22 27										22 57	22 57						
Shenfield 3	a			22 35	22 35										23 05	23 05						
Shenfield 3	d	22 29	22 34		22 35		22 38	22 38	22 44	22 51		22 51	22 54	22 59		23 05	23 08	23 08	23 14	23 20	23 20	23 27
Brentwood	d	22 32	22 37						22 47				22 57	23 02					23 17			23 30
Harold Wood	d	22 37	22 42						22 52				23 02	23 07					23 22			23 35
Gidea Park 2	d	22 41	22 46						22 56				23 06	23 11					23 26			23 39
Romford	d	22 43	22 48						22 58				23 08	23 13				23 19	23 28	23 28	23 31	23 41
Chadwell Heath	d	22 47	22 52						23 02				23 12	23 17					23 32			23 45
Goodmayes	d	22 49	22 54						23 04				23 14	23 19					23 34			23 47
Seven Kings	d	22 51	22 56						23 06				23 16	23 21					23 36			23 49
Ilford 2	d	22 54	22 59						23 09				23 19	23 24					23 39			23 52
Manor Park	d	22 57	23 02						23 12				23 22	23 27					23 42			23 55
Forest Gate	d	22 59	23 04						23 14				23 24	23 29					23 44			23 57
Maryland	d	23 01	23 06						23 16				23 26	23 31					23 46			23 59
Stratford 7 ⊖	d	23 04	23 09		22 49		22 52	22 54	23 19	23 05	23 06	23 11	23 29	23 34		23 19	23 22	23 31	23 49	23 36	23 41	00 02
London Liverpool Street 15 ⊖	a	23 12	23 18		22 58		23 01	23 03	23 27	23 15	23 15	23 20	23 38	23 42		23 28	23 31	23 40	23 57	23 45	23 50	00 11

		LE A	LE ■ B	LE ■ A	LE ◇■ B	LE ■ A	LE A	LE ■ B	LE B
Southend Victoria	d		23 00	23 00					
Prittlewell	d		23 02	23 02					
Southend Airport ✈	d		23 05	23 05					
Rochford	d		23 08	23 08					
Hockley	d		23 11	23 11					
Rayleigh	d		23 16	23 16					
Southminster	d					22 56		23 06	
Burnham-on-Crouch	d					23 00		23 10	
Althorne	d					23 05		23 15	
North Fambridge	d					23 11		23 21	
South Woodham Ferrers	d					23 16		23 26	
Battlesbridge	d					23 20		23 30	
Wickford 2	d		23 21	23 21		23 26		23 36	
Billericay	d		23 27	23 27		23 32		23 42	
Shenfield 3	a		23 35	23 35		23 39		23 49	
Shenfield 3	d	23 29		23 35	23 38	23 39	23 44	23 52	23 54
Brentwood	d	23 32					23 47		23 57
Harold Wood	d	23 37					23 52		00 02
Gidea Park 2	d	23 41					23 56		00 06
Romford	d	23 43				23 47	23 58	00 03	00 08
Chadwell Heath	d	23 47					00 02		00 12
Goodmayes	d	23 49					00 04		00 14
Seven Kings	d	23 51					00 06		00 16
Ilford 2	d	23 54					00 09		00 19
Manor Park	d	23 57					00 12		00 22
Forest Gate	d	23 59					00 14		00 24
Maryland	d	00 01					00 16		00 26
Stratford 7 ⊖	d	00 04		23 49	00s04	23 56	00 19	00 13	00 29
London Liverpool Street 15 ⊖	a	00 12		23 58	00 14	00 05	00 27	00 22	00 38

A ThFO, also from 10 September until 12 September

B MTWO from 17 September

Saturdays
until 21 July

Southend Victoria, Southminster and Shenfield - London

Network Diagram - see first Page of Table 5

		LE ◇■ A	LE ◇■ B	LE	LE ■	CC	LE	LE ■	LE	LE ■	LE ■	LE ■	LE	LE ■	LE ■	LE	LE ■	LE ■	LE	LE	LE ■	LE
Southend Victoria	d							04 00			04 30			05 00				05 30				
Prittlewell	d							04 02			04 32			05 02				05 32				
Southend Airport ✈	d							04 05			04 35			05 05				05 35				
Rochford	d							04 08			04 38			05 08				05 38				
Hockley	d							04 12			04 42			05 11				05 41				
Rayleigh	d							04 16			04 46			05 16				05 46				
Southminster	d				22p56																	
Burnham-on-Crouch	d				23p00																	
Althorne	d				23p05																	
North Fambridge	d				23p11																	
South Woodham Ferrers	d				23p16																	
Battlesbridge	d				23p20																	
Wickford 2	d				23p26			04 21			04 51			05 21				05 51				
Billericay	d				23p32			04 28			04 58			05 27				05 57				
Shenfield 3	a				23p39			04 39			05 09			05 35				06 05				
Shenfield 3	d			23p29	23p39		23p44	04 39			05 09	05 24		05 35		05 44	05 53	06 05		06 14	06 24	
Brentwood	d			23p32			23p47	04 42			05 12					05 47				06 17		
Harold Wood	d			23p37			23p52	04 47			05 17					05 52				06 22		
Gidea Park 2	d			23p41			23p56	04 51			05 21	05 31				05 56			06 16	06 26		06 36
Romford	d			23p43	23p47		23p58	04 53			05 23			05 43		05 58			06 18	06 28		06 38
Chadwell Heath	d			23p47			00 02	04 57			05 27					06 02			06 22	06 32		06 42
Goodmayes	d			23p49			00 04	04 59			05 29					06 04			06 24	06 34		06 44
Seven Kings	d			23p51			00 06	05 01			05 31	05 36				06 06			06 26	06 36		06 46
Ilford 2	d			23p54			00 09	05 04	05 09		05 34		05 39			06 09			06 29	06 39		06 49
Manor Park	d			23p57			00 12		05 11				05 41			06 12			06 32	06 42		06 52
Forest Gate	d			23p59			00 14		05 14				05 44			06 14			06 34	06 44		06 54
Maryland	d			00 01			00 16		05 16				05 46			06 16			06 36	06 46		06 56
Stratford 7 ⊖	d	23b52	23b52	00 04	23p56	00 09	00 19	05 10	05 18	05 30	05 40	05 42	05 48	05 51	06 05	06 19	06 07	06 19	06 39	06 49	06 38	06 59
London Liverpool Street 15 ⊖	a	00 02	00 02	00 12	00 05	00 20	00 27	05 18	05 26	08 13	05 48	05 55	05 56	06 00	06 14	06 27	06 16	06 28	06 47	06 57	06 47	07 07

		LE ■	LE ■	LE	LE	LE ■	LE	LE	LE ■	LE ■	LE	LE ■	LE	LE ■	LE ■	LE	LE ■	LE	LE ■	LE ■	LE	LE
Southend Victoria	d	06 00							06 30					06 50					07 10			
Prittlewell	d	06 02							06 32					06 52					07 12			
Southend Airport ✈	d	06 05							06 35					06 55					07 15			
Rochford	d	06 08							06 38					06 58					07 18			
Hockley	d	06 11							06 41					07 01					07 21			
Rayleigh	d	06 16							06 46					07 06					07 26			
Southminster	d		06 16												06 56							
Burnham-on-Crouch	d		06 20												07 00							
Althorne	d		06 25												07 05							
North Fambridge	d		06 31												07 11							
South Woodham Ferrers	d		06 36												07 16							
Battlesbridge	d		06 40												07 20							
Wickford 2	d	06 21	06a46						06 51					07 11	07a26				07 31			
Billericay	d	06 27							06 57					07 17					07 37			
Shenfield 3	a	06 35							07 05					07 25					07 45			
Shenfield 3	d	06 35			06 44	06 51		07 04	07 05	07 08	07 14	07 20	07 24	07 25		07 34	07 38	07 44	07 45	07 51	07 54	08 04
Brentwood	d				06 47			07 07			07 17		07 27			07 37		07 47			07 57	08 07
Harold Wood	d				06 52			07 12			07 22		07 32			07 42		07 52			08 02	08 12
Gidea Park 2	d			06 46	06 56		07 06	07 16			07 26		07 36			07 46		07 56			08 06	08 16
Romford	d	06 43		06 48	06 58		07 08	07 18			07 28	07 28	07 38			07 48		07 58	07 53		08 08	08 18
Chadwell Heath	d			06 52	07 02		07 12	07 22			07 32		07 42			07 52		08 02			08 12	08 22
Goodmayes	d			06 54	07 04		07 14	07 24			07 34		07 44			07 54		08 04			08 14	08 24
Seven Kings	d			06 56	07 06		07 16	07 26			07 36		07 46			07 56		08 06			08 16	08 26
Ilford 2	d			06 59	07 09		07 19	07 29			07 39		07 49			07 59		08 09			08 19	08 29
Manor Park	d			07 02	07 12		07 22	07 32			07 42		07 52			08 02		08 12			08 22	08 32
Forest Gate	d			07 04	07 14		07 24	07 34			07 44		07 54			08 04		08 14			08 24	08 34
Maryland	d			07 06	07 16		07 26	07 36			07 46		07 56			08 06		08 16			08 26	08 36
Stratford 7 ⊖	d	06 51		07 09	07 19	07 05	07 29	07 39	07 19	07 22	07 49	07 36	07 59	07 39		08 09	07 52	08 19	08 01	08 05	08 29	08 39
London Liverpool Street 15 ⊖	a	07 00		07 17	07 27	07 14	07 37	07 47	07 28	07 31	07 57	07 45	08 07	07 48		08 17	08 01	08 27	08 10	08 14	08 37	08 47

A from 30 June until 21 July

B until 23 June

b Previous night, stops to set down only

Southend Victoria, Southminster and Shenfield - London

Network Diagram - see first Page of Table 5

Station		LE ■		LE ■	LE ■	LE	LE ■	LE	LE ■	LE ◇■	LE	LE ■		LE	LE ■	LE ■	LE ■	LE	LE	LE ■	LE ■	LE		LE ■	LE
Southend Victoria	d	07 30							07 50						08 10					08 30					
Prittlewell	d	07 32							07 52						08 12					08 32					
Southend Airport ✈	d	07 35							07 55						08 15					08 35					
Rochford	d	07 38							07 58						08 18					08 38					
Hockley	d	07 41							08 01						08 21					08 41					
Rayleigh	d	07 46							08 06						08 26					08 46					
Southminster	d			07 36												08 16									
Burnham-on-Crouch	d			07 40												08 20									
Althorne	d			07 45												08 25									
North Fambridge	d			07 51												08 31									
South Woodham Ferrers	d			07 56												08 36									
Battlesbridge	d			08 00												08 40									
Wickford 2	d	07 51		08a06					08 11						08 31	08a46				08 51					
Billericay	d	07 57							08 17						08 37					08 57					
Shenfield 3	a	08 05							08 25						08 45					09 05					
Shenfield 3	d	08 05			08 08	08 14	08 20	08 24	08 25		08 34	08 38		08 44	08 45		08 51	08 54	09 04	09 05	09 08	09 14		09 20	09 24
Brentwood	d					08 17		08 27			08 37			08 47				08 57	09 07			09 17			09 27
Harold Wood	d					08 22		08 32			08 42			08 52				09 02	09 12			09 22			09 32
Gidea Park 2	d					08 26		08 36			08 46			08 56				09 06	09 16			09 26			09 36
Romford	d					08 28	08 28	08 38			08 48			08 58	08 53			09 08	09 18			09 28		09 28	09 38
Chadwell Heath	d					08 32		08 42			08 52			09 02				09 12	09 22			09 32			09 42
Goodmayes	d					08 34		08 44			08 54			09 04				09 14	09 24			09 34			09 44
Seven Kings	d					08 36		08 46			08 56			09 06				09 16	09 26			09 36			09 46
Ilford 2	d					08 39		08 49			08 59			09 09				09 19	09 29			09 39			09 49
Manor Park	d					08 42		08 52			09 02			09 12				09 22	09 32			09 42			09 52
Forest Gate	d					08 44		08 54			09 04			09 14				09 24	09 34			09 44			09 54
Maryland	d					08 46		08 56			09 06			09 16				09 26	09 36			09 46			09 56
Stratford 7 ⊖	d	08 19			08 22	08 49	08 36	08 59	08 39		09 09	08 52		09 19	09 01		09 05	09 29	09 39	09 19	09 22	09 49		09 36	09 59
London Liverpool Street 15 ⊖	a	08 28			08 31	08 57	08 45	09 07	08 48	08 55	09 17	09 01		09 27	09 10		09 14	09 37	09 47	09 28	09 31	09 57		09 45	10 07

Station		LE ■	LE ■		LE	LE ■	LE	LE ■		LE ■	LE	LE	LE ■	LE ■	LE ■	LE	LE ■	LE		LE ■		LE	LE ■	LE	LE ■
Southend Victoria	d	08 50						09 10					09 30							09 50					10 10
Prittlewell	d	08 52						09 12					09 32							09 52					10 12
Southend Airport ✈	d	08 55						09 15					09 35							09 55					10 15
Rochford	d	08 58						09 18					09 38							09 58					10 18
Hockley	d	09 01						09 21					09 41							10 01					10 21
Rayleigh	d	09 06						09 26					09 46							10 06					10 26
Southminster	d		08 56											09 36											
Burnham-on-Crouch	d		09 00											09 40											
Althorne	d		09 05											09 45											
North Fambridge	d		09 11											09 51											
South Woodham Ferrers	d		09 16											09 56											
Battlesbridge	d		09 20											10 00											
Wickford 2	d	09 11	09a26					09 31					09 51	10a06						10 11					10 31
Billericay	d	09 17						09 37					09 57							10 17					10 37
Shenfield 3	a	09 25						09 45					10 05							10 25					10 45
Shenfield 3	d	09 25			09 34	09 38	09 44	09 45		09 51	09 54	10 04	10 05		10 08	10 14	10 20	10 24		10 25		10 34	10 38	10 44	10 45
Brentwood	d				09 37		09 47				09 57	10 07				10 17		10 27				10 37		10 47	
Harold Wood	d				09 42		09 52				10 02	10 12				10 22		10 32				10 42		10 52	
Gidea Park 2	d				09 46		09 56				10 06	10 16				10 26		10 36				10 46		10 56	
Romford	d				09 48		09 58	09 53			10 08	10 18				10 28	10 28	10 38				10 48		10 58	10 53
Chadwell Heath	d				09 52		10 02				10 12	10 22				10 32		10 42				10 52		11 02	
Goodmayes	d				09 54		10 04				10 14	10 24				10 34		10 44				10 54		11 04	
Seven Kings	d				09 56		10 06				10 16	10 26				10 36		10 46				10 56		11 06	
Ilford 2	d				09 59		10 09				10 19	10 29				10 39		10 49				10 59		11 09	
Manor Park	d				10 02		10 12				10 22	10 32				10 42		10 52				11 02		11 12	
Forest Gate	d				10 04		10 14				10 24	10 34				10 44		10 54				11 04		11 14	
Maryland	d				10 06		10 16				10 26	10 36				10 46		10 56				11 06		11 16	
Stratford 7 ⊖	d	09 39			10 09	09 52	10 19	10 01		10 05	10 29	10 39	10 19		10 22	10 49	10 36	10 59		10 39		11 09	10 52	11 19	11 01
London Liverpool Street 15 ⊖	a	09 48			10 17	10 01	10 27	10 10		10 14	10 37	10 47	10 28		10 31	10 57	10 45	11 07		10 48		11 17	11 01	11 27	11 10

Southend Victoria, Southminster and Shenfield - London

Network Diagram - see first Page of Table 5

Station		LE ■	LE ■	LE		LE	LE ■	LE ■	LE	LE ■	LE	LE ■	LE ■			LE	LE ■	LE	LE ■	LE ■	LE	LE	LE ■	LE ■	
Southend Victoria	d						10 30					10 50							11 10				11 30		
Prittlewell	d						10 32					10 52							11 12				11 32		
Southend Airport ✈	d						10 35					10 55							11 15				11 35		
Rochford	d						10 38					10 58							11 18				11 38		
Hockley	d						10 41					11 01							11 21				11 41		
Rayleigh	d						10 46					11 06							11 26				11 46		
Southminster	d	10 16											10 56											11 36	
Burnham-on-Crouch	d	10 20											11 00											11 40	
Althorne	d	10 25											11 05											11 45	
North Fambridge	d	10 31											11 11											11 51	
South Woodham Ferrers	d	10 36											11 16											11 56	
Battlesbridge	d	10 40											11 20											12 00	
Wickford 2	d	10a46					10 51					11 11	11a26						11 31				11 51	12a06	
Billericay	d						10 57					11 17							11 37				11 57		
Shenfield 3	a						11 05					11 25							11 45				12 05		
Shenfield 3	d		10 51	10 54		11 04	11 05	11 08	11 14	11 20	11 24	11 25				11 34	11 38	11 44	11 45	11 51	11 54	12 04	12 05		
Brentwood	d			10 57		11 07			11 17		11 27					11 37		11 47			11 57	12 07			
Harold Wood	d			11 02		11 12			11 22		11 32					11 42		11 52			12 02	12 12			
Gidea Park 2	d			11 06		11 16			11 26		11 36					11 46		11 56			12 06	12 16			
Romford	d			11 08		11 18			11 28	11 28	11 38					11 48		11 58	11 53		12 08	12 18			
Chadwell Heath	d			11 12		11 22			11 32		11 42					11 52		12 02			12 12	12 22			
Goodmayes	d			11 14		11 24			11 34		11 44					11 54		12 04			12 14	12 24			
Seven Kings	d			11 16		11 26			11 36		11 46					11 56		12 06			12 16	12 26			
Ilford 2	d			11 19		11 29			11 39		11 49					11 59		12 09			12 19	12 29			
Manor Park	d			11 22		11 32			11 42		11 52					12 02		12 12			12 22	12 32			
Forest Gate	d			11 24		11 34			11 44		11 54					12 04		12 14			12 24	12 34			
Maryland	d			11 26		11 36			11 46		11 56					12 06		12 16			12 26	12 36			
Stratford 7 ⊖	d		11 05	11 29		11 39	11 19	11 22	11 49	11 36	11 59	11 39				12 09	11 52	12 19	12 01	12 05	12 29	12 39	12 19		
London Liverpool Street 15 ⊖	a		11 14	11 37		11 47	11 28	11 31	11 57	11 45	12 07	11 48				12 17	12 01	12 27	12 10	12 14	12 37	12 47	12 28		

Station		LE ■	LE	LE ■	LE	LE ■		LE	LE ■	LE		LE ■	LE ■	LE ■	LE	LE	LE ■	LE ■	LE	LE ■		LE	LE ■	LE ■	
Southend Victoria	d					11 50						12 10					12 30						12 50		
Prittlewell	d					11 52						12 12					12 32						12 52		
Southend Airport ✈	d					11 55						12 15					12 35						12 55		
Rochford	d					11 58						12 18					12 38						12 58		
Hockley	d					12 01						12 21					12 41						13 01		
Rayleigh	d					12 06						12 26					12 46						13 06		
Southminster	d												12 16											12 56	
Burnham-on-Crouch	d												12 20											13 00	
Althorne	d												12 25											13 05	
North Fambridge	d												12 31											13 11	
South Woodham Ferrers	d												12 36											13 16	
Battlesbridge	d												12 40											13 20	
Wickford 2	d					12 11						12 31	12a46				12 51						13 11	13a26	
Billericay	d					12 17						12 37					12 57						13 17		
Shenfield 3	a					12 25						12 45					13 05						13 25		
Shenfield 3	d	12 08	12 14	12 20	12 24	12 25		12 34	12 38	12 44		12 45		12 51	12 54	13 04	13 05	13 08	13 14	13 20		13 24	13 25		
Brentwood	d		12 17		12 27			12 37		12 47					12 57	13 07			13 17			13 27			
Harold Wood	d		12 22		12 32			12 42		12 52					13 02	13 12			13 22			13 32			
Gidea Park 2	d		12 26		12 36			12 46		12 56					13 06	13 16			13 26			13 36			
Romford	d		12 28	12 28	12 38			12 48		12 58		12 53			13 08	13 18			13 28	13 28		13 38			
Chadwell Heath	d		12 32		12 42			12 52		13 02					13 12	13 22			13 32			13 42			
Goodmayes	d		12 34		12 44			12 54		13 04					13 14	13 24			13 34			13 44			
Seven Kings	d		12 36		12 46			12 56		13 06					13 16	13 26			13 36			13 46			
Ilford 2	d		12 39		12 49			12 59		13 09					13 19	13 29			13 39			13 49			
Manor Park	d		12 42		12 52			13 02		13 12					13 22	13 32			13 42			13 52			
Forest Gate	d		12 44		12 54			13 04		13 14					13 24	13 34			13 44			13 54			
Maryland	d		12 46		12 56			13 06		13 16					13 26	13 36			13 46			13 56			
Stratford 7 ⊖	d	12 22	12 49	12 36	12 59	12 39		13 09	12 52	13 19		13 01		13 05	13 29	13 39	13 19	13 22	13 49	13 36		13 59	13 39		
London Liverpool Street 15 ⊖	a	12 31	12 57	12 45	13 07	12 48		13 17	13 01	13 27		13 10		13 14	13 37	13 47	13 28	13 31	13 57	13 45		14 07	13 48		

Table 5

Saturdays until 21 July

Southend Victoria, Southminster and Shenfield - London

Network Diagram - see first Page of Table 5

	LE	LE ■	LE	LE ■	LE ■		LE	LE	LE ■	LE ■	LE ■	LE	LE ■	LE	LE ■			LE	LE ■	LE	LE ■	LE ■	LE ■	LE
Southend Victoria d				13 10					13 30						13 50						14 10			
Prittlewell d				13 12					13 32						13 52						14 12			
Southend Airport ✈ d				13 15					13 35						13 55						14 15			
Rochford d				13 18					13 38						13 58						14 18			
Hockley d				13 21					13 41						14 01						14 21			
Rayleigh d				13 26					13 46						14 06						14 26			
Southminster d										13 36												14 16		
Burnham-on-Crouch d										13 40												14 20		
Althorne d										13 45												14 25		
North Fambridge d										13 51												14 31		
South Woodham Ferrers d										13 56												14 36		
Battlesbridge d										14 00												14 40		
Wickford ■ d				13 31					13 51	14a06					14 11						14 31	14a46		
Billericay d				13 37					13 57						14 17						14 37			
Shenfield ■ a				13 45					14 05						14 25						14 45			
Shenfield ■ d	13 34	13 38	13 44	13 45	13 51		13 54	14 04	14 05		14 08	14 14	14 20	14 24	14 25			14 34	14 38	14 44	14 45		14 51	14 54
Brentwood d	13 37		13 47				13 57	14 07				14 17		14 27				14 37		14 47				14 57
Harold Wood d	13 42		13 52				14 02	14 12				14 22		14 32				14 42		14 52				15 02
Gidea Park ■ d	13 46		13 56				14 06	14 16				14 26		14 36				14 46		14 56				15 06
Romford d	13 48		13 58	13 53			14 08	14 18				14 28	14 28	14 38				14 48		14 58	14 53			15 08
Chadwell Heath d	13 52		14 02				14 12	14 22				14 32		14 42				14 52		15 02				15 12
Goodmayes d	13 54		14 04				14 14	14 24				14 34		14 44				14 54		15 04				15 14
Seven Kings d	13 56		14 06				14 16	14 26				14 36		14 46				14 56		15 06				15 16
Ilford ■ d	13 59		14 09				14 19	14 29				14 39		14 49				14 59		15 09				15 19
Manor Park d	14 02		14 12				14 22	14 32				14 42		14 52				15 02		15 12				15 22
Forest Gate d	14 04		14 14				14 24	14 34				14 44		14 54				15 04		15 14				15 24
Maryland d	14 06		14 16				14 26	14 36				14 46		14 56				15 06		15 16				15 26
Stratford ■ ⊖ d	14 09	13 52	14 19	14 01	14 05		14 29	14 39	14 19		14 22	14 49	14 36	14 59	14 39			15 09	14 52	15 19	15 01		15 05	15 29
London Liverpool Street ■ ⊖ a	14 17	14 01	14 27	14 10	14 14		14 37	14 47	14 28		14 31	14 57	14 45	15 07	14 48			15 17	15 01	15 27	15 10		15 14	15 37

	LE		LE ■	LE ■	LE	LE ■	LE	LE ■	LE ■		LE		LE ■	LE	LE ■	LE ■	LE	LE	LE ■	LE ■	LE ■		LE	LE ■
Southend Victoria d			14 30					14 50							15 10				15 30					
Prittlewell d			14 32					14 52							15 12				15 32					
Southend Airport ✈ d			14 35					14 55							15 15				15 35					
Rochford d			14 38					14 58							15 18				15 38					
Hockley d			14 41					15 01							15 21				15 41					
Rayleigh d			14 46					15 06							15 26				15 46					
Southminster d									14 56											15 36				
Burnham-on-Crouch d									15 00											15 40				
Althorne d									15 05											15 45				
North Fambridge d									15 11											15 51				
South Woodham Ferrers d									15 16											15 56				
Battlesbridge d									15 20											16 00				
Wickford ■ d			14 51					15 11	15a26						15 31				15 51	16a06				
Billericay d			14 57					15 17							15 37				15 57					
Shenfield ■ a			15 05					15 25							15 45				16 05					
Shenfield ■ d	15 04		15 05	15 08	15 14	15 20	15 24	15 25			15 34		15 38	15 44	15 45	15 51	15 54	16 04	16 05		16 08		16 14	16 20
Brentwood d	15 07				15 17		15 27				15 37			15 47			15 57	16 07					16 17	
Harold Wood d	15 12				15 22		15 32				15 42			15 52			16 02	16 12					16 22	
Gidea Park ■ d	15 16				15 26		15 36				15 46			15 56			16 06	16 16					16 26	
Romford d	15 18				15 28	15 28	15 38				15 48			15 58	15 53		16 08	16 18					16 28	16 28
Chadwell Heath d	15 22				15 32		15 42				15 52			16 02			16 12	16 22					16 32	
Goodmayes d	15 24				15 34		15 44				15 54			16 04			16 14	16 24					16 34	
Seven Kings d	15 26				15 36		15 46				15 56			16 06			16 16	16 26					16 36	
Ilford ■ d	15 29				15 39		15 49				15 59			16 09			16 19	16 29					16 39	
Manor Park d	15 32				15 42		15 52				16 02			16 12			16 22	16 32					16 42	
Forest Gate d	15 34				15 44		15 54				16 04			16 14			16 24	16 34					16 44	
Maryland d	15 36				15 46		15 56				16 06			16 16			16 26	16 36					16 46	
Stratford ■ ⊖ d	15 39		15 19	15 22	15 49	15 36	15 59	15 39			16 09		15 52	16 19	16 01	16 05	16 29	16 39	16 19		16 22		16 49	16 36
London Liverpool Street ■ ⊖ a	15 47		15 28	15 31	15 57	15 45	16 07	15 48			16 17		16 01	16 27	16 10	16 14	16 37	16 47	16 28		16 31		16 57	16 45

Table 5

Saturdays until 21 July

Southend Victoria, Southminster and Shenfield - London

Network Diagram - see first Page of Table 5

	LE	LE ■		LE	LE ■	LE	LE ■		LE ■	LE ■	LE	LE	LE ■	LE ■	LE	LE ■	LE		LE ■	LE ■		LE	LE ■	LE ■
Southend Victoria d		15 50					16 10						16 30						16 50					17 10
Prittlewell d		15 52					16 12						16 32						16 52					17 12
Southend Airport ✈ d		15 55					16 15						16 35						16 55					17 15
Rochford d		15 58					16 18						16 38						16 58					17 18
Hockley d		16 01					16 21						16 41						17 01					17 21
Rayleigh d		16 06					16 26						16 46						17 06					17 26
Southminster d									16 16											16 56				
Burnham-on-Crouch d									16 20											17 00				
Althorne d									16 25											17 05				
North Fambridge d									16 31											17 11				
South Woodham Ferrers d									16 36											17 16				
Battlesbridge d									16 40											17 20				
Wickford ■ d		16 11					16 31		16a46				16 51						17 11	17a26				17 31
Billericay d		16 17					16 37						16 57						17 17					17 37
Shenfield ■ a		16 25					16 45						17 05						17 25					17 44
Shenfield ■ d	16 24	16 25		16 34	16 38	16 44	16 45			16 51	16 54	17 04	17 05	17 08	17 14	17 20	17 24		17 25			17 34	17 38	17 45
Brentwood d	16 27			16 37		16 47					16 57	17 07			17 17		17 27					17 37		
Harold Wood d	16 32			16 42		16 52					17 02	17 12			17 22		17 32					17 42		
Gidea Park ■ d	16 36			16 46		16 56					17 06	17 16			17 26		17 36					17 46		
Romford d	16 38			16 48		16 58	16 53				17 08	17 18			17 28	17 28	17 38					17 48		17 53
Chadwell Heath d	16 42			16 52		17 02					17 12	17 22			17 32		17 42					17 52		
Goodmayes d	16 44			16 54		17 04					17 14	17 24			17 34		17 44					17 54		
Seven Kings d	16 46			16 56		17 06					17 16	17 26			17 36		17 46					17 56		
Ilford ■ d	16 49			16 59		17 09					17 19	17 29			17 39		17 49					17 59		
Manor Park d	16 52			17 02		17 12					17 22	17 32			17 42		17 52					18 02		
Forest Gate d	16 54			17 04		17 14					17 24	17 34			17 44		17 54					18 04		
Maryland d	16 56			17 06		17 16					17 26	17 36			17 46		17 56					18 06		
Stratford ■ ⊖ d	16 59	16 39		17 09	16 52	17 19	17 01			17 05	17 29	17 39	17 19	17 22	17 49	17 36	17 59		17 39			18 09	17 52	18 01
London Liverpool Street ■ ⊖ a	17 07	16 48		17 17	17 01	17 27	17 10			17 14	17 37	17 47	17 28	17 31	17 57	17 45	18 07		17 48			18 17	18 01	18 10

	LE	LE ■	LE		LE	LE ■	LE ■	LE ■	LE	LE ■	LE	LE ■			LE	LE ■	LE	LE ■	LE ■	LE ■	LE	LE	LE ■	
Southend Victoria d						17 30						17 50						18 10					18 30	
Prittlewell d						17 32						17 52						18 12					18 32	
Southend Airport ✈ d						17 35						17 55						18 15					18 35	
Rochford d						17 38						17 58						18 18					18 38	
Hockley d						17 41						18 01						18 21					18 41	
Rayleigh d						17 46						18 06						18 26					18 46	
Southminster d							17 36												18 16					
Burnham-on-Crouch d							17 40												18 20					
Althorne d							17 45												18 25					
North Fambridge d							17 51												18 31					
South Woodham Ferrers d							17 56												18 36					
Battlesbridge d							18 00												18 40					
Wickford ■ d						17 51	18a06					18 11						18 31	18a46				18 51	
Billericay d						17 57						18 17						18 37					18 57	
Shenfield ■ a						18 05						18 25						18 45					19 05	
Shenfield ■ d	17 44	17 51	17 54		18 04	18 05		18 08	18 14	18 20	18 24	18 25			18 34	18 38	18 44	18 45		18 51	18 54	19 04	19 05	
Brentwood d	17 47		17 57		18 07				18 17		18 27				18 37		18 47				18 57	19 07		
Harold Wood d	17 52		18 02		18 12				18 22		18 32				18 42		18 52				19 02	19 12		
Gidea Park ■ d	17 56		18 06		18 16				18 26		18 36				18 46		18 56				19 06	19 16		
Romford d	17 58		18 08		18 18				18 28	18 28	18 38				18 48		18 58	18 53			19 08	19 18		
Chadwell Heath d	18 02		18 12		18 22				18 32		18 42				18 52		19 02				19 12	19 22		
Goodmayes d	18 04		18 14		18 24				18 34		18 44				18 54		19 04				19 14	19 24		
Seven Kings d	18 06		18 16		18 26				18 36		18 46				18 56		19 06				19 16	19 26		
Ilford ■ d	18 09		18 19		18 29				18 39		18 49				18 59		19 09				19 19	19 29		
Manor Park d	18 12		18 22		18 32				18 42		18 52				19 02		19 12				19 22	19 32		
Forest Gate d	18 14		18 24		18 34				18 44		18 54				19 04		19 14				19 24	19 34		
Maryland d	18 16		18 26		18 36				18 46		18 56				19 06		19 16				19 26	19 36		
Stratford ■ ⊖ d	18 19	18 05	18 29		18 39	18 19		18 22	18 49	18 36	18 59	18 39			19 09	18 52	19 19	19 01		19 05	19 29	19 39	19 19	
London Liverpool Street ■ ⊖ a	18 27	18 14	18 37		18 47	18 28		18 31	18 57	18 45	19 07	18 48			19 17	19 01	19 27	19 10		19 14	19 37	19 47	19 28	

Southend Victoria, Southminster and Shenfield - London

Network Diagram - see first Page of Table 5

		LE 1	LE	LE 1	LE	LE 1	LE 1		LE	LE 1		LE	LE 1	LE 1	LE	LE	LE 1	LE 1	LE 1	LE		LE 1	LE	LE 1	
Southend Victoria	d					18 50							19 10				19 30							19 50	
Prittlewell	d					18 52							19 12				19 32							19 52	
Southend Airport ✈	d					18 55							19 15				19 35							19 55	
Rochford	d					18 58							19 18				19 38							19 58	
Hockley	d					19 01							19 21				19 41							20 01	
Rayleigh	d					19 06							19 26				19 46							20 06	
Southminster	d						18 56											19 36							
Burnham-on-Crouch	d						19 00											19 40							
Althorne	d						19 05											19 45							
North Fambridge	d						19 11											19 51							
South Woodham Ferrers	d						19 16											19 56							
Battlesbridge	d						19 20											20 00							
Wickford 2	d					19 11	19a26						19 31				19 51	20a06						20 11	
Billericay	d					19 17							19 37				19 57							20 17	
Shenfield 3	a					19 25							19 45				20 05							20 25	
Shenfield 3	d	19 08	19 14	19 20	19 24	19 25			19 34	19 38		19 44	19 45	19 51	19 54	20 04	20 05		20 08	20 14		20 20	20 24	20 25	
Brentwood	d		19 17		19 27				19 37			19 47			19 57	20 07				20 17			20 27		
Harold Wood	d		19 22		19 32				19 42			19 52			20 02	20 12				20 22			20 32		
Gidea Park 2	d		19 26		19 36				19 46			19 56			20 06	20 16				20 26			20 36		
Romford	d		19 28	19 28	19 38				19 48			19 58	19 53		20 08	20 18				20 28		20 28	20 38		
Chadwell Heath	d		19 32		19 42				19 52			20 02			20 12	20 22				20 32			20 42		
Goodmayes	d		19 34		19 44				19 54			20 04			20 14	20 24				20 34			20 44		
Seven Kings	d		19 36		19 46				19 56			20 06			20 16	20 26				20 36			20 46		
Ilford 2	d		19 39		19 49				19 59			20 09			20 19	20 29				20 39			20 49		
Manor Park	d		19 42		19 52				20 02			20 12			20 22	20 32				20 42			20 52		
Forest Gate	d		19 44		19 54				20 04			20 14			20 24	20 34				20 44			20 54		
Maryland	d		19 46		19 56				20 06			20 16			20 26	20 36				20 46			20 56		
Stratford 7 ⊖	d	19 22	19 49	19 36	19 59	19 39			20 09	19 52		20 19	20 01	20 05	20 29	20 39	20s19		20 22	20 49		20 36	20 59	20 39	
London Liverpool Street 15 ⊖	a	19 31	19 57	19 45	20 07	19 48			20 17	20 01		20 27	20 10	20 14	20 37	20 47	20 28		20 31	20 57		20 45	21 07	20 48	

		LE	LE 1	LE	LE 1	LE 1		LE 1	LE	LE 1	LE 1	LE	LE 1	LE 1	LE 1			LE	LE 1	LE	LE 1	LE 1	LE	LE 1	LE 1
Southend Victoria	d				20 10					20 30				20 50							21 10			21 30	
Prittlewell	d				20 12					20 32				20 52							21 12			21 32	
Southend Airport ✈	d				20 15					20 35				20 55							21 15			21 35	
Rochford	d				20 18					20 38				20 58							21 18			21 38	
Hockley	d				20 21					20 41				21 01							21 21			21 41	
Rayleigh	d				20 26					20 46				21 06							21 26			21 46	
Southminster	d					20 16									20 56										21 36
Burnham-on-Crouch	d					20 20									21 00										21 40
Althorne	d					20 25									21 05										21 45
North Fambridge	d					20 31									21 11										21 51
South Woodham Ferrers	d					20 36									21 16										21 56
Battlesbridge	d					20 40									21 20										22 00
Wickford 2	d				20 31	20a46				20 51				21 11	21a26						21 31			21 51	22a06
Billericay	d				20 37					20 57				21 17							21 37			21 57	
Shenfield 3	a				20 45					21 05				21 25							21 45			22 05	
Shenfield 3	d	20 34	20 38	20 44	20 45			20 51	20 59	21 05	21 08	21 14	21 20	21 25				21 29	21 38	21 44	21 45	21 51	21 59	22 05	
Brentwood	d	20 37		20 47					21 02			21 17						21 32		21 47			22 02		
Harold Wood	d	20 42		20 52					21 07			21 22						21 37		21 52			22 07		
Gidea Park 2	d	20 46		20 56					21 11			21 26						21 41		21 56			22 11		
Romford	d	20 48		20 58	20 53				21 13			21 28	21 28					21 43		21 58	21 53		22 13		
Chadwell Heath	d	20 52		21 02					21 17			21 32						21 47		22 02			22 17		
Goodmayes	d	20 54		21 04					21 19			21 34						21 49		22 04			22 19		
Seven Kings	d	20 56		21 06					21 21			21 36						21 51		22 06			22 21		
Ilford 2	d	20 59		21 09					21 24			21 39						21 54		22 09			22 24		
Manor Park	d	21 02		21 12					21 27			21 42						21 57		22 12			22 27		
Forest Gate	d	21 04		21 14					21 29			21 44						21 59		22 14			22 29		
Maryland	d	21 06		21 16					21 31			21 46						22 01		22 16			22 31		
Stratford 7 ⊖	d	21 09	20 52	21 19	21 01			21 05	21 34	21 19	21 22	21 49	21 36	21 39				22 04	21 52	22 19	22 01	22 05	22 34	22 19	
London Liverpool Street 15 ⊖	a	21 17	21 01	21 27	21 10			21 14	21 42	21 28	21 31	21 57	21 45	21 48				22 12	22 01	22 27	22 10	22 14	22 42	22 28	

Table 5

Saturdays
until 21 July

Southend Victoria, Southminster and Shenfield - London

Network Diagram - see first Page of Table 5

		LE 1		LE	LE 1		LE	LE 1	LE 1	LE 1	LE	LE 1		LE 1	LE	LE 1	LE 1	LE	LE 1	LE	LE 1	LE 1		LE	
Southend Victoria	d							22 00								22 30					23 00				
Prittlewell	d							22 02								22 32					23 02				
Southend Airport ✈	d							22 05								22 35					23 05				
Rochford	d							22 08								22 38					23 08				
Hockley	d							22 11								22 41					23 11				
Rayleigh	d							22 16								22 46					23 16				
Southminster	d								22 16													22 56			
Burnham-on-Crouch	d								22 20													23 00			
Althorne	d								22 25													23 05			
North Fambridge	d								22 31													23 11			
South Woodham Ferrers	d								22 36													23 16			
Battlesbridge	d								22 40													23 20			
Wickford 2	d							22 21	22a46							22 51					23 21	23 26			
Billericay	d							22 27								22 57					23 27	23 32			
Shenfield 3	a							22 35								23 05					23 35	23 39			
Shenfield 3	d	22 08		22 14	22 20		22 29	22 35		22 38	22 44	22 51			22 59	23 05	23 08	23 14	23 20	23 29	23 35	23 39		23 44	
Brentwood	d			22 17			22 32				22 47				23 02			23 17		23 32				23 47	
Harold Wood	d			22 22			22 37				22 52				23 07			23 22		23 37				23 52	
Gidea Park 2	d			22 26			22 41				22 56				23 11			23 26		23 41				23 56	
Romford	d			22 28	22 28		22 43				22 58				23 13			23 28	23 28	23 43		23 47		23 58	
Chadwell Heath	d			22 32			22 47				23 02				23 17			23 32		23 47				00 02	
Goodmayes	d			22 34			22 49				23 04				23 19			23 34		23 49				00 04	
Seven Kings	d			22 36			22 51				23 06				23 21			23 36		23 51				00 06	
Ilford 2	d			22 39			22 54				23 09				23 24			23 39		23 54				00 09	
Manor Park	d			22 42			22 57				23 12				23 27			23 42		23 57				00 12	
Forest Gate	d			22 44			22 59				23 14				23 29			23 44		23 59				00 14	
Maryland	d			22 46			23 01				23 16				23 31			23 46		00 01				00 16	
Stratford 7 ⊖	d	22 22		22 49	22 36		23 04	22 49		22 52	23 19	23 05		23 07	23 34	23 19	23 22	23 49	23 36	00 04	23 49	23 56		00 19	
London Liverpool Street 15 ⊖	a	22 31		22 57	22 46		23 12	22 58		23 01	23 27	23 14		23 18	23 42	23 28	23 31	23 57	23 45	00 12	23 58	00 05		00 27	

Saturdays
28 July to 11 August

		LE		LE	LE	LE 1	LE 1	LE	LE	LE		LE	LE	LE	LE	LE	LE	LE 1	LE	LE 1		LE 1	LE	LE 1	LE 1
Southend Victoria	d					23p10												04 00		04 30				05 00	
Prittlewell	d					23p12												04 02		04 32				05 02	
Southend Airport ✈	d					23p15												04 05		04 35				05 05	
Rochford	d					23p18												04 08		04 38				05 08	
Hockley	d					23p21												04 12		04 42				05 11	
Rayleigh	d					23p26												04 16		04 46				05 16	
Southminster	d																								
Burnham-on-Crouch	d																								
Althorne	d																								
North Fambridge	d																								
South Woodham Ferrers	d																								
Battlesbridge	d																								
Wickford 2	d					23p31												04 21		04 51				05 21	
Billericay	d					23p37												04 28		04 58				05 27	
Shenfield 3	a					23p45												04 39		05 09				05 35	
Shenfield 3	d			23p29	23p44	23p45			23p59	00 14			00 29	00 44				04 39		05 09		05 24		05 35	
Brentwood	d			23p32	23p47				00 02	00 17			00 32	00 47				04 42		05 12					
Harold Wood	d			23p37	23p52				00 07	00 22			00 37	00 52				04 47		05 17					
Gidea Park 2	d			23p41	23p56				00 11	00 26			00 41	00 56				04 51		05 21		05 31			
Romford	d			23p43	23p58				00 13	00 28			00 43	00 58				04 53		05 23				05 43	
Chadwell Heath	d			23p47	00 02				00 17	00 32			00 47	01 02				04 57		05 27					
Goodmayes	d			23p49	00 04				00 19	00 34			00 49	01 04				04 59		05 29					
Seven Kings	d			23p51	00 06				00 21	00 36			00 51	01 06				05 01		05 31		05 36			
Ilford 2	d			23p54	00 09				00 24	00 39			00 54	01 09				05 04	05 09	05 34			05 39		
Manor Park	d			23p57	00 12				00 27	00 42			00 57	01 12					05 11				05 41		
Forest Gate	d			23p59	00 14				00 29	00 44			00 59	01 14					05 14				05 44		
Maryland	d																								
Stratford 7 ⊖	d	23p54		00 04	00 20	00 08	00 12	00 30	00 40	00 50		01 00	01 10	01 20	01 30	01 40	01 50	05 10	05 18	05 40		05 42	05 48	05 51	06 05
London Liverpool Street 15 ⊖	a	00 02		00 12	00 28	00 16	00 20	00 38	00 48	00 58		01 08	01 18	01 28	01 38	01 48	01 58	05 18	05 26	05 48		05 55	05 56	06 00	06 14

Table 5

Saturdays

28 July to 11 August

Southend Victoria, Southminster and Shenfield - London

Network Diagram - see first Page of Table 5

		LE	LE ■	LE ■	LE	LE		LE ■		LE	LE ■	LE ■	LE	LE	LE ■	LE		LE	LE ■	LE ■	LE	LE ■	LE	LE ■	LE ■
Southend Victoria	d			05 30							06 00								06 30					06 50	
Prittlewell	d			05 32							06 02								06 32					06 52	
Southend Airport ✈	d			05 35							06 05								06 35					06 55	
Rochford	d			05 38							06 08								06 38					06 58	
Hockley	d			05 41							06 11								06 41					07 01	
Rayleigh	d			05 46							06 16								06 46					07 06	
Southminster	d											06 16													06 56
Burnham-on-Crouch	d											06 20													07 00
Althorne	d											06 25													07 05
North Fambridge	d											06 31													07 11
South Woodham Ferrers	d											06 36													07 16
Battlesbridge	d											06 40													07 20
Wickford [2]	d			05 51							06 21	06a46							06 51					07 11	07a26
Billericay	d			05 57							06 27								06 57					07 17	
Shenfield [3]	a			06 05							06 35								07 05					07 25	
Shenfield [3]	d	05 44	05 53	06 05		06 14		06 24			06 35			06 44	06 51			07 04	07 05	07 08	07 14	07 20	07 24	07 25	
Brentwood	d	05 47				06 17								06 47				07 07			07 17		07 27		
Harold Wood	d	05 52				06 22								06 52				07 12			07 22		07 32		
Gidea Park [2]	d	05 56			06 16	06 26				06 36			06 46	06 56		07 06		07 16			07 26		07 36		
Romford	d	05 58			06 18	06 28				06 38	06 43		06 48	06 58		07 08		07 18			07 28		07 38		
Chadwell Heath	d	06 02			06 22	06 32				06 42			06 52	07 02		07 12		07 22			07 32		07 42		
Goodmayes	d	06 04			06 24	06 34				06 44			06 54	07 04		07 14		07 24			07 34		07 44		
Seven Kings	d	06 06			06 26	06 36				06 46			06 56	07 06		07 16		07 26			07 36		07 46		
Ilford [2]	d	06 09			06 29	06 39				06 49			06 59	07 09		07 19		07 29			07 39		07 49		
Manor Park	d	06 12			06 32	06 42				06 52			07 02	07 12		07 22		07 32			07 42		07 52		
Forest Gate	d	06 14			06 34	06 44				06 54			07 04	07 14		07 24		07 34			07 44		07 54		
Maryland	d																								
Stratford [7] ⊖	d	06 19	06 07	06 19	06 39	06 49		06 38		06 59	06 51		07 09	07 19	07 05	07 29		07 39	07 19	07 22	07 49	07s36	07 59	07 39	
London Liverpool Street [15] ⊖	a	06 27	06 16	06 28	06 47	06 57		06 47		07 07	07 00		07 17	07 27	07 14	07 37		07 47	07 28	07 31	07 57	07 47	08 07	07 48	

				LE	LE ■	LE	LE ■	LE ■	LE	LE	LE ■	LE ■		LE ■	LE	LE ■	LE	LE ■	LE ◇■	LE	LE ■	LE		LE ■	LE ■
Southend Victoria	d						07 10				07 30							07 50						08 10	
Prittlewell	d						07 12				07 32							07 52						08 12	
Southend Airport ✈	d						07 15				07 35							07 55						08 15	
Rochford	d						07 18				07 38							07 58						08 18	
Hockley	d						07 21				07 41							08 01						08 21	
Rayleigh	d						07 26				07 46							08 06						08 26	
Southminster	d											07 36													08 16
Burnham-on-Crouch	d											07 40													08 20
Althorne	d											07 45													08 25
North Fambridge	d											07 51													08 31
South Woodham Ferrers	d											07 56													08 36
Battlesbridge	d											08 00													08 40
Wickford [2]	d						07 31				07 51	08a06						08 11						08 31	08a46
Billericay	d						07 37				07 57							08 17						08 37	
Shenfield [3]	a						07 45				08 05							08 25						08 45	
Shenfield [3]	d			07 34	07 38	07 44	07 45	07 51	07 54	08 04	08 05			08 08	08 14	08 20	08 24	08 25		08 34	08 38	08 44		08 45	
Brentwood	d			07 37		07 47			07 57	08 07					08 17		08 27			08 37		08 47			
Harold Wood	d			07 42		07 52			08 02	08 12					08 22		08 32			08 42		08 52			
Gidea Park [2]	d			07 46		07 56			08 06	08 16					08 26		08 36			08 46		08 56			
Romford	d			07 48		07 58	07 53		08 08	08 18					08 28		08 38			08 48		08 58		08 53	
Chadwell Heath	d			07 52		08 02			08 12	08 22					08 32		08 42			08 52		09 02			
Goodmayes	d			07 54		08 04			08 14	08 24					08 34		08 44			08 54		09 04			
Seven Kings	d			07 56		08 06			08 16	08 26					08 36		08 46			08 56		09 06			
Ilford [2]	d			07 59		08 09			08 19	08 29					08 39		08 49			08 59		09 09			
Manor Park	d			08 02		08 12			08 22	08 32					08 42		08 52			09 02		09 12			
Forest Gate	d			08 04		08 14			08 24	08 34					08 44		08 54			09 04		09 14			
Maryland	d																								
Stratford [7] ⊖	d			08 09	07 52	08 19	08 01	08 05	08 29	08 39	08 19			08 22	08 49	08 36	08 59	08 39		09 09	08 52	09 19		09 01	
London Liverpool Street [15] ⊖	a			08 17	08 01	08 27	08 10	08 14	08 37	08 47	08 28			08 31	08 57	08 45	09 07	08 48	08 55	09 17	09 01	09 27		09 10	

Table 5

Saturdays

28 July to 11 August

Southend Victoria, Southminster and Shenfield - London

Network Diagram - see first Page of Table 5

		LE ■	LE	LE	LE ■	LE ■	LE	LE ■		LE	LE ■	LE ■		LE	LE ■	LE	LE ■	LE ■		LE	LE	LE ■	LE ■	LE ■	LE
Southend Victoria	d				08 30						08 50						09 10					09 30			
Prittlewell	d				08 32						08 52						09 12					09 32			
Southend Airport ✈	d				08 35						08 55						09 15					09 35			
Rochford	d				08 38						08 58						09 18					09 38			
Hockley	d				08 41						09 01						09 21					09 41			
Rayleigh	d				08 46						09 06						09 26					09 46			
Southminster	d											08 56											09 36		
Burnham-on-Crouch	d											09 00											09 40		
Althorne	d											09 05											09 45		
North Fambridge	d											09 11											09 51		
South Woodham Ferrers	d											09 16											09 56		
Battlesbridge	d											09 20											10 00		
Wickford [2]	d				08 51						09 11	09a26					09 31					09 51	10a06		
Billericay	d				08 57						09 17						09 37					09 57			
Shenfield [3]	a				09 05						09 25						09 45					10 05			
Shenfield [3]	d	08 51	08 54	09 04	09 05	09 08	09 14	09 20		09 24	09 25			09 34	09 38	09 44	09 45	09 51		09 54	10 04	10 05		10 08	10 14
Brentwood	d		08 57	09 07			09 17			09 27				09 37		09 47				09 57	10 07				10 17
Harold Wood	d		09 02	09 12			09 22			09 32				09 42		09 52				10 02	10 12				10 22
Gidea Park [2]	d		09 06	09 16			09 26			09 36				09 46		09 56				10 06	10 16				10 26
Romford	d		09 08	09 18			09 28	09 28		09 38				09 48		09 58	09 53			10 08	10 18				10 28
Chadwell Heath	d		09 12	09 22			09 32			09 42				09 52		10 02				10 12	10 22				10 32
Goodmayes	d		09 14	09 24			09 34			09 44				09 54		10 04				10 14	10 24				10 34
Seven Kings	d		09 16	09 26			09 36			09 46				09 56		10 06				10 16	10 26				10 36
Ilford [2]	d		09 19	09 29			09 39			09 49				09 59		10 09				10 19	10 29				10 39
Manor Park	d		09 22	09 32			09 42			09 52				10 02		10 12				10 22	10 32				10 42
Forest Gate	d		09 24	09 34			09 44			09 54				10 04		10 14				10 24	10 34				10 44
Maryland	d																								
Stratford [7] ⊖	d	09 05	09 29	09 39	09 19	09 22	09 49	09 36		09 59	09 39			10 09	09 52	10 19	10 01	10 05		10 29	10 39	10 19		10 22	10 49
London Liverpool Street [15] ⊖	a	09 14	09 37	09 47	09 28	09 31	09 57	09 45		10 07	09 48			10 17	10 01	10 27	10 10	10 14		10 37	10 47	10 28		10 31	10 57

		LE ■	LE	LE ■			LE	LE ■	LE	LE ■	LE ■	LE ■	LE	LE		LE ■	LE ■	LE	LE ■	LE	LE ■	LE ■		LE	
Southend Victoria	d			09 50						10 10						10 30					10 50				
Prittlewell	d			09 52						10 12						10 32					10 52				
Southend Airport ✈	d			09 55						10 15						10 35					10 55				
Rochford	d			09 58						10 18						10 38					10 58				
Hockley	d			10 01						10 21						10 41					11 01				
Rayleigh	d			10 06						10 26						10 46					11 06				
Southminster	d										10 16											10 56			
Burnham-on-Crouch	d										10 20											11 00			
Althorne	d										10 25											11 05			
North Fambridge	d										10 31											11 11			
South Woodham Ferrers	d										10 36											11 16			
Battlesbridge	d										10 40											11 20			
Wickford [2]	d			10 11						10 31	10a46					10 51					11 11	11a26			
Billericay	d			10 17						10 37						10 57					11 17				
Shenfield [3]	a			10 25						10 45						11 05					11 25				
Shenfield [3]	d	10 20	10 24	10 25			10 34	10 38	10 44	10 45		10 51	10 54	11 04		11 05	11 08	11 14	11 20	11 24	11 25			11 34	
Brentwood	d		10 27				10 37		10 47				10 57	11 07				11 17		11 27				11 37	
Harold Wood	d		10 32				10 42		10 52				11 02	11 12				11 22		11 32				11 42	
Gidea Park [2]	d		10 36				10 46		10 56				11 06	11 16				11 26		11 36				11 46	
Romford	d	10 28	10 38				10 48		10 58	10 53			11 08	11 18				11 28	11 28	11 38				11 48	
Chadwell Heath	d		10 42				10 52		11 02				11 12	11 22				11 32		11 42				11 52	
Goodmayes	d		10 44				10 54		11 04				11 14	11 24				11 34		11 44				11 54	
Seven Kings	d		10 46				10 56		11 06				11 16	11 26				11 36		11 46				11 56	
Ilford [2]	d		10 49				10 59		11 09				11 19	11 29				11 39		11 49				11 59	
Manor Park	d		10 52				11 02		11 12				11 22	11 32				11 42		11 52				12 02	
Forest Gate	d		10 54				11 04		11 14				11 24	11 34				11 44		11 54				12 04	
Maryland	d																								
Stratford [7] ⊖	d	10 36	10 59	10 39			11 09	10 52	11 19	11 01		11 05	11 29	11 39		11 19	11 22	11 49	11 36	11 59	11 39			12 09	
London Liverpool Street [15] ⊖	a	10 45	11 07	10 48			11 17	11 01	11 27	11 10		11 14	11 37	11 47		11 28	11 31	11 57	11 45	12 07	11 48			12 17	

Southend Victoria, Southminster and Shenfield - London

Network Diagram - see first Page of Table 5

		LE ■	LE	LE ■	LE ■	LE	LE	LE ■	LE ■	LE ■		LE	LE ■	LE	LE ■		LE	LE ■	LE	LE ■		LE ■	LE ■	LE	LE
Southend Victoria	d			11 10				11 30							11 50					12 10					
Prittlewell	d			11 12				11 32							11 52					12 12					
Southend Airport ✈	d			11 15				11 35							11 55					12 15					
Rochford	d			11 18				11 38							11 58					12 18					
Hockley	d			11 21				11 41							12 01					12 21					
Rayleigh	d			11 26				11 46							12 06					12 26					
Southminster	d								11 36													12 16			
Burnham-on-Crouch	d								11 40													12 20			
Althorne	d								11 45													12 25			
North Fambridge	d								11 51													12 31			
South Woodham Ferrers	d								11 56													12 36			
Battlesbridge	d								12 00													12 40			
Wickford [2]	d			11 31				11 51	12a06						12 11					12 31		12a46			
Billericay	d			11 37				11 57							12 17					12 37					
Shenfield [3]	a			11 45				12 05							12 25					12 45					
Shenfield [3]	d	11 38	11 44	11 45	11 51	11 54	12 04	12 05		12 08		12 14	12 20	12 24	12 25		12 34	12 38	12 44	12 45			12 51	12 54	13 04
Brentwood	d		11 47			11 57	12 07					12 17		12 27			12 37		12 47					12 57	13 07
Harold Wood	d		11 52			12 02	12 12					12 22		12 32			12 42		12 52					13 02	13 12
Gidea Park [2]	d		11 56			12 06	12 16					12 26		12 36			12 46		12 56					13 06	13 16
Romford	d		11 58	11 53		12 08	12 18					12 28	12 28	12 38			12 48		12 58	12 53				13 08	13 18
Chadwell Heath	d		12 02			12 12	12 22					12 32		12 42			12 52		13 02					13 12	13 22
Goodmayes	d		12 04			12 14	12 24					12 34		12 44			12 54		13 04					13 14	13 24
Seven Kings	d		12 06			12 16	12 26					12 36		12 46			12 56		13 06					13 16	13 26
Ilford [2]	d		12 09			12 19	12 29					12 39		12 49			12 59		13 09					13 19	13 29
Manor Park	d		12 12			12 22	12 32					12 42		12 52			13 02		13 12					13 22	13 32
Forest Gate	d		12 14			12 24	12 34					12 44		12 54			13 04		13 14					13 24	13 34
Maryland	d																								
Stratford [7] ⊖	d	11 52	12 19	12 01	12 05	12 29	12 39	12 19		12 22		12 49	12 36	12 59	12 39		13 09	12 52	13 19	13 01			13 05	13 29	13 39
London Liverpool Street [15] ⊖	a	12 01	12 27	12 10	12 14	12 37	12 47	12 28		12 31		12 57	12 45	13 07	12 48		13 17	13 01	13 27	13 10			13 14	13 37	13 47

		LE ■	LE ■	LE	LE ■	LE		LE ■	LE ■		LE	LE ■	LE	LE ■	LE ■	LE		LE	LE ■	LE ■	LE ■	LE	LE ■	LE	LE ■
Southend Victoria	d	12 30						12 50						13 10					13 30						13 50
Prittlewell	d	12 32						12 52						13 12					13 32						13 52
Southend Airport ✈	d	12 35						12 55						13 15					13 35						13 55
Rochford	d	12 38						12 58						13 18					13 38						13 58
Hockley	d	12 41						13 01						13 21					13 41						14 01
Rayleigh	d	12 46						13 06						13 26					13 46						14 06
Southminster	d								12 56											13 36					
Burnham-on-Crouch	d								13 00											13 40					
Althorne	d								13 05											13 45					
North Fambridge	d								13 11											13 51					
South Woodham Ferrers	d								13 16											13 56					
Battlesbridge	d								13 20											14 00					
Wickford [2]	d	12 51						13 11	13a26					13 31					13 51	14a06					14 11
Billericay	d	12 57						13 17						13 37					13 57						14 17
Shenfield [3]	a	13 05						13 25						13 45					14 05						14 25
Shenfield [3]	d	13 05	13 08	13 14	13 20	13 24		13 25			13 34	13 38	13 44	13 45	13 51	13 54		14 04	14 05		14 08	14 14	14 20	14 24	14 25
Brentwood	d			13 17		13 27					13 37		13 47			13 57		14 07				14 17		14 27	
Harold Wood	d			13 22		13 32					13 42		13 52			14 02		14 12				14 22		14 32	
Gidea Park [2]	d			13 26		13 36					13 46		13 56			14 06		14 16				14 26		14 36	
Romford	d			13 28	13 28	13 38					13 48		13 58	13 53		14 08		14 18				14 28	14 28	14 38	
Chadwell Heath	d			13 32		13 42					13 52		14 02			14 12		14 22				14 32		14 42	
Goodmayes	d			13 34		13 44					13 54		14 04			14 14		14 24				14 34		14 44	
Seven Kings	d			13 36		13 46					13 56		14 06			14 16		14 26				14 36		14 46	
Ilford [2]	d			13 39		13 49					13 59		14 09			14 19		14 29				14 39		14 49	
Manor Park	d			13 42		13 52					14 02		14 12			14 22		14 32				14 42		14 52	
Forest Gate	d			13 44		13 54					14 04		14 14			14 24		14 34				14 44		14 54	
Maryland	d																								
Stratford [7] ⊖	d	13 19	13 22	13 49	13 36	13 59		13 39			14 09	13 52	14 19	14 01	14 05	14 29		14 39	14 19		14 22	14 49	14 36	14 59	14 39
London Liverpool Street [15] ⊖	a	13 28	13 31	13 57	13 45	14 07		13 48			14 17	14 01	14 27	14 10	14 14	14 37		14 47	14 28		14 31	14 57	14 45	15 07	14 48

Southend Victoria, Southminster and Shenfield - London

Network Diagram - see first Page of Table 5

		LE	LE ■	LE			LE ■	LE ■	LE ■	LE	LE	LE ■		LE ■	LE	LE	LE ■	LE ■		LE	LE ■	LE		LE ■	LE ■
Southend Victoria	d						14 10					14 30					14 50							15 10	
Prittlewell	d						14 12					14 32					14 52							15 12	
Southend Airport ✈	d						14 15					14 35					14 55							15 15	
Rochford	d						14 18					14 38					14 58							15 18	
Hockley	d						14 21					14 41					15 01							15 21	
Rayleigh	d						14 26					14 46					15 06							15 26	
Southminster	d							14 16										14 56							
Burnham-on-Crouch	d							14 20										15 00							
Althorne	d							14 25										15 05							
North Fambridge	d							14 31										15 11							
South Woodham Ferrers	d							14 36										15 16							
Battlesbridge	d							14 40										15 20							
Wickford [2]	d						14 31	14a46				14 51					15 11	15a26						15 31	
Billericay	d						14 37					14 57					15 17							15 37	
Shenfield [3]	a						14 45					15 05					15 25							15 45	
Shenfield [3]	d	14 34	14 38	14 44			14 45		14 51	14 54	15 04	15 05		15 08	15 14	15 24	15 25			15 34	15 38	15 44		15 45	15 51
Brentwood	d	14 37		14 47						14 57	15 07				15 17	15 27				15 37		15 47			
Harold Wood	d	14 42		14 52						15 02	15 12				15 22	15 32				15 42		15 52			
Gidea Park [2]	d	14 46		14 56						15 06	15 16				15 26	15 36				15 46		15 56			
Romford	d	14 48		14 58			14 53			15 08	15 18				15 28	15 38				15 48		15 58		15 53	
Chadwell Heath	d	14 52		15 02						15 12	15 22				15 32	15 42				15 52		16 02			
Goodmayes	d	14 54		15 04						15 14	15 24				15 34	15 44				15 54		16 04			
Seven Kings	d	14 56		15 06						15 16	15 26				15 36	15 46				15 56		16 06			
Ilford [2]	d	14 59		15 09						15 19	15 29				15 39	15 49				15 59		16 09			
Manor Park	d	15 02		15 12						15 22	15 32				15 42	15 52				16 02		16 12			
Forest Gate	d	15 04		15 14						15 24	15 34				15 44	15 54				16 04		16 14			
Maryland	d																								
Stratford [7] ⊖	d	15 09	14 52	15 19			15 01		15 05	15 29	15 39	15 19		15 22	15 49	15 59	15 39			16 09	15 52	16 19		16 01	16 05
London Liverpool Street [15] ⊖	a	15 17	15 01	15 27			15 10		15 14	15 37	15 47	15 28		15 31	15 57	16 07	15 48			16 17	16 01	16 27		16 10	16 14

		LE	LE	LE ■	LE ■	LE ■	LE	LE ■		LE	LE ■	LE ◇■	LE	LE ■	LE	LE ■	LE ■	LE ■		LE	LE	LE ■	LE ■	LE	LE
Southend Victoria	d			15 30							15 50					16 10						16 30			
Prittlewell	d			15 32							15 52					16 12						16 32			
Southend Airport ✈	d			15 35							15 55					16 15						16 35			
Rochford	d			15 38							15 58					16 18						16 38			
Hockley	d			15 41							16 01					16 21						16 41			
Rayleigh	d			15 46							16 06					16 26						16 46			
Southminster	d				15 36												16 16								
Burnham-on-Crouch	d				15 40												16 20								
Althorne	d				15 45												16 25								
North Fambridge	d				15 51												16 31								
South Woodham Ferrers	d				15 56												16 36								
Battlesbridge	d				16 00												16 40								
Wickford [2]	d			15 51	16a06						16 11					16 31	16a46					16 51			
Billericay	d			15 57							16 17					16 37						16 57			
Shenfield [3]	a			16 05							16 25					16 45						17 05			
Shenfield [3]	d	15 54	16 04	16 05		16 08	16 14	16 20		16 24	16 25		16 34	16 38	16 44	16 45		16 51		16 54	17 04	17 05	17 08	17 14	17 24
Brentwood	d	15 57	16 07				16 17			16 27			16 37		16 47					16 57	17 07			17 17	17 27
Harold Wood	d	16 02	16 12				16 22			16 32			16 42		16 52					17 02	17 12			17 22	17 32
Gidea Park [2]	d	16 06	16 16				16 26			16 36			16 46		16 56					17 06	17 16			17 26	17 36
Romford	d	16 08	16 18				16 28	16 28		16 38			16 48		16 58	16 53				17 08	17 18			17 28	17 38
Chadwell Heath	d	16 12	16 22				16 32			16 42			16 52		17 02					17 12	17 22			17 32	17 42
Goodmayes	d	16 14	16 24				16 34			16 44			16 54		17 04					17 14	17 24			17 34	17 44
Seven Kings	d	16 16	16 26				16 36			16 46			16 56		17 06					17 16	17 26			17 36	17 46
Ilford [2]	d	16 19	16 29				16 39			16 49			16 59		17 09					17 19	17 29			17 39	17 49
Manor Park	d	16 22	16 32				16 42			16 52			17 02		17 12					17 22	17 32			17 42	17 52
Forest Gate	d	16 24	16 34				16 44			16 54			17 04		17 14					17 24	17 34			17 44	17 54
Maryland	d																								
Stratford [7] ⊖	d	16 29	16 39	16 19		16 22	16 49	16 36		16 59	16 39		17 09	16 52	17 19	17 01		17 05		17 29	17 39	17 19	17 22	17 49	17 59
London Liverpool Street [15] ⊖	a	16 37	16 47	16 28		16 31	16 57	16 45		17 07	16 48	16 55	17 17	17 01	17 27	17 10		17 14		17 37	17 47	17 28	17 31	17 57	18 07

Saturdays

28 July to 11 August

Southend Victoria, Southminster and Shenfield - London

Network Diagram - see first Page of Table 5

Station		LE 1	LE 1			LE	LE 1	LE 1	LE	LE 1	LE	LE	LE 1	LE 1		LE 1	LE	LE 1	LE	LE 1		LE	LE 1	LE
Southend Victoria	d	16 50						17 10					17 30							17 50				
Prittlewell	d	16 52						17 12					17 32							17 52				
Southend Airport ✈	d	16 55						17 15					17 35							17 55				
Rochford	d	16 58						17 18					17 38							17 58				
Hockley	d	17 01						17 21					17 41							18 01				
Rayleigh	d	17 06						17 26					17 46							18 06				
Southminster	d		16 56											17 36										
Burnham-on-Crouch	d		17 00											17 40										
Althorne	d		17 05											17 45										
North Fambridge	d		17 11											17 51										
South Woodham Ferrers	d		17 16											17 56										
Battlesbridge	d		17 20											18 00										
Wickford 2	d	17 11	17a26					17 31					17 51	18a06						18 11				
Billericay	d	17 17						17 37					17 57							18 17				
Shenfield 3	a	17 25						17 44					18 05							18 25				
Shenfield 3	d	17 25				17 34	17 38	17 45	17 44	17 51	17 54	18 04	18 05			18 08	18 14	18 20	18 24	18 25		18 34	18 38	18 44
Brentwood	d					17 37			17 47		17 57	18 07					18 17		18 27			18 37		18 47
Harold Wood	d					17 42			17 52		18 02	18 12					18 22		18 32			18 42		18 52
Gidea Park 2	d					17 46			17 56		18 06	18 16					18 26		18 36			18 46		18 56
Romford	d					17 48		17 53	17 58		18 08	18 18					18 28	18 28	18 38			18 48		18 58
Chadwell Heath	d					17 52			18 02		18 12	18 22					18 32		18 42			18 52		19 02
Goodmayes	d					17 54			18 04		18 14	18 24					18 34		18 44			18 54		19 04
Seven Kings	d					17 56			18 06		18 16	18 26					18 36		18 46			18 56		19 06
Ilford 2	d					17 59			18 09		18 19	18 29					18 39		18 49			18 59		19 09
Manor Park	d					18 02			18 12		18 22	18 32					18 42		18 52			19 02		19 12
Forest Gate	d					18 04			18 14		18 24	18 34					18 44		18 54			19 04		19 14
Maryland	d																							
Stratford 7 ⊖	d	17 39				18 09	17 52	18 01	18 19	18 05	18 29	18 39	18 19			18 22	18 49	18 36	18 59	18 39		19 09	18 52	19 19
London Liverpool Street 15 ⊖	a	17 48				18 17	18 01	18 10	18 27	18 14	18 37	18 47	18 28			18 31	18 57	18 45	19 07	18 48		19 17	19 01	19 27

Station		LE 1	LE 1	LE 1	LE	LE	LE 1	LE 1	LE	LE		LE 1	LE 1		LE	LE 1	LE	LE 1	LE 1	LE		LE	LE 1	LE 1	LE 1
Southend Victoria	d	18 10					18 30					18 50						19 10					19 30		
Prittlewell	d	18 12					18 32					18 52						19 12					19 32		
Southend Airport ✈	d	18 15					18 35					18 55						19 15					19 35		
Rochford	d	18 18					18 38					18 58						19 18					19 38		
Hockley	d	18 21					18 41					19 01						19 21					19 41		
Rayleigh	d	18 26					18 46					19 06						19 26					19 46		
Southminster	d		18 16										18 56											19 36	
Burnham-on-Crouch	d		18 20										19 00											19 40	
Althorne	d		18 25										19 05											19 45	
North Fambridge	d		18 31										19 11											19 51	
South Woodham Ferrers	d		18 36										19 16											19 56	
Battlesbridge	d		18 40										19 20											20 00	
Wickford 2	d	18 31	18a46				18 51					19 11	19a26					19 31					19 51	20a06	
Billericay	d	18 37					18 57					19 17						19 37					19 57		
Shenfield 3	a	18 45					19 05					19 25						19 45					20 05		
Shenfield 3	d	18 45		18 51	18 54	19 04	19 05	19 08	19 14	19 24		19 25			19 34	19 38	19 44	19 45	19 51	19 54		20 04	20 05		20 08
Brentwood	d				18 57	19 07			19 17	19 27					19 37		19 47			19 57		20 07			
Harold Wood	d				19 02	19 12			19 22	19 32					19 42		19 52			20 02		20 12			
Gidea Park 2	d				19 06	19 16			19 26	19 36					19 46		19 56			20 06		20 16			
Romford	d				19 08	19 18			19 28	19 38					19 48		19 58			20 08		20 18			
Chadwell Heath	d				19 12	19 22			19 32	19 42					19 52		20 02			20 12		20 22			
Goodmayes	d				19 14	19 24			19 34	19 44					19 54		20 04			20 14		20 24			
Seven Kings	d				19 16	19 26			19 36	19 46					19 56		20 06			20 16		20 26			
Ilford 2	d				19 19	19 29			19 39	19 49					19 59		20 09			20 19		20 29			
Manor Park	d				19 22	19 32			19 42	19 52					20 02		20 12			20 22		20 32			
Forest Gate	d				19 24	19 34			19 44	19 54					20 04		20 14			20 24		20 34			
Maryland	d																								
Stratford 7 ⊖	d	19 01		19 05	19 29	19 39	19 19	19 22	19 49	19 59		19 39			20 09	19 52	20 19	20 01	20 05	20 29		20 39	20s19		20 22
London Liverpool Street 15 ⊖	a	19 10		19 14	19 37	19 47	19 28	19 31	19 57	20 07		19 48			20 17	20 01	20 27	20 10	20 14	20 37		20 47	20 28		20 33

Table 5

Saturdays

28 July to 11 August

Southend Victoria, Southminster and Shenfield - London

Network Diagram - see first Page of Table 5

Station		LE	LE 1	LE	LE 1			LE	LE 1	LE	LE 1	LE 1	LE 1	LE	LE 1	LE 1		LE	LE 1	LE	LE 1	LE 1		LE	LE 1
Southend Victoria	d				19 50						20 10				20 30						20 50				
Prittlewell	d				19 52						20 12				20 32						20 52				
Southend Airport ✈	d				19 55						20 15				20 35						20 55				
Rochford	d				19 58						20 18				20 38						20 58				
Hockley	d				20 01						20 21				20 41						21 01				
Rayleigh	d				20 06						20 26				20 46						21 06				
Southminster	d											20 16										20 56			
Burnham-on-Crouch	d											20 20										21 00			
Althorne	d											20 25										21 05			
North Fambridge	d											20 31										21 11			
South Woodham Ferrers	d											20 36										21 16			
Battlesbridge	d											20 40										21 20			
Wickford 2	d				20 11						20 31	20a46			20 51						21 11	21a26			
Billericay	d				20 17						20 37				20 57						21 17				
Shenfield 3	a				20 25						20 45				21 05						21 25				
Shenfield 3	d	20 14	20 20	20 24	20 25			20 34	20 38	20 44	20 45		20 51	20 59	21 05	21 08		21 14	21 20	21 24	21 25			21 34	21 38
Brentwood	d	20 17		20 27				20 37		20 47				21 02				21 17		21 27				21 37	
Harold Wood	d	20 22		20 32				20 42		20 52				21 07				21 22		21 32				21 42	
Gidea Park 2	d	20 26		20 36				20 46		20 56				21 11				21 26		21 36				21 46	
Romford	d	20 28	20 28	20 38				20 48		20 58	20 53			21 13				21 28		21 38				21 48	
Chadwell Heath	d	20 32		20 42				20 52		21 02				21 17				21 32		21 42				21 52	
Goodmayes	d	20 34		20 44				20 54		21 04				21 19				21 34		21 44				21 54	
Seven Kings	d	20 36		20 46				20 56		21 06				21 21				21 36		21 46				21 56	
Ilford 2	d	20 39		20 49				20 59		21 09				21 24				21 39		21 49				21 59	
Manor Park	d	20 42		20 52				21 02		21 12				21 27				21 42		21 52				22 02	
Forest Gate	d	20 44		20 54				21 04		21 14				21 29				21 44		21 54				22 04	
Maryland	d																								
Stratford 7 ⊖	d	20 49	20 36	20 59	20 39			21 09	20 52	21 19	21 01		21 05	21 34	21 19	21 22		21 49	21 36	21 59	21 39			22 09	21 52
London Liverpool Street 15 ⊖	a	20 57	20 45	21 07	20 48			21 17	21 01	21 27	21 10		21 14	21 42	21 28	21 31		21 57	21 45	22 07	21 48			22 20	22 01

Station		LE		LE 1	LE 1	LE	LE 1	LE 1	LE 1	LE	LE 1	LE		LE	LE	LE 1	LE	LE 1	LE 1	LE 1	LE	LE 1		LE 1	LE
Southend Victoria	d			21 10			21 30					21 50						22 10				22 30			
Prittlewell	d			21 12			21 32					21 52						22 12				22 32			
Southend Airport ✈	d			21 15			21 35					21 55						22 15				22 35			
Rochford	d			21 18			21 38					21 58						22 18				22 38			
Hockley	d			21 21			21 41					22 01						22 21				22 41			
Rayleigh	d			21 26			21 46					22 06						22 26				22 46			
Southminster	d							21 36											22 16						
Burnham-on-Crouch	d							21 40											22 20						
Althorne	d							21 45											22 25						
North Fambridge	d							21 51											22 31						
South Woodham Ferrers	d							21 56											22 36						
Battlesbridge	d							22 00											22 40						
Wickford 2	d			21 31			21 51	22a06				22 11						22 31	22a46			22 51			
Billericay	d			21 37			21 57					22 17						22 37				22 57			
Shenfield 3	a			21 45			22 05					22 25						22 45				23 05			
Shenfield 3	d	21 44		21 45	21 51	21 59	22 05		22 08	22 14	22 20	22 25			22 29	22 38	22 44	22 45		22 51	22 59	23 05		23 08	
Brentwood	d	21 47				22 02				22 17					22 32		22 47				23 02				
Harold Wood	d	21 52				22 07				22 22					22 37		22 52				23 07				
Gidea Park 2	d	21 56				22 11				22 26					22 41		22 56				23 11				
Romford	d	21 58				22 13				22 28					22 43		22 58				23 13				
Chadwell Heath	d	22 02				22 17				22 32					22 47		23 02				23 17				
Goodmayes	d	22 04				22 19				22 34					22 49		23 04				23 19				
Seven Kings	d	22 06				22 21				22 36					22 51		23 06				23 21				
Ilford 2	d	22 09				22 24				22 41					22 54		23 09				23 24				
Manor Park	d	22 12				22 27				22 44					22 57		23 12				23 27				
Forest Gate	d	22 14				22 29				22 46					22 59		23 14				23 29				
Maryland	d																								
Stratford 7 ⊖	d	22 19		22 04	22 13	22 34	22 24		22 28	22 52	22 40	22 44		22 48	23 04	22 58	23 19	23 08		23 12	23 36	23 24		23 28	23 32
London Liverpool Street 15 ⊖	a	22 27		22 13	22 21	22 42	22 32		22 36	23 00	22 48	22 52		22 56	23 12	23 06	23 27	23 16		23 20	23 44	23 32		23 36	23 40

Table 5

Saturdays

28 July to 11 August

Southend Victoria, Southminster and Shenfield - London

Network Diagram - see first Page of Table 5

		LE	LE ■	LE ■	LE ■	LE	LE	LE	LE ■	LE
Southend Victoria	d			22 50					23 10	
Prittlewell	d			22 52					23 12	
Southend Airport ✈	d			22 55					23 15	
Rochford	d			22 58					23 18	
Hockley	d			23 01					23 21	
Rayleigh	d			23 06					23 26	
Southminster	d				22 56					
Burnham-on-Crouch	d				23 00					
Althorne	d				23 05					
North Fambridge	d				23 11					
South Woodham Ferrers	d				23 16					
Battlesbridge	d				23 20					
Wickford ■	d			23 11	23a26				23 31	
Billericay	d			23 17					23 37	
Shenfield ■	a			23 25					23 45	
Shenfield ■	d	23 14	23 20	23 25			23 29	23 44	23 45	23 59
Brentwood	d	23 17					23 32	23 47		00 02
Harold Wood	d	23 22					23 37	23 52		00 07
Gidea Park ■	d	23 26					23 41	23 56		00 11
Romford	d	23 28					23 43	23 58		00 13
Chadwell Heath	d	23 32					23 47	00 02		00 17
Goodmayes	d	23 34					23 49	00 04		00 19
Seven Kings	d	23 36					23 51	00 06		00 21
Ilford ■	d	23 39					23 54	00 09		00 24
Manor Park	d	23 42					23 57	00 12		00 27
Forest Gate	d	23 45					23 59	00 14		00 29
Maryland	d									
Stratford ■ ⊖	d	23 50	23 40	23 44		23 54	00 04	00 20	00 08	00 40
London Liverpool Street ■ ⊖	a	23 58	23 48	23 52		00 02	00 12	00 28	00 16	00 48

Saturdays

18 August to 25 August

		LE ◇■	LE	LE ■	CC	LE	LE ■	LE	LE ■	LE ■	LE ■	LE	LE ■	LE ■	LE	LE ■	LE ■	LE	LE	LE ■	LE	LE ■
Southend Victoria	d						04 00			04 30			05 00				05 30					06 00
Prittlewell	d						04 02			04 32			05 02				05 32					06 02
Southend Airport ✈	d						04 05			04 35			05 05				05 35					06 05
Rochford	d						04 08			04 38			05 08				05 38					06 08
Hockley	d						04 12			04 42			05 11				05 41					06 11
Rayleigh	d						04 16			04 46			05 16				05 46					06 16
Southminster	d			22p56																		
Burnham-on-Crouch	d			23p00																		
Althorne	d			23p05																		
North Fambridge	d			23p11																		
South Woodham Ferrers	d			23p16																		
Battlesbridge	d			23p20																		
Wickford ■	d			23p26			04 21			04 51			05 21				05 51					06 21
Billericay	d			23p32			04 28			04 58			05 27				05 57					06 27
Shenfield ■	a			23p39			04 39			05 09			05 35				06 05					06 35
Shenfield ■	d		23p29	23p39		23p44	04 39			05 09	05 24		05 35		05 44	05 53	06 05		06 14	06 24		06 35
Brentwood	d		23p32			23p47	04 42			05 12					05 47				06 17			
Harold Wood	d		23p37			23p52	04 47			05 17					05 52				06 22			
Gidea Park ■	d		23p41			23p56	04 51			05 21	05 31				05 56			06 16	06 26		06 36	
Romford	d		23p43	23p47		23p58	04 53			05 23			05 43		05 58			06 18	06 28		06 38	06 43
Chadwell Heath	d		23p47			00 02	04 57			05 27					06 02			06 22	06 32		06 42	
Goodmayes	d		23p49			00 04	04 59			05 29					06 04			06 24	06 34		06 44	
Seven Kings	d		23p51			00 06	05 01			05 31	05 36				06 06			06 26	06 36		06 46	
Ilford ■	d		23p54			00 09	05 04	05 09		05 34		05 39			06 09			06 29	06 39		06 49	
Manor Park	d		23p57			00 12		05 11				05 41			06 12			06 32	06 42		06 52	
Forest Gate	d		23p59			00 14		05 14				05 44			06 14			06 34	06 44		06 54	
Maryland	d		00 01			00 16		05 16				05 46			06 16			06 36	06 46		06 56	
Stratford ■ ⊖	d	23b52	00 04	23p56	00 09	00 19	05 10	05 18	05 30	05 40	05 42	05 48	05 51	06 05	06 19	06 07	06 19	06 39	06 49	06 38	06 59	06 51
London Liverpool Street ■ ⊖	a	00 02	00 12	00 05	00 20	00 27	05 18	05 26	08 13	05 48	05 55	05 56	06 00	06 14	06 27	06 16	06 28	06 47	06 57	06 47	07 07	07 00

b Previous night, stops to set down only

Table 5

Saturdays

18 August to 25 August

Southend Victoria, Southminster and Shenfield - London

Network Diagram - see first Page of Table 5

		LE ■	LE	LE	LE ■	LE	LE	LE ■	LE ■	LE	LE ■	LE	LE ■	LE ■	LE	LE ■	LE	LE ■	LE ■	LE	LE	LE ■
Southend Victoria	d							06 30					06 50					07 10				07 30
Prittlewell	d							06 32					06 52					07 12				07 32
Southend Airport ✈	d							06 35					06 55					07 15				07 35
Rochford	d							06 38					06 58					07 18				07 38
Hockley	d							06 41					07 01					07 21				07 41
Rayleigh	d							06 46					07 06					07 26				07 46
Southminster	d	06 16												06 56								
Burnham-on-Crouch	d	06 20												07 00								
Althorne	d	06 25												07 05								
North Fambridge	d	06 31												07 11								
South Woodham Ferrers	d	06 36												07 16								
Battlesbridge	d	06 40												07 20								
Wickford ■	d	06a46						06 51					07 11	07a26				07 31				07 51
Billericay	d							06 57					07 17					07 37				07 57
Shenfield ■	a							07 05					07 25					07 45				08 05
Shenfield ■	d			06 44	06 51		07 04	07 05	07 08	07 14	07 20	07 24	07 25		07 34	07 38	07 44	07 45	07 51	07 54	08 04	08 05
Brentwood	d			06 47			07 07			07 17		07 27			07 37		07 47			07 57	08 07	
Harold Wood	d			06 52			07 12			07 22		07 32			07 42		07 52			08 02	08 12	
Gidea Park ■	d		06 46	06 56		07 06	07 16			07 26		07 36			07 46		07 56			08 06	08 16	
Romford	d		06 48	06 58		07 08	07 18			07 28	07 28	07 38			07 48		07 58	07 53		08 08	08 18	
Chadwell Heath	d		06 52	07 02		07 12	07 22			07 32		07 42			07 52		08 02			08 12	08 22	
Goodmayes	d		06 54	07 04		07 14	07 24			07 34		07 44			07 54		08 04			08 14	08 24	
Seven Kings	d		06 56	07 06		07 16	07 26			07 36		07 46			07 56		08 06			08 16	08 26	
Ilford ■	d		06 59	07 09		07 19	07 29			07 39		07 49			07 59		08 09			08 19	08 29	
Manor Park	d		07 02	07 12		07 22	07 32			07 42		07 52			08 02		08 12			08 22	08 32	
Forest Gate	d		07 04	07 14		07 24	07 34			07 44		07 54			08 04		08 14			08 24	08 34	
Maryland	d		07 06	07 16		07 26	07 36			07 46		07 56			08 06		08 16			08 26	08 36	
Stratford ■ ⊖	d		07 09	07 19	07 05	07 29	07 39	07 19	07 22	07 49	07 36	07 59	07 39		08 09	07 52	08 19	08 01	08 05	08 29	08 39	08 19
London Liverpool Street ■ ⊖	a		07 17	07 27	07 14	07 37	07 47	07 28	07 31	07 57	07 45	08 07	07 48		08 17	08 01	08 27	08 10	08 14	08 37	08 47	08 28

		LE ■	LE ■	LE	LE ■	LE	LE ■	LE	LE ■	LE	LE ■	LE ■	LE ■	LE	LE	LE ■	LE ■	LE	LE ■	LE	LE ■
Southend Victoria	d						07 50				08 10					08 30					08 50
Prittlewell	d						07 52				08 12					08 32					08 52
Southend Airport ✈	d						07 55				08 15					08 35					08 55
Rochford	d						07 58				08 18					08 38					08 58
Hockley	d						08 01				08 21					08 41					09 01
Rayleigh	d						08 06				08 26					08 46					09 06
Southminster	d	07 36										08 16									
Burnham-on-Crouch	d	07 40										08 20									
Althorne	d	07 45										08 25									
North Fambridge	d	07 51										08 31									
South Woodham Ferrers	d	07 56										08 36									
Battlesbridge	d	08 00										08 40									
Wickford ■	d	08a06					08 11				08 31	08a46				08 51					09 11
Billericay	d						08 17				08 37					08 57					09 17
Shenfield ■	a						08 25				08 45					09 05					09 25
Shenfield ■	d		08 08	08 14	08 20	08 24	08 25	08 34	08 38	08 44	08 45		08 51	08 54	09 04	09 05	09 08	09 14	09 20	09 24	09 25
Brentwood	d			08 17		08 27		08 37		08 47				08 57	09 07			09 17		09 27	
Harold Wood	d			08 22		08 32		08 42		08 52				09 02	09 12			09 22		09 32	
Gidea Park ■	d			08 26		08 36		08 46		08 56				09 06	09 16			09 26		09 36	
Romford	d			08 28	08 28	08 38		08 48		08 58	08 53			09 08	09 18			09 28	09 28	09 38	
Chadwell Heath	d			08 32		08 42		08 52		09 02				09 12	09 22			09 32		09 42	
Goodmayes	d			08 34		08 44		08 54		09 04				09 14	09 24			09 34		09 44	
Seven Kings	d			08 36		08 46		08 56		09 06				09 16	09 26			09 36		09 46	
Ilford ■	d			08 39		08 49		08 59		09 09				09 19	09 29			09 39		09 49	
Manor Park	d			08 42		08 52		09 02		09 12				09 22	09 32			09 42		09 52	
Forest Gate	d			08 44		08 54		09 04		09 14				09 24	09 34			09 44		09 54	
Maryland	d			08 46		08 56		09 06		09 16				09 26	09 36			09 46		09 56	
Stratford ■ ⊖	d		08 22	08 49	08 36	08 59	08 39	09 09	08 52	09 19	09 01		09 05	09 29	09 39	09 19	09 22	09 49	09 36	09 59	09 39
London Liverpool Street ■ ⊖	a		08 31	08 57	08 45	09 07	08 48	09 17	09 01	09 27	09 10		09 14	09 37	09 47	09 28	09 31	09 57	09 45	10 07	09 48

18 August to 25 August

Southend Victoria, Southminster and Shenfield - London

Network Diagram - see first Page of Table 5

		LE 1		LE	LE 1	LE	LE 1	LE 1		LE	LE	LE 1	LE 1	LE 1	LE	LE 1	LE	LE 1			LE	LE 1	LE	LE 1	LE 1
Southend Victoria	d						09 10					09 30						09 50						10 10	
Prittlewell	d						09 12					09 32						09 52						10 12	
Southend Airport ✈	d						09 15					09 35						09 55						10 15	
Rochford	d						09 18					09 38						09 58						10 18	
Hockley	d						09 21					09 41						10 01						10 21	
Rayleigh	d						09 26					09 46						10 06						10 26	
Southminster	d	08 56											09 36												10 16
Burnham-on-Crouch	d	09 00											09 40												10 20
Althorne	d	09 05											09 45												10 25
North Fambridge	d	09 11											09 51												10 31
South Woodham Ferrers	d	09 16											09 56												10 36
Battlesbridge	d	09 20											10 00												10 40
Wickford 2	d	09a26					09 31					09 51	10a06					10 11						10 31	10a46
Billericay	d						09 37					09 57						10 17						10 37	
Shenfield 3	a						09 45					10 05						10 25						10 45	
Shenfield 3	d			09 34	09 38	09 44	09 45	09 51		09 54	10 04	10 05		10 08	10 14	10 20	10 24	10 25			10 34	10 38	10 44	10 45	
Brentwood	d			09 37		09 47				09 57	10 07				10 17		10 27				10 37		10 47		
Harold Wood	d			09 42		09 52				10 02	10 12				10 22		10 32				10 42		10 52		
Gidea Park 2	d			09 46		09 56				10 06	10 16				10 26		10 36				10 46		10 56		
Romford	d			09 48		09 58	09 53			10 08	10 18				10 28	10 28	10 38				10 48		10 58	10 53	
Chadwell Heath	d			09 52		10 02				10 12	10 22				10 32		10 42				10 52		11 02		
Goodmayes	d			09 54		10 04				10 14	10 24				10 34		10 44				10 54		11 04		
Seven Kings	d			09 56		10 06				10 16	10 26				10 36		10 46				10 56		11 06		
Ilford 2	d			09 59		10 09				10 19	10 29				10 39		10 49				10 59		11 09		
Manor Park	d			10 02		10 12				10 22	10 32				10 42		10 52				11 02		11 12		
Forest Gate	d			10 04		10 14				10 24	10 34				10 44		10 54				11 04		11 14		
Maryland	d			10 06		10 16				10 26	10 36				10 46		10 56				11 06		11 16		
Stratford 7 ⊖	d			10 09	09 52	10 19	10 01	10 05		10 29	10 39	10 19		10 22	10 49	10 36	10 59	10 39			11 09	10 52	11 19	11 01	
London Liverpool Street 15 ⊖	a			10 17	10 01	10 27	10 10	10 14		10 37	10 47	10 28		10 31	10 57	10 45	11 07	10 48			11 17	11 01	11 27	11 10	

		LE 1	LE	LE		LE 1	LE 1	LE	LE 1	LE	LE 1	LE 1		LE		LE 1	LE	LE 1	LE 1	LE	LE	LE 1	LE 1	LE 1	
Southend Victoria	d					10 30					10 50							11 10				11 30			
Prittlewell	d					10 32					10 52							11 12				11 32			
Southend Airport ✈	d					10 35					10 55							11 15				11 35			
Rochford	d					10 38					10 58							11 18				11 38			
Hockley	d					10 41					11 01							11 21				11 41			
Rayleigh	d					10 46					11 06							11 26				11 46			
Southminster	d											10 56											11 36		
Burnham-on-Crouch	d											11 00											11 40		
Althorne	d											11 05											11 45		
North Fambridge	d											11 11											11 51		
South Woodham Ferrers	d											11 16											11 56		
Battlesbridge	d											11 20											12 00		
Wickford 2	d					10 51					11 11	11a26						11 31				11 51	12a06		
Billericay	d					10 57					11 17							11 37				11 57			
Shenfield 3	a					11 05					11 25							11 45				12 05			
Shenfield 3	d	10 51	10 54	11 04		11 05	11 08	11 14	11 20	11 24	11 25			11 34		11 38	11 44	11 45	11 51	11 54	12 04	12 05		12 08	
Brentwood	d		10 57	11 07				11 17		11 27				11 37			11 47			11 57	12 07				
Harold Wood	d		11 02	11 12				11 22		11 32				11 42			11 52			12 02	12 12				
Gidea Park 2	d		11 06	11 16				11 26		11 36				11 46			11 56			12 06	12 16				
Romford	d		11 08	11 18				11 28	11 28	11 38				11 48			11 58	11 53		12 08	12 18				
Chadwell Heath	d		11 12	11 22				11 32		11 42				11 52			12 02			12 12	12 22				
Goodmayes	d		11 14	11 24				11 34		11 44				11 54			12 04			12 14	12 24				
Seven Kings	d		11 16	11 26				11 36		11 46				11 56			12 06			12 16	12 26				
Ilford 2	d		11 19	11 29				11 39		11 49				11 59			12 09			12 19	12 29				
Manor Park	d		11 22	11 32				11 42		11 52				12 02			12 12			12 22	12 32				
Forest Gate	d		11 24	11 34				11 44		11 54				12 04			12 14			12 24	12 34				
Maryland	d		11 26	11 36				11 46		11 56				12 06			12 16			12 26	12 36				
Stratford 7 ⊖	d	11 05	11 29	11 39		11 19	11 22	11 49	11 36	11 59	11 39			12 09		11 52	12 19	12 01	12 05	12 29	12 39	12 19		12 22	
London Liverpool Street 15 ⊖	a	11 14	11 37	11 47		11 28	11 31	11 57	11 45	12 07	11 48			12 17		12 01	12 27	12 10	12 14	12 37	12 47	12 28		12 31	

18 August to 25 August

Southend Victoria, Southminster and Shenfield - London

Network Diagram - see first Page of Table 5

		LE	LE 1	LE	LE 1		LE	LE 1	LE	LE 1		LE 1	LE 1	LE	LE	LE 1	LE 1	LE	LE 1	LE		LE 1	LE 1		LE
Southend Victoria	d				11 50					12 10						12 30						12 50			
Prittlewell	d				11 52					12 12						12 32						12 52			
Southend Airport ✈	d				11 55					12 15						12 35						12 55			
Rochford	d				11 58					12 18						12 38						12 58			
Hockley	d				12 01					12 21						12 41						13 01			
Rayleigh	d				12 06					12 26						12 46						13 06			
Southminster	d											12 16											12 56		
Burnham-on-Crouch	d											12 20											13 00		
Althorne	d											12 25											13 05		
North Fambridge	d											12 31											13 11		
South Woodham Ferrers	d											12 36											13 16		
Battlesbridge	d											12 40											13 20		
Wickford 2	d				12 11					12 31		12a46				12 51						13 11	13a26		
Billericay	d				12 17					12 37						12 57						13 17			
Shenfield 3	a				12 25					12 45						13 05						13 25			
Shenfield 3	d	12 14	12 20	12 24	12 25		12 34	12 38	12 44	12 45			12 51	12 54	13 04	13 05	13 08	13 14	13 20	13 24		13 25			13 34
Brentwood	d	12 17		12 27			12 37		12 47					12 57	13 07			13 17		13 27					13 37
Harold Wood	d	12 22		12 32			12 42		12 52					13 02	13 12			13 22		13 32					13 42
Gidea Park 2	d	12 26		12 36			12 46		12 56					13 06	13 16			13 26		13 36					13 46
Romford	d	12 28	12 28	12 38			12 48		12 58	12 53				13 08	13 18			13 28	13 28	13 38					13 48
Chadwell Heath	d	12 32		12 42			12 52		13 02					13 12	13 22			13 32		13 42					13 52
Goodmayes	d	12 34		12 44			12 54		13 04					13 14	13 24			13 34		13 44					13 54
Seven Kings	d	12 36		12 46			12 56		13 06					13 16	13 26			13 36		13 46					13 56
Ilford 2	d	12 39		12 49			12 59		13 09					13 19	13 29			13 39		13 49					13 59
Manor Park	d	12 42		12 52			13 02		13 12					13 22	13 32			13 42		13 52					14 02
Forest Gate	d	12 44		12 54			13 04		13 14					13 24	13 34			13 44		13 54					14 04
Maryland	d	12 46		12 56			13 06		13 16					13 26	13 36			13 46		13 56					14 06
Stratford 7 ⊖	d	12 49	12 36	12 59	12 39		13 09	12 52	13 19	13 01			13 05	13 29	13 39	13 19	13 22	13 49	13 36	13 59		13 39			14 09
London Liverpool Street 15 ⊖	a	12 57	12 45	13 07	12 48		13 17	13 01	13 27	13 10			13 14	13 37	13 47	13 28	13 31	13 57	13 45	14 07		13 48			14 17

		LE 1	LE	LE 1	LE 1	LE		LE	LE 1	LE 1	LE 1	LE	LE 1	LE	LE 1			LE	LE 1	LE	LE 1	LE 1	LE 1	LE	LE
Southend Victoria	d			13 10					13 30						13 50						14 10				
Prittlewell	d			13 12					13 32						13 52						14 12				
Southend Airport ✈	d			13 15					13 35						13 55						14 15				
Rochford	d			13 18					13 38						13 58						14 18				
Hockley	d			13 21					13 41						14 01						14 21				
Rayleigh	d			13 26					13 46						14 06						14 26				
Southminster	d									13 36												14 16			
Burnham-on-Crouch	d									13 40												14 20			
Althorne	d									13 45												14 25			
North Fambridge	d									13 51												14 31			
South Woodham Ferrers	d									13 56												14 36			
Battlesbridge	d									14 00												14 40			
Wickford 2	d			13 31					13 51	14a06					14 11						14 31	14a46			
Billericay	d			13 37					13 57						14 17						14 37				
Shenfield 3	a			13 45					14 05						14 25						14 45				
Shenfield 3	d	13 38	13 44	13 45	13 51	13 54		14 04	14 05		14 08	14 14	14 20	14 24	14 25			14 34	14 38	14 44	14 45		14 51	14 54	15 04
Brentwood	d		13 47			13 57		14 07				14 17		14 27				14 37		14 47				14 57	15 07
Harold Wood	d		13 52			14 02		14 12				14 22		14 32				14 42		14 52				15 02	15 12
Gidea Park 2	d		13 56			14 06		14 16				14 26		14 36				14 46		14 56				15 06	15 16
Romford	d		13 58	13 53		14 08		14 18				14 28	14 28	14 38				14 48		14 58	14 53			15 08	15 18
Chadwell Heath	d		14 02			14 12		14 22				14 32		14 42				14 52		15 02				15 12	15 22
Goodmayes	d		14 04			14 14		14 24				14 34		14 44				14 54		15 04				15 14	15 24
Seven Kings	d		14 06			14 16		14 26				14 36		14 46				14 56		15 06				15 16	15 26
Ilford 2	d		14 09			14 19		14 29				14 39		14 49				14 59		15 09				15 19	15 29
Manor Park	d		14 12			14 22		14 32				14 42		14 52				15 02		15 12				15 22	15 32
Forest Gate	d		14 14			14 24		14 34				14 44		14 54				15 04		15 14				15 24	15 34
Maryland	d		14 16			14 26		14 36				14 46		14 56				15 06		15 16				15 26	15 36
Stratford 7 ⊖	d	13 52	14 19	14 01	14 05	14 29		14 39	14 19		14 22	14 49	14 36	14 59	14 39			15 09	14 52	15 19	15 01		15 05	15 29	15 39
London Liverpool Street 15 ⊖	a	14 01	14 27	14 10	14 14	14 37		14 47	14 28		14 31	14 57	14 45	15 07	14 48			15 17	15 01	15 27	15 10		15 14	15 37	15 47

Saturdays
18 August to 25 August

Southend Victoria, Southminster and Shenfield - London

Network Diagram - see first Page of Table 5

		LE 1	LE 1	LE	LE 1	LE	LE 1	LE 1	LE	LE 1	LE	LE 1	LE 1	LE	LE	LE 1	LE 1	LE 1	LE	LE 1	LE
Southend Victoria	d	14 30					14 50					15 10				15 30					
Prittlewell	d	14 32					14 52					15 12				15 32					
Southend Airport ✈	d	14 35					14 55					15 15				15 35					
Rochford	d	14 38					14 58					15 18				15 38					
Hockley	d	14 41					15 01					15 21				15 41					
Rayleigh	d	14 46					15 06					15 26				15 46					
Southminster	d							14 56									15 36				
Burnham-on-Crouch	d							15 00									15 40				
Althorne	d							15 05									15 45				
North Fambridge	d							15 11									15 51				
South Woodham Ferrers	d							15 16									15 56				
Battlesbridge	d							15 20									16 00				
Wickford 2	d	14 51					15 11	15a26				15 31				15 51	16a06				
Billericay	d	14 57					15 17					15 37				15 57					
Shenfield 3	a	15 05					15 25					15 45				16 05					
Shenfield 3	d	15 05	15 08	15 14	15 20	15 24	15 25		15 34	15 38	15 44	15 45	15 51	15 54	16 04	16 05		16 08	16 14	16 20	16 24
Brentwood	d			15 17		15 27			15 37		15 47			15 57	16 07				16 17		16 27
Harold Wood	d			15 22		15 32			15 42		15 52			16 02	16 12				16 22		16 32
Gidea Park 2	d			15 26		15 36			15 46		15 56			16 06	16 16				16 26		16 36
Romford	d			15 28	15 28	15 38			15 48		15 58	15 53		16 08	16 18				16 28	16 28	16 38
Chadwell Heath	d			15 32		15 42			15 52		16 02			16 12	16 22				16 32		16 42
Goodmayes	d			15 34		15 44			15 54		16 04			16 14	16 24				16 34		16 44
Seven Kings	d			15 36		15 46			15 56		16 06			16 16	16 26				16 36		16 46
Ilford 2	d			15 39		15 49			15 59		16 09			16 19	16 29				16 39		16 49
Manor Park	d			15 42		15 52			16 02		16 12			16 22	16 32				16 42		16 52
Forest Gate	d			15 44		15 54			16 04		16 14			16 24	16 34				16 44		16 54
Maryland	d			15 46		15 56			16 06		16 16			16 26	16 36				16 46		16 56
Stratford 7 ⊖	d	15 19	15 22	15 49	15 36	15 59	15 39		16 09	15 52	16 19	16 01	16 05	16 29	16 39	16 19		16 22	16 49	16 36	16 59
London Liverpool Street 15 ⊖	a	15 28	15 31	15 57	15 45	16 07	15 48		16 17	16 01	16 27	16 10	16 14	16 37	16 47	16 28		16 31	16 57	16 45	17 07

		LE 1	LE	LE 1	LE	LE 1	LE 1	LE 1	LE	LE	LE 1	LE 1	LE	LE 1	LE	LE 1	LE 1	LE	LE 1	LE 1	LE
Southend Victoria	d	15 50				16 10					16 30					16 50				17 10	
Prittlewell	d	15 52				16 12					16 32					16 52				17 12	
Southend Airport ✈	d	15 55				16 15					16 35					16 55				17 15	
Rochford	d	15 58				16 18					16 38					16 58				17 18	
Hockley	d	16 01				16 21					16 41					17 01				17 21	
Rayleigh	d	16 06				16 26					16 46					17 06				17 26	
Southminster	d						16 16										16 56				
Burnham-on-Crouch	d						16 20										17 00				
Althorne	d						16 25										17 05				
North Fambridge	d						16 31										17 11				
South Woodham Ferrers	d						16 36										17 16				
Battlesbridge	d						16 40										17 20				
Wickford 2	d	16 11				16 31	16a46				16 51					17 11	17a26			17 31	
Billericay	d	16 17				16 37					16 57					17 17				17 37	
Shenfield 3	a	16 25				16 45					17 05					17 25				17 44	
Shenfield 3	d	16 25	16 34	16 38	16 44	16 45		16 51	16 54	17 04	17 05	17 08	17 14	17 20	17 24	17 25		17 34	17 38	17 45	17 44
Brentwood	d		16 37		16 47				16 57	17 07			17 17		17 27			17 37			17 47
Harold Wood	d		16 42		16 52				17 02	17 12			17 22		17 32			17 42			17 52
Gidea Park 2	d		16 46		16 56				17 06	17 16			17 26		17 36			17 46			17 56
Romford	d		16 48		16 58	16 53			17 08	17 18			17 28	17 28	17 38			17 48		17 53	17 58
Chadwell Heath	d		16 52		17 02				17 12	17 22			17 32		17 42			17 52			18 02
Goodmayes	d		16 54		17 04				17 14	17 24			17 34		17 44			17 54			18 04
Seven Kings	d		16 56		17 06				17 16	17 26			17 36		17 46			17 56			18 06
Ilford 2	d		16 59		17 09				17 19	17 29			17 39		17 49			17 59			18 09
Manor Park	d		17 02		17 12				17 22	17 32			17 42		17 52			18 02			18 12
Forest Gate	d		17 04		17 14				17 24	17 34			17 44		17 54			18 04			18 14
Maryland	d		17 06		17 16				17 26	17 36			17 46		17 56			18 06			18 16
Stratford 7 ⊖	d	16 39	17 09	16 52	17 19	17 01		17 05	17 29	17 39	17 19	17 22	17 49	17 36	17 59	17 39		18 09	17 52	18 01	18 19
London Liverpool Street 15 ⊖	a	16 48	17 17	17 01	17 27	17 10		17 14	17 37	17 47	17 28	17 31	17 57	17 45	18 07	17 48		18 17	18 01	18 10	18 27

Saturdays
18 August to 25 August

Southend Victoria, Southminster and Shenfield - London

Network Diagram - see first Page of Table 5

		LE 1	LE	LE	LE 1	LE 1	LE 1	LE	LE 1	LE	LE 1	LE ◇1 🅿	LE	LE 1	LE	LE 1	LE 1	LE 1	LE	LE	LE 1	LE 1
Southend Victoria	d				17 30						17 50					18 10					18 30	
Prittlewell	d				17 32						17 52					18 12					18 32	
Southend Airport ✈	d				17 35						17 55					18 15					18 35	
Rochford	d				17 38						17 58					18 18					18 38	
Hockley	d				17 41						18 01					18 21					18 41	
Rayleigh	d				17 46						18 06					18 26					18 46	
Southminster	d					17 36											18 16					
Burnham-on-Crouch	d					17 40											18 20					
Althorne	d					17 45											18 25					
North Fambridge	d					17 51											18 31					
South Woodham Ferrers	d					17 56											18 36					
Battlesbridge	d					18 00											18 40					
Wickford 2	d				17 51	18a06					18 11					18 31	18a46				18 51	
Billericay	d				17 57						18 17					18 37					18 57	
Shenfield 3	a				18 05						18 25					18 45					19 05	
Shenfield 3	d	17 51	17 54	18 04	18 05		18 08	18 14	18 20	18 24	18 25		18 34	18 38	18 44	18 45		18 51	18 54	19 04	19 05	19 08
Brentwood	d		17 57	18 07				18 17		18 27			18 37		18 47				18 57	19 07		
Harold Wood	d		18 02	18 12				18 22		18 32			18 42		18 52				19 02	19 12		
Gidea Park 2	d		18 06	18 16				18 26		18 36			18 46		18 56				19 06	19 16		
Romford	d		18 08	18 18				18 28	18 28	18 38			18 48		18 58	18 53			19 08	19 18		
Chadwell Heath	d		18 12	18 22				18 32		18 42			18 52		19 02				19 12	19 22		
Goodmayes	d		18 14	18 24				18 34		18 44			18 54		19 04				19 14	19 24		
Seven Kings	d		18 16	18 26				18 36		18 46			18 56		19 06				19 16	19 26		
Ilford 2	d		18 19	18 29				18 39		18 49			18 59		19 09				19 19	19 29		
Manor Park	d		18 22	18 32				18 42		18 52			19 02		19 12				19 22	19 32		
Forest Gate	d		18 24	18 34				18 44		18 54			19 04		19 14				19 24	19 34		
Maryland	d		18 26	18 36				18 46		18 56			19 06		19 16				19 26	19 36		
Stratford 7 ⊖	d	18 05	18 29	18 39	18 19		18 22	18 49	18 36	18 59	18 39		19 09	18 52	19 19	19 01		19 05	19 29	19 39	19 19	19 22
London Liverpool Street 15 ⊖	a	18 14	18 37	18 47	18 28		18 31	18 57	18 45	19 07	18 48	18 55	19 17	19 01	19 27	19 10		19 14	19 37	19 47	19 28	19 31

		LE	LE 1	LE	LE 1	LE 1	LE	LE 1	LE	LE 1	LE 1	LE	LE	LE 1	LE 1	LE 1	LE	LE 1	LE	LE 1	LE
Southend Victoria	d				18 50					19 10				19 30						19 50	
Prittlewell	d				18 52					19 12				19 32						19 52	
Southend Airport ✈	d				18 55					19 15				19 35						19 55	
Rochford	d				18 58					19 18				19 38						19 58	
Hockley	d				19 01					19 21				19 41						20 01	
Rayleigh	d				19 06					19 26				19 46						20 06	
Southminster	d					18 56									19 36						
Burnham-on-Crouch	d					19 00									19 40						
Althorne	d					19 05									19 45						
North Fambridge	d					19 11									19 51						
South Woodham Ferrers	d					19 16									19 56						
Battlesbridge	d					19 20									20 00						
Wickford 2	d				19 11	19a26				19 31				19 51	20a06					20 11	
Billericay	d				19 17					19 37				19 57						20 17	
Shenfield 3	a				19 25					19 45				20 05						20 25	
Shenfield 3	d	19 14	19 20	19 24	19 25		19 34	19 38	19 44	19 45	19 51	19 54	20 04	20 05		20 08	20 14	20 20	20 24	20 25	20 34
Brentwood	d	19 17		19 27			19 37		19 47			19 57	20 07				20 17		20 27		20 37
Harold Wood	d	19 22		19 32			19 42		19 52			20 02	20 12				20 22		20 32		20 42
Gidea Park 2	d	19 26		19 36			19 46		19 56			20 06	20 16				20 26		20 36		20 46
Romford	d	19 28	19 28	19 38			19 48		19 58	19 53		20 08	20 18				20 28	20 28	20 38		20 48
Chadwell Heath	d	19 32		19 42			19 52		20 02			20 12	20 22				20 32		20 42		20 52
Goodmayes	d	19 34		19 44			19 54		20 04			20 14	20 24				20 34		20 44		20 54
Seven Kings	d	19 36		19 46			19 56		20 06			20 16	20 26				20 36		20 46		20 56
Ilford 2	d	19 39		19 49			19 59		20 09			20 19	20 29				20 39		20 49		20 59
Manor Park	d	19 42		19 52			20 02		20 12			20 22	20 32				20 42		20 52		21 02
Forest Gate	d	19 44		19 54			20 04		20 14			20 24	20 34				20 44		20 54		21 04
Maryland	d	19 46		19 56			20 06		20 16			20 26	20 36				20 46		20 56		21 06
Stratford 7 ⊖	d	19 49	19 36	19 59	19 39		20 09	19 52	20 19	20 01	20 05	20 29	20 39	20s19		20 22	20 49	20 36	20 59	20 39	21 09
London Liverpool Street 15 ⊖	a	19 57	19 45	20 07	19 48		20 17	20 01	20 27	20 10	20 14	20 37	20 47	20 28		20 31	20 57	20 45	21 07	20 48	21 17

Table 5

Saturdays

18 August to 25 August

Southend Victoria, Southminster and Shenfield - London

Network Diagram - see first Page of Table 5

		LE 1	LE	LE 1	LE 1	LE 1		LE	LE 1	LE 1	LE	LE 1	LE 1	LE 1		LE		LE 1	LE	LE 1	LE 1	LE	LE 1	LE 1	LE 1
Southend Victoria	d			20 10					20 30				20 50							21 10			21 30		
Prittlewell	d			20 12					20 32				20 52							21 12			21 32		
Southend Airport ✈	d			20 15					20 35				20 55							21 15			21 35		
Rochford	d			20 18					20 38				20 58							21 18			21 38		
Hockley	d			20 21					20 41				21 01							21 21			21 41		
Rayleigh	d			20 26					20 46				21 06							21 26			21 46		
Southminster	d				20 16									20 56										21 36	
Burnham-on-Crouch	d				20 20									21 00										21 40	
Althorne	d				20 25									21 05										21 45	
North Fambridge	d				20 31									21 11										21 51	
South Woodham Ferrers	d				20 36									21 16										21 56	
Battlesbridge	d				20 40									21 20										22 00	
Wickford 2	d			20 31	20a46				20 51				21 11	21a26						21 31			21 51	22a06	
Billericay	d			20 37					20 57				21 17							21 37			21 57		
Shenfield 3	a			20 45					21 05				21 25							21 45			22 05		
Shenfield 3	d	20 38	20 44	20 45		20 51		20 59	21 05	21 08	21 14	21 20	21 25			21 29		21 38	21 44	21 45	21 51	21 59	22 05		22 08
Brentwood	d		20 47					21 02			21 17					21 32			21 47			22 02			
Harold Wood	d		20 52					21 07			21 22					21 37			21 52			22 07			
Gidea Park 2	d		20 56					21 11			21 26					21 41			21 56			22 11			
Romford	d		20 58	20 53				21 13			21 28	21 28				21 43			21 58	21 53		22 13			
Chadwell Heath	d		21 02					21 17			21 32					21 47			22 02			22 17			
Goodmayes	d		21 04					21 19			21 34					21 49			22 04			22 19			
Seven Kings	d		21 06					21 21			21 36					21 51			22 06			22 21			
Ilford 2	d		21 09					21 24			21 39					21 54			22 09			22 24			
Manor Park	d		21 12					21 27			21 42					21 57			22 12			22 27			
Forest Gate	d		21 14					21 29			21 44					21 59			22 14			22 29			
Maryland	d		21 16					21 31			21 46					22 01			22 16			22 31			
Stratford 7 ⊖	d	20 52	21 19	21 01		21 05		21 34	21 19	21 22	21 49	21 36	21 39			22 04		21 52	22 19	22 01	22 05	22 34	22 19		22 22
London Liverpool Street 15 ⊖	a	21 01	21 27	21 10		21 14		21 42	21 28	21 31	21 57	21 45	21 48			22 12		22 01	22 27	22 10	22 14	22 42	22 28		22 31

		LE		LE 1		LE	LE 1	LE 1	LE 1	LE	LE 1	LE 1		LE	LE 1	LE 1	LE	LE 1	LE	LE 1	LE 1	LE			
Southend Victoria	d						22 00								22 30					23 00					
Prittlewell	d						22 02								22 32					23 02					
Southend Airport ✈	d						22 05								22 35					23 05					
Rochford	d						22 08								22 38					23 08					
Hockley	d						22 11								22 41					23 11					
Rayleigh	d						22 16								22 46					23 16					
Southminster	d							22 16													22 56				
Burnham-on-Crouch	d							22 20													23 00				
Althorne	d							22 25													23 05				
North Fambridge	d							22 31													23 11				
South Woodham Ferrers	d							22 36													23 16				
Battlesbridge	d							22 40													23 20				
Wickford 2	d						22 21	22a46							22 51					23 21	23 26				
Billericay	d						22 27								22 57					23 27	23 32				
Shenfield 3	a						22 35								23 05					23 35	23 39				
Shenfield 3	d	22 14		22 20		22 29	22 35		22 38	22 44	22 51			22 59	23 05	23 08	23 14	23 20	23 29	23 35	23 39	23 44			
Brentwood	d	22 17				22 32				22 47				23 02			23 17		23 32			23 47			
Harold Wood	d	22 22				22 37				22 52				23 07			23 22		23 37			23 52			
Gidea Park 2	d	22 26				22 41				22 56				23 11			23 26		23 41			23 56			
Romford	d	22 28		22 28		22 43				22 58				23 13			23 28	23 28	23 43		23 47	23 58			
Chadwell Heath	d	22 32				22 47				23 02				23 17			23 32		23 47			00 02			
Goodmayes	d	22 34				22 49				23 04				23 19			23 34		23 49			00 04			
Seven Kings	d	22 36				22 51				23 06				23 21			23 36		23 51			00 06			
Ilford 2	d	22 39				22 54				23 09				23 24			23 39		23 54			00 09			
Manor Park	d	22 42				22 57				23 12				23 27			23 42		23 57			00 12			
Forest Gate	d	22 44				22 59				23 14				23 29			23 44		23 59			00 14			
Maryland	d	22 46				23 01				23 16				23 31			23 46		00 01			00 16			
Stratford 7 ⊖	d	22 49		22 36		23 04	22 49		22 52	23 19	23 05	23 07		23 34	23 19	23 22	23 49	23 36	00 04	23 49	23 56	00 19			
London Liverpool Street 15 ⊖	a	22 57		22 46		23 12	22 58		23 01	23 27	23 14	23 18		23 42	23 28	23 31	23 57	23 45	00 12	23 58	00 05	00 27			

Table 5

Saturdays

1 September to 8 September

Southend Victoria, Southminster and Shenfield - London

Network Diagram - see first Page of Table 5

		LE		LE	LE	LE 1	LE 1	LE	LE	LE		LE	LE	LE	LE	LE	LE	LE 1	LE	LE 1		LE 1	LE	LE 1	LE 1
Southend Victoria	d					23p10												04 00		04 30				05 00	
Prittlewell	d					23p12												04 02		04 32				05 02	
Southend Airport ✈	d					23p15												04 05		04 35				05 05	
Rochford	d					23p18												04 08		04 38				05 08	
Hockley	d					23p21												04 12		04 42				05 11	
Rayleigh	d					23p26												04 16		04 46				05 16	
Southminster	d																								
Burnham-on-Crouch	d																								
Althorne	d																								
North Fambridge	d																								
South Woodham Ferrers	d																								
Battlesbridge	d																								
Wickford 2	d					23p31												04 21		04 51				05 21	
Billericay	d					23p37												04 28		04 58				05 27	
Shenfield 3	a					23p45												04 39		05 09				05 35	
Shenfield 3	d			23p29	23p44	23p45			23p59	00 14			00 29	00 44				04 39		05 09		05 24		05 35	
Brentwood	d			23p32	23p47				00 02	00 17			00 32	00 47				04 42		05 12					
Harold Wood	d			23p37	23p52				00 07	00 22			00 37	00 52				04 47		05 17					
Gidea Park 2	d			23p41	23p56				00 11	00 26			00 41	00 56				04 51		05 21		05 31			
Romford	d			23p43	23p58				00 13	00 28			00 43	00 58				04 53		05 23				05 43	
Chadwell Heath	d			23p47	00 02				00 17	00 32			00 47	01 02				04 57		05 27					
Goodmayes	d			23p49	00 04				00 19	00 34			00 49	01 04				04 59		05 29					
Seven Kings	d			23p51	00 06				00 21	00 36			00 51	01 06				05 01		05 31		05 36			
Ilford 2	d			23p54	00 09				00 24	00 39			00 54	01 09				05 04	05 09	05 34			05 39		
Manor Park	d			23p57	00 12				00 27	00 42			00 57	01 12					05 11				05 41		
Forest Gate	d			23p59	00 14				00 29	00 44			00 59	01 14					05 14				05 44		
Maryland	d			00 01	00 16														05 16				05 46		
Stratford 7 ⊖	d	23p54		00 04	00 20	00 08	00 12	00 30	00 40	00 50		01 00	01 10	01 20	01 30	01 40	01 50	05 10	05 18	05 40		05 42	05 48	05 51	06 05
London Liverpool Street 15 ⊖	a	00 02		00 12	00 28	00 16	00 20	00 38	00 48	00 58		01 08	01 18	01 28	01 38	01 48	01 58	05 18	05 26	05 48		05 55	05 56	06 00	06 14

		LE	LE 1	LE 1	LE	LE		LE 1		LE	LE 1	LE 1	LE	LE	LE 1	LE		LE	LE 1	LE 1	LE	LE 1	LE	LE 1	LE 1
Southend Victoria	d			05 30							06 00								06 30					06 50	
Prittlewell	d			05 32							06 02								06 32					06 52	
Southend Airport ✈	d			05 35							06 05								06 35					06 55	
Rochford	d			05 38							06 08								06 38					06 58	
Hockley	d			05 41							06 11								06 41					07 01	
Rayleigh	d			05 46							06 16								06 46					07 06	
Southminster	d											06 16													06 56
Burnham-on-Crouch	d											06 20													07 00
Althorne	d											06 25													07 05
North Fambridge	d											06 31													07 11
South Woodham Ferrers	d											06 36													07 16
Battlesbridge	d											06 40													07 20
Wickford 2	d			05 51							06 21	06a46							06 51					07 11	07a26
Billericay	d			05 57							06 27								06 57					07 17	
Shenfield 3	a			06 05							06 35								07 05					07 25	
Shenfield 3	d	05 44	05 53	06 05		06 14		06 24			06 35			06 44	06 51			07 04	07 05	07 08	07 14	07 20	07 24	07 25	
Brentwood	d	05 47				06 17								06 47				07 07			07 17		07 27		
Harold Wood	d	05 52				06 22								06 52				07 12			07 22		07 32		
Gidea Park 2	d	05 56			06 16	06 26				06 36			06 46	06 56		07 06		07 16			07 26		07 36		
Romford	d	05 58			06 18	06 28				06 38	06 43		06 48	06 58		07 08		07 18			07 28	07 28	07 38		
Chadwell Heath	d	06 02			06 22	06 32				06 42			06 52	07 02		07 12		07 22			07 32		07 42		
Goodmayes	d	06 04			06 24	06 34				06 44			06 54	07 04		07 14		07 24			07 34		07 44		
Seven Kings	d	06 06			06 26	06 36				06 46			06 56	07 06		07 16		07 26			07 36		07 46		
Ilford 2	d	06 09			06 29	06 39				06 49			06 59	07 09		07 19		07 29			07 39		07 49		
Manor Park	d	06 12			06 32	06 42				06 52			07 02	07 12		07 22		07 32			07 42		07 52		
Forest Gate	d	06 14			06 34	06 44				06 54			07 04	07 14		07 24		07 34			07 44		07 54		
Maryland	d	06 16			06 36	06 46				06 56			07 06	07 16		07 26		07 36			07 46		07 56		
Stratford 7 ⊖	d	06 19	06 07	06 19	06 39	06 49		06 38		06 59	06 51		07 09	07 19	07 05	07 29		07 39	07 19	07 22	07 49	07 36	07 59	07 39	
London Liverpool Street 15 ⊖	a	06 27	06 16	06 28	06 47	06 57		06 47		07 07	07 00		07 17	07 27	07 14	07 37		07 47	07 28	07 31	07 57	07 45	08 07	07 48	

Southend Victoria, Southminster and Shenfield - London

Network Diagram - see first Page of Table 5

		LE	LE 1			LE	LE 1	LE 1	LE	LE	LE 1	LE 1		LE 1	LE	LE 1	LE	LE 1		LE	LE 1	LE		LE 1	LE 1
Southend Victoria	d						07 10				07 30							07 50						08 10	
Prittlewell	d						07 12				07 32							07 52						08 12	
Southend Airport	d						07 15				07 35							07 55						08 15	
Rochford	d						07 18				07 38							07 58						08 18	
Hockley	d						07 21				07 41							08 01						08 21	
Rayleigh	d						07 26				07 46							08 06						08 26	
Southminster	d											07 36													08 16
Burnham-on-Crouch	d											07 40													08 20
Althorne	d											07 45													08 25
North Fambridge	d											07 51													08 31
South Woodham Ferrers	d											07 56													08 36
Battlesbridge	d											08 00													08 40
Wickford 2	d						07 31				07 51	08a06						08 11						08 31	08a46
Billericay	d						07 37				07 57							08 17						08 37	
Shenfield 3	a						07 45				08 05							08 25						08 45	
Shenfield 3	d	07 34	07 38			07 44	07 45	07 51	07 54	08 04	08 05			08 08	08 14	08 20	08 24	08 25		08 34	08 38	08 44		08 45	
Brentwood	d	07 37				07 47			07 57	08 07					08 17		08 27			08 37		08 47			
Harold Wood	d	07 42				07 52			08 02	08 12					08 22		08 32			08 42		08 52			
Gidea Park 2	d	07 46				07 56			08 06	08 16					08 26		08 36			08 46		08 56			
Romford	d	07 48				07 58	07 53		08 08	08 18					08 28	08 28	08 38			08 48		08 58		08 53	
Chadwell Heath	d	07 52				08 02			08 12	08 22					08 32		08 42			08 52		09 02			
Goodmayes	d	07 54				08 04			08 14	08 24					08 34		08 44			08 54		09 04			
Seven Kings	d	07 56				08 06			08 16	08 26					08 36		08 46			08 56		09 06			
Ilford 2	d	07 59				08 09			08 19	08 29					08 39		08 49			08 59		09 09			
Manor Park	d	08 02				08 12			08 22	08 32					08 42		08 52			09 02		09 12			
Forest Gate	d	08 04				08 14			08 24	08 34					08 44		08 54			09 04		09 14			
Maryland	d	08 06				08 16			08 26	08 36					08 46		08 56			09 06		09 16			
Stratford 7 ⊖	d	08 09	07 52			08 19	08 01	08 05	08 29	08 39	08 19			08 22	08 49	08 36	08 59	08 39		09 09	08 52	09 19		09 01	
London Liverpool Street 15 ⊖	a	08 17	08 01			08 27	08 10	08 14	08 37	08 47	08 28			08 31	08 57	08 45	09 07	08 48		09 17	09 01	09 27		09 10	

		LE 1	LE	LE	LE 1	LE 1	LE	LE 1		LE	LE 1	LE 1		LE	LE 1	LE	LE 1	LE 1		LE	LE	LE 1	LE 1	LE 1	LE
Southend Victoria	d				08 30						08 50						09 10					09 30			
Prittlewell	d				08 32						08 52						09 12					09 32			
Southend Airport	d				08 35						08 55						09 15					09 35			
Rochford	d				08 38						08 58						09 18					09 38			
Hockley	d				08 41						09 01						09 21					09 41			
Rayleigh	d				08 46						09 06						09 26					09 46			
Southminster	d											08 56											09 36		
Burnham-on-Crouch	d											09 00											09 40		
Althorne	d											09 05											09 45		
North Fambridge	d											09 11											09 51		
South Woodham Ferrers	d											09 16											09 56		
Battlesbridge	d											09 20											10 00		
Wickford 2	d				08 51						09 11	09a26					09 31					09 51	10a06		
Billericay	d				08 57						09 17						09 37					09 57			
Shenfield 3	a				09 05						09 25						09 45					10 05			
Shenfield 3	d	08 51	08 54	09 04	09 05	09 08	09 14	09 20		09 24	09 25			09 34	09 38	09 44	09 45	09 51		09 54	10 04	10 05		10 08	10 14
Brentwood	d		08 57	09 07			09 17			09 27				09 37		09 47				09 57	10 07				10 17
Harold Wood	d		09 02	09 12			09 22			09 32				09 42		09 52				10 02	10 12				10 22
Gidea Park 2	d		09 06	09 16			09 26			09 36				09 46		09 56				10 06	10 16				10 26
Romford	d		09 08	09 18			09 28	09 28		09 38				09 48		09 58	09 53			10 08	10 18				10 28
Chadwell Heath	d		09 12	09 22			09 32			09 42				09 52		10 02				10 12	10 22				10 32
Goodmayes	d		09 14	09 24			09 34			09 44				09 54		10 04				10 14	10 24				10 34
Seven Kings	d		09 16	09 26			09 36			09 46				09 56		10 06				10 16	10 26				10 36
Ilford 2	d		09 19	09 29			09 39			09 49				09 59		10 09				10 19	10 29				10 39
Manor Park	d		09 22	09 32			09 42			09 52				10 02		10 12				10 22	10 32				10 42
Forest Gate	d		09 24	09 34			09 44			09 54				10 04		10 14				10 24	10 34				10 44
Maryland	d		09 26	09 36			09 46			09 56				10 06		10 16				10 26	10 36				10 46
Stratford 7 ⊖	d	09 05	09 29	09 39	09 19	09 22	09 49	09 36		09 59	09 39			10 09	09 52	10 19	10 01	10 05		10 29	10 39	10 19		10 22	10 49
London Liverpool Street 15 ⊖	a	09 14	09 37	09 47	09 28	09 31	09 57	09 45		10 07	09 48			10 17	10 01	10 27	10 10	10 14		10 37	10 47	10 28		10 31	10 57

Table 5

Saturdays

1 September to 8 September

Southend Victoria, Southminster and Shenfield - London

Network Diagram - see first Page of Table 5

		LE 1	LE	LE 1			LE	LE 1	LE	LE 1	LE 1	LE 1	LE	LE		LE 1	LE 1	LE	LE 1	LE	LE 1	LE 1		LE	
Southend Victoria	d			09 50						10 10						10 30					10 50				
Prittlewell	d			09 52						10 12						10 32					10 52				
Southend Airport	d			09 55						10 15						10 35					10 55				
Rochford	d			09 58						10 18						10 38					10 58				
Hockley	d			10 01						10 21						10 41					11 01				
Rayleigh	d			10 06						10 26						10 46					11 06				
Southminster	d										10 16											10 56			
Burnham-on-Crouch	d										10 20											11 00			
Althorne	d										10 25											11 05			
North Fambridge	d										10 31											11 11			
South Woodham Ferrers	d										10 36											11 16			
Battlesbridge	d										10 40											11 20			
Wickford 2	d			10 11						10 31	10a46					10 51					11 11	11a26			
Billericay	d			10 17						10 37						10 57					11 17				
Shenfield 3	a			10 25						10 45						11 05					11 25				
Shenfield 3	d	10 20	10 24	10 25			10 34	10 38	10 44	10 45		10 51	10 54	11 04		11 05	11 08	11 14	11 20	11 24	11 25			11 34	
Brentwood	d		10 27				10 37		10 47				10 57	11 07				11 17		11 27				11 37	
Harold Wood	d		10 32				10 42		10 52				11 02	11 12				11 22		11 32				11 42	
Gidea Park 2	d		10 36				10 46		10 56				11 06	11 16				11 26		11 36				11 46	
Romford	d	10 28	10 38				10 48		10 58	10 53			11 08	11 18				11 28	11 28	11 38				11 48	
Chadwell Heath	d		10 42				10 52		11 02				11 12	11 22				11 32		11 42				11 52	
Goodmayes	d		10 44				10 54		11 04				11 14	11 24				11 34		11 44				11 54	
Seven Kings	d		10 46				10 56		11 06				11 16	11 26				11 36		11 46				11 56	
Ilford 2	d		10 49				10 59		11 09				11 19	11 29				11 39		11 49				11 59	
Manor Park	d		10 52				11 02		11 12				11 22	11 32				11 42		11 52				12 02	
Forest Gate	d		10 54				11 04		11 14				11 24	11 34				11 44		11 54				12 04	
Maryland	d		10 56				11 06		11 16				11 26	11 36				11 46		11 56				12 06	
Stratford 7 ⊖	d	10 36	10 59	10 39			11 09	10 52	11 19	11 01		11 05	11 29	11 39		11 19	11 22	11 49	11 36	11 59	11 39			12 09	
London Liverpool Street 15 ⊖	a	10 45	11 07	10 48			11 17	11 01	11 27	11 10		11 14	11 37	11 47		11 28	11 31	11 57	11 45	12 07	11 48			12 17	

		LE 1	LE	LE 1	LE 1	LE	LE	LE 1	LE 1	LE 1		LE	LE 1	LE	LE 1		LE	LE 1	LE	LE 1		LE 1	LE 1	LE	LE
Southend Victoria	d			11 10				11 30							11 50					12 10					
Prittlewell	d			11 12				11 32							11 52					12 12					
Southend Airport	d			11 15				11 35							11 55					12 15					
Rochford	d			11 18				11 38							11 58					12 18					
Hockley	d			11 21				11 41							12 01					12 21					
Rayleigh	d			11 26				11 46							12 06					12 26					
Southminster	d								11 36													12 16			
Burnham-on-Crouch	d								11 40													12 20			
Althorne	d								11 45													12 25			
North Fambridge	d								11 51													12 31			
South Woodham Ferrers	d								11 56													12 36			
Battlesbridge	d								12 00													12 40			
Wickford 2	d			11 31				11 51	12a06						12 11					12 31		12a46			
Billericay	d			11 37				11 57							12 17					12 37					
Shenfield 3	a			11 45				12 05							12 25					12 45					
Shenfield 3	d	11 38	11 44	11 45	11 51	11 54	12 04	12 05		12 08		12 14	12 20	12 24	12 25		12 34	12 38	12 44	12 45			12 51	12 54	13 04
Brentwood	d		11 47			11 57	12 07					12 17		12 27			12 37		12 47					12 57	13 07
Harold Wood	d		11 52			12 02	12 12					12 22		12 32			12 42		12 52					13 02	13 12
Gidea Park 2	d		11 56			12 06	12 16					12 26		12 36			12 46		12 56					13 06	13 16
Romford	d		11 58	11 53		12 08	12 18					12 28	12 28	12 38			12 48		12 58	12 53				13 08	13 18
Chadwell Heath	d		12 02			12 12	12 22					12 32		12 42			12 52		13 02					13 12	13 22
Goodmayes	d		12 04			12 14	12 24					12 34		12 44			12 54		13 04					13 14	13 24
Seven Kings	d		12 06			12 16	12 26					12 36		12 46			12 56		13 06					13 16	13 26
Ilford 2	d		12 09			12 19	12 29					12 39		12 49			12 59		13 09					13 19	13 29
Manor Park	d		12 12			12 22	12 32					12 42		12 52			13 02		13 12					13 22	13 32
Forest Gate	d		12 14			12 24	12 34					12 44		12 54			13 04		13 14					13 24	13 34
Maryland	d		12 16			12 26	12 36					12 46		12 56			13 06		13 16					13 26	13 36
Stratford 7 ⊖	d	11 52	12 19	12 01	12 05	12 29	12 39	12 19		12 22		12 49	12 36	12 59	12 39		13 09	12 52	13 19	13 01			13 05	13 29	13 39
London Liverpool Street 15 ⊖	a	12 01	12 27	12 10	12 14	12 37	12 47	12 28		12 31		12 57	12 45	13 07	12 48		13 17	13 01	13 27	13 10			13 14	13 37	13 47

Southend Victoria, Southminster and Shenfield - London

Network Diagram - see first Page of Table 5

		LE [1]	LE [1]	LE	LE [1]	LE		LE [1]	LE [1]		LE	LE [1]	LE	LE [1]	LE [1]	LE		LE	LE [1]	LE [1]	LE [1]	LE	LE [1]	LE	LE [1]
Southend Victoria	d	12 30						12 50						13 10					13 30						13 50
Prittlewell	d	12 32						12 52						13 12					13 32						13 52
Southend Airport ✈	d	12 35						12 55						13 15					13 35						13 55
Rochford	d	12 38						12 58						13 18					13 38						13 58
Hockley	d	12 41						13 01						13 21					13 41						14 01
Rayleigh	d	12 46						13 06						13 26					13 46						14 06
Southminster	d								12 56											13 36					
Burnham-on-Crouch	d								13 00											13 40					
Althorne	d								13 05											13 45					
North Fambridge	d								13 11											13 51					
South Woodham Ferrers	d								13 16											13 56					
Battlesbridge	d								13 20											14 00					
Wickford [2]	d	12 51						13 11	13a26					13 31					13 51	14a06					14 11
Billericay	d	12 57						13 17						13 37					13 57						14 17
Shenfield [3]	a	13 05						13 25						13 45					14 05						14 25
Shenfield [3]	d	13 05	13 08	13 14	13 20	13 24		13 25			13 34	13 38	13 44	13 45	13 51	13 54		14 04	14 05		14 08	14 14	14 20	14 24	14 25
Brentwood	d			13 17		13 27					13 37		13 47			13 57		14 07				14 17		14 27	
Harold Wood	d			13 22		13 32					13 42		13 52			14 02		14 12				14 22		14 32	
Gidea Park [2]	d			13 26		13 36					13 46		13 56			14 06		14 16				14 26		14 36	
Romford	d			13 28	13 28	13 38					13 48		13 58	13 53		14 08		14 18				14 28	14 28	14 38	
Chadwell Heath	d			13 32		13 42					13 52		14 02			14 12		14 22				14 32		14 42	
Goodmayes	d			13 34		13 44					13 54		14 04			14 14		14 24				14 34		14 44	
Seven Kings	d			13 36		13 46					13 56		14 06			14 16		14 26				14 36		14 46	
Ilford [2]	d			13 39		13 49					13 59		14 09			14 19		14 29				14 39		14 49	
Manor Park	d			13 42		13 52					14 02		14 12			14 22		14 32				14 42		14 52	
Forest Gate	d			13 44		13 54					14 04		14 14			14 24		14 34				14 44		14 54	
Maryland	d			13 46		13 56					14 06		14 16			14 26		14 36				14 46		14 56	
Stratford [7] ⊖	d	13 19	13 22	13 49	13 36	13 59		13 39			14 09	13 52	14 19	14 01	14 05	14 29		14 39	14 19		14 22	14 49	14 36	14 59	14 39
London Liverpool Street [15] ⊖	a	13 28	13 31	13 57	13 45	14 07		13 48			14 17	14 01	14 27	14 10	14 14	14 37		14 47	14 28		14 31	14 57	14 45	15 07	14 48

				LE	LE [1]	LE	LE [1]	LE [1]	LE [1]	LE	LE	LE [1]		LE [1]	LE	LE	LE [1]	LE [1]		LE	LE [1]	LE		LE [1]	LE [1]
Southend Victoria	d						14 10					14 30					14 50							15 10	
Prittlewell	d						14 12					14 32					14 52							15 12	
Southend Airport ✈	d						14 15					14 35					14 55							15 15	
Rochford	d						14 18					14 38					14 58							15 18	
Hockley	d						14 21					14 41					15 01							15 21	
Rayleigh	d						14 26					14 46					15 06							15 26	
Southminster	d							14 16										14 56							
Burnham-on-Crouch	d							14 20										15 00							
Althorne	d							14 25										15 05							
North Fambridge	d							14 31										15 11							
South Woodham Ferrers	d							14 36										15 16							
Battlesbridge	d							14 40										15 20							
Wickford [2]	d						14 31	14a46				14 51					15 11	15a26						15 31	
Billericay	d						14 37					14 57					15 17							15 37	
Shenfield [3]	a						14 45					15 05					15 25							15 45	
Shenfield [3]	d			14 34	14 38	14 44	14 45		14 51	14 54	15 04	15 05		15 08	15 14	15 24	15 25			15 34	15 38	15 44		15 45	15 51
Brentwood	d			14 37		14 47				14 57	15 07				15 17	15 27				15 37		15 47			
Harold Wood	d			14 42		14 52				15 02	15 12				15 22	15 32				15 42		15 52			
Gidea Park [2]	d			14 46		14 56				15 06	15 16				15 26	15 36				15 46		15 56			
Romford	d			14 48		14 58	14 53			15 08	15 18				15 28	15 38				15 48		15 58		15 53	
Chadwell Heath	d			14 52		15 02				15 12	15 22				15 32	15 42				15 52		16 02			
Goodmayes	d			14 54		15 04				15 14	15 24				15 34	15 44				15 54		16 04			
Seven Kings	d			14 56		15 06				15 16	15 26				15 36	15 46				15 56		16 06			
Ilford [2]	d			14 59		15 09				15 19	15 29				15 39	15 49				15 59		16 09			
Manor Park	d			15 02		15 12				15 22	15 32				15 42	15 52				16 02		16 12			
Forest Gate	d			15 04		15 14				15 24	15 34				15 44	15 54				16 04		16 14			
Maryland	d			15 06		15 16				15 26	15 36				15 46	15 56				16 06		16 16			
Stratford [7] ⊖	d			15 09	14 52	15 19	15 01		15 05	15 29	15 39	15 19		15 22	15 49	15 59	15 39			16 09	15 52	16 19		16 01	16 05
London Liverpool Street [15] ⊖	a			15 17	15 01	15 27	15 10		15 14	15 37	15 47	15 28		15 31	15 57	16 07	15 48			16 17	16 01	16 27		16 10	16 14

Southend Victoria, Southminster and Shenfield - London

Network Diagram - see first Page of Table 5

		LE	LE	LE [1]	LE [1]	LE [1]	LE	LE [1]		LE	LE [1]		LE	LE [1]	LE	LE [1]	LE [1]	LE [1]		LE	LE	LE [1]	LE [1]	LE	LE
Southend Victoria	d			15 30							15 50					16 10						16 30			
Prittlewell	d			15 32							15 52					16 12						16 32			
Southend Airport ✈	d			15 35							15 55					16 15						16 35			
Rochford	d			15 38							15 58					16 18						16 38			
Hockley	d			15 41							16 01					16 21						16 41			
Rayleigh	d			15 46							16 06					16 26						16 46			
Southminster	d				15 36												16 16								
Burnham-on-Crouch	d				15 40												16 20								
Althorne	d				15 45												16 25								
North Fambridge	d				15 51												16 31								
South Woodham Ferrers	d				15 56												16 36								
Battlesbridge	d				16 00												16 40								
Wickford [2]	d			15 51	16a06						16 11					16 31	16a46					16 51			
Billericay	d			15 57							16 17					16 37						16 57			
Shenfield [3]	a			16 05							16 25					16 45						17 05			
Shenfield [3]	d	15 54	16 04	16 05		16 08	16 14	16 20		16 24	16 25		16 34	16 38	16 44	16 45		16 51		16 54	17 04	17 05	17 08	17 14	17 24
Brentwood	d	15 57	16 07				16 17			16 27			16 37		16 47					16 57	17 07			17 17	17 27
Harold Wood	d	16 02	16 12				16 22			16 32			16 42		16 52					17 02	17 12			17 22	17 32
Gidea Park [2]	d	16 06	16 16				16 26			16 36			16 46		16 56					17 06	17 16			17 26	17 36
Romford	d	16 08	16 18				16 28	16 28		16 38			16 48		16 58	16 53				17 08	17 18			17 28	17 38
Chadwell Heath	d	16 12	16 22				16 32			16 42			16 52		17 02					17 12	17 22			17 32	17 42
Goodmayes	d	16 14	16 24				16 34			16 44			16 54		17 04					17 14	17 24			17 34	17 44
Seven Kings	d	16 16	16 26				16 36			16 46			16 56		17 06					17 16	17 26			17 36	17 46
Ilford [2]	d	16 19	16 29				16 39			16 49			16 59		17 09					17 19	17 29			17 39	17 49
Manor Park	d	16 22	16 32				16 42			16 52			17 02		17 12					17 22	17 32			17 42	17 52
Forest Gate	d	16 24	16 34				16 44			16 54			17 04		17 14					17 24	17 34			17 44	17 54
Maryland	d	16 26	16 36				16 46			16 56			17 06		17 16					17 26	17 36			17 46	17 56
Stratford [7] ⊖	d	16 29	16 39	16 19		16 22	16 49	16 36		16 59	16 39		17 09	16 52	17 19	17 01		17 05		17 29	17 39	17 19	17 22	17 49	17 59
London Liverpool Street [15] ⊖	a	16 37	16 47	16 28		16 31	16 57	16 45		17 07	16 48		17 17	17 01	17 27	17 10		17 14		17 37	17 47	17 28	17 31	17 57	18 07

		LE [1]	LE [1]			LE	LE [1]	LE [1]	LE	LE [1]	LE	LE	LE [1]	LE [1]		LE [1]	LE	LE [1]	LE	LE [1]		LE	LE [1]	LE	
Southend Victoria	d	16 50						17 10					17 30							17 50					
Prittlewell	d	16 52						17 12					17 32							17 52					
Southend Airport ✈	d	16 55						17 15					17 35							17 55					
Rochford	d	16 58						17 18					17 38							17 58					
Hockley	d	17 01						17 21					17 41							18 01					
Rayleigh	d	17 06						17 26					17 46							18 06					
Southminster	d		16 56											17 36											
Burnham-on-Crouch	d		17 00											17 40											
Althorne	d		17 05											17 45											
North Fambridge	d		17 11											17 51											
South Woodham Ferrers	d		17 16											17 56											
Battlesbridge	d		17 20											18 00											
Wickford [2]	d	17 11	17a26					17 31					17 51	18a06						18 11					
Billericay	d	17 17						17 37					17 57							18 17					
Shenfield [3]	a	17 25						17 44					18 05							18 25					
Shenfield [3]	d	17 25				17 34	17 38	17 45	17 44	17 51	17 54	18 04	18 05			18 08	18 14	18 20	18 24	18 25		18 34	18 38	18 44	
Brentwood	d					17 37			17 47		17 57	18 07					18 17		18 27			18 37		18 47	
Harold Wood	d					17 42			17 52		18 02	18 12					18 22		18 32			18 42		18 52	
Gidea Park [2]	d					17 46			17 56		18 06	18 16					18 26		18 36			18 46		18 56	
Romford	d					17 48		17 53	17 58		18 08	18 18					18 28	18 28	18 38			18 48		18 58	
Chadwell Heath	d					17 52			18 02		18 12	18 22					18 32		18 42			18 52		19 02	
Goodmayes	d					17 54			18 04		18 14	18 24					18 34		18 44			18 54		19 04	
Seven Kings	d					17 56			18 06		18 16	18 26					18 36		18 46			18 56		19 06	
Ilford [2]	d					17 59			18 09		18 19	18 29					18 39		18 49			18 59		19 09	
Manor Park	d					18 02			18 12		18 22	18 32					18 42		18 52			19 02		19 12	
Forest Gate	d					18 04			18 14		18 24	18 34					18 44		18 54			19 04		19 14	
Maryland	d					18 06			18 16		18 26	18 36					18 46		18 56			19 06		19 16	
Stratford [7] ⊖	d	17 39				18 09	17 52	18 01	18 19	18 05	18 29	18 39	18 19			18 22	18 49	18 36	18 59	18 39		19 09	18 52	19 19	
London Liverpool Street [15] ⊖	a	17 48				18 17	18 01	18 10	18 27	18 14	18 37	18 47	18 28			18 31	18 57	18 45	19 07	18 48		19 17	19 01	19 27	

Table 5

Saturdays

1 September to 8 September

Southend Victoria, Southminster and Shenfield - London

Network Diagram - see first Page of Table 5

		LE ■	LE ■	LE ■	LE	LE	LE ■	LE ■	LE	LE		LE ■	LE ■		LE	LE ■	LE	LE ■	LE ■	LE		LE	LE ■	LE ■	LE ■
Southend Victoria	d	18 10					18 30					18 50						19 10					19 30		
Prittlewell	d	18 12					18 32					18 52						19 12					19 32		
Southend Airport ✈	d	18 15					18 35					18 55						19 15					19 35		
Rochford	d	18 18					18 38					18 58						19 18					19 38		
Hockley	d	18 21					18 41					19 01						19 21					19 41		
Rayleigh	d	18 26					18 46					19 06						19 26					19 46		
Southminster	d		18 16										18 56											19 36	
Burnham-on-Crouch	d		18 20										19 00											19 40	
Althorne	d		18 25										19 05											19 45	
North Fambridge	d		18 31										19 11											19 51	
South Woodham Ferrers	d		18 36										19 16											19 56	
Battlesbridge	d		18 40										19 20											20 00	
Wickford ■	d	18 31	18a46				18 51					19 11	19a26					19 31					19 51	20a06	
Billericay	d	18 37					18 57					19 17						19 37					19 57		
Shenfield ■	a	18 45					19 05					19 25						19 45					20 05		
Shenfield ■	d	18 45		18 51	18 54	19 04	19 05	19 08	19 14	19 24		19 25			19 34	19 38	19 44	19 45	19 51	19 54		20 04	20 05		20 08
Brentwood	d				18 57	19 07			19 17	19 27					19 37		19 47			19 57		20 07			
Harold Wood	d				19 02	19 12			19 22	19 32					19 42		19 52			20 02		20 12			
Gidea Park ■	d				19 06	19 16			19 26	19 36					19 46		19 56			20 06		20 16			
Romford	d				19 08	19 18			19 28	19 38					19 48		19 58			20 08		20 18			
Chadwell Heath	d				19 12	19 22			19 32	19 42					19 52		20 02			20 12		20 22			
Goodmayes	d				19 14	19 24			19 34	19 44					19 54		20 04			20 14		20 24			
Seven Kings	d				19 16	19 26			19 36	19 46					19 56		20 06			20 16		20 26			
Ilford ■	d				19 19	19 29			19 39	19 49					19 59		20 09			20 19		20 29			
Manor Park	d				19 22	19 32			19 42	19 52					20 02		20 12			20 22		20 32			
Forest Gate	d				19 24	19 34			19 44	19 54					20 04		20 14			20 24		20 34			
Maryland	d				19 26	19 36			19 46	19 56					20 06		20 16			20 26		20 36			
Stratford ■ ⊖	d	19 01		19 05	19 29	19 39	19 19	19 22	19 49	19 59		19 39			20 09	19 52	20 19	20 01	20 05	20 29		20 39	20s19		20 22
London Liverpool Street ■ ⊖	a	19 10		19 14	19 37	19 47	19 28	19 31	19 57	20 07		19 48			20 17	20 01	20 27	20 10	20 14	20 37		20 47	20 28		20 33

		LE	LE ■	LE	LE ■			LE	LE ■	LE	LE ■	LE ■	LE ■	LE	LE ■	LE ■		LE	LE ■	LE	LE ■	LE ■		LE	LE ■
Southend Victoria	d				19 50						20 10				20 30						20 50				
Prittlewell	d				19 52						20 12				20 32						20 52				
Southend Airport ✈	d				19 55						20 15				20 35						20 55				
Rochford	d				19 58						20 18				20 38						20 58				
Hockley	d				20 01						20 21				20 41						21 01				
Rayleigh	d				20 06						20 26				20 46						21 06				
Southminster	d											20 16										20 56			
Burnham-on-Crouch	d											20 20										21 00			
Althorne	d											20 25										21 05			
North Fambridge	d											20 31										21 11			
South Woodham Ferrers	d											20 36										21 16			
Battlesbridge	d											20 40										21 20			
Wickford ■	d				20 11						20 31	20a46			20 51						21 11	21a26			
Billericay	d				20 17						20 37				20 57						21 17				
Shenfield ■	a				20 25						20 45				21 05						21 25				
Shenfield ■	d	20 14	20 20	20 24	20 25			20 34	20 38	20 44	20 45		20 51	20 59	21 05	21 08		21 14	21 20	21 24	21 25			21 34	21 38
Brentwood	d	20 17		20 27				20 37		20 47				21 02				21 17		21 27				21 37	
Harold Wood	d	20 22		20 32				20 42		20 52				21 07				21 22		21 32				21 42	
Gidea Park ■	d	20 26		20 36				20 46		20 56				21 11				21 26		21 36				21 46	
Romford	d	20 28	20 28	20 38				20 48		20 58	20 53			21 13				21 28		21 38				21 48	
Chadwell Heath	d	20 32		20 42				20 52		21 02				21 17				21 32		21 42				21 52	
Goodmayes	d	20 34		20 44				20 54		21 04				21 19				21 34		21 44				21 54	
Seven Kings	d	20 36		20 46				20 56		21 06				21 21				21 36		21 46				21 56	
Ilford ■	d	20 39		20 49				20 59		21 09				21 24				21 39		21 49				21 59	
Manor Park	d	20 42		20 52				21 02		21 12				21 27				21 42		21 52				22 02	
Forest Gate	d	20 44		20 54				21 04		21 14				21 29				21 44		21 54				22 04	
Maryland	d	20 46		20 56				21 06		21 16				21 31				21 46		21 56				22 06	
Stratford ■ ⊖	d	20 49	20 36	20 59	20 39			21 09	20 52	21 19	21 01		21 05	21 34	21 19	21 22		21 49	21 36	21 59	21 39			22 09	21 52
London Liverpool Street ■ ⊖	a	20 57	20 45	21 07	20 48			21 17	21 01	21 27	21 10		21 14	21 42	21 28	21 31		21 57	21 45	22 07	21 48			22 20	22 01

Table 5

Saturdays

1 September to 8 September

Southend Victoria, Southminster and Shenfield - London

Network Diagram - see first Page of Table 5

		LE		LE ■	LE ■	LE	LE ■	LE ■	LE ■	LE	LE ■	LE		LE	LE	LE ■	LE	LE ■	LE ■	LE ■	LE	LE ■		LE ■	LE
Southend Victoria	d			21 10			21 30					21 50						22 10				22 30			
Prittlewell	d			21 12			21 32					21 52						22 12				22 32			
Southend Airport ✈	d			21 15			21 35					21 55						22 15				22 35			
Rochford	d			21 18			21 38					21 58						22 18				22 38			
Hockley	d			21 21			21 41					22 01						22 21				22 41			
Rayleigh	d			21 26			21 46					22 06						22 26				22 46			
Southminster	d							21 36											22 16						
Burnham-on-Crouch	d							21 40											22 20						
Althorne	d							21 45											22 25						
North Fambridge	d							21 51											22 31						
South Woodham Ferrers	d							21 56											22 36						
Battlesbridge	d							22 00											22 40						
Wickford ■	d			21 31			21 51	22a06				22 11						22 31	22a46			22 51			
Billericay	d			21 37			21 57					22 17						22 37				22 57			
Shenfield ■	a			21 45			22 05					22 25						22 45				23 05			
Shenfield ■	d	21 44		21 45	21 51	21 59	22 05		22 08	22 14	22 20	22 25			22 29	22 38	22 44	22 45		22 51	22 59	23 05		23 08	
Brentwood	d	21 47				22 02				22 17					22 32		22 47				23 02				
Harold Wood	d	21 52				22 07				22 22					22 37		22 52				23 07				
Gidea Park ■	d	21 56				22 11				22 26					22 41		22 56				23 11				
Romford	d	21 58				22 13				22 28					22 43		22 58				23 13				
Chadwell Heath	d	22 02				22 17				22 32					22 47		23 02				23 17				
Goodmayes	d	22 04				22 19				22 34					22 49		23 04				23 19				
Seven Kings	d	22 06				22 21				22 36					22 51		23 06				23 21				
Ilford ■	d	22 09				22 24				22 41					22 54		23 09				23 24				
Manor Park	d	22 12				22 27				22 44					22 57		23 12				23 27				
Forest Gate	d	22 14				22 29				22 46					22 59		23 14				23 29				
Maryland	d	22 16				22 31				22 48					23 01		23 16				23 31				
Stratford ■ ⊖	d	22 19		22 04	22 13	22 34	22 24		22 28	22 52	22 40	22 44		22 48	23 04	22 58	23 19	23 08		23 12	23 36	23 24		23 28	23 32
London Liverpool Street ■ ⊖	a	22 27		22 13	22 21	22 42	22 32		22 36	23 00	22 48	22 52		22 56	23 12	23 06	23 27	23 16		23 20	23 44	23 32		23 36	23 40

		LE	LE ■	LE ■	LE ■	LE	LE	LE		LE ■	LE
Southend Victoria	d			22 50						23 10	
Prittlewell	d			22 52						23 12	
Southend Airport ✈	d			22 55						23 15	
Rochford	d			22 58						23 18	
Hockley	d			23 01						23 21	
Rayleigh	d			23 06						23 26	
Southminster	d				22 56						
Burnham-on-Crouch	d				23 00						
Althorne	d				23 05						
North Fambridge	d				23 11						
South Woodham Ferrers	d				23 16						
Battlesbridge	d				23 20						
Wickford ■	d			23 11	23a26					23 31	
Billericay	d			23 17						23 37	
Shenfield ■	a			23 25						23 45	
Shenfield ■	d	23 14	23 20	23 25			23 29	23 44		23 45	23 59
Brentwood	d	23 17					23 32	23 47			00 02
Harold Wood	d	23 22					23 37	23 52			00 07
Gidea Park ■	d	23 26					23 41	23 56			00 11
Romford	d	23 28					23 43	23 58			00 13
Chadwell Heath	d	23 32					23 47	00 02			00 17
Goodmayes	d	23 34					23 49	00 04			00 19
Seven Kings	d	23 36					23 51	00 06			00 21
Ilford ■	d	23 39					23 54	00 09			00 24
Manor Park	d	23 42					23 57	00 12			00 27
Forest Gate	d	23 45					23 59	00 14			00 29
Maryland	d	23 47					00 01	00 16			
Stratford ■ ⊖	d	23 50	23 40	23 44		23 54	00 04	00 20		00 08	00 40
London Liverpool Street ■ ⊖	a	23 58	23 48	23 52		00 02	00 12	00 28		00 16	00 48

Southend Victoria, Southminster and Shenfield - London

Network Diagram - see first Page of Table 5

	LE ◇1 A	LE ◇1 B	LE	LE 1	CC	LE	LE 1	LE	LE 1		LE 1	LE 1	LE	LE 1	LE 1	LE	LE 1	LE 1	LE		LE	LE 1		LE
Southend Victoria d							04 00				04 30			05 00				05 30						
Prittlewell d							04 02				04 32			05 02				05 32						
Southend Airport ✈ d							04 05				04 35			05 05				05 35						
Rochford d							04 08				04 38			05 08				05 38						
Hockley d							04 12				04 42			05 11				05 41						
Rayleigh d							04 16				04 46			05 16				05 46						
Southminster d				22p56																				
Burnham-on-Crouch d				23p00																				
Althorne d				23p05																				
North Fambridge d				23p11																				
South Woodham Ferrers d				23p16																				
Battlesbridge d				23p20																				
Wickford 2 d				23p26			04 21				04 51			05 21				05 51						
Billericay d				23p32			04 28				04 58			05 27				05 57						
Shenfield 3 a				23p39			04 39				05 09			05 35				06 05						
Shenfield 3 d			23p29	23p39		23p44	04 39				05 09	05 24		05 35		05 44	05 53	06 05			06 14	06 24		
Brentwood d			23p32			23p47	04 42				05 12					05 47					06 17			
Harold Wood d			23p37			23p52	04 47				05 17					05 52					06 22			
Gidea Park 2 d			23p41			23p56	04 51				05 21	05 31				05 56			06 16		06 26			06 36
Romford d			23p43	23p47		23p58	04 53				05 23			05 43		05 58			06 18		06 28			06 38
Chadwell Heath d			23p47			00 02	04 57				05 27					06 02			06 22		06 32			06 42
Goodmayes d			23p49			00 04	04 59				05 29					06 04			06 24		06 34			06 44
Seven Kings d			23p51			00 06	05 01				05 31	05 36				06 06			06 26		06 36			06 46
Ilford 2 d			23p54			00 09	05 04	05 09			05 34		05 39			06 09			06 29		06 39			06 49
Manor Park d			23p57			00 12		05 11					05 41			06 12			06 32		06 42			06 52
Forest Gate d			23p59			00 14		05 14					05 44			06 14			06 34		06 44			06 54
Maryland d			00 01			00 16		05 16					05 46			06 16			06 36		06 46			06 56
Stratford 7 ⊖ d	23b52	23b52	00 04	23p56	00 09	00 19	05 10	05 18	05 30		05 40	05 42	05 48	05 51	06 05	06 19	06 07	06 19	06 39		06 49	06 38		06 59
London Liverpool Street 15 ⊖ a	00 02	00 02	00 12	00 05	00 20	00 27	05 18	05 26	08 13		05 48	05 55	05 56	06 00	06 14	06 27	06 16	06 28	06 47		06 57	06 47		07 07

	LE 1	LE 1	LE	LE	LE 1		LE	LE	LE 1	LE 1	LE	LE 1	LE	LE 1	LE 1			LE	LE 1	LE	LE 1	LE 1	LE	LE
Southend Victoria d	06 00								06 30					06 50							07 10			
Prittlewell d	06 02								06 32					06 52							07 12			
Southend Airport ✈ d	06 05								06 35					06 55							07 15			
Rochford d	06 08								06 38					06 58							07 18			
Hockley d	06 11								06 41					07 01							07 21			
Rayleigh d	06 16								06 46					07 06							07 26			
Southminster d		06 16													06 56									
Burnham-on-Crouch d		06 20													07 00									
Althorne d		06 25													07 05									
North Fambridge d		06 31													07 11									
South Woodham Ferrers d		06 36													07 16									
Battlesbridge d		06 40													07 20									
Wickford 2 d	06 21	06a46							06 51					07 11	07a26						07 31			
Billericay d	06 27								06 57					07 17							07 37			
Shenfield 3 a	06 35								07 05					07 25							07 45			
Shenfield 3 d	06 35			06 44	06 51			07 04	07 05	07 08	07 14	07 20	07 24	07 25				07 34	07 38	07 44	07 45	07 51	07 54	08 04
Brentwood d				06 47				07 07			07 17		07 27					07 37		07 47			07 57	08 07
Harold Wood d				06 52				07 12			07 22		07 32					07 42		07 52			08 02	08 12
Gidea Park 2 d			06 46	06 56			07 06	07 16			07 26		07 36					07 46		07 56			08 06	08 16
Romford d	06 43		06 48	06 58			07 08	07 18			07 28	07 28	07 38					07 48		07 58	07 53		08 08	08 18
Chadwell Heath d			06 52	07 02			07 12	07 22			07 32		07 42					07 52		08 02			08 12	08 22
Goodmayes d			06 54	07 04			07 14	07 24			07 34		07 44					07 54		08 04			08 14	08 24
Seven Kings d			06 56	07 06			07 16	07 26			07 36		07 46					07 56		08 06			08 16	08 26
Ilford 2 d			06 59	07 09			07 19	07 29			07 39		07 49					07 59		08 09			08 19	08 29
Manor Park d			07 02	07 12			07 22	07 32			07 42		07 52					08 02		08 12			08 22	08 32
Forest Gate d			07 04	07 14			07 24	07 34			07 44		07 54					08 04		08 14			08 24	08 34
Maryland d			07 06	07 16			07 26	07 36			07 46		07 56					08 06		08 16			08 26	08 36
Stratford 7 ⊖ d	06 51		07 09	07 19	07 05		07 29	07 39	07 19	07 22	07 49	07 36	07 59	07 39				08 09	07 52	08 19	08 01	08 05	08 29	08 39
London Liverpool Street 15 ⊖ a	07 00		07 17	07 27	07 14		07 37	07 47	07 28	07 31	07 57	07 45	08 07	07 48				08 17	08 01	08 27	08 10	08 14	08 37	08 47

A 15 September
B not 15 September
b Previous night, stops to set down only

Table 5

Saturdays
from 15 September

Southend Victoria, Southminster and Shenfield - London

Network Diagram - see first Page of Table 5

	LE 1		LE 1	LE 1	LE	LE 1	LE	LE 1	LE ◇1	LE	LE 1		LE	LE 1	LE 1	LE 1	LE	LE	LE 1	LE 1	LE		LE 1	LE
Southend Victoria d	07 30							07 50						08 10					08 30					
Prittlewell d	07 32							07 52						08 12					08 32					
Southend Airport ✈ d	07 35							07 55						08 15					08 35					
Rochford d	07 38							07 58						08 18					08 38					
Hockley d	07 41							08 01						08 21					08 41					
Rayleigh d	07 46							08 06						08 26					08 46					
Southminster d			07 36												08 16									
Burnham-on-Crouch d			07 40												08 20									
Althorne d			07 45												08 25									
North Fambridge d			07 51												08 31									
South Woodham Ferrers d			07 56												08 36									
Battlesbridge d			08 00												08 40									
Wickford 2 d	07 51		08a06					08 11						08 31	08a46				08 51					
Billericay d	07 57							08 17						08 37					08 57					
Shenfield 3 a	08 05							08 25						08 45					09 05					
Shenfield 3 d	08 05			08 08	08 14	08 20	08 24	08 25		08 34	08 38		08 44	08 45		08 51	08 54	09 04	09 05	09 08	09 14		09 20	09 24
Brentwood d					08 17		08 27			08 37			08 47				08 57	09 07			09 17			09 27
Harold Wood d					08 22		08 32			08 42			08 52				09 02	09 12			09 22			09 32
Gidea Park 2 d					08 26		08 36			08 46			08 56				09 06	09 16			09 26			09 36
Romford d					08 28	08 28	08 38			08 48			08 58	08 53			09 08	09 18			09 28		09 28	09 38
Chadwell Heath d					08 32		08 42			08 52			09 02				09 12	09 22			09 32			09 42
Goodmayes d					08 34		08 44			08 54			09 04				09 14	09 24			09 34			09 44
Seven Kings d					08 36		08 46			08 56			09 06				09 16	09 26			09 36			09 46
Ilford 2 d					08 39		08 49			08 59			09 09				09 19	09 29			09 39			09 49
Manor Park d					08 42		08 52			09 02			09 12				09 22	09 32			09 42			09 52
Forest Gate d					08 44		08 54			09 04			09 14				09 24	09 34			09 44			09 54
Maryland d					08 46		08 56			09 06			09 16				09 26	09 36			09 46			09 56
Stratford 7 ⊖ d	08 19			08 22	08 49	08 36	08 59	08 39		09 09	08 52		09 19	09 01		09 05	09 29	09 39	09 19	09 22	09 49		09 36	09 59
London Liverpool Street 15 ⊖ a	08 28			08 31	08 57	08 45	09 07	08 48	08 55	09 17	09 01		09 27	09 10		09 14	09 37	09 47	09 28	09 31	09 57		09 45	10 07

	LE 1	LE 1		LE	LE 1	LE	LE 1		LE 1	LE	LE	LE 1	LE 1	LE 1	LE	LE 1	LE		LE 1		LE	LE 1	LE	LE 1
Southend Victoria d	08 50						09 10					09 30							09 50					10 10
Prittlewell d	08 52						09 12					09 32							09 52					10 12
Southend Airport ✈ d	08 55						09 15					09 35							09 55					10 15
Rochford d	08 58						09 18					09 38							09 58					10 18
Hockley d	09 01						09 21					09 41							10 01					10 21
Rayleigh d	09 06						09 26					09 46							10 06					10 26
Southminster d		08 56											09 36											
Burnham-on-Crouch d		09 00											09 40											
Althorne d		09 05											09 45											
North Fambridge d		09 11											09 51											
South Woodham Ferrers d		09 16											09 56											
Battlesbridge d		09 20											10 00											
Wickford 2 d	09 11	09a26					09 31					09 51	10a06						10 11					10 31
Billericay d	09 17						09 37					09 57							10 17					10 37
Shenfield 3 a	09 25						09 45					10 05							10 25					10 45
Shenfield 3 d	09 25			09 34	09 38	09 44	09 45		09 51	09 54	10 04	10 05		10 08	10 14	10 20	10 24		10 25		10 34	10 38	10 44	10 45
Brentwood d				09 37		09 47				09 57	10 07				10 17		10 27				10 37		10 47	
Harold Wood d				09 42		09 52				10 02	10 12				10 22		10 32				10 42		10 52	
Gidea Park 2 d				09 46		09 56				10 06	10 16				10 26		10 36				10 46		10 56	
Romford d				09 48		09 58	09 53			10 08	10 18				10 28	10 28	10 38				10 48		10 58	10 53
Chadwell Heath d				09 52		10 02				10 12	10 22				10 32		10 42				10 52		11 02	
Goodmayes d				09 54		10 04				10 14	10 24				10 34		10 44				10 54		11 04	
Seven Kings d				09 56		10 06				10 16	10 26				10 36		10 46				10 56		11 06	
Ilford 2 d				09 59		10 09				10 19	10 29				10 39		10 49				10 59		11 09	
Manor Park d				10 02		10 12				10 22	10 32				10 42		10 52				11 02		11 12	
Forest Gate d				10 04		10 14				10 24	10 34				10 44		10 54				11 04		11 14	
Maryland d				10 06		10 16				10 26	10 36				10 46		10 56				11 06		11 16	
Stratford 7 ⊖ d	09 39			10 09	09 52	10 19	10 01		10 05	10 29	10 39	10 19		10 22	10 49	10 36	10 59		10 39		11 09	10 52	11 19	11 01
London Liverpool Street 15 ⊖ a	09 48			10 17	10 01	10 27	10 10		10 14	10 37	10 47	10 28		10 31	10 57	10 45	11 07		10 48		11 17	11 01	11 27	11 10

Southend Victoria, Southminster and Shenfield - London

Saturdays from 15 September

Network Diagram - see first Page of Table 5

		LE [1]	LE [1]	LE	LE	LE [1]	LE [1]	LE	LE [1]	LE	LE [1]	LE [1]	LE	LE [1]	LE	LE [1]	LE [1]	LE	LE	LE [1]	LE [1]
Southend Victoria	d					10 30					10 50					11 10				11 30	
Prittlewell	d					10 32					10 52					11 12				11 32	
Southend Airport ✈	d					10 35					10 55					11 15				11 35	
Rochford	d					10 38					10 58					11 18				11 38	
Hockley	d					10 41					11 01					11 21				11 41	
Rayleigh	d					10 46					11 06					11 26				11 46	
Southminster	d	10 16										10 56									11 36
Burnham-on-Crouch	d	10 20										11 00									11 40
Althorne	d	10 25										11 05									11 45
North Fambridge	d	10 31										11 11									11 51
South Woodham Ferrers	d	10 36										11 16									11 56
Battlesbridge	d	10 40										11 20									12 00
Wickford [2]	d	10a46				10 51					11 11	11a26				11 31				11 51	12a06
Billericay	d					10 57					11 17					11 37				11 57	
Shenfield [3]	a					11 05					11 25					11 45				12 05	
Shenfield [3]	d		10 51	10 54	11 04	11 05	11 08	11 14	11 20	11 24	11 25		11 34	11 38	11 44	11 45	11 51	11 54	12 04	12 05	
Brentwood	d			10 57	11 07			11 17		11 27			11 37		11 47			11 57	12 07		
Harold Wood	d			11 02	11 12			11 22		11 32			11 42		11 52			12 02	12 12		
Gidea Park [2]	d			11 06	11 16			11 26		11 36			11 46		11 56			12 06	12 16		
Romford	d			11 08	11 18			11 28	11 28	11 38			11 48		11 58	11 53		12 08	12 18		
Chadwell Heath	d			11 12	11 22			11 32		11 42			11 52		12 02			12 12	12 22		
Goodmayes	d			11 14	11 24			11 34		11 44			11 54		12 04			12 14	12 24		
Seven Kings	d			11 16	11 26			11 36		11 46			11 56		12 06			12 16	12 26		
Ilford [2]	d			11 19	11 29			11 39		11 49			11 59		12 09			12 19	12 29		
Manor Park	d			11 22	11 32			11 42		11 52			12 02		12 12			12 22	12 32		
Forest Gate	d			11 24	11 34			11 44		11 54			12 04		12 14			12 24	12 34		
Maryland	d			11 26	11 36			11 46		11 56			12 06		12 16			12 26	12 36		
Stratford [7] ⊖	d		11 05	11 29	11 39	11 19	11 22	11 49	11 36	11 59	11 39		12 09	11 52	12 19	12 01	12 05	12 29	12 39	12 19	
London Liverpool Street [15] ⊖	a		11 14	11 37	11 47	11 28	11 31	11 57	11 45	12 07	11 48		12 17	12 01	12 27	12 10	12 14	12 37	12 47	12 28	

		LE [1]	LE	LE [1]	LE	LE [1]	LE	LE [1]	LE	LE [1]	LE [1]	LE [1]	LE	LE	LE [1]	LE [1]	LE	LE [1]	LE	LE [1]	LE [1]
Southend Victoria	d					11 50				12 10					12 30					12 50	
Prittlewell	d					11 52				12 12					12 32					12 52	
Southend Airport ✈	d					11 55				12 15					12 35					12 55	
Rochford	d					11 58				12 18					12 38					12 58	
Hockley	d					12 01				12 21					12 41					13 01	
Rayleigh	d					12 06				12 26					12 46					13 06	
Southminster	d										12 16										12 56
Burnham-on-Crouch	d										12 20										13 00
Althorne	d										12 25										13 05
North Fambridge	d										12 31										13 11
South Woodham Ferrers	d										12 36										13 16
Battlesbridge	d										12 40										13 20
Wickford [2]	d					12 11				12 31	12a46				12 51					13 11	13a26
Billericay	d					12 17				12 37					12 57					13 17	
Shenfield [3]	a					12 25				12 45					13 05					13 25	
Shenfield [3]	d	12 08	12 14	12 20	12 24	12 25	12 34	12 38	12 44	12 45		12 51	12 54	13 04	13 05	13 08	13 14	13 20	13 24	13 25	
Brentwood	d		12 17		12 27		12 37		12 47				12 57	13 07			13 17		13 27		
Harold Wood	d		12 22		12 32		12 42		12 52				13 02	13 12			13 22		13 32		
Gidea Park [2]	d		12 26		12 36		12 46		12 56				13 06	13 16			13 26		13 36		
Romford	d		12 28	12 28	12 38		12 48		12 58	12 53			13 08	13 18			13 28	13 28	13 38		
Chadwell Heath	d		12 32		12 42		12 52		13 02				13 12	13 22			13 32		13 42		
Goodmayes	d		12 34		12 44		12 54		13 04				13 14	13 24			13 34		13 44		
Seven Kings	d		12 36		12 46		12 56		13 06				13 16	13 26			13 36		13 46		
Ilford [2]	d		12 39		12 49		12 59		13 09				13 19	13 29			13 39		13 49		
Manor Park	d		12 42		12 52		13 02		13 12				13 22	13 32			13 42		13 52		
Forest Gate	d		12 44		12 54		13 04		13 14				13 24	13 34			13 44		13 54		
Maryland	d		12 46		12 56		13 06		13 16				13 26	13 36			13 46		13 56		
Stratford [7] ⊖	d	12 22	12 49	12 36	12 59	12 39	13 09	12 52	13 19	13 01		13 05	13 29	13 39	13 19	13 22	13 49	13 36	13 59	13 39	
London Liverpool Street [15] ⊖	a	12 31	12 57	12 45	13 07	12 48	13 17	13 01	13 27	13 10		13 14	13 37	13 47	13 28	13 31	13 57	13 45	14 07	13 48	

Southend Victoria, Southminster and Shenfield - London

Saturdays from 15 September

Network Diagram - see first Page of Table 5

		LE	LE [1]	LE	LE [1]	LE [1]	LE	LE	LE [1]	LE [1]	LE [1]	LE	LE [1]	LE	LE [1]	LE	LE [1]	LE	LE [1]	LE [1]	LE [1]	LE
Southend Victoria	d				13 10				13 30						13 50				14 10			
Prittlewell	d				13 12				13 32						13 52				14 12			
Southend Airport ✈	d				13 15				13 35						13 55				14 15			
Rochford	d				13 18				13 38						13 58				14 18			
Hockley	d				13 21				13 41						14 01				14 21			
Rayleigh	d				13 26				13 46						14 06				14 26			
Southminster	d									13 36										14 16		
Burnham-on-Crouch	d									13 40										14 20		
Althorne	d									13 45										14 25		
North Fambridge	d									13 51										14 31		
South Woodham Ferrers	d									13 56										14 36		
Battlesbridge	d									14 00										14 40		
Wickford [2]	d				13 31				13 51	14a06					14 11				14 31	14a46		
Billericay	d				13 37				13 57						14 17				14 37			
Shenfield [3]	a				13 45				14 05						14 25				14 45			
Shenfield [3]	d	13 34	13 38	13 44	13 45	13 51	13 54	14 04	14 05		14 08	14 14	14 20	14 24	14 25	14 34	14 38	14 44	14 45		14 51	14 54
Brentwood	d	13 37		13 47			13 57	14 07				14 17		14 27		14 37		14 47				14 57
Harold Wood	d	13 42		13 52			14 02	14 12				14 22		14 32		14 42		14 52				15 02
Gidea Park [2]	d	13 46		13 56			14 06	14 16				14 26		14 36		14 46		14 56				15 06
Romford	d	13 48		13 58	13 53		14 08	14 18				14 28	14 28	14 38		14 48		14 58	14 53			15 08
Chadwell Heath	d	13 52		14 02			14 12	14 22				14 32		14 42		14 52		15 02				15 12
Goodmayes	d	13 54		14 04			14 14	14 24				14 34		14 44		14 54		15 04				15 14
Seven Kings	d	13 56		14 06			14 16	14 26				14 36		14 46		14 56		15 06				15 16
Ilford [2]	d	13 59		14 09			14 19	14 29				14 39		14 49		14 59		15 09				15 19
Manor Park	d	14 02		14 12			14 22	14 32				14 42		14 52		15 02		15 12				15 22
Forest Gate	d	14 04		14 14			14 24	14 34				14 44		14 54		15 04		15 14				15 24
Maryland	d	14 06		14 16			14 26	14 36				14 46		14 56		15 06		15 16				15 26
Stratford [7] ⊖	d	14 09	13 52	14 19	14 01	14 05	14 29	14 39	14 19		14 22	14 49	14 36	14 59	14 39	15 09	14 52	15 19	15 01		15 05	15 29
London Liverpool Street [15] ⊖	a	14 17	14 01	14 27	14 10	14 14	14 37	14 47	14 28		14 31	14 57	14 45	15 07	14 48	15 17	15 01	15 27	15 10		15 14	15 37

		LE	LE [1]	LE [1]	LE	LE [1]	LE	LE [1]	LE [1]	LE	LE [1]	LE	LE [1]	LE [1]	LE	LE	LE [1]	LE [1]	LE [1]	LE	LE [1]
Southend Victoria	d		14 30					14 50					15 10				15 30				
Prittlewell	d		14 32					14 52					15 12				15 32				
Southend Airport ✈	d		14 35					14 55					15 15				15 35				
Rochford	d		14 38					14 58					15 18				15 38				
Hockley	d		14 41					15 01					15 21				15 41				
Rayleigh	d		14 46					15 06					15 26				15 46				
Southminster	d								14 56									15 36			
Burnham-on-Crouch	d								15 00									15 40			
Althorne	d								15 05									15 45			
North Fambridge	d								15 11									15 51			
South Woodham Ferrers	d								15 16									15 56			
Battlesbridge	d								15 20									16 00			
Wickford [2]	d		14 51					15 11	15a26				15 31				15 51	16a06			
Billericay	d		14 57					15 17					15 37				15 57				
Shenfield [3]	a		15 05					15 25					15 45				16 05				
Shenfield [3]	d	15 04	15 05	15 08	15 14	15 20	15 24	15 25		15 34	15 38	15 44	15 45	15 51	15 54	16 04	16 05		16 08	16 14	16 20
Brentwood	d	15 07			15 17		15 27			15 37		15 47			15 57	16 07				16 17	
Harold Wood	d	15 12			15 22		15 32			15 42		15 52			16 02	16 12				16 22	
Gidea Park [2]	d	15 16			15 26		15 36			15 46		15 56			16 06	16 16				16 26	
Romford	d	15 18			15 28	15 28	15 38			15 48		15 58	15 53		16 08	16 18				16 28	16 28
Chadwell Heath	d	15 22			15 32		15 42			15 52		16 02			16 12	16 22				16 32	
Goodmayes	d	15 24			15 34		15 44			15 54		16 04			16 14	16 24				16 34	
Seven Kings	d	15 26			15 36		15 46			15 56		16 06			16 16	16 26				16 36	
Ilford [2]	d	15 29			15 39		15 49			15 59		16 09			16 19	16 29				16 39	
Manor Park	d	15 32			15 42		15 52			16 02		16 12			16 22	16 32				16 42	
Forest Gate	d	15 34			15 44		15 54			16 04		16 14			16 24	16 34				16 44	
Maryland	d	15 36			15 46		15 56			16 06		16 16			16 26	16 36				16 46	
Stratford [7] ⊖	d	15 39	15 19	15 22	15 49	15 36	15 59	15 39		16 09	15 52	16 19	16 01	16 05	16 29	16 39	16 19		16 22	16 49	16 36
London Liverpool Street [15] ⊖	a	15 47	15 28	15 31	15 57	15 45	16 07	15 48		16 17	16 01	16 27	16 10	16 14	16 37	16 47	16 28		16 31	16 57	16 45

Southend Victoria, Southminster and Shenfield - London

Network Diagram - see first Page of Table 5

		LE	LE ■		LE	LE ■	LE	LE ■		LE ■	LE ■	LE	LE	LE ■	LE ■	LE	LE ■	LE		LE ■	LE ■		LE	LE ■	LE ■
Southend Victoria	d		15 50					16 10						16 30						16 50					17 10
Prittlewell	d		15 52					16 12						16 32						16 52					17 12
Southend Airport ✈	d		15 55					16 15						16 35						16 55					17 15
Rochford	d		15 58					16 18						16 38						16 58					17 18
Hockley	d		16 01					16 21						16 41						17 01					17 21
Rayleigh	d		16 06					16 26						16 46						17 06					17 26
Southminster	d									16 16											16 56				
Burnham-on-Crouch	d									16 20											17 00				
Althorne	d									16 25											17 05				
North Fambridge	d									16 31											17 11				
South Woodham Ferrers	d									16 36											17 16				
Battlesbridge	d									16 40											17 20				
Wickford 2	d		16 11					16 31		16a46				16 51						17 11	17a26				17 31
Billericay	d		16 17					16 37						16 57						17 17					17 37
Shenfield 3	a		16 25					16 45						17 05						17 25					17 44
Shenfield 3	d	16 24	16 25		16 34	16 38	16 44	16 45			16 51	16 54	17 04	17 05	17 08	17 14	17 20	17 24		17 25			17 34	17 38	17 45
Brentwood	d	16 27			16 37		16 47					16 57	17 07			17 17		17 27					17 37		
Harold Wood	d	16 32			16 42		16 52					17 02	17 12			17 22		17 32					17 42		
Gidea Park 2	d	16 36			16 46		16 56					17 06	17 16			17 26		17 36					17 46		
Romford	d	16 38			16 48		16 58	16 53				17 08	17 18			17 28	17 28	17 38					17 48		17 53
Chadwell Heath	d	16 42			16 52		17 02					17 12	17 22			17 32		17 42					17 52		
Goodmayes	d	16 44			16 54		17 04					17 14	17 24			17 34		17 44					17 54		
Seven Kings	d	16 46			16 56		17 06					17 16	17 26			17 36		17 46					17 56		
Ilford 2	d	16 49			16 59		17 09					17 19	17 29			17 39		17 49					17 59		
Manor Park	d	16 52			17 02		17 12					17 22	17 32			17 42		17 52					18 02		
Forest Gate	d	16 54			17 04		17 14					17 24	17 34			17 44		17 54					18 04		
Maryland	d	16 56			17 06		17 16					17 26	17 36			17 46		17 56					18 06		
Stratford 7 ⊖	d	16 59	16 39		17 09	16 52	17 19	17 01			17 05	17 29	17 39	17 19	17 22	17 49	17 36	17 59		17 39			18 09	17 52	18 01
London Liverpool Street 15 ⊖	a	17 07	16 48		17 17	17 01	17 27	17 10			17 14	17 37	17 47	17 28	17 31	17 57	17 45	18 07		17 48			18 17	18 01	18 10

		LE	LE ■	LE		LE	LE ■	LE ■		LE	LE ■	LE	LE ■			LE	LE ■	LE	LE ■	LE ■	LE ■	LE	LE	LE ■	
Southend Victoria	d						17 30						17 50						18 10					18 30	
Prittlewell	d						17 32						17 52						18 12					18 32	
Southend Airport ✈	d						17 35						17 55						18 15					18 35	
Rochford	d						17 38						17 58						18 18					18 38	
Hockley	d						17 41						18 01						18 21					18 41	
Rayleigh	d						17 46						18 06						18 26					18 46	
Southminster	d							17 36												18 16					
Burnham-on-Crouch	d							17 40												18 20					
Althorne	d							17 45												18 25					
North Fambridge	d							17 51												18 31					
South Woodham Ferrers	d							17 56												18 36					
Battlesbridge	d							18 00												18 40					
Wickford 2	d						17 51	18a06					18 11						18 31	18a46				18 51	
Billericay	d						17 57						18 17						18 37					18 57	
Shenfield 3	a						18 05						18 25						18 45					19 05	
Shenfield 3	d	17 44	17 51	17 54		18 04	18 05			18 14	18 20	18 24	18 25			18 34	18 38	18 44	18 45		18 51	18 54	19 04	19 05	
Brentwood	d	17 47		17 57		18 07				18 17		18 27				18 37		18 47				18 57	19 07		
Harold Wood	d	17 52		18 02		18 12				18 22		18 32				18 42		18 52				19 02	19 12		
Gidea Park 2	d	17 56		18 06		18 16				18 26		18 36				18 46		18 56				19 06	19 16		
Romford	d	17 58		18 08		18 18				18 28	18 28	18 38				18 48		18 58	18 53			19 08	19 18		
Chadwell Heath	d	18 02		18 12		18 22				18 32		18 42				18 52		19 02				19 12	19 22		
Goodmayes	d	18 04		18 14		18 24				18 34		18 44				18 54		19 04				19 14	19 24		
Seven Kings	d	18 06		18 16		18 26				18 36		18 46				18 56		19 06				19 16	19 26		
Ilford 2	d	18 09		18 19		18 29				18 39		18 49				18 59		19 09				19 19	19 29		
Manor Park	d	18 12		18 22		18 32				18 42		18 52				19 02		19 12				19 22	19 32		
Forest Gate	d	18 14		18 24		18 34				18 44		18 54				19 04		19 14				19 24	19 34		
Maryland	d	18 16		18 26		18 36				18 46		18 56				19 06		19 16				19 26	19 36		
Stratford 7 ⊖	d	18 19	18 05	18 29		18 39	18 19			18 49	18 36	18 59	18 39			19 09	18 52	19 19	19 01		19 05	19 29	19 39	19 19	
London Liverpool Street 15 ⊖	a	18 27	18 14	18 37		18 47	18 28			18 57	18 45	19 07	18 48			19 17	19 01	19 27	19 10		19 14	19 37	19 47	19 28	

Southend Victoria, Southminster and Shenfield - London

Network Diagram - see first Page of Table 5

		LE ■	LE	LE ■	LE	LE ■	LE ■		LE	LE ■		LE	LE ■	LE ■	LE	LE	LE ■	LE ■	LE ■	LE		LE ■	LE	LE ■	
Southend Victoria	d					18 50							19 10				19 30							19 50	
Prittlewell	d					18 52							19 12				19 32							19 52	
Southend Airport ✈	d					18 55							19 15				19 35							19 55	
Rochford	d					18 58							19 18				19 38							19 58	
Hockley	d					19 01							19 21				19 41							20 01	
Rayleigh	d					19 06							19 26				19 46							20 06	
Southminster	d						18 56											19 36							
Burnham-on-Crouch	d						19 00											19 40							
Althorne	d						19 05											19 45							
North Fambridge	d						19 11											19 51							
South Woodham Ferrers	d						19 16											19 56							
Battlesbridge	d						19 20											20 00							
Wickford 2	d					19 11	19a26						19 31				19 51	20a06						20 11	
Billericay	d					19 17							19 37				19 57							20 17	
Shenfield 3	a					19 25							19 45				20 05							20 25	
Shenfield 3	d	19 08	19 14	19 20	19 24	19 25			19 34	19 38		19 44	19 45	19 51	19 54	20 04	20 05		20 08	20 14		20 20	20 24	20 25	
Brentwood	d		19 17		19 27				19 37			19 47			19 57	20 07				20 17			20 27		
Harold Wood	d		19 22		19 32				19 42			19 52			20 02	20 12				20 22			20 32		
Gidea Park 2	d		19 26		19 36				19 46			19 56			20 06	20 16				20 26			20 36		
Romford	d		19 28	19 28	19 38				19 48			19 58	19 53		20 08	20 18				20 28		20 28	20 38		
Chadwell Heath	d		19 32		19 42				19 52			20 02			20 12	20 22				20 32			20 42		
Goodmayes	d		19 34		19 44				19 54			20 04			20 14	20 24				20 34			20 44		
Seven Kings	d		19 36		19 46				19 56			20 06			20 16	20 26				20 36			20 46		
Ilford 2	d		19 39		19 49				19 59			20 09			20 19	20 29				20 39			20 49		
Manor Park	d		19 42		19 52				20 02			20 12			20 22	20 32				20 42			20 52		
Forest Gate	d		19 44		19 54				20 04			20 14			20 24	20 34				20 44			20 54		
Maryland	d		19 46		19 56				20 06			20 16			20 26	20 36				20 46			20 56		
Stratford 7 ⊖	d	19 22	19 49	19 36	19 59	19 39			20 09	19 52		20 19	20 01	20 05	20 29	20 39	20s19		20 22	20 49		20 36	20 59	20 39	
London Liverpool Street 15 ⊖	a	19 31	19 57	19 45	20 07	19 48			20 17	20 01		20 27	20 10	20 14	20 37	20 47	20 28		20 31	20 57		20 45	21 07	20 48	

		LE	LE ■	LE	LE ■	LE ■		LE ■	LE	LE ■	LE ■	LE	LE ■	LE ■	LE ■			LE	LE ■	LE	LE ■	LE ■	LE	LE ■	LE ■
Southend Victoria	d				20 10					20 30				20 50							21 10			21 30	
Prittlewell	d				20 12					20 32				20 52							21 12			21 32	
Southend Airport ✈	d				20 15					20 35				20 55							21 15			21 35	
Rochford	d				20 18					20 38				20 58							21 18			21 38	
Hockley	d				20 21					20 41				21 01							21 21			21 41	
Rayleigh	d				20 26					20 46				21 06							21 26			21 46	
Southminster	d					20 16									20 56										21 36
Burnham-on-Crouch	d					20 20									21 00										21 40
Althorne	d					20 25									21 05										21 45
North Fambridge	d					20 31									21 11										21 51
South Woodham Ferrers	d					20 36									21 16										21 56
Battlesbridge	d					20 40									21 20										22 00
Wickford 2	d				20 31	20a46				20 51				21 11	21a26						21 31			21 51	22a06
Billericay	d				20 37					20 57				21 17							21 37			21 57	
Shenfield 3	a				20 45					21 05				21 25							21 45			22 05	
Shenfield 3	d	20 34	20 38	20 44	20 45			20 51	20 59	21 05	21 08	21 14	21 20	21 25				21 29	21 38	21 44	21 45	21 51	21 59	22 05	
Brentwood	d	20 37		20 47					21 02			21 17						21 32		21 47			22 02		
Harold Wood	d	20 42		20 52					21 07			21 22						21 37		21 52			22 07		
Gidea Park 2	d	20 46		20 56					21 11			21 26						21 41		21 56			22 11		
Romford	d	20 48		20 58	20 53				21 13			21 28	21 28					21 43		21 58	21 53		22 13		
Chadwell Heath	d	20 52		21 02					21 17			21 32						21 47		22 02			22 17		
Goodmayes	d	20 54		21 04					21 19			21 34						21 49		22 04			22 19		
Seven Kings	d	20 56		21 06					21 21			21 36						21 51		22 06			22 21		
Ilford 2	d	20 59		21 09					21 24			21 39						21 54		22 09			22 24		
Manor Park	d	21 02		21 12					21 27			21 42						21 57		22 12			22 27		
Forest Gate	d	21 04		21 14					21 29			21 44						21 59		22 14			22 29		
Maryland	d	21 06		21 16					21 31			21 46						22 01		22 16			22 31		
Stratford 7 ⊖	d	21 09	20 52	21 19	21 01			21 05	21 34	21 19	21 22	21 49	21 36	21 39				22 04	21 52	22 19	22 01	22 05	22 34	22 19	
London Liverpool Street 15 ⊖	a	21 17	21 01	21 27	21 10			21 14	21 42	21 28	21 31	21 57	21 45	21 48				22 12	22 01	22 27	22 10	22 14	22 42	22 28	

Table 5

Saturdays from 15 September

Southend Victoria, Southminster and Shenfield - London

Network Diagram - see first Page of Table 5

		LE ■	LE	LE ■	LE ◇■	LE	LE ■	LE ■	LE ■	LE	LE ■	LE ■	LE	LE ■	LE ■	LE	LE ■	LE	LE ■	LE ■	LE
Southend Victoria	d						22 00							22 30					23 00		
Prittlewell	d						22 02							22 32					23 02		
Southend Airport ✈	d						22 05							22 35					23 05		
Rochford	d						22 08							22 38					23 08		
Hockley	d						22 11							22 41					23 11		
Rayleigh	d						22 16							22 46					23 16		
Southminster	d							22 16												22 56	
Burnham-on-Crouch	d							22 20												23 00	
Althorne	d							22 25												23 05	
North Fambridge	d							22 31												23 11	
South Woodham Ferrers	d							22 36												23 16	
Battlesbridge	d							22 40												23 20	
Wickford 2	d						22 21	22a46						22 51					23 21	23 26	
Billericay	d						22 27							22 57					23 27	23 32	
Shenfield 3	a						22 35							23 05					23 35	23 39	
Shenfield 3	d	22 08	22 14	22 20		22 29	22 35		22 38	22 44	22 51		22 59	23 05	23 08	23 14	23 20	23 29	23 35	23 39	23 44
Brentwood	d		22 17			22 32				22 47			23 02			23 17		23 32			23 47
Harold Wood	d		22 22			22 37				22 52			23 07			23 22		23 37			23 52
Gidea Park 2	d		22 26			22 41				22 56			23 11			23 26		23 41			23 56
Romford	d		22 28	22 28		22 43				22 58			23 13			23 28	23 28	23 43		23 47	23 58
Chadwell Heath	d		22 32			22 47				23 02			23 17			23 32		23 47			00 02
Goodmayes	d		22 34			22 49				23 04			23 19			23 34		23 49			00 04
Seven Kings	d		22 36			22 51				23 06			23 21			23 36		23 51			00 06
Ilford 2	d		22 39			22 54				23 09			23 24			23 39		23 54			00 09
Manor Park	d		22 42			22 57				23 12			23 27			23 42		23 57			00 12
Forest Gate	d		22 44			22 59				23 14			23 29			23 44		23 59			00 14
Maryland	d		22 46			23 01				23 16			23 31			23 46		00 01			00 16
Stratford 7 ⊖	d	22 22	22 49	22 36		23 04	22 49		22 52	23 19	23 05	23 07	23 34	23 19	23 22	23 49	23 36	00 04	23 49	23 56	00 19
London Liverpool Street 15 ⊖	a	22 31	22 57	22 46	22 55	23 12	22 58		23 01	23 27	23 14	23 18	23 42	23 28	23 31	23 57	23 45	00 12	23 58	00 05	00 27

Sundays until 22 July

		LE ◇■	LE	LE ■	LE	LE A 🚌	LE B	LE A 🚌	LE B	LE B	LE ■ A	LE ■ B	LE B	LE A 🚌	LE ■ B	LE B	LE ■ A	LE ■ B	LE B	LE ■ B	LE B	LE A 🚌	LE ■ B
Southend Victoria	d										06 15	06 15					06 45	06 45					07 15
Prittlewell	d																						
Southend Airport ✈	d										06 19	06 19					06 49	06 49					07 19
Rochford	d										06 22	06 22					06 52	06 52					07 22
Hockley	d										06 25	06 25					06 55	06 55					07 25
Rayleigh	d										06 30	06 30					07 00	07 00					07 30
Southminster	d			22p56																			
Burnham-on-Crouch	d			23p00																			
Althorne	d			23p05																			
North Fambridge	d			23p11																			
South Woodham Ferrers	d			23p16																			
Battlesbridge	d			23p20																			
Wickford 2	d			23p26							06 35	06 35					07 05	07 05					07 35
Billericay	d			23p32							06 41	06 41					07 11	07 11					07 41
Shenfield 3	a			23p39							06 53	06 52					07 22	07 22					07 52
Shenfield 3	d		23p29	23p39	23p44					06 43		06 53		06 58	07 07	07 13		07 23		07 37	07 43	07 45	07 53
Brentwood	d		23p32		23p47					06 46		06 56		07 08		07 16		07 26			07 46		07 56
Harold Wood	d		23p37		23p52					06 51		07 01		07 23		07 21		07 31			07 51		08 01
Gidea Park 2	d		23p41		23p56	05 25	05 55	05 55	06 25	06 55		07 05	07 11	07 30		07 25		07 35	07 41		07 55		08 05
Romford	d		23p43	23p47	23p58	05 32	05 57	06 02	06 27	06 57		07 07	07 13	07 37		07 27		07 37	07 43		07 57		08 07
Chadwell Heath	d		23p47		00 02		06 01		06 31	07 01			07 17			07 31			07 47		08 01		
Goodmayes	d		23p49		00 04		06 03		06 33	07 03			07 19			07 33			07 49		08 03		
Seven Kings	d		23p51		00 06		06 05		06 35	07 05			07 21			07 35			07 51		08 05		
Ilford 2	d		23p54		00 09	05 52	06 08	06 22	06 38	07 08			07 24	07 57		07 38			07 54		08 08		
Manor Park	d		23p57		00 12		06 10		06 40	07 10			07 26			07 40			07 56		08 10		
Forest Gate	d		23p59		00 14		06 12		06 42	07 12			07 28			07 42			07 58		08 12		
Maryland	d		00 01		00 16		06 14		06 44	07 14						07 44					08 14		
Stratford 7 ⊖	d	23b52	00 04	23p56	00 19	06 07	06 16	06 37	06 46	07 16		07 19	07 31	08 12	07s34	07 46		07 49	08 01	08s04	08 16		08 19
London Liverpool Street 15 ⊖	a	00 02	00 12	00 05	00 27	06 27	06 26	06 57	06 56	07 26		07 27	07 41	08 32	07 42	07 56		07 58	08 11	08 12	08 26	08 35	08 27

A until 24 June

B from 1 July until 22 July

b Previous night, stops to set down only

Table 5

Sundays until 22 July

Southend Victoria, Southminster and Shenfield - London

Network Diagram - see first Page of Table 5

		LE ■ A	LE B	LE ■	LE	LE ■	LE ■ B	LE ■ A	LE ■	LE	LE ■	LE	LE ■	LE	LE ■	LE	LE ■	LE ■	LE	LE ■	LE	LE ■	LE
Southend Victoria	d	07 19					07 49	07 49					08 19				08 49					09 19	
Prittlewell	d																						
Southend Airport ✈	d	07 23					07 53	07 53					08 23				08 53					09 23	
Rochford	d	07 26					07 56	07 56					08 26				08 56					09 26	
Hockley	d	07 29					07 59	07 59					08 29				08 59					09 29	
Rayleigh	d	07 34					08 04	08 04					08 34				09 04					09 34	
Southminster	d								08 05									09 05					
Burnham-on-Crouch	d								08 09									09 09					
Althorne	d								08 14									09 14					
North Fambridge	d								08 20									09 20					
South Woodham Ferrers	d								08 25									09 25					
Battlesbridge	d								08 29									09 29					
Wickford 2	d	07 39					08 09	08 09	08a35				08 39				09 09	09a35				09 39	
Billericay	d	07 45					08 15	08 15					08 45				09 15					09 45	
Shenfield 3	a	07 53					08 22	08 23					08 52				09 22					09 52	
Shenfield 3	d			08 07	08 13	08 20	08 23	08 24			08 41	08 43	08 53		09 11	09 13	09 23			09 41	09 43	09 53	
Brentwood	d				08 16		08 26	08 27				08 46	08 56			09 16	09 26				09 46	09 56	
Harold Wood	d				08 21		08 31	08 32				08 51	09 01			09 21	09 31				09 51	10 01	
Gidea Park 2	d		08 11		08 25		08 35	08 36		08 41		08 55	09 05	09 11		09 25	09 35		09 41		09 55	10 05	10 11
Romford	d		08 13		08 27		08 37	08 38		08 43		08 57	09 07	09 13		09 27	09 37		09 43		09 57	10 07	10 13
Chadwell Heath	d		08 17		08 31					08 47		09 01		09 17		09 31			09 47		10 01		10 17
Goodmayes	d		08 19		08 33					08 49		09 03		09 19		09 33			09 49		10 03		10 19
Seven Kings	d		08 21		08 35					08 51		09 05		09 21		09 35			09 51		10 05		10 21
Ilford 2	d		08 24		08 38					08 54		09 08		09 24		09 38			09 54		10 08		10 24
Manor Park	d		08 26		08 40					08 56		09 10		09 26		09 40			09 56		10 10		10 26
Forest Gate	d		08 28		08 42					08 58		09 12		09 28		09 42			09 58		10 12		10 28
Maryland	d				08 44							09 14				09 44					10 14		
Stratford 7 ⊖	d		08 31	08s34	08 46	08s49	08 49	08 49		09 01	09s04	09 16	09 19	09 31	09s34	09 46	09 49		10 01	10s04	10 16	10 21	10 31
London Liverpool Street 15 ⊖	a		08 41	08 42	08 56	08 59	08 59	08 59		09 11	09 12	09 26	09 29	09 41	09 42	09 56	09 59		10 11	10 12	10 26	10 31	10 41

		LE ■	LE	LE ■	LE ■	LE	LE ■	LE	LE ■	and at the same minutes past each hour until	LE ■	LE	LE ■	LE	LE ■	LE ■	LE	LE ■	LE	LE ■	LE
Southend Victoria	d			09 49					10 19		16 19				16 49					17 19	
Prittlewell	d																				
Southend Airport ✈	d			09 53					10 23		16 23				16 53					17 23	
Rochford	d			09 56					10 26		16 26				16 56					17 26	
Hockley	d			09 59					10 29		16 29				16 59					17 29	
Rayleigh	d			10 04					10 34		16 34				17 04					17 34	
Southminster	d				10 05											17 05					
Burnham-on-Crouch	d				10 09											17 09					
Althorne	d				10 14											17 14					
North Fambridge	d				10 20											17 20					
South Woodham Ferrers	d				10 25											17 25					
Battlesbridge	d				10 29											17 29					
Wickford 2	d			10 09	10a35				10 39		16 39				17 09	17a35				17 39	
Billericay	d			10 15					10 45		16 45				17 15					17 45	
Shenfield 3	a			10 22					10 52		16 52				17 22					17 52	
Shenfield 3	d	10 11	10 13	10 23			10 41	10 43	10 53		16 53		17 11	17 13	17 23			17 41	17 43	17 53	
Brentwood	d		10 16	10 26				10 46	10 56		16 56			17 16	17 26				17 46	17 56	
Harold Wood	d		10 21	10 31				10 51	11 01		17 01			17 21	17 31				17 51	18 01	
Gidea Park 2	d		10 25	10 35		10 41		10 55	11 05		17 05	17 11		17 25	17 35		17 41		17 55	18 05	18 11
Romford	d		10 27	10 37		10 43		10 57	11 07		17 07	17 13		17 27	17 37		17 43		17 57	18 07	18 13
Chadwell Heath	d		10 31			10 47		11 01				17 17		17 31			17 47		18 01		18 17
Goodmayes	d		10 33			10 49		11 03				17 19		17 33			17 49		18 03		18 19
Seven Kings	d		10 35			10 51		11 05				17 21		17 35			17 51		18 05		18 21
Ilford 2	d		10 38			10 54		11 08				17 24		17 38			17 54		18 08		18 24
Manor Park	d		10 40			10 56		11 10				17 26		17 40			17 56		18 10		18 26
Forest Gate	d		10 42			10 58		11 12				17 28		17 42			17 58		18 12		18 28
Maryland	d		10 44					11 14						17 44					18 14		
Stratford 7 ⊖	d	10s34	10 46	10 49		11 01	11s04	11 16	11 19		17 19	17 31	17s34	17 46	17 49		18 01	18s04	18 16	18 19	18 31
London Liverpool Street 15 ⊖	a	10 42	10 56	10 59		11 11	11 12	11 26	11 29		17 29	17 41	17 42	17 56	17 59		18 11	18 12	18 26	18 31	18 41

A until 24 June

B from 1 July until 22 July

Table 5

Sundays
until 22 July

Southend Victoria, Southminster and Shenfield - London

Network Diagram - see first Page of Table 5

		LE 1	LE	LE 1	LE 1	LE	LE 1	LE	LE 1		LE	LE 1	LE	LE 1	LE 1	LE	LE 1	LE	LE 1		LE	LE 1	LE	LE 1	LE 1
Southend Victoria	d			17 49					18 19					18 49					19 19					19 49	
Prittlewell	d																								
Southend Airport ✈	d			17 53					18 23					18 53					19 23					19 53	
Rochford	d			17 56					18 26					18 56					19 26					19 56	
Hockley	d			17 59					18 29					18 59					19 29					19 59	
Rayleigh	d			18 04					18 34					19 04					19 34					20 04	
Southminster	d				18 05										19 05										20 05
Burnham-on-Crouch	d				18 09										19 09										20 09
Althorne	d				18 14										19 14										20 14
North Fambridge	d				18 20										19 20										20 20
South Woodham Ferrers	d				18 25										19 25										20 25
Battlesbridge	d				18 29										19 29										20 29
Wickford 2	d			18 09	18a35				18 39					19 09	19a35				19 39					20 09	20a35
Billericay	d			18 15					18 45					19 15					19 45					20 15	
Shenfield 3	a			18 22					18 52					19 22					19 52					20 22	
Shenfield 3	d	18 11	18 13	18 23			18 41	18 43	18 53			19 11	19 13	19 23			19 41	19 43	19 53			20 11	20 13	20 23	
Brentwood	d		18 16	18 26				18 46	18 56				19 16	19 26				19 46	19 56				20 16	20 26	
Harold Wood	d		18 21	18 31				18 51	19 01				19 21	19 31				19 51	20 01				20 21	20 31	
Gidea Park 2	d		18 25	18 35		18 41		18 55	19 05		19 11		19 25	19 35		19 41		19 55	20 05		20 11		20 25	20 35	
Romford	d		18 27	18 37		18 43		18 57	19 07		19 13		19 27	19 37		19 43		19 57	20 07		20 13		20 27	20 37	
Chadwell Heath	d		18 31			18 47		19 01			19 17		19 31			19 47		20 01			20 17		20 31		
Goodmayes	d		18 33			18 49		19 03			19 19		19 33			19 49		20 03			20 19		20 33		
Seven Kings	d		18 35			18 51		19 05			19 21		19 35			19 51		20 05			20 21		20 35		
Ilford 2	d		18 38			18 54		19 08			19 24		19 38			19 54		20 08			20 24		20 38		
Manor Park	d		18 40			18 56		19 10			19 26		19 40			19 56		20 10			20 26		20 40		
Forest Gate	d		18 42			18 58		19 12			19 28		19 42			19 58		20 12			20 28		20 42		
Maryland	d		18 44					19 14					19 44					20 14					20 44		
Stratford 7 ⊖	d	18s34	18 46	18 49		19 01	19s04	19 16	19 19		19 31	19s34	19 46	19 49		20 01	20s04	20 16	20 19		20 31	20s34	20 46	20 49	
London Liverpool Street 15 ⊖	a	18 42	18 56	18 59		19 11	19 12	19 26	19 29		19 41	19 42	19 56	19 59		20 11	20 12	20 26	20 29		20 41	20 42	20 56	20 59	

		LE	LE 1	LE	LE 1		LE	LE 1	LE	LE 1	LE 1	LE 1	LE 1	LE	LE 1		LE 1	LE	LE 1	LE 1	LE 1	LE	LE 1	LE 1	LE
Southend Victoria	d				20 19					20 49					21 19				21 49				22 19		
Prittlewell	d																								
Southend Airport ✈	d				20 23					20 53					21 23				21 53				22 23		
Rochford	d				20 26					20 56					21 26				21 56				22 26		
Hockley	d				20 29					20 59					21 29				21 59				22 29		
Rayleigh	d				20 34					21 04					21 34				22 04				22 34		
Southminster	d										21 05									22 05					
Burnham-on-Crouch	d										21 09									22 09					
Althorne	d										21 14									22 14					
North Fambridge	d										21 20									22 20					
South Woodham Ferrers	d										21 25									22 25					
Battlesbridge	d										21 29									22 29					
Wickford 2	d				20 39					21 09	21a35				21 39				22 09	22a35			22 39		
Billericay	d				20 45					21 15					21 45				22 15				22 45		
Shenfield 3	a				20 52					21 22					21 52				22 22				22 52		
Shenfield 3	d		20 41	20 43	20 53			21 11	21 13	21 23		21 26	21 41	21 43	21 53		22 11	22 13	22 23		22 41	22 43	22 53	23 11	23 13
Brentwood	d			20 46	20 56				21 16	21 26				21 46	21 56			22 16	22 26			22 46	22 56		23 16
Harold Wood	d			20 51	21 01				21 21	21 31				21 51	22 01			22 21	22 31			22 51	23 01		23 21
Gidea Park 2	d	20 41		20 55	21 05		21 11		21 25	21 35				21 55	22 05			22 25	22 35			22 55	23 05		23 25
Romford	d	20 43		20 57	21 07		21 13		21 27	21 37				21 57	22 07			22 27	22 37			22 57	23 07		23 27
Chadwell Heath	d	20 47		21 01			21 17		21 31					22 01				22 31				23 01			23 31
Goodmayes	d	20 49		21 03			21 19		21 33					22 03				22 33				23 03			23 33
Seven Kings	d	20 51		21 05			21 21		21 35					22 05				22 35				23 05			23 35
Ilford 2	d	20 54		21 08			21 24		21 38					22 08				22 38				23 08			23 38
Manor Park	d	20 56		21 10			21 26		21 40					22 10				22 40				23 10			23 40
Forest Gate	d	20 58		21 12			21 28		21 42					22 12				22 42				23 12			23 42
Maryland	d			21 14					21 44					22 14				22 44				23 14			23 44
Stratford 7 ⊖	d	21 01	21s04	21 16	21 19		21 31	21s34	21 46	21 49		21s51	22s04	22 16	22 19		22s34	22 46	22 49		23s04	23 16	23 19	23s34	23 46
London Liverpool Street 15 ⊖	a	21 11	21 12	21 26	21 29		21 41	21 42	21 56	21 59		21 59	22 12	22 26	22 29		22 42	22 56	22 59		23 12	23 26	23 31	23 42	23 56

Table 5

Sundays
until 22 July

Southend Victoria, Southminster and Shenfield - London

Network Diagram - see first Page of Table 5

			LE 1	LE 1	LE
Southend Victoria	d		22 49		
Prittlewell	d				
Southend Airport ✈	d		22 53		
Rochford	d		22 56		
Hockley	d		22 59		
Rayleigh	d		23 04		
Southminster	d			22 45	
Burnham-on-Crouch	d			22 49	
Althorne	d			22 54	
North Fambridge	d			23 00	
South Woodham Ferrers	d			23 05	
Battlesbridge	d			23 09	
Wickford 2	d		23 09	23 15	
Billericay	d		23 15		
Shenfield 3	a		23 22	23 26	
Shenfield 3	d		23 23		23 43
Brentwood	d		23 26		23 46
Harold Wood	d		23 31		23 51
Gidea Park 2	d		23 35		23 55
Romford	d		23 37		23 57
Chadwell Heath	d				00 01
Goodmayes	d				00 03
Seven Kings	d				00 05
Ilford 2	d				00 08
Manor Park	d				00 10
Forest Gate	d				00 12
Maryland	d				00 14
Stratford 7 ⊖	d		23 49		00 16
London Liverpool Street 15 ⊖	a		23 59		00 26

Sundays
29 July to 12 August

		LE		LE	LE	LE 1	LE 1	LE	LE	LE		LE	LE	LE	LE	LE	LE	LE	LE	LE		LE 1	LE	LE	LE 1
Southend Victoria	d					23p10																05 30			06 00
Prittlewell	d					23p12																05 32			06 02
Southend Airport ✈	d					23p15																05 35			06 05
Rochford	d					23p18																05 38			06 08
Hockley	d					23p21																05 41			06 11
Rayleigh	d					23p26																05 46			06 16
Southminster	d																								
Burnham-on-Crouch	d																								
Althorne	d																								
North Fambridge	d																								
South Woodham Ferrers	d																								
Battlesbridge	d																								
Wickford 2	d					23p31																05 51			06 21
Billericay	d					23p37																05 57			06 27
Shenfield 3	a					23p45																06 05			06 35
Shenfield 3	d			23p29	23p44	23p45			23p59	00 14			00 29	00 44						05 59		06 05		06 29	06 35
Brentwood	d			23p32	23p47				00 02	00 17			00 32	00 47						06 02				06 32	
Harold Wood	d			23p37	23p52				00 07	00 22			00 37	00 52						06 07				06 37	
Gidea Park 2	d			23p41	23p56				00 11	00 26			00 41	00 56				05 11	05 41	06 11			06 26	06 41	
Romford	d			23p43	23p58				00 13	00 28			00 43	00 58				05 13	05 43	06 13			06 28	06 43	
Chadwell Heath	d			23p47	00 02				00 17	00 32			00 47	01 02				05 17	05 47	06 17			06 32	06 47	
Goodmayes	d			23p49	00 04				00 19	00 34			00 49	01 04				05 19	05 49	06 19			06 34	06 49	
Seven Kings	d			23p51	00 06				00 21	00 36			00 51	01 06				05 21	05 51	06 21			06 36	06 51	
Ilford 2	d			23p54	00 09				00 24	00 39			00 54	01 09				05 24	05 54	06 24			06 39	06 54	
Manor Park	d			23p57	00 12				00 27	00 42			00 57	01 12				05 27	05 57	06 27			06 42	06 57	
Forest Gate	d			23p59	00 14				00 29	00 44			00 59	01 14				05 29	05 59	06 29			06 44	06 59	
Maryland	d																								
Stratford 7 ⊖	d	23p54		00 04	00 20	00 08	00 12	00 30	00 40	00 50		01 00	01 10	01 20	01 30	01 40	01 50	05 34	06 04	06 34		06 19	06 49	07 04	06 49
London Liverpool Street 15 ⊖	a	00 02		00 12	00 28	00 16	00 20	00 38	00 48	00 58		01 08	01 18	01 28	01 38	01 48	01 58	05 42	06 12	06 42		06 28	06 57	07 12	06 58

29 July to 12 August

Southend Victoria, Southminster and Shenfield - London

Network Diagram - see first Page of Table 5

		LE	LE ■	LE	LE ■	LE ■		LE	LE ■	LE ■	LE	LE	LE ■	LE ■	LE ◇■	LE		LE ■	LE ■	LE	LE ■	LE ■	LE ◇■	LE	LE
Southend Victoria	d				06 30					06 50			07 10					07 30				07 50			
Prittlewell	d				06 32					06 52			07 12					07 32				07 52			
Southend Airport ✈	d				06 35					06 55			07 15					07 35				07 55			
Rochford	d				06 38					06 58			07 18					07 38				07 58			
Hockley	d				06 41					07 01			07 21					07 41				08 01			
Rayleigh	d				06 46					07 06			07 26					07 46				08 06			
Southminster	d																								
Burnham-on-Crouch	d																								
Althorne	d																								
North Fambridge	d																								
South Woodham Ferrers	d																								
Battlesbridge	d																								
Wickford ■	d				06 51					07 11			07 31					07 51				08 11			
Billericay	d				06 57					07 17			07 37					07 57				08 17			
Shenfield ■	a				07 05					07 25			07 45					08 05				08 25			
Shenfield ■	d	06 44	06 51	06 59	07 05	07 08		07 14	07 20	07 25	07 29	07 44	07 45	07 51		07 59		08 05	08 08	08 14	08 20	08 25		08 29	08 44
Brentwood	d	06 47		07 02				07 17			07 32	07 47				08 02				08 17				08 32	08 47
Harold Wood	d	06 52		07 07				07 22			07 37	07 52				08 07				08 22				08 37	08 52
Gidea Park ■	d	06 56		07 11				07 26			07 41	07 56				08 11				08 26				08 41	08 56
Romford	d	06 58		07 13				07 28			07 43	07 58				08 13				08 28				08 43	08 58
Chadwell Heath	d	07 02		07 17				07 32			07 47	08 02				08 17				08 32				08 47	09 02
Goodmayes	d	07 04		07 19				07 34			07 49	08 04				08 19				08 34				08 49	09 04
Seven Kings	d	07 06		07 21				07 36			07 51	08 06				08 21				08 36				08 51	09 06
Ilford ■	d	07 09		07 24				07 39			07 54	08 09				08 24				08 39				08 54	09 09
Manor Park	d	07 12		07 27				07 42			07 57	08 12				08 27				08 42				08 57	09 12
Forest Gate	d	07 14		07 29				07 44			07 59	08 14				08 29				08 44				08 59	09 14
Maryland	d																								
Stratford ■ ⊖	d	07 19	07 05	07 34	07 19	07 22		07 49	07s36	07 39	08 04	08 19	07 59	08 05	08 12	08 34		08 19	08 22	08 49	08 36	08 39	08 48	09 04	09 19
London Liverpool Street ■ ⊖	a	07 27	07 14	07 42	07 28	07 31		07 57	07 47	07 48	08 12	08 27	08 08	08 14	08 22	08 42		08 28	08 31	08 57	08 45	08 48	08 59	09 12	09 27

		LE ■		LE ■	LE ■	LE ◇■	LE	LE ■	LE ■	LE	LE ■	LE ■		LE ◇■	LE	LE	LE ■	LE ■	LE ■	LE ◇■	LE	LE ■		LE ■	LE
Southend Victoria	d	08 10						08 30				08 50					09 10					09 30			
Prittlewell	d	08 12						08 32				08 52					09 12					09 32			
Southend Airport ✈	d	08 15						08 35				08 55					09 15					09 35			
Rochford	d	08 18						08 38				08 58					09 18					09 38			
Hockley	d	08 21						08 41				09 01					09 21					09 41			
Rayleigh	d	08 26						08 46				09 06					09 26					09 46			
Southminster	d			08 16														09 16							
Burnham-on-Crouch	d			08 20														09 20							
Althorne	d			08 25														09 25							
North Fambridge	d			08 31														09 31							
South Woodham Ferrers	d			08 36														09 36							
Battlesbridge	d			08 40														09 40							
Wickford ■	d	08 31		08a46				08 51				09 11					09 31	09a46				09 51			
Billericay	d	08 37						08 57				09 17					09 37					09 57			
Shenfield ■	a	08 45						09 05				09 25					09 45					10 05			
Shenfield ■	d	08 45			08 51		08 59	09 05	09 08	09 14	09 20	09 25			09 29	09 44	09 45		09 51		09 59	10 05		10 08	10 14
Brentwood	d						09 02			09 17					09 32	09 47					10 02				10 17
Harold Wood	d						09 07			09 22					09 37	09 52					10 07				10 22
Gidea Park ■	d						09 11			09 26					09 41	09 56					10 11				10 26
Romford	d						09 13			09 28					09 43	09 58					10 13				10 28
Chadwell Heath	d						09 17			09 32					09 47	10 02					10 17				10 32
Goodmayes	d						09 19			09 34					09 49	10 04					10 19				10 34
Seven Kings	d						09 21			09 36					09 51	10 06					10 21				10 36
Ilford ■	d						09 24			09 39					09 54	10 09					10 24				10 39
Manor Park	d						09 27			09 42					09 57	10 12					10 27				10 42
Forest Gate	d						09 29			09 44					09 59	10 14					10 29				10 44
Maryland	d																								
Stratford ■ ⊖	d	08 59			09 05	09 12	09 34	09 19	09 22	09 49	09 36	09 39		09 48	10 04	10 19	09 59		10 05	10 12	10 34	10 19		10 22	10 49
London Liverpool Street ■ ⊖	a	09 08			09 14	09 22	09 42	09 28	09 31	09 57	09 45	09 48		09 59	10 12	10 27	10 08		10 14	10 22	10 42	10 28		10 31	10 57

Table 5

Sundays

29 July to 12 August

Southend Victoria, Southminster and Shenfield - London

Network Diagram - see first Page of Table 5

		LE ■	LE ■	LE ◇■	LE	LE	LE ■	LE ■		LE ■	LE ◇■	LE	LE ■	LE ■	LE	LE ■	LE ■	LE ◇■		LE	LE	LE ■	LE ■	LE ■	LE ◇■
Southend Victoria	d		09 50				10 10						10 30				10 50					11 10			
Prittlewell	d		09 52				10 12						10 32				10 52					11 12			
Southend Airport ✈	d		09 55				10 15						10 35				10 55					11 15			
Rochford	d		09 58				10 18						10 38				10 58					11 18			
Hockley	d		10 01				10 21						10 41				11 01					11 21			
Rayleigh	d		10 06				10 26						10 46				11 06					11 26			
Southminster	d							10 16															11 16		
Burnham-on-Crouch	d							10 20															11 20		
Althorne	d							10 25															11 25		
North Fambridge	d							10 31															11 31		
South Woodham Ferrers	d							10 36															11 36		
Battlesbridge	d							10 40															11 40		
Wickford ■	d		10 11				10 31	10a46					10 51				11 11					11 31	11a46		
Billericay	d		10 17				10 37						10 57				11 17					11 37			
Shenfield ■	a		10 25				10 45						11 05				11 25					11 45			
Shenfield ■	d	10 20	10 25		10 29	10 44	10 45			10 51		10 59	11 05	11 08	11 14	11 20	11 25			11 29	11 44	11 45		11 51	
Brentwood	d				10 32	10 47						11 02			11 17					11 32	11 47				
Harold Wood	d				10 37	10 52						11 07			11 22					11 37	11 52				
Gidea Park ■	d				10 41	10 56						11 11			11 26					11 41	11 56				
Romford	d				10 43	10 58						11 13			11 28					11 43	11 58				
Chadwell Heath	d				10 47	11 02						11 17			11 32					11 47	12 02				
Goodmayes	d				10 49	11 04						11 19			11 34					11 49	12 04				
Seven Kings	d				10 51	11 06						11 21			11 36					11 51	12 06				
Ilford ■	d				10 54	11 09						11 24			11 39					11 54	12 09				
Manor Park	d				10 57	11 12						11 27			11 42					11 57	12 12				
Forest Gate	d				10 59	11 14						11 29			11 44					11 59	12 14				
Maryland	d																								
Stratford ■ ⊖	d	10 36	10 39	10 48	11 04	11 19	10 59			11 05	11 12	11 34	11 19	11 22	11 49	11 36	11 39	11 48		12 04	12 19	11 59		12 05	12 12
London Liverpool Street ■ ⊖	a	10 45	10 48	10 59	11 12	11 27	11 08			11 14	11 22	11 42	11 28	11 31	11 57	11 45	11 48	11 59		12 12	12 27	12 08		12 14	12 22

		LE	LE ■	LE ■		LE	LE ■	LE ■	LE ◇■	LE	LE	LE ■	LE ■	LE ■		LE ■2 ■1	LE	LE ■	LE ■	LE	LE ■	LE ■	LE ◇■	LE	
Southend Victoria	d		11 30					11 50				12 10						12 30				12 50			
Prittlewell	d		11 32					11 52				12 12						12 32				12 52			
Southend Airport ✈	d		11 35					11 55				12 15						12 35				12 55			
Rochford	d		11 38					11 58				12 18						12 38				12 58			
Hockley	d		11 41					12 01				12 21						12 41				13 01			
Rayleigh	d		11 46					12 06				12 26						12 46				13 06			
Southminster	d												12 16												
Burnham-on-Crouch	d												12 20												
Althorne	d												12 25												
North Fambridge	d												12 31												
South Woodham Ferrers	d												12 36												
Battlesbridge	d												12 40												
Wickford ■	d		11 51					12 11				12 31	12a46					12 51				13 11			
Billericay	d		11 57					12 17				12 37						12 57				13 17			
Shenfield ■	a		12 05					12 25				12 45						13 05				13 25			
Shenfield ■	d	11 59	12 05	12 08		12 14	12 20	12 25		12 29	12 44	12 45		12 51			12 59	13 05	13 08	13 14	13 20	13 25		13 29	
Brentwood	d	12 02				12 17				12 32	12 47						13 02			13 17				13 32	
Harold Wood	d	12 07				12 22				12 37	12 52						13 07			13 22				13 37	
Gidea Park ■	d	12 11				12 26				12 41	12 56						13 11			13 26				13 41	
Romford	d	12 13				12 28				12 43	12 58						13 13			13 28				13 43	
Chadwell Heath	d	12 17				12 32				12 47	13 02						13 17			13 32				13 47	
Goodmayes	d	12 19				12 34				12 49	13 04						13 19			13 34				13 49	
Seven Kings	d	12 21				12 36				12 51	13 06						13 21			13 36				13 51	
Ilford ■	d	12 24				12 39				12 54	13 09						13 24			13 39				13 54	
Manor Park	d	12 27				12 42				12 57	13 12						13 27			13 42				13 57	
Forest Gate	d	12 29				12 44				12 59	13 14						13 29			13 44				13 59	
Maryland	d																								
Stratford ■ ⊖	d	12 34	12 19	12 22		12 49	12 36	12 39	12 48	13 04	13 19	12 59		13 05		13 12	13 34	13 19	13 22	13 49	13 36	13 39	13 48	14 04	
London Liverpool Street ■ ⊖	a	12 42	12 28	12 31		12 57	12 45	12 48	12 59	13 12	13 27	13 08		13 14		13 22	13 42	13 28	13 31	13 57	13 45	13 48	13 59	14 12	

Table 5

Sundays

29 July to 12 August

Southend Victoria, Southminster and Shenfield - London

Network Diagram - see first Page of Table 5

		LE	LE 1	LE 1	LE 1	LE ◇1 🛒	LE	LE 1	LE 1	LE		LE 1	LE 1	LE ◇1 🛒	LE	LE	LE 1	LE 1	LE 1	LE ◇1 🛒		LE	LE 1	LE 1	LE
Southend Victoria	d		13 10					13 30					13 50				14 10						14 30		
Prittlewell	d		13 12					13 32					13 52				14 12						14 32		
Southend Airport ✈	d		13 15					13 35					13 55				14 15						14 35		
Rochford	d		13 18					13 38					13 58				14 18						14 38		
Hockley	d		13 21					13 41					14 01				14 21						14 41		
Rayleigh	d		13 26					13 46					14 06				14 26						14 46		
Southminster	d			13 16														14 16							
Burnham-on-Crouch	d			13 20														14 20							
Althorne	d			13 25														14 25							
North Fambridge	d			13 31														14 31							
South Woodham Ferrers	d			13 36														14 36							
Battlesbridge	d			13 40														14 40							
Wickford 2	d		13 31	13a46				13 51					14 11				14 31	14a46					14 51		
Billericay	d		13 37					13 57					14 17				14 37						14 57		
Shenfield 3	a		13 45					14 05					14 25				14 45						15 05		
Shenfield 3	d	13 44	13 45		13 51		13 59	14 05	14 08	14 14		14 20	14 25		14 29	14 44	14 45		14 51			14 59	15 05	15 08	15 14
Brentwood	d	13 47					14 02			14 17					14 32	14 47						15 02			15 17
Harold Wood	d	13 52					14 07			14 22					14 37	14 52						15 07			15 22
Gidea Park 2	d	13 56					14 11			14 26					14 41	14 56						15 11			15 26
Romford	d	13 58					14 13			14 28					14 43	14 58						15 13			15 28
Chadwell Heath	d	14 02					14 17			14 32					14 47	15 02						15 17			15 32
Goodmayes	d	14 04					14 19			14 34					14 49	15 04						15 19			15 34
Seven Kings	d	14 06					14 21			14 36					14 51	15 06						15 21			15 36
Ilford 2	d	14 09					14 24			14 39					14 54	15 09						15 24			15 39
Manor Park	d	14 12					14 27			14 42					14 57	15 12						15 27			15 42
Forest Gate	d	14 14					14 29			14 44					14 59	15 14						15 29			15 44
Maryland	d																								
Stratford 7 ⊖	d	14 19	13 59		14 05	14 12	14 34	14 19	14 22	14 49		14 36	14 39	14 48	15 04	15 19	14 59		15 05	15 12		15 34	15 19	15 22	15 49
London Liverpool Street 15 ⊖	a	14 27	14 08		14 14	14 22	14 42	14 28	14 31	14 57		14 45	14 48	14 59	15 12	15 27	15 08		15 14	15 22		15 42	15 28	15 31	15 57

		LE 1	LE 1	LE ◇1 🛒	LE	LE		LE 1	LE 1	LE 1	LE ◇1 🛒	LE	LE 1	LE 1	LE	LE 1		LE 1	LE ◇1 🛒	LE	LE	LE 1	LE 1	LE 1	LE ◇1 🛒
Southend Victoria	d		14 50					15 10					15 30					15 50				16 10			
Prittlewell	d		14 52					15 12					15 32					15 52				16 12			
Southend Airport ✈	d		14 55					15 15					15 35					15 55				16 15			
Rochford	d		14 58					15 18					15 38					15 58				16 18			
Hockley	d		15 01					15 21					15 41					16 01				16 21			
Rayleigh	d		15 06					15 26					15 46					16 06				16 26			
Southminster	d								15 16														16 16		
Burnham-on-Crouch	d								15 20														16 20		
Althorne	d								15 25														16 25		
North Fambridge	d								15 31														16 31		
South Woodham Ferrers	d								15 36														16 36		
Battlesbridge	d								15 40														16 40		
Wickford 2	d		15 11					15 31	15a46				15 51					16 11				16 31	16a46		
Billericay	d		15 17					15 37					15 57					16 17				16 37			
Shenfield 3	a		15 25					15 45					16 05					16 25				16 45			
Shenfield 3	d	15 20	15 25		15 29	15 44		15 45		15 51		15 59	16 05	16 08	16 14	16 20		16 25		16 29	16 44	16 45		16 51	
Brentwood	d				15 32	15 47						16 02			16 17					16 32	16 47				
Harold Wood	d				15 37	15 52						16 07			16 22					16 37	16 52				
Gidea Park 2	d				15 41	15 56						16 11			16 26					16 41	16 56				
Romford	d				15 43	15 58						16 13			16 28					16 43	16 58				
Chadwell Heath	d				15 47	16 02						16 17			16 32					16 47	17 02				
Goodmayes	d				15 49	16 04						16 19			16 34					16 49	17 04				
Seven Kings	d				15 51	16 06						16 21			16 36					16 51	17 06				
Ilford 2	d				15 54	16 09						16 24			16 39					16 54	17 09				
Manor Park	d				15 57	16 12						16 27			16 42					16 57	17 12				
Forest Gate	d				15 59	16 14						16 29			16 44					16 59	17 14				
Maryland	d																								
Stratford 7 ⊖	d	15 36	15 39	15 48	16 04	16 19		15 59		16 05	16 12	16 34	16 19	16 22	16 49	16 36		16 39	16 48	17 04	17 19	16 59		17 05	17 12
London Liverpool Street 15 ⊖	a	15 45	15 48	15 59	16 12	16 27		16 08		16 14	16 22	16 42	16 28	16 31	16 57	16 45		16 48	16 59	17 12	17 27	17 08		17 14	17 22

Table 5

Sundays

29 July to 12 August

Southend Victoria, Southminster and Shenfield - London

Network Diagram - see first Page of Table 5

		LE		LE 1	LE 1	LE	LE 1	LE 1	LE ◇1 🛒	LE	LE	LE 1		LE 1	LE 1	LE ◇1 🛒	LE	LE 1	LE 1	LE	LE 1	LE 1		LE ◇1 🛒	LE
Southend Victoria	d			16 30				16 50				17 10						17 30				17 50			
Prittlewell	d			16 32				16 52				17 12						17 32				17 52			
Southend Airport ✈	d			16 35				16 55				17 15						17 35				17 55			
Rochford	d			16 38				16 58				17 18						17 38				17 58			
Hockley	d			16 41				17 01				17 21						17 41				18 01			
Rayleigh	d			16 46				17 06				17 26						17 46				18 06			
Southminster	d													17 16											
Burnham-on-Crouch	d													17 20											
Althorne	d													17 25											
North Fambridge	d													17 31											
South Woodham Ferrers	d													17 36											
Battlesbridge	d													17 40											
Wickford 2	d			16 51				17 11				17 31		17a46				17 51				18 11			
Billericay	d			16 57				17 17				17 37						17 57				18 17			
Shenfield 3	a			17 05				17 25				17 45						18 05				18 25			
Shenfield 3	d	16 59		17 05	17 08	17 14	17 20	17 25		17 29	17 44	17 45			17 51		17 59	18 05	18 08	18 14	18 20	18 25			18 29
Brentwood	d	17 02				17 17				17 32	17 47						18 02			18 17					18 32
Harold Wood	d	17 07				17 22				17 37	17 52						18 07			18 22					18 37
Gidea Park 2	d	17 11				17 26				17 41	17 56						18 11			18 26					18 41
Romford	d	17 13				17 28				17 43	17 58						18 13			18 28					18 43
Chadwell Heath	d	17 17				17 32				17 47	18 02						18 17			18 32					18 47
Goodmayes	d	17 19				17 34				17 49	18 04						18 19			18 34					18 49
Seven Kings	d	17 21				17 36				17 51	18 06						18 21			18 36					18 51
Ilford 2	d	17 24				17 39				17 54	18 09						18 24			18 39					18 54
Manor Park	d	17 27				17 42				17 57	18 12						18 27			18 42					18 57
Forest Gate	d	17 29				17 44				17 59	18 14						18 29			18 44					18 59
Maryland	d																								
Stratford 7 ⊖	d	17 34		17 19	17 22	17 49	17 36	17 39	17 48	18 04	18 19	17 59			18 05	18 12	18 34	18 19	18 22	18 49	18 36	18 39		18 48	19 04
London Liverpool Street 15 ⊖	a	17 42		17 28	17 31	17 57	17 45	17 48	17 59	18 12	18 27	18 08			18 14	18 22	18 42	18 28	18 31	18 57	18 45	18 48		18 59	19 12

		LE	LE 1	LE 1	LE 1	LE ◇1 🛒	LE	LE 1		LE 1	LE	LE 1	LE 1	LE ◇1 🛒	LE	LE	LE 1	LE 1		LE 1	LE ◇1 🛒	LE	LE 1	LE 1	LE
Southend Victoria	d		18 10					18 30					18 50				19 10						19 30		
Prittlewell	d		18 12					18 32					18 52				19 12						19 32		
Southend Airport ✈	d		18 15					18 35					18 55				19 15						19 35		
Rochford	d		18 18					18 38					18 58				19 18						19 38		
Hockley	d		18 21					18 41					19 01				19 21						19 41		
Rayleigh	d		18 26					18 46					19 06				19 26						19 46		
Southminster	d			18 16														19 16							
Burnham-on-Crouch	d			18 20														19 20							
Althorne	d			18 25														19 25							
North Fambridge	d			18 31														19 31							
South Woodham Ferrers	d			18 36														19 36							
Battlesbridge	d			18 40														19 40							
Wickford 2	d		18 31	18a46				18 51					19 11				19 31	19a46					19 51		
Billericay	d		18 37					18 57					19 17				19 37						19 57		
Shenfield 3	a		18 45					19 05					19 25				19 45						20 05		
Shenfield 3	d	18 44	18 45		18 51		18 59	19 05		19 08	19 14	19 20	19 25		19 29	19 44	19 45			19 51		19 59	20 05	20 08	20 14
Brentwood	d	18 47					19 02				19 17				19 32	19 47						20 02			20 17
Harold Wood	d	18 52					19 07				19 22				19 37	19 52						20 07			20 22
Gidea Park 2	d	18 56					19 11				19 26				19 41	19 56						20 11			20 26
Romford	d	18 58					19 13				19 28				19 43	19 58						20 13			20 28
Chadwell Heath	d	19 02					19 17				19 32				19 47	20 02						20 17			20 32
Goodmayes	d	19 04					19 19				19 34				19 49	20 04						20 19			20 34
Seven Kings	d	19 06					19 21				19 36				19 51	20 06						20 21			20 36
Ilford 2	d	19 09					19 24				19 39				19 54	20 09						20 24			20 39
Manor Park	d	19 12					19 27				19 42				19 57	20 12						20 27			20 42
Forest Gate	d	19 14					19 29				19 44				19 59	20 14						20 29			20 44
Maryland	d																								
Stratford 7 ⊖	d	19 19	18 59		19 05	19 12	19 34	19 19		19 22	19 49	19 36	19 39	19 48	20 04	20 19	19 59			20 05	20 12	20 34	20 19	20 22	20 49
London Liverpool Street 15 ⊖	a	19 27	19 08		19 14	19 22	19 42	19 28		19 31	19 57	19 45	19 48	19 59	20 12	20 27	20 08			20 14	20 22	20 42	20 28	20 31	20 57

Table 5

Sundays
29 July to 12 August

Southend Victoria, Southminster and Shenfield - London

Network Diagram - see first Page of Table 5

Station		LE 1	LE 1	LE ◇1	LE	LE	LE 1	LE 1	LE 1	LE 1	LE	LE 1	LE 1	LE	LE 1	LE 1	LE ◇1	LE 1	LE 1	LE	LE	LE 1
Southend Victoria	d		19 50				20 10					20 30				20 50						21 10
Prittlewell	d		19 52				20 12					20 32				20 52						21 12
Southend Airport	d		19 55				20 15					20 35				20 55						21 15
Rochford	d		19 58				20 18					20 38				20 58						21 18
Hockley	d		20 01				20 21					20 41				21 01						21 21
Rayleigh	d		20 06				20 26					20 46				21 06						21 26
Southminster	d							20 16														
Burnham-on-Crouch	d							20 20														
Althorne	d							20 25														
North Fambridge	d							20 31														
South Woodham Ferrers	d							20 36														
Battlesbridge	d							20 40														
Wickford 2	d		20 11				20 31	20a46				20 51				21 11						21 31
Billericay	d		20 17				20 37					20 57				21 17						21 37
Shenfield 3	a		20 25				20 45					21 05				21 25						21 45
Shenfield 3	d	20 20	20 25		20 29	20 44	20 45		20 51		20 59	21 05	21 08	21 14	21 20	21 25				21 29	21 44	21 45
Brentwood	d				20 32	20 47					21 02			21 17						21 32	21 47	
Harold Wood	d				20 37	20 52					21 07			21 22						21 37	21 52	
Gidea Park 2	d				20 41	20 56					21 11			21 26						21 41	21 56	
Romford	d				20 43	20 58					21 13			21 28						21 43	21 58	
Chadwell Heath	d				20 47	21 02					21 17			21 32						21 47	22 02	
Goodmayes	d				20 49	21 04					21 19			21 34						21 49	22 04	
Seven Kings	d				20 51	21 06					21 21			21 36						21 51	22 06	
Ilford 2	d				20 54	21 09					21 24			21 39						21 54	22 09	
Manor Park	d				20 57	21 12					21 27			21 42						21 57	22 12	
Forest Gate	d				20 59	21 14					21 29			21 44						21 59	22 14	
Maryland	d																					
Stratford 7 ⊖	d	20 36	20 39	20 48	21 04	21 19	20 59		21 05	21 10	21 34	21 19	21 22	21 49	21 34	21 39	21 48	21 53	22 00	22 04	22 19	22 08
London Liverpool Street 15 ⊖	a	20 45	20 48	20 59	21 12	21 27	21 08		21 14	21 19	21 42	21 28	21 31	21 57	21 43	21 48	21 59	22 01	22 08	22 12	22 27	22 16

Station		LE 1	LE 1	LE	LE 1	LE 1	LE	LE 1	LE 1	LE 1	LE 1	LE	LE	LE 1	LE 1	LE 1	LE	LE	LE 1	LE 1	LE	LE	LE 1
Southend Victoria	d				21 30				21 50					22 10					22 30				
Prittlewell	d				21 32				21 52					22 12					22 32				
Southend Airport	d				21 35				21 55					22 15					22 35				
Rochford	d				21 38				21 58					22 18					22 38				
Hockley	d				21 41				22 01					22 21					22 41				
Rayleigh	d				21 46				22 06					22 26					22 46				
Southminster	d	21 16													22 16								
Burnham-on-Crouch	d	21 20													22 20								
Althorne	d	21 25													22 25								
North Fambridge	d	21 31													22 31								
South Woodham Ferrers	d	21 36													22 36								
Battlesbridge	d	21 40													22 40								
Wickford 2	d	21a46			21 51				22 11					22 31	22a46				22 51				
Billericay	d				21 57				22 17					22 37					22 57				
Shenfield 3	a				22 05				22 25					22 45					23 05				
Shenfield 3	d		21 47	21 59	22 05	22 08	22 14	22 20	22 25			22 29	22 44	22 45		22 51		22 59	23 05	23 08		23 14	23 21
Brentwood	d			22 02			22 17					22 32	22 47					23 02				23 17	
Harold Wood	d			22 07			22 22					22 37	22 52					23 07				23 22	
Gidea Park 2	d			22 11			22 26					22 41	22 56					23 11				23 26	
Romford	d			22 13			22 28					22 43	22 58					23 13				23 28	
Chadwell Heath	d			22 17			22 32					22 47	23 02					23 17				23 32	
Goodmayes	d			22 19			22 34					22 49	23 04					23 19				23 34	
Seven Kings	d			22 21			22 36					22 51	23 06					23 21				23 36	
Ilford 2	d			22 24			22 41					22 54	23 09					23 24				23 39	
Manor Park	d			22 27			22 44					22 57	23 12					23 27				23 42	
Forest Gate	d			22 29			22 46					22 59	23 14					23 29				23 44	
Maryland	d																						
Stratford 7 ⊖	d		22 13	22 34	22 24	22 28	22 52	22 40	22 44	22 48	22 58	23 04	23 20	23 08		23 12	23 16	23 36	23 24	23 28	23 32	23 50	23 40
London Liverpool Street 15 ⊖	a		22 21	22 42	22 32	22 36	23 00	22 48	22 52	22 56	23 06	23 12	23 28	23 16		23 20	23 24	23 44	23 32	23 36	23 40	23 58	23 48

Table 5

Sundays
29 July to 12 August

Southend Victoria, Southminster and Shenfield - London

Network Diagram - see first Page of Table 5

Station		LE 1	LE 1	LE 1	LE	LE	LE 1	LE
Southend Victoria	d	22 50					23 10	
Prittlewell	d	22 52					23 12	
Southend Airport	d	22 55					23 15	
Rochford	d	22 58					23 18	
Hockley	d	23 01					23 21	
Rayleigh	d	23 06					23 26	
Southminster	d		22 56					
Burnham-on-Crouch	d		23 00					
Althorne	d		23 05					
North Fambridge	d		23 11					
South Woodham Ferrers	d		23 16					
Battlesbridge	d		23 20					
Wickford 2	d	23 11	23a26				23 31	
Billericay	d	23 17					23 37	
Shenfield 3	a	23 25					23 45	
Shenfield 3	d	23 25			23 29	23 44	23 45	23 59
Brentwood	d				23 32	23 47		00 02
Harold Wood	d				23 37	23 52		00 07
Gidea Park 2	d				23 41	23 56		00 11
Romford	d				23 43	23 58		00 13
Chadwell Heath	d				23 47	00 02		00 17
Goodmayes	d				23 49	00 04		00 19
Seven Kings	d				23 51	00 06		00 21
Ilford 2	d				23 54	00 09		00 24
Manor Park	d				23 57	00 12		00 27
Forest Gate	d				23 59	00 14		00 29
Maryland	d							
Stratford 7 ⊖	d	23 44		23 54	00 04	00 20	00 08	00 40
London Liverpool Street 15 ⊖	a	23 52		00 02	00 12	00 28	00 16	00 48

Sundays
19 August to 26 August

Station		LE ◇1	LE	LE 1	LE	LE	LE	LE	LE 1	LE	LE 1	LE	LE 1	LE	LE 1	LE	LE 1	LE	LE 1	LE	LE 1	LE 1	LE 1
Southend Victoria	d								06 15				06 45				07 15					07 49	
Prittlewell	d																						
Southend Airport	d								06 19				06 49				07 19					07 53	
Rochford	d								06 22				06 52				07 22					07 56	
Hockley	d								06 25				06 55				07 25					07 59	
Rayleigh	d								06 30				07 00				07 30					08 04	
Southminster	d			22p56																			08 05
Burnham-on-Crouch	d			23p00																			08 09
Althorne	d			23p05																			08 14
North Fambridge	d			23p11																			08 20
South Woodham Ferrers	d			23p16																			08 25
Battlesbridge	d			23p20																			08 29
Wickford 2	d			23p26					06 35				07 05				07 35					08 09	08a35
Billericay	d			23p32					06 41				07 11				07 41					08 15	
Shenfield 3	a			23p39					06 52				07 22				07 52					08 22	
Shenfield 3	d		23p29	23p39	23p44			06 43	06 53		07 07	07 13	07 23		07 37	07 43	07 53		08 07	08 13	08 20	08 23	
Brentwood	d		23p32		23p47			06 46	06 56			07 16	07 26			07 46	07 56			08 16		08 26	
Harold Wood	d		23p37		23p52			06 51	07 01			07 21	07 31			07 51	08 01			08 21		08 31	
Gidea Park 2	d		23p41		23p56	05 55	06 25	06 55	07 05	07 11		07 25	07 35	07 41		07 55	08 05	08 11		08 25		08 35	
Romford	d		23p43	23p47	23p58	05 57	06 27	06 57	07 07	07 13		07 27	07 37	07 43		07 57	08 07	08 13		08 27		08 37	
Chadwell Heath	d		23p47		00 02	06 01	06 31	07 01		07 17		07 31		07 47		08 01		08 17		08 31			
Goodmayes	d		23p49		00 04	06 03	06 33	07 03		07 19		07 33		07 49		08 03		08 19		08 33			
Seven Kings	d		23p51		00 06	06 05	06 35	07 05		07 21		07 35		07 51		08 05		08 21		08 35			
Ilford 2	d		23p54		00 09	06 08	06 38	07 08		07 24		07 38		07 54		08 08		08 24		08 38			
Manor Park	d		23p57		00 12	06 10	06 40	07 10		07 26		07 40		07 56		08 10		08 26		08 40			
Forest Gate	d		23p59		00 14	06 12	06 42	07 12		07 28		07 42		07 58		08 12		08 28		08 42			
Maryland	d		00 01		00 16	06 14	06 44	07 14				07 44				08 14				08 44			
Stratford 7 ⊖	d	23b52	00 04	23p56	00 19	06 16	06 46	07 16	07 19	07 31	07s34	07 46	07 49	08 01	08s04	08 16	08 19	08 31	08s34	08 46	08s49	08 49	
London Liverpool Street 15 ⊖	a	00 02	00 12	00 05	00 27	06 26	06 56	07 26	07 27	07 41	07 42	07 56	07 58	08 11	08 12	08 26	08 27	08 41	08 42	08 56	08 59	08 59	

b Previous night, stops to set down only

Table 5

Sundays

19 August to 26 August

Southend Victoria, Southminster and Shenfield - London

Network Diagram - see first Page of Table 5

		LE	LE 1	LE	LE 1	LE	LE 1	LE	LE 1	LE 1	LE	LE 1	LE	LE 1	LE	LE 1	LE	LE 1	LE 1	LE	LE 1	LE
Southend Victoria	d				08 19				08 49					09 19				09 49				
Prittlewell	d																					
Southend Airport ✈	d				08 23				08 53					09 23				09 53				
Rochford	d				08 26				08 56					09 26				09 56				
Hockley	d				08 29				08 59					09 29				09 59				
Rayleigh	d				08 34				09 04					09 34				10 04				
Southminster	d									09 05									10 05			
Burnham-on-Crouch	d									09 09									10 09			
Althorne	d									09 14									10 14			
North Fambridge	d									09 20									10 20			
South Woodham Ferrers	d									09 25									10 25			
Battlesbridge	d									09 29									10 29			
Wickford 2	d				08 39				09 09	09a35				09 39				10 09	10a35			
Billericay	d				08 45				09 15					09 45				10 15				
Shenfield 3	a				08 52				09 22					09 52				10 22				
Shenfield 3	d		08 41	08 43	08 53		09 11	09 13	09 23			09 41	09 43	09 53		10 11	10 13	10 23			10 41	10 43
Brentwood	d			08 46	08 56			09 16	09 26				09 46	09 56			10 16	10 26				10 46
Harold Wood	d			08 51	09 01			09 21	09 31				09 51	10 01			10 21	10 31				10 51
Gidea Park 2	d	08 41		08 55	09 05	09 11		09 25	09 35		09 41		09 55	10 05	10 11		10 25	10 35		10 41		10 55
Romford	d	08 43		08 57	09 07	09 13		09 27	09 37		09 43		09 57	10 07	10 13		10 27	10 37		10 43		10 57
Chadwell Heath	d	08 47		09 01		09 17		09 31			09 47		10 01		10 17		10 31			10 47		11 01
Goodmayes	d	08 49		09 03		09 19		09 33			09 49		10 03		10 19		10 33			10 49		11 03
Seven Kings	d	08 51		09 05		09 21		09 35			09 51		10 05		10 21		10 35			10 51		11 05
Ilford 2	d	08 54		09 08		09 24		09 38			09 54		10 08		10 24		10 38			10 54		11 08
Manor Park	d	08 56		09 10		09 26		09 40			09 56		10 10		10 26		10 40			10 56		11 10
Forest Gate	d	08 58		09 12		09 28		09 42			09 58		10 12		10 28		10 42			10 58		11 12
Maryland	d			09 14				09 44					10 14				10 44					11 14
Stratford 7 ⊖	d	09 01	09s04	09 16	09 19	09 31	09s34	09 46	09 49		10 01	10s04	10 16	10 21	10 31	10s34	10 46	10 49		11 01	11s04	11 16
London Liverpool Street 15 ⊖	a	09 11	09 12	09 26	09 29	09 41	09 42	09 56	09 59		10 11	10 12	10 26	10 31	10 41	10 42	10 56	10 59		11 11	11 12	11 26

		LE 1		LE 1	LE	LE 1	LE	LE 1	LE 1	LE	LE 1	LE	LE 1	LE	LE 1	LE	LE 1	LE 1	LE	LE 1	LE	LE 1
Southend Victoria	d	10 19	and at the same minutes past each hour until	16 19				16 49					17 19				17 49					18 19
Prittlewell	d																					
Southend Airport ✈	d	10 23		16 23				16 53					17 23				17 53					18 23
Rochford	d	10 26		16 26				16 56					17 26				17 56					18 26
Hockley	d	10 29		16 29				16 59					17 29				17 59					18 29
Rayleigh	d	10 34		16 34				17 04					17 34				18 04					18 34
Southminster	d								17 05									18 05				
Burnham-on-Crouch	d								17 09									18 09				
Althorne	d								17 14									18 14				
North Fambridge	d								17 20									18 20				
South Woodham Ferrers	d								17 25									18 25				
Battlesbridge	d								17 29									18 29				
Wickford 2	d	10 39		16 39				17 09	17a35				17 39				18 09	18a35				18 39
Billericay	d	10 45		16 45				17 15					17 45				18 15					18 45
Shenfield 3	a	10 52		16 52				17 22					17 52				18 22					18 52
Shenfield 3	d	10 53		16 53		17 11	17 13	17 23			17 41	17 43	17 53		18 11	18 13	18 23			18 41	18 43	18 53
Brentwood	d	10 56		16 56			17 16	17 26				17 46	17 56			18 16	18 26				18 46	18 56
Harold Wood	d	11 01		17 01			17 21	17 31				17 51	18 01			18 21	18 31				18 51	19 01
Gidea Park 2	d	11 05		17 05	17 11		17 25	17 35		17 41		17 55	18 05	18 11		18 25	18 35		18 41		18 55	19 05
Romford	d	11 07		17 07	17 13		17 27	17 37		17 43		17 57	18 07	18 13		18 27	18 37		18 43		18 57	19 07
Chadwell Heath	d				17 17		17 31			17 47		18 01		18 17		18 31			18 47		19 01	
Goodmayes	d				17 19		17 33			17 49		18 03		18 19		18 33			18 49		19 03	
Seven Kings	d				17 21		17 35			17 51		18 05		18 21		18 35			18 51		19 05	
Ilford 2	d				17 24		17 38			17 54		18 08		18 24		18 38			18 54		19 08	
Manor Park	d				17 26		17 40			17 56		18 10		18 26		18 40			18 56		19 10	
Forest Gate	d				17 28		17 42			17 58		18 12		18 28		18 42			18 58		19 12	
Maryland	d						17 44					18 14				18 44					19 14	
Stratford 7 ⊖	d	11 19		17 19	17 31	17s34	17 46	17 49		18 01	18s04	18 16	18 19	18 31	18s34	18 46	18 49		19 01	19s04	19 16	19 19
London Liverpool Street 15 ⊖	a	11 29		17 29	17 41	17 42	17 56	17 59		18 11	18 12	18 26	18 31	18 41	18 42	18 56	18 59		19 11	19 12	19 26	19 29

Table 5

Sundays

19 August to 26 August

Southend Victoria, Southminster and Shenfield - London

Network Diagram - see first Page of Table 5

		LE	LE 1	LE	LE 1	LE 1	LE	LE 1	LE	LE 1	LE	LE 1	LE	LE 1	LE 1	LE	LE 1	LE	LE 1	LE	LE 1	LE
Southend Victoria	d				18 49					19 19				19 49					20 19			
Prittlewell	d																					
Southend Airport ✈	d				18 53					19 23				19 53					20 23			
Rochford	d				18 56					19 26				19 56					20 26			
Hockley	d				18 59					19 29				19 59					20 29			
Rayleigh	d				19 04					19 34				20 04					20 34			
Southminster	d					19 05									20 05							
Burnham-on-Crouch	d					19 09									20 09							
Althorne	d					19 14									20 14							
North Fambridge	d					19 20									20 20							
South Woodham Ferrers	d					19 25									20 25							
Battlesbridge	d					19 29									20 29							
Wickford 2	d				19 09	19a35				19 39				20 09	20a35				20 39			
Billericay	d				19 15					19 45				20 15					20 45			
Shenfield 3	a				19 22					19 52				20 22					20 52			
Shenfield 3	d		19 11	19 13	19 23			19 41	19 43	19 53		20 11	20 13	20 23			20 41	20 43	20 53		21 11	21 13
Brentwood	d			19 16	19 26				19 46	19 56			20 16	20 26				20 46	20 56			21 16
Harold Wood	d			19 21	19 31				19 51	20 01			20 21	20 31				20 51	21 01			21 21
Gidea Park 2	d	19 11		19 25	19 35		19 41		19 55	20 05	20 11		20 25	20 35		20 41		20 55	21 05	21 11		21 25
Romford	d	19 13		19 27	19 37		19 43		19 57	20 07	20 13		20 27	20 37		20 43		20 57	21 07	21 13		21 27
Chadwell Heath	d	19 17		19 31			19 47		20 01		20 17		20 31			20 47		21 01		21 17		21 31
Goodmayes	d	19 19		19 33			19 49		20 03		20 19		20 33			20 49		21 03		21 19		21 33
Seven Kings	d	19 21		19 35			19 51		20 05		20 21		20 35			20 51		21 05		21 21		21 35
Ilford 2	d	19 24		19 38			19 54		20 08		20 24		20 38			20 54		21 08		21 24		21 38
Manor Park	d	19 26		19 40			19 56		20 10		20 26		20 40			20 56		21 10		21 26		21 40
Forest Gate	d	19 28		19 42			19 58		20 12		20 28		20 42			20 58		21 12		21 28		21 42
Maryland	d			19 44					20 14				20 44					21 14				21 44
Stratford 7 ⊖	d	19 31	19s34	19 46	19 49		20 01	20s04	20 16	20 19	20 31	20s34	20 46	20 49		21 01	21s04	21 16	21 19	21 31	21s34	21 46
London Liverpool Street 15 ⊖	a	19 41	19 42	19 56	19 59		20 11	20 12	20 26	20 29	20 41	20 42	20 56	20 59		21 11	21 12	21 26	21 29	21 41	21 42	21 56

		LE 1	LE 1	LE 1	LE 1	LE	LE 1	LE 1	LE	LE 1	LE 1	LE 1	LE	LE 1	LE 1	LE	LE 1	LE 1	LE
Southend Victoria	d	20 49					21 19			21 49				22 19			22 49		
Prittlewell	d																		
Southend Airport ✈	d	20 53					21 23			21 53				22 23			22 53		
Rochford	d	20 56					21 26			21 56				22 26			22 56		
Hockley	d	20 59					21 29			21 59				22 29			22 59		
Rayleigh	d	21 04					21 34			22 04				22 34			23 04		
Southminster	d		21 05								22 05							22 45	
Burnham-on-Crouch	d		21 09								22 09							22 49	
Althorne	d		21 14								22 14							22 54	
North Fambridge	d		21 20								22 20							23 00	
South Woodham Ferrers	d		21 25								22 25							23 05	
Battlesbridge	d		21 29								22 29							23 09	
Wickford 2	d	21 09	21a35				21 39			22 09	22a35			22 39			23 09	23 15	
Billericay	d	21 15					21 45			22 15				22 45			23 15		
Shenfield 3	a	21 22					21 52			22 22				22 52			23 22	23 26	
Shenfield 3	d	21 23		21 26	21 41	21 43	21 53	22 11	22 13	22 23		22 41	22 43	22 53	23 11	23 13	23 23		23 43
Brentwood	d	21 26				21 46	21 56		22 16	22 26			22 46	22 56		23 16	23 26		23 46
Harold Wood	d	21 31				21 51	22 01		22 21	22 31			22 51	23 01		23 21	23 31		23 51
Gidea Park 2	d	21 35				21 55	22 05		22 25	22 35			22 55	23 05		23 25	23 35		23 55
Romford	d	21 37				21 57	22 07		22 27	22 37			22 57	23 07		23 27	23 37		23 57
Chadwell Heath	d					22 01			22 31				23 01			23 31			00 01
Goodmayes	d					22 03			22 33				23 03			23 33			00 03
Seven Kings	d					22 05			22 35				23 05			23 35			00 05
Ilford 2	d					22 08			22 38				23 08			23 38			00 08
Manor Park	d					22 10			22 40				23 10			23 40			00 10
Forest Gate	d					22 12			22 42				23 12			23 42			00 12
Maryland	d					22 14			22 44				23 14			23 44			00 14
Stratford 7 ⊖	d	21 49		21s51	22s04	22 16	22 19	22s34	22 46	22 49		23s04	23 16	23 19	23s34	23 46	23 49		00 16
London Liverpool Street 15 ⊖	a	21 59		21 59	22 12	22 26	22 29	22 42	22 56	22 59		23 12	23 26	23 31	23 42	23 56	23 59		00 26

Southend Victoria, Southminster and Shenfield - London

Network Diagram - see first Page of Table 5

		LE		LE	LE	LE [1]	LE [1]	LE	LE	LE		LE	LE	LE	LE	LE	LE	LE	LE	LE		LE [1]	LE	LE	LE [1]
Southend Victoria	d					23p10																05 30			06 00
Prittlewell	d					23p12																05 32			06 02
Southend Airport ✈	d					23p15																05 35			06 05
Rochford	d					23p18																05 38			06 08
Hockley	d					23p21																05 41			06 11
Rayleigh	d					23p26																05 46			06 16
Southminster	d																							
Burnham-on-Crouch	d																							
Althorne	d																							
North Fambridge	d																							
South Woodham Ferrers	d																							
Battlesbridge	d																							
Wickford [2]	d					23p31																05 51			06 21
Billericay	d					23p37																05 57			06 27
Shenfield [3]	a					23p45																06 05			06 35
Shenfield [3]	d			23p29	23p44	23p45			23p59	00 14			00 29	00 44						05 59		06 05		06 29	06 35
Brentwood	d			23p32	23p47				00 02	00 17			00 32	00 47						06 02				06 32	
Harold Wood	d			23p37	23p52				00 07	00 22			00 37	00 52						06 07				06 37	
Gidea Park [2]	d			23p41	23p56				00 11	00 26			00 41	00 56				05 11	05 41	06 11			06 26	06 41	
Romford	d			23p43	23p58				00 13	00 28			00 43	00 58				05 13	05 43	06 13			06 28	06 43	
Chadwell Heath	d			23p47	00 02				00 17	00 32			00 47	01 02				05 17	05 47	06 17			06 32	06 47	
Goodmayes	d			23p49	00 04				00 19	00 34			00 49	01 04				05 19	05 49	06 19			06 34	06 49	
Seven Kings	d			23p51	00 06				00 21	00 36			00 51	01 06				05 21	05 51	06 21			06 36	06 51	
Ilford [2]	d			23p54	00 09				00 24	00 39			00 54	01 09				05 24	05 54	06 24			06 39	06 54	
Manor Park	d			23p57	00 12				00 27	00 42			00 57	01 12				05 27	05 57	06 27			06 42	06 57	
Forest Gate	d			23p59	00 14				00 29	00 44			00 59	01 14				05 29	05 59	06 29			06 44	06 59	
Maryland	d			00 01	00 16													05 31	06 01	06 31			06 46	07 01	
Stratford [7] ⊖	d	23p54		00 04	00 20	00 08	00 12	00 30	00 40	00 50		01 00	01 10	01 20	01 30	01 40	01 50	05 34	06 04	06 34		06 19	06 49	07 04	06 49
London Liverpool Street [15] ⊖	a	00 02		00 12	00 28	00 16	00 20	00 38	00 48	00 58		01 08	01 18	01 28	01 38	01 48	01 58	05 42	06 12	06 42		06 28	06 57	07 12	06 58

		LE	LE [1]	LE	LE [1]	LE [1]		LE	LE [1]	LE [1]	LE	LE	LE [1]	LE [1]	LE ◇[1]	LE		LE [1]	LE [1]	LE	LE [1]	LE [1]	LE ◇[1]	LE	LE
Southend Victoria	d				06 30					06 50			07 10					07 30				07 50			
Prittlewell	d				06 32					06 52			07 12					07 32				07 52			
Southend Airport ✈	d				06 35					06 55			07 15					07 35				07 55			
Rochford	d				06 38					06 58			07 18					07 38				07 58			
Hockley	d				06 41					07 01			07 21					07 41				08 01			
Rayleigh	d				06 46					07 06			07 26					07 46				08 06			
Southminster	d																							
Burnham-on-Crouch	d																							
Althorne	d																							
North Fambridge	d																							
South Woodham Ferrers	d																							
Battlesbridge	d																							
Wickford [2]	d				06 51					07 11			07 31					07 51				08 11			
Billericay	d				06 57					07 17			07 37					07 57				08 17			
Shenfield [3]	a				07 05					07 25			07 45					08 05				08 25			
Shenfield [3]	d	06 44	06 51	06 59	07 05	07 08		07 14	07 20	07 25	07 29	07 44	07 45	07 51		07 59		08 05	08 08	08 14	08 20	08 25		08 29	08 44
Brentwood	d	06 47		07 02				07 17			07 32	07 47				08 02				08 17				08 32	08 47
Harold Wood	d	06 52		07 07				07 22			07 37	07 52				08 07				08 22				08 37	08 52
Gidea Park [2]	d	06 56		07 11				07 26			07 41	07 56				08 11				08 26				08 41	08 56
Romford	d	06 58		07 13				07 28			07 43	07 58				08 13				08 28				08 43	08 58
Chadwell Heath	d	07 02		07 17				07 32			07 47	08 02				08 17				08 32				08 47	09 02
Goodmayes	d	07 04		07 19				07 34			07 49	08 04				08 19				08 34				08 49	09 04
Seven Kings	d	07 06		07 21				07 36			07 51	08 06				08 21				08 36				08 51	09 06
Ilford [2]	d	07 09		07 24				07 39			07 54	08 09				08 24				08 39				08 54	09 09
Manor Park	d	07 12		07 27				07 42			07 57	08 12				08 27				08 42				08 57	09 12
Forest Gate	d	07 14		07 29				07 44			07 59	08 14				08 29				08 44				08 59	09 14
Maryland	d	07 16		07 31				07 46			08 01	08 16				08 31				08 46				09 01	09 16
Stratford [7] ⊖	d	07 19	07 05	07 34	07 19	07 22		07 49	07 34	07 39	08 04	08 19	07 59	08 05	08 12	08 34		08 19	08 22	08 49	08 36	08 39	08 48	09 04	09 19
London Liverpool Street [15] ⊖	a	07 27	07 14	07 42	07 28	07 31		07 57	07 43	07 48	08 12	08 27	08 08	08 14	08 22	08 42		08 28	08 31	08 57	08 45	08 48	08 59	09 12	09 27

Table 5

Sundays

2 September to 9 September

Southend Victoria, Southminster and Shenfield - London

Network Diagram - see first Page of Table 5

		LE [1]		LE [1]	LE [1]	LE ◇[1]	LE	LE [1]	LE [1]	LE	LE [1]	LE [1]		LE ◇[1]	LE	LE	LE [1]	LE [1]	LE [1]	LE ◇[1]	LE	LE [1]		LE [1]	LE
Southend Victoria	d	08 10						08 30				08 50					09 10					09 30			
Prittlewell	d	08 12						08 32				08 52					09 12					09 32			
Southend Airport ✈	d	08 15						08 35				08 55					09 15					09 35			
Rochford	d	08 18						08 38				08 58					09 18					09 38			
Hockley	d	08 21						08 41				09 01					09 21					09 41			
Rayleigh	d	08 26						08 46				09 06					09 26					09 46			
Southminster	d			08 16														09 16							
Burnham-on-Crouch	d			08 20														09 20							
Althorne	d			08 25														09 25							
North Fambridge	d			08 31														09 31							
South Woodham Ferrers	d			08 36														09 36							
Battlesbridge	d			08 40														09 40							
Wickford [2]	d	08 31		08a46				08 51				09 11					09 31	09a46				09 51			
Billericay	d	08 37						08 57				09 17					09 37					09 57			
Shenfield [3]	a	08 45						09 05				09 25					09 45					10 05			
Shenfield [3]	d	08 45			08 51		08 59	09 05	09 08	09 14	09 20	09 25			09 29	09 44	09 45		09 51		09 59	10 05		10 08	10 14
Brentwood	d						09 02			09 17					09 32	09 47					10 02				10 17
Harold Wood	d						09 07			09 22					09 37	09 52					10 07				10 22
Gidea Park [2]	d						09 11			09 26					09 41	09 56					10 11				10 26
Romford	d						09 13			09 28					09 43	09 58					10 13				10 28
Chadwell Heath	d						09 17			09 32					09 47	10 02					10 17				10 32
Goodmayes	d						09 19			09 34					09 49	10 04					10 19				10 34
Seven Kings	d						09 21			09 36					09 51	10 06					10 21				10 36
Ilford [2]	d						09 24			09 39					09 54	10 09					10 24				10 39
Manor Park	d						09 27			09 42					09 57	10 12					10 27				10 42
Forest Gate	d						09 29			09 44					09 59	10 14					10 29				10 44
Maryland	d						09 31			09 46					10 01	10 16					10 31				10 46
Stratford [7] ⊖	d	08 59			09 05	09 12	09 34	09 19	09 22	09 49	09 36	09 39		09 48	10 04	10 19	09 59		10 05	10 12	10 34	10 19		10 22	10 49
London Liverpool Street [15] ⊖	a	09 08			09 14	09 22	09 42	09 28	09 31	09 57	09 45	09 48		09 59	10 12	10 27	10 08		10 14	10 22	10 42	10 28		10 31	10 57

		LE [1]	LE [1]	LE ◇[1]	LE	LE	LE [1]	LE [1]		LE [1]	LE ◇[1]	LE	LE [1]	LE [1]	LE	LE [1]	LE [1]	LE ◇[1]		LE	LE	LE [1]	LE [1]	LE [1]	LE ◇[1]
Southend Victoria	d		09 50				10 10						10 30				10 50					11 10			
Prittlewell	d		09 52				10 12						10 32				10 52					11 12			
Southend Airport ✈	d		09 55				10 15						10 35				10 55					11 15			
Rochford	d		09 58				10 18						10 38				10 58					11 18			
Hockley	d		10 01				10 21						10 41				11 01					11 21			
Rayleigh	d		10 06				10 26						10 46				11 06					11 26			
Southminster	d							10 16															11 16		
Burnham-on-Crouch	d							10 20															11 20		
Althorne	d							10 25															11 25		
North Fambridge	d							10 31															11 31		
South Woodham Ferrers	d							10 36															11 36		
Battlesbridge	d							10 40															11 40		
Wickford [2]	d		10 11				10 31	10a46					10 51				11 11					11 31	11a46		
Billericay	d		10 17				10 37						10 57				11 17					11 37			
Shenfield [3]	a		10 25				10 45						11 05				11 25					11 45			
Shenfield [3]	d	10 20	10 25		10 29	10 44	10 45			10 51		10 59	11 05	11 08	11 14	11 20	11 25			11 29	11 44	11 45		11 51	
Brentwood	d				10 32	10 47						11 02			11 17					11 32	11 47				
Harold Wood	d				10 37	10 52						11 07			11 22					11 37	11 52				
Gidea Park [2]	d				10 41	10 56						11 11			11 26					11 41	11 56				
Romford	d				10 43	10 58						11 13			11 28					11 43	11 58				
Chadwell Heath	d				10 47	11 02						11 17			11 32					11 47	12 02				
Goodmayes	d				10 49	11 04						11 19			11 34					11 49	12 04				
Seven Kings	d				10 51	11 06						11 21			11 36					11 51	12 06				
Ilford [2]	d				10 54	11 09						11 24			11 39					11 54	12 09				
Manor Park	d				10 57	11 12						11 27			11 42					11 57	12 12				
Forest Gate	d				10 59	11 14						11 29			11 44					11 59	12 14				
Maryland	d				11 01	11 16						11 31			11 46					12 01	12 16				
Stratford [7] ⊖	d	10 36	10 39	10 48	11 04	11 19	10 59			11 05	11 12	11 34	11 19	11 22	11 49	11 36	11 39	11 48		12 04	12 19	11 59		12 05	12 12
London Liverpool Street [15] ⊖	a	10 45	10 48	10 59	11 12	11 27	11 08			11 14	11 22	11 42	11 28	11 31	11 57	11 45	11 48	11 59		12 12	12 27	12 08		12 14	12 22

Southend Victoria, Southminster and Shenfield - London

Network Diagram - see first Page of Table 5

		LE	LE ■	LE ■		LE	LE ■	LE ■	LE ◇■ ⊡	LE	LE	LE ■	LE ■	LE ■		LE ■ ⊡	LE	LE ■	LE ■	LE	LE ■	LE ■	LE ◇■ ⊡	LE
Southend Victoria	d		11 30					11 50				12 10						12 30				12 50		
Prittlewell	d		11 32					11 52				12 12						12 32				12 52		
Southend Airport ✈	d		11 35					11 55				12 15						12 35				12 55		
Rochford	d		11 38					11 58				12 18						12 38				12 58		
Hockley	d		11 41					12 01				12 21						12 41				13 01		
Rayleigh	d		11 46					12 06				12 26						12 46				13 06		
Southminster	d												12 16											
Burnham-on-Crouch	d												12 20											
Althorne	d												12 25											
North Fambridge	d												12 31											
South Woodham Ferrers	d												12 36											
Battlesbridge	d												12 40											
Wickford 2	d		11 51					12 11				12 31	12a46					12 51				13 11		
Billericay	d		11 57					12 17				12 37						12 57				13 17		
Shenfield 3	a		12 05					12 25				12 45						13 05				13 25		
Shenfield 3	d	11 59	12 05	12 08		12 14	12 20	12 25		12 29	12 44	12 45		12 51			12 59	13 05	13 08	13 14	13 20	13 25		13 29
Brentwood	d	12 02				12 17				12 32	12 47						13 02			13 17				13 32
Harold Wood	d	12 07				12 22				12 37	12 52						13 07			13 22				13 37
Gidea Park 2	d	12 11				12 26				12 41	12 56						13 11			13 26				13 41
Romford	d	12 13				12 28				12 43	12 58						13 13			13 28				13 43
Chadwell Heath	d	12 17				12 32				12 47	13 02						13 17			13 32				13 47
Goodmayes	d	12 19				12 34				12 49	13 04						13 19			13 34				13 49
Seven Kings	d	12 21				12 36				12 51	13 06						13 21			13 36				13 51
Ilford 2	d	12 24				12 39				12 54	13 09						13 24			13 39				13 54
Manor Park	d	12 27				12 42				12 57	13 12						13 27			13 42				13 57
Forest Gate	d	12 29				12 44				12 59	13 14						13 29			13 44				13 59
Maryland	d	12 31				12 46				13 01	13 16						13 31			13 46				14 01
Stratford 7 ⊖	d	12 34	12 19	12 22		12 49	12 36	12 39	12 48	13 04	13 19	12 59		13 05		13 12	13 34	13 19	13 22	13 49	13 36	13 39	13 48	14 04
London Liverpool Street 15 ⊖	a	12 42	12 28	12 31		12 57	12 45	12 48	12 59	13 12	13 27	13 08		13 14		13 22	13 42	13 28	13 31	13 57	13 45	13 48	13 59	14 12

		LE	LE ■	LE ■	LE ■	LE ◇■ ⊡	LE	LE ■	LE ■	LE		LE ■	LE ■	LE ◇■ ⊡	LE	LE	LE ■	LE ■	LE ■	LE ◇■ ⊡		LE	LE ■	LE ■	LE
Southend Victoria	d		13 10					13 30					13 50				14 10						14 30		
Prittlewell	d		13 12					13 32					13 52				14 12						14 32		
Southend Airport ✈	d		13 15					13 35					13 55				14 15						14 35		
Rochford	d		13 18					13 38					13 58				14 18						14 38		
Hockley	d		13 21					13 41					14 01				14 21						14 41		
Rayleigh	d		13 26					13 46					14 06				14 26						14 46		
Southminster	d			13 16														14 16							
Burnham-on-Crouch	d			13 20														14 20							
Althorne	d			13 25														14 25							
North Fambridge	d			13 31														14 31							
South Woodham Ferrers	d			13 36														14 36							
Battlesbridge	d			13 40														14 40							
Wickford 2	d		13 31	13a46				13 51					14 11				14 31	14a46					14 51		
Billericay	d		13 37					13 57					14 17				14 37						14 57		
Shenfield 3	a		13 45					14 05					14 25				14 45						15 05		
Shenfield 3	d	13 44	13 45		13 51		13 59	14 05	14 08	14 14		14 20	14 25		14 29	14 44	14 45		14 51			14 59	15 05	15 08	15 14
Brentwood	d	13 47					14 02			14 17					14 32	14 47						15 02			15 17
Harold Wood	d	13 52					14 07			14 22					14 37	14 52						15 07			15 22
Gidea Park 2	d	13 56					14 11			14 26					14 41	14 56						15 11			15 26
Romford	d	13 58					14 13			14 28					14 43	14 58						15 13			15 28
Chadwell Heath	d	14 02					14 17			14 32					14 47	15 02						15 17			15 32
Goodmayes	d	14 04					14 19			14 34					14 49	15 04						15 19			15 34
Seven Kings	d	14 06					14 21			14 36					14 51	15 06						15 21			15 36
Ilford 2	d	14 09					14 24			14 39					14 54	15 09						15 24			15 39
Manor Park	d	14 12					14 27			14 42					14 57	15 12						15 27			15 42
Forest Gate	d	14 14					14 29			14 44					14 59	15 14						15 29			15 44
Maryland	d	14 16					14 31			14 46					15 01	15 16						15 31			15 46
Stratford 7 ⊖	d	14 19	13 59		14 05	14 12	14 34	14 19	14 22	14 49		14 36	14 39	14 48	15 04	15 19	14 59		15 05	15 12		15 34	15 19	15 22	15 49
London Liverpool Street 15 ⊖	a	14 27	14 08		14 14	14 22	14 42	14 28	14 31	14 57		14 45	14 48	14 59	15 12	15 27	15 08		15 14	15 22		15 42	15 28	15 31	15 57

Table 5

Sundays

2 September to 9 September

Southend Victoria, Southminster and Shenfield - London

Network Diagram - see first Page of Table 5

		LE ■	LE ■	LE ◇■ ⊡	LE	LE		LE ■	LE ■	LE ■	LE ◇■ ⊡	LE	LE ■	LE ■	LE	LE ■		LE ■	LE ◇■ ⊡	LE	LE	LE ■	LE ■	LE ■	LE ◇■ ⊡
Southend Victoria	d		14 50					15 10					15 30					15 50				16 10			
Prittlewell	d		14 52					15 12					15 32					15 52				16 12			
Southend Airport ✈	d		14 55					15 15					15 35					15 55				16 15			
Rochford	d		14 58					15 18					15 38					15 58				16 18			
Hockley	d		15 01					15 21					15 41					16 01				16 21			
Rayleigh	d		15 06					15 26					15 46					16 06				16 26			
Southminster	d								15 16														16 16		
Burnham-on-Crouch	d								15 20														16 20		
Althorne	d								15 25														16 25		
North Fambridge	d								15 31														16 31		
South Woodham Ferrers	d								15 36														16 36		
Battlesbridge	d								15 40														16 40		
Wickford 2	d		15 11					15 31	15a46				15 51					16 11				16 31	16a46		
Billericay	d		15 17					15 37					15 57					16 17				16 37			
Shenfield 3	a		15 25					15 45					16 05					16 25				16 45			
Shenfield 3	d	15 20	15 25		15 29	15 44		15 45		15 51		15 59	16 05	16 08	16 14	16 20		16 25		16 29	16 44	16 45		16 51	
Brentwood	d				15 32	15 47						16 02			16 17					16 32	16 47				
Harold Wood	d				15 37	15 52						16 07			16 22					16 37	16 52				
Gidea Park 2	d				15 41	15 56						16 11			16 26					16 41	16 56				
Romford	d				15 43	15 58						16 13			16 28					16 43	16 58				
Chadwell Heath	d				15 47	16 02						16 17			16 32					16 47	17 02				
Goodmayes	d				15 49	16 04						16 19			16 34					16 49	17 04				
Seven Kings	d				15 51	16 06						16 21			16 36					16 51	17 06				
Ilford 2	d				15 54	16 09						16 24			16 39					16 54	17 09				
Manor Park	d				15 57	16 12						16 27			16 42					16 57	17 12				
Forest Gate	d				15 59	16 14						16 29			16 44					16 59	17 14				
Maryland	d				16 01	16 16						16 31			16 46					17 01	17 16				
Stratford 7 ⊖	d	15 36	15 39	15 48	16 04	16 19		15 59		16 05	16 12	16 34	16 19	16 22	16 49	16 36		16 39	16 48	17 04	17 19	16 59		17 05	17 12
London Liverpool Street 15 ⊖	a	15 45	15 48	15 59	16 12	16 27		16 08		16 14	16 22	16 42	16 28	16 31	16 57	16 45		16 48	16 59	17 12	17 27	17 08		17 14	17 22

		LE		LE ■	LE ■	LE	LE ■	LE ■	LE ◇■ ⊡	LE	LE	LE ■		LE ■	LE ■	LE ◇■ ⊡	LE	LE ■	LE ■	LE	LE ■	LE ■		LE ◇■ ⊡	LE
Southend Victoria	d			16 30				16 50				17 10						17 30				17 50			
Prittlewell	d			16 32				16 52				17 12						17 32				17 52			
Southend Airport ✈	d			16 35				16 55				17 15						17 35				17 55			
Rochford	d			16 38				16 58				17 18						17 38				17 58			
Hockley	d			16 41				17 01				17 21						17 41				18 01			
Rayleigh	d			16 46				17 06				17 26						17 46				18 06			
Southminster	d													17 16											
Burnham-on-Crouch	d													17 20											
Althorne	d													17 25											
North Fambridge	d													17 31											
South Woodham Ferrers	d													17 36											
Battlesbridge	d													17 40											
Wickford 2	d			16 51				17 11				17 31		17a46				17 51				18 11			
Billericay	d			16 57				17 17				17 37						17 57				18 17			
Shenfield 3	a			17 05				17 25				17 45						18 05				18 25			
Shenfield 3	d	16 59		17 05	17 08	17 14	17 20	17 25		17 29	17 44	17 45			17 51		17 59	18 05	18 08	18 14	18 20	18 25			18 29
Brentwood	d	17 02				17 17				17 32	17 47						18 02			18 17					18 32
Harold Wood	d	17 07				17 22				17 37	17 52						18 07			18 22					18 37
Gidea Park 2	d	17 11				17 26				17 41	17 56						18 11			18 26					18 41
Romford	d	17 13				17 28				17 43	17 58						18 13			18 28					18 43
Chadwell Heath	d	17 17				17 32				17 47	18 02						18 17			18 32					18 47
Goodmayes	d	17 19				17 34				17 49	18 04						18 19			18 34					18 49
Seven Kings	d	17 21				17 36				17 51	18 06						18 21			18 36					18 51
Ilford 2	d	17 24				17 39				17 54	18 09						18 24			18 39					18 54
Manor Park	d	17 27				17 42				17 57	18 12						18 27			18 42					18 57
Forest Gate	d	17 29				17 44				17 59	18 14						18 29			18 44					18 59
Maryland	d	17 31				17 46				18 01	18 16						18 31			18 46					19 01
Stratford 7 ⊖	d	17 34		17 19	17 22	17 49	17 36	17 39	17 48	18 04	18 19	17 59			18 05	18 12	18 34	18 19	18 22	18 49	18 36	18 39		18 48	19 04
London Liverpool Street 15 ⊖	a	17 42		17 28	17 31	17 57	17 45	17 48	17 59	18 12	18 27	18 08			18 14	18 22	18 42	18 28	18 31	18 57	18 45	18 48		18 59	19 12

Southend Victoria, Southminster and Shenfield - London

Network Diagram - see first Page of Table 5

		LE	LE [1]	LE [1]	LE [1]	LE ◇[1] 🍴	LE	LE [1]		LE [1]	LE	LE [1]	LE [1]	LE ◇[1] 🍴	LE	LE	LE [1]	LE [1]		LE [1]	LE ◇[1] 🍴	LE	LE [1]	LE [1]	LE
Southend Victoria	d		18 10					18 30					18 50				19 10						19 30		
Prittlewell	d		18 12					18 32					18 52				19 12						19 32		
Southend Airport ✈	d		18 15					18 35					18 55				19 15						19 35		
Rochford	d		18 18					18 38					18 58				19 18						19 38		
Hockley	d		18 21					18 41					19 01				19 21						19 41		
Rayleigh	d		18 26					18 46					19 06				19 26						19 46		
Southminster	d			18 16														19 16							
Burnham-on-Crouch	d			18 20														19 20							
Althorne	d			18 25														19 25							
North Fambridge	d			18 31														19 31							
South Woodham Ferrers	d			18 36														19 36							
Battlesbridge	d			18 40														19 40							
Wickford [2]	d		18 31	18a46				18 51					19 11				19 31	19a46					19 51		
Billericay	d		18 37					18 57					19 17				19 37						19 57		
Shenfield [3]	a		18 45					19 05					19 25				19 45						20 05		
Shenfield [3]	d	18 44	18 45		18 51		18 59	19 05		19 08	19 14	19 20	19 25		19 29	19 44	19 45			19 51		19 59	20 05	20 08	20 14
Brentwood	d	18 47					19 02				19 17				19 32	19 47						20 02			20 17
Harold Wood	d	18 52					19 07				19 22				19 37	19 52						20 07			20 22
Gidea Park [2]	d	18 56					19 11				19 26				19 41	19 56						20 11			20 26
Romford	d	18 58					19 13				19 28				19 43	19 58						20 13			20 28
Chadwell Heath	d	19 02					19 17				19 32				19 47	20 02						20 17			20 32
Goodmayes	d	19 04					19 19				19 34				19 49	20 04						20 19			20 34
Seven Kings	d	19 06					19 21				19 36				19 51	20 06						20 21			20 36
Ilford [2]	d	19 09					19 24				19 39				19 54	20 09						20 24			20 39
Manor Park	d	19 12					19 27				19 42				19 57	20 12						20 27			20 42
Forest Gate	d	19 14					19 29				19 44				19 59	20 14						20 29			20 44
Maryland	d	19 16					19 31				19 46				20 01	20 16						20 31			20 46
Stratford [7] ⊖	d	19 19	18 59		19 05	19 12	19 34	19 19		19 22	19 49	19 36	19 39	19 48	20 04	20 19	19 59			20 05	20 12	20 34	20 19	20 22	20 49
London Liverpool Street [15] ⊖	a	19 27	19 08		19 14	19 22	19 42	19 28		19 31	19 57	19 45	19 48	19 59	20 12	20 27	20 08			20 14	20 22	20 42	20 28	20 31	20 57

		LE [1]	LE [1]	LE ◇[1] 🍴		LE	LE	LE [1]	LE [1]	LE [1]	LE [1]	LE	LE [1]	LE [1]		LE	LE [1]	LE [1]	LE ◇[1] 🍴	LE [1]	LE [1]	LE	LE	LE [1]	
Southend Victoria	d		19 50					20 10					20 30					20 50						21 10	
Prittlewell	d		19 52					20 12					20 32					20 52						21 12	
Southend Airport ✈	d		19 55					20 15					20 35					20 55						21 15	
Rochford	d		19 58					20 18					20 38					20 58						21 18	
Hockley	d		20 01					20 21					20 41					21 01						21 21	
Rayleigh	d		20 06					20 26					20 46					21 06						21 26	
Southminster	d								20 16																
Burnham-on-Crouch	d								20 20																
Althorne	d								20 25																
North Fambridge	d								20 31																
South Woodham Ferrers	d								20 36																
Battlesbridge	d								20 40																
Wickford [2]	d		20 11					20 31	20a46				20 51					21 11						21 31	
Billericay	d		20 17					20 37					20 57					21 17						21 37	
Shenfield [3]	a		20 25					20 45					21 05					21 25						21 45	
Shenfield [3]	d	20 20	20 25			20 29	20 44	20 45		20 51		20 59	21 05	21 08		21 14	21 20	21 25				21 29	21 44	21 45	
Brentwood	d					20 32	20 47					21 02				21 17						21 32	21 47		
Harold Wood	d					20 37	20 52					21 07				21 22						21 37	21 52		
Gidea Park [2]	d					20 41	20 56					21 11				21 26						21 41	21 56		
Romford	d					20 43	20 58					21 13				21 28						21 43	21 58		
Chadwell Heath	d					20 47	21 02					21 17				21 32						21 47	22 02		
Goodmayes	d					20 49	21 04					21 19				21 34						21 49	22 04		
Seven Kings	d					20 51	21 06					21 21				21 36						21 51	22 06		
Ilford [2]	d					20 54	21 09					21 24				21 39						21 54	22 09		
Manor Park	d					20 57	21 12					21 27				21 42						21 57	22 12		
Forest Gate	d					20 59	21 14					21 29				21 44						21 59	22 14		
Maryland	d					21 01	21 16					21 31				21 46						22 01	22 16		
Stratford [7] ⊖	d	20 36	20 39	20 48		21 04	21 19	20 59		21 05	21 10	21 34	21 19	21 22		21 49	21 34	21 39	21 48	21 53	22 00	22 04	22 19	22 08	
London Liverpool Street [15] ⊖	a	20 45	20 48	20 59		21 12	21 27	21 08		21 14	21 19	21 42	21 28	21 31		21 57	21 43	21 48	21 59	22 01	22 08	22 12	22 27	22 16	

Southend Victoria, Southminster and Shenfield - London

Network Diagram - see first Page of Table 5

		LE [1]	LE [1]	LE	LE [1]	LE [1]	LE	LE [1]	LE [1]	LE [1]		LE [1]	LE	LE	LE [1]	LE [1]	LE [1]	LE	LE	LE [1]		LE [1]	LE	LE	LE [1]
Southend Victoria	d				21 30				21 50						22 10					22 30					
Prittlewell	d				21 32				21 52						22 12					22 32					
Southend Airport ✈	d				21 35				21 55						22 15					22 35					
Rochford	d				21 38				21 58						22 18					22 38					
Hockley	d				21 41				22 01						22 21					22 41					
Rayleigh	d				21 46				22 06						22 26					22 46					
Southminster	d	21 16														22 16									
Burnham-on-Crouch	d	21 20														22 20									
Althorne	d	21 25														22 25									
North Fambridge	d	21 31														22 31									
South Woodham Ferrers	d	21 36														22 36									
Battlesbridge	d	21 40														22 40									
Wickford [2]	d	21a46			21 51				22 11						22 31	22a46				22 51					
Billericay	d				21 57				22 17						22 37					22 57					
Shenfield [3]	a				22 05				22 25						22 45					23 05					
Shenfield [3]	d		21 47	21 59	22 05	22 08	22 14	22 20	22 25				22 29	22 44	22 45		22 51		22 59	23 05		23 08		23 14	23 21
Brentwood	d			22 02			22 17						22 32	22 47					23 02					23 17	
Harold Wood	d			22 07			22 22						22 37	22 52					23 07					23 22	
Gidea Park [2]	d			22 11			22 26						22 41	22 56					23 11					23 26	
Romford	d			22 13			22 28						22 43	22 58					23 13					23 28	
Chadwell Heath	d			22 17			22 32						22 47	23 02					23 17					23 32	
Goodmayes	d			22 19			22 34						22 49	23 04					23 19					23 34	
Seven Kings	d			22 21			22 36						22 51	23 06					23 21					23 36	
Ilford [2]	d			22 24			22 41						22 54	23 09					23 24					23 39	
Manor Park	d			22 27			22 44						22 57	23 12					23 27					23 42	
Forest Gate	d			22 29			22 46						22 59	23 14					23 29					23 44	
Maryland	d			22 31			22 48						23 01	23 16					23 31					23 46	
Stratford [7] ⊖	d		22 13	22 34	22 24	22 28	22 52	22 40	22 44	22 48		22 58	23 04	23 20	23 08		23 12	23 16	23 36	23 24		23 28	23 32	23 50	23 40
London Liverpool Street [15] ⊖	a		22 21	22 42	22 32	22 36	23 00	22 48	22 52	22 56		23 06	23 12	23 28	23 16		23 20	23 24	23 44	23 32		23 36	23 40	23 58	23 48

		LE [1]	LE [1]	LE [1]	LE	LE		LE [1]	LE
Southend Victoria	d	22 50						23 10	
Prittlewell	d	22 52						23 12	
Southend Airport ✈	d	22 55						23 15	
Rochford	d	22 58						23 18	
Hockley	d	23 01						23 21	
Rayleigh	d	23 06						23 26	
Southminster	d		22 56						
Burnham-on-Crouch	d		23 00						
Althorne	d		23 05						
North Fambridge	d		23 11						
South Woodham Ferrers	d		23 16						
Battlesbridge	d		23 20						
Wickford [2]	d	23 11	23a26					23 31	
Billericay	d	23 17						23 37	
Shenfield [3]	a	23 25						23 45	
Shenfield [3]	d	23 25			23 29	23 44		23 45	23 59
Brentwood	d				23 32	23 47			00 02
Harold Wood	d				23 37	23 52			00 07
Gidea Park [2]	d				23 41	23 56			00 11
Romford	d				23 43	23 58			00 13
Chadwell Heath	d				23 47	00 02			00 17
Goodmayes	d				23 49	00 04			00 19
Seven Kings	d				23 51	00 06			00 21
Ilford [2]	d				23 54	00 09			00 24
Manor Park	d				23 57	00 12			00 27
Forest Gate	d				23 59	00 14			00 29
Maryland	d				00 01	00 16			
Stratford [7] ⊖	d	23 44		23 54	00 04	00 20		00 08	00 40
London Liverpool Street [15] ⊖	a	23 52		00 02	00 12	00 28		00 16	00 48

Table 5

Sundays
from 16 September

Southend Victoria, Southminster and Shenfield - London

Network Diagram - see first Page of Table 5

Station		LE	LE	LE	LE	LE	LE	LE	LE	LE		LE	LE	LE	LE	LE	LE	LE	LE	LE		LE	LE	LE	LE
		◇1		1				1		1			1	1		1	1	1		1			1		1
						═	═		═			═													
Southend Victoria	d							06 15		06 45			07 19				07 49						08 19		
Prittlewell	d																								
Southend Airport ✈	d							06 19		06 49			07 23				07 53						08 23		
Rochford	d							06 22		06 52			07 26				07 56						08 26		
Hockley	d							06 25		06 55			07 29				07 59						08 29		
Rayleigh	d							06 30		07 00			07 34				08 04						08 34		
Southminster	d			22p56														08 05							
Burnham-on-Crouch	d			23p00														08 09							
Althorne	d			23p05														08 14							
North Fambridge	d			23p11														08 20							
South Woodham Ferrers	d			23p16														08 25							
Battlesbridge	d			23p20														08 29							
Wickford 2	d			23p26				06 35		07 05			07 39				08 09	08a35					08 39		
Billericay	d			23p32				06 41		07 11			07 45				08 15						08 45		
Shenfield 3	a			23p39				06 53		07 22			07 53				08 23						08 52		
Shenfield 3	d		23p29	23p39	23p44				06 58			07 45		08 07	08 13	08 20	08 24			08 41		08 43	08 53		09 11
Brentwood	d		23p32		23p47				07 08						08 16		08 27					08 46	08 56		
Harold Wood	d		23p37		23p52				07 23						08 21		08 32					08 51	09 01		
Gidea Park 2	d		23p41		23p56	05 25	05 55		07 30						08 25		08 36		08 41			08 55	09 05	09 11	
Romford	d		23p43	23p47	23p58	05 32	06 02		07 37					08 22	08 27		08 38		08 43			08 57	09 07	09 13	
Chadwell Heath	d		23p47		00 02										08 31				08 47			09 01		09 17	
Goodmayes	d		23p49		00 04										08 33				08 49			09 03		09 19	
Seven Kings	d		23p51		00 06										08 35				08 51			09 05		09 21	
Ilford 2	d		23p54		00 09	05 52	06 22		07 57					08 29	08 38				08 54			09 08		09 24	
Manor Park	d		23p57		00 12										08 40				08 56			09 10		09 26	
Forest Gate	d		23p59		00 14										08 42				08 58			09 12		09 28	
Maryland	d		00 01		00 16										08 44							09 14			
Stratford 7 ⊖	d	23b52	00 04	23p56	00 19	06 07	06 37		08 12					08s34	08 46	08s49	08 49		09 01	09s04		09 16	09 19	09 31	09s34
London Liverpool Street 15 ⊖	a	00 02	00 12	00 05	00 27	06 27	06 57		08 32			08 35		08 42	08 56	08 59	08 59		09 11	09 12		09 26	09 29	09 41	09 42

Station		LE	LE	LE	LE	LE		LE	LE	LE	LE	LE	LE	LE	LE	LE		LE	LE		LE	LE	LE	LE
			1	1		1			1		1		1	1		1			1		1		1	
Southend Victoria	d		08 49						09 19				09 49						10 19		16 19			
Prittlewell	d																							
Southend Airport ✈	d		08 53						09 23				09 53						10 23		16 23			
Rochford	d		08 56						09 26				09 56						10 26		16 26			
Hockley	d		08 59						09 29				09 59						10 29		16 29			
Rayleigh	d		09 04						09 34				10 04						10 34		16 34			
Southminster	d			09 05										10 05										
Burnham-on-Crouch	d			09 09										10 09										
Althorne	d			09 14										10 14										
North Fambridge	d			09 20										10 20										
South Woodham Ferrers	d			09 25										10 25										
Battlesbridge	d			09 29										10 29										
Wickford 2	d		09 09	09a35					09 39				10 09	10a35					10 39	and at the same minutes past each hour until	16 39			
Billericay	d		09 15						09 45				10 15						10 45		16 45			
Shenfield 3	a		09 22						09 52				10 22						10 52		16 52			
Shenfield 3	d	09 13	09 23			09 41		09 43	09 53		10 11	10 13	10 23			10 41		10 43	10 53		16 53		17 11	17 13
Brentwood	d	09 16	09 26					09 46	09 56			10 16	10 26					10 46	10 56		16 56			17 16
Harold Wood	d	09 21	09 31					09 51	10 01			10 21	10 31					10 51	11 01		17 01			17 21
Gidea Park 2	d	09 25	09 35		09 41			09 55	10 05	10 11		10 25	10 35		10 41			10 55	11 05		17 05	17 11		17 25
Romford	d	09 27	09 37		09 43			09 57	10 07	10 13		10 27	10 37		10 43			10 57	11 07		17 07	17 13		17 27
Chadwell Heath	d	09 31			09 47			10 01		10 17		10 31			10 47			11 01				17 17		17 31
Goodmayes	d	09 33			09 49			10 03		10 19		10 33			10 49			11 03				17 19		17 33
Seven Kings	d	09 35			09 51			10 05		10 21		10 35			10 51			11 05				17 21		17 35
Ilford 2	d	09 38			09 54			10 08		10 24		10 38			10 54			11 08				17 24		17 38
Manor Park	d	09 40			09 56			10 10		10 26		10 40			10 56			11 10				17 26		17 40
Forest Gate	d	09 42			09 58			10 12		10 28		10 42			10 58			11 12				17 28		17 42
Maryland	d	09 44						10 14				10 44						11 14						17 44
Stratford 7 ⊖	d	09 46	09 49		10 01	10s04		10 16	10 21	10 31	10s34	10 46	10 49		11 01	11s04		11 16	11 19		17 19	17 31	17s34	17 46
London Liverpool Street 15 ⊖	a	09 56	09 59		10 11	10 12		10 26	10 31	10 41	10 42	10 56	10 59		11 11	11 12		11 26	11 29		17 29	17 41	17 42	17 56

b Previous night, stops to set down only

Table 5

Sundays
from 16 September

Southend Victoria, Southminster and Shenfield - London

Network Diagram - see first Page of Table 5

Station		LE		LE	LE	LE	LE	LE	LE	LE	LE	LE		LE	LE	LE	LE	LE	LE	LE	LE	LE		LE	LE
		1		1		1		1		1		1		1		1		1		1		1		1	
Southend Victoria	d	16 49						17 19				17 49						18 19				18 49			
Prittlewell	d																								
Southend Airport ✈	d	16 53						17 23				17 53						18 23				18 53			
Rochford	d	16 56						17 26				17 56						18 26				18 56			
Hockley	d	16 59						17 29				17 59						18 29				18 59			
Rayleigh	d	17 04						17 34				18 04						18 34				19 04			
Southminster	d			17 05										18 05										19 05	
Burnham-on-Crouch	d			17 09										18 09										19 09	
Althorne	d			17 14										18 14										19 14	
North Fambridge	d			17 20										18 20										19 20	
South Woodham Ferrers	d			17 25										18 25										19 25	
Battlesbridge	d			17 29										18 29										19 29	
Wickford 2	d	17 09		17a35				17 39				18 09		18a35				18 39				19 09		19a35	
Billericay	d	17 15						17 45				18 15						18 45				19 15			
Shenfield 3	a	17 22						17 52				18 22						18 52				19 22			
Shenfield 3	d	17 23				17 41	17 43	17 53		18 11	18 13	18 23				18 41	18 43	18 53		19 11	19 13	19 23			
Brentwood	d	17 26					17 46	17 56			18 16	18 26					18 46	18 56			19 16	19 26			
Harold Wood	d	17 31					17 51	18 01			18 21	18 31					18 51	19 01			19 21	19 31			
Gidea Park 2	d	17 35			17 41		17 55	18 05	18 11		18 25	18 35			18 41		18 55	19 05	19 11		19 25	19 35			19 41
Romford	d	17 37			17 43		17 57	18 07	18 13		18 27	18 37			18 43		18 57	19 07	19 13		19 27	19 37			19 43
Chadwell Heath	d				17 47		18 01		18 17		18 31				18 47		19 01		19 17		19 31				19 47
Goodmayes	d				17 49		18 03		18 19		18 33				18 49		19 03		19 19		19 33				19 49
Seven Kings	d				17 51		18 05		18 21		18 35				18 51		19 05		19 21		19 35				19 51
Ilford 2	d				17 54		18 08		18 24		18 38				18 54		19 08		19 24		19 38				19 54
Manor Park	d				17 56		18 10		18 26		18 40				18 56		19 10		19 26		19 40				19 56
Forest Gate	d				17 58		18 12		18 28		18 42				18 58		19 12		19 28		19 42				19 58
Maryland	d						18 14				18 44						19 14				19 44				
Stratford 7 ⊖	d	17 49			18 01	18s04	18 16	18 19	18 31	18s34	18 46	18 49			19 01	19s04	19 16	19 19	19 31	19s34	19 46	19 49			20 01
London Liverpool Street 15 ⊖	a	17 59			18 11	18 12	18 26	18 31	18 41	18 42	18 56	18 59			19 11	19 12	19 26	19 29	19 41	19 42	19 56	19 59			20 11

Station		LE	LE	LE	LE	LE	LE	LE		LE	LE	LE	LE	LE	LE	LE	LE	LE		LE	LE	LE	LE	LE	LE
		1		1		1		1		1		1		1		1		1		1	1	1		1	1
Southend Victoria	d			19 19				19 49						20 19				20 49						21 19	
Prittlewell	d																								
Southend Airport ✈	d			19 23				19 53						20 23				20 53						21 23	
Rochford	d			19 26				19 56						20 26				20 56						21 26	
Hockley	d			19 29				19 59						20 29				20 59						21 29	
Rayleigh	d			19 34				20 04						20 34				21 04						21 34	
Southminster	d									20 05										21 05					
Burnham-on-Crouch	d									20 09										21 09					
Althorne	d									20 14										21 14					
North Fambridge	d									20 20										21 20					
South Woodham Ferrers	d									20 25										21 25					
Battlesbridge	d									20 29										21 29					
Wickford 2	d			19 39				20 09		20a35				20 39				21 09		21a35				21 39	
Billericay	d			19 45				20 15						20 45				21 15						21 45	
Shenfield 3	a			19 52				20 22						20 52				21 22						21 52	
Shenfield 3	d	19 41	19 43	19 53		20 11	20 13	20 23				20 41	20 43	20 53		21 11	21 13	21 23			21 26	21 41	21 43	21 53	22 11
Brentwood	d		19 46	19 56			20 16	20 26					20 46	20 56			21 16	21 26					21 46	21 56	
Harold Wood	d		19 51	20 01			20 21	20 31					20 51	21 01			21 21	21 31					21 51	22 01	
Gidea Park 2	d		19 55	20 05	20 11		20 25	20 35			20 41		20 55	21 05	21 11		21 25	21 35					21 55	22 05	
Romford	d		19 57	20 07	20 13		20 27	20 37			20 43		20 57	21 07	21 13		21 27	21 37					21 57	22 07	
Chadwell Heath	d		20 01		20 17		20 31				20 47		21 01		21 17		21 31						22 01		
Goodmayes	d		20 03		20 19		20 33				20 49		21 03		21 19		21 33						22 03		
Seven Kings	d		20 05		20 21		20 35				20 51		21 05		21 21		21 35						22 05		
Ilford 2	d		20 08		20 24		20 38				20 54		21 08		21 24		21 38						22 08		
Manor Park	d		20 10		20 26		20 40				20 56		21 10		21 26		21 40						22 10		
Forest Gate	d		20 12		20 28		20 42				20 58		21 12		21 28		21 42						22 12		
Maryland	d		20 14				20 44						21 14				21 44						22 14		
Stratford 7 ⊖	d	20s04	20 16	20 19	20 31	20s34	20 46	20 49			21 01	21s04	21 16	21 19	21 31	21s34	21 46	21 49			21s51	22s04	22 16	22 19	22s34
London Liverpool Street 15 ⊖	a	20 12	20 26	20 29	20 41	20 42	20 56	20 59			21 11	21 12	21 26	21 29	21 41	21 42	21 56	21 59			21 59	22 12	22 26	22 29	22 42

Sundays
from 16 September

Southend Victoria, Southminster and Shenfield - London

Network Diagram - see first Page of Table 5

		LE	LE 1	LE 1		LE 1	LE	LE 1	LE 1	LE	LE 1	LE 1	LE
Southend Victoria	d		21 49					22 19			22 49		
Prittlewell	d												
Southend Airport ✈	d		21 53					22 23			22 53		
Rochford	d		21 56					22 26			22 56		
Hockley	d		21 59					22 29			22 59		
Rayleigh	d		22 04					22 34			23 04		
Southminster	d			22 05								22 45	
Burnham-on-Crouch	d			22 09								22 49	
Althorne	d			22 14								22 54	
North Fambridge	d			22 20								23 00	
South Woodham Ferrers	d			22 25								23 05	
Battlesbridge	d			22 29								23 09	
Wickford 2	d		22 09	22a35				22 39			23 09	23 15	
Billericay	d		22 15					22 45			23 15		
Shenfield 3	a		22 22					22 52			23 22	23 26	
Shenfield 3	d	22 13	22 23			22 41	22 43	22 53	23 11	23 13	23 23		23 43
Brentwood	d	22 16	22 26				22 46	22 56		23 16	23 26		23 46
Harold Wood	d	22 21	22 31				22 51	23 01		23 21	23 31		23 51
Gidea Park 2	d	22 25	22 35				22 55	23 05		23 25	23 35		23 55
Romford	d	22 27	22 37				22 57	23 07		23 27	23 37		23 57
Chadwell Heath	d	22 31					23 01			23 31			00 01
Goodmayes	d	22 33					23 03			23 33			00 03
Seven Kings	d	22 35					23 05			23 35			00 05
Ilford 2	d	22 38					23 08			23 38			00 08
Manor Park	d	22 40					23 10			23 40			00 10
Forest Gate	d	22 42					23 12			23 42			00 12
Maryland	d	22 44					23 14			23 44			00 14
Stratford 7 ⊖	d	22 46	22 49			23s04	23 16	23 19	23s34	23 46	23 49		00 16
London Liverpool Street 15 ⊖	a	22 56	22 59			23 12	23 26	23 31	23 42	23 56	23 59		00 26

Mondays to Fridays

Marks Tey - Sudbury

Miles			LE	LE	LE	LE	LE	LE	LE	LE	LE		LE	LE	LE	LE	LE	LE	LE	LE	LE		LE
0	**Colchester 4**	d																					
5	Marks Tey 2	d	06 01	06 52	07 39	08 22	09 09	10 01	11 01	12 01	13 01		14 01	15 01	16 01	17 07	18 05	19 11	20 05	21 01	22 01		23 01
8½	Chappel & Wakes Colne	d	06 07	06 58		08 28	09 15	10 07	11 07	12 07	13 07		14 07	15 07	16 07	17 13	18 11	19 17	20 11	21 07	22 07		23 07
11¾	Bures	d	06 13	07 04		08 34	09 21	10 13	11 13	12 13	13 13		14 13	15 13	16 13	17 19	18 17	19 23	20 17	21 13	22 13		23 13
16¾	**Sudbury**	a	06 21	07 12	07 55	08 42	09 29	10 21	11 21	12 21	13 21		14 21	15 21	16 21	17 27	18 25	19 31	20 25	21 21	22 21		23 21

Saturdays

		LE	LE	LE	LE	LE	LE	LE	LE	LE		LE	LE	LE	LE	LE	LE	LE	LE	LE
Colchester 4	d	05 50																		
Marks Tey 2	d	06 01	07 01	08 01	09 01	10 01	11 01	12 01	13 01	14 01		15 01	16 01	17 01	18 01	19 01	20 01	21 01	22 01	23 01
Chappel & Wakes Colne	d	06 07	07 07	08 07	09 07	10 07	11 07	12 07	13 07	14 07		15 07	16 07	17 07	18 07	19 07	20 07	21 07	22 07	23 07
Bures	d	06 13	07 13	08 13	09 13	10 13	11 13	12 13	13 13	14 13		15 13	16 13	17 13	18 13	19 13	20 13	21 13	22 13	23 13
Sudbury	a	06 21	07 21	08 21	09 21	10 21	11 21	12 21	13 21	14 21		15 21	16 21	17 21	18 21	19 21	20 21	21 21	22 21	23 21

Sundays
until 22 July

		LE	LE	LE	LE	LE	LE	LE	LE	LE		LE	LE	LE	LE	LE	LE
Colchester 4	d	07 07															
Marks Tey 2	d	07 15	08 15	09 15	10 15	11 15	12 15	13 15	14 15	15 15		16 15	17 15	18 15	19 15	20 15	21 15
Chappel & Wakes Colne	d	07 21	08 21	09 21	10 21	11 21	12 21	13 21	14 21	15 21		16 21	17 21	18 21	19 21	20 21	21 21
Bures	d	07 27	08 27	09 27	10 27	11 27	12 27	13 27	14 27	15 27		16 27	17 27	18 27	19 27	20 27	21 27
Sudbury	a	07 35	08 35	09 35	10 35	11 35	12 35	13 35	14 35	15 35		16 35	17 35	18 35	19 35	20 35	21 35

Sundays
29 July to 12 August

		LE	LE	LE	LE	LE	LE	LE	LE	LE		LE	LE	LE	LE	LE	LE	LE
Colchester 4	d	06 53																
Marks Tey 2	d	07 01	08 01	09 01	10 01	11 01	12 01	13 01	14 01	15 01		16 01	17 01	18 01	19 01	20 01	21 01	22 01
Chappel & Wakes Colne	d	07 07	08 07	09 07	10 07	11 07	12 07	13 07	14 07	15 07		16 07	17 07	18 07	19 07	20 07	21 07	22 07
Bures	d	07 13	08 13	09 13	10 13	11 13	12 13	13 13	14 13	15 13		16 13	17 13	18 13	19 13	20 13	21 13	22 13
Sudbury	a	07 21	08 21	09 21	10 21	11 21	12 21	13 21	14 21	15 21		16 21	17 21	18 21	19 21	20 21	21 21	22 21

Sundays
19 August to 26 August

		LE	LE	LE	LE	LE	LE	LE	LE	LE		LE	LE	LE	LE	LE	LE
Colchester 4	d	07 07															
Marks Tey 2	d	07 15	08 15	09 15	10 15	11 15	12 15	13 15	14 15	15 15		16 15	17 15	18 15	19 15	20 15	21 15
Chappel & Wakes Colne	d	07 21	08 21	09 21	10 21	11 21	12 21	13 21	14 21	15 21		16 21	17 21	18 21	19 21	20 21	21 21
Bures	d	07 27	08 27	09 27	10 27	11 27	12 27	13 27	14 27	15 27		16 27	17 27	18 27	19 27	20 27	21 27
Sudbury	a	07 35	08 35	09 35	10 35	11 35	12 35	13 35	14 35	15 35		16 35	17 35	18 35	19 35	20 35	21 35

Sundays
2 September to 9 September

		LE	LE	LE	LE	LE	LE	LE	LE	LE		LE	LE	LE	LE	LE	LE	LE
Colchester 4	d	06 53																
Marks Tey 2	d	07 01	08 01	09 01	10 01	11 01	12 01	13 01	14 01	15 01		16 01	17 01	18 01	19 01	20 01	21 01	22 01
Chappel & Wakes Colne	d	07 07	08 07	09 07	10 07	11 07	12 07	13 07	14 07	15 07		16 07	17 07	18 07	19 07	20 07	21 07	22 07
Bures	d	07 13	08 13	09 13	10 13	11 13	12 13	13 13	14 13	15 13		16 13	17 13	18 13	19 13	20 13	21 13	22 13
Sudbury	a	07 21	08 21	09 21	10 21	11 21	12 21	13 21	14 21	15 21		16 21	17 21	18 21	19 21	20 21	21 21	22 21

Sundays
from 16 September

		LE	LE	LE	LE	LE	LE	LE	LE	LE		LE	LE	LE	LE	LE	LE
Colchester 4	d	07 07															
Marks Tey 2	d	07 15	08 15	09 15	10 15	11 15	12 15	13 15	14 15	15 15		16 15	17 15	18 15	19 15	20 15	21 15
Chappel & Wakes Colne	d	07 21	08 21	09 21	10 21	11 21	12 21	13 21	14 21	15 21		16 21	17 21	18 21	19 21	20 21	21 21
Bures	d	07 27	08 27	09 27	10 27	11 27	12 27	13 27	14 27	15 27		16 27	17 27	18 27	19 27	20 27	21 27
Sudbury	a	07 35	08 35	09 35	10 35	11 35	12 35	13 35	14 35	15 35		16 35	17 35	18 35	19 35	20 35	21 35

Table 10

Mondays to Fridays

Sudbury - Marks Tey

Miles			LE	LE	LE	LE	LE	LE	LE	LE	LE	LE	LE	LE	LE	LE	LE	LE	LE	LE	LE	LE
0	**Sudbury**	d	05 30	06 29	07 16	07 59	08 46	09 33	10 26	11 26	12 26	13 26	14 26	15 26	16 32	17 32	18 37	19 37	20 32	21 26	22 26	23 26
5	Bures	d	05 37	06 36	07 23	08 06	08 53	09 40	10 33	11 33	12 33	13 33	14 33	15 33	16 39	17 39	18 44	19 44	20 39	21 33	22 33	23 33
8¾	Chappel & Wakes Colne	d	05 43	06 42	07 29	08 12	08 59	09 46	10 39	11 39	12 39	13 39	14 39	15 39	16 45	17 45	18 50	19 50	20 45	21 39	22 39	23 39
11¾	Marks Tey ■	a	05 49	06 48	07 35	08 18	09 05	09 52	10 45	11 45	12 45	13 45	14 45	15 45	16 51	17 51	18 56	19 56	20 51	21 45	22 45	23 45
16¾	**Colchester ■**	a																				23 55

Saturdays

		LE	LE	LE	LE	LE	LE	LE	LE	LE	LE	LE	LE	LE	LE	LE	LE	LE	LE A	LE B
Sudbury	d	06 26	07 26	08 26	09 26	10 26	11 26	12 26	13 26	14 26	15 26	16 26	17 26	18 26	19 26	20 26	21 26	22 26	23 26	23 26
Bures	d	06 33	07 33	08 33	09 33	10 33	11 33	12 33	13 33	14 33	15 33	16 33	17 33	18 33	19 33	20 33	21 33	22 33	23 33	23 33
Chappel & Wakes Colne	d	06 39	07 39	08 39	09 39	10 39	11 39	12 39	13 39	14 39	15 39	16 39	17 39	18 39	19 39	20 39	21 39	22 39	23 39	23 39
Marks Tey ■	a	06 45	07 45	08 45	09 45	10 45	11 45	12 45	13 45	14 45	15 45	16 45	17 45	18 45	19 45	20 45	21 45	22 45	23 45	23 45
Colchester ■	a																		23 55	23 59

Sundays
until 22 July

		LE	LE	LE	LE	LE	LE	LE	LE	LE	LE	LE	LE	LE	LE	LE
Sudbury	d	07 40	08 40	09 40	10 40	11 40	12 40	13 40	14 40	15 40	16 40	17 40	18 40	19 40	20 40	21 40
Bures	d	07 47	08 47	09 47	10 47	11 47	12 47	13 47	14 47	15 47	16 47	17 47	18 47	19 47	20 47	21 47
Chappel & Wakes Colne	d	07 53	08 53	09 53	10 53	11 53	12 53	13 53	14 53	15 53	16 53	17 53	18 53	19 53	20 53	21 53
Marks Tey ■	a	07 59	08 59	09 59	10 59	11 59	12 59	13 59	14 59	15 59	16 59	17 59	18 59	19 59	20 59	21 59
Colchester ■	a															22 08

Sundays
29 July to 12 August

		LE	LE	LE	LE	LE	LE	LE	LE	LE	LE	LE	LE	LE	LE	LE	LE
Sudbury	d	07 26	08 26	09 26	10 26	11 26	12 26	13 26	14 26	15 26	16 26	17 26	18 26	19 26	20 26	21 26	22 26
Bures	d	07 33	08 33	09 33	10 33	11 33	12 33	13 33	14 33	15 33	16 33	17 33	18 33	19 33	20 33	21 33	22 33
Chappel & Wakes Colne	d	07 39	08 39	09 39	10 39	11 39	12 39	13 39	14 39	15 39	16 39	17 39	18 39	19 39	20 39	21 39	22 39
Marks Tey ■	a	07 45	08 45	09 45	10 45	11 45	12 45	13 45	14 45	15 45	16 45	17 45	18 45	19 45	20 45	21 45	22 45
Colchester ■	a																22 55

Sundays
19 August to 26 August

		LE	LE	LE	LE	LE	LE	LE	LE	LE	LE	LE	LE	LE	LE	LE
Sudbury	d	07 40	08 40	09 40	10 40	11 40	12 40	13 40	14 40	15 40	16 40	17 40	18 40	19 40	20 40	21 40
Bures	d	07 47	08 47	09 47	10 47	11 47	12 47	13 47	14 47	15 47	16 47	17 47	18 47	19 47	20 47	21 47
Chappel & Wakes Colne	d	07 53	08 53	09 53	10 53	11 53	12 53	13 53	14 53	15 53	16 53	17 53	18 53	19 53	20 53	21 53
Marks Tey ■	a	07 59	08 59	09 59	10 59	11 59	12 59	13 59	14 59	15 59	16 59	17 59	18 59	19 59	20 59	21 59
Colchester ■	a															22 08

Sundays
2 September to 9 September

		LE	LE	LE	LE	LE	LE	LE	LE	LE	LE	LE	LE	LE	LE	LE	LE
Sudbury	d	07 26	08 26	09 26	10 26	11 26	12 26	13 26	14 26	15 26	16 26	17 26	18 26	19 26	20 26	21 26	22 26
Bures	d	07 33	08 33	09 33	10 33	11 33	12 33	13 33	14 33	15 33	16 33	17 33	18 33	19 33	20 33	21 33	22 33
Chappel & Wakes Colne	d	07 39	08 39	09 39	10 39	11 39	12 39	13 39	14 39	15 39	16 39	17 39	18 39	19 39	20 39	21 39	22 39
Marks Tey ■	a	07 45	08 45	09 45	10 45	11 45	12 45	13 45	14 45	15 45	16 45	17 45	18 45	19 45	20 45	21 45	22 45
Colchester ■	a																22 55

Sundays
from 16 September

		LE	LE	LE	LE	LE	LE	LE	LE	LE	LE	LE	LE	LE	LE	LE
Sudbury	d	07 40	08 40	09 40	10 40	11 40	12 40	13 40	14 40	15 40	16 40	17 40	18 40	19 40	20 40	21 40
Bures	d	07 47	08 47	09 47	10 47	11 47	12 47	13 47	14 47	15 47	16 47	17 47	18 47	19 47	20 47	21 47
Chappel & Wakes Colne	d	07 53	08 53	09 53	10 53	11 53	12 53	13 53	14 53	15 53	16 53	17 53	18 53	19 53	20 53	21 53
Marks Tey ■	a	07 59	08 59	09 59	10 59	11 59	12 59	13 59	14 59	15 59	16 59	17 59	18 59	19 59	20 59	21 59
Colchester ■	a															22 08

A 28 July, 4 August, 11 August, 1 September, 8 September

B until 21 July, from 18 August, not 1 September, 8 September

Table 11

Mondays to Fridays
until 26 July

London - Chelmsford, Colchester, Walton-on-Naze, Clacton, Harwich, Ipswich and Norwich

Network Diagram - see first Page of Table 5

Miles	Miles	Miles	Miles	Miles			LE	LE	LE	LE	LE	LE	LE	LE	LE	LE	LE	LE	LE	LE	LE	LE	LE	LE
							MX	MO	MO	TW ThO	TW ThO		MO	TW ThO			MO		TW ThO	MO	TW ThO	TW ThO		TW ThO
							◇■	◇■	■	■	■	■	■	■	■	◇■	◇■	■	◇■	■	◇■	■	■	■
								A	A	B	B	C	A	B	C	C	A	C	B	A	B	B	C	B
							⊐	⊐								⊐			⊐		⊐			
0	—	—	—	—	**London Liverpool Street ■ ⊖**	d	22p30	22p30	22p32	22p50		23p02	23p02	23p10	23p18	23p30	23p30		23p30	23p32			23p48	23p50
4	—	—	—	—	Stratford ■ ⊖	d	22b38		22p39	22p57		23p09	23p09	23p17	23p25	23b38			23b39	23p39			23p55	23p57
12¼	—	—	—	—	Romford	d																		
20¼	—	—	—	—	Shenfield ■	d			23p01	23p21		23p25	23p31	23p41	23p41				00 02	00 01			00 11	00 21
23½	—	—	—	—	Ingatestone	d				23p25			23p35		23p45								00 15	00 25
29¾	—	—	—	—	**Chelmsford ■**	d	23p03		23p10	23p32		23p34	23p42	23p50	23p52	00 03			00 13	00 10			00 22	00 32
36	—	—	—	—	Hatfield Peverel	d						23p40	23p48	23p56							←		00 28	00 38
38½	0	—	—	—	**Witham ■**	d			23p21	23p43	23p45	23p47	23p55	00 03	00 03			00 05	00 24	00 21	00 24	00 26	00 35	00 45
—	3	—	—	—	White Notley	d					23p52							00 12	→			00 33		
—	4¼	—	—	—	Cressing	d					23p54							00 14				00 35		
—	5½	—	—	—	Braintree Freeport	d					23p57							00 17				00 38		
—	6¼	—	—	—	**Braintree**	a					00 01							00 21				00 42		
42¼	—	—	—	—	Kelvedon	d				23p47		23p51	23p59	00 07									00 39	00 49
46¾	—	—	—	—	Marks Tey ■	d			23p28	23p53		23p57	00 05	00 13						00 28			00 45	00 55
51¾	—	—	—	—	**Colchester ■**	a	23p22	23p23	23p36	00 05		00 04	00 12	00 20	00 15	00 22	00 27			00 39	00 36		00 57	01 07
—	0	0	—	—	**Colchester ■**	d	23p23	23p23	23p36			00 04	00 12	00 20	00 16	00 23	00 27				00 37			
—	—	2¼	—	—	Colchester Town	a																		
—	—	—	—	—		d																		
—	2¾	3¼	—	—	Hythe	d																		
—	—	5¾	—	—	Wivenhoe ■	d			23p44						00 23									
—	—	7½	—	—	Alresford (Essex)	d			23p47						00 27									
—	—	9¾	—	—	Great Bentley	d			23p51						00 31									
—	—	12½	—	—	Weeley	d																		
—	—	14¾	0	—	Thorpe-le-Soken ■	a			23p58						00 38									
—	—	—	—	—		d			23p58						00 38									
—	—	—	4¾	—	**Clacton-on-Sea**	a			00 07						00 51									
—	—	17¾	—	—	Kirby Cross	d																		
—	—	18½	—	—	Frinton-on-Sea	d																		
—	—	19¾	—	—	**Walton-on-the-Naze**	a																		
59½	—	—	—	0	Manningtree ■	d	23p31	23p31				00 12	00 20	00 28		00 31	00 35				00 45			
—	—	—	—	1¾	Mistley	d																		
—	—	—	—	5¾	Wrabness	d																		
—	—	—	—	9½	Harwich International	d																		
—	—	—	—	10¾	Dovercourt	d																		
—	—	—	—	11¼	**Harwich Town**	a																		
68¾	—	—	—	—	**Ipswich**	a	23p43	23p43				00 28	00 36	00 44		00 43	00 47				00 57			
—	—	—	—	—		d	23p44	23p44								00 44	00 48				00 58			
77	—	—	—	—	Needham Market	d																		
80¾	—	—	—	—	Stowmarket	d	23p55	23p55								00 55	00 59				01 09			
—	—	—	—	—	**Peterborough ■**	a																		
95	—	—	—	—	Diss	d	00 08	00 08								01 08	01 12				01 22			
115	—	—	—	—	**Norwich**	a	00 39	00 41								01 43	01 45				01 57			

A from 21 May until 23 July

B until 21 June

C FO until 15 June, MX from 22 June until 26 July

b Previous night, stops to pick up only

London - Chelmsford, Colchester, Walton-on-Naze, Clacton, Harwich, Ipswich and Norwich

Network Diagram - see first Page of Table 5

		LE MO ■	LE ■ A	LE TW ThO ■ B	LE TW ThO ■ B	LE	LE ■	LE ◇■	LE ■	LE ■	LE ■	LE ■	LE ■	LE ■	LE ■	LE ■	LE ■	LE ■	LE ■	LE ■	LE ◇■	LE ■
London Liverpool Street ⊖	d	00 02	00 18	00 18												05 23					06 00	06 02
Stratford ⊖	d	00 09	00 25	00 25												05 30						06 09
Romford	d			00 37												05 38						
Shenfield	d	00 31	00 47	00 51												05 48						06 25
Ingatestone	d	00 35	00 51	00 55												05 52						
Chelmsford	d	00 42	00 58	01 02												05 59					06 30	06 34
Hatfield Peverel	d	00 48	01 04	01 08												06 05						
Witham	d	00 55	01 11	01 15			05 21									06 12	06 16					06 45
White Notley	d						05 28										06 23					
Cressing	d						05 30										06 25					
Braintree Freeport	d						05 33										06 28					
Braintree	a						05 37										06 32					
Kelvedon	d	00 59	01 15	01 19												06 16						06 49
Marks Tey	d	01 05	01 21	01 25												06 22						06 55
Colchester	a	01 18	01 41	01 45												06 29					06 49	07 02
Colchester	d				00 41			05 40			06 10		06 15	06 20		06 30					06 50	07 02
Colchester Town	a													06 27								
	d																					
Hythe	d																					07 07
Wivenhoe	d				00 48											06 37						07 11
Alresford (Essex)	d				00 52																	07 14
Great Bentley	d				00 56																	07 18
Weeley	d																					07 22
Thorpe-le-Soken	a				01 03											06 50						07 28
	d				01 03					06 03					06 31	06 50			06 56			07 28
Clacton-on-Sea	a				01 16											06 59						07 37
Kirby Cross	d									06 12					06 39				07 06			
Frinton-on-Sea	d									06 15					06 42				07 09			
Walton-on-the-Naze	a									06 19					06 46				07 13			
Manningtree	d							05 49	05 56		06 18		06 23								06 58	
Mistley	d								06 00		06 22											
Wrabness	d								06 05		06 27											
Harwich International	d								06 13		06 35											
Dovercourt	d								06 16		06 38											
Harwich Town	a								06 18		06 40											
Ipswich	a							05 59					06 34								07 10	
	d					05 10		06 00				06 16						06 39		06 56	07 11	
Needham Market	d					05 20						06 25								07 05		
Stowmarket	d					05a26		06 12				06a30						06 51		07a10	07 22	
Peterborough	a							07 38														
Diss	d																	07 04			07 35	
Norwich	a																	07 24			07 54	

A FO until 15 June, MX from 22 June until 26 July B until 21 June

London - Chelmsford, Colchester, Walton-on-Naze, Clacton, Harwich, Ipswich and Norwich

Network Diagram - see first Page of Table 5

		LE ■	LE ■	LE ■	LE ◇■	LE ■	LE ■	LE ■	LE ■	LE ■	LE ◇■	LE ■	LE ■ A	LE ■	LE ■	LE ■	LE ■	LE ◇■	LE ■	LE ■		LE ◇■	LE ■
London Liverpool Street ⊖	d	06 12			06 25			06 38	06 48		07 00	07 02			07 08	07 18		07 30	07 36	07 46		07 55	
Stratford ⊖	d	06 19			06u33			06 45	06 55			07 09			07 15	07 25		07u38	07 45	07 54			
Romford	d																						
Shenfield	d	06 36						07 01	07 11		07u22	07 25			07 31	07 41			08 01	08 11			
Ingatestone	d	06 40							07 15							07 45			08 05				
Chelmsford	d	06 47			06 58			07 10	07 22			07 34			07 40	07 52		08 03	08 12	08 20			
Hatfield Peverel	d	06 53										07 40											
Witham	d	07 03			07 09			07 21	07 33			07 48			07 51	08 03			08 23	08 35	08 38		
White Notley	d	07 10										07 55								08 42			
Cressing	d	07 12										07 57								08 44			
Braintree Freeport	d	07 15										08 00								08 47			
Braintree	a	07 19										08 04								08 51			
Kelvedon	d							07 25							07 55				08 27				
Marks Tey	d							07 31	07 40						08 01	08 11			08 33				
Colchester	a				07 22			07 38	07 47		07 50				08 08	08 18		08 22	08 40		08 53	08 45	
Colchester	d		07 10		07 23		07 26	07 43	07 48		07 51			07 56	08 08	08 19		08 23	08 41		08 56	08 47	
Colchester Town	a						07 34		07 56					08 03					08 49		09 03		
	d						07 38							08 07							09 07		
Hythe	d						07 42							08 11		08 23					09 11		
Wivenhoe	d						07 46							08 15		08 27					09 15		
Alresford (Essex)	d													08 19							09 19		
Great Bentley	d													08 23							09 23		
Weeley	d													08 26			←				09 26		
Thorpe-le-Soken	a						07 57							08 31		08 38	08 31				09 31		
	d					07 38	07 57							08 40		08 38	08 40				09 38		
Clacton-on-Sea	a						08 06							→		08 47					→		
Kirby Cross	d					07 47											08 45						
Frinton-on-Sea	d					07 50											08 48						
Walton-on-the-Naze	a					07 54											08 52						
Manningtree	d		07 18	07 24	07 31			07 51			07 59				08 16			08 31				08 55	09 00
Mistley	d			07 28				07 55															09 04
Wrabness	d			07 33				08 01															09 09
Harwich International	d			07 41				08 10					07 50										09 17
Dovercourt	d			07 44				08 13															09 20
Harwich Town	a			07 46				08 15															09 22
Ipswich	a		07 30		07 42						08 11		08 17		08 29			08 43				09 07	
	d				07 44					08 03	08 12		08 19					08 44				09 08	
Needham Market	d												08 28										
Stowmarket	d				07 55					08 15	08 23		08a33					08 55					
Peterborough	a									09 39													
Diss	d				08 08						08 36							09 08				09 29	
Norwich	a				08 27						08 55							09 27				09 48	

		LE ■	LE ■	LE ■	LE ■	LE ■	LE ■	LE ◇■	LE ■	LE ■	LE ■	LE ◇■	LE ■	LE ■	LE ■	LE ■	LE ■	LE ■	LE ■	LE ◇■	LE ■	LE ■
London Liverpool Street ⊖	d		08 00	08 06		08 17		08 30	08 36	08 48		09 00				09 02	09 18			09 30	09 38	09 48
Stratford ⊖	d		08 08	08 14		08 25		08u38	08 45	08 55						09 09	09 25			09u38	09 45	09 55
Romford	d																				09 53	
Shenfield	d		08 25	08 30		08 41			09 03	09 11						09 25	09 41				10 03	10 11
Ingatestone	d			08 34		08 45				09 15							09 45					10 15
Chelmsford	d		08 34	08 41		08 52		09 03	09 12	09 22						09 34	09 52			10 03	10 12	10 22
Hatfield Peverel	d			08 47												09 40						
Witham	d		08 45	08 54		09 03			09 23	09 35						09 47	10 03				10 23	10 34
White Notley	d									09 42												10 41
Cressing	d									09 44												10 43
Braintree Freeport	d									09 47												10 46
Braintree	a									09 51												10 50
Kelvedon	d		08 49						09 27							09 51					10 27	
Marks Tey	d		08 55			09 10			09 33							09 57					10 33	
Colchester	a		09 02	09 06		09 17		09 22	09 40			09 46				10 04	10 15			10 22	10 40	
Colchester	d		09 02	09 06	09 14	09 18		09 23	09 41			09 47			09 56	10 04	10 16		10 20	10 23	10 41	
Colchester Town	a				09 21				09 49						10 03				10 27		10 49	
	d														10 07							
Hythe	d														10 11							
Wivenhoe	d					09 25									10 15		10 23					
Alresford (Essex)	d														10 19							
Great Bentley	d														10 23							
Weeley	d						←								10 26			←				
Thorpe-le-Soken	a					09 36	09 31								10 31		10 35	10 31				
	d					09 36	09 38								10 37		10 35	10 37				
Clacton-on-Sea	a					09 45									→		10 44					
Kirby Cross	d						09 43											10 42				
Frinton-on-Sea	d						09 46											10 45				
Walton-on-the-Naze	a						09 50											10 49				
Manningtree	d			09 14				09 31				09 55	10 00			10 12				10 31		
Mistley	d												10 04									
Wrabness	d												10 09									
Harwich International	d												10 17									
Dovercourt	d												10 20									
Harwich Town	a												10 22									
Ipswich	a		09 20	09 26				09 43				10 07				10 25				10 43		
	d	09 19						09 44			10 00	10 08		10 19						10 44		
Needham Market	d	09 28												10 28								
Stowmarket	d	09a33						09 55			10 12			10a33						10 55		
Peterborough	a										11 37											
Diss	d							10 08				10 29								11 08		
Norwich	a							10 27				10 50								11 27		

A To Cambridge

London - Chelmsford, Colchester, Walton-on-Naze, Clacton, Harwich, Ipswich and Norwich

Network Diagram - see first Page of Table 5

		LE ◇[1] ⊏	LE [1]	LE [1]	LE [1]	LE [1]	LE [1]	LE [1]	LE [1]	LE ◇[1] ⊏	LE [1]	LE [1]	LE [1]	LE ◇[1] ⊏	LE [1]	LE [1]	LE [1]	LE [1]	LE [1]	LE [1]	LE [1]	LE ◇[1] ⊏	LE [1]
London Liverpool Street [15] ⊖	d	10 00				10 02	10 18			10 30	10 38	10 48		11 00				11 02	11 18			11 30	11 38
Stratford [7] ⊖	d					10 09	10 25			10u38	10 45	10 55						11 09	11 25			11u38	11 45
Romford	d										10 53												11 53
Shenfield [3]	d					10 25	10 41				11 03	11 11						11 25	11 41				12 03
Ingatestone	d						10 45					11 15							11 45				
Chelmsford [3]	d					10 34	10 52			11 03	11 12	11 22						11 34	11 52			12 03	12 12
Hatfield Peverel	d					10 40												11 40					
Witham [2]	d					10 47	11 03				11 23	11 34						11 47	12 03				12 23
White Notley	d											11 41											
Cressing	d											11 43											
Braintree Freeport	d											11 46											
Braintree	a											11 50											
Kelvedon	d					10 51					11 27							11 51					12 27
Marks Tey [2]	d					10 57					11 33							11 57					12 33
Colchester [4]	a	10 46				11 04	11 15			11 22	11 40			11 46				12 04	12 15			12 22	12 40
Colchester [4]	d	10 47			10 56	11 04	11 16		11 20	11 23	11 41			11 47			11 56	12 04	12 16		12 20	12 23	12 41
Colchester Town	a				11 03				11 27		11 49						12 03				12 27		12 49
	d				11 07												12 07						
Hythe	d				11 11												12 11						
Wivenhoe [3]	d				11 15		11 23										12 15		12 23				
Alresford (Essex)	d				11 19												12 19						
Great Bentley	d				11 23												12 23						
Weeley	d				11 26			←									12 26			←			
Thorpe-le-Soken [1]	a				11 31		11 35	11 31									12 31		12 35	12 31			
	d				11 37		11 35	11 37									12 37		12 35	12 37			
Clacton-on-Sea	a				→		11 44										→		12 44				
Kirby Cross	d							11 42												12 42			
Frinton-on-Sea	d							11 45												12 45			
Walton-on-the-Naze	a							11 49												12 49			
Manningtree [2]	d	10 55	11 00			11 12				11 31				11 55	12 00			12 12				12 31	
Mistley	d		11 04												12 04								
Wrabness	d		11 09												12 09								
Harwich International	d		11 17												12 17								
Dovercourt	d		11 20												12 20								
Harwich Town	a		11 22												12 22								
Ipswich	a	11 07				11 25				11 43				12 07				12 25				12 43	
	d	11 08		11 19						11 44			12 00	12 08		12 19						12 44	
Needham Market	d			11 28												12 28							
Stowmarket	d			11a33						11 55			12 12			12a33						12 55	
Peterborough [8]	a												13 37										
Diss	d	11 29								12 08				12 29								13 08	
Norwich	a	11 50								12 27				12 50								13 27	

		LE [1]	LE ◇[1] ⊏	LE [1]	LE [1]	LE [1]	LE [1]	LE [1]	LE [1]	LE [1]	LE ◇[1] ⊏	LE [1]	LE [1]	LE [1]	LE ◇[1] ⊏	LE [1]	LE [1]	LE [1]	LE [1]	LE [1]	LE [1]	LE [1]	LE ◇[1] ⊏
London Liverpool Street [15] ⊖	d	11 48	12 00				12 02	12 18			12 30	12 38	12 48		13 00				13 02	13 18			13 30
Stratford [7] ⊖	d	11 55					12 09	12 25			12u38	12 45	12 55						13 09	13 25			13u38
Romford	d											12 53											
Shenfield [3]	d	12 11					12 25	12 41				13 03	13 11						13 25	13 41			
Ingatestone	d	12 15						12 45					13 15							13 45			
Chelmsford [3]	d	12 22					12 34	12 52			13 03	13 12	13 22						13 34	13 52			14 03
Hatfield Peverel	d						12 40												13 40				
Witham [2]	d	12 34					12 47	13 03				13 23	13 34						13 47	14 03			
White Notley	d	12 41											13 41										
Cressing	d	12 43											13 43										
Braintree Freeport	d	12 46											13 46										
Braintree	a	12 50											13 50										
Kelvedon	d						12 51					13 27							13 51				
Marks Tey [2]	d						12 57					13 33							13 57				
Colchester [4]	a		12 46				13 04	13 15			13 22	13 40			13 46				14 04	14 15			14 22
Colchester [4]	d		12 47			12 56	13 04	13 16		13 20	13 23	13 41			13 47			13 56	14 04	14 16		14 20	14 23
Colchester Town	a					13 03				13 27		13 49						14 03				14 27	
	d					13 07												14 07					
Hythe	d					13 11												14 11					
Wivenhoe [3]	d					13 15		13 23										14 15		14 23			
Alresford (Essex)	d					13 19												14 19					
Great Bentley	d					13 23												14 23					
Weeley	d					13 26			←									14 26			←		
Thorpe-le-Soken [1]	a					13 31		13 35	13 31									14 31		14 35	14 31		
	d					13 37		13 35	13 37									14 37		14 35	14 37		
Clacton-on-Sea	a					→		13 44										→		14 44			
Kirby Cross	d								13 42												14 42		
Frinton-on-Sea	d								13 45												14 45		
Walton-on-the-Naze	a								13 49												14 49		
Manningtree [2]	d		12 55	13 00			13 12				13 31				13 55	14 00			14 12				14 31
Mistley	d			13 04												14 04							
Wrabness	d			13 09												14 09							
Harwich International	d			13 17												14 17							
Dovercourt	d			13 20												14 20							
Harwich Town	a			13 22												14 22							
Ipswich	a		13 07				13 25				13 43				14 07				14 25				14 43
	d		13 08		13 19						13 44			14 00	14 08		14 19						14 44
Needham Market	d				13 28												14 28						
Stowmarket	d				13a33						13 55			14 12			14a33						14 55
Peterborough [8]	a													15 37									
Diss	d		13 29								14 08				14 29								15 08
Norwich	a		13 50								14 27				14 50								15 27

Table 11 — Mondays to Fridays until 26 July

London - Chelmsford, Colchester, Walton-on-Naze, Clacton, Harwich, Ipswich and Norwich

Network Diagram - see first Page of Table 5

		LE [1]	LE [1]	LE ◇[1] ⊏	LE [1]	LE [1]	LE [1]	LE [1]	LE [1]	LE [1]	LE [1]	LE ◇[1] ⊏	LE [1]	LE [1]	LE [1]	LE ◇[1] ⊏	LE [1]	LE [1]	LE [1]	LE [1]	LE [1]	LE [1]
London Liverpool Street [15] ⊖	d	13 38	13 48	14 00				14 02	14 18			14 30	14 38	14 48		15 00				15 02		15 18
Stratford [7] ⊖	d	13 45	13 55					14 09	14 25			14u38	14 45	14 55						15 09		15 25
Romford	d	13 53											14 53									
Shenfield [3]	d	14 03	14 11					14 25	14 41				15 03	15 11						15 25		15 41
Ingatestone	d		14 15						14 45					15 15								15 45
Chelmsford [3]	d	14 12	14 22					14 34	14 52			15 03	15 12	15 22						15 34		15 52
Hatfield Peverel	d							14 40												15 40		
Witham [2]	d	14 23	14 34					14 47	15 03				15 23	15 35						15 47		16 03
White Notley	d		14 41											15 42								
Cressing	d		14 43											15 44								
Braintree Freeport	d		14 46											15 47								
Braintree	a		14 50											15 51								
Kelvedon	d	14 27						14 51					15 27							15 51		
Marks Tey [2]	d	14 33						14 57					15 33							15 57		
Colchester [4]	a	14 40		14 46				15 04	15 15			15 22	15 40			15 46				16 04		16 15
Colchester [4]	d	14 41		14 47			14 56	15 04	15 16		15 20	15 23	15 41			15 47			15 56	16 04	16 14	16 16
Colchester Town	a	14 49					15 03				15 27		15 49						16 03			
	d						15 07												16 07			
Hythe	d						15 11												16 11			
Wivenhoe [3]	d						15 15		15 23										16 15			16 23
Alresford (Essex)	d						15 19												16 19			
Great Bentley	d						15 23												16 23			
Weeley	d						15 26			←									16 26			
Thorpe-le-Soken [1]	a						15 31		15 35	15 31									16 31			16 35
	d						15 37		15 35	15 37									16 37			16 35
Clacton-on-Sea	a						→		15 44										→			16 44
Kirby Cross	d									15 42												
Frinton-on-Sea	d									15 45												
Walton-on-the-Naze	a									15 49												
Manningtree [2]	d			14 55	15 00			15 12				15 31				15 55	16 00			16 12	16 23	
Mistley	d				15 04												16 04				16 27	
Wrabness	d				15 09												16 09				16 32	
Harwich International	d				15 17												16 17				16 41	
Dovercourt	d				15 20												16 20				16 44	
Harwich Town	a				15 22												16 22				16 46	
Ipswich	a			15 07				15 25				15 43				16 07				16 25		
	d			15 08		15 19						15 44			16 00	16 08		16 19				
Needham Market	d					15 28												16 28				
Stowmarket	d					15a33						15 55			16 12			16a33				
Peterborough [8]	a														17 37							
Diss	d			15 31								16 08				16 29						
Norwich	a			15 48								16 27				16 50						

		LE [1]	LE [1]	LE ■ [1] ⊏	LE [1]	LE [1]	LE [1]	LE ■ [1] ⊏	LE [1]	LE [1]	LE [1]	LE [1]	LE [1]	LE [1]	LE [1]	LE [1]	LE ■ [1] ⊏	LE [1]	LE [1]	LE [1]	LE [1]	LE [1]	LE [1]
London Liverpool Street [15] ⊖	d			15 30		15 38	15 48	16 00				16 02		16 14		16 17	16 30				16 32	16 34	
Stratford [7] ⊖	d					15 45	15 55					16 09		16 22		16 25						16 42	
Romford	d					15 53																	
Shenfield [3]	d					16 03	16 11					16 25		16 38		16 41					16 54	16 58	
Ingatestone	d				16 00		16 15									16 46							
Chelmsford [3]	d			16 00	16 07	16 12	16 22					16 34		16 48		16 53					17 04	17 08	
Hatfield Peverel	d				16 13							16 40										17 14	
Witham [2]	d				16 20	16 24	16 35					16 47				17a06					17 14	17 21	
White Notley	d						16 42															17 28	
Cressing	d						16 44															17 30	
Braintree Freeport	d						16 47															17 33	
Braintree	a						16 51															17 39	
Kelvedon	d				16 24	16 28						16 51		16 59									
Marks Tey [2]	d				16 30	16 34						16 57		17 05									
Colchester [4]	a			16 21	16 38	16 41		16 46				17 04		17 12			17 16				17 26		
Colchester [4]	d		16 20	16 21		16 42		16 47			16 56	17 04	17 09	17 16			17 17			17 24	17 27		
Colchester Town	a		16 27			16 50					17 03		17 16							17 33			
	d										17 07									17 37			
Hythe	d										17 11			17 20						17 41			
Wivenhoe [3]	d										17 15			17 24						17 45			
Alresford (Essex)	d										17 19									17 49			
Great Bentley	d										17 23									17 53			
Weeley	d	←									17 26				←					17 56			←
Thorpe-le-Soken [1]	a	16 31									17 31			17 35	17 31					18 01			18 01
	d	16 37									17 37			17 35	17 37					18 10			18 10
Clacton-on-Sea	a										→			17 46						→			
Kirby Cross	d	16 42													17 42								18 15
Frinton-on-Sea	d	16 45													17 45								18 18
Walton-on-the-Naze	a	16 49													17 49								18 22
Manningtree [2]	d			16 29				16 55	17 00			17 12						17 24			17 35		
Mistley	d								17 04									17 28					
Wrabness	d								17 09									17 33					
Harwich International	d								17 17									17 41					
Dovercourt	d								17 20									17 44					
Harwich Town	a								17 22									17 46					
Ipswich	a			16 40				17 07				17 27					17 34				17 49		
	d			16 41				17 08		17 19							17 36		17 49				
Needham Market	d									17 28									17 58				
Stowmarket	d			16 52				17 19		17a33							17 47		18 04				
Peterborough [8]	a																		19 38				
Diss	d			17 05				17 32									18 00						
Norwich	a			17 24				17 53									18 22						

London - Chelmsford, Colchester, Walton-on-Naze, Clacton, Harwich, Ipswich and Norwich

Network Diagram - see first Page of Table 5

		LE ■		LE ■	LE ■ ■ A ⊏	LE ■	LE ■	LE ◇■	LE ■	LE ■	LE ■	LE ■	LE ■ B	LE ■ ■ ⊏	LE ■	LE ■	LE ■	LE ■	LE ■	LE ■	LE ■ B	LE ■ ■ ⊏
London Liverpool Street 15 ⊖	d	16 44		16 47	17 00			17 02	17 08		17 12	17 18	17 20	17 30		17 32		17 38			17 40	17 50
Stratford 7 ⊖	d	16 52		16 55				17 10	17 16		17 20	17 26	17 29			17 40		17 47			17 49	
Romford	d																					
Shenfield 3	d			17 11				17u26					17 45								18 05	
Ingatestone	d			17 16									17 49								18 09	
Chelmsford 3	d	17 15		17 23				17 36	17 40		17 44	17 50	17 57			18 05		18 12			18 17	
Hatfield Peverel	d										17 50					18 11						
Witham 2	d			17a36				17 46	17 50		17a59		18 10			18 17					18 31	
White Notley	d												18 17									
Cressing	d												18 19									
Braintree Freeport	d												18 22									
Braintree	a												18 28									
Kelvedon	d	17 27							17 55			18 02						18 25			18 37	
Marks Tey 2	d	17 32						17 54	18 00							18 25						
Colchester 4	a	17 40						18 01	18 08			18 12				18 32		18 36			18 48	18 42
Colchester 4	d	17 44	17 47				17 56	18 01	18 12			18 12			18 16	18 32		18 36		18 40	18 49	18 43
Colchester Town	a						18 03								18 26						18 59	
	d						18 07															
Hythe	d						18 11		18 16											18 44		
Wivenhoe 3	d	17 51					18 15		18 20							18 40				18 48		
Alresford (Essex)	d	17 55					18 19		18 24											18 52		
Great Bentley	d	17 59					18 23		18 28											18 56		
Weeley	d						18 26			←										18 59		
Thorpe-le-Soken 1	a	18 06					18 31		18 35	18 31						18 51				19 04		
	d	18 06					18 37		18 35	18 37						18 51			18 53	19 04		
Clacton-on-Sea	a	18 17					→		18 46							19 02				19 13		
Kirby Cross	d									18 42									19 01			
Frinton-on-Sea	d									18 45									19 04			
Walton-on-the-Naze	a									18 49									19 08			
Manningtree 2	d		17 57					18 09				18 20		18 27			18 35	18 44				18 52
Mistley	d		18 01														18 39					
Wrabness	d		18 06														18 44					
Harwich International	d		18 15														18 52					
Dovercourt	d		18 18														18 55					
Harwich Town	a		18 22														18 57					
Ipswich	a				17 59			18 20				18 35		18 37				18 59				19 03
	d				18 00	18 16		18 24						18 39								19 04
Needham Market	d					18 25																
Stowmarket	d					18a30		18 35						18 50								19 16
Peterborough 8	a																					
Diss	d				18 21			18 47						19 03								19 29
Norwich	a				18 42			19 09						19 25								19 50

		LE ■	LE ■	LE ■	LE ■	LE ■	LE ■ ■ ⊏	LE ■	LE ■	LE ■	LE ■	LE ■	LE ■	LE ■ ■ ⊏	LE ■	LE ■	LE ■	LE ■	LE ■		LE ■	LE ■	LE ■
London Liverpool Street 15 ⊖	d	17 52			17 58	18 00	18 10		18 12		18 18		18 20	18 30					18 32		18 38	18 48	
Stratford 7 ⊖	d	18 01			18 06	18 09			18 21		18 27		18 29						18 40		18 46	18 56	
Romford	d																						
Shenfield 3	d					18 25							18 45								19 02		
Ingatestone	d					18 29							18 49								19 07		
Chelmsford 3	d	18 25				18 37			18 46		18 52		18 57						19 05		19 14	19 20	
Hatfield Peverel	d	18 31							18 52	←									19 11				
Witham 2	d	18 37			18 41	19c01			18 58	19 01			19 11						19 17		19 24	19 30	
White Notley	d					→				19 08													
Cressing	d									19 10													
Braintree Freeport	d									19 13													
Braintree	a									19 19													
Kelvedon	d				18 46						19 06		19 17						19 22				
Marks Tey 2	d	18 46							19 06				19 23								19 32		
Colchester 4	a	18 53			18 56		19 00		19 13		19 17		19 30	19 21					19 33		19 39	19 43	
Colchester 4	d	18 54			18 57		19 02	19 06	19 13		19 17	19 20	19 30	19 23					19 37	19 39	19 39	19 44	
Colchester Town	a							19 13				19 27				←				19 50			
	d							19 19															
Hythe	d	18 58						19 23	19 18							19 23						19 48	
Wivenhoe 3	d	19 02						→	19 22							19 27			19 44			19 52	
Alresford (Essex)	d															19 31			19 48				
Great Bentley	d															19 35			19 52				
Weeley	d															19 38			19 55				←
Thorpe-le-Soken 1	a	19 13							19 33							19 43			20 00			20 04	20 00
	d	19 13							19 33						19 35	19 43			20 08			20 04	20 08
Clacton-on-Sea	a	19 24							19 44							19 52			→			20 15	
Kirby Cross	d														19 40								20 13
Frinton-on-Sea	d														19 43								20 16
Walton-on-the-Naze	a														19 47								20 22
Manningtree 2	d		19 00		19 05		19 11				19 25		19 40	19 32			19 38				19 47		
Mistley	d		19 04														19 42						
Wrabness	d		19 09														19 47						
Harwich International	d		19 17										20a01				19 55						
Dovercourt	d		19 20														19 58						
Harwich Town	a		19 22														20 00						
Ipswich	a				19 19		19 21				19 39			19 42							20 04		
	d			19 10			19 23							19 44				20 00					
Needham Market	d			19 19																			
Stowmarket	d			19a24			19 34							19 55				20 12					
Peterborough 8	a																	21 39					
Diss	d						19 47							20 08									
Norwich	a						20 09							20 30									

A The East Anglian

B The Stratford call is subject to introduction during the currency of the timetable.

c arr 1854

London - Chelmsford, Colchester, Walton-on-Naze, Clacton, Harwich, Ipswich and Norwich

Network Diagram - see first Page of Table 5

		LE ■ ■ ⊏	LE ■	LE ■	LE ■	LE ■	LE ■	LE ■	LE ■	LE ■ ■ ⊏	LE ■	LE ■	LE ■	LE ■	LE ■	LE ◇■ ⊏	LE ■	LE ■	LE	LE ■	LE ■	LE ■	LE ■
London Liverpool Street 15 ⊖	d	19 00	19 02				19 08	19 18		19 30		19 32	19 38	19 48		20 00					20 02	20 18	
Stratford 7 ⊖	d		19 09				19 15	19 25				19 39	19 45	19 55							20 09	20 25	
Romford	d																						
Shenfield 3	d		19 25					19 41					20 01	20 11							20 25	20 41	
Ingatestone	d							19 45						20 15								20 45	
Chelmsford 3	d		19 34				19 38	19 52				20 02	20 10	20 22							20 34	20 52	
Hatfield Peverel	d		19 40										20 16								20 40		
Witham 2	d		19 49				19 50	20 03				20 13	20 23	20 34							20 47	21 03	
White Notley	d		19 56											20 41									
Cressing	d		19 58											20 43									
Braintree Freeport	d		20 01											20 46									
Braintree	a		20 05											20 50									
Kelvedon	d						19 55						20 27								20 51		
Marks Tey 2	d						20 00						20 33								20 57		
Colchester 4	a	19 47					20 07	20 15		20 19		20 25	20 40			20 46					21 04	21 15	
Colchester 4	d	19 47				19 56	20 08	20 16		20 20	20 20	20 25	20 41			20 47				20 56	21 04	21 16	
Colchester Town	a					20 03					20 27		20 49							21 03			
	d					20 07														21 07			
Hythe	d					20 11														21 11			
Wivenhoe 3	d					20 15		20 23												21 15		21 23	
Alresford (Essex)	d					20 19														21 19			
Great Bentley	d					20 23														21 23			
Weeley	d					20 26			←											21 26			←
Thorpe-le-Soken 1	a					20 31		20 35	20 31											21 31		21 35	21 31
	d					20 37		20 35	20 37								20 54			21 37		21 35	21 37
Clacton-on-Sea	a					→		20 44									21 03			→		21 44	
Kirby Cross	d								20 42														21 42
Frinton-on-Sea	d								20 45														21 45
Walton-on-the-Naze	a								20 49														21 49
Manningtree 2	d	19 55		20 00			20 16			20 28		20 34			20 38	20 55		21 00			21 12		
Mistley	d			20 04											20 42			21 04					
Wrabness	d			20 09											20 47			21 09					
Harwich International	d			20 17								20a54			20 55			21 17					
Dovercourt	d			20 20											20 58			21 20					
Harwich Town	a			20 22											21 00			21 22					
Ipswich	a	20 07					20 28			20 40						21 07					21 25		
	d	20 08			20 19					20 41						21 08			21 16				
Needham Market	d				20 28														21 26				
Stowmarket	d	20 19			20a33					20 52						21 19			21a32				
Peterborough 8	a																						
Diss	d	20 32								21 05						21 32							
Norwich	a	20 51								21 24						21 51							

		LE ■	LE ◇■ ⊏	LE ■	LE ■	LE ■	LE ◇■ ⊏	LE ■	LE	LE ■	LE ■	LE ■	LE ■	LE ◇■ ⊏	LE ■	LE ■	LE ■	LE ■	LE ■	LE ■	LE ■	LE ■
London Liverpool Street 15 ⊖	d		20 30	20 38	20 48		21 00				21 02	21 18		21 30	21 38	21 48	22 00	22 02				22 18
Stratford 7 ⊖	d		20u38	20 45	20 55						21 09	21 25		21u38	21 45	21 55		22 09				22 25
Romford	d			20 53											21 53							
Shenfield 3	d			21 03	21 11						21 25	21 41			22 03	22 11		22 25				22 41
Ingatestone	d				21 15							21 45				22 15						22 45
Chelmsford 3	d		21 03	21 12	21 22						21 34	21 52		22 03	22 12	22 22	22 28	22 34				22 52
Hatfield Peverel	d										21 40							22 40				
Witham 2	d			21 23	21 34						21 47	22 03			22 23	22 34		22 47				23 03
White Notley	d				21 41											22 41						
Cressing	d				21 43											22 43						
Braintree Freeport	d				21 46											22 46						
Braintree	a				21 50											22 50						
Kelvedon	d			21 27							21 51				22 27			22 51				
Marks Tey 2	d			21 33							21 57				22 33			22 57				
Colchester 4	a		21 22	21 40			21 46				22 04	22 15		22 22	22 40		22 47	23 05				23 15
Colchester 4	d	21 20	21 23	21 41			21 47			21 56	22 04	22 16		22 23	22 41		22 47				22 56	23 16
Colchester Town	a	21 27		21 49						22 03					22 49						23 03	
	d									22 07											23 07	
Hythe	d									22 11											23 11	
Wivenhoe 3	d									22 15		22 23									23 15	23 23
Alresford (Essex)	d									22 19											23 19	
Great Bentley	d									22 23											23 23	
Weeley	d									22 26			←								23 26	
Thorpe-le-Soken 1	a									22 31		22 35	22 31								23 31	23 35
	d									22 37		22 35	22 37							23 16	23 37	23 35
Clacton-on-Sea	a									→		22 44								23 25	→	23 44
Kirby Cross	d												22 42									
Frinton-on-Sea	d												22 45									
Walton-on-the-Naze	a												22 49									
Manningtree 2	d		21 31				21 55	22 00			22 12			22 31			22 55		23 00			
Mistley	d							22 04											23 04			
Wrabness	d							22 09											23 09			
Harwich International	d					21 38		22 17			22a28								23 17			
Dovercourt	d							22 20											23 20			
Harwich Town	a							22 22											23 22			
Ipswich	a		21 43			22 03	22 07							22 43			23 08					
	d		21 44				22 08		22 16					22 44								
Needham Market	d								22 26													
Stowmarket	d		21 55				22 19		22a32					22 55								
Peterborough 8	a																					
Diss	d		22 08				22 32							23 08								
Norwich	a		22 27				22 51							23 27								

Table 11

Mondays to Fridays
until 26 July

London - Chelmsford, Colchester, Walton-on-Naze, Clacton, Harwich, Ipswich and Norwich

Network Diagram - see first Page of Table 5

		LE 1	LE ◇1 ☕	LE 1 A	LE 1 A	LE 1	LE	LE 1 MT WO B	LE 1 MT WO B	LE 1 A	LE 1 MT WO B	LE 1 A	LE ◇1 A ☕	LE ◇1 MT WO B ☕	LE 1 A	LE 1 MT WO B
London Liverpool Street ⊖	d		22 30	22 38				22 50		23 02	23 10	23 18	23 30	23 30	23 48	23 50
Stratford ⊖	d		22u38	22 45				22 57		23 09	23 17	23 25	23u38	23u39	23 55	23 57
Romford	d															
Shenfield	d			23 01				23 21		23 25	23 41	23 41		00 02	00 11	00 21
Ingatestone	d			23 05				23 25				23 45			00 15	00 25
Chelmsford	d		23 03	23 12				23 32		23 34	23 50	23 52	00 03	00 13	00 22	00 32
Hatfield Peverel	d									23 40	23 56				00 28	00 38
Witham	d			23 23	23 25			23 43	23 45	23 47	00 03	00 03		00 24	00 35	00 45
White Notley	d				23 32				23 52							
Cressing	d				23 34				23 54							
Braintree Freeport	d				23 37				23 57							
Braintree	a				23 41				00 01							
Kelvedon	d			23 27				23 47		23 51	00 07				00 39	00 49
Marks Tey	d			23 33			23 46	23 53		23 57	00 13				00 45	00 55
Colchester	a		23 22	23 45			23 55	00 05		00 04	00 20	00 15	00 22	00 36	00 57	01 07
Colchester	d		23 23							00 04	00 20	00 16	00 23	00 37		
Colchester Town	a															
	d															
Hythe	d															
Wivenhoe	d											00 23				
Alresford (Essex)	d											00 27				
Great Bentley	d											00 31				
Weeley	d	←														
Thorpe-le-Soken	a	23 31										00 38				
	d	23 37										00 38				
Clacton-on-Sea	a											00 51				
Kirby Cross	d	23 42														
Frinton-on-Sea	d	23 45														
Walton-on-the-Naze	a	23 49														
Manningtree	d		23 31			23 36				00 12	00 28		00 31	00 45		
Mistley	d					23 40										
Wrabness	d					23 45										
Harwich International	d					23 53										
Dovercourt	d					23 56										
Harwich Town	a					23 58										
Ipswich	a		23 43							00 28	00 44		00 43	00 57		
	d		23 44										00 44	00 58		
Needham Market	d															
Stowmarket	d		23 55										00 55	01 09		
Peterborough	a															
Diss	d		00 08										01 08	01 22		
Norwich	a		00 39										01 43	01 57		

A ThFO until 15 June, from 21 June until 26 July B until 20 June

Table 11

Mondays to Fridays
27 July to 10 August

London - Chelmsford, Colchester, Walton-on-Naze, Clacton, Harwich, Ipswich and Norwich

Network Diagram - see first Page of Table 5

		LE ◇1 A ☕	LE MX ◇1 B ☕	LE MO ◇1 ☕	LE MO 1	LE MX 1 B	LE MO ◇1 ☕	LE MX ◇1 B ☕	LE MO 1	LE 1 A	LE 1 C	LE MO 1	LE MX 1 B	LE MX 1 B	LE 1 A	LE MX 1 B	LE 1 A	LE ◇1 A ☕	LE MX ◇1 B ☕	LE 🚌 C	LE MO ◇1 ☕	LE 1 D	LE MX 1 B	LE 1 C	LE MO 1
London Liverpool Street ⊖	d	22p30	22p30	22p30	22p45	22p45	23p00	23p00		23p02	23p07	23p15		23p15	23p18			23p30	23p30		23p30			23p35	23p45
Stratford ⊖	d	22b38	22b40	22b40	22p54	22p54	23b10	23b10		23p09	23p17	23p25		23p25	23p25			23b38	23b40		23b40			23p45	23p54
Romford	d																								
Shenfield	d				23p11	23p12				23p25	23p34	23p41		23p43	23p41									00 01	00 11
Ingatestone	d				23p15	23p16						23p46		23p48	23p45									00 05	00 15
Chelmsford	d	23p03	23p05	23p06	23p22	23p23	23p36	23p37		23p34	23p43	23p53		23p55	23p52			00 03	00 06		00 06			00 12	00 22
Hatfield Peverel	d									23p40	23p49					←								00 18	
Witham	d				23p33	23p34				23p47	23p56	00 03		00 05	00 03	00 05						00 05	00 07	00 25	00 33
White Notley	d													→								00 12	00 14		
Cressing	d																					00 14	00 16		
Braintree Freeport	d																					00 17	00 19		
Braintree	a																					00 21	00 23		
Kelvedon	d									23p51	00 01													00 29	
Marks Tey	d									23p57	00 06													00 35	
Colchester	a	23p22	23p24	23p25	23p45	23p46	23p55	23p58		00 04	00 14	00 17			00 15	00 17		00 22	00 25		00 25			00 43	00 46
Colchester	d	23p23	23p25	23p25	23p46	23p47	23p55	23p59		00 04		00 18			00 16	00 18		00 23	00 25		00 25				00 47
Colchester Town	a																								
	d																								
Hythe	d																								
Wivenhoe	d				23p54	23p54						00 26			00 23	00 25				00 30					00 55
Alresford (Essex)	d														00 27					00 40					
Great Bentley	d														00 31					00 50					
Weeley	d																←								
Thorpe-le-Soken	a				00 05	00 06						00 37			00 38	00 37	00 38			01 00					01 06
	d				00 05	00 06						00 37			00 38	00 37	00 38			01 10					01 06
Clacton-on-Sea	a				00 14	00 15						00 46			→	00 46	00 51			→					01 15
Kirby Cross	d																								
Frinton-on-Sea	d																								
Walton-on-the-Naze	a																								
Manningtree	d	23p31	23p33	23p34			00 04	00 09	00 08	00 12			00 12					00 31	00 33		00 34				
Mistley	d								00 12				00 16												
Wrabness	d								00 17				00 21												
Harwich International	d								00 24				00 29												
Dovercourt	d								00 27				00 32												
Harwich Town	a								00 30				00 34												
Ipswich	a	23p43	23p45	23p45			00 15	00 19		00 28								00 43	00 45		00 45				
	d	23p44	23p46	23p47			00 17	00 21										00 44	00 46		00 47				
Needham Market	d																								
Stowmarket	d	23p55	23p58	23p58			00 28	00 32										00 55	00 58		00 58				
Peterborough	a																								
Diss	d	00 08	00 10	00 11			00 41	00 45										01 08	01 10		01 11				
Norwich	a	00 39	00 30	00 30			01 00	01 04										01 43	01 30		01 30				

A 27 July
B from 31 July until 10 August
C not 27 July
D 27 July, 30 July, 6 August
b Previous night, stops to pick up only

London - Chelmsford, Colchester, Walton-on-Naze, Clacton, Harwich, Ipswich and Norwich

Network Diagram - see first Page of Table 5

		LE	LE	LE	LE	LE	LE	LE	LE	LE	LE	LE	LE	LE	LE	LE	LE	LE	LE	LE	LE	LE	LE	LE
		bus	1	1	MO ◇1	◇1	1	1	◇1	1		1	◇1	1	1	1	1	1	1	1	1	1	1	1
		C	MX A	B		MX A	C	B	C	C														
London Liverpool Street ⊖	d		23p45	23p48	23p59	23p59	00 12	00 18	00 30	00 46											05 23			
Stratford ⊖	d		23p54	23p55	00u10	00u10	00 24	00 25	00u40	01 00											05 30			
Romford	d																				05 38			
Shenfield	d		00 12	00 11			00 41	00 47		01 17											05 48			
Ingatestone	d		00 16	00 15			00 45	00 51		01 22											05 52			
Chelmsford	d		00 23	00 22	00 36	00 37	00 52	00 58	01 07	01 29											05 59			
Hatfield Peverel	d			00 28			00 58	01 04		01 35											06 05			
Witham	d		00 34	00 35			01 05	01 11		01 41		05 21									06 12	06 16		
White Notley	d											05 28										06 23		
Cressing	d											05 30										06 25		
Braintree Freeport	d											05 33										06 28		
Braintree	a											05 37										06 32		
Kelvedon	d			00 39			01 09	01 15		01 46											06 16			
Marks Tey	d			00 45			01 15	01 21		01 51											06 22			
Colchester	a		00 46	00 57	00 55	00 56	01 23	01 41	01 29	02 00											06 29			
Colchester	d		00 47		00 56	00 57			01 30				05 40			06 10		06 15	06 25		06 30			
Colchester Town	a																		06 32					
	d																							
Hythe	d																							
Wivenhoe	d		00 54																		06 37			
Alresford (Essex)	d																							
Great Bentley	d																							
Weeley	d																							
Thorpe-le-Soken	a	←	01 06																		06 50			
	d	01 10	01 06												06 03					06 31	06 50			06 56
Clacton-on-Sea	a		01 15																		06 59			
Kirby Cross	d	01 17													06 12					06 39				07 06
Frinton-on-Sea	d	01 22													06 15					06 42				07 09
Walton-on-the-Naze	a	01 27													06 19					06 46				07 13
Manningtree	d				01 05	01 07			01 40				05 49	05 56		06 18		06 23						
Mistley	d													06 00		06 22								
Wrabness	d													06 05		06 27								
Harwich International	d													06 13		06 35								
Dovercourt	d													06 16		06 38								
Harwich Town	a													06 20		06 40								
Ipswich	a				01 15	01 17			01 50				05 59					06 34						
	d				01 17	01 19			01 52		05 10		06 00				06 16						06 39	
Needham Market	d										05 20						06 25							
Stowmarket	d				01 28	01 30			02 03		05a26		06 12				06a30						06 51	
Peterborough	a												07 38											
Diss	d				01 41	01 43			02 16														07 04	
Norwich	a				02 00	02 03			02 35														07 24	

A from 31 July until 10 August B 27 July C not 27 July

Table 11

Mondays to Fridays

27 July to 10 August

London - Chelmsford, Colchester, Walton-on-Naze, Clacton, Harwich, Ipswich and Norwich

Network Diagram - see first Page of Table 5

		LE	LE	LE	LE	LE	LE	LE	LE	LE	LE	LE	LE	LE	LE	LE	LE	LE	LE	LE	LE	LE
		1	◇1	1	1	1	1	◇1	1	1	1	1	1	◇1	1	1	1	1	1	1	◇1	1
London Liverpool Street ⊖	d		06 00	06 02	06 12			06 25			06 38	06 48		07 00	07 02			07 08	07 18		07 30	07 36
Stratford ⊖	d			06 09	06 19			06u33			06 45	06 55			07 09			07 15	07 25		07u38	07 45
Romford	d																					
Shenfield	d			06 25	06 36						07 01	07 11		07u22	07 25			07 31	07 41			08 01
Ingatestone	d				06 40							07 15							07 45			08 05
Chelmsford	d		06 30	06 34	06 47			06 58			07 10	07 22			07 34			07 40	07 52		08 03	08 12
Hatfield Peverel	d				06 53										07 40							
Witham	d			06 45	07 03			07 09			07 21	07 33			07 48			07 51	08 03			08 23
White Notley	d				07 10										07 55							
Cressing	d				07 12										07 57							
Braintree Freeport	d				07 15										08 00							
Braintree	a				07 19										08 04							
Kelvedon	d			06 49							07 25							07 55				08 27
Marks Tey	d			06 55							07 31	07 40						08 01	08 11			08 33
Colchester	a		06 49	07 02				07 22			07 38	07 47		07 50				08 08	08 18		08 22	08 40
Colchester	d		06 50	07 02		07 10		07 23		07 26	07 43	07 48		07 51			07 56	08 08	08 19		08 23	08 41
Colchester Town	a									07 34		07 56					08 03					08 49
	d									07 38							08 07					
Hythe	d			07 07						07 42							08 11		08 23			
Wivenhoe	d			07 11						07 46							08 15		08 27			
Alresford (Essex)	d			07 14													08 19					
Great Bentley	d			07 18													08 23					
Weeley	d			07 22													08 26			←		
Thorpe-le-Soken	a			07 28						07 57							08 31		08 38	08 31		
	d			07 28					07 38	07 57							08 40		08 38	08 40		
Clacton-on-Sea	a			07 37						08 06							→		08 47			
Kirby Cross	d								07 47											08 45		
Frinton-on-Sea	d								07 50											08 48		
Walton-on-the-Naze	a								07 54											08 52		
Manningtree	d		06 58			07 18	07 24	07 31			07 51			07 59				08 16			08 31	
Mistley	d						07 28				07 55					08 02						
Wrabness	d						07 33				08 01											
Harwich International	d						07 41				08 10											
Dovercourt	d						07 44				08 13											
Harwich Town	a						07 46				08 15											
Ipswich	a		07 10			07 30		07 42						08 11		08 17		08 29			08 43	
	d	06 56	07 11					07 44					08 03	08 12		08 19					08 44	
Needham Market	d	07 05														08 28						
Stowmarket	d	07a10	07 22					07 55					08 15	08 23		08a33					08 55	
Peterborough	a												09 39									
Diss	d		07 35					08 08						08 36							09 08	
Norwich	a		07 54					08 27						08 55							09 27	

		LE		LE	LE	LE	LE	LE	LE	LE	LE	LE	LE	LE	LE	LE	LE	LE	LE	LE	LE	LE	LE
		1		◇1	1	1	1	1		1	1	1		◇1	1	1		1	◇1	1	1	1	1
London Liverpool Street ⊖	d	07 46		07 55			08 00	08 06	08 17		08 17		08 27	08 30	08 36	08 48	08 55		09 00				09 02
Stratford ⊖	d	07 54					08 08	08 14	08a24		08 25		08a34	08u38	08 45	08 55	09a04						09 09
Romford	d																						
Shenfield	d	08 11					08 25	08 30			08 41				09 03	09 11							09 25
Ingatestone	d							08 34			08 45					09 15							
Chelmsford	d	08 20					08 34	08 41			08 52			09 03	09 12	09 22							09 34
Hatfield Peverel	d							08 47															09 40
Witham	d	08 35	08 38				08 45	08 54			09 03				09 23	09 35							09 47
White Notley	d	08 42														09 42							
Cressing	d	08 44														09 44							
Braintree Freeport	d	08 47														09 47							
Braintree	a	08 51														09 51							
Kelvedon	d						08 49								09 27								09 51
Marks Tey	d						08 55				09 10				09 33								09 57
Colchester	a		08 53	08 45			09 02	09 06			09 17			09 22	09 40				09 46				10 04
Colchester	d		08 56	08 47			09 02	09 06		09 14	09 18			09 23	09 41				09 47			09 56	10 04
Colchester Town	a		09 03							09 21					09 49							10 03	
	d		09 07																			10 07	
Hythe	d		09 11																			10 11	
Wivenhoe	d		09 15								09 25											10 15	
Alresford (Essex)	d		09 19																			10 19	
Great Bentley	d		09 23																			10 23	
Weeley	d		09 26									←										10 26	
Thorpe-le-Soken	a		09 31								09 36	09 31										10 31	
	d		09 38								09 36	09 38										10 37	
Clacton-on-Sea	a		→								09 45											→	
Kirby Cross	d											09 43											
Frinton-on-Sea	d											09 46											
Walton-on-the-Naze	a											09 50											
Manningtree	d			08 55	09 00			09 14						09 31					09 55	10 00			10 12
Mistley	d				09 04															10 04			
Wrabness	d				09 09															10 09			
Harwich International	d				09 17															10 17			
Dovercourt	d				09 20															10 20			
Harwich Town	a				09 22															10 22			
Ipswich	a			09 07			09 20	09 27						09 43					10 07				10 25
	d			09 08		09 19								09 44				10 00	10 08		10 19		
Needham Market	d					09 28															10 28		
Stowmarket	d					09a33								09 55				10 12			10a33		
Peterborough	a																	11 37					
Diss	d			09 29										10 08					10 29				
Norwich	a			09 48										10 27					10 50				

London - Chelmsford, Colchester, Walton-on-Naze, Clacton, Harwich, Ipswich and Norwich

Network Diagram - see first Page of Table 5

	LE 1	LE 1	LE 1	LE ◇1 ☕	LE 1	LE 1	LE ◇1 ☕	LE 1	LE 1	LE 1	LE 1	LE 1	LE 1	LE 1	LE ◇1 ☕	LE 1	LE 1	LE 1	LE ◇1 ☕	LE 1	LE 1
London Liverpool Street 15 ⊖ d	09 18			09 30	09 38	09 48	10 00				10 02	10 18			10 30	10 38	10 48		11 00		
Stratford 7 ⊖ d	09 25			09u38	09 45	09 55					10 09	10 25			10u38	10 45	10 55				
Romford d					09 53											10 53					
Shenfield 3 d	09 41				10 03	10 11					10 25	10 41				11 03	11 11				
Ingatestone d	09 45					10 15						10 45					11 15				
Chelmsford 3 d	09 52			10 03	10 12	10 22					10 34	10 52			11 03	11 12	11 22				
Hatfield Peverel d											10 40										
Witham 2 d	10 03				10 23	10 34					10 47	11 03				11 23	11 34				
White Notley d						10 41											11 41				
Cressing d						10 43											11 43				
Braintree Freeport d						10 46											11 46				
Braintree a						10 50											11 50				
Kelvedon d					10 27						10 51					11 27					
Marks Tey 2 d					10 33						10 57					11 33					
Colchester 4 a	10 15			10 22	10 40		10 46				11 04	11 15			11 22	11 40			11 46		
Colchester 4 d	10 16		10 20	10 23	10 41		10 47			10 56	11 04	11 16		11 20	11 23	11 41			11 47		
Colchester Town a			10 27		10 49					11 03				11 27		11 49					
d										11 07											
Hythe d										11 11											
Wivenhoe 3 d	10 23									11 15		11 23									
Alresford (Essex) d										11 19											
Great Bentley d										11 23											
Weeley d		←								11 26			←								
Thorpe-le-Soken 1 a	10 35	10 31								11 31		11 35	11 31								
d	10 35	10 37								11 37		11 35	11 37								
Clacton-on-Sea a	10 44									→		11 44									
Kirby Cross d		10 42											11 42								
Frinton-on-Sea d		10 45											11 45								
Walton-on-the-Naze a		10 49											11 49								
Manningtree 2 d				10 31			10 55	11 00			11 12				11 31				11 55	12 00	
Mistley d								11 04												12 04	
Wrabness d								11 09												12 09	
Harwich International d								11 17												12 17	
Dovercourt d								11 20												12 20	
Harwich Town a								11 22												12 22	
Ipswich a				10 43			11 07				11 25				11 43				12 07		
d				10 44			11 08		11 19						11 44			12 00	12 08		12 19
Needham Market d									11 28												12 28
Stowmarket d				10 55					11a33						11 55			12 12			12a33
Peterborough 8 a																		13 37			
Diss d				11 08			11 29								12 08				12 29		
Norwich a				11 27			11 50								12 27				12 50		

	LE 1	LE 1	LE 1	LE 1	LE 1	LE ◇1 ☕	LE 1	LE 1	LE ◇1 ☕	LE 1	LE 1	LE 1	LE 1	LE 1	LE 1	LE 1	LE ◇1 ☕	LE 1	LE 1	LE 1	LE ◇1 ☕	LE 1
London Liverpool Street 15 ⊖ d		11 02	11 18			11 30	11 38	11 48	12 00				12 02	12 18			12 30	12 38	12 48		13 00	
Stratford 7 ⊖ d		11 09	11 25			11u38	11 45	11 55					12 09	12 25			12u38	12 45	12 55			
Romford d							11 53											12 53				
Shenfield 3 d		11 25	11 41				12 03	12 11					12 25	12 41				13 03	13 11			
Ingatestone d			11 45					12 15						12 45					13 15			
Chelmsford 3 d		11 34	11 52			12 03	12 12	12 22					12 34	12 52			13 03	13 12	13 22			
Hatfield Peverel d		11 40											12 40									
Witham 2 d		11 47	12 03				12 23	12 34					12 47	13 03				13 23	13 34			
White Notley d								12 41											13 41			
Cressing d								12 43											13 43			
Braintree Freeport d								12 46											13 46			
Braintree a								12 50											13 50			
Kelvedon d		11 51					12 27						12 51					13 27				
Marks Tey 2 d		11 57					12 33						12 57					13 33				
Colchester 4 a		12 04	12 15			12 22	12 40		12 46				13 04	13 15			13 22	13 40			13 46	
Colchester 4 d	11 56	12 04	12 16		12 20	12 23	12 41		12 47			12 56	13 04	13 16		13 20	13 23	13 41			13 47	
Colchester Town a	12 03				12 27		12 49					13 03				13 27		13 49				
d	12 07											13 07										
Hythe d	12 11											13 11										
Wivenhoe 3 d	12 15		12 23									13 15		13 23								
Alresford (Essex) d	12 19											13 19										
Great Bentley d	12 23											13 23										
Weeley d	12 26			←								13 26			←							
Thorpe-le-Soken 1 a	12 31		12 35	12 31								13 31		13 35	13 31							
d	12 37		12 35	12 37								13 37		13 35	13 37							
Clacton-on-Sea a	→		12 44									→		13 44								
Kirby Cross d				12 42											13 42							
Frinton-on-Sea d				12 45											13 45							
Walton-on-the-Naze a				12 49											13 49							
Manningtree 2 d		12 12				12 31			12 55	13 00			13 12				13 31				13 55	14 00
Mistley d										13 04												14 04
Wrabness d										13 09												14 09
Harwich International d										13 17												14 17
Dovercourt d										13 20												14 20
Harwich Town a										13 22												14 22
Ipswich a		12 25				12 43			13 07				13 25				13 43				14 07	
d						12 44			13 08		13 19						13 44			14 00	14 08	
Needham Market d											13 28											
Stowmarket d						12 55					13a33						13 55			14 12		
Peterborough 8 a																				15 37		
Diss d						13 08			13 29								14 08				14 29	
Norwich a						13 27			13 50								14 27				14 50	

London - Chelmsford, Colchester, Walton-on-Naze, Clacton, Harwich, Ipswich and Norwich

Network Diagram - see first Page of Table 5

	LE 1	LE 1	LE 1	LE 1	LE 1	LE 1	LE ◇1 ☕	LE 1	LE 1	LE ◇1 ☕	LE 1	LE 1	LE 1	LE 1	LE 1	LE 1	LE 1	LE ◇1 ☕	LE 1	LE 1	LE 1	LE ◇1 ☕
London Liverpool Street 15 ⊖ d			13 02	13 18			13 30	13 38	13 48	14 00				14 02	14 18			14 30	14 38	14 48		15 00
Stratford 7 ⊖ d			13 09	13 25			13u38	13 45	13 55					14 09	14 25			14u38	14 45	14 55		
Romford d								13 53											14 53			
Shenfield 3 d			13 25	13 41				14 03	14 11					14 25	14 41				15 03	15 11		
Ingatestone d				13 45					14 15						14 45					15 15		
Chelmsford 3 d			13 34	13 52			14 03	14 12	14 22					14 34	14 52			15 03	15 12	15 22		
Hatfield Peverel d			13 40											14 40								
Witham 2 d			13 47	14 03				14 23	14 34					14 47	15 03				15 23	15 35		
White Notley d									14 41											15 42		
Cressing d									14 43											15 44		
Braintree Freeport d									14 46											15 47		
Braintree a									14 50											15 51		
Kelvedon d			13 51					14 27						14 51					15 27			
Marks Tey 2 d			13 57					14 33						14 57					15 33			
Colchester 4 a			14 04	14 15			14 22	14 40		14 46				15 04	15 15			15 22	15 40			15 46
Colchester 4 d		13 56	14 04	14 16		14 20	14 23	14 41		14 47			14 56	15 04	15 16		15 20	15 23	15 41			15 47
Colchester Town a		14 03				14 27		14 49					15 03				15 27		15 49			
d		14 07											15 07									
Hythe d		14 11											15 11									
Wivenhoe 3 d		14 15		14 23									15 15		15 23							
Alresford (Essex) d		14 19											15 19									
Great Bentley d		14 23											15 23									
Weeley d		14 26			←								15 26			←						
Thorpe-le-Soken 1 a		14 31		14 35	14 31								15 31		15 35	15 31						
d		14 37		14 35	14 37								15 37		15 35	15 37						
Clacton-on-Sea a		→		14 44									→		15 44							
Kirby Cross d					14 42											15 42						
Frinton-on-Sea d					14 45											15 45						
Walton-on-the-Naze a					14 49											15 49						
Manningtree 2 d			14 12				14 31			14 55	15 00			15 12				15 31				15 55
Mistley d											15 04											
Wrabness d											15 09											
Harwich International d											15 17											
Dovercourt d											15 20											
Harwich Town a											15 22											
Ipswich a			14 25				14 43			15 07				15 25				15 43				16 07
d	14 19						14 44			15 08		15 19						15 44			16 00	16 08
Needham Market d	14 28											15 28										
Stowmarket d	14a33						14 55					15a33						15 55			16 12	
Peterborough 8 a																					17 37	
Diss d							15 08			15 29								16 08				16 29
Norwich a							15 27			15 48								16 27				16 50

	LE 1	LE 1	LE 1	LE 1	LE 1	LE 1	LE 1	LE 1	LE ■ 1 ☕	LE 1	LE 1	LE 1	LE ■ 1 ☕	LE 1	LE 1	LE 1	LE 1	LE 1	LE 1	LE 1	LE 1
London Liverpool Street 15 ⊖ d				15 02		15 18			15 30		15 38	15 48	16 00				16 02		16 14		16 17
Stratford 7 ⊖ d				15 09		15 25					15 45	15 55					16 09		16 22		16 25
Romford d											15 53										
Shenfield 3 d				15 25		15 41					16 03	16 11					16 25		16 38		16 41
Ingatestone d						15 45				16 00		16 15									16 46
Chelmsford 3 d				15 34		15 52			16 00	16 07	16 12	16 22					16 34		16 48		16 53
Hatfield Peverel d				15 40						16 13							16 40				
Witham 2 d				15 47		16 03				16 20	16 24	16 35					16 47				17a06
White Notley d												16 42									
Cressing d												16 44									
Braintree Freeport d												16 47									
Braintree a												16 51									
Kelvedon d				15 51						16 24	16 28						16 51		16 59		
Marks Tey 2 d				15 57						16 30	16 34						16 57		17 05		
Colchester 4 a				16 04		16 15			16 21	16 38	16 41		16 46				17 04		17 12		
Colchester 4 d			15 56	16 04	16 14	16 16		16 20	16 21		16 42		16 47			16 56	17 04	17 09	17 16		
Colchester Town a			16 03					16 27			16 50					17 03		17 16			
d			16 07													17 07					
Hythe d			16 11													17 11			17 20		
Wivenhoe 3 d			16 15			16 23										17 15			17 24		
Alresford (Essex) d			16 19													17 19					
Great Bentley d			16 23													17 23					
Weeley d			16 26				←									17 26				←	
Thorpe-le-Soken 1 a			16 31			16 35	16 31									17 31			17 35	17 31	
d			16 37			16 35	16 37									17 37			17 35	17 37	
Clacton-on-Sea a			→			16 44										→			17 46		
Kirby Cross d							16 42													17 42	
Frinton-on-Sea d							16 45													17 45	
Walton-on-the-Naze a							16 49													17 49	
Manningtree 2 d	16 00			16 12	16 23				16 29				16 55	17 00			17 12				
Mistley d	16 04				16 27									17 04							
Wrabness d	16 09				16 32									17 09							
Harwich International d	16 17				16 41									17 17							
Dovercourt d	16 20				16 44									17 20							
Harwich Town a	16 22				16 46									17 22							
Ipswich a				16 25					16 40				17 07				17 27				
d		16 19							16 41				17 08		17 19						
Needham Market d		16 28													17 28						
Stowmarket d		16a33							16 52				17 19		17a33						
Peterborough 8 a																					
Diss d									17 05				17 32								
Norwich a									17 24				17 53								

Table 11

Mondays to Fridays
27 July to 10 August

London - Chelmsford, Colchester, Walton-on-Naze, Clacton, Harwich, Ipswich and Norwich

Network Diagram - see first Page of Table 5

	LE	LE	LE	LE	LE	LE	LE	LE		LE	LE	LE	LE	LE	LE	LE	LE	LE	LE	LE	LE	LE
											B			◇					A			
London Liverpool Street ⊖ d	16 30				16 32	16 34		16 44		16 47	17 00			17 02	17 08		17 12	17 18	17 20	17 30		17 32
Stratford ⊖ d						16 42		16 52		16 55				17 10	17 16		17 20	17 26	17 29			17 40
Romford d																						
Shenfield d					16 54	16 58				17 11				17u26					17 45			
Ingatestone d										17 16									17 49			
Chelmsford d					17 04	17 08		17 15		17 23				17 36	17 40		17 44	17 50	17 57			18 05
Hatfield Peverel d						17 14											17 50					18 11
Witham d					17 14	17 21				17a36				17 46	17 50		17a59		18 10			18 17
White Notley d						17 28													18 17			
Cressing d						17 30													18 19			
Braintree Freeport d						17 33													18 22			
Braintree a						17 39													18 28			
Kelvedon d								17 27							17 55			18 02				
Marks Tey d								17 32						17 54	18 00							18 25
Colchester a	17 16				17 26			17 40						18 01	18 08			18 12				18 32
Colchester d	17 17			17 24	17 27			17 44	17 47				17 56	18 01	18 12			18 12			18 16	18 32
Colchester Town a				17 33									18 03								18 26	
Colchester Town d				17 37									18 07									
Hythe d				17 41									18 11		18 16							
Wivenhoe d				17 45				17 51					18 15		18 20							18 40
Alresford (Essex) d				17 49				17 55					18 19		18 24							
Great Bentley d				17 53				17 59					18 23		18 28							
Weeley d				17 56			←						18 26			←						
Thorpe-le-Soken a				18 01			18 01	18 06					18 31		18 35	18 31						18 51
Thorpe-le-Soken d				18 10			18 10	18 06					18 37		18 35	18 37						18 51
Clacton-on-Sea a				→				18 17					→		18 46							19 02
Kirby Cross d							18 15									18 42						
Frinton-on-Sea d							18 18									18 45						
Walton-on-the-Naze a							18 22									18 49						
Manningtree d		17 24			17 35				17 57					18 09				18 20		18 27		
Mistley d		17 28							18 01													
Wrabness d		17 33							18 06													
Harwich International d		17 41							18 15													
Dovercourt d		17 44							18 18													
Harwich Town a		17 46							18 22													
Ipswich a	17 34				17 49						17 59			18 20				18 35		18 37		
Ipswich d	17 36		17 49								18 00	18 16		18 24						18 39		
Needham Market d			17 58									18 25										
Stowmarket d	17 47		18 04									18a30		18 35						18 50		
Peterborough a			19 38																			
Diss d	18 00										18 21			18 47						19 03		
Norwich a	18 22										18 42			19 09						19 25		

	LE	LE	LE	LE	LE	LE	LE	LE	LE	LE	LE	LE	LE	LE	LE	LE	LE	LE	LE	LE	LE
					A																
London Liverpool Street ⊖ d		17 38			17 40	17 50	17 52			17 58	18 00	18 10		18 12		18 18		18 20	18 30		
Stratford ⊖ d		17 47			17 49		18 01			18 06	18 09			18 21		18 27		18 29			
Romford d																					
Shenfield d					18 05						18 25							18 45			
Ingatestone d					18 09						18 29							18 49			
Chelmsford d		18 12			18 17		18 25				18 37			18 46		18 52		18 57			
Hatfield Peverel d							18 31							18 52	←						
Witham d					18 31		18 37			18 41	19c01			18 58	19 01			19 11			
White Notley d											→				19 08						
Cressing d															19 10						
Braintree Freeport d															19 13						
Braintree a															19 19						
Kelvedon d		18 25			18 37					18 46						19 06		19 17			
Marks Tey d							18 46							19 06				19 23			
Colchester a		18 36			18 48	18 42	18 53			18 56		19 00		19 13		19 17		19 30	19 21		
Colchester d		18 36		18 40	18 49	18 43	18 54			18 57		19 02	19 06	19 13		19 17	19 20	19 30	19 23		
Colchester Town a					18 59								19 13				19 27				
Colchester Town d													19 19								←
Hythe d				18 44			18 58						19 23	19 18							19 23
Wivenhoe d				18 48			19 02						→	19 22							19 27
Alresford (Essex) d				18 52																	19 31
Great Bentley d				18 56																	19 35
Weeley d				18 59																	19 38
Thorpe-le-Soken a				19 04			19 13							19 33							19 43
Thorpe-le-Soken d			18 53	19 04			19 13							19 33						19 35	19 43
Clacton-on-Sea a				19 13			19 24							19 44							19 52
Kirby Cross d			19 01																	19 40	
Frinton-on-Sea d			19 04																	19 43	
Walton-on-the-Naze a			19 08																	19 47	
Manningtree d	18 35	18 44				18 52		19 00		19 05		19 11				19 25		19 40	19 32		
Mistley d	18 39							19 04													
Wrabness d	18 44							19 09													
Harwich International d	18 52							19 17										20a01			
Dovercourt d	18 55							19 20													
Harwich Town a	18 57							19 22													
Ipswich a		18 59				19 03				19 19		19 21				19 39			19 42		
Ipswich d						19 04			19 10			19 23							19 44		
Needham Market d									19 19												
Stowmarket d						19 16			19a24			19 34							19 55		
Peterborough a																					
Diss d						19 29						19 47							20 08		
Norwich a						19 50						20 09							20 30		

B The East Anglian

A The Stratford call is subject to introduction during the currency of the timetable.

c arr 1854

Table 11

Mondays to Fridays
27 July to 10 August

London - Chelmsford, Colchester, Walton-on-Naze, Clacton, Harwich, Ipswich and Norwich

Network Diagram - see first Page of Table 5

	LE	LE	LE		LE	LE	LE	LE	LE	LE	LE	LE	LE	LE	LE	LE	LE	LE	LE	LE	LE	LE
																						◇
London Liverpool Street ⊖ d			18 32		18 38	18 48		19 00	19 02				19 08	19 18		19 30		19 32	19 38	19 48		20 00
Stratford ⊖ d			18 40		18 46	18 56			19 09				19 15	19 25				19 39	19 45	19 55		
Romford d																						
Shenfield d					19 02				19 25					19 41					20 01	20 11		
Ingatestone d					19 07									19 45						20 15		
Chelmsford d			19 05		19 14	19 20			19 34				19 38	19 52				20 02	20 10	20 22		
Hatfield Peverel d			19 11						19 40										20 16			
Witham d			19 17		19 24	19 30			19 49				19 50	20 03				20 13	20 23	20 34		
White Notley d									19 56											20 41		
Cressing d									19 58											20 43		
Braintree Freeport d									20 01											20 46		
Braintree a									20 05											20 50		
Kelvedon d			19 22										19 55						20 27			
Marks Tey d					19 32								20 00						20 33			
Colchester a			19 33		19 39	19 43		19 47					20 07	20 15		20 19		20 25	20 40			20 46
Colchester d			19 37	19 39	19 39	19 44		19 47				19 56	20 08	20 16		20 20	20 20	20 25	20 41			20 47
Colchester Town a				19 50								20 03					20 27		20 49			
Colchester Town d												20 07										
Hythe d						19 48						20 11										
Wivenhoe d			19 44			19 52						20 15		20 23								
Alresford (Essex) d			19 48									20 19										
Great Bentley d			19 52									20 23										
Weeley d			19 55				←					20 26			←							
Thorpe-le-Soken a			20 00			20 04	20 00					20 31		20 35	20 31							
Thorpe-le-Soken d			20 08			20 04	20 08					20 37		20 35	20 37							
Clacton-on-Sea a			→			20 15						→		20 44								
Kirby Cross d							20 13								20 42							
Frinton-on-Sea d							20 16								20 45							
Walton-on-the-Naze a							20 22								20 49							
Manningtree d	19 38				19 47			19 55		20 00			20 16			20 28		20 34			20 38	20 55
Mistley d	19 42									20 04											20 42	
Wrabness d	19 47									20 09											20 47	
Harwich International d	19 55									20 17								20a54			20 55	
Dovercourt d	19 58									20 20											20 58	
Harwich Town a	20 00									20 22											21 00	
Ipswich a					20 04			20 07					20 28			20 40						21 07
Ipswich d		20 00						20 08			20 19					20 41						21 08
Needham Market d											20 28											
Stowmarket d		20 12						20 19			20a33					20 52						21 19
Peterborough a		21 39																				
Diss d								20 32								21 05						21 32
Norwich a								20 51								21 24						21 51

	LE	LE	LE	LE	LE	LE	LE	LE	LE	LE	LE	LE	LE	LE	LE	LE	LE	LE	LE	LE	LE	LE
									◇				◇							◇		
London Liverpool Street ⊖ d					20 02	20 18			20 30	20 38	20 48		21 00				21 02	21 18		21 30	21 38	21 48
Stratford ⊖ d					20 09	20 25			20u38	20 45	20 55						21 09	21 25		21u38	21 45	21 55
Romford d																						
Shenfield d					20 25	20 41				21 03	21 11						21 25	21 41			22 03	22 11
Ingatestone d						20 45					21 15							21 45				22 15
Chelmsford d					20 34	20 52			21 03	21 12	21 22						21 34	21 52		22 03	22 12	22 22
Hatfield Peverel d					20 40												21 40					
Witham d					20 47	21 03				21 23	21 34						21 47	22 03			22 23	22 34
White Notley d											21 41											22 41
Cressing d											21 43											22 43
Braintree Freeport d											21 46											22 46
Braintree a											21 50											22 50
Kelvedon d					20 51					21 27							21 51				22 27	
Marks Tey d					20 57					21 33							21 57				22 33	
Colchester a					21 04	21 15			21 22	21 40			21 46				22 04	22 15		22 22	22 40	
Colchester d				20 56	21 04	21 16		21 20	21 23	21 41			21 47			21 56	22 04	22 16		22 23	22 41	
Colchester Town a				21 03				21 27		21 49						22 03					22 49	
Colchester Town d				21 07												22 07						
Hythe d				21 11												22 11						
Wivenhoe d				21 15		21 23										22 15		22 23				
Alresford (Essex) d				21 19												22 19						
Great Bentley d				21 23												22 23						
Weeley d				21 26			←									22 26			←			
Thorpe-le-Soken a				21 31		21 35	21 31									22 31		22 35	22 31			
Thorpe-le-Soken d	20 54			21 37		21 35	21 37									22 37		22 35	22 37			
Clacton-on-Sea a	21 03			→		21 44										→		22 44				
Kirby Cross d							21 42												22 42			
Frinton-on-Sea d							21 45												22 45			
Walton-on-the-Naze a							21 49												22 49			
Manningtree d		21 00			21 12				21 31				21 55	22 00			22 12			22 31		
Mistley d		21 04												22 04								
Wrabness d		21 09												22 09								
Harwich International d		21 17										21 38		22 17			22a28					
Dovercourt d		21 20												22 20								
Harwich Town a		21 22												22 22								
Ipswich a					21 25				21 43			22 03	22 07							22 43		
Ipswich d			21 16						21 44				22 08		22 16					22 44		
Needham Market d			21 26												22 26							
Stowmarket d			21a32						21 55				22 19		22a32					22 55		
Peterborough a																						
Diss d									22 08				22 32							23 08		
Norwich a									22 27				22 51							23 27		

Table 11

Mondays to Fridays

27 July to 10 August

London - Chelmsford, Colchester, Walton-on-Naze, Clacton, Harwich, Ipswich and Norwich

Network Diagram - see first Page of Table 5

		LE 1	LE 1	LE 1	LE 1	LE 1	LE 1	LE 1	LE ◇1 ⊐	LE 1	LE 1	LE 1	LE ◇1 ⊐	LE	LE 1	LE 1	LE ◇1 ⊐	LE 1	LE 1	LE ◇1 ⊐ A
London Liverpool Street 15 ⊖	d	21 56				22 02	22 15		22 30	22 35		22 45	23 00		23 07	23 15	23 30	23 35	23 45	23 59
Stratford 7 ⊖	d	22 05				22 10	22 24		22u40	22 44		22 54	23u10		23 17	23 25	23u40	23 45	23 54	00u10
Romford	d																			
Shenfield 3	d					22 27	22 41			23 01		23 12			23 34	23 43		00 01	00 12	
Ingatestone	d						22 45			23 05		23 16				23 48		00 05	00 16	
Chelmsford 3	d	22 28				22 36	22 52		23 05	23 12		23 23	23 37		23 43	23 55	00 06	00 12	00 23	00 37
Hatfield Peverel	d					22 42									23 49			00 18		
Witham 2	d					22 49	23 03			23 23	23 25	23 34			23 56	00 05		00 25	00 34	
White Notley	d										23 32									
Cressing	d										23 34									
Braintree Freeport	d										23 37									
Braintree	a										23 41									
Kelvedon	d					22 53				23 27					00 01			00 29		
Marks Tey 2	d					22 59				23 33				23 46	00 06			00 35		
Colchester 4	a	22 47				23 06	23 15		23 24	23 41		23 46	23 58	23 55	00 14	00 17	00 25	00 43	00 46	00 56
Colchester 4	d	22 47			22 56	23 07	23 16		23 25			23 47	23 59			00 18	00 25		00 47	00 57
Colchester Town	a				23 03															
	d				23 07															
Hythe	d				23 11															
Wivenhoe 3	d				23 15		23 23					23 54				00 25			00 54	
Alresford (Essex)	d				23 19															
Great Bentley	d				23 23															
Weeley	d				23 26			←												
Thorpe-le-Soken 1	a				23 31		23 35	23 31				00 06				00 37			01 06	
	d			23 16	23 37		23 35	23 37				00 06				00 37			01 06	
Clacton-on-Sea	a			23 25	→		23 44					00 15				00 46			01 15	
Kirby Cross	d							23 42												
Frinton-on-Sea	d							23 45												
Walton-on-the-Naze	a							23 49												
Manningtree 2	d	22 56	23 00			23 15			23 33				00 09				00 33			01 07
Mistley	d		23 04																	
Wrabness	d		23 09																	
Harwich International	d	23a11	23 17																	
Dovercourt	d		23 20																	
Harwich Town	a		23 22																	
Ipswich	a					23 27			23 45				00 19				00 45			01 17
	d								23 46				00 21				00 46			01 19
Needham Market	d																			
Stowmarket	d								23 58				00 32				00 58			01 30
Peterborough 8	a																			
Diss	d								00 10				00 45				01 10			01 43
Norwich	a								00 30				01 04				01 30			02 03

A not 27 July

Table 11

Mondays to Fridays

13 August to 28 August

London - Chelmsford, Colchester, Walton-on-Naze, Clacton, Harwich, Ipswich and Norwich

Network Diagram - see first Page of Table 5

		LE MX ◇1 ⊐	LE ◇1 A ⊐	LE ◇1 B ⊐	LE 1 A	LE 1 B	LE ◇1 B ⊐	LE 1 B	LE MX 1	LE 1 A	LE 1 B	LE 1 B	LE MX 1	LE MX ◇1 ⊐	LE ◇1 B ⊐	LE ═ B	LE ◇1 A	LE 1 C	LE 1 A	LE 1 B	LE 1 B	LE MX 1	LE ═ B	LE ◇1 B ⊐	LE 1 A
London Liverpool Street 15 ⊖	d	22p30	22p30	22p30	22p32	22p45	23p00		23p02	23p02	23p07	23p15	23p18	23p30	23p30		23p30		23p32	23p35	23p45	23p48		23p59	00 02
Stratford 7 ⊖	d	22b38		22b40	22p39	22p54	23b10		23p09	23p09	23p17	23p25	23p25	23b38	23b40				23p39	23p45	23p54	23p55		00u10	00 09
Romford	d																								
Shenfield 3	d				23p01	23p11			23p25	23p31	23p34	23p41	23p41						00 01	00 01	00 11	00 11			00 31
Ingatestone	d					23p15				23p35		23p46	23p45							00 05	00 15	00 15			00 35
Chelmsford 3	d	23p03		23p06	23p10	23p22	23p36		23p34	23p42	23p43	23p53	23p52	00 03	00 06				00 10	00 12	00 22	00 22		00 36	00 42
Hatfield Peverel	d								23p40	23p48	23p49									00 18		00 28			00 48
Witham 2	d				23p21	23p33			23p47	23p55	23p56	00 03	00 03					00 05	00 21	00 25	00 33	00 35			00 55
White Notley	d																	00 12							
Cressing	d																	00 14							
Braintree Freeport	d																	00 17							
Braintree	a																	00 21							
Kelvedon	d								23p51	23p59	00 01									00 29		00 39			00 59
Marks Tey 2	d				23p28				23p57	00 05	00 06								00 28	00 35		00 45			01 05
Colchester 4	a	23p22	23p23	23p25	23p36	23p45	23p55		00 04	00 12	00 14	00 17	00 15	00 22	00 25		00 27		00 39	00 43	00 46	00 57		00 55	01 18
Colchester 4	d	23p23	23p23	23p25	23p36	23p46	23p55		00 04	00 12		00 18	00 16	00 23	00 25		00 27				00 47			00 56	
Colchester Town	a																								
	d																								
Hythe	d																								
Wivenhoe 3	d				23p44	23p54						00 26	00 23			00 30					00 55				
Alresford (Essex)	d				23p47								00 27			00 40									
Great Bentley	d				23p51								00 31			00 50									
Weeley	d																								
Thorpe-le-Soken 1	a				23p58	00 05						00 37	00 38			01 00					01 06		←		
	d				23p58	00 05						00 37	00 38			01 10					01 06		01 10		
Clacton-on-Sea	a				00 07	00 14						00 46	00 51			→					01 15				
Kirby Cross	d																						01 17		
Frinton-on-Sea	d																						01 22		
Walton-on-the-Naze	a																						01 27		
Manningtree 2	d	23p31	23p31	23p34			00 04	00 08	00 12	00 20				00 31	00 34		00 35							01 05	
Mistley	d							00 12																	
Wrabness	d							00 17																	
Harwich International	d							00 24																	
Dovercourt	d							00 27																	
Harwich Town	a							00 30																	
Ipswich	a	23p43	23p43	23p45			00 15		00 28	00 36				00 43	00 45		00 47							01 15	
	d	23p44	23p44	23p47			00 17							00 44	00 47		00 48							01 17	
Needham Market	d																								
Stowmarket	d	23p55	23p55	23p58			00 28							00 55	00 58		00 59							01 28	
Peterborough 8	a																								
Diss	d	00 08	00 08	00 11			00 41							01 08	01 11		01 12							01 41	
Norwich	a	00 39	00 41	00 30			01 00							01 43	01 30		01 45							02 00	

		LE 1 B	LE MX 1	LE ◇1 B ⊐	LE 1 B	LE	LE 1	LE ◇1	LE 1	LE 1	LE 1	LE 1	LE 1	LE 1	LE 1	LE 1	LE 1	LE 1	LE 1	LE 1	LE ◇1	LE 1	LE 1
London Liverpool Street 15 ⊖	d	00 12	00 18	00 30	00 46											05 23					06 00	06 02	06 12
Stratford 7 ⊖	d	00 24	00 25	00u40	01 00											05 30						06 09	06 19
Romford	d															05 38							
Shenfield 3	d	00 41	00 47		01 17											05 48						06 25	06 36
Ingatestone	d	00 45	00 51		01 22											05 52							06 40
Chelmsford 3	d	00 52	00 58	01 07	01 29											05 59					06 30	06 34	06 47
Hatfield Peverel	d	00 58	01 04		01 35											06 05							06 53
Witham 2	d	01 05	01 11		01 41		05 21									06 12	06 16					06 45	07 03
White Notley	d						05 28										06 23						07 10
Cressing	d						05 30										06 25						07 12
Braintree Freeport	d						05 33										06 28						07 15
Braintree	a						05 37										06 32						07 19
Kelvedon	d	01 09	01 15		01 46											06 16						06 49	
Marks Tey 2	d	01 15	01 21		01 51											06 22						06 55	
Colchester 4	a	01 23	01 41	01 29	02 00											06 29					06 49	07 02	
Colchester 4	d			01 30				05 40			06 10		06 15	06 20		06 30					06 50	07 02	
Colchester Town	a													06 27									
	d																						
Hythe	d																					07 07	
Wivenhoe 3	d															06 37						07 11	
Alresford (Essex)	d																					07 14	
Great Bentley	d																					07 18	
Weeley	d																					07 22	
Thorpe-le-Soken 1	a															06 50						07 28	
	d									06 03					06 31	06 50			06 56			07 28	
Clacton-on-Sea	a															06 59						07 37	
Kirby Cross	d									06 12					06 39				07 06				
Frinton-on-Sea	d									06 15					06 42				07 09				
Walton-on-the-Naze	a									06 19					06 46				07 13				
Manningtree 2	d			01 40				05 49	05 56		06 18		06 23								06 58		
Mistley	d								06 00		06 22												
Wrabness	d								06 05		06 27												
Harwich International	d								06 13		06 35												
Dovercourt	d								06 16		06 38												
Harwich Town	a								06 20		06 40												
Ipswich	a			01 50				05 59					06 34								07 10		
	d			01 52		05 10		06 00				06 16						06 39		06 56	07 11		
Needham Market	d					05 20						06 25								07 05			
Stowmarket	d			02 03		05a26		06 12				06a30						06 51		07a10	07 22		
Peterborough 8	a							07 38															
Diss	d			02 16														07 04			07 35		
Norwich	a			02 35														07 24			07 54		

A 20 August, 27 August
B 13 August
C not 20 August, 27 August
b Previous night, stops to pick up only

London - Chelmsford, Colchester, Walton-on-Naze, Clacton, Harwich, Ipswich and Norwich

Network Diagram - see first Page of Table 5

Station		LE 1		LE 1	LE ◇1	LE 1	LE 1	LE 1	LE 1	LE 1	LE ◇1	LE 1		LE 1	LE 1	LE 1	LE 1	LE 1	LE ◇1 ☕	LE 1	LE 1			LE ◇1 ☕	LE 1
London Liverpool Street 15 ⊖	d				06 25			06 38	06 48		07 00	07 02				07 08	07 18		07 30	07 36	07 46			07 55	
Stratford 7 ⊖	d				06u33			06 45	06 55			07 09				07 15	07 25		07u38	07 45	07 54				
Romford	d																								
Shenfield 3	d							07 01	07 11		07u22	07 25				07 31	07 41			08 01	08 11				
Ingatestone	d								07 15								07 45			08 05					
Chelmsford 3	d				06 58			07 10	07 22			07 34				07 40	07 52		08 03	08 12	08 20				
Hatfield Peverel	d											07 40													
Witham 2	d				07 09			07 21	07 33			07 48				07 51	08 03			08 23	08 35	08 38			
White Notley	d											07 55									08 42				
Cressing	d											07 57									08 44				
Braintree Freeport	d											08 00									08 47				
Braintree	a											08 04									08 51				
Kelvedon	d							07 25								07 55				08 27					
Marks Tey 2	d							07 31	07 40							08 01	08 11			08 33					
Colchester 4	a				07 22			07 38	07 47		07 50					08 08	08 18		08 22	08 40		08 53		08 45	
Colchester 4	d	07 10			07 23		07 26	07 43	07 48		07 51				07 56	08 08	08 19		08 23	08 41		08 56		08 47	
Colchester Town	a						07 34		07 56						08 03					08 49		09 03			
	d						07 38								08 07							09 07			
Hythe	d						07 42								08 11		08 23					09 11			
Wivenhoe 3	d						07 46								08 15		08 27					09 15			
Alresford (Essex)	d														08 19							09 19			
Great Bentley	d														08 23							09 23			
Weeley	d														08 26							09 26			
Thorpe-le-Soken 1	a						07 57								08 31		08 38	← 08 31				09 31			
	d					07 38	07 57								08 40		08 38	08 40				09 38			
Clacton-on-Sea	a						08 06								→		08 47					→			
Kirby Cross	d					07 47												08 45							
Frinton-on-Sea	d					07 50												08 48							
Walton-on-the-Naze	a					07 54												08 52							
Manningtree 2	d	07 18		07 24	07 31			07 51			07 59					08 16			08 31					08 55	09 00
Mistley	d			07 28				07 55						08 02											09 04
Wrabness	d			07 33				08 01																	09 09
Harwich International	d			07 41				08 10																	09 17
Dovercourt	d			07 44				08 13																	09 20
Harwich Town	a			07 46				08 15																	09 22
Ipswich	a	07 30			07 42						08 11			08 17		08 29			08 43					09 07	
	d				07 44					08 03	08 12			08 19					08 44					09 08	
Needham Market	d													08 28											
Stowmarket	d				07 55					08 15	08 23			08a33					08 55						
Peterborough 8	a									09 39															
Diss	d				08 08						08 36								09 08					09 29	
Norwich	a				08 27						08 55								09 27					09 48	

Station		LE 1	LE 1	LE 1	LE 1	LE 1	LE 1	LE ◇1 ☕		LE 1	LE 1	LE 1	LE ◇1 ☕	LE 1	LE 1	LE 1	LE 1	LE 1		LE 1	LE 1	LE ◇1 ☕	LE 1	LE 1	LE ◇1 ☕
London Liverpool Street 15 ⊖	d		08 00	08 06		08 17		08 30		08 36	08 48		09 00				09 02	09 18				09 30	09 38	09 48	10 00
Stratford 7 ⊖	d		08 08	08 14		08 25		08u38		08 45	08 55						09 09	09 25				09u38	09 45	09 55	
Romford	d																						09 53		
Shenfield 3	d		08 25	08 30		08 41				09 03	09 11						09 25	09 41					10 03	10 11	
Ingatestone	d			08 34		08 45					09 15							09 45						10 15	
Chelmsford 3	d		08 34	08 41		08 52		09 03		09 12	09 22						09 34	09 52				10 03	10 12	10 22	
Hatfield Peverel	d			08 47													09 40								
Witham 2	d		08 45	08 54		09 03				09 23	09 35						09 47	10 03					10 23	10 34	
White Notley	d										09 42													10 41	
Cressing	d										09 44													10 43	
Braintree Freeport	d										09 47													10 46	
Braintree	a										09 51													10 50	
Kelvedon	d		08 49							09 27							09 51						10 27		
Marks Tey 2	d		08 55			09 10				09 33							09 57						10 33		
Colchester 4	a		09 02	09 06		09 17		09 22		09 40			09 46				10 04	10 15				10 22	10 40		10 46
Colchester 4	d		09 02	09 06	09 14	09 18		09 23		09 41			09 47			09 56	10 04	10 16			10 20	10 23	10 41		10 47
Colchester Town	a				09 21					09 49						10 03					10 27		10 49		
	d															10 07									
Hythe	d															10 11									
Wivenhoe 3	d					09 25										10 15		10 23							
Alresford (Essex)	d															10 19									
Great Bentley	d															10 23									
Weeley	d															10 26									
Thorpe-le-Soken 1	a					09 36	← 09 31									10 31		10 35		← 10 31					
	d					09 36	09 38									10 37		10 35		10 37					
Clacton-on-Sea	a					09 45										→		10 44							
Kirby Cross	d						09 43													10 42					
Frinton-on-Sea	d						09 46													10 45					
Walton-on-the-Naze	a						09 50													10 49					
Manningtree 2	d			09 14				09 31					09 55	10 00			10 12					10 31			10 55
Mistley	d													10 04											
Wrabness	d													10 09											
Harwich International	d													10 17											
Dovercourt	d													10 20											
Harwich Town	a													10 22											
Ipswich	a		09 20	09 27				09 43					10 07				10 25					10 43			11 07
	d	09 19						09 44				10 00	10 08		10 19							10 44			11 08
Needham Market	d	09 28													10 28										
Stowmarket	d	09a33						09 55				10 12			10a33							10 55			
Peterborough 8	a											11 37													
Diss	d							10 08					10 29									11 08			11 29
Norwich	a							10 27					10 50									11 27			11 50

London - Chelmsford, Colchester, Walton-on-Naze, Clacton, Harwich, Ipswich and Norwich

Network Diagram - see first Page of Table 5

Station		LE 1	LE 1	LE 1		LE 1	LE 1	LE 1	LE 1	LE ◇1 ☕	LE 1	LE 1	LE 1	LE ◇1 ☕		LE 1	LE 1	LE 1	LE 1	LE 1	LE 1	LE 1	LE ◇1 ☕	LE 1	
London Liverpool Street 15 ⊖	d					10 02	10 18			10 30	10 38	10 48		11 00					11 02	11 18			11 30	11 38	
Stratford 7 ⊖	d					10 09	10 25			10u38	10 45	10 55							11 09	11 25			11u38	11 45	
Romford	d										10 53													11 53	
Shenfield 3	d					10 25	10 41				11 03	11 11							11 25	11 41				12 03	
Ingatestone	d						10 45					11 15								11 45					
Chelmsford 3	d					10 34	10 52			11 03	11 12	11 22							11 34	11 52			12 03	12 12	
Hatfield Peverel	d					10 40													11 40						
Witham 2	d					10 47	11 03				11 23	11 34							11 47	12 03				12 23	
White Notley	d											11 41													
Cressing	d											11 43													
Braintree Freeport	d											11 46													
Braintree	a											11 50													
Kelvedon	d					10 51					11 27								11 51					12 27	
Marks Tey 2	d					10 57					11 33								11 57					12 33	
Colchester 4	a					11 04	11 15			11 22	11 40			11 46					12 04	12 15			12 22	12 40	
Colchester 4	d			10 56		11 04	11 16		11 20	11 23	11 41			11 47				11 56	12 04	12 16		12 20	12 23	12 41	
Colchester Town	a			11 03					11 27		11 49							12 03				12 27		12 49	
	d			11 07														12 07							
Hythe	d			11 11														12 11							
Wivenhoe 3	d			11 15			11 23											12 15		12 23					
Alresford (Essex)	d			11 19														12 19							
Great Bentley	d			11 23														12 23							
Weeley	d			11 26														12 26							
Thorpe-le-Soken 1	a			11 31			11 35	← 11 31										12 31		12 35	← 12 31				
	d			11 37			11 35	11 37										12 37		12 35	12 37				
Clacton-on-Sea	a			→			11 44											→		12 44					
Kirby Cross	d							11 42													12 42				
Frinton-on-Sea	d							11 45													12 45				
Walton-on-the-Naze	a							11 49													12 49				
Manningtree 2	d	11 00				11 12				11 31				11 55		12 00			12 12				12 31		
Mistley	d	11 04														12 04									
Wrabness	d	11 09														12 09									
Harwich International	d	11 17														12 17									
Dovercourt	d	11 20														12 20									
Harwich Town	a	11 22														12 22									
Ipswich	a					11 25				11 43				12 07					12 25				12 43		
	d		11 19							11 44			12 00	12 08			12 19						12 44		
Needham Market	d		11 28														12 28								
Stowmarket	d		11a33							11 55			12 12				12a33						12 55		
Peterborough 8	a												13 37												
Diss	d									12 08				12 29									13 08		
Norwich	a									12 27				12 50									13 27		

Station		LE 1	LE ◇1 ☕	LE 1	LE 1	LE 1	LE 1	LE 1	LE 1	LE 1		LE ◇1 ☕	LE 1	LE 1	LE 1	LE ◇1 ☕	LE 1	LE 1	LE 1	LE 1		LE 1	LE 1	LE 1	LE ◇1 ☕
London Liverpool Street 15 ⊖	d	11 48	12 00				12 02	12 18				12 30	12 38	12 48		13 00				13 02		13 18			13 30
Stratford 7 ⊖	d	11 55					12 09	12 25				12u38	12 45	12 55						13 09		13 25			13u38
Romford	d												12 53												
Shenfield 3	d	12 11					12 25	12 41					13 03	13 11						13 25		13 41			
Ingatestone	d	12 15						12 45						13 15								13 45			
Chelmsford 3	d	12 22					12 34	12 52				13 03	13 12	13 22						13 34		13 52			14 03
Hatfield Peverel	d						12 40													13 40					
Witham 2	d	12 34					12 47	13 03					13 23	13 34						13 47		14 03			
White Notley	d	12 41												13 41											
Cressing	d	12 43												13 43											
Braintree Freeport	d	12 46												13 46											
Braintree	a	12 50												13 50											
Kelvedon	d						12 51						13 27							13 51					
Marks Tey 2	d						12 57						13 33							13 57					
Colchester 4	a		12 46				13 04	13 15				13 22	13 40			13 46				14 04		14 15			14 22
Colchester 4	d		12 47			12 56	13 04	13 16		13 20		13 23	13 41			13 47			13 56	14 04		14 16		14 20	14 23
Colchester Town	a					13 03				13 27			13 49						14 03					14 27	
	d					13 07													14 07						
Hythe	d					13 11													14 11						
Wivenhoe 3	d					13 15		13 23											14 15			14 23			
Alresford (Essex)	d					13 19													14 19						
Great Bentley	d					13 23													14 23						
Weeley	d					13 26													14 26						
Thorpe-le-Soken 1	a					13 31		13 35	← 13 31										14 31			14 35	← 14 31		
	d					13 37		13 35	13 37										14 37			14 35	14 37		
Clacton-on-Sea	a					→		13 44											→			14 44			
Kirby Cross	d								13 42														14 42		
Frinton-on-Sea	d								13 45														14 45		
Walton-on-the-Naze	a								13 49														14 49		
Manningtree 2	d		12 55	13 00			13 12					13 31				13 55	14 00			14 12					14 31
Mistley	d			13 04													14 04								
Wrabness	d			13 09													14 09								
Harwich International	d			13 17													14 17								
Dovercourt	d			13 20													14 20								
Harwich Town	a			13 22													14 22								
Ipswich	a		13 07				13 25					13 43				14 07				14 25					14 43
	d		13 08		13 19							13 44			14 00	14 08		14 19							14 44
Needham Market	d				13 28													14 28							
Stowmarket	d				13a33							13 55			14 12			14a33							14 55
Peterborough 8	a														15 37										
Diss	d		13 29									14 08				14 29									15 08
Norwich	a		13 50									14 27				14 50									15 27

Table 11

Mondays to Fridays

13 August to 28 August

London - Chelmsford, Colchester, Walton-on-Naze, Clacton, Harwich, Ipswich and Norwich

Network Diagram - see first Page of Table 5

		LE 1	LE 1	LE ◇1 ⊐	LE 1	LE 1	LE 1	LE 1	LE 1	LE 1	LE 1	LE ◇1 ⊐	LE 1	LE 1	LE 1	LE ◇1 ⊐	LE 1	LE 1	LE 1	LE 1	LE 1	LE 1	LE 1
London Liverpool Street 15 ⊖	d	13 38	13 48	14 00				14 02	14 18			14 30	14 38	14 48		15 00				15 02		15 18	
Stratford 7 ⊖	d	13 45	13 55					14 09	14 25			14u38	14 45	14 55						15 09		15 25	
Romford	d	13 53											14 53										
Shenfield 3	d	14 03	14 11					14 25	14 41				15 03	15 11						15 25		15 41	
Ingatestone	d		14 15						14 45					15 15								15 45	
Chelmsford 3	d	14 12	14 22					14 34	14 52			15 03	15 12	15 22						15 34		15 52	
Hatfield Peverel	d							14 40												15 40			
Witham 2	d	14 23	14 34					14 47	15 03				15 23	15 35						15 47		16 03	
White Notley	d		14 41											15 42									
Cressing	d		14 43											15 44									
Braintree Freeport	d		14 46											15 47									
Braintree	a		14 50											15 51									
Kelvedon	d	14 27						14 51					15 27							15 51			
Marks Tey 2	d	14 33						14 57					15 33							15 57			
Colchester 4	a	14 40		14 46				15 04	15 15			15 22	15 40			15 46				16 04		16 15	
Colchester 4	d	14 41		14 47			14 56	15 04	15 16		15 20	15 23	15 41			15 47			15 56	16 04	16 14	16 16	
Colchester Town	a	14 49					15 03				15 27		15 49						16 03				
	d						15 07												16 07				
Hythe	d						15 11												16 11				
Wivenhoe 3	d						15 15		15 23										16 15			16 23	
Alresford (Essex)	d						15 19												16 19				
Great Bentley	d						15 23												16 23				
Weeley	d						15 26			←									16 26				←
Thorpe-le-Soken 1	a						15 31		15 35	15 31									16 31			16 35	16 31
	d						15 37		15 35	15 37									16 37			16 35	16 37
Clacton-on-Sea	a						→		15 44										→			16 44	
Kirby Cross	d									15 42													16 42
Frinton-on-Sea	d									15 45													16 45
Walton-on-the-Naze	a									15 49													16 49
Manningtree 2	d			14 55	15 00			15 12				15 31				15 55	16 00			16 12	16 23		
Mistley	d				15 04												16 04				16 27		
Wrabness	d				15 09												16 09				16 32		
Harwich International	d				15 17												16 17				16 41		
Dovercourt	d				15 20												16 20				16 44		
Harwich Town	a				15 22												16 22				16 46		
Ipswich	a			15 07				15 25				15 43				16 07				16 25			
	d			15 08		15 19						15 44			16 00	16 08		16 19					
Needham Market	d					15 28												16 28					
Stowmarket	d					15a33						15 55			16 12			16a33					
Peterborough 8	a														17 37								
Diss	d			15 29								16 08				16 29							
Norwich	a			15 48								16 27				16 50							

		LE 1	LE ▪1 ⊐	LE 1	LE 1	LE 1	LE ▪1 ⊐	LE 1	LE 1	LE 1	LE 1	LE 1	LE 1	LE 1	LE 1	LE ▪1 ⊐	LE 1	LE 1	LE 1	LE 1	LE 1	LE 1
London Liverpool Street 15 ⊖	d		15 30		15 38	15 48	16 00				16 02		16 14		16 17	16 30				16 32	16 34	
Stratford 7 ⊖	d				15 45	15 55					16 09		16 22		16 25						16 42	
Romford	d				15 53																	
Shenfield 3	d				16 03	16 11					16 25		16 38		16 41					16 54	16 58	
Ingatestone	d			16 00		16 15									16 46							
Chelmsford 3	d		16 00	16 07	16 12	16 22					16 34		16 48		16 53					17 04	17 08	
Hatfield Peverel	d			16 13							16 40										17 14	
Witham 2	d			16 20	16 24	16 35					16 47				17a06					17 14	17 21	
White Notley	d					16 42															17 28	
Cressing	d					16 44															17 30	
Braintree Freeport	d					16 47															17 33	
Braintree	a					16 51															17 39	
Kelvedon	d			16 24	16 28						16 51		16 59									
Marks Tey 2	d			16 30	16 34						16 57		17 05									
Colchester 4	a		16 21	16 38	16 41		16 46				17 04		17 12			17 16				17 26		
Colchester 4	d	16 20	16 21		16 42		16 47			16 56	17 04	17 09	17 16			17 17			17 24	17 27		
Colchester Town	a	16 27			16 50					17 03		17 16							17 33			
	d									17 07									17 37			
Hythe	d									17 11			17 20						17 41			
Wivenhoe 3	d									17 15			17 24						17 45			
Alresford (Essex)	d									17 19									17 49			
Great Bentley	d									17 23									17 53			
Weeley	d									17 26				←					17 56			←
Thorpe-le-Soken 1	a									17 31			17 35	17 31					18 01			18 01
	d									17 37			17 35	17 37					18 10			18 10
Clacton-on-Sea	a									→			17 46						→			
Kirby Cross	d													17 42								18 15
Frinton-on-Sea	d													17 45								18 18
Walton-on-the-Naze	a													17 49								18 22
Manningtree 2	d		16 29				16 55	17 00			17 12						17 24			17 35		
Mistley	d							17 04									17 28					
Wrabness	d							17 09									17 33					
Harwich International	d							17 17									17 41					
Dovercourt	d							17 20									17 44					
Harwich Town	a							17 22									17 46					
Ipswich	a		16 40				17 07				17 27					17 34				17 49		
	d		16 41				17 08		17 19							17 36		17 49				
Needham Market	d								17 28									17 58				
Stowmarket	d		16 52				17 19		17a33							17 47		18 04				
Peterborough 8	a																	19 38				
Diss	d		17 05				17 32									18 00						
Norwich	a		17 24				17 53									18 22						

Table 11

Mondays to Fridays

13 August to 28 August

London - Chelmsford, Colchester, Walton-on-Naze, Clacton, Harwich, Ipswich and Norwich

Network Diagram - see first Page of Table 5

		LE 1	LE 1	LE 1	LE ▪1 A ⊐	LE 1	LE 1	LE ◇1	LE 1	LE 1	LE 1	LE 1	LE 1 B	LE ▪1 ⊐	LE 1	LE 1	LE 1	LE 1	LE 1	LE 1	LE 1 B	LE ▪1 ⊐	LE 1
London Liverpool Street 15 ⊖	d	16 44		16 47	17 00			17 02	17 08		17 12	17 18	17 20	17 30		17 32		17 38			17 40	17 50	17 52
Stratford 7 ⊖	d	16 52		16 55				17 10	17 16		17 20	17 26	17 29			17 40		17 47			17 49		18 01
Romford	d																						
Shenfield 3	d			17 11				17u26					17 45								18 05		
Ingatestone	d			17 16									17 49								18 09		
Chelmsford 3	d	17 15		17 23				17 36	17 40		17 44	17 50	17 57			18 05		18 12			18 17		18 25
Hatfield Peverel	d										17 50					18 11							18 31
Witham 2	d			17a36				17 46	17 50		17a59		18 10			18 17					18 31		18 37
White Notley	d												18 17										
Cressing	d												18 19										
Braintree Freeport	d												18 22										
Braintree	a												18 28										
Kelvedon	d	17 27							17 55			18 02						18 25			18 37		
Marks Tey 2	d	17 32						17 54	18 00							18 25							18 46
Colchester 4	a	17 40						18 01	18 08			18 12				18 32		18 36			18 48	18 42	18 53
Colchester 4	d	17 44	17 47				17 56	18 01	18 12			18 12			18 16	18 32		18 36		18 40	18 49	18 43	18 54
Colchester Town	a						18 03								18 26						18 59		
	d						18 07																
Hythe	d						18 11		18 16											18 44			18 58
Wivenhoe 3	d	17 51					18 15		18 20							18 40				18 48			19 02
Alresford (Essex)	d	17 55					18 19		18 24											18 52			
Great Bentley	d	17 59					18 23		18 28											18 56			
Weeley	d						18 26			←										18 59			
Thorpe-le-Soken 1	a	18 06					18 31		18 35	18 31						18 51				19 04			19 13
	d	18 06					18 37		18 35	18 37						18 51			18 53	19 04			19 13
Clacton-on-Sea	a	18 17					→		18 46							19 02				19 13			19 24
Kirby Cross	d									18 42									19 01				
Frinton-on-Sea	d									18 45									19 04				
Walton-on-the-Naze	a									18 49									19 08				
Manningtree 2	d		17 57					18 09				18 20		18 27			18 35	18 44				18 52	
Mistley	d		18 01														18 39						
Wrabness	d		18 06														18 44						
Harwich International	d		18 15														18 52						
Dovercourt	d		18 18														18 55						
Harwich Town	a		18 22														18 57						
Ipswich	a				17 59			18 20				18 35		18 37				18 59				19 03	
	d				18 00	18 16		18 24						18 39								19 04	
Needham Market	d					18 25																	
Stowmarket	d					18a30		18 35						18 50								19 16	
Peterborough 8	a																						
Diss	d				18 21			18 47						19 03								19 29	
Norwich	a				18 42			19 09						19 25								19 50	

		LE 1	LE 1	LE 1	LE 1	LE ▪1 ⊐	LE 1	LE 1	LE 1	LE 1	LE 1	LE 1	LE ▪1 ⊐	LE 1	LE 1	LE 1	LE 1	LE 1	LE 1	LE 1	LE 1	LE 1
London Liverpool Street 15 ⊖	d			17 58	18 00	18 10		18 12		18 18		18 20	18 30					18 32		18 38	18 48	
Stratford 7 ⊖	d			18 06	18 09			18 21		18 27		18 29						18 40		18 46	18 56	
Romford	d																					
Shenfield 3	d				18 25							18 45								19 02		
Ingatestone	d				18 29							18 49								19 07		
Chelmsford 3	d				18 37			18 46		18 52		18 57						19 05		19 14	19 20	
Hatfield Peverel	d							18 52	←									19 11				
Witham 2	d			18 41	19c01			18 58	19 01			19 11						19 17		19 24	19 30	
White Notley	d				→				19 08													
Cressing	d								19 10													
Braintree Freeport	d								19 13													
Braintree	a								19 19													
Kelvedon	d			18 46						19 06		19 17						19 22				
Marks Tey 2	d							19 06				19 23								19 32		
Colchester 4	a			18 56		19 00		19 13		19 17		19 30	19 21					19 33		19 39	19 43	
Colchester 4	d			18 57		19 02	19 06	19 13		19 17	19 20	19 30	19 23					19 37	19 39	19 39	19 44	
Colchester Town	a						19 13				19 27				←				19 50			
	d						19 19															
Hythe	d						19 23	19 18							19 23						19 48	
Wivenhoe 3	d						→	19 22							19 27			19 44			19 52	
Alresford (Essex)	d														19 31			19 48				
Great Bentley	d														19 35			19 52				
Weeley	d														19 38			19 55				←
Thorpe-le-Soken 1	a							19 33							19 43			20 00			20 04	20 00
	d							19 33						19 35	19 43			20 08			20 04	20 08
Clacton-on-Sea	a							19 44							19 52			→			20 15	
Kirby Cross	d													19 40								20 13
Frinton-on-Sea	d													19 43								20 16
Walton-on-the-Naze	a													19 47								20 22
Manningtree 2	d	19 00		19 05		19 11				19 25		19 40	19 32			19 38				19 47		
Mistley	d	19 04														19 42						
Wrabness	d	19 09														19 47						
Harwich International	d	19 17										20a01				19 55						
Dovercourt	d	19 20														19 58						
Harwich Town	a	19 22														20 00						
Ipswich	a			19 19		19 21				19 39			19 42							20 04		
	d		19 10			19 23							19 44				20 00					
Needham Market	d		19 19																			
Stowmarket	d		19a24			19 34							19 55				20 12					
Peterborough 8	a																21 39					
Diss	d					19 47							20 08									
Norwich	a					20 09							20 30									

A The East Anglian

B The Stratford call is subject to introduction during the currency of the timetable.

c arr 1854

London - Chelmsford, Colchester, Walton-on-Naze, Clacton, Harwich, Ipswich and Norwich

Network Diagram - see first Page of Table 5

		LE	LE	LE	LE	LE	LE	LE	LE	LE		LE	LE	LE	LE	LE	LE	LE	LE	LE		LE	LE	LE	LE
		■ ■ ⊏	■	■	■	■	■	■	■	■ ■ ⊏		■	■	■	■	■	◇■ ⊏	■	■			■	■	■	■
London Liverpool Street ⊖	d	19 00	19 02				19 08	19 18		19 30			19 32	19 38	19 48		20 00						20 02	20 18	
Stratford ⊖	d		19 09				19 15	19 25					19 39	19 45	19 55								20 09	20 25	
Romford	d																								
Shenfield	d		19 25					19 41						20 01	20 11								20 25	20 41	
Ingatestone	d							19 45							20 15									20 45	
Chelmsford	d		19 34				19 38	19 52					20 02	20 10	20 22								20 34	20 52	
Hatfield Peverel	d		19 40											20 16									20 40		
Witham	d		19 49				19 50	20 03					20 13	20 23	20 34								20 47	21 03	
White Notley	d		19 56												20 41										
Cressing	d		19 58												20 43										
Braintree Freeport	d		20 01												20 46										
Braintree	a		20 05												20 50										
Kelvedon	d						19 55							20 27									20 51		
Marks Tey	d						20 00							20 33									20 57		
Colchester	a	19 47					20 07	20 15		20 19			20 25	20 40			20 46						21 04	21 15	
Colchester	d	19 47				19 56	20 08	20 16		20 20		20 20	20 25	20 41			20 47					20 56	21 04	21 16	
Colchester Town	a					20 03						20 27		20 49								21 03			
	d					20 07																21 07			
Hythe	d					20 11																21 11			
Wivenhoe	d					20 15		20 23														21 15		21 23	
Alresford (Essex)	d					20 19																21 19			
Great Bentley	d					20 23																21 23			
Weeley	d					20 26			←													21 26			←
Thorpe-le-Soken	a					20 31		20 35	20 31													21 31		21 35	21 31
	d					20 37		20 35	20 37									20 54				21 37		21 35	21 37
Clacton-on-Sea	a					→		20 44										21 03				→		21 44	
Kirby Cross	d								20 42																21 42
Frinton-on-Sea	d								20 45																21 45
Walton-on-the-Naze	a								20 49																21 49
Manningtree	d	19 55		20 00			20 16			20 28			20 34			20 38	20 55		21 00				21 12		
Mistley	d			20 04												20 42			21 04						
Wrabness	d			20 09												20 47			21 09						
Harwich International	d			20 17									20a54			20 55			21 17						
Dovercourt	d			20 20												20 58			21 20						
Harwich Town	a			20 22												21 00			21 22						
Ipswich	a	20 07					20 28			20 40							21 07						21 25		
	d	20 08			20 19					20 41							21 08			21 16					
Needham Market	d				20 28															21 26					
Stowmarket	d	20 19			20a33					20 52							21 19			21a32					
Peterborough	a																								
Diss	d	20 32								21 05							21 32								
Norwich	a	20 51								21 24							21 51								

		LE	LE	LE	LE	LE		LE	LE	LE	LE	LE	LE	LE	LE	LE		LE	LE	LE	LE	LE	LE	LE	LE
		■	◇■ ⊏	■	■	■		◇■ ⊏	■		■	■	■	■	◇■ ⊏	■		■	■	■	■	■	■	■	■
London Liverpool Street ⊖	d		20 30	20 38	20 48			21 00				21 02	21 18		21 30	21 38		21 48	22 00	22 02				22 18	
Stratford ⊖	d		20u38	20 45	20 55							21 09	21 25		21u38	21 45		21 55		22 09				22 25	
Romford	d			20 53												21 53									
Shenfield	d			21 03	21 11							21 25	21 41			22 03		22 11		22 25				22 41	
Ingatestone	d				21 15								21 45					22 15						22 45	
Chelmsford	d		21 03	21 12	21 22							21 34	21 52		22 03	22 12		22 22	22 28	22 34				22 52	
Hatfield Peverel	d											21 40								22 40					
Witham	d			21 23	21 34							21 47	22 03			22 23		22 34		22 47				23 03	
White Notley	d				21 41													22 41							
Cressing	d				21 43													22 43							
Braintree Freeport	d				21 46													22 46							
Braintree	a				21 50													22 50							
Kelvedon	d			21 27								21 51				22 27				22 51					
Marks Tey	d			21 33								21 57				22 33				22 57					
Colchester	a		21 22	21 40				21 46				22 04	22 15		22 22	22 40			22 47	23 05				23 15	
Colchester	d	21 20	21 23	21 41				21 47			21 56	22 04	22 16		22 23	22 41			22 47				22 56	23 16	
Colchester Town	a	21 27		21 49							22 03					22 49							23 03		
	d										22 07												23 07		
Hythe	d										22 11												23 11		
Wivenhoe	d										22 15		22 23										23 15	23 23	
Alresford (Essex)	d										22 19												23 19		
Great Bentley	d										22 23												23 23		
Weeley	d										22 26			←									23 26		←
Thorpe-le-Soken	a										22 31		22 35	22 31									23 31	23 35	23 31
	d										22 37		22 35	22 37								23 16	23 37	23 35	23 37
Clacton-on-Sea	a										→		22 44									23 25	→	23 44	
Kirby Cross	d													22 42											23 42
Frinton-on-Sea	d													22 45											23 45
Walton-on-the-Naze	a													22 49											23 49
Manningtree	d		21 31					21 55	22 00			22 12			22 31				22 55		23 00				
Mistley	d								22 04												23 04				
Wrabness	d								22 09												23 09				
Harwich International	d					21 38			22 17			22a28									23 17				
Dovercourt	d								22 20												23 20				
Harwich Town	a								22 22												23 22				
Ipswich	a		21 43			22 03		22 07							22 43				23 08						
	d		21 44					22 08		22 16					22 44										
Needham Market	d									22 26															
Stowmarket	d		21 55					22 19		22a32					22 55										
Peterborough	a																								
Diss	d		22 08					22 32							23 08										
Norwich	a		22 27					22 51							23 27										

London - Chelmsford, Colchester, Walton-on-Naze, Clacton, Harwich, Ipswich and Norwich

Network Diagram - see first Page of Table 5

		LE		LE	LE	LE	LE	LE	LE	LE	LE
		◇■ ⊏		■	■	■		■	■	◇■ ⊏	■
London Liverpool Street ⊖	d	22 30		22 38				23 02	23 18	23 30	23 48
Stratford ⊖	d	22u38		22 45				23 09	23 25	23u38	23 55
Romford	d										
Shenfield	d			23 01				23 25	23 41		00 11
Ingatestone	d			23 05					23 45		00 15
Chelmsford	d	23 03		23 12				23 34	23 52	00 03	00 22
Hatfield Peverel	d							23 40			00 28
Witham	d			23 23	23 25			23 47	00 03		00 35
White Notley	d				23 32						
Cressing	d				23 34						
Braintree Freeport	d				23 37						
Braintree	a				23 41						
Kelvedon	d			23 27				23 51			00 39
Marks Tey	d			23 33			23 46	23 57			00 45
Colchester	a	23 22		23 45			23 55	00 04	00 15	00 22	00 57
Colchester	d	23 23						00 04	00 16	00 23	
Colchester Town	a										
	d										
Hythe	d										
Wivenhoe	d								00 23		
Alresford (Essex)	d								00 27		
Great Bentley	d								00 31		
Weeley	d										
Thorpe-le-Soken	a								00 38		
	d								00 38		
Clacton-on-Sea	a								00 51		
Kirby Cross	d										
Frinton-on-Sea	d										
Walton-on-the-Naze	a										
Manningtree	d	23 31				23 36		00 12		00 31	
Mistley	d					23 40					
Wrabness	d					23 45					
Harwich International	d					23 53					
Dovercourt	d					23 56					
Harwich Town	a					23 58					
Ipswich	a	23 43						00 28		00 43	
	d	23 44								00 44	
Needham Market	d										
Stowmarket	d	23 55								00 55	
Peterborough	a										
Diss	d	00 08								01 08	
Norwich	a	00 39								01 43	

Table 11

Mondays to Fridays
29 August to 7 September

London - Chelmsford, Colchester, Walton-on-Naze, Clacton, Harwich, Ipswich and Norwich

Network Diagram - see first Page of Table 5

Station		LE	LE	LE	LE	LE	LE	LE	LE	LE	LE	LE	LE	LE	LE	LE	LE	LE	LE	LE	LE	LE	LE	LE
		◇■	◇■	◇■	■	■	◇■	◇■	■	■	■	■	■	■	■	■	■	◇■	◇■	◇■	■	■	■	■
		A	B	C	C	B	C	B	C	A	D	C	B	B	A	B	A	A	B	C	E	B	D	C
London Liverpool Street ⊖	d	22p30	22p30	22p30	22p45	22p45	23p00	23p00		23p02	23p07	23p15		23p15	23p18			23p30	23p30	23p30			23p35	23p45
Stratford ⊖	d	22b38	22b40	22b40	22p54	22p54	23b10	23b10		23p09	23p17	23p25		23p25	23p25			23b38	23b40	23b40			23p45	23p54
Romford	d																							
Shenfield	d				23p11	23p12				23p25	23p34	23p41		23p43	23p41								00 01	00 11
Ingatestone	d				23p15	23p16						23p46		23p48	23p45								00 05	00 15
Chelmsford	d	23p03	23p05	23p06	23p22	23p23	23p36	23p37		23p34	23p43	23p53		23p55	23p52			00 03	00 06	00 06			00 12	00 22
Hatfield Peverel	d									23p40	23p49					←							00 18	
Witham	d				23p33	23p34				23p47	23p56	00 03		00 05 →	00 03	00 05					00 05	00 07	00 25	00 33
White Notley	d																				00 12	00 14		
Cressing	d																				00 14	00 16		
Braintree Freeport	d																				00 17	00 19		
Braintree	a																				00 21	00 23		
Kelvedon	d									23p51	00 01												00 29	
Marks Tey	d									23p57	00 06												00 35	
Colchester	a	23p22	23p24	23p25	23p45	23p46	23p55	23p58		00 04	00 14	00 17			00 15	00 17		00 22	00 25	00 25			00 43	00 46
Colchester	d	23p23	23p25	23p25	23p46	23p47	23p55	23p59		00 04		00 18			00 16	00 18		00 23	00 25	00 25				00 47
Colchester Town	a																							
	d																							
Hythe	d																							
Wivenhoe	d				23p54	23p54						00 26			00 23	00 25								00 55
Alresford (Essex)	d														00 27									
Great Bentley	d														00 31									
Weeley	d																←							
Thorpe-le-Soken	a				00 05	00 06						00 37			00 38	00 37	00 38							01 06
	d				00 05	00 06						00 37			00 38	00 37	00 38							01 06
Clacton-on-Sea	a				00 14	00 15						00 46			→	00 46	00 51							01 15
Kirby Cross	d																							
Frinton-on-Sea	d																							
Walton-on-the-Naze	a																							
Manningtree	d	23p31	23p33	23p34			00 04	00 09	00 08	00 12			00 12					00 31	00 33	00 34				
Mistley	d								00 12				00 16											
Wrabness	d								00 17				00 21											
Harwich International	d								00 24				00 29											
Dovercourt	d								00 27				00 32											
Harwich Town	a								00 30				00 34											
Ipswich	a	23p43	23p45	23p45			00 15	00 19		00 28								00 43	00 45	00 45				
	d	23p44	23p46	23p47			00 17	00 21										00 44	00 46	00 47				
Needham Market	d																							
Stowmarket	d	23p55	23p58	23p58			00 28	00 32										00 55	00 58	00 58				
Peterborough	a																							
Diss	d	00 08	00 10	00 11			00 41	00 45										01 08	01 10	01 11				
Norwich	a	00 39	00 30	00 30			01 00	01 04										01 43	01 30	01 30				

A 29 August
B not 29 August, 3 September
C 3 September
D not 29 August
b Previous night, stops to pick up only
E 29 August, 3 September

Table 11

Mondays to Fridays
29 August to 7 September

London - Chelmsford, Colchester, Walton-on-Naze, Clacton, Harwich, Ipswich and Norwich

Network Diagram - see first Page of Table 5

Station		LE	LE	LE	LE	LE	LE	LE	LE	LE	LE	LE	LE	LE	LE	LE	LE	LE	LE	LE	LE	LE	LE
		■	■	◇■	◇■	■	■	◇■	■		■	◇■	■	■	■	■	■	■	■	■	■	■	■
		A	B	C	A	D	B	D	D														
London Liverpool Street ⊖	d	23p45	23p48	23p59	23p59	00 12	00 18	00 30	00 46											05 23			
Stratford ⊖	d	23p54	23p55	00u10	00u10	00 24	00 25	00u40	01 00											05 30			
Romford	d																			05 38			
Shenfield	d	00 12	00 11			00 41	00 47		01 17											05 48			
Ingatestone	d	00 16	00 15			00 45	00 51		01 22											05 52			
Chelmsford	d	00 23	00 22	00 36	00 37	00 52	00 58	01 07	01 29											05 59			
Hatfield Peverel	d		00 28			00 58	01 04		01 35											06 05			
Witham	d	00 34	00 35			01 05	01 11		01 41		05 21									06 12	06 16		
White Notley	d										05 28										06 23		
Cressing	d										05 30										06 25		
Braintree Freeport	d										05 33										06 28		
Braintree	a										05 37										06 32		
Kelvedon	d		00 39			01 09	01 15		01 46											06 16			
Marks Tey	d		00 45			01 15	01 21		01 51											06 22			
Colchester	a	00 46	00 57	00 55	00 56	01 23	01 41	01 29	02 00											06 29			
Colchester	d	00 47		00 56	00 57			01 30				05 40			06 10		06 15	06 20		06 30			
Colchester Town	a																	06 27					
	d																						
Hythe	d																						
Wivenhoe	d	00 54																		06 37			
Alresford (Essex)	d																						
Great Bentley	d																						
Weeley	d																						
Thorpe-le-Soken	a	01 06																		06 50			
	d	01 06												06 03					06 31	06 50			06 56
Clacton-on-Sea	a	01 15																		06 59			
Kirby Cross	d													06 12					06 39				07 06
Frinton-on-Sea	d													06 15					06 42				07 09
Walton-on-the-Naze	a													06 19					06 46				07 13
Manningtree	d			01 05	01 07			01 40				05 49	05 56		06 18		06 23						
Mistley	d												06 00		06 22								
Wrabness	d												06 05		06 27								
Harwich International	d												06 13		06 35								
Dovercourt	d												06 16		06 38								
Harwich Town	a												06 20		06 40								
Ipswich	a			01 15	01 17			01 50				05 59					06 34						
	d			01 17	01 19			01 52		05 10		06 00				06 16						06 39	
Needham Market	d									05 20						06 25							
Stowmarket	d			01 28	01 30			02 03		05a26		06 12				06a30						06 51	
Peterborough	a											07 38											
Diss	d			01 41	01 43			02 16														07 04	
Norwich	a			02 00	02 03			02 35														07 24	

A not 29 August, 3 September
B 29 August
C 3 September
D not 29 August

London - Chelmsford, Colchester, Walton-on-Naze, Clacton, Harwich, Ipswich and Norwich

Network Diagram - see first Page of Table 5

		LE 1		LE ◇1	LE 1	LE 1	LE 1	LE 1	LE ◇1	LE 1	LE 1	LE 1		LE 1	LE 1	LE ◇1	LE 1	LE 1	LE 1	LE 1	LE 1	LE 1		LE ◇1 ☕	LE 1
London Liverpool Street 15 ⊖	d			06 00	06 02	06 12			06 25			06 38		06 48		07 00	07 02			07 08	07 18			07 30	07 36
Stratford 7 ⊖	d				06 09	06 19			06u33			06 45		06 55			07 09			07 15	07 25			07u38	07 45
Romford	d																								
Shenfield 3	d				06 25	06 36						07 01		07 11		07u22	07 25			07 31	07 41				08 01
Ingatestone	d					06 40								07 15							07 45				08 05
Chelmsford 3	d			06 30	06 34	06 47			06 58			07 10		07 22			07 34			07 40	07 52			08 03	08 12
Hatfield Peverel	d					06 53											07 40								
Witham 2	d				06 45	07 03			07 09			07 21		07 33			07 48			07 51	08 03				08 23
White Notley	d					07 10											07 55								
Cressing	d					07 12											07 57								
Braintree Freeport	d					07 15											08 00								
Braintree	a					07 19											08 04								
Kelvedon	d				06 49							07 25								07 55					08 27
Marks Tey 2	d				06 55							07 31		07 40						08 01	08 11				08 33
Colchester 4	a			06 49	07 02				07 22			07 38		07 47		07 50				08 08	08 18			08 22	08 40
Colchester 4	d			06 50	07 02		07 10		07 23		07 26	07 43		07 48		07 51			07 56	08 08	08 19			08 23	08 41
Colchester Town	a										07 34			07 56					08 03						08 49
	d										07 38								08 07						
Hythe	d				07 07						07 42								08 11		08 23				
Wivenhoe 3	d				07 11						07 46								08 15		08 27				
Alresford (Essex)	d				07 14														08 19						
Great Bentley	d				07 18														08 23						
Weeley	d				07 22														08 26			←			
Thorpe-le-Soken 1	a				07 28						07 57								08 31		08 38	08 31			
	d				07 28					07 38	07 57								08 40		08 38	08 40			
Clacton-on-Sea	a				07 37						08 06								→		08 47				
Kirby Cross	d									07 47												08 45			
Frinton-on-Sea	d									07 50												08 48			
Walton-on-the-Naze	a									07 54												08 52			
Manningtree 2	d			06 58			07 18	07 24	07 31			07 51				07 59				08 16				08 31	
Mistley	d							07 28				07 55						08 02							
Wrabness	d							07 33				08 01													
Harwich International	d							07 41				08 10													
Dovercourt	d							07 44				08 13													
Harwich Town	a							07 46				08 15													
Ipswich	a			07 10			07 30		07 42							08 11		08 17		08 29				08 43	
	d	06 56		07 11					07 44						08 03	08 12		08 19						08 44	
Needham Market	d	07 05																08 28							
Stowmarket	d	07a10		07 22					07 55						08 15	08 23		08a33						08 55	
Peterborough 8	a														09 39										
Diss	d			07 35					08 08							08 36								09 08	
Norwich	a			07 54					08 27							08 55								09 27	

		LE 1		LE ◇1 ☕	LE 1	LE 1	LE 1	LE 1		LE	LE 1	LE 1	LE 1	LE	LE ◇1 ☕	LE 1	LE 1	LE		LE 1	LE ◇1 ☕	LE 1	LE 1	LE 1	LE 1
London Liverpool Street 15 ⊖	d	07 46		07 55			08 00	08 06		08 17		08 17		08 27	08 30	08 36	08 48	08 55			09 00				09 02
Stratford 7 ⊖	d	07 54					08 08	08 14		08a24		08 25		08a34	08u38	08 45	08 55	09a04							09 09
Romford	d																								
Shenfield 3	d	08 11					08 25	08 30				08 41				09 03	09 11								09 25
Ingatestone	d							08 34				08 45					09 15								
Chelmsford 3	d	08 20					08 34	08 41				08 52			09 03	09 12	09 22								09 34
Hatfield Peverel	d							08 47																	09 40
Witham 2	d	08 35	08 38				08 45	08 54				09 03				09 23	09 35								09 47
White Notley	d	08 42															09 42								
Cressing	d	08 44															09 44								
Braintree Freeport	d	08 47															09 47								
Braintree	a	08 51															09 51								
Kelvedon	d						08 49									09 27									09 51
Marks Tey 2	d						08 55					09 10				09 33									09 57
Colchester 4	a		08 53	08 45			09 02	09 06				09 17			09 22	09 40					09 46				10 04
Colchester 4	d		08 56	08 47			09 02	09 06			09 14	09 18			09 23	09 41					09 47			09 56	10 04
Colchester Town	a		09 03								09 21					09 49								10 03	
	d		09 07																					10 07	
Hythe	d		09 11																					10 11	
Wivenhoe 3	d		09 15									09 25												10 15	
Alresford (Essex)	d		09 19																					10 19	
Great Bentley	d		09 23																					10 23	
Weeley	d		09 26										←											10 26	
Thorpe-le-Soken 1	a		09 31									09 36	09 31											10 31	
	d		09 38									09 36	09 38											10 37	
Clacton-on-Sea	a		→									09 45												→	
Kirby Cross	d												09 43												
Frinton-on-Sea	d												09 46												
Walton-on-the-Naze	a												09 50												
Manningtree 2	d			08 55	09 00			09 14							09 31						09 55	10 00			10 12
Mistley	d				09 04																	10 04			
Wrabness	d				09 09																	10 09			
Harwich International	d				09 17																	10 17			
Dovercourt	d				09 20																	10 20			
Harwich Town	a				09 22																	10 22			
Ipswich	a			09 07			09 20	09 26							09 43						10 07				10 25
	d			09 08		09 19									09 44					10 00	10 08		10 19		
Needham Market	d					09 28																	10 28		
Stowmarket	d					09a33									09 55					10 12			10a33		
Peterborough 8	a																			11 37					
Diss	d			09 29											10 08						10 29				
Norwich	a			09 48											10 27						10 50				

London - Chelmsford, Colchester, Walton-on-Naze, Clacton, Harwich, Ipswich and Norwich

Network Diagram - see first Page of Table 5

		LE 1	LE 1	LE 1		LE ◇1 ☕	LE 1	LE 1	LE ◇1 ☕	LE 1	LE 1	LE 1	LE 1	LE 1		LE 1	LE 1	LE ◇1 ☕	LE 1	LE 1	LE 1	LE ◇1 ☕	LE 1	LE 1
London Liverpool Street 15 ⊖	d	09 18				09 30	09 38	09 48	10 00				10 02	10 18				10 30	10 38	10 48		11 00		
Stratford 7 ⊖	d	09 25				09u38	09 45	09 55					10 09	10 25				10u38	10 45	10 55				
Romford	d						09 53												10 53					
Shenfield 3	d	09 41					10 03	10 11					10 25	10 41					11 03	11 11				
Ingatestone	d	09 45						10 15						10 45						11 15				
Chelmsford 3	d	09 52				10 03	10 12	10 22					10 34	10 52				11 03	11 12	11 22				
Hatfield Peverel	d												10 40											
Witham 2	d	10 03					10 23	10 34					10 47	11 03					11 23	11 34				
White Notley	d							10 41												11 41				
Cressing	d							10 43												11 43				
Braintree Freeport	d							10 46												11 46				
Braintree	a							10 50												11 50				
Kelvedon	d						10 27						10 51						11 27					
Marks Tey 2	d						10 33						10 57						11 33					
Colchester 4	a	10 15				10 22	10 40		10 46				11 04	11 15				11 22	11 40			11 46		
Colchester 4	d	10 16		10 20		10 23	10 41		10 47			10 56	11 04	11 16			11 20	11 23	11 41			11 47		
Colchester Town	a			10 27			10 49					11 03					11 27		11 49					
	d											11 07												
Hythe	d											11 11												
Wivenhoe 3	d	10 23										11 15		11 23										
Alresford (Essex)	d											11 19												
Great Bentley	d											11 23												
Weeley	d		←									11 26				←								
Thorpe-le-Soken 1	a	10 35	10 31									11 31		11 35		11 31								
	d	10 35	10 37									11 37		11 35		11 37								
Clacton-on-Sea	a	10 44										→		11 44										
Kirby Cross	d		10 42													11 42								
Frinton-on-Sea	d		10 45													11 45								
Walton-on-the-Naze	a		10 49													11 49								
Manningtree 2	d					10 31			10 55	11 00			11 12					11 31				11 55	12 00	
Mistley	d									11 04													12 04	
Wrabness	d									11 09													12 09	
Harwich International	d									11 17													12 17	
Dovercourt	d									11 20													12 20	
Harwich Town	a									11 22													12 22	
Ipswich	a					10 43			11 07				11 25					11 43				12 07		
	d					10 44			11 08		11 19							11 44			12 00	12 08		12 19
Needham Market	d										11 28													12 28
Stowmarket	d					10 55					11a33							11 55			12 12			12a33
Peterborough 8	a																				13 37			
Diss	d					11 08			11 29									12 08				12 29		
Norwich	a					11 27			11 50									12 27				12 50		

		LE 1	LE 1	LE 1	LE 1	LE 1	LE ◇1 ☕	LE 1	LE 1	LE ◇1 ☕		LE 1	LE 1	LE 1	LE 1	LE 1	LE 1	LE 1	LE ◇1 ☕	LE 1		LE 1	LE 1	LE ◇1 ☕	LE 1
London Liverpool Street 15 ⊖	d		11 02	11 18			11 30	11 38	11 48	12 00					12 02	12 18			12 30	12 38		12 48		13 00	
Stratford 7 ⊖	d		11 09	11 25			11u38	11 45	11 55						12 09	12 25			12u38	12 45		12 55			
Romford	d							11 53												12 53					
Shenfield 3	d		11 25	11 41				12 03	12 11						12 25	12 41				13 03		13 11			
Ingatestone	d			11 45					12 15							12 45						13 15			
Chelmsford 3	d		11 34	11 52			12 03	12 12	12 22						12 34	12 52			13 03	13 12		13 22			
Hatfield Peverel	d		11 40												12 40										
Witham 2	d		11 47	12 03				12 23	12 34						12 47	13 03				13 23		13 34			
White Notley	d								12 41													13 41			
Cressing	d								12 43													13 43			
Braintree Freeport	d								12 46													13 46			
Braintree	a								12 50													13 50			
Kelvedon	d		11 51					12 27							12 51					13 27					
Marks Tey 2	d		11 57					12 33							12 57					13 33					
Colchester 4	a		12 04	12 15			12 22	12 40		12 46					13 04	13 15			13 22	13 40				13 46	
Colchester 4	d	11 56	12 04	12 16		12 20	12 23	12 41		12 47				12 56	13 04	13 16		13 20	13 23	13 41				13 47	
Colchester Town	a	12 03				12 27		12 49						13 03				13 27		13 49					
	d	12 07												13 07											
Hythe	d	12 11												13 11											
Wivenhoe 3	d	12 15		12 23										13 15		13 23									
Alresford (Essex)	d	12 19												13 19											
Great Bentley	d	12 23												13 23											
Weeley	d	12 26			←									13 26			←								
Thorpe-le-Soken 1	a	12 31		12 35	12 31									13 31		13 35	13 31								
	d	12 37		12 35	12 37									13 37		13 35	13 37								
Clacton-on-Sea	a	→		12 44										→		13 44									
Kirby Cross	d				12 42												13 42								
Frinton-on-Sea	d				12 45												13 45								
Walton-on-the-Naze	a				12 49												13 49								
Manningtree 2	d		12 12				12 31			12 55		13 00			13 12				13 31					13 55	14 00
Mistley	d											13 04													14 04
Wrabness	d											13 09													14 09
Harwich International	d											13 17													14 17
Dovercourt	d											13 20													14 20
Harwich Town	a											13 22													14 22
Ipswich	a		12 25				12 43			13 07					13 25				13 43					14 07	
	d						12 44			13 08			13 19						13 44				14 00	14 08	
Needham Market	d												13 28												
Stowmarket	d						12 55						13a33						13 55				14 12		
Peterborough 8	a																						15 37		
Diss	d						13 08			13 29									14 08					14 29	
Norwich	a						13 27			13 50									14 27					14 50	

London - Chelmsford, Colchester, Walton-on-Naze, Clacton, Harwich, Ipswich and Norwich

Network Diagram - see first Page of Table 5

		LE	LE	LE	LE	LE		LE	LE	LE	LE	LE	LE	LE	LE	LE		LE	LE	LE	LE	LE	LE	LE	LE
		■	■	■	■	■		■	◇■ ⊡	■	■	◇■ ⊡	■	■	■	■		■	■	■	◇■ ⊡	■	■	■	◇■ ⊡
London Liverpool Street ⊖	d			13 02	13 18				13 30	13 38	13 48	14 00				14 02		14 18			14 30	14 38	14 48		15 00
Stratford ⊖	d			13 09	13 25				13u38	13 45	13 55					14 09		14 25			14u38	14 45	14 55		
Romford	d									13 53												14 53			
Shenfield	d			13 25	13 41					14 03	14 11					14 25		14 41				15 03	15 11		
Ingatestone	d				13 45						14 15							14 45					15 15		
Chelmsford	d			13 34	13 52				14 03	14 12	14 22					14 34		14 52			15 03	15 12	15 22		
Hatfield Peverel	d			13 40												14 40									
Witham	d			13 47	14 03					14 23	14 34					14 47		15 03				15 23	15 35		
White Notley	d										14 41												15 42		
Cressing	d										14 43												15 44		
Braintree Freeport	d										14 46												15 47		
Braintree	a										14 50												15 51		
Kelvedon	d			13 51						14 27						14 51						15 27			
Marks Tey	d			13 57						14 33						14 57						15 33			
Colchester	a			14 04	14 15				14 22	14 40		14 46				15 04		15 15			15 22	15 40			15 46
Colchester	d		13 56	14 04	14 16			14 20	14 23	14 41		14 47			14 56	15 04		15 16		15 20	15 23	15 41			15 47
Colchester Town	a		14 03					14 27		14 49					15 03					15 27		15 49			
	d		14 07												15 07										
Hythe	d		14 11												15 11										
Wivenhoe	d		14 15		14 23										15 15			15 23							
Alresford (Essex)	d		14 19												15 19										
Great Bentley	d		14 23												15 23										
Weeley	d		14 26			←									15 26				←						
Thorpe-le-Soken	a		14 31		14 35	14 31									15 31			15 35	15 31						
	d		14 37		14 35	14 37									15 37			15 35	15 37						
Clacton-on-Sea	a		→		14 44										→			15 44							
Kirby Cross	d					14 42													15 42						
Frinton-on-Sea	d					14 45													15 45						
Walton-on-the-Naze	a					14 49													15 49						
Manningtree	d			14 12					14 31			14 55	15 00			15 12					15 31				15 55
Mistley	d												15 04												
Wrabness	d												15 09												
Harwich International	d												15 17												
Dovercourt	d												15 20												
Harwich Town	a												15 22												
Ipswich	a			14 25					14 43			15 07				15 25					15 43				16 07
	d	14 19							14 44			15 08		15 19							15 44			16 00	16 08
Needham Market	d	14 28												15 28											
Stowmarket	d	14a33							14 55					15a33							15 55			16 12	
Peterborough	a																							17 37	
Diss	d								15 08			15 29									16 08				16 29
Norwich	a								15 27			15 48									16 27				16 50

		LE		LE	LE	LE	LE	LE	LE	LE	LE	LE		LE	LE	LE	LE	LE	LE	LE	LE	LE		LE	LE
		■		■	■	■	■	■	■	■	■ ■ ⊡	■		■	■	■ ■ ⊡	■	■	■	■	■	■		■	■
London Liverpool Street ⊖	d					15 02		15 18			15 30			15 38	15 48	16 00				16 02		16 14			16 17
Stratford ⊖	d					15 09		15 25						15 45	15 55					16 09		16 22			16 25
Romford	d													15 53											
Shenfield	d					15 25		15 41						16 03	16 11					16 25		16 38			16 41
Ingatestone	d							15 45				16 00			16 15										16 46
Chelmsford	d					15 34		15 52			16 00	16 07		16 12	16 22					16 34		16 48			16 53
Hatfield Peverel	d					15 40						16 13								16 40					
Witham	d					15 47		16 03				16 20		16 24	16 35					16 47					17a06
White Notley	d														16 42										
Cressing	d														16 44										
Braintree Freeport	d														16 47										
Braintree	a														16 51										
Kelvedon	d					15 51						16 24		16 28						16 51		16 59			
Marks Tey	d					15 57						16 30		16 34						16 57		17 05			
Colchester	a					16 04		16 15			16 21	16 38		16 41		16 46				17 04		17 12			
Colchester	d				15 56	16 04	16 14	16 16		16 20	16 21			16 42		16 47			16 56	17 04	17 09	17 16			
Colchester Town	a				16 03					16 27				16 50					17 03		17 16				
	d				16 07														17 07						
Hythe	d				16 11														17 11			17 20			
Wivenhoe	d				16 15			16 23											17 15			17 24			
Alresford (Essex)	d				16 19														17 19						
Great Bentley	d				16 23														17 23						
Weeley	d				16 26				←										17 26					←	
Thorpe-le-Soken	a				16 31			16 35	16 31										17 31			17 35		17 31	
	d				16 37			16 35	16 37										17 37			17 35		17 37	
Clacton-on-Sea	a				→			16 44											→			17 46			
Kirby Cross	d								16 42															17 42	
Frinton-on-Sea	d								16 45															17 45	
Walton-on-the-Naze	a								16 49															17 49	
Manningtree	d	16 00				16 12	16 23				16 29					16 55	17 00			17 12					
Mistley	d	16 04					16 27										17 04								
Wrabness	d	16 09					16 32										17 09								
Harwich International	d	16 17					16 41										17 17								
Dovercourt	d	16 20					16 44										17 20								
Harwich Town	a	16 22					16 46										17 22								
Ipswich	a					16 25					16 40					17 07				17 27					
	d			16 19							16 41					17 08		17 19							
Needham Market	d			16 28														17 28							
Stowmarket	d			16a33							16 52					17 19		17a33							
Peterborough	a																								
Diss	d										17 05					17 32									
Norwich	a										17 24					17 53									

Table 11

Mondays to Fridays
29 August to 7 September

London - Chelmsford, Colchester, Walton-on-Naze, Clacton, Harwich, Ipswich and Norwich

Network Diagram - see first Page of Table 5

		LE	LE	LE	LE	LE	LE	LE		LE		LE	LE	LE	LE	LE	LE	LE		LE	LE	LE	LE	LE	LE
		■ ■ ⊡	■	■	■	■	■	■		■		■	■ ■ A ⊡	■	■	◇■	■	■		■	■	■ B	■ ■ ⊡	■	■
London Liverpool Street ⊖	d	16 30				16 32	16 34			16 44		16 47	17 00			17 02	17 08			17 12	17 18	17 20	17 30		17 32
Stratford ⊖	d						16 42			16 52		16 55				17 10	17 16			17 20	17 26	17 29			17 40
Romford	d																								
Shenfield	d					16 54	16 58					17 11				17u26						17 45			
Ingatestone	d											17 16										17 49			
Chelmsford	d					17 04	17 08			17 15		17 23				17 36	17 40			17 44	17 50	17 57			18 05
Hatfield Peverel	d						17 14													17 50					18 11
Witham	d					17 14	17 21					17a36				17 46	17 50			17a59		18 10			18 17
White Notley	d						17 28															18 17			
Cressing	d						17 30															18 19			
Braintree Freeport	d						17 33															18 22			
Braintree	a						17 39															18 28			
Kelvedon	d									17 27							17 55				18 02				
Marks Tey	d									17 32						17 54	18 00								18 25
Colchester	a	17 16				17 26				17 40						18 01	18 08				18 12				18 32
Colchester	d	17 17			17 24	17 27				17 44	17 47				17 56	18 01	18 12				18 12			18 16	18 32
Colchester Town	a				17 33										18 03									18 26	
	d				17 37										18 07										
Hythe	d				17 41										18 11		18 16								
Wivenhoe	d				17 45					17 51					18 15		18 20								18 40
Alresford (Essex)	d				17 49					17 55					18 19		18 24								
Great Bentley	d				17 53					17 59					18 23		18 28								
Weeley	d				17 56			←							18 26			←							
Thorpe-le-Soken	a				18 01			18 01		18 06					18 31		18 35	18 31							18 51
	d				18 10			18 10		18 06					18 37		18 35	18 37							18 51
Clacton-on-Sea	a				→					18 17					→		18 46								19 02
Kirby Cross	d							18 15										18 42							
Frinton-on-Sea	d							18 18										18 45							
Walton-on-the-Naze	a							18 22										18 49							
Manningtree	d		17 24			17 35					17 57					18 09					18 20		18 27		
Mistley	d		17 28								18 01														
Wrabness	d		17 33								18 06														
Harwich International	d		17 41								18 15														
Dovercourt	d		17 44								18 18														
Harwich Town	a		17 46								18 22														
Ipswich	a	17 34				17 49							17 59			18 20					18 35		18 37		
	d	17 36		17 49									18 00	18 16		18 24							18 39		
Needham Market	d			17 58										18 25											
Stowmarket	d	17 47		18 04										18a30		18 35							18 50		
Peterborough	a			19 38																					
Diss	d	18 00											18 21			18 47							19 03		
Norwich	a	18 22											18 42			19 09							19 25		

		LE	LE	LE		LE	LE	LE	LE	LE	LE	LE	LE	LE		LE	LE	LE	LE	LE	LE	LE	LE	LE	
		■	■	■		■	■ B	■ ■ ⊡	■	■	■	■	■	■ ■ ⊡		■	■	■	■	■	■	■ ■ ⊡	■	■	
London Liverpool Street ⊖	d		17 38				17 40	17 50	17 52			17 58	18 00	18 10			18 12		18 18		18 20	18 30			
Stratford ⊖	d		17 47				17 49		18 01			18 06	18 09				18 21		18 27		18 29				
Romford	d																								
Shenfield	d						18 05						18 25								18 45				
Ingatestone	d						18 09						18 29								18 49				
Chelmsford	d		18 12				18 17		18 25				18 37				18 46		18 52		18 57				
Hatfield Peverel	d								18 31								18 52	←							
Witham	d						18 31		18 37			18 41	19c01				18 58	19 01			19 11				
White Notley	d												→					19 08							
Cressing	d																	19 10							
Braintree Freeport	d																	19 13							
Braintree	a																	19 19							
Kelvedon	d		18 25				18 37					18 46							19 06		19 17				
Marks Tey	d								18 46								19 06				19 23				
Colchester	a		18 36				18 48	18 42	18 53			18 56		19 00			19 13		19 17		19 30	19 21			
Colchester	d		18 36			18 40	18 49	18 43	18 54			18 57		19 02		19 06	19 13		19 17	19 20	19 30	19 23			
Colchester Town	a						18 59									19 13				19 27				←	
	d															19 19									
Hythe	d					18 44			18 58							19 23	19 18							19 23	
Wivenhoe	d					18 48			19 02							→	19 22							19 27	
Alresford (Essex)	d					18 52																		19 31	
Great Bentley	d					18 56																		19 35	
Weeley	d					18 59																		19 38	
Thorpe-le-Soken	a					19 04			19 13								19 33							19 43	
	d			18 53		19 04			19 13								19 33						19 35	19 43	
Clacton-on-Sea	a					19 13			19 24								19 44							19 52	
Kirby Cross	d			19 01																			19 40		
Frinton-on-Sea	d			19 04																			19 43		
Walton-on-the-Naze	a			19 08																			19 47		
Manningtree	d	18 35	18 44					18 52		19 00		19 05		19 11					19 25		19 40	19 32			
Mistley	d	18 39								19 04															
Wrabness	d	18 44								19 09															
Harwich International	d	18 52								19 17											20a01				
Dovercourt	d	18 55								19 20															
Harwich Town	a	18 57								19 22															
Ipswich	a		18 59					19 03				19 19		19 21					19 39			19 42			
	d							19 04			19 10			19 23								19 44			
Needham Market	d										19 19														
Stowmarket	d							19 16			19a24			19 34								19 55			
Peterborough	a																								
Diss	d							19 29						19 47								20 08			
Norwich	a							19 50						20 09								20 30			

A The East Anglian

B The Stratford call is subject to introduction during the currency of the timetable.

c arr 1854

London - Chelmsford, Colchester, Walton-on-Naze, Clacton, Harwich, Ipswich and Norwich

Network Diagram - see first Page of Table 5

Station		LE ■	LE ■	LE ■		LE ■	LE ■	LE ■	LE ■ ■ ⊡	LE ■		LE ■	LE ■	LE ■	LE ■	LE ■	LE ■	LE ■ ■ ⊡	LE ■	LE ■		LE ■	LE ■	LE ■	LE ◇■ ⊡
London Liverpool Street ■15 ⊖	d			18 32		18 38	18 48		19 00	19 02					19 08	19 18		19 30		19 32		19 38	19 48		20 00
Stratford ■7 ⊖	d			18 40		18 46	18 56			19 09					19 15	19 25				19 39		19 45	19 55		
Romford	d																								
Shenfield ■3	d					19 02				19 25						19 41						20 01	20 11		
Ingatestone	d					19 07										19 45							20 15		
Chelmsford ■3	d			19 05		19 14	19 20			19 34					19 38	19 52				20 02		20 10	20 22		
Hatfield Peverel	d			19 11						19 40												20 16			
Witham ■2	d			19 17		19 24	19 30			19 49					19 50	20 03				20 13		20 23	20 34		
White Notley	d									19 56													20 41		
Cressing	d									19 58													20 43		
Braintree Freeport	d									20 01													20 46		
Braintree	a									20 05													20 50		
Kelvedon	d			19 22											19 55							20 27			
Marks Tey ■2	d					19 32									20 00							20 33			
Colchester ■4	a			19 33		19 39	19 43		19 47						20 07	20 15		20 19		20 25		20 40			20 46
Colchester ■4	d			19 37	19 39	19 39	19 44		19 47					19 56	20 08	20 16		20 20	20 20	20 25		20 41			20 47
Colchester Town	a				19 50									20 03					20 27			20 49			
	d													20 07											
Hythe	d						19 48							20 11											
Wivenhoe ■3	d			19 44			19 52							20 15		20 23									
Alresford (Essex)	d			19 48										20 19											
Great Bentley	d			19 52										20 23											
Weeley	d			19 55				←						20 26			←								
Thorpe-le-Soken ■1	a			20 00			20 04	20 00						20 31		20 35	20 31								
	d			20 08			20 04	20 08						20 37		20 35	20 37								
Clacton-on-Sea	a			→			20 15							→		20 44									
Kirby Cross	d							20 13									20 42								
Frinton-on-Sea	d							20 16									20 45								
Walton-on-the-Naze	a							20 22									20 49								
Manningtree ■2	d	19 38				19 47			19 55			20 00			20 16			20 28		20 34				20 38	20 55
Mistley	d	19 42										20 04												20 42	
Wrabness	d	19 47										20 09												20 47	
Harwich International	d	19 55										20 17								20a54				20 55	
Dovercourt	d	19 58										20 20												20 58	
Harwich Town	a	20 00										20 22												21 00	
Ipswich	a					20 04			20 07						20 28			20 40							21 07
	d		20 00						20 08				20 19					20 41							21 08
Needham Market	d												20 28												
Stowmarket	d		20 12						20 19				20a33					20 52							21 19
Peterborough ■8	a		21 39																						
Diss	d								20 32									21 05							21 32
Norwich	a								20 51									21 24							21 51

Station		LE ■	LE ■	LE	LE ■	LE ■		LE ■	LE ■	LE ■	LE ◇■ ⊡	LE ■	LE ■	LE ■	LE ◇■ ⊡	LE ■		LE	LE ■	LE ■	LE ■	LE ■	LE ◇■ ⊡	LE ■	LE ■
London Liverpool Street ■15 ⊖	d					20 02		20 18			20 30	20 38	20 48		21 00					21 02	21 18		21 30	21 38	21 48
Stratford ■7 ⊖	d					20 09		20 25			20u38	20 45	20 55							21 09	21 25		21u38	21 45	21 55
Romford	d																								
Shenfield ■3	d					20 25		20 41				21 03	21 11							21 25	21 41			22 03	22 11
Ingatestone	d							20 45					21 15								21 45				22 15
Chelmsford ■3	d					20 34		20 52			21 03	21 12	21 22							21 34	21 52		22 03	22 12	22 22
Hatfield Peverel	d					20 40														21 40					
Witham ■2	d					20 47		21 03				21 23	21 34							21 47	22 03			22 23	22 34
White Notley	d												21 41												22 41
Cressing	d												21 43												22 43
Braintree Freeport	d												21 46												22 46
Braintree	a												21 50												22 50
Kelvedon	d					20 51						21 27								21 51				22 27	
Marks Tey ■2	d					20 57						21 33								21 57				22 33	
Colchester ■4	a					21 04		21 15			21 22	21 40			21 46					22 04	22 15		22 22	22 40	
Colchester ■4	d				20 56	21 04		21 16		21 20	21 23	21 41			21 47				21 56	22 04	22 16		22 23	22 41	
Colchester Town	a				21 03					21 27		21 49							22 03					22 49	
	d				21 07														22 07						
Hythe	d				21 11														22 11						
Wivenhoe ■3	d				21 15			21 23											22 15		22 23				
Alresford (Essex)	d				21 19														22 19						
Great Bentley	d				21 23														22 23						
Weeley	d				21 26				←										22 26			←			
Thorpe-le-Soken ■1	a				21 31			21 35	21 31										22 31		22 35	22 31			
	d	20 54			21 37			21 35	21 37										22 37		22 35	22 37			
Clacton-on-Sea	a	21 03			→			21 44											→		22 44				
Kirby Cross	d								21 42													22 42			
Frinton-on-Sea	d								21 45													22 45			
Walton-on-the-Naze	a								21 49													22 49			
Manningtree ■2	d		21 00			21 12					21 31				21 55	22 00				22 12			22 31		
Mistley	d		21 04													22 04									
Wrabness	d		21 09													22 09									
Harwich International	d		21 17											21 38		22 17				22a28					
Dovercourt	d		21 20													22 20									
Harwich Town	a		21 22													22 22									
Ipswich	a					21 25					21 43			22 03	22 07								22 43		
	d			21 16							21 44				22 08			22 16					22 44		
Needham Market	d			21 26														22 26							
Stowmarket	d			21a32							21 55				22 19			22a32					22 55		
Peterborough ■8	a																								
Diss	d										22 08				22 32								23 08		
Norwich	a										22 27				22 51								23 27		

London - Chelmsford, Colchester, Walton-on-Naze, Clacton, Harwich, Ipswich and Norwich

Network Diagram - see first Page of Table 5

Station		LE ■		LE ■	LE ■	LE ■	LE ■	LE ■	LE ■	LE ◇■ ⊡	LE ■	LE ■		LE ■	LE ◇■ ⊡	LE	LE ■	LE ■	LE ◇■ ⊡	LE ■	LE ■	LE ◇■ ⊡			
London Liverpool Street ■15 ⊖	d	22 00		22 02				22 15		22 30	22 35			22 45	23 00		23 07	23 15	23 30	23 35	23 45	23 59			
Stratford ■7 ⊖	d			22 10				22 24		22u40	22 44			22 54	23u10		23 17	23 25	23u40	23 45	23 54	00u10			
Romford	d																								
Shenfield ■3	d			22 27				22 41			23 01			23 12			23 34	23 43		00 01	00 12				
Ingatestone	d							22 45			23 05			23 16				23 48		00 05	00 16				
Chelmsford ■3	d	22 28		22 36				22 52		23 05	23 12			23 23	23 37		23 43	23 55	00 06	00 12	00 23	00 37			
Hatfield Peverel	d			22 42													23 49			00 18					
Witham ■2	d			22 49				23 03			23 23	23 25		23 34			23 56	00 05		00 25	00 34				
White Notley	d											23 32													
Cressing	d											23 34													
Braintree Freeport	d											23 37													
Braintree	a											23 41													
Kelvedon	d			22 53							23 27						00 01			00 29					
Marks Tey ■2	d			22 59							23 33					23 46	00 06			00 35					
Colchester ■4	a	22 47		23 07				23 15		23 24	23 41			23 46	23 58	23 55	00 14	00 17	00 25	00 43	00 46	00 56			
Colchester ■4	d	22 47					22 56	23 16		23 25				23 47	23 59			00 18	00 25		00 47	00 57			
Colchester Town	a						23 03																		
	d						23 07																		
Hythe	d						23 11																		
Wivenhoe ■3	d						23 15	23 23						23 54				00 25			00 54				
Alresford (Essex)	d						23 19																		
Great Bentley	d						23 23																		
Weeley	d						23 26		←																
Thorpe-le-Soken ■1	a						23 31	23 35	23 31					00 06				00 37			01 06				
	d					23 16	23 37	23 35	23 37					00 06				00 37			01 06				
Clacton-on-Sea	a					23 25	→	23 44						00 15				00 46			01 15				
Kirby Cross	d								23 42																
Frinton-on-Sea	d								23 45																
Walton-on-the-Naze	a								23 49																
Manningtree ■2	d	22 55			23 00					23 33					00 09				00 33			01 07			
Mistley	d				23 04																				
Wrabness	d				23 09																				
Harwich International	d				23 17																				
Dovercourt	d				23 20																				
Harwich Town	a				23 22																				
Ipswich	a	23 08								23 45					00 19				00 45			01 17			
	d									23 46					00 21				00 46			01 19			
Needham Market	d																								
Stowmarket	d									23 58					00 32				00 58			01 30			
Peterborough ■8	a																								
Diss	d									00 10					00 45				01 10			01 43			
Norwich	a									00 30					01 04				01 30			02 03			

Table 11

Mondays to Fridays
from 10 September

London - Chelmsford, Colchester, Walton-on-Naze, Clacton, Harwich, Ipswich and Norwich

Network Diagram - see first Page of Table 5

		LE	LE	LE	LE	LE	LE	LE	LE	LE	LE	LE	LE	LE	LE	LE	LE	LE	LE	LE	LE	LE	LE
		MX									FO					FO	FO	FO					
		◇■	◇■	◇■	■	■	■	◇■	■	■	■	■	■	■	■	■	◇■	■	◇■	◇■	◇■	■	◇■
			MO		MO		TW ThO		TW ThO			MO		TW ThO					TW ThO		MO	MO	TW ThO
			A	B	A	B	C	B	C	B	D	A	B	C	B	D	D	E	C	B	A	A	C
		⊡	⊡	⊡				⊡									⊡		⊡	⊡			⊡
London Liverpool Street ■ ⊖	d	22p30	22p30	22p30	22p32	22p45	22p50	23p00			23p02	23p02	23p07	23p10	23p15	23p18	23p30		23p30	23p30	23p30	23p32	
Stratford ■ ⊖	d	22b38		22b40	22p39	22p54	22p57	23b10			23p09	23p09	23p17	23p17	23p25	23p25	23b38		23b39	23b40		23p39	
Romford	d																						
Shenfield ■	d				23p01	23p11	23p21				23p25	23p31	23p34	23p41	23p41	23p41			00 02			00 01	
Ingatestone	d					23p15	23p25					23p35			23p46	23p45							
Chelmsford ■	d	23p03		23p06	23p10	23p22	23p32	23p36			23p34	23p42	23p43	23p50	23p53	23p52	00 03		00 13	00 06		00 10	
Hatfield Peverel	d										23p40	23p48	23p49	23p56									←
Witham ■	d				23p21	23p33	23p43		23p45		23p47	23p55	23p56	00 03	00 03	00 03		00 05	00 24			00 21	00 24
White Notley	d								23p52									00 12	→				
Cressing	d								23p54									00 14					
Braintree Freeport	d								23p57									00 17					
Braintree	a								00 01									00 21					
Kelvedon	d						23p47				23p51	23p59	00 01	00 07								00 28	
Marks Tey ■	d				23p28		23p53				23p57	00 05	00 06	00 13									
Colchester ■	a	23p22	23p23	23p25	23p36	23p45	00 05	23p55			00 04	00 12	00 14	00 20	00 17	00 15	00 22			00 25	00 27	00 39	00 36
Colchester ■	d	23p23	23p23	23p25	23p36	23p46		23p55			00 04	00 12		00 20	00 18	00 16	00 23			00 25	00 27		00 37
Colchester Town	a																						
	d																						
Hythe	d																						
Wivenhoe ■	d				23p44	23p54									00 26	00 23							
Alresford (Essex)	d				23p47											00 27							
Great Bentley	d				23p51											00 31							
Weeley	d																						
Thorpe-le-Soken ■	a				23p58	00 05									00 37	00 38							
	d				23p58	00 05									00 37	00 38							
Clacton-on-Sea	a				00 07	00 14									00 46	00 51							
Kirby Cross	d																						
Frinton-on-Sea	d																						
Walton-on-the-Naze	a																						
Manningtree ■	d	23p31	23p31	23p34				00 04		00 08	00 12	00 20		00 28			00 31			00 34	00 35		00 45
Mistley	d									00 12													
Wrabness	d									00 17													
Harwich International	d									00 24													
Dovercourt	d									00 27													
Harwich Town	a									00 30													
Ipswich	a	23p43	23p43	23p45				00 15			00 28	00 36		00 44			00 43			00 45	00 47		00 57
	d	23p44	23p44	23p47				00 17									00 44			00 47	00 48		00 58
Needham Market	d																						
Stowmarket	d	23p55	23p55	23p58				00 28									00 55			00 58	00 59		01 09
Peterborough ■	a																						
Diss	d	00 08	00 08	00 11				00 41									01 08			01 11	01 12		01 22
Norwich	a	00 39	00 41	00 30				01 00									01 43			01 30	01 45		01 57

A from 17 September
B 10 September
C from 18 September
D also from 11 September until 13 September
E also from 10 September until 13 September
b Previous night, stops to pick up only

Table 11

Mondays to Fridays
from 10 September

London - Chelmsford, Colchester, Walton-on-Naze, Clacton, Harwich, Ipswich and Norwich

Network Diagram - see first Page of Table 5

		LE	LE	LE	LE	LE	LE	LE	LE	LE	LE	LE	LE	LE	LE	LE	LE	LE	LE	LE	LE	LE	LE
						FO					FO												
		■	■	■	■	■	■	◇■	■	■	■	■	◇■	■		■	◇■	■	■	■	■	■	■
			TW ThO	TW ThO			TW ThO		MO			TW ThO											
		A	B	B	A	C	B	A	D	A	C	B	A	A									
								⊡					⊡										
London Liverpool Street ■ ⊖	d	23p35			23p45	23p48	23p50	23p59	00 02	00 12	00 18	00 18	00 30	00 46									
Stratford ■ ⊖	d	23p45			23p54	23p55	23p57	00u10	00 09	00 24	00 25	00 25	00u40	01 00									
Romford	d											00 37											
Shenfield ■	d	00 01			00 11	00 11	00 21		00 31	00 41	00 47	00 51		01 17									
Ingatestone	d	00 05			00 15	00 15	00 25		00 35	00 45	00 51	00 55		01 22									
Chelmsford ■	d	00 12			00 22	00 22	00 32	00 36	00 42	00 52	00 58	01 02	01 07	01 29									
Hatfield Peverel	d	00 18				00 28	00 38		00 48	00 58	01 04	01 08		01 35									
Witham ■	d	00 25	00 26		00 33	00 35	00 45		00 55	01 05	01 11	01 15		01 41		05 21							
White Notley	d		00 33													05 28							
Cressing	d		00 35													05 30							
Braintree Freeport	d		00 38													05 33							
Braintree	a		00 42													05 37							
Kelvedon	d	00 29				00 39	00 49		00 59	01 09	01 15	01 19		01 46									
Marks Tey ■	d	00 35				00 45	00 55		01 05	01 15	01 21	01 25		01 51									
Colchester ■	a	00 43			00 46	00 57	01 07	00 55	01 18	01 23	01 41	01 45	01 29	02 00									
Colchester ■	d			00 41	00 47			00 56					01 30				05 40			06 10		06 15	06 20
Colchester Town	a																						06 27
	d																						
Hythe	d																						
Wivenhoe ■	d			00 48	00 55																		
Alresford (Essex)	d			00 52																			
Great Bentley	d			00 56																			
Weeley	d																						
Thorpe-le-Soken ■	a			01 03	01 06																		
	d			01 03	01 06														06 03				
Clacton-on-Sea	a			01 16	01 15																		
Kirby Cross	d																		06 12				
Frinton-on-Sea	d																		06 15				
Walton-on-the-Naze	a																		06 19				
Manningtree ■	d							01 05					01 40				05 49	05 56		06 18		06 23	
Mistley	d																	06 00		06 22			
Wrabness	d																	06 05		06 27			
Harwich International	d																	06 13		06 35			
Dovercourt	d																	06 16		06 38			
Harwich Town	a																	06 20		06 40			
Ipswich	a							01 15					01 50				05 59					06 34	
	d							01 17					01 52		05 10		06 00				06 16		
Needham Market	d														05 20						06 25		
Stowmarket	d							01 28					02 03		05a26		06 12				06a30		
Peterborough ■	a																07 38						
Diss	d							01 41					02 16										
Norwich	a							02 00					02 35										

A 10 September
B from 18 September
C also from 11 September until 13 September
D from 17 September

London - Chelmsford, Colchester, Walton-on-Naze, Clacton, Harwich, Ipswich and Norwich

Network Diagram - see first Page of Table 5

		LE ■		LE ■	LE ■	LE ■	LE ■	LE ■	LE ◇■	LE ■	LE ■	LE ■		LE ■	LE ◇■	LE ■	LE ■	LE ■	LE ■	LE ■	LE ◇■	LE ■		LE ■	LE ■
London Liverpool Street ⊖	d			05 23					06 00	06 02	06 12				06 25			06 38	06 48		07 00	07 02			
Stratford ⊖	d			05 30						06 09	06 19				06u33			06 45	06 55			07 09			
Romford	d			05 38																					
Shenfield	d			05 48						06 25	06 36							07 01	07 11		07u22	07 25			
Ingatestone	d			05 52							06 40								07 15						
Chelmsford	d			05 59					06 30	06 34	06 47				06 58			07 10	07 22			07 34			
Hatfield Peverel	d			06 05							06 53											07 40			
Witham	d			06 12	06 16					06 45	07 03				07 09			07 21	07 33			07 48			
White Notley	d				06 23						07 10											07 55			
Cressing	d				06 25						07 12											07 57			
Braintree Freeport	d				06 28						07 15											08 00			
Braintree	a				06 32						07 19											08 04			
Kelvedon	d			06 16						06 49								07 25							
Marks Tey	d			06 22						06 55								07 31	07 40						
Colchester	a			06 29					06 49	07 02					07 22			07 38	07 47		07 50				
Colchester	d			06 30					06 50	07 02		07 10			07 23		07 26	07 43	07 48		07 51				07 56
Colchester Town	a																07 34		07 56						08 03
	d																07 38								08 07
Hythe	d									07 07							07 42								08 11
Wivenhoe	d			06 37						07 11							07 46								08 15
Alresford (Essex)	d									07 14															08 19
Great Bentley	d									07 18															08 23
Weeley	d									07 22															08 26
Thorpe-le-Soken	a			06 50						07 28							07 57								08 31
	d	06 31		06 50			06 56			07 28						07 38	07 57								08 40
Clacton-on-Sea	a			06 59						07 37							08 06								→
Kirby Cross	d	06 39					07 06									07 47									
Frinton-on-Sea	d	06 42					07 09									07 50									
Walton-on-the-Naze	a	06 46					07 13									07 54									
Manningtree	d								06 58			07 18		07 24	07 31			07 51			07 59				
Mistley	d													07 28				07 55						08 02	
Wrabness	d													07 33				08 01							
Harwich International	d													07 41				08 10							
Dovercourt	d													07 44				08 13							
Harwich Town	a													07 46				08 15							
Ipswich	a								07 10			07 30			07 42						08 11			08 17	
	d					06 39		06 56	07 11						07 44					08 03	08 12			08 19	
Needham Market	d							07 05																08 28	
Stowmarket	d					06 51		07a10	07 22						07 55					08 15	08 23			08a33	
Peterborough	a																			09 39					
Diss	d					07 04			07 35						08 08						08 36				
Norwich	a					07 24			07 54						08 27						08 55				

		LE ■	LE ■	LE ■	LE ◇■	LE ■	LE ■			LE ◇■	LE ■	LE ■	LE ■	LE ■	LE ■	LE ■	LE ■	LE ◇■		LE ■	LE ■	LE ■	LE ◇■	LE ■	LE ■
London Liverpool Street ⊖	d	07 08	07 18		07 30	07 36	07 46			07 55			08 00	08 06		08 17		08 30		08 36	08 48		09 00		
Stratford ⊖	d	07 15	07 25		07u38	07 45	07 54						08 08	08 14		08 25		08u38		08 45	08 55				
Romford	d																								
Shenfield	d	07 31	07 41			08 01	08 11						08 25	08 30		08 41				09 03	09 11				
Ingatestone	d		07 45			08 05								08 34		08 45					09 15				
Chelmsford	d	07 40	07 52		08 03	08 12	08 20						08 34	08 41		08 52		09 03		09 12	09 22				
Hatfield Peverel	d													08 47											
Witham	d	07 51	08 03			08 23	08 35	08 38					08 45	08 54		09 03				09 23	09 35				
White Notley	d						08 42														09 42				
Cressing	d						08 44														09 44				
Braintree Freeport	d						08 47														09 47				
Braintree	a						08 51														09 51				
Kelvedon	d	07 55				08 27							08 49							09 27					
Marks Tey	d	08 01	08 11			08 33							08 55			09 10				09 33					
Colchester	a	08 08	08 18		08 22	08 40		08 53		08 45			09 02	09 06		09 17		09 22		09 40			09 46		
Colchester	d	08 08	08 19		08 23	08 41		08 56		08 47			09 02	09 06	09 14	09 18		09 23		09 41			09 47		
Colchester Town	a					08 49		09 03							09 21					09 49					
	d							09 07																	
Hythe	d		08 23					09 11																	
Wivenhoe	d		08 27					09 15								09 25									
Alresford (Essex)	d							09 19																	
Great Bentley	d							09 23																	
Weeley	d			←				09 26									←								
Thorpe-le-Soken	a		08 38	08 31				09 31								09 36	09 31								
	d		08 38	08 40				09 38								09 36	09 38								
Clacton-on-Sea	a		08 47					→								09 45									
Kirby Cross	d			08 45													09 43								
Frinton-on-Sea	d			08 48													09 46								
Walton-on-the-Naze	a			08 52													09 50								
Manningtree	d	08 16			08 31					08 55	09 00			09 14				09 31					09 55	10 00	
Mistley	d										09 04													10 04	
Wrabness	d										09 09													10 09	
Harwich International	d										09 17													10 17	
Dovercourt	d										09 20													10 20	
Harwich Town	a										09 22													10 22	
Ipswich	a	08 29			08 43					09 07			09 20	09 27				09 43					10 07		
	d				08 44					09 08		09 19						09 44				10 00	10 08		10 19
Needham Market	d											09 28													10 28
Stowmarket	d				08 55							09a33						09 55				10 12			10a33
Peterborough	a																					11 37			
Diss	d				09 08					09 29								10 08					10 29		
Norwich	a				09 27					09 48								10 27					10 50		

London - Chelmsford, Colchester, Walton-on-Naze, Clacton, Harwich, Ipswich and Norwich

Network Diagram - see first Page of Table 5

		LE ■	LE ■	LE ■		LE ■	LE ■	LE ◇■	LE ■	LE ■	LE ◇■	LE ■	LE ■	LE ■		LE ■	LE ■	LE ■	LE ■	LE ◇■	LE ■	LE ■	LE ■	LE ◇■
London Liverpool Street ⊖	d		09 02	09 18				09 30	09 38	09 48	10 00					10 02	10 18			10 30	10 38	10 48		11 00
Stratford ⊖	d		09 09	09 25				09u38	09 45	09 55						10 09	10 25			10u38	10 45	10 55		
Romford	d								09 53												10 53			
Shenfield	d		09 25	09 41					10 03	10 11						10 25	10 41				11 03	11 11		
Ingatestone	d			09 45						10 15							10 45					11 15		
Chelmsford	d		09 34	09 52				10 03	10 12	10 22						10 34	10 52			11 03	11 12	11 22		
Hatfield Peverel	d		09 40													10 40								
Witham	d		09 47	10 03					10 23	10 34						10 47	11 03				11 23	11 34		
White Notley	d									10 41												11 41		
Cressing	d									10 43												11 43		
Braintree Freeport	d									10 46												11 46		
Braintree	a									10 50												11 50		
Kelvedon	d		09 51						10 27							10 51					11 27			
Marks Tey	d		09 57						10 33							10 57					11 33			
Colchester	a		10 04	10 15				10 22	10 40		10 46					11 04	11 15			11 22	11 40			11 46
Colchester	d	09 56	10 04	10 16			10 20	10 23	10 41		10 47			10 56		11 04	11 16		11 20	11 23	11 41			11 47
Colchester Town	a	10 03					10 27		10 49					11 03					11 27		11 49			
	d	10 07												11 07										
Hythe	d	10 11												11 11										
Wivenhoe	d	10 15		10 23										11 15			11 23							
Alresford (Essex)	d	10 19												11 19										
Great Bentley	d	10 23												11 23										
Weeley	d	10 26				←								11 26				←						
Thorpe-le-Soken	a	10 31		10 35		10 31								11 31			11 35	11 31						
	d	10 37		10 35		10 37								11 37			11 35	11 37						
Clacton-on-Sea	a	→		10 44										→			11 44							
Kirby Cross	d					10 42												11 42						
Frinton-on-Sea	d					10 45												11 45						
Walton-on-the-Naze	a					10 49												11 49						
Manningtree	d		10 12					10 31			10 55	11 00				11 12				11 31				11 55
Mistley	d											11 04												
Wrabness	d											11 09												
Harwich International	d											11 17												
Dovercourt	d											11 20												
Harwich Town	a											11 22												
Ipswich	a		10 25					10 43			11 07					11 25				11 43				12 07
	d							10 44			11 08		11 19							11 44			12 00	12 08
Needham Market	d												11 28											
Stowmarket	d							10 55					11a33							11 55			12 12	
Peterborough	a																						13 37	
Diss	d							11 08			11 29									12 08				12 29
Norwich	a							11 27			11 50									12 27				12 50

		LE ■	LE ■	LE ■	LE ■	LE ■	LE ■	LE ■	LE ◇■	LE ■		LE ■	LE ◇■	LE ■	LE ■	LE ■	LE ■	LE ■	LE ■	LE ■		LE ◇■	LE ■	LE ■	LE ■
London Liverpool Street ⊖	d				11 02	11 18			11 30	11 38		11 48	12 00				12 02	12 18				12 30	12 38	12 48	
Stratford ⊖	d				11 09	11 25			11u38	11 45		11 55					12 09	12 25				12u38	12 45	12 55	
Romford	d									11 53													12 53		
Shenfield	d				11 25	11 41				12 03		12 11					12 25	12 41					13 03	13 11	
Ingatestone	d					11 45						12 15						12 45						13 15	
Chelmsford	d				11 34	11 52			12 03	12 12		12 22					12 34	12 52				13 03	13 12	13 22	
Hatfield Peverel	d				11 40												12 40								
Witham	d				11 47	12 03				12 23		12 34					12 47	13 03					13 23	13 34	
White Notley	d											12 41												13 41	
Cressing	d											12 43												13 43	
Braintree Freeport	d											12 46												13 46	
Braintree	a											12 50												13 50	
Kelvedon	d				11 51					12 27							12 51						13 27		
Marks Tey	d				11 57					12 33							12 57						13 33		
Colchester	a				12 04	12 15			12 22	12 40			12 46				13 04	13 15				13 22	13 40		
Colchester	d			11 56	12 04	12 16		12 20	12 23	12 41			12 47			12 56	13 04	13 16		13 20		13 23	13 41		
Colchester Town	a			12 03				12 27		12 49						13 03				13 27			13 49		
	d			12 07												13 07									
Hythe	d			12 11												13 11									
Wivenhoe	d			12 15		12 23										13 15		13 23							
Alresford (Essex)	d			12 19												13 19									
Great Bentley	d			12 23												13 23									
Weeley	d			12 26			←									13 26			←						
Thorpe-le-Soken	a			12 31		12 35	12 31									13 31		13 35	13 31						
	d			12 37		12 35	12 37									13 37		13 35	13 37						
Clacton-on-Sea	a			→		12 44										→		13 44							
Kirby Cross	d						12 42												13 42						
Frinton-on-Sea	d						12 45												13 45						
Walton-on-the-Naze	a						12 49												13 49						
Manningtree	d	12 00			12 12				12 31				12 55	13 00			13 12					13 31			
Mistley	d	12 04												13 04											
Wrabness	d	12 09												13 09											
Harwich International	d	12 17												13 17											
Dovercourt	d	12 20												13 20											
Harwich Town	a	12 22												13 22											
Ipswich	a				12 25				12 43				13 07				13 25					13 43			
	d		12 19						12 44				13 08		13 19							13 44			14 00
Needham Market	d		12 28												13 28										
Stowmarket	d		12a33						12 55						13a33							13 55			14 12
Peterborough	a																								15 37
Diss	d								13 08				13 29									14 08			
Norwich	a								13 27				13 50									14 27			

Table 11

Mondays to Fridays
from 10 September

London - Chelmsford, Colchester, Walton-on-Naze, Clacton, Harwich, Ipswich and Norwich

Network Diagram - see first Page of Table 5

		LE ◇1 🍴	LE 1	LE 1	LE 1	LE 1	LE 1	LE 1	LE 1	LE ◇1 🍴	LE 1	LE 1	LE ◇1 🍴	LE 1	LE 1	LE 1	LE 1	LE 1	LE 1	LE 1	LE ◇1 🍴	LE 1	LE 1
London Liverpool Street 15 ⊖	d	13 00				13 02	13 18			13 30	13 38	13 48	14 00				14 02	14 18			14 30	14 38	14 48
Stratford 7 ⊖	d					13 09	13 25			13u38	13 45	13 55					14 09	14 25			14u38	14 45	14 55
Romford	d										13 53											14 53	
Shenfield 3	d					13 25	13 41				14 03	14 11					14 25	14 41				15 03	15 11
Ingatestone	d						13 45					14 15						14 45					15 15
Chelmsford 3	d					13 34	13 52			14 03	14 12	14 22					14 34	14 52			15 03	15 12	15 22
Hatfield Peverel	d					13 40											14 40						
Witham 2	d					13 47	14 03				14 23	14 34					14 47	15 03				15 23	15 35
White Notley	d											14 41											15 42
Cressing	d											14 43											15 44
Braintree Freeport	d											14 46											15 47
Braintree	a											14 50											15 51
Kelvedon	d					13 51					14 27						14 51					15 27	
Marks Tey 2	d					13 57					14 33						14 57					15 33	
Colchester 4	a	13 46				14 04	14 15			14 22	14 40		14 46				15 04	15 15			15 22	15 40	
Colchester 4	d	13 47			13 56	14 04	14 16		14 20	14 23	14 41		14 47			14 56	15 04	15 16		15 20	15 23	15 41	
Colchester Town	a				14 03				14 27		14 49					15 03				15 27		15 49	
	d				14 07											15 07							
Hythe	d				14 11											15 11							
Wivenhoe 3	d				14 15		14 23									15 15		15 23					
Alresford (Essex)	d				14 19											15 19							
Great Bentley	d				14 23											15 23							
Weeley	d				14 26			←								15 26			←				
Thorpe-le-Soken 1	a				14 31		14 35	14 31								15 31		15 35	15 31				
	d				14 37		14 35	14 37								15 37		15 35	15 37				
Clacton-on-Sea	a				→		14 44									→		15 44					
Kirby Cross	d							14 42											15 42				
Frinton-on-Sea	d							14 45											15 45				
Walton-on-the-Naze	a							14 49											15 49				
Manningtree 2	d	13 55	14 00			14 12				14 31			14 55	15 00			15 12				15 31		
Mistley	d		14 04											15 04									
Wrabness	d		14 09											15 09									
Harwich International	d		14 17											15 17									
Dovercourt	d		14 20											15 20									
Harwich Town	a		14 22											15 22									
Ipswich	a	14 07				14 25				14 43			15 07				15 25				15 43		
	d	14 08		14 19						14 44			15 08		15 19						15 44		
Needham Market	d			14 28											15 28								
Stowmarket	d			14a33						14 55					15a33						15 55		
Peterborough 8	a																						
Diss	d	14 29								15 08			15 29								16 08		
Norwich	a	14 50								15 27			15 48								16 27		

		LE 1	LE ◇1 🍴	LE 1	LE 1	LE 1	LE 1	LE 1	LE 1	LE 1	LE 1	LE ■ 1 🍴	LE 1	LE 1	LE 1	LE ■ 1 🍴	LE 1	LE 1	LE 1	LE 1	LE 1	LE 1
London Liverpool Street 15 ⊖	d		15 00				15 02		15 18			15 30		15 38	15 48	16 00				16 02		16 14
Stratford 7 ⊖	d						15 09		15 25					15 45	15 55					16 09		16 22
Romford	d													15 53								
Shenfield 3	d						15 25		15 41					16 03	16 11					16 25		16 38
Ingatestone	d								15 45				16 00		16 15							
Chelmsford 3	d						15 34		15 52			16 00	16 07	16 12	16 22					16 34		16 48
Hatfield Peverel	d						15 40						16 13							16 40		
Witham 2	d						15 47		16 03				16 20	16 24	16 35					16 47		
White Notley	d														16 42							
Cressing	d														16 44							
Braintree Freeport	d														16 47							
Braintree	a														16 51							
Kelvedon	d						15 51						16 24	16 28						16 51		16 59
Marks Tey 2	d						15 57						16 30	16 34						16 57		17 05
Colchester 4	a		15 46				16 04		16 15			16 21	16 38	16 41		16 46				17 04		17 12
Colchester 4	d		15 47			15 56	16 04	16 14	16 16		16 20	16 21		16 42		16 47			16 56	17 04	17 09	17 16
Colchester Town	a					16 03					16 27			16 50					17 03		17 16	
	d					16 07													17 07			
Hythe	d					16 11													17 11			17 20
Wivenhoe 3	d					16 15			16 23										17 15			17 24
Alresford (Essex)	d					16 19													17 19			
Great Bentley	d					16 23													17 23			
Weeley	d					16 26				←									17 26			
Thorpe-le-Soken 1	a					16 31			16 35	16 31									17 31			17 35
	d					16 37			16 35	16 37									17 37			17 35
Clacton-on-Sea	a					→			16 44										→			17 46
Kirby Cross	d									16 42												
Frinton-on-Sea	d									16 45												
Walton-on-the-Naze	a									16 49												
Manningtree 2	d		15 55	16 00			16 12	16 23				16 29				16 55	17 00			17 12		
Mistley	d			16 04				16 27									17 04					
Wrabness	d			16 09				16 32									17 09					
Harwich International	d			16 17				16 41									17 17					
Dovercourt	d			16 20				16 44									17 20					
Harwich Town	a			16 22				16 46									17 22					
Ipswich	a		16 07				16 25					16 40				17 07				17 27		
	d	16 00	16 08		16 19							16 41				17 08		17 19				
Needham Market	d				16 28													17 28				
Stowmarket	d	16 12			16a33							16 52				17 19		17a33				
Peterborough 8	a	17 37																				
Diss	d		16 29									17 05				17 32						
Norwich	a		16 50									17 24				17 53						

Table 11

Mondays to Fridays
from 10 September

London - Chelmsford, Colchester, Walton-on-Naze, Clacton, Harwich, Ipswich and Norwich

Network Diagram - see first Page of Table 5

		LE 1	LE 1	LE ■ 1 🍴	LE 1	LE 1	LE 1	LE 1	LE 1	LE 1	LE 1		LE 1	LE ■ 1 A 🍴	LE 1	LE 1	LE ◇1	LE 1	LE 1	LE 1	LE 1	LE 1 B	LE ■ 1 🍴
London Liverpool Street 15 ⊖	d		16 17	16 30				16 32	16 34		16 44		16 47	17 00			17 02	17 08		17 12	17 18	17 20	17 30
Stratford 7 ⊖	d		16 25						16 42		16 52		16 55				17 10	17 16		17 20	17 26	17 29	
Romford	d																						
Shenfield 3	d		16 41					16 54	16 58				17 11				17u26					17 45	
Ingatestone	d		16 46										17 16									17 49	
Chelmsford 3	d		16 53					17 04	17 08		17 15		17 23				17 36	17 40		17 44	17 50	17 57	
Hatfield Peverel	d								17 14											17 50			
Witham 2	d		17a06					17 14	17 21				17a36				17 46	17 50		17a59		18 10	
White Notley	d								17 28													18 17	
Cressing	d								17 30													18 19	
Braintree Freeport	d								17 33													18 22	
Braintree	a								17 39													18 28	
Kelvedon	d										17 27							17 55			18 02		
Marks Tey 2	d										17 32						17 54	18 00					
Colchester 4	a			17 16				17 26			17 40						18 01	18 08			18 12		
Colchester 4	d			17 17			17 24	17 27			17 44	17 47				17 56	18 01	18 12			18 12		
Colchester Town	a						17 33									18 03							
	d						17 37									18 07							
Hythe	d						17 41									18 11		18 16					
Wivenhoe 3	d						17 45				17 51					18 15		18 20					
Alresford (Essex)	d						17 49				17 55					18 19		18 24					
Great Bentley	d						17 53				17 59					18 23		18 28					
Weeley	d	←					17 56			←						18 26			←				
Thorpe-le-Soken 1	a	17 31					18 01			18 01	18 06					18 31		18 35	18 31				
	d	17 37					18 10			18 10	18 06					18 37		18 35	18 37				
Clacton-on-Sea	a						→				18 17					→		18 46					
Kirby Cross	d	17 42								18 15									18 42				
Frinton-on-Sea	d	17 45								18 18									18 45				
Walton-on-the-Naze	a	17 49								18 22									18 49				
Manningtree 2	d				17 24			17 35				17 57					18 09				18 20		18 27
Mistley	d				17 28							18 01											
Wrabness	d				17 33							18 06											
Harwich International	d				17 41							18 15											
Dovercourt	d				17 44							18 18											
Harwich Town	a				17 46							18 22											
Ipswich	a			17 34				17 49						17 59			18 20				18 35		18 37
	d			17 36		17 49								18 00	18 16		18 24						18 39
Needham Market	d					17 58									18 25								
Stowmarket	d			17 47		18 04									18a30		18 35						18 50
Peterborough 8	a					19 38																	
Diss	d			18 00										18 21			18 47						19 03
Norwich	a			18 22										18 42			19 09						19 25

		LE 1	LE 1	LE 1	LE 1	LE 1	LE 1	LE 1 B	LE ■ 1 🍴	LE 1	LE 1	LE 1	LE 1	LE 1	LE ■ 1 🍴	LE 1	LE 1	LE 1	LE 1	LE 1	LE 1	LE ■ 1 🍴
London Liverpool Street 15 ⊖	d		17 32		17 38			17 40	17 50	17 52			17 58	18 00	18 10		18 12		18 18		18 20	18 30
Stratford 7 ⊖	d		17 40		17 47			17 49		18 01			18 06	18 09			18 21		18 27		18 29	
Romford	d																					
Shenfield 3	d							18 05						18 25							18 45	
Ingatestone	d							18 09						18 29							18 49	
Chelmsford 3	d		18 05		18 12			18 17		18 25				18 37			18 46		18 52		18 57	
Hatfield Peverel	d		18 11							18 31							18 52	←				
Witham 2	d		18 17					18 31		18 37			18 41	19c01			18 58	19 01			19 11	
White Notley	d													→				19 08				
Cressing	d																	19 10				
Braintree Freeport	d																	19 13				
Braintree	a																	19 19				
Kelvedon	d				18 25			18 37					18 46						19 06		19 17	
Marks Tey 2	d		18 25							18 46							19 06				19 23	
Colchester 4	a		18 32		18 36			18 48	18 42	18 53			18 56		19 00		19 13		19 17		19 30	19 21
Colchester 4	d	18 16	18 32		18 36		18 40	18 49	18 43	18 54			18 57		19 02	19 06	19 13		19 17	19 20	19 30	19 23
Colchester Town	a	18 26						18 59								19 13				19 27		
	d															19 19						
Hythe	d						18 44			18 58						19 23	19 18					
Wivenhoe 3	d		18 40				18 48			19 02						→	19 22					
Alresford (Essex)	d						18 52															
Great Bentley	d						18 56															
Weeley	d						18 59															
Thorpe-le-Soken 1	a		18 51				19 04			19 13							19 33					
	d		18 51			18 53	19 04			19 13							19 33					
Clacton-on-Sea	a		19 02				19 13			19 24							19 44					
Kirby Cross	d					19 01																
Frinton-on-Sea	d					19 04																
Walton-on-the-Naze	a					19 08																
Manningtree 2	d			18 35	18 44				18 52		19 00		19 05		19 11				19 25		19 40	19 32
Mistley	d			18 39							19 04											
Wrabness	d			18 44							19 09											
Harwich International	d			18 52							19 17										20a01	
Dovercourt	d			18 55							19 20											
Harwich Town	a			18 57							19 22											
Ipswich	a				18 59				19 03				19 19		19 21				19 39			19 42
	d								19 04			19 10			19 23							19 44
Needham Market	d											19 19										
Stowmarket	d								19 16			19a24			19 34							19 55
Peterborough 8	a																					
Diss	d								19 29						19 47							20 08
Norwich	a								19 50						20 09							20 30

A The East Anglian

B The Stratford call is subject to introduction during the currency of the timetable.

c arr 1854

London - Chelmsford, Colchester, Walton-on-Naze, Clacton, Harwich, Ipswich and Norwich

Network Diagram - see first Page of Table 5

		LE	LE	LE	LE	LE		LE	LE	LE		LE	LE	LE	LE	LE	LE	LE	LE	LE		LE	LE	LE	LE
		1	1	1	1	1		1	1	1		1 ⊏⊐	1	1	1	1	1	1	1	1 ⊏⊐		1	1	1	1
London Liverpool Street 15 ⊖	d					18 32		18 38	18 48			19 00	19 02				19 08	19 18		19 30			19 32	19 38	19 48
Stratford 7 ⊖	d					18 40		18 46	18 56				19 09				19 15	19 25					19 39	19 45	19 55
Romford	d																								
Shenfield 3	d							19 02					19 25					19 41						20 01	20 11
Ingatestone	d							19 07										19 45							20 15
Chelmsford 3	d					19 05		19 14	19 20				19 34				19 38	19 52					20 02	20 10	20 22
Hatfield Peverel	d					19 11							19 40											20 16	
Witham 2	d					19 17		19 24	19 30				19 49				19 50	20 03					20 13	20 23	20 34
White Notley	d												19 56												20 41
Cressing	d												19 58												20 43
Braintree Freeport	d												20 01												20 46
Braintree	a												20 05												20 50
Kelvedon	d					19 22											19 55							20 27	
Marks Tey 2	d							19 32									20 00							20 33	
Colchester 4	a					19 33		19 39	19 43			19 47					20 07	20 15		20 19			20 25	20 40	
Colchester 4	d					19 37	19 39	19 39	19 44			19 47				19 56	20 08	20 16		20 20		20 20	20 25	20 41	
Colchester Town	a		←				19 50									20 03						20 27		20 49	
	d															20 07									
Hythe	d		19 23						19 48							20 11									
Wivenhoe 3	d		19 27			19 44			19 52							20 15		20 23							
Alresford (Essex)	d		19 31			19 48										20 19									
Great Bentley	d		19 35			19 52										20 23									
Weeley	d		19 38			19 55				←						20 26			←						
Thorpe-le-Soken 1	a		19 43			20 00			20 04	20 00						20 31		20 35	20 31						
	d	19 35	19 43			20 08			20 04	20 08						20 37		20 35	20 37						
Clacton-on-Sea	a		19 52			→			20 15							→		20 44							
Kirby Cross	d	19 40								20 13									20 42						
Frinton-on-Sea	d	19 43								20 16									20 45						
Walton-on-the-Naze	a	19 47								20 22									20 49						
Manningtree 2	d			19 38				19 47				19 55		20 00			20 16			20 28			20 34		
Mistley	d			19 42										20 04											
Wrabness	d			19 47										20 09											
Harwich International	d			19 55										20 17									20a54		
Dovercourt	d			19 58										20 20											
Harwich Town	a			20 00										20 22											
Ipswich	a							20 04				20 07					20 28			20 40					
	d				20 00							20 08			20 19					20 41					
Needham Market	d														20 28										
Stowmarket	d				20 12							20 19			20a33					20 52					
Peterborough 8	a				21 39																				
Diss	d											20 32								21 05					
Norwich	a											20 51								21 24					

		LE	LE	LE	LE	LE		LE	LE	LE	LE	LE	LE	LE	LE	LE		LE	LE	LE	LE	LE	LE	LE	LE
		1	◇1 ⊏⊐	1	1			1	1	1	1	1	◇1 ⊏⊐	1	1	1		◇1 ⊏⊐	1		1	1	1	1	◇1 ⊏⊐
London Liverpool Street 15 ⊖	d		20 00						20 02	20 18			20 30	20 38	20 48			21 00				21 02	21 18		21 30
Stratford 7 ⊖	d								20 09	20 25			20u38	20 45	20 55							21 09	21 25		21u38
Romford	d													20 53											
Shenfield 3	d								20 25	20 41				21 03	21 11							21 25	21 41		
Ingatestone	d									20 45					21 15								21 45		
Chelmsford 3	d								20 34	20 52			21 03	21 12	21 22							21 34	21 52		22 03
Hatfield Peverel	d								20 40													21 40			
Witham 2	d								20 47	21 03				21 23	21 34							21 47	22 03		
White Notley	d														21 41										
Cressing	d														21 43										
Braintree Freeport	d														21 46										
Braintree	a														21 50										
Kelvedon	d								20 51					21 27								21 51			
Marks Tey 2	d								20 57					21 33								21 57			
Colchester 4	a		20 46						21 04	21 15			21 22	21 40				21 46				22 04	22 15		22 22
Colchester 4	d		20 47					20 56	21 04	21 16		21 20	21 23	21 41				21 47			21 56	22 04	22 16		22 23
Colchester Town	a							21 03				21 27		21 49							22 03				
	d							21 07													22 07				
Hythe	d							21 11													22 11				
Wivenhoe 3	d							21 15		21 23											22 15		22 23		
Alresford (Essex)	d							21 19													22 19				
Great Bentley	d							21 23													22 23				
Weeley	d							21 26			←										22 26			←	
Thorpe-le-Soken 1	a							21 31		21 35	21 31										22 31		22 35	22 31	
	d			20 54				21 37		21 35	21 37										22 37		22 35	22 37	
Clacton-on-Sea	a			21 03				→		21 44											→		22 44		
Kirby Cross	d										21 42													22 42	
Frinton-on-Sea	d										21 45													22 45	
Walton-on-the-Naze	a										21 49													22 49	
Manningtree 2	d	20 38	20 55		21 00				21 12				21 31					21 55	22 00			22 12			22 31
Mistley	d	20 42			21 04														22 04						
Wrabness	d	20 47			21 09														22 09						
Harwich International	d	20 55			21 17											21 38			22 17			22a28			
Dovercourt	d	20 58			21 20														22 20						
Harwich Town	a	21 00			21 22														22 22						
Ipswich	a		21 07						21 25				21 43			22 03		22 07							22 43
	d		21 08			21 16							21 44					22 08		22 16					22 44
Needham Market	d					21 26														22 26					
Stowmarket	d		21 19			21a32							21 55					22 19		22a32					22 55
Peterborough 8	a																								
Diss	d		21 32										22 08					22 32							23 08
Norwich	a		21 51										22 27					22 51							23 27

London - Chelmsford, Colchester, Walton-on-Naze, Clacton, Harwich, Ipswich and Norwich

Network Diagram - see first Page of Table 5

		LE		LE	LE	LE	LE	LE	LE	LE	LE	LE		LE	LE	LE	LE	LE	LE	LE	LE	LE		LE	LE
		1		1	1	1	1	1	1	1	1	◇1 ⊏⊐		1 A	1 A	1		1 MT WO B	1 MT WO B	1 A	1 MT WO B	1 A		◇1 A ⊏⊐	◇1 MT WO B ⊏⊐
London Liverpool Street 15 ⊖	d	21 38		21 48	22 00	22 02				22 18		22 30		22 38				22 50		23 02	23 10	23 18		23 30	23 30
Stratford 7 ⊖	d	21 45		21 55		22 09				22 25		22u38		22 45				22 57		23 09	23 17	23 25		23u38	23u39
Romford	d	21 53																							
Shenfield 3	d	22 03		22 11		22 25				22 41				23 01				23 21		23 25	23 41	23 41			00 02
Ingatestone	d			22 15						22 45				23 05				23 25				23 45			
Chelmsford 3	d	22 12		22 22	22 28	22 34				22 52		23 03		23 12				23 32		23 34	23 50	23 52		00 03	00 13
Hatfield Peverel	d					22 40														23 40	23 56				
Witham 2	d	22 23		22 34		22 47				23 03				23 23	23 25			23 43	23 45	23 47	00 03	00 03			00 24
White Notley	d			22 41											23 32				23 52						
Cressing	d			22 43											23 34				23 54						
Braintree Freeport	d			22 46											23 37				23 57						
Braintree	a			22 50											23 41				00 01						
Kelvedon	d	22 27				22 51								23 27				23 47		23 51	00 07				
Marks Tey 2	d	22 33				22 57								23 33			23 46	23 53		23 57	00 13				
Colchester 4	a	22 40			22 47	23 05				23 15		23 22		23 45			23 55	00 05		00 04	00 20	00 15		00 22	00 36
Colchester 4	d	22 41			22 47				22 56	23 16		23 23								00 04	00 20	00 16		00 23	00 37
Colchester Town	a	22 49							23 03																
	d								23 07																
Hythe	d								23 11																
Wivenhoe 3	d								23 15	23 23												00 23			
Alresford (Essex)	d								23 19													00 27			
Great Bentley	d								23 23													00 31			
Weeley	d								23 26		←														
Thorpe-le-Soken 1	a								23 31	23 35	23 31											00 38			
	d							23 16	23 37	23 35	23 37											00 38			
Clacton-on-Sea	a							23 25	→	23 44												00 51			
Kirby Cross	d										23 42														
Frinton-on-Sea	d										23 45														
Walton-on-the-Naze	a										23 49														
Manningtree 2	d				22 55		23 00					23 31				23 36				00 12	00 28			00 31	00 45
Mistley	d						23 04									23 40									
Wrabness	d						23 09									23 45									
Harwich International	d						23 17									23 53									
Dovercourt	d						23 20									23 56									
Harwich Town	a						23 22									23 58									
Ipswich	a				23 08							23 43								00 28	00 44			00 43	00 57
	d											23 44												00 44	00 58
Needham Market	d																								
Stowmarket	d											23 55												00 55	01 09
Peterborough 8	a																								
Diss	d											00 08												01 08	01 22
Norwich	a											00 39												01 43	01 57

		LE	LE
		1 ThFO A	1 MT WO B
London Liverpool Street 15 ⊖	d	23 48	23 50
Stratford 7 ⊖	d	23 55	23 57
Romford	d		
Shenfield 3	d	00 11	00 21
Ingatestone	d	00 15	00 25
Chelmsford 3	d	00 22	00 32
Hatfield Peverel	d	00 28	00 38
Witham 2	d	00 35	00 45
White Notley	d		
Cressing	d		
Braintree Freeport	d		
Braintree	a		
Kelvedon	d	00 39	00 49
Marks Tey 2	d	00 45	00 55
Colchester 4	a	00 57	01 07
Colchester 4	d		
Colchester Town	a		
	d		
Hythe	d		
Wivenhoe 3	d		
Alresford (Essex)	d		
Great Bentley	d		
Weeley	d		
Thorpe-le-Soken 1	a		
	d		
Clacton-on-Sea	a		
Kirby Cross	d		
Frinton-on-Sea	d		
Walton-on-the-Naze	a		
Manningtree 2	d		
Mistley	d		
Wrabness	d		
Harwich International	d		
Dovercourt	d		
Harwich Town	a		
Ipswich	a		
	d		
Needham Market	d		
Stowmarket	d		
Peterborough 8	a		
Diss	d		
Norwich	a		

A also from 10 September until 12 September

B from 17 September

London - Chelmsford, Colchester, Walton-on-Naze, Clacton, Harwich, Ipswich and Norwich

Network Diagram - see first Page of Table 5

		LE ◇1	LE 1	LE 1	LE ◇1	LE 1	LE 1	LE 1	LE	LE 1		LE ◇1	LE 1	LE 1	LE 1	LE 1	LE 1	LE 1	LE 1	LE 1		LE ◇1	LE 1	LE 1	LE 1
London Liverpool Street 15 ⊖	d	22p30	23p02	23p18	23p30		23p48	00 18									05 34								06 02
Stratford 7 ⊖	d	22b38	23p09	23p25	23b38		23p55	00 25									05 41								06 09
Romford	d																05 49								
Shenfield 3	d		23p25	23p41			00 11	00 47									05 59								06 25
Ingatestone	d			23p45			00 15	00 51									06 03								
Chelmsford 3	d	23p03	23p34	23p52	00 03		00 22	00 58									06 10								06 34
Hatfield Peverel	d		23p40				00 28	01 04									06 16								06 40
Witham 2	d		23p47	00 03		00 05	00 35	01 11		05 34							06 23	06 34							06 47
White Notley	d					00 12				05 41								06 41							
Cressing	d					00 14				05 43								06 43							
Braintree Freeport	d					00 17				05 46								06 46							
Braintree	a					00 21				05 50								06 50							
Kelvedon	d		23p51				00 39	01 15									06 27								06 51
Marks Tey 2	d		23p57				00 45	01 21									06 33								06 57
Colchester 4	a	23p22	00 04	00 15	00 22		00 57	01 41									06 40								07 04
Colchester 4	d	23p23	00 04	00 16	00 23							05 40	05 52		06 20	06 24	06 40							06 56	07 04
Colchester Town	a														06 27									07 03	
	d																							07 07	
Hythe	d																							07 11	
Wivenhoe 3	d			00 23																				07 15	
Alresford (Essex)	d			00 27																				07 19	
Great Bentley	d			00 31																				07 23	
Weeley	d																							07 26	
Thorpe-le-Soken 1	a			00 38																				07 31	
	d			00 38															06 37					07 37	
Clacton-on-Sea	a			00 51																				→	
Kirby Cross	d																		06 42						
Frinton-on-Sea	d																		06 45						
Walton-on-the-Naze	a																		06 49						
Manningtree 2	d	23p31	00 12		00 31							05 49	06 00			06 32	06 48			07 00					07 12
Mistley	d												06 04							07 04					
Wrabness	d												06 09							07 09					
Harwich International	d												06 17							07 17					
Dovercourt	d												06 20							07 20					
Harwich Town	a												06 22							07 22					
Ipswich	a	23p43	00 28		00 43							05 59				06 44	07 00								07 25
	d	23p44			00 44				05 10			06 00		06 16								07 10	07 19		
Needham Market	d								05 20					06 25									07 28		
Stowmarket	d	23p55			00 55				05a26			06 12		06a30								07 21	07a33		
Peterborough 8	a											07 38													
Diss	d	00 08			01 08																	07 34			
Norwich	a	00 39			01 43																	07 53			

		LE 1	LE 1	LE ◇1	LE 1	LE 1		LE 1	LE 1	LE ◇1	LE 1	LE 1	LE 1	LE 1	LE 1	LE 1		LE 1	LE ◇1	LE 1	LE 1	LE ◇1	LE 1	LE 1	LE 1
London Liverpool Street 15 ⊖	d	06 18		06 30	06 38	06 48				07 00				07 02	07 18				07 30	07 38	07 48	08 00			
Stratford 7 ⊖	d	06 25		06u38	06 45	06 55								07 09	07 25				07u38	07 45	07 55				
Romford	d				06 53															07 53					
Shenfield 3	d	06 41			07 03	07 11								07 25	07 41					08 03	08 11				
Ingatestone	d	06 45				07 15									07 45						08 15				
Chelmsford 3	d	06 52		07 03	07 12	07 22								07 34	07 52				08 03	08 12	08 22				
Hatfield Peverel	d													07 40											
Witham 2	d	07 03			07 23	07 34								07 47	08 03					08 23	08 34				
White Notley	d					07 41															08 41				
Cressing	d					07 43															08 43				
Braintree Freeport	d					07 46															08 46				
Braintree	a					07 50															08 50				
Kelvedon	d				07 27									07 51						08 27					
Marks Tey 2	d				07 33									07 57						08 33					
Colchester 4	a	07 15		07 22	07 40					07 46				08 04	08 15				08 22	08 40		08 46			
Colchester 4	d	07 16		07 23	07 40			07 44		07 47			07 56	08 04	08 16			08 20	08 23	08 41		08 47			08 56
Colchester Town	a							07 51					08 03					08 27		08 49					09 03
	d												08 07												09 07
Hythe	d												08 11												09 11
Wivenhoe 3	d	07 23											08 15		08 23										09 15
Alresford (Essex)	d												08 19												09 19
Great Bentley	d												08 23												09 23
Weeley	d		←										08 26			←									09 26
Thorpe-le-Soken 1	a	07 35	07 31										08 31		08 35	08 31									09 31
	d	07 35	07 37										08 37		08 35	08 37									09 37
Clacton-on-Sea	a	07 44											→		08 44										→
Kirby Cross	d		07 42													08 42									
Frinton-on-Sea	d		07 45													08 45									
Walton-on-the-Naze	a		07 49													08 49									
Manningtree 2	d			07 31	07 48					07 55		08 00		08 12					08 31			08 55	09 00		
Mistley	d										08 02	08 04											09 04		
Wrabness	d											08 09											09 09		
Harwich International	d				08a09							08 17											09 17		
Dovercourt	d											08 20											09 20		
Harwich Town	a											08 22											09 22		
Ipswich	a			07 43						08 07	08 17			08 25					08 43			09 07			
	d			07 44					08 00	08 08	08 19								08 44			09 08		09 19	
Needham Market	d										08 28													09 28	
Stowmarket	d			07 55					08 12		08a33								08 55					09a33	
Peterborough 8	a								09 38																
Diss	d			08 08						08 29									09 08			09 29			
Norwich	a			08 27						08 50									09 27			09 50			

b Previous night, stops to pick up only

London - Chelmsford, Colchester, Walton-on-Naze, Clacton, Harwich, Ipswich and Norwich

Network Diagram - see first Page of Table 5

		LE 1		LE 1	LE 1	LE 1	LE ◇1	LE 1	LE 1	LE 1	LE ◇1	LE 1		LE 1	LE 1	LE 1	LE 1	LE 1	LE 1	LE ◇1	LE 1	LE 1		LE ◇1 A	LE 1 B
London Liverpool Street 15 ⊖	d	08 02		08 18			08 30	08 38	08 48		09 00					09 02	09 18			09 30	09 38	09 48		10 00	10 00
Stratford 7 ⊖	d	08 09		08 25			08u38	08 45	08 55							09 09	09 25			09u38	09 45	09 55			
Romford	d							08 53													09 53				
Shenfield 3	d	08 25		08 41				09 03	09 11							09 25	09 41				10 03	10 11			
Ingatestone	d			08 45					09 15								09 45					10 15			
Chelmsford 3	d	08 34		08 52			09 03	09 12	09 22							09 34	09 52			10 03	10 12	10 22			
Hatfield Peverel	d	08 40														09 40									
Witham 2	d	08 47		09 03				09 23	09 34							09 47	10 03				10 23	10 34			
White Notley	d								09 41													10 41			
Cressing	d								09 43													10 43			
Braintree Freeport	d								09 46													10 46			
Braintree	a								09 50													10 50			
Kelvedon	d	08 51						09 27								09 51					10 27				
Marks Tey 2	d	08 57						09 33								09 57					10 33				
Colchester 4	a	09 04		09 15			09 22	09 40			09 46					10 04	10 15			10 22	10 40			10 46	10 46
Colchester 4	d	09 04		09 16		09 20	09 23	09 41			09 47				09 56	10 04	10 16		10 20	10 23	10 41			10 47	10 47
Colchester Town	a					09 27		09 49							10 03				10 27		10 49				
	d														10 07										
Hythe	d														10 11										
Wivenhoe 3	d			09 23											10 15		10 23								
Alresford (Essex)	d														10 19										
Great Bentley	d														10 23										
Weeley	d				←										10 26			←							
Thorpe-le-Soken 1	a			09 35	09 31										10 31		10 35	10 31							
	d			09 35	09 37										10 37		10 35	10 37							
Clacton-on-Sea	a			09 44											→		10 44								
Kirby Cross	d				09 42													10 42							
Frinton-on-Sea	d				09 45													10 45							
Walton-on-the-Naze	a				09 49													10 49							
Manningtree 2	d	09 12					09 31				09 55	10 00				10 12				10 31				10 55	10 55
Mistley	d											10 04													
Wrabness	d											10 09													
Harwich International	d											10 17													
Dovercourt	d											10 20													
Harwich Town	a											10 22													
Ipswich	a	09 25					09 43				10 07					10 25				10 43				11 07	11 07
	d						09 44			10 00	10 08			10 19						10 44				11 08	11 08
Needham Market	d													10 28											
Stowmarket	d						09 55			10 12				10a33						10 55					
Peterborough 8	a									11 37															
Diss	d						10 08				10 29									11 08				11 29	11 29
Norwich	a						10 27				10 50									11 27				11 50	11 50

		LE 1	LE 1	LE 1	LE 1	LE 1	LE 1	LE 1		LE ◇1	LE 1	LE 1	LE 1	LE ◇1	LE 1	LE 1	LE 1	LE 1		LE 1	LE 1	LE 1	LE ◇1	LE 1	LE 1
London Liverpool Street 15 ⊖	d				10 02	10 18				10 30	10 38	10 48		11 00				11 02		11 18			11 30	11 38	11 48
Stratford 7 ⊖	d				10 09	10 25				10u38	10 45	10 55						11 09		11 25			11u38	11 45	11 55
Romford	d										10 53													11 53	
Shenfield 3	d				10 25	10 41					11 03	11 11						11 25		11 41				12 03	12 11
Ingatestone	d					10 45						11 15								11 45					12 15
Chelmsford 3	d				10 34	10 52				11 03	11 12	11 22						11 34		11 52			12 03	12 12	12 22
Hatfield Peverel	d				10 40													11 40							
Witham 2	d				10 47	11 03					11 23	11 34						11 47		12 03				12 23	12 34
White Notley	d											11 41													12 41
Cressing	d											11 43													12 43
Braintree Freeport	d											11 46													12 46
Braintree	a											11 50													12 50
Kelvedon	d				10 51						11 27							11 51						12 27	
Marks Tey 2	d				10 57						11 33							11 57						12 33	
Colchester 4	a				11 04	11 15				11 22	11 40			11 46				12 04		12 15			12 22	12 40	
Colchester 4	d			10 56	11 04	11 16		11 20		11 23	11 41			11 47			11 56	12 04		12 16		12 20	12 23	12 41	
Colchester Town	a			11 03				11 27			11 49						12 03					12 27		12 49	
	d			11 07													12 07								
Hythe	d			11 11													12 11								
Wivenhoe 3	d			11 15		11 23											12 15			12 23					
Alresford (Essex)	d			11 19													12 19								
Great Bentley	d			11 23													12 23								
Weeley	d			11 26			←										12 26				←				
Thorpe-le-Soken 1	a			11 31		11 35	11 31										12 31			12 35	12 31				
	d			11 37		11 35	11 37										12 37			12 35	12 37				
Clacton-on-Sea	a			→		11 44											→			12 44					
Kirby Cross	d						11 42														12 42				
Frinton-on-Sea	d						11 45														12 45				
Walton-on-the-Naze	a						11 49														12 49				
Manningtree 2	d	11 00			11 12					11 31				11 55	12 00			12 12					12 31		
Mistley	d	11 04													12 04										
Wrabness	d	11 09													12 09										
Harwich International	d	11 17													12 17										
Dovercourt	d	11 20													12 20										
Harwich Town	a	11 22													12 22										
Ipswich	a				11 25					11 43				12 07				12 25					12 43		
	d		11 19							11 44			12 00	12 08		12 19							12 44		
Needham Market	d		11 28													12 28									
Stowmarket	d		11a33							11 55			12 12			12a33							12 55		
Peterborough 8	a												13 37												
Diss	d									12 08				12 29									13 08		
Norwich	a									12 27				12 50									13 27		

A 19 May

B not 19 May

London - Chelmsford, Colchester, Walton-on-Naze, Clacton, Harwich, Ipswich and Norwich

Network Diagram - see first Page of Table 5

		LE ◇■ ☕	LE ■	LE ■	LE ■	LE ■	LE ■	LE ■	LE ■	LE ◇■ A ☕	LE ■ B ☕	LE ■	LE ■	LE ■	LE ◇■ ☕	LE ■	LE ■	LE ■	LE ■	LE ■	LE ■	LE ■
London Liverpool Street ⊖	d	12 00				12 02	12 18			12 30	12 30	12 38	12 48		13 00				13 02	13 18		
Stratford ⊖	d					12 09	12 25			12u38	12u38	12 45	12 55						13 09	13 25		
Romford	d											12 53										
Shenfield	d					12 25	12 41					13 03	13 11						13 25	13 41		
Ingatestone	d						12 45						13 15							13 45		
Chelmsford	d					12 34	12 52			13 03	13 03	13 12	13 22						13 34	13 52		
Hatfield Peverel	d					12 40													13 40			
Witham	d					12 47	13 03					13 23	13 34						13 47	14 03		
White Notley	d												13 41									
Cressing	d												13 43									
Braintree Freeport	d												13 46									
Braintree	a												13 50									
Kelvedon	d					12 51						13 27							13 51			
Marks Tey	d					12 57						13 33							13 57			
Colchester	a	12 46				13 04	13 15			13 22	13 22	13 40			13 46				14 04	14 15		
Colchester	d	12 47			12 56	13 04	13 16		13 20	13 23	13 23	13 41			13 47			13 56	14 04	14 16		14 20
Colchester Town	a				13 03				13 27			13 49						14 03				14 27
	d				13 07													14 07				
Hythe	d				13 11													14 11				
Wivenhoe	d				13 15		13 23											14 15		14 23		
Alresford (Essex)	d				13 19													14 19				
Great Bentley	d				13 23													14 23				
Weeley	d				13 26			←										14 26			←	
Thorpe-le-Soken	a				13 31		13 35	13 31										14 31		14 35	14 31	
	d				13 37		13 35	13 37										14 37		14 35	14 37	
Clacton-on-Sea	a				→		13 44											→		14 44		
Kirby Cross	d							13 42													14 42	
Frinton-on-Sea	d							13 45													14 45	
Walton-on-the-Naze	a							13 49													14 49	
Manningtree	d	12 55	13 00			13 12				13 31	13 31				13 55	14 00			14 12			
Mistley	d		13 04													14 04						
Wrabness	d		13 09													14 09						
Harwich International	d		13 17													14 17						
Dovercourt	d		13 20													14 20						
Harwich Town	a		13 22													14 22						
Ipswich	a	13 07				13 25				13 43	13 43				14 07				14 25			
	d	13 08		13 19						13 44	13 44			14 00	14 08		14 19					
Needham Market	d			13 28													14 28					
Stowmarket	d			13a33						13 55	13 55			14 12			14a33					
Peterborough	a													15 37								
Diss	d	13 29								14 08	14 08				14 29							
Norwich	a	13 50								14 27	14 27				14 50							

A 19 May

B not 19 May

London - Chelmsford, Colchester, Walton-on-Naze, Clacton, Harwich, Ipswich and Norwich

Network Diagram - see first Page of Table 5

		LE ◇■ ☕	LE ■	LE ■	LE ◇■ ☕	LE ■	LE ■	LE ■	LE ■	LE ■	LE ■	LE ■	LE ◇■ ☕	LE ■	LE ■	LE ■	LE ◇■ ☕	LE ■	LE ■	LE ■	LE ■	LE ■	LE ■
London Liverpool Street ⊖	d	13 30	13 38	13 48	14 00				14 02	14 18			14 30	14 38	14 48		15 00				15 02	15 18	
Stratford ⊖	d	13u38	13 45	13 55					14 09	14 25			14u38	14 45	14 55						15 09	15 25	
Romford	d		13 53											14 53									
Shenfield	d		14 03	14 11					14 25	14 41				15 03	15 11						15 25	15 41	
Ingatestone	d			14 15						14 45					15 15							15 45	
Chelmsford	d	14 03	14 12	14 22					14 34	14 52			15 03	15 12	15 22						15 34	15 52	
Hatfield Peverel	d								14 40												15 40		
Witham	d		14 23	14 34					14 47	15 03				15 23	15 34						15 47	16 03	
White Notley	d			14 41											15 41								
Cressing	d			14 43											15 43								
Braintree Freeport	d			14 46											15 46								
Braintree	a			14 50											15 50								
Kelvedon	d		14 27						14 51					15 27							15 51		
Marks Tey	d		14 33						14 57					15 33							15 57		
Colchester	a	14 22	14 40		14 46				15 04	15 15			15 22	15 40			15 46				16 04	16 15	
Colchester	d	14 23	14 41		14 47			14 56	15 04	15 16		15 20	15 23	15 41			15 47			15 56	16 04	16 16	
Colchester Town	a		14 49					15 03				15 27		15 49						16 03			
	d							15 07												16 07			
Hythe	d							15 11												16 11			
Wivenhoe	d							15 15		15 23										16 15		16 23	
Alresford (Essex)	d							15 19												16 19			
Great Bentley	d							15 23												16 23			
Weeley	d							15 26			←									16 26			←
Thorpe-le-Soken	a							15 31		15 35	15 31									16 31		16 35	16 31
	d							15 37		15 35	15 37									16 37		16 35	16 37
Clacton-on-Sea	a							→		15 44										→		16 44	
Kirby Cross	d										15 42												16 42
Frinton-on-Sea	d										15 45												16 45
Walton-on-the-Naze	a										15 49												16 49
Manningtree	d	14 31			14 55	15 00			15 12				15 31				15 55	16 00			16 12		
Mistley	d					15 04												16 04					
Wrabness	d					15 09												16 09					
Harwich International	d					15 17												16 17					
Dovercourt	d					15 20												16 20					
Harwich Town	a					15 22												16 22					
Ipswich	a	14 43			15 07				15 25				15 43				16 07				16 25		
	d	14 44			15 08		15 19						15 44			16 00	16 08		16 19				
Needham Market	d						15 28												16 28				
Stowmarket	d	14 55					15a33						15 55			16 12			16a33				
Peterborough	a															17 37							
Diss	d	15 08			15 29								16 08				16 29						
Norwich	a	15 27			15 48								16 27				16 50						

		LE ■	LE ◇■ ☕	LE ■	LE ■	LE ◇■ ☕	LE ■	LE ■	LE ■	LE ■	LE ■	LE ■	LE ■	LE ◇■ ☕	LE ■	LE ■	LE ■	LE ◇■ ☕	LE ■	LE ■	LE ■	LE ■	LE ■
London Liverpool Street ⊖	d		15 30	15 38	15 48	16 00				16 02	16 18			16 30	16 38	16 48		17 00				17 02	17 18
Stratford ⊖	d		15u38	15 45	15 55					16 09	16 25			16u38	16 45	16 55						17 09	17 25
Romford	d			15 53											16 53								
Shenfield	d			16 03	16 11					16 25	16 41				17 03	17 11						17 25	17 41
Ingatestone	d				16 15						16 45					17 15							17 45
Chelmsford	d		16 03	16 12	16 22					16 34	16 52			17 03	17 12	17 22						17 34	17 52
Hatfield Peverel	d									16 40												17 40	
Witham	d			16 23	16 34					16 47	17 03				17 23	17 34						17 47	18 03
White Notley	d				16 41											17 41							
Cressing	d				16 43											17 43							
Braintree Freeport	d				16 46											17 46							
Braintree	a				16 50											17 50							
Kelvedon	d			16 27						16 51					17 27							17 51	
Marks Tey	d			16 33						16 57					17 33							17 57	
Colchester	a		16 22	16 40		16 46				17 04	17 15			17 22	17 40			17 46				18 04	18 15
Colchester	d	16 20	16 23	16 41		16 47			16 56	17 04	17 16		17 20	17 23	17 41			17 47			17 56	18 04	18 16
Colchester Town	a	16 27		16 49					17 03				17 27		17 49						18 03		
	d								17 07												18 07		
Hythe	d								17 11												18 11		
Wivenhoe	d								17 15		17 23										18 15		18 23
Alresford (Essex)	d								17 19												18 19		
Great Bentley	d								17 23												18 23		
Weeley	d								17 26			←									18 26		
Thorpe-le-Soken	a								17 31		17 35	17 31									18 31		18 35
	d								17 37		17 35	17 37									18 37		18 35
Clacton-on-Sea	a								→		17 44										→		18 44
Kirby Cross	d											17 42											
Frinton-on-Sea	d											17 45											
Walton-on-the-Naze	a											17 49											
Manningtree	d		16 31			16 55	17 00			17 12				17 31				17 55	18 00			18 12	
Mistley	d						17 04												18 04				
Wrabness	d						17 09												18 09				
Harwich International	d						17 17												18 17				
Dovercourt	d						17 20												18 20				
Harwich Town	a						17 22												18 22				
Ipswich	a		16 43			17 07				17 25				17 43				18 07				18 25	
	d		16 44			17 08		17 19						17 44			18 00	18 08		18 19			
Needham Market	d							17 28												18 28			
Stowmarket	d		16 55			17 19		17a33						17 55			18 12			18a33			
Peterborough	a																19 38						
Diss	d		17 08			17 32								18 08				18 29					
Norwich	a		17 27			17 51								18 27				18 50					

London - Chelmsford, Colchester, Walton-on-Naze, Clacton, Harwich, Ipswich and Norwich

Network Diagram - see first Page of Table 5

		LE ■	LE ■	LE ◇■	LE ■	LE ■	LE ◇■	LE ■	LE ■	LE ■	LE ■	LE ■	LE ■	LE ■	LE ◇■	LE ■	LE ■	LE ■	LE ◇■	LE ■	LE ■	LE ■
London Liverpool Street ⊖	d			17 30	17 38	17 48	18 00				18 02	18 18			18 30	18 38	18 48		19 00			
Stratford ⊖	d			17u38	17 45	17 55					18 09	18 25			18u38	18 45	18 55					
Romford	d				17 53											18 53						
Shenfield	d				18 03	18 11					18 25	18 41				19 03	19 11					
Ingatestone	d					18 15						18 45					19 15					
Chelmsford	d			18 03	18 12	18 22					18 34	18 52			19 03	19 12	19 22					
Hatfield Peverel	d										18 40											
Witham	d				18 23	18 34					18 47	19 03				19 23	19 34					
White Notley	d					18 41											19 41					
Cressing	d					18 43											19 43					
Braintree Freeport	d					18 46											19 46					
Braintree	a					18 50											19 50					
Kelvedon	d				18 27						18 51					19 27						
Marks Tey	d				18 33						18 57					19 33						
Colchester	a			18 22	18 40		18 46				19 04	19 15			19 22	19 40			19 46			
Colchester	d		18 20	18 23	18 41		18 47			18 56	19 04	19 16		19 20	19 23	19 41			19 47			19 56
Colchester Town	a		18 27		18 49					19 03				19 27		19 49						20 03
	d									19 07												20 07
Hythe	d									19 11												20 11
Wivenhoe	d									19 15		19 23										20 15
Alresford (Essex)	d									19 19												20 19
Great Bentley	d									19 23												20 23
Weeley	d	←								19 26			←									20 26
Thorpe-le-Soken	a	18 31								19 31		19 35	19 31									20 31
	d	18 37								19 37		19 35	19 37									20 37
Clacton-on-Sea	a									→		19 44										→
Kirby Cross	d	18 42											19 42									
Frinton-on-Sea	d	18 45											19 45									
Walton-on-the-Naze	a	18 49											19 49									
Manningtree	d			18 31			18 55	19 00			19 12				19 31				19 55	20 00		
Mistley	d							19 04												20 04		
Wrabness	d							19 09												20 09		
Harwich International	d							19 17												20 17		
Dovercourt	d							19 20												20 20		
Harwich Town	a							19 22												20 22		
Ipswich	a			18 43			19 07				19 25				19 43				20 07			
	d			18 44			19 08		19 19						19 44			20 00	20 08		20 19	
Needham Market	d								19 28												20 28	
Stowmarket	d			18 55					19a33						19 55			20 12			20a33	
Peterborough	a																	21 37				
Diss	d			19 08			19 29								20 08				20 29			
Norwich	a			19 27			19 50								20 27				20 50			

		LE ■	LE ■	LE ■	LE ■	LE ◇■	LE ■	LE ■	LE ■	LE ◇■	LE ■	LE	LE ■	LE ■	LE ■	LE ■	LE ■	LE ◇■	LE ■	LE ■	LE ■	LE ■	LE ■
London Liverpool Street ⊖	d	19 02	19 18			19 30	19 32	19 38	19 48	20 00				20 02	20 18			20 30	20 38	20 48		21 00	
Stratford ⊖	d	19 09	19 25			19u38	19 39	19 46	19 55					20 09	20 25			20u38	20 45	20 55			
Romford	d							19 54											20 53				
Shenfield	d	19 25	19 41				19 57	20 04	20 11					20 25	20 41				21 03	21 11			
Ingatestone	d		19 45						20 15						20 45					21 15			
Chelmsford	d	19 34	19 52			20 03	20 07	20 13	20 22					20 34	20 52			21 03	21 12	21 22			
Hatfield Peverel	d	19 40												20 40									
Witham	d	19 47	20 03				20 18	20 24	20 34					20 47	21 03				21 23	21 34			
White Notley	d								20 41											21 41			
Cressing	d								20 43											21 43			
Braintree Freeport	d								20 46											21 46			
Braintree	a								20 50											21 50			
Kelvedon	d	19 51						20 28						20 51					21 27				
Marks Tey	d	19 57						20 34						20 57					21 33				
Colchester	a	20 04	20 15			20 22	20 30	20 41		20 46				21 04	21 15			21 22	21 40			21 46	
Colchester	d	20 04	20 16		20 20	20 23	20 30	20 42		20 47			20 56	21 04	21 16		21 20	21 23	21 41			21 47	
Colchester Town	a				20 27			20 50					21 03				21 27		21 49				
	d												21 07										
Hythe	d												21 11										
Wivenhoe	d		20 23										21 15		21 23								
Alresford (Essex)	d												21 19										
Great Bentley	d												21 23										
Weeley	d			←									21 26			←							
Thorpe-le-Soken	a		20 35	20 31									21 31		21 35	21 31							
	d		20 35	20 37									21 37		21 35	21 37							
Clacton-on-Sea	a		20 44										→		21 44								
Kirby Cross	d			20 42												21 42							
Frinton-on-Sea	d			20 45												21 45							
Walton-on-the-Naze	a			20 49												21 49							
Manningtree	d	20 12				20 31	20 39			20 55	21 00			21 12				21 31				21 55	22 00
Mistley	d										21 04												22 04
Wrabness	d										21 09												22 09
Harwich International	d						20a54				21 17										21 38		22 17
Dovercourt	d										21 20												22 20
Harwich Town	a										21 22												22 22
Ipswich	a	20 25				20 43				21 07				21 25				21 43			22 03	22 08	
	d					20 44				21 08		21 16						21 44					
Needham Market	d											21 26											
Stowmarket	d					20 55						21a32						21 55					
Peterborough	a																						
Diss	d					21 08				21 29								22 08					
Norwich	a					21 27				21 50								22 27					

London - Chelmsford, Colchester, Walton-on-Naze, Clacton, Harwich, Ipswich and Norwich

Network Diagram - see first Page of Table 5

		LE	LE ■	LE ■	LE ■	LE ■	LE ◇■	LE ■	LE ■	LE ■	LE ■	LE ■	LE ■	LE ■	LE ■	LE ■	LE ◇■	LE ■	LE ■	LE ■	LE	LE ■
London Liverpool Street ⊖	d			21 02	21 18		21 30	21 38	21 48	22 00	22 02				22 18		22 30	22 38				23 02
Stratford ⊖	d			21 09	21 25		21u38	21 45	21 55		22 09				22 25		22u38	22 45				23 09
Romford	d							21 53										22 53				
Shenfield	d			21 25	21 41			22 03	22 11		22 25				22 41			23 03				23 25
Ingatestone	d				21 45				22 15						22 45							
Chelmsford	d			21 34	21 52		22 03	22 12	22 22	22 28	22 34				22 52		23 03	23 12				23 34
Hatfield Peverel	d			21 40							22 40											23 40
Witham	d			21 47	22 03			22 23	22 34		22 47				23 03			23 23	23 25			23 47
White Notley	d								22 41										23 32			
Cressing	d								22 43										23 34			
Braintree Freeport	d								22 46										23 37			
Braintree	a								22 50										23 41			
Kelvedon	d			21 51				22 27			22 51							23 27				23 51
Marks Tey	d			21 57				22 33			22 57							23 33			23 46	23 57
Colchester	a			22 04	22 15		22 22	22 40		22 47	23 05				23 15		23 22	23 45			23 59	00 04
Colchester	d		21 56	22 04	22 16		22 23	22 41		22 48				22 56	23 16		23 23					00 04
Colchester Town	a		22 03					22 49						23 03								
	d		22 07											23 07								
Hythe	d		22 11											23 11								
Wivenhoe	d		22 15		22 23									23 15	23 23							
Alresford (Essex)	d		22 19											23 19								
Great Bentley	d		22 23											23 23								
Weeley	d		22 26			←								23 26		←						
Thorpe-le-Soken	a		22 31		22 35	22 31								23 31	23 35	23 31						
	d		22 37		22 35	22 37							23 16	23 37	23 35	23 37						
Clacton-on-Sea	a		→		22 44								23 25	→	23 44							
Kirby Cross	d					22 42										23 42						
Frinton-on-Sea	d					22 45										23 45						
Walton-on-the-Naze	a					22 49										23 49						
Manningtree	d			22 12			22 31			22 56		23 00					23 31			23 36		00 12
Mistley	d											23 04								23 40		
Wrabness	d											23 09								23 45		
Harwich International	d			22a28								23 17								23 53		
Dovercourt	d											23 20								23 56		
Harwich Town	a											23 22								23 58		
Ipswich	a						22 43			23 08							23 43					00 28
	d	22 16					22 44										23 44					
Needham Market	d	22 26																				
Stowmarket	d	22a32					22 55										23 55					
Peterborough	a																					
Diss	d						23 08										00 08					
Norwich	a						23 27										00 27					

		LE ■	LE ◇■	LE ■
London Liverpool Street ⊖	d	23 18	23 30	23 48
Stratford ⊖	d	23 25	23u38	23 55
Romford	d			
Shenfield	d	23 41		00 11
Ingatestone	d	23 45		00 15
Chelmsford	d	23 52	00 03	00 22
Hatfield Peverel	d			00 28
Witham	d	00 03		00 35
White Notley	d			
Cressing	d			
Braintree Freeport	d			
Braintree	a			
Kelvedon	d			00 39
Marks Tey	d			00 45
Colchester	a	00 15	00 22	00 57
Colchester	d	00 16	00 23	
Colchester Town	a			
	d			
Hythe	d			
Wivenhoe	d	00 23		
Alresford (Essex)	d	00 27		
Great Bentley	d	00 31		
Weeley	d			
Thorpe-le-Soken	a	00 38		
	d	00 38		
Clacton-on-Sea	a	00 51		
Kirby Cross	d			
Frinton-on-Sea	d			
Walton-on-the-Naze	a			
Manningtree	d		00 31	
Mistley	d			
Wrabness	d			
Harwich International	d			
Dovercourt	d			
Harwich Town	a			
Ipswich	a		00 43	
	d		00 44	
Needham Market	d			
Stowmarket	d		00 55	
Peterborough	a			
Diss	d		01 08	
Norwich	a		01 31	

London - Chelmsford, Colchester, Walton-on-Naze, Clacton, Harwich, Ipswich and Norwich

Network Diagram - see first Page of Table 5

		LE	LE	LE	LE	LE	LE	LE	LE	LE	LE	LE	LE	LE	LE	LE	LE	LE	LE	LE	LE	LE	LE	LE	LE
		◇1 ⊐	1	◇1 ⊐	1	1	1	[bus]	1	◇1 ⊐	1	[bus]	1	A ◇1 ⊐	1	◇1 ⊐	1	B 1	B ◇1		1	◇1	1	1	1
London Liverpool Street 15 ⊖	d	22p30	22p45	23p00	23p07	23p15				23p30	23p35		23p45	23p59	00 12	00 30	00 46	01 12	01 30						
Stratford 7 ⊖	d	22b40	22p54	23b10	23p17	23p25				23b40	23p45		23p54	00u10	00 24	00u40	01 00	01 24	01u41						
Romford	d																								
Shenfield 3	d		23p12		23p34	23p43					00 01		00 12		00 41		01 17	01 41							
Ingatestone	d		23p16			23p48					00 05		00 16		00 45		01 22	01 45							
Chelmsford 3	d	23p05	23p23	23p37	23p43	23p55				00 06	00 12		00 23	00 37	00 52	01 07	01 29	01 52	02 08						
Hatfield Peverel	d				23p49						00 18				00 58		01 35	01 58							
Witham 2	d		23p34		23p56	00 05	00 07				00 25		00 34		01 05		01 41	02 05	02 19		05 34				
White Notley	d						00 14														05 41				
Cressing	d						00 16														05 43				
Braintree Freeport	d						00 19														05 46				
Braintree	a						00 23														05 50				
Kelvedon	d				00 01						00 29				01 09		01 46	02 09							
Marks Tey 2	d				00 06						00 35				01 15		01 51	02 15							
Colchester 4	a	23p24	23p46	23p58	00 14	00 17				00 25	00 43		00 46	00 56	01 23	01 29	02 00	02 23	02 32						
Colchester 4	d	23p25	23p47	23p59		00 18				00 25			00 47	00 57		01 30			02 33			05 40	05 52		06 24
Colchester Town	a																								
	d																								
Hythe	d																								
Wivenhoe 3	d		23p54			00 25		00 30					00 54												
Alresford (Essex)	d							00 40																	
Great Bentley	d							00 50																	
Weeley	d																								
Thorpe-le-Soken 1	a		00 06			00 37		01 00				←	01 06												
	d		00 06			00 37		01 10				01 10	01 06												
Clacton-on-Sea	a		00 15			00 46		→					01 15												
Kirby Cross	d											01 17													
Frinton-on-Sea	d											01 22													
Walton-on-the-Naze	a											01 27													
Manningtree 2	d	23p33		00 09					00 12	00 33				01 07		01 40			02 43			05 49	06 00		06 32
Mistley	d								00 16														06 04		
Wrabness	d								00 21														06 09		
Harwich International	d								00 29														06 17		
Dovercourt	d								00 32														06 20		
Harwich Town	a								00 34														06 22		
Ipswich	a	23p45		00 19						00 45				01 17		01 50			02 53			05 59			06 44
	d	23p46		00 21						00 46				01 19		01 52			02 55	05 10		06 00		06 16	
Needham Market	d																			05 20				06 25	
Stowmarket	d	23p58		00 32						00 58				01 30		02 03			03 06	05a26		06 12		06a30	
Peterborough 8	a																					07 38			
Diss	d	00 10		00 45						01 10				01 43		02 16			03 19						
Norwich	a	00 30		01 04						01 30				02 03		02 35			03 39						

		LE	LE	LE	LE	LE	LE	LE	LE	LE	LE	LE	LE	LE	LE	LE	LE	LE	LE	LE	LE	LE	LE	LE	LE
		1	1	1	1	◇1	1	1	1	1	1	◇1	1	1	1	1	◇1	1	1	1	1	1	1	1	◇1 ⊐
London Liverpool Street 15 ⊖	d	05 34							06 02	06 18		06 30	06 38	06 48			07 00				07 02	07 18			07 30
Stratford 7 ⊖	d	05 41							06 09	06 25		06u38	06 45	06 55							07 09	07 25			07u38
Romford	d	05 49											06 53												
Shenfield 3	d	05 59							06 25	06 41			07 03	07 11							07 25	07 41			
Ingatestone	d	06 03								06 45				07 15								07 45			
Chelmsford 3	d	06 10							06 34	06 52		07 03	07 12	07 22							07 34	07 52			08 03
Hatfield Peverel	d	06 16							06 40												07 40				
Witham 2	d	06 23	06 34						06 47	07 03			07 23	07 34							07 47	08 03			
White Notley	d		06 41											07 41											
Cressing	d		06 43											07 43											
Braintree Freeport	d		06 46											07 46											
Braintree	a		06 50											07 50											
Kelvedon	d	06 27							06 51				07 27								07 51				
Marks Tey 2	d	06 33							06 57				07 33								07 57				
Colchester 4	a	06 40							07 04	07 15		07 22	07 40				07 46				08 04	08 15			08 22
Colchester 4	d	06 40						06 56	07 04	07 16		07 23	07 40		07 44		07 47			07 56	08 04	08 16		08 20	08 23
Colchester Town	a							07 03							07 51					08 03				08 27	
	d							07 07												08 07					
Hythe	d							07 11												08 11					
Wivenhoe 3	d							07 15		07 23										08 15		08 23			
Alresford (Essex)	d							07 19												08 19					
Great Bentley	d							07 23												08 23					
Weeley	d							07 26			←									08 26			←		
Thorpe-le-Soken 1	a							07 31		07 35	07 31									08 31		08 35	08 31		
	d			06 37				07 37		07 35	07 37									08 37		08 35	08 37		
Clacton-on-Sea	a							→		07 44										→		08 44			
Kirby Cross	d			06 42							07 42												08 42		
Frinton-on-Sea	d			06 45							07 45												08 45		
Walton-on-the-Naze	a			06 49							07 49												08 49		
Manningtree 2	d	06 48			07 00				07 12			07 31	07 48				07 55		08 00		08 12				08 31
Mistley	d				07 04													08 02	08 04						
Wrabness	d				07 09														08 09						
Harwich International	d				07 17								08a09						08 17						
Dovercourt	d				07 20														08 20						
Harwich Town	a				07 22														08 22						
Ipswich	a	07 00							07 25			07 43					08 07	08 17			08 25				08 43
	d					07 10	07 19					07 44				08 00	08 08	08 19							08 44
Needham Market	d						07 28											08 28							
Stowmarket	d					07 21	07a33					07 55				08 12		08a33							08 55
Peterborough 8	a															09 38									
Diss	d					07 34						08 08					08 29								09 08
Norwich	a					07 53						08 27					08 50								09 27

b Previous night, stops to pick up only
B 28 July only
A not 28 July

London - Chelmsford, Colchester, Walton-on-Naze, Clacton, Harwich, Ipswich and Norwich

Network Diagram - see first Page of Table 5

		LE	LE	LE	LE	LE	LE	LE	LE	LE	LE	LE	LE	LE	LE	LE	LE	LE	LE	LE	LE	LE
		1	1	◇1 ⊐	1	1	1	1	1	1	1	◇1 ⊐	1	1	1	◇1 ⊐	1	1	1	1	1	1
London Liverpool Street 15 ⊖	d	07 38	07 48	08 00				08 02	08 18			08 30	08 38	08 48		09 00				09 02	09 18	
Stratford 7 ⊖	d	07 45	07 55					08 09	08 25			08u38	08 45	08 55						09 09	09 25	
Romford	d	07 53											08 53									
Shenfield 3	d	08 03	08 11					08 25	08 41				09 03	09 11						09 25	09 41	
Ingatestone	d		08 15						08 45					09 15							09 45	
Chelmsford 3	d	08 12	08 22					08 34	08 52			09 03	09 12	09 22						09 34	09 52	
Hatfield Peverel	d							08 40												09 40		
Witham 2	d	08 23	08 34					08 47	09 03				09 23	09 34						09 47	10 03	
White Notley	d		08 41											09 41								
Cressing	d		08 43											09 43								
Braintree Freeport	d		08 46											09 46								
Braintree	a		08 50											09 50								
Kelvedon	d	08 27						08 51					09 27							09 51		
Marks Tey 2	d	08 33						08 57					09 33							09 57		
Colchester 4	a	08 40		08 46				09 04	09 15			09 22	09 40			09 46				10 04	10 15	
Colchester 4	d	08 41		08 47			08 56	09 04	09 16		09 20	09 23	09 41			09 47			09 56	10 04	10 16	
Colchester Town	a	08 49					09 03				09 27		09 49						10 03			
	d						09 07												10 07			
Hythe	d						09 11												10 11			
Wivenhoe 3	d						09 15		09 23										10 15		10 23	
Alresford (Essex)	d						09 19												10 19			
Great Bentley	d						09 23												10 23			
Weeley	d						09 26			←									10 26			←
Thorpe-le-Soken 1	a						09 31		09 35	09 31									10 31		10 35	10 31
	d						09 37		09 35	09 37									10 37		10 35	10 37
Clacton-on-Sea	a						→		09 44										→		10 44	
Kirby Cross	d									09 42												10 42
Frinton-on-Sea	d									09 45												10 45
Walton-on-the-Naze	a									09 49												10 49
Manningtree 2	d			08 55	09 00			09 12				09 31				09 55	10 00			10 12		
Mistley	d				09 04												10 04					
Wrabness	d				09 09												10 09					
Harwich International	d				09 17												10 17					
Dovercourt	d				09 20												10 20					
Harwich Town	a				09 22												10 22					
Ipswich	a			09 07				09 25				09 43				10 07				10 25		
	d			09 08		09 19						09 44			10 00	10 08		10 19				
Needham Market	d					09 28												10 28				
Stowmarket	d					09a33						09 55			10 12			10a33				
Peterborough 8	a														11 37							
Diss	d			09 29								10 08				10 29						
Norwich	a			09 50								10 27				10 50						

		LE	LE	LE	LE	LE	LE	LE	LE	LE	LE	LE	LE	LE	LE	LE	LE	LE	LE	LE	LE	LE	LE
		1	◇1 ⊐	1	1	1 ⊐	1	1	1	1	1	1	1	◇1 ⊐	1	1	1	◇1 ⊐	1	1	1	1	1
London Liverpool Street 15 ⊖	d		09 30	09 38	09 48	10 00				10 02	10 18			10 30	10 38	10 48		11 00				11 02	11 18
Stratford 7 ⊖	d		09u38	09 45	09 55					10 09	10 25			10u38	10 45	10 55						11 09	11 25
Romford	d			09 53																			
Shenfield 3	d			10 03	10 11					10 25	10 41				11 03	11 11						11 25	11 41
Ingatestone	d				10 15						10 45					11 15							11 45
Chelmsford 3	d		10 03	10 12	10 22					10 34	10 52			11 03	11 12	11 22						11 34	11 52
Hatfield Peverel	d									10 40												11 40	
Witham 2	d			10 23	10 34					10 47	11 03				11 23	11 34						11 47	12 03
White Notley	d				10 41											11 41							
Cressing	d				10 43											11 43							
Braintree Freeport	d				10 46											11 46							
Braintree	a				10 50											11 50							
Kelvedon	d			10 27						10 51					11 27							11 51	
Marks Tey 2	d			10 33						10 57					11 33							11 57	
Colchester 4	a		10 22	10 40		10 46				11 04	11 15			11 22	11 40			11 46				12 04	12 15
Colchester 4	d	10 20	10 23	10 41		10 47			10 56	11 04	11 16		11 20	11 23	11 41			11 47			11 56	12 04	12 16
Colchester Town	a	10 27		10 49					11 03				11 27		11 49						12 03		
	d								11 07												12 07		
Hythe	d								11 11												12 11		
Wivenhoe 3	d								11 15		11 23										12 15		12 23
Alresford (Essex)	d								11 19												12 19		
Great Bentley	d								11 23												12 23		
Weeley	d								11 26			←									12 26		
Thorpe-le-Soken 1	a								11 31		11 35	11 31									12 31		12 35
	d								11 37		11 35	11 37									12 37		12 35
Clacton-on-Sea	a								→		11 44										→		12 44
Kirby Cross	d											11 42											
Frinton-on-Sea	d											11 45											
Walton-on-the-Naze	a											11 49											
Manningtree 2	d		10 31			10 55	11 00			11 12				11 31				11 55	12 00			12 12	
Mistley	d						11 04												12 04				
Wrabness	d						11 09												12 09				
Harwich International	d						11 17												12 17				
Dovercourt	d						11 20												12 20				
Harwich Town	a						11 22												12 22				
Ipswich	a		10 43			11 07				11 25				11 43				12 07				12 25	
	d		10 44			11 08		11 19						11 44			12 00	12 08		12 19			
Needham Market	d							11 28												12 28			
Stowmarket	d		10 55					11a33						11 55			12 12			12a33			
Peterborough 8	a																13 37						
Diss	d		11 08			11 29								12 08				12 29					
Norwich	a		11 27			11 50								12 27				12 50					

London - Chelmsford, Colchester, Walton-on-Naze, Clacton, Harwich, Ipswich and Norwich

Network Diagram - see first Page of Table 5

		LE	LE	LE		LE	LE	LE	LE	LE	LE	LE	LE	LE		LE	LE	LE	LE	LE	LE	LE	LE	LE	LE
		■	■	◇■ 🍴		■	■	◇■ 🍴	■	■	■	■	■	■		■	■ 🍴	■	■	■	◇■ 🍴	■	■	■	■
London Liverpool Street ⊖	d			11 30		11 38	11 48	12 00				12 02	12 18				12 30	12 38	12 48		13 00				13 02
Stratford ⊖	d			11u38		11 45	11 55					12 09	12 25				12u38	12 45	12 55						13 09
Romford	d					11 53																			
Shenfield	d					12 03	12 11					12 25	12 41					13 03	13 11						13 25
Ingatestone	d						12 15						12 45						13 15						
Chelmsford	d			12 03		12 12	12 22					12 34	12 52				13 03	13 12	13 22						13 34
Hatfield Peverel	d											12 40													13 40
Witham	d					12 23	12 34					12 47	13 03					13 23	13 34						13 47
White Notley	d						12 41												13 41						
Cressing	d						12 43												13 43						
Braintree Freeport	d						12 46												13 46						
Braintree	a						12 50												13 50						
Kelvedon	d					12 27						12 51						13 27							13 51
Marks Tey	d					12 33						12 57						13 33							13 57
Colchester	a			12 22		12 40		12 46				13 04	13 15				13 22	13 40			13 46				14 04
Colchester	d		12 20	12 23		12 41		12 47			12 56	13 04	13 16			13 20	13 23	13 41			13 47			13 56	14 04
Colchester Town	a		12 27			12 49					13 03					13 27		13 49						14 03	
	d										13 07													14 07	
Hythe	d										13 11													14 11	
Wivenhoe	d										13 15		13 23											14 15	
Alresford (Essex)	d										13 19													14 19	
Great Bentley	d										13 23													14 23	
Weeley	d	←									13 26			←										14 26	
Thorpe-le-Soken	a	12 31									13 31		13 35	13 31										14 31	
	d	12 37									13 37		13 35	13 37										14 37	
Clacton-on-Sea	a										→		13 44											→	
Kirby Cross	d	12 42												13 42											
Frinton-on-Sea	d	12 45												13 45											
Walton-on-the-Naze	a	12 49												13 49											
Manningtree	d			12 31				12 55	13 00			13 12					13 31				13 55	14 00			14 12
Mistley	d								13 04													14 04			
Wrabness	d								13 09													14 09			
Harwich International	d								13 17													14 17			
Dovercourt	d								13 20													14 20			
Harwich Town	a								13 22													14 22			
Ipswich	a			12 43				13 07				13 25					13 43				14 07				14 25
	d			12 44				13 08		13 19							13 44			14 00	14 08		14 19		
Needham Market	d									13 28													14 28		
Stowmarket	d			12 55						13a33							13 55			14 12			14a33		
Peterborough	a																			15 37					
Diss	d			13 08				13 29									14 08				14 29				
Norwich	a			13 27				13 50									14 27				14 50				

		LE	LE	LE	LE	LE	LE	LE	LE	LE		LE	LE	LE	LE	LE	LE	LE	LE	LE	LE	LE	LE	LE	LE
		■	■	■	◇■ 🍴	■	■	◇■ 🍴	■	■		■	■	■	■	■	◇■ 🍴	■	■	■	◇■ 🍴	■	■	■	■
London Liverpool Street ⊖	d	13 18			13 30	13 38	13 48	14 00					14 02	14 18			14 30	14 38	14 48		15 00				15 02
Stratford ⊖	d	13 25			13u38	13 45	13 55						14 09	14 25			14u38	14 45	14 55						15 09
Romford	d					13 53																			
Shenfield	d	13 41				14 03	14 11						14 25	14 41				15 03	15 11						15 25
Ingatestone	d	13 45					14 15							14 45					15 15						
Chelmsford	d	13 52			14 03	14 12	14 22						14 34	14 52			15 03	15 12	15 22						15 34
Hatfield Peverel	d												14 40												15 40
Witham	d	14 03				14 23	14 34						14 47	15 03				15 23	15 34						15 47
White Notley	d						14 41												15 41						
Cressing	d						14 43												15 43						
Braintree Freeport	d						14 46												15 46						
Braintree	a						14 50												15 50						
Kelvedon	d					14 27							14 51					15 27							15 51
Marks Tey	d					14 33							14 57					15 33							15 57
Colchester	a	14 15			14 22	14 40		14 46					15 04	15 15			15 22	15 40			15 46				16 04
Colchester	d	14 16		14 20	14 23	14 41		14 47				14 56	15 04	15 16		15 20	15 23	15 41			15 47			15 56	16 04
Colchester Town	a			14 27		14 49						15 03				15 27		15 49						16 03	
	d											15 07												16 07	
Hythe	d											15 11												16 11	
Wivenhoe	d	14 23										15 15		15 23										16 15	
Alresford (Essex)	d											15 19												16 19	
Great Bentley	d											15 23												16 23	
Weeley	d		←									15 26			←									16 26	
Thorpe-le-Soken	a	14 35	14 31									15 31		15 35	15 31									16 31	
	d	14 35	14 37									15 37		15 35	15 37									16 37	
Clacton-on-Sea	a	14 44										→		15 44										→	
Kirby Cross	d		14 42												15 42										
Frinton-on-Sea	d		14 45												15 45										
Walton-on-the-Naze	a		14 49												15 49										
Manningtree	d				14 31			14 55	15 00				15 12				15 31				15 55	16 00			16 12
Mistley	d								15 04													16 04			
Wrabness	d								15 09													16 09			
Harwich International	d								15 17													16 17			
Dovercourt	d								15 20													16 20			
Harwich Town	a								15 22													16 22			
Ipswich	a				14 43			15 07					15 25				15 43				16 07				16 25
	d				14 44			15 08		15 19							15 44			16 00	16 08		16 19		
Needham Market	d									15 28													16 28		
Stowmarket	d				14 55					15a33							15 55			16 12			16a33		
Peterborough	a																			17 37					
Diss	d				15 08			15 29									16 08				16 29				
Norwich	a				15 27			15 48									16 27				16 50				

Table 11 — Saturdays — 28 July to 11 August

London - Chelmsford, Colchester, Walton-on-Naze, Clacton, Harwich, Ipswich and Norwich

Network Diagram - see first Page of Table 5

		LE	LE	LE	LE	LE		LE	LE	LE	LE	LE	LE	LE	LE	LE	LE	LE	LE	LE	LE	LE	LE	LE	LE
		■	■	■	◇■ 🍴	■		■	◇■ 🍴	■	■	■	■	■	■	■	◇■ 🍴	■	■	■	◇■ 🍴	■	■	■	■
London Liverpool Street ⊖	d	15 18			15 30	15 38		15 48	16 00				16 02	16 18			16 30	16 38	16 48		17 00				17 02
Stratford ⊖	d	15 25			15u38	15 45		15 55					16 09	16 25			16u38	16 45	16 55						17 09
Romford	d					15 53																			
Shenfield	d	15 41				16 03		16 11					16 25	16 41				17 03	17 11						17 25
Ingatestone	d	15 45						16 15						16 45					17 15						
Chelmsford	d	15 52			16 03	16 12		16 22					16 34	16 52			17 03	17 12	17 22						17 34
Hatfield Peverel	d												16 40												17 40
Witham	d	16 03				16 23		16 34					16 47	17 03				17 23	17 34						17 47
White Notley	d							16 41											17 41						
Cressing	d							16 43											17 43						
Braintree Freeport	d							16 46											17 46						
Braintree	a							16 50											17 50						
Kelvedon	d					16 27							16 51					17 27							17 51
Marks Tey	d					16 33							16 57					17 33							17 57
Colchester	a	16 15			16 22	16 40			16 46				17 04	17 15			17 22	17 40			17 46				18 04
Colchester	d	16 16		16 20	16 23	16 41			16 47			16 56	17 04	17 16		17 20	17 23	17 41			17 47			17 56	18 04
Colchester Town	a			16 27		16 49						17 03				17 27		17 49						18 03	
	d											17 07												18 07	
Hythe	d											17 11												18 11	
Wivenhoe	d	16 23										17 15		17 23										18 15	
Alresford (Essex)	d											17 19												18 19	
Great Bentley	d											17 23												18 23	
Weeley	d		←									17 26			←									18 26	
Thorpe-le-Soken	a	16 35	16 31									17 31		17 35	17 31									18 31	
	d	16 35	16 37									17 37		17 35	17 37									18 37	
Clacton-on-Sea	a	16 44										→		17 44										→	
Kirby Cross	d		16 42												17 42										
Frinton-on-Sea	d		16 45												17 45										
Walton-on-the-Naze	a		16 49												17 49										
Manningtree	d				16 31				16 55	17 00			17 12				17 31				17 55	18 00			18 12
Mistley	d									17 04												18 04			
Wrabness	d									17 09												18 09			
Harwich International	d									17 17												18 17			
Dovercourt	d									17 20												18 20			
Harwich Town	a									17 22												18 22			
Ipswich	a				16 43				17 07				17 25				17 43				18 07				18 25
	d				16 44				17 08		17 19						17 44			18 00	18 08		18 19		
Needham Market	d										17 28												18 28		
Stowmarket	d				16 55				17 19		17a33						17 55			18 12			18a33		
Peterborough	a																			19 38					
Diss	d				17 08				17 32								18 08				18 29				
Norwich	a				17 27				17 51								18 27				18 50				

		LE		LE	LE	LE	LE	LE	LE	LE	LE	LE		LE	LE	LE	LE	LE	LE	LE	LE	LE	LE	LE	LE
		■		■	■	◇■ 🍴	■	■	◇■ 🍴	■	■	■		■	■	■	■	◇■ 🍴	■	■	■	◇■ 🍴	■	■	■
London Liverpool Street ⊖	d	17 18				17 30	17 38	17 48	18 00					18 02	18 18			18 30	18 38	18 48		19 00			
Stratford ⊖	d	17 25				17u38	17 45	17 55						18 09	18 25			18u38	18 45	18 55					
Romford	d						17 53																		
Shenfield	d	17 41					18 03	18 11						18 25	18 41				19 03	19 11					
Ingatestone	d	17 45						18 15							18 45					19 15					
Chelmsford	d	17 52				18 03	18 12	18 22						18 34	18 52			19 03	19 12	19 22					
Hatfield Peverel	d													18 40											
Witham	d	18 03					18 23	18 34						18 47	19 03				19 23	19 34					
White Notley	d							18 41												19 41					
Cressing	d							18 43												19 43					
Braintree Freeport	d							18 46												19 46					
Braintree	a							18 50												19 50					
Kelvedon	d						18 27							18 51					19 27						
Marks Tey	d						18 33							18 57					19 33						
Colchester	a	18 15				18 22	18 40		18 46					19 04	19 15			19 22	19 40			19 46			
Colchester	d	18 16			18 20	18 23	18 41		18 47			18 56		19 04	19 16		19 20	19 23	19 41			19 47			19 56
Colchester Town	a				18 27		18 49					19 03					19 27		19 49						20 03
	d											19 07													20 07
Hythe	d											19 11													20 11
Wivenhoe	d	18 23										19 15			19 23										20 15
Alresford (Essex)	d											19 19													20 19
Great Bentley	d											19 23													20 23
Weeley	d			←								19 26				←									20 26
Thorpe-le-Soken	a	18 35		18 31								19 31			19 35	19 31									20 31
	d	18 35		18 37								19 37			19 35	19 37									20 37
Clacton-on-Sea	a	18 44										→			19 44										→
Kirby Cross	d			18 42												19 42									
Frinton-on-Sea	d			18 45												19 45									
Walton-on-the-Naze	a			18 49												19 49									
Manningtree	d					18 31			18 55	19 00				19 12				19 31				19 55	20 00		
Mistley	d									19 04													20 04		
Wrabness	d									19 09													20 09		
Harwich International	d									19 17													20 17		
Dovercourt	d									19 20													20 20		
Harwich Town	a									19 22													20 22		
Ipswich	a					18 43			19 07					19 25				19 43				20 07			
	d					18 44			19 08		19 19							19 44			20 00	20 08		20 19	
Needham Market	d										19 28													20 28	
Stowmarket	d					18 55					19a33							19 55			20 12			20a33	
Peterborough	a																				21 37				
Diss	d					19 08			19 29									20 08				20 29			
Norwich	a					19 27			19 50									20 27				20 50			

London - Chelmsford, Colchester, Walton-on-Naze, Clacton, Harwich, Ipswich and Norwich

Network Diagram - see first Page of Table 5

		LE 1	LE 1	LE 1	LE 1	LE ◇1	LE 1	LE 1	LE ◇1	LE 1	LE	LE 1	LE 1	LE 1	LE 1	LE 1	LE ◇1	LE 1	LE 1	LE 1	LE 1	LE 1	LE
London Liverpool Street 15 ⊖	d	19 02	19 18			19 30	19 38	19 48	20 00				20 02	20 18			20 30	20 38	20 48		21 00		
Stratford 7 ⊖	d	19 09	19 25			19u38	19 46	19 55					20 09	20 25			20u38	20 45	20 55				
Romford	d						19 54											20 53					
Shenfield 3	d	19 25	19 41				20 04	20 11					20 25	20 41				21 03	21 11				
Ingatestone	d		19 45					20 15						20 45					21 15				
Chelmsford 3	d	19 34	19 52			20 03	20 13	20 22					20 34	20 52			21 03	21 12	21 22				
Hatfield Peverel	d	19 40											20 40										
Witham 2	d	19 47	20 03				20 24	20 34					20 47	21 03				21 23	21 34				
White Notley	d							20 41											21 41				
Cressing	d							20 43											21 43				
Braintree Freeport	d							20 46											21 46				
Braintree	a							20 50											21 50				
Kelvedon	d	19 51					20 28						20 51					21 27					
Marks Tey 2	d	19 57					20 34						20 57					21 33					
Colchester 4	a	20 04	20 15			20 22	20 41		20 46				21 04	21 15			21 22	21 40			21 46		
Colchester 4	d	20 04	20 16		20 20	20 23	20 42		20 47			20 56	21 04	21 16		21 20	21 23	21 41			21 47		
Colchester Town	a				20 27		20 50					21 03				21 27		21 49					
	d											21 07											
Hythe	d											21 11											
Wivenhoe 3	d		20 23									21 15		21 23									
Alresford (Essex)	d											21 19											
Great Bentley	d											21 23											
Weeley	d			←								21 26			←								
Thorpe-le-Soken 1	a		20 35	20 31								21 31		21 35	21 31								
	d		20 35	20 37								21 37		21 35	21 37								
Clacton-on-Sea	a		20 44									→		21 44									
Kirby Cross	d			20 42											21 42								
Frinton-on-Sea	d			20 45											21 45								
Walton-on-the-Naze	a			20 49											21 49								
Manningtree 2	d	20 12				20 31			20 55	21 00			21 12				21 31				21 55	22 00	
Mistley	d									21 04												22 04	
Wrabness	d									21 09												22 09	
Harwich International	d									21 17										21 38		22 17	
Dovercourt	d									21 20												22 20	
Harwich Town	a									21 22												22 22	
Ipswich	a	20 25				20 43			21 07				21 25				21 43			22 03	22 08		
	d					20 44			21 08		21 16						21 44						22 16
Needham Market	d										21 26												22 26
Stowmarket	d					20 55					21a32						21 55						22a32
Peterborough 8	a																						
Diss	d					21 08			21 29								22 08						
Norwich	a					21 27			21 50								22 27						

		LE 1	LE 1	LE 1	LE 1	LE ◇1	LE 1	LE 1	LE 1	LE 1	LE 1	LE 1	LE 1	LE 1	LE 1	LE ◇1	LE 1	LE 1	LE 1	LE ◇1	LE	LE 1
London Liverpool Street 15 ⊖	d		21 02	21 18		21 30	21 38	21 48	21 56				22 02	22 15		22 30	22 35		22 45	23 00		23 07
Stratford 7 ⊖	d		21 09	21 25		21u38	21 45	21 55	22 05				22 10	22 24		22u40	22 44		22 54	23u10		23 17
Romford	d						21 53															
Shenfield 3	d		21 25	21 41			22 03	22 11					22 27	22 41			23 01		23 12			23 34
Ingatestone	d			21 45				22 15						22 45			23 05		23 16			
Chelmsford 3	d		21 34	21 52		22 03	22 12	22 22	22 28				22 36	22 52		23 05	23 12		23 23	23 37		23 43
Hatfield Peverel	d		21 40										22 42									23 49
Witham 2	d		21 47	22 03			22 23	22 34					22 49	23 03			23 23	23 25	23 34			23 56
White Notley	d							22 41										23 32				
Cressing	d							22 43										23 34				
Braintree Freeport	d							22 46										23 37				
Braintree	a							22 50										23 41				
Kelvedon	d		21 51				22 27						22 53				23 27					
Marks Tey 2	d		21 57				22 33						22 59				23 33					00 01
Colchester 4	a		22 04	22 15		22 22	22 40		22 47				23 06	23 15		23 24	23 41		23 46	23 58	23 46	00 06
Colchester 4	d	21 56	22 04	22 16		22 23	22 41		22 47			22 56	23 07	23 16		23 25			23 47	23 59	23 55	00 14
Colchester Town	a	22 03					22 49					23 03										
	d	22 07										23 07										
Hythe	d	22 11										23 11										
Wivenhoe 3	d	22 15		22 23								23 15		23 23					23 54			
Alresford (Essex)	d	22 19										23 19										
Great Bentley	d	22 23										23 23										
Weeley	d	22 26			←							23 26			←							
Thorpe-le-Soken 1	a	22 31		22 35	22 31							23 31		23 35	23 31				00 06			
	d	22 37		22 35	22 37						23 16	23 37		23 35	23 37				00 06			
Clacton-on-Sea	a	→		22 44							23 25	→		23 44					00 15			
Kirby Cross	d				22 42										23 42							
Frinton-on-Sea	d				22 45										23 45							
Walton-on-the-Naze	a				22 49										23 49							
Manningtree 2	d		22 12			22 31			22 56	23 00			23 15			23 34				00 09		
Mistley	d									23 04												
Wrabness	d									23 09												
Harwich International	d		22a28						23a11	23 17												
Dovercourt	d									23 20												
Harwich Town	a									23 22												
Ipswich	a					22 43							23 27			23 45				00 19		
	d					22 44										23 46				00 21		
Needham Market	d																					
Stowmarket	d					22 55										23 58				00 32		
Peterborough 8	a																					
Diss	d					23 08										00 10				00 45		
Norwich	a					23 27										00 30				01 05		

London - Chelmsford, Colchester, Walton-on-Naze, Clacton, Harwich, Ipswich and Norwich

Network Diagram - see first Page of Table 5

		LE 1	LE ◇1	LE 1	LE 1	LE ◇1
London Liverpool Street 15 ⊖	d	23 15	23 30	23 35	23 45	23 59
Stratford 7 ⊖	d	23 25	23u40	23 45	23 54	00u10
Romford	d					
Shenfield 3	d	23 43		00 02	00 12	
Ingatestone	d	23 48		00 05	00 16	
Chelmsford 3	d	23 55	00 06	00 12	00 23	00 37
Hatfield Peverel	d			00 18		
Witham 2	d	00 05		00 25	00 34	
White Notley	d					
Cressing	d					
Braintree Freeport	d					
Braintree	a					
Kelvedon	d			00 29		
Marks Tey 2	d			00 35		
Colchester 4	a	00 17	00 25	00 43	00 46	00 56
Colchester 4	d	00 18	00 25		00 47	00 57
Colchester Town	a					
	d					
Hythe	d					
Wivenhoe 3	d	00 25			00 54	
Alresford (Essex)	d					
Great Bentley	d					
Weeley	d					
Thorpe-le-Soken 1	a	00 37			01 06	
	d	00 37			01 06	
Clacton-on-Sea	a	00 46			01 15	
Kirby Cross	d					
Frinton-on-Sea	d					
Walton-on-the-Naze	a					
Manningtree 2	d		00 34			01 07
Mistley	d					
Wrabness	d					
Harwich International	d					
Dovercourt	d					
Harwich Town	a					
Ipswich	a		00 45			01 17
	d		00 46			01 19
Needham Market	d					
Stowmarket	d		00 58			01 30
Peterborough 8	a					
Diss	d		01 10			01 43
Norwich	a		01 30			02 03

Table 11

Saturdays

18 August to 25 August

London - Chelmsford, Colchester, Walton-on-Naze, Clacton, Harwich, Ipswich and Norwich

Network Diagram - see first Page of Table 5

Station		LE ◇■ 🍽	LE ■	LE ■	LE ◇■ 🍽	LE ■	LE ■	LE ■	LE	LE ■	LE ◇■	LE ■	LE ■	LE ■	LE ■	LE ■	LE ■	LE ■	LE ■	LE ◇■ 🍽	LE ■	LE ■	LE ■
London Liverpool Street ⊖	d	22p30	23p02	23p18	23p30		23p48	00 18								05 34							06 02
Stratford ⊖	d	22b38	23p09	23p25	23b38		23p55	00 25								05 41							06 09
Romford	d															05 49							
Shenfield	d		23p25	23p41			00 11	00 47								05 59							06 25
Ingatestone	d			23p45			00 15	00 51								06 03							
Chelmsford	d	23p03	23p34	23p52	00 03		00 22	00 58								06 10							06 34
Hatfield Peverel	d		23p40				00 28	01 04								06 16							06 40
Witham	d		23p47	00 03		00 05	00 35	01 11		05 34						06 23	06 34						06 47
White Notley	d					00 12				05 41							06 41						
Cressing	d					00 14				05 43							06 43						
Braintree Freeport	d					00 17				05 46							06 46						
Braintree	a					00 21				05 50							06 50						
Kelvedon	d		23p51				00 39	01 15								06 27							06 51
Marks Tey	d		23p57				00 45	01 21								06 33							06 57
Colchester	a	23p22	00 04	00 15	00 22		00 57	01 41								06 40							07 04
Colchester	d	23p23	00 04	00 16	00 23						05 40	05 52		06 20	06 24	06 40						06 56	07 04
Colchester Town	a													06 27								07 03	
	d																					07 07	
Hythe	d																					07 11	
Wivenhoe	d			00 23																		07 15	
Alresford (Essex)	d			00 27																		07 19	
Great Bentley	d			00 31																		07 23	
Weeley	d																					07 26	
Thorpe-le-Soken	a			00 38																		07 31	
	d			00 38														06 37				07 37	
Clacton-on-Sea	a			00 51																		→	
Kirby Cross	d																	06 42					
Frinton-on-Sea	d																	06 45					
Walton-on-the-Naze	a																	06 49					
Manningtree	d	23p31	00 12		00 31						05 49	06 00			06 32	06 48			07 00				07 12
Mistley	d											06 04							07 04				
Wrabness	d											06 09							07 09				
Harwich International	d											06 17							07 17				
Dovercourt	d											06 20							07 20				
Harwich Town	a											06 22							07 22				
Ipswich	a	23p43	00 28		00 43						05 59				06 44	07 00							07 25
	d	23p44			00 44				05 10		06 00		06 16							07 10	07 19		
Needham Market	d								05 20				06 25								07 28		
Stowmarket	d	23p55			00 55				05a26		06 12		06a30							07 21	07a33		
Peterborough	a										07 38												
Diss	d	00 08			01 08															07 34			
Norwich	a	00 39			01 43															07 53			

Station		LE ■	LE ■	LE ◇■ 🍽	LE ■	LE ■	LE ■	LE ■	LE ◇■ 🍽	LE ■	LE ■	LE ■	LE ■	LE ■	LE ■	LE ■	LE ◇■ 🍽	LE ■	LE ■	LE ◇■ 🍽	LE ■	LE ■	LE ■
London Liverpool Street ⊖	d	06 18		06 30	06 38	06 48			07 00				07 02	07 18			07 30	07 38	07 48	08 00			
Stratford ⊖	d	06 25		06u38	06 45	06 55							07 09	07 25			07u38	07 45	07 55				
Romford	d				06 53													07 53					
Shenfield	d	06 41			07 03	07 11							07 25	07 41				08 03	08 11				
Ingatestone	d	06 45				07 15								07 45					08 15				
Chelmsford	d	06 52		07 03	07 12	07 22							07 34	07 52			08 03	08 12	08 22				
Hatfield Peverel	d												07 40										
Witham	d	07 03			07 23	07 34							07 47	08 03				08 23	08 34				
White Notley	d					07 41													08 41				
Cressing	d					07 43													08 43				
Braintree Freeport	d					07 46													08 46				
Braintree	a					07 50													08 50				
Kelvedon	d				07 27								07 51					08 27					
Marks Tey	d				07 33								07 57					08 33					
Colchester	a	07 15		07 22	07 40				07 46				08 04	08 15			08 22	08 40		08 46			
Colchester	d	07 16		07 23	07 40		07 44		07 47			07 56	08 04	08 16		08 20	08 23	08 41		08 47			08 56
Colchester Town	a						07 51					08 03				08 27		08 49					09 03
	d											08 07											09 07
Hythe	d											08 11											09 11
Wivenhoe	d	07 23										08 15		08 23									09 15
Alresford (Essex)	d											08 19											09 19
Great Bentley	d											08 23											09 23
Weeley	d		←									08 26			←								09 26
Thorpe-le-Soken	a	07 35	07 31									08 31		08 35	08 31								09 31
	d	07 35	07 37									08 37		08 35	08 37								09 37
Clacton-on-Sea	a	07 44										→		08 44									→
Kirby Cross	d		07 42												08 42								
Frinton-on-Sea	d		07 45												08 45								
Walton-on-the-Naze	a		07 49												08 49								
Manningtree	d			07 31	07 48				07 55		08 00		08 12				08 31			08 55	09 00		
Mistley	d									08 02	08 04										09 04		
Wrabness	d										08 09										09 09		
Harwich International	d				08a09						08 17										09 17		
Dovercourt	d										08 20										09 20		
Harwich Town	a										08 22										09 22		
Ipswich	a			07 43					08 07	08 17			08 25				08 43			09 07			
	d			07 44				08 00	08 08	08 19							08 44			09 08		09 19	
Needham Market	d									08 28												09 28	
Stowmarket	d			07 55				08 12		08a33							08 55					09a33	
Peterborough	a							09 38															
Diss	d			08 08					08 29								09 08			09 29			
Norwich	a			08 27					08 50								09 27			09 50			

b Previous night, stops to pick up only

Table 11

Saturdays

18 August to 25 August

London - Chelmsford, Colchester, Walton-on-Naze, Clacton, Harwich, Ipswich and Norwich

Network Diagram - see first Page of Table 5

Station		LE ■	LE ■	LE ■	LE ■	LE ◇■ 🍽	LE ■	LE ■	LE ■	LE ◇■ 🍽	LE ■	LE ■	LE ■	LE ■	LE ■	LE ■	LE ■	LE ◇■ 🍽	LE ■	LE ■	LE ■ ■ 🍽	LE ■
London Liverpool Street ⊖	d	08 02	08 18			08 30	08 38	08 48		09 00				09 02	09 18			09 30	09 38	09 48	10 00	
Stratford ⊖	d	08 09	08 25			08u38	08 45	08 55						09 09	09 25			09u38	09 45	09 55		
Romford	d						08 53												09 53			
Shenfield	d	08 25	08 41				09 03	09 11						09 25	09 41				10 03	10 11		
Ingatestone	d		08 45					09 15							09 45					10 15		
Chelmsford	d	08 34	08 52			09 03	09 12	09 22						09 34	09 52			10 03	10 12	10 22		
Hatfield Peverel	d	08 40												09 40								
Witham	d	08 47	09 03				09 23	09 34						09 47	10 03				10 23	10 34		
White Notley	d							09 41												10 41		
Cressing	d							09 43												10 43		
Braintree Freeport	d							09 46												10 46		
Braintree	a							09 50												10 50		
Kelvedon	d	08 51					09 27							09 51					10 27			
Marks Tey	d	08 57					09 33							09 57					10 33			
Colchester	a	09 04	09 15			09 22	09 40			09 46				10 04	10 15			10 22	10 40		10 46	
Colchester	d	09 04	09 16		09 20	09 23	09 41			09 47			09 56	10 04	10 16		10 20	10 23	10 41		10 47	
Colchester Town	a				09 27		09 49						10 03				10 27		10 49			
	d												10 07									
Hythe	d												10 11									
Wivenhoe	d		09 23										10 15		10 23							
Alresford (Essex)	d												10 19									
Great Bentley	d												10 23									
Weeley	d			←									10 26			←						
Thorpe-le-Soken	a		09 35	09 31									10 31		10 35	10 31						
	d		09 35	09 37									10 37		10 35	10 37						
Clacton-on-Sea	a		09 44										→		10 44							
Kirby Cross	d			09 42												10 42						
Frinton-on-Sea	d			09 45												10 45						
Walton-on-the-Naze	a			09 49												10 49						
Manningtree	d	09 12				09 31				09 55	10 00			10 12				10 31			10 55	11 00
Mistley	d										10 04											11 04
Wrabness	d										10 09											11 09
Harwich International	d										10 17											11 17
Dovercourt	d										10 20											11 20
Harwich Town	a										10 22											11 22
Ipswich	a	09 25				09 43				10 07				10 25				10 43			11 07	
	d					09 44			10 00	10 08		10 19						10 44			11 08	
Needham Market	d											10 28										
Stowmarket	d					09 55			10 12			10a33						10 55				
Peterborough	a								11 37													
Diss	d					10 08				10 29								11 08			11 29	
Norwich	a					10 27				10 50								11 27			11 50	

Station		LE ■	LE ■	LE ■	LE ■	LE ■	LE ■	LE ◇■ 🍽	LE ■	LE ■	LE ■	LE ◇■ 🍽	LE ■	LE ■	LE ■	LE ■	LE ■	LE ■	LE ■	LE ◇■ 🍽	LE ■	LE ■	LE ◇■ 🍽
London Liverpool Street ⊖	d			10 02	10 18			10 30	10 38	10 48		11 00				11 02	11 18			11 30	11 38	11 48	12 00
Stratford ⊖	d			10 09	10 25			10u38	10 45	10 55						11 09	11 25			11u38	11 45	11 55	
Romford	d								10 53												11 53		
Shenfield	d			10 25	10 41				11 03	11 11						11 25	11 41				12 03	12 11	
Ingatestone	d				10 45					11 15							11 45					12 15	
Chelmsford	d			10 34	10 52			11 03	11 12	11 22						11 34	11 52			12 03	12 12	12 22	
Hatfield Peverel	d			10 40												11 40							
Witham	d			10 47	11 03				11 23	11 34						11 47	12 03				12 23	12 34	
White Notley	d									11 41												12 41	
Cressing	d									11 43												12 43	
Braintree Freeport	d									11 46												12 46	
Braintree	a									11 50												12 50	
Kelvedon	d			10 51					11 27							11 51					12 27		
Marks Tey	d			10 57					11 33							11 57					12 33		
Colchester	a			11 04	11 15			11 22	11 40			11 46				12 04	12 15			12 22	12 40		12 46
Colchester	d		10 56	11 04	11 16		11 20	11 23	11 41			11 47			11 56	12 04	12 16		12 20	12 23	12 41		12 47
Colchester Town	a		11 03				11 27		11 49						12 03				12 27		12 49		
	d		11 07												12 07								
Hythe	d		11 11												12 11								
Wivenhoe	d		11 15		11 23										12 15		12 23						
Alresford (Essex)	d		11 19												12 19								
Great Bentley	d		11 23												12 23								
Weeley	d		11 26			←									12 26			←					
Thorpe-le-Soken	a		11 31		11 35	11 31									12 31		12 35	12 31					
	d		11 37		11 35	11 37									12 37		12 35	12 37					
Clacton-on-Sea	a		→		11 44										→		12 44						
Kirby Cross	d					11 42												12 42					
Frinton-on-Sea	d					11 45												12 45					
Walton-on-the-Naze	a					11 49												12 49					
Manningtree	d			11 12				11 31				11 55	12 00			12 12				12 31			12 55
Mistley	d												12 04										
Wrabness	d												12 09										
Harwich International	d												12 17										
Dovercourt	d												12 20										
Harwich Town	a												12 22										
Ipswich	a			11 25				11 43				12 07				12 25				12 43			13 07
	d	11 19						11 44			12 00	12 08		12 19						12 44			13 08
Needham Market	d	11 28												12 28									
Stowmarket	d	11a33						11 55			12 12			12a33						12 55			
Peterborough	a										13 37												
Diss	d							12 08				12 29								13 08			13 29
Norwich	a							12 27				12 50								13 27			13 50

London - Chelmsford, Colchester, Walton-on-Naze, Clacton, Harwich, Ipswich and Norwich

Network Diagram - see first Page of Table 5

		LE	LE	LE	LE	LE	LE	LE	LE	LE	LE	LE	LE	LE	LE	LE	LE	LE	LE	LE	LE	LE
		1	1	1	1	1	1	1	1 ⊡	1	1	1	◇1 ⊡	1	1	1	1	1	1	1	◇1 ⊡	1
London Liverpool Street ⊖	d				12 02	12 18			12 30	12 38	12 48		13 00				13 02	13 18			13 30	13 38
Stratford ⊖	d				12 09	12 25			12u38	12 45	12 55						13 09	13 25			13u38	13 45
Romford	d									12 53												13 53
Shenfield	d				12 25	12 41				13 03	13 11						13 25	13 41				14 03
Ingatestone	d					12 45					13 15							13 45				
Chelmsford	d				12 34	12 52			13 03	13 12	13 22						13 34	13 52			14 03	14 12
Hatfield Peverel	d				12 40												13 40					
Witham	d				12 47	13 03				13 23	13 34						13 47	14 03				14 23
White Notley	d										13 41											
Cressing	d										13 43											
Braintree Freeport	d										13 46											
Braintree	a										13 50											
Kelvedon	d				12 51					13 27							13 51					14 27
Marks Tey	d				12 57					13 33							13 57					14 33
Colchester	a				13 04	13 15			13 22	13 40			13 46				14 04	14 15			14 22	14 40
Colchester	d			12 56	13 04	13 16		13 20	13 23	13 41			13 47			13 56	14 04	14 16		14 20	14 23	14 41
Colchester Town	a			13 03				13 27		13 49						14 03				14 27		14 49
	d			13 07												14 07						
Hythe	d			13 11												14 11						
Wivenhoe	d			13 15		13 23										14 15		14 23				
Alresford (Essex)	d			13 19												14 19						
Great Bentley	d			13 23												14 23						
Weeley	d			13 26			←									14 26			←			
Thorpe-le-Soken	a			13 31		13 35	13 31									14 31		14 35	14 31			
	d			13 37		13 35	13 37									14 37		14 35	14 37			
Clacton-on-Sea	a			→		13 44										→		14 44				
Kirby Cross	d						13 42												14 42			
Frinton-on-Sea	d						13 45												14 45			
Walton-on-the-Naze	a						13 49												14 49			
Manningtree	d	13 00			13 12				13 31				13 55	14 00			14 12				14 31	
Mistley	d	13 04												14 04								
Wrabness	d	13 09												14 09								
Harwich International	d	13 17												14 17								
Dovercourt	d	13 20												14 20								
Harwich Town	a	13 22												14 22								
Ipswich	a				13 25				13 43				14 07				14 25				14 43	
	d		13 19						13 44			14 00	14 08		14 19						14 44	
Needham Market	d		13 28												14 28							
Stowmarket	d		13a33						13 55			14 12			14a33						14 55	
Peterborough	a											15 37										
Diss	d								14 08				14 29								15 08	
Norwich	a								14 27				14 50								15 27	

		LE	LE	LE	LE	LE	LE	LE	LE	LE	LE	LE	LE	LE	LE	LE	LE	LE	LE	LE	LE	LE	LE
		1	◇1 ⊡	1	1	1	1	1	1	1	◇1 ⊡	1	1	1	◇1 ⊡	1	1	1	1	1	1	1	◇1 ⊡
London Liverpool Street ⊖	d	13 48	14 00				14 02	14 18			14 30	14 38	14 48		15 00				15 02	15 18			15 30
Stratford ⊖	d	13 55					14 09	14 25			14u38	14 45	14 55						15 09	15 25			15u38
Romford	d											14 53											
Shenfield	d	14 11					14 25	14 41				15 03	15 11						15 25	15 41			
Ingatestone	d	14 15						14 45					15 15							15 45			
Chelmsford	d	14 22					14 34	14 52			15 03	15 12	15 22						15 34	15 52			16 03
Hatfield Peverel	d						14 40												15 40				
Witham	d	14 34					14 47	15 03				15 23	15 34						15 47	16 03			
White Notley	d	14 41											15 41										
Cressing	d	14 43											15 43										
Braintree Freeport	d	14 46											15 46										
Braintree	a	14 50											15 50										
Kelvedon	d						14 51					15 27							15 51				
Marks Tey	d						14 57					15 33							15 57				
Colchester	a		14 46				15 04	15 15			15 22	15 40			15 46				16 04	16 15			16 22
Colchester	d		14 47			14 56	15 04	15 16		15 20	15 23	15 41			15 47			15 56	16 04	16 16		16 20	16 23
Colchester Town	a					15 03				15 27		15 49						16 03				16 27	
	d					15 07												16 07					
Hythe	d					15 11												16 11					
Wivenhoe	d					15 15		15 23										16 15		16 23			
Alresford (Essex)	d					15 19												16 19					
Great Bentley	d					15 23												16 23					
Weeley	d					15 26			←									16 26			←		
Thorpe-le-Soken	a					15 31		15 35	15 31									16 31		16 35	16 31		
	d					15 37		15 35	15 37									16 37		16 35	16 37		
Clacton-on-Sea	a					→		15 44										→		16 44			
Kirby Cross	d								15 42												16 42		
Frinton-on-Sea	d								15 45												16 45		
Walton-on-the-Naze	a								15 49												16 49		
Manningtree	d		14 55	15 00			15 12				15 31				15 55	16 00			16 12				16 31
Mistley	d			15 04												16 04							
Wrabness	d			15 09												16 09							
Harwich International	d			15 17												16 17							
Dovercourt	d			15 20												16 20							
Harwich Town	a			15 22												16 22							
Ipswich	a		15 07				15 25				15 43				16 07				16 25				16 43
	d		15 08		15 19						15 44			16 00	16 08		16 19						16 44
Needham Market	d				15 28												16 28						
Stowmarket	d				15a33						15 55			16 12			16a33						16 55
Peterborough	a													17 37									
Diss	d		15 29								16 08				16 29								17 08
Norwich	a		15 48								16 27				16 50								17 27

Table 11

Saturdays
18 August to 25 August

London - Chelmsford, Colchester, Walton-on-Naze, Clacton, Harwich, Ipswich and Norwich

Network Diagram - see first Page of Table 5

		LE	LE	LE	LE	LE	LE	LE	LE	LE	LE	LE	LE	LE	LE	LE	LE	LE	LE	LE	LE	LE	LE
		1	1	◇1 ⊡	1	1	1	1	1	1	1	◇1 ⊡	1	1	1	◇1 ⊡	1	1	1	1	1	1	1
London Liverpool Street ⊖	d	15 38	15 48	16 00				16 02	16 18			16 30	16 38	16 48		17 00				17 02	17 18		
Stratford ⊖	d	15 45	15 55					16 09	16 25			16u38	16 45	16 55						17 09	17 25		
Romford	d	15 53											16 53										
Shenfield	d	16 03	16 11					16 25	16 41				17 03	17 11						17 25	17 41		
Ingatestone	d		16 15						16 45					17 15							17 45		
Chelmsford	d	16 12	16 22					16 34	16 52			17 03	17 12	17 22						17 34	17 52		
Hatfield Peverel	d							16 40												17 40			
Witham	d	16 23	16 34					16 47	17 03				17 23	17 34						17 47	18 03		
White Notley	d		16 41											17 41									
Cressing	d		16 43											17 43									
Braintree Freeport	d		16 46											17 46									
Braintree	a		16 50											17 50									
Kelvedon	d	16 27						16 51					17 27							17 51			
Marks Tey	d	16 33						16 57					17 33							17 57			
Colchester	a	16 40		16 46				17 04	17 15			17 22	17 40			17 46				18 04	18 15		
Colchester	d	16 41		16 47			16 56	17 04	17 16		17 20	17 23	17 41			17 47			17 56	18 04	18 16		18 20
Colchester Town	a	16 49					17 03				17 27		17 49						18 03				18 27
	d						17 07												18 07				
Hythe	d						17 11												18 11				
Wivenhoe	d						17 15		17 23										18 15		18 23		
Alresford (Essex)	d						17 19												18 19				
Great Bentley	d						17 23												18 23				
Weeley	d						17 26			←									18 26			←	
Thorpe-le-Soken	a						17 31		17 35	17 31									18 31		18 35	18 31	
	d						17 37		17 35	17 37									18 37		18 35	18 37	
Clacton-on-Sea	a						→		17 44										→		18 44		
Kirby Cross	d									17 42												18 42	
Frinton-on-Sea	d									17 45												18 45	
Walton-on-the-Naze	a									17 49												18 49	
Manningtree	d			16 55	17 00			17 12				17 31				17 55	18 00			18 12			
Mistley	d				17 04												18 04						
Wrabness	d				17 09												18 09						
Harwich International	d				17 17												18 17						
Dovercourt	d				17 20												18 20						
Harwich Town	a				17 22												18 22						
Ipswich	a			17 07				17 25				17 43				18 07				18 25			
	d			17 08		17 19						17 44			18 00	18 08		18 19					
Needham Market	d					17 28												18 28					
Stowmarket	d			17 19		17a33						17 55			18 12			18a33					
Peterborough	a														19 38								
Diss	d			17 32								18 08				18 29							
Norwich	a			17 51								18 27				18 50							

		LE	LE	LE	LE	LE	LE	LE	LE	LE	LE	LE	LE	LE	LE	LE	LE	LE	LE	LE	LE	LE
		◇1 ⊡	1	1	◇1 ⊡	1	1	1	1	1	1	1	◇1 ⊡	1	1	1	◇1 ⊡	1	1	1	1	1
London Liverpool Street ⊖	d	17 30	17 38	17 48	18 00				18 02	18 18			18 30	18 38	18 48		19 00				19 02	19 18
Stratford ⊖	d	17u38	17 45	17 55					18 09	18 25			18u38	18 45	18 55						19 09	19 25
Romford	d		17 53											18 53								
Shenfield	d		18 03	18 11					18 25	18 41				19 03	19 11						19 25	19 41
Ingatestone	d			18 15						18 45					19 15							19 45
Chelmsford	d	18 03	18 12	18 22					18 34	18 52			19 03	19 12	19 22						19 34	19 52
Hatfield Peverel	d								18 40												19 40	
Witham	d		18 23	18 34					18 47	19 03				19 23	19 34						19 47	20 03
White Notley	d			18 41											19 41							
Cressing	d			18 43											19 43							
Braintree Freeport	d			18 46											19 46							
Braintree	a			18 50											19 50							
Kelvedon	d		18 27						18 51					19 27							19 51	
Marks Tey	d		18 33						18 57					19 33							19 57	
Colchester	a	18 22	18 40		18 46				19 04	19 15			19 22	19 40			19 46				20 04	20 15
Colchester	d	18 23	18 41		18 47			18 56	19 04	19 16		19 20	19 23	19 41			19 47			19 56	20 04	20 16
Colchester Town	a		18 49					19 03				19 27		19 49						20 03		
	d							19 07												20 07		
Hythe	d							19 11												20 11		
Wivenhoe	d							19 15		19 23										20 15		20 23
Alresford (Essex)	d							19 19												20 19		
Great Bentley	d							19 23												20 23		
Weeley	d							19 26			←									20 26		
Thorpe-le-Soken	a							19 31		19 35	19 31									20 31		20 35
	d							19 37		19 35	19 37									20 37		20 35
Clacton-on-Sea	a							→		19 44										→		20 44
Kirby Cross	d										19 42											
Frinton-on-Sea	d										19 45											
Walton-on-the-Naze	a										19 49											
Manningtree	d	18 31			18 55	19 00			19 12				19 31				19 55	20 00			20 12	
Mistley	d					19 04												20 04				
Wrabness	d					19 09												20 09				
Harwich International	d					19 17												20 17				
Dovercourt	d					19 20												20 20				
Harwich Town	a					19 22												20 22				
Ipswich	a	18 43			19 07				19 25				19 43				20 07				20 25	
	d	18 44			19 08		19 19						19 44			20 00	20 08		20 19			
Needham Market	d						19 28												20 28			
Stowmarket	d	18 55					19a33						19 55			20 12			20a33			
Peterborough	a															21 37						
Diss	d	19 08			19 29								20 08				20 29					
Norwich	a	19 27			19 50								20 27				20 50					

18 August to 25 August

London - Chelmsford, Colchester, Walton-on-Naze, Clacton, Harwich, Ipswich and Norwich

Network Diagram - see first Page of Table 5

		LE 1	LE 1	LE ◇1 ☕	LE 1	LE 1	LE 1	LE ◇1 ☕		LE 1	LE	LE 1	LE 1	LE 1	LE 1	LE 1	LE ◇1 ☕	LE 1		LE 1	LE 1	LE 1	LE 1	LE	LE 1
London Liverpool Street 15 ⊖	d			19 30	19 32	19 38	19 48	20 00					20 02	20 18			20 30	20 38		20 48		21 00			
Stratford 7 ⊖	d			19u38	19 39	19 46	19 55						20 09	20 25			20u38	20 45		20 55					
Romford	d					19 54												20 53							
Shenfield 3	d				19 57	20 04	20 11						20 25	20 41				21 03		21 11					
Ingatestone	d						20 15							20 45						21 15					
Chelmsford 3	d			20 03	20 07	20 13	20 22						20 34	20 52			21 03	21 12		21 22					
Hatfield Peverel	d												20 40												
Witham 2	d				20 18	20 24	20 34						20 47	21 03				21 23		21 34					
White Notley	d						20 41													21 41					
Cressing	d						20 43													21 43					
Braintree Freeport	d						20 46													21 46					
Braintree	a						20 50													21 50					
Kelvedon	d					20 28							20 51					21 27							
Marks Tey 2	d					20 34							20 57					21 33							
Colchester 4	a			20 22	20 30	20 41		20 46					21 04	21 15			21 22	21 40				21 46			
Colchester 4	d		20 20	20 23	20 30	20 42		20 47				20 56	21 04	21 16		21 20	21 23	21 41				21 47			21 56
Colchester Town	a		20 27			20 50						21 03				21 27		21 49							22 03
	d											21 07													22 07
Hythe	d											21 11													22 11
Wivenhoe 3	d											21 15		21 23											22 15
Alresford (Essex)	d											21 19													22 19
Great Bentley	d											21 23													22 23
Weeley	d	←										21 26			←										22 26
Thorpe-le-Soken 1	a	20 31										21 31		21 35	21 31										22 31
	d	20 37										21 37		21 35	21 37										22 37
Clacton-on-Sea	a											→		21 44											→
Kirby Cross	d	20 42													21 42										
Frinton-on-Sea	d	20 45													21 45										
Walton-on-the-Naze	a	20 49													21 49										
Manningtree 2	d			20 31	20 39			20 55		21 00			21 12				21 31					21 55	22 00		
Mistley	d									21 04													22 04		
Wrabness	d									21 09													22 09		
Harwich International	d				20a54					21 17											21 38		22 17		
Dovercourt	d									21 20													22 20		
Harwich Town	a									21 22													22 22		
Ipswich	a			20 43				21 07					21 25				21 43				22 03	22 08			
	d			20 44				21 08			21 16						21 44							22 16	
Needham Market	d										21 26													22 26	
Stowmarket	d			20 55							21a32						21 55							22a32	
Peterborough 8	a																								
Diss	d			21 08				21 29									22 08								
Norwich	a			21 27				21 50									22 27								

		LE 1	LE 1	LE 1		LE ◇1 ☕	LE 1	LE 1	LE 1	LE 1	LE 1	LE 1	LE 1	LE 1		LE 1	LE ◇1 ☕	LE 1	LE 1	LE 1	LE	LE 1	LE 1	LE ◇1 ☕	LE 1
London Liverpool Street 15 ⊖	d	21 02	21 18			21 30	21 38	21 48	22 00	22 02				22 18			22 30	22 38				23 02	23 18	23 30	23 48
Stratford 7 ⊖	d	21 09	21 25			21u38	21 45	21 55		22 09				22 25			22u38	22 45				23 09	23 25	23u38	23 55
Romford	d						21 53											22 53							
Shenfield 3	d	21 25	21 41				22 03	22 11		22 25				22 41				23 03				23 25	23 41		00 11
Ingatestone	d		21 45					22 15						22 45									23 45		00 15
Chelmsford 3	d	21 34	21 52			22 03	22 12	22 22	22 28	22 34				22 52			23 03	23 12				23 34	23 52	00 03	00 22
Hatfield Peverel	d	21 40								22 40												23 40			00 28
Witham 2	d	21 47	22 03				22 23	22 34		22 47				23 03				23 23	23 25			23 47	00 03		00 35
White Notley	d							22 41											23 32						
Cressing	d							22 43											23 34						
Braintree Freeport	d							22 46											23 37						
Braintree	a							22 50											23 41						
Kelvedon	d	21 51					22 27			22 51								23 27				23 51			00 39
Marks Tey 2	d	21 57					22 33			22 57								23 33			23 46	23 57			00 45
Colchester 4	a	22 04	22 15			22 22	22 40		22 47	23 05				23 15			23 22	23 45			23 59	00 04	00 15	00 22	00 57
Colchester 4	d	22 04	22 16			22 23	22 41		22 48				22 56	23 16			23 23					00 04	00 16	00 23	
Colchester Town	a						22 49						23 03												
	d												23 07												
Hythe	d												23 11												
Wivenhoe 3	d		22 23										23 15	23 23									00 23		
Alresford (Essex)	d												23 19										00 27		
Great Bentley	d												23 23										00 31		
Weeley	d			←									23 26			←									
Thorpe-le-Soken 1	a		22 35	22 31									23 31	23 35		23 31							00 38		
	d		22 35	22 37								23 16	23 37	23 35		23 37							00 38		
Clacton-on-Sea	a		22 44									23 25	→	23 44									00 51		
Kirby Cross	d			22 42												23 42									
Frinton-on-Sea	d			22 45												23 45									
Walton-on-the-Naze	a			22 49												23 49									
Manningtree 2	d	22 12				22 31			22 56		23 00						23 31			23 36		00 12		00 31	
Mistley	d										23 04									23 40					
Wrabness	d										23 09									23 45					
Harwich International	d	22a28									23 17									23 53					
Dovercourt	d										23 20									23 56					
Harwich Town	a										23 22									23 58					
Ipswich	a					22 43			23 08								23 43					00 28		00 43	
	d					22 44											23 44							00 44	
Needham Market	d																								
Stowmarket	d					22 55											23 55							00 55	
Peterborough 8	a																								
Diss	d					23 08											00 08							01 08	
Norwich	a					23 27											00 27							01 31	

1 September to 8 September

London - Chelmsford, Colchester, Walton-on-Naze, Clacton, Harwich, Ipswich and Norwich

Network Diagram - see first Page of Table 5

		LE ◇1 ☕	LE 1	LE ◇1 ☕	LE 1	LE 1	LE 1	LE 1	LE ◇1 ☕	LE 1		LE 1	LE ◇1 ☕	LE 1	LE ◇1 ☕	LE 1	LE	LE 1	LE ◇1	LE 1		LE 1	LE 1	LE 1	LE 1
London Liverpool Street 15 ⊖	d	22p30	22p45	23p00	23p07	23p15			23p30	23p35		23p45	23p59	00 12	00 30	00 46									05 34
Stratford 7 ⊖	d	22b40	22p54	23b10	23p17	23p25			23b40	23p45		23p54	00u10	00 24	00u40	01 00									05 41
Romford	d																								05 49
Shenfield 3	d		23p12		23p34	23p43				00 01		00 12		00 41		01 17									05 59
Ingatestone	d		23p16			23p48				00 05		00 16		00 45		01 22									06 03
Chelmsford 3	d	23p05	23p23	23p37	23p43	23p55			00 06	00 12		00 23	00 37	00 52	01 07	01 29									06 10
Hatfield Peverel	d				23p49					00 18				00 58		01 35									06 16
Witham 2	d		23p34		23p56	00 05	00 07			00 25		00 34		01 05		01 41		05 34							06 23
White Notley	d						00 14											05 41							
Cressing	d						00 16											05 43							
Braintree Freeport	d						00 19											05 46							
Braintree	a						00 23											05 50							
Kelvedon	d				00 01					00 29				01 09		01 46									06 27
Marks Tey 2	d				00 06					00 35				01 15		01 51									06 33
Colchester 4	a	23p24	23p46	23p58	00 14	00 17			00 25	00 43		00 46	00 56	01 23	01 29	02 00									06 40
Colchester 4	d	23p25	23p47	23p59		00 18			00 25			00 47	00 57		01 30				05 40	05 52			06 20	06 24	06 40
Colchester Town	a																						06 27		
	d																								
Hythe	d																								
Wivenhoe 3	d		23p54			00 25						00 54													
Alresford (Essex)	d																								
Great Bentley	d																								
Weeley	d																								
Thorpe-le-Soken 1	a		00 06			00 37						01 06													
	d		00 06			00 37						01 06													
Clacton-on-Sea	a		00 15			00 46						01 15													
Kirby Cross	d																								
Frinton-on-Sea	d																								
Walton-on-the-Naze	a																								
Manningtree 2	d	23p33		00 09				00 12	00 33				01 07		01 40				05 49	06 00				06 32	06 48
Mistley	d							00 16												06 04					
Wrabness	d							00 21												06 09					
Harwich International	d							00 29												06 17					
Dovercourt	d							00 32												06 20					
Harwich Town	a							00 34												06 22					
Ipswich	a	23p45		00 19					00 45				01 17		01 50				05 59					06 44	07 00
	d	23p46		00 21					00 46				01 19		01 52		05 10		06 00			06 16			
Needham Market	d																05 20					06 25			
Stowmarket	d	23p58		00 32					00 58				01 30		02 03		05a26		06 12			06a30			
Peterborough 8	a																		07 38						
Diss	d	00 10		00 45					01 10				01 43		02 16										
Norwich	a	00 30		01 04					01 30				02 03		02 35										

		LE 1	LE 1	LE 1	LE ◇1	LE 1		LE 1	LE 1	LE 1	LE 1	LE ◇1	LE 1	LE 1	LE 1	LE 1		LE ◇1	LE 1	LE 1	LE 1	LE 1	LE 1	LE 1	LE 1
London Liverpool Street 15 ⊖	d								06 02	06 18		06 30	06 38	06 48				07 00				07 02	07 18		
Stratford 7 ⊖	d								06 09	06 25		06u38	06 45	06 55								07 09	07 25		
Romford	d												06 53												
Shenfield 3	d								06 25	06 41			07 03	07 11								07 25	07 41		
Ingatestone	d									06 45				07 15									07 45		
Chelmsford 3	d								06 34	06 52		07 03	07 12	07 22								07 34	07 52		
Hatfield Peverel	d								06 40													07 40			
Witham 2	d	06 34							06 47	07 03			07 23	07 34								07 47	08 03		
White Notley	d	06 41												07 41											
Cressing	d	06 43												07 43											
Braintree Freeport	d	06 46												07 46											
Braintree	a	06 50												07 50											
Kelvedon	d								06 51				07 27									07 51			
Marks Tey 2	d								06 57				07 33									07 57			
Colchester 4	a								07 04	07 15		07 22	07 40					07 46				08 04	08 15		
Colchester 4	d							06 56	07 04	07 16		07 23	07 40		07 44			07 47			07 56	08 04	08 16		08 20
Colchester Town	a							07 03							07 51						08 03				08 27
	d							07 07													08 07				
Hythe	d							07 11													08 11				
Wivenhoe 3	d							07 15		07 23											08 15		08 23		
Alresford (Essex)	d							07 19													08 19				
Great Bentley	d							07 23													08 23				
Weeley	d							07 26			←										08 26			←	
Thorpe-le-Soken 1	a							07 31		07 35	07 31										08 31		08 35	08 31	
	d		06 37					07 37		07 35	07 37										08 37		08 35	08 37	
Clacton-on-Sea	a							→		07 44											→		08 44		
Kirby Cross	d		06 42								07 42													08 42	
Frinton-on-Sea	d		06 45								07 45													08 45	
Walton-on-the-Naze	a		06 49								07 49													08 49	
Manningtree 2	d			07 00					07 12			07 31	07 48					07 55		08 00		08 12			
Mistley	d			07 04															08 02	08 04					
Wrabness	d			07 09																08 09					
Harwich International	d			07 17									08a09							08 17					
Dovercourt	d			07 20																08 20					
Harwich Town	a			07 22																08 22					
Ipswich	a								07 25			07 43						08 07	08 17			08 25			
	d				07 10	07 19						07 44				08 00		08 08	08 19						
Needham Market	d					07 28													08 28						
Stowmarket	d				07 21	07a33						07 55				08 12			08a33						
Peterborough 8	a															09 38									
Diss	d				07 34							08 08						08 29							
Norwich	a				07 53							08 27						08 50							

b Previous night, stops to pick up only

London - Chelmsford, Colchester, Walton-on-Naze, Clacton, Harwich, Ipswich and Norwich

Network Diagram - see first Page of Table 5

	LE ◇1 ☕	LE 1	LE 1	LE ◇1 ☕	LE 1	LE 1	LE 1	LE 1	LE 1	LE 1	LE 1	LE ◇1 ☕	LE 1	LE 1	LE 1	LE ◇1 ☕	LE 1	LE 1	LE 1	LE 1	LE 1
London Liverpool Street 15 ⊖ d	07 30	07 38	07 48	08 00				08 02	08 18			08 30	08 38	08 48		09 00				09 02	09 18
Stratford 7 ⊖ d	07u38	07 45	07 55					08 09	08 25			08u38	08 45	08 55						09 09	09 25
Romford d		07 53											08 53								
Shenfield 3 d		08 03	08 11					08 25	08 41				09 03	09 11						09 25	09 41
Ingatestone d			08 15						08 45					09 15							09 45
Chelmsford 3 d	08 03	08 12	08 22					08 34	08 52			09 03	09 12	09 22						09 34	09 52
Hatfield Peverel d								08 40												09 40	
Witham 2 d		08 23	08 34					08 47	09 03				09 23	09 34						09 47	10 03
White Notley d			08 41											09 41							
Cressing d			08 43											09 43							
Braintree Freeport d			08 46											09 46							
Braintree a			08 50											09 50							
Kelvedon d		08 27						08 51					09 27							09 51	
Marks Tey 2 d		08 33						08 57					09 33							09 57	
Colchester 4 a	08 22	08 40		08 46				09 04	09 15			09 22	09 40			09 46				10 04	10 15
Colchester 4 d	08 23	08 41		08 47			08 56	09 04	09 16		09 20	09 23	09 41			09 47			09 56	10 04	10 16
Colchester Town a		08 49					09 03				09 27		09 49						10 03		
d							09 07												10 07		
Hythe d							09 11												10 11		
Wivenhoe 3 d							09 15		09 23										10 15		10 23
Alresford (Essex) d							09 19												10 19		
Great Bentley d							09 23												10 23		
Weeley d							09 26			←									10 26		
Thorpe-le-Soken 1 a							09 31		09 35	09 31									10 31		10 35
d							09 37		09 35	09 37									10 37		10 35
Clacton-on-Sea a							→		09 44										→		10 44
Kirby Cross d										09 42											
Frinton-on-Sea d										09 45											
Walton-on-the-Naze a										09 49											
Manningtree 2 d	08 31			08 55	09 00			09 12				09 31				09 55	10 00			10 12	
Mistley d					09 04												10 04				
Wrabness d					09 09												10 09				
Harwich International d					09 17												10 17				
Dovercourt d					09 20												10 20				
Harwich Town a					09 22												10 22				
Ipswich a	08 43			09 07				09 25				09 43				10 07				10 25	
d	08 44			09 08		09 19						09 44			10 00	10 08		10 19			
Needham Market d						09 28												10 28			
Stowmarket d	08 55					09a33						09 55			10 12			10a33			
Peterborough 8 a															11 37						
Diss d	09 08			09 29								10 08				10 29					
Norwich a	09 27			09 50								10 27				10 50					

	LE 1	LE 1	LE ◇1 ☕	LE 1	LE 1	LE 1 ☕	LE 1	LE 1	LE 1	LE 1	LE 1	LE 1	LE 1	LE ◇1 ☕	LE 1	LE 1	LE 1	LE ◇1 ☕	LE 1	LE 1	LE 1	LE 1
London Liverpool Street 15 ⊖ d			09 30	09 38	09 48	10 00				10 02	10 18			10 30	10 38	10 48		11 00				11 02
Stratford 7 ⊖ d			09u38	09 45	09 55					10 09	10 25			10u38	10 45	10 55						11 09
Romford d				09 53																		
Shenfield 3 d				10 03	10 11					10 25	10 41				11 03	11 11						11 25
Ingatestone d					10 15						10 45					11 15						
Chelmsford 3 d			10 03	10 12	10 22					10 34	10 52			11 03	11 12	11 22						11 34
Hatfield Peverel d										10 40												11 40
Witham 2 d				10 23	10 34					10 47	11 03				11 23	11 34						11 47
White Notley d					10 41											11 41						
Cressing d					10 43											11 43						
Braintree Freeport d					10 46											11 46						
Braintree a					10 50											11 50						
Kelvedon d				10 27						10 51					11 27							11 51
Marks Tey 2 d				10 33						10 57					11 33							11 57
Colchester 4 a			10 22	10 40		10 46				11 04	11 15			11 22	11 40			11 46				12 04
Colchester 4 d		10 20	10 23	10 41		10 47			10 56	11 04	11 16		11 20	11 23	11 41			11 47			11 56	12 04
Colchester Town a		10 27		10 49					11 03				11 27		11 49						12 03	
d									11 07												12 07	
Hythe d									11 11												12 11	
Wivenhoe 3 d									11 15		11 23										12 15	
Alresford (Essex) d									11 19												12 19	
Great Bentley d									11 23												12 23	
Weeley d	←								11 26			←									12 26	
Thorpe-le-Soken 1 a	10 31								11 31		11 35	11 31									12 31	
d	10 37								11 37		11 35	11 37									12 37	
Clacton-on-Sea a									→		11 44										→	
Kirby Cross d	10 42											11 42										
Frinton-on-Sea d	10 45											11 45										
Walton-on-the-Naze a	10 49											11 49										
Manningtree 2 d			10 31			10 55	11 00			11 12				11 31				11 55	12 00			12 12
Mistley d							11 04												12 04			
Wrabness d							11 09												12 09			
Harwich International d							11 17												12 17			
Dovercourt d							11 20												12 20			
Harwich Town a							11 22												12 22			
Ipswich a			10 43			11 07				11 25				11 43				12 07				12 25
d			10 44			11 08		11 19						11 44			12 00	12 08		12 19		
Needham Market d								11 28												12 28		
Stowmarket d			10 55					11a33						11 55			12 12			12a33		
Peterborough 8 a																	13 37					
Diss d			11 08			11 29								12 08				12 29				
Norwich a			11 27			11 50								12 27				12 50				

London - Chelmsford, Colchester, Walton-on-Naze, Clacton, Harwich, Ipswich and Norwich

Network Diagram - see first Page of Table 5

	LE 1	LE 1	LE 1	LE ◇1 ☕	LE 1	LE 1	LE ◇1 ☕	LE 1	LE 1	LE 1	LE 1	LE 1	LE 1	LE 1	LE 1 ☕	LE 1	LE 1	LE 1	LE ◇1 ☕	LE 1	LE 1	LE 1
London Liverpool Street 15 ⊖ d	11 18			11 30	11 38	11 48	12 00				12 02	12 18			12 30	12 48	12 48		13 00			
Stratford 7 ⊖ d	11 25			11u38	11 45	11 55					12 09	12 25			12u38	12 55	12 55					
Romford d					11 53																	
Shenfield 3 d	11 41				12 03	12 11					12 25	12 41				13 11	13 11					
Ingatestone d	11 45					12 15						12 45				13 15	13 15					
Chelmsford 3 d	11 52			12 03	12 12	12 22					12 34	12 52			13 03	13 22	13 22					
Hatfield Peverel d											12 40											
Witham 2 d	12 03				12 23	12 34					12 47	13 03				13 34	13 34					
White Notley d						12 41										13 41	13 41					
Cressing d						12 43										13 43	13 43					
Braintree Freeport d						12 46										13 46	13 46					
Braintree a						12 50										13 50	13 50					
Kelvedon d					12 27						12 51											
Marks Tey 2 d					12 33						12 57											
Colchester 4 a	12 15			12 22	12 40		12 46				13 04	13 15			13 22				13 46			
Colchester 4 d	12 16		12 20	12 23	12 41		12 47			12 56	13 04	13 16		13 20	13 23				13 47			13 56
Colchester Town a			12 27		12 49					13 03				13 27								14 03
d										13 07												14 07
Hythe d										13 11												14 11
Wivenhoe 3 d	12 23									13 15		13 23										14 15
Alresford (Essex) d										13 19												14 19
Great Bentley d										13 23												14 23
Weeley d		←								13 26			←									14 26
Thorpe-le-Soken 1 a	12 35	12 31								13 31		13 35	13 31									14 31
d	12 35	12 37								13 37		13 35	13 37									14 37
Clacton-on-Sea a	12 44									→		13 44										→
Kirby Cross d		12 42											13 42									
Frinton-on-Sea d		12 45											13 45									
Walton-on-the-Naze a		12 49											13 49									
Manningtree 2 d				12 31			12 55	13 00			13 12				13 31				13 55	14 00		
Mistley d								13 04												14 04		
Wrabness d								13 09												14 09		
Harwich International d								13 17												14 17		
Dovercourt d								13 20												14 20		
Harwich Town a								13 22												14 22		
Ipswich a				12 43			13 07				13 25				13 43				14 07			
d				12 44			13 08		13 19						13 44			14 00	14 08		14 19	
Needham Market d									13 28												14 28	
Stowmarket d				12 55					13a33						13 55			14 12			14a33	
Peterborough 8 a																		15 37				
Diss d				13 08			13 29								14 08				14 29			
Norwich a				13 27			13 50								14 27				14 50			

	LE 1	LE 1	LE 1	LE 1	LE ◇1 ☕	LE 1	LE 1	LE ◇1 ☕	LE 1	LE 1	LE 1	LE 1	LE 1	LE 1	LE 1	LE ◇1 ☕	LE 1	LE 1	LE 1	LE ◇1 ☕	LE 1	LE 1	LE 1
London Liverpool Street 15 ⊖ d	13 02	13 18			13 30	13 38	13 48	14 00				14 02	14 18			14 30	14 38	14 48		15 00			
Stratford 7 ⊖ d	13 09	13 25			13u38	13 45	13 55					14 09	14 25			14u38	14 45	14 55					
Romford d						13 53																	
Shenfield 3 d	13 25	13 41				14 03	14 11					14 25	14 41				15 03	15 11					
Ingatestone d		13 45					14 15						14 45					15 15					
Chelmsford 3 d	13 34	13 52			14 03	14 12	14 22					14 34	14 52			15 03	15 12	15 22					
Hatfield Peverel d	13 40											14 40											
Witham 2 d	13 47	14 03				14 23	14 34					14 47	15 03				15 23	15 34					
White Notley d							14 41											15 41					
Cressing d							14 43											15 43					
Braintree Freeport d							14 46											15 46					
Braintree a							14 50											15 50					
Kelvedon d	13 51					14 27						14 51					15 27						
Marks Tey 2 d	13 57					14 33						14 57					15 33						
Colchester 4 a	14 04	14 15			14 22	14 40		14 46				15 04	15 15			15 22	15 40			15 46			
Colchester 4 d	14 04	14 16		14 20	14 23	14 41		14 47			14 56	15 04	15 16		15 20	15 23	15 41			15 47			15 56
Colchester Town a				14 27		14 49					15 03				15 27		15 49						16 03
d											15 07												16 07
Hythe d											15 11												16 11
Wivenhoe 3 d		14 23									15 15		15 23										16 15
Alresford (Essex) d											15 19												16 19
Great Bentley d											15 23												16 23
Weeley d			←								15 26			←									16 26
Thorpe-le-Soken 1 a		14 35	14 31								15 31		15 35	15 31									16 31
d		14 35	14 37								15 37		15 35	15 37									16 37
Clacton-on-Sea a		14 44									→		15 44										→
Kirby Cross d			14 42											15 42									
Frinton-on-Sea d			14 45											15 45									
Walton-on-the-Naze a			14 49											15 49									
Manningtree 2 d	14 12				14 31			14 55	15 00			15 12				15 31				15 55	16 00		
Mistley d									15 04												16 04		
Wrabness d									15 09												16 09		
Harwich International d									15 17												16 17		
Dovercourt d									15 20												16 20		
Harwich Town a									15 22												16 22		
Ipswich a	14 25				14 43			15 07				15 25				15 43				16 07			
d					14 44			15 08		15 19						15 44			16 00	16 08		16 19	
Needham Market d										15 28												16 28	
Stowmarket d					14 55					15a33						15 55			16 12			16a33	
Peterborough 8 a																			17 37				
Diss d					15 08			15 29								16 08				16 29			
Norwich a					15 27			15 48								16 27				16 50			

Table 11

Saturdays

1 September to 8 September

London - Chelmsford, Colchester, Walton-on-Naze, Clacton, Harwich, Ipswich and Norwich

Network Diagram - see first Page of Table 5

		LE	LE	LE	LE	LE ◇	LE	LE	LE ◇	LE	LE	LE	LE	LE	LE	LE	LE ◇	LE	LE	LE	LE ◇	LE	LE	LE
London Liverpool Street ⊖	d	15 02	15 18			15 30	15 38	15 48	16 00				16 02	16 18			16 30	16 38	16 48		17 00			
Stratford ⊖	d	15 09	15 25			15u38	15 45	15 55					16 09	16 25			16u38	16 45	16 55					
Romford	d						15 53																	
Shenfield	d	15 25	15 41				16 03	16 11					16 25	16 41				17 03	17 11					
Ingatestone	d		15 45					16 15						16 45					17 15					
Chelmsford	d	15 34	15 52			16 03	16 12	16 22					16 34	16 52			17 03	17 12	17 22					
Hatfield Peverel	d	15 40											16 40											
Witham	d	15 47	16 03				16 23	16 34					16 47	17 03				17 23	17 34					
White Notley	d							16 41											17 41					
Cressing	d							16 43											17 43					
Braintree Freeport	d							16 46											17 46					
Braintree	a							16 50											17 50					
Kelvedon	d	15 51					16 27						16 51					17 27						
Marks Tey	d	15 57					16 33						16 57					17 33						
Colchester	a	16 04	16 15			16 22	16 40		16 46				17 04	17 15			17 22	17 40			17 46			
Colchester	d	16 04	16 16		16 20	16 23	16 41		16 47			16 56	17 04	17 16		17 20	17 23	17 41			17 47			17 56
Colchester Town	a				16 27		16 49					17 03				17 27		17 49						18 03
	d											17 07												18 07
Hythe	d											17 11												18 11
Wivenhoe	d		16 23									17 15		17 23										18 15
Alresford (Essex)	d											17 19												18 19
Great Bentley	d											17 23												18 23
Weeley	d			←								17 26			←									18 26
Thorpe-le-Soken	a		16 35	16 31								17 31		17 35	17 31									18 31
	d		16 35	16 37								17 37		17 35	17 37									18 37
Clacton-on-Sea	a		16 44									→		17 44										→
Kirby Cross	d			16 42											17 42									
Frinton-on-Sea	d			16 45											17 45									
Walton-on-the-Naze	a			16 49											17 49									
Manningtree	d	16 12				16 31			16 55	17 00			17 12				17 31				17 55	18 00		
Mistley	d									17 04												18 04		
Wrabness	d									17 09												18 09		
Harwich International	d									17 17												18 17		
Dovercourt	d									17 20												18 20		
Harwich Town	a									17 22												18 22		
Ipswich	a	16 25				16 43			17 07				17 25				17 43				18 07			
	d					16 44			17 08		17 19						17 44			18 00	18 08		18 19	
Needham Market	d										17 28												18 28	
Stowmarket	d					16 55			17 19		17a33						17 55			18 12			18a33	
Peterborough	a																			19 38				
Diss	d					17 08			17 32								18 08				18 29			
Norwich	a					17 27			17 51								18 27				18 50			

		LE	LE	LE	LE	LE ◇	LE	LE	LE ◇	LE	LE	LE	LE	LE	LE	LE	LE ◇	LE	LE	LE	LE ◇	LE	LE
London Liverpool Street ⊖	d	17 02	17 18			17 30	17 38	17 48	18 00				18 02	18 18			18 30	18 38	18 48		19 00		
Stratford ⊖	d	17 09	17 25			17u38	17 45	17 55					18 09	18 25			18u38	18 45	18 55				
Romford	d						17 53																
Shenfield	d	17 25	17 41				18 03	18 11					18 25	18 41				19 03	19 11				
Ingatestone	d		17 45					18 15						18 45					19 15				
Chelmsford	d	17 34	17 52			18 03	18 12	18 22					18 34	18 52			19 03	19 12	19 22				
Hatfield Peverel	d	17 40											18 40										
Witham	d	17 47	18 03				18 23	18 34					18 47	19 03				19 23	19 34				
White Notley	d							18 41											19 41				
Cressing	d							18 43											19 43				
Braintree Freeport	d							18 46											19 46				
Braintree	a							18 50											19 50				
Kelvedon	d	17 51					18 27						18 51					19 27					
Marks Tey	d	17 57					18 33						18 57					19 33					
Colchester	a	18 04	18 15			18 22	18 40		18 46				19 04	19 15			19 22	19 40			19 46		
Colchester	d	18 04	18 16		18 20	18 23	18 41		18 47			18 56	19 04	19 16		19 20	19 23	19 41			19 47		
Colchester Town	a				18 27		18 49					19 03				19 27		19 49					
	d											19 07											
Hythe	d											19 11											
Wivenhoe	d		18 23									19 15		19 23									
Alresford (Essex)	d											19 19											
Great Bentley	d											19 23											
Weeley	d			←								19 26			←								
Thorpe-le-Soken	a		18 35	18 31								19 31		19 35	19 31								
	d		18 35	18 37								19 37		19 35	19 37								
Clacton-on-Sea	a		18 44									→		19 44									
Kirby Cross	d			18 42											19 42								
Frinton-on-Sea	d			18 45											19 45								
Walton-on-the-Naze	a			18 49											19 49								
Manningtree	d	18 12				18 31			18 55	19 00			19 12				19 31				19 55	20 00	
Mistley	d									19 04												20 04	
Wrabness	d									19 09												20 09	
Harwich International	d									19 17												20 17	
Dovercourt	d									19 20												20 20	
Harwich Town	a									19 22												20 22	
Ipswich	a	18 25				18 43			19 07				19 25				19 43				20 07		
	d					18 44			19 08		19 19						19 44			20 00	20 08		20 19
Needham Market	d										19 28												20 28
Stowmarket	d					18 55					19a33						19 55			20 12			20a33
Peterborough	a																			21 37			
Diss	d					19 08			19 29								20 08				20 29		
Norwich	a					19 27			19 50								20 27				20 50		

Table 11

Saturdays

1 September to 8 September

London - Chelmsford, Colchester, Walton-on-Naze, Clacton, Harwich, Ipswich and Norwich

Network Diagram - see first Page of Table 5

		LE	LE	LE	LE	LE	LE ◇	LE	LE	LE	LE ◇	LE	LE	LE	LE	LE	LE	LE	LE ◇	LE	LE	LE	LE
London Liverpool Street ⊖	d		19 02	19 18			19 30	19 32	19 38	19 48	20 00				20 02	20 18			20 30	20 38	20 48		21 00
Stratford ⊖	d		19 09	19 25			19u38	19 39	19 46	19 55					20 09	20 25			20u38	20 45	20 55		
Romford	d								19 54											20 53			
Shenfield	d		19 25	19 41				19 57	20 04	20 11					20 25	20 41				21 03	21 11		
Ingatestone	d			19 45						20 15						20 45					21 15		
Chelmsford	d		19 34	19 52			20 03	20 07	20 13	20 22					20 34	20 52			21 03	21 12	21 22		
Hatfield Peverel	d		19 40												20 40								
Witham	d		19 47	20 03				20 18	20 24	20 34					20 47	21 03				21 23	21 34		
White Notley	d									20 41											21 41		
Cressing	d									20 43											21 43		
Braintree Freeport	d									20 46											21 46		
Braintree	a									20 50											21 50		
Kelvedon	d		19 51						20 28						20 51					21 27			
Marks Tey	d		19 57						20 34						20 57					21 33			
Colchester	a		20 04	20 15			20 22	20 30	20 41		20 46				21 04	21 15			21 22	21 40			21 46
Colchester	d	19 56	20 04	20 16		20 20	20 23	20 30	20 42		20 47			20 56	21 04	21 16		21 20	21 23	21 41			21 47
Colchester Town	a	20 03				20 27			20 50					21 03				21 27		21 49			
	d	20 07												21 07									
Hythe	d	20 11												21 11									
Wivenhoe	d	20 15		20 23										21 15		21 23							
Alresford (Essex)	d	20 19												21 19									
Great Bentley	d	20 23												21 23									
Weeley	d	20 26			←									21 26			←						
Thorpe-le-Soken	a	20 31		20 35	20 31									21 31		21 35	21 31						
	d	20 37		20 35	20 37									21 37		21 35	21 37						
Clacton-on-Sea	a	→		20 44										→		21 44							
Kirby Cross	d				20 42												21 42						
Frinton-on-Sea	d				20 45												21 45						
Walton-on-the-Naze	a				20 49												21 49						
Manningtree	d		20 12				20 31	20 39			20 55	21 00			21 12				21 31				21 55
Mistley	d											21 04											
Wrabness	d											21 09											
Harwich International	d							20a54				21 17										21 38	
Dovercourt	d											21 20											
Harwich Town	a											21 22											
Ipswich	a		20 25				20 43				21 07				21 25				21 43			22 03	22 08
	d						20 44				21 08		21 16						21 44				
Needham Market	d												21 26										
Stowmarket	d						20 55						21a32						21 55				
Peterborough	a																						
Diss	d						21 08				21 29								22 08				
Norwich	a						21 27				21 50								22 27				

		LE	LE	LE	LE	LE	LE	LE ◇	LE	LE	LE	LE	LE	LE	LE	LE	LE	LE ◇	LE	LE	LE	LE ◇
London Liverpool Street ⊖	d				21 02	21 18		21 30	21 38	21 48	22 00	22 02				22 15		22 30	22 35		22 45	23 00
Stratford ⊖	d				21 09	21 25		21u38	21 45	21 55		22 09				22 24		22u40	22 44		22 54	23u10
Romford	d								21 53													
Shenfield	d				21 25	21 41			22 03	22 11		22 25				22 41			23 01		23 12	
Ingatestone	d					21 45				22 15						22 45			23 05		23 16	
Chelmsford	d				21 34	21 52		22 03	22 12	22 22	22 28	22 34				22 52		23 05	23 12		23 23	23 37
Hatfield Peverel	d				21 40							22 40										
Witham	d				21 47	22 03			22 23	22 34		22 47				23 03			23 23	23 25	23 34	
White Notley	d									22 41										23 32		
Cressing	d									22 43										23 34		
Braintree Freeport	d									22 46										23 37		
Braintree	a									22 50										23 41		
Kelvedon	d				21 51				22 27			22 51							23 27			
Marks Tey	d				21 57				22 33			22 57							23 33			
Colchester	a				22 04	22 15		22 22	22 40		22 47	23 05				23 15		23 24	23 41		23 46	23 58
Colchester	d			21 56	22 04	22 16		22 23	22 41		22 48				22 56	23 16		23 25			23 47	23 59
Colchester Town	a			22 03					22 49						23 03							
	d			22 07											23 07							
Hythe	d			22 11											23 11							
Wivenhoe	d			22 15		22 23									23 15	23 23					23 54	
Alresford (Essex)	d			22 19											23 19							
Great Bentley	d			22 23											23 23							
Weeley	d			22 26			←								23 26		←					
Thorpe-le-Soken	a			22 31		22 35	22 31								23 31	23 35	23 31				00 06	
	d			22 37		22 35	22 37							23 16	23 37	23 35	23 37				00 06	
Clacton-on-Sea	a			→		22 44								23 25	→	23 44					00 15	
Kirby Cross	d						22 42										23 42					
Frinton-on-Sea	d						22 45										23 45					
Walton-on-the-Naze	a						22 49										23 49					
Manningtree	d	22 00			22 12			22 31			22 56		23 00					23 34				00 09
Mistley	d	22 04											23 04									
Wrabness	d	22 09											23 09									
Harwich International	d	22 17			22a28								23 17									
Dovercourt	d	22 20											23 20									
Harwich Town	a	22 22											23 22									
Ipswich	a							22 43			23 08							23 45				00 19
	d		22 16					22 44										23 46				00 21
Needham Market	d		22 26																			
Stowmarket	d		22a32					22 55										23 58				00 32
Peterborough	a																					
Diss	d							23 08										00 10				00 45
Norwich	a							23 27										00 30				01 05

Saturdays

1 September to 8 September

London - Chelmsford, Colchester, Walton-on-Naze, Clacton, Harwich, Ipswich and Norwich

Network Diagram - see first Page of Table 5

		LE	LE ■	LE ■	LE ◇■ ☕	LE ■	LE ■	LE ◇■ ☕
London Liverpool Street 15 ⊖	d		23 07	23 15	23 30	23 35	23 45	23 59
Stratford 7 ⊖	d		23 17	23 25	23u40	23 45	23 54	00u10
Romford	d							
Shenfield 3	d		23 34	23 43		00 02	00 12	
Ingatestone	d			23 48		00 05	00 16	
Chelmsford 3	d		23 43	23 55	00 06	00 12	00 23	00 37
Hatfield Peverel	d		23 49			00 18		
Witham 2	d		23 56	00 05		00 25	00 34	
White Notley	d							
Cressing	d							
Braintree Freeport	d							
Braintree	a							
Kelvedon	d		00 01			00 29		
Marks Tey 2	d	23 46	00 06			00 35		
Colchester 4	a	23 55	00 14	00 17	00 25	00 43	00 46	00 56
Colchester 4	d			00 18	00 25		00 47	00 57
Colchester Town	a							
	d							
Hythe	d							
Wivenhoe 3	d			00 25			00 54	
Alresford (Essex)	d							
Great Bentley	d							
Weeley	d							
Thorpe-le-Soken 1	a			00 37			01 06	
	d			00 37			01 06	
Clacton-on-Sea	a			00 46			01 15	
Kirby Cross	d							
Frinton-on-Sea	d							
Walton-on-the-Naze	a							
Manningtree 2	d				00 34			01 07
Mistley	d							
Wrabness	d							
Harwich International	d							
Dovercourt	d							
Harwich Town	a							
Ipswich	a				00 45			01 17
	d				00 46			01 19
Needham Market	d							
Stowmarket	d				00 58			01 30
Peterborough 8	a							
Diss	d				01 10			01 43
Norwich	a				01 30			02 03

Saturdays

from 15 September

London - Chelmsford, Colchester, Walton-on-Naze, Clacton, Harwich, Ipswich and Norwich

Network Diagram - see first Page of Table 5

		LE ◇■ ☕	LE ■	LE ■	LE ◇■ ☕	LE ■	LE ■	LE ■	LE	LE ■		LE ◇■	LE ■	LE ■	LE ■	LE ■	LE ■	LE ■	LE ■	LE ■		LE ◇■ ☕	LE ■	LE ■	LE ■
London Liverpool Street 15 ⊖	d	22p30	23p02	23p18	23p30		23p48	00 18									05 34								06 02
Stratford 7 ⊖	d	22b38	23p09	23p25	23b38		23p55	00 25									05 41								06 09
Romford	d																05 49								
Shenfield 3	d		23p25	23p41			00 11	00 47									05 59								06 25
Ingatestone	d			23p45			00 15	00 51									06 03								
Chelmsford 3	d	23p03	23p34	23p52	00 03		00 22	00 58									06 10								06 34
Hatfield Peverel	d		23p40				00 28	01 04									06 16								06 40
Witham 2	d		23p47	00 03		00 05	00 35	01 11		05 34							06 23	06 34							06 47
White Notley	d					00 12				05 41								06 41							
Cressing	d					00 14				05 43								06 43							
Braintree Freeport	d					00 17				05 46								06 46							
Braintree	a					00 21				05 50								06 50							
Kelvedon	d		23p51				00 39	01 15									06 27								06 51
Marks Tey 2	d		23p57				00 45	01 21									06 33								06 57
Colchester 4	a	23p22	00 04	00 15	00 22		00 57	01 41									06 40								07 04
Colchester 4	d	23p23	00 04	00 16	00 23							05 40	05 52		06 20	06 24	06 40							06 56	07 04
Colchester Town	a														06 27									07 03	
	d																							07 07	
Hythe	d																							07 11	
Wivenhoe 3	d			00 23																				07 15	
Alresford (Essex)	d			00 27																				07 19	
Great Bentley	d			00 31																				07 23	
Weeley	d																							07 26	
Thorpe-le-Soken 1	a			00 38																				07 31	
	d			00 38															06 37					07 37	
Clacton-on-Sea	a			00 51																				→	
Kirby Cross	d																		06 42						
Frinton-on-Sea	d																		06 45						
Walton-on-the-Naze	a																		06 49						
Manningtree 2	d	23p31	00 12		00 31							05 49	06 00			06 32	06 48			07 00					07 12
Mistley	d												06 04							07 04					
Wrabness	d												06 09							07 09					
Harwich International	d												06 17							07 17					
Dovercourt	d												06 20							07 20					
Harwich Town	a												06 22							07 22					
Ipswich	a	23p43	00 28		00 43							05 59				06 44	07 00								07 25
	d	23p44			00 44				05 10			06 00		06 16								07 10	07 19		
Needham Market	d								05 20					06 25									07 28		
Stowmarket	d	23p55			00 55				05a26			06 12		06a30								07 21	07a33		
Peterborough 8	a											07 38													
Diss	d	00 08			01 08																	07 34			
Norwich	a	00 39			01 43																	07 53			

		LE ■	LE ■	LE ◇■ ☕	LE ■	LE ■		LE ■	LE ■	LE ◇■ ☕	LE ■	LE ■	LE ■	LE ■	LE ■	LE ■		LE ■	LE ◇■ ☕	LE ■	LE ■	LE ◇■ ☕	LE ■	LE ■	LE ■
London Liverpool Street 15 ⊖	d	06 18		06 30	06 38	06 48				07 00				07 02	07 18				07 30	07 38	07 48	08 00			
Stratford 7 ⊖	d	06 25		06u38	06 45	06 55								07 09	07 25				07u38	07 45	07 55				
Romford	d				06 53															07 53					
Shenfield 3	d	06 41			07 03	07 11								07 25	07 41					08 03	08 11				
Ingatestone	d	06 45				07 15									07 45						08 15				
Chelmsford 3	d	06 52		07 03	07 12	07 22								07 34	07 52				08 03	08 12	08 22				
Hatfield Peverel	d													07 40											
Witham 2	d	07 03			07 23	07 34								07 47	08 03					08 23	08 34				
White Notley	d					07 41															08 41				
Cressing	d					07 43															08 43				
Braintree Freeport	d					07 46															08 46				
Braintree	a					07 50															08 50				
Kelvedon	d				07 27									07 51						08 27					
Marks Tey 2	d				07 33									07 57						08 33					
Colchester 4	a	07 15		07 22	07 40					07 46				08 04	08 15				08 22	08 40		08 46			
Colchester 4	d	07 16		07 23	07 40			07 44		07 47			07 56	08 04	08 16			08 20	08 23	08 41		08 47			08 56
Colchester Town	a							07 51					08 03					08 27		08 49					09 03
	d												08 07												09 07
Hythe	d												08 11												09 11
Wivenhoe 3	d	07 23											08 15		08 23										09 15
Alresford (Essex)	d												08 19												09 19
Great Bentley	d												08 23												09 23
Weeley	d		←										08 26			←									09 26
Thorpe-le-Soken 1	a	07 35	07 31										08 31		08 35	08 31									09 31
	d	07 35	07 37										08 37		08 35	08 37									09 37
Clacton-on-Sea	a	07 44											→		08 44										→
Kirby Cross	d		07 42													08 42									
Frinton-on-Sea	d		07 45													08 45									
Walton-on-the-Naze	a		07 49													08 49									
Manningtree 2	d			07 31	07 48					07 55		08 00		08 12					08 31			08 55	09 00		
Mistley	d										08 02	08 04											09 04		
Wrabness	d											08 09											09 09		
Harwich International	d				08a09							08 17											09 17		
Dovercourt	d											08 20											09 20		
Harwich Town	a											08 22											09 22		
Ipswich	a			07 43						08 07	08 17			08 25					08 43			09 07			
	d			07 44					08 00	08 08	08 19								08 44			09 08		09 19	
Needham Market	d										08 28													09 28	
Stowmarket	d			07 55					08 12		08a33								08 55					09a33	
Peterborough 8	a								09 38																
Diss	d			08 08						08 29									09 08			09 29			
Norwich	a			08 27						08 50									09 27			09 50			

b Previous night, stops to pick up only

Table 11

Saturdays from 15 September

London - Chelmsford, Colchester, Walton-on-Naze, Clacton, Harwich, Ipswich and Norwich

Network Diagram - see first Page of Table 5

Station		LE ■	LE ■	LE ■	LE ■	LE ◇■	LE ■	LE ■	LE ■	LE ◇■	LE ■	LE ■	LE ■	LE ■	LE ■	LE ■	LE ■	LE ◇■	LE ■	LE ■	LE ◇■ A	LE ■ B
London Liverpool Street [15] ⊖	d	08 02	08 18			08 30	08 38	08 48		09 00				09 02	09 18			09 30	09 38	09 48	10 00	10 00
Stratford [7] ⊖	d	08 09	08 25			08u38	08 45	08 55						09 09	09 25			09u38	09 45	09 55		
Romford	d						08 53												09 53			
Shenfield [3]	d	08 25	08 41				09 03	09 11						09 25	09 41				10 03	10 11		
Ingatestone	d		08 45					09 15							09 45					10 15		
Chelmsford [3]	d	08 34	08 52			09 03	09 12	09 22						09 34	09 52			10 03	10 12	10 22		
Hatfield Peverel	d	08 40												09 40								
Witham [2]	d	08 47	09 03				09 23	09 34						09 47	10 03				10 23	10 34		
White Notley	d							09 41												10 41		
Cressing	d							09 43												10 43		
Braintree Freeport	d							09 46												10 46		
Braintree	a							09 50												10 50		
Kelvedon	d	08 51					09 27							09 51					10 27			
Marks Tey [2]	d	08 57					09 33							09 57					10 33			
Colchester [4]	a	09 04	09 15			09 22	09 40			09 46				10 04	10 15			10 22	10 40		10 46	10 46
Colchester [4]	d	09 04	09 16		09 20	09 23	09 41			09 47			09 56	10 04	10 16		10 20	10 23	10 41		10 47	10 47
Colchester Town	a				09 27		09 49						10 03				10 27		10 49			
	d												10 07									
Hythe	d												10 11									
Wivenhoe [3]	d		09 23										10 15		10 23							
Alresford (Essex)	d												10 19									
Great Bentley	d												10 23									
Weeley	d			←									10 26			←						
Thorpe-le-Soken [1]	a		09 35	09 31									10 31		10 35	10 31						
	d		09 35	09 37									10 37		10 35	10 37						
Clacton-on-Sea	a		09 44										→		10 44							
Kirby Cross	d			09 42												10 42						
Frinton-on-Sea	d			09 45												10 45						
Walton-on-the-Naze	a			09 49												10 49						
Manningtree [2]	d	09 12				09 31				09 55	10 00			10 12				10 31			10 55	10 55
Mistley	d										10 04											
Wrabness	d										10 09											
Harwich International	d										10 17											
Dovercourt	d										10 20											
Harwich Town	a										10 22											
Ipswich	a	09 25				09 43				10 07				10 25				10 43			11 07	11 07
	d					09 44			10 00	10 08		10 19						10 44			11 08	11 08
Needham Market	d											10 28										
Stowmarket	d					09 55			10 12			10a33						10 55				
Peterborough [8]	a								11 37													
Diss	d					10 08				10 29								11 08			11 29	11 29
Norwich	a					10 27				10 50								11 27			11 50	11 50

Station		LE ■	LE ■	LE ■	LE ■	LE ■	LE ■	LE ■	LE ◇■	LE ■	LE ■	LE ■	LE ◇■	LE ■	LE ■	LE ■	LE ■	LE ■	LE ■	LE ■	LE ◇■	LE ■	LE ■
London Liverpool Street [15] ⊖	d				10 02	10 18			10 30	10 38	10 48		11 00				11 02	11 18			11 30	11 38	11 48
Stratford [7] ⊖	d				10 09	10 25			10u38	10 45	10 55						11 09	11 25			11u38	11 45	11 55
Romford	d									10 53												11 53	
Shenfield [3]	d				10 25	10 41				11 03	11 11						11 25	11 41				12 03	12 11
Ingatestone	d					10 45					11 15							11 45					12 15
Chelmsford [3]	d				10 34	10 52			11 03	11 12	11 22						11 34	11 52			12 03	12 12	12 22
Hatfield Peverel	d				10 40												11 40						
Witham [2]	d				10 47	11 03				11 23	11 34						11 47	12 03				12 23	12 34
White Notley	d										11 41												12 41
Cressing	d										11 43												12 43
Braintree Freeport	d										11 46												12 46
Braintree	a										11 50												12 50
Kelvedon	d				10 51					11 27							11 51					12 27	
Marks Tey [2]	d				10 57					11 33							11 57					12 33	
Colchester [4]	a				11 04	11 15			11 22	11 40			11 46				12 04	12 15			12 22	12 40	
Colchester [4]	d			10 56	11 04	11 16		11 20	11 23	11 41			11 47			11 56	12 04	12 16		12 20	12 23	12 41	
Colchester Town	a			11 03				11 27		11 49						12 03				12 27		12 49	
	d			11 07												12 07							
Hythe	d			11 11												12 11							
Wivenhoe [3]	d			11 15		11 23										12 15		12 23					
Alresford (Essex)	d			11 19												12 19							
Great Bentley	d			11 23												12 23							
Weeley	d			11 26			←									12 26			←				
Thorpe-le-Soken [1]	a			11 31		11 35	11 31									12 31		12 35	12 31				
	d			11 37		11 35	11 37									12 37		12 35	12 37				
Clacton-on-Sea	a			→		11 44										→		12 44					
Kirby Cross	d						11 42												12 42				
Frinton-on-Sea	d						11 45												12 45				
Walton-on-the-Naze	a						11 49												12 49				
Manningtree [2]	d	11 00			11 12				11 31				11 55	12 00			12 12				12 31		
Mistley	d	11 04												12 04									
Wrabness	d	11 09												12 09									
Harwich International	d	11 17												12 17									
Dovercourt	d	11 20												12 20									
Harwich Town	a	11 22												12 22									
Ipswich	a				11 25				11 43				12 07				12 25				12 43		
	d		11 19						11 44			12 00	12 08		12 19						12 44		
Needham Market	d		11 28												12 28								
Stowmarket	d		11a33						11 55			12 12			12a33						12 55		
Peterborough [8]	a											13 37											
Diss	d								12 08				12 29								13 08		
Norwich	a								12 27				12 50								13 27		

A from 6 October

B 15 September, 22 September, 29 September

Table 11

Saturdays from 15 September

London - Chelmsford, Colchester, Walton-on-Naze, Clacton, Harwich, Ipswich and Norwich

Network Diagram - see first Page of Table 5

Station		LE ◇■	LE ■	LE ■	LE ■	LE ■	LE ■	LE ■	LE ■	LE ◇■ A	LE ■ B	LE ■	LE ■	LE ■	LE ◇■	LE ■	LE ■	LE ■	LE ■	LE ■	LE ■	LE ■
London Liverpool Street [15] ⊖	d	12 00				12 02	12 18			12 30	12 30	12 38	12 48		13 00				13 02	13 18		
Stratford [7] ⊖	d					12 09	12 25			12u38	12u38	12 45	12 55						13 09	13 25		
Romford	d											12 53										
Shenfield [3]	d					12 25	12 41					13 03	13 11						13 25	13 41		
Ingatestone	d						12 45						13 15							13 45		
Chelmsford [3]	d					12 34	12 52			13 03	13 03	13 12	13 22						13 34	13 52		
Hatfield Peverel	d					12 40													13 40			
Witham [2]	d					12 47	13 03					13 23	13 34						13 47	14 03		
White Notley	d												13 41									
Cressing	d												13 43									
Braintree Freeport	d												13 46									
Braintree	a												13 50									
Kelvedon	d					12 51						13 27							13 51			
Marks Tey [2]	d					12 57						13 33							13 57			
Colchester [4]	a	12 46				13 04	13 15			13 22	13 22	13 40			13 46				14 04	14 15		
Colchester [4]	d	12 47			12 56	13 04	13 16		13 20	13 23	13 23	13 41			13 47			13 56	14 04	14 16		14 20
Colchester Town	a				13 03				13 27			13 49						14 03				14 27
	d				13 07													14 07				
Hythe	d				13 11													14 11				
Wivenhoe [3]	d				13 15		13 23											14 15		14 23		
Alresford (Essex)	d				13 19													14 19				
Great Bentley	d				13 23													14 23				
Weeley	d				13 26			←										14 26			←	
Thorpe-le-Soken [1]	a				13 31		13 35	13 31										14 31		14 35	14 31	
	d				13 37		13 35	13 37										14 37		14 35	14 37	
Clacton-on-Sea	a				→		13 44											→		14 44		
Kirby Cross	d							13 42													14 42	
Frinton-on-Sea	d							13 45													14 45	
Walton-on-the-Naze	a							13 49													14 49	
Manningtree [2]	d	12 55	13 00			13 12				13 31	13 31				13 55	14 00			14 12			
Mistley	d		13 04													14 04						
Wrabness	d		13 09													14 09						
Harwich International	d		13 17													14 17						
Dovercourt	d		13 20													14 20						
Harwich Town	a		13 22													14 22						
Ipswich	a	13 07				13 25				13 43	13 43				14 07				14 25			
	d	13 08		13 19						13 44	13 44			14 00	14 08		14 19					
Needham Market	d			13 28													14 28					
Stowmarket	d			13a33						13 55	13 55			14 12			14a33					
Peterborough [8]	a													15 37								
Diss	d	13 29								14 08	14 08				14 29							
Norwich	a	13 50								14 27	14 27				14 50							

A from 6 October

B 15 September, 22 September, 29 September

London - Chelmsford, Colchester, Walton-on-Naze, Clacton, Harwich, Ipswich and Norwich

Network Diagram - see first Page of Table 5

		LE ◇■ ⊡	LE ■	LE ■	LE ◇■ ⊡	LE ■	LE ■	LE ■	LE ■	LE ■	LE ■	LE ■	LE ◇■ ⊡	LE ■	LE ■	LE ■	LE ◇■ ⊡	LE ■	LE ■	LE ■	LE ■	LE ■	LE ■
London Liverpool Street ⊖	d	13 30	13 38	13 48	14 00				14 02	14 18			14 30	14 38	14 48		15 00				15 02	15 18	
Stratford ⊖	d	13u38	13 45	13 55					14 09	14 25			14u38	14 45	14 55						15 09	15 25	
Romford	d		13 53											14 53									
Shenfield	d		14 03	14 11					14 25	14 41				15 03	15 11						15 25	15 41	
Ingatestone	d			14 15						14 45					15 15							15 45	
Chelmsford	d	14 03	14 12	14 22					14 34	14 52			15 03	15 12	15 22						15 34	15 52	
Hatfield Peverel	d								14 40												15 40		
Witham	d		14 23	14 34					14 47	15 03				15 23	15 34						15 47	16 03	
White Notley	d			14 41											15 41								
Cressing	d			14 43											15 43								
Braintree Freeport	d			14 46											15 46								
Braintree	a			14 50											15 50								
Kelvedon	d		14 27						14 51					15 27							15 51		
Marks Tey	d		14 33						14 57					15 33							15 57		
Colchester	a	14 22	14 40		14 46				15 04	15 15			15 22	15 40			15 46				16 04	16 15	
Colchester	d	14 23	14 41		14 47			14 56	15 04	15 16		15 20	15 23	15 41			15 47			15 56	16 04	16 16	
Colchester Town	a		14 49					15 03				15 27		15 49						16 03			
	d							15 07												16 07			
Hythe	d							15 11												16 11			
Wivenhoe	d							15 15		15 23										16 15		16 23	
Alresford (Essex)	d							15 19												16 19			
Great Bentley	d							15 23												16 23			
Weeley	d							15 26			←									16 26			←
Thorpe-le-Soken	a							15 31		15 35	15 31									16 31		16 35	16 31
	d							15 37		15 35	15 37									16 37		16 35	16 37
Clacton-on-Sea	a							→		15 44										→		16 44	
Kirby Cross	d										15 42												16 42
Frinton-on-Sea	d										15 45												16 45
Walton-on-the-Naze	a										15 49												16 49
Manningtree	d	14 31			14 55	15 00			15 12				15 31				15 55	16 00			16 12		
Mistley	d					15 04												16 04					
Wrabness	d					15 09												16 09					
Harwich International	d					15 17												16 17					
Dovercourt	d					15 20												16 20					
Harwich Town	a					15 22												16 22					
Ipswich	a	14 43			15 07				15 25				15 43				16 07				16 25		
	d	14 44			15 08		15 19						15 44			16 00	16 08		16 19				
Needham Market	d						15 28												16 28				
Stowmarket	d	14 55					15a33						15 55			16 12			16a33				
Peterborough	a															17 37							
Diss	d	15 08			15 29								16 08				16 29						
Norwich	a	15 27			15 48								16 27				16 50						

		LE ■	LE ◇■ ⊡	LE ■	LE ■	LE ◇■ ⊡	LE ■	LE ■	LE ■	LE ■	LE ■	LE ■	LE ■	LE ◇■ ⊡	LE ■	LE ■	LE ■	LE ◇■ ⊡	LE ■	LE ■	LE ■	LE ■	LE ■
London Liverpool Street ⊖	d		15 30	15 38	15 48	16 00				16 02	16 18			16 30	16 38	16 48		17 00				17 02	17 18
Stratford ⊖	d		15u38	15 45	15 55					16 09	16 25			16u38	16 45	16 55						17 09	17 25
Romford	d			15 53											16 53								
Shenfield	d			16 03	16 11					16 25	16 41				17 03	17 11						17 25	17 41
Ingatestone	d				16 15						16 45					17 15							17 45
Chelmsford	d		16 03	16 12	16 22					16 34	16 52			17 03	17 12	17 22						17 34	17 52
Hatfield Peverel	d									16 40												17 40	
Witham	d			16 23	16 34					16 47	17 03				17 23	17 34						17 47	18 03
White Notley	d				16 41											17 41							
Cressing	d				16 43											17 43							
Braintree Freeport	d				16 46											17 46							
Braintree	a				16 50											17 50							
Kelvedon	d			16 27						16 51					17 27							17 51	
Marks Tey	d			16 33						16 57					17 33							17 57	
Colchester	a		16 22	16 40		16 46				17 04	17 15			17 22	17 40			17 46				18 04	18 15
Colchester	d	16 20	16 23	16 41		16 47			16 56	17 04	17 16		17 20	17 23	17 41			17 47			17 56	18 04	18 16
Colchester Town	a	16 27		16 49					17 03				17 27		17 49						18 03		
	d								17 07												18 07		
Hythe	d								17 11												18 11		
Wivenhoe	d								17 15		17 23										18 15		18 23
Alresford (Essex)	d								17 19												18 19		
Great Bentley	d								17 23												18 23		
Weeley	d								17 26			←									18 26		
Thorpe-le-Soken	a								17 31		17 35	17 31									18 31		18 35
	d								17 37		17 35	17 37									18 37		18 35
Clacton-on-Sea	a								→		17 44										→		18 44
Kirby Cross	d											17 42											
Frinton-on-Sea	d											17 45											
Walton-on-the-Naze	a											17 49											
Manningtree	d		16 31			16 55	17 00			17 12				17 31				17 55	18 00			18 12	
Mistley	d						17 04												18 04				
Wrabness	d						17 09												18 09				
Harwich International	d						17 17												18 17				
Dovercourt	d						17 20												18 20				
Harwich Town	a						17 22												18 22				
Ipswich	a		16 43			17 07				17 25				17 43				18 07				18 25	
	d		16 44			17 08		17 19						17 44			18 00	18 08		18 19			
Needham Market	d							17 28												18 28			
Stowmarket	d		16 55			17 19		17a33						17 55			18 12			18a33			
Peterborough	a																19 38						
Diss	d		17 08			17 32								18 08				18 29					
Norwich	a		17 27			17 51								18 27				18 50					

London - Chelmsford, Colchester, Walton-on-Naze, Clacton, Harwich, Ipswich and Norwich

Network Diagram - see first Page of Table 5

		LE ■	LE ■	LE ◇■ ⊡	LE ■	LE ■	LE ◇■ ⊡	LE ■	LE ■	LE ■	LE ■	LE ■	LE ■	LE ■	LE ◇■ ⊡	LE ■	LE ■	LE ■	LE ◇■ ⊡	LE ■	LE ■	LE ■
London Liverpool Street ⊖	d			17 30	17 38	17 48	18 00				18 02	18 18			18 30	18 38	18 48		19 00			
Stratford ⊖	d			17u38	17 45	17 55					18 09	18 25			18u38	18 45	18 55					
Romford	d				17 53											18 53						
Shenfield	d				18 03	18 11					18 25	18 41				19 03	19 11					
Ingatestone	d					18 15						18 45					19 15					
Chelmsford	d			18 03	18 12	18 22					18 34	18 52			19 03	19 12	19 22					
Hatfield Peverel	d										18 40											
Witham	d				18 23	18 34					18 47	19 03				19 23	19 34					
White Notley	d					18 41											19 41					
Cressing	d					18 43											19 43					
Braintree Freeport	d					18 46											19 46					
Braintree	a					18 50											19 50					
Kelvedon	d				18 27						18 51					19 27						
Marks Tey	d				18 33						18 57					19 33						
Colchester	a			18 22	18 40		18 46				19 04	19 15			19 22	19 40			19 46			
Colchester	d		18 20	18 23	18 41		18 47			18 56	19 04	19 16		19 20	19 23	19 41			19 47			19 56
Colchester Town	a		18 27		18 49					19 03				19 27		19 49						20 03
	d									19 07												20 07
Hythe	d									19 11												20 11
Wivenhoe	d									19 15		19 23										20 15
Alresford (Essex)	d									19 19												20 19
Great Bentley	d									19 23												20 23
Weeley	d	←								19 26			←									20 26
Thorpe-le-Soken	a	18 31								19 31		19 35	19 31									20 31
	d	18 37								19 37		19 35	19 37									20 37
Clacton-on-Sea	a									→		19 44										→
Kirby Cross	d	18 42											19 42									
Frinton-on-Sea	d	18 45											19 45									
Walton-on-the-Naze	a	18 49											19 49									
Manningtree	d			18 31			18 55	19 00			19 12				19 31				19 55	20 00		
Mistley	d							19 04												20 04		
Wrabness	d							19 09												20 09		
Harwich International	d							19 17												20 17		
Dovercourt	d							19 20												20 20		
Harwich Town	a							19 22												20 22		
Ipswich	a			18 43			19 07				19 25				19 43				20 07			
	d			18 44			19 08		19 19						19 44			20 00	20 08		20 19	
Needham Market	d								19 28												20 28	
Stowmarket	d			18 55					19a33						19 55			20 12			20a33	
Peterborough	a																	21 37				
Diss	d			19 08			19 29								20 08				20 29			
Norwich	a			19 27			19 50								20 27				20 50			

		LE ■	LE ■	LE ■	LE ■	LE ◇■ ⊡	LE ■	LE ■	LE ■	LE ◇■ ⊡	LE ■	LE	LE ■	LE ■	LE ■	LE ■	LE ■	LE ◇■ ⊡	LE ■	LE ■	LE ■	LE ■	LE ■
London Liverpool Street ⊖	d	19 02	19 18			19 30	19 32	19 38	19 48	20 00				20 02	20 18			20 30	20 38	20 48		21 00	
Stratford ⊖	d	19 09	19 25			19u38	19 39	19 46	19 55					20 09	20 25			20u38	20 45	20 55			
Romford	d							19 54											20 53				
Shenfield	d	19 25	19 41				19 57	20 04	20 11					20 25	20 41				21 03	21 11			
Ingatestone	d		19 45						20 15						20 45					21 15			
Chelmsford	d	19 34	19 52			20 03	20 07	20 13	20 22					20 34	20 52			21 03	21 12	21 22			
Hatfield Peverel	d	19 40												20 40									
Witham	d	19 47	20 03				20 18	20 24	20 34					20 47	21 03				21 23	21 34			
White Notley	d								20 41											21 41			
Cressing	d								20 43											21 43			
Braintree Freeport	d								20 46											21 46			
Braintree	a								20 50											21 50			
Kelvedon	d	19 51						20 28						20 51					21 27				
Marks Tey	d	19 57						20 34						20 57					21 33				
Colchester	a	20 04	20 15			20 22	20 30	20 41		20 46				21 04	21 15			21 22	21 40			21 46	
Colchester	d	20 04	20 16		20 20	20 23	20 30	20 42		20 47			20 56	21 04	21 16		21 20	21 23	21 41			21 47	
Colchester Town	a				20 27			20 50					21 03				21 27		21 49				
	d												21 07										
Hythe	d												21 11										
Wivenhoe	d		20 23										21 15		21 23								
Alresford (Essex)	d												21 19										
Great Bentley	d												21 23										
Weeley	d			←									21 26			←							
Thorpe-le-Soken	a		20 35	20 31									21 31		21 35	21 31							
	d		20 35	20 37									21 37		21 35	21 37							
Clacton-on-Sea	a		20 44										→		21 44								
Kirby Cross	d			20 42												21 42							
Frinton-on-Sea	d			20 45												21 45							
Walton-on-the-Naze	a			20 49												21 49							
Manningtree	d	20 12				20 31	20 39			20 55	21 00			21 12				21 31				21 55	22 00
Mistley	d										21 04												22 04
Wrabness	d										21 09												22 09
Harwich International	d						20a54				21 17										21 38		22 17
Dovercourt	d										21 20												22 20
Harwich Town	a										21 22												22 22
Ipswich	a	20 25				20 43				21 07				21 25				21 43			22 03	22 08	
	d					20 44				21 08		21 16						21 44					
Needham Market	d											21 26											
Stowmarket	d					20 55						21a32						21 55					
Peterborough	a																						
Diss	d					21 08				21 29								22 08					
Norwich	a					21 27				21 50								22 27					

London - Chelmsford, Colchester, Walton-on-Naze, Clacton, Harwich, Ipswich and Norwich

Saturdays from 15 September

Network Diagram - see first Page of Table 5

		LE	LE 1	LE 1	LE 1	LE 1	LE ◇1	LE 1	LE 1	LE 1	LE 1	LE 1	LE 1	LE 1	LE 1	LE 1	LE ◇1	LE 1	LE 1	LE 1	LE	LE 1
London Liverpool Street 15 ⊖	d			21 02	21 18		21 30	21 38	21 48	22 00	22 02				22 18		22 30	22 38				23 02
Stratford 7 ⊖	d			21 09	21 25		21u38	21 45	21 55		22 09				22 25		22u38	22 45				23 09
Romford	d							21 53										22 53				
Shenfield 3	d			21 25	21 41			22 03	22 11		22 25				22 41			23 03				23 25
Ingatestone	d				21 45				22 15						22 45							
Chelmsford 3	d			21 34	21 52		22 03	22 12	22 22	22 28	22 34				22 52		23 03	23 12				23 34
Hatfield Peverel	d			21 40							22 40											23 40
Witham 2	d			21 47	22 03			22 23	22 34		22 47				23 03			23 23	23 25			23 47
White Notley	d								22 41										23 32			
Cressing	d								22 43										23 34			
Braintree Freeport	d								22 46										23 37			
Braintree	a								22 50										23 41			
Kelvedon	d			21 51				22 27			22 51							23 27				23 51
Marks Tey 2	d			21 57				22 33			22 57							23 33			23 46	23 57
Colchester 4	a			22 04	22 15		22 22	22 40		22 47	23 05				23 15		23 22	23 45			23 59	00 04
Colchester 4	d		21 56	22 04	22 16		22 23	22 41		22 48				22 56	23 16		23 23					00 04
Colchester Town	a		22 03					22 49						23 03								
	d		22 07											23 07								
Hythe	d		22 11											23 11								
Wivenhoe 3	d		22 15		22 23									23 15	23 23							
Alresford (Essex)	d		22 19											23 19								
Great Bentley	d		22 23											23 23								
Weeley	d		22 26			←								23 26		←						
Thorpe-le-Soken 1	a		22 31		22 35	22 31								23 31	23 35	23 31						
	d		22 37		22 35	22 37							23 16	23 37	23 35	23 37						
Clacton-on-Sea	a		→		22 44								23 25	→	23 44							
Kirby Cross	d					22 42										23 42						
Frinton-on-Sea	d					22 45										23 45						
Walton-on-the-Naze	a					22 49										23 49						
Manningtree 2	d			22 12			22 31			22 56		23 00					23 31			23 36		00 12
Mistley	d											23 04								23 40		
Wrabness	d											23 09								23 45		
Harwich International	d			22a28								23 17								23 53		
Dovercourt	d											23 20								23 56		
Harwich Town	a											23 22								23 58		
Ipswich	a						22 43			23 08							23 43					00 28
	d	22 16					22 44										23 44					
Needham Market	d	22 26																				
Stowmarket	d	22a32					22 55										23 55					
Peterborough 8	a																					
Diss	d						23 08										00 08					
Norwich	a						23 27										00 27					

		LE 1	LE ◇1	LE 1
London Liverpool Street 15 ⊖	d	23 18	23 30	23 48
Stratford 7 ⊖	d	23 25	23u38	23 55
Romford	d			
Shenfield 3	d	23 41		00 11
Ingatestone	d	23 45		00 15
Chelmsford 3	d	23 52	00 03	00 22
Hatfield Peverel	d			00 28
Witham 2	d	00 03		00 35
White Notley	d			
Cressing	d			
Braintree Freeport	d			
Braintree	a			
Kelvedon	d			00 39
Marks Tey 2	d			00 45
Colchester 4	a	00 15	00 22	00 57
Colchester 4	d	00 16	00 23	
Colchester Town	a			
	d			
Hythe	d			
Wivenhoe 3	d	00 23		
Alresford (Essex)	d	00 27		
Great Bentley	d	00 31		
Weeley	d			
Thorpe-le-Soken 1	a	00 38		
	d	00 38		
Clacton-on-Sea	a	00 51		
Kirby Cross	d			
Frinton-on-Sea	d			
Walton-on-the-Naze	a			
Manningtree 2	d		00 31	
Mistley	d			
Wrabness	d			
Harwich International	d			
Dovercourt	d			
Harwich Town	a			
Ipswich	a		00 43	
	d		00 44	
Needham Market	d			
Stowmarket	d		00 55	
Peterborough 8	a			
Diss	d		01 08	
Norwich	a		01 31	

London - Chelmsford, Colchester, Walton-on-Naze, Clacton, Harwich, Ipswich and Norwich

Sundays until 22 July

Network Diagram - see first Page of Table 5

		LE ◇1	LE 1	LE 1	LE ◇1	LE 1	LE 1	LE 1	LE 1	LE 1	LE 1	LE 1	LE 1	LE	LE 1	LE 1	LE 1	LE 1	LE 1 A	LE 1 B	LE 1	LE 1	LE ◇1 A
London Liverpool Street 15 ⊖	d	22p30	23p02	23p18	23p30		23p48	00 18										07 55	08 02				08 30
Stratford 7 ⊖	d	22b38	23p09	23p25	23b38		23p55	00 25										08 02	08 09				
Romford	d																						
Shenfield 3	d		23p25	23p41			00 11	00 47										08 24	08 31	08 31			
Ingatestone	d			23p45			00 15	00 51											08 35	08 36			
Chelmsford 3	d	23p03	23p34	23p52	00 03		00 22	00 58										08 34	08 42	08 43			
Hatfield Peverel	d		23p40				00 28	01 04											08 48	08 49			
Witham 2	d		23p47	00 03		00 05	00 35	01 11	07 34				08 24					08 44	08 55	08 55			
White Notley	d					00 12			07 41				08 31										
Cressing	d					00 14			07 43				08 33										
Braintree Freeport	d					00 17			07 46				08 36										
Braintree	a					00 21			07 50				08 40										
Kelvedon	d		23p51				00 39	01 15											08 59	08 59			
Marks Tey 2	d		23p57				00 45	01 21											09 05	09 05			
Colchester 4	a	23p22	00 04	00 15	00 22		00 57	01 32										08 56	09 12	09 12			09 23
Colchester 4	d	23p23	00 04	00 16	00 23						07 40	08 12				08 18	08 36	08 57	09 12	09 15			09 23
Colchester Town	a																						
	d																						
Hythe	d																						
Wivenhoe 3	d			00 23													08 44						
Alresford (Essex)	d			00 27													08 47						
Great Bentley	d			00 31													08 51						
Weeley	d																						
Thorpe-le-Soken 1	a			00 38													08 58						
	d			00 38													08 58				09 00		
Clacton-on-Sea	a			00 51													09 07						
Kirby Cross	d																				09 05		
Frinton-on-Sea	d																				09 08		
Walton-on-the-Naze	a																				09 12		
Manningtree 2	d	23p31	00 12		00 31						07 48	08 20				08 26		09 05	09 20	09 23		09 26	09 31
Mistley	d															08 30						09 30	
Wrabness	d															08 35						09 35	
Harwich International	d														08 30	08 43		09a25				09 43	
Dovercourt	d															08 46						09 46	
Harwich Town	a															08 48						09 48	
Ipswich	a	23p43	00 28		00 43						08 00	08 32			08 53				09 32	09 35			09 43
	d	23p44			00 44					07 55				08 45	09 02								09 44
Needham Market	d														09 12								
Stowmarket	d	23p55			00 55					08 07				08a59	09a17								09 55
Peterborough 8	a									09 36													
Diss	d	00 08			01 08																		10 08
Norwich	a	00 27			01 31																		10 29

		LE ◇1 B	LE ◇1	LE 1 A	LE 1 B	LE 1	LE 1	LE 1	LE 1	LE ◇1	LE 1	LE 1	LE 1	LE 1	LE 1	LE 1	LE ◇1	LE 1	LE 1	LE 1	LE 1	LE 1	LE 1
London Liverpool Street 15 ⊖	d	08 30		08 32			09 02			09 30	09 32				10 02		10 30	10 32			11 02		
Stratford 7 ⊖	d			08 39			09 09				09 39				10 09			10 39			11 09		
Romford	d																						
Shenfield 3	d	08 58		09 01	09 01		09 31				10 01				10 31			11 01			11 31		
Ingatestone	d						09 35								10 35						11 35		
Chelmsford 3	d			09 10	09 11		09 42				10 10				10 42			11 10			11 42		
Hatfield Peverel	d						09 48								10 48						11 48		
Witham 2	d			09 21	09 21	09 24	09 55				10 21	10 24			10 55			11 21	11 24		11 55		
White Notley	d					09 31						10 31							11 31				
Cressing	d					09 33						10 33							11 33				
Braintree Freeport	d					09 36						10 36							11 36				
Braintree	a					09 40						10 40							11 40				
Kelvedon	d						09 59								10 59						11 59		
Marks Tey 2	d			09 28	09 28		10 05				10 28				11 05			11 28			12 05		
Colchester 4	a	09 24		09 36	09 36		10 12			10 23	10 36				11 12		11 23	11 36			12 12		
Colchester 4	d	09 25	09 32	09 36	09 36		10 12			10 23	10 36				11 12		11 23	11 36			12 12		
Colchester Town	a																						
	d																						
Hythe	d																						
Wivenhoe 3	d			09 44	09 44						10 44							11 44					
Alresford (Essex)	d			09 47	09 47						10 47							11 47					
Great Bentley	d			09 51	09 51						10 51							11 51					
Weeley	d																						
Thorpe-le-Soken 1	a			09 58	09 58						10 58							11 58					
	d			09 58	09 58			10 00			10 58		11 00					11 58				12 00	
Clacton-on-Sea	a			10 07	10 07						11 07							12 07					
Kirby Cross	d							10 05					11 05									12 05	
Frinton-on-Sea	d							10 08					11 08									12 08	
Walton-on-the-Naze	a							10 12					11 12									12 12	
Manningtree 2	d	09 33	09 40				10 20		10 26	10 31					11 20	11 26	11 31				12 20		12 26
Mistley	d								10 30							11 30							12 30
Wrabness	d								10 35							11 35							12 35
Harwich International	d								10 43							11 43							12 43
Dovercourt	d								10 46							11 46							12 46
Harwich Town	a								10 48							11 48							12 48
Ipswich	a	09 45	09 51				10 32			10 43					11 32		11 43				12 32		
	d	09 46	09 55							10 44				11 02			11 44			11 55			
Needham Market	d													11 12									
Stowmarket	d	09 57	10 07							10 55				11a18			11 55			12 07			
Peterborough 8	a		11 36																	13 31			
Diss	d	10 10								11 08							12 08						
Norwich	a	10 31								11 29							12 29						

A from 1 July until 22 July

B until 24 June

b Previous night, stops to pick up only

London - Chelmsford, Colchester, Walton-on-Naze, Clacton, Harwich, Ipswich and Norwich

Network Diagram - see first Page of Table 5

		LE ◇1	LE 1	LE 1	LE 1	LE 1	LE 1	LE 1	LE ◇1	LE 1	LE 1	LE 1	LE 1	LE 1	LE 1	LE ◇1	LE 1	LE 1	LE 1	LE 1	LE 1	LE 1
London Liverpool Street 15 ⊖	d	11 30	11 32				12 02		12 30	12 32			13 02			13 30	13 32				14 02	
Stratford 7 ⊖	d		11 39				12 09			12 39			13 09				13 39				14 09	
Romford	d																					
Shenfield 3	d		12 01				12 31			13 01			13 31				14 01				14 31	
Ingatestone	d						12 35						13 35								14 35	
Chelmsford 3	d		12 10				12 42			13 10			13 42				14 10				14 42	
Hatfield Peverel	d						12 48						13 48								14 48	
Witham 2	d		12 21	12 24			12 55			13 21	13 24		13 55				14 21	14 24			14 55	
White Notley	d			12 31							13 31							14 31				
Cressing	d			12 33							13 33							14 33				
Braintree Freeport	d			12 36							13 36							14 36				
Braintree	a			12 40							13 40							14 40				
Kelvedon	d						12 59						13 59								14 59	
Marks Tey 2	d		12 28				13 05			13 28			14 05				14 28				15 05	
Colchester 4	a	12 23	12 36				13 12		13 23	13 36			14 12			14 23	14 36				15 12	
Colchester 4	d	12 23	12 36				13 12		13 23	13 36			14 12			14 23	14 36				15 12	
Colchester Town	a																					
	d																					
Hythe	d																					
Wivenhoe 3	d		12 44							13 44							14 44					
Alresford (Essex)	d		12 47							13 47							14 47					
Great Bentley	d		12 51							13 51							14 51					
Weeley	d																					
Thorpe-le-Soken 1	a		12 58							13 58							14 58					
	d		12 58		13 00					13 58				14 00			14 58		15 00			
Clacton-on-Sea	a		13 07							14 07							15 07					
Kirby Cross	d				13 05									14 05					15 05			
Frinton-on-Sea	d				13 08									14 08					15 08			
Walton-on-the-Naze	a				13 12									14 12					15 12			
Manningtree 2	d	12 31					13 20	13 26	13 31				14 20		14 26	14 31					15 20	15 26
Mistley	d							13 30							14 30							15 30
Wrabness	d							13 35							14 35							15 35
Harwich International	d							13 43							14 43							15 43
Dovercourt	d							13 46							14 46							15 46
Harwich Town	a							13 48							14 48							15 48
Ipswich	a	12 43					13 32		13 43				14 32			14 43					15 32	
	d	12 44				13 02			13 44			13 55				14 44				15 02		
Needham Market	d					13 12														15 12		
Stowmarket	d	12 55				13a18			13 55			14 07				14 55				15a18		
Peterborough 8	a											15 31										
Diss	d	13 08							14 08							15 08						
Norwich	a	13 29							14 29							15 29						

		LE ◇1	LE 1	LE 1	LE 1	LE 1	LE 1	LE 1	LE ◇1	LE 1	LE 1	LE 1	LE 1	LE 1	LE 1	LE ◇1	LE 1	LE 1	LE 1	LE 1	LE 1	LE 1	LE ◇1
London Liverpool Street 15 ⊖	d	14 30	14 32			15 02			15 30	15 32				16 02		16 30	16 32			17 02			17 30
Stratford 7 ⊖	d		14 39			15 09				15 39				16 09			16 39			17 09			
Romford	d																						
Shenfield 3	d		15 01			15 31				16 01				16 31			17 01			17 31			
Ingatestone	d					15 35								16 35						17 35			
Chelmsford 3	d		15 10			15 42				16 10				16 42			17 10			17 42			
Hatfield Peverel	d					15 48								16 48						17 48			
Witham 2	d		15 21	15 24		15 55				16 21	16 24			16 55			17 21	17 24		17 55			
White Notley	d			15 31							16 31							17 31					
Cressing	d			15 33							16 33							17 33					
Braintree Freeport	d			15 36							16 36							17 36					
Braintree	a			15 40							16 40							17 40					
Kelvedon	d					15 59								16 59						17 59			
Marks Tey 2	d		15 28			16 05				16 28				17 05			17 28			18 05			
Colchester 4	a	15 23	15 36			16 12			16 23	16 36				17 12		17 23	17 36			18 12			18 23
Colchester 4	d	15 23	15 36			16 12			16 23	16 36				17 12		17 23	17 36			18 12			18 23
Colchester Town	a																						
	d																						
Hythe	d																						
Wivenhoe 3	d		15 44							16 44							17 44						
Alresford (Essex)	d		15 47							16 47							17 47						
Great Bentley	d		15 51							16 51							17 51						
Weeley	d																						
Thorpe-le-Soken 1	a		15 58							16 58							17 58						
	d		15 58				16 00			16 58		17 00					17 58				18 00		
Clacton-on-Sea	a		16 07							17 07							18 07						
Kirby Cross	d						16 05					17 05									18 05		
Frinton-on-Sea	d						16 08					17 08									18 08		
Walton-on-the-Naze	a						16 12					17 12									18 12		
Manningtree 2	d	15 31				16 20		16 26	16 31					17 20	17 26	17 31				18 20		18 26	18 31
Mistley	d							16 30							17 30							18 30	
Wrabness	d							16 35							17 35							18 35	
Harwich International	d							16 43							17 43							18 43	
Dovercourt	d							16 46							17 46							18 46	
Harwich Town	a							16 48							17 48							18 48	
Ipswich	a	15 43				16 32			16 43					17 32		17 43				18 32			18 43
	d	15 44			15 55				16 44				17 02			17 44			17 55				18 44
Needham Market	d												17 12										
Stowmarket	d	15 55			16 07				16 55				17a18			17 55			18 07				18 55
Peterborough 8	a				17 31														19 32				
Diss	d	16 08							17 08							18 08							19 08
Norwich	a	16 29							17 29							18 30							19 29

Table 11

Sundays
until 22 July

London - Chelmsford, Colchester, Walton-on-Naze, Clacton, Harwich, Ipswich and Norwich

Network Diagram - see first Page of Table 5

		LE 1	LE 1	LE 1	LE 1	LE 1	LE 1	LE ◇1	LE 1	LE ◇1	LE 1	LE 1	LE 1	LE 1	LE ◇1	LE 1	LE 1	LE 1	LE	LE 1	LE 1	LE 1
London Liverpool Street 15 ⊖	d	17 32				18 02		18 30	18 32	19 00		19 02			19 30	19 32				20 02		
Stratford 7 ⊖	d	17 39				18 09			18 39			19 09				19 39				20 09		
Romford	d																					
Shenfield 3	d	18 01				18 31			19 01			19 31				20 01				20 31		
Ingatestone	d					18 35						19 35								20 35		
Chelmsford 3	d	18 10				18 42			19 10	19 37		19 42				20 10				20 42		
Hatfield Peverel	d					18 48						19 48								20 48		
Witham 2	d	18 21	18 24			18 55			19 21		19 24	19 55				20 21	20 24			20 55		
White Notley	d		18 31								19 31						20 31					
Cressing	d		18 33								19 33						20 33					
Braintree Freeport	d		18 36								19 36						20 36					
Braintree	a		18 40								19 40						20 40					
Kelvedon	d					18 59						19 59								20 59		
Marks Tey 2	d	18 28				19 05			19 28			20 05				20 28				21 05		
Colchester 4	a	18 36				19 12		19 23	19 36	19 56		20 12			20 23	20 36				21 12		
Colchester 4	d	18 36				19 12		19 23	19 36	19 56		20 12			20 23	20 39		20 46		21 12		
Colchester Town	a																					
	d																					
Hythe	d																					
Wivenhoe 3	d	18 44							19 44							20 47						
Alresford (Essex)	d	18 47							19 47							20 50						
Great Bentley	d	18 51							19 51							20 54						
Weeley	d																					
Thorpe-le-Soken 1	a	18 58							19 58							21 01						
	d	18 58		19 00					19 58				20 00			21 01					21 03	
Clacton-on-Sea	a	19 07							20 07							21 10						
Kirby Cross	d			19 05									20 05								21 08	
Frinton-on-Sea	d			19 08									20 08								21 11	
Walton-on-the-Naze	a			19 12									20 12								21 15	
Manningtree 2	d					19 20	19 26	19 31		20 04		20 20		20 26	20 31			20 55		21 20		
Mistley	d						19 30							20 30								
Wrabness	d						19 35							20 35								
Harwich International	d						19 43							20 43				21a14				21 10
Dovercourt	d						19 46							20 46								
Harwich Town	a						19 48							20 48								
Ipswich	a					19 32		19 43		20 16		20 32			20 43					21 32		21 36
	d				19 02			19 44		20 17					20 44				21 02			
Needham Market	d				19 12														21 12			
Stowmarket	d				19a18			19 55		20 28					20 55				21a18			
Peterborough 8	a																					
Diss	d							20 08		20 41					21 08							
Norwich	a							20 29		21 02					21 29							

		LE 1	LE ◇1	LE 1	LE 1	LE	LE 1	LE 1	LE 1	LE ◇1	LE 1	LE 1	LE 1	LE ◇1	LE 1	LE 1	LE 1	LE 1	LE ◇1	LE 1
London Liverpool Street 15 ⊖	d		20 30	20 32			21 02			21 30	21 32		22 02	22 30		22 32		23 02	23 30	23 32
Stratford 7 ⊖	d			20 39			21 09				21 39		22 09			22 39		23 09		23 39
Romford	d																			
Shenfield 3	d			21 01			21 31				22 01		22 31			23 01		23 31		00 01
Ingatestone	d						21 35						22 35					23 35		
Chelmsford 3	d			21 10			21 42				22 10		22 42			23 10		23 42		00 10
Hatfield Peverel	d						21 48						22 48					23 48		
Witham 2	d			21 21	21 24		21 55				22 21	22 24	22 55			23 21	23 24	23 55		00 21
White Notley	d				21 31							22 31					23 31			
Cressing	d				21 33							22 33					23 33			
Braintree Freeport	d				21 36							22 36					23 36			
Braintree	a				21 40							22 40					23 40			
Kelvedon	d						21 59						22 59					23 59		
Marks Tey 2	d			21 28		22 00	22 05				22 28		23 05			23 28		00 05		00 28
Colchester 4	a		21 23	21 36		22 08	22 12			22 23	22 36		23 12	23 23		23 36		00 12	00 27	00 39
Colchester 4	d		21 23	21 36			22 12			22 23	22 36		23 12	23 23		23 36		00 12	00 27	
Colchester Town	a																			
	d																			
Hythe	d																			
Wivenhoe 3	d			21 44							22 44					23 44				
Alresford (Essex)	d			21 47							22 47					23 47				
Great Bentley	d			21 51							22 51					23 51				
Weeley	d																			
Thorpe-le-Soken 1	a			21 58							22 58					23 58				
	d			21 58				22 00			22 58				23 00	23 58				
Clacton-on-Sea	a			22 07							23 07					00 07				
Kirby Cross	d							22 05							23 05					
Frinton-on-Sea	d							22 08							23 08					
Walton-on-the-Naze	a							22 12							23 12					
Manningtree 2	d	21 26	21 31				22 20		22 26	22 31			23 20	23 31				00 20	00 35	
Mistley	d	21 30							22 30											
Wrabness	d	21 35							22 35											
Harwich International	d	21 43							22 43											
Dovercourt	d	21 46							22 46											
Harwich Town	a	21 48							22 48											
Ipswich	a		21 43				22 32			22 43			23 32	23 43				00 36	00 47	
	d		21 44							22 44				23 44					00 48	
Needham Market	d																			
Stowmarket	d		21 55							22 55				23 55					00 59	
Peterborough 8	a																			
Diss	d		22 08							23 08				00 08					01 12	
Norwich	a		22 29							23 29				00 41					01 45	

London - Chelmsford, Colchester, Walton-on-Naze, Clacton, Harwich, Ipswich and Norwich

Network Diagram - see first Page of Table 5

		LE	LE	LE	LE	LE	LE	LE	LE	LE	LE	LE	LE	LE	LE	LE	LE	LE	LE	LE	LE	LE	LE	LE	LE
		◇1 ⊡	1	◇1 ⊡	1	1	1	1	◇1 ⊡	1	Bus	1	Bus	◇1 ⊡	1	◇1 ⊡	1	1	1	1	1	1	1		1
London Liverpool Street [15] ⊖	d	22p30	22p45	23p00	23p07	23p15			23p30	23p35		23p45		23p59	00 12	00 30	00 46				07 38				
Stratford [7] ⊖	d	22b40	22p54	23b10	23p17	23p25			23b40	23p45		23p54		00u10	00 24	00u40	01 00				07 47				
Romford	d																								
Shenfield [3]	d		23p12		23p34	23p43				00 02		00 12			00 41		01 17				08 03				
Ingatestone	d		23p16			23p48				00 05		00 16			00 45		01 22								
Chelmsford [3]	d	23p05	23p23	23p37	23p43	23p55			00 06	00 12		00 23		00 37	00 52	01 07	01 29				08 12				
Hatfield Peverel	d				23p49					00 18					00 58		01 35								
Witham [2]	d		23p34		23p56	00 05	00 07			00 25		00 34			01 05		01 41			07 34	08 23				
White Notley	d						00 14													07 41					
Cressing	d						00 16													07 43					
Braintree Freeport	d						00 19													07 46					
Braintree	a						00 23													07 50					
Kelvedon	d				00 01					00 29					01 09		01 46				08 27				
Marks Tey [2]	d				00 06					00 35					01 15		01 51				08 33				
Colchester [4]	a	23p24	23p46	23p58	00 14	00 17			00 25	00 43		00 46		00 56	01 23	01 29	02 00				08 40				
Colchester [4]	d	23p25	23p47	23p59		00 18			00 25			00 47		00 57		01 30			07 04				07 54	08 04	08 16
Colchester Town	a																								
	d																								
Hythe	d																								
Wivenhoe [3]	d		23p54			00 25					00 30	00 54													08 24
Alresford (Essex)	d										00 40														08 27
Great Bentley	d										00 50														08 31
Weeley	d																								
Thorpe-le-Soken [1]	a		00 06			00 37					01 00	01 06	←												08 38
	d		00 06			00 37					00 10	01 06	00 10												08 38
Clacton-on-Sea	a		00 15			00 46					→	01 15													08 47
Kirby Cross	d												01 17												
Frinton-on-Sea	d												01 22												
Walton-on-the-Naze	a												01 27												
Manningtree [2]	d	23p34		00 09				00 12	00 34					01 07		01 40			07 12				08 02	08 12	
Mistley	d							00 16															08 06		
Wrabness	d							00 21															08 11		
Harwich International	d							00 29															08 19		
Dovercourt	d							00 32															08 22		
Harwich Town	a							00 34															08 24		
Ipswich	a	23p45		00 19					00 45					01 17		01 50			07 25					08 25	
	d	23p46		00 21					00 46					01 19		01 52		07 17				08 17			
Needham Market	d																	07 26				08 26			
Stowmarket	d	23p58		00 32					00 58					01 30		02 03		07a31				08a31			
Peterborough [8]	a																								
Diss	d	00 10		00 45					01 10					01 43		02 16									
Norwich	a	00 30		01 05					01 30					02 03		02 35									

		LE	LE	LE	LE	LE	LE	LE	LE	LE	LE	LE	LE	LE	LE	LE	LE	LE	LE	LE	LE	LE	LE	LE	LE
		1	1	1	1	1	1	1	1	1	◇1 ⊡	1	◇1 ⊡	1	1	1	1	1	1	1	◇1 ⊡	1	1 ⊡	1	1
London Liverpool Street [15] ⊖	d				07 55			08 02	08 18		08 30	08 38	09 00					09 02	09 18		09 30	09 38	10 00		
Stratford [7] ⊖	d				08 02			08 09	08 25		08u38	08 47						09 09	09 25		09u38	09 47			
Romford	d																								
Shenfield [3]	d				08 22			08 25	08 41			09 03						09 25	09 41			10 03			
Ingatestone	d								08 45										09 45						
Chelmsford [3]	d				08 31			08 34	08 52		09 03	09 12						09 34	09 52		10 03	10 12			
Hatfield Peverel	d							08 40										09 40							
Witham [2]	d	08 34			08 42			08 47	09 03			09 23		09 34				09 47	10 03			10 23		10 34	
White Notley	d	08 41												09 41										10 41	
Cressing	d	08 43												09 43										10 43	
Braintree Freeport	d	08 46												09 46										10 46	
Braintree	a	08 50												09 50										10 50	
Kelvedon	d							08 51				09 27						09 51				10 27			
Marks Tey [2]	d							08 57				09 33						09 57				10 33			
Colchester [4]	a				08 54			09 04	09 15		09 22	09 40	09 45					10 04	10 15		10 22	10 40	10 45		
Colchester [4]	d				08 54	08 56		09 04	09 16		09 23		09 47				09 56	10 04	10 16		10 23		10 47		
Colchester Town	a					09 03											10 03								
	d					09 07											10 07								
Hythe	d					09 11											10 11								
Wivenhoe [3]	d					09 15			09 24								10 15		10 24						
Alresford (Essex)	d					09 19											10 19								
Great Bentley	d					09 23											10 23								
Weeley	d					09 26				←							10 26			←					
Thorpe-le-Soken [1]	a					09 31			09 35	09 31							10 31		10 35	10 31					
	d		08 42			09 37			09 35	09 37							10 37		10 35	10 37					
Clacton-on-Sea	a					→			09 44								→		10 44						
Kirby Cross	d		08 47							09 42										10 42					
Frinton-on-Sea	d		08 50							09 45										10 45					
Walton-on-the-Naze	a		08 54							09 49										10 49					
Manningtree [2]	d			09 00	09 03			09 12			09 31		09 55		10 00			10 12			10 31		10 55		11 00
Mistley	d			09 04											10 04										11 04
Wrabness	d			09 09											10 09										11 09
Harwich International	d			09 17	09a23										10 17										11 17
Dovercourt	d			09 20											10 20										11 20
Harwich Town	a			09 22											10 22										11 22
Ipswich	a							09 25			09 43		10 07					10 25			10 43		11 07		
	d						09 17				09 44		10 08			10 17					10 44		11 08		
Needham Market	d						09 26									10 26									
Stowmarket	d						09a31				09 55					10a31					10 55				
Peterborough [8]	a																								
Diss	d										10 08		10 29								11 08		11 29		
Norwich	a										10 27		10 48								11 27		11 48		

b Previous night, stops to pick up only

London - Chelmsford, Colchester, Walton-on-Naze, Clacton, Harwich, Ipswich and Norwich

Network Diagram - see first Page of Table 5

		LE	LE	LE	LE	LE	LE	LE	LE	LE	LE	LE	LE	LE	LE	LE	LE	LE	LE	LE	LE	LE	LE	LE	LE
		1	1	1	1	1	◇1 ⊡	1	◇1 ⊡	1	1	1	1	1	1	1	◇1 ⊡	1	◇1 ⊡	1	1	1	1	1	1
London Liverpool Street [15] ⊖	d			10 02	10 18		10 30	10 38	11 00					11 02	11 18		11 30	11 38	12 00					12 02	12 18
Stratford [7] ⊖	d			10 09	10 25		10u38	10 47						11 09	11 25		11u38	11 47						12 09	12 25
Romford	d																								
Shenfield [3]	d			10 25	10 41			11 03						11 25	11 41			12 03						12 25	12 41
Ingatestone	d				10 45										11 45										12 45
Chelmsford [3]	d			10 34	10 52		11 03	11 12						11 34	11 52		12 03	12 12						12 34	12 52
Hatfield Peverel	d			10 40										11 40										12 40	
Witham [2]	d			10 47	11 03			11 23		11 34				11 47	12 03			12 23		12 34				12 47	13 03
White Notley	d									11 41										12 41					
Cressing	d									11 43										12 43					
Braintree Freeport	d									11 46										12 46					
Braintree	a									11 50										12 50					
Kelvedon	d			10 51				11 27						11 51				12 27						12 51	
Marks Tey [2]	d			10 57				11 33						11 57				12 33						12 57	
Colchester [4]	a			11 04	11 15		11 22	11 40	11 45					12 04	12 15		12 22	12 40	12 45					13 04	13 15
Colchester [4]	d	10 56		11 04	11 16		11 23		11 47			11 56		12 04	12 16		12 23		12 47			12 56		13 04	13 16
Colchester Town	a	11 03										12 03										13 03			
	d	11 07										12 07										13 07			
Hythe	d	11 11										12 11										13 11			
Wivenhoe [3]	d	11 15			11 24							12 15			12 24							13 15			13 24
Alresford (Essex)	d	11 19										12 19										13 19			
Great Bentley	d	11 23										12 23										13 23			
Weeley	d	11 26				←						12 26				←						13 26			
Thorpe-le-Soken [1]	a	11 31			11 35	11 31						12 31			12 35	12 31						13 31			13 35
	d	11 37			11 35	11 37						12 37			12 35	12 37						13 37			13 35
Clacton-on-Sea	a	→			11 44							→			12 44							→			13 44
Kirby Cross	d					11 42										12 42									
Frinton-on-Sea	d					11 45										12 45									
Walton-on-the-Naze	a					11 49										12 49									
Manningtree [2]	d			11 12			11 31		11 55		12 00			12 12			12 31		12 55		13 00			13 12	
Mistley	d										12 04										13 04				
Wrabness	d										12 09										13 09				
Harwich International	d										12 17										13 17				
Dovercourt	d										12 20										13 20				
Harwich Town	a										12 22										13 22				
Ipswich	a			11 25			11 43		12 07					12 25			12 43		13 07					13 25	
	d		11 17				11 44		12 08				12 17				12 44		13 08				13 17		
Needham Market	d		11 26										12 26										13 26		
Stowmarket	d		11a31				11 55						12a31				12 55						13a31		
Peterborough [8]	a																								
Diss	d						12 08		12 29								13 08		13 29						
Norwich	a						12 27		12 48								13 27		13 48						

		LE	LE	LE	LE	LE	LE	LE	LE	LE	LE	LE	LE	LE	LE	LE	LE	LE	LE	LE	LE	LE	LE	LE	LE
		1	◇1 ⊡	1	◇1 ⊡	1	1	1	1	1	1	1	◇1 ⊡	1	◇1 ⊡	1	1	1	1	1	1	1	◇1 ⊡	1	◇1 ⊡
London Liverpool Street [15] ⊖	d		12 30	12 38	13 00					13 02	13 18		13 30	13 38	14 00					14 02	14 18		14 30	14 38	15 00
Stratford [7] ⊖	d		12u38	12 47						13 09	13 25		13u38	13 47						14 09	14 25		14u38	14 47	
Romford	d																								
Shenfield [3]	d			13 03						13 25	13 41			14 03						14 25	14 41			15 03	
Ingatestone	d										13 45										14 45				
Chelmsford [3]	d		13 03	13 12						13 34	13 52		14 03	14 12						14 34	14 52		15 03	15 12	
Hatfield Peverel	d									13 40										14 40					
Witham [2]	d			13 23		13 34				13 47	14 03			14 23		14 34				14 47	15 03			15 23	
White Notley	d					13 41										14 41									
Cressing	d					13 43										14 43									
Braintree Freeport	d					13 46										14 46									
Braintree	a					13 50										14 50									
Kelvedon	d			13 27						13 51				14 27						14 51				15 27	
Marks Tey [2]	d			13 33						13 57				14 33						14 57				15 33	
Colchester [4]	a		13 22	13 40	13 45					14 04	14 15		14 22	14 40	14 45					15 04	15 15		15 22	15 40	15 45
Colchester [4]	d		13 23		13 47			13 56		14 04	14 16		14 23		14 47			14 56		15 04	15 16		15 23		15 47
Colchester Town	a							14 03										15 03							
	d							14 07										15 07							
Hythe	d							14 11										15 11							
Wivenhoe [3]	d							14 15			14 24							15 15			15 24				
Alresford (Essex)	d							14 19										15 19							
Great Bentley	d							14 23										15 23							
Weeley	d	←						14 26				←						15 26				←			
Thorpe-le-Soken [1]	a	13 31						14 31			14 35	14 31						15 31			15 35	15 31			
	d	13 37						14 37			14 35	14 37						15 37			15 35	15 37			
Clacton-on-Sea	a							→			14 44							→			15 44				
Kirby Cross	d	13 42										14 42										15 42			
Frinton-on-Sea	d	13 45										14 45										15 45			
Walton-on-the-Naze	a	13 49										14 49										15 49			
Manningtree [2]	d		13 31		13 55		14 00			14 12			14 31		14 55		15 00			15 12			15 31		15 55
Mistley	d						14 04										15 04								
Wrabness	d						14 09										15 09								
Harwich International	d						14 17										15 17								
Dovercourt	d						14 20										15 20								
Harwich Town	a						14 22										15 22								
Ipswich	a		13 43		14 07					14 25			14 43		15 07					15 25			15 43		16 07
	d		13 44		14 08				14 17				14 44		15 08				15 17				15 44		16 08
Needham Market	d								14 26										15 26						
Stowmarket	d		13 55						14a31				14 55						15a31				15 55		
Peterborough [8]	a																								
Diss	d		14 08		14 29								15 08		15 29								16 08		16 29
Norwich	a		14 27		14 48								15 27		15 48								16 27		16 48

Table 11

Sundays
29 July to 12 August

London - Chelmsford, Colchester, Walton-on-Naze, Clacton, Harwich, Ipswich and Norwich

Network Diagram - see first Page of Table 5

		LE	LE	LE	LE	LE	LE	LE	LE ◇	LE	LE ◇	LE	LE	LE	LE	LE	LE	LE	LE ◇	LE	LE ◇	LE	LE	LE	LE
London Liverpool Street	d					15 02	15 18		15 30	15 38	16 00					16 02	16 18		16 30	16 38	17 00				
Stratford	d					15 09	15 25		15u38	15 47						16 09	16 25		16u38	16 47					
Romford	d																								
Shenfield	d					15 25	15 41			16 03						16 25	16 41			17 03					
Ingatestone	d						15 45										16 45								
Chelmsford	d					15 34	15 52		16 03	16 12						16 34	16 52		17 03	17 12					
Hatfield Peverel	d					15 40										16 40									
Witham	d	15 34				15 47	16 03			16 23		16 34				16 47	17 03			17 23		17 34			
White Notley	d	15 41										16 41										17 41			
Cressing	d	15 43										16 43										17 43			
Braintree Freeport	d	15 46										16 46										17 46			
Braintree	a	15 50										16 50										17 50			
Kelvedon	d					15 51				16 27						16 51				17 27					
Marks Tey	d					15 57				16 33						16 57				17 33					
Colchester	a					16 04	16 15		16 22	16 40	16 45					17 04	17 15		17 22	17 40	17 45				
Colchester	d			15 56		16 04	16 16		16 23		16 47			16 56		17 04	17 16		17 23		17 47			17 56	
Colchester Town	a			16 03										17 03										18 03	
	d			16 07										17 07										18 07	
Hythe	d			16 11										17 11										18 11	
Wivenhoe	d			16 15			16 24							17 15			17 24							18 15	
Alresford (Essex)	d			16 19										17 19										18 19	
Great Bentley	d			16 23										17 23										18 23	
Weeley	d			16 26				←						17 26				←						18 26	
Thorpe-le-Soken	a			16 31			16 35	16 31						17 31			17 35	17 31						18 31	
	d			16 37			16 35	16 37						17 37			17 35	17 37						18 37	
Clacton-on-Sea	a			→			16 44							→			17 44							→	
Kirby Cross	d							16 42										17 42							
Frinton-on-Sea	d							16 45										17 45							
Walton-on-the-Naze	a							16 49										17 49							
Manningtree	d		16 00			16 12			16 31		16 55		17 00			17 12			17 31		17 55		18 00		
Mistley	d		16 04										17 04										18 04		
Wrabness	d		16 09										17 09										18 09		
Harwich International	d		16 17										17 17										18 17		
Dovercourt	d		16 20										17 20										18 20		
Harwich Town	a		16 22										17 22										18 22		
Ipswich	a					16 25			16 43		17 07					17 25			17 43		18 07				
	d				16 17				16 44		17 08				17 17				17 44		18 08				18 17
Needham Market	d				16 26										17 26										18 26
Stowmarket	d				16a31				16 55		17 19				17a31				17 55						18a31
Peterborough	a																								
Diss	d								17 08		17 32								18 08		18 29				
Norwich	a								17 27		17 51								18 27		18 48				

		LE	LE	LE	LE ◇	LE	LE ◇	LE	LE	LE	LE	LE	LE	LE	LE ◇	LE	LE ◇	LE	LE	LE	LE	LE	LE	LE	LE ◇
London Liverpool Street	d	17 02	17 18		17 30	17 38	18 00					18 02	18 18		18 30	18 38	19 00					19 02	19 18		19 30
Stratford	d	17 09	17 25		17u38	17 47						18 09	18 25		18u38	18 47						19 09	19 25		19u38
Romford	d																								
Shenfield	d	17 25	17 41			18 03						18 25	18 41			19 03						19 25	19 41		
Ingatestone	d		17 45										18 45										19 45		
Chelmsford	d	17 34	17 52		18 03	18 12						18 34	18 52		19 03	19 12						19 34	19 52		20 03
Hatfield Peverel	d	17 40										18 40										19 40			
Witham	d	17 47	18 03			18 23		18 34				18 47	19 03			19 23		19 34				19 47	20 03		
White Notley	d							18 41										19 41							
Cressing	d							18 43										19 43							
Braintree Freeport	d							18 46										19 46							
Braintree	a							18 50										19 50							
Kelvedon	d	17 51				18 27						18 51				19 27						19 51			
Marks Tey	d	17 57				18 33						18 57				19 33						19 57			
Colchester	a	18 04	18 15		18 22	18 40	18 45					19 04	19 15		19 22	19 40	19 45					20 04	20 15		20 22
Colchester	d	18 04	18 16		18 23		18 47			18 56		19 04	19 16		19 23		19 47			19 56		20 04	20 16		20 23
Colchester Town	a									19 03										20 03					
	d									19 07										20 07					
Hythe	d									19 11										20 11					
Wivenhoe	d		18 24							19 15			19 24							20 15			20 24		
Alresford (Essex)	d									19 19										20 19					
Great Bentley	d									19 23										20 23					
Weeley	d			←						19 26				←						20 26				←	
Thorpe-le-Soken	a		18 35	18 31						19 31			19 35	19 31						20 31			20 35	20 31	
	d		18 35	18 37						19 37			19 35	19 37						20 37			20 35	20 37	
Clacton-on-Sea	a		18 44							→			19 44							→			20 44		
Kirby Cross	d			18 42										19 42										20 42	
Frinton-on-Sea	d			18 45										19 45										20 45	
Walton-on-the-Naze	a			18 49										19 49										20 49	
Manningtree	d	18 12			18 31		18 55		19 00			19 12			19 31		19 55		20 00			20 12			20 31
Mistley	d								19 04										20 04						
Wrabness	d								19 09										20 09						
Harwich International	d								19 17										20 17						
Dovercourt	d								19 20										20 20						
Harwich Town	a								19 22										20 22						
Ipswich	a	18 25			18 43		19 07					19 25			19 43		20 07					20 25			20 43
	d				18 44		19 08				19 17				19 44		20 08				20 17				20 44
Needham Market	d										19 26										20 26				
Stowmarket	d				18 55						19a31				19 55		20 19				20a31				20 55
Peterborough	a																								
Diss	d				19 08		19 29								20 08		20 32								21 08
Norwich	a				19 27		19 48								20 27		20 51								21 27

Table 11

Sundays
29 July to 12 August

London - Chelmsford, Colchester, Walton-on-Naze, Clacton, Harwich, Ipswich and Norwich

Network Diagram - see first Page of Table 5

		LE	LE ◇	LE	LE	LE		LE	LE	LE	LE	LE ◇	LE	LE	LE	LE	LE	LE	LE	LE	LE	LE ◇	LE	LE	LE
London Liverpool Street	d	19 38	20 00						20 02	20 18		20 30	20 38	21 00					21 02	21 18		21 30	21 38	21 56	
Stratford	d	19 47							20 09	20 25		20u38	20 47						21 09	21 25		21u38	21 47	22 05	
Romford	d																								
Shenfield	d	20 03							20 25	20 41			21 03						21 25	21 41			22 03		
Ingatestone	d									20 45										21 45					
Chelmsford	d	20 12							20 34	20 52		21 03	21 12						21 34	21 52		22 03	22 12	22 28	
Hatfield Peverel	d								20 40										21 40						
Witham	d	20 23		20 34					20 47	21 03			21 23		21 34				21 47	22 03			22 23		22 34
White Notley	d			20 41											21 41										22 41
Cressing	d			20 43											21 43										22 43
Braintree Freeport	d			20 46											21 46										22 46
Braintree	a			20 50											21 50										22 50
Kelvedon	d	20 27							20 51				21 27						21 51				22 27		
Marks Tey	d	20 33							20 57				21 33						21 57				22 33		
Colchester	a	20 40	20 45						21 04	21 15		21 22	21 40	21 46					22 04	22 15		22 22	22 40	22 47	
Colchester	d		20 47					20 56	21 04	21 16		21 23		21 47				21 56	22 04	22 16		22 23		22 47	
Colchester Town	a							21 03										22 03							
	d							21 07										22 07							
Hythe	d							21 11										22 11							
Wivenhoe	d							21 15		21 24								22 15		22 24					
Alresford (Essex)	d							21 19										22 19							
Great Bentley	d							21 23										22 23							
Weeley	d							21 26			←							22 26			←				
Thorpe-le-Soken	a							21 31		21 35	21 31							22 31		22 35	22 31				
	d							21 37		21 35	21 37							22 37		22 35	22 37				
Clacton-on-Sea	a							→		21 44								→		22 44					
Kirby Cross	d										21 42										22 42				
Frinton-on-Sea	d										21 45										22 45				
Walton-on-the-Naze	a										21 49										22 49				
Manningtree	d		20 55		21 00				21 12			21 31		21 55		22 00			22 12			22 31		22 56	
Mistley	d				21 04											22 04									
Wrabness	d				21 09											22 09									
Harwich International	d				21 17											22 17			22a28					23a11	
Dovercourt	d				21 20											22 20									
Harwich Town	a				21 22											22 22									
Ipswich	a		21 07						21 25			21 43		22 08								22 43			
	d		21 08			21 17						21 44					22 17					22 44			
Needham Market	d					21 26											22 26								
Stowmarket	d					21a31						21 55					22a33					22 55			
Peterborough	a																								
Diss	d		21 29									22 08										23 08			
Norwich	a		21 48									22 27										23 27			

		LE	LE	LE	LE	LE	LE	LE	LE	LE ◇	LE	LE		LE	LE ◇	LE	LE	LE ◇	LE	LE	LE ◇
London Liverpool Street	d						22 02	22 15		22 30	22 35			22 45	23 00	23 07	23 15	23 30	23 35	23 45	23 59
Stratford	d						22 10	22 24		22u40	22 44			22 54	23u10	23 17	23 25	23u40	23 45	23 54	00u10
Romford	d																				
Shenfield	d						22 27	22 41			23 01			23 11		23 34	23 41		00 01	00 11	
Ingatestone	d							22 45			23 05			23 15			23 46		00 05	00 15	
Chelmsford	d						22 36	22 52		23 06	23 12			23 22	23 36	23 43	23 53	00 06	00 12	00 22	00 36
Hatfield Peverel	d						22 42									23 49			00 18		
Witham	d						22 49	23 03			23 23	23 25		23 33		23 56	00 03		00 25	00 33	
White Notley	d											23 32									
Cressing	d											23 34									
Braintree Freeport	d											23 37									
Braintree	a											23 41									
Kelvedon	d						22 53				23 27					00 01			00 29		
Marks Tey	d	22 46					22 59				23 33					00 06			00 35		
Colchester	a	22 55					23 06	23 15		23 25	23 41			23 45	23 55	00 14	00 17	00 25	00 43	00 46	00 55
Colchester	d					22 56	23 07	23 16		23 25				23 46	23 55		00 18	00 25		00 47	00 56
Colchester Town	a					23 03															
	d					23 07															
Hythe	d					23 11															
Wivenhoe	d					23 15		23 24						23 54			00 26			00 55	
Alresford (Essex)	d					23 19															
Great Bentley	d					23 23															
Weeley	d					23 26			←												
Thorpe-le-Soken	a					23 31		23 35	23 31					00 05			00 37			01 06	
	d				23 16	23 37		23 35	23 37					00 05			00 37			01 06	
Clacton-on-Sea	a				23 25	→		23 44						00 14			00 46			01 15	
Kirby Cross	d								23 42												
Frinton-on-Sea	d								23 45												
Walton-on-the-Naze	a								23 49												
Manningtree	d			23 00			23 15			23 34					00 04			00 34			01 05
Mistley	d			23 04																	
Wrabness	d			23 09																	
Harwich International	d			23 17																	
Dovercourt	d			23 20																	
Harwich Town	a			23 22																	
Ipswich	a						23 27			23 45					00 15			00 45			01 15
	d		23 17							23 47					00 17			00 47			01 17
Needham Market	d		21326																		
Stowmarket	d		23a31							23 58					00 28			00 58			01 28
Peterborough	a																				
Diss	d									00 11					00 41			01 11			01 41
Norwich	a									00 30					01 00			01 30			02 00

Table 11

London - Chelmsford, Colchester, Walton-on-Naze, Clacton, Harwich, Ipswich and Norwich

Network Diagram - see first Page of Table 5

		LE ◇1 🛒	LE 1	LE 1	LE ◇1 🛒	LE 1	LE 1	LE 1	LE 1	LE 1		LE 1	LE 1	LE 1	LE 1	LE 1	LE 1	LE 1	LE 1	LE ◇1		LE ◇1	LE 1	LE 1	LE 1
London Liverpool Street ⊖	d	22p30	23p02	23p18	23p30		23p48	00 18								07 55	08 02			08 30			08 32		09 02
Stratford ⊖	d	22b38	23p09	23p25	23b38		23p55	00 25								08 02	08 09						08 39		09 09
Romford	d																								
Shenfield	d		23p25	23p41			00 11	00 47								08 24	08 31						09 01		09 31
Ingatestone	d			23p45			00 15	00 51									08 35								09 35
Chelmsford	d	23p03	23p34	23p52	00 03		00 22	00 58								08 34	08 42						09 10		09 42
Hatfield Peverel	d		23p40				00 28	01 04									08 48								09 48
Witham	d		23p47	00 03		00 05	00 35	01 11	07 34					08 24		08 44	08 55						09 21	09 24	09 55
White Notley	d					00 12			07 41					08 31										09 31	
Cressing	d					00 14			07 43					08 33										09 33	
Braintree Freeport	d					00 17			07 46					08 36										09 36	
Braintree	a					00 21			07 50					08 40										09 40	
Kelvedon	d		23p51				00 39	01 15									08 59								09 59
Marks Tey	d		23p57				00 45	01 21									09 05						09 28		10 05
Colchester	a	23p22	00 04	00 15	00 22		00 57	01 32								08 56	09 12			09 23			09 36		10 12
Colchester	d	23p23	00 04	00 16	00 23					07 40		08 12	08 18		08 36	08 57	09 12			09 23		09 32	09 36		10 12
Colchester Town	a																								
	d																								
Hythe	d																								
Wivenhoe	d			00 23											08 44								09 44		
Alresford (Essex)	d			00 27											08 47								09 47		
Great Bentley	d			00 31											08 51								09 51		
Weeley	d																								
Thorpe-le-Soken	a			00 38											08 58								09 58		
	d			00 38											08 58			09 00					09 58		
Clacton-on-Sea	a			00 51											09 07								10 07		
Kirby Cross	d																	09 05							
Frinton-on-Sea	d																	09 08							
Walton-on-the-Naze	a																	09 12							
Manningtree	d	23p31	00 12		00 31					07 48		08 20	08 26			09 05	09 20		09 26	09 31		09 40			10 20
Mistley	d												08 30						09 30						
Wrabness	d												08 35						09 35						
Harwich International	d												08 43			09a25			09 43						
Dovercourt	d												08 46						09 46						
Harwich Town	a												08 48						09 48						
Ipswich	a	23p43	00 28		00 43					08 00		08 32					09 32			09 43		09 51			10 32
	d	23p44			00 44															09 44		09 55			
Needham Market	d																								
Stowmarket	d	23p55			00 55															09 55		10 07			
Peterborough	a																					11 36			
Diss	d	00 08			01 08															10 08					
Norwich	a	00 27			01 31															10 29					

		LE 1	LE 1	LE ◇1 🛒	LE 1	LE 1		LE 1	LE 1	LE 1	LE 1	LE ◇1 🛒	LE 1	LE 1	LE 1	LE 1		LE 1	LE 1	LE ◇1 🛒	LE 1	LE 1	LE 1	LE 1	LE 1
London Liverpool Street ⊖	d			09 30	09 32					10 02		10 30	10 32			11 02				11 30	11 32				12 02
Stratford ⊖	d				09 39					10 09			10 39			11 09					11 39				12 09
Romford	d																								
Shenfield	d				10 01					10 31			11 01			11 31					12 01				12 31
Ingatestone	d									10 35						11 35									12 35
Chelmsford	d				10 10					10 42			11 10			11 42					12 10				12 42
Hatfield Peverel	d									10 48						11 48									12 48
Witham	d				10 21	10 24				10 55			11 21	11 24		11 55					12 21	12 24			12 55
White Notley	d					10 31								11 31								12 31			
Cressing	d					10 33								11 33								12 33			
Braintree Freeport	d					10 36								11 36								12 36			
Braintree	a					10 40								11 40								12 40			
Kelvedon	d									10 59						11 59									12 59
Marks Tey	d				10 28					11 05			11 28			12 05					12 28				13 05
Colchester	a			10 23	10 36					11 12		11 23	11 36			12 12				12 23	12 36				13 12
Colchester	d			10 23	10 36					11 12		11 23	11 36			12 12				12 23	12 36				13 12
Colchester Town	a																								
	d																								
Hythe	d																								
Wivenhoe	d				10 44								11 44								12 44				
Alresford (Essex)	d				10 47								11 47								12 47				
Great Bentley	d				10 51								11 51								12 51				
Weeley	d																								
Thorpe-le-Soken	a				10 58								11 58								12 58				
	d	10 00			10 58			11 00					11 58					12 00			12 58		13 00		
Clacton-on-Sea	a				11 07								12 07								13 07				
Kirby Cross	d	10 05						11 05										12 05					13 05		
Frinton-on-Sea	d	10 08						11 08										12 08					13 08		
Walton-on-the-Naze	a	10 12						11 12										12 12					13 12		
Manningtree	d		10 26	10 31						11 20	11 26	11 31				12 20			12 26	12 31					13 20
Mistley	d		10 30								11 30								12 30						
Wrabness	d		10 35								11 35								12 35						
Harwich International	d		10 43								11 43								12 43						
Dovercourt	d		10 46								11 46								12 46						
Harwich Town	a		10 48								11 48								12 48						
Ipswich	a			10 43						11 32		11 43				12 32				12 43					13 32
	d			10 44					11 02			11 44			11 55					12 44				13 02	
Needham Market	d								11 12															13 12	
Stowmarket	d			10 55					11a18			11 55			12 07					12 55				13a18	
Peterborough	a														13 31										
Diss	d			11 08								12 08								13 08					
Norwich	a			11 29								12 29								13 29					

b Previous night, stops to pick up only

Table 11

London - Chelmsford, Colchester, Walton-on-Naze, Clacton, Harwich, Ipswich and Norwich

Network Diagram - see first Page of Table 5

		LE 1		LE ◇1 🛒	LE 1	LE 1	LE 1	LE 1	LE 1	LE 1	LE ◇1 🛒	LE 1		LE 1	LE 1	LE 1	LE 1	LE 1	LE ◇1 🛒	LE 1	LE 1	LE 1		LE 1	LE 1
London Liverpool Street ⊖	d			12 30	12 32			13 02			13 30	13 32					14 02		14 30	14 32				15 02	
Stratford ⊖	d				12 39			13 09				13 39					14 09			14 39				15 09	
Romford	d																								
Shenfield	d				13 01			13 31				14 01					14 31			15 01				15 31	
Ingatestone	d							13 35									14 35							15 35	
Chelmsford	d				13 10			13 42				14 10					14 42			15 10				15 42	
Hatfield Peverel	d							13 48									14 48							15 48	
Witham	d				13 21	13 24		13 55				14 21		14 24			14 55			15 21	15 24			15 55	
White Notley	d					13 31								14 31							15 31				
Cressing	d					13 33								14 33							15 33				
Braintree Freeport	d					13 36								14 36							15 36				
Braintree	a					13 40								14 40							15 40				
Kelvedon	d							13 59									14 59							15 59	
Marks Tey	d				13 28			14 05				14 28					15 05			15 28				16 05	
Colchester	a			13 23	13 36			14 12			14 23	14 36					15 12		15 23	15 36				16 12	
Colchester	d			13 23	13 36			14 12			14 23	14 36					15 12		15 23	15 36				16 12	
Colchester Town	a																								
	d																								
Hythe	d																								
Wivenhoe	d				13 44							14 44								15 44					
Alresford (Essex)	d				13 47							14 47								15 47					
Great Bentley	d				13 51							14 51								15 51					
Weeley	d																								
Thorpe-le-Soken	a				13 58							14 58								15 58					
	d				13 58				14 00			14 58				15 00				15 58					16 00
Clacton-on-Sea	a				14 07							15 07								16 07					
Kirby Cross	d								14 05							15 05									16 05
Frinton-on-Sea	d								14 08							15 08									16 08
Walton-on-the-Naze	a								14 12							15 12									16 12
Manningtree	d	13 26		13 31				14 20		14 26	14 31						15 20	15 26	15 31					16 20	
Mistley	d	13 30								14 30								15 30							
Wrabness	d	13 35								14 35								15 35							
Harwich International	d	13 43								14 43								15 43							
Dovercourt	d	13 46								14 46								15 46							
Harwich Town	a	13 48								14 48								15 48							
Ipswich	a			13 43				14 32			14 43						15 32		15 43					16 32	
	d			13 44			13 55				14 44					15 02			15 44			15 55			
Needham Market	d															15 12									
Stowmarket	d			13 55			14 07				14 55					15a18			15 55			16 07			
Peterborough	a						15 31															17 31			
Diss	d			14 08							15 08								16 08						
Norwich	a			14 29							15 29								16 29						

		LE 1	LE ◇1 🛒	LE 1	LE 1	LE 1	LE 1	LE 1		LE 1	LE ◇1 🛒	LE 1	LE 1	LE 1	LE 1	LE 1	LE 1	LE ◇1 🛒		LE 1	LE 1	LE 1	LE 1	LE 1	LE 1
London Liverpool Street ⊖	d		15 30	15 32				16 02			16 30	16 32			17 02			17 30		17 32				18 02	
Stratford ⊖	d			15 39				16 09				16 39			17 09					17 39				18 09	
Romford	d																								
Shenfield	d			16 01				16 31				17 01			17 31					18 01				18 31	
Ingatestone	d							16 35							17 35									18 35	
Chelmsford	d			16 10				16 42				17 10			17 42					18 10				18 42	
Hatfield Peverel	d							16 48							17 48									18 48	
Witham	d			16 21	16 24			16 55				17 21	17 24		17 55					18 21	18 24			18 55	
White Notley	d				16 31								17 31								18 31				
Cressing	d				16 33								17 33								18 33				
Braintree Freeport	d				16 36								17 36								18 36				
Braintree	a				16 40								17 40								18 40				
Kelvedon	d							16 59							17 59									18 59	
Marks Tey	d			16 28				17 05				17 28			18 05					18 28				19 05	
Colchester	a		16 23	16 36				17 12			17 23	17 36			18 12			18 23		18 36				19 12	
Colchester	d		16 23	16 36				17 12			17 23	17 36			18 12			18 23		18 36				19 12	
Colchester Town	a																								
	d																								
Hythe	d																								
Wivenhoe	d			16 44								17 44								18 44					
Alresford (Essex)	d			16 47								17 47								18 47					
Great Bentley	d			16 51								17 51								18 51					
Weeley	d																								
Thorpe-le-Soken	a			16 58								17 58								18 58					
	d			16 58		17 00						17 58				18 00				18 58		19 00			
Clacton-on-Sea	a			17 07								18 07								19 07					
Kirby Cross	d					17 05										18 05						19 05			
Frinton-on-Sea	d					17 08										18 08						19 08			
Walton-on-the-Naze	a					17 12										18 12						19 12			
Manningtree	d	16 26	16 31					17 20		17 26	17 31				18 20		18 26	18 31						19 20	19 26
Mistley	d	16 30								17 30							18 30								19 30
Wrabness	d	16 35								17 35							18 35								19 35
Harwich International	d	16 43								17 43							18 43								19 43
Dovercourt	d	16 46								17 46							18 46								19 46
Harwich Town	a	16 48								17 48							18 48								19 48
Ipswich	a		16 43					17 32			17 43				18 32			18 43						19 32	
	d		16 44				17 02				17 44			17 55				18 44					19 02		
Needham Market	d						17 12																19 12		
Stowmarket	d		16 55				17a18				17 55			18 07				18 55					19a18		
Peterborough	a													19 32											
Diss	d		17 08								18 08							19 08							
Norwich	a		17 29								18 30							19 29							

19 August to 26 August

London - Chelmsford, Colchester, Walton-on-Naze, Clacton, Harwich, Ipswich and Norwich

Network Diagram - see first Page of Table 5

		LE ◇1	LE 1	LE ◇1	LE 1	LE 1	LE 1	LE 1	LE ◇1	LE 1	LE 1	LE 1	LE 1	LE 1	LE 1	LE 1	LE ◇1	LE 1	LE 1	LE	LE 1	LE 1
London Liverpool Street 15 ⊖	d	18 30	18 32	19 00		19 02			19 30	19 32			20 02				20 30	20 32			21 02	
Stratford 7 ⊖	d		18 39			19 09				19 39			20 09					20 39			21 09	
Romford	d																					
Shenfield 3	d		19 01			19 31				20 01			20 31					21 01			21 31	
Ingatestone	d					19 35							20 35								21 35	
Chelmsford 3	d		19 10	19 37		19 42				20 10			20 42					21 10			21 42	
Hatfield Peverel	d					19 48							20 48								21 48	
Witham 2	d		19 21		19 24	19 55				20 21	20 24		20 55					21 21	21 24		21 55	
White Notley	d				19 31						20 31								21 31			
Cressing	d				19 33						20 33								21 33			
Braintree Freeport	d				19 36						20 36								21 36			
Braintree	a				19 40						20 40								21 40			
Kelvedon	d					19 59							20 59								21 59	
Marks Tey 2	d		19 28			20 05				20 28			21 05					21 28		22 00	22 05	
Colchester 4	a	19 23	19 36	19 56		20 12			20 23	20 36			21 12				21 23	21 36		22 08	22 12	
Colchester 4	d	19 23	19 36	19 56		20 12			20 23	20 39		20 46	21 12				21 23	21 36			22 12	
Colchester Town	a																					
	d																					
Hythe	d																					
Wivenhoe 3	d		19 44							20 47								21 44				
Alresford (Essex)	d		19 47							20 50								21 47				
Great Bentley	d		19 51							20 54								21 51				
Weeley	d																					
Thorpe-le-Soken 1	a		19 58							21 01								21 58				
	d		19 58				20 00			21 01				21 03				21 58				22 00
Clacton-on-Sea	a		20 07							21 10								22 07				
Kirby Cross	d						20 05							21 08								22 05
Frinton-on-Sea	d						20 08							21 11								22 08
Walton-on-the-Naze	a						20 12							21 15								22 12
Manningtree 2	d	19 31		20 04		20 20		20 26	20 31			20 55	21 20			21 26	21 31				22 20	
Mistley	d							20 30								21 30						
Wrabness	d							20 35								21 35						
Harwich International	d							20 43				21a14			21 10	21 43						
Dovercourt	d							20 46								21 46						
Harwich Town	a							20 48								21 48						
Ipswich	a	19 43		20 16		20 32			20 43				21 32		21 36		21 43				22 32	
	d	19 44		20 17					20 44								21 44					
Needham Market	d																					
Stowmarket	d	19 55		20 28					20 55								21 55					
Peterborough 8	a																					
Diss	d	20 08		20 41					21 08								22 08					
Norwich	a	20 29		21 02					21 29								22 29					

		LE 1	LE ◇1	LE 1	LE 1	LE 1	LE ◇1	LE 1	LE 1	LE 1	LE 1	LE ◇1	LE 1
London Liverpool Street 15 ⊖	d		21 30	21 32		22 02	22 30		22 32		23 02	23 30	23 32
Stratford 7 ⊖	d			21 39		22 09			22 39		23 09		23 39
Romford	d												
Shenfield 3	d			22 01		22 31			23 01		23 31		00 01
Ingatestone	d					22 35					23 35		
Chelmsford 3	d			22 10		22 42			23 10		23 42		00 10
Hatfield Peverel	d					22 48					23 48		
Witham 2	d			22 21	22 24	22 55			23 21	23 24	23 55		00 21
White Notley	d				22 31					23 31			
Cressing	d				22 33					23 33			
Braintree Freeport	d				22 36					23 36			
Braintree	a				22 40					23 40			
Kelvedon	d					22 59					23 59		
Marks Tey 2	d			22 28		23 05			23 28		00 05		00 28
Colchester 4	a		22 23	22 36		23 12	23 23		23 36		00 12	00 27	00 39
Colchester 4	d		22 23	22 36		23 12	23 23		23 36		00 12	00 27	
Colchester Town	a												
	d												
Hythe	d												
Wivenhoe 3	d			22 44					23 44				
Alresford (Essex)	d			22 47					23 47				
Great Bentley	d			22 51					23 51				
Weeley	d												
Thorpe-le-Soken 1	a			22 58					23 58				
	d			22 58				23 00	23 58				
Clacton-on-Sea	a			23 07					00 07				
Kirby Cross	d							23 05					
Frinton-on-Sea	d							23 08					
Walton-on-the-Naze	a							23 12					
Manningtree 2	d	22 26	22 31			23 20	23 31				00 20	00 35	
Mistley	d	22 30											
Wrabness	d	22 35											
Harwich International	d	22 43											
Dovercourt	d	22 46											
Harwich Town	a	22 48											
Ipswich	a		22 43			23 32	23 43				00 36	00 47	
	d		22 44				23 44					00 48	
Needham Market	d												
Stowmarket	d		22 55				23 55					00 59	
Peterborough 8	a												
Diss	d		23 08				00 08					01 12	
Norwich	a		23 29				00 41					01 45	

2 September to 9 September

London - Chelmsford, Colchester, Walton-on-Naze, Clacton, Harwich, Ipswich and Norwich

Network Diagram - see first Page of Table 5

		LE ◇1	LE 1	LE ◇1	LE 1	LE 1	LE 1	LE 🚌	LE 1	LE ◇1	LE 1	LE 1	LE 🚌	LE ◇1	LE 1	LE ◇1	LE 1	LE 1	LE 1	LE 1	LE 1	LE 1	LE 1	LE	LE 1
London Liverpool Street 15 ⊖	d	22p30	22p45	23p00	23p07	23p15				23p30	23p35	23p45		23p59	00 12	00 30	00 46				07 38				
Stratford 7 ⊖	d	22b40	22p54	23b10	23p17	23p25				23b40	23p45	23p54		00u10	00 24	00u40	01 00				07 47				
Romford	d																								
Shenfield 3	d		23p12		23p34	23p43					00 02	00 12			00 41		01 17				08 03				
Ingatestone	d		23p16			23p48					00 05	00 16			00 45		01 22								
Chelmsford 3	d	23p05	23p23	23p37	23p43	23p55				00 06	00 12	00 23		00 37	00 52	01 07	01 29				08 12				
Hatfield Peverel	d				23p49						00 18				00 58		01 35								
Witham 2	d		23p34		23p56	00 05	00 07				00 25	00 34			01 05		01 41			07 34	08 23				
White Notley	d						00 14													07 41					
Cressing	d						00 16													07 43					
Braintree Freeport	d						00 19													07 46					
Braintree	a						00 23													07 50					
Kelvedon	d				00 01						00 29				01 09		01 46				08 27				
Marks Tey 2	d				00 06						00 35				01 15		01 51				08 33				
Colchester 4	a	23p24	23p46	23p58	00 14	00 17				00 25	00 43	00 46		00 56	01 23	01 29	02 00				08 40				
Colchester 4	d	23p25	23p47	23p59		00 18				00 25		00 47		00 57		01 30			07 04			07 54		08 04	08 16
Colchester Town	a																								
	d																								
Hythe	d																								
Wivenhoe 3	d		23p54			00 25		00 30				00 54													08 24
Alresford (Essex)	d							00 40																	08 27
Great Bentley	d							00 50																	08 31
Weeley	d																								
Thorpe-le-Soken 1	a		00 06			00 37		01 00				01 06	←												08 38
	d		00 06			00 37		00 10				01 06	00 10												08 38
Clacton-on-Sea	a		00 15			00 46		→				01 15													08 47
Kirby Cross	d												01 17												
Frinton-on-Sea	d												01 22												
Walton-on-the-Naze	a												01 27												
Manningtree 2	d	23p34		00 09					00 12	00 34				01 07		01 40			07 12			08 02		08 12	
Mistley	d								00 16													08 06			
Wrabness	d								00 21													08 11			
Harwich International	d								00 29													08 19			
Dovercourt	d								00 32													08 22			
Harwich Town	a								00 34													08 24			
Ipswich	a	23p45		00 19						00 45				01 17		01 50			07 25					08 25	
	d	23p46		00 21						00 46				01 19		01 52		07 17					08 17		
Needham Market	d																	07 26					08 26		
Stowmarket	d	23p58		00 32						00 58				01 30		02 03		07a31					08a31		
Peterborough 8	a																								
Diss	d	00 10		00 45						01 10				01 43		02 16									
Norwich	a	00 30		01 05						01 30				02 03		02 35									

		LE 1	LE 1	LE 1	LE 1	LE 1	LE 1	LE 1	LE 1	LE 1	LE ◇1	LE 1	LE ◇1	LE 1	LE 1	LE 1	LE 1	LE 1	LE 1	LE 1	LE ◇1	LE 1	LE 1	LE 1	LE 1
London Liverpool Street 15 ⊖	d					07 55		08 02	08 18		08 30	08 38	09 00					09 02	09 18		09 30	09 38	10 00		
Stratford 7 ⊖	d					08 02		08 09	08 25		08u38	08 47						09 09	09 25		09u38	09 47			
Romford	d																								
Shenfield 3	d					08 22		08 25	08 41			09 03						09 25	09 41			10 03			
Ingatestone	d								08 45										09 45						
Chelmsford 3	d					08 31		08 34	08 52		09 03	09 12						09 34	09 52		10 03	10 12			
Hatfield Peverel	d							08 40										09 40							
Witham 2	d	08 34				08 42		08 47	09 03			09 23		09 34				09 47	10 03			10 23		10 34	
White Notley	d	08 41												09 41										10 41	
Cressing	d	08 43												09 43										10 43	
Braintree Freeport	d	08 46												09 46										10 46	
Braintree	a	08 50												09 50										10 50	
Kelvedon	d							08 51				09 27						09 51				10 27			
Marks Tey 2	d							08 57				09 33						09 57				10 33			
Colchester 4	a					08 54		09 04	09 15		09 22	09 40	09 45					10 04	10 15		10 22	10 40	10 45		
Colchester 4	d					08 54	08 56	09 04	09 16		09 23		09 47			09 56		10 04	10 16		10 23		10 47		
Colchester Town	a						09 03									10 03									
	d						09 07									10 07									
Hythe	d						09 11									10 11									
Wivenhoe 3	d						09 15		09 24							10 15			10 24						
Alresford (Essex)	d						09 19									10 19									
Great Bentley	d						09 23									10 23									
Weeley	d						09 26			←						10 26				←					
Thorpe-le-Soken 1	a						09 31		09 35	09 31						10 31			10 35	10 31					
	d		08 42				09 37		09 35	09 37						10 37			10 35	10 37					
Clacton-on-Sea	a						→		09 44							→			10 44						
Kirby Cross	d		08 47							09 42										10 42					
Frinton-on-Sea	d		08 50							09 45										10 45					
Walton-on-the-Naze	a		08 54							09 49										10 49					
Manningtree 2	d			09 00		09 03		09 12			09 31		09 55		10 00			10 12			10 31		10 55		
Mistley	d			09 04											10 04										
Wrabness	d			09 09											10 09										
Harwich International	d			09 17		09a25									10 17										
Dovercourt	d			09 20											10 20										
Harwich Town	a			09 22											10 22										
Ipswich	a							09 25			09 43		10 07					10 25			10 43		11 07		
	d				09 17						09 45		10 08				10 17				10 45		11 08		11 17
Needham Market	d				09 26												10 26								11 26
Stowmarket	d				09a31						09 56						10a31				10 56				11a31
Peterborough 8	a																								
Diss	d										10 09		10 29								11 09		11 29		
Norwich	a										10 28		10 48								11 28		11 48		

b Previous night, stops to pick up only

Table 11

Sundays

2 September to 9 September

London - Chelmsford, Colchester, Walton-on-Naze, Clacton, Harwich, Ipswich and Norwich

Network Diagram - see first Page of Table 5

		LE 1	LE 1	LE 1		LE 1	LE 1	LE ◇1 ⊏	LE 1	LE ◇1 ⊏	LE 1	LE 1	LE 1	LE 1	LE 1	LE 1	LE 1	LE ◇1 ⊏	LE 1	LE ◇1 ⊏	LE 1	LE 1	LE 1	LE 1	LE 1
London Liverpool Street 15 ⊖	d			10 02		10 18		10 30	10 38	11 00					11 02	11 18		11 30	11 38	12 00				12 02	12 18
Stratford 7 ⊖	d			10 09		10 25		10u38	10 47						11 09	11 25		11u38	11 47					12 09	12 25
Romford	d																								
Shenfield 3	d			10 25		10 41			11 03						11 25	11 41			12 03					12 25	12 41
Ingatestone	d					10 45										11 45									12 45
Chelmsford 3	d			10 34		10 52		11 03	11 12						11 34	11 52		12 03	12 12					12 34	12 52
Hatfield Peverel	d			10 40											11 40									12 40	
Witham 2	d			10 47		11 03			11 23		11 34				11 47	12 03			12 23		12 34			12 47	13 03
White Notley	d										11 41										12 41				
Cressing	d										11 43										12 43				
Braintree Freeport	d										11 46										12 46				
Braintree	a										11 50										12 50				
Kelvedon	d			10 51					11 27						11 51				12 27					12 51	
Marks Tey 2	d			10 57					11 33						11 57				12 33					12 57	
Colchester 4	a			11 04		11 15		11 22	11 40	11 45					12 04	12 15		12 22	12 40	12 45				13 04	13 15
Colchester 4	d		10 56	11 04		11 16		11 23		11 47				11 56	12 04	12 16		12 23		12 47			12 56	13 04	13 16
Colchester Town	a		11 03											12 03									13 03		
	d		11 07											12 07									13 07		
Hythe	d		11 11											12 11									13 11		
Wivenhoe 3	d		11 15			11 24								12 15		12 24							13 15		13 24
Alresford (Essex)	d		11 19											12 19									13 19		
Great Bentley	d		11 23											12 23									13 23		
Weeley	d		11 26				←							12 26			←						13 26		
Thorpe-le-Soken 1	a		11 31			11 35	11 31							12 31		12 35	12 31						13 31		13 35
	d		11 37			11 35	11 37							12 37		12 35	12 37						13 37		13 35
Clacton-on-Sea	a		→			11 44								→		12 44							→		13 44
Kirby Cross	d						11 42										12 42								
Frinton-on-Sea	d						11 45										12 45								
Walton-on-the-Naze	a						11 49										12 49								
Manningtree 2	d	11 00		11 12				11 31		11 55			12 00		12 12			12 31		12 55		13 00		13 12	
Mistley	d	11 04											12 04									13 04			
Wrabness	d	11 09											12 09									13 09			
Harwich International	d	11 17											12 17									13 17			
Dovercourt	d	11 20											12 20									13 20			
Harwich Town	a	11 22											12 22									13 22			
Ipswich	a			11 25				11 43		12 07					12 25			12 43		13 07				13 25	
	d							11 45		12 08		12 17						12 45		13 08					
Needham Market	d											12 26													
Stowmarket	d							11 56				12a31						12 56							
Peterborough 8	a																								
Diss	d							12 09		12 29								13 09		13 29					
Norwich	a							12 28		12 48								13 28		13 48					

		LE 1	LE 1	LE ◇1 ⊏	LE 1	LE ◇1 ⊏	LE 1	LE 1	LE 1	LE 1	LE 1	LE 1	LE 1	LE ◇1 ⊏	LE 1	LE ◇1 ⊏	LE 1	LE 1	LE 1	LE 1	LE 1	LE 1	LE 1	LE ◇1 ⊏	LE 1
London Liverpool Street 15 ⊖	d			12 30	12 38	13 00					13 02	13 18		13 30	13 38	14 00					14 02	14 18		14 30	14 38
Stratford 7 ⊖	d			12u38	12 47						13 09	13 25		13u38	13 47						14 09	14 25		14u38	14 47
Romford	d																								
Shenfield 3	d				13 03						13 25	13 41			14 03						14 25	14 41			15 03
Ingatestone	d											13 45										14 45			
Chelmsford 3	d			13 03	13 12						13 34	13 52		14 03	14 12						14 34	14 52		15 03	15 12
Hatfield Peverel	d										13 40										14 40				
Witham 2	d				13 23		13 34				13 47	14 03			14 23		14 34				14 47	15 03			15 23
White Notley	d						13 41										14 41								
Cressing	d						13 43										14 43								
Braintree Freeport	d						13 46										14 46								
Braintree	a						13 50										14 50								
Kelvedon	d				13 27						13 51				14 27						14 51				15 27
Marks Tey 2	d				13 33						13 57				14 33						14 57				15 33
Colchester 4	a			13 22	13 40	13 45					14 04	14 15		14 22	14 40	14 45					15 04	15 15		15 22	15 40
Colchester 4	d			13 23		13 47				13 56	14 04	14 16		14 23		14 47				14 56	15 04	15 16		15 23	
Colchester Town	a									14 03										15 03					
	d									14 07										15 07					
Hythe	d									14 11										15 11					
Wivenhoe 3	d									14 15		14 24								15 15		15 24			
Alresford (Essex)	d									14 19										15 19					
Great Bentley	d									14 23										15 23					
Weeley	d	←								14 26			←							15 26			←		
Thorpe-le-Soken 1	a	13 31								14 31		14 35	14 31							15 31		15 35	15 31		
	d	13 37								14 37		14 35	14 37							15 37		15 35	15 37		
Clacton-on-Sea	a									→		14 44								→		15 44			
Kirby Cross	d	13 42											14 42										15 42		
Frinton-on-Sea	d	13 45											14 45										15 45		
Walton-on-the-Naze	a	13 49											14 49										15 49		
Manningtree 2	d			13 31		13 55			14 00		14 12			14 31		14 55			15 00		15 12			15 31	
Mistley	d								14 04										15 04						
Wrabness	d								14 09										15 09						
Harwich International	d								14 17										15 17						
Dovercourt	d								14 20										15 20						
Harwich Town	a								14 22										15 22						
Ipswich	a			13 43		14 07					14 25			14 43		15 07					15 25			15 43	
	d		13 17	13 45		14 08		14 17						14 45		15 08		15 17						15 45	
Needham Market	d		13 26					14 26										15 26							
Stowmarket	d		13a31	13 56				14a31						14 56				15a31						15 56	
Peterborough 8	a																								
Diss	d			14 09		14 29								15 09		15 29								16 09	
Norwich	a			14 28		14 48								15 28		15 48								16 28	

Table 11

Sundays

2 September to 9 September

London - Chelmsford, Colchester, Walton-on-Naze, Clacton, Harwich, Ipswich and Norwich

Network Diagram - see first Page of Table 5

		LE ◇1 ⊏	LE 1	LE 1	LE 1	LE 1	LE 1	LE 1	LE 1	LE ◇1 ⊏	LE 1	LE ◇1 ⊏	LE 1	LE 1	LE 1	LE 1	LE 1	LE 1	LE 1	LE ◇1 ⊏	LE 1	LE ◇1 ⊏	LE 1	LE 1	LE 1
London Liverpool Street 15 ⊖	d	15 00					15 02	15 18		15 30	15 38	16 00					16 02	16 18		16 30	16 38	17 00			
Stratford 7 ⊖	d						15 09	15 25		15u38	15 47						16 09	16 25		16u38	16 47				
Romford	d																								
Shenfield 3	d						15 25	15 41			16 03						16 25	16 41			17 03				
Ingatestone	d							15 45										16 45							
Chelmsford 3	d						15 34	15 52		16 03	16 12						16 34	16 52		17 03	17 12				
Hatfield Peverel	d						15 40										16 40								
Witham 2	d		15 34				15 47	16 03			16 23		16 34				16 47	17 03			17 23		17 34		
White Notley	d		15 41										16 41										17 41		
Cressing	d		15 43										16 43										17 43		
Braintree Freeport	d		15 46										16 46										17 46		
Braintree	a		15 50										16 50										17 50		
Kelvedon	d						15 51				16 27						16 51				17 27				
Marks Tey 2	d						15 57				16 33						16 57				17 33				
Colchester 4	a	15 45					16 04	16 15		16 22	16 40	16 45					17 04	17 15		17 22	17 40	17 45			
Colchester 4	d	15 47				15 56	16 04	16 16		16 23		16 47				16 56	17 04	17 16		17 23		17 47			
Colchester Town	a					16 03										17 03									
	d					16 07										17 07									
Hythe	d					16 11										17 11									
Wivenhoe 3	d					16 15		16 24								17 15		17 24							
Alresford (Essex)	d					16 19										17 19									
Great Bentley	d					16 23										17 23									
Weeley	d					16 26			←							17 26			←						
Thorpe-le-Soken 1	a					16 31		16 35	16 31							17 31		17 35	17 31						
	d					16 37		16 35	16 37							17 37		17 35	17 37						
Clacton-on-Sea	a					→		16 44								→		17 44							
Kirby Cross	d								16 42										17 42						
Frinton-on-Sea	d								16 45										17 45						
Walton-on-the-Naze	a								16 49										17 49						
Manningtree 2	d	15 55			16 00		16 12			16 31		16 55			17 00		17 12			17 31		17 55		18 00	
Mistley	d				16 04										17 04									18 04	
Wrabness	d				16 09										17 09									18 09	
Harwich International	d				16 17										17 17									18 17	
Dovercourt	d				16 20										17 20									18 20	
Harwich Town	a				16 22										17 22									18 22	
Ipswich	a	16 07					16 25			16 43		17 07					17 25			17 43		18 07			
	d	16 08		16 17						16 45		17 08		17 17						17 45		18 08			18 17
Needham Market	d			16 26										17 26											18 26
Stowmarket	d			16a31						16 56		17 19		17a31						17 56					18a31
Peterborough 8	a																								
Diss	d	16 29								17 09		17 32								18 09		18 29			
Norwich	a	16 48								17 28		17 51								18 28		18 48			

		LE 1	LE 1	LE 1	LE 1	LE ◇1 ⊏	LE 1	LE ◇1 ⊏	LE 1	LE 1	LE 1	LE 1	LE 1	LE 1	LE 1	LE ◇1 ⊏	LE 1	LE ◇1 ⊏	LE 1	LE 1	LE 1	LE 1	LE 1	LE 1	LE 1
London Liverpool Street 15 ⊖	d		17 02	17 18		17 30	17 38	18 00					18 02	18 18		18 30	18 38	19 00					19 02	19 18	
Stratford 7 ⊖	d		17 09	17 25		17u38	17 47						18 09	18 25		18u38	18 47						19 09	19 25	
Romford	d																								
Shenfield 3	d		17 25	17 41			18 03						18 25	18 41			19 03						19 25	19 41	
Ingatestone	d			17 45										18 45										19 45	
Chelmsford 3	d		17 34	17 52		18 03	18 12						18 34	18 52		19 03	19 12						19 34	19 52	
Hatfield Peverel	d		17 40										18 40										19 40		
Witham 2	d		17 47	18 03			18 23		18 34				18 47	19 03			19 23		19 34				19 47	20 03	
White Notley	d								18 41										19 41						
Cressing	d								18 43										19 43						
Braintree Freeport	d								18 46										19 46						
Braintree	a								18 50										19 50						
Kelvedon	d		17 51				18 27						18 51				19 27						19 51		
Marks Tey 2	d		17 57				18 33						18 57				19 33						19 57		
Colchester 4	a		18 04	18 15		18 22	18 40	18 45					19 04	19 15		19 22	19 40	19 45					20 04	20 15	
Colchester 4	d	17 56	18 04	18 16		18 23		18 47				18 56	19 04	19 16		19 23		19 47				19 56	20 04	20 16	
Colchester Town	a	18 03										19 03										20 03			
	d	18 07										19 07										20 07			
Hythe	d	18 11										19 11										20 11			
Wivenhoe 3	d	18 15		18 24								19 15		19 24								20 15		20 24	
Alresford (Essex)	d	18 19										19 19										20 19			
Great Bentley	d	18 23										19 23										20 23			
Weeley	d	18 26			←							19 26			←							20 26			←
Thorpe-le-Soken 1	a	18 31		18 35	18 31							19 31		19 35	19 31							20 31		20 35	20 31
	d	18 37		18 35	18 37							19 37		19 35	19 37							20 37		20 35	20 37
Clacton-on-Sea	a	→		18 44								→		19 44								→		20 44	
Kirby Cross	d				18 42										19 42										20 42
Frinton-on-Sea	d				18 45										19 45										20 45
Walton-on-the-Naze	a				18 49										19 49										20 49
Manningtree 2	d		18 12			18 31		18 55			19 00		19 12			19 31		19 55			20 00		20 12		
Mistley	d										19 04										20 04				
Wrabness	d										19 09										20 09				
Harwich International	d										19 17										20 17				
Dovercourt	d										19 20										20 20				
Harwich Town	a										19 22										20 22				
Ipswich	a		18 25			18 43		19 07					19 25			19 43		20 07					20 25		
	d					18 45		19 08		19 17						19 45		20 08		20 17					
Needham Market	d									19 26										20 26					
Stowmarket	d					18 56				19a31						19 56		20 19		20a31					
Peterborough 8	a																								
Diss	d					19 09		19 29								20 09		20 32							
Norwich	a					19 28		19 48								20 28		20 51							

Sundays
2 September to 9 September

London - Chelmsford, Colchester, Walton-on-Naze, Clacton, Harwich, Ipswich and Norwich

Network Diagram - see first Page of Table 5

		LE ◇1	LE 1	LE 1	LE ◇1	LE 1	LE 1	LE 1	LE 1	LE 1	LE 1	LE 1	LE ◇1	LE 1	LE 1	LE 1	LE 1	LE 1	LE 1	LE 1	LE 1	LE 1	LE ◇1	LE 1	LE 1
London Liverpool Street 15 ⊖	d	19 30	19 32	19 38	20 00					20 02	20 18		20 30	20 38	21 00					21 02	21 18		21 30	21 38	22 00
Stratford 7 ⊖	d	19u38	19 41	19 47						20 09	20 25		20u38	20 47						21 09	21 25		21u38	21 47	
Romford	d																								
Shenfield 3	d		19 57	20 03						20 25	20 41			21 03						21 25	21 41			22 03	
Ingatestone	d										20 45										21 45				
Chelmsford 3	d	20 03	20 07	20 12						20 34	20 52		21 03	21 12						21 34	21 52		22 03	22 12	22 28
Hatfield Peverel	d									20 40										21 40					
Witham 2	d		20 18	20 23		20 34				20 47	21 03			21 23		21 34				21 47	22 03			22 23	
White Notley	d					20 41										21 41									
Cressing	d					20 43										21 43									
Braintree Freeport	d					20 46										21 46									
Braintree	a					20 50										21 50									
Kelvedon	d			20 27						20 51				21 27						21 51				22 27	
Marks Tey 2	d			20 33						20 57				21 33						21 57				22 33	
Colchester 4	a	20 22	20 30	20 40	20 45					21 04	21 15		21 22	21 40	21 46					22 04	22 15		22 22	22 40	22 47
Colchester 4	d	20 23	20 30		20 47			20 56		21 04	21 16		21 23		21 47			21 56		22 04	22 16		22 23		22 48
Colchester Town	a							21 03										22 03							
	d							21 07										22 07							
Hythe	d							21 11										22 11							
Wivenhoe 3	d							21 15			21 24							22 15			22 24				
Alresford (Essex)	d							21 19										22 19							
Great Bentley	d							21 23										22 23							
Weeley	d							21 26				←						22 26				←			
Thorpe-le-Soken 1	a							21 31			21 35	21 31						22 31			22 35	22 31			
	d							21 37			21 35	21 37						22 37			22 35	22 37			
Clacton-on-Sea	a							→			21 44							→			22 44				
Kirby Cross	d											21 42										22 42			
Frinton-on-Sea	d											21 45										22 45			
Walton-on-the-Naze	a											21 49										22 49			
Manningtree 2	d	20 31	20 39		20 55		21 00			21 12			21 31		21 55		22 00			22 12			22 31		22 56
Mistley	d						21 04										22 04								
Wrabness	d						21 09										22 09								
Harwich International	d		20a54				21 17										22 17			22a28					
Dovercourt	d						21 20										22 20								
Harwich Town	a						21 22										22 22								
Ipswich	a	20 43			21 07					21 25			21 43		22 08								22 43		23 08
	d	20 45			21 08				21 17				21 45						22 17				22 44		
Needham Market	d								21 26										22 26						
Stowmarket	d	20 56							21a31				21 56						22a31				22 55		
Peterborough 8	a																								
Diss	d	21 09			21 29								22 09										23 08		
Norwich	a	21 28			21 48								22 28										23 27		

		LE 1	LE	LE 1	LE 1	LE 1	LE 1	LE 1	LE 1	LE 1	LE ◇1	LE 1	LE 1	LE 1	LE ◇1	LE 1	LE 1	LE ◇1	LE 1	LE 1	LE ◇1
London Liverpool Street 15 ⊖	d				22 02				22 15		22 30	22 35		22 45	23 00	23 07	23 15	23 30	23 35	23 45	23 59
Stratford 7 ⊖	d				22 09				22 24		22u40	22 44		22 54	23u10	23 17	23 25	23u40	23 45	23 54	00u10
Romford	d																				
Shenfield 3	d				22 25				22 41			23 01		23 11		23 34	23 41		00 01	00 11	
Ingatestone	d								22 45			23 05		23 15			23 46		00 05	00 15	
Chelmsford 3	d				22 34				22 52		23 06	23 12		23 22	23 36	23 43	23 53	00 06	00 12	00 22	00 36
Hatfield Peverel	d				22 40											23 49			00 18		
Witham 2	d	22 34			22 47				23 03			23 23	23 25	23 33		23 56	00 03		00 25	00 33	
White Notley	d	22 41											23 32								
Cressing	d	22 43											23 34								
Braintree Freeport	d	22 46											23 37								
Braintree	a	22 50											23 41								
Kelvedon	d				22 51							23 27				00 01			00 29		
Marks Tey 2	d		22 46		22 57							23 33				00 06			00 35		
Colchester 4	a		22 55		23 05				23 15		23 25	23 41		23 45	23 55	00 14	00 17	00 25	00 43	00 46	00 55
Colchester 4	d							22 56	23 16		23 25			23 46	23 55		00 18	00 25		00 47	00 56
Colchester Town	a							23 03													
	d							23 07													
Hythe	d							23 11													
Wivenhoe 3	d							23 15	23 24					23 54			00 26			00 55	
Alresford (Essex)	d							23 19													
Great Bentley	d							23 23													
Weeley	d							23 26		←											
Thorpe-le-Soken 1	a							23 31	23 35	23 31				00 05			00 37			01 06	
	d						23 16	23 37	23 35	23 37				00 05			00 37			01 06	
Clacton-on-Sea	a						23 25	→	23 44					00 14			00 46			01 15	
Kirby Cross	d									23 42											
Frinton-on-Sea	d									23 45											
Walton-on-the-Naze	a									23 49											
Manningtree 2	d					23 00					23 34				00 04			00 34			01 05
Mistley	d					23 04															
Wrabness	d					23 09															
Harwich International	d					23 17															
Dovercourt	d					23 20															
Harwich Town	a					23 22															
Ipswich	a										23 45				00 15			00 45			01 15
	d			23 17							23 47				00 17			00 47			01 17
Needham Market	d			23 26																	
Stowmarket	d			23a31							23 58				00 28			00 58			01 28
Peterborough 8	a																				
Diss	d										00 11				00 41			01 11			01 41
Norwich	a										00 30				01 00			01 30			02 00

Sundays
from 16 September

London - Chelmsford, Colchester, Walton-on-Naze, Clacton, Harwich, Ipswich and Norwich

Network Diagram - see first Page of Table 5

		LE ◇1	LE 1	LE 1	LE ◇1	LE 1	LE 1	LE 1	LE 1	LE 1	LE 1	LE 1	LE	LE 1	LE 1	LE 1	LE 1	LE 1	LE 1	LE 1	LE ◇1	LE ◇1	LE 1
London Liverpool Street 15 ⊖	d	22p30	23p02	23p18	23p30		23p48	00 18									07 55				08 30		
Stratford 7 ⊖	d	22b38	23p09	23p25	23b38		23p55	00 25									08 02						
Romford	d																						
Shenfield 3	d		23p25	23p41			00 11	00 47									08 24	08 31			08 58		09 01
Ingatestone	d			23p45			00 15	00 51										08 36					
Chelmsford 3	d	23p03	23p34	23p52	00 03		00 22	00 58									08 34	08 43					09 11
Hatfield Peverel	d		23p40				00 28	01 04										08 49					
Witham 2	d		23p47	00 03		00 05	00 35	01 11	07 34			08 24					08 44	08 55					09 21
White Notley	d					00 12			07 41			08 31											
Cressing	d					00 14			07 43			08 33											
Braintree Freeport	d					00 17			07 46			08 36											
Braintree	a					00 21			07 50			08 40											
Kelvedon	d		23p51				00 39	01 15										08 59					
Marks Tey 2	d		23p57				00 45	01 21										09 05					09 28
Colchester 4	a	23p22	00 04	00 15	00 22		00 57	01 32									08 56	09 12			09 24		09 36
Colchester 4	d	23p23	00 04	00 16	00 23					07 40	08 12				08 18	08 36	08 57	09 15			09 25	09 32	09 36
Colchester Town	a																						
	d																						
Hythe	d																						
Wivenhoe 3	d			00 23												08 44							09 44
Alresford (Essex)	d			00 27												08 47							09 47
Great Bentley	d			00 31												08 51							09 51
Weeley	d																						
Thorpe-le-Soken 1	a			00 38												08 58							09 58
	d			00 38												08 58			09 00				09 58
Clacton-on-Sea	a			00 51												09 07							10 07
Kirby Cross	d																		09 05				
Frinton-on-Sea	d																		09 08				
Walton-on-the-Naze	a																		09 12				
Manningtree 2	d	23p31	00 12		00 31					07 48	08 20				08 26		09 05	09 23		09 26	09 33	09 40	
Mistley	d														08 30					09 30			
Wrabness	d														08 35					09 35			
Harwich International	d													08 30	08 43		09a25			09 43			
Dovercourt	d														08 46					09 46			
Harwich Town	a														08 48					09 48			
Ipswich	a	23p43	00 28		00 43					08 00	08 32			08 53				09 35			09 45	09 51	
	d	23p44			00 44								08 45	09 02							09 46	09 55	
Needham Market	d													09 12									
Stowmarket	d	23p55			00 55								08a59	09a17							09 57	10 07	
Peterborough 8	a																					11 36	
Diss	d	00 08			01 08																10 10		
Norwich	a	00 27			01 31																10 31		

		LE 1	LE 1	LE 1	LE 1	LE ◇1	LE 1	LE 1	LE 1	LE 1	LE 1	LE 1	LE ◇1	LE 1	LE 1	LE 1	LE 1	LE 1	LE 1	LE ◇1	LE 1	LE 1	LE 1
London Liverpool Street 15 ⊖	d		09 02			09 30	09 32				10 02		10 30	10 32			11 02			11 30	11 32		
Stratford 7 ⊖	d		09 09				09 39				10 09			10 39			11 09				11 39		
Romford	d																						
Shenfield 3	d		09 31				10 01				10 31			11 01			11 31				12 01		
Ingatestone	d		09 35								10 35						11 35						
Chelmsford 3	d		09 42				10 10				10 42			11 10			11 42				12 10		
Hatfield Peverel	d		09 48								10 48						11 48						
Witham 2	d	09 24	09 55				10 21	10 24			10 55			11 21	11 24		11 55				12 21	12 24	
White Notley	d	09 31						10 31							11 31							12 31	
Cressing	d	09 33						10 33							11 33							12 33	
Braintree Freeport	d	09 36						10 36							11 36							12 36	
Braintree	a	09 40						10 40							11 40							12 40	
Kelvedon	d		09 59								10 59						11 59						
Marks Tey 2	d		10 05				10 28				11 05			11 28			12 05				12 28		
Colchester 4	a		10 12			10 23	10 36				11 12		11 23	11 36			12 12			12 23	12 36		
Colchester 4	d		10 12			10 23	10 36				11 12		11 23	11 36			12 12			12 23	12 36		
Colchester Town	a																						
	d																						
Hythe	d																						
Wivenhoe 3	d						10 44							11 44							12 44		
Alresford (Essex)	d						10 47							11 47							12 47		
Great Bentley	d						10 51							11 51							12 51		
Weeley	d																						
Thorpe-le-Soken 1	a						10 58							11 58							12 58		
	d			10 00			10 58		11 00					11 58				12 00			12 58		13 00
Clacton-on-Sea	a						11 07							12 07							13 07		
Kirby Cross	d			10 05					11 05									12 05					13 05
Frinton-on-Sea	d			10 08					11 08									12 08					13 08
Walton-on-the-Naze	a			10 12					11 12									12 12					13 12
Manningtree 2	d		10 20		10 26	10 31					11 20	11 26	11 31				12 20		12 26	12 31			
Mistley	d				10 30							11 30							12 30				
Wrabness	d				10 35							11 35							12 35				
Harwich International	d				10 43							11 43							12 43				
Dovercourt	d				10 46							11 46							12 46				
Harwich Town	a				10 48							11 48							12 48				
Ipswich	a		10 32			10 43					11 32		11 43				12 32			12 43			
	d					10 44				11 02			11 44			11 55				12 44			
Needham Market	d									11 12													
Stowmarket	d					10 55				11a18			11 55			12 07				12 55			
Peterborough 8	a															13 31							
Diss	d					11 08							12 08							13 08			
Norwich	a					11 29							12 29							13 29			

b Previous night, stops to pick up only

Sundays
from 16 September

London - Chelmsford, Colchester, Walton-on-Naze, Clacton, Harwich, Ipswich and Norwich

Network Diagram - see first Page of Table 5

		LE ■		LE ■	LE ■	LE ◇■	LE ■	LE ■	LE ■	LE ■	LE ■	LE ■		LE ◇■	LE ■	LE ■	LE ■	LE ■	LE ■	LE ■	LE ◇■	LE ■		LE ■	LE ■
London Liverpool Street ■ ⊖	d			12 02		12 30	12 32			13 02				13 30	13 32				14 02		14 30	14 32			
Stratford ■ ⊖	d			12 09			12 39			13 09					13 39				14 09			14 39			
Romford	d																								
Shenfield ■	d			12 31			13 01			13 31					14 01				14 31			15 01			
Ingatestone	d			12 35						13 35									14 35						
Chelmsford ■	d			12 42			13 10			13 42					14 10				14 42			15 10			
Hatfield Peverel	d			12 48						13 48									14 48						
Witham ■	d			12 55			13 21	13 24		13 55					14 21	14 24			14 55			15 21		15 24	
White Notley	d							13 31								14 31								15 31	
Cressing	d							13 33								14 33								15 33	
Braintree Freeport	d							13 36								14 36								15 36	
Braintree	a							13 40								14 40								15 40	
Kelvedon	d			12 59						13 59									14 59						
Marks Tey ■	d			13 05			13 28			14 05					14 28				15 05			15 28			
Colchester ■	a			13 12		13 23	13 36			14 12				14 23	14 36				15 12		15 23	15 36			
Colchester ■	d			13 12		13 23	13 36			14 12				14 23	14 36				15 12		15 23	15 36			
Colchester Town	a																								
	d																								
Hythe	d																								
Wivenhoe ■	d						13 44								14 44							15 44			
Alresford (Essex)	d						13 47								14 47							15 47			
Great Bentley	d						13 51								14 51							15 51			
Weeley	d																								
Thorpe-le-Soken ■	a						13 58								14 58							15 58			
	d						13 58				14 00				14 58		15 00					15 58			
Clacton-on-Sea	a						14 07								15 07							16 07			
Kirby Cross	d										14 05						15 05								
Frinton-on-Sea	d										14 08						15 08								
Walton-on-the-Naze	a										14 12						15 12								
Manningtree ■	d			13 20	13 26	13 31				14 20		14 26		14 31					15 20	15 26	15 31				
Mistley	d				13 30							14 30								15 30					
Wrabness	d				13 35							14 35								15 35					
Harwich International	d				13 43							14 43								15 43					
Dovercourt	d				13 46							14 46								15 46					
Harwich Town	a				13 48							14 48								15 48					
Ipswich	a			13 32		13 43				14 32				14 43					15 32		15 43				
	d	13 02				13 44			13 55					14 44				15 02			15 44				15 55
Needham Market	d	13 12																15 12							
Stowmarket	d	13a18				13 55			14 07					14 55				15a18			15 55				16 07
Peterborough ■	a								15 31																17 31
Diss	d					14 08								15 08							16 08				
Norwich	a					14 29								15 29							16 29				

		LE ■	LE ■	LE ■	LE ◇■	LE ■	LE ■	LE ■		LE ■	LE ■	LE ■	LE ◇■	LE ■	LE ■	LE ■	LE ■	LE ■		LE ■	LE ◇■	LE ■	LE ■	LE ■	LE ■
London Liverpool Street ■ ⊖	d	15 02			15 30	15 32					16 02		16 30	16 32			17 02				17 30	17 32			
Stratford ■ ⊖	d	15 09				15 39					16 09			16 39			17 09					17 39			
Romford	d																								
Shenfield ■	d	15 31				16 01					16 31			17 01			17 31					18 01			
Ingatestone	d	15 35									16 35						17 35								
Chelmsford ■	d	15 42				16 10					16 42			17 10			17 42					18 10			
Hatfield Peverel	d	15 48									16 48						17 48								
Witham ■	d	15 55				16 21	16 24				16 55			17 21	17 24		17 55					18 21	18 24		
White Notley	d						16 31								17 31								18 31		
Cressing	d						16 33								17 33								18 33		
Braintree Freeport	d						16 36								17 36								18 36		
Braintree	a						16 40								17 40								18 40		
Kelvedon	d	15 59									16 59						17 59								
Marks Tey ■	d	16 05				16 28					17 05			17 28			18 05					18 28			
Colchester ■	a	16 12			16 23	16 36					17 12		17 23	17 36			18 12				18 23	18 36			
Colchester ■	d	16 12			16 23	16 36					17 12		17 23	17 36			18 12				18 23	18 36			
Colchester Town	a																								
	d																								
Hythe	d																								
Wivenhoe ■	d					16 44								17 44								18 44			
Alresford (Essex)	d					16 47								17 47								18 47			
Great Bentley	d					16 51								17 51								18 51			
Weeley	d																								
Thorpe-le-Soken ■	a					16 58								17 58								18 58			
	d		16 00			16 58		17 00						17 58				18 00				18 58		19 00	
Clacton-on-Sea	a					17 07								18 07								19 07			
Kirby Cross	d		16 05					17 05										18 05						19 05	
Frinton-on-Sea	d		16 08					17 08										18 08						19 08	
Walton-on-the-Naze	a		16 12					17 12										18 12						19 12	
Manningtree ■	d	16 20		16 26	16 31						17 20	17 26	17 31				18 20			18 26	18 31				
Mistley	d			16 30								17 30								18 30					
Wrabness	d			16 35								17 35								18 35					
Harwich International	d			16 43								17 43								18 43					
Dovercourt	d			16 46								17 46								18 46					
Harwich Town	a			16 48								17 48								18 48					
Ipswich	a	16 32			16 43						17 32		17 43				18 32				18 43				
	d				16 44					17 02			17 44			17 55					18 44				19 02
Needham Market	d									17 12															19 12
Stowmarket	d				16 55					17a18			17 55			18 07					18 55				19a18
Peterborough ■	a															19 32									
Diss	d				17 08								18 08								19 08				
Norwich	a				17 29								18 30								19 29				

Sundays
from 16 September

London - Chelmsford, Colchester, Walton-on-Naze, Clacton, Harwich, Ipswich and Norwich

Network Diagram - see first Page of Table 5

		LE ■	LE ■	LE ◇■		LE ■	LE ◇■	LE ■	LE ■	LE ■	LE ■	LE ◇■	LE ■	LE ■		LE ■	LE	LE ■	LE ■	LE ■	LE ■	LE ◇■	LE ■	LE ■
London Liverpool Street ■ ⊖	d	18 02		18 30		18 32	19 00		19 02			19 30	19 32					20 02				20 30	20 32	
Stratford ■ ⊖	d	18 09				18 39			19 09				19 39					20 09					20 39	
Romford	d																							
Shenfield ■	d	18 31				19 01			19 31				20 01					20 31					21 01	
Ingatestone	d	18 35							19 35									20 35						
Chelmsford ■	d	18 42				19 10	19 37		19 42				20 10					20 42					21 10	
Hatfield Peverel	d	18 48							19 48									20 48						
Witham ■	d	18 55				19 21		19 24	19 55				20 21	20 24				20 55					21 21	21 24
White Notley	d							19 31						20 31										21 31
Cressing	d							19 33						20 33										21 33
Braintree Freeport	d							19 36						20 36										21 36
Braintree	a							19 40						20 40										21 40
Kelvedon	d	18 59							19 59									20 59						
Marks Tey ■	d	19 05				19 28			20 05				20 28					21 05					21 28	
Colchester ■	a	19 12		19 23		19 36	19 56		20 12			20 23	20 36					21 12				21 23	21 36	
Colchester ■	d	19 12		19 23		19 36	19 56		20 12			20 23	20 39			20 46		21 12				21 23	21 36	
Colchester Town	a																							
	d																							
Hythe	d																							
Wivenhoe ■	d					19 44							20 47										21 44	
Alresford (Essex)	d					19 47							20 50										21 47	
Great Bentley	d					19 51							20 54										21 51	
Weeley	d																							
Thorpe-le-Soken ■	a					19 58							21 01										21 58	
	d					19 58				20 00			21 01						21 03				21 58	
Clacton-on-Sea	a					20 07							21 10										22 07	
Kirby Cross	d									20 05									21 08					
Frinton-on-Sea	d									20 08									21 11					
Walton-on-the-Naze	a									20 12									21 15					
Manningtree ■	d	19 20	19 26	19 31			20 04		20 20		20 26	20 31				20 55		21 20			21 26	21 31		
Mistley	d		19 30								20 30										21 30			
Wrabness	d		19 35								20 35										21 35			
Harwich International	d		19 43								20 43					21a14				21 10	21 43			
Dovercourt	d		19 46								20 46										21 46			
Harwich Town	a		19 48								20 48										21 48			
Ipswich	a	19 32		19 43			20 16		20 32			20 43						21 32		21 36		21 43		
	d			19 44			20 17					20 44					21 02					21 44		
Needham Market	d																21 12							
Stowmarket	d			19 55			20 28					20 55					21a18					21 55		
Peterborough ■	a																							
Diss	d			20 08			20 41					21 08										22 08		
Norwich	a			20 29			21 02					21 29										22 29		

		LE	LE ■	LE ■	LE ■	LE ◇■	LE ■	LE ■	LE ■	LE ◇■		LE ■	LE ■	LE ■	LE ■	LE ◇■	LE ■
London Liverpool Street ■ ⊖	d		21 02			21 30	21 32		22 02	22 30			22 32		23 02	23 30	23 32
Stratford ■ ⊖	d		21 09				21 39		22 09				22 39		23 09		23 39
Romford	d																
Shenfield ■	d		21 31				22 01		22 31				23 01		23 31		00 01
Ingatestone	d		21 35						22 35						23 35		
Chelmsford ■	d		21 42				22 10		22 42				23 10		23 42		00 10
Hatfield Peverel	d		21 48						22 48						23 48		
Witham ■	d		21 55				22 21	22 24	22 55				23 21	23 24	23 55		00 21
White Notley	d							22 31						23 31			
Cressing	d							22 33						23 33			
Braintree Freeport	d							22 36						23 36			
Braintree	a							22 40						23 40			
Kelvedon	d		21 59						22 59						23 59		
Marks Tey ■	d	22 00	22 05				22 28		23 05				23 28		00 05		00 28
Colchester ■	a	22 08	22 12			22 23	22 36		23 12	23 23			23 36		00 12	00 27	00 39
Colchester ■	d		22 12			22 23	22 36		23 12	23 23			23 36		00 12	00 27	
Colchester Town	a																
	d																
Hythe	d																
Wivenhoe ■	d						22 44						23 44				
Alresford (Essex)	d						22 47						23 47				
Great Bentley	d						22 51						23 51				
Weeley	d																
Thorpe-le-Soken ■	a						22 58						23 58				
	d			22 00			22 58					23 00	23 58				
Clacton-on-Sea	a						23 07						00 07				
Kirby Cross	d			22 05								23 05					
Frinton-on-Sea	d			22 08								23 08					
Walton-on-the-Naze	a			22 12								23 12					
Manningtree ■	d		22 20		22 26	22 31			23 20	23 31					00 20	00 35	
Mistley	d				22 30												
Wrabness	d				22 35												
Harwich International	d				22 43												
Dovercourt	d				22 46												
Harwich Town	a				22 48												
Ipswich	a		22 32			22 43			23 32	23 43					00 36	00 47	
	d					22 44				23 44						00 48	
Needham Market	d																
Stowmarket	d					22 55				23 55						00 59	
Peterborough ■	a																
Diss	d					23 08				00 08						01 12	
Norwich	a					23 29				00 41						01 45	

Norwich, Ipswich, Harwich, Clacton, Walton-on-Naze, Colchester and Chelmsford - London

Network Diagram - see first Page of Table 5

Miles	Miles	Miles	Miles	Miles			LE ◇1 A	LE MO ◇1 B	LE TW ThO ◇1 C	LE MX	LE TW ThO 1 C	LE MO B	LE 1 A	LE TW ThO 1 C	LE 1	LE ◇1	LE 1	LE 1	LE 1	LE ◇1 ☕	LE 1	LE 1	LE 1	LE 1
0	—	—	—	—	**Norwich**	d	22p00	22p00	22p00											05 00				
20	—	—	—	—	Diss	d	22p17	22p17	22p17											05 18				
—	—	—	—	—	**Peterborough 8**	d																		
34¼	—	—	—	—	Stowmarket	d	22p29	22p29	22p29	23p47		00 06								05 30				
38	—	—	—	—	Needham Market	d				23p52		00 11												
46¾	—	—	—	—	**Ipswich**	a	22p41	22p41	22p41	00 05		00 23								05 42				
—	—	—	—	—		d	22p43	22p43	22p43							05 14				05 44				06 00
—	0	—	—	—	**Harwich Town**	d											05 24							
—	0½	—	—	—	Dovercourt	d											05 26							
—	1¾	—	—	—	Harwich International	d											05 29							
—	5½	—	—	—	Wrabness	d											05 35							
—	9½	—	—	—	Mistley	d											05 41							
55½	11¼	—	—	—	Manningtree 2	d	22p53	22p53	22p53							05 25	05a46			05 54				06 10
—	—	0	—	—	**Walton-on-the-Naze**	d															05 35			
—	—	1¼	—	—	Frinton-on-Sea	d															05 38			
—	—	2½	—	—	Kirby Cross	d															05 41			
—	—	—	0	—	**Clacton-on-Sea**	d													05 20				05 40	
—	—	5	4¾	—	Thorpe-le-Soken 1	a													05 28		05 47		05 48	
—	—	—	—	—		d													05 28				05 48	
—	—	7¼	—	—	Weeley	d																	05 52	
—	—	10	—	—	Great Bentley	d																	05 56	
—	—	12¼	—	—	Alresford (Essex)	d																	06 00	
—	—	14	—	—	Wivenhoe 3	d													05 38				06 04	
—	—	16½	—	—	Hythe	d																	06 08	
—	—	18	—	—	Colchester Town	a																		
—	—	—	—	—		d																		
63¼	—	—	—	—	**Colchester 4**	a	23p02	23p02	23p02							05 34			05 46	06 03			06 14	06 19
—	0	19¾	—	—	**Colchester 4**	d	23p03	23p03	23p03						05 12	05 35			05 47	06 05			06 15	06 20
68¼	—	—	—	—	Marks Tey 2	d									05 18				05 53					06 26
72¾	—	—	—	—	Kelvedon	d									05 23				05 59				06 25	06 32
—	—	—	—	0	**Braintree**	d					00 05		00 25	00 46				05 45						
—	—	—	—	0¾	Braintree Freeport	d					00 07		00 27	00 48				05 47						
—	—	—	—	2	Cressing	d					00 10		00 30	00 51				05 50						
—	—	—	—	3¼	White Notley	d					00 13		00 33	00 54				05 53						
76½	—	—	—	6¼	**Witham 2**	d	23p16	23p16	23p16		00a21		00a41	01a02	05 29	05 48		06a02	06 05			06 18	06 31	06 38
79	—	—	—	—	Hatfield Peverel	d									05 33							06 22		
85¾	—	—	—	—	**Chelmsford 3**	d	23p25	23p25	23p25						05 40	05 58			06 14			06 29	06 40	06 47
91½	—	—	—	—	Ingatestone	d									05 47							06 36		
94¾	—	—	—	—	Shenfield 3	a	23b36	23b36	23p36						05 52				06 24			06 41	06 50	
102¾	—	—	—	—	Romford	a																		
111¾	—	—	—	—	Stratford 7 ⊖	a	23b52	23b57	00s04						06 07	06s22			06 39	06s44		06s57	07s06	
115	—	—	—	—	**London Liverpool Street 15** ⊖	a	00 02	00 08	00 14						06 16	06 34			06 48	06 54		07 09	07 18	07 24

A FO until 15 June, MX from 22 June until 26 July
B from 21 May until 23 July
C until 21 June
b Previous night, stops to set down only

Norwich, Ipswich, Harwich, Clacton, Walton-on-Naze, Colchester and Chelmsford - London

Network Diagram - see first Page of Table 5

		LE 1	LE 1	LE 1	LE ■ 1 ☕	LE 1	LE 1	LE 1	LE 1	LE 1	LE ■ 1 ☕	LE 1	LE 1	LE 1	LE 1	LE 1	LE 1	LE 1	LE	LE 1	LE 1	LE ■ 1 ☕
Norwich	d				05 30						06 00											06 25
Diss	d				05 48						06 18											06 43
Peterborough 8	d																					
Stowmarket	d	05 54			06 00						06 30								06 44			06 55
Needham Market	d	05 59																	06 49			
Ipswich	a	06 09			06 12						06 42								07 01			07 07
	d				06 14			06 29			06 44					06 52		06 59				07 09
Harwich Town	d								06 24								06 52					
Dovercourt	d								06 26								06 54					
Harwich International	d								06 29								06 57	07a28				
Wrabness	d								06 35								07 03					
Mistley	d								06 41								07 09					
Manningtree 2	d				06 24			06 39	06a46		06 54					07 02	07a14					07 19
Walton-on-the-Naze	d		06 05										06 32									
Frinton-on-Sea	d		06 08										06 35									
Kirby Cross	d		06 11										06 38									
Clacton-on-Sea	d					06 10						06 28			06 38						06 47	
Thorpe-le-Soken 1	a		06 17			06 18						06 36	06 44		06 46						06 55	
	d					06 18						06 36			06 46						06 55	
Weeley	d											06 40										
Great Bentley	d											06 43										
Alresford (Essex)	d											06 47										
Wivenhoe 3	d					06 29						06 51			06 57						07 06	
Hythe	d					06 33						06 55			07 01						07 10	
Colchester Town	a											06 59										
	d			06 19						06 47		07 03										
Colchester 4	a			06 26	06 33	06 39		06 48		06 54	07 03	07 13			07 07	07 12					07 16	07 28
Colchester 4	d			06 27	06 35	06 40		06 49		06 55	07 05				07 08	07 13					07 17	07 30
Marks Tey 2	d			06 33				06 55		07 01						07 19					07 23	
Kelvedon	d					06 50		07 00							07 18						07 29	
Braintree	d						06 40															
Braintree Freeport	d						06 42															
Cressing	d						06 45															
White Notley	d						06 48															
Witham 2	d			06 47			06 57	07 06		07 10				07 17						07 29	07 35	
Hatfield Peverel	d						07 02													07 33		
Chelmsford 3	d			06 56		07 03	07 09			07 19				07 27	07 31	07 35				07 40		
Ingatestone	d			07 03										07 33		07 42						
Shenfield 3	a			07 07			07 19							07 38	07 41					07 50		
Romford	a																					
Stratford 7 ⊖	a			07s23	07s15	07s27	07s35	07s38		07 44				07s55	07s58	08s01				08s07	08s09	
London Liverpool Street 15 ⊖	a			07 35	07 27	07 38	07 46	07 50		07 56	07 58			08 07	08 09	08 13				08 19	08 21	08 23

		LE 1	LE 1	LE 1	LE 1	LE 1	LE ◇1	LE 1	LE 1	LE ■ 1 ☕	LE 1	LE 1	LE 1	LE ■ 1 ☕	LE	LE 1	LE C	LE 1	LE 1	LE 1	LE ■ 1 A ☕	LE 1	LE 1	LE 1
Norwich	d									06 50				07 05							07 40			
Diss	d									07 08				07 23							07 58			
Peterborough 8	d																							
Stowmarket	d						07 05			07 20				07 35	07 45									
Needham Market	d														07 50									
Ipswich	a						07 18			07 32				07 47	08 03						08 18			
	d						07 18			07 34			07 38	07 49							08 20			
Harwich Town	d										07 16												07 58	
Dovercourt	d										07 18												08 00	
Harwich International	d								07 15		07 21						07 50						08 03	
Wrabness	d										07 27						07 56						08 09	
Mistley	d										07 33						08 02						08 15	
Manningtree 2	d						07 28		07 32	07 44	07 38		07 49	07 59									08 20	
Walton-on-the-Naze	d		06 59																			07 40		08 00
Frinton-on-Sea	d		07 02																			07 43		08 03
Kirby Cross	d		07 05																			07 46		08 06
Clacton-on-Sea	d	06 51				07 05						07 16							07 45					
Thorpe-le-Soken 1	a	06 59	07 11			07 13						07 24							07 53			07 52		08 11
	d	06 59				07 13						07 24							07 53			07 58		08 12
Weeley	d	07 03										07 28										08 02		
Great Bentley	d	07 06										07 31										08 05		
Alresford (Essex)	d	07 10										07 35										08 09		
Wivenhoe 3	d	07 14				07 24						07 39							08 03			08 13		08 22
Hythe	d	07 18										07 43										08 17		08 26
Colchester Town	a	07 22																				08 21		
	d	07 27																		08 00		08 32		
Colchester 4	a	07 35				07 32	07 37		07 41		07 47	07 50	07 58	08 08					08 16	08 09		08 40	08 29	08 35
Colchester 4	d					07 33	07 38		07 42		07 54		07 59	08 10					08 18			08 48	08 37	
Marks Tey 2	d						07 44		07 48				08 05						08 24			→		
Kelvedon	d					07 43	07 49				08 04		08 10						08 30					
Braintree	d				07 26													08 12						
Braintree Freeport	d				07 29													08 14						
Cressing	d				07 32													08 17						
White Notley	d				07 35													08 20						
Witham 2	d				07 44	07 50	07 55		08 03		08 10		08 16					08 28	08 36				08 50	
Hatfield Peverel	d				07 48				08 07									08 32						
Chelmsford 3	d			07 49	07 55	07 59		08 09	08 14		08 19					08 30		08 39	08 45				08 59	
Ingatestone	d			07 56				08 16								08 37		08 46						
Shenfield 3	a			08 01		08 09		08 21	08 23		08 29					08 42		08 51	08 55					
Romford	a																							
Stratford 7 ⊖	a			08s18	08s20	08s25	08s28	08s38	08s41		08s45		08s48	08s52		08s59		09s08					09s23	
London Liverpool Street 15 ⊖	a			08 30	08 32	08 38	08 40	08 50	08 54	08 42	08 58		09 01	09 04		09 11		09 19	09 21		09 24		09 36	

A The East Anglian
C To Cambridge

Table 11

Mondays to Fridays

until 26 July

Norwich, Ipswich, Harwich, Clacton, Walton-on-Naze, Colchester and Chelmsford - London

Network Diagram - see first Page of Table 5

		LE ◇1	LE 1	LE 1	LE 1	LE 1	LE ■1 ☕	LE 1	LE 1	LE 1	LE 1	LE ■1 ☕	LE 1	LE 1	LE 1	LE 1	LE 1	LE 1	LE ■1 ☕	LE 1	LE 1	LE 1
Norwich	d						08 00					08 30							09 00			
Diss	d						08 17					08 47							09 17			
Peterborough 8	d													07 45										
Stowmarket	d	08 11					08 29		08 44				09 14					09 29			
Needham Market	d								08 49													
Ipswich	a	08 24					08 41		09 00			09 08	09 28					09 41			
	d	08 26					08 43			08 48		09 09				09 30			09 43			09 52
Harwich Town	d		08 28															09 28				
Dovercourt	d		08 30															09 30				
Harwich International	d		08 33															09 33				
Wrabness	d		08 39															09 39				
Mistley	d		08 45															09 45				
Manningtree 2	d	08 36	08a50				08 53			08 58		09 19				09 40		09a50	09 53			10 02
Walton-on-the-Naze	d																09 00					
Frinton-on-Sea	d																09 03					
Kirby Cross	d																09 06					
Clacton-on-Sea	d					08 11								09 05									
Thorpe-le-Soken 1	a					08 19								09 13			09 12					
	d					08 19								09 13			09 17					
Weeley	d					08 23											09 21					
Great Bentley	d					08 26											09 24					
Alresford (Essex)	d					08 30											09 28					
Wivenhoe 3	d					08 34								09 23			09 32					
Hythe	d					08 38											09 36					
Colchester Town	a				←												09 40					
	d											08 58				09 35		09 44			10 00		
Colchester 4	a	08 45			08 40	08 46	09 02			09 08	09 05	09 28		09 31	09 42	09 49	09 52		10 02	10 07			10 11
Colchester 4	d	08 45			08 48		09 03			09 12		09 30		09 33	09 43	09 50			10 03				10 12
Marks Tey 2	d				08 54						09 18						09 56						10 18
Kelvedon	d				09 00						09 23						09 52						10 23
Braintree	d							09 00														10 00	
Braintree Freeport	d							09 02														10 02	
Cressing	d							09 05														10 05	
White Notley	d							09 08														10 08	
Witham 2	d			08 58	09 06			09 16		09 29				09 46	09 58	10 05					10 16	10 29
Hatfield Peverel	d			09 02							09 33													10 33
Chelmsford 3	d	09 04		09 09	09 15		09 21	09 26		09 40				09 56	10 07	10 14			10 21		10 26	10 40
Ingatestone	d			09 16				09 32						10 02							10 32	
Shenfield 3	a			09 21	09 25			09 38		09 50				10 08	10 17						10 38	10 50
Romford	a														10 26							
Stratford 7 ⊖	a	09s28		09s37	09s41			09 52		10 05				10 22	10 34				10s45		10 52	11 05
London Liverpool Street 15 ⊖	a	09 40		09 49	09 53		09 56	10 01		10 14		10 19		10 31	10 43	10 44			10 55		11 01	11 14

		LE 1	LE ◇1 ☕	LE 1	LE 1	LE 1	LE 1	LE ◇1 ☕	LE 1	LE 1	LE 1	LE 1	LE ◇1 ☕	LE 1	LE 1	LE 1	LE 1	LE 1	LE ◇1 ☕	LE 1	LE 1	LE 1	LE 1
Norwich	d		09 30					10 00					10 30						11 00				
Diss	d		09 47					10 17					10 47						11 17				
Peterborough 8	d													09 45										
Stowmarket	d	09 44					10 29				10 44		11 14					11 29				11 44
Needham Market	d	09 49									10 49											11 49
Ipswich	a	10 02	10 08					10 41				11 00	11 08	11 28					11 41				12 00
	d		10 09					10 43			10 52		11 09						11 43			11 52	
Harwich Town	d				10 28											11 28						
Dovercourt	d				10 30											11 30						
Harwich International	d				10 33											11 33						
Wrabness	d				10 39											11 39						
Mistley	d				10 45											11 45						
Manningtree 2	d		10 19		10a50			10 53			11 02		11 19			11a50			11 53			12 02	
Walton-on-the-Naze	d						10 00											11 00				
Frinton-on-Sea	d						10 03											11 03				
Kirby Cross	d						10 06											11 06				
Clacton-on-Sea	d			10 05											11 05							
Thorpe-le-Soken 1	a			10 13			10 12								11 13			11 12				
	d			10 13			10 17								11 13			11 17				
Weeley	d						10 21											11 21				
Great Bentley	d						10 24											11 24				
Alresford (Essex)	d						10 28											11 28				
Wivenhoe 3	d			10 23			10 32								11 23			11 32				
Hythe	d						10 36											11 36				
Colchester Town	a						10 40											11 40				
	d					10 35	10 44		11 00								11 35	11 44		12 00			
Colchester 4	a		10 28	10 31		10 42	10 52	11 02	11 07		11 11		11 28		11 31		11 42	11 52	12 02	12 07		12 11	
Colchester 4	d		10 30	10 33		10 43		11 03			11 12		11 30		11 33		11 43		12 03			12 12	
Marks Tey 2	d					10 49					11 18						11 49					12 18	
Kelvedon	d					10 54					11 23						11 54					12 23	
Braintree	d									11 00												12 00		
Braintree Freeport	d									11 02												12 02		
Cressing	d									11 05												12 05		
White Notley	d									11 08												12 08		
Witham 2	d			10 46		11 00				11 16	11 29				11 46		12 00				12 16	12 29	
Hatfield Peverel	d										11 33											11 33	
Chelmsford 3	d			10 56		11 09		11 21		11 26	11 40				11 56		12 09		12 21		12 26	12 40	
Ingatestone	d			11 02						11 32					12 02							12 32		
Shenfield 3	a			11 08		11 19				11 38	11 50				12 08		12 19				12 38	12 50	
Romford	a					11 28											12 28						
Stratford 7 ⊖	a			11 22		11 36		11s45		11 52	12 05				12 22		12 36		12s45		12 52	13 05	
London Liverpool Street 15 ⊖	a		11 19	11 31		11 45		11 55		12 01	12 14		12 19		12 31		12 45		12 55		13 01	13 14	

Table 11

Mondays to Fridays

until 26 July

Norwich, Ipswich, Harwich, Clacton, Walton-on-Naze, Colchester and Chelmsford - London

Network Diagram - see first Page of Table 5

		LE ◇1 ☕	LE 1	LE 1	LE 1	LE 1	LE ◇1 ☕	LE 1	LE 1	LE 1	LE 1	LE ◇1 ☕	LE 1	LE 1	LE 1	LE 1	LE 1	LE ◇1 ☕	LE 1	LE 1	LE 1	LE 1	LE ◇1 ☕
Norwich	d	11 30					12 00					12 30						13 00					13 30
Diss	d	11 47					12 17					12 47						13 17					13 47
Peterborough 8	d												11 45											
Stowmarket	d						12 29				12 44		13 13						13 29				13 44	
Needham Market	d										12 49											13 49	
Ipswich	a	12 08					12 41				13 00	13 08	13 28						13 41				14 00	14 08
	d	12 09					12 43			12 52		13 09							13 43			13 52		14 09
Harwich Town	d			12 28											13 28							
Dovercourt	d			12 30											13 30							
Harwich International	d			12 33											13 33							
Wrabness	d			12 39											13 39							
Mistley	d			12 45											13 45							
Manningtree 2	d	12 19		12a50			12 53			13 02		13 19			13a50			13 53			14 02		14 19
Walton-on-the-Naze	d					12 00											13 00					
Frinton-on-Sea	d					12 03											13 03					
Kirby Cross	d					12 06											13 06					
Clacton-on-Sea	d		12 05											13 05								
Thorpe-le-Soken 1	a		12 13			12 12								13 13			13 12					
	d		12 13			12 17								13 13			13 17					
Weeley	d					12 21											13 21					
Great Bentley	d					12 24											13 24					
Alresford (Essex)	d					12 28											13 28					
Wivenhoe 3	d		12 23			12 32								13 23			13 32					
Hythe	d					12 36											13 36					
Colchester Town	a					12 40											13 40					
	d				12 35	12 44		13 00								13 35	13 44		14 00				
Colchester 4	a	12 28	12 31		12 42	12 52	13 02	13 07		13 11		13 28		13 31		13 42	13 52	14 02	14 07		14 11		14 28
Colchester 4	d	12 30	12 33		12 43		13 03			13 12		13 30		13 33		13 43		14 03			14 12		14 30
Marks Tey 2	d				12 49					13 18						13 49					14 18		
Kelvedon	d				12 54					13 23						13 54					14 23		
Braintree	d								13 00											14 00			
Braintree Freeport	d								13 02											14 02			
Cressing	d								13 05											14 05			
White Notley	d								13 08											14 08			
Witham 2	d		12 46		13 00				13 16	13 29				13 46		14 00				14 16	14 29		
Hatfield Peverel	d									13 33												14 33		
Chelmsford 3	d		12 56		13 09		13 21		13 26	13 40				13 56		14 09		14 21		14 26	14 40		
Ingatestone	d		13 02						13 32					14 02						14 32			
Shenfield 3	a		13 08		13 19				13 38	13 50				14 08		14 19				14 38	14 50		
Romford	a				13 28											14 28						
Stratford 7 ⊖	a		13 22		13 36		13s45		13 52	14 05				14 22		14 36		14s45		14 52	15 05		
London Liverpool Street 15 ⊖	a	13 19	13 31		13 45		13 55		14 01	14 14		14 19		14 31		14 45		14 55		15 01	15 15		15 19

		LE 1	LE 1	LE 1	LE 1	LE ◇1 ☕	LE 1	LE 1	LE 1	LE 1	LE ◇1 ☕	LE 1	LE 1	LE 1	LE 1	LE 1	LE ◇1 ☕	LE 1	LE 1	LE 1	LE 1	LE ◇1 ☕
Norwich	d					14 00					14 30						15 00					15 30
Diss	d					14 17					14 47						15 17					15 47
Peterborough 8	d											13 45										
Stowmarket	d					14 29				14 44		15 13					15 29				15 44	
Needham Market	d										14 49											15 49	
Ipswich	a					14 41				15 00	15 08	15 28					15 41				16 00	16 08
	d					14 43			14 52		15 09						15 43			15 52		16 09
Harwich Town	d		14 28											15 28							
Dovercourt	d		14 30											15 30							
Harwich International	d		14 33											15 33							
Wrabness	d		14 39											15 39							
Mistley	d		14 45											15 45							
Manningtree 2	d		14a50			14 53			15 02		15 19			15a50			15 53			16 02		16 19
Walton-on-the-Naze	d				14 00											15 00					
Frinton-on-Sea	d				14 03											15 03					
Kirby Cross	d				14 06											15 06					
Clacton-on-Sea	d	14 05											15 05								
Thorpe-le-Soken 1	a	14 13			14 12								15 13			15 12					
	d	14 13			14 17								15 13			15 17					
Weeley	d				14 21											15 21					
Great Bentley	d				14 24											15 24					
Alresford (Essex)	d				14 28											15 28					
Wivenhoe 3	d	14 23			14 32								15 23			15 32					
Hythe	d				14 36											15 36					
Colchester Town	a				14 40											15 40					
	d			14 35	14 44		15 00								15 35	15 44		16 00				
Colchester 4	a	14 31		14 42	14 52	15 02	15 07		15 11		15 28		15 31		15 42	15 52	16 02	16 07		16 11		16 28
Colchester 4	d	14 33		14 43		15 03			15 12		15 30		15 33		15 43		16 03			16 12		16 30
Marks Tey 2	d			14 49					15 18						15 49					16 18		
Kelvedon	d			14 54					15 23						15 54					16 23		
Braintree	d							15 00											16 00			
Braintree Freeport	d							15 02											16 02			
Cressing	d							15 05											16 05			
White Notley	d							15 08											16 08			
Witham 2	d	14 46		15 00				15 16	15 29				15 46		16 00				16 16	16 29		
Hatfield Peverel	d								15 33												16 33		
Chelmsford 3	d	14 56		15 09		15 21		15 26	15 40				15 56		16 09		16 21		16 26	16 40		
Ingatestone	d	15 02						15 32					16 02						16 32			
Shenfield 3	a	15 08		15 19				15 38	15 50				16 08		16 19				16 38	16 50		
Romford	a			15 28																			
Stratford 7 ⊖	a	15 22		15 36		15s45		15 52	16 05				16 22		16 34		16s45		16 52	17 05		
London Liverpool Street 15 ⊖	a	15 33		15 45		15 55		16 01	16 14			16 17	16 31		16 44		16 55		17 03	17 16		17 19

Norwich, Ipswich, Harwich, Clacton, Walton-on-Naze, Colchester and Chelmsford - London

Network Diagram - see first Page of Table 5

		LE 1	LE 1	LE 1	LE 1	LE 1	LE ◇1		LE 1	LE 1	LE 1	LE 1	LE 1	LE ◇1	LE 1	LE 1	LE 1		LE 1	LE 1	LE 1	LE 1	LE ◇1	LE 1	LE 1
Norwich	d						16 00							16 30									17 00		
Diss	d						16 17							16 47									17 17		
Peterborough 8	d														15 45										
Stowmarket	d						16 29					16 44			17 13								17 29	17 45	
Needham Market	d											16 49												17 50	
Ipswich	a						16 41					17 00		17 08	17 28								17 41	18 04	
	d						16 43				16 52			17 09							17 33		17 43		
Harwich Town	d		16 28										16 53									17 28			18 00
Dovercourt	d		16 30										16 55									17 30			18 02
Harwich International	d		16 33										16 58									17 33			18 05
Wrabness	d		16 39										17 04									17 39			18 11
Mistley	d		16 45										17 10									17 45			18 17
Manningtree 2	d		16a50				16 53				17 02		17a15	17 19							17 43	17a50	17 53		18a22
Walton-on-the-Naze	d					16 00														17 00					
Frinton-on-Sea	d					16 03														17 03					
Kirby Cross	d					16 06														17 06					
Clacton-on-Sea	d	16 05														17 05									
Thorpe-le-Soken 1	a	16 13				16 12										17 13				17 12					
	d	16 13				16 17										17 13				17 17					
Weeley	d					16 21														17 21					
Great Bentley	d					16 24														17 24					
Alresford (Essex)	d					16 28														17 28					
Wivenhoe 3	d	16 23				16 32										17 23				17 32					
Hythe	d					16 36														17 36					
Colchester Town	a					16 40														17 40					
	d			16 35		16 44			16 56										17 30	17 44					
Colchester 4	a	16 31		16 42		16 54	17 02		17 05		17 11			17 28		17 31			17 37	17 52	17 52		18 02		
Colchester 4	d	16 33		16 43	16 53		17 03				17 12			17 30		17 33			17 48				18 03		
Marks Tey 2	d				16 59						17 18								17 54						
Kelvedon	d			16 52							17 23								17 59						
Braintree	d									17 00							17 44								
Braintree Freeport	d									17 02							17 46								
Cressing	d									17 05							17 49								
White Notley	d									17 08							17 52								
Witham 2	d	16 46		16 58	17 08					17 16	17 29					17 46	18 00		18 05						
Hatfield Peverel	d			17 02							17 33								18 09						
Chelmsford 3	d	16 56		17 09	17 17		17 21			17 26	17 40					17 56	18 09		18 16				18 21		
Ingatestone	d	17 02								17 32						18 02									
Shenfield 3	a	17 08		17 19	17 27					17 38	17 50					18 08	18 19		18 26						
Romford	a																18 28								
Stratford 7 ⊖	a	17 22		17 36	17 42		17s45			17 52	18 06					18 22	18 36		18 42				18s45		
London Liverpool Street 15 ⊖	a	17 34		17 46	17 53		17 58			18 01	18 15			18 19		18 31	18 45		18 51				18 55		

		LE 1	LE 1		LE ◇1	LE 1	LE 1	LE 1	LE 1	LE 1	LE 1	LE 1	LE 1		LE ◇1	LE 1	LE 1	LE 1	LE 1	LE ◇1	LE 1	LE 1	LE 1		LE 1
Norwich	d				17 30										18 00					18 30					
Diss	d				17 47										18 17					18 47					
Peterborough 8	d																								
Stowmarket	d				17 59										18 29			18 45							
Needham Market	d																	18 50							
Ipswich	a				18 11										18 41			19 02		19 08					
	d				18 13				18 22						18 43		18 47			19 09					
Harwich Town	d										18 26										19 05				
Dovercourt	d										18 28										19 07				
Harwich International	d										18 31										19 10				
Wrabness	d										18 37										19 16				
Mistley	d										18 43										19 22				
Manningtree 2	d								18 33		18a48				18 53		18 57			19 19	19a27				
Walton-on-the-Naze	d									17 57		18 33													
Frinton-on-Sea	d									18 00		18 36													
Kirby Cross	d									18 03		18 42													
Clacton-on-Sea	d					18 05																	19 02		
Thorpe-le-Soken 1	a					18 13				18 09		18 48											19 10		
	d					18 13				18 17													19 10		
Weeley	d									18 21															
Great Bentley	d									18 24															
Alresford (Essex)	d									18 28															
Wivenhoe 3	d					18 23				18 32													19 23		
Hythe	d									18 36															
Colchester Town	a									18 40															
	d						18 32			18 44									19 08						19 35
Colchester 4	a				18 28	18 33	18 39		18 42	18 52					19 02		19 06		19 15	19 28			19 31		19 42
Colchester 4	d		18 12		18 30	18 33			18 43				18 55		19 03		19 12			19 30			19 33		19 43
Marks Tey 2	d		18 18						18 49				19 01				19 18								19 49
Kelvedon	d		18 23						18 54								19 23								19 54
Braintree	d							18 33														19 24			
Braintree Freeport	d							18 36														19 27			
Cressing	d							18 39														19 30			
White Notley	d							18 42														19 33			
Witham 2	d	18 16	18 29			18 46		18 51	19 00				19 16				19 29					19 42	19 46		20 00
Hatfield Peverel	d		18 33					18 55								←	19 33								
Chelmsford 3	d	18 26	18 40			18 56		19 02	19 09				19 26		19 21	19 26	19 40					19 51	19 56		20 09
Ingatestone	d	18 32				19 02							→			19 32							20 02		
Shenfield 3	a	18 38	18 50			19 08		19 13	19 19							19 38	19 50						20 08		20 19
Romford	a								19 28																20 28
Stratford 7 ⊖	a	18 52	19 05			19 22		19 27	19 36						19s45	19 52	20 05					20 14	20 22		20 36
London Liverpool Street 15 ⊖	a	19 01	19 14		19 17	19 31		19 36	19 45						19 55	20 01	20 14			20 19		20 23	20 31		20 45

Norwich, Ipswich, Harwich, Clacton, Walton-on-Naze, Colchester and Chelmsford - London

Network Diagram - see first Page of Table 5

		LE 1	LE 1	LE 1	LE 1	LE 1	LE 1	LE ◇1	LE 1		LE 1	LE 1	LE 1	LE 1	LE ◇1	LE 1	LE 1	LE 1	LE 1		LE 1	LE 1	LE ◇1	LE 1	LE 1
Norwich	d							19 00							19 30								20 00		
Diss	d							19 17							19 47								20 17		
Peterborough 8	d		17 45																						
Stowmarket	d		19 13					19 29						19 44									20 29		
Needham Market	d													19 49											
Ipswich	a		19 28					19 41						20 00	20 09								20 41		
	d	19 23				19 35		19 43					19 52		20 09			20 20					20 43		
Harwich Town	d						19 28									20 05			20 28						
Dovercourt	d						19 30									20 07			20 30						
Harwich International	d						19 33									20 10			20 33						
Wrabness	d						19 39									20 16			20 39						
Mistley	d						19 45									20 22			20 45						
Manningtree 2	d	19 36				19 45	19a50	19 53					20 02		20 19	20a27		20 33	20a50				20 53		
Walton-on-the-Naze	d			18 54	19 15																	19 55		20 33	
Frinton-on-Sea	d			18 57	19 18																	19 58		20 36	
Kirby Cross	d			19 00	19 21																	20 01		20 42	
Clacton-on-Sea	d																20 05								
Thorpe-le-Soken 1	a			19 08	19 27												20 13					20 07		20 48	
	d			19 17													20 13					20 17			
Weeley	d			19 21																		20 21			
Great Bentley	d			19 24																		20 24			
Alresford (Essex)	d			19 28																		20 28			
Wivenhoe 3	d			19 32													20 23					20 32			
Hythe	d			19 36																		20 36			
Colchester Town	a			19 40																		20 40			
	d			19 44							20 00										20 35	20 44			21 00
Colchester 4	a	19 46		19 52		19 54		20 02			20 07		20 11		20 29		20 31	20 45			20 42	20 52	21 02		21 07
Colchester 4	d					19 55		20 03					20 12		20 30		20 33				20 50		21 03		
Marks Tey 2	d					20 01							20 18								20 56				
Kelvedon	d												20 23								21 01				
Braintree	d											20 11													
Braintree Freeport	d											20 13													
Cressing	d											20 16													
White Notley	d											20 19													
Witham 2	d					20 16						20 27	20 31				20 46				21 07				
Hatfield Peverel	d								←				20 35												
Chelmsford 3	d					20 26		20 21	20 26			20 36	20 42				20 56				21 16		21 21		
Ingatestone	d					→			20 32								21 02								
Shenfield 3	a								20 38			20 46	20 52				21 08				21 26				
Romford	a																								
Stratford 7 ⊖	a							20s45	20 52				21 07				21 22				21 42		21s45		
London Liverpool Street 15 ⊖	a							20 55	21 01			21 12	21 16		21 19		21 31				21 51		21 55		

		LE 1	LE 1	LE 1	LE ◇1		LE 1	LE 1	LE 1	LE ◇1	LE 1	LE 1	LE ◇1 A	LE ◇1 MT WO B	LE 1		LE 1 A	LE 1 MT WO B	LE 1 A	LE 1 MT WO B	LE 1 A	LE 1 MT WO B	LE 1 A	LE 1 MT WO B	LE 1
Norwich	d				20 30								21 00	21 00											
Diss	d				20 47								21 17	21 17											
Peterborough 8	d									19 45															
Stowmarket	d			20 44						21 09			21 29	21 29	21 44										
Needham Market	d			20 49											21 49										
Ipswich	a			21 00	21 08					21 23			21 41	21 41	22 00										
	d			21 00	21 09					21 25			21 43	21 43									22 23	22 23	
Harwich Town	d							21 05				21 28													
Dovercourt	d							21 07				21 30													
Harwich International	d		20 45	21a29				21 10				21 33													
Wrabness	d							21 16				21 39													
Mistley	d							21 22				21 45													
Manningtree 2	d		20 58		21 19			21 27		21 35		21a50	21 53	21 53									22 33	22 33	
Walton-on-the-Naze	d										21 00														22 00
Frinton-on-Sea	d										21 03														22 03
Kirby Cross	d										21 06														22 06
Clacton-on-Sea	d						21 05														22 05	22 05			
Thorpe-le-Soken 1	a						21 13				21 12										22 13	22 13			22 12
	d						21 13				21 17										22 13	22 13			22 17
Weeley	d										21 21														22 21
Great Bentley	d										21 24														22 24
Alresford (Essex)	d										21 28														22 28
Wivenhoe 3	d						21 23				21 32										22 23	22 23			22 32
Hythe	d										21 36														22 36
Colchester Town	a										21 40														22 40
	d								21 35		21 44								22 00	22 00					22 44
Colchester 4	a		21 07		21 28		21 31	21 36	21 42	21 46	21 52		22 02	22 02					22 07	22 07	22 31	22 31	22 42	22 42	22 52
Colchester 4	d		21 12		21 30		21 33		21 43				22 03	22 03					22 12	22 12	22 33	22 33	22 43	22 43	
Marks Tey 2	d		21 18						21 49										22 18	22 18			22 49	22 49	
Kelvedon	d		21 23						21 54										22 23	22 23			22 54	22 54	
Braintree	d	21 00															22 00	22 00							
Braintree Freeport	d	21 02															22 02	22 02							
Cressing	d	21 05															22 05	22 05							
White Notley	d	21 08															22 08	22 08							
Witham 2	d	21 16	21 29				21 46		22 00								22 16	22 16	22 29	22 29	22 46	22 46	23 00	23 00	
Hatfield Peverel	d		21 33																22 33	22 33					
Chelmsford 3	d	21 26	21 40				21 56		22 09				22 21	22 21			22 26	22 26	22 40	22 40	22 56	22 56	23 09	23 09	
Ingatestone	d	21 32					22 02										22 32	22 32			23 02	23 02			
Shenfield 3	a	21 38	21 50				22 08		22 19								22 38	22 38	22 50	22 50	23 08	23 08	23 19	23 19	
Romford	a								22 28													23 19	23 28	23 31	
Stratford 7 ⊖	a	21 52	22 05				22 22		22 36				22s45	22s51			22 52	22 54	23 05	23 11	23 22	23 31	23 36	23 41	
London Liverpool Street 15 ⊖	a	22 01	22 14		22 19		22 31		22 45				22 55	23 00			23 01	23 03	23 15	23 20	23 31	23 40	23 45	23 50	

A ThFO until 15 June, from 21 June until 26 July B until 20 June

Table 11

Mondays to Fridays

until 26 July

Norwich, Ipswich, Harwich, Clacton, Walton-on-Naze, Colchester and Chelmsford - London

Network Diagram - see first Page of Table 5

		LE	LE	LE	LE	LE	LE	LE	LE	LE		LE	LE	LE	LE
		[1]	[1]	◇[1]	◇[1]	[1]	[1]	[1]	[1]	◇[1]		[1]	[1]	[1]	
				A	MT WO B									A	
Norwich	d			22 00	22 00							23 05			
Diss	d			22 17	22 17							23 22			
Peterborough [8]	d									21 45					
Stowmarket	d			22 29	22 29	22 44				23 06		23 34			23 47
Needham Market	d					22 49									23 52
Ipswich	a			22 41	22 41	23 00				23 18		23 48			00 05
	d			22 43	22 43					23 19					
Harwich Town	d	22 28											23 28		
Dovercourt	d	22 30											23 30		
Harwich International	d	22 33											23 33		
Wrabness	d	22 39											23 39		
Mistley	d	22 45											23 45		
Manningtree [2]	d	22a50		22 53	22 53					23 29			23 50		
Walton-on-the-Naze	d							23 00							
Frinton-on-Sea	d							23 03							
Kirby Cross	d							23 06							
Clacton-on-Sea	d								23 05						
Thorpe-le-Soken [1]	a							23 12	23 13						
	d								23 13						
Weeley	d								23 17						
Great Bentley	d								23 20						
Alresford (Essex)	d								23 24						
Wivenhoe [3]	d								23 28						
Hythe	d								23 32						
Colchester Town	a														
	d						23 00								
Colchester [4]	a			23 02	23 02		23 07		23 38	23 40			23 59		
Colchester [4]	d			23 03	23 03										
Marks Tey [2]	d														
Kelvedon	d														
Braintree	d		22 56											23 45	
Braintree Freeport	d		22 58											23 47	
Cressing	d		23 01											23 50	
White Notley	d		23 04											23 53	
Witham [2]	d		23a12	23 16	23 16									00a01	
Hatfield Peverel	d														
Chelmsford [3]	d			23 25	23 25										
Ingatestone	d														
Shenfield [3]	a			23s36	23 36										
Romford	a														
Stratford [7] ⊖	a			23s52	00s04										
London Liverpool Street [15] ⊖	a			00 02	00 14										

A ThFO until 15 June, from 21 June until 26 July B until 20 June

Table 11

Mondays to Fridays

27 July to 10 August

Norwich, Ipswich, Harwich, Clacton, Walton-on-Naze, Colchester and Chelmsford - London

Network Diagram - see first Page of Table 5

		LE	LE	LE	LE	LE	LE	LE	LE	LE	LE	LE	LE	LE	LE	LE	LE	LE	LE	LE	LE	LE	LE	LE	LE
		◇[1]	◇[1]	◇[1]		[1]	[1]	[1]	[1]	◇[1]	[1]	[1]	[1]	◇[1]	[1]	[1]	[1]	[1]	[1]	[1]	[1]	[2] [1]	[1]	[1]	[1]
		A	MX B	MO ⊡	C	D	MX B	MO						⊡								⊡			
Norwich	d	22p00	22p00	22p00										05 00								05 30			
Diss	d	22p17	22p17	22p17										05 18								05 48			
Peterborough [8]	d																								
Stowmarket	d	22p29	22p29	22p29	23p47			00 47						05 30					05 54			06 00			
Needham Market	d				23p52			00 52											05 59						
Ipswich	a	22p41	22p41	22p41	00 05			01 03						05 42					06 09			06 12			
	d	22p43	22p43	22p43						05 14				05 44				06 00				06 14			
Harwich Town	d										05 24														
Dovercourt	d										05 26														
Harwich International	d										05 29														06 25
Wrabness	d										05 35														
Mistley	d										05 41														
Manningtree [2]	d	22p53	22p53	22p53						05 25	05a46			05 54				06 11				06 24			06 39
Walton-on-the-Naze	d														05 35					06 05					
Frinton-on-Sea	d														05 38					06 08					
Kirby Cross	d														05 41					06 11					
Clacton-on-Sea	d												05 20				05 40						06 10		
Thorpe-le-Soken [1]	a												05 28		05 47		05 48			06 17			06 18		
	d												05 28				05 48						06 18		
Weeley	d																05 52								
Great Bentley	d																05 56								
Alresford (Essex)	d																06 00								
Wivenhoe [3]	d												05 38				06 04						06 29		
Hythe	d																06 08						06 33		
Colchester Town	a																								
	d																				06 19				
Colchester [4]	a	23p02	23p02	23p02						05 34			05 46	06 03			06 14	06 20			06 26	06 33	06 39		06 48
Colchester [4]	d	23p03	23p03	23p03					05 12	05 35			05 47	06 05			06 15	06 20			06 27	06 35	06 40		06 49
Marks Tey [2]	d								05 18				05 53					06 26			06 33				06 55
Kelvedon	d								05 23				05 59				06 25	06 32					06 50		07 00
Braintree	d					00 25	00 27					05 45												06 40	
Braintree Freeport	d					00 27	00 29					05 47												06 42	
Cressing	d					00 30	00 32					05 50												06 45	
White Notley	d					00 33	00 35					05 53												06 48	
Witham [2]	d	23p16	23p16	23p16		00a41	00a43		05 29	05 48		06a02	06 05			06 18	06 31	06 38			06 47			06 57	07 06
Hatfield Peverel	d								05 33							06 22								07 02	
Chelmsford [3]	d	23p25	23p25	23p25					05 40	05 58			06 14			06 29	06 40	06 47			06 56		07 03	07 09	
Ingatestone	d								05 47							06 36					07 03				
Shenfield [3]	a	23b36	23b36	23b36					05 52				06 24			06 41	06 50				07 07			07 19	
Romford	a																								
Stratford [7] ⊖	a	23b52							06 07	06s22			06 39	06s44		06s57	07s06				07s23	07s15	07s27	07s35	07s38
London Liverpool Street [15] ⊖	a	00 02	00 03	00 03					06 16	06 34			06 48	06 54		07 09	07 18	07 24			07 35	07 27	07 38	07 46	07 50

		LE	LE	LE	LE	LE		LE	LE	LE	LE	LE	LE	LE	LE	LE		LE	LE	LE	LE	LE	LE	LE	LE
		[1]	[1]	[1]	[2] [1]	[1]		[1]	[1]	[1]	[1]	[1]	[1]		[1]	[1]		[2] [1]	[1]	[1]	[1]	[1]	[1]	◇[1]	[1]
					⊡													⊡							
Norwich	d				06 00													06 25							
Diss	d				06 18													06 43							
Peterborough [8]	d																								
Stowmarket	d				06 30									06 44				06 55						07 05	
Needham Market	d													06 49											
Ipswich	a				06 42									07 01				07 07						07 18	
	d		06 35		06 44						06 52		06 59					07 09						07 18	
Harwich Town	d			06 24								06 52													
Dovercourt	d			06 26								06 54													
Harwich International	d			06 29								06 57	07a28												
Wrabness	d			06 35								07 03													
Mistley	d			06 41								07 09													
Manningtree [2]	d		06 45	06a46	06 54						07 02	07a14						07 19						07 28	
Walton-on-the-Naze	d							06 32												06 59					
Frinton-on-Sea	d							06 35												07 02					
Kirby Cross	d							06 38												07 05					
Clacton-on-Sea	d					06 28				06 38						06 47			06 51				07 05		
Thorpe-le-Soken [1]	a					06 36		06 44		06 46						06 55			06 59	07 11			07 13		
	d					06 36				06 46						06 55			06 59				07 13		
Weeley	d					06 40													07 03						
Great Bentley	d					06 43													07 06						
Alresford (Essex)	d					06 47													07 10						
Wivenhoe [3]	d					06 51				06 57						07 06			07 14				07 24		
Hythe	d					06 55				07 01						07 10			07 18						
Colchester Town	a					06 59													07 22						
	d	06 43				07 03													07 27						
Colchester [4]	a	06 50	06 54		07 03	07 13				07 07	07 12					07 16		07 28	07 35				07 32	07 37	
Colchester [4]	d		06 55		07 05					07 08	07 13					07 17		07 30					07 33	07 38	
Marks Tey [2]	d		07 01								07 19					07 23								07 44	
Kelvedon	d									07 18						07 29							07 43	07 49	
Braintree	d																					07 26			
Braintree Freeport	d																					07 29			
Cressing	d																					07 32			
White Notley	d																					07 35			
Witham [2]	d		07 10						07 17						07 29	07 35						07 44	07 50	07 55	
Hatfield Peverel	d														07 33							07 48			
Chelmsford [3]	d		07 19						07 27	07 31	07 35				07 40						07 49	07 55	07 59		08 09
Ingatestone	d								07 33		07 42										07 56				08 16
Shenfield [3]	a								07 38	07 41					07 50						08 01		08 09		08 21
Romford	a																								
Stratford [7] ⊖	a		07 44						07s55	07s58	08s01				08s07	08s09					08s18	08s20	08s25	08s28	08s38
London Liverpool Street [15] ⊖	a		07 56		07 58				08 07	08 09	08 13				08 19	08 21		08 23			08 30	08 32	08 38	08 40	08 50

A 27 July
B from 31 July until 10 August
C not 30 July, 6 August
D 27 July, 30 July, 6 August
b Previous night, stops to set down only

27 July to 10 August

Norwich, Ipswich, Harwich, Clacton, Walton-on-Naze, Colchester and Chelmsford - London

Network Diagram - see first Page of Table 5

		LE		LE	LE	LE	LE	LE	LE	LE	LE	LE	LE		LE	LE	LE	LE	LE	LE	LE	LE	LE		LE
		1		■ 1 ☕	1	1	1	■ 1 ☕		1	1	1	1		■ 1 A ☕	1	1	1	◇1	1	1	1	1		■ 1 ☕
Norwich	d			06 50				07 05							07 40										08 00
Diss	d			07 08				07 23							07 58										08 17
Peterborough	d																								
Stowmarket	d			07 20				07 35	07 45										08 11						08 29
Needham Market	d								07 50																
Ipswich	a			07 32				07 47	08 03						08 18				08 24						08 41
	d			07 34			07 38	07 49							08 20				08 26						08 43
Harwich Town	d				07 16												07 58			08 28					
Dovercourt	d				07 18												08 00			08 30					
Harwich International	d	07 15			07 21												08 03			08 33					
Wrabness	d				07 27												08 09			08 39					
Mistley	d				07 33												08 15			08 45					
Manningtree	d	07 32		07 44	07 38		07 49	07 59									08 20		08 36	08a50					08 53
Walton-on-the-Naze	d															07 40		08 00							
Frinton-on-Sea	d															07 43		08 03							
Kirby Cross	d															07 46		08 06							
Clacton-on-Sea	d					07 16						07 45											08 11		
Thorpe-le-Soken	a					07 24						07 53				07 52		08 11					08 19		
	d					07 24						07 53				07 58		08 12					08 19		
Weeley	d					07 28										08 02							08 23		
Great Bentley	d					07 31										08 05							08 26		
Alresford (Essex)	d					07 35										08 09							08 30		
Wivenhoe	d					07 39						08 03				08 13		08 22					08 34		
Hythe	d					07 43										08 17		08 26					08 38		
Colchester Town	a															08 21						←			
	d												08 00			08 32									
Colchester	a	07 41			07 47	07 50	07 58	08 08				08 16	08 09			08 40	08 29	08 35	08 45			08 40	08 46		09 02
Colchester	d	07 42			07 54		07 59	08 10				08 18				08 48	08 37		08 45			08 48			09 03
Marks Tey	d	07 48					08 05					08 24				→						08 54			
Kelvedon	d				08 04		08 10					08 30										09 00			
Braintree	d										08 12														
Braintree Freeport	d										08 14														
Cressing	d										08 17														
White Notley	d										08 20														
Witham	d	08 03			08 10		08 16				08 28	08 36					08 50				08 58	09 06			
Hatfield Peverel	d	08 07									08 32										09 02				
Chelmsford	d	08 14			08 19					08 30	08 39	08 45					08 59		09 04		09 09	09 15			09 21
Ingatestone	d									08 37	08 46										09 16				
Shenfield	a	08 23			08 29					08 42	08 51	08 55									09 21	09 25			
Romford	a																								
Stratford ⊖	a	08s41			08s45		08s48	08s52		08s59	09s08				09s14		09s23		09s28		09s37	09s41			
London Liverpool Street ⊖	a	08 54		08 42	08 58		09 01	09 04		09 11	09 19	09 21			09 26		09 36		09 40		09 49	09 53			09 56

A The East Anglian

27 July to 10 August

Norwich, Ipswich, Harwich, Clacton, Walton-on-Naze, Colchester and Chelmsford - London

Network Diagram - see first Page of Table 5

		LE	LE	LE	LE	LE	LE	LE	LE		LE	LE	LE	LE	LE	LE	LE	LE	LE		LE	LE	LE	LE	LE
		1	1	1	1	■ 1 ☕	1	1	1		1	1	1	■ 1 ☕	1	1	1	1	◇1 ☕		1	1	1	1	◇1 ☕
Norwich	d					08 30								09 00					09 30						10 00
Diss	d					08 47								09 17					09 47						10 17
Peterborough	d						07 45																		
Stowmarket	d		08 44				09 14							09 29				09 44							10 29
Needham Market	d		08 49															09 49							
Ipswich	a		09 00			09 08	09 28							09 41				10 02	10 08						10 41
	d			08 48		09 09					09 30			09 43			09 52		10 09						10 43
Harwich Town	d												09 28									10 28			
Dovercourt	d												09 30									10 30			
Harwich International	d												09 33									10 33			
Wrabness	d												09 39									10 39			
Mistley	d												09 45									10 45			
Manningtree	d			08 58		09 19					09 40		09a50	09 53			10 02		10 19			10a50			10 53
Walton-on-the-Naze	d											09 00												10 00	
Frinton-on-Sea	d											09 03												10 03	
Kirby Cross	d											09 06												10 06	
Clacton-on-Sea	d							09 05													10 05				
Thorpe-le-Soken	a							09 13				09 12									10 13			10 12	
	d							09 13				09 17									10 13			10 17	
Weeley	d											09 21												10 21	
Great Bentley	d											09 24												10 24	
Alresford (Essex)	d											09 28												10 28	
Wivenhoe	d							09 23				09 32									10 23			10 32	
Hythe	d											09 36												10 36	
Colchester Town	a											09 40												10 40	
	d				08 58				09 35			09 44			10 00								10 35	10 44	
Colchester	a			09 08	09 05	09 28		09 31	09 42		09 49	09 52		10 02	10 07		10 11		10 28		10 31		10 42	10 52	11 02
Colchester	d			09 12		09 30		09 33	09 43		09 50			10 03			10 12		10 30		10 33		10 43		11 03
Marks Tey	d			09 18							09 56						10 18						10 49		
Kelvedon	d			09 23					09 52								10 23						10 54		
Braintree	d	09 00														10 00									
Braintree Freeport	d	09 02														10 02									
Cressing	d	09 05														10 05									
White Notley	d	09 08														10 08									
Witham	d	09 16		09 29				09 46	09 58		10 05					10 16	10 29				10 46		11 00		
Hatfield Peverel	d			09 33													10 33								
Chelmsford	d	09 26		09 40				09 56	10 07		10 14			10 21		10 26	10 40				10 56		11 09		11 21
Ingatestone	d	09 32						10 02								10 32					11 02				
Shenfield	a	09 38		09 50				10 08	10 17							10 38	10 50				11 08		11 19		
Romford	a								10 26														11 28		
Stratford ⊖	a	09 52		10 05				10 22	10 34					10s45		10 52	11 05				11 22		11 36		11s45
London Liverpool Street ⊖	a	10 01		10 14		10 19		10 31	10 43		10 44			10 55		11 01	11 14		11 19		11 31		11 45		11 55

		LE	LE	LE	LE		LE	LE	LE	LE	LE	LE	LE	LE	LE		LE	LE	LE	LE	LE	LE	LE	LE	LE
		1	1	1	1		◇1 ☕	1	1	1	1	1	◇1 ☕	1	1		1	1	◇1 ☕	1	1	1	1	◇1 ☕	1
Norwich	d						10 30						11 00						11 30					12 00	
Diss	d						10 47						11 17						11 47					12 17	
Peterborough	d							09 45																	
Stowmarket	d				10 44			11 14					11 29					11 44						12 29	
Needham Market	d				10 49													11 49							
Ipswich	a				11 00		11 08	11 28					11 41					12 00	12 08					12 41	
	d			10 52			11 09						11 43				11 52		12 09					12 43	
Harwich Town	d									11 28											12 28				
Dovercourt	d									11 30											12 30				
Harwich International	d									11 33											12 33				
Wrabness	d									11 39											12 39				
Mistley	d									11 45											12 45				
Manningtree	d			11 02			11 19			11a50			11 53				12 02		12 19		12a50			12 53	
Walton-on-the-Naze	d											11 00											12 00		
Frinton-on-Sea	d											11 03											12 03		
Kirby Cross	d											11 06											12 06		
Clacton-on-Sea	d								11 05											12 05					
Thorpe-le-Soken	a								11 13			11 12								12 13			12 12		
	d								11 13			11 17								12 13			12 17		
Weeley	d											11 21											12 21		
Great Bentley	d											11 24											12 24		
Alresford (Essex)	d											11 28											12 28		
Wivenhoe	d								11 23			11 32								12 23			12 32		
Hythe	d											11 36											12 36		
Colchester Town	a											11 40											12 40		
	d	11 00									11 35	11 44		12 00								12 35	12 44		13 00
Colchester	a	11 07		11 11			11 28		11 31		11 42	11 52	12 02	12 07			12 11		12 28	12 31		12 42	12 52	13 02	13 07
Colchester	d			11 12			11 30		11 33		11 43		12 03				12 12		12 30	12 33		12 43		13 03	
Marks Tey	d			11 18							11 49						12 18					12 49			
Kelvedon	d			11 23							11 54						12 23					12 54			
Braintree	d		11 00												12 00										
Braintree Freeport	d		11 02												12 02										
Cressing	d		11 05												12 05										
White Notley	d		11 08												12 08										
Witham	d		11 16	11 29					11 46		12 00				12 16		12 29			12 46		13 00			
Hatfield Peverel	d			11 33													12 33								
Chelmsford	d		11 26	11 40					11 56		12 09		12 21		12 26		12 40			12 56		13 09		13 21	
Ingatestone	d		11 32						12 02						12 32					13 02					
Shenfield	a		11 38	11 50					12 08		12 19				12 38		12 50			13 08		13 19			
Romford	a										12 28											13 28			
Stratford ⊖	a		11 52	12 05					12 22		12 36		12s45		12 52		13 05			13 22		13 36		13s45	
London Liverpool Street ⊖	a		12 01	12 14			12 19		12 31		12 45		12 55		13 01		13 14		13 19	13 31		13 45		13 55	

Norwich, Ipswich, Harwich, Clacton, Walton-on-Naze, Colchester and Chelmsford - London

Network Diagram - see first Page of Table 5

		LE 1	LE 1	LE 1	LE ◇1 ⊡	LE 1	LE 1	LE 1	LE 1	LE 1	LE ◇1 ⊡	LE 1	LE 1	LE 1	LE 1	LE ◇1 ⊡	LE 1	LE 1	LE 1	LE 1	LE ◇1 ⊡	LE 1
Norwich	d				12 30						13 00					13 30					14 00	
Diss	d				12 47						13 17					13 47					14 17	
Peterborough 8	d					11 45																
Stowmarket	d			12 44		13 13					13 29				13 44						14 29	
Needham Market	d			12 49											13 49							
Ipswich	a			13 00	13 08	13 28					13 41				14 00	14 08					14 41	
	d		12 52		13 09						13 43			13 52		14 09					14 43	
Harwich Town	d							13 28										14 28				
Dovercourt	d							13 30										14 30				
Harwich International	d							13 33										14 33				
Wrabness	d							13 39										14 39				
Mistley	d							13 45										14 45				
Manningtree 2	d		13 02		13 19			13a50			13 53			14 02		14 19		14a50			14 53	
Walton-on-the-Naze	d									13 00										14 00		
Frinton-on-Sea	d									13 03										14 03		
Kirby Cross	d									13 06										14 06		
Clacton-on-Sea	d						13 05										14 05					
Thorpe-le-Soken 1	a						13 13			13 12							14 13			14 12		
	d						13 13			13 17							14 13			14 17		
Weeley	d									13 21										14 21		
Great Bentley	d									13 24										14 24		
Alresford (Essex)	d									13 28										14 28		
Wivenhoe 3	d						13 23			13 32							14 23			14 32		
Hythe	d									13 36										14 36		
Colchester Town	a									13 40										14 40		
	d								13 35	13 44		14 00							14 35	14 44		15 00
Colchester 4	a		13 11		13 28		13 31		13 42	13 52	14 02	14 07		14 11		14 28	14 31		14 42	14 52	15 02	15 07
Colchester 4	d		13 12		13 30		13 33		13 43		14 03			14 12		14 30	14 33		14 43		15 03	
Marks Tey 2	d		13 18						13 49					14 18					14 49			
Kelvedon	d		13 23						13 54					14 23					14 54			
Braintree	d	13 00											14 00									
Braintree Freeport	d	13 02											14 02									
Cressing	d	13 05											14 05									
White Notley	d	13 08											14 08									
Witham 2	d	13 16	13 29				13 46		14 00				14 16	14 29			14 46		15 00			
Hatfield Peverel	d		13 33											14 33								
Chelmsford 3	d	13 26	13 40				13 56		14 09		14 21		14 26	14 40			14 56		15 09		15 21	
Ingatestone	d	13 32					14 02						14 32				15 02					
Shenfield 3	a	13 38	13 50				14 08		14 19				14 38	14 50			15 08		15 19			
Romford	a								14 28										15 28			
Stratford 7 ⊖	a	13 52	14 05				14 22		14 36		14s45		14 52	15 05			15 22		15 36		15s45	
London Liverpool Street 15 ⊖	a	14 01	14 14		14 19		14 31		14 45		14 55		15 01	15 15		15 19	15 33		15 45		15 55	

		LE 1	LE 1	LE 1	LE ◇1 ⊡	LE 1	LE 1	LE 1	LE 1	LE 1	LE ◇1 ⊡	LE 1	LE 1	LE 1	LE 1	LE ◇1 ⊡	LE 1	LE 1	LE 1	LE 1	LE 1	LE ◇1 ⊡	LE 1
Norwich	d				14 30						15 00					15 30						16 00	
Diss	d				14 47						15 17					15 47						16 17	
Peterborough 8	d					13 45																	
Stowmarket	d			14 44		15 13					15 29				15 44							16 29	
Needham Market	d			14 49											15 49								
Ipswich	a			15 00	15 08	15 28					15 41				16 00	16 08						16 41	
	d		14 52		15 09						15 43			15 52		16 09						16 43	
Harwich Town	d							15 28										16 28					
Dovercourt	d							15 30										16 30					
Harwich International	d							15 33										16 33					
Wrabness	d							15 39										16 39					
Mistley	d							15 45										16 45					
Manningtree 2	d		15 02		15 19			15a50			15 53			16 02		16 19		16a50				16 53	
Walton-on-the-Naze	d									15 00											16 00		
Frinton-on-Sea	d									15 03											16 03		
Kirby Cross	d									15 06											16 06		
Clacton-on-Sea	d						15 05										16 05						
Thorpe-le-Soken 1	a						15 13			15 12							16 13				16 12		
	d						15 13			15 17							16 13				16 17		
Weeley	d									15 21											16 21		
Great Bentley	d									15 24											16 24		
Alresford (Essex)	d									15 28											16 28		
Wivenhoe 3	d						15 23			15 32							16 23				16 32		
Hythe	d									15 36											16 36		
Colchester Town	a									15 40											16 40		
	d								15 35	15 44		16 00							16 35		16 44		16 56
Colchester 4	a		15 11		15 28		15 31		15 42	15 52	16 02	16 07		16 11		16 28	16 31		16 42		16 54	17 02	17 05
Colchester 4	d		15 12		15 30		15 33		15 43		16 03			16 12		16 30	16 33		16 43	16 53		17 03	
Marks Tey 2	d		15 18						15 49					16 18						16 59			
Kelvedon	d		15 23						15 54					16 23					16 52				
Braintree	d	15 00											16 00										
Braintree Freeport	d	15 02											16 02										
Cressing	d	15 05											16 05										
White Notley	d	15 08											16 08										
Witham 2	d	15 16	15 29				15 46		16 00				16 16	16 29			16 46		16 58	17 08			
Hatfield Peverel	d		15 33											16 33					17 02				
Chelmsford 3	d	15 26	15 40				15 56		16 09		16 21		16 26	16 40			16 56		17 09	17 17		17 21	
Ingatestone	d	15 32					16 02						16 32				17 02						
Shenfield 3	a	15 38	15 50				16 08		16 19				16 38	16 50			17 08		17 19	17 27			
Romford	a																						
Stratford 7 ⊖	a	15 52	16 05				16 22		16 34		16s45		16 52	17 05			17 22		17 36	17 42		17s45	
London Liverpool Street 15 ⊖	a	16 01	16 14		16 17		16 31		16 44		16 55		17 03	17 16		17 19	17 34		17 46	17 53		17 58	

Norwich, Ipswich, Harwich, Clacton, Walton-on-Naze, Colchester and Chelmsford - London

Network Diagram - see first Page of Table 5

		LE 1	LE 1	LE 1	LE 1	LE ◇1 ⊡	LE 1	LE 1	LE 1	LE 1	LE 1	LE 1	LE 1	LE ◇1 ⊡	LE 1	LE 1	LE 1	LE 1	LE ◇1 ⊡	LE 1	LE 1	LE 1
Norwich	d					16 30								17 00					17 30			
Diss	d					16 47								17 17					17 47			
Peterborough 8	d						15 45															
Stowmarket	d			16 44			17 13							17 29	17 45				17 59			
Needham Market	d			16 49											17 50							
Ipswich	a			17 00		17 08	17 28							17 41	18 04				18 11			
	d		16 52			17 09						17 33		17 43					18 13			
Harwich Town	d				16 53								17 28			18 00						
Dovercourt	d				16 55								17 30			18 02						
Harwich International	d				16 58								17 33			18 05						
Wrabness	d				17 04								17 39			18 11						
Mistley	d				17 10								17 45			18 17						
Manningtree 2	d		17 02		17a15	17 19						17 43	17a50	17 53		18a22						
Walton-on-the-Naze	d										17 00											
Frinton-on-Sea	d										17 03											
Kirby Cross	d										17 06											
Clacton-on-Sea	d							17 05												18 05		
Thorpe-le-Soken 1	a							17 13			17 12									18 13		
	d							17 13			17 17									18 13		
Weeley	d										17 21											
Great Bentley	d										17 24											
Alresford (Essex)	d										17 28											
Wivenhoe 3	d							17 23			17 32									18 23		
Hythe	d										17 36											
Colchester Town	a										17 40											
	d									17 30	17 44										18 32	
Colchester 4	a		17 11			17 28		17 31		17 37	17 52	17 52		18 02					18 28	18 33	18 39	
Colchester 4	d		17 12			17 30		17 33		17 48				18 03				18 12	18 30	18 33		
Marks Tey 2	d		17 18							17 54								18 18				
Kelvedon	d		17 23							17 59								18 23				
Braintree	d	17 00							17 44													18 33
Braintree Freeport	d	17 02							17 46													18 36
Cressing	d	17 05							17 49													18 39
White Notley	d	17 08							17 52													18 42
Witham 2	d	17 16	17 29					17 46	18 00	18 05							18 16	18 29		18 46		18 51
Hatfield Peverel	d		17 33							18 09								18 33				18 55
Chelmsford 3	d	17 26	17 40					17 56	18 09	18 16				18 21			18 26	18 40		18 56		19 02
Ingatestone	d	17 32						18 02									18 32			19 02		
Shenfield 3	a	17 38	17 50					18 08	18 19	18 26							18 38	18 50		19 08		19 13
Romford	a								18 28													
Stratford 7 ⊖	a	17 52	18 06					18 22	18 36	18 42				18s45			18 52	19 05		19 22		19 27
London Liverpool Street 15 ⊖	a	18 01	18 15			18 19		18 31	18 45	18 51				18 55			19 01	19 14	19 17	19 31		19 36

		LE 1	LE 1	LE 1	LE 1	LE 1	LE ◇1 ⊡	LE 1	LE 1	LE 1	LE 1	LE ◇1 ⊡	LE 1	LE 1	LE 1	LE 1	LE 1	LE 1	LE 1	LE 1	LE 1	LE 1	LE ◇1 ⊡
Norwich	d						18 00					18 30											19 00
Diss	d						18 17					18 47											19 17
Peterborough 8	d																	17 45					
Stowmarket	d						18 29			18 45								19 13					19 29
Needham Market	d									18 50													
Ipswich	a						18 41			19 02		19 08						19 28					19 41
	d	18 22					18 43		18 47			19 09					19 23				19 35		19 43
Harwich Town	d			18 26									19 05									19 28	
Dovercourt	d			18 28									19 07									19 30	
Harwich International	d			18 31									19 10									19 33	
Wrabness	d			18 37									19 16									19 39	
Mistley	d			18 43									19 22									19 45	
Manningtree 2	d	18 33		18a48			18 53		18 57			19 19	19a27				19 36				19 45	19a50	19 53
Walton-on-the-Naze	d		17 57		18 33														18 54	19 15			
Frinton-on-Sea	d		18 00		18 36														18 57	19 18			
Kirby Cross	d		18 03		18 42														19 00	19 21			
Clacton-on-Sea	d														19 02								
Thorpe-le-Soken 1	a		18 09		18 48										19 10				19 08	19 27			
	d		18 17												19 10				19 17				
Weeley	d		18 21																19 21				
Great Bentley	d		18 24																19 24				
Alresford (Essex)	d		18 28																19 28				
Wivenhoe 3	d		18 32												19 23				19 32				
Hythe	d		18 36																19 36				
Colchester Town	a		18 40																19 40				
	d		18 44								19 08					19 35			19 44				
Colchester 4	a	18 42	18 52				19 02		19 06		19 15	19 28			19 31	19 42	19 46		19 52		19 54		20 02
Colchester 4	d	18 43				18 55	19 03		19 12			19 30			19 33	19 43					19 55		20 03
Marks Tey 2	d	18 49				19 01			19 18							19 49					20 01		
Kelvedon	d	18 54							19 23							19 54							
Braintree	d													19 24									
Braintree Freeport	d													19 27									
Cressing	d													19 30									
White Notley	d													19 33									
Witham 2	d	19 00				19 16			19 29					19 42	19 46	20 00					20 16		
Hatfield Peverel	d							←	19 33														
Chelmsford 3	d	19 09				19 26	19 21	19 26	19 40					19 51	19 56	20 09					20 26		20 21
Ingatestone	d					→		19 32							20 02						→		
Shenfield 3	a	19 19						19 38	19 50						20 08	20 19							
Romford	a	19 28														20 28							
Stratford 7 ⊖	a	19 36					19s45	19 52	20 05					20 14	20 22	20 36							20s45
London Liverpool Street 15 ⊖	a	19 45					19 55	20 01	20 14			20 19		20 23	20 31	20 45							20 55

27 July to 10 August

Norwich, Ipswich, Harwich, Clacton, Walton-on-Naze, Colchester and Chelmsford - London

Network Diagram - see first Page of Table 5

		LE [1]	LE [1]	LE [1]	LE [1]		LE [1]	LE ◇[1]	LE [1]	LE [1]	LE [1]	LE [1]	LE [1]	LE [1]	LE ◇[1] ☕		LE [1]	LE [1]	LE [1]	LE [1]	LE [1]	LE ◇[1]	LE [1]	LE [1]	LE [1]
Norwich	d							19 30							20 00							20 30			
Diss	d							19 47							20 17							20 47			
Peterborough [8]	d																								
Stowmarket	d						19 44								20 29						20 44				
Needham Market	d						19 49														20 49				
Ipswich	a						20 00	20 09							20 41						21 00	21 08			
	d				19 52			20 09			20 20				20 43						21 00	21 09			
Harwich Town	d								20 05			20 28												21 05	
Dovercourt	d								20 07			20 30												21 07	
Harwich International	d								20 10			20 33								20 45	21a29			21 10	
Wrabness	d								20 16			20 39												21 16	
Mistley	d								20 22			20 45												21 22	
Manningtree [2]	d				20 02			20 19	20a27		20 33	20a50			20 53					20 58		21 19		21 27	
Walton-on-the-Naze	d													19 55			20 33								
Frinton-on-Sea	d													19 58			20 36								
Kirby Cross	d													20 01			20 42								
Clacton-on-Sea	d									20 05													21 05		
Thorpe-le-Soken [1]	a									20 13				20 07			20 48						21 13		
	d									20 13				20 17									21 13		
Weeley	d													20 21											
Great Bentley	d													20 24											
Alresford (Essex)	d													20 28											
Wivenhoe [3]	d									20 23				20 32									21 23		
Hythe	d													20 36											
Colchester Town	a													20 40											
	d		20 00										20 35	20 44				21 00							21 35
Colchester [4]	a		20 07		20 11			20 29		20 31	20 45		20 42	20 52	21 02			21 07		21 07		21 28	21 31	21 36	21 42
Colchester [4]	d				20 12			20 30		20 33			20 50		21 03					21 12		21 30	21 33		21 43
Marks Tey [2]	d				20 18								20 56							21 18					21 49
Kelvedon	d				20 23								21 01							21 23					21 54
Braintree	d			20 11															21 00						
Braintree Freeport	d			20 13															21 02						
Cressing	d			20 16															21 05						
White Notley	d			20 19															21 08						
Witham [2]	d			20 27	20 31					20 46			21 07						21 16	21 29			21 46		22 00
Hatfield Peverel	d	←			20 35															21 33					
Chelmsford [3]	d	20 26		20 36	20 42					20 56			21 16		21 21				21 26	21 40			21 56		22 09
Ingatestone	d	20 32								21 02									21 32				22 02		
Shenfield [3]	a	20 38		20 46	20 52					21 08			21 26						21 38	21 50			22 08		22 19
Romford	a																								
Stratford [7] ⊖	a	20 52			21 07					21 22			21 42		21s45				21 52	22 11			22 26		22 38
London Liverpool Street [15] ⊖	a	21 01		21 12	21 16			21 19		21 31			21 51		21 55				22 01	22 21		22 20	22 36		22 48

			LE ◇[1]	LE [1]	LE [1]	LE ◇[1] ☕	LE [1]	LE [1]	LE [1]	LE [1]	LE [1]		LE [1]	LE [1]	LE [1]	LE ◇[1]	LE [1]	LE [1]	LE [1]	LE [1]	LE ◇[1]	LE [1]	LE [1]	LE [1]	LE
Norwich	d					21 00										22 00						23 05			
Diss	d					21 17										22 17						23 22			
Peterborough [8]	d		19 45																		21 45				
Stowmarket	d		21 09			21 29	21 44									22 29	22 44				23 06	23 34			23 47
Needham Market	d						21 49										22 49								23 52
Ipswich	a		21 23			21 41	22 00									22 41	23 00				23 18	23 48			00 05
	d		21 25			21 43					22 23					22 43					23 19				
Harwich Town	d				21 28									22 28									23 28		
Dovercourt	d				21 30									22 30									23 30		
Harwich International	d				21 33									22 33									23 33		
Wrabness	d				21 39									22 39									23 39		
Mistley	d				21 45									22 45									23 45		
Manningtree [2]	d		21 35		21a50	21 53					22 33			22a50		22 53					23 29		23a50		
Walton-on-the-Naze	d			21 00									22 00						23 00						
Frinton-on-Sea	d			21 03									22 03						23 03						
Kirby Cross	d			21 06									22 06						23 06						
Clacton-on-Sea	d									22 05										23 05					
Thorpe-le-Soken [1]	a			21 12						22 13			22 12						23 12	23 13					
	d			21 17						22 13			22 17							23 13					
Weeley	d			21 21									22 21							23 17					
Great Bentley	d			21 24									22 24							23 20					
Alresford (Essex)	d			21 28									22 28							23 24					
Wivenhoe [3]	d			21 32						22 23			22 32							23 28					
Hythe	d			21 36									22 36							23 32					
Colchester Town	a			21 40									22 40												
	d			21 44					22 00				22 44					23 00							
Colchester [4]	a		21 46	21 52		22 02			22 07	22 31	22 42		22 52			23 02		23 07		23 38	23 40				
Colchester [4]	d					22 03			22 12	22 33	22 43					23 03									
Marks Tey [2]	d								22 18		22 49														
Kelvedon	d								22 23		22 54														
Braintree	d							22 00							22 56									23 45	
Braintree Freeport	d							22 02							22 58									23 47	
Cressing	d							22 05							23 01									23 50	
White Notley	d							22 08							23 04									23 53	
Witham [2]	d							22 16	22 29	22 46	23 00				23a12	23 16								00a01	
Hatfield Peverel	d								22 33																
Chelmsford [3]	d					22 21		22 26	22 40	22 56	23 09					23 25									
Ingatestone	d							22 32		23 02															
Shenfield [3]	a							22 38	22 50	23 08	23 19					23s36									
Romford	a																								
Stratford [7] ⊖	a							22 56	23 10	23 26	23 38														
London Liverpool Street [15] ⊖	a					22 54		23 06	23 20	23 36	23 48					00 03									

13 August to 28 August

Norwich, Ipswich, Harwich, Clacton, Walton-on-Naze, Colchester and Chelmsford - London

Network Diagram - see first Page of Table 5

		LE MX ◇[1]	LE ◇[1] A ☕	LE ◇[1] B	LE MX	LE B	LE [1] C	LE [1] A	LE [1]	LE ◇[1]	LE [1]		LE [1]	LE [1]	LE ◇[1] ☕	LE [1]	LE [1]	LE [1]	LE [1]	LE [1]	LE [1]	LE [1]	LE [1] ☕	LE [1]	LE [1]
Norwich	d	22p00	22p00	22p00											05 00								05 30		
Diss	d	22p17	22p17	22p17											05 18								05 48		
Peterborough [8]	d																								
Stowmarket	d	22p29	22p29	22p29	23p47	00 06		00 47							05 30					05 54			06 00		
Needham Market	d				23p52	00 11		00 52												05 59					
Ipswich	a	22p41	22p41	22p41	00 05	00 23		01 03							05 42					06 09			06 12		
	d	22p43	22p43	22p43						05 14					05 44				06 00				06 14		
Harwich Town	d										05 24														
Dovercourt	d										05 26														
Harwich International	d										05 29														
Wrabness	d										05 35														
Mistley	d										05 41														
Manningtree [2]	d	22p53	22p53	22p53						05 25	05a46				05 54				06 11				06 24		
Walton-on-the-Naze	d															05 35					06 05				
Frinton-on-Sea	d															05 38					06 08				
Kirby Cross	d															05 41					06 11				
Clacton-on-Sea	d													05 20				05 40						06 10	
Thorpe-le-Soken [1]	a													05 28		05 47		05 48			06 17			06 18	
	d													05 28				05 48						06 18	
Weeley	d																	05 52							
Great Bentley	d																	05 56							
Alresford (Essex)	d																	06 00							
Wivenhoe [3]	d													05 38				06 04						06 29	
Hythe	d																	06 08						06 33	
Colchester Town	a																								
	d																					06 19			
Colchester [4]	a	23p02	23p02	23p02						05 34				05 46	06 03			06 14	06 20			06 26	06 33	06 39	
Colchester [4]	d	23p03	23p03	23p03					05 12	05 35				05 47	06 05			06 15	06 20			06 27	06 35	06 40	
Marks Tey [2]	d								05 18					05 53					06 26			06 33			
Kelvedon	d								05 23					05 59				06 25	06 32					06 50	
Braintree	d						00 25						05 45												06 40
Braintree Freeport	d						00 27						05 47												06 42
Cressing	d						00 30						05 50												06 45
White Notley	d						00 33						05 53												06 48
Witham [2]	d	23p16	23p16	23p16			00a41		05 29	05 48			06a02	06 05			06 18	06 31	06 38			06 47			06 57
Hatfield Peverel	d								05 33								06 22								07 02
Chelmsford [3]	d	23p25	23p25	23p25					05 40	05 58				06 14			06 29	06 40	06 47			06 56		07 03	07 09
Ingatestone	d								05 47								06 36					07 03			
Shenfield [3]	a	23b36	23b36	23b36					05 52					06 24			06 41	06 50				07 07			07 19
Romford	a																								
Stratford [7] ⊖	a	23b52		23b57					06 07	06s22				06 39	06s44		06s57	07s06				07s23	07s15	07s27	07s35
London Liverpool Street [15] ⊖	a	00 02	00 03	00 08					06 16	06 34				06 48	06 54		07 09	07 18	07 24			07 35	07 27	07 38	07 46

		LE [1]	LE [1]	LE [1]	LE [1] ☕	LE [1]		LE [1]	LE [1]	LE [1]	LE [1]	LE [1]	LE [1]	LE	LE [1]	LE [1]		LE [1] ☕	LE [1]	LE [1]	LE [1]	LE [1]	LE [1]	LE ◇[1]	LE [1]
Norwich	d				06 00													06 25							
Diss	d				06 18													06 43							
Peterborough [8]	d																								
Stowmarket	d				06 30									06 44				06 55						07 05	
Needham Market	d													06 49											
Ipswich	a				06 42									07 01				07 07						07 18	
	d	06 29			06 44						06 52		06 59					07 09						07 18	
Harwich Town	d		06 24									06 52													
Dovercourt	d		06 26									06 54													
Harwich International	d		06 29									06 57	07a28												
Wrabness	d		06 35									07 03													
Mistley	d		06 41									07 09													
Manningtree [2]	d	06 39	06a46		06 54						07 02	07a14						07 19						07 28	
Walton-on-the-Naze	d							06 32												06 59					
Frinton-on-Sea	d							06 35												07 02					
Kirby Cross	d							06 38												07 05					
Clacton-on-Sea	d					06 28				06 38						06 47			06 51				07 05		
Thorpe-le-Soken [1]	a					06 36		06 44		06 46						06 55			06 59	07 11			07 13		
	d					06 36				06 46						06 55			06 59				07 13		
Weeley	d					06 40													07 03						
Great Bentley	d					06 43													07 06						
Alresford (Essex)	d					06 47													07 10						
Wivenhoe [3]	d					06 51				06 57						07 06			07 14				07 24		
Hythe	d					06 55				07 01						07 10			07 18						
Colchester Town	a					06 59													07 22						
	d			06 47		07 03													07 27						
Colchester [4]	a	06 48		06 54	07 03	07 13				07 07	07 12					07 16		07 28	07 35				07 32	07 37	
Colchester [4]	d	06 49		06 55	07 05					07 08	07 13					07 17		07 30					07 33	07 38	
Marks Tey [2]	d	06 55		07 01							07 19					07 23								07 44	
Kelvedon	d	07 00								07 18						07 29							07 43	07 49	
Braintree	d																					07 26			
Braintree Freeport	d																					07 29			
Cressing	d																					07 32			
White Notley	d																					07 35			
Witham [2]	d	07 06		07 10					07 17						07 29	07 35						07 44	07 50	07 55	
Hatfield Peverel	d														07 33							07 48			
Chelmsford [3]	d			07 19					07 27	07 31	07 35				07 40						07 49	07 55	07 59		08 09
Ingatestone	d								07 33		07 42										07 56				08 16
Shenfield [3]	a								07 38	07 41					07 50						08 01		08 09		08 21
Romford	a																								
Stratford [7] ⊖	a	07s38		07s44					07s55	07s58	08s01				08s07	08s09					08s18	08s20	08s25	08s28	08s38
London Liverpool Street [15] ⊖	a	07 50		07 56	07 58				08 07	08 09	08 13				08 19	08 21		08 23			08 30	08 32	08 38	08 40	08 50

A 13 August
B 20 August, 27 August
C not 20 August, 27 August
b Previous night, stops to set down only

Table 11

Mondays to Fridays

13 August to 28 August

Norwich, Ipswich, Harwich, Clacton, Walton-on-Naze, Colchester and Chelmsford - London

Network Diagram - see first Page of Table 5

		LE		LE	LE	LE	LE	LE	LE	LE	LE	LE	LE
		■		▪ ■ ⊡	■	■	■	▪ ■ ⊡		■	■	■	■
Norwich	d			06 50				07 05					
Diss	d			07 08				07 23					
Peterborough ■	d												
Stowmarket	d			07 20				07 35	07 45				
Needham Market	d								07 50				
Ipswich	a			07 32				07 47	08 03				
	d			07 34			07 38	07 49					
Harwich Town	d				07 16								
Dovercourt	d				07 18								
Harwich International	d	07 15			07 21								
Wrabness	d				07 27								
Mistley	d				07 33								
Manningtree 2	d	07 32		07 44	07 38		07 49	07 59					
Walton-on-the-Naze	d												
Frinton-on-Sea	d												
Kirby Cross	d												
Clacton-on-Sea	d					07 16						07 45	
Thorpe-le-Soken 1	a					07 24						07 53	
	d					07 24						07 53	
Weeley	d					07 28							
Great Bentley	d					07 31							
Alresford (Essex)	d					07 35							
Wivenhoe 3	d					07 39						08 03	
Hythe	d					07 43							
Colchester Town	a												
	d												08 00
Colchester 4	a	07 41			07 47	07 50	07 58	08 08				08 16	08 09
Colchester 4	d	07 42			07 54		07 59	08 10				08 18	
Marks Tey 2	d	07 48					08 05					08 24	
Kelvedon	d				08 04		08 10					08 30	
Braintree	d										08 12		
Braintree Freeport	d										08 14		
Cressing	d										08 17		
White Notley	d										08 20		
Witham 2	d	08 03			08 10		08 16				08 28	08 36	
Hatfield Peverel	d	08 07									08 32		
Chelmsford 3	d	08 14			08 19					08 30	08 39	08 45	
Ingatestone	d									08 37	08 46		
Shenfield 3	a	08 23			08 29					08 42	08 51	08 55	
Romford	a												
Stratford 7 ⊖	a	08s41			08s45		08s48	08s52		08s59	09s08		
London Liverpool Street 15 ⊖	a	08 54		08 42	08 58		09 01	09 04		09 11	09 19	09 21	

			LE	LE	LE	LE	LE	LE	LE	LE	LE		LE
			▪ ■ A ⊡	■	■	■	◇■	■	■	■	■		▪ ■ ⊡
Norwich	d		07 40										08 00
Diss	d		07 58										08 17
Peterborough ■	d												
Stowmarket	d						08 11						08 29
Needham Market	d												
Ipswich	a		08 18				08 24						08 41
	d		08 20				08 26						08 43
Harwich Town	d				07 58			08 28					
Dovercourt	d				08 00			08 30					
Harwich International	d				08 03			08 33					
Wrabness	d				08 09			08 39					
Mistley	d				08 15			08 45					
Manningtree 2	d				08 20		08 36	08a50					08 53
Walton-on-the-Naze	d			07 40		08 00							
Frinton-on-Sea	d			07 43		08 03							
Kirby Cross	d			07 46		08 06							
Clacton-on-Sea	d										08 11		
Thorpe-le-Soken 1	a			07 52		08 11					08 19		
	d			07 58		08 12					08 19		
Weeley	d			08 02							08 23		
Great Bentley	d			08 05							08 26		
Alresford (Essex)	d			08 09							08 30		
Wivenhoe 3	d			08 13		08 22					08 34		
Hythe	d			08 17		08 26					08 38		
Colchester Town	a			08 21						←			
	d			08 32									
Colchester 4	a			08 40	08 29	08 35	08 45			08 40	08 46		09 02
Colchester 4	d			08 48	08 37		08 45			08 48			09 03
Marks Tey 2	d			→						08 54			
Kelvedon	d									09 00			
Braintree	d												
Braintree Freeport	d												
Cressing	d												
White Notley	d												
Witham 2	d				08 50				08 58	09 06			
Hatfield Peverel	d								09 02				
Chelmsford 3	d				08 59		09 04		09 09	09 15			09 21
Ingatestone	d								09 16				
Shenfield 3	a								09 21	09 25			
Romford	a												
Stratford 7 ⊖	a				09s23		09s28		09s37	09s41			
London Liverpool Street 15 ⊖	a		09 24		09 36		09 40		09 49	09 53			09 56

A The East Anglian

Table 11

Mondays to Fridays

13 August to 28 August

Norwich, Ipswich, Harwich, Clacton, Walton-on-Naze, Colchester and Chelmsford - London

Network Diagram - see first Page of Table 5

		LE	LE	LE	LE	LE	LE	LE	LE		LE	LE	LE
		■	■	■	■	▪ ■ ⊡	■	■	■		■	■	■
Norwich	d					08 30							
Diss	d					08 47							
Peterborough ■	d						07 45						
Stowmarket	d		08 44				09 14						
Needham Market	d		08 49										
Ipswich	a		09 00			09 08	09 28						
	d			08 48		09 09					09 30		
Harwich Town	d												09 28
Dovercourt	d												09 30
Harwich International	d												09 33
Wrabness	d												09 39
Mistley	d												09 45
Manningtree 2	d			08 58		09 19					09 40		09a50
Walton-on-the-Naze	d											09 00	
Frinton-on-Sea	d											09 03	
Kirby Cross	d											09 06	
Clacton-on-Sea	d							09 05					
Thorpe-le-Soken 1	a							09 13				09 12	
	d							09 13				09 17	
Weeley	d											09 21	
Great Bentley	d											09 24	
Alresford (Essex)	d											09 28	
Wivenhoe 3	d							09 23				09 32	
Hythe	d											09 36	
Colchester Town	a											09 40	
	d				08 58				09 35			09 44	
Colchester 4	a			09 08	09 05	09 28		09 31	09 42		09 49	09 52	
Colchester 4	d			09 12		09 30		09 33	09 43		09 50		
Marks Tey 2	d			09 18							09 56		
Kelvedon	d			09 23					09 52				
Braintree	d	09 00											
Braintree Freeport	d	09 02											
Cressing	d	09 05											
White Notley	d	09 08											
Witham 2	d	09 16		09 29				09 46	09 58		10 05		
Hatfield Peverel	d			09 33									
Chelmsford 3	d	09 26		09 40				09 56	10 07		10 14		
Ingatestone	d	09 32						10 02					
Shenfield 3	a	09 38		09 50				10 08	10 17				
Romford	a								10 26				
Stratford 7 ⊖	a	09 52		10 05				10 22	10 34				
London Liverpool Street 15 ⊖	a	10 01		10 14		10 19		10 31	10 43		10 44		

		LE	LE	LE	LE	LE	LE		LE	LE	LE	LE	LE
		▪ ■ ⊡	■	■	■	■	◇■ ⊡		■	■	■	■	◇■ ⊡
Norwich	d	09 00					09 30						10 00
Diss	d	09 17					09 47						10 17
Peterborough ■	d												
Stowmarket	d	09 29				09 44							10 29
Needham Market	d					09 49							
Ipswich	a	09 41				10 02	10 08						10 41
	d	09 43			09 52		10 09						10 43
Harwich Town	d									10 28			
Dovercourt	d									10 30			
Harwich International	d									10 33			
Wrabness	d									10 39			
Mistley	d									10 45			
Manningtree 2	d	09 53			10 02		10 19			10a50			10 53
Walton-on-the-Naze	d											10 00	
Frinton-on-Sea	d											10 03	
Kirby Cross	d											10 06	
Clacton-on-Sea	d								10 05				
Thorpe-le-Soken 1	a								10 13			10 12	
	d								10 13			10 17	
Weeley	d											10 21	
Great Bentley	d											10 24	
Alresford (Essex)	d											10 28	
Wivenhoe 3	d								10 23			10 32	
Hythe	d											10 36	
Colchester Town	a											10 40	
	d		10 00								10 35	10 44	
Colchester 4	a	10 02	10 07		10 11		10 28		10 31		10 42	10 52	11 02
Colchester 4	d	10 03			10 12		10 30		10 33		10 43		11 03
Marks Tey 2	d				10 18						10 49		
Kelvedon	d				10 23						10 54		
Braintree	d			10 00									
Braintree Freeport	d			10 02									
Cressing	d			10 05									
White Notley	d			10 08									
Witham 2	d			10 16	10 29				10 46		11 00		
Hatfield Peverel	d				10 33								
Chelmsford 3	d	10 21		10 26	10 40				10 56		11 09		11 21
Ingatestone	d			10 32					11 02				
Shenfield 3	a			10 38	10 50				11 08		11 19		
Romford	a										11 28		
Stratford 7 ⊖	a	10s45		10 52	11 05				11 22		11 36		11s45
London Liverpool Street 15 ⊖	a	10 55		11 01	11 14		11 19		11 31		11 45		11 55

		LE	LE	LE	LE		LE	LE	LE	LE	LE	LE	LE
		■	■	■	■		◇■ ⊡	■	■	■	■	■	◇■ ⊡
Norwich	d						10 30						11 00
Diss	d						10 47						11 17
Peterborough ■	d							09 45					
Stowmarket	d				10 44			11 14					11 29
Needham Market	d				10 49								
Ipswich	a				11 00		11 08	11 28					11 41
	d			10 52			11 09						11 43
Harwich Town	d									11 28			
Dovercourt	d									11 30			
Harwich International	d									11 33			
Wrabness	d									11 39			
Mistley	d									11 45			
Manningtree 2	d			11 02			11 19			11a50			11 53
Walton-on-the-Naze	d											11 00	
Frinton-on-Sea	d											11 03	
Kirby Cross	d											11 06	
Clacton-on-Sea	d								11 05				
Thorpe-le-Soken 1	a								11 13			11 12	
	d								11 13			11 17	
Weeley	d											11 21	
Great Bentley	d											11 24	
Alresford (Essex)	d											11 28	
Wivenhoe 3	d								11 23			11 32	
Hythe	d											11 36	
Colchester Town	a											11 40	
	d	11 00									11 35	11 44	
Colchester 4	a	11 07		11 11			11 28		11 31		11 42	11 52	12 02
Colchester 4	d			11 12			11 30		11 33		11 43		12 03
Marks Tey 2	d			11 18							11 49		
Kelvedon	d			11 23							11 54		
Braintree	d		11 00										
Braintree Freeport	d		11 02										
Cressing	d		11 05										
White Notley	d		11 08										
Witham 2	d		11 16	11 29					11 46		12 00		
Hatfield Peverel	d			11 33									
Chelmsford 3	d		11 26	11 40					11 56		12 09		12 21
Ingatestone	d		11 32						12 02				
Shenfield 3	a		11 38	11 50					12 08		12 19		
Romford	a										12 28		
Stratford 7 ⊖	a		11 52	12 05					12 22		12 36		12s45
London Liverpool Street 15 ⊖	a		12 01	12 14			12 19		12 31		12 45		12 55

		LE	LE		LE	LE	LE	LE	LE	LE	LE	LE	LE
		■	■		■	■	◇■ ⊡	■	■	■	■	◇■ ⊡	■
Norwich	d						11 30					12 00	
Diss	d						11 47					12 17	
Peterborough ■	d												
Stowmarket	d					11 44						12 29	
Needham Market	d					11 49							
Ipswich	a					12 00	12 08					12 41	
	d				11 52		12 09					12 43	
Harwich Town	d								12 28				
Dovercourt	d								12 30				
Harwich International	d								12 33				
Wrabness	d								12 39				
Mistley	d								12 45				
Manningtree 2	d				12 02		12 19		12a50			12 53	
Walton-on-the-Naze	d										12 00		
Frinton-on-Sea	d										12 03		
Kirby Cross	d										12 06		
Clacton-on-Sea	d							12 05					
Thorpe-le-Soken 1	a							12 13			12 12		
	d							12 13			12 17		
Weeley	d										12 21		
Great Bentley	d										12 24		
Alresford (Essex)	d										12 28		
Wivenhoe 3	d							12 23			12 32		
Hythe	d										12 36		
Colchester Town	a										12 40		
	d	12 00								12 35	12 44		13 00
Colchester 4	a	12 07			12 11		12 28	12 31		12 42	12 52	13 02	13 07
Colchester 4	d				12 12		12 30	12 33		12 43		13 03	
Marks Tey 2	d				12 18					12 49			
Kelvedon	d				12 23					12 54			
Braintree	d		12 00										
Braintree Freeport	d		12 02										
Cressing	d		12 05										
White Notley	d		12 08										
Witham 2	d		12 16		12 29			12 46		13 00			
Hatfield Peverel	d				12 33								
Chelmsford 3	d		12 26		12 40			12 56		13 09		13 21	
Ingatestone	d		12 32					13 02					
Shenfield 3	a		12 38		12 50			13 08		13 19			
Romford	a									13 28			
Stratford 7 ⊖	a		12 52		13 05			13 22		13 36		13s45	
London Liverpool Street 15 ⊖	a		13 01		13 14		13 19	13 31		13 45		13 55	

Table 11

Mondays to Fridays

13 August to 28 August

Norwich, Ipswich, Harwich, Clacton, Walton-on-Naze, Colchester and Chelmsford - London

Network Diagram - see first Page of Table 5

Station		LE 1	LE 1	LE 1	LE ◇1 🍴	LE 1	LE 1	LE 1	LE 1	LE 1	LE ◇1 🍴	LE 1	LE 1	LE 1	LE 1	LE ◇1 🍴	LE 1	LE 1	LE 1	LE 1	LE ◇1 🍴	LE 1
Norwich	d				12 30						13 00					13 30					14 00	
Diss	d				12 47						13 17					13 47					14 17	
Peterborough 8	d					11 45																
Stowmarket	d			12 44		13 13					13 29				13 44						14 29	
Needham Market	d			12 49											13 49							
Ipswich	a			13 00	13 08	13 28					13 41				14 00	14 08					14 41	
	d		12 52		13 09						13 43			13 52		14 09					14 43	
Harwich Town	d							13 28										14 28				
Dovercourt	d							13 30										14 30				
Harwich International	d							13 33										14 33				
Wrabness	d							13 39										14 39				
Mistley	d							13 45										14 45				
Manningtree 2	d		13 02		13 19			13a50			13 53			14 02		14 19		14a50			14 53	
Walton-on-the-Naze	d									13 00										14 00		
Frinton-on-Sea	d									13 03										14 03		
Kirby Cross	d									13 06										14 06		
Clacton-on-Sea	d						13 05										14 05					
Thorpe-le-Soken 1	a						13 13			13 12							14 13			14 12		
	d						13 13			13 17							14 13			14 17		
Weeley	d									13 21										14 21		
Great Bentley	d									13 24										14 24		
Alresford (Essex)	d									13 28										14 28		
Wivenhoe 3	d						13 23			13 32							14 23			14 32		
Hythe	d									13 36										14 36		
Colchester Town	a									13 40										14 40		
	d								13 35	13 44		14 00							14 35	14 44		15 00
Colchester 4	a		13 11		13 28		13 31		13 42	13 52	14 02	14 07		14 11		14 28	14 31		14 42	14 52	15 02	15 07
Colchester 4	d		13 12		13 30		13 33		13 43		14 03			14 12		14 30	14 33		14 43		15 03	
Marks Tey 2	d		13 18						13 49					14 18					14 49			
Kelvedon	d		13 23						13 54					14 23					14 54			
Braintree	d	13 00											14 00									
Braintree Freeport	d	13 02											14 02									
Cressing	d	13 05											14 05									
White Notley	d	13 08											14 08									
Witham 2	d	13 16	13 29				13 46		14 00				14 16	14 29			14 46		15 00			
Hatfield Peverel	d		13 33											14 33								
Chelmsford 3	d	13 26	13 40				13 56		14 09		14 21		14 26	14 40			14 56		15 09		15 21	
Ingatestone	d	13 32					14 02						14 32				15 02					
Shenfield 3	a	13 38	13 50				14 08		14 19				14 38	14 50			15 08		15 19			
Romford	a								14 28										15 28			
Stratford 7 ⊖	a	13 52	14 05				14 22		14 36		14s45		14 52	15 05			15 22		15 36		15s45	
London Liverpool Street 15 ⊖	a	14 01	14 14		14 19		14 31		14 45		14 55		15 01	15 15		15 19	15 33		15 45		15 55	

Station		LE 1	LE 1	LE 1	LE ◇1 🍴	LE 1	LE 1	LE 1	LE 1	LE 1	LE ◇1 🍴	LE 1	LE 1	LE 1	LE 1	LE ◇1 🍴	LE 1	LE 1	LE 1	LE 1	LE 1	LE ◇1 🍴	LE 1
Norwich	d				14 30						15 00					15 30						16 00	
Diss	d				14 47						15 17					15 47						16 17	
Peterborough 8	d					13 45																	
Stowmarket	d			14 44		15 13					15 29				15 44							16 29	
Needham Market	d			14 49											15 49								
Ipswich	a			15 00	15 08	15 28					15 41				16 00	16 08						16 41	
	d		14 52		15 09						15 43			15 52		16 09						16 43	
Harwich Town	d							15 28										16 28					
Dovercourt	d							15 30										16 30					
Harwich International	d							15 33										16 33					
Wrabness	d							15 39										16 39					
Mistley	d							15 45										16 45					
Manningtree 2	d		15 02		15 19			15a50			15 53			16 02		16 19		16a50				16 53	
Walton-on-the-Naze	d									15 00											16 00		
Frinton-on-Sea	d									15 03											16 03		
Kirby Cross	d									15 06											16 06		
Clacton-on-Sea	d						15 05										16 05						
Thorpe-le-Soken 1	a						15 13			15 12							16 13				16 12		
	d						15 13			15 17							16 13				16 17		
Weeley	d									15 21											16 21		
Great Bentley	d									15 24											16 24		
Alresford (Essex)	d									15 28											16 28		
Wivenhoe 3	d						15 23			15 32							16 23				16 32		
Hythe	d									15 36											16 36		
Colchester Town	a									15 40											16 40		
	d								15 35	15 44		16 00							16 35		16 44		16 56
Colchester 4	a		15 11		15 28		15 31		15 42	15 52	16 02	16 07		16 11		16 28	16 31		16 42		16 54	17 02	17 05
Colchester 4	d		15 12		15 30		15 33		15 43		16 03			16 12		16 30	16 33		16 43	16 53		17 03	
Marks Tey 2	d		15 18						15 49					16 18						16 59			
Kelvedon	d		15 23						15 54					16 23					16 52				
Braintree	d	15 00											16 00										
Braintree Freeport	d	15 02											16 02										
Cressing	d	15 05											16 05										
White Notley	d	15 08											16 08										
Witham 2	d	15 16	15 29				15 46		16 00				16 16	16 29			16 46		16 58	17 08			
Hatfield Peverel	d		15 33											16 33					17 02				
Chelmsford 3	d	15 26	15 40				15 56		16 09		16 21		16 26	16 40			16 56		17 09	17 17		17 21	
Ingatestone	d	15 32					16 02						16 32				17 02						
Shenfield 3	a	15 38	15 50				16 08		16 19				16 38	16 50			17 08		17 19	17 27			
Romford	a																						
Stratford 7 ⊖	a	15 52	16 05				16 22		16 34		16s45		16 52	17 05			17 22		17 36	17 42		17s45	
London Liverpool Street 15 ⊖	a	16 01	16 14		16 17		16 31		16 44		16 55		17 03	17 16		17 19	17 34		17 46	17 53		17 58	

Table 11

Mondays to Fridays

13 August to 28 August

Norwich, Ipswich, Harwich, Clacton, Walton-on-Naze, Colchester and Chelmsford - London

Network Diagram - see first Page of Table 5

Station		LE 1	LE 1	LE 1	LE 1	LE ◇1 🍴	LE 1	LE 1	LE 1	LE 1	LE 1	LE 1	LE 1	LE ◇1 🍴	LE 1	LE 1	LE 1	LE 1	LE ◇1 🍴	LE 1	LE 1	LE 1
Norwich	d					16 30								17 00					17 30			
Diss	d					16 47								17 17					17 47			
Peterborough 8	d						15 45															
Stowmarket	d			16 44			17 13							17 29	17 45				17 59			
Needham Market	d			16 49											17 50							
Ipswich	a			17 00		17 08	17 28							17 41	18 04				18 11			
	d		16 52			17 09						17 33		17 43					18 13			
Harwich Town	d				16 53								17 28			18 00						
Dovercourt	d				16 55								17 30			18 02						
Harwich International	d				16 58								17 33			18 05						
Wrabness	d				17 04								17 39			18 11						
Mistley	d				17 10								17 45			18 17						
Manningtree 2	d		17 02		17a15	17 19						17 43	17a50	17 53		18a22						
Walton-on-the-Naze	d										17 00											
Frinton-on-Sea	d										17 03											
Kirby Cross	d										17 06											
Clacton-on-Sea	d							17 05												18 05		
Thorpe-le-Soken 1	a							17 13			17 12									18 13		
	d							17 13			17 17									18 13		
Weeley	d										17 21											
Great Bentley	d										17 24											
Alresford (Essex)	d										17 28											
Wivenhoe 3	d							17 23			17 32									18 23		
Hythe	d										17 36											
Colchester Town	a										17 40											
	d									17 30	17 44										18 32	
Colchester 4	a		17 11			17 28		17 31		17 37	17 52	17 52		18 02					18 28	18 33	18 39	
Colchester 4	d		17 12			17 30		17 33		17 48				18 03				18 12	18 30	18 33		
Marks Tey 2	d		17 18							17 54								18 18				
Kelvedon	d		17 23							17 59								18 23				
Braintree	d	17 00							17 44													18 33
Braintree Freeport	d	17 02							17 46													18 36
Cressing	d	17 05							17 49													18 39
White Notley	d	17 08							17 52													18 42
Witham 2	d	17 16	17 29					17 46	18 00	18 05							18 16	18 29		18 46		18 51
Hatfield Peverel	d		17 33							18 09								18 33				18 55
Chelmsford 3	d	17 26	17 40					17 56	18 09	18 16				18 21			18 26	18 40		18 56		19 02
Ingatestone	d	17 32						18 02									18 32			19 02		
Shenfield 3	a	17 38	17 50					18 08	18 19	18 26							18 38	18 50		19 08		19 13
Romford	a								18 28													
Stratford 7 ⊖	a	17 52	18 06					18 22	18 36	18 42				18s45			18 52	19 05		19 22		19 27
London Liverpool Street 15 ⊖	a	18 01	18 15			18 19		18 31	18 45	18 51				18 55			19 01	19 14	19 17	19 31		19 36

Station		LE 1	LE 1	LE 1	LE 1	LE 1	LE ◇1 🍴	LE 1	LE 1	LE 1	LE 1	LE ◇1 🍴	LE 1	LE 1	LE 1	LE 1	LE 1	LE 1	LE 1	LE 1	LE 1	LE 1	LE ◇1 🍴
Norwich	d						18 00					18 30											19 00
Diss	d						18 17					18 47											19 17
Peterborough 8	d																	17 45					
Stowmarket	d						18 29			18 45								19 13					19 29
Needham Market	d									18 50													
Ipswich	a						18 41			19 02		19 08						19 28					19 41
	d	18 22					18 43		18 47			19 09					19 23				19 35		19 43
Harwich Town	d			18 26									19 05									19 28	
Dovercourt	d			18 28									19 07									19 30	
Harwich International	d			18 31									19 10									19 33	
Wrabness	d			18 37									19 16									19 39	
Mistley	d			18 43									19 22									19 45	
Manningtree 2	d	18 32		18a48			18 53		18 57			19 19	19a27				19 36				19 45	19a50	19 53
Walton-on-the-Naze	d		17 57		18 33														18 54	19 15			
Frinton-on-Sea	d		18 00		18 36														18 57	19 18			
Kirby Cross	d		18 03		18 42														19 00	19 21			
Clacton-on-Sea	d														19 02								
Thorpe-le-Soken 1	a		18 09		18 48										19 10				19 08	19 27			
	d		18 17												19 10				19 17				
Weeley	d		18 21																19 21				
Great Bentley	d		18 24																19 24				
Alresford (Essex)	d		18 28																19 28				
Wivenhoe 3	d		18 32												19 23				19 32				
Hythe	d		18 36																19 36				
Colchester Town	a		18 40																19 40				
	d		18 44								19 08					19 35			19 44				
Colchester 4	a	18 42	18 52				19 02		19 06		19 15	19 28			19 31	19 42	19 46		19 52		19 54		20 02
Colchester 4	d	18 42				18 55	19 03		19 12			19 30			19 33	19 43					19 55		20 03
Marks Tey 2	d	18 48				19 01			19 18							19 49					20 01		
Kelvedon	d	18 54							19 23							19 54							
Braintree	d													19 24									
Braintree Freeport	d													19 27									
Cressing	d													19 30									
White Notley	d													19 33									
Witham 2	d	19 00				19 16			19 29					19 42	19 46	20 00					20 16		
Hatfield Peverel	d							←	19 33														
Chelmsford 3	d	19 09				19 26	19 21	19 26	19 40					19 51	19 56	20 09					20 26		20 21
Ingatestone	d					→		19 32							20 02						→		
Shenfield 3	a	19 19						19 38	19 50						20 08	20 19							
Romford	a	19 27														20 28							
Stratford 7 ⊖	a	19 36					19s45	19 52	20 05					20 14	20 22	20 36							20s45
London Liverpool Street 15 ⊖	a	19 45					19 55	20 01	20 14			20 19		20 23	20 31	20 45							20 55

Table 11

Mondays to Fridays
13 August to 28 August

Norwich, Ipswich, Harwich, Clacton, Walton-on-Naze, Colchester and Chelmsford - London

Network Diagram - see first Page of Table 5

		LE	LE	LE	LE	LE	LE	LE	LE	LE	LE	LE	LE	LE	LE	LE	LE	LE	LE	LE	LE	LE	LE
		■	■	■	■	■	◇■	■	■	■	■	■	■	◇■	■	■	■	■	■	◇■	■	■	■
Norwich	d						19 30							20 00						20 30			
Diss	d						19 47							20 17						20 47			
Peterborough ■	d																						
Stowmarket	d					19 44								20 29					20 44				
Needham Market	d					19 49													20 49				
Ipswich	a					20 00	20 09							20 41					21 00	21 08			
	d				19 52		20 09			20 20				20 43					21 00	21 09			
Harwich Town	d							20 05			20 28											21 05	
Dovercourt	d							20 07			20 30											21 07	
Harwich International	d							20 10			20 33							20 45	21a29			21 10	
Wrabness	d							20 16			20 39											21 16	
Mistley	d							20 22			20 45											21 22	
Manningtree ■	d				20 02		20 19	20a27		20 33	20a50			20 53				20 58		21 19		21 27	
Walton-on-the-Naze	d												19 55		20 33								
Frinton-on-Sea	d												19 58		20 36								
Kirby Cross	d												20 01		20 42								
Clacton-on-Sea	d								20 05												21 05		
Thorpe-le-Soken ■	a								20 13				20 07		20 48						21 13		
	d								20 13				20 17								21 13		
Weeley	d												20 21										
Great Bentley	d												20 24										
Alresford (Essex)	d												20 28										
Wivenhoe ■	d								20 23				20 32								21 23		
Hythe	d												20 36										
Colchester Town	a												20 40										
	d		20 00									20 35	20 44			21 00							21 35
Colchester ■	a		20 07		20 11		20 29		20 31	20 45		20 42	20 52	21 02		21 07		21 07		21 28	21 31	21 36	21 42
Colchester ■	d				20 12		20 30		20 33			20 50		21 03				21 12		21 30	21 33		21 43
Marks Tey ■	d				20 18							20 56						21 18					21 49
Kelvedon	d				20 23							21 01						21 23					21 54
Braintree	d			20 11													21 00						
Braintree Freeport	d			20 13													21 02						
Cressing	d			20 16													21 05						
White Notley	d			20 19													21 08						
Witham ■	d			20 27	20 31				20 46			21 07					21 16	21 29			21 46		22 00
Hatfield Peverel	d	←			20 35													21 33					
Chelmsford ■	d	20 26		20 36	20 42				20 56			21 16		21 21			21 26	21 40			21 56		22 09
Ingatestone	d	20 32							21 02								21 32				22 02		
Shenfield ■	a	20 38		20 46	20 52				21 08			21 26					21 38	21 50			22 08		22 19
Romford	a																						22 28
Stratford ■ ⊖	a	20 52			21 07				21 22			21 42		21s45			21 52	22 05			22 22		22 36
London Liverpool Street ■ ⊖	a	21 01		21 12	21 16		21 19		21 31			21 51		21 55			22 01	22 14		22 19	22 31		22 45

		LE	LE	LE	LE	LE	LE	LE	LE	LE	LE	LE	LE	LE	LE	LE	LE	LE	LE	LE	LE	LE	LE
		◇■	■	■	◇■	■	■	■	■	■	■	■	■	◇■	■	■	■	■	◇■	■	■	■	
Norwich	d				21 00									22 00						23 05			
Diss	d				21 17									22 17						23 22			
Peterborough ■	d	19 45																	21 45				
Stowmarket	d	21 09			21 29	21 44								22 29	22 44				23 06	23 34			23 47
Needham Market	d					21 49									22 49								23 52
Ipswich	a	21 23			21 41	22 00								22 41	23 00				23 18	23 48			00 05
	d	21 25			21 43					22 23				22 43					23 19				
Harwich Town	d			21 28								22 28									23 28		
Dovercourt	d			21 30								22 30									23 30		
Harwich International	d			21 33								22 33									23 33		
Wrabness	d			21 39								22 39									23 39		
Mistley	d			21 45								22 45									23 45		
Manningtree ■	d	21 35		21a50	21 53					22 33		22a50		22 53					23 29		23 50		
Walton-on-the-Naze	d		21 00								22 00						23 00						
Frinton-on-Sea	d		21 03								22 03						23 03						
Kirby Cross	d		21 06								22 06						23 06						
Clacton-on-Sea	d								22 05									23 05					
Thorpe-le-Soken ■	a		21 12						22 13		22 12						23 12	23 13					
	d		21 17						22 13		22 17							23 13					
Weeley	d		21 21								22 21							23 17					
Great Bentley	d		21 24								22 24							23 20					
Alresford (Essex)	d		21 28								22 28							23 24					
Wivenhoe ■	d		21 32						22 23		22 32							23 28					
Hythe	d		21 36								22 36							23 32					
Colchester Town	a		21 40								22 40												
	d		21 44					22 00			22 44					23 00							
Colchester ■	a	21 46	21 52		22 02			22 07	22 31	22 42	22 52			23 02		23 07		23 38	23 40		23 59		
Colchester ■	d				22 03			22 12	22 33	22 43				23 03									
Marks Tey ■	d							22 18		22 49													
Kelvedon	d							22 23		22 54													
Braintree	d						22 00						22 56									23 45	
Braintree Freeport	d						22 02						22 58									23 47	
Cressing	d						22 05						23 01									23 50	
White Notley	d						22 08						23 04									23 53	
Witham ■	d						22 16	22 29	22 46	23 00			23a12	23 16								00a01	
Hatfield Peverel	d							22 33															
Chelmsford ■	d				22 21		22 26	22 40	22 56	23 09				23 25									
Ingatestone	d						22 32		23 02														
Shenfield ■	a						22 38	22 50	23 08	23 19				23s36									
Romford	a									23 28													
Stratford ■ ⊖	a				22s45		22 52	23 05	23 22	23 36				23s52									
London Liverpool Street ■ ⊖	a				22 55		23 01	23 15	23 31	23 45				00 02									

Table 11

Mondays to Fridays
29 August to 7 September

Norwich, Ipswich, Harwich, Clacton, Walton-on-Naze, Colchester and Chelmsford - London

Network Diagram - see first Page of Table 5

		LE	LE	LE	LE	LE	LE	LE	LE	LE	LE	LE	LE	LE	LE	LE	LE	LE	LE	LE	LE	LE	LE	LE	LE
		◇■	◇■	◇■		■	■	■	■	◇■	■	■	■	◇■	■	■	■	■	■	■	■	■	■	■	■
		A	B	C	D	C	B	C																	
Norwich	d	22p00	22p00	22p00										05 00								05 30			
Diss	d	22p17	22p17	22p17										05 18								05 48			
Peterborough ■	d																								
Stowmarket	d	22p29	22p29	22p29	23p47			00 47						05 30					05 54			06 00			
Needham Market	d				23p52			00 52											05 59						
Ipswich	a	22p41	22p41	22p41	00 05			00 05						05 42					06 09			06 12			
	d	22p43	22p43	22p43						05 14				05 44				06 00				06 14			06 29
Harwich Town	d										05 24														
Dovercourt	d										05 26														
Harwich International	d										05 29														
Wrabness	d										05 35														
Mistley	d										05 41														
Manningtree ■	d	22p53	22p53	22p53						05 25	05a46			05 54				06 11				06 24			06 39
Walton-on-the-Naze	d														05 35					06 05					
Frinton-on-Sea	d														05 38					06 08					
Kirby Cross	d														05 41					06 11					
Clacton-on-Sea	d												05 20				05 40						06 10		
Thorpe-le-Soken ■	a												05 28		05 47		05 48			06 17			06 18		
	d												05 28				05 48						06 18		
Weeley	d																05 52								
Great Bentley	d																05 56								
Alresford (Essex)	d																06 00								
Wivenhoe ■	d												05 38				06 04						06 29		
Hythe	d																06 08						06 33		
Colchester Town	a																								
	d																				06 19				
Colchester ■	a	23p02	23p02	23p02						05 34			05 46	06 03			06 14	06 20			06 26	06 33	06 39		06 48
Colchester ■	d	23p03	23p03	23p03					05 12	05 35			05 47	06 05			06 15	06 20			06 27	06 35	06 40		06 49
Marks Tey ■	d								05 18				05 53					06 26			06 33				06 55
Kelvedon	d								05 23				05 59				06 25	06 32					06 50		07 00
Braintree	d					00 25	00 27					05 45												06 40	
Braintree Freeport	d					00 27	00 29					05 47												06 42	
Cressing	d					00 30	00 32					05 50												06 45	
White Notley	d					00 33	00 35					05 53												06 48	
Witham ■	d	23p16	23p16	23p16		00a41	00a43		05 29	05 48		06a02	06 05			06 18	06 31	06 38			06 47			06 57	07 06
Hatfield Peverel	d								05 33							06 22								07 02	
Chelmsford ■	d	23p25	23p25	23p25					05 40	05 58			06 14			06 29	06 40	06 47			06 56		07 03	07 09	
Ingatestone	d								05 47							06 36					07 03				
Shenfield ■	a	23b36	23b36	23b36					05 52				06 24			06 41	06 50				07 07			07 19	
Romford	a																								
Stratford ■ ⊖	a	23b52							06 07	06s22			06 39	06s44		06s57	07s06				07s23	07s15	07s27	07s35	07s38
London Liverpool Street ■ ⊖	a	00 02	00 03	00 03					06 16	06 34			06 48	06 54		07 09	07 18	07 24			07 35	07 27	07 38	07 46	07 50

		LE	LE	LE	LE	LE	LE	LE	LE	LE	LE	LE	LE	LE	LE	LE	LE	LE	LE	LE	LE	LE	LE
		■	■	■	■	■	■	■	■	■	■		■	■	■	■	■	■	■	■	◇■	■	■
Norwich	d			06 00											06 25								
Diss	d			06 18											06 43								
Peterborough ■	d																						
Stowmarket	d			06 30								06 44			06 55						07 05		
Needham Market	d											06 49											
Ipswich	a			06 42								07 01			07 07						07 18		
	d			06 44					06 52		06 59				07 09						07 18		
Harwich Town	d	06 24								06 52													
Dovercourt	d	06 26								06 54													
Harwich International	d	06 29								06 57	07a28												07 15
Wrabness	d	06 35								07 03													
Mistley	d	06 41								07 09													
Manningtree ■	d	06a46		06 54					07 02	07a14					07 19						07 28		07 32
Walton-on-the-Naze	d					06 32											06 59						
Frinton-on-Sea	d					06 35											07 02						
Kirby Cross	d					06 38											07 05						
Clacton-on-Sea	d				06 28			06 38						06 47		06 51				07 05			
Thorpe-le-Soken ■	a				06 36	06 44		06 46						06 55		06 59	07 11			07 13			
	d				06 36			06 46						06 55		06 59				07 13			
Weeley	d				06 40											07 03							
Great Bentley	d				06 43											07 06							
Alresford (Essex)	d				06 47											07 10							
Wivenhoe ■	d				06 51			06 57						07 06		07 14				07 24			
Hythe	d				06 55			07 01						07 10		07 18							
Colchester Town	a				06 59											07 22							
	d		06 47		07 03											07 27							
Colchester ■	a		06 54	07 03	07 13			07 07	07 12					07 16	07 28	07 35				07 32	07 37		07 41
Colchester ■	d		06 55	07 05				07 08	07 13					07 17	07 30					07 33	07 38		07 42
Marks Tey ■	d		07 01						07 19					07 23							07 44		07 48
Kelvedon	d							07 18						07 29						07 43	07 49		
Braintree	d																		07 26				
Braintree Freeport	d																		07 29				
Cressing	d																		07 32				
White Notley	d																		07 35				
Witham ■	d		07 10				07 17						07 29	07 35					07 44	07 50	07 55		08 03
Hatfield Peverel	d												07 33						07 48				08 07
Chelmsford ■	d		07 19				07 27	07 31	07 35				07 40					07 49	07 55	07 59		08 09	08 14
Ingatestone	d						07 33		07 42									07 56				08 16	
Shenfield ■	a						07 38	07 41					07 50					08 01		08 09		08 21	08 23
Romford	a																						
Stratford ■ ⊖	a		07 44				07s55	07s58	08s01				08s07	08s09				08s18	08s20	08s25	08s28	08s38	08s41
London Liverpool Street ■ ⊖	a		07 56	07 58			08 07	08 09	08 13				08 19	08 21	08 23			08 30	08 32	08 38	08 40	08 50	08 54

A 29 August
B not 29 August, 3 September
C 3 September
D not 3 September
b Previous night, stops to set down only

Norwich, Ipswich, Harwich, Clacton, Walton-on-Naze, Colchester and Chelmsford - London

Network Diagram - see first Page of Table 5

		LE	LE	LE	LE	LE	LE	LE	LE	LE	LE	LE	LE	LE	LE	LE	LE	LE	LE	LE	LE	LE
		▪ ■ ⊐	■	■	■	▪ ■ ⊐		■	■	■	■	▪ ■ A ⊐	■	■	■	◇■	■	■	■	■	▪ ■ ⊐	■
Norwich	d	06 50				07 05						07 40									08 00	
Diss	d	07 08				07 23						07 58									08 17	
Peterborough ■	d																					
Stowmarket	d	07 20				07 35	07 45									08 11					08 29	
Needham Market	d						07 50															
Ipswich	a	07 32				07 47	08 03					08 18				08 24					08 41	
	d	07 34			07 38	07 49						08 20				08 26					08 43	
Harwich Town	d		07 16											07 58			08 28					
Dovercourt	d		07 18											08 00			08 30					
Harwich International	d		07 21											08 03			08 33					
Wrabness	d		07 27											08 09			08 39					
Mistley	d		07 33											08 15			08 45					
Manningtree ■	d	07 44	07 38		07 49	07 59								08 20		08 36	08a50				08 53	
Walton-on-the-Naze	d												07 40		08 00							
Frinton-on-Sea	d												07 43		08 03							
Kirby Cross	d												07 46		08 06							
Clacton-on-Sea	d			07 16						07 45										08 11		
Thorpe-le-Soken ■	a			07 24						07 53			07 52		08 11					08 19		
	d			07 24						07 53			07 58		08 12					08 19		
Weeley	d			07 28									08 02							08 23		
Great Bentley	d			07 31									08 05							08 26		
Alresford (Essex)	d			07 35									08 09							08 30		
Wivenhoe ■	d			07 39						08 03			08 13		08 22					08 34		
Hythe	d			07 43									08 17		08 26					08 38		
Colchester Town	a												08 21						←			
	d										08 00		08 32									
Colchester ■	a		07 47	07 50	07 58	08 08				08 16	08 09		08 40	08 29	08 35	08 45			08 40	08 46	09 02	
Colchester ■	d		07 54		07 59	08 10				08 18			08 48	08 37		08 45			08 48		09 03	
Marks Tey ■	d				08 05					08 24			→						08 54			
Kelvedon	d		08 04		08 10					08 30									09 00			
Braintree	d								08 12													09 00
Braintree Freeport	d								08 14													09 02
Cressing	d								08 17													09 05
White Notley	d								08 20													09 08
Witham ■	d		08 10		08 16				08 28	08 36				08 50				08 58	09 06			09 16
Hatfield Peverel	d								08 32									09 02				
Chelmsford ■	d		08 19					08 30	08 39	08 45				08 59		09 04		09 09	09 15		09 21	09 26
Ingatestone	d							08 37	08 46									09 16				09 32
Shenfield ■	a		08 29					08 42	08 51	08 55								09 21	09 25			09 38
Romford	a																					
Stratford ■ ⊖	a		08s45		08s48	08s52		08s59	09s08			09s14		09s23		09s28		09s37	09s41			09 52
London Liverpool Street ■ ⊖	a	08 42	08 58		09 01	09 04		09 11	09 19	09 21		09 26		09 36		09 40		09 49	09 53		09 56	10 01

A The East Anglian

Table 11

Mondays to Fridays

29 August to 7 September

Norwich, Ipswich, Harwich, Clacton, Walton-on-Naze, Colchester and Chelmsford - London

Network Diagram - see first Page of Table 5

		LE	LE	LE	LE	LE	LE	LE	LE	LE	LE	LE	LE	LE	LE	LE	LE	LE	LE	LE	LE	LE	LE
		■	■	■	▪ ■ ⊐	■	■	■	■	■	■	▪ ■ ⊐	■	■	■	■	◇■ ⊐	■	■	■	■	◇■ ⊐	■
Norwich	d				08 30							09 00					09 30					10 00	
Diss	d				08 47							09 17					09 47					10 17	
Peterborough ■	d					07 45																	
Stowmarket	d	08 44				09 14						09 29				09 44						10 29	
Needham Market	d	08 49														09 49							
Ipswich	a	09 00			09 08	09 28						09 41				10 02	10 08					10 41	
	d		08 48		09 09				09 30			09 43			09 52		10 09					10 43	
Harwich Town	d										09 28								10 28				
Dovercourt	d										09 30								10 30				
Harwich International	d										09 33								10 33				
Wrabness	d										09 39								10 39				
Mistley	d										09 45								10 45				
Manningtree ■	d		08 58		09 19				09 40		09a50	09 53			10 02		10 19		10a50			10 53	
Walton-on-the-Naze	d									09 00											10 00		
Frinton-on-Sea	d									09 03											10 03		
Kirby Cross	d									09 06											10 06		
Clacton-on-Sea	d						09 05											10 05					
Thorpe-le-Soken ■	a						09 13			09 12								10 13			10 12		
	d						09 13			09 17								10 13			10 17		
Weeley	d									09 21											10 21		
Great Bentley	d									09 24											10 24		
Alresford (Essex)	d									09 28											10 28		
Wivenhoe ■	d						09 23			09 32								10 23			10 32		
Hythe	d									09 36											10 36		
Colchester Town	a									09 40											10 40		
	d			08 58				09 35		09 44			10 00							10 35	10 44		11 00
Colchester ■	a		09 08	09 05	09 28		09 31	09 42	09 49	09 52		10 02	10 07		10 11		10 28	10 31		10 42	10 52	11 02	11 07
Colchester ■	d		09 12		09 30		09 33	09 43	09 50			10 03			10 12		10 30	10 33		10 43		11 03	
Marks Tey ■	d		09 18						09 56						10 18					10 49			
Kelvedon	d		09 23					09 52							10 23					10 54			
Braintree	d													10 00									
Braintree Freeport	d													10 02									
Cressing	d													10 05									
White Notley	d													10 08									
Witham ■	d		09 29				09 46	09 58	10 05					10 16	10 29			10 46		11 00			
Hatfield Peverel	d		09 33												10 33								
Chelmsford ■	d		09 40				09 56	10 07	10 14			10 21		10 26	10 40			10 56		11 09		11 21	
Ingatestone	d						10 02							10 32				11 02					
Shenfield ■	a		09 50				10 08	10 17						10 38	10 50			11 08		11 19			
Romford	a							10 26												11 28			
Stratford ■ ⊖	a		10 05				10 22	10 34				10s45		10 52	11 05			11 22		11 36		11s45	
London Liverpool Street ■ ⊖	a		10 14		10 19		10 31	10 43	10 44			10 55		11 01	11 14		11 19	11 31		11 45		11 55	

		LE	LE	LE	LE	LE	LE	LE	LE	LE	LE	LE	LE	LE	LE	LE	LE	LE	LE	LE	LE	LE
		■	■	■	◇■ ⊐	■	■	■	■	■	◇■ ⊐	■	■	■	■	◇■ ⊐	■	■	■	■	◇■ ⊐	■
Norwich	d				10 30						11 00					11 30					12 00	
Diss	d				10 47						11 17					11 47					12 17	
Peterborough ■	d					09 45																
Stowmarket	d			10 44		11 14					11 29				11 44						12 29	
Needham Market	d			10 49											11 49							
Ipswich	a			11 00	11 08	11 28					11 41				12 00	12 08					12 41	
	d		10 52		11 09						11 43			11 52		12 09					12 43	
Harwich Town	d							11 28										12 28				
Dovercourt	d							11 30										12 30				
Harwich International	d							11 33										12 33				
Wrabness	d							11 39										12 39				
Mistley	d							11 45										12 45				
Manningtree ■	d		11 02		11 19			11a50			11 53			12 02		12 19		12a50			12 53	
Walton-on-the-Naze	d									11 00										12 00		
Frinton-on-Sea	d									11 03										12 03		
Kirby Cross	d									11 06										12 06		
Clacton-on-Sea	d						11 05										12 05					
Thorpe-le-Soken ■	a						11 13			11 12							12 13			12 12		
	d						11 13			11 17							12 13			12 17		
Weeley	d									11 21										12 21		
Great Bentley	d									11 24										12 24		
Alresford (Essex)	d									11 28										12 28		
Wivenhoe ■	d						11 23			11 32							12 23			12 32		
Hythe	d									11 36										12 36		
Colchester Town	a									11 40										12 40		
	d								11 35	11 44		12 00							12 35	12 44		13 00
Colchester ■	a		11 11		11 28		11 31		11 42	11 52	12 02	12 07		12 11		12 28	12 31		12 42	12 52	13 02	13 07
Colchester ■	d		11 12		11 30		11 33		11 43		12 03			12 12		12 30	12 33		12 43		13 03	
Marks Tey ■	d		11 18						11 49					12 18					12 49			
Kelvedon	d		11 23						11 54					12 23					12 54			
Braintree	d	11 00											12 00									
Braintree Freeport	d	11 02											12 02									
Cressing	d	11 05											12 05									
White Notley	d	11 08											12 08									
Witham ■	d	11 16	11 29				11 46		12 00				12 16	12 29			12 46		13 00			
Hatfield Peverel	d		11 33											12 33								
Chelmsford ■	d	11 26	11 40				11 56		12 09		12 21		12 26	12 40			12 56		13 09		13 21	
Ingatestone	d	11 32					12 02						12 32				13 02					
Shenfield ■	a	11 38	11 50				12 08		12 19				12 38	12 50			13 08		13 19			
Romford	a								12 28										13 28			
Stratford ■ ⊖	a	11 52	12 05				12 22		12 36		12s45		12 52	13 05			13 22		13 36		13s45	
London Liverpool Street ■ ⊖	a	12 01	12 14		12 19		12 31		12 45		12 55		13 01	13 14		13 19	13 31		13 45		13 55	

Norwich, Ipswich, Harwich, Clacton, Walton-on-Naze, Colchester and Chelmsford - London

Network Diagram - see first Page of Table 5

		LE 1	LE 1	LE 1	LE ◇1 ⊡	LE 1	LE 1	LE 1	LE 1	LE 1	LE ◇1 ⊡	LE 1	LE 1	LE 1	LE 1	LE ◇1 ⊡	LE 1	LE 1	LE 1	LE 1	LE ◇1 ⊡	LE 1	LE 1
Norwich	d				12 30						13 00					13 30					14 00		
Diss	d				12 47						13 17					13 47					14 17		
Peterborough 8	d					11 45																	
Stowmarket	d			12 44		13 13					13 29				13 44						14 29		
Needham Market	d			12 49											13 49								
Ipswich	a			13 00	13 08	13 28					13 41				14 00	14 08					14 41		
	d		12 52		13 09						13 43			13 52		14 09					14 43		
Harwich Town	d							13 28										14 28					
Dovercourt	d							13 30										14 30					
Harwich International	d							13 33										14 33					
Wrabness	d							13 39										14 39					
Mistley	d							13 45										14 45					
Manningtree 2	d		13 02		13 19			13a50			13 53			14 02		14 19		14a50			14 53		
Walton-on-the-Naze	d									13 00										14 00			
Frinton-on-Sea	d									13 03										14 03			
Kirby Cross	d									13 06										14 06			
Clacton-on-Sea	d						13 05										14 05						
Thorpe-le-Soken 1	a						13 13			13 12							14 13			14 12			
	d						13 13			13 17							14 13			14 17			
Weeley	d									13 21										14 21			
Great Bentley	d									13 24										14 24			
Alresford (Essex)	d									13 28										14 28			
Wivenhoe 3	d						13 23			13 32							14 23			14 32			
Hythe	d									13 36										14 36			
Colchester Town	a									13 40										14 40			
	d								13 35	13 44		14 00							14 35	14 44		15 00	
Colchester 4	a		13 11		13 28		13 31		13 42	13 52	14 02	14 07		14 11		14 28	14 31		14 42	14 52	15 02	15 07	
Colchester 4	d		13 12		13 30		13 33		13 43		14 03			14 12		14 30	14 33		14 43		15 03		
Marks Tey 2	d		13 18						13 49					14 18					14 49				
Kelvedon	d		13 23						13 54					14 23					14 54				
Braintree	d	13 00											14 00										15 00
Braintree Freeport	d	13 02											14 02										15 02
Cressing	d	13 05											14 05										15 05
White Notley	d	13 08											14 08										15 08
Witham 2	d	13 16	13 29				13 46		14 00				14 16	14 29			14 46		15 00				15 16
Hatfield Peverel	d		13 33											14 33									
Chelmsford 3	d	13 26	13 40				13 56		14 09		14 21		14 26	14 40			14 56		15 09		15 21		15 26
Ingatestone	d	13 32					14 02						14 32				15 02						15 32
Shenfield 3	a	13 38	13 50				14 08		14 19				14 38	14 50			15 08		15 19				15 38
Romford	a								14 28										15 28				
Stratford 7 ⊖	a	13 52	14 05				14 22		14 36		14s45		14 52	15 05			15 22		15 36		15s45		15 52
London Liverpool Street 15 ⊖	a	14 01	14 14		14 19		14 31		14 45		14 55		15 01	15 15		15 19	15 33		15 45		15 55		16 01

		LE 1	LE 1	LE ◇1 ⊡	LE 1	LE 1	LE 1	LE 1	LE 1	LE ◇1 ⊡	LE 1	LE 1	LE 1	LE 1	LE ◇1 ⊡	LE 1	LE 1	LE 1	LE 1	LE 1	LE ◇1 ⊡	LE 1	LE 1
Norwich	d			14 30						15 00					15 30						16 00		
Diss	d			14 47						15 17					15 47						16 17		
Peterborough 8	d				13 45																		
Stowmarket	d		14 44		15 13					15 29				15 44							16 29		
Needham Market	d		14 49											15 49									
Ipswich	a		15 00	15 08	15 28					15 41				16 00	16 08						16 41		
	d	14 52		15 09						15 43			15 52		16 09						16 43		
Harwich Town	d						15 28										16 28						
Dovercourt	d						15 30										16 30						
Harwich International	d						15 33										16 33						
Wrabness	d						15 39										16 39						
Mistley	d						15 45										16 45						
Manningtree 2	d	15 02		15 19			15a50			15 53			16 02		16 19		16a50				16 53		
Walton-on-the-Naze	d								15 00											16 00			
Frinton-on-Sea	d								15 03											16 03			
Kirby Cross	d								15 06											16 06			
Clacton-on-Sea	d					15 05										16 05							
Thorpe-le-Soken 1	a					15 13			15 12							16 13				16 12			
	d					15 13			15 17							16 13				16 17			
Weeley	d								15 21											16 21			
Great Bentley	d								15 24											16 24			
Alresford (Essex)	d								15 28											16 28			
Wivenhoe 3	d					15 23			15 32							16 23				16 32			
Hythe	d								15 36											16 36			
Colchester Town	a								15 40											16 40			
	d							15 35	15 44		16 00							16 35		16 44		16 56	
Colchester 4	a	15 11		15 28		15 31		15 42	15 52	16 02	16 07		16 11		16 28	16 31		16 42		16 54	17 02	17 05	
Colchester 4	d	15 12		15 30		15 33		15 43		16 03			16 12		16 30	16 33		16 43	16 53		17 03		
Marks Tey 2	d	15 18						15 49					16 18						16 59				
Kelvedon	d	15 23						15 54					16 23					16 52					
Braintree	d											16 00											17 00
Braintree Freeport	d											16 02											17 02
Cressing	d											16 05											17 05
White Notley	d											16 08											17 08
Witham 2	d	15 29				15 46		16 00				16 16	16 29			16 46		16 58	17 08				17 16
Hatfield Peverel	d	15 33											16 33					17 02					
Chelmsford 3	d	15 40				15 56		16 09		16 21		16 26	16 40			16 56		17 09	17 17		17 21		17 26
Ingatestone	d					16 02						16 32				17 02							17 32
Shenfield 3	a	15 50				16 08		16 19				16 38	16 50			17 08		17 19	17 27				17 38
Romford	a																						
Stratford 7 ⊖	a	16 05				16 22		16 34		16s45		16 52	17 05			17 22		17 36	17 42		17s45		17 52
London Liverpool Street 15 ⊖	a	16 14		16 17		16 31		16 44		16 55		17 03	17 16		17 19	17 34		17 46	17 53		17 58		18 01

Table 11 Mondays to Fridays
29 August to 7 September

Norwich, Ipswich, Harwich, Clacton, Walton-on-Naze, Colchester and Chelmsford - London

Network Diagram - see first Page of Table 5

		LE 1	LE 1	LE 1	LE ◇1 ⊡	LE 1	LE 1	LE 1	LE 1	LE 1	LE 1	LE 1	LE ◇1 ⊡	LE 1	LE 1	LE 1	LE 1	LE ◇1 ⊡	LE 1	LE 1	LE 1	LE 1
Norwich	d				16 30								17 00					17 30				
Diss	d				16 47								17 17					17 47				
Peterborough 8	d					15 45																
Stowmarket	d		16 44			17 13							17 29	17 45				17 59				
Needham Market	d		16 49											17 50								
Ipswich	a		17 00		17 08	17 28							17 41	18 04				18 11				
	d	16 52			17 09						17 33		17 43					18 13				18 22
Harwich Town	d			16 53								17 28			18 00							
Dovercourt	d			16 55								17 30			18 02							
Harwich International	d			16 58								17 33			18 05							
Wrabness	d			17 04								17 39			18 11							
Mistley	d			17 10								17 45			18 17							
Manningtree 2	d	17 02		17a15	17 19						17 43	17a50	17 53		18a22							18 33
Walton-on-the-Naze	d									17 00												
Frinton-on-Sea	d									17 03												
Kirby Cross	d									17 06												
Clacton-on-Sea	d						17 05												18 05			
Thorpe-le-Soken 1	a						17 13			17 12									18 13			
	d						17 13			17 17									18 13			
Weeley	d									17 21												
Great Bentley	d									17 24												
Alresford (Essex)	d									17 28												
Wivenhoe 3	d						17 23			17 32									18 23			
Hythe	d									17 36												
Colchester Town	a									17 40												
	d								17 30	17 44										18 32		
Colchester 4	a	17 11			17 28		17 31		17 37	17 52	17 52		18 02					18 28	18 33	18 39		18 42
Colchester 4	d	17 12			17 30		17 33		17 48				18 03				18 12	18 30	18 33			18 43
Marks Tey 2	d	17 18							17 54								18 18					18 49
Kelvedon	d	17 23							17 59								18 23					18 54
Braintree	d							17 44													18 33	
Braintree Freeport	d							17 46													18 36	
Cressing	d							17 49													18 39	
White Notley	d							17 52													18 42	
Witham 2	d	17 29					17 46	18 00	18 05							18 16	18 29		18 46		18 51	19 00
Hatfield Peverel	d	17 33							18 09								18 33				18 55	
Chelmsford 3	d	17 40					17 56	18 09	18 16				18 21			18 26	18 40		18 56		19 02	19 09
Ingatestone	d						18 02									18 32			19 02			
Shenfield 3	a	17 50					18 08	18 19	18 26							18 38	18 50		19 08		19 13	19 19
Romford	a							18 28														19 28
Stratford 7 ⊖	a	18 06					18 22	18 36	18 42				18s45			18 52	19 05		19 22		19 27	19 36
London Liverpool Street 15 ⊖	a	18 15			18 19		18 31	18 45	18 51				18 55			19 01	19 14	19 17	19 31		19 36	19 45

		LE 1	LE 1	LE 1	LE 1	LE ◇1 ⊡	LE 1	LE 1	LE 1	LE 1	LE ◇1 ⊡	LE 1	LE 1	LE 1	LE 1	LE 1	LE 1	LE 1	LE 1	LE 1	LE 1	LE ◇1 ⊡	LE 1
Norwich	d					18 00					18 30											19 00	
Diss	d					18 17					18 47											19 17	
Peterborough 8	d																17 45						
Stowmarket	d					18 29			18 45								19 13					19 29	
Needham Market	d								18 50														
Ipswich	a					18 41			19 02		19 08						19 28					19 41	
	d					18 43		18 47			19 09					19 23				19 35		19 43	
Harwich Town	d		18 26									19 05									19 28		
Dovercourt	d		18 28									19 07									19 30		
Harwich International	d		18 31									19 10									19 33		
Wrabness	d		18 37									19 16									19 39		
Mistley	d		18 43									19 22									19 45		
Manningtree 2	d		18a48			18 53		18 57			19 19	19a27				19 36				19 45	19a50	19 53	
Walton-on-the-Naze	d	17 57		18 33														18 54	19 15				
Frinton-on-Sea	d	18 00		18 36														18 57	19 18				
Kirby Cross	d	18 03		18 42														19 00	19 21				
Clacton-on-Sea	d													19 02									
Thorpe-le-Soken 1	a	18 09		18 48										19 10				19 08	19 27				
	d	18 17												19 10				19 17					
Weeley	d	18 21																19 21					
Great Bentley	d	18 24																19 24					
Alresford (Essex)	d	18 28																19 28					
Wivenhoe 3	d	18 32												19 23				19 32					
Hythe	d	18 36																19 36					
Colchester Town	a	18 40																19 40					
	d	18 44								19 08					19 35			19 44					
Colchester 4	a	18 52				19 02		19 06		19 15	19 28			19 31	19 42	19 46		19 52		19 54		20 02	
Colchester 4	d				18 55	19 03		19 12			19 30			19 33	19 43					19 55		20 03	
Marks Tey 2	d				19 01			19 18							19 49					20 01			
Kelvedon	d							19 23							19 54								
Braintree	d												19 24										
Braintree Freeport	d												19 27										
Cressing	d												19 30										
White Notley	d												19 33										
Witham 2	d				19 16			19 29					19 42	19 46	20 00					20 16			
Hatfield Peverel	d						←	19 33															←
Chelmsford 3	d				19 26	19 21	19 26	19 40					19 51	19 56	20 09					20 26		20 21	20 26
Ingatestone	d				→		19 32							20 02						→			20 32
Shenfield 3	a						19 38	19 50						20 08	20 19								20 38
Romford	a														20 28								
Stratford 7 ⊖	a					19s45	19 52	20 05					20 14	20 22	20 36							20s45	20 52
London Liverpool Street 15 ⊖	a					19 55	20 01	20 14			20 19		20 23	20 31	20 45							20 55	21 01

29 August to 7 September

Norwich, Ipswich, Harwich, Clacton, Walton-on-Naze, Colchester and Chelmsford - London

Network Diagram - see first Page of Table 5

		LE 1	LE 1	LE 1	LE 1	LE ◇1	LE 1	LE 1	LE 1	LE 1	LE 1	LE 1	LE ◇1	LE 1	LE 1	LE 1	LE 1	LE 1	LE ◇1	LE 1	LE 1	LE 1
Norwich	d					19 30							20 00						20 30			
Diss	d					19 47							20 17						20 47			
Peterborough 8	d																					
Stowmarket	d				19 44								20 29					20 44				
Needham Market	d				19 49													20 49				
Ipswich	a				20 00	20 09							20 41					21 00	21 08			
	d			19 52		20 09			20 20				20 43					21 00	21 09			
Harwich Town	d						20 05			20 28											21 05	
Dovercourt	d						20 07			20 30											21 07	
Harwich International	d						20 10			20 33							20 45	21a29			21 10	
Wrabness	d						20 16			20 39											21 16	
Mistley	d						20 22			20 45											21 22	
Manningtree 2	d			20 02		20 19	20a27		20 33	20a50			20 53				20 58		21 19		21 27	
Walton-on-the-Naze	d											19 55		20 33								
Frinton-on-Sea	d											19 58		20 36								
Kirby Cross	d											20 01		20 42								
Clacton-on-Sea	d							20 05												21 05		
Thorpe-le-Soken 1	a							20 13				20 07		20 48						21 13		
	d							20 13				20 17								21 13		
Weeley	d											20 21										
Great Bentley	d											20 24										
Alresford (Essex)	d											20 28										
Wivenhoe 3	d							20 23				20 32								21 23		
Hythe	d											20 36										
Colchester Town	a											20 40										
	d	20 00									20 35	20 44			21 00							21 35
Colchester 4	a	20 07		20 11		20 29		20 31	20 45		20 42	20 52	21 02		21 07		21 07		21 28	21 31	21 36	21 42
Colchester 4	d			20 12		20 30		20 33			20 50		21 03				21 12		21 30	21 33		21 43
Marks Tey 2	d			20 18							20 56						21 18					21 49
Kelvedon	d			20 23							21 01						21 23					21 54
Braintree	d		20 11													21 00						
Braintree Freeport	d		20 13													21 02						
Cressing	d		20 16													21 05						
White Notley	d		20 19													21 08						
Witham 2	d		20 27	20 31				20 46			21 07					21 16	21 29			21 46		22 00
Hatfield Peverel	d			20 35													21 33					
Chelmsford 3	d		20 36	20 42				20 56			21 16		21 21			21 26	21 40			21 56		22 09
Ingatestone	d							21 02								21 32				22 02		
Shenfield 3	a		20 46	20 52				21 08			21 26					21 38	21 50			22 08		22 19
Romford	a																					
Stratford 7 ⊖	a			21 07				21 22			21 42		21s45			21 52	22 11			22 26		22 38
London Liverpool Street 15 ⊖	a		21 12	21 16		21 19		21 31			21 51		21 55			22 01	22 21		22 20	22 36		22 48

		LE ◇1	LE 1	LE 1	LE ◇1	LE 1	LE 1	LE 1	LE 1	LE 1	LE 1	LE 1	LE 1	LE ◇1	LE 1	LE 1	LE 1	LE 1	LE ◇1	LE 1	LE 1	LE 1	LE
Norwich	d				21 00									22 00						23 05			
Diss	d				21 17									22 17						23 22			
Peterborough 8	d	19 45																	21 45				
Stowmarket	d	21 09			21 29	21 44								22 29	22 44				23 06	23 34			23 47
Needham Market	d					21 49									22 49								23 52
Ipswich	a	21 23			21 41	22 00								22 41	23 00				23 18	23 48			00 05
	d	21 25			21 43					22 23				22 43					23 19				
Harwich Town	d			21 28								22 28									23 28		
Dovercourt	d			21 30								22 30									23 30		
Harwich International	d			21 33								22 33									23 33		
Wrabness	d			21 39								22 39									23 39		
Mistley	d			21 45								22 45									23 45		
Manningtree 2	d	21 35		21a50	21 53					22 33		22a50		22 53					23 29		23a50		
Walton-on-the-Naze	d		21 00								22 00						23 00						
Frinton-on-Sea	d		21 03								22 03						23 03						
Kirby Cross	d		21 06								22 06						23 06						
Clacton-on-Sea	d								22 05									23 05					
Thorpe-le-Soken 1	a		21 12						22 13		22 12						23 12	23 13					
	d		21 17						22 13		22 17							23 13					
Weeley	d		21 21								22 21							23 17					
Great Bentley	d		21 24								22 24							23 20					
Alresford (Essex)	d		21 28								22 28							23 24					
Wivenhoe 3	d		21 32						22 23		22 32							23 28					
Hythe	d		21 36								22 36							23 32					
Colchester Town	a		21 40								22 40												
	d		21 44					22 00			22 44					23 00							
Colchester 4	a	21 46	21 52		22 02			22 07	22 31	22 42	22 52			23 02		23 07		23 38	23 40				
Colchester 4	d				22 03			22 12	22 33	22 43				23 03									
Marks Tey 2	d							22 18		22 49													
Kelvedon	d							22 23		22 54													
Braintree	d						22 00						22 56									23 45	
Braintree Freeport	d						22 02						22 58									23 47	
Cressing	d						22 05						23 01									23 50	
White Notley	d						22 08						23 04									23 53	
Witham 2	d						22 16	22 29	22 46	23 00			23a12	23 16								00a01	
Hatfield Peverel	d							22 33															
Chelmsford 3	d				22 21		22 26	22 40	22 56	23 09				23 25									
Ingatestone	d						22 32		23 02														
Shenfield 3	a						22 38	22 50	23 08	23 19				23s36									
Romford	a																						
Stratford 7 ⊖	a						22 56	23 10	23 26	23 38													
London Liverpool Street 15 ⊖	a				22 54		23 06	23 20	23 36	23 48				00 03									

from 10 September

Norwich, Ipswich, Harwich, Clacton, Walton-on-Naze, Colchester and Chelmsford - London

Network Diagram - see first Page of Table 5

		LE FO ◇1 A	LE ◇1 B	LE MO ◇1 C	LE TW ThO ◇1 D	LE B	LE MX	LE TW ThO 1 D	LE MO C	LE FO 1 E	LE TW ThO 1 D	LE 1 B	LE 1	LE ◇1	LE 1	LE 1	LE 1	LE ◇1	LE 1	LE 1	LE 1	LE 1	LE 1	LE 1	LE 1
Norwich	d	22p00	22p00	22p00	22p00													05 00							
Diss	d	22p17	22p17	22p17	22p17													05 18							
Peterborough 8	d																								
Stowmarket	d	22p29	22p29	22p29	22p29	23p47	23p47		00 06			00 47						05 30					05 54		
Needham Market	d					23p52	23p52		00 11			00 52											05 59		
Ipswich	a	22p41	22p41	22p41	22p41	00 03	00 05		00 23			01 03						05 42					06 09		
	d	22p43	22p43	22p43	22p43									05 14				05 44				06 00			
Harwich Town	d														05 24										
Dovercourt	d														05 26										
Harwich International	d														05 29										
Wrabness	d														05 35										
Mistley	d														05 41										
Manningtree 2	d	22p53	22p53	22p53	22p53									05 25	05a46			05 54				06 11			
Walton-on-the-Naze	d																		05 35					06 05	
Frinton-on-Sea	d																		05 38					06 08	
Kirby Cross	d																		05 41					06 11	
Clacton-on-Sea	d																05 20				05 40				
Thorpe-le-Soken 1	a																05 28		05 47		05 48			06 17	
	d																05 28				05 48				
Weeley	d																				05 52				
Great Bentley	d																				05 56				
Alresford (Essex)	d																				06 00				
Wivenhoe 3	d																05 38				06 04				
Hythe	d																				06 08				
Colchester Town	a																								
	d																								06 19
Colchester 4	a	23p02	23p02	23p02	23p02									05 34			05 46	06 03			06 14	06 20			06 26
Colchester 4	d	23p03	23p03	23p03	23p03								05 12	05 35			05 47	06 05			06 15	06 20			06 27
Marks Tey 2	d												05 18				05 53					06 26			06 33
Kelvedon	d												05 23				05 59				06 25	06 32			
Braintree	d							00 05		00 25	00 46					05 45									
Braintree Freeport	d							00 07		00 27	00 48					05 47									
Cressing	d							00 10		00 30	00 51					05 50									
White Notley	d							00 13		00 33	00 54					05 53									
Witham 2	d	23p16	23p16	23p16	23p16			00a21		00a41	01a02		05 29	05 48		06a02	06 05			06 18	06 31	06 38			06 47
Hatfield Peverel	d												05 33							06 22					
Chelmsford 3	d	23p25	23p25	23p25	23p25								05 40	05 58			06 14			06 29	06 40	06 47			06 56
Ingatestone	d												05 47							06 36					07 03
Shenfield 3	a	23b36	23b36	23b36	23p36								05 52				06 24			06 41	06 50				07 07
Romford	a																								
Stratford 7 ⊖	a	23b52		23b57	00s04								06 07	06s22			06 39	06s44		06s57	07s06				07s23
London Liverpool Street 15 ⊖	a	00 02	00 03	00 08	00 14								06 16	06 34			06 48	06 54		07 09	07 18	07 24			07 35

A also from 11 September until 13 September
B 10 September
C from 17 September
D from 18 September
E also from 10 September until 13 September
b Previous night, stops to set down only

Table 11

Mondays to Fridays
from 10 September

Norwich, Ipswich, Harwich, Clacton, Walton-on-Naze, Colchester and Chelmsford - London

Network Diagram - see first Page of Table 5

		LE	LE	LE	LE	LE	LE	LE	LE	LE	LE	LE	LE	LE	LE	LE	LE	LE	LE	LE	LE	LE	LE
		■ 1 ⊡	1	1	1	1	1	■ 1 ⊡	1	1	1	1	1	1	1		1	1	■ 1 ⊡	1	1	1	1
Norwich	d	05 30						06 00											06 25				
Diss	d	05 48						06 18											06 43				
Peterborough 8	d																						
Stowmarket	d	06 00						06 30								06 44			06 55				
Needham Market	d															06 49							
Ipswich	a	06 12						06 42								07 01			07 07				
	d	06 14			06 29			06 44					06 52		06 59				07 09				
Harwich Town	d					06 24								06 52									
Dovercourt	d					06 26								06 54									
Harwich International	d					06 29								06 57	07a28								
Wrabness	d					06 35								07 03									
Mistley	d					06 41								07 09									
Manningtree 2	d	06 24			06 39	06a46		06 54					07 02	07a14					07 19				
Walton-on-the-Naze	d									06 32											06 59		
Frinton-on-Sea	d									06 35											07 02		
Kirby Cross	d									06 38											07 05		
Clacton-on-Sea	d		06 10						06 28			06 38						06 47		06 51			
Thorpe-le-Soken 1	a		06 18						06 36	06 44		06 46						06 55		06 59	07 11		
	d		06 18						06 36			06 46						06 55		06 59			
Weeley	d								06 40											07 03			
Great Bentley	d								06 43											07 06			
Alresford (Essex)	d								06 47											07 10			
Wivenhoe 3	d		06 29						06 51			06 57						07 06		07 14			
Hythe	d		06 33						06 55			07 01						07 10		07 18			
Colchester Town	a								06 59											07 22			
	d						06 47		07 03											07 27			
Colchester 4	a	06 33	06 39		06 48		06 54	07 03	07 13			07 07	07 12					07 16	07 28	07 35			
Colchester 4	d	06 35	06 40		06 49		06 55	07 05				07 08	07 13					07 17	07 30				
Marks Tey 2	d				06 55		07 01						07 19					07 23					
Kelvedon	d		06 50		07 00							07 18						07 29					
Braintree	d			06 40																			07 26
Braintree Freeport	d			06 42																			07 29
Cressing	d			06 45																			07 32
White Notley	d			06 48																			07 35
Witham 2	d			06 57	07 06		07 10				07 17						07 29	07 35					07 44
Hatfield Peverel	d			07 02													07 33						07 48
Chelmsford 3	d		07 03	07 09			07 19				07 27	07 31	07 35				07 40					07 49	07 55
Ingatestone	d										07 33		07 42									07 56	
Shenfield 3	a			07 19							07 38	07 41					07 50					08 01	
Romford	a																						
Stratford 7 ⊖	a	07s15	07s27	07s35	07s38		07 44				07s55	07s58	08s01				08s07	08s09				08s18	08s20
London Liverpool Street 15 ⊖	a	07 27	07 38	07 46	07 50		07 56	07 58			08 07	08 09	08 13				08 19	08 21	08 23			08 30	08 32

		LE	LE	LE	LE	LE	LE	LE	LE	LE	LE	LE	LE	LE	LE	LE	LE	LE	LE	LE	LE	LE
		1	◇1	1	1	■ 1 ⊡	1	1	1	■ 1 ⊡		1	1	1	1	■ 1 A ⊡	1	1	1	◇1	1	1
Norwich	d					06 50				07 05						07 40						
Diss	d					07 08				07 23						07 58						
Peterborough 8	d																					
Stowmarket	d		07 05			07 20				07 35	07 45									08 11		
Needham Market	d										07 50											
Ipswich	a		07 18			07 32				07 47	08 03					08 18				08 24		
	d		07 18			07 34			07 38	07 49						08 20				08 26		
Harwich Town	d						07 16											07 58			08 28	
Dovercourt	d						07 18											08 00			08 30	
Harwich International	d				07 15		07 21											08 03			08 33	
Wrabness	d						07 27											08 09			08 39	
Mistley	d						07 33											08 15			08 45	
Manningtree 2	d		07 28		07 32	07 44	07 38		07 49	07 59								08 20		08 36	08a50	
Walton-on-the-Naze	d																07 40		08 00			
Frinton-on-Sea	d																07 43		08 03			
Kirby Cross	d																07 46		08 06			
Clacton-on-Sea	d	07 05						07 16						07 45								
Thorpe-le-Soken 1	a	07 13						07 24						07 53			07 52		08 11			
	d	07 13						07 24						07 53			07 58		08 12			
Weeley	d							07 28									08 02					
Great Bentley	d							07 31									08 05					
Alresford (Essex)	d							07 35									08 09					
Wivenhoe 3	d	07 24						07 39						08 03			08 13		08 22			
Hythe	d							07 43									08 17		08 26			
Colchester Town	a																08 21					
	d														08 00		08 32					
Colchester 4	a	07 32	07 37		07 41		07 47	07 50	07 58	08 08				08 16	08 09		08 40	08 29	08 35	08 45		
Colchester 4	d	07 33	07 38		07 42		07 54		07 59	08 10					08 18		08 48	08 37		08 45		
Marks Tey 2	d		07 44		07 48				08 05						08 24		→					
Kelvedon	d	07 43	07 49				08 04		08 10						08 30							
Braintree	d												08 12									
Braintree Freeport	d												08 14									
Cressing	d												08 17									
White Notley	d												08 20									
Witham 2	d	07 50	07 55		08 03		08 10		08 16				08 28		08 36			08 50				08 58
Hatfield Peverel	d				08 07								08 32									09 02
Chelmsford 3	d	07 59		08 09	08 14		08 19					08 30	08 39		08 45			08 59		09 04		09 09
Ingatestone	d			08 16								08 37	08 46									09 16
Shenfield 3	a	08 09		08 21	08 23		08 29					08 42	08 51		08 55							09 21
Romford	a																					
Stratford 7 ⊖	a	08s25	08s28	08s38	08s41		08s45		08s48	08s52		08s59	09s08					09s23		09s28		09s37
London Liverpool Street 15 ⊖	a	08 38	08 40	08 50	08 54	08 42	08 58		09 01	09 04		09 11	09 19		09 21	09 24		09 36		09 40		09 49

A The East Anglian

Table 11

Mondays to Fridays
from 10 September

Norwich, Ipswich, Harwich, Clacton, Walton-on-Naze, Colchester and Chelmsford - London

Network Diagram - see first Page of Table 5

		LE	LE	LE	LE	LE	LE	LE	LE	LE	LE	LE	LE	LE	LE	LE	LE	LE	LE	LE	LE	LE	LE
		1	1	■ 1 ⊡	1	1	1	1	■ 1 ⊡	1	1	1	1	1	1	■ 1 ⊡	1	1	1	1	◇1 ⊡	1	1
Norwich	d			08 00					08 30							09 00					09 30		
Diss	d			08 17					08 47							09 17					09 47		
Peterborough 8	d									07 45													
Stowmarket	d			08 29		08 44				09 14						09 29				09 44			
Needham Market	d					08 49														09 49			
Ipswich	a			08 41		09 00			09 08	09 28						09 41				10 02	10 08		
	d			08 43			08 48		09 09				09 30			09 43			09 52		10 09		
Harwich Town	d														09 28								10 28
Dovercourt	d														09 30								10 30
Harwich International	d														09 33								10 33
Wrabness	d														09 39								10 39
Mistley	d														09 45								10 45
Manningtree 2	d			08 53			08 58		09 19				09 40		09a50	09 53			10 02		10 19		10a50
Walton-on-the-Naze	d													09 00									
Frinton-on-Sea	d													09 03									
Kirby Cross	d													09 06									
Clacton-on-Sea	d		08 11								09 05											10 05	
Thorpe-le-Soken 1	a		08 19								09 13			09 12								10 13	
	d		08 19								09 13			09 17								10 13	
Weeley	d		08 23											09 21									
Great Bentley	d		08 26											09 24									
Alresford (Essex)	d		08 30											09 28									
Wivenhoe 3	d		08 34								09 23			09 32								10 23	
Hythe	d		08 38											09 36									
Colchester Town	a	←												09 40									
	d							08 58				09 35		09 44			10 00						
Colchester 4	a	08 40	08 46	09 02			09 08	09 05	09 28		09 31	09 42	09 49	09 52		10 02	10 07		10 11		10 28	10 31	
Colchester 4	d	08 48		09 03			09 12		09 30		09 33	09 43	09 50			10 03			10 12		10 30	10 33	
Marks Tey 2	d	08 54					09 18						09 56						10 18				
Kelvedon	d	09 00					09 23					09 52							10 23				
Braintree	d				09 00													10 00					
Braintree Freeport	d				09 02													10 02					
Cressing	d				09 05													10 05					
White Notley	d				09 08													10 08					
Witham 2	d	09 06			09 16		09 29				09 46	09 58	10 05					10 16	10 29			10 46	
Hatfield Peverel	d						09 33												10 33				
Chelmsford 3	d	09 15		09 21	09 26		09 40				09 56	10 07	10 14			10 21		10 26	10 40			10 56	
Ingatestone	d				09 32						10 02							10 32				11 02	
Shenfield 3	a	09 25			09 38		09 50				10 08	10 17						10 38	10 50			11 08	
Romford	a											10 26											
Stratford 7 ⊖	a	09s41			09 52		10 05				10 22	10 34				10s45		10 52	11 05			11 22	
London Liverpool Street 15 ⊖	a	09 53		09 56	10 01		10 14		10 19		10 31	10 43	10 44			10 55		11 01	11 14		11 19	11 31	

		LE	LE	LE	LE	LE	LE	LE	LE	LE	LE	LE	LE	LE	LE	LE	LE	LE	LE	LE	LE	LE
		1	1	◇1 ⊡	1	1	1	1	◇1 ⊡	1	1	1	1	1	◇1 ⊡	1	1	1	1	◇1 ⊡	1	1
Norwich	d			10 00					10 30						11 00					11 30		
Diss	d			10 17					10 47						11 17					11 47		
Peterborough 8	d									09 45												
Stowmarket	d			10 29				10 44		11 14					11 29				11 44			
Needham Market	d							10 49											11 49			
Ipswich	a			10 41				11 00	11 08	11 28					11 41				12 00	12 08		
	d			10 43			10 52		11 09						11 43			11 52		12 09		
Harwich Town	d											11 28										12 28
Dovercourt	d											11 30										12 30
Harwich International	d											11 33										12 33
Wrabness	d											11 39										12 39
Mistley	d											11 45										12 45
Manningtree 2	d			10 53			11 02		11 19			11a50			11 53			12 02		12 19		12a50
Walton-on-the-Naze	d		10 00											11 00								
Frinton-on-Sea	d		10 03											11 03								
Kirby Cross	d		10 06											11 06								
Clacton-on-Sea	d										11 05										12 05	
Thorpe-le-Soken 1	a		10 12								11 13			11 12							12 13	
	d		10 17								11 13			11 17							12 13	
Weeley	d		10 21											11 21								
Great Bentley	d		10 24											11 24								
Alresford (Essex)	d		10 28											11 28								
Wivenhoe 3	d		10 32								11 23			11 32							12 23	
Hythe	d		10 36											11 36								
Colchester Town	a		10 40											11 40								
	d	10 35	10 44		11 00								11 35	11 44		12 00						
Colchester 4	a	10 42	10 52	11 02	11 07		11 11		11 28		11 31		11 42	11 52	12 02	12 07		12 11		12 28	12 31	
Colchester 4	d	10 43		11 03			11 12		11 30		11 33		11 43		12 03			12 12		12 30	12 33	
Marks Tey 2	d	10 49					11 18						11 49					12 18				
Kelvedon	d	10 54					11 23						11 54					12 23				
Braintree	d					11 00											12 00					
Braintree Freeport	d					11 02											12 02					
Cressing	d					11 05											12 05					
White Notley	d					11 08											12 08					
Witham 2	d	11 00				11 16	11 29				11 46		12 00				12 16	12 29			12 46	
Hatfield Peverel	d						11 33											12 33				
Chelmsford 3	d	11 09		11 21		11 26	11 40				11 56		12 09		12 21		12 26	12 40			12 56	
Ingatestone	d					11 32					12 02						12 32				13 02	
Shenfield 3	a	11 19				11 38	11 50				12 08		12 19				12 38	12 50			13 08	
Romford	a	11 28											12 28									
Stratford 7 ⊖	a	11 36		11s45		11 52	12 05				12 22		12 36		12s45		12 52	13 05			13 22	
London Liverpool Street 15 ⊖	a	11 45		11 55		12 01	12 14		12 19		12 31		12 45		12 55		13 01	13 14		13 19	13 31	

Norwich, Ipswich, Harwich, Clacton, Walton-on-Naze, Colchester and Chelmsford - London

Network Diagram - see first Page of Table 5

		LE 1	LE 1	LE ◇1 ☕	LE 1	LE 1	LE 1	LE 1	LE ◇1 ☕	LE 1	LE 1	LE 1	LE 1	LE 1	LE ◇1 ☕	LE 1	LE 1	LE 1	LE 1	LE ◇1 ☕	LE 1	LE 1	LE 1
Norwich	d			12 00					12 30						13 00					13 30			
Diss	d			12 17					12 47						13 17					13 47			
Peterborough 8	d									11 45													
Stowmarket	d			12 29				12 44		13 13					13 29				13 44				
Needham Market	d							12 49											13 49				
Ipswich	a			12 41				13 00	13 08	13 28					13 41				14 00	14 08			
	d			12 43			12 52		13 09						13 43			13 52		14 09			
Harwich Town	d											13 28										14 28	
Dovercourt	d											13 30										14 30	
Harwich International	d											13 33										14 33	
Wrabness	d											13 39										14 39	
Mistley	d											13 45										14 45	
Manningtree 2	d			12 53			13 02		13 19			13a50			13 53			14 02		14 19		14a50	
Walton-on-the-Naze	d		12 00											13 00									
Frinton-on-Sea	d		12 03											13 03									
Kirby Cross	d		12 06											13 06									
Clacton-on-Sea	d										13 05										14 05		
Thorpe-le-Soken 1	a		12 12								13 13			13 12							14 13		
	d		12 17								13 13			13 17							14 13		
Weeley	d		12 21											13 21									
Great Bentley	d		12 24											13 24									
Alresford (Essex)	d		12 28											13 28									
Wivenhoe 3	d		12 32								13 23			13 32							14 23		
Hythe	d		12 36											13 36									
Colchester Town	a		12 40											13 40									
	d	12 35	12 44		13 00								13 35	13 44		14 00							14 35
Colchester 4	a	12 42	12 52	13 02	13 07		13 11		13 28		13 31		13 42	13 52	14 02	14 07		14 11		14 28	14 31		14 42
Colchester 4	d	12 43		13 03			13 12		13 30		13 33		13 43		14 03			14 12		14 30	14 33		14 43
Marks Tey 2	d	12 49					13 18						13 49					14 18					14 49
Kelvedon	d	12 54					13 23						13 54					14 23					14 54
Braintree	d					13 00											14 00						
Braintree Freeport	d					13 02											14 02						
Cressing	d					13 05											14 05						
White Notley	d					13 08											14 08						
Witham 2	d	13 00				13 16	13 29				13 46		14 00				14 16	14 29			14 46		15 00
Hatfield Peverel	d						13 33											14 33					
Chelmsford 3	d	13 09		13 21		13 26	13 40				13 56		14 09		14 21		14 26	14 40			14 56		15 09
Ingatestone	d					13 32					14 02						14 32				15 02		
Shenfield 3	a	13 19				13 38	13 50				14 08		14 19				14 38	14 50			15 08		15 19
Romford	a	13 28											14 28										15 28
Stratford 7 ⊖	a	13 36		13s45		13 52	14 05				14 22		14 36		14s45		14 52	15 05			15 22		15 36
London Liverpool Street 15 ⊖	a	13 45		13 55		14 01	14 14		14 19		14 31		14 45		14 55		15 01	15 15		15 19	15 33		15 45

		LE 1	LE ◇1 ☕	LE 1	LE 1	LE 1	LE 1	LE ◇1 ☕	LE 1	LE 1	LE 1	LE 1	LE 1	LE ◇1 ☕	LE 1	LE 1	LE 1	LE 1	LE ◇1 ☕	LE 1	LE 1	LE 1	LE 1
Norwich	d		14 00					14 30						15 00					15 30				
Diss	d		14 17					14 47						15 17					15 47				
Peterborough 8	d								13 45														
Stowmarket	d		14 29				14 44		15 13					15 29				15 44					
Needham Market	d						14 49											15 49					
Ipswich	a		14 41				15 00	15 08	15 28					15 41				16 00	16 08				
	d		14 43			14 52		15 09						15 43			15 52		16 09				
Harwich Town	d										15 28										16 28		
Dovercourt	d										15 30										16 30		
Harwich International	d										15 33										16 33		
Wrabness	d										15 39										16 39		
Mistley	d										15 45										16 45		
Manningtree 2	d		14 53			15 02		15 19			15a50			15 53			16 02		16 19		16a50		
Walton-on-the-Naze	d	14 00											15 00										
Frinton-on-Sea	d	14 03											15 03										
Kirby Cross	d	14 06											15 06										
Clacton-on-Sea	d									15 05										16 05			
Thorpe-le-Soken 1	a	14 12								15 13			15 12							16 13			
	d	14 17								15 13			15 17							16 13			
Weeley	d	14 21											15 21										
Great Bentley	d	14 24											15 24										
Alresford (Essex)	d	14 28											15 28										
Wivenhoe 3	d	14 32								15 23			15 32							16 23			
Hythe	d	14 36											15 36										
Colchester Town	a	14 40											15 40										
	d	14 44		15 00								15 35	15 44		16 00							16 35	
Colchester 4	a	14 52	15 02	15 07		15 11		15 28		15 31		15 42	15 52	16 02	16 07		16 11		16 28	16 31		16 42	
Colchester 4	d		15 03			15 12		15 30		15 33		15 43		16 03			16 12		16 30	16 33		16 43	16 53
Marks Tey 2	d					15 18						15 49					16 18						16 59
Kelvedon	d					15 23						15 54					16 23					16 52	
Braintree	d				15 00											16 00							
Braintree Freeport	d				15 02											16 02							
Cressing	d				15 05											16 05							
White Notley	d				15 08											16 08							
Witham 2	d				15 16	15 29				15 46		16 00				16 16	16 29			16 46		16 58	17 08
Hatfield Peverel	d					15 33											16 33					17 02	
Chelmsford 3	d		15 21		15 26	15 40				15 56		16 09		16 21		16 26	16 40			16 56		17 09	17 17
Ingatestone	d				15 32					16 02						16 32				17 02			
Shenfield 3	a				15 38	15 50				16 08		16 19				16 38	16 50			17 08		17 19	17 27
Romford	a																						
Stratford 7 ⊖	a		15s45		15 52	16 05				16 22		16 34		16s45		16 52	17 05			17 22		17 36	17 42
London Liverpool Street 15 ⊖	a		15 55		16 01	16 14		16 17		16 31		16 44		16 55		17 03	17 16		17 19	17 34		17 46	17 53

Norwich, Ipswich, Harwich, Clacton, Walton-on-Naze, Colchester and Chelmsford - London

Network Diagram - see first Page of Table 5

		LE 1	LE ◇1 ☕	LE 1	LE 1	LE 1	LE 1	LE 1	LE ◇1 ☕	LE 1	LE 1	LE 1	LE 1	LE 1	LE 1	LE 1	LE ◇1 ☕	LE 1	LE 1	LE 1	LE 1	LE ◇1 ☕
Norwich	d		16 00						16 30								17 00					17 30
Diss	d		16 17						16 47								17 17					17 47
Peterborough 8	d									15 45												
Stowmarket	d		16 29				16 44			17 13							17 29	17 45				17 59
Needham Market	d						16 49											17 50				
Ipswich	a		16 41				17 00		17 08	17 28							17 41	18 04				18 11
	d		16 43			16 52			17 09						17 33		17 43					18 13
Harwich Town	d							16 53								17 28			18 00			
Dovercourt	d							16 55								17 30			18 02			
Harwich International	d							16 58								17 33			18 05			
Wrabness	d							17 04								17 39			18 11			
Mistley	d							17 10								17 45			18 17			
Manningtree 2	d		16 53			17 02		17a15	17 19						17 43	17a50	17 53		18a22			
Walton-on-the-Naze	d	16 00												17 00								
Frinton-on-Sea	d	16 03												17 03								
Kirby Cross	d	16 06												17 06								
Clacton-on-Sea	d										17 05											
Thorpe-le-Soken 1	a	16 12									17 13			17 12								
	d	16 17									17 13			17 17								
Weeley	d	16 21												17 21								
Great Bentley	d	16 24												17 24								
Alresford (Essex)	d	16 28												17 28								
Wivenhoe 3	d	16 32									17 23			17 32								
Hythe	d	16 36												17 36								
Colchester Town	a	16 40												17 40								
	d	16 44		16 56									17 30	17 44								
Colchester 4	a	16 54	17 02	17 05		17 11			17 28		17 31		17 37	17 52	17 52		18 02					18 28
Colchester 4	d		17 03			17 12			17 30		17 33		17 48				18 03				18 12	18 30
Marks Tey 2	d					17 18							17 54								18 18	
Kelvedon	d					17 23							17 59								18 23	
Braintree	d				17 00							17 44										
Braintree Freeport	d				17 02							17 46										
Cressing	d				17 05							17 49										
White Notley	d				17 08							17 52										
Witham 2	d				17 16	17 29					17 46	18 00	18 05							18 16	18 29	
Hatfield Peverel	d					17 33							18 09								18 33	
Chelmsford 3	d		17 21		17 26	17 40					17 56	18 09	18 16				18 21			18 26	18 40	
Ingatestone	d				17 32						18 02									18 32		
Shenfield 3	a				17 38	17 50					18 08	18 19	18 26							18 38	18 50	
Romford	a											18 28										
Stratford 7 ⊖	a		17s45		17 52	18 06					18 22	18 36	18 42				18s45			18 52	19 05	
London Liverpool Street 15 ⊖	a		17 58		18 01	18 15			18 19		18 31	18 45	18 51				18 55			19 01	19 14	19 17

		LE 1	LE 1	LE 1	LE 1	LE 1	LE 1	LE 1	LE 1	LE ◇1 ☕	LE 1	LE 1	LE 1	LE 1	LE ◇1 ☕	LE 1	LE 1	LE 1	LE 1	LE 1	LE 1	LE 1	LE 1
Norwich	d									18 00					18 30								
Diss	d									18 17					18 47								
Peterborough 8	d																				17 45		
Stowmarket	d									18 29			18 45								19 13		
Needham Market	d												18 50										
Ipswich	a									18 41			19 02		19 08						19 28		
	d				18 22					18 43		18 47			19 09					19 23			
Harwich Town	d						18 26									19 05							
Dovercourt	d						18 28									19 07							
Harwich International	d						18 31									19 10							
Wrabness	d						18 37									19 16							
Mistley	d						18 43									19 22							
Manningtree 2	d				18 33		18a48			18 53		18 57			19 19	19a27				19 36			
Walton-on-the-Naze	d					17 57		18 33														18 54	19 15
Frinton-on-Sea	d					18 00		18 36														18 57	19 18
Kirby Cross	d					18 03		18 42														19 00	19 21
Clacton-on-Sea	d	18 05																19 02					
Thorpe-le-Soken 1	a	18 13				18 09		18 48										19 10				19 08	19 27
	d	18 13				18 17												19 10				19 17	
Weeley	d					18 21																19 21	
Great Bentley	d					18 24																19 24	
Alresford (Essex)	d					18 28																19 28	
Wivenhoe 3	d	18 23				18 32												19 23				19 32	
Hythe	d					18 36																19 36	
Colchester Town	a					18 40																19 40	
	d		18 32			18 44								19 08					19 35			19 44	
Colchester 4	a	18 33	18 39		18 42	18 52				19 02		19 06		19 15	19 28			19 31	19 42	19 46		19 52	
Colchester 4	d	18 33			18 43				18 55	19 03		19 12			19 30			19 33	19 43				
Marks Tey 2	d				18 49				19 01			19 18							19 49				
Kelvedon	d				18 54							19 23							19 54				
Braintree	d			18 33													19 24						
Braintree Freeport	d			18 36													19 27						
Cressing	d			18 39													19 30						
White Notley	d			18 42													19 33						
Witham 2	d	18 46		18 51	19 00				19 16			19 29					19 42	19 46	20 00				
Hatfield Peverel	d			18 55							←	19 33											
Chelmsford 3	d	18 56		19 02	19 09				19 26	19 21	19 26	19 40					19 51	19 56	20 09				
Ingatestone	d	19 02							→		19 32							20 02					
Shenfield 3	a	19 08		19 13	19 19						19 38	19 50						20 08	20 19				
Romford	a				19 28														20 28				
Stratford 7 ⊖	a	19 22		19 27	19 36					19s45	19 52	20 05					20 14	20 22	20 36				
London Liverpool Street 15 ⊖	a	19 31		19 36	19 45					19 55	20 01	20 14			20 19		20 23	20 31	20 45				

Table 11

Mondays to Fridays

from 10 September

Norwich, Ipswich, Harwich, Clacton, Walton-on-Naze, Colchester and Chelmsford - London

Network Diagram - see first Page of Table 5

		LE ■	LE ■	LE ◇■ ⊡		LE ■	LE ■	LE ■	LE ■	LE ■	LE ◇■	LE ■	LE ■	LE ■		LE ■	LE ■	LE ■	LE ◇■ ⊡	LE ■	LE ■	LE ■	LE ■	LE ■
Norwich	d			19 00							19 30								20 00					
Diss	d			19 17							19 47								20 17					
Peterborough 8	d																							
Stowmarket	d			19 29						19 44									20 29					20 44
Needham Market	d									19 49														20 49
Ipswich	a			19 41						20 00	20 09								20 41					21 00
	d	19 35		19 43					19 52		20 09			20 20					20 43					21 00
Harwich Town	d		19 28									20 05				20 28								
Dovercourt	d		19 30									20 07				20 30								
Harwich International	d		19 33									20 10				20 33							20 45	21a29
Wrabness	d		19 39									20 16				20 39								
Mistley	d		19 45									20 22				20 45								
Manningtree 2	d	19 45	19a50	19 53					20 02		20 19	20a27		20 33		20a50			20 53				20 58	
Walton-on-the-Naze	d																	19 55		20 33				
Frinton-on-Sea	d																	19 58		20 36				
Kirby Cross	d																	20 01		20 42				
Clacton-on-Sea	d												20 05											
Thorpe-le-Soken 1	a												20 13					20 07		20 48				
	d												20 13					20 17						
Weeley	d																	20 21						
Great Bentley	d																	20 24						
Alresford (Essex)	d																	20 28						
Wivenhoe 3	d												20 23					20 32						
Hythe	d																	20 36						
Colchester Town	a																	20 40						
	d						20 00										20 35	20 44			21 00			
Colchester 4	a	19 54		20 02			20 07		20 11		20 29		20 31	20 45			20 42	20 52	21 02		21 07		21 07	
Colchester 4	d	19 55		20 03					20 12		20 30		20 33				20 50		21 03				21 12	
Marks Tey 2	d	20 01							20 18								20 56						21 18	
Kelvedon	d								20 23								21 01						21 23	
Braintree	d							20 11														21 00		
Braintree Freeport	d							20 13														21 02		
Cressing	d							20 16														21 05		
White Notley	d							20 19														21 08		
Witham 2	d	20 16						20 27	20 31				20 46				21 07					21 16	21 29	
Hatfield Peverel	d					←			20 35														21 33	
Chelmsford 3	d	20 26		20 21		20 26		20 36	20 42				20 56				21 16		21 21			21 26	21 40	
Ingatestone	d	→				20 32							21 02									21 32		
Shenfield 3	a					20 38		20 46	20 52				21 08				21 26					21 38	21 50	
Romford	a																							
Stratford 7 ⊖	a			20s45		20 52			21 07				21 22				21 42		21s45			21 52	22 05	
London Liverpool Street 15 ⊖	a			20 55		21 01		21 12	21 16		21 19		21 31				21 51		21 55			22 01	22 14	

Table 11

Mondays to Fridays

from 10 September

Norwich, Ipswich, Harwich, Clacton, Walton-on-Naze, Colchester and Chelmsford - London

Network Diagram - see first Page of Table 5

		LE ◇■	LE ■	LE ■	LE ■	LE ◇■	LE ■	LE ■	LE ◇■ A ⊡	LE ◇■ MT WO B ⊡		LE ■	LE ■ A	LE ■ MT WO B	LE ■ A	LE ■ MT WO B	LE ■ A	LE ■ MT WO B	LE ■ A	LE ■ MT WO B		LE ■	LE ■	LE ■	LE ◇■ A
Norwich	d	20 30							21 00	21 00															22 00
Diss	d	20 47							21 17	21 17															22 17
Peterborough 8	d					19 45																			
Stowmarket	d					21 09			21 29	21 29		21 44													22 29
Needham Market	d											21 49													
Ipswich	a	21 08				21 23			21 41	21 41		22 00													22 41
	d	21 09				21 25			21 43	21 43									22 23	22 23					22 43
Harwich Town	d			21 05				21 28															22 28		
Dovercourt	d			21 07				21 30															22 30		
Harwich International	d			21 10				21 33															22 33		
Wrabness	d			21 16				21 39															22 39		
Mistley	d			21 22				21 45															22 45		
Manningtree 2	d	21 19		21 27		21 35		21a50	21 53	21 53									22 33	22 33			22a50		22 53
Walton-on-the-Naze	d						21 00															22 00			
Frinton-on-Sea	d						21 03															22 03			
Kirby Cross	d						21 06															22 06			
Clacton-on-Sea	d		21 05														22 05	22 05							
Thorpe-le-Soken 1	a		21 13				21 12										22 13	22 13				22 12			
	d		21 13				21 17										22 13	22 13				22 17			
Weeley	d						21 21															22 21			
Great Bentley	d						21 24															22 24			
Alresford (Essex)	d						21 28															22 28			
Wivenhoe 3	d		21 23				21 32										22 23	22 23				22 32			
Hythe	d						21 36															22 36			
Colchester Town	a						21 40															22 40			
	d				21 35		21 44								22 00	22 00						22 44			
Colchester 4	a	21 28	21 31	21 36	21 42	21 46	21 52		22 02	22 02					22 07	22 07	22 31	22 31	22 42	22 42		22 52			23 02
Colchester 4	d	21 30	21 33		21 43				22 03	22 03					22 12	22 12	22 33	22 33	22 43	22 43					23 03
Marks Tey 2	d				21 49										22 18	22 18			22 49	22 49					
Kelvedon	d				21 54										22 23	22 23			22 54	22 54					
Braintree	d												22 00	22 00										22 56	
Braintree Freeport	d												22 02	22 02										22 58	
Cressing	d												22 05	22 05										23 01	
White Notley	d												22 08	22 08										23 04	
Witham 2	d		21 46		22 00								22 16	22 16	22 29	22 29	22 46	22 46	23 00	23 00				23a12	23 16
Hatfield Peverel	d														22 33	22 33									
Chelmsford 3	d		21 56		22 09				22 21	22 21			22 26	22 26	22 40	22 40	22 56	22 56	23 09	23 09					23 25
Ingatestone	d		22 02										22 32	22 32			23 02	23 02							
Shenfield 3	a		22 08		22 19								22 38	22 38	22 50	22 50	23 08	23 08	23 19	23 19					23s36
Romford	a				22 28													23 19	23 28	23 31					
Stratford 7 ⊖	a		22 22		22 36				22s45	22s51			22 52	22 54	23 05	23 11	23 22	23 31	23 36	23 41					23s52
London Liverpool Street 15 ⊖	a	22 19	22 31		22 45				22 55	23 00			23 01	23 03	23 15	23 20	23 31	23 40	23 45	23 50					00 02

A ThFO, also from 10 September until 12 September

B from 17 September

Norwich, Ipswich, Harwich, Clacton, Walton-on-Naze, Colchester and Chelmsford - London

Network Diagram - see first Page of Table 5

		LE ◇■ MT WO A	LE ■	LE ■	LE ■	LE ■	LE ◇■	LE ■	LE ■	LE ■ B	LE
Norwich	d	22 00						23 05			
Diss	d	22 17						23 22			
Peterborough ■	d						21 45				
Stowmarket	d	22 29	22 44				23 06	23 34			23 47
Needham Market	d		22 49								23 52
Ipswich	a	22 41	23 00				23 18	23 48			00 05
	d	22 43					23 19				
Harwich Town	d								23 28		
Dovercourt	d								23 30		
Harwich International	d								23 33		
Wrabness	d								23 39		
Mistley	d								23 45		
Manningtree ■	d	22 53					23 29		23 50		
Walton-on-the-Naze	d				23 00						
Frinton-on-Sea	d				23 03						
Kirby Cross	d				23 06						
Clacton-on-Sea	d					23 05					
Thorpe-le-Soken ■	a				23 12	23 13					
	d					23 13					
Weeley	d					23 17					
Great Bentley	d					23 20					
Alresford (Essex)	d					23 24					
Wivenhoe ■	d					23 28					
Hythe	d					23 32					
Colchester Town	a										
	d			23 00							
Colchester ■	a	23 02		23 07		23 38	23 40		23 59		
Colchester ■	d	23 03									
Marks Tey ■	d										
Kelvedon	d										
Braintree	d									23 45	
Braintree Freeport	d									23 47	
Cressing	d									23 50	
White Notley	d									23 53	
Witham ■	d	23 16								00a01	
Hatfield Peverel	d										
Chelmsford ■	d	23 25									
Ingatestone	d										
Shenfield ■	a	23 36									
Romford	a										
Stratford ■ ⊖	a	00s04									
London Liverpool Street ■ ⊖	a	00 14									

A from 17 September

B ThFO, also from 10 September until 12 September

Norwich, Ipswich, Harwich, Clacton, Walton-on-Naze, Colchester and Chelmsford - London

Network Diagram - see first Page of Table 5

		LE ◇■	LE	LE ■	LE ■	LE ■	LE	LE ■	LE ◇■ 🍴	LE ■	LE ■	LE ◇■ 🍴	LE ■	LE ■	LE ■	LE ■	LE ◇■ 🍴	LE ■	LE ■	LE ■	LE ■	LE	LE ◇■ 🍴
Norwich	d	22p00							05 00			05 30					06 00						06 30
Diss	d	22p17							05 17			05 47					06 17						06 47
Peterborough ■	d																						
Stowmarket	d	22p29	23p47						05 29								06 29					06 44	
Needham Market	d		23p52																			06 49	
Ipswich	a	22p41	00 05						05 41			06 08					06 41					07 02	07 08
	d	22p43							05 43			06 09					06 43			06 52	06 59		07 09
Harwich Town	d													06 28									
Dovercourt	d													06 30									
Harwich International	d													06 33							07a28		
Wrabness	d													06 39									
Mistley	d													06 45									
Manningtree ■	d	22p53							05 53			06 19		06a50			06 53			07 02			07 19
Walton-on-the-Naze	d															06 00							
Frinton-on-Sea	d															06 03							
Kirby Cross	d															06 06							
Clacton-on-Sea	d							05 30					06 05					06 24					
Thorpe-le-Soken ■	a							05 38					06 13			06 12		06 32					
	d							05 38					06 13			06 17							
Weeley	d															06 21							
Great Bentley	d															06 24							
Alresford (Essex)	d															06 28							
Wivenhoe ■	d							05 48					06 23			06 32							
Hythe	d															06 36							
Colchester Town	a															06 40							
	d														06 35	06 44							
Colchester ■	a	23p02						05 57	06 02			06 28	06 31		06 42	06 52	07 02			07 11			07 28
Colchester ■	d	23p03			05 12	05 43	05 50		06 03		06 12	06 30	06 33		06 43		07 03			07 12			07 30
Marks Tey ■	d				05 18	05 49	05a57				06 18				06 49					07 18			
Kelvedon	d				05 23	05 54					06 23				06 54					07 23			
Braintree	d			00 25						06 00									07 00				
Braintree Freeport	d			00 27						06 02									07 02				
Cressing	d			00 30						06 05									07 05				
White Notley	d			00 33						06 08									07 08				
Witham ■	d	23p16		00a41	05 29	06 00				06a16	06 29		06 46		07 00				07 16	07 29			
Hatfield Peverel	d				05 33	06 04					06 33									07 33			
Chelmsford ■	d	23p25			05 40	06 11			06 21		06 40		06 56		07 09		07 21		07 26	07 40			
Ingatestone	d				05 47	06 18							07 02						07 32				
Shenfield ■	a	23b36			05 52	06 23					06 50		07 08		07 19				07 38	07 50			
Romford	a														07 28								
Stratford ■ ⊖	a	23b52			06 07	06 38			06s45		07 05		07 22		07 36		07s45		07 52	08 05			
London Liverpool Street ■ ⊖	a	00 02			06 16	06 47			06 55		07 14	07 19	07 31		07 45		07 55		08 01	08 14			08 19

		LE ■	LE ■	LE ■	LE ■	LE ◇■ 🍴	LE ■	LE ■	LE ■	LE	LE ◇■ 🍴	LE ■	LE ■	LE ■	LE ■	LE ◇■ 🍴	LE ■	LE ■	LE ■	LE ■	LE ◇■ 🍴	LE ■	LE ■
Norwich	d					07 00					07 30					08 00					08 30		
Diss	d					07 17					07 47					08 17					08 47		
Peterborough ■	d																					07 45	
Stowmarket	d					07 29				07 45						08 29				08 44		09 13	
Needham Market	d									07 50										08 49			
Ipswich	a					07 41				08 03	08 08					08 41				09 00	09 08	09 28	
	d					07 43			07 52		08 09					08 43			08 52		09 09		
Harwich Town	d				07 28								08 28										
Dovercourt	d				07 30								08 30										
Harwich International	d		07 20		07 33								08 33										
Wrabness	d				07 39								08 39										
Mistley	d				07 45								08 45										
Manningtree ■	d		07 33		07a50	07 53			08 02		08 19		08a50			08 53			09 02		09 19		
Walton-on-the-Naze	d			07 00											08 00								
Frinton-on-Sea	d			07 03											08 03								
Kirby Cross	d			07 06											08 06								
Clacton-on-Sea	d	07 05										08 05											09 05
Thorpe-le-Soken ■	a	07 13		07 12								08 13			08 12								09 13
	d	07 13		07 17								08 13			08 17								09 13
Weeley	d			07 21											08 21								
Great Bentley	d			07 24											08 24								
Alresford (Essex)	d			07 28											08 28								
Wivenhoe ■	d	07 23		07 32								08 23			08 32								09 23
Hythe	d			07 36											08 36								
Colchester Town	a			07 40											08 40								
	d			07 44			08 00							08 35	08 44		09 00						
Colchester ■	a	07 31	07 42	07 52		08 02	08 07		08 11		08 28	08 31		08 42	08 52	09 02	09 07		09 11		09 28		09 31
Colchester ■	d	07 33	07 43			08 03			08 12		08 30	08 33		08 43		09 03			09 12		09 30		09 33
Marks Tey ■	d		07 49						08 18					08 49					09 18				
Kelvedon	d		07 54						08 23					08 54					09 23				
Braintree	d							08 00										09 00					
Braintree Freeport	d							08 02										09 02					
Cressing	d							08 05										09 05					
White Notley	d							08 08										09 08					
Witham ■	d	07 46	08 00					08 16	08 29			08 46		09 00				09 16	09 29				09 46
Hatfield Peverel	d								08 33										09 33				
Chelmsford ■	d	07 56	08 09			08 21		08 26	08 40			08 56		09 09		09 21		09 26	09 40				09 56
Ingatestone	d	08 02						08 32				09 02						09 32					10 02
Shenfield ■	a	08 08	08 19					08 38	08 50			09 08		09 19				09 38	09 50				10 08
Romford	a		08 28											09 28									
Stratford ■ ⊖	a	08 22	08 36			08s45		08 52	09 05			09 22		09 36		09s45		09 52	10 05				10 22
London Liverpool Street ■ ⊖	a	08 31	08 45			08 55		09 01	09 14		09 19	09 31		09 45		09 55		10 01	10 14		10 19		10 31

b Previous night, stops to set down only

Table 11

Norwich, Ipswich, Harwich, Clacton, Walton-on-Naze, Colchester and Chelmsford - London

Saturdays until 21 July

Network Diagram - see first Page of Table 5

		LE 1		LE 1	LE 1	LE ◇1 🍴	LE 1	LE 1	LE 1	LE 1	LE ◇1 🍴	LE 1		LE 1	LE 1	LE 1	LE ◇1 🍴	LE 1	LE 1	LE 1	LE 1	LE ◇1 🍴		LE 1	LE 1
Norwich	d					09 00					09 30						10 00					10 30			
Diss	d					09 17					09 47						10 17					10 47			
Peterborough 8	d																							09 47	
Stowmarket	d					09 29				09 44							10 29				10 44			11 13	
Needham Market	d									09 49											10 49				
Ipswich	a					09 41				10 00	10 08						10 41				11 00	11 08		11 28	
	d					09 43			09 52		10 09						10 43			10 52		11 09			
Harwich Town	d	09 28												10 28											
Dovercourt	d	09 30												10 30											
Harwich International	d	09 33												10 33											
Wrabness	d	09 39												10 39											
Mistley	d	09 45												10 45											
Manningtree 2	d	09a50				09 53			10 02		10 19			10a50			10 53			11 02		11 19			
Walton-on-the-Naze	d				09 00											10 00									
Frinton-on-Sea	d				09 03											10 03									
Kirby Cross	d				09 06											10 06									
Clacton-on-Sea	d											10 05													11 05
Thorpe-le-Soken 1	a				09 12							10 13				10 12									11 13
	d				09 17							10 13				10 17									11 13
Weeley	d				09 21											10 21									
Great Bentley	d				09 24											10 24									
Alresford (Essex)	d				09 28											10 28									
Wivenhoe 3	d				09 32							10 23				10 32									11 23
Hythe	d				09 36											10 36									
Colchester Town	a				09 40											10 40									
	d			09 35	09 44		10 00								10 35	10 44		11 00							
Colchester 4	a			09 42	09 52	10 02	10 07		10 11		10 28	10 31			10 42	10 52	11 02	11 07		11 11		11 28			11 31
Colchester 4	d			09 43		10 03			10 12		10 30	10 33			10 43		11 03			11 12		11 30			11 33
Marks Tey 2	d			09 49					10 18						10 49					11 18					
Kelvedon	d			09 54					10 23						10 54					11 23					
Braintree	d							10 00											11 00						
Braintree Freeport	d							10 02											11 02						
Cressing	d							10 05											11 05						
White Notley	d							10 08											11 08						
Witham 2	d			10 00				10 16	10 29			10 46			11 00				11 16	11 29					11 46
Hatfield Peverel	d								10 33											11 33					
Chelmsford 3	d			10 09		10 21		10 26	10 40			10 56			11 09		11 21		11 26	11 40					11 56
Ingatestone	d							10 32				11 02							11 32						12 02
Shenfield 3	a			10 19				10 38	10 50			11 08			11 19				11 38	11 50					12 08
Romford	a			10 28											11 28										
Stratford 7 ⊖	a			10 36		10s45		10 52	11 05			11 22			11 36		11s45		11 52	12 05					12 22
London Liverpool Street 15 ⊖	a			10 45		10 55		11 01	11 14		11 19	11 31			11 45		11 55		12 01	12 14		12 19			12 31

Table 11

Norwich, Ipswich, Harwich, Clacton, Walton-on-Naze, Colchester and Chelmsford - London

Saturdays until 21 July

Network Diagram - see first Page of Table 5

		LE 1	LE 1	LE 1	LE ◇1 🍴	LE 1	LE 1	LE 1		LE 1	LE ■ 1 A 🍴	LE ◇1 B 🍴	LE 1	LE 1	LE 1	LE 1	LE ◇1 🍴	LE 1		LE 1	LE 1	LE 1	LE ◇1 🍴	LE 1	LE 1
Norwich	d				11 00						11 30	11 30					12 00						12 30		
Diss	d				11 17						11 47	11 47					12 17						12 47		
Peterborough 8	d																							11 45	
Stowmarket	d				11 29					11 44							12 29					12 44		13 13	
Needham Market	d									11 49												12 49			
Ipswich	a				11 41					12 00	12 08	12 08					12 41					13 00	13 08	13 28	
	d				11 43			11 52			12 09	12 09					12 43				12 52		13 09		
Harwich Town	d	11 28												12 28											
Dovercourt	d	11 30												12 30											
Harwich International	d	11 33												12 33											
Wrabness	d	11 39												12 39											
Mistley	d	11 45												12 45											
Manningtree 2	d	11a50			11 53			12 02			12 19	12 19		12a50			12 53				13 02		13 19		
Walton-on-the-Naze	d			11 00												12 00									
Frinton-on-Sea	d			11 03												12 03									
Kirby Cross	d			11 06												12 06									
Clacton-on-Sea	d												12 05												13 05
Thorpe-le-Soken 1	a			11 12									12 13			12 12									13 13
	d			11 17									12 13			12 17									13 13
Weeley	d			11 21												12 21									
Great Bentley	d			11 24												12 24									
Alresford (Essex)	d			11 28												12 28									
Wivenhoe 3	d			11 32									12 23			12 32									13 23
Hythe	d			11 36												12 36									
Colchester Town	a			11 40												12 40									
	d		11 35	11 44		12 00									12 35	12 44		13 00							
Colchester 4	a		11 42	11 52	12 02	12 07		12 11			12 28	12 28	12 31		12 42	12 52	13 02	13 07			13 11		13 28		13 31
Colchester 4	d		11 43		12 03			12 12			12 30	12 30	12 33		12 43		13 03				13 12		13 30		13 33
Marks Tey 2	d		11 49					12 18							12 49						13 18				
Kelvedon	d		11 54					12 23							12 54						13 23				
Braintree	d						12 00													13 00					
Braintree Freeport	d						12 02													13 02					
Cressing	d						12 05													13 05					
White Notley	d						12 08													13 08					
Witham 2	d		12 00				12 16	12 29					12 46		13 00					13 16	13 29				13 46
Hatfield Peverel	d							12 33													13 33				
Chelmsford 3	d		12 09		12 21		12 26	12 40					12 56		13 09		13 21			13 26	13 40				13 56
Ingatestone	d						12 32						13 02							13 32					14 02
Shenfield 3	a		12 19				12 38	12 50					13 08		13 19					13 38	13 50				14 08
Romford	a		12 28												13 28										
Stratford 7 ⊖	a		12 36		12s45		12 52	13 05					13 22		13 36		13s45			13 52	14 05				14 22
London Liverpool Street 15 ⊖	a		12 45		12 55		13 01	13 14			13 19	13 19	13 31		13 45		13 55			14 01	14 14		14 19		14 31

		LE 1	LE 1	LE 1		LE ◇1 🍴	LE 1	LE 1	LE 1	LE 1	LE ◇1 🍴	LE 1	LE 1	LE 1		LE 1	LE ■ 1 A 🍴	LE ◇1 B 🍴	LE 1	LE 1	LE 1	LE 1	LE ◇1 🍴	LE 1	
Norwich	d					13 00					13 30						14 00	14 00					14 30		
Diss	d					13 17					13 47						14 17	14 17					14 47		
Peterborough 8	d																							13 45	
Stowmarket	d					13 29				13 44							14 29	14 29				14 44		15 13	
Needham Market	d									13 49												14 49			
Ipswich	a					13 41				14 00	14 08						14 41	14 41				15 00	15 08	15 28	
	d					13 43			13 52		14 09						14 43	14 43			14 52		15 09		
Harwich Town	d	13 28											14 28												
Dovercourt	d	13 30											14 30												
Harwich International	d	13 33											14 33												
Wrabness	d	13 39											14 39												
Mistley	d	13 45											14 45												
Manningtree 2	d	13a50				13 53			14 02		14 19		14a50				14 53	14 53			15 02		15 19		
Walton-on-the-Naze	d			13 00												14 00									
Frinton-on-Sea	d			13 03												14 03									
Kirby Cross	d			13 06												14 06									
Clacton-on-Sea	d											14 05													
Thorpe-le-Soken 1	a			13 12								14 13				14 12									
	d			13 17								14 13				14 17									
Weeley	d			13 21												14 21									
Great Bentley	d			13 24												14 24									
Alresford (Essex)	d			13 28												14 28									
Wivenhoe 3	d			13 32								14 23				14 32									
Hythe	d			13 36												14 36									
Colchester Town	a			13 40												14 40									
	d		13 35	13 44			14 00							14 35		14 44			15 00						
Colchester 4	a		13 42	13 52		14 02	14 07		14 11		14 28	14 31		14 42		14 52	15 02	15 02	15 07		15 11		15 28		
Colchester 4	d		13 43			14 03			14 12		14 30	14 33		14 43			15 03	15 03			15 12		15 30		
Marks Tey 2	d		13 49						14 18					14 49							15 18				
Kelvedon	d		13 54						14 23					14 54							15 23				
Braintree	d							14 00												15 00					
Braintree Freeport	d							14 02												15 02					
Cressing	d							14 05												15 05					
White Notley	d							14 08												15 08					
Witham 2	d		14 00					14 16	14 29			14 46		15 00						15 16	15 29				
Hatfield Peverel	d								14 33												15 33				
Chelmsford 3	d		14 09			14 21		14 26	14 40			14 56		15 09			15 21	15 21		15 26	15 40				
Ingatestone	d							14 32				15 02								15 32					
Shenfield 3	a		14 19					14 38	14 50			15 08		15 19						15 38	15 50				
Romford	a		14 28											15 28											
Stratford 7 ⊖	a		14 36			14s45		14 52	15 05			15 22		15 36			15s45	15s45		15 52	16 05				
London Liverpool Street 15 ⊖	a		14 45			14 55		15 01	15 14		15 19	15 31		15 45			15 55	15 55		16 01	16 14		16 19		

A not 19 May

B 19 May

Norwich, Ipswich, Harwich, Clacton, Walton-on-Naze, Colchester and Chelmsford - London

Network Diagram - see first Page of Table 5

		LE 1	LE 1	LE 1	LE 1	LE ◇1	LE 1	LE 1	LE 1	LE 1		LE ◇1	LE 1	LE 1	LE 1	LE 1	LE ◇1	LE 1	LE 1	LE 1		LE 1	LE ◇1	LE 1	LE 1
Norwich	d					15 00						15 30					16 00						16 30		
Diss	d					15 17						15 47					16 17						16 47		
Peterborough 8	d																							15 45	
Stowmarket	d					15 29				15 44							16 29					16 44		17 13	
Needham Market	d									15 49												16 49			
Ipswich	a					15 41				16 00		16 08					16 41					17 00	17 08	17 28	
	d					15 43			15 52			16 09					16 43			16 52			17 09		
Harwich Town	d		15 28											16 28											
Dovercourt	d		15 30											16 30											
Harwich International	d		15 33											16 33											
Wrabness	d		15 39											16 39											
Mistley	d		15 45											16 45											
Manningtree 2	d		15a50			15 53			16 02			16 19		16a50			16 53			17 02			17 19		
Walton-on-the-Naze	d				15 00											16 00									
Frinton-on-Sea	d				15 03											16 03									
Kirby Cross	d				15 06											16 06									
Clacton-on-Sea	d	15 05											16 05												17 05
Thorpe-le-Soken 1	a	15 13			15 12								16 13			16 12									17 13
	d	15 13			15 17								16 13			16 17									17 13
Weeley	d				15 21											16 21									
Great Bentley	d				15 24											16 24									
Alresford (Essex)	d				15 28											16 28									
Wivenhoe 3	d	15 23			15 32								16 23			16 32									17 23
Hythe	d				15 36											16 36									
Colchester Town	a				15 40											16 40									
	d			15 35	15 44		16 00								16 35	16 44		17 00							
Colchester 4	a	15 31		15 42	15 52	16 02	16 07		16 11			16 28	16 31		16 42	16 52	17 02	17 07		17 11			17 28		17 31
Colchester 4	d	15 33		15 43		16 03			16 12			16 30	16 33		16 43		17 03			17 12			17 30		17 33
Marks Tey 2	d			15 49					16 18						16 49					17 18					
Kelvedon	d			15 54					16 23						16 54					17 23					
Braintree	d							16 00											17 00						
Braintree Freeport	d							16 02											17 02						
Cressing	d							16 05											17 05						
White Notley	d							16 08											17 08						
Witham 2	d	15 46		16 00				16 16	16 29				16 46		17 00				17 16	17 29					17 46
Hatfield Peverel	d								16 33											17 33					
Chelmsford 3	d	15 56		16 09		16 21		16 26	16 40				16 56		17 09		17 21		17 26	17 40					17 56
Ingatestone	d	16 02						16 32					17 02						17 32						18 02
Shenfield 3	a	16 08		16 19				16 38	16 50				17 08		17 19				17 38	17 50					18 08
Romford	a			16 28											17 28										
Stratford 7 ⊖	a	16 22		16 36		16s45		16 52	17 05				17 22		17 36		17s45		17 52	18 05					18 22
London Liverpool Street 15 ⊖	a	16 31		16 45		16 55		17 01	17 14			17 19	17 31		17 45		17 55		18 01	18 14			18 19		18 31

		LE 1	LE 1	LE 1	LE ◇1	LE 1		LE 1	LE 1	LE 1	LE ◇1	LE 1	LE 1	LE 1	LE 1	LE ◇1		LE 1	LE 1	LE 1	LE 1	LE ◇1	LE 1	LE 1	LE 1
Norwich	d				17 00						17 30					18 00						18 30			
Diss	d				17 17						17 47					18 17						18 47			
Peterborough 8	d																						17 45		
Stowmarket	d				17 29					17 45	17 59					18 29					18 45		19 13		
Needham Market	d									17 50											18 50				
Ipswich	a				17 41					18 01	18 11					18 41					19 01	19 08	19 28		
	d				17 43				17 52		18 13					18 43				18 52		19 09			
Harwich Town	d	17 28											18 28												19 28
Dovercourt	d	17 30											18 30												19 30
Harwich International	d	17 33											18 33												19 33
Wrabness	d	17 39											18 39												19 39
Mistley	d	17 45											18 45												19 45
Manningtree 2	d	17a50			17 53				18 02				18a50			18 53				19 02		19 19			19a50
Walton-on-the-Naze	d			17 00											18 00										
Frinton-on-Sea	d			17 03											18 03										
Kirby Cross	d			17 06											18 06										
Clacton-on-Sea	d											18 05												19 05	
Thorpe-le-Soken 1	a			17 12								18 13			18 12									19 13	
	d			17 17								18 13			18 17									19 13	
Weeley	d			17 21											18 21										
Great Bentley	d			17 24											18 24										
Alresford (Essex)	d			17 28											18 28										
Wivenhoe 3	d			17 32								18 23			18 32									19 23	
Hythe	d			17 36											18 36										
Colchester Town	a			17 40											18 40										
	d		17 35	17 44		18 00								18 35	18 44			19 00							
Colchester 4	a		17 42	17 52	18 02	18 07			18 11		18 28	18 31		18 42	18 52	19 02		19 07		19 11		19 28		19 31	
Colchester 4	d		17 43		18 03				18 12		18 30	18 33		18 43		19 03				19 12		19 30		19 33	
Marks Tey 2	d		17 49						18 18					18 49						19 18					
Kelvedon	d		17 54						18 23					18 54						19 23					
Braintree	d							18 00											19 00						
Braintree Freeport	d							18 02											19 02						
Cressing	d							18 05											19 05						
White Notley	d							18 08											19 08						
Witham 2	d		18 00					18 16	18 29			18 46		19 00					19 16	19 29				19 46	
Hatfield Peverel	d								18 33											19 33					
Chelmsford 3	d		18 09		18 21			18 26	18 40			18 56		19 09		19 21			19 26	19 40				19 56	
Ingatestone	d							18 32				19 02							19 32					20 02	
Shenfield 3	a		18 19					18 38	18 50			19 08		19 19					19 38	19 50				20 08	
Romford	a		18 28											19 28											
Stratford 7 ⊖	a		18 36		18s45			18 52	19 05			19 22		19 36		19s45			19 52	20 05				20 22	
London Liverpool Street 15 ⊖	a		18 45		18 55			19 01	19 14		19 19	19 31		19 45		19 55			20 01	20 14		20 19		20 31	

Table 11
Saturdays until 21 July

Norwich, Ipswich, Harwich, Clacton, Walton-on-Naze, Colchester and Chelmsford - London

Network Diagram - see first Page of Table 5

		LE 1		LE 1	LE ◇1	LE 1	LE 1	LE 1	LE 1	LE 1	LE 1	LE 1		LE 1	LE 1	LE ◇1	LE 1	LE 1	LE 1	LE 1	LE 1	LE 1		LE 1	LE ◇1
Norwich	d				19 00											20 00									
Diss	d				19 17											20 17									
Peterborough 8	d																								19 45
Stowmarket	d				19 29				19 44							20 29				20 44					21 09
Needham Market	d								19 49											20 49					
Ipswich	a				19 41				20 00							20 41				21 00					21 22
	d				19 43			19 52		20 09						20 43				21 00	21 09				21 25
Harwich Town	d											20 28													
Dovercourt	d											20 30													
Harwich International	d											20 33							20 45	21a29					
Wrabness	d											20 39													
Mistley	d											20 45													
Manningtree 2	d				19 53			20 02		20 20		20a50				20 53			20 58		21 19				21 35
Walton-on-the-Naze	d			19 00											20 00										
Frinton-on-Sea	d			19 03											20 03										
Kirby Cross	d			19 06											20 06										
Clacton-on-Sea	d										20 05											21 05			
Thorpe-le-Soken 1	a			19 12							20 13				20 12							21 13			
	d			19 17							20 13				20 17							21 13			
Weeley	d			19 21											20 21										
Great Bentley	d			19 24											20 24										
Alresford (Essex)	d			19 28											20 28										
Wivenhoe 3	d			19 32							20 23				20 32							21 23			
Hythe	d			19 36											20 36										
Colchester Town	a			19 40											20 40										
	d	19 35		19 44		20 00								20 35	20 44		21 00							21 35	
Colchester 4	a	19 42		19 52	20 02	20 07		20 11		20 29	20 31			20 42	20 52	21 02	21 07		21 07		21 28	21 31		21 42	21 46
Colchester 4	d	19 43			20 03			20 12		20 30	20 33			20 43		21 03			21 12		21 30	21 33		21 43	
Marks Tey 2	d	19 49						20 18						20 49					21 18					21 49	
Kelvedon	d	19 54						20 23						20 54					21 23					21 54	
Braintree	d						20 00											21 00							
Braintree Freeport	d						20 02											21 02							
Cressing	d						20 05											21 05							
White Notley	d						20 08											21 08							
Witham 2	d	20 00					20 16	20 29			20 46			21 00				21 16	21 29			21 46		22 00	
Hatfield Peverel	d							20 33											21 33						
Chelmsford 3	d	20 09			20 21		20 26	20 40			20 56			21 09		21 21		21 26	21 40			21 56		22 09	
Ingatestone	d						20 32				21 02							21 32				22 02			
Shenfield 3	a	20 19					20 38	20 50			21 08			21 19				21 38	21 50			22 08		22 19	
Romford	a	20 28												21 28										22 28	
Stratford 7 ⊖	a	20 36			20s45		20 52	21 05			21 22			21 36		21s45		21 52	22 05			22 22		22 36	
London Liverpool Street 15 ⊖	a	20 45			20 55		21 01	21 14		21 17	21 31			21 45		21 55		22 01	22 14		22 17	22 31		22 46	

		LE 1	LE 1	LE ◇1	LE 1	LE 1	LE 1	LE 1		LE 1	LE 1	LE 1	LE 1	LE 1	LE ◇1	LE 1	LE 1	LE 1	LE 1	LE 1	LE ◇1	LE 1	LE 1	LE 1	LE
Norwich	d			21 00											22 00							23 05			
Diss	d			21 17											22 17							23 22			
Peterborough 8	d																				21 45				
Stowmarket	d			21 29				21 44							22 29	22 44					23 06	23 36			23 47
Needham Market	d							21 49								22 49									23 52
Ipswich	a			21 41				22 00							22 41	23 00					23 18	23 50			00 05
	d			21 43			21 52				22 23				22 43				23 15		23 19				
Harwich Town	d		21 28										22 28										23 28		
Dovercourt	d		21 30										22 30										23 30		
Harwich International	d		21 33										22 33										23 33		
Wrabness	d		21 39										22 39										23 39		
Mistley	d		21 45										22 45										23 45		
Manningtree 2	d		21a50	21 53			22 02				22 33		22a50		22 53				23 25		23 29		23 50		
Walton-on-the-Naze	d	21 00										22 00						23 00							
Frinton-on-Sea	d	21 03										22 03						23 03							
Kirby Cross	d	21 06										22 06						23 06							
Clacton-on-Sea	d									22 05										23 05					
Thorpe-le-Soken 1	a	21 12								22 13		22 12						23 12		23 13					
	d	21 17								22 13		22 17								23 13					
Weeley	d	21 21										22 21								23 17					
Great Bentley	d	21 24										22 24								23 20					
Alresford (Essex)	d	21 28										22 28								23 24					
Wivenhoe 3	d	21 32								22 23		22 32								23 28					
Hythe	d	21 36										22 36								23 32					
Colchester Town	a	21 40										22 40													
	d	21 44			22 00							22 44					23 00								
Colchester 4	a	21 52		22 02	22 07		22 11			22 31	22 42	22 52			23 02		23 07		23 35	23 38	23 40		23 59		
Colchester 4	d			22 03			22 12			22 33	22 43				23 03										
Marks Tey 2	d						22 18				22 49														
Kelvedon	d						22 23				22 54														
Braintree	d					22 00								22 56										23 45	
Braintree Freeport	d					22 02								22 58										23 47	
Cressing	d					22 05								23 01										23 50	
White Notley	d					22 08								23 04										23 53	
Witham 2	d					22 16	22 29			22 46	23 00			23a12	23 16									00a01	
Hatfield Peverel	d						22 33																		
Chelmsford 3	d			22 21		22 26	22 40			22 56	23 09				23 25										
Ingatestone	d					22 32				23 02															
Shenfield 3	a					22 38	22 50			23 08	23 19				23s36										
Romford	a										23 28														
Stratford 7 ⊖	a			22s45		22 52	23 05			23 22	23 36				23s52										
London Liverpool Street 15 ⊖	a			22 55		23 01	23 14			23 31	23 45				00 02										

Norwich, Ipswich, Harwich, Clacton, Walton-on-Naze, Colchester and Chelmsford - London

Network Diagram - see first Page of Table 5

		LE ◇1	LE	LE 1	LE 1	LE 1	LE	LE 1	LE ◇1	LE 1		LE 1	LE ◇1	LE 1	LE 1	LE 1	LE 1	LE 1	LE ◇1	LE 1		LE 1	LE 1	LE	LE ◇1
Norwich	d	22p00							05 00				05 30						06 00						06 30
Diss	d	22p17							05 17				05 47						06 17						06 47
Peterborough	d																								
Stowmarket	d	22p29	23p47						05 29										06 29					06 44	
Needham Market	d		23p52																					06 49	
Ipswich	a	22p41	00 05						05 41				06 08						06 41					07 02	07 08
	d	22p43							05 43				06 09						06 43			06 52	06 59		07 09
Harwich Town	d																	06 28							
Dovercourt	d																	06 30					07a28		
Harwich International	d														06 20			06 33							
Wrabness	d																	06 39							
Mistley	d																	06 45							
Manningtree	d	22p53							05 53				06 19		06 33			06a50	06 53			07 02			07 19
Walton-on-the-Naze	d															06 00									
Frinton-on-Sea	d															06 03									
Kirby Cross	d															06 06									
Clacton-on-Sea	d							05 30						06 05			06 24								
Thorpe-le-Soken	a							05 38						06 13		06 12	06 32								
	d							05 38						06 13		06 17									
Weeley	d															06 21									
Great Bentley	d															06 24									
Alresford (Essex)	d															06 28									
Wivenhoe	d							05 48						06 23		06 32									
Hythe	d															06 36									
Colchester Town	a															06 40									
	d															06 44									
Colchester	a	23p02						05 57	06 02				06 28	06 31	06 42	06 52			07 02			07 11			07 28
Colchester	d	23p03			05 12	05 43	05 50		06 03			06 12	06 30	06 33	06 43				07 03			07 12			07 30
Marks Tey	d				05 18	05 49	05a57					06 18			06 49							07 18			
Kelvedon	d				05 23	05 54						06 23			06 54							07 23			
Braintree	d			00 27						06 00										07 00					
Braintree Freeport	d			00 29						06 02										07 02					
Cressing	d			00 32						06 05										07 05					
White Notley	d			00 35						06 08										07 08					
Witham	d	23p16		00a43	05 29	06 00				06a16		06 29		06 46	07 00					07 16		07 29			
Hatfield Peverel	d				05 33	06 04						06 33										07 33			
Chelmsford	d	23p25			05 40	06 11			06 21			06 40		06 56	07 09				07 21	07 26		07 40			
Ingatestone	d				05 47	06 18								07 02						07 32					
Shenfield	a	23b36			05 52	06 23						06 50		07 08	07 19					07 38		07 50			
Romford	a																								
Stratford ⊖	a				06 07	06 38			06s45			07 05		07 22	07s36				07s45	07 52		08 05			
London Liverpool Street ⊖	a	00 03			06 16	06 47			06 55			07 14	07 19	07 31	07 47				07 55	08 01		08 14			08 19

		LE 1	LE 1	LE 1	LE 1	LE ◇1		LE 1	LE 1	LE 1	LE	LE ◇1	LE 1	LE 1	LE 1	LE 1		LE ◇1	LE 1	LE 1	LE 1	LE 1	LE ◇1	LE 1	LE 1
Norwich	d					07 00						07 30						08 00					08 30		
Diss	d					07 17						07 47						08 17					08 47		
Peterborough	d																							07 45	
Stowmarket	d					07 29					07 45							08 29				08 44		09 13	
Needham Market	d										07 50											08 49			
Ipswich	a					07 41					08 03	08 08						08 41				09 00	09 08	09 28	
	d					07 43				07 52		08 09						08 43			08 52		09 09		
Harwich Town	d				07 28									08 28											
Dovercourt	d				07 30									08 30											
Harwich International	d		07 20		07 33									08 33											
Wrabness	d				07 39									08 39											
Mistley	d				07 45									08 45											
Manningtree	d		07 33		07a50	07 53				08 02		08 19		08a50				08 53			09 02		09 19		
Walton-on-the-Naze	d			07 00												08 00									
Frinton-on-Sea	d			07 03												08 03									
Kirby Cross	d			07 06												08 06									
Clacton-on-Sea	d	07 05											08 05												09 05
Thorpe-le-Soken	a	07 13		07 12									08 13			08 12									09 13
	d	07 13		07 17									08 13			08 17									09 13
Weeley	d			07 21												08 21									
Great Bentley	d			07 24												08 24									
Alresford (Essex)	d			07 28												08 28									
Wivenhoe	d	07 23		07 32									08 23			08 32									09 23
Hythe	d			07 36												08 36									
Colchester Town	a			07 40												08 40									
	d			07 44				08 00							08 35	08 44			09 00						
Colchester	a	07 31	07 42	07 52		08 02		08 07		08 11		08 28	08 31		08 42	08 52		09 02	09 07		09 11		09 28		09 31
Colchester	d	07 33	07 43			08 03				08 12		08 30	08 33		08 43			09 03			09 12		09 30		09 33
Marks Tey	d		07 49							08 18					08 49						09 18				
Kelvedon	d		07 54							08 23					08 54						09 23				
Braintree	d								08 00											09 00					
Braintree Freeport	d								08 02											09 02					
Cressing	d								08 05											09 05					
White Notley	d								08 08											09 08					
Witham	d	07 46	08 00						08 16	08 29			08 46		09 00					09 16	09 29				09 46
Hatfield Peverel	d									08 33											09 33				
Chelmsford	d	07 56	08 09			08 21			08 26	08 40			08 56		09 09			09 21		09 26	09 40				09 56
Ingatestone	d	08 02							08 32				09 02							09 32					10 02
Shenfield	a	08 08	08 19						08 38	08 50			09 08		09 19					09 38	09 50				10 08
Romford	a														09 28										
Stratford ⊖	a	08 22	08 36			08s45			08 52	09 05			09 22		09 36			09s45		09 52	10 05				10 22
London Liverpool Street ⊖	a	08 31	08 45			08 55			09 01	09 14		09 19	09 31		09 45			09 55		10 01	10 14		10 19		10 31

b Previous night, stops to set down only

Norwich, Ipswich, Harwich, Clacton, Walton-on-Naze, Colchester and Chelmsford - London

Network Diagram - see first Page of Table 5

		LE 1		LE 1	LE 1	LE ◇1	LE 1	LE 1	LE 1	LE 1	LE ◇1	LE 1		LE 1	LE 1	LE 1	LE ◇1	LE 1	LE 1	LE 1	LE 1	LE ◇1		LE 1	LE 1
Norwich	d					09 00					09 30						10 00					10 30			
Diss	d					09 17					09 47						10 17					10 47			
Peterborough	d																							09 47	
Stowmarket	d					09 29				09 44							10 29				10 44			11 13	
Needham Market	d									09 49											10 49				
Ipswich	a					09 41				10 00	10 08						10 41				11 00	11 08		11 28	
	d					09 43			09 52		10 09						10 43			10 52		11 09			
Harwich Town	d	09 28												10 28											
Dovercourt	d	09 30												10 30											
Harwich International	d	09 33												10 33											
Wrabness	d	09 39												10 39											
Mistley	d	09 45												10 45											
Manningtree	d	09a50				09 53			10 02		10 19			10a50			10 53			11 02		11 19			
Walton-on-the-Naze	d				09 00											10 00									
Frinton-on-Sea	d				09 03											10 03									
Kirby Cross	d				09 06											10 06									
Clacton-on-Sea	d											10 05													11 05
Thorpe-le-Soken	a				09 12							10 13				10 12									11 13
	d				09 17							10 13				10 17									11 13
Weeley	d				09 21											10 21									
Great Bentley	d				09 24											10 24									
Alresford (Essex)	d				09 28											10 28									
Wivenhoe	d				09 32							10 23				10 32									11 23
Hythe	d				09 36											10 36									
Colchester Town	a				09 40											10 40									
	d			09 35	09 44		10 00								10 35	10 44		11 00							
Colchester	a			09 42	09 52	10 02	10 07		10 11		10 28	10 31			10 42	10 52	11 02	11 07		11 11		11 28			11 31
Colchester	d			09 43		10 03			10 12		10 30	10 33			10 43		11 03			11 12		11 30			11 33
Marks Tey	d			09 49					10 18						10 49					11 18					
Kelvedon	d			09 54					10 23						10 54					11 23					
Braintree	d							10 00											11 00						
Braintree Freeport	d							10 02											11 02						
Cressing	d							10 05											11 05						
White Notley	d							10 08											11 08						
Witham	d			10 00				10 16	10 29			10 46			11 00				11 16	11 29					11 46
Hatfield Peverel	d								10 33											11 33					
Chelmsford	d			10 09		10 21		10 26	10 40			10 56			11 09		11 21		11 26	11 40					11 56
Ingatestone	d							10 32				11 02							11 32						12 02
Shenfield	a			10 19				10 38	10 50			11 08			11 19				11 38	11 50					12 08
Romford	a			10 28											11 28										
Stratford ⊖	a			10 36		10s45		10 52	11 05			11 22			11 36		11s45		11 52	12 05					12 22
London Liverpool Street ⊖	a			10 45		10 55		11 01	11 14		11 19	11 31			11 45		11 55		12 01	12 14		12 19			12 31

		LE 1	LE 1	LE 1	LE ◇1	LE 1	LE 1	LE 1		LE 1	LE 1	LE 1	LE 1	LE 1	LE 1	LE ◇1	LE 1	LE 1		LE 1	LE 1	LE ◇1	LE 1	LE 1	LE 1
Norwich	d				11 00						11 30					12 00						12 30			
Diss	d				11 17						11 47					12 17						12 47			
Peterborough	d																						11 45		
Stowmarket	d				11 29					11 44						12 29					12 44		13 13		
Needham Market	d									11 49											12 49				
Ipswich	a				11 41					12 00	12 08					12 41					13 00	13 08	13 28		
	d				11 43			11 52			12 09					12 43				12 52		13 09			
Harwich Town	d	11 28											12 28												13 28
Dovercourt	d	11 30											12 30												13 30
Harwich International	d	11 33											12 33												13 33
Wrabness	d	11 39											12 39												13 39
Mistley	d	11 45											12 45												13 45
Manningtree	d	11a50			11 53			12 02			12 19		12a50			12 53				13 02		13 19			13a50
Walton-on-the-Naze	d			11 00											12 00										
Frinton-on-Sea	d			11 03											12 03										
Kirby Cross	d			11 06											12 06										
Clacton-on-Sea	d											12 05												13 05	
Thorpe-le-Soken	a			11 12								12 13			12 12									13 13	
	d			11 17								12 13			12 17									13 13	
Weeley	d			11 21											12 21										
Great Bentley	d			11 24											12 24										
Alresford (Essex)	d			11 28											12 28										
Wivenhoe	d			11 32								12 23			12 32									13 23	
Hythe	d			11 36											12 36										
Colchester Town	a			11 40											12 40										
	d		11 35	11 44		12 00								12 35	12 44		13 00								
Colchester	a		11 42	11 52	12 02	12 07		12 11			12 28	12 31		12 42	12 52	13 02	13 07			13 11		13 28		13 31	
Colchester	d		11 43		12 03			12 12			12 30	12 33		12 43		13 03				13 12		13 30		13 33	
Marks Tey	d		11 49					12 18						12 49						13 18					
Kelvedon	d		11 54					12 23						12 54						13 23					
Braintree	d						12 00											13 00							
Braintree Freeport	d						12 02											13 02							
Cressing	d						12 05											13 05							
White Notley	d						12 08											13 08							
Witham	d		12 00				12 16	12 29				12 46		13 00				13 16		13 29				13 46	
Hatfield Peverel	d							12 33												13 33					
Chelmsford	d		12 09		12 21		12 26	12 40				12 56		13 09		13 21		13 26		13 40				13 56	
Ingatestone	d						12 32					13 02						13 32						14 02	
Shenfield	a		12 19				12 38	12 50				13 08		13 19				13 38		13 50				14 08	
Romford	a		12 28											13 28											
Stratford ⊖	a		12 36		12s45		12 52	13 05				13 22		13 36		13s45		13 52		14 05				14 22	
London Liverpool Street ⊖	a		12 45		12 55		13 01	13 14			13 19	13 31		13 45		13 55		14 01		14 14		14 19		14 31	

Norwich, Ipswich, Harwich, Clacton, Walton-on-Naze, Colchester and Chelmsford - London

Network Diagram - see first Page of Table 5

		LE	LE	LE	LE	LE	LE	LE	LE	LE	LE	LE	LE	LE	LE	LE	LE	LE	LE	LE	LE	LE	LE
		1	1	◇1 ☕	1	1	1	1	◇1 ☕	1	1	1	1	1 ☕	1	1	1	1	◇1 ☕	1	1	1	1
Norwich	d			13 00					13 30					14 00					14 30				
Diss	d			13 17					13 47					14 17					14 47				
Peterborough	d																			13 45			
Stowmarket	d			13 29				13 44						14 29				14 44		15 13			
Needham Market	d							13 49										14 49					
Ipswich	a			13 41				14 00	14 08					14 41				15 00	15 08	15 28			
	d			13 43			13 52		14 09					14 43			14 52		15 09				
Harwich Town	d												14 28									15 28	
Dovercourt	d												14 30									15 30	
Harwich International	d												14 33									15 33	
Wrabness	d												14 39									15 39	
Mistley	d												14 45									15 45	
Manningtree	d			13 53			14 02		14 19				14a50	14 53			15 02		15 19			15a50	
Walton-on-the-Naze	d		13 00									14 00											
Frinton-on-Sea	d		13 03									14 03											
Kirby Cross	d		13 06									14 06											
Clacton-on-Sea	d									14 05											15 05		
Thorpe-le-Soken	a		13 12							14 13		14 12									15 13		
	d		13 17							14 13		14 17									15 13		
Weeley	d		13 21									14 21											
Great Bentley	d		13 24									14 24											
Alresford (Essex)	d		13 28									14 28											
Wivenhoe	d		13 32							14 23		14 32									15 23		
Hythe	d		13 36									14 36											
Colchester Town	a		13 40									14 40											
	d	13 35	13 44		14 00						14 35	14 44			15 00								15 35
Colchester	a	13 42	13 52	14 02	14 07		14 11		14 28	14 31	14 42	14 52		15 02	15 07		15 11		15 28		15 31		15 42
Colchester	d	13 43		14 03			14 12		14 30	14 33	14 43			15 03			15 12		15 30		15 33		15 43
Marks Tey	d	13 49					14 18				14 49						15 18						15 49
Kelvedon	d	13 54					14 23				14 54						15 23						15 54
Braintree	d					14 00										15 00							
Braintree Freeport	d					14 02										15 02							
Cressing	d					14 05										15 05							
White Notley	d					14 08										15 08							
Witham	d	14 00				14 16	14 29			14 46	15 00					15 16	15 29				15 46		16 00
Hatfield Peverel	d						14 33										15 33						
Chelmsford	d	14 09		14 21		14 26	14 40			14 56	15 09			15 21		15 26	15 40				15 56		16 09
Ingatestone	d					14 32				15 02						15 32					16 02		
Shenfield	a	14 19				14 38	14 50			15 08	15 19					15 38	15 50				16 08		16 19
Romford	a	14 28																					16 28
Stratford ⊖	a	14 36		14s45		14 52	15 05			15 22	15 36			15s45		15 52	16 05				16 22		16 36
London Liverpool Street ⊖	a	14 45		14 55		15 01	15 14		15 19	15 31	15 45			15 55		16 01	16 14		16 19		16 31		16 45

		LE	LE	LE	LE	LE	LE	LE	LE	LE	LE	LE	LE	LE	LE	LE	LE	LE	LE	LE	LE	LE	LE	LE
		1	◇1 ☕	1	1	1	1	◇1 ☕	1	1	1	1	◇1 ☕	1	1	1	1	◇1 ☕	1	1	1	1	1	◇1 ☕
Norwich	d		15 00					15 30					16 00					16 30						17 00
Diss	d		15 17					15 47					16 17					16 47						17 17
Peterborough	d																		15 45					
Stowmarket	d		15 29				15 44						16 29				16 44		17 13					17 29
Needham Market	d						15 49										16 49							
Ipswich	a		15 41				16 00	16 08					16 41				17 00	17 08	17 28					17 41
	d		15 43			15 52		16 09					16 43			16 52		17 09						17 43
Harwich Town	d											16 28									17 28			
Dovercourt	d											16 30									17 30			
Harwich International	d											16 33									17 33			
Wrabness	d											16 39									17 39			
Mistley	d											16 45									17 45			
Manningtree	d		15 53			16 02		16 19				16a50	16 53			17 02		17 19			17a50			17 53
Walton-on-the-Naze	d	15 00									16 00												17 00	
Frinton-on-Sea	d	15 03									16 03												17 03	
Kirby Cross	d	15 06									16 06												17 06	
Clacton-on-Sea	d								16 05											17 05				
Thorpe-le-Soken	a	15 12							16 13		16 12									17 13			17 12	
	d	15 17							16 13		16 17									17 13			17 17	
Weeley	d	15 21									16 21												17 21	
Great Bentley	d	15 24									16 24												17 24	
Alresford (Essex)	d	15 28									16 28												17 28	
Wivenhoe	d	15 32							16 23		16 32									17 23			17 32	
Hythe	d	15 36									16 36												17 36	
Colchester Town	a	15 40									16 40												17 40	
	d	15 44		16 00						16 35	16 44			17 00								17 35	17 44	
Colchester	a	15 52	16 02	16 07		16 11		16 28	16 31	16 42	16 52		17 02	17 07		17 11		17 28		17 31		17 42	17 52	18 02
Colchester	d		16 03			16 12		16 30	16 33	16 43			17 03			17 12		17 30		17 33		17 43		18 03
Marks Tey	d					16 18				16 49						17 18						17 49		
Kelvedon	d					16 23				16 54						17 23						17 54		
Braintree	d				16 00										17 00									
Braintree Freeport	d				16 02										17 02									
Cressing	d				16 05										17 05									
White Notley	d				16 08										17 08									
Witham	d				16 16	16 29			16 46	17 00					17 16	17 29				17 46		18 00		
Hatfield Peverel	d					16 33										17 33								
Chelmsford	d		16 21		16 26	16 40			16 56	17 09			17 21		17 26	17 40				17 56		18 09		18 21
Ingatestone	d				16 32				17 02						17 32					18 02				
Shenfield	a				16 38	16 50			17 08	17 19					17 38	17 50				18 08		18 19		
Romford	a																					18 28		
Stratford ⊖	a		16s45		16 52	17 05			17 22	17 36			17s45		17 52	18 05				18 22		18 36		18s45
London Liverpool Street ⊖	a		16 55		17 01	17 14		17 19	17 31	17 45			17 55		18 01	18 14		18 19		18 31		18 45		18 55

		LE	LE	LE	LE	LE	LE	LE	LE	LE	LE	LE	LE	LE	LE	LE	LE	LE	LE	LE	LE	LE	LE	LE
		1	1	1	1	◇1 ☕	1	1	1	1	◇1 ☕	1	1	1	1	◇1 ☕	1	1	1	1	1	◇1 ☕	1	1
Norwich	d					17 30					18 00					18 30						19 00		
Diss	d					17 47					18 17					18 47						19 17		
Peterborough	d																17 45							
Stowmarket	d				17 45	17 59					18 29				18 45		19 13					19 29		
Needham Market	d				17 50										18 50									
Ipswich	a				18 01	18 11					18 41				19 01	19 08	19 28					19 41		
	d			17 52		18 13					18 43			18 52		19 09						19 43		
Harwich Town	d									18 28									19 28					
Dovercourt	d									18 30									19 30					
Harwich International	d									18 33									19 33					
Wrabness	d									18 39									19 39					
Mistley	d									18 45									19 45					
Manningtree	d			18 02						18a50	18 53			19 02		19 19			19a50			19 53		
Walton-on-the-Naze	d								18 00												19 00			
Frinton-on-Sea	d								18 03												19 03			
Kirby Cross	d								18 06												19 06			
Clacton-on-Sea	d						18 05											19 05						
Thorpe-le-Soken	a						18 13		18 12									19 13			19 12			
	d						18 13		18 17									19 13			19 17			
Weeley	d								18 21												19 21			
Great Bentley	d								18 24												19 24			
Alresford (Essex)	d								18 28												19 28			
Wivenhoe	d						18 23		18 32									19 23			19 32			
Hythe	d								18 36												19 36			
Colchester Town	a								18 40												19 40			
	d	18 00						18 35	18 44			19 00								19 35	19 44		20 00	
Colchester	a	18 07		18 11		18 28	18 31	18 42	18 52		19 02	19 07		19 11		19 28		19 31		19 42	19 52	20 02	20 07	
Colchester	d			18 12		18 30	18 33	18 43			19 03			19 12		19 30		19 33		19 43		20 03		
Marks Tey	d			18 18				18 49						19 18						19 49				
Kelvedon	d			18 23				18 54						19 23						19 54				
Braintree	d		18 00										19 00											20 00
Braintree Freeport	d		18 02										19 02											20 02
Cressing	d		18 05										19 05											20 05
White Notley	d		18 08										19 08											20 08
Witham	d		18 16	18 29			18 46	19 00					19 16	19 29				19 46		20 00				20 16
Hatfield Peverel	d			18 33										19 33										
Chelmsford	d		18 26	18 40			18 56	19 09			19 21		19 26	19 40				19 56		20 09		20 21		20 26
Ingatestone	d		18 32				19 02						19 32					20 02						20 32
Shenfield	a		18 38	18 50			19 08	19 19					19 38	19 50				20 08		20 19				20 38
Romford	a																			20 28				
Stratford ⊖	a		18 52	19 05			19 22	19 36			19s45		19 52	20 05				20 22		20 36		20s45		20 52
London Liverpool Street ⊖	a		19 01	19 14		19 19	19 31	19 45			19 55		20 01	20 14		20 19		20 33		20 45		20 55		21 01

		LE	LE	LE	LE	LE	LE	LE	LE	LE	LE	LE	LE	LE	LE	LE	LE	LE	LE	LE	LE	LE
		1	1	1	1	1	1	1	◇1 ☕	1	1	1	1	1	1	1	◇1	1	1	◇1 ☕	1	1
Norwich	d								20 00					20 30						21 00		
Diss	d								20 17					20 47						21 17		
Peterborough	d																19 45					
Stowmarket	d		19 44						20 29				20 44				21 09			21 29		
Needham Market	d		19 49										20 49									
Ipswich	a		20 00						20 41				21 00	21 08			21 22			21 41		
	d	19 52		20 09					20 43				21 00	21 09			21 25			21 43		
Harwich Town	d					20 28													21 28			
Dovercourt	d					20 30													21 30			
Harwich International	d					20 33						20 45	21a29						21 33			
Wrabness	d					20 39													21 39			
Mistley	d					20 45													21 45			
Manningtree	d	20 02		20 20		20a50			20 53			20 58		21 19			21 35		21a50	21 53		
Walton-on-the-Naze	d							20 00										21 00				
Frinton-on-Sea	d							20 03										21 03				
Kirby Cross	d							20 06										21 06				
Clacton-on-Sea	d				20 05										21 05							
Thorpe-le-Soken	a				20 13			20 12							21 13			21 12				
	d				20 13			20 17							21 13			21 17				
Weeley	d							20 21										21 21				
Great Bentley	d							20 24										21 24				
Alresford (Essex)	d							20 28										21 28				
Wivenhoe	d				20 23			20 32							21 23			21 32				
Hythe	d							20 36										21 36				
Colchester Town	a							20 40										21 40				
	d						20 35	20 44		21 00						21 35		21 44			22 00	
Colchester	a	20 11		20 29	20 31		20 42	20 52	21 02	21 07		21 07		21 28	21 31	21 42	21 46	21 52		22 02	22 07	
Colchester	d	20 12		20 30	20 33		20 43		21 03			21 12		21 30	21 33	21 43				22 03		
Marks Tey	d	20 18					20 49					21 18				21 49						
Kelvedon	d	20 23					20 54					21 23				21 54						
Braintree	d										21 00											22 00
Braintree Freeport	d										21 02											22 02
Cressing	d										21 05											22 05
White Notley	d										21 08											22 08
Witham	d	20 29			20 46		21 00				21 16	21 29			21 46	22 00						22 16
Hatfield Peverel	d	20 33										21 33										
Chelmsford	d	20 40			20 56		21 09		21 21		21 26	21 40			21 56	22 09				22 21		22 26
Ingatestone	d				21 02						21 32				22 02							22 32
Shenfield	a	20 50			21 08		21 19				21 38	21 50			22 08	22 19						22 38
Romford	a																					
Stratford ⊖	a	21 05			21 22		21 34		21s45		21 52	22 11			22 26	22 38						22 56
London Liverpool Street ⊖	a	21 14		21 19	21 31		21 45		21 55		22 01	22 21		22 20	22 36	22 48				22 55		23 06

Table 11

Saturdays
28 July to 11 August

Norwich, Ipswich, Harwich, Clacton, Walton-on-Naze, Colchester and Chelmsford - London

Network Diagram - see first Page of Table 5

		LE 1	LE 1	LE 1	LE 1	LE 1	LE 1	LE 1		LE ◇1	LE 1	LE 1	LE 1	LE 1	LE ◇1	LE 1	LE 1	LE 1		LE
Norwich	d									22 00						23 05				
Diss	d									22 17						23 22				
Peterborough	d														21 45					
Stowmarket	d		21 44							22 29	22 44				23 06	23 36				23 47
Needham Market	d		21 49								22 49									23 52
Ipswich	a		22 00							22 41	23 00				23 18	23 50				00 05
	d	21 52			22 23					22 43					23 19					
Harwich Town	d						22 28										23 28			
Dovercourt	d						22 30										23 30			
Harwich International	d						22 33										23 33			
Wrabness	d						22 39										23 39			
Mistley	d						22 45										23 45			
Manningtree	d	22 02			22 33		22a50			22 53					23 29		23a50			
Walton-on-the-Naze	d					22 00							23 00							
Frinton-on-Sea	d					22 03							23 03							
Kirby Cross	d					22 06							23 06							
Clacton-on-Sea	d			22 05										23 05						
Thorpe-le-Soken	a			22 13		22 12							23 12	23 13						
	d			22 13		22 17								23 13						
Weeley	d					22 21								23 17						
Great Bentley	d					22 24								23 20						
Alresford (Essex)	d					22 28								23 24						
Wivenhoe	d			22 23		22 32								23 28						
Hythe	d					22 36								23 32						
Colchester Town	a					22 40														
	d					22 44						23 00								
Colchester	a	22 11		22 31	22 42	22 52				23 02		23 07		23 38	23 40					
Colchester	d	22 12		22 33	22 43					23 03										
Marks Tey	d	22 18			22 49															
Kelvedon	d	22 23			22 54															
Braintree	d							22 56										23 45		
Braintree Freeport	d							22 58										23 47		
Cressing	d							23 01										23 50		
White Notley	d							23 04										23 53		
Witham	d	22 29		22 46	23 00			23a12		23 16								00a01		
Hatfield Peverel	d	22 33																		
Chelmsford	d	22 40		22 56	23 09					23 25										
Ingatestone	d			23 02																
Shenfield	a	22 50		23 08	23 19					23s36										
Romford	a																			
Stratford ⊖	a	23 10		23 26	23 38															
London Liverpool Street ⊖	a	23 20		23 36	23 48					00 03										

Table 11

Saturdays
18 August to 25 August

Norwich, Ipswich, Harwich, Clacton, Walton-on-Naze, Colchester and Chelmsford - London

Network Diagram - see first Page of Table 5

		LE ◇1	LE	LE 1	LE 1	LE 1	LE	LE 1	LE ◇1 ☕	LE 1		LE 1	LE ◇1 ☕	LE 1	LE 1	LE 1	LE 1	LE ◇1 ☕	LE 1	LE 1		LE 1	LE 1	LE	LE ◇1 ☕
Norwich	d	22p00							05 00				05 30					06 00							06 30
Diss	d	22p17							05 17				05 47					06 17							06 47
Peterborough	d																								
Stowmarket	d	22p29	23p47						05 29									06 29						06 44	
Needham Market	d		23p52																					06 49	
Ipswich	a	22p41	00 05						05 41				06 08					06 41						07 02	07 08
	d	22p43							05 43				06 09					06 43				06 52	06 59		07 09
Harwich Town	d														06 28										
Dovercourt	d														06 30										
Harwich International	d														06 33								07a28		
Wrabness	d														06 39										
Mistley	d														06 45										
Manningtree	d	22p53							05 53				06 19		06a50			06 53				07 02			07 19
Walton-on-the-Naze	d																06 00								
Frinton-on-Sea	d																06 03								
Kirby Cross	d																06 06								
Clacton-on-Sea	d							05 30						06 05					06 24						
Thorpe-le-Soken	a							05 38						06 13			06 12		06 32						
	d							05 38						06 13			06 17								
Weeley	d																06 21								
Great Bentley	d																06 24								
Alresford (Essex)	d																06 28								
Wivenhoe	d							05 48						06 23			06 32								
Hythe	d																06 36								
Colchester Town	a																06 40								
	d															06 35	06 44								
Colchester	a	23p02						05 57	06 02				06 28	06 31		06 42	06 52	07 02				07 11			07 28
Colchester	d	23p03			05 12	05 43	05 50		06 03			06 12	06 30	06 33		06 43		07 03				07 12			07 30
Marks Tey	d				05 18	05 49	05a57					06 18				06 49						07 18			
Kelvedon	d				05 23	05 54						06 23				06 54						07 23			
Braintree	d			00 25						06 00										07 00					
Braintree Freeport	d			00 27						06 02										07 02					
Cressing	d			00 30						06 05										07 05					
White Notley	d			00 33						06 08										07 08					
Witham	d	23p16		00a41	05 29	06 00				06a16		06 29		06 46		07 00				07 16		07 29			
Hatfield Peverel	d				05 33	06 04						06 33										07 33			
Chelmsford	d	23p25			05 40	06 11			06 21			06 40		06 56		07 09		07 21		07 26		07 40			
Ingatestone	d				05 47	06 18								07 02						07 32					
Shenfield	a	23b36			05 52	06 23						06 50		07 08		07 19				07 38		07 50			
Romford	a															07 28									
Stratford ⊖	a	23b52			06 07	06 38			06s45			07 05		07 22		07 36		07s45		07 52		08 05			
London Liverpool Street ⊖	a	00 02			06 16	06 47			06 55			07 14	07 19	07 31		07 45		07 55		08 01		08 14			08 19

		LE 1	LE 1	LE 1	LE 1	LE ◇1 ☕		LE 1	LE 1	LE 1	LE	LE ◇1 ☕	LE 1	LE 1	LE 1	LE 1		LE ◇1 ☕	LE 1	LE 1	LE 1	LE 1	LE ◇1 ☕	LE 1	LE 1
Norwich	d					07 00						07 30						08 00					08 30		
Diss	d					07 17						07 47						08 17					08 47		
Peterborough	d																							07 45	
Stowmarket	d					07 29					07 45							08 29				08 44		09 13	
Needham Market	d										07 50											08 49			
Ipswich	a					07 41					08 03	08 08						08 41				09 00	09 08	09 28	
	d					07 43				07 52		08 09						08 43			08 52		09 09		
Harwich Town	d				07 28									08 28											
Dovercourt	d				07 30									08 30											
Harwich International	d		07 20		07 33									08 33											
Wrabness	d				07 39									08 39											
Mistley	d				07 45									08 45											
Manningtree	d		07 33		07a50	07 53				08 02		08 19		08a50				08 53			09 02		09 19		
Walton-on-the-Naze	d			07 00												08 00									
Frinton-on-Sea	d			07 03												08 03									
Kirby Cross	d			07 06												08 06									
Clacton-on-Sea	d	07 05											08 05												09 05
Thorpe-le-Soken	a	07 13		07 12									08 13			08 12									09 13
	d	07 13		07 17									08 13			08 17									09 13
Weeley	d			07 21												08 21									
Great Bentley	d			07 24												08 24									
Alresford (Essex)	d			07 28												08 28									
Wivenhoe	d	07 23		07 32									08 23			08 32									09 23
Hythe	d			07 36												08 36									
Colchester Town	a			07 40												08 40									
	d			07 44				08 00							08 35	08 44			09 00						
Colchester	a	07 31	07 42	07 52		08 02		08 07		08 11		08 28	08 31		08 42	08 52		09 02	09 07		09 11		09 28		09 31
Colchester	d	07 33	07 43			08 03				08 12		08 30	08 33		08 43			09 03			09 12		09 30		09 33
Marks Tey	d		07 49							08 18					08 49						09 18				
Kelvedon	d		07 54							08 23					08 54						09 23				
Braintree	d								08 00											09 00					
Braintree Freeport	d								08 02											09 02					
Cressing	d								08 05											09 05					
White Notley	d								08 08											09 08					
Witham	d	07 46	08 00						08 16	08 29			08 46		09 00					09 16	09 29				09 46
Hatfield Peverel	d									08 33											09 33				
Chelmsford	d	07 56	08 09			08 21			08 26	08 40			08 56		09 09			09 21		09 26	09 40				09 56
Ingatestone	d	08 02							08 32				09 02							09 32					10 02
Shenfield	a	08 08	08 19						08 38	08 50			09 08		09 19					09 38	09 50				10 08
Romford	a		08 28												09 28										
Stratford ⊖	a	08 22	08 36			08s45			08 52	09 05			09 22		09 36			09s45		09 52	10 05				10 22
London Liverpool Street ⊖	a	08 31	08 45			08 55			09 01	09 14		09 19	09 31		09 45			09 55		10 01	10 14		10 19		10 31

b Previous night, stops to set down only

Norwich, Ipswich, Harwich, Clacton, Walton-on-Naze, Colchester and Chelmsford - London

Network Diagram - see first Page of Table 5

	LE 1		LE 1	LE 1	LE ◇1 ⊡	LE 1	LE 1	LE 1	LE 1	LE ◇1 ⊡	LE 1		LE 1	LE 1	LE 1	LE ◇1 ⊡	LE 1	LE 1	LE 1	LE 1	LE ◇1 ⊡		LE 1	LE 1
Norwich d					09 00					09 30						10 00					10 30			
Diss d					09 17					09 47						10 17					10 47			
Peterborough 8 d																							09 47	
Stowmarket d					09 29				09 44							10 29				10 44			11 13	
Needham Market d									09 49											10 49				
Ipswich a					09 41				10 00	10 08						10 41				11 00	11 08		11 28	
Ipswich d					09 43			09 52		10 09						10 43			10 52		11 09			
Harwich Town d	09 28												10 28											
Dovercourt d	09 30												10 30											
Harwich International d	09 33												10 33											
Wrabness d	09 39												10 39											
Mistley d	09 45												10 45											
Manningtree 2 d	09a50				09 53			10 02		10 19			10a50			10 53			11 02		11 19			
Walton-on-the-Naze d				09 00											10 00									
Frinton-on-Sea d				09 03											10 03									
Kirby Cross d				09 06											10 06									
Clacton-on-Sea d											10 05													11 05
Thorpe-le-Soken 1 a				09 12							10 13				10 12									11 13
Thorpe-le-Soken 1 d				09 17							10 13				10 17									11 13
Weeley d				09 21											10 21									
Great Bentley d				09 24											10 24									
Alresford (Essex) d				09 28											10 28									
Wivenhoe 3 d				09 32							10 23				10 32									11 23
Hythe d				09 36											10 36									
Colchester Town a				09 40											10 40									
Colchester Town d			09 35	09 44		10 00								10 35	10 44		11 00							
Colchester 4 a			09 42	09 52	10 02	10 07		10 11		10 28	10 31			10 42	10 52	11 02	11 07		11 11		11 28			11 31
Colchester 4 d			09 43		10 03			10 12		10 30	10 33			10 43		11 03			11 12		11 30			11 33
Marks Tey 2 d			09 49					10 18						10 49					11 18					
Kelvedon d			09 54					10 23						10 54					11 23					
Braintree d							10 00											11 00						
Braintree Freeport d							10 02											11 02						
Cressing d							10 05											11 05						
White Notley d							10 08											11 08						
Witham 2 d			10 00				10 16	10 29			10 46			11 00				11 16	11 29					11 46
Hatfield Peverel d								10 33											11 33					
Chelmsford 3 d			10 09		10 21		10 26	10 40			10 56			11 09		11 21		11 26	11 40					11 56
Ingatestone d							10 32				11 02							11 32						12 02
Shenfield 3 a			10 19				10 38	10 50			11 08			11 19				11 38	11 50					12 08
Romford a			10 28											11 28										
Stratford 7 ⊖ a			10 36		10s45		10 52	11 05			11 22			11 36		11s45		11 52	12 05					12 22
London Liverpool Street 15 ⊖ a			10 45		10 55		11 01	11 14		11 19	11 31			11 45		11 55		12 01	12 14		12 19			12 31

	LE 1	LE 1	LE 1	LE ◇1 ⊡	LE 1	LE 1	LE 1		LE 1	LE 1 ⊡	LE 1	LE 1	LE 1	LE 1	LE ◇1 ⊡	LE 1	LE 1		LE 1	LE 1	LE ◇1 ⊡	LE 1	LE 1	LE 1
Norwich d				11 00						11 30					12 00						12 30			
Diss d				11 17						11 47					12 17						12 47			
Peterborough 8 d																						11 45		
Stowmarket d				11 29					11 44						12 29					12 44		13 13		
Needham Market d									11 49											12 49				
Ipswich a				11 41					12 00	12 08					12 41					13 00	13 08	13 28		
Ipswich d				11 43			11 52			12 09					12 43				12 52		13 09			
Harwich Town d	11 28											12 28												13 28
Dovercourt d	11 30											12 30												13 30
Harwich International d	11 33											12 33												13 33
Wrabness d	11 39											12 39												13 39
Mistley d	11 45											12 45												13 45
Manningtree 2 d	11a50			11 53			12 02			12 19		12a50			12 53				13 02		13 19			13a50
Walton-on-the-Naze d			11 00											12 00										
Frinton-on-Sea d			11 03											12 03										
Kirby Cross d			11 06											12 06										
Clacton-on-Sea d											12 05												13 05	
Thorpe-le-Soken 1 a			11 12								12 13			12 12									13 13	
Thorpe-le-Soken 1 d			11 17								12 13			12 17									13 13	
Weeley d			11 21											12 21										
Great Bentley d			11 24											12 24										
Alresford (Essex) d			11 28											12 28										
Wivenhoe 3 d			11 32								12 23			12 32									13 23	
Hythe d			11 36											12 36										
Colchester Town a			11 40											12 40										
Colchester Town d		11 35	11 44		12 00								12 35	12 44		13 00								
Colchester 4 a		11 42	11 52	12 02	12 07		12 11			12 28	12 31		12 42	12 52	13 02	13 07			13 11		13 28		13 31	
Colchester 4 d		11 43		12 03			12 12			12 30	12 33		12 43		13 03				13 12		13 30		13 33	
Marks Tey 2 d		11 49					12 18						12 49						13 18					
Kelvedon d		11 54					12 23						12 54						13 23					
Braintree d						12 00											13 00							
Braintree Freeport d						12 02											13 02							
Cressing d						12 05											13 05							
White Notley d						12 08											13 08							
Witham 2 d		12 00				12 16	12 29				12 46		13 00				13 16		13 29				13 46	
Hatfield Peverel d							12 33												13 33					
Chelmsford 3 d		12 09		12 21		12 26	12 40				12 56		13 09		13 21		13 26		13 40				13 56	
Ingatestone d						12 32					13 02						13 32						14 02	
Shenfield 3 a		12 19				12 38	12 50				13 08		13 19				13 38		13 50				14 08	
Romford a		12 28											13 28											
Stratford 7 ⊖ a		12 36		12s45		12 52	13 05				13 22		13 36		13s45		13 52		14 05				14 22	
London Liverpool Street 15 ⊖ a		12 45		12 55		13 01	13 14			13 19	13 31		13 45		13 55		14 01		14 14		14 19		14 31	

	LE 1	LE 1	LE ◇1 ⊡		LE 1	LE 1	LE 1	LE 1	LE ◇1 ⊡	LE 1	LE 1	LE 1	LE 1		LE 1 ⊡	LE 1	LE 1	LE 1	LE 1	LE ◇1 ⊡	LE 1	LE 1	LE 1
Norwich d			13 00						13 30						14 00					14 30			
Diss d			13 17						13 47						14 17					14 47			
Peterborough 8 d																					13 45		
Stowmarket d			13 29					13 44							14 29				14 44		15 13		
Needham Market d								13 49											14 49				
Ipswich a			13 41					14 00	14 08						14 41				15 00	15 08	15 28		
Ipswich d			13 43				13 52		14 09						14 43			14 52		15 09			
Harwich Town d											14 28												15 28
Dovercourt d											14 30												15 30
Harwich International d											14 33												15 33
Wrabness d											14 39												15 39
Mistley d											14 45												15 45
Manningtree 2 d			13 53				14 02		14 19		14a50				14 53			15 02		15 19			15a50
Walton-on-the-Naze d		13 00											14 00										
Frinton-on-Sea d		13 03											14 03										
Kirby Cross d		13 06											14 06										
Clacton-on-Sea d										14 05												15 05	
Thorpe-le-Soken 1 a		13 12								14 13			14 12									15 13	
Thorpe-le-Soken 1 d		13 17								14 13			14 17									15 13	
Weeley d		13 21											14 21										
Great Bentley d		13 24											14 24										
Alresford (Essex) d		13 28											14 28										
Wivenhoe 3 d		13 32								14 23			14 32									15 23	
Hythe d		13 36											14 36										
Colchester Town a		13 40											14 40										
Colchester Town d	13 35	13 44			14 00							14 35	14 44			15 00							
Colchester 4 a	13 42	13 52	14 02		14 07		14 11		14 28	14 31		14 42	14 52		15 02	15 07		15 11		15 28		15 31	
Colchester 4 d	13 43		14 03				14 12		14 30	14 33		14 43			15 03			15 12		15 30		15 33	
Marks Tey 2 d	13 49						14 18					14 49						15 18					
Kelvedon d	13 54						14 23					14 54						15 23					
Braintree d						14 00											15 00						
Braintree Freeport d						14 02											15 02						
Cressing d						14 05											15 05						
White Notley d						14 08											15 08						
Witham 2 d	14 00					14 16	14 29			14 46		15 00					15 16	15 29				15 46	
Hatfield Peverel d							14 33											15 33					
Chelmsford 3 d	14 09		14 21			14 26	14 40			14 56		15 09			15 21		15 26	15 40				15 56	
Ingatestone d						14 32				15 02							15 32					16 02	
Shenfield 3 a	14 19					14 38	14 50			15 08		15 19					15 38	15 50				16 08	
Romford a	14 28											15 28											
Stratford 7 ⊖ a	14 36		14s45			14 52	15 05			15 22		15 36			15s45		15 52	16 05				16 22	
London Liverpool Street 15 ⊖ a	14 45		14 55			15 01	15 14		15 19	15 31		15 45			15 55		16 01	16 14		16 19		16 31	

	LE 1	LE 1	LE ◇1 ⊡	LE 1	LE 1	LE 1	LE 1	LE ◇1 ⊡	LE 1		LE 1	LE 1	LE 1	LE ◇1 ⊡	LE 1	LE 1	LE 1	LE 1	LE ◇1 ⊡		LE 1	LE 1	LE 1	LE 1
Norwich d			15 00					15 30						16 00					16 30					
Diss d			15 17					15 47						16 17					16 47					
Peterborough 8 d																					15 45			
Stowmarket d			15 29				15 44							16 29				16 44			17 13			
Needham Market d							15 49											16 49						
Ipswich a			15 41				16 00	16 08						16 41				17 00	17 08		17 28			
Ipswich d			15 43			15 52		16 09						16 43			16 52		17 09					
Harwich Town d											16 28												17 28	
Dovercourt d											16 30												17 30	
Harwich International d											16 33												17 33	
Wrabness d											16 39												17 39	
Mistley d											16 45												17 45	
Manningtree 2 d			15 53			16 02		16 19			16a50			16 53			17 02		17 19				17a50	
Walton-on-the-Naze d		15 00											16 00											
Frinton-on-Sea d		15 03											16 03											
Kirby Cross d		15 06											16 06											
Clacton-on-Sea d									16 05													17 05		
Thorpe-le-Soken 1 a		15 12							16 13				16 12									17 13		
Thorpe-le-Soken 1 d		15 17							16 13				16 17									17 13		
Weeley d		15 21											16 21											
Great Bentley d		15 24											16 24											
Alresford (Essex) d		15 28											16 28											
Wivenhoe 3 d		15 32							16 23				16 32									17 23		
Hythe d		15 36											16 36											
Colchester Town a		15 40											16 40											
Colchester Town d	15 35	15 44		16 00								16 35	16 44		17 00									17 35
Colchester 4 a	15 42	15 52	16 02	16 07		16 11		16 28	16 31			16 42	16 52	17 02	17 07		17 11		17 28			17 31		17 42
Colchester 4 d	15 43		16 03			16 12		16 30	16 33			16 43		17 03			17 12		17 30			17 33		17 43
Marks Tey 2 d	15 49					16 18						16 49					17 18							17 49
Kelvedon d	15 54					16 23						16 54					17 23							17 54
Braintree d					16 00											17 00								
Braintree Freeport d					16 02											17 02								
Cressing d					16 05											17 05								
White Notley d					16 08											17 08								
Witham 2 d	16 00				16 16	16 29			16 46			17 00				17 16	17 29					17 46		18 00
Hatfield Peverel d						16 33											17 33							
Chelmsford 3 d	16 09		16 21		16 26	16 40			16 56			17 09		17 21		17 26	17 40					17 56		18 09
Ingatestone d					16 32				17 02							17 32						18 02		
Shenfield 3 a	16 19				16 38	16 50			17 08			17 19				17 38	17 50					18 08		18 19
Romford a	16 28											17 28												18 28
Stratford 7 ⊖ a	16 36		16s45		16 52	17 05			17 22			17 36		17s45		17 52	18 05					18 22		18 36
London Liverpool Street 15 ⊖ a	16 45		16 55		17 01	17 14		17 19	17 31			17 45		17 55		18 01	18 14		18 19			18 31		18 45

Table 11

Saturdays
18 August to 25 August

Norwich, Ipswich, Harwich, Clacton, Walton-on-Naze, Colchester and Chelmsford - London

Network Diagram - see first Page of Table 5

Station		LE 1	LE ◇1	LE 1	LE 1	LE 1	LE 1	LE ◇1	LE 1	LE 1	LE 1	LE 1	LE ◇1	LE 1	LE 1	LE 1	LE 1	LE ◇1	LE 1	LE 1	LE 1	LE 1	LE 1
Norwich	d		17 00					17 30					18 00					18 30					
Diss	d		17 17					17 47					18 17					18 47					
Peterborough 8	d																		17 45				
Stowmarket	d		17 29				17 45	17 59					18 29				18 45		19 13				
Needham Market	d						17 50										18 50						
Ipswich	a		17 41				18 01	18 11					18 41				19 01	19 08	19 28				
	d		17 43			17 52		18 13					18 43			18 52		19 09					
Harwich Town	d									18 28											19 28		
Dovercourt	d									18 30											19 30		
Harwich International	d									18 33											19 33		
Wrabness	d									18 39											19 39		
Mistley	d									18 45											19 45		
Manningtree 2	d		17 53			18 02				18a50			18 53			19 02		19 19			19a50		
Walton-on-the-Naze	d	17 00										18 00											19 00
Frinton-on-Sea	d	17 03										18 03											19 03
Kirby Cross	d	17 06										18 06											19 06
Clacton-on-Sea	d								18 05											19 05			
Thorpe-le-Soken 1	a	17 12							18 13			18 12								19 13			19 12
	d	17 17							18 13			18 17								19 13			19 17
Weeley	d	17 21										18 21											19 21
Great Bentley	d	17 24										18 24											19 24
Alresford (Essex)	d	17 28										18 28											19 28
Wivenhoe 3	d	17 32							18 23			18 32								19 23			19 32
Hythe	d	17 36										18 36											19 36
Colchester Town	a	17 40										18 40											19 40
	d	17 44		18 00							18 35	18 44		19 00								19 35	19 44
Colchester 4	a	17 52	18 02	18 07		18 11		18 28	18 31		18 42	18 52	19 02	19 07		19 11		19 28		19 31		19 42	19 52
Colchester 4	d		18 03			18 12		18 30	18 33		18 43		19 03			19 12		19 30		19 33		19 43	
Marks Tey 2	d					18 18					18 49					19 18						19 49	
Kelvedon	d					18 23					18 54					19 23						19 54	
Braintree	d				18 00										19 00								
Braintree Freeport	d				18 02										19 02								
Cressing	d				18 05										19 05								
White Notley	d				18 08										19 08								
Witham 2	d				18 16	18 29			18 46		19 00				19 16	19 29				19 46		20 00	
Hatfield Peverel	d					18 33										19 33							
Chelmsford 3	d		18 21		18 26	18 40			18 56		19 09		19 21		19 26	19 40				19 56		20 09	
Ingatestone	d				18 32				19 02						19 32					20 02			
Shenfield 3	a				18 38	18 50			19 08		19 19				19 38	19 50				20 08		20 19	
Romford	a										19 28											20 28	
Stratford 7 ⊖	a		18s45		18 52	19 05			19 22		19 36		19s45		19 52	20 05				20 22		20 36	
London Liverpool Street 15 ⊖	a		18 55		19 01	19 14		19 19	19 31		19 45		19 55		20 01	20 14		20 19		20 31		20 45	

Station		LE ◇1	LE 1	LE 1	LE 1	LE 1	LE 1	LE 1	LE 1	LE 1	LE 1	LE ◇1	LE 1	LE 1	LE 1	LE 1	LE 1	LE 1	LE 1	LE ◇1	LE 1	LE 1
Norwich	d	19 00										20 00										
Diss	d	19 17										20 17										
Peterborough 8	d																			19 45		
Stowmarket	d	19 29				19 44						20 29				20 44				21 09		
Needham Market	d					19 49										20 49						
Ipswich	a	19 41				20 00						20 41				21 00				21 22		
	d	19 43			19 52		20 09					20 43				21 00	21 09			21 25		
Harwich Town	d								20 28													21 28
Dovercourt	d								20 30													21 30
Harwich International	d								20 33						20 45	21a29						21 33
Wrabness	d								20 39													21 39
Mistley	d								20 45													21 45
Manningtree 2	d	19 53			20 02		20 20		20a50			20 53			20 58		21 19			21 35		21a50
Walton-on-the-Naze	d										20 00										21 00	
Frinton-on-Sea	d										20 03										21 03	
Kirby Cross	d										20 06										21 06	
Clacton-on-Sea	d							20 05										21 05				
Thorpe-le-Soken 1	a							20 13			20 12							21 13			21 12	
	d							20 13			20 17							21 13			21 17	
Weeley	d										20 21										21 21	
Great Bentley	d										20 24										21 24	
Alresford (Essex)	d										20 28										21 28	
Wivenhoe 3	d							20 23			20 32							21 23			21 32	
Hythe	d										20 36										21 36	
Colchester Town	a										20 40										21 40	
	d		20 00							20 35	20 44		21 00						21 35		21 44	
Colchester 4	a	20 02	20 07		20 11		20 29	20 31		20 42	20 52	21 02	21 07		21 07		21 28	21 31	21 42	21 46	21 52	
Colchester 4	d	20 03			20 12		20 30	20 33		20 43		21 03			21 12		21 30	21 33	21 43			
Marks Tey 2	d				20 18					20 49					21 18				21 49			
Kelvedon	d				20 23					20 54					21 23				21 54			
Braintree	d			20 00										21 00								
Braintree Freeport	d			20 02										21 02								
Cressing	d			20 05										21 05								
White Notley	d			20 08										21 08								
Witham 2	d			20 16	20 29			20 46		21 00				21 16	21 29			21 46	22 00			
Hatfield Peverel	d				20 33										21 33							
Chelmsford 3	d	20 21		20 26	20 40			20 56		21 09		21 21		21 26	21 40			21 56	22 09			
Ingatestone	d			20 32				21 02						21 32				22 02				
Shenfield 3	a			20 38	20 50			21 08		21 19				21 38	21 50			22 08	22 19			
Romford	a									21 28									22 28			
Stratford 7 ⊖	a	20s45		20 52	21 05			21 22		21 36		21s45		21 52	22 05			22 22	22 36			
London Liverpool Street 15 ⊖	a	20 55		21 01	21 14		21 17	21 31		21 45		21 55		22 01	22 14		22 17	22 31	22 46			

Table 11

Saturdays
18 August to 25 August

Norwich, Ipswich, Harwich, Clacton, Walton-on-Naze, Colchester and Chelmsford - London

Network Diagram - see first Page of Table 5

Station		LE ◇1	LE 1	LE 1	LE 1	LE 1	LE 1	LE 1	LE 1	LE 1	LE 1	LE ◇1	LE 1	LE 1	LE 1	LE 1	LE 1	LE ◇1	LE 1	LE 1	LE 1	LE
Norwich	d	21 00										22 00							23 05			
Diss	d	21 17										22 17							23 22			
Peterborough 8	d																	21 45				
Stowmarket	d	21 29				21 44						22 29	22 44					23 06	23 36			23 47
Needham Market	d					21 49							22 49									23 52
Ipswich	a	21 41				22 00						22 41	23 00					23 18	23 50			00 05
	d	21 43			21 52			22 23				22 43				23 15		23 19				
Harwich Town	d									22 28										23 28		
Dovercourt	d									22 30										23 30		
Harwich International	d									22 33										23 33		
Wrabness	d									22 39										23 39		
Mistley	d									22 45										23 45		
Manningtree 2	d	21 53			22 02			22 33		22a50		22 53				23 25		23 29		23 50		
Walton-on-the-Naze	d								22 00						23 00							
Frinton-on-Sea	d								22 03						23 03							
Kirby Cross	d								22 06						23 06							
Clacton-on-Sea	d						22 05										23 05					
Thorpe-le-Soken 1	a						22 13		22 12						23 12		23 13					
	d						22 13		22 17								23 13					
Weeley	d								22 21								23 17					
Great Bentley	d								22 24								23 20					
Alresford (Essex)	d								22 28								23 24					
Wivenhoe 3	d						22 23		22 32								23 28					
Hythe	d								22 36								23 32					
Colchester Town	a								22 40													
	d		22 00						22 44					23 00								
Colchester 4	a	22 02	22 07		22 11		22 31	22 42	22 52			23 02		23 07		23 35	23 38	23 40		23 59		
Colchester 4	d	22 03			22 12		22 33	22 43				23 03										
Marks Tey 2	d				22 18			22 49														
Kelvedon	d				22 23			22 54														
Braintree	d			22 00							22 56										23 45	
Braintree Freeport	d			22 02							22 58										23 47	
Cressing	d			22 05							23 01										23 50	
White Notley	d			22 08							23 04										23 53	
Witham 2	d			22 16	22 29		22 46	23 00			23a12	23 16									00a01	
Hatfield Peverel	d				22 33																	
Chelmsford 3	d	22 21		22 26	22 40		22 56	23 09				23 25										
Ingatestone	d			22 32			23 02															
Shenfield 3	a			22 38	22 50		23 08	23 19				23s36										
Romford	a							23 28														
Stratford 7 ⊖	a	22s45		22 52	23 05		23 22	23 36				23s52										
London Liverpool Street 15 ⊖	a	22 55		23 01	23 14		23 31	23 45				00 02										

Norwich, Ipswich, Harwich, Clacton, Walton-on-Naze, Colchester and Chelmsford - London

Network Diagram - see first Page of Table 5

		LE ◇1	LE	LE 1	LE 1	LE 1	LE	LE 1	LE ◇1 ☕	LE 1	LE 1	LE ◇1 ☕	LE 1	LE 1	LE 1	LE 1	LE ◇1 ☕	LE 1	LE 1	LE 1	LE 1	LE	LE ◇1 ☕
Norwich	d	22p00							05 00			05 30					06 00						06 30
Diss	d	22p17							05 17			05 47					06 17						06 47
Peterborough 8	d																						
Stowmarket	d	22p29	23p47						05 29								06 29					06 44	
Needham Market	d		23p52																			06 49	
Ipswich	a	22p41	00 05						05 41			06 08					06 41					07 02	07 08
	d	22p43							05 43			06 09					06 43			06 52	06 59		07 09
Harwich Town	d													06 28									
Dovercourt	d													06 30									
Harwich International	d													06 33							07a28		
Wrabness	d													06 39									
Mistley	d													06 45									
Manningtree 2	d	22p53							05 53			06 19		06a50			06 53			07 02			07 19
Walton-on-the-Naze	d															06 00							
Frinton-on-Sea	d															06 03							
Kirby Cross	d															06 06							
Clacton-on-Sea	d							05 30					06 05					06 24					
Thorpe-le-Soken 1	a							05 38					06 13			06 12		06 32					
	d							05 38					06 13			06 17							
Weeley	d															06 21							
Great Bentley	d															06 24							
Alresford (Essex)	d															06 28							
Wivenhoe 3	d							05 48					06 23			06 32							
Hythe	d															06 36							
Colchester Town	a															06 40							
	d														06 35	06 44							
Colchester 4	a	23p02						05 57	06 02			06 28	06 31		06 42	06 52	07 02			07 11			07 28
Colchester 4	d	23p03			05 12	05 43	05 50		06 03		06 12	06 30	06 33		06 43		07 03			07 12			07 30
Marks Tey 2	d				05 18	05 49	05a57				06 18				06 49					07 18			
Kelvedon	d				05 23	05 54					06 23				06 54					07 23			
Braintree	d			00 27						06 00									07 00				
Braintree Freeport	d			00 29						06 02									07 02				
Cressing	d			00 32						06 05									07 05				
White Notley	d			00 35						06 08									07 08				
Witham 2	d	23p16		00a43	05 29	06 00				06a16	06 29		06 46		07 00				07 16	07 29			
Hatfield Peverel	d				05 33	06 04					06 33									07 33			
Chelmsford 3	d	23p25			05 40	06 11			06 21		06 40		06 56		07 09		07 21		07 26	07 40			
Ingatestone	d				05 47	06 18							07 02						07 32				
Shenfield 3	a	23b36			05 52	06 23					06 50		07 08		07 19				07 38	07 50			
Romford	a																						
Stratford 7 ⊖	a				06 07	06 38			06s45		07 05		07 22		07 36		07s45		07 52	08 05			
London Liverpool Street 15 ⊖	a	00 03			06 16	06 47			06 55		07 14	07 19	07 31		07 45		07 55		08 01	08 14			08 19

		LE 1	LE 1	LE 1	LE 1	LE ◇1 ☕	LE 1	LE 1	LE 1	LE	LE ◇1 ☕	LE 1	LE 1	LE 1	LE 1	LE ◇1 ☕	LE 1	LE 1	LE 1	LE 1	LE ◇1 ☕	LE 1	LE 1
Norwich	d					07 00					07 30					08 00					08 30		
Diss	d					07 17					07 47					08 17					08 47		
Peterborough 8	d																					07 45	
Stowmarket	d					07 29				07 45						08 29				08 44		09 13	
Needham Market	d									07 50										08 49			
Ipswich	a					07 41				08 03	08 08					08 41				09 00	09 08	09 28	
	d					07 43			07 52		08 09					08 43			08 52		09 09		
Harwich Town	d				07 28								08 28										
Dovercourt	d				07 30								08 30										
Harwich International	d		07 20		07 33								08 33										
Wrabness	d				07 39								08 39										
Mistley	d				07 45								08 45										
Manningtree 2	d		07 33		07a50	07 53			08 02		08 19		08a50			08 53			09 02		09 19		
Walton-on-the-Naze	d			07 00											08 00								
Frinton-on-Sea	d			07 03											08 03								
Kirby Cross	d			07 06											08 06								
Clacton-on-Sea	d	07 05										08 05											09 05
Thorpe-le-Soken 1	a	07 13		07 12								08 13			08 12								09 13
	d	07 13		07 17								08 13			08 17								09 13
Weeley	d			07 21											08 21								
Great Bentley	d			07 24											08 24								
Alresford (Essex)	d			07 28											08 28								
Wivenhoe 3	d	07 23		07 32								08 23			08 32								09 23
Hythe	d			07 36											08 36								
Colchester Town	a			07 40											08 40								
	d			07 44			08 00							08 35	08 44		09 00						
Colchester 4	a	07 31	07 42	07 52		08 02	08 07		08 11		08 28	08 31		08 42	08 52	09 02	09 07		09 11		09 28		09 31
Colchester 4	d	07 33	07 43			08 03			08 12		08 30	08 33		08 43		09 03			09 12		09 30		09 33
Marks Tey 2	d		07 49						08 18					08 49					09 18				
Kelvedon	d		07 54						08 23					08 54					09 23				
Braintree	d							08 00										09 00					
Braintree Freeport	d							08 02										09 02					
Cressing	d							08 05										09 05					
White Notley	d							08 08										09 08					
Witham 2	d	07 46	08 00					08 16	08 29			08 46		09 00				09 16	09 29				09 46
Hatfield Peverel	d								08 33										09 33				
Chelmsford 3	d	07 56	08 09			08 21		08 26	08 40			08 56		09 09		09 21		09 26	09 40				09 56
Ingatestone	d	08 02						08 32				09 02						09 32					10 02
Shenfield 3	a	08 08	08 19					08 38	08 50			09 08		09 19				09 38	09 50				10 08
Romford	a													09 28									
Stratford 7 ⊖	a	08 22	08 36			08s45		08 52	09 05			09 22		09 36		09s45		09 52	10 05				10 22
London Liverpool Street 15 ⊖	a	08 31	08 45			08 55		09 01	09 14		09 19	09 31		09 45		09 55		10 01	10 14		10 19		10 31

b Previous night, stops to set down only

		LE 1	LE 1	LE 1	LE ◇1 ☕	LE 1	LE 1	LE 1	LE 1	LE ◇1 ☕	LE 1	LE 1	LE 1	LE 1	LE ◇1 ☕	LE 1	LE 1	LE 1	LE 1	LE ◇1 ☕	LE 1	LE 1
Norwich	d				09 00					09 30					10 00					10 30		
Diss	d				09 17					09 47					10 17					10 47		
Peterborough 8	d																				09 47	
Stowmarket	d				09 29				09 44						10 29				10 44		11 13	
Needham Market	d								09 49										10 49			
Ipswich	a				09 41				10 00	10 08					10 41				11 00	11 08	11 28	
	d				09 43			09 52		10 09					10 43			10 52		11 09		
Harwich Town	d	09 28										10 28										
Dovercourt	d	09 30										10 30										
Harwich International	d	09 33										10 33										
Wrabness	d	09 39										10 39										
Mistley	d	09 45										10 45										
Manningtree 2	d	09a50			09 53			10 02		10 19		10a50			10 53			11 02		11 19		
Walton-on-the-Naze	d			09 00										10 00								
Frinton-on-Sea	d			09 03										10 03								
Kirby Cross	d			09 06										10 06								
Clacton-on-Sea	d										10 05											11 05
Thorpe-le-Soken 1	a			09 12							10 13			10 12								11 13
	d			09 17							10 13			10 17								11 13
Weeley	d			09 21										10 21								
Great Bentley	d			09 24										10 24								
Alresford (Essex)	d			09 28										10 28								
Wivenhoe 3	d			09 32							10 23			10 32								11 23
Hythe	d			09 36										10 36								
Colchester Town	a			09 40										10 40								
	d		09 35	09 44		10 00							10 35	10 44		11 00						
Colchester 4	a		09 42	09 52	10 02	10 07		10 11		10 28	10 31		10 42	10 52	11 02	11 07		11 11		11 28		11 31
Colchester 4	d		09 43		10 03			10 12		10 30	10 33		10 43		11 03			11 12		11 30		11 33
Marks Tey 2	d		09 49					10 18					10 49					11 18				
Kelvedon	d		09 54					10 23					10 54					11 23				
Braintree	d						10 00										11 00					
Braintree Freeport	d						10 02										11 02					
Cressing	d						10 05										11 05					
White Notley	d						10 08										11 08					
Witham 2	d		10 00				10 16	10 29			10 46		11 00				11 16	11 29				11 46
Hatfield Peverel	d							10 33										11 33				
Chelmsford 3	d		10 09		10 21		10 26	10 40			10 56		11 09		11 21		11 26	11 40				11 56
Ingatestone	d						10 32				11 02						11 32					12 02
Shenfield 3	a		10 19				10 38	10 50			11 08		11 19				11 38	11 50				12 08
Romford	a		10 28										11 28									
Stratford 7 ⊖	a		10 36		10s45		10 52	11 05			11 22		11 36		11s45		11 52	12 05				12 22
London Liverpool Street 15 ⊖	a		10 45		10 55		11 01	11 14		11 19	11 31		11 45		11 55		12 01	12 14		12 19		12 31

		LE 1	LE 1	LE 1	LE ◇1 ☕	LE 1	LE 1	LE 1	LE 1	LE 8 1 ☕	LE 1	LE 1	LE 1	LE 1	LE ◇1 ☕	LE 1	LE 1	LE 1	LE 1	LE ◇1 ☕	LE 1	LE 1	LE 1
Norwich	d				11 00					11 30					12 00					12 30			
Diss	d				11 17					11 47					12 17					12 47			
Peterborough 8	d																				11 45		
Stowmarket	d				11 29				11 44						12 29				12 44		13 13		
Needham Market	d								11 49										12 49				
Ipswich	a				11 41				12 00	12 08					12 41				13 00	13 08	13 28		
	d				11 43			11 52		12 09					12 43			12 52		13 09			
Harwich Town	d	11 28										12 28											13 28
Dovercourt	d	11 30										12 30											13 30
Harwich International	d	11 33										12 33											13 33
Wrabness	d	11 39										12 39											13 39
Mistley	d	11 45										12 45											13 45
Manningtree 2	d	11a50			11 53			12 02		12 19		12a50			12 53			13 02		13 19			13a50
Walton-on-the-Naze	d			11 00										12 00									
Frinton-on-Sea	d			11 03										12 03									
Kirby Cross	d			11 06										12 06									
Clacton-on-Sea	d										12 05											13 05	
Thorpe-le-Soken 1	a			11 12							12 13			12 12								13 13	
	d			11 17							12 13			12 17								13 13	
Weeley	d			11 21										12 21									
Great Bentley	d			11 24										12 24									
Alresford (Essex)	d			11 28										12 28									
Wivenhoe 3	d			11 32							12 23			12 32								13 23	
Hythe	d			11 36										12 36									
Colchester Town	a			11 40										12 40									
	d		11 35	11 44		12 00							12 35	12 44		13 00							
Colchester 4	a		11 42	11 52	12 02	12 07		12 11		12 28	12 31		12 42	12 52	13 02	13 07		13 11		13 28		13 31	
Colchester 4	d		11 43		12 03			12 12		12 30	12 33		12 43		13 03			13 12		13 30		13 33	
Marks Tey 2	d		11 49					12 18					12 49					13 18					
Kelvedon	d		11 54					12 23					12 54					13 23					
Braintree	d						12 00										13 00						
Braintree Freeport	d						12 02										13 02						
Cressing	d						12 05										13 05						
White Notley	d						12 08										13 08						
Witham 2	d		12 00				12 16	12 29			12 46		13 00				13 16	13 29				13 46	
Hatfield Peverel	d							12 33										13 33					
Chelmsford 3	d		12 09		12 21		12 26	12 40			12 56		13 09		13 21		13 26	13 40				13 56	
Ingatestone	d						12 32				13 02						13 32					14 02	
Shenfield 3	a		12 19				12 38	12 50			13 08		13 19				13 38	13 50				14 08	
Romford	a		12 28										13 28										
Stratford 7 ⊖	a		12 36		12s45		12 52	13 05			13 22		13 36		13s45		13 52	14 05				14 22	
London Liverpool Street 15 ⊖	a		12 45		12 55		13 01	13 14		13 19	13 31		13 45		13 55		14 01	14 14		14 19		14 31	

Table 11

Saturdays

1 September to 8 September

Norwich, Ipswich, Harwich, Clacton, Walton-on-Naze, Colchester and Chelmsford - London

Network Diagram - see first Page of Table 5

		LE	LE	LE	LE	LE	LE	LE	LE	LE	LE	LE	LE	LE	LE	LE	LE	LE	LE	LE	LE	LE	LE
		■	■	◇■ ⊐	■	■	■	■	◇■ ⊐	■	■	■	■	■ ■ ⊐	■	■	■	■	◇■ ⊐	■	■	■	■
Norwich	d			13 00					13 30					14 00					14 30				
Diss	d			13 17					13 47					14 17					14 47				
Peterborough ■	d																			13 45			
Stowmarket	d			13 29				13 44						14 29				14 44		15 13			
Needham Market	d							13 49										14 49					
Ipswich	a			13 41				14 00	14 08					14 41				15 00	15 08	15 28			
	d			13 43			13 52		14 09					14 43			14 52		15 09				
Harwich Town	d												14 28									15 28	
Dovercourt	d												14 30									15 30	
Harwich International	d												14 33									15 33	
Wrabness	d												14 39									15 39	
Mistley	d												14 45									15 45	
Manningtree ■	d			13 53			14 02		14 19				14a50	14 53			15 02		15 19			15a50	
Walton-on-the-Naze	d		13 00									14 00											
Frinton-on-Sea	d		13 03									14 03											
Kirby Cross	d		13 06									14 06											
Clacton-on-Sea	d									14 05											15 05		
Thorpe-le-Soken ■	a		13 12							14 13		14 12									15 13		
	d		13 17							14 13		14 17									15 13		
Weeley	d		13 21									14 21											
Great Bentley	d		13 24									14 24											
Alresford (Essex)	d		13 28									14 28											
Wivenhoe ■	d		13 32							14 23		14 32									15 23		
Hythe	d		13 36									14 36											
Colchester Town	a		13 40									14 40											
	d	13 35	13 44		14 00						14 35	14 44			15 00								15 35
Colchester ■	a	13 42	13 52	14 02	14 07		14 11		14 28	14 31	14 42	14 52		15 02	15 07		15 11		15 28		15 31		15 42
Colchester ■	d	13 43		14 03			14 12		14 30	14 33	14 43			15 03			15 12		15 30		15 33		15 43
Marks Tey ■	d	13 49					14 18				14 49						15 18						15 49
Kelvedon	d	13 54					14 23				14 54						15 23						15 54
Braintree	d					14 00										15 00							
Braintree Freeport	d					14 02										15 02							
Cressing	d					14 05										15 05							
White Notley	d					14 08										15 08							
Witham ■	d	14 00				14 16	14 29			14 46	15 00					15 16	15 29				15 46		16 00
Hatfield Peverel	d						14 33										15 33						
Chelmsford ■	d	14 09		14 21		14 26	14 40			14 56	15 09			15 21		15 26	15 40				15 56		16 09
Ingatestone	d					14 32				15 02						15 32					16 02		
Shenfield ■	a	14 19				14 38	14 50			15 08	15 19					15 38	15 50				16 08		16 19
Romford	a	14 28																					16 28
Stratford ■ ⊖	a	14 36		14s45		14 52	15 05			15 22	15 36			15s45		15 52	16 05				16 22		16 36
London Liverpool Street ■ ⊖	a	14 45		14 55		15 01	15 14		15 19	15 31	15 45			15 55		16 01	16 14		16 19		16 31		16 45

		LE	LE	LE	LE	LE	LE	LE	LE	LE	LE	LE	LE	LE	LE	LE	LE	LE	LE	LE	LE	LE	LE	LE
		■	◇■ ⊐	■	■	■	■	◇■ ⊐	■	■	■	■	◇■ ⊐	■	■	■	■	◇■ ⊐	■	■	■	■	■	◇■ ⊐
Norwich	d		15 00					15 30					16 00					16 30						17 00
Diss	d		15 17					15 47					16 17					16 47						17 17
Peterborough ■	d																		15 45					
Stowmarket	d		15 29				15 44						16 29				16 44		17 13					17 29
Needham Market	d						15 49										16 49							
Ipswich	a		15 41				16 00	16 08					16 41				17 00	17 08	17 28					17 41
	d		15 43			15 52		16 09					16 43			16 52		17 09						17 43
Harwich Town	d											16 28									17 28			
Dovercourt	d											16 30									17 30			
Harwich International	d											16 33									17 33			
Wrabness	d											16 39									17 39			
Mistley	d											16 45									17 45			
Manningtree ■	d		15 53			16 02		16 19				16a50	16 53			17 02		17 19			17a50			17 53
Walton-on-the-Naze	d	15 00									16 00												17 00	
Frinton-on-Sea	d	15 03									16 03												17 03	
Kirby Cross	d	15 06									16 06												17 06	
Clacton-on-Sea	d								16 05											17 05				
Thorpe-le-Soken ■	a	15 12							16 13		16 12									17 13			17 12	
	d	15 17							16 13		16 17									17 13			17 17	
Weeley	d	15 21									16 21												17 21	
Great Bentley	d	15 24									16 24												17 24	
Alresford (Essex)	d	15 28									16 28												17 28	
Wivenhoe ■	d	15 32							16 23		16 32									17 23			17 32	
Hythe	d	15 36									16 36												17 36	
Colchester Town	a	15 40									16 40												17 40	
	d	15 44		16 00						16 35	16 44			17 00								17 35	17 44	
Colchester ■	a	15 52	16 02	16 07		16 11		16 28	16 31	16 42	16 52		17 02	17 07		17 11		17 28		17 31		17 42	17 52	18 02
Colchester ■	d		16 03			16 12		16 30	16 33	16 43			17 03			17 12		17 30		17 33		17 43		18 03
Marks Tey ■	d					16 18				16 49						17 18						17 49		
Kelvedon	d					16 23				16 54						17 23						17 54		
Braintree	d				16 00										17 00									
Braintree Freeport	d				16 02										17 02									
Cressing	d				16 05										17 05									
White Notley	d				16 08										17 08									
Witham ■	d				16 16	16 29			16 46	17 00					17 16	17 29				17 46		18 00		
Hatfield Peverel	d					16 33										17 33								
Chelmsford ■	d		16 21		16 26	16 40			16 56	17 09			17 21		17 26	17 40				17 56		18 09		18 21
Ingatestone	d				16 32				17 02						17 32					18 02				
Shenfield ■	a				16 38	16 50			17 08	17 19					17 38	17 50				18 08		18 19		
Romford	a																					18 28		
Stratford ■ ⊖	a		16s45		16 52	17 05			17 22	17 36			17s45		17 52	18 05				18 22		18 36		18s45
London Liverpool Street ■ ⊖	a		16 55		17 01	17 14		17 19	17 31	17 45			17 55		18 01	18 14		18 19		18 31		18 45		18 55

Table 11

Saturdays

1 September to 8 September

Norwich, Ipswich, Harwich, Clacton, Walton-on-Naze, Colchester and Chelmsford - London

Network Diagram - see first Page of Table 5

		LE	LE	LE	LE	LE	LE	LE	LE	LE	LE	LE	LE	LE	LE	LE	LE	LE	LE	LE	LE	LE	LE	LE
		■	■	■	■	◇■ ⊐	■	■	■	■	◇■ ⊐	■	■	■	■	◇■ ⊐	■	■	■	■	■	◇■ ⊐	■	■
Norwich	d					17 30					18 00					18 30						19 00		
Diss	d					17 47					18 17					18 47						19 17		
Peterborough ■	d																17 45							
Stowmarket	d				17 45	17 59					18 29				18 45		19 13					19 29		
Needham Market	d				17 50										18 50									
Ipswich	a				18 01	18 11					18 41				19 01	19 08	19 28					19 41		
	d			17 52		18 13					18 43			18 52		19 09						19 43		
Harwich Town	d									18 28									19 28					
Dovercourt	d									18 30									19 30					
Harwich International	d									18 33									19 33					
Wrabness	d									18 39									19 39					
Mistley	d									18 45									19 45					
Manningtree ■	d			18 02						18a50	18 53			19 02		19 19			19a50			19 53		
Walton-on-the-Naze	d								18 00												19 00			
Frinton-on-Sea	d								18 03												19 03			
Kirby Cross	d								18 06												19 06			
Clacton-on-Sea	d						18 05											19 05						
Thorpe-le-Soken ■	a						18 13		18 12									19 13			19 12			
	d						18 13		18 17									19 13			19 17			
Weeley	d								18 21												19 21			
Great Bentley	d								18 24												19 24			
Alresford (Essex)	d								18 28												19 28			
Wivenhoe ■	d						18 23		18 32									19 23			19 32			
Hythe	d								18 36												19 36			
Colchester Town	a								18 40												19 40			
	d	18 00						18 35	18 44			19 00								19 35	19 44		20 00	
Colchester ■	a	18 07		18 11		18 28	18 31	18 42	18 52		19 02	19 07		19 11		19 28		19 31		19 42	19 52	20 02	20 07	
Colchester ■	d			18 12		18 30	18 33	18 43			19 03			19 12		19 30		19 33		19 43		20 03		
Marks Tey ■	d			18 18				18 49						19 18						19 49				
Kelvedon	d			18 23				18 54						19 23						19 54				
Braintree	d		18 00										19 00											20 00
Braintree Freeport	d		18 02										19 02											20 02
Cressing	d		18 05										19 05											20 05
White Notley	d		18 08										19 08											20 08
Witham ■	d		18 16	18 29			18 46	19 00					19 16	19 29				19 46		20 00				20 16
Hatfield Peverel	d			18 33										19 33										
Chelmsford ■	d		18 26	18 40			18 56	19 09			19 21		19 26	19 40				19 56		20 09		20 21		20 26
Ingatestone	d		18 32				19 02						19 32					20 02						20 32
Shenfield ■	a		18 38	18 50			19 08	19 19					19 38	19 50				20 08		20 19				20 38
Romford	a																			20 28				
Stratford ■ ⊖	a		18 52	19 05			19 22	19 36			19s45		19 52	20 05				20 22		20 36		20s45		20 52
London Liverpool Street ■ ⊖	a		19 01	19 14		19 19	19 31	19 45			19 55		20 01	20 14		20 19		20 33		20 45		20 55		21 01

		LE	LE	LE	LE	LE	LE	LE	LE	LE	LE	LE	LE	LE	LE	LE	LE	LE	LE	LE	LE	LE
		■	■	■	■	■	■	■	◇■ ⊐	■	■	■	■	■	■	■	◇■	■	■	◇■ ⊐	■	■
Norwich	d								20 00					20 30						21 00		
Diss	d								20 17					20 47						21 17		
Peterborough ■	d																19 45					
Stowmarket	d		19 44						20 29				20 44				21 09			21 29		
Needham Market	d		19 49										20 49									
Ipswich	a		20 00						20 41				21 00	21 08			21 22			21 41		
	d	19 52		20 09					20 43				21 00	21 09			21 25			21 43		
Harwich Town	d					20 28													21 28			
Dovercourt	d					20 30													21 30			
Harwich International	d					20 33						20 45	21a29						21 33			
Wrabness	d					20 39													21 39			
Mistley	d					20 45													21 45			
Manningtree ■	d	20 02		20 20		20a50			20 53			20 58		21 19			21 35		21a50	21 53		
Walton-on-the-Naze	d							20 00										21 00				
Frinton-on-Sea	d							20 03										21 03				
Kirby Cross	d							20 06										21 06				
Clacton-on-Sea	d				20 05										21 05							
Thorpe-le-Soken ■	a				20 13			20 12							21 13			21 12				
	d				20 13			20 17							21 13			21 17				
Weeley	d							20 21										21 21				
Great Bentley	d							20 24										21 24				
Alresford (Essex)	d							20 28										21 28				
Wivenhoe ■	d				20 23			20 32							21 23			21 32				
Hythe	d							20 36										21 36				
Colchester Town	a							20 40										21 40				
	d						20 35	20 44		21 00						21 35		21 44			22 00	
Colchester ■	a	20 11		20 29	20 31		20 42	20 52	21 02	21 07		21 07		21 28	21 31	21 42	21 46	21 52		22 02	22 07	
Colchester ■	d	20 12		20 30	20 33		20 43		21 03			21 12		21 30	21 33	21 43				22 03		
Marks Tey ■	d	20 18					20 49					21 18				21 49						
Kelvedon	d	20 23					20 54					21 23				21 54						
Braintree	d										21 00											22 00
Braintree Freeport	d										21 02											22 02
Cressing	d										21 05											22 05
White Notley	d										21 08											22 08
Witham ■	d	20 29			20 46		21 00				21 16	21 29			21 46	22 00						22 16
Hatfield Peverel	d	20 33										21 33										
Chelmsford ■	d	20 40			20 56		21 09		21 21		21 26	21 40			21 56	22 09				22 21		22 26
Ingatestone	d				21 02						21 32				22 02							22 32
Shenfield ■	a	20 50			21 08		21 19				21 38	21 50			22 08	22 19						22 38
Romford	a																					
Stratford ■ ⊖	a	21 05			21 22		21 34		21s45		21 52	22 11			22 26	22 38						22 56
London Liverpool Street ■ ⊖	a	21 14		21 19	21 31		21 45		21 55		22 01	22 21		22 20	22 36	22 48				22 55		23 06

Norwich, Ipswich, Harwich, Clacton, Walton-on-Naze, Colchester and Chelmsford - London

Network Diagram - see first Page of Table 5

		LE ■	LE ■	LE ■	LE ■	LE ■	LE ■	LE ■	LE ◇■	LE ■	LE ■	LE ■	LE ■	LE ◇■	LE ■	LE ■	LE ■	LE
Norwich	d								22 00						23 05			
Diss	d								22 17						23 22			
Peterborough ■	d													21 45				
Stowmarket	d		21 44						22 29	22 44				23 06	23 36			23 47
Needham Market	d		21 49							22 49								23 52
Ipswich	a		22 00						22 41	23 00				23 18	23 50			00 05
	d	21 52			22 23				22 43					23 19				
Harwich Town	d						22 28									23 28		
Dovercourt	d						22 30									23 30		
Harwich International	d						22 33									23 33		
Wrabness	d						22 39									23 39		
Mistley	d						22 45									23 45		
Manningtree ■	d	22 02			22 33		22a50		22 53					23 29		23a50		
Walton-on-the-Naze	d					22 00						23 00						
Frinton-on-Sea	d					22 03						23 03						
Kirby Cross	d					22 06						23 06						
Clacton-on-Sea	d			22 05									23 05					
Thorpe-le-Soken ■	a			22 13		22 12						23 12	23 13					
	d			22 13		22 17							23 13					
Weeley	d					22 21							23 17					
Great Bentley	d					22 24							23 20					
Alresford (Essex)	d					22 28							23 24					
Wivenhoe ■	d			22 23		22 32							23 28					
Hythe	d					22 36							23 32					
Colchester Town	a					22 40												
	d					22 44					23 00							
Colchester ■	a	22 11		22 31	22 42	22 52			23 02		23 07		23 38	23 40				
Colchester ■	d	22 12		22 33	22 43				23 03									
Marks Tey ■	d	22 18			22 49													
Kelvedon	d	22 23			22 54													
Braintree	d							22 56									23 45	
Braintree Freeport	d							22 58									23 47	
Cressing	d							23 01									23 50	
White Notley	d							23 04									23 53	
Witham ■	d	22 29		22 46	23 00			23a12	23 16								00a01	
Hatfield Peverel	d	22 33																
Chelmsford ■	d	22 40		22 56	23 09				23 25									
Ingatestone	d			23 02														
Shenfield ■	a	22 50		23 08	23 19				23s36									
Romford	a																	
Stratford ■ ⊖	a	23 10		23 26	23 38													
London Liverpool Street ■ ⊖	a	23 20		23 36	23 48				00 03									

Saturdays

from 15 September

		LE ◇■	LE	LE ■	LE ■	LE ■	LE	LE ■	LE ◇■	LE ■	LE ■	LE ◇■	LE ■	LE ■	LE ■	LE ■	LE ◇■	LE ■	LE ■	LE ■	LE ■	LE	LE ◇■
Norwich	d	22p00							05 00			05 30					06 00						06 30
Diss	d	22p17							05 17			05 47					06 17						06 47
Peterborough ■	d																						
Stowmarket	d	22p29	23p47						05 29								06 29					06 44	
Needham Market	d		23p52																			06 49	
Ipswich	a	22p41	00 05						05 41			06 08					06 41					07 02	07 08
	d	22p43							05 43			06 09					06 43			06 52	06 59		07 09
Harwich Town	d													06 28									
Dovercourt	d													06 30									
Harwich International	d													06 33							07a28		
Wrabness	d													06 39									
Mistley	d													06 45									
Manningtree ■	d	22p53							05 53			06 19		06a50			06 53			07 02			07 19
Walton-on-the-Naze	d															06 00							
Frinton-on-Sea	d															06 03							
Kirby Cross	d															06 06							
Clacton-on-Sea	d							05 30					06 05					06 24					
Thorpe-le-Soken ■	a							05 38					06 13			06 12		06 32					
	d							05 38					06 13			06 17							
Weeley	d															06 21							
Great Bentley	d															06 24							
Alresford (Essex)	d															06 28							
Wivenhoe ■	d							05 48					06 23			06 32							
Hythe	d															06 36							
Colchester Town	a															06 40							
	d														06 35	06 44							
Colchester ■	a	23p02						05 57	06 02			06 28	06 31		06 42	06 52	07 02			07 11			07 28
Colchester ■	d	23p03			05 12	05 43	05 50		06 03		06 12	06 30	06 33		06 43		07 03			07 12			07 30
Marks Tey ■	d				05 18	05 49	05a57				06 18				06 49					07 18			
Kelvedon	d				05 23	05 54					06 23				06 54					07 23			
Braintree	d			00 25						06 00									07 00				
Braintree Freeport	d			00 27						06 02									07 02				
Cressing	d			00 30						06 05									07 05				
White Notley	d			00 33						06 08									07 08				
Witham ■	d	23p16		00a41	05 29	06 00				06a16	06 29		06 46		07 00				07 16	07 29			
Hatfield Peverel	d				05 33	06 04					06 33									07 33			
Chelmsford ■	d	23p25			05 40	06 11			06 21		06 40		06 56		07 09		07 21		07 26	07 40			
Ingatestone	d				05 47	06 18							07 02						07 32				
Shenfield ■	a	23b36			05 52	06 23					06 50		07 08		07 19				07 38	07 50			
Romford	a														07 28								
Stratford ■ ⊖	a	23b52			06 07	06 38			06s45		07 05		07 22		07 36		07s45		07 52	08 05			
London Liverpool Street ■ ⊖	a	00 02			06 16	06 47			06 55		07 14	07 19	07 31		07 45		07 55		08 01	08 14			08 19

Norwich, Ipswich, Harwich, Clacton, Walton-on-Naze, Colchester and Chelmsford - London

Network Diagram - see first Page of Table 5

		LE ■	LE ■	LE ■	LE ■	LE ◇■	LE ■	LE ■	LE ■	LE	LE ◇■	LE ■	LE ■	LE ■	LE ■	LE ◇■	LE ■	LE ■	LE ■	LE ■	LE ◇■	LE ■	LE ■
Norwich	d					07 00					07 30					08 00					08 30		
Diss	d					07 17					07 47					08 17					08 47		
Peterborough ■	d																					07 45	
Stowmarket	d					07 29				07 45						08 29				08 44		09 13	
Needham Market	d									07 50										08 49			
Ipswich	a					07 41				08 03	08 08					08 41				09 00	09 08	09 28	
	d					07 43			07 52		08 09					08 43			08 52		09 09		
Harwich Town	d				07 28								08 28										
Dovercourt	d				07 30								08 30										
Harwich International	d		07 20		07 33								08 33										
Wrabness	d				07 39								08 39										
Mistley	d				07 45								08 45										
Manningtree ■	d		07 33		07a50	07 53			08 02		08 19		08a50			08 53			09 02		09 19		
Walton-on-the-Naze	d			07 00											08 00								
Frinton-on-Sea	d			07 03											08 03								
Kirby Cross	d			07 06											08 06								
Clacton-on-Sea	d	07 05										08 05											09 05
Thorpe-le-Soken ■	a	07 13		07 12								08 13			08 12								09 13
	d	07 13		07 17								08 13			08 17								09 13
Weeley	d			07 21											08 21								
Great Bentley	d			07 24											08 24								
Alresford (Essex)	d			07 28											08 28								
Wivenhoe ■	d	07 23		07 32								08 23			08 32								09 23
Hythe	d			07 36											08 36								
Colchester Town	a			07 40											08 40								
	d			07 44			08 00							08 35	08 44		09 00						
Colchester ■	a	07 31	07 42	07 52		08 02	08 07		08 11		08 28	08 31		08 42	08 52	09 02	09 07		09 11		09 28		09 31
Colchester ■	d	07 33	07 43			08 03			08 12		08 30	08 33		08 43		09 03			09 12		09 30		09 33
Marks Tey ■	d		07 49						08 18					08 49					09 18				
Kelvedon	d		07 54						08 23					08 54					09 23				
Braintree	d							08 00										09 00					
Braintree Freeport	d							08 02										09 02					
Cressing	d							08 05										09 05					
White Notley	d							08 08										09 08					
Witham ■	d	07 46	08 00					08 16	08 29			08 46		09 00				09 16	09 29				09 46
Hatfield Peverel	d								08 33										09 33				
Chelmsford ■	d	07 56	08 09			08 21		08 26	08 40			08 56		09 09		09 21		09 26	09 40				09 56
Ingatestone	d	08 02						08 32				09 02						09 32					10 02
Shenfield ■	a	08 08	08 19					08 38	08 50			09 08		09 19				09 38	09 50				10 08
Romford	a		08 28											09 28									
Stratford ■ ⊖	a	08 22	08 36			08s45		08 52	09 05			09 22		09 36		09s45		09 52	10 05				10 22
London Liverpool Street ■ ⊖	a	08 31	08 45			08 55		09 01	09 14		09 19	09 31		09 45		09 55		10 01	10 14		10 19		10 31

		LE ■	LE ■	LE ■	LE ◇■	LE ■	LE ■	LE ■	LE ■	LE ◇■	LE ■	LE ■	LE ■	LE ■	LE ◇■	LE ■	LE ■	LE ■	LE ■	LE ◇■	LE ■	LE ■
Norwich	d				09 00					09 30					10 00					10 30		
Diss	d				09 17					09 47					10 17					10 47		
Peterborough ■	d																				09 47	
Stowmarket	d				09 29				09 44						10 29				10 44		11 13	
Needham Market	d								09 49										10 49			
Ipswich	a				09 41				10 00	10 08					10 41				11 00	11 08	11 28	
	d				09 43			09 52		10 09					10 43			10 52		11 09		
Harwich Town	d	09 28										10 28										
Dovercourt	d	09 30										10 30										
Harwich International	d	09 33										10 33										
Wrabness	d	09 39										10 39										
Mistley	d	09 45										10 45										
Manningtree ■	d	09a50			09 53			10 02		10 19		10a50			10 53			11 02		11 19		
Walton-on-the-Naze	d			09 00										10 00								
Frinton-on-Sea	d			09 03										10 03								
Kirby Cross	d			09 06										10 06								
Clacton-on-Sea	d										10 05											11 05
Thorpe-le-Soken ■	a			09 12							10 13			10 12								11 13
	d			09 17							10 13			10 17								11 13
Weeley	d			09 21										10 21								
Great Bentley	d			09 24										10 24								
Alresford (Essex)	d			09 28										10 28								
Wivenhoe ■	d			09 32							10 23			10 32								11 23
Hythe	d			09 36										10 36								
Colchester Town	a			09 40										10 40								
	d		09 35	09 44		10 00							10 35	10 44		11 00						
Colchester ■	a		09 42	09 52	10 02	10 07		10 11		10 28	10 31		10 42	10 52	11 02	11 07		11 11		11 28		11 31
Colchester ■	d		09 43		10 03			10 12		10 30	10 33		10 43		11 03			11 12		11 30		11 33
Marks Tey ■	d		09 49					10 18					10 49					11 18				
Kelvedon	d		09 54					10 23					10 54					11 23				
Braintree	d						10 00										11 00					
Braintree Freeport	d						10 02										11 02					
Cressing	d						10 05										11 05					
White Notley	d						10 08										11 08					
Witham ■	d		10 00				10 16	10 29			10 46		11 00				11 16	11 29				11 46
Hatfield Peverel	d							10 33										11 33				
Chelmsford ■	d		10 09		10 21		10 26	10 40			10 56		11 09		11 21		11 26	11 40				11 56
Ingatestone	d						10 32				11 02						11 32					12 02
Shenfield ■	a		10 19				10 38	10 50			11 08		11 19				11 38	11 50				12 08
Romford	a		10 28										11 28									
Stratford ■ ⊖	a		10 36		10s45		10 52	11 05			11 22		11 36		11s45		11 52	12 05				12 22
London Liverpool Street ■ ⊖	a		10 45		10 55		11 01	11 14		11 19	11 31		11 45		11 55		12 01	12 14		12 19		12 31

b Previous night, stops to set down only

Norwich, Ipswich, Harwich, Clacton, Walton-on-Naze, Colchester and Chelmsford - London

Network Diagram - see first Page of Table 5

		LE	LE	LE	LE	LE	LE	LE	LE	LE	LE	LE	LE	LE	LE	LE	LE	LE	LE	LE	LE	LE	LE
		■	■	■	◇■ 🍴	■	■	■	■	■ A 🍴	◇■ B 🍴	■	■	■	■	◇■ 🍴	■	■	■	■	◇■ 🍴	■	■
Norwich	d				11 00					11 30	11 30					12 00					12 30		
Diss	d				11 17					11 47	11 47					12 17					12 47		
Peterborough	d																					11 45	
Stowmarket	d				11 29				11 44							12 29				12 44		13 13	
Needham Market	d								11 49											12 49			
Ipswich	a				11 41				12 00	12 08	12 08					12 41				13 00	13 08	13 28	
	d				11 43			11 52		12 09	12 09					12 43			12 52		13 09		
Harwich Town	d	11 28											12 28										
Dovercourt	d	11 30											12 30										
Harwich International	d	11 33											12 33										
Wrabness	d	11 39											12 39										
Mistley	d	11 45											12 45										
Manningtree	d	11a50			11 53			12 02		12 19	12 19		12a50			12 53			13 02		13 19		
Walton-on-the-Naze	d			11 00											12 00								
Frinton-on-Sea	d			11 03											12 03								
Kirby Cross	d			11 06											12 06								
Clacton-on-Sea	d											12 05											13 05
Thorpe-le-Soken	a			11 12								12 13			12 12								13 13
	d			11 17								12 13			12 17								13 13
Weeley	d			11 21											12 21								
Great Bentley	d			11 24											12 24								
Alresford (Essex)	d			11 28											12 28								
Wivenhoe	d			11 32								12 23			12 32								13 23
Hythe	d			11 36											12 36								
Colchester Town	a			11 40											12 40								
	d		11 35	11 44		12 00								12 35	12 44		13 00						
Colchester	a		11 42	11 52	12 02	12 07		12 11		12 28	12 28	12 31		12 42	12 52	13 02	13 07		13 11		13 28		13 31
Colchester	d		11 43		12 03			12 12		12 30	12 30	12 33		12 43		13 03			13 12		13 30		13 33
Marks Tey	d		11 49					12 18						12 49					13 18				
Kelvedon	d		11 54					12 23						12 54					13 23				
Braintree	d						12 00											13 00					
Braintree Freeport	d						12 02											13 02					
Cressing	d						12 05											13 05					
White Notley	d						12 08											13 08					
Witham	d		12 00				12 16	12 29				12 46		13 00				13 16	13 29				13 46
Hatfield Peverel	d							12 33											13 33				
Chelmsford	d		12 09		12 21		12 26	12 40				12 56		13 09		13 21		13 26	13 40				13 56
Ingatestone	d						12 32					13 02						13 32					14 02
Shenfield	a		12 19				12 38	12 50				13 08		13 19				13 38	13 50				14 08
Romford	a		12 28											13 28									
Stratford ⊖	a		12 36		12s45		12 52	13 05				13 22		13 36		13s45		13 52	14 05				14 22
London Liverpool Street ⊖	a		12 45		12 55		13 01	13 14		13 19	13 19	13 31		13 45		13 55		14 01	14 14		14 19		14 31

		LE	LE	LE	LE	LE	LE	LE	LE	LE	LE	LE	LE	LE	LE	LE	LE	LE	LE	LE	LE	LE
		■	■	■	◇■ 🍴	■	■	■	■	◇■ 🍴	■	■	■	■	■ A 🍴	◇■ B 🍴	■	■	■	■	◇■ 🍴	■
Norwich	d				13 00					13 30					14 00	14 00					14 30	
Diss	d				13 17					13 47					14 17	14 17					14 47	
Peterborough	d																					13 45
Stowmarket	d				13 29				13 44						14 29	14 29				14 44		15 13
Needham Market	d								13 49											14 49		
Ipswich	a				13 41				14 00	14 08					14 41	14 41				15 00	15 08	15 28
	d				13 43			13 52		14 09					14 43	14 43			14 52		15 09	
Harwich Town	d	13 28										14 28										
Dovercourt	d	13 30										14 30										
Harwich International	d	13 33										14 33										
Wrabness	d	13 39										14 39										
Mistley	d	13 45										14 45										
Manningtree	d	13a50			13 53			14 02		14 19		14a50			14 53	14 53			15 02		15 19	
Walton-on-the-Naze	d			13 00										14 00								
Frinton-on-Sea	d			13 03										14 03								
Kirby Cross	d			13 06										14 06								
Clacton-on-Sea	d										14 05											
Thorpe-le-Soken	a			13 12							14 13			14 12								
	d			13 17							14 13			14 17								
Weeley	d			13 21										14 21								
Great Bentley	d			13 24										14 24								
Alresford (Essex)	d			13 28										14 28								
Wivenhoe	d			13 32							14 23			14 32								
Hythe	d			13 36										14 36								
Colchester Town	a			13 40										14 40								
	d		13 35	13 44		14 00							14 35	14 44			15 00					
Colchester	a		13 42	13 52	14 02	14 07		14 11		14 28	14 31		14 42	14 52	15 02	15 02	15 07		15 11		15 28	
Colchester	d		13 43		14 03			14 12		14 30	14 33		14 43		15 03	15 03			15 12		15 30	
Marks Tey	d		13 49					14 18					14 49						15 18			
Kelvedon	d		13 54					14 23					14 54						15 23			
Braintree	d						14 00											15 00				
Braintree Freeport	d						14 02											15 02				
Cressing	d						14 05											15 05				
White Notley	d						14 08											15 08				
Witham	d		14 00				14 16	14 29			14 46		15 00					15 16	15 29			
Hatfield Peverel	d							14 33											15 33			
Chelmsford	d		14 09		14 21		14 26	14 40			14 56		15 09		15 21	15 21		15 26	15 40			
Ingatestone	d						14 32				15 02							15 32				
Shenfield	a		14 19				14 38	14 50			15 08		15 19					15 38	15 50			
Romford	a		14 28										15 28									
Stratford ⊖	a		14 36		14s45		14 52	15 05			15 22		15 36		15s45	15s45		15 52	16 05			
London Liverpool Street ⊖	a		14 45		14 55		15 01	15 14		15 19	15 31		15 45		15 55	15 55		16 01	16 14		16 19	

A 15 September, 22 September, 29 September B from 6 October

Norwich, Ipswich, Harwich, Clacton, Walton-on-Naze, Colchester and Chelmsford - London

Network Diagram - see first Page of Table 5

		LE	LE	LE	LE	LE	LE	LE	LE	LE	LE	LE	LE	LE	LE	LE	LE	LE	LE	LE	LE	LE	LE
		■	■	■	■	◇■ 🍴	■	■	■	■	◇■ 🍴	■	■	■	■	◇■ 🍴	■	■	■	■	◇■ 🍴	■	■
Norwich	d					15 00					15 30					16 00					16 30		
Diss	d					15 17					15 47					16 17					16 47		
Peterborough	d																					15 45	
Stowmarket	d					15 29				15 44						16 29				16 44		17 13	
Needham Market	d									15 49										16 49			
Ipswich	a					15 41				16 00	16 08					16 41				17 00	17 08	17 28	
	d					15 43			15 52		16 09					16 43			16 52		17 09		
Harwich Town	d		15 28										16 28										
Dovercourt	d		15 30										16 30										
Harwich International	d		15 33										16 33										
Wrabness	d		15 39										16 39										
Mistley	d		15 45										16 45										
Manningtree	d		15a50			15 53			16 02		16 19		16a50			16 53			17 02		17 19		
Walton-on-the-Naze	d				15 00										16 00								
Frinton-on-Sea	d				15 03										16 03								
Kirby Cross	d				15 06										16 06								
Clacton-on-Sea	d	15 05										16 05											17 05
Thorpe-le-Soken	a	15 13			15 12							16 13			16 12								17 13
	d	15 13			15 17							16 13			16 17								17 13
Weeley	d				15 21										16 21								
Great Bentley	d				15 24										16 24								
Alresford (Essex)	d				15 28										16 28								
Wivenhoe	d	15 23			15 32							16 23			16 32								17 23
Hythe	d				15 36										16 36								
Colchester Town	a				15 40										16 40								
	d			15 35	15 44		16 00							16 35	16 44		17 00						
Colchester	a	15 31		15 42	15 52	16 02	16 07		16 11		16 28	16 31		16 42	16 52	17 02	17 07		17 11		17 28		17 31
Colchester	d	15 33		15 43		16 03			16 12		16 30	16 33		16 43		17 03			17 12		17 30		17 33
Marks Tey	d			15 49					16 18					16 49					17 18				
Kelvedon	d			15 54					16 23					16 54					17 23				
Braintree	d							16 00										17 00					
Braintree Freeport	d							16 02										17 02					
Cressing	d							16 05										17 05					
White Notley	d							16 08										17 08					
Witham	d	15 46		16 00				16 16	16 29			16 46		17 00				17 16	17 29				17 46
Hatfield Peverel	d								16 33										17 33				
Chelmsford	d	15 56		16 09		16 21		16 26	16 40			16 56		17 09		17 21		17 26	17 40				17 56
Ingatestone	d	16 02						16 32				17 02						17 32					18 02
Shenfield	a	16 08		16 19				16 38	16 50			17 08		17 19				17 38	17 50				18 08
Romford	a			16 28										17 28									
Stratford ⊖	a	16 22		16 36		16s45		16 52	17 05			17 22		17 36		17s45		17 52	18 05				18 22
London Liverpool Street ⊖	a	16 31		16 45		16 55		17 01	17 14		17 19	17 31		17 45		17 55		18 01	18 14		18 19		18 31

		LE	LE	LE	LE	LE	LE	LE	LE	LE	LE	LE	LE	LE	LE	LE	LE	LE	LE	LE	LE	LE	LE
		■	■	■	◇■ 🍴	■	■	■	■	◇■ 🍴	■	■	■	■	◇■ 🍴	■	■	■	■	◇■ 🍴	■	■	■
Norwich	d				17 00					17 30					18 00					18 30			
Diss	d				17 17					17 47					18 17					18 47			
Peterborough	d																				17 45		
Stowmarket	d				17 29				17 45	17 59					18 29				18 45		19 13		
Needham Market	d								17 50										18 50				
Ipswich	a				17 41				18 01	18 11					18 41				19 01	19 08	19 28		
	d				17 43			17 52		18 13					18 43			18 52		19 09			
Harwich Town	d	17 28										18 28											19 28
Dovercourt	d	17 30										18 30											19 30
Harwich International	d	17 33										18 33											19 33
Wrabness	d	17 39										18 39											19 39
Mistley	d	17 45										18 45											19 45
Manningtree	d	17a50			17 53			18 02				18a50			18 53			19 02		19 19			19a50
Walton-on-the-Naze	d			17 00										18 00									
Frinton-on-Sea	d			17 03										18 03									
Kirby Cross	d			17 06										18 06									
Clacton-on-Sea	d										18 05											19 05	
Thorpe-le-Soken	a			17 12							18 13			18 12								19 13	
	d			17 17							18 13			18 17								19 13	
Weeley	d			17 21										18 21									
Great Bentley	d			17 24										18 24									
Alresford (Essex)	d			17 28										18 28									
Wivenhoe	d			17 32							18 23			18 32								19 23	
Hythe	d			17 36										18 36									
Colchester Town	a			17 40										18 40									
	d		17 35	17 44		18 00							18 35	18 44		19 00							
Colchester	a		17 42	17 52	18 02	18 07		18 11		18 28	18 31		18 42	18 52	19 02	19 07		19 11		19 28		19 31	
Colchester	d		17 43		18 03			18 12		18 30	18 33		18 43		19 03			19 12		19 30		19 33	
Marks Tey	d		17 49					18 18					18 49					19 18					
Kelvedon	d		17 54					18 23					18 54					19 23					
Braintree	d						18 00										19 00						
Braintree Freeport	d						18 02										19 02						
Cressing	d						18 05										19 05						
White Notley	d						18 08										19 08						
Witham	d		18 00				18 16	18 29			18 46		19 00				19 16	19 29				19 46	
Hatfield Peverel	d							18 33										19 33					
Chelmsford	d		18 09		18 21		18 26	18 40			18 56		19 09		19 21		19 26	19 40				19 56	
Ingatestone	d						18 32				19 02						19 32					20 02	
Shenfield	a		18 19				18 38	18 50			19 08		19 19				19 38	19 50				20 08	
Romford	a		18 28										19 28										
Stratford ⊖	a		18 36		18s45		18 52	19 05			19 22		19 36		19s45		19 52	20 05				20 22	
London Liverpool Street ⊖	a		18 45		18 55		19 01	19 14		19 19	19 31		19 45		19 55		20 01	20 14		20 19		20 31	

Norwich, Ipswich, Harwich, Clacton, Walton-on-Naze, Colchester and Chelmsford - London

Network Diagram - see first Page of Table 5

Station		LE ■	LE ■	LE ◇■ 🍴	LE ■	LE ■	LE ■	LE ■	LE ■	LE ■	LE ■	LE ■	LE ■	LE ◇■ 🍴	LE ■	LE ■	LE ■	LE ■	LE ■	LE ■	LE ■	LE ◇■
Norwich	d			19 00										20 00								
Diss	d			19 17										20 17								
Peterborough ■	d																					19 45
Stowmarket	d			19 29				19 44						20 29				20 44				21 09
Needham Market	d							19 49										20 49				
Ipswich	a			19 41				20 00						20 41				21 00				21 22
	d			19 43			19 52		20 09					20 43				21 00	21 09			21 25
Harwich Town	d										20 28											
Dovercourt	d										20 30											
Harwich International	d										20 33						20 45	21a29				
Wrabness	d										20 39											
Mistley	d										20 45											
Manningtree ■	d			19 53			20 02		20 20		20a50			20 53			20 58		21 19			21 35
Walton-on-the-Naze	d		19 00										20 00									
Frinton-on-Sea	d		19 03										20 03									
Kirby Cross	d		19 06										20 06									
Clacton-on-Sea	d									20 05										21 05		
Thorpe-le-Soken ■	a		19 12							20 13			20 12							21 13		
	d		19 17							20 13			20 17							21 13		
Weeley	d		19 21										20 21									
Great Bentley	d		19 24										20 24									
Alresford (Essex)	d		19 28										20 28									
Wivenhoe ■	d		19 32							20 23			20 32							21 23		
Hythe	d		19 36										20 36									
Colchester Town	a		19 40										20 40									
	d	19 35	19 44		20 00							20 35	20 44		21 00						21 35	
Colchester ■	a	19 42	19 52	20 02	20 07		20 11		20 29	20 31		20 42	20 52	21 02	21 07		21 07		21 28	21 31	21 42	21 46
Colchester ■	d	19 43		20 03			20 12		20 30	20 33		20 43		21 03			21 12		21 30	21 33	21 43	
Marks Tey ■	d	19 49					20 18					20 49					21 18				21 49	
Kelvedon	d	19 54					20 23					20 54					21 23				21 54	
Braintree	d					20 00										21 00						
Braintree Freeport	d					20 02										21 02						
Cressing	d					20 05										21 05						
White Notley	d					20 08										21 08						
Witham ■	d	20 00				20 16	20 29			20 46		21 00				21 16	21 29			21 46	22 00	
Hatfield Peverel	d						20 33										21 33					
Chelmsford ■	d	20 09		20 21		20 26	20 40			20 56		21 09		21 21		21 26	21 40			21 56	22 09	
Ingatestone	d					20 32				21 02						21 32				22 02		
Shenfield ■	a	20 19				20 38	20 50			21 08		21 19				21 38	21 50			22 08	22 19	
Romford	a	20 28										21 28									22 28	
Stratford ■ ⊖	a	20 36		20s45		20 52	21 05			21 22		21 36		21s45		21 52	22 05			22 22	22 36	
London Liverpool Street ■ ⊖	a	20 45		20 55		21 01	21 14		21 17	21 31		21 45		21 55		22 01	22 14		22 17	22 31	22 46	

Station		LE ■	LE ■	LE ◇■ 🍴	LE ■	LE ■	LE ■	LE ■	LE ■	LE ■	LE ■	LE ■	LE ■	LE ◇■	LE ■	LE ■	LE ■	LE ■	LE ■	LE ◇■	LE ■	LE ■	LE ■	LE
Norwich	d			21 00										22 00							23 05			
Diss	d			21 17										22 17							23 22			
Peterborough ■	d																			21 45				
Stowmarket	d			21 29				21 44						22 29	22 44					23 06	23 36			23 47
Needham Market	d							21 49							22 49									23 52
Ipswich	a			21 41				22 00						22 41	23 00					23 18	23 50			00 05
	d			21 43			21 52			22 23				22 43				23 15		23 19				
Harwich Town	d		21 28									22 28										23 28		
Dovercourt	d		21 30									22 30										23 30		
Harwich International	d		21 33									22 33										23 33		
Wrabness	d		21 39									22 39										23 39		
Mistley	d		21 45									22 45										23 45		
Manningtree ■	d		21a50	21 53			22 02			22 33		22a50		22 53				23 25		23 29		23 50		
Walton-on-the-Naze	d	21 00									22 00						23 00							
Frinton-on-Sea	d	21 03									22 03						23 03							
Kirby Cross	d	21 06									22 06						23 06							
Clacton-on-Sea	d								22 05										23 05					
Thorpe-le-Soken ■	a	21 12							22 13		22 12						23 12		23 13					
	d	21 17							22 13		22 17								23 13					
Weeley	d	21 21									22 21								23 17					
Great Bentley	d	21 24									22 24								23 20					
Alresford (Essex)	d	21 28									22 28								23 24					
Wivenhoe ■	d	21 32							22 23		22 32								23 28					
Hythe	d	21 36									22 36								23 32					
Colchester Town	a	21 40									22 40													
	d	21 44			22 00						22 44					23 00								
Colchester ■	a	21 52		22 02	22 07		22 11		22 31	22 42	22 52			23 02		23 07		23 35	23 38	23 40		23 59		
Colchester ■	d			22 03			22 12		22 33	22 43				23 03										
Marks Tey ■	d						22 18			22 49														
Kelvedon	d						22 23			22 54														
Braintree	d					22 00							22 56										23 45	
Braintree Freeport	d					22 02							22 58										23 47	
Cressing	d					22 05							23 01										23 50	
White Notley	d					22 08							23 04										23 53	
Witham ■	d					22 16	22 29		22 46	23 00			23a12	23 16									00a01	
Hatfield Peverel	d						22 33																	
Chelmsford ■	d			22 21		22 26	22 40		22 56	23 09				23 25										
Ingatestone	d					22 32			23 02															
Shenfield ■	a					22 38	22 50		23 08	23 19				23s36										
Romford	a									23 28														
Stratford ■ ⊖	a			22s45		22 52	23 05		23 22	23 36				23s52										
London Liverpool Street ■ ⊖	a			22 55		23 01	23 14		23 31	23 45				00 02										

Norwich, Ipswich, Harwich, Clacton, Walton-on-Naze, Colchester and Chelmsford - London

Network Diagram - see first Page of Table 5

Station		LE ◇■	LE	LE ■	LE ■ A	LE ■ B	LE ■ A	LE	LE ■	LE ■	LE ◇■ 🍴	LE ■	LE ■	LE ■	LE ■	LE ◇■ 🍴	LE ■	LE ■	LE ■	LE ■	LE ■	LE ◇■ 🍴	LE ■
Norwich	d	22p00									07 00					08 00						09 00	
Diss	d	22p17									07 17					08 17						09 17	
Peterborough ■	d																						
Stowmarket	d	22p29	23p47								07 29					08 29						09 29	
Needham Market	d		23p52																				
Ipswich	a	22p41	00 05								07 41					08 41						09 41	
	d	22p43									07 43	07 46			08 09	08 43					09 09	09 43	
Harwich Town	d																	08 53					
Dovercourt	d																	08 55					
Harwich International	d									07 20		08a14						08 58					
Wrabness	d																	09 04					
Mistley	d																	09 10					
Manningtree ■	d	22p53								07 33	07 53				08 19	08 53		09a15			09 19	09 53	
Walton-on-the-Naze	d																08 30						09 30
Frinton-on-Sea	d																08 33						09 33
Kirby Cross	d																08 36						09 36
Clacton-on-Sea	d													07 36						08 36			
Thorpe-le-Soken ■	a													07 44			08 42			08 44			09 42
	d													07 44						08 44			
Weeley	d																						
Great Bentley	d													07 49						08 49			
Alresford (Essex)	d													07 53						08 53			
Wivenhoe ■	d													07 57						08 57			
Hythe	d																						
Colchester Town	a																						
	d																						
Colchester ■	a	23p02								07 42	08 02			08 05	08 29	09 02				09 05	09 29	10 02	
Colchester ■	d	23p03				06 56	06 56	07 07	07 26	07 43	08 03			08 06	08 30	09 03				09 06	09 30	10 03	
Marks Tey ■	d					07 02	07 02	07a14	07 32	07 49				08 12	08 36					09 12	09 36		
Kelvedon	d					07 07	07 07		07 37	07 54					08 41						09 41		
Braintree	d			00 25									08 00						09 00				
Braintree Freeport	d			00 27									08 02						09 02				
Cressing	d			00 30									08 05						09 05				
White Notley	d			00 33									08 08						09 08				
Witham ■	d	23p16		00a41		07 13	07 13		07 43	08 00			08a16	08 21	08 47				09a16	09 21	09 47		
Hatfield Peverel	d					07 17	07 17		07 47						08 51						09 51		
Chelmsford ■	d	23p25			06 54	07 24	07 24		07 54	08 09				08 30	08 58					09 30	09 58		
Ingatestone	d				07 01	07 31	07 31		08 01						09 05						10 05		
Shenfield ■	a	23b36			07 06	07 36	07 36		08 06	08 19				08 40	09 10					09 40	10 10		
Romford	a																						
Stratford ■ ⊖	a	23b52			07s34		08s04		08s34	08s49				09s04	09s34					10s04	10s34		
London Liverpool Street ■ ⊖	a	00 02			07 42		08 12		08 42	08 59	09 03			09 12	09 42	10 01				10 12	10 42	11 01	

Station		LE ■	LE ■	LE ■	LE ■	LE	LE ◇■ 🍴	LE ■	LE ■	LE ■	LE ■	LE ■	LE ■	LE ◇■ 🍴	LE ■	LE ■	LE ■	LE ■	LE ■	LE ■	LE ◇■ 🍴	LE ■	LE ■
Norwich	d						10 00							11 00							12 00		
Diss	d						10 17							11 17							12 17		
Peterborough ■	d												09 45										
Stowmarket	d					10 18	10 29						11 13	11 29						12 18	12 29		
Needham Market	d					10 23														12 23			
Ipswich	a					10 35	10 41						11 28	11 41						12 35	12 41		
	d				10 09		10 43					11 09		11 43					12 09		12 43		
Harwich Town	d	09 53							10 53							11 53							12 53
Dovercourt	d	09 55							10 55							11 55							12 55
Harwich International	d	09 58							10 58							11 58							12 58
Wrabness	d	10 04							11 04							12 04							13 04
Mistley	d	10 10							11 10							12 10							13 10
Manningtree ■	d	10a15			10 19		10 53		11a15			11 19		11 53		12a15			12 19		12 53		13a15
Walton-on-the-Naze	d							10 30							11 30							12 30	
Frinton-on-Sea	d							10 33							11 33							12 33	
Kirby Cross	d							10 36							11 36							12 36	
Clacton-on-Sea	d			09 36							10 36							11 36					
Thorpe-le-Soken ■	a			09 44				10 42			10 44				11 42			11 44				12 42	
	d			09 44							10 44							11 44					
Weeley	d																						
Great Bentley	d			09 49							10 49							11 49					
Alresford (Essex)	d			09 53							10 53							11 53					
Wivenhoe ■	d			09 57							10 57							11 57					
Hythe	d																						
Colchester Town	a																						
	d																						
Colchester ■	a			10 05	10 29		11 02				11 05	11 29		12 02				12 05	12 29		13 02		
Colchester ■	d			10 06	10 30		11 03				11 06	11 30		12 03				12 06	12 30		13 03		
Marks Tey ■	d			10 12	10 36						11 12	11 36						12 12	12 36				
Kelvedon	d				10 41							11 41							12 41				
Braintree	d		10 00							11 00							12 00						
Braintree Freeport	d		10 02							11 02							12 02						
Cressing	d		10 05							11 05							12 05						
White Notley	d		10 08							11 08							12 08						
Witham ■	d		10a16	10 21	10 47					11a16	11 21	11 47					12a16	12 21	12 47				
Hatfield Peverel	d				10 51							11 51							12 51				
Chelmsford ■	d			10 30	10 58						11 30	11 58						12 30	12 58				
Ingatestone	d				11 05							12 05							13 05				
Shenfield ■	a			10 40	11 10						11 40	12 10						12 40	13 10				
Romford	a																						
Stratford ■ ⊖	a			11s04	11s34						12s04	12s34						13s04	13s34				
London Liverpool Street ■ ⊖	a			11 12	11 42		12 01				12 12	12 42		13 01				13 12	13 42		14 01		

A from 1 July until 22 July

B until 24 June

b Previous night, stops to set down only

Table 11

Sundays until 22 July

Norwich, Ipswich, Harwich, Clacton, Walton-on-Naze, Colchester and Chelmsford - London

Network Diagram - see first Page of Table 5

		LE 1	LE 1	LE 1	LE 1	LE ◇1 ⊡	LE 1	LE 1	LE 1	LE 1	LE 1	LE 1	LE ◇1 ⊡	LE 1	LE 1	LE 1	LE 1	LE 1	LE 1	LE ◇1 ⊡	LE 1	LE 1
Norwich	d					13 00							14 00							15 00		
Diss	d					13 17							14 17							15 17		
Peterborough 8	d				11 46														13 46			
Stowmarket	d				13 13	13 29						14 18	14 29						15 13	15 29		
Needham Market	d											14 23										
Ipswich	a				13 28	13 41						14 35	14 41						15 28	15 41		
	d			13 09		13 43					14 09		14 43					15 09		15 43		
Harwich Town	d							13 53							14 53							15 53
Dovercourt	d							13 55							14 55							15 55
Harwich International	d							13 58							14 58							15 58
Wrabness	d							14 04							15 04							16 04
Mistley	d							14 10							15 10							16 10
Manningtree 2	d			13 19		13 53		14a15			14 19		14 53		15a15			15 19		15 53		16a15
Walton-on-the-Naze	d						13 30							14 30							15 30	
Frinton-on-Sea	d						13 33							14 33							15 33	
Kirby Cross	d						13 36							14 36							15 36	
Clacton-on-Sea	d		12 36							13 36							14 36					
Thorpe-le-Soken 1	a		12 44				13 42			13 44				14 42			14 44				15 42	
	d		12 44							13 44							14 44					
Weeley	d																					
Great Bentley	d		12 49							13 49							14 49					
Alresford (Essex)	d		12 53							13 53							14 53					
Wivenhoe 3	d		12 57							13 57							14 57					
Hythe	d																					
Colchester Town	a																					
	d																					
Colchester 4	a		13 05	13 29		14 02				14 05	14 29		15 02				15 05	15 29		16 02		
Colchester 4	d		13 06	13 30		14 03				14 06	14 30		15 03				15 06	15 30		16 03		
Marks Tey 2	d		13 12	13 36						14 12	14 36						15 12	15 36				
Kelvedon	d			13 41							14 41							15 41				
Braintree	d	13 00							14 00							15 00						
Braintree Freeport	d	13 02							14 02							15 02						
Cressing	d	13 05							14 05							15 05						
White Notley	d	13 08							14 08							15 08						
Witham 2	d	13a16	13 21	13 47					14a16	14 21	14 47					15a16	15 21	15 47				
Hatfield Peverel	d			13 51							14 51							15 51				
Chelmsford 3	d		13 30	13 58						14 30	14 58						15 30	15 58				
Ingatestone	d			14 05							15 05							16 05				
Shenfield 3	a		13 40	14 10						14 40	15 10						15 40	16 10				
Romford	a																					
Stratford 7 ⊖	a		14s04	14s34						15s04	15s34						16s04	16s34				
London Liverpool Street 15 ⊖	a		14 12	14 42		15 01				15 12	15 42		16 01				16 12	16 42		17 01		

		LE 1	LE 1	LE 1	LE 1	LE 1 ⊡	LE 1	LE 1	LE 1	LE 1	LE ◇1 ⊡	LE 1	LE 1	LE ◇1 ⊡	LE 1	LE 1	LE 1	LE 1	LE 1	LE 1	LE ◇1 ⊡	LE 1	LE 1
Norwich	d					16 00					16 20			17 00							18 00		
Diss	d					16 17					16 37			17 17							18 17		
Peterborough 8	d												15 45										
Stowmarket	d				16 18	16 29					16 49		17 13	17 29						18 18	18 29		
Needham Market	d				16 23															18 23			
Ipswich	a				16 35	16 41					17 01		17 28	17 41						18 35	18 41		
	d			16 09		16 43					17 03	17 09		17 43					18 09		18 43		
Harwich Town	d							16 53								17 53							18 53
Dovercourt	d							16 55								17 55							18 55
Harwich International	d							16 58								17 58							18 58
Wrabness	d							17 04								18 04							19 04
Mistley	d							17 10								18 10							19 10
Manningtree 2	d			16 19		16 53		17a15				17 19		17 53		18a15			18 19		18 53		19a15
Walton-on-the-Naze	d						16 30								17 30							18 30	
Frinton-on-Sea	d						16 33								17 33							18 33	
Kirby Cross	d						16 36								17 36							18 36	
Clacton-on-Sea	d		15 36							16 36								17 36					
Thorpe-le-Soken 1	a		15 44				16 42			16 44					17 42			17 44				18 42	
	d		15 44							16 44								17 44					
Weeley	d																						
Great Bentley	d		15 49							16 49								17 49					
Alresford (Essex)	d		15 53							16 53								17 53					
Wivenhoe 3	d		15 57							16 57								17 57					
Hythe	d																						
Colchester Town	a																						
	d																						
Colchester 4	a		16 05	16 29		17 02				17 05	17 18	17 29		18 02				18 05	18 29		19 02		
Colchester 4	d		16 06	16 30		17 03				17 06	17 21	17 30		18 03				18 06	18 30		19 03		
Marks Tey 2	d		16 12	16 36						17 12		17 36						18 12	18 36				
Kelvedon	d			16 41								17 41							18 41				
Braintree	d	16 00							17 00								18 00						
Braintree Freeport	d	16 02							17 02								18 02						
Cressing	d	16 05							17 05								18 05						
White Notley	d	16 08							17 08								18 08						
Witham 2	d	16a16	16 21	16 47					17a16	17 21		17 47					18a16	18 21	18 47				
Hatfield Peverel	d			16 51								17 51							18 51				
Chelmsford 3	d		16 30	16 58						17 30		17 58						18 30	18 58				
Ingatestone	d			17 05								18 05							19 05				
Shenfield 3	a		16 40	17 10						17 40		18 10						18 40	19 10				
Romford	a																						
Stratford 7 ⊖	a		17s04	17s34						18s04		18s34						19s04	19s34				
London Liverpool Street 15 ⊖	a		17 12	17 42		18 01				18 12	18 28	18 42		19 01				19 12	19 42		20 01		

Table 11

Sundays until 22 July

Norwich, Ipswich, Harwich, Clacton, Walton-on-Naze, Colchester and Chelmsford - London

Network Diagram - see first Page of Table 5

		LE 1	LE 1	LE 1	LE ◇1	LE ◇1 ⊡	LE 1	LE 1	LE 1	LE 1	LE 1	LE 1	LE 1	LE 1	LE ◇1 ⊡	LE 1	LE 1	LE 1	LE 1	LE ◇1	LE ◇1	LE 1
Norwich	d					19 00									20 00						21 00	
Diss	d					19 17									20 17						21 17	
Peterborough 8	d				17 45															19 45		
Stowmarket	d				19 13	19 29								20 18	20 29					21 06	21 29	
Needham Market	d													20 23								
Ipswich	a				19 28	19 41								20 35	20 41					21 18	21 41	
	d			19 09	19 28	19 43					20 09			20 35	20 43				21 09	21 19	21 43	
Harwich Town	d							19 53								20 53						
Dovercourt	d							19 55								20 55						
Harwich International	d							19 58					20 35	21a04		20 58						
Wrabness	d							20 04								21 04						
Mistley	d							20 10								21 10						
Manningtree 2	d			19 19	19 38	19 53		20a15			20 19		20 48		20 53	21a15			21 19	21 29	21 53	
Walton-on-the-Naze	d						19 30					20 30										21 30
Frinton-on-Sea	d						19 33					20 33										21 33
Kirby Cross	d						19 36					20 36										21 36
Clacton-on-Sea	d		18 36							19 36								20 36				
Thorpe-le-Soken 1	a		18 44				19 42			19 44		20 42						20 44				21 42
	d		18 44							19 44								20 44				
Weeley	d																					
Great Bentley	d		18 49							19 49								20 49				
Alresford (Essex)	d		18 53							19 53								20 53				
Wivenhoe 3	d		18 57							19 57								20 57				
Hythe	d																					
Colchester Town	a																					
	d																					
Colchester 4	a		19 05	19 29	19 49	20 02				20 05	20 29		20 57		21 02			21 05	21 29	21 40	22 02	
Colchester 4	d		19 06	19 30		20 03				20 06	20 30		20 57		21 03			21 06	21 30		22 03	
Marks Tey 2	d		19 12	19 36						20 12	20 36							21 12	21 36			
Kelvedon	d			19 41							20 41								21 41			
Braintree	d	19 00							20 00								21 00					
Braintree Freeport	d	19 02							20 02								21 02					
Cressing	d	19 05							20 05								21 05					
White Notley	d	19 08							20 08								21 08					
Witham 2	d	19a16	19 21	19 47					20a16	20 21	20 47						21a16	21 21	21 47			
Hatfield Peverel	d			19 51							20 51								21 51			
Chelmsford 3	d		19 30	19 58						20 30	20 58		21 15					21 30	21 58			
Ingatestone	d			20 05							21 05								22 05			
Shenfield 3	a		19 40	20 10						20 40	21 10		21 25					21 40	22 10			
Romford	a																					
Stratford 7 ⊖	a		20s04	20s34						21s04	21s34		21s51					22s04	22s34			
London Liverpool Street 15 ⊖	a		20 12	20 42		21 01				21 12	21 42		21 59		22 01			22 12	22 42		23 01	

		LE 1	LE 1	LE 1	LE 1	LE 1	LE 1	LE 1	LE 1	LE ◇1	LE 1	LE 1
Norwich	d									22 00		23 05
Diss	d									22 17		23 22
Peterborough 8	d											
Stowmarket	d						22 18			22 29		23 34
Needham Market	d						22 23					
Ipswich	a						22 35			22 41		23 48
	d				22 09					22 43		
Harwich Town	d	21 53									22 53	
Dovercourt	d	21 55									22 55	
Harwich International	d	21 58									22 58	
Wrabness	d	22 04									23 04	
Mistley	d	22 10									23 10	
Manningtree 2	d	22a15			22 19					22 53	23 15	
Walton-on-the-Naze	d					22 16						
Frinton-on-Sea	d					22 19						
Kirby Cross	d					22 22						
Clacton-on-Sea	d			21 36				22 22				
Thorpe-le-Soken 1	a			21 44		22 28		22 30				
	d			21 44				22 30				
Weeley	d											
Great Bentley	d			21 49								
Alresford (Essex)	d			21 53								
Wivenhoe 3	d			21 57				22 40				
Hythe	d											
Colchester Town	a											
	d											
Colchester 4	a			22 05	22 29			22 48		23 02	23 24	
Colchester 4	d			22 06	22 30					23 03		
Marks Tey 2	d			22 12	22 36							
Kelvedon	d				22 41							
Braintree	d		22 00						22 56			
Braintree Freeport	d		22 02						22 58			
Cressing	d		22 05						23 01			
White Notley	d		22 08						23 04			
Witham 2	d		22a16	22 21	22 47				23a12	23 16		
Hatfield Peverel	d				22 51							
Chelmsford 3	d			22 30	22 58					23 25		
Ingatestone	d				23 05							
Shenfield 3	a			22 40	23 10					23s36		
Romford	a											
Stratford 7 ⊖	a			23s04	23s34					23s57		
London Liverpool Street 15 ⊖	a			23 12	23 42					00 08		

Norwich, Ipswich, Harwich, Clacton, Walton-on-Naze, Colchester and Chelmsford - London

Network Diagram - see first Page of Table 5

		LE ◇1	LE	LE 1	LE 1	LE 1	LE 1	LE	LE 1	LE ◇1 ☕	LE 1	LE 1	LE ◇1 ☕	LE 1	LE 1	LE 1	LE ◇1 ☕	LE 1	LE 1	LE 1	LE 1	LE ◇1 ☕	LE 1	LE 1
Norwich	d	22p00								06 30			07 00				07 30					08 00		
Diss	d	22p17								06 47			07 17				07 47					08 17		
Peterborough 8	d																							
Stowmarket	d	22p29	23p47										07 29									08 29		
Needham Market	d		23p52																					
Ipswich	a	22p41	00 05							07 08			07 41				08 08					08 41		
	d	22p43								07 09			07 43	07 46		07 52	08 09					08 43		
Harwich Town	d																		08 28					
Dovercourt	d																		08 30					
Harwich International	d						06 20					07 20		08a14					08 33					
Wrabness	d																		08 39					
Mistley	d																		08 45					
Manningtree 2	d	22p53					06 33			07 19		07 33	07 53			08 02	08 19		08a50			08 53		
Walton-on-the-Naze	d																				08 00			
Frinton-on-Sea	d																				08 03			
Kirby Cross	d																				08 06			
Clacton-on-Sea	d										07 05							08 05					08 30	
Thorpe-le-Soken 1	a										07 13							08 13			08 12		08 38	
	d										07 13							08 13			08 17			
Weeley	d																				08 21			
Great Bentley	d																				08 24			
Alresford (Essex)	d																				08 28			
Wivenhoe 3	d										07 24							08 24			08 32			
Hythe	d																				08 36			
Colchester Town	a																				08 40			
	d																				08 44			
Colchester 4	a	23p02					06 42			07 28	07 32	07 42	08 02			08 11	08 28	08 32			08 52	09 02		
Colchester 4	d	23p03				06 33	06 43	06 53	07 12	07 30	07 33	07 43	08 03			08 12	08 30	08 33		08 43		09 03		
Marks Tey 2	d						06 49	07a00	07 18			07 49				08 18				08 49				
Kelvedon	d						06 54		07 23			07 54				08 23				08 54				
Braintree	d			00 27											08 04									09 04
Braintree Freeport	d			00 29											08 06									09 06
Cressing	d			00 32											08 09									09 09
White Notley	d			00 35											08 12									09 12
Witham 2	d	23p16		00a43		06 46	07 00		07 29		07 46	08 00			08a20	08 29		08 46		09 00				09a20
Hatfield Peverel	d								07 33							08 33								
Chelmsford 3	d	23p25			06 40	06 56	07 09		07 40		07 56	08 09	08 21			08 40		08 56		09 09		09 21		
Ingatestone	d					07 02					08 02							09 02						
Shenfield 3	a	23b36			06 50	07 08	07 19		07 50		08 08	08 19				08 50		09 08		09 19				
Romford	a																							
Stratford 7 ⊖	a				07 05	07 22	07s36		08 05	08 09	08 22	08 36	08 45			09 05	09 09	09 22		09 36		09 45		
London Liverpool Street 15 ⊖	a	00 03			07 14	07 31	07 47		08 14	08 22	08 31	08 45	08 59			09 14	09 22	09 31		09 45		09 59		

		LE 1	LE 1	LE ◇1 ☕	LE 1	LE 1	LE 1	LE 1	LE ◇1 ☕	LE 1	LE 1	LE 1	LE ◇1 ☕	LE 1	LE 1	LE 1	LE 1	LE ◇1 ☕	LE 1	LE 1	LE 1	LE ◇1 ☕	LE 1	LE 1	LE 1
Norwich	d			08 30					09 00				09 30					10 00				10 30			
Diss	d			08 47					09 17				09 47					10 17				10 47			
Peterborough 8	d																								
Stowmarket	d		08 47						09 29			09 47						10 29			10 47				
Needham Market	d		08 52									09 52									10 52				
Ipswich	a		09 03	09 08					09 41			10 03	10 08					10 41			11 03	11 08			
	d	08 52		09 09					09 43		09 52		10 09					10 43		10 52		11 09			
Harwich Town	d					09 28									10 28									11 28	
Dovercourt	d					09 30									10 30									11 30	
Harwich International	d					09 33									10 33									11 33	
Wrabness	d					09 39									10 39									11 39	
Mistley	d					09 45									10 45									11 45	
Manningtree 2	d	09 02		09 19		09a50			09 53		10 02		10 19		10a50			10 53		11 02		11 19		11a50	
Walton-on-the-Naze	d							09 00									10 00								
Frinton-on-Sea	d							09 03									10 03								
Kirby Cross	d							09 06									10 06								
Clacton-on-Sea	d				09 05									10 05									11 05		
Thorpe-le-Soken 1	a				09 13			09 12						10 13			10 12						11 13		
	d				09 13			09 17						10 13			10 17						11 13		
Weeley	d							09 21									10 21								
Great Bentley	d							09 24									10 24								
Alresford (Essex)	d							09 28									10 28								
Wivenhoe 3	d				09 24			09 32						10 24			10 32						11 24		
Hythe	d							09 36									10 36								
Colchester Town	a							09 40									10 40								
	d							09 44									10 44								
Colchester 4	a	09 11		09 28	09 32			09 52	10 02		10 11		10 28	10 32			10 52	11 02		11 11		11 28	11 32		
Colchester 4	d	09 12		09 30	09 33		09 43		10 03		10 12		10 30	10 33		10 43		11 03		11 12		11 30	11 33		11 43
Marks Tey 2	d	09 18					09 49				10 18					10 49				11 18					11 49
Kelvedon	d	09 23					09 54				10 23					10 54				11 23					11 54
Braintree	d									10 04									11 04						
Braintree Freeport	d									10 06									11 06						
Cressing	d									10 09									11 09						
White Notley	d									10 12									11 12						
Witham 2	d	09 29			09 46		10 00			10a20	10 29			10 46		11 00			11a20	11 29			11 46		12 00
Hatfield Peverel	d	09 33									10 33									11 33					
Chelmsford 3	d	09 40			09 56		10 09		10 21		10 40			10 56		11 09		11 21		11 40			11 56		12 09
Ingatestone	d				10 02									11 02									12 02		
Shenfield 3	a	09 50			10 08		10 19				10 50			11 08		11 19				11 50			12 08		12 19
Romford	a																								
Stratford 7 ⊖	a	10 05		10 09	10 22		10 36		10 45		11 05		11 09	11 22		11 36		11 45		12 05		12 09	12 22		12 36
London Liverpool Street 15 ⊖	a	10 14		10 22	10 31		10 45		10 59		11 14		11 22	11 31		11 45		11 59		12 14		12 22	12 31		12 45

b Previous night, stops to set down only

Norwich, Ipswich, Harwich, Clacton, Walton-on-Naze, Colchester and Chelmsford - London

Network Diagram - see first Page of Table 5

		LE 1	LE ◇1 ☕	LE 1	LE 1	LE 1	LE ■ 1 ☕	LE 1	LE 1	LE 1	LE 1	LE ◇1 ☕	LE 1	LE 1	LE 1	LE ◇1 ☕	LE 1	LE 1	LE 1	LE 1	LE ◇1 ☕	LE 1	LE 1	LE 1
Norwich	d		11 00				11 30					12 00				12 30					13 00			
Diss	d		11 17				11 47					12 17				12 47					13 17			
Peterborough 8	d																							
Stowmarket	d		11 29			11 47						12 29	12 47								13 29			13 47
Needham Market	d					11 52							12 52											13 52
Ipswich	a		11 41			12 03	12 08					12 41	13 03			13 08					13 41			14 03
	d		11 43		11 52		12 09					12 43			12 52	13 09					13 43		13 52	
Harwich Town	d								12 28									13 28						
Dovercourt	d								12 30									13 30						
Harwich International	d								12 33									13 33						
Wrabness	d								12 39									13 39						
Mistley	d								12 45									13 45						
Manningtree 2	d		11 53		12 02		12 19		12a50			12 53			13 02	13 19		13a50			13 53		14 02	
Walton-on-the-Naze	d	11 00									12 00									13 00				
Frinton-on-Sea	d	11 03									12 03									13 03				
Kirby Cross	d	11 06									12 06									13 06				
Clacton-on-Sea	d							12 05									13 05							
Thorpe-le-Soken 1	a	11 12						12 13			12 12						13 13			13 12				
	d	11 17						12 13			12 17						13 13			13 17				
Weeley	d	11 21									12 21									13 21				
Great Bentley	d	11 24									12 24									13 24				
Alresford (Essex)	d	11 28									12 28									13 28				
Wivenhoe 3	d	11 32						12 24			12 32						13 24			13 32				
Hythe	d	11 36									12 36									13 36				
Colchester Town	a	11 40									12 40									13 40				
	d	11 44									12 44									13 44				
Colchester 4	a	11 52	12 02		12 11		12 28	12 32			12 52	13 02			13 11	13 28	13 32			13 52	14 02		14 11	
Colchester 4	d		12 03		12 12		12 30	12 33		12 43		13 03			13 12	13 30	13 33		13 43		14 03		14 12	
Marks Tey 2	d				12 18					12 49					13 18				13 49				14 18	
Kelvedon	d				12 23					12 54					13 23				13 54				14 23	
Braintree	d			12 04										13 04								14 04		
Braintree Freeport	d			12 06										13 06								14 06		
Cressing	d			12 09										13 09								14 09		
White Notley	d			12 12										13 12								14 12		
Witham 2	d			12a20	12 29			12 46		13 00				13a20	13 29		13 46		14 00			14a20	14 29	
Hatfield Peverel	d				12 33										13 33								14 33	
Chelmsford 3	d		12 21		12 40			12 56		13 09		13 21			13 40		13 56		14 09		14 21		14 40	
Ingatestone	d							13 02									14 02							
Shenfield 3	a				12 50			13 08		13 19					13 50		14 08		14 19				14 50	
Romford	a																							
Stratford 7 ⊖	a		12 45		13 05		13 09	13 22		13 36		13 45			14 05	14 09	14 22		14 36		14 45		15 05	
London Liverpool Street 15 ⊖	a		12 59		13 14		13 22	13 31		13 45		13 59			14 14	14 22	14 31		14 45		14 59		15 14	

		LE ◇1 ☕	LE 1	LE 1	LE 1	LE 1	LE ◇1 ☕	LE 1	LE 1	LE 1	LE ◇1 ☕	LE 1	LE 1	LE 1	LE 1	LE ◇1 ☕	LE 1	LE 1	LE 1	LE ◇1 ☕	LE 1	LE 1	LE 1	LE 1	LE ◇1 ☕
Norwich	d	13 30					14 00				14 30					15 00				15 30					16 00
Diss	d	13 47					14 17				14 47					15 17				15 47					16 17
Peterborough 8	d																								
Stowmarket	d						14 29			14 47						15 29			15 47						16 29
Needham Market	d									14 52									15 52						
Ipswich	a	14 08					14 41			15 03	15 08					15 41			16 03	16 08					16 41
	d	14 09					14 43		14 52		15 09					15 43		15 52		16 09					16 43
Harwich Town	d			14 28									15 28									16 28			
Dovercourt	d			14 30									15 30									16 30			
Harwich International	d			14 33									15 33									16 33			
Wrabness	d			14 39									15 39									16 39			
Mistley	d			14 45									15 45									16 45			
Manningtree 2	d	14 19		14a50			14 53		15 02		15 19		15a50			15 53		16 02		16 19		16a50			16 53
Walton-on-the-Naze	d					14 00									15 00									16 00	
Frinton-on-Sea	d					14 03									15 03									16 03	
Kirby Cross	d					14 06									15 06									16 06	
Clacton-on-Sea	d		14 05									15 05									16 05				
Thorpe-le-Soken 1	a		14 13			14 12						15 13			15 12						16 13			16 12	
	d		14 13			14 17						15 13			15 17						16 13			16 17	
Weeley	d					14 21									15 21									16 21	
Great Bentley	d					14 24									15 24									16 24	
Alresford (Essex)	d					14 28									15 28									16 28	
Wivenhoe 3	d		14 24			14 32						15 24			15 32						16 24			16 32	
Hythe	d					14 36									15 36									16 36	
Colchester Town	a					14 40									15 40									16 40	
	d					14 44									15 44									16 44	
Colchester 4	a	14 28	14 32			14 52	15 02		15 11		15 28	15 32			15 52	16 02		16 11		16 28	16 32			16 52	17 02
Colchester 4	d	14 30	14 33		14 43		15 03		15 12		15 30	15 33		15 43		16 03		16 12		16 30	16 33		16 43		17 03
Marks Tey 2	d				14 49				15 18					15 49				16 18					16 49		
Kelvedon	d				14 54				15 23					15 54				16 23					16 54		
Braintree	d							15 04									16 04								
Braintree Freeport	d							15 06									16 06								
Cressing	d							15 09									16 09								
White Notley	d							15 12									16 12								
Witham 2	d		14 46		15 00			15a20	15 29			15 46		16 00			16a20	16 29			16 46		17 00		
Hatfield Peverel	d								15 33									16 33							
Chelmsford 3	d		14 56		15 09		15 21		15 40			15 56		16 09		16 21		16 40			16 56		17 09		17 21
Ingatestone	d		15 02									16 02									17 02				
Shenfield 3	a		15 08		15 19				15 50			16 08		16 19				16 50			17 08		17 19		
Romford	a																								
Stratford 7 ⊖	a	15 09	15 22		15 36		15 45		16 05		16 09	16 22		16 36		16 45		17 05		17 09	17 22		17 36		17 45
London Liverpool Street 15 ⊖	a	15 22	15 31		15 45		15 59		16 14		16 22	16 31		16 45		16 59		17 14		17 22	17 31		17 45		17 59

Table 11

Sundays
29 July to 12 August

Norwich, Ipswich, Harwich, Clacton, Walton-on-Naze, Colchester and Chelmsford - London

Network Diagram - see first Page of Table 5

		LE 1	LE 1	LE 1	LE ◇1 ⊐P	LE 1	LE 1	LE 1	LE 1	LE ◇1 ⊐P	LE 1	LE 1	LE 1
Norwich	d				16 30					17 00			
Diss	d				16 47					17 17			
Peterborough 8	d												
Stowmarket	d			16 47	16 59					17 29			17 47
Needham Market	d			16 52									17 52
Ipswich	a			17 03	17 11					17 41			18 03
	d		16 52		17 13					17 43		17 52	
Harwich Town	d						17 28						
Dovercourt	d						17 30						
Harwich International	d						17 33						
Wrabness	d						17 39						
Mistley	d						17 45						
Manningtree 2	d		17 02				17a50			17 53		18 02	
Walton-on-the-Naze	d								17 00				
Frinton-on-Sea	d								17 03				
Kirby Cross	d								17 06				
Clacton-on-Sea	d					17 05							
Thorpe-le-Soken 1	a					17 13			17 12				
	d					17 13			17 17				
Weeley	d								17 21				
Great Bentley	d								17 24				
Alresford (Essex)	d								17 28				
Wivenhoe 3	d					17 24			17 32				
Hythe	d								17 36				
Colchester Town	a								17 40				
	d								17 44				
Colchester 4	a		17 11		17 28	17 32			17 52	18 02		18 11	
Colchester 4	d		17 12		17 30	17 33		17 43		18 03		18 12	
Marks Tey 2	d		17 18					17 49				18 18	
Kelvedon	d		17 23					17 54				18 23	
Braintree	d	17 04									18 04		
Braintree Freeport	d	17 06									18 06		
Cressing	d	17 09									18 09		
White Notley	d	17 12									18 12		
Witham 2	d	17a20	17 29			17 46		18 00			18a20	18 29	
Hatfield Peverel	d		17 33									18 33	
Chelmsford 3	d		17 40			17 56		18 09		18 21		18 40	
Ingatestone	d					18 02							
Shenfield 3	a		17 50			18 08		18 19				18 50	
Romford	a												
Stratford 7 ⊖	a		18 05		18 09	18 22		18 36		18 45		19 05	
London Liverpool Street 15 ⊖	a		18 14		18 22	18 31		18 45		18 59		19 14	

		LE ◇1 ⊐P	LE 1	LE 1	LE 1	LE 1	LE ◇1 ⊐P	LE 1	LE 1	LE 1	LE ◇1 ⊐P	LE 1	LE 1
Norwich	d	17 30					18 00				18 30		
Diss	d	17 47					18 17				18 47		
Peterborough 8	d												
Stowmarket	d	17 59					18 29			18 47			
Needham Market	d									18 52			
Ipswich	a	18 11					18 41			19 03	19 08		
	d	18 13					18 43		18 52		19 09		
Harwich Town	d			18 28									19 28
Dovercourt	d			18 30									19 30
Harwich International	d			18 33									19 33
Wrabness	d			18 39									19 39
Mistley	d			18 45									19 45
Manningtree 2	d			18a50			18 53		19 02		19 19		19a50
Walton-on-the-Naze	d					18 00							
Frinton-on-Sea	d					18 03							
Kirby Cross	d					18 06							
Clacton-on-Sea	d		18 05									19 05	
Thorpe-le-Soken 1	a		18 13			18 12						19 13	
	d		18 13			18 17						19 13	
Weeley	d					18 21							
Great Bentley	d					18 24							
Alresford (Essex)	d					18 28							
Wivenhoe 3	d		18 24			18 32						19 24	
Hythe	d					18 36							
Colchester Town	a					18 40							
	d					18 44							
Colchester 4	a	18 28	18 32			18 52	19 02		19 11		19 28	19 32	
Colchester 4	d	18 30	18 33		18 43		19 03		19 12		19 30	19 33	
Marks Tey 2	d				18 49				19 18				
Kelvedon	d				18 54				19 23				
Braintree	d							19 04					
Braintree Freeport	d							19 06					
Cressing	d							19 09					
White Notley	d							19 12					
Witham 2	d		18 46		19 00			19a20	19 29			19 46	
Hatfield Peverel	d								19 33				
Chelmsford 3	d		18 56		19 09		19 21		19 40			19 56	
Ingatestone	d		19 02									20 02	
Shenfield 3	a		19 08		19 19				19 50			20 08	
Romford	a												
Stratford 7 ⊖	a	19 09	19 22		19 36		19 45		20 05		20 09	20 22	
London Liverpool Street 15 ⊖	a	19 22	19 31		19 45		19 59		20 14		20 22	20 31	

		LE 1	LE 1	LE ◇1 ⊐P	LE 1	LE 1	LE 1	LE 1	LE 1	LE 1	LE 1	LE 1	LE ◇1 ⊐P
Norwich	d			19 00									20 00
Diss	d			19 17									20 17
Peterborough 8	d												
Stowmarket	d			19 29			19 47						20 29
Needham Market	d						19 52						
Ipswich	a			19 41			20 03						20 41
	d			19 43		19 52		20 09					20 43
Harwich Town	d									20 28			
Dovercourt	d									20 30			
Harwich International	d									20 33			
Wrabness	d									20 39			
Mistley	d									20 45			
Manningtree 2	d			19 53		20 02		20 20		20a50			20 53
Walton-on-the-Naze	d		19 00									20 00	
Frinton-on-Sea	d		19 03									20 03	
Kirby Cross	d		19 06									20 06	
Clacton-on-Sea	d								20 05				
Thorpe-le-Soken 1	a		19 12						20 13			20 12	
	d		19 17						20 13			20 17	
Weeley	d		19 21									20 21	
Great Bentley	d		19 24									20 24	
Alresford (Essex)	d		19 28									20 28	
Wivenhoe 3	d		19 32						20 24			20 32	
Hythe	d		19 36									20 36	
Colchester Town	a		19 40									20 40	
	d		19 44									20 44	
Colchester 4	a		19 52	20 02		20 11		20 29	20 32			20 52	21 02
Colchester 4	d	19 43		20 03		20 12		20 30	20 33		20 43		21 03
Marks Tey 2	d	19 49				20 18					20 49		
Kelvedon	d	19 54				20 23					20 54		
Braintree	d				20 04								
Braintree Freeport	d				20 06								
Cressing	d				20 09								
White Notley	d				20 12								
Witham 2	d	20 00			20a20	20 29			20 46		21 00		
Hatfield Peverel	d					20 33							
Chelmsford 3	d	20 09		20 21		20 40			20 56		21 09		21 21
Ingatestone	d								21 02				
Shenfield 3	a	20 19				20 50			21 08		21 19		
Romford	a												
Stratford 7 ⊖	a	20 36		20 45		21 05		21 09	21 22		21 34		21 45
London Liverpool Street 15 ⊖	a	20 45		20 59		21 14		21 19	21 31		21 43		21 59

		LE 1	LE 1	LE 1	LE 1	LE 1	LE ◇1	LE 1	LE 1	LE 1	LE ◇1 ⊐P	LE 1	LE 1
Norwich	d				20 30						21 00		
Diss	d				20 47						21 17		
Peterborough 8	d						19 45						
Stowmarket	d		20 47				21 06				21 29		
Needham Market	d		20 52										
Ipswich	a		21 03		21 08		21 18				21 41		
	d				21 09		21 19				21 43		21 52
Harwich Town	d							21 28					
Dovercourt	d							21 30					
Harwich International	d			20 45				21 33					
Wrabness	d							21 39					
Mistley	d							21 45					
Manningtree 2	d			20 58	21 19		21 29	21a50			21 53		22 02
Walton-on-the-Naze	d									21 00			
Frinton-on-Sea	d									21 03			
Kirby Cross	d									21 06			
Clacton-on-Sea	d					21 05							
Thorpe-le-Soken 1	a					21 13				21 12			
	d					21 13				21 17			
Weeley	d									21 21			
Great Bentley	d									21 24			
Alresford (Essex)	d									21 28			
Wivenhoe 3	d					21 24				21 32			
Hythe	d									21 36			
Colchester Town	a									21 40			
	d									21 44			
Colchester 4	a			21 07	21 28	21 32	21 40			21 52	22 02		22 11
Colchester 4	d			21 08	21 30	21 33			21 43		22 03		22 12
Marks Tey 2	d			21 14					21 49				22 18
Kelvedon	d			21 19					21 54				22 23
Braintree	d	21 04										22 04	
Braintree Freeport	d	21 06										22 06	
Cressing	d	21 09										22 09	
White Notley	d	21 12										22 12	
Witham 2	d	21a20		21 25		21 46			22 00			22a20	22 29
Hatfield Peverel	d			21 29									22 33
Chelmsford 3	d			21 36		21 56			22 09		22 21		22 40
Ingatestone	d					22 02							
Shenfield 3	a			21 46		22 08			22 19				22 50
Romford	a												
Stratford 7 ⊖	a			22 11		22 26			22 37				23 10
London Liverpool Street 15 ⊖	a			22 21	22 18	22 36			22 48		22 54		23 20

Table 11

Sundays
29 July to 12 August

Norwich, Ipswich, Harwich, Clacton, Walton-on-Naze, Colchester and Chelmsford - London

Network Diagram - see first Page of Table 5

		LE 1	LE 1	LE 1	LE 1	LE 1	LE 1	LE ◇1 ⊐P	LE 1	LE 1	LE 1	LE ◇1 ⊐P	LE 1	LE 1	LE 1
Norwich	d							22 00				23 05			
Diss	d							22 17				23 22			
Peterborough 8	d														
Stowmarket	d		21 47					22 29		22 47		23 34			23 47
Needham Market	d		21 52							22 52					23 52
Ipswich	a		22 03					22 41		23 03		23 48			23 03
	d			22 23				22 43							
Harwich Town	d					22 28							23 28		
Dovercourt	d					22 30							23 30		
Harwich International	d					22 33							23 33		
Wrabness	d					22 39							23 39		
Mistley	d					22 45							23 45		
Manningtree 2	d			22 33		22a50		22 53					23a50		
Walton-on-the-Naze	d				22 00				23 00						
Frinton-on-Sea	d				22 03				23 03						
Kirby Cross	d				22 06				23 06						
Clacton-on-Sea	d	22 05									23 05				
Thorpe-le-Soken 1	a	22 13			22 12				23 12		23 13				
	d	22 13			22 17						23 13				
Weeley	d				22 21						23 17				
Great Bentley	d				22 24						23 20				
Alresford (Essex)	d				22 28						23 24				
Wivenhoe 3	d	22 24			22 32						23 28				
Hythe	d				22 36						23 32				
Colchester Town	a				22 40										
	d				22 44										
Colchester 4	a	22 32		22 42	22 52			23 02			23 38				
Colchester 4	d	22 33		22 43				23 03							
Marks Tey 2	d			22 49											
Kelvedon	d			22 54											
Braintree	d						22 56							23 45	
Braintree Freeport	d						22 58							23 47	
Cressing	d						23 01							23 50	
White Notley	d						23 04							23 53	
Witham 2	d	22 46		23 00			23a12	23 16						00a01	
Hatfield Peverel	d														
Chelmsford 3	d	22 56		23 09				23 25							
Ingatestone	d	23 02													
Shenfield 3	a	23 08		23 19				23s36							
Romford	a														
Stratford 7 ⊖	a	23 26		23 38											
London Liverpool Street 15 ⊖	a	23 36		23 48				00 03							

Table 11

Sundays

19 August to 26 August

Norwich, Ipswich, Harwich, Clacton, Walton-on-Naze, Colchester and Chelmsford - London

Network Diagram - see first Page of Table 5

	LE ◇1	LE	LE 1	LE 1	LE 1	LE	LE 1	LE 1	LE ◇1 ☕	LE 1	LE 1	LE 1	LE 1	LE ◇1 ☕	LE 1	LE 1	LE 1	LE 1	LE 1	LE ◇1 ☕	LE 1	LE 1
Norwich d	22p00								07 00					08 00						09 00		
Diss d	22p17								07 17					08 17						09 17		
Peterborough 8 d																						
Stowmarket d	22p29	23p47							07 29					08 29						09 29		
Needham Market d		23p52																				
Ipswich a	22p41	00 05							07 41					08 41						09 41		
d	22p43								07 43	07 46			08 09	08 43					09 09	09 43		
Harwich Town d																08 53						09 53
Dovercourt d																08 55						09 55
Harwich International d								07 20		08a14						08 58						09 58
Wrabness d																09 04						10 04
Mistley d																09 10						10 10
Manningtree 2 d	22p53							07 33	07 53				08 19	08 53		09a15			09 19	09 53		10a15
Walton-on-the-Naze d															08 30						09 30	
Frinton-on-Sea d															08 33						09 33	
Kirby Cross d															08 36						09 36	
Clacton-on-Sea d												07 36						08 36				
Thorpe-le-Soken 1 a												07 44			08 42			08 44			09 42	
d												07 44						08 44				
Weeley d																						
Great Bentley d												07 49						08 49				
Alresford (Essex) d												07 53						08 53				
Wivenhoe 3 d												07 57						08 57				
Hythe d																						
Colchester Town a																						
d																						
Colchester 4 a	23p02							07 42	08 02			08 05	08 29	09 02				09 05	09 29	10 02		
Colchester 4 d	23p03				06 56	07 07	07 26	07 43	08 03			08 06	08 30	09 03				09 06	09 30	10 03		
Marks Tey 2 d					07 02	07a14	07 32	07 49				08 12	08 36					09 12	09 36			
Kelvedon d					07 07		07 37	07 54					08 41						09 41			
Braintree d			00 25								08 00						09 00					
Braintree Freeport d			00 27								08 02						09 02					
Cressing d			00 30								08 05						09 05					
White Notley d			00 33								08 08						09 08					
Witham 2 d	23p16		00a41		07 13		07 43	08 00			08a16	08 21	08 47				09a16	09 21	09 47			
Hatfield Peverel d					07 17		07 47						08 51						09 51			
Chelmsford 3 d	23p25			06 54	07 24		07 54	08 09				08 30	08 58					09 30	09 58			
Ingatestone d				07 01	07 31		08 01						09 05						10 05			
Shenfield 3 a	23b36			07 06	07 36		08 06	08 19				08 40	09 10					09 40	10 10			
Romford a																						
Stratford 7 ⊖ a	23b52			07s34	08s04		08s34	08s49				09s04	09s34					10s04	10s34			
London Liverpool Street 15 ⊖ a	00 02			07 42	08 12		08 42	08 59	09 03			09 12	09 42	10 01				10 12	10 42	11 01		

	LE 1	LE 1	LE 1	LE	LE ◇1 ☕	LE 1	LE 1	LE 1	LE 1	LE 1	LE ◇1 ☕	LE 1	LE 1	LE 1	LE 1	LE 1	LE 1	LE ◇1 ☕	LE 1	LE 1	LE 1	LE 1
Norwich d					10 00						11 00							12 00				
Diss d					10 17						11 17							12 17				
Peterborough 8 d																						
Stowmarket d				10 18	10 29						11 29						12 18	12 29				
Needham Market d				10 23													12 23					
Ipswich a				10 35	10 41						11 41						12 35	12 41				
d			10 09		10 43					11 09	11 43					12 09		12 43				
Harwich Town d							10 53						11 53							12 53		
Dovercourt d							10 55						11 55							12 55		
Harwich International d							10 58						11 58							12 58		
Wrabness d							11 04						12 04							13 04		
Mistley d							11 10						12 10							13 10		
Manningtree 2 d			10 19		10 53		11a15			11 19	11 53		12a15			12 19		12 53		13a15		
Walton-on-the-Naze d						10 30						11 30							12 30			
Frinton-on-Sea d						10 33						11 33							12 33			
Kirby Cross d						10 36						11 36							12 36			
Clacton-on-Sea d		09 36							10 36						11 36							12 36
Thorpe-le-Soken 1 a		09 44				10 42			10 44			11 42			11 44				12 42			12 44
d		09 44							10 44						11 44							12 44
Weeley d																						
Great Bentley d		09 49							10 49						11 49							12 49
Alresford (Essex) d		09 53							10 53						11 53							12 53
Wivenhoe 3 d		09 57							10 57						11 57							12 57
Hythe d																						
Colchester Town a																						
d																						
Colchester 4 a		10 05	10 29		11 02				11 05	11 29	12 02				12 05	12 29		13 02				13 05
Colchester 4 d		10 06	10 30		11 03				11 06	11 30	12 03				12 06	12 30		13 03				13 06
Marks Tey 2 d		10 12	10 36						11 12	11 36					12 12	12 36						13 12
Kelvedon d			10 41							11 41						12 41						
Braintree d	10 00							11 00						12 00							13 00	
Braintree Freeport d	10 02							11 02						12 02							13 02	
Cressing d	10 05							11 05						12 05							13 05	
White Notley d	10 08							11 08						12 08							13 08	
Witham 2 d	10a16	10 21	10 47					11a16	11 21	11 47				12a16	12 21	12 47					13a16	13 21
Hatfield Peverel d			10 51							11 51						12 51						
Chelmsford 3 d		10 30	10 58						11 30	11 58					12 30	12 58						13 30
Ingatestone d			11 05							12 05						13 05						
Shenfield 3 a		10 40	11 10						11 40	12 10					12 40	13 10						13 40
Romford a																						
Stratford 7 ⊖ a		11s04	11s34						12s04	12s34					13s04	13s34						14s04
London Liverpool Street 15 ⊖ a		11 12	11 42		12 01				12 12	12 42	13 01				13 12	13 42		14 01				14 12

b Previous night, stops to set down only

Table 11

Sundays

19 August to 26 August

Norwich, Ipswich, Harwich, Clacton, Walton-on-Naze, Colchester and Chelmsford - London

Network Diagram - see first Page of Table 5

	LE 1	LE 1	LE ◇1 ☕	LE 1	LE 1	LE 1	LE 1	LE 1	LE 1	LE ◇1 ☕	LE 1	LE 1	LE 1	LE 1	LE 1	LE 1	LE ◇1 ☕	LE 1	LE 1	LE 1	LE 1
Norwich d			13 00							14 00							15 00				
Diss d			13 17							14 17							15 17				
Peterborough 8 d		11 46														13 46					
Stowmarket d		13 13	13 29						14 18	14 29						15 13	15 29				
Needham Market d									14 23												
Ipswich a		13 28	13 41						14 35	14 41						15 28	15 41				
d	13 09		13 43					14 09		14 43					15 09		15 43				
Harwich Town d					13 53							14 53							15 53		
Dovercourt d					13 55							14 55							15 55		
Harwich International d					13 58							14 58							15 58		
Wrabness d					14 04							15 04							16 04		
Mistley d					14 10							15 10							16 10		
Manningtree 2 d	13 19		13 53		14a15			14 19		14 53		15a15			15 19		15 53		16a15		
Walton-on-the-Naze d				13 30							14 30							15 30			
Frinton-on-Sea d				13 33							14 33							15 33			
Kirby Cross d				13 36							14 36							15 36			
Clacton-on-Sea d							13 36							14 36							15 36
Thorpe-le-Soken 1 a				13 42			13 44				14 42			14 44				15 42			15 44
d							13 44							14 44							15 44
Weeley d																					
Great Bentley d							13 49							14 49							15 49
Alresford (Essex) d							13 53							14 53							15 53
Wivenhoe 3 d							13 57							14 57							15 57
Hythe d																					
Colchester Town a																					
d																					
Colchester 4 a	13 29		14 02				14 05	14 29		15 02				15 05	15 29		16 02				16 05
Colchester 4 d	13 30		14 03				14 06	14 30		15 03				15 06	15 30		16 03				16 06
Marks Tey 2 d	13 36						14 12	14 36						15 12	15 36						16 12
Kelvedon d	13 41							14 41							15 41						
Braintree d						14 00							15 00							16 00	
Braintree Freeport d						14 02							15 02							16 02	
Cressing d						14 05							15 05							16 05	
White Notley d						14 08							15 08							16 08	
Witham 2 d	13 47					14a16	14 21	14 47					15a16	15 21	15 47					16a16	16 21
Hatfield Peverel d	13 51							14 51							15 51						
Chelmsford 3 d	13 58						14 30	14 58						15 30	15 58						16 30
Ingatestone d	14 05							15 05							16 05						
Shenfield 3 a	14 10						14 40	15 10						15 40	16 10						16 40
Romford a																					
Stratford 7 ⊖ a	14s34						15s04	15s34						16s04	16s34						17s04
London Liverpool Street 15 ⊖ a	14 42		15 01				15 12	15 42		16 01				16 12	16 42		17 01				17 12

	LE 1	LE 1	LE ■ 1 ☕	LE 1	LE 1	LE 1	LE 1	LE ◇1 ☕	LE 1	LE 1	LE ◇1 ☕	LE 1	LE 1	LE 1	LE 1	LE 1	LE 1	LE ◇1 ☕	LE 1	LE 1	LE 1	LE 1
Norwich d			16 00					16 20			17 00							18 00				
Diss d			16 17					16 37			17 17							18 17				
Peterborough 8 d										15 45												
Stowmarket d		16 18	16 29					16 49		17 13	17 29						18 18	18 29				
Needham Market d		16 23															18 23					
Ipswich a		16 35	16 41					17 01		17 28	17 41						18 35	18 41				
d	16 09		16 43					17 03	17 09		17 43					18 09		18 43				
Harwich Town d					16 53								17 53							18 53		
Dovercourt d					16 55								17 55							18 55		
Harwich International d					16 58								17 58							18 58		
Wrabness d					17 04								18 04							19 04		
Mistley d					17 10								18 10							19 10		
Manningtree 2 d	16 19		16 53		17a15				17 19		17 53		18a15			18 19		18 53		19a15		
Walton-on-the-Naze d				16 30								17 30							18 30			
Frinton-on-Sea d				16 33								17 33							18 33			
Kirby Cross d				16 36								17 36							18 36			
Clacton-on-Sea d							16 36								17 36							18 36
Thorpe-le-Soken 1 a				16 42			16 44					17 42			17 44				18 42			18 44
d							16 44								17 44							18 44
Weeley d																						
Great Bentley d							16 49								17 49							18 49
Alresford (Essex) d							16 53								17 53							18 53
Wivenhoe 3 d							16 57								17 57							18 57
Hythe d																						
Colchester Town a																						
d																						
Colchester 4 a	16 29		17 02				17 05	17 18	17 29		18 02				18 05	18 29		19 02				19 05
Colchester 4 d	16 30		17 03				17 06	17 21	17 30		18 03				18 06	18 30		19 03				19 06
Marks Tey 2 d	16 36						17 12		17 36						18 12	18 36						19 12
Kelvedon d	16 41								17 41							18 41						
Braintree d						17 00								18 00							19 00	
Braintree Freeport d						17 02								18 02							19 02	
Cressing d						17 05								18 05							19 05	
White Notley d						17 08								18 08							19 08	
Witham 2 d	16 47					17a16	17 21		17 47					18a16	18 21	18 47					19a16	19 21
Hatfield Peverel d	16 51								17 51							18 51						
Chelmsford 3 d	16 58						17 30		17 58						18 30	18 58						19 30
Ingatestone d	17 05								18 05							19 05						
Shenfield 3 a	17 10						17 40		18 10						18 40	19 10						19 40
Romford a																						
Stratford 7 ⊖ a	17s34						18s04		18s34						19s04	19s34						20s04
London Liverpool Street 15 ⊖ a	17 42		18 01				18 12	18 28	18 42		19 01				19 12	19 42		20 01				20 12

19 August to 26 August

Norwich, Ipswich, Harwich, Clacton, Walton-on-Naze, Colchester and Chelmsford - London

Network Diagram - see first Page of Table 5

Station		LE 1	LE ◇1	LE ◇1 ⊡	LE 1	LE 1	LE 1	LE 1	LE 1	LE 1	LE 1	LE 1	LE ◇1 ⊡	LE 1	LE 1	LE 1	LE 1	LE ◇1	LE 1	LE 1	LE 1	LE 1
Norwich	d			19 00									20 00					21 00				
Diss	d			19 17									20 17					21 17				
Peterborough 8	d		17 45																			
Stowmarket	d		19 13	19 29								20 18	20 29					21 29				
Needham Market	d											20 23										
Ipswich	a		19 28	19 41								20 35	20 41					21 41				
	d	19 09	19 28	19 43					20 09			20 35	20 43				21 09	21 43				
Harwich Town	d					19 53								20 53						21 53		
Dovercourt	d					19 55								20 55						21 55		
Harwich International	d					19 58					20 35	21a04		20 58						21 58		
Wrabness	d					20 04								21 04						22 04		
Mistley	d					20 10								21 10						22 10		
Manningtree 2	d	19 19	19 38	19 53		20a15			20 19		20 48		20 53	21a15			21 19	21 53		22a15		
Walton-on-the-Naze	d				19 30					20 30									21 30			
Frinton-on-Sea	d				19 33					20 33									21 33			
Kirby Cross	d				19 36					20 36									21 36			
Clacton-on-Sea	d							19 36								20 36						21 36
Thorpe-le-Soken 1	a				19 42			19 44		20 42						20 44			21 42			21 44
	d							19 44								20 44						21 44
Weeley	d																					
Great Bentley	d							19 49								20 49						21 49
Alresford (Essex)	d							19 53								20 53						21 53
Wivenhoe 3	d							19 57								20 57						21 57
Hythe	d																					
Colchester Town	a																					
	d																					
Colchester 4	a	19 29	19 49	20 02				20 05	20 29		20 57		21 02			21 05	21 29	22 02				22 05
Colchester 4	d	19 30		20 03				20 06	20 30		20 57		21 03			21 06	21 30	22 03				22 06
Marks Tey 2	d	19 36						20 12	20 36							21 12	21 36					22 12
Kelvedon	d	19 41							20 41								21 41					
Braintree	d						20 00								21 00						22 00	
Braintree Freeport	d						20 02								21 02						22 02	
Cressing	d						20 05								21 05						22 05	
White Notley	d						20 08								21 08						22 08	
Witham 2	d	19 47					20a16	20 21	20 47						21a16	21 21	21 47				22a16	22 21
Hatfield Peverel	d	19 51							20 51								21 51					
Chelmsford 3	d	19 58						20 30	20 58		21 15					21 30	21 58					22 30
Ingatestone	d	20 05							21 05								22 05					
Shenfield 3	a	20 10						20 40	21 10		21 25					21 40	22 10					22 40
Romford	a																					
Stratford 7 ⊖	a	20s34						21s04	21s34		21s51					22s04	22s34					23s04
London Liverpool Street 15 ⊖	a	20 42		21 01				21 12	21 42		21 59		22 01			22 12	22 42	23 01				23 12

Station		LE 1	LE 1	LE 1	LE 1	LE 1	LE ◇1	LE 1	LE 1
Norwich	d						22 00		23 05
Diss	d						22 17		23 22
Peterborough 8	d								
Stowmarket	d			22 18			22 29		23 34
Needham Market	d			22 23					
Ipswich	a			22 35			22 41		23 48
	d	22 09					22 43		
Harwich Town	d							22 53	
Dovercourt	d							22 55	
Harwich International	d							22 58	
Wrabness	d							23 04	
Mistley	d							23 10	
Manningtree 2	d	22 19					22 53	23 15	
Walton-on-the-Naze	d		22 16						
Frinton-on-Sea	d		22 19						
Kirby Cross	d		22 22						
Clacton-on-Sea	d				22 22				
Thorpe-le-Soken 1	a		22 28		22 30				
	d				22 30				
Weeley	d								
Great Bentley	d								
Alresford (Essex)	d								
Wivenhoe 3	d				22 40				
Hythe	d								
Colchester Town	a								
	d								
Colchester 4	a	22 29			22 48		23 02	23 24	
Colchester 4	d	22 30					23 03		
Marks Tey 2	d	22 36							
Kelvedon	d	22 41							
Braintree	d					22 56			
Braintree Freeport	d					22 58			
Cressing	d					23 01			
White Notley	d					23 04			
Witham 2	d	22 47				23a12	23 16		
Hatfield Peverel	d	22 51							
Chelmsford 3	d	22 58					23 25		
Ingatestone	d	23 05							
Shenfield 3	a	23 10					23s36		
Romford	a								
Stratford 7 ⊖	a	23s34					23s57		
London Liverpool Street 15 ⊖	a	23 42					00 08		

2 September to 9 September

Norwich, Ipswich, Harwich, Clacton, Walton-on-Naze, Colchester and Chelmsford - London

Network Diagram - see first Page of Table 5

Station		LE ◇1	LE	LE 1	LE 1	LE 1	LE 1	LE	LE 1	LE ◇1 ⊡	LE 1	LE 1	LE ◇1 ⊡	LE 1	LE 1	LE ◇1 ⊡	LE 1	LE 1	LE 1	LE 1	LE ◇1 ⊡	LE 1	LE 1
Norwich	d	22p00								06 30			07 00			07 30					08 00		
Diss	d	22p17								06 47			07 17			07 47					08 17		
Peterborough 8	d																						
Stowmarket	d	22p29	23p47										07 29								08 29		08 47
Needham Market	d		23p52																				08 52
Ipswich	a	22p41	00 05							07 08			07 41			08 08					08 41		09 03
	d	22p43								07 09			07 43		07 52	08 09					08 43		
Harwich Town	d																	08 28					
Dovercourt	d																	08 30					
Harwich International	d											07 20						08 33					
Wrabness	d																	08 39					
Mistley	d																	08 45					
Manningtree 2	d	22p53								07 19		07 33	07 53		08 02	08 19		08a50			08 53		
Walton-on-the-Naze	d																			08 00			
Frinton-on-Sea	d																			08 03			
Kirby Cross	d																			08 06			
Clacton-on-Sea	d										07 05						08 05					08 30	
Thorpe-le-Soken 1	a										07 13						08 13			08 12		08 38	
	d										07 13						08 13			08 17			
Weeley	d																			08 21			
Great Bentley	d																			08 24			
Alresford (Essex)	d																			08 28			
Wivenhoe 3	d										07 24						08 24			08 32			
Hythe	d																			08 36			
Colchester Town	a																			08 40			
	d																			08 44			
Colchester 4	a	23p02								07 28	07 32	07 42	08 02		08 11	08 28	08 32			08 52	09 02		
Colchester 4	d	23p03				06 33	06 43	06 53	07 12	07 30	07 33	07 43	08 03		08 12	08 30	08 33		08 43		09 03		
Marks Tey 2	d						06 49	07a00	07 18			07 49			08 18				08 49				
Kelvedon	d						06 54		07 23			07 54			08 23				08 54				
Braintree	d			00 27										08 04									
Braintree Freeport	d			00 29										08 06									
Cressing	d			00 32										08 09									
White Notley	d			00 35										08 12									
Witham 2	d	23p16		00a43		06 46	07 00		07 29		07 46	08 00		08a20	08 29		08 46		09 00				
Hatfield Peverel	d								07 33						08 33								
Chelmsford 3	d	23p25			06 40	06 56	07 09		07 40		07 56	08 09	08 21		08 40		08 56		09 09		09 21		
Ingatestone	d					07 02					08 02						09 02						
Shenfield 3	a	23b36			06 50	07 08	07 19		07 50		08 08	08 19			08 50		09 08		09 19				
Romford	a																						
Stratford 7 ⊖	a				07 05	07 22	07 34		08 05	08 09	08 22	08 36	08 45		09 05	09 09	09 22		09 36		09 45		
London Liverpool Street 15 ⊖	a	00 03			07 14	07 31	07 43		08 14	08 22	08 31	08 45	08 59		09 14	09 22	09 31		09 45		09 59		

Station		LE 1	LE 1	LE ◇1 ⊡	LE 1	LE 1	LE 1	LE 1	LE ◇1 ⊡	LE 1	LE 1	LE 1	LE ◇1 ⊡	LE 1	LE 1	LE 1	LE 1	LE ◇1 ⊡	LE 1	LE 1	LE 1	LE ◇1 ⊡	LE 1
Norwich	d			08 30					09 00				09 30					10 00				10 30	
Diss	d			08 47					09 17				09 47					10 17				10 47	
Peterborough 8	d																						
Stowmarket	d								09 29			09 47						10 29			10 47		
Needham Market	d											09 52									10 52		
Ipswich	a			09 08					09 41			10 03	10 08					10 41			11 03	11 08	
	d		08 52	09 09					09 43		09 52		10 09					10 43		10 52		11 09	
Harwich Town	d					09 28									10 28								
Dovercourt	d					09 30									10 30								
Harwich International	d					09 33									10 33								
Wrabness	d					09 39									10 39								
Mistley	d					09 45									10 45								
Manningtree 2	d		09 02	09 19		09a50			09 53		10 02		10 19		10a50			10 53		11 02		11 19	
Walton-on-the-Naze	d							09 00									10 00						
Frinton-on-Sea	d							09 03									10 03						
Kirby Cross	d							09 06									10 06						
Clacton-on-Sea	d				09 05									10 05									11 05
Thorpe-le-Soken 1	a				09 13			09 12						10 13			10 12						11 13
	d				09 13			09 17						10 13			10 17						11 13
Weeley	d							09 21									10 21						
Great Bentley	d							09 24									10 24						
Alresford (Essex)	d							09 28									10 28						
Wivenhoe 3	d				09 24			09 32						10 24			10 32						11 24
Hythe	d							09 36									10 36						
Colchester Town	a							09 40									10 40						
	d							09 44									10 44						
Colchester 4	a		09 11	09 28	09 32			09 52	10 02		10 11		10 28	10 32			10 52	11 02		11 11		11 28	11 32
Colchester 4	d		09 12	09 30	09 33		09 43		10 03		10 12		10 30	10 33		10 43		11 03		11 12		11 30	11 33
Marks Tey 2	d		09 18				09 49				10 18					10 49				11 18			
Kelvedon	d		09 23				09 54				10 23					10 54				11 23			
Braintree	d	09 04								10 04									11 04				
Braintree Freeport	d	09 06								10 06									11 06				
Cressing	d	09 09								10 09									11 09				
White Notley	d	09 12								10 12									11 12				
Witham 2	d	09a20	09 29		09 46		10 00			10a20	10 29			10 46		11 00			11a20	11 29			11 46
Hatfield Peverel	d		09 33								10 33									11 33			
Chelmsford 3	d		09 40		09 56		10 09		10 21		10 40			10 56		11 09		11 21		11 40			11 56
Ingatestone	d				10 02									11 02									12 02
Shenfield 3	a		09 50		10 08		10 19				10 50			11 08		11 19				11 50			12 08
Romford	a																						
Stratford 7 ⊖	a		10 05	10 09	10 22		10 36		10 45		11 05		11 09	11 22		11 36		11 45		12 05		12 09	12 22
London Liverpool Street 15 ⊖	a		10 14	10 22	10 31		10 45		10 59		11 14		11 22	11 31		11 45		11 59		12 14		12 22	12 31

b Previous night, stops to set down only

2 September to 9 September

Norwich, Ipswich, Harwich, Clacton, Walton-on-Naze, Colchester and Chelmsford - London

Network Diagram - see first Page of Table 5

		LE		LE	LE	LE	LE	LE	LE	LE	LE	LE	LE	LE	LE	LE	LE	LE	LE	LE	LE	LE	LE	LE	LE
		1		1	1	◇1	1	1	1	1	1	1	1	1	◇1	1	1	1	◇1	1	1	1	1	◇1	1
Norwich	d					11 00				11 30					12 00				12 30					13 00	
Diss	d					11 17				11 47					12 17				12 47					13 17	
Peterborough 8	d																								
Stowmarket	d					11 29			11 47						12 29			12 47						13 29	
Needham Market	d								11 52									12 52							
Ipswich	a					11 41			12 03	12 08					12 41			13 03	13 08					13 41	
	d					11 43		11 52		12 09					12 43		12 52		13 09					13 43	
Harwich Town	d	11 28										12 28									13 28				
Dovercourt	d	11 30										12 30									13 30				
Harwich International	d	11 33										12 33									13 33				
Wrabness	d	11 39										12 39									13 39				
Mistley	d	11 45										12 45									13 45				
Manningtree 2	d	11a50				11 53		12 02		12 19		12a50			12 53		13 02		13 19		13a50			13 53	
Walton-on-the-Naze	d				11 00									12 00									13 00		
Frinton-on-Sea	d				11 03									12 03									13 03		
Kirby Cross	d				11 06									12 06									13 06		
Clacton-on-Sea	d										12 05									13 05					
Thorpe-le-Soken 1	a				11 12						12 13			12 12						13 13			13 12		
	d				11 17						12 13			12 17						13 13			13 17		
Weeley	d				11 21									12 21									13 21		
Great Bentley	d				11 24									12 24									13 24		
Alresford (Essex)	d				11 28									12 28									13 28		
Wivenhoe 3	d				11 32						12 24			12 32						13 24			13 32		
Hythe	d				11 36									12 36									13 36		
Colchester Town	a				11 40									12 40									13 40		
	d				11 44									12 44									13 44		
Colchester 4	a				11 52	12 02		12 11		12 28	12 32			12 52	13 02		13 11		13 28	13 32			13 52	14 02	
Colchester 4	d			11 43		12 03		12 12		12 30	12 33		12 43		13 03		13 12		13 30	13 33		13 43		14 03	
Marks Tey 2	d			11 49				12 18					12 49				13 18					13 49			
Kelvedon	d			11 54				12 23					12 54				13 23					13 54			
Braintree	d						12 04									13 04									14 04
Braintree Freeport	d						12 06									13 06									14 06
Cressing	d						12 09									13 09									14 09
White Notley	d						12 12									13 12									14 12
Witham 2	d			12 00			12a20	12 29			12 46		13 00			13a20	13 29			13 46		14 00			14a20
Hatfield Peverel	d							12 33									13 33								
Chelmsford 3	d			12 09		12 21		12 40			12 56		13 09		13 21		13 40			13 56		14 09		14 21	
Ingatestone	d										13 02									14 02					
Shenfield 3	a			12 19				12 50			13 08		13 19				13 50			14 08		14 19			
Romford	a																								
Stratford 7 ⊖	a			12 36		12 45		13 05		13 09	13 22		13 36		13 45		14 05		14 09	14 22		14 36		14 45	
London Liverpool Street 15 ⊖	a			12 45		12 59		13 14		13 22	13 31		13 45		13 59		14 14		14 22	14 31		14 45		14 59	

		LE	LE	LE	LE	LE	LE	LE	LE	LE	LE	LE	LE	LE	LE	LE	LE	LE	LE	LE	LE	LE	LE	LE	LE
		1	1	◇1	1	1	1	1	◇1	1	1	1	◇1	1	1	1	1	◇1	1	1	1	◇1	1	1	1
Norwich	d			13 30					14 00				14 30					15 00				15 30			
Diss	d			13 47					14 17				14 47					15 17				15 47			
Peterborough 8	d																								
Stowmarket	d		13 47						14 29			14 47						15 29			15 47				
Needham Market	d		13 52									14 52									15 52				
Ipswich	a		14 03	14 08					14 41			15 03	15 08					15 41			16 03	16 08			
	d	13 52		14 09					14 43		14 52		15 09					15 43		15 52		16 09			
Harwich Town	d					14 28									15 28									16 28	
Dovercourt	d					14 30									15 30									16 30	
Harwich International	d					14 33									15 33									16 33	
Wrabness	d					14 39									15 39									16 39	
Mistley	d					14 45									15 45									16 45	
Manningtree 2	d	14 02		14 19		14a50			14 53		15 02		15 19		15a50			15 53		16 02		16 19		16a50	
Walton-on-the-Naze	d							14 00									15 00								
Frinton-on-Sea	d							14 03									15 03								
Kirby Cross	d							14 06									15 06								
Clacton-on-Sea	d				14 05									15 05									16 05		
Thorpe-le-Soken 1	a				14 13			14 12						15 13			15 12						16 13		
	d				14 13			14 17						15 13			15 17						16 13		
Weeley	d							14 21									15 21								
Great Bentley	d							14 24									15 24								
Alresford (Essex)	d							14 28									15 28								
Wivenhoe 3	d				14 24			14 32						15 24			15 32						16 24		
Hythe	d							14 36									15 36								
Colchester Town	a							14 40									15 40								
	d							14 44									15 44								
Colchester 4	a	14 11		14 28	14 32			14 52	15 02		15 11		15 28	15 32			15 52	16 02		16 11		16 28	16 32		
Colchester 4	d	14 12		14 30	14 33		14 43		15 03		15 12		15 30	15 33		15 43		16 03		16 12		16 30	16 33		16 43
Marks Tey 2	d	14 18					14 49				15 18					15 49				16 18					16 49
Kelvedon	d	14 23					14 54				15 23					15 54				16 23					16 54
Braintree	d									15 04									16 04						
Braintree Freeport	d									15 06									16 06						
Cressing	d									15 09									16 09						
White Notley	d									15 12									16 12						
Witham 2	d	14 29			14 46		15 00			15a20	15 29			15 46		16 00			16a20	16 29			16 46		17 00
Hatfield Peverel	d	14 33									15 33									16 33					
Chelmsford 3	d	14 40			14 56		15 09		15 21		15 40			15 56		16 09		16 21		16 40			16 56		17 09
Ingatestone	d				15 02									16 02									17 02		
Shenfield 3	a	14 50			15 08		15 19				15 50			16 08		16 19				16 50			17 08		17 19
Romford	a																								
Stratford 7 ⊖	a	15 05		15 09	15 22		15 36		15 45		16 05		16 09	16 22		16 36		16 45		17 05		17 09	17 22		17 36
London Liverpool Street 15 ⊖	a	15 14		15 22	15 31		15 45		15 59		16 14		16 22	16 31		16 45		16 59		17 14		17 22	17 31		17 45

2 September to 9 September

Norwich, Ipswich, Harwich, Clacton, Walton-on-Naze, Colchester and Chelmsford - London

Network Diagram - see first Page of Table 5

		LE	LE	LE	LE	LE	LE	LE	LE	LE	LE	LE	LE	LE	LE	LE	LE	LE	LE	LE	LE	LE	LE	LE	LE
		1	◇1	1	1	1	◇1	1	1	1	1	◇1	1	1	1	◇1	1	1	1	1	◇1	1	1	1	◇1
Norwich	d		16 00				16 30					17 00				17 30					18 00				18 30
Diss	d		16 17				16 47					17 17				17 47					18 17				18 47
Peterborough 8	d																								
Stowmarket	d		16 29			16 47	16 59					17 29			17 47	17 59					18 29			18 47	
Needham Market	d					16 52									17 52									18 52	
Ipswich	a		16 41			17 03	17 11					17 41			18 03	18 11					18 41			19 03	19 08
	d		16 43		16 52		17 13					17 43		17 52		18 13					18 43		18 52		19 09
Harwich Town	d								17 28									18 28							
Dovercourt	d								17 30									18 30							
Harwich International	d								17 33									18 33							
Wrabness	d								17 39									18 39							
Mistley	d								17 45									18 45							
Manningtree 2	d		16 53		17 02				17a50			17 53		18 02				18a50			18 53		19 02		19 19
Walton-on-the-Naze	d	16 00									17 00									18 00					
Frinton-on-Sea	d	16 03									17 03									18 03					
Kirby Cross	d	16 06									17 06									18 06					
Clacton-on-Sea	d							17 05									18 05								
Thorpe-le-Soken 1	a	16 12						17 13			17 12						18 13			18 12					
	d	16 17						17 13			17 17						18 13			18 17					
Weeley	d	16 21									17 21									18 21					
Great Bentley	d	16 24									17 24									18 24					
Alresford (Essex)	d	16 28									17 28									18 28					
Wivenhoe 3	d	16 32						17 24			17 32						18 24			18 32					
Hythe	d	16 36									17 36									18 36					
Colchester Town	a	16 40									17 40									18 40					
	d	16 44									17 44									18 44					
Colchester 4	a	16 52	17 02		17 11		17 28	17 32			17 52	18 02		18 11		18 28	18 32			18 52	19 02		19 11		19 28
Colchester 4	d		17 03		17 12		17 30	17 33		17 43		18 03		18 12		18 30	18 33		18 43		19 03		19 12		19 30
Marks Tey 2	d				17 18					17 49				18 18					18 49				19 18		
Kelvedon	d				17 23					17 54				18 23					18 54				19 23		
Braintree	d			17 04									18 04									19 04			
Braintree Freeport	d			17 06									18 06									19 06			
Cressing	d			17 09									18 09									19 09			
White Notley	d			17 12									18 12									19 12			
Witham 2	d			17a20	17 29			17 46		18 00			18a20	18 29			18 46		19 00			19a20	19 29		
Hatfield Peverel	d				17 33									18 33									19 33		
Chelmsford 3	d		17 21		17 40			17 56		18 09		18 21		18 40			18 56		19 09		19 21		19 40		
Ingatestone	d							18 02									19 02								
Shenfield 3	a				17 50			18 08		18 19				18 50			19 08		19 19				19 50		
Romford	a																								
Stratford 7 ⊖	a		17 45		18 05		18 09	18 22		18 36		18 45		19 05		19 09	19 22		19 36		19 45		20 05		20 09
London Liverpool Street 15 ⊖	a		17 59		18 14		18 22	18 31		18 45		18 59		19 14		19 22	19 31		19 45		19 59		20 14		20 22

		LE	LE	LE	LE	LE	LE	LE	LE	LE	LE	LE		LE	LE	LE	LE	LE	LE	LE	LE		LE	LE	LE
		1	1	1	1	◇1	1	1	1	1	1	1		1	1	◇1	1	1	1	1	1		1	1	◇1
Norwich	d					19 00										20 00			20 30						21 00
Diss	d					19 17										20 17			20 47						21 17
Peterborough 8	d																								
Stowmarket	d					19 29			19 47							20 29									21 29
Needham Market	d								19 52																
Ipswich	a					19 41			20 03							20 41			21 08						21 41
	d					19 43		19 52		20 09						20 43			21 09						21 43
Harwich Town	d		19 28									20 28									21 28				
Dovercourt	d		19 30									20 30									21 30				
Harwich International	d		19 33									20 33						20 45			21 33				
Wrabness	d		19 39									20 39									21 39				
Mistley	d		19 45									20 45									21 45				
Manningtree 2	d		19a50			19 53		20 02		20 20		20a50				20 53		20 58	21 19		21a50				21 53
Walton-on-the-Naze	d				19 00										20 00									21 00	
Frinton-on-Sea	d				19 03										20 03									21 03	
Kirby Cross	d				19 06										20 06									21 06	
Clacton-on-Sea	d	19 05									20 05									21 05					
Thorpe-le-Soken 1	a	19 13			19 12						20 13				20 12					21 13				21 12	
	d	19 13			19 17						20 13				20 17					21 13				21 17	
Weeley	d				19 21										20 21									21 21	
Great Bentley	d				19 24										20 24									21 24	
Alresford (Essex)	d				19 28										20 28									21 28	
Wivenhoe 3	d	19 24			19 32						20 24				20 32					21 24				21 32	
Hythe	d				19 36										20 36									21 36	
Colchester Town	a				19 40										20 40									21 40	
	d				19 44										20 44									21 44	
Colchester 4	a	19 32			19 52	20 02		20 11		20 29	20 32				20 52	21 02		21 07	21 28	21 32				21 52	22 02
Colchester 4	d	19 33		19 43		20 03		20 12		20 30	20 33			20 43		21 03		21 08	21 30	21 33			21 43		22 03
Marks Tey 2	d			19 49				20 18						20 49				21 14					21 49		
Kelvedon	d			19 54				20 23						20 54				21 19					21 54		
Braintree	d						20 04										21 04								
Braintree Freeport	d						20 06										21 06								
Cressing	d						20 09										21 09								
White Notley	d						20 12										21 12								
Witham 2	d	19 46		20 00			20a20	20 29			20 46			21 00			21a20	21 25		21 46			22 00		
Hatfield Peverel	d							20 33										21 29							
Chelmsford 3	d	19 56		20 09		20 21		20 40			20 56			21 09		21 21		21 36		21 56			22 09		22 21
Ingatestone	d	20 02									21 02									22 02					
Shenfield 3	a	20 08		20 19				20 50			21 08			21 19				21 46		22 08			22 19		
Romford	a																								
Stratford 7 ⊖	a	20 22		20 36		20 45		21 05		21 09	21 22			21 34		21 45		22 11		22 26			22 37		
London Liverpool Street 15 ⊖	a	20 31		20 45		20 59		21 14		21 19	21 31			21 43		21 59		22 21	22 18	22 36			22 48		22 54

Sundays
2 September to 9 September

Norwich, Ipswich, Harwich, Clacton, Walton-on-Naze, Colchester and Chelmsford - London

Network Diagram - see first Page of Table 5

		LE 1	LE 1	LE 1	LE 1	LE 1	LE 1	LE 1	LE 1	LE ◇1 ⊡	LE 1	LE 1	LE 1	LE ◇1 ⊡	LE 1	LE 1	LE 1
Norwich	d									22 00				23 05			
Diss	d									22 17				23 22			
Peterborough 8	d																
Stowmarket	d				21 47					22 29		22 47		23 34			23 47
Needham Market	d				21 52							22 52					23 52
Ipswich	a				22 03					22 41		23 03		23 48			00 03
	d		21 52			22 23				22 43							
Harwich Town	d							22 28							23 28		
Dovercourt	d							22 30							23 30		
Harwich International	d							22 33							23 33		
Wrabness	d							22 39							23 39		
Mistley	d							22 45							23 45		
Manningtree 2	d		22 02			22 33		22a50		22 53					23a50		
Walton-on-the-Naze	d						22 00				23 00						
Frinton-on-Sea	d						22 03				23 03						
Kirby Cross	d						22 06				23 06						
Clacton-on-Sea	d			22 05									23 05				
Thorpe-le-Soken 1	a			22 13			22 12				23 12		23 13				
	d			22 13			22 17						23 13				
Weeley	d						22 21						23 17				
Great Bentley	d						22 24						23 20				
Alresford (Essex)	d						22 28						23 24				
Wivenhoe 3	d			22 24			22 32						23 28				
Hythe	d						22 36						23 32				
Colchester Town	a						22 40										
	d						22 44										
Colchester 4	a		22 11	22 32		22 42	22 52			23 02			23 38				
Colchester 4	d		22 12	22 33		22 43				23 03							
Marks Tey 2	d		22 18			22 49											
Kelvedon	d		22 23			22 54											
Braintree	d	22 04							22 56							23 45	
Braintree Freeport	d	22 06							22 58							23 47	
Cressing	d	22 09							23 01							23 50	
White Notley	d	22 12							23 04							23 53	
Witham 2	d	22a20	22 29	22 46		23 00			23a12	23 16						00a01	
Hatfield Peverel	d		22 33														
Chelmsford 3	d		22 40	22 56		23 09				23 25							
Ingatestone	d			23 02													
Shenfield 3	a		22 50	23 08		23 19				23s36							
Romford	a																
Stratford 7 ⊖	a		23 10	23 26		23 38											
London Liverpool Street 15 ⊖	a		23 20	23 36		23 48				00 03							

Sundays
from 16 September

Norwich, Ipswich, Harwich, Clacton, Walton-on-Naze, Colchester and Chelmsford - London

Network Diagram - see first Page of Table 5

		LE ◇1	LE	LE 1	LE 1	LE	LE 1	LE 1	LE ◇1 ⊡	LE 1	LE 1	LE 1	LE 1	LE ◇1 ⊡	LE 1	LE 1	LE 1	LE 1	LE 1	LE ◇1 ⊡	LE 1	LE 1	LE 1
Norwich	d	22p00							07 00					08 00						09 00			
Diss	d	22p17							07 17					08 17						09 17			
Peterborough 8	d																						
Stowmarket	d	22p29	23p47						07 29					08 29						09 29			
Needham Market	d		23p52																				
Ipswich	a	22p41	00 05						07 41					08 41						09 41			
	d	22p43							07 43	07 46			08 09	08 43					09 09	09 43			
Harwich Town	d															08 53						09 53	
Dovercourt	d															08 55						09 55	
Harwich International	d							07 20		08a14						08 58						09 58	
Wrabness	d															09 04						10 04	
Mistley	d															09 10						10 10	
Manningtree 2	d	22p53						07 33	07 53				08 19	08 53		09a15			09 19	09 53		10a15	
Walton-on-the-Naze	d														08 30						09 30		
Frinton-on-Sea	d														08 33						09 33		
Kirby Cross	d														08 36						09 36		
Clacton-on-Sea	d											07 36						08 36					
Thorpe-le-Soken 1	a											07 44			08 42			08 44			09 42		
	d											07 44						08 44					
Weeley	d																						
Great Bentley	d											07 49						08 49					
Alresford (Essex)	d											07 53						08 53					
Wivenhoe 3	d											07 57						08 57					
Hythe	d																						
Colchester Town	a																						
	d																						
Colchester 4	a	23p02						07 42	08 02			08 05	08 29	09 02				09 05	09 29	10 02			
Colchester 4	d	23p03			06 56	07 07	07 26	07 43	08 03			08 06	08 30	09 03				09 06	09 30	10 03			
Marks Tey 2	d				07 02	07a14	07 32	07 49				08 12	08 36					09 12	09 36				
Kelvedon	d				07 07		07 37	07 54					08 41						09 41				
Braintree	d			00 25							08 00						09 00						10 00
Braintree Freeport	d			00 27							08 02						09 02						10 02
Cressing	d			00 30							08 05						09 05						10 05
White Notley	d			00 33							08 08						09 08						10 08
Witham 2	d	23p16		00a41	07 13		07 43	08 00			08a16	08 21	08 47				09a16	09 21	09 47				10a16
Hatfield Peverel	d				07 17		07 47						08 51						09 51				
Chelmsford 3	d	23p25			07 24		07 54	08 09				08 30	08 58					09 30	09 58				
Ingatestone	d				07 31		08 01						09 05						10 05				
Shenfield 3	a	23b36			07 36		08 06	08 19				08 40	09 10					09 40	10 10				
Romford	a						08 22																
Stratford 7 ⊖	a	23b52					08s34	08s49				09s04	09s34					10s04	10s34				
London Liverpool Street 15 ⊖	a	00 02					08 42	08 59	09 03			09 12	09 42	10 01				10 12	10 42	11 01			

		LE 1	LE 1	LE	LE ◇1 ⊡	LE 1	LE 1	LE 1	LE 1	LE 1	LE ◇1 ⊡	LE 1	LE 1	LE 1	LE 1	LE 1	LE 1	LE ◇1 ⊡	LE 1	LE 1	LE 1	LE 1	LE 1
Norwich	d				10 00						11 00							12 00					
Diss	d				10 17						11 17							12 17					
Peterborough 8	d																						
Stowmarket	d			10 18	10 29						11 29						12 18	12 29					
Needham Market	d			10 23													12 23						
Ipswich	a			10 35	10 41						11 41						12 35	12 41					
	d		10 09		10 43					11 09	11 43					12 09		12 43					13 09
Harwich Town	d						10 53						11 53							12 53			
Dovercourt	d						10 55						11 55							12 55			
Harwich International	d						10 58						11 58							12 58			
Wrabness	d						11 04						12 04							13 04			
Mistley	d						11 10						12 10							13 10			
Manningtree 2	d		10 19		10 53		11a15			11 19	11 53		12a15			12 19		12 53		13a15			13 19
Walton-on-the-Naze	d					10 30						11 30							12 30				
Frinton-on-Sea	d					10 33						11 33							12 33				
Kirby Cross	d					10 36						11 36							12 36				
Clacton-on-Sea	d	09 36							10 36						11 36							12 36	
Thorpe-le-Soken 1	a	09 44				10 42			10 44			11 42			11 44				12 42			12 44	
	d	09 44							10 44						11 44							12 44	
Weeley	d																						
Great Bentley	d	09 49							10 49						11 49							12 49	
Alresford (Essex)	d	09 53							10 53						11 53							12 53	
Wivenhoe 3	d	09 57							10 57						11 57							12 57	
Hythe	d																						
Colchester Town	a																						
	d																						
Colchester 4	a	10 05	10 29		11 02				11 05	11 29	12 02				12 05	12 29		13 02				13 05	13 29
Colchester 4	d	10 06	10 30		11 03				11 06	11 30	12 03				12 06	12 30		13 03				13 06	13 30
Marks Tey 2	d	10 12	10 36						11 12	11 36					12 12	12 36						13 12	13 36
Kelvedon	d		10 41							11 41						12 41							13 41
Braintree	d							11 00						12 00							13 00		
Braintree Freeport	d							11 02						12 02							13 02		
Cressing	d							11 05						12 05							13 05		
White Notley	d							11 08						12 08							13 08		
Witham 2	d	10 21	10 47					11a16	11 21	11 47				12a16	12 21	12 47					13a16	13 21	13 47
Hatfield Peverel	d		10 51							11 51						12 51							13 51
Chelmsford 3	d	10 30	10 58						11 30	11 58					12 30	12 58						13 30	13 58
Ingatestone	d		11 05							12 05						13 05							14 05
Shenfield 3	a	10 40	11 10						11 40	12 10					12 40	13 10						13 40	14 10
Romford	a																						
Stratford 7 ⊖	a	11s04	11s34						12s04	12s34					13s04	13s34						14s04	14s34
London Liverpool Street 15 ⊖	a	11 12	11 42		12 01				12 12	12 42	13 01				13 12	13 42		14 01				14 12	14 42

b Previous night, stops to set down only

Sundays from 16 September

Norwich, Ipswich, Harwich, Clacton, Walton-on-Naze, Colchester and Chelmsford - London

Network Diagram - see first Page of Table 5

		LE 1	LE ◇1 ⊡	LE 1	LE 1	LE 1	LE 1	LE 1	LE 1	LE ◇1 ⊡	LE 1	LE 1	LE 1	LE 1	LE 1	LE 1	LE ◇1 ⊡	LE 1	LE 1	LE 1	LE 1	LE 1
Norwich	d		13 00							14 00							15 00					
Diss	d		13 17							14 17							15 17					
Peterborough 8	d	11 46														13 46						
Stowmarket	d	13 13	13 29						14 18	14 29						15 13	15 29					
Needham Market	d								14 23													
Ipswich	a	13 28	13 41						14 35	14 41						15 28	15 41					
	d		13 43					14 09		14 43					15 09		15 43					16 09
Harwich Town	d				13 53							14 53							15 53			
Dovercourt	d				13 55							14 55							15 55			
Harwich International	d				13 58							14 58							15 58			
Wrabness	d				14 04							15 04							16 04			
Mistley	d				14 10							15 10							16 10			
Manningtree 2	d		13 53		14a15			14 19		14 53		15a15			15 19		15 53		16a15			16 19
Walton-on-the-Naze	d			13 30							14 30							15 30				
Frinton-on-Sea	d			13 33							14 33							15 33				
Kirby Cross	d			13 36							14 36							15 36				
Clacton-on-Sea	d						13 36							14 36							15 36	
Thorpe-le-Soken 1	a			13 42			13 44				14 42			14 44				15 42			15 44	
	d						13 44							14 44							15 44	
Weeley	d																					
Great Bentley	d						13 49							14 49							15 49	
Alresford (Essex)	d						13 53							14 53							15 53	
Wivenhoe 3	d						13 57							14 57							15 57	
Hythe	d																					
Colchester Town	a																					
	d																					
Colchester 4	a		14 02				14 05	14 29		15 02				15 05	15 29		16 02				16 05	16 29
Colchester 4	d		14 03				14 06	14 30		15 03				15 06	15 30		16 03				16 06	16 30
Marks Tey 2	d						14 12	14 36						15 12	15 36						16 12	16 36
Kelvedon	d							14 41							15 41							16 41
Braintree	d					14 00							15 00							16 00		
Braintree Freeport	d					14 02							15 02							16 02		
Cressing	d					14 05							15 05							16 05		
White Notley	d					14 08							15 08							16 08		
Witham 2	d					14a16	14 21	14 47					15a16	15 21	15 47					16a16	16 21	16 47
Hatfield Peverel	d							14 51							15 51							16 51
Chelmsford 3	d						14 30	14 58						15 30	15 58						16 30	16 58
Ingatestone	d							15 05							16 05							17 05
Shenfield 3	a						14 40	15 10						15 40	16 10						16 40	17 10
Romford	a																					
Stratford 7 ⊖	a						15s04	15s34						16s04	16s34						17s04	17s34
London Liverpool Street 15 ⊖	a		15 01				15 12	15 42		16 01				16 12	16 42		17 01				17 12	17 42

		LE 1	LE 2 1 ⊡	LE 1	LE 1	LE 1	LE 1	LE ◇1 ⊡		LE 1	LE 1	LE ◇1 ⊡	LE 1	LE 1	LE 1	LE 1	LE 1	LE 1	LE ◇1 ⊡	LE 1	LE 1	LE 1	LE 1	LE 1
Norwich	d		16 00					16 20				17 00							18 00					
Diss	d		16 17					16 37				17 17							18 17					
Peterborough 8	d										15 45													
Stowmarket	d	16 18	16 29					16 49			17 13	17 29						18 18	18 29					
Needham Market	d	16 23																18 23						
Ipswich	a	16 35	16 41					17 01			17 28	17 41						18 35	18 41					
	d		16 43					17 03		17 09		17 43					18 09		18 43					19 09
Harwich Town	d				16 53									17 53							18 53			
Dovercourt	d				16 55									17 55							18 55			
Harwich International	d				16 58									17 58							18 58			
Wrabness	d				17 04									18 04							19 04			
Mistley	d				17 10									18 10							19 10			
Manningtree 2	d		16 53		17a15					17 19		17 53		18a15			18 19		18 53		19a15			19 19
Walton-on-the-Naze	d			16 30									17 30							18 30				
Frinton-on-Sea	d			16 33									17 33							18 33				
Kirby Cross	d			16 36									17 36							18 36				
Clacton-on-Sea	d						16 36									17 36							18 36	
Thorpe-le-Soken 1	a			16 42			16 44						17 42			17 44				18 42			18 44	
	d						16 44									17 44							18 44	
Weeley	d																							
Great Bentley	d						16 49									17 49							18 49	
Alresford (Essex)	d						16 53									17 53							18 53	
Wivenhoe 3	d						16 57									17 57							18 57	
Hythe	d																							
Colchester Town	a																							
	d																							
Colchester 4	a		17 02				17 05		17 18	17 29		18 02				18 05	18 29		19 02				19 05	19 29
Colchester 4	d		17 03				17 06		17 21	17 30		18 03				18 06	18 30		19 03				19 06	19 30
Marks Tey 2	d						17 12			17 36						18 12	18 36						19 12	19 36
Kelvedon	d									17 41							18 41							19 41
Braintree	d					17 00									18 00							19 00		
Braintree Freeport	d					17 02									18 02							19 02		
Cressing	d					17 05									18 05							19 05		
White Notley	d					17 08									18 08							19 08		
Witham 2	d					17a16	17 21			17 47					18a16	18 21	18 47					19a16	19 21	19 47
Hatfield Peverel	d									17 51							18 51							19 51
Chelmsford 3	d						17 30			17 58						18 30	18 58						19 30	19 58
Ingatestone	d									18 05							19 05							20 05
Shenfield 3	a						17 40			18 10						18 40	19 10						19 40	20 10
Romford	a																							
Stratford 7 ⊖	a						18s04			18s34						19s04	19s34						20s04	20s34
London Liverpool Street 15 ⊖	a		18 01				18 12		18 28	18 42		19 01				19 12	19 42		20 01				20 12	20 42

Sundays from 16 September

Norwich, Ipswich, Harwich, Clacton, Walton-on-Naze, Colchester and Chelmsford - London

Network Diagram - see first Page of Table 5

		LE ◇1	LE ◇1 ⊡	LE 1	LE 1	LE 1	LE 1	LE 1	LE 1	LE 1	LE 1	LE ◇1 ⊡	LE 1	LE 1	LE 1	LE 1	LE ◇1	LE ◇1	LE 1	LE 1	LE 1	LE 1
Norwich	d		19 00									20 00						21 00				
Diss	d		19 17									20 17						21 17				
Peterborough 8	d	17 45															19 45					
Stowmarket	d	19 13	19 29								20 18	20 29					21 06	21 29				
Needham Market	d										20 23											
Ipswich	a	19 28	19 41								20 35	20 41					21 18	21 41				
	d	19 28	19 43					20 09			20 35	20 43				21 09	21 19	21 43				
Harwich Town	d				19 53								20 53							21 53		
Dovercourt	d				19 55								20 55							21 55		
Harwich International	d				19 58					20 35	21a04		20 58							21 58		
Wrabness	d				20 04								21 04							22 04		
Mistley	d				20 10								21 10							22 10		
Manningtree 2	d	19 38	19 53		20a15			20 19		20 48		20 53	21a15			21 19	21 29	21 53		22a15		
Walton-on-the-Naze	d			19 30					20 30										21 30			
Frinton-on-Sea	d			19 33					20 33										21 33			
Kirby Cross	d			19 36					20 36										21 36			
Clacton-on-Sea	d						19 36								20 36							21 36
Thorpe-le-Soken 1	a			19 42			19 44		20 42						20 44				21 42			21 44
	d						19 44								20 44							21 44
Weeley	d																					
Great Bentley	d						19 49								20 49							21 49
Alresford (Essex)	d						19 53								20 53							21 53
Wivenhoe 3	d						19 57								20 57							21 57
Hythe	d																					
Colchester Town	a																					
	d																					
Colchester 4	a	19 49	20 02				20 05	20 29		20 57		21 02			21 05	21 29	21 40	22 02				22 05
Colchester 4	d		20 03				20 06	20 30		20 57		21 03			21 06	21 30		22 03				22 06
Marks Tey 2	d						20 12	20 36							21 12	21 36						22 12
Kelvedon	d							20 41								21 41						
Braintree	d					20 00								21 00							22 00	
Braintree Freeport	d					20 02								21 02							22 02	
Cressing	d					20 05								21 05							22 05	
White Notley	d					20 08								21 08							22 08	
Witham 2	d					20a16	20 21	20 47						21a16	21 21	21 47					22a16	22 21
Hatfield Peverel	d							20 51								21 51						
Chelmsford 3	d						20 30	20 58		21 15					21 30	21 58						22 30
Ingatestone	d							21 05								22 05						
Shenfield 3	a						20 40	21 10		21 25					21 40	22 10						22 40
Romford	a																					
Stratford 7 ⊖	a						21s04	21s34		21s51					22s04	22s34						23s04
London Liverpool Street 15 ⊖	a		21 01				21 12	21 42		21 59		22 01			22 12	22 42		23 01				23 12

		LE 1	LE 1	LE 1	LE 1	LE 1	LE ◇1	LE 1	LE 1
Norwich	d						22 00		23 05
Diss	d						22 17		23 22
Peterborough 8	d								
Stowmarket	d			22 18			22 29		23 34
Needham Market	d			22 23					
Ipswich	a			22 35			22 41		23 48
	d	22 09					22 43		
Harwich Town	d							22 53	
Dovercourt	d							22 55	
Harwich International	d							22 58	
Wrabness	d							23 04	
Mistley	d							23 10	
Manningtree 2	d	22 19					22 53	23 15	
Walton-on-the-Naze	d		22 16						
Frinton-on-Sea	d		22 19						
Kirby Cross	d		22 22						
Clacton-on-Sea	d				22 22				
Thorpe-le-Soken 1	a		22 28		22 30				
	d				22 30				
Weeley	d								
Great Bentley	d								
Alresford (Essex)	d								
Wivenhoe 3	d				22 40				
Hythe	d								
Colchester Town	a								
	d								
Colchester 4	a	22 29			22 48		23 02	23 24	
Colchester 4	d	22 30					23 03		
Marks Tey 2	d	22 36							
Kelvedon	d	22 41							
Braintree	d					22 56			
Braintree Freeport	d					22 58			
Cressing	d					23 01			
White Notley	d					23 04			
Witham 2	d	22 47				23a12	23 16		
Hatfield Peverel	d	22 51							
Chelmsford 3	d	22 58					23 25		
Ingatestone	d	23 05							
Shenfield 3	a	23 10					23s36		
Romford	a								
Stratford 7 ⊖	a	23s34					23s57		
London Liverpool Street 15 ⊖	a	23 42					00 08		

Network Diagram for Tables 13, 14, 15, 16, 17

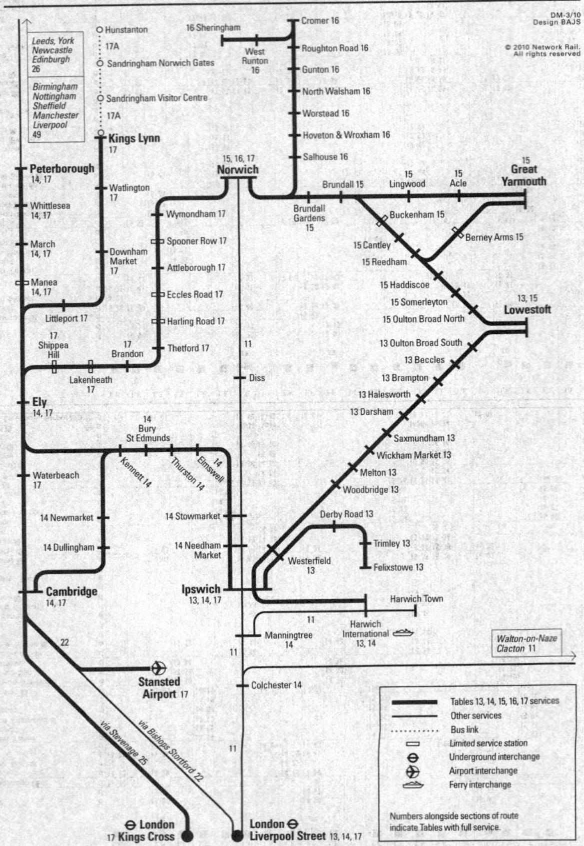

Ipswich - Felixstowe and Lowestoft

Network Diagram - see first Page of Table 13

Mondays to Fridays

Miles	Miles			LE	LE	LE		LE	LE	LE	LE [1]	LE		LE	LE [1]	LE	LE	LE	LE [1]	LE	LE	LE		LE [1]	LE
—	—	London Liverpool Street ⊖	d																						
—	—	Harwich International	d								07 50														
0	—	**Ipswich**	d	05 04	06 04	06 20		07 14		07 35	08a17	08 25		08 58	09 13	09 58	10 13	10 58	11 13	11 58	12 13	12 58		13 13	13 58
3½	0	Westerfield	d	05 10	06 10	06 27		07 20		07 42		08 31		09 04	09 20	10 04	10 20	11 04	11 20	12 04	12 20	13 04		13 20	14 04
—	2½	Derby Road	d	05 15	06 15			07 25				08 36		09 09		10 09		11 09		12 09		13 09			14 09
—	10½	Trimley	d	05 24	06 24			07 34				08 45		09 18		10 18		11 18		12 18		13 18			14 18
—	12¼	**Felixstowe**	a	05 30	06 30			07 40				08 51		09 24		10 24		11 24		12 24		13 24			14 24
10¼	—	Woodbridge	d			06 39				07 54					09 32		10 32		11 32		12 32			13 32	
11½	—	Melton	d			06 43				07 58					09 36		10 36		11 36		12 36			13 36	
15¾	—	Wickham Market	d			06 49				08 04					09 42		10 42		11 42		12 42			13 42	
22½	—	Saxmundham	d			07a00			07 45	08 16					09 54		10a53		11 54		12a53			13 54	
26¾	—	Darsham	d						07 52	08 22					10 00				12 00					14 00	
32	—	Halesworth	d						08 02	08 32					10 10				12 10					14 10	
36	—	Brampton (Suffolk)	d						08 09	08 39					10 17				12 17					14 17	
40¼	—	Beccles	d						08 17	08 47					10 25				12 25					14 25	
46¾	—	Oulton Broad South	d						08 27	08 57					10 35				12 35					14 35	
49	—	**Lowestoft**	a						08 35	09 06					10 44				12 44					14 44	

		LE A	LE	LE [1]	LE	LE		LE		LE [1]	LE	LE	LE	LE [1]	LE	LE	LE	LE [1]		LE [1]	LE
London Liverpool Street ⊖	d																				
Harwich International	d																			21 38	
Ipswich	d	14 13	14 58	15 13	15 54	15 58		16 58		17 13	17 58	18 13	18 58	19 13	19 58	20 13	20 58	21 13		22 13	22 28
Westerfield	d	14 20	15 04	15 20	16 01	16 04		17 04		17 20	18 04	18 20	19 04	19 20	20 04	20 20	21 04	21 20		22 20	22 37
Derby Road	d		15 09			16 09		17 09			18 09		19 09		20 09		21 09				22 42
Trimley	d		15 18			16 18		17 18			18 18		19 18		20 18		21 18				22 51
Felixstowe	a		15 24			16 24		17 24			18 24		19 24		20 24		21 24				22 57
Woodbridge	d	14 32		15 32	16 20					17 32		18 32		19 32		20 32		21 32		22 32	
Melton	d	14 36		15 36	16 24					17 36		18 36		19 36		20 36		21 36		22 36	
Wickham Market	d	14 42		15 42	16 30					17 42		18 42		19 42		20 42		21 42		22 42	
Saxmundham	d	14a53		15 54	16a41					17 54		18 54		19 54		20a53		21 54		22 54	
Darsham	d			16 00						18 00		19 00		20 00				22 00		23 00	
Halesworth	d			16 10						18 10		19 22		20 10				22 10		23 10	
Brampton (Suffolk)	d			16 17						18 17		19 29		20 17				22 17		23 17	
Beccles	d			16 25						18 25		19 37		20 25				22 25		23 25	
Oulton Broad South	d			16 35						18 35		19 47		20 35				22 35		23 35	
Lowestoft	a			16 44						18 44		19 56		20 44				22 44		23 44	

Saturdays

		LE	LE	LE	LE	LE	LE [1]	LE	LE [1]	LE		LE	LE	LE [1]	LE	LE	LE	LE [1]	LE	LE		LE	LE [1]	LE	LE
London Liverpool Street ⊖	d																								
Harwich International	d						07 50																		
Ipswich	d	05 58	06 58	07 13	07 58	08 13	08a17	08 58	09 13	09 58		10 13	10 58	11 13	11 58	12 13	12 58	13 13	13 58	14 13		14 58	15 13	15 58	16 13
Westerfield	d	06 04	07 04	07 20	08 04	08 20		09 04	09 20	10 04		10 20	11 04	11 20	12 04	12 20	13 04	13 20	14 04	14 20		15 04	15 20	16 04	16 20
Derby Road	d	06 09	07 09		08 09			09 09		10 09			11 09		12 09		13 09		14 09			15 09		16 09	
Trimley	d	06 18	07 18		08 18			09 18		10 18			11 18		12 18		13 18		14 18			15 18		16 18	
Felixstowe	a	06 24	07 24		08 24			09 24		10 24			11 24		12 24		13 24		14 24			15 24		16 24	
Woodbridge	d			07 32		08 32			09 32			10 32		11 32		12 32		13 32		14 32			15 32		16 32
Melton	d			07 36		08 36			09 36			10 36		11 36		12 36		13 36		14 36			15 36		16 36
Wickham Market	d			07 42		08 42			09 42			10 42		11 42		12 42		13 42		14 42			15 42		16 42
Saxmundham	d			07 54		08a53			09 54			10a53		11 54		12a53		13 54		14a53			15 54		16a53
Darsham	d			08 00					10 00					12 00				14 00					16 00		
Halesworth	d			08 10					10 10					12 10				14 10					16 10		
Brampton (Suffolk)	d			08 17					10 17					12 17				14 17					16 17		
Beccles	d			08 25					10 25					12 25				14 25					16 25		
Oulton Broad South	d			08 35					10 35					12 35				14 35					16 35		
Lowestoft	a			08 44					10 44					12 44				14 44					16 44		

		LE	LE [1]	LE	LE	LE		LE [1]	LE	LE	LE	LE [1]	LE [1]	LE B	LE C
London Liverpool Street ⊖	d														
Harwich International	d												21 38		
Ipswich	d	16 58	17 13	17 58	18 13	18 58		19 13	19 58	20 13	20 58	21 13	22 13	22 28	22 48
Westerfield	d	17 04	17 20	18 04	18 20	19 04		19 20	20 04	20 20	21 04	21 20	22 20	22 34	22 54
Derby Road	d	17 09		18 09		19 09			20 09		21 09			22 39	22 59
Trimley	d	17 18		18 18		19 18			20 18		21 18			22 48	22 08
Felixstowe	a	17 24		18 24		19 24			20 24		21 24			22 54	22 14
Woodbridge	d		17 32		18 32			19 32		20 32		21 32	22 32		
Melton	d		17 36		18 36			19 36		20 36		21 36	22 36		
Wickham Market	d		17 42		18 42			19 42		20 42		21 42	22 42		
Saxmundham	d		17 54		18a53			19 54		20a53		21 54	22 54		
Darsham	d		18 00					20 00				22 00	23 00		
Halesworth	d		18 10					20 10				22 10	23 10		
Brampton (Suffolk)	d		18 17					20 17				22 17	23 17		
Beccles	d		18 25					20 25				22 25	23 25		
Oulton Broad South	d		18 35					20 35				22 35	23 35		
Lowestoft	a		18 44					20 44				22 44	23 44		

A From 1 October may be subject to bus replacement
B Not 28 July to 11 August, 1 and 8 September
C 28 July to 11 August, 1 and 8 September

Sundays

Ipswich - Felixstowe and Lowestoft

Network Diagram - see first Page of Table 13

		LE ■ A	LE B	LE ■	LE	LE	LE ■	LE	LE	LE	LE	LE	LE ■	LE	LE	LE ■	LE	LE	LE	LE ■ C	LE ■
London Liverpool Street ⊖	d																				
Harwich International	d	08§30																		21§10	
Ipswich	d	08a53	09§55	10 00	10 55	11 55	12 00	12 55	13 55	14 00	14 55	15 55	16 00	16 55	17 55	18 00	18 55	19 55	20 00	21a36	22 00
Westerfield	d		10§01	10 07	11 01	12 01	12 07	13 01	14 01	14 07	15 01	16 01	16 07	17 01	18 01	18 07	19 01	20 01	20 07		22 07
Derby Road	d		10§06		11 06	12 06		13 06	14 06		15 06	16 06		17 06	18 06		19 06	20 06			
Trimley	d		10§15		11 15	12 15		13 15	14 15		15 15	16 15		17 15	18 15		19 15	20 15			
Felixstowe	a		10§21		11 21	12 21		13 21	14 21		15 21	16 21		17 21	18 21		19 21	20 21			
Woodbridge	d			10 19			12 19			14 19			16 19			18 19			20 19		22 19
Melton	d			10 23			12 23			14 23			16 23			18 23			20 23		22 23
Wickham Market	d			10 29			12 29			14 29			16 29			18 29			20 29		22 29
Saxmundham	d			10 41			12 41			14 41			16 41			18 41			20 41		22 41
Darsham	d			10 47			12 47			14 47			16 47			18 47			20 47		22 47
Halesworth	d			10 57			12 57			14 57			16 57			18 57			20 57		22 57
Brampton (Suffolk)	d			11 04			13 04			15 04			17 04			19 04			21 04		23 04
Beccles	d			11 12			13 12			15 12			17 12			19 12			21 12		23 12
Oulton Broad South	d			11 22			13 22			15 22			17 22			19 22			21 22		23 22
Lowestoft	a			11 31			13 31			15 31			17 31			19 31			21 31		23 31

A until 12 August, from 16 September

B until 9 September

C until 22 July, from 19 August, not 2 September, 9 September

Mondays to Fridays

Lowestoft and Felixstowe - Ipswich

Network Diagram - see first Page of Table 13

Miles	Miles			LE	LE ■	LE	LE ■	LE ■	LE	LE	LE	LE	LE ■	LE	LE A	LE	LE ■	LE	LE	LE	LE ■	LE	LE A
0	—	**Lowestoft**	d		05 25		06 11	06 42		07 27			09 08				11 08				13 08		
2¼	—	Oulton Broad South	d		05 32		06 18	06 49		07 34			09 15				11 15				13 15		
8½	—	Beccles	d		05 41		06 27	06 58		07 43			09 24				11 24				13 24		
13	—	Brampton (Suffolk)	d		05 49		06 35	07 06		07 51			09 32				11 32				13 32		
17	—	Halesworth	d		05 57		06 43	07 14		07 59			09 40				11 40				13 40		
22¼	—	Darsham	d		06 05		06 51	07 22		08 07			09 48				11 48				13 48		
26½	—	Saxmundham	d		06 14		07 05	07 31		08 18			09 57		10 57		11 57		12 57		13 57		14 57
33¼	—	Wickham Market	d		06 23		07 14	07 40		08 27			10 06		11 06		12 06		13 06		14 06		15 06
37¼	—	Melton	d		06 30		07 21	07 47		08 34			10 13		11 13		12 13		13 13		14 13		15 13
38¾	—	Woodbridge	d		06 35		07 26	07 52		08 39			10 18		11 18		12 18		13 18		14 18		15 18
—	0	**Felixstowe**	d	05 34		06 38			07 48		08 54	09 28		10 28		11 28		12 28		13 28		14 28	
—	1¾	Trimley	d	05 37		06 41			07 51		08 57	09 31		10 31		11 31		12 31		13 31		14 31	
—	9¾	Derby Road	d	05 47		06 51			08 01		09 10	09 41		10 41		11 41		12 41		13 41		14 41	
45½	12¼	Westerfield	d	05 52	06 46	06 56	07 37	08 03	08 07	08 50	09 15	09 46	10 29	10 46	11 29	11 46	12 29	12 46	13 29	13 46	14 29	14 46	15 29
49	—	**Ipswich**	a	06 00	06 53	07 04	07 44	08 10	08 15	08 57	09 25	09 54	10 36	10 54	11 36	11 54	12 36	12 54	13 36	13 54	14 36	14 54	15 36
—	—		d		06 59																		
—	—	Harwich International	a		07 28																		
—	—	London Liverpool Street ⊖	a																				

		LE	LE ■	LE	LE	LE	LE ■	LE	LE	LE ■	LE	LE ■	LE	LE	LE	LE
Lowestoft	d		15 08				17 08			18 49					21 08	
Oulton Broad South	d		15 15				17 15			18 56					21 15	
Beccles	d		15 24				17 24			19 05					21 24	
Brampton (Suffolk)	d		15 32				17 32			19 13					21 32	
Halesworth	d		15 40				17 40			19 21					21 40	
Darsham	d		15 48				17 48			19 29					21 48	
Saxmundham	d		15 57		17 09		17 57			19 57			20 57		21 57	
Wickham Market	d		16 06		17 18		18 06			20 06			21 06		22 06	
Melton	d		16 13		17 25		18 13			20 13			21 13		22 13	
Woodbridge	d		16 18		17 30		18 18			20 18			21 18		22 18	
Felixstowe	d	15 28		16 28		17 28		18 28	19 28		20 28			21 28		23 01
Trimley	d	15 31		16 31		17 31		18 31	19 31		20 31			21 31		23 04
Derby Road	d	15 41		16 41		17 41		18 41	19 41		20 41			21 41		23 14
Westerfield	d	15 46	16 29	16 46	17 41	17 46	18 29	18 46	19 46	20 29	20 46		21 29	21 46	22 29	23 19
Ipswich	a	15 54	16 36	16 54	17 49	17 54	18 36	18 54	19 54	20 37	20 54		21 36	21 54	22 36	23 27
	d											21 00				
Harwich International	a											21 29				
London Liverpool Street ⊖	a															

Saturdays

		LE	LE ■	LE ■	LE	LE ■	LE	LE	LE	LE ■	LE	LE	LE	LE ■	LE	LE	LE	LE ■	LE	LE	LE	LE ■	LE
Lowestoft	d			06 08		07 08				09 08				11 08				13 08				15 08	
Oulton Broad South	d			06 15		07 15				09 15				11 15				13 15				15 15	
Beccles	d			06 24		07 24				09 24				11 24				13 24				15 24	
Brampton (Suffolk)	d			06 32		07 32				09 32				11 32				13 32				15 32	
Halesworth	d			06 40		07 40				09 40				11 40				13 40				15 40	
Darsham	d			06 48		07 48				09 48				11 48				13 48				15 48	
Saxmundham	d			06 57		07 57		08 57		09 57		10 57		11 57		12 57		13 57		14 57		15 57	
Wickham Market	d			07 06		08 06		09 06		10 06		11 06		12 06		13 06		14 06		15 06		16 06	
Melton	d			07 13		08 13		09 13		10 13		11 13		12 13		13 13		14 13		15 13		16 13	
Woodbridge	d			07 18		08 18		09 18		10 18		11 18		12 18		13 18		14 18		15 18		16 18	
Felixstowe	d	06 28			07 28		08 28		09 28		10 28		11 28		12 28		13 28		14 28		15 28		16 28
Trimley	d	06 31			07 31		08 31		09 31		10 31		11 31		12 31		13 31		14 31		15 31		16 31
Derby Road	d	06 41			07 41		08 41		09 41		10 41		11 41		12 41		13 41		14 41		15 41		16 41
Westerfield	d	06 46		07 29	07 46	08 29	08 46	09 29	09 46	10 29	10 46	11 29	11 46	12 29	12 46	13 29	13 46	14 29	14 46	15 29	15 46	16 29	16 46
Ipswich	a	06 54		07 36	07 54	08 36	08 54	09 36	09 54	10 36	10 54	11 36	11 54	12 36	12 54	13 36	13 54	14 36	14 54	15 36	15 54	16 36	16 54
	d		06 59																				
Harwich International	a		07 28																				
London Liverpool Street ⊖	a																						

		LE	LE	LE ■	LE	LE	LE	LE ■	LE	LE ■	LE	LE	LE	LE B	LE C
Lowestoft	d			17 08				19 08					21 08		
Oulton Broad South	d			17 15				19 15					21 15		
Beccles	d			17 24				19 24					21 24		
Brampton (Suffolk)	d			17 32				19 32					21 32		
Halesworth	d			17 40				19 40					21 40		
Darsham	d			17 48				19 48					21 48		
Saxmundham	d	16 57		17 57		18 57		19 57			20 57		21 57		
Wickham Market	d	17 06		18 06		19 06		20 06			21 06		22 06		
Melton	d	17 13		18 13		19 13		20 13			21 13		22 13		
Woodbridge	d	17 18		18 18		19 18		20 18			21 18		22 18		
Felixstowe	d		17 28		18 28		19 28		20 28			21 28		22§58	23§18
Trimley	d		17 31		18 31		19 31		20 31			21 31		23§01	23§21
Derby Road	d		17 41		18 41		19 41		20 41			21 41		23§11	23§31
Westerfield	d	17 29	17 46	18 29	18 46	19 29	19 46	20 29	20 46		21 29	21 46	22 29	23§16	23§36
Ipswich	a	17 36	17 54	18 36	18 54	19 36	19 54	20 36	20 54		21 36	21 54	22 36	23§24	23§44
	d									21 00					
Harwich International	a									21 29					
London Liverpool Street ⊖	a														

A From 1 October may be subject to bus replacement

B 28 July to 11 August, 1 and 8 September

C 28 July to 11 August, 1 and 8 September

Table 13

Sundays

Lowestoft and Felixstowe - Ipswich

Network Diagram - see first Page of Table 13

		LE	LE	LE	LE	LE	LE	LE	LE	LE		LE	LE	LE	LE	LE	LE	LE	LE	LE	LE		LE
		■	■	A	■							■			■					■			■
Lowestoft	d		08 05		10 05			12 05				14 05			16 05			18 05					20 05
Oulton Broad South	d		08 12		10 12			12 12				14 12			16 12			18 12					20 12
Beccles	d		08 21		10 21			12 21				14 21			16 21			18 21					20 21
Brampton (Suffolk)	d		08 29		10 29			12 29				14 29			16 29			18 29					20 29
Halesworth	d		08 37		10 37			12 37				14 37			16 37			18 37					20 37
Darsham	d		08 45		10 45			12 45				14 45			16 45			18 45					20 45
Saxmundham	d		08 54		10 54			12 54				14 54			16 54			18 54					20 54
Wickham Market	d		09 03		11 03			13 03				15 03			17 03			19 03					21 03
Melton	d		09 10		11 10			13 10				15 10			17 10			19 10					21 10
Woodbridge	d		09 15		11 15			13 15				15 15			17 15			19 15					21 15
Felixstowe	d			10 25		11 25	12 25		13 25	14 25			15 25	16 25		17 25	18 25		19 25		20 25		
Trimley	d			10 28		11 28	12 28		13 28	14 28			15 28	16 28		17 28	18 28		19 28		20 28		
Derby Road	d			10 38		11 38	12 38		13 38	14 38			15 38	16 38		17 38	18 38		19 38		20 38		
Westerfield	d		09 26	10 43	11 26	11 43	12 43	13 26	13 43	14 43		15 26	15 43	16 43	17 26	17 43	18 43	19 26	19 43		20 43		21 26
Ipswich	a		09 33	10 50	11 33	11 50	12 50	13 33	13 50	14 50		15 33	15 50	16 50	17 33	17 50	18 50	19 33	19 50		20 50		21 33
	d	07 46																		20 35			
Harwich International	a	08 14																		21 04			
London Liverpool Street ⊖	a																						

A until 9 September

Table 14

Mondays to Fridays

Ipswich - Bury St. Edmunds, Cambridge, Ely and Peterborough

Network Diagram - see first Page of Table 13

Miles	Miles	Miles			LE	XC	LE	LE	LE	LE	LE	LE	LE	LE	LE	LE	LE	LE	LE	LE	LE	LE	LE
						◇■	◇■	■	■	■	■	■	■	■	■	■	■	■	■	■	■	■	■
—	—	—	London Liverpool Street ⊖	d																			
—	—	—	Colchester	d			05 40																
—	—	—	Manningtree	d			05 49																
—	—	0	Harwich International	d							07 50												
0	0	18	**Ipswich**	d	05 10		06 00	06 16	06 56	08 03	08 19	09 19	10 00	10 19	11 19	12 00	12 19	13 19	14 00	14 19	15 19	16 00	16 19
8¼	—	—	Needham Market	d	05 20			06 25	07 05		08 28	09 28		10 28	11 28		12 28	13 28		14 28	15 28		16 28
11¾	11¾	—	Stowmarket	d	05 26		06 12	06 31	07 11	08 15	08 34	09 34	10 12	10 34	11 34	12 12	12 34	13 34	14 12	14 34	15 34	16 12	16 34
17¾	—	—	Elmswell	d	05 35			06 39	07 19		08 42	09 42		10 42	11 42		12 42	13 42		14 42	15 42		16 42
22¼	—	—	Thurston	d	05 41			06 45	07 25		08 48	09 48		10 48	11 48		12 48	13 48		14 48	15 48		16 48
—	—	—	**Bury St Edmunds**	a	05 48		06 28	06 51	07 31	08 31	08 54	09 54	10 28	10 54	11 54	12 28	12 54	13 54	14 28	14 54	15 54	16 28	16 54
26¼	26¼	—	**Bury St Edmunds**	d	05 49		06 29	06 53	07 32	08 31	08 56	09 56	10 29	10 56	11 56	12 29	12 56	13 56	14 29	14 56	15 56	16 29	16 56
36	—	—	Kennett	d	06 00			07 03	07 42			10 06			12 06			14 06			16 06		17 06
41	—	—	Newmarket	d	06 09			07 13	07 51		09 15	10 16		11 15	12 16		13 15	14 16		15 15	16 16		17 16
44¼	—	—	Dullingham	d	06 14			07 18	08 00		09 20			11 20			13 20			15 20			
55½	—	—	**Cambridge**	a	06 36			07 39	08 19		09 39	10 39		11 39	12 39		13 39	14 39		15 39	16 39		17 39
—	50¾	—	**Ely** ■	a			06 59			09 00			10 58			12 58			14 58			16 58	
—	—	—		d		05 30	07 00			09 00			10 58			12 58			14 58			16 58	
—	—	—	Manea	d																			
—	66¼	—	March	d		05 46	07 16			09 17			11 15			13 15			15 15			17 15	
—	74	—	Whittlesea	d		05 58	07 27			09 28			11 26			13 26			15 26			17 26	
—	81¼	—	**Peterborough** ■	a		06 08	07 38			09 39			11 37			13 37			15 37			17 37	

		LE	LE	LE	LE	LE	LE	LE	LE
		■	■	■	■	■	■		
London Liverpool Street ⊖	d								
Colchester	d								
Manningtree	d								
Harwich International	d								
Ipswich	d	17 19	17 49	18 16	19 10	20 00	20 19	21 16	22 16
Needham Market	d	17 28	17 58	18 25	19 19		20 28	21 26	22 26
Stowmarket	d	17 34	18 04	18 31	19 25	20 12	20 34	21 32	22 32
Elmswell	d	17 42	18 12	18 39	19 33		20 42	21 41	22 41
Thurston	d	17 48	18 18	18 45	19 39		20 48	21 47	22 47
Bury St Edmunds	a	17 54	18 24	18 51	19 45	20 28	20 54	21 54	22 54
Bury St Edmunds	d	17 56	18 25	18 56	19 56	20 29	20 56	21 55	
Kennett	d	18 06			20 06			22 06	
Newmarket	d	18 16		19 15	20 16		21 15	22 16	
Dullingham	d			19 20			21 20	22 22	
Cambridge	a	18 39		19 39	20 39		21 39	22 39	
Ely ■	a		18 52			21 00			
	d		19 00			21 00			
Manea	d								
March	d		19 16			21 17			
Whittlesea	d		19 28			21 28			
Peterborough ■	a		19 38			21 39			

Saturdays

		LE	XC	LE	LE	LE	LE	LE	LE	LE	LE	LE	LE	LE	LE	LE	LE	LE	LE	LE	LE	LE	LE
			◇■	◇■	■	■	■	■	■	■	■	■	■	■	■	■	■	■	■	■	■	■	■
London Liverpool Street ⊖	d																						
Colchester	d			05 40																			
Manningtree	d			05 49																			
Harwich International	d							07 50															
Ipswich	d	05 10		06 00	06 16	07 19	08 00	08 19	09 19	10 00	10 19	11 19	12 00	12 19	13 19	14 00	14 19	15 19	16 00	16 19	17 19	18 00	18 19
Needham Market	d	05 20			06 25	07 28		08 28	09 28		10 28	11 28		12 28	13 28		14 28	15 28		16 28	17 28		18 28
Stowmarket	d	05 26		06 12	06 31	07 34	08 12	08 34	09 34	10 12	10 34	11 34	12 12	12 34	13 34	14 12	14 34	15 34	16 12	16 34	17 34	18 12	18 34
Elmswell	d	05 35			06 39	07 42		08 42	09 42		10 42	11 42		12 42	13 42		14 42	15 42		16 42	17 42		18 42
Thurston	d	05 41			06 45	07 48		08 48	09 48		10 48	11 48		12 48	13 48		14 48	15 48		16 48	17 48		18 48
Bury St Edmunds	a	05 48		06 28	06 51	07 54	08 28	08 54	09 54	10 28	10 54	11 54	12 28	12 54	13 54	14 28	14 54	15 54	16 28	16 54	17 54	18 28	18 54
Bury St Edmunds	d	05 49		06 29	06 53	07 56	08 29	08 56	09 56	10 29	10 56	11 56	12 29	12 56	13 56	14 29	14 56	15 56	16 29	16 56	17 56	18 29	18 56
Kennett	d	06 00			07 03	08 06			10 06			12 06			14 06			16 06		17 06	18 06		
Newmarket	d	06 09			07 13	08 16		09 15	10 16		11 15	12 16		13 15	14 16		15 15	16 16		17 16	18 16		19 15
Dullingham	d	06 14			07 18	08 21		09 20			11 20			13 20			15 20						19 20
Cambridge	a	06 36			07 39	08 39		09 39	10 39		11 39	12 39		13 39	14 39		15 39	16 39		17 39	18 39		19 39
Ely ■	a			06 59			08 58			10 58			12 58			14 58			16 58			18 58	
	d		05 30	07 00			08 58			10 58			12 58			14 58			16 58			19 00	
Manea	d																						
March	d		05 46	07 16			09 15			11 15			13 15			15 15			17 15			19 16	
Whittlesea	d		05 58	07 27			09 26			11 26			13 26			15 26			17 26			19 28	
Peterborough ■	a		06 08	07 38			09 38			11 37			13 37			15 37			17 37			19 38	

Ipswich - Bury St. Edmunds, Cambridge, Ely and Peterborough

Saturdays

Network Diagram - see first Page of Table 13

	LE [1]	LE [1] A	LE [1] B	LE [1]	LE	LE
London Liverpool Street [15] ⊖ d						
Colchester d						
Manningtree d						
Harwich International d						
Ipswich d	19 19	20 00	20 00	20 19	21 16	22 16
Needham Market d	19 28			20 28	21 26	22 26
Stowmarket d	19 34	20 12	20 12	20 34	21 32	22 32
Elmswell d	19 42			20 42	21 41	22 41
Thurston d	19 48			20 48	21 47	22 47
Bury St Edmunds a	19 54	20 28	20 28	20 54	21 54	22 54
Bury St Edmunds d	19 56	20 29	20 29	20 56	21 55	
Kennett d	20 06				22 06	
Newmarket d	20 16			21 15	22 16	
Dullingham d				21 20	22 22	
Cambridge a	20 39			21 39	22 39	
Ely [4] a		20 58	20 58			
d		20 58	20 59			
Manea d						
March d		21 15	21 15			
Whittlesea d		21 26	21 27			
Peterborough [8] a		21 37	21 37			

Sundays
until 22 July

	LE [1]	LE	LE [1]	LE ◇[1]	LE [1]	LE [1]	LE [1]	LE [1]	LE [1]	LE [1]	LE [1]	LE [1]	LE [1]	LE
London Liverpool Street [15] ⊖ d														
Colchester d				09 32										
Manningtree d				09 40										
Harwich International d			08 30											
Ipswich d	07 55	08 45	09 02	09 55	11 02	11 55	13 02	13 55	15 02	15 55	17 02	17 55	19 02	21 02
Needham Market d			09 12		11 12		13 12		15 12		17 12		19 12	21 12
Stowmarket d	08 07	08 59	09 18	10 07	11 18	12 07	13 18	14 07	15 18	16 07	17 18	18 07	19 18	21 18
Elmswell d			09 27		11 27		13 27		15 27		17 27		19 27	21 27
Thurston d			09 33		11 33		13 33		15 33		17 33		19 33	21 33
Bury St Edmunds a	08 23	09 17	09 40	10 23	11 40	12 23	13 40	14 23	15 40	16 23	17 40	18 23	19 40	21 40
Bury St Edmunds d	08 24		09 41	10 24	11 41	12 24	13 41	14 24	15 41	16 24	17 41	18 24	19 41	21 41
Kennett d			09 52		11 52		13 52		15 52		17 52		19 52	21 52
Newmarket d			10 01		12 01		14 01		16 01		18 01		20 01	22 01
Dullingham d			10 06		12 06		14 06		16 06		18 06		20 06	22 06
Cambridge a			10 24		12 24		14 25		16 25		18 25		20 24	22 24
Ely [4] a	08 51			10 51		12 51		14 51		16 51		18 51		
d	08 52			10 52		12 52		14 52		16 52		18 52		
Manea d														
March d	09 09			11 09		13 09		15 09		17 09		19 09		
Whittlesea d	09 20			11 20		13 20		15 20		17 20		19 20		
Peterborough [8] a	09 36			11 36		13 31		15 31		17 31		19 32		

Sundays
29 July to 12 August

	LE [1]	LE Bus	LE [1]	LE [1]	LE Bus	LE	LE [1]	LE Bus	LE [1]	LE [1]	LE Bus	LE	LE [1]	LE Bus	LE [1]	LE [1]	LE Bus	LE	LE [1]	LE Bus	LE [1]	LE [1]	LE Bus
London Liverpool Street [15] ⊖ d																							
Colchester d																							
Manningtree d																							
Harwich International d																							
Ipswich d	07 17			08 17			09 17			10 17			11 17			12 17			13 17			14 17	
Needham Market d	07 26			08 26			09 26			10 26			11 26			12 26			13 26			14 26	
Stowmarket d	07 32			08 32			09 32			10 32			11 32			12 32			13 32			14 32	
Elmswell d	07 40			08 40			09 40			10 40			11 40			12 40			13 40			14 40	
Thurston d	07 46			08 46			09 46			10 46			11 46			12 46			13 46			14 46	
Bury St Edmunds a	07 52			08 52			09 52			10 52			11 52			12 52			13 52			14 52	
Bury St Edmunds d		07 57			08 57			09 57			10 57			11 57			12 57			13 57			14 57
Kennett d					09 17						11 17						13 17						15 17
Newmarket d					09a32	09 40					11a32	11 40					13a32	13 40					15a32
Dullingham d						09 46						11 46						13 46					
Cambridge a						10 03						12 03						14 03					
Ely [4] a		08 42						10 42						12 42						14 42			
d			08 52						10 52						12 52						14 52		
Manea d																							
March d			09 09						11 09						13 09						15 09		
Whittlesea d			09 20						11 20						13 20						15 20		
Peterborough [8] a			09 36						11 36						13 31						15 31		

A 28 July, 4 August, 11 August, 1 September, 8 September

B until 21 July, from 18 August, not 1 September, 8 September

Ipswich - Bury St. Edmunds, Cambridge, Ely and Peterborough

Sundays
29 July to 12 August

Network Diagram - see first Page of Table 13

	LE	LE [1]	LE Bus	LE [1]	LE [1]	LE Bus	LE	LE [1]	LE Bus	LE [1]	LE [1]	LE Bus	LE	LE [1]	LE Bus	LE [1]	LE [1]	LE Bus	LE	LE [1]	LE Bus	LE	LE [1]
London Liverpool Street [15] ⊖ d																							
Colchester d																							
Manningtree d																							
Harwich International d																							
Ipswich d		15 17			16 17			17 17			18 17			19 17			20 17			21 17		22 17	23 17
Needham Market d		15 26			16 26			17 26			18 26			19 26			20 26			21 26		22 27	23 26
Stowmarket d		15 32			16 32			17 32			18 32			19 32			20 32			21 32		22 33	23 32
Elmswell d		15 40			16 40			17 40			18 40			19 40			20 40			21 40		22 42	23 40
Thurston d		15 46			16 46			17 46			18 46			19 46			20 46			21 46		22 48	23 46
Bury St Edmunds a		15 52			16 52			17 52			18 52			19 52			20 52			21 52		22 55	23 52
Bury St Edmunds d			15 57			16 57			18 57			18 57			19 57			20 57			21 57		
Kennett d						17 17						19 17						21 17			22 17		
Newmarket d	15 40					17a32	17 40					19a32	19 40					21a32	21 40		22 32		
Dullingham d	15 46						17 46						19 46						21 46		22 42		
Cambridge a	16 03						18 03						20 03						22 03		23 12		
Ely [4] a			16 42						18 42						20 42								
d				16 52						18 52						20 52							
Manea d																							
March d				17 09						19 09						21 09							
Whittlesea d				17 20						19 20						21 20							
Peterborough [8] a				17 31						19 32						21 31							

Sundays
19 August to 26 August

	LE ◇[1]	LE [1]	LE [1]	LE [1]	LE [1]	LE [1]	LE [1]	LE [1]	LE [1]	LE [1]
London Liverpool Street [15] ⊖ d										
Colchester d	09 32									
Manningtree d	09 40									
Harwich International d										
Ipswich d	09 55	11 02	11 55	13 02	13 55	15 02	15 55	17 02	17 55	19 02
Needham Market d		11 12		13 12		15 12		17 12		19 12
Stowmarket d	10 07	11 18	12 07	13 18	14 07	15 18	16 07	17 18	18 07	19 18
Elmswell d		11 27		13 27		15 27		17 27		19 27
Thurston d		11 33		13 33		15 33		17 33		19 33
Bury St Edmunds a	10 23	11 40	12 23	13 40	14 23	15 40	16 23	17 40	18 23	19 40
Bury St Edmunds d	10 24	11 41	12 24	13 41	14 24	15 41	16 24	17 41	18 24	19 41
Kennett d		11 52		13 52		15 52		17 52		19 52
Newmarket d		12 01		14 01		16 01		18 01		20 01
Dullingham d		12 06		14 06		16 06		18 06		20 06
Cambridge a		12 24		14 25		16 25		18 25		20 24
Ely [4] a	10 51		12 51		14 51		16 51		18 51	
d	10 52		12 52		14 52		16 52		18 52	
Manea d										
March d	11 09		13 09		15 09		17 09		19 09	
Whittlesea d	11 20		13 20		15 20		17 20		19 20	
Peterborough [8] a	11 36		13 31		15 31		17 31		19 32	

Sundays
2 September to 9 September

	LE [1]	LE Bus	LE [1]	LE [1]	LE Bus	LE	LE [1]	LE Bus	LE [1]	LE [1]	LE Bus	LE	LE [1]	LE Bus	LE [1]	LE [1]	LE Bus	LE	LE [1]	LE Bus	LE [1]	LE [1]	LE Bus
London Liverpool Street [15] ⊖ d																							
Colchester d																							
Manningtree d																							
Harwich International d																							
Ipswich d	07 17			08 17			09 17			10 17			11 17			12 17			13 17			14 17	
Needham Market d	07 26			08 26			09 26			10 26			11 26			12 26			13 26			14 26	
Stowmarket d	07 32			08 32			09 32			10 32			11 32			12 32			13 32			14 32	
Elmswell d	07 40			08 40			09 40			10 40			11 40			12 40			13 40			14 40	
Thurston d	07 46			08 46			09 46			10 46			11 46			12 46			13 46			14 46	
Bury St Edmunds a	07 52			08 52			09 52			10 52			11 52			12 52			13 52			14 52	
Bury St Edmunds d		07 57			08 57			09 57			10 57			11 57			12 57			13 57			14 57
Kennett d					09 17						11 17						13 17						15 17
Newmarket d					09a32	09 40					11a32	11 40					13a32	13 40					15a32
Dullingham d						09 46						11 46						13 46					
Cambridge a						10 03						12 03						14 03					
Ely [4] a		08 42						10 42						12 42						14 42			
d			08 52						10 52						12 52						14 52		
Manea d																							
March d			09 09						11 09						13 09						15 09		
Whittlesea d			09 20						11 20						13 20						15 20		
Peterborough [8] a			09 36						11 36						13 31						15 31		

Sundays

2 September to 9 September

Ipswich - Bury St. Edmunds, Cambridge, Ely and Peterborough

Network Diagram - see first Page of Table 13

		LE	LE ■	LE 🚌	LE ■	LE ■	LE 🚌	LE	LE ■	LE 🚌	LE ■	LE ■	LE 🚌
London Liverpool Street ⊖	d												
Colchester	d												
Manningtree	d												
Harwich International	d												
Ipswich	d		15 17			16 17			17 17			18 17	
Needham Market	d		15 26			16 26			17 26			18 26	
Stowmarket	d		15 32			16 32			17 32			18 32	
Elmswell	d		15 40			16 40			17 40			18 40	
Thurston	d		15 46			16 46			17 46			18 46	
Bury St Edmunds	a		15 52			16 52			17 52			18 52	
Bury St Edmunds	d			15 57			16 57			18 57			18 57
Kennett	d						17 17						19 17
Newmarket	d	15 40					17a32	17 40					19a32
Dullingham	d	15 46						17 46					
Cambridge	a	16 03						18 03					
Ely ■	a			16 42						18 42			
	d				16 52						18 52		
Manea	d												
March	d				17 09						19 09		
Whittlesea	d				17 20						19 20		
Peterborough ■	a				17 31						19 32		

		LE	LE ■	LE 🚌	LE ■	LE ■	LE 🚌	LE	LE ■	LE 🚌	LE	LE ■
London Liverpool Street ⊖	d											
Colchester	d											
Manningtree	d											
Harwich International	d											
Ipswich	d		19 17			20 17			21 17		22 17	23 17
Needham Market	d		19 26			20 26			21 26		22 27	23 26
Stowmarket	d		19 32			20 32			21 32		22 33	23 32
Elmswell	d		19 40			20 40			21 40		22 42	23 40
Thurston	d		19 46			20 46			21 46		22 48	23 46
Bury St Edmunds	a		19 52			20 52			21 52		22 55	23 52
Bury St Edmunds	d			19 57			20 57			21 57		
Kennett	d						21 17			22 17		
Newmarket	d	19 40					21a32	21 40		22 32		
Dullingham	d	19 46						21 46		22 42		
Cambridge	a	20 03						22 03		23 12		
Ely ■	a			20 42								
	d				20 52							
Manea	d											
March	d				21 09							
Whittlesea	d				21 20							
Peterborough ■	a				21 31							

Sundays

from 16 September

		LE	LE ■	LE ◇■	LE ■	LE ■	LE ■	LE ■	LE ■	LE ■	LE ■	LE ■	LE ■	LE
London Liverpool Street ⊖	d													
Colchester	d			09 32										
Manningtree	d			09 40										
Harwich International	d		08 30											
Ipswich	d	08 45	09 02	09 55	11 02	11 55	13 02	13 55	15 02	15 55	17 02	17 55	19 02	21 02
Needham Market	d		09 12		11 12		13 12		15 12		17 12		19 12	21 12
Stowmarket	d	08 59	09 18	10 07	11 18	12 07	13 18	14 07	15 18	16 07	17 18	18 07	19 18	21 18
Elmswell	d		09 27		11 27		13 27		15 27		17 27		19 27	21 27
Thurston	d		09 33		11 33		13 33		15 33		17 33		19 33	21 33
Bury St Edmunds	a	09 17	09 40	10 23	11 40	12 23	13 40	14 23	15 40	16 23	17 40	18 23	19 40	21 40
Bury St Edmunds	d		09 41	10 24	11 41	12 24	13 41	14 24	15 41	16 24	17 41	18 24	19 41	21 41
Kennett	d		09 52		11 52		13 52		15 52		17 52		19 52	21 52
Newmarket	d		10 01		12 01		14 01		16 01		18 01		20 01	22 01
Dullingham	d		10 06		12 06		14 06		16 06		18 06		20 06	22 06
Cambridge	a		10 24		12 24		14 25		16 25		18 25		20 24	22 24
Ely ■	a			10 51		12 51		14 51		16 51		18 51		
	d			10 52		12 52		14 52		16 52		18 52		
Manea	d													
March	d			11 09		13 09		15 09		17 09		19 09		
Whittlesea	d			11 20		13 20		15 20		17 20		19 20		
Peterborough ■	a			11 36		13 31		15 31		17 31		19 32		

Mondays to Fridays

Peterborough, Ely, Cambridge and Bury St. Edmunds - Ipswich

Network Diagram - see first Page of Table 13

Miles	Miles	Miles			LE MX	LE MO A	LE ■	LE	LE ■ B	LE ■	LE ◇■	LE	LE ■
0	—	—	**Peterborough** ■	d									
7	—	—	Whittlesea	d									
14¾	—	—	March	d									
—	—	—	Manea	d									
30¼	—	—	**Ely** ■	a									
—	—	—		d									
—	0	—	**Cambridge**	d	22p43	23p00						06 41	
—	11¼	—	Dullingham	d	22p59	23p16							
—	14½	—	Newmarket	d	23p05	23p22						07 01	
—	19½	—	Kennett	d	23p13	23p30						07 09	
—	—	—	**Bury St Edmunds**	a	23p25	23p42						07 22	
54½	29¼	—	**Bury St Edmunds**	d	23p26	23p43	05 33	06 23				07 23	
—	33¼	—	Thurston	d	23p32	23p49	05 39	06 29				07 29	
—	37¾	—	Elmswell	d	23p38	23p55	05 45	06 36				07 36	
69	43¾	—	Stowmarket	d	23p47	00 06	05 54	06 44			07 05	07 45	
—	47¼	—	Needham Market	d	23p52	00 11	05 59	06 49				07 50	
81¼	55½	0	**Ipswich**	a	00 05	00 23	06 09	07 01			07 18	08 03	
—	—	—		d					06 29	06 59	07 18		07 38
—	—	18	Harwich International	a						07 28			
—	—	—	Manningtree	a					06 39		07 28		07 48
—	—	—	Colchester	a					06 48		07 37		07 58
—	—	—	London Liverpool Street ⊖	a					07 50		08 40		09 01

		LE ■	LE ■	LE ■	LE ■	LE ■	LE ■	LE ■	LE ■	LE ■	LE ■
Peterborough ■	d		07 45			09 45			11 45		
Whittlesea	d		07 53			09 53			11 53		
March	d		08 04			10 04			12 04		
Manea	d										
Ely ■	a		08 31			10 25			12 29		
	d		08 31			10 32			12 31		
Cambridge	d	07 43		08 43	09 43		10 43	11 43		12 43	13 43
Dullingham	d	07 59			09 59			11 59			13 59
Newmarket	d	08 04		09 03	10 04		11 03	12 04		13 03	14 04
Kennett	d			09 11			11 11			13 11	
Bury St Edmunds	a	08 22	08 57	09 23	10 22	10 58	11 23	12 22	12 57	13 23	14 22
Bury St Edmunds	d	08 23	08 58	09 23	10 23	10 58	11 23	12 23	12 57	13 23	14 23
Thurston	d	08 29		09 29	10 29		11 29	12 29		13 29	14 29
Elmswell	d	08 35		09 35	10 35		11 35	12 35		13 35	14 35
Stowmarket	d	08 44	09 14	09 44	10 44	11 14	11 44	12 44	13 13	13 44	14 44
Needham Market	d	08 49		09 49	10 49		11 49	12 49		13 49	14 49
Ipswich	a	09 00	09 28	10 02	11 00	11 28	12 00	13 00	13 28	14 00	15 00
	d										
Harwich International	a										
Manningtree	a										
Colchester	a										
London Liverpool Street ⊖	a										

		LE ■	LE ■	LE ■	LE ■	LE ■	LE ■	LE ■	LE ■	LE ■
Peterborough ■	d	13 45			15 45				17 45	
Whittlesea	d	13 53			15 53				17 53	
March	d	14 04			16 04				18 04	
Manea	d									
Ely ■	a	14 29			16 28				18 28	
	d	14 31			16 31				18 31	
Cambridge	d		14 43	15 43		16 43		17 43		18 43
Dullingham	d			15 59		16 59		17 59		
Newmarket	d		15 03	16 04		17 04		18 04		19 03
Kennett	d		15 11			17 12		18 12		19 11
Bury St Edmunds	a	14 57	15 23	16 22	16 57	17 24		18 24	18 57	19 23
Bury St Edmunds	d	14 57	15 23	16 23	16 57	17 25		18 25	18 57	19 23
Thurston	d		15 29	16 29		17 31		18 31		19 29
Elmswell	d		15 35	16 35		17 37		18 37		19 35
Stowmarket	d	15 13	15 44	16 44	17 13	17 45		18 45	19 13	19 44
Needham Market	d		15 49	16 49		17 50		18 50		19 49
Ipswich	a	15 28	16 00	17 00	17 28	18 04		19 02	19 28	20 00
	d						17 33			
Harwich International	a									
Manningtree	a						17 42			
Colchester	a						17 52			
London Liverpool Street ⊖	a									

		LE ■	LE ■	LE ■	LE ◇■	LE ■	LE ■	LE ◇■	LE
Peterborough ■	d				19 45			21 45	
Whittlesea	d				19 53			21 53	
March	d				20 04			22 04	
Manea	d								
Ely ■	a				20 26			22 23	
	d				20 27			22 23	
Cambridge	d		19 43			20 43	21 43		22 43
Dullingham	d		19 59				21 59		22 59
Newmarket	d		20 04			21 03	22 04		23 05
Kennett	d					21 11			23 13
Bury St Edmunds	a		20 22		20 53	21 23	22 22	22 49	23 25
Bury St Edmunds	d		20 23		20 53	21 23	22 23	22 50	23 26
Thurston	d		20 29			21 29	22 29		23 32
Elmswell	d		20 35			21 35	22 35		23 38
Stowmarket	d		20 44		21 09	21 44	22 44	23 06	23 47
Needham Market	d		20 49			21 49	22 49		23 52
Ipswich	a		21 00		21 23	22 00	23 00	23 18	00 05
	d	19 23	21 00	20 20	21 25			23 19	
Harwich International	a		21 29						
Manningtree	a	19 36		20 33	21 35			23 29	
Colchester	a	19 46		20 45	21 46			23 40	
London Liverpool Street ⊖	a								

Saturdays

		LE	LE	LE	LE ■	LE ■	LE ■	LE ■	LE ■	LE ■	LE ■	LE ■
Peterborough ■	d						07 45			09 47		
Whittlesea	d						07 53			09 55		
March	d						08 04			10 06		
Manea	d											
Ely ■	a						08 22			10 29		
	d						08 31			10 31		
Cambridge	d	22p43		06 41		07 43		08 43	09 43		10 43	11 43
Dullingham	d	22p59				07 59			09 59			11 59
Newmarket	d	23p05		07 01		08 04		09 03	10 04		11 03	12 04
Kennett	d	23p13		07 09				09 11			11 11	
Bury St Edmunds	a	23p25		07 22		08 22	08 57	09 23	10 22	10 57	11 23	12 22
Bury St Edmunds	d	23p26	06 23	07 23		08 23	08 57	09 23	10 23	10 57	11 23	12 23
Thurston	d	23p32	06 29	07 29		08 29		09 29	10 29		11 29	12 29
Elmswell	d	23p38	06 36	07 36		08 35		09 35	10 35		11 35	12 35
Stowmarket	d	23p47	06 44	07 45		08 44	09 13	09 44	10 44	11 13	11 44	12 44
Needham Market	d	23p52	06 49	07 50		08 49		09 49	10 49		11 49	12 49
Ipswich	a	00 05	07 02	08 03		09 00	09 28	10 00	11 00	11 28	12 00	13 00
	d				06 59							
Harwich International	a				07 28							
Manningtree	a											
Colchester	a											
London Liverpool Street ⊖	a											

		LE ■	LE ■	LE ■	LE ■	LE ■	LE ■	LE ■	LE ■	LE ■	LE ■	LE ■
Peterborough ■	d	11 45			13 45			15 45			17 45	
Whittlesea	d	11 53			13 53			15 53			17 53	
March	d	12 04			14 04			16 04			18 04	
Manea	d											
Ely ■	a	12 28			14 28			16 28			18 28	
	d	12 31			14 31			16 31			18 31	
Cambridge	d		12 43	13 43		14 43	15 43		16 43	17 43		18 43
Dullingham	d			13 59			15 59		16 59	17 59		
Newmarket	d		13 03	14 04		15 03	16 04		17 04	18 04		19 03
Kennett	d		13 11			15 11			17 12	18 12		19 11
Bury St Edmunds	a	12 57	13 23	14 22	14 57	15 23	16 22	16 57	17 24	18 24	18 57	19 23
Bury St Edmunds	d	12 57	13 23	14 23	14 57	15 23	16 23	16 57	17 25	18 25	18 57	19 23
Thurston	d		13 29	14 29		15 29	16 29		17 31	18 31		19 29
Elmswell	d		13 35	14 35		15 35	16 35		17 37	18 37		19 35
Stowmarket	d	13 13	13 44	14 44	15 13	15 44	16 44	17 13	17 45	18 45	19 13	19 44
Needham Market	d		13 49	14 49		15 49	16 49		17 50	18 50		19 49
Ipswich	a	13 28	14 00	15 00	15 28	16 00	17 00	17 28	18 01	19 01	19 28	20 00
	d											
Harwich International	a											
Manningtree	a											
Colchester	a											
London Liverpool Street ⊖	a											

A from 21 May until 23 July, MO from 20 August, not 3 September, 10 September

B not from 27 July until 10 August

Peterborough, Ely, Cambridge and Bury St. Edmunds - Ipswich

Network Diagram - see first Page of Table 13

		LE	LE	LE	LE	LE	LE	LE	LE	LE	LE
		■	■	■	■	◇■	■	■	■	◇■	
			A	B	A				A		
Peterborough ■	d					19 45				21 45	
Whittlesea	d					19 53				21 53	
March	d					20 04				22 04	
Manea	d										
Ely ■	a					20 26				22 23	
	d					20 27				22 23	
Cambridge	d	19 43					20 43	21 43			22 43
Dullingham	d	19 59						21 59			22 59
Newmarket	d	20 04					21 03	22 04			23 05
Kennett	d						21 11				23 13
Bury St Edmunds	a	20 22				20 53	21 23	22 22		22 49	23 25
Bury St Edmunds	d	20 23				20 53	21 23	22 23		22 50	23 26
Thurston	d	20 29					21 29	22 29			23 32
Elmswell	d	20 35					21 35	22 35			23 38
Stowmarket	d	20 44				21 09	21 44	22 44		23 06	23 47
Needham Market	d	20 49					21 49	22 49			23 52
Ipswich	a	21 00				21 22	22 00	23 00		23 18	00 05
	d	21 00	20 09	20 09	21 09	21 25			23 15	23 19	
Harwich International	a	21 29									
Manningtree	a		20 19	20 19	21 19	21 35			23 25	23 29	
Colchester	a		20 29	20 29	21 28	21 46			23 35	23 40	
London Liverpool Street ■ ⊖	a		21 17	21 19	22 17						

Sundays
until 22 July

		LE	LE	LE	LE	LE	LE	LE	LE	LE	LE	LE	LE	LE	LE	LE	LE
			■		■	■	■	■	■	■	■	■	◇■	■	◇■	■	
Peterborough ■	d				09 45		11 46		13 46		15 45		17 45		19 45		
Whittlesea	d				09 53		11 54		13 55		15 53		17 53		19 53		
March	d				10 04		12 05		14 06		16 04		18 04		20 04		
Manea	d																
Ely ■	a				10 28		12 29		14 29		16 23		18 23		20 23		
	d				10 31		12 31		14 31		16 31		18 31		20 23		
Cambridge	d	22p43				11 12		13 12		15 12		17 12		19 12		21 12	23 00
Dullingham	d	22p59				11 28		13 28		15 28		17 28		19 28		21 28	23 16
Newmarket	d	23p05				11 34		13 34		15 34		17 34		19 34		21 34	23 22
Kennett	d	23p13				11 42		13 42		15 42		17 42		19 42		21 42	23 30
Bury St Edmunds	a	23p25			10 57	11 54	12 57	13 54	14 57	15 54	16 57	17 54	18 57	19 54	20 49	21 54	23 42
Bury St Edmunds	d	23p26		09 55	10 57	11 55	12 57	13 55	14 57	15 55	16 57	17 55	18 57	19 55	20 50	21 55	23 43
Thurston	d	23p32		10 01		12 01		14 01		16 01		18 01		20 01		22 01	23 49
Elmswell	d	23p38		10 07		12 07		14 07		16 07		18 07		20 07		22 07	23 55
Stowmarket	d	23p47		10 18	11 13	12 18	13 13	14 18	15 13	16 18	17 13	18 18	19 13	20 18	21 06	22 18	00 06
Needham Market	d	23p52		10 23		12 23		14 23		16 23		18 23		20 23		22 23	00 11
Ipswich	a	00 05		10 35	11 28	12 35	13 28	14 35	15 28	16 35	17 28	18 35	19 28	20 35	21 18	22 35	00 23
	d		07 46										19 28	20 35	21 19		
Harwich International	a		08 14											21 04			
Manningtree	a												19 38		21 29		
Colchester	a												19 49		21 40		
London Liverpool Street ■ ⊖	a																

Sundays
29 July to 12 August

		LE	LE	LE	LE	LE	LE	LE	LE	LE	LE	LE	LE	LE	LE	LE	LE	LE	LE	LE	LE	LE	LE
		■	■	■	■	🚌	■		🚌	■	■	🚌	■		🚌	■	■	🚌	■		🚌	■	■
Peterborough ■	d				09 45						11 46						13 46						15 45
Whittlesea	d				09 53						11 54						13 54						15 53
March	d				10 04						12 05						14 05						16 04
Manea	d																						
Ely ■	a				10 28						12 29						14 29						16 22
	d					10 34						12 34						14 34					
Cambridge	d							11 12						13 12						15 12			
Dullingham	d							11 28						13 28						15 28			
Newmarket	d							11a34	11 39					13a34	13 39					15a34	15 39		
Kennett	d								11 54						13 54						15 54		
Bury St Edmunds	a					11 19			12 14			13 19			14 14			15 19			16 14		
Bury St Edmunds	d	08 24	09 24	10 24			11 24			12 24			13 24			14 24			15 24			16 24	
Thurston	d	08 30	09 30	10 30			11 30			12 30			13 30			14 30			15 30			16 30	
Elmswell	d	08 36	09 36	10 36			11 36			12 36			13 36			14 36			15 36			16 36	
Stowmarket	d	08 47	09 47	10 47			11 47			12 47			13 47			14 47			15 47			16 47	
Needham Market	d	08 52	09 52	10 52			11 52			12 52			13 52			14 52			15 52			16 52	
Ipswich	a	09 03	10 03	11 03			12 03			13 03			14 03			15 03			16 03			17 03	
	d																						
Harwich International	a																						
Manningtree	a																						
Colchester	a																						
London Liverpool Street ■ ⊖	a																						

A until 21 July, from 18 August, not 1 September, 8 September

B 28 July, 4 August, 11 August, 1 September, 8 September

29 July to 12 August

Peterborough, Ely, Cambridge and Bury St. Edmunds - Ipswich

Network Diagram - see first Page of Table 13

		LE	LE	LE	LE	LE	LE	LE	LE	LE	LE	LE	LE	LE	LE	LE	LE	LE	LE	LE	LE	LE	LE	LE
		🚌	■		🚌	■	■	🚌	■		🚌	■	■	🚌	■		🚌	■	■	🚌			🚌	■
Peterborough ■	d						17 45						19 45						21 45					
Whittlesea	d						17 53						19 53						21 53					
March	d						18 04						20 04						22 04					
Manea	d																							
Ely ■	a						18 22						20 22						22 22					
	d	16 29						18 29						20 29						22 29				
Cambridge	d			17 12						19 12						21 12						23 12		
Dullingham	d			17 28						19 28						21 28						23 28		
Newmarket	d			17a34	17 39					19a34	19 39					21a34	21 39					23a34	23 39	
Kennett	d				17 54						19 54						21 54						23 54	
Bury St Edmunds	a	17 14			18 14			19 14			20 14			21 14			22 14			23 14			00 14	
Bury St Edmunds	d		17 24			18 24			19 24			20 24			21 24			22 24			23 24			00 24
Thurston	d		17 30			18 30			19 30			20 30			21 30			22 30			23 30			00 30
Elmswell	d		17 36			18 36			19 36			20 36			21 36			22 36			23 36			00 36
Stowmarket	d		17 47			18 47			19 47			20 47			21 47			22 47			23 47			00 47
Needham Market	d		17 52			18 52			19 52			20 52			21 52			22 52			23 52			00 52
Ipswich	a		18 03			19 03			20 03			21 03			22 03			23 03			00 03			01 03
	d																							
Harwich International	a																							
Manningtree	a																							
Colchester	a																							
London Liverpool Street ■ ⊖	a																							

Sundays
19 August to 26 August

		LE	LE	LE	LE	LE	LE	LE	LE	LE	LE	LE	LE	LE	LE
			■		■	■	■	■	■	■	■	◇■	■	■	
Peterborough ■	d					11 46		13 46		15 45		17 45			
Whittlesea	d					11 54		13 55		15 53		17 53			
March	d					12 05		14 06		16 04		18 04			
Manea	d														
Ely ■	a					12 29		14 29		16 23		18 23			
	d					12 31		14 31		16 31		18 31			
Cambridge	d	22p43			11 12		13 12		15 12		17 12		19 12	21 12	23 00
Dullingham	d	22p59			11 28		13 28		15 28		17 28		19 28	21 28	23 16
Newmarket	d	23p05			11 34		13 34		15 34		17 34		19 34	21 34	23 22
Kennett	d	23p13			11 42		13 42		15 42		17 42		19 42	21 42	23 30
Bury St Edmunds	a	23p25			11 54	12 57	13 54	14 57	15 54	16 57	17 54	18 57	19 54	21 54	23 42
Bury St Edmunds	d	23p26		09 55	11 55	12 57	13 55	14 57	15 55	16 57	17 55	18 57	19 55	21 55	23 43
Thurston	d	23p32		10 01	12 01		14 01		16 01		18 01		20 01	22 01	23 49
Elmswell	d	23p38		10 07	12 07		14 07		16 07		18 07		20 07	22 07	23 55
Stowmarket	d	23p47		10 18	12 18	13 13	14 18	15 13	16 18	17 13	18 18	19 13	20 18	22 18	00 06
Needham Market	d	23p52		10 23	12 23		14 23		16 23		18 23		20 23	22 23	00 11
Ipswich	a	00 05		10 35	12 35	13 28	14 35	15 28	16 35	17 28	18 35	19 28	20 35	22 35	00 23
	d		07 46									19 28	20 35		
Harwich International	a		08 14										21 04		
Manningtree	a											19 38			
Colchester	a											19 49			
London Liverpool Street ■ ⊖	a														

Sundays
2 September to 9 September

		LE	LE	LE	LE	LE	LE	LE	LE	LE	LE	LE	LE	LE	LE	LE	LE	LE	LE	LE	LE	LE	LE
		■	■	■	■	🚌	■		🚌	■	■	🚌	■		🚌	■	■	🚌	■		🚌	■	■
Peterborough ■	d				09 45						11 46						13 46						15 45
Whittlesea	d				09 53						11 54						13 54						15 53
March	d				10 04						12 05						14 05						16 04
Manea	d																						
Ely ■	a				10 28						12 29						14 29						16 22
	d					10 34						12 34						14 34					
Cambridge	d							11 12						13 12						15 12			
Dullingham	d							11 28						13 28						15 28			
Newmarket	d							11a34	11 39					13a34	13 39					15a34	15 39		
Kennett	d								11 54						13 54						15 54		
Bury St Edmunds	a					11 19			12 14			13 19			14 14			15 19			16 14		
Bury St Edmunds	d	08 24	09 24	10 24			11 24			12 24			13 24			14 24			15 24			16 24	
Thurston	d	08 30	09 30	10 30			11 30			12 30			13 30			14 30			15 30			16 30	
Elmswell	d	08 36	09 36	10 36			11 36			12 36			13 36			14 36			15 36			16 36	
Stowmarket	d	08 47	09 47	10 47			11 47			12 47			13 47			14 47			15 47			16 47	
Needham Market	d	08 52	09 52	10 52			11 52			12 52			13 52			14 52			15 52			16 52	
Ipswich	a	09 03	10 03	11 03			12 03			13 03			14 03			15 03			16 03			17 03	
	d																						
Harwich International	a																						
Manningtree	a																						
Colchester	a																						
London Liverpool Street ■ ⊖	a																						

Table 14

Ipswich - Bury St. Edmunds, Cambridge, Ely and Peterborough

Sundays

2 September to 9 September

Network Diagram - see first Page of Table 13

		LE (bus)	LE [1]	LE	LE (bus)	LE [1]	LE [1]	LE (bus)	LE [1]	LE	LE (bus)	LE [1]	LE [1]	LE (bus)	LE [1]	LE	LE (bus)	LE [1]	LE [1]	LE (bus)	LE	LE	LE (bus)	LE [1]
Peterborough [8]	d						17 45						19 45						21 45					
Whittlesea	d						17 53						19 53						21 53					
March	d						18 04						20 04						22 04					
Manea	d																							
Ely [4]	a						18 22						20 22						22 22					
	d	16 29						18 29						20 29						22 29				
Cambridge	d			17 12						19 12						21 12						23 12		
Dullingham	d			17 28						19 28						21 28						23 28		
Newmarket	d			17a34	17 39					19a34	19 39					21a34	21 39					23a34	23 39	
Kennett	d				17 54						19 54						21 54						23 54	
Bury St Edmunds	a	17 14			18 14			19 14			20 14			21 14			22 14			23 14			00 14	
Bury St Edmunds	d		17 24			18 24			19 24			20 24			21 24			22 24			23 24			00 24
Thurston	d		17 30			18 30			19 30			20 30			21 30			22 30			23 30			00 30
Elmswell	d		17 36			18 36			19 36			20 36			21 36			22 36			23 36			00 36
Stowmarket	d		17 47			18 47			19 47			20 47			21 47			22 47			23 47			00 47
Needham Market	d		17 52			18 52			19 52			20 52			21 52			22 52			23 52			00 52
Ipswich	a		18 03			19 03			20 03			21 03			22 03			23 03			00 03			01 03
	d																							
Harwich International	a																							
Manningtree	a																							
Colchester	a																							
London Liverpool Street [15] ⊖	a																							

Sundays

from 16 September

		LE	LE [1]	LE	LE [1]	LE [1]	LE [1]	LE [1]	LE [1]	LE [1]	LE [1]	LE ◇[1]	LE [1]	LE ◇[1]	LE [1]	LE
Peterborough [8]	d					11 46		13 46		15 45		17 45		19 45		
Whittlesea	d					11 54		13 55		15 53		17 53		19 53		
March	d					12 05		14 06		16 04		18 04		20 04		
Manea	d															
Ely [4]	a					12 29		14 29		16 23		18 23		20 23		
	d					12 31		14 31		16 31		18 31		20 23		
Cambridge	d	22p43			11 12		13 12		15 12		17 12		19 12		21 12	23 00
Dullingham	d	22p59			11 28		13 28		15 28		17 28		19 28		21 28	23 16
Newmarket	d	23p05			11 34		13 34		15 34		17 34		19 34		21 34	23 22
Kennett	d	23p13			11 42		13 42		15 42		17 42		19 42		21 42	23 30
Bury St Edmunds	a	23p25			11 54	12 57	13 54	14 57	15 54	16 57	17 54	18 57	19 54	20 49	21 54	23 42
Bury St Edmunds	d	23p26		09 55	11 55	12 57	13 55	14 57	15 55	16 57	17 55	18 57	19 55	20 50	21 55	23 43
Thurston	d	23p32		10 01	12 01		14 01		16 01		18 01		20 01		22 01	23 49
Elmswell	d	23p38		10 07	12 07		14 07		16 07		18 07		20 07		22 07	23 55
Stowmarket	d	23p47		10 18	12 18	13 13	14 18	15 13	16 18	17 13	18 18	19 13	20 18	21 06	22 18	00 06
Needham Market	d	23p52		10 23	12 23		14 23		16 23		18 23		20 23		22 23	00 11
Ipswich	a	00 05		10 35	12 35	13 28	14 35	15 28	16 35	17 28	18 35	19 28	20 35	21 18	22 35	00 23
	d		07 46									19 28	20 35	21 19		
Harwich International	a		08 14										21 04			
Manningtree	a											19 38		21 29		
Colchester	a											19 49		21 40		
London Liverpool Street [15] ⊖	a															

Table 15

Norwich - Great Yarmouth and Lowestoft

Mondays to Fridays

Network Diagram - see first Page of Table 13

Miles	Miles	Miles			LE	LE	LE	LE	LE	LE [1]	LE	LE	LE	LE	LE	LE	LE	LE	LE	LE	LE	LE
—	—	—	London Liverpool Street [15] ⊖	d																		
0	0	0	**Norwich**	d	05 10	05 40	06 15	06 30	06 50	07 00	07 36	08 00	08 09	08 39	09 06	09 36	10 06	10 36	11 06	11 36	12 06	12 36
4¾	4¾	4¾	Brundall Gardens	d		05 47	06 22		06 57			08 07		08 46		09 43		10 43		11 43		12 43
5¾	5¾	5¾	Brundall	d	05 19	05 50	06 25	06 39	07 00	07 09	07 45	08 10		08 49		09 46	10 15	10 46		11 46	12 15	12 46
8	—	—	Lingwood	d			06 30		07 05				08 21	08 54		09 51		10 51				12 51
10½	—	—	Acle	d			06 38		07 13				08 28	09 00		09 56		10 56				12 56
—	7¾	7¾	Buckenham	d																		
—	10	10	Cantley	d		05 56				07 15	07 51	08 16					10 21			11 52	12 21	
—	12¼	12¼	Reedham (Norfolk)	d		06 00		06 47		07 19	07 55	08 21					10 25			11 57	12 25	
—	16	—	Berney Arms	d							08x01									12x03		
18¼	20½	—	**Great Yarmouth**	a	05 40		06 51		07 26		08 12		08 41	09 13		10 09		11 09		12 13		13 09
—	—	16¼	Haddiscoe	d		06 09				07 28		08 29					10 34				12 34	
—	—	18	Somerleyton	d		06 13				07 32		08 33					10 38				12 38	
—	—	22	Oulton Broad North	d		06 19		07 02		07 38		08 40			09 36		10 44		11 36		12 44	
—	—	23½	**Lowestoft**	a		06 26		07 09		07 45		08 46			09 43		10 51		11 43		12 51	

		LE	LE	LE	LE	LE	LE	LE	LE [1]	LE	LE	LE	LE	LE [1]	LE	LE	LE	LE	LE	LE	LE	LE	LE	LE
London Liverpool Street [15] ⊖	d																							
Norwich	d	13 06	13 36	14 06	14 36	15 06	15 36	15 50	16 40	16 58	17 06	17 36	17 50	18 06	18 40	18 58	19 33	20 06	20 40	21 06	21 40	22 06	22 40	23 00
Brundall Gardens	d		13 43		14 43		15 43		16 47		17 13	17 43		18 13	18 47		19 40		20 47		21 47			
Brundall	d		13 46	14 15	14 46		15 46	15 59	16 50	17 07	17 16	17 46	17 59	18 16	18 50	19 07	19 43	20 15	20 50	21 15	21 50	22 15	22 49	23 09
Lingwood	d		13 51		14 51		15 51		16 55		17 21	17 51		18 21	18 55		19 48		20 55		21 55			23 14
Acle	d		13 56		14 56		15 56		17 00		17 28	17 56		18 28	19 00		19 53		21 00		22 00			23 18
Buckenham	d																							
Cantley	d			14 21		15 18		16 05		17 13			18 05			19 13		20 21		21 21		22 21	22 55	
Reedham (Norfolk)	d			14 25		15 23		16 09		17 17			18 09			19 17		20 25		21 25		22 25	22 59	
Berney Arms	d																							
Great Yarmouth	a		14 09		15 09		16 09		17 13		17 41	18 09		18 41	19 13		20 06		21 13		22 13			23 31
Haddiscoe	d			14 34				16 18		17 26			18 18			19 26		20 34				22 34	23 08	
Somerleyton	d			14 38				16 22		17 30			18 22			19 30		20 38				22 38	23 12	
Oulton Broad North	d	13 36		14 44		15 38		16 28		17 36			18 28			19 36		20 44		21 40		22 44	23 18	
Lowestoft	a	13 43		14 51		15 44		16 35		17 43			18 35			19 43		20 51		21 47		22 51	23 25	

Saturdays

until 19 May

		LE	LE	LE	LE	LE	LE	LE [1]	LE	LE	LE	LE	LE	LE	LE	LE	LE	LE	LE	LE	LE	LE	LE
London Liverpool Street [15] ⊖	d																						
Norwich	d	05 30	05 40	06 36	06 50	07 06	07 36	07 50	08 09	08 36	09 06	09 36	10 06	10 36	11 06	11 36	12 06	12 36	13 06	13 36	14 06	14 36	15 06
Brundall Gardens	d		05 47	06 43		07 13		07 57		08 43		09 43		10 43		11 43		12 43		13 43		14 43	
Brundall	d	05 39	05 50	06 46	06 59	07 16	07 45	08 00		08 46		09 46	10 15	10 46		11 46	12 15	12 46		13 46	14 15	14 46	
Lingwood	d			06 51		07 21			08 21	08 51		09 51		10 51				12 51		13 51		14 51	
Acle	d			06 56		07 28			08 28	08 58		09 56		10 56				12 56		13 56		14 56	
Buckenham	d												10x19										
Cantley	d		05 56		07 05		07 51	08 06					10 23			11 52	12 21				14 21		15 18
Reedham (Norfolk)	d	05 47	06 01		07 09		07 55	08 11					10 27			11 57	12 25				14 26		15 23
Berney Arms	d						08x01									12x03							
Great Yarmouth	a	06 02		07 09		07 41	08 12		08 41	09 11		10 09		11 09		12 13		13 09		14 09		15 09	
Haddiscoe	d		06 09		07 18			08 19					10 36				12 34				14 34		
Somerleyton	d		06 13		07 22			08 23					10 40				12 38				14 38		
Oulton Broad North	d		06 20		07 28			08 30			09 36		10 46		11 36		12 44		13 36		14 45		15 38
Lowestoft	a		06 26		07 35			08 36			09 43		10 53		11 43		12 51		13 43		14 51		15 44

		LE	LE	LE	LE	LE	LE	LE	LE	LE	LE	LE	LE	LE	LE	LE	LE	LE	LE
London Liverpool Street [15] ⊖	d																		
Norwich	d	15 36	15 50	16 40	16 58	17 06	17 36	17 50	18 06	18 40	18 58	19 33	20 06	20 40	21 06	21 40	22 06	22 40	23 00
Brundall Gardens	d	15 43		16 47		17 13	17 43		18 13	18 47		19 40		20 47		21 47			
Brundall	d	15 46	15 59	16 50	17 07	17 16	17 46	17 59	18 16	18 50	19 07	19 43	20 15	20 50	21 15	21 50	22 15	22 49	23 09
Lingwood	d	15 51		16 55		17 21	17 51		18 21	18 55		19 48		20 55		21 55			23 14
Acle	d	15 56		17 00		17 28	17 56		18 28	19 00		19 53		21 00		22 00			23 18
Buckenham	d																		
Cantley	d		16 05		17 13			18 05			19 13		20 21		21 21		22 21	22 55	
Reedham (Norfolk)	d		16 09		17 17			18 09			19 17		20 25		21 25		22 25	22 59	
Berney Arms	d																		
Great Yarmouth	a	16 09		17 13		17 41	18 09		18 41	19 13		20 06		21 13		22 13			23 31
Haddiscoe	d		16 18		17 26			18 18			19 26		20 34				22 34	23 08	
Somerleyton	d		16 22		17 30			18 22			19 30		20 38				22 38	23 12	
Oulton Broad North	d		16 28		17 36			18 28			19 36		20 44		21 40		22 44	23 18	
Lowestoft	a		16 35		17 43			18 35			19 43		20 51		21 47		22 51	23 25	

Saturdays

26 May to 29 September

Norwich - Great Yarmouth and Lowestoft

Network Diagram - see first Page of Table 13

		LE	LE	LE	LE	LE	LE	LE	LE	LE		LE	LE	LE	LE	LE	LE	LE	LE	LE		LE	LE	LE	LE
								■												■ A ⊡					
London Liverpool Street ⊖	d																			10 00					
Norwich	d	05 30	05 40	06 36	06 50	07 06	07 36	07 50	08 09	08 36		08 55	09 06	09 36	10 06	10 15	10 36	11 06	11 36	12 03		12 10	12 36	13 06	13 18
Brundall Gardens	d		05 47	06 43		07 13		07 57		08 43				09 43			10 43		11 43				12 43		
Brundall	d	05 39	05 50	06 46	06 59	07 16	07 45	08 00		08 46				09 46	10 15		10 46		11 46			12 19	12 46		
Lingwood	d			06 51		07 21			08 21	08 51				09 51			10 51						12 51		
Acle	d			06 56		07 28			08 28	08 58				09 56			10 56						12 56		
Buckenham	d														10x19										
Cantley	d		05 56		07 05		07 51	08 06							10 23				11 52			12 25			
Reedham (Norfolk)	d	05 47	06 01		07 09		07 55	08 11							10 27				11 57			12 29			
Berney Arms	d						08x01												12x03						
Great Yarmouth	a	06 02		07 09		07 41	08 12		08 41	09 11		09 24		10 09		10 41	11 09		12 13	12 40			13 09		13 47
Haddiscoe	d		06 09		07 18			08 19							10 36							12 38			
Somerleyton	d		06 13		07 22			08 23							10 40							12 42			
Oulton Broad North	d		06 20		07 28			08 30					09 36		10 46			11 36				12 48		13 36	
Lowestoft	a		06 26		07 35			08 36					09 43		10 53			11 43				12 55		13 43	

		LE	LE	LE	LE	LE		LE	LE	LE	LE	LE	LE	LE	LE	LE		LE	LE	LE	LE	LE	LE	LE	LE
					■ A ⊡																				
London Liverpool Street ⊖	d				12 30																				
Norwich	d	13 36	14 10	14 36	14 50	15 06		15 18	15 36	15 50	16 40	16 58	17 06	17 36	17 50	18 06		18 40	18 58	19 33	20 06	20 40	21 06	21 40	22 06
Brundall Gardens	d	13 43		14 43					15 43		16 47		17 13	17 43		18 13		18 47		19 40		20 47		21 47	
Brundall	d	13 46	14 19	14 46					15 46	15 59	16 50	17 07	17 16	17 46	17 59	18 16		18 50	19 07	19 43	20 15	20 50	21 15	21 50	22 15
Lingwood	d	13 51		14 51					15 51		16 55		17 21	17 51		18 21		18 55		19 48		20 55		21 55	
Acle	d	13 56		14 56					15 56		17 00		17 28	17 56		18 28		19 00		19 53		21 00		22 00	
Buckenham	d																								
Cantley	d		14 25			15 18				16 05		17 13			18 05				19 13		20 21		21 21		22 21
Reedham (Norfolk)	d		14 30			15 23				16 09		17 17			18 09				19 17		20 25		21 25		22 25
Berney Arms	d																								
Great Yarmouth	a	14 09		15 09	15 28			15 47	16 09		17 13		17 41	18 09		18 41		19 13		20 06		21 13		22 13	
Haddiscoe	d		14 38							16 18		17 26			18 18				19 26		20 34				22 34
Somerleyton	d		14 42							16 22		17 30			18 22				19 30		20 38				22 38
Oulton Broad North	d		14 49			15 38				16 28		17 36			18 28				19 36		20 44		21 40		22 44
Lowestoft	a		14 55			15 44				16 35		17 43			18 35				19 43		20 51		21 47		22 51

		LE		LE
London Liverpool Street ⊖	d			
Norwich	d	22 40		23 00
Brundall Gardens	d			
Brundall	d	22 49		23 09
Lingwood	d			23 14
Acle	d			23 18
Buckenham	d			
Cantley	d	22 55		
Reedham (Norfolk)	d	22 59		
Berney Arms	d			
Great Yarmouth	a			23 31
Haddiscoe	d	23 08		
Somerleyton	d	23 12		
Oulton Broad North	d	23 18		
Lowestoft	a	23 25		

Saturdays

from 6 October

		LE	LE	LE	LE	LE	LE	LE	LE	LE		LE	LE	LE	LE	LE	LE	LE	LE	LE		LE	LE	LE	LE
								■																	
London Liverpool Street ⊖	d																								
Norwich	d	05 30	05 40	06 36	06 50	07 06	07 36	07 50	08 09	08 36		09 06	09 36	10 06	10 36	11 06	11 36	12 06	12 36	13 06		13 36	14 06	14 36	15 06
Brundall Gardens	d		05 47	06 43		07 13		07 57		08 43			09 43		10 43		11 43		12 43			13 43		14 43	
Brundall	d	05 39	05 50	06 46	06 59	07 16	07 45	08 00		08 46			09 46	10 15	10 46		11 46	12 15	12 46			13 46	14 15	14 46	
Lingwood	d			06 51		07 21			08 21	08 51			09 51		10 51				12 51			13 51		14 51	
Acle	d			06 56		07 28			08 28	08 58			09 56		10 56				12 56			13 56		14 56	
Buckenham	d													10x19											
Cantley	d		05 56		07 05		07 51	08 06						10 23			11 52	12 21					14 21		15 18
Reedham (Norfolk)	d	05 47	06 01		07 09		07 55	08 11						10 27			11 57	12 25					14 26		15 23
Berney Arms	d						08x01										12x03								
Great Yarmouth	a	06 02		07 09		07 41	08 12		08 41	09 11			10 09		11 09		12 13		13 09			14 09		15 09	
Haddiscoe	d		06 09		07 18			08 19						10 36				12 34					14 34		
Somerleyton	d		06 13		07 22			08 23						10 40				12 38					14 38		
Oulton Broad North	d		06 20		07 28			08 30				09 36		10 46		11 36		12 44		13 36			14 45		15 38
Lowestoft	a		06 26		07 35			08 36				09 43		10 53		11 43		12 51		13 43			14 51		15 44

A ⊡ to Norwich

Saturdays

from 6 October

Norwich - Great Yarmouth and Lowestoft

Network Diagram - see first Page of Table 13

		LE	LE	LE	LE	LE		LE	LE	LE	LE	LE	LE	LE	LE	LE		LE	LE	LE	LE
London Liverpool Street ⊖	d																				
Norwich	d	15 36	15 50	16 40	16 58	17 06		17 36	17 50	18 06	18 40	18 58	19 33	20 06	20 40	21 06		21 40	22 06	22 40	23 00
Brundall Gardens	d	15 43		16 47		17 13		17 43		18 13	18 47		19 40		20 47			21 47			
Brundall	d	15 46	15 59	16 50	17 07	17 16		17 46	17 59	18 16	18 50	19 07	19 43	20 15	20 50	21 15		21 50	22 15	22 49	23 09
Lingwood	d	15 51		16 55		17 21		17 51		18 21	18 55		19 48		20 55			21 55			23 14
Acle	d	15 56		17 00		17 28		17 56		18 28	19 00		19 53		21 00			22 00			23 18
Buckenham	d																				
Cantley	d		16 05		17 13				18 05			19 13		20 21		21 21			22 21	22 55	
Reedham (Norfolk)	d		16 09		17 17				18 09			19 17		20 25		21 25			22 25	22 59	
Berney Arms	d																				
Great Yarmouth	a	16 09		17 13		17 41		18 09		18 41	19 13		20 06		21 13			22 13			23 31
Haddiscoe	d		16 18		17 26				18 18			19 26		20 34					22 34	23 08	
Somerleyton	d		16 22		17 30				18 22			19 30		20 38					22 38	23 12	
Oulton Broad North	d		16 28		17 36				18 28			19 36		20 44		21 40			22 44	23 18	
Lowestoft	a		16 35		17 43				18 35			19 43		20 51		21 47			22 51	23 25	

Sundays

		LE	LE	LE	LE	LE	LE	LE	LE	LE		LE	LE	LE	LE	LE	LE	LE	LE	LE		LE	LE	LE	LE
		■										■			■	A	B		C	D				■	
London Liverpool Street ⊖	d																								
Norwich	d	07 25	07 36	08 45	08 57	09 36	10 45	10 57	11 36	12 45		12 57	13 36	14 45	14 57	15 36	15 36	16 45	16 57	16 57		17 36	18 45	18 57	19 36
Brundall Gardens	d			08 52			10 52			12 52				14 52				16 52					18 52		
Brundall	d		07 45	08 55	09 06	09 45	10 55	11 06	11 45	12 55		13 06	13 45	14 55	15 06	15 45	15 45	16 55	17 06	17 06		17 45	18 55	19 06	19 45
Lingwood	d			09 00			11 00			13 00				15 00				17 00					19 00		
Acle	d			09 05			11 05			13 05				15 05				17 05					19 05		
Buckenham	d					09x49			11x49							15x49	15x49			17x10					
Cantley	d		07 51		09 12	09 53		11 12	11 53			13 12	13 51		15 12	15 53	15 53		17 14	17 14		17 51		19 12	19 51
Reedham (Norfolk)	d		07 55		09 16	09 57		11 16	11 57			13 16	13 55		15 16	15 57	15 57		17 18	17 18		17 55		19 16	19 55
Berney Arms	d		08x01			10x03			12x03				14x01			16x03									
Great Yarmouth	a		08 12	09 18		10 14	11 18		12 14	13 18			14 12	15 18		16 14	16 14	17 18				18 10	19 18		20 10
Haddiscoe	d				09 25			11 25				13 25			15 25				17 27	17 27				19 25	
Somerleyton	d				09 29			11 29				13 29			15 29				17 31	17 31				19 29	
Oulton Broad North	d	07 53			09 35			11 35				13 35			15 35				17 37	17 37				19 35	
Lowestoft	a	08 00			09 42			11 42				13 42			15 42				17 44	17 44				19 42	

		LE	LE	LE	LE
			■		
London Liverpool Street ⊖	d				
Norwich	d	20 45	20 57	21 36	22 36
Brundall Gardens	d	20 52			22 43
Brundall	d	20 55	21 06	21 45	22 46
Lingwood	d	21 00			22 51
Acle	d	21 05			22 56
Buckenham	d				
Cantley	d		21 12	21 51	
Reedham (Norfolk)	d		21 16	21 55	
Berney Arms	d				
Great Yarmouth	a	21 18		22 10	23 09
Haddiscoe	d		21 25		
Somerleyton	d		21 29		
Oulton Broad North	d		21 35		
Lowestoft	a		21 42		

A until 9 September
B from 16 September
C until 22 July, from 16 September
D from 29 July until 9 September

Table 15

Mondays to Fridays

Lowestoft and Great Yarmouth - Norwich

Network Diagram - see first Page of Table 13

Miles	Miles	Miles			LE MX	LE MX	LE ■ A	LE	LE ■	LE	LE	LE	LE	LE ■	LE ■	LE	LE	LE	LE	LE	LE	LE	LE
0	—	—	**Lowestoft**	d		23p30	23p35		05 42		06 35			07 35	07 55			08 50		09 50		11 00	
1½	—	—	Oulton Broad North	d		23p34	23p39		05 46		06 39			07 39	07 59			08 54		09 54		11 04	
5½	—	—	Somerleyton	d					05 52		06 45			07 45				09 00		10 00			
7¼	—	—	Haddiscoe	d					05 56		06 49			07 49				09 04		10 04			
—	0	0	**Great Yarmouth**	d	23p34			05 47		06 27		07 02	07 32			08 17	08 49		09 17		10 17		11 17
—	—	4½	Berney Arms	d																			
11¼	—	8¼	Reedham (Norfolk)	d	23p47	23p52	23p54		06 05		06 58			07 58	08 14			09 13		10 13			
13½	—	10½	Cantley	d		23p56			06 09		07 02			08 02	08 19			09 17		10 17			
15¾	—	12¾	Buckenham	d																			
—	8	—	Acle	d				05 58		06 38		07 13	07 43			08 28	09 00		09 28		10 28		11 28
—	10½	—	Lingwood	d				06 03		06 43		07 18	07 48			08 33	09 05		09 33		10 33		11 33
17¾	12¾	14¾	Brundall	d	23p55	00 03	00 03	06 07	06 16	06 47	07 09	07 22	07 52	08 09		08 37		09 24	09 37	10 24	10 37		11 37
18¾	13¾	15¾	Brundall Gardens	d				06 10		06 50		07 25	07 55			08 40			09 40		10 40		11 40
23½	18½	20½	**Norwich**	a	00 07	00 14	00 13	06 20	06 27	07 00	07 20	07 35	08 06	08 20	08 34	08 50	09 19	09 35	09 50	10 35	10 50	11 35	11 50
—	—	—	London Liverpool Street ⊖	a																			

		LE	LE	LE	LE	LE	LE	LE	LE	LE	LE	LE	LE ■	LE B	LE C	LE	LE	LE	LE	LE	LE	LE	LE ■
Lowestoft	d	11 50		13 00		13 50		15 00		15 50		16 50				17 50			18 55		19 55		21 00
Oulton Broad North	d	11 54		13 04		13 54		15 04		15 54		16 54				17 54			18 59		19 59		21 04
Somerleyton	d	12 00				14 00				16 00		17 00				18 00			19 05		20 05		
Haddiscoe	d	12 04				14 04				16 04		17 04				18 04			19 09		20 09		
Great Yarmouth	d		12 17		13 17		14 17		15 13		16 17		17 17	17 47	17 47		18 17	18 47		19 17		20 17	
Berney Arms	d								15x20					17x54									
Reedham (Norfolk)	d	12 13				14 13			15 28	16 13		17 13		18 01	18 01	18 13		19 01	19 18		20 18		
Cantley	d	12 17				14 17			15 32	16 17		17 17		18 05	18 05	18 17		19 05	19 22		20 22		
Buckenham	d																						
Acle	d		12 28		13 28		14 28				16 28		17 28				18 28			19 28		20 28	
Lingwood	d		12 33		13 33		14 33				16 33		17 33				18 33			19 33		20 33	
Brundall	d	12 24	12 37		13 37	14 24	14 37		15 38	16 24	16 37	17 24	17 37	18 12	18 12	18 24	18 37	19 12	19 29	19 37	20 29	20 37	
Brundall Gardens	d		12 40		13 40		14 40		15 41		16 40		17 40				18 40			19 40		20 40	
Norwich	a	12 35	12 50	13 35	13 50	14 35	14 50	15 35	15 50	16 35	16 50	17 35	17 50	18 23	18 23	18 35	18 50	19 23	19 40	19 50	20 40	20 50	21 35
London Liverpool Street ⊖	a																						

		LE	LE	LE	LE ■	LE	LE
Lowestoft	d		21 50		22 50		23 30
Oulton Broad North	d		21 54		22 54		23 34
Somerleyton	d		22 00		23 00		
Haddiscoe	d		22 04		23 04		
Great Yarmouth	d	21 17		22 17		23 34	
Berney Arms	d						
Reedham (Norfolk)	d		22 13		23 13	23 47	23 52
Cantley	d		22 17		23 17		23 56
Buckenham	d						
Acle	d	21 28		22 28			
Lingwood	d	21 33		22 33			
Brundall	d	21 37	22 24	22 37	23 24	23 55	00 03
Brundall Gardens	d	21 40		22 40			
Norwich	a	21 50	22 35	22 50	23 35	00 07	00 14
London Liverpool Street ⊖	a						

Saturdays

until 19 May

		LE	LE	LE	LE	LE	LE	LE	LE	LE	LE	LE	LE	LE	LE	LE	LE	LE	LE	LE	LE	LE	LE
Lowestoft	d		23p30		06 38			07 40			08 50		09 50		11 00		11 50		13 00		13 50		15 00
Oulton Broad North	d		23p34		06 42			07 44			08 54		09 54		11 04		11 54		13 04		13 54		15 04
Somerleyton	d				06 48			07 50			09 00		10 00				12 00				14 00		
Haddiscoe	d				06 52			07 54			09 04		10 04				12 04				14 04		
Great Yarmouth	d	23p34		06 17		07 17	07 45		08 17	08 47		09 17		10 17		11 17		12 17		13 17		14 17	
Berney Arms	d																						
Reedham (Norfolk)	d	23p47	23p52		07 01			08 03			09 13		10 13				12 13				14 13		
Cantley	d		23p56		07 05			08 07			09 17		10 17				12 17				14 17		
Buckenham	d																						
Acle	d			06 28		07 28	07 56		08 28	08 58		09 28		10 28		11 28		12 28		13 28		14 28	
Lingwood	d			06 33		07 33	08 01		08 33	09 03		09 33		10 33		11 33		12 33		13 33		14 33	
Brundall	d	23p55	00 03	06 37	07 12	07 37	08 05	08 14	08 37		09 24	09 37	10 24	10 37		11 37	12 24	12 37		13 37	14 24	14 37	
Brundall Gardens	d			06 40		07 40	08 08		08 40			09 40		10 40		11 40		12 40		13 40		14 40	
Norwich	a	00 07	00 14	06 50	07 24	07 50	08 18	08 25	08 50	09 17	09 35	09 50	10 35	10 52	11 35	11 50	12 35	12 50	13 35	13 52	14 35	14 50	15 35
London Liverpool Street ⊖	a																						

A MO from 21 May

B until 7 September

C from 10 September

Table 15

Saturdays

until 19 May

Lowestoft and Great Yarmouth - Norwich

Network Diagram - see first Page of Table 13

		LE	LE	LE	LE	LE	LE	LE	LE	LE	LE	LE	LE	LE	LE ■	LE	LE	LE	LE ■	LE	LE
Lowestoft	d		15 50		16 50			17 50			18 55		19 55		21 00		21 50		22 50		23 30
Oulton Broad North	d		15 54		16 54			17 54			18 59		19 59		21 04		21 54		22 54		23 34
Somerleyton	d		16 00		17 00			18 00			19 05		20 05				22 00		23 00		
Haddiscoe	d		16 04		17 04			18 04			19 09		20 09				22 04		23 04		
Great Yarmouth	d	15 13		16 17		17 17	17 47		18 17	18 47		19 17		20 17		21 17		22 17		23 34	
Berney Arms	d	15x20					17x54														
Reedham (Norfolk)	d	15 28	16 13		17 13		18 01	18 13		19 01	19 18		20 18				22 13		23 13	23 47	23 52
Cantley	d	15 32	16 17		17 17		18 05	18 17		19 05	19 22		20 22				22 17		23 17		23 56
Buckenham	d		16x21																		
Acle	d			16 28		17 28			18 28			19 28		20 28		21 28		22 28			
Lingwood	d			16 33		17 33			18 33			19 33		20 33		21 33		22 33			
Brundall	d	15 38	16 24	16 37	17 24	17 37	18 12	18 24	18 37	19 12	19 29	19 37	20 29	20 37		21 37	22 24	22 37	23 24	23 55	00 03
Brundall Gardens	d	15 41		16 40		17 40			18 40			19 40		20 40		21 40		22 40			
Norwich	a	15 50	16 35	16 50	17 35	17 50	18 23	18 35	18 50	19 23	19 40	19 50	20 40	20 50	21 35	21 50	22 35	22 50	23 35	00 07	00 14
London Liverpool Street ⊖	a																				

Saturdays

26 May to 29 September

		LE	LE	LE	LE	LE	LE	LE	LE	LE	LE	LE	LE	LE	LE	LE ■ A ⊡	LE	LE	LE	LE	LE	LE	LE ■ A ⊡
Lowestoft	d		23p30		06 38			07 40			08 50			09 50			11 00			11 50		13 00	
Oulton Broad North	d		23p34		06 42			07 44			08 54			09 54			11 04			11 54		13 04	
Somerleyton	d				06 48			07 50			09 00			10 00						12 00			
Haddiscoe	d				06 52			07 54			09 04			10 04						12 04			
Great Yarmouth	d	23p34		06 17		07 17	07 45		08 17	08 47		09 17	09 55		10 17	10 40		11 17	11 53		12 17		13 10
Berney Arms	d																						
Reedham (Norfolk)	d	23p47	23p52		07 01			08 03			09 13			10 13						12 13			
Cantley	d		23p56		07 05			08 07			09 17			10 17						12 17			
Buckenham	d																						
Acle	d			06 28		07 28	07 56		08 28	08 58		09 28			10 28			11 28			12 28		
Lingwood	d			06 33		07 33	08 01		08 33	09 03		09 33			10 33			11 33			12 33		
Brundall	d	23p55	00 03	06 37	07 12	07 37	08 05	08 14	08 37		09 24	09 37		10 24	10 37			11 37		12 24	12 37		
Brundall Gardens	d			06 40		07 40	08 08		08 40			09 40			10 40			11 40			12 40		
Norwich	a	00 07	00 14	06 50	07 24	07 50	08 18	08 25	08 50	09 17	09 35	09 50	10 23	10 35	10 52	11 14	11 35	11 50	12 19	12 35	12 50	13 35	13 44
London Liverpool Street ⊖	a															13 19							15 55

		LE B	LE C	LE	LE	LE	LE	LE D	LE E	LE	LE	LE	LE	LE	LE	LE	LE	LE	LE	LE	LE	LE	LE ■
Lowestoft	d			13 50			15 00				15 50		16 50			17 50			18 55		19 55		21 00
Oulton Broad North	d			13 54			15 04				15 54		16 54			17 54			18 59		19 59		21 04
Somerleyton	d			14 00							16 00		17 00			18 00			19 05		20 05		
Haddiscoe	d			14 04							16 04		17 04			18 04			19 09		20 09		
Great Yarmouth	d	13 17	13 17		14 17	14 55		15 13	15 13	15 55		16 17		17 17	17 47		18 17	18 47		19 17		20 17	
Berney Arms	d							15x20	15x20						17x54								
Reedham (Norfolk)	d			14 13				15 28	15 28		16 13		17 13		18 01	18 13		19 01	19 18		20 18		
Cantley	d			14 17				15 32	15 32		16 17		17 17		18 05	18 17		19 05	19 22		20 22		
Buckenham	d										16x21												
Acle	d	13 28	13 28		14 28							16 28		17 28			18 28			19 28		20 28	
Lingwood	d	13 33	13 33		14 33							16 33		17 33			18 33			19 33		20 33	
Brundall	d	13 37	13 37	14 24	14 37			15 38	15 38		16 24	16 37	17 24	17 37	18 12	18 24	18 37	19 12	19 29	19 37	20 29	20 37	
Brundall Gardens	d	13 40	13 40		14 40			15 41	15 41			16 40		17 40			18 40			19 40		20 40	
Norwich	a	13 50	13 52	14 35	14 50	15 23	15 35	15 50	15 51	16 23	16 35	16 50	17 35	17 50	18 23	18 35	18 50	19 23	19 40	19 50	20 40	20 50	21 35
London Liverpool Street ⊖	a																						

		LE	LE	LE	LE ■	LE	LE
Lowestoft	d		21 50		22 50		23 30
Oulton Broad North	d		21 54		22 54		23 34
Somerleyton	d		22 00		23 00		
Haddiscoe	d		22 04		23 04		
Great Yarmouth	d	21 17		22 17		23 34	
Berney Arms	d						
Reedham (Norfolk)	d		22 13		23 13	23 47	23 52
Cantley	d		22 17		23 17		23 56
Buckenham	d						
Acle	d	21 28		22 28			
Lingwood	d	21 33		22 33			
Brundall	d	21 37	22 24	22 37	23 24	23 55	00 03
Brundall Gardens	d	21 40		22 40			
Norwich	a	21 50	22 35	22 50	23 35	00 07	00 14
London Liverpool Street ⊖	a						

A ⊡ from Norwich

B from 26 May until 21 July, 15 September, 22 September, 29 September

C from 28 July until 8 September

D from 26 May until 21 July, 18 August, 25 August, 15 September, 22 September, 29 September

E 28 July, 4 August, 11 August, 1 September, 8 September

Lowestoft and Great Yarmouth - Norwich

Network Diagram - see first Page of Table 13

		LE	LE	LE	LE	LE	LE	LE	LE	LE	LE	LE	LE	LE	LE	LE	LE	LE	LE	LE	LE	LE	LE
Lowestoft	d		23p30		06 38			07 40			08 50		09 50		11 00		11 50		13 00		13 50		15 00
Oulton Broad North	d		23p34		06 42			07 44			08 54		09 54		11 04		11 54		13 04		13 54		15 04
Somerleyton	d				06 48			07 50			09 00		10 00				12 00				14 00		
Haddiscoe	d				06 52			07 54			09 04		10 04				12 04				14 04		
Great Yarmouth	d	23p34		06 17		07 17	07 45		08 17	08 47		09 17		10 17		11 17		12 17		13 17		14 17	
Berney Arms	d																						
Reedham (Norfolk)	d	23p47	23p52		07 01			08 03			09 13		10 13				12 13				14 13		
Cantley	d		23p56		07 05			08 07			09 17		10 17				12 17				14 17		
Buckenham	d																						
Acle	d			06 28		07 28	07 56		08 28	08 58		09 28		10 28		11 28		12 28		13 28		14 28	
Lingwood	d			06 33		07 33	08 01		08 33	09 03		09 33		10 33		11 33		12 33		13 33		14 33	
Brundall	d	23p55	00 03	06 37	07 12	07 37	08 05	08 14	08 37		09 24	09 37	10 24	10 37		11 37	12 24	12 37		13 37	14 24	14 37	
Brundall Gardens	d			06 40		07 40	08 08		08 40			09 40		10 40		11 40		12 40		13 40		14 40	
Norwich	a	00 07	00 14	06 50	07 24	07 50	08 18	08 25	08 50	09 17	09 35	09 50	10 35	10 52	11 35	11 50	12 35	12 50	13 35	13 52	14 35	14 50	15 35
London Liverpool Street 15 ⊖	a																						

		LE	LE	LE	LE	LE	LE	LE	LE	LE	LE	LE	LE	LE	LE 1	LE	LE	LE	LE 1	LE	LE
Lowestoft	d		15 50		16 50			17 50			18 55		19 55		21 00		21 50		22 50		23 30
Oulton Broad North	d		15 54		16 54			17 54			18 59		19 59		21 04		21 54		22 54		23 34
Somerleyton	d		16 00		17 00			18 00			19 05		20 05				22 00		23 00		
Haddiscoe	d		16 04		17 04			18 04			19 09		20 09				22 04		23 04		
Great Yarmouth	d	15 13		16 17		17 17	17 47		18 17	18 47		19 17		20 17		21 17		22 17		23 34	
Berney Arms	d	15x20																			
Reedham (Norfolk)	d	15 28	16 13		17 13		18 01	18 13		19 01	19 18		20 18				22 13		23 13	23 47	23 52
Cantley	d	15 32	16 17		17 17		18 05	18 17		19 05	19 22		20 22				22 17		23 17		23 56
Buckenham	d		16x21																		
Acle	d			16 28		17 28			18 28			19 28		20 28		21 28		22 28			
Lingwood	d			16 33		17 33			18 33			19 33		20 33		21 33		22 33			
Brundall	d	15 38	16 24	16 37	17 24	17 37	18 12	18 24	18 37	19 12	19 29	19 37	20 29	20 37		21 37	22 24	22 37	23 24	23 55	00 03
Brundall Gardens	d	15 41		16 40		17 40			18 40			19 40		20 40		21 40		22 40			
Norwich	a	15 50	16 35	16 50	17 35	17 50	18 23	18 35	18 50	19 23	19 40	19 50	20 40	20 50	21 35	21 50	22 35	22 50	23 35	00 07	00 14
London Liverpool Street 15 ⊖	a																				

Sundays

		LE	LE	LE	LE	LE	LE	LE	LE 1	LE	LE	LE 1	LE	LE	LE	LE A	LE B	LE C	LE	LE 1	LE	LE	LE 1
Lowestoft	d		23p30			09 50			11 50			13 50			15 50					17 50			19 50
Oulton Broad North	d		23p34			09 54			11 54			13 54			15 54					17 54			19 54
Somerleyton	d					10 00			12 00			14 00			16 00					18 00			20 00
Haddiscoe	d					10 04			12 04			14 04			16 04					18 04			20 04
Great Yarmouth	d	23p34		08 20	09 22		10 18	11 22		12 18	13 22		14 20	15 22		16 18	16 18	16 18	17 22		18 18	19 22	
Berney Arms	d			08x27			10x25			12x25			14x27			16x25		16x25					
Reedham (Norfolk)	d	23p47	23p52	08 34		10 13	10 32		12 13	12 32		14 13	14 34		16 13	16 32	16 32	16 32		18 13	18 31		20 13
Cantley	d		23p56	08 38		10 17	10 36		12 17	12 36		14 17	14 38		16 17	16 36	16 36	16 36		18 17	18 35		20 17
Buckenham	d					10x21	10x40			12x40								16x40					
Acle	d				09 33			11 33			13 33			15 33					17 33			19 33	
Lingwood	d				09 38			11 38			13 38			15 38					17 38			19 38	
Brundall	d	23p55	00 03	08 45	09 42	10 24	10 44	11 42	12 24	12 44	13 42	14 24	14 45	15 42	16 24	16 44	16 44	16 44	17 42	18 24	18 41	19 42	20 24
Brundall Gardens	d				09 45			11 45			13 45			15 45					17 45			19 45	
Norwich	a	00 07	00 14	08 55	09 55	10 35	10 55	11 55	12 35	12 55	13 55	14 35	14 55	15 55	16 35	16 55	16 55	16 55	17 55	18 35	18 52	19 55	20 35
London Liverpool Street 15 ⊖	a																						

		LE	LE	LE 1	LE	LE	LE 1
Lowestoft	d			21 50			23 35
Oulton Broad North	d			21 54			23 39
Somerleyton	d			22 00			
Haddiscoe	d			22 04			
Great Yarmouth	d	20 20	21 22		22 20	23 20	
Berney Arms	d						
Reedham (Norfolk)	d	20 33		22 13	22 33	23 33	23 54
Cantley	d	20 37		22 17	22 37	23 37	
Buckenham	d						
Acle	d		21 33				
Lingwood	d		21 38				
Brundall	d	20 43	21 42	22 24	22 43	23 43	00 03
Brundall Gardens	d		21 45			23 46	
Norwich	a	20 55	21 55	22 35	22 55	23 55	00 13
London Liverpool Street 15 ⊖	a						

A until 22 July, 19 August, 26 August

B from 16 September

C 29 July, 5 August, 12 August, 2 September, 9 September

Norwich - Cromer and Sheringham

Network Diagram - see first Page of Table 13

Miles			LE SX	LE SO	LE SO	LE SX	LE	LE	LE	LE	LE	LE	LE	LE	LE	LE	LE	LE	LE	LE	LE
0	**Norwich**	d	05 15	05 20	05 45	05 45	07 15	08 21	09 45	10 45	11 45	12 45	13 45	14 45	15 45	16 45	17 45	18 51	19 55	21 15	22 45
6	Salhouse	d			05 55	05 55	07 25	08 31	09 55		11 55		13 55		15 55	16 55	17 55		20 05	21 25	22 55
8¾	Hoveton & Wroxham	d	05 29	05 34	06 00	06 00	07 30	08 36	10 00	10 59	12 00	12 59	14 00	14 59	16 00	17 00	18 00	19 05	20 10	21 30	23 00
13	Worstead	d			06 07	06 07	07 37	08 43		11 05		13 05		15 05	16 07	17 07	18 07	19 11	20 17	21 37	23 07
—	**North Walsham**	a	05 39	05 44	06 12	06 12	07 42	08 48	10 10	11 11	12 10	13 11	14 10	15 11	16 12	17 12	18 12	19 17	20 22	21 42	23 12
16	**North Walsham**	d	05 39	05 44	06 13	06 15	07 45	08 51	10 13	11 13	12 13	13 13	14 13	15 13	16 15	17 15	18 17	19 20	20 25	21 43	23 13
19¾	Gunton	d			06 19	06 21	07 51	08 57	10 19		12 19		14 19		16 21	17 21	18 23	19 26	20 31	21 49	23 19
23½	Roughton Road	d			06 25	06 28	07 57	09 04		11 24		13 24		15 24	16 27	17 27	18 30	19 33	20 38	21 55	23 25
—	**Cromer**	a	05 54	05 59	06 31	06 33	08 03	09 09	10 30	11 30	12 30	13 30	14 30	15 30	16 33	17 33	18 36	19 39	20 43	22 01	23 31
26½	**Cromer**	d	06 01	06 01	06 36	06 46	08 05	09 12	10 32	11 32	12 32	13 32	14 32	15 32	16 35	17 35	18 38	19 41	20 46	22 03	23 33
28¾	West Runton	d	06 05	06 06	06 40	06 50	08 10	09 16	10 37	11 37	12 37	13 37	14 37	15 37	16 40	17 40	18 43	19 46	20 50	22 08	23 38
30½	**Sheringham**	a	06 12	06 12	06 46	06 56	08 15	09 22	10 43	11 43	12 43	13 43	14 43	15 43	16 46	17 46	18 49	19 52	20 56	22 14	23 44

Sundays

until 30 September

		LE	LE	LE	LE	LE	LE	LE	LE	LE	LE	LE	LE	LE
Norwich	d	08 36	09 45	10 36	11 45	12 36	13 45	14 36	15 45	16 36	17 45	18 36	19 45	20 36
Salhouse	d	08 46		10 46		12 46		14 46		16 46		18 46		20 46
Hoveton & Wroxham	d	08 51	09 59	10 51	11 59	12 51	13 59	14 51	15 59	16 51	17 59	18 51	19 59	20 51
Worstead	d	08 58		10 58		12 58		14 58		16 58		18 58		20 58
North Walsham	a	09 03	10 09	11 03	12 09	13 03	14 09	15 03	16 09	17 03	18 09	19 03	20 09	21 03
North Walsham	d	09 04	10 11	11 06	12 11	13 06	14 11	15 06	16 11	17 06	18 11	19 06	20 11	21 06
Gunton	d	09 10		11 12		13 12		15 12		17 12		19 12		21 12
Roughton Road	d	09 16		11 19		13 19		15 19		17 19		19 19		21 19
Cromer	a	09 22	10 26	11 24	12 26	13 24	14 26	15 24	16 26	17 24	18 26	19 24	20 26	21 24
Cromer	d	09 25	10 29	11 27	12 29	13 27	14 29	15 27	16 29	17 27	18 29	19 27	20 29	21 27
West Runton	d	09 30		11 31		13 31		15 31		17 31		19 31		21 31
Sheringham	a	09 36	10 38	11 38	12 38	13 38	14 38	15 38	16 38	17 38	18 38	19 38	20 38	21 38

Sundays

from 7 October

		LE	LE	LE	LE	LE	LE	LE
Norwich	d	08 36	10 36	12 36	14 36	16 36	18 36	20 36
Salhouse	d	08 46	10 46	12 46	14 46	16 46	18 46	20 46
Hoveton & Wroxham	d	08 51	10 51	12 51	14 51	16 51	18 51	20 51
Worstead	d	08 58	10 58	12 58	14 58	16 58	18 58	20 58
North Walsham	a	09 03	11 03	13 03	15 03	17 03	19 03	21 03
North Walsham	d	09 04	11 06	13 06	15 06	17 06	19 06	21 06
Gunton	d	09 10	11 12	13 12	15 12	17 12	19 12	21 12
Roughton Road	d	09 16	11 19	13 19	15 19	17 19	19 19	21 19
Cromer	a	09 22	11 24	13 24	15 24	17 24	19 24	21 24
Cromer	d	09 25	11 27	13 27	15 27	17 27	19 27	21 27
West Runton	d	09 30	11 31	13 31	15 31	17 31	19 31	21 31
Sheringham	a	09 36	11 38	13 38	15 38	17 38	19 38	21 38

Table 16

Mondays to Saturdays

Sheringham and Cromer - Norwich

Network Diagram - see first Page of Table 13

Miles			LE MX	LE SX	LE SO	LE SX	LE	LE	LE	LE	LE	LE	LE	LE	LE	LE	LE	LE	LE	LE	LE	LE
0	Sheringham	d	23p47		06 22	06 32	07 16	08 23	09 46	10 46	11 46	12 46	13 46	14 46	15 46	16 49	17 49	18 55	19 57	21 10	22 17	23 47
1¾	West Runton	d	23p51		06 26	06 36	07 20	08 27	09 50	10 50	11 50	12 50	13 50	14 50	15 50	16 53	17 53	18 59	20 01	21 14	22 21	23 51
—	Cromer	a	23p55		06 30	06 40	07 24	08 31	09 54	10 54	11 54	12 54	13 54	14 54	15 54	16 57	17 57	19 03	20 05	21 18	22 25	23 55
4	Cromer	d	23p58	05 58	06 33	06 43	07 27	08 34	09 57	10 57	11 57	12 57	13 57	14 57	15 57	17 00	18 00	19 06	20 08	21 21	22 28	23 58
7	Roughton Road	d		06 04	06 39	06 49	07 33	08 40	10 03		12 03		14 03	15 03	16 03		18 06		20 14	21 27	22 34	
10¾	Gunton	d		06 10	06 45	06 55	07 39	08 46		11 08		13 08			16 09		18 12		20 20	21 33	22 40	
—	North Walsham	a	00 12	06 15	06 50	07 00	07 45	08 51	10 13	11 13	12 13	13 13	14 13	15 13	16 15	17 15	18 17	19 20	20 25	21 38	22 45	00 12
14½	North Walsham	d	00 13	06 16	06 51	07 01	07 45	08 52	10 13	11 14	12 13	13 14	14 13	15 14	16 15	17 15	18 18	19 21	20 26	21 43	22 46	00 13
17½	Worstead	d		06 21	06 56	07 06	07 50	08 57	10 18		12 18		14 18		16 20		18 23		20 31	21 48	22 51	
21¾	Hoveton & Wroxham	d	00 22	06 28	07 03	07 13	07 57	09 04	10 25	11 24	12 25	13 24	14 25	15 24	16 27	17 25	18 30	19 31	20 38	21 55	22 58	00 22
24½	Salhouse	d		06 32	07 07	07 17	08 02	09 08		11 28		13 28		15 28	16 32		18 34		20 42	21 59	23 02	
30½	Norwich	a	00 37	06 45	07 20	07 30	08 14	09 23	10 41	11 41	12 41	13 41	14 41	15 41	16 44	17 41	18 47	19 46	20 55	22 12	23 15	00 37

Sundays

until 30 September

		LE	LE	LE	LE	LE	LE	LE	LE	LE	LE	LE	LE	LE	LE
Sheringham	d	23p47	09 42	10 42	11 42	12 42	13 42	14 42	15 42	16 42	17 42	18 42	19 42	20 42	21 42
West Runton	d	23p51	09 46		11 46		13 46		15 46		17 46		19 46		21 46
Cromer	a	23p55	09 50	10 48	11 50	12 48	13 50	14 48	15 50	16 48	17 50	18 48	19 50	20 48	21 50
Cromer	d	23p58	09 54	10 52	11 54	12 52	13 54	14 52	15 54	16 52	17 54	18 52	19 54	20 52	21 54
Roughton Road	d		10 00		12 00		14 00		16 00		18 00		20 00		22 00
Gunton	d		10 06		12 06		14 06		16 06		18 06		20 06		22 06
North Walsham	a	00 12	10 11	11 06	12 11	13 06	14 11	15 06	16 11	17 06	18 11	19 06	20 11	21 06	22 11
North Walsham	d	00 13	10 12	11 07	12 12	13 07	14 12	15 07	16 12	17 07	18 12	19 07	20 12	21 07	22 12
Worstead	d		10 17		12 17		14 17		16 17		18 17		20 17		22 17
Hoveton & Wroxham	d	00 22	10 24	11 17	12 24	13 17	14 24	15 17	16 24	17 17	18 24	19 17	20 24	21 17	22 24
Salhouse	d		10 28		12 28		14 28		16 28		18 28		20 28		22 28
Norwich	a	00 37	10 40	11 31	12 40	13 31	14 40	15 31	16 40	17 31	18 40	19 31	20 40	21 31	22 40

Sundays

from 7 October

		LE	LE	LE	LE	LE	LE	LE	LE
Sheringham	d	23p47	09 42	11 42	13 42	15 42	17 42	19 42	21 42
West Runton	d	23p51	09 46	11 46	13 46	15 46	17 46	19 46	21 46
Cromer	a	23p55	09 50	11 50	13 50	15 50	17 50	19 50	21 50
Cromer	d	23p58	09 54	11 54	13 54	15 54	17 54	19 54	21 54
Roughton Road	d		10 00	12 00	14 00	16 00	18 00	20 00	22 00
Gunton	d		10 06	12 06	14 06	16 06	18 06	20 06	22 06
North Walsham	a	00 12	10 11	12 11	14 11	16 11	18 11	20 11	22 11
North Walsham	d	00 13	10 12	12 12	14 12	16 12	18 12	20 12	22 12
Worstead	d		10 17	12 17	14 17	16 17	18 17	20 17	22 17
Hoveton & Wroxham	d	00 22	10 24	12 24	14 24	16 24	18 24	20 24	22 24
Salhouse	d		10 28	12 28	14 28	16 28	18 28	20 28	22 28
Norwich	a	00 37	10 40	12 40	14 40	16 40	18 40	20 40	22 40

Table 17

Mondays to Fridays

London and Cambridge - Ely, Kings Lynn, Peterborough and Norwich

Network Diagram - see first Page of Table 13

Miles	Miles	Miles			LE MX ■	FC MO ■ A	FC MX ■	XC ◇■	XC ◇■	LE ■	FC ■	EM ◇	LE ◇■	FC ■	XC ◇■	EM ◇	LE ■	LE ■	FC ■	EM ◇	XC ◇■	FC ■	EM ◇
—	—	—	London Liverpool Street	d																			
—	—	0	London Kings Cross	d		23p15	23p15							05 45					06 45			07 15	
—	0	—	Ipswich	d									06 00										
—	—	—	Stansted Airport	d					05 16						06 06						07 21		
0	—	58	Cambridge	d	22p55	00 13	00 14	05 15	05 55	06 05	06 18			06 52	06 55		07 04	07 22	07 33		08 00	08 03	
5¼	—	63¼	Waterbeach	d		00 19	00 20				06 24			06 58					07 39			08 09	
14¾	50¾	72¾	Ely ■	a	23p09	00 29	00 30	05 29	06 09	06 19	06 33		06 59	07 07	07 10		07 18	07 38	07 48		08 14	08 20	
—	—	—		d	23p10			05 30	06 10	06 20	06 33	06 51	07 00	07 08	07 12	07 05	07 19		07 48	07 45	08 15	08 21	08 15
—	—	78¼	Littleport	d							06 43			07 15					07 55			08 28	
—	—	88½	Downham Market	d							06 54			07 24					08 04			08 37	
—	—	93¼	Watlington	d							07 00			07 31					08 10			08 43	
—	—	99¼	Kings Lynn	a							07 09			07 42					08 20			08 53	
—	—	—	Manea	d					06x20														
—	66¼	—	March	d				05 46	06 28			07 07	07 16		07 28					08 01	08 31		
—	74	—	Whittlesea	d				05 58	06 39				07 27		07 39					08 13			
—	81¼	—	Peterborough ■	a				06 08	06 50			07 25	07 38		07 51					08 24	08 50		
—	—	—	Shippea Hill	d													07x28						
—	—	—	Lakenheath	d																			
30¾	—	—	Brandon	d	23p26					06 36						07 20	07 38						
38	—	—	Thetford	d	23p34					06 44						07 29	07 47						08 37
45¾	—	—	Harling Road	d						06 53							07 55						
48¾	—	—	Eccles Road	d						06 58							08 00						
52¼	—	—	Attleborough	d	23p49					07 04						07 43	08 06						08 51
—	—	—	Spooner Row	d													08x11						
58¼	—	—	Wymondham	d	23p57					07 11						07 50	08 16						08 58
68¼	—	—	Norwich	a	00 11					07 27						08 13	08 30						09 13

		LE ■	FC ■	EM ◇	LE ■	XC ◇■	LE ■	FC ■	EM ◇	EM ◇	XC ◇■	EM ◇	LE ■	FC ■	EM ◇	LE ■	XC ◇■	EM ◇	LE ■	FC ■	EM ◇	XC ◇■	EM ◇
London Liverpool Street	d																						
London Kings Cross	d		07 45					08 45						09 45						10 45			
Ipswich	d				08 03											10 00							
Stansted Airport	d					08 21					09 21						10 27					11 27	
Cambridge	d	08 12	08 38			09 00	09 12	09 38			10 00		10 12	10 37			11 00		11 12	11 35		12 00	
Waterbeach	d		08 44					09 44						10 43						11 41			
Ely ■	a	08 26	08 53		09 00	09 14	09 26	09 53			10 14		10 26	10 52		10 58	11 14		11 26	11 50		12 14	
	d	08 29	08 54	08 50	09 00	09 15	09 27	09 54	09 45	09 49	10 15	10 17	10 27	10 52	10 54	10 58	11 15	11 19	11 27	11 50	11 53	12 15	12 18
Littleport	d		09 01					10 01						10 59						11 57			
Downham Market	d		09 10					10 10						11 08						12 06			
Watlington	d		09 16					10 16						11 14						12 11			
Kings Lynn	a		09 25					10 25						11 22						12 20			
Manea	d																						
March	d			09 07	09 17	09 31					10 31					11 15	11 31					12 31	
Whittlesea	d				09 28											11 26							
Peterborough ■	a			09 25	09 39	09 50				10 26	10 50				11 27	11 37	11 50				12 24	12 50	
Shippea Hill	d																						
Lakenheath	d																						
Brandon	d	08 45					09 43						10 43						11 43				
Thetford	d	08 53					09 51		10 06			10 41	10 51					11 41	11 51				12 39
Harling Road	d																						
Eccles Road	d																						
Attleborough	d	09 08					10 06						11 06						12 06				
Spooner Row	d						10x11																
Wymondham	d	09 16					10 16						11 14						12 14				
Norwich	a	09 30					10 30		10 44			11 14	11 30					12 13	12 30				13 13

		LE ■	FC ■	EM ◇	LE ■	XC ◇■	EM ◇	LE ■	FC ■	EM ◇	XC ◇■	EM ◇	LE ■	FC ■	EM ◇	LE ■	XC ◇■	EM ◇	LE ■	FC ■	FC ■	EM ◇	XC ◇■
London Liverpool Street	d																						
London Kings Cross	d		11 45						12 45					13 45							14 45		
Ipswich	d				12 00											14 00							
Stansted Airport	d					12 27					13 27						14 27						15 27
Cambridge	d	12 12	12 33			13 00		13 12	13 34		14 00		14 12	14 35			15 00		15 12	15 24	15 35		16 00
Waterbeach	d		12 39						13 40					14 41						15 30	15 41		
Ely ■	a	12 26	12 48		12 58	13 14		13 26	13 49		14 14		14 26	14 50		14 58	15 14		15 26	15 40	15 50		16 14
	d	12 27	12 48	12 52	12 58	13 15	13 20	13 27	13 49	13 52	14 15	14 17	14 27	14 50	14 53	14 58	15 15	15 17	15 27		15 50	15 52	16 15
Littleport	d		12 55						13 57					14 57							15 57		
Downham Market	d		13 04						14 06					15 06							16 06		
Watlington	d		13 10						14 11					15 11							16 11		
Kings Lynn	a		13 20						14 21					15 20							16 20		
Manea	d																						
March	d				13 15	13 31					14 31					15 15	15 31						16 31
Whittlesea	d				13 26											15 26							
Peterborough ■	a			13 25	13 37	13 50				14 25	14 50				15 27	15 37	15 50					16 27	16 50
Shippea Hill	d																						
Lakenheath	d																						
Brandon	d	12 43						13 43					14 43						15 43				
Thetford	d	12 51					13 41	13 51				14 38	14 51					15 38	15 51				
Harling Road	d																						
Eccles Road	d																						
Attleborough	d	13 06						14 06					15 06						16 06				
Spooner Row	d																						
Wymondham	d	13 14						14 14					15 14						16 14				
Norwich	a	13 30					14 13	14 30				15 13	15 30					16 14	16 30				

A from 21 May

London and Cambridge - Ely, Kings Lynn, Peterborough and Norwich

Network Diagram - see first Page of Table 13

		EM ◇	LE ■	FC ■	FC ■	EM ◇	LE ■	XC ◇■	EM ◇	LE ■	LE ■	FC ■	EM ◇	XC ◇■	FC ■	EM ◇	LE ■	LE ■ A	LE ■	EM ◇	LE ■	FC ■
London Liverpool Street	d										15 58							17 07				
London Kings Cross	d				15 44							16 44			17 14							17 44
Ipswich	d						16 00														17 49	
Stansted Airport	d							16 27						17 27								
Cambridge	d		16 12	16 21	16 39			17 00		17 12	17 22	17 39		18 00	18 05		18 12	18 17	18 24			18 39
Waterbeach	d			16 27	16 45						17 28	17 45						18 23	18 30			18 45
Ely ■	a		16 26	16 36	16 55		16 58	17 14		17 26	17 38	17 55		18 14	18 19		18 26	18 32	18 40		18 52	18 55
	d	16 16	16 27	16 36	16 55	16 51	16 58	17 15	17 17	17 27		17 56	17 52	18 15		18 20	18 27	18 33		18 52	19 00	18 56
Littleport	d				17 02							18 03						18 40				19 03
Downham Market	d			16a50	17 11							18 12						18 50				19 12
Watlington	d				17 17							18 18						18 56				19 18
Kings Lynn	a				17 26							18 28						19 08				19 28
Manea	d													18x25								
March	d						17 15	17 31						18 33						19 08	19 16	
Whittlesea	d						17 26														19 28	
Peterborough ■	a					17 26	17 37	17 51					18 25	18 50						19 26	19 38	
Shippea Hill	d																					
Lakenheath	d																					
Brandon	d		16 43							17 43							18 43					
Thetford	d	16 37	16 51						17 38	17 51						18 41	18 51					
Harling Road	d																					
Eccles Road	d																					
Attleborough	d		17 06							18 06							19 06					
Spooner Row	d																					
Wymondham	d		17 14							18 14							19 14					
Norwich	a	17 13	17 28						18 18	18 28						19 15	19 28					

		XC ◇■	FC ■	LE ■	EM ◇	LE ■	FC ■	EM ◇	XC ◇■	LE ■	EM ◇	LE ■	FC ■	LE ■	XC ◇■	FC ■	LE ■	FC ■	FC ■	FC ■	EM ◇	LE ■	FC ■
London Liverpool Street	d			18 07						19 07													
London Kings Cross	d		18 14				18 44						19 45			20 15		20 45	21 15	21 45			22 15
Ipswich	d													20 00									
Stansted Airport	d	18 21							19 21						20 21								
Cambridge	d	19 00	19 09	19 19		19 25	19 39		20 00	20 15		20 20	20 40		21 00	21 10	21 15	21 38	22 08	22 38		22 55	23 08
Waterbeach	d			19 25			19 45			20 21			20 46			21 16		21 44	22 14	22 44			23 14
Ely ■	a	19 14	19 23	19 34		19 39	19 55		20 14	20 30		20 35	20 55	21 00	21 14	21 25	21 30	21 53	22 23	22 54		23 09	23 23
	d	19 15	19 24	19 35	19 27	19 40	19 56	19 52	20 15	20 31	20 16	20 37	20 55	21 00	21 15	21 25	21 30	21 53	22 23		22 15	23 10	23 23
Littleport	d			19 42			20 03			20 38			21 02			21 32		22 00	22 30				23 30
Downham Market	d		19 39	19 52			20 12			20 48			21 11			21 41		22 09	22 39				23 39
Watlington	d			19 58			20 18			20 54			21 17			21 47		22 15	22 45				23 45
Kings Lynn	a		19 53	20 10			20 28			21 05			21 26			21 56		22 24	22 54				23 54
Manea	d																						
March	d	19 31							20 31					21 17	21 31								
Whittlesea	d													21 28									
Peterborough ■	a	19 50						20 26	20 50					21 39	21 51								
Shippea Hill	d																						
Lakenheath	d																						
Brandon	d					19 56						20 53					21 46					23 26	
Thetford	d				19 50	20 04					20 37	21 01					21 55				22 36	23 34	
Harling Road	d																						
Eccles Road	d																						
Attleborough	d					20 19						21 16					22 10				22 50	23 49	
Spooner Row	d																						
Wymondham	d					20 27						21 24					22 17				22 57	23 57	
Norwich	a				20 22	20 41					21 14	21 38					22 31				23 18	00 11	

		FC FO ■	FC FX ■
London Liverpool Street	d		
London Kings Cross	d	23 15	23 15
Ipswich	d		
Stansted Airport	d		
Cambridge	d	00 14	00 14
Waterbeach	d	00 20	00 20
Ely ■	a	00 29	00 30
	d	00 29	
Littleport	d	00 36	
Downham Market	d	00 45	
Watlington	d	00 51	
Kings Lynn	a	01 00	
Manea	d		
March	d		
Whittlesea	d		
Peterborough ■	a		
Shippea Hill	d		
Lakenheath	d		
Brandon	d		
Thetford	d		
Harling Road	d		
Eccles Road	d		
Attleborough	d		
Spooner Row	d		
Wymondham	d		
Norwich	a		

A The Fenman

London and Cambridge - Ely, Kings Lynn, Peterborough and Norwich

Network Diagram - see first Page of Table 13

		LE ■	FC ■	XC ◇■	XC ◇■	LE ■	FC ■	EM ◇	LE ◇■	XC ◇■	EM ◇	LE ■	FC ■	EM ◇	XC ◇■	EM ◇	LE ■	FC ■	EM ◇	LE ■	XC ◇■	LE ■	FC ■
London Liverpool Street	d																						
London Kings Cross	d		23p15										06 45					07 45					08 45
Ipswich	d								06 00											08 00			
Stansted Airport	d				05 25					06 27					07 27						08 27		
Cambridge	d	22p55	00 14	05 15	05 55	06 08	06 32			06 57		07 00	07 35		08 00		08 12	08 35			09 00	09 12	09 35
Waterbeach	d		00 20				06 38						07 41					08 41					09 41
Ely ■	a	23p09	00 29	05 29	06 09	06 22	06 47		06 59	07 11		07 14	07 50		08 14		08 26	08 50		08 58	09 14	09 26	09 50
	d	23p10	00 29	05 30	06 10	06 23	06 47	06 51	07 00	07 12	07 06	07 15	07 50	07 53	08 15	08 14	08 27	08 50	08 54	08 58	09 15	09 27	09 50
Littleport	d		00 36				06 54						07 57					08 57					09 57
Downham Market	d		00 45				07 03						08 06					09 06					10 06
Watlington	d		00 51				07 09						08 11					09 11					10 11
Kings Lynn	a		01 00				07 20						08 20					09 20					10 20
Manea	d				06x20																		
March	d			05 46	06 28			07 07	07 16	07 29				08 08	08 31				09 11	09 15	09 31		
Whittlesea	d			05 58	06 39				07 27	07 40				08 19						09 26			
Peterborough ■	a			06 08	06 50			07 25	07 38	07 50				08 31	08 50				09 28	09 38	09 50		
Shippea Hill	d											07x24											
Lakenheath	d																						
Brandon	d	23p26				06 39					07 22	07 34					08 43					09 43	
Thetford	d	23p34				06 48					07 30	07 42				08 36	08 51					09 51	
Harling Road	d					06 56						07 51											
Eccles Road	d					07 01						07 56											
Attleborough	d	23p49				07 07					07 44	08 02				08 50	09 06					10 06	
Spooner Row	d											08x07											
Wymondham	d	23p57				07 15					07 51	08 12				08 57	09 14					10 14	
Norwich	a	00 11				07 29					08 13	08 30				09 15	09 30					10 30	

		EM ◇	EM ◇	XC ◇■	EM ◇	LE ■	FC ■	EM ◇	LE ■	XC ◇■	EM ◇	LE ■	FC ■	EM ◇	XC ◇■	EM ◇	LE ■	FC ■	EM ◇	LE ■	XC ◇■	EM ◇	LE ■
London Liverpool Street	d																						
London Kings Cross	d						09 45						10 45					11 45					
Ipswich	d								10 00											12 00			
Stansted Airport	d			09 27						10 27					11 27						12 27		
Cambridge	d			10 00		10 12	10 35			11 00		11 12	11 35		12 00		12 12	12 35			13 00		13 12
Waterbeach	d						10 41						11 41					12 41					
Ely ■	a			10 14		10 26	10 50		10 58	11 14		11 26	11 50		12 14		12 26	12 50		12 58	13 14		13 26
	d	09 39	09 51	10 15	10 17	10 29	10 50	10 53	10 58	11 15	11 22	11 29	11 50	11 53	12 15	12 17	12 27	12 50	12 54	12 58	13 15	13 17	13 27
Littleport	d						10 57						11 57					12 57					
Downham Market	d						11 06						12 06					13 06					
Watlington	d						11 11						12 11					13 11					
Kings Lynn	a						11 20						12 20					13 20					
Manea	d																						
March	d			10 31					11 15	11 31					12 31					13 15	13 31		
Whittlesea	d								11 26											13 26			
Peterborough ■	a		10 25	10 50				11 24	11 37	11 50				12 24	12 50				13 26	13 37	13 50		
Shippea Hill	d																						
Lakenheath	d																						
Brandon	d					10 45						11 45					12 43						13 43
Thetford	d	10 04			10 40	10 54					11 44	11 54				12 39	12 51					13 39	13 51
Harling Road	d																						
Eccles Road	d																						
Attleborough	d					11 09						12 09					13 06						14 06
Spooner Row	d																						
Wymondham	d					11 16						12 16					13 14						14 14
Norwich	a	10 43			11 15	11 30					12 18	12 30				13 13	13 30					14 13	14 30

		FC ■	EM ◇	XC ◇■	EM ◇	LE ■	FC ■	EM ◇	LE ■	XC ◇■	EM ◇	LE ■	FC ■	EM ◇	XC ◇■	EM ◇	LE ■	FC ■	EM ◇	LE ■	XC ◇■	EM ◇
London Liverpool Street	d																					
London Kings Cross	d	12 45					13 45						14 45					15 45				
Ipswich	d								14 00											16 00		
Stansted Airport	d			13 27						14 27					15 27						16 27	
Cambridge	d	13 35		14 00		14 12	14 35			15 00		15 12	15 35		16 00		16 12	16 35			17 00	
Waterbeach	d	13 41					14 41						15 41					16 41				
Ely ■	a	13 50		14 14		14 26	14 50		14 58	15 14		15 26	15 50		16 14		16 26	16 50		16 58	17 14	
	d	13 50	13 53	14 15	14 17	14 27	14 50	14 53	14 58	15 15	15 17	15 27	15 50	15 52	16 15	16 17	16 27	16 50	16 52	16 58	17 15	17 17
Littleport	d	13 57					14 57						15 57					16 57				
Downham Market	d	14 06					15 06						16 06					17 06				
Watlington	d	14 11					15 11						16 11					17 11				
Kings Lynn	a	14 20					15 20						16 20					17 20				
Manea	d																					
March	d			14 31					15 15	15 31					16 31					17 15	17 31	
Whittlesea	d								15 26											17 26		
Peterborough ■	a		14 25	14 50				15 25	15 37	15 50				16 25	16 50				17 26	17 37	17 50	
Shippea Hill	d																					
Lakenheath	d											15x40										
Brandon	d					14 43						15 45					16 43					
Thetford	d				14 38	14 51					15 40	15 54				16 38	16 51					17 40
Harling Road	d																					
Eccles Road	d																					
Attleborough	d					15 06						16 09					17 06					
Spooner Row	d																					
Wymondham	d					15 14						16 16					17 14					
Norwich	a				15 13	15 30					16 15	16 30				17 13	17 30					18 18

Table 17

London and Cambridge - Ely, Kings Lynn, Peterborough and Norwich

Saturdays

Network Diagram - see first Page of Table 13

		LE ■	FC ■	EM ◇	XC ◇■	EM ◇	LE ■	FC ■	EM ◇	LE ■	XC ◇■	FC ■	EM ◇	LE ■	FC ■	EM ◇	XC ◇■	EM ◇	LE ■	FC ■	LE ■ A	LE ■ B	LE ■
London Liverpool Street	d																						
London Kings Cross	d		16 45					17 45				18 15			18 45					19 45			
Ipswich	d									18 00											20 00	20 00	
Stansted Airport	d				17 27						18 27						19 27						
Cambridge	d	17 12	17 35		18 00		18 12	18 35			19 00	19 04		19 12	19 40		20 00		20 12	20 40			21 12
Waterbeach	d		17 41					18 41							19 46					20 46			
Ely	a	17 26	17 50		18 14		18 26	18 50		18 58	19 14	19 18		19 26	19 55		20 14		20 26	20 55	20 58	20 58	21 26
	d	17 27	17 50	17 52	18 15	18 15	18 27	18 50	18 53	19 00	19 15	19 19	19 23	19 29	19 55	19 51	20 15	20 16	20 27	20 55	20 58	20 59	21 27
Littleport	d		17 57					18 57							20 02					21 02			
Downham Market	d		18 06					19 06				19 35			20 11					21 11			
Watlington	d		18 11					19 11				19 44			20 17					21 17			
Kings Lynn	a		18 20					19 20				19 52			20 25					21 25			
Manea	d				18x25																		
March	d				18 33				19 09	19 16	19 31						20 31				21 15	21 15	
Whittlesea	d									19 28											21 26	21 27	
Peterborough	a			18 25	18 50				19 29	19 38	19 50					20 25	20 50				21 37	21 37	
Shippea Hill	d																						
Lakenheath	d																						
Brandon	d	17 43					18 43							19 45					20 43				21 43
Thetford	d	17 51				18 37	18 51						19 44	19 54				20 37	20 51				21 51
Harling Road	d																						
Eccles Road	d																						
Attleborough	d	18 06					19 06							20 09					21 06				22 06
Spooner Row	d																						
Wymondham	d	18 14					19 14							20 16					21 14				22 14
Norwich	a	18 30				19 19	19 30						20 18	20 30				21 14	21 30				22 30

		FC ■	EM ◇	LE ■	FC ■	FC ■
London Liverpool Street	d					
London Kings Cross	d	20 45			22 15	23 15
Ipswich	d					
Stansted Airport	d					
Cambridge	d	21 40		22 30	23 11	00 14
Waterbeach	d	21 46			23 17	00 20
Ely	a	21 55		22 44	23 26	00 29
	d	21 55	22 16	22 45	23 26	00 29
Littleport	d	22 02			23 33	00 36
Downham Market	d	22 11			23 43	00 45
Watlington	d	22 17			23 48	00 51
Kings Lynn	a	22 25			23 58	01 00
Manea	d					
March	d					
Whittlesea	d					
Peterborough	a					
Shippea Hill	d					
Lakenheath	d					
Brandon	d			23 01		
Thetford	d		22 37	23 09		
Harling Road	d					
Eccles Road	d					
Attleborough	d		22 51	23 24		
Spooner Row	d					
Wymondham	d		22 58	23 32		
Norwich	a		23 20	23 46		

A 28 July, 4 August, 11 August, 1 September, 8 September

B until 21 July, from 18 August, not 1 September, 8 September

Table 17

London and Cambridge - Ely, Kings Lynn, Peterborough and Norwich

Sundays

until 9 September

Network Diagram - see first Page of Table 13

		FC ■	LE ■ A	LE ■ B	LE ■	FC ■	FC ■	EM ◇	LE ◇■ A	LE ◇■ B	LE ■	XC ◇■	FC ■ B	FC ■ D	EM ◇	EM ◇	LE ■	XC ◇■	FC ■	LE ■ A	LE ■ B	LE ■	XC ◇■	FC ■	EM ◇
London Liverpool Street	d																								
London Kings Cross	d	23p15				07 53	09 15						10 15	10 15					11 15					12 15	
Ipswich	d		07 17	07 55					09 17	09 55										11 17	11 55				
Stansted Airport	d											10 25						11 25					12 25		
Cambridge	d	00 14			08 48	09 05	10 05				10 48	11 00	11 05	11 05			11 52	12 00	12 05			12 52	13 00	13 05	
Waterbeach	d	00 20				09 11	10 11						11 11	11 11					12 11					13 11	
Ely	a	00 29	08 42	08 51	09 02	09 20	10 20		10 42	10 51	11 02	11 14	11 20	11 20			12 06	12 15	12 20	12 42	12 51	13 06	13 15	13 20	
	d	00 29	08 55	08 52	09 03	09 20	10 20	10 32	10 52	10 52	11 03	11 15	11 20	11 20	11 39	11 59	12 07	12 15	12 20	12 52	12 52	13 07	13 15	13 20	13 36
Littleport	d	00 36				09 27	10 27						11 27	11 27					12 27					13 27	
Downham Market	d	00 45				09 36	10 36						11 36	11 36					12 36					13 36	
Watlington	d	00 51				09 41	10 41						11 41	11 42					12 41					13 41	
Kings Lynn	a	01 00				09 50	10 50						11 50	11 50					12 50					13 50	
Manea	d																								
March	d		09 09	09 09					11 09	11 09		11 31						12 31		13 09	13 09		13 31		
Whittlesea	d		09 20	09 20					11 20	11 20										13 20	13 20				
Peterborough	a		09 36	09 36				11 09	11 36	11 36		11 50			12 16			12 50		13 31	13 31		13 50		
Shippea Hill	d																								
Lakenheath	d				09x17						11x17											13x20			
Brandon	d				09 22						11 22					12 15	12 23					13 25			
Thetford	d				09 31						11 31					12 23	12 31					13 34			13 57
Harling Road	d																								
Eccles Road	d																								
Attleborough	d				09 46						11 46					12 37	12 46					13 49			
Spooner Row	d																								
Wymondham	d				09 53						11 53					12 44	12 54					13 56			
Norwich	a				10 13						12 13					13 06	13 13					14 13			14 35

		LE ■	XC ◇■	FC ■	EM ◇	EM ◇	LE ■ A	LE ■ B	LE ■	XC ◇■	FC ■	EM ◇	EM ◇	LE ■	XC ◇■	FC ■	LE ■ A	LE ■ B	EM ◇	LE ■	XC ◇■	FC ■	EM ◇	EM ◇	LE ■
London Liverpool Street	d																								
London Kings Cross	d			13 15							14 15					15 15						16 15			
Ipswich	d						13 17	13 55									15 17	15 55							
Stansted Airport	d		13 25							14 25					15 25						16 25				
Cambridge	d	13 52	14 00	14 05					14 52	15 00	15 05			15 52	16 00	16 05				16 52	17 00	17 05			17 52
Waterbeach	d			14 11							15 11					16 11						17 11			
Ely	a	14 06	14 14	14 20			14 42	14 51	15 06	15 14	15 20			16 06	16 15	16 20	16 42	16 51		17 06	17 15	17 20			18 06
	d	14 07	14 15	14 20	14 24	14 45	14 52	14 52	15 07	15 15	15 20	15 33	15 48	16 07	16 15	16 20	16 52	16 52	16 41	17 07	17 15	17 20	17 36	17 48	18 07
Littleport	d			14 27							15 27					16 27						17 27			
Downham Market	d			14 36							15 36					16 36						17 36			
Watlington	d			14 41							15 41					16 41						17 41			
Kings Lynn	a			14 50							15 50					16 50						17 50			
Manea	d																								
March	d		14 31				15 09	15 09		15 31					16 31		17 09	17 09			17 31				
Whittlesea	d						15 20	15 20									17 20	17 20							
Peterborough	a		14 50			15 24	15 31	15 31		15 50			16 22		16 50		17 31	17 31			17 50			18 23	
Shippea Hill	d																								
Lakenheath	d													16x20											
Brandon	d	14 23			14 42				15 23					16 25						17 23					18 23
Thetford	d	14 31			14 50				15 31			15 54		16 34					17 02	17 31			17 57		18 31
Harling Road	d																								
Eccles Road	d																								
Attleborough	d	14 46			15 04				15 46					16 49						17 46					18 46
Spooner Row	d																								
Wymondham	d	14 54			15 11				15 54					16 56						17 54					18 54
Norwich	a	15 13			15 30				16 13			16 35		17 13					17 35	18 13			18 30		19 10

		XC ◇■	FC ■	EM ◇	EM ◇	LE ■ A	LE ■ B	LE ■	XC ◇■ C	FC ■	EM ◇	EM ◇	LE ■	XC ◇■ C	FC ■	LE ■ A	EM ◇	FC ■	EM ◇	LE ■	FC ■	FC ■	EM ◇	FC ■
London Liverpool Street	d																							
London Kings Cross	d		17 15							18 15					19 15			20 15			21 15	22 15		23 15
Ipswich	d					17 17	17 55									19 17								
Stansted Airport	d	17 25							18 25					19 25										
Cambridge	d	18 00	18 05					18 52	19 00	19 05			19 52	20 00	20 05			21 05		21 52	22 05	23 05		00 13
Waterbeach	d		18 11							19 11					20 11			21 11			22 11	23 11		00 19
Ely	a	18 15	18 20			18 42	18 51	19 06	19 15	19 20			20 06	20 15	20 20	20 42		21 20		22 06	22 20	23 20		00 29
	d	18 15	18 20	18 36	18 48	18 52	18 52	19 07	19 15	19 20	19 26	19 48	20 07	20 15	20 20	20 52	20 35	21 20	21 44	22 07	22 20	23 20	22 32	
Littleport	d		18 27							19 27					20 27			21 27			22 27	23 27		
Downham Market	d		18 36							19 36					20 36			21 36			22 36	23 36		
Watlington	d		18 41							19 41					20 41			21 41			22 41	23 41		
Kings Lynn	a		18 50							19 50					20 50			21 50			22 50	23 50		
Manea	d																							
March	d	18 31				19 09	19 09		19 31					20 31		21 09								
Whittlesea	d					19 20	19 20									21 20								
Peterborough	a	18 50			19 24	19 32	19 32		19 50			20 29		20 50		21 32			22 20					
Shippea Hill	d																							
Lakenheath	d																							
Brandon	d							19 23					20 23							22 23				
Thetford	d			18 57				19 31			19 50		20 31				20 56			22 31			22 53	
Harling Road	d																							
Eccles Road	d																							
Attleborough	d							19 46					20 46				21 10			22 46			23 07	
Spooner Row	d																							
Wymondham	d							19 54					20 54				21 17			22 54			23 14	
Norwich	a			19 29				20 13			20 29		21 10				21 35			23 13			23 28	

A 29 July, 5 August, 12 August, 2 September, 9 September. Train service operates between Ipswich and Bury St Edmunds (Table 14) and Ely and Peterborough. Bus replacement service operates between Bury St Edmunds and Ely (Table 14)

B until 22 July, 19 August, 26 August

C until 24 June

D 29 July, 5 August, 12 August, 2 September, 9 September

16 September to 21 October

London and Cambridge - Ely, Kings Lynn, Peterborough and Norwich

Network Diagram - see first Page of Table 13

		FC ■	LE ■	FC ■	FC ■	LE ◇■	LE ■	FC ■	XC ◇■	EM ◇	LE ■	XC ◇■	FC ■	LE ■	LE ■	XC ◇■	FC ■	LE ■	XC ◇■	FC ■	EM ◇	EM ◇	LE ■
London Liverpool Street	d																						
London Kings Cross	d	23p15		07 53	09 12			10 12					11 12				12 12			13 12			
Ipswich	d					09 55								11 55									13 55
Stansted Airport	d								10 25			11 25				12 25			13 25				
Cambridge	d	00 14	08 48	09 05	10 05		10 48	11 05	11 00		11 52	12 00	12 05		12 52	13 00	13 05	13 52	14 00	14 05			
Waterbeach	d	00 20		09 11	10 11			11 11					12 11				13 11			14 11			
Ely ■	a	00 29	09 02	09 20	10 20	10 51	11 02	11 20	11 14		12 06	12 15	12 20	12 51	13 06	13 15	13 20	14 06	14 14	14 20			14 51
	d	00 29	09 03	09 20	10 20	10 52	11 03	11 20	11 15	11 39	12 07	12 15	12 20	12 52	13 07	13 15	13 20	14 07	14 15	14 20	14 24	14 45	14 52
Littleport	d	00 36		09 27	10 27			11 27					12 27				13 27			14 27			
Downham Market	d	00 45		09 36	10 36			11 36					12 36				13 36			14 36			
Watlington	d	00 51		09 41	10 41			11 41					12 41				13 41			14 41			
Kings Lynn	a	01 00		09 50	10 50			11 50					12 50				13 50			14 50			
Manea	d																						
March	d					11 09			11 31			12 31		13 09		13 31			14 31				15 09
Whittlesea	d					11 20								13 20									15 20
Peterborough ■	a					11 36			11 50	12 16		12 50		13 31		13 50			14 50			15 24	15 31
Shippea Hill	d																						
Lakenheath	d		09x17				11x17								13x20								
Brandon	d		09 22				11 22				12 23				13 25			14 23			14 42		
Thetford	d		09 31				11 31				12 31				13 34			14 31			14 50		
Harling Road	d																						
Eccles Road	d																						
Attleborough	d		09 46				11 46				12 46				13 49			14 46			15 04		
Spooner Row	d																						
Wymondham	d		09 53				11 53				12 54				13 56			14 54			15 11		
Norwich	a		10 13				12 13				13 13				14 13			15 13			15 30		

		LE ■	XC ◇■	FC ■	EM ◇	EM ◇	LE ■	XC ◇■	FC ■	LE ■	EM ◇	LE ■	XC ◇■	FC ■	EM ◇	EM ◇	LE ■	XC ◇■	FC ■	EM ◇	EM ◇	LE ■	LE ■
London Liverpool Street	d																						
London Kings Cross	d			14 15					15 15					16 15					17 15				
Ipswich	d									15 55												17 55	
Stansted Airport	d		14 25					15 25					16 25					17 25					
Cambridge	d	14 52	15 00	15 05			15 52	16 00	16 05			16 52	17 00	17 05			17 52	18 00	18 05				18 52
Waterbeach	d			15 11					16 11					17 11					18 11				
Ely ■	a	15 06	15 14	15 20			16 06	16 15	16 20	16 51		17 06	17 15	17 20			18 06	18 15	18 20			18 51	19 06
	d	15 07	15 15	15 20	15 33	15 48	16 07	16 15	16 20	16 52	16 41	17 07	17 15	17 20	17 36	17 48	18 07	18 15	18 20	18 36	18 48	18 52	19 07
Littleport	d			15 27					16 27					17 27					18 27				
Downham Market	d			15 36					16 36					17 36					18 36				
Watlington	d			15 41					16 41					17 41					18 41				
Kings Lynn	a			15 50					16 50					17 50					18 50				
Manea	d																						
March	d		15 31					16 31		17 09			17 31					18 31				19 09	
Whittlesea	d									17 20												19 20	
Peterborough ■	a		15 50			16 22		16 50		17 31			17 50			18 23		18 50			19 24	19 32	
Shippea Hill	d																						
Lakenheath	d						16x20																
Brandon	d	15 23					16 25					17 23					18 23						19 23
Thetford	d	15 31			15 54		16 34				17 02	17 31			17 57		18 31			18 57			19 31
Harling Road	d																						
Eccles Road	d																						
Attleborough	d	15 46					16 49					17 46					18 46						19 46
Spooner Row	d																						
Wymondham	d	15 54					16 56					17 54					18 54						19 54
Norwich	a	16 13			16 35		17 13				17 35	18 13			18 30		19 10			19 29			20 13

		FC ■	EM ◇	EM ◇	LE ■	FC ■	FC ■	EM ◇	EM ◇	LE ■	FC ■	FC ■	EM ◇	FC ■
London Liverpool Street	d													
London Kings Cross	d	18 15				19 15	20 15				21 15	22 15		23 15
Ipswich	d													
Stansted Airport	d													
Cambridge	d	19 05			19 52	20 05	21 05			21 52	22 05	23 05		00 13
Waterbeach	d	19 11				20 11	21 11				22 11	23 11		00 19
Ely ■	a	19 20			20 06	20 20	21 20			22 06	22 20	23 20		00 29
	d	19 20	19 26	19 48	20 07	20 20	21 20	20 35	21 44	22 07	22 20	23 20	22 32	
Littleport	d	19 27				20 27	21 27				22 27	23 27		
Downham Market	d	19 36				20 36	21 36				22 36	23 36		
Watlington	d	19 41				20 41	21 41				22 41	23 41		
Kings Lynn	a	19 50				20 50	21 50				22 50	23 50		
Manea	d													
March	d													
Whittlesea	d													
Peterborough ■	a			20 29					22 20					
Shippea Hill	d													
Lakenheath	d													
Brandon	d				20 23					22 23				
Thetford	d		19 50		20 31			20 56		22 31			22 53	
Harling Road	d													
Eccles Road	d													
Attleborough	d				20 46			21 10		22 46			23 07	
Spooner Row	d													
Wymondham	d				20 54			21 17		22 54			23 14	
Norwich	a		20 29		21 10			21 35		23 13			23 28	

from 28 October

London and Cambridge - Ely, Kings Lynn, Peterborough and Norwich

Network Diagram - see first Page of Table 13

		FC ■	LE ■	FC ■	FC ■	LE ◇■	LE ■	XC ◇■	FC ■	EM ◇	LE ■	XC ◇■	FC ■	LE ■	LE ■	XC ◇■	FC ■	LE ■	XC ◇■	FC ■	EM ◇	EM ◇	LE ■
London Liverpool Street	d																						
London Kings Cross	d	23p15		07 53	09 15				10 15				11 15				12 15			13 15			
Ipswich	d					09 55								11 55									13 55
Stansted Airport	d							10 25				11 25				12 25			13 25				
Cambridge	d	00 14	08 48	09 05	10 05		10 48	11 00	11 05		11 52	12 00	12 05		12 52	13 00	13 05	13 52	14 00	14 05			
Waterbeach	d	00 20		09 11	10 11				11 11				12 11				13 11			14 11			
Ely ■	a	00 29	09 02	09 20	10 20	10 51	11 02	11 14	11 20		12 06	12 15	12 20	12 51	13 06	13 15	13 20	14 06	14 14	14 20			14 51
	d	00 29	09 03	09 20	10 20	10 52	11 03	11 15	11 20	11 39	12 07	12 15	12 20	12 52	13 07	13 15	13 20	14 07	14 15	14 20	14 24	14 45	14 52
Littleport	d	00 36		09 27	10 27				11 27				12 27				13 27			14 27			
Downham Market	d	00 45		09 36	10 36				11 36				12 36				13 36			14 36			
Watlington	d	00 51		09 41	10 41				11 41				12 41				13 41			14 41			
Kings Lynn	a	01 00		09 50	10 50				11 50				12 50				13 50			14 50			
Manea	d																						
March	d					11 09		11 31				12 31		13 09		13 31			14 31				15 09
Whittlesea	d					11 20								13 20									15 20
Peterborough ■	a					11 36		11 50		12 16		12 50		13 31		13 50			14 50			15 24	15 31
Shippea Hill	d																						
Lakenheath	d		09x17				11x17								13x20								
Brandon	d		09 22				11 22				12 23				13 25			14 23			14 42		
Thetford	d		09 31				11 31				12 31				13 34			14 31			14 50		
Harling Road	d																						
Eccles Road	d																						
Attleborough	d		09 46				11 46				12 46				13 49			14 46			15 04		
Spooner Row	d																						
Wymondham	d		09 53				11 53				12 54				13 56			14 54			15 11		
Norwich	a		10 13				12 13				13 13				14 13			15 13			15 30		

		LE ■	XC ◇■	FC ■	EM ◇	EM ◇	LE ■	XC ◇■	FC ■	LE ■	EM ◇	LE ■	XC ◇■	FC ■	EM ◇	EM ◇	LE ■	XC ◇■	FC ■	EM ◇	EM ◇	LE ■	LE ■
London Liverpool Street	d																						
London Kings Cross	d			14 15					15 15					16 15					17 15				
Ipswich	d									15 55												17 55	
Stansted Airport	d		14 25					15 25					16 25					17 25					
Cambridge	d	14 52	15 00	15 05			15 52	16 00	16 05			16 52	17 00	17 05			17 52	18 00	18 05				18 52
Waterbeach	d			15 11					16 11					17 11					18 11				
Ely ■	a	15 06	15 14	15 20			16 06	16 15	16 20	16 51		17 06	17 15	17 20			18 06	18 15	18 20			18 51	19 06
	d	15 07	15 15	15 20	15 33	15 48	16 07	16 15	16 20	16 52	16 41	17 07	17 15	17 20	17 36	17 48	18 07	18 15	18 20	18 36	18 48	18 52	19 07
Littleport	d			15 27					16 27					17 27					18 27				
Downham Market	d			15 36					16 36					17 36					18 36				
Watlington	d			15 41					16 41					17 41					18 41				
Kings Lynn	a			15 50					16 50					17 50					18 50				
Manea	d																						
March	d		15 31					16 31		17 09			17 31					18 31				19 09	
Whittlesea	d									17 20												19 20	
Peterborough ■	a		15 50			16 22		16 50		17 31			17 50			18 23		18 50			19 24	19 32	
Shippea Hill	d																						
Lakenheath	d						16x20																
Brandon	d	15 23					16 25					17 23					18 23						19 23
Thetford	d	15 31			15 54		16 34				17 02	17 31			17 57		18 31			18 57			19 31
Harling Road	d																						
Eccles Road	d																						
Attleborough	d	15 46					16 49					17 46					18 46						19 46
Spooner Row	d																						
Wymondham	d	15 54					16 56					17 54					18 54						19 54
Norwich	a	16 13			16 35		17 13				17 35	18 13			18 30		19 10			19 29			20 13

		FC ■	EM ◇	EM ◇	LE ■	FC ■	FC ■	EM ◇	EM ◇	LE ■	FC ■	FC ■	EM ◇	FC ■
London Liverpool Street	d													
London Kings Cross	d	18 15				19 15	20 15				21 15	22 15		23 15
Ipswich	d													
Stansted Airport	d													
Cambridge	d	19 05			19 52	20 05	21 05			21 52	22 05	23 05		00 13
Waterbeach	d	19 11				20 11	21 11				22 11	23 11		00 19
Ely ■	a	19 20			20 06	20 20	21 20			22 06	22 20	23 20		00 29
	d	19 20	19 26	19 48	20 07	20 20	21 20	20 35	21 44	22 07	22 20	23 20	22 32	
Littleport	d	19 27				20 27	21 27				22 27	23 27		
Downham Market	d	19 36				20 36	21 36				22 36	23 36		
Watlington	d	19 41				20 41	21 41				22 41	23 41		
Kings Lynn	a	19 50				20 50	21 50				22 50	23 50		
Manea	d													
March	d													
Whittlesea	d													
Peterborough ■	a			20 29					22 20					
Shippea Hill	d													
Lakenheath	d													
Brandon	d				20 23					22 23				
Thetford	d		19 50		20 31			20 56		22 31			22 53	
Harling Road	d													
Eccles Road	d													
Attleborough	d				20 46			21 10		22 46			23 07	
Spooner Row	d													
Wymondham	d				20 54			21 17		22 54			23 14	
Norwich	a		20 29		21 10			21 35		23 13			23 28	

Norwich, Peterborough, Kings Lynn and Ely - Cambridge and London

Network Diagram - see first Page of Table 13

Miles	Miles	Miles			LE	FC	FC	FC	LE	FC	LE	EM	LE	EM		FC	LE	EM	XC	FC	EM	FC	LE	LE	EM
					MO	MO	MX																		
					■	■	■	■	■	■	■	◇	■	◇		■	■	◇	◇■	■	◇	■	■	■	◇
					C	A							B												
0	—	—	**Norwich**	d							05 33	05 50					06 33	06 52						07 37	07 57
10	—	—	Wymondham	d							05 45	06 02					06 45							07 49	
—	—	—	Spooner Row	d																					
16	—	—	Attleborough	d							05 52	06 09					06 52							07 56	
—	—	—	Eccles Road	d																					
—	—	—	Harling Road	d																					
30½	—	—	Thetford	d							06 06	06 23					07 06	07 20						08 10	08 24
37½	—	—	Brandon	d							06 14						07 14							08 18	
—	—	—	Lakenheath	d																					
—	—	—	Shippea Hill	d																					
—	0	—	**Peterborough ■**	d	21p45									06 27					07 12		07 35		07 45		
—	—	—	Whittlesea	d	21p53														07 20				07 53		
—	15	—	March	d	22p04									06 43					07 31		07 51		08 04		
—	—	—	Manea	d															07x38						
—	—	0	**Kings Lynn**	d		22p28	22p28	04 56	05 19	05 51			06 17			06 51				07 25		07 55			
—	—	6	Watlington	d		22p35	22p35	05 03	05 26	05 58			06 24			06 58				07 32		08 02			
—	—	10¾	Downham Market	d		22p41	22p41	05 09	05 33	06 04			06 31			07 04				07 38		08 08			
—	—	21	Littleport	d		22p50	22p50	05 18	05 42	06 13			06 40			07 13				07 47		08 17			
53½	30½	26½	**Ely ■**	a	22p22	22p58	22p58	05 26	05 51	06 21	06 31	06 45	06 49	07 01		07 21	07 31	07 41	07 51	07 56	08 11	08 26	08 31	08 37	08 46
—	—	—		d	22p29	22p58	22p58	05 26	05 52	06 21	06 32		06 50			07 21	07 33		07 52	07 56		08 26	08 31	08 39	
—	—	36	Waterbeach	d		23p07	23p07	05 35	06 01	06 31			06 59			07 31						08 36			
68¼	—	41¼	**Cambridge**	a		23p15	23p14	05 44	06 10	06 39	06 51		07 08			07 39	07 52		08 07	08 12		08 45		08 59	
—	55	—	Stansted Airport	a															08 39						
—	—	—	Ipswich	a	00 03																		09 28		
—	—	99¼	**London Kings Cross**	a		00 39	00 40	06 38		07 39						08 39				09 09		09 44			
—	—	—	London Liverpool Street	a					07 25				08 25												

		XC	FC	FC	LE	EM	EM	XC	EM		LE	FC	LE	EM	XC	EM	FC	LE	EM		XC	EM	FC	LE	LE
		◇■	■	■	■	◇	◇	◇■	◇		■	■	■	◇	◇■	◇	■	■	◇		◇■	◇	■	■	■
Norwich	d				08 40		08 57						09 40	09 57				10 40	10 57						11 40
Wymondham	d				08 52								09 52					10 52							11 52
Spooner Row	d																								
Attleborough	d				08 59								09 59					10 59							11 59
Eccles Road	d																								
Harling Road	d																								
Thetford	d				09 13		09 24						10 13	10 24				11 13	11 24						12 13
Brandon	d				09 21								10 21					11 21							12 21
Lakenheath	d																								
Shippea Hill	d																								
Peterborough ■	d	08 18				08 59		09 18	09 40		09 45				10 18	10 44					11 17	11 41		11 45	
Whittlesea	d										09 53													11 53	
March	d	08 34						09 34			10 04				10 34						11 34			12 04	
Manea	d																								
Kings Lynn	d		08 27	08 59								09 59					10 56						11 56		
Watlington	d		08 34	09 06								10 06					11 03						12 03		
Downham Market	d		08 40	09 12								10 12					11 09						12 09		
Littleport	d		08 49	09 21								10 21					11 18						12 18		
Ely ■	a	08 52	08 57	09 29	09 38	09 41	09 45	09 52	10 13		10 25	10 29	10 38	10 48	10 52	11 16	11 26	11 38	11 48		11 52	12 14	12 26	12 29	12 38
	d	08 52	08 57	09 29	09 39			09 53			10 32	10 29	10 39		10 52		11 26	11 39			11 52		12 26	12 31	12 39
Waterbeach	d		09 07	09 38								10 38					11 35						12 35		
Cambridge	a	09 08	09 15	09 47	09 59			10 08				10 47	10 59		11 08		11 44	11 59			12 08		12 44		12 59
Stansted Airport	a	09 39						10 40							11 40						12 40				
Ipswich	a										11 28													13 28	
London Kings Cross	a		10 14	10 46								11 44					12 35						13 35		
London Liverpool Street	a																								

		EM	XC	EM	FC		LE	EM	XC	EM	FC	LE	LE	EM	XC		EM	FC	LE	EM	XC	EM	FC	LE	LE
		◇	◇■	◇	■		■	◇	◇■	◇	■	■	■	◇	◇■		◇	■	■	◇	◇■	◇	■	■	■
Norwich	d	11 57					12 40	12 57					13 40	13 57					14 40	14 57					15 40
Wymondham	d						12 52						13 52						14 52						15 52
Spooner Row	d																								
Attleborough	d						12 59						13 59						14 59						15 59
Eccles Road	d																								
Harling Road	d																								
Thetford	d	12 24					13 13	13 24					14 13	14 24					15 13	15 24					16 13
Brandon	d						13 21						14 21						15 21						16 21
Lakenheath	d																								
Shippea Hill	d																								
Peterborough ■	d		12 18	12 43					13 18	13 41		13 45			14 18		14 41				15 18	15 40		15 45	
Whittlesea	d											13 53												15 53	
March	d		12 34						13 34			14 04			14 34						15 34			16 04	
Manea	d																								
Kings Lynn	d				12 56						13 56							14 56					15 55		
Watlington	d				13 03						14 03							15 03					16 02		
Downham Market	d				13 09						14 09							15 09					16 08		
Littleport	d				13 18						14 18							15 18					16 17		
Ely ■	a	12 47	12 52	13 16	13 26		13 38	13 49	13 52	14 14	14 26	14 29	14 38	14 47	14 52		15 14	15 26	15 38	15 47	15 52	16 13	16 24	16 28	16 38
	d		12 52		13 26		13 39		13 52		14 26	14 31	14 39		14 52			15 26	15 39		15 52		16 24	16 31	16 39
Waterbeach	d				13 35						14 35							15 35					16 33		
Cambridge	a		13 08		13 44		13 59		14 08		14 44		14 59		15 08			15 44	15 59		16 08		16 43		16 59
Stansted Airport	a		13 40						14 40						15 40						16 40				
Ipswich	a											15 28												17 28	
London Kings Cross	a				14 34						15 34							16 34					17 35		
London Liverpool Street	a																								

A from 21 May
B The Fenman
C 30 July, 6 August, 13 August, 3 September, 10 September. Train service operates between Peterborough and Ely and Bury St Edmunds and Ipswich (Table 14) Bus replacement service operates between Ely and Bury St Edmunds (Table 14)

Norwich, Peterborough, Kings Lynn and Ely - Cambridge and London

Network Diagram - see first Page of Table 13

			EM	XC	FC	EM	FC	LE	EM	XC	FC		EM	LE	LE	EM	XC	FC	EM	XC	LE		EM	XC	FC
			◇	◇■	■	◇	■	■	◇	◇■	■		◇	■	■	◇	◇■	■	◇	◇■	■		◇	◇■	■
Norwich	d		15 52					16 38	16 57						17 35	17 54					18 40		18 57		
Wymondham	d							16 50	17 09						17 47	18 06					18 52				
Spooner Row	d							16x54																	
Attleborough	d		16 09					16 59							17 54	18 13					18 59				
Eccles Road	d		16 14												17 59										
Harling Road	d		16 18												18 03										
Thetford	d		16 27					17 13	17 27						18 13	18 27					19 13		19 24		
Brandon	d							17 21							18 21						19 21				
Lakenheath	d																								
Shippea Hill	d																								
Peterborough ■	d			16 18		16 41				17 18			17 42	17 45			18 18		18 45	18 59				19 18	
Whittlesea	d									17 26				17 53											
March	d			16 34						17 37				18 04			18 34		19 01	19 15				19 35	
Manea	d									17x44															
Kings Lynn	d				16 37						17 37							18 37							19 37
Watlington	d				16 44						17 44							18 44							19 44
Downham Market	d				16 50		17 12				17 50							18 50							19 50
Littleport	d				17 00						17 59							18 59							19 59
Ely ■	a		16 48	16 52	17 08	17 14	17 28	17 38	17 48	17 58	18 07		18 16	18 28	18 38	18 48	18 52	19 08	19 24	19 33	19 38		19 48	19 53	20 08
	d			16 52	17 08		17 28	17 39		17 59	18 08			18 31	18 39		18 52	19 08		19 33	19 39			19 53	20 08
Waterbeach	d				17 17						18 17							19 17							20 17
Cambridge	a			17 08	17 24		17 44	17 59		18 16	18 24				18 59		19 08	19 24		19 50	19 59			20 08	20 26
Stansted Airport	a			17 40						18 54							19 39							20 39	
Ipswich	a													19 28											
London Kings Cross	a				18 32		18 38				19 36							20 33							21 32
London Liverpool Street	a																								

		EM	LE	LE	XC	FC	XC		FC	EM	LE	LE	XC	FC	LE
		◇	◇■	■	◇■	■	◇■		■	◇	■	◇■	◇■	■	■
Norwich	d			19 40							21 15				22 40
Wymondham	d			19 52							21 27				22 52
Spooner Row	d														
Attleborough	d			19 59							21 34				22 59
Eccles Road	d														
Harling Road	d														
Thetford	d			20 13							21 48				23 13
Brandon	d			20 21							21 56				23 21
Lakenheath	d														
Shippea Hill	d														
Peterborough ■	d	19 40	19 45		20 18		21 18			21 38		21 45	22 18		
Whittlesea	d		19 53									21 53			
March	d		20 04		20 35		21 34					22 04	22 35		
Manea	d														
Kings Lynn	d					20 37			21 37					22 28	
Watlington	d					20 44			21 44					22 35	
Downham Market	d					20 50			21 50					22 41	
Littleport	d					20 59			21 59					22 50	
Ely ■	a	20 13	20 26	20 38	20 53	21 08	21 52		22 08	22 11	22 14	22 23	22 53	22 58	23 38
	d		20 27	20 39	20 53	21 08	21 52		22 08		22 15	22 23	22 53	22 58	23 39
Waterbeach	d					21 17			22 17					23 07	
Cambridge	a			20 56	21 08	21 26	22 08		22 24		22 34		23 10	23 14	23 56
Stansted Airport	a				21 40		22 52								
Ipswich	a		21 23									23 18			
London Kings Cross	a					22 32			23 32					00 40	
London Liverpool Street	a														

Saturdays

		FC	FC	LE	EM	EM	FC	LE	EM	XC		EM	LE	FC	LE	EM	XC	FC	EM	LE		EM	XC	FC	EM
		■	■	■	◇	◇	■	■	◇	◇■		◇	■	■	■	◇	◇■	■	◇	■		◇	◇■	■	◇
Norwich	d			05 37	05 52			06 40	06 53						07 40	07 57				08 40		08 57			
Wymondham	d			05 49	06 04			06 52							07 52					08 52					
Spooner Row	d																								
Attleborough	d			05 56	06 11			06 59							07 59					08 59					
Eccles Road	d																								
Harling Road	d																								
Thetford	d			06 10	06 25			07 13	07 22						08 13	08 24				09 13		09 24			
Brandon	d			06 18				07 21							08 21					09 21					
Lakenheath	d																								
Shippea Hill	d																								
Peterborough ■	d					06 27				07 13		07 35	07 45				08 18		09 00				09 18		09 43
Whittlesea	d									07 21			07 53												
March	d					06 43				07 32		07 51	08 04				08 34						09 34		
Manea	d									07x39															
Kings Lynn	d	22p28	05 56				06 56							07 56				08 56						09 30	
Watlington	d	22p35	06 03				07 03							08 03				09 03							
Downham Market	d	22p41	06 09				07 09							08 09				09 09						09 41	
Littleport	d	22p50	06 18				07 18							08 18				09 18							
Ely ■	a	22p58	06 26	06 35	06 46	07 01	07 26	07 38	07 45	07 52		08 11	08 22	08 26	08 38	08 47	08 52	09 26	09 35	09 38		09 48	09 52	09 58	10 14
	d	22p58	06 26	06 36			07 26	07 39		07 52			08 31	08 26	08 39		08 52	09 26		09 39			09 52	09 58	
Waterbeach	d	23p07	06 35				07 35							08 35				09 35							
Cambridge	a	23p14	06 44	06 56			07 44	07 59		08 08				08 44	08 59		09 07	09 44		09 59			10 07	10 13	
Stansted Airport	a									08 39							09 40						10 40		
Ipswich	a												09 28												
London Kings Cross	a	00 40	07 36				08 36							09 39				10 35						11 04	
London Liverpool Street	a																								

Norwich, Peterborough, Kings Lynn and Ely - Cambridge and London

Network Diagram - see first Page of Table 13

		FC ■	LE ■	LE ■	EM ◇	XC ◇■		EM ◇	FC ■	LE ■	EM ◇	XC ◇■	EM ◇	FC ■	LE ■	LE ■		EM ◇	XC ◇■	EM ◇	FC ■	LE ■	EM ◇	XC ◇■	EM ◇
Norwich	d			09 40	09 57					10 40	10 57					11 40		11 57				12 40	12 57		
Wymondham	d			09 52						10 52						11 52						12 52			
Spooner Row	d																								
Attleborough	d			09 59						10 59						11 59						12 59			
Eccles Road	d																								
Harling Road	d																								
Thetford	d			10 13	10 24					11 13	11 24					12 13		12 24				13 13	13 24		
Brandon	d			10 21						11 21						12 21						13 21			
Lakenheath	d			10x26																					
Shippea Hill	d																								
Peterborough 8	d		09 47			10 18		10 41				11 18	11 41		11 45				12 18	12 40				13 18	13 41
Whittlesea	d		09 55												11 53										
March	d		10 06			10 34						11 34			12 04				12 34					13 34	
Manea	d																								
Kings Lynn	d	09 56							10 56					11 56							12 56				
Watlington	d	10 03							11 03					12 03							13 03				
Downham Market	d	10 09							11 09					12 09							13 09				
Littleport	d	10 18							11 18					12 18							13 18				
Ely 4	a	10 26	10 29	10 39	10 47	10 52		11 17	11 26	11 38	11 48	11 52	12 14	12 26	12 28	12 38		12 47	12 52	13 13	13 26	13 38	13 47	13 52	14 14
	d	10 26	10 31	10 39		10 52			11 26	11 39		11 52		12 26	12 31	12 39			12 52		13 26	13 39		13 52	
Waterbeach	d	10 35							11 35					12 35							13 35				
Cambridge	a	10 44		10 59		11 07			11 44	11 59		12 07		12 44		12 59			13 07		13 44	13 59		14 07	
Stansted Airport	a					11 40						12 40							13 40					14 40	
Ipswich	a		11 28												13 28										
London Kings Cross	a	11 37							12 35					13 35							14 35				
London Liverpool Street	a																								

		FC ■		LE ■	LE ■	EM ◇	XC ◇■	EM ◇	FC ■	LE ■	EM ◇	XC ◇■		EM ◇	FC ■	LE ■	LE ■	EM ◇	XC ◇■	EM ◇	FC ■	LE ■		EM ◇	XC ◇■
Norwich	d				13 40	13 57				14 40	14 57						15 35	15 52				16 38		16 57	
Wymondham	d				13 52					14 52							15 47					16 50		17 09	
Spooner Row	d																					16x54			
Attleborough	d				13 59					14 59							15 54	16 09				16 59			
Eccles Road	d																15 59								
Harling Road	d																16 03								
Thetford	d				14 13	14 24				15 13	15 24						16 13	16 23				17 13		17 27	
Brandon	d				14 21					15 21							16 21					17 21			
Lakenheath	d																								
Shippea Hill	d																								
Peterborough 8	d			13 45			14 18	14 43				15 18		15 41		15 45			16 18	16 41					17 19
Whittlesea	d			13 53												15 53									17 27
March	d			14 04			14 34					15 34				16 04			16 34						17 38
Manea	d																								17x46
Kings Lynn	d	13 56							14 56						15 56						16 56				
Watlington	d	14 03							15 03						16 03						17 03				
Downham Market	d	14 09							15 09						16 09						17 09				
Littleport	d	14 18							15 18						16 18						17 18				
Ely 4	a	14 26		14 28	14 38	14 47	14 52	15 14	15 26	15 38	15 48	15 52		16 14	16 26	16 28	16 38	16 47	16 52	17 13	17 26	17 38		17 48	17 59
	d	14 26		14 31	14 39		14 52		15 26	15 39		15 52			16 26	16 31	16 39		16 52		17 26	17 39			18 00
Waterbeach	d	14 35							15 35						16 35						17 35				
Cambridge	a	14 44			14 59		15 07		15 44	15 59		16 07			16 44		16 59		17 07		17 44	17 59			18 17
Stansted Airport	a						15 40					16 40							17 40						18 53
Ipswich	a			15 28												17 28									
London Kings Cross	a	15 35							16 35						17 35						18 35				
London Liverpool Street	a																								

		EM ◇	FC ■	LE ■	LE ■	EM ◇	XC ◇■	FC ■		EM ◇	LE ■	EM ◇	XC ◇■	FC ■	EM ◇	LE ◇■	LE ■	XC ◇■		FC ■	LE ■	XC ◇■ A	XC ◇■ B	FC ■ A	FC ■ B
Norwich	d				17 35	17 54					18 40	18 57					19 40				20 40				
Wymondham	d				17 47	18 06					18 52						19 52				20 52				
Spooner Row	d																								
Attleborough	d				17 54	18 13					18 59						19 59				20 59				
Eccles Road	d				17 59																				
Harling Road	d				18 03																				
Thetford	d				18 13	18 27					19 13	19 24					20 13				21 13				
Brandon	d				18 21						19 21						20 21				21 21				
Lakenheath	d																								
Shippea Hill	d										19x29														
Peterborough 8	d	17 39		17 45			18 18			18 44			19 18		19 41	19 45		20 18				21 18	21 18		
Whittlesea	d			17 53												19 53									
March	d			18 04			18 34			19 01			19 34			20 04		20 34				21 34	21 34		
Manea	d																								
Kings Lynn	d		17 56					18 35						19 35						20 35				21 35	21 35
Watlington	d		18 03					18 42						19 42						20 42				21 42	21 42
Downham Market	d		18 09					18 48						19 48						20 48				21 48	21 48
Littleport	d		18 18					18 57						19 57						20 57				21 57	21 57
Ely 4	a	18 12	18 26	18 28	18 38	18 48	18 52	19 05		19 19	19 39	19 46	19 51	20 05	20 14	20 26	20 38	20 51		21 05	21 38	21 51	21 51	22 05	22 05
	d		18 26	18 31	18 39		18 53	19 05			19 39		19 52	20 05		20 27	20 39	20 51		21 05	21 39	21 51	21 51	22 05	22 05
Waterbeach	d		18 35					19 15						20 15						21 15				22 15	22 15
Cambridge	a		18 44		18 59		19 09	19 21			19 59		20 08	20 21			20 59	21 07		21 21	21 59	22 07	22 07	22 21	22 21
Stansted Airport	a						19 40						20 40					21 40				22 40	22 42		
Ipswich	a			19 28												21 22									
London Kings Cross	a		19 35					20 30						21 32						22 31				23 31	23 32
London Liverpool Street	a																								

A until 21 July, from 18 August, not 1 September, 8 September

B 28 July, 4 August, 11 August, 1 September, 8 September

Norwich, Peterborough, Kings Lynn and Ely - Cambridge and London

Network Diagram - see first Page of Table 13

		EM ◇	LE ◇■	XC ◇■		LE ■	FC ■
Norwich	d					22 40	
Wymondham	d					22 52	
Spooner Row	d						
Attleborough	d					22 59	
Eccles Road	d						
Harling Road	d						
Thetford	d					23 13	
Brandon	d					23 21	
Lakenheath	d						
Shippea Hill	d						
Peterborough 8	d	21 38	21 45	22 18			
Whittlesea	d		21 53				
March	d		22 04	22 34			
Manea	d						
Kings Lynn	d						23 10
Watlington	d						23 17
Downham Market	d						23 23
Littleport	d						23 32
Ely 4	a	22 12	22 23	22 53		23 38	23 41
	d		22 23	22 55		23 39	23 43
Waterbeach	d						23 52
Cambridge	a			23 10		23 59	23 59
Stansted Airport	a						
Ipswich	a		23 18				
London Kings Cross	a						
London Liverpool Street	a						

Sundays

until 9 September

		FC ■	FC ■	LE ■	EM ◇	LE ■ A	LE ■ B	FC ■	LE ■	EM ◇	EM ◇	FC ■	LE ■	LE ■ A	LE ■ B	FC ■	LE ■	EM ◇	XC ◇■	FC ■	LE ■	EM ◇	LE ■ A	LE ■ B	EM ◇
Norwich	d			09 03	09 33				10 03	10 47			11 03				12 03				13 03				13 49
Wymondham	d			09 15					10 15				11 15				12 15				13 15				
Spooner Row	d																								
Attleborough	d			09 22					10 22				11 22				12 22				13 22				
Eccles Road	d																								
Harling Road	d																								
Thetford	d			09 36	10 00				10 36	11 14			11 36				12 36				13 36				14 16
Brandon	d			09 44					10 44				11 44				12 44				13 44				
Lakenheath	d			09x49									11x49												
Shippea Hill	d																								
Peterborough 8	d					09 45	09 45				11 09			11 46	11 46			12 53	13 18			13 43	13 46	13 46	
Whittlesea	d					09 53	09 53							11 54	11 54								13 55	13 55	
March	d					10 04	10 04				11 25			12 05	12 05				13 34				14 06	14 06	
Manea	d																								
Kings Lynn	d	08 28	09 28					10 28				11 28				12 28				13 28					
Watlington	d	08 35	09 35					10 35				11 35				12 35				13 35					
Downham Market	d	08 41	09 41					10 41				11 41				12 41				13 41					
Littleport	d	08 50	09 50					10 50				11 50				12 50				13 50					
Ely 4	a	08 58	09 58	10 08	10 22	10 28	10 28	10 58	11 06	11 35	11 48	11 58	12 08	12 29	12 29	12 58	13 01	13 32	13 52	13 58	14 01	14 16	14 29	14 29	14 42
	d	08 58	09 58	10 09		10 31	10 34	10 58	11 07			11 58	12 09	12 31	12 34	12 58	13 04		13 52	13 58	14 04		14 31	14 34	
Waterbeach	d	09 07	10 07					11 07				12 07				13 07				14 07					
Cambridge	a	09 15	10 15	10 27				11 15	11 25			12 15	12 27			13 15	13 22		14 08	14 15	14 22				
Stansted Airport	a																		14 45						
Ipswich	a					11 28	12 03							13 28	14 03								15 28	16 03	
London Kings Cross	a	10 09	11 08					12 08				13 08				14 08				15 08					
London Liverpool Street	a																								

A until 22 July, 19 August, 26 August

B 29 July, 5 August, 12 August, 2 September, 9 September. Train service operates between Peterborough and Ely and Bury St Edmunds and Ipswich. Bus replacement service operates between Ely and Bury St Edmunds (Table 14)

Table 17

Sundays
until 9 September

Norwich, Peterborough, Kings Lynn and Ely - Cambridge and London

Network Diagram - see first Page of Table 13

		XC	FC	LE	EM	EM	XC	FC	LE	LE	LE	EM	XC	EM	FC	LE	EM	EM	XC	FC	LE	LE	LE	FC	EM
		◇■	■	■	◇	◇	◇■	■	■	■	■	◇	◇■	◇	■	■	◇	◇	◇■	■	■	◇■	◇■	■	◇
										A	B											A	B		
Norwich	d			14 03		14 49			15 03					15 53		16 03		16 54			17 03				
Wymondham	d			14 15					15 15							16 15					17 15				
Spooner Row	d																								
Attleborough	d			14 22					15 22							16 22					17 22				
Eccles Road	d																								
Harling Road	d																								
Thetford	d			14 36		15 16			15 36					16 20		16 36		17 21			17 36				
Brandon	d			14 44					15 44							16 44					17 44				
Lakenheath	d								15x49																
Shippea Hill	d																								
Peterborough ■	d	14 18			14 53		15 18			15 45	15 45	16 03	16 18	17a10			16 59		17 18			17 45	17 45		17 56
Whittlesea	d									15 53	15 53											17 53	17 53		
March	d	14 34					15 34			16 04	16 04		16 34						17 34			18 04	18 04		18 12
Manea	d																								
Kings Lynn	d		14 28					15 28							16 28					17 28				17 58	
Watlington	d		14 35					15 35							16 35					17 35				18 05	
Downham Market	d		14 41					15 41							16 41					17 41				18 11	
Littleport	d		14 50					15 50							16 50					17 50				18 20	
Ely ■	a	14 52	14 58	15 01	15 29	15 42	15 52	15 58	16 03	16 23	16 22	16 38	16 52		16 58	17 01	17 32	17 45	17 52	17 58	18 01	18 23	18 22	18 28	18 32
	d	14 52	14 58	15 04			15 52	15 58	16 04	16 31	16 29		16 52		16 58	17 04			17 52	17 58	18 04	18 31	18 29	18 28	
Waterbeach	d		15 07					16 07							17 07					18 07				18 37	
Cambridge	a	15 08	15 15	15 22			16 08	16 15	16 22				17 07		17 15	17 22			18 07	18 15	18 22			18 45	
Stansted Airport	a	15 45					16 45						17 45						18 45						
Ipswich	a									17 28	18 03											19 28	20 03		
London Kings Cross	a		16 08					17 08							18 08					19 11				19 36	
London Liverpool Street	a																								

		EM	XC		FC	LE	EM	EM	XC	FC	LE	LE	EM	XC		FC	LE	EM	XC	LE	FC	EM	XC	FC	LE
		◇	◇■		■	■	◇	◇	◇■	■	◇■	◇■	◇	◇■		■	■	◇	◇■	◇■	■	◇	◇■	■	■
											A	B								B			C		
Norwich	d	17 54				18 03		18 56									20 03	20 52							22 03
Wymondham	d					18 15											20 15								22 15
Spooner Row	d																								
Attleborough	d					18 22											20 22								22 22
Eccles Road	d																								
Harling Road	d																								
Thetford	d	18 21				18 36		19 23									20 36	21 19							22 36
Brandon	d					18 44											20 44								22 44
Lakenheath	d																								
Shippea Hill	d																								
Peterborough ■	d		18 18				18 48		19 18		19 45	19 45	19 58	20 18					21 18	21 45		21 53	22 18		
Whittlesea	d										19 53	19 53								21 53					
March	d		18 34						19 34		20 04	20 04		20 34					21 34	22 04			22 34		
Manea	d																								
Kings Lynn	d				18 28					19 28						20 28					21 28			22 28	
Watlington	d				18 35					19 35						20 35					21 35			22 35	
Downham Market	d				18 41					19 41						20 41					21 41			22 41	
Littleport	d				18 50					19 50						20 50					21 50			22 50	
Ely ■	a	18 44	18 52		18 58	19 01	19 21	19 44	19 52	19 58	20 23	20 22	20 31	20 52		20 58	21 01	21 40	21 52	22 22	21 58	22 28	22 52	22 58	23 01
	d		18 52		18 58	19 04			19 52	19 58	20 23	20 29		20 52		20 58	21 04		21 52	22 29	21 58		22 52	22 58	23 04
Waterbeach	d				19 07					20 07						21 07					22 07			23 07	
Cambridge	a		19 07		19 15	19 22			20 07	20 15				21 07		21 15	21 22		22 07		22 15		23 07	23 15	23 22
Stansted Airport	a		19 45						20 45					21 45					22 45						
Ipswich	a										21 18	22 03								00 03					
London Kings Cross	a				20 11					21 11						22 10					23 08			00 39	
London Liverpool Street	a																								

A until 22 July, 19 August, 26 August

B 29 July, 5 August, 12 August, 2 September, 9 September. Train service operates between Peterborough and Ely and Bury St Edmund and Ipswich. Bus replacement service operates between Ely and Bury St Edmunds (Table 14)

C until 24 June

Table 17

Sundays
16 September to 21 October

Norwich, Peterborough, Kings Lynn and Ely - Cambridge and London

Network Diagram - see first Page of Table 13

		FC	FC	LE	FC	LE	EM	FC	LE	LE		FC	LE	XC	FC	LE	EM	LE	EM	XC		FC	LE	EM	EM
		■	■	■	■	■	◇	■	■	■		■	■	◇■	■	■	◇	■	◇	◇■		■	■	◇	◇
Norwich	d			09 03		10 03	10 47		11 03				12 03			13 03			13 49				14 03		14 49
Wymondham	d			09 15		10 15			11 15				12 15			13 15							14 15		
Spooner Row	d																								
Attleborough	d			09 22		10 22			11 22				12 22			13 22							14 22		
Eccles Road	d																								
Harling Road	d																								
Thetford	d			09 36		10 36	11 14		11 36				12 36			13 36			14 16				14 36		15 16
Brandon	d			09 44		10 44			11 44				12 44			13 44							14 44		
Lakenheath	d			09x49					11x49																
Shippea Hill	d																								
Peterborough ■	d									11 46				13 18			13 43	13 46		14 18				14 53	
Whittlesea	d									11 54								13 55							
March	d									12 05				13 34				14 06		14 34					
Manea	d																								
Kings Lynn	d	08 28	09 28		10 28			11 28				12 28			13 28							14 28			
Watlington	d	08 35	09 35		10 35			11 35				12 35			13 35							14 35			
Downham Market	d	08 41	09 41		10 41			11 41				12 41			13 41							14 41			
Littleport	d	08 50	09 50		10 50			11 50				12 50			13 50							14 50			
Ely ■	a	08 58	09 58	10 08	10 58	11 06	11 35	11 58	12 08	12 29		12 58	13 01	13 52	13 58	14 01	14 16	14 29	14 42	14 52		14 58	15 01	15 29	15 42
	d	08 58	09 58	10 09	10 58	11 07		11 58	12 09	12 31		12 58	13 04	13 52	13 58	14 04		14 31		14 52		14 58	15 04		
Waterbeach	d	09 07	10 07		11 07			12 07				13 07			14 07							15 07			
Cambridge	a	09 15	10 15	10 27	11 15	11 25		12 15	12 27			13 14	13 22	14 08	14 15	14 22				15 08		15 15	15 22		
Stansted Airport	a													14 45						15 45					
Ipswich	a									13 28								15 28							
London Kings Cross	a	10 12	11 09		12 08			13 08				14 08			15 08							16 08			
London Liverpool Street	a																								

		XC	FC	LE	LE	EM		XC	EM	FC	LE	EM	EM	XC	FC	LE		LE	FC	EM	EM	XC	FC	LE	EM
		◇■	■	■	■	◇		◇■	◇	■	■	◇	◇	◇■	■	■		◇■	■	◇	◇	◇■	■	■	◇
Norwich	d			15 03					15 53		16 03		16 54			17 03					17 54			18 03	
Wymondham	d			15 15							16 15					17 15								18 15	
Spooner Row	d																								
Attleborough	d			15 22							16 22					17 22								18 22	
Eccles Road	d																								
Harling Road	d																								
Thetford	d			15 36					16 20		16 36		17 21			17 36					18 21			18 36	
Brandon	d			15 44							16 44					17 44								18 44	
Lakenheath	d			15x49																					
Shippea Hill	d																								
Peterborough ■	d	15 18			15 45	16 03		16 18	17a10			16 59		17 18				17 45		17 56		18 18			18 48
Whittlesea	d				15 53													17 53							
March	d	15 34			16 04			16 34						17 34				18 04		18 12		18 34			
Manea	d																								
Kings Lynn	d		15 28							16 28					17 28				17 58				18 28		
Watlington	d		15 35							16 35					17 35				18 05				18 35		
Downham Market	d		15 41							16 41					17 41				18 11				18 41		
Littleport	d		15 50							16 50					17 50				18 20				18 50		
Ely ■	a	15 52	15 58	16 03	16 23	16 38		16 52		16 58	17 01	17 32	17 45	17 52	17 58	18 01		18 23	18 28	18 32	18 44	18 52	18 58	19 01	19 21
	d	15 52	15 58	16 04	16 31			16 52		16 58	17 04			17 52	17 58	18 04		18 31	18 28			18 52	18 58	19 04	
Waterbeach	d		16 07							17 07					18 07				18 37				19 07		
Cambridge	a	16 08	16 15	16 22				17 07		17 15	17 22			18 07	18 15	18 22			18 45			19 07	19 15	19 22	
Stansted Airport	a	16 45						17 45						18 45								19 45			
Ipswich	a				17 28													19 28							
London Kings Cross	a		17 08							18 08					19 11				19 36				20 11		
London Liverpool Street	a																								

		EM		XC	FC	LE	EM	XC	FC	LE	EM	XC		FC	EM	XC	FC	LE
		◇		◇■	■	◇■	◇	◇■	■	■	◇	◇■		■	◇	◇■	■	■
Norwich	d	18 56								20 03	20 52							22 03
Wymondham	d									20 15								22 15
Spooner Row	d																	
Attleborough	d									20 22								22 22
Eccles Road	d																	
Harling Road	d																	
Thetford	d	19 23								20 36	21 19							22 36
Brandon	d									20 44								22 44
Lakenheath	d																	
Shippea Hill	d																	
Peterborough ■	d			19 18		19 45	19 58	20 18				21 18			21 53	22 18		
Whittlesea	d					19 53												
March	d			19 34		20 04		20 34				21 34				22 34		
Manea	d																	
Kings Lynn	d				19 28				20 28					21 28			22 28	
Watlington	d				19 35				20 35					21 35			22 35	
Downham Market	d				19 41				20 41					21 41			22 41	
Littleport	d				19 50				20 50					21 50			22 50	
Ely ■	a	19 44		19 52	19 58	20 23	20 31	20 52	20 58	21 01	21 40	21 52		21 58	22 28	22 52	22 58	23 01
	d			19 52	19 58	20 23		20 52	20 58	21 04		21 52		21 58		22 52	22 58	23 04
Waterbeach	d				20 07				21 07					22 07			23 07	
Cambridge	a			20 07	20 15			21 07	21 15	21 22		22 07		22 15		23 07	23 15	23 22
Stansted Airport	a			20 45				21 45				22 45						
Ipswich	a					21 18												
London Kings Cross	a				21 11				22 10					23 08			00 39	
London Liverpool Street	a																	

Norwich, Peterborough, Kings Lynn and Ely - Cambridge and London

Network Diagram - see first Page of Table 13

		FC ■	FC ■	LE ■	FC ■	LE ■	EM ◇	FC ■	LE ■	LE ■		FC ■	LE ■	XC ◇■	FC ■	LE ■	EM ◇	LE ■	EM ◇	XC ◇■		FC ■	LE ■	EM ◇	EM ◇
Norwich	d			09 03		10 03	10 47		11 03				12 03			13 03			13 49				14 03		14 49
Wymondham	d			09 15		10 15			11 15				12 15			13 15							14 15		
Spooner Row	d																								
Attleborough	d			09 22		10 22			11 22				12 22			13 22							14 22		
Eccles Road	d																								
Harling Road	d																								
Thetford	d			09 36		10 36	11 14		11 36				12 36			13 36			14 16				14 36		15 16
Brandon	d			09 44		10 44			11 44				12 44			13 44							14 44		
Lakenheath	d			09x49					11x49																
Shippea Hill	d																								
Peterborough ■	d									11 46				13 18			13 43	13 46		14 18				14 53	
Whittlesea	d									11 54								13 55							
March	d									12 05				13 34				14 06		14 34					
Manea	d																								
Kings Lynn	d	08 28	09 28		10 28			11 28				12 28			13 28							14 28			
Watlington	d	08 35	09 35		10 35			11 35				12 35			13 35							14 35			
Downham Market	d	08 41	09 41		10 41			11 41				12 41			13 41							14 41			
Littleport	d	08 50	09 50		10 50			11 50				12 50			13 50							14 50			
Ely ■	a	08 58	09 58	10 08	10 58	11 06	11 35	11 58	12 08	12 29		12 58	13 01	13 52	13 58	14 01	14 16	14 29	14 42	14 52		14 58	15 01	15 29	15 42
	d	08 58	09 58	10 09	10 58	11 07		11 58	12 09	12 31		12 58	13 04	13 52	13 58	14 04		14 31		14 52		14 58	15 04		
Waterbeach	d	09 07	10 07		11 07			12 07				13 07			14 07							15 07			
Cambridge	a	09 15	10 15	10 27	11 15	11 25		12 15	12 27			13 15	13 22	14 08	14 15	14 22				15 08		15 15	15 22		
Stansted Airport	a													14 45						15 45					
Ipswich	a									13 28								15 28							
London Kings Cross	a	10 09	11 08		12 08			13 08				14 08			15 08							16 08			
London Liverpool Street	a																								

		XC ◇■	FC ■	LE ■	LE ■	EM ◇		XC ◇■	EM ◇	FC ■	LE ■	EM ◇	EM ◇	XC ◇■	FC ■	LE ■		LE ◇■	FC ■	EM ◇	EM ◇	XC ◇■	FC ■	LE ■	EM ◇
Norwich	d			15 03					15 53		16 03		16 54			17 03					17 54			18 03	
Wymondham	d			15 15							16 15					17 15								18 15	
Spooner Row	d																								
Attleborough	d			15 22							16 22					17 22								18 22	
Eccles Road	d																								
Harling Road	d																								
Thetford	d			15 36					16 20		16 36		17 21			17 36					18 21			18 36	
Brandon	d			15 44							16 44					17 44								18 44	
Lakenheath	d			15x49																					
Shippea Hill	d																								
Peterborough ■	d	15 18			15 45	16 03		16 18	17a10			16 59		17 18				17 45		17 56		18 18			18 48
Whittlesea	d				15 53													17 53							
March	d	15 34			16 04			16 34						17 34				18 04		18 12		18 34			
Manea	d																								
Kings Lynn	d		15 28							16 28					17 28				17 58				18 28		
Watlington	d		15 35							16 35					17 35				18 05				18 35		
Downham Market	d		15 41							16 41					17 41				18 11				18 41		
Littleport	d		15 50							16 50					17 50				18 20				18 50		
Ely ■	a	15 52	15 58	16 03	16 23	16 38		16 52		16 58	17 01	17 32	17 45	17 52	17 58	18 01		18 23	18 28	18 32	18 44	18 52	18 58	19 01	19 21
	d	15 52	15 58	16 04	16 31			16 52		16 58	17 04			17 52	17 58	18 04		18 31	18 28			18 52	18 58	19 04	
Waterbeach	d		16 07							17 07					18 07				18 37				19 07		
Cambridge	a	16 08	16 15	16 22				17 07		17 15	17 22			18 07	18 15	18 22			18 45			19 07	19 15	19 22	
Stansted Airport	a	16 45						17 45						18 45								19 45			
Ipswich	a				17 28													19 28							
London Kings Cross	a		17 08							18 08					19 11				19 36				20 11		
London Liverpool Street	a																								

		EM ◇		XC ◇■	FC ■	LE ◇■	EM ◇	XC ◇■	FC ■	LE ■	EM ◇	XC ◇■		FC ■	EM ◇	XC ◇■	FC ■	LE ■
Norwich	d	18 56								20 03	20 52							22 03
Wymondham	d									20 15								22 15
Spooner Row	d																	
Attleborough	d									20 22								22 22
Eccles Road	d																	
Harling Road	d																	
Thetford	d	19 23								20 36	21 19							22 36
Brandon	d									20 44								22 44
Lakenheath	d																	
Shippea Hill	d																	
Peterborough ■	d			19 18		19 45	19 58	20 18				21 18			21 53	22 18		
Whittlesea	d					19 53												
March	d			19 34		20 04		20 34				21 34				22 34		
Manea	d																	
Kings Lynn	d				19 28				20 28					21 28			22 28	
Watlington	d				19 35				20 35					21 35			22 35	
Downham Market	d				19 41				20 41					21 41			22 41	
Littleport	d				19 50				20 50					21 50			22 50	
Ely ■	a	19 44		19 52	19 58	20 23	20 31	20 52	20 58	21 01	21 40	21 52		21 58	22 28	22 52	22 58	23 01
	d			19 52	19 58	20 23		20 52	20 58	21 04		21 52		21 58		22 52	22 58	23 04
Waterbeach	d				20 07				21 07					22 07			23 07	
Cambridge	a			20 07	20 15			21 07	21 15	21 22		22 07		22 15		23 07	23 15	23 22
Stansted Airport	a			20 45				21 45				22 45						
Ipswich	a					21 18												
London Kings Cross	a				21 11				22 10					23 08			00 39	
London Liverpool Street	a																	

Kings Lynn - Sandringham and Hunstanton

Bus Service

		FC A 🚌	FC A 🚌	FC B 🚌	FC C 🚌	FC D 🚌	FC A 🚌	FC A 🚌	FC A 🚌	FC D 🚌		FC A 🚌	FC D 🚌	FC A 🚌	FC A 🚌	FC A 🚌	FC D 🚌	FC A 🚌	FC A 🚌	FC A 🚌		FC D 🚌	FC A 🚌	FC D 🚌	FC A 🚌
Kings Lynn	d	06 20	06 50	07 30	07 30	08 05	08 35	09 00	09 00	09 15		09 25	09 30	09 30	09 40	10 05	10 15	10 25	10 30	10 40		11 00	11 05	11 15	11 25
Sandringham Visitor Centre	a						09 03								10 06		10 39			11 06					
Sandringham Norwich Gates	a																								
Hunstanton Bus Station	a	07 07	07 37	08 22	08 27	08 51	09 36	09 39	09 56	10 07		10 18	10 00	10 04	10 38	10 59	11 08	11 18	11 04	11 38		11 33	11 59	12 07	12 18

		FC A 🚌	FC A 🚌	FC D 🚌	FC A 🚌	FC D 🚌		FC A 🚌	FC A 🚌	FC A 🚌	FC D 🚌	FC A 🚌	FC D 🚌	FC A 🚌	FC A 🚌	FC A 🚌		FC A 🚌	FC D 🚌	FC A 🚌	FC A 🚌	FC B 🚌	FC D 🚌	FC A 🚌	FC D 🚌
Kings Lynn	d	11 30	11 40	12 00	12 05	12 15		12 25	12 30	12 40	13 00	13 05	13 15	13 25	13 30	13 40		14 05	14 15	14 25	14 30	14 40	15 00	15 05	15 15
Sandringham Visitor Centre	a		12 06			12 39				13 06						14 06			14 39			15 06			
Sandringham Norwich Gates	a																								
Hunstanton Bus Station	a	12 04	12 38	12 33	12 59	13 08		13 18	13 04	13 38	13 33	13 59	14 07	14 18	14 04	14 38		14 59	15 08	15 18	15 04	15 38	15 33	16 04	16 07

		FC A 🚌		FC A 🚌	FC A 🚌	FC D 🚌	FC A 🚌	FC A 🚌	FC C 🚌	FC A 🚌	FC D 🚌	FC D 🚌		FC A 🚌	FC A 🚌	FC A 🚌	FC D 🚌	FC A 🚌	FC D 🚌	FC A 🚌	FC A 🚌	FC D 🚌		FC A 🚌	
Kings Lynn	d	15 25		15 30	15 45	16 15	16 15	16 30	16 30	16 40	17 00	17 15		17 15	17 35	17 45	18 20	18 35	19 20	20 00	21 30	21 35		23 07	
Sandringham Visitor Centre	a				16 12	16 39				17 08															
Sandringham Norwich Gates	a																								
Hunstanton Bus Station	a	16 20		16 04	16 40	17 08	17 15	17 13	17 29	17 38	17 33	18 07		18 15	18 15	18 40	19 08	19 23	20 04	20 48	22 20	22 19		23 54	

Saturdays

		FC 🚌	FC 🚌	FC 🚌	FC 🚌	FC 🚌	FC 🚌	FC 🚌	FC 🚌	FC 🚌		FC 🚌	FC 🚌	FC 🚌	FC 🚌	FC 🚌	FC 🚌	FC 🚌	FC 🚌	FC 🚌		FC 🚌	FC 🚌	FC 🚌	FC 🚌
Kings Lynn	d	06 50	07 30	08 40	09 00	09 00	09 25	09 30	09 40	10 05		10 25	10 30	10 40	11 05	11 25	11 30	11 40	12 05	12 25		12 30	12 40	13 05	13 25
Sandringham Visitor Centre	a			09 06					10 06					11 06				12 06					13 06		
Sandringham Norwich Gates	a																								
Hunstanton Bus Station	a	07 37	08 22	09 38	09 39	09 56	10 18	10 04	10 38	10 59		11 18	11 04	11 38	11 59	12 18	12 04	12 38	12 59	13 18		13 04	13 38	13 59	14 18

		FC 🚌	FC 🚌	FC 🚌	FC 🚌	FC 🚌		FC 🚌	FC 🚌	FC 🚌	FC 🚌	FC 🚌	FC 🚌	FC 🚌	FC 🚌	FC 🚌		FC 🚌	FC 🚌	FC 🚌	FC 🚌	FC 🚌	FC 🚌
Kings Lynn	d	13 30	13 40	14 05	14 25	14 30		14 40	15 05	15 25	15 30	15 40	16 15	16 30	16 40	17 15		17 35	17 45	18 35	20 00	21 30	23 07
Sandringham Visitor Centre	a		14 06					15 06				16 06			17 06								
Sandringham Norwich Gates	a																						
Hunstanton Bus Station	a	14 04	14 38	14 59	15 18	15 04		15 38	15 59	16 18	16 04	16 37	17 10	17 13	17 37	18 10		18 15	18 38	19 23	20 48	22 20	23 54

Sundays

		FC 🚌	FC 🚌	FC 🚌	FC 🚌	FC 🚌	FC 🚌	FC 🚌	FC 🚌	FC 🚌		FC 🚌	FC 🚌	FC 🚌	FC 🚌	FC 🚌	FC 🚌	FC 🚌	FC 🚌	FC 🚌		FC 🚌
Kings Lynn	d	08 05	09 15	09 30	10 15	11 00	11 15	12 00	12 15	13 00		13 15	14 15	15 00	15 15	16 15	17 00	17 15	18 20	19 20		21 35
Sandringham Visitor Centre	a				10 39				12 39				14 39			16 39						
Sandringham Norwich Gates	a																					
Hunstanton Bus Station	a	08 51	10 07	10 00	11 08	11 33	12 07	12 33	13 08	13 33		14 07	15 08	15 33	16 07	17 08	17 33	18 07	19 08	20 04		22 19

A not 4 June, 5 June, 27 August
B from 6 June until 8 June, 28 June, from 23 July until 5 September, not 27 August, also from 29 October until 2 November
C until 20 July, not from 4 June until 8 June, 28 June, also from 6 September, not from 29 October until 2 November
D 4 June, 5 June, 27 August

Services are subject to variation on Bank Holidays

Table 17A

Mondays to Fridays

Hunstanton and Sandringham - Kings Lynn

Bus Service

		FC	FC	FC	FC	FC	FC	FC	FC	FC	FC	FC	FC	FC	FC	FC	FC	FC	FC	FC	FC	FC	FC
		FO	A	A	A	A	A	A	A	B	A	A	A	A	A	A	B	A	B	A	A	B	A
Hunstanton Bus Station	d	23p55	06 15	06 45	07 10	07 40	08 00	08 25	08 47	09 00	09 06	09 10	09 25	09 47	10 06	10 10	10 13	10 25	10 40	10 47	11 06	11 13	11 15
Sandringham Norwich Gates	d																						
Sandringham Visitor Centre	d							09 00					10 00				10 43	11 00					
Kings Lynn	a	00 41	07 08	07 34	08 07	08 41	08 42	09 23	09 40	09 50	10 00	09 41	10 23	10 40	11 00	10 41	11 07	11 23	11 10	11 40	12 00	12 07	11 46

		FC	FC	FC	FC	FC	FC	FC	FC	FC	FC	FC	FC	FC	FC	FC	FC	FC	FC	FC	FC	FC	FC
		A	B	A	A	B	A	A	A	A	B	A	A	B	A	A	B	A	A	B	C	C	B
Hunstanton Bus Station	d	11 25	11 40	11 47	12 06	12 13	12 15	12 25	12 47	13 06	13 13	13 15	13 25	13 40	13 47	14 06	14 13	14 15	14 25	14 40	14 47	15 06	15 13
Sandringham Norwich Gates	d																						
Sandringham Visitor Centre	d	12 00				12 43		13 00					14 00				14 43		15 00				
Kings Lynn	a	12 23	12 10	12 40	13 00	13 07	12 46	13 23	13 40	14 00	14 07	13 46	14 23	14 10	14 40	15 00	15 07	14 46	15 23	15 10	15 40	16 00	16 07

		FC	FC	FC	FC	FC	FC	FC	FC	FC	FC	FC	FC	FC	FC	FC	FC	FC	FC	FC	FC	FC
		A	C	D	B	C	A	B	A	A	A	B	A	A	B	A	B	A	A	A	B	A
Hunstanton Bus Station	d	15 15	15 25	15 25	15 40	15 47	16 10	16 13	16 25	16 30	16 45	17 13	17 20	17 30	17 40	17 45	18 13	18 20	18 40	18 45	20 05	20 50
Sandringham Norwich Gates	d																					
Sandringham Visitor Centre	d		16 00	16 00				16 43	17 00													
Kings Lynn	a	15 52	16 23	16 25	16 10	16 42	17 06	17 07	17 28	17 00	17 44	18 07	18 13	18 00	18 07	18 40	19 01	19 10	19 08	19 33	20 49	21 36

		FC	FC	FC
		B	A	E
Hunstanton Bus Station	d	22 20	22 23	23 55
Sandringham Norwich Gates	d			
Sandringham Visitor Centre	d			
Kings Lynn	a	23 01	23 07	00 41

Saturdays

		FC	FC	FC	FC	FC	FC	FC	FC	FC	FC	FC	FC	FC	FC	FC	FC	FC	FC	FC	FC	FC	FC
Hunstanton Bus Station	d	23p55	06 45	07 40	08 47	09 10	09 25	09 47	10 06	10 10	10 25	10 47	11 06	11 15	11 25	11 45	11 47	12 06	12 15	12 25	12 47	13 06	13 15
Sandringham Norwich Gates	d																						
Sandringham Visitor Centre	d						10 00				11 00				12 00					13 00			
Kings Lynn	a	00 41	07 34	08 31	09 40	09 41	10 23	10 40	11 00	10 41	11 23	11 40	12 00	11 46	12 23	12 16	12 40	13 00	12 46	13 23	13 40	14 00	13 46

		FC	FC	FC	FC	FC	FC	FC	FC	FC	FC	FC	FC	FC	FC	FC	FC	FC	FC	FC	FC	FC	FC
Hunstanton Bus Station	d	13 25	13 47	14 06	14 15	14 25	14 47	15 06	15 15	15 25	15 47	16 06	16 25	16 30	16 47	17 20	17 30	17 45	18 20	18 40	18 45	20 50	22 23
Sandringham Norwich Gates	d																						
Sandringham Visitor Centre	d	14 00				15 00				16 00			17 00										
Kings Lynn	a	14 23	14 40	15 00	14 46	15 23	15 40	16 00	15 52	16 23	16 40	17 00	17 23	17 00	17 40	18 13	18 00	18 40	19 10	19 08	19 33	21 36	23 07

		FC
Hunstanton Bus Station	d	23 55
Sandringham Norwich Gates	d	
Sandringham Visitor Centre	d	
Kings Lynn	a	00 41

Sundays

		FC	FC	FC	FC	FC	FC	FC	FC	FC	FC	FC	FC	FC	FC	FC	FC	FC	FC	FC
Hunstanton Bus Station	d	23p55	09 00	10 13	10 40	11 13	11 40	12 13	13 13	13 40	14 13	14 40	15 13	15 40	16 13	17 13	17 40	18 13	20 05	22 20
Sandringham Norwich Gates	d																			
Sandringham Visitor Centre	d			10 43				12 43			14 43				16 43					
Kings Lynn	a	00 41	09 50	11 07	11 10	12 07	12 10	13 07	14 07	14 10	15 07	15 10	16 07	16 10	17 07	18 07	18 07	19 01	20 49	23 01

A not 4 June, 5 June, 27 August
B 4 June, 5 June, 27 August
C from 6 June until 8 June, 28 June, from 23 July until 5 September, not 27 August, also from 29 October until 2 November
D until 20 July, not from 4 June until 8 June, 28 June, also from 6 September, not from 29 October until 2 November
E ThFO

Services are subject to variation on Bank Holidays

Network Diagram for Tables 18, 19, 27, 29, 30

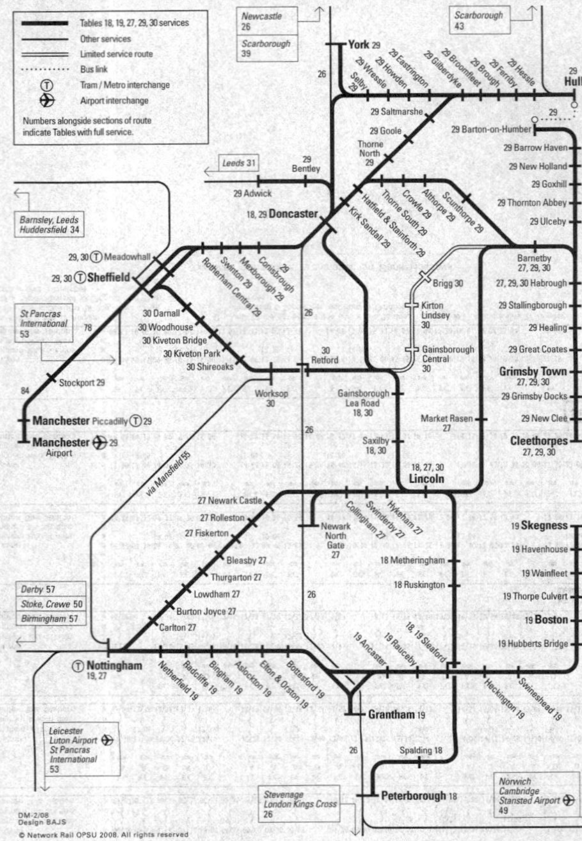

Peterborough - Sleaford, Lincoln and Doncaster

Network Diagram - see first Page of Table 18

Miles			EM	NT	EM	EM	EM	NT	EM	NT	EM	NT	EM	NT	EM	EM	NT	EM	NT	EM	NT	EM	NT
0	Peterborough 8	d	06 30			07 30					08 33		09 35			10 38		11 48		12 41		13 40	
16½	Spalding	d	06a56			07a56					08 57		09 57			11 01		12 10		13 03		14 02	
35½	Sleaford	a									09 25		10 25			11 29		12 38		13 31		14 30	
—		d			06 50		07 42		08 40		09 25		10 25			11 30		12 42		13 32		14 31	
40	Ruskington	d			06 58		07 50		08 48		09 34		10 34			11 38		12 50		13 40		14 39	
47½	Metheringham	d			07 09		08 00		08 59		09 44		10 44			11 48		12 59		13 50		14 49	
56¾	Lincoln	a			07 22		08 13		09 13		09 59		10 59			12 04		13 14		14 06		15 05	
—		d		07 00				08 25	09 15	09 25		10 25		11 25	11 54		12 27	13 15	13 26		14 25		15 24
62¾	Saxilby	d		07 10				08 34	09 24	09 34		10 34		11 34	12 04		12 36	13 24	13 35		14 34		15 33
72¼	Gainsborough Lea Road	d		07a22				08 48	09 37	09 48		10 48		11 48	12 17		12a48	13 37	13 48		14 48		15 48
93½	Doncaster 7	a						10 32	10 03	11 32		12 32		13 33	12 47			14 06	15 33		16 32		17 32

		NT	EM	NT	EM	EM	NT	EM	EM	EM	NT	NT	EM	EM	NT
Peterborough 8	d		15 10		16 25	17 32			18 36					20 30	
Spalding	d		15 32		16 48	17a58			19a02					20a56	
Sleaford	a		16 00		17 16										
	d		16 14		17 19			17 56		19 00			20 07		
Ruskington	d		16 22		17 27			18 04		19 07			20 14		
Metheringham	d		16 32		17 37			18 14		19 17			20 24		
Lincoln	a		16 47		17 51			18 29		19 32			20 41		
	d	16 25		17 22			18 24	18 31		19 32	19 43	20 27			21 27
Saxilby	d	16 35		17 31			18 33	18 42		19 41	19 52	20 36			21 36
Gainsborough Lea Road	d	16 48		17a43			18a45	18 57		19 53	20a04	20a48			21a48
Doncaster 7	a	18 35						19 25		20 23					

Saturdays

		EM	NT	EM	EM	EM	NT	EM	NT	EM	NT	EM	NT	EM	NT	EM	NT	EM	EM	NT	EM	NT	NT
Peterborough 8	d	06 30			07 30					08 33		09 33				11 48		12 41					
Spalding	d	06a56			07a56					08 57		09 57				12 10		13 03					
Sleaford	a									09 25		10 25				12 38		13 31					
	d			06 50		07 42				09 25		10 25				12 42		13 32					
Ruskington	d			06 58		07 50				09 34		10 34				12 50		13 40					
Metheringham	d			07 09		08 00				09 44		10 44				12 59		13 50					
Lincoln	a			07 22		08 13				09 59		10 59				13 14		14 06					
	d		07 00				08 25	09 15	09 25		10 25		11 25	11 54	12 27		13 25		14 10	14 25	15 10	15 24	16 25
Saxilby	d		07 10				08 34	09 24	09 34		10 34		11 34	12 04	12 36		13 34		14 19	14 34	15 20	15 33	16 35
Gainsborough Lea Road	d		07a22				08 48	09 37	09 48		10 48		11 48	12 17	12 49		13 48		14 32	14 48	15 32	15 48	16 48
Doncaster 7	a						10 32	10 11	11 32		12 33		13 32	12 47	14 32		15 34		15 01	16 32	16 01	17 32	18 38

		EM	NT	EM	EM	NT	EM	EM	EM	NT	NT	EM	EM	NT
Peterborough 8	d	15 11		16 25	17 30			18 36					20 28	
Spalding	d	15 33		16 48	17a56			19a02					20a54	
Sleaford	a	16 02		17 16										
	d	16 14		17 19			17 54		19 00			20 10		
Ruskington	d	16 22		17 27			18 02		19 07			20 17		
Metheringham	d	16 32		17 37			18 12		19 17			20 27		
Lincoln	a	16 48		17 51			18 27		19 32			20 40		
	d		17 22			18 24			19 32	19 43	20 27			21 27
Saxilby	d		17 31			18 33			19 41	19 52	20 36			21 36
Gainsborough Lea Road	d		17a43			18a45			19 54	20a04	20a48			21a48
Doncaster 7	a								20 23					

Sundays

		NT	NT	NT	NT
Peterborough 8	d				
Spalding	d				
Sleaford	a				
	d				
Ruskington	d				
Metheringham	d				
Lincoln	a				
	d	15 15	17 15	19 15	21 10
Saxilby	d	15 25	17 25	19 25	21 20
Gainsborough Lea Road	d	15a37	17a37	19a37	21a32
Doncaster 7	a				

For connections from London Kings Cross please refer to Table 25

Doncaster, Lincoln and Sleaford - Peterborough

Network Diagram - see first Page of Table 18

Miles			NT	EM	EM	EM	EM	NT	NT	EM	NT	EM	NT	EM	EM	NT	EM	NT	EM	EM	NT	EM	NT
0	Doncaster 7	d											09 01		10 24	10 04		11 04		13 05	12 03		13 02
21¼	Gainsborough Lea Road	d	06 25					07 38	08 24		09 38		10 38		10 52	11 38		12 38		13 31	13 39		14 38
30¾	Saxilby	d	06 37					07 51	08 37		09 51		10 51		11 05	11 51		12 51		13 44	13 52		14 51
36¾	Lincoln	a	06 53					08 06	08 52		10 06		11 06		11 17	12 06		13 06		13 55	14 06		15 06
—		d			07 05		08 00			09 10		10 15		11 10			12 10		13 30			14 41	
46¼	Metheringham	d			07 17		08 12			09 22		10 28		11 23			12 22		13 43			14 54	
53½	Ruskington	d			07 27		08 22			09 32		10 38		11 33			12 32		13 53			15 04	
58	Sleaford	a			07 36		08 31			09 41		10 50		11 42			12 41		14 02			15 13	
—		d					08 34			09 42		10 50		11 42			12 42		14 03			15 16	
77	Spalding	d		07 00		08 00	09 02			10 07		11 16		12 07			13 07		14 28			15 43	
93½	Peterborough 8	a		07 25		08 25	09 27			10 31		11 42		12 33			13 32		14 53			16 09	

		EM	EM	EM	NT	NT	EM	NT	EM	EM	NT	EM	NT	EM	EM	EM	NT	EM	EM
Doncaster 7	d		14 27		14 03	15 04		16 03			17 01			19 34				20 33	
Gainsborough Lea Road	d		14 54		15 38	16 38		17 38			18 38		19 39	20 00			20 42	21 00	
Saxilby	d		15 07		15 51	16 51		17 51			18 51		19 52	20 13			20 55	21 14	
Lincoln	a		15 18		16 10	17 06		18 06			19 07		20 06	20 25			21 10	21 26	
	d	15 12		16 01			17 20			18 10		19 10				20 48			
Metheringham	d	15 25		16 14			17 33			18 23		19 22				21 01			
Ruskington	d	15 35		16 24			17 42			18 33		19 32				21 10			
Sleaford	a	15 44		16 34			17 51			18 42		19 41				21 19			
	d			16 34															
Spalding	d			16 59					18 02						19 56				21 00
Peterborough 8	a			17 25					18 28						20 21				21 26

Saturdays

		NT	EM	EM	EM	EM	NT	NT	NT	EM	NT	EM	EM	NT	NT	EM	EM	NT	EM	NT	EM	EM	NT
Doncaster 7	d										09 03		10 24	10 04	11 04		13 05	12 03		13 04	15 07		14 01
Gainsborough Lea Road	d	06 25					07 38	08 24	09 38		10 38		10 52	11 38	12 38		13 31	13 37		14 36	15 33		15 40
Saxilby	d	06 37					07 51	08 37	09 51		10 51		11 05	11 51	12 51		13 44	13 50		14 49	15 46		15 53
Lincoln	a	06 53					08 06	08 52	10 06		11 06		11 16	12 06	13 06		13 55	14 07		15 06	15 57		16 10
	d			07 05		08 00				10 15		11 10				13 30			14 41			16 01	
Metheringham	d			07 17		08 12				10 28		11 23				13 43			14 54			16 14	
Ruskington	d			07 27		08 22				10 38		11 33				13 53			15 04			16 24	
Sleaford	a			07 36		08 31				10 50		11 42				14 02			15 13			16 34	
	d					08 34				10 50		11 42				14 03			15 16			16 34	
Spalding	d		07 00		08 00	09 02				11 16		12 07				14 28			15 41			16 59	
Peterborough 8	a		07 25		08 25	09 27				11 42		12 33				14 53			16 07			17 25	

		NT	EM	EM	NT	EM	EM	EM	NT	NT	EM	EM	NT	EM	EM
Doncaster 7	d	15 04		16 27	16 01				17 00	18 02				20 33	
Gainsborough Lea Road	d	16 38		16 56	17 38				18 38	19 39			20 42	21 00	
Saxilby	d	16 51		17 09	17 51				18 51	19 52			20 55	21 14	
Lincoln	a	17 06		17 20	18 06				19 07	20 06			21 10	21 26	
	d		17 15				18 10	19 05				20 49			
Metheringham	d		17 28				18 23	19 17				21 02			
Ruskington	d		17 38				18 33	19 27				21 11			
Sleaford	a		17 47				18 42	19 36				21 20			
	d														
Spalding	d					18 02					19 56				20 58
Peterborough 8	a					18 28					20 21				21 23

Sundays

		NT	NT	NT	NT
Doncaster 7	d				
Gainsborough Lea Road	d	14 26	16 35	18 35	20 24
Saxilby	d	14 39	16 48	18 48	20 37
Lincoln	a	14 54	17 02	19 03	20 51
	d				
Metheringham	d				
Ruskington	d				
Sleaford	a				
	d				
Spalding	d				
Peterborough 8	a				

For connections to London Kings Cross please refer to Table 25

Skegness - Grantham and Nottingham

Network Diagram - see first Page of Table 18

Miles	Miles			EM	EM	EM ◇	EM	EM ◇	EM	EM ◇	EM	EM ◇	EM	EM ◇	EM	EM ◇	EM	EM ◇	EM	EM ◇	EM
0	—	**Skegness**	d				07 09		08 10		09 06		10 15		11 15		12 15		13 15		14 15
3¼	—	Havenhouse	d				07 15														
5	—	Wainfleet	d				07 19		08 18		09 14		10 23		11 23		12 23		13 23		14 23
7	—	Thorpe Culvert	d				07 23														
23¾	—	**Boston**	d		06 13		07 46		08 45		09 41		10 50		11 50		12 50		13 50		14 50
27½	—	Hubberts Bridge	d				07 52														
30¾	—	Swineshead	d				07 57														
35¾	—	Heckington	d		06 27		08 02		08 59		09 55		11 04		12 04		13 04		14 04		15 04
40¼	—	**Sleaford**	d		06 35		08 11		09 07		10 03		11 12		12 12		13 12		14 13		15 12
42½	—	Rauceby	d		06 39		08 15														
46¼	0	Ancaster	d		06 45		08 21						11 21								
57¾	—	**Grantham**	a		07 04		08 42		09 35		10 31		11 41		12 41		13 41		14 42		15 41
—	—		d	06 10	07 10	07 58	08 45	08 55	09 40	09 58	10 36	11 00	11 45	12 00	12 45	12 59	13 45	13 58	14 45	14 58	15 45
65¼	12¾	Bottesford	d	06 21	07 21	08 11			09 52				11 56				13 56				15 56
67¾	—	Elton & Orston	d	06 25																	
69½	—	Aslockton	d	06 29	07 27	08 18	09 00				10 52				13 00				15 00		
71¾	—	Bingham	d	06 33	07 31	08 22	09 05		10 00		10 57		12 04		13 04		14 04		15 05		16 04
75¼	—	Radcliffe (Notts)	d	06 39	07 37	08 28							12 09								
77	—	Netherfield	d		07 42	08 33															
80¼	—	**Nottingham**	a	06 54	07 54	08 40	09 20	09 36	10 18	10 36	11 14	11 35	12 23	12 36	13 23	13 36	14 23	14 36	15 23	15 36	16 22

		EM ◇	EM	EM ◇	EM	EM ◇	EM	EM ◇	EM	EM ◇	EM	EM ◇	EM	EM
Skegness	d		15 09		16 11		17 30		18 14		19 14		20 15	21 02
Havenhouse	d				16 17									
Wainfleet	d		15 17		16 21		17 38		18 22		19 22		20 23	21 10
Thorpe Culvert	d				16 25									
Boston	d		15 44		16 48		18 05		18 49		19 49		20 50	21 37
Hubberts Bridge	d		15 50											
Swineshead	d		15 55											
Heckington	d		16 01		17 04		18 19		19 04		20 05		21 04	21 51
Sleaford	d		16 10		17 13		18 27		19 13		20 13		21 12	22 00
Rauceby	d		16 14											
Ancaster	d		16 20											
Grantham	a		16 41		17 42				19 41		20 40		21 43	
	d	16 01	16 45	17 00	17 45	17 58		18 56	19 45	19 59	20 44	20 59	21 47	
Bottesford	d				17 56				19 56				21 58	
Elton & Orston	d													
Aslockton	d				18 02				20 02				22 04	
Bingham	d		17 02		18 07		19 03	19 13	20 06		21 01		22 08	22 35
Radcliffe (Notts)	d								20 12					
Netherfield	d								20 16					
Nottingham	a	16 36	17 20	17 36	18 22	18 36	19 22	19 36	20 25	20 31	21 21	21 35	22 25	22 54

Saturdays

		EM	EM	EM ◇	EM	EM ◇	EM	EM ◇	EM	EM ◇	EM	EM ◇	EM	EM ◇	EM A	EM	EM ◇	EM	EM ◇	EM	EM ◇
Skegness	d				07 09		08 15		09 15		10 15		11 15		11 40	12 15		13 15		14 15	
Havenhouse	d				07 15																
Wainfleet	d				07 19		08 23		09 23		10 23		11 23			12 23		13 23		14 23	
Thorpe Culvert	d				07 23																
Boston	d		06 13		07 46		08 50		09 50		10 50		11 50		12 25	12 50		13 50		14 50	
Hubberts Bridge	d				07 52																
Swineshead	d				07 57																
Heckington	d		06 27		08 02		09 04		10 05		11 04		12 04			13 04		14 04		15 04	
Sleaford	d		06 35		08 11		09 12		10 14		11 12		12 12		12 47	13 12		14 13		15 12	
Rauceby	d		06 39		08 15																
Ancaster	d		06 45		08 21						11 21										
Grantham	a		07 07		08 42		09 41		10 43		11 41		12 41			13 41		14 42		15 41	
	d	06 10	07 10	07 58	08 45	09 09	09 45	09 58	10 46	10 58	11 45	11 58	12 45	12 58		13 45	13 58	14 45	14 58	15 45	15 58
Bottesford	d	06 21	07 21	08 11			09 56				11 56					13 56				15 56	
Elton & Orston	d	06 25																			
Aslockton	d	06 29	07 27	08 17	09 00				11 01				13 00					15 00			
Bingham	d	06 33	07 31	08 21	09 05		10 04		11 06		12 04		13 04			14 04		15 05		16 04	
Radcliffe (Notts)	d	06 39	07 37	08 27							12 09										
Netherfield	d		07 41	08 31																	
Nottingham	a	06 54	07 53	08 39	09 20	09 40	10 22	10 40	11 24	11 35	12 23	12 36	13 23	13 36	13 42	14 23	14 36	15 23	15 36	16 22	16 36

A from 21 July until 8 September

For connections to London Kings Cross please refer to Table 26

Skegness - Grantham and Nottingham

Network Diagram - see first Page of Table 18

		EM	EM ◇	EM	EM ◇	EM	EM ◇	EM	EM ◇	EM	EM ◇	EM	EM	EM
Skegness	d	15 09		16 11		17 30		18 14		19 19		20 15		21 02
Havenhouse	d			16 17										
Wainfleet	d	15 17		16 21		17 38		18 22		19 27		20 23		21 10
Thorpe Culvert	d			16 25										
Boston	d	15 44		16 48		18 05		18 49		19 54		20 50		21 37
Hubberts Bridge	d	15 50												
Swineshead	d	15 55												
Heckington	d	16 01		17 04		18 19		19 04		20 10		21 04		21 51
Sleaford	d	16 10		17 13		18 27		19 13		20 18		21 12		22 00
Rauceby	d	16 14												
Ancaster	d	16 20												
Grantham	a	16 41		17 42				19 41		20 45		21 43		
	d	16 45	16 56	17 45	18 03		18 58	19 45	20 03	20 48	20 58	21 47	22 02	
Bottesford	d			17 56				19 56				21 58		
Elton & Orston	d													
Aslockton	d			18 02				20 02				22 04		
Bingham	d	17 02		18 07		19 03	19 15	20 06		21 05		22 08		22 35
Radcliffe (Notts)	d							20 12						
Netherfield	d							20 16						
Nottingham	a	17 20	17 36	18 22	18 36	19 23	19 36	20 25	20 37	21 24	21 32	22 25	22 32	22 54

Sundays

until 9 September

		EM	EM	EM ◇	EM	EM ◇	EM	EM	EM ◇	EM	EM ◇	EM	EM ◇	EM ◇	EM	EM ◇	EM	EM ◇	EM	EM ◇
Skegness	d		10 14		11 15		12 27	14 10		15 04		16 22			18 07		19 15		20 43	
Havenhouse	d																			
Wainfleet	d		10 22		11 23		12 35	14 18		15 12		16 30			18 15		19 23		20 51	
Thorpe Culvert	d																			
Boston	d	09 06	10 49		11 49		13 02	14 45		15 40		16 57			18 42		19 50		21 18	
Hubberts Bridge	d																			
Swineshead	d																			
Heckington	d	09 20	11 03		12 03		13 16	14 59		15 54		17 11			18 56		20 04		21 32	
Sleaford	d	09 28	11 11		12 11		13 24	15 07		16 03		17 19			19 04		20 12		21 41	
Rauceby	d																			
Ancaster	d																			
Grantham	a	09 57	11 40		12 40			15 35		16 32					19 33		20 41		22 10	
	d	10 01	11 45	11 56	12 44	12 54		15 40	15 59	16 36	16 56		17 55	18 58	19 37	19 57	20 45	21 03	22 13	22 54
Bottesford	d		11 56			13 05														
Elton & Orston	d																			
Aslockton	d		12 02			13 11														
Bingham	d	10 18	12 06		13 01	13 16	14 00	15 57		16 53		17 55	18 14		19 54		21 02		22 30	
Radcliffe (Notts)	d		12 12			13 21														
Netherfield	d		12 16			13 25														
Nottingham	a	10 37	12 27	12 29	13 21	13 33	14 16	16 17	16 28	17 13	17 25	18 11	18 29	19 33	20 14	20 31	21 21	21 35	22 49	23 28

Sundays

16 September to 21 October

		EM ◇	EM	EM	EM ◇	EM ◇	EM	EM ◇	EM ◇	EM	EM ◇	EM	EM ◇	EM	EM ◇
Skegness	d			14 10			16 17			18 07		19 15			
Havenhouse	d														
Wainfleet	d			14 18			16 25			18 15		19 23			
Thorpe Culvert	d														
Boston	d		12 13	14 45			16 52			18 42		19 50			
Hubberts Bridge	d														
Swineshead	d														
Heckington	d		12 27	14 59			17 06			18 56		20 04			
Sleaford	d		12 35	15 07			17 14			19 04		20 12		21 41	
Rauceby	d														
Ancaster	d														
Grantham	a		13 04	15 35			17 43			19 33		20 41		22 10	
	d	12 54		15 40	15 59	16 56	17 47	17 55	18 58	19 37	19 57	20 45	21 03	22 13	22 54
Bottesford	d	13 05													
Elton & Orston	d														
Aslockton	d	13 11													
Bingham	d	13 16		15 57			18 04	18 14		19 54		21 02		22 30	
Radcliffe (Notts)	d	13 21													
Netherfield	d	13 25													
Nottingham	a	13 33		16 17	16 28	17 25	18 23	18 29	19 33	20 14	20 31	21 21	21 35	22 49	23 28

For connections to London Kings Cross please refer to Table 26

Skegness - Grantham and Nottingham

Sundays from 28 October

Network Diagram - see first Page of Table 18

		EM	EM (bus)	EM	EM (bus)	EM	EM (bus)	EM	EM (bus)	EM	EM (bus)	EM (bus)
Skegness	d			14 10		16 17		18 07		19 15		
Havenhouse	d											
Wainfleet	d			14 18		16 25		18 15		19 23		
Thorpe Culvert	d											
Boston	d	12 13		14 45		16 52		18 42		19 50		
Hubberts Bridge	d											
Swineshead	d											
Heckington	d	12 27		14 59		17 06		18 56		20 04		
Sleaford	d	12a34	12 45	15a07	15 17	17a14	17 25	19a04	19 15	20a12	20 23	21 41
Rauceby	d											
Ancaster	d											
Grantham	a		13 25		15 57		18 05		19 55		21 03	22 21
	d		13 26		15 58		18 06		19 56		21 04	22 22
Bottesford	d		13 42									
Elton & Orston	d											
Aslockton	d		13 48									
Bingham	d		13 57		16 24		18 32		20 22		21 30	22 48
Radcliffe (Notts)	d		14 10									
Netherfield	d											
Nottingham	a		14 30		16 54		19 02		20 52		22 00	23 18

For connections to London Kings Cross please refer to Table 26

Nottingham and Grantham - Skegness

Mondays to Fridays

Network Diagram - see first Page of Table 18

Miles	Miles			EM	EM	EM	EM	EM	EM ◇	EM ◇	EM	EM ◇	EM	EM ◇	EM	EM ◇	EM	EM ◇	EM	EM ◇	EM	EM ◇
0	—	**Nottingham**	d	05 10		05 50	06 41	07 34	07 52	08 34	08 50	09 34	09 55	10 34	10 45	11 34	11 45	12 34	12 45	13 34	13 45	14 34
4½	—	Netherfield	d								08 56											
5	—	Radcliffe (Notts)	d								09 01								12 55			
8½	—	Bingham	d	05 24		06 04	06 55	07 48			09 07		10 09		10 59		11 59		13 01		13 59	
10¾	—	Aslockton	d	05 28				07 52			09 11				11 03						14 03	
14½	—	Elton & Orston	d																			
15	0	Bottesford	d	05 35		06 13	07 04	07 59			09 17				11 10				13 09			
22½	—	**Grantham**	a	05 49		06 27	07 18	08 12	08 23	09 07	09 31	10 06		11 07	11 23	12 08	12 19	13 07	13 23	14 05	14 23	15 07
—	—		d			06 31	07 24	08 16			09 36				11 27		12 25		13 27		14 27	
34	12¾	Ancaster	d					08 34											13 45			
37¾	—	Rauceby	d					08 40														
40	—	**Sleaford**	d			06 57	07 50	08 45			10 04		10 44		11 53		12 50		13 55		14 52	
44½	—	Heckington	d			07 04	07 57	08 52			10 11		10 51		12 00		12 57		14 02		14 59	
49½	—	Swineshead	d				08 03															
52¾	—	Hubberts Bridge	d				08 08															
56½	—	**Boston**	d		06 25	07 24	08 18	09 12			10 28		11 11		12 19		13 15		14 21		15 17	
73¼	—	Thorpe Culvert	d			07 46																
75¼	—	Wainfleet	d		06 49	07 51	08 43	09 36			10 52		11 35		12 44		13 40		14 46		15 42	
77	—	Havenhouse	d			07 54																
80¼	—	**Skegness**	a		07 03	08 05	08 56	09 49			11 05		11 50		12 58		13 54		15 00		15 56	

		EM	EM ◇	EM	EM	EM ◇	EM	EM ◇	EM	EM ◇	EM	EM ◇	EM	EM
Nottingham	d	14 45	15 34	15 45	16 14	16 34	16 45	17 34	17 45	18 37	18 45	20 34		20 51
Netherfield	d			15 51			16 51							
Radcliffe (Notts)	d			15 56			16 56		17 55					21 01
Bingham	d	14 59		16 02			17 02	17 48	18 01		18 59			21 07
Aslockton	d			16 06			17 06	17 52	18 05		19 03			21 11
Elton & Orston	d						17 10							
Bottesford	d	15 08		16 12			17 14		18 12		19 10			21 17
Grantham	a	15 22	16 08	16 25		17 08	17 28	18 09	18 25	19 08	19 23	21 07		21 32
	d	15 26		16 29			17 32		18 29		19 26			21 36
Ancaster	d						17 50				19 44			
Rauceby	d						17 56				19 50			
Sleaford	d	15 52		16 55	17a51		18 01		18 55		19 55		21 20	22 01
Heckington	d	15 59		17 02			18 08		19 02		20 02		21 28	22 08
Swineshead	d	16 05												
Hubberts Bridge	d	16 10											21 43	
Boston	d	16 20		17 21			18 26		19 21		20 19		21a53	22a29
Thorpe Culvert	d			17 43										
Wainfleet	d	16 45		17 48			18 51		19 46		20 43			
Havenhouse	d			17 51										
Skegness	a	16 59		18 00			19 05		20 00		20 57			

Saturdays

		EM	EM	EM	EM	EM	EM ◇	EM A	EM ◇	EM	EM ◇	EM	EM ◇	EM	EM ◇	EM	EM ◇	EM	EM ◇	EM	EM ◇
Nottingham	d	05 10		05 50	06 41	07 28	07 45	08 24	08 32	08 45	09 34	09 55	10 34	10 45	11 34	11 45	12 34	12 45	13 34	13 45	14 34
Netherfield	d									08 51											
Radcliffe (Notts)	d									08 56								12 55			
Bingham	d	05 24		06 04	06 55	07 42				09 02		10 09		10 59		11 59		13 01		13 59	
Aslockton	d	05 28				07 46				09 06				11 03						14 03	
Elton & Orston	d																				
Bottesford	d	05 35		06 13	07 04	07 53				09 12				11 10				13 09			
Grantham	a	05 49		06 27	07 18	08 07	08 15		09 02	09 26	10 07		11 06	11 23	12 06	12 19	13 07	13 25	14 05	14 23	15 07
	d			06 31	07 24	08 16				09 30				11 27		12 25		13 29		14 27	
Ancaster	d					08 34															
Rauceby	d					08 40															
Sleaford	d			06 57	07 50	08 45		09 17		09 56		10 44		11 53		12 50		13 55		14 52	
Heckington	d			07 04	07 57	08 52				10 03		10 51		12 00		12 57		14 02		14 59	
Swineshead	d				08 03																
Hubberts Bridge	d				08 08																
Boston	d		06 25	07 24	08 18	09 11		09 49		10 22		11 11		12 19		13 15		14 21		15 17	
Thorpe Culvert	d			07 46																	
Wainfleet	d		06 49	07 51	08 43	09 35				10 47		11 35		12 44		13 40		14 46		15 42	
Havenhouse	d			07 54																	
Skegness	a		07 03	08 05	08 56	09 48		10 26		11 00		11 50		12 58		13 54		15 00		15 56	

A from 21 July until 8 September

For connections from London Kings Cross please refer to Table 26

Table 19

Saturdays

Nottingham and Grantham - Skegness

Network Diagram - see first Page of Table 18

		EM	EM	EM	EM	EM	EM	EM	EM	EM	EM	EM	EM
			◇		◇				◇		◇		
Nottingham	d	14 45	15 34	15 45	16 34	16 45	17 34	17 45	18 34	18 45	20 34		20 51
Netherfield	d			15 51		16 51							
Radcliffe (Notts)	d			15 56		16 56		17 55					21 01
Bingham	d	14 59		16 02		17 02	17 48	18 01		18 59			21 07
Aslockton	d			16 06		17 06	17 52	18 05		19 03			21 11
Elton & Orston	d					17 10							
Bottesford	d	15 08		16 12		17 14		18 12		19 10			21 17
Grantham	a	15 22	16 06	16 25	17 04	17 28	18 10	18 25	19 07	19 23	21 05		21 31
	d	15 26		16 29		17 32		18 29		19 26			21 36
Ancaster	d					17 50				19 44			
Rauceby	d					17 56				19 50			
Sleaford	d	15 52		16 55		18 01		18 55		19 55		21 21	22 01
Heckington	d	15 59		17 02		18 08		19 02		20 02		21 29	22 08
Swineshead	d	16 05											
Hubberts Bridge	d	16 10										21 43	
Boston	d	16 20		17 21		18 26		19 21		20 19		21a53	22a29
Thorpe Culvert	d			17 43									
Wainfleet	d	16 45		17 48		18 51		19 46		20 43			
Havenhouse	d			17 51									
Skegness	a	16 59		18 00		19 05		20 00		20 57			

Sundays

until 9 September

		EM	EM	EM	EM	EM	EM	EM	EM	EM	EM	EM	EM	EM	EM	EM	EM	EM	EM	EM	EM
					◇		◇		◇	◇		◇		◇		◇	◇		◇		◇
Nottingham	d		09 00	09 41	09 52	11 09	11 45	11 55	12 37	13 49	14 03	14 45	14 56	15 49	16 23	16 45	17 36	18 17	18 47	19 48	20 44
Netherfield	d														16 29		17 42				
Radcliffe (Notts)	d														16 34		17 46				
Bingham	d		09 14	09 55		11 23		12 11	12 51		14 17		15 10		16 40		17 52	18 31	19 01	20 02	20 58
Aslockton	d														16 44		17 56				
Elton & Orston	d																				
Bottesford	d														16 50		18 03				
Grantham	a			10 15	10 25	11 44	12 16	12 29	13 11	14 20	14 37	15 18	15 31	16 20	17 03	17 15	18 16	18 51	19 21	20 22	21 18
	d			10 20		11 49		12 33			14 41		15 36		17 07			18 55		20 27	
Ancaster	d																				
Rauceby	d																				
Sleaford	d		09 49	10 46		12 15		12 59			15 09		16 04		17 36			19 21		20 52	
Heckington	d		09 56	10 53		12 22		13 06			15 16		16 11		17 43			19 28		20 59	
Swineshead	d																				
Hubberts Bridge	d																				
Boston	d	09 31	10 16	11 11		12 41		13 24			15 39		16 31		18 02			19 50		21a20	
Thorpe Culvert	d																				
Wainfleet	d	09 55	10 40	11 36		13 06		13 49			16 03		16 55		18 27			20 14			
Havenhouse	d																				
Skegness	a	10 07	10 55	11 50		13 20		14 00			16 18		17 10		18 38			20 26			

Sundays

16 September to 21 October

		EM	EM	EM	EM	EM	EM	EM	EM	EM	EM	EM	EM	EM	EM
			◇		◇	◇		◇		◇	◇		◇		◇
Nottingham	d	11 55	12 37		13 49	14 45	14 56	15 49	16 23	16 45	17 36	18 31	18 47	19 48	20 44
Netherfield	d								16 29						
Radcliffe (Notts)	d								16 34		17 46				
Bingham	d	12 11	12 51				15 10		16 40		17 52	18 45	19 01	20 02	20 58
Aslockton	d								16 44		17 56				
Elton & Orston	d														
Bottesford	d								16 50		18 03				
Grantham	a	12 29	13 11		14 20	15 18	15 31	16 20	17 03	17 15	18 16	19 08	19 21	20 22	21 18
	d	12 33		13 50			15 36		17 07			19 13		20 27	
Ancaster	d														
Rauceby	d														
Sleaford	d	12 59		14 16			16 04		17 36			19 41		20a55	
Heckington	d	13 06		14 23			16 11		17 43			19 48			
Swineshead	d														
Hubberts Bridge	d														
Boston	d	13 24		14 45			16 31		18 02			20a10			
Thorpe Culvert	d														
Wainfleet	d	13 49		15 09			16 55		18 27						
Havenhouse	d														
Skegness	a	14 00		15 24			17 10		18 38						

For connections from London Kings Cross please refer to Table 26

Table 19

Sundays

from 28 October

Nottingham and Grantham - Skegness

Network Diagram - see first Page of Table 18

		EM	EM	EM	EM	EM	EM	EM	EM	EM	EM	EM	EM
							◇						
		🚌		🚌		🚌			🚌		🚌		🚌
Nottingham	d	11 12		12 28		14 17	14 45		15 41		17 45		19 48
Netherfield	d												
Radcliffe (Notts)	d								15 57		18 01		
Bingham	d	11 43		12 59		14 48			16 10		18 14		20 19
Aslockton	d								16 19		18 23		
Elton & Orston	d												
Bottesford	d								16 25		18 29		
Grantham	a	12 08		13 24		15 13	15 18		16 45		18 49		20 44
	d	12 09		13 25		15 14			16 46		18 50		20 45
Ancaster	d												
Rauceby	d												
Sleaford	d	12a49	12 59	14a05	14 16	15a54		16 04	17a26	17 36	19a30	19 41	21a25
Heckington	d		13 06		14 23			16 11		17 43		19 48	
Swineshead	d												
Hubberts Bridge	d												
Boston	d		13 24		14 45			16 31		18 02		20a10	
Thorpe Culvert	d												
Wainfleet	d		13 49		15 09			16 55		18 27			
Havenhouse	d												
Skegness	a		14 00		15 24			17 10		18 38			

For connections from London Kings Cross please refer to Table 26

Network Diagram for Tables 20, 21, 22

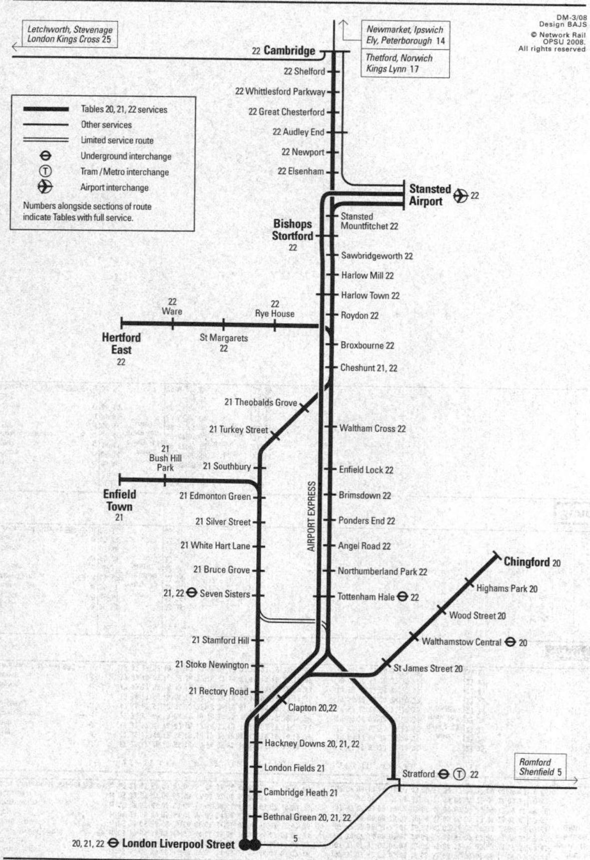

London - Chingford

Network Diagram - see first Page of Table 20

Miles			LE	LE	LE	LE	LE	LE	LE	LE	LE		LE	LE	LE	LE	LE	LE	LE	LE		LE
			A				MX															
0	**London Liverpool Street** 15 ⊖	d	23p48	00 03	00 18	00 33	00 48	01 03	06 03	06 33	06 48		07 03	07 18	07 33	07 48	08 05	08 18	08 35	08 48	and every 15 minutes until	15 48
1¼	Bethnal Green	d	23p51	00 06	00 21	00 36			06 06	06 36	06 51		07 06	07 21	07 36	07 51		08 21		08 51		15 51
3	Hackney Downs	d	23p55	00 10	00 25	00 40	00 55	01 10	06 10	06 40	06 55		07 10	07 25	07 40	07 55	08 12	08 25	08 42	08 55		15 55
4	Clapton	d	23p58	00 13	00 28	00 43	00 58	01 13	06 13	06 43	06 58		07 13	07 28	07 43	07 58	08 15	08 28	08 45	08 58		15 58
5¾	St James Street	d	00 01	00 16	00 32	00 47	01 02	01 17	06 16	06 46	07 01		07 17	07 32	07 47	08 02	08 18	08 31	08 48	09 01		16 01
6¼	Walthamstow Central ⊖	d	00 03	00 18	00 34	00 49	01 04	01 19	06 18	06 48	07 03		07 19	07 34	07 49	08 04	08 20	08 33	08 50	09 03		16 03
7	Wood Street	d	00 05	00 20	00 36	00 51	01 06	01 21	06 20	06 50	07 05		07 21	07 36	07 51	08 06	08 22	08 35	08 52	09 05		16 05
8½	Highams Park	d	00 08	00 23	00 39	00 54	01 09	01 24	06 23	06 53	07 08		07 24	07 39	07 54	08 09	08 25	08 38	08 55	09 08		16 08
10½	**Chingford**	a	00 14	00 29	00 44	00 59	01 14	01 29	06 29	06 59	07 17		07 29	07 44	08 02	08 14	08 32	08 44	09 01	09 14		16 14

		LE		LE		LE	LE	LE	LE	LE	LE	LE	LE	LE	LE		LE		LE	LE
London Liverpool Street 15 ⊖	d	16 03	and every 15 minutes until	16 48		17 03	17 18	17 33	17 48	18 03	18 18	18 33	18 48	19 03	19 18	and every 15 minutes until	23 18		23 33	23 48
Bethnal Green	d	16 06		16 51			17 21		17 51		18 21		18 51		19 21		23 21			23 51
Hackney Downs	d	16 10		16 55		17 10	17 25	17 40	17 55	18 10	18 25	18 40	18 55	19 10	19 25		23 25			23 55
Clapton	d	16 13		16 58		17 12	17 28	17 42	17 58	18 12	18 28	18 42	18 58	19 12	19 28		23 28			23 58
St James Street	d	16 16		17 01		17 16	17 31	17 46	18 01	18 16	18 31	18 46	19 01	19 16	19 31		23 31			00 01
Walthamstow Central ⊖	d	16 19		17 04		17 18	17 34	17 48	18 04	18 18	18 34	18 48	19 04	19 18	19 33		23 33		23 44	00 03
Wood Street	d	16 21		17 06		17 20	17 36	17 50	18 06	18 20	18 36	18 50	19 06	19 20	19 35		23 35			00 05
Highams Park	d	16 24		17 09		17 23	17 39	17 53	18 09	18 23	18 39	18 53	19 09	19 23	19 38		23 38			00 08
Chingford	a	16 31		17 16		17 31	17 46	18 01	18 16	18 31	18 46	19 01	19 16	19 29	19 44		23 44		23 54	00 14

Saturdays

		LE	LE	LE	LE	LE	LE	LE	LE		LE		LE	LE
London Liverpool Street 15 ⊖	d	23p48	00 03	00 18	00 33	00 48	01 03	06 03	06 33	and every 15 minutes until	23 18		23 33	23 48
Bethnal Green	d	23p51	00 06	00 21	00 36			06 06	06 36		23 21			23 51
Hackney Downs	d	23p55	00 10	00 25	00 40	00 55	01 10	06 10	06 40		23 25			23 55
Clapton	d	23p58	00 13	00 28	00 43	00 58	01 13	06 13	06 43		23 28			23 58
St James Street	d	00 01	00 16	00 32	00 47	01 02	01 17	06 16	06 46		23 31			00 01
Walthamstow Central ⊖	d	00 03	00 18	00 34	00 49	01 04	01 19	06 18	06 48		23 33		23 44	00 03
Wood Street	d	00 05	00 20	00 36	00 51	01 06	01 21	06 20	06 50		23 35			00 05
Highams Park	d	00 08	00 23	00 39	00 54	01 09	01 24	06 23	06 53		23 38			00 08
Chingford	a	00 14	00 29	00 44	00 59	01 14	01 29	06 29	06 59		23 44		23 54	00 14

Sundays

		LE	LE	LE	LE	LE	LE	LE	LE	LE		LE	LE	LE		LE	LE
London Liverpool Street 15 ⊖	d	23p48	00 03	00 18	00 33	00 48	01 03	07 33	08 03	08 33		08 48	09 03	09 18	and every 15 minutes until	23 33	23 48
Bethnal Green	d	23p51	00 06	00 21	00 36									09 21		23 36	23 51
Hackney Downs	d	23p55	00 10	00 25	00 40	00 55	01 10	07 40	08 10	08 40		08 55	09 10	09 25		23 40	23 55
Clapton	d	23p58	00 13	00 28	00 43	00 58	01 13	07 43	08 13	08 43		08 58	09 13	09 28		23 43	23 58
St James Street	d	00 01	00 16	00 32	00 47	01 02	01 17	07 46	08 16	08 46		09 01	09 16	09 31		23 46	00 01
Walthamstow Central ⊖	d	00 03	00 18	00 34	00 49	01 04	01 19	07 48	08 18	08 48		09 03	09 18	09 33		23 48	00 03
Wood Street	d	00 05	00 20	00 36	00 51	01 06	01 21	07 50	08 20	08 50		09 05	09 20	09 35		23 50	00 05
Highams Park	d	00 08	00 23	00 39	00 54	01 09	01 24	07 53	08 23	08 53		09 08	09 23	09 38		23 53	00 08
Chingford	a	00 14	00 29	00 44	00 59	01 14	01 29	07 59	08 29	08 59		09 14	09 29	09 44		23 59	00 14

A not 14 May

Table 20

Chingford - London

Network Diagram - see first Page of Table 20

Miles			LE	LE	LE	LE	LE	LE	LE	LE	LE	LE	LE	LE	LE	LE	LE	LE	LE	LE	LE		LE
0	Chingford	d	05 10	05 25	05 40	05 55	06 10	06 29	06 44	06 59	07 14	07 29	07 44	07 59	08 14	08 29	08 44	08 57	09 12	09 27	09 40	and every 15 minutes until	17 10
2	Highams Park	d	05 14	05 29	05 44	05 59	06 14	06 33	06 48	07 03	07 18	07 33	07 48	08 03	08 18	08 33	08 48	09 01	09 16	09 31	09 44		17 14
3½	Wood Street	d	05 17	05 32	05 47	06 02	06 17	06 37	06 52	07 07	07 22	07 37	07 52	08 07	08 22	08 37	08 52	09 05	09 20	09 35	09 47		17 17
4¼	Walthamstow Central ⊖	d	05 19	05 34	05 49	06 04	06 19	06 39	06 54	07 09	07 24	07 39	07 54	08 09	08 24	08 39	08 54	09 07	09 22	09 37	09 49		17 19
4¾	St James Street	d	05 21	05 36	05 51	06 06	06 21	06 42	06 56	07 12	07 26	07 42	07 56	08 12	08 26	08 42	08 56	09 10	09 25	09 40	09 51		17 21
6½	Clapton	d	05 24	05 39	05 54	06 09	06 24	06 45	07 00	07 15	07 30	07 45	08 00	08 15	08 30	08 45	09 00	09 13	09 28	09 43	09 54		17 24
7½	Hackney Downs	d	05 28	05 43	05 58	06 13	06 28	06 49	07 03	07 19	07 33	07 49	08 03	08 19	08 33	08 49	09 03	09 17	09 32	09 47	09 58		17 28
9¼	Bethnal Green	d	05 32	05 47	06 02	06 17	06 32	06 53	07 07		07 37		08 07		08 37		09 07	09 21	09 36	09 51	10 02		17 32
10½	London Liverpool Street 15 ⊖	a	05 36	05 51	06 07	06 21	06 36	06 58	07 13	07 28	07 43	07 58	08 13	08 28	08 43	08 57	09 13	09 27	09 42	09 57	10 06		17 36

		LE	LE	LE	LE	LE	LE	LE	LE	LE	LE	LE	LE	LE		LE
Chingford	d	17 25	17 40	17 55	18 10	18 25	18 40	18 55	19 10	19 25	19 40	19 55	20 10	20 25	and every 15 minutes until	23 25
Highams Park	d	17 29	17 44	17 59	18 14	18 29	18 44	18 59	19 14	19 29	19 44	19 59	20 14	20 29		23 29
Wood Street	d	17 32	17 47	18 02	18 17	18 32	18 47	19 02	19 17	19 32	19 47	20 02	20 17	20 32		23 32
Walthamstow Central ⊖	d	17 34	17 49	18 04	18 19	18 34	18 49	19 04	19 19	19 34	19 49	20 04	20 19	20 34		23 34
St James Street	d	17 36	17 51	18 06	18 21	18 36	18 51	19 06	19 21	19 36	19 51	20 06	20 21	20 36		23 36
Clapton	d	17 39	17 54	18 09	18 24	18 39	18 54	19 09	19 24	19 39	19 54	20 09	20 24	20 39		23 39
Hackney Downs	d	17 43	17 58	18 13	18 28	18 43	18 58	19 13	19 28	19 43	19 58	20 13	20 28	20 43		23 43
Bethnal Green	d	17 47	18 02	18 17	18 32	18 47	19 02	19 17	19 32	19 47	20 02	20 17	20 32	20 47		23 47
London Liverpool Street 15 ⊖	a	17 52	18 07	18 21	18 37	18 51	19 07	19 21	19 37	19 51	20 06	20 21	20 37	20 51		23 51

Saturdays

		LE		LE
Chingford	d	05 10	and every 15 minutes until	23 25
Highams Park	d	05 14		23 29
Wood Street	d	05 17		23 32
Walthamstow Central ⊖	d	05 19		23 34
St James Street	d	05 21		23 36
Clapton	d	05 24		23 39
Hackney Downs	d	05 28		23 43
Bethnal Green	d	05 32		23 47
London Liverpool Street 15 ⊖	a	05 36		23 51

Sundays

		LE		LE	LE		LE
Chingford	d	06 40	and every 15 minutes until	08 40	08 55	and every 15 minutes until	23 10
Highams Park	d	06 44		08 44	08 59		23 14
Wood Street	d	06 47		08 47	09 02		23 17
Walthamstow Central ⊖	d	06 49		08 49	09 04		23 19
St James Street	d	06 51		08 51	09 06		23 21
Clapton	d	06 54		08 54	09 09		23 24
Hackney Downs	d	06 58		08 58	09 13		23 28
Bethnal Green	d				09 17		23 32
London Liverpool Street 15 ⊖	a	07 06		09 06	09 21		23 36

Table 21

London - Cheshunt (via Seven Sisters) and Enfield Town

Network Diagram - see first Page of Table 20

Miles	Miles			LE A	LE MX	LE MX	LE	LE	LE	LE	LE	LE	LE	LE	LE	LE	LE	LE	LE	LE	LE	LE	LE
0	0	London Liverpool Street 15 ⊖	d	23p30	23p45	00 01	05 45	06 00	06 15	06 21	06 36	06 45	06 51	07 06	07 15	07 21	07 36	07 45	07 51	08 00	08 07	08 15	08 30
1¼	1¼	Bethnal Green	d	23p33	23p48	00 03	05 48	06 03		06 24	06 39		06 54	07 09		07 24	07 39		07 54		08 10	08 18	08 33
1¾	1¾	Cambridge Heath	d	23p35	23p50	00 05	05 50	06 05		06 26	06 41		06 56	07 11		07 26	07 41		07 56		08 12	08 20	08 35
2½	2½	London Fields	d	23p37	23p52	00 07	05 52	06 07		06 28	06 43		06 58	07 13		07 28	07 43		07 58		08 14	08 22	08 37
3	3	Hackney Downs	d	23p39	23p54	00 09	05 54	06 09	06 22	06 30	06 45	06 52	07 00	07 15	07 22	07 30	07 45	07 52	08 00	08 07	08 16	08 24	08 39
3¾	3¾	Rectory Road	d	23p42	23p57	00 12	05 57	06 12		06 33	06 48	06 55	07 03	07 18	07 25	07 33	07 48	07 55	08 03		08 19	08 27	08 42
4¼	4¼	Stoke Newington	d	23p43	23p58	00 13	05 58	06 13		06 34	06 49	06 56	07 04	07 19	07 26	07 34	07 49	07 56	08 04		08 20	08 28	08 43
5	5	Stamford Hill	d	23p45	23p59	00 15	06 00	06 15		06 36	06 51	06 58	07 06	07 21	07 28	07 36	07 51	07 58	08 06		08 22	08 30	08 45
5½	5½	Seven Sisters ⊖	d	23p47	00 02	00 17	06 02	06 17	06 27	06 38	06 53	07 00	07 08	07 23	07 30	07 38	07 53	08 00	08 08	08 15	08 24	08 32	08 47
6¼	6¼	Bruce Grove	d	23p49	00 04	00 19	06 04	06 19		06 40	06 55	07 02	07 10	07 25	07 32	07 40	07 55	08 02	08 10		08 26	08 34	08 49
7¼	7¼	White Hart Lane	d	23p51	00 06	00 21	06 06	06 21		06 42	06 57	07 04	07 12	07 27	07 34	07 42	07 57	08 04	08 12		08 28	08 36	08 51
8	8	Silver Street	d	23p53	00 08	00 23	06 08	06 23		06 44	06 59	07 06	07 14	07 29	07 36	07 44	07 59	08 06	08 14		08 30	08 38	08 53
8½	8½	Edmonton Green	d	23p55	00 10	00 25	06 10	06 25	06 32	06 46	07 01	07 08	07 16	07 31	07 38	07 46	08 01	08 08	08 16	08 20	08 32	08 44	08 55
—	9¾	Bush Hill Park	d	23p58		00 28		06 28		06 49		07 11	07 19		07 41	07 49		08 11	08 19		08 35		08 58
—	10¾	Enfield Town	a	00 03		00 33		06 33		06 54		07 16	07 24		07 46	07 54		08 16	08 24		08 40		09 03
10½	—	Southbury	d		00 14		06 14		06 36		07 05			07 35			08 05			08 24		08 48	
12¼	—	Turkey Street	d		00 17		06 17		06 39		07 08			07 38			08 08			08 27		08 51	
13½	—	Theobalds Grove	d		00 19		06 19		06 41		07 10			07 40			08 10			08 29		08 53	
14½	—	Cheshunt	a		00 22		06 24		06 46		07 15			07 45			08 15			08 34		08 58	

		LE	LE	LE	LE	LE	LE		LE	LE	LE	LE	LE	LE	LE	LE	LE	LE	LE	LE	LE	LE
London Liverpool Street 15 ⊖	d	08 38	08 45	09 00	09 15	09 30	09 45	and at the same minutes past each hour until	15 45	16 00	16 15	16 21	16 30	16 41	16 45	16 52	17 00	17 11	17 15	17 22	17 30	17 41
Bethnal Green	d		08 48	09 03	09 18	09 33	09 48		15 48	16 03	16 18	16 24	16 33		16 48		17 03		17 18		17 33	
Cambridge Heath	d	08 43	08 50	09 05	09 20	09 35	09 50		15 50	16 05	16 20	16 26	16 35		16 50	16 57	17 05		17 20	17 27	17 35	
London Fields	d	08 45	08 52	09 07	09 22	09 37	09 52		15 52	16 07	16 22	16 28	16 37		16 52	16 59	17 07		17 22	17 29	17 37	
Hackney Downs	d	08 47	08 54	09 09	09 24	09 39	09 54		15 54	16 09	16 24	16 30	16 39	16 48	16 54	17 01	17 09	17 18	17 24	17 31	17 39	17 48
Rectory Road	d	08 49	08 57	09 12	09 27	09 42	09 57		15 57	16 12	16 27	16 33	16 42		16 57	17 03	17 12		17 27	17 33	17 42	
Stoke Newington	d	08 51	08 58	09 13	09 28	09 43	09 58		15 58	16 13	16 28	16 34	16 43		16 58	17 05	17 13		17 28	17 35	17 43	
Stamford Hill	d	08 53	09 00	09 15	09 30	09 45	10 00		16 00	16 15	16 30	16 36	16 45		17 00		17 15		17 30		17 45	
Seven Sisters ⊖	d	08 55	09 02	09 17	09 32	09 47	10 02		16 02	16 18	16 33	16 39	16 48	16 54	17 03	17 09	17 18	17 24	17 33	17 39	17 48	17 54
Bruce Grove	d	08 57	09 04	09 19	09 34	09 49	10 04		16 04	16 20	16 35	16 41	16 50		17 05	17 11	17 20		17 35	17 41	17 50	
White Hart Lane	d	08 59	09 06	09 21	09 36	09 51	10 06		16 06	16 22	16 37	16 43	16 52		17 07	17 13	17 22		17 37	17 43	17 52	
Silver Street	d	09 01	09 08	09 23	09 38	09 53	10 08		16 08	16 24	16 39	16 45	16 54		17 09	17 15	17 24		17 39	17 45	17 54	
Edmonton Green	d	09 03	09 10	09 25	09 40	09 55	10 10		16 10	16 26	16 41	16 47	16 56	17 00	17 11	17 17	17 26	17 30	17 41	17 47	17 56	18 00
Bush Hill Park	d		09 13	09 28		09 58				16 29		16 50	16 59		17 14		17 29		17 44		17 59	
Enfield Town	a		09 18	09 33		10 03				16 35		16 56	17 05		17 20		17 35		17 50		18 05	
Southbury	d	09 07			09 44		10 14		16 14		16 45					17 21				17 51		
Turkey Street	d	09 10			09 47		10 17		16 17		16 48					17 24				17 54		
Theobalds Grove	d	09 12			09 49		10 19		16 19		16 50					17 26				17 56		
Cheshunt	a	09 17			09 54		10 24		16 24		16 56			17 08		17 32		17 38		18 02		18 08

		LE	LE	LE	LE	LE	LE	LE	LE	LE	LE	LE	LE	LE	LE	LE	LE		LE	LE	LE
London Liverpool Street 15 ⊖	d	17 45	17 52	18 00	18 11	18 15	18 22	18 30	18 41	18 45	19 00	19 15	19 22	19 30	19 45	20 00	20 15	and at the same minutes past each hour until	23 15	23 30	23 45
Bethnal Green	d	17 48		18 03		18 18		18 33		18 48	19 03	19 18		19 33	19 48	20 03	20 18		23 18	23 33	23 48
Cambridge Heath	d	17 50	17 57	18 05		18 20	18 27	18 35		18 50	19 05	19 20		19 35	19 50	20 05	20 20		23 20	23 35	23 50
London Fields	d	17 52	17 59	18 07		18 22	18 29	18 37		18 52	19 07	19 22	19 28	19 37	19 52	20 07	20 22		23 22	23 37	23 52
Hackney Downs	d	17 54	18 01	18 09	18 18	18 24	18 31	18 39	18 48	18 54	19 09	19 24	19 30	19 39	19 54	20 09	20 24		23 24	23 39	23 54
Rectory Road	d	17 57	18 03	18 12		18 27	18 33	18 42		18 57	19 12	19 27	19 32	19 42	19 57	20 12	20 27		23 27	23 42	23 57
Stoke Newington	d	17 58	18 05	18 13		18 28	18 35	18 43		18 58	19 13	19 28	19 34	19 43	19 58	20 13	20 28		23 28	23 43	23 58
Stamford Hill	d	18 00		18 15		18 30		18 45		19 00	19 15	19 30		19 45	20 00	20 15	20 30		23 30	23 45	23 59
Seven Sisters ⊖	d	18 03	18 09	18 18	18 24	18 33	18 39	18 48	18 54	19 03	19 17	19 32	19 37	19 47	20 02	20 17	20 32		23 32	23 47	00 02
Bruce Grove	d	18 05	18 11	18 20		18 35	18 41	18 50		19 05	19 19	19 34	19 39	19 49	20 04	20 19	20 34		23 34	23 49	00 04
White Hart Lane	d	18 07	18 13	18 22		18 37	18 43	18 52		19 07	19 21	19 36	19 41	19 51	20 06	20 21	20 36		23 36	23 51	00 06
Silver Street	d	18 09	18 15	18 24		18 39	18 45	18 54		19 09	19 23	19 38	19 43	19 53	20 08	20 23	20 38		23 38	23 53	00 08
Edmonton Green	d	18 11	18 17	18 26	18 30	18 41	18 47	18 56	19 00	19 11	19 25	19 40	19 45	19 55	20 10	20 25	20 40		23 40	23 55	00 10
Bush Hill Park	d	18 14		18 29		18 44		18 59			19 28		19 48	19 58		20 28				23 58	
Enfield Town	a	18 20		18 35		18 50		19 05			19 33		19 53	20 03		20 33				00 03	
Southbury	d		18 21				18 51			19 15		19 44			20 14		20 44		23 44		00 14
Turkey Street	d		18 24				18 54			19 18		19 47			20 17		20 47		23 47		00 17
Theobalds Grove	d		18 26				18 56			19 21		19 50			20 19		20 49		23 49		00 19
Cheshunt	a		18 32		18 38		19 02		19 08	19 26		19 54			20 24		20 54		23 54		00 22

Saturdays

		LE	LE	LE	LE	LE	LE	LE	LE	LE		LE	LE
London Liverpool Street 15 ⊖	d	23p30	23p45	00 01	05 15	05 31	05 45	06 00	06 15	06 30	and at the same minutes past each hour until	23 30	23 45
Bethnal Green	d	23p33	23p48	00 03	05 18		05 48	06 03	06 18	06 33		23 33	23 48
Cambridge Heath	d	23p35	23p50	00 05	05 20		05 50	06 05	06 20	06 35		23 35	23 50
London Fields	d	23p37	23p52	00 07	05 22		05 52	06 07	06 22	06 37		23 37	23 52
Hackney Downs	d	23p39	23p54	00 09	05 24	05 38	05 54	06 09	06 24	06 39		23 39	23 54
Rectory Road	d	23p42	23p57	00 12	05 27		05 57	06 12	06 27	06 42		23 42	23 57
Stoke Newington	d	23p43	23p58	00 13	05 28		05 58	06 13	06 28	06 43		23 43	23 58
Stamford Hill	d	23p45	23p59	00 15	05 30		06 00	06 15	06 30	06 45		23 45	23 59
Seven Sisters ⊖	d	23p47	00 02	00 17	05 32	05 47	06 02	06 17	06 32	06 47		23 47	00 02
Bruce Grove	d	23p49	00 04	00 19	05 34	05 49	06 04	06 19	06 34	06 49		23 49	00 04
White Hart Lane	d	23p51	00 06	00 21	05 36	05 51	06 06	06 21	06 36	06 51		23 51	00 06
Silver Street	d	23p53	00 08	00 23	05 38	05 53	06 08	06 23	06 38	06 53		23 53	00 08
Edmonton Green	d	23p55	00 10	00 25	05 40	05 55	06 10	06 25	06 40	06 55		23 55	00 10
Bush Hill Park	d	23p58		00 28		05 58		06 28		06 58		23 58	
Enfield Town	a	00 03		00 33		06 03		06 33		07 03		00 03	
Southbury	d		00 14		05 44		06 14		06 44				00 14
Turkey Street	d		00 17		05 47		06 17		06 47				00 17
Theobalds Grove	d		00 19		05 49		06 19		06 49				00 19
Cheshunt	a		00 22		05 54		06 24		06 54				00 24

A not 14 May

London - Cheshunt (via Seven Sisters) and Enfield Town

Sundays until 22 July

Network Diagram - see first Page of Table 20

		LE	LE	LE	LE	LE	LE	LE	LE	LE		LE	LE	LE	LE	LE		LE	LE		LE
London Liverpool Street 15 ⊖	d	23p30	23p45	00 01	07 30	07 52	08 00	08 22	08 30	08 52		09 00	09 22	09 30	09 52	10 00	and at the same minutes past each hour until	23 00	23 22		23 30
Bethnal Green	d	23p33	23p48	00 03										09 33		10 03		23 03			23 33
Cambridge Heath	d	23p35	23p50	00 05										09 35		10 05		23 05			23 35
London Fields	d	23p37	23p52	00 07										09 37		10 07		23 07			23 37
Hackney Downs	d	23p39	23p54	00 09	07 39	07 59	08 09	08 29	08 39	08 59		09 09	09 29	09 39	09 59	10 09		23 09	23 29		23 39
Rectory Road	d	23p42	23p57	00 12	07 42		08 12		08 42			09 12		09 42		10 12		23 12			23 42
Stoke Newington	d	23p43	23p58	00 13	07 43		08 13		08 43			09 13		09 43		10 13		23 13			23 43
Stamford Hill	d	23p45	23p59	00 15	07 45		08 15		08 45			09 15		09 45		10 15		23 15			23 45
Seven Sisters ⊖	d	23p47	00 02	00 17	07 47	08 04	08 17	08 34	08 47	09 04		09 17	09 34	09 47	10 04	10 17		23 17	23 34		23 47
Bruce Grove	d	23p49	00 04	00 19	07 49		08 19		08 49			09 19		09 49		10 19		23 19			23 49
White Hart Lane	d	23p51	00 06	00 21	07 51		08 21		08 51			09 21		09 51		10 21		23 21			23 51
Silver Street	d	23p53	00 08	00 23	07 53		08 23		08 53			09 23		09 53		10 23		23 23			23 53
Edmonton Green	d	23p55	00 10	00 25	07 55	08 08	08 25	08 38	08 55	09 08		09 25	09 38	09 55	10 08	10 25		23 25	23 38		23 55
Bush Hill Park	d	23p58		00 28	07 58		08 28		08 58			09 28		09 58		10 28		23 28			23 58
Enfield Town	a	00 03		00 33	08 03		08 33		09 03			09 33		10 03		10 33		23 33			00 03
Southbury	d		00 14			08 12		08 42		09 12			09 42		10 12				23 42		
Turkey Street	d		00 17			08 15		08 45		09 15			09 45		10 15				23 45		
Theobalds Grove	d		00 19			08 17		08 47		09 17			09 47		10 17				23 47		
Cheshunt	a		00 24			08 20		08 52		09 20			09 52		10 20				23 50		

Sundays 29 July to 12 August

		LE	LE	LE	LE	LE	LE	LE	LE	LE		LE	LE	LE	LE	LE		LE	LE		LE
London Liverpool Street 15 ⊖	d	23p30	23p45	00 01	07 30	07 52	08 00	08 22	08 30	08 52		09 00	09 22	09 30	09 52	10 00	C and at the same minutes past each hour until	23 00	23 22		23 30
Bethnal Green	d	23p33	23p48	00 03										09 33		10 03		23 03			23 33
Cambridge Heath	d	23p35	23p50	00 05										09 35		10 05		23 05			23 35
London Fields	d	23p37	23p52	00 07										09 37		10 07		23 07			23 37
Hackney Downs	d	23p39	23p54	00 09	07 39	07 59	08 09	08 29	08 39	08 59		09 09	09 29	09 39	09 59	10 09		23 09	23 29		23 39
Rectory Road	d	23p42	23p57	00 12	07 42		08 12		08 42			09 12		09 42		10 12		23 12			23 42
Stoke Newington	d	23p43	23p58	00 13	07 43		08 13		08 43			09 13		09 43		10 13		23 13			23 43
Stamford Hill	d	23p45	23p59	00 15	07 45		08 15		08 45			09 15		09 45		10 15		23 15			23 45
Seven Sisters ⊖	d	23p47	00 02	00 17	07 47	08 04	08 17	08 34	08 47	09 04		09 17	09 34	09 47	10 04	10 17		23 17	23 34		23 47
Bruce Grove	d	23p49	00 04	00 19	07 49		08 19		08 49			09 19		09 49		10 19		23 19			23 49
White Hart Lane	d	23p51	00 06	00 21	07 51		08 21		08 51			09 21		09 51		10 21		23 21			23 51
Silver Street	d	23p53	00 08	00 23	07 53		08 23		08 53			09 23		09 53		10 23		23 23			23 53
Edmonton Green	d	23p55	00 10	00 25	07 55	08 08	08 25	08 38	08 55	09 08		09 25	09 38	09 55	10 08	10 25		23 25	23 38		23 55
Bush Hill Park	d	23p58		00 28	07 58		08 28		08 58			09 28		09 58		10 28		23 28			23 58
Enfield Town	a	00 03		00 33	08 03		08 33		09 03			09 33		10 03		10 33		23 33			00 03
Southbury	d		00 14			08 12		08 42		09 12			09 42		10 12				23 42		
Turkey Street	d		00 17			08 15		08 45		09 15			09 45		10 15				23 45		
Theobalds Grove	d		00 19			08 17		08 47		09 17			09 47		10 17				23 47		
Cheshunt	a		00 24			08 22		08 52		09 22			09 52		10 22				23 52		

Sundays from 19 August

		LE	LE	LE	LE	LE A	LE B	LE	LE	LE		LE A	LE B	LE	LE	LE	LE A	LE B	LE		LE	LE A	LE B	LE
London Liverpool Street 15 ⊖	d	23p30	23p45	00 01	07 30	07 52	07 52	08 00	08 22	08 30		08 52	08 52	09 00	09 22	09 30	09 52	09 52	10 00	and at the same minutes past each hour until	23 00	23 22	23 22	23 30
Bethnal Green	d	23p33	23p48	00 03												09 33			10 03		23 03			23 33
Cambridge Heath	d	23p35	23p50	00 05												09 35			10 05		23 05			23 35
London Fields	d	23p37	23p52	00 07												09 37			10 07		23 07			23 37
Hackney Downs	d	23p39	23p54	00 09	07 39	07 59	07 59	08 09	08 29	08 39		08 59	08 59	09 09	09 29	09 39	09 59	09 59	10 09		23 09	23 29	23 29	23 39
Rectory Road	d	23p42	23p57	00 12	07 42			08 12		08 42				09 12		09 42			10 12		23 12			23 42
Stoke Newington	d	23p43	23p58	00 13	07 43			08 13		08 43				09 13		09 43			10 13		23 13			23 43
Stamford Hill	d	23p45	23p59	00 15	07 45			08 15		08 45				09 15		09 45			10 15		23 15			23 45
Seven Sisters ⊖	d	23p47	00 02	00 17	07 47	08 04	08 04	08 17	08 34	08 47		09 04	09 04	09 17	09 34	09 47	10 04	10 04	10 17		23 17	23 34	23 34	23 47
Bruce Grove	d	23p49	00 04	00 19	07 49			08 19		08 49				09 19		09 49			10 19		23 19			23 49
White Hart Lane	d	23p51	00 06	00 21	07 51			08 21		08 51				09 21		09 51			10 21		23 21			23 51
Silver Street	d	23p53	00 08	00 23	07 53			08 23		08 53				09 23		09 53			10 23		23 23			23 53
Edmonton Green	d	23p55	00 10	00 25	07 55	08 08	08 08	08 25	08 38	08 55		09 08	09 08	09 25	09 38	09 55	10 08	10 08	10 25		23 25	23 38	23 38	23 55
Bush Hill Park	d	23p58		00 28	07 58			08 28		08 58				09 28		09 58			10 28		23 28			23 58
Enfield Town	a	00 03		00 33	08 03			08 33		09 03				09 33		10 03			10 33		23 33			00 03
Southbury	d		00 14			08 12	08 12		08 42			09 12	09 12		09 42		10 12	10 12				23 42	23 42	
Turkey Street	d		00 17			08 15	08 15		08 45			09 15	09 15		09 45		10 15	10 15				23 45	23 45	
Theobalds Grove	d		00 19			08 17	08 17		08 47			09 17	09 17		09 47		10 17	10 17				23 47	23 47	
Cheshunt	a		00 24			08 20	08 22		08 52			09 20	09 22		09 52		10 20	10 22				23 50	23 52	

A not from 2 September until 9 September
B 2 September, 9 September
C 29 July only. Additional services operate from London Liverpool Street to Cheshunt departing 10 43, 11 13, 11 43 and 12 13 calling at Seven Sisters 10 55, 11 25, 11 55 and 12 25 and Cheshunt arriving at 11 09, 1139, 1209 and 12 39

Mondays to Fridays

Cheshunt (via Seven Sisters) and Enfield Town - London

Network Diagram - see first Page of Table 20

Miles	Miles			LE MX	LE MX 1	LE MX 1	LE	LE	LE	LE	LE	LE		LE	LE	LE	LE	LE	LE	LE	LE	LE		LE	LE
0	—	**Cheshunt**	d	23p31	23p52	23p58	05 16		06 01			06 33		06 48		06 52		07 18		07 22		07 48			07 52
1	—	Theobalds Grove	d	23p34			05 19		06 04			06 36				06 55				07 25					07 55
2¼	—	Turkey Street	d	23p36			05 21		06 06			06 38				06 57				07 27					07 57
4	—	Southbury	d	23p39			05 24		06 09			06 41				07 00				07 30					08 00
—	0	**Enfield Town**	d					05 52		06 18	06 33				06 54		07 09		07 24		07 39			07 54	
—	1	Bush Hill Park	d					05 55		06 21	06 36				06 57		07 12		07 27		07 42			07 57	
6	2¼	Edmonton Green	d	23p43			05 28	05 58	06 13	06 24	06 39	06 45		06 56	07 00	07 05	07 15	07 26	07 30	07 35	07 45	07 56		08 00	08 05
6½	2¾	Silver Street	d	23p45			05 30	06 00	06 15	06 26	06 41	06 47			07 02	07 07	07 17		07 32	07 37	07 47			08 02	08 07
7¼	3½	White Hart Lane	d	23p47			05 32	06 02	06 17	06 28	06 43	06 49			07 04	07 09	07 19		07 34	07 39	07 49			08 04	08 09
8¼	4½	Bruce Grove	d	23p49			05 34	06 04	06 19	06 30	06 45	06 51			07 06	07 11	07 21		07 36	07 41	07 51			08 06	08 11
9	5¼	Seven Sisters ⊖	d	23p51	00 04	00 11	05 36	06 06	06 21	06 33	06 48	06 54		07 02	07 09	07 14	07 24	07 32	07 39	07 44	07 54	08 02		08 09	08 14
9½	5¾	Stamford Hill	d	23p53			05 38	06 08	06 23	06 35	06 50	06 56			07 11		07 26		07 41		07 56			08 11	
10¼	6½	Stoke Newington	d	23p55			05 40	06 10	06 25	06 37	06 52	06 58			07 13	07 17	07 28		07 43	07 47	07 58			08 13	08 17
10¾	7	Rectory Road	d	23p56			05 41	06 11	06 26	06 39	06 54	07 00			07 15	07 18	07 30		07 45	07 48	08 00			08 15	08 18
11½	7¾	Hackney Downs	d	23p59		00 16	05 44	06 14	06 29	06 43	06 58	07 04		07 08	07 19	07 22	07 34	07 38	07 49	07 52	08 04	08 08		08 19	08 22
12	8¼	London Fields	d	00 01			05 46	06 16	06 31	06 45	07 00	07 06			07 21	07 24	07 36		07 51	07 54	08 06			08 21	08 24
12¾	9	Cambridge Heath	d	00 03			05 48	06 18	06 33	06 47	07 02	07 08			07 23		07 38		07 53		08 08			08 23	
13¼	9½	Bethnal Green	d	00 05			05 50	06 20	06 35	06 49		07 10			07 25		07 40		07 55		08 10			08 25	
14½	10¾	**London Liverpool Street** 15 ⊖	a	00 10	00 18	00 26	05 55	06 25	06 40	06 54	07 10	07 16		07 18	07 31	07 33	07 46	07 48	08 01	08 03	08 16	08 18		08 31	08 33

		LE	LE	LE	LE	LE	LE	LE		LE	LE	LE	LE	LE	LE	LE		LE		LE	LE	LE	LE	LE
Cheshunt	d		08 18		08 22		08 43				09 07		09 31		10 01		and at the same minutes past each hour until			16 31			17 04	
Theobalds Grove	d				08 25		08 46				09 10		09 34		10 04					16 34			17 07	
Turkey Street	d				08 27		08 48				09 12		09 36		10 06					16 36			17 09	
Southbury	d				08 30		08 51				09 15		09 39		10 09					16 39			17 12	
Enfield Town	d	08 09		08 24		08 39		08 54		09 09		09 24		09 52		10 22		16 22			16 52	17 07		17 22
Bush Hill Park	d	08 12		08 27		08 42		08 57		09 12		09 27		09 55		10 25		16 25			16 55	17 10		17 25
Edmonton Green	d	08 15	08 26	08 30	08 35	08 45	08 56	09 00		09 15	09 20	09 30	09 43	09 58	10 13	10 28		16 28		16 43	16 58	17 13	17 17	17 28
Silver Street	d	08 17		08 32	08 37	08 47		09 02		09 17	09 22	09 32	09 45	10 00	10 15	10 30		16 30		16 45	17 00	17 15	17 19	17 30
White Hart Lane	d	08 19		08 34	08 39	08 49		09 04		09 19	09 24	09 34	09 47	10 02	10 17	10 32		16 32		16 47	17 02	17 17	17 21	17 32
Bruce Grove	d	08 21		08 36	08 41	08 51		09 06		09 21	09 26	09 36	09 49	10 04	10 19	10 34		16 34		16 49	17 04	17 19	17 23	17 34
Seven Sisters ⊖	d	08 24	08 32	08 39	08 44	08 54	09 02	09 09		09 24	09 29	09 39	09 51	10 06	10 21	10 36		16 36		16 51	17 06	17 21	17 25	17 36
Stamford Hill	d	08 26		08 41		08 56		09 11		09 26		09 41	09 53	10 08	10 23	10 38		16 38		16 53	17 08	17 23	17 27	17 38
Stoke Newington	d	08 28		08 43	08 47	08 58		09 13		09 28	09 32	09 43	09 55	10 10	10 25	10 40		16 40		16 55	17 10	17 25	17 29	17 40
Rectory Road	d	08 30		08 45	08 48	09 00		09 15		09 30	09 33	09 45	09 56	10 11	10 26	10 41		16 41		16 56	17 11	17 26	17 30	17 41
Hackney Downs	d	08 34	08 38	08 49	08 52	09 04	09 08	09 19		09 34	09 37	09 49	09 59	10 14	10 29	10 44		16 44		16 59	17 14	17 29	17 33	17 44
London Fields	d	08 36		08 51	08 54	09 06		09 21		09 36	09 39	09 51	10 01	10 16	10 31	10 46		16 46		17 01	17 16	17 31		17 46
Cambridge Heath	d	08 38		08 53		09 08		09 23		09 38		09 53	10 03	10 18	10 33	10 48		16 48		17 03	17 18	17 33		17 48
Bethnal Green	d	08 40		08 55		09 10		09 25		09 40		09 55	10 05	10 20	10 35	10 50		16 50		17 05	17 20	17 35		17 50
London Liverpool Street 15 ⊖	a	08 46	08 48	08 59	09 03	09 16	09 18	09 31		09 46	09 48	10 01	10 10	10 25	10 40	10 55		16 55		17 10	17 25	17 40	17 42	17 55

		LE	LE	LE	LE		LE	LE	LE	LE	LE	LE	LE	LE	LE		LE	LE	LE	LE	LE	LE	LE	LE	LE
Cheshunt	d		17 39				18 09			18 39			19 09		19 31			20 01		20 31		21 01		21 31	
Theobalds Grove	d		17 42				18 12			18 42			19 12		19 34			20 04		20 34		21 04		21 34	
Turkey Street	d		17 44				18 14			18 44			19 14		19 36			20 06		20 36		21 06		21 36	
Southbury	d		17 47				18 17			18 47			19 17		19 39			20 09		20 39		21 09		21 39	
Enfield Town	d	17 37		17 52	18 07			18 22	18 37		18 52	19 07		19 22			19 52		20 22		20 52		21 22		21 52
Bush Hill Park	d	17 40		17 55	18 10			18 25	18 40		18 55	19 10		19 25			19 55		20 25		20 55		21 25		21 55
Edmonton Green	d	17 43	17 51	17 58	18 13		18 21	18 28	18 43	18 51	18 58	19 13	19 21	19 28	19 43		19 58	20 13	20 28	20 43	20 58	21 13	21 28	21 43	21 58
Silver Street	d	17 45		18 00	18 15			18 30	18 45		19 00	19 15		19 30	19 45		20 00	20 15	20 30	20 45	21 00	21 15	21 30	21 45	22 00
White Hart Lane	d	17 47		18 02	18 17			18 32	18 47		19 02	19 17		19 32	19 47		20 02	20 17	20 32	20 47	21 02	21 17	21 32	21 47	22 02
Bruce Grove	d	17 49		18 04	18 19			18 34	18 49		19 04	19 19		19 34	19 49		20 04	20 19	20 34	20 49	21 04	21 19	21 34	21 49	22 04
Seven Sisters ⊖	d	17 51	17 57	18 06	18 21		18 27	18 36	18 51	18 57	19 06	19 21	19 27	19 36	19 51		20 06	20 21	20 36	20 51	21 06	21 21	21 36	21 51	22 06
Stamford Hill	d	17 53		18 08	18 23			18 38	18 53		19 08	19 23		19 38	19 53		20 08	20 23	20 38	20 53	21 08	21 23	21 38	21 53	22 08
Stoke Newington	d	17 55	18 00	18 10	18 25		18 30	18 40	18 55	19 00	19 10	19 25	19 30	19 40	19 55		20 10	20 25	20 40	20 55	21 10	21 25	21 40	21 55	22 10
Rectory Road	d	17 56		18 11	18 26			18 41	18 56		19 11	19 26		19 41	19 56		20 11	20 26	20 41	20 56	21 11	21 26	21 41	21 56	22 11
Hackney Downs	d	17 59	18 03	18 14	18 29		18 33	18 44	18 59	19 03	19 14	19 29	19 33	19 44	19 59		20 14	20 29	20 44	20 59	21 14	21 29	21 44	21 59	22 14
London Fields	d	18 01		18 16	18 31			18 46	19 01		19 16	19 31		19 46	20 01		20 16	20 31	20 46	21 01	21 16	21 31	21 46	22 01	22 16
Cambridge Heath	d	18 03		18 18	18 33			18 48	19 03		19 18	19 33		19 48	20 03		20 18	20 33	20 48	21 03	21 18	21 33	21 48	22 03	22 18
Bethnal Green	d	18 05		18 20	18 35			18 50	19 05		19 20	19 35		19 50	20 05		20 20	20 35	20 50	21 05	21 20	21 35	21 50	22 05	22 20
London Liverpool Street 15 ⊖	a	18 10	18 12	18 25	18 40		18 42	18 55	19 10	19 12	19 25	19 40	19 43	19 55	20 09		20 25	20 40	20 55	21 10	21 25	21 40	21 55	22 10	22 25

			LE	LE	LE	LE	LE	LE	LE	LE 1	LE 1
Cheshunt	d		22 01		22 31		23 01		23 31	23 52	23 58
Theobalds Grove	d		22 04		22 34		23 04		23 34		
Turkey Street	d		22 06		22 36		23 06		23 36		
Southbury	d		22 09		22 39		23 09		23 39		
Enfield Town	d			22 22		22 52		23 22			
Bush Hill Park	d			22 25		22 55		23 25			
Edmonton Green	d		22 13	22 28	22 43	22 58	23 13	23 28	23 43		
Silver Street	d		22 15	22 30	22 45	23 00	23 15	23 30	23 45		
White Hart Lane	d		22 17	22 32	22 47	23 02	23 17	23 32	23 47		
Bruce Grove	d		22 19	22 34	22 49	23 04	23 19	23 34	23 49		
Seven Sisters ⊖	d		22 21	22 36	22 51	23 06	23 21	23 36	23 51	00 04	00 11
Stamford Hill	d		22 23	22 38	22 53	23 08	23 23	23 38	23 53		
Stoke Newington	d		22 25	22 40	22 55	23 10	23 25	23 40	23 55		
Rectory Road	d		22 26	22 41	22 56	23 11	23 26	23 41	23 56		
Hackney Downs	d		22 29	22 44	22 59	23 14	23 29	23 44	23 59		00 16
London Fields	d		22 31	22 46	23 01	23 16	23 31	23 46	00 01		
Cambridge Heath	d		22 33	22 48	23 03	23 18	23 33	23 48	00 03		
Bethnal Green	d		22 35	22 50	23 05	23 20	23 35	23 50	00 05		
London Liverpool Street 15 ⊖	a		22 40	22 55	23 10	23 25	23 40	23 55	00 10	00 18	00 26

Table 21

Saturdays

Cheshunt (via Seven Sisters) and Enfield Town - London

Network Diagram - see first Page of Table 20

		LE	LE ■	LE ■	LE ■	LE	LE	LE	LE		LE	LE	LE	LE	LE	LE	LE	LE	LE
Cheshunt	d	23p31	23p52	23p58	05 16	06 01		06 31		and at the same minutes past each hour until		22 01		22 31		23 01		23 31	
Theobalds Grove	d	23p34			05 19	06 04		06 34				22 04		22 34		23 04		23 34	
Turkey Street	d	23p36			05 21	06 06		06 36				22 06		22 36		23 06		23 36	
Southbury	d	23p39			05 24	06 09		06 39				22 09		22 39		23 09		23 39	
Enfield Town	d						06 22		06 52		21 52		22 22		22 52		23 22		23 52
Bush Hill Park	d						06 25		06 55		21 55		22 25		22 55		23 25		23 55
Edmonton Green	d	23p43			05 28	06 13	06 28	06 43	06 58		21 58	22 13	22 28	22 43	22 58	23 13	23 28	23 43	23 58
Silver Street	d	23p45			05 30	06 15	06 30	06 45	07 00		22 00	22 15	22 30	22 45	23 00	23 15	23 30	23 45	23 59
White Hart Lane	d	23p47			05 32	06 17	06 32	06 47	07 02		22 02	22 17	22 32	22 47	23 02	23 17	23 32	23 47	00 02
Bruce Grove	d	23p49			05 34	06 19	06 34	06 49	07 04		22 04	22 19	22 34	22 49	23 04	23 19	23 34	23 49	00 04
Seven Sisters ⊖	d	23p51	00 04	00 11	05 36	06 21	06 36	06 51	07 06		22 06	22 21	22 36	22 51	23 06	23 21	23 36	23 51	00 06
Stamford Hill	d	23p53			05 38	06 23	06 38	06 53	07 08		22 08	22 23	22 38	22 53	23 08	23 23	23 38	23 53	00 08
Stoke Newington	d	23p55			05 40	06 25	06 40	06 55	07 10		22 10	22 25	22 40	22 55	23 10	23 25	23 40	23 55	00 10
Rectory Road	d	23p56			05 41	06 26	06 41	06 56	07 11		22 11	22 26	22 41	22 56	23 11	23 26	23 41	23 56	00 11
Hackney Downs	d	23p59		00 16	05 45	06 29	06 44	06 59	07 14		22 14	22 29	22 44	22 59	23 14	23 29	23 44	23 59	00 14
London Fields	d	00 01				06 31	06 46	07 01	07 16		22 16	22 31	22 46	23 01	23 16	23 31	23 46	00 01	00 16
Cambridge Heath	d	00 03				06 33	06 48	07 03	07 18		22 18	22 33	22 48	23 03	23 18	23 33	23 48	00 03	00 18
Bethnal Green	d	00 05			05 49	06 35	06 50	07 05	07 20		22 20	22 35	22 50	23 05	23 20	23 35	23 50	00 05	00 20
London Liverpool Street 15 ⊖	a	00 10	00 18	00 26	05 54	06 40	06 55	07 10	07 25		22 25	22 40	22 55	23 10	23 24	23 40	23 55	00 10	00 25

Sundays

until 22 July

		LE	LE	LE	LE	LE	LE	LE	LE	LE	LE		LE	LE	LE	LE	LE
Cheshunt	d	23p31		07 45		08 15		08 45		09 15		and at the same minutes past each hour until		22 45		23 15	
Theobalds Grove	d	23p34		07 48		08 18		08 48		09 18				22 48		23 18	
Turkey Street	d	23p36		07 51		08 21		08 51		09 21				22 51		23 21	
Southbury	d	23p39		07 54		08 24		08 54		09 24				22 54		23 24	
Enfield Town	d		23p52		07 57		08 27		08 57		09 27		22 27		22 57		23 27
Bush Hill Park	d		23p55		08 00		08 30		09 00		09 30		22 30		23 00		23 30
Edmonton Green	d	23p43	23p58	07 57	08 03	08 27	08 33	08 57	09 03	09 27	09 33		22 33	22 57	23 03	23 27	23 33
Silver Street	d	23p45	23p59		08 05		08 35		09 05		09 35		22 35		23 05		23 35
White Hart Lane	d	23p47	00 02		08 07		08 37		09 07		09 37		22 37		23 07		23 37
Bruce Grove	d	23p49	00 04		08 09		08 39		09 09		09 39		22 39		23 09		23 39
Seven Sisters ⊖	d	23p51	00 06	08 03	08 11	08 33	08 41	09 03	09 11	09 33	09 41		22 41	23 03	23 11	23 33	23 41
Stamford Hill	d	23p53	00 08		08 13		08 43		09 13		09 43		22 43		23 13		23 43
Stoke Newington	d	23p55	00 10		08 15		08 45		09 15		09 45		22 45		23 15		23 45
Rectory Road	d	23p56	00 11		08 16		08 46		09 16		09 46		22 46		23 16		23 46
Hackney Downs	d	23p59	00 14	08 09	08 19	08 39	08 49	09 09	09 19	09 39	09 49		22 49	23 09	23 19	23 39	23 49
London Fields	d	00 01	00 16						09 21		09 51		22 51		23 21		23 51
Cambridge Heath	d	00 03	00 18						09 23		09 53		22 53		23 23		23 53
Bethnal Green	d	00 05	00 20						09 25		09 55		22 55		23 25		23 55
London Liverpool Street 15 ⊖	a	00 10	00 25	08 18	08 30	08 48	09 00	09 18	09 30	09 48	10 00		23 00	23 18	23 30	23 48	23 58

Sundays

29 July to 12 August

		LE	LE	LE	LE	LE	LE	LE	LE	LE	LE		LE	LE	LE	LE	LE
Cheshunt	d	23p31		07 45		08 15		08 45		09 15		A		22 45		23 15	
Theobalds Grove	d	23p34		07 48		08 18		08 48		09 18		and at the same minutes past each hour until		22 48		23 18	
Turkey Street	d	23p36		07 51		08 21		08 51		09 21				22 51		23 21	
Southbury	d	23p39		07 54		08 24		08 54		09 24				22 54		23 24	
Enfield Town	d		23p52		07 57		08 27		08 57		09 27		22 27		22 57		23 27
Bush Hill Park	d		23p55		08 00		08 30		09 00		09 30		22 30		23 00		23 30
Edmonton Green	d	23p43	23p58	07 57	08 03	08 27	08 33	08 57	09 03	09 27	09 33		22 33	22 57	23 03	23 27	23 33
Silver Street	d	23p45	23p59		08 05		08 35		09 05		09 35		22 35		23 05		23 35
White Hart Lane	d	23p47	00 02		08 07		08 37		09 07		09 37		22 37		23 07		23 37
Bruce Grove	d	23p49	00 04		08 09		08 39		09 09		09 39		22 39		23 09		23 39
Seven Sisters ⊖	d	23p51	00 06	08 03	08 11	08 33	08 41	09 03	09 11	09 33	09 41		22 41	23 03	23 11	23 33	23 41
Stamford Hill	d	23p53	00 08		08 13		08 43		09 13		09 43		22 43		23 13		23 43
Stoke Newington	d	23p55	00 10		08 15		08 45		09 15		09 45		22 45		23 15		23 45
Rectory Road	d	23p56	00 11		08 16		08 46		09 16		09 46		22 46		23 16		23 46
Hackney Downs	d	23p59	00 14	08 09	08 19	08 39	08 49	09 09	09 19	09 39	09 49		22 49	23 09	23 19	23 39	23 49
London Fields	d	00 01	00 16						09 21		09 51		22 51		23 21		23 51
Cambridge Heath	d	00 03	00 18						09 23		09 53		22 53		23 23		23 53
Bethnal Green	d	00 05	00 20						09 25		09 55		22 55		23 25		23 55
London Liverpool Street 15 ⊖	a	00 10	00 25	08 19	08 29	08 48	08 59	09 19	09 30	09 48	10 00		23 00	23 19	23 30	23 48	23 59

A 29 July only. Additional services operate from Cheshunt to London Liverpool Street departing at 17 34, 18 04, 18 34, 19 04 and 19 34 calling at Seven Sisters 17 46, 18 16, 18 46, 19 16 and 19 46 and London Liverpool Street arriving at 18 04, 18 34, 19 04, 1934 and 20 04

Table 21

Sundays

from 19 August

Cheshunt (via Seven Sisters) and Enfield Town - London

Network Diagram - see first Page of Table 20

		LE	LE	LE A	LE B	LE B	LE A	LE	LE B	LE A	LE A	LE B	LE	LE	LE		LE	LE A	LE B	LE	LE	LE A
Cheshunt	d	23p31		07 45	07 45			08 15			08 45	08 45		09 15		and at the same minutes past each hour until		22 45	22 45		23 15	
Theobalds Grove	d	23p34		07 48	07 48			08 18			08 48	08 48		09 18				22 48	22 48		23 18	
Turkey Street	d	23p36		07 51	07 51			08 21			08 51	08 51		09 21				22 51	22 51		23 21	
Southbury	d	23p39		07 54	07 54			08 24			08 54	08 54		09 24				22 54	22 54		23 24	
Enfield Town	d		23p52			07 57	07 57		08 27	08 27			08 57		09 27		22 27			22 57		23 27
Bush Hill Park	d		23p55			08 00	08 00		08 30	08 30			09 00		09 30		22 30			23 00		23 30
Edmonton Green	d	23p43	23p58	07 57	07 57	08 03	08 03	08 27	08 33	08 33	08 57	08 57	09 03	09 27	09 33		22 33	22 57	22 57	23 03	23 27	23 33
Silver Street	d	23p45	23p59			08 05	08 05		08 35	08 35			09 05		09 35		22 35			23 05		23 35
White Hart Lane	d	23p47	00 02			08 07	08 07		08 37	08 37			09 07		09 37		22 37			23 07		23 37
Bruce Grove	d	23p49	00 04			08 09	08 09		08 39	08 39			09 09		09 39		22 39			23 09		23 39
Seven Sisters ⊖	d	23p51	00 06	08 03	08 03	08 11	08 11	08 33	08 41	08 41	09 03	09 03	09 11	09 33	09 41		22 41	23 03	23 03	23 11	23 33	23 41
Stamford Hill	d	23p53	00 08			08 13	08 13		08 43	08 43			09 13		09 43		22 43			23 13		23 43
Stoke Newington	d	23p55	00 10			08 15	08 15		08 45	08 45			09 15		09 45		22 45			23 15		23 45
Rectory Road	d	23p56	00 11			08 16	08 16		08 46	08 46			09 16		09 46		22 46			23 16		23 46
Hackney Downs	d	23p59	00 14	08 09	08 09	08 19	08 19	08 39	08 49	08 49	09 09	09 09	09 19	09 39	09 49		22 49	23 09	23 09	23 19	23 39	23 49
London Fields	d	00 01	00 16										09 21		09 51		22 51			23 21		23 51
Cambridge Heath	d	00 03	00 18										09 23		09 53		22 53			23 23		23 53
Bethnal Green	d	00 05	00 20										09 25		09 55		22 55			23 25		23 55
London Liverpool Street 15 ⊖	a	00 10	00 25	08 18	08 19	08 29	08 30	08 48	08 59	09 00	09 18	09 19	09 30	09 48	10 00		23 00	23 18	23 19	23 30	23 48	23 58

		LE B
Cheshunt	d	
Theobalds Grove	d	
Turkey Street	d	
Southbury	d	
Enfield Town	d	23 27
Bush Hill Park	d	23 30
Edmonton Green	d	23 33
Silver Street	d	23 35
White Hart Lane	d	23 37
Bruce Grove	d	23 39
Seven Sisters ⊖	d	23 41
Stamford Hill	d	23 43
Stoke Newington	d	23 45
Rectory Road	d	23 46
Hackney Downs	d	23 49
London Fields	d	23 51
Cambridge Heath	d	23 53
Bethnal Green	d	23 55
London Liverpool Street 15 ⊖	a	23 59

A not from 2 September until 9 September

B 2 September, 9 September

London - Broxbourne, Hertford East, Bishops Stortford, Stansted Airport and Cambridge

Network Diagram - see first Page of Table 20

Miles	Miles			LE MO A	LE MX B	LE MX C	LE MO A	LE D	LE MX C	LE E	LE MX B	LE MO A	LE MX B	LE MO A	LE MX	LE D	LE MX B	LE MX C	LE D	LE MO A	LE MO A	LE MX B	LE MO A
0	—	**London Liverpool Street** ⊖	d		22p42	22p58			23p12		23p12	23p22	23p22	23p25	23p25	23p25		23p28			23p28		
1¼	—	Bethnal Green	d																				
3	—	Hackney Downs	d						23p18			23p29											
—	0	Stratford ⊖	d	22p45	22p55			23p00		23p15	23p25		23p35						23p30				
4	—	Clapton	d																				
—	6¾	Seven Sisters ⊖	d									23p34					←					←	
6	—	Tottenham Hale ⊖	d	22p55	23p10	23p10		23p10	23p25	23p25	23p40		23p45	23p37	23b37	23p37	23p40	23p40	23p40		23p40	23p45	
7	—	Northumberland Park	d								→		→										
7¾	—	Angel Road	d																				
10	—	Ponders End	d	22p59					23p29	23p29											23p44		
10¾	—	Brimsdown	d	23p02					23p32	23p32											23p47		
11¾	—	Enfield Lock	d	23p04					23p34	23p34											23p49		
12¾	—	Waltham Cross	d	23p07					23p37	23p37										←	23p52	23p52	
14	—	Cheshunt	d	23p09	23p18	23p18		23p18	23p39	23p39		23p50					23p48	23p48	23p49	23p50	23p54	23p55	←
17¼	—	**Broxbourne**	a	23p14	23p22	23p22		23p23	23p44	23p44		→					23p52	23p52	23p53	23p55	23p59	23p59	23p55
—	0	**Broxbourne**	d	23p19	23p22	23p22		23p23	23p44	23p44							23p52	23p52	23p53	00 02	23p59	23p59	00 02
—	1¾	Rye House	d						23p47	23p47										→			00 06
—	3	St Margarets (Herts)	d						23p50	23p50													00 09
—	5	Ware	d						23p54	23p54													00 13
—	7	**Hertford East**	a						00 01	00 01													00 19
20	—	Roydon	d	23p24				23p27									23p56	23p56	23p57				
22¾	—	Harlow Town	d	23p28	23p28	23p28		23p31						23p52	23p54	23p53	23p59	23p59	00 01		00 05	00 09	
24½	—	Harlow Mill	d	23p31				23p34									00 03	00 03	00 04				
26¾	—	Sawbridgeworth	d	23p34			←	23p37									00 07	00 07	00 08				
30¼	—	**Bishops Stortford**	a	23p41	23p38	23p38	23p41	23p44						00 02	00 04	00 03	00 14	00 14	00 15		00 10	00 15	
—	—		d	23p42	23p39	23p39	23p42	23p44						00 03	00 04	00 04	00 14	00 14	00 15		00 17	00 22	
33¾	0	Stansted Mountfitchet	d	→			23p46	23p49									00 18	00 18	00 19				
—	—	**Stansted Airport**	a											00 12	00 13	00 13							
—	3¾	**Stansted Airport**	d																				
35½	8¼	Elsenham	d				23p50	23p52									00 22	00 22	00 23				
40	—	Newport (Essex)	d				23p55	23p58									00 27	00 27	00 28				
41¾	—	Audley End	d		23p51	23p51	23p58	00 01									00 30	00 30	00 31				
45¾	—	Great Chesterford	d				00 03	00 06									00 35	00 35	00 36				
49	—	Whittlesford Parkway	d		23p58	23p58	00 08	00 10									00 40	00 40	00 41				
52½	—	Shelford	d				00 12	00 15									00 44	00 44	00 45				
55¾	—	**Cambridge**	a		00 08	00 08	00 19	00 22									00 51	00 51	00 52				

		LE MX C	LE D	LE MX B	LE MX B	LE F	LE D	LE D	LE MX B	LE MX B	LE D	LE MO	LE MFO G	XC ◇	LE H	LE TWO I	LE	LE	LE	XC ◇	LE	LE	LE
London Liverpool Street ⊖	d	23p40			23p42	23p58		00 02		00 18	00 18	03 40	04 10		04 40	04 40	05 10				05 25	05 28	05 40
Bethnal Green	d																						
Hackney Downs	d	23p46																					
Stratford ⊖	d		23p45	23p45	23p55		23p59	00 15	00 15	00 30	00 30												
Clapton	d	23p49																					
Seven Sisters ⊖	d																						
Tottenham Hale ⊖	d	23p53	23p55	23p55	00 10	00 10	00 10	00 25	00 25	00 40	00 40				04u52	04u59	05u22				05u37	05 40	05u52
Northumberland Park	d	23p55		23p57																			
Angel Road	d																						
Ponders End	d	23p59	23p59	00 01				00 29	00 29														
Brimsdown	d	00 02	00 02	00 04				00 32	00 32														
Enfield Lock	d	00 04	00 04	00 06				00 34	00 34														
Waltham Cross	d	00 07	00 07	00 09				00 37	00 37														
Cheshunt	d	00 09	00 09	00 11	00 18	00 18	00 18	00 39	00 39	00 48	00 48				05 00	05 07						05 48	
Broxbourne	a	00 14	00 14	00 16	00 22	00 22	00 22	00 44	00 44	00 52	00 52				05 04	05 11						05 52	
Broxbourne	d	00 14	00 14	00 16	00 22	00 22	00 22	00 44	00 44	00 52	00 52				05 04	05 11		05 40				05 52	
Rye House	d	00 17	00 17	00 19				00 47	00 47									05 43					
St Margarets (Herts)	d	00 20	00 20	00 22				00 50	00 50									05 46					
Ware	d	00 24	00 24	00 26				00 54	00 54									05 50					
Hertford East	a	00 31	00 31	00 33				01 01	01 01									05 56					
Roydon	d				00 26	00 26	00 26				00 56											05 56	
Harlow Town	d				00 30	00 30	00 30			00 58	01 00				05 10	05 17	05 37				05 52	06 00	
Harlow Mill	d				00 33	00 33	00 33				01 03											06 03	
Sawbridgeworth	d				00 37	00 37	00 37			01 03	01 07						05 42					06 07	
Bishops Stortford	a				00 44	00 44	00 44			01 10	01 14				05 20	05 27	05 49				06 02	06 14	06 17
	d				00 44		00 44			01 11	01 14				05 20	05 27	05 50		05 55		06 02	06 14	06 18
Stansted Mountfitchet	d				00 48		00 48			01 15	01 18				05 24	05 31			05 59			06 18	06 23
Stansted Airport	a											04 30	05 00		05 39	05 39	05 59				06 15		06 29
Stansted Airport	d													05 16						06 06			
Elsenham	d				00 52		00 52			01 19	01 22								06 03			06 22	
Newport (Essex)	d				00 57		00 57			01 24	01 27								06 08			06 27	
Audley End	d				01 00		01 00			01 27	01 30			05 37					06 11	06 23		06 30	
Great Chesterford	d				01 05		01 05			01 32	01 35								06 16			06 35	
Whittlesford Parkway	d				01 10		01 10			01 37	01 40								06 21			06 40	
Shelford	d									01 41	01 44								06 25			06 44	
Cambridge	a				01 19		01 19			01 49	01 51			05 53					06 32	06 38		06 56	

A from 21 May until 23 July, MO from 20 August, not 3 September, 10 September
B from 31 July until 7 September, not from 14 August until 29 August
C not from 31 July until 10 August, from 30 August until 7 September
D 30 July, 6 August, 13 August, 3 September, 10 September
E from 30 July until 10 September, not from 14 August until 29 August
F not 14 May, from 30 July until 13 August, from 30 August until 10 September
G also from 31 July until 9 August, from 29 August until 6 September
H MThFO, also from 31 July until 8 August, from 29 August until 5 September
I not from 31 July until 8 August, from 29 August until 5 September
b Previous night, stops to pick up only

London - Broxbourne, Hertford East, Bishops Stortford, Stansted Airport and Cambridge

Network Diagram - see first Page of Table 20

		LE	LE	LE	LE	LE	LE	LE	LE	XC ◇	LE	LE	LE	LE	LE	LE	LE	LE	LE 🚲	LE	LE 🚲	LE
London Liverpool Street ⊖	d	05 42	05 52	05 55	05 58		06 10	06 12	06 25		06 28		06 40		06 42		06 55	06 58	07 10	07 12	07 25	07 28
Bethnal Green	d																					
Hackney Downs	d	05 48						06 18							06 48					07 18		
Stratford ⊖	d		06 03									06 35				06 50						
Clapton	d																					
Seven Sisters ⊖	d					←																
Tottenham Hale ⊖	d	05 55	06 15	06u07	06 10	06 15	06u22	06 25	06u37		06 40	06 45	06u52		06 55	07 00	07u07	07 10	07u22	07 25	07u37	07 40
Northumberland Park	d		→			06 17						06 48										
Angel Road	d					06 19																
Ponders End	d	05 59						06 29								07 04				07 29		
Brimsdown	d	06 02						06 32								07 07				07 32		
Enfield Lock	d	06 04				06 24		06 34							07 01					07 34		
Waltham Cross	d	06 07						06 37							07 04					07 37		
Cheshunt	d	06 09			06 18	06 28		06 39			06 48	06 55			07 06	07 11		07 18		07 39		07 48
Broxbourne	a	06 14			06 22	06 32		06 44			06 52	06 59			07 11	07 16		07 22		07 44		07 52
Broxbourne	d	06 14			06 24	06 36		06 44			06 52	06 59			07 14			07 22		07 44		07 52
Rye House	d	06 17				06 39		06 47							07 17					07 47		
St Margarets (Herts)	d	06 20				06 42		06 50							07 20					07 50		
Ware	d	06 24				06 46		06 54							07 24					07 54		
Hertford East	a	06 31				06 53		07 01							07 31					08 01		
Roydon	d				06 28						06 56							07 26				07 56
Harlow Town	d			06 26	06 32				06 54		07 09						07 24	07 30			07 55	08 00
Harlow Mill	d				06 35						07 13							07 33				08 03
Sawbridgeworth	d				06 38						07 16			←				07 37				08 07
Bishops Stortford	a				06 45		06 49				07 23	07 13	07 16	07 23				07 44	07 47			08 14
	d				06 45		06 49				07 26		07 17	07 26				07 44	07 48			08 14
Stansted Mountfitchet	d				06 50						→			07 30			07 35	07 48				08 18
Stansted Airport	a			06 44			06 59		07 12				07 30				07 43		07 59		08 13	
Stansted Airport	d									07 21												
Elsenham	d				06 53									07 34				07 52				08 22
Newport (Essex)	d				06 59									07 39				07 57				08 27
Audley End	d				07 02					07 37				07 42				08 00				08 30
Great Chesterford	d				07 07									07 47				08 05				08 35
Whittlesford Parkway	d				07 11									07 52				08 10				08 40
Shelford	d				07 16									07 56				08 14				08 44
Cambridge	a				07 26					07 58				08 07				08 23				08 52

		LE	XC ◇	LE 🚲	LE A	LE B	LE 🚲	LE	LE	LE	LE 🚲	LE	LE 🚲	LE	LE	LE	XC ◇	LE 🚲	LE	LE 🚲	LE	LE	LE 🚲
London Liverpool Street ⊖	d			07 40	07 42	07 42	07 55	07 58	08 03		08 10	08 12	08 25	08 28	08 33			08 40	08 42	08 55	08 58		09 10
Bethnal Green	d																						
Hackney Downs	d				07 48	07 49						08 18							08 48				
Stratford ⊖	d	07 34								08 04						08 34						09 00	
Clapton	d																						
Seven Sisters ⊖	d																						
Tottenham Hale ⊖	d	07 47		07u52	07 55	07 55	08u07	08 10	08 15	08 18	08u22	08 25	08u37	08 40	08 45	08 48		08u52	08 55	09u07	09 10	09 13	09u22
Northumberland Park	d	07 49								08 20						08 50						09 15	
Angel Road	d	07 51														08 52							
Ponders End	d				07 59	07 59						08 29							08 59				
Brimsdown	d				08 02	08 02						08 32							09 02				
Enfield Lock	d				08 04	08 04				08 26		08 34							09 04			09 21	
Waltham Cross	d				08 07	08 07						08 37							09 07				
Cheshunt	d	07 58			08 09	08 09		08 18		08 29		08 39		08 48		08 59			09 09		09 18	09 25	
Broxbourne	a	08 04			08 14	08 14		08 22		08 34		08 44		08 52		09 04			09 14		09 22	09 30	
Broxbourne	d	08 10			08 14	08 14		08 22		08 38		08 44		08 52		09 08			09 14		09 22	09 33	
Rye House	d				08 17	08 17						08 47							09 17				
St Margarets (Herts)	d				08 20	08 20						08 50							09 20				
Ware	d				08 24	08 24						08 54							09 24				
Hertford East	a				08 31	08 31						09 01							09 31				
Roydon	d	08 15								08 42				08 56		09 12						09 38	
Harlow Town	d	08 19					08 25	08 33		08 46			08 54	09 04		09 16				09 24	09 28	09 42	
Harlow Mill	d							08 36		08 49						09 19						09 45	
Sawbridgeworth	d	08 24						08 40		08 53				09 10		09 23						09 48	
Bishops Stortford	a	08 32		08 19				08 47		09 02	08 50			09 17		09 32		09 20			09 38	09 56	09 45
	d			08 20				08 47			08 51			09 17				09 21			09 39		09 45
Stansted Mountfitchet	d						08 37	08 51						09 21						09 37			
Stansted Airport	a			08 30			08 45				09 00		09 14					09 30		09 45			09 55
Stansted Airport	d		08 21														09 21						
Elsenham	d							08 55						09 25									
Newport (Essex)	d							09 00						09 30									
Audley End	d		08 37					09 03	08 52					09 33	09 22		09 39				09 51		
Great Chesterford	d							09 08						09 38									
Whittlesford Parkway	d							09 13						09 43							09 58		
Shelford	d							09 17						09 47									
Cambridge	a		08 58					09 25	09 07					09 54	09 41		09 58				10 08		

A not from 27 July until 10 August, from 29 August until 7 September
B from 27 July until 7 September, not from 13 August until 28 August

London - Broxbourne, Hertford East, Bishops Stortford, Stansted Airport and Cambridge

Network Diagram - see first Page of Table 20

		LE	LE ✈	LE	LE	LE ✈	LE	XC ◇	LE ✈	LE	LE	LE ✈	LE	LE ✈	LE	LE	LE ✈	LE	XC ◇	LE ✈	LE	LE	LE ✈
London Liverpool Street 15 ⊖	d	09 12	09 25	09 28		09 40	09 42		09 55	09 58		10 10	10 12	10 25	10 28		10 40	10 42		10 55	10 58		11 10
Bethnal Green	d																						
Hackney Downs	d	09 18					09 48						10 18					10 48					
Stratford 7 ⊖	d			09 30						10 00					10 30						11 00	
Clapton	d																						
Seven Sisters ⊖	d																						
Tottenham Hale ⊖	d	09 25	09u37	09 40	09 43	09u52	09 55		10u07	10 10	10 13	10u22	10 25	10u37	10 40	10 43	10u52	10 55		11u07	11 10	11 13	11u22
Northumberland Park	d			09 46						10 15											11 15	
Angel Road	d			09 48																		
Ponders End	d	09 29					09 59						10 29					10 59					
Brimsdown	d	09 32					10 02						10 32					11 02					
Enfield Lock	d	09 34					10 04				10 21		10 34					11 04				11 21	
Waltham Cross	d	09 37			09 53		10 07						10 37			10 50		11 07					
Cheshunt	d	09 39		09 48	09 56		10 09			10 18	10 25		10 39		10 48	10 53		11 09			11 18	11 25	
Broxbourne 3	a	09 44		09 52	10 00		10 14			10 22	10 29		10 44		10 52	10 57		11 14			11 22	11 29	
Broxbourne 3	d	09 44		09 52	10 04		10 14			10 22	10 33		10 44		10 52	10 57		11 14			11 22	11 33	
Rye House	d	09 47					10 17						10 47					11 17					
St Margarets (Herts)	d	09 50					10 20						10 50					11 20					
Ware	d	09 54					10 24						10 54					11 24					
Hertford East	a	10 01					10 31						11 01					11 31					
Roydon	d			09 56							10 38				10 56							11 38	
Harlow Town	d		09 54	10 00	10 10				10 24	10 28	10 42			10 54	11 00	11 09				11 24	11 28	11 42	
Harlow Mill	d			10 03							10 45				11 03							11 45	
Sawbridgeworth	d			10 07	10 15						10 48				11 07	11 15						11 48	
Bishops Stortford	a			10 14	10 22	10 17				10 38	10 56	10 45			11 14	11 22	11 17				11 38	11 56	11 45
	d			10 14		10 18				10 39		10 45			11 14		11 18				11 39		11 45
Stansted Mountfitchet	d			10 18					10 35						11 18					11 35			
Stansted Airport	a		10 12			10 27			10 44			10 55		11 13			11 27			11 44			11 55
Stansted Airport	d							10 27											11 27				
Elsenham	d			10 22											11 22								
Newport (Essex)	d			10 27											11 27								
Audley End	d			10 30				10 40		10 51					11 30				11 40		11 51		
Great Chesterford	d			10 35											11 35								
Whittlesford Parkway	d			10 40						10 58					11 40						11 58		
Shelford	d			10 44											11 44								
Cambridge	a			10 51				10 58		11 08					11 51				11 58		12 08		

		LE A	LE B	LE ✈	LE	LE	LE ✈	LE	XC ◇	LE ✈	LE	LE	LE ✈	LE	LE ✈	LE	LE	LE ✈	LE	XC ◇	LE ✈	LE
London Liverpool Street 15 ⊖	d	11 12	11 12	11 25	11 28		11 40	11 42		11 55	11 58		12 10	12 12	12 25	12 28		12 40	12 42		12 55	12 58
Bethnal Green	d																					
Hackney Downs	d	11 18	11 19					11 48						12 18					12 48			
Stratford 7 ⊖	d					11 30						12 00					12 30					
Clapton	d																					
Seven Sisters ⊖	d																					
Tottenham Hale ⊖	d	11 25	11 25	11u37	11 40	11 43	11u52	11 55		12u07	12 10	12 13	12u22	12 25	12u37	12 40	12 43	12u52	12 55		13u07	13 10
Northumberland Park	d											12 15										
Angel Road	d																					
Ponders End	d	11 29	11 29					11 59						12 29					12 59			
Brimsdown	d	11 32	11 32					12 02						12 32					13 02			
Enfield Lock	d	11 34	11 34					12 04				12 21		12 34					13 04			
Waltham Cross	d	11 37	11 37			11 50		12 07						12 37			12 50		13 07			
Cheshunt	d	11 39	11 39		11 48	11 53		12 09			12 18	12 25		12 39		12 48	12 53		13 09			13 18
Broxbourne 3	a	11 44	11 44		11 52	11 57		12 14			12 22	12 29		12 44		12 52	12 57		13 14			13 22
Broxbourne 3	d	11 44	11 44		11 52	11 57		12 14			12 22	12 33		12 44		12 52	12 57		13 14			13 22
Rye House	d	11 47	11 47					12 17						12 47					13 17			
St Margarets (Herts)	d	11 50	11 50					12 20						12 50					13 20			
Ware	d	11 54	11 54					12 24						12 54					13 24			
Hertford East	a	12 01	12 01					12 31						13 01					13 31			
Roydon	d				11 56							12 38				12 56						
Harlow Town	d			11 54	12 00	12 09				12 24	12 28	12 42			12 54	13 00	13 09				13 24	13 28
Harlow Mill	d				12 03							12 45				13 03						
Sawbridgeworth	d				12 07	12 15						12 48				13 07	13 15					
Bishops Stortford	a				12 14	12 22	12 17				12 38	12 56	12 45			13 14	13 22	13 17				13 38
	d				12 14		12 18				12 39		12 45			13 14		13 18				13 39
Stansted Mountfitchet	d				12 18					12 35						13 18					13 35	
Stansted Airport	a			12 12			12 27			12 44			12 55		13 12			13 27			13 44	
Stansted Airport	d								12 27											13 27		
Elsenham	d				12 22											13 22						
Newport (Essex)	d				12 27											13 27						
Audley End	d				12 30				12 40		12 51					13 30				13 40		13 51
Great Chesterford	d				12 35											13 35						
Whittlesford Parkway	d				12 40						12 58					13 40						13 58
Shelford	d				12 44											13 44						
Cambridge	a				12 51				12 58		13 08					13 51				13 58		14 08

A not from 27 July until 10 August, from 29 August until 7 September

B from 27 July until 7 September, not from 13 August until 28 August

London - Broxbourne, Hertford East, Bishops Stortford, Stansted Airport and Cambridge

Network Diagram - see first Page of Table 20

		LE	LE ✈	LE	LE ✈	LE	LE	LE ✈	LE	XC ◇	LE ✈	LE	LE	LE ✈	LE	LE ✈	LE	LE	LE ✈	LE A	LE B	XC ◇	LE ✈
London Liverpool Street 15 ⊖	d		13 10	13 12	13 25	13 28		13 40	13 42		13 55	13 58		14 10	14 12	14 25	14 28		14 40	14 42	14 42		14 55
Bethnal Green	d																						
Hackney Downs	d			13 18					13 48						14 18					14 48	14 49		
Stratford 7 ⊖	d	13 00					13 30						14 00					14 30					
Clapton	d																						
Seven Sisters ⊖	d																						
Tottenham Hale ⊖	d	13 13	13u22	13 25	13u37	13 40	13 43	13u52	13 55		14u07	14 10	14 13	14u22	14 25	14u37	14 40	14 43	14u52	14 55	14 55		15u07
Northumberland Park	d	13 15											14 15										
Angel Road	d																						
Ponders End	d			13 29					13 59						14 29					14 59	14 59		
Brimsdown	d			13 32					14 02						14 32					15 02	15 02		
Enfield Lock	d	13 21		13 34					14 04				14 21		14 34					15 04	15 04		
Waltham Cross	d			13 37			13 50		14 07						14 37			14 50		15 07	15 07		
Cheshunt	d	13 25		13 39		13 48	13 53		14 09			14 18	14 25		14 39		14 48	14 53		15 09	15 09		
Broxbourne 3	a	13 29		13 44		13 52	13 57		14 14			14 22	14 29		14 44		14 52	14 57		15 14	15 14		
Broxbourne 3	d	13 33		13 44		13 52	13 57		14 14			14 22	14 33		14 44		14 52	14 57		15 14	15 14		
Rye House	d			13 47					14 17						14 47					15 17	15 17		
St Margarets (Herts)	d			13 50					14 20						14 50					15 20	15 20		
Ware	d			13 54					14 24						14 54					15 24	15 24		
Hertford East	a			14 01					14 31						15 01					15 31	15 31		
Roydon	d	13 38				13 56							14 38				14 56					
Harlow Town	d	13 42			13 54	14 00	14 09				14 24	14 28	14 42			14 54	15 00	15 09					15 24
Harlow Mill	d	13 45				14 03							14 45				15 03					
Sawbridgeworth	d	13 48				14 07	14 15						14 48				15 07	15 15				
Bishops Stortford	a	13 56	13 45			14 14	14 22	14 17				14 38	14 56	14 45			15 14	15 22	15 17			
	d		13 45			14 14		14 18				14 39		14 45			15 14		15 18			
Stansted Mountfitchet	d					14 18					14 35						15 18						15 35
Stansted Airport	a		13 55		14 12			14 27			14 44			14 55		15 13			15 27				15 44
Stansted Airport	d									14 27													15 27	
Elsenham	d					14 22											15 22					
Newport (Essex)	d					14 27											15 27					
Audley End	d					14 30				14 40		14 51					15 30					15 40	
Great Chesterford	d					14 35											15 35					
Whittlesford Parkway	d					14 40						14 58					15 40					
Shelford	d					14 44											15 44					
Cambridge	a					14 51				14 58		15 09					15 51					15 58	

		LE	LE	LE ✈	LE	LE ✈	LE	LE	LE ✈	LE	XC ◇	LE ✈	LE	LE	LE ✈	LE	LE ✈	LE	LE	XC ◇	LE ✈	LE
London Liverpool Street 15 ⊖	d	14 58		15 10	15 12	15 25	15 28		15 40	15 42		15 55	15 58		16 10	16 12	16 25	16 28			16 39	16 41
Bethnal Green	d																					
Hackney Downs	d				15 18					15 48						16 18						16 48
Stratford 7 ⊖	d		15 00					15 30						16 00					16 30			
Clapton	d																					
Seven Sisters ⊖	d																					16 54
Tottenham Hale ⊖	d	15 10	15 13	15u22	15 25	15u37	15 40	15 43	15u52	15 55		16u07	16 10	16 13	16u22	16 25	16u37	16 40	16 43		16u52	
Northumberland Park	d		15 15											16 15								
Angel Road	d													16 17								
Ponders End	d				15 29					15 59						16 29			16 47			
Brimsdown	d				15 32					16 02						16 32			16 50			
Enfield Lock	d		15 21		15 34					16 04				16 22		16 34			16 52			
Waltham Cross	d				15 37			15 50		16 07						16 37			16 55			
Cheshunt	d	15 18	15 25		15 39		15 48	15 53		16 09			16 18	16 26		16 39			16 57			17 08
Broxbourne 3	a	15 22	15 29		15 44		15 52	15 57		16 14			16 22	16 30		16 44		16 51	17 02			→
Broxbourne 3	d	15 22	15 33		15 44		15 52	15 57		16 14			16 22	16 34		16 44		16 52	17 03			
Rye House	d				15 47					16 17						16 48						
St Margarets (Herts)	d				15 50					16 20						16 51						
Ware	d				15 54					16 24						16 55						
Hertford East	a				16 01					16 31						17 03						
Roydon	d		15 38				15 56						16 26	16 38								
Harlow Town	d	15 28	15 42			15 54	16 00	16 09				16 24	16 30	16 42			16 54	16 59	17 12			
Harlow Mill	d		15 45				16 03						16 33	16 45								
Sawbridgeworth	d		15 48				16 07	16 15					16 37	16 49				17 04				
Bishops Stortford	a	15 38	15 56	15 45			16 14	16 22	16 17				16 44	16 58	16 47			17 11	17 24		17 17	
	d	15 41		15 45			16 14		16 18				16 44		16 48			17 11			17 18	
Stansted Mountfitchet	d	15 45					16 18					16 35	16 48					17 15				
Stansted Airport	a			15 55		16 12			16 27			16 44			17 01		17 14				17 29	
Stansted Airport	d										16 27									17 27		
Elsenham	d	15 49					16 22						16 52									
Newport (Essex)	d	15 55					16 27						16 57									
Audley End	d	15 59					16 30				16 40		17 00					17 25		17 40		
Great Chesterford	d	16 04					16 35						17 05									
Whittlesford Parkway	d	16 09					16 40						17 10					17 33				
Shelford	d	16 13					16 44						17 14									
Cambridge	a	16 20					16 51				16 58		17 21					17 44		17 58		

A not from 27 July until 10 August, from 29 August until 7 September

B from 27 July until 7 September, not from 13 August until 28 August

London - Broxbourne, Hertford East, Bishops Stortford, Stansted Airport and Cambridge

Network Diagram - see first Page of Table 20

		LE 1	LE	LE 1	LE 1 T	LE	LE 1 A	LE 1 T	LE 1	LE		LE 1	LE	LE 1	LE 1 T	LE	LE 1	XC ◇1	LE 1 T	LE		LE 1	LE	LE 1	LE 1 T
London Liverpool Street 15 ⊖	d	16 43			16 54	16 56	17 07	17 09		17 11		17 13			17 24	17 26	17 37		17 39	17 41		17 43			17 54
Bethnal Green	d																								
Hackney Downs	d					17 02				17 18						17 32				17 48					
Stratford 7 ⊖	d			16 47										17 17										17 47	
Clapton	d																								
Seven Sisters ⊖	d									17 24										17 54					
Tottenham Hale ⊖	d	16 55		16 58	17u06	17 09	17 19	17u22				17 25		17 28	17u36	17 39	17 49		17u52			17 55		17 58	18u06
Northumberland Park	d			17 00										17 30										18 00	
Angel Road	d			17 02										17 32										18 02	
Ponders End	d					17 13										17 43									
Brimsdown	d					17 16										17 46									
Enfield Lock	d			17 07		17 18								17 37		17 48								18 07	
Waltham Cross	d		←	17 10		17 21							←	17 40		17 51							←	18 10	
Cheshunt	d	17 04	17 08	17 12		17 23				17 38		17 34	17 38	17 42		17 53				18 08		18 04	18 08	18 12	
Broxbourne 3	a	17 08	17 13	17 17		17 30				→		17 38	17 43	17 47		18 00				→		18 08	18 13	18 17	
Broxbourne 3	d	17 09	17 13	17 22								17 39	17 43	17 50								18 09	18 13	18 22	
Rye House	d		17 17										17 47	17 54									18 17		
St Margarets (Herts)	d		17 20										17 50	17 57									18 20		
Ware	d		17 24										17 54	18 01									18 24		
Hertford East	a		17 32										18 02	18 09									18 32		
Roydon	d	17 13		17 26					←			17 43										18 13		18 26	
Harlow Town	d	17 17		17 42	17 24			17 39	17 42			17 47			17 54				18 09			18 17		18 42	18 24
Harlow Mill	d	17 20		→					17 45			17 50										18 20		→	
Sawbridgeworth	d	17 24							17 49			17 54							18 14			18 24			
Bishops Stortford	a	17 31			17 35		17 43		17 58			18 01			18 05		18 13					18 31			18 35
	d	17 31			17 35		17 44					18 01			18 05		18 14					18 31			18 35
Stansted Mountfitchet	d	17 36						17 52				18 06										18 36			
Stansted Airport	a				17 47			18 01							18 17				18 32						18 47
Stansted Airport	d																	18 21							
Elsenham	d	17 39										18 09										18 39			
Newport (Essex)	d	17 45										18 15										18 45			
Audley End	d	17 48					17 56					18 18					18 26	18 38				18 48			
Great Chesterford	d	17 53										18 23										18 53			
Whittlesford Parkway	d	17 58					18 04					18 28					18 34					18 58			
Shelford	d	18 02										18 32										19 02			
Cambridge	a	18 11					18 15					18 41					18 45	18 58				19 14			

		LE	LE 1	LE 1 T	LE 1	LE		LE 1	LE	LE 1	LE 1 T	LE	LE 1	XC ◇1	LE 1 T	LE		LE 1	LE	LE	LE 1 T	LE	LE 1	LE 1 T	LE
London Liverpool Street 15 ⊖	d	17 56	18 07	18 09		18 11		18 13			18 24	18 26	18 37		18 39	18 41		18 43			18 54	18 56	19 07	19 09	
Bethnal Green	d																								
Hackney Downs	d	18 02				18 18						18 32				18 48						19 02			
Stratford 7 ⊖	d									18 17										18 47					
Clapton	d																								
Seven Sisters ⊖	d					18 24										18 54									
Tottenham Hale ⊖	d	18 09	18 19	18u22				18 25		18 28	18u36	18 39	18 49		18u52			18 55		18 58	19u06	19 09	19 19	19u22	
Northumberland Park	d									18 30										19 00					
Angel Road	d									18 32										19 02					
Ponders End	d	18 13										18 43										19 13			
Brimsdown	d	18 16										18 46										19 16			
Enfield Lock	d	18 18								18 37		18 48								19 07		19 18			
Waltham Cross	d	18 21							←	18 40		18 51							←	19 10		19 21			
Cheshunt	d	18 23				18 38		18 34	18 38	18 42		18 53				19 08		19 04	19 08	19 12		19 23			
Broxbourne 3	a	18 30				→		18 38	18 43	18 47		19 00				→		19 08	19 13	19 17		19 30			
Broxbourne 3	d							18 39	18 43	18 50								19 09	19 13	19 22		19 35			
Rye House	d								18 47	18 54									19 17			19 38			
St Margarets (Herts)	d								18 50	18 57									19 20			19 41			
Ware	d								18 54	19 01									19 24			19 47			
Hertford East	a								19 02	19 09									19 32			19 55			
Roydon	d				←			18 43										19 13		19 26					←
Harlow Town	d			18 39	18 42			18 47			18 54				19 09			19 17		19 42	19 24			19 39	19 42
Harlow Mill	d				18 45			18 50										19 20		→					19 45
Sawbridgeworth	d				18 49			18 54							19 14			19 24							19 49
Bishops Stortford	a		18 43		18 58			19 01			19 05		19 13					19 31			19 35		19 43		19 56
	d		18 44					19 01			19 05		19 14					19 31			19 35		19 44		
Stansted Mountfitchet	d			18 52				19 06										19 36						19 52	
Stansted Airport	a			19 01							19 17				19 32						19 47			19 59	
Stansted Airport	d													19 21											
Elsenham	d							19 09										19 39							
Newport (Essex)	d							19 15										19 45							
Audley End	d		18 56					19 18					19 26	19 38				19 48					19 56		
Great Chesterford	d							19 23										19 53							
Whittlesford Parkway	d		19 04					19 28					19 34					19 58					20 04		
Shelford	d							19 32										20 02							
Cambridge	a		19 17					19 43					19 46	19 58				20 12					20 13		

A The Fenman

London - Broxbourne, Hertford East, Bishops Stortford, Stansted Airport and Cambridge

Network Diagram - see first Page of Table 20

		LE 1		LE 1	LE 1 T	LE 1	LE 1	XC ◇1	LE 1 T	LE 1	LE 1 T	LE 1		LE 1	LE 1 T	LE 1	LE 1 T	LE 1	LE 1	LE 1 T	LE 1	XC 1		LE 1 T	LE 1
London Liverpool Street 15 ⊖	d	19 11		19 13	19 25	19 28			19 40	19 42	19 55	19 58			20 10	20 12	20 25	20 28		20 40	20 42			20 55	20 58
Bethnal Green	d																								
Hackney Downs	d			19 19						19 48						20 18					20 48				
Stratford 7 ⊖	d						19 30							20 00					20 30						
Clapton	d																								
Seven Sisters ⊖	d																								
Tottenham Hale ⊖	d	19 25		19 28	19u37	19 40	19 43		19u52	19 55	20u07	20 10		20 13	20u22	20 25	20u37	20 40	20 43	20u52	20 55			21u07	21 10
Northumberland Park	d						19 45							20 15											
Angel Road	d						19 47																		
Ponders End	d			19 32						19 59						20 29					20 59				
Brimsdown	d			19 35						20 02						20 32					21 02				
Enfield Lock	d			19 37						20 04				20 21		20 34					21 04				
Waltham Cross	d			19 40			19 53			20 07						20 37			20 50		21 07				
Cheshunt	d	19 34		19 42		19 49	19 55			20 09		20 18		20 25		20 39		20 48	20 53		21 09				21 18
Broxbourne 3	a	19 39		19 47		19 54	20 00			20 14		20 22		20 29		20 44		20 52	20 57		21 14				21 22
Broxbourne 3	d	19 39		19 47		19 54	20 03			20 14		20 22		20 33		20 44		20 52	20 57		21 14				21 22
Rye House	d			19 50						20 17						20 47					21 17				
St Margarets (Herts)	d			19 53						20 20						20 50					21 20				
Ware	d			19 57						20 24						20 54					21 24				
Hertford East	a			20 04						20 31						21 01					21 31				
Roydon	d	19 43				19 59	20 08							20 38				20 56							
Harlow Town	d	19 47			19 57	20 03	20 12				20 24	20 28		20 42			20 54	21 00	21 09					21 24	21 28
Harlow Mill	d	19 50				20 06	20 15							20 45				21 03							
Sawbridgeworth	d	19 54				20 09	20 18							20 48				21 07	21 15						
Bishops Stortford	a	20 01				20 16	20 28		20 20			20 38		20 56	20 45			21 14	21 22	21 17					21 38
	d	20 01				20 17			20 21			20 39			20 45			21 14		21 18					21 39
Stansted Mountfitchet	d	20 06				20 21					20 36							21 18						21 35	
Stansted Airport	a				20 15				20 30		20 43				20 55		21 12			21 27				21 44	
Stansted Airport	d							20 21														21 27			
Elsenham	d	20 09				20 25												21 22							
Newport (Essex)	d	20 15				20 30												21 27							
Audley End	d	20 18				20 33		20 39				20 51						21 30				21 40			21 51
Great Chesterford	d	20 23				20 38												21 35							
Whittlesford Parkway	d	20 28				20 43						20 58						21 40							21 58
Shelford	d	20 32				20 47												21 44							
Cambridge	a	20 41				20 56		20 59				21 09						21 51				21 58			22 09

		LE 1	LE 1 T	LE 1	LE 1 T	LE 1	LE 1	LE 1 T		LE 1	XC 1	LE 1 A	LE 1 T	LE 1 A	LE 1 B	LE 1 B	XC 1	LE 1 A	LE 1 A	LE 1 B T	LE 1 A	LE 1 B	LE 1 A	LE 1 A	LE 1 A
London Liverpool Street 15 ⊖	d		21 10	21 12	21 25	21 28		21 40		21 42		21 42	21 55		21 58			21 58	22 10	22 10		22 12		22 12	22 22
Bethnal Green	d																								
Hackney Downs	d			21 18						21 48												22 18			
Stratford 7 ⊖	d	21 00					21 30					21 55				22 00							22 15	22 25	22 35
Clapton	d																								
Seven Sisters ⊖	d													←											
Tottenham Hale ⊖	d	21 13	21u22	21 25	21u37	21 40	21 43	21u52		21 55		22 10	22u07	22 10	22 10	22 13		22 13	22 22	22u22		22 25	22 25	22 40	22 45
Northumberland Park	d	21 15										→				22 15		22 15						→	→
Angel Road	d																								
Ponders End	d			21 29						21 59												22 29	22 29		
Brimsdown	d			21 32						22 02												22 32	22 32		
Enfield Lock	d	21 21		21 34						22 04						22 21		22 21				22 34	22 34		
Waltham Cross	d			21 37			21 50			22 07												22 37	22 37		
Cheshunt	d	21 25		21 39		21 48	21 53			22 09				22 18	22 18	22 25		22 25				22 39	22 39		
Broxbourne 3	a	21 29		21 44		21 52	21 57			22 14				22 22	22 22	22 29		22 29				22 44	22 44		
Broxbourne 3	d	21 33		21 44		21 52	21 57			22 14				22 22	22 22	22 33		22 33				22 44	22 44		
Rye House	d			21 47						22 17												22 47	22 47		
St Margarets (Herts)	d			21 50						22 20												22 50	22 50		
Ware	d			21 54						22 24												22 54	22 54		
Hertford East	a			22 01						22 31												23 01	23 01		
Roydon	d	21 38				21 56										22 38		22 38							
Harlow Town	d	21 42			21 54	22 00	22 09						22 24	22 28	22 28	22 42		22 42							
Harlow Mill	d	21 45				22 03										22 45		22 45							
Sawbridgeworth	d	21 48				22 07	22 15									22 48		22 48			←				
Bishops Stortford	a	21 56	21 45			22 14	22 22	22 17						22 38	22 38	22 56		22 55	22 45	22 45	22 55				
	d		21 45			22 14		22 18						22 39	22 39			22 56	22 45	22 45	22 56				
Stansted Mountfitchet	d					22 18							22 35					→							
Stansted Airport	a		21 55		22 12			22 27					22 44						22 57	22 57	23 09				
Stansted Airport	d										22 27						22 57								
Elsenham	d					22 22																			
Newport (Essex)	d					22 27																			
Audley End	d					22 30					22 40			22 51	22 51		23 10								
Great Chesterford	d					22 35																			
Whittlesford Parkway	d					22 40								22 58	22 58										
Shelford	d					22 44																			
Cambridge	a					22 51					22 56			23 09	23 09		23 30								

A from 27 July until 7 September, not from 13 August until 28 August

B not from 27 July until 10 August, from 29 August until 7 September

Table 22

Mondays to Fridays

London - Broxbourne, Hertford East, Bishops Stortford, Stansted Airport and Cambridge

Network Diagram - see first Page of Table 20

		LE	LE	LE	LE	LE	LE	LE	LE	LE	LE	LE	LE	LE	LE	LE	LE	LE	LE	LE	LE	LE	LE	LE
		1	1	1	1	1	1	1	1	1	1	1	1	1	1	1	1	1	1	1	1	1	1	1
		A	B	B	A	A	B	A	B	A	B	B	B	A	B	B	A	A	B	A	B	B	B	A
		⌶	⌶					⌶						⌶										
London Liverpool Street 15 ⊖	d	22 25	22 25		22 28			22 40	22 40	22 42		22 42	22 52	22 55	22 55		22 58			23 12		23 12	23 22	23 25
Bethnal Green	d																							
Hackney Downs	d									22 48										23 18				
Stratford 7 ⊖	d					22 30					22 45	22 55	23 05					23 00			23 15	23 25	23 35	
Clapton	d																							
Seven Sisters ⊖	d			←			←									←			←					
Tottenham Hale ⊖	d	22u37	22u37	22 40	22 40	22 43	22 45	22u52	22 52	22 55	22 55	23 10	23 15	23u07	23 07	23 10	23 10	23 13	23 15	23 25	23 25	23 40	23 45	23u37
Northumberland Park	d											→	→					23 15	23 17			→	→	
Angel Road	d																							
Ponders End	d									22 59	22 59									23 29	23 29			
Brimsdown	d									23 02	23 02									23 32	23 32			
Enfield Lock	d									23 04	23 04							23 21	23 23	23 34	23 34			
Waltham Cross	d					22 50	22 52			23 07	23 07									23 37	23 37			
Cheshunt	d			22 48	22 48	22 53	22 55			23 09	23 09					23 18	23 18	23 25	23 27	23 39	23 39			
Broxbourne 3	a			22 52	22 52	22 57	22 59			23 14	23 14					23 22	23 22	23 29	23 31	23 44	23 44			
Broxbourne 3	d			22 52	22 52	22 57	22 59			23 14	23 14					23 22	23 22	23 29	23 31	23 44	23 44			
Rye House	d									23 17	23 17									23 47	23 47			
St Margarets (Herts)	d									23 20	23 20									23 50	23 50			
Ware	d									23 24	23 24									23 54	23 54			
Hertford East	a									23 31	23 31									00 01	00 01			
Roydon	d			22 56	22 56													23 33	23 35					
Harlow Town	d	22 54	22 54	23 00	23 00	23 09	23 09							23 24	23 24	23 28	23 28	23 37	23 39					23 54
Harlow Mill	d			23 03	23 03													23 40	23 42					
Sawbridgeworth	d			23 07	23 07	23 15	23 15											23 44	23 46					
Bishops Stortford	a			23 14	23 14	23 22	23 22	23 17	23 17							23 38	23 38	23 51	23 56					00 04
	d			23 14	23 14			23 18	23 18						23 35	23 39	23 39							00 04
Stansted Mountfitchet	d			23 18	23 18									23 35	23 35									
Stansted Airport	a	23 12	23 13					23 30	23 30					23 43	23 43									00 13
Stansted Airport	d																							
Elsenham	d			23 22	23 22																			
Newport (Essex)	d			23 27	23 27																			
Audley End	d			23 30	23 30											23 51	23 51							
Great Chesterford	d			23 35	23 35																			
Whittlesford Parkway	d			23 40	23 40											23 58	23 58							
Shelford	d			23 44	23 44																			
Cambridge	a			23 51	23 51											00 08	00 08							

		LE	LE	LE	LE	LE	LE	LE	LE FX	LE FO
		1	1	1	1	1	1	1	1	1
		B	B	A	B	A	B	B	C	D
London Liverpool Street 15 ⊖	d	23 25		23 28		23 40		23 42	23 58	23 58
Bethnal Green	d									
Hackney Downs	d					23 46				
Stratford 7 ⊖	d						23 45	23 55		
Clapton	d					23 49				
Seven Sisters ⊖	d		←		←					
Tottenham Hale ⊖	d	23 37	23 40	23 40	23 45	23 53	23 55	00 10	00 10	00 10
Northumberland Park	d					23 55	23 57			
Angel Road	d									
Ponders End	d					23 59	00 01			
Brimsdown	d					00 02	00 04			
Enfield Lock	d					00 04	00 06			
Waltham Cross	d				23 52	00 07	00 09			
Cheshunt	d		23 48	23 48	23 55	00 09	00 11	00 18	00 18	00 18
Broxbourne 3	a		23 52	23 52	23 59	00 14	00 16	00 22	00 22	00 22
Broxbourne 3	d		23 52	23 52	23 59	00 14	00 16	00 22	00 22	00 22
Rye House	d					00 17	00 19			
St Margarets (Herts)	d					00 20	00 22			
Ware	d					00 24	00 26			
Hertford East	a					00 31	00 33			
Roydon	d		23 56	23 56				00 26	00 26	00 26
Harlow Town	d	23 54	23 59	23 59	00 09			00 30	00 30	00 30
Harlow Mill	d		00 03	00 03				00 33	00 33	00 33
Sawbridgeworth	d		00 07	00 07	00 15			00 37	00 37	00 37
Bishops Stortford	a	00 04	00 14	00 14	00 22			00 44	00 44	00 44
	d	00 04	00 14	00 14				00 44		00 44
Stansted Mountfitchet	d		00 18	00 18				00 48		00 48
Stansted Airport	a	00 13								
Stansted Airport	d									
Elsenham	d		00 22	00 22				00 52		00 52
Newport (Essex)	d		00 27	00 27				00 57		00 57
Audley End	d		00 30	00 30				01 00		01 00
Great Chesterford	d		00 35	00 35				01 05		01 05
Whittlesford Parkway	d		00 40	00 40				01 10		01 10
Shelford	d		00 44	00 44						
Cambridge	a		00 51	00 51				01 19		01 19

A not from 27 July until 10 August, from 29 August until 7 September

B from 27 July until 7 September, not from 13 August until 28 August

C not from 30 July until 9 August, from 29 August until 6 September

D until 20 July, FO from 17 August, not 31 August, 7 September

Table 22

Saturdays
until 21 July

London - Broxbourne, Hertford East, Bishops Stortford, Stansted Airport and Cambridge

Network Diagram - see first Page of Table 20

		LE	LE	LE	LE	LE	LE	LE	XC	LE	LE	LE	LE	LE	LE	LE	XC	LE	LE	LE	LE	LE	LE
		1	1	1	1	1	1	1	◇1	1	1	1	1	1	1	1	◇1	1	1	1	1	1	1
London Liverpool Street 15 ⊖	d	22p58	23p12	23p25	23p28	23p40	23p58	04 10		04 40	05 10	05 21	05 25		05 40	05 42		05 51	05 55	05 58		06 10	06 12
Bethnal Green	d																						
Hackney Downs	d		23p18			23p46										05 48							06 18
Stratford 7 ⊖	d											05 30						06 00					
Clapton	d					23p49																	
Seven Sisters ⊖	d													←							←		
Tottenham Hale ⊖	d	23p10	23p25	23b37	23p40	23p53	00 10			04u52	05u22	05 40	05u37	05 40	05u52	05 55		06 13	06u07	06 10	06 13	06u22	06 25
Northumberland Park	d					23p55						→						→			06 15		
Angel Road	d																						
Ponders End	d		23p29			23p59										05 59							06 29
Brimsdown	d		23p32			00 02										06 02							06 32
Enfield Lock	d		23p34			00 04										06 04					06 21		06 34
Waltham Cross	d		23p37			00 07										06 07							06 37
Cheshunt	d	23p18	23p39		23p48	00 09	00 18			05 00				05 48		06 09				06 18	06 25		06 39
Broxbourne 3	a	23p22	23p44		23p52	00 14	00 22			05 04				05 52		06 14				06 22	06 29		06 44
Broxbourne 3	d	23p22	23p44		23p52	00 14	00 22			05 04				05 52		06 14				06 22	06 33		06 44
Rye House	d		23p47			00 17										06 17							06 47
St Margarets (Herts)	d		23p50			00 20										06 20							06 50
Ware	d		23p54			00 24										06 24							06 54
Hertford East	a		00 01			00 31										06 31							07 01
Roydon	d				23p56		00 26							05 56							06 38		
Harlow Town	d	23p28		23p54	23p59		00 30			05 10	05 37		05 52	06 00					06 24	06 28	06 42		
Harlow Mill	d				00 03		00 33							06 03							06 45		
Sawbridgeworth	d				00 07		00 37				05 42			06 07							06 48		
Bishops Stortford	a	23p38		00 04	00 14		00 44			05 20	05 49		06 02	06 14	06 17					06 38	06 56	06 45	
	d	23p39		00 04	00 14		00 44			05 20	05 50		06 02	06 14	06 18					06 39		06 45	
Stansted Mountfitchet	d				00 18		00 48			05 24			06 05	06 18					06 35				
Stansted Airport	a			00 13				05 00		05 39	05 59		06 13		06 27				06 44			06 57	
Stansted Airport	d								05 25								06 27						
Elsenham	d				00 22		00 52							06 22									
Newport (Essex)	d				00 27		00 57							06 27									
Audley End	d	23p51			00 30		01 00		05 37					06 30			06 40			06 51			
Great Chesterford	d				00 35		01 05							06 35									
Whittlesford Parkway	d	23p58			00 40		01 10							06 40						06 58			
Shelford	d				00 44									06 44									
Cambridge	a	00 08			00 51		01 19		05 54					06 51			06 56			07 08			

		LE	LE	LE	LE	LE	LE	XC	LE	LE	LE	LE	LE	LE	LE	LE	LE	LE	XC	LE	LE	LE	LE
		1	1	1	1	1	1	◇1	1	1	1	1	1	1	1	1	1	1	◇1	1	1	1	1
												⌶		⌶			⌶			⌶			⌶
London Liverpool Street 15 ⊖	d	06 21	06 25	06 28		06 40	06 42		06 55	06 58		07 10	07 12	07 25	07 28		07 40	07 42		07 55	07 58		08 10
Bethnal Green	d																						
Hackney Downs	d						06 48						07 18					07 48					
Stratford 7 ⊖	d	06 30									07 00					07 30						08 00	
Clapton	d																						
Seven Sisters ⊖	d				←																		
Tottenham Hale ⊖	d	06 43	06u37	06 40	06 43	06u52	06 55		07u07	07 10	07 13	07u22	07 25	07u37	07 40	07 43	07u52	07 55		08u07	08 10	08 13	08u22
Northumberland Park	d	→									07 15											08 15	
Angel Road	d																						
Ponders End	d						06 59						07 29					07 59					
Brimsdown	d						07 02						07 32					08 02					
Enfield Lock	d						07 04				07 21		07 34					08 04				08 21	
Waltham Cross	d				06 50		07 07						07 37			07 50		08 07					
Cheshunt	d			06 48	06 53		07 09			07 18	07 25		07 39		07 48	07 53		08 09			08 18	08 25	
Broxbourne 3	a			06 52	06 57		07 14			07 22	07 29		07 44		07 52	07 57		08 14			08 22	08 29	
Broxbourne 3	d			06 52	06 57		07 14			07 22	07 33		07 44		07 52	07 57		08 14			08 22	08 33	
Rye House	d						07 17						07 47					08 17					
St Margarets (Herts)	d						07 20						07 50					08 20					
Ware	d						07 24						07 54					08 24					
Hertford East	a						07 31						08 01					08 31					
Roydon	d			06 56							07 38				07 56							08 38	
Harlow Town	d		06 54	07 00	07 09				07 24	07 28	07 42			07 54	08 00	08 09				08 24	08 28	08 42	
Harlow Mill	d			07 03							07 45				08 03							08 45	
Sawbridgeworth	d			07 07	07 15						07 48				08 07	08 15						08 48	
Bishops Stortford	a			07 14	07 22	07 17				07 38	07 56	07 45			08 14	08 22	08 17				08 38	08 56	08 45
	d			07 14		07 18				07 39		07 45			08 14		08 18				08 39		08 45
Stansted Mountfitchet	d			07 18					07 35						08 18					08 35			
Stansted Airport	a		07 12			07 27			07 44			07 57		08 12			08 27			08 44			08 57
Stansted Airport	d							07 27											08 27				
Elsenham	d			07 22											08 22								
Newport (Essex)	d			07 27											08 27								
Audley End	d			07 30				07 40		07 51					08 30				08 40		08 51		
Great Chesterford	d			07 35											08 35								
Whittlesford Parkway	d			07 40						07 58					08 40						08 58		
Shelford	d			07 44											08 44								
Cambridge	a			07 51				07 58		08 08					08 51				08 58		09 08		

b Previous night, stops to pick up only

London - Broxbourne, Hertford East, Bishops Stortford, Stansted Airport and Cambridge

Network Diagram - see first Page of Table 20

		LE 1	LE 1 🚲	LE 1	LE 1	LE 1 🚲	LE 1	XC ◇1	LE 1 🚲	LE 1	LE 1	LE 1 🚲	LE 1	LE 1 🚲	LE 1	LE 1	LE 1 🚲	LE 1	XC ◇1	LE 1 🚲	LE 1	LE 1
London Liverpool Street 15 ⊖	d	08 12	08 25	08 28		08 40	08 42		08 55	08 58		09 10	09 12	09 25	09 28		09 40	09 42		09 55	09 58	
Bethnal Green	d																					
Hackney Downs	d	08 18					08 48						09 18					09 48				
Stratford 7 ⊖	d				08 30						09 00					09 30						10 00
Clapton	d																					
Seven Sisters ⊖	d																					
Tottenham Hale ⊖	d	08 25	08u37	08 40	08 43	08u52	08 55		09u07	09 10	09 13	09u22	09 25	09u37	09 40	09 43	09u52	09 55		10u07	10 10	10 13
Northumberland Park	d										09 15											10 15
Angel Road	d																					
Ponders End	d	08 29					08 59						09 29					09 59				
Brimsdown	d	08 32					09 02						09 32					10 02				
Enfield Lock	d	08 34					09 04				09 21		09 34					10 04				10 21
Waltham Cross	d	08 37			08 50		09 07						09 37			09 50		10 07				
Cheshunt	d	08 39		08 48	08 53		09 09			09 18	09 25		09 39		09 48	09 53		10 09			10 18	10 25
Broxbourne 3	a	08 44		08 52	08 57		09 14			09 22	09 29		09 44		09 52	09 57		10 14			10 22	10 29
Broxbourne 3	d	08 44		08 52	08 57		09 14			09 22	09 33		09 44		09 52	09 57		10 14			10 22	10 33
Rye House	d	08 47					09 17						09 47					10 17				
St Margarets (Herts)	d	08 50					09 20						09 50					10 20				
Ware	d	08 54					09 24						09 54					10 24				
Hertford East	a	09 01					09 31						10 01					10 31				
Roydon	d			08 56							09 38				09 56							10 38
Harlow Town	d		08 54	09 00	09 09				09 24	09 28	09 42			09 54	10 00	10 09				10 24	10 28	10 42
Harlow Mill	d			09 03							09 45				10 03							10 45
Sawbridgeworth	d			09 07	09 15						09 48				10 07	10 15						10 48
Bishops Stortford	a			09 14	09 22	09 17				09 38	09 56	09 45			10 14	10 22	10 17				10 38	10 56
	d			09 14		09 18				09 39		09 45			10 14		10 18				10 39	
Stansted Mountfitchet	d			09 18					09 35						10 18					10 35		
Stansted Airport	a		09 12			09 27			09 44			09 57		10 12			10 27			10 44		
Stansted Airport	d							09 27											10 27			
Elsenham	d			09 22											10 22							
Newport (Essex)	d			09 27											10 27							
Audley End	d			09 30				09 40		09 51					10 30				10 40		10 51	
Great Chesterford	d			09 35											10 35							
Whittlesford Parkway	d			09 40						09 58					10 40						10 58	
Shelford	d			09 44											10 44							
Cambridge	a			09 51				09 58		10 08					10 51				10 58		11 08	

		LE 1 🚲	LE 1	LE 1 🚲	LE 1	LE 1	LE 1 🚲	LE 1	XC ◇1	LE 1 🚲	LE 1	LE 1	LE 1 🚲	LE 1	LE 1 🚲	LE 1	LE 1	LE 1 🚲	LE 1	XC ◇1	LE 1 🚲	LE 1	LE 1
London Liverpool Street 15 ⊖	d	10 10	10 12	10 25	10 28		10 40	10 42		10 55	10 58		11 10	11 12	11 25	11 28		11 40	11 42		11 55	11 58	
Bethnal Green	d																						
Hackney Downs	d		10 18					10 48						11 18					11 48				
Stratford 7 ⊖	d					10 30						11 00					11 30						12 00
Clapton	d																						
Seven Sisters ⊖	d																						
Tottenham Hale ⊖	d	10u22	10 25	10u37	10 40	10 43	10u52	10 55		11u07	11 10	11 13	11u22	11 25	11u37	11 40	11 43	11u52	11 55		12u07	12 10	12 13
Northumberland Park	d											11 15											12 15
Angel Road	d																						
Ponders End	d		10 29					10 59						11 29					11 59				
Brimsdown	d		10 32					11 02						11 32					12 02				
Enfield Lock	d		10 34					11 04				11 21		11 34					12 04				12 21
Waltham Cross	d		10 37			10 50		11 07						11 37			11 50		12 07				
Cheshunt	d		10 39		10 48	10 53		11 09			11 18	11 25		11 39		11 48	11 53		12 09			12 18	12 25
Broxbourne 3	a		10 44		10 52	10 57		11 14			11 22	11 29		11 44		11 52	11 57		12 14			12 22	12 29
Broxbourne 3	d		10 44		10 52	10 57		11 14			11 22	11 33		11 44		11 52	11 57		12 14			12 22	12 33
Rye House	d		10 47					11 17						11 47					12 17				
St Margarets (Herts)	d		10 50					11 20						11 50					12 20				
Ware	d		10 54					11 24						11 54					12 24				
Hertford East	a		11 01					11 31						12 01					12 31				
Roydon	d				10 56							11 38				11 56							12 38
Harlow Town	d			10 54	11 00	11 09				11 24	11 28	11 42			11 54	12 00	12 09				12 24	12 28	12 42
Harlow Mill	d				11 03							11 45				12 03							12 45
Sawbridgeworth	d				11 07	11 15						11 48				12 07	12 15						12 48
Bishops Stortford	a	10 45			11 14	11 22	11 17				11 38	11 56	11 45			12 14	12 22	12 17				12 38	12 56
	d	10 45			11 14		11 18				11 39		11 45			12 14		12 18				12 39	
Stansted Mountfitchet	d				11 18					11 35						12 18					12 35		
Stansted Airport	a	10 57		11 13			11 27			11 44			11 57		12 12			12 27			12 44		
Stansted Airport	d								11 27											12 27			
Elsenham	d				11 22											12 22							
Newport (Essex)	d				11 27											12 27							
Audley End	d				11 30				11 40		11 51					12 30				12 40		12 51	
Great Chesterford	d				11 35											12 35							
Whittlesford Parkway	d				11 40						11 58					12 40						12 58	
Shelford	d				11 44											12 44							
Cambridge	a				11 51				11 58		12 08					12 51				12 58		13 08	

London - Broxbourne, Hertford East, Bishops Stortford, Stansted Airport and Cambridge

Network Diagram - see first Page of Table 20

		LE 1 🚲	LE 1	LE 1 🚲	LE 1	LE 1	LE 1 🚲	LE 1	XC ◇1	LE 1 🚲	LE 1	LE 1	LE 1 🚲	LE 1	LE 1 🚲	LE 1	LE 1	LE 1 🚲	LE 1	XC ◇1	LE 1 🚲	LE 1
London Liverpool Street 15 ⊖	d	12 10	12 12	12 25	12 28		12 40	12 42		12 55	12 58		13 10	13 12	13 25	13 28		13 40	13 42		13 55	13 58
Bethnal Green	d																					
Hackney Downs	d		12 18					12 48						13 18					13 48			
Stratford 7 ⊖	d					12 30						13 00					13 30					
Clapton	d																					
Seven Sisters ⊖	d																					
Tottenham Hale ⊖	d	12u22	12 25	12u37	12 40	12 43	12u52	12 55		13u07	13 10	13 13	13u22	13 25	13u37	13 40	13 43	13u52	13 55		14u07	14 10
Northumberland Park	d											13 15										
Angel Road	d																					
Ponders End	d		12 29					12 59						13 29					13 59			
Brimsdown	d		12 32					13 02						13 32					14 02			
Enfield Lock	d		12 34					13 04				13 21		13 34					14 04			
Waltham Cross	d		12 37			12 50		13 07						13 37			13 50		14 07			
Cheshunt	d		12 39		12 48	12 53		13 09			13 18	13 25		13 39		13 48	13 53		14 09			14 18
Broxbourne 3	a		12 44		12 52	12 57		13 14			13 22	13 29		13 44		13 52	13 57		14 14			14 22
Broxbourne 3	d		12 44		12 52	12 57		13 14			13 22	13 33		13 44		13 52	13 57		14 14			14 22
Rye House	d		12 47					13 17						13 47					14 17			
St Margarets (Herts)	d		12 50					13 20						13 50					14 20			
Ware	d		12 54					13 24						13 54					14 24			
Hertford East	a		13 01					13 31						14 01					14 31			
Roydon	d				12 56							13 38				13 56						
Harlow Town	d			12 54	13 00	13 09				13 24	13 28	13 42			13 54	14 00	14 09				14 24	14 28
Harlow Mill	d				13 03							13 45				14 03						
Sawbridgeworth	d				13 07	13 15						13 48				14 07	14 15					
Bishops Stortford	a	12 45			13 14	13 22	13 17				13 38	13 56	13 45			14 14	14 22	14 17				14 38
	d	12 45			13 14		13 18				13 39		13 45			14 14		14 18				14 39
Stansted Mountfitchet	d				13 18					13 35						14 18					14 35	
Stansted Airport	a	12 57		13 12			13 27			13 44			13 57		14 12			14 27			14 44	
Stansted Airport	d								13 27											14 27		
Elsenham	d				13 22											14 22						
Newport (Essex)	d				13 27											14 27						
Audley End	d				13 30				13 40		13 51					14 30				14 40		14 51
Great Chesterford	d				13 35											14 35						
Whittlesford Parkway	d				13 40						13 58					14 40						14 58
Shelford	d				13 44											14 44						
Cambridge	a				13 51				13 58		14 08					14 51				14 58		15 08

		LE 1	LE 1 🚲	LE 1	LE 1 🚲	LE 1	LE 1	LE 1 🚲	LE 1	XC ◇1	LE 1 🚲	LE 1	LE 1	LE 1 🚲	LE 1	LE 1 🚲	LE 1	LE 1	LE 1 🚲	LE 1	XC ◇1	LE 1 🚲	LE 1
London Liverpool Street 15 ⊖	d		14 10	14 12	14 25	14 28		14 40	14 42		14 55	14 58		15 10	15 12	15 25	15 28		15 40	15 42		15 55	15 58
Bethnal Green	d																						
Hackney Downs	d			14 18					14 48						15 18					15 48			
Stratford 7 ⊖	d	14 00					14 30						15 00					15 30					
Clapton	d																						
Seven Sisters ⊖	d																						
Tottenham Hale ⊖	d	14 13	14u22	14 25	14u37	14 40	14 43	14u52	14 55		15u07	15 10	15 13	15u22	15 25	15u37	15 40	15 43	15u52	15 55		16u07	16 10
Northumberland Park	d	14 15											15 15										
Angel Road	d																						
Ponders End	d			14 29					14 59						15 29					15 59			
Brimsdown	d			14 32					15 02						15 32					16 02			
Enfield Lock	d	14 21		14 34					15 04				15 21		15 34					16 04			
Waltham Cross	d			14 37			14 50		15 07						15 37			15 50		16 07			
Cheshunt	d	14 25		14 39		14 48	14 53		15 09			15 18	15 25		15 39		15 48	15 53		16 09			16 18
Broxbourne 3	a	14 29		14 44		14 52	14 57		15 14			15 22	15 29		15 44		15 52	15 57		16 14			16 22
Broxbourne 3	d	14 33		14 44		14 52	14 57		15 14			15 22	15 33		15 44		15 52	15 57		16 14			16 22
Rye House	d			14 47					15 17						15 47					16 17			
St Margarets (Herts)	d			14 50					15 20						15 50					16 20			
Ware	d			14 54					15 24						15 54					16 24			
Hertford East	a			15 01					15 31						16 01					16 31			
Roydon	d	14 38				14 56							15 38				15 56						
Harlow Town	d	14 42			14 54	15 00	15 09				15 24	15 28	15 42			15 54	16 00	16 09				16 24	16 28
Harlow Mill	d	14 45				15 03							15 45				16 03						
Sawbridgeworth	d	14 48				15 07	15 15						15 48				16 07	16 15					
Bishops Stortford	a	14 56	14 45			15 14	15 22	15 17				15 38	15 56	15 45			16 14	16 22	16 17				16 38
	d		14 45			15 14		15 18				15 39		15 45			16 14		16 18				16 39
Stansted Mountfitchet	d					15 18					15 35						16 18					16 35	
Stansted Airport	a		14 57		15 12			15 27			15 44			15 57		16 12			16 27			16 44	
Stansted Airport	d									15 27											16 27		
Elsenham	d					15 22											16 22						
Newport (Essex)	d					15 27											16 27						
Audley End	d					15 30				15 40		15 51					16 30				16 40		16 51
Great Chesterford	d					15 35											16 35						
Whittlesford Parkway	d					15 40						15 58					16 40						16 58
Shelford	d					15 44											16 44						
Cambridge	a					15 51				15 58		16 08					16 51				16 58		17 08

London - Broxbourne, Hertford East, Bishops Stortford, Stansted Airport and Cambridge

Network Diagram - see first Page of Table 20

Station		LE ■	LE ■ ⊼	LE ■	LE ■ ⊼	LE ■	LE ■	LE ■ ⊼	LE ■	XC ◇■	LE ■ ⊼	LE ■	LE ■	LE ■ ⊼	LE ■	LE ■ ⊼	LE ■	LE ■	LE ■ ⊼	LE ■	XC ◇■	LE ■ ⊼	LE ■
London Liverpool Street ■ ⊖	d		16 10	16 12	16 25	16 28		16 40	16 42		16 55	16 58		17 10	17 12	17 25	17 28		17 40	17 42		17 55	17 58
Bethnal Green	d																						
Hackney Downs	d			16 18					16 48						17 18					17 48			
Stratford ■ ⊖	d	16 00					16 30						17 00					17 30					
Clapton	d																						
Seven Sisters ⊖	d																						
Tottenham Hale ⊖	d	16 13	16u22	16 25	16u37	16 40	16 43	16u52	16 55		17u07	17 10	17 13	17u22	17 25	17u37	17 40	17 43	17u52	17 55		18u07	18 10
Northumberland Park	d	16 15											17 15										
Angel Road	d																						
Ponders End	d			16 29					16 59						17 29					17 59			
Brimsdown	d			16 32					17 02						17 32					18 02			
Enfield Lock	d	16 21		16 34					17 04				17 21		17 34					18 04			
Waltham Cross	d			16 37			16 50		17 07						17 37			17 50		18 07			
Cheshunt	d	16 25		16 39		16 48	16 53		17 09			17 18	17 25		17 39		17 48	17 53		18 09			18 18
Broxbourne ■	a	16 29		16 44		16 52	16 57		17 14			17 22	17 29		17 44		17 52	17 57		18 14			18 22
Broxbourne ■	d	16 33		16 44		16 52	16 57		17 14			17 22	17 33		17 44		17 52	17 57		18 14			18 22
Rye House	d			16 47					17 17						17 47					18 17			
St Margarets (Herts)	d			16 50					17 20						17 50					18 20			
Ware	d			16 54					17 24						17 54					18 24			
Hertford East	a			17 01					17 31						18 01					18 31			
Roydon	d	16 38				16 56							17 38				17 56						
Harlow Town	d	16 42			16 54	17 00	17 09				17 24	17 28	17 42			17 54	18 00	18 09				18 24	18 28
Harlow Mill	d	16 45				17 03							17 45				18 03						
Sawbridgeworth	d	16 48				17 07	17 15						17 48				18 07	18 15					
Bishops Stortford	a	16 56	16 45			17 14	17 22	17 17				17 38	17 56	17 45			18 14	18 22	18 17				18 38
	d		16 45			17 14		17 18				17 39		17 45			18 14		18 18				18 39
Stansted Mountfitchet	d					17 18					17 35						18 18					18 35	
Stansted Airport	a		16 57		17 12			17 27			17 44			17 57		18 12			18 27			18 44	
Stansted Airport	d									17 27											18 27		
Elsenham	d					17 22											18 22						
Newport (Essex)	d					17 27											18 27						
Audley End	d					17 30				17 40		17 51					18 30				18 40		18 51
Great Chesterford	d					17 35											18 35						
Whittlesford Parkway	d					17 40						17 58					18 40						18 58
Shelford	d					17 44											18 44						
Cambridge	a					17 51				17 58		18 08					18 51				18 58		19 08

Station		LE ■	LE ■ ⊼	LE ■	LE ■ ⊼	LE ■	LE ■	LE ■ ⊼	LE ■	XC ◇■	LE ■ ⊼	LE ■	LE ■	LE ■ ⊼	LE ■	LE ■ ⊼	LE ■	LE ■	LE ■ ⊼	LE ■	XC ■	LE ■ ⊼
London Liverpool Street ■ ⊖	d		18 10	18 12	18 25	18 28		18 40	18 42		18 55	18 58		19 10	19 12	19 25	19 28		19 40	19 42		19 55
Bethnal Green	d																					
Hackney Downs	d			18 18					18 48						19 18					19 48		
Stratford ■ ⊖	d	18 00					18 30						19 00					19 30				
Clapton	d																					
Seven Sisters ⊖	d																					
Tottenham Hale ⊖	d	18 13	18u22	18 25	18u37	18 40	18 43	18u52	18 55		19u07	19 10	19 13	19u22	19 25	19u37	19 40	19 43	19u52	19 55		20u07
Northumberland Park	d	18 15											19 15									
Angel Road	d																					
Ponders End	d			18 29					18 59						19 29					19 59		
Brimsdown	d			18 32					19 02						19 32					20 02		
Enfield Lock	d	18 21		18 34					19 04				19 21		19 34					20 04		
Waltham Cross	d			18 37			18 50		19 07						19 37			19 50		20 07		
Cheshunt	d	18 25		18 39		18 48	18 53		19 09			19 18	19 25		19 39		19 48	19 53		20 09		
Broxbourne ■	a	18 29		18 44		18 52	18 57		19 14			19 22	19 29		19 44		19 52	19 57		20 14		
Broxbourne ■	d	18 33		18 44		18 52	18 57		19 14			19 22	19 33		19 44		19 52	19 57		20 14		
Rye House	d			18 47					19 17						19 47					20 17		
St Margarets (Herts)	d			18 50					19 20						19 50					20 20		
Ware	d			18 54					19 24						19 54					20 24		
Hertford East	a			19 01					19 31						20 01					20 31		
Roydon	d	18 38				18 56							19 38				19 56					
Harlow Town	d	18 42			18 54	19 00	19 09				19 24	19 28	19 42			19 54	20 00	20 09				20 24
Harlow Mill	d	18 45				19 03							19 45				20 03					
Sawbridgeworth	d	18 48				19 07	19 15						19 48				20 07	20 15				
Bishops Stortford	a	18 56	18 45			19 14	19 22	19 17				19 38	19 56	19 45			20 14	20 22	20 17			
	d		18 45			19 14		19 18				19 39		19 45			20 14		20 18			
Stansted Mountfitchet	d					19 18					19 35						20 18					20 35
Stansted Airport	a		18 57		19 12			19 27			19 44			19 57		20 12			20 27			20 44
Stansted Airport	d									19 27											20 27	
Elsenham	d					19 22											20 22					
Newport (Essex)	d					19 27											20 27					
Audley End	d					19 30				19 40		19 51					20 30				20 40	
Great Chesterford	d					19 35											20 35					
Whittlesford Parkway	d					19 40						19 58					20 40					
Shelford	d					19 44											20 44					
Cambridge	a					19 51				19 58		20 08					20 51				20 57	

Table 22

Saturdays
until 21 July

London - Broxbourne, Hertford East, Bishops Stortford, Stansted Airport and Cambridge

Network Diagram - see first Page of Table 20

Station		LE ■	LE ■	LE ■ ⊼	LE ■	LE ■ ⊼	LE ■	LE ■	LE ■ ⊼	LE ■	XC ■	LE ■ ⊼	LE ■	LE ■	LE ■ ⊼	LE ■	LE ■ ⊼	LE ■	LE ■	LE ■ ⊼	LE ■	XC ■	LE ■ ⊼
London Liverpool Street ■ ⊖	d	19 58		20 10	20 12	20 25	20 28		20 40	20 42		20 55	20 58		21 10	21 12	21 25	21 28		21 40	21 42		21 55
Bethnal Green	d																						
Hackney Downs	d				20 18					20 48						21 18					21 48		
Stratford ■ ⊖	d		20 00					20 30						21 00					21 30				
Clapton	d																						
Seven Sisters ⊖	d																						
Tottenham Hale ⊖	d	20 10	20 13	20u22	20 25	20u37	20 40	20 43	20u52	20 55		21u07	21 10	21 13	21u22	21 25	21u37	21 40	21 43	21u52	21 55		22u07
Northumberland Park	d		20 15											21 15									
Angel Road	d																						
Ponders End	d				20 29					20 59						21 29					21 59		
Brimsdown	d				20 32					21 02						21 32					22 02		
Enfield Lock	d		20 21		20 34					21 04				21 21		21 34					22 04		
Waltham Cross	d				20 37			20 50		21 07						21 37			21 50		22 07		
Cheshunt	d	20 18	20 25		20 39		20 48	20 53		21 09			21 18	21 25		21 39		21 48	21 53		22 09		
Broxbourne ■	a	20 22	20 29		20 44		20 52	20 57		21 14			21 22	21 29		21 44		21 52	21 57		22 14		
Broxbourne ■	d	20 22	20 33		20 44		20 52	20 57		21 14			21 22	21 33		21 44		21 52	21 57		22 14		
Rye House	d				20 47					21 17						21 47					22 17		
St Margarets (Herts)	d				20 50					21 20						21 50					22 20		
Ware	d				20 54					21 24						21 54					22 24		
Hertford East	a				21 01					21 31						22 01					22 31		
Roydon	d		20 38				20 56							21 38				21 56					
Harlow Town	d	20 28	20 42			20 54	21 00	21 09				21 24	21 28	21 42			21 54	22 00	22 09				22 24
Harlow Mill	d		20 45				21 03							21 45				22 03					
Sawbridgeworth	d		20 48				21 07	21 15						21 48				22 07	22 15				
Bishops Stortford	a	20 38	20 56	20 45			21 14	21 22	21 17				21 38	21 56	21 45			22 14	22 22	22 17			
	d	20 39		20 45			21 14		21 18				21 39		21 45			22 14		22 18			
Stansted Mountfitchet	d						21 18					21 35						22 18					22 35
Stansted Airport	a			20 57		21 12			21 27			21 44			21 57		22 12			22 27			22 44
Stansted Airport	d										21 27											22 27	
Elsenham	d						21 22											22 22					
Newport (Essex)	d						21 27											22 27					
Audley End	d	20 51					21 30				21 40		21 51					22 30				22 40	
Great Chesterford	d						21 35											22 35					
Whittlesford Parkway	d	20 58					21 40						21 58					22 40					
Shelford	d						21 44											22 44					
Cambridge	a	21 08					21 51				22 01		22 08					22 51				23 01	

Station		LE ■	LE ■	LE ■ ⊼	LE ■	LE ■ ⊼	LE ■	LE ■	LE ■ ⊼	LE ■	XC ■	LE ■ ⊼	LE ■	LE ■	LE ■	LE ■	LE ■	LE ■	LE ■
London Liverpool Street ■ ⊖	d	21 58		22 10	22 12	22 25	22 28		22 40	22 42		22 55	22 58		23 12	23 25	23 28	23 40	23 58
Bethnal Green	d																		
Hackney Downs	d				22 18					22 48					23 18			23 46	
Stratford ■ ⊖	d		22 00					22 30						23 00					
Clapton	d																	23 49	
Seven Sisters ⊖	d																		
Tottenham Hale ⊖	d	22 10	22 13	22u22	22 25	22u37	22 40	22 43	22u52	22 55		23u07	23 10	23 13	23 25	23u37	23 40	23 53	00 10
Northumberland Park	d		22 15											23 15				23 55	
Angel Road	d																		
Ponders End	d				22 29					22 59					23 29			23 59	
Brimsdown	d				22 32					23 02					23 32			00 02	
Enfield Lock	d		22 21		22 34					23 04				23 21	23 34			00 04	
Waltham Cross	d				22 37			22 50		23 07					23 37			00 07	
Cheshunt	d	22 18	22 25		22 39		22 48	22 53		23 09			23 18	23 25	23 39		23 48	00 09	00 18
Broxbourne ■	a	22 22	22 29		22 44		22 52	22 57		23 14			23 22	23 29	23 44		23 52	00 14	00 22
Broxbourne ■	d	22 22	22 33		22 44		22 52	22 57		23 14			23 22	23 29	23 44		23 52	00 14	00 22
Rye House	d				22 47					23 17					23 47			00 17	
St Margarets (Herts)	d				22 50					23 20					23 50			00 20	
Ware	d				22 54					23 24					23 54			00 24	
Hertford East	a				23 01					23 31					00 01			00 31	
Roydon	d		22 38				22 56							23 33			23 56		00 26
Harlow Town	d	22 28	22 42			22 54	23 00	23 09				23 24	23 28	23 37		23 54	00 01		00 30
Harlow Mill	d		22 45				23 03							23 40			00 03		00 33
Sawbridgeworth	d		22 48				23 07	23 15						23 44			00 07		00 37
Bishops Stortford	a	22 38	22 56	22 45			23 14	23 22	23 17				23 38	23 51		00 04	00 14		00 44
	d	22 39		22 45			23 14		23 18				23 39			00 04	00 14		00 44
Stansted Mountfitchet	d						23 18					23 35					00 18		00 48
Stansted Airport	a			22 57		23 12			23 27			23 44				00 13			
Stansted Airport	d										23 27								
Elsenham	d						23 22										00 22		00 52
Newport (Essex)	d						23 27										00 27		00 57
Audley End	d	22 51					23 30				23 40		23 51				00 30		01 00
Great Chesterford	d						23 35										00 35		01 05
Whittlesford Parkway	d	22 58					23 40						23 58				00 40		01 10
Shelford	d						23 44										00 44		
Cambridge	a	23 09					23 51				23 55		00 08				00 51		01 19

London - Broxbourne, Hertford East, Bishops Stortford, Stansted Airport and Cambridge

Network Diagram - see first Page of Table 20

		LE	LE	LE	LE	LE	LE	LE	LE	LE	LE	LE	LE	LE	LE	LE	LE	XC	LE	LE	LE	LE	LE	LE	LE
		■	■	■	■	■	■	■	■	■	■	■	■	■	■	■	■	◇■	■	■	■	■	■	■	■
												A	A	A	A									
London Liverpool Street	d	22p42		23p12	23p22	23p25				23p42		00 18	00 33	00 48	01 03	01 18	04 10		04 40	05 10	05 21	05 25		05 40	05 42
Bethnal Green	d																								
Hackney Downs	d																								05 48
Stratford	d	22p55	23p15	23p25	23p35				23p45	23p55	00 15	00 30	00 45	01 00	01 15	01 03					05 30				
Clapton	d																								
Seven Sisters	d						←	←															←		
Tottenham Hale	d	23p10	23p25	23p40	23p45	23p37	23p40	23p45	23p55	00 10	00 25	00 40	0055	01 10	01 25	01 40			04u52	05u22	05 40	05u37	05 40	05u52	05 55
Northumberland Park	d			→	→				23p57												→				
Angel Road	d																								
Ponders End	d		23p29						00 01		00 29		00 59		01 29										05 59
Brimsdown	d		23p32						00 04		00 32		01 02		01 32										06 02
Enfield Lock	d		23p34						00 06		00 34		01 04		01 34										06 04
Waltham Cross	d		23p37					23p52	00 09		00 37		01 07		01 37										06 07
Cheshunt	d	23p18	23p39				23p48	23p55	00 11	00 18	00 39	00 48	01 09	01 18	01 39	01 48			05 00				05 48		06 09
Broxbourne	a	23p22	23p44				23p52	23p59	00 16	00 22	00 44	00 52	01 14	01 22	01 44	01 52			05 04				05 52		06 14
Broxbourne	d	23p22	23p44				23p52	23p59	00 16	00 22	00 44	00 52	01 14	01 22	01 44	01 52			05 04				05 52		06 14
Rye House	d		23p47						00 19		00 47		01 17		01 47										06 17
St Margarets (Herts)	d		23p50						00 22		00 50		01 20		01 50										06 20
Ware	d		23p54						00 26		00 54		01 24		01 54										06 24
Hertford East	a		00 01						00 33		01 01		01 31		02 01										06 31
Roydon	d						23p56			00 26													05 56		
Harlow Town	d	23p28				23p54	23p59	00 09		00 30		00 58		01 28		01 58			05 10	05 37		05 52	06 00		
Harlow Mill	d						00 03			00 33													06 03		
Sawbridgeworth	d						00 07	00 15		00 37		01 03		01 33		02 03				05 42			06 07		
Bishops Stortford	a	23p38				00 04	00 14	00 22		00 44		01 10		01 40		02 10			05 20	05 49		06 02	06 14	06 17	
	d	23p39				00 04	00 14			00 44		01 11		01 41		02 11			05 20	05 50		06 02	06 14	06 18	
Stansted Mountfitchet	d						00 18			00 48		01 15		01 45		02 15			05 24			06 05	06 18		
Stansted Airport	a					00 13											05 00		05 39	05 59		06 13		06 27	
Stansted Airport	d																	05 25							
Elsenham	d						00 22			00 52		01 19		01 49		02 19							06 22		
Newport (Essex)	d						00 27			00 57		01 24		01 54		02 24							06 27		
Audley End	d	23p51					00 30			01 00		01 27		01 57		02 27		05 37					06 30		
Great Chesterford	d						00 35			01 05		01 32		02 02		02 32							06 35		
Whittlesford Parkway	d	23p58					00 40			01 10		01 37		02 07		02 37							06 40		
Shelford	d						00 44					01 41		02 11		02 41							06 44		
Cambridge	a	00 08					00 51			01 19		01 49		02 19		02 49		05 54					06 51		

		XC	LE	LE	LE	LE	LE	LE	LE	LE	LE	LE	LE	LE	XC	LE	LE	LE	LE	LE	LE	LE	LE	LE	LE
		◇■	■	■	■	■	■	■	■	■	■	■	■	■	◇■	■	■	■	■	■	■	■	■	■	■
																			🛒		🛒			🛒	
London Liverpool Street	d		05 51	05 55	05 58		06 10	06 12	06 21	06 25	06 28		06 40	06 42		06 55	06 58		07 10	07 12	07 25	07 28		07 40	07 42
Bethnal Green	d																								
Hackney Downs	d							06 18						06 48						07 18					07 48
Stratford	d		06 00						06 30								07 00					07 30		
Clapton	d																								
Seven Sisters	d					←						←													
Tottenham Hale	d		06 13	06u07	06 10	06 13	06u22	06 25	06 43	06u37	06 40	06 43	06u52	06 55		07u07	07 10	07 13	07u22	07 25	07u37	07 40	07 43	07u52	07 55
Northumberland Park	d		→			06 15			→									07 15							
Angel Road	d																								
Ponders End	d							06 29						06 59						07 29					07 59
Brimsdown	d							06 32						07 02						07 32					08 02
Enfield Lock	d					06 21		06 34						07 04				07 21		07 34					08 04
Waltham Cross	d							06 37				06 50		07 07						07 37			07 50		08 07
Cheshunt	d				06 18	06 25		06 39			06 48	06 53		07 09			07 18	07 25		07 39		07 48	07 53		08 09
Broxbourne	a				06 22	06 29		06 44			06 52	06 57		07 14			07 22	07 29		07 44		07 52	07 57		08 14
Broxbourne	d				06 22	06 33		06 44			06 52	06 57		07 14			07 22	07 33		07 44		07 52	07 57		08 14
Rye House	d							06 47						07 17						07 47					08 17
St Margarets (Herts)	d							06 50						07 20						07 50					08 20
Ware	d							06 54						07 24						07 54					08 24
Hertford East	a							07 01						07 31						08 01					08 31
Roydon	d					06 38					06 56							07 38				07 56			
Harlow Town	d			06 24	06 28	06 42				06 54	07 00	07 09				07 24	07 28	07 42			07 54	08 00	08 09		
Harlow Mill	d					06 45					07 03							07 45				08 03			
Sawbridgeworth	d					06 48					07 07	07 15						07 48				08 07	08 15		
Bishops Stortford	a				06 38	06 56	06 45				07 14	07 22	07 17				07 38	07 56	07 45			08 14	08 22	08 17	
	d				06 39		06 45				07 14		07 18				07 39		07 45			08 14		08 18	
Stansted Mountfitchet	d			06 35							07 18					07 35						08 18			
Stansted Airport	a			06 44			06 57			07 12			07 27			07 44			07 57		08 12			08 27	
Stansted Airport	d	06 27													07 27									
Elsenham	d										07 22										08 22			
Newport (Essex)	d										07 27										08 27			
Audley End	d	06 40			06 51						07 30				07 40		07 51					08 30			
Great Chesterford	d										07 35										08 35			
Whittlesford Parkway	d				06 58						07 40						07 58					08 40			
Shelford	d										07 44										08 44			
Cambridge	a	06 56			07 08						07 51				07 58		08 08					08 51			

A 28 July only

London - Broxbourne, Hertford East, Bishops Stortford, Stansted Airport and Cambridge

Network Diagram - see first Page of Table 20

		XC		LE	LE	LE	LE	LE	LE	LE	LE	LE		LE	XC	LE	LE	LE	LE	LE	LE	LE		LE	LE
		◇■		■	■	■	■	■	■	■	■	■		■	◇■	■	■	■	■	■	■	■		■	■
				🛒			🛒		🛒			🛒				🛒			🛒		🛒				🛒
London Liverpool Street	d			07 55	07 58		08 10	08 12	08 25	08 28		08 40		08 42		08 55	08 58		09 10	09 12	09 25	09 28			09 40
Bethnal Green	d																								
Hackney Downs	d							08 18						08 48						09 18					
Stratford	d					08 00					08 30							09 00						09 30	
Clapton	d																								
Seven Sisters	d																								
Tottenham Hale	d			08u07	08 10	08 13	08u22	08 25	08u37	08 40	08 43	08u52		08 55		09u07	09 10	09 13	09u22	09 25	09u37	09 40		09 43	09u52
Northumberland Park	d					08 15											09 15						
Angel Road	d																								
Ponders End	d							08 29						08 59						09 29					
Brimsdown	d							08 32						09 02						09 32					
Enfield Lock	d					08 21		08 34						09 04				09 21		09 34					
Waltham Cross	d							08 37			08 50			09 07						09 37				09 50	
Cheshunt	d				08 18	08 25		08 39		08 48	08 53			09 09			09 18	09 25		09 39		09 48		09 53	
Broxbourne	a				08 22	08 29		08 44		08 52	08 57			09 14			09 22	09 29		09 44		09 52		09 57	
Broxbourne	d				08 22	08 33		08 44		08 52	08 57			09 14			09 22	09 33		09 44		09 52		09 57	
Rye House	d							08 47						09 17						09 47					
St Margarets (Herts)	d							08 50						09 20						09 50					
Ware	d							08 54						09 24						09 54					
Hertford East	a							09 01						09 31						10 01					
Roydon	d					08 38				08 56								09 38				09 56			
Harlow Town	d			08 24	08 28	08 42			08 54	09 00	09 09					09 24	09 28	09 42			09 54	10 00		10 09	
Harlow Mill	d					08 45				09 03								09 45				10 03			
Sawbridgeworth	d					08 48				09 07	09 15							09 48				10 07		10 15	
Bishops Stortford	a				08 38	08 56	08 45			09 14	09 22	09 17					09 38	09 56	09 45			10 14		10 22	10 17
	d				08 39		08 45			09 14		09 18					09 39		09 45			10 14			10 18
Stansted Mountfitchet	d			08 35						09 18						09 35						10 18			
Stansted Airport	a			08 44			08 57		09 12			09 27				09 44			09 57		10 12				10 27
Stansted Airport	d	08 27													09 27									
Elsenham	d									09 22												10 22			
Newport (Essex)	d									09 27												10 27			
Audley End	d	08 40			08 51					09 30					09 40		09 51					10 30			
Great Chesterford	d									09 35												10 35			
Whittlesford Parkway	d				08 58					09 40						09 58					10 40			
Shelford	d									09 44												10 44			
Cambridge	a	08 58			09 08					09 51					09 58		10 08					10 51			

		LE	XC	LE	LE	LE	LE	LE		LE	LE	LE	LE	LE	XC	LE	LE	LE		LE	LE	LE	LE	LE	LE
		■	◇■	■	■	■	■	■		■	■	■	■	■	◇■	■	■	■		■	■	■	■	■	■
				🛒			🛒			🛒			🛒			🛒				🛒		🛒			🛒
London Liverpool Street	d	09 42		09 55	09 58		10 10	10 12		10 25	10 28		10 40	10 42		10 55	10 58			11 10	11 12	11 25	11 28		11 40
Bethnal Green	d																								
Hackney Downs	d	09 48						10 18						10 48							11 18				
Stratford	d					10 00						10 30						11 00						11 30	
Clapton	d																								
Seven Sisters	d																								
Tottenham Hale	d	09 55		10u07	10 10	10 13	10u22	10 25		10u37	10 40	10 43	10u52	10 55		11u07	11 10	11 13		11u22	11 25	11u37	11 40	11 43	11u52
Northumberland Park	d					10 15											11 15						
Angel Road	d																								
Ponders End	d	09 59						10 29						10 59							11 29				
Brimsdown	d	10 02						10 32						11 02							11 32				
Enfield Lock	d	10 04				10 21		10 34						11 04				11 21			11 34				
Waltham Cross	d	10 07						10 37				10 50		11 07							11 37			11 50	
Cheshunt	d	10 09			10 18	10 25		10 39			10 48	10 53		11 09			11 18	11 25			11 39		11 48	11 53	
Broxbourne	a	10 14			10 22	10 29		10 44			10 52	10 57		11 14			11 22	11 29			11 44		11 52	11 57	
Broxbourne	d	10 14			10 22	10 33		10 44			10 52	10 57		11 14			11 22	11 33			11 44		11 52	11 57	
Rye House	d	10 17						10 47						11 17							11 47				
St Margarets (Herts)	d	10 20						10 50						11 20							11 50				
Ware	d	10 24						10 54						11 24							11 54				
Hertford East	a	10 31						11 01						11 31							12 01				
Roydon	d					10 38					10 56							11 38					11 56		
Harlow Town	d			10 24	10 28	10 42				10 54	11 00	11 09				11 24	11 28	11 42				11 54	12 00	12 09	
Harlow Mill	d					10 45					11 03							11 45					12 03		
Sawbridgeworth	d					10 48					11 07	11 15						11 48					12 07	12 15	
Bishops Stortford	a				10 38	10 56	10 45				11 14	11 22	11 17				11 38	11 56		11 45			12 14	12 22	12 17
	d				10 39		10 45				11 14		11 18				11 39			11 45			12 14		12 18
Stansted Mountfitchet	d			10 35							11 18					11 35							12 18		
Stansted Airport	a			10 44			10 57			11 13			11 27			11 44				11 57		12 12			12 27
Stansted Airport	d		10 27											11 27									
Elsenham	d										11 22											12 22		
Newport (Essex)	d										11 27											12 27		
Audley End	d		10 40		10 51						11 30				11 40		11 51						12 30		
Great Chesterford	d										11 35											12 35		
Whittlesford Parkway	d				10 58						11 40						11 58						12 40		
Shelford	d										11 44											12 44		
Cambridge	a		10 58		11 08						11 51				11 58		12 08						12 51		

Table 22

Saturdays
28 July to 11 August

London - Broxbourne, Hertford East, Bishops Stortford, Stansted Airport and Cambridge

Network Diagram - see first Page of Table 20

		LE 1	XC ◇1	LE 1 🚲	LE 1	LE 1	LE 1 🚲	LE 1	LE 1 🚲	LE 1	LE 1	LE 1 🚲	LE 1	XC ◇1	LE 1 🚲	LE 1	LE 1	LE 1 🚲	LE 1	LE 1 🚲	LE 1	LE 1
London Liverpool Street 15 ⊖	d	11 42		11 55	11 58		12 10	12 12	12 25	12 28		12 40	12 42		12 55	12 58		13 10	13 12	13 25	13 28	
Bethnal Green	d																					
Hackney Downs	d	11 48						12 18					12 48						13 18			
Stratford 7 ⊖	d					12 00					12 30						13 00					13 30
Clapton	d																					
Seven Sisters ⊖	d																					
Tottenham Hale ⊖	d	11 55		12u07	12 10	12 13	12u22	12 25	12u37	12 40	12 43	12u52	12 55		13u07	13 10	13 13	13u22	13 25	13u37	13 40	13 43
Northumberland Park	d					12 15											13 15					
Angel Road	d																					
Ponders End	d	11 59						12 29					12 59						13 29			
Brimsdown	d	12 02						12 32					13 02						13 32			
Enfield Lock	d	12 04				12 21		12 34					13 04				13 21		13 34			
Waltham Cross	d	12 07						12 37			12 50		13 07						13 37			13 50
Cheshunt	d	12 09			12 18	12 25		12 39		12 48	12 53		13 09			13 18	13 25		13 39		13 48	13 53
Broxbourne 3	a	12 14			12 22	12 29		12 44		12 52	12 57		13 14			13 22	13 29		13 44		13 52	13 57
Broxbourne 3	d	12 14			12 22	12 33		12 44		12 52	12 57		13 14			13 22	13 33		13 44		13 52	13 57
Rye House	d	12 17						12 47					13 17						13 47			
St Margarets (Herts)	d	12 20						12 50					13 20						13 50			
Ware	d	12 24						12 54					13 24						13 54			
Hertford East	a	12 31						13 01					13 31						14 01			
Roydon	d					12 38				12 56							13 38				13 56	
Harlow Town	d			12 24	12 28	12 42			12 54	13 00	13 09				13 24	13 28	13 42			13 54	14 00	14 09
Harlow Mill	d					12 45				13 03							13 45				14 03	
Sawbridgeworth	d					12 48				13 07	13 15						13 48				14 07	14 15
Bishops Stortford	a				12 38	12 56	12 45			13 14	13 22	13 17				13 38	13 56	13 45			14 14	14 22
	d				12 39		12 45			13 14		13 18				13 39		13 45			14 14	
Stansted Mountfitchet	d			12 35						13 18					13 35						14 18	
Stansted Airport	a			12 44			12 57		13 12			13 27			13 44			13 57		14 12		
Stansted Airport	d		12 27											13 27								
Elsenham	d									13 22											14 22	
Newport (Essex)	d									13 27											14 27	
Audley End	d		12 40		12 51					13 30				13 40		13 51					14 30	
Great Chesterford	d									13 35											14 35	
Whittlesford Parkway	d				12 58					13 40						13 58					14 40	
Shelford	d									13 44											14 44	
Cambridge	a		12 58		13 08					13 51				13 58		14 08					14 51	

		LE 1 🚲	LE 1	XC ◇1	LE 1 🚲	LE 1	LE 1	LE 1 🚲	LE 1	LE 1 🚲	LE 1	LE 1	LE 1 🚲	LE 1	XC ◇1	LE 1 🚲	LE 1	LE 1	LE 1 🚲	LE 1	LE 1 🚲	LE 1	LE 1
London Liverpool Street 15 ⊖	d	13 40	13 42		13 55	13 58		14 10	14 12	14 25	14 28		14 40	14 42		14 55	14 58		15 10	15 12	15 25	15 28	
Bethnal Green	d																						
Hackney Downs	d		13 48						14 18					14 48						15 18			
Stratford 7 ⊖	d						14 00					14 30						15 00					15 30
Clapton	d																						
Seven Sisters ⊖	d																						
Tottenham Hale ⊖	d	13u52	13 55		14u07	14 10	14 13	14u22	14 25	14u37	14 40	14 43	14u52	14 55		15u07	15 10	15 13	15u22	15 25	15u37	15 40	15 43
Northumberland Park	d						14 15											15 15					
Angel Road	d																						
Ponders End	d		13 59						14 29					14 59						15 29			
Brimsdown	d		14 02						14 32					15 02						15 32			
Enfield Lock	d		14 04				14 21		14 34					15 04				15 21		15 34			
Waltham Cross	d		14 07						14 37			14 50		15 07						15 37			15 50
Cheshunt	d		14 09			14 18	14 25		14 39		14 48	14 53		15 09			15 18	15 25		15 39		15 48	15 53
Broxbourne 3	a		14 14			14 22	14 29		14 44		14 52	14 57		15 14			15 22	15 29		15 44		15 52	15 57
Broxbourne 3	d		14 14			14 22	14 33		14 44		14 52	14 57		15 14			15 22	15 33		15 44		15 52	15 57
Rye House	d		14 17						14 47					15 17						15 47			
St Margarets (Herts)	d		14 20						14 50					15 20						15 50			
Ware	d		14 24						14 54					15 24						15 54			
Hertford East	a		14 31						15 01					15 31						16 01			
Roydon	d						14 38				14 56							15 38				15 56	
Harlow Town	d				14 24	14 28	14 42			14 54	15 00	15 09				15 24	15 28	15 42			15 54	16 00	16 09
Harlow Mill	d						14 45				15 03							15 45				16 03	
Sawbridgeworth	d						14 48				15 07	15 15						15 48				16 07	16 15
Bishops Stortford	a	14 17				14 38	14 56	14 45			15 14	15 22	15 17				15 38	15 56	15 45			16 14	16 22
	d	14 18				14 39		14 45			15 14		15 18				15 39		15 45			16 14	
Stansted Mountfitchet	d				14 35						15 18					15 35						16 18	
Stansted Airport	a	14 27			14 44			14 57		15 12			15 27			15 44			15 57		16 12		
Stansted Airport	d			14 27											15 27								
Elsenham	d										15 22											16 22	
Newport (Essex)	d										15 27											16 27	
Audley End	d			14 40		14 51					15 30				15 40		15 51					16 30	
Great Chesterford	d										15 35											16 35	
Whittlesford Parkway	d					14 58					15 40						15 58					16 40	
Shelford	d										15 44											16 44	
Cambridge	a			14 58		15 08					15 51				15 58		16 08					16 51	

Table 22

Saturdays
28 July to 11 August

London - Broxbourne, Hertford East, Bishops Stortford, Stansted Airport and Cambridge

Network Diagram - see first Page of Table 20

		LE 1 🚲	LE 1	XC ◇1	LE 1 🚲	LE 1	LE 1	LE 1 🚲	LE 1	LE 1 🚲	LE 1	LE 1	LE 1 🚲	LE 1	XC ◇1	LE 1 🚲	LE 1	LE 1	LE 1 🚲	LE 1	LE 1 🚲	LE 1	LE 1
London Liverpool Street 15 ⊖	d	15 40	15 42		15 55	15 58		16 10	16 12	16 25	16 28		16 40	16 42		16 55	16 58		17 10	17 12	17 25	17 28	
Bethnal Green	d																						
Hackney Downs	d		15 48						16 18					16 48						17 18			
Stratford 7 ⊖	d						16 00					16 30						17 00					17 30
Clapton	d																						
Seven Sisters ⊖	d																						
Tottenham Hale ⊖	d	15u52	15 55		16u07	16 10	16 13	16u22	16 25	16u37	16 40	16 43	16u52	16 55		17u07	17 10	17 13	17u22	17 25	17u37	17 40	17 43
Northumberland Park	d						16 15											17 15					
Angel Road	d																						
Ponders End	d		15 59						16 29					16 59						17 29			
Brimsdown	d		16 02						16 32					17 02						17 32			
Enfield Lock	d		16 04				16 21		16 34					17 04				17 21		17 34			
Waltham Cross	d		16 07						16 37			16 50		17 07						17 37			17 50
Cheshunt	d		16 09			16 18	16 25		16 39		16 48	16 53		17 09			17 18	17 25		17 39		17 48	17 53
Broxbourne 3	a		16 14			16 22	16 29		16 44		16 52	16 57		17 14			17 22	17 29		17 44		17 52	17 57
Broxbourne 3	d		16 14			16 22	16 33		16 44		16 52	16 57		17 14			17 22	17 33		17 44		17 52	17 57
Rye House	d		16 17						16 47					17 17						17 47			
St Margarets (Herts)	d		16 20						16 50					17 20						17 50			
Ware	d		16 24						16 54					17 24						17 54			
Hertford East	a		16 31						17 01					17 31						18 01			
Roydon	d						16 38				16 56							17 38				17 56	
Harlow Town	d				16 24	16 28	16 42			16 54	17 00	17 09				17 24	17 28	17 42			17 54	18 00	18 09
Harlow Mill	d						16 45				17 03							17 45				18 03	
Sawbridgeworth	d						16 48				17 07	17 15						17 48				18 07	18 15
Bishops Stortford	a	16 17				16 38	16 56	16 45			17 14	17 22	17 17				17 38	17 56	17 45			18 14	18 22
	d	16 18				16 39		16 45			17 14		17 18				17 39		17 45			18 14	
Stansted Mountfitchet	d				16 35						17 18					17 35						18 18	
Stansted Airport	a	16 27			16 44			16 57		17 12			17 27			17 44			17 57		18 12		
Stansted Airport	d			16 27											17 27								
Elsenham	d										17 22											18 22	
Newport (Essex)	d										17 27											18 27	
Audley End	d			16 40		16 51					17 30				17 40		17 51					18 30	
Great Chesterford	d										17 35											18 35	
Whittlesford Parkway	d					16 58					17 40						17 58					18 40	
Shelford	d										17 44											18 44	
Cambridge	a			16 58		17 08					17 51				17 58		18 08					18 51	

		LE 1 🚲	LE 1	XC ◇1	LE 1 🚲	LE 1	LE 1	LE 1 🚲	LE 1	LE 1 🚲	LE 1	LE 1	LE 1 🚲	LE 1	XC ◇1	LE 1 🚲	LE 1	LE 1	LE 1 🚲	LE 1	LE 1 🚲	LE 1
London Liverpool Street 15 ⊖	d	17 40	17 42		17 55	17 58		18 10	18 12	18 25	18 28		18 40	18 42		18 55	18 58		19 10	19 12	19 25	19 28
Bethnal Green	d																					
Hackney Downs	d		17 48						18 18					18 48						19 18		
Stratford 7 ⊖	d						18 00					18 30						19 00				
Clapton	d																					
Seven Sisters ⊖	d																					
Tottenham Hale ⊖	d	17u52	17 55		18u07	18 10	18 13	18u22	18 25	18u37	18 40	18 43	18u52	18 55		19u07	19 10	19 13	19u22	19 25	19u37	19 40
Northumberland Park	d						18 15											19 15				
Angel Road	d																					
Ponders End	d		17 59						18 29					18 59						19 29		
Brimsdown	d		18 02						18 32					19 02						19 32		
Enfield Lock	d		18 04				18 21		18 34					19 04				19 21		19 34		
Waltham Cross	d		18 07						18 37			18 50		19 07						19 37		
Cheshunt	d		18 09			18 18	18 25		18 39		18 48	18 53		19 09			19 18	19 25		19 39		19 48
Broxbourne 3	a		18 14			18 22	18 29		18 44		18 52	18 57		19 14			19 22	19 29		19 44		19 52
Broxbourne 3	d		18 14			18 22	18 33		18 44		18 52	18 57		19 14			19 22	19 33		19 44		19 52
Rye House	d		18 17						18 47					19 17						19 47		
St Margarets (Herts)	d		18 20						18 50					19 20						19 50		
Ware	d		18 24						18 54					19 24						19 54		
Hertford East	a		18 31						19 01					19 31						20 01		
Roydon	d						18 38				18 56							19 38				19 56
Harlow Town	d				18 24	18 28	18 42			18 54	19 00	19 09				19 24	19 28	19 42			19 54	20 00
Harlow Mill	d						18 45				19 03							19 45				20 03
Sawbridgeworth	d						18 48				19 07	19 15						19 48				20 07
Bishops Stortford	a	18 17				18 38	18 56	18 45			19 14	19 22	19 17				19 38	19 56	19 45			20 14
	d	18 18				18 39		18 45			19 14		19 18				19 39		19 45			20 14
Stansted Mountfitchet	d				18 35						19 18					19 35						20 18
Stansted Airport	a	18 27			18 44			18 57		19 12			19 27			19 44			19 57		20 12	
Stansted Airport	d			18 27											19 27							
Elsenham	d										19 22											20 22
Newport (Essex)	d										19 27											20 27
Audley End	d			18 40		18 51					19 30				19 40		19 51					20 30
Great Chesterford	d										19 35											20 35
Whittlesford Parkway	d					18 58					19 40						19 58					20 40
Shelford	d										19 44											20 44
Cambridge	a			18 58		19 08					19 51				19 58		20 08					20 51

London - Broxbourne, Hertford East, Bishops Stortford, Stansted Airport and Cambridge

Saturdays
28 July to 11 August

Network Diagram - see first Page of Table 20

		LE ■	LE ■ 🚲	LE ■	XC ■	LE ■ 🚲	LE ■	LE ■	LE ■ 🚲	LE ■	LE ■ 🚲	LE ■	LE ■	LE ■ 🚲	LE ■	XC ■	LE ■ 🚲	LE ■	LE ■	LE ■ 🚲	LE ■	LE ■ 🚲	LE ■
London Liverpool Street [15] ⊖	d		19 40	19 42		19 55	19 58		20 10	20 12	20 25	20 28		20 40	20 42		20 55	20 58		21 10	21 12	21 25	21 28
Bethnal Green	d																						
Hackney Downs	d			19 48						20 18					20 48						21 18		
Stratford [7] ⊖	d	19 30						20 00					20 30						21 00				
Clapton	d																						
Seven Sisters ⊖	d																						
Tottenham Hale ⊖	d	19 43	19u52	19 55		20u07	20 10	20 13	20u22	20 25	20u37	20 40	20 43	20u52	20 55		21u07	21 10	21 13	21u22	21 25	21u37	21 40
Northumberland Park	d							20 15											21 15				
Angel Road	d																						
Ponders End	d			19 59						20 29					20 59						21 29		
Brimsdown	d			20 02						20 32					21 02						21 32		
Enfield Lock	d			20 04				20 21		20 34					21 04				21 21		21 34		
Waltham Cross	d	19 50		20 07						20 37			20 50		21 07						21 37		
Cheshunt	d	19 53		20 09			20 18	20 25		20 39		20 48	20 53		21 09			21 18	21 25		21 39		21 48
Broxbourne [3]	a	19 57		20 14			20 22	20 29		20 44		20 52	20 57		21 14			21 22	21 29		21 44		21 52
Broxbourne [3]	d	19 57		20 14			20 22	20 33		20 44		20 52	20 57		21 14			21 22	21 33		21 44		21 52
Rye House	d			20 17						20 47					21 17						21 47		
St Margarets (Herts)	d			20 20						20 50					21 20						21 50		
Ware	d			20 24						20 54					21 24						21 54		
Hertford East	a			20 31						21 01					21 31						22 01		
Roydon	d							20 38				20 56							21 38				21 56
Harlow Town	d	20 09				20 24	20 28	20 42			20 54	21 00	21 09				21 24	21 28	21 42			21 54	22 00
Harlow Mill	d							20 45				21 03							21 45				22 03
Sawbridgeworth	d	20 15						20 48				21 07	21 15						21 48				22 07
Bishops Stortford	a	20 22	20 17				20 38	20 56	20 45			21 14	21 22	21 17				21 38	21 56	21 45			22 14
	d		20 18				20 39		20 45			21 14		21 18				21 39		21 45			22 14
Stansted Mountfitchet	d					20 35						21 18					21 35						22 18
Stansted Airport	a		20 27			20 44			20 57		21 12			21 27			21 44			21 57		22 12	
Stansted Airport	d				20 27											21 27							
Elsenham	d											21 22											22 22
Newport (Essex)	d											21 27											22 27
Audley End	d				20 40		20 51					21 30				21 40		21 51					22 30
Great Chesterford	d											21 35											22 35
Whittlesford Parkway	d						20 58					21 40						21 58					22 40
Shelford	d											21 44											22 44
Cambridge	a				20 57		21 08					21 51				22 01		22 08					22 51

		XC ■	LE ■	LE ■ 🚲	LE ■	LE ■	LE ■	LE ■ 🚲	LE ■	LE ■	LE ■ 🚲	LE ■	LE ■	LE ■	LE ■ 🚲	LE ■	LE ■	LE ■ 🚲	LE ■	XC ■	LE ■	LE ■
London Liverpool Street [15] ⊖	d			21 40		21 42	21 42	21 55		21 58	22 10		22 12	22 22	22 25			22 40			22 42	22 52
Bethnal Green	d																					
Hackney Downs	d					21 48																
Stratford [7] ⊖	d		21 30				21 55					22 15	22 25	22 35					22 45		22 55	23 05
Clapton	d																					
Seven Sisters ⊖	d								←							←	←					
Tottenham Hale ⊖	d		21 43	21u52		21 55	22 10	22u07	22 10	22 13	22 22	22 25	22 40	22 45	22u37	22 40	22 45	22 52	22 55		23 10	23 15
Northumberland Park	d						→			22 15			→	→							→	→
Angel Road	d																					
Ponders End	d					21 59						22 29							22 59			
Brimsdown	d					22 02						22 32							23 02			
Enfield Lock	d					22 04				22 21		22 34							23 04			
Waltham Cross	d		21 50			22 07						22 37					22 52		23 07			
Cheshunt	d		21 53			22 09			22 18	22 25		22 39				22 48	22 55		23 09			
Broxbourne [3]	a		21 57			22 14			22 22	22 29		22 44				22 52	22 59		23 14			
Broxbourne [3]	d		21 57			22 14			22 22	22 33		22 44				22 52	22 59		23 14			
Rye House	d					22 17						22 47							23 17			
St Margarets (Herts)	d					22 20						22 50							23 20			
Ware	d					22 24						22 54							23 24			
Hertford East	a					22 31						23 01							23 31			
Roydon	d									22 38						22 56						
Harlow Town	d		22 09					22 24	22 28	22 42					22 54	23 00	23 09					
Harlow Mill	d									22 45						23 03						
Sawbridgeworth	d		22 15		←					22 48						23 07	23 15					
Bishops Stortford	a		22 22	22 17	22 22				22 38	22 56	22 45					23 14	23 22	23 17				
	d		22 23	22 18	22 23				22 39		22 45					23 14		23 18				
Stansted Mountfitchet	d		→					22 35								23 18						
Stansted Airport	a			22 27	22 39			22 45			22 57				23 12			23 27				
Stansted Airport	d	22 27																		23 27		
Elsenham	d															23 22						
Newport (Essex)	d															23 27						
Audley End	d	22 40							22 51							23 30				23 40		
Great Chesterford	d															23 35						
Whittlesford Parkway	d								22 58							23 40						
Shelford	d															23 44						
Cambridge	a	23 01							23 09							23 51				23 55		

London - Broxbourne, Hertford East, Bishops Stortford, Stansted Airport and Cambridge

Saturdays
28 July to 11 August

Network Diagram - see first Page of Table 20

		LE ■ 🚲	LE ■	LE ■	LE ■	LE ■	LE ■	LE ■	LE ■	LE ■
London Liverpool Street [15] ⊖	d	22 55				23 12	23 25			23 42
Bethnal Green	d									
Hackney Downs	d									
Stratford [7] ⊖	d				23 15	23 25			23 45	23 55
Clapton	d									
Seven Sisters ⊖	d		←	←				←		
Tottenham Hale ⊖	d	23 07	23 10	23 15	23 25	23 40	23 37	23 40	23 55	00 10
Northumberland Park	d			23 17		→			23 57	
Angel Road	d									
Ponders End	d				23 29				00 01	
Brimsdown	d				23 32				00 04	
Enfield Lock	d			23 23	23 34				00 06	
Waltham Cross	d				23 37				00 09	
Cheshunt	d		23 18	23 27	23 39			23 48	00 11	00 18
Broxbourne [3]	a		23 22	23 31	23 44			23 52	00 16	00 22
Broxbourne [3]	d		23 22	23 31	23 44			23 52	00 16	00 22
Rye House	d				23 47				00 19	
St Margarets (Herts)	d				23 50				00 22	
Ware	d				23 54				00 26	
Hertford East	a				00 01				00 33	
Roydon	d			23 35				23 56		00 26
Harlow Town	d	23 24	23 28	23 39			23 54	00 01		00 30
Harlow Mill	d			23 42				00 03		00 33
Sawbridgeworth	d			23 46				00 07		00 37
Bishops Stortford	a		23 38	23 56			00 04	00 14		00 44
	d		23 39				00 04	00 14		00 44
Stansted Mountfitchet	d	23 35						00 18		00 48
Stansted Airport	a	23 44					00 13			
Stansted Airport	d									
Elsenham	d							00 22		00 52
Newport (Essex)	d							00 27		00 57
Audley End	d		23 51					00 30		01 00
Great Chesterford	d							00 35		01 05
Whittlesford Parkway	d		23 58					00 40		01 10
Shelford	d							00 44		
Cambridge	a		00 08					00 51		01 19

Saturdays
18 August to 25 August

		LE ■	LE ■	LE ■	LE ■	LE ■	LE ■	LE ■	XC ◇■	LE ■	LE ■	LE ■	LE ■	LE ■	LE ■	LE ■	XC ◇■	LE ■	LE ■	LE ■	LE ■	LE ■	LE ■
London Liverpool Street [15] ⊖	d	22p58	23p12	23p25	23p28	23p40	23p58	04 10		04 40	05 10	05 21	05 25		05 40	05 42		05 51	05 55	05 58		06 10	06 12
Bethnal Green	d																						
Hackney Downs	d		23p18			23p46										05 48							06 18
Stratford [7] ⊖	d											05 30						06 00					
Clapton	d					23p49																	
Seven Sisters ⊖	d													←							←		
Tottenham Hale ⊖	d	23p10	23p25	23b37	23p40	23p53	00 10			04u52	05u22	05 40	05u37	05 40	05u52	05 55		06 13	06u07	06 10	06 13	06u22	06 25
Northumberland Park	d					23p55						→						→			06 15		
Angel Road	d																						
Ponders End	d		23p29			23p59										05 59							06 29
Brimsdown	d		23p32			00 02										06 02							06 32
Enfield Lock	d		23p34			00 04										06 04					06 21		06 34
Waltham Cross	d		23p37			00 07										06 07							06 37
Cheshunt	d	23p18	23p39		23p48	00 09	00 18			05 00				05 48		06 09				06 18	06 25		06 39
Broxbourne [3]	a	23p22	23p44		23p52	00 14	00 22			05 04				05 52		06 14				06 22	06 29		06 44
Broxbourne [3]	d	23p22	23p44		23p52	00 14	00 22			05 04				05 52		06 14				06 22	06 33		06 44
Rye House	d		23p47			00 17										06 17							06 47
St Margarets (Herts)	d		23p50			00 20										06 20							06 50
Ware	d		23p54			00 24										06 24							06 54
Hertford East	a		00 01			00 31										06 31							07 01
Roydon	d				23p56		00 26							05 56							06 38		
Harlow Town	d	23p28		23p54	23p59		00 30			05 10	05 37		05 52	06 00					06 24	06 28	06 42		
Harlow Mill	d				00 03		00 33							06 03							06 45		
Sawbridgeworth	d				00 07		00 37				05 42			06 07							06 48		
Bishops Stortford	a	23p38		00 04	00 14		00 44			05 20	05 49		06 02	06 14	06 17					06 38	06 56	06 45	
	d	23p39		00 04	00 14		00 44			05 20	05 50		06 02	06 14	06 18					06 39		06 45	
Stansted Mountfitchet	d				00 18		00 48			05 24			06 05	06 18					06 35				
Stansted Airport	a			00 13				05 00		05 39	05 59		06 13		06 27				06 44			06 57	
Stansted Airport	d								05 25								06 27						
Elsenham	d				00 22		00 52							06 22									
Newport (Essex)	d				00 27		00 57							06 27									
Audley End	d	23p51			00 30		01 00		05 37					06 30			06 40			06 51			
Great Chesterford	d				00 35		01 05							06 35									
Whittlesford Parkway	d	23p58			00 40		01 10							06 40						06 58			
Shelford	d				00 44									06 44									
Cambridge	a	00 08			00 51		01 19		05 54					06 51			06 56			07 08			

b Previous night, stops to pick up only

Table 22

Saturdays

18 August to 25 August

London - Broxbourne, Hertford East, Bishops Stortford, Stansted Airport and Cambridge

Network Diagram - see first Page of Table 20

		LE 1	LE 1	LE 1	LE 1	LE 1		LE 1	XC ◇1	LE 1	LE 1	LE 1	LE 1 🛒	LE 1	LE 1 🛒	LE 1		LE 1	LE 1 🛒	LE 1	XC ◇1	LE 1 🛒	LE 1	LE 1	LE 1 🛒
London Liverpool Street 15 ⊖	d	06 21	06 25	06 28		06 40		06 42		06 55	06 58		07 10	07 12	07 25	07 28			07 40	07 42		07 55	07 58		08 10
Bethnal Green	d																								
Hackney Downs	d							06 48						07 18						07 48					
Stratford 7 ⊖	d	06 30										07 00						07 30						08 00	
Clapton	d																								
Seven Sisters ⊖	d				←																				
Tottenham Hale ⊖	d	06 43	06u37	06 40	06 43	06u52		06 55		07u07	07 10	07 13	07u22	07 25	07u37	07 40		07 43	07u52	07 55		08u07	08 10	08 13	08u22
Northumberland Park	d	→										07 15												08 15	
Angel Road	d																								
Ponders End	d							06 59						07 29						07 59					
Brimsdown	d							07 02						07 32						08 02					
Enfield Lock	d							07 04				07 21		07 34						08 04				08 21	
Waltham Cross	d				06 50			07 07						07 37				07 50		08 07					
Cheshunt	d			06 48	06 53			07 09			07 18	07 25		07 39		07 48		07 53		08 09			08 18	08 25	
Broxbourne 3	a			06 52	06 57			07 14			07 22	07 29		07 44		07 52		07 57		08 14			08 22	08 29	
Broxbourne 3	d			06 52	06 57			07 14			07 22	07 33		07 44		07 52		07 57		08 14			08 22	08 33	
Rye House	d							07 17						07 47						08 17					
St Margarets (Herts)	d							07 20						07 50						08 20					
Ware	d							07 24						07 54						08 24					
Hertford East	a							07 31						08 01						08 31					
Roydon	d			06 56								07 38				07 56								08 38	
Harlow Town	d		06 54	07 00	07 09					07 24	07 28	07 42			07 54	08 00		08 09				08 24	08 28	08 42	
Harlow Mill	d			07 03								07 45				08 03								08 45	
Sawbridgeworth	d			07 07	07 15							07 48				08 07		08 15						08 48	
Bishops Stortford	a			07 14	07 22	07 17					07 38	07 56	07 45			08 14		08 22	08 17				08 38	08 56	08 45
	d			07 14		07 18					07 39		07 45			08 14			08 18				08 39		08 45
Stansted Mountfitchet	d			07 18						07 35						08 18						08 35			
Stansted Airport	a		07 12			07 27				07 44			07 57		08 12				08 27			08 44			08 57
Stansted Airport	d								07 27												08 27				
Elsenham	d			07 22												08 22									
Newport (Essex)	d			07 27												08 27									
Audley End	d			07 30					07 40		07 51					08 30					08 40		08 51		
Great Chesterford	d			07 35												08 35									
Whittlesford Parkway	d			07 40							07 58					08 40							08 58		
Shelford	d			07 44												08 44									
Cambridge	a			07 51					07 58		08 08					08 51					08 58		09 08		

		LE 1		LE 1 🛒	LE 1	LE 1	LE 1 🛒	LE 1	XC ◇1	LE 1 🛒	LE 1	LE 1		LE 1 🛒	LE 1	LE 1 🛒	LE 1	LE 1	LE 1 🛒	LE 1	XC ◇1	LE 1 🛒		LE 1	LE 1
London Liverpool Street 15 ⊖	d	08 12		08 25	08 28		08 40	08 42		08 55	08 58			09 10	09 12	09 25	09 28		09 40	09 42		09 55		09 58	
Bethnal Green	d																								
Hackney Downs	d	08 18						08 48							09 18					09 48					
Stratford 7 ⊖	d					08 30						09 00						09 30							10 00
Clapton	d																								
Seven Sisters ⊖	d																								
Tottenham Hale ⊖	d	08 25		08u37	08 40	08 43	08u52	08 55		09u07	09 10	09 13		09u22	09 25	09u37	09 40	09 43	09u52	09 55		10u07		10 10	10 13
Northumberland Park	d											09 15													10 15
Angel Road	d																								
Ponders End	d	08 29						08 59							09 29					09 59					
Brimsdown	d	08 32						09 02							09 32					10 02					
Enfield Lock	d	08 34						09 04				09 21			09 34					10 04					10 21
Waltham Cross	d	08 37				08 50		09 07							09 37			09 50		10 07					
Cheshunt	d	08 39			08 48	08 53		09 09			09 18	09 25			09 39		09 48	09 53		10 09				10 18	10 25
Broxbourne 3	a	08 44			08 52	08 57		09 14			09 22	09 29			09 44		09 52	09 57		10 14				10 22	10 29
Broxbourne 3	d	08 44			08 52	08 57		09 14			09 22	09 33			09 44		09 52	09 57		10 14				10 22	10 33
Rye House	d	08 47						09 17							09 47					10 17					
St Margarets (Herts)	d	08 50						09 20							09 50					10 20					
Ware	d	08 54						09 24							09 54					10 24					
Hertford East	a	09 01						09 31							10 01					10 31					
Roydon	d				08 56							09 38					09 56								10 38
Harlow Town	d			08 54	09 00	09 09				09 24	09 28	09 42				09 54	10 00	10 09				10 24		10 28	10 42
Harlow Mill	d				09 03							09 45					10 03								10 45
Sawbridgeworth	d				09 07	09 15						09 48					10 07	10 15							10 48
Bishops Stortford	a				09 14	09 22	09 17				09 38	09 56		09 45			10 14	10 22	10 17					10 38	10 56
	d				09 14		09 18				09 39			09 45			10 14		10 18					10 39	
Stansted Mountfitchet	d				09 18					09 35							10 18					10 35			
Stansted Airport	a			09 12			09 27			09 44				09 57		10 12			10 27			10 44			
Stansted Airport	d								09 27												10 27				
Elsenham	d				09 22												10 22								
Newport (Essex)	d				09 27												10 27								
Audley End	d				09 30				09 40		09 51						10 30				10 40			10 51	
Great Chesterford	d				09 35												10 35								
Whittlesford Parkway	d				09 40						09 58						10 40							10 58	
Shelford	d				09 44												10 44								
Cambridge	a				09 51				09 58		10 08						10 51				10 58			11 08	

Table 22

Saturdays

18 August to 25 August

London - Broxbourne, Hertford East, Bishops Stortford, Stansted Airport and Cambridge

Network Diagram - see first Page of Table 20

		LE 1 🛒	LE 1	LE 1 🛒	LE 1	LE 1	LE 1 🛒	LE 1		XC ◇1	LE 1 🛒	LE 1	LE 1	LE 1 🛒	LE 1	LE 1 🛒	LE 1	LE 1		LE 1 🛒	LE 1	XC ◇1	LE 1 🛒	LE 1	LE 1
London Liverpool Street 15 ⊖	d	10 10	10 12	10 25	10 28		10 40	10 42			10 55	10 58		11 10	11 12	11 25	11 28			11 40	11 42		11 55	11 58	
Bethnal Green	d																								
Hackney Downs	d		10 18					10 48							11 18						11 48				
Stratford 7 ⊖	d					10 30							11 00					11 30							12 00
Clapton	d																								
Seven Sisters ⊖	d																								
Tottenham Hale ⊖	d	10u22	10 25	10u37	10 40	10 43	10u52	10 55			11u07	11 10	11 13	11u22	11 25	11u37	11 40	11 43		11u52	11 55		12u07	12 10	12 13
Northumberland Park	d												11 15												12 15
Angel Road	d																								
Ponders End	d		10 29					10 59							11 29						11 59				
Brimsdown	d		10 32					11 02							11 32						12 02				
Enfield Lock	d		10 34					11 04					11 21		11 34						12 04				12 21
Waltham Cross	d		10 37			10 50		11 07							11 37			11 50			12 07				
Cheshunt	d		10 39		10 48	10 53		11 09				11 18	11 25		11 39		11 48	11 53			12 09			12 18	12 25
Broxbourne 3	a		10 44		10 52	10 57		11 14				11 22	11 29		11 44		11 52	11 57			12 14			12 22	12 29
Broxbourne 3	d		10 44		10 52	10 57		11 14				11 22	11 33		11 44		11 52	11 57			12 14			12 22	12 33
Rye House	d		10 47					11 17							11 47						12 17				
St Margarets (Herts)	d		10 50					11 20							11 50						12 20				
Ware	d		10 54					11 24							11 54						12 24				
Hertford East	a		11 01					11 31							12 01						12 31				
Roydon	d				10 56								11 38				11 56								12 38
Harlow Town	d			10 54	11 00	11 09					11 24	11 28	11 42			11 54	12 00	12 09					12 24	12 28	12 42
Harlow Mill	d				11 03								11 45				12 03								12 45
Sawbridgeworth	d				11 07	11 15							11 48				12 07	12 15							12 48
Bishops Stortford	a	10 45			11 14	11 22	11 17					11 38	11 56	11 45			12 14	12 22		12 17				12 38	12 56
	d	10 45			11 14		11 18					11 39		11 45			12 14			12 18				12 39	
Stansted Mountfitchet	d				11 18						11 35						12 18						12 35		
Stansted Airport	a	10 57		11 13			11 27				11 44			11 57		12 12				12 27			12 44		
Stansted Airport	d									11 27												12 27			
Elsenham	d				11 22												12 22								
Newport (Essex)	d				11 27												12 27								
Audley End	d				11 30					11 40		11 51					12 30					12 40		12 51	
Great Chesterford	d				11 35												12 35								
Whittlesford Parkway	d				11 40							11 58					12 40							12 58	
Shelford	d				11 44												12 44								
Cambridge	a				11 51					11 58		12 08					12 51					12 58		13 08	

		LE 1 🛒	LE 1	LE 1 🛒		LE 1	LE 1	LE 1 🛒	LE 1	XC ◇1	LE 1 🛒	LE 1	LE 1	LE 1 🛒		LE 1	LE 1 🛒	LE 1	LE 1	LE 1 🛒	LE 1	XC ◇1	LE 1 🛒	LE 1	
London Liverpool Street 15 ⊖	d	12 10	12 12	12 25		12 28		12 40	12 42		12 55	12 58		13 10		13 12	13 25	13 28		13 40	13 42		13 55	13 58	
Bethnal Green	d																								
Hackney Downs	d		12 18						12 48							13 18					13 48				
Stratford 7 ⊖	d						12 30						13 00						13 30						
Clapton	d																								
Seven Sisters ⊖	d																								
Tottenham Hale ⊖	d	12u22	12 25	12u37		12 40	12 43	12u52	12 55		13u07	13 10	13 13	13u22		13 25	13u37	13 40	13 43	13u52	13 55		14u07	14 10	
Northumberland Park	d												13 15												
Angel Road	d																								
Ponders End	d		12 29						12 59							13 29					13 59				
Brimsdown	d		12 32						13 02							13 32					14 02				
Enfield Lock	d		12 34						13 04				13 21			13 34					14 04				
Waltham Cross	d		12 37				12 50		13 07							13 37			13 50		14 07				
Cheshunt	d		12 39			12 48	12 53		13 09			13 18	13 25			13 39		13 48	13 53		14 09			14 18	
Broxbourne 3	a		12 44			12 52	12 57		13 14			13 22	13 29			13 44		13 52	13 57		14 14			14 22	
Broxbourne 3	d		12 44			12 52	12 57		13 14			13 22	13 33			13 44		13 52	13 57		14 14			14 22	
Rye House	d		12 47						13 17							13 47					14 17				
St Margarets (Herts)	d		12 50						13 20							13 50					14 20				
Ware	d		12 54						13 24							13 54					14 24				
Hertford East	a		13 01						13 31							14 01					14 31				
Roydon	d					12 56							13 38					13 56							
Harlow Town	d			12 54		13 00	13 09				13 24	13 28	13 42				13 54	14 00	14 09				14 24	14 28	
Harlow Mill	d					13 03							13 45					14 03							
Sawbridgeworth	d					13 07	13 15						13 48					14 07	14 15						
Bishops Stortford	a	12 45				13 14	13 22	13 17				13 38	13 56	13 45				14 14	14 22	14 17				14 38	
	d	12 45				13 14		13 18				13 39		13 45				14 14		14 18				14 39	
Stansted Mountfitchet	d					13 18					13 35							14 18					14 35		
Stansted Airport	a	12 57		13 12				13 27			13 44			13 57			14 12			14 27			14 44		
Stansted Airport	d									13 27												14 27			
Elsenham	d					13 22												14 22							
Newport (Essex)	d					13 27												14 27							
Audley End	d					13 30				13 40		13 51						14 30				14 40		14 51	
Great Chesterford	d					13 35												14 35							
Whittlesford Parkway	d					13 40						13 58						14 40						14 58	
Shelford	d					13 44												14 44							
Cambridge	a					13 51				13 58		14 08						14 51				14 58		15 08	

18 August to 25 August

London - Broxbourne, Hertford East, Bishops Stortford, Stansted Airport and Cambridge

Network Diagram - see first Page of Table 20

		LE	LE	LE	LE	LE	LE	LE	LE	XC	LE	LE	LE	LE	LE	LE	LE	LE	LE	LE	XC	LE	LE
London Liverpool Street	d		14 10	14 12	14 25	14 28		14 40	14 42		14 55	14 58		15 10	15 12	15 25	15 28		15 40	15 42		15 55	15 58
Bethnal Green	d																						
Hackney Downs	d			14 18					14 48						15 18					15 48			
Stratford	d	14 00					14 30						15 00					15 30					
Clapton	d																						
Seven Sisters	d																						
Tottenham Hale	d	14 13	14u22	14 25	14u37	14 40	14 43	14u52	14 55		15u07	15 10	15 13	15u22	15 25	15u37	15 40	15 43	15u52	15 55		16u07	16 10
Northumberland Park	d	14 15											15 15										
Angel Road	d																						
Ponders End	d			14 29					14 59						15 29					15 59			
Brimsdown	d			14 32					15 02						15 32					16 02			
Enfield Lock	d	14 21		14 34					15 04				15 21		15 34					16 04			
Waltham Cross	d			14 37			14 50		15 07						15 37			15 50		16 07			
Cheshunt	d	14 25		14 39		14 48	14 53		15 09			15 18	15 25		15 39		15 48	15 53		16 09			16 18
Broxbourne	a	14 29		14 44		14 52	14 57		15 14			15 22	15 29		15 44		15 52	15 57		16 14			16 22
Broxbourne	d	14 33		14 44		14 52	14 57		15 14			15 22	15 33		15 44		15 52	15 57		16 14			16 22
Rye House	d			14 47					15 17						15 47					16 17			
St Margarets (Herts)	d			14 50					15 20						15 50					16 20			
Ware	d			14 54					15 24						15 54					16 24			
Hertford East	a			15 01					15 31						16 01					16 31			
Roydon	d	14 38				14 56							15 38				15 56						
Harlow Town	d	14 42			14 54	15 00	15 09				15 24	15 28	15 42			15 54	16 00	16 09				16 24	16 28
Harlow Mill	d	14 45				15 03							15 45				16 03						
Sawbridgeworth	d	14 48				15 07	15 15						15 48				16 07	16 15					
Bishops Stortford	a	14 56	14 45			15 14	15 22	15 17				15 38	15 56	15 45			16 14	16 22	16 17				16 38
	d		14 45			15 14		15 18				15 39		15 45			16 14		16 18				16 39
Stansted Mountfitchet	d					15 18					15 35						16 18					16 35	
Stansted Airport	a		14 57		15 12			15 27			15 44			15 57		16 12			16 27			16 44	
Stansted Airport	d									15 27											16 27		
Elsenham	d					15 22											16 22						
Newport (Essex)	d					15 27											16 27						
Audley End	d					15 30				15 40		15 51					16 30				16 40		16 51
Great Chesterford	d					15 35											16 35						
Whittlesford Parkway	d					15 40						15 58					16 40						16 58
Shelford	d					15 44											16 44						
Cambridge	a					15 51				15 58		16 08					16 51				16 58		17 08

		LE	LE	LE	LE	LE	LE	LE	LE	XC	LE	LE	LE	LE	LE	LE	LE	LE	LE	LE	XC	LE	LE
London Liverpool Street	d		16 10	16 12	16 25	16 28		16 40	16 42		16 55	16 58		17 10	17 12	17 25	17 28		17 40	17 42		17 55	17 58
Bethnal Green	d																						
Hackney Downs	d			16 18					16 48						17 18					17 48			
Stratford	d	16 00					16 30						17 00					17 30					
Clapton	d																						
Seven Sisters	d																						
Tottenham Hale	d	16 13	16u22	16 25	16u37	16 40	16 43	16u52	16 55		17u07	17 10	17 13	17u22	17 25	17u37	17 40	17 43	17u52	17 55		18u07	18 10
Northumberland Park	d	16 15											17 15										
Angel Road	d																						
Ponders End	d			16 29					16 59						17 29					17 59			
Brimsdown	d			16 32					17 02						17 32					18 02			
Enfield Lock	d	16 21		16 34					17 04				17 21		17 34					18 04			
Waltham Cross	d			16 37			16 50		17 07						17 37			17 50		18 07			
Cheshunt	d	16 25		16 39		16 48	16 53		17 09			17 18	17 25		17 39		17 48	17 53		18 09			18 18
Broxbourne	a	16 29		16 44		16 52	16 57		17 14			17 22	17 29		17 44		17 52	17 57		18 14			18 22
Broxbourne	d	16 33		16 44		16 52	16 57		17 14			17 22	17 33		17 44		17 52	17 57		18 14			18 22
Rye House	d			16 47					17 17						17 47					18 17			
St Margarets (Herts)	d			16 50					17 20						17 50					18 20			
Ware	d			16 54					17 24						17 54					18 24			
Hertford East	a			17 01					17 31						18 01					18 31			
Roydon	d	16 38				16 56							17 38				17 56						
Harlow Town	d	16 42			16 54	17 00	17 09				17 24	17 28	17 42			17 54	18 00	18 09				18 24	18 28
Harlow Mill	d	16 45				17 03							17 45				18 03						
Sawbridgeworth	d	16 48				17 07	17 15						17 48				18 07	18 15					
Bishops Stortford	a	16 56	16 45			17 14	17 22	17 17				17 38	17 56	17 45			18 14	18 22	18 17				18 38
	d		16 45			17 14		17 18				17 39		17 45			18 14		18 18				18 39
Stansted Mountfitchet	d					17 18					17 35						18 18					18 35	
Stansted Airport	a		16 57		17 12			17 27			17 44			17 57		18 12			18 27			18 44	
Stansted Airport	d									17 27											18 27		
Elsenham	d					17 22											18 22						
Newport (Essex)	d					17 27											18 27						
Audley End	d					17 30				17 40		17 51					18 30				18 40		18 51
Great Chesterford	d					17 35											18 35						
Whittlesford Parkway	d					17 40						17 58					18 40						18 58
Shelford	d					17 44											18 44						
Cambridge	a					17 51				17 58		18 08					18 51				18 58		19 08

18 August to 25 August

London - Broxbourne, Hertford East, Bishops Stortford, Stansted Airport and Cambridge

Network Diagram - see first Page of Table 20

		LE	LE	LE	LE	LE	LE	LE	LE	XC	LE	LE	LE	LE	LE	LE	LE	LE	LE	LE	XC	LE	LE
London Liverpool Street	d		18 10	18 12	18 25	18 28		18 40	18 42		18 55	18 58		19 10	19 12	19 25	19 28		19 40	19 42		19 55	
Bethnal Green	d																						
Hackney Downs	d			18 18					18 48						19 18					19 48			
Stratford	d	18 00					18 30						19 00					19 30					
Clapton	d																						
Seven Sisters	d																						
Tottenham Hale	d	18 13	18u22	18 25	18u37	18 40	18 43	18u52	18 55		19u07	19 10	19 13	19u22	19 25	19u37	19 40	19 43	19u52	19 55		20u07	
Northumberland Park	d	18 15											19 15										
Angel Road	d																						
Ponders End	d			18 29					18 59						19 29					19 59			
Brimsdown	d			18 32					19 02						19 32					20 02			
Enfield Lock	d	18 21		18 34					19 04				19 21		19 34					20 04			
Waltham Cross	d			18 37			18 50		19 07						19 37			19 50		20 07			
Cheshunt	d	18 25		18 39		18 48	18 53		19 09			19 18	19 25		19 39		19 48	19 53		20 09			
Broxbourne	a	18 29		18 44		18 52	18 57		19 14			19 22	19 29		19 44		19 52	19 57		20 14			
Broxbourne	d	18 33		18 44		18 52	18 57		19 14			19 22	19 33		19 44		19 52	19 57		20 14			
Rye House	d			18 47					19 17						19 47					20 17			
St Margarets (Herts)	d			18 50					19 20						19 50					20 20			
Ware	d			18 54					19 24						19 54					20 24			
Hertford East	a			19 01					19 31						20 01					20 31			
Roydon	d	18 38				18 56							19 38				19 56						
Harlow Town	d	18 42			18 54	19 00	19 09				19 24	19 28	19 42			19 54	20 00	20 09				20 24	
Harlow Mill	d	18 45				19 03							19 45				20 03						
Sawbridgeworth	d	18 48				19 07	19 15						19 48				20 07	20 15					
Bishops Stortford	a	18 56	18 45			19 14	19 22	19 17				19 38	19 56	19 45			20 14	20 22	20 17				
	d		18 45			19 14		19 18				19 39		19 45			20 14		20 18				
Stansted Mountfitchet	d					19 18					19 35						20 18					20 35	
Stansted Airport	a		18 57		19 12			19 27			19 44			19 57		20 12			20 27			20 44	
Stansted Airport	d									19 27											20 27		
Elsenham	d					19 22											20 22						
Newport (Essex)	d					19 27											20 27						
Audley End	d					19 30				19 40		19 51					20 30				20 40		
Great Chesterford	d					19 35											20 35						
Whittlesford Parkway	d					19 40						19 58					20 40						
Shelford	d					19 44											20 44						
Cambridge	a					19 51				19 58		20 08					20 51				20 57		

		LE	LE	LE	LE	LE	LE	LE	LE	LE	XC	LE	LE	LE	LE	LE	LE	LE	LE	LE	LE	XC	LE
London Liverpool Street	d	19 58		20 10	20 12	20 25	20 28		20 40	20 42		20 55	20 58		21 10	21 12	21 25	21 28		21 40	21 42		21 55
Bethnal Green	d																						
Hackney Downs	d				20 18					20 48						21 18					21 48		
Stratford	d		20 00					20 30						21 00					21 30				
Clapton	d																						
Seven Sisters	d																						
Tottenham Hale	d	20 10	20 13	20u22	20 25	20u37	20 40	20 43	20u52	20 55		21u07	21 10	21 13	21u22	21 25	21u37	21 40	21 43	21u52	21 55		22u07
Northumberland Park	d		20 15											21 15									
Angel Road	d																						
Ponders End	d				20 29					20 59						21 29					21 59		
Brimsdown	d				20 32					21 02						21 32					22 02		
Enfield Lock	d		20 21		20 34					21 04				21 21		21 34					22 04		
Waltham Cross	d				20 37			20 50		21 07						21 37			21 50		22 07		
Cheshunt	d	20 18	20 25		20 39		20 48	20 53		21 09			21 18	21 25		21 39		21 48	21 53		22 09		
Broxbourne	a	20 22	20 29		20 44		20 52	20 57		21 14			21 22	21 29		21 44		21 52	21 57		22 14		
Broxbourne	d	20 22	20 33		20 44		20 52	20 57		21 14			21 22	21 33		21 44		21 52	21 57		22 14		
Rye House	d				20 47					21 17						21 47					22 17		
St Margarets (Herts)	d				20 50					21 20						21 50					22 20		
Ware	d				20 54					21 24						21 54					22 24		
Hertford East	a				21 01					21 31						22 01					22 31		
Roydon	d		20 38				20 56							21 38				21 56					
Harlow Town	d	20 28	20 42			20 54	21 00	21 09				21 24	21 28	21 42			21 54	22 00	22 09				22 24
Harlow Mill	d		20 45				21 03							21 45				22 03					
Sawbridgeworth	d		20 48				21 07	21 15						21 48				22 07	22 15				
Bishops Stortford	a	20 38	20 56	20 45			21 14	21 22	21 17				21 38	21 56	21 45			22 14	22 22	22 17			
	d	20 39		20 45			21 14		21 18				21 39		21 45			22 14		22 18			
Stansted Mountfitchet	d						21 18					21 35						22 18					22 35
Stansted Airport	a			20 57		21 12			21 27			21 44			21 57		22 12			22 27			22 44
Stansted Airport	d										21 27											22 27	
Elsenham	d						21 22											22 22					
Newport (Essex)	d						21 27											22 27					
Audley End	d	20 51					21 30				21 40		21 51					22 30				22 40	
Great Chesterford	d						21 35											22 35					
Whittlesford Parkway	d	20 58					21 40						21 58					22 40					
Shelford	d						21 44											22 44					
Cambridge	a	21 08					21 51				22 01		22 08					22 51				23 01	

Table 22

Saturdays
18 August to 25 August

London - Broxbourne, Hertford East, Bishops Stortford, Stansted Airport and Cambridge

Network Diagram - see first Page of Table 20

		LE ■	LE ■	LE ■ ⌶	LE ■	LE ■ ⌶	LE ■	LE ■	LE ■ ⌶	LE ■	XC ■	LE ■ ⌶	LE ■	LE ■	LE ■	LE ■	LE ■	LE ■	LE ■
London Liverpool Street ⊖	d	21 58		22 10	22 12	22 25	22 28		22 40	22 42		22 55	22 58		23 12	23 25	23 28	23 40	23 58
Bethnal Green	d																		
Hackney Downs	d				22 18					22 48					23 18			23 46	
Stratford ⊖	d		22 00					22 30						23 00					
Clapton	d																	23 49	
Seven Sisters ⊖	d																		
Tottenham Hale ⊖	d	22 10	22 13	22u22	22 25	22u37	22 40	22 43	22u52	22 55		23u07	23 10	23 13	23 25	23u37	23 40	23 53	00 10
Northumberland Park	d		22 15											23 15				23 55	
Angel Road	d																		
Ponders End	d				22 29					22 59					23 29			23 59	
Brimsdown	d				22 32					23 02					23 32			00 02	
Enfield Lock	d		22 21		22 34					23 04				23 21	23 34			00 04	
Waltham Cross	d				22 37			22 50		23 07					23 37			00 07	
Cheshunt	d	22 18	22 25		22 39		22 48	22 53		23 09			23 18	23 25	23 39		23 48	00 09	00 18
Broxbourne ■	a	22 22	22 29		22 44		22 52	22 57		23 14			23 22	23 29	23 44		23 52	00 14	00 22
Broxbourne ■	d	22 22	22 33		22 44		22 52	22 57		23 14			23 22	23 29	23 44		23 52	00 14	00 22
Rye House	d				22 47					23 17					23 47			00 17	
St Margarets (Herts)	d				22 50					23 20					23 50			00 20	
Ware	d				22 54					23 24					23 54			00 24	
Hertford East	a				23 01					23 31					00 01			00 31	
Roydon	d		22 38				22 56							23 33			23 56		00 26
Harlow Town	d	22 28	22 42			22 54	23 00	23 09				23 24	23 28	23 37		23 54	00 01		00 30
Harlow Mill	d		22 45				23 03							23 40			00 03		00 33
Sawbridgeworth	d		22 48				23 07	23 15						23 44			00 07		00 37
Bishops Stortford	a	22 38	22 56	22 45			23 14	23 22	23 17				23 38	23 51		00 04	00 14		00 44
	d	22 39		22 45			23 14		23 18				23 39			00 04	00 14		00 44
Stansted Mountfitchet	d						23 18					23 35					00 18		00 48
Stansted Airport	a			22 57		23 12			23 27			23 44				00 13			
Stansted Airport	d										23 27								
Elsenham	d						23 22										00 22		00 52
Newport (Essex)	d						23 27										00 27		00 57
Audley End	d	22 51					23 30				23 40		23 51				00 30		01 00
Great Chesterford	d						23 35										00 35		01 05
Whittlesford Parkway	d	22 58					23 40						23 58				00 40		01 10
Shelford	d						23 44										00 44		
Cambridge	a	23 09					23 51				23 55		00 08				00 51		01 19

Saturdays
1 September to 8 September

		LE ■	LE ■	LE ■	LE ■	LE ■	LE ■	LE ■	LE ■	LE ■	LE ■	LE ■	LE ■	XC ◇■	LE ■	LE ■	LE ■	LE ■	LE ■	LE ■	LE ■	XC ◇■	LE ■
London Liverpool Street ⊖	d	22p42		23p12	23p22	23p25				23p42		00 18	04 10		04 40	05 10	05 21	05 25		05 40	05 42		05 51
Bethnal Green	d																						
Hackney Downs	d																				05 48		
Stratford ⊖	d	22p55	23p15	23p25	23p35				23p45	23p55	00 15	00 30					05 30						06 00
Clapton	d																						
Seven Sisters ⊖	d						←	←											←				
Tottenham Hale ⊖	d	23p10	23p25	23p40	23p45	23 37	23p40	23p45	23p55	00 10	00 25	00 40			04u52	05u22	05 40	05u37	05 40	05u52	05 55		06 13
Northumberland Park	d			→	→				23p57								→						→
Angel Road	d																						
Ponders End	d		23p29						00 01		00 29										05 59		
Brimsdown	d		23p32						00 04		00 32										06 02		
Enfield Lock	d		23p34						00 06		00 34										06 04		
Waltham Cross	d		23p37					23p52	00 09		00 37										06 07		
Cheshunt	d	23p18	23p39				23p48	23p55	00 11	00 18	00 39	00 48			05 00				05 48		06 09		
Broxbourne ■	a	23p22	23p44				23p52	23p59	00 16	00 22	00 44	00 52			05 04				05 52		06 14		
Broxbourne ■	d	23p22	23p44				23p52	23p59	00 16	00 22	00 44	00 52			05 04				05 52		06 14		
Rye House	d		23p47						00 19		00 47										06 17		
St Margarets (Herts)	d		23p50						00 22		00 50										06 20		
Ware	d		23p54						00 26		00 54										06 24		
Hertford East	a		00 01						00 33		01 01										06 31		
Roydon	d						23p56			00 26									05 56				
Harlow Town	d	23p28				23p54	23p59	00 09		00 30		00 58			05 10	05 37		05 52	06 00				
Harlow Mill	d						00 03			00 33									06 03				
Sawbridgeworth	d						00 07	00 15		00 37		01 03				05 42			06 07				
Bishops Stortford	a	23p38				00 04	00 14	00 22		00 44		01 10			05 20	05 49		06 02	06 14	06 17			
	d	23p39				00 04	00 14			00 44		01 11			05 20	05 50		06 02	06 14	06 18			
Stansted Mountfitchet	d						00 18			00 48		01 15			05 24			06 05	06 18				
Stansted Airport	a					00 13							05 00		05 39	05 59		06 13		06 27			
Stansted Airport	d													05 25								06 27	
Elsenham	d						00 22			00 52		01 19							06 22				
Newport (Essex)	d						00 27			00 57		01 24							06 27				
Audley End	d	23p51					00 30			01 00		01 27		05 37					06 30			06 40	
Great Chesterford	d						00 35			01 05		01 32							06 35				
Whittlesford Parkway	d	23p58					00 40			01 10		01 37							06 40				
Shelford	d						00 44					01 41							06 44				
Cambridge	a	00 08					00 51			01 19		01 49		05 54					06 51			06 56	

Table 22

Saturdays
1 September to 8 September

London - Broxbourne, Hertford East, Bishops Stortford, Stansted Airport and Cambridge

Network Diagram - see first Page of Table 20

		LE ■	LE ■	LE ■	LE ■	LE ■	LE ■	LE ■	LE ■	LE ■	LE ■	LE ■	XC ◇■	LE ■	LE ■	LE ■	LE ■ ⌶	LE ■	LE ■ ⌶	LE ■	LE ■	LE ■ ⌶	LE ■
London Liverpool Street ⊖	d	05 55	05 58		06 10	06 12	06 21	06 25	06 28		06 40	06 42		06 55	06 58		07 10	07 12	07 25	07 28		07 40	07 42
Bethnal Green	d																						
Hackney Downs	d					06 18						06 48						07 18					07 48
Stratford ⊖	d						06 30									07 00					07 30		
Clapton	d																						
Seven Sisters ⊖	d			←						←													
Tottenham Hale ⊖	d	06u07	06 10	06 13	06u22	06 25	06 43	06u37	06 40	06 43	06u52	06 55		07u07	07 10	07 13	07u22	07 25	07u37	07 40	07 43	07u52	07 55
Northumberland Park	d			06 15			→									07 15							
Angel Road	d																						
Ponders End	d					06 29						06 59						07 29					07 59
Brimsdown	d					06 32						07 02						07 32					08 02
Enfield Lock	d			06 21		06 34						07 04				07 21		07 34					08 04
Waltham Cross	d					06 37				06 50		07 07						07 37			07 50		08 07
Cheshunt	d		06 18	06 25		06 39			06 48	06 53		07 09			07 18	07 25		07 39		07 48	07 53		08 09
Broxbourne ■	a		06 22	06 29		06 44			06 52	06 57		07 14			07 22	07 29		07 44		07 52	07 57		08 14
Broxbourne ■	d		06 22	06 33		06 44			06 52	06 57		07 14			07 22	07 33		07 44		07 52	07 57		08 14
Rye House	d					06 47						07 17						07 47					08 17
St Margarets (Herts)	d					06 50						07 20						07 50					08 20
Ware	d					06 54						07 24						07 54					08 24
Hertford East	a					07 01						07 31						08 01					08 31
Roydon	d			06 38					06 56							07 38				07 56			
Harlow Town	d	06 24	06 28	06 42				06 54	07 00	07 09				07 24	07 28	07 42			07 54	08 00	08 09		
Harlow Mill	d			06 45					07 03							07 45				08 03			
Sawbridgeworth	d			06 48					07 07	07 15						07 48				08 07	08 15		
Bishops Stortford	a		06 38	06 56	06 45				07 14	07 22	07 17				07 38	07 56	07 45			08 14	08 22	08 17	
	d		06 39		06 45				07 14		07 18				07 39		07 45			08 14		08 18	
Stansted Mountfitchet	d	06 35							07 18					07 35						08 18			
Stansted Airport	a	06 44			06 57			07 12			07 27			07 44			07 57		08 12			08 27	
Stansted Airport	d												07 27										
Elsenham	d								07 22											08 22			
Newport (Essex)	d								07 27											08 27			
Audley End	d		06 51						07 30				07 40		07 51					08 30			
Great Chesterford	d								07 35											08 35			
Whittlesford Parkway	d		06 58						07 40						07 58					08 40			
Shelford	d								07 44											08 44			
Cambridge	a		07 08						07 51				07 58		08 08					08 51			

		XC ◇■	LE ■ ⌶	LE ■	LE ■	LE ■ ⌶	LE ■	LE ■ ⌶	LE ■	LE ■	LE ■ ⌶	LE ■	XC ◇■	LE ■ ⌶	LE ■	LE ■	LE ■ ⌶	LE ■	LE ■ ⌶	LE ■	LE ■	LE ■ ⌶
London Liverpool Street ⊖	d		07 55	07 58		08 10	08 12	08 25	08 28		08 40	08 42		08 55	08 58		09 10	09 12	09 25	09 28		09 40
Bethnal Green	d																					
Hackney Downs	d						08 18					08 48						09 18				
Stratford ⊖	d				08 00					08 30						09 00					09 30	
Clapton	d																					
Seven Sisters ⊖	d																					
Tottenham Hale ⊖	d		08u07	08 10	08 13	08u22	08 25	08u37	08 40	08 43	08u52	08 55		09u07	09 10	09 13	09u22	09 25	09u37	09 40	09 43	09u52
Northumberland Park	d				08 15											09 15						
Angel Road	d																					
Ponders End	d						08 29					08 59						09 29				
Brimsdown	d						08 32					09 02						09 32				
Enfield Lock	d				08 21		08 34					09 04				09 21		09 34				
Waltham Cross	d						08 37			08 50		09 07						09 37			09 50	
Cheshunt	d			08 18	08 25		08 39		08 48	08 53		09 09			09 18	09 25		09 39		09 48	09 53	
Broxbourne ■	a			08 22	08 29		08 44		08 52	08 57		09 14			09 22	09 29		09 44		09 52	09 57	
Broxbourne ■	d			08 22	08 33		08 44		08 52	08 57		09 14			09 22	09 33		09 44		09 52	09 57	
Rye House	d						08 47					09 17						09 47				
St Margarets (Herts)	d						08 50					09 20						09 50				
Ware	d						08 54					09 24						09 54				
Hertford East	a						09 01					09 31						10 01				
Roydon	d				08 38				08 56							09 38				09 56		
Harlow Town	d		08 24	08 28	08 42			08 54	09 00	09 09				09 24	09 28	09 42			09 54	10 00	10 09	
Harlow Mill	d				08 45				09 03							09 45				10 03		
Sawbridgeworth	d				08 48				09 07	09 15						09 48				10 07	10 15	
Bishops Stortford	a			08 38	08 56	08 45			09 14	09 22	09 17				09 38	09 56	09 45			10 14	10 22	10 17
	d			08 39		08 45			09 14		09 18				09 39		09 45			10 14		10 18
Stansted Mountfitchet	d		08 35						09 18					09 35						10 18		
Stansted Airport	a		08 44			08 57		09 12			09 27			09 44			09 57		10 12			10 27
Stansted Airport	d	08 27											09 27									
Elsenham	d								09 22											10 22		
Newport (Essex)	d								09 27											10 27		
Audley End	d	08 40		08 51					09 30				09 40		09 51					10 30		
Great Chesterford	d								09 35											10 35		
Whittlesford Parkway	d			08 58					09 40						09 58					10 40		
Shelford	d								09 44											10 44		
Cambridge	a	08 58		09 08					09 51				09 58		10 08					10 51		

London - Broxbourne, Hertford East, Bishops Stortford, Stansted Airport and Cambridge

Network Diagram - see first Page of Table 20

		LE 1	XC ◇1	LE 1 ⊼	LE 1	LE 1	LE 1 ⊼	LE 1	LE 1 ⊼	LE 1	LE 1	LE 1 ⊼	LE 1	XC ◇1	LE 1 ⊼	LE 1	LE 1	LE 1 ⊼	LE 1	LE 1 ⊼	LE 1	LE 1	LE 1 ⊼
London Liverpool Street 15 ⊖	d	09 42		09 55	09 58		10 10	10 12	10 25	10 28		10 40	10 42		10 55	10 58		11 10	11 12	11 25	11 28		11 40
Bethnal Green	d																						
Hackney Downs	d	09 48						10 18					10 48						11 18				
Stratford 7 ⊖	d					10 00					10 30						11 00					11 30	
Clapton	d																						
Seven Sisters ⊖	d																						
Tottenham Hale ⊖	d	09 55		10u07	10 10	10 13	10u22	10 25	10u37	10 40	10 43	10u52	10 55		11u07	11 10	11 13	11u22	11 25	11u37	11 40	11 43	11u52
Northumberland Park	d					10 15											11 15						
Angel Road	d																						
Ponders End	d	09 59						10 29					10 59						11 29				
Brimsdown	d	10 02						10 32					11 02						11 32				
Enfield Lock	d	10 04				10 21		10 34					11 04				11 21		11 34				
Waltham Cross	d	10 07						10 37			10 50		11 07						11 37			11 50	
Cheshunt	d	10 09			10 18	10 25		10 39		10 48	10 53		11 09			11 18	11 25		11 39		11 48	11 53	
Broxbourne 3	a	10 14			10 22	10 29		10 44		10 52	10 57		11 14			11 22	11 29		11 44		11 52	11 57	
Broxbourne 3	d	10 14			10 22	10 33		10 44		10 52	10 57		11 14			11 22	11 33		11 44		11 52	11 57	
Rye House	d	10 17						10 47					11 17						11 47				
St Margarets (Herts)	d	10 20						10 50					11 20						11 50				
Ware	d	10 24						10 54					11 24						11 54				
Hertford East	a	10 31						11 01					11 31						12 01				
Roydon	d					10 38				10 56							11 38				11 56		
Harlow Town	d			10 24	10 28	10 42			10 54	11 00	11 09				11 24	11 28	11 42			11 54	12 00	12 09	
Harlow Mill	d					10 45				11 03							11 45				12 03		
Sawbridgeworth	d					10 48				11 07	11 15						11 48				12 07	12 15	
Bishops Stortford	a				10 38	10 56	10 45			11 14	11 22	11 17				11 38	11 56	11 45			12 14	12 22	12 17
	d				10 39		10 45			11 14		11 18				11 39		11 45			12 14		12 18
Stansted Mountfitchet	d			10 35						11 18					11 35						12 18		
Stansted Airport	a			10 44			10 57		11 13			11 27			11 44			11 57		12 12			12 27
Stansted Airport	d		10 27											11 27									
Elsenham	d									11 22											12 22		
Newport (Essex)	d									11 27											12 27		
Audley End	d		10 40		10 51					11 30				11 40		11 51					12 30		
Great Chesterford	d									11 35											12 35		
Whittlesford Parkway	d				10 58					11 40						11 58					12 40		
Shelford	d									11 44											12 44		
Cambridge	a		10 58		11 08					11 51				11 58		12 08					12 51		

		LE 1	XC ◇1	LE 1 ⊼	LE 1	LE 1	LE 1 ⊼	LE 1	LE 1 ⊼	LE 1	LE 1	LE 1 ⊼	LE 1	XC ◇1	LE 1 ⊼	LE 1	LE 1	LE 1 ⊼	LE 1	LE 1 ⊼	LE 1	LE 1
London Liverpool Street 15 ⊖	d	11 42		11 55	11 58		12 10	12 12	12 25	12 28		12 40	12 42		12 55	12 58		13 10	13 12	13 25	13 28	
Bethnal Green	d																					
Hackney Downs	d	11 48						12 18					12 48						13 18			
Stratford 7 ⊖	d					12 00					12 30						13 00					13 30
Clapton	d																					
Seven Sisters ⊖	d																					
Tottenham Hale ⊖	d	11 55		12u07	12 10	12 13	12u22	12 25	12u37	12 40	12 43	12u52	12 55		13u07	13 10	13 13	13u22	13 25	13u37	13 40	13 43
Northumberland Park	d					12 15											13 15					
Angel Road	d																					
Ponders End	d	11 59						12 29					12 59						13 29			
Brimsdown	d	12 02						12 32					13 02						13 32			
Enfield Lock	d	12 04				12 21		12 34					13 04				13 21		13 34			
Waltham Cross	d	12 07						12 37			12 50		13 07						13 37			13 50
Cheshunt	d	12 09			12 18	12 25		12 39		12 48	12 53		13 09			13 18	13 25		13 39		13 48	13 53
Broxbourne 3	a	12 14			12 22	12 29		12 44		12 52	12 57		13 14			13 22	13 29		13 44		13 52	13 57
Broxbourne 3	d	12 14			12 22	12 33		12 44		12 52	12 57		13 14			13 22	13 33		13 44		13 52	13 57
Rye House	d	12 17						12 47					13 17						13 47			
St Margarets (Herts)	d	12 20						12 50					13 20						13 50			
Ware	d	12 24						12 54					13 24						13 54			
Hertford East	a	12 31						13 01					13 31						14 01			
Roydon	d					12 38				12 56							13 38				13 56	
Harlow Town	d			12 24	12 28	12 42			12 54	13 00	13 09				13 24	13 28	13 42			13 54	14 00	14 09
Harlow Mill	d					12 45				13 03							13 45				14 03	
Sawbridgeworth	d					12 48				13 07	13 15						13 48				14 07	14 15
Bishops Stortford	a				12 38	12 56	12 45			13 14	13 22	13 17				13 38	13 56	13 45			14 14	14 22
	d				12 39		12 45			13 14		13 18				13 39		13 45			14 14	
Stansted Mountfitchet	d			12 35						13 18					13 35						14 18	
Stansted Airport	a			12 44			12 57		13 12			13 27			13 44			13 57		14 12		
Stansted Airport	d		12 27											13 27								
Elsenham	d									13 22											14 22	
Newport (Essex)	d									13 27											14 27	
Audley End	d		12 40		12 51					13 30				13 40		13 51					14 30	
Great Chesterford	d									13 35											14 35	
Whittlesford Parkway	d				12 58					13 40						13 58					14 40	
Shelford	d									13 44											14 44	
Cambridge	a		12 58		13 08					13 51				13 58		14 08					14 51	

London - Broxbourne, Hertford East, Bishops Stortford, Stansted Airport and Cambridge

Network Diagram - see first Page of Table 20

		LE 1 ⊼	LE 1	XC ◇1	LE 1 ⊼	LE 1	LE 1	LE 1 ⊼	LE 1	LE 1 ⊼	LE 1	LE 1	LE 1 ⊼	LE 1	XC ◇1	LE 1 ⊼	LE 1	LE 1	LE 1 ⊼	LE 1	LE 1 ⊼	LE 1	LE 1
London Liverpool Street 15 ⊖	d	13 40	13 42		13 55	13 58		14 10	14 12	14 25	14 28		14 40	14 42		14 55	14 58		15 10	15 12	15 25	15 28	
Bethnal Green	d																						
Hackney Downs	d		13 48						14 18					14 48						15 18			
Stratford 7 ⊖	d						14 00					14 30						15 00					15 30
Clapton	d																						
Seven Sisters ⊖	d																						
Tottenham Hale ⊖	d	13u52	13 55		14u07	14 10	14 13	14u22	14 25	14u37	14 40	14 43	14u52	14 55		15u07	15 10	15 13	15u22	15 25	15u37	15 40	15 43
Northumberland Park	d						14 15											15 15					
Angel Road	d																						
Ponders End	d		13 59						14 29					14 59						15 29			
Brimsdown	d		14 02						14 32					15 02						15 32			
Enfield Lock	d		14 04				14 21		14 34					15 04				15 21		15 34			
Waltham Cross	d		14 07						14 37			14 50		15 07						15 37			15 50
Cheshunt	d		14 09			14 18	14 25		14 39		14 48	14 53		15 09			15 18	15 25		15 39		15 48	15 53
Broxbourne 3	a		14 14			14 22	14 29		14 44		14 52	14 57		15 14			15 22	15 29		15 44		15 52	15 57
Broxbourne 3	d		14 14			14 22	14 33		14 44		14 52	14 57		15 14			15 22	15 33		15 44		15 52	15 57
Rye House	d		14 17						14 47					15 17						15 47			
St Margarets (Herts)	d		14 20						14 50					15 20						15 50			
Ware	d		14 24						14 54					15 24						15 54			
Hertford East	a		14 31						15 01					15 31						16 01			
Roydon	d						14 38				14 56							15 38				15 56	
Harlow Town	d				14 24	14 28	14 42			14 54	15 00	15 09				15 24	15 28	15 42			15 54	16 00	16 09
Harlow Mill	d						14 45				15 03							15 45				16 03	
Sawbridgeworth	d						14 48				15 07	15 15						15 48				16 07	16 15
Bishops Stortford	a	14 17				14 38	14 56	14 45			15 14	15 22	15 17				15 38	15 56	15 45			16 14	16 22
	d	14 18				14 39		14 45			15 14		15 18				15 39		15 45			16 14	
Stansted Mountfitchet	d				14 35						15 18					15 35						16 18	
Stansted Airport	a	14 27			14 44			14 57		15 12			15 27			15 44			15 57		16 12		
Stansted Airport	d			14 27											15 27								
Elsenham	d										15 22											16 22	
Newport (Essex)	d										15 27											16 27	
Audley End	d			14 40		14 51					15 30				15 40		15 51					16 30	
Great Chesterford	d										15 35											16 35	
Whittlesford Parkway	d					14 58					15 40						15 58					16 40	
Shelford	d										15 44											16 44	
Cambridge	a			14 58		15 08					15 51				15 58		16 08					16 51	

		LE 1 ⊼	LE 1	XC ◇1	LE 1 ⊼	LE 1	LE 1	LE 1 ⊼	LE 1	LE 1 ⊼	LE 1	LE 1	LE 1 ⊼	LE 1	XC ◇1	LE 1 ⊼	LE 1	LE 1	LE 1 ⊼	LE 1	LE 1 ⊼	LE 1	LE 1
London Liverpool Street 15 ⊖	d	15 40	15 42		15 55	15 58		16 10	16 12	16 25	16 28		16 40	16 42		16 55	16 58		17 10	17 12	17 25	17 28	
Bethnal Green	d																						
Hackney Downs	d		15 48						16 18					16 48						17 18			
Stratford 7 ⊖	d						16 00					16 30						17 00					17 30
Clapton	d																						
Seven Sisters ⊖	d																						
Tottenham Hale ⊖	d	15u52	15 55		16u07	16 10	16 13	16u22	16 25	16u37	16 40	16 43	16u52	16 55		17u07	17 10	17 13	17u22	17 25	17u37	17 40	17 43
Northumberland Park	d						16 15											17 15					
Angel Road	d																						
Ponders End	d		15 59						16 29					16 59						17 29			
Brimsdown	d		16 02						16 32					17 02						17 32			
Enfield Lock	d		16 04				16 21		16 34					17 04				17 21		17 34			
Waltham Cross	d		16 07						16 37			16 50		17 07						17 37			17 50
Cheshunt	d		16 09			16 18	16 25		16 39		16 48	16 53		17 09			17 18	17 25		17 39		17 48	17 53
Broxbourne 3	a		16 14			16 22	16 29		16 44		16 52	16 57		17 14			17 22	17 29		17 44		17 52	17 57
Broxbourne 3	d		16 14			16 22	16 33		16 44		16 52	16 57		17 14			17 22	17 33		17 44		17 52	17 57
Rye House	d		16 17						16 47					17 17						17 47			
St Margarets (Herts)	d		16 20						16 50					17 20						17 50			
Ware	d		16 24						16 54					17 24						17 54			
Hertford East	a		16 31						17 01					17 31						18 01			
Roydon	d						16 38				16 56							17 38				17 56	
Harlow Town	d				16 24	16 28	16 42			16 54	17 00	17 09				17 24	17 28	17 42			17 54	18 00	18 09
Harlow Mill	d						16 45				17 03							17 45				18 03	
Sawbridgeworth	d						16 48				17 07	17 15						17 48				18 07	18 15
Bishops Stortford	a	16 17				16 38	16 56	16 45			17 14	17 22	17 17				17 38	17 56	17 45			18 14	18 22
	d	16 18				16 39		16 45			17 14		17 18				17 39		17 45			18 14	
Stansted Mountfitchet	d				16 35						17 18					17 35						18 18	
Stansted Airport	a	16 27			16 44			16 57		17 12			17 27			17 44			17 57		18 12		
Stansted Airport	d			16 27											17 27								
Elsenham	d										17 22											18 22	
Newport (Essex)	d										17 27											18 27	
Audley End	d			16 40		16 51					17 30				17 40		17 51					18 30	
Great Chesterford	d										17 35											18 35	
Whittlesford Parkway	d					16 58					17 40						17 58					18 40	
Shelford	d										17 44											18 44	
Cambridge	a			16 58		17 08					17 51				17 58		18 08					18 51	

Table 22

Saturdays

1 September to 8 September

London - Broxbourne, Hertford East, Bishops Stortford, Stansted Airport and Cambridge

Network Diagram - see first Page of Table 20

		LE 1 ✠	LE 1	XC ◇1	LE 1 ✠	LE 1	LE 1	LE 1 ✠	LE 1	LE 1 ✠	LE 1	LE 1	LE 1 ✠	LE 1	XC ◇1	LE 1 ✠	LE 1	LE 1	LE 1 ✠	LE 1	LE 1 ✠	LE 1
London Liverpool Street 15 ⊖	d	17 40	17 42		17 55	17 58		18 10	18 12	18 25	18 28		18 40	18 42		18 55	18 58		19 10	19 12	19 25	19 28
Bethnal Green	d																					
Hackney Downs	d		17 48						18 18					18 48						19 18		
Stratford 7 ⊖	d						18 00					18 30						19 00				
Clapton	d																					
Seven Sisters ⊖	d																					
Tottenham Hale ⊖	d	17u52	17 55		18u07	18 10	18 13	18u22	18 25	18u37	18 40	18 43	18u52	18 55		19u07	19 10	19 13	19u22	19 25	19u37	19 40
Northumberland Park	d						18 15											19 15				
Angel Road	d																					
Ponders End	d		17 59						18 29					18 59						19 29		
Brimsdown	d		18 02						18 32					19 02						19 32		
Enfield Lock	d		18 04				18 21		18 34					19 04				19 21		19 34		
Waltham Cross	d		18 07						18 37			18 50		19 07						19 37		
Cheshunt	d		18 09			18 18	18 25		18 39		18 48	18 53		19 09			19 18	19 25		19 39		19 48
Broxbourne 3	a		18 14			18 22	18 29		18 44		18 52	18 57		19 14			19 22	19 29		19 44		19 52
Broxbourne 3	d		18 14			18 22	18 33		18 44		18 52	18 57		19 14			19 22	19 33		19 44		19 52
Rye House	d		18 17						18 47					19 17						19 47		
St Margarets (Herts)	d		18 20						18 50					19 20						19 50		
Ware	d		18 24						18 54					19 24						19 54		
Hertford East	a		18 31						19 01					19 31						20 01		
Roydon	d						18 38				18 56							19 38				19 56
Harlow Town	d				18 24	18 28	18 42			18 54	19 00	19 09				19 24	19 28	19 42			19 54	20 00
Harlow Mill	d						18 45				19 03							19 45				20 03
Sawbridgeworth	d						18 48				19 07	19 15						19 48				20 07
Bishops Stortford	a	18 17				18 38	18 56	18 45			19 14	19 22	19 17				19 38	19 56	19 45			20 14
	d	18 18				18 39		18 45			19 14		19 18				19 39		19 45			20 14
Stansted Mountfitchet	d				18 35						19 18					19 35						20 18
Stansted Airport	a	18 27			18 44			18 57		19 12			19 27			19 44			19 57		20 12	
Stansted Airport	d			18 27											19 27							
Elsenham	d										19 22											20 22
Newport (Essex)	d										19 27											20 27
Audley End	d			18 40		18 51					19 30				19 40		19 51					20 30
Great Chesterford	d										19 35											20 35
Whittlesford Parkway	d					18 58					19 40						19 58					20 40
Shelford	d										19 44											20 44
Cambridge	a			18 58		19 08					19 51				19 58		20 08					20 51

		LE 1	LE 1 ✠	LE 1	XC 1	LE 1 ✠	LE 1	LE 1	LE 1 ✠	LE 1	LE 1 ✠	LE 1	LE 1	LE 1 ✠	LE 1	XC 1	LE 1 ✠	LE 1	LE 1	LE 1 ✠	LE 1	LE 1 ✠	LE 1
London Liverpool Street 15 ⊖	d		19 40	19 42		19 55	19 58		20 10	20 12	20 25	20 28		20 40	20 42		20 55	20 58		21 10	21 12	21 25	21 28
Bethnal Green	d																						
Hackney Downs	d			19 48						20 18					20 48						21 18		
Stratford 7 ⊖	d	19 30						20 00					20 30						21 00				
Clapton	d																						
Seven Sisters ⊖	d																						
Tottenham Hale ⊖	d	19 43	19u52	19 55		20u07	20 10	20 13	20u22	20 25	20u37	20 40	20 43	20u52	20 55		21u07	21 10	21 13	21u22	21 25	21u37	21 40
Northumberland Park	d							20 15											21 15				
Angel Road	d																						
Ponders End	d			19 59						20 29					20 59						21 29		
Brimsdown	d			20 02						20 32					21 02						21 32		
Enfield Lock	d			20 04				20 21		20 34					21 04				21 21		21 34		
Waltham Cross	d	19 50		20 07						20 37			20 50		21 07						21 37		
Cheshunt	d	19 53		20 09			20 18	20 25		20 39		20 48	20 53		21 09			21 18	21 25		21 39		21 48
Broxbourne 3	a	19 57		20 14			20 22	20 29		20 44		20 52	20 57		21 14			21 22	21 29		21 44		21 52
Broxbourne 3	d	19 57		20 14			20 22	20 33		20 44		20 52	20 57		21 14			21 22	21 33		21 44		21 52
Rye House	d			20 17						20 47					21 17						21 47		
St Margarets (Herts)	d			20 20						20 50					21 20						21 50		
Ware	d			20 24						20 54					21 24						21 54		
Hertford East	a			20 31						21 01					21 31						22 01		
Roydon	d							20 38				20 56							21 38				21 56
Harlow Town	d	20 09				20 24	20 28	20 42			20 54	21 00	21 09				21 24	21 28	21 42			21 54	22 00
Harlow Mill	d							20 45				21 03							21 45				22 03
Sawbridgeworth	d	20 15						20 48				21 07	21 15						21 48				22 07
Bishops Stortford	a	20 22	20 17				20 38	20 56	20 45			21 14	21 22	21 17				21 38	21 56	21 45			22 14
	d		20 18				20 39		20 45			21 14		21 18				21 39		21 45			22 14
Stansted Mountfitchet	d					20 35						21 18					21 35						22 18
Stansted Airport	a		20 27			20 44			20 57		21 12			21 27			21 44			21 57		22 12	
Stansted Airport	d				20 27											21 27							
Elsenham	d											21 22											22 22
Newport (Essex)	d											21 27											22 27
Audley End	d				20 40		20 51					21 30				21 40		21 51					22 30
Great Chesterford	d											21 35											22 35
Whittlesford Parkway	d						20 58					21 40						21 58					22 40
Shelford	d											21 44											22 44
Cambridge	a				20 57		21 08					21 51				22 01		22 08					22 51

Table 22

Saturdays

1 September to 8 September

London - Broxbourne, Hertford East, Bishops Stortford, Stansted Airport and Cambridge

Network Diagram - see first Page of Table 20

		XC 1	LE 1	LE 1 ✠	LE 1	LE 1	LE 1	LE 1 ✠	LE 1	LE 1	LE 1 ✠	LE 1	LE 1	LE 1	LE 1 ✠	LE 1	LE 1	LE 1 ✠	LE 1	XC 1	LE 1	LE 1
London Liverpool Street 15 ⊖	d			21 40		21 42	21 42	21 55		21 58	22 10		22 12	22 22	22 25			22 40			22 42	22 52
Bethnal Green	d																					
Hackney Downs	d					21 48																
Stratford 7 ⊖	d		21 30				21 55					22 15	22 25	22 35					22 45		22 55	23 05
Clapton	d																					
Seven Sisters ⊖	d								←							←	←					
Tottenham Hale ⊖	d		21 43	21u52		21 55	22 10	22u07	22 10	22 13	22 22	22 25	22 40	22 45	22u37	22 40	22 45	22 52	22 55		23 10	23 15
Northumberland Park	d						→			22 15			→	→							→	→
Angel Road	d																					
Ponders End	d					21 59						22 29							22 59			
Brimsdown	d					22 02						22 32							23 02			
Enfield Lock	d					22 04				22 21		22 34							23 04			
Waltham Cross	d		21 50			22 07						22 37					22 52		23 07			
Cheshunt	d		21 53			22 09			22 18	22 25		22 39				22 48	22 55		23 09			
Broxbourne 3	a		21 57			22 14			22 22	22 29		22 44				22 52	22 59		23 14			
Broxbourne 3	d		21 57			22 14			22 22	22 33		22 44				22 52	22 59		23 14			
Rye House	d					22 17						22 47							23 17			
St Margarets (Herts)	d					22 20						22 50							23 20			
Ware	d					22 24						22 54							23 24			
Hertford East	a					22 31						23 01							23 31			
Roydon	d									22 38						22 56						
Harlow Town	d		22 09					22 24	22 28	22 42					22 54	23 00	23 09					
Harlow Mill	d									22 45						23 03						
Sawbridgeworth	d		22 15		←					22 48						23 07	23 15					
Bishops Stortford	a		22 22	22 17	22 22				22 38	22 56	22 45					23 14	23 22	23 17				
	d		22 23	22 18	22 23				22 39		22 45					23 14		23 18				
Stansted Mountfitchet	d		→					22 35								23 18						
Stansted Airport	a			22 27	22 39			22 45			22 57				23 12			23 27				
Stansted Airport	d	22 27																		23 27		
Elsenham	d															23 22						
Newport (Essex)	d															23 27						
Audley End	d	22 40							22 51							23 30				23 40		
Great Chesterford	d															23 35						
Whittlesford Parkway	d								22 58							23 40						
Shelford	d															23 44						
Cambridge	a	23 01							23 09							23 51				23 55		

		LE 1 ✠	LE 1	LE 1	LE 1	LE 1	LE 1	LE 1	LE 1	LE 1
London Liverpool Street 15 ⊖	d	22 55				23 12	23 25			23 42
Bethnal Green	d									
Hackney Downs	d									
Stratford 7 ⊖	d				23 15	23 25			23 45	23 55
Clapton	d									
Seven Sisters ⊖	d		←	←				←		
Tottenham Hale ⊖	d	23 07	23 10	23 15	23 25	23 40	23u37	23 40	23 55	00 10
Northumberland Park	d			23 17		→			23 57	
Angel Road	d									
Ponders End	d				23 29				00 01	
Brimsdown	d				23 32				00 04	
Enfield Lock	d			23 23	23 34				00 06	
Waltham Cross	d				23 37				00 09	
Cheshunt	d		23 18	23 27	23 39			23 48	00 11	00 18
Broxbourne 3	a		23 22	23 31	23 44			23 52	00 16	00 22
Broxbourne 3	d		23 22	23 31	23 44			23 52	00 16	00 22
Rye House	d				23 47				00 19	
St Margarets (Herts)	d				23 50				00 22	
Ware	d				23 54				00 26	
Hertford East	a				00 01				00 33	
Roydon	d			23 35				23 56		00 26
Harlow Town	d	23 24	23 28	23 39			23 54	00 01		00 30
Harlow Mill	d			23 42				00 03		00 33
Sawbridgeworth	d			23 46				00 07		00 37
Bishops Stortford	a		23 38	23 56			00 04	00 14		00 44
	d		23 39				00 04	00 14		00 44
Stansted Mountfitchet	d	23 35						00 18		00 48
Stansted Airport	a	23 44					00 13			
Stansted Airport	d									
Elsenham	d							00 22		00 52
Newport (Essex)	d							00 27		00 57
Audley End	d		23 51					00 30		01 00
Great Chesterford	d							00 35		01 05
Whittlesford Parkway	d		23 58					00 40		01 10
Shelford	d							00 44		
Cambridge	a		00 08					00 51		01 19

London - Broxbourne, Hertford East, Bishops Stortford, Stansted Airport and Cambridge

Network Diagram - see first Page of Table 20

		LE	LE	LE	LE	LE	LE	LE	XC ◇	LE	LE	LE	LE	LE	LE	LE	XC ◇	LE	LE	LE	LE	LE	LE
London Liverpool Street 15 ⊖	d	22p58	23p12	23p25	23p28	23p40	23p58	04 10		04 40	05 10	05 21	05 25		05 40	05 42		05 51	05 55	05 58		06 10	06 12
Bethnal Green	d																						
Hackney Downs	d		23p18			23p46										05 48							06 18
Stratford 7 ⊖	d											05 30						06 00					
Clapton	d					23p49																	
Seven Sisters ⊖	d													←							←		
Tottenham Hale ⊖	d	23p10	23p25	23b37	23p40	23p53	00 10			04u52	05u22	05 40	05u37	05 40	05u52	05 55		06 13	06u07	06 10	06 13	06u22	06 25
Northumberland Park	d					23p55						→						→			06 15		
Angel Road	d																						
Ponders End	d		23p29			23p59										05 59							06 29
Brimsdown	d		23p32			00 02										06 02							06 32
Enfield Lock	d		23p34			00 04										06 04					06 21		06 34
Waltham Cross	d		23p37			00 07										06 07							06 37
Cheshunt	d	23p18	23p39		23p48	00 09	00 18			05 00				05 48		06 09				06 18	06 25		06 39
Broxbourne 3	a	23p22	23p44		23p52	00 14	00 22			05 04				05 52		06 14				06 22	06 29		06 44
Broxbourne 3	d	23p22	23p44		23p52	00 14	00 22			05 04				05 52		06 14				06 22	06 33		06 44
Rye House	d		23p47			00 17										06 17							06 47
St Margarets (Herts)	d		23p50			00 20										06 20							06 50
Ware	d		23p54			00 24										06 24							06 54
Hertford East	a		00 01			00 31										06 31							07 01
Roydon	d				23p56		00 26							05 56							06 38		
Harlow Town	d	23p28		23p54	23p59		00 30			05 10	05 37		05 52	06 00					06 24	06 28	06 42		
Harlow Mill	d				00 03		00 33							06 03							06 45		
Sawbridgeworth	d				00 07		00 37				05 42			06 07							06 48		
Bishops Stortford	a	23p38		00 04	00 14		00 44			05 20	05 49		06 02	06 14	06 17					06 38	06 56	06 45	
	d	23p39		00 04	00 14		00 44			05 20	05 50		06 02	06 14	06 18					06 39		06 45	
Stansted Mountfitchet	d				00 18		00 48			05 24			06 05	06 18					06 35				
Stansted Airport	a			00 13				05 00		05 39	05 59		06 13		06 27				06 44			06 57	
Stansted Airport	d								05 25								06 27						
Elsenham	d				00 22		00 52							06 22									
Newport (Essex)	d				00 27		00 57							06 27									
Audley End	d	23p51			00 30		01 00		05 37					06 30			06 40			06 51			
Great Chesterford	d				00 35		01 05							06 35									
Whittlesford Parkway	d	23p58			00 40		01 10							06 40									
Shelford	d				00 44									06 44						06 58			
Cambridge	a	00 08			00 51		01 19		05 54					06 51			06 56			07 08			

		LE	LE	LE	LE	LE	LE	XC ◇	LE	LE	LE	LE ⌶	LE	LE ⌶	LE	LE	LE ⌶	LE	XC ◇	LE ⌶	LE	LE	LE ⌶
London Liverpool Street 15 ⊖	d	06 21	06 25	06 28		06 40	06 42		06 55	06 58		07 10	07 12	07 25	07 28		07 40	07 42		07 55	07 58		08 10
Bethnal Green	d																						
Hackney Downs	d						06 48						07 18					07 48					
Stratford 7 ⊖	d	06 30									07 00					07 30						08 00	
Clapton	d																						
Seven Sisters ⊖	d				←																		
Tottenham Hale ⊖	d	06 43	06u37	06 40	06 43	06u52	06 55		07u07	07 10	07 13	07u22	07 25	07u37	07 40	07 43	07u52	07 55		08u07	08 10	08 13	08u22
Northumberland Park	d	→									07 15											08 15	
Angel Road	d																						
Ponders End	d						06 59						07 29					07 59					
Brimsdown	d						07 02						07 32					08 02					
Enfield Lock	d						07 04				07 21		07 34					08 04				08 21	
Waltham Cross	d				06 50		07 07						07 37			07 50		08 07					
Cheshunt	d			06 48	06 53		07 09			07 18	07 25		07 39		07 48	07 53		08 09			08 18	08 25	
Broxbourne 3	a			06 52	06 57		07 14			07 22	07 29		07 44		07 52	07 57		08 14			08 22	08 29	
Broxbourne 3	d			06 52	06 57		07 14			07 22	07 33		07 44		07 52	07 57		08 14			08 22	08 33	
Rye House	d						07 17						07 47					08 17					
St Margarets (Herts)	d						07 20						07 50					08 20					
Ware	d						07 24						07 54					08 24					
Hertford East	a						07 31						08 01					08 31					
Roydon	d			06 56							07 38				07 56							08 38	
Harlow Town	d		06 54	07 00	07 09				07 24	07 28	07 42			07 54	08 00	08 09				08 24	08 28	08 42	
Harlow Mill	d			07 03							07 45				08 03							08 45	
Sawbridgeworth	d			07 07	07 15						07 48				08 07	08 15						08 48	
Bishops Stortford	a			07 14	07 22	07 17				07 38	07 56	07 45			08 14	08 22	08 17				08 38	08 56	08 45
	d			07 14		07 18				07 39		07 45			08 14		08 18				08 39		08 45
Stansted Mountfitchet	d			07 18					07 35						08 18					08 35			
Stansted Airport	a		07 12			07 27			07 44			07 57		08 12			08 27			08 44			08 57
Stansted Airport	d							07 27											08 27				
Elsenham	d			07 22											08 22								
Newport (Essex)	d			07 27											08 27								
Audley End	d			07 30				07 40		07 51					08 30				08 40		08 51		
Great Chesterford	d			07 35											08 35								
Whittlesford Parkway	d			07 40						07 58					08 40						08 58		
Shelford	d			07 44											08 44								
Cambridge	a			07 51				07 58		08 08					08 51				08 58		09 08		

b Previous night, stops to pick up only

London - Broxbourne, Hertford East, Bishops Stortford, Stansted Airport and Cambridge

Network Diagram - see first Page of Table 20

		LE	LE ⌶	LE	LE	LE ⌶	LE	XC ◇	LE ⌶	LE	LE	LE ⌶	LE	LE ⌶	LE	LE	LE ⌶	LE	XC ◇	LE ⌶	LE	LE
London Liverpool Street 15 ⊖	d	08 12	08 25	08 28		08 40	08 42		08 55	08 58		09 10	09 12	09 25	09 28		09 40	09 42		09 55	09 58	
Bethnal Green	d																					
Hackney Downs	d	08 18					08 48						09 18					09 48				
Stratford 7 ⊖	d				08 30						09 00					09 30						10 00
Clapton	d																					
Seven Sisters ⊖	d																					
Tottenham Hale ⊖	d	08 25	08u37	08 40	08 43	08u52	08 55		09u07	09 10	09 13	09u22	09 25	09u37	09 40	09 43	09u52	09 55		10u07	10 10	10 13
Northumberland Park	d										09 15											10 15
Angel Road	d																					
Ponders End	d	08 29					08 59						09 29					09 59				
Brimsdown	d	08 32					09 02						09 32					10 02				
Enfield Lock	d	08 34					09 04				09 21		09 34					10 04				10 21
Waltham Cross	d	08 37			08 50		09 07						09 37			09 50		10 07				
Cheshunt	d	08 39		08 48	08 53		09 09			09 18	09 25		09 39		09 48	09 53		10 09			10 18	10 25
Broxbourne 3	a	08 44		08 52	08 57		09 14			09 22	09 29		09 44		09 52	09 57		10 14			10 22	10 29
Broxbourne 3	d	08 44		08 52	08 57		09 14			09 22	09 33		09 44		09 52	09 57		10 14			10 22	10 33
Rye House	d	08 47					09 17						09 47					10 17				
St Margarets (Herts)	d	08 50					09 20						09 50					10 20				
Ware	d	08 54					09 24						09 54					10 24				
Hertford East	a	09 01					09 31						10 01					10 31				
Roydon	d			08 56							09 38				09 56							10 38
Harlow Town	d		08 54	09 00	09 09				09 24	09 28	09 42			09 54	10 00	10 09				10 24	10 28	10 42
Harlow Mill	d			09 03							09 45				10 03							10 45
Sawbridgeworth	d			09 07	09 15						09 48				10 07	10 15						10 48
Bishops Stortford	a			09 14	09 22	09 17				09 38	09 56	09 45			10 14	10 22	10 17				10 38	10 56
	d			09 14		09 18				09 39		09 45			10 14		10 18				10 39	
Stansted Mountfitchet	d			09 18					09 35						10 18					10 35		
Stansted Airport	a		09 12			09 27			09 44			09 57		10 12			10 27			10 44		
Stansted Airport	d							09 27											10 27			
Elsenham	d			09 22											10 22							
Newport (Essex)	d			09 27											10 27							
Audley End	d			09 30				09 40		09 51					10 30				10 40		10 51	
Great Chesterford	d			09 35											10 35							
Whittlesford Parkway	d			09 40						09 58					10 40						10 58	
Shelford	d			09 44											10 44							
Cambridge	a			09 51				09 58		10 08					10 51				10 58		11 08	

		LE ⌶	LE	LE ⌶	LE	LE	LE ⌶	LE	XC ◇	LE ⌶	LE	LE	LE ⌶	LE	LE ⌶	LE	LE	LE ⌶	LE	XC ◇	LE ⌶	LE	LE
London Liverpool Street 15 ⊖	d	10 10	10 12	10 25	10 28		10 40	10 42		10 55	10 58		11 10	11 12	11 25	11 28		11 40	11 42		11 55	11 58	
Bethnal Green	d																						
Hackney Downs	d		10 18					10 48						11 18					11 48				
Stratford 7 ⊖	d					10 30						11 00					11 30						12 00
Clapton	d																						
Seven Sisters ⊖	d																						
Tottenham Hale ⊖	d	10u22	10 25	10u37	10 40	10 43	10u52	10 55		11u07	11 10	11 13	11u22	11 25	11u37	11 40	11 43	11u52	11 55		12u07	12 10	12 13
Northumberland Park	d											11 15											12 15
Angel Road	d																						
Ponders End	d		10 29					10 59						11 29					11 59				
Brimsdown	d		10 32					11 02						11 32					12 02				
Enfield Lock	d		10 34					11 04				11 21		11 34					12 04				12 21
Waltham Cross	d		10 37			10 50		11 07						11 37			11 50		12 07				
Cheshunt	d		10 39		10 48	10 53		11 09			11 18	11 25		11 39		11 48	11 53		12 09			12 18	12 25
Broxbourne 3	a		10 44		10 52	10 57		11 14			11 22	11 29		11 44		11 52	11 57		12 14			12 22	12 29
Broxbourne 3	d		10 44		10 52	10 57		11 14			11 22	11 33		11 44		11 52	11 57		12 14			12 22	12 33
Rye House	d		10 47					11 17						11 47					12 17				
St Margarets (Herts)	d		10 50					11 20						11 50					12 20				
Ware	d		10 54					11 24						11 54					12 24				
Hertford East	a		11 01					11 31						12 01					12 31				
Roydon	d				10 56							11 38				11 56							12 38
Harlow Town	d			10 54	11 00	11 09				11 24	11 28	11 42			11 54	12 00	12 09				12 24	12 28	12 42
Harlow Mill	d				11 03							11 45				12 03							12 45
Sawbridgeworth	d				11 07	11 15						11 48				12 07	12 15						12 48
Bishops Stortford	a	10 45			11 14	11 22	11 17				11 38	11 56	11 45			12 14	12 22	12 17				12 38	12 56
	d	10 45			11 14		11 18				11 39		11 45			12 14		12 18				12 39	
Stansted Mountfitchet	d				11 18					11 35						12 18					12 35		
Stansted Airport	a	10 57		11 13			11 27			11 44			11 57		12 12			12 27			12 44		
Stansted Airport	d								11 27											12 27			
Elsenham	d				11 22											12 22							
Newport (Essex)	d				11 27											12 27							
Audley End	d				11 30				11 40		11 51					12 30				12 40		12 51	
Great Chesterford	d				11 35											12 35							
Whittlesford Parkway	d				11 40						11 58					12 40						12 58	
Shelford	d				11 44											12 44							
Cambridge	a				11 51				11 58		12 08					12 51				12 58		13 08	

Table 22

Saturdays from 15 September

London - Broxbourne, Hertford East, Bishops Stortford, Stansted Airport and Cambridge

Network Diagram - see first Page of Table 20

		LE 1 ⊼	LE 1	LE 1 ⊼	LE 1	LE 1	LE 1 ⊼	LE 1	XC ◇1	LE 1 ⊼	LE 1	LE 1	LE 1 ⊼	LE 1	LE 1 ⊼	LE 1	LE 1	LE 1 ⊼	LE 1	XC ◇1	LE 1 ⊼	LE 1
London Liverpool Street 15 ⊖	d	12 10	12 12	12 25	12 28		12 40	12 42		12 55	12 58		13 10	13 12	13 25	13 28		13 40	13 42		13 55	13 58
Bethnal Green	d																					
Hackney Downs	d		12 18					12 48						13 18					13 48			
Stratford 7 ⊖	d					12 30						13 00					13 30					
Clapton	d																					
Seven Sisters ⊖	d																					
Tottenham Hale ⊖	d	12u22	12 25	12u37	12 40	12 43	12u52	12 55		13u07	13 10	13 13	13u22	13 25	13u37	13 40	13 43	13u52	13 55		14u07	14 10
Northumberland Park	d											13 15										
Angel Road	d																					
Ponders End	d		12 29					12 59						13 29					13 59			
Brimsdown	d		12 32					13 02						13 32					14 02			
Enfield Lock	d		12 34					13 04				13 21		13 34					14 04			
Waltham Cross	d		12 37			12 50		13 07						13 37			13 50		14 07			
Cheshunt	d		12 39		12 48	12 53		13 09			13 18	13 25		13 39		13 48	13 53		14 09			14 18
Broxbourne 8	a		12 44		12 52	12 57		13 14			13 22	13 29		13 44		13 52	13 57		14 14			14 22
Broxbourne 8	d		12 44		12 52	12 57		13 14			13 22	13 33		13 44		13 52	13 57		14 14			14 22
Rye House	d		12 47					13 17						13 47					14 17			
St Margarets (Herts)	d		12 50					13 20						13 50					14 20			
Ware	d		12 54					13 24						13 54					14 24			
Hertford East	a		13 01					13 31						14 01					14 31			
Roydon	d				12 56							13 38				13 56						
Harlow Town	d			12 54	13 00	13 09				13 24	13 28	13 42			13 54	14 00	14 09				14 24	14 28
Harlow Mill	d				13 03							13 45				14 03						
Sawbridgeworth	d				13 07	13 15						13 48				14 07	14 15					
Bishops Stortford	a	12 45			13 14	13 22	13 17				13 38	13 56	13 45			14 14	14 22	14 17				14 38
	d	12 45			13 14		13 18				13 39		13 45			14 14		14 18				14 39
Stansted Mountfitchet	d				13 18					13 35						14 18					14 35	
Stansted Airport	a	12 57		13 12			13 27			13 44			13 57		14 12			14 27			14 44	
Stansted Airport	d								13 27											14 27		
Elsenham	d				13 22											14 22						
Newport (Essex)	d				13 27											14 27						
Audley End	d				13 30				13 40		13 51					14 30				14 40		14 51
Great Chesterford	d				13 35											14 35						
Whittlesford Parkway	d				13 40						13 58					14 40						14 58
Shelford	d				13 44											14 44						
Cambridge	a				13 51				13 58		14 08					14 51				14 58		15 08

		LE 1	LE 1 ⊼	LE 1	LE 1 ⊼	LE 1	LE 1	LE 1 ⊼	LE 1	XC ◇1	LE 1 ⊼	LE 1	LE 1	LE 1 ⊼	LE 1	LE 1 ⊼	LE 1	LE 1	LE 1 ⊼	LE 1	XC ◇1	LE 1 ⊼	LE 1
London Liverpool Street 15 ⊖	d		14 10	14 12	14 25	14 28		14 40	14 42		14 55	14 58		15 10	15 12	15 25	15 28		15 40	15 42		15 55	15 58
Bethnal Green	d																						
Hackney Downs	d			14 18					14 48						15 18					15 48			
Stratford 7 ⊖	d	14 00					14 30						15 00					15 30					
Clapton	d																						
Seven Sisters ⊖	d																						
Tottenham Hale ⊖	d	14 13	14u22	14 25	14u37	14 40	14 43	14u52	14 55		15u07	15 10	15 13	15u22	15 25	15u37	15 40	15 43	15u52	15 55		16u07	16 10
Northumberland Park	d	14 15											15 15										
Angel Road	d																						
Ponders End	d			14 29					14 59						15 29					15 59			
Brimsdown	d			14 32					15 02						15 32					16 02			
Enfield Lock	d	14 21		14 34					15 04				15 21		15 34					16 04			
Waltham Cross	d			14 37			14 50		15 07						15 37			15 50		16 07			
Cheshunt	d	14 25		14 39		14 48	14 53		15 09			15 18	15 25		15 39		15 48	15 53		16 09			16 18
Broxbourne 8	a	14 29		14 44		14 52	14 57		15 14			15 22	15 29		15 44		15 52	15 57		16 14			16 22
Broxbourne 8	d	14 33		14 44		14 52	14 57		15 14			15 22	15 33		15 44		15 52	15 57		16 14			16 22
Rye House	d			14 47					15 17						15 47					16 17			
St Margarets (Herts)	d			14 50					15 20						15 50					16 20			
Ware	d			14 54					15 24						15 54					16 24			
Hertford East	a			15 01					15 31						16 01					16 31			
Roydon	d	14 38				14 56							15 38				15 56						
Harlow Town	d	14 42			14 54	15 00	15 09				15 24	15 28	15 42			15 54	16 00	16 09				16 24	16 28
Harlow Mill	d	14 45				15 03							15 45				16 03						
Sawbridgeworth	d	14 48				15 07	15 15						15 48				16 07	16 15					
Bishops Stortford	a	14 56	14 45			15 14	15 22	15 17				15 38	15 56	15 45			16 14	16 22	16 17				16 38
	d		14 45			15 14		15 18				15 39		15 45			16 14		16 18				16 39
Stansted Mountfitchet	d					15 18					15 35						16 18					16 35	
Stansted Airport	a		14 57		15 12			15 27			15 44			15 57		16 12			16 27			16 44	
Stansted Airport	d									15 27											16 27		
Elsenham	d					15 22											16 22						
Newport (Essex)	d					15 27											16 27						
Audley End	d					15 30				15 40		15 51					16 30				16 40		16 51
Great Chesterford	d					15 35											16 35						
Whittlesford Parkway	d					15 40						15 58					16 40						16 58
Shelford	d					15 44											16 44						
Cambridge	a					15 51				15 58		16 08					16 51				16 58		17 08

Table 22

Saturdays from 15 September

London - Broxbourne, Hertford East, Bishops Stortford, Stansted Airport and Cambridge

Network Diagram - see first Page of Table 20

		LE 1	LE 1 ⊼	LE 1	LE 1 ⊼	LE 1	LE 1	LE 1 ⊼	LE 1	XC ◇1	LE 1 ⊼	LE 1	LE 1	LE 1 ⊼	LE 1	LE 1 ⊼	LE 1	LE 1	LE 1 ⊼	LE 1	XC ◇1	LE 1 ⊼	LE 1
London Liverpool Street 15 ⊖	d		16 10	16 12	16 25	16 28		16 40	16 42		16 55	16 58		17 10	17 12	17 25	17 28		17 40	17 42		17 55	17 58
Bethnal Green	d																						
Hackney Downs	d			16 18					16 48						17 18					17 48			
Stratford 7 ⊖	d	16 00					16 30						17 00					17 30					
Clapton	d																						
Seven Sisters ⊖	d																						
Tottenham Hale ⊖	d	16 13	16u22	16 25	16u37	16 40	16 43	16u52	16 55		17u07	17 10	17 13	17u22	17 25	17u37	17 40	17 43	17u52	17 55		18u07	18 10
Northumberland Park	d	16 15											17 15										
Angel Road	d																						
Ponders End	d			16 29					16 59						17 29					17 59			
Brimsdown	d			16 32					17 02						17 32					18 02			
Enfield Lock	d	16 21		16 34					17 04				17 21		17 34					18 04			
Waltham Cross	d			16 37			16 50		17 07						17 37			17 50		18 07			
Cheshunt	d	16 25		16 39		16 48	16 53		17 09			17 18	17 25		17 39		17 48	17 53		18 09			18 18
Broxbourne 8	a	16 29		16 44		16 52	16 57		17 14			17 22	17 29		17 44		17 52	17 57		18 14			18 22
Broxbourne 8	d	16 33		16 44		16 52	16 57		17 14			17 22	17 33		17 44		17 52	17 57		18 14			18 22
Rye House	d			16 47					17 17						17 47					18 17			
St Margarets (Herts)	d			16 50					17 20						17 50					18 20			
Ware	d			16 54					17 24						17 54					18 24			
Hertford East	a			17 01					17 31						18 01					18 31			
Roydon	d	16 38				16 56							17 38				17 56						
Harlow Town	d	16 42			16 54	17 00	17 09				17 24	17 28	17 42			17 54	18 00	18 09				18 24	18 28
Harlow Mill	d	16 45				17 03							17 45				18 03						
Sawbridgeworth	d	16 48				17 07	17 15						17 48				18 07	18 15					
Bishops Stortford	a	16 56	16 45			17 14	17 22	17 17				17 38	17 56	17 45			18 14	18 22	18 17				18 38
	d		16 45			17 14		17 18				17 39		17 45			18 14		18 18				18 39
Stansted Mountfitchet	d					17 18					17 35						18 18					18 35	
Stansted Airport	a		16 57		17 12			17 27			17 44			17 57		18 12			18 27			18 44	
Stansted Airport	d									17 27											18 27		
Elsenham	d					17 22											18 22						
Newport (Essex)	d					17 27											18 27						
Audley End	d					17 30				17 40		17 51					18 30				18 40		18 51
Great Chesterford	d					17 35											18 35						
Whittlesford Parkway	d					17 40						17 58					18 40						18 58
Shelford	d					17 44											18 44						
Cambridge	a					17 51				17 58		18 08					18 51				18 58		19 08

		LE 1	LE 1 ⊼	LE 1	LE 1 ⊼	LE 1	LE 1	LE 1 ⊼	LE 1	XC ◇1	LE 1 ⊼	LE 1	LE 1	LE 1 ⊼	LE 1	LE 1 ⊼	LE 1	LE 1	LE 1 ⊼	LE 1	XC 1	LE 1 ⊼
London Liverpool Street 15 ⊖	d		18 10	18 12	18 25	18 28		18 40	18 42		18 55	18 58		19 10	19 12	19 25	19 28		19 40	19 42		19 55
Bethnal Green	d																					
Hackney Downs	d			18 18					18 48						19 18					19 48		
Stratford 7 ⊖	d	18 00					18 30						19 00					19 30				
Clapton	d																					
Seven Sisters ⊖	d																					
Tottenham Hale ⊖	d	18 13	18u22	18 25	18u37	18 40	18 43	18u52	18 55		19u07	19 10	19 13	19u22	19 25	19u37	19 40	19 43	19u52	19 55		20u07
Northumberland Park	d	18 15											19 15									
Angel Road	d																					
Ponders End	d			18 29					18 59						19 29					19 59		
Brimsdown	d			18 32					19 02						19 32					20 02		
Enfield Lock	d	18 21		18 34					19 04				19 21		19 34					20 04		
Waltham Cross	d			18 37			18 50		19 07						19 37			19 50		20 07		
Cheshunt	d	18 25		18 39		18 48	18 53		19 09			19 18	19 25		19 39		19 48	19 53		20 09		
Broxbourne 8	a	18 29		18 44		18 52	18 57		19 14			19 22	19 29		19 44		19 52	19 57		20 14		
Broxbourne 8	d	18 33		18 44		18 52	18 57		19 14			19 22	19 33		19 44		19 52	19 57		20 14		
Rye House	d			18 47					19 17						19 47					20 17		
St Margarets (Herts)	d			18 50					19 20						19 50					20 20		
Ware	d			18 54					19 24						19 54					20 24		
Hertford East	a			19 01					19 31						20 01					20 31		
Roydon	d	18 38				18 56							19 38				19 56					
Harlow Town	d	18 42			18 54	19 00	19 09				19 24	19 28	19 42			19 54	20 00	20 09				20 24
Harlow Mill	d	18 45				19 03							19 45				20 03					
Sawbridgeworth	d	18 48				19 07	19 15						19 48				20 07	20 15				
Bishops Stortford	a	18 56	18 45			19 14	19 22	19 17				19 38	19 56	19 45			20 14	20 22	20 17			
	d		18 45			19 14		19 18				19 39		19 45			20 14		20 18			
Stansted Mountfitchet	d					19 18					19 35						20 18					20 35
Stansted Airport	a		18 57		19 12			19 27			19 44			19 57		20 12			20 27			20 44
Stansted Airport	d									19 27											20 27	
Elsenham	d					19 22											20 22					
Newport (Essex)	d					19 27											20 27					
Audley End	d					19 30				19 40		19 51					20 30				20 40	
Great Chesterford	d					19 35											20 35					
Whittlesford Parkway	d					19 40						19 58					20 40					
Shelford	d					19 44											20 44					
Cambridge	a					19 51				19 58		20 08					20 51				20 57	

Table 22

Saturdays from 15 September

London - Broxbourne, Hertford East, Bishops Stortford, Stansted Airport and Cambridge

Network Diagram - see first Page of Table 20

		LE	LE	LE 🚲	LE	LE 🚲	LE	LE		LE 🚲	LE	XC	LE 🚲	LE	LE	LE 🚲	LE	LE 🚲		LE	LE	LE 🚲	LE	XC	LE 🚲
London Liverpool Street ⊖	d	19 58		20 10	20 12	20 25	20 28			20 40	20 42		20 55	20 58		21 10	21 12	21 25		21 28		21 40	21 42		21 55
Bethnal Green	d																								
Hackney Downs	d				20 18						20 48						21 18						21 48		
Stratford ⊖	d		20 00					20 30							21 00						21 30				
Clapton	d																								
Seven Sisters ⊖	d																								
Tottenham Hale ⊖	d	20 10	20 13	20u22	20 25	20u37	20 40	20 43		20u52	20 55		21u07	21 10	21 13	21u22	21 25	21u37		21 40	21 43	21u52	21 55		22u07
Northumberland Park	d		20 15												21 15										
Angel Road	d																								
Ponders End	d				20 29						20 59						21 29						21 59		
Brimsdown	d				20 32						21 02						21 32						22 02		
Enfield Lock	d		20 21		20 34						21 04				21 21		21 34						22 04		
Waltham Cross	d				20 37			20 50			21 07						21 37				21 50		22 07		
Cheshunt	d	20 18	20 25		20 39		20 48	20 53			21 09			21 18	21 25		21 39			21 48	21 53		22 09		
Broxbourne	a	20 22	20 29		20 44		20 52	20 57			21 14			21 22	21 29		21 44			21 52	21 57		22 14		
Broxbourne	d	20 22	20 33		20 44		20 52	20 57			21 14			21 22	21 33		21 44			21 52	21 57		22 14		
Rye House	d				20 47						21 17						21 47						22 17		
St Margarets (Herts)	d				20 50						21 20						21 50						22 20		
Ware	d				20 54						21 24						21 54						22 24		
Hertford East	a				21 01						21 31						22 01						22 31		
Roydon	d		20 38				20 56								21 38					21 56					
Harlow Town	d	20 28	20 42			20 54	21 00	21 09					21 24	21 28	21 42			21 54		22 00	22 09				22 24
Harlow Mill	d		20 45				21 03								21 45					22 03					
Sawbridgeworth	d		20 48				21 07	21 15							21 48					22 07	22 15				
Bishops Stortford	a	20 38	20 56	20 45			21 14	21 22		21 17				21 38	21 56	21 45				22 14	22 22	22 17			
	d	20 39		20 45			21 14			21 18				21 39		21 45				22 14		22 18			
Stansted Mountfitchet	d						21 18						21 35							22 18					22 35
Stansted Airport	a			20 57		21 12				21 27			21 44			21 57		22 12				22 27			22 44
Stansted Airport	d											21 27												22 27	
Elsenham	d						21 22													22 22					
Newport (Essex)	d						21 27													22 27					
Audley End	d	20 51					21 30					21 40		21 51						22 30				22 40	
Great Chesterford	d						21 35													22 35					
Whittlesford Parkway	d	20 58					21 40							21 58						22 40					
Shelford	d						21 44													22 44					
Cambridge	a	21 08					21 51					22 01		22 08						22 51				23 01	

		LE	LE	LE 🚲		LE	LE 🚲	LE	LE	LE 🚲	LE	XC	LE 🚲	LE		LE	LE	LE	LE	LE	LE
London Liverpool Street ⊖	d	21 58		22 10		22 12	22 25	22 28		22 40	22 42		22 55	22 58			23 12	23 25	23 28	23 40	23 58
Bethnal Green	d																				
Hackney Downs	d					22 18					22 48						23 18			23 46	
Stratford ⊖	d		22 00						22 30							23 00					
Clapton	d																				
Seven Sisters ⊖	d																			23 49	
Tottenham Hale ⊖	d	22 10	22 13	22u22		22 25	22u37	22 40	22 43	22u52	22 55		23u07	23 10		23 13	23 25	23u37	23 40	23 53	00 10
Northumberland Park	d		22 15													23 15				23 55	
Angel Road	d																				
Ponders End	d					22 29					22 59						23 29			23 59	
Brimsdown	d					22 32					23 02						23 32			00 02	
Enfield Lock	d		22 21			22 34					23 04					23 21	23 34			00 04	
Waltham Cross	d					22 37			22 50		23 07						23 37			00 07	
Cheshunt	d	22 18	22 25			22 39		22 48	22 53		23 09			23 18		23 25	23 39		23 48	00 09	00 18
Broxbourne	a	22 22	22 29			22 44		22 52	22 57		23 14			23 22		23 29	23 44		23 52	00 14	00 22
Broxbourne	d	22 22	22 33			22 44		22 52	22 57		23 14			23 22		23 29	23 44		23 52	00 14	00 22
Rye House	d					22 47					23 17						23 47			00 17	
St Margarets (Herts)	d					22 50					23 20						23 50			00 20	
Ware	d					22 54					23 24						23 54			00 24	
Hertford East	a					23 01					23 31						00 01			00 31	
Roydon	d		22 38					22 56								23 33			23 56		00 26
Harlow Town	d	22 28	22 42				22 54	23 00	23 09				23 24	23 28		23 37		23 54	00 01		00 30
Harlow Mill	d		22 45					23 03								23 40			00 03		00 33
Sawbridgeworth	d		22 48					23 07	23 15							23 44			00 07		00 37
Bishops Stortford	a	22 38	22 56	22 45				23 14	23 22	23 17				23 38		23 51		00 04	00 14		00 44
	d	22 39		22 45				23 14		23 18				23 39				00 04	00 14		00 44
Stansted Mountfitchet	d							23 18					23 35						00 18		00 48
Stansted Airport	a			22 57			23 12			23 27			23 44					00 13			
Stansted Airport	d											23 27									
Elsenham	d							23 22											00 22		00 52
Newport (Essex)	d							23 27											00 27		00 57
Audley End	d	22 51						23 30				23 40		23 51					00 30		01 00
Great Chesterford	d							23 35											00 35		01 05
Whittlesford Parkway	d	22 58						23 40						23 58					00 40		01 10
Shelford	d							23 44											00 44		
Cambridge	a	23 09						23 51				23 55		00 08					00 51		01 19

Table 22

Sundays until 22 July

London - Broxbourne, Hertford East, Bishops Stortford, Stansted Airport and Cambridge

Network Diagram - see first Page of Table 20

		LE	LE	LE	LE	LE	LE	LE	LE	LE		LE	LE	LE	LE	LE	LE 🚲	LE 🚲	LE 🚲	LE		LE	LE	LE 🚲	LE
London Liverpool Street ⊖	d	22p58	23p12	23p25	23p28	23p40	23p58	04 10	04 40	05 10		05 40	06 10	06 25	06 40	06 55	07 10	07 25	07 40			07 43	07 52	07 55	
Bethnal Green	d																								
Hackney Downs	d		23p18			23p46																	07 59		
Stratford ⊖	d																								
Clapton	d					23p49																			
Seven Sisters ⊖	d																						08 04		
Tottenham Hale ⊖	d	23p10	23p25	23b37	23p40	23p53	00 10		04u52	05u22		05u52	06u22	06u37	06u52	07 07	07 22	07 37	07 52			07 55		08 07	
Northumberland Park	d					23p55																			
Angel Road	d																								
Ponders End	d		23p29			23p59																07 59			
Brimsdown	d		23p32			00 02																08 02			
Enfield Lock	d		23p34			00 04																08 04			
Waltham Cross	d		23p37			00 07																08 07			
Cheshunt	d	23p18	23p39		23p48	00 09	00 18					06 00										08 09	08 20		
Broxbourne	a	23p22	23p44		23p52	00 14	00 22					06 04										08 14	08 25		
Broxbourne	d	23p22	23p44		23p52	00 14	00 22					06 04								07 57		08 19	08 25		
Rye House	d		23p47			00 17														08 00			08 28		
St Margarets (Herts)	d		23p50			00 20														08 03			08 31		
Ware	d		23p54			00 24														08 07			08 35		
Hertford East	a		00 01			00 31														08 14			08 42		
Roydon	d				23p56		00 26															08 24			←
Harlow Town	d	23p28		23p54	00 01		00 30		05 07	05 37		06 10		06 52		07 22		07 52				08 28		08 22	08 28
Harlow Mill	d				00 03		00 33															→			08 31
Sawbridgeworth	d				00 07		00 37																		08 34
Bishops Stortford	a	23p38		00 04	00 14		00 44		05 17	05 47		06 20	06 45		07 15		07 45		08 15						08 41
	d	23p39		00 04	00 14		00 44		05 18	05 48		06 21	06 46		07 16		07 46		08 16						08 42
Stansted Mountfitchet	d				00 18		00 48		05 22					07 03				08 03							08 46
Stansted Airport	a			00 13				04 58	05 29	05 57		06 30	06 55	07 12	07 25	07 40	07 55	08 13	08 25					08 40	
Stansted Airport	d																								
Elsenham	d				00 22		00 52																		08 50
Newport (Essex)	d				00 27		00 57																		08 55
Audley End	d	23p51			00 30		01 00																		08 58
Great Chesterford	d				00 35		01 05																		09 03
Whittlesford Parkway	d	23p58			00 40		01 10																		09 08
Shelford	d				00 44																				09 12
Cambridge	a	00 08			00 51		01 19																		09 19

		LE 🚲	LE	LE 🚲	LE	LE		LE 🚲	LE	LE	LE 🚲	LE	LE 🚲	LE	LE 🚲	LE		LE	LE 🚲	XC ◇ A	LE	LE	LE 🚲	LE	LE 🚲
London Liverpool Street ⊖	d	08 10	08 22	08 25	08 28			08 40		08 52	08 55		09 10	09 22	09 25	09 28			09 40			09 52	09 55		10 10
Bethnal Green	d																								
Hackney Downs	d		08 29							08 59				09 29								09 59			
Stratford ⊖	d								08 45												09 45				
Clapton	d																								
Seven Sisters ⊖	d		08 34							09 04				09 34								10 04			
Tottenham Hale ⊖	d	08 22		08 37	08 40			08 52	08 55		09 07		09 22		09 37	09 40			09 52		09 55		10 07		10 22
Northumberland Park	d																								
Angel Road	d																								
Ponders End	d								08 59												09 59				
Brimsdown	d								09 02												10 02				
Enfield Lock	d								09 04												10 04				
Waltham Cross	d					←			09 07									←			10 07				
Cheshunt	d		08 52		08 49	08 52			09 09	09 20				09 52		09 49		09 52			10 09	10 20			
Broxbourne	a		→		08 53	08 57			09 14	09 25				→		09 53		09 57			10 14	10 25			
Broxbourne	d				08 53	08 57			09 19	09 25						09 53		09 57			10 19	10 25			
Rye House	d					09 00				09 28								10 00				10 28			
St Margarets (Herts)	d					09 03				09 31								10 03				10 31			
Ware	d					09 07				09 35								10 07				10 35			
Hertford East	a					09 14				09 42								10 14				10 42			
Roydon	d								09 24			←									10 24			←	
Harlow Town	d			08 52	08 59				09 28		09 22	09 28			09 52	09 59					10 28		10 22	10 28	
Harlow Mill	d								→			09 31									→			10 31	
Sawbridgeworth	d				09 04							09 34				10 04								10 34	
Bishops Stortford	a	08 45			09 11			09 15				09 41	09 45			10 11			10 15					10 41	10 45
	d	08 46			09 12			09 16				09 42	09 46			10 12			10 16					10 42	10 46
Stansted Mountfitchet	d			09 03								09 46			10 03									10 46	
Stansted Airport	a	08 55		09 12				09 25			09 40		09 55		10 12				10 25				10 40		10 55
Stansted Airport	d																			10 25					
Elsenham	d											09 50												10 50	
Newport (Essex)	d											09 55												10 55	
Audley End	d				09 24							09 58				10 24				10 39				10 58	
Great Chesterford	d											10 03												11 03	
Whittlesford Parkway	d				09 31							10 08				10 31								11 08	
Shelford	d											10 12												11 12	
Cambridge	a				09 41							10 19				10 41				10 58				11 19	

A until 24 June

b Previous night, stops to pick up only

Table 22

Sundays until 22 July

London - Broxbourne, Hertford East, Bishops Stortford, Stansted Airport and Cambridge

Network Diagram - see first Page of Table 20

		LE		LE ■ ⊼	LE ■	LE	LE ■ ⊼	XC ◇■	LE ■	LE	LE ■ ⊼	LE ■		LE ■ ⊼	LE	LE ■ ⊼	LE ■	LE	LE ■ ⊼	XC ◇■	LE ■	LE		LE ■ ⊼	LE ■
London Liverpool Street ⊖	d	10 22		10 25	10 28		10 40			10 52	10 55			11 10	11 22	11 25	11 28		11 40			11 52		11 55	
Bethnal Green	d																								
Hackney Downs	d	10 29								10 59					11 29							11 59			
Stratford ⊖	d								10 45												11 45				
Clapton	d																								
Seven Sisters ⊖	d	10 34								11 04					11 34							12 04			
Tottenham Hale ⊖	d			10 37	10 40		10 52		10 55		11 07			11 22		11 37	11 40		11 52		11 55			12 07	
Northumberland Park	d																								
Angel Road	d																								
Ponders End	d								10 59												11 59				
Brimsdown	d								11 02												12 02				
Enfield Lock	d								11 04												12 04				
Waltham Cross	d					←			11 07									←			12 07				
Cheshunt	d	10 52			10 49	10 52			11 09	11 20					11 52		11 49	11 52			12 09	12 20			
Broxbourne	a	→			10 53	10 57			11 14	11 25					→		11 53	11 57			12 14	12 25			
Broxbourne	d				10 53	10 57			11 19	11 25							11 53	11 57			12 19	12 25			
Rye House	d					11 00				11 28								12 00				12 28			
St Margarets (Herts)	d					11 03				11 31								12 03				12 31			
Ware	d					11 07				11 35								12 07				12 35			
Hertford East	a					11 14				11 42								12 14				12 42			
Roydon	d								11 24			←									12 24				←
Harlow Town	d			10 52	10 59				11 28		11 22	11 28				11 52	11 59				12 28			12 22	12 28
Harlow Mill	d								→			11 31									→				12 31
Sawbridgeworth	d				11 04							11 34					12 04								12 34
Bishops Stortford	a				11 11		11 15					11 41		11 45			12 11		12 15						12 41
	d				11 12		11 16					11 42		11 46			12 12		12 16						12 42
Stansted Mountfitchet	d			11 03								11 46				12 03									12 46
Stansted Airport	a			11 12			11 25				11 40			11 55		12 12			12 25					12 40	
Stansted Airport	d							11 25												12 25					
Elsenham	d											11 50													12 50
Newport (Essex)	d											11 55													12 55
Audley End	d				11 24			11 39				11 58					12 24			12 39					12 58
Great Chesterford	d											12 03													13 03
Whittlesford Parkway	d				11 31							12 08					12 31								13 08
Shelford	d											12 12													13 12
Cambridge	a				11 41			11 57				12 19					12 41			12 58					13 19

		LE ■ ⊼	LE	LE ■ ⊼	LE ■	LE	LE ■ ⊼	XC ◇■		LE ■	LE	LE ■ ⊼	LE ■	LE ■ ⊼	LE	LE ■ ⊼	LE ■	LE		LE ■ ⊼	XC ◇■	LE ■	LE	LE ■ ⊼	LE ■
London Liverpool Street ⊖	d	12 10	12 22	12 25	12 28		12 40				12 52	12 55		13 10	13 22	13 25	13 28			13 40			13 52	13 55	
Bethnal Green	d																								
Hackney Downs	d		12 29								12 59				13 29								13 59		
Stratford ⊖	d									12 45												13 45			
Clapton	d																								
Seven Sisters ⊖	d		12 34								13 04				13 34								14 04		
Tottenham Hale ⊖	d	12 22		12 37	12 40		12 52			12 55		13 07		13 22		13 37	13 40			13 52		13 55		14 07	
Northumberland Park	d																								
Angel Road	d																								
Ponders End	d									12 59												13 59			
Brimsdown	d									13 02												14 02			
Enfield Lock	d									13 04												14 04			
Waltham Cross	d					←				13 07								←				14 07			
Cheshunt	d		12 52		12 49	12 52				13 09	13 20				13 52		13 49	13 52				14 09	14 20		
Broxbourne	a		→		12 53	12 57				13 14	13 25				→		13 53	13 57				14 14	14 25		
Broxbourne	d				12 53	12 57				13 19	13 25						13 53	13 57				14 19	14 25		
Rye House	d					13 00					13 28							14 00					14 28		
St Margarets (Herts)	d					13 03					13 31							14 03					14 31		
Ware	d					13 07					13 35							14 07					14 35		
Hertford East	a					13 14					13 42							14 14					14 42		
Roydon	d									13 24			←									14 24			←
Harlow Town	d			12 52	12 59					13 28		13 22	13 28			13 52	13 59					14 28		14 22	14 28
Harlow Mill	d									→			13 31									→			14 31
Sawbridgeworth	d				13 04								13 34				14 04								14 34
Bishops Stortford	a	12 45			13 11		13 15						13 41	13 45			14 11			14 15					14 41
	d	12 46			13 12		13 16						13 42	13 46			14 12			14 16					14 42
Stansted Mountfitchet	d			13 03									13 46			14 03									14 46
Stansted Airport	a	12 55		13 12			13 25					13 40		13 55		14 12				14 25				14 40	
Stansted Airport	d							13 25													14 25				
Elsenham	d												13 50												14 50
Newport (Essex)	d												13 55												14 55
Audley End	d				13 24			13 39					13 58				14 24				14 39				14 58
Great Chesterford	d												14 03												15 03
Whittlesford Parkway	d				13 31								14 08				14 31								15 08
Shelford	d												14 12												15 12
Cambridge	a				13 41			13 58					14 19				14 41				14 57				15 19

Table 22

Sundays until 22 July

London - Broxbourne, Hertford East, Bishops Stortford, Stansted Airport and Cambridge

Network Diagram - see first Page of Table 20

		LE ■ ⊼	LE	LE ■ ⊼		LE ■	LE	LE ■ ⊼	XC ◇■	LE ■	LE	LE ■ ⊼	LE ■	LE ■ ⊼		LE	LE ■ ⊼	LE ■	LE	LE ■ ⊼	XC ◇■	LE ■	LE	LE ■ ⊼	
London Liverpool Street ⊖	d	14 10	14 22	14 25		14 28		14 40			14 52	14 55		15 10		15 22	15 25	15 28		15 40			15 52	15 55	
Bethnal Green	d																								
Hackney Downs	d		14 29								14 59					15 29							15 59		
Stratford ⊖	d									14 45												15 45			
Clapton	d																								
Seven Sisters ⊖	d		14 34								15 04					15 34							16 04		
Tottenham Hale ⊖	d	14 22		14 37		14 40		14 52		14 55		15 07		15 22			15 37	15 40		15 52		15 55		16 07	
Northumberland Park	d																								
Angel Road	d																								
Ponders End	d									14 59												15 59			
Brimsdown	d									15 02												16 02			
Enfield Lock	d									15 04												16 04			
Waltham Cross	d						←			15 07									←			16 07			
Cheshunt	d		14 52			14 49	14 52			15 09	15 20					15 52		15 49	15 52			16 09	16 20		
Broxbourne	a		→			14 53	14 57			15 14	15 25					→		15 53	15 57			16 14	16 25		
Broxbourne	d					14 53	14 57			15 19	15 25							15 53	15 57			16 19	16 25		
Rye House	d						15 00				15 28								16 00				16 28		
St Margarets (Herts)	d						15 03				15 31								16 03				16 31		
Ware	d						15 07				15 35								16 07				16 35		
Hertford East	a						15 14				15 42								16 14				16 42		
Roydon	d									15 24			←									16 24			
Harlow Town	d			14 52		14 59				15 28		15 22	15 28				15 52	15 59				16 28		16 22	
Harlow Mill	d									→			15 31									→			
Sawbridgeworth	d					15 04							15 34					16 04							
Bishops Stortford	a	14 45				15 11		15 15					15 41	15 45				16 11		16 15					
	d	14 46				15 12		15 16					15 42	15 46				16 12		16 16					
Stansted Mountfitchet	d			15 03									15 46				16 03								
Stansted Airport	a	14 55		15 12				15 25				15 40		15 55			16 12			16 25				16 40	
Stansted Airport	d								15 25												16 25				
Elsenham	d												15 50												
Newport (Essex)	d												15 55												
Audley End	d					15 24			15 39				15 58					16 24			16 39				
Great Chesterford	d												16 03												
Whittlesford Parkway	d					15 31							16 08					16 31							
Shelford	d												16 12												
Cambridge	a					15 41			15 58				16 19					16 41			16 58				

		LE ■	LE ■ ⊼	LE	LE ■ ⊼	LE ■	LE	LE ■ ⊼	XC ◇■	LE ■		LE	LE ■ ⊼	LE ■	LE ■ ⊼	LE	LE ■ ⊼	LE ■	LE	LE ■ ⊼		XC ◇■ A	LE ■	LE	LE ■ ⊼
London Liverpool Street ⊖	d		16 10	16 22	16 25	16 28		16 40				16 52	16 55		17 10	17 22	17 25	17 28		17 40				17 52	17 55
Bethnal Green	d																								
Hackney Downs	d			16 29								16 59				17 29								17 59	
Stratford ⊖	d									16 45													17 45		
Clapton	d																								
Seven Sisters ⊖	d			16 34								17 04				17 34								18 04	
Tottenham Hale ⊖	d		16 22		16 37	16 40		16 52		16 55			17 07		17 22		17 37	17 40		17 52			17 55		18 07
Northumberland Park	d																								
Angel Road	d																								
Ponders End	d									16 59													17 59		
Brimsdown	d									17 02													18 02		
Enfield Lock	d									17 04													18 04		
Waltham Cross	d						←			17 07									←				18 07		
Cheshunt	d			16 52		16 49	16 52			17 09		17 20				17 52		17 49	17 52				18 09	18 20	
Broxbourne	a			→		16 53	16 57			17 14		17 25				→		17 53	17 57				18 14	18 25	
Broxbourne	d					16 53	16 57			17 19		17 25						17 53	17 57				18 19	18 25	
Rye House	d						17 00					17 28							18 00					18 28	
St Margarets (Herts)	d						17 03					17 31							18 03					18 31	
Ware	d						17 07					17 35							18 07					18 35	
Hertford East	a						17 14					17 42							18 14					18 42	
Roydon	d	←								17 24				←									18 24		
Harlow Town	d	16 28			16 52	16 59				17 28			17 22	17 28			17 52	17 59					18 28		18 22
Harlow Mill	d	16 31								→				17 31									→		
Sawbridgeworth	d	16 34				17 04								17 34				18 04							
Bishops Stortford	a	16 41	16 45			17 11		17 15						17 41	17 45			18 11		18 15					
	d	16 42	16 46			17 12		17 16						17 42	17 46			18 12		18 16					
Stansted Mountfitchet	d	16 46			17 03									17 46			18 03								
Stansted Airport	a		16 55		17 12			17 25					17 40		17 55		18 12			18 25					18 40
Stansted Airport	d								17 25													18 25			
Elsenham	d	16 50												17 50											
Newport (Essex)	d	16 55												17 55											
Audley End	d	16 58				17 24			17 39					17 58				18 24				18 39			
Great Chesterford	d	17 03												18 03											
Whittlesford Parkway	d	17 08				17 31								18 08				18 31							
Shelford	d	17 12												18 12											
Cambridge	a	17 19				17 41			17 58					18 19				18 41				18 58			

A until 24 June

Table 22

Sundays
until 22 July

London - Broxbourne, Hertford East, Bishops Stortford, Stansted Airport and Cambridge

Network Diagram - see first Page of Table 20

		LE ■	LE ■ (trolley)	LE	LE ■ (trolley)	LE ■	LE	LE ■ (trolley)	XC ◇■ A	LE ■	LE	LE ■ (trolley)	LE ■	LE ■ (trolley)	LE	LE ■ (trolley)	LE ■	LE	LE ■ (trolley)	XC ■	LE ■	LE	LE ■ (trolley)
London Liverpool Street ■ ⊖	d		18 10	18 22	18 25	18 28		18 40			18 52	18 55		19 10	19 22	19 25	19 28		19 40			19 52	19 55
Bethnal Green	d																						
Hackney Downs	d			18 29							18 59				19 29							19 59	
Stratford ■ ⊖	d									18 45											19 45		
Clapton	d																						
Seven Sisters ⊖	d			18 34							19 04				19 34							20 04	
Tottenham Hale ⊖	d		18 22		18 37	18 40		18 52		18 55		19 07		19 22		19 37	19 40		19 52		19 55		20 07
Northumberland Park	d																						
Angel Road	d																						
Ponders End	d									18 59											19 59		
Brimsdown	d									19 02											20 02		
Enfield Lock	d									19 04											20 04		
Waltham Cross	d						←			19 07								←			20 07		
Cheshunt	d			18 52		18 49	18 52			19 09	19 20				19 52		19 49	19 52			20 09	20 20	
Broxbourne ■	a			→		18 53	18 57			19 14	19 25				→		19 53	19 57			20 14	20 25	
Broxbourne ■	d					18 53	18 57			19 19	19 25						19 53	19 57			20 19	20 25	
Rye House	d						19 00				19 28							20 00				20 28	
St Margarets (Herts)	d						19 03				19 31							20 03				20 31	
Ware	d						19 07				19 35							20 07				20 35	
Hertford East	a						19 14				19 42							20 14				20 42	
Roydon	d	←								19 24			←								20 24		
Harlow Town	d	18 28			18 52	18 59				19 28		19 22	19 28			19 52	19 59				20 28		20 22
Harlow Mill	d	18 31								→			19 31								→		
Sawbridgeworth	d	18 34				19 04							19 34				20 04						
Bishops Stortford	a	18 41	18 45			19 11		19 15					19 41	19 45			20 11		20 15				
	d	18 42	18 46			19 12		19 16					19 42	19 46			20 12		20 16				
Stansted Mountfitchet	d	18 46			19 03								19 46			20 03							
Stansted Airport	a		18 55		19 12			19 25				19 40		19 55		20 12			20 25				20 40
Stansted Airport	d								19 25											20 25			
Elsenham	d	18 50											19 50										
Newport (Essex)	d	18 55											19 55										
Audley End	d	18 58				19 24			19 39				19 58				20 24			20 39			
Great Chesterford	d	19 03											20 03										
Whittlesford Parkway	d	19 08				19 31							20 08				20 31						
Shelford	d	19 12											20 12										
Cambridge	a	19 19				19 41			19 58				20 19				20 41			20 57			

		LE ■	LE ■ (trolley)	LE	LE ■ (trolley)	LE ■	LE	XC ■	LE ■ (trolley)	LE ■	LE	LE ■ (trolley)	LE ■	LE ■ (trolley)	LE	LE ■ (trolley)	LE ■	LE	LE ■ (trolley)	XC ■	LE ■	LE
London Liverpool Street ■ ⊖	d		20 10	20 22	20 25	20 28			20 40		20 52	20 55		21 10	21 22	21 25	21 28		21 40			21 52
Bethnal Green	d																					
Hackney Downs	d			20 29							20 59				21 29							21 59
Stratford ■ ⊖	d									20 45											21 45	
Clapton	d																					
Seven Sisters ⊖	d			20 34							21 04				21 34							22 04
Tottenham Hale ⊖	d		20 22		20 37	20 40			20 52	20 55		21 07		21 22		21 37	21 40		21 52		21 55	
Northumberland Park	d																					
Angel Road	d																					
Ponders End	d									20 59											21 59	
Brimsdown	d									21 02											22 02	
Enfield Lock	d									21 04											22 04	
Waltham Cross	d						←			21 07								←			22 07	
Cheshunt	d			20 52		20 49	20 52			21 09	21 20				21 52		21 49	21 52			22 09	22 20
Broxbourne ■	a			→		20 53	20 57			21 14	21 25				→		21 53	21 57			22 14	22 25
Broxbourne ■	d					20 53	20 57			21 19	21 25						21 53	21 57			22 19	22 25
Rye House	d						21 00				21 28							22 00				22 28
St Margarets (Herts)	d						21 03				21 31							22 03				22 31
Ware	d						21 07				21 35							22 07				22 35
Hertford East	a						21 14				21 42							22 14				22 42
Roydon	d	←								21 24			←								22 24	
Harlow Town	d	20 28			20 52	20 59				21 28		21 22	21 28			21 52	21 59				22 28	
Harlow Mill	d	20 31								→			21 31								→	
Sawbridgeworth	d	20 34				21 04							21 34				22 04					
Bishops Stortford	a	20 41	20 45			21 11			21 15				21 41	21 45			22 11		22 15			
	d	20 42	20 46			21 12			21 16				21 42	21 46			22 12		22 16			
Stansted Mountfitchet	d	20 46			21 03								21 46			22 03						
Stansted Airport	a		20 55		21 12				21 27			21 40		21 55		22 12			22 25			
Stansted Airport	d							21 19												22 25		
Elsenham	d	20 50											21 50									
Newport (Essex)	d	20 55											21 55									
Audley End	d	20 58				21 24		21 33					21 58				22 24			22 40		
Great Chesterford	d	21 03											22 03									
Whittlesford Parkway	d	21 08				21 31							22 08				22 31					
Shelford	d	21 12											22 12									
Cambridge	a	21 19				21 41		21 47					22 19				22 41			22 57		

A until 24 June

Table 22

Sundays
until 22 July

London - Broxbourne, Hertford East, Bishops Stortford, Stansted Airport and Cambridge

Network Diagram - see first Page of Table 20

		LE ■ (trolley)	LE ■	LE ■ (trolley)	XC ■	LE	LE ■ (trolley)	LE ■	LE	LE ■ (trolley)	LE ■	LE	LE ■ (trolley)	LE ■	LE	LE	LE ■	LE ■	LE	LE ■
London Liverpool Street ■ ⊖	d	21 55		22 10		22 22	22 25	22 28		22 40		22 52	22 55			23 22	23 25	23 28		23 58
Bethnal Green	d																			
Hackney Downs	d					22 29						22 59				23 29				
Stratford ■ ⊖	d										22 45									
Clapton	d																			
Seven Sisters ⊖	d					22 34						23 04				23 34				
Tottenham Hale ⊖	d	22 07		22 22			22 37	22 40		22 52	22 55		23 07				23 37	23 40		00 10
Northumberland Park	d																			
Angel Road	d																			
Ponders End	d										22 59							23 44		
Brimsdown	d										23 02							23 47		
Enfield Lock	d										23 04							23 49		
Waltham Cross	d								←		23 07							23 52		
Cheshunt	d					22 52		22 49	22 52		23 09	23 20				23 50		23 54	←	00 18
Broxbourne ■	a					→		22 53	22 57		23 14	23 25				23 55		23 59	23 55	00 22
Broxbourne ■	d							22 53	22 57		23 19	23 25				00 02		23 59	00 02	00 22
Rye House	d								23 00							→			00 06	
St Margarets (Herts)	d								23 03										00 09	
Ware	d								23 07										00 13	
Hertford East	a								23 14										00 19	
Roydon	d		←								23 24			←	←					00 26
Harlow Town	d	22 22	22 28				22 52	22 59			23 28	23 32	23 22	23 28	23 32		23 52	00 05		00 30
Harlow Mill	d		22 31								→	→		23 31						00 33
Sawbridgeworth	d		22 34					23 04						23 34				00 10		00 37
Bishops Stortford	a		22 41	22 45				23 11		23 15				23 41	23 45		00 02	00 17		00 44
	d		22 42	22 46				23 12		23 16				23 42			00 03			
Stansted Mountfitchet	d		22 46				23 03							23 46						
Stansted Airport	a	22 40		22 55			23 12			23 25			23 40				00 12			
Stansted Airport	d				23 04															
Elsenham	d		22 50											23 50						
Newport (Essex)	d		22 55											23 55						
Audley End	d		22 58		23 18			23 24						23 58						
Great Chesterford	d		23 03											00 03						
Whittlesford Parkway	d		23 08					23 31						00 08						
Shelford	d		23 12											00 12						
Cambridge	a		23 19		23 34			23 41						00 19						

Sundays
29 July to 12 August

		LE ■	LE ■	LE ■	LE ■	LE ■	LE ■	LE ■	LE ■	LE ■	LE ■	LE ■	LE ■	LE ■	LE ■	LE ■	LE ■	LE ■	LE ■ (trolley)	LE ■ (trolley)	LE ■ (trolley)	LE	LE ■
London Liverpool Street ■ ⊖	d	22p42		23p12	23p25			23p42		00 18	04 10	04 40	05 10	05 40	06 10	06 25	06 40	06 55	07 10	07 25	07 40		07 43
Bethnal Green	d																						
Hackney Downs	d																						
Stratford ■ ⊖	d	22p55	23p15	23p25			23p45	23p55	00 15	00 30													
Clapton	d																						
Seven Sisters ⊖	d					←																	
Tottenham Hale ⊖	d	23p10	23p25	23p40	23p37	23p40	23p55	00 10	00 25	00 40		04u52	05u22	05u52	06u22	06u37	06u52	07 07	07 22	07 37	07 52		07 55
Northumberland Park	d			→			23p57																
Angel Road	d																						
Ponders End	d		23p29				00 01		00 29														07 59
Brimsdown	d		23p32				00 04		00 32														08 02
Enfield Lock	d		23p34				00 06		00 34														08 04
Waltham Cross	d		23p37				00 09		00 37														08 07
Cheshunt	d	23p18	23p39			23p48	00 11	00 18	00 39	00 48				06 00									08 09
Broxbourne ■	a	23p22	23p44			23p52	00 16	00 22	00 44	00 52				06 04									08 14
Broxbourne ■	d	23p22	23p44			23p52	00 16	00 22	00 44	00 52				06 04								07 57	08 18
Rye House	d		23p47				00 19		00 47													08 00	
St Margarets (Herts)	d		23p50				00 22		00 50													08 03	
Ware	d		23p54				00 26		00 54													08 07	
Hertford East	a		00 01				00 33		01 01													08 14	
Roydon	d					23p56		00 26															08 22
Harlow Town	d	23p28			23p54	00 01		00 30		00 58		05 07	05 37	06 10		06 52		07 22		07 52			08 26
Harlow Mill	d					00 03		00 33															→
Sawbridgeworth	d					00 07		00 37		01 03													
Bishops Stortford	a	23p38			00 04	00 14		00 44		01 10		05 17	05 47	06 20	06 45		07 15		07 45		08 15		
	d	23p39			00 04	00 14		00 44		01 11		05 18	05 48	06 21	06 46		07 16		07 46		08 16		
Stansted Mountfitchet	d					00 18		00 48		01 15		05 22				07 03				08 03			
Stansted Airport	a				00 13						04 58	05 29	05 57	06 30	06 55	07 12	07 25	07 40	07 55	08 13	08 25		
Stansted Airport	d																						
Elsenham	d					00 22		00 52		01 19													
Newport (Essex)	d					00 27		00 57		01 24													
Audley End	d	23p51				00 30		01 00		01 27													
Great Chesterford	d					00 35		01 05		01 32													
Whittlesford Parkway	d	23p58				00 40		01 10		01 37													
Shelford	d					00 44				01 41													
Cambridge	a	00 08				00 51		01 19		01 49													

London - Broxbourne, Hertford East, Bishops Stortford, Stansted Airport and Cambridge

Network Diagram - see first Page of Table 20

Station		LE ■ ⌶	LE ■	LE ■ ⌶	LE ■	LE ■ ⌶	LE ■	LE ■ ⌶	LE ■	LE ■ ⌶	LE ■	LE ■ ⌶	LE ■	LE ■ ⌶	LE ■	LE ■ ⌶	LE ■	LE ■ ⌶	LE ■	LE ■ ⌶	LE ■	LE ■ ⌶	LE ■
London Liverpool Street ■ ⊖	d	07 55		08 10	08 19	08 25		08 40		08 55		09 10		09 25		09 40		09 55		10 10		10 25	
Bethnal Green	d																						
Hackney Downs	d																						
Stratford ■ ⊖	d						08 30		08 45		09 00		09 15		09 30		09 45		10 00		10 15		10 30
Clapton	d																						
Seven Sisters ⊖	d																						
Tottenham Hale ⊖	d	08 07		08 22	08 31	08 37	08 40	08 52	08 55	09 07	09 10	09 22	09 25	09 37	09 40	09 52	09 55	10 07	10 10	10 22	10 25	10 37	10 40
Northumberland Park	d																						
Angel Road	d																						
Ponders End	d								08 59				09 29				09 59				10 29		
Brimsdown	d								09 02				09 32				10 02				10 32		
Enfield Lock	d								09 04				09 34				10 04				10 34		
Waltham Cross	d								09 07				09 37				10 07				10 37		
Cheshunt	d				08 39		08 49		09 09		09 18		09 39		09 49		10 09		10 18		10 39		10 49
Broxbourne ■	a				08 44		08 53		09 14		09 23		09 44		09 53		10 14		10 23		10 44		10 53
Broxbourne ■	d				08 44		08 53		09 14		09 23		09 44		09 53		10 14		10 23		10 44		10 53
Rye House	d				08 47				09 17				09 47				10 17				10 47		
St Margarets (Herts)	d				08 50				09 20				09 50				10 20				10 50		
Ware	d				08 54				09 24				09 54				10 24				10 54		
Hertford East	a				09 01				09 31				10 01				10 31				11 01		
Roydon	d		←								09 27								10 27				
Harlow Town	d	08 22	08 26			08 53	08 59			09 23	09 31			09 53	09 59			10 23	10 31			10 53	10 59
Harlow Mill	d		08 29								09 34								10 34				
Sawbridgeworth	d		08 33				09 04				09 37				10 04				10 37				11 04
Bishops Stortford	a		08 40	08 45			09 11	09 15			09 44	09 48			10 11	10 15			10 44	10 48			11 11
	d		08 40	08 46			09 12	09 16			09 44	09 48			10 12	10 16			10 44	10 48			11 12
Stansted Mountfitchet	d		08 44			09 04					09 49			10 04					10 49			11 04	
Stansted Airport	a	08 40		08 55		09 13		09 25		09 41		09 58		10 13		10 25		10 41		10 58		11 13	
Stansted Airport	d																						
Elsenham	d		08 48								09 52								10 52				
Newport (Essex)	d		08 53								09 58								10 58				
Audley End	d		08 56				09 24				10 01				10 24				11 01				11 24
Great Chesterford	d		09 01								10 06								11 06				
Whittlesford Parkway	d		09 06				09 31				10 10				10 31				11 10				11 31
Shelford	d		09 10								10 15								11 15				
Cambridge	a		09 18				09 41				10 22				10 41				11 23				11 41

Station		LE ■ ⌶	LE ■	XC ◇■	LE ■ ⌶	LE ■	LE ■ ⌶	LE ■	LE ■ ⌶ A	LE ■ ⌶ B	LE ■	LE ■ ⌶	LE ■	XC ◇■	LE ■ ⌶	LE ■	LE ■ ⌶	LE ■	LE ■ ⌶	LE ■	LE ■ ⌶	LE ■	XC ◇■
London Liverpool Street ■ ⊖	d	10 40			10 55		11 10		11 25	11 25		11 40			11 55		12 10		12 25		12 40		
Bethnal Green	d																						
Hackney Downs	d																						
Stratford ■ ⊖	d		10 45			11 00		11 15			11 30		11 45			12 00		12 15		12 30		12 45	
Clapton	d																						
Seven Sisters ⊖	d																						
Tottenham Hale ⊖	d	10 52	10 55		11 07	11 10	11 22	11 25	11 37	11 37	11 40	11 52	11 55		12 07	12 10	12 22	12 25	12 37	12 40	12 52	12 55	
Northumberland Park	d																						
Angel Road	d																						
Ponders End	d		10 59					11 29					11 59					12 29				12 59	
Brimsdown	d		11 02					11 32					12 02					12 32				13 02	
Enfield Lock	d		11 04					11 34					12 04					12 34				13 04	
Waltham Cross	d		11 07					11 37					12 07					12 37				13 07	
Cheshunt	d		11 09			11 18		11 39	11 45		11 49		12 09			12 18		12 39		12 49		13 09	
Broxbourne ■	a		11 14			11 23		11 44			11 53		12 14			12 23		12 44		12 53		13 14	
Broxbourne ■	d		11 14			11 23		11 44			11 53		12 14			12 23		12 44		12 53		13 14	
Rye House	d		11 17					11 47					12 17					12 47				13 17	
St Margarets (Herts)	d		11 20					11 50					12 20					12 50				13 20	
Ware	d		11 24					11 54					12 24					12 54				13 24	
Hertford East	a		11 31					12 01					12 31					13 01				13 31	
Roydon	d					11 27										12 27							
Harlow Town	d				11 23	11 31			11 55	11 53	11 59				12 23	12 31			12 53	12 59			
Harlow Mill	d					11 34										12 34							
Sawbridgeworth	d					11 37					12 04					12 37				13 04			
Bishops Stortford	a	11 15				11 44	11 48				12 11	12 15				12 44	12 48			13 11	13 15		
	d	11 16				11 44	11 48				12 12	12 16				12 44	12 48			13 12	13 16		
Stansted Mountfitchet	d					11 49			12 06	12 04						12 49			13 04				
Stansted Airport	a	11 25			11 41		11 58		12 14	12 13		12 25			12 41		12 58		13 13		13 25		
Stansted Airport	d			11 25										12 25									13 25
Elsenham	d					11 52										12 52							
Newport (Essex)	d					11 58										12 58							
Audley End	d			11 39		12 01					12 24			12 39		13 01				13 24			13 39
Great Chesterford	d					12 06										13 06							
Whittlesford Parkway	d					12 10					12 31					13 10				13 31			
Shelford	d					12 15										13 15							
Cambridge	a			11 57		12 23					12 41			12 58		13 23				13 41			13 58

A 29 July

B from 5 to 12 August

London - Broxbourne, Hertford East, Bishops Stortford, Stansted Airport and Cambridge

Network Diagram - see first Page of Table 20

Station		LE ■ ⌶	LE ■	LE ■ ⌶	LE ■	LE ■ ⌶	LE ■	LE ■ ⌶	LE ■	XC ◇■	LE ■ ⌶	LE ■	LE ■ ⌶	LE ■	LE ■ ⌶	LE ■	LE ■ ⌶	LE ■	XC ◇■	LE ■ ⌶	LE ■	LE ■ ⌶	LE ■
London Liverpool Street ■ ⊖	d	12 55		13 10		13 25		13 40			13 55		14 10		14 25		14 40			14 55		15 10	
Bethnal Green	d																						
Hackney Downs	d																						
Stratford ■ ⊖	d		13 00		13 15		13 30		13 45			14 00		14 15		14 30		14 45			15 00		15 15
Clapton	d																						
Seven Sisters ⊖	d																						
Tottenham Hale ⊖	d	13 07	13 10	13 22	13 25	13 37	13 40	13 52	13 55		14 07	14 10	14 22	14 25	14 37	14 40	14 52	14 55		15 07	15 10	15 22	15 25
Northumberland Park	d																						
Angel Road	d																						
Ponders End	d				13 29				13 59					14 29				14 59					15 29
Brimsdown	d				13 32				14 02					14 32				15 02					15 32
Enfield Lock	d				13 34				14 04					14 34				15 04					15 34
Waltham Cross	d				13 37				14 07					14 37				15 07					15 37
Cheshunt	d		13 18		13 39		13 49		14 09			14 18		14 39		14 49		15 09			15 18		15 39
Broxbourne ■	a		13 23		13 44		13 53		14 14			14 23		14 44		14 53		15 14			15 23		15 44
Broxbourne ■	d		13 23		13 44		13 53		14 14			14 23		14 44		14 53		15 14			15 23		15 44
Rye House	d				13 47				14 17					14 47				15 17					15 47
St Margarets (Herts)	d				13 50				14 20					14 50				15 20					15 50
Ware	d				13 54				14 24					14 54				15 24					15 54
Hertford East	a				14 01				14 31					15 01				15 31					16 01
Roydon	d		13 27									14 27									15 27		
Harlow Town	d	13 23	13 31			13 53	13 59				14 23	14 31			14 53	14 59				15 23	15 31		
Harlow Mill	d		13 34									14 34									15 34		
Sawbridgeworth	d		13 37				14 04					14 37				15 04					15 37		
Bishops Stortford	a		13 44	13 48			14 11	14 15				14 44	14 48			15 11	15 15				15 44	15 48	
	d		13 44	13 48			14 12	14 16				14 44	14 48			15 12	15 16				15 44	15 48	
Stansted Mountfitchet	d		13 49			14 04						14 49			15 04						15 49		
Stansted Airport	a	13 41		13 58		14 13		14 25			14 41		14 58		15 13		15 25			15 41		15 58	
Stansted Airport	d									14 25									15 25				
Elsenham	d		13 52									14 52									15 52		
Newport (Essex)	d		13 58									14 58									15 58		
Audley End	d		14 01				14 24			14 39		15 01				15 24			15 39		16 01		
Great Chesterford	d		14 06									15 06									16 06		
Whittlesford Parkway	d		14 10				14 31					15 10				15 31					16 10		
Shelford	d		14 15									15 15									16 15		
Cambridge	a		14 23				14 41			14 57		15 23				15 41			15 58		16 23		

Station		LE ■ ⌶	LE ■	LE ■ ⌶	LE ■	XC ◇■	LE ■ ⌶	LE ■	LE ■ ⌶	LE ■	LE ■ ⌶	LE ■	LE ■ ⌶	LE ■	XC ◇■	LE ■ ⌶	LE ■	LE ■ ⌶	LE ■	LE ■ ⌶	LE ■	LE ■ ⌶
London Liverpool Street ■ ⊖	d	15 25		15 40			15 55		16 10		16 25		16 40			16 55		17 10		17 25		17 40
Bethnal Green	d																					
Hackney Downs	d																					
Stratford ■ ⊖	d		15 30		15 45			16 00		16 15		16 30		16 45			17 00		17 15		17 30	
Clapton	d																					
Seven Sisters ⊖	d																					
Tottenham Hale ⊖	d	15 37	15 40	15 52	15 55		16 07	16 10	16 22	16 25	16 37	16 40	16 52	16 55		17 07	17 10	17 22	17 25	17 37	17 40	17 52
Northumberland Park	d																					
Angel Road	d																					
Ponders End	d				15 59					16 29				16 59					17 29			
Brimsdown	d				16 02					16 32				17 02					17 32			
Enfield Lock	d				16 04					16 34				17 04					17 34			
Waltham Cross	d				16 07					16 37				17 07					17 37			
Cheshunt	d		15 49		16 09			16 18		16 39		16 49		17 09			17 18		17 39		17 49	
Broxbourne ■	a		15 53		16 14			16 23		16 44		16 53		17 14			17 23		17 44		17 53	
Broxbourne ■	d		15 53		16 14			16 23		16 44		16 53		17 14			17 23		17 44		17 53	
Rye House	d				16 17					16 47				17 17					17 47			
St Margarets (Herts)	d				16 20					16 50				17 20					17 50			
Ware	d				16 24					16 54				17 24					17 54			
Hertford East	a				16 31					17 01				17 31					18 01			
Roydon	d							16 27									17 27					
Harlow Town	d	15 53	15 59				16 23	16 31			16 53	16 59				17 23	17 31			17 53	17 59	
Harlow Mill	d							16 34									17 34					
Sawbridgeworth	d		16 04					16 37				17 04					17 37				18 04	
Bishops Stortford	a		16 11	16 15				16 44	16 48			17 11	17 15				17 44	17 48			18 11	18 15
	d		16 12	16 16				16 44	16 48			17 12	17 16				17 44	17 48			18 12	18 16
Stansted Mountfitchet	d	16 04						16 49			17 04						17 49			18 04		
Stansted Airport	a	16 13		16 25			16 41		16 58		17 13		17 25			17 41		17 58		18 13		18 25
Stansted Airport	d					16 25									17 25							
Elsenham	d							16 52									17 52					
Newport (Essex)	d							16 58									17 58					
Audley End	d		16 24			16 39		17 01				17 24			17 39		18 01				18 24	
Great Chesterford	d							17 06									18 06					
Whittlesford Parkway	d		16 31					17 10				17 31					18 10				18 31	
Shelford	d							17 15									18 15					
Cambridge	a		16 41			16 58		17 23				17 41			17 58		18 23				18 41	

Sundays
29 July to 12 August

London - Broxbourne, Hertford East, Bishops Stortford, Stansted Airport and Cambridge

Network Diagram - see first Page of Table 20

		LE 1	LE 1 ⊼	LE 1	LE 1 ⊼	LE 1	LE 1 ⊼	LE 1	LE 1 ⊼	LE 1	LE 1 ⊼	LE 1	LE 1 ⊼	LE 1	LE 1 ⊼	LE 1	LE 1 ⊼	LE 1	XC 1	LE 1 ⊼	LE 1	LE 1 ⊼	LE 1
London Liverpool Street 15 ⊖	d		17 55		18 10		18 25		18 40		18 55		19 10		19 25		19 40			19 55		20 10	
Bethnal Green	d																						
Hackney Downs	d																						
Stratford 7 ⊖	d	17 45		18 00		18 15		18 30		18 45		19 00		19 15		19 30		19 45			20 00		20 15
Clapton	d																						
Seven Sisters ⊖	d																						
Tottenham Hale ⊖	d	17 55	18 07	18 10	18 22	18 25	18 37	18 40	18 52	18 55	19 07	19 10	19 22	19 25	19 37	19 40	19 52	19 55		20 07	20 10	20 22	20 25
Northumberland Park	d																						
Angel Road	d																						
Ponders End	d	17 59				18 29				18 59				19 29				19 59					20 29
Brimsdown	d	18 02				18 32				19 02				19 32				20 02					20 32
Enfield Lock	d	18 04				18 34				19 04				19 34				20 04					20 34
Waltham Cross	d	18 07				18 37				19 07				19 37				20 07					20 37
Cheshunt	d	18 09		18 18		18 39		18 49		19 09		19 18		19 39		19 49		20 09			20 18		20 39
Broxbourne 3	a	18 14		18 23		18 44		18 53		19 14		19 23		19 44		19 53		20 14			20 23		20 44
Broxbourne 3	d	18 14		18 23		18 44		18 53		19 14		19 23		19 44		19 53		20 14			20 23		20 44
Rye House	d	18 17				18 47				19 17				19 47				20 17					20 47
St Margarets (Herts)	d	18 20				18 50				19 20				19 50				20 20					20 50
Ware	d	18 24				18 54				19 24				19 54				20 24					20 54
Hertford East	a	18 31				19 01				19 31				20 01				20 31					21 01
Roydon	d			18 27								19 27									20 27		
Harlow Town	d		18 23	18 31			18 53	18 59			19 23	19 31			19 52	19 59				20 23	20 31		
Harlow Mill	d			18 34								19 34									20 34		
Sawbridgeworth	d			18 37				19 04				19 37				20 04					20 37		
Bishops Stortford	a			18 44	18 48			19 11	19 15			19 44	19 48			20 11	20 15				20 44	20 48	
	d			18 44	18 48			19 12	19 16			19 44	19 48			20 12	20 16				20 44	20 48	
Stansted Mountfitchet	d			18 49			19 04					19 49			20 03						20 49		
Stansted Airport	a		18 41		18 58		19 13		19 25		19 41		19 58		20 12		20 25			20 41		20 58	
Stansted Airport	d																		20 25				
Elsenham	d			18 52								19 52									20 52		
Newport (Essex)	d			18 58								19 58									20 58		
Audley End	d			19 01				19 24				20 01				20 24			20 39		21 01		
Great Chesterford	d			19 06								20 06									21 06		
Whittlesford Parkway	d			19 10				19 31				20 10				20 31					21 10		
Shelford	d			19 15								20 15									21 15		
Cambridge	a			19 24				19 41				20 22				20 41			20 57		21 22		

		LE 1 ⊼	LE 1	XC 1	LE 1 ⊼	LE 1	LE 1 ⊼	LE 1	LE 1 ⊼	LE 1	LE 1 ⊼	LE 1	LE 1 ⊼	LE 1	XC 1	LE 1 ⊼	LE 1	LE 1 ⊼	LE 1	XC 1	LE 1 ⊼	LE 1	LE 1 ⊼
London Liverpool Street 15 ⊖	d	20 25			20 40		20 55		21 10		21 25		21 40			21 55		22 10			22 25		22 40
Bethnal Green	d																						
Hackney Downs	d																						
Stratford 7 ⊖	d		20 30			20 45		21 00		21 15		21 30		21 45			22 00		22 15			22 30	
Clapton	d																						
Seven Sisters ⊖	d																						
Tottenham Hale ⊖	d	20 37	20 40		20 52	20 55	21 07	21 10	21 22	21 25	21 37	21 40	21 52	21 55		22 07	22 10	22 22	22 25		22 37	22 40	22 52
Northumberland Park	d																						
Angel Road	d																						
Ponders End	d					20 59				21 29				21 59					22 29				
Brimsdown	d					21 02				21 32				22 02					22 32				
Enfield Lock	d					21 04				21 34				22 04					22 34				
Waltham Cross	d					21 07				21 37				22 07					22 37				
Cheshunt	d		20 49			21 09		21 18		21 39		21 49		22 09			22 18		22 39			22 49	
Broxbourne 3	a		20 53			21 14		21 23		21 44		21 53		22 14			22 23		22 44			22 53	
Broxbourne 3	d		20 53			21 14		21 23		21 44		21 53		22 14			22 23		22 44			22 53	
Rye House	d					21 17				21 47				22 17					22 47				
St Margarets (Herts)	d					21 20				21 50				22 20					22 50				
Ware	d					21 24				21 54				22 24					22 54				
Hertford East	a					21 31				22 01				22 31					23 01				
Roydon	d							21 27									22 27						
Harlow Town	d	20 53	20 59				21 23	21 31			21 53	21 59				22 23	22 31				22 53	22 59	
Harlow Mill	d							21 34									22 34						
Sawbridgeworth	d		21 04					21 37				22 04					22 37					23 04	
Bishops Stortford	a		21 11		21 15			21 44	21 48			22 11	22 15				22 44	22 48				23 11	23 15
	d		21 12		21 16			21 44	21 48			22 12	22 16				22 44	22 48				23 12	23 16
Stansted Mountfitchet	d	21 04						21 49			22 04						22 49				23 04		
Stansted Airport	a	21 13			21 27		21 41		21 58		22 13		22 25			22 41		22 58			23 13		23 25
Stansted Airport	d			21 19											22 25					23 04			
Elsenham	d							21 52									22 52						
Newport (Essex)	d							21 58									22 58						
Audley End	d		21 24	21 33				22 01				22 24			22 40		23 01			23 18		23 24	
Great Chesterford	d							22 06									23 06						
Whittlesford Parkway	d		21 31					22 10				22 31					23 10					23 31	
Shelford	d							22 15									23 15						
Cambridge	a		21 41	21 47				22 22				22 41			22 57		23 23			23 34		23 41	

Sundays
29 July to 12 August

London - Broxbourne, Hertford East, Bishops Stortford, Stansted Airport and Cambridge

Network Diagram - see first Page of Table 20

		LE 1	LE	LE 1 ⊼	LE 1	LE	LE 1	LE 1	LE 1	LE 1	LE 1
London Liverpool Street 15 ⊖	d		22 52	22 55				23 25			
Bethnal Green	d										
Hackney Downs	d		22 59								
Stratford 7 ⊖	d	22 45			23 00		23 15		23 30	23 45	23 59
Clapton	d										
Seven Sisters ⊖	d		23 04								
Tottenham Hale ⊖	d	22 55		23 07	23 10		23 25	23 37	23 40	23 55	00 10
Northumberland Park	d										
Angel Road	d										
Ponders End	d	22 59					23 29			23 59	
Brimsdown	d	23 02					23 32			00 02	
Enfield Lock	d	23 04					23 34			00 04	
Waltham Cross	d	23 07				←	23 37			00 07	
Cheshunt	d	23 09	23 22		23 18	23 22	23 39		23 49	00 09	00 18
Broxbourne 3	a	23 14	→		23 23	23 27	23 44		23 53	00 14	00 22
Broxbourne 3	d	23 14			23 23	23 27	23 44		23 53	00 14	00 22
Rye House	d	23 17					23 47			00 17	
St Margarets (Herts)	d	23 20					23 50			00 20	
Ware	d	23 24					23 54			00 24	
Hertford East	a	23 31					00 01			00 31	
Roydon	d				23 27				23 57		00 26
Harlow Town	d			23 23	23 31	23 34		23 53	00 01		00 30
Harlow Mill	d				23 34				00 04		00 33
Sawbridgeworth	d				23 37				00 08		00 37
Bishops Stortford	a				23 44	23 47		00 03	00 15		00 44
	d				23 44			00 04	00 15		00 44
Stansted Mountfitchet	d				23 49				00 19		00 48
Stansted Airport	a			23 41				00 13			
Stansted Airport	d										
Elsenham	d				23 52				00 23		00 52
Newport (Essex)	d				23 58				00 28		00 57
Audley End	d				00 01				00 31		01 00
Great Chesterford	d				00 06				00 36		01 05
Whittlesford Parkway	d				00 10				00 41		01 10
Shelford	d				00 15				00 45		
Cambridge	a				00 22				00 52		01 19

Sundays
19 August to 26 August

		LE 1	LE 1	LE 1	LE 1	LE 1	LE 1	LE 1	LE 1	LE 1	LE 1	LE 1	LE 1	LE 1	LE 1	LE 1 ⊼	LE 1 ⊼	LE 1 ⊼	LE	LE 1	LE	LE 1 ⊼	LE 1
London Liverpool Street 15 ⊖	d	22p58	23p12	23p25	23p28	23p40	23p58	04 10	04 40	05 10	05 40	06 10	06 25	06 40	06 55	07 10	07 25	07 40		07 43	07 52	07 55	
Bethnal Green	d																						
Hackney Downs	d		23p18			23p46															07 59		
Stratford 7 ⊖	d																						
Clapton	d					23p49																	
Seven Sisters ⊖	d																				08 04		
Tottenham Hale ⊖	d	23p10	23p25	23b37	23p40	23p53	00 10		04u52	05u22	05u52	06u22	06u37	06u52	07 07	07 22	07 37	07 52		07 55		08 07	
Northumberland Park	d					23p55																	
Angel Road	d																						
Ponders End	d		23p29			23p59														07 59			
Brimsdown	d		23p32			00 02														08 02			
Enfield Lock	d		23p34			00 04														08 04			
Waltham Cross	d		23p37			00 07														08 07			
Cheshunt	d	23p18	23p39		23p48	00 09	00 18				06 00									08 09	08 20		
Broxbourne 3	a	23p22	23p44		23p52	00 14	00 22				06 04									08 14	08 25		
Broxbourne 3	d	23p22	23p44		23p52	00 14	00 22				06 04								07 57	08 19	08 25		
Rye House	d		23p47			00 17													08 00		08 28		
St Margarets (Herts)	d		23p50			00 20													08 03		08 31		
Ware	d		23p54			00 24													08 07		08 35		
Hertford East	a		00 01			00 31													08 14		08 42		
Roydon	d				23p56		00 26													08 24			←
Harlow Town	d	23p28		23p54	00 01		00 30		05 07	05 37	06 10		06 52		07 22		07 52			08 28		08 22	08 28
Harlow Mill	d				00 03		00 33																08 31
Sawbridgeworth	d				00 07		00 37													→			08 34
Bishops Stortford	a	23p38		00 04	00 14		00 44		05 17	05 47	06 20	06 45		07 15		07 45		08 15					08 41
	d	23p39		00 04	00 14		00 44		05 18	05 48	06 21	06 46		07 16		07 46		08 16					08 42
Stansted Mountfitchet	d				00 18		00 48		05 22				07 03				08 03						08 46
Stansted Airport	a			00 13				04 58	05 29	05 57	06 30	06 55	07 12	07 25	07 40	07 55	08 13	08 25				08 40	
Stansted Airport	d																						
Elsenham	d				00 22		00 52																08 50
Newport (Essex)	d				00 27		00 57																08 55
Audley End	d	23p51			00 30		01 00																08 58
Great Chesterford	d				00 35		01 05																09 03
Whittlesford Parkway	d	23p58			00 40		01 10																09 08
Shelford	d				00 44																		09 12
Cambridge	a	00 08			00 51		01 19																09 19

b Previous night, stops to pick up only

Table 22

Sundays

19 August to 26 August

London - Broxbourne, Hertford East, Bishops Stortford, Stansted Airport and Cambridge

Network Diagram - see first Page of Table 20

		LE	LE	LE	LE	LE	LE	LE	LE	LE	LE	LE	LE	LE	LE	LE	LE	LE	LE	LE	LE	LE	LE
		1		1	1		1	1		1	1	1		1	1		1	1		1	1	1	
		⊼		⊼			⊼			⊼		⊼		⊼			⊼			⊼		⊼	
London Liverpool Street 15 ⊖	d	08 10	08 22	08 25	08 28		08 40		08 52	08 55		09 10	09 22	09 25	09 28		09 40		09 52	09 55		10 10	10 22
Bethnal Green	d																						
Hackney Downs	d		08 29						08 59				09 29						09 59				10 29
Stratford 7 ⊖	d							08 45										09 45					
Clapton	d																						
Seven Sisters ⊖	d		08 34						09 04				09 34						10 04				10 34
Tottenham Hale ⊖	d	08 22		08 37	08 40		08 52	08 55		09 07		09 22		09 37	09 40		09 52	09 55		10 07		10 22	
Northumberland Park	d																						
Angel Road	d																						
Ponders End	d							08 59										09 59					
Brimsdown	d							09 02										10 02					
Enfield Lock	d							09 04										10 04					
Waltham Cross	d					←		09 07								←		10 07					
Cheshunt	d		08 52		08 49	08 52		09 09	09 20				09 52		09 49	09 52		10 09	10 20				10 52
Broxbourne 3	a		→		08 53	08 57		09 14	09 25				→		09 53	09 57		10 14	10 25				→
Broxbourne 3	d				08 53	08 57		09 19	09 25						09 53	09 57		10 19	10 25				
Rye House	d					09 00			09 28							10 00			10 28				
St Margarets (Herts)	d					09 03			09 31							10 03			10 31				
Ware	d					09 07			09 35							10 07			10 35				
Hertford East	a					09 14			09 42							10 14			10 42				
Roydon	d							09 24			←							10 24			←		
Harlow Town	d			08 52	08 59			09 28		09 22	09 28			09 52	09 59			10 28		10 22	10 28		
Harlow Mill	d							→			09 31							→			10 31		
Sawbridgeworth	d				09 04						09 34				10 04						10 34		
Bishops Stortford	a	08 45			09 11		09 15				09 41	09 45			10 11		10 15				10 41	10 45	
	d	08 46			09 12		09 16				09 42	09 46			10 12		10 16				10 42	10 46	
Stansted Mountfitchet	d			09 03							09 46			10 03							10 46		
Stansted Airport	a	08 55		09 12			09 25			09 40		09 55		10 12			10 25			10 40		10 55	
Stansted Airport	d																						
Elsenham	d										09 50										10 50		
Newport (Essex)	d										09 55										10 55		
Audley End	d				09 24						09 58				10 24						10 58		
Great Chesterford	d										10 03										11 03		
Whittlesford Parkway	d				09 31						10 08				10 31						11 08		
Shelford	d										10 12										11 12		
Cambridge	a				09 41						10 19				10 41						11 19		

		LE	LE	LE	LE	XC	LE	LE	LE	LE	LE	LE	LE	LE	LE	LE	XC	LE	LE	LE	LE	LE
		1	1		1	◇1	1		1	1	1		1	1		1	◇1	1		1	1	1
		⊼			⊼				⊼		⊼		⊼			⊼				⊼		⊼
London Liverpool Street 15 ⊖	d	10 25	10 28		10 40			10 52	10 55		11 10	11 22	11 25	11 28		11 40			11 52	11 55		12 10
Bethnal Green	d																					
Hackney Downs	d							10 59				11 29							11 59			
Stratford 7 ⊖	d						10 45											11 45				
Clapton	d																					
Seven Sisters ⊖	d							11 04				11 34							12 04			
Tottenham Hale ⊖	d	10 37	10 40		10 52		10 55		11 07		11 22		11 37	11 40		11 52		11 55		12 07		12 22
Northumberland Park	d																					
Angel Road	d																					
Ponders End	d						10 59											11 59				
Brimsdown	d						11 02											12 02				
Enfield Lock	d						11 04											12 04				
Waltham Cross	d			←			11 07								←			12 07				
Cheshunt	d		10 49	10 52			11 09	11 20				11 52		11 49	11 52			12 09	12 20			
Broxbourne 3	a		10 53	10 57			11 14	11 25				→		11 53	11 57			12 14	12 25			
Broxbourne 3	d		10 53	10 57			11 19	11 25						11 53	11 57			12 19	12 25			
Rye House	d			11 00				11 28							12 00				12 28			
St Margarets (Herts)	d			11 03				11 31							12 03				12 31			
Ware	d			11 07				11 35							12 07				12 35			
Hertford East	a			11 14				11 42							12 14				12 42			
Roydon	d						11 24			←								12 24			←	
Harlow Town	d	10 52	10 59				11 28		11 22	11 28			11 52	11 59				12 28		12 22	12 28	
Harlow Mill	d						→			11 31								→			12 31	
Sawbridgeworth	d		11 04							11 34				12 04							12 34	
Bishops Stortford	a		11 11		11 15					11 41	11 45			12 11		12 15					12 41	12 45
	d		11 12		11 16					11 42	11 46			12 12		12 16					12 42	12 46
Stansted Mountfitchet	d	11 03								11 46			12 03								12 46	
Stansted Airport	a	11 12			11 25				11 40		11 55		12 12			12 25				12 40		12 55
Stansted Airport	d					11 25											12 25					
Elsenham	d									11 50											12 50	
Newport (Essex)	d									11 55											12 55	
Audley End	d		11 24			11 39				11 58				12 24			12 39				12 58	
Great Chesterford	d									12 03											13 03	
Whittlesford Parkway	d		11 31							12 08				12 31							13 08	
Shelford	d									12 12											13 12	
Cambridge	a		11 41			11 57				12 19				12 41			12 58				13 19	

Table 22

Sundays

19 August to 26 August

London - Broxbourne, Hertford East, Bishops Stortford, Stansted Airport and Cambridge

Network Diagram - see first Page of Table 20

		LE	LE	LE	LE	LE	XC	LE	LE	LE	LE	LE	LE	LE	LE	LE	LE	XC	LE	LE	LE	LE	LE
			1	1		1	◇1	1		1	1	1		1	1		1	◇1	1		1	1	1
			⊼			⊼				⊼		⊼		⊼			⊼				⊼		⊼
London Liverpool Street 15 ⊖	d	12 22	12 25	12 28		12 40			12 52	12 55		13 10	13 22	13 25	13 28		13 40			13 52	13 55		14 10
Bethnal Green	d																						
Hackney Downs	d	12 29							12 59				13 29							13 59			
Stratford 7 ⊖	d							12 45											13 45				
Clapton	d																						
Seven Sisters ⊖	d	12 34							13 04				13 34							14 04			
Tottenham Hale ⊖	d		12 37	12 40		12 52		12 55		13 07		13 22		13 37	13 40		13 52		13 55		14 07		14 22
Northumberland Park	d																						
Angel Road	d																						
Ponders End	d							12 59											13 59				
Brimsdown	d							13 02											14 02				
Enfield Lock	d							13 04											14 04				
Waltham Cross	d				←			13 07								←			14 07				
Cheshunt	d	12 52		12 49	12 52			13 09	13 20				13 52		13 49	13 52			14 09	14 20			
Broxbourne 3	a	→		12 53	12 57			13 14	13 25				→		13 53	13 57			14 14	14 25			
Broxbourne 3	d			12 53	12 57			13 19	13 25						13 53	13 57			14 19	14 25			
Rye House	d				13 00				13 28							14 00				14 28			
St Margarets (Herts)	d				13 03				13 31							14 03				14 31			
Ware	d				13 07				13 35							14 07				14 35			
Hertford East	a				13 14				13 42							14 14				14 42			
Roydon	d							13 24			←								14 24			←	
Harlow Town	d		12 52	12 59				13 28		13 22	13 28			13 52	13 59				14 28		14 22	14 28	
Harlow Mill	d							→			13 31								→			14 31	
Sawbridgeworth	d			13 04							13 34				14 04							14 34	
Bishops Stortford	a			13 11		13 15					13 41	13 45			14 11		14 15					14 41	14 45
	d			13 12		13 16					13 42	13 46			14 12		14 16					14 42	14 46
Stansted Mountfitchet	d		13 03								13 46			14 03								14 46	
Stansted Airport	a		13 12			13 25				13 40		13 55		14 12			14 25				14 40		14 55
Stansted Airport	d						13 25											14 25					
Elsenham	d										13 50											14 50	
Newport (Essex)	d										13 55											14 55	
Audley End	d			13 24			13 39				13 58				14 24			14 39				14 58	
Great Chesterford	d										14 03											15 03	
Whittlesford Parkway	d			13 31							14 08				14 31							15 08	
Shelford	d										14 12											15 12	
Cambridge	a			13 41			13 58				14 19				14 41			14 57				15 19	

		LE	LE	LE	LE	LE	XC	LE	LE	LE	LE	LE	LE	LE	LE	LE	LE	XC	LE	LE	LE	LE
			1	1		1	◇1	1		1	1	1		1	1		1	◇1	1		1	1
			⊼			⊼				⊼		⊼		⊼			⊼				⊼	
London Liverpool Street 15 ⊖	d	14 22	14 25	14 28		14 40			14 52	14 55		15 10	15 22	15 25	15 28		15 40			15 52	15 55	
Bethnal Green	d																					
Hackney Downs	d	14 29							14 59				15 29							15 59		
Stratford 7 ⊖	d							14 45											15 45			
Clapton	d																					
Seven Sisters ⊖	d	14 34							15 04				15 34							16 04		
Tottenham Hale ⊖	d		14 37	14 40		14 52		14 55		15 07		15 22		15 37	15 40		15 52		15 55		16 07	
Northumberland Park	d																					
Angel Road	d																					
Ponders End	d							14 59											15 59			
Brimsdown	d							15 02											16 02			
Enfield Lock	d							15 04											16 04			
Waltham Cross	d				←			15 07								←			16 07			
Cheshunt	d	14 52		14 49	14 52			15 09	15 20				15 52		15 49	15 52			16 09	16 20		
Broxbourne 3	a	→		14 53	14 57			15 14	15 25				→		15 53	15 57			16 14	16 25		
Broxbourne 3	d			14 53	14 57			15 19	15 25						15 53	15 57			16 19	16 25		
Rye House	d				15 00				15 28							16 00				16 28		
St Margarets (Herts)	d				15 03				15 31							16 03				16 31		
Ware	d				15 07				15 35							16 07				16 35		
Hertford East	a				15 14				15 42							16 14				16 42		
Roydon	d							15 24			←								16 24			←
Harlow Town	d		14 52	14 59				15 28		15 22	15 28			15 52	15 59				16 28		16 22	16 28
Harlow Mill	d							→			15 31								→			16 31
Sawbridgeworth	d			15 04							15 34				16 04							16 34
Bishops Stortford	a			15 11		15 15					15 41	15 45			16 11		16 15					16 41
	d			15 12		15 16					15 42	15 46			16 12		16 16					16 42
Stansted Mountfitchet	d		15 03								15 46			16 03								16 46
Stansted Airport	a		15 12			15 25				15 40		15 55		16 12			16 25				16 40	
Stansted Airport	d						15 25											16 25				
Elsenham	d										15 50											16 50
Newport (Essex)	d										15 55											16 55
Audley End	d			15 24			15 39				15 58				16 24			16 39				16 58
Great Chesterford	d										16 03											17 03
Whittlesford Parkway	d			15 31							16 08				16 31							17 08
Shelford	d										16 12											17 12
Cambridge	a			15 41			15 58				16 19				16 41			16 58				17 19

London - Broxbourne, Hertford East, Bishops Stortford, Stansted Airport and Cambridge

Network Diagram - see first Page of Table 20

Station		LE ■ ⊼	LE	LE ■ ⊼	LE ■	LE	LE ■ ⊼	XC ◇■	LE ■	LE		LE ■ ⊼	LE ■	LE ■ ⊼	LE	LE ■ ⊼	LE ■	LE	LE ■ ⊼	LE ■		LE	LE ■ ⊼	LE ■	LE ■ ⊼
London Liverpool Street ⊖	d	16 10	16 22	16 25	16 28		16 40			16 52		16 55		17 10	17 22	17 25	17 28		17 40			17 52	17 55		18 10
Bethnal Green	d																								
Hackney Downs	d		16 29							16 59					17 29							17 59			
Stratford ⊖	d								16 45											17 45					
Clapton	d																								
Seven Sisters ⊖	d		16 34							17 04					17 34							18 04			
Tottenham Hale ⊖	d	16 22		16 37	16 40		16 52		16 55			17 07		17 22		17 37	17 40		17 52	17 55			18 07		18 22
Northumberland Park	d																								
Angel Road	d																								
Ponders End	d								16 59											17 59					
Brimsdown	d								17 02											18 02					
Enfield Lock	d								17 04											18 04					
Waltham Cross	d					←			17 07									←		18 07					
Cheshunt	d		16 52		16 49	16 52			17 09	17 20					17 52		17 49	17 52		18 09		18 20			
Broxbourne	a		→		16 53	16 57			17 14	17 25					→		17 53	17 57		18 14		18 25			
Broxbourne	d				16 53	16 57			17 19	17 25							17 53	17 57		18 19		18 25			
Rye House	d					17 00				17 28								18 00				18 28			
St Margarets (Herts)	d					17 03				17 31								18 03				18 31			
Ware	d					17 07				17 35								18 07				18 35			
Hertford East	a					17 14				17 42								18 14				18 42			
Roydon	d								17 24				←							18 24				←	
Harlow Town	d			16 52	16 59				17 28			17 22	17 28			17 52	17 59			18 28			18 22	18 28	
Harlow Mill	d								→				17 31							→				18 31	
Sawbridgeworth	d				17 04								17 34				18 04							18 34	
Bishops Stortford	a	16 45			17 11		17 15						17 41	17 45			18 11		18 15					18 41	18 45
	d	16 46			17 12		17 16						17 42	17 46			18 12		18 16					18 42	18 46
Stansted Mountfitchet	d			17 03									17 46			18 03								18 46	
Stansted Airport	a	16 55		17 12			17 25					17 40		17 55		18 12			18 25				18 40		18 55
Stansted Airport	d							17 25																	
Elsenham	d												17 50											18 50	
Newport (Essex)	d												17 55											18 55	
Audley End	d				17 24			17 39					17 58				18 24							18 58	
Great Chesterford	d												18 03											19 03	
Whittlesford Parkway	d				17 31								18 08				18 31							19 08	
Shelford	d												18 12											19 12	
Cambridge	a				17 41			17 58					18 19				18 41							19 19	

Station		LE	LE ■ ⊼	LE ■	LE	LE ■ ⊼		LE ■	LE	LE ■ ⊼	LE ■	LE ■ ⊼	LE	LE ■ ⊼	LE ■	LE		LE ■ ⊼	XC ■	LE ■	LE	LE ■ ⊼	LE ■	LE ■ ⊼	LE
London Liverpool Street ⊖	d	18 22	18 25	18 28		18 40			18 52	18 55		19 10	19 22	19 25	19 28			19 40			19 52	19 55		20 10	20 22
Bethnal Green	d																								
Hackney Downs	d	18 29							18 59				19 29								19 59				20 29
Stratford ⊖	d							18 45												19 45					
Clapton	d																								
Seven Sisters ⊖	d	18 34							19 04				19 34								20 04				20 34
Tottenham Hale ⊖	d		18 37	18 40		18 52		18 55		19 07		19 22		19 37	19 40			19 52		19 55		20 07		20 22	
Northumberland Park	d																								
Angel Road	d																								
Ponders End	d							18 59												19 59					
Brimsdown	d							19 02												20 02					
Enfield Lock	d							19 04												20 04					
Waltham Cross	d				←			19 07								←				20 07					
Cheshunt	d	18 52		18 49	18 52			19 09	19 20				19 52		19 49	19 52				20 09	20 20				20 52
Broxbourne	a	→		18 53	18 57			19 14	19 25				→		19 53	19 57				20 14	20 25				→
Broxbourne	d			18 53	18 57			19 19	19 25						19 53	19 57				20 19	20 25				
Rye House	d				19 00				19 28							20 00					20 28				
St Margarets (Herts)	d				19 03				19 31							20 03					20 31				
Ware	d				19 07				19 35							20 07					20 35				
Hertford East	a				19 14				19 42							20 14					20 42				
Roydon	d							19 24			←									20 24			←		
Harlow Town	d		18 52	18 59				19 28		19 22	19 28			19 52	19 59					20 28		20 22	20 28		
Harlow Mill	d							→			19 31									→			20 31		
Sawbridgeworth	d			19 04							19 34				20 04								20 34		
Bishops Stortford	a			19 11		19 15					19 41	19 45			20 11			20 15					20 41	20 45	
	d			19 12		19 16					19 42	19 46			20 12			20 16					20 42	20 46	
Stansted Mountfitchet	d		19 03								19 46			20 03									20 46		
Stansted Airport	a		19 12			19 25				19 40		19 55		20 12				20 25				20 40		20 55	
Stansted Airport	d																		20 25						
Elsenham	d										19 50												20 50		
Newport (Essex)	d										19 55												20 55		
Audley End	d			19 24							19 58				20 24				20 39				20 58		
Great Chesterford	d										20 03												21 03		
Whittlesford Parkway	d			19 31							20 08				20 31								21 08		
Shelford	d										20 12												21 12		
Cambridge	a			19 41							20 19				20 41				20 57				21 19		

Table 22

Sundays

19 August to 26 August

London - Broxbourne, Hertford East, Bishops Stortford, Stansted Airport and Cambridge

Network Diagram - see first Page of Table 20

Station		LE ■ ⊼		LE ■	LE	XC ■	LE ■ ⊼	LE ■	LE	LE ■ ⊼	LE ■	LE ■ ⊼		LE	LE ■ ⊼	LE ■	LE	LE ■ ⊼	XC ■	LE ■	LE	LE ■ ⊼		LE ■	LE ■ ⊼
London Liverpool Street ⊖	d	20 25		20 28			20 40		20 52	20 55		21 10		21 22	21 25	21 28		21 40			21 52	21 55			22 10
Bethnal Green	d																								
Hackney Downs	d								20 59					21 29							21 59				
Stratford ⊖	d							20 45												21 45					
Clapton	d																								
Seven Sisters ⊖	d								21 04					21 34							22 04				
Tottenham Hale ⊖	d	20 37		20 40			20 52	20 55		21 07		21 22			21 37	21 40		21 52		21 55		22 07			22 22
Northumberland Park	d																								
Angel Road	d																								
Ponders End	d							20 59												21 59					
Brimsdown	d							21 02												22 02					
Enfield Lock	d							21 04												22 04					
Waltham Cross	d				←			21 07									←			22 07					
Cheshunt	d			20 49	20 52			21 09	21 20					21 52		21 49	21 52			22 09	22 20				
Broxbourne	a			20 53	20 57			21 14	21 25					→		21 53	21 57			22 14	22 25				
Broxbourne	d			20 53	20 57			21 19	21 25							21 53	21 57			22 19	22 25				
Rye House	d				21 00				21 28								22 00				22 28				
St Margarets (Herts)	d				21 03				21 31								22 03				22 31				
Ware	d				21 07				21 35								22 07				22 35				
Hertford East	a				21 14				21 42								22 14				22 42				
Roydon	d							21 24			←									22 24				←	
Harlow Town	d	20 52		20 59				21 28		21 22	21 28				21 52	21 59				22 28		22 22		22 28	
Harlow Mill	d							→			21 31									→				22 31	
Sawbridgeworth	d			21 04							21 34					22 04								22 34	
Bishops Stortford	a			21 11			21 15				21 41	21 45				22 11		22 15						22 41	22 45
	d			21 12			21 16				21 42	21 46				22 12		22 16						22 42	22 46
Stansted Mountfitchet	d	21 03									21 46				22 03									22 46	
Stansted Airport	a	21 12					21 27			21 40		21 55			22 12			22 25				22 40			22 55
Stansted Airport	d					21 19													22 25						
Elsenham	d										21 50													22 50	
Newport (Essex)	d										21 55													22 55	
Audley End	d			21 24		21 33					21 58					22 24			22 40					22 58	
Great Chesterford	d										22 03													23 03	
Whittlesford Parkway	d			21 31							22 08					22 31								23 08	
Shelford	d										22 12													23 12	
Cambridge	a			21 41		21 47					22 19					22 41			22 57					23 19	

Station		XC ■	LE	LE ■ ⊼	LE ■	LE	LE ■ ⊼	LE ■		LE	LE ■ ⊼	LE ■	LE	LE	LE ■	LE ■	LE	LE ■
London Liverpool Street ⊖	d		22 22	22 25	22 28		22 40			22 52	22 55			23 22	23 25	23 28		23 58
Bethnal Green	d																	
Hackney Downs	d		22 29							22 59				23 29				
Stratford ⊖	d							22 45										
Clapton	d																	
Seven Sisters ⊖	d		22 34							23 04				23 34				
Tottenham Hale ⊖	d			22 37	22 40		22 52	22 55			23 07				23 37	23 40		00 10
Northumberland Park	d																	
Angel Road	d																	
Ponders End	d							22 59								23 44		
Brimsdown	d							23 02								23 47		
Enfield Lock	d							23 04								23 49		
Waltham Cross	d					←		23 07								23 52		
Cheshunt	d		22 52		22 49	22 52		23 09		23 20				23 50		23 54	←	00 18
Broxbourne	a		→		22 53	22 57		23 14		23 25				23 55		23 59	23 55	00 22
Broxbourne	d				22 53	22 57		23 19		23 25				00 02		23 59	00 02	00 22
Rye House	d					23 00								→			00 06	
St Margarets (Herts)	d					23 03											00 09	
Ware	d					23 07											00 13	
Hertford East	a					23 14											00 19	
Roydon	d							23 24				←	←					00 26
Harlow Town	d			22 52	22 59			23 28		23 32	23 22	23 28	23 32		23 52	00 05		00 30
Harlow Mill	d							→		→		23 31						00 33
Sawbridgeworth	d				23 04							23 34				00 10		00 37
Bishops Stortford	a				23 11		23 15					23 41	23 45		00 02	00 17		00 44
	d				23 12		23 16					23 42			00 03			
Stansted Mountfitchet	d			23 03								23 46						
Stansted Airport	a			23 12			23 25				23 40				00 12			
Stansted Airport	d	23 04																
Elsenham	d											23 50						
Newport (Essex)	d											23 55						
Audley End	d	23 18			23 24							23 58						
Great Chesterford	d											00 03						
Whittlesford Parkway	d				23 31							00 08						
Shelford	d											00 12						
Cambridge	a	23 34			23 41							00 19						

Table 22 **Sundays**

2 September to 9 September

London - Broxbourne, Hertford East, Bishops Stortford, Stansted Airport and Cambridge

Network Diagram - see first Page of Table 20

		LE	LE	LE	LE	LE	LE	LE	LE	LE	LE	LE	LE	LE	LE	LE	LE	LE	LE	LE	LE	LE	LE
																			🚌	🚌	🚌		
London Liverpool Street ⊖	d	22p42		23p12	23p25			23p42		00 18	04 10	04 40	05 10	05 40	06 10	06 25	06 40	06 55	07 10	07 25	07 40		07 43
Bethnal Green	d																						
Hackney Downs	d																						
Stratford ⊖	d	22p55	23p15	23p25			23p45	23p55	00 15	00 30													
Clapton	d																						
Seven Sisters ⊖	d					←																	
Tottenham Hale ⊖	d	23p10	23p25	23p40	23p37	23p40	23p55	00 10	00 25	00 40		04u52	05u22	05u52	06u22	06u37	06u52	07 07	07 22	07 37	07 52		07 55
Northumberland Park	d			→			23p57																
Angel Road	d																						
Ponders End	d		23p29				00 01		00 29														07 59
Brimsdown	d		23p32				00 04		00 32														08 02
Enfield Lock	d		23p34				00 06		00 34														08 04
Waltham Cross	d		23p37				00 09		00 37														08 07
Cheshunt	d	23p18	23p39			23p48	00 11	00 18	00 39	00 48				06 00									08 09
Broxbourne	a	23p22	23p44			23p52	00 16	00 22	00 44	00 52				06 04									08 14
Broxbourne	d	23p22	23p44			23p52	00 16	00 22	00 44	00 52				06 04								07 57	08 18
Rye House	d		23p47				00 19		00 47													08 00	
St Margarets (Herts)	d		23p50				00 22		00 50													08 03	
Ware	d		23p54				00 26		00 54													08 07	
Hertford East	a		00 01				00 33		01 01													08 14	
Roydon	d					23p56		00 26															08 22
Harlow Town	d	23p28			23p54	00 01		00 30		00 58		05 07	05 37	06 10		06 52		07 22		07 52			08 26
Harlow Mill	d					00 03		00 33															→
Sawbridgeworth	d					00 07		00 37		01 03													
Bishops Stortford	a	23p38			00 04	00 14		00 44		01 10		05 17	05 47	06 20	06 45		07 15		07 45		08 15		
	d	23p39			00 04	00 14		00 44		01 11		05 18	05 48	06 21	06 46		07 16		07 46		08 16		
Stansted Mountfitchet	d					00 18		00 48		01 15		05 22				07 03				08 03			
Stansted Airport	a				00 13						04 58	05 29	05 57	06 30	06 55	07 12	07 25	07 40	07 55	08 13	08 25		
Stansted Airport	d																						
Elsenham	d					00 22		00 52		01 19													
Newport (Essex)	d					00 27		00 57		01 24													
Audley End	d	23p51				00 30		01 00		01 27													
Great Chesterford	d					00 35		01 05		01 32													
Whittlesford Parkway	d	23p58				00 40		01 10		01 37													
Shelford	d					00 44				01 41													
Cambridge	a	00 08				00 51		01 19		01 49													

		LE	LE	LE	LE	LE	LE	LE	LE	LE	LE	LE	LE	LE	LE	LE	LE	LE	LE	LE	LE	LE	LE
		🚌		🚌		🚌		🚌		🚌		🚌		🚌		🚌		🚌		🚌		🚌	
London Liverpool Street ⊖	d	07 55		08 10	08 19	08 25		08 40		08 55		09 10		09 25		09 40		09 55		10 10		10 25	
Bethnal Green	d																						
Hackney Downs	d																						
Stratford ⊖	d						08 30		08 45		09 00		09 15		09 30		09 45		10 00		10 15		10 30
Clapton	d																						
Seven Sisters ⊖	d																						
Tottenham Hale ⊖	d	08 07		08 22	08 31	08 37	08 40	08 52	08 55	09 07	09 10	09 22	09 25	09 37	09 40	09 52	09 55	10 07	10 10	10 22	10 25	10 37	10 40
Northumberland Park	d																						
Angel Road	d																						
Ponders End	d								08 59				09 29				09 59				10 29		
Brimsdown	d								09 02				09 32				10 02				10 32		
Enfield Lock	d								09 04				09 34				10 04				10 34		
Waltham Cross	d								09 07				09 37				10 07				10 37		
Cheshunt	d				08 39		08 49		09 09		09 18		09 39		09 49		10 09		10 18		10 39		10 49
Broxbourne	a				08 44		08 53		09 14		09 23		09 44		09 53		10 14		10 23		10 44		10 53
Broxbourne	d				08 44		08 53		09 14		09 23		09 44		09 53		10 14		10 23		10 44		10 53
Rye House	d				08 47				09 17				09 47				10 17				10 47		
St Margarets (Herts)	d				08 50				09 20				09 50				10 20				10 50		
Ware	d				08 54				09 24				09 54				10 24				10 54		
Hertford East	a				09 01				09 31				10 01				10 31				11 01		
Roydon	d		←								09 27								10 27				
Harlow Town	d	08 22	08 26			08 53	08 59			09 23	09 31			09 53	09 59			10 23	10 31			10 53	10 59
Harlow Mill	d		08 29								09 34								10 34				
Sawbridgeworth	d		08 33				09 04				09 37				10 04				10 37				11 04
Bishops Stortford	a		08 40	08 45			09 11	09 15			09 44	09 48			10 11	10 15			10 44	10 48			11 11
	d		08 40	08 46			09 12	09 16			09 44	09 48			10 12	10 16			10 44	10 48			11 12
Stansted Mountfitchet	d		08 44			09 04					09 49			10 04					10 49			11 04	
Stansted Airport	a	08 40		08 55		09 13		09 25		09 41		09 58		10 13		10 25		10 41		10 58		11 13	
Stansted Airport	d																						
Elsenham	d		08 48								09 52								10 52				
Newport (Essex)	d		08 53								09 58								10 58				
Audley End	d		08 56				09 24				10 01				10 24				11 01				11 24
Great Chesterford	d		09 01								10 06								11 06				
Whittlesford Parkway	d		09 06				09 31				10 10				10 31				11 10				11 31
Shelford	d		09 10								10 15								11 15				
Cambridge	a		09 18				09 41				10 22				10 41				11 23				11 41

Table 22 **Sundays**

2 September to 9 September

London - Broxbourne, Hertford East, Bishops Stortford, Stansted Airport and Cambridge

Network Diagram - see first Page of Table 20

		LE	LE	XC ◇	LE	LE	LE	LE	LE	LE	LE	LE	XC ◇	LE	LE	LE	LE	LE	LE	LE	LE	XC ◇
		🚌			🚌		🚌		🚌		🚌			🚌		🚌		🚌		🚌		
London Liverpool Street ⊖	d	10 40			10 55		11 10		11 25		11 40			11 55		12 10		12 25		12 40		
Bethnal Green	d																					
Hackney Downs	d																					
Stratford ⊖	d		10 45			11 00		11 15		11 30		11 45			12 00		12 15		12 30		12 45	
Clapton	d																					
Seven Sisters ⊖	d																					
Tottenham Hale ⊖	d	10 52	10 55		11 07	11 10	11 22	11 25	11 37	11 40	11 52	11 55		12 07	12 10	12 22	12 25	12 37	12 40	12 52	12 55	
Northumberland Park	d																					
Angel Road	d																					
Ponders End	d		10 59					11 29				11 59					12 29				12 59	
Brimsdown	d		11 02					11 32				12 02					12 32				13 02	
Enfield Lock	d		11 04					11 34				12 04					12 34				13 04	
Waltham Cross	d		11 07					11 37				12 07					12 37				13 07	
Cheshunt	d		11 09			11 18		11 39		11 49		12 09			12 18		12 39		12 49		13 09	
Broxbourne	a		11 14			11 23		11 44		11 53		12 14			12 23		12 44		12 53		13 14	
Broxbourne	d		11 14			11 23		11 44		11 53		12 14			12 23		12 44		12 53		13 14	
Rye House	d		11 17					11 47				12 17					12 47				13 17	
St Margarets (Herts)	d		11 20					11 50				12 20					12 50				13 20	
Ware	d		11 24					11 54				12 24					12 54				13 24	
Hertford East	a		11 31					12 01				12 31					13 01				13 31	
Roydon	d					11 27									12 27							
Harlow Town	d				11 23	11 31			11 53	11 59				12 23	12 31			12 53	12 59			
Harlow Mill	d					11 34									12 34							
Sawbridgeworth	d					11 37				12 04					12 37				13 04			
Bishops Stortford	a	11 15				11 44	11 48			12 11	12 15				12 44	12 48			13 11	13 15		
	d	11 16				11 44	11 48			12 12	12 16				12 44	12 48			13 12	13 16		
Stansted Mountfitchet	d					11 49			12 04						12 49			13 04				
Stansted Airport	a	11 25			11 41		11 58		12 13		12 25			12 41		12 58		13 13		13 25		
Stansted Airport	d			11 25									12 25									13 25
Elsenham	d					11 52									12 52							
Newport (Essex)	d					11 58									12 58							
Audley End	d			11 39		12 01				12 24			12 39		13 01				13 24			13 39
Great Chesterford	d					12 06									13 06							
Whittlesford Parkway	d					12 10				12 31					13 10				13 31			
Shelford	d					12 15									13 15							
Cambridge	a			11 57		12 23				12 41			12 58		13 23				13 41			13 58

		LE	LE	LE	LE	LE	LE	LE	LE	XC ◇	LE	LE	LE	LE	LE	LE	LE	LE	XC ◇	LE	LE	LE	LE
		🚌		🚌		🚌		🚌			🚌		🚌		🚌		🚌			🚌		🚌	
London Liverpool Street ⊖	d	12 55		13 10		13 25		13 40			13 55		14 10		14 25		14 40			14 55		15 10	
Bethnal Green	d																						
Hackney Downs	d																						
Stratford ⊖	d		13 00		13 15		13 30		13 45			14 00		14 15		14 30		14 45			15 00		15 15
Clapton	d																						
Seven Sisters ⊖	d																						
Tottenham Hale ⊖	d	13 07	13 10	13 22	13 25	13 37	13 40	13 52	13 55		14 07	14 10	14 22	14 25	14 37	14 40	14 52	14 55		15 07	15 10	15 22	15 25
Northumberland Park	d																						
Angel Road	d																						
Ponders End	d				13 29				13 59					14 29				14 59					15 29
Brimsdown	d				13 32				14 02					14 32				15 02					15 32
Enfield Lock	d				13 34				14 04					14 34				15 04					15 34
Waltham Cross	d				13 37				14 07					14 37				15 07					15 37
Cheshunt	d		13 18		13 39		13 49		14 09			14 18		14 39		14 49		15 09			15 18		15 39
Broxbourne	a		13 23		13 44		13 53		14 14			14 23		14 44		14 53		15 14			15 23		15 44
Broxbourne	d		13 23		13 44		13 53		14 14			14 23		14 44		14 53		15 14			15 23		15 44
Rye House	d				13 47				14 17					14 47				15 17					15 47
St Margarets (Herts)	d				13 50				14 20					14 50				15 20					15 50
Ware	d				13 54				14 24					14 54				15 24					15 54
Hertford East	a				14 01				14 31					15 01				15 31					16 01
Roydon	d		13 27									14 27									15 27		
Harlow Town	d	13 23	13 31			13 53	13 59				14 23	14 31			14 53	14 59				15 23	15 31		
Harlow Mill	d		13 34									14 34									15 34		
Sawbridgeworth	d		13 37				14 04					14 37				15 04					15 37		
Bishops Stortford	a		13 44	13 48			14 11	14 15				14 44	14 48			15 11	15 15				15 44	15 48	
	d		13 44	13 48			14 12	14 16				14 44	14 48			15 12	15 16				15 44	15 48	
Stansted Mountfitchet	d		13 49			14 04						14 49			15 04						15 49		
Stansted Airport	a	13 41		13 58		14 13		14 25			14 41		14 58		15 13		15 25			15 41		15 58	
Stansted Airport	d									14 25									15 25				
Elsenham	d		13 52									14 52									15 52		
Newport (Essex)	d		13 58									14 58									15 58		
Audley End	d		14 01				14 24			14 39		15 01				15 24			15 39		16 01		
Great Chesterford	d		14 06									15 06									16 06		
Whittlesford Parkway	d		14 10				14 31					15 10				15 31					16 10		
Shelford	d		14 15									15 15									16 15		
Cambridge	a		14 23				14 41			14 57		15 23				15 41			15 58		16 23		

London - Broxbourne, Hertford East, Bishops Stortford, Stansted Airport and Cambridge

Network Diagram - see first Page of Table 20

		LE 1 🚲	LE 1	LE 1 🚲	LE 1	XC ◇1	LE 1 🚲	LE 1	LE 1 🚲	LE 1	LE 1 🚲	LE 1	LE 1 🚲	LE 1	XC ◇1	LE 1 🚲	LE 1	LE 1 🚲	LE 1	LE 1 🚲	LE 1	LE 1 🚲
London Liverpool Street 15 ⊖	d	15 25		15 40			15 55		16 10		16 25		16 40			16 55		17 10		17 25		17 40
Bethnal Green	d																					
Hackney Downs	d																					
Stratford 7 ⊖	d		15 30		15 45			16 00		16 15		16 30		16 45			17 00		17 15		17 30	
Clapton	d																					
Seven Sisters ⊖	d																					
Tottenham Hale ⊖	d	15 37	15 40	15 52	15 55		16 07	16 10	16 22	16 25	16 37	16 40	16 52	16 55		17 07	17 10	17 22	17 25	17 37	17 40	17 52
Northumberland Park	d																					
Angel Road	d																					
Ponders End	d				15 59					16 29				16 59					17 29			
Brimsdown	d				16 02					16 32				17 02					17 32			
Enfield Lock	d				16 04					16 34				17 04					17 34			
Waltham Cross	d				16 07					16 37				17 07					17 37			
Cheshunt	d		15 49		16 09			16 18		16 39		16 49		17 09			17 18		17 39		17 49	
Broxbourne 3	a		15 53		16 14			16 23		16 44		16 53		17 14			17 23		17 44		17 53	
Broxbourne 3	d		15 53		16 14			16 23		16 44		16 53		17 14			17 23		17 44		17 53	
Rye House	d				16 17					16 47				17 17					17 47			
St Margarets (Herts)	d				16 20					16 50				17 20					17 50			
Ware	d				16 24					16 54				17 24					17 54			
Hertford East	a				16 31					17 01				17 31					18 01			
Roydon	d							16 27									17 27					
Harlow Town	d	15 53	15 59				16 23	16 31			16 53	16 59				17 23	17 31			17 53	17 59	
Harlow Mill	d							16 34									17 34					
Sawbridgeworth	d		16 04					16 37				17 04					17 37				18 04	
Bishops Stortford	a		16 11	16 15				16 44	16 48			17 11	17 15				17 44	17 48			18 11	18 15
	d		16 12	16 16				16 44	16 48			17 12	17 16				17 44	17 48			18 12	18 16
Stansted Mountfitchet	d	16 04						16 49			17 04						17 49			18 04		
Stansted Airport	a	16 13		16 25			16 41		16 58		17 13		17 25			17 41		17 58		18 13		18 25
Stansted Airport	d					16 25									17 25							
Elsenham	d							16 52									17 52					
Newport (Essex)	d							16 58									17 58					
Audley End	d		16 24			16 39		17 01				17 24			17 39		18 01				18 24	
Great Chesterford	d							17 06									18 06					
Whittlesford Parkway	d		16 31					17 10				17 31					18 10				18 31	
Shelford	d							17 15									18 15					
Cambridge	a		16 41			16 58		17 23				17 41			17 58		18 23				18 41	

		LE 1	LE 1 🚲	LE 1	LE 1 🚲	LE 1	LE 1 🚲	LE 1	LE 1 🚲	LE 1	LE 1 🚲	LE 1	LE 1 🚲	LE 1	LE 1 🚲	LE 1	LE 1 🚲	LE 1	XC 1	LE 1 🚲	LE 1	LE 1 🚲	LE 1
London Liverpool Street 15 ⊖	d		17 55		18 10		18 25		18 40		18 55		19 10		19 25		19 40			19 55		20 10	
Bethnal Green	d																						
Hackney Downs	d																						
Stratford 7 ⊖	d	17 45		18 00		18 15		18 30		18 45		19 00		19 15		19 30		19 45			20 00		20 15
Clapton	d																						
Seven Sisters ⊖	d																						
Tottenham Hale ⊖	d	17 55	18 07	18 10	18 22	18 25	18 37	18 40	18 52	18 55	19 07	19 10	19 22	19 25	19 37	19 40	19 52	19 55		20 07	20 10	20 22	20 25
Northumberland Park	d																						
Angel Road	d																						
Ponders End	d	17 59				18 29				18 59				19 29				19 59					20 29
Brimsdown	d	18 02				18 32				19 02				19 32				20 02					20 32
Enfield Lock	d	18 04				18 34				19 04				19 34				20 04					20 34
Waltham Cross	d	18 07				18 37				19 07				19 37				20 07					20 37
Cheshunt	d	18 09		18 18		18 39		18 49		19 09		19 18		19 39		19 49		20 09			20 18		20 39
Broxbourne 3	a	18 14		18 23		18 44		18 53		19 14		19 23		19 44		19 53		20 14			20 23		20 44
Broxbourne 3	d	18 14		18 23		18 44		18 53		19 14		19 23		19 44		19 53		20 14			20 23		20 44
Rye House	d	18 17				18 47				19 17				19 47				20 17					20 47
St Margarets (Herts)	d	18 20				18 50				19 20				19 50				20 20					20 50
Ware	d	18 24				18 54				19 24				19 54				20 24					20 54
Hertford East	a	18 31				19 01				19 31				20 01				20 31					21 01
Roydon	d			18 27								19 27									20 27		
Harlow Town	d		18 23	18 31			18 53	18 59			19 23	19 31			19 52	19 59				20 23	20 31		
Harlow Mill	d			18 34								19 34									20 34		
Sawbridgeworth	d			18 37				19 04				19 37				20 04					20 37		
Bishops Stortford	a			18 44	18 48			19 11	19 15			19 44	19 48			20 11	20 15				20 44	20 48	
	d			18 44	18 48			19 12	19 16			19 44	19 48			20 12	20 16				20 44	20 48	
Stansted Mountfitchet	d			18 49			19 04					19 49			20 03						20 49		
Stansted Airport	a		18 41		18 58		19 13		19 25		19 41		19 58		20 12		20 25			20 41		20 58	
Stansted Airport	d																		20 25				
Elsenham	d			18 52								19 52									20 52		
Newport (Essex)	d			18 58								19 58									20 58		
Audley End	d			19 01				19 24				20 01				20 24			20 39		21 01		
Great Chesterford	d			19 06								20 06									21 06		
Whittlesford Parkway	d			19 10				19 31				20 10				20 31					21 10		
Shelford	d			19 15								20 15									21 15		
Cambridge	a			19 24				19 41				20 22				20 41			20 57		21 22		

London - Broxbourne, Hertford East, Bishops Stortford, Stansted Airport and Cambridge

Network Diagram - see first Page of Table 20

		LE 1 🚲	LE 1	XC 1	LE 1 🚲	LE 1	LE 1 🚲	LE 1	LE 1 🚲	LE 1	LE 1 🚲	LE 1	LE 1 🚲	LE 1	XC 1	LE 1 🚲	LE 1	LE 1 🚲	LE 1	XC 1	LE 1 🚲	LE 1	LE 1 🚲
London Liverpool Street 15 ⊖	d	20 25			20 40		20 55		21 10		21 25		21 40			21 55		22 10			22 25		22 40
Bethnal Green	d																						
Hackney Downs	d																						
Stratford 7 ⊖	d		20 30			20 45		21 00		21 15		21 30		21 45			22 00		22 15			22 30	
Clapton	d																						
Seven Sisters ⊖	d																						
Tottenham Hale ⊖	d	20 37	20 40		20 52	20 55	21 07	21 10	21 22	21 25	21 37	21 40	21 52	21 55		22 07	22 10	22 22	22 25		22 37	22 40	22 52
Northumberland Park	d																						
Angel Road	d																						
Ponders End	d					20 59				21 29				21 59					22 29				
Brimsdown	d					21 02				21 32				22 02					22 32				
Enfield Lock	d					21 04				21 34				22 04					22 34				
Waltham Cross	d					21 07				21 37				22 07					22 37				
Cheshunt	d		20 49			21 09		21 18		21 39		21 49		22 09			22 18		22 39			22 49	
Broxbourne 3	a		20 53			21 14		21 23		21 44		21 53		22 14			22 23		22 44			22 53	
Broxbourne 3	d		20 53			21 14		21 23		21 44		21 53		22 14			22 23		22 44			22 53	
Rye House	d					21 17				21 47				22 17					22 47				
St Margarets (Herts)	d					21 20				21 50				22 20					22 50				
Ware	d					21 24				21 54				22 24					22 54				
Hertford East	a					21 31				22 01				22 31					23 01				
Roydon	d							21 27									22 27						
Harlow Town	d	20 53	20 59				21 23	21 31			21 53	21 59				22 23	22 31				22 53	22 59	
Harlow Mill	d							21 34									22 34						
Sawbridgeworth	d		21 04					21 37				22 04					22 37					23 04	
Bishops Stortford	a		21 11		21 15			21 44	21 48			22 11	22 15				22 44	22 48				23 11	23 15
	d		21 12		21 16			21 44	21 48			22 12	22 16				22 44	22 48				23 12	23 16
Stansted Mountfitchet	d	21 04						21 49			22 04						22 49				23 04		
Stansted Airport	a	21 13			21 27		21 41		21 58		22 13		22 25			22 41		22 58			23 13		23 25
Stansted Airport	d			21 19											22 25					23 04			
Elsenham	d							21 52									22 52						
Newport (Essex)	d							21 58									22 58						
Audley End	d		21 24	21 33				22 01				22 24			22 40		23 01			23 18		23 24	
Great Chesterford	d							22 06									23 06						
Whittlesford Parkway	d		21 31					22 10				22 31					23 10					23 31	
Shelford	d							22 15									23 15						
Cambridge	a		21 41	21 47				22 22				22 41			22 57		23 23			23 34		23 41	

		LE 1	LE	LE 1 🚲	LE 1	LE	LE 1	LE 1	LE 1	LE 1	LE 1
London Liverpool Street 15 ⊖	d		22 52	22 55				23 25			
Bethnal Green	d										
Hackney Downs	d		22 59								
Stratford 7 ⊖	d	22 45			23 00		23 15		23 30	23 45	23 59
Clapton	d										
Seven Sisters ⊖	d		23 04								
Tottenham Hale ⊖	d	22 55		23 07	23 10		23 25	23 37	23 40	23 55	00 10
Northumberland Park	d										
Angel Road	d										
Ponders End	d	22 59					23 29			23 59	
Brimsdown	d	23 02					23 32			00 02	
Enfield Lock	d	23 04					23 34			00 04	
Waltham Cross	d	23 07				←	23 37			00 07	
Cheshunt	d	23 09	23 22		23 18	23 22	23 39		23 49	00 09	00 18
Broxbourne 3	a	23 14	→		23 23	23 27	23 44		23 53	00 14	00 22
Broxbourne 3	d	23 14			23 23	23 27	23 44		23 53	00 14	00 22
Rye House	d	23 17					23 47			00 17	
St Margarets (Herts)	d	23 20					23 50			00 20	
Ware	d	23 24					23 54			00 24	
Hertford East	a	23 31					00 01			00 31	
Roydon	d				23 27				23 57		00 26
Harlow Town	d			23 23	23 31	23 34		23 53	00 01		00 30
Harlow Mill	d				23 34				00 04		00 33
Sawbridgeworth	d				23 37				00 08		00 37
Bishops Stortford	a				23 44	23 47		00 03	00 15		00 44
	d				23 44			00 04	00 15		00 44
Stansted Mountfitchet	d				23 49				00 19		00 48
Stansted Airport	a			23 41				00 13			
Stansted Airport	d										
Elsenham	d				23 52				00 23		00 52
Newport (Essex)	d				23 58				00 28		00 57
Audley End	d				00 01				00 31		01 00
Great Chesterford	d				00 06				00 36		01 05
Whittlesford Parkway	d				00 10				00 41		01 10
Shelford	d				00 15				00 45		
Cambridge	a				00 22				00 52		01 19

Table 22

Sundays
from 16 September

London - Broxbourne, Hertford East, Bishops Stortford, Stansted Airport and Cambridge

Network Diagram - see first Page of Table 20

		LE ■	LE ■	LE ■	LE ■	LE ■	LE ■	LE ■	LE ■	LE ■		LE ■	LE ■	LE ■	LE ■	LE ■	LE ■ ⊼	LE ■ ⊼	LE ■ ⊼	LE		LE ■	LE	LE ■ ⊼	LE ■
London Liverpool Street ⊖	d	22p58	23p12	23p25	23p28	23p40	23p58	04 10	04 40	05 10		05 40	06 10	06 25	06 40	06 55	07 10	07 25	07 40			07 43	07 52	07 55	
Bethnal Green	d																								
Hackney Downs	d		23p18			23p46																	07 59		
Stratford	⊖ d																								
Clapton	d					23p49																			
Seven Sisters	⊖ d																						08 04		
Tottenham Hale	⊖ d	23p10	23p25	23b37	23p40	23p53	00 10		04u52	05u22		05u52	06u22	06u37	06u52	07 07	07 22	07 37	07 52			07 55		08 07	
Northumberland Park	d					23p55																			
Angel Road	d																								
Ponders End	d		23p29			23p59																07 59			
Brimsdown	d		23p32			00 02																08 02			
Enfield Lock	d		23p34			00 04																08 04			
Waltham Cross	d		23p37			00 07																08 07			
Cheshunt	d	23p18	23p39		23p48	00 09	00 18					06 00										08 09	08 20		
Broxbourne	a	23p22	23p44		23p52	00 14	00 22					06 04										08 14	08 25		
Broxbourne	d	23p22	23p44		23p52	00 14	00 22					06 04								07 57		08 19	08 25		
Rye House	d		23p47			00 17														08 00			08 28		
St Margarets (Herts)	d		23p50			00 20														08 03			08 31		
Ware	d		23p54			00 24														08 07			08 35		
Hertford East	a		00 01			00 31														08 14			08 42		
Roydon	d				23p56		00 26															08 24			←
Harlow Town	d	23p28		23p54	00 01		00 30		05 07	05 37		06 10		06 52		07 22		07 52				08 28		08 22	08 28
Harlow Mill	d				00 03		00 33															→			08 31
Sawbridgeworth	d				00 07		00 37																		08 34
Bishops Stortford	a	23p38		00 04	00 14		00 44		05 17	05 47		06 20	06 45		07 15		07 45		08 15						08 41
	d	23p39		00 04	00 14		00 44		05 18	05 48		06 21	06 46		07 16		07 46		08 16						08 42
Stansted Mountfitchet	d				00 18		00 48		05 22					07 03				08 03							08 46
Stansted Airport	a			00 13				04 58	05 29	05 57		06 30	06 55	07 12	07 25	07 40	07 55	08 13	08 25					08 40	
Stansted Airport	d																								
Elsenham	d				00 22		00 52																		08 50
Newport (Essex)	d				00 27		00 57																		08 55
Audley End	d	23p51			00 30		01 00																		08 58
Great Chesterford	d				00 35		01 05																		09 03
Whittlesford Parkway	d	23p58			00 40		01 10																		09 08
Shelford	d				00 44																				09 12
Cambridge	a	00 08			00 51		01 19																		09 19

		LE ■ ⊼	LE	LE ■ ⊼	LE ■	LE		LE ■ ⊼	LE ■	LE	LE ■ ⊼	LE ■	LE ■ ⊼	LE	LE ■ ⊼	LE ■		LE	LE ■ ⊼	LE ■	LE	LE ■ ⊼	LE ■	LE ■ ⊼	LE
London Liverpool Street ⊖	d	08 10	08 22	08 25	08 28			08 40		08 52	08 55		09 10	09 22	09 25	09 28			09 40		09 52	09 55		10 10	10 22
Bethnal Green	d																								
Hackney Downs	d		08 29							08 59				09 29							09 59				10 29
Stratford	⊖ d								08 45											09 45					
Clapton	d																								
Seven Sisters	⊖ d		08 34							09 04				09 34							10 04				10 34
Tottenham Hale	⊖ d	08 22		08 37	08 40			08 52	08 55		09 07		09 22		09 37	09 40			09 52	09 55		10 07		10 22	
Northumberland Park	d																								
Angel Road	d																								
Ponders End	d								08 59											09 59					
Brimsdown	d								09 02											10 02					
Enfield Lock	d								09 04											10 04					
Waltham Cross	d					←			09 07									←		10 07					
Cheshunt	d		08 52		08 49	08 52			09 09	09 20				09 52		09 49		09 52		10 09	10 20				10 52
Broxbourne	a		→		08 53	08 57			09 14	09 25				→		09 53		09 57		10 14	10 25				→
Broxbourne	d				08 53	08 57			09 19	09 25						09 53		09 57		10 19	10 25				
Rye House	d					09 00				09 28								10 00			10 28				
St Margarets (Herts)	d					09 03				09 31								10 03			10 31				
Ware	d					09 07				09 35								10 07			10 35				
Hertford East	a					09 14				09 42								10 14			10 42				
Roydon	d								09 24			←								10 24			←		
Harlow Town	d			08 52	08 59				09 28		09 22	09 28			09 52	09 59				10 28		10 22	10 28		
Harlow Mill	d								→			09 31								→			10 31		
Sawbridgeworth	d				09 04							09 34				10 04							10 34		
Bishops Stortford	a	08 45			09 11			09 15				09 41	09 45			10 11			10 15				10 41	10 45	
	d	08 46			09 12			09 16				09 42	09 46			10 12			10 16				10 42	10 46	
Stansted Mountfitchet	d			09 03								09 46			10 03								10 46		
Stansted Airport	a	08 55		09 12				09 25			09 40		09 55		10 12				10 25			10 40		10 55	
Stansted Airport	d																								
Elsenham	d											09 50											10 50		
Newport (Essex)	d											09 55											10 55		
Audley End	d				09 24							09 58				10 24							10 58		
Great Chesterford	d											10 03											11 03		
Whittlesford Parkway	d				09 31							10 08				10 31							11 08		
Shelford	d											10 12											11 12		
Cambridge	a				09 41							10 19				10 41							11 19		

b Previous night, stops to pick up only

Table 22

Sundays
from 16 September

London - Broxbourne, Hertford East, Bishops Stortford, Stansted Airport and Cambridge

Network Diagram - see first Page of Table 20

		LE ■ ⊼		LE ■	LE	LE ■ ⊼	XC ◇■	LE ■	LE	LE ■ ⊼	LE ■	LE ■ ⊼		LE	LE ■ ⊼	LE ■	LE	LE ■ ⊼	XC ◇■	LE ■	LE	LE ■ ⊼		LE ■	LE ■ ⊼
London Liverpool Street ⊖	d	10 25		10 28		10 40			10 52	10 55		11 10		11 22	11 25	11 28		11 40			11 52	11 55			12 10
Bethnal Green	d																								
Hackney Downs	d								10 59					11 29							11 59				
Stratford	⊖ d							10 45												11 45					
Clapton	d																								
Seven Sisters	⊖ d								11 04					11 34							12 04				
Tottenham Hale	⊖ d	10 37		10 40		10 52		10 55		11 07		11 22			11 37	11 40		11 52		11 55		12 07			12 22
Northumberland Park	d																								
Angel Road	d																								
Ponders End	d							10 59												11 59					
Brimsdown	d							11 02												12 02					
Enfield Lock	d							11 04												12 04					
Waltham Cross	d				←			11 07									←			12 07					
Cheshunt	d			10 49	10 52			11 09	11 20					11 52		11 49	11 52			12 09	12 20				
Broxbourne	a			10 53	10 57			11 14	11 25					→		11 53	11 57			12 14	12 25				
Broxbourne	d			10 53	10 57			11 19	11 25							11 53	11 57			12 19	12 25				
Rye House	d				11 00				11 28								12 00				12 28				
St Margarets (Herts)	d				11 03				11 31								12 03				12 31				
Ware	d				11 07				11 35								12 07				12 35				
Hertford East	a				11 14				11 42								12 14				12 42				
Roydon	d							11 24			←									12 24				←	
Harlow Town	d	10 52		10 59				11 28		11 22	11 28				11 52	11 59				12 28		12 22		12 28	
Harlow Mill	d							→			11 31									→				12 31	
Sawbridgeworth	d			11 04							11 34					12 04								12 34	
Bishops Stortford	a			11 11		11 15					11 41	11 45				12 11		12 15						12 41	12 45
	d			11 12		11 16					11 42	11 46				12 12		12 16						12 42	12 46
Stansted Mountfitchet	d	11 03									11 46				12 03									12 46	
Stansted Airport	a	11 12				11 25				11 40		11 55			12 12			12 25				12 40			12 55
Stansted Airport	d						11 25												12 25						
Elsenham	d										11 50													12 50	
Newport (Essex)	d										11 55													12 55	
Audley End	d			11 24			11 39				11 58					12 24			12 39					12 58	
Great Chesterford	d										12 03													13 03	
Whittlesford Parkway	d			11 31							12 08					12 31								13 08	
Shelford	d										12 12													13 12	
Cambridge	a			11 41			11 57				12 19					12 41			12 58					13 19	

		LE	LE ■ ⊼	LE ■	LE	LE ■ ⊼	XC ◇■	LE ■		LE	LE ■ ⊼	LE ■	LE ■ ⊼	LE	LE ■ ⊼	LE ■	LE	LE ■ ⊼		XC ◇■	LE ■	LE	LE ■ ⊼	LE ■	LE ■ ⊼
London Liverpool Street ⊖	d	12 22	12 25	12 28		12 40				12 52	12 55		13 10	13 22	13 25	13 28		13 40				13 52	13 55		14 10
Bethnal Green	d																								
Hackney Downs	d	12 29								12 59				13 29								13 59			
Stratford	⊖ d							12 45													13 45				
Clapton	d																								
Seven Sisters	⊖ d	12 34								13 04				13 34								14 04			
Tottenham Hale	⊖ d		12 37	12 40		12 52		12 55			13 07		13 22		13 37	13 40		13 52			13 55		14 07		14 22
Northumberland Park	d																								
Angel Road	d																								
Ponders End	d							12 59													13 59				
Brimsdown	d							13 02													14 02				
Enfield Lock	d							13 04													14 04				
Waltham Cross	d				←			13 07									←				14 07				
Cheshunt	d	12 52		12 49	12 52			13 09		13 20				13 52		13 49	13 52				14 09	14 20			
Broxbourne	a	→		12 53	12 57			13 14		13 25				→		13 53	13 57				14 14	14 25			
Broxbourne	d			12 53	12 57			13 19		13 25						13 53	13 57				14 19	14 25			
Rye House	d				13 00					13 28							14 00					14 28			
St Margarets (Herts)	d				13 03					13 31							14 03					14 31			
Ware	d				13 07					13 35							14 07					14 35			
Hertford East	a				13 14					13 42							14 14					14 42			
Roydon	d							13 24				←									14 24			←	
Harlow Town	d		12 52	12 59				13 28			13 22	13 28			13 52	13 59					14 28		14 22	14 28	
Harlow Mill	d							→				13 31									→			14 31	
Sawbridgeworth	d			13 04								13 34				14 04								14 34	
Bishops Stortford	a			13 11		13 15						13 41	13 45			14 11		14 15						14 41	14 45
	d			13 12		13 16						13 42	13 46			14 12		14 16						14 42	14 46
Stansted Mountfitchet	d		13 03									13 46			14 03									14 46	
Stansted Airport	a		13 12			13 25					13 40		13 55		14 12			14 25					14 40		14 55
Stansted Airport	d						13 25													14 25					
Elsenham	d											13 50												14 50	
Newport (Essex)	d											13 55												14 55	
Audley End	d			13 24			13 39					13 58				14 24				14 39				14 58	
Great Chesterford	d											14 03												15 03	
Whittlesford Parkway	d			13 31								14 08				14 31								15 08	
Shelford	d											14 12												15 12	
Cambridge	a			13 41			13 58					14 19				14 41				14 57				15 19	

London - Broxbourne, Hertford East, Bishops Stortford, Stansted Airport and Cambridge

Network Diagram - see first Page of Table 20

		LE	LE ■ ✠	LE ■	LE	LE ■ ✠	XC ◇■	LE ■	LE	LE ■ ✠	LE ■	LE ■ ✠	LE	LE ■ ✠	LE ■	LE	LE ■ ✠	XC ◇■	LE ■	LE	LE ■ ✠	LE ■
London Liverpool Street 15 ⊖	d	14 22	14 25	14 28		14 40			14 52	14 55		15 10	15 22	15 25	15 28		15 40			15 52	15 55	
Bethnal Green	d																					
Hackney Downs	d	14 29							14 59				15 29							15 59		
Stratford 7 ⊖	d							14 45											15 45			
Clapton	d																					
Seven Sisters ⊖	d	14 34							15 04				15 34							16 04		
Tottenham Hale ⊖	d		14 37	14 40		14 52		14 55		15 07		15 22		15 37	15 40		15 52		15 55		16 07	
Northumberland Park	d																					
Angel Road	d																					
Ponders End	d							14 59											15 59			
Brimsdown	d							15 02											16 02			
Enfield Lock	d							15 04											16 04			
Waltham Cross	d				←			15 07								←			16 07			
Cheshunt	d	14 52		14 49	14 52			15 09	15 20				15 52		15 49	15 52			16 09	16 20		
Broxbourne 3	a	→		14 53	14 57			15 14	15 25				→		15 53	15 57			16 14	16 25		
Broxbourne 3	d			14 53	14 57			15 19	15 25						15 53	15 57			16 19	16 25		
Rye House	d				15 00				15 28							16 00				16 28		
St Margarets (Herts)	d				15 03				15 31							16 03				16 31		
Ware	d				15 07				15 35							16 07				16 35		
Hertford East	a				15 14				15 42							16 14				16 42		
Roydon	d							15 24			←								16 24			←
Harlow Town	d		14 52	14 59				15 28		15 22	15 28			15 52	15 59				16 28		16 22	16 28
Harlow Mill	d							→			15 31								→			16 31
Sawbridgeworth	d			15 04							15 34				16 04							16 34
Bishops Stortford	a			15 11		15 15					15 41	15 45			16 11		16 15					16 41
	d			15 12		15 16					15 42	15 46			16 12		16 16					16 42
Stansted Mountfitchet	d		15 03								15 46			16 03								16 46
Stansted Airport	a		15 12			15 25				15 40		15 55		16 12			16 25				16 40	
Stansted Airport	d						15 25											16 25				
Elsenham	d										15 50											16 50
Newport (Essex)	d										15 55											16 55
Audley End	d			15 24			15 39				15 58				16 24			16 39				16 58
Great Chesterford	d										16 03											17 03
Whittlesford Parkway	d			15 31							16 08				16 31							17 08
Shelford	d										16 12											17 12
Cambridge	a			15 41			15 58				16 19				16 41			16 58				17 19

		LE ■ ✠	LE	LE ■ ✠	LE ■	LE	LE ■ ✠	XC ◇■	LE ■	LE	LE ■ ✠	LE ■	LE ■ ✠	LE	LE ■ ✠	LE ■	LE	LE ■ ✠	LE ■	LE	LE ■ ✠	LE ■	LE ■ ✠
London Liverpool Street 15 ⊖	d	16 10	16 22	16 25	16 28		16 40			16 52	16 55		17 10	17 22	17 25	17 28		17 40		17 52	17 55		18 10
Bethnal Green	d																						
Hackney Downs	d		16 29							16 59				17 29						17 59			
Stratford 7 ⊖	d								16 45										17 45				
Clapton	d																						
Seven Sisters ⊖	d		16 34							17 04				17 34						18 04			
Tottenham Hale ⊖	d	16 22		16 37	16 40		16 52		16 55		17 07		17 22		17 37	17 40		17 52	17 55		18 07		18 22
Northumberland Park	d																						
Angel Road	d																						
Ponders End	d								16 59										17 59				
Brimsdown	d								17 02										18 02				
Enfield Lock	d								17 04										18 04				
Waltham Cross	d					←			17 07								←		18 07				
Cheshunt	d		16 52		16 49	16 52			17 09	17 20				17 52		17 49	17 52		18 09	18 20			
Broxbourne 3	a		→		16 53	16 57			17 14	17 25				→		17 53	17 57		18 14	18 25			
Broxbourne 3	d				16 53	16 57			17 19	17 25						17 53	17 57		18 19	18 25			
Rye House	d					17 00				17 28							18 00			18 28			
St Margarets (Herts)	d					17 03				17 31							18 03			18 31			
Ware	d					17 07				17 35							18 07			18 35			
Hertford East	a					17 14				17 42							18 14			18 42			
Roydon	d								17 24			←							18 24			←	
Harlow Town	d			16 52	16 59				17 28		17 22	17 28			17 52	17 59			18 28		18 22	18 28	
Harlow Mill	d								→			17 31							→			18 31	
Sawbridgeworth	d				17 04							17 34				18 04						18 34	
Bishops Stortford	a	16 45			17 11		17 15					17 41	17 45			18 11		18 15				18 41	18 45
	d	16 46			17 12		17 16					17 42	17 46			18 12		18 16				18 42	18 46
Stansted Mountfitchet	d			17 03								17 46			18 03							18 46	
Stansted Airport	a	16 55		17 12			17 25				17 40		17 55		18 12			18 25			18 40		18 55
Stansted Airport	d							17 25															
Elsenham	d											17 50										18 50	
Newport (Essex)	d											17 55										18 55	
Audley End	d				17 24			17 39				17 58				18 24						18 58	
Great Chesterford	d											18 03										19 03	
Whittlesford Parkway	d				17 31							18 08				18 31						19 08	
Shelford	d											18 12										19 12	
Cambridge	a				17 41			17 58				18 19				18 41						19 19	

London - Broxbourne, Hertford East, Bishops Stortford, Stansted Airport and Cambridge

Network Diagram - see first Page of Table 20

		LE	LE ■ ✠	LE ■	LE	LE ■ ✠	LE ■	LE	LE ■ ✠	LE ■	LE ■ ✠	LE	LE ■ ✠	LE ■	LE	LE ■ ✠	XC ■	LE ■	LE	LE ■ ✠	LE ■	LE ■ ✠	LE
London Liverpool Street 15 ⊖	d	18 22	18 25	18 28		18 40		18 52	18 55		19 10	19 22	19 25	19 28		19 40			19 52	19 55		20 10	20 22
Bethnal Green	d																						
Hackney Downs	d	18 29						18 59				19 29							19 59				20 29
Stratford 7 ⊖	d						18 45											19 45					
Clapton	d																						
Seven Sisters ⊖	d	18 34						19 04				19 34							20 04				20 34
Tottenham Hale ⊖	d		18 37	18 40		18 52	18 55		19 07		19 22		19 37	19 40		19 52		19 55		20 07		20 22	
Northumberland Park	d																						
Angel Road	d																						
Ponders End	d						18 59											19 59					
Brimsdown	d						19 02											20 02					
Enfield Lock	d						19 04											20 04					
Waltham Cross	d				←		19 07								←			20 07					
Cheshunt	d	18 52		18 49	18 52		19 09	19 20				19 52		19 49	19 52			20 09	20 20				20 52
Broxbourne 3	a	→		18 53	18 57		19 14	19 25				→		19 53	19 57			20 14	20 25				→
Broxbourne 3	d			18 53	18 57		19 19	19 25						19 53	19 57			20 19	20 25				
Rye House	d				19 00			19 28							20 00				20 28				
St Margarets (Herts)	d				19 03			19 31							20 03				20 31				
Ware	d				19 07			19 35							20 07				20 35				
Hertford East	a				19 14			19 42							20 14				20 42				
Roydon	d						19 24			←								20 24			←		
Harlow Town	d		18 52	18 59			19 28		19 22	19 28			19 52	19 59				20 28		20 22	20 28		
Harlow Mill	d						→			19 31								→			20 31		
Sawbridgeworth	d			19 04						19 34				20 04							20 34		
Bishops Stortford	a			19 11		19 15				19 41	19 45			20 11		20 15					20 41	20 45	
	d			19 12		19 16				19 42	19 46			20 12		20 16					20 42	20 46	
Stansted Mountfitchet	d		19 03							19 46			20 03								20 46		
Stansted Airport	a		19 12			19 25			19 40		19 55		20 12			20 25				20 40		20 55	
Stansted Airport	d																20 25						
Elsenham	d									19 50											20 50		
Newport (Essex)	d									19 55											20 55		
Audley End	d			19 24						19 58				20 24			20 39				20 58		
Great Chesterford	d									20 03											21 03		
Whittlesford Parkway	d			19 31						20 08				20 31							21 08		
Shelford	d									20 12											21 12		
Cambridge	a			19 41						20 19				20 41			20 57				21 19		

		LE ■ ✠	LE ■	LE	XC ■	LE ■ ✠	LE ■	LE	LE ■ ✠	LE ■	LE ■ ✠	LE	LE ■ ✠	LE ■	LE	LE ■ ✠	XC ■	LE ■	LE	LE ■ ✠	LE ■	LE ■ ✠
London Liverpool Street 15 ⊖	d	20 25	20 28			20 40		20 52	20 55		21 10	21 22	21 25	21 28		21 40			21 52	21 55		22 10
Bethnal Green	d																					
Hackney Downs	d							20 59				21 29							21 59			
Stratford 7 ⊖	d						20 45											21 45				
Clapton	d																					
Seven Sisters ⊖	d							21 04				21 34							22 04			
Tottenham Hale ⊖	d	20 37	20 40			20 52	20 55		21 07		21 22		21 37	21 40		21 52		21 55		22 07		22 22
Northumberland Park	d																					
Angel Road	d																					
Ponders End	d						20 59											21 59				
Brimsdown	d						21 02											22 02				
Enfield Lock	d						21 04											22 04				
Waltham Cross	d			←			21 07								←			22 07				
Cheshunt	d		20 49	20 52			21 09	21 20				21 52		21 49	21 52			22 09	22 20			
Broxbourne 3	a		20 53	20 57			21 14	21 25				→		21 53	21 57			22 14	22 25			
Broxbourne 3	d		20 53	20 57			21 19	21 25						21 53	21 57			22 19	22 25			
Rye House	d			21 00				21 28							22 00				22 28			
St Margarets (Herts)	d			21 03				21 31							22 03				22 31			
Ware	d			21 07				21 35							22 07				22 35			
Hertford East	a			21 14				21 42							22 14				22 42			
Roydon	d						21 24			←								22 24			←	
Harlow Town	d	20 52	20 59				21 28		21 22	21 28			21 52	21 59				22 28		22 22	22 28	
Harlow Mill	d						→			21 31								→			22 31	
Sawbridgeworth	d		21 04							21 34				22 04							22 34	
Bishops Stortford	a		21 11			21 15				21 41	21 45			22 11		22 15					22 41	22 45
	d		21 12			21 16				21 42	21 46			22 12		22 16					22 42	22 46
Stansted Mountfitchet	d	21 03								21 46			22 03								22 46	
Stansted Airport	a	21 12				21 27			21 40		21 55		22 12			22 25				22 40		22 55
Stansted Airport	d				21 19												22 25					
Elsenham	d									21 50											22 50	
Newport (Essex)	d									21 55											22 55	
Audley End	d		21 24		21 33					21 58				22 24			22 40				22 58	
Great Chesterford	d									22 03											23 03	
Whittlesford Parkway	d		21 31							22 08				22 31							23 08	
Shelford	d									22 12											23 12	
Cambridge	a		21 41		21 47					22 19				22 41			22 57				23 19	

Table 22

Sundays

from 16 September

London - Broxbourne, Hertford East, Bishops Stortford, Stansted Airport and Cambridge

Network Diagram - see first Page of Table 20

		XC	LE	LE	LE	LE	LE	LE	LE	LE	LE	LE	LE	LE	LE	LE	LE
		■		■	■		■	■		■	■			■	■		■
				H			H			H							
London Liverpool Street 15 ⊖	d		22 22	22 25	22 28		22 40		22 52	22 55			23 22	23 25	23 28		23 58
Bethnal Green	d																
Hackney Downs	d		22 29						22 59				23 29				
Stratford 7 ⊖	d							22 45									
Clapton	d																
Seven Sisters ⊖	d		22 34						23 04				23 34				
Tottenham Hale ⊖	d			22 37	22 40		22 52	22 55		23 07				23 37	23 40		00 10
Northumberland Park	d																
Angel Road	d																
Ponders End	d							22 59							23 44		
Brimsdown	d							23 02							23 47		
Enfield Lock	d							23 04							23 49		
Waltham Cross	d					←		23 07							23 52		
Cheshunt	d		22 52		22 49	22 52		23 09	23 20				23 50		23 54	←	00 18
Broxbourne 3	a		→		22 53	22 57		23 14	23 25				23 55		23 59	23 55	00 22
Broxbourne 3	d				22 53	22 57		23 19	23 25				00 02		23 59	00 02	00 22
Rye House	d					23 00							→			00 06	
St Margarets (Herts)	d					23 03										00 09	
Ware	d					23 07										00 13	
Hertford East	a					23 14										00 19	
Roydon	d							23 24			←	←					00 26
Harlow Town	d			22 52	22 59			23 28	23 32	23 22	23 28	23 32		23 52	00 05		00 30
Harlow Mill	d							→	→		23 31						00 33
Sawbridgeworth	d				23 04						23 34				00 10		00 37
Bishops Stortford	a				23 11		23 15				23 41	23 45		00 02	00 17		00 44
	d				23 12		23 16				23 42			00 03			
Stansted Mountfitchet	d			23 03							23 46						
Stansted Airport	a			23 12			23 25			23 40				00 12			
Stansted Airport	d	23 04															
Elsenham	d										23 50						
Newport Essex	d										23 55						
Audley End	d	23 18			23 24						23 58						
Great Chesterford	d										00 03						
Whittlesford Parkway	d				23 31						00 08						
Shelford	d										00 12						
Cambridge	a	23 34			23 41						00 19						

Table 22

Mondays to Fridays

Cambridge, Stansted Airport, Bishops Stortford, Hertford East and Broxbourne - London

Network Diagram - see first Page of Table 20

Miles	Miles			LE	LE	LE	LE	LE	LE	LE	LE	LE	LE	LE	LE	LE	LE	XC	LE	LE	LE	LE	XC
				MO		MX	MX	MX	MO	MX	MO	MX	MX			MFO	MFO					MFO	
				■	■	■	■	■	■	■	■	■	■	■	■	■	■	■	■	■	■	■	■
				A	B				C		C			D		E	E					F	
0	—	Cambridge	d				22p51											04 44	04 48				05 17
3¼	—	Shelford	d				22p56																
6¾	—	Whittlesford Parkway	d				23p00												04 55				
10	—	Great Chesterford	d				23p04																
14	—	Audley End	d				23p10											04 58	05 03				05 35
15¾	—	Newport Essex	d				23p13																
20¼	0	Elsenham	d				23p19																
—	—	Stansted Airport	a															05 12					05 49
—	4½	Stansted Airport	d	23p15	23p15	23p15		23p30	23p30		23p45	23p45		23p59	00 30	01 00	01 30					05 30	
22½	8¼	Stansted Mountfitchet	d			23p21	23p24																
25½	—	Bishops Stortford	a				23p29	23p39	23p39					00 08	00 39				05 16			05 39	
—	—		d				23p29	23p39	23p39					00 08	00 39				05 16		05 30	05 39	
29	—	Sawbridgeworth	d				23p33												05 21		05 35		
31¼	—	Harlow Mill	d				23p37												05 24		05 38		
33	—	Harlow Town	d	23p30	23p30	23p32	23p40		23p47		23p59	23p59		00 16	00 47				05 27		05 41	05 47	
35¾	—	Roydon	d				23p44												05 31		05 45		
—	0	Hertford East	d							23p39			00 07							05 25			
—	2	Ware	d							23p43										05 29			
—	4	St Margarets (Herts)	d							23p47										05 33			
—	5¼	Rye House	d							23p50										05 36			
38½	—	Broxbourne 3	a				23p48			23p54			00 19						05 36	05 40	05 50	05 53	
—	7	Broxbourne 3	d				23p48			23p54			00 19						05 36	05 40	05 56	05 53	
41¾	—	Cheshunt	d				23p52			23p58									05 41	05 44	→	05 57	
43	—	Waltham Cross	d																	05 47			
44	—	Enfield Lock	d																	05 49			
45	—	Brimsdown	d																	05 52			
45¾	—	Ponders End	d																	05 54			
48	—	Angel Road	d																	05 57			
48¾	—	Northumberland Park	d																	05 59			
49½	—	Tottenham Hale ⊖	d	23p46	23p47	23p48													05 49	06 03		06 07	
—	0	Seven Sisters ⊖	d				00 04	00 08	00 08	00 11	00 21	00 21											
51¾	—	Clapton	d																				
—	6¾	Stratford 7 ⊖	a																				
52¾	—	Hackney Downs	d							00 16			00 41							06 08			
54½	—	Bethnal Green	d																				
55¾	—	London Liverpool Street 15 ⊖	a	00 01	00 01	00 01	00 18	00 22	00 22	00 26	00 35	00 36	00 49	00 51	01 21	01 50	02 20		06 03	06 18		06 23	

		LE	LE	LE	LE	LE	LE	LE	LE	LE	LE	LE	LE	LE	LE	LE	LE	LE	LE	LE	LE	LE	XC
		■	■	■	■	■	■	■	■	■		■		■	■	■		■	■		■	■	■
		TW ThO G																					
						H			H						H			H				H	
Cambridge	d			05 20	05 32			05 48				05 51				06 18					06 21		06 32
Shelford	d			05 25								05 56									06 26		
Whittlesford Parkway	d			05 29	05 39			05 55				06 00				06 25					06 30		
Great Chesterford	d			05 33								06 04									06 34		
Audley End	d			05 39	05 48			06 04				06 10				06 34					06 40		06 46
Newport Essex	d			05 42								06 13									06 43		
Elsenham	d			05 48								06 19									06 49		
Stansted Airport	a																						07 09
Stansted Airport	d					06 00			06 15						06 30			06 45				07 00	
Stansted Mountfitchet	d			05 51		06 06						06 22			06 36						06 52		
Bishops Stortford	a			05 57	06 01	06 10		06 17	06 24			06 28			06 40	06 47		06 54			06 58	07 09	
	d	05 39		05 57	06 01	06 10		06 18	06 24			06 29		06 34	06 41	06 47		06 54			06 58	07 09	
Sawbridgeworth	d			06 01	06 05							06 33		06 39							07 03	07 14	
Harlow Mill	d			06 05								06 37		06 42							07 06		
Harlow Town	d	05 47		06 08	06 13	06 18		06 27	06 33			06 40		06 56	06 50			07 03			07 10	07 20	
Roydon	d			06 12								06 44		07 00							07 14		
Hertford East	d						06 06				06 28									06 58			
Ware	d						06 10				06 32									07 02			
St Margarets (Herts)	d						06 14				06 36									07 06			
Rye House	d		←				06 17				06 39									07 09			
Broxbourne 3	a	05 53	05 50	06 16	06 19		06 22	06 33			06 43	06 48		07 05						07 13	07 18		
Broxbourne 3	d	05 53	05 56	06 16	06 20		06 26	06 34		06 40	06 44	06 49	07 00	07 10						07 14	07 18		
Cheshunt	d	05 57	06 01	06 20			06 30			06 44	06 48	06 53	07 04	07 14						07 18	07 23		
Waltham Cross	d		06 03				06 33			06 47			07 07	07 17				07 12					
Enfield Lock	d		06 06				06 35			06 49			07 09	07 19									
Brimsdown	d		06 08				06 38			06 52			07 12					07 17					
Ponders End	d		06 10				06 40						07 14										
Angel Road	d		06 14											07 24									
Northumberland Park	d		06 16							06 57				07 26			←		←				
Tottenham Hale ⊖	d	06 07	06 20	06 28	06 31	06 34	06 45	06 48	06 51	06 59		07 02	07 19	07 29	07 05	07 08	07 19	07 23	07 29		07 32	07 35	
Seven Sisters ⊖	d										07 02		→	→						07 32			
Clapton	d																						
Stratford 7 ⊖	a		06 32		06 45					07 13									07 43				
Hackney Downs	d						06 52				07 08						07 26			07 38			
Bethnal Green	d																						
London Liverpool Street 15 ⊖	a	06 23		06 43		06 49	07 02	07 05	07 08		07 18	07 20			07 23	07 25	07 38	07 41		07 48	07 50	07 53	

A from 21 May until 23 July, MO from 20 August, not 3 September, 10 September

B 30 July, 6 August, 13 August, 3 September, 10 September

C from 21 May

D not 14 May

E also from 31 July until 9 August, from 30 August until 6 September

F also from 31 July until 9 August, from 29 August until 6 September

G not from 31 July until 9 August, from 29 August until 6 September

Cambridge, Stansted Airport, Bishops Stortford, Hertford East and Broxbourne - London

Network Diagram - see first Page of Table 20

		LE 1	LE	LE 1 A ⊼	LE 1 B ⊼	LE 1	LE	LE 1	LE	LE 1	LE 1 ⊼	LE 1 C	LE	LE 1 A ⊼	LE 1 B ⊼	LE 1	LE	LE 1	LE 1 ⊼	XC 1	LE 1	LE
Cambridge	d	06 47						06 51				07 17						07 21		07 30	07 47	
Shelford	d							06 56										07 26				
Whittlesford Parkway	d	06 55						07 00				07 25						07 30			07 55	
Great Chesterford	d							07 04										07 34				
Audley End	d	07 04						07 10				07 34						07 40		07 44	08 04	
Newport (Essex)	d							07 13										07 43				
Elsenham	d							07 19										07 49				
Stansted Airport	a																			08 09		
Stansted Airport	d			07 15	07 15						07 30			07 43	07 43				08 00			
Stansted Mountfitchet	d							07 22						07 49	07 49			07 52				
Bishops Stortford	a	07 17		07 24	07 24			07 28			07 39	07 47		07 53	07 53			07 58	08 09		08 17	
	d	07 17		07 24	07 24			07 28		07 34	07 41	07 47		07 54	07 54			07 58	08 09		08 17	
Sawbridgeworth	d							07 33		07 39								08 03	08 14			
Harlow Mill	d							07 36		07 42								08 06				
Harlow Town	d			07 33	07 33			07 40		07 56	07 50			08 03	08 03			08 10	08 20			
Roydon	d							07 44		08 00								08 14				
Hertford East	d					07 16	07 28										07 58					
Ware	d					07 20	07 32										08 02					
St Margarets (Herts)	d					07 24	07 36										08 06					
Rye House	d					07 28	07 39										08 09					
Broxbourne [3]	a					07 32	07 43	07 48		08 05							08 13	08 18				
Broxbourne [3]	d		07 30			07 40	07 44	07 48	08 00	08 10							08 14	08 18				08 30
Cheshunt	d		07 34			07 44	07 48	07 53	08 04	08 14							08 18	08 23				08 34
Waltham Cross	d		07 37			07 47			08 07	08 17				08 12	08 12							08 37
Enfield Lock	d		07 39	07 44	07 44	07 49			08 09	08 19												08 39
Brimsdown	d		07 42	07 47	07 47	07 52			08 12					08 17	08 17							08 42
Ponders End	d		07 44						08 14													08 44
Angel Road	d									08 24												
Northumberland Park	d					07 57				08 26												
Tottenham Hale ⊖	d	07 38	07 49	07 53	07 54	07 59		08 02	08 19	08 29	08 05	08 08	← 08 19	08 23	08 24	← 08 29		08 32	08 35		08 38	08 49
Seven Sisters ⊖	d						08 02		→	→												
Clapton	d																08 32					
Stratford [7] ⊖	a					08 13										08 43						
Hackney Downs	d		07 56				08 08						08 26				08 38					08 56
Bethnal Green	d																					
London Liverpool Street [15] ⊖	a	07 55	08 08	08 10	08 10		08 18	08 20			08 23	08 25	08 37	08 40	08 40		08 48	08 50	08 53		08 55	09 07

		LE 1 ⊼	LE 1	LE 1	LE 1 ⊼	XC ◇1	LE 1	LE	LE 1	LE 1 ⊼	LE	LE 1	LE 1 ⊼	LE 1	LE 1 ⊼	LE 1	LE 1	LE 1 ⊼	XC ◇1	LE 1	LE 1 ⊼	LE 1	LE 1
Cambridge	d			07 51		08 10			08 18			08 21					08 48		09 10				09 18
Shelford	d			07 56								08 26					08 53						09 23
Whittlesford Parkway	d			08 00					08 25			08 30					09 00						09 30
Great Chesterford	d			08 04								08 34					09 04						09 34
Audley End	d			08 10		08 25			08 34			08 40					09 10		09 24				09 40
Newport (Essex)	d			08 13								08 43					09 13						09 43
Elsenham	d			08 19								08 49					09 19						09 49
Stansted Airport	a					08 39													09 39				
Stansted Airport	d	08 15			08 30					08 45			09 00		09 15			09 30			09 45		
Stansted Mountfitchet	d			08 22						08 51		08 53			09 21		09 24						09 52
Bishops Stortford	a	08 24		08 28	08 39				08 48			08 58	09 09				09 29	09 39					09 58
	d	08 24		08 28	08 39			08 43	08 48			08 58	09 09			09 15	09 29	09 39				09 47	09 58
Sawbridgeworth	d			08 33				08 48				09 03				09 20	09 33					09 52	10 03
Harlow Mill	d			08 36								09 06				09 23	09 37						10 06
Harlow Town	d	08 33		08 40				08 53	08 57	09 02		09 10			09 32	09 26	09 40				10 00	10 05	10 09
Roydon	d			08 44								09 14				09 30							10 13
Hertford East	d		08 16				08 39							09 09						09 39			
Ware	d		08 20				08 43							09 13						09 43			
St Margarets (Herts)	d		08 24				08 47							09 17						09 47			
Rye House	d		08 28				08 50							09 20						09 50			
Broxbourne [3]	a		08 33	08 48			08 55	09 00	09 03		← 09 00	09 18		09 25		09 35	09 46			09 54		10 11	10 17
Broxbourne [3]	d		08 40	08 48			08 55	09 09	09 04		09 09	09 18		09 25		09 39	09 46			09 54		10 12	10 17
Cheshunt	d		08 44	08 53			09 00	→			09 14	09 23		09 30		09 43	09 50			09 58		10 16	10 21
Waltham Cross	d		08 47				09 02				09 16			09 32						10 01		10 19	
Enfield Lock	d		08 49				09 05				09 19			09 35		09 47				10 03			
Brimsdown	d		08 52				09 07							09 37						10 06			
Ponders End	d						09 09							09 39						10 08			
Angel Road	d										09 24					09 52							
Northumberland Park	d		08 57								09 26					09 54							
Tottenham Hale ⊖	d	08 52	08 59	09 02	09 05		09 15		09 18	09 21	09 29	09 32	09 35	09 45	09 48	09 57	10 00	10 03		10 14	10 17	10 27	10 30
Seven Sisters ⊖	d																						
Clapton	d																						
Stratford [7] ⊖	a		09 13								09 42					10 08						10 37	
Hackney Downs	d						09 22							09 51						10 20			
Bethnal Green	d																						
London Liverpool Street [15] ⊖	a	09 09		09 20	09 23		09 33		09 35	09 38		09 50	09 53	10 01	10 03		10 14	10 17		10 28	10 31		10 44

A not from 27 July until 10 August, from 29 August until 7 September

B from 27 July until 7 September, not from 13 August until 28 August

C The Fenman

Cambridge, Stansted Airport, Bishops Stortford, Hertford East and Broxbourne - London

Network Diagram - see first Page of Table 20

		LE 1 ⊼	LE 1	LE 1 ⊼	LE 1	LE 1	LE 1 ⊼	XC ◇1	LE 1	LE 1 ⊼	LE 1	LE 1	LE 1 ⊼	LE 1	LE 1 ⊼	LE 1	LE 1	LE 1 ⊼	XC ◇1	LE 1	LE 1 ⊼	LE 1	LE 1
Cambridge	d					10 04		10 10				10 21					11 04		11 10				11 21
Shelford	d											10 26											11 26
Whittlesford Parkway	d					10 11						10 30					11 11						11 30
Great Chesterford	d											10 34											11 34
Audley End	d					10 19		10 25				10 40					11 19		11 24				11 40
Newport (Essex)	d											10 43											11 43
Elsenham	d											10 49											11 49
Stansted Airport	a							10 40											11 40				
Stansted Airport	d	10 00		10 15			10 30			10 45			11 00		11 15			11 30			11 45		
Stansted Mountfitchet	d			10 21								10 52			11 21								11 52
Bishops Stortford	a	10 09				10 32	10 39					10 58	11 09				11 32	11 39					11 58
	d	10 09			10 15	10 32	10 39				10 47	10 58	11 09			11 15	11 32	11 39				11 47	11 58
Sawbridgeworth	d				10 20						10 52	11 03				11 20						11 52	12 03
Harlow Mill	d				10 23							11 06				11 23							12 06
Harlow Town	d			10 32	10 26	10 40				11 00	11 05	11 09			11 32	11 26	11 40				12 00	12 05	12 09
Roydon	d				10 30							11 13				11 30							12 13
Hertford East	d		10 09						10 39					11 09						11 39			
Ware	d		10 13						10 43					11 13						11 43			
St Margarets (Herts)	d		10 17						10 47					11 17						11 47			
Rye House	d		10 20						10 50					11 20						11 50			
Broxbourne [3]	a		10 24		10 35	10 46			10 54		11 11	11 17		11 24		11 35	11 46			11 54		12 11	12 17
Broxbourne [3]	d		10 24		10 39	10 46			10 54		11 12	11 17		11 24		11 39	11 46			11 54		12 12	12 17
Cheshunt	d		10 28		10 43	10 50			10 58		11 16	11 21		11 28		11 43	11 50			11 58		12 16	12 21
Waltham Cross	d		10 31						11 01		11 19			11 31						12 01		12 19	
Enfield Lock	d		10 33		10 47				11 03					11 33		11 47				12 03			
Brimsdown	d		10 36						11 06					11 36						12 06			
Ponders End	d		10 38						11 08					11 38						12 08			
Angel Road	d																						
Northumberland Park	d				10 52											11 52							
Tottenham Hale ⊖	d	10 33	10 44	10 48	10 56	11 00	11 03		11 14	11 17	11 27	11 30	11 33	11 44	11 48	11 56	12 00	12 03		12 14	12 17	12 27	12 30
Seven Sisters ⊖	d																						
Clapton	d																						
Stratford [7] ⊖	a				11 07						11 37					12 07						12 37	
Hackney Downs	d		10 50						11 20					11 50						12 20			
Bethnal Green	d																						
London Liverpool Street [15] ⊖	a	10 47	10 58	11 01		11 13	11 16		11 28	11 31		11 44	11 47	11 58	12 01		12 13	12 16		12 31	12 33		12 44

		LE 1 ⊼	LE 1	LE 1 ⊼	LE 1	LE 1	LE 1 ⊼	XC ◇1	LE 1	LE 1 ⊼	LE 1	LE 1	LE 1 ⊼	LE 1	LE 1 ⊼	LE 1	LE 1	LE 1 ⊼	XC ◇1	LE 1	LE 1 ⊼	LE 1
Cambridge	d					12 04		12 10				12 21					13 04		13 10			
Shelford	d											12 26										
Whittlesford Parkway	d					12 11						12 30					13 11					
Great Chesterford	d											12 34										
Audley End	d					12 19		12 24				12 40					13 19		13 24			
Newport (Essex)	d											12 43										
Elsenham	d											12 49										
Stansted Airport	a							12 40											13 40			
Stansted Airport	d	12 00		12 15			12 30			12 45			13 00		13 15			13 30			13 45	
Stansted Mountfitchet	d			12 21								12 52			13 21							
Bishops Stortford	a	12 09				12 32	12 39					12 58	13 09				13 32	13 39				
	d	12 09			12 15	12 32	12 39				12 47	12 58	13 09			13 15	13 32	13 39				13 47
Sawbridgeworth	d				12 20						12 52	13 03				13 20						13 52
Harlow Mill	d				12 23							13 06				13 23						
Harlow Town	d			12 32	12 26	12 40				13 00	13 05	13 09			13 32	13 26	13 40				14 00	14 05
Roydon	d				12 30							13 13				13 30						
Hertford East	d		12 09						12 39					13 09						13 39		
Ware	d		12 13						12 43					13 13						13 43		
St Margarets (Herts)	d		12 17						12 47					13 17						13 47		
Rye House	d		12 20						12 50					13 20						13 50		
Broxbourne [3]	a		12 24		12 35	12 46			12 54		13 11	13 17		13 24		13 35	13 46			13 54		14 11
Broxbourne [3]	d		12 24		12 39	12 46			12 54		13 12	13 17		13 24		13 39	13 46			13 54		14 12
Cheshunt	d		12 28		12 43	12 50			12 58		13 16	13 21		13 28		13 43	13 50			13 58		14 16
Waltham Cross	d		12 31						13 01		13 19			13 31						14 01		14 19
Enfield Lock	d		12 33		12 47				13 03					13 33		13 47				14 03		
Brimsdown	d		12 36						13 06					13 36						14 06		
Ponders End	d		12 38						13 08					13 38						14 08		
Angel Road	d																					
Northumberland Park	d				12 52											13 52						
Tottenham Hale ⊖	d	12 33	12 44	12 48	12 56	13 00	13 03		13 14	13 17	13 27	13 30	13 33	13 44	13 48	13 56	14 00	14 03		14 14	14 17	14 27
Seven Sisters ⊖	d																					
Clapton	d																					
Stratford [7] ⊖	a				13 07						13 37					14 07						14 37
Hackney Downs	d		12 50						13 20					13 50						14 20		
Bethnal Green	d																					
London Liverpool Street [15] ⊖	a	12 47	12 58	13 01		13 13	13 16		13 28	13 31		13 44	13 47	13 58	14 01		14 13	14 16		14 28	14 31	

Cambridge, Stansted Airport, Bishops Stortford, Hertford East and Broxbourne - London

Network Diagram - see first Page of Table 20

Station		LE	LE	LE	LE	LE	LE	LE	XC	LE	LE	LE	LE	LE	LE	LE	LE	LE	LE	XC	LE	LE	LE
		1	1	1	1	1	1	1	◇1	1	1	1	1	1	1	1	1	1	1	◇1	1	1	1
			🛒		🛒			🛒			🛒			🛒		🛒			🛒			🛒	
Cambridge	d	13 21					14 04		14 10				14 21					15 04		15 10			
Shelford	d	13 26											14 26										
Whittlesford Parkway	d	13 30					14 11						14 30					15 11					
Great Chesterford	d	13 34											14 34										
Audley End	d	13 40					14 19		14 24				14 40					15 19		15 24			
Newport (Essex)	d	13 43											14 43										
Elsenham	d	13 49											14 49										
Stansted Airport	a								14 40											15 40			
Stansted Airport	d		14 00		14 15			14 30			14 45			15 00		15 15			15 30			15 45	
Stansted Mountfitchet	d	13 52			14 21								14 52			15 21							
Bishops Stortford	a	13 58	14 09				14 32	14 39					14 58	15 09				15 32	15 39				
	d	13 58	14 09			14 15	14 32	14 39				14 47	14 58	15 09			15 15	15 32	15 39				15 47
Sawbridgeworth	d	14 03				14 20						14 52	15 03				15 20						15 52
Harlow Mill	d	14 06				14 23							15 06				15 23						
Harlow Town	d	14 09			14 32	14 26	14 40				15 00	15 05	15 09			15 32	15 26	15 40				16 00	16 03
Roydon	d	14 13				14 30							15 13				15 30						
Hertford East	d			14 09						14 39					15 09						15 39		
Ware	d			14 13						14 43					15 13						15 43		
St Margarets (Herts)	d			14 17						14 47					15 17						15 47		
Rye House	d			14 20						14 50					15 20						15 50		
Broxbourne 3	a	14 17		14 24		14 35	14 46			14 54		15 11	15 17		15 24		15 35	15 46			15 54		16 10
Broxbourne 3	d	14 17		14 24		14 39	14 46			14 54		15 12	15 17		15 24		15 39	15 46			15 54		16 10
Cheshunt	d	14 21		14 28		14 43	14 50			14 58		15 16	15 21		15 28		15 43	15 50			15 58		16 14
Waltham Cross	d			14 31						15 01		15 19			15 31						16 01		16 16
Enfield Lock	d			14 33		14 47				15 03					15 33		15 47				16 03		
Brimsdown	d			14 36						15 06					15 36						16 06		
Ponders End	d			14 38						15 08					15 38						16 08		
Angel Road	d																15 52						
Northumberland Park	d					14 52											15 54						16 23
Tottenham Hale ⊖	d	14 30	14 33	14 44	14 48	14 56	15 00	15 03		15 14	15 17	15 27	15 30	15 33	15 44	15 48	15 57	16 00	16 03		16 14	16 17	16 27
Seven Sisters ⊖	d																						
Clapton	d																						
Stratford 7 ⊖	a					15 07						15 37					16 08						16 37
Hackney Downs	d			14 50						15 20					15 50						16 20		
Bethnal Green	d																						
London Liverpool Street 15 ⊖	a	14 44	14 47	14 58	15 01		15 13	15 18		15 28	15 31		15 45	15 47	15 58	16 03		16 15	16 18		16 31	16 33	

Station		LE	LE	LE	LE	LE	LE	LE	XC	LE	LE	LE	LE	LE	LE	LE	LE	LE	LE	LE	XC	LE
		1	1	1	1	1	1	1	◇1	1	1	1	1	1	1	1	1	1	1	1	◇1	1
			🛒		🛒			🛒			🛒				🛒		🛒			🛒		
Cambridge	d	15 21					15 51		16 10				16 21	16 40					16 51		17 10	
Shelford	d	15 26					15 56						16 26						16 56			
Whittlesford Parkway	d	15 30					16 00						16 30						17 00			
Great Chesterford	d	15 34					16 04						16 34						17 04			
Audley End	d	15 40					16 10		16 24				16 40	16 53					17 10		17 24	
Newport (Essex)	d	15 43					16 13						16 43						17 13			
Elsenham	d	15 49					16 19						16 49						17 19			
Stansted Airport	a								16 40												17 40	
Stansted Airport	d		16 00		16 15			16 30			16 45				17 00		17 15			17 30		
Stansted Mountfitchet	d	15 52			16 21		16 24						16 52				17 21		17 24			
Bishops Stortford	a	15 58	16 09				16 30	16 39					16 58		17 09				17 30	17 39		
	d	15 58	16 09			16 15	16 30	16 39				16 43	16 58		17 09			17 15	17 30	17 39		
Sawbridgeworth	d	16 03				16 20						16 48	17 03					17 20	17 35			
Harlow Mill	d	16 06				16 23						16 51						17 23	17 38			
Harlow Town	d	16 09			16 32	16 26	16 38				17 00	16 54	17 08				17 32	17 26	17 41			
Roydon	d	16 13				16 30						16 58						17 30				
Hertford East	d			16 09						16 39						17 09						17 39
Ware	d			16 13						16 43						17 13						17 43
St Margarets (Herts)	d			16 17						16 47						17 17						17 47
Rye House	d			16 20						16 50						17 20						17 50
Broxbourne 3	a	16 17		16 24		16 35	16 44			16 54		17 03	17 14			17 24		17 35	17 47			17 54
Broxbourne 3	d	16 17		16 24		16 39	16 44			16 54		17 07	17 14			17 24		17 39	17 47			17 54
Cheshunt	d	16 21		16 28		16 43	16 48			16 58		17 12	17 18			17 28		17 43	17 51			17 58
Waltham Cross	d			16 31						17 01		17 14				17 31						18 01
Enfield Lock	d			16 33		16 47				17 03						17 33		17 47				18 03
Brimsdown	d			16 36						17 06						17 36						18 06
Ponders End	d			16 38						17 08						17 38						18 08
Angel Road	d					16 52												17 52				
Northumberland Park	d					16 54						17 21						17 54				
Tottenham Hale ⊖	d	16 30	16 33	16 44	16 48	16 57	17 00	17 03		17 14	17 18	17 24	17 27	17 30	17 33	17 44	17 49	17 57	18 01	18 03		18 14
Seven Sisters ⊖	d																					
Clapton	d																					
Stratford 7 ⊖	a					17 08						17 35						18 08				
Hackney Downs	d			16 50						17 20						17 50						18 20
Bethnal Green	d																					
London Liverpool Street 15 ⊖	a	16 44	16 47	16 59	17 01		17 16	17 18		17 30	17 32		17 44	17 46	17 48	17 59	18 03		18 17	18 18		18 28

Table 22 | Mondays to Fridays

Cambridge, Stansted Airport, Bishops Stortford, Hertford East and Broxbourne - London

Network Diagram - see first Page of Table 20

Station		LE	LE	LE	LE	LE	LE	LE	LE	LE	LE	LE	XC	LE	LE	LE	LE	LE	LE	LE	LE	LE	XC
		1	1	1	1	1	1	1	1	1	1	1	◇1	1	1	1	1	1	1	1	1	1	◇1
																				A	B		
		🛒			🛒		🛒			🛒		🛒				🛒		🛒				🛒	
Cambridge	d			17 21					17 51				18 18		18 21					18 51	18 51		19 10
Shelford	d			17 26					17 56						18 26					18 56	18 56		
Whittlesford Parkway	d			17 30					18 00						18 30					19 00	19 00		
Great Chesterford	d			17 34					18 04						18 34					19 04	19 04		
Audley End	d			17 40					18 10				18 32		18 40					19 10	19 10		19 24
Newport (Essex)	d			17 43					18 13						18 43					19 13	19 13		
Elsenham	d			17 49					18 19						18 49					19 19	19 19		
Stansted Airport	a												18 54										19 39
Stansted Airport	d	17 45			18 00		18 15			18 30		18 45				19 00		19 15				19 30	
Stansted Mountfitchet	d			17 52			18 21		18 24						18 52			19 21		19 24	19 24		
Bishops Stortford	a			17 58	18 09				18 29	18 39					18 58	19 09				19 29	19 29	19 39	
	d		17 47	17 58	18 09			18 15	18 30	18 39					18 58	19 09			19 15	19 30	19 30	19 39	
Sawbridgeworth	d		17 52	18 03				18 20	18 35						19 03				19 20	19 35	19 35		
Harlow Mill	d			18 06				18 23							19 06				19 23				
Harlow Town	d	18 00	18 03	18 09			18 32	18 26	18 40			19 00			19 09			19 32	19 26	19 40	19 40		
Roydon	d			18 13				18 30							19 13				19 30				
Hertford East	d					18 09					18 39			18 25			19 09						
Ware	d					18 13					18 43			18 29			19 13						
St Margarets (Herts)	d					18 17					18 47			18 33			19 17						
Rye House	d					18 20					18 50			18 36			19 20						
Broxbourne 3	a		18 10	18 17		18 24		18 35	18 46		18 54			18 42	19 17		19 24		19 35	19 46	19 46		
Broxbourne 3	d		18 10	18 17		18 24		18 39	18 46		18 54			19 10	19 17		19 24		19 39	19 46	19 46		
Cheshunt	d		18 14	18 21		18 28		18 43	18 50		18 58			19 14	19 21		19 28		19 43	19 50	19 50		
Waltham Cross	d		18 17			18 31					19 01			19 17			19 31						
Enfield Lock	d					18 33		18 47			19 03						19 33		19 47				
Brimsdown	d					18 36					19 06						19 36						
Ponders End	d					18 38					19 08						19 38						
Angel Road	d							18 52											19 52				
Northumberland Park	d		18 23					18 54						19 23					19 54				
Tottenham Hale ⊖	d	18 19	18 27	18 30	18 33	18 44	18 49	18 57	19 00	19 03	19 14	19 19		19 27	19 30	19 33	19 44	19 48	19 57	20 00	20 00	20 03	
Seven Sisters ⊖	d																						
Clapton	d																						
Stratford 7 ⊖	a		18 38					19 08						19 38					20 08				
Hackney Downs	d					18 50					19 20						19 50						
Bethnal Green	d																						
London Liverpool Street 15 ⊖	a	18 33		18 44	18 47	18 58	19 03		19 16	19 18	19 28	19 33			19 45	19 48	19 58	20 01		20 14	20 15	20 17	

Station		LE	LE	LE	LE	LE	LE	LE	LE	LE	LE	LE	LE	XC	LE	LE	LE	LE	LE	LE	LE	LE	LE
		1	1	1	1	1	1	1	1	1	1	1	1	◇1	1	1	1	1	1	1	1	1	1
					B	A						A	B				A	B	A	B		B	A
			🛒				🛒		🛒			🛒	🛒			🛒					🛒		
Cambridge	d				19 21	19 21					20 04			20 10					20 21	20 21			
Shelford	d				19 26	19 26													20 26	20 26			
Whittlesford Parkway	d				19 30	19 30					20 11								20 30	20 30			
Great Chesterford	d				19 34	19 34													20 34	20 34			
Audley End	d				19 40	19 40					20 19			20 24					20 40	20 40			
Newport (Essex)	d				19 43	19 43													20 43	20 43			
Elsenham	d				19 49	19 49													20 49	20 49			
Stansted Airport	a													20 39									
Stansted Airport	d		19 45				20 00		20 15			20 30	20 30			20 45					21 00		
Stansted Mountfitchet	d				19 52	19 52			20 21										20 52	20 52			
Bishops Stortford	a				19 58	19 58	20 09				20 32	20 39	20 39						20 58	20 58	21 09		
	d				19 58	19 58	20 09			20 15	20 32	20 39	20 39				20 47	20 47	20 58	20 58	21 09		
Sawbridgeworth	d				20 03	20 03				20 20							20 52	20 52	21 03	21 03			
Harlow Mill	d				20 06	20 06				20 23									21 06	21 06			
Harlow Town	d		20 00		20 09	20 09			20 32	20 26	20 40					21 00	20 57	20 57	21 09	21 09			
Roydon	d				20 13	20 13				20 30									21 13	21 13			
Hertford East	d	19 39		19 25				20 10							20 39							21 09	21 09
Ware	d	19 43		19 29				20 14							20 43							21 13	21 13
St Margarets (Herts)	d	19 47		19 33				20 18							20 47							21 17	21 17
Rye House	d	19 50		19 36				20 21							20 50							21 20	21 20
Broxbourne 3	a	19 57		19 42	20 17	20 17		20 25		20 35	20 46				20 54		21 04	21 04	21 17	21 17		21 24	21 24
Broxbourne 3	d	19 57		20 12	20 17	20 17		20 25		20 39	20 46				20 54		21 07	21 07	21 17	21 17		21 24	21 24
Cheshunt	d	20 01		20 16	20 21	20 21		20 29		20 43	20 50				20 58		21 12	21 12	21 21	21 21		21 28	21 28
Waltham Cross	d	20 03		20 19				20 32							21 01		21 14	21 14				21 31	21 31
Enfield Lock	d	20 06						20 34		20 47					21 03							21 33	21 33
Brimsdown	d	20 08						20 37							21 06							21 36	21 36
Ponders End	d	20 10						20 39							21 08							21 38	21 38
Angel Road	d																						
Northumberland Park	d									20 52													
Tottenham Hale ⊖	d	20 15	20 18	20 27	20 30	20 30	20 33	20 44	20 48	20 56	21 00	21 03	21 03		21 14	21 17	21 23	21 23	21 30	21 30	21 33	21 44	21 44
Seven Sisters ⊖	d																						
Clapton	d																						
Stratford 7 ⊖	a			20 37						21 07							21 37					21 55	
Hackney Downs	d	20 22						20 50							21 20								21 50
Bethnal Green	d																						
London Liverpool Street 15 ⊖	a	20 31	20 33		20 44	20 45	20 47	20 59	21 03		21 13	21 16	21 18		21 28	21 31		21 43	21 44	21 45	21 47		21 58

A not from 27 July until 10 August, from 29 August until 7 September

B from 27 July until 7 September, not from 13 August until 28 August

Cambridge, Stansted Airport, Bishops Stortford, Hertford East and Broxbourne - London

Network Diagram - see first Page of Table 20

		LE ✠	LE A	LE B	LE A	LE B	LE A ✠	LE B ✠	XC ◇	LE B	LE A	LE ✠	LE A	LE B	LE A	LE B	LE	LE B	LE A	LE	LE B	LE A
Cambridge	d				21 04	21 04			21 10						21 21	21 21						
Shelford	d														21 26	21 26						
Whittlesford Parkway	d				21 11	21 11									21 30	21 30						
Great Chesterford	d														21 34	21 34						
Audley End	d				21 19	21 19			21 24						21 40	21 40						
Newport (Essex)	d														21 43	21 43						
Elsenham	d														21 49	21 49						
Stansted Airport	a								21 40													
Stansted Airport	d	21 15					21 30	21 30				21 45					22 00			22 15		
Stansted Mountfitchet	d	21 21													21 52	21 52				22 21		
Bishops Stortford	a				21 32	21 32	21 39	21 39							21 58	21 58	22 09					
	d		21 15	21 15	21 32	21 32	21 39	21 39					21 47	21 47	21 58	21 58	22 09				22 15	22 15
Sawbridgeworth	d		21 20	21 20									21 52	21 52	22 03	22 03					22 20	22 20
Harlow Mill	d		21 23	21 23											22 06	22 06					22 23	22 23
Harlow Town	d	21 32	21 26	21 26	21 40	21 40						22 00	22 05	22 05	22 09	22 09				22 32	22 26	22 26
Roydon	d		21 30	21 30											22 13	22 13					22 30	22 30
Hertford East	d									21 39	21 39							22 09	22 09			
Ware	d									21 43	21 43							22 13	22 13			
St Margarets (Herts)	d									21 47	21 47							22 17	22 17			
Rye House	d									21 50	21 50							22 20	22 20			
Broxbourne	a		21 35	21 35	21 46	21 46				21 54	21 54		22 11	22 11	22 17	22 17		22 24	22 24		22 35	22 35
Broxbourne	d		21 39	21 39	21 46	21 46				21 54	21 54		22 12	22 12	22 17	22 17		22 24	22 24		22 39	22 39
Cheshunt	d		21 43	21 43	21 50	21 50				21 58	21 58		22 16	22 16	22 21	22 21		22 28	22 28		22 43	22 43
Waltham Cross	d									22 01	22 01							22 31	22 31			
Enfield Lock	d		21 47	21 47						22 03	22 03		22 19	22 19				22 33	22 33		22 47	22 47
Brimsdown	d									22 06	22 06							22 36	22 36			
Ponders End	d									22 08	22 08							22 38	22 38			
Angel Road	d																					
Northumberland Park	d		21 52	21 52																	22 52	22 52
Tottenham Hale ⊖	d	21 48	21 56	21 56	22 00	22 00	22 03	22 03		22 14	22 14	22 17	22 27	22 27	22 30	22 30	22 33	22 44	22 44	22 48	22 56	22 56
Seven Sisters ⊖	d																					
Clapton	d																					
Stratford ⊖	a		22 07							22 25			22 37					22 55				23 06
Hackney Downs	d										22 20											
Bethnal Green	d																		22 50			
London Liverpool Street ⊖	a	22 01		22 12	22 13	22 15	22 16	22 17			22 28	22 31		22 42	22 44	22 45	22 47		22 58	23 01	23 12	23 15

		LE A	LE B	LE	LE B	LE A	LE	XC ◇	LE A	LE B	LE	LE B	LE A	LE	LE	LE	LE	LE	LE
Cambridge	d	22 04	22 04					22 10	22 21	22 21					22 51				
Shelford	d								22 26	22 26					22 56				
Whittlesford Parkway	d	22 11	22 11						22 30	22 30					23 00				
Great Chesterford	d								22 34	22 34					23 04				
Audley End	d	22 19	22 19					22 24	22 40	22 40					23 10				
Newport (Essex)	d								22 43	22 43					23 13				
Elsenham	d								22 49	22 49					23 19				
Stansted Airport	a							22 52											
Stansted Airport	d			22 30			22 45				23 00			23 15		23 30		23 45	23 59
Stansted Mountfitchet	d								22 52	22 52				23 21	23 24				
Bishops Stortford	a	22 32	22 32	22 39					22 58	22 58	23 09				23 29	23 39			00 08
	d	22 32	22 32	22 39					22 58	22 58	23 09				23 29	23 39			00 08
Sawbridgeworth	d								23 03	23 03					23 33				
Harlow Mill	d								23 06	23 06					23 37				
Harlow Town	d	22 40	22 40				23 00		23 09	23 09				23 32	23 40			23 59	00 16
Roydon	d								23 13	23 13					23 44				
Hertford East	d				22 39	22 39						23 09	23 09				23 39		
Ware	d				22 43	22 43						23 13	23 13				23 43		
St Margarets (Herts)	d				22 47	22 47						23 17	23 17				23 47		
Rye House	d				22 50	22 50						23 20	23 20				23 50		
Broxbourne	a	22 46	22 46		22 54	22 54			23 17	23 17		23 24	23 24		23 48		23 54		
Broxbourne	d	22 46	22 46		22 54	22 54			23 17	23 17		23 24	23 24		23 48		23 54		
Cheshunt	d	22 50	22 50		22 58	22 58			23 21	23 21		23 28	23 28		23 52		23 58		
Waltham Cross	d				23 01	23 01						23 31	23 31						
Enfield Lock	d				23 03	23 03						23 33	23 33						
Brimsdown	d				23 06	23 06						23 36	23 36						
Ponders End	d				23 08	23 08						23 38	23 38						
Angel Road	d																		
Northumberland Park	d																		
Tottenham Hale ⊖	d	23 00	23 00	23 03	23 14	23 14	23 17		23 30	23 30	23 33	23 44	23 44	23 48					
Seven Sisters ⊖	d														00 04	00 08	00 11	00 21	
Clapton	d																		
Stratford ⊖	a				23 25							23 55							
Hackney Downs	d					23 20							23 50				00 16		
Bethnal Green	d																		
London Liverpool Street ⊖	a	23 13	23 14	23 16		23 28	23 31		23 44	23 45	23 47		23 58	00 01	00 18	00 22	00 26	00 36	00 51

A not from 27 July until 10 August, from 29 August until 7 September

B from 27 July until 7 September, not from 13 August until 28 August

Cambridge, Stansted Airport, Bishops Stortford, Hertford East and Broxbourne - London

Network Diagram - see first Page of Table 20

		LE	LE	LE	LE	LE	LE	LE	LE	LE	LE	XC	LE	LE	LE	LE	LE	LE ✠	XC	LE	LE ✠	LE	LE
Cambridge	d		22p51									04 56					05 21		05 42				06 04
Shelford	d		22p56														05 26						
Whittlesford Parkway	d		23p00														05 30						06 11
Great Chesterford	d		23p04														05 34						
Audley End	d		23p10														05 40		05 56				06 19
Newport (Essex)	d		23p13														05 43						
Elsenham	d		23p19														05 49						
Stansted Airport	a											05 20							06 08				
Stansted Airport	d	23p15		23p30		23p45		23p59	00 30	01 00	01 30			05 30				06 00			06 15		
Stansted Mountfitchet	d	23p21	23p24														05 52				06 21		
Bishops Stortford	a		23p29	23p39				00 08	00 39					05 39			05 58	06 09					06 32
	d		23p29	23p39				00 08	00 39				05 15	05 39		05 47	05 58	06 09				06 15	06 32
Sawbridgeworth	d		23p33										05 20			05 52	06 03					06 20	
Harlow Mill	d		23p37										05 23				06 06					06 23	
Harlow Town	d	23p32	23p40			23p59		00 16	00 47				05 26			06 05	06 09				06 32	06 26	06 40
Roydon	d		23p44										05 30				06 13					06 30	
Hertford East	d				23p39		00 07													06 09			
Ware	d				23p43															06 13			
St Margarets (Herts)	d				23p47															06 17			
Rye House	d				23p50															06 20			
Broxbourne	a		23p48		23p54		00 19						05 34			06 11	06 17			06 24		06 35	06 46
Broxbourne	d		23p48		23p54		00 19						05 34		05 54	06 12	06 17			06 24		06 39	06 46
Cheshunt	d		23p52		23p58								05 38		05 58	06 16	06 21			06 28		06 43	06 50
Waltham Cross	d												05 41		06 01	06 19				06 31			
Enfield Lock	d												05 43		06 03					06 33		06 47	
Brimsdown	d												05 46		06 06					06 36			
Ponders End	d												05 48		06 08					06 38			
Angel Road	d																						
Northumberland Park	d												05 52									06 52	
Tottenham Hale ⊖	d	23p48											05 55	06 01	06 14	06 27	06 30	06 33		06 44	06 48	06 56	07 00
Seven Sisters ⊖	d		00 04	00 08	00 11	00 21																	
Clapton	d																						
Stratford ⊖	a												06 05			06 37						07 07	
Hackney Downs	d				00 16		00 41								06 20					06 50			
Bethnal Green	d																						
London Liverpool Street ⊖	a	00 01	00 18	00 22	00 26	00 36	00 49	00 51	01 21	01 50	02 20		06 14	06 14	06 28		06 44	06 47		06 58	07 01		07 13

		LE ✠	LE	LE ✠	LE	LE	LE ✠	XC	LE	LE ✠	LE	LE	LE ✠	LE	LE ✠	LE	LE	LE ✠	XC	LE	LE ✠	LE	LE
Cambridge	d					06 21		06 40				07 04					07 21		07 40				08 04
Shelford	d					06 26											07 26						
Whittlesford Parkway	d					06 30						07 11					07 30						08 11
Great Chesterford	d					06 34											07 34						
Audley End	d					06 40		06 54				07 19					07 40		07 54				08 19
Newport (Essex)	d					06 43											07 43						
Elsenham	d					06 49											07 49						
Stansted Airport	a							07 09											08 08				
Stansted Airport	d	06 30		06 45			07 00			07 15			07 30		07 45			08 00			08 15		
Stansted Mountfitchet	d					06 52				07 21							07 52				08 21		
Bishops Stortford	a	06 39				06 58	07 09					07 32	07 39				07 58	08 09					08 32
	d	06 39			06 47	06 58	07 09				07 15	07 32	07 39			07 47	07 58	08 09				08 15	08 32
Sawbridgeworth	d				06 52	07 03					07 20					07 52	08 03					08 20	
Harlow Mill	d					07 06					07 23						08 06					08 23	
Harlow Town	d			07 00	07 05	07 09				07 32	07 26	07 40			08 00	08 05	08 09				08 32	08 26	08 40
Roydon	d					07 13					07 30						08 13					08 30	
Hertford East	d		06 39						07 09					07 39						08 09			
Ware	d		06 43						07 13					07 43						08 13			
St Margarets (Herts)	d		06 47						07 17					07 47						08 17			
Rye House	d		06 50						07 20					07 50						08 20			
Broxbourne	a		06 54		07 11	07 17			07 24		07 35	07 46		07 54		08 11	08 17			08 24		08 35	08 46
Broxbourne	d		06 54		07 12	07 17			07 24		07 39	07 46		07 54		08 12	08 17			08 24		08 39	08 46
Cheshunt	d		06 58		07 16	07 21			07 28		07 43	07 50		07 58		08 16	08 21			08 28		08 43	08 50
Waltham Cross	d		07 01		07 19				07 31					08 01		08 19				08 31			
Enfield Lock	d		07 03						07 33		07 47			08 03						08 33		08 47	
Brimsdown	d		07 06						07 36					08 06						08 36			
Ponders End	d		07 08						07 38					08 08						08 38			
Angel Road	d																						
Northumberland Park	d										07 52											08 52	
Tottenham Hale ⊖	d	07 03	07 14	07 17	07 27	07 30	07 33		07 44	07 48	07 56	08 00	08 03	08 14	08 17	08 27	08 30	08 33		08 44	08 48	08 56	09 00
Seven Sisters ⊖	d																						
Clapton	d																						
Stratford ⊖	a				07 37						08 07					08 37						09 07	
Hackney Downs	d		07 20						07 50					08 20						08 50			
Bethnal Green	d																						
London Liverpool Street ⊖	a	07 16	07 28	07 31		07 44	07 47		07 58	08 01		08 13	08 16	08 28	08 31		08 44	08 47		08 58	09 01		09 13

Table 22

Saturdays
until 21 July

Cambridge, Stansted Airport, Bishops Stortford, Hertford East and Broxbourne - London

Network Diagram - see first Page of Table 20

	LE [1] ⌶	XC ◇[1]	LE [1]	LE [1] ⌶	LE [1]	LE [1]	LE [1] ⌶	LE [1]	LE [1] ⌶	LE [1]	LE [1]	LE [1] ⌶	XC ◇[1]	LE [1]	LE [1] ⌶	LE [1]	LE [1]	LE [1] ⌶	LE [1]	LE [1] ⌶	LE [1]
Cambridge d		08 10				08 21					09 04		09 10				09 21				
Shelford d						08 26											09 26				
Whittlesford Parkway d						08 30					09 11						09 30				
Great Chesterford d						08 34											09 34				
Audley End d		08 24				08 40					09 19		09 24				09 40				
Newport (Essex) d						08 43											09 43				
Elsenham d						08 49											09 49				
Stansted Airport a		08 39											09 40								
Stansted Airport d	08 30			08 45			09 00		09 15			09 30			09 45			10 00		10 15	
Stansted Mountfitchet d						08 52			09 21								09 52			10 21	
Bishops Stortford a	08 39					08 58	09 09				09 32	09 39					09 58	10 09			
d	08 39				08 47	08 58	09 09			09 15	09 32	09 39				09 47	09 58	10 09			10 15
Sawbridgeworth d					08 52	09 03				09 20						09 52	10 03				10 20
Harlow Mill d						09 06				09 23							10 06				10 23
Harlow Town d				09 00	09 05	09 09			09 32	09 26	09 40				10 00	10 05	10 09			10 32	10 26
Roydon d						09 13				09 30							10 13				10 30
Hertford East d			08 39					09 09						09 39					10 09		
Ware d			08 43					09 13						09 43					10 13		
St Margarets (Herts) d			08 47					09 17						09 47					10 17		
Rye House d			08 50					09 20						09 50					10 20		
Broxbourne a			08 54		09 11	09 17		09 24		09 35	09 46			09 54		10 11	10 17		10 24		10 35
Broxbourne d			08 54		09 12	09 17		09 24		09 39	09 46			09 54		10 12	10 17		10 24		10 39
Cheshunt d			08 58		09 16	09 21		09 28		09 43	09 50			09 58		10 16	10 21		10 28		10 43
Waltham Cross d			09 01		09 19			09 31						10 01		10 19			10 31		
Enfield Lock d			09 03					09 33		09 47				10 03					10 33		10 47
Brimsdown d			09 06					09 36						10 06					10 36		
Ponders End d			09 08					09 38						10 08					10 38		
Angel Road d																					
Northumberland Park d										09 52											10 52
Tottenham Hale ⊖ d	09 03		09 14	09 17	09 27	09 30	09 33	09 44	09 48	09 56	10 00	10 03		10 14	10 17	10 27	10 30	10 33	10 44	10 48	10 56
Seven Sisters ⊖ d																					
Clapton d																					
Stratford [7] ⊖ a					09 37					10 07						10 37					11 07
Hackney Downs d			09 20					09 50						10 20					10 50		
Bethnal Green d																					
London Liverpool Street [15] ⊖ a	09 16		09 28	09 31		09 44	09 47	09 58	10 01		10 13	10 16		10 28	10 31		10 44	10 47	10 58	11 01	

	LE [1]	LE [1] ⌶	XC ◇[1]	LE [1]	LE [1] ⌶	LE [1]	LE [1]	LE [1] ⌶	LE [1]	LE [1] ⌶	LE [1]	LE [1]	LE [1] ⌶	XC ◇[1]	LE [1]	LE [1] ⌶	LE [1]	LE [1]	LE [1] ⌶	LE [1]	LE [1] ⌶	LE [1]
Cambridge d	10 04		10 10				10 21					11 04		11 10				11 21				
Shelford d							10 26											11 26				
Whittlesford Parkway d	10 11						10 30					11 11						11 30				
Great Chesterford d							10 34											11 34				
Audley End d	10 19		10 24				10 40					11 19		11 24				11 40				
Newport (Essex) d							10 43											11 43				
Elsenham d							10 49											11 49				
Stansted Airport a			10 40											11 40								
Stansted Airport d		10 30			10 45			11 00		11 15			11 30			11 45			12 00		12 15	
Stansted Mountfitchet d							10 52			11 21								11 52			12 21	
Bishops Stortford a	10 32	10 39					10 58	11 09				11 32	11 39					11 58	12 09			
d	10 32	10 39				10 47	10 58	11 09			11 15	11 32	11 39				11 47	11 58	12 09			12 15
Sawbridgeworth d						10 52	11 03				11 20						11 52	12 03				12 20
Harlow Mill d							11 06				11 23							12 06				12 23
Harlow Town d	10 40				11 00	11 05	11 09			11 32	11 26	11 40				12 00	12 05	12 09			12 32	12 26
Roydon d							11 13				11 30							12 13				12 30
Hertford East d				10 39					11 09						11 39					12 09		
Ware d				10 43					11 13						11 43					12 13		
St Margarets (Herts) d				10 47					11 17						11 47					12 17		
Rye House d				10 50					11 20						11 50					12 20		
Broxbourne a	10 46			10 54		11 11	11 17		11 24		11 35	11 46			11 54		12 11	12 17		12 24		12 35
Broxbourne d	10 46			10 54		11 12	11 17		11 24		11 39	11 46			11 54		12 12	12 17		12 24		12 39
Cheshunt d	10 50			10 58		11 16	11 21		11 28		11 43	11 50			11 58		12 16	12 21		12 28		12 43
Waltham Cross d				11 01		11 19			11 31						12 01		12 19			12 31		
Enfield Lock d				11 03					11 33		11 47				12 03					12 33		12 47
Brimsdown d				11 06					11 36						12 06					12 36		
Ponders End d				11 08					11 38						12 08					12 38		
Angel Road d																						
Northumberland Park d											11 52											12 52
Tottenham Hale ⊖ d	11 00	11 03		11 14	11 17	11 27	11 30	11 33	11 44	11 48	11 56	12 00	12 03		12 14	12 17	12 27	12 30	12 33	12 44	12 48	12 56
Seven Sisters ⊖ d																						
Clapton d																						
Stratford [7] ⊖ a						11 37					12 07						12 37					13 07
Hackney Downs d				11 20					11 50						12 20					12 50		
Bethnal Green d																						
London Liverpool Street [15] ⊖ a	11 13	11 16		11 28	11 31		11 44	11 47	11 58	12 01		12 13	12 16		12 28	12 31		12 44	12 47	12 58	13 01	

Table 22

Saturdays
until 21 July

Cambridge, Stansted Airport, Bishops Stortford, Hertford East and Broxbourne - London

Network Diagram - see first Page of Table 20

	LE [1]	LE [1] ⌶	XC ◇[1]	LE [1]	LE [1] ⌶	LE [1]	LE [1]	LE [1] ⌶	LE [1]	LE [1] ⌶	LE [1]	LE [1]	LE [1] ⌶	XC ◇[1]	LE [1]	LE [1] ⌶	LE [1]	LE [1]	LE [1] ⌶	LE [1]	LE [1] ⌶
Cambridge d	12 04		12 10				12 21					13 04		13 10				13 21			
Shelford d							12 26											13 26			
Whittlesford Parkway d	12 11						12 30					13 11						13 30			
Great Chesterford d							12 34											13 34			
Audley End d	12 19		12 24				12 40					13 19		13 24				13 40			
Newport (Essex) d							12 43											13 43			
Elsenham d							12 49											13 49			
Stansted Airport a			12 40											13 40							
Stansted Airport d		12 30			12 45			13 00		13 15			13 30			13 45			14 00		14 15
Stansted Mountfitchet d							12 52			13 21								13 52			14 21
Bishops Stortford a	12 32	12 39					12 58	13 09				13 32	13 39					13 58	14 09		
d	12 32	12 39				12 47	12 58	13 09			13 15	13 32	13 39				13 47	13 58	14 09		
Sawbridgeworth d						12 52	13 03				13 20						13 52	14 03			
Harlow Mill d							13 06				13 23							14 06			
Harlow Town d	12 40				13 00	13 05	13 09			13 32	13 26	13 40				14 00	14 05	14 09			14 32
Roydon d							13 13				13 30							14 13			
Hertford East d				12 39					13 09						13 39					14 09	
Ware d				12 43					13 13						13 43					14 13	
St Margarets (Herts) d				12 47					13 17						13 47					14 17	
Rye House d				12 50					13 20						13 50					14 20	
Broxbourne a	12 46			12 54		13 11	13 17		13 24		13 35	13 46			13 54		14 11	14 17		14 24	
Broxbourne d	12 46			12 54		13 12	13 17		13 24		13 39	13 46			13 54		14 12	14 17		14 24	
Cheshunt d	12 50			12 58		13 16	13 21		13 28		13 43	13 50			13 58		14 16	14 21		14 28	
Waltham Cross d				13 01		13 19			13 31						14 01		14 19			14 31	
Enfield Lock d				13 03					13 33		13 47				14 03					14 33	
Brimsdown d				13 06					13 36						14 06					14 36	
Ponders End d				13 08					13 38						14 08					14 38	
Angel Road d																					
Northumberland Park d											13 52										
Tottenham Hale ⊖ d	13 00	13 03		13 14	13 17	13 27	13 30	13 33	13 44	13 48	13 56	14 00	14 03		14 14	14 17	14 27	14 30	14 33	14 44	14 48
Seven Sisters ⊖ d																					
Clapton d																					
Stratford [7] ⊖ a						13 37					14 07						14 37				
Hackney Downs d				13 20					13 50						14 20					14 50	
Bethnal Green d																					
London Liverpool Street [15] ⊖ a	13 13	13 16		13 28	13 31		13 44	13 47	13 58	14 01		14 13	14 16		14 28	14 31		14 44	14 47	14 58	15 01

	LE [1]	LE [1]	LE [1] ⌶	XC ◇[1]	LE [1]	LE [1] ⌶	LE [1]	LE [1]	LE [1] ⌶	LE [1]	LE [1] ⌶	LE [1]	LE [1]	LE [1] ⌶	XC ◇[1]	LE [1]	LE [1] ⌶	LE [1]	LE [1]	LE [1] ⌶	LE [1]	LE [1] ⌶
Cambridge d		14 04		14 10				14 21					15 04		15 10				15 21			
Shelford d								14 26											15 26			
Whittlesford Parkway d		14 11						14 30					15 11						15 30			
Great Chesterford d								14 34											15 34			
Audley End d		14 19		14 24				14 40					15 19		15 24				15 40			
Newport (Essex) d								14 43											15 43			
Elsenham d								14 49											15 49			
Stansted Airport a				14 40											15 40							
Stansted Airport d			14 30			14 45			15 00		15 15			15 30			15 45			16 00		16 15
Stansted Mountfitchet d								14 52			15 21								15 52			16 21
Bishops Stortford a		14 32	14 39					14 58	15 09				15 32	15 39					15 58	16 09		
d	14 15	14 32	14 39				14 47	14 58	15 09			15 15	15 32	15 39				15 47	15 58	16 09		
Sawbridgeworth d	14 20						14 52	15 03				15 20						15 52	16 03			
Harlow Mill d	14 23							15 06				15 23							16 06			
Harlow Town d	14 26	14 40				15 00	15 05	15 09			15 32	15 26	15 40				16 00	16 05	16 09			16 32
Roydon d	14 30							15 13				15 30							16 13			
Hertford East d					14 39					15 09						15 39					16 09	
Ware d					14 43					15 13						15 43					16 13	
St Margarets (Herts) d					14 47					15 17						15 47					16 17	
Rye House d					14 50					15 20						15 50					16 20	
Broxbourne a	14 35	14 46			14 54		15 11	15 17		15 24		15 35	15 46			15 54		16 11	16 17		16 24	
Broxbourne d	14 39	14 46			14 54		15 12	15 17		15 24		15 39	15 46			15 54		16 12	16 17		16 24	
Cheshunt d	14 43	14 50			14 58		15 16	15 21		15 28		15 43	15 50			15 58		16 16	16 21		16 28	
Waltham Cross d					15 01		15 19			15 31						16 01		16 19			16 31	
Enfield Lock d	14 47				15 03					15 33		15 47				16 03					16 33	
Brimsdown d					15 06					15 36						16 06					16 36	
Ponders End d					15 08					15 38						16 08					16 38	
Angel Road d																						
Northumberland Park d	14 52											15 52										
Tottenham Hale ⊖ d	14 56	15 00	15 03		15 14	15 17	15 27	15 30	15 33	15 44	15 48	15 56	16 00	16 03		16 14	16 17	16 27	16 30	16 33	16 44	16 48
Seven Sisters ⊖ d																						
Clapton d																						
Stratford [7] ⊖ a	15 07						15 37					16 07						16 37				
Hackney Downs d					15 20					15 50						16 20					16 50	
Bethnal Green d																						
London Liverpool Street [15] ⊖ a		15 13	15 16		15 28	15 31		15 44	15 47	15 58	16 01		16 13	16 16		16 28	16 31		16 44	16 47	16 58	17 01

Cambridge, Stansted Airport, Bishops Stortford, Hertford East and Broxbourne - London

Network Diagram - see first Page of Table 20

		LE ■	LE ■	LE ■ 🚲	XC ◇■	LE ■		LE ■ 🚲	LE ■	LE ■	LE ■ 🚲	LE ■	LE ■ 🚲	LE ■	LE ■	LE ■ 🚲		XC ◇■	LE ■	LE ■ 🚲	LE ■	LE ■	LE ■ 🚲	LE ■	LE ■ 🚲
Cambridge	d		16 04		16 10					16 21					17 04			17 10				17 21			
Shelford	d									16 26												17 26			
Whittlesford Parkway	d		16 11							16 30					17 11							17 30			
Great Chesterford	d									16 34												17 34			
Audley End	d		16 19		16 24					16 40					17 19			17 24				17 40			
Newport (Essex)	d									16 43												17 43			
Elsenham	d									16 49												17 49			
Stansted Airport	a				16 40													17 40							
Stansted Airport	d			16 30				16 45			17 00		17 15			17 30				17 45			18 00		18 15
Stansted Mountfitchet	d									16 52			17 21									17 52			18 21
Bishops Stortford	a		16 32	16 39						16 58	17 09				17 32	17 39						17 58	18 09		
	d	16 15	16 32	16 39					16 47	16 58	17 09			17 15	17 32	17 39					17 47	17 58	18 09		
Sawbridgeworth	d	16 20							16 52	17 03				17 20							17 52	18 03			
Harlow Mill	d	16 23								17 06				17 23								18 06			
Harlow Town	d	16 26	16 40					17 00	17 05	17 09			17 32	17 26	17 40					18 00	18 05	18 09			18 32
Roydon	d	16 30								17 13				17 30								18 13			
Hertford East	d					16 39						17 09							17 39					18 09	
Ware	d					16 43						17 13							17 43					18 13	
St Margarets (Herts)	d					16 47						17 17							17 47					18 17	
Rye House	d					16 50						17 20							17 50					18 20	
Broxbourne ■	a	16 35	16 46			16 54			17 11	17 17		17 24		17 35	17 46				17 54		18 11	18 17		18 24	
Broxbourne ■	d	16 39	16 46			16 54			17 12	17 17		17 24		17 39	17 46				17 54		18 12	18 17		18 24	
Cheshunt	d	16 43	16 50			16 58			17 16	17 21		17 28		17 43	17 50				17 58		18 16	18 21		18 28	
Waltham Cross	d					17 01			17 19			17 31							18 01		18 19			18 31	
Enfield Lock	d	16 47				17 03						17 33		17 47					18 03					18 33	
Brimsdown	d					17 06						17 36							18 06					18 36	
Ponders End	d					17 08						17 38							18 08					18 38	
Angel Road	d																								
Northumberland Park	d	16 52												17 52											
Tottenham Hale ⊖	d	16 56	17 00	17 03		17 14		17 17	17 27	17 30	17 33	17 44	17 48	17 56	18 00	18 03			18 14	18 17	18 27	18 30	18 33	18 44	18 48
Seven Sisters ⊖	d																								
Clapton	d																								
Stratford ■ ⊖	a	17 07							17 37					18 07							18 37				
Hackney Downs	d					17 20						17 50							18 20					18 50	
Bethnal Green	d																								
London Liverpool Street ■ ⊖	a		17 13	17 16		17 28		17 31		17 44	17 47	17 58	18 01		18 13	18 16			18 28	18 31		18 44	18 47	18 58	19 01

		LE ■		LE ■	LE ■ 🚲	LE ■	LE ■ 🚲	XC ◇■	LE ■	LE ■	LE ■ 🚲	LE ■		LE ■ 🚲	LE ■	LE ■	LE ■ 🚲	XC ◇■	LE ■	LE ■ 🚲	LE ■	LE ■		LE ■ 🚲	LE ■
Cambridge	d			18 04				18 18		18 21						19 04		19 10				19 21			
Shelford	d									18 26												19 26			
Whittlesford Parkway	d			18 11						18 30						19 11						19 30			
Great Chesterford	d									18 34												19 34			
Audley End	d			18 19				18 34		18 40						19 19		19 25				19 40			
Newport (Essex)	d									18 43												19 43			
Elsenham	d									18 49												19 49			
Stansted Airport	a							18 53										19 40							
Stansted Airport	d				18 30		18 45				19 00			19 15			19 30			19 45				20 00	
Stansted Mountfitchet	d									18 52				19 21								19 52			
Bishops Stortford	a			18 32	18 39					18 58	19 09					19 32	19 39					19 58		20 09	
	d	18 15		18 32	18 39				18 47	18 58	19 09				19 15	19 32	19 39				19 47	19 58		20 09	
Sawbridgeworth	d	18 20							18 52	19 03					19 20						19 52	20 03			
Harlow Mill	d	18 23								19 06					19 23							20 06			
Harlow Town	d	18 26		18 40			19 00		19 05	19 09				19 32	19 26	19 40				20 00	20 05	20 09			
Roydon	d	18 30								19 13					19 30							20 13			
Hertford East	d					18 39						19 09							19 39						20 09
Ware	d					18 43						19 13							19 43						20 13
St Margarets (Herts)	d					18 47						19 17							19 47						20 17
Rye House	d					18 50						19 20							19 50						20 20
Broxbourne ■	a	18 35		18 46		18 54			19 11	19 17		19 24			19 35	19 46			19 54		20 11	20 17			20 24
Broxbourne ■	d	18 39		18 46		18 54			19 12	19 17		19 24			19 39	19 46			19 54		20 12	20 17			20 24
Cheshunt	d	18 43		18 50		18 58			19 16	19 21		19 28			19 43	19 50			19 58		20 16	20 21			20 28
Waltham Cross	d					19 01			19 19			19 31							20 01		20 19				20 31
Enfield Lock	d	18 47				19 03						19 33			19 47				20 03						20 33
Brimsdown	d					19 06						19 36							20 06						20 36
Ponders End	d					19 08						19 38							20 08						20 38
Angel Road	d																								
Northumberland Park	d	18 52													19 52										
Tottenham Hale ⊖	d	18 56		19 00	19 03	19 14	19 17		19 27	19 30	19 33	19 44		19 48	19 56	20 00	20 03		20 14	20 17	20 27	20 30		20 33	20 44
Seven Sisters ⊖	d																								
Clapton	d																								
Stratford ■ ⊖	a	19 07							19 37						20 07						20 37				
Hackney Downs	d					19 20						19 50							20 20						20 50
Bethnal Green	d																								
London Liverpool Street ■ ⊖	a			19 13	19 16	19 28	19 31			19 44	19 47	19 58		20 01		20 13	20 16		20 28	20 31		20 44		20 47	20 58

Table 22

Saturdays
until 21 July

Cambridge, Stansted Airport, Bishops Stortford, Hertford East and Broxbourne - London

Network Diagram - see first Page of Table 20

		LE ■ 🚲	LE ■	LE ■	LE ■ 🚲	XC ◇■	LE ■	LE ■ 🚲		LE ■	LE ■	LE ■ 🚲	LE ■	LE ■ 🚲	LE ■	LE ■	LE ■ 🚲	XC ◇■		LE ■	LE ■ 🚲	LE ■	LE ■	LE ■	LE ■
Cambridge	d			20 04		20 10					20 21					21 04		21 10					21 21		
Shelford	d										20 26												21 26		
Whittlesford Parkway	d			20 11							20 30					21 11							21 30		
Great Chesterford	d										20 34												21 34		
Audley End	d			20 19		20 24					20 40					21 19		21 24					21 40		
Newport (Essex)	d										20 43												21 43		
Elsenham	d										20 49												21 49		
Stansted Airport	a					20 40												21 40							
Stansted Airport	d	20 15			20 30			20 45				21 00		21 15			21 30				21 45			22 00	
Stansted Mountfitchet	d	20 21									20 52			21 21									21 52		
Bishops Stortford	a			20 32	20 39						20 58	21 09				21 32	21 39						21 58	22 09	
	d		20 15	20 32	20 39					20 47	20 58	21 09			21 15	21 32	21 39					21 47	21 58	22 09	
Sawbridgeworth	d		20 20							20 52	21 03				21 20							21 52	22 03		
Harlow Mill	d		20 23								21 06				21 23								22 06		
Harlow Town	d	20 32	20 26	20 40				21 00		21 05	21 09			21 32	21 26	21 40					22 00	22 05	22 09		
Roydon	d		20 30								21 13				21 30								22 13		
Hertford East	d						20 39						21 09							21 39					22 09
Ware	d						20 43						21 13							21 43					22 13
St Margarets (Herts)	d						20 47						21 17							21 47					22 17
Rye House	d						20 50						21 20							21 50					22 20
Broxbourne ■	a		20 35	20 46			20 54			21 11	21 17		21 24		21 35	21 46				21 54		22 11	22 17		22 24
Broxbourne ■	d		20 39	20 46			20 54			21 12	21 17		21 24		21 39	21 46				21 54		22 12	22 17		22 24
Cheshunt	d		20 43	20 50			20 58			21 16	21 21		21 28		21 43	21 50				21 58		22 16	22 21		22 28
Waltham Cross	d						21 01			21 19			21 31							22 01		22 19			22 31
Enfield Lock	d		20 47				21 03						21 33		21 47					22 03					22 33
Brimsdown	d						21 06						21 36							22 06					22 36
Ponders End	d						21 08						21 38							22 08					22 38
Angel Road	d																								
Northumberland Park	d		20 52												21 52										
Tottenham Hale ⊖	d	20 48	20 56	21 00	21 03		21 14	21 17		21 27	21 30	21 33	21 44	21 48	21 56	22 00	22 03			22 14	22 17	22 27	22 30	22 33	22 44
Seven Sisters ⊖	d																								
Clapton	d																								
Stratford ■ ⊖	a		21 07							21 37					22 07							22 37			
Hackney Downs	d						21 20						21 50							22 20					22 50
Bethnal Green	d																								
London Liverpool Street ■ ⊖	a	21 01		21 13	21 16		21 28	21 31			21 44	21 47	21 58	22 01		22 13	22 16			22 28	22 31		22 44	22 47	22 58

		LE ■	LE ■	LE ■		LE ■	XC ◇■	LE ■	LE ■	LE ■	LE ■	LE ■	LE ■	LE ■		LE ■	LE ■	LE ■	LE ■
Cambridge	d			22 04			22 10			22 21				22 51					
Shelford	d									22 26				22 56					
Whittlesford Parkway	d			22 11						22 30				23 00					
Great Chesterford	d									22 34				23 04					
Audley End	d			22 19			22 24			22 40				23 10					
Newport (Essex)	d									22 43				23 13					
Elsenham	d									22 49				23 19					
Stansted Airport	a						22 40												
Stansted Airport	d	22 15				22 30			22 45		23 00		23 15			23 30		23 45	23 59
Stansted Mountfitchet	d	22 21								22 52			23 21	23 22					
Bishops Stortford	a			22 32		22 39				22 58	23 09			23 28		23 39			00 08
	d		22 15	22 32		22 39				22 58	23 09			23 28		23 39			00 08
Sawbridgeworth	d		22 20							23 03				23 32					
Harlow Mill	d		22 23							23 06				23 36					
Harlow Town	d	22 32	22 26	22 40					23 00	23 09			23 32	23 39				23 59	00 16
Roydon	d		22 30							23 13				23 43					
Hertford East	d							22 39				23 09					23 39		
Ware	d							22 43				23 13					23 43		
St Margarets (Herts)	d							22 47				23 17					23 47		
Rye House	d							22 50				23 20					23 50		
Broxbourne ■	a		22 35	22 46				22 54		23 17		23 24		23 47			23 54		
Broxbourne ■	d		22 39	22 46				22 54		23 17		23 24		23 47			23 54		
Cheshunt	d		22 43	22 50				22 58		23 21		23 28		23 51			23 58		
Waltham Cross	d							23 01				23 31					00 01		
Enfield Lock	d		22 47					23 03				23 33					00 03		
Brimsdown	d							23 06				23 36					00 06		
Ponders End	d							23 08				23 38					00 08		
Angel Road	d																		
Northumberland Park	d		22 52																
Tottenham Hale ⊖	d	22 48	22 56	23 00		23 03		23 14	23 17	23 30	23 33	23 44	23 48	23 59		00 03	00 14	00 17	
Seven Sisters ⊖	d																		
Clapton	d																		
Stratford ■ ⊖	a		23 07																
Hackney Downs	d							23 20				23 50					00 20		
Bethnal Green	d																		
London Liverpool Street ■ ⊖	a	23 01	23 18	23 13		23 16		23 28	23 31	23 45	23 47	23 58	00 01	00 13		00 16	00 28	00 32	00 51

Table 22

Saturdays

28 July to 11 August

Cambridge, Stansted Airport, Bishops Stortford, Hertford East and Broxbourne - London

Network Diagram - see first Page of Table 20

		LE ■	LE ■	LE ■	LE ■	LE ■	LE ■	LE ■	LE ■	LE ■	LE ■	XC ■	LE ■	LE ■	LE ■	LE ■	LE ■	LE ■ 🛒	XC ■	LE ■	LE ■ 🛒	LE ■	LE ■
Cambridge	d		22p51									04 56					05 21		05 42				06 04
Shelford	d		22p56														05 26						
Whittlesford Parkway	d		23p00														05 30						06 11
Great Chesterford	d		23p04														05 34						
Audley End	d		23p10														05 40		05 56				06 19
Newport (Essex)	d		23p13														05 43						
Elsenham	d		23p19														05 49						
Stansted Airport	a											05 20							06 08				
Stansted Airport	d	23p15		23p30		23p45		23p59	00 30	01 00	01 30			05 30				06 00			06 15		
Stansted Mountfitchet	d	23p21	23p24														05 52				06 21		
Bishops Stortford	a		23p29	23p39				00 08	00 39					05 39			05 58	06 09					06 32
	d		23p29	23p39				00 08	00 39				05 15	05 39		05 47	05 58	06 09				06 15	06 32
Sawbridgeworth	d		23p33										05 20			05 52	06 03					06 20	
Harlow Mill	d		23p37										05 23				06 06					06 23	
Harlow Town	d	23p32	23p40			23p59		00 16	00 47				05 26			06 05	06 09				06 32	06 26	06 40
Roydon	d		23p44										05 30				06 13					06 30	
Hertford East	d				23p39		00 07													06 09			
Ware	d				23p43															06 13			
St Margarets (Herts)	d				23p47															06 17			
Rye House	d				23p50															06 20			
Broxbourne ■	a		23p48		23p54		00 19						05 34			06 11	06 17			06 24		06 35	06 46
Broxbourne ■	d		23p48		23p54		00 19						05 34		05 54	06 12	06 17			06 24		06 39	06 46
Cheshunt	d		23p52		23p58								05 38		05 58	06 16	06 21			06 28		06 43	06 50
Waltham Cross	d												05 41		06 01	06 19				06 31			
Enfield Lock	d												05 43		06 03					06 33		06 47	
Brimsdown	d												05 46		06 06					06 36			
Ponders End	d												05 48		06 08					06 38			
Angel Road	d																						
Northumberland Park	d												05 52									06 52	
Tottenham Hale ⊖	d	23p48											05 55	06 01	06 14	06 27	06 30	06 33		06 44	06 48	06 56	07 00
Seven Sisters ⊖	d		00 04	00 08	00 11	00 21																	
Clapton	d																						
Stratford ■ ⊖	a												06 05			06 37						07 07	
Hackney Downs	d				00 16		00 41								06 20					06 50			
Bethnal Green	d																						
London Liverpool Street ■ ⊖	a	00 01	00 18	00 22	00 26	00 36	00 49	00 51	01 21	01 50	02 20		06 14	06 14	06 28		06 45	06 47		06 58	07 01		07 13

		LE ■ 🛒	LE ■	LE ■ 🛒	LE ■	LE ■	LE ■ 🛒	XC ■	LE ■	LE ■ 🛒	LE ■	LE ■	LE ■ 🛒	LE ■	LE ■ 🛒	LE ■	LE ■	LE ■ 🛒	XC ■	LE ■	LE ■ 🛒	LE ■	LE ■
Cambridge	d					06 21		06 40				07 04					07 21		07 40				08 04
Shelford	d					06 26											07 26						
Whittlesford Parkway	d					06 30						07 11					07 30						08 11
Great Chesterford	d					06 34											07 34						
Audley End	d					06 40		06 54				07 19					07 40		07 54				08 19
Newport (Essex)	d					06 43											07 43						
Elsenham	d					06 49											07 49						
Stansted Airport	a							07 09											08 08				
Stansted Airport	d	06 30		06 45			07 00			07 15			07 30		07 45			08 00			08 15		
Stansted Mountfitchet	d					06 52				07 21							07 52				08 21		
Bishops Stortford	a	06 39				06 58	07 09					07 32	07 39				07 58	08 09					08 32
	d	06 39			06 47	06 58	07 09				07 15	07 32	07 39			07 47	07 58	08 09				08 15	08 32
Sawbridgeworth	d				06 52	07 03					07 20					07 52	08 03					08 20	
Harlow Mill	d					07 06					07 23						08 06					08 23	
Harlow Town	d			07 00	07 05	07 09				07 32	07 26	07 40			08 00	08 05	08 09				08 32	08 26	08 40
Roydon	d					07 13					07 30						08 13					08 30	
Hertford East	d		06 39						07 09					07 39						08 09			
Ware	d		06 43						07 13					07 43						08 13			
St Margarets (Herts)	d		06 47						07 17					07 47						08 17			
Rye House	d		06 50						07 20					07 50						08 20			
Broxbourne ■	a		06 54		07 11	07 17			07 24		07 35	07 46		07 54		08 11	08 17			08 24		08 35	08 46
Broxbourne ■	d		06 54		07 12	07 17			07 24		07 39	07 46		07 54		08 12	08 17			08 24		08 39	08 46
Cheshunt	d		06 58		07 16	07 21			07 28		07 43	07 50		07 58		08 16	08 21			08 28		08 43	08 50
Waltham Cross	d		07 01		07 19				07 31					08 01		08 19				08 31			
Enfield Lock	d		07 03						07 33		07 47			08 03						08 33		08 47	
Brimsdown	d		07 06						07 36					08 06						08 36			
Ponders End	d		07 08						07 38					08 08						08 38			
Angel Road	d																						
Northumberland Park	d										07 52											08 52	
Tottenham Hale ⊖	d	07 03	07 14	07 17	07 27	07 30	07 33		07 44	07 48	07 56	08 00	08 03	08 14	08 17	08 27	08 30	08 33		08 44	08 48	08 56	09 00
Seven Sisters ⊖	d																						
Clapton	d																						
Stratford ■ ⊖	a				07 37						08 07					08 37						09 07	
Hackney Downs	d		07 20						07 50					08 20						08 50			
Bethnal Green	d																						
London Liverpool Street ■ ⊖	a	07 16	07 28	07 31		07 44	07 47		07 58	08 01		08 13	08 16	08 28	08 31		08 44	08 47		08 58	09 01		09 13

Table 22

Saturdays

28 July to 11 August

Cambridge, Stansted Airport, Bishops Stortford, Hertford East and Broxbourne - London

Network Diagram - see first Page of Table 20

		LE ■ 🛒	XC ◇■	LE ■	LE ■ 🛒	LE ■	LE ■	LE ■ 🛒	LE ■	LE ■ 🛒	LE ■	LE ■	LE ■ 🛒	XC ◇■	LE ■	LE ■ 🛒	LE ■	LE ■	LE ■ 🛒	LE ■	LE ■ 🛒	LE ■
Cambridge	d		08 10				08 21					09 04		09 10				09 21				
Shelford	d						08 26											09 26				
Whittlesford Parkway	d						08 30					09 11						09 30				
Great Chesterford	d						08 34											09 34				
Audley End	d		08 24				08 40					09 19		09 24				09 40				
Newport (Essex)	d						08 43											09 43				
Elsenham	d						08 49											09 49				
Stansted Airport	a		08 39											09 40								
Stansted Airport	d	08 30			08 45			09 00		09 15			09 30			09 45			10 00		10 15	
Stansted Mountfitchet	d						08 52			09 21								09 52			10 21	
Bishops Stortford	a	08 39					08 58	09 09				09 32	09 39					09 58	10 09			
	d	08 39				08 47	08 58	09 09			09 15	09 32	09 39				09 47	09 58	10 09			10 15
Sawbridgeworth	d					08 52	09 03				09 20						09 52	10 03				10 20
Harlow Mill	d						09 06				09 23							10 06				10 23
Harlow Town	d				09 00	09 05	09 09			09 32	09 26	09 40				10 00	10 05	10 09			10 32	10 26
Roydon	d						09 13				09 30							10 13				10 30
Hertford East	d			08 39					09 09						09 39					10 09		
Ware	d			08 43					09 13						09 43					10 13		
St Margarets (Herts)	d			08 47					09 17						09 47					10 17		
Rye House	d			08 50					09 20						09 50					10 20		
Broxbourne ■	a			08 54		09 11	09 17		09 24		09 35	09 46			09 54		10 11	10 17		10 24		10 35
Broxbourne ■	d			08 54		09 12	09 17		09 24		09 39	09 46			09 54		10 12	10 17		10 24		10 39
Cheshunt	d			08 58		09 16	09 21		09 28		09 43	09 50			09 58		10 16	10 21		10 28		10 43
Waltham Cross	d			09 01		09 19			09 31						10 01		10 19			10 31		
Enfield Lock	d			09 03					09 33		09 47				10 03					10 33		10 47
Brimsdown	d			09 06					09 36						10 06					10 36		
Ponders End	d			09 08					09 38						10 08					10 38		
Angel Road	d																					
Northumberland Park	d										09 52											10 52
Tottenham Hale ⊖	d	09 03		09 14	09 17	09 27	09 30	09 33	09 44	09 48	09 56	10 00	10 03		10 14	10 17	10 27	10 30	10 33	10 44	10 48	10 56
Seven Sisters ⊖	d																					
Clapton	d																					
Stratford ■ ⊖	a					09 37					10 07						10 37					11 07
Hackney Downs	d			09 20					09 50						10 20					10 50		
Bethnal Green	d																					
London Liverpool Street ■ ⊖	a	09 16		09 28	09 31		09 44	09 47	09 58	10 01		10 13	10 16		10 28	10 31		10 44	10 47	10 58	11 01	

		LE ■	LE ■ 🛒	XC ◇■	LE ■	LE ■ 🛒	LE ■	LE ■	LE ■ 🛒	LE ■	LE ■ 🛒	LE ■	LE ■	LE ■ 🛒	XC ◇■	LE ■	LE ■ 🛒	LE ■	LE ■	LE ■ 🛒	LE ■	LE ■ 🛒	LE ■
Cambridge	d	10 04		10 10				10 21					11 04		11 10				11 21				
Shelford	d							10 26											11 26				
Whittlesford Parkway	d	10 11						10 30					11 11						11 30				
Great Chesterford	d							10 34											11 34				
Audley End	d	10 19		10 24				10 40					11 19		11 24				11 40				
Newport (Essex)	d							10 43											11 43				
Elsenham	d							10 49											11 49				
Stansted Airport	a			10 40											11 40								
Stansted Airport	d		10 30			10 45			11 00		11 15			11 30			11 45			12 00		12 15	
Stansted Mountfitchet	d							10 52			11 21								11 52			12 21	
Bishops Stortford	a	10 32	10 39					10 58	11 09				11 32	11 39					11 58	12 09			
	d	10 32	10 39				10 47	10 58	11 09			11 15	11 32	11 39				11 47	11 58	12 09			12 15
Sawbridgeworth	d						10 52	11 03				11 20						11 52	12 03				12 20
Harlow Mill	d							11 06				11 23							12 06				12 23
Harlow Town	d	10 40				11 00	11 05	11 09			11 32	11 26	11 40				12 00	12 05	12 09			12 32	12 26
Roydon	d							11 13				11 30							12 13				12 30
Hertford East	d				10 39					11 09						11 39					12 09		
Ware	d				10 43					11 13						11 43					12 13		
St Margarets (Herts)	d				10 47					11 17						11 47					12 17		
Rye House	d				10 50					11 20						11 50					12 20		
Broxbourne ■	a	10 46			10 54		11 11	11 17		11 24		11 35	11 46			11 54		12 11	12 17		12 24		12 35
Broxbourne ■	d	10 46			10 54		11 12	11 17		11 24		11 39	11 46			11 54		12 12	12 17		12 24		12 39
Cheshunt	d	10 50			10 58		11 16	11 21		11 28		11 43	11 50			11 58		12 16	12 21		12 28		12 43
Waltham Cross	d				11 01		11 19			11 31						12 01		12 19			12 31		
Enfield Lock	d				11 03					11 33		11 47				12 03					12 33		12 47
Brimsdown	d				11 06					11 36						12 06					12 36		
Ponders End	d				11 08					11 38						12 08					12 38		
Angel Road	d																						
Northumberland Park	d											11 52											12 52
Tottenham Hale ⊖	d	11 00	11 03		11 14	11 17	11 27	11 30	11 33	11 44	11 48	11 56	12 00	12 03		12 14	12 17	12 27	12 30	12 33	12 44	12 48	12 56
Seven Sisters ⊖	d																						
Clapton	d																						
Stratford ■ ⊖	a						11 37					12 07						12 37					13 07
Hackney Downs	d				11 20					11 50						12 20					12 50		
Bethnal Green	d																						
London Liverpool Street ■ ⊖	a	11 13	11 16		11 28	11 31		11 44	11 47	11 58	12 01		12 13	12 16		12 28	12 31		12 44	12 47	12 58	13 01	

Cambridge, Stansted Airport, Bishops Stortford, Hertford East and Broxbourne - London

Network Diagram - see first Page of Table 20

		LE 1	LE 1 🚲	XC ◇1	LE 1	LE 1 🚲	LE 1	LE 1	LE 1 🚲	LE 1	LE 1 🚲	LE 1	LE 1	LE 1 🚲	XC ◇1	LE 1	LE 1 🚲	LE 1	LE 1	LE 1 🚲	LE 1	LE 1 🚲
Cambridge	d	12 04		12 10				12 21					13 04		13 10				13 21			
Shelford	d							12 26											13 26			
Whittlesford Parkway	d	12 11						12 30					13 11						13 30			
Great Chesterford	d							12 34											13 34			
Audley End	d	12 19		12 24				12 40					13 19		13 24				13 40			
Newport (Essex)	d							12 43											13 43			
Elsenham	d							12 49											13 49			
Stansted Airport	a			12 40											13 40							
Stansted Airport	d		12 30			12 45			13 00		13 15			13 30			13 45			14 00		14 15
Stansted Mountfitchet	d							12 52			13 21								13 52			14 21
Bishops Stortford	a	12 32	12 39					12 58	13 09				13 32	13 39					13 58	14 09		
	d	12 32	12 39				12 47	12 58	13 09			13 15	13 32	13 39				13 47	13 58	14 09		
Sawbridgeworth	d						12 52	13 03				13 20						13 52	14 03			
Harlow Mill	d							13 06				13 23							14 06			
Harlow Town	d	12 40				13 00	13 05	13 09			13 32	13 26	13 40				14 00	14 05	14 09			14 32
Roydon	d							13 13				13 30							14 13			
Hertford East	d				12 39					13 09						13 39					14 09	
Ware	d				12 43					13 13						13 43					14 13	
St Margarets (Herts)	d				12 47					13 17						13 47					14 17	
Rye House	d				12 50					13 20						13 50					14 20	
Broxbourne 3	a	12 46			12 54		13 11	13 17		13 24		13 35	13 46			13 54		14 11	14 17		14 24	
Broxbourne 3	d	12 46			12 54		13 12	13 17		13 24		13 39	13 46			13 54		14 12	14 17		14 24	
Cheshunt	d	12 50			12 58		13 16	13 21		13 28		13 43	13 50			13 58		14 16	14 21		14 28	
Waltham Cross	d				13 01		13 19			13 31						14 01		14 19			14 31	
Enfield Lock	d				13 03					13 33		13 47				14 03					14 33	
Brimsdown	d				13 06					13 36						14 06					14 36	
Ponders End	d				13 08					13 38						14 08					14 38	
Angel Road	d																					
Northumberland Park	d											13 52										
Tottenham Hale ⊖	d	13 00	13 03		13 14	13 17	13 27	13 30	13 33	13 44	13 48	13 56	14 00	14 03		14 14	14 17	14 27	14 30	14 33	14 44	14 48
Seven Sisters ⊖	d																					
Clapton	d																					
Stratford 7 ⊖	a						13 37					14 07						14 37				
Hackney Downs	d				13 20					13 50						14 20					14 50	
Bethnal Green	d																					
London Liverpool Street 15 ⊖	a	13 13	13 16		13 28	13 31		13 44	13 47	13 58	14 01		14 13	14 16		14 28	14 31		14 44	14 47	14 58	15 01

		LE 1	LE 1	LE 1 🚲	XC ◇1	LE 1	LE 1 🚲	LE 1	LE 1	LE 1 🚲	LE 1	LE 1 🚲	LE 1	LE 1	LE 1 🚲	XC ◇1	LE 1	LE 1 🚲	LE 1	LE 1	LE 1 🚲	LE 1	LE 1 🚲
Cambridge	d		14 04		14 10				14 21					15 04		15 10				15 21			
Shelford	d								14 26											15 26			
Whittlesford Parkway	d		14 11						14 30					15 11						15 30			
Great Chesterford	d								14 34											15 34			
Audley End	d		14 19		14 24				14 40					15 19		15 24				15 40			
Newport (Essex)	d								14 43											15 43			
Elsenham	d								14 49											15 49			
Stansted Airport	a				14 40											15 40							
Stansted Airport	d			14 30			14 45			15 00		15 15			15 30			15 45			16 00		16 15
Stansted Mountfitchet	d								14 52			15 21								15 52			16 21
Bishops Stortford	a		14 32	14 39					14 58	15 09				15 32	15 39					15 58	16 09		
	d	14 15	14 32	14 39				14 47	14 58	15 09			15 15	15 32	15 39				15 47	15 58	16 09		
Sawbridgeworth	d	14 20						14 52	15 03				15 20						15 52	16 03			
Harlow Mill	d	14 23							15 06				15 23							16 06			
Harlow Town	d	14 26	14 40				15 00	15 05	15 09			15 32	15 26	15 40				16 00	16 05	16 09			16 32
Roydon	d	14 30							15 13				15 30							16 13			
Hertford East	d					14 39					15 09						15 39					16 09	
Ware	d					14 43					15 13						15 43					16 13	
St Margarets (Herts)	d					14 47					15 17						15 47					16 17	
Rye House	d					14 50					15 20						15 50					16 20	
Broxbourne 3	a	14 35	14 46			14 54		15 11	15 17		15 24		15 35	15 46			15 54		16 11	16 17		16 24	
Broxbourne 3	d	14 39	14 46			14 54		15 12	15 17		15 24		15 39	15 46			15 54		16 12	16 17		16 24	
Cheshunt	d	14 43	14 50			14 58		15 16	15 21		15 28		15 43	15 50			15 58		16 16	16 21		16 28	
Waltham Cross	d					15 01		15 19			15 31						16 01		16 19			16 31	
Enfield Lock	d	14 47				15 03					15 33		15 47				16 03					16 33	
Brimsdown	d					15 06					15 36						16 06					16 36	
Ponders End	d					15 08					15 38						16 08					16 38	
Angel Road	d																						
Northumberland Park	d	14 52											15 52										
Tottenham Hale ⊖	d	14 56	15 00	15 03		15 14	15 17	15 27	15 30	15 33	15 44	15 48	15 56	16 00	16 03		16 14	16 17	16 27	16 30	16 33	16 44	16 48
Seven Sisters ⊖	d																						
Clapton	d																						
Stratford 7 ⊖	a	15 07						15 37					16 07						16 37				
Hackney Downs	d					15 20					15 50						16 20					16 50	
Bethnal Green	d																						
London Liverpool Street 15 ⊖	a		15 13	15 16		15 28	15 31		15 44	15 47	15 58	16 01		16 13	16 16		16 28	16 31		16 44	16 47	16 58	17 01

Cambridge, Stansted Airport, Bishops Stortford, Hertford East and Broxbourne - London

Network Diagram - see first Page of Table 20

		LE 1	LE 1	LE 1 🚲	XC ◇1	LE 1	LE 1 🚲	LE 1	LE 1	LE 1 🚲	LE 1	LE 1 🚲	LE 1	LE 1	LE 1 🚲	XC ◇1	LE 1	LE 1 🚲	LE 1	LE 1	LE 1 🚲	LE 1	LE 1 🚲
Cambridge	d		16 04		16 10				16 21					17 04		17 10				17 21			
Shelford	d								16 26											17 26			
Whittlesford Parkway	d		16 11						16 30					17 11						17 30			
Great Chesterford	d								16 34											17 34			
Audley End	d		16 19		16 24				16 40					17 19		17 24				17 40			
Newport (Essex)	d								16 43											17 43			
Elsenham	d								16 49											17 49			
Stansted Airport	a				16 40											17 40							
Stansted Airport	d			16 30			16 45			17 00		17 15			17 30			17 45			18 00		18 15
Stansted Mountfitchet	d								16 52			17 21								17 52			18 21
Bishops Stortford	a		16 32	16 39					16 58	17 09				17 32	17 39					17 58	18 09		
	d	16 15	16 32	16 39				16 47	16 58	17 09			17 15	17 32	17 39				17 47	17 58	18 09		
Sawbridgeworth	d	16 20						16 52	17 03				17 20						17 52	18 03			
Harlow Mill	d	16 23							17 06				17 23							18 06			
Harlow Town	d	16 26	16 40				17 00	17 05	17 09			17 32	17 26	17 40				18 00	18 05	18 09			18 32
Roydon	d	16 30							17 13				17 30							18 13			
Hertford East	d					16 39					17 09						17 39					18 09	
Ware	d					16 43					17 13						17 43					18 13	
St Margarets (Herts)	d					16 47					17 17						17 47					18 17	
Rye House	d					16 50					17 20						17 50					18 20	
Broxbourne 3	a	16 35	16 46			16 54		17 11	17 17		17 24		17 35	17 46			17 54		18 11	18 17		18 24	
Broxbourne 3	d	16 39	16 46			16 54		17 12	17 17		17 24		17 39	17 46			17 54		18 12	18 17		18 24	
Cheshunt	d	16 43	16 50			16 58		17 16	17 21		17 28		17 43	17 50			17 58		18 16	18 21		18 28	
Waltham Cross	d					17 01		17 19			17 31						18 01		18 19			18 31	
Enfield Lock	d	16 47				17 03					17 33		17 47				18 03					18 33	
Brimsdown	d					17 06					17 36						18 06					18 36	
Ponders End	d					17 08					17 38						18 08					18 38	
Angel Road	d																						
Northumberland Park	d	16 52											17 52										
Tottenham Hale ⊖	d	16 56	17 00	17 03		17 14	17 17	17 27	17 30	17 33	17 44	17 48	17 56	18 00	18 03		18 14	18 17	18 27	18 30	18 33	18 44	18 48
Seven Sisters ⊖	d																						
Clapton	d																						
Stratford 7 ⊖	a	17 07						17 37					18 07						18 37				
Hackney Downs	d					17 20					17 50						18 20					18 50	
Bethnal Green	d																						
London Liverpool Street 15 ⊖	a		17 13	17 16		17 28	17 31		17 44	17 47	17 58	18 01		18 13	18 16		18 28	18 31		18 44	18 47	18 58	19 01

		LE 1	LE 1	LE 1 🚲	LE 1	LE 1 🚲	XC ◇1	LE 1	LE 1	LE 1 🚲	LE 1	LE 1 🚲	LE 1	LE 1	LE 1 🚲	XC ◇1	LE 1	LE 1 🚲	LE 1	LE 1	LE 1 🚲	LE 1
Cambridge	d		18 04				18 18		18 21					19 04		19 10				19 21		
Shelford	d								18 26											19 26		
Whittlesford Parkway	d		18 11						18 30					19 11						19 30		
Great Chesterford	d								18 34											19 34		
Audley End	d		18 19				18 34		18 40					19 19		19 25				19 40		
Newport (Essex)	d								18 43											19 43		
Elsenham	d								18 49											19 49		
Stansted Airport	a						18 53									19 40						
Stansted Airport	d			18 30		18 45				19 00		19 15			19 30			19 45			20 00	
Stansted Mountfitchet	d								18 52			19 21								19 52		
Bishops Stortford	a		18 32	18 39					18 58	19 09				19 32	19 39					19 58	20 09	
	d	18 15	18 32	18 39				18 47	18 58	19 09			19 15	19 32	19 39				19 47	19 58	20 09	
Sawbridgeworth	d	18 20						18 52	19 03				19 20						19 52	20 03		
Harlow Mill	d	18 23							19 06				19 23							20 06		
Harlow Town	d	18 26	18 40			19 00		19 05	19 09			19 32	19 26	19 40				20 00	20 05	20 09		
Roydon	d	18 30							19 13				19 30							20 13		
Hertford East	d				18 39						19 09						19 39					20 09
Ware	d				18 43						19 13						19 43					20 13
St Margarets (Herts)	d				18 47						19 17						19 47					20 17
Rye House	d				18 50						19 20						19 50					20 20
Broxbourne 3	a	18 35	18 46		18 54			19 11	19 17		19 24		19 35	19 46			19 54		20 11	20 17		20 24
Broxbourne 3	d	18 39	18 46		18 54			19 12	19 17		19 24		19 39	19 46			19 54		20 12	20 17		20 24
Cheshunt	d	18 43	18 50		18 58			19 16	19 21		19 28		19 43	19 50			19 58		20 16	20 21		20 28
Waltham Cross	d				19 01			19 19			19 31						20 01		20 19			20 31
Enfield Lock	d	18 47			19 03						19 33		19 47				20 03					20 33
Brimsdown	d				19 06						19 36						20 06					20 36
Ponders End	d				19 08						19 38						20 08					20 38
Angel Road	d																					
Northumberland Park	d	18 52											19 52									
Tottenham Hale ⊖	d	18 56	19 00	19 03	19 14	19 17		19 27	19 30	19 33	19 44	19 48	19 56	20 00	20 03		20 14	20 17	20 27	20 30	20 33	20 44
Seven Sisters ⊖	d																					
Clapton	d																					
Stratford 7 ⊖	a	19 07						19 37					20 07						20 37			
Hackney Downs	d				19 20						19 50						20 20					20 50
Bethnal Green	d																					
London Liverpool Street 15 ⊖	a		19 13	19 16	19 28	19 31			19 44	19 47	19 58	20 01		20 13	20 16		20 28	20 31		20 44	20 47	20 58

Table 22 — Saturdays, 28 July to 11 August

Cambridge, Stansted Airport, Bishops Stortford, Hertford East and Broxbourne - London

Network Diagram - see first Page of Table 20

Station		LE 1 trolley	LE 1	LE 1	LE 1 trolley	XC ◇1	LE 1	LE 1 trolley	LE 1	LE 1	LE 1 trolley	LE 1	LE 1 trolley	LE 1	LE 1	LE 1 trolley	XC ◇1	LE 1	LE 1 trolley	LE 1	LE 1	LE 1	LE 1
Cambridge	d			20 04		20 10				20 21					21 04		21 10				21 21		
Shelford	d									20 26											21 26		
Whittlesford Parkway	d			20 11						20 30					21 11						21 30		
Great Chesterford	d									20 34											21 34		
Audley End	d			20 19		20 24				20 40					21 19		21 24				21 40		
Newport (Essex)	d									20 43											21 43		
Elsenham	d									20 49											21 49		
Stansted Airport	a					20 40											21 40						
Stansted Airport	d	20 15			20 30			20 45			21 00		21 15			21 30			21 45			22 00	
Stansted Mountfitchet	d	20 21								20 52			21 21								21 52		
Bishops Stortford	a			20 32	20 39					20 58	21 09				21 32	21 39					21 58	22 09	
	d		20 15	20 32	20 39				20 47	20 58	21 09			21 15	21 32	21 39				21 47	21 58	22 09	
Sawbridgeworth	d		20 20						20 52	21 03				21 20						21 52	22 03		
Harlow Mill	d		20 23							21 06				21 23							22 06		
Harlow Town	d	20 32	20 26	20 40				21 00	21 05	21 09			21 32	21 26	21 40				22 00	22 05	22 09		
Roydon	d		20 30							21 13				21 30							22 13		
Hertford East	d						20 39					21 09						21 39					22 09
Ware	d						20 43					21 13						21 43					22 13
St Margarets (Herts)	d						20 47					21 17						21 47					22 17
Rye House	d						20 50					21 20						21 50					22 20
Broxbourne 3	a		20 35	20 46			20 54		21 11	21 17		21 24		21 35	21 46			21 54		22 11	22 17		22 24
Broxbourne 3	d		20 39	20 46			20 54		21 12	21 17		21 24		21 39	21 46			21 54		22 12	22 17		22 24
Cheshunt	d		20 43	20 50			20 58		21 16	21 21		21 28		21 43	21 50			21 58		22 16	22 21		22 28
Waltham Cross	d						21 01		21 19			21 31						22 01		22 19			22 31
Enfield Lock	d		20 47				21 03					21 33		21 47				22 03					22 33
Brimsdown	d						21 06					21 36						22 06					22 36
Ponders End	d						21 08					21 38						22 08					22 38
Angel Road	d																						
Northumberland Park	d		20 52											21 52									
Tottenham Hale ⊖	d	20 48	20 56	21 00	21 03		21 14	21 17	21 27	21 30	21 33	21 44	21 48	21 56	22 00	22 03		22 14	22 17	22 27	22 30	22 33	22 44
Seven Sisters ⊖	d																						
Clapton	d																						
Stratford 7 ⊖	a		21 07									21 55						22 25					22 55
Hackney Downs	d						21 20																
Bethnal Green	d																						
London Liverpool Street 15 ⊖	a	21 01		21 13	21 16		21 28	21 31	21 42	21 44	21 47		22 01	22 12	22 14	22 16			22 31	22 42	22 44	22 47	

Station		LE 1	LE 1	LE 1	LE 1	XC ◇1	LE 1	LE 1	LE 1	LE 1	LE 1	LE 1	LE 1	LE 1	LE 1	LE 1	LE 1
Cambridge	d			22 04		22 10			22 21				22 51				
Shelford	d								22 26				22 56				
Whittlesford Parkway	d			22 11					22 30				23 00				
Great Chesterford	d								22 34				23 04				
Audley End	d			22 19		22 24			22 40				23 10				
Newport (Essex)	d								22 43				23 13				
Elsenham	d								22 49				23 19				
Stansted Airport	a					22 42											
Stansted Airport	d	22 15			22 30			22 45		23 00		23 15		23 30		23 45	23 59
Stansted Mountfitchet	d	22 21							22 52			23 21	23 22				
Bishops Stortford	a			22 32	22 39				22 58	23 09			23 28	23 39			00 08
	d		22 15	22 32	22 39				23 01	23 09			23 28	23 39			00 08
Sawbridgeworth	d		22 20						23 05				23 32				
Harlow Mill	d		22 23						23 09				23 36				
Harlow Town	d	22 32	22 26	22 40				23 00	23 12			23 32	23 39			23 59	00 16
Roydon	d		22 30						23 16				23 43				
Hertford East	d						22 39				23 09				23 39		
Ware	d						22 43				23 13				23 43		
St Margarets (Herts)	d						22 47				23 17				23 47		
Rye House	d						22 50				23 20				23 50		
Broxbourne 3	a		22 35	22 46			22 54		23 20		23 24		23 47		23 54		
Broxbourne 3	d		22 39	22 46			22 54		23 20		23 24		23 47		23 54		
Cheshunt	d		22 43	22 50			22 58		23 24		23 28		23 51		23 58		
Waltham Cross	d						23 01				23 31				00 01		
Enfield Lock	d		22 47				23 03				23 33				00 03		
Brimsdown	d						23 06				23 36				00 06		
Ponders End	d						23 08				23 38				00 08		
Angel Road	d																
Northumberland Park	d		22 52														
Tottenham Hale ⊖	d	22 48	22 56	23 00	23 03		23 14	23 17	23 33	23 33	23 44	23 48	23 59	00 03	00 14	00 17	
Seven Sisters ⊖	d																
Clapton	d																
Stratford 7 ⊖	a						23 25				23 55						
Hackney Downs	d														00 20		
Bethnal Green	d																
London Liverpool Street 15 ⊖	a	23 01	23 12	23 14	23 16			23 31	23 47	23 47		00 01	00 13	00 16	00 28	00 32	00 51

Table 22 — Saturdays, 18 August to 25 August

Cambridge, Stansted Airport, Bishops Stortford, Hertford East and Broxbourne - London

Network Diagram - see first Page of Table 20

Station		LE 1	LE 1	LE 1	LE 1	LE 1	LE 1	LE 1	LE 1	LE 1	LE 1	XC 1	LE 1	LE 1	LE 1	LE 1	LE 1	LE 1 trolley	XC 1	LE 1	LE 1 trolley	LE 1	LE 1
Cambridge	d		22p51									04 56					05 21		05 42				06 04
Shelford	d		22p56														05 26						
Whittlesford Parkway	d		23p00														05 30						06 11
Great Chesterford	d		23p04														05 34						
Audley End	d		23p10														05 40		05 56				06 19
Newport (Essex)	d		23p13														05 43						
Elsenham	d		23p19														05 49						
Stansted Airport	a											05 20							06 08				
Stansted Airport	d	23p15		23p30		23p45		23p59	00 30	01 00	01 30			05 30				06 00			06 15		
Stansted Mountfitchet	d	23p21	23p24														05 52				06 21		
Bishops Stortford	a		23p29	23p39				00 08	00 39					05 39			05 58	06 09					06 32
	d		23p29	23p39				00 08	00 39				05 15	05 39		05 47	05 58	06 09				06 15	06 32
Sawbridgeworth	d		23p33										05 20			05 52	06 03					06 20	
Harlow Mill	d		23p37										05 23				06 06					06 23	
Harlow Town	d	23p32	23p40			23p59		00 16	00 47				05 26			06 05	06 09				06 32	06 26	06 40
Roydon	d		23p44										05 30				06 13					06 30	
Hertford East	d				23p39		00 07													06 09			
Ware	d				23p43															06 13			
St Margarets (Herts)	d				23p47															06 17			
Rye House	d				23p50															06 20			
Broxbourne 3	a		23p48		23p54		00 19						05 34			06 11	06 17			06 24		06 35	06 46
Broxbourne 3	d		23p48		23p54		00 19						05 34		05 54	06 12	06 17			06 24		06 39	06 46
Cheshunt	d		23p52		23p58								05 38		05 58	06 16	06 21			06 28		06 43	06 50
Waltham Cross	d												05 41		06 01	06 19				06 31			
Enfield Lock	d												05 43		06 03					06 33		06 47	
Brimsdown	d												05 46		06 06					06 36			
Ponders End	d												05 48		06 08					06 38			
Angel Road	d																						
Northumberland Park	d												05 52									06 52	
Tottenham Hale ⊖	d	23p48											05 55	06 01	06 14	06 27	06 30	06 33		06 44	06 48	06 56	07 00
Seven Sisters ⊖	d		00 04	00 08	00 11	00 21																	
Clapton	d																						
Stratford 7 ⊖	a												06 05			06 37						07 07	
Hackney Downs	d				00 16		00 41								06 20					06 50			
Bethnal Green	d																						
London Liverpool Street 15 ⊖	a	00 01	00 18	00 22	00 26	00 36	00 49	00 51	01 21	01 50	02 20		06 14	06 14	06 28		06 44	06 47		06 58	07 01		07 13

Station		LE 1 trolley	LE 1	LE 1 trolley	LE 1	LE 1	LE 1 trolley	XC 1	LE 1	LE 1 trolley	LE 1	LE 1	LE 1 trolley	LE 1	LE 1 trolley	LE 1	LE 1	LE 1 trolley	XC 1	LE 1	LE 1 trolley	LE 1	LE 1
Cambridge	d					06 21		06 40				07 04					07 21		07 40				08 04
Shelford	d					06 26											07 26						
Whittlesford Parkway	d					06 30						07 11					07 30						08 11
Great Chesterford	d					06 34											07 34						
Audley End	d					06 40		06 54				07 19					07 40		07 54				08 19
Newport (Essex)	d					06 43											07 43						
Elsenham	d					06 49											07 49						
Stansted Airport	a							07 09											08 08				
Stansted Airport	d	06 30		06 45			07 00			07 15			07 30		07 45			08 00			08 15		
Stansted Mountfitchet	d					06 52				07 21							07 52				08 21		
Bishops Stortford	a	06 39				06 58	07 09					07 32	07 39				07 58	08 09					08 32
	d	06 39			06 47	06 58	07 09				07 15	07 32	07 39			07 47	07 58	08 09				08 15	08 32
Sawbridgeworth	d				06 52	07 03					07 20					07 52	08 03					08 20	
Harlow Mill	d					07 06					07 23						08 06					08 23	
Harlow Town	d			07 00	07 05	07 09				07 32	07 26	07 40			08 00	08 05	08 09				08 32	08 26	08 40
Roydon	d					07 13					07 30						08 13					08 30	
Hertford East	d		06 39						07 09					07 39						08 09			
Ware	d		06 43						07 13					07 43						08 13			
St Margarets (Herts)	d		06 47						07 17					07 47						08 17			
Rye House	d		06 50						07 20					07 50						08 20			
Broxbourne 3	a		06 54		07 11	07 17			07 24		07 35	07 46		07 54		08 11	08 17			08 24		08 35	08 46
Broxbourne 3	d		06 54		07 12	07 17			07 24		07 39	07 46		07 54		08 12	08 17			08 24		08 39	08 46
Cheshunt	d		06 58		07 16	07 21			07 28		07 43	07 50		07 58		08 16	08 21			08 28		08 43	08 50
Waltham Cross	d		07 01		07 19				07 31					08 01		08 19				08 31			
Enfield Lock	d		07 03						07 33		07 47			08 03						08 33		08 47	
Brimsdown	d		07 06						07 36					08 06						08 36			
Ponders End	d		07 08						07 38					08 08						08 38			
Angel Road	d																						
Northumberland Park	d										07 52											08 52	
Tottenham Hale ⊖	d	07 03	07 14	07 17	07 27	07 30	07 33		07 44	07 48	07 56	08 00	08 03	08 14	08 17	08 27	08 30	08 33		08 44	08 48	08 56	09 00
Seven Sisters ⊖	d																						
Clapton	d																						
Stratford 7 ⊖	a				07 37						08 07					08 37						09 07	
Hackney Downs	d		07 20						07 50					08 20						08 50			
Bethnal Green	d																						
London Liverpool Street 15 ⊖	a	07 16	07 28	07 31		07 44	07 47		07 58	08 01		08 13	08 16	08 28	08 31		08 44	08 47		08 58	09 01		09 13

Cambridge, Stansted Airport, Bishops Stortford, Hertford East and Broxbourne - London

Network Diagram - see first Page of Table 20

		LE 1 🛒	XC ◇1	LE 1	LE 1 🛒	LE 1	LE 1	LE 1 🛒	LE 1	LE 1 🛒	LE 1	LE 1	LE 1 🛒	XC ◇1	LE 1	LE 1 🛒	LE 1	LE 1	LE 1 🛒	LE 1	LE 1 🛒	LE 1
Cambridge	d		08 10				08 21					09 04		09 10				09 21				
Shelford	d						08 26											09 26				
Whittlesford Parkway	d						08 30					09 11						09 30				
Great Chesterford	d						08 34											09 34				
Audley End	d		08 24				08 40					09 19		09 24				09 40				
Newport (Essex)	d						08 43											09 43				
Elsenham	d						08 49											09 49				
Stansted Airport	a		08 39											09 40								
Stansted Airport	d	08 30			08 45			09 00		09 15			09 30			09 45			10 00		10 15	
Stansted Mountfitchet	d						08 52			09 21								09 52			10 21	
Bishops Stortford	a	08 39					08 58	09 09				09 32	09 39					09 58	10 09			
	d	08 39				08 47	08 58	09 09			09 15	09 32	09 39				09 47	09 58	10 09			10 15
Sawbridgeworth	d					08 52	09 03				09 20						09 52	10 03				10 20
Harlow Mill	d						09 06				09 23							10 06				10 23
Harlow Town	d				09 00	09 05	09 09			09 32	09 26	09 40				10 00	10 05	10 09			10 32	10 26
Roydon	d						09 13				09 30							10 13				10 30
Hertford East	d			08 39					09 09						09 39					10 09		
Ware	d			08 43					09 13						09 43					10 13		
St Margarets (Herts)	d			08 47					09 17						09 47					10 17		
Rye House	d			08 50					09 20						09 50					10 20		
Broxbourne 3	a			08 54		09 11	09 17		09 24		09 35	09 46			09 54		10 11	10 17		10 24		10 35
Broxbourne 3	d			08 54		09 12	09 17		09 24		09 39	09 46			09 54		10 12	10 17		10 24		10 39
Cheshunt	d			08 58		09 16	09 21		09 28		09 43	09 50			09 58		10 16	10 21		10 28		10 43
Waltham Cross	d			09 01		09 19			09 31						10 01		10 19			10 31		
Enfield Lock	d			09 03					09 33		09 47				10 03					10 33		10 47
Brimsdown	d			09 06					09 36						10 06					10 36		
Ponders End	d			09 08					09 38						10 08					10 38		
Angel Road	d																					
Northumberland Park	d										09 52											10 52
Tottenham Hale ⊖	d	09 03		09 14	09 17	09 27	09 30	09 33	09 44	09 48	09 56	10 00	10 03		10 14	10 17	10 27	10 30	10 33	10 44	10 48	10 56
Seven Sisters ⊖	d																					
Clapton	d																					
Stratford 7 ⊖	a					09 37					10 07						10 37					11 07
Hackney Downs	d			09 20					09 50						10 20					10 50		
Bethnal Green	d																					
London Liverpool Street 15 ⊖	a	09 16		09 28	09 31		09 44	09 47	09 58	10 01		10 13	10 16		10 28	10 31		10 44	10 47	10 58	11 01	

		LE 1	LE 1 🛒	XC ◇1	LE 1	LE 1 🛒	LE 1	LE 1	LE 1 🛒	LE 1	LE 1 🛒	LE 1	LE 1	LE 1 🛒	XC ◇1	LE 1	LE 1 🛒	LE 1	LE 1	LE 1 🛒	LE 1	LE 1 🛒	LE 1
Cambridge	d	10 04		10 10				10 21					11 04		11 10				11 21				
Shelford	d							10 26											11 26				
Whittlesford Parkway	d	10 11						10 30					11 11						11 30				
Great Chesterford	d							10 34											11 34				
Audley End	d	10 19		10 24				10 40					11 19		11 24				11 40				
Newport (Essex)	d							10 43											11 43				
Elsenham	d							10 49											11 49				
Stansted Airport	a			10 40											11 40								
Stansted Airport	d		10 30			10 45			11 00		11 15			11 30			11 45			12 00		12 15	
Stansted Mountfitchet	d							10 52			11 21								11 52			12 21	
Bishops Stortford	a	10 32	10 39					10 58	11 09				11 32	11 39					11 58	12 09			
	d	10 32	10 39				10 47	10 58	11 09			11 15	11 32	11 39				11 47	11 58	12 09			12 15
Sawbridgeworth	d						10 52	11 03				11 20						11 52	12 03				12 20
Harlow Mill	d							11 06				11 23							12 06				12 23
Harlow Town	d	10 40				11 00	11 05	11 09			11 32	11 26	11 40				12 00	12 05	12 09			12 32	12 26
Roydon	d							11 13				11 30							12 13				12 30
Hertford East	d				10 39					11 09						11 39					12 09		
Ware	d				10 43					11 13						11 43					12 13		
St Margarets (Herts)	d				10 47					11 17						11 47					12 17		
Rye House	d				10 50					11 20						11 50					12 20		
Broxbourne 3	a	10 46			10 54		11 11	11 17		11 24		11 35	11 46			11 54		12 11	12 17		12 24		12 35
Broxbourne 3	d	10 46			10 54		11 12	11 17		11 24		11 39	11 46			11 54		12 12	12 17		12 24		12 39
Cheshunt	d	10 50			10 58		11 16	11 21		11 28		11 43	11 50			11 58		12 16	12 21		12 28		12 43
Waltham Cross	d				11 01		11 19			11 31						12 01		12 19			12 31		
Enfield Lock	d				11 03					11 33		11 47				12 03					12 33		12 47
Brimsdown	d				11 06					11 36						12 06					12 36		
Ponders End	d				11 08					11 38						12 08					12 38		
Angel Road	d																						
Northumberland Park	d											11 52											12 52
Tottenham Hale ⊖	d	11 00	11 03		11 14	11 17	11 27	11 30	11 33	11 44	11 48	11 56	12 00	12 03		12 14	12 17	12 27	12 30	12 33	12 44	12 48	12 56
Seven Sisters ⊖	d																						
Clapton	d																						
Stratford 7 ⊖	a						11 37					12 07						12 37					13 07
Hackney Downs	d				11 20					11 50						12 20					12 50		
Bethnal Green	d																						
London Liverpool Street 15 ⊖	a	11 13	11 16		11 28	11 31		11 44	11 47	11 58	12 01		12 13	12 16		12 28	12 31		12 44	12 47	12 58	13 01	

Cambridge, Stansted Airport, Bishops Stortford, Hertford East and Broxbourne - London

Network Diagram - see first Page of Table 20

		LE 1	LE 1 🛒	XC ◇1	LE 1	LE 1 🛒	LE 1	LE 1	LE 1 🛒	LE 1	LE 1 🛒	LE 1	LE 1	LE 1 🛒	XC ◇1	LE 1	LE 1 🛒	LE 1	LE 1	LE 1 🛒	LE 1	LE 1 🛒
Cambridge	d	12 04		12 10				12 21					13 04		13 10				13 21			
Shelford	d							12 26											13 26			
Whittlesford Parkway	d	12 11						12 30					13 11						13 30			
Great Chesterford	d							12 34											13 34			
Audley End	d	12 19		12 24				12 40					13 19		13 24				13 40			
Newport (Essex)	d							12 43											13 43			
Elsenham	d							12 49											13 49			
Stansted Airport	a			12 40											13 40							
Stansted Airport	d		12 30			12 45			13 00		13 15			13 30			13 45			14 00		14 15
Stansted Mountfitchet	d							12 52			13 21								13 52			14 21
Bishops Stortford	a	12 32	12 39					12 58	13 09				13 32	13 39					13 58	14 09		
	d	12 32	12 39				12 47	12 58	13 09			13 15	13 32	13 39				13 47	13 58	14 09		
Sawbridgeworth	d						12 52	13 03				13 20						13 52	14 03			
Harlow Mill	d							13 06				13 23							14 06			
Harlow Town	d	12 40				13 00	13 05	13 09			13 32	13 26	13 40				14 00	14 05	14 09			14 32
Roydon	d							13 13				13 30							14 13			
Hertford East	d				12 39					13 09						13 39					14 09	
Ware	d				12 43					13 13						13 43					14 13	
St Margarets (Herts)	d				12 47					13 17						13 47					14 17	
Rye House	d				12 50					13 20						13 50					14 20	
Broxbourne 3	a	12 46			12 54		13 11	13 17		13 24		13 35	13 46			13 54		14 11	14 17		14 24	
Broxbourne 3	d	12 46			12 54		13 12	13 17		13 24		13 39	13 46			13 54		14 12	14 17		14 24	
Cheshunt	d	12 50			12 58		13 16	13 21		13 28		13 43	13 50			13 58		14 16	14 21		14 28	
Waltham Cross	d				13 01		13 19			13 31						14 01		14 19			14 31	
Enfield Lock	d				13 03					13 33		13 47				14 03					14 33	
Brimsdown	d				13 06					13 36						14 06					14 36	
Ponders End	d				13 08					13 38						14 08					14 38	
Angel Road	d																					
Northumberland Park	d											13 52										
Tottenham Hale ⊖	d	13 00	13 03		13 14	13 17	13 27	13 30	13 33	13 44	13 48	13 56	14 00	14 03		14 14	14 17	14 27	14 30	14 33	14 44	14 48
Seven Sisters ⊖	d																					
Clapton	d																					
Stratford 7 ⊖	a						13 37					14 07						14 37				
Hackney Downs	d				13 20					13 50						14 20					14 50	
Bethnal Green	d																					
London Liverpool Street 15 ⊖	a	13 13	13 16		13 28	13 31		13 44	13 47	13 58	14 01		14 13	14 16		14 28	14 31		14 44	14 47	14 58	15 01

		LE 1	LE 1	LE 1 🛒	XC ◇1	LE 1	LE 1 🛒	LE 1	LE 1	LE 1 🛒	LE 1	LE 1 🛒	LE 1	LE 1	LE 1 🛒	XC ◇1	LE 1	LE 1 🛒	LE 1	LE 1	LE 1 🛒	LE 1	LE 1 🛒
Cambridge	d		14 04		14 10				14 21					15 04		15 10				15 21			
Shelford	d								14 26											15 26			
Whittlesford Parkway	d		14 11						14 30					15 11						15 30			
Great Chesterford	d								14 34											15 34			
Audley End	d		14 19		14 24				14 40					15 19		15 24				15 40			
Newport (Essex)	d								14 43											15 43			
Elsenham	d								14 49											15 49			
Stansted Airport	a				14 40											15 40							
Stansted Airport	d			14 30			14 45			15 00		15 15			15 30			15 45			16 00		16 15
Stansted Mountfitchet	d								14 52			15 21								15 52			16 21
Bishops Stortford	a		14 32	14 39					14 58	15 09				15 32	15 39					15 58	16 09		
	d	14 15	14 32	14 39				14 47	14 58	15 09			15 15	15 32	15 39				15 47	15 58	16 09		
Sawbridgeworth	d	14 20						14 52	15 03				15 20						15 52	16 03			
Harlow Mill	d	14 23							15 06				15 23							16 06			
Harlow Town	d	14 26	14 40				15 00	15 05	15 09			15 32	15 26	15 40				16 00	16 05	16 09			16 32
Roydon	d	14 30							15 13				15 30							16 13			
Hertford East	d					14 39					15 09						15 39					16 09	
Ware	d					14 43					15 13						15 43					16 13	
St Margarets (Herts)	d					14 47					15 17						15 47					16 17	
Rye House	d					14 50					15 20						15 50					16 20	
Broxbourne 3	a	14 35	14 46			14 54		15 11	15 17		15 24		15 35	15 46			15 54		16 11	16 17		16 24	
Broxbourne 3	d	14 39	14 46			14 54		15 12	15 17		15 24		15 39	15 46			15 54		16 12	16 17		16 24	
Cheshunt	d	14 43	14 50			14 58		15 16	15 21		15 28		15 43	15 50			15 58		16 16	16 21		16 28	
Waltham Cross	d					15 01		15 19			15 31						16 01		16 19			16 31	
Enfield Lock	d	14 47				15 03					15 33		15 47				16 03					16 33	
Brimsdown	d					15 06					15 36						16 06					16 36	
Ponders End	d					15 08					15 38						16 08					16 38	
Angel Road	d																						
Northumberland Park	d	14 52											15 52										
Tottenham Hale ⊖	d	14 56	15 00	15 03		15 14	15 17	15 27	15 30	15 33	15 44	15 48	15 56	16 00	16 03		16 14	16 17	16 27	16 30	16 33	16 44	16 48
Seven Sisters ⊖	d																						
Clapton	d																						
Stratford 7 ⊖	a	15 07						15 37					16 07						16 37				
Hackney Downs	d					15 20					15 50						16 20					16 50	
Bethnal Green	d																						
London Liverpool Street 15 ⊖	a		15 13	15 16		15 28	15 31		15 44	15 47	15 58	16 01		16 13	16 16		16 28	16 31		16 44	16 47	16 58	17 01

Table 22

Saturdays
18 August to 25 August

Cambridge, Stansted Airport, Bishops Stortford, Hertford East and Broxbourne - London

Network Diagram - see first Page of Table 20

		LE 1	LE 1	LE 1 H	XC ◇1	LE 1	LE 1 H	LE 1	LE 1	LE 1 H	LE 1	LE 1 H	LE 1	LE 1	LE 1 H	XC ◇1	LE 1	LE 1 H	LE 1	LE 1	LE 1 H	LE 1	LE 1 H
Cambridge	d		16 04		16 10				16 21					17 04		17 10				17 21			
Shelford	d								16 26											17 26			
Whittlesford Parkway	d		16 11						16 30					17 11						17 30			
Great Chesterford	d								16 34											17 34			
Audley End	d		16 19		16 24				16 40					17 19		17 24				17 40			
Newport (Essex)	d								16 43											17 43			
Elsenham	d								16 49											17 49			
Stansted Airport	a				16 40											17 40							
Stansted Airport	d			16 30			16 45			17 00		17 15			17 30			17 45			18 00		18 15
Stansted Mountfitchet	d								16 52			17 21								17 52			18 21
Bishops Stortford	a		16 32	16 39					16 58	17 09				17 32	17 39					17 58	18 09		
	d	16 15	16 32	16 39				16 47	16 58	17 09			17 15	17 32	17 39				17 47	17 58	18 09		
Sawbridgeworth	d	16 20						16 52	17 03				17 20						17 52	18 03			
Harlow Mill	d	16 23							17 06				17 23							18 06			
Harlow Town	d	16 26	16 40				17 00	17 05	17 09			17 32	17 26	17 40				18 00	18 05	18 09			18 32
Roydon	d	16 30							17 13				17 30							18 13			
Hertford East	d					16 39					17 09						17 39					18 09	
Ware	d					16 43					17 13						17 43					18 13	
St Margarets (Herts)	d					16 47					17 17						17 47					18 17	
Rye House	d					16 50					17 20						17 50					18 20	
Broxbourne 3	a	16 35	16 46			16 54		17 11	17 17		17 24		17 35	17 46			17 54		18 11	18 17		18 24	
Broxbourne 3	d	16 39	16 46			16 54		17 12	17 17		17 24		17 39	17 46			17 54		18 12	18 17		18 24	
Cheshunt	d	16 43	16 50			16 58		17 16	17 21		17 28		17 43	17 50			17 58		18 16	18 21		18 28	
Waltham Cross	d					17 01		17 19			17 31						18 01		18 19			18 31	
Enfield Lock	d	16 47				17 03					17 33		17 47				18 03					18 33	
Brimsdown	d					17 06					17 36						18 06					18 36	
Ponders End	d					17 08					17 38						18 08					18 38	
Angel Road	d																						
Northumberland Park	d	16 52											17 52										
Tottenham Hale ⊖	d	16 56	17 00	17 03		17 14	17 17	17 27	17 30	17 33	17 44	17 48	17 56	18 00	18 03		18 14	18 17	18 27	18 30	18 33	18 44	18 48
Seven Sisters ⊖	d																						
Clapton	d																						
Stratford 7 ⊖	a	17 07						17 37					18 07						18 37				
Hackney Downs	d					17 20					17 50						18 20					18 50	
Bethnal Green	d																						
London Liverpool Street 15 ⊖	a		17 13	17 16		17 28	17 31		17 44	17 47	17 58	18 01		18 13	18 16		18 28	18 31		18 44	18 47	18 58	19 01

		LE 1	LE 1	LE 1 H	LE 1	LE 1 H	XC ◇1	LE 1	LE 1	LE 1 H	LE 1	LE 1 H	LE 1	LE 1	LE 1 H	XC ◇1	LE 1	LE 1 H	LE 1	LE 1	LE 1 H	LE 1
Cambridge	d		18 04				18 18		18 21					19 04		19 10				19 21		
Shelford	d								18 26											19 26		
Whittlesford Parkway	d		18 11						18 30					19 11						19 30		
Great Chesterford	d								18 34											19 34		
Audley End	d		18 19				18 34		18 40					19 19		19 25				19 40		
Newport (Essex)	d								18 43											19 43		
Elsenham	d								18 49											19 49		
Stansted Airport	a						18 53									19 40						
Stansted Airport	d			18 30		18 45				19 00		19 15			19 30			19 45			20 00	
Stansted Mountfitchet	d								18 52			19 21								19 52		
Bishops Stortford	a		18 32	18 39					18 58	19 09				19 32	19 39					19 58	20 09	
	d	18 15	18 32	18 39				18 47	18 58	19 09			19 15	19 32	19 39				19 47	19 58	20 09	
Sawbridgeworth	d	18 20						18 52	19 03				19 20						19 52	20 03		
Harlow Mill	d	18 23							19 06				19 23							20 06		
Harlow Town	d	18 26	18 40			19 00		19 05	19 09			19 32	19 26	19 40				20 00	20 05	20 09		
Roydon	d	18 30							19 13				19 30							20 13		
Hertford East	d				18 39						19 09						19 39					20 09
Ware	d				18 43						19 13						19 43					20 13
St Margarets (Herts)	d				18 47						19 17						19 47					20 17
Rye House	d				18 50						19 20						19 50					20 20
Broxbourne 3	a	18 35	18 46		18 54			19 11	19 17		19 24		19 35	19 46			19 54		20 11	20 17		20 24
Broxbourne 3	d	18 39	18 46		18 54			19 12	19 17		19 24		19 39	19 46			19 54		20 12	20 17		20 24
Cheshunt	d	18 43	18 50		18 58			19 16	19 21		19 28		19 43	19 50			19 58		20 16	20 21		20 28
Waltham Cross	d				19 01			19 19			19 31						20 01		20 19			20 31
Enfield Lock	d	18 47			19 03						19 33		19 47				20 03					20 33
Brimsdown	d				19 06						19 36						20 06					20 36
Ponders End	d				19 08						19 38						20 08					20 38
Angel Road	d																					
Northumberland Park	d	18 52											19 52									
Tottenham Hale ⊖	d	18 56	19 00	19 03	19 14	19 17		19 27	19 30	19 33	19 44	19 48	19 56	20 00	20 03		20 14	20 17	20 27	20 30	20 33	20 44
Seven Sisters ⊖	d																					
Clapton	d																					
Stratford 7 ⊖	a	19 07						19 37					20 07						20 37			
Hackney Downs	d				19 20						19 50						20 20					20 50
Bethnal Green	d																					
London Liverpool Street 15 ⊖	a		19 13	19 16	19 28	19 31			19 44	19 47	19 58	20 01		20 13	20 16		20 28	20 31		20 44	20 47	20 58

Table 22

Saturdays
18 August to 25 August

Cambridge, Stansted Airport, Bishops Stortford, Hertford East and Broxbourne - London

Network Diagram - see first Page of Table 20

		LE 1 H	LE 1	LE 1	LE 1 H	XC ◇1	LE 1	LE 1 H	LE 1	LE 1	LE 1 H	LE 1	LE 1 H	LE 1	LE 1	LE 1 H	XC ◇1	LE 1	LE 1 H	LE 1	LE 1	LE 1	LE 1
Cambridge	d			20 04		20 10				20 21					21 04		21 10				21 21		
Shelford	d									20 26											21 26		
Whittlesford Parkway	d			20 11						20 30					21 11						21 30		
Great Chesterford	d									20 34											21 34		
Audley End	d			20 19		20 24				20 40					21 19		21 24				21 40		
Newport (Essex)	d									20 43											21 43		
Elsenham	d									20 49											21 49		
Stansted Airport	a					20 40											21 40						
Stansted Airport	d	20 15			20 30			20 45			21 00		21 15			21 30			21 45			22 00	
Stansted Mountfitchet	d	20 21								20 52			21 21								21 52		
Bishops Stortford	a			20 32	20 39					20 58	21 09				21 32	21 39					21 58	22 09	
	d		20 15	20 32	20 39				20 47	20 58	21 09			21 15	21 32	21 39				21 47	21 58	22 09	
Sawbridgeworth	d		20 20						20 52	21 03				21 20						21 52	22 03		
Harlow Mill	d		20 23							21 06				21 23							22 06		
Harlow Town	d	20 32	20 26	20 40				21 00	21 05	21 09			21 32	21 26	21 40				22 00	22 05	22 09		
Roydon	d		20 30							21 13				21 30							22 13		
Hertford East	d						20 39					21 09						21 39					22 09
Ware	d						20 43					21 13						21 43					22 13
St Margarets (Herts)	d						20 47					21 17						21 47					22 17
Rye House	d						20 50					21 20						21 50					22 20
Broxbourne 3	a		20 35	20 46			20 54		21 11	21 17		21 24		21 35	21 46			21 54		22 11	22 17		22 24
Broxbourne 3	d		20 39	20 46			20 54		21 12	21 17		21 24		21 39	21 46			21 54		22 12	22 17		22 24
Cheshunt	d		20 43	20 50			20 58		21 16	21 21		21 28		21 43	21 50			21 58		22 16	22 21		22 28
Waltham Cross	d						21 01		21 19			21 31						22 01		22 19			22 31
Enfield Lock	d		20 47				21 03					21 33		21 47				22 03					22 33
Brimsdown	d						21 06					21 36						22 06					22 36
Ponders End	d						21 08					21 38						22 08					22 38
Angel Road	d																						
Northumberland Park	d		20 52											21 52									
Tottenham Hale ⊖	d	20 48	20 56	21 00	21 03		21 14	21 17	21 27	21 30	21 33	21 44	21 48	21 56	22 00	22 03		22 14	22 17	22 27	22 30	22 33	22 44
Seven Sisters ⊖	d																						
Clapton	d																						
Stratford 7 ⊖	a		21 07						21 37					22 07						22 37			
Hackney Downs	d						21 20					21 50						22 20					22 50
Bethnal Green	d																						
London Liverpool Street 15 ⊖	a	21 01		21 13	21 16		21 28	21 31		21 44	21 47	21 58	22 01		22 13	22 16		22 28	22 31		22 44	22 47	22 58

		LE 1	LE 1	LE 1	LE 1	XC ◇1	LE 1	LE 1	LE 1	LE 1	LE 1	LE 1	LE 1	LE 1	LE 1	LE 1	LE 1
Cambridge	d			22 04		22 10			22 21				22 51				
Shelford	d								22 26				22 56				
Whittlesford Parkway	d			22 11					22 30				23 00				
Great Chesterford	d								22 34				23 04				
Audley End	d			22 19		22 24			22 40				23 10				
Newport (Essex)	d								22 43				23 13				
Elsenham	d								22 49				23 19				
Stansted Airport	a					22 40											
Stansted Airport	d	22 15			22 30			22 45		23 00		23 15		23 30		23 45	23 59
Stansted Mountfitchet	d	22 21							22 52			23 21	23 22				
Bishops Stortford	a			22 32	22 39				22 58	23 09			23 28	23 39			00 08
	d		22 15	22 32	22 39				23 01	23 09			23 28	23 39			00 08
Sawbridgeworth	d		22 20						23 05				23 32				
Harlow Mill	d		22 23						23 09				23 36				
Harlow Town	d	22 32	22 26	22 40				23 00	23 12			23 32	23 39			23 59	00 16
Roydon	d		22 30						23 16				23 43				
Hertford East	d						22 39				23 09				23 39		
Ware	d						22 43				23 13				23 43		
St Margarets (Herts)	d						22 47				23 17				23 47		
Rye House	d						22 50				23 20				23 50		
Broxbourne 3	a		22 35	22 46			22 54		23 20		23 24		23 47		23 54		
Broxbourne 3	d		22 39	22 46			22 54		23 20		23 24		23 47		23 54		
Cheshunt	d		22 43	22 50			22 58		23 24		23 28		23 51		23 58		
Waltham Cross	d						23 01				23 31				00 01		
Enfield Lock	d		22 47				23 03				23 33				00 03		
Brimsdown	d						23 06				23 36				00 06		
Ponders End	d						23 08				23 38				00 08		
Angel Road	d																
Northumberland Park	d		22 52														
Tottenham Hale ⊖	d	22 48	22 56	23 00	23 03		23 14	23 17	23 33	23 33	23 44	23 48	23 59	00 03	00 14	00 17	
Seven Sisters ⊖	d																
Clapton	d																
Stratford 7 ⊖	a		23 07														
Hackney Downs	d						23 20				23 50				00 20		
Bethnal Green	d																
London Liverpool Street 15 ⊖	a	23 01	23 18	23 13	23 16		23 28	23 31	23 48	23 47	23 58	00 01	00 13	00 16	00 28	00 32	00 51

Cambridge, Stansted Airport, Bishops Stortford, Hertford East and Broxbourne - London

Network Diagram - see first Page of Table 20

Station		LE	LE	LE	LE	LE	LE	LE	LE	LE	LE	XC	LE	LE	LE	LE	LE	LE	XC	LE	LE	LE	LE
		1	1	1	1	1	1	1	1	1	1	1	1	1	1	1	1	1 🚲	1	1	1 🚲	1	1
Cambridge	d		22p51									04 56					05 21		05 42				06 04
Shelford	d		22p56														05 26						
Whittlesford Parkway	d		23p00														05 30						06 11
Great Chesterford	d		23p04														05 34						
Audley End	d		23p10														05 40		05 56				06 19
Newport (Essex)	d		23p13														05 43						
Elsenham	d		23p19														05 49						
Stansted Airport	a											05 20							06 08				
Stansted Airport	d	23p15		23p30		23p45		23p59	00 30	01 00	01 30			05 30				06 00			06 15		
Stansted Mountfitchet	d	23p21	23p24														05 52				06 21		
Bishops Stortford	a		23p29	23p39				00 08	00 39					05 39			05 58	06 09					06 32
	d		23p29	23p39				00 08	00 39				05 15	05 39		05 47	05 58	06 09				06 15	06 32
Sawbridgeworth	d		23p33										05 20			05 52	06 03					06 20	
Harlow Mill	d		23p37										05 23				06 06					06 23	
Harlow Town	d	23p32	23p40			23p59		00 16	00 47				05 26			06 05	06 09				06 32	06 26	06 40
Roydon	d		23p44										05 30				06 13					06 30	
Hertford East	d				23p39		00 07													06 09			
Ware	d				23p43															06 13			
St Margarets (Herts)	d				23p47															06 17			
Rye House	d				23p50															06 20			
Broxbourne 5	a		23p48		23p54		00 19						05 34			06 11	06 17			06 24		06 35	06 46
Broxbourne 5	d		23p48		23p54		00 19						05 34		05 54	06 12	06 17			06 24		06 39	06 46
Cheshunt	d		23p52		23p58								05 38		05 58	06 16	06 21			06 28		06 43	06 50
Waltham Cross	d												05 41		06 01	06 19				06 31			
Enfield Lock	d												05 43		06 03					06 33		06 47	
Brimsdown	d												05 46		06 06					06 36			
Ponders End	d												05 48		06 08					06 38			
Angel Road	d																						
Northumberland Park	d												05 52									06 52	
Tottenham Hale ⊖	d	23p48											05 55	06 01	06 14	06 27	06 30	06 33		06 44	06 48	06 56	07 00
Seven Sisters ⊖	d		00 04	00 08	00 11	00 21																	
Clapton	d																						
Stratford 7 ⊖	a												06 05			06 37						07 07	
Hackney Downs	d				00 16		00 41								06 20					06 50			
Bethnal Green	d																						
London Liverpool Street 15 ⊖	a	00 01	00 18	00 22	00 26	00 36	00 49	00 51	01 21	01 50	02 20		06 14	06 14	06 28		06 45	06 47		06 58	07 01		07 13

Station		LE	LE	LE	LE	LE	LE	XC	LE	LE	LE	LE	LE	LE	LE	LE	LE	LE	XC	LE	LE	LE	LE
		1 🚲	1	1 🚲	1	1	1 🚲	1	1	1 🚲	1	1	1 🚲	1	1 🚲	1	1	1 🚲	1	1	1 🚲	1	1
Cambridge	d					06 21		06 40				07 04					07 21		07 40				08 04
Shelford	d					06 26											07 26						
Whittlesford Parkway	d					06 30						07 11					07 30						08 11
Great Chesterford	d					06 34											07 34						
Audley End	d					06 40		06 54				07 19					07 40		07 54				08 19
Newport (Essex)	d					06 43											07 43						
Elsenham	d					06 49											07 49						
Stansted Airport	a							07 09											08 08				
Stansted Airport	d	06 30		06 45			07 00			07 15			07 30		07 45			08 00			08 15		
Stansted Mountfitchet	d					06 52				07 21							07 52				08 21		
Bishops Stortford	a	06 39				06 58	07 09					07 32	07 39				07 58	08 09					08 32
	d	06 39			06 47	06 58	07 09				07 15	07 32	07 39			07 47	07 58	08 09				08 15	08 32
Sawbridgeworth	d				06 52	07 03					07 20					07 52	08 03					08 20	
Harlow Mill	d					07 06					07 23						08 06					08 23	
Harlow Town	d			07 00	07 05	07 09				07 32	07 26	07 40			08 00	08 05	08 09				08 32	08 26	08 40
Roydon	d					07 13					07 30						08 13					08 30	
Hertford East	d		06 39						07 09					07 39						08 09			
Ware	d		06 43						07 13					07 43						08 13			
St Margarets (Herts)	d		06 47						07 17					07 47						08 17			
Rye House	d		06 50						07 20					07 50						08 20			
Broxbourne 5	a		06 54		07 11	07 17			07 24		07 35	07 46		07 54		08 11	08 17			08 24		08 35	08 46
Broxbourne 5	d		06 54		07 12	07 17			07 24		07 39	07 46		07 54		08 12	08 17			08 24		08 39	08 46
Cheshunt	d		06 58		07 16	07 21			07 28		07 43	07 50		07 58		08 16	08 21			08 28		08 43	08 50
Waltham Cross	d		07 01		07 19				07 31					08 01		08 19				08 31			
Enfield Lock	d		07 03						07 33		07 47			08 03						08 33		08 47	
Brimsdown	d		07 06						07 36					08 06						08 36			
Ponders End	d		07 08						07 38					08 08						08 38			
Angel Road	d																						
Northumberland Park	d										07 52											08 52	
Tottenham Hale ⊖	d	07 03	07 14	07 17	07 27	07 30	07 33		07 44	07 48	07 56	08 00	08 03	08 14	08 17	08 27	08 30	08 33		08 44	08 48	08 56	09 00
Seven Sisters ⊖	d																						
Clapton	d																						
Stratford 7 ⊖	a				07 37						08 07					08 37						09 07	
Hackney Downs	d		07 20						07 50					08 20						08 50			
Bethnal Green	d																						
London Liverpool Street 15 ⊖	a	07 16	07 28	07 31		07 44	07 47		07 58	08 01		08 13	08 16	08 28	08 31		08 44	08 47		08 58	09 01		09 13

Cambridge, Stansted Airport, Bishops Stortford, Hertford East and Broxbourne - London

Network Diagram - see first Page of Table 20

Station		LE	XC	LE	LE	LE	LE	LE	LE	LE	LE	LE	LE	XC	LE	LE	LE	LE	LE	LE	LE	LE
		1 🚲	◇1	1	1 🚲	1	1	1 🚲	1	1 🚲	1	1	1 🚲	◇1	1	1 🚲	1	1	1 🚲	1	1 🚲	1
Cambridge	d		08 10				08 21					09 04		09 10				09 21				
Shelford	d						08 26											09 26				
Whittlesford Parkway	d						08 30					09 11						09 30				
Great Chesterford	d						08 34											09 34				
Audley End	d		08 24				08 40					09 19		09 24				09 40				
Newport (Essex)	d						08 43											09 43				
Elsenham	d						08 49											09 49				
Stansted Airport	a		08 39											09 40								
Stansted Airport	d	08 30			08 45			09 00		09 15			09 30			09 45			10 00		10 15	
Stansted Mountfitchet	d						08 52			09 21								09 52			10 21	
Bishops Stortford	a	08 39					08 58	09 09				09 32	09 39					09 58	10 09			
	d	08 39				08 47	08 58	09 09			09 15	09 32	09 39				09 47	09 58	10 09			10 15
Sawbridgeworth	d					08 52	09 03				09 20						09 52	10 03				10 20
Harlow Mill	d						09 06				09 23							10 06				10 23
Harlow Town	d				09 00	09 05	09 09			09 32	09 26	09 40				10 00	10 05	10 09			10 32	10 26
Roydon	d						09 13				09 30							10 13				10 30
Hertford East	d			08 39					09 09						09 39					10 09		
Ware	d			08 43					09 13						09 43					10 13		
St Margarets (Herts)	d			08 47					09 17						09 47					10 17		
Rye House	d			08 50					09 20						09 50					10 20		
Broxbourne 5	a			08 54		09 11	09 17		09 24		09 35	09 46			09 54		10 11	10 17		10 24		10 35
Broxbourne 5	d			08 54		09 12	09 17		09 24		09 39	09 46			09 54		10 12	10 17		10 24		10 39
Cheshunt	d			08 58		09 16	09 21		09 28		09 43	09 50			09 58		10 16	10 21		10 28		10 43
Waltham Cross	d			09 01		09 19			09 31						10 01		10 19			10 31		
Enfield Lock	d			09 03					09 33		09 47				10 03					10 33		10 47
Brimsdown	d			09 06					09 36						10 06					10 36		
Ponders End	d			09 08					09 38						10 08					10 38		
Angel Road	d																					
Northumberland Park	d										09 52											10 52
Tottenham Hale ⊖	d	09 03		09 14	09 17	09 27	09 30	09 33	09 44	09 48	09 56	10 00	10 03		10 14	10 17	10 27	10 30	10 33	10 44	10 48	10 56
Seven Sisters ⊖	d																					
Clapton	d																					
Stratford 7 ⊖	a					09 37					10 07						10 37					11 07
Hackney Downs	d			09 20					09 50						10 20					10 50		
Bethnal Green	d																					
London Liverpool Street 15 ⊖	a	09 16		09 28	09 31		09 44	09 47	09 58	10 01		10 13	10 16		10 28	10 31		10 44	10 47	10 58	11 01	

Station		LE	LE	XC	LE	LE	LE	LE	LE	LE	LE	LE	LE	LE	XC	LE	LE	LE	LE	LE	LE	LE	LE
		1	1 🚲	◇1	1	1 🚲	1	1	1 🚲	1	1 🚲	1	1	1 🚲	◇1	1	1 🚲	1	1	1 🚲	1	1 🚲	1
Cambridge	d	10 04		10 10				10 21					11 04		11 10				11 21				
Shelford	d							10 26											11 26				
Whittlesford Parkway	d	10 11						10 30					11 11						11 30				
Great Chesterford	d							10 34											11 34				
Audley End	d	10 19		10 24				10 40					11 19		11 24				11 40				
Newport (Essex)	d							10 43											11 43				
Elsenham	d							10 49											11 49				
Stansted Airport	a			10 40											11 40								
Stansted Airport	d		10 30			10 45			11 00		11 15			11 30			11 45			12 00		12 15	
Stansted Mountfitchet	d							10 52			11 21								11 52			12 21	
Bishops Stortford	a	10 32	10 39					10 58	11 09				11 32	11 39					11 58	12 09			
	d	10 32	10 39				10 47	10 58	11 09			11 15	11 32	11 39				11 47	11 58	12 09			12 15
Sawbridgeworth	d						10 52	11 03				11 20						11 52	12 03				12 20
Harlow Mill	d							11 06				11 23							12 06				12 23
Harlow Town	d	10 40				11 00	11 05	11 09			11 32	11 26	11 40				12 00	12 05	12 09			12 32	12 26
Roydon	d							11 13				11 30							12 13				12 30
Hertford East	d				10 39					11 09						11 39					12 09		
Ware	d				10 43					11 13						11 43					12 13		
St Margarets (Herts)	d				10 47					11 17						11 47					12 17		
Rye House	d				10 50					11 20						11 50					12 20		
Broxbourne 5	a	10 46			10 54		11 11	11 17		11 24		11 35	11 46			11 54		12 11	12 17		12 24		12 35
Broxbourne 5	d	10 46			10 54		11 12	11 17		11 24		11 39	11 46			11 54		12 12	12 17		12 24		12 39
Cheshunt	d	10 50			10 58		11 16	11 21		11 28		11 43	11 50			11 58		12 16	12 21		12 28		12 43
Waltham Cross	d				11 01		11 19			11 31						12 01		12 19			12 31		
Enfield Lock	d				11 03					11 33		11 47				12 03					12 33		12 47
Brimsdown	d				11 06					11 36						12 06					12 36		
Ponders End	d				11 08					11 38						12 08					12 38		
Angel Road	d																						
Northumberland Park	d											11 52											12 52
Tottenham Hale ⊖	d	11 00	11 03		11 14	11 17	11 27	11 30	11 33	11 44	11 48	11 56	12 00	12 03		12 14	12 17	12 27	12 30	12 33	12 44	12 48	12 56
Seven Sisters ⊖	d																						
Clapton	d																						
Stratford 7 ⊖	a						11 37					12 07						12 37					13 07
Hackney Downs	d				11 20					11 50						12 20					12 50		
Bethnal Green	d																						
London Liverpool Street 15 ⊖	a	11 13	11 16		11 28	11 31		11 44	11 47	11 58	12 01		12 13	12 16		12 28	12 31		12 44	12 47	12 58	13 01	

Cambridge, Stansted Airport, Bishops Stortford, Hertford East and Broxbourne - London

Network Diagram - see first Page of Table 20

		LE 1	LE 1 bus	XC ◇1	LE 1	LE 1 bus	LE 1	LE 1	LE 1 bus	LE 1	LE 1 bus	LE 1	LE 1	LE 1 bus	XC ◇1	LE 1	LE 1 bus	LE 1	LE 1	LE 1 bus	LE 1	LE 1 bus
Cambridge	d	12 04		12 10				12 21					13 04		13 10				13 21			
Shelford	d							12 26											13 26			
Whittlesford Parkway	d	12 11						12 30					13 11						13 30			
Great Chesterford	d							12 34											13 34			
Audley End	d	12 19		12 24				12 40					13 19		13 24				13 40			
Newport Essex	d							12 43											13 43			
Elsenham	d							12 49											13 49			
Stansted Airport	a			12 40											13 40							
Stansted Airport	d		12 30			12 45			13 00		13 15			13 30			13 45			14 00		14 15
Stansted Mountfitchet	d							12 52			13 21								13 52			14 21
Bishops Stortford	a	12 32	12 39					12 58	13 09				13 32	13 39					13 58	14 09		
	d	12 32	12 39				12 47	12 58	13 09			13 15	13 32	13 39				13 47	13 58	14 09		
Sawbridgeworth	d						12 52	13 03				13 20						13 52	14 03			
Harlow Mill	d							13 06				13 23							14 06			
Harlow Town	d	12 40				13 00	13 05	13 09			13 32	13 26	13 40				14 00	14 05	14 09			14 32
Roydon	d							13 13				13 30							14 13			
Hertford East	d				12 39					13 09						13 39					14 09	
Ware	d				12 43					13 13						13 43					14 13	
St Margarets (Herts)	d				12 47					13 17						13 47					14 17	
Rye House	d				12 50					13 20						13 50					14 20	
Broxbourne 3	a	12 46			12 54		13 11	13 17		13 24		13 35	13 46			13 54		14 11	14 17		14 24	
Broxbourne 3	d	12 46			12 54		13 12	13 17		13 24		13 39	13 46			13 54		14 12	14 17		14 24	
Cheshunt	d	12 50			12 58		13 16	13 21		13 28		13 43	13 50			13 58		14 16	14 21		14 28	
Waltham Cross	d				13 01		13 19			13 31						14 01		14 19			14 31	
Enfield Lock	d				13 03					13 33		13 47				14 03					14 33	
Brimsdown	d				13 06					13 36						14 06					14 36	
Ponders End	d				13 08					13 38						14 08					14 38	
Angel Road	d																					
Northumberland Park	d											13 52										
Tottenham Hale ⊖	d	13 00	13 03		13 14	13 17	13 27	13 30	13 33	13 44	13 48	13 56	14 00	14 03		14 14	14 17	14 27	14 30	14 33	14 44	14 48
Seven Sisters ⊖	d																					
Clapton	d																					
Stratford 7 ⊖	a						13 37					14 07						14 37				
Hackney Downs	d				13 20					13 50						14 20					14 50	
Bethnal Green	d																					
London Liverpool Street 15 ⊖	a	13 13	13 16		13 28	13 31		13 44	13 47	13 58	14 01		14 13	14 16		14 28	14 31		14 44	14 47	14 58	15 01

		LE 1	LE 1	LE 1 bus	XC ◇1	LE 1	LE 1 bus	LE 1	LE 1	LE 1 bus	LE 1	LE 1 bus	LE 1	LE 1	LE 1 bus	XC ◇1	LE 1	LE 1 bus	LE 1	LE 1	LE 1 bus	LE 1	LE 1 bus
Cambridge	d		14 04		14 10				14 21					15 04		15 10				15 21			
Shelford	d								14 26											15 26			
Whittlesford Parkway	d		14 11						14 30					15 11						15 30			
Great Chesterford	d								14 34											15 34			
Audley End	d		14 19		14 24				14 40					15 19		15 24				15 40			
Newport Essex	d								14 43											15 43			
Elsenham	d								14 49											15 49			
Stansted Airport	a				14 40											15 40							
Stansted Airport	d			14 30			14 45			15 00		15 15			15 30			15 45			16 00		16 15
Stansted Mountfitchet	d								14 52			15 21								15 52			16 21
Bishops Stortford	a		14 32	14 39					14 58	15 09				15 32	15 39					15 58	16 09		
	d	14 15	14 32	14 39				14 47	14 58	15 09			15 15	15 32	15 39				15 47	15 58	16 09		
Sawbridgeworth	d	14 20						14 52	15 03				15 20						15 52	16 03			
Harlow Mill	d	14 23							15 06				15 23							16 06			
Harlow Town	d	14 26	14 40				15 00	15 05	15 09			15 32	15 26	15 40				16 00	16 05	16 09			16 32
Roydon	d	14 30							15 13				15 30							16 13			
Hertford East	d					14 39					15 09						15 39					16 09	
Ware	d					14 43					15 13						15 43					16 13	
St Margarets (Herts)	d					14 47					15 17						15 47					16 17	
Rye House	d					14 50					15 20						15 50					16 20	
Broxbourne 3	a	14 35	14 46			14 54		15 11	15 17		15 24		15 35	15 46			15 54		16 11	16 17		16 24	
Broxbourne 3	d	14 39	14 46			14 54		15 12	15 17		15 24		15 39	15 46			15 54		16 12	16 17		16 24	
Cheshunt	d	14 43	14 50			14 58		15 16	15 21		15 28		15 43	15 50			15 58		16 16	16 21		16 28	
Waltham Cross	d					15 01		15 19			15 31						16 01		16 19			16 31	
Enfield Lock	d	14 47				15 03					15 33		15 47				16 03					16 33	
Brimsdown	d					15 06					15 36						16 06					16 36	
Ponders End	d					15 08					15 38						16 08					16 38	
Angel Road	d																						
Northumberland Park	d	14 52											15 52										
Tottenham Hale ⊖	d	14 56	15 00	15 03		15 14	15 17	15 27	15 30	15 33	15 44	15 48	15 56	16 00	16 03		16 14	16 17	16 27	16 30	16 33	16 44	16 48
Seven Sisters ⊖	d																						
Clapton	d																						
Stratford 7 ⊖	a	15 07						15 37					16 07						16 37				
Hackney Downs	d					15 20					15 50						16 20					16 50	
Bethnal Green	d																						
London Liverpool Street 15 ⊖	a		15 13	15 16		15 28	15 31		15 44	15 47	15 58	16 01		16 13	16 16		16 28	16 31		16 44	16 47	16 58	17 01

Cambridge, Stansted Airport, Bishops Stortford, Hertford East and Broxbourne - London

Network Diagram - see first Page of Table 20

		LE 1	LE 1	LE 1 bus	XC ◇1	LE 1	LE 1 bus	LE 1	LE 1	LE 1 bus	LE 1	LE 1 bus	LE 1	LE 1	LE 1 bus	XC ◇1	LE 1	LE 1 bus	LE 1	LE 1	LE 1 bus	LE 1	LE 1 bus
Cambridge	d		16 04		16 10				16 21					17 04		17 10				17 21			
Shelford	d								16 26											17 26			
Whittlesford Parkway	d		16 11						16 30					17 11						17 30			
Great Chesterford	d								16 34											17 34			
Audley End	d		16 19		16 24				16 40					17 19		17 24				17 40			
Newport Essex	d								16 43											17 43			
Elsenham	d								16 49											17 49			
Stansted Airport	a				16 40											17 40							
Stansted Airport	d			16 30			16 45			17 00		17 15			17 30			17 45			18 00		18 15
Stansted Mountfitchet	d								16 52			17 21								17 52			18 21
Bishops Stortford	a		16 32	16 39					16 58	17 09				17 32	17 39					17 58	18 09		
	d	16 15	16 32	16 39				16 47	16 58	17 09			17 15	17 32	17 39				17 47	17 58	18 09		
Sawbridgeworth	d	16 20						16 52	17 03				17 20						17 52	18 03			
Harlow Mill	d	16 23							17 06				17 23							18 06			
Harlow Town	d	16 26	16 40				17 00	17 05	17 09			17 32	17 26	17 40				18 00	18 05	18 09			18 32
Roydon	d	16 30							17 13				17 30							18 13			
Hertford East	d					16 39					17 09						17 39					18 09	
Ware	d					16 43					17 13						17 43					18 13	
St Margarets (Herts)	d					16 47					17 17						17 47					18 17	
Rye House	d					16 50					17 20						17 50					18 20	
Broxbourne 3	a	16 35	16 46			16 54		17 11	17 17		17 24		17 35	17 46			17 54		18 11	18 17		18 24	
Broxbourne 3	d	16 39	16 46			16 54		17 12	17 17		17 24		17 39	17 46			17 54		18 12	18 17		18 24	
Cheshunt	d	16 43	16 50			16 58		17 16	17 21		17 28		17 43	17 50			17 58		18 16	18 21		18 28	
Waltham Cross	d					17 01		17 19			17 31						18 01		18 19			18 31	
Enfield Lock	d	16 47				17 03					17 33		17 47				18 03					18 33	
Brimsdown	d					17 06					17 36						18 06					18 36	
Ponders End	d					17 08					17 38						18 08					18 38	
Angel Road	d																						
Northumberland Park	d	16 52											17 52										
Tottenham Hale ⊖	d	16 56	17 00	17 03		17 14	17 17	17 27	17 30	17 33	17 44	17 48	17 56	18 00	18 03		18 14	18 17	18 27	18 30	18 33	18 44	18 48
Seven Sisters ⊖	d																						
Clapton	d																						
Stratford 7 ⊖	a	17 07						17 37					18 07						18 37				
Hackney Downs	d					17 20					17 50						18 20					18 50	
Bethnal Green	d																						
London Liverpool Street 15 ⊖	a		17 13	17 16		17 28	17 31		17 44	17 47	17 58	18 01		18 13	18 16		18 28	18 31		18 44	18 47	18 58	19 01

		LE 1	LE 1	LE 1 bus	LE 1	LE 1 bus	XC ◇1	LE 1	LE 1	LE 1 bus	LE 1	LE 1 bus	LE 1	LE 1	LE 1 bus	XC ◇1	LE 1	LE 1 bus	LE 1	LE 1	LE 1 bus	LE 1
Cambridge	d		18 04				18 18		18 21					19 04		19 10				19 21		
Shelford	d								18 26											19 26		
Whittlesford Parkway	d		18 11						18 30					19 11						19 30		
Great Chesterford	d								18 34											19 34		
Audley End	d		18 19				18 34		18 40					19 19		19 25				19 40		
Newport Essex	d								18 43											19 43		
Elsenham	d								18 49											19 49		
Stansted Airport	a						18 53									19 40						
Stansted Airport	d			18 30		18 45				19 00		19 15			19 30			19 45			20 00	
Stansted Mountfitchet	d								18 52			19 21								19 52		
Bishops Stortford	a		18 32	18 39					18 58	19 09				19 32	19 39					19 58	20 09	
	d	18 15	18 32	18 39				18 47	18 58	19 09			19 15	19 32	19 39				19 47	19 58	20 09	
Sawbridgeworth	d	18 20						18 52	19 03				19 20						19 52	20 03		
Harlow Mill	d	18 23							19 06				19 23							20 06		
Harlow Town	d	18 26	18 40			19 00		19 05	19 09			19 32	19 26	19 40				20 00	20 05	20 09		
Roydon	d	18 30							19 13				19 30							20 13		
Hertford East	d				18 39						19 09						19 39					20 09
Ware	d				18 43						19 13						19 43					20 13
St Margarets (Herts)	d				18 47						19 17						19 47					20 17
Rye House	d				18 50						19 20						19 50					20 20
Broxbourne 3	a	18 35	18 46		18 54			19 11	19 17		19 24		19 35	19 46			19 54		20 11	20 17		20 24
Broxbourne 3	d	18 39	18 46		18 54			19 12	19 17		19 24		19 39	19 46			19 54		20 12	20 17		20 24
Cheshunt	d	18 43	18 50		18 58			19 16	19 21		19 28		19 43	19 50			19 58		20 16	20 21		20 28
Waltham Cross	d				19 01			19 19			19 31						20 01		20 19			20 31
Enfield Lock	d	18 47			19 03						19 33		19 47				20 03					20 33
Brimsdown	d				19 06						19 36						20 06					20 36
Ponders End	d				19 08						19 38						20 08					20 38
Angel Road	d																					
Northumberland Park	d	18 52											19 52									
Tottenham Hale ⊖	d	18 56	19 00	19 03	19 14	19 17		19 27	19 30	19 33	19 44	19 48	19 56	20 00	20 03		20 14	20 17	20 27	20 30	20 33	20 44
Seven Sisters ⊖	d																					
Clapton	d																					
Stratford 7 ⊖	a	19 07						19 37					20 07						20 37			
Hackney Downs	d				19 20						19 50						20 20					20 50
Bethnal Green	d																					
London Liverpool Street 15 ⊖	a		19 13	19 16	19 28	19 31			19 44	19 47	19 58	20 01		20 13	20 16		20 28	20 31		20 44	20 47	20 58

1 September to 8 September

Cambridge, Stansted Airport, Bishops Stortford, Hertford East and Broxbourne - London

Network Diagram - see first Page of Table 20

		LE ■ ⌶	LE ■	LE ■	LE ■ ⌶	XC ◇■	LE ■	LE ■ ⌶	LE ■	LE ■	LE ■ ⌶	LE ■	LE ■ ⌶	LE ■	LE ■	LE ■ ⌶	XC ◇■	LE ■	LE ■ ⌶	LE ■	LE ■	LE ■	LE ■
Cambridge	d			20 04		20 10				20 21					21 04		21 10				21 21		
Shelford	d									20 26											21 26		
Whittlesford Parkway	d			20 11						20 30					21 11						21 30		
Great Chesterford	d									20 34											21 34		
Audley End	d			20 19		20 24				20 40					21 19		21 24				21 40		
Newport (Essex)	d									20 43											21 43		
Elsenham	d									20 49											21 49		
Stansted Airport	a					20 40											21 40						
Stansted Airport	d	20 15			20 30			20 45			21 00		21 15			21 30			21 45			22 00	
Stansted Mountfitchet	d	20 21								20 52			21 21								21 52		
Bishops Stortford	a			20 32	20 39					20 58	21 09				21 32	21 39					21 58	22 09	
	d		20 15	20 32	20 39				20 47	20 58	21 09			21 15	21 32	21 39				21 47	21 58	22 09	
Sawbridgeworth	d		20 20						20 52	21 03				21 20						21 52	22 03		
Harlow Mill	d		20 23							21 06				21 23							22 06		
Harlow Town	d	20 32	20 26	20 40				21 00	21 05	21 09			21 32	21 26	21 40				22 00	22 05	22 09		
Roydon	d		20 30							21 13				21 30							22 13		
Hertford East	d						20 39					21 09						21 39					22 09
Ware	d						20 43					21 13						21 43					22 13
St Margarets (Herts)	d						20 47					21 17						21 47					22 17
Rye House	d						20 50					21 20						21 50					22 20
Broxbourne 3	a		20 35	20 46			20 54		21 11	21 17		21 24		21 35	21 46			21 54		22 11	22 17		22 24
Broxbourne 3	d		20 39	20 46			20 54		21 12	21 17		21 24		21 39	21 46			21 54		22 12	22 17		22 24
Cheshunt	d		20 43	20 50			20 58		21 16	21 21		21 28		21 43	21 50			21 58		22 16	22 21		22 28
Waltham Cross	d						21 01		21 19			21 31						22 01		22 19			22 31
Enfield Lock	d		20 47				21 03					21 33		21 47				22 03					22 33
Brimsdown	d						21 06					21 36						22 06					22 36
Ponders End	d						21 08					21 38						22 08					22 38
Angel Road	d																						
Northumberland Park	d		20 52											21 52									
Tottenham Hale ⊖	d	20 48	20 56	21 00	21 03		21 14	21 17	21 27	21 30	21 33	21 44	21 48	21 56	22 00	22 03		22 14	22 17	22 27	22 30	22 33	22 44
Seven Sisters ⊖	d																						
Clapton	d																						
Stratford 7 ⊖	a		21 07									21 55						22 25					22 55
Hackney Downs	d						21 20																
Bethnal Green	d																						
London Liverpool Street 15 ⊖	a	21 01		21 13	21 16		21 28	21 31	21 42	21 44	21 47		22 01	22 12	22 14	22 16			22 31	22 42	22 44	22 47	

		LE ■	LE ■	LE ■	LE ■	XC ◇■	LE ■	LE ■	LE ■	LE ■	LE ■	LE ■	LE ■	LE ■	LE ■	LE ■	LE ■
Cambridge	d			22 04		22 10			22 21				22 51				
Shelford	d								22 26				22 56				
Whittlesford Parkway	d			22 11					22 30				23 00				
Great Chesterford	d								22 34				23 04				
Audley End	d			22 19		22 24			22 40				23 10				
Newport (Essex)	d								22 43				23 13				
Elsenham	d								22 49				23 19				
Stansted Airport	a					22 42											
Stansted Airport	d	22 15			22 30			22 45		23 00		23 15		23 30		23 45	23 59
Stansted Mountfitchet	d	22 21							22 52			23 21	23 22				
Bishops Stortford	a			22 32	22 39				22 58	23 09			23 28	23 39			00 08
	d		22 15	22 32	22 39				23 01	23 09			23 28	23 39			00 08
Sawbridgeworth	d		22 20						23 05				23 32				
Harlow Mill	d		22 23						23 09				23 36				
Harlow Town	d	22 32	22 26	22 40				23 00	23 12			23 32	23 39			23 59	00 16
Roydon	d		22 30						23 16				23 43				
Hertford East	d						22 39				23 09				23 39		
Ware	d						22 43				23 13				23 43		
St Margarets (Herts)	d						22 47				23 17				23 47		
Rye House	d						22 50				23 20				23 50		
Broxbourne 3	a		22 35	22 46			22 54		23 20		23 24		23 47		23 54		
Broxbourne 3	d		22 39	22 46			22 54		23 20		23 24		23 47		23 54		
Cheshunt	d		22 43	22 50			22 58		23 24		23 28		23 51		23 58		
Waltham Cross	d						23 01				23 31				00 01		
Enfield Lock	d		22 47				23 03				23 33				00 03		
Brimsdown	d						23 06				23 36				00 06		
Ponders End	d						23 08				23 38				00 08		
Angel Road	d																
Northumberland Park	d		22 52														
Tottenham Hale ⊖	d	22 48	22 56	23 00	23 03		23 14	23 17	23 33	23 33	23 44	23 48	23 59	00 03	00 14	00 17	
Seven Sisters ⊖	d																
Clapton	d																
Stratford 7 ⊖	a						23 25				23 55						
Hackney Downs	d														00 20		
Bethnal Green	d																
London Liverpool Street 15 ⊖	a	23 01	23 12	23 14	23 16			23 31	23 47	23 47		00 01	00 13	00 16	00 28	00 32	00 51

from 15 September

Cambridge, Stansted Airport, Bishops Stortford, Hertford East and Broxbourne - London

Network Diagram - see first Page of Table 20

		LE ■	LE ■	LE ■	LE ■	LE ■	LE ■	LE ■	LE ■	LE ■	LE ■	XC ■	LE ■	LE ■	LE ■	LE ■	LE ■	LE ■ ⌶	XC ■	LE ■	LE ■ ⌶	LE ■	LE ■
Cambridge	d		22p51									04 56					05 21		05 42				06 04
Shelford	d		22p56														05 26						
Whittlesford Parkway	d		23p00														05 30						06 11
Great Chesterford	d		23p04														05 34						
Audley End	d		23p10														05 40		05 56				06 19
Newport (Essex)	d		23p13														05 43						
Elsenham	d		23p19														05 49						
Stansted Airport	a											05 20							06 08				
Stansted Airport	d	23p15		23p30		23p45		23p59	00 30	01 00	01 30			05 30				06 00			06 15		
Stansted Mountfitchet	d	23p21	23p24														05 52				06 21		
Bishops Stortford	a		23p29	23p39				00 08	00 39					05 39			05 58	06 09					06 32
	d		23p29	23p39				00 08	00 39				05 15	05 39		05 47	05 58	06 09				06 15	06 32
Sawbridgeworth	d		23p33										05 20			05 52	06 03					06 20	
Harlow Mill	d		23p37										05 23				06 06					06 23	
Harlow Town	d	23p32	23p40			23p59		00 16	00 47				05 26			06 05	06 09				06 32	06 26	06 40
Roydon	d		23p44										05 30				06 13					06 30	
Hertford East	d				23p39		00 07													06 09			
Ware	d				23p43															06 13			
St Margarets (Herts)	d				23p47															06 17			
Rye House	d				23p50															06 20			
Broxbourne 3	a		23p48		23p54		00 19						05 34			06 11	06 17			06 24		06 35	06 46
Broxbourne 3	d		23p48		23p54		00 19						05 34		05 54	06 12	06 17			06 24		06 39	06 46
Cheshunt	d		23p52		23p58								05 38		05 58	06 16	06 21			06 28		06 43	06 50
Waltham Cross	d												05 41		06 01	06 19				06 31			
Enfield Lock	d												05 43		06 03					06 33		06 47	
Brimsdown	d												05 46		06 06					06 36			
Ponders End	d												05 48		06 08					06 38			
Angel Road	d																						
Northumberland Park	d												05 52									06 52	
Tottenham Hale ⊖	d	23p48											05 55	06 01	06 14	06 27	06 30	06 33		06 44	06 48	06 56	07 00
Seven Sisters ⊖	d		00 04	00 08	00 11	00 21																	
Clapton	d																						
Stratford 7 ⊖	a												06 05			06 37						07 07	
Hackney Downs	d				00 16		00 41								06 20					06 50			
Bethnal Green	d																						
London Liverpool Street 15 ⊖	a	00 01	00 18	00 22	00 26	00 36	00 49	00 51	01 21	01 50	02 20		06 14	06 14	06 28		06 44	06 47		06 58	07 01		07 13

		LE ■ ⌶	LE ■	LE ■ ⌶	LE ■	LE ■	LE ■ ⌶	XC ■	LE ■	LE ■ ⌶	LE ■	LE ■	LE ■ ⌶	LE ■	LE ■ ⌶	LE ■	LE ■	LE ■ ⌶	XC ■	LE ■	LE ■ ⌶	LE ■	LE ■
Cambridge	d					06 21		06 40				07 04					07 21		07 40				08 04
Shelford	d					06 26											07 26						
Whittlesford Parkway	d					06 30						07 11					07 30						08 11
Great Chesterford	d					06 34											07 34						
Audley End	d					06 40		06 54				07 19					07 40		07 54				08 19
Newport (Essex)	d					06 43											07 43						
Elsenham	d					06 49											07 49						
Stansted Airport	a							07 09											08 08				
Stansted Airport	d	06 30		06 45			07 00			07 15			07 30		07 45			08 00			08 15		
Stansted Mountfitchet	d					06 52				07 21							07 52				08 21		
Bishops Stortford	a	06 39				06 58	07 09					07 32	07 39				07 58	08 09					08 32
	d	06 39			06 47	06 58	07 09				07 15	07 32	07 39			07 47	07 58	08 09				08 15	08 32
Sawbridgeworth	d				06 52	07 03					07 20					07 52	08 03					08 20	
Harlow Mill	d					07 06					07 23						08 06					08 23	
Harlow Town	d			07 00	07 05	07 09				07 32	07 26	07 40			08 00	08 05	08 09				08 32	08 26	08 40
Roydon	d					07 13					07 30						08 13					08 30	
Hertford East	d		06 39						07 09					07 39						08 09			
Ware	d		06 43						07 13					07 43						08 13			
St Margarets (Herts)	d		06 47						07 17					07 47						08 17			
Rye House	d		06 50						07 20					07 50						08 20			
Broxbourne 3	a		06 54		07 11	07 17			07 24		07 35	07 46		07 54		08 11	08 17			08 24		08 35	08 46
Broxbourne 3	d		06 54		07 12	07 17			07 24		07 39	07 46		07 54		08 12	08 17			08 24		08 39	08 46
Cheshunt	d		06 58		07 16	07 21			07 28		07 43	07 50		07 58		08 16	08 21			08 28		08 43	08 50
Waltham Cross	d		07 01		07 19				07 31					08 01		08 19				08 31			
Enfield Lock	d		07 03						07 33		07 47			08 03						08 33		08 47	
Brimsdown	d		07 06						07 36					08 06						08 36			
Ponders End	d		07 08						07 38					08 08						08 38			
Angel Road	d																						
Northumberland Park	d										07 52											08 52	
Tottenham Hale ⊖	d	07 03	07 14	07 17	07 27	07 30	07 33		07 44	07 48	07 56	08 00	08 03	08 14	08 17	08 27	08 30	08 33		08 44	08 48	08 56	09 00
Seven Sisters ⊖	d																						
Clapton	d																						
Stratford 7 ⊖	a				07 37						08 07					08 37						09 07	
Hackney Downs	d		07 20						07 50					08 20						08 50			
Bethnal Green	d																						
London Liverpool Street 15 ⊖	a	07 16	07 28	07 31		07 44	07 47		07 58	08 01		08 13	08 16	08 28	08 31		08 44	08 47		08 58	09 01		09 13

Saturdays
from 15 September

Cambridge, Stansted Airport, Bishops Stortford, Hertford East and Broxbourne - London

Network Diagram - see first Page of Table 20

	LE 1 ⚲	XC ◇1	LE 1	LE 1 ⚲	LE 1	LE 1	LE 1 ⚲	LE 1	LE 1 ⚲	LE 1	LE 1	LE 1 ⚲	XC ◇1	LE 1	LE 1 ⚲	LE 1	LE 1	LE 1 ⚲	LE 1	LE 1 ⚲	LE 1
Cambridge d		08 10				08 21					09 04		09 10				09 21				
Shelford d						08 26											09 26				
Whittlesford Parkway d						08 30					09 11						09 30				
Great Chesterford d						08 34											09 34				
Audley End d		08 24				08 40					09 19		09 24				09 40				
Newport (Essex) d						08 43											09 43				
Elsenham d						08 49											09 49				
Stansted Airport a		08 39											09 40								
Stansted Airport d	08 30			08 45			09 00		09 15			09 30			09 45			10 00		10 15	
Stansted Mountfitchet d						08 52			09 21								09 52			10 21	
Bishops Stortford a	08 39					08 58	09 09				09 32	09 39					09 58	10 09			
d	08 39				08 47	08 58	09 09			09 15	09 32	09 39				09 47	09 58	10 09			10 15
Sawbridgeworth d					08 52	09 03				09 20						09 52	10 03				10 20
Harlow Mill d						09 06				09 23							10 06				10 23
Harlow Town d				09 00	09 05	09 09			09 32	09 26	09 40				10 00	10 05	10 09			10 32	10 26
Roydon d						09 13				09 30							10 13				10 30
Hertford East d			08 39					09 09						09 39					10 09		
Ware d			08 43					09 13						09 43					10 13		
St Margarets (Herts) d			08 47					09 17						09 47					10 17		
Rye House d			08 50					09 20						09 50					10 20		
Broxbourne a			08 54		09 11	09 17		09 24		09 35	09 46			09 54		10 11	10 17		10 24		10 35
Broxbourne d			08 54		09 12	09 17		09 24		09 39	09 46			09 54		10 12	10 17		10 24		10 39
Cheshunt d			08 58		09 16	09 21		09 28		09 43	09 50			09 58		10 16	10 21		10 28		10 43
Waltham Cross d			09 01		09 19			09 31						10 01		10 19			10 31		
Enfield Lock d			09 03					09 33		09 47				10 03					10 33		10 47
Brimsdown d			09 06					09 36						10 06					10 36		
Ponders End d			09 08					09 38						10 08					10 38		
Angel Road d																					
Northumberland Park d										09 52											10 52
Tottenham Hale ⊖ d	09 03		09 14	09 17	09 27	09 30	09 33	09 44	09 48	09 56	10 00	10 03		10 14	10 17	10 27	10 30	10 33	10 44	10 48	10 56
Seven Sisters ⊖ d																					
Clapton d																					
Stratford ⊖ a					09 37					10 07						10 37					11 07
Hackney Downs d			09 20					09 50						10 20					10 50		
Bethnal Green d																					
London Liverpool Street ⊖ a	09 16		09 28	09 31		09 44	09 47	09 58	10 01		10 13	10 16		10 28	10 31		10 44	10 47	10 58	11 01	

	LE 1	LE 1 ⚲	XC ◇1	LE 1	LE 1 ⚲	LE 1	LE 1	LE 1 ⚲	LE 1	LE 1 ⚲	LE 1	LE 1	LE 1 ⚲	XC ◇1	LE 1	LE 1 ⚲	LE 1	LE 1	LE 1 ⚲	LE 1	LE 1 ⚲	LE 1
Cambridge d	10 04		10 10				10 21					11 04		11 10				11 21				
Shelford d							10 26											11 26				
Whittlesford Parkway d	10 11						10 30					11 11						11 30				
Great Chesterford d							10 34											11 34				
Audley End d	10 19		10 24				10 40					11 19		11 24				11 40				
Newport (Essex) d							10 43											11 43				
Elsenham d							10 49											11 49				
Stansted Airport a			10 40											11 40								
Stansted Airport d		10 30			10 45			11 00		11 15			11 30			11 45			12 00		12 15	
Stansted Mountfitchet d							10 52			11 21								11 52			12 21	
Bishops Stortford a	10 32	10 39					10 58	11 09				11 32	11 39					11 58	12 09			
d	10 32	10 39				10 47	10 58	11 09			11 15	11 32	11 39				11 47	11 58	12 09			12 15
Sawbridgeworth d						10 52	11 03				11 20						11 52	12 03				12 20
Harlow Mill d							11 06				11 23							12 06				12 23
Harlow Town d	10 40				11 00	11 05	11 09			11 32	11 26	11 40				12 00	12 05	12 09			12 32	12 26
Roydon d							11 13				11 30							12 13				12 30
Hertford East d				10 39					11 09						11 39					12 09		
Ware d				10 43					11 13						11 43					12 13		
St Margarets (Herts) d				10 47					11 17						11 47					12 17		
Rye House d				10 50					11 20						11 50					12 20		
Broxbourne a	10 46			10 54		11 11	11 17		11 24		11 35	11 46			11 54		12 11	12 17		12 24		12 35
Broxbourne d	10 46			10 54		11 12	11 17		11 24		11 39	11 46			11 54		12 12	12 17		12 24		12 39
Cheshunt d	10 50			10 58		11 16	11 21		11 28		11 43	11 50			11 58		12 16	12 21		12 28		12 43
Waltham Cross d				11 01		11 19			11 31						12 01		12 19			12 31		
Enfield Lock d				11 03					11 33		11 47				12 03					12 33		12 47
Brimsdown d				11 06					11 36						12 06					12 36		
Ponders End d				11 08					11 38						12 08					12 38		
Angel Road d																						
Northumberland Park d											11 52											12 52
Tottenham Hale ⊖ d	11 00	11 03		11 14	11 17	11 27	11 30	11 33	11 44	11 48	11 56	12 00	12 03		12 14	12 17	12 27	12 30	12 33	12 44	12 48	12 56
Seven Sisters ⊖ d																						
Clapton d																						
Stratford ⊖ a						11 37					12 07						12 37					13 07
Hackney Downs d				11 20					11 50						12 20					12 50		
Bethnal Green d																						
London Liverpool Street ⊖ a	11 13	11 16		11 28	11 31		11 44	11 47	11 58	12 01		12 13	12 16		12 28	12 31		12 44	12 47	12 58	13 01	

Saturdays
from 15 September

Cambridge, Stansted Airport, Bishops Stortford, Hertford East and Broxbourne - London

Network Diagram - see first Page of Table 20

	LE 1	LE 1 ⚲	XC ◇1	LE 1	LE 1 ⚲	LE 1	LE 1	LE 1 ⚲	LE 1	LE 1 ⚲	LE 1	LE 1	LE 1 ⚲	XC ◇1	LE 1	LE 1 ⚲	LE 1	LE 1	LE 1 ⚲	LE 1	LE 1 ⚲
Cambridge d	12 04		12 10				12 21					13 04		13 10				13 21			
Shelford d							12 26											13 26			
Whittlesford Parkway d	12 11						12 30					13 11						13 30			
Great Chesterford d							12 34											13 34			
Audley End d	12 19		12 24				12 40					13 19		13 24				13 40			
Newport (Essex) d							12 43											13 43			
Elsenham d							12 49											13 49			
Stansted Airport a			12 40											13 40							
Stansted Airport d		12 30			12 45			13 00		13 15			13 30			13 45			14 00		14 15
Stansted Mountfitchet d							12 52			13 21								13 52			14 21
Bishops Stortford a	12 32	12 39					12 58	13 09				13 32	13 39					13 58	14 09		
d	12 32	12 39				12 47	12 58	13 09			13 15	13 32	13 39				13 47	13 58	14 09		
Sawbridgeworth d						12 52	13 03				13 20						13 52	14 03			
Harlow Mill d							13 06				13 23							14 06			
Harlow Town d	12 40				13 00	13 05	13 09			13 32	13 26	13 40				14 00	14 05	14 09			14 32
Roydon d							13 13				13 30							14 13			
Hertford East d				12 39					13 09						13 39					14 09	
Ware d				12 43					13 13						13 43					14 13	
St Margarets (Herts) d				12 47					13 17						13 47					14 17	
Rye House d				12 50					13 20						13 50					14 20	
Broxbourne a	12 46			12 54		13 11	13 17		13 24		13 35	13 46			13 54		14 11	14 17		14 24	
Broxbourne d	12 46			12 54		13 12	13 17		13 24		13 39	13 46			13 54		14 12	14 17		14 24	
Cheshunt d	12 50			12 58		13 16	13 21		13 28		13 43	13 50			13 58		14 16	14 21		14 28	
Waltham Cross d				13 01		13 19			13 31						14 01		14 19			14 31	
Enfield Lock d				13 03					13 33		13 47				14 03					14 33	
Brimsdown d				13 06					13 36						14 06					14 36	
Ponders End d				13 08					13 38						14 08					14 38	
Angel Road d																					
Northumberland Park d											13 52										
Tottenham Hale ⊖ d	13 00	13 03		13 14	13 17	13 27	13 30	13 33	13 44	13 48	13 56	14 00	14 03		14 14	14 17	14 27	14 30	14 33	14 44	14 48
Seven Sisters ⊖ d																					
Clapton d																					
Stratford ⊖ a						13 37					14 07						14 37				
Hackney Downs d				13 20					13 50						14 20					14 50	
Bethnal Green d																					
London Liverpool Street ⊖ a	13 13	13 16		13 28	13 31		13 44	13 47	13 58	14 01		14 13	14 16		14 28	14 31		14 44	14 47	14 58	15 01

	LE 1	LE 1	LE 1 ⚲	XC ◇1	LE 1	LE 1 ⚲	LE 1	LE 1	LE 1 ⚲	LE 1	LE 1 ⚲	LE 1	LE 1	LE 1 ⚲	XC ◇1	LE 1	LE 1 ⚲	LE 1	LE 1	LE 1 ⚲	LE 1	LE 1 ⚲
Cambridge d		14 04		14 10				14 21					15 04		15 10				15 21			
Shelford d								14 26											15 26			
Whittlesford Parkway d		14 11						14 30					15 11						15 30			
Great Chesterford d								14 34											15 34			
Audley End d		14 19		14 24				14 40					15 19		15 24				15 40			
Newport (Essex) d								14 43											15 43			
Elsenham d								14 49											15 49			
Stansted Airport a				14 40											15 40							
Stansted Airport d			14 30			14 45			15 00		15 15			15 30			15 45			16 00		16 15
Stansted Mountfitchet d								14 52			15 21								15 52			16 21
Bishops Stortford a		14 32	14 39					14 58	15 09				15 32	15 39					15 58	16 09		
d	14 15	14 32	14 39				14 47	14 58	15 09			15 15	15 32	15 39				15 47	15 58	16 09		
Sawbridgeworth d	14 20						14 52	15 03				15 20						15 52	16 03			
Harlow Mill d	14 23							15 06				15 23							16 06			
Harlow Town d	14 26	14 40				15 00	15 05	15 09			15 32	15 26	15 40				16 00	16 05	16 09			16 32
Roydon d	14 30							15 13				15 30							16 13			
Hertford East d					14 39					15 09						15 39					16 09	
Ware d					14 43					15 13						15 43					16 13	
St Margarets (Herts) d					14 47					15 17						15 47					16 17	
Rye House d					14 50					15 20						15 50					16 20	
Broxbourne a	14 35	14 46			14 54		15 11	15 17		15 24		15 35	15 46			15 54		16 11	16 17		16 24	
Broxbourne d	14 39	14 46			14 54		15 12	15 17		15 24		15 39	15 46			15 54		16 12	16 17		16 24	
Cheshunt d	14 43	14 50			14 58		15 16	15 21		15 28		15 43	15 50			15 58		16 16	16 21		16 28	
Waltham Cross d					15 01		15 19			15 31						16 01		16 19			16 31	
Enfield Lock d	14 47				15 03					15 33		15 47				16 03					16 33	
Brimsdown d					15 06					15 36						16 06					16 36	
Ponders End d					15 08					15 38						16 08					16 38	
Angel Road d																						
Northumberland Park d	14 52											15 52										
Tottenham Hale ⊖ d	14 56	15 00	15 03		15 14	15 17	15 27	15 30	15 33	15 44	15 48	15 56	16 00	16 03		16 14	16 17	16 27	16 30	16 33	16 44	16 48
Seven Sisters ⊖ d																						
Clapton d																						
Stratford ⊖ a	15 07						15 37					16 07						16 37				
Hackney Downs d					15 20					15 50						16 20					16 50	
Bethnal Green d																						
London Liverpool Street ⊖ a		15 13	15 16		15 28	15 31		15 44	15 47	15 58	16 01		16 13	16 16		16 28	16 31		16 44	16 47	16 58	17 01

Cambridge, Stansted Airport, Bishops Stortford, Hertford East and Broxbourne - London

Network Diagram - see first Page of Table 20

		LE 1	LE 1	LE 1	XC ◇1	LE 1	LE 1	LE 1	LE 1	LE 1	LE 1	LE 1	LE 1	LE 1	LE 1	XC ◇1	LE 1	LE 1	LE 1	LE 1	LE 1	LE 1	LE 1
				🚌			🚌			🚌		🚌			🚌			🚌			🚌		🚌
Cambridge	d		16 04		16 10				16 21					17 04		17 10				17 21			
Shelford	d								16 26											17 26			
Whittlesford Parkway	d		16 11						16 30					17 11						17 30			
Great Chesterford	d								16 34											17 34			
Audley End	d		16 19		16 24				16 40					17 19		17 24				17 40			
Newport (Essex)	d								16 43											17 43			
Elsenham	d								16 49											17 49			
Stansted Airport	a				16 40											17 40							
Stansted Airport	d			16 30			16 45			17 00		17 15			17 30			17 45			18 00		18 15
Stansted Mountfitchet	d								16 52			17 21								17 52			18 21
Bishops Stortford	a		16 32	16 39					16 58	17 09				17 32	17 39					17 58	18 09		
	d	16 15	16 32	16 39				16 47	16 58	17 09			17 15	17 32	17 39				17 47	17 58	18 09		
Sawbridgeworth	d	16 20						16 52	17 03				17 20						17 52	18 03			
Harlow Mill	d	16 23							17 06				17 23							18 06			
Harlow Town	d	16 26	16 40				17 00	17 05	17 09			17 32	17 26	17 40				18 00	18 05	18 09			18 32
Roydon	d	16 30							17 13				17 30							18 13			
Hertford East	d					16 39					17 09						17 39					18 09	
Ware	d					16 43					17 13						17 43					18 13	
St Margarets (Herts)	d					16 47					17 17						17 47					18 17	
Rye House	d					16 50					17 20						17 50					18 20	
Broxbourne 3	a	16 35	16 46			16 54		17 11	17 17		17 24		17 35	17 46			17 54		18 11	18 17		18 24	
Broxbourne 3	d	16 39	16 46			16 54		17 12	17 17		17 24		17 39	17 46			17 54		18 12	18 17		18 24	
Cheshunt	d	16 43	16 50			16 58		17 16	17 21		17 28		17 43	17 50			17 58		18 16	18 21		18 28	
Waltham Cross	d					17 01		17 19			17 31						18 01		18 19			18 31	
Enfield Lock	d	16 47				17 03					17 33		17 47				18 03					18 33	
Brimsdown	d					17 06					17 36						18 06					18 36	
Ponders End	d					17 08					17 38						18 08					18 38	
Angel Road	d																						
Northumberland Park	d	16 52											17 52										
Tottenham Hale ⊖	d	16 56	17 00	17 03		17 14	17 17	17 27	17 30	17 33	17 44	17 48	17 56	18 00	18 03		18 14	18 17	18 27	18 30	18 33	18 44	18 48
Seven Sisters ⊖	d																						
Clapton	d																						
Stratford 7 ⊖	a	17 07						17 37					18 07						18 37				
Hackney Downs	d					17 20					17 50						18 20					18 50	
Bethnal Green	d																						
London Liverpool Street 15 ⊖	a		17 13	17 16		17 28	17 31		17 44	17 47	17 58	18 01		18 13	18 16		18 28	18 31		18 44	18 47	18 58	19 01

		LE 1	LE 1	LE 1	LE 1	LE 1	XC ◇1	LE 1	LE 1	LE 1	LE 1	LE 1	LE 1	LE 1	LE 1	XC ◇1	LE 1	LE 1	LE 1	LE 1	LE 1	LE 1
				🚌		🚌				🚌		🚌			🚌			🚌			🚌	
Cambridge	d		18 04				18 18		18 21					19 04		19 10				19 21		
Shelford	d								18 26											19 26		
Whittlesford Parkway	d		18 11						18 30					19 11						19 30		
Great Chesterford	d								18 34											19 34		
Audley End	d		18 19				18 34		18 40					19 19		19 25				19 40		
Newport (Essex)	d								18 43											19 43		
Elsenham	d								18 49											19 49		
Stansted Airport	a						18 53									19 40						
Stansted Airport	d			18 30		18 45				19 00		19 15			19 30			19 45			20 00	
Stansted Mountfitchet	d								18 52			19 21								19 52		
Bishops Stortford	a		18 32	18 39					18 58	19 09				19 32	19 39					19 58	20 09	
	d	18 15	18 32	18 39				18 47	18 58	19 09			19 15	19 32	19 39				19 47	19 58	20 09	
Sawbridgeworth	d	18 20						18 52	19 03				19 20						19 52	20 03		
Harlow Mill	d	18 23							19 06				19 23							20 06		
Harlow Town	d	18 26	18 40			19 00		19 05	19 09			19 32	19 26	19 40				20 00	20 05	20 09		
Roydon	d	18 30							19 13				19 30							20 13		
Hertford East	d				18 39						19 09						19 39					20 09
Ware	d				18 43						19 13						19 43					20 13
St Margarets (Herts)	d				18 47						19 17						19 47					20 17
Rye House	d				18 50						19 20						19 50					20 20
Broxbourne 3	a	18 35	18 46		18 54			19 11	19 17		19 24		19 35	19 46			19 54		20 11	20 17		20 24
Broxbourne 3	d	18 39	18 46		18 54			19 12	19 17		19 24		19 39	19 46			19 54		20 12	20 17		20 24
Cheshunt	d	18 43	18 50		18 58			19 16	19 21		19 28		19 43	19 50			19 58		20 16	20 21		20 28
Waltham Cross	d				19 01			19 19			19 31						20 01		20 19			20 31
Enfield Lock	d	18 47			19 03						19 33		19 47				20 03					20 33
Brimsdown	d				19 06						19 36						20 06					20 36
Ponders End	d				19 08						19 38						20 08					20 38
Angel Road	d																					
Northumberland Park	d	18 52											19 52									
Tottenham Hale ⊖	d	18 56	19 00	19 03	19 14	19 17		19 27	19 30	19 33	19 44	19 48	19 56	20 00	20 03		20 14	20 17	20 27	20 30	20 33	20 44
Seven Sisters ⊖	d																					
Clapton	d																					
Stratford 7 ⊖	a	19 07						19 37					20 07						20 37			
Hackney Downs	d				19 20						19 50						20 20					20 50
Bethnal Green	d																					
London Liverpool Street 15 ⊖	a		19 13	19 16	19 28	19 31			19 44	19 47	19 58	20 01		20 13	20 16		20 28	20 31		20 44	20 47	20 58

Cambridge, Stansted Airport, Bishops Stortford, Hertford East and Broxbourne - London

Network Diagram - see first Page of Table 20

		LE 1	LE 1	LE 1	LE 1	XC ◇1	LE 1	LE 1	LE 1	LE 1	LE 1	LE 1	LE 1	LE 1	LE 1	LE 1	XC ◇1	LE 1	LE 1	LE 1	LE 1	LE 1	LE 1
		🚌			🚌			🚌			🚌		🚌			🚌			🚌				
Cambridge	d			20 04		20 10				20 21					21 04		21 10				21 21		
Shelford	d									20 26											21 26		
Whittlesford Parkway	d			20 11						20 30					21 11						21 30		
Great Chesterford	d									20 34											21 34		
Audley End	d			20 19		20 24				20 40					21 19		21 24				21 40		
Newport (Essex)	d									20 43											21 43		
Elsenham	d									20 49											21 49		
Stansted Airport	a					20 40											21 40						
Stansted Airport	d	20 15			20 30			20 45			21 00		21 15			21 30			21 45			22 00	
Stansted Mountfitchet	d	20 21								20 52			21 21								21 52		
Bishops Stortford	a			20 32	20 39					20 58	21 09				21 32	21 39					21 58	22 09	
	d		20 15	20 32	20 39				20 47	20 58	21 09			21 15	21 32	21 39				21 47	21 58	22 09	
Sawbridgeworth	d		20 20						20 52	21 03				21 20						21 52	22 03		
Harlow Mill	d		20 23							21 06				21 23							22 06		
Harlow Town	d	20 32	20 26	20 40				21 00	21 05	21 09			21 32	21 26	21 40				22 00	22 05	22 09		
Roydon	d		20 30							21 13				21 30							22 13		
Hertford East	d						20 39					21 09						21 39					22 09
Ware	d						20 43					21 13						21 43					22 13
St Margarets (Herts)	d						20 47					21 17						21 47					22 17
Rye House	d						20 50					21 20						21 50					22 20
Broxbourne 3	a		20 35	20 46			20 54		21 11	21 17		21 24		21 35	21 46			21 54		22 11	22 17		22 24
Broxbourne 3	d		20 39	20 46			20 54		21 12	21 17		21 24		21 39	21 46			21 54		22 12	22 17		22 24
Cheshunt	d		20 43	20 50			20 58		21 16	21 21		21 28		21 43	21 50			21 58		22 16	22 21		22 28
Waltham Cross	d						21 01		21 19			21 31						22 01		22 19			22 31
Enfield Lock	d		20 47				21 03					21 33		21 47				22 03					22 33
Brimsdown	d						21 06					21 36						22 06					22 36
Ponders End	d						21 08					21 38						22 08					22 38
Angel Road	d																						
Northumberland Park	d		20 52											21 52									
Tottenham Hale ⊖	d	20 48	20 56	21 00	21 03		21 14	21 17	21 27	21 30	21 33	21 44	21 48	21 56	22 00	22 03		22 14	22 17	22 27	22 30	22 33	22 44
Seven Sisters ⊖	d																						
Clapton	d																						
Stratford 7 ⊖	a		21 07						21 37					22 07						22 37			
Hackney Downs	d						21 20					21 50						22 20					22 50
Bethnal Green	d																						
London Liverpool Street 15 ⊖	a	21 01		21 13	21 16		21 28	21 31		21 44	21 47	21 58	22 01		22 13	22 16		22 28	22 31		22 44	22 47	22 58

		LE 1	LE 1	LE 1	LE 1	XC ◇1	LE 1	LE 1	LE 1	LE 1	LE 1	LE 1	LE 1	LE 1	LE 1	LE 1	LE 1
Cambridge	d			22 04		22 10			22 21				22 51				
Shelford	d								22 26				22 56				
Whittlesford Parkway	d			22 11					22 30				23 00				
Great Chesterford	d								22 34				23 04				
Audley End	d			22 19		22 24			22 40				23 10				
Newport (Essex)	d								22 43				23 13				
Elsenham	d								22 49				23 19				
Stansted Airport	a					22 40											
Stansted Airport	d	22 15			22 30			22 45		23 00		23 15		23 30		23 45	23 59
Stansted Mountfitchet	d	22 21							22 52			23 21	23 22				
Bishops Stortford	a			22 32	22 39				22 58	23 09			23 28	23 39			00 08
	d		22 15	22 32	22 39				23 01	23 09			23 28	23 39			00 08
Sawbridgeworth	d		22 20						23 05				23 32				
Harlow Mill	d		22 23						23 09				23 36				
Harlow Town	d	22 32	22 26	22 40				23 00	23 12			23 32	23 39			23 59	00 16
Roydon	d		22 30						23 16				23 43				
Hertford East	d						22 39				23 09				23 39		
Ware	d						22 43				23 13				23 43		
St Margarets (Herts)	d						22 47				23 17				23 47		
Rye House	d						22 50				23 20				23 50		
Broxbourne 3	a		22 35	22 46			22 54		23 20		23 24		23 47		23 54		
Broxbourne 3	d		22 39	22 46			22 54		23 20		23 24		23 47		23 54		
Cheshunt	d		22 43	22 50			22 58		23 24		23 28		23 51		23 58		
Waltham Cross	d						23 01				23 31				00 01		
Enfield Lock	d		22 47				23 03				23 33				00 03		
Brimsdown	d						23 06				23 36				00 06		
Ponders End	d						23 08				23 38				00 08		
Angel Road	d																
Northumberland Park	d		22 52														
Tottenham Hale ⊖	d	22 48	22 56	23 00	23 03		23 14	23 17	23 33	23 33	23 44	23 48	23 59	00 03	00 14	00 17	
Seven Sisters ⊖	d																
Clapton	d																
Stratford 7 ⊖	a		23 07														
Hackney Downs	d						23 20				23 50				00 20		
Bethnal Green	d																
London Liverpool Street 15 ⊖	a	23 01	23 18	23 13	23 16		23 28	23 31	23 48	23 47	23 58	00 01	00 13	00 16	00 28	00 32	00 51

Table 22

Sundays until 15 July

Cambridge, Stansted Airport, Bishops Stortford, Hertford East and Broxbourne - London

Network Diagram - see first Page of Table 20

		LE ■	LE ■	LE ■	LE ■	LE ■	LE ■	LE ■	LE ■	LE ■	LE ■ ⌶	LE ■ ⌶	LE ■	LE ■ ⌶	LE ■ ⌶	LE	LE ■	LE ■ ⌶	LE ■	LE ■ ⌶	LE	LE ■	LE ■ ⌶
Cambridge	d		22p51																			07 32	
Shelford	d		22p56																				
Whittlesford Parkway	d		23p00																			07 39	
Great Chesterford	d		23p04																				
Audley End	d		23p10																			07 47	
Newport (Essex)	d		23p13																				
Elsenham	d		23p19																				
Stansted Airport	a																						
Stansted Airport	d	23p15		23p30		23p45	23p59		00 30	05 30	06 00	06 30		07 00	07 15			07 30		07 45			08 00
Stansted Mountfitchet	d	23p21	23p22																	07 51			
Bishops Stortford	a		23p28	23p39			00 08		00 39	05 39	06 09	06 39		07 09				07 39				08 00	08 09
	d		23p28	23p39			00 08		00 39	05 39	06 09	06 39	06 42	07 09			07 28	07 39				08 00	08 09
Sawbridgeworth	d		23p32										06 46				07 32					08 05	
Harlow Mill	d		23p36														07 36						
Harlow Town	d	23p32	23p39			23p59	00 16		00 47	05 47	06 17	06 47	06 51	07 17	07 30		07 39			08 02		08 10	
Roydon	d		23p43														07 43						
Hertford East	d				23p39			00 07													07 55		
Ware	d				23p43																07 59		
St Margarets (Herts)	d				23p47																08 03		
Rye House	d				23p50																08 06		
Broxbourne ■	a		23p47		23p54			00 19					06 57				07 48				08 11	08 16	
Broxbourne ■	d		23p47		23p54								06 57			07 41	07 52				08 11	08 16	
Cheshunt	d		23p51		23p58								07 01			07 45	07 57				08 15	08 20	
Waltham Cross	d				00 01								07 04				07 59						
Enfield Lock	d				00 03								07 06				08 02						
Brimsdown	d				00 06								07 09				08 04						
Ponders End	d				00 08								07 11				08 06						
Angel Road	d																						
Northumberland Park	d																		←				
Tottenham Hale ⊖	d	23p48	23p59	00 03	00 14	00 17				06 04	06 33	07 03	07 17	07 33	07 46		08 12	08 01	08 12	08 17		08 29	08 32
Seven Sisters ⊖	d															08 03	→				08 33		
Clapton	d																						
Stratford ■ ⊖	a																		08 23				
Hackney Downs	d				00 20											08 09					08 39		
Bethnal Green	d																						
London Liverpool Street ■ ⊖	a	00 01	00 13	00 16	00 28	00 32	00 51		01 21	06 18	06 46	07 16	07 30	07 46	08 01	08 18		08 15		08 31	08 48	08 43	08 46

		LE ■ ⌶	LE	LE ■	LE ■ ⌶	LE ■	LE ■ ⌶	LE	LE ■	LE ■ ⌶	LE ■ ⌶	LE	LE ■	LE ■ ⌶	LE ■	XC ■	LE ■ ⌶	LE	LE ■	LE ■ ⌶	LE ■ ⌶	LE	LE ■
Cambridge	d			07 51					08 32				08 51			09 15			09 32				09 51
Shelford	d			07 56									08 56										09 56
Whittlesford Parkway	d			08 00					08 39				09 00						09 39				10 00
Great Chesterford	d			08 04									09 04										10 04
Audley End	d			08 10					08 47				09 10			09 28			09 47				10 10
Newport (Essex)	d			08 13									09 13										10 13
Elsenham	d			08 19									09 19										10 19
Stansted Airport	a															09 45							
Stansted Airport	d	08 15			08 30		08 45			09 00	09 15			09 30			09 45			10 00	10 15		
Stansted Mountfitchet	d			08 22			08 51						09 22				09 51						10 22
Bishops Stortford	a			08 28	08 39				09 00	09 09			09 28	09 39					10 00	10 09			10 28
	d			08 28	08 39				09 00	09 09			09 28	09 39					10 00	10 09			10 28
Sawbridgeworth	d			08 32					09 05				09 32						10 05				10 32
Harlow Mill	d			08 36									09 36										10 36
Harlow Town	d	08 30		08 39			09 02		09 10		09 30		09 39				10 02		10 10		10 30		10 39
Roydon	d			08 43									09 43										10 43
Hertford East	d		08 25					08 55				09 25						09 55				10 25	
Ware	d		08 29					08 59				09 29						09 59				10 29	
St Margarets (Herts)	d		08 33					09 03				09 33						10 03				10 33	
Rye House	d		08 36					09 06				09 36						10 06				10 36	
Broxbourne ■	a		08 41	08 48				09 11	09 16			09 41	09 48					10 11	10 16			10 41	10 48
Broxbourne ■	d		08 41	08 52				09 11	09 16			09 41	09 52					10 11	10 16			10 41	10 52
Cheshunt	d		08 45	08 57				09 15	09 20			09 45	09 57					10 15	10 20			10 45	10 57
Waltham Cross	d			08 59									09 59										10 59
Enfield Lock	d			09 02									10 02										11 02
Brimsdown	d			09 04									10 04										11 04
Ponders End	d			09 06									10 06										11 06
Angel Road	d																						
Northumberland Park	d					←									←								
Tottenham Hale ⊖	d	08 46		09 12	09 01	09 12	09 17		09 29	09 32	09 46		10 12	10 01	10 12		10 17		10 29	10 32	10 46		11 12
Seven Sisters ⊖	d		09 03	→				09 33				10 03	→					10 33				11 03	→
Clapton	d																						
Stratford ■ ⊖	a					09 23									10 23								
Hackney Downs	d		09 09					09 39				10 09						10 39				11 09	
Bethnal Green	d																						
London Liverpool Street ■ ⊖	a	09 00	09 18		09 15		09 31	09 48	09 43	09 46	10 01	10 18		10 15			10 31	10 48	10 43	10 46	11 01	11 18	

Table 22

Sundays until 15 July

Cambridge, Stansted Airport, Bishops Stortford, Hertford East and Broxbourne - London

Network Diagram - see first Page of Table 20

		LE ■ ⌶	LE ■	XC ■	LE ■ ⌶	LE	LE ■	LE ■ ⌶	LE ■ ⌶	LE	LE ■	LE ■ ⌶	LE ■	XC ■	LE ■ ⌶	LE	LE ■	LE ■ ⌶	LE ■ ⌶	LE	LE ■	LE ■ ⌶
Cambridge	d			10 15			10 32				10 51			11 15			11 32				11 51	
Shelford	d										10 56										11 56	
Whittlesford Parkway	d						10 39				11 00						11 39				12 00	
Great Chesterford	d										11 04										12 04	
Audley End	d			10 28			10 47				11 10			11 28			11 47				12 10	
Newport (Essex)	d										11 13										12 13	
Elsenham	d										11 19										12 19	
Stansted Airport	a			10 45										11 45								
Stansted Airport	d	10 30			10 45			11 00	11 15			11 30			11 45			12 00	12 15			12 30
Stansted Mountfitchet	d				10 51						11 22				11 51						12 22	
Bishops Stortford	a	10 39					11 00	11 09			11 28	11 39					12 00	12 09			12 28	12 39
	d	10 39					11 00	11 09			11 28	11 39					12 00	12 09			12 28	12 39
Sawbridgeworth	d						11 05				11 32						12 05				12 32	
Harlow Mill	d										11 36										12 36	
Harlow Town	d				11 02		11 10		11 30		11 39				12 02		12 10		12 30		12 39	
Roydon	d										11 43										12 43	
Hertford East	d					10 55				11 25						11 55				12 25		
Ware	d					10 59				11 29						11 59				12 29		
St Margarets (Herts)	d					11 03				11 33						12 03				12 33		
Rye House	d					11 06				11 36						12 06				12 36		
Broxbourne ■	a					11 11	11 16			11 41	11 48					12 11	12 16			12 41	12 48	
Broxbourne ■	d					11 11	11 16			11 41	11 52					12 11	12 16			12 41	12 52	
Cheshunt	d					11 15	11 20			11 45	11 57					12 15	12 20			12 45	12 57	
Waltham Cross	d										11 59										12 59	
Enfield Lock	d										12 02										13 02	
Brimsdown	d										12 04										13 04	
Ponders End	d										12 06										13 06	
Angel Road	d																					
Northumberland Park	d		←										←									
Tottenham Hale ⊖	d	11 01	11 12		11 17		11 29	11 32	11 46		12 12	12 01	12 12		12 17		12 29	12 32	12 46		13 12	13 01
Seven Sisters ⊖	d					11 33				12 03	→					12 33				13 03	→	
Clapton	d																					
Stratford ■ ⊖	a		11 23										12 23									
Hackney Downs	d					11 39				12 09						12 39				13 09		
Bethnal Green	d																					
London Liverpool Street ■ ⊖	a	11 15			11 31	11 48	11 43	11 46	12 01	12 18		12 15			12 31	12 48	12 43	12 46	13 01	13 18		13 15

		LE ■	XC ■	LE ■ ⌶	LE	LE ■	LE ■ ⌶	LE ■ ⌶	LE	LE ■	LE ■ ⌶	LE ■	XC ■	LE ■ ⌶	LE	LE ■	LE ■ ⌶	LE ■ ⌶	LE	LE ■	LE ■ ⌶	LE ■	XC ◇■
Cambridge	d		12 15			12 32				12 51			13 15			13 32				13 51			14 10
Shelford	d									12 56										13 56			
Whittlesford Parkway	d					12 39				13 00						13 39				14 00			
Great Chesterford	d									13 04										14 04			
Audley End	d		12 28			12 47				13 10			13 28			13 47				14 10			14 24
Newport (Essex)	d									13 13										14 13			
Elsenham	d									13 19										14 19			
Stansted Airport	a		12 45										13 45										14 45
Stansted Airport	d			12 45			13 00	13 15			13 30			13 45			14 00	14 15			14 30		
Stansted Mountfitchet	d			12 51						13 22				13 51						14 22			
Bishops Stortford	a					13 00	13 09			13 28	13 39					14 00	14 09			14 28	14 39		
	d					13 00	13 09			13 28	13 39					14 00	14 09			14 28	14 39		
Sawbridgeworth	d					13 05				13 32						14 05				14 32			
Harlow Mill	d									13 36										14 36			
Harlow Town	d			13 02		13 10		13 30		13 39				14 02		14 10		14 30		14 39			
Roydon	d									13 43										14 43			
Hertford East	d				12 55				13 25						13 55				14 25				
Ware	d				12 59				13 29						13 59				14 29				
St Margarets (Herts)	d				13 03				13 33						14 03				14 33				
Rye House	d				13 06				13 36						14 06				14 36				
Broxbourne ■	a				13 11	13 16			13 41	13 48					14 11	14 16			14 41	14 48			
Broxbourne ■	d				13 11	13 16			13 41	13 52					14 11	14 16			14 41	14 52			
Cheshunt	d				13 15	13 20			13 45	13 57					14 15	14 20			14 45	14 57			
Waltham Cross	d									13 59										14 59			
Enfield Lock	d									14 02										15 02			
Brimsdown	d									14 04										15 04			
Ponders End	d									14 06										15 06			
Angel Road	d																						
Northumberland Park	d	←										←										←	
Tottenham Hale ⊖	d	13 12		13 17		13 29	13 32	13 46		14 12	14 01	14 12		14 17		14 29	14 32	14 46		15 12	15 01	15 12	
Seven Sisters ⊖	d				13 33				14 03	→					14 33				15 03	→			
Clapton	d																						
Stratford ■ ⊖	a	13 23										14 23										15 23	
Hackney Downs	d				13 39				14 09						14 39				15 09				
Bethnal Green	d																						
London Liverpool Street ■ ⊖	a			13 31	13 48	13 43	13 46	14 01	14 18		14 15			14 31	14 48	14 43	14 46	15 01	15 18		15 15		

Cambridge, Stansted Airport, Bishops Stortford, Hertford East and Broxbourne - London

Network Diagram - see first Page of Table 20

		LE 1 ⌶	LE	LE 1	LE 1 ⌶	LE 1 ⌶	LE	LE 1	LE 1 ⌶	LE 1	XC ◇1	LE 1 ⌶	LE	LE 1	LE 1 ⌶	LE 1 ⌶	LE	LE 1	LE 1 ⌶	LE 1	XC ◇1	LE 1 ⌶
Cambridge	d			14 32				14 51			15 10			15 32				15 51			16 10	
Shelford	d							14 56										15 56				
Whittlesford Parkway	d			14 39				15 00						15 39				16 00				
Great Chesterford	d							15 04										16 04				
Audley End	d			14 47				15 10			15 24			15 47				16 10			16 23	
Newport (Essex)	d							15 13										16 13				
Elsenham	d							15 19										16 19				
Stansted Airport	a										15 45										16 45	
Stansted Airport	d	14 45			15 00	15 15			15 30			15 45			16 00	16 15			16 30			16 45
Stansted Mountfitchet	d	14 51						15 22				15 51						16 22				16 51
Bishops Stortford	a			15 00	15 09			15 28	15 39					16 00	16 09			16 28	16 39			
	d			15 00	15 09			15 28	15 39					16 00	16 09			16 28	16 39			
Sawbridgeworth	d			15 05				15 32						16 05				16 32				
Harlow Mill	d							15 36										16 36				
Harlow Town	d	15 02		15 10		15 30		15 39				16 02		16 10		16 30		16 39				17 02
Roydon	d							15 43										16 43				
Hertford East	d		14 55				15 25						15 55				16 25					
Ware	d		14 59				15 29						15 59				16 29					
St Margarets (Herts)	d		15 03				15 33						16 03				16 33					
Rye House	d		15 06				15 36						16 06				16 36					
Broxbourne ■	a		15 11	15 16			15 41	15 48					16 11	16 16			16 41	16 48				
Broxbourne ■	d		15 11	15 16			15 41	15 52					16 11	16 16			16 41	16 52				
Cheshunt	d		15 15	15 20			15 45	15 57					16 15	16 20			16 45	16 57				
Waltham Cross	d							15 59										16 59				
Enfield Lock	d							16 02										17 02				
Brimsdown	d							16 04										17 04				
Ponders End	d							16 06										17 06				
Angel Road	d																					
Northumberland Park	d									←										←		
Tottenham Hale ⊖	d	15 17		15 29	15 32	15 46		16 12	16 01	16 12		16 17		16 29	16 32	16 46		17 12	17 01	17 12		17 17
Seven Sisters ⊖	d		15 33				16 03	→					16 33				17 03	→				
Clapton	d																					
Stratford ■ ⊖	a									16 23										17 23		
Hackney Downs	d		15 39				16 09						16 39				17 09					
Bethnal Green	d																					
London Liverpool Street 15 ⊖	a	15 31	15 48	15 43	15 46	16 01	16 18		16 15			16 31	16 48	16 43	16 46	17 01	17 18		17 15			17 31

		LE	LE 1	LE 1 ⌶	LE 1 ⌶	LE	LE 1	LE 1 ⌶	LE 1	XC ◇1	LE 1 ⌶	LE	LE 1	LE 1 ⌶	LE 1 ⌶	LE	LE 1	LE 1 ⌶	LE 1	XC ◇1	LE 1 ⌶	LE	LE 1
Cambridge	d		16 32				16 51			17 10			17 32				17 51			18 10			18 32
Shelford	d						16 56										17 56						
Whittlesford Parkway	d		16 39				17 00						17 39				18 00						18 39
Great Chesterford	d						17 04										18 04						
Audley End	d		16 47				17 10			17 24			17 47				18 10			18 24			18 47
Newport (Essex)	d						17 13										18 13						
Elsenham	d						17 19										18 19						
Stansted Airport	a									17 45										18 45			
Stansted Airport	d			17 00	17 15			17 30			17 45			18 00	18 15			18 30			18 45		
Stansted Mountfitchet	d						17 22				17 51						18 22				18 51		
Bishops Stortford	a		17 00	17 09			17 28	17 39					18 00	18 09			18 28	18 39					19 00
	d		17 00	17 09			17 28	17 39					18 00	18 09			18 28	18 39					19 00
Sawbridgeworth	d		17 05				17 32						18 05				18 32						19 05
Harlow Mill	d						17 36										18 36						
Harlow Town	d		17 10		17 30		17 39				18 02		18 10		18 30		18 39				19 02		19 10
Roydon	d						17 43										18 43						
Hertford East	d	16 55				17 25						17 55				18 25						18 55	
Ware	d	16 59				17 29						17 59				18 29						18 59	
St Margarets (Herts)	d	17 03				17 33						18 03				18 33						19 03	
Rye House	d	17 06				17 36						18 06				18 36						19 06	
Broxbourne ■	a	17 11	17 16			17 41	17 48					18 11	18 16			18 41	18 48					19 11	19 16
Broxbourne ■	d	17 11	17 16			17 41	17 52					18 11	18 16			18 41	18 52					19 11	19 16
Cheshunt	d	17 15	17 20			17 45	17 57					18 15	18 20			18 45	18 57					19 15	19 20
Waltham Cross	d						17 59										18 59						
Enfield Lock	d						18 02										19 02						
Brimsdown	d						18 04										19 04						
Ponders End	d						18 06										19 06						
Angel Road	d																						
Northumberland Park	d								←										←				
Tottenham Hale ⊖	d		17 29	17 32	17 46		18 12	18 01	18 12		18 17		18 29	18 32	18 46		19 12	19 01	19 12		19 17		19 29
Seven Sisters ⊖	d	17 33				18 03	→					18 33				19 03	→					19 33	
Clapton	d																						
Stratford ■ ⊖	a								18 23										19 23				
Hackney Downs	d	17 39				18 09						18 39				19 09						19 39	
Bethnal Green	d																						
London Liverpool Street 15 ⊖	a	17 48	17 43	17 46	18 01	18 18		18 15			18 31	18 48	18 43	18 46	19 01	19 18		19 15			19 31	19 48	19 43

Cambridge, Stansted Airport, Bishops Stortford, Hertford East and Broxbourne - London

Network Diagram - see first Page of Table 20

		LE 1 ⌶	LE 1 ⌶	LE	LE 1	LE 1 ⌶	LE 1	XC ◇1	LE 1 ⌶	LE	LE 1	LE 1 ⌶	LE 1 ⌶	LE	LE 1	LE 1 ⌶	LE 1	XC ◇1	LE 1 ⌶	LE	LE 1	LE 1 ⌶	LE 1 ⌶
Cambridge	d				18 51			19 10			19 32				19 51			20 10			20 32		
Shelford	d				18 56										19 56								
Whittlesford Parkway	d				19 00						19 39				20 00						20 39		
Great Chesterford	d				19 04										20 04								
Audley End	d				19 10			19 24			19 47				20 10			20 24			20 47		
Newport (Essex)	d				19 13										20 13								
Elsenham	d				19 19										20 19								
Stansted Airport	a							19 45										20 45					
Stansted Airport	d	19 00	19 15			19 30			19 45			20 00	20 15			20 30			20 45			21 00	21 15
Stansted Mountfitchet	d				19 22				19 51						20 22				20 51				
Bishops Stortford	a	19 09			19 28	19 39					20 00	20 09			20 28	20 39					21 00	21 09	
	d	19 09			19 28	19 39					20 00	20 09			20 28	20 39					21 00	21 09	
Sawbridgeworth	d				19 32						20 05				20 32						21 05		
Harlow Mill	d				19 36										20 36								
Harlow Town	d		19 30		19 39				20 02		20 10		20 30		20 39				21 02		21 10		21 30
Roydon	d				19 43										20 43								
Hertford East	d			19 25						19 55				20 25						20 55			
Ware	d			19 29						19 59				20 29						20 59			
St Margarets (Herts)	d			19 33						20 03				20 33						21 03			
Rye House	d			19 36						20 06				20 36						21 06			
Broxbourne ■	a			19 41	19 48					20 11	20 16			20 41	20 48					21 11	21 16		
Broxbourne ■	d			19 41	19 52					20 11	20 16			20 41	20 52					21 11	21 16		
Cheshunt	d			19 45	19 57					20 15	20 20			20 45	20 57					21 15	21 20		
Waltham Cross	d				19 59										20 59								
Enfield Lock	d				20 02										21 02								
Brimsdown	d				20 04										21 04								
Ponders End	d				20 06										21 06								
Angel Road	d																						
Northumberland Park	d						←										←						
Tottenham Hale ⊖	d	19 32	19 46		20 12	20 01	20 12		20 17		20 29	20 32	20 46		21 12	21 01	21 12		21 17		21 29	21 32	21 46
Seven Sisters ⊖	d			20 03	→					20 33				21 03	→					21 33			
Clapton	d																						
Stratford ■ ⊖	a						20 23										21 23						
Hackney Downs	d			20 09						20 39				21 09						21 39			
Bethnal Green	d																						
London Liverpool Street 15 ⊖	a	19 46	20 01	20 18		20 15			20 31	20 48	20 43	20 46	21 01	21 18		21 15			21 31	21 48	21 43	21 46	22 01

		LE	LE 1	LE 1 ⌶	LE 1	XC ◇1	LE 1 ⌶	LE	LE 1	LE 1	LE 1	LE	LE 1	LE 1	LE 1	XC ◇1	LE 1	LE	LE 1	LE 1	LE 1	LE 1
Cambridge	d		20 51			21 10			21 32				21 51			22 10			22 32	22 51		
Shelford	d		20 56										21 56							22 56		
Whittlesford Parkway	d		21 00						21 39				22 00						22 39	23 00		
Great Chesterford	d		21 04										22 04							23 04		
Audley End	d		21 10			21 24			21 47				22 10			22 24			22 47	23 10		
Newport (Essex)	d		21 13										22 13							23 13		
Elsenham	d		21 19										22 19							23 19		
Stansted Airport	a					21 45										22 45						
Stansted Airport	d			21 30			21 45			22 00	22 15			22 30			22 45				23 00	23 15
Stansted Mountfitchet	d		21 22				21 51						22 22				22 51			23 22		
Bishops Stortford	a		21 28	21 39					22 00	22 09			22 28	22 39					23 00	23 28	23 09	
	d		21 28	21 39					22 00	22 09			22 28	22 39					23 00		23 09	
Sawbridgeworth	d		21 32						22 05				22 32						23 05			
Harlow Mill	d		21 36										22 36									
Harlow Town	d		21 39				22 02		22 10		22 30		22 39				23 02		23 10			23 30
Roydon	d		21 43										22 43									
Hertford East	d	21 25						21 55				22 25						22 55				
Ware	d	21 29						21 59				22 29						22 59				
St Margarets (Herts)	d	21 33						22 03				22 33						23 03				
Rye House	d	21 36						22 06				22 36						23 06				
Broxbourne ■	a	21 41	21 48					22 11	22 16			22 41	22 48					23 11	23 16			
Broxbourne ■	d	21 41	21 52					22 11	22 16			22 41	22 52					23 11	23 16			
Cheshunt	d	21 45	21 57					22 15	22 20			22 45	22 57					23 15	23 20			
Waltham Cross	d		21 59										22 59									
Enfield Lock	d		22 02										23 02									
Brimsdown	d		22 04										23 04									
Ponders End	d		22 06										23 06									
Angel Road	d																					
Northumberland Park	d				←										←							
Tottenham Hale ⊖	d		22 12	22 01	22 12		22 17		22 29	22 32	22 46		23 12	23 01	23 12		23 17		23 29		23 32	23 46
Seven Sisters ⊖	d	22 03	→					22 33				23 03	→					23 33				
Clapton	d																					
Stratford ■ ⊖	a				22 23										23 23							
Hackney Downs	d	22 09						22 39				23 09						23 39				
Bethnal Green	d																					
London Liverpool Street 15 ⊖	a	22 18		22 15			22 31	22 48	22 43	22 46	23 01	23 18		23 15			23 31	23 48	23 43		23 46	00 01

Table 22

Sundays until 15 July

Cambridge, Stansted Airport, Bishops Stortford, Hertford East and Broxbourne - London

Network Diagram - see first Page of Table 20

Station		LE ■	LE ■	LE ■
Cambridge	d			
Shelford	d			
Whittlesford Parkway	d			
Great Chesterford	d			
Audley End	d			
Newport (Essex)	d			
Elsenham	d			
Stansted Airport	a			
Stansted Airport	d	23 30	23 45	23 59
Stansted Mountfitchet	d			
Bishops Stortford	a	23 39		00 08
	d	23 39		00 08
Sawbridgeworth	d			
Harlow Mill	d			
Harlow Town	d	23 47	23 59	00 16
Roydon	d			
Hertford East	d			
Ware	d			
St Margarets (Herts)	d			
Rye House	d			
Broxbourne ■	a			
Broxbourne ■	d			
Cheshunt	d			
Waltham Cross	d			
Enfield Lock	d			
Brimsdown	d			
Ponders End	d			
Angel Road	d			
Northumberland Park	d			
Tottenham Hale ⊖	d			
Seven Sisters ⊖	d	00 08	00 21	
Clapton	d			
Stratford ■ ⊖	a			
Hackney Downs	d			
Bethnal Green	d			
London Liverpool Street ■ ⊖	a	00 22	00 35	00 51

Sundays 29 July to 12 August

Station		LE ■	LE ■	LE ■	LE ■	LE ■	LE ■	LE ■	LE ■	LE ■	LE ■	LE ■	LE ■ H	LE ■ H	LE ■	LE ■ H	LE ■ H	LE	LE ■	LE ■ H	LE ■	LE ■ H	LE ■
Cambridge	d		22p51																				07 32
Shelford	d		22p56																				
Whittlesford Parkway	d		23p00																				07 39
Great Chesterford	d		23p04																				
Audley End	d		23p10																				07 47
Newport (Essex)	d		23p13																				
Elsenham	d		23p19																				
Stansted Airport	a																						
Stansted Airport	d	23p15		23p30		23p45	23p59		00 30	01 00	01 30	05 30	06 00	06 30		07 00	07 15			07 30		07 45	
Stansted Mountfitchet	d	23p21	23p22																			07 51	
Bishops Stortford	a		23p28	23p39			00 08		00 39			05 39	06 09	06 39		07 09				07 39			08 00
	d		23p28	23p39			00 08		00 39			05 39	06 09	06 39	06 42	07 09			07 28	07 39			08 00
Sawbridgeworth	d		23p32												06 46				07 32				08 05
Harlow Mill	d		23p36																07 36				
Harlow Town	d	23p32	23p39			23p59	00 16		00 47			05 47	06 17	06 47	06 51	07 17	07 30		07 39			08 02	08 10
Roydon	d		23p43																07 43				
Hertford East	d				23p39			00 07													07 39		
Ware	d				23p43																07 43		
St Margarets (Herts)	d				23p47																07 47		
Rye House	d				23p50																07 50		
Broxbourne ■	a		23p47		23p54			00 19							06 57				07 47		07 54		08 16
Broxbourne ■	d		23p47		23p54										06 57			07 41	07 47		07 54		08 16
Cheshunt	d		23p51		23p58										07 01			07 45	07 51		07 58		08 20
Waltham Cross	d				00 01										07 04						08 01		
Enfield Lock	d				00 03										07 06						08 03		
Brimsdown	d				00 06										07 09						08 06		
Ponders End	d				00 08										07 11						08 08		
Angel Road	d																						
Northumberland Park	d																						
Tottenham Hale ⊖	d	23p48	23p59	00 03	00 14	00 17						06 04	06 33	07 03	07 17	07 33	07 46		08 00	08 03	08 14	08 17	08 29
Seven Sisters ⊖	d																	08 03					
Clapton	d																						
Stratford ■ ⊖	a																		08 11		08 25		08 40
Hackney Downs	d				00 20													08 09					
Bethnal Green	d																						
London Liverpool Street ■ ⊖	a	00 01	00 13	00 16	00 28	00 32	00 51		01 21	01 50	02 20	06 18	06 46	07 16	07 31	07 46	08 01	08 19		08 17		08 31	

Table 22

Sundays 29 July to 12 August

Cambridge, Stansted Airport, Bishops Stortford, Hertford East and Broxbourne - London

Network Diagram - see first Page of Table 20

Station		LE ■ H	LE ■	LE ■ H	LE ■	LE ■ H	LE ■	LE ■ H	LE ■	LE ■ H	LE ■	LE ■ H	LE ■	LE ■ H	XC ■	LE ■	LE ■ H	LE ■	LE ■ H	LE ■	LE ■ H	LE ■	LE ■ H
Cambridge	d				07 51				08 32				08 51		09 15			09 32				09 51	
Shelford	d				07 56								08 56									09 56	
Whittlesford Parkway	d				08 00				08 39				09 00					09 39				10 00	
Great Chesterford	d				08 04								09 04									10 04	
Audley End	d				08 10				08 47				09 10		09 28			09 47				10 10	
Newport (Essex)	d				08 13								09 13									10 13	
Elsenham	d				08 19								09 19									10 19	
Stansted Airport	a														09 45								
Stansted Airport	d	08 00		08 15		08 30		08 45		09 00		09 15		09 30			09 45		10 00		10 15		10 30
Stansted Mountfitchet	d				08 22			08 51					09 22				09 51					10 22	
Bishops Stortford	a	08 09			08 28	08 39			09 00	09 09			09 28	09 39				10 00	10 09			10 28	10 39
	d	08 09			08 28	08 39			09 00	09 09			09 28	09 39				10 00	10 09			10 28	10 39
Sawbridgeworth	d				08 32				09 05				09 32					10 05				10 32	
Harlow Mill	d				08 36								09 36									10 36	
Harlow Town	d			08 30	08 39			09 02	09 10			09 30	09 39				10 02	10 10			10 30	10 39	
Roydon	d				08 43								09 43									10 43	
Hertford East	d		08 09				08 39				09 09					09 39				10 09			
Ware	d		08 13				08 43				09 13					09 43				10 13			
St Margarets (Herts)	d		08 17				08 47				09 17					09 47				10 17			
Rye House	d		08 20				08 50				09 20					09 50				10 20			
Broxbourne ■	a		08 24		08 47		08 54		09 16		09 24		09 47			09 54		10 16		10 24		10 47	
Broxbourne ■	d		08 24		08 47		08 54		09 16		09 24		09 47			09 54		10 16		10 24		10 47	
Cheshunt	d		08 28		08 51		08 58		09 20		09 28		09 51			09 58		10 20		10 28		10 51	
Waltham Cross	d		08 31				09 01				09 31					10 01				10 31			
Enfield Lock	d		08 33				09 03				09 33					10 03				10 33			
Brimsdown	d		08 36				09 06				09 36					10 06				10 36			
Ponders End	d		08 38				09 08				09 38					10 08				10 38			
Angel Road	d																						
Northumberland Park	d																						
Tottenham Hale ⊖	d	08 32	08 44	08 47	09 00	09 03	09 14	09 17	09 29	09 32	09 44	09 47	10 00	10 03		10 14	10 17	10 29	10 32	10 44	10 47	11 00	11 03
Seven Sisters ⊖	d																						
Clapton	d																						
Stratford ■ ⊖	a		08 55		09 11		09 25		09 40		09 55		10 11			10 25		10 40		10 55		11 11	
Hackney Downs	d																						
Bethnal Green	d																						
London Liverpool Street ■ ⊖	a	08 46		09 01		09 17		09 31		09 46		10 01		10 17			10 31		10 46		11 01		11 17

Station		XC ■	LE ■	LE ■ H	LE ■	LE ■ H	LE ■	LE ■ H	LE ■	LE ■ H	XC ■	LE ■	LE ■ H	LE ■	LE ■ H	LE ■	LE ■ H	LE ■	LE ■ H	XC ■	LE ■	LE ■ H
Cambridge	d	10 15			10 32				10 51		11 15			11 32				11 51		12 15		
Shelford	d								10 56									11 56				
Whittlesford Parkway	d				10 39				11 00					11 39				12 00				
Great Chesterford	d								11 04									12 04				
Audley End	d	10 28			10 47				11 10		11 28			11 47				12 10		12 28		
Newport (Essex)	d								11 13									12 13				
Elsenham	d								11 19									12 19				
Stansted Airport	a	10 45									11 45									12 45		
Stansted Airport	d			10 45		11 00		11 15		11 30			11 45		12 00		12 15		12 30			12 45
Stansted Mountfitchet	d			10 51					11 22				11 51					12 23				12 51
Bishops Stortford	a				11 00	11 09			11 28	11 39				12 00	12 09			12 28	12 39			
	d				11 00	11 09			11 28	11 39				12 00	12 09			12 28	12 39			
Sawbridgeworth	d				11 05				11 32					12 05				12 32				
Harlow Mill	d								11 36									12 36				
Harlow Town	d			11 02	11 10			11 30	11 39				12 02	12 10			12 30	12 39				13 02
Roydon	d								11 43									12 43				
Hertford East	d		10 39				11 09					11 39				12 09					12 39	
Ware	d		10 43				11 13					11 43				12 13					12 43	
St Margarets (Herts)	d		10 47				11 17					11 47				12 17					12 47	
Rye House	d		10 50				11 20					11 50				12 20					12 50	
Broxbourne ■	a		10 54		11 16		11 24		11 47			11 54		12 16		12 24		12 47			12 54	
Broxbourne ■	d		10 54		11 16		11 24		11 47			11 54		12 16		12 24		12 47			12 54	
Cheshunt	d		10 58		11 20		11 28		11 51			11 58		12 20		12 28		12 51			12 58	
Waltham Cross	d		11 01				11 31					12 01				12 31					13 01	
Enfield Lock	d		11 03				11 33					12 03				12 33					13 03	
Brimsdown	d		11 06				11 36					12 06				12 36					13 06	
Ponders End	d		11 08				11 38					12 08				12 38					13 08	
Angel Road	d																					
Northumberland Park	d																					
Tottenham Hale ⊖	d		11 14	11 17	11 29	11 32	11 44	11 47	12 00	12 03		12 14	12 17	12 29	12 32	12 44	12 47	13 00	13 03		13 14	13 17
Seven Sisters ⊖	d																					
Clapton	d																					
Stratford ■ ⊖	a		11 25		11 40		11 55		12 11			12 25		12 40		12 55		13 11			13 25	
Hackney Downs	d																					
Bethnal Green	d																					
London Liverpool Street ■ ⊖	a			11 31		11 46		12 01		12 17			12 31		12 46		13 01		13 17			13 31

Cambridge, Stansted Airport, Bishops Stortford, Hertford East and Broxbourne - London

Network Diagram - see first Page of Table 20

	LE	LE ⌶	LE	LE ⌶	LE	LE ⌶	XC	LE	LE ⌶	LE	LE ⌶	LE	LE ⌶	LE	LE ⌶	XC ◇	LE	LE ⌶	LE	LE ⌶	LE	LE ⌶
Cambridge d	12 32				12 51		13 15			13 32				13 51		14 10			14 32			
Shelford d					12 56									13 56								
Whittlesford Parkway d	12 39				13 00					13 39				14 00					14 39			
Great Chesterford d					13 04									14 04								
Audley End d	12 47				13 10		13 28			13 47				14 10		14 24			14 47			
Newport (Essex) d					13 13									14 13								
Elsenham d					13 19									14 19								
Stansted Airport a							13 45									14 45						
Stansted Airport d		13 00		13 15		13 30			13 45		14 00		14 15		14 30			14 45		15 00		15 15
Stansted Mountfitchet d					13 23				13 51					14 23				14 51				
Bishops Stortford a	13 00	13 09			13 28	13 39				14 00	14 09			14 28	14 39				15 00	15 09		
d	13 00	13 09			13 28	13 39				14 00	14 09			14 28	14 39				15 00	15 09		
Sawbridgeworth d	13 05				13 32					14 05				14 32					15 05			
Harlow Mill d					13 36									14 36								
Harlow Town d	13 10			13 30	13 39				14 02	14 10			14 30	14 39				15 02	15 10			15 30
Roydon d					13 43									14 43								
Hertford East d			13 09					13 39				14 09					14 39				15 09	
Ware d			13 13					13 43				14 13					14 43				15 13	
St Margarets (Herts) d			13 17					13 47				14 17					14 47				15 17	
Rye House d			13 20					13 50				14 20					14 50				15 20	
Broxbourne a	13 16		13 24		13 47			13 54		14 16		14 24		14 47			14 54		15 16		15 24	
Broxbourne d	13 16		13 24		13 47			13 54		14 16		14 24		14 47			14 54		15 16		15 24	
Cheshunt d	13 20		13 28		13 51			13 58		14 20		14 28		14 51			14 58		15 20		15 28	
Waltham Cross d			13 31					14 01				14 31					15 01				15 31	
Enfield Lock d			13 33					14 03				14 33					15 03				15 33	
Brimsdown d			13 36					14 06				14 36					15 06				15 36	
Ponders End d			13 38					14 08				14 38					15 08				15 38	
Angel Road d																						
Northumberland Park d																						
Tottenham Hale ⊖ d	13 29	13 32	13 44	13 47	14 00	14 03		14 14	14 17	14 29	14 32	14 44	14 47	15 00	15 03		15 14	15 17	15 29	15 32	15 44	15 47
Seven Sisters ⊖ d																						
Clapton d																						
Stratford ⊖ a	13 40		13 55		14 11			14 25		14 40		14 55		15 11			15 25		15 40		15 55	
Hackney Downs d																						
Bethnal Green d																						
London Liverpool Street ⊖ a		13 46		14 01		14 17			14 31		14 46		15 01		15 17			15 31		15 46		16 01

	LE	LE ⌶	XC ◇	LE	LE ⌶	LE	LE ⌶	LE	LE ⌶	LE	LE ⌶	XC ◇	LE	LE ⌶	LE	LE ⌶	LE	LE ⌶	LE	LE ⌶	XC ◇
Cambridge d	14 51		15 10			15 32				15 51		16 10			16 32				16 51		17 10
Shelford d	14 56									15 56									16 56		
Whittlesford Parkway d	15 00					15 39				16 00					16 39				17 00		
Great Chesterford d	15 04									16 04									17 04		
Audley End d	15 10		15 24			15 47				16 10		16 23			16 47				17 10		17 24
Newport (Essex) d	15 13									16 13									17 13		
Elsenham d	15 19									16 19									17 19		
Stansted Airport a			15 45									16 45									17 45
Stansted Airport d		15 30			15 45		16 00		16 15		16 30			16 45		17 00		17 15		17 30	
Stansted Mountfitchet d	15 23				15 51					16 23				16 51					17 23		
Bishops Stortford a	15 28	15 39				16 00	16 09			16 28	16 39				17 00	17 09			17 28	17 39	
d	15 28	15 39				16 00	16 09			16 28	16 39				17 00	17 09			17 28	17 39	
Sawbridgeworth d	15 32					16 05				16 32					17 05				17 32		
Harlow Mill d	15 36									16 36									17 36		
Harlow Town d	15 39				16 02	16 10			16 30	16 39				17 02	17 10			17 30	17 39		
Roydon d	15 43									16 43									17 43		
Hertford East d				15 39				16 09					16 39				17 09				
Ware d				15 43				16 13					16 43				17 13				
St Margarets (Herts) d				15 47				16 17					16 47				17 17				
Rye House d				15 50				16 20					16 50				17 20				
Broxbourne a	15 47			15 54		16 16		16 24		16 47			16 54		17 16		17 24		17 47		
Broxbourne d	15 47			15 54		16 16		16 24		16 47			16 54		17 16		17 24		17 47		
Cheshunt d	15 51			15 58		16 20		16 28		16 51			16 58		17 20		17 28		17 51		
Waltham Cross d				16 01				16 31					17 01				17 31				
Enfield Lock d				16 03				16 33					17 03				17 33				
Brimsdown d				16 06				16 36					17 06				17 36				
Ponders End d				16 08				16 38					17 08				17 38				
Angel Road d																					
Northumberland Park d																					
Tottenham Hale ⊖ d	16 00	16 03		16 14	16 17	16 29	16 32	16 44	16 47	17 00	17 03		17 14	17 17	17 29	17 32	17 44	17 47	18 00	18 03	
Seven Sisters ⊖ d																					
Clapton d																					
Stratford ⊖ a	16 11			16 25		16 40		16 55		17 11			17 25		17 40		17 55		18 11		
Hackney Downs d																					
Bethnal Green d																					
London Liverpool Street ⊖ a		16 17			16 31		16 46		17 01		17 17			17 31		17 46		18 01		18 17	

Cambridge, Stansted Airport, Bishops Stortford, Hertford East and Broxbourne - London

Network Diagram - see first Page of Table 20

	LE	LE ⌶	LE	LE ⌶	LE	LE ⌶	LE	LE ⌶	XC ◇	LE	LE ⌶	LE	LE ⌶	LE	LE ⌶	LE	LE ⌶	XC ◇	LE	LE ⌶	LE	LE ⌶
Cambridge d			17 32				17 51		18 10			18 32				18 51		19 10			19 32	
Shelford d							17 56									18 56						
Whittlesford Parkway d			17 39				18 00					18 39				19 00					19 39	
Great Chesterford d							18 04									19 04						
Audley End d			17 47				18 10		18 24			18 47				19 10		19 24			19 47	
Newport (Essex) d							18 13									19 13						
Elsenham d							18 19									19 19						
Stansted Airport a									18 45									19 45				
Stansted Airport d		17 45		18 00		18 15		18 30			18 45		19 00		19 15		19 30			19 45		20 00
Stansted Mountfitchet d		17 51					18 23				18 51					19 23				19 51		
Bishops Stortford a			18 00	18 09			18 28	18 39				19 00	19 09			19 28	19 39				20 00	20 09
d			18 00	18 09			18 28	18 39				19 00	19 09			19 28	19 39				20 00	20 09
Sawbridgeworth d			18 05				18 32					19 05				19 32					20 05	
Harlow Mill d							18 36									19 36						
Harlow Town d		18 02	18 10			18 30	18 39				19 02	19 10			19 30	19 39				20 02	20 10	
Roydon d							18 43									19 43						
Hertford East d	17 39				18 09					18 39				19 09					19 39			
Ware d	17 43				18 13					18 43				19 13					19 43			
St Margarets (Herts) d	17 47				18 17					18 47				19 17					19 47			
Rye House d	17 50				18 20					18 50				19 20					19 50			
Broxbourne a	17 54		18 16		18 24		18 47			18 54		19 16		19 24		19 47			19 54		20 16	
Broxbourne d	17 54		18 16		18 24		18 47			18 54		19 16		19 24		19 47			19 54		20 16	
Cheshunt d	17 58		18 20		18 28		18 51			18 58		19 20		19 28		19 51			19 58		20 20	
Waltham Cross d	18 01				18 31					19 01				19 31					20 01			
Enfield Lock d	18 03				18 33					19 03				19 33					20 03			
Brimsdown d	18 06				18 36					19 06				19 36					20 06			
Ponders End d	18 08				18 38					19 08				19 38					20 08			
Angel Road d																						
Northumberland Park d																						
Tottenham Hale ⊖ d	18 14	18 17	18 29	18 32	18 44	18 47	19 00	19 03		19 14	19 17	19 29	19 32	19 44	19 47	20 00	20 03		20 14	20 17	20 29	20 32
Seven Sisters ⊖ d																						
Clapton d																						
Stratford ⊖ a	18 25		18 40		18 55		19 11			19 25		19 40		19 55		20 11			20 25		20 40	
Hackney Downs d																						
Bethnal Green d																						
London Liverpool Street ⊖ a		18 31		18 46		19 01		19 17			19 31		19 46		20 01		20 17			20 31		20 46

	LE	LE ⌶	LE	LE ⌶	XC ◇	LE	LE ⌶	LE	LE ⌶	LE	LE ⌶	LE	LE ⌶	XC ◇	LE	LE ⌶	LE	LE	LE	LE	LE	LE
Cambridge d			19 51		20 10			20 32				20 51		21 10			21 32				21 51	
Shelford d			19 56									20 56									21 56	
Whittlesford Parkway d			20 00					20 39				21 00					21 39				22 00	
Great Chesterford d			20 04									21 04									22 04	
Audley End d			20 10		20 24			20 47				21 10		21 24			21 47				22 10	
Newport (Essex) d			20 13									21 13									22 13	
Elsenham d			20 19									21 19									22 19	
Stansted Airport a					20 45									21 45								
Stansted Airport d		20 15		20 30			20 45		21 00		21 15		21 30			21 45		22 00		22 15		22 30
Stansted Mountfitchet d			20 23				20 51					21 23				21 51					22 22	
Bishops Stortford a			20 28	20 39				21 00	21 09			21 28	21 39				22 00	22 09			22 28	22 39
d			20 28	20 39				21 00	21 09			21 28	21 39				22 00	22 09			22 28	22 39
Sawbridgeworth d			20 32					21 05				21 32					22 05				22 32	
Harlow Mill d			20 36									21 36									22 36	
Harlow Town d		20 30	20 39				21 02	21 10			21 30	21 39				22 02	22 10			22 30	22 39	
Roydon d			20 43									21 43									22 43	
Hertford East d	20 09					20 39				21 09					21 39				22 09			
Ware d	20 13					20 43				21 13					21 43				22 13			
St Margarets (Herts) d	20 17					20 47				21 17					21 47				22 17			
Rye House d	20 20					20 50				21 20					21 50				22 20			
Broxbourne a	20 24		20 47			20 54		21 16		21 24		21 47			21 54		22 16		22 24		22 47	
Broxbourne d	20 24		20 47			20 54		21 16		21 24		21 47			21 54		22 16		22 24		22 47	
Cheshunt d	20 28		20 51			20 58		21 20		21 28		21 51			21 58		22 20		22 28		22 51	
Waltham Cross d	20 31					21 01				21 31					22 01				22 31			
Enfield Lock d	20 33					21 03				21 33					22 03				22 33			
Brimsdown d	20 36					21 06				21 36					22 06				22 36			
Ponders End d	20 38					21 08				21 38					22 08				22 38			
Angel Road d																						
Northumberland Park d																						
Tottenham Hale ⊖ d	20 44	20 47	21 00	21 03		21 14	21 17	21 29	21 32	21 44	21 47	22 00	22 03		22 14	22 17	22 29	22 32	22 44	22 47	23 00	23 03
Seven Sisters ⊖ d																						
Clapton d																						
Stratford ⊖ a	20 55		21 11			21 25		21 40		21 55		22 11			22 25		22 40		22 55		23 11	
Hackney Downs d																						
Bethnal Green d																						
London Liverpool Street ⊖ a		21 01		21 17			21 31		21 46		22 01		22 17			22 31		22 46		23 01		23 17

Table 22

Sundays
29 July to 12 August

Cambridge, Stansted Airport, Bishops Stortford, Hertford East and Broxbourne - London

Network Diagram - see first Page of Table 20

		XC ◇1		LE 1	LE 1	LE 1	LE 1	LE 1	LE 1	LE 1	LE 1	LE 1		LE 1
Cambridge	d	22 10				22 32	22 51							
Shelford	d						22 56							
Whittlesford Parkway	d					22 39	23 00							
Great Chesterford	d						23 04							
Audley End	d	22 24				22 47	23 10							
Newport (Essex)	d						23 13							
Elsenham	d						23 19							
Stansted Airport	a	22 45												
Stansted Airport	d				22 45			23 00		23 15	23 30	23 45		23 59
Stansted Mountfitchet	d				22 51		23 22							
Bishops Stortford	a					23 00	23 28	23 09			23 39			00 08
	d					23 00		23 09			23 39			00 08
Sawbridgeworth	d					23 05								
Harlow Mill	d													
Harlow Town	d				23 02	23 10				23 30	23 47	23 59		00 16
Roydon	d													
Hertford East	d			22 39					23 09					
Ware	d			22 43					23 13					
St Margarets (Herts)	d			22 47					23 17					
Rye House	d			22 50					23 20					
Broxbourne 3	a			22 54		23 16			23 24					
Broxbourne 3	d			22 54		23 16			23 24					
Cheshunt	d			22 58		23 20			23 28					
Waltham Cross	d			23 01										
Enfield Lock	d			23 03										
Brimsdown	d			23 06										
Ponders End	d			23 08										
Angel Road	d													
Northumberland Park	d													
Tottenham Hale ⊖	d			23 14	23 17	23 29		23 32	23 37	23 47				
Seven Sisters ⊖	d										00 08	00 21		
Clapton	d													
Stratford 7 ⊖	a			23 25		23 40								
Hackney Downs	d								23 44					
Bethnal Green	d													
London Liverpool Street 15 ⊖	a				23 31			23 46	23 51	00 01	00 22	00 35		00 51

Sundays
19 August to 26 August

		LE 1	LE 1	LE 1	LE 1	LE 1	LE 1	LE 1	LE 1	LE 1		LE 1 ✕	LE 1 ✕	LE 1	LE 1 ✕	LE 1 ✕	LE	LE 1	LE 1 ✕	LE 1		LE 1 ✕	LE	LE 1	LE 1 ✕
Cambridge	d		22p51																					07 32	
Shelford	d		22p56																						
Whittlesford Parkway	d		23p00																					07 39	
Great Chesterford	d		23p04																						
Audley End	d		23p10																					07 47	
Newport (Essex)	d		23p13																						
Elsenham	d		23p19																						
Stansted Airport	a																								
Stansted Airport	d	23p15		23p30		23p45	23p59		00 30	05 30		06 00	06 30		07 00	07 15			07 30			07 45			08 00
Stansted Mountfitchet	d	23p21	23p22																			07 51			
Bishops Stortford	a		23p28	23p39			00 08		00 39	05 39		06 09	06 39		07 09				07 39					08 00	08 09
	d		23p28	23p39			00 08		00 39	05 39		06 09	06 39	06 42	07 09			07 28	07 39					08 00	08 09
Sawbridgeworth	d		23p32											06 46				07 32						08 05	
Harlow Mill	d		23p36															07 36							
Harlow Town	d	23p32	23p39			23p59	00 16		00 47	05 47		06 17	06 47	06 51	07 17	07 30		07 39				08 02		08 10	
Roydon	d		23p43															07 43							
Hertford East	d				23p39			00 07															07 55		
Ware	d				23p43																		07 59		
St Margarets (Herts)	d				23p47																		08 03		
Rye House	d				23p50																		08 06		
Broxbourne 3	a		23p47		23p54			00 19						06 57				07 48					08 11	08 16	
Broxbourne 3	d		23p47		23p54									06 57			07 41	07 52					08 11	08 16	
Cheshunt	d		23p51		23p58									07 01			07 45	07 57					08 15	08 20	
Waltham Cross	d				00 01									07 04				07 59							
Enfield Lock	d				00 03									07 06				08 02							
Brimsdown	d				00 06									07 09				08 04							
Ponders End	d				00 08									07 11				08 06							
Angel Road	d																								
Northumberland Park	d																			←					
Tottenham Hale ⊖	d	23p48	23p59	00 03	00 14	00 17				06 04		06 33	07 03	07 17	07 33	07 46		08 12	08 01	08 12		08 17		08 29	08 32
Seven Sisters ⊖	d																08 03	→					08 33		
Clapton	d																								
Stratford 7 ⊖	a																			08 23					
Hackney Downs	d				00 20												08 09						08 39		
Bethnal Green	d																								
London Liverpool Street 15 ⊖	a	00 01	00 13	00 16	00 28	00 32	00 51		01 21	06 18		06 46	07 16	07 30	07 46	08 01	08 18		08 15			08 31	08 48	08 43	08 46

Table 22

Sundays
19 August to 26 August

Cambridge, Stansted Airport, Bishops Stortford, Hertford East and Broxbourne - London

Network Diagram - see first Page of Table 20

		LE 1 ✕	LE	LE 1	LE 1 ✕	LE 1		LE 1 ✕	LE	LE 1	LE 1 ✕	LE 1 ✕	LE	LE 1	LE 1 ✕	LE 1		XC 1	LE 1 ✕	LE	LE 1	LE 1 ✕	LE 1 ✕	LE	LE 1
Cambridge	d			07 51						08 32				08 51				09 15			09 32				09 51
Shelford	d			07 56										08 56											09 56
Whittlesford Parkway	d			08 00						08 39				09 00							09 39				10 00
Great Chesterford	d			08 04										09 04											10 04
Audley End	d			08 10						08 47				09 10				09 28			09 47				10 10
Newport (Essex)	d			08 13										09 13											10 13
Elsenham	d			08 19										09 19											10 19
Stansted Airport	a																	09 45							
Stansted Airport	d	08 15			08 30			08 45			09 00	09 15			09 30				09 45			10 00	10 15		
Stansted Mountfitchet	d			08 22				08 51						09 22					09 51						10 22
Bishops Stortford	a			08 28	08 39					09 00	09 09			09 28	09 39						10 00	10 09			10 28
	d			08 28	08 39					09 00	09 09			09 28	09 39						10 00	10 09			10 28
Sawbridgeworth	d			08 32						09 05				09 32							10 05				10 32
Harlow Mill	d			08 36										09 36											10 36
Harlow Town	d	08 30		08 39				09 02		09 10		09 30		09 39					10 02		10 10		10 30		10 39
Roydon	d			08 43										09 43											10 43
Hertford East	d		08 25						08 55				09 25							09 55				10 25	
Ware	d		08 29						08 59				09 29							09 59				10 29	
St Margarets (Herts)	d		08 33						09 03				09 33							10 03				10 33	
Rye House	d		08 36						09 06				09 36							10 06				10 36	
Broxbourne 3	a		08 41	08 48					09 11	09 16			09 41	09 48						10 11	10 16			10 41	10 48
Broxbourne 3	d		08 41	08 52					09 11	09 16			09 41	09 52						10 11	10 16			10 41	10 52
Cheshunt	d		08 45	08 57					09 15	09 20			09 45	09 57						10 15	10 20			10 45	10 57
Waltham Cross	d			08 59										09 59											10 59
Enfield Lock	d			09 02										10 02											11 02
Brimsdown	d			09 04										10 04											11 04
Ponders End	d			09 06										10 06											11 06
Angel Road	d																								
Northumberland Park	d					←										←									
Tottenham Hale ⊖	d	08 46		09 12	09 01	09 12		09 17		09 29	09 32	09 46		10 12	10 01	10 12			10 17		10 29	10 32	10 46		11 12
Seven Sisters ⊖	d		09 03	→					09 33				10 03	→						10 33				11 03	→
Clapton	d																								
Stratford 7 ⊖	a					09 23										10 23									
Hackney Downs	d		09 09						09 39				10 09							10 39				11 09	
Bethnal Green	d																								
London Liverpool Street 15 ⊖	a	09 00	09 18		09 15			09 31	09 48	09 43	09 46	10 01	10 18		10 15				10 31	10 48	10 43	10 46	11 01	11 18	

		LE 1 ✕		LE 1	XC 1	LE 1 ✕	LE	LE 1	LE 1 ✕	LE 1 ✕	LE	LE 1		LE 1 ✕	LE 1	XC 1	LE 1 ✕	LE	LE 1	LE 1 ✕	LE 1 ✕	LE		LE 1	LE 1 ✕
Cambridge	d				10 15			10 32				10 51				11 15			11 32					11 51	
Shelford	d											10 56												11 56	
Whittlesford Parkway	d							10 39				11 00							11 39					12 00	
Great Chesterford	d											11 04												12 04	
Audley End	d				10 28			10 47				11 10				11 28			11 47					12 10	
Newport (Essex)	d											11 13												12 13	
Elsenham	d											11 19												12 19	
Stansted Airport	a				10 45											11 45									
Stansted Airport	d	10 30				10 45			11 00	11 15				11 30			11 45			12 00	12 15				12 30
Stansted Mountfitchet	d					10 51						11 22					11 51							12 22	
Bishops Stortford	a	10 39						11 00	11 09			11 28		11 39					12 00	12 09				12 28	12 39
	d	10 39						11 00	11 09			11 28		11 39					12 00	12 09				12 28	12 39
Sawbridgeworth	d							11 05				11 32							12 05					12 32	
Harlow Mill	d											11 36												12 36	
Harlow Town	d					11 02		11 10		11 30		11 39					12 02		12 10		12 30			12 39	
Roydon	d											11 43												12 43	
Hertford East	d						10 55				11 25							11 55				12 25			
Ware	d						10 59				11 29							11 59				12 29			
St Margarets (Herts)	d						11 03				11 33							12 03				12 33			
Rye House	d						11 06				11 36							12 06				12 36			
Broxbourne 3	a						11 11	11 16			11 41	11 48						12 11	12 16			12 41		12 48	
Broxbourne 3	d						11 11	11 16			11 41	11 52						12 11	12 16			12 41		12 52	
Cheshunt	d						11 15	11 20			11 45	11 57						12 15	12 20			12 45		12 57	
Waltham Cross	d											11 59												12 59	
Enfield Lock	d											12 02												13 02	
Brimsdown	d											12 04												13 04	
Ponders End	d											12 06												13 06	
Angel Road	d																								
Northumberland Park	d			←											←										
Tottenham Hale ⊖	d	11 01		11 12		11 17		11 29	11 32	11 46		12 12		12 01	12 12		12 17		12 29	12 32	12 46			13 12	13 01
Seven Sisters ⊖	d						11 33				12 03	→						12 33				13 03		→	
Clapton	d																								
Stratford 7 ⊖	a			11 23											12 23										
Hackney Downs	d						11 39				12 09							12 39				13 09			
Bethnal Green	d																								
London Liverpool Street 15 ⊖	a	11 15				11 31	11 48	11 43	11 46	12 01	12 18			12 15			12 31	12 48	12 43	12 46	13 01	13 18			13 15

Cambridge, Stansted Airport, Bishops Stortford, Hertford East and Broxbourne - London

Network Diagram - see first Page of Table 20

		LE ■	XC ■	LE ■ 🚲	LE	LE ■	LE ■ 🚲	LE ■ 🚲		LE	LE ■	LE ■ 🚲	LE ■	XC ■	LE ■ 🚲	LE	LE ■	LE ■ 🚲		LE ■ 🚲	LE	LE ■	LE ■ 🚲	LE ■	XC ◇■
Cambridge	d		12 15			12 32					12 51			13 15			13 32					13 51			14 10
Shelford	d										12 56											13 56			
Whittlesford Parkway	d					12 39					13 00						13 39					14 00			
Great Chesterford	d										13 04											14 04			
Audley End	d		12 28			12 47					13 10			13 28			13 47					14 10			14 24
Newport (Essex)	d										13 13											14 13			
Elsenham	d										13 19											14 19			
Stansted Airport	a		12 45											13 45											14 45
Stansted Airport	d			12 45			13 00	13 15				13 30			13 45			14 00		14 15			14 30		
Stansted Mountfitchet	d			12 51							13 22				13 51							14 22			
Bishops Stortford	a					13 00	13 09				13 28	13 39					14 00	14 09				14 28	14 39		
	d					13 00	13 09				13 28	13 39					14 00	14 09				14 28	14 39		
Sawbridgeworth	d					13 05					13 32						14 05					14 32			
Harlow Mill	d										13 36											14 36			
Harlow Town	d			13 02		13 10		13 30			13 39				14 02		14 10			14 30		14 39			
Roydon	d										13 43											14 43			
Hertford East	d				12 55					13 25						13 55					14 25				
Ware	d				12 59					13 29						13 59					14 29				
St Margarets (Herts)	d				13 03					13 33						14 03					14 33				
Rye House	d				13 06					13 36						14 06					14 36				
Broxbourne ■	a				13 11	13 16				13 41	13 48					14 11	14 16				14 41	14 48			
Broxbourne ■	d				13 11	13 16				13 41	13 52					14 11	14 16				14 41	14 52			
Cheshunt	d				13 15	13 20				13 45	13 57					14 15	14 20				14 45	14 57			
Waltham Cross	d										13 59											14 59			
Enfield Lock	d										14 02											15 02			
Brimsdown	d										14 04											15 04			
Ponders End	d										14 06											15 06			
Angel Road	d																								
Northumberland Park	d	←											←											←	
Tottenham Hale ⊖	d	13 12		13 17		13 29	13 32	13 46			14 12	14 01	14 12		14 17		14 29	14 32		14 46		15 12	15 01	15 12	
Seven Sisters ⊖	d				13 33					14 03	→					14 33					15 03	→			
Clapton	d																								
Stratford ■ ⊖	a	13 23											14 23											15 23	
Hackney Downs	d				13 39					14 09						14 39					15 09				
Bethnal Green	d																								
London Liverpool Street ■ ⊖	a			13 31	13 48	13 43	13 46	14 01		14 18		14 15			14 31	14 48	14 43	14 46		15 01	15 18		15 15		

		LE ■ 🚲	LE	LE ■		LE ■ 🚲	LE ■ 🚲	LE	LE ■	LE ■ 🚲	LE ■	XC ◇■	LE ■ 🚲	LE		LE ■	LE ■ 🚲	LE ■ 🚲	LE	LE ■	LE ■ 🚲	LE ■	XC ◇■	LE ■ 🚲
Cambridge	d			14 32					14 51			15 10				15 32				15 51			16 10	
Shelford	d								14 56											15 56				
Whittlesford Parkway	d			14 39					15 00							15 39				16 00				
Great Chesterford	d								15 04											16 04				
Audley End	d			14 47					15 10			15 24				15 47				16 10			16 23	
Newport (Essex)	d								15 13											16 13				
Elsenham	d								15 19											16 19				
Stansted Airport	a											15 45											16 45	
Stansted Airport	d	14 45				15 00	15 15			15 30			15 45				16 00	16 15			16 30			16 45
Stansted Mountfitchet	d	14 51							15 22				15 51							16 22				16 51
Bishops Stortford	a			15 00		15 09			15 28	15 39						16 00	16 09			16 28	16 39			
	d			15 00		15 09			15 28	15 39						16 00	16 09			16 28	16 39			
Sawbridgeworth	d			15 05					15 32							16 05				16 32				
Harlow Mill	d								15 36											16 36				
Harlow Town	d	15 02		15 10			15 30		15 39				16 02			16 10		16 30		16 39				17 02
Roydon	d								15 43											16 43				
Hertford East	d		14 55					15 25						15 55					16 25					
Ware	d		14 59					15 29						15 59					16 29					
St Margarets (Herts)	d		15 03					15 33						16 03					16 33					
Rye House	d		15 06					15 36						16 06					16 36					
Broxbourne ■	a		15 11	15 16				15 41	15 48					16 11		16 16			16 41	16 48				
Broxbourne ■	d		15 11	15 16				15 41	15 52					16 11		16 16			16 41	16 52				
Cheshunt	d		15 15	15 20				15 45	15 57					16 15		16 20			16 45	16 57				
Waltham Cross	d								15 59											16 59				
Enfield Lock	d								16 02											17 02				
Brimsdown	d								16 04											17 04				
Ponders End	d								16 06											17 06				
Angel Road	d																							
Northumberland Park	d										←											←		
Tottenham Hale ⊖	d	15 17		15 29		15 32	15 46		16 12	16 01	16 12		16 17			16 29	16 32	16 46		17 12	17 01	17 12		17 17
Seven Sisters ⊖	d		15 33					16 03	→					16 33					17 03	→				
Clapton	d																							
Stratford ■ ⊖	a										16 23											17 23		
Hackney Downs	d		15 39					16 09						16 39					17 09					
Bethnal Green	d																							
London Liverpool Street ■ ⊖	a	15 31	15 48	15 43		15 46	16 01	16 18		16 15			16 31	16 48		16 43	16 46	17 01	17 18		17 15			17 31

Table 22

Sundays

19 August to 26 August

Cambridge, Stansted Airport, Bishops Stortford, Hertford East and Broxbourne - London

Network Diagram - see first Page of Table 20

		LE	LE ■	LE ■ 🚲	LE ■ 🚲	LE	LE ■	LE ■ 🚲	LE ■	XC ◇■		LE ■ 🚲	LE	LE ■	LE ■ 🚲	LE ■ 🚲	LE	LE ■	LE ■ 🚲	LE ■		XC ◇■	LE ■ 🚲	LE	LE ■
Cambridge	d		16 32				16 51			17 10				17 32				17 51				18 10			18 32
Shelford	d						16 56											17 56							
Whittlesford Parkway	d		16 39				17 00							17 39				18 00							18 39
Great Chesterford	d						17 04											18 04							
Audley End	d		16 47				17 10			17 24				17 47				18 10				18 24			18 47
Newport (Essex)	d						17 13											18 13							
Elsenham	d						17 19											18 19							
Stansted Airport	a									17 45												18 45			
Stansted Airport	d			17 00	17 15			17 30				17 45			18 00	18 15			18 30				18 45		
Stansted Mountfitchet	d						17 22					17 51						18 22					18 51		
Bishops Stortford	a		17 00	17 09			17 28	17 39						18 00	18 09			18 28	18 39						19 00
	d		17 00	17 09			17 28	17 39						18 00	18 09			18 28	18 39						19 00
Sawbridgeworth	d		17 05				17 32							18 05				18 32							19 05
Harlow Mill	d						17 36											18 36							
Harlow Town	d		17 10		17 30		17 39					18 02		18 10		18 30		18 39					19 02		19 10
Roydon	d						17 43											18 43							
Hertford East	d	16 55				17 25							17 55				18 25							18 55	
Ware	d	16 59				17 29							17 59				18 29							18 59	
St Margarets (Herts)	d	17 03				17 33							18 03				18 33							19 03	
Rye House	d	17 06				17 36							18 06				18 36							19 06	
Broxbourne ■	a	17 11	17 16			17 41	17 48						18 11	18 16			18 41	18 48						19 11	19 16
Broxbourne ■	d	17 11	17 16			17 41	17 52						18 11	18 16			18 41	18 52						19 11	19 16
Cheshunt	d	17 15	17 20			17 45	17 57						18 15	18 20			18 45	18 57						19 15	19 20
Waltham Cross	d						17 59											18 59							
Enfield Lock	d						18 02											19 02							
Brimsdown	d						18 04											19 04							
Ponders End	d						18 06											19 06							
Angel Road	d																								
Northumberland Park	d								←											←					
Tottenham Hale ⊖	d		17 29	17 32	17 46		18 12	18 01	18 12			18 17		18 29	18 32	18 46		19 12	19 01	19 12			19 17		19 29
Seven Sisters ⊖	d	17 33				18 03	→						18 33				19 03	→						19 33	
Clapton	d																								
Stratford ■ ⊖	a								18 23											19 23					
Hackney Downs	d	17 39				18 09							18 39				19 09							19 39	
Bethnal Green	d																								
London Liverpool Street ■ ⊖	a	17 48	17 43	17 46	18 01	18 18		18 15				18 31	18 48	18 43	18 46	19 01	19 18		19 15				19 31	19 48	19 43

		LE ■ 🚲	LE ■ 🚲	LE	LE ■	LE ■ 🚲		LE ■	XC ◇■	LE ■ 🚲	LE	LE ■	LE ■ 🚲	LE ■ 🚲	LE	LE ■		LE ■ 🚲	LE ■	XC ◇■	LE ■ 🚲	LE	LE ■	LE ■ 🚲	LE ■ 🚲
Cambridge	d				18 51				19 10			19 32				19 51				20 10			20 32		
Shelford	d				18 56											19 56									
Whittlesford Parkway	d				19 00							19 39				20 00							20 39		
Great Chesterford	d				19 04											20 04									
Audley End	d				19 10				19 24			19 47				20 10				20 24			20 47		
Newport (Essex)	d				19 13											20 13									
Elsenham	d				19 19											20 19									
Stansted Airport	a								19 45											20 45					
Stansted Airport	d	19 00	19 15			19 30				19 45			20 00	20 15				20 30			20 45			21 00	21 15
Stansted Mountfitchet	d				19 22					19 51						20 22					20 51				
Bishops Stortford	a	19 09			19 28	19 39						20 00	20 09			20 28		20 39					21 00	21 09	
	d	19 09			19 28	19 39						20 00	20 09			20 28		20 39					21 00	21 09	
Sawbridgeworth	d				19 32							20 05				20 32							21 05		
Harlow Mill	d				19 36											20 36									
Harlow Town	d		19 30		19 39					20 02		20 10		20 30		20 39					21 02		21 10		21 30
Roydon	d				19 43											20 43									
Hertford East	d			19 25							19 55				20 25							20 55			
Ware	d			19 29							19 59				20 29							20 59			
St Margarets (Herts)	d			19 33							20 03				20 33							21 03			
Rye House	d			19 36							20 06				20 36							21 06			
Broxbourne ■	a			19 41	19 48						20 11	20 16			20 41	20 48						21 11	21 16		
Broxbourne ■	d			19 41	19 52						20 11	20 16			20 41	20 52						21 11	21 16		
Cheshunt	d			19 45	19 57						20 15	20 20			20 45	20 57						21 15	21 20		
Waltham Cross	d				19 59											20 59									
Enfield Lock	d				20 02											21 02									
Brimsdown	d				20 04											21 04									
Ponders End	d				20 06											21 06									
Angel Road	d																								
Northumberland Park	d							←											←						
Tottenham Hale ⊖	d	19 32	19 46		20 12	20 01		20 12		20 17		20 29	20 32	20 46		21 12		21 01	21 12		21 17		21 29	21 32	21 46
Seven Sisters ⊖	d			20 03	→						20 33				21 03	→						21 33			
Clapton	d																								
Stratford ■ ⊖	a							20 23											21 23						
Hackney Downs	d			20 09							20 39				21 09							21 39			
Bethnal Green	d																								
London Liverpool Street ■ ⊖	a	19 46	20 01	20 18		20 15				20 31	20 48	20 43	20 46	21 01	21 18			21 15			21 31	21 48	21 43	21 46	22 01

Table 22

Sundays 19 August to 26 August

Cambridge, Stansted Airport, Bishops Stortford, Hertford East and Broxbourne - London

Network Diagram - see first Page of Table 20

		LE	LE	LE	LE	XC	LE	LE	LE	LE	LE	LE	LE	LE	LE	XC	LE	LE	LE	LE	LE	LE
			1	1	1	◇1	1		1	1	1		1	1	1	◇1	1		1	1	1	1
				🚲			🚲															
Cambridge	d		20 51			21 10			21 32				21 51			22 10			22 32	22 51		
Shelford	d		20 56										21 56							22 56		
Whittlesford Parkway	d		21 00						21 39				22 00						22 39	23 00		
Great Chesterford	d		21 04										22 04							23 04		
Audley End	d		21 10			21 24			21 47				22 10			22 24			22 47	23 10		
Newport (Essex)	d		21 13										22 13							23 13		
Elsenham	d		21 19										22 19							23 19		
Stansted Airport	a					21 45										22 45						
Stansted Airport	d			21 30			21 45			22 00	22 15			22 30			22 45				23 00	23 15
Stansted Mountfitchet	d		21 22				21 51						22 22				22 51			23 22		
Bishops Stortford	a		21 28	21 39					22 00	22 09			22 28	22 39					23 00	23 28	23 09	
	d		21 28	21 39					22 00	22 09			22 28	22 39					23 00		23 09	
Sawbridgeworth	d		21 32						22 05				22 32						23 05			
Harlow Mill	d		21 36										22 36									
Harlow Town	d		21 39				22 02		22 10		22 30		22 39				23 02		23 10			23 30
Roydon	d		21 43										22 43									
Hertford East	d	21 25						21 55				22 25						22 55				
Ware	d	21 29						21 59				22 29						22 59				
St Margarets (Herts)	d	21 33						22 03				22 33						23 03				
Rye House	d	21 36						22 06				22 36						23 06				
Broxbourne 3	a	21 41	21 48					22 11	22 16			22 41	22 48					23 11	23 16			
Broxbourne 3	d	21 41	21 52					22 11	22 16			22 41	22 52					23 11	23 16			
Cheshunt	d	21 45	21 57					22 15	22 20			22 45	22 57					23 15	23 20			
Waltham Cross	d		21 59										22 59									
Enfield Lock	d		22 02										23 02									
Brimsdown	d		22 04										23 04									
Ponders End	d		22 06										23 06									
Angel Road	d																					
Northumberland Park	d				←										←							
Tottenham Hale ⊖	d		22 12	22 01	22 12		22 17		22 29	22 32	22 46		23 12	23 01	23 12		23 17		23 29		23 32	23 46
Seven Sisters ⊖	d	22 03	→					22 33				23 03	→					23 33				
Clapton	d																					
Stratford 7 ⊖	a				22 23										23 23							
Hackney Downs	d	22 09						22 39				23 09						23 39				
Bethnal Green	d																					
London Liverpool Street 15 ⊖	a	22 18		22 15			22 31	22 48	22 43	22 46	23 01	23 18		23 15			23 31	23 48	23 43		23 46	00 01

		LE	LE	LE
		1	1	1
Cambridge	d			
Shelford	d			
Whittlesford Parkway	d			
Great Chesterford	d			
Audley End	d			
Newport (Essex)	d			
Elsenham	d			
Stansted Airport	a			
Stansted Airport	d	23 30	23 45	23 59
Stansted Mountfitchet	d			
Bishops Stortford	a	23 39		00 08
	d	23 39		00 08
Sawbridgeworth	d			
Harlow Mill	d			
Harlow Town	d	23 47	23 59	00 16
Roydon	d			
Hertford East	d			
Ware	d			
St Margarets (Herts)	d			
Rye House	d			
Broxbourne 3	a			
Broxbourne 3	d			
Cheshunt	d			
Waltham Cross	d			
Enfield Lock	d			
Brimsdown	d			
Ponders End	d			
Angel Road	d			
Northumberland Park	d			
Tottenham Hale ⊖	d			
Seven Sisters ⊖	d	00 08	00 21	
Clapton	d			
Stratford 7 ⊖	a			
Hackney Downs	d			
Bethnal Green	d			
London Liverpool Street 15 ⊖	a	00 22	00 35	00 51

Table 22

Sundays 2 September to 9 September

Cambridge, Stansted Airport, Bishops Stortford, Hertford East and Broxbourne - London

Network Diagram - see first Page of Table 20

		LE	LE	LE	LE	LE	LE	LE	LE	LE	LE	LE	LE	LE	LE	LE	LE	LE	LE	LE	LE	LE	LE
		1	1	1	1	1	1	1	1	1	1	1	1	1	1	1	1		1	1	1	1	1
													🚲	🚲		🚲	🚲			🚲		🚲	
Cambridge	d		22p51																				07 32
Shelford	d		22p56																				
Whittlesford Parkway	d		23p00																				07 39
Great Chesterford	d		23p04																				
Audley End	d		23p10																				07 47
Newport (Essex)	d		23p13																				
Elsenham	d		23p19																				
Stansted Airport	a																						
Stansted Airport	d	23p15		23p30		23p45	23p59		00 30	01 00	01 30	05 30	06 00	06 30		07 00	07 15			07 30		07 45	
Stansted Mountfitchet	d	23p21	23p22																			07 51	
Bishops Stortford	a		23p28	23p39			00 08		00 39			05 39	06 09	06 39		07 09				07 39			08 00
	d		23p28	23p39			00 08		00 39			05 39	06 09	06 39	06 42	07 09			07 28	07 39			08 00
Sawbridgeworth	d		23p32												06 46				07 32				08 05
Harlow Mill	d		23p36																07 36				
Harlow Town	d	23p32	23p39			23p59	00 16		00 47			05 47	06 17	06 47	06 51	07 17	07 30		07 39			08 02	08 10
Roydon	d		23p43																07 43				
Hertford East	d				23p39			00 07													07 39		
Ware	d				23p43																07 43		
St Margarets (Herts)	d				23p47																07 47		
Rye House	d				23p50																07 50		
Broxbourne 3	a		23p47		23p54			00 19							06 57				07 47		07 54		08 16
Broxbourne 3	d		23p47		23p54										06 57			07 41	07 47		07 54		08 16
Cheshunt	d		23p51		23p58										07 01			07 45	07 51		07 58		08 20
Waltham Cross	d				00 01										07 04						08 01		
Enfield Lock	d				00 03										07 06						08 03		
Brimsdown	d				00 06										07 09						08 06		
Ponders End	d				00 08										07 11						08 08		
Angel Road	d																						
Northumberland Park	d																						
Tottenham Hale ⊖	d	23p48	23p59	00 03	00 14	00 17						06 04	06 33	07 03	07 17	07 33	07 46		08 00	08 03	08 14	08 17	08 29
Seven Sisters ⊖	d																	08 03					
Clapton	d																						
Stratford 7 ⊖	a																		08 11		08 25		08 40
Hackney Downs	d				00 20													08 09					
Bethnal Green	d																						
London Liverpool Street 15 ⊖	a	00 01	00 13	00 16	00 28	00 32	00 51		01 21	01 50	02 20	06 18	06 46	07 16	07 31	07 46	08 01	08 19		08 17		08 31	

		LE	LE	LE	LE	LE	LE	LE	LE	LE	LE	LE	LE	LE	XC	LE	LE	LE	LE	LE	LE	LE	LE
		1	1	1	1	1	1	1	1	1	1	1	1	1	1	1	1	1	1	1	1	1	1
		🚲		🚲		🚲		🚲		🚲		🚲		🚲			🚲		🚲		🚲		🚲
Cambridge	d				07 51				08 32				08 51		09 15			09 32				09 51	
Shelford	d				07 56								08 56									09 56	
Whittlesford Parkway	d				08 00				08 39				09 00					09 39				10 00	
Great Chesterford	d				08 04								09 04									10 04	
Audley End	d				08 10				08 47				09 10		09 28			09 47				10 10	
Newport (Essex)	d				08 13								09 13									10 13	
Elsenham	d				08 19								09 19									10 19	
Stansted Airport	a														09 45								
Stansted Airport	d	08 00		08 15		08 30		08 45		09 00		09 15		09 30			09 45		10 00		10 15		10 30
Stansted Mountfitchet	d				08 22			08 51					09 22				09 51					10 22	
Bishops Stortford	a	08 09			08 28	08 39			09 00	09 09			09 28	09 39				10 00	10 09			10 28	10 39
	d	08 09			08 28	08 39			09 00	09 09			09 28	09 39				10 00	10 09			10 28	10 39
Sawbridgeworth	d				08 32				09 05				09 32					10 05				10 32	
Harlow Mill	d				08 36								09 36									10 36	
Harlow Town	d			08 30	08 39			09 02	09 10			09 30	09 39				10 02	10 10			10 30	10 39	
Roydon	d				08 43								09 43									10 43	
Hertford East	d		08 09				08 39				09 09					09 39				10 09			
Ware	d		08 13				08 43				09 13					09 43				10 13			
St Margarets (Herts)	d		08 17				08 47				09 17					09 47				10 17			
Rye House	d		08 20				08 50				09 20					09 50				10 20			
Broxbourne 3	a		08 24		08 47		08 54		09 16		09 24		09 47			09 54		10 16		10 24		10 47	
Broxbourne 3	d		08 24		08 47		08 54		09 16		09 24		09 47			09 54		10 16		10 24		10 47	
Cheshunt	d		08 28		08 51		08 58		09 20		09 28		09 51			09 58		10 20		10 28		10 51	
Waltham Cross	d		08 31				09 01				09 31					10 01				10 31			
Enfield Lock	d		08 33				09 03				09 33					10 03				10 33			
Brimsdown	d		08 36				09 06				09 36					10 06				10 36			
Ponders End	d		08 38				09 08				09 38					10 08				10 38			
Angel Road	d																						
Northumberland Park	d																						
Tottenham Hale ⊖	d	08 32	08 44	08 47	09 00	09 03	09 14	09 17	09 29	09 32	09 44	09 47	10 00	10 03		10 14	10 17	10 29	10 32	10 44	10 47	11 00	11 03
Seven Sisters ⊖	d																						
Clapton	d																						
Stratford 7 ⊖	a		08 55		09 11		09 25		09 40		09 55		10 11			10 25		10 40		10 55		11 11	
Hackney Downs	d																						
Bethnal Green	d																						
London Liverpool Street 15 ⊖	a	08 46		09 01		09 17		09 31		09 46		10 01		10 17			10 31		10 46		11 01		11 17

2 September to 9 September

Cambridge, Stansted Airport, Bishops Stortford, Hertford East and Broxbourne - London

Network Diagram - see first Page of Table 20

		XC 1	LE 1	LE 1 🛒	LE 1	LE 1 🛒	LE 1	LE 1 🛒	LE 1	LE 1 🛒	XC 1	LE 1	LE 1 🛒	LE 1	LE 1 🛒	LE 1	LE 1 🛒	LE 1	LE 1 🛒	XC 1	LE 1	LE 1 🛒
Cambridge	d	10 15			10 32				10 51		11 15			11 32				11 51		12 15		
Shelford	d								10 56									11 56				
Whittlesford Parkway	d				10 39				11 00					11 39				12 00				
Great Chesterford	d								11 04									12 04				
Audley End	d	10 28			10 47				11 10		11 28			11 47				12 10		12 28		
Newport (Essex)	d								11 13									12 13				
Elsenham	d								11 19									12 19				
Stansted Airport	a	10 45									11 45									12 45		
Stansted Airport	d			10 45		11 00		11 15		11 30			11 45		12 00		12 15		12 30			12 45
Stansted Mountfitchet	d			10 51					11 22				11 51					12 23				12 51
Bishops Stortford	a				11 00	11 09			11 28	11 39				12 00	12 09			12 28	12 39			
	d				11 00	11 09			11 28	11 39				12 00	12 09			12 28	12 39			
Sawbridgeworth	d				11 05				11 32					12 05				12 32				
Harlow Mill	d								11 36									12 36				
Harlow Town	d			11 02	11 10			11 30	11 39				12 02	12 10			12 30	12 39				13 02
Roydon	d								11 43									12 43				
Hertford East	d		10 39				11 09					11 39				12 09					12 39	
Ware	d		10 43				11 13					11 43				12 13					12 43	
St Margarets (Herts)	d		10 47				11 17					11 47				12 17					12 47	
Rye House	d		10 50				11 20					11 50				12 20					12 50	
Broxbourne 3	a		10 54		11 16		11 24		11 47			11 54		12 16		12 24		12 47			12 54	
Broxbourne 3	d		10 54		11 16		11 24		11 47			11 54		12 16		12 24		12 47			12 54	
Cheshunt	d		10 58		11 20		11 28		11 51			11 58		12 20		12 28		12 51			12 58	
Waltham Cross	d		11 01				11 31					12 01				12 31					13 01	
Enfield Lock	d		11 03				11 33					12 03				12 33					13 03	
Brimsdown	d		11 06				11 36					12 06				12 36					13 06	
Ponders End	d		11 08				11 38					12 08				12 38					13 08	
Angel Road	d																					
Northumberland Park	d																					
Tottenham Hale ⊖	d		11 14	11 17	11 29	11 32	11 44	11 47	12 00	12 03		12 14	12 17	12 29	12 32	12 44	12 47	13 00	13 03		13 14	13 17
Seven Sisters ⊖	d																					
Clapton	d																					
Stratford 7 ⊖	a		11 25		11 40		11 55		12 11			12 25		12 40		12 55		13 11			13 25	
Hackney Downs	d																					
Bethnal Green	d																					
London Liverpool Street 15 ⊖	a			11 31		11 46		12 01		12 17			12 31		12 46		13 01		13 17			13 31

		LE 1	LE 1 🛒	LE 1	LE 1 🛒	LE 1	LE 1 🛒	XC 1	LE 1	LE 1 🛒	LE 1	LE 1 🛒	LE 1	LE 1 🛒	LE 1	LE 1 🛒	XC ◇1	LE 1	LE 1 🛒	LE 1	LE 1 🛒	LE 1	LE 1 🛒
Cambridge	d	12 32				12 51		13 15			13 32				13 51		14 10			14 32			
Shelford	d					12 56									13 56								
Whittlesford Parkway	d	12 39				13 00					13 39				14 00					14 39			
Great Chesterford	d					13 04									14 04								
Audley End	d	12 47				13 10		13 28			13 47				14 10		14 24			14 47			
Newport (Essex)	d					13 13									14 13								
Elsenham	d					13 19									14 19								
Stansted Airport	a							13 45									14 45						
Stansted Airport	d		13 00		13 15		13 30			13 45		14 00		14 15		14 30			14 45		15 00		15 15
Stansted Mountfitchet	d					13 23				13 51					14 23				14 51				
Bishops Stortford	a	13 00	13 09			13 28	13 39				14 00	14 09			14 28	14 39				15 00	15 09		
	d	13 00	13 09			13 28	13 39				14 00	14 09			14 28	14 39				15 00	15 09		
Sawbridgeworth	d	13 05				13 32					14 05				14 32					15 05			
Harlow Mill	d					13 36									14 36								
Harlow Town	d	13 10			13 30	13 39				14 02	14 10			14 30	14 39				15 02	15 10			15 30
Roydon	d					13 43									14 43								
Hertford East	d			13 09					13 39				14 09					14 39				15 09	
Ware	d			13 13					13 43				14 13					14 43				15 13	
St Margarets (Herts)	d			13 17					13 47				14 17					14 47				15 17	
Rye House	d			13 20					13 50				14 20					14 50				15 20	
Broxbourne 3	a	13 16		13 24		13 47			13 54		14 16		14 24		14 47			14 54		15 16		15 24	
Broxbourne 3	d	13 16		13 24		13 47			13 54		14 16		14 24		14 47			14 54		15 16		15 24	
Cheshunt	d	13 20		13 28		13 51			13 58		14 20		14 28		14 51			14 58		15 20		15 28	
Waltham Cross	d			13 31					14 01				14 31					15 01				15 31	
Enfield Lock	d			13 33					14 03				14 33					15 03				15 33	
Brimsdown	d			13 36					14 06				14 36					15 06				15 36	
Ponders End	d			13 38					14 08				14 38					15 08				15 38	
Angel Road	d																						
Northumberland Park	d																						
Tottenham Hale ⊖	d	13 29	13 32	13 44	13 47	14 00	14 03		14 14	14 17	14 29	14 32	14 44	14 47	15 00	15 03		15 14	15 17	15 29	15 32	15 44	15 47
Seven Sisters ⊖	d																						
Clapton	d																						
Stratford 7 ⊖	a	13 40		13 55		14 11			14 25		14 40		14 55		15 11			15 25		15 40		15 55	
Hackney Downs	d																						
Bethnal Green	d																						
London Liverpool Street 15 ⊖	a		13 46		14 01		14 17			14 31		14 46		15 01		15 17			15 31		15 46		16 01

2 September to 9 September

Cambridge, Stansted Airport, Bishops Stortford, Hertford East and Broxbourne - London

Network Diagram - see first Page of Table 20

		LE 1	LE 1 🛒	XC ◇1	LE 1	LE 1 🛒	LE 1	LE 1 🛒	LE 1	LE 1 🛒	LE 1	LE 1 🛒	XC ◇1	LE 1	LE 1 🛒	LE 1	LE 1 🛒	LE 1	LE 1 🛒	LE 1	LE 1 🛒	XC ◇1
Cambridge	d	14 51		15 10			15 32				15 51		16 10			16 32				16 51		17 10
Shelford	d	14 56									15 56									16 56		
Whittlesford Parkway	d	15 00					15 39				16 00					16 39				17 00		
Great Chesterford	d	15 04									16 04									17 04		
Audley End	d	15 10		15 24			15 47				16 10		16 23			16 47				17 10		17 24
Newport (Essex)	d	15 13									16 13									17 13		
Elsenham	d	15 19									16 19									17 19		
Stansted Airport	a			15 45									16 45									17 45
Stansted Airport	d		15 30			15 45		16 00		16 15		16 30			16 45		17 00		17 15		17 30	
Stansted Mountfitchet	d	15 23				15 51					16 23				16 51					17 23		
Bishops Stortford	a	15 28	15 39				16 00	16 09			16 28	16 39				17 00	17 09			17 28	17 39	
	d	15 28	15 39				16 00	16 09			16 28	16 39				17 00	17 09			17 28	17 39	
Sawbridgeworth	d	15 32					16 05				16 32					17 05				17 32		
Harlow Mill	d	15 36									16 36									17 36		
Harlow Town	d	15 39				16 02	16 10			16 30	16 39				17 02	17 10			17 30	17 39		
Roydon	d	15 43									16 43									17 43		
Hertford East	d				15 39				16 09					16 39				17 09				
Ware	d				15 43				16 13					16 43				17 13				
St Margarets (Herts)	d				15 47				16 17					16 47				17 17				
Rye House	d				15 50				16 20					16 50				17 20				
Broxbourne 3	a	15 47			15 54		16 16		16 24		16 47			16 54		17 16		17 24		17 47		
Broxbourne 3	d	15 47			15 54		16 16		16 24		16 47			16 54		17 16		17 24		17 47		
Cheshunt	d	15 51			15 58		16 20		16 28		16 51			16 58		17 20		17 28		17 51		
Waltham Cross	d				16 01				16 31					17 01				17 31				
Enfield Lock	d				16 03				16 33					17 03				17 33				
Brimsdown	d				16 06				16 36					17 06				17 36				
Ponders End	d				16 08				16 38					17 08				17 38				
Angel Road	d																					
Northumberland Park	d																					
Tottenham Hale ⊖	d	16 00	16 03		16 14	16 17	16 29	16 32	16 44	16 47	17 00	17 03		17 14	17 17	17 29	17 32	17 44	17 47	18 00	18 03	
Seven Sisters ⊖	d																					
Clapton	d																					
Stratford 7 ⊖	a	16 11			16 25		16 40		16 55		17 11			17 25		17 40		17 55		18 11		
Hackney Downs	d																					
Bethnal Green	d																					
London Liverpool Street 15 ⊖	a		16 17			16 31		16 46		17 01		17 17			17 31		17 46		18 01		18 17	

		LE 1	LE 1 🛒	LE 1	LE 1 🛒	LE 1	LE 1 🛒	LE 1	LE 1 🛒	XC ◇1	LE 1	LE 1 🛒	LE 1	LE 1 🛒	LE 1	LE 1 🛒	LE 1	LE 1 🛒	XC ◇1	LE 1	LE 1 🛒	LE 1	LE 1 🛒
Cambridge	d			17 32				17 51		18 10			18 32				18 51		19 10			19 32	
Shelford	d							17 56									18 56						
Whittlesford Parkway	d			17 39				18 00					18 39				19 00					19 39	
Great Chesterford	d							18 04									19 04						
Audley End	d			17 47				18 10		18 24			18 47				19 10		19 24			19 47	
Newport (Essex)	d							18 13									19 13						
Elsenham	d							18 19									19 19						
Stansted Airport	a									18 45									19 45				
Stansted Airport	d		17 45		18 00		18 15		18 30			18 45		19 00		19 15		19 30			19 45		20 00
Stansted Mountfitchet	d		17 51					18 23				18 51					19 23				19 51		
Bishops Stortford	a			18 00	18 09			18 28	18 39				19 00	19 09			19 28	19 39				20 00	20 09
	d			18 00	18 09			18 28	18 39				19 00	19 09			19 28	19 39				20 00	20 09
Sawbridgeworth	d			18 05				18 32					19 05				19 32					20 05	
Harlow Mill	d							18 36									19 36						
Harlow Town	d		18 02	18 10			18 30	18 39				19 02	19 10			19 30	19 39				20 02	20 10	
Roydon	d							18 43									19 43						
Hertford East	d	17 39				18 09					18 39				19 09					19 39			
Ware	d	17 43				18 13					18 43				19 13					19 43			
St Margarets (Herts)	d	17 47				18 17					18 47				19 17					19 47			
Rye House	d	17 50				18 20					18 50				19 20					19 50			
Broxbourne 3	a	17 54		18 16		18 24		18 47			18 54		19 16		19 24		19 47			19 54		20 16	
Broxbourne 3	d	17 54		18 16		18 24		18 47			18 54		19 16		19 24		19 47			19 54		20 16	
Cheshunt	d	17 58		18 20		18 28		18 51			18 58		19 20		19 28		19 51			19 58		20 20	
Waltham Cross	d	18 01				18 31					19 01				19 31					20 01			
Enfield Lock	d	18 03				18 33					19 03				19 33					20 03			
Brimsdown	d	18 06				18 36					19 06				19 36					20 06			
Ponders End	d	18 08				18 38					19 08				19 38					20 08			
Angel Road	d																						
Northumberland Park	d																						
Tottenham Hale ⊖	d	18 14	18 17	18 29	18 32	18 44	18 47	19 00	19 03		19 14	19 17	19 29	19 32	19 44	19 47	20 00	20 03		20 14	20 17	20 29	20 32
Seven Sisters ⊖	d																						
Clapton	d																						
Stratford 7 ⊖	a	18 25		18 40		18 55		19 11			19 25		19 40		19 55		20 11			20 25		20 40	
Hackney Downs	d																						
Bethnal Green	d																						
London Liverpool Street 15 ⊖	a		18 31		18 46		19 01		19 17			19 31		19 46		20 01		20 17			20 31		20 46

Table 22

Sundays

2 September to 9 September

Cambridge, Stansted Airport, Bishops Stortford, Hertford East and Broxbourne - London

Network Diagram - see first Page of Table 20

		LE ■	LE ■ ⌶	LE ■	LE ■ ⌶	XC ◇■	LE ■	LE ■ ⌶	LE ■	LE ■ ⌶	LE ■	LE ■ ⌶	LE ■	LE ■ ⌶	XC ◇■	LE ■	LE ■ ⌶	LE ■	LE ■	LE ■	LE ■	LE ■	LE ■
Cambridge	d			19 51		20 10			20 32				20 51		21 10			21 32				21 51	
Shelford	d			19 56									20 56									21 56	
Whittlesford Parkway	d			20 00					20 39				21 00					21 39				22 00	
Great Chesterford	d			20 04									21 04									22 04	
Audley End	d			20 10		20 24			20 47				21 10		21 24			21 47				22 10	
Newport (Essex)	d			20 13									21 13									22 13	
Elsenham	d			20 19									21 19									22 19	
Stansted Airport	a					20 45									21 45								
Stansted Airport	d		20 15		20 30			20 45		21 00		21 15		21 30			21 45		22 00		22 15		22 30
Stansted Mountfitchet	d			20 23				20 51					21 23				21 51					22 22	
Bishops Stortford	a			20 28	20 39				21 00	21 09			21 28	21 39				22 00	22 09			22 28	22 39
	d			20 28	20 39				21 00	21 09			21 28	21 39				22 00	22 09			22 28	22 39
Sawbridgeworth	d			20 32					21 05				21 32					22 05				22 32	
Harlow Mill	d			20 36									21 36									22 36	
Harlow Town	d		20 30	20 39				21 02	21 10			21 30	21 39				22 02	22 10			22 30	22 39	
Roydon	d			20 43									21 43									22 43	
Hertford East	d	20 09					20 39				21 09					21 39				22 09			
Ware	d	20 13					20 43				21 13					21 43				22 13			
St Margarets (Herts)	d	20 17					20 47				21 17					21 47				22 17			
Rye House	d	20 20					20 50				21 20					21 50				22 20			
Broxbourne ■	a	20 24		20 47			20 54		21 16		21 24		21 47			21 54		22 16		22 24		22 47	
Broxbourne ■	d	20 24		20 47			20 54		21 16		21 24		21 47			21 54		22 16		22 24		22 47	
Cheshunt	d	20 28		20 51			20 58		21 20		21 28		21 51			21 58		22 20		22 28		22 51	
Waltham Cross	d	20 31					21 01				21 31					22 01				22 31			
Enfield Lock	d	20 33					21 03				21 33					22 03				22 33			
Brimsdown	d	20 36					21 06				21 36					22 06				22 36			
Ponders End	d	20 38					21 08				21 38					22 08				22 38			
Angel Road	d																						
Northumberland Park	d																						
Tottenham Hale ⊖	d	20 44	20 47	21 00	21 03		21 14	21 17	21 29	21 32	21 44	21 47	22 00	22 03		22 14	22 17	22 29	22 32	22 44	22 47	23 00	23 03
Seven Sisters ⊖	d																						
Clapton	d																						
Stratford ■ ⊖	a	20 55		21 11			21 25		21 40		21 55		22 11			22 25		22 40		22 55		23 11	
Hackney Downs	d																						
Bethnal Green	d																						
London Liverpool Street ■ ⊖	a		21 01		21 17			21 31		21 46		22 01		22 17			22 31		22 46		23 01		23 17

		XC ◇■	LE ■	LE ■	LE ■	LE ■	LE ■	LE ■	LE ■	LE ■	LE ■	LE ■
Cambridge	d	22 10			22 32	22 51						
Shelford	d					22 56						
Whittlesford Parkway	d				22 39	23 00						
Great Chesterford	d					23 04						
Audley End	d	22 24			22 47	23 10						
Newport (Essex)	d					23 13						
Elsenham	d					23 19						
Stansted Airport	a	22 45										
Stansted Airport	d			22 45			23 00		23 15	23 30	23 45	23 59
Stansted Mountfitchet	d			22 51		23 22						
Bishops Stortford	a				23 00	23 28	23 09			23 39		00 08
	d				23 00		23 09			23 39		00 08
Sawbridgeworth	d				23 05							
Harlow Mill	d											
Harlow Town	d			23 02	23 10				23 30	23 47	23 59	00 16
Roydon	d											
Hertford East	d		22 39					23 09				
Ware	d		22 43					23 13				
St Margarets (Herts)	d		22 47					23 17				
Rye House	d		22 50					23 20				
Broxbourne ■	a		22 54		23 16			23 24				
Broxbourne ■	d		22 54		23 16			23 24				
Cheshunt	d		22 58		23 20			23 28				
Waltham Cross	d		23 01									
Enfield Lock	d		23 03									
Brimsdown	d		23 06									
Ponders End	d		23 08									
Angel Road	d											
Northumberland Park	d											
Tottenham Hale ⊖	d		23 14	23 17	23 29		23 32	23 37	23 47			
Seven Sisters ⊖	d									00 08	00 21	
Clapton	d											
Stratford ■ ⊖	a		23 25		23 40							
Hackney Downs	d							23 44				
Bethnal Green	d											
London Liverpool Street ■ ⊖	a			23 31			23 46	23 51	00 01	00 22	00 35	00 51

Table 22

Sundays

from 16 September

Cambridge, Stansted Airport, Bishops Stortford, Hertford East and Broxbourne - London

Network Diagram - see first Page of Table 20

		LE ■	LE ■	LE ■	LE ■	LE ■	LE ■	LE ■	LE ■	LE ■	LE ■ ⌶	LE ■ ⌶	LE ■	LE ■ ⌶	LE ■ ⌶	LE	LE ■	LE ■ ⌶	LE ■	LE ■ ⌶	LE	LE ■	LE ■ ⌶
Cambridge	d		22p51																			07 32	
Shelford	d		22p56																				
Whittlesford Parkway	d		23p00																			07 39	
Great Chesterford	d		23p04																				
Audley End	d		23p10																			07 47	
Newport (Essex)	d		23p13																				
Elsenham	d		23p19																				
Stansted Airport	a																						
Stansted Airport	d	23p15		23p30		23p45	23p59		00 30	05 30	06 00	06 30		07 00	07 15			07 30		07 45			08 00
Stansted Mountfitchet	d	23p21	23p22																	07 51			
Bishops Stortford	a		23p28	23p39			00 08		00 39	05 39	06 09	06 39		07 09				07 39				08 00	08 09
	d		23p28	23p39			00 08		00 39	05 39	06 09	06 39	06 42	07 09			07 28	07 39				08 00	08 09
Sawbridgeworth	d		23p32										06 46				07 32					08 05	
Harlow Mill	d		23p36														07 36						
Harlow Town	d	23p32	23p39			23p59	00 16		00 47	05 47	06 17	06 47	06 51	07 17	07 30		07 39			08 02		08 10	
Roydon	d		23p43														07 43						
Hertford East	d				23p39			00 07													07 55		
Ware	d				23p43																07 59		
St Margarets (Herts)	d				23p47																08 03		
Rye House	d				23p50																08 06		
Broxbourne ■	a		23p47		23p54			00 19					06 57				07 48				08 11	08 16	
Broxbourne ■	d		23p47		23p54								06 57			07 41	07 52				08 11	08 16	
Cheshunt	d		23p51		23p58								07 01			07 45	07 57				08 15	08 20	
Waltham Cross	d				00 01								07 04				07 59						
Enfield Lock	d				00 03								07 06				08 02						
Brimsdown	d				00 06								07 09				08 04						
Ponders End	d				00 08								07 11				08 06						
Angel Road	d																						
Northumberland Park	d																		←				
Tottenham Hale ⊖	d	23p48	23p59	00 03	00 14	00 17				06 04	06 33	07 03	07 17	07 33	07 46		08 12	08 01	08 12	08 17		08 29	08 32
Seven Sisters ⊖	d															08 03	→				08 33		
Clapton	d																						
Stratford ■ ⊖	a																		08 23				
Hackney Downs	d				00 20											08 09					08 39		
Bethnal Green	d																						
London Liverpool Street ■ ⊖	a	00 01	00 13	00 16	00 28	00 32	00 51		01 21	06 18	06 46	07 16	07 30	07 46	08 01	08 18		08 15		08 31	08 48	08 43	08 46

		LE ■ ⌶	LE	LE ■	LE ■ ⌶	LE ■	LE ■ ⌶	LE	LE ■	LE ■ ⌶	LE ■ ⌶	LE	LE ■	LE ■ ⌶	LE ■	XC ■	LE ■ ⌶	LE	LE ■	LE ■ ⌶	LE ■ ⌶	LE	LE ■
Cambridge	d			07 51					08 32				08 51			09 15			09 32				09 51
Shelford	d			07 56									08 56										09 56
Whittlesford Parkway	d			08 00					08 39				09 00						09 39				10 00
Great Chesterford	d			08 04									09 04										10 04
Audley End	d			08 10					08 47				09 10			09 28			09 47				10 10
Newport (Essex)	d			08 13									09 13										10 13
Elsenham	d			08 19									09 19										10 19
Stansted Airport	a															09 45							
Stansted Airport	d	08 15			08 30		08 45			09 00	09 15			09 30			09 45			10 00	10 15		
Stansted Mountfitchet	d			08 22			08 51						09 22				09 51						10 22
Bishops Stortford	a			08 28	08 39				09 00	09 09			09 28	09 39					10 00	10 09			10 28
	d			08 28	08 39				09 00	09 09			09 28	09 39					10 00	10 09			10 28
Sawbridgeworth	d			08 32					09 05				09 32						10 05				10 32
Harlow Mill	d			08 36									09 36										10 36
Harlow Town	d	08 30		08 39			09 02		09 10		09 30		09 39				10 02		10 10		10 30		10 39
Roydon	d			08 43									09 43										10 43
Hertford East	d		08 25					08 55				09 25						09 55				10 25	
Ware	d		08 29					08 59				09 29						09 59				10 29	
St Margarets (Herts)	d		08 33					09 03				09 33						10 03				10 33	
Rye House	d		08 36					09 06				09 36						10 06				10 36	
Broxbourne ■	a		08 41	08 48				09 11	09 16			09 41	09 48					10 11	10 16			10 41	10 48
Broxbourne ■	d		08 41	08 52				09 11	09 16			09 41	09 52					10 11	10 16			10 41	10 52
Cheshunt	d		08 45	08 57				09 15	09 20			09 45	09 57					10 15	10 20			10 45	10 57
Waltham Cross	d			08 59									09 59										10 59
Enfield Lock	d			09 02									10 02										11 02
Brimsdown	d			09 04									10 04										11 04
Ponders End	d			09 06									10 06										11 06
Angel Road	d																						
Northumberland Park	d					←									←								
Tottenham Hale ⊖	d	08 46		09 12	09 01	09 12	09 17		09 29	09 32	09 46		10 12	10 01	10 12		10 17		10 29	10 32	10 46		11 12
Seven Sisters ⊖	d		09 03	→				09 33				10 03	→					10 33				11 03	→
Clapton	d																						
Stratford ■ ⊖	a					09 23									10 23								
Hackney Downs	d		09 09					09 39				10 09						10 39				11 09	
Bethnal Green	d																						
London Liverpool Street ■ ⊖	a	09 00	09 18		09 15		09 31	09 48	09 43	09 46	10 01	10 18		10 15			10 31	10 48	10 43	10 46	11 01	11 18	

Cambridge, Stansted Airport, Bishops Stortford, Hertford East and Broxbourne - London

Network Diagram - see first Page of Table 20

		LE 1 ⊼	LE 1	XC 1	LE 1 ⊼	LE	LE 1	LE 1 ⊼	LE 1 ⊼	LE	LE 1	LE 1 ⊼	LE 1	XC 1	LE 1 ⊼	LE	LE 1	LE 1 ⊼	LE 1 ⊼	LE	LE 1	LE 1 ⊼
Cambridge	d			10 15			10 32				10 51			11 15			11 32				11 51	
Shelford	d										10 56										11 56	
Whittlesford Parkway	d						10 39				11 00						11 39				12 00	
Great Chesterford	d										11 04										12 04	
Audley End	d			10 28			10 47				11 10			11 28			11 47				12 10	
Newport (Essex)	d										11 13										12 13	
Elsenham	d										11 19										12 19	
Stansted Airport	a			10 45										11 45								
Stansted Airport	d	10 30			10 45			11 00	11 15			11 30			11 45			12 00	12 15			12 30
Stansted Mountfitchet	d				10 51						11 22				11 51						12 22	
Bishops Stortford	a	10 39					11 00	11 09			11 28	11 39					12 00	12 09			12 28	12 39
	d	10 39					11 00	11 09			11 28	11 39					12 00	12 09			12 28	12 39
Sawbridgeworth	d						11 05				11 32						12 05				12 32	
Harlow Mill	d										11 36										12 36	
Harlow Town	d				11 02		11 10		11 30		11 39				12 02		12 10		12 30		12 39	
Roydon	d										11 43										12 43	
Hertford East	d					10 55				11 25						11 55				12 25		
Ware	d					10 59				11 29						11 59				12 29		
St Margarets (Herts)	d					11 03				11 33						12 03				12 33		
Rye House	d					11 06				11 36						12 06				12 36		
Broxbourne 3	a					11 11	11 16			11 41	11 48					12 11	12 16			12 41	12 48	
Broxbourne 3	d					11 11	11 16			11 41	11 52					12 11	12 16			12 41	12 52	
Cheshunt	d					11 15	11 20			11 45	11 57					12 15	12 20			12 45	12 57	
Waltham Cross	d										11 59										12 59	
Enfield Lock	d										12 02										13 02	
Brimsdown	d										12 04										13 04	
Ponders End	d										12 06										13 06	
Angel Road	d																					
Northumberland Park	d		←										←									
Tottenham Hale ⊖	d	11 01	11 12		11 17		11 29	11 32	11 46		12 12	12 01	12 12		12 17		12 29	12 32	12 46		13 12	13 01
Seven Sisters ⊖	d					11 33				12 03	→					12 33				13 03	→	
Clapton	d																					
Stratford 7 ⊖	a		11 23										12 23									
Hackney Downs	d					11 39				12 09						12 39				13 09		
Bethnal Green	d																					
London Liverpool Street 15 ⊖	a	11 15			11 31	11 48	11 43	11 46	12 01	12 18		12 15			12 31	12 48	12 43	12 46	13 01	13 18		13 15

		LE 1	XC 1	LE 1 ⊼	LE	LE 1	LE 1 ⊼	LE 1 ⊼	LE	LE 1	LE 1 ⊼	LE 1	XC 1	LE 1 ⊼	LE	LE 1	LE 1 ⊼	LE 1 ⊼	LE	LE 1	LE 1 ⊼	LE 1	XC ◇1
Cambridge	d		12 15			12 32				12 51			13 15			13 32				13 51			14 10
Shelford	d									12 56										13 56			
Whittlesford Parkway	d					12 39				13 00						13 39				14 00			
Great Chesterford	d									13 04										14 04			
Audley End	d		12 28			12 47				13 10			13 28			13 47				14 10			14 24
Newport (Essex)	d									13 13										14 13			
Elsenham	d									13 19										14 19			
Stansted Airport	a		12 45										13 45										14 45
Stansted Airport	d			12 45			13 00	13 15			13 30			13 45			14 00	14 15			14 30		
Stansted Mountfitchet	d			12 51						13 22				13 51						14 22			
Bishops Stortford	a					13 00	13 09			13 28	13 39					14 00	14 09			14 28	14 39		
	d					13 00	13 09			13 28	13 39					14 00	14 09			14 28	14 39		
Sawbridgeworth	d					13 05				13 32						14 05				14 32			
Harlow Mill	d									13 36										14 36			
Harlow Town	d			13 02		13 10		13 30		13 39				14 02		14 10		14 30		14 39			
Roydon	d									13 43										14 43			
Hertford East	d				12 55				13 25						13 55				14 25				
Ware	d				12 59				13 29						13 59				14 29				
St Margarets (Herts)	d				13 03				13 33						14 03				14 33				
Rye House	d				13 06				13 36						14 06				14 36				
Broxbourne 3	a				13 11	13 16			13 41	13 48					14 11	14 16			14 41	14 48			
Broxbourne 3	d				13 11	13 16			13 41	13 52					14 11	14 16			14 41	14 52			
Cheshunt	d				13 15	13 20			13 45	13 57					14 15	14 20			14 45	14 57			
Waltham Cross	d									13 59										14 59			
Enfield Lock	d									14 02										15 02			
Brimsdown	d									14 04										15 04			
Ponders End	d									14 06										15 06			
Angel Road	d																						
Northumberland Park	d	←										←										←	
Tottenham Hale ⊖	d	13 12		13 17		13 29	13 32	13 46		14 12	14 01	14 12		14 17		14 29	14 32	14 46		15 12	15 01	15 12	
Seven Sisters ⊖	d				13 33				14 03	→					14 33				15 03	→			
Clapton	d																						
Stratford 7 ⊖	a	13 23										14 23										15 23	
Hackney Downs	d				13 39				14 09						14 39				15 09				
Bethnal Green	d																						
London Liverpool Street 15 ⊖	a			13 31	13 48	13 43	13 46	14 01	14 18		14 15			14 31	14 48	14 43	14 46	15 01	15 18		15 15		

Cambridge, Stansted Airport, Bishops Stortford, Hertford East and Broxbourne - London

Network Diagram - see first Page of Table 20

		LE 1 ⊼	LE	LE 1	LE 1 ⊼	LE 1 ⊼	LE	LE 1	LE 1 ⊼	LE 1	XC ◇1	LE 1 ⊼	LE	LE 1	LE 1 ⊼	LE 1 ⊼	LE	LE 1	LE 1 ⊼	LE 1	XC ◇1	LE 1 ⊼
Cambridge	d			14 32				14 51			15 10			15 32				15 51			16 10	
Shelford	d							14 56										15 56				
Whittlesford Parkway	d			14 39				15 00						15 39				16 00				
Great Chesterford	d							15 04										16 04				
Audley End	d			14 47				15 10			15 24			15 47				16 10			16 23	
Newport (Essex)	d							15 13										16 13				
Elsenham	d							15 19										16 19				
Stansted Airport	a										15 45										16 45	
Stansted Airport	d	14 45			15 00	15 15			15 30			15 45			16 00	16 15			16 30			16 45
Stansted Mountfitchet	d	14 51						15 22				15 51						16 22				16 51
Bishops Stortford	a			15 00	15 09			15 28	15 39					16 00	16 09			16 28	16 39			
	d			15 00	15 09			15 28	15 39					16 00	16 09			16 28	16 39			
Sawbridgeworth	d			15 05				15 32						16 05				16 32				
Harlow Mill	d							15 36										16 36				
Harlow Town	d	15 02		15 10		15 30		15 39				16 02		16 10		16 30		16 39				17 02
Roydon	d							15 43										16 43				
Hertford East	d		14 55				15 25						15 55				16 25					
Ware	d		14 59				15 29						15 59				16 29					
St Margarets (Herts)	d		15 03				15 33						16 03				16 33					
Rye House	d		15 06				15 36						16 06				16 36					
Broxbourne 3	a		15 11	15 16			15 41	15 48					16 11	16 16			16 41	16 48				
Broxbourne 3	d		15 11	15 16			15 41	15 52					16 11	16 16			16 41	16 52				
Cheshunt	d		15 15	15 20			15 45	15 57					16 15	16 20			16 45	16 57				
Waltham Cross	d							15 59										16 59				
Enfield Lock	d							16 02										17 02				
Brimsdown	d							16 04										17 04				
Ponders End	d							16 06										17 06				
Angel Road	d																					
Northumberland Park	d									←										←		
Tottenham Hale ⊖	d	15 17		15 29	15 32	15 46		16 12	16 01	16 12		16 17		16 29	16 32	16 46		17 12	17 01	17 12		17 17
Seven Sisters ⊖	d		15 33				16 03	→					16 33				17 03	→				
Clapton	d																					
Stratford 7 ⊖	a									16 23										17 23		
Hackney Downs	d		15 39				16 09						16 39				17 09					
Bethnal Green	d																					
London Liverpool Street 15 ⊖	a	15 31	15 48	15 43	15 46	16 01	16 18		16 15			16 31	16 48	16 43	16 46	17 01	17 18		17 15			17 31

		LE	LE 1	LE 1 ⊼	LE 1 ⊼	LE	LE 1	LE 1 ⊼	LE 1	XC ◇1	LE 1 ⊼	LE	LE 1	LE 1 ⊼	LE 1 ⊼	LE	LE 1	LE 1 ⊼	LE 1	XC ◇1	LE 1 ⊼	LE	LE 1
Cambridge	d		16 32				16 51			17 10			17 32				17 51			18 10			18 32
Shelford	d						16 56										17 56						
Whittlesford Parkway	d		16 39				17 00						17 39				18 00						18 39
Great Chesterford	d						17 04										18 04						
Audley End	d		16 47				17 10			17 24			17 47				18 10			18 24			18 47
Newport (Essex)	d						17 13										18 13						
Elsenham	d						17 19										18 19						
Stansted Airport	a									17 45										18 45			
Stansted Airport	d			17 00	17 15			17 30			17 45			18 00	18 15			18 30			18 45		
Stansted Mountfitchet	d						17 22				17 51						18 22				18 51		
Bishops Stortford	a		17 00	17 09			17 28	17 39					18 00	18 09			18 28	18 39					19 00
	d		17 00	17 09			17 28	17 39					18 00	18 09			18 28	18 39					19 00
Sawbridgeworth	d		17 05				17 32						18 05				18 32						19 05
Harlow Mill	d						17 36										18 36						
Harlow Town	d		17 10		17 30		17 39				18 02		18 10		18 30		18 39				19 02		19 10
Roydon	d						17 43										18 43						
Hertford East	d	16 55				17 25						17 55				18 25						18 55	
Ware	d	16 59				17 29						17 59				18 29						18 59	
St Margarets (Herts)	d	17 03				17 33						18 03				18 33						19 03	
Rye House	d	17 06				17 36						18 06				18 36						19 06	
Broxbourne 3	a	17 11	17 16			17 41	17 48					18 11	18 16			18 41	18 48					19 11	19 16
Broxbourne 3	d	17 11	17 16			17 41	17 52					18 11	18 16			18 41	18 52					19 11	19 16
Cheshunt	d	17 15	17 20			17 45	17 57					18 15	18 20			18 45	18 57					19 15	19 20
Waltham Cross	d						17 59										18 59						
Enfield Lock	d						18 02										19 02						
Brimsdown	d						18 04										19 04						
Ponders End	d						18 06										19 06						
Angel Road	d																						
Northumberland Park	d								←										←				
Tottenham Hale ⊖	d		17 29	17 32	17 46		18 12	18 01	18 12		18 17		18 29	18 32	18 46		19 12	19 01	19 12		19 17		19 29
Seven Sisters ⊖	d	17 33				18 03	→					18 33				19 03	→					19 33	
Clapton	d																						
Stratford 7 ⊖	a								18 23										19 23				
Hackney Downs	d	17 39				18 09						18 39				19 09						19 39	
Bethnal Green	d																						
London Liverpool Street 15 ⊖	a	17 48	17 43	17 46	18 01	18 18		18 15			18 31	18 48	18 43	18 46	19 01	19 18		19 15			19 31	19 48	19 43

Table 22

Sundays from 16 September

Cambridge, Stansted Airport, Bishops Stortford, Hertford East and Broxbourne - London

Network Diagram - see first Page of Table 20

		LE ■ ✈	LE ■ ✈	LE	LE ■	LE ■ ✈		LE ■	XC ◇■	LE ■ ✈	LE	LE ■	LE ■ ✈	LE ■ ✈	LE	LE ■		LE ■ ✈	LE ■	XC ◇■	LE ■ ✈	LE	LE ■	LE ■ ✈	LE ■ ✈
Cambridge	d				18 51				19 10			19 32				19 51				20 10			20 32		
Shelford	d				18 56											19 56									
Whittlesford Parkway	d				19 00							19 39				20 00							20 39		
Great Chesterford	d				19 04											20 04									
Audley End	d				19 10				19 24			19 47				20 10				20 24			20 47		
Newport (Essex)	d				19 13											20 13									
Elsenham	d				19 19											20 19									
Stansted Airport	a								19 45											20 45					
Stansted Airport	d	19 00	19 15			19 30				19 45			20 00	20 15				20 30			20 45			21 00	21 15
Stansted Mountfitchet	d				19 22					19 51						20 22					20 51				
Bishops Stortford	a	19 09			19 28	19 39						20 00	20 09			20 28		20 39					21 00	21 09	
	d	19 09			19 28	19 39						20 00	20 09			20 28		20 39					21 00	21 09	
Sawbridgeworth	d				19 32							20 05				20 32							21 05		
Harlow Mill	d				19 36											20 36									
Harlow Town	d		19 30		19 39					20 02		20 10		20 30		20 39					21 02		21 10		21 30
Roydon	d				19 43											20 43									
Hertford East	d			19 25							19 55				20 25							20 55			
Ware	d			19 29							19 59				20 29							20 59			
St Margarets (Herts)	d			19 33							20 03				20 33							21 03			
Rye House	d			19 36							20 06				20 36							21 06			
Broxbourne ■	a			19 41	19 48						20 11	20 16			20 41	20 48						21 11	21 16		
Broxbourne ■	d			19 41	19 52						20 11	20 16			20 41	20 52						21 11	21 16		
Cheshunt	d			19 45	19 57						20 15	20 20			20 45	20 57						21 15	21 20		
Waltham Cross	d				19 59											20 59									
Enfield Lock	d				20 02											21 02									
Brimsdown	d				20 04											21 04									
Ponders End	d				20 06											21 06									
Angel Road	d																								
Northumberland Park	d							←											←						
Tottenham Hale ⊖	d	19 32	19 46		20 12	20 01		20 12		20 17		20 29	20 32	20 46		21 12		21 01	21 12		21 17		21 29	21 32	21 46
Seven Sisters ⊖	d			20 03	→						20 33				21 03	→						21 33			
Clapton	d																								
Stratford ■ ⊖	a							20 23											21 23						
Hackney Downs	d			20 09							20 39				21 09							21 39			
Bethnal Green	d																								
London Liverpool Street ■ ⊖	a	19 46	20 01	20 18		20 15				20 31	20 48	20 43	20 46	21 01	21 18			21 15			21 31	21 48	21 43	21 46	22 01

		LE		LE ■	LE ■ ✈	LE ■	XC ◇■	LE ■ ✈	LE	LE ■	LE ■	LE ■		LE	LE ■	LE ■	LE ■	XC ◇■	LE ■	LE	LE ■	LE ■		LE ■	LE ■
Cambridge	d			20 51			21 10			21 32					21 51			22 10			22 32	22 51			
Shelford	d			20 56											21 56							22 56			
Whittlesford Parkway	d			21 00						21 39					22 00						22 39	23 00			
Great Chesterford	d			21 04											22 04							23 04			
Audley End	d			21 10			21 24			21 47					22 10			22 24			22 47	23 10			
Newport (Essex)	d			21 13											22 13							23 13			
Elsenham	d			21 19											22 19							23 19			
Stansted Airport	a						21 45											22 45							
Stansted Airport	d				21 30			21 45			22 00	22 15				22 30			22 45					23 00	23 15
Stansted Mountfitchet	d			21 22				21 51							22 22				22 51			23 22			
Bishops Stortford	a			21 28	21 39					22 00	22 09				22 28	22 39					23 00	23 28		23 09	
	d			21 28	21 39					22 00	22 09				22 28	22 39					23 00			23 09	
Sawbridgeworth	d			21 32						22 05					22 32						23 05				
Harlow Mill	d			21 36											22 36										
Harlow Town	d			21 39				22 02		22 10		22 30			22 39				23 02		23 10				23 30
Roydon	d			21 43											22 43										
Hertford East	d	21 25							21 55					22 25						22 55					
Ware	d	21 29							21 59					22 29						22 59					
St Margarets (Herts)	d	21 33							22 03					22 33						23 03					
Rye House	d	21 36							22 06					22 36						23 06					
Broxbourne ■	a	21 41		21 48					22 11	22 16				22 41	22 48					23 11	23 16				
Broxbourne ■	d	21 41		21 52					22 11	22 16				22 41	22 52					23 11	23 16				
Cheshunt	d	21 45		21 57					22 15	22 20				22 45	22 57					23 15	23 20				
Waltham Cross	d			21 59											22 59										
Enfield Lock	d			22 02											23 02										
Brimsdown	d			22 04											23 04										
Ponders End	d			22 06											23 06										
Angel Road	d																								
Northumberland Park	d					←											←								
Tottenham Hale ⊖	d			22 12	22 01	22 12		22 17		22 29	22 32	22 46			23 12	23 01	23 12		23 17		23 29			23 32	23 46
Seven Sisters ⊖	d	22 03		→					22 33					23 03	→					23 33					
Clapton	d																								
Stratford ■ ⊖	a					22 23											23 23								
Hackney Downs	d	22 09							22 39					23 09						23 39					
Bethnal Green	d																								
London Liverpool Street ■ ⊖	a	22 18			22 15			22 31	22 48	22 43	22 46	23 01		23 18		23 15			23 31	23 48	23 43			23 46	00 01

Table 22

Sundays from 16 September

Cambridge, Stansted Airport, Bishops Stortford, Hertford East and Broxbourne - London

Network Diagram - see first Page of Table 20

		LE ■	LE ■	LE ■
Cambridge	d			
Shelford	d			
Whittlesford Parkway	d			
Great Chesterford	d			
Audley End	d			
Newport (Essex)	d			
Elsenham	d			
Stansted Airport	a			
Stansted Airport	d	23 30	23 45	23 59
Stansted Mountfitchet	d			
Bishops Stortford	a	23 39		00 08
	d	23 39		00 08
Sawbridgeworth	d			
Harlow Mill	d			
Harlow Town	d	23 47	23 59	00 16
Roydon	d			
Hertford East	d			
Ware	d			
St Margarets (Herts)	d			
Rye House	d			
Broxbourne ■	a			
Broxbourne ■	d			
Cheshunt	d			
Waltham Cross	d			
Enfield Lock	d			
Brimsdown	d			
Ponders End	d			
Angel Road	d			
Northumberland Park	d			
Tottenham Hale ⊖	d			
Seven Sisters ⊖	d	00 08	00 21	
Clapton	d			
Stratford ■ ⊖	a			
Hackney Downs	d			
Bethnal Green	d			
London Liverpool Street ■ ⊖	a	00 22	00 35	00 51

Network Diagram for Tables 24, 25

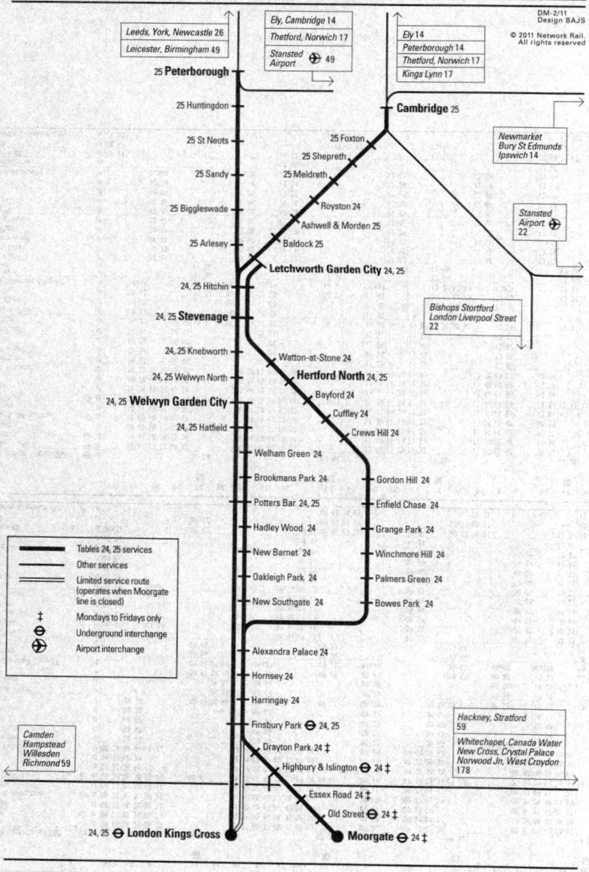

London - Welwyn Garden City, Hertford North and Letchworth Garden City

Network Diagram - see first Page of Table 24

Miles	Miles		FC MO A 🚌	FC MO A 🚌	FC MO B	FC MX	FC MX 1	FC MX	FC MO C	FC MX	FC MO A 🚌	FC MO 1 D	FC MX	FC	FC 1	FC MO A 🚌	FC 1 E	FC MX 1 F	FC MO 1 G	FC 1	FC MO A 🚌	FC 1
0	—	London Kings Cross 15 ⊖ d			23p26	23p26	23p36		23p41	23p41		00 07	00 06	00 11	00 36		01 06	01 06	01 06	01 36		05 23
—	0	**Moorgate** ⊖ d																				
—	0½	Old Street ⊖ d																				
—	1¾	Essex Road d																				
—	2¼	Highbury & Islington ⊖ d																				
—	2¾	Drayton Park d																				
2½	3½	Finsbury Park ⊖ d			23p32	23p32	23p41		23p47	23p47		00 12	00 12	00 17	00 41		01 11	01 11	01 11	01 41		05 28
3½	4½	Harringay d			23p34	23p34			23p49	23p49			00 14	00 19								
4	5	Hornsey d			23p36	23p36			23p51	23p51			00 16	00 21								
5	6	Alexandra Palace d			23p38	23p38			23p53	23p53		00 17	00 18	00 23		00 25	01 16	01 16	01 16	01 45	01 25	
6½	—	New Southgate d							23p56	23p56				00 26						01 48		
8½	—	Oakleigh Park d							23p59	23p59				00 29						01 51		
9¼	—	New Barnet d							00 01	00 01				00 31						01 53		
10½	—	Hadley Wood d							00 04	00 04				00 34						01 56		
12¾	—	Potters Bar d					23p51		00 08	00 08				00 38	00 51					01 59		05 38
14½	—	Brookmans Park d							00 11	00 11				00 41								
15½	—	Welham Green d							00 13	00 13				00 43								
17¾	—	Hatfield d					23p57		00 16	00 16				00 46	00 57					02 05		05 44
20¼	—	**Welwyn Garden City** 4 d					00 01		00 20	00a24				00a54	01 01					02 09		05 48
22	—	Welwyn North d					00 04		00 23						01s04					02s12		05 51
25	—	Knebworth d					00 08		00 28						01s08					02s16		05 55
—	6¾	Bowes Park d			23p41	23p41							00 21									
—	7¾	Palmers Green d			23p43	23p43						00 20	00 23			00 36	01 19	01 19	01 19		01 36	
—	8¾	Winchmore Hill d			23p45	23p45						00 22	00 25			00 44	01 21	01 21	01 21		01 44	
—	9½	Grange Park d			23p47	23p47							00 27									
—	10¼	Enfield Chase d			23p49	23p49						00 25	00 29			00 54	01 24	01 24	01 24		01 54	
—	11	Gordon Hill d	23p00	23p30	23p51	23p51					23p59	00 27	00 31			01 00	01 26	01 26	01 26		02 00	
—	12½	Crews Hill d	23p10	23p40	23p54	23p54					00 10		00 34									
—	14¼	Cuffley d	23p18	23p48	23p57	23p57					00 18	00 31	00 37			01 15	01 30	01 30	01 30		02 15	
—	17¾	Bayford d	23p33	00 03	00 02	00 02					00 33		00 42									
—	20¼	**Hertford North** d	23p50	00a18	00 07	00 07					00 50	00 39	00 47			01 40	01 38	01 38	01 38		02 40	
—	25	Watton-at-Stone d	00 04		00 13	00 13		←			01 04		00 53									
27½	30	**Stevenage** 4 d	00a21		00a20	00 20	00 12	00 20	00 31		01a21	00 48	01 00		01 12	02a02	01 47	01 47	01 47	02 20	03s02	05 59
31¾	34¼	Hitchin 4 d				→	00 20	00 26	00 37			00 56	01 06		01a17		01 52	01 52	01 52	02a25	03s22	06a07
34¾	37¼	**Letchworth Garden City** a					00 29	00 36	00 52			01 00	01 15				01 56	02 01	02 06		03 37	

	FC	FC	FC	FC 1	FC	FC	FC 1	FC	FC	FC 1	FC	FC	FC 1	FC	FC	FC	FC 1	FC	FC	FC H	FC I	FC
London Kings Cross 15 ⊖ d		05 26	05 56	06 06	06 11	06 26	06 36			07 06			07 36				08 03					
Moorgate ⊖ d								06 35	06 50		07 05	07 20		07 33	07 38	07 48			07 58	08 03	08 03	08 08
Old Street ⊖ d								06 37	06 52		07 07	07 22		07 35	07 40	07 50			08 00	08 05	08 05	08 10
Essex Road d								06 40	06 55		07 10	07 25		07 38	07 43	07 53			08 03	08 08	08 08	08 13
Highbury & Islington ⊖ d								06 42	06 57		07 12	07 27		07 40	07 45	07 55			08 05	08 10	08 10	08 15
Drayton Park d								06 44	06 59		07 14	07 29		07 42	07 47	07 57			08 07	08 12	08 12	08 17
Finsbury Park ⊖ d		05 32	06 02	06 11	06 17	06 32	06 41	06 47	07 02	07 11	07 17	07 32	07 41	07 45	07 50	08 00	08 08		08 10	08 15	08 15	08 20
Harringay d		05 34	06 04		06 19	06 34		06 49	07 04		07 19	07 34			07 52	08 02				08 17		08 22
Hornsey d		05 36	06 06		06 21	06 36		06 51	07 06		07 21	07 36			07 54	08 04				08 19		08 24
Alexandra Palace d		05 38	06 08		06 23	06 38		06 53	07 08		07 23	07 38		07 51	07 56	08 06			08 14	08 21	08 21	08 26
New Southgate d					06 26			06 56			07 26				07 59							08 29
Oakleigh Park d					06 29			06 59			07 29				08 02							08 32
New Barnet d					06 31			07 01			07 31				08 04							08 34
Hadley Wood d					06 34			07 04			07 34				08 07							08 37
Potters Bar d				06 21	06 38		06 51	07 08		07 21	07 38		07 51		08 11		08 18					08 41
Brookmans Park d					06 41			07 11			07 41				08 14							08 44
Welham Green d					06 43			07 13			07 43				08 16							08 46
Hatfield d				06 27	06 46		06 57	07 16		07 27	07 46		07 57		08 19		08 25					08 49
Welwyn Garden City 4 d				06 31	06a53		07 01	07a21		07 31	07a51		08 01		08a24		08 30					08a54
Welwyn North d				06 34			07 04			07 34			08 04				08 33					
Knebworth d				06 38			07 08			07 38			08 08				08 37					
Bowes Park d		05 41	06 11			06 41			07 11			07 41				08 09			08 17			
Palmers Green d		05 43	06 13			06 43			07 13			07 43		07 55		08 11			08 19	08 25	08 25	
Winchmore Hill d		05 45	06 15			06 45			07 15			07 45		07 57		08 13			08 21	08 27	08 27	
Grange Park d		05 47	06 17			06 47			07 17			07 47				08 15			08 23			
Enfield Chase d		05 49	06 19			06 49			07 19			07 49		08 01		08 17			08 25	08 31	08 31	
Gordon Hill d		05 51	06 21			06 51			07 21			07 51		08 03		08 19			08a29	08 33	08 33	
Crews Hill d		05 54	06 24			06 54			07 24			07 54				08 22						
Cuffley d		05 57	06 27			06 57			07 27			07 57		08 08		08 25				08 38	08 38	
Bayford d		06 02	06 32			07 02			07 32			08 02				08 30						
Hertford North d	05 50	06a10	06 40			07 10			07 40			08 10		08a16		08 37				08a46	08a46	
Watton-at-Stone d	05 55		06 45			07 15			07 45			08 15				08 43		←				
Stevenage 4 d	06a04		06a55	06 42		07a25	07 12		07a55	07 42		08a25	08 12			08 51	08 41	08 51				
Hitchin 4 d				06 47			07a17			07 47			08a17			→	08 46	08 57				
Letchworth Garden City a				06 51						07 51							08 50	09 03				

A from 17 September until 22 October
B from 21 May until 10 September, from 29 October
C from 21 May
D until 10 September, from 29 October
E from 30 July until 10 September, not from 14 August until 29 August
F not from 31 July until 10 August, from 30 August until 7 September
G until 23 July, 20 August, 27 August, from 29 October
H from 27 July
I until 26 July

London - Welwyn Garden City, Hertford North and Letchworth Garden City

Network Diagram - see first Page of Table 24

		FC	FC	FC		FC 1	FC	FC	FC	FC	FC	FC 1	FC	FC		FC	FC	FC 1	FC	FC	FC	FC	FC	FC 1
London Kings Cross 15	⊖ d					08 36						09 06						09 36						10 06
Moorgate	⊖ d	08 18	08 23	08 28				08 33	08 38	08 43	08 52			09 02		09 12	09 22				09 32	09 42	09 52	
Old Street	⊖ d	08 20	08 25	08 30				08 35	08 40	08 45	08 54			09 04		09 14	09 24				09 34	09 44	09 54	
Essex Road	d	08 23	08 28	08 33				08 38	08 43	08 48	08 57			09 07		09 17	09 27				09 37	09 47	09 57	
Highbury & Islington	⊖ d	08 25	08 30	08 35				08 40	08 45	08 50	08 59			09 09		09 19	09 29				09 39	09 49	09 59	
Drayton Park	d	08 27	08 32	08 37				08 42	08 47	08 52	09 01			09 11		09 21	09 31				09 41	09 51	10 01	
Finsbury Park	⊖ d	08 30	08 35	08 40		08 41		08 45	08 50	08 55	09 04	09 11		09 14		09 24	09 34	09 41			09 44	09 54	10 04	10 11
Harringay	d	08 32	08 37					08 47	08 52	08 57	09 06			09 16		09 26	09 36				09 46	09 56	10 06	
Hornsey	d	08 34	08 39					08 49	08 54	08 59	09 08			09 18		09 28	09 38				09 48	09 58	10 08	
Alexandra Palace	d	08 36	08 41	08 45				08 51	08 56	09 01	09 10			09 20		09 30	09 40				09 50	10 00	10 10	
New Southgate	d		08 44						08 59					09 23			09 43					10 03		
Oakleigh Park	d		08 47						09 02					09 26			09 46					10 06		
New Barnet	d		08 49						09 04					09 28			09 48					10 08		
Hadley Wood	d		08 52				←		09 07					09 31			09 51			←		10 11		
Potters Bar	d		08 56			08 51	08 56		09 11			09 21		09 35			09 55	09 51		09 55		10 15		10 21
Brookmans Park	d		→				08 59		09 14					09 38			→			09 58		10 18		
Welham Green	d						09 01		09 16					09 40						10 00		10 20		
Hatfield	d					08 57	09 04		09 19			09 27		09 43				09 57		10 03		10 23		10 27
Welwyn Garden City 4	d					09 01	09a09		09a27			09 31		09a49				10 01		10a09		10a29		10 31
Welwyn North	d					09 04						09 34						10 04						10 34
Knebworth	d					09 08						09 38						10 08						10 38
Bowes Park	d	08 39		08 48						09 04	09 13					09 33					09 53		10 13	
Palmers Green	d	08 41		08 50				08 55		09 06	09 15					09 35					09 55		10 15	
Winchmore Hill	d	08 43		08 52				08 57		09 08	09 17					09 37					09 57		10 17	
Grange Park	d	08 45		08 54						09 10	09 19					09 39					09 59		10 19	
Enfield Chase	d	08 47		08 56				09 01		09 12	09 21					09 41					10 01		10 21	
Gordon Hill	d	08 49		08a59				09 03		09a16	09 23					09 43					10 03		10 23	
Crews Hill	d	08 52									09 26					09 46					10 06		10 26	
Cuffley	d	08 55						09 08			09 29					09 49					10 09		10 29	
Bayford	d	09 00									09 34					09 54					10 14		10 34	
Hertford North	d	09 07						09a16			09 39					10 09					10a20		10 39	
Watton-at-Stone	d	09 13									09 45		←			10 15			←				10 45	
Stevenage 4	d	09a22				09 12					09 51	09 42	09 51			10 21		10 12	10 21				10 51	10 42
Hitchin 4	d					09a17					→	09 47	09 57			→		10a17	10 27				→	10 47
Letchworth Garden City	a											09 51	10 03						10 33					10 51

		FC	FC	FC	FC	FC 1	FC	FC	FC	FC		FC 1	FC	FC	FC	FC	FC 1	FC	FC	FC		FC	FC 1	FC	FC
London Kings Cross 15	⊖ d					10 36						11 06					11 36						12 06		
Moorgate	⊖ d		10 02	10 12	10 22			10 32	10 42	10 52				11 02	11 12	11 22			11 32	11 42		11 52			12 02
Old Street	⊖ d		10 04	10 14	10 24			10 34	10 44	10 54				11 04	11 14	11 24			11 34	11 44		11 54			12 04
Essex Road	d		10 07	10 17	10 27			10 37	10 47	10 57				11 07	11 17	11 27			11 37	11 47		11 57			12 07
Highbury & Islington	⊖ d		10 09	10 19	10 29			10 39	10 49	10 59				11 09	11 19	11 29			11 39	11 49		11 59			12 09
Drayton Park	d		10 11	10 21	10 31			10 41	10 51	11 01				11 11	11 21	11 31			11 41	11 51		12 01			12 11
Finsbury Park	⊖ d		10 14	10 24	10 34	10 41		10 44	10 54	11 04		11 11		11 14	11 24	11 34	11 41		11 44	11 54		12 04	12 11		12 14
Harringay	d		10 16	10 26	10 36			10 46	10 56	11 06				11 16	11 26	11 36			11 46	11 56		12 06			12 16
Hornsey	d		10 18	10 28	10 38			10 48	10 58	11 08				11 18	11 28	11 38			11 48	11 58		12 08			12 18
Alexandra Palace	d		10 20	10 30	10 40			10 50	11 00	11 10				11 20	11 30	11 40			11 50	12 00		12 10			12 20
New Southgate	d		10 23		10 43				11 03					11 23		11 43				12 03					12 23
Oakleigh Park	d		10 26		10 46				11 06					11 26		11 46				12 06					12 26
New Barnet	d		10 28		10 48				11 08					11 28		11 48				12 08					12 28
Hadley Wood	d		10 31		10 51		←		11 11					11 31		11 51		←		12 11					12 31
Potters Bar	d		10 35		10 55	10 51	10 55		11 15			11 21		11 35		11 55	11 51	11 55		12 15			12 21		12 35
Brookmans Park	d		10 38		→		10 58		11 18					11 38		→		11 58		12 18					12 38
Welham Green	d		10 40				11 00		11 20					11 40				12 00		12 20					12 40
Hatfield	d		10 43			10 57	11 03		11 23			11 27		11 43			11 57	12 03		12 23			12 27		12 43
Welwyn Garden City 4	d		10a49			11 01	11a09		11a29			11 31		11a49			12 01	12a09		12a29			12 31		12a49
Welwyn North	d					11 04						11 34					12 04						12 34		
Knebworth	d					11 08						11 38					12 08						12 38		
Bowes Park	d			10 33				10 53		11 13					11 33				11 53			12 13			
Palmers Green	d			10 35				10 55		11 15					11 35				11 55			12 15			
Winchmore Hill	d			10 37				10 57		11 17					11 37				11 57			12 17			
Grange Park	d			10 39				10 59		11 19					11 39				11 59			12 19			
Enfield Chase	d			10 41				11 01		11 21					11 41				12 01			12 21			
Gordon Hill	d			10 43				11 03		11 23					11 43				12 03			12 23			
Crews Hill	d			10 46				11 06		11 26					11 46				12 06			12 26			
Cuffley	d			10 49				11 09		11 29					11 49				12 09			12 29			
Bayford	d			10 54				11 14		11 34					11 54				12 14			12 34			
Hertford North	d			11a00				11a20		11 39					12a00				12a20			12 39			
Watton-at-Stone	d	←								11 45			←									12 45		←	
Stevenage 4	d	10 51				11 12				11 51		11 42	11 51				12 12					12 51	12 42	12 51	
Hitchin 4	d	10 57				11a17				→		11 47	11 57				12a17					→	12 47	12 57	
Letchworth Garden City	a	11 03										11 51	12 03										12 51	13 03	

London - Welwyn Garden City, Hertford North and Letchworth Garden City

Network Diagram - see first Page of Table 24

		FC	FC	FC 1	FC	FC		FC	FC	FC 1	FC	FC	FC	FC	FC 1	FC		FC	FC	FC	FC 1	FC	FC	FC	FC
London Kings Cross 15	⊖ d			12 36						13 06					13 36						14 06				
Moorgate	⊖ d	12 12	12 22			12 32		12 42	12 52			13 02	13 12	13 22				13 32	13 42	13 52			14 02	14 12	14 22
Old Street	⊖ d	12 14	12 24			12 34		12 44	12 54			13 04	13 14	13 24				13 34	13 44	13 54			14 04	14 14	14 24
Essex Road	d	12 17	12 27			12 37		12 47	12 57			13 07	13 17	13 27				13 37	13 47	13 57			14 07	14 17	14 27
Highbury & Islington	⊖ d	12 19	12 29			12 39		12 49	12 59			13 09	13 19	13 29				13 39	13 49	13 59			14 09	14 19	14 29
Drayton Park	d	12 21	12 31			12 41		12 51	13 01			13 11	13 21	13 31				13 41	13 51	14 01			14 11	14 21	14 31
Finsbury Park	⊖ d	12 24	12 34	12 41		12 44		12 54	13 04	13 11		13 14	13 24	13 34	13 41			13 44	13 54	14 04	14 11		14 14	14 24	14 34
Harringay	d	12 26	12 36			12 46		12 56	13 06			13 16	13 26	13 36				13 46	13 56	14 06			14 16	14 26	14 36
Hornsey	d	12 28	12 38			12 48		12 58	13 08			13 18	13 28	13 38				13 48	13 58	14 08			14 18	14 28	14 38
Alexandra Palace	d	12 30	12 40			12 50		13 00	13 10			13 20	13 30	13 40				13 50	14 00	14 10			14 20	14 30	14 40
New Southgate	d		12 43					13 03				13 23		13 43					14 03				14 23		14 43
Oakleigh Park	d		12 46					13 06				13 26		13 46					14 06				14 26		14 46
New Barnet	d		12 48					13 08				13 28		13 48					14 08				14 28		14 48
Hadley Wood	d		12 51		←			13 11				13 31		13 51		←			14 11				14 31		14 51
Potters Bar	d		12 55	12 51	12 55			13 15		13 21		13 35		13 55	13 51	13 55			14 15		14 21		14 35		14 55
Brookmans Park	d		→		12 58			13 18				13 38		→		13 58			14 18				14 38		→
Welham Green	d				13 00			13 20				13 40				14 00			14 20				14 40		
Hatfield	d			12 57	13 03			13 23		13 27		13 43			13 57	14 03			14 23		14 27		14 43		
Welwyn Garden City 4	d			13 01	13a09			13a29		13 31		13a49			14 01	14a09			14a29		14 31		14a49		
Welwyn North	d			13 04						13 34					14 04						14 34				
Knebworth	d			13 08						13 38					14 08						14 38				
Bowes Park	d	12 33				12 53			13 13				13 33					13 53		14 13				14 33	
Palmers Green	d	12 35				12 55			13 15				13 35					13 55		14 15				14 35	
Winchmore Hill	d	12 37				12 57			13 17				13 37					13 57		14 17				14 37	
Grange Park	d	12 39				12 59			13 19				13 39					13 59		14 19				14 39	
Enfield Chase	d	12 41				13 01			13 21				13 41					14 01		14 21				14 41	
Gordon Hill	d	12 43				13 03			13 23				13 43					14 03		14 23				14 43	
Crews Hill	d	12 46				13 06			13 26				13 46					14 06		14 26				14 46	
Cuffley	d	12 49				13 09			13 29				13 49					14 09		14 29				14 49	
Bayford	d	12 54				13 14			13 34				13 54					14 14		14 34				14 54	
Hertford North	d	13a00				13a20			13 39				14a00					14a20		14 39				15a00	
Watton-at-Stone	d								13 45		←									14 45		←			
Stevenage 4	d			13 12					13 51	13 42	13 51				14 12					14 51	14 42	14 51			
Hitchin 4	d			13a17					→	13 47	13 57				14a17					→	14 47	14 57			
Letchworth Garden City	a									13 51	14 03										14 51	15 03			

		FC 1		FC	FC	FC	FC	FC 1	FC	FC	FC	FC		FC 1	FC	FC	FC	FC	FC	FC 1	FC	FC		FC	FC
London Kings Cross 15	⊖ d	14 36						15 06						15 36			15 44			16 06					
Moorgate	⊖ d				14 32	14 42	14 52			15 02	15 12	15 22				15 32		15 42	15 52		16 02	16 08		16 18	16 23
Old Street	⊖ d				14 34	14 44	14 54			15 04	15 14	15 24				15 34		15 44	15 54		16 04	16 10		16 20	16 25
Essex Road	d				14 37	14 47	14 57			15 07	15 17	15 27				15 37		15 47	15 57		16 07	16 13		16 23	16 28
Highbury & Islington	⊖ d				14 39	14 49	14 59			15 09	15 19	15 29				15 39		15 49	15 59		16 09	16 16		16 26	16 31
Drayton Park	d				14 41	14 51	15 01			15 11	15 21	15 31				15 41		15 51	16 01		16 11	16 17		16 27	16 32
Finsbury Park	⊖ d	14 41			14 44	14 54	15 04	15 11		15 14	15 24	15 34		15 41		15 44	15 50	15 54	16 04	16 11	16 14	16 20		16 30	16 35
Harringay	d				14 46	14 56	15 06			15 16	15 26	15 36				15 46		15 56	16 06		16 16	16 23		16 33	
Hornsey	d				14 48	14 58	15 08			15 18	15 28	15 38				15 48		15 58	16 08		16 18	16 25		16 35	
Alexandra Palace	d				14 50	15 00	15 10			15 20	15 30	15 40				15 50		16 00	16 10		16 20	16 28		16 38	16 41
New Southgate	d					15 03				15 23		15 43					15 55	16 03			16 23				
Oakleigh Park	d					15 06				15 26		15 46					15 58	16 06			16 26				
New Barnet	d					15 08				15 28		15 48					16 00	16 08			16 28				
Hadley Wood	d			←		15 11				15 31		15 51			←			16 11			16 31				
Potters Bar	d	14 51		14 55		15 15		15 21		15 35		15 55		15 51	15 55		16 05	16 15		16 21	16 35				
Brookmans Park	d			14 58		15 18				15 38		→			15 58			16 18			16 38				
Welham Green	d			15 00		15 20				15 40					16 00			16 20			16 40				
Hatfield	d	14 57		15 03		15 23		15 27		15 43				15 58	16 03		16 11	16 23		16 28	16 43				
Welwyn Garden City 4	d	15 01		15a09		15a29		15 31		15a49				16 02	16a09		16a16	16a29		16 32	16a49				
Welwyn North	d	15 04						15 34						16 05						16 35					
Knebworth	d	15 08						15 38						16 09						16 39					
Bowes Park	d				14 53		15 13				15 33					15 53			16 13			16 30			16 44
Palmers Green	d				14 55		15 15				15 35					15 55			16 15			16 32		16 41	16 46
Winchmore Hill	d				14 57		15 17				15 37					15 57			16 17			16 35		16 44	16 49
Grange Park	d				14 59		15 19				15 39					15 59			16 19			16 37			16 51
Enfield Chase	d				15 01		15 21				15 41					16 01			16 21			16 39		16 47	16 53
Gordon Hill	d				15 03		15 23				15 43					16 03			16 23			16 41		16a51	16 55
Crews Hill	d				15 06		15 26				15 46					16 06			16 26			16 44			
Cuffley	d				15 09		15 29				15 49					16 09			16 29			16 47			17 00
Bayford	d				15 14		15 34				15 54					16 14			16 34			16 52			
Hertford North	d				15a20		15 39				16 09					16a20			16 39			16a58			17 09
Watton-at-Stone	d						15 45		←		16 15								16 45						17 15
Stevenage 4	d	15 12					15 51	15 42	15 51		16a23			16 12					16a53	16 45					17a23
Hitchin 4	d	15a17					→	15 47	15 57					16a17						16 50					
Letchworth Garden City	a							15 51	16 03											16 55					

London - Welwyn Garden City, Hertford North and Letchworth Garden City

Network Diagram - see first Page of Table 24

		FC ■	FC	FC	FC	FC ■	FC	FC	FC	FC	FC	FC	FC	FC ■	FC	FC	FC	FC	FC	FC	FC	FC	FC ■
London Kings Cross 15 ⊖	d	16 32				16 54	16 54							17 22			17 27						17 52
Moorgate ⊖	d		16 28	16 33	16 38			16 48	16 53	16 58	17 03	17 08	17 13			17 18		17 23	17 28	17 33	17 38	17 43	
Old Street ⊖	d		16 30	16 35	16 40			16 50	16 55	17 00	17 05	17 10	17 15			17 20		17 25	17 30	17 35	17 40	17 45	
Essex Road	d		16 33	16 38	16 43			16 53	16 58	17 03	17 08	17 13	17 18			17 23		17 28	17 33	17 38	17 43	17 48	
Highbury & Islington ⊖	d		16 36	16 41	16 46			16 56	17 01	17 06	17 11	17 16	17 21			17 26		17 31	17 36	17 41	17 46	17 51	
Drayton Park	d		16 37	16 42	16 47			16 57	17 02	17 07	17 12	17 17	17 22			17 27		17 32	17 37	17 42	17 47	17 52	
Finsbury Park ⊖	d	16 37	16 40	16 45	16 50	16 59	16 59	17 00	17 05	17 10	17 15	17 20	17 25	17 28		17 30	17 33	17 35	17 40	17 45	17 50	17 55	17 58
Harringay	d		16 43		16 53				17 08		17 18	17 23						17 38		17 48	17 53		
Hornsey	d		16 45		16 55				17 10		17 20	17 25						17 40		17 50	17 55		
Alexandra Palace	d		16 47	16 51	16 58				17 12	17 16	17 23	17 27	17 31					17 42	17 46	17 53	17 57	18 01	
New Southgate	d		16 50				17 04		17 15			17 30					17 38	17 45			18 00		
Oakleigh Park	d		16 54				17 08		17 19			17 34					17 41	17 49			18 04		
New Barnet	d		16 56				17 10		17 21			17 36					17 43	17 51			18 06		
Hadley Wood	d		16 59				17 12		17 24			17 39						17 54			18 09		
Potters Bar	d	16 47	17 03				17 16		17 28			17 43					17 49	17 58			18 13		
Brookmans Park	d		17 06						17 31			17 46						18 01			18 16		
Welham Green	d		17 08						17 33			17 48			←			18 03			18 18		
Hatfield	d	16 54	17 11			17 15	17 22		17 36			17 51		17 44	17 51		17 55	18 06			18 21		18 14
Welwyn Garden City 4	d	16 58	17a16			17 19	17a27		17a41			→		17 48	17a56		18a00	18a11			→		18 18
Welwyn North	d	17 01				17 22								17 52									18 22
Knebworth	d	17 06				17 26								17 56									18 26
Bowes Park	d				17 00			17 07			17 25					17 37				17 55			
Palmers Green	d			16 54	17 02			17 09		17 19	17 27		17 34			17 39			17 49	17 57		18 04	
Winchmore Hill	d			16 57	17 05			17 12		17 22	17 30		17 37			17 42			17 52	18 00		18 07	
Grange Park	d				17 07			17 14			17 32					17 44				18 02			
Enfield Chase	d			17 01	17 09			17 16		17 26	17 34		17 41			17 46			17 56	18 04		18 11	
Gordon Hill	d			17 03	17a12			17 18		17a31	17 37		17a44			17 49			17 58	18 07		18a14	
Crews Hill	d			17 06							17 40									18 10			
Cuffley	d			17 09				17 23			17 43					17 53			18 03	18 13			
Bayford	d			17 14							17 48									18 18			
Hertford North	d			17a20				17 33			17a53					18 03			18a12	18a23			
Watton-at-Stone	d							17 38								18 08							
Stevenage 4	d	17 10				17 36		17a46						18 04		18a16							18 34
Hitchin 4	d	17 17				17 42								18 10									18 40
Letchworth Garden City	a	17 21				17 47								18 16									18 46

		FC	FC	FC	FC	FC	FC	FC	FC	FC ■	FC	FC	FC	FC	FC	FC	FC	FC ■	FC	FC	FC	FC
London Kings Cross 15 ⊖	d			17 57						18 22			18 27					18 52		18 57		
Moorgate ⊖	d		17 48		17 53	17 58	18 03	18 08	18 13			18 18		18 23	18 28	18 37	18 42				18 52	18 57
Old Street ⊖	d		17 50		17 55	18 00	18 05	18 10	18 15			18 20		18 25	18 30	18 39	18 44				18 54	18 59
Essex Road	d		17 53		17 58	18 03	18 08	18 13	18 18			18 23		18 28	18 33	18 42	18 47				18 57	19 02
Highbury & Islington ⊖	d		17 56		18 01	18 06	18 11	18 16	18 21			18 26		18 31	18 36	18 45	18 50				19 00	19 05
Drayton Park	d		17 57		18 02	18 07	18 12	18 17	18 22			18 27		18 32	18 37	18 46	18 51				19 01	19 06
Finsbury Park ⊖	d		18 00	18 03	18 05	18 10	18 15	18 20	18 25	18 28		18 30	18 33	18 35	18 40	18 49	18 54	18 58		19 03	19 04	19 09
Harringay	d				18 08		18 18	18 23						18 38		18 52	18 57					19 12
Hornsey	d				18 10		18 20	18 25						18 40		18 54	18 59					19 14
Alexandra Palace	d				18 12	18 16	18 23	18 27	18 31					18 42	18 46	18 57	19 01					19 16
New Southgate	d			18 08	18 15			18 30					18 38	18 45			19 04			19 08		19 19
Oakleigh Park	d			18 11	18 19			18 34					18 41	18 49			19 08			19 11		19 23
New Barnet	d				18 21			18 36					18 43	18 51			19 10			19 13		19 25
Hadley Wood	d			18 15	18 24			18 39						18 54			19 13			19 16		19 28
Potters Bar	d			18 19	18 28			18 43					18 49	18 58			19 17			19 21		19 32
Brookmans Park	d				18 31			18 46						19 01			19 20					19 35
Welham Green	d	←			18 33			18 48			←			19 03			19 22		←			19 37
Hatfield	d	18 21		18 25	18 36			18 51		18 44	18 51		18 55	19 06			19 25	19 14	19 25	19 28		19 40
Welwyn Garden City 4	d	18a26		18a30	18a41			→		18 49	18a56		19a00	19a11			→	19 19	19a30	19a33		19a45
Welwyn North	d									18 51								19 24				
Knebworth	d									18 55								19 28				
Bowes Park	d		18 07				18 25					18 37				18 59					19 11	
Palmers Green	d		18 09			18 19	18 27		18 34			18 39			18 49	19 01					19 13	
Winchmore Hill	d		18 12			18 22	18 30		18 37			18 42			18 52	19 04					19 16	
Grange Park	d		18 14				18 32					18 44				19 06					19 18	
Enfield Chase	d		18 16			18 26	18 34		18 41			18 46			18 56	19 08					19 20	
Gordon Hill	d		18 19			18 28	18 37		18a44			18 49			18 58	19 11					19 23	
Crews Hill	d						18 40									19 14						
Cuffley	d		18 23			18 33	18 43					18 53			19 03	19 17					19 27	
Bayford	d						18 48									19 22						
Hertford North	d		18 33			18a42	18a53					19 03			19a12	19a27					19 37	
Watton-at-Stone	d		18 38									19 08									19 42	
Stevenage 4	d		18a46							19 04		19 16						19 35			19a52	
Hitchin 4	d									19 10		19 22						19 42				
Letchworth Garden City	a									19 16		19 27						19 46				

London - Welwyn Garden City, Hertford North and Letchworth Garden City

Network Diagram - see first Page of Table 24

		FC	FC ■	FC	FC	FC ■	FC	FC	FC	FC	FC	FC	FC	FC ■	FC	FC	FC ■	FC	FC	FC	FC	FC ■	FC
London Kings Cross 15 ⊖	d		19 18			19 34				19 40				20 06			20 36					21 06	
Moorgate ⊖	d	19 02		19 12	19 22				19 32		19 37	19 42	19 52		20 07	20 12			20 32	20 37	20 52		21 07
Old Street ⊖	d	19 04		19 14	19 24				19 34		19 39	19 44	19 54		20 09	20 14			20 34	20 39	20 54		21 09
Essex Road	d	19 07		19 17	19 27				19 37		19 42	19 47	19 57		20 12	20 17			20 37	20 42	20 57		21 12
Highbury & Islington ⊖	d	19 10		19 20	19 30				19 40		19 45	19 50	19 59		20 14	20 19			20 39	20 44	20 59		21 14
Drayton Park	d	19 11		19 21	19 31				19 41		19 46	19 51	20 01		20 16	20 21			20 41	20 46	21 01		21 16
Finsbury Park ⊖	d	19 14	19 23	19 24	19 34	19 39			19 44	19 46	19 49	19 54	20 04	20 11	20 19	20 24	20 41		20 44	20 49	21 04	21 11	21 19
Harringay	d	19 17		19 27	19 37						19 52	19 57	20 06		20 21	20 26			20 46	20 51	21 06		21 21
Hornsey	d	19 19		19 29	19 39						19 54	19 59	20 08		20 23	20 28			20 48	20 53	21 08		21 23
Alexandra Palace	d	19 22		19 31	19 42						19 56	20 02	20 10		20 25	20 30			20 50	20 55	21 10		21 25
New Southgate	d			19 34						19 51	19 59				20 28					20 58			21 28
Oakleigh Park	d			19 38						19 54	20 03				20 31					21 01			21 31
New Barnet	d			19 40						19 56	20 05				20 33					21 03			21 33
Hadley Wood	d			19 43							20 08				20 36					21 06			21 36
Potters Bar	d		19 37	19 47						20 02	20 12			20 21	20 40		20 51			21 10		21 21	21 40
Brookmans Park	d			19 50							20 15				20 43					21 13			21 43
Welham Green	d			19 52			←				20 17				20 45					21 15			21 45
Hatfield	d		19 44	19 55		19 53	19 55			20 08	20 20			20 27	20 48		20 57			21 18		21 27	21 48
Welwyn Garden City 4	d		19 49	→		20 00	20a00			20a13	20a25			20 31	20a54		21 01			21a24		21 31	21a54
Welwyn North	d		19 53			20 03								20 34			21 04					21 34	
Knebworth	d		19 57			20 07								20 38			21 08					21 38	
Bowes Park	d	19 24			19 44				19 51			20 04	20 13			20 33			20 53		21 13		
Palmers Green	d	19 26			19 46				19 53			20 06	20 15			20 35			20 55		21 15		
Winchmore Hill	d	19 29			19 49				19 56			20 09	20 17			20 37			20 57		21 17		
Grange Park	d	19 31			19 51				19 58			20 11	20 19			20 39			20 59		21 19		
Enfield Chase	d	19 33			19 53				20 00			20 13	20 21			20 41			21 01		21 21		
Gordon Hill	d	19 36			19 56				20 03			20 16	20 23			20 43			21 03		21 23		
Crews Hill	d	19 39							20 06				20 26			20 46			21 06		21 26		
Cuffley	d	19 42			20 00				20 09			20 20	20 29			20 49			21 09		21 29		
Bayford	d	19 47							20 14				20 34			20 54			21 14		21 34		
Hertford North	d	19a52			20 09				20a19			20a30	20 40			21 10			21a20		21a40		
Watton-at-Stone	d				20 15			←					20 45			21 15		←					
Stevenage 4	d		20 04		20 21	20 12		20 21					20a53	20 42		21 23	21 12	21 23				21 42	
Hitchin 4	d		20 13		→	20 17		20 27						20 47		→	21 17	21 28				21 47	
Letchworth Garden City	a		20 17			20 23		20 32						20 51			21 23	21 34				21 51	

		FC	FC ■	FC	FC	FC	FC	FC ■	FC	FC	FC ■	FC	FC	FC	FC ■	FC	FC	FC ■	FC	FC
London Kings Cross 15 ⊖	d		21 36					22 06	22 11	22 26	22 36		22 41	22 56	23 06	23 11	23 26	23 36		23 41
Moorgate ⊖	d	21 12			21 32	21 37	21 52													
Old Street ⊖	d	21 14			21 34	21 39	21 54													
Essex Road	d	21 17			21 37	21 42	21 57													
Highbury & Islington ⊖	d	21 19			21 39	21 44	21 59													
Drayton Park	d	21 21			21 41	21 46	22 01													
Finsbury Park ⊖	d	21 24	21 41		21 44	21 49	22 04	22 11	22 17	22 32	22 41		22 47	23 02	23 11	23 17	23 32	23 41		23 47
Harringay	d	21 26			21 46	21 51	22 06		22 19	22 34			22 49	23 04		23 19	23 34			23 49
Hornsey	d	21 28			21 48	21 53	22 08		22 21	22 36			22 51	23 06		23 21	23 36			23 51
Alexandra Palace	d	21 30			21 50	21 55	22 10		22 23	22 38			22 53	23 08		23 23	23 38			23 53
New Southgate	d					21 58			22 26				22 56			23 26				23 56
Oakleigh Park	d					22 01			22 29				22 59			23 29				23 59
New Barnet	d					22 03			22 31				23 01			23 31				00 01
Hadley Wood	d					22 06			22 34				23 04			23 34				00 04
Potters Bar	d		21 51			22 10		22 21	22 38		22 51		23 08		23 21	23 38		23 51		00 08
Brookmans Park	d					22 13			22 41				23 11			23 41				00 11
Welham Green	d					22 15			22 43				23 13			23 43				00 13
Hatfield	d		21 57			22 18		22 27	22 46		22 57		23 16		23 27	23 46		23 57		00 16
Welwyn Garden City 4	d		22 01			22a24		22 31	22a51		23 01		23a24		23 31	23a54		00 01		00a24
Welwyn North	d		22 04					22 34			23 04				23 34			00 04		
Knebworth	d		22 08					22 38			23 08				23 38			00 08		
Bowes Park	d	21 33			21 53		22 13			22 41				23 11			23 41			
Palmers Green	d	21 35			21 55		22 15			22 43				23 13			23 43			
Winchmore Hill	d	21 37			21 57		22 17			22 45				23 15			23 45			
Grange Park	d	21 39			21 59		22 19			22 47				23 17			23 47			
Enfield Chase	d	21 41			22 01		22 21			22 49				23 19			23 49			
Gordon Hill	d	21 43			22 03		22 23			22 51				23 21			23 51			
Crews Hill	d	21 46			22 06		22 26			22 54				23 24			23 54			
Cuffley	d	21 49			22 09		22 29			22 57				23 27			23 57			
Bayford	d	21 54			22 14		22 34			23 02				23 32			00 02			
Hertford North	d	22 10			22a20		22a40			23 07				23a38			00 07			
Watton-at-Stone	d	22 15		←						23 13		←					00 13		←	
Stevenage 4	d	22 23	22 12	22 23				22 42		23 21	23 12	23 21			23 42		00 20	00 12	00 20	
Hitchin 4	d	→	22 17	22 28				22 47		→	23 17	23 30			23 50		→	00 20	00 26	
Letchworth Garden City	a		22 23	22 34				22 51			23 26	23 36			23 54			00 29	00 36	

London - Welwyn Garden City, Hertford North and Letchworth Garden City

Network Diagram - see first Page of Table 24

		FC	FC ■	FC	FC	FC	FC	FC ■	FC ■ A	FC ■ B	FC	FC ■	FC ■	FC	FC	FC ■	FC	FC	FC ■	FC	FC	FC ■	FC
London Kings Cross ⊖	d	23p26	23p36		23p41	00 06	00 11	00 36	01 06	01 06	01 11	01 36	05 23	05 26	05 56	06 06	06 11	06 26	06 36	06 41	06 56	07 06	07 11
Moorgate ⊖	d																						
Old Street ⊖	d																						
Essex Road	d																						
Highbury & Islington ⊖	d																						
Drayton Park	d																						
Finsbury Park ⊖	d	23p32	23p41		23p47	00 12	00 17	00 41	01 11	01 11	01 17	01 41	05 28	05 32	06 02	06 11	06 17	06 32	06 41	06 47	07 02	07 11	07 17
Harringay	d	23p34			23p49	00 14	00 19				01 19			05 34	06 04		06 19	06 34		06 49	07 04		07 19
Hornsey	d	23p36			23p51	00 16	00 21				01 21			05 36	06 06		06 21	06 36		06 51	07 06		07 21
Alexandra Palace	d	23p38			23p53	00 18	00 23		01 16	01 16	01 23	01 45		05 38	06 08		06 23	06 38		06 53	07 08		07 23
New Southgate	d				23p56		00 26				01 26	01 48					06 26			06 56			07 26
Oakleigh Park	d				23p59		00 29				01 29	01 51					06 29			06 59			07 29
New Barnet	d				00 01		00 31				01 31	01 53					06 31			07 01			07 31
Hadley Wood	d				00 04		00 34				01 34	01 56					06 34			07 04			07 34
Potters Bar	d		23p51		00 08		00 38	00 51			01 38	01 59	05 38			06 21	06 38		06 51	07 08		07 21	07 38
Brookmans Park	d				00 11		00 41				01 41						06 41			07 11			07 41
Welham Green	d				00 13		00 43				01 43						06 43			07 13			07 43
Hatfield	d		23p57		00 16		00 46	00 57			01 46	02 05	05 44			06 27	06 46		06 57	07 16		07 27	07 46
Welwyn Garden City ■	d		00 01		00a24		00a54	01 01			01a54	02 09	05 48			06 31	06a51		07 01	07a21		07 31	07a51
Welwyn North	d		00 04					01s04				02s12	05 51			06 34			07 04			07 34	
Knebworth	d		00 08					01s08				02s16	05 55			06 38			07 08			07 38	
Bowes Park	d	23p41				00 21								05 41	06 11			06 41			07 11		
Palmers Green	d	23p43				00 23			01 19	01 19				05 43	06 13			06 43			07 13		
Winchmore Hill	d	23p45				00 25			01 21	01 21				05 45	06 15			06 45			07 15		
Grange Park	d	23p47				00 27								05 47	06 17			06 47			07 17		
Enfield Chase	d	23p49				00 29			01 24	01 24				05 49	06 19			06 49			07 19		
Gordon Hill	d	23p51				00 31			01 26	01 26				05 51	06 21			06 51			07 21		
Crews Hill	d	23p54				00 34								05 54	06 24			06 54			07 24		
Cuffley	d	23p57				00 37			01 30	01 30				05 57	06 27			06 57			07 27		
Bayford	d	00 02				00 42								06 02	06 32			07 02			07 32		
Hertford North	d	00 07				00 47			01 38	01 38				06a07	06a37			07 07			07a37		
Watton-at-Stone	d	00 13		←		00 53												07 13					
Stevenage ■	d	00 20	00 12	00 20		01 00		01 12	01 47	01 47		02 20	05 59			06 41		07a20	07 12			07 42	
Hitchin ■	d	→	00 20	00 26		01 06		01a17	01 52	01 52		02a25	06a07			06 47			07a17			07 47	
Letchworth Garden City	a		00 29	00 36		01 15			01 56	02 01						06 51						07 51	

		FC	FC ■	FC	FC	FC ■	FC	FC	FC ■	FC	FC	FC ■	FC	FC	FC ■	FC	FC	FC ■	FC	FC	FC ■	FC	FC
London Kings Cross ⊖	d	07 26	07 36	07 41	07 56	08 06	08 11	08 26	08 36	08 41	08 56	09 06	09 11	09 26	09 36	09 41	09 56	10 06	10 11	10 26	10 36	10 41	10 56
Moorgate ⊖	d																						
Old Street ⊖	d																						
Essex Road	d																						
Highbury & Islington ⊖	d																						
Drayton Park	d																						
Finsbury Park ⊖	d	07 32	07 41	07 47	08 02	08 11	08 17	08 32	08 41	08 47	09 02	09 11	09 17	09 32	09 41	09 47	10 02	10 11	10 17	10 32	10 41	10 47	11 02
Harringay	d	07 34		07 49	08 04		08 19	08 34		08 49	09 04		09 19	09 34		09 49	10 04		10 19	10 34		10 49	11 04
Hornsey	d	07 36		07 51	08 06		08 21	08 36		08 51	09 06		09 21	09 36		09 51	10 06		10 21	10 36		10 51	11 06
Alexandra Palace	d	07 38		07 53	08 08		08 23	08 38		08 53	09 08		09 23	09 38		09 53	10 08		10 23	10 38		10 53	11 08
New Southgate	d			07 56			08 26			08 56			09 26			09 56			10 26			10 56	
Oakleigh Park	d			07 59			08 29			08 59			09 29			09 59			10 29			10 59	
New Barnet	d			08 01			08 31			09 01			09 31			10 01			10 31			11 01	
Hadley Wood	d			08 04			08 34			09 04			09 34			10 04			10 34			11 04	
Potters Bar	d		07 51	08 08		08 21	08 38		08 51	09 08		09 21	09 38		09 51	10 08		10 21	10 38		10 51	11 08	
Brookmans Park	d			08 11			08 41			09 11			09 41			10 11			10 41			11 11	
Welham Green	d			08 13			08 43			09 13			09 43			10 13			10 43			11 13	
Hatfield	d		07 57	08 16		08 27	08 46		08 57	09 16		09 27	09 46		09 57	10 16		10 27	10 46		10 57	11 16	
Welwyn Garden City ■	d		08 01	08a21		08 31	08a51		09 01	09a21		09 31	09a51		10 01	10a21		10 31	10a51		11 01	11a21	
Welwyn North	d		08 04			08 34			09 04			09 34			10 04			10 34			11 04		
Knebworth	d		08 08			08 38			09 08			09 38			10 08			10 38			11 08		
Bowes Park	d	07 41			08 11			08 41			09 11			09 41			10 11			10 41			11 11
Palmers Green	d	07 43			08 13			08 43			09 13			09 43			10 13			10 43			11 13
Winchmore Hill	d	07 45			08 15			08 45			09 15			09 45			10 15			10 45			11 15
Grange Park	d	07 47			08 17			08 47			09 17			09 47			10 17			10 47			11 17
Enfield Chase	d	07 49			08 19			08 49			09 19			09 49			10 19			10 49			11 19
Gordon Hill	d	07 51			08 21			08 51			09 21			09 51			10 21			10 51			11 21
Crews Hill	d	07 54			08 24			08 54			09 24			09 54			10 24			10 54			11 24
Cuffley	d	07 57			08 27			08 57			09 27			09 57			10 27			10 57			11 27
Bayford	d	08 02			08 32			09 02			09 32			10 02			10 32			11 02			11 32
Hertford North	d	08 07			08a37			09 07			09a37			10 07			10a37			11 07			11a37
Watton-at-Stone	d	08 13						09 13						10 13						11 13			
Stevenage ■	d	08a20	08 12			08 42		09a20	09 12			09 42		10a20	10 12			10 42		11a20	11 12		
Hitchin ■	d		08a17			08 47			09a17			09 47			10a17			10 47			11a17		
Letchworth Garden City	a					08 51						09 51						10 51					

A 28 July, 4 August, 11 August, 1 September, 8 September

B until 21 July, from 18 August, not 1 September, 8 September

London - Welwyn Garden City, Hertford North and Letchworth Garden City

Network Diagram - see first Page of Table 24

		FC ■	FC	FC	FC ■	FC	FC	FC ■	FC	FC	FC ■	FC	FC	FC ■	FC	FC	FC ■	FC	FC	FC ■	FC	FC
London Kings Cross ⊖	d	11 06	11 11	11 26	11 36	11 41	11 56	12 06	12 11	12 26	12 36	12 41	12 56	13 06	13 11	13 26	13 36	13 41	13 56	14 06	14 11	14 26
Moorgate ⊖	d																					
Old Street ⊖	d																					
Essex Road	d																					
Highbury & Islington ⊖	d																					
Drayton Park	d																					
Finsbury Park ⊖	d	11 11	11 17	11 32	11 41	11 47	12 02	12 11	12 17	12 32	12 41	12 47	13 02	13 11	13 17	13 32	13 41	13 47	14 02	14 11	14 17	14 32
Harringay	d		11 19	11 34		11 49	12 04		12 19	12 34		12 49	13 04		13 19	13 34		13 49	14 04		14 19	14 34
Hornsey	d		11 21	11 36		11 51	12 06		12 21	12 36		12 51	13 06		13 21	13 36		13 51	14 06		14 21	14 36
Alexandra Palace	d		11 23	11 38		11 53	12 08		12 23	12 38		12 53	13 08		13 23	13 38		13 53	14 08		14 23	14 38
New Southgate	d		11 26			11 56			12 26			12 56			13 26			13 56			14 26	
Oakleigh Park	d		11 29			11 59			12 29			12 59			13 29			13 59			14 29	
New Barnet	d		11 31			12 01			12 31			13 01			13 31			14 01			14 31	
Hadley Wood	d		11 34			12 04			12 34			13 04			13 34			14 04			14 34	
Potters Bar	d	11 21	11 38		11 51	12 08		12 21	12 38		12 51	13 08		13 21	13 38		13 51	14 08		14 21	14 38	
Brookmans Park	d		11 41			12 11			12 41			13 11			13 41			14 11			14 41	
Welham Green	d		11 43			12 13			12 43			13 13			13 43			14 13			14 43	
Hatfield	d	11 27	11 46		11 57	12 16		12 27	12 46		12 57	13 16		13 27	13 46		13 57	14 16		14 27	14 46	
Welwyn Garden City ■	d	11 31	11a51		12 01	12a21		12 31	12a51		13 01	13a21		13 31	13a51		14 01	14a21		14 31	14a51	
Welwyn North	d	11 34			12 04			12 34			13 04			13 34			14 04			14 34		
Knebworth	d	11 38			12 08			12 38			13 08			13 38			14 08			14 38		
Bowes Park	d			11 41			12 11			12 41			13 11			13 41			14 11			14 41
Palmers Green	d			11 43			12 13			12 43			13 13			13 43			14 13			14 43
Winchmore Hill	d			11 45			12 15			12 45			13 15			13 45			14 15			14 45
Grange Park	d			11 47			12 17			12 47			13 17			13 47			14 17			14 47
Enfield Chase	d			11 49			12 19			12 49			13 19			13 49			14 19			14 49
Gordon Hill	d			11 51			12 21			12 51			13 21			13 51			14 21			14 51
Crews Hill	d			11 54			12 24			12 54			13 24			13 54			14 24			14 54
Cuffley	d			11 57			12 27			12 57			13 27			13 57			14 27			14 57
Bayford	d			12 02			12 32			13 02			13 32			14 02			14 32			15 02
Hertford North	d			12 07			12a37			13 07			13a37			14 07			14a37			15 07
Watton-at-Stone	d			12 13						13 13						14 13						15 13
Stevenage ■	d	11 42		12a20	12 12			12 42		13a20	13 12			13 42		14a20	14 12			14 42		15a20
Hitchin ■	d	11 47			12a17			12 47			13a17			13 47			14a17			14 47		
Letchworth Garden City	a	11 51						12 51						13 51						14 51		

		FC ■	FC	FC	FC ■	FC	FC	FC ■	FC	FC	FC ■	FC	FC	FC ■	FC	FC	FC ■	FC	FC	FC ■	FC	FC	FC ■
London Kings Cross ⊖	d	14 36	14 41	14 56	15 06	15 11	15 26	15 36	15 41	15 56	16 06	16 11	16 26	16 36	16 41	16 56	17 06	17 11	17 26	17 36	17 41	17 56	18 06
Moorgate ⊖	d																						
Old Street ⊖	d																						
Essex Road	d																						
Highbury & Islington ⊖	d																						
Drayton Park	d																						
Finsbury Park ⊖	d	14 41	14 47	15 02	15 11	15 17	15 32	15 41	15 47	16 02	16 11	16 17	16 32	16 41	16 47	17 02	17 11	17 17	17 32	17 41	17 47	18 02	18 11
Harringay	d		14 49	15 04		15 19	15 34		15 49	16 04		16 19	16 34		16 49	17 04		17 19	17 34		17 49	18 04	
Hornsey	d		14 51	15 06		15 21	15 36		15 51	16 06		16 21	16 36		16 51	17 06		17 21	17 36		17 51	18 06	
Alexandra Palace	d		14 53	15 08		15 23	15 38		15 53	16 08		16 23	16 38		16 53	17 08		17 23	17 38		17 53	18 08	
New Southgate	d		14 56			15 26			15 56			16 26			16 56			17 26			17 56		
Oakleigh Park	d		14 59			15 29			15 59			16 29			16 59			17 29			17 59		
New Barnet	d		15 01			15 31			16 01			16 31			17 01			17 31			18 01		
Hadley Wood	d		15 04			15 34			16 04			16 34			17 04			17 34			18 04		
Potters Bar	d	14 51	15 08		15 21	15 38		15 51	16 08		16 21	16 38		16 51	17 08		17 21	17 38		17 51	18 08		18 21
Brookmans Park	d		15 11			15 41			16 11			16 41			17 11			17 41			18 11		
Welham Green	d		15 13			15 43			16 13			16 43			17 13			17 43			18 13		
Hatfield	d	14 57	15 16		15 27	15 46		15 57	16 16		16 27	16 46		16 57	17 16		17 27	17 46		17 57	18 16		18 27
Welwyn Garden City ■	d	15 01	15a21		15 31	15a51		16 01	16a21		16 31	16a51		17 01	17a21		17 31	17a51		18 01	18a21		18 31
Welwyn North	d	15 04			15 34			16 04			16 34			17 04			17 34			18 04			18 34
Knebworth	d	15 08			15 38			16 08			16 38			17 08			17 38			18 08			18 38
Bowes Park	d			15 11			15 41			16 11			16 41			17 11			17 41			18 11	
Palmers Green	d			15 13			15 43			16 13			16 43			17 13			17 43			18 13	
Winchmore Hill	d			15 15			15 45			16 15			16 45			17 15			17 45			18 15	
Grange Park	d			15 17			15 47			16 17			16 47			17 17			17 47			18 17	
Enfield Chase	d			15 19			15 49			16 19			16 49			17 19			17 49			18 19	
Gordon Hill	d			15 21			15 51			16 21			16 51			17 21			17 51			18 21	
Crews Hill	d			15 24			15 54			16 24			16 54			17 24			17 54			18 24	
Cuffley	d			15 27			15 57			16 27			16 57			17 27			17 57			18 27	
Bayford	d			15 32			16 02			16 32			17 02			17 32			18 02			18 32	
Hertford North	d			15a37			16 07			16a37			17 07			17a37			18 07			18a37	
Watton-at-Stone	d						16 13						17 13						18 13				
Stevenage ■	d	15 12			15 42		16a20	16 12			16 42		17a20	17 12			17 42		18a20	18 12			18 42
Hitchin ■	d	15a17			15 47			16a17			16 47			17a17			17 47			18a17			18 47
Letchworth Garden City	a				15 51						16 51						17 51						18 51

London - Welwyn Garden City, Hertford North and Letchworth Garden City

Network Diagram - see first Page of Table 24

Station		FC	FC	FC 1	FC	FC	FC 1	FC	FC	FC 1	FC	FC	FC 1	FC	FC	FC 1	FC	FC	FC 1	FC	FC	FC 1
London Kings Cross 15 ⊖	d	18 11	18 26	18 36	18 41	18 56	19 06	19 11	19 26	19 36	19 41	19 56	20 06	20 11	20 26	20 36	20 41	20 56	21 06	21 11	21 26	21 36
Moorgate ⊖	d																					
Old Street ⊖	d																					
Essex Road	d																					
Highbury & Islington ⊖	d																					
Drayton Park	d																					
Finsbury Park ⊖	d	18 17	18 32	18 41	18 47	19 02	19 11	19 17	19 32	19 41	19 47	20 02	20 11	20 17	20 32	20 41	20 47	21 02	21 11	21 17	21 32	21 41
Harringay	d	18 19	18 34		18 49	19 04		19 19	19 34		19 49	20 04		20 19	20 34		20 49	21 04		21 19	21 34	
Hornsey	d	18 21	18 36		18 51	19 06		19 21	19 36		19 51	20 06		20 21	20 36		20 51	21 06		21 21	21 36	
Alexandra Palace	d	18 23	18 38		18 53	19 08		19 23	19 38		19 53	20 08		20 23	20 38		20 53	21 08		21 23	21 38	
New Southgate	d	18 26			18 56			19 26			19 56			20 26			20 56			21 26		
Oakleigh Park	d	18 29			18 59			19 29			19 59			20 29			20 59			21 29		
New Barnet	d	18 31			19 01			19 31			20 01			20 31			21 01			21 31		
Hadley Wood	d	18 34			19 04			19 34			20 04			20 34			21 04			21 34		
Potters Bar	d	18 38		18 51	19 08		19 21	19 38		19 51	20 08		20 21	20 38		20 51	21 08		21 21	21 38		21 51
Brookmans Park	d	18 41			19 11			19 41			20 11			20 41			21 11			21 41		
Welham Green	d	18 43			19 13			19 43			20 13			20 43			21 13			21 43		
Hatfield	d	18 46		18 57	19 16		19 27	19 46		19 57	20 16		20 27	20 46		20 57	21 16		21 27	21 46		21 57
Welwyn Garden City 4	d	18a51		19 01	19a21		19 31	19a51		20 01	20a21		20 31	20a51		21 01	21a21		21 31	21a51		22 01
Welwyn North	d			19 04			19 34			20 04			20 34			21 04			21 34			22 04
Knebworth	d			19 08			19 38			20 08			20 38			21 08			21 38			22 08
Bowes Park	d		18 41			19 11			19 41			20 11			20 41			21 11			21 41	
Palmers Green	d		18 43			19 13			19 43			20 13			20 43			21 13			21 43	
Winchmore Hill	d		18 45			19 15			19 45			20 15			20 45			21 15			21 45	
Grange Park	d		18 47			19 17			19 47			20 17			20 47			21 17			21 47	
Enfield Chase	d		18 49			19 19			19 49			20 19			20 49			21 19			21 49	
Gordon Hill	d		18 51			19 21			19 51			20 21			20 51			21 21			21 51	
Crews Hill	d		18 54			19 24			19 54			20 24			20 54			21 24			21 54	
Cuffley	d		18 57			19 27			19 57			20 27			20 57			21 27			21 57	
Bayford	d		19 02			19 32			20 02			20 32			21 02			21 32			22 02	
Hertford North	d		19 07			19a37			20 07			20a37			21 07			21a37			22 07	
Watton-at-Stone	d		19 13						20 13						21 13						22 13	
Stevenage 4	d		19a20	19 12			19 42		20a20	20 12			20 42		21a20	21 12			21 42		22a20	22 12
Hitchin 4	d			19a17			19 47			20a17			20 47			21a17			21 47			22a17
Letchworth Garden City	a						19 51						20 51						21 51			

Station		FC	FC	FC 1	FC	FC	FC 1	FC	FC	FC 1	FC	FC	FC 1	FC	FC	FC
London Kings Cross 15 ⊖	d	21 41	21 56	22 06	22 11	22 26	22 36	22 41	22 56	23 06	23 11	23 26	23 36		23 41	23 56
Moorgate ⊖	d															
Old Street ⊖	d															
Essex Road	d															
Highbury & Islington ⊖	d															
Drayton Park	d															
Finsbury Park ⊖	d	21 47	22 02	22 11	22 17	22 32	22 41	22 47	23 02	23 11	23 17	23 32	23 41		23 47	00 02
Harringay	d	21 49	22 04		22 19	22 34		22 49	23 04		23 19	23 34			23 49	00 04
Hornsey	d	21 51	22 06		22 21	22 36		22 51	23 06		23 21	23 36			23 51	00 06
Alexandra Palace	d	21 53	22 08		22 23	22 38		22 53	23 08		23 23	23 38			23 53	00 08
New Southgate	d	21 56			22 26			22 56			23 26				23 56	
Oakleigh Park	d	21 59			22 29			22 59			23 29				23 59	
New Barnet	d	22 01			22 31			23 01			23 31				00 01	
Hadley Wood	d	22 04			22 34			23 04			23 34				00 04	
Potters Bar	d	22 08		22 21	22 38		22 51	23 08		23 21	23 38		23 53		00 08	
Brookmans Park	d	22 11			22 41			23 11			23 41				00 11	
Welham Green	d	22 13			22 43			23 13			23 43				00 13	
Hatfield	d	22 16		22 27	22 46		22 57	23 16		23 27	23 46		23 59		00 16	
Welwyn Garden City 4	d	22a21		22 31	22a51		23 01	23a21		23 31	23a53		00 06		00a25	
Welwyn North	d			22 34			23 04			23 34			00 09			
Knebworth	d			22 38			23 08			23 38			00 13			
Bowes Park	d		22 11			22 41			23 11			23 41				00 11
Palmers Green	d		22 13			22 43			23 13			23 43				00 13
Winchmore Hill	d		22 15			22 45			23 15			23 45				00 15
Grange Park	d		22 17			22 47			23 17			23 47				00 17
Enfield Chase	d		22 19			22 49			23 19			23 49				00 19
Gordon Hill	d		22 21			22 51			23 21			23 51				00 21
Crews Hill	d		22 24			22 54			23 24			23 54				00 24
Cuffley	d		22 27			22 57			23 27			23 57				00 27
Bayford	d		22 32			23 02			23 32			00 02				00 32
Hertford North	d		22a37			23 07			23a37			00 07				00a39
Watton-at-Stone	d					23 13						00 13		←		
Stevenage 4	d			22 42		23a20	23 12			23 42		00 22	00 18	00 22		
Hitchin 4	d			22 47			23 20			23 50		→	00 25	00 29		
Letchworth Garden City	a			22 51			23 26			23 54			00 30	00 37		

London - Welwyn Garden City, Hertford North and Letchworth Garden City

Network Diagram - see first Page of Table 24

Station		FC	FC 1	FC	FC	FC	FC 1	FC	FC	FC 1	FC	FC	FC	FC	FC	FC	FC 1	FC	FC	FC	FC	FC 1	FC
London Kings Cross 15 ⊖	d	23p26	23p36		23p41	23p56	00 06	00 26	00 32	00 53	00 56	01 11	05 56	06 26	06 41	06 56	07 06	07 11	07 26	07 41	07 56	08 06	08 11
Moorgate ⊖	d																						
Old Street ⊖	d																						
Essex Road	d																						
Highbury & Islington ⊖	d																						
Drayton Park	d																						
Finsbury Park ⊖	d	23p32	23p41		23p47	00 02	00 11	00 32	00 38	00 58	01 02	01 17	06 02	06 32	06 47	07 02	07 11	07 17	07 32	07 47	08 02	08 11	08 17
Harringay	d	23p34			23p49	00 04		00 34	00 40		01 04	01 19	06 04	06 34	06 49	07 04		07 19	07 34	07 49	08 04		08 19
Hornsey	d	23p36			23p51	00 06		00 36	00 42		01 06	01 21	06 06	06 36	06 51	07 06		07 21	07 36	07 51	08 06		08 21
Alexandra Palace	d	23p38			23p53	00 08		00 38	00 44		01 08	01 23	06 08	06 38	06 53	07 08		07 23	07 38	07 53	08 08		08 23
New Southgate	d				23p56				00 47			01 26			06 56			07 26		07 56			08 26
Oakleigh Park	d				23p59				00 50			01 29			06 59			07 29		07 59			08 29
New Barnet	d				00 01				00 52			01 31			07 01			07 31		08 01			08 31
Hadley Wood	d				00 04				00 55			01 34			07 04			07 34		08 04			08 34
Potters Bar	d		23p53		00 08		00 23		00 59	01 10		01 38			07 08		07 21	07 38		08 08		08 21	08 38
Brookmans Park	d				00 11				01 02			01 41			07 11			07 41		08 11			08 41
Welham Green	d				00 13				01 04			01 43			07 13			07 43		08 13			08 43
Hatfield	d		23p59		00 16		00 29		01 07	01 16		01 46			07 16		07 27	07 46		08 16		08 27	08 46
Welwyn Garden City 4	d		00 06		00a25		00 41		01a16	01 20		01a55			07a25		07 33	07a55		08a25		08 31	08a53
Welwyn North	d		00 09				00 44			01s24							07 36					08 34	
Knebworth	d		00 13				00 48			01s28							07 40					08 38	
Bowes Park	d	23p41				00 11		00 41			01 11		06 11	06 41		07 11			07 41		08 11		
Palmers Green	d	23p43				00 13		00 43			01 13		06 13	06 43		07 13			07 43		08 13		
Winchmore Hill	d	23p45				00 15		00 45			01 15		06 15	06 45		07 15			07 45		08 15		
Grange Park	d	23p47				00 17		00 47			01 17		06 17	06 47		07 17			07 47		08 17		
Enfield Chase	d	23p49				00 19		00 49			01 19		06 19	06 49		07 19			07 49		08 19		
Gordon Hill	d	23p51				00 21		00 51			01 21		06 21	06 51		07 21			07 51		08 21		
Crews Hill	d	23p54				00 24		00 54			01 24		06 24	06 54		07 24			07 54		08 24		
Cuffley	d	23p57				00 27		00 57			01 27		06 27	06 57		07 27			07 57		08 27		
Bayford	d	00 02				00 32		01 02			01 32		06 32	07 02		07 32			08 02		08 32		
Hertford North	d	00 07				00a39		01a09			01 37		06a39	07 07		07a39			08 07		08a37		
Watton-at-Stone	d	00 13		←							01 43			07 13					08 13				
Stevenage 4	d	00 22	00 18	00 22			00 53			01 32	01 51			07a22			07 45		08a23			08 42	
Hitchin 4	d	→	00 25	00 29			01 00			01a39	01 59						07 52					08 47	
Letchworth Garden City	a		00 30	00 37			01 04				02 05						07 56					08 51	

Station		FC	FC	FC	FC 1	FC	FC	FC	FC	FC 1	FC	FC	FC	FC	FC 1	FC	FC	FC	FC	FC 1	FC	FC	FC
London Kings Cross 15 ⊖	d	08 26	08 41	08 56	09 06	09 11	09 26	09 41	09 56	10 06	10 11	10 26	10 41	10 56	11 06	11 11	11 26	11 41	11 56	12 06	12 11	12 26	12 41
Moorgate ⊖	d																						
Old Street ⊖	d																						
Essex Road	d																						
Highbury & Islington ⊖	d																						
Drayton Park	d																						
Finsbury Park ⊖	d	08 32	08 47	09 02	09 11	09 17	09 32	09 47	10 02	10 11	10 17	10 32	10 47	11 02	11 11	11 17	11 32	11 47	12 02	12 11	12 17	12 32	12 47
Harringay	d	08 34	08 49	09 04		09 19	09 34	09 49	10 04		10 19	10 34	10 49	11 04		11 19	11 34	11 49	12 04		12 19	12 34	12 49
Hornsey	d	08 36	08 51	09 06		09 21	09 36	09 51	10 06		10 21	10 36	10 51	11 06		11 21	11 36	11 51	12 06		12 21	12 36	12 51
Alexandra Palace	d	08 38	08 53	09 08		09 23	09 38	09 53	10 08		10 23	10 38	10 53	11 08		11 23	11 38	11 53	12 08		12 23	12 38	12 53
New Southgate	d		08 56			09 26		09 56			10 26		10 56			11 26		11 56			12 26		12 56
Oakleigh Park	d		08 59			09 29		09 59			10 29		10 59			11 29		11 59			12 29		12 59
New Barnet	d		09 01			09 31		10 01			10 31		11 01			11 31		12 01			12 31		13 01
Hadley Wood	d		09 04			09 34		10 04			10 34		11 04			11 34		12 04			12 34		13 04
Potters Bar	d		09 08		09 21	09 38		10 08		10 21	10 38		11 08		11 21	11 38		12 08		12 21	12 38		13 08
Brookmans Park	d		09 11			09 41		10 11			10 41		11 11			11 41		12 11			12 41		13 11
Welham Green	d		09 13			09 43		10 13			10 43		11 13			11 43		12 13			12 43		13 13
Hatfield	d		09 16		09 27	09 46		10 16		10 27	10 46		11 16		11 27	11 46		12 16		12 27	12 46		13 16
Welwyn Garden City 4	d		09a21		09 31	09a51		10a21		10 31	10a51		11a21		11 31	11a51		12a21		12 31	12a51		13a21
Welwyn North	d				09 34					10 34					11 34					12 34			
Knebworth	d				09 38					10 38					11 38					12 38			
Bowes Park	d	08 41		09 11			09 41		10 11			10 41		11 11			11 41		12 11			12 41	
Palmers Green	d	08 43		09 13			09 43		10 13			10 43		11 13			11 43		12 13			12 43	
Winchmore Hill	d	08 45		09 15			09 45		10 15			10 45		11 15			11 45		12 15			12 45	
Grange Park	d	08 47		09 17			09 47		10 17			10 47		11 17			11 47		12 17			12 47	
Enfield Chase	d	08 49		09 19			09 49		10 19			10 49		11 19			11 49		12 19			12 49	
Gordon Hill	d	08 51		09 21			09 51		10 21			10 51		11 21			11 51		12 21			12 51	
Crews Hill	d	08 54		09 24			09 54		10 24			10 54		11 24			11 54		12 24			12 54	
Cuffley	d	08 57		09 27			09 57		10 27			10 57		11 27			11 57		12 27			12 57	
Bayford	d	09 02		09 32			10 02		10 32			11 02		11 32			12 02		12 32			13 02	
Hertford North	d	09 07		09a37			10 07		10a37			11 07		11a37			12 07		12a37			13 07	
Watton-at-Stone	d	09 13					10 13					11 13					12 13					13 13	
Stevenage 4	d	09a20			09 42		10a20			10 42		11a20			11 42		12a20			12 42		13a20	
Hitchin 4	d				09 47					10 47					11 47					12 47			
Letchworth Garden City	a				09 51					10 51					11 51					12 51			

Table 24

London - Welwyn Garden City, Hertford North and Letchworth Garden City

Sundays
until 9 September

Network Diagram - see first Page of Table 24

		FC		FC ■	FC	FC	FC	FC	FC ■	FC	FC	FC		FC	FC ■	FC	FC	FC	FC	FC ■	FC	FC		FC ■	FC
London Kings Cross ⊖	d	12 56		13 06	13 11	13 26	13 41	13 56	14 06	14 11	14 26	14 41		14 56	15 06	15 11	15 26	15 41	15 56	16 06	16 11	16 26		16 36	16 41
Moorgate ⊖	d																								
Old Street ⊖	d																								
Essex Road	d																								
Highbury & Islington ⊖	d																								
Drayton Park	d																								
Finsbury Park ⊖	d	13 02		13 11	13 17	13 32	13 47	14 02	14 11	14 17	14 32	14 47		15 02	15 11	15 17	15 32	15 47	16 02	16 11	16 17	16 32		16 41	16 47
Harringay	d	13 04			13 19	13 34	13 49	14 04		14 19	14 34	14 49		15 04		15 19	15 34	15 49	16 04		16 19	16 34			16 49
Hornsey	d	13 06			13 21	13 36	13 51	14 06		14 21	14 36	14 51		15 06		15 21	15 36	15 51	16 06		16 21	16 36			16 51
Alexandra Palace	d	13 08			13 23	13 38	13 53	14 08		14 23	14 38	14 53		15 08		15 23	15 38	15 53	16 08		16 23	16 38			16 53
New Southgate	d				13 26		13 56			14 26		14 56				15 26		15 56			16 26				16 56
Oakleigh Park	d				13 29		13 59			14 29		14 59				15 29		15 59			16 29				16 59
New Barnet	d				13 31		14 01			14 31		15 01				15 31		16 01			16 31				17 01
Hadley Wood	d				13 34		14 04			14 34		15 04				15 34		16 04			16 34				17 04
Potters Bar	d			13 21	13 38		14 08		14 21	14 38		15 08			15 21	15 38		16 08		16 21	16 38			16 51	17 08
Brookmans Park	d				13 41		14 11			14 41		15 11				15 41		16 11			16 41				17 11
Welham Green	d				13 43		14 13			14 43		15 13				15 43		16 13			16 43				17 13
Hatfield	d			13 27	13 46		14 16		14 27	14 46		15 16			15 27	15 46		16 16		16 27	16 46			16 57	17 16
Welwyn Garden City	d			13 31	13a51		14a21		14 31	14a51		15a21			15 31	15a51		16a21		16 31	16a51			17 01	17a21
Welwyn North	d			13 34					14 34						15 34					16 34				17 04	
Knebworth	d			13 38					14 38						15 38					16 38				17 08	
Bowes Park	d	13 11				13 41		14 11			14 41			15 11			15 41		16 11			16 41			
Palmers Green	d	13 13				13 43		14 13			14 43			15 13			15 43		16 13			16 43			
Winchmore Hill	d	13 15				13 45		14 15			14 45			15 15			15 45		16 15			16 45			
Grange Park	d	13 17				13 47		14 17			14 47			15 17			15 47		16 17			16 47			
Enfield Chase	d	13 19				13 49		14 19			14 49			15 19			15 49		16 19			16 49			
Gordon Hill	d	13 21				13 51		14 21			14 51			15 21			15 51		16 21			16 51			
Crews Hill	d	13 24				13 54		14 24			14 54			15 24			15 54		16 24			16 54			
Cuffley	d	13 27				13 57		14 27			14 57			15 27			15 57		16 27			16 57			
Bayford	d	13 32				14 02		14 32			15 02			15 32			16 02		16 32			17 02			
Hertford North	d	13a37				14 07		14a37			15 07			15a37			16 07		16a37			17 07			
Watton-at-Stone	d					14 13					15 13						16 13					17 13			
Stevenage	d			13 42		14a20			14 42		15a20				15 42		16a20			16 42		17a20		17 12	
Hitchin	d			13 47					14 47						15 47					16 47				17a17	
Letchworth Garden City	a			13 51					14 51						15 51					16 51					

		FC	FC ■	FC	FC	FC ■	FC	FC		FC ■	FC	FC	FC ■	FC	FC	FC ■	FC	FC		FC	FC	FC ■	FC	FC	FC
London Kings Cross ⊖	d	16 56	17 06	17 11	17 26	17 36	17 41	17 56		18 06	18 11	18 26	18 36	18 41	18 56	19 06	19 11	19 26		19 41	19 56	20 06	20 11	20 26	20 41
Moorgate ⊖	d																								
Old Street ⊖	d																								
Essex Road	d																								
Highbury & Islington ⊖	d																								
Drayton Park	d																								
Finsbury Park ⊖	d	17 02	17 11	17 17	17 32	17 41	17 47	18 02		18 11	18 17	18 32	18 41	18 47	19 02	19 11	19 17	19 32		19 47	20 02	20 11	20 17	20 32	20 47
Harringay	d	17 04		17 19	17 34		17 49	18 04			18 19	18 34		18 49	19 04		19 19	19 34		19 49	20 04		20 19	20 34	20 49
Hornsey	d	17 06		17 21	17 36		17 51	18 06			18 21	18 36		18 51	19 06		19 21	19 36		19 51	20 06		20 21	20 36	20 51
Alexandra Palace	d	17 08		17 23	17 38		17 53	18 08			18 23	18 38		18 53	19 08		19 23	19 38		19 53	20 08		20 23	20 38	20 53
New Southgate	d			17 26			17 56				18 26			18 56			19 26			19 56			20 26		20 56
Oakleigh Park	d			17 29			17 59				18 29			18 59			19 29			19 59			20 29		20 59
New Barnet	d			17 31			18 01				18 31			19 01			19 31			20 01			20 31		21 01
Hadley Wood	d			17 34			18 04				18 34			19 04			19 34			20 04			20 34		21 04
Potters Bar	d		17 21	17 38		17 51	18 08			18 21	18 38		18 51	19 08		19 21	19 38			20 08		20 21	20 38		21 08
Brookmans Park	d			17 41			18 11				18 41			19 11			19 41			20 11			20 41		21 11
Welham Green	d			17 43			18 13				18 43			19 13			19 43			20 13			20 43		21 13
Hatfield	d		17 27	17 46		17 57	18 16			18 27	18 46		18 57	19 16		19 27	19 46			20 16		20 27	20 46		21 16
Welwyn Garden City	d		17 31	17a51		18 01	18a21			18 31	18a51		19 01	19a21		19 31	19a51			20a21		20 31	20a51		21a21
Welwyn North	d		17 34			18 04				18 34			19 04			19 34						20 34			
Knebworth	d		17 38			18 08				18 38			19 08			19 38						20 38			
Bowes Park	d	17 11			17 41			18 11				18 41			19 11			19 41			20 11			20 41	
Palmers Green	d	17 13			17 43			18 13				18 43			19 13			19 43			20 13			20 43	
Winchmore Hill	d	17 15			17 45			18 15				18 45			19 15			19 45			20 15			20 45	
Grange Park	d	17 17			17 47			18 17				18 47			19 17			19 47			20 17			20 47	
Enfield Chase	d	17 19			17 49			18 19				18 49			19 19			19 49			20 19			20 49	
Gordon Hill	d	17 21			17 51			18 21				18 51			19 21			19 51			20 21			20 51	
Crews Hill	d	17 24			17 54			18 24				18 54			19 24			19 54			20 24			20 54	
Cuffley	d	17 27			17 57			18 27				18 57			19 27			19 57			20 27			20 57	
Bayford	d	17 32			18 02			18 32				19 02			19 32			20 02			20 32			21 02	
Hertford North	d	17a37			18 07			18a37				19 07			19a37			20 07			20a37			21 07	
Watton-at-Stone	d				18 13							19 13						20 13						21 13	
Stevenage	d		17 42		18a20	18 12				18 42		19a20	19 12			19 42		20a20				20 42		21a20	
Hitchin	d		17 47			18a17				18 47			19 17			19 47						20 47			
Letchworth Garden City	a		17 51							18 51			19 21			19 51						20 51			

Table 24

London - Welwyn Garden City, Hertford North and Letchworth Garden City

Sundays
until 9 September

Network Diagram - see first Page of Table 24

		FC	FC ■	FC		FC	FC	FC	FC ■	FC	FC	FC	FC	FC ■		FC	FC	FC
London Kings Cross ⊖	d	20 56	21 06	21 11		21 26	21 41	21 56	22 06	22 11	22 26	22 41	22 56	23 06		23 11	23 26	23 41
Moorgate ⊖	d																	
Old Street ⊖	d																	
Essex Road	d																	
Highbury & Islington ⊖	d																	
Drayton Park	d																	
Finsbury Park ⊖	d	21 02	21 11	21 17		21 32	21 47	22 02	22 11	22 17	22 32	22 47	23 02	23 11		23 17	23 32	23 47
Harringay	d	21 04		21 19		21 34	21 49	22 04		22 19	22 34	22 49	23 04			23 19	23 34	23 49
Hornsey	d	21 06		21 21		21 36	21 51	22 06		22 21	22 36	22 51	23 06			23 21	23 36	23 51
Alexandra Palace	d	21 08		21 23		21 38	21 53	22 08		22 23	22 38	22 53	23 08			23 23	23 38	23 53
New Southgate	d			21 26			21 56			22 26		22 56				23 26		23 56
Oakleigh Park	d			21 29			21 59			22 29		22 59				23 29		23 59
New Barnet	d			21 31			22 01			22 31		23 01				23 31		00 01
Hadley Wood	d			21 34			22 04			22 34		23 04				23 34		00 04
Potters Bar	d		21 21	21 38			22 08		22 21	22 38		23 08		23 21		23 38		00 08
Brookmans Park	d			21 41			22 11			22 41		23 11				23 41		00 11
Welham Green	d			21 43			22 13			22 43		23 13				23 43		00 13
Hatfield	d		21 27	21 46			22 16		22 27	22 46		23 16		23 27		23 46		00 16
Welwyn Garden City	d		21 31	21a51			22a21		22 31	22a51		23a21		23 31		23a51		00 20
Welwyn North	d		21 34						22 34					23 34				00 23
Knebworth	d		21 38						22 38					23 38				00 28
Bowes Park	d	21 11				21 41		22 11			22 41		23 11				23 41	
Palmers Green	d	21 13				21 43		22 13			22 43		23 13				23 43	
Winchmore Hill	d	21 15				21 45		22 15			22 45		23 15				23 45	
Grange Park	d	21 17				21 47		22 17			22 47		23 17				23 47	
Enfield Chase	d	21 19				21 49		22 19			22 49		23 19				23 49	
Gordon Hill	d	21 21				21 51		22 21			22 51		23 21				23 51	
Crews Hill	d	21 24				21 54		22 24			22 54		23 24				23 54	
Cuffley	d	21 27				21 57		22 27			22 57		23 27				23 57	
Bayford	d	21 32				22 02		22 32			23 02		23 32				00 02	
Hertford North	d	21a37				22 07		22a37			23 07		23a37				00 07	
Watton-at-Stone	d					22 13					23 13						00 13	
Stevenage	d		21 42			22a20			22 42		23a20			23 42			00a20	00 31
Hitchin	d		21 47						22 47					23 47				00 37
Letchworth Garden City	a		21 51						22 51					23 51				00 52

Sundays
16 September to 21 October

		FC	FC ■	FC	FC	FC	FC ■	FC	FC	FC ■		FC	FC	FC Bus	FC	FC Bus	FC Bus	FC ■	FC Bus	FC		FC Bus	FC	FC ■	FC Bus
London Kings Cross ⊖	d	23p26	23p36		23p41	23p56	00 06	00 26	00 32	00 53		00 56	01 11		06 41			07 06		07 11			07 41	08 06	
Moorgate ⊖	d																								
Old Street ⊖	d																								
Essex Road	d																								
Highbury & Islington ⊖	d																								
Drayton Park	d																								
Finsbury Park ⊖	d	23p32	23p41		23p47	00 02	00 11	00 32	00 38	00 58		01 02	01 17		06 47			07 11		07 17			07 47	08 11	
Harringay	d	23p34			23p49	00 04		00 34	00 40			01 04	01 19		06 49					07 19			07 49		
Hornsey	d	23p36			23p51	00 06		00 36	00 42			01 06	01 21		06 51					07 21			07 51		
Alexandra Palace	d	23p38			23p53	00 08		00 38	00 44			01 08	01 23		06 53					07 23			07 53		
New Southgate	d				23p56				00 47				01 26		06 56					07 26			07 56		
Oakleigh Park	d				23p59				00 50				01 29		06 59					07 29			07 59		
New Barnet	d				00 01				00 52				01 31		07 01					07 31			08 01		
Hadley Wood	d				00 04				00 55				01 34		07 04					07 34			08 04		
Potters Bar	d		23p53		00 08		00 23		00 59	01 10			01 38		07 08			07 21		07 38			08 08	08 21	
Brookmans Park	d				00 11				01 02				01 41		07 11					07 41			08 11		
Welham Green	d				00 13				01 04				01 43		07 13					07 43			08 13		
Hatfield	d		23p59		00 16		00 29		01 07	01 16			01 46		07 16			07 27		07 46			08 16	08 27	
Welwyn Garden City	d		00 06		00a25		00 41		01a16	01 20			01a55		07a25			07 33		07a55			08a25	08 31	
Welwyn North	d		00 09				00 44			01s24								07 36						08 34	
Knebworth	d		00 13				00 48			01s28								07 40						08 38	
Bowes Park	d	23p41				00 11		00 41				01 11													
Palmers Green	d	23p43				00 13		00 43				01 13													
Winchmore Hill	d	23p45				00 15		00 45				01 15													
Grange Park	d	23p47				00 17		00 47				01 17													
Enfield Chase	d	23p49				00 19		00 49				01 19													
Gordon Hill	d	23p51				00 21		00 51				01 21					06 30		07 00			07 30			08 00
Crews Hill	d	23p54				00 24		00 54				01 24					06 40		07 10			07 40			08 10
Cuffley	d	23p57				00 27		00 57				01 27					06 48		07 18			07 48			08 18
Bayford	d	00 02				00 32		01 02				01 32					07 03		07 33			08 03			08 33
Hertford North	d	00 07				00a39		01a09				01a39		01 45		06 50	07a18		07 50			08a18			08 50
Watton-at-Stone	d	00 13		←												07 04			08 04						09 04
Stevenage	d	00 22	00 18	00 22			00 53			01 32						07a21		07 45	08a21					08 42	09a21
Hitchin	d	→	00 25	00 29			01 00			01a39								07 52						08 47	
Letchworth Garden City	a		00 30	00 37			01 04							02 51				07 56						08 51	

London - Welwyn Garden City, Hertford North and Letchworth Garden City

Network Diagram - see first Page of Table 24

		FC	FC 🚌	FC	FC ■	FC 🚌	FC	FC 🚌	FC	FC ■	FC 🚌	FC	FC 🚌	FC	FC ■	FC 🚌	FC	FC 🚌	FC	FC ■	FC 🚌	FC	FC 🚌
London Kings Cross ⊖	d	08 11		08 41	09 03		09 11		09 41	10 03		10 11		10 41	11 03		11 11		11 41	12 03		12 11	
Moorgate ⊖	d																						
Old Street ⊖	d																						
Essex Road	d																						
Highbury & Islington ⊖	d																						
Drayton Park	d																						
Finsbury Park ⊖	d	08 17		08 47	09 08		09 17		09 47	10 08		10 17		10 47	11 08		11 17		11 47	12 08		12 17	
Harringay	d	08 19		08 49			09 19		09 49			10 19		10 49			11 19		11 49			12 19	
Hornsey	d	08 21		08 51			09 21		09 51			10 21		10 51			11 21		11 51			12 21	
Alexandra Palace	d	08 23		08 53			09 23		09 53			10 23		10 53			11 23		11 53			12 23	
New Southgate	d	08 26		08 56			09 26		09 56			10 26		10 56			11 26		11 56			12 26	
Oakleigh Park	d	08 29		08 59			09 29		09 59			10 29		10 59			11 29		11 59			12 29	
New Barnet	d	08 31		09 01			09 31		10 01			10 31		11 01			11 31		12 01			12 31	
Hadley Wood	d	08 34		09 04			09 34		10 04			10 34		11 04			11 34		12 04			12 34	
Potters Bar	d	08 38		09 08	09 18		09 38		10 08	10 18		10 38		11 08	11 18		11 38		12 08	12 18		12 38	
Brookmans Park	d	08 41		09 11			09 41		10 11			10 41		11 11			11 41		12 11			12 41	
Welham Green	d	08 43		09 13			09 43		10 13			10 43		11 13			11 43		12 13			12 43	
Hatfield	d	08 46		09 16	09 24		09 46		10 16	10 24		10 46		11 16	11 24		11 46		12 16	12 24		12 46	
Welwyn Garden City ■	d	08a53		09a21	09 28		09a51		10a21	10 28		10a51		11a21	11 28		11a51		12a21	12 28		12a51	
Welwyn North	d				09 31					10 31					11 31					12 31			
Knebworth	d				09 35					10 35					11 35					12 35			
Bowes Park	d																						
Palmers Green	d																						
Winchmore Hill	d																						
Grange Park	d																						
Enfield Chase	d																						
Gordon Hill	d		08 30			09 00		09 30			10 00		10 30			11 00		11 30			12 00		12 30
Crews Hill	d		08 40			09 10		09 40			10 10		10 40			11 10		11 40			12 10		12 40
Cuffley	d		08 48			09 18		09 48			10 18		10 48			11 18		11 48			12 18		12 48
Bayford	d		09 03			09 33		10 03			10 33		11 03			11 33		12 03			12 33		13 03
Hertford North	d		09a18			09 50		10a18			10 50		11a18			11 50		12a18			12 50		13a18
Watton-at-Stone	d					10 04					11 04					12 04					13 04		
Stevenage ■	d				09 39	10a21				10 39	11a21				11 39	12a21				12 39	13a21		
Hitchin ■	d				09 44					10 44					11 44					12 44			
Letchworth Garden City	a				09 48					10 48					11 48					12 49			

		FC	FC ■	FC 🚌	FC	FC 🚌	FC	FC ■	FC 🚌	FC	FC 🚌	FC	FC ■	FC 🚌	FC	FC 🚌	FC	FC ■	FC	FC ■	FC 🚌	FC 🚌
London Kings Cross ⊖	d	12 41	13 03		13 11		13 41	14 03		14 11		14 41	15 06		15 11		15 41	16 06	16 11	16 36		
Moorgate ⊖	d																					
Old Street ⊖	d																					
Essex Road	d																					
Highbury & Islington ⊖	d																					
Drayton Park	d																					
Finsbury Park ⊖	d	12 47	13 08		13 17		13 47	14 08		14 17		14 47	15 11		15 17		15 47	16 11	16 17	16 41		
Harringay	d	12 49			13 19		13 49			14 19		14 49			15 19		15 49		16 19			
Hornsey	d	12 51			13 21		13 51			14 21		14 51			15 21		15 51		16 21			
Alexandra Palace	d	12 53			13 23		13 53			14 23		14 53			15 23		15 53		16 23			
New Southgate	d	12 56			13 26		13 56			14 26		14 56			15 26		15 56		16 26			
Oakleigh Park	d	12 59			13 29		13 59			14 29		14 59			15 29		15 59		16 29			
New Barnet	d	13 01			13 31		14 01			14 31		15 01			15 31		16 01		16 31			
Hadley Wood	d	13 04			13 34		14 04			14 34		15 04			15 34		16 04		16 34			
Potters Bar	d	13 08	13 18		13 38		14 08	14 18		14 38		15 08	15 21		15 38		16 08	16 21	16 38	16 51		
Brookmans Park	d	13 11			13 41		14 11			14 41		15 11			15 41		16 11		16 41			
Welham Green	d	13 13			13 43		14 13			14 43		15 13			15 43		16 13		16 43			
Hatfield	d	13 16	13 24		13 46		14 16	14 24		14 46		15 16	15 27		15 46		16 16	16 27	16 46	16 57		
Welwyn Garden City ■	d	13a21	13 28		13a51		14a21	14 28		14a51		15a21	15 31		15a51		16a21	16 31	16a51	17 01		
Welwyn North	d		13 31					14 31					15 34					16 34		17 04		
Knebworth	d		13 35					14 35					15 38					16 38		17 08		
Bowes Park	d																					
Palmers Green	d																					
Winchmore Hill	d																					
Grange Park	d																					
Enfield Chase	d																					
Gordon Hill	d			13 00		13 30			14 00		14 30			15 00		15 30					16 00	16 30
Crews Hill	d			13 10		13 40			14 10		14 40			15 10		15 40					16 10	16 40
Cuffley	d			13 18		13 48			14 18		14 48			15 18		15 48					16 18	16 48
Bayford	d			13 33		14 03			14 33		15 03			15 33		16 03					16 33	17 03
Hertford North	d			13 50		14a18			14 50		15a18			15 50		16a18					16 50	17a18
Watton-at-Stone	d			14 04					15 04					16 04							17 04	
Stevenage ■	d		13 39	14a21				14 39	15a21				15 42	16a21				16 42		17 12	17a21	
Hitchin ■	d		13 44					14 44					15 47					16 47		17a17		
Letchworth Garden City	a		13 48					14 49					15 51					16 51				

London - Welwyn Garden City, Hertford North and Letchworth Garden City

Network Diagram - see first Page of Table 24

		FC	FC ■	FC	FC ■	FC 🚌	FC 🚌	FC	FC ■	FC	FC ■	FC 🚌	FC 🚌	FC	FC ■	FC 🚌	FC	FC 🚌	FC	FC ■	FC 🚌	FC	FC 🚌
London Kings Cross ⊖	d	16 41	17 06	17 11	17 36			17 41	18 06	18 11	18 36			18 41	19 06		19 11		19 41	20 06		20 11	
Moorgate ⊖	d																						
Old Street ⊖	d																						
Essex Road	d																						
Highbury & Islington ⊖	d																						
Drayton Park	d																						
Finsbury Park ⊖	d	16 47	17 11	17 17	17 41			17 47	18 11	18 17	18 41			18 47	19 11		19 17		19 47	20 11		20 17	
Harringay	d	16 49		17 19				17 49		18 19				18 49			19 19		19 49			20 19	
Hornsey	d	16 51		17 21				17 51		18 21				18 51			19 21		19 51			20 21	
Alexandra Palace	d	16 53		17 23				17 53		18 23				18 53			19 23		19 53			20 23	
New Southgate	d	16 56		17 26				17 56		18 26				18 56			19 26		19 56			20 26	
Oakleigh Park	d	16 59		17 29				17 59		18 29				18 59			19 29		19 59			20 29	
New Barnet	d	17 01		17 31				18 01		18 31				19 01			19 31		20 01			20 31	
Hadley Wood	d	17 04		17 34				18 04		18 34				19 04			19 34		20 04			20 34	
Potters Bar	d	17 08	17 21	17 38	17 51			18 08	18 21	18 38	18 51			19 08	19 21		19 38		20 08	20 21		20 38	
Brookmans Park	d	17 11		17 41				18 11		18 41				19 11			19 41		20 11			20 41	
Welham Green	d	17 13		17 43				18 13		18 43				19 13			19 43		20 13			20 43	
Hatfield	d	17 16	17 27	17 46	17 57			18 16	18 27	18 46	18 57			19 16	19 27		19 46		20 16	20 27		20 46	
Welwyn Garden City ■	d	17a21	17 31	17a51	18 01			18a21	18 31	18a51	19 01			19a21	19 31		19a51		20a21	20 31		20a51	
Welwyn North	d		17 34		18 04				18 34		19 04				19 34					20 34			
Knebworth	d		17 38		18 08				18 38		19 08				19 38					20 38			
Bowes Park	d																						
Palmers Green	d																						
Winchmore Hill	d																						
Grange Park	d																						
Enfield Chase	d																						
Gordon Hill	d					17 00	17 30					18 00	18 30			19 00		19 30			20 00		20 30
Crews Hill	d					17 10	17 40					18 10	18 40			19 10		19 40			20 10		20 40
Cuffley	d					17 18	17 48					18 18	18 48			19 18		19 48			20 18		20 48
Bayford	d					17 33	18 03					18 33	19 03			19 33		20 03			20 33		21 03
Hertford North	d					17 50	18a18					18 50	19a18			19 50		20a18			20 50		21a18
Watton-at-Stone	d					18 04						19 04				20 04					21 04		
Stevenage ■	d		17 42		18 12	18a21			18 42		19 12	19a21			19 42	20a21				20 42	21a21		
Hitchin ■	d		17 47		18a17				18 47		19 17				19 47					20 47			
Letchworth Garden City	a		17 51						18 51		19 21				19 51					20 51			

		FC	FC ■	FC 🚌	FC	FC 🚌	FC	FC ■	FC 🚌	FC	FC 🚌	FC	FC ■	FC 🚌	FC	FC 🚌	FC	FC 🚌
London Kings Cross ⊖	d	20 41	21 06		21 11		21 41	22 06		22 11		22 41	23 06		23 11		23 41	
Moorgate ⊖	d																	
Old Street ⊖	d																	
Essex Road	d																	
Highbury & Islington ⊖	d																	
Drayton Park	d																	
Finsbury Park ⊖	d	20 47	21 11		21 17		21 47	22 11		22 17		22 47	23 11		23 17		23 47	
Harringay	d	20 49			21 19		21 49			22 19		22 49			23 19		23 49	
Hornsey	d	20 51			21 21		21 51			22 21		22 51			23 21		23 51	
Alexandra Palace	d	20 53			21 23		21 53			22 23		22 53			23 23		23 53	
New Southgate	d	20 56			21 26		21 56			22 26		22 56			23 26		23 56	
Oakleigh Park	d	20 59			21 29		21 59			22 29		22 59			23 29		23 59	
New Barnet	d	21 01			21 31		22 01			22 31		23 01			23 31		00 01	
Hadley Wood	d	21 04			21 34		22 04			22 34		23 04			23 34		00 04	
Potters Bar	d	21 08	21 21		21 38		22 08	22 21		22 38		23 08	23 21		23 38		00 08	
Brookmans Park	d	21 11			21 41		22 11			22 41		23 11			23 41		00 11	
Welham Green	d	21 13			21 43		22 13			22 43		23 13			23 43		00 13	
Hatfield	d	21 16	21 27		21 46		22 16	22 27		22 46		23 16	23 27		23 46		00 16	
Welwyn Garden City ■	d	21a21	21 31		21a51		22a21	22 31		22a51		23a21	23 31		23a51		00 20	
Welwyn North	d		21 34					22 34					23 34				00 23	
Knebworth	d		21 38					22 38					23 38				00 28	
Bowes Park	d																	
Palmers Green	d																	
Winchmore Hill	d																	
Grange Park	d																	
Enfield Chase	d																	
Gordon Hill	d			21 00		21 30			22 00		22 30			23 00		23 30		23 59
Crews Hill	d			21 10		21 40			22 10		22 40			23 10		23 40		00 10
Cuffley	d			21 18		21 48			22 18		22 48			23 18		23 48		00 18
Bayford	d			21 33		22 03			22 33		23 03			23 33		00 03		00 33
Hertford North	d			21 50		22a18			22 50		23a18			23 50		00a18		00 50
Watton-at-Stone	d			22 04					23 04					00 04				01 04
Stevenage ■	d		21 42	22a21				22 42	23a21				23 42	00a21			00 31	01a21
Hitchin ■	d		21 47					22 47					23 47				00 37	
Letchworth Garden City	a		21 51					22 51					23 51				00 52	

Table 24

Sundays from 28 October

London - Welwyn Garden City, Hertford North and Letchworth Garden City

Network Diagram - see first Page of Table 24

	FC	FC 1	FC	FC	FC	FC 1	FC	FC	FC 1	FC	FC	FC	FC	FC	FC	FC 1	FC	FC	FC	FC	FC 1	FC
London Kings Cross [15] ⊖ d	23p26	23p36		23p41	23p56	00 06	00 26	00 32	00 53	00 56	01 11	05 56	06 26	06 41	06 56	07 06	07 11	07 26	07 41	07 56	08 06	08 11
Moorgate ⊖ d																						
Old Street ⊖ d																						
EssexRoad d																						
Highbury & Islington ⊖ d																						
Drayton Park d																						
Finsbury Park ⊖ d	23p32	23p41		23p47	00 02	00 11	00 32	00 38	00 58	01 02	01 17	06 02	06 32	06 47	07 02	07 11	07 17	07 32	07 47	08 02	08 11	08 17
Harringay d	23p34			23p49	00 04		00 34	00 40		01 04	01 19	06 04	06 34	06 49	07 04		07 19	07 34	07 49	08 04		08 19
Hornsey d	23p36			23p51	00 06		00 36	00 42		01 06	01 21	06 06	06 36	06 51	07 06		07 21	07 36	07 51	08 06		08 21
Alexandra Palace d	23p38			23p53	00 08		00 38	00 44		01 08	01 23	06 08	06 38	06 53	07 08		07 23	07 38	07 53	08 08		08 23
New Southgate d				23p56				00 47			01 26			06 56			07 26		07 56			08 26
Oakleigh Park d				23p59				00 50			01 29			06 59			07 29		07 59			08 29
New Barnet d				00 01				00 52			01 31			07 01			07 31		08 01			08 31
Hadley Wood d				00 04				00 55			01 34			07 04			07 34		08 04			08 34
Potters Bar d		23p53		00 08		00 23		00 59	01 10		01 38			07 08		07 21	07 38		08 08		08 21	08 38
Brookmans Park d				00 11				01 02			01 41			07 11			07 41		08 11			08 41
Welham Green d				00 13				01 04			01 43			07 13			07 43		08 13			08 43
Hatfield d		23p59		00 16		00 29		01 07	01 16		01 46			07 16		07 27	07 46		08 16		08 27	08 46
Welwyn Garden City [4] d		00 06		00a25		00 41		01a16	01 20		01a55			07a25		07 33	07a55		08a25		08 31	08a53
Welwyn North d		00 09				00 44			01s24							07 36					08 34	
Knebworth d		00 13				00 48			01s28							07 40					08 38	
Bowes Park d	23p41				00 11		00 41			01 11		06 11	06 41		07 11			07 41		08 11		
Palmers Green d	23p43				00 13		00 43			01 13		06 13	06 43		07 13			07 43		08 13		
Winchmore Hill d	23p45				00 15		00 45			01 15		06 15	06 45		07 15			07 45		08 15		
Grange Park d	23p47				00 17		00 47			01 17		06 17	06 47		07 17			07 47		08 17		
Enfield Chase d	23p49				00 19		00 49			01 19		06 19	06 49		07 19			07 49		08 19		
Gordon Hill d	23p51				00 21		00 51			01 21		06 21	06 51		07 21			07 51		08 21		
Crews Hill d	23p54				00 24		00 54			01 24		06 24	06 54		07 24			07 54		08 24		
Cuffley d	23p57				00 27		00 57			01 27		06 27	06 57		07 27			07 57		08 27		
Bayford d	00 02				00 32		01 02			01 32		06 32	07 02		07 32			08 02		08 32		
Hertford North d	00 07				00a39		01a09			01 37		06a39	07 07		07a39			08 07		08a37		
Watton-at-Stone d	00 13		←							01 43			07 13					08 13				
Stevenage [4] d	00 22	00 18	00 22			00 53			01 32	01 51			07a22			07 45		08a23			08 42	
Hitchin [4] d	→	00 25	00 29			01 00			01a39	01 59						07 52					08 47	
Letchworth Garden City a		00 30	00 37			01 04				02 05						07 56					08 51	

	FC	FC	FC	FC 1	FC	FC	FC	FC	FC 1	FC	FC	FC	FC	FC 1	FC	FC	FC	FC	FC 1	FC	FC	FC
London Kings Cross [15] ⊖ d	08 26	08 41	08 56	09 06	09 11	09 26	09 41	09 56	10 06	10 11	10 26	10 41	10 56	11 06	11 11	11 26	11 41	11 56	12 06	12 11	12 26	12 41
Moorgate ⊖ d																						
Old Street ⊖ d																						
EssexRoad d																						
Highbury & Islington ⊖ d																						
Drayton Park d																						
Finsbury Park ⊖ d	08 32	08 47	09 02	09 11	09 17	09 32	09 47	10 02	10 11	10 17	10 32	10 47	11 02	11 11	11 17	11 32	11 47	12 02	12 11	12 17	12 32	12 47
Harringay d	08 34	08 49	09 04		09 19	09 34	09 49	10 04		10 19	10 34	10 49	11 04		11 19	11 34	11 49	12 04		12 19	12 34	12 49
Hornsey d	08 36	08 51	09 06		09 21	09 36	09 51	10 06		10 21	10 36	10 51	11 06		11 21	11 36	11 51	12 06		12 21	12 36	12 51
Alexandra Palace d	08 38	08 53	09 08		09 23	09 38	09 53	10 08		10 23	10 38	10 53	11 08		11 23	11 38	11 53	12 08		12 23	12 38	12 53
New Southgate d		08 56			09 26		09 56			10 26		10 56			11 26		11 56			12 26		12 56
Oakleigh Park d		08 59			09 29		09 59			10 29		10 59			11 29		11 59			12 29		12 59
New Barnet d		09 01			09 31		10 01			10 31		11 01			11 31		12 01			12 31		13 01
Hadley Wood d		09 04			09 34		10 04			10 34		11 04			11 34		12 04			12 34		13 04
Potters Bar d		09 08		09 21	09 38		10 08		10 21	10 38		11 08		11 21	11 38		12 08		12 21	12 38		13 08
Brookmans Park d		09 11			09 41		10 11			10 41		11 11			11 41		12 11			12 41		13 11
Welham Green d		09 13			09 43		10 13			10 43		11 13			11 43		12 13			12 43		13 13
Hatfield d		09 16		09 27	09 46		10 16		10 27	10 46		11 16		11 27	11 46		12 16		12 27	12 46		13 16
Welwyn Garden City [4] d		09a21		09 31	09a51		10a21		10 31	10a51		11a21		11 31	11a51		12a21		12 31	12a51		13a21
Welwyn North d				09 34					10 34					11 34					12 34			
Knebworth d				09 38					10 38					11 38					12 38			
Bowes Park d	08 41		09 11			09 41		10 11			10 41		11 11			11 41		12 11			12 41	
Palmers Green d	08 43		09 13			09 43		10 13			10 43		11 13			11 43		12 13			12 43	
Winchmore Hill d	08 45		09 15			09 45		10 15			10 45		11 15			11 45		12 15			12 45	
Grange Park d	08 47		09 17			09 47		10 17			10 47		11 17			11 47		12 17			12 47	
Enfield Chase d	08 49		09 19			09 49		10 19			10 49		11 19			11 49		12 19			12 49	
Gordon Hill d	08 51		09 21			09 51		10 21			10 51		11 21			11 51		12 21			12 51	
Crews Hill d	08 54		09 24			09 54		10 24			10 54		11 24			11 54		12 24			12 54	
Cuffley d	08 57		09 27			09 57		10 27			10 57		11 27			11 57		12 27			12 57	
Bayford d	09 02		09 32			10 02		10 32			11 02		11 32			12 02		12 32			13 02	
Hertford North d	09 07		09a37			10 07		10a37			11 07		11a37			12 07		12a37			13 07	
Watton-at-Stone d	09 13					10 13					11 13					12 13					13 13	
Stevenage [4] d	09a20			09 42		10a20			10 42		11a20			11 42		12a20			12 42		13a20	
Hitchin [4] d				09 47					10 47					11 47					12 47			
Letchworth Garden City a				09 51					10 51					11 51					12 51			

Table 24

Sundays from 28 October

London - Welwyn Garden City, Hertford North and Letchworth Garden City

Network Diagram - see first Page of Table 24

	FC	FC 1	FC	FC	FC	FC	FC 1	FC	FC	FC	FC	FC 1	FC	FC	FC	FC	FC 1	FC	FC	FC 1	FC
London Kings Cross [15] ⊖ d	12 56	13 06	13 11	13 26	13 41	13 56	14 06	14 11	14 26	14 41	14 56	15 06	15 11	15 26	15 41	15 56	16 06	16 11	16 26	16 36	16 41
Moorgate ⊖ d																					
Old Street ⊖ d																					
EssexRoad d																					
Highbury & Islington ⊖ d																					
Drayton Park d																					
Finsbury Park ⊖ d	13 02	13 11	13 17	13 32	13 47	14 02	14 11	14 17	14 32	14 47	15 02	15 11	15 17	15 32	15 47	16 02	16 11	16 17	16 32	16 41	16 47
Harringay d	13 04		13 19	13 34	13 49	14 04		14 19	14 34	14 49	15 04		15 19	15 34	15 49	16 04		16 19	16 34		16 49
Hornsey d	13 06		13 21	13 36	13 51	14 06		14 21	14 36	14 51	15 06		15 21	15 36	15 51	16 06		16 21	16 36		16 51
Alexandra Palace d	13 08		13 23	13 38	13 53	14 08		14 23	14 38	14 53	15 08		15 23	15 38	15 53	16 08		16 23	16 38		16 53
New Southgate d			13 26		13 56			14 26		14 56			15 26		15 56			16 26			16 56
Oakleigh Park d			13 29		13 59			14 29		14 59			15 29		15 59			16 29			16 59
New Barnet d			13 31		14 01			14 31		15 01			15 31		16 01			16 31			17 01
Hadley Wood d			13 34		14 04			14 34		15 04			15 34		16 04			16 34			17 04
Potters Bar d		13 21	13 38		14 08		14 21	14 38		15 08		15 21	15 38		16 08		16 21	16 38		16 51	17 08
Brookmans Park d			13 41		14 11			14 41		15 11			15 41		16 11			16 41			17 11
Welham Green d			13 43		14 13			14 43		15 13			15 43		16 13			16 43			17 13
Hatfield d		13 27	13 46		14 16		14 27	14 46		15 16		15 27	15 46		16 16		16 27	16 46		16 57	17 16
Welwyn Garden City [4] d		13 31	13a51		14a21		14 31	14a51		15a21		15 31	15a51		16a21		16 31	16a51		17 01	17a21
Welwyn North d		13 34					14 34					15 34					16 34			17 04	
Knebworth d		13 38					14 38					15 38					16 38			17 08	
Bowes Park d	13 11			13 41		14 11			14 41		15 11			15 41		16 11			16 41		
Palmers Green d	13 13			13 43		14 13			14 43		15 13			15 43		16 13			16 43		
Winchmore Hill d	13 15			13 45		14 15			14 45		15 15			15 45		16 15			16 45		
Grange Park d	13 17			13 47		14 17			14 47		15 17			15 47		16 17			16 47		
Enfield Chase d	13 19			13 49		14 19			14 49		15 19			15 49		16 19			16 49		
Gordon Hill d	13 21			13 51		14 21			14 51		15 21			15 51		16 21			16 51		
Crews Hill d	13 24			13 54		14 24			14 54		15 24			15 54		16 24			16 54		
Cuffley d	13 27			13 57		14 27			14 57		15 27			15 57		16 27			16 57		
Bayford d	13 32			14 02		14 32			15 02		15 32			16 02		16 32			17 02		
Hertford North d	13a37			14 07		14a37			15 07		15a37			16 07		16a37			17 07		
Watton-at-Stone d				14 13					15 13					16 13					17 13		
Stevenage [4] d		13 42		14a20			14 42		15a20			15 42		16a20			16 42		17a20	17 12	
Hitchin [4] d		13 47					14 47					15 47					16 47			17a17	
Letchworth Garden City a		13 51					14 51					15 51					16 51				

	FC	FC 1	FC	FC	FC 1	FC	FC	FC 1	FC	FC	FC 1	FC	FC	FC 1	FC	FC	FC	FC	FC 1	FC	FC	FC
London Kings Cross [15] ⊖ d	16 56	17 06	17 11	17 26	17 36	17 41	17 56	18 06	18 11	18 26	18 36	18 41	18 56	19 06	19 11	19 26	19 41	19 56	20 06	20 11	20 26	20 41
Moorgate ⊖ d																						
Old Street ⊖ d																						
EssexRoad d																						
Highbury & Islington ⊖ d																						
Drayton Park d																						
Finsbury Park ⊖ d	17 02	17 11	17 17	17 32	17 41	17 47	18 02	18 11	18 17	18 32	18 41	18 47	19 02	19 11	19 17	19 32	19 47	20 02	20 11	20 17	20 32	20 47
Harringay d	17 04		17 19	17 34		17 49	18 04		18 19	18 34		18 49	19 04		19 19	19 34	19 49	20 04		20 19	20 34	20 49
Hornsey d	17 06		17 21	17 36		17 51	18 06		18 21	18 36		18 51	19 06		19 21	19 36	19 51	20 06		20 21	20 36	20 51
Alexandra Palace d	17 08		17 23	17 38		17 53	18 08		18 23	18 38		18 53	19 08		19 23	19 38	19 53	20 08		20 23	20 38	20 53
New Southgate d			17 26			17 56			18 26			18 56			19 26		19 56			20 26		20 56
Oakleigh Park d			17 29			17 59			18 29			18 59			19 29		19 59			20 29		20 59
New Barnet d			17 31			18 01			18 31			19 01			19 31		20 01			20 31		21 01
Hadley Wood d			17 34			18 04			18 34			19 04			19 34		20 04			20 34		21 04
Potters Bar d		17 21	17 38		17 51	18 08		18 21	18 38		18 51	19 08		19 21	19 38		20 08		20 21	20 38		21 08
Brookmans Park d			17 41			18 11			18 41			19 11			19 41		20 11			20 41		21 11
Welham Green d			17 43			18 13			18 43			19 13			19 43		20 13			20 43		21 13
Hatfield d		17 27	17 46		17 57	18 16		18 27	18 46		18 57	19 16		19 27	19 46		20 16		20 27	20 46		21 16
Welwyn Garden City [4] d		17 31	17a51		18 01	18a21		18 31	18a51		19 01	19a21		19 31	19a51		20a21		20 31	20a51		21a21
Welwyn North d		17 34			18 04			18 34			19 04			19 34					20 34			
Knebworth d		17 38			18 08			18 38			19 08			19 38					20 38			
Bowes Park d	17 11			17 41			18 11			18 41			19 11			19 41		20 11			20 41	
Palmers Green d	17 13			17 43			18 13			18 43			19 13			19 43		20 13			20 43	
Winchmore Hill d	17 15			17 45			18 15			18 45			19 15			19 45		20 15			20 45	
Grange Park d	17 17			17 47			18 17			18 47			19 17			19 47		20 17			20 47	
Enfield Chase d	17 19			17 49			18 19			18 49			19 19			19 49		20 19			20 49	
Gordon Hill d	17 21			17 51			18 21			18 51			19 21			19 51		20 21			20 51	
Crews Hill d	17 24			17 54			18 24			18 54			19 24			19 54		20 24			20 54	
Cuffley d	17 27			17 57			18 27			18 57			19 27			19 57		20 27			20 57	
Bayford d	17 32			18 02			18 32			19 02			19 32			20 02		20 32			21 02	
Hertford North d	17a37			18 07			18a37			19 07			19a37			20 07		20a37			21 07	
Watton-at-Stone d				18 13						19 13						20 13					21 13	
Stevenage [4] d		17 42		18a20	18 12			18 42		19a20	19 12			19 42		20a20			20 42		21a20	
Hitchin [4] d		17 47			18a17			18 47			19 17			19 47					20 47			
Letchworth Garden City a		17 51						18 51			19 21			19 51					20 51			

London - Welwyn Garden City, Hertford North and Letchworth Garden City

Sundays from 28 October

Network Diagram - see first Page of Table 24

		FC	FC ■	FC	FC	FC	FC	FC ■	FC	FC	FC	FC	FC ■	FC	FC	FC
London Kings Cross ⊖	d	20 56	21 06	21 11	21 26	21 41	21 56	22 06	22 11	22 26	22 41	22 56	23 06	23 11	23 26	23 41
Moorgate ⊖	d															
Old Street ⊖	d															
Essex Road	d															
Highbury & Islington ⊖	d															
Drayton Park	d															
Finsbury Park ⊖	d	21 02	21 11	21 17	21 32	21 47	22 02	22 11	22 17	22 32	22 47	23 02	23 11	23 17	23 32	23 47
Harringay	d	21 04		21 19	21 34	21 49	22 04		22 19	22 34	22 49	23 04		23 19	23 34	23 49
Hornsey	d	21 06		21 21	21 36	21 51	22 06		22 21	22 36	22 51	23 06		23 21	23 36	23 51
Alexandra Palace	d	21 08		21 23	21 38	21 53	22 08		22 23	22 38	22 53	23 08		23 23	23 38	23 53
New Southgate	d			21 26		21 56			22 26		22 56			23 26		23 56
Oakleigh Park	d			21 29		21 59			22 29		22 59			23 29		23 59
New Barnet	d			21 31		22 01			22 31		23 01			23 31		00 01
Hadley Wood	d			21 34		22 04			22 34		23 04			23 34		00 04
Potters Bar	d		21 21	21 38		22 08		22 21	22 38		23 08		23 21	23 38		00 08
Brookmans Park	d			21 41		22 11			22 41		23 11			23 41		00 11
Welham Green	d			21 43		22 13			22 43		23 13			23 43		00 13
Hatfield	d		21 27	21 46		22 16		22 27	22 46		23 16		23 27	23 46		00 16
Welwyn Garden City ■	d		21 31	21a51		22a21		22 31	22a51		23a21		23 31	23a51		00 20
Welwyn North	d		21 34					22 34					23 34			00 23
Knebworth	d		21 38					22 38					23 38			00 28
Bowes Park	d	21 11			21 41		22 11			22 41		23 11			23 41	
Palmers Green	d	21 13			21 43		22 13			22 43		23 13			23 43	
Winchmore Hill	d	21 15			21 45		22 15			22 45		23 15			23 45	
Grange Park	d	21 17			21 47		22 17			22 47		23 17			23 47	
Enfield Chase	d	21 19			21 49		22 19			22 49		23 19			23 49	
Gordon Hill	d	21 21			21 51		22 21			22 51		23 21			23 51	
Crews Hill	d	21 24			21 54		22 24			22 54		23 24			23 54	
Cuffley	d	21 27			21 57		22 27			22 57		23 27			23 57	
Bayford	d	21 32			22 02		22 32			23 02		23 32			00 02	
Hertford North	d	21a37			22 07		22a37			23 07		23a37			00 07	
Watton-at-Stone	d				22 13					23 13					00 13	
Stevenage ■	d		21 42		22a20			22 42		23a20			23 42		00a20	00 31
Hitchin ■	d		21 47					22 47					23 47			00 37
Letchworth Garden City	a		21 51					22 51					23 51			00 52

Letchworth Garden City, Hertford North and Welwyn Garden City - London

Mondays to Fridays

Network Diagram - see first Page of Table 24

Miles	Miles			FC MX ■	FC MX	FC MO A	FC MO B (bus)	FC MO ■ C	FC MX ■	FC MO B (bus)	FC	FC ■	FC D	FC E	FC ■	FC D	FC E	FC D	FC E	FC D	FC E	FC ■ D	FC E
0	0	**Letchworth Garden City**	d		23p20			23p46	23p47				04 47	04 50						05 17	05 20	05 26	
3	3	Hitchin ■	d	23p16	23p24			23p50	23p54			04 08	04 51	04 54	04 57					05 21	05 24	05 31	
7¼	7¼	**Stevenage** ■	d	23p22	23p29	23p30	23p30	23p55	23p59			04 13	04 56	04 59	05 02					05 26	05 29	05 36	
—	12¼	Watton-at-Stone	d		23p36	23p37	23p47						05 03	05 06						05 33	05 36		
—	16½	**Hertford North**	d		23p42	23p43	00 01					04 23	05 09	05 12						05 39	05 42		
—	19½	Bayford	d		23p46	23p47	00 16						05 13	05 16						05 43	05 46		
—	23	Cuffley	d		23p51	23p52	00 31					04 30	05 18	05 21						05 48	05 51		
—	24¾	Crews Hill	d		23p54	23p55	00 39						05 21	05 24						05 51	05 54		
—	26¼	Gordon Hill	d		23p57	23p58	00s49					04 34	05 24	05 27						05 54	05 57		
—	27	Enfield Chase	d		23p59	23p59	00s55					04 36	05 26	05 29						05 56	05 59		
—	27¾	Grange Park	d		00 01	00 02	01s00						05 28	05 31						05 58	06 01		
—	28½	Winchmore Hill	d		00 03	00 04	01s06					04 38	05 30	05 33						06 00	06 03		
—	29½	Palmers Green	d		00 05	00 06	01s14					04 40	05 32	05 35						06 02	06 05		
—	30½	Bowes Park	d		00 08	00 09	01s24						05 38	05 38						06 05	06 08		
9¾	—	Knebworth	d	23p25				23p58	00 02						05 06							05 40	
12¾	—	Welwyn North	d	23p29				00 02	00 06						05 10							05 44	
14½	—	**Welwyn Garden City** ■	d	23p32				00 05	00 09		04 10				05 13			05 30	05 33			05 47	
17	—	Hatfield	d	23p35				00 08	00 12		04 14				05 16			05 34	05 37			05 51	
19¼	—	Welham Green	d															05 38	05 41				
20¼	—	Brookmans Park	d								04 19							05 40	05 43				
22	—	Potters Bar	d	23p41				00 14	00 18		04 22				05 22			05 43	05 46			05 57	
24¼	—	Hadley Wood	d								04 25							05 47	05 50				
25½	—	New Barnet	d								04 28				05 27			05 49	05 52				
26¼	—	Oakleigh Park	d								04 30				05 29			05 51	05 54				
28¼	—	New Southgate	d								04 33				05 32			05 54	05 57				
29¾	31¼	Alexandra Palace	d		00 10	00 11	01s29				04 36		05 41	05 41	05 35			05 57	06 00	06 07	06 10		
30¾	32¼	Hornsey	d		00 12	00 13					04 38		05 43	05 43				05 59	06 02	06 09	06 12		
31¼	32¾	Harringay	d		00 14	00 15				←	04 40		05 45	05 45		←	←	06 01	06 04	06 11	06 14		←
32¼	33¾	Finsbury Park ⊖	d	23b51	00 17	00 18	01s59	00 27	00 29	01s59	04 42	04s47	05 47	05 47	05 39	05 47	05 47	06 04	06 07	06 14	06 17	06 06	06 07
—	34½	Drayton Park	d				→						→	→					→	→	→		
—	35	Highbury & Islington ⊖	d																				
—	35½	Essex Road	d																				
—	36¾	Old Street ⊖	d																				
—	37¼	**Moorgate** ⊖	a																				
34¾	—	London Kings Cross ⊖	a	00 01	00 26	00 27		00 39	00 40	02 14	04 51	05 00			05 48	05 55	05 55	06 15				06 19	06 15

		FC ■ F	FC ■ G	FC D	FC E	FC D	FC E	FC D	FC E	FC ■ D	FC D	FC ■ E	FC D	FC E	FC D	FC E	FC ■ E	FC	FC D	FC E	FC D	FC E	FC
Letchworth Garden City	d	05 29	05 29					05 45	05 48	05 56		05 59					06 19						06 23
Hitchin ■	d	05 34	05 34					05 49	05 52	06 01		06 04					06 23						06 27
Stevenage ■	d	05 39	05 39					05 54	05 57	06 06	06 08	06 09				06 10	06 29						06 33
Watton-at-Stone	d							06 01	06 04		06 15					06 17							06 40
Hertford North	d							06 09	06 12		06 24					06 26					06 30	06 33	06 46
Bayford	d							06 13	06 16												06 34	06 37	
Cuffley	d							06 18	06 21		06 32					06 34					06 39	06 42	06 54
Crews Hill	d							06 21	06 24												06 42	06 45	
Gordon Hill	d							06 24	06 27		06 36					06 38					06 45	06 48	06 58
Enfield Chase	d							06 26	06 29		06 39					06 41					06 48	06 51	07 01
Grange Park	d							06 28	06 31												06 50	06 53	
Winchmore Hill	d							06 30	06 33		06 42					06 44					06 52	06 55	07 04
Palmers Green	d							06 32	06 35		06 44					06 46					06 55	06 58	07 06
Bowes Park	d							06 35	06 38												06 57	07 00	
Knebworth	d	05 43	05 43							06 10		06 13					06 33						
Welwyn North	d	05 47	05 47							06 14		06 17					06 37						
Welwyn Garden City ■	d	05 50	05 50			05 55	05 58			06 17		06 20					06 40	06 25	06 32	06 35			
Hatfield	d	05 54	05 54			05 59	06 02			06 21		06 24					06 44	06 29	06 36	06 39			
Welham Green	d					06 03	06 06											06 33					
Brookmans Park	d					06 05	06 08											06 35					
Potters Bar	d	06 00	06 00			06 08	06 11			06 27		06 30					06 49	06 38	06 43	06 46			
Hadley Wood	d					06 12	06 15											06 42	06 46	06 49			
New Barnet	d					06 14	06 17											06 45	06 49	06 52			
Oakleigh Park	d					06 16	06 19											06 47	06 51	06 54			
New Southgate	d					06 19	06 22											06 50	06 54	06 57			
Alexandra Palace	d					06 22	06 25	06 37	06 40									06 53			07 00	07 03	
Hornsey	d					06 24	06 27	06 39	06 42									06 55			07 02	07 05	
Harringay	d			←	←	06 26	06 29	06 41	06 44				←	←	←			06 57			07 04	07 07	
Finsbury Park ⊖	d	06 09	06 09	06 14	06 17	06 29	06 32	06 44	06 47	06 36	06 54	06 39	06 44	06 47	06 54	06 54	06 58	07 00	07 03	07 03	07 09	07 09	07 14
Drayton Park	d			06 16	06 19	06 31	06 34	→	→		→		06 46	06 49	06 56	06 56		07 02			07 11	07 11	07 16
Highbury & Islington ⊖	d			06 17	06 20	06 32	06 35						06 47	06 50	06 58	06 58		07 04			07 13	07 13	07 18
Essex Road	d			06 19	06 22	06 34	06 37						06 49	06 52	07 00	07 00		07 06			07 15	07 15	07 20
Old Street ⊖	d			06 22	06 25	06 37	06 40						06 52	06 55	07 03	07 03		07 09			07 18	07 18	07 23
Moorgate ⊖	a			06 30	06 30	06 45	06 45						07 00	07 00	07 08	07 08		07 14			07 23	07 23	07 28
London Kings Cross ⊖	a	06 18	06 19							06 48		06 48					07 07		07 10	07 10			

A MO from 21 May until 10 September, MO from 29 October
B MO from 17 September until 22 October
C MO from 21 May
D from 8 October
E until 5 October
F until 18 May
G from 21 May until 5 October
b Previous night, stops to set down only

Letchworth Garden City, Hertford North and Welwyn Garden City - London

Network Diagram - see first Page of Table 24

	FC	FC	FC	FC	FC	FC	FC	FC	FC	FC	FC	FC ■	FC ■	FC	FC	FC	FC	FC	FC	FC	FC
		A	B			A	B	A	B	A	B	A	B	A	B	A	B	A	B		
Letchworth Garden City d					06 46							07 02	07 04								07 20
Hitchin ■ d					06 50							07 06	07 08								07 24
Stevenage ■ d					06 55			07 01	07 03			07 12	07 14								07 30
Watton-at-Stone d								07 08	07 10												
Hertford North d						07 00	07 03	07 14	07 16							07 21	07 24	07 31	07 33		
Bayford d						07 04	07 07									07 25	07 28				
Cuffley d						07 09	07 12	07 22	07 24							07 30	07 33	07 39	07 41		
Crews Hill d						07 12	07 15									07 33	07 36				
Gordon Hill d		07 03	07 06			07 15	07 18	07 26	07 28					07 31	07 33	07 36	07 39	07 43	07 45		
Enfield Chase d		07 05	07 08			07 18	07 21	07 29	07 31					07 33	07 35	07 39	07 42	07 46	07 48		
Grange Park d		07 07	07 10			07 20	07 23							07 35	07 37	07 41	07 44				
Winchmore Hill d		07 09	07 12			07 22	07 25	07 32	07 34					07 38	07 40	07 43	07 46	07 49	07 51		
Palmers Green d		07 12	07 15			07 25	07 28	07 34	07 36					07 40	07 42	07 45	07 48	07 51	07 53		
Bowes Park d		07 14	07 17			07 27	07 30							07 43	07 45	07 48	07 51				
Knebworth d												07 16	07 18								
Welwyn North d												07 24	07 24								
Welwyn Garden City ■ d	06 45			06 57	07 07					07 14	07 17	07 27	07 27							07 32	07 42
Hatfield d	06 49			07 01	07 11					07 18	07 21	07 31	07 31							07 36	07 46
Welham Green d	06 53			07 05						07 22	07 25									07 40	
Brookmans Park d	06 55			07 07						07 24	07 27									07 42	
Potters Bar d	06 58			07 10	07 18					07 27	07 30									07 45	07 52
Hadley Wood d	07 02			07 14						07 31	07 34									07 49	
New Barnet d	07 05			07 17	07 23					07 34	07 37									07 52	07 57
Oakleigh Park d	07 07			07 19	07 25					07 36	07 39									07 54	07 59
New Southgate d	07 10			07 22	07 28					07 39	07 42									07 57	08 02
Alexandra Palace d	07 13	07 17	07 20	07 25		07 33	07 33							07 45	07 47	07 50	07 53			08 00	
Hornsey d	07 15	07 19	07 22	07 27		07 35	07 35							07 47	07 49					08 02	
Harringay d	07 17	07 21	07 24	07 29		07 37	07 37							07 49	07 51					08 04	
Finsbury Park ⊖ d	07 20	07 24	07 27	07 32	07 35	07 39	07 39	07 44	07 44	07 48	07 48	07 47	07 47	07 54	07 54	07 58	07 58	08 02	08 02	08 06	08 10
Drayton Park d	07 22	07 26	07 29	07 34		07 41	07 41	07 46	07 46	07 50	07 50			07 56	07 56	08 00	08 00	08 04	08 04	08 08	
Highbury & Islington ⊖ d	07 24	07 28	07 31	07 36		07 43	07 43	07 48	07 48	07 52	07 52			07 58	07 58	08 02	08 02	08 06	08 06	08 10	
Essex Road d	07 26	07 30	07 33	07 38		07 45	07 45	07 50	07 50	07 54	07 54			08 00	08 00	08 04	08 04	08 08	08 08	08 12	
Old Street ⊖ d	07 29	07 33	07 36	07 41		07 48	07 48	07 53	07 53	07 57	07 57			08 03	08 03	08 07	08 07	08 11	08 11	08 15	
Moorgate ⊖ a	07 34	07 41	07 41	07 46		07 53	07 53	07 58	07 58	08 02	08 02			08 08	08 08	08 12	08 12	08 17	08 17	08 22	
London Kings Cross ■ ⊖ a					07 43							07 57	07 57								08 17

	FC	FC	FC	FC	FC	FC	FC	FC	FC	FC	FC	FC	FC	FC	FC	FC	FC	FC	FC	FC	FC	FC ■
	A	B	A	B		A	B		A	B	A	B										
Letchworth Garden City d																						
Hitchin ■ d																						08 39
Stevenage ■ d			07 32	07 35										08 05							08 34	08 45
Watton-at-Stone d			07 39	07 42										08 12							08 41	
Hertford North d	07 35	07 38	07 47	07 50		07 52	07 55				08 03	08 05		08 20			08 30				08 50	
Bayford d	07 39	07 42									08 07	08 09					08 34				08 54	
Cuffley d	07 44	07 47	07 54	07 57		07 59	08 02				08 12	08 14		08 27			08 39				08 59	
Crews Hill d	07 47	07 50									08 15	08 17					08 42				09 02	
Gordon Hill d	07 50	07 53	07 59	08 02		08 04	08 07		08 13	08 15	08 18	08 20		08 32		08 37	08 45			08 55	09 05	
Enfield Chase d	07 53	07 56	08 01	08 04		08 06	08 09		08 15	08 17	08 20	08 22		08 34		08 39	08 47			08 57	09 07	
Grange Park d	07 55	07 58				08 08	08 11		08 17	08 19	08 22	08 24				08 41				08 59	09 09	
Winchmore Hill d	07 57	08 00				08 10	08 13		08 19	08 21	08 24	08 26				08 43				09 01	09 11	
Palmers Green d	08 00	08 03				08 13	08 16		08 22	08 24	08 27	08 29				08 46				09 04	09 14	
Bowes Park d	08 02	08 05	08 06	08 09		08 15	08 18		08 24	08 26	08 29	08 31		08 38		08 48	08 52			09 06	09 16	
Knebworth d																						08 49
Welwyn North d																						08 53
Welwyn Garden City ■ d					07 47			07 58					08 14		08 18			08 32	08 42			08 58
Hatfield d					07 51			08 02					08 18		08 22			08 36	08 46			09 02
Welham Green d					07 55			08 06							08 26			08 40				
Brookmans Park d					07 57			08 08							08 28			08 42				
Potters Bar d					08 00			08 11					08 25		08 31			08 46	08 53			
Hadley Wood d					08 04			08 15							08 35			08 49				
New Barnet d					08 07			08 18					08 30		08 38			08 52	08 57			
Oakleigh Park d					08 09			08 20					08 32		08 40			08 54	08 59			
New Southgate d					08 12			08 23					08 35		08 43			08 57	09 02			
Alexandra Palace d	08 08	08 08	08 11	08 11	08 15	08 21	08 21		08 29	08 29	08 34	08 34	08 38	08 41	08 46	08 51	08 55	09 00	09 05	09 09	09 19	
Hornsey d	08 10	08 10	08 13	08 13	08 17	08 23	08 23	08 27	08 31	08 31				08 43	08 48		08 57	09 02		09 11	09 21	
Harringay d	08 12	08 12	08 15	08 15	08 19	08 25	08 25	08 29	08 33	08 33				08 45	08 50		08 59	09 04		09 13	09 23	
Finsbury Park ⊖ d	08 14	08 14	08 18	08 18	08 22	08 28	08 28	08 32	08 36	08 36	08 40	08 40	08 43	08 48	08 53	08 57	09 02	09 07	09 10	09 16	09 26	09 19
Drayton Park d	08 16	08 16	08 20	08 20	08 24	08 30	08 30	08 34	08 38	08 38	08 42	08 42		08 50	08 55	08 59	09 04	09 09		09 18	→	
Highbury & Islington ⊖ d	08 18	08 18	08 22	08 22	08 26	08 32	08 32	08 36	08 40	08 40	08 44	08 44		08 52	08 57	09 01	09 06	09 11		09 20		
Essex Road d	08 20	08 20	08 24	08 24	08 28	08 34	08 34	08 38	08 42	08 42	08 46	08 46		08 54	08 59	09 03	09 08	09 13		09 22		
Old Street ⊖ d	08 23	08 23	08 27	08 27	08 31	08 37	08 37	08 41	08 45	08 45	08 49	08 49		08 57	09 02	09 06	09 11	09 16		09 25		
Moorgate ⊖ a	08 28	08 28	08 32	08 32	08 37	08 42	08 42	08 46	08 50	08 50	08 55	08 55		09 02	09 07	09 11	09 16	09 21		09 30		
London Kings Cross ■ ⊖ a													08 51						09 16			09 28

A from 8 October

B until 5 October

Table 24

Mondays to Fridays

Letchworth Garden City, Hertford North and Welwyn Garden City - London

Network Diagram - see first Page of Table 24

	FC	FC	FC	FC	FC	FC ■	FC	FC	FC	FC	FC	FC	FC	FC ■	FC	FC	FC	FC	FC ■	FC	FC	FC
Letchworth Garden City d						08 59								09 29				09 50	09 59			
Hitchin ■ d						09 05								09 34				09 54	10 04			
Stevenage ■ d					09 04	09 11							09 34	09 40				10 00	10 10			
Watton-at-Stone d					09 11								09 41					10 06				
Hertford North d					09 17						09 33		09 53					10 13				10 33
Bayford d					09 21						09 37		09 57					10 17				10 37
Cuffley d					09 26						09 42		10 02					10 22				10 42
Crews Hill d					09 29						09 45		10 05					10 25				10 45
Gordon Hill d		09 12		09 27	09 32						09 48		10 08					10 28				10 48
Enfield Chase d		09 14		09 29	09 34						09 50		10 10					10 30				10 50
Grange Park d		09 16		09 31	09 36						09 52		10 12					10 32				10 52
Winchmore Hill d		09 18		09 33	09 38						09 54		10 14					10 34				10 54
Palmers Green d		09 21		09 36	09 41						09 56		10 16					10 36				10 56
Bowes Park d		09 23		09 38	09 43						09 59		10 19					10 39				10 59
Knebworth d						09 14								09 44					10 14			
Welwyn North d						09 18								09 48					10 18			
Welwyn Garden City ■ d			09 04			09 21			09 24	09 40		09 44		09 51			10 04		10 21		10 24	
Hatfield d			09 08			09 25			09 28	09 43		09 48		09 55			10 08		10 25		10 28	
Welham Green d			09 12						09 32			09 52					10 12				10 32	
Brookmans Park d			09 14						09 34			09 54					10 14				10 34	
Potters Bar d			09 17			09 31			09 37	09 49		09 57		10 01			10 17		10 31		10 37	
Hadley Wood d			09 21						09 41			10 01					10 21				10 41	
New Barnet d			09 23						09 43			10 03					10 23				10 43	
Oakleigh Park d			09 25						09 45			10 05					10 25				10 45	
New Southgate d			09 28						09 48			10 08					10 28				10 48	
Alexandra Palace d		09 26	09 31	09 42	09 46				09 51		10 01	10 11	10 21				10 31	10 41			10 51	11 01
Hornsey d		09 28	09 33		09 48				09 53		10 03	10 13	10 23				10 33	10 43			10 53	11 03
Harringay d	←	09 30	09 35		09 50		←	←	09 55		10 05	10 15	10 25		←	←	10 35	10 45		←	10 55	11 05
Finsbury Park ⊖ d	09 26	09 33	09 38	09 46	09 53	09 40	09 46	09 53	09 58	10 01	10 08	10 18	10 28	10 10	10 18	10 28	10 38	10 48	10 40	10 48	10 58	11 08
Drayton Park d	09 28	09 35	09 40	→	→		09 48	09 55	10 00		10 10	→	→		10 20	10 30	10 40	→		10 50	11 00	11 10
Highbury & Islington ⊖ d	09 30	09 36	09 41				09 49	09 56	10 01		10 11				10 21	10 31	10 41			10 51	11 01	11 11
Essex Road d	09 32	09 38	09 43				09 51	09 58	10 03		10 13				10 23	10 33	10 43			10 53	11 03	11 13
Old Street ⊖ d	09 35	09 41	09 46				09 54	10 01	10 06		10 16				10 26	10 36	10 46			10 56	11 06	11 16
Moorgate ⊖ a	09 40	09 46	09 51				09 59	10 06	10 11		10 21				10 31	10 41	10 51			11 01	11 11	11 21
London Kings Cross ■ ⊖ a						09 49				10 08				10 19					10 49			

	FC ■	FC	FC	FC	FC	FC ■	FC	FC	FC	FC ■	FC	FC	FC	FC	FC ■	FC	FC	FC	FC ■	FC	FC
Letchworth Garden City d	10 29				10 50					11 29				11 50					12 29		
Hitchin ■ d	10 34				10 54	11 04				11 34				11 54	12 04				12 34		
Stevenage ■ d	10 40				11 00	11 10				11 40				12 00	12 10				12 40		
Watton-at-Stone d					11 06									12 06							
Hertford North d			10 53		11 13				11 33			11 53		12 13				12 33			12 53
Bayford d			10 57		11 17				11 37			11 57		12 17				12 37			12 57
Cuffley d			11 02		11 22				11 42			12 02		12 22				12 42			13 02
Crews Hill d			11 05		11 25				11 45			12 05		12 25				12 45			13 05
Gordon Hill d			11 08		11 28				11 48			12 08		12 28				12 48			13 08
Enfield Chase d			11 10		11 30				11 50			12 10		12 30				12 50			13 10
Grange Park d			11 12		11 32				11 52			12 12		12 32				12 52			13 12
Winchmore Hill d			11 14		11 34				11 54			12 14		12 34				12 54			13 14
Palmers Green d			11 16		11 36				11 56			12 16		12 36				12 56			13 16
Bowes Park d			11 19		11 39				11 59			12 19		12 39				12 59			13 19
Knebworth d	10 44					11 14				11 44					12 14				12 44		
Welwyn North d	10 48					11 18				11 48					12 18				12 48		
Welwyn Garden City ■ d	10 51	10 44		11 04		11 21		11 24		11 51	11 44		12 04		12 21		12 24		12 51	12 44	
Hatfield d	10 55	10 48		11 08		11 25		11 28		11 55	11 48		12 08		12 25		12 28		12 55	12 48	
Welham Green d		10 52		11 12				11 32			11 52		12 12				12 32			12 52	
Brookmans Park d		10 54		11 14				11 34			11 54		12 14				12 34			12 54	
Potters Bar d	11 01	10 57		11 17		11 31		11 37		12 01	11 57		12 17		12 31		12 37		13 01	12 57	
Hadley Wood d		11 01		11 21				11 41			12 01		12 21				12 41			13 01	
New Barnet d		11 03		11 23				11 43			12 03		12 23				12 43			13 03	
Oakleigh Park d		11 05		11 25				11 45			12 05		12 25				12 45			13 05	
New Southgate d		11 08		11 28				11 48			12 08		12 28				12 48			13 08	
Alexandra Palace d		11 11	11 21	11 31	11 41			11 51	12 01		12 11	12 21	12 31	12 41			12 51	13 01		13 11	13 21
Hornsey d		11 13	11 23	11 33	11 43			11 53	12 03		12 13	12 23	12 33	12 43			12 53	13 03		13 13	13 23
Harringay d		11 15	11 25	11 35	11 45		←	11 55	12 05		12 15	12 25	12 35	12 45		←	12 55	13 05		13 15	13 25
Finsbury Park ⊖ d	11 10	11 18	11 28	11 38	11 48	11 40	11 48	11 58	12 08	12 10	12 18	12 28	12 38	12 48	12 40	12 48	12 58	13 08	13 10	13 18	13 28
Drayton Park d		11 20	11 30	11 40	→		11 50	12 00	12 10		12 20	12 30	12 40	→		12 50	13 00	13 10		13 20	13 30
Highbury & Islington ⊖ d		11 21	11 31	11 41			11 51	12 01	12 11		12 21	12 31	12 41			12 51	13 01	13 11		13 21	13 31
Essex Road d		11 23	11 33	11 43			11 53	12 03	12 13		12 23	12 33	12 43			12 53	13 03	13 13		13 23	13 33
Old Street ⊖ d		11 26	11 36	11 46			11 56	12 06	12 16		12 26	12 36	12 46			12 56	13 06	13 16		13 26	13 36
Moorgate ⊖ a		11 31	11 41	11 51			12 01	12 11	12 21		12 31	12 41	12 51			13 01	13 11	13 21		13 31	13 41
London Kings Cross ■ ⊖ a	11 19					11 49				12 19					12 49				13 19		

Letchworth Garden City, Hertford North and Welwyn Garden City - London

Network Diagram - see first Page of Table 24

		FC	FC	FC [1]	FC	FC	FC	FC [1]		FC	FC	FC	FC	FC [1]	FC	FC	FC	FC [1]		FC	FC	FC	FC	FC [1]	FC
Letchworth Garden City	d		12 50					13 29					13 50					14 29					14 50		
Hitchin [4]	d		12 54	13 04				13 34					13 54	14 04				14 34					14 54	15 04	
Stevenage [4]	d		13 00	13 10				13 40					14 00	14 10				14 40					15 00	15 10	
Watton at Stone	d		13 06										14 06										15 06		
Hertford North	d		13 13				13 33				13 53		14 13				14 33				14 53		15 13		
Bayford	d		13 17				13 37				13 57		14 17				14 37				14 57		15 17		
Cuffley	d		13 22				13 42				14 02		14 22				14 42				15 02		15 22		
Crews Hill	d		13 25				13 45				14 05		14 25				14 45				15 05		15 25		
Gordon Hill	d		13 28				13 48				14 08		14 28				14 48				15 08		15 28		
Enfield Chase	d		13 30				13 50				14 10		14 30				14 50				15 10		15 30		
Grange Park	d		13 32				13 52				14 12		14 32				14 52				15 12		15 32		
Winchmore Hill	d		13 34				13 54				14 14		14 34				14 54				15 14		15 34		
Palmers Green	d		13 36				13 56				14 16		14 36				14 56				15 16		15 36		
Bowes Park	d		13 39				13 59				14 19		14 39				14 59				15 19		15 39		
Knebworth	d			13 14				13 44						14 14				14 44						15 14	
Welwyn North	d			13 18				13 48						14 18				14 48						15 18	
Welwyn Garden City [4]	d	13 04		13 21		13 24		13 51		13 44		14 04		14 21		14 24		14 51		14 44		15 04		15 21	
Hatfield	d	13 08		13 25		13 28		13 55		13 48		14 08		14 25		14 28		14 55		14 48		15 08		15 25	
Welham Green	d	13 12				13 32				13 52		14 12				14 32				14 52		15 12			
Brookmans Park	d	13 14				13 34				13 54		14 14				14 34				14 54		15 14			
Potters Bar	d	13 17		13 31		13 37		14 01		13 57		14 17		14 31		14 37		15 01		14 57		15 17		15 31	
Hadley Wood	d	13 21				13 41				14 01		14 21				14 41				15 01		15 21			
New Barnet	d	13 23				13 43				14 03		14 23				14 43				15 03		15 23			
Oakleigh Park	d	13 25				13 45				14 05		14 25				14 45				15 05		15 25			
New Southgate	d	13 28				13 48				14 08		14 28				14 48				15 08		15 28			
Alexandra Palace	d	13 31	13 41			13 51	14 01			14 11	14 21	14 31	14 41			14 51	15 01			15 11	15 21	15 31	15 41		
Hornsey	d	13 33	13 43			13 53	14 03			14 13	14 23	14 33	14 43			14 53	15 03			15 13	15 23	15 33	15 43		
Harringay	d	13 35	13 45		←	13 55	14 05			14 15	14 25	14 35	14 45		←	14 55	15 05			15 15	15 25	15 35	15 45		←
Finsbury Park ⊖	d	13 38	13 48	13 40	13 48	13 58	14 08	14 10		14 18	14 28	14 38	14 48	14 40	14 48	14 58	15 08	15 10		15 18	15 28	15 38	15 48	15 40	15 48
Drayton Park	d	13 40	→		13 50	14 00	14 10			14 20	14 30	14 40	→		14 50	15 00	15 10			15 20	15 30	15 40	→		15 50
Highbury & Islington ⊖	d	13 41			13 51	14 01	14 11			14 21	14 31	14 41			14 51	15 01	15 11			15 21	15 31	15 41			15 51
Essex Road	d	13 43			13 53	14 03	14 13			14 23	14 33	14 43			14 53	15 03	15 13			15 23	15 33	15 43			15 53
Old Street ⊖	d	13 46			13 56	14 06	14 16			14 26	14 36	14 46			14 56	15 06	15 16			15 26	15 36	15 46			15 56
Moorgate ⊖	a	13 51			14 01	14 11	14 21			14 31	14 41	14 51			15 01	15 11	15 21			15 31	15 41	15 51			16 01
London Kings Cross [15] ⊖	a			13 49				14 19						14 49				15 19						15 49	

		FC	FC	FC		FC	FC [1]	FC	FC	FC	FC	FC [1]	FC	FC		FC	FC	FC	FC [1]	FC	FC	FC	FC	FC
Letchworth Garden City	d					15 20	15 29				15 50							16 20	16 29					
Hitchin [4]	d					15 24	15 34				15 54	16 04						16 24	16 34					
Stevenage [4]	d					15 30	15 40				16 00	16 10						16 30	16 40					
Watton at Stone	d					15 36					16 06							16 36						
Hertford North	d		15 33			15 53					16 13						16 33	16 43				16 53		
Bayford	d		15 37			15 57					16 17						16 37	16 47				16 57		
Cuffley	d		15 42			16 02					16 22						16 42	16 52				17 02		
Crews Hill	d		15 45			16 05					16 25						16 45	16 55				17 05		
Gordon Hill	d		15 48			16 08					16 28						16 48	16 58				17 08	17 18	
Enfield Chase	d		15 50			16 10					16 30						16 50	17 00				17 10	17 20	
Grange Park	d		15 52			16 12					16 32						16 52					17 12		
Winchmore Hill	d		15 54			16 14					16 34						16 54	17 02				17 14	17 22	
Palmers Green	d		15 56			16 16					16 36						16 56	17 05				17 16	17 25	
Bowes Park	d		15 59			16 19					16 39						16 59					17 19		
Knebworth	d						15 44					16 14							16 44					
Welwyn North	d						15 48					16 18							16 48					
Welwyn Garden City [4]	d	15 24		15 44			15 51			16 04		16 21		16 24		16 40			16 51		16 44			17 04
Hatfield	d	15 28		15 48			15 55			16 08		16 25		16 28		16 44			16 55		16 48			17 08
Welham Green	d	15 32		15 52						16 12				16 32							16 52			17 12
Brookmans Park	d	15 34		15 54						16 14				16 34							16 54			17 14
Potters Bar	d	15 37		15 57			16 01			16 17		16 31		16 37		16 50			17 01		16 57			17 17
Hadley Wood	d	15 41		16 01						16 21				16 41							17 01			17 21
New Barnet	d	15 43		16 03						16 23				16 43							17 03			17 23
Oakleigh Park	d	15 45		16 05						16 25				16 45							17 05			17 25
New Southgate	d	15 48		16 08						16 28				16 48							17 08			17 28
Alexandra Palace	d	15 51	16 01	16 11		16 21				16 31	16 41			16 51			17 01				17 11	17 21		17 31
Hornsey	d	15 53	16 03	16 13		16 23				16 33	16 43			16 53			17 03				17 13	17 23		17 33
Harringay	d	15 55	16 05	16 15		16 25		←	←	16 35	16 45		←	16 55			17 05			←	17 15	17 25		17 35
Finsbury Park ⊖	d	15 58	16 08	16 18		16 28	16 10	16 18	16 28	16 38	16 48	16 40	16 48	16 58		17 02	17 08	17 13	17 10	17 13	17 18	17 28	17 33	17 38
Drayton Park	d	16 00	16 10	→		→		16 20	16 30	16 40	→		16 50	17 00			17 10	→		17 15	17 20	17 30	17 35	17 40
Highbury & Islington ⊖	d	16 01	16 11					16 21	16 31	16 41			16 51	17 01			17 11			17 16	17 21	17 31	17 36	17 41
Essex Road	d	16 03	16 13					16 23	16 33	16 43			16 53	17 03			17 13			17 18	17 23	17 33	17 38	17 43
Old Street ⊖	d	16 06	16 16					16 26	16 36	16 46			16 56	17 06			17 16			17 21	17 26	17 36	17 41	17 46
Moorgate ⊖	a	16 11	16 21					16 31	16 41	16 51			17 01	17 11			17 21			17 26	17 31	17 41	17 46	17 51
London Kings Cross [15] ⊖	a						16 19					16 49				17 10			17 19					

Table 24

Mondays to Fridays

Letchworth Garden City, Hertford North and Welwyn Garden City - London

Network Diagram - see first Page of Table 24

		FC	FC [1]	FC	FC	FC	FC	FC	FC	FC [1]		FC	FC	FC	FC	FC	FC [1]	FC	FC	FC		FC [1]	FC	FC	FC
Letchworth Garden City	d									17 29												18 29			
Hitchin [4]	d		17 04							17 34							18 04					18 34			
Stevenage [4]	d	16 59	17 10						17 29	17 40			17 53				18 10		18 23			18 40			18 53
Watton at Stone	d	17 06							17 36				18 00						18 30						19 00
Hertford North	d	17 13				17 36			17 43				18 06					18 18	18 36					18 48	19 06
Bayford	d	17 17							17 47									18 22						18 52	
Cuffley	d	17 22				17 43			17 52				18 13					18 27	18 43					18 57	19 13
Crews Hill	d	17 25							17 55									18 30						19 00	
Gordon Hill	d	17 28			17 38	17 48			17 58				18 18			18 23		18 33	18 48				18 53	19 03	19 18
Enfield Chase	d	17 30			17 40	17 50			18 00				18 20			18 25		18 35	18 50				18 55	19 05	19 20
Grange Park	d	17 32			17 42				18 02							18 27		18 37					18 57	19 07	
Winchmore Hill	d	17 34			17 44	17 52			18 04				18 22			18 29		18 39	18 52				18 59	19 09	19 22
Palmers Green	d	17 36			17 46	17 55			18 06				18 25			18 31		18 41	18 55				19 01	19 11	19 25
Bowes Park	d	17 39			17 49				18 09							18 34		18 44					19 04	19 14	
Knebworth	d		17 14							17 44							18 14					18 44			
Welwyn North	d		17 18							17 48							18 18					18 48			
Welwyn Garden City [4]	d		17 21				17 34	17 46		17 51				18 04	18 16		18 28			18 34		18 51			
Hatfield	d		17 25				17 38	17 50		17 55				18 08	18 20		18 32			18 38		18 55			
Welham Green	d						17 42							18 12						18 42					
Brookmans Park	d						17 44							18 14						18 44					
Potters Bar	d		17 31				17 47	17 57		18 01				18 17	18 27		18 38			18 47		19 01			
Hadley Wood	d						17 51							18 21						18 51					
New Barnet	d						17 53							18 23						18 53					
Oakleigh Park	d						17 55							18 25						18 55					
New Southgate	d						17 58							18 28						18 58					
Alexandra Palace	d	17 41			17 51		18 01		18 11					18 31		18 36		18 46		19 01			19 06	19 16	
Hornsey	d	17 43			17 53		18 03		18 13					18 33		18 38		18 48		19 03			19 08	19 18	
Harringay	d	17 45		←	17 55		18 05		18 15			←		18 35		18 40		18 50		19 05			19 10	19 20	
Finsbury Park ⊖	d	17 48	17 40	17 48	17 58	18 03	18 08	18 07	18 18	18 10		18 18	18 32	18 38	18 38	18 43	18 47	18 53	19 02	19 08		19 10	19 13	19 23	19 32
Drayton Park	d	→		17 50	18 00	18 05	18 10		→			18 20	18 34	18 40		18 45		18 55	19 04	19 10			19 15	19 25	19 34
Highbury & Islington ⊖	d			17 51	18 01	18 06	18 11					18 21	18 35	18 41		18 46		18 56	19 05	19 11			19 16	19 26	19 35
Essex Road	d			17 53	18 03	18 08	18 13					18 23	18 37	18 43		18 48		18 58	19 07	19 13			19 18	19 28	19 37
Old Street ⊖	d			17 56	18 06	18 11	18 16					18 26	18 40	18 46		18 51		19 01	19 10	19 16			19 21	19 31	19 40
Moorgate ⊖	a			18 01	18 11	18 16	18 21					18 31	18 45	18 51		18 56		19 06	19 15	19 21			19 26	19 36	19 45
London Kings Cross [15] ⊖	a		17 49					18 17		18 19					18 47		18 56					19 22			

		FC	FC [1]	FC	FC	FC		FC [1]	FC	FC	FC	FC [1]	FC	FC	FC	FC [1]		FC	FC	FC	FC [1]	FC	FC	FC	FC [1]
Letchworth Garden City	d							19 29						20 20	20 29									21 20	21 29
Hitchin [4]	d		19 11					19 34				20 04		20 24	20 34						21 04			21 24	21 34
Stevenage [4]	d		19 17					19 40			19 59	20 10		20 29	20 40					20 59	21 10			21 29	21 40
Watton at Stone	d										20 06				20 36					21 06				21 36	
Hertford North	d			19 18	19 36				19 48		20 12				20 42					21 12				21 42	
Bayford	d			19 22					19 52		20 16				20 46					21 16				21 46	
Cuffley	d			19 27	19 43				19 57		20 21				20 51					21 21				21 51	
Crews Hill	d			19 30					20 00		20 24				20 54					21 24				21 54	
Gordon Hill	d			19 33	19 48				20 03		20 27				20 57					21 27				21 57	
Enfield Chase	d			19 35	19 50				20 05		20 29				20 59					21 29				21 59	
Grange Park	d			19 37					20 07		20 31				21 01					21 31				22 01	
Winchmore Hill	d			19 39	19 52				20 09		20 33				21 03					21 33				22 03	
Palmers Green	d			19 41	19 55				20 11		20 35				21 05					21 35				22 05	
Bowes Park	d			19 44					20 14		20 38				21 08					21 38				22 08	
Knebworth	d		19 20					19 44				20 14				20 44					21 14				21 44
Welwyn North	d		19 24					19 48				20 18				20 48					21 18				21 48
Welwyn Garden City [4]	d	19 04	19 28			19 34		19 51		19 58		20 21		20 28		20 51			20 58		21 21		21 28		21 51
Hatfield	d	19 08	19 32			19 38		19 55		20 02		20 25		20 32		20 55			21 02		21 25		21 32		21 55
Welham Green	d	19 12				19 42				20 06				20 36					21 06				21 36		
Brookmans Park	d	19 14				19 44				20 08				20 38					21 08				21 38		
Potters Bar	d	19 17	19 38			19 47		20 01		20 11		20 31		20 41		21 01			21 11		21 31		21 41		22 01
Hadley Wood	d	19 21				19 51				20 15				20 45					21 15				21 45		
New Barnet	d	19 23				19 53				20 17				20 47					21 17				21 47		
Oakleigh Park	d	19 25				19 55				20 19				20 49					21 19				21 49		
New Southgate	d	19 28				19 58				20 22				20 52					21 22				21 52		
Alexandra Palace	d	19 31		19 46		20 01			20 16	20 25	20 40			20 55	21 10				21 25	21 40			21 55	22 10	
Hornsey	d	19 33		19 48		20 03			20 18	20 27	20 42			20 57	21 12				21 27	21 42			21 57	22 12	
Harringay	d	19 35		19 50		20 05			20 20	20 29	20 44		←	20 59	21 14			←	21 29	21 44		←	21 59	22 14	
Finsbury Park ⊖	d	19 38	19 47	19 53	20 02	20 08		20 10	20 23	20 32	20 47	20 40	20 47	21 02	21 17	21 10		21 17	21 32	21 47	21 40	21 47	22 02	22 17	22 10
Drayton Park	d	19 40		19 55	20 04	20 10			20 25	20 34	→		20 49	21 04	→			21 19	21 34	→		21 49		→	
Highbury & Islington ⊖	d	19 41		19 56	20 05	20 11			20 26	20 35			20 50	21 05				21 20	21 35			21 50			
Essex Road	d	19 43		19 58	20 07	20 13			20 28	20 37			20 52	21 07				21 22	21 37			21 52			
Old Street ⊖	d	19 46		20 01	20 10	20 16			20 31	20 40			20 55	21 10				21 25	21 40			21 55			
Moorgate ⊖	a	19 51		20 06	20 15	20 21			20 36	20 45			21 00	21 15				21 30	21 45			22 00			
London Kings Cross [15] ⊖	a		19 56					20 19				20 49				21 19					21 49		22 10		22 19

Letchworth Garden City, Hertford North and Welwyn Garden City - London

Network Diagram - see first Page of Table 24

		FC		FC	FC 1	FC	FC	FC	FC 1	FC	FC	FC		FC 1	FC	FC 1
Letchworth Garden City	d							22 20	22 29						23 20	23 47
Hitchin 4	d				22 13			22 24	22 34					23 16	23 24	23 54
Stevenage 4	d				22 18			22 29	22 40					23 22	23 29	23 59
Watton-at-Stone	d							22 36							23 36	
Hertford North	d					22 12		22 42				23 12			23 42	
Bayford	d					22 16		22 46				23 16			23 46	
Cuffley	d					22 21		22 51				23 21			23 51	
Crews Hill	d					22 24		22 54				23 24			23 54	
Gordon Hill	d					22 27		22 57				23 27			23 57	
Enfield Chase	d					22 29		22 59				23 29			23 59	
Grange Park	d					22 31		23 01				23 31			00 01	
Winchmore Hill	d					22 33		23 03				23 33			00 03	
Palmers Green	d					22 35		23 05				23 35			00 05	
Bowes Park	d					22 38		23 08				23 38			00 08	
Knebworth	d				22 22				22 44					23 25		00 02
Welwyn North	d				22 25				22 48					23 29		00 06
Welwyn Garden City 4	d			21 58	22 28		22 30		22 51		23 00			23 32		00 09
Hatfield	d			22 02	22 32		22 34		22 55		23 04			23 35		00 12
Welham Green	d			22 06			22 38				23 08					
Brookmans Park	d			22 08			22 40				23 10					
Potters Bar	d			22 11	22 37		22 43		23 01		23 13			23 41		00 18
Hadley Wood	d			22 15			22 47				23 17					
New Barnet	d			22 17			22 49				23 19					
Oakleigh Park	d			22 19			22 51				23 21					
New Southgate	d			22 22			22 54				23 24					
Alexandra Palace	d			22 25		22 40	22 57	23 10			23 27	23 40			00 10	
Hornsey	d			22 27		22 42	22 59	23 12			23 29	23 42			00 12	
Harringay	d	←		22 29		22 44	23 01	23 14		←	23 31	23 44			00 14	
Finsbury Park ⊖	d	22 17		22 32	22 46	22 47	23 04	23 17	23 10	23 17	23 34	23 47		23s51	00 17	00 29
Drayton Park	d							→								
Highbury & Islington ⊖	d															
Essex Road	d															
Old Street ⊖	d															
Moorgate ⊖	a															
London Kings Cross 15 ⊖	a	22 25		22 40	22 52	22 55	23 10		23 20	23 25	23 40	23 55		00 01	00 26	00 40

Saturdays

		FC 1	FC	FC 1	FC	FC 1	FC	FC 1	FC	FC		FC 1	FC	FC	FC 1	FC	FC	FC	FC 1	FC		FC	FC 1	FC	FC
Letchworth Garden City	d		23p20	23p47			04 50			05 20		05 29						06 20	06 29						
Hitchin 4	d	23p16	23p24	23p54		04 08	04 54	04 57		05 24		05 34			06 04			06 24	06 34				07 04		
Stevenage 4	d	23p22	23p29	23p59		04 13	04 59	05 02		05 30		05 40			06 10			06 30	06 40				07 10		
Watton-at-Stone	d		23p36				05 06			05 37								06 37							
Hertford North	d		23p42			04 23	05 12			05 43						06 13		06 43						07 13	
Bayford	d		23p46				05 16			05 47						06 17		06 47						07 17	
Cuffley	d		23p51			04 30	05 21			05 52						06 22		06 52						07 22	
Crews Hill	d		23p54				05 24			05 55						06 25		06 55						07 25	
Gordon Hill	d		23p57			04 34	05 27			05 58						06 28		06 58						07 28	
Enfield Chase	d		23p59			04 36	05 29			06 00						06 30		07 00						07 30	
Grange Park	d		00 01				05 31			06 02						06 32		07 02						07 32	
Winchmore Hill	d		00 03			04 38	05 33			06 04						06 34		07 04						07 34	
Palmers Green	d		00 05			04 40	05 35			06 06						06 36		07 06						07 36	
Bowes Park	d		00 08				05 38			06 09						06 39		07 09						07 39	
Knebworth	d	23p25		00 02				05 06				05 44			06 14				06 44				07 14		
Welwyn North	d	23p29		00 06				05 10				05 48			06 18				06 48				07 18		
Welwyn Garden City 4	d	23p32		00 09	04 10			05 13				05 51		05 58	06 21		06 28		06 51			06 58	07 21		07 28
Hatfield	d	23p35		00 12	04 14			05 16				05 55		06 02	06 25		06 32		06 55			07 02	07 25		07 32
Welham Green	d													06 06			06 36					07 06			07 36
Brookmans Park	d				04 19									06 08			06 38					07 08			07 38
Potters Bar	d	23p41		00 18	04 22			05 22				06 01		06 11	06 31		06 41		07 01			07 11	07 31		07 41
Hadley Wood	d				04 25									06 15			06 45					07 15			07 45
New Barnet	d				04 28			05 27						06 17			06 47					07 17			07 47
Oakleigh Park	d				04 30			05 29						06 19			06 49					07 19			07 49
New Southgate	d				04 33			05 32						06 22			06 52					07 22			07 52
Alexandra Palace	d		00 10		04 36		05 40	05 35		06 11				06 25		06 41	06 55	07 11				07 25		07 41	07 55
Hornsey	d		00 12		04 38		05 42			06 13				06 27		06 43	06 57	07 13				07 27		07 43	07 57
Harringay	d		00 14		04 40		05 44		←	06 15			←	06 29		06 45	06 59	07 15		←		07 29		07 45	07 59
Finsbury Park ⊖	d	23b51	00 17	00 29	04 42	04s50	05 47	05 39	05 47	06 18		06 10	06 18	06 32	06 40	06 48	07 02	07 18	07 10	07 18		07 32	07 40	07 48	08 02
Drayton Park	d						→			→								→							
Highbury & Islington ⊖	d																								
Essex Road	d																								
Old Street ⊖	d																								
Moorgate ⊖	a																								
London Kings Cross 15 ⊖	a	00 01	00 26	00 40	04 51	05 00		05 48	05 55			06 20	06 25	06 40	06 47	06 55	07 10		07 19	07 25		07 40	07 49	07 55	08 10

b Previous night, stops to set down only

Letchworth Garden City, Hertford North and Welwyn Garden City - London

Network Diagram - see first Page of Table 24

		FC	FC 1	FC	FC	FC 1		FC	FC	FC	FC 1	FC	FC	FC 1	FC	FC		FC	FC 1	FC	FC	FC 1	FC	FC	FC
Letchworth Garden City	d		07 29								08 29								09 29						
Hitchin 4	d		07 34			08 04					08 34			09 04					09 34			10 04			
Stevenage 4	d	07 30	07 40			08 10				08 30	08 40			09 10				09 30	09 40			10 10			10 30
Watton-at-Stone	d	07 37								08 37								09 37							10 37
Hertford North	d	07 43						08 13		08 43					09 13			09 43					10 13		10 43
Bayford	d	07 47						08 17		08 47					09 17			09 47					10 17		10 47
Cuffley	d	07 52						08 22		08 52					09 22			09 52					10 22		10 52
Crews Hill	d	07 55						08 25		08 55					09 25			09 55					10 25		10 55
Gordon Hill	d	07 58						08 28		08 58					09 28			09 58					10 28		10 58
Enfield Chase	d	08 00						08 30		09 00					09 30			10 00					10 30		11 00
Grange Park	d	08 02						08 32		09 02					09 32			10 02					10 32		11 02
Winchmore Hill	d	08 04						08 34		09 04					09 34			10 04					10 34		11 04
Palmers Green	d	08 06						08 36		09 06					09 36			10 06					10 36		11 06
Bowes Park	d	08 09						08 39		09 09					09 39			10 09					10 39		11 09
Knebworth	d		07 44			08 14					08 44			09 14					09 44			10 14			
Welwyn North	d		07 48			08 18					08 48			09 18					09 48			10 18			
Welwyn Garden City 4	d		07 51		07 58	08 21			08 28		08 51		08 58	09 21		09 28			09 51		09 58	10 21		10 28	
Hatfield	d		07 55		08 02	08 25			08 32		08 55		09 02	09 25		09 32			09 55		10 02	10 25		10 32	
Welham Green	d				08 06				08 36				09 06			09 36					10 06			10 36	
Brookmans Park	d				08 08				08 38				09 08			09 38					10 08			10 38	
Potters Bar	d		08 01		08 11	08 31			08 41		09 01		09 11	09 31		09 41			10 01		10 11	10 31		10 41	
Hadley Wood	d				08 15				08 45				09 15			09 45					10 15			10 45	
New Barnet	d				08 17				08 47				09 17			09 47					10 17			10 47	
Oakleigh Park	d				08 19				08 49				09 19			09 49					10 19			10 49	
New Southgate	d				08 22				08 52				09 22			09 52					10 22			10 52	
Alexandra Palace	d	08 11			08 25			08 41	08 55	09 11			09 25		09 41	09 55		10 11			10 25		10 41	10 55	11 11
Hornsey	d	08 13			08 27			08 43	08 57	09 13			09 27		09 43	09 57		10 13			10 27		10 43	10 57	11 13
Harringay	d	08 15		←	08 29			08 45	08 59	09 15		←	09 29		09 45	09 59		10 15		←	10 29		10 45	10 59	11 15
Finsbury Park ⊖	d	08 18	08 10	08 18	08 32	08 40		08 48	09 02	09 18	09 10	09 18	09 32	09 40	09 48	10 02		10 18	10 10	10 18	10 32	10 40	10 48	11 02	11 18
Drayton Park	d	→								→								→							→
Highbury & Islington ⊖	d																								
Essex Road	d																								
Old Street ⊖	d																								
Moorgate ⊖	a																								
London Kings Cross 15 ⊖	a		08 19	08 25	08 40	08 49		08 55	09 10		09 20	09 25	09 40	09 49	09 55	10 10			10 20	10 25	10 40	10 49	10 55	11 10	

		FC 1		FC	FC	FC 1	FC	FC	FC	FC 1	FC	FC		FC 1	FC	FC	FC	FC 1	FC	FC	FC 1	FC		FC	FC
Letchworth Garden City	d	10 29								11 29								12 29							
Hitchin 4	d	10 34				11 04				11 34				12 04				12 34			13 04				
Stevenage 4	d	10 40				11 10			11 30	11 40				12 10			12 30	12 40			13 10				13 30
Watton-at-Stone	d								11 37								12 37								13 37
Hertford North	d						11 13		11 43						12 13		12 43					13 13			13 43
Bayford	d						11 17		11 47						12 17		12 47					13 17			13 47
Cuffley	d						11 22		11 52						12 22		12 52					13 22			13 52
Crews Hill	d						11 25		11 55						12 25		12 55					13 25			13 55
Gordon Hill	d						11 28		11 58						12 28		12 58					13 28			13 58
Enfield Chase	d						11 30		12 00						12 30		13 00					13 30			14 00
Grange Park	d						11 32		12 02						12 32		13 02					13 32			14 02
Winchmore Hill	d						11 34		12 04						12 34		13 04					13 34			14 04
Palmers Green	d						11 36		12 06						12 36		13 06					13 36			14 06
Bowes Park	d						11 39		12 09						12 39		13 09					13 39			14 09
Knebworth	d	10 44				11 14				11 44				12 14				12 44			13 14				
Welwyn North	d	10 48				11 18				11 48				12 18				12 48			13 18				
Welwyn Garden City 4	d	10 51			10 58	11 21		11 28		11 51		11 58		12 21		12 28		12 51		12 58	13 21			13 28	
Hatfield	d	10 55			11 02	11 25		11 32		11 55		12 02		12 25		12 32		12 55		13 02	13 25			13 32	
Welham Green	d				11 06			11 36				12 06				12 36				13 06				13 36	
Brookmans Park	d				11 08			11 38				12 08				12 38				13 08				13 38	
Potters Bar	d	11 01			11 11	11 31		11 41		12 01		12 11		12 31		12 41		13 01		13 11	13 31			13 41	
Hadley Wood	d				11 15			11 45				12 15				12 45				13 15				13 45	
New Barnet	d				11 17			11 47				12 17				12 47				13 17				13 47	
Oakleigh Park	d				11 19			11 49				12 19				12 49				13 19				13 49	
New Southgate	d				11 22			11 52				12 22				12 52				13 22				13 52	
Alexandra Palace	d				11 25		11 41	11 55	12 11			12 25			12 41	12 55	13 11			13 25		13 41		13 55	14 11
Hornsey	d				11 27		11 43	11 57	12 13			12 27			12 43	12 57	13 13			13 27		13 43		13 57	14 13
Harringay	d			←	11 29		11 45	11 59	12 15		←	12 29			12 45	12 59	13 15		←	13 29		13 45		13 59	14 15
Finsbury Park ⊖	d	11 10		11 18	11 32	11 40	11 48	12 02	12 18	12 10	12 18	12 32		12 40	12 48	13 02	13 18	13 10	13 18	13 32	13 40	13 48		14 02	14 18
Drayton Park	d								→								→								→
Highbury & Islington ⊖	d																								
Essex Road	d																								
Old Street ⊖	d																								
Moorgate ⊖	a																								
London Kings Cross 15 ⊖	a	11 20		11 25	11 40	11 49	11 55	12 10		12 19	12 25	12 40		12 49	12 55	13 10		13 19	13 25	13 40	13 49	13 55		14 10	

Letchworth Garden City, Hertford North and Welwyn Garden City - London

Network Diagram - see first Page of Table 24

		FC 1	FC	FC	FC 1	FC	FC	FC	FC 1	FC	FC	FC 1	FC	FC	FC	FC 1	FC	FC	FC 1	FC	FC	FC	FC 1
Letchworth Garden City	d	13 29							14 29							15 29							16 29
Hitchin [4]	d	13 34			14 04				14 34			15 04				15 34			16 04				16 34
Stevenage [4]	d	13 40			14 10			14 30	14 40			15 10			15 30	15 40			16 10			16 30	16 40
Watton-at-Stone	d							14 37							15 37							16 37	
Hertford North	d					14 13		14 43					15 13		15 43					16 13		16 43	
Bayford	d					14 17		14 47					15 17		15 47					16 17		16 47	
Cuffley	d					14 22		14 52					15 22		15 52					16 22		16 52	
Crews Hill	d					14 25		14 55					15 25		15 55					16 25		16 55	
Gordon Hill	d					14 28		14 58					15 28		15 58					16 28		16 58	
Enfield Chase	d					14 30		15 00					15 30		16 00					16 30		17 00	
Grange Park	d					14 32		15 02					15 32		16 02					16 32		17 02	
Winchmore Hill	d					14 34		15 04					15 34		16 04					16 34		17 04	
Palmers Green	d					14 36		15 06					15 36		16 06					16 36		17 06	
Bowes Park	d					14 39		15 09					15 39		16 09					16 39		17 09	
Knebworth	d	13 44			14 14				14 44			15 14				15 44			16 14				16 44
Welwyn North	d	13 48			14 18				14 48			15 18				15 48			16 18				16 48
Welwyn Garden City [4]	d	13 51		13 58	14 21		14 28		14 51		14 58	15 21		15 28		15 51		15 58	16 21		16 28		16 51
Hatfield	d	13 55		14 02	14 25		14 32		14 55		15 02	15 25		15 32		15 55		16 02	16 25		16 32		16 55
Welham Green	d			14 06			14 36				15 06			15 36				16 06			16 36		
Brookmans Park	d			14 08			14 38				15 08			15 38				16 08			16 38		
Potters Bar	d	14 01		14 11	14 31		14 41		15 01		15 11	15 31		15 41		16 01		16 11	16 31		16 41		17 01
Hadley Wood	d			14 15			14 45				15 15			15 45				16 15			16 45		
New Barnet	d			14 17			14 47				15 17			15 47				16 17			16 47		
Oakleigh Park	d			14 19			14 49				15 19			15 49				16 19			16 49		
New Southgate	d			14 22			14 52				15 22			15 52				16 22			16 52		
Alexandra Palace	d			14 25		14 41	14 55	15 11			15 25		15 41	15 55	16 11			16 25		16 41	16 55	17 11	
Hornsey	d			14 27		14 43	14 57	15 13			15 27		15 43	15 57	16 13			16 27		16 43	16 57	17 13	
Harringay	d		←	14 29		14 45	14 59	15 15		←	15 29		15 45	15 59	16 15		←	16 29		16 45	16 59	17 15	
Finsbury Park ⊖	d	14 10	14 18	14 32	14 40	14 48	15 02	15 18	15 10	15 18	15 32	15 40	15 48	16 02	16 18	16 10	16 18	16 32	16 40	16 48	17 02	17 18	17 10
Drayton Park	d							→							→							→	
Highbury & Islington ⊖	d																						
Essex Road	d																						
Old Street ⊖	d																						
Moorgate ⊖	a																						
London Kings Cross [15] ⊖	a	14 19	14 25	14 40	14 49	14 55	15 10		15 19	15 25	15 40	15 49	15 55	16 10		16 19	16 25	16 40	16 49	16 55	17 10		17 19

		FC	FC	FC 1	FC	FC	FC	FC 1	FC	FC	FC 1	FC	FC	FC	FC 1	FC	FC	FC 1	FC	FC	FC	FC 1
Letchworth Garden City	d							17 29							18 29							19 29
Hitchin [4]	d			17 04				17 34			18 04				18 34			19 04				19 34
Stevenage [4]	d			17 10			17 30	17 40			18 10			18 30	18 40			19 10			19 30	19 40
Watton-at-Stone	d						17 37							18 37							19 37	
Hertford North	d				17 13		17 43					18 13		18 43					19 13		19 43	
Bayford	d				17 17		17 47					18 17		18 47					19 17		19 47	
Cuffley	d				17 22		17 52					18 22		18 52					19 22		19 52	
Crews Hill	d				17 25		17 55					18 25		18 55					19 25		19 55	
Gordon Hill	d				17 28		17 58					18 28		18 58					19 28		19 58	
Enfield Chase	d				17 30		18 00					18 30		19 00					19 30		20 00	
Grange Park	d				17 32		18 02					18 32		19 02					19 32		20 02	
Winchmore Hill	d				17 34		18 04					18 34		19 04					19 34		20 04	
Palmers Green	d				17 36		18 06					18 36		19 06					19 36		20 06	
Bowes Park	d				17 39		18 09					18 39		19 09					19 39		20 09	
Knebworth	d			17 14				17 44			18 14				18 44			19 14				19 44
Welwyn North	d			17 18				17 48			18 18				18 48			19 18				19 48
Welwyn Garden City [4]	d		16 58	17 21		17 28		17 51		17 58	18 21		18 28		18 51		18 58	19 21		19 28		19 51
Hatfield	d		17 02	17 25		17 32		17 55		18 02	18 25		18 32		18 55		19 02	19 25		19 32		19 55
Welham Green	d		17 06			17 36				18 06			18 36				19 06			19 36		
Brookmans Park	d		17 08			17 38				18 08			18 38				19 08			19 38		
Potters Bar	d		17 11	17 31		17 41		18 01		18 11	18 31		18 41		19 01		19 11	19 31		19 41		20 01
Hadley Wood	d		17 15			17 45				18 15			18 45				19 15			19 45		
New Barnet	d		17 17			17 47				18 17			18 47				19 17			19 47		
Oakleigh Park	d		17 19			17 49				18 19			18 49				19 19			19 49		
New Southgate	d		17 22			17 52				18 22			18 52				19 22			19 52		
Alexandra Palace	d		17 25		17 41	17 55	18 11			18 25		18 41	18 55	19 11			19 25		19 41	19 55	20 11	
Hornsey	d		17 27		17 43	17 57	18 13			18 27		18 43	18 57	19 13			19 27		19 43	19 57	20 13	
Harringay	d	←	17 29		17 45	17 59	18 15		←	18 29		18 45	18 59	19 15		←	19 29		19 45	19 59	20 15	
Finsbury Park ⊖	d	17 18	17 32	17 40	17 48	18 02	18 18	18 10	18 18	18 32	18 40	18 48	19 02	19 18	19 10	19 18	19 32	19 40	19 48	20 02	20 18	20 10
Drayton Park	d						→							→							→	
Highbury & Islington ⊖	d																					
Essex Road	d																					
Old Street ⊖	d																					
Moorgate ⊖	a																					
London Kings Cross [15] ⊖	a	17 25	17 40	17 49	17 55	18 10		18 19	18 25	18 40	18 49	18 55	19 10		19 19	19 25	19 40	19 49	19 55	20 10		20 19

Letchworth Garden City, Hertford North and Welwyn Garden City - London

Network Diagram - see first Page of Table 24

		FC	FC	FC 1	FC	FC	FC	FC 1	FC	FC	FC 1	FC	FC	FC	FC 1	FC	FC	FC 1	FC	FC	FC	FC 1	FC
Letchworth Garden City	d							20 29							21 29							22 29	
Hitchin [4]	d			20 04				20 34			21 04				21 34			22 04				22 34	
Stevenage [4]	d			20 10			20 30	20 40			21 10			21 30	21 40			22 10			22 30	22 40	
Watton-at-Stone	d						20 37							21 37							22 37		
Hertford North	d				20 13		20 43					21 13		21 43					22 13		22 43		
Bayford	d				20 17		20 47					21 17		21 47					22 17		22 47		
Cuffley	d				20 22		20 52					21 22		21 52					22 22		22 52		
Crews Hill	d				20 25		20 55					21 25		21 55					22 25		22 55		
Gordon Hill	d				20 28		20 58					21 28		21 58					22 28		22 58		
Enfield Chase	d				20 30		21 00					21 30		22 00					22 30		23 00		
Grange Park	d				20 32		21 02					21 32		22 02					22 32		23 02		
Winchmore Hill	d				20 34		21 04					21 34		22 04					22 34		23 04		
Palmers Green	d				20 36		21 06					21 36		22 06					22 36		23 06		
Bowes Park	d				20 39		21 09					21 39		22 09					22 39		23 09		
Knebworth	d			20 14				20 44			21 14				21 44			22 14				22 44	
Welwyn North	d			20 18				20 48			21 18				21 48			22 18				22 48	
Welwyn Garden City [4]	d		19 58	20 21		20 28		20 51		20 58	21 21		21 28		21 51		21 58	22 21		22 28		22 51	
Hatfield	d		20 02	20 25		20 32		20 55		21 02	21 25		21 32		21 55		22 02	22 25		22 32		22 55	
Welham Green	d		20 06			20 36				21 06			21 36				22 06			22 36			
Brookmans Park	d		20 08			20 38				21 08			21 38				22 08			22 38			
Potters Bar	d		20 11	20 31		20 41		21 01		21 11	21 31		21 41		22 01		22 11	22 31		22 41		23 01	
Hadley Wood	d		20 15			20 45				21 15			21 45				22 15			22 45			
New Barnet	d		20 17			20 47				21 17			21 47				22 17			22 47			
Oakleigh Park	d		20 19			20 49				21 19			21 49				22 19			22 49			
New Southgate	d		20 22			20 52				21 22			21 52				22 22			22 52			
Alexandra Palace	d		20 25		20 41	20 55	21 11			21 25		21 41	21 55	22 11			22 25		22 41	22 55	23 11		
Hornsey	d		20 27		20 43	20 57	21 13			21 27		21 43	21 57	22 13			22 27		22 43	22 57	23 13		
Harringay	d	←	20 29		20 45	20 59	21 15		←	21 29		21 45	21 59	22 15		←	22 29		22 45	22 59	23 15		←
Finsbury Park ⊖	d	20 18	20 32	20 40	20 48	21 02	21 18	21 10	21 18	21 32	21 40	21 48	22 02	22 18	22 10	22 18	22 32	22 40	22 48	23 02	23 18	23 10	23 18
Drayton Park	d						→							→							→		
Highbury & Islington ⊖	d																						
Essex Road	d																						
Old Street ⊖	d																						
Moorgate ⊖	a																						
London Kings Cross [15] ⊖	a	20 25	20 40	20 49	20 55	21 10		21 19	21 25	21 40	21 49	21 55	22 10		22 19	22 25	22 40	22 49	22 55	23 10		23 19	23 25

		FC	FC 1	FC	FC	FC 1 A
Letchworth Garden City	d					23 46
Hitchin [4]	d		23 04			23 50
Stevenage [4]	d		23 10		23 30	23 55
Watton-at-Stone	d				23 37	
Hertford North	d			23 13	23 43	
Bayford	d			23 17	23 47	
Cuffley	d			23 22	23 52	
Crews Hill	d			23 25	23 55	
Gordon Hill	d			23 28	23 58	
Enfield Chase	d			23 30	23 59	
Grange Park	d			23 32	00 02	
Winchmore Hill	d			23 34	00 04	
Palmers Green	d			23 36	00 06	
Bowes Park	d			23 39	00 09	
Knebworth	d		23 14			23 59
Welwyn North	d		23 18			00 02
Welwyn Garden City [4]	d	22 58	23 21			00 06
Hatfield	d	23 02	23 25			00 10
Welham Green	d	23 06				
Brookmans Park	d	23 08				
Potters Bar	d	23 11	23 31			00 15
Hadley Wood	d	23 15				
New Barnet	d	23 17				
Oakleigh Park	d	23 19				
New Southgate	d	23 22				
Alexandra Palace	d	23 25		23 41	00 11	
Hornsey	d	23 27		23 43	00 13	
Harringay	d	23 29		23 45	00 15	
Finsbury Park ⊖	d	23 32	23 40	23 48	00 18	00s32
Drayton Park	d					
Highbury & Islington ⊖	d					
Essex Road	d					
Old Street ⊖	d					
Moorgate ⊖	a					
London Kings Cross [15] ⊖	a	23 40	23 50	23 56	00 26	00 40

A until 8 September, from 27 October

Table 24

Sundays until 9 September

Letchworth Garden City, Hertford North and Welwyn Garden City - London

Network Diagram - see first Page of Table 24

		FC	FC ■	FC	FC	FC ■	FC	FC	FC	FC		FC	FC ■	FC	FC	FC	FC	FC	FC ■	FC		FC	FC	FC	FC
Letchworth Garden City	d		23p46																08 29						
Hitchin ■	d		23p50			06 33							07 33						08 34						
Stevenage ■	d	23p30	23p55			06 39						07 30	07 39					08 30	08 39						09 30
Watton-at-Stone	d	23p37										07 37						08 37							09 37
Hertford North	d	23p43		06 13			06 43		07 13			07 43				08 13		08 43					09 13		09 43
Bayford	d	23p47		06 17			06 47		07 17			07 47				08 17		08 47					09 17		09 47
Cuffley	d	23p52		06 22			06 52		07 22			07 52				08 22		08 52					09 22		09 52
Crews Hill	d	23p55		06 25			06 55		07 25			07 55				08 25		08 55					09 25		09 55
Gordon Hill	d	23p58		06 28			06 58		07 28			07 58				08 28		08 58					09 28		09 58
Enfield Chase	d	23p59		06 30			07 00		07 30			08 00				08 30		09 00					09 30		10 00
Grange Park	d	00 02		06 32			07 02		07 32			08 02				08 32		09 02					09 32		10 02
Winchmore Hill	d	00 04		06 34			07 04		07 34			08 04				08 34		09 04					09 34		10 04
Palmers Green	d	00 06		06 36			07 06		07 36			08 06				08 36		09 06					09 36		10 06
Bowes Park	d	00 09		06 39			07 09		07 39			08 09				08 39		09 09					09 39		10 09
Knebworth	d		23p59			06 43							07 43						08 43						
Welwyn North	d		00 02			06 47							07 47						08 47						
Welwyn Garden City ■	d		00 06		06 28	06 51		06 58		07 28			07 51		07 58		08 28		08 51			08 58		09 28	
Hatfield	d		00 10		06 32	06 54		07 02		07 32			07 54		08 02		08 32		08 54			09 02		09 32	
Welham Green	d				06 36			07 06		07 36					08 06		08 36					09 06		09 36	
Brookmans Park	d				06 38			07 08		07 38					08 08		08 38					09 08		09 38	
Potters Bar	d		00 15		06 41	07 00		07 11		07 41			08 00		08 11		08 41		09 00			09 11		09 41	
Hadley Wood	d				06 45			07 15		07 45					08 15		08 45					09 15		09 45	
New Barnet	d				06 47			07 17		07 47					08 17		08 47					09 17		09 47	
Oakleigh Park	d				06 49			07 19		07 49					08 19		08 49					09 19		09 49	
New Southgate	d				06 52			07 22		07 52					08 22		08 52					09 22		09 52	
Alexandra Palace	d	00 11		06 41	06 55		07 11	07 25	07 41	07 55		08 11			08 25	08 41	08 55	09 11				09 25	09 41	09 55	10 11
Hornsey	d	00 13		06 43	06 57		07 13	07 27	07 43	07 57		08 13			08 27	08 43	08 57	09 13				09 27	09 43	09 57	10 13
Harringay	d	00 15		06 45	06 59		07 15	07 29	07 45	07 59		08 15		←	08 29	08 45	08 59	09 15		←		09 29	09 45	09 59	10 15
Finsbury Park ⊖	d	00 18	00s32	06 48	07 02	07 10	07 18	07 32	07 48	08 02		08 18	08 10	08 18	08 32	08 48	09 02	09 18	09 10	09 18		09 32	09 48	10 02	10 18
Drayton Park	d											→						→							→
Highbury & Islington ⊖	d																								
Essex Road	d																								
Old Street ⊖	d																								
Moorgate ⊖	a																								
London Kings Cross ■ ⊖	a	00 26	00 40	06 56	07 13	07 20	07 27	07 45	07 56	08 15			08 20	08 26	08 40	08 55	09 10		09 19	09 25		09 40	09 55	10 10	

		FC ■	FC	FC	FC ■	FC		FC	FC	FC ■ A	FC	FC	FC	FC	FC	FC ■		FC	FC	FC	FC	FC	FC ■	FC	FC
Letchworth Garden City	d	09 29			09 59					10 29						11 29							12 29		
Hitchin ■	d	09 34			10 04					10 34						11 34							12 34		
Stevenage ■	d	09 39			10 09				10 30	10 39					11 30	11 39						12 30	12 39		
Watton-at-Stone	d								10 37						11 37							12 37			
Hertford North	d					10 13			10 43				11 13		11 43					12 13		12 43			
Bayford	d					10 17			10 47				11 17		11 47					12 17		12 47			
Cuffley	d					10 22			10 52				11 22		11 52					12 22		12 52			
Crews Hill	d					10 25			10 55				11 25		11 55					12 25		12 55			
Gordon Hill	d					10 28			10 58				11 28		11 58					12 28		12 58			
Enfield Chase	d					10 30			11 00				11 30		12 00					12 30		13 00			
Grange Park	d					10 32			11 02				11 32		12 02					12 32		13 02			
Winchmore Hill	d					10 34			11 04				11 34		12 04					12 34		13 04			
Palmers Green	d					10 36			11 06				11 36		12 06					12 36		13 06			
Bowes Park	d					10 39			11 09				11 39		12 09					12 39		13 09			
Knebworth	d	09 43			10 13					10 43						11 43							12 43		
Welwyn North	d	09 47			10 17					10 47						11 47							12 47		
Welwyn Garden City ■	d	09 51		09 58	10 21			10 28		10 51		10 58		11 28		11 51			11 58		12 28		12 51		12 58
Hatfield	d	09 54		10 02	10 24			10 32		10 54		11 02		11 32		11 54			12 02		12 32		12 54		13 02
Welham Green	d			10 06				10 36				11 06		11 36					12 06		12 36				13 06
Brookmans Park	d			10 08				10 38				11 08		11 38					12 08		12 38				13 08
Potters Bar	d	10 00		10 11	10 30			10 41		11 00		11 11		11 41		12 00			12 11		12 41		13 00		13 11
Hadley Wood	d			10 15				10 45				11 15		11 45					12 15		12 45				13 15
New Barnet	d			10 17				10 47				11 17		11 47					12 17		12 47				13 17
Oakleigh Park	d			10 19				10 49				11 19		11 49					12 19		12 49				13 19
New Southgate	d			10 22				10 52				11 22		11 52					12 22		12 52				13 22
Alexandra Palace	d			10 25		10 41		10 55	11 11			11 25	11 41	11 55	12 11				12 25	12 41	12 55	13 11			13 25
Hornsey	d			10 27		10 43		10 57	11 13			11 27	11 43	11 57	12 13				12 27	12 43	12 57	13 13			13 27
Harringay	d		←	10 29		10 45		10 59	11 15		←	11 29	11 45	11 59	12 15			←	12 29	12 45	12 59	13 15		←	13 29
Finsbury Park ⊖	d	10 10	10 18	10 32	10 40	10 48		11 02	11 18	11 10	11 18	11 32	11 48	12 02	12 18	12 10		12 18	12 32	12 48	13 02	13 18	13 10	13 18	13 32
Drayton Park	d								→						→							→			
Highbury & Islington ⊖	d																								
Essex Road	d																								
Old Street ⊖	d																								
Moorgate ⊖	a																								
London Kings Cross ■ ⊖	a	10 19	10 25	10 40	10 49	10 55		11 10		11 19	11 25	11 40	11 55	12 10		12 19		12 25	12 40	12 55	13 10		13 19	13 25	13 40

A until 22 July, 19 August, 26 August

Table 24

Sundays until 9 September

Letchworth Garden City, Hertford North and Welwyn Garden City - London

Network Diagram - see first Page of Table 24

		FC		FC	FC	FC ■	FC	FC	FC	FC	FC	FC ■		FC	FC	FC	FC	FC	FC ■	FC	FC	FC		FC	FC
Letchworth Garden City	d					13 29						14 29							15 29						
Hitchin ■	d					13 34						14 34							15 34						
Stevenage ■	d				13 30	13 39					14 30	14 39						15 30	15 39						16 30
Watton-at-Stone	d				13 37						14 37							15 37							16 37
Hertford North	d	13 13			13 43				14 13		14 43					15 13		15 43				16 13			16 43
Bayford	d	13 17			13 47				14 17		14 47					15 17		15 47				16 17			16 47
Cuffley	d	13 22			13 52				14 22		14 52					15 22		15 52				16 22			16 52
Crews Hill	d	13 25			13 55				14 25		14 55					15 25		15 55				16 25			16 55
Gordon Hill	d	13 28			13 58				14 28		14 58					15 28		15 58				16 28			16 58
Enfield Chase	d	13 30			14 00				14 30		15 00					15 30		16 00				16 30			17 00
Grange Park	d	13 32			14 02				14 32		15 02					15 32		16 02				16 32			17 02
Winchmore Hill	d	13 34			14 04				14 34		15 04					15 34		16 04				16 34			17 04
Palmers Green	d	13 36			14 06				14 36		15 06					15 36		16 06				16 36			17 06
Bowes Park	d	13 39			14 09				14 39		15 09					15 39		16 09				16 39			17 09
Knebworth	d					13 43						14 43							15 43						
Welwyn North	d					13 47						14 47							15 47						
Welwyn Garden City ■	d			13 28		13 51		13 58		14 28		14 51			14 58		15 28		15 51		15 58			16 28	
Hatfield	d			13 32		13 54		14 02		14 32		14 54			15 02		15 32		15 54		16 02			16 32	
Welham Green	d			13 36				14 06		14 36					15 06		15 36				16 06			16 36	
Brookmans Park	d			13 38				14 08		14 38					15 08		15 38				16 08			16 38	
Potters Bar	d			13 41		14 00		14 11		14 41		15 00			15 11		15 41		16 00		16 11			16 41	
Hadley Wood	d			13 45				14 15		14 45					15 15		15 45				16 15			16 45	
New Barnet	d			13 47				14 17		14 47					15 17		15 47				16 17			16 47	
Oakleigh Park	d			13 49				14 19		14 49					15 19		15 49				16 19			16 49	
New Southgate	d			13 52				14 22		14 52					15 22		15 52				16 22			16 52	
Alexandra Palace	d	13 41		13 55	14 11			14 25	14 41	14 55	15 11				15 25	15 41	15 55	16 11			16 25	16 41		16 55	17 11
Hornsey	d	13 43		13 57	14 13			14 27	14 43	14 57	15 13				15 27	15 43	15 57	16 13			16 27	16 43		16 57	17 13
Harringay	d	13 45		13 59	14 15		←	14 29	14 45	14 59	15 15			←	15 29	15 45	15 59	16 15		←	16 29	16 45		16 59	17 15
Finsbury Park ⊖	d	13 48		14 02	14 18	14 10	14 18	14 32	14 48	15 02	15 18	15 10		15 18	15 32	15 48	16 02	16 18	16 10	16 18	16 32	16 48		17 02	17 18
Drayton Park	d				→						→							→							→
Highbury & Islington ⊖	d																								
Essex Road	d																								
Old Street ⊖	d																								
Moorgate ⊖	a																								
London Kings Cross ■ ⊖	a	13 55		14 10		14 19	14 25	14 40	14 55	15 10		15 19		15 25	15 40	15 55	16 10		16 19	16 25	16 40	16 55		17 10	

		FC ■	FC	FC	FC	FC	FC	FC ■		FC	FC	FC	FC	FC	FC ■	FC	FC	FC		FC	FC	FC ■	FC	FC	FC
Letchworth Garden City	d	16 29						17 29							18 29							19 29			
Hitchin ■	d	16 34						17 34							18 34							19 34			
Stevenage ■	d	16 39					17 30	17 39						18 30	18 39						19 30	19 39			
Watton-at-Stone	d						17 37							18 37							19 37				
Hertford North	d				17 13		17 43					18 13		18 43				19 13			19 43				20 13
Bayford	d				17 17		17 47					18 17		18 47				19 17			19 47				20 17
Cuffley	d				17 22		17 52					18 22		18 52				19 22			19 52				20 22
Crews Hill	d				17 25		17 55					18 25		18 55				19 25			19 55				20 25
Gordon Hill	d				17 28		17 58					18 28		18 58				19 28			19 58				20 28
Enfield Chase	d				17 30		18 00					18 30		19 00				19 30			20 00				20 30
Grange Park	d				17 32		18 02					18 32		19 02				19 32			20 02				20 32
Winchmore Hill	d				17 34		18 04					18 34		19 04				19 34			20 04				20 34
Palmers Green	d				17 36		18 06					18 36		19 06				19 36			20 06				20 36
Bowes Park	d				17 39		18 09					18 39		19 09				19 39			20 09				20 39
Knebworth	d	16 43						17 43							18 43							19 43			
Welwyn North	d	16 47						17 47							18 47							19 47			
Welwyn Garden City ■	d	16 51		16 58		17 28		17 51			17 58		18 28		18 51		18 58			19 28		19 51		19 58	
Hatfield	d	16 54		17 02		17 32		17 54			18 02		18 32		18 54		19 02			19 32		19 54		20 02	
Welham Green	d			17 06		17 36					18 06		18 36				19 06			19 36				20 06	
Brookmans Park	d			17 08		17 38					18 08		18 38				19 08			19 38				20 08	
Potters Bar	d	17 00		17 11		17 41		18 00			18 11		18 41		19 00		19 11			19 41		20 00		20 11	
Hadley Wood	d			17 15		17 45					18 15		18 45				19 15			19 45				20 15	
New Barnet	d			17 17		17 47					18 17		18 47				19 17			19 47				20 17	
Oakleigh Park	d			17 19		17 49					18 19		18 49				19 19			19 49				20 19	
New Southgate	d			17 22		17 52					18 22		18 52				19 22			19 52				20 22	
Alexandra Palace	d			17 25	17 41	17 55	18 11				18 25	18 41	18 55	19 11			19 25	19 41		19 55	20 11			20 25	20 41
Hornsey	d			17 27	17 43	17 57	18 13				18 27	18 43	18 57	19 13			19 27	19 43		19 57	20 13			20 27	20 43
Harringay	d		←	17 29	17 45	17 59	18 15			←	18 29	18 45	18 59	19 15		←	19 29	19 45		19 59	20 15		←	20 29	20 45
Finsbury Park ⊖	d	17 10	17 18	17 32	17 48	18 02	18 18	18 10		18 18	18 32	18 48	19 02	19 18	19 10	19 18	19 32	19 48		20 02	20 18	20 10	20 18	20 32	20 48
Drayton Park	d						→							→							→				
Highbury & Islington ⊖	d																								
Essex Road	d																								
Old Street ⊖	d																								
Moorgate ⊖	a																								
London Kings Cross ■ ⊖	a	17 19	17 25	17 40	17 55	18 10		18 19		18 25	18 40	18 55	19 10		19 19	19 25	19 40	19 55		20 10		20 19	20 25	20 40	20 55

Sundays
until 9 September

Letchworth Garden City, Hertford North and Welwyn Garden City - London

Network Diagram - see first Page of Table 24

		FC	FC	FC ■		FC	FC	FC	FC	FC	FC ■	FC	FC	FC		FC	FC	FC ■	FC	FC	FC	FC	FC ■
Letchworth Garden City	d			20 29							21 29							22 29					23 46
Hitchin ■	d			20 34							21 34							22 34					23 50
Stevenage ■	d		20 30	20 39						21 30	21 39						22 30	22 39				23 30	23 55
Watton at Stone	d		20 37							21 37							22 37					23 37	
Hertford North	d		20 43					21 13		21 43				22 13			22 43				23 13	23 43	
Bayford	d		20 47					21 17		21 47				22 17			22 47				23 17	23 47	
Cuffley	d		20 52					21 22		21 52				22 22			22 52				23 22	23 52	
Crews Hill	d		20 55					21 25		21 55				22 25			22 55				23 25	23 55	
Gordon Hill	d		20 58					21 28		21 58				22 28			22 58				23 28	23 58	
Enfield Chase	d		21 00					21 30		22 00				22 30			23 00				23 30	23 59	
Grange Park	d		21 02					21 32		22 02				22 32			23 02				23 32	00 02	
Winchmore Hill	d		21 04					21 34		22 04				22 34			23 04				23 34	00 04	
Palmers Green	d		21 06					21 36		22 06				22 36			23 06				23 36	00 06	
Bowes Park	d		21 09					21 39		22 09				22 39			23 09				23 39	00 09	
Knebworth	d			20 43							21 43							22 43					23 58
Welwyn North	d			20 47							21 47							22 47					00 02
Welwyn Garden City ■	d	20 28		20 51			20 58		21 28		21 51		21 58			22 28		22 51		22 58			00 05
Hatfield	d	20 32		20 54			21 02		21 32		21 54		22 02			22 32		22 54		23 02			00 08
Welham Green	d	20 36					21 06		21 36				22 06			22 36				23 06			
Brookmans Park	d	20 38					21 08		21 38				22 08			22 38				23 08			
Potters Bar	d	20 41		21 00			21 11		21 41		22 00		22 11			22 41		23 00		23 11			00 14
Hadley Wood	d	20 45					21 15		21 45				22 15			22 45				23 15			
New Barnet	d	20 47					21 17		21 47				22 17			22 47				23 17			
Oakleigh Park	d	20 49					21 19		21 49				22 19			22 49				23 19			
New Southgate	d	20 52					21 22		21 52				22 22			22 52				23 22			
Alexandra Palace	d	20 55	21 11				21 25	21 41	21 55	22 11			22 25	22 41		22 55	23 11			23 25	23 41	00 11	
Hornsey	d	20 57	21 13				21 27	21 43	21 57	22 13			22 27	22 43		22 57	23 13			23 27	23 43	00 13	
Harringay	d	20 59	21 15			←	21 29	21 45	21 59	22 15		←	22 29	22 45		22 59	23 15		←	23 29	23 45	00 15	
Finsbury Park ⊖	d	21 02	21 18	21 10		21 18	21 32	21 48	22 02	22 18	22 10	22 18	22 32	22 48		23 02	23 18	23 10	23 18	23 32	23 48	00 18	00 27
Drayton Park	d		→							→							→						
Highbury & Islington ⊖	d																						
Essex Road	d																						
Old Street ⊖	d																						
Moorgate ⊖	a																						
London Kings Cross ■ ⊖	a	21 10		21 19		21 25	21 40	21 55	22 10		22 19	22 25	22 40	22 55		23 12		23 19	23 26	23 44	23 56	00 27	00 39

Sundays
16 September to 21 October

		FC	FC bus	FC bus	FC	FC bus	FC bus	FC ■	FC	FC		FC bus	FC bus	FC ■	FC	FC	FC bus	FC bus	FC ■	FC		FC	FC bus	FC bus	FC ■
Letchworth Garden City	d																		08 29						09 29
Hitchin ■	d							06 33						07 33					08 34						09 37
Stevenage ■	d	23p30					06 30	06 39					07 30	07 39				08 30	08 39					09 30	09 43
Watton at Stone	d	23p37					06 47						07 47					08 47						09 47	
Hertford North	d	23p43	05 33	06 03		06 33	07 03					07 33	08 03				08 33	09 03					09 33	10 03	
Bayford	d	23p47	05 48	06 18		06 48	07 18					07 48	08 18				08 48	09 18					09 48	10 18	
Cuffley	d	23p52	06 03	06 33		07 03	07 33					08 03	08 33				09 03	09 33					10 03	10 33	
Crews Hill	d	23p55	06 11	06 41		07 11	07 41					08 11	08 41				09 11	09 41					10 11	10 41	
Gordon Hill	d	23p58	06a21	06a51		07a21	07a51					08a21	08a51				09a21	09a51					10a21	10a51	
Enfield Chase	d	23p59																							
Grange Park	d	00 02																							
Winchmore Hill	d	00 04																							
Palmers Green	d	00 06																							
Bowes Park	d	00 09																							
Knebworth	d							06 43						07 43					08 43						09 46
Welwyn North	d							06 47						07 47					08 47						09 50
Welwyn Garden City ■	d				06 28			06 51	06 58	07 28				07 51	07 58	08 28			08 51	08 58		09 28			09 53
Hatfield	d				06 32			06 54	07 02	07 32				07 54	08 02	08 32			08 54	09 02		09 32			09 57
Welham Green	d				06 36				07 06	07 36					08 06	08 36				09 06		09 36			
Brookmans Park	d				06 38				07 08	07 38					08 08	08 38				09 08		09 38			
Potters Bar	d				06 41			07 00	07 11	07 41				08 00	08 11	08 41			09 00	09 11		09 41			10 03
Hadley Wood	d				06 45				07 15	07 45					08 15	08 45				09 15		09 45			
New Barnet	d				06 47				07 17	07 47					08 17	08 47				09 17		09 47			
Oakleigh Park	d				06 49				07 19	07 49					08 19	08 49				09 19		09 49			
New Southgate	d				06 52				07 22	07 52					08 22	08 52				09 22		09 52			
Alexandra Palace	d	00 11			06 55				07 25	07 55					08 25	08 55				09 25		09 55			
Hornsey	d	00 13			06 57				07 27	07 57					08 27	08 57				09 27		09 57			
Harringay	d	00 15			06 59				07 29	07 59					08 29	08 59				09 29		09 59			
Finsbury Park ⊖	d	00 18			07 02			07 10	07 32	08 02				08 10	08 32	09 02			09 10	09 32		10 02			10 14
Drayton Park	d																								
Highbury & Islington ⊖	d																								
Essex Road	d																								
Old Street ⊖	d																								
Moorgate ⊖	a																								
London Kings Cross ■ ⊖	a	00 26			07 13			07 20	07 45	08 15				08 20	08 40	09 10			09 19	09 40		10 10			10 21

Sundays
16 September to 21 October

Letchworth Garden City, Hertford North and Welwyn Garden City - London

Network Diagram - see first Page of Table 24

		FC	FC ■	FC	FC bus	FC bus		FC ■	FC	FC	FC bus	FC bus	FC ■	FC	FC	FC bus		FC bus	FC ■	FC	FC	FC bus	FC bus	FC ■	FC
Letchworth Garden City	d		10 04					10 29					11 29						12 29					13 29	
Hitchin ■	d		10 08					10 34					11 34						12 34					13 34	
Stevenage ■	d		10 13			10 30		10 39				11 30	11 39					12 30	12 39				13 30	13 39	
Watton at Stone	d					10 47						11 47						12 47					13 47		
Hertford North	d				10 33	11 03					11 33	12 03				12 33		13 03				13 33	14 03		
Bayford	d				10 48	11 18					11 48	12 18				12 48		13 18				13 48	14 18		
Cuffley	d				11 03	11 33					12 03	12 33				13 03		13 33				14 03	14 33		
Crews Hill	d				11 11	11 41					12 11	12 41				13 11		13 41				14 11	14 41		
Gordon Hill	d				11a21	11a51					12a21	12a51				13a21		13a51				14a21	14a51		
Enfield Chase	d																								
Grange Park	d																								
Winchmore Hill	d																								
Palmers Green	d																								
Bowes Park	d																								
Knebworth	d		10 17					10 43					11 43						12 43					13 43	
Welwyn North	d		10 21					10 47					11 47						12 47					13 47	
Welwyn Garden City ■	d	09 58	10 24	10 28				10 51	10 58	11 28			11 51	11 58	12 28				12 51	12 58	13 28			13 51	13 58
Hatfield	d	10 02	10 27	10 32				10 54	11 02	11 32			11 54	12 02	12 32				12 54	13 02	13 32			13 54	14 02
Welham Green	d	10 06		10 36					11 06	11 36				12 06	12 36					13 06	13 36				14 06
Brookmans Park	d	10 08		10 38					11 08	11 38				12 08	12 38					13 08	13 38				14 08
Potters Bar	d	10 11	10 33	10 41				11 00	11 11	11 41			12 02	12 11	12 41				13 00	13 11	13 41			14 00	14 11
Hadley Wood	d	10 15		10 45					11 15	11 45				12 15	12 45					13 15	13 45				14 15
New Barnet	d	10 17		10 47					11 17	11 47				12 17	12 47					13 17	13 47				14 17
Oakleigh Park	d	10 19		10 49					11 19	11 49				12 19	12 49					13 19	13 49				14 19
New Southgate	d	10 22		10 52					11 22	11 52				12 22	12 52					13 22	13 52				14 22
Alexandra Palace	d	10 25		10 55					11 25	11 55				12 25	12 55					13 25	13 55				14 25
Hornsey	d	10 27		10 57					11 27	11 57				12 27	12 57					13 27	13 57				14 27
Harringay	d	10 29		10 59					11 29	11 59				12 29	12 59					13 29	13 59				14 29
Finsbury Park ⊖	d	10 32	10 40	11 02				11 12	11 32	12 02			12 10	12 32	13 02				13 10	13 32	14 02			14 10	14 32
Drayton Park	d																								
Highbury & Islington ⊖	d																								
Essex Road	d																								
Old Street ⊖	d																								
Moorgate ⊖	a																								
London Kings Cross ■ ⊖	a	10 40	10 50	11 10				11 19	11 40	12 10			12 19	12 40	13 10				13 19	13 40	14 10			14 19	14 40

		FC		FC bus	FC bus	FC ■	FC	FC	FC bus	FC bus	FC ■	FC		FC	FC bus	FC bus	FC ■	FC	FC	FC bus	FC bus	FC ■		FC	FC
Letchworth Garden City	d					14 29					15 29						16 29					17 29			
Hitchin ■	d					14 34					15 34						16 34					17 34			
Stevenage ■	d				14 30	14 39				15 30	15 39					16 30	16 39				17 30	17 39			
Watton at Stone	d				14 47					15 47						16 47					17 47				
Hertford North	d			14 33	15 03				15 33	16 03					16 33	17 03				17 33	18 03				
Bayford	d			14 48	15 18				15 48	16 18					16 48	17 18				17 48	18 18				
Cuffley	d			15 03	15 33				16 03	16 33					17 03	17 33				18 03	18 33				
Crews Hill	d			15 11	15 41				16 11	16 41					17 11	17 41				18 11	18 41				
Gordon Hill	d			15a21	15a51				16a21	16a51					17a21	17a51				18a21	18a51				
Enfield Chase	d																								
Grange Park	d																								
Winchmore Hill	d																								
Palmers Green	d																								
Bowes Park	d																								
Knebworth	d					14 43					15 43						16 43					17 43			
Welwyn North	d					14 47					15 47						16 47					17 47			
Welwyn Garden City ■	d	14 28				14 51	14 58	15 28			15 51	15 58		16 28			16 51	16 58	17 28			17 51		17 58	18 28
Hatfield	d	14 32				14 54	15 02	15 32			15 54	16 02		16 32			16 54	17 02	17 32			17 54		18 02	18 32
Welham Green	d	14 36					15 06	15 36				16 06		16 36				17 06	17 36					18 06	18 36
Brookmans Park	d	14 38					15 08	15 38				16 08		16 38				17 08	17 38					18 08	18 38
Potters Bar	d	14 41				15 00	15 11	15 41			16 00	16 11		16 41			17 00	17 11	17 41			18 00		18 11	18 41
Hadley Wood	d	14 45					15 15	15 45				16 15		16 45				17 15	17 45					18 15	18 45
New Barnet	d	14 47					15 17	15 47				16 17		16 47				17 17	17 47					18 17	18 47
Oakleigh Park	d	14 49					15 19	15 49				16 19		16 49				17 19	17 49					18 19	18 49
New Southgate	d	14 52					15 22	15 52				16 22		16 52				17 22	17 52					18 22	18 52
Alexandra Palace	d	14 55					15 25	15 55				16 25		16 55				17 25	17 55					18 25	18 55
Hornsey	d	14 57					15 27	15 57				16 27		16 57				17 27	17 57					18 27	18 57
Harringay	d	14 59					15 29	15 59				16 29		16 59				17 29	17 59					18 29	18 59
Finsbury Park ⊖	d	15 02				15 10	15 32	16 02			16 10	16 32		17 02			17 10	17 32	18 02			18 10		18 32	19 02
Drayton Park	d																								
Highbury & Islington ⊖	d																								
Essex Road	d																								
Old Street ⊖	d																								
Moorgate ⊖	a																								
London Kings Cross ■ ⊖	a	15 10				15 19	15 40	16 10			16 19	16 40		17 10			17 19	17 40	18 10			18 19		18 40	19 10

Table 24

Sundays
16 September to 21 October

Letchworth Garden City, Hertford North and Welwyn Garden City - London

Network Diagram - see first Page of Table 24

		FC	FC	FC	FC	FC	FC	FC	FC	FC	FC	FC	FC	FC	FC	FC	FC	FC	FC	FC	FC	FC	FC
		🚌	🚌	1			🚌	🚌	1			🚌	🚌	1			🚌	🚌	1			🚌	🚌
Letchworth Garden City	d			18 29					19 29					20 29					21 29				
Hitchin 4	d			18 34					19 34					20 34					21 34				
Stevenage 4	d		18 30	18 39				19 30	19 39				20 30	20 39				21 30	21 39				22 30
Watton-at-Stone	d		18 47					19 47					20 47					21 47					22 47
Hertford North	d	18 33	19 03				19 33	20 03				20 33	21 03				21 33	22 03				22 33	23 03
Bayford	d	18 48	19 18				19 48	20 18				20 48	21 18				21 48	22 18				22 48	23 18
Cuffley	d	19 03	19 33				20 03	20 33				21 03	21 33				22 03	22 33				23 03	23 33
Crews Hill	d	19 11	19 41				20 11	20 41				21 11	21 41				22 11	22 41				23 11	23 41
Gordon Hill	d	19a21	19a51				20a21	20a51				21a21	21a51				22a21	22a51				23a21	23a51
Enfield Chase	d																						
Grange Park	d																						
Winchmore Hill	d																						
Palmers Green	d																						
Bowes Park	d																						
Knebworth	d			18 43					19 43					20 43					21 43				
Welwyn North	d			18 47					19 47					20 47					21 47				
Welwyn Garden City 4	d			18 51	18 58	19 28			19 51	19 58	20 28			20 51	20 58	21 28			21 51	21 58	22 28		
Hatfield	d			18 54	19 02	19 32			19 54	20 02	20 32			20 54	21 02	21 32			21 54	22 02	22 32		
Welham Green	d				19 06	19 36				20 06	20 36				21 06	21 36				22 06	22 36		
Brookmans Park	d				19 08	19 38				20 08	20 38				21 08	21 38				22 08	22 38		
Potters Bar	d			19 00	19 11	19 41			20 00	20 11	20 41			21 00	21 11	21 41			22 00	22 11	22 41		
Hadley Wood	d				19 15	19 45				20 15	20 45				21 15	21 45				22 15	22 45		
New Barnet	d				19 17	19 47				20 17	20 47				21 17	21 47				22 17	22 47		
Oakleigh Park	d				19 19	19 49				20 19	20 49				21 19	21 49				22 19	22 49		
New Southgate	d				19 22	19 52				20 22	20 52				21 22	21 52				22 22	22 52		
Alexandra Palace	d				19 25	19 55				20 25	20 55				21 25	21 55				22 25	22 55		
Hornsey	d				19 27	19 57				20 27	20 57				21 27	21 57				22 27	22 57		
Harringay	d				19 29	19 59				20 29	20 59				21 29	21 59				22 29	22 59		
Finsbury Park ⊖	d			19 10	19 32	20 02			20 10	20 32	21 02			21 10	21 32	22 02			22 10	22 32	23 02		
Drayton Park	d																						
Highbury & Islington ⊖	d																						
Essex Road	d																						
Old Street ⊖	d																						
Moorgate ⊖	a																						
London Kings Cross 15 ⊖	a			19 19	19 40	20 10			20 19	20 40	21 10			21 19	21 40	22 10			22 19	22 40	23 12		

		FC	FC	FC	FC	FC
		1		🚌	1	🚌
Letchworth Garden City	d	22 29			23 46	
Hitchin 4	d	22 34			23 50	
Stevenage 4	d	22 39		23 30	23 55	
Watton-at-Stone	d			23 47		
Hertford North	d			00 01		
Bayford	d			00 16		
Cuffley	d			00 31		
Crews Hill	d			00 39		
Gordon Hill	d			00s49		
Enfield Chase	d			00s55		
Grange Park	d			01s00		
Winchmore Hill	d			01s06		
Palmers Green	d			01s14		
Bowes Park	d			01s24		
Knebworth	d	22 43			23 58	
Welwyn North	d	22 47			00 02	
Welwyn Garden City 4	d	22 51	22 58		00 05	
Hatfield	d	22 54	23 02		00 08	
Welham Green	d		23 06			
Brookmans Park	d		23 08			
Potters Bar	d	23 00	23 11		00 14	
Hadley Wood	d		23 15			
New Barnet	d		23 17			
Oakleigh Park	d		23 19			
New Southgate	d		23 22			
Alexandra Palace	d		23 25	01s29		
Hornsey	d		23 27			
Harringay	d		23 29			←
Finsbury Park ⊖	d	23 10	23 32	01s59	00 27	01s59
Drayton Park	d			→		
Highbury & Islington ⊖	d					
Essex Road	d					
Old Street ⊖	d					
Moorgate ⊖	a					
London Kings Cross 15 ⊖	a	23 19	23 44		00 39	02 14

Table 24

Sundays
from 28 October

Letchworth Garden City, Hertford North and Welwyn Garden City - London

Network Diagram - see first Page of Table 24

		FC	FC	FC	FC	FC	FC	FC	FC	FC	FC	FC	FC	FC	FC	FC	FC	FC	FC	FC	FC	FC	FC
			1			1						1						1					
Letchworth Garden City	d		23p46															08 29					
Hitchin 4	d		23p50			06 33						07 33						08 34					
Stevenage 4	d	23p30	23p55			06 39					07 30	07 39					08 30	08 39					09 30
Watton-at-Stone	d	23p37									07 37						08 37						09 37
Hertford North	d	23p43		06 13			06 43		07 13		07 43				08 13		08 43				09 13		09 43
Bayford	d	23p47		06 17			06 47		07 17		07 47				08 17		08 47				09 17		09 47
Cuffley	d	23p52		06 22			06 52		07 22		07 52				08 22		08 52				09 22		09 52
Crews Hill	d	23p55		06 25			06 55		07 25		07 55				08 25		08 55				09 25		09 55
Gordon Hill	d	23p58		06 28			06 58		07 28		07 58				08 28		08 58				09 28		09 58
Enfield Chase	d	23p59		06 30			07 00		07 30		08 00				08 30		09 00				09 30		10 00
Grange Park	d	00 02		06 32			07 02		07 32		08 02				08 32		09 02				09 32		10 02
Winchmore Hill	d	00 04		06 34			07 04		07 34		08 04				08 34		09 04				09 34		10 04
Palmers Green	d	00 06		06 36			07 06		07 36		08 06				08 36		09 06				09 36		10 06
Bowes Park	d	00 09		06 39			07 09		07 39		08 09				08 39		09 09				09 39		10 09
Knebworth	d		23p59			06 43						07 43						08 43					
Welwyn North	d		00 02			06 47						07 47						08 47					
Welwyn Garden City 4	d		00 06		06 28	06 51		06 58		07 28		07 51		07 58		08 28		08 51		08 58		09 28	
Hatfield	d		00 10		06 32	06 54		07 02		07 32		07 54		08 02		08 32		08 54		09 02		09 32	
Welham Green	d				06 36			07 06		07 36				08 06		08 36				09 06		09 36	
Brookmans Park	d				06 38			07 08		07 38				08 08		08 38				09 08		09 38	
Potters Bar	d		00 15		06 41	07 00		07 11		07 41		08 00		08 11		08 41		09 00		09 11		09 41	
Hadley Wood	d				06 45			07 15		07 45				08 15		08 45				09 15		09 45	
New Barnet	d				06 47			07 17		07 47				08 17		08 47				09 17		09 47	
Oakleigh Park	d				06 49			07 19		07 49				08 19		08 49				09 19		09 49	
New Southgate	d				06 52			07 22		07 52				08 22		08 52				09 22		09 52	
Alexandra Palace	d	00 11		06 41	06 55		07 11	07 25	07 41	07 55	08 11			08 25	08 41	08 55	09 11			09 25	09 41	09 55	10 11
Hornsey	d	00 13		06 43	06 57		07 13	07 27	07 43	07 57	08 13			08 27	08 43	08 57	09 13			09 27	09 43	09 57	10 13
Harringay	d	00 15		06 45	06 59		07 15	07 29	07 45	07 59	08 15		←	08 29	08 45	08 59	09 15		←	09 29	09 45	09 59	10 15
Finsbury Park ⊖	d	00 18	00s32	06 48	07 02	07 10	07 18	07 32	07 48	08 02	08 18	08 10	08 18	08 32	08 48	09 02	09 18	09 10	09 18	09 32	09 48	10 02	10 18
Drayton Park	d										→						→						→
Highbury & Islington ⊖	d																						
Essex Road	d																						
Old Street ⊖	d																						
Moorgate ⊖	a																						
London Kings Cross 15 ⊖	a	00 26	00 40	06 56	07 13	07 20	07 27	07 45	07 56	08 15		08 20	08 26	08 40	08 55	09 10		09 19	09 25	09 40	09 55	10 10	

		FC	FC	FC	FC	FC	FC	FC	FC	FC	FC	FC	FC	FC	FC	FC	FC	FC	FC	FC	FC	FC	FC
		1			1				1						1						1		
Letchworth Garden City	d	09 29			09 59				10 29						11 29						12 29		
Hitchin 4	d	09 34			10 04				10 34						11 34						12 34		
Stevenage 4	d	09 39			10 09			10 30	10 39					11 30	11 39					12 30	12 39		
Watton-at-Stone	d							10 37						11 37						12 37			
Hertford North	d					10 13		10 43				11 13		11 43				12 13		12 43			
Bayford	d					10 17		10 47				11 17		11 47				12 17		12 47			
Cuffley	d					10 22		10 52				11 22		11 52				12 22		12 52			
Crews Hill	d					10 25		10 55				11 25		11 55				12 25		12 55			
Gordon Hill	d					10 28		10 58				11 28		11 58				12 28		12 58			
Enfield Chase	d					10 30		11 00				11 30		12 00				12 30		13 00			
Grange Park	d					10 32		11 02				11 32		12 02				12 32		13 02			
Winchmore Hill	d					10 34		11 04				11 34		12 04				12 34		13 04			
Palmers Green	d					10 36		11 06				11 36		12 06				12 36		13 06			
Bowes Park	d					10 39		11 09				11 39		12 09				12 39		13 09			
Knebworth	d	09 43			10 13				10 43						11 43						12 43		
Welwyn North	d	09 47			10 17				10 47						11 47						12 47		
Welwyn Garden City 4	d	09 51		09 58	10 21		10 28		10 51		10 58		11 28		11 51		11 58		12 28		12 51		12 58
Hatfield	d	09 54		10 02	10 24		10 32		10 54		11 02		11 32		11 54		12 02		12 32		12 54		13 02
Welham Green	d			10 06			10 36				11 06		11 36				12 06		12 36				13 06
Brookmans Park	d			10 08			10 38				11 08		11 38				12 08		12 38				13 08
Potters Bar	d	10 00		10 11	10 30		10 41		11 00		11 11		11 41		12 00		12 11		12 41		13 00		13 11
Hadley Wood	d			10 15			10 45				11 15		11 45				12 15		12 45				13 15
New Barnet	d			10 17			10 47				11 17		11 47				12 17		12 47				13 17
Oakleigh Park	d			10 19			10 49				11 19		11 49				12 19		12 49				13 19
New Southgate	d			10 22			10 52				11 22		11 52				12 22		12 52				13 22
Alexandra Palace	d			10 25		10 41	10 55	11 11			11 25	11 41	11 55	12 11			12 25	12 41	12 55	13 11			13 25
Hornsey	d			10 27		10 43	10 57	11 13			11 27	11 43	11 57	12 13			12 27	12 43	12 57	13 13			13 27
Harringay	d		←	10 29		10 45	10 59	11 15		←	11 29	11 45	11 59	12 15		←	12 29	12 45	12 59	13 15		←	13 29
Finsbury Park ⊖	d	10 10	10 18	10 32	10 40	10 48	11 02	11 18	11 10	11 18	11 32	11 48	12 02	12 18	12 10	12 18	12 32	12 48	13 02	13 18	13 10	13 18	13 32
Drayton Park	d							→						→						→			
Highbury & Islington ⊖	d																						
Essex Road	d																						
Old Street ⊖	d																						
Moorgate ⊖	a																						
London Kings Cross 15 ⊖	a	10 19	10 25	10 40	10 49	10 55	11 10		11 19	11 25	11 40	11 55	12 10		12 19	12 25	12 40	12 55	13 10		13 19	13 25	13 40

Sundays
from 28 October

Letchworth Garden City, Hertford North and Welwyn Garden City - London

Network Diagram - see first Page of Table 24

		FC		FC	FC	FC ■	FC	FC	FC	FC	FC	FC ■		FC	FC	FC	FC	FC	FC ■	FC	FC	FC		FC	FC
Letchworth Garden City	d					13 29						14 29							15 29						
Hitchin ■	d					13 34						14 34							15 34						
Stevenage ■	d				13 30	13 39					14 30	14 39						15 30	15 39						16 30
Watton at Stone	d				13 37						14 37							15 37							16 37
Hertford North	d	13 13			13 43				14 13		14 43					15 13		15 43				16 13			16 43
Bayford	d	13 17			13 47				14 17		14 47					15 17		15 47				16 17			16 47
Cuffley	d	13 22			13 52				14 22		14 52					15 22		15 52				16 22			16 52
Crews Hill	d	13 25			13 55				14 25		14 55					15 25		15 55				16 25			16 55
Gordon Hill	d	13 28			13 58				14 28		14 58					15 28		15 58				16 28			16 58
Enfield Chase	d	13 30			14 00				14 30		15 00					15 30		16 00				16 30			17 00
Grange Park	d	13 32			14 02				14 32		15 02					15 32		16 02				16 32			17 02
Winchmore Hill	d	13 34			14 04				14 34		15 04					15 34		16 04				16 34			17 04
Palmers Green	d	13 36			14 06				14 36		15 06					15 36		16 06				16 36			17 06
Bowes Park	d	13 39			14 09				14 39		15 09					15 39		16 09				16 39			17 09
Knebworth	d					13 43						14 43							15 43						
Welwyn North	d					13 47						14 47							15 47						
Welwyn Garden City ■	d			13 28		13 51		13 58		14 28		14 51			14 58		15 28		15 51		15 58			16 28	
Hatfield	d			13 32		13 54		14 02		14 32		14 54			15 02		15 32		15 54		16 02			16 32	
Welham Green	d			13 36				14 06		14 36					15 06		15 36				16 06			16 36	
Brookmans Park	d			13 38				14 08		14 38					15 08		15 38				16 08			16 38	
Potters Bar	d			13 41		14 00		14 11		14 41		15 00			15 11		15 41		16 00		16 11			16 41	
Hadley Wood	d			13 45				14 15		14 45					15 15		15 45				16 15			16 45	
New Barnet	d			13 47				14 17		14 47					15 17		15 47				16 17			16 47	
Oakleigh Park	d			13 49				14 19		14 49					15 19		15 49				16 19			16 49	
New Southgate	d			13 52				14 22		14 52					15 22		15 52				16 22			16 52	
Alexandra Palace	d	13 41		13 55	14 11			14 25	14 41	14 55	15 11				15 25	15 41	15 55	16 11			16 25	16 41		16 55	17 11
Hornsey	d	13 43		13 57	14 13			14 27	14 43	14 57	15 13				15 27	15 43	15 57	16 13			16 27	16 43		16 57	17 13
Harringay	d	13 45		13 59	14 15		←	14 29	14 45	14 59	15 15			←	15 29	15 45	15 59	16 15		←	16 29	16 45		16 59	17 15
Finsbury Park ⊖	d	13 48		14 02	14 18	14 10	14 18	14 32	14 48	15 02	15 18	15 10		15 18	15 32	15 48	16 02	16 18	16 10	16 18	16 32	16 48		17 02	17 18
Drayton Park	d				→						→							→							→
Highbury & Islington ⊖	d																								
Essex Road	d																								
Old Street ⊖	d																								
Moorgate ⊖	a																								
London Kings Cross ■ ⊖	a	13 55		14 10		14 19	14 25	14 40	14 55	15 10		15 19		15 25	15 40	15 55	16 10		16 19	16 25	16 40	16 55		17 10	

		FC ■	FC	FC	FC	FC	FC	FC ■		FC	FC	FC	FC	FC	FC ■	FC	FC	FC		FC	FC	FC ■	FC	FC	FC
Letchworth Garden City	d	16 29						17 29							18 29							19 29			
Hitchin ■	d	16 34						17 34							18 34							19 34			
Stevenage ■	d	16 39					17 30	17 39					18 30	18 39					19 30	19 39			
Watton at Stone	d						17 37							18 37							19 37				
Hertford North	d				17 13		17 43					18 13		18 43				19 13			19 43				20 13
Bayford	d				17 17		17 47					18 17		18 47				19 17			19 47				20 17
Cuffley	d				17 22		17 52					18 22		18 52				19 22			19 52				20 22
Crews Hill	d				17 25		17 55					18 25		18 55				19 25			19 55				20 25
Gordon Hill	d				17 28		17 58					18 28		18 58				19 28			19 58				20 28
Enfield Chase	d				17 30		18 00					18 30		19 00				19 30			20 00				20 30
Grange Park	d				17 32		18 02					18 32		19 02				19 32			20 02				20 32
Winchmore Hill	d				17 34		18 04					18 34		19 04				19 34			20 04				20 34
Palmers Green	d				17 36		18 06					18 36		19 06				19 36			20 06				20 36
Bowes Park	d				17 39		18 09					18 39		19 09				19 39			20 09				20 39
Knebworth	d	16 43						17 43							18 43							19 43			
Welwyn North	d	16 47						17 47							18 47							19 47			
Welwyn Garden City ■	d	16 51		16 58		17 28		17 51			17 58		18 28		18 51		18 58			19 28		19 51		19 58	
Hatfield	d	16 54		17 02		17 32		17 54			18 02		18 32		18 54		19 02			19 32		19 54		20 02	
Welham Green	d			17 06		17 36					18 06		18 36				19 06			19 36				20 06	
Brookmans Park	d			17 08		17 38					18 08		18 38				19 08			19 38				20 08	
Potters Bar	d	17 00		17 11		17 41		18 00			18 11		18 41		19 00		19 11			19 41		20 00		20 11	
Hadley Wood	d			17 15		17 45					18 15		18 45				19 15			19 45				20 15	
New Barnet	d			17 17		17 47					18 17		18 47				19 17			19 47				20 17	
Oakleigh Park	d			17 19		17 49					18 19		18 49				19 19			19 49				20 19	
New Southgate	d			17 22		17 52					18 22		18 52				19 22			19 52				20 22	
Alexandra Palace	d			17 25	17 41	17 55	18 11				18 25	18 41	18 55	19 11			19 25	19 41		19 55	20 11			20 25	20 41
Hornsey	d			17 27	17 43	17 57	18 13				18 27	18 43	18 57	19 13			19 27	19 43		19 57	20 13			20 27	20 43
Harringay	d		←	17 29	17 45	17 59	18 15			←	18 29	18 45	18 59	19 15		←	19 29	19 45		19 59	20 15		←	20 29	20 45
Finsbury Park ⊖	d	17 10	17 18	17 32	17 48	18 02	18 18	18 10		18 18	18 32	18 48	19 02	19 18	19 10	19 18	19 32	19 48		20 02	20 18	20 10	20 18	20 32	20 48
Drayton Park	d						→							→							→				
Highbury & Islington ⊖	d																								
Essex Road	d																								
Old Street ⊖	d																								
Moorgate ⊖	a																								
London Kings Cross ■ ⊖	a	17 19	17 25	17 40	17 55	18 10		18 19		18 25	18 40	18 55	19 10		19 19	19 25	19 40	19 55		20 10		20 19	20 25	20 40	20 55

Sundays
from 28 October

Letchworth Garden City, Hertford North and Welwyn Garden City - London

Network Diagram - see first Page of Table 24

		FC	FC	FC ■		FC	FC	FC	FC	FC	FC ■	FC	FC	FC		FC	FC	FC ■	FC	FC	FC	FC	FC ■
Letchworth Garden City	d			20 29							21 29							22 29					23 46
Hitchin ■	d			20 34							21 34							22 34					23 50
Stevenage ■	d		20 30	20 39						21 30	21 39						22 30	22 39				23 30	23 55
Watton at Stone	d		20 37							21 37							22 37					23 37	
Hertford North	d		20 43					21 13		21 43				22 13			22 43				23 13	23 43	
Bayford	d		20 47					21 17		21 47				22 17			22 47				23 17	23 47	
Cuffley	d		20 52					21 22		21 52				22 22			22 52				23 22	23 52	
Crews Hill	d		20 55					21 25		21 55				22 25			22 55				23 25	23 55	
Gordon Hill	d		20 58					21 28		21 58				22 28			22 58				23 28	23 58	
Enfield Chase	d		21 00					21 30		22 00				22 30			23 00				23 30	23 59	
Grange Park	d		21 02					21 32		22 02				22 32			23 02				23 32	00 02	
Winchmore Hill	d		21 04					21 34		22 04				22 34			23 04				23 34	00 04	
Palmers Green	d		21 06					21 36		22 06				22 36			23 06				23 36	00 06	
Bowes Park	d		21 09					21 39		22 09				22 39			23 09				23 39	00 09	
Knebworth	d			20 43							21 43							22 43					23 58
Welwyn North	d			20 47							21 47							22 47					00 02
Welwyn Garden City ■	d	20 28		20 51			20 58		21 28		21 51		21 58			22 28		22 51		22 58			00 05
Hatfield	d	20 32		20 54			21 02		21 32		21 54		22 02			22 32		22 54		23 02			00 08
Welham Green	d	20 36					21 06		21 36				22 06			22 36				23 06			
Brookmans Park	d	20 38					21 08		21 38				22 08			22 38				23 08			
Potters Bar	d	20 41		21 00			21 11		21 41		22 00		22 11			22 41		23 00		23 11			00 14
Hadley Wood	d	20 45					21 15		21 45				22 15			22 45				23 15			
New Barnet	d	20 47					21 17		21 47				22 17			22 47				23 17			
Oakleigh Park	d	20 49					21 19		21 49				22 19			22 49				23 19			
New Southgate	d	20 52					21 22		21 52				22 22			22 52				23 22			
Alexandra Palace	d	20 55	21 11				21 25	21 41	21 55	22 11			22 25	22 41		22 55	23 11			23 25	23 41	00 11	
Hornsey	d	20 57	21 13				21 27	21 43	21 57	22 13			22 27	22 43		22 57	23 13			23 27	23 43	00 13	
Harringay	d	20 59	21 15			←	21 29	21 45	21 59	22 15		←	22 29	22 45		22 59	23 15		←	23 29	23 45	00 15	
Finsbury Park ⊖	d	21 02	21 18	21 10		21 18	21 32	21 48	22 02	22 18	22 10	22 18	22 32	22 48		23 02	23 18	23 10	23 18	23 32	23 48	00 18	00 27
Drayton Park	d		→							→							→						
Highbury & Islington ⊖	d																						
Essex Road	d																						
Old Street ⊖	d																						
Moorgate ⊖	a																						
London Kings Cross ■ ⊖	a	21 10		21 19		21 25	21 40	21 55	22 10		22 19	22 25	22 40	22 55		23 12		23 19	23 26	23 44	23 56	00 27	00 39

London - Stevenage, Cambridge and Peterborough

Network Diagram - see first Page of Table 24

Miles	Miles			FC	FC	FC	FC	FC	FC	FC	FC	FC	FC	FC	FC	FC	FC	FC	FC	FC	FC	FC	FC
				MX ■	MO ■ A	MX ■	■ B	MO ■ A	MX ■	MO ■ A	MX ■	MO C	MX	MX ■	MX	MO A	MX ■	MX	MO ■ D	MO ■ E	■ F	MO A	MX ■
0	0	London Kings Cross ⊖	d	23p01	23p06	23p06	23p15			23p23	23p23	23p26	23p26	23p36		23p41	00 04	00 06	00 07	00 07	00 10		
2½	2½	Finsbury Park ⊖	d		23p11	23p11				23p28	23p28	23p32	23p32	23p41		23p47	00 09	00 12	00 12	00 12			
12¾	12¾	Potters Bar	d		23p21	23p21								23p51		00 08			00s25				
17¾	17¾	Hatfield	d		23p27	23p27								23p57		00 16							
20¼	20¼	Welwyn Garden City ■	d		23p31	23p31								00 01		00 20			00s34				
22	22	Welwyn North	d		23p34	23p34								00 04		00 23							
25	25	Knebworth	d		23p38	23p38								00 08		00 28							
—	—	Hertford North	d									00 07	00 07		←			00 47		00 39		←	
27½	27½	Stevenage ■	d		23p42	23p42				23p47	23p47	00a20	00 20	00 12	00 20	00 31	00 31	01 00	00 48	00 48	00 30	00 31	←
31¾	31¾	Hitchin ■	d		23p47	23p50		←	←	23p52	23p53		→	00 20	00 26	→	00 39	→	→	→	00 35	00 37	00 39
34¾	—	Letchworth Garden City	d		23p51	23p54	23p44	23p51	23p54					00a29	00a36		→				00 39	00a52	00 43
36¾	—	Baldock	d		→	→		23p54	23p58												00 42		00 46
41	—	Ashwell & Morden	d					23p59	00 03														00 51
45	—	Royston	d				23p54	00 04	00 07												00 50		00 56
48	—	Meldreth	d					00 08	00 11														00 59
50	—	Shepreth	d					00 11	00 14														01 02
51	—	Foxton	d					00 14	00 17														01 05
58	—	Cambridge	a				00 10	00 29	00 29												01 09		01 22
—	37	Arlesey	d							23p57	23p59												
—	41	Biggleswade	d	23p29						00 02	00 04												
—	44	Sandy	d							00 06	00 08												
—	51½	St Neots	d	23p38						00 13	00 15												
—	58¾	Huntingdon	d	23p45						00 21	00 23												
—	76¼	Peterborough ■	a	00 12						00 43	00 42												

		FC	FC	FC	FC	FC	FC	FC	FC	FC	FC	FC	FC	FC	FC	FC	FC	FC	FC	FC	GR	FC	FC
		■ G	MO ■ D	MO ■ E	MX ■ H	■ F	MX	MO ■	MX ■	MO D	■ G	■ G	■ I	MO ■ D	MO D	■	MO D	■		■	■ ■		■
London Kings Cross ⊖	d	00 23			00 31	00 31		00 36	00 36		01 01	01 06	01 06	01 06		01 36		05 23		05 45	05 50	05 56	06 06
Finsbury Park ⊖	d	00 28						00 41	00 41			01 11	01 11	01 11		01 41		05 28		05 50		06 02	06 11
Potters Bar	d							00 51	00 51					01s27		01 59		05 38					06 21
Hatfield	d							00 57	00 57							02 05		05 44					06 27
Welwyn Garden City ■	d							01 01	01 01					01s35		02 09		05 48					06 31
Welwyn North	d							01s04	01s04							02s12		05 51					06 34
Knebworth	d							01s08	01s08							02s16		05 55					06 38
Hertford North	d		←	←			←			00 50		01 38	01 38		01 40		02 40		05 50			06 40	
Stevenage ■	d	00 46	00 48	00 48	00s55	00s55	01 00	01 12	01 12	01a21	01 21	01 47	01 47	01 47	02a02	02 20	03s02	05 59	06a04	06 08	06 11	06a55	06 42
Hitchin ■	d	00 54	00 56	00 56	01s02	01s02	01 06	01 17	01 17		01 29	01 52	01 52	01 52		02 25	03s22	06 07		06 12			→
Letchworth Garden City	d		01 00	01 00	01s06	01s06	01a15					01 56	02a01	02a06			03a37			06 16			
Baldock	d		01 04	01 04	01s09	01s09						02 00								06 19			
Ashwell & Morden	d		01 09	01 09								02 05								06 24			
Royston	d		01 13	01 13	01s17	01s17						02 09								06 29			
Meldreth	d		01 17	01 17								02 13								06 33			
Shepreth	d		01 20	01 20								02 16								06 36			
Foxton	d		01 23	01 23								02 19								06 38			
Cambridge	a		01 39	01 39	01 32	01 38						02 34								06 50			
Arlesey	d	00 59						01s25	01s25									06 13					
Biggleswade	d	01 04						01s30	01s30		01 38					02s37		06 18					
Sandy	d	01 08						01s34	01s34									06 22					
St Neots	d	01 15						01s42	01s42		01 47					02s47		06 29					
Huntingdon	d	01 23						01s52	01s52		01 55					02s57		06 37					
Peterborough ■	a	01 42						02 11	02 13		02 17					03 16		06 54			06 41		

A from 21 May
B not 14 May
C from 21 May until 10 Septemberfrom 29 October
D from 17 September until 22 October
E until 10 September, MO from 29 October
F 30 July, 6 August, 13 August, 3 September, 10 September
G from 30 July until 10 September, not from 14 August until 29 August
H from 31 July until 7 September, not from 14 August until 29 August
I until 29 August, not from 30 July until 13 August, also MXfrom 11 September until 19 October, from 23 October

Table 25 Mondays to Fridays

London - Stevenage, Cambridge and Peterborough

Network Diagram - see first Page of Table 24

		GR	FC	FC	FC	GR	FC	FC	FC	FC	GR	FC	FC	FC	GR	FC	FC	FC	FC	FC	FC	GR
		■ ■	■	■		■ ■	■	■	■	■	■ ■	■	■	■	■ ■	■	■	■	■	■	■	■ ■
London Kings Cross ⊖	d	06 15		06 23	06 26	06 30	06 36	06 45	06 53	07 06	07 08	07 15		07 23	07 35	07 36	07 45	07 53	08 03	08 15	08 23	08 35
Finsbury Park ⊖	d			06 28	06 32		06 41		06 58	07 11				07 28		07 41		07 58	08 08		08 28	
Potters Bar	d						06 51			07 21						07 51			08 18			
Hatfield	d						06 57			07 27						07 57			08 25			
Welwyn Garden City ■	d						07 01			07 31						08 01			08 30			
Welwyn North	d						07 04			07 34						08 04			08 33			
Knebworth	d						07 08			07 38						08 08			08 37			
Hertford North	d		←		07 10								←									
Stevenage ■	d	06 34	06 42	06 47	07a25	06 49	07 12		07 17	07 42	07 27		07 42	07 47	07a54	08 12		08 17	08 41		08 47	08a54
Hitchin ■	d		06 47	06 52			07 17		07 22	→			07 47	07 52		08 17		08 22	08 46		08 52	
Letchworth Garden City	d		06 51						07 26				07 51					08 26	08 54			
Baldock	d		06 55						07 29				07 55					08 29	08 58			
Ashwell & Morden	d		07 00						07 35				08 00					08 35	09 03			
Royston	d		07 06						07 39				08 06					08 39	09 07			
Meldreth	d		07 10						07 43				08 10					08 43	09 11			
Shepreth	d		07 13						07 46				08 13					08 46	09 14			
Foxton	d		07 16						07 49				08 16					08 49	09 17			
Cambridge	a		07 29					07 31	08 02			08 02	08 29				08 32	09 02	09 29	09 03		
Arlesey	d			06 57			07 23							07 57		08 23					08 57	
Biggleswade	d			07 02			07 28							08 02		08 28					09 02	
Sandy	d			07 06			07 32							08 06		08 32					09 06	
St Neots	d			07 13			07 39							08 13		08 39					09 13	
Huntingdon	d			07 21			07 47							08 21		08 47					09 21	
Peterborough ■	a	07 04		07 38		07 19	08 06				07 57			08 38		09 06					09 38	

		FC	FC	FC	FC	GR	FC	FC	FC	GR	FC	FC	FC	FC	GR	FC	FC	FC	GR	FC	FC	FC	FC
		■	■	■	■	■ ■	■	■	■	■ ■	■	■	■	■	■ ■	■	■	■	■ ■	■	■	■	■
London Kings Cross ⊖	d	08 36	08 45	08 53	09 06	09 08	09 15		09 23	09 35	09 36	09 45	09 53	10 06	10 08	10 15		10 23	10 35	10 36	10 45	10 53	11 06
Finsbury Park ⊖	d	08 41		08 58	09 11				09 28		09 41		09 58	10 11				10 28		10 41		10 58	11 11
Potters Bar	d	08 51			09 21						09 51			10 21						10 51			11 21
Hatfield	d	08 57			09 27						09 57			10 27						10 57			11 27
Welwyn Garden City ■	d	09 01			09 31						10 01			10 31						11 01			11 31
Welwyn North	d	09 04			09 34						10 04			10 34						11 04			11 34
Knebworth	d	09 08			09 38						10 08			10 38						11 08			11 38
Hertford North	d							←									←						
Stevenage ■	d	09 12		09 17	09 42	09 28		09 42	09 47	09a54	10 12		10 17	10 42	10 28		10 42	10 47	10a54	11 12		11 17	11 42
Hitchin ■	d	09 17		09 22	→			09 47	09 52		10 17		10 22	→			10 47	10 52		11 17		11 22	→
Letchworth Garden City	d			09 26				09 51					10 26				10 51					11 26	
Baldock	d			09 29				09 55					10 29				10 55					11 29	
Ashwell & Morden	d			09 35				10 00									11 00						
Royston	d			09 39				10 04					10 37				11 04					11 37	
Meldreth	d			09 43				10 08									11 08						
Shepreth	d			09 46				10 11									11 11						
Foxton	d			09 49				10 14									11 14						
Cambridge	a		09 31	10 02			10 03	10 27				10 31	10 54			11 01	11 27				11 30	11 54	
Arlesey	d	09 23							09 57		10 23							10 57		11 23			
Biggleswade	d	09 28							10 02		10 28							11 02		11 28			
Sandy	d	09 32							10 06		10 32							11 06		11 32			
St Neots	d	09 39							10 13		10 39							11 13		11 39			
Huntingdon	d	09 47							10 21		10 47							11 21		11 47			
Peterborough ■	a	10 06				10 00			10 38		11 06				10 59			11 38		12 06			

		GR	FC	FC	FC	GR	FC	FC	FC	FC	GR	FC	FC	FC	GR	FC	FC	FC	FC	GR	FC	FC	FC
		■ ■	■	■	■	■ ■	■	■	■	■	■ ■	■	■	■	■ ■	■	■	■	■	■ ■	■	■	■
London Kings Cross ⊖	d	11 08	11 15		11 23	11 35	11 36	11 45	11 53	12 06	12 08	12 15		12 23	12 35	12 36	12 45	12 53	13 06	13 08	13 15		13 23
Finsbury Park ⊖	d				11 28		11 41		11 58	12 11				12 28		12 41		12 58	13 11				13 28
Potters Bar	d						11 51			12 21						12 51			13 21				
Hatfield	d						11 57			12 27						12 57			13 27				
Welwyn Garden City ■	d						12 01			12 31						13 01			13 31				
Welwyn North	d						12 04			12 34						13 04			13 34				
Knebworth	d						12 08			12 38						13 08			13 38				
Hertford North	d			←									←									←	
Stevenage ■	d	11 27		11 42	11 47	11a54	12 12		12 17	12 42	12 28		12 42	12 47	12a54	13 12		13 17	13 42	13 28		13 42	13 47
Hitchin ■	d			11 47	11 52		12 17		12 22	→			12 47	12 52		13 17		13 22	→			13 47	13 52
Letchworth Garden City	d			11 51					12 26				12 51					13 26				13 51	
Baldock	d			11 55					12 29				12 55					13 29				13 55	
Ashwell & Morden	d			12 00									13 00									14 00	
Royston	d			12 04					12 37				13 04					13 37				14 04	
Meldreth	d			12 08									13 08									14 08	
Shepreth	d			12 11									13 11									14 11	
Foxton	d			12 14									13 14									14 14	
Cambridge	a		12 01	12 27				12 31	12 54			13 01	13 27				13 30	13 54			14 01	14 27	
Arlesey	d				11 57		12 23							12 57		13 23							13 57
Biggleswade	d				12 02		12 28							13 02		13 28							14 02
Sandy	d				12 06		12 32							13 06		13 32							14 06
St Neots	d				12 13		12 39							13 13		13 39							14 13
Huntingdon	d				12 21		12 47							13 21		13 47							14 21
Peterborough ■	a	11 57			12 38		13 06				12 59			13 38		14 06				13 59			14 38

London - Stevenage, Cambridge and Peterborough

Network Diagram - see first Page of Table 24

		GR	FC	FC	FC	FC	GR	FC	FC	FC	GR	FC	FC	FC	FC	GR	FC	FC	FC	GR	FC	FC
London Kings Cross ⊖	d	13 35	13 36	13 45	13 53	14 06	14 08	14 15		14 23	14 35	14 36	14 45	14 53	15 06	15 08	15 15		15 23	15 35	15 36	15 44
Finsbury Park ⊖	d		13 41		13 58	14 11				14 28		14 41		14 58	15 11				15 28		15 41	
Potters Bar	d		13 51			14 21						14 51			15 21						15 51	
Hatfield	d		13 57			14 27						14 57			15 27						15 58	
Welwyn Garden City	d		14 01			14 31						15 01			15 31						16 02	
Welwyn North	d		14 04			14 34						15 04			15 34						16 05	
Knebworth	d		14 08			14 38						15 08			15 38						16 09	
Hertford North	d								←									←				
Stevenage	d	13a54	14 12		14 17	14 42	14 27		14 42	14 47	14a54	15 12		15 17	15 42	15 28		15 42	15 47	15a54	16 12	
Hitchin	d		14 17		14 22	→			14 47	14 52		15 17		15 22	→			15 47	15 52		16 17	
Letchworth Garden City	d				14 26				14 51					15 26				15 51				16 09
Baldock	d				14 29				14 55					15 29				15 55				
Ashwell & Morden	d								15 00									16 00				
Royston	d				14 37				15 04					15 37				16 04				16 19
Meldreth	d								15 08									16 08				
Shepreth	d								15 11									16 11				
Foxton	d								15 14									16 14				
Cambridge	a			14 30	14 54			15 01	15 27				15 30	15 54			16 03	16 28				16 34
Arlesey	d		14 23							14 57		15 23							15 57		16 23	
Biggleswade	d		14 28							15 02		15 28							16 02		16 28	
Sandy	d		14 32							15 06		15 32							16 06		16 32	
St Neots	d		14 39							15 13		15 39							16 13		16 39	
Huntingdon	d		14 47							15 21		15 47							16 21		16 47	
Peterborough	a		15 06				14 58			15 38		16 06				15 59			16 38		17 06	

		FC	FC	GR	FC	FC	FC	FC	FC	GR	FC	FC	FC	FC	FC	FC	FC	FC	FC	FC	FC	GR	FC
London Kings Cross ⊖	d	15 53	16 06	16 08	16 14	16 17		16 22	16 32	16 33	16 40	16 44		16 50	16 54	17 10	17 14		17 14	17 22	17 23	17 33	17 40
Finsbury Park ⊖	d	15 58	16 11					16 27	16 37					16 55	16 59				17 19	17 28			
Potters Bar	d		16 21						16 47														
Hatfield	d		16 28						16 54						17 15					17 44			
Welwyn Garden City	d		16 32						16 58						17 19					17 48			
Welwyn North	d		16 35						17 01						17 22					17 52			
Knebworth	d		16 39					16 45	17 06					17 11	17 26				17 35	17 56			
Hertford North	d						←																
Stevenage	d	16 17	16 45	16 29		16 40	16 45	16 49	17 10	16a52				17 18	17 36			←	17 40	18 04	17 43	17a53	
Hitchin	d	16 22	→				16 50	16 54	17 17				←	17 23	17 42	17 34		17 42	17 46	→			18 04
Letchworth Garden City	d	16 26				16 48	16 55		17 26			17 09	17 26		→			17 47			17 52		
Baldock	d	16 29				16 52	16 59		→				17 30					17 51			17 55		
Ashwell & Morden	d	16 34				16 57	17 04						17 35					17 56			18 00		
Royston	d	16 38				17a03	17 08					17 19	17 39				17 48	18 01			18a07		
Meldreth	d						17 12						17 43					18 05					
Shepreth	d						17 15						17 46					18 08					
Foxton	d						17 18						17 49					18 10					
Cambridge	a	16 54			17 01		17 30					17 34	18 02				18 03	18 24					
Arlesey	d							17 00						17 29					17 51				
Biggleswade	d							17 05			17 07			17 34					17 56				
Sandy	d							17 09						17 38					18 00				
St Neots	d							17 22			17 17			17 45		17 51			18 08				18 21
Huntingdon	d							17a30			17 26			17 53		17 59			18 16				18 29
Peterborough	a			16 59							17 42			18 12		18 22			18 32				18 50

		FC	FC	FC	FC	FC	FC	FC	FC	FC	FC	FC	FC	GR	FC	FC	FC	FC	FC	FC	GR A	GR B
London Kings Cross ⊖	d	17 44		17 44	17 52	17 53	18 10	18 14			18 14	18 22	18 23	18 33	18 40	18 44		18 44	18 52	18 53	19 06	19 06
Finsbury Park ⊖	d			17 49	17 58						18 19	18 28						18 49	18 58			
Potters Bar	d																					
Hatfield	d				18 14							18 44							19 14			
Welwyn Garden City	d				18 18							18 49							19 19			
Welwyn North	d				18 22							18 51	18 41						19 24			
Knebworth	d				18 26							18 55						19 05	19 28			
Hertford North	d		←							←												
Stevenage	d		18 04	18 09	18 34	18 13				18 34	18 39	19 04		18a52			←	19 10	19 35	19 13	19 26	19 27
Hitchin	d		18 10	18 16	→		18 34			18 40	18 46	19 10	18 53				19 10	19 16	→			
Letchworth Garden City	d		18 16			18 22				18 48		→	18 57				19 16			19 22		
Baldock	d					18 26				18 52			19 01							19 26		
Ashwell & Morden	d					18 31				18 57			19 06							19 31		
Royston	d	18 18	18 30			18a37		18 52	18 56	19 02			19a13			19 18	19 31			19a38		
Meldreth	d		18 34						18 59								19 35					
Shepreth	d		18 37						19 02								19 38					
Foxton	d		18 39						19 05								19 41					
Cambridge	a	18 34	18 54					19 08	19 20	19 24						19 34	19 56					
Arlesey	d			18 21							18 51							19 21				
Biggleswade	d			18 26							18 56				19 07			19 26				
Sandy	d			18 30							19 00							19 30				
St Neots	d			18 38			18 51				19 08				19 17			19 38				
Huntingdon	d			18 46			18 59				19 16				19 26			19 46				
Peterborough	a			19 04			19 21				19 40				19 44			20 03			19 57	19 57

A until 22 June B from 25 June

London - Stevenage, Cambridge and Peterborough

Network Diagram - see first Page of Table 24

		FC	FC	FC	FC	FC	GR	FC	FC	FC	FC	FC	FC	FC	FC	FC	FC	GR	FC	FC	FC	GR	FC
London Kings Cross ⊖	d	19 10	19 15		19 18	19 23	19 33		19 34	19 45		19 53	20 06	20 10	20 15		20 23	20 35	20 36	20 45	20 53	21 00	21 06
Finsbury Park ⊖	d				19 23	19 28			19 39			19 58	20 11				20 28		20 41		20 58		21 11
Potters Bar	d				19 37								20 21						20 51				21 21
Hatfield	d				19 44				19 53				20 27						20 57				21 27
Welwyn Garden City	d				19 49				20 00				20 31						21 01				21 31
Welwyn North	d				19 53				20 03				20 34						21 04				21 34
Knebworth	d				19 57				20 07				20 38						21 08				21 38
Hertford North	d			←				←															
Stevenage	d			19 35	20 04	19 47	19a52	20 04	20 12			20 17	20 42				20 47	20 54	21 12		21 17	21 20	21 42
Hitchin	d	19 36		19 42	→	19 53		20 13	20 17		←	20 23	20 47			←	20 53		21 17		21 22		21 47
Letchworth Garden City	d		19 40	19 52				20 17	20a23	20 10	20 17		20 51		20 40	20 51			21a23		21 29		21 51
Baldock	d			19 55				→			20 21		→			20 55					21 32		→
Ashwell & Morden	d			20 00							20 26					21 00					21 37		
Royston	d		19 50	20 05						20 20	20 31				20 50	21 04				21 19	21 42		
Meldreth	d			20 09							20 35					21 08					21 45		
Shepreth	d			20 12							20 38					21 11					21 48		
Foxton	d			20 15							20 40					21 14					21 51		
Cambridge	a		20 07	20 27						20 35	20 54				21 05	21 27				21 34	22 03		
Arlesey	d					19 59						20 29					20 59						
Biggleswade	d					20 04						20 34					21 04						
Sandy	d					20 08						20 38					21 08						
St Neots	d	19 54				20 15						20 45		20 45			21 15						
Huntingdon	d	20 02				20 23						20 58		20 53			21 23						
Peterborough	a	20 22				20 41						21 21		21 12			21 41	21 24				21 50	

		FC	FC	FC	FC	GR	FC	FC	FC	FC	FC	FC	FC	FC	FC	FC	FC	FC	FC	FC	FC	FC	FC
London Kings Cross ⊖	d	21 07	21 15		21 23	21 35	21 36	21 45	21 53	22 06	22 07	22 15		22 23	22 26	22 36	22 53		23 01	23 06	23 15		23 23
Finsbury Park ⊖	d				21 28		21 41		21 58	22 11				22 28	22 32	22 41	22 58			23 11			23 28
Potters Bar	d						21 51			22 21						22 51				23 21			
Hatfield	d						21 57			22 27						22 57				23 27			
Welwyn Garden City	d						22 01			22 31						23 01				23 31			
Welwyn North	d						22 04			22 34						23 04				23 34			
Knebworth	d						22 08			22 38						23 08				23 38			
Hertford North	d														23 07			←					
Stevenage	d				21 47	21 55	22 12		22 17	22 42				22 47	23 21	23 12	23 17	23 21		23 42			23 47
Hitchin	d			←	21 53		22 17		22 22	22 47			←	22 53	→	23 17	23 25	23 30		23 50		←	23 53
Letchworth Garden City	d		21 40	21 51			22a23	22 10	22 29	22 51		22 40	22 51			23a26	23 31	23a36		23 54	23 44	23 54	
Baldock	d			21 55					22 32	→			22 55				23 34			→		23 58	
Ashwell & Morden	d			22 00					22 37				23 00				23 39					00 03	
Royston	d		21 50	22 04				22 20	22 42			22 50	23 04				23 44				23 54	00 07	
Meldreth	d			22 08					22 45				23 08									00 11	
Shepreth	d			22 11					22 48				23 11									00 14	
Foxton	d			22 14					22 51				23 14									00 17	
Cambridge	a		22 05	22 27				22 35	23 03			23 05	23 27				23 59				00 10	00 29	
Arlesey	d				21 59									22 59									23 59
Biggleswade	d	21 35			22 04						22 35			23 04					23 29				00 04
Sandy	d				22 08									23 08									00 08
St Neots	d	21 44			22 15						22 44			23 15					23 38				00 15
Huntingdon	d	21 51			22 23						22 51			23 23					23 45				00 23
Peterborough	a	22 07			22 41	22 26					23 07			23 43					00 12				00 42

		FC	FC	FC
London Kings Cross ⊖	d	23 26	23 36	
Finsbury Park ⊖	d	23 32	23 41	
Potters Bar	d		23 51	
Hatfield	d		23 57	
Welwyn Garden City	d		00 01	
Welwyn North	d		00 04	
Knebworth	d		00 08	
Hertford North	d	00 07		←
Stevenage	d	00 20	00 12	00 20
Hitchin	d	→	00 20	00 26
Letchworth Garden City	d		00a29	00a36
Baldock	d			
Ashwell & Morden	d			
Royston	d			
Meldreth	d			
Shepreth	d			
Foxton	d			
Cambridge	a			
Arlesey	d			
Biggleswade	d			
Sandy	d			
St Neots	d			
Huntingdon	d			
Peterborough	a			

Table 25

Saturdays

London - Stevenage, Cambridge and Peterborough

Network Diagram - see first Page of Table 24

		FC	FC	FC	FC	FC	FC	FC	FC	FC	FC	FC	FC	FC	FC	FC	FC	FC	FC	FC	FC	FC	FC
													A				A	B	C				
London Kings Cross ⊖	d	23p01	23p06	23p15		23p23	23p26	23p36		00 01	00 04	00 06	00 23	00 31		00 36	01 01	01 06	01 06	01 36	05 23	05 45	06 06
Finsbury Park ⊖	d		23p11			23p28	23p32	23p41			00 09	00 12	00 28			00 41		01 11	01 11	01 41	05 28	05 50	06 11
Potters Bar	d		23p21					23p51								00 51				01 59	05 38		06 21
Hatfield	d		23p27					23p57								00 57				02 05	05 44		06 27
Welwyn Garden City	d		23p31					00 01								01 01				02 09	05 48		06 31
Welwyn North	d		23p34					00 04								01s04				02s12	05 51		06 34
Knebworth	d		23p38					00 08								01s08				02s16	05 55		06 38
Hertford North	d						00 07		←			00 47			←			01 38	01 38				
Stevenage	d		23p42			23p47	00 20	00 12	00 20	00s20	00 31	01 00	00 46	00s50	01 00	01 12	01 21	01 47	01 47	02 20	05 59	06 08	06 41
Hitchin	d		23p50		←	23p53	→	00 20	00 26	00s35	00 39	→	00 54	01s05	01 06	01 17	01 29	01 52	01 52	02 25	06 07	06 13	→
Letchworth Garden City	d		23p54	23p44	23p54			00a29	00a36		00 43			01s09	01a15			01 56	02a01			06 17	
Baldock	d		→		23p58						00 46			01s12				02 00				06 20	
Ashwell & Morden	d				00 03						00 51							02 05				06 25	
Royston	d			23p54	00 07						00 56			01s20				02 09				06 29	
Meldreth	d				00 11						00 59							02 13				06 33	
Shepreth	d				00 14						01 02							02 16				06 36	
Foxton	d				00 17						01 05							02 19				06 38	
Cambridge	a			00 10	00 29						01 22			01 35				02 34				06 53	
Arlesey	d					23p59							00 59			01s25					06 13		
Biggleswade	d	23p29				00 04				00 43			01 04			01s30	01 38			02s37	06 18		
Sandy	d					00 08							01 08			01s34					06 22		
St Neots	d	23p38				00 15				00s53			01 15			01s42	01 47			02s47	06 29		
Huntingdon	d	23p45				00 23				01s03			01 23			01s52	01 55			02s57	06 37		
Peterborough	a	00 12				00 42				01 19			01 42			02 13	02 17			03 16	06 54		

		GR	FC	FC	FC	FC	FC	FC	GR	FC	FC	FC	FC	FC	FC	FC	FC	FC	FC	FC	FC	FC	GR
London Kings Cross ⊖	d	06 15		06 23	06 26	06 36	06 45	06 53	07 03	07 06	07 23	07 26	07 36	07 45	07 53	08 06	08 15	08 23	08 26	08 36	08 45	08 53	09 03
Finsbury Park ⊖	d			06 28	06 32	06 41		06 58		07 11	07 28	07 32	07 41		07 58	08 11		08 28	08 32	08 41		08 58	
Potters Bar	d					06 51				07 21			07 51			08 21				08 51			
Hatfield	d					06 57				07 27			07 57			08 27				08 57			
Welwyn Garden City	d					07 01				07 31			08 01			08 31				09 01			
Welwyn North	d					07 04				07 34			08 04			08 34				09 04			
Knebworth	d					07 08				07 38			08 08			08 38				09 08			
Hertford North	d		←		07 07							08 07							09 07				
Stevenage	d	06 34	06 41	06 47	07a20	07 12		07 17	07 22	07 42	07 47	08a20	08 12		08 17	08 42		08 47	09a20	09 12		09 17	09 22
Hitchin	d		06 47	06 52		07 17		07 22		07 47	07 52		08 17		08 22	08 47		08 52		09 17		09 22	
Letchworth Garden City	d		06 51					07 26		07 51					08 26	08 51						09 26	
Baldock	d		06 54					07 29		07 55					08 29	08 55						09 29	
Ashwell & Morden	d		06 59					07 34		08 00						09 00							
Royston	d		07 04					07 39		08 04					08 37	09 04						09 37	
Meldreth	d		07 08					07 42		08 08						09 08							
Shepreth	d		07 11					07 45		08 11						09 11							
Foxton	d		07 14					07 48		08 14						09 14							
Cambridge	a		07 27				07 30	08 00		08 27				08 30	08 54	09 27	09 01				09 30	09 54	
Arlesey	d			06 57		07 23					07 57		08 23					08 57		09 23			
Biggleswade	d			07 02		07 28					08 02		08 28					09 02		09 28			
Sandy	d			07 06		07 32					08 06		08 32					09 06		09 32			
St Neots	d			07 13		07 39					08 13		08 39					09 13		09 39			
Huntingdon	d			07 21		07 47					08 21		08 47					09 21		09 47			
Peterborough	a	07 04		07 38		08 06			07 52		08 38		09 08					09 37		10 06			09 52

		FC	FC	FC	FC	FC	FC	FC	FC	FC	FC	FC	FC	FC	FC	GR	FC	FC	FC	FC	FC	FC
London Kings Cross ⊖	d	09 06	09 15	09 23	09 26	09 36	09 45	09 53	10 06	10 15	10 23	10 26	10 36	10 45	10 53	11 03	11 06	11 15	11 23	11 26	11 36	11 45
Finsbury Park ⊖	d	09 11		09 28	09 32	09 41		09 58	10 11		10 28	10 32	10 41		10 58		11 11		11 28	11 32	11 41	
Potters Bar	d	09 21				09 51			10 21				10 51				11 21				11 51	
Hatfield	d	09 27				09 57			10 27				10 57				11 27				11 57	
Welwyn Garden City	d	09 31				10 01			10 31				11 01				11 31				12 01	
Welwyn North	d	09 34				10 04			10 34				11 04				11 34				12 04	
Knebworth	d	09 38				10 08			10 38				11 08				11 38				12 08	
Hertford North	d				10 07							11 07								12 07		
Stevenage	d	09 42		09 47	10a20	10 12		10 17	10 42		10 47	11a20	11 12		11 17	11 22	11 42		11 47	12a20	12 12	
Hitchin	d	09 47		09 52		10 17		10 22	10 47		10 52		11 17		11 22		11 47		11 52		12 17	
Letchworth Garden City	d	09 51						10 26	10 51						11 26		11 51					
Baldock	d	09 55						10 29	10 55						11 29		11 55					
Ashwell & Morden	d	10 00							11 00								12 00					
Royston	d	10 04						10 37	11 04						11 37		12 04					
Meldreth	d	10 08							11 08								12 08					
Shepreth	d	10 11							11 11								12 11					
Foxton	d	10 14							11 14								12 14					
Cambridge	a	10 27	10 01				10 30	10 54	11 27	11 01				11 30	11 54		12 27	12 01				12 30
Arlesey	d			09 57		10 23					10 57		11 23						11 57		12 23	
Biggleswade	d			10 02		10 28					11 02		11 28						12 02		12 28	
Sandy	d			10 06		10 32					11 06		11 32						12 06		12 32	
St Neots	d			10 13		10 39					11 13		11 39						12 13		12 39	
Huntingdon	d			10 21		10 47					11 21		11 47						12 21		12 47	
Peterborough	a			10 38		11 06					11 38		12 06			11 52			12 39		13 05	

A 4 August, 11 August, 1 September, 8 September

B 28 July, 4 August, 11 August, 1 September, 8 September

C until 21 July, from 18 August, not 1 September, 8 September

Table 25

Saturdays

London - Stevenage, Cambridge and Peterborough

Network Diagram - see first Page of Table 24

		FC	FC	FC	FC	FC	FC	FC	FC	GR	FC	FC	FC	FC	FC	FC	FC	FC	FC	FC	FC	FC	FC
London Kings Cross ⊖	d	11 53	12 06	12 15	12 23	12 26	12 36	12 45	12 53	13 03	13 06	13 15	13 23	13 26	13 36	13 45	13 53	14 06	14 15	14 23	14 26	14 36	14 45
Finsbury Park ⊖	d	11 58	12 11		12 28	12 32	12 41		12 58		13 11		13 28	13 32	13 41		13 58	14 11		14 28	14 32	14 41	
Potters Bar	d		12 21				12 51				13 21				13 51			14 21				14 51	
Hatfield	d		12 27				12 57				13 27				13 57			14 27				14 57	
Welwyn Garden City	d		12 31				13 01				13 31				14 01			14 31				15 01	
Welwyn North	d		12 34				13 04				13 34				14 04			14 34				15 04	
Knebworth	d		12 38				13 08				13 38				14 08			14 38				15 08	
Hertford North	d					13 07								14 07							15 07		
Stevenage	d	12 17	12 42		12 47	13a20	13 12		13 17	13 22	13 42		13 47	14a20	14 12		14 17	14 42		14 47	15a20	15 12	
Hitchin	d	12 22	12 47		12 52		13 17		13 22		13 47		13 52		14 17		14 22	14 47		14 52		15 17	
Letchworth Garden City	d	12 26	12 51						13 26		13 51						14 26	14 51					
Baldock	d	12 29	12 55						13 29		13 55						14 29	14 55					
Ashwell & Morden	d		13 00								14 00							15 00					
Royston	d	12 37	13 04						13 37		14 04						14 37	15 04					
Meldreth	d		13 08								14 08							15 08					
Shepreth	d		13 11								14 11							15 11					
Foxton	d		13 14								14 14							15 14					
Cambridge	a	12 54	13 27	13 01				13 30	13 54		14 27	14 01				14 30	14 54	15 27	15 01				15 30
Arlesey	d				12 57		13 23						13 57		14 23					14 57		15 23	
Biggleswade	d				13 02		13 28						14 02		14 28					15 02		15 28	
Sandy	d				13 06		13 32						14 06		14 32					15 06		15 32	
St Neots	d				13 13		13 39						14 13		14 39					15 13		15 39	
Huntingdon	d				13 21		13 47						14 21		14 47					15 21		15 47	
Peterborough	a				13 37		14 06			13 52			14 38		15 07					15 38		16 06	

		FC	GR	FC	FC	FC	FC	FC	FC	FC	FC	FC	FC	FC	FC	FC	FC	FC	GR	FC	FC	FC
London Kings Cross ⊖	d	14 53	15 03	15 06	15 15	15 23	15 26	15 36	15 45	15 53	16 06	16 15	16 23	16 26	16 36	16 40	16 45	16 53	17 03	17 06	17 15	17 23
Finsbury Park ⊖	d	14 58		15 11		15 28	15 32	15 41		15 58	16 11		16 28	16 32	16 41			16 58		17 11		17 28
Potters Bar	d			15 21				15 51			16 21				16 51					17 21		
Hatfield	d			15 27				15 57			16 27				16 57					17 27		
Welwyn Garden City	d			15 31				16 01			16 31				17 01					17 31		
Welwyn North	d			15 34				16 04			16 34				17 04					17 34		
Knebworth	d			15 38				16 08			16 38				17 08					17 38		
Hertford North	d						16 07							17 07								
Stevenage	d	15 17	15 22	15 42		15 47	16a20	16 12		16 17	16 42		16 47	17a20	17 12			17 17	17 22	17 42		17 47
Hitchin	d	15 22		15 47		15 52		16 17		16 22	16 47		16 52		17 17			17 22		17 47		17 52
Letchworth Garden City	d	15 26		15 51						16 26	16 51							17 26		17 51		
Baldock	d	15 29		15 55						16 29	16 55							17 29		17 55		
Ashwell & Morden	d			16 00							17 00									18 00		
Royston	d	15 37		16 04						16 37	17 04							17 37		18 04		
Meldreth	d			16 08							17 08									18 08		
Shepreth	d			16 11							17 11									18 11		
Foxton	d			16 14							17 14									18 14		
Cambridge	a	15 54		16 27	16 01				16 30	16 54	17 27	17 01					17 30	17 54		18 27	18 01	
Arlesey	d					15 57		16 23					16 57		17 23							17 57
Biggleswade	d					16 02		16 28					17 02		17 28	17 08						18 02
Sandy	d					16 06		16 32					17 06		17 32							18 06
St Neots	d					16 13		16 39					17 13		17 39	17 18						18 13
Huntingdon	d					16 21		16 47					17 21		17 47	17 26						18 21
Peterborough	a		15 52			16 38		17 06					17 38		18 06	17 42			17 52			18 38

		FC	FC	FC	FC	FC	FC	GR	FC	FC	FC	FC	FC	FC	FC	FC	FC	FC	FC	FC	GR	FC	FC
London Kings Cross ⊖	d	17 26	17 36	17 40	17 45	17 53	18 06	18 08	18 15		18 23	18 26	18 36	18 40	18 45	18 53	19 06	19 15	19 23	19 26	19 30	19 36	19 45
Finsbury Park ⊖	d	17 32	17 41			17 58	18 11				18 28	18 32	18 41			18 58	19 11		19 28	19 32		19 41	
Potters Bar	d		17 51				18 21						18 51				19 21					19 51	
Hatfield	d		17 57				18 27						18 57				19 27					19 57	
Welwyn Garden City	d		18 01				18 31						19 01				19 31					20 01	
Welwyn North	d		18 04				18 34						19 04				19 34					20 04	
Knebworth	d		18 08				18 38						19 08				19 38					20 08	
Hertford North	d	18 07								←		19 07								20 07			
Stevenage	d	18a20	18 12			18 17	18 42	18 28		18 42	18 47	19a20	19 12			19 17	19 42		19 47	20a20	19 49	20 12	
Hitchin	d		18 17			18 22	→			18 47	18 52		19 17			19 22	19 47		19 52			20 17	
Letchworth Garden City	d					18 26				18 51						19 26	19 51						
Baldock	d					18 29				18 55						19 29	19 55						
Ashwell & Morden	d									19 00							20 00						
Royston	d					18 37				19 04					19 19	19 37	20 04						20 19
Meldreth	d									19 08							20 08						
Shepreth	d									19 11							20 11						
Foxton	d									19 14							20 14						
Cambridge	a				18 30	18 54			19 01	19 27					19 35	19 54	20 27	20 01					20 35
Arlesey	d		18 23								18 57		19 23						19 57			20 23	
Biggleswade	d		18 28	18 08							19 02		19 28	19 08					20 02			20 28	
Sandy	d		18 32								19 06		19 32						20 06			20 32	
St Neots	d		18 39	18 18							19 13		19 39	19 18					20 13			20 39	
Huntingdon	d		18 47	18 26							19 21		19 47	19 26					20 21			20 47	
Peterborough	a		19 06	18 42				18 58			19 38		20 06	19 44					20 39		20 19	21 06	

London - Stevenage, Cambridge and Peterborough

Saturdays

Network Diagram - see first Page of Table 24

		FC ■	FC ■	FC ■	FC	FC ■		FC ■	FC ■	FC ■	FC ■	FC	FC ■	FC ■	FC ■	FC ■		FC ■	FC ■	FC	FC ■	FC ■	FC ■	FC ■	FC ■
London Kings Cross ⊖	d	19 53	20 06	20 23	20 26	20 36		20 45	20 53	21 06	21 23	21 26	21 36	21 53	22 06	22 15			22 23	22 26	22 36	22 53	23 06	23 15	
Finsbury Park ⊖	d	19 58	20 11	20 28	20 32	20 41			20 58	21 11	21 28	21 32	21 41	21 58	22 11				22 28	22 32	22 41	22 58	23 11		
Potters Bar	d		20 21			20 51				21 21			21 51		22 21						22 51		23 21		
Hatfield	d		20 27			20 57				21 27			21 57		22 27						22 57		23 27		
Welwyn Garden City	d		20 31			21 01				21 31			22 01		22 31						23 01		23 31		
Welwyn North	d		20 34			21 04				21 34			22 04		22 34						23 04		23 34		
Knebworth	d		20 38			21 08				21 38			22 08		22 38						23 08		23 38		
Hertford North	d				21 07							22 07								23 07					
Stevenage	d	20 17	20 42	20 47	21a20	21 12			21 17	21 42	21 47	22a20	22 12	22 17	22 42				22 47	23a20	23 12	23 17	23 42		
Hitchin	d	20 22	20 47	20 52		21 17			21 22	21 47	21 52		22 17	22 22	22 47			←	22 54		23 20	23 24	23 50		←
Letchworth Garden City	d	20 26	20 51						21 26	21 51				22 26	22 51	22 40		22 51			23a26		23 54	23 43	23 54
Baldock	d	20 29	20 55						21 29	21 55				22 29	→			22 55					→		23 57
Ashwell & Morden	d		21 00							22 00								23 00							00 02
Royston	d	20 37	21 04					21 19	21 37	22 04				22 37		22 50		23 04						23 53	00 07
Meldreth	d		21 08							22 08								23 08							00 11
Shepreth	d		21 11							22 11								23 11							00 14
Foxton	d		21 14							22 14								23 14							00 16
Cambridge	a	20 54	21 27					21 35	21 54	22 27				22 54		23 05		23 27						00 10	00 29
Arlesey	d			20 57		21 23					21 57		22 23						22 59			23 29			
Biggleswade	d			21 02		21 28					22 02		22 28						23 04			23 34			
Sandy	d			21 06		21 32					22 06		22 32						23 08			23 38			
St Neots	d			21 13		21 39					22 13		22 39						23 15			23 45			
Huntingdon	d			21 21		21 47					22 21		22 47						23 23			23 53			
Peterborough	a			21 37		22 06					22 37		23 06						23 43			00 13			

		FC ■		FC	FC ■	FC	FC ■
London Kings Cross ⊖	d	23 23		23 26	23 36		23 53
Finsbury Park ⊖	d	23 28		23 32	23 41		23 58
Potters Bar	d				23 53		
Hatfield	d				23 59		
Welwyn Garden City	d				00 06		
Welwyn North	d				00 09		
Knebworth	d				00 13		
Hertford North	d			00 07		←	
Stevenage	d	23 47		00 22	00 18	00 22	00 29
Hitchin	d	23 54		→	00 25	00 29	00 36
Letchworth Garden City	d				00a30	00a37	
Baldock	d						
Ashwell & Morden	d						
Royston	d						
Meldreth	d						
Shepreth	d						
Foxton	d						
Cambridge	a						
Arlesey	d	23 59					00s43
Biggleswade	d	00 04					00s48
Sandy	d	00 08					00s51
St Neots	d	00 15					00s59
Huntingdon	d	00 23					01s06
Peterborough	a	00 43					01 25

Sundays
until 9 September

		FC ■	FC ■	FC ■	FC ■	FC ■	FC	FC ■	FC	FC ■		FC ■	FC ■	FC ■	FC ■	FC ■ A	FC ■	FC	FC ■ A	FC ■ A		FC	FC ■ A	FC	FC ■
London Kings Cross ⊖	d	22p53	23p06	23p15		23p23	23p26	23p36		23p53		00 06	00 15		00 23	00 31	00 53	00 56	01 01	01 15			01 23	06 26	06 53
Finsbury Park ⊖	d	22p58	23p11			23p28	23p32	23p41		23p58		00 11			00 28		00 58	01 02					01 28	06 32	06 58
Potters Bar	d		23p21					23p53				00 23					01 10								
Hatfield	d		23p27					23p59				00 29					01 16								
Welwyn Garden City	d		23p31					00 06				00 41					01 20								
Welwyn North	d		23p34					00 09				00 44					01s24								
Knebworth	d		23p38					00 13				00 48					01s28								
Hertford North	d						00 07		←					←				01 37				←		07 07	
Stevenage	d	23p17	23p42			23p47	00 22	00 18	00 22	00 29		00 53	00 47	00 53	00 58	01s02	01 32	01 51	01 40	01 47		01 51	01 57	07a22	07 17
Hitchin	d	23p24	23p50		←	23p54	→	00 25	00 29	00 36		→	00 54	01 00	01 05	01s09	01 39	→	01 48	01 55		01 59	02 05		07 27
Letchworth Garden City	d		23p54	23p43	23p54			00a30	00a37				00 58	01 04		01s13				02 02		02a05			07 36
Baldock	d		→		23p57								01 01	01 08		01s16				02 05					07 39
Ashwell & Morden	d				00 02									01 13											
Royston	d			23p53	00 07								01 09	01 17		01s24				02 13					07 47
Meldreth	d				00 11									01 21											
Shepreth	d				00 14									01 24											
Foxton	d				00 16									01 27											
Cambridge	a			00 10	00 29								01 25	01 40		01 42				02 28					08 04
Arlesey	d	23p29				23p59				00s43					01s10		01s46						02s10		
Biggleswade	d	23p34				00 04				00s48					01s15		01s51		01 56				02s15		
Sandy	d	23p38				00 08				00s51					01s19		01s55						02s19		
St Neots	d	23p45				00 15				00s59					01s26		02s02		02 06				02s26		
Huntingdon	d	23p53				00 23				01s06					01s34		02s10		02 13				02s34		
Peterborough	a	00 13				00 43				01 25					01 54		02 30		02 32				02 54		

A 29 July, 5 August, 12 August, 2 September, 9 September

London - Stevenage, Cambridge and Peterborough

Sundays
until 9 September

Network Diagram - see first Page of Table 24

		FC ■	FC ■	FC	FC ■	FC ■		FC ■	FC	FC ■	GR ■	FC ■	FC ■	FC ■	FC	FC ■		FC ■	FC ■ A	FC ■ B	FC ■	FC	FC ■	GR ■	FC ■
London Kings Cross ⊖	d	07 06	07 23	07 26	07 53	08 06		08 23	08 26	08 53	09 03	09 06	09 15	09 23	09 26	09 53		10 06	10 15	10 15	10 23	10 26	10 53	11 03	11 06
Finsbury Park ⊖	d	07 11	07 28	07 32	07 58	08 11		08 28	08 32	08 58		09 11		09 28	09 32	09 58		10 11			10 28	10 32	10 58		11 11
Potters Bar	d	07 21				08 21						09 21						10 21							11 21
Hatfield	d	07 27				08 27						09 27						10 27							11 27
Welwyn Garden City	d	07 33				08 31						09 31						10 31							11 31
Welwyn North	d	07 36				08 34						09 34						10 34							11 34
Knebworth	d	07 40				08 38						09 38						10 38							11 38
Hertford North	d			08 07					09 07						10 07							11 07			
Stevenage	d	07 45	07 51	08a23	08 17	08 42		08 47	09a20	09 17	09 22	09 42		09 47	10a20	10 17		10 42			10 47	11a20	11 17	11 22	11 42
Hitchin	d	07 52	08 01		08 22	08 47		08 52		09 22		09 47		09 52		10 22		10 47			10 52		11 22		11 47
Letchworth Garden City	d	07 56			08 26	08 51				09 26		09 51				10 26		10 51					11 26		11 51
Baldock	d	07 59			08 29	08 55				09 29		09 55				10 29		10 55					11 29		11 55
Ashwell & Morden	d	08 04				09 00						10 00						11 00							12 00
Royston	d	08 09			08 37	09 04				09 37		10 04				10 37		11 04					11 37		12 04
Meldreth	d	08 13				09 08						10 08						11 08							12 08
Shepreth	d	08 16				09 11						10 11						11 11							12 11
Foxton	d	08 18				09 14						10 14						11 14							12 14
Cambridge	a	08 34			08 54	09 27				09 54		10 27	10 00			10 54		11 27	11 00	11 01			11 54		12 27
Arlesey	d		08 06					08 57						09 57							10 57				
Biggleswade	d		08 11					09 02						10 02							11 02				
Sandy	d		08 15					09 06						10 06							11 06				
St Neots	d		08 22					09 13						10 13							11 13				
Huntingdon	d		08 30					09 21						10 21							11 21				
Peterborough	a		08 51					09 38			09 52			10 38							11 38			11 52	

		FC ■		FC ■	FC	FC ■	FC ■	FC ■	FC ■	FC	FC ■	GR ■		FC ■	FC ■	FC ■	FC	FC ■	FC ■	FC ■	FC ■	FC		FC ■	GR ■
London Kings Cross ⊖	d	11 15		11 23	11 26	11 53	12 06	12 15	12 23	12 26	12 53	13 03		13 06	13 15	13 23	13 26	13 53	14 06	14 15	14 23	14 26		14 53	15 03
Finsbury Park ⊖	d			11 28	11 32	11 58	12 11		12 28	12 32	12 58			13 11		13 28	13 32	13 58	14 11		14 28	14 32		14 58	
Potters Bar	d						12 21							13 21					14 21						
Hatfield	d						12 27							13 27					14 27						
Welwyn Garden City	d						12 31							13 31					14 31						
Welwyn North	d						12 34							13 34					14 34						
Knebworth	d						12 38							13 38					14 38						
Hertford North	d				12 07					13 07							14 07					15 07			
Stevenage	d			11 47	12a20	12 17	12 42		12 47	13a20	13 17	13 22		13 42		13 47	14a20	14 17	14 42		14 47	15a20		15 17	15 22
Hitchin	d			11 52		12 22	12 47		12 52		13 22			13 47		13 52		14 22	14 47		14 52			15 22	
Letchworth Garden City	d					12 26	12 51				13 26			13 51				14 26	14 51					15 26	
Baldock	d					12 29	12 55				13 29			13 55				14 29	14 55					15 29	
Ashwell & Morden	d						13 00							14 00					15 00						
Royston	d					12 37	13 04				13 37			14 04				14 37	15 04					15 37	
Meldreth	d						13 08							14 08					15 08						
Shepreth	d						13 11							14 11					15 11						
Foxton	d						13 14							14 14					15 14						
Cambridge	a	12 00				12 54	13 27	13 00			13 54			14 27	14 00			14 54	15 27	15 00				15 54	
Arlesey	d			11 57					12 57							13 57					14 57				
Biggleswade	d			12 02					13 02							14 02					15 02				
Sandy	d			12 06					13 06							14 06					15 06				
St Neots	d			12 13					13 13							14 13					15 13				
Huntingdon	d			12 21					13 21							14 21					15 21				
Peterborough	a			12 39					13 38			13 52				14 38					15 38				15 52

		FC ■	FC ■	FC ■	FC	FC ■	FC ■	FC ■		FC ■	FC	GR ■	FC ■	FC ■	FC ■	FC ■	FC ■	FC		GR ■	FC ■	FC ■	FC ■	FC ■	FC ■
London Kings Cross ⊖	d	15 06	15 15	15 23	15 26	15 53	16 06	16 15		16 23	16 26	16 35	16 36	16 53	17 06	17 15	17 23	17 26		17 35	17 36	17 53	18 06	18 10	18 15
Finsbury Park ⊖	d	15 11		15 28	15 32	15 58	16 11			16 28	16 32		16 41	16 58	17 11		17 28	17 32			17 41	17 58	18 11		
Potters Bar	d	15 21					16 21						16 51		17 21						17 51		18 21		
Hatfield	d	15 27					16 27						16 57		17 27						17 57		18 27		
Welwyn Garden City	d	15 31					16 31						17 01		17 31						18 01		18 31		
Welwyn North	d	15 34					16 34						17 04		17 34						18 04		18 34		
Knebworth	d	15 38					16 38						17 08		17 38						18 08		18 38		
Hertford North	d				16 07						17 07							18 07							
Stevenage	d	15 42		15 47	16a20	16 17	16 42			16 47	17a20	16a54	17 12	17 17	17 42		17 47	18a20		17a54	18 12	18 17	18 42		
Hitchin	d	15 47		15 52		16 22	16 47			16 52			17 17	17 22	17 47		17 52				18 17	18 22	18 47		
Letchworth Garden City	d	15 51				16 26	16 51							17 26	17 51							18 26	18 51		
Baldock	d	15 55				16 29	16 55							17 29	17 55							18 29	18 55		
Ashwell & Morden	d	16 00					17 00								18 00								19 00		
Royston	d	16 04				16 37	17 04							17 37	18 04							18 37	19 04		
Meldreth	d	16 08					17 08								18 08								19 08		
Shepreth	d	16 11					17 11								18 11								19 11		
Foxton	d	16 14					17 14								18 14								19 14		
Cambridge	a	16 27	16 00			16 54	17 27	17 00						17 54	18 27	18 00						18 54	19 27		19 00
Arlesey	d			15 57						16 57			17 23				17 57				18 23				
Biggleswade	d			16 02						17 02			17 28				18 02				18 28			18 37	
Sandy	d			16 06						17 06			17 32				18 06				18 32				
St Neots	d			16 13						17 13			17 39				18 13				18 39			18 47	
Huntingdon	d			16 21						17 21			17 47				18 21				18 47			18 54	
Peterborough	a			16 38						17 39			18 06				18 38				19 05			19 12	

A until 22 July, 19 August, 26 August

B 29 July, 5 August, 12 August, 2 September, 9 September

Table 25

Sundays until 9 September

London - Stevenage, Cambridge and Peterborough

Network Diagram - see first Page of Table 24

		FC	FC	GR		FC	FC	FC	GR	FC	FC	FC	FC	GR		HT	FC	FC	FC	FC	FC	GR	FC	FC	
		1		1		1	1	1	1	1	1	1		1		◇1 ⊠	1	1	1	1		1	1	1	
London Kings Cross ⊖	d	18 23	18 26	18 35		18 36	18 53	19 06	19 08	19 15		19 23	19 26	19 35		19 45	19 53	20 06	20 15	20 23	20 26	20 35	20 53	21 06	
Finsbury Park ⊖	d	18 28	18 32			18 41	18 58	19 11				19 28	19 32				19 58	20 11		20 28	20 32		20 58	21 11	
Potters Bar	d					18 51		19 21										20 21						21 21	
Hatfield	d					18 57		19 27										20 27						21 27	
Welwyn Garden City	d					19 01		19 31										20 31						21 31	
Welwyn North	d					19 04		19 34										20 34						21 34	
Knebworth	d					19 08		19 38										20 38						21 38	
Hertford North	d		19 07								←		20 07								21 07				
Stevenage	d	18 47	19a20	18a54		19 12	19 17	19 42	19 28		19 42	19 47	20a20	19 54		20a04	20 17	20 42		20 47	21a20	20 54	21 17	21 42	
Hitchin	d	18 52				19 17	19 22	→			19 47	19 52					20 22	20 47		20 52			21 22	21 47	
Letchworth Garden City	d					19 22	19 26				19 51						20 26	20 51					21 26	21 51	
Baldock	d						19 29				19 55						20 29	20 55					21 29	21 55	
Ashwell & Morden	d										20 00							21 00						22 00	
Royston	d					19a33	19 37				20 04						20 37	21 04					21 37	22 04	
Meldreth	d										20 08							21 08						22 08	
Shepreth	d										20 11							21 11						22 11	
Foxton	d										20 14							21 14						22 14	
Cambridge	a						19 54			20 00	20 27						20 54	21 27	21 00				21 54	22 27	
Arlesey	d	18 57										19 57								20 57					
Biggleswade	d	19 02										20 02								21 02					
Sandy	d	19 06										20 06								21 06					
St Neots	d	19 13										20 13								21 13					
Huntingdon	d	19 21										20 21								21 21					
Peterborough	a	19 39							19 58			20 38		20 24						21 37		21 24			

		FC	FC	FC	GR	FC	FC	FC	FC	FC		FC	FC	FC	FC	FC	FC	FC
		1	1		1	1	1	1	1			1	1	1	1	1		
London Kings Cross ⊖	d	21 15	21 23	21 26	21 35	21 53	22 06	22 15	22 23	22 26		22 53	23 06	23 15		23 23	23 26	23 41
Finsbury Park ⊖	d		21 28	21 32		21 58	22 11		22 28	22 32		22 58	23 11			23 28	23 32	23 47
Potters Bar	d						22 21						23 21					00 08
Hatfield	d						22 27						23 27					00 16
Welwyn Garden City	d						22 31						23 31					00 20
Welwyn North	d						22 34						23 34					00 23
Knebworth	d						22 38						23 38					00 28
Hertford North	d			22 07						23 07							00 07	
Stevenage	d		21 47	22a20	21 55	22 17	22 42		22 47	23a20		23 17	23 42			23 47	00a20	00 31
Hitchin	d		21 52			22 22	22 47		22 52			23 22	23 47		←	23 52		00 37
Letchworth Garden City	d					22 26	22 51					23 26	23 51	23 44	23 51			00a52
Baldock	d					22 29	22 55					23 29	→		23 54			
Ashwell & Morden	d						23 00								23 59			
Royston	d					22 37	23 04					23 37		23 54	00 04			
Meldreth	d						23 08								00 08			
Shepreth	d						23 11								00 11			
Foxton	d						23 14								00 14			
Cambridge	a	22 00				22 54	23 27	23 00				23 54		00 10	00 29			
Arlesey	d		21 57						22 57							23 57		
Biggleswade	d		22 02						23 02							00 02		
Sandy	d		22 06						23 06							00 06		
St Neots	d		22 13						23 13							00 13		
Huntingdon	d		22 21						23 21							00 21		
Peterborough	a		22 37		22 25				23 41							00 43		

Sundays 16 September to 21 October

		FC	FC	FC	FC	FC	FC	FC	FC	FC		FC	FC	FC	FC	FC	FC	FC	FC	FC		FC	FC	FC	FC
		1	1	1	1	1		1		1		1	1	1	1	1	1		1	1		1		1	1
London Kings Cross ⊖	d	22p53	23p06	23p15		23p23	23p26	23p36		23p53		00 06	00 15		00 23	00 53	06 53		07 06	07 23		07 53		08 06	08 23
Finsbury Park ⊖	d	22p58	23p11			23p28	23p32	23p41		23p58		00 11			00 28	00 58	06 58		07 11	07 28		07 58		08 11	08 28
Potters Bar	d		23p21					23p53				00 23				01 10			07 21					08 21	
Hatfield	d		23p27					23p59				00 29				01 16			07 27					08 27	
Welwyn Garden City	d		23p31					00 06				00 41				01 20			07 33					08 31	
Welwyn North	d		23p34					00 09				00 44				01s24			07 36					08 34	
Knebworth	d		23p38					00 13				00 48				01s28			07 40					08 38	
Hertford North	d						00 07		←					←				06 50					07 50		
Stevenage	d	23p17	23p42			23p47	00 22	00 18	00 22	00 29		00 53	00 47	00 53	00 58	01 32	07 17	07a21	07 45	07 51		08 17	08a21	08 42	08 47
Hitchin	d	23p24	23p50		←	23p54	→	00 25	00 29	00 36		→	00 54	01 00	01 05	01 39	07 27		07 52	08 01		08 22		08 47	08 52
Letchworth Garden City	d		23p54	23p43	23p54			00a30	00a37				00 58	01 04			07 36		07 56			08 26		08 51	
Baldock	d		→		23p57								01 01	01 08			07 39		07 59			08 29		08 55	
Ashwell & Morden	d				00 02									01 13					08 04					09 00	
Royston	d			23p53	00 07								01 09	01 17			07 47		08 09			08 37		09 04	
Meldreth	d				00 11									01 21					08 13					09 08	
Shepreth	d				00 14									01 24					08 16					09 11	
Foxton	d				00 16									01 27					08 18					09 14	
Cambridge	a			00 10	00 29								01 25	01 40			08 04		08 34			08 54		09 27	
Arlesey	d	23p29				23p59				00s43					01s10	01s46				08 06					08 57
Biggleswade	d	23p34				00 04				00s48					01s15	01s51				08 11					09 02
Sandy	d	23p38				00 08				00s51					01s19	01s55				08 15					09 06
St Neots	d	23p45				00 15				00s59					01s26	02s02				08 22					09 13
Huntingdon	d	23p53				00 23				01s06					01s34	02s10				08 30					09 21
Peterborough	a	00 13				00 43				01 25					01 54	02 30				08 51					09 38

Table 25

Sundays 16 September to 21 October

London - Stevenage, Cambridge and Peterborough

Network Diagram - see first Page of Table 24

		FC	FC	GR	FC	FC		FC	FC	FC	FC	FC	FC	FC	FC	GR		FC	FC	FC	FC	FC	FC	FC	FC
		1		1	1	1		1	1		1	1	1	1		1		1	1	1	1		1	1	1
London Kings Cross ⊖	d	08 52		09 03	09 03	09 12		09 22	09 52		10 03	10 12	10 22	10 52		11 03		11 03	11 12	11 22	11 52		12 03	12 12	12 22
Finsbury Park ⊖	d	08 56			09 08			09 26	09 56		10 08		10 26	10 56				11 08		11 26	11 56		12 08		12 26
Potters Bar	d				09 18						10 18							11 18					12 18		
Hatfield	d				09 24						10 24							11 24					12 24		
Welwyn Garden City	d				09 28						10 28							11 28					12 28		
Welwyn North	d				09 31						10 31							11 31					12 31		
Knebworth	d				09 35						10 35							11 35					12 35		
Hertford North	d		08 50							09 50					10 50							11 50			
Stevenage	d	09 14	09a21	09 22	09 39			09 44	10 14	10a21	10 39		10 44	11 14	11a21	11 22		11 39		11 44	12 14	12a21	12 39		12 44
Hitchin	d	09 22			09 44			09 52	10 22		10 44		10 52	11 22				11 44		11 52	12 22		12 44		12 52
Letchworth Garden City	d	09 26			09 51				10 26		10 51			11 26				11 51			12 26		12 51		
Baldock	d	09 29			09 55				10 29		10 55			11 29				11 55			12 29		12 55		
Ashwell & Morden	d				10 00						11 00							12 00					13 00		
Royston	d	09 37			10 04				10 37		11 04			11 37				12 04			12 37		13 04		
Meldreth	d				10 08						11 08							12 08					13 08		
Shepreth	d				10 11						11 11							12 11					13 11		
Foxton	d				10 14						11 14							12 14					13 14		
Cambridge	a	09 54			10 27	10 02			10 54		11 27	11 00		11 54				12 27	12 00		12 54		13 27	13 00	
Arlesey	d							09 57					10 57							11 57					12 57
Biggleswade	d							10 02					11 02							12 02					13 02
Sandy	d							10 06					11 06							12 06					13 06
St Neots	d							10 13					11 13							12 13					13 13
Huntingdon	d							10 21					11 21							12 21					13 21
Peterborough	a			09 52				10 38					11 38			11 52				12 39					13 38

		FC		FC	GR	FC	FC	FC	FC	FC	FC	FC		FC	FC	FC	GR	FC	FC	FC	FC	FC		FC	FC
		1			1	1	1	1	1		1	1		1	1		1	1	1	1	1			1	1
London Kings Cross ⊖	d	12 52			13 03	13 03	13 12	13 22	13 52		14 03	14 15		14 22	14 52		15 03	15 06	15 15	15 22	15 52			16 06	16 15
Finsbury Park ⊖	d	12 56				13 08		13 26	13 56		14 08			14 26	14 56			15 11		15 26	15 56			16 11	
Potters Bar	d					13 18					14 18							15 21						16 21	
Hatfield	d					13 24					14 24							15 27						16 27	
Welwyn Garden City	d					13 28					14 28							15 31						16 31	
Welwyn North	d					13 31					14 31							15 34						16 34	
Knebworth	d					13 35					14 35							15 38						16 38	
Hertford North	d			12 50						13 50						14 50						15 50			
Stevenage	d	13 14		13a21	13 22	13 39		13 44	14 14	14a21	14 39			14 44	15 14	15a21	15 22	15 42		15 44	16 14	16a21		16 42	
Hitchin	d	13 22				13 44		13 52	14 22		14 44			14 52	15 22			15 47		15 52	16 22			16 47	
Letchworth Garden City	d	13 26				13 51			14 26		14 51				15 26			15 51			16 26			16 51	
Baldock	d	13 29				13 55			14 29		14 55				15 29			15 55			16 29			16 55	
Ashwell & Morden	d					14 00					15 00							16 00						17 00	
Royston	d	13 37				14 04			14 37		15 04				15 37			16 04			16 37			17 04	
Meldreth	d					14 08					15 08							16 08						17 08	
Shepreth	d					14 11					15 11							16 11						17 11	
Foxton	d					14 14					15 14							16 14						17 14	
Cambridge	a	13 54				14 27	14 00		14 54		15 27	15 00			15 54			16 27	16 00		16 54			17 27	17 00
Arlesey	d							13 57						14 57						15 57					
Biggleswade	d							14 02						15 02						16 02					
Sandy	d							14 06						15 06						16 06					
St Neots	d							14 13						15 13						16 13					
Huntingdon	d							14 21						15 21						16 21					
Peterborough	a				13 52			14 38						15 38			15 52			16 38					

		FC	GR	FC	FC	FC	FC	FC		FC	GR	FC	FC	FC	FC	FC	FC	FC		GR	FC	FC	FC	FC	GR
		1	1	1	1		1	1		1	1	1	1		1	1	1	1		1	1	1		1	1
London Kings Cross ⊖	d	16 22	16 35	16 36	16 53		17 06	17 15		17 23	17 35	17 36	17 53		18 06	18 10	18 15	18 23		18 35	18 36	18 53		19 06	19 08
Finsbury Park ⊖	d	16 26		16 41	16 58		17 11			17 28		17 41	17 58		18 11			18 28			18 41	18 58		19 11	
Potters Bar	d			16 51			17 21					17 51			18 21						18 51			19 21	
Hatfield	d			16 57			17 27					17 57			18 27						18 57			19 27	
Welwyn Garden City	d			17 01			17 31					18 01			18 31						19 01			19 31	
Welwyn North	d			17 04			17 34					18 04			18 34						19 04			19 34	
Knebworth	d			17 08			17 38					18 08			18 38						19 08			19 38	
Hertford North	d					16 50								17 50									18 50		
Stevenage	d	16 44	16a54	17 12	17 17	17a21	17 42			17 47	17a54	18 12	18 17	18a21	18 42			18 47		18a54	19 12	19 17	19a21	19 42	19 28
Hitchin	d	16 52		17 17	17 22		17 47			17 52		18 17	18 22		18 47			18 52			19 17	19 22		→	
Letchworth Garden City	d				17 26		17 51						18 26		18 51						19 22	19 26			
Baldock	d				17 29		17 55						18 29		18 55							19 29			
Ashwell & Morden	d						18 00								19 00										
Royston	d				17 37		18 04						18 37		19 04						19a33	19 37			
Meldreth	d						18 08								19 08										
Shepreth	d						18 11								19 11										
Foxton	d						18 14								19 14										
Cambridge	a				17 54		18 27	18 00					18 54		19 27		19 00					19 54			
Arlesey	d	16 57		17 23						17 57		18 23						18 57							
Biggleswade	d	17 02		17 28						18 02		18 28				18 37		19 02							
Sandy	d	17 06		17 32						18 06		18 32						19 06							
St Neots	d	17 13		17 39						18 13		18 39				18 47		19 13							
Huntingdon	d	17 21		17 47						18 21		18 47				18 54		19 21							
Peterborough	a	17 39		18 06						18 38		19 05				19 12		19 39							19 58

London - Stevenage, Cambridge and Peterborough

Sundays
16 September to 21 October

Network Diagram - see first Page of Table 24

Station		FC	FC	FC	GR	HT	FC	FC	FC	FC	FC	GR	FC	FC	FC	FC	FC	GR	FC	FC	FC	FC
London Kings Cross ⊖	d	19 15		19 23	19 35	19 45	19 53		20 06	20 15	20 23	20 35	20 53		21 06	21 15	21 23	21 35	21 53		22 06	22 15
Finsbury Park ⊖	d			19 28			19 58		20 11		20 28		20 58		21 11		21 28		21 58		22 11	
Potters Bar	d								20 21						21 21						22 21	
Hatfield	d								20 27						21 27						22 27	
Welwyn Garden City	d								20 31						21 31						22 31	
Welwyn North	d								20 34						21 34						22 34	
Knebworth	d								20 38						21 38						22 38	
Hertford North	d		←					19 50						20 50						21 50		
Stevenage	d		19 42	19 47	19 54	20a04	20 17	20a21	20 42		20 47	20 54	21 17	21a21	21 42		21 47	21 55	22 17	22a21	22 42	
Hitchin	d		19 47	19 52			20 22		20 47		20 52		21 22		21 47		21 52		22 22		22 47	
Letchworth Garden City	d		19 51				20 26		20 51				21 26		21 51				22 26		22 51	
Baldock	d		19 55				20 29		20 55				21 29		21 55				22 29		22 55	
Ashwell & Morden	d		20 00						21 00						22 00						23 00	
Royston	d		20 04				20 37		21 04				21 37		22 04				22 37		23 04	
Meldreth	d		20 08						21 08						22 08						23 08	
Shepreth	d		20 11						21 11						22 11						23 11	
Foxton	d		20 14						21 14						22 14						23 14	
Cambridge	a	20 00	20 27				20 54		21 27	21 00			21 54		22 27	22 00			22 54		23 27	23 00
Arlesey	d			19 57							20 57						21 57					
Biggleswade	d			20 02							21 02						22 02					
Sandy	d			20 06							21 06						22 06					
St Neots	d			20 13							21 13						22 13					
Huntingdon	d			20 21							21 21						22 21					
Peterborough	a			20 38	20 24						21 37	21 24					22 37	22 25				

Station		FC	FC	FC	FC	FC	FC	FC	FC	FC
London Kings Cross ⊖	d	22 23	22 53		23 06	23 15		23 23		23 41
Finsbury Park ⊖	d	22 28	22 58		23 11			23 28		23 47
Potters Bar	d				23 21					00 08
Hatfield	d				23 27					00 16
Welwyn Garden City	d				23 31					00 20
Welwyn North	d				23 34					00 23
Knebworth	d				23 38					00 28
Hertford North	d			22 50					23 50	
Stevenage	d	22 47	23 17	23a21	23 42			23 47	00a21	00 31
Hitchin	d	22 52	23 22		23 47		←	23 52		00 37
Letchworth Garden City	d		23 26		23 51	23 44	23 51			00a52
Baldock	d		23 29		→		23 54			
Ashwell & Morden	d						23 59			
Royston	d		23 37			23 54	00 04			
Meldreth	d						00 08			
Shepreth	d						00 11			
Foxton	d						00 14			
Cambridge	a		23 54			00 10	00 29			
Arlesey	d	22 57						23 57		
Biggleswade	d	23 02						00 02		
Sandy	d	23 06						00 06		
St Neots	d	23 13						00 13		
Huntingdon	d	23 21						00 21		
Peterborough	a	23 41						00 43		

Sundays
from 28 October

Station		FC	FC	FC	FC	FC	FC	FC	FC	FC	FC	FC	FC	FC	FC	FC	FC	FC	FC	FC	FC	FC	FC
London Kings Cross ⊖	d	22p53	23p06	23p15		23p23	23p26	23p36		23p53	00 06	00 15		00 23	00 53	00 56	06 26	06 53	07 06	07 23	07 26	07 53	08 06
Finsbury Park ⊖	d	22p58	23p11			23p28	23p32	23p41		23p58	00 11			00 28	00 58	01 02	06 32	06 58	07 11	07 28	07 32	07 58	08 11
Potters Bar	d		23p21					23p53			00 23				01 10				07 21				08 21
Hatfield	d		23p27					23p59			00 29				01 16				07 27				08 27
Welwyn Garden City	d		23p31					00 06			00 41				01 20				07 33				08 31
Welwyn North	d		23p34					00 09			00 44				01s24				07 36				08 34
Knebworth	d		23p38					00 13			00 48				01s28				07 40				08 38
Hertford North	d						00 07		←				←			01 37	07 07				08 07		
Stevenage	d	23p17	23p42			23p47	00 22	00 18	00 22	00 29	00 53	00 47	00 53	00 58	01 32	01 51	07a22	07 17	07 45	07 51	08a23	08 17	08 42
Hitchin	d	23p24	23p50		←	23p54	→	00 25	00 29	00 36	→	00 54	01 00	01 05	01 39	01 59		07 27	07 52	08 01		08 22	08 47
Letchworth Garden City	d		23p54	23p43	23p54			00a30	00a37			00 58	01 04			02a05		07 36	07 56			08 26	08 51
Baldock	d		→		23p57							01 01	01 08					07 39	07 59			08 29	08 55
Ashwell & Morden	d				00 02								01 13						08 04				09 00
Royston	d			23p53	00 07							01 09	01 17					07 47	08 09			08 37	09 04
Meldreth	d				00 11								01 21						08 13				09 08
Shepreth	d				00 14								01 24						08 16				09 11
Foxton	d				00 16								01 27						08 18				09 14
Cambridge	a			00 10	00 29							01 25	01 40					08 04	08 34			08 54	09 27
Arlesey	d	23p29				23p59				00s43				01s10	01s46					08 06			
Biggleswade	d	23p34				00 04				00s48				01s15	01s51					08 11			
Sandy	d	23p38				00 08				00s51				01s19	01s55					08 15			
St Neots	d	23p45				00 15				00s59				01s26	02s02					08 22			
Huntingdon	d	23p53				00 23				01s06				01s34	02s10					08 30			
Peterborough	a	00 13				00 43				01 25				01 54	02 30					08 51			

London - Stevenage, Cambridge and Peterborough

Sundays
from 28 October

Network Diagram - see first Page of Table 24

Station		FC	FC	FC	GR	FC	FC	FC	FC	FC	FC	FC	FC	FC	FC	GR	FC	FC	FC	FC	FC	FC	FC
London Kings Cross ⊖	d	08 23	08 26	08 53	09 03	09 06	09 15	09 23	09 26	09 53	10 06	10 15	10 23	10 26	10 53	11 03	11 06	11 15	11 23	11 26	11 53	12 06	12 15
Finsbury Park ⊖	d	08 28	08 32	08 58		09 11		09 28	09 32	09 58	10 11		10 28	10 32	10 58		11 11		11 28	11 32	11 58	12 11	
Potters Bar	d					09 21					10 21						11 21					12 21	
Hatfield	d					09 27					10 27						11 27					12 27	
Welwyn Garden City	d					09 31					10 31						11 31					12 31	
Welwyn North	d					09 34					10 34						11 34					12 34	
Knebworth	d					09 38					10 38						11 38					12 38	
Hertford North	d		09 07						10 07					11 07						12 07			
Stevenage	d	08 47	09a20	09 17	09 22	09 42		09 47	10a20	10 17	10 42		10 47	11a20	11 17	11 22	11 42		11 47	12a20	12 17	12 42	
Hitchin	d	08 52		09 22		09 47		09 52		10 22	10 47		10 52		11 22		11 47		11 52		12 22	12 47	
Letchworth Garden City	d			09 26		09 51				10 26	10 51				11 26		11 51				12 26	12 51	
Baldock	d			09 29		09 55				10 29	10 55				11 29		11 55				12 29	12 55	
Ashwell & Morden	d					10 00					11 00						12 00					13 00	
Royston	d			09 37		10 04				10 37	11 04				11 37		12 04				12 37	13 04	
Meldreth	d					10 08					11 08						12 08					13 08	
Shepreth	d					10 11					11 11						12 11					13 11	
Foxton	d					10 14					11 14						12 14					13 14	
Cambridge	a			09 54		10 27	10 00			10 54	11 27	11 00			11 54		12 27	12 00			12 54	13 27	13 00
Arlesey	d	08 57						09 57					10 57						11 57				
Biggleswade	d	09 02						10 02					11 02						12 02				
Sandy	d	09 06						10 06					11 06						12 06				
St Neots	d	09 13						10 13					11 13						12 13				
Huntingdon	d	09 21						10 21					11 21						12 21				
Peterborough	a	09 38			09 52			10 38					11 38			11 52			12 39				

Station		FC	FC	FC	GR	FC	FC	FC	FC	FC	FC	FC	FC	FC	FC	GR	FC	FC	FC	FC	FC	FC
London Kings Cross ⊖	d	12 23	12 26	12 53	13 03	13 06	13 15	13 23	13 26	13 53	14 06	14 15	14 23	14 26	14 53	15 03	15 06	15 15	15 23	15 26	15 53	16 06
Finsbury Park ⊖	d	12 28	12 32	12 58		13 11		13 28	13 32	13 58	14 11		14 28	14 32	14 58		15 11		15 28	15 32	15 58	16 11
Potters Bar	d					13 21					14 21						15 21					16 21
Hatfield	d					13 27					14 27						15 27					16 27
Welwyn Garden City	d					13 31					14 31						15 31					16 31
Welwyn North	d					13 34					14 34						15 34					16 34
Knebworth	d					13 38					14 38						15 38					16 38
Hertford North	d		13 07						14 07					15 07						16 07		
Stevenage	d	12 47	13a20	13 17	13 22	13 42		13 47	14a20	14 17	14 42		14 47	15a20	15 17	15 22	15 42		15 47	16a20	16 17	16 42
Hitchin	d	12 52		13 22		13 47		13 52		14 22	14 47		14 52		15 22		15 47		15 52		16 22	16 47
Letchworth Garden City	d			13 26		13 51				14 26	14 51				15 26		15 51				16 26	16 51
Baldock	d			13 29		13 55				14 29	14 55				15 29		15 55				16 29	16 55
Ashwell & Morden	d					14 00					15 00						16 00					17 00
Royston	d			13 37		14 04				14 37	15 04				15 37		16 04				16 37	17 04
Meldreth	d					14 08					15 08						16 08					17 08
Shepreth	d					14 11					15 11						16 11					17 11
Foxton	d					14 14					15 14						16 14					17 14
Cambridge	a			13 54		14 27	14 00			14 54	15 27	15 00			15 54		16 27	16 00			16 54	17 27
Arlesey	d	12 57						13 57					14 57						15 57			
Biggleswade	d	13 02						14 02					15 02						16 02			
Sandy	d	13 06						14 06					15 06						16 06			
St Neots	d	13 13						14 13					15 13						16 13			
Huntingdon	d	13 21						14 21					15 21						16 21			
Peterborough	a	13 38			13 52			14 38					15 38			15 52			16 38			

Station		FC	FC	FC	GR	FC	FC	FC	FC	FC	FC	GR	FC	FC	FC	FC	FC	FC	FC	GR	FC	FC	FC
London Kings Cross ⊖	d	16 15	16 23	16 26	16 35	16 36	16 53	17 06	17 15	17 23	17 26	17 35	17 36	17 53	18 06	18 10	18 15	18 23	18 26	18 35	18 36	18 53	19 06
Finsbury Park ⊖	d		16 28	16 32		16 41	16 58	17 11		17 28	17 32		17 41	17 58	18 11			18 28	18 32		18 41	18 58	19 11
Potters Bar	d					16 51		17 21					17 51		18 21						18 51		19 21
Hatfield	d					16 57		17 27					17 57		18 27						18 57		19 27
Welwyn Garden City	d					17 01		17 31					18 01		18 31						19 01		19 31
Welwyn North	d					17 04		17 34					18 04		18 34						19 04		19 34
Knebworth	d					17 08		17 38					18 08		18 38						19 08		19 38
Hertford North	d			17 07							18 07								19 07				
Stevenage	d		16 47	17a20	16a54	17 12	17 17	17 42		17 47	18a20	17a54	18 12	18 17	18 42			18 47	19a20	18a54	19 12	19 17	19 42
Hitchin	d		16 52			17 17	17 22	17 47		17 52			18 17	18 22	18 47			18 52			19 17	19 22	→
Letchworth Garden City	d						17 26	17 51						18 26	18 51						19 22	19 26	
Baldock	d						17 29	17 55						18 29	18 55							19 29	
Ashwell & Morden	d							18 00							19 00								
Royston	d						17 37	18 04						18 37	19 04						19a33	19 37	
Meldreth	d							18 08							19 08								
Shepreth	d							18 11							19 11								
Foxton	d							18 14							19 14								
Cambridge	a	17 00					17 54	18 27	18 00					18 54	19 27		19 00					19 54	
Arlesey	d		16 57			17 23				17 57			18 23					18 57					
Biggleswade	d		17 02			17 28				18 02			18 28			18 37		19 02					
Sandy	d		17 06			17 32				18 06			18 32					19 06					
St Neots	d		17 13			17 39				18 13			18 39			18 47		19 13					
Huntingdon	d		17 21			17 47				18 21			18 47			18 54		19 21					
Peterborough	a		17 39			18 06				18 38			19 05			19 12		19 39					

Table 25

London - Stevenage, Cambridge and Peterborough

Network Diagram - see first Page of Table 24

Station		GR	FC	FC		FC	FC	GR	HT	FC	FC	FC	FC	FC		GR	FC	FC	FC	FC	FC	GR	FC	FC
London Kings Cross 15 ⊖	d	19 08	19 15			19 23	19 26	19 35	19 45	19 53	20 06	20 15	20 23	20 26		20 35	20 53	21 06	21 15	21 23	21 26	21 35	21 53	22 06
Finsbury Park ⊖	d					19 28	19 32			19 58	20 11		20 28	20 32			20 58	21 11		21 28	21 32		21 58	22 11
Potters Bar	d										20 21							21 21						22 21
Hatfield	d										20 27							21 27						22 27
Welwyn Garden City 4	d										20 31							21 31						22 31
Welwyn North	d										20 34							21 34						22 34
Knebworth	d										20 38							21 38						22 38
Hertford North	d			←			20 07							21 07							22 07			
Stevenage 4	d	19 28		19 42		19 47	20a20	19 54	20a04	20 17	20 42		20 47	21a20		20 54	21 17	21 42		21 47	22a20	21 55	22 17	22 42
Hitchin 4	d			19 47		19 52				20 22	20 47		20 52				21 22	21 47		21 52			22 22	22 47
Letchworth Garden City	d			19 51						20 26	20 51						21 26	21 51					22 26	22 51
Baldock	d			19 55						20 29	20 55						21 29	21 55					22 29	22 55
Ashwell & Morden	d			20 00							21 00							22 00						23 00
Royston	d			20 04						20 37	21 04						21 37	22 04					22 37	23 04
Meldreth	d			20 08							21 08							22 08						23 08
Shepreth	d			20 11							21 11							22 11						23 11
Foxton	d			20 14							21 14							22 14						23 14
Cambridge	a		20 00	20 27						20 54	21 27	21 00					21 54	22 27	22 00				22 54	23 27
Arlesey	d					19 57							20 57							21 57				
Biggleswade	d					20 02							21 02							22 02				
Sandy	d					20 06							21 06							22 06				
St Neots	d					20 13							21 13							22 13				
Huntingdon	d					20 21							21 21							22 21				
Peterborough 8	a	19 58				20 38		20 24					21 37			21 24				22 37		22 25		

Station		FC	FC	FC	FC	FC	FC	FC	FC	FC		FC
London Kings Cross 15 ⊖	d	22 15	22 23	22 26	22 53	23 06	23 15		23 23	23 26		23 41
Finsbury Park ⊖	d		22 28	22 32	22 58	23 11			23 28	23 32		23 47
Potters Bar	d					23 21						00 08
Hatfield	d					23 27						00 16
Welwyn Garden City 4	d					23 31						00 20
Welwyn North	d					23 34						00 23
Knebworth	d					23 38						00 28
Hertford North	d			23 07						00 07		
Stevenage 4	d		22 47	23a20	23 17	23 42			23 47	00a20		00 31
Hitchin 4	d		22 52		23 22	23 47		←	23 52			00 37
Letchworth Garden City	d				23 26	23 51	23 44	23 51				00a52
Baldock	d				23 29	→		23 54				
Ashwell & Morden	d							23 59				
Royston	d				23 37		23 54	00 04				
Meldreth	d							00 08				
Shepreth	d							00 11				
Foxton	d							00 14				
Cambridge	a	23 00			23 54		00 10	00 29				
Arlesey	d		22 57						23 57			
Biggleswade	d		23 02						00 02			
Sandy	d		23 06						00 06			
St Neots	d		23 13						00 13			
Huntingdon	d		23 21						00 21			
Peterborough 8	a		23 41						00 43			

Table 25

Peterborough, Cambridge and Stevenage - London

Network Diagram - see first Page of Table 24

Miles	Miles	Station		FC MX	GR MO A	FC MX	FC MO B	FC MO C	FC MO A	FC MO A	FC MX	GR MX		FC	FC D	FC E	FC	FC D	FC F	FC G	FC	FC D		FC E	FC
0	—	**Peterborough 8**	d	22p30	22p53				23p01			23p40		03 25			04 10				05 10				05 40
17½	—	Huntingdon	d	22p44					23p15					03 39			04 24				05 24				05 55
24¾	—	St Neots	d	22p51					23p22					03 46			04 32				05 32				06 02
32¼	—	Sandy	d	22p59					23p30								04 39				05 39				
35¼	—	Biggleswade	d	23p02					23p33					03 56			04 43				05 43				
39¼	—	Arlesey	d	23p07					23p38								04 48				05 48				
—	0	**Cambridge**	d							23p15	23p15														
—	7	Foxton	d							23p24	23p25														
—	8	Shepreth	d							23p26	23p27														
—	10	Meldreth	d							23p29	23p30														
—	13	Royston	d							23p34	23p35							05 13	05 16	05 16		05 43		05 46	
—	17	Ashwell & Morden	d							23p38	23p39							05 18	05 21	05 21		05 48		05 51	
—	21¼	Baldock	d							23p43	23p44							05 23	05 26	05 26		05 53		05 56	
—	23¼	Letchworth Garden City	d			23p20				23p46	23p47				04 47	04 50		05 26	05 29	05 29		05 56		05 59	
44½	26	Hitchin 4	d	23p16		23p24			23p46	23p50	23p54			04 08	04 51	04 54	04 57	05 31	05 34	05 34	05 57	06 01		06 04	06 18
48¾	30¼	**Stevenage 4**	d	23p22	23b24	23p29	23p30	23p30	23p51	23p55	23p59	00s21		04 13	04 56	04 59	05 02	05 36	05 39	05 39	06 02	06 06		06 09	06 24
—	—	Hertford North	a			23p42	23p43	00 01						04 23	05 09	05 12									
51¼	33	Knebworth	d	23p25						23p58	00 02						05 06	05 40	05 43	05 43		06 10		06 13	
54¼	36	Welwyn North	d	23p29						00 02	00 06						05 10	05 44	05 47	05 47		06 14		06 17	
56	37¾	Welwyn Garden City 4	d	23p32						00 05	00 09						05 13	05 47	05 50	05 50		06 17		06 20	
58½	40¼	Hatfield	d	23p35						00 08	00 12						05 16	05 51	05 54	05 54		06 21		06 24	
63½	45¼	Potters Bar	d	23p41						00 14	00 18						05 22	05 57	06 00	06 00		06 27		06 30	
73¾	55½	Finsbury Park ⊖	d	23b51		00 17	00 18	01s59	00s13	00 27	00 29			04s47	05 47	05 47	05 39	06 06	06 09	06 09	06 22	06 36		06 39	06 43
76¼	58	**London Kings Cross 15** ⊖	a	00 01	00 01	00 26	00 27	02 14	00 24	00 39	00 40	00 57		05 00	05 55	05 55	05 48	06 19	06 18	06 19	06 29	06 48		06 48	06 50

Station		FC E	FC	FC	FC	FC	FC	FC D		FC E	FC	FC D	FC E	FC	FC	FC	FC D	FC		FC E	FC D	FC E	FC	FC	FC
Peterborough 8	d			05 50			06 17								06 32			06 53							07 06
Huntingdon	d			06 05			06 32				06 40				06 47			07 09							07 24
St Neots	d			06 13			06 40				06 48				06 55			07 17							07 33
Sandy	d			06 21							06 55				07 03										07 41
Biggleswade	d			06 25							06 59				07 07										07 45
Arlesey	d			06 30							07 04				07 12										07 50
Cambridge	d	05 35	05 45		06 15							06 24	06 27	06 45							06 54	06 57	07 15		
Foxton	d	05 44										06 35	06 37								07 04	07 07			
Shepreth	d	05 46										06 38	06 40								07 07	07 10			
Meldreth	d	05 49										06 41	06 43								07 10	07 13			
Royston	d	06 05	05 59		06 29			06 41		06 43		06 48	06 50	06 59			07 10			07 13	07 18	07 21	07 29	07 34	
Ashwell & Morden	d	06 10						06 46		06 48		06 53	06 55				07 15			07 18				07 38	
Baldock	d	06 15						06 51		06 53		06 58	07 00				07 20			07 23				07 43	
Letchworth Garden City	d	06 19	06 09		06 39	06 46		06 55		06 57		07 02	07 04	07 09		07 20	07 24			07 27	07 29	07 32		07 47	
Hitchin 4	d	06 23		06 36	06 43	06 50		06 59		07 01		07 06	07 08		07 18	07 24	07 28			07 31	07 33	07 36		07 51	07 56
Stevenage 4	d	06 29		06 42	06 48	06 55	06 59	07 05		07 07		07 12	07 14		07 23	07 30	07 34	07 36		07 37	07 39	07 42			08 01
Hertford North	a																								→
Knebworth	d	06 33		06 46				07 09		07 11		07 16	07 18								07 43	07 46			
Welwyn North	d	06 37		06 50								07 24	07 24								07 50	07 50		07 59	
Welwyn Garden City 4	d	06 40		06 54		07 07						07 27	07 27			07 42					07 54	07 54			
Hatfield	d	06 44				07 11						07 31	07 31			07 46									
Potters Bar	d	06 49				07 18										07 52									
Finsbury Park ⊖	d	06 58		07 11	07 06	07 35		07 26		07 26		07 47	07 47		07 41	08 10	07 57			07 57	08 09	08 06			
London Kings Cross 15 ⊖	a	07 07	06 38	07 19	07 15	07 43	07 24	07 35		07 35	07 38	07 57	07 57	07 39	07 49	08 17	08 04	08 00		08 04	08 17	08 17	08 07	08 20	

A from 21 May
B from 21 May until 10 September, from 29 October
C from 17 September until 22 October
D from 8 October
E until 5 October
F until 18 May
G from 21 May until 5 October
b Previous night, stops to set down only

Peterborough, Cambridge and Stevenage - London

Network Diagram - see first Page of Table 24

		FC	FC	FC	FC	FC	FC	FC	FC	FC	FC	FC	FC	FC	FC	GR	GR	FC	FC	FC
					A	B														
Peterborough	d	07 14		07 25					07 33	07 46					08 16	08 26				
Huntingdon	d	07 32		07 40					07 51	08 06					08 30					
St Neots	d	07 40		07 47					07 59	08 14					08 38					
Sandy	d								08 06						08 45					
Biggleswade	d			07 55					08 10						08 49					
Arlesey	d								08 15						08 54					
Cambridge	d						07 27	07 45			07 55	08 15							08 25	08 50
Foxton	d						07 37				08 05								08 35	
Shepreth	d						07 40				08 07								08 37	
Meldreth	d						07 43				08 10								08 40	
Royston	d				07 40	07 43	07 51	07 59			08 15	08 29		08 34					08 45	09 04
Ashwell & Morden	d				07 45	07 48					08 19			08 38					08 50	
Baldock	d				07 50	07 53					08 24			08 43					08 55	
Letchworth Garden City	d				07 54	07 57	08 02				08 28	08 39		08 47					08 59	09 14
Hitchin	d		←		08 01	08 01	08 06		08 21		08 32		08 39	08 51	09 00			←	09 05	
Stevenage	d	07 59	08 01		08 07	08 07	08 12		08 27	08 33			08 45	08 56	09 07	08 58	09 00	09 07	09 11	
Hertford North	a														→					
Knebworth	d				08 11	08 11	08 16						08 49						09 14	
Welwyn North	d						08 20						08 53						09 18	
Welwyn Garden City	d						08 24						08 58						09 21	
Hatfield	d												09 02						09 25	
Potters Bar	d																		09 31	
Finsbury Park	d		08 19				08 36		08 47				09 19	09 14				09 26	09 40	
London Kings Cross	a	08 23	08 28	08 30	08 35	08 35	08 47	08 39	08 55	08 58	09 02	09 09	09 28	09 21		09 26	09 29	09 35	09 49	09 44

		FC	FC	FC	FC	FC	GR	FC	FC	FC	FC	FC	FC	GR	FC	FC	FC	FC	FC	FC	FC
Peterborough	d	08 46			09 16				09 26		09 46						10 16	10 46			11 16
Huntingdon	d	09 00			09 30				09 41		10 00						10 34	11 00			11 34
St Neots	d	09 08			09 38				09 49		10 08						10 41	11 08			11 41
Sandy	d	09 15							09 57		10 15						10 49	11 15			11 49
Biggleswade	d	09 19			09 47				10 01		10 19						10 53	11 19			11 53
Arlesey	d	09 24							10 06		10 24						10 58	11 24			11 58
Cambridge	d		08 55	09 20		09 30				09 50		09 55	10 15		10 30	10 50			10 55	11 15	
Foxton	d		09 05									10 05							11 05		
Shepreth	d		09 07									10 07							11 07		
Meldreth	d		09 10									10 10							11 10		
Royston	d		09 15	09 34		09 44				10 04		10 15			10 44	11 04			11 15		
Ashwell & Morden	d		09 20									10 20							11 20		
Baldock	d		09 25			09 52						10 25			10 52				11 25		
Letchworth Garden City	d		09 29	09 44		09 55		09 59		10 14		10 29			10 55	11 14			11 29		
Hitchin	d	09 30	09 34			10 00		10 04	10 12		10 30	10 34			11 00		11 04	11 30	11 34		12 04
Stevenage	d	09 36	09 40		09 58	10 06	10 09	10 10	10 18		10 36	10 40		11 00	11 06		11 10	11 36	11 40		12 10
Hertford North	a																				→
Knebworth	d		09 44					10 14				10 44					11 14		11 44		
Welwyn North	d		09 48					10 18				10 48					11 18		11 48		
Welwyn Garden City	d		09 51					10 21				10 51					11 21		11 51		
Hatfield	d		09 55					10 25				10 55					11 25		11 55		
Potters Bar	d		10 01					10 31				11 01					11 31		12 01		
Finsbury Park	d	09 56	10 10			10 24		10 40			10 54	11 10			11 24		11 40	11 54	12 10		
London Kings Cross	a	10 04	10 19	10 14	10 22	10 32	10 37	10 49	10 44	10 46	11 02	11 19	11 05	11 28	11 32	11 44	11 49	12 02	12 19	12 04	

		GR	GR	FC	FC	FC	FC	FC	FC	FC	GR	GR	FC	FC	FC	FC	FC	FC	FC	GR
Peterborough	d	11 27					11 46			12 16	12 27					12 46			13 16	13 28
Huntingdon	d						12 00			12 34						13 00			13 34	
St Neots	d						12 08			12 41						13 08			13 41	
Sandy	d						12 15			12 49						13 15			13 49	
Biggleswade	d						12 19			12 53						13 19			13 53	
Arlesey	d						12 24			12 58						13 24			13 58	
Cambridge	d			11 30	11 45			11 55	12 15				12 30	12 45			12 55	13 15		
Foxton	d							12 05									13 05			
Shepreth	d							12 07									13 07			
Meldreth	d							12 10									13 10			
Royston	d			11 44				12 15					12 44				13 15			
Ashwell & Morden	d							12 20									13 20			
Baldock	d			11 52				12 25					12 52				13 25			
Letchworth Garden City	d			11 55				12 29					12 55				13 29			
Hitchin	d			12 00		←	12 30	12 34		13 04			13 00		←	13 30	13 34		14 04	
Stevenage	d	11 56	12 00	12 06		12 10	12 36	12 40		13 10	12 57	13 02	13 06		13 10	13 36	13 40		14 10	13 58
Hertford North	a									→									→	
Knebworth	d					12 14		12 44							13 14		13 44			
Welwyn North	d					12 18		12 48							13 18		13 48			
Welwyn Garden City	d					12 21		12 51							13 21		13 51			
Hatfield	d					12 25		12 55							13 25		13 55			
Potters Bar	d					12 31		13 01							13 31		14 01			
Finsbury Park	d			12 24		12 40	12 54	13 10					13 24		13 40	13 54	14 10			
London Kings Cross	a	12 24	12 28	12 32	12 35	12 49	13 03	13 19	13 04		13 26	13 29	13 33	13 35	13 49	14 02	14 19	14 04		14 26

A from 8 October

B until 5 October

Peterborough, Cambridge and Stevenage - London

Network Diagram - see first Page of Table 24

		GR	FC	FC	FC	FC	FC	FC	FC	GR	GR	FC	FC	FC	FC	FC	FC	FC	GR	GR
Peterborough	d					13 46			14 16	14 26					14 46			15 16	15 27	
Huntingdon	d					14 00			14 34						15 00			15 34		
St Neots	d					14 08			14 41						15 08			15 41		
Sandy	d					14 15			14 49						15 15			15 49		
Biggleswade	d					14 19			14 53						15 19			15 53		
Arlesey	d					14 24			14 58						15 24			15 58		
Cambridge	d		13 30	13 45			13 55	14 15				14 30	14 45			14 55	15 15			
Foxton	d						14 05									15 05				
Shepreth	d						14 07									15 07				
Meldreth	d						14 10									15 10				
Royston	d		13 44				14 15					14 44				15 15				
Ashwell & Morden	d						14 20									15 20				
Baldock	d		13 52				14 25					14 52				15 25				
Letchworth Garden City	d		13 55				14 29					14 55				15 29				
Hitchin	d		14 00		←	14 30	14 34		15 04			15 00		←	15 30	15 34		16 04		
Stevenage	d	14 02	14 06		14 10	14 36	14 40		15 10	14 56	15 00	15 06		15 10	15 36	15 40		16 10	15 57	16 02
Hertford North	a								→									→		
Knebworth	d				14 14		14 44							15 14		15 44				
Welwyn North	d				14 18		14 48							15 18		15 48				
Welwyn Garden City	d				14 21		14 51							15 21		15 51				
Hatfield	d				14 25		14 55							15 25		15 55				
Potters Bar	d				14 31		15 01							15 31		16 01				
Finsbury Park	d		14 24		14 40	14 54	15 10					15 24		15 40	15 54	16 10				
London Kings Cross	a	14 29	14 32	14 34	14 49	15 03	15 19	15 05		15 25	15 28	15 32	15 34	15 49	16 03	16 19	16 06		16 25	16 28

		FC	FC	FC	FC	FC	FC	FC	GR	GR	FC	FC	FC	FC	FC	FC	FC	GR	GR	FC	FC
Peterborough	d				15 46			16 16	16 25					16 46			17 16	17 28			
Huntingdon	d				16 00			16 34						17 00			17 34				
St Neots	d				16 08			16 41						17 08			17 41				
Sandy	d				16 15			16 49						17 15			17 49				
Biggleswade	d				16 19			16 53						17 19			17 53				
Arlesey	d				16 24			16 58						17 24			17 58				
Cambridge	d	15 30	15 45			15 55	16 15				16 25	16 45			16 55	17 15				17 25	17 45
Foxton	d					16 05					16 34				17 05					17 34	
Shepreth	d					16 07					16 36				17 07					17 36	
Meldreth	d					16 10					16 39				17 10					17 39	
Royston	d	15 44				16 15					16 44				17 15					17 44	
Ashwell & Morden	d					16 20					16 48				17 20					17 48	
Baldock	d	15 52				16 25					16 53				17 25					17 53	
Letchworth Garden City	d	15 55				16 29					16 56				17 29					17 56	
Hitchin	d	16 00		←	16 30	16 34		17 04			17 00		←	17 30	17 34		18 04			18 00	
Stevenage	d	16 06		16 10	16 36	16 40		17 10	16 54	17 00	17 06		17 10	17 36	17 40		18 10	17 58	18 03	18 06	
Hertford North	a							→									→				
Knebworth	d			16 14		16 44							17 14		17 44						
Welwyn North	d			16 18		16 48							17 18		17 48						
Welwyn Garden City	d			16 21		16 51							17 21		17 51						
Hatfield	d			16 25		16 55							17 25		17 55						
Potters Bar	d			16 31		17 01							17 31		18 01						
Finsbury Park	d	16 24		16 40	16 54	17 10					17 24		17 40	17 54	18 10					18 24	
London Kings Cross	a	16 32	16 34	16 49	17 01	17 19	17 04		17 22	17 29	17 32	17 35	17 49	18 02	18 19	18 05		18 27	18 30	18 32	18 38

		FC	FC	FC	FC	FC	FC	GR	GR	FC	FC	FC	FC	FC	FC	FC	GR	GR	FC	FC
Peterborough	d					17 55	18 21	18 26					18 45			19 16	19 27			
Huntingdon	d		18 04			18 14	18 41						19 00			19 34				
St Neots	d		18 11			18 21	18 48						19 08			19 41				
Sandy	d					18 29	18 56						19 15			19 49				
Biggleswade	d					18 32	19 00						19 19			19 53				
Arlesey	d					18 37	19 05						19 24			19 58				
Cambridge	d			17 55	18 15					18 25	18 45			18 55	19 15				19 25	19 45
Foxton	d			18 05						18 34				19 05					19 34	
Shepreth	d			18 07						18 36				19 07					19 36	
Meldreth	d			18 10						18 39				19 10					19 39	
Royston	d			18 15						18 46				19 15					19 44	
Ashwell & Morden	d			18 20						18 51				19 20					19 48	
Baldock	d			18 25						18 56				19 25					19 53	
Letchworth Garden City	d			18 29						18 59				19 29					19 56	
Hitchin	d	←	18 29	18 34		18 43	19 11			19 03		←	19 30	19 34		20 04			20 00	
Stevenage	d	18 10	18 35	18 40		18 49	19 17	18 56	19 07	19 09		19 17	19 36	19 40		20 10	19 56	20 01	20 06	
Hertford North	a						→									→				
Knebworth	d	18 14		18 44								19 20		19 44						
Welwyn North	d	18 18		18 48								19 24		19 48						
Welwyn Garden City	d	18 28		18 51								19 28		19 51						
Hatfield	d	18 32		18 55								19 32		19 55						
Potters Bar	d	18 38		19 01								19 38		20 01						
Finsbury Park	d	18 47	18 54	19 10		19 07				19 29		19 47	19 54	20 10					20 25	
London Kings Cross	a	18 56	19 02	19 22	19 08	19 14		19 25	19 35	19 36	19 38	19 56	20 00	20 19	20 11		20 26	20 29	20 33	20 34

Table 25

Mondays to Fridays

Peterborough, Cambridge and Stevenage - London

Network Diagram - see first Page of Table 24

		FC	FC	GR	GR	FC	FC	GR	FC	FC	FC	GR	FC	FC	FC	GR	FC	FC	FC	FC	FC
Peterborough	d		19 46	19 50							20 16	20 46			20 57	21 16			21 30		
Huntingdon	d		20 00								20 34				21 12				21 44		
St Neots	d		20 08								20 41				21 19				21 51		
Sandy	d		20 15								20 49				21 27				21 59		
Biggleswade	d		20 19								20 53				21 30				22 02		
Arlesey	d		20 24								20 58				21 35				22 07		
Cambridge	d						19 55		20 30	20 45				20 55			21 30	21 45			21 55
Foxton	d						20 05							21 05							22 05
Shepreth	d						20 07							21 07							22 07
Meldreth	d						20 10							21 10							22 10
Royston	d						20 15		20 44					21 15			21 44				22 15
Ashwell & Morden	d						20 20							21 20							22 20
Baldock	d						20 25		20 52					21 25			21 52				22 25
Letchworth Garden City	d						20 29		20 55				21 20	21 29			21 55			22 20	22 29
Hitchin	d	←	20 30			←	20 34		21 00		21 04		21 24	21 34	21 41		22 00		22 13	22 24	22 34
Stevenage	d	20 10	20 36	20 21	20 23	20 36	20 40	20 59	21 06		21 10	21 15	21 29	21 40	21 47	21 48	22 06		22 18	22 29	22 40
Hertford North	a		→										21 42							22 42	
Knebworth	d	20 14					20 44				21 14			21 44					22 22		22 44
Welwyn North	d	20 18					20 48				21 18			21 48					22 25		22 48
Welwyn Garden City	d	20 21					20 51				21 21			21 51					22 28		22 51
Hatfield	d	20 25					20 55				21 25			21 55					22 32		22 55
Potters Bar	d	20 31					21 01				21 31			22 01					22 37		23 01
Finsbury Park ⊖	d	20 40				20 54	21 10		21 24		21 40		22 17	22 10	22 05		22 24		22 46	23 17	23 10
London Kings Cross ⊖	a	20 49		20 48	20 55	21 02	21 19	21 28	21 32	21 34	21 49	21 45	22 25	22 19	22 11	22 20	22 32	22 34	22 52	23 25	23 20

		GR	FC	FC	GR	FC	FC	FC	GR
Peterborough	d	22 16		22 30	22 35				23 40
Huntingdon	d			22 44					
St Neots	d			22 51					
Sandy	d			22 59					
Biggleswade	d			23 02					
Arlesey	d			23 07					
Cambridge	d		22 30					23 15	
Foxton	d							23 25	
Shepreth	d							23 27	
Meldreth	d							23 30	
Royston	d		22 44					23 35	
Ashwell & Morden	d							23 39	
Baldock	d		22 52					23 44	
Letchworth Garden City	d		22 55				23 20	23 47	
Hitchin	d		23 00	23 16		←	23 24	23 54	
Stevenage	d	22 47	23 06	23 22	23 05	23 22	23 29	23 59	00s21
Hertford North	a			→			23 42		
Knebworth	d					23 25		00 02	
Welwyn North	d					23 29		00 06	
Welwyn Garden City	d					23 32		00 09	
Hatfield	d					23 35		00 12	
Potters Bar	d					23 41		00 18	
Finsbury Park ⊖	d		23 24			23s51	00 17	00 29	
London Kings Cross ⊖	a	23 13	23 32		23 36	00 01	00 26	00 40	00 57

Saturdays

		FC	FC	FC	GR	FC	FC	FC	FC	FC	FC	FC	FC	FC	FC	FC	FC	FC	GR	FC	FC	FC	FC
Peterborough	d	22p30			23p40	03 25		04 10				05 16		05 46				06 16	06 37			06 46	
Huntingdon	d	22p44				03 39		04 24				05 34		06 00				06 34				07 00	
St Neots	d	22p51				03 46		04 32				05 41		06 08				06 41				07 08	
Sandy	d	22p59						04 39				05 49		06 15				06 49				07 15	
Biggleswade	d	23p02				03 56		04 43				05 53		06 19				06 53				07 19	
Arlesey	d	23p07						04 48				05 58		06 24				06 58				07 24	
Cambridge	d			23p15							05 45				05 55	06 30	06 45						06 55
Foxton	d			23p25											06 05								07 05
Shepreth	d			23p27											06 07								07 07
Meldreth	d			23p30											06 10								07 10
Royston	d			23p35						05 15	06 00				06 15	06 44							07 15
Ashwell & Morden	d			23p39						05 20					06 20								07 20
Baldock	d			23p44						05 25					06 25	06 52							07 25
Letchworth Garden City	d		23p20	23p47			04 50		05 20	05 29	06 09		06 20		06 29	06 55							07 29
Hitchin	d	23p16	23p24	23p54		04 08	04 54	04 57	05 24	05 34		06 04	06 24	06 30	06 34	07 00		07 04		←		07 30	07 34
Stevenage	d	23p22	23p29	23p59	00s21	04 13	04 59	05 02	05 30	05 40		06 10	06 30	06 36	06 40	07 06		07 10	07 06	07 10	07 30	07 36	07 40
Hertford North	a		23p42			04 23	05 12		05 43				06 43					→			07 43		
Knebworth	d	23p25		00 02				05 06		05 44		06 14			06 44					07 14			07 44
Welwyn North	d	23p29		00 06				05 10		05 48		06 18			06 48					07 18			07 48
Welwyn Garden City	d	23p32		00 09				05 13		05 51		06 21			06 51					07 21			07 51
Hatfield	d	23p35		00 12				05 16		05 55		06 25			06 55					07 25			07 55
Potters Bar	d	23p41		00 18				05 22		06 01		06 31			07 01					07 31			08 01
Finsbury Park ⊖	d	23b51	00 17	00 29		04s50	05 47	05 39	06 18	06 10		06 40	07 18	06 54	07 10	07 24				07 40	08 18	07 54	08 10
London Kings Cross ⊖	a	00 01	00 26	00 40	00 57	05 00	05 55	05 48	06 25	06 20	06 39	06 47	07 25	07 01	07 19	07 31	07 36		07 36	07 49	08 25	08 01	08 19

b Previous night, stops to set down only

Table 25

Saturdays

Peterborough, Cambridge and Stevenage - London

Network Diagram - see first Page of Table 24

		FC	FC	FC	GR	FC	FC	FC	FC	FC	FC	FC	GR	FC	FC	FC	FC	FC	FC	FC	FC
Peterborough	d			07 18	07 37			07 46			08 09	08 18	08 32					08 46			09 09
Huntingdon	d			07 34				08 00			08 24	08 34						09 00			09 23
St Neots	d			07 41				08 08			08 33	08 41						09 08			09 31
Sandy	d			07 49				08 15				08 49						09 15			
Biggleswade	d			07 53				08 19			08 42	08 53						09 19			09 39
Arlesey	d			07 58				08 24				08 58						09 24			
Cambridge	d	07 30	07 45						07 55	08 15				08 30	08 45				08 55	09 15	
Foxton	d								08 05										09 05		
Shepreth	d								08 07										09 07		
Meldreth	d								08 10										09 10		
Royston	d	07 44							08 15					08 44					09 15		
Ashwell & Morden	d								08 20										09 20		
Baldock	d	07 52							08 25					08 52					09 25		
Letchworth Garden City	d	07 55							08 29					08 55					09 29		
Hitchin	d	08 00		08 04		←		08 30	08 34			09 04		09 00		←		09 30	09 34		
Stevenage	d	08 06		08 10	08 06	08 10	08 30	08 36	08 40			09 10	09 01	09 06		09 10	09 30	09 36	09 40		
Hertford North	a			→			08 43					→					09 43				
Knebworth	d					08 14			08 44							09 14			09 44		
Welwyn North	d					08 18			08 48							09 18			09 48		
Welwyn Garden City	d					08 21			08 51							09 21			09 51		
Hatfield	d					08 25			08 55							09 25			09 55		
Potters Bar	d					08 31			09 01							09 31			10 01		
Finsbury Park ⊖	d	08 24				08 40	09 18	08 54	09 10					09 24		09 40	10 18	09 54	10 10		
London Kings Cross ⊖	a	08 31	08 36		08 36	08 49	09 25	09 01	09 20	09 04	09 13		09 29	09 31	09 39	09 49	10 25	10 01	10 20	10 04	10 11

		FC	FC	FC	FC	FC	FC	FC	FC	FC	GR	FC	GR	FC	FC	FC	FC	FC	FC
Peterborough	d			09 16		09 46			10 10	10 18	10 27		10 36				10 46		
Huntingdon	d			09 34		10 00			10 25	10 34							11 00		
St Neots	d			09 41		10 08			10 33	10 41							11 08		
Sandy	d			09 49		10 15				10 49							11 15		
Biggleswade	d			09 53		10 19			10 41	10 53							11 19		
Arlesey	d			09 58		10 24				10 58							11 24		
Cambridge	d	09 30	09 45				09 55	10 15				10 30		10 45				10 55	11 15
Foxton	d						10 05											11 05	
Shepreth	d						10 07											11 07	
Meldreth	d						10 10											11 10	
Royston	d	09 44					10 15					10 44						11 15	
Ashwell & Morden	d						10 20											11 20	
Baldock	d	09 52					10 25					10 52						11 25	
Letchworth Garden City	d	09 55					10 29					10 55						11 29	
Hitchin	d	10 00		10 04		10 30	10 34			11 04		11 00			←		11 30	11 34	
Stevenage	d	10 06		10 10	10 30	10 36	10 40			11 10	10 59	11 06	11 07		11 10	11 30	11 36	11 40	
Hertford North	a				10 43					→						11 43			
Knebworth	d			10 14			10 44								11 14			11 44	
Welwyn North	d			10 18			10 48								11 18			11 48	
Welwyn Garden City	d			10 21			10 51								11 21			11 51	
Hatfield	d			10 25			10 55								11 25			11 55	
Potters Bar	d			10 31			11 01								11 31			12 01	
Finsbury Park ⊖	d	10 24		10 40	11 18	10 54	11 10					11 24			11 40	12 18	11 54	12 10	
London Kings Cross ⊖	a	10 31	10 35	10 49	11 25	11 01	11 20	11 04	11 14		11 27	11 31	11 37	11 37	11 49	12 25	12 01	12 19	12 04

		FC	FC	FC	FC	FC	FC	FC	FC	GR	FC	FC	FC	FC	FC	FC	FC	FC	FC	FC	FC
Peterborough	d			11 18		11 46			12 19	12 33					12 46					13 16	
Huntingdon	d			11 34		12 00			12 34						13 00					13 34	
St Neots	d			11 41		12 08			12 41						13 08					13 41	
Sandy	d			11 49		12 15			12 49						13 15					13 49	
Biggleswade	d			11 53		12 19			12 53						13 19					13 53	
Arlesey	d			11 58		12 24			12 58						13 24					13 58	
Cambridge	d	11 30	11 45				11 55	12 15			12 30	12 45				12 55	13 15	13 30	13 45		
Foxton	d						12 05									13 05					
Shepreth	d						12 07									13 07					
Meldreth	d						12 10									13 10					
Royston	d	11 44					12 15				12 44					13 15		13 44			
Ashwell & Morden	d						12 20									13 20					
Baldock	d	11 52					12 25				12 52					13 25		13 52			
Letchworth Garden City	d	11 55					12 29				12 55					13 29		13 55			
Hitchin	d	12 00		12 04		12 30	12 34		13 04		13 00		←		13 30	13 34		14 00		14 04	
Stevenage	d	12 06		12 10	12 30	12 36	12 40		13 10	13 02	13 06		13 10	13 30	13 36	13 40		14 06		14 10	14 30
Hertford North	a				12 43				→					13 43							14 43
Knebworth	d			12 14			12 44						13 14			13 44				14 14	
Welwyn North	d			12 18			12 48						13 18			13 48				14 18	
Welwyn Garden City	d			12 21			12 51						13 21			13 51				14 21	
Hatfield	d			12 25			12 55						13 25			13 55				14 25	
Potters Bar	d			12 31			13 01						13 31			14 01				14 31	
Finsbury Park ⊖	d	12 24		12 40	13 18	12 54	13 10				13 24		13 40	14 18	13 54	14 10		14 24		14 40	15 18
London Kings Cross ⊖	a	12 32	12 35	12 49	13 25	13 01	13 19	13 04		13 30	13 31	13 35	13 49	14 25	14 01	14 19	14 04	14 31	14 35	14 49	15 25

Peterborough, Cambridge and Stevenage - London

Network Diagram - see first Page of Table 24

		FC ■	FC ■	FC ■	FC ■	GR ■	FC ■	FC ■	FC ■	FC	FC ■	FC ■	FC ■	FC ■	FC ■	FC ■	FC	FC ■	FC ■	FC ■
Peterborough ■	d	13 46			14 16	14 32					14 46					15 19		15 46		
Huntingdon	d	14 00			14 34						15 00					15 34		16 00		
St Neots	d	14 08			14 41						15 08					15 41		16 08		
Sandy	d	14 15			14 49						15 15					15 49		16 15		
Biggleswade	d	14 19			14 53						15 19					15 53		16 19		
Arlesey	d	14 24			14 58						15 24					15 58		16 24		
Cambridge	d		13 55	14 15			14 30	14 45				14 55	15 15	15 30	15 45				15 55	16 15
Foxton	d		14 05									15 05							16 05	
Shepreth	d		14 07									15 07							16 07	
Meldreth	d		14 10									15 10							16 10	
Royston	d		14 15				14 44					15 15		15 44					16 15	
Ashwell & Morden	d		14 20									15 20							16 20	
Baldock	d		14 25				14 52					15 25		15 52					16 25	
Letchworth Garden City	d		14 29				14 55					15 29		15 55					16 29	
Hitchin ■	d	14 30	14 34		15 04		15 00		←		15 30	15 34		16 00		16 04		16 30	16 34	
Stevenage ■	d	14 36	14 40		15 10	15 01	15 06		15 10	15 30	15 36	15 40		16 06		16 10	16 30	16 36	16 40	
Hertford North	a				→					15 43							16 43			
Knebworth	d		14 44						15 14			15 44				16 14			16 44	
Welwyn North	d		14 48						15 18			15 48				16 18			16 48	
Welwyn Garden City ■	d		14 51						15 21			15 51				16 21			16 51	
Hatfield	d		14 55						15 25			15 55				16 25			16 55	
Potters Bar	d		15 01						15 31			16 01				16 31			17 01	
Finsbury Park ⊖	d	14 54	15 10				15 24		15 40	16 18	15 54	16 10		16 24		16 40	17 18	16 54	17 10	
London Kings Cross ■ ⊖	a	15 01	15 19	15 04		15 30	15 31	15 35	15 49	16 25	16 01	16 19	16 04	16 31	16 35	16 49	17 25	17 01	17 19	17 04

		FC ■	GR ■	FC ■	FC ■	FC ■	FC	FC ■	FC ■	FC ■	FC ■	FC ■	FC ■	FC	FC ■	FC ■	FC ■	FC ■	GR ■	FC ■
Peterborough ■	d	16 16	16 33					16 46					17 18		17 46			18 16	18 32	
Huntingdon	d	16 34						17 00					17 34		18 00			18 34		
St Neots	d	16 41						17 08					17 41		18 08			18 41		
Sandy	d	16 49						17 15					17 49		18 15			18 49		
Biggleswade	d	16 53						17 19					17 53		18 19			18 53		
Arlesey	d	16 58						17 24					17 58		18 24			18 58		
Cambridge	d			16 30	16 45				16 55	17 15	17 30	17 45				17 55	18 15			18 30
Foxton	d								17 05							18 05				
Shepreth	d								17 07							18 07				
Meldreth	d								17 10							18 10				
Royston	d			16 44					17 15		17 44					18 15				18 44
Ashwell & Morden	d								17 20							18 20				
Baldock	d			16 52					17 25		17 52					18 25				18 52
Letchworth Garden City	d			16 55					17 29		17 55					18 29				18 55
Hitchin ■	d	17 04		17 00		←		17 30	17 34		18 00		18 04		18 30	18 34		19 04		19 00
Stevenage ■	d	17 10	17 03	17 06		17 10	17 30	17 36	17 40		18 06		18 10	18 30	18 36	18 40		19 10	19 01	19 06
Hertford North	a	→					17 43							18 43				→		
Knebworth	d					17 14			17 44				18 14			18 44				
Welwyn North	d					17 18			17 48				18 18			18 48				
Welwyn Garden City ■	d					17 21			17 51				18 21			18 51				
Hatfield	d					17 25			17 55				18 25			18 55				
Potters Bar	d					17 31			18 01				18 31			19 01				
Finsbury Park ⊖	d			17 24		17 40	18 18	17 54	18 10		18 24		18 40	19 18	18 54	19 10				19 24
London Kings Cross ■ ⊖	a		17 32	17 32	17 35	17 49	18 25	18 01	18 19	18 04	18 31	18 35	18 49	19 25	19 01	19 19	19 05		19 29	19 31

		FC ■	FC ■	FC	FC ■	FC ■	FC ■	FC ■	FC ■	FC ■	FC	FC ■	FC ■	FC ■	FC ■	GR ■	FC ■	FC ■	FC ■	FC	FC ■
Peterborough ■	d				18 46					19 16		19 46			20 16	20 33					20 46
Huntingdon	d				19 00					19 34		20 00			20 34						21 00
St Neots	d				19 08					19 41		20 08			20 41						21 08
Sandy	d				19 15					19 49		20 15			20 49						21 15
Biggleswade	d				19 19					19 53		20 19			20 53						21 19
Arlesey	d				19 24					19 58		20 24			20 58						21 24
Cambridge	d	18 45				18 55	19 15	19 30	19 45				19 55	20 15			20 30	20 45			
Foxton	d					19 05							20 05								
Shepreth	d					19 07							20 07								
Meldreth	d					19 10							20 10								
Royston	d					19 15		19 44					20 15				20 44				
Ashwell & Morden	d					19 20							20 20								
Baldock	d					19 25		19 52					20 25				20 52				
Letchworth Garden City	d					19 29		19 55					20 29				20 55				
Hitchin ■	d		←		19 30	19 34		20 00		20 04		20 30	20 34		21 04		21 00		←		21 30
Stevenage ■	d		19 10	19 30	19 36	19 40		20 06		20 10	20 30	20 36	20 40		21 10	21 02	21 06		21 10	21 30	21 36
Hertford North	a			19 43							20 43				→					21 43	
Knebworth	d		19 14			19 44				20 14			20 44						21 14		
Welwyn North	d		19 18			19 48				20 18			20 48						21 18		
Welwyn Garden City ■	d		19 21			19 51				20 21			20 51						21 21		
Hatfield	d		19 25			19 55				20 25			20 55						21 25		
Potters Bar	d		19 31			20 01				20 31			21 01						21 31		
Finsbury Park ⊖	d		19 40	20 18	19 54	20 10		20 24		20 40	21 18	20 54	21 10				21 24		21 40	22 18	21 54
London Kings Cross ■ ⊖	a	19 35	19 49	20 25	20 01	20 19	20 05	20 30	20 33	20 49	21 25	21 01	21 19	21 04		21 30	21 32	21 34	21 49	22 25	22 01

Peterborough, Cambridge and Stevenage - London

Network Diagram - see first Page of Table 24

		FC ■	FC ■	GR ■	FC ■	FC ■	FC ■	FC	FC ■	FC ■	FC ■ A	FC ■ B	FC ■	FC	FC ■	FC ■ C
Peterborough ■	d		21 16	21 21					21 46				22 16		22 46	
Huntingdon	d		21 34						22 00				22 34		23 00	
St Neots	d		21 41						22 08				22 41		23 08	
Sandy	d		21 49						22 15				22 49		23 15	
Biggleswade	d		21 53						22 19				22 53		23 19	
Arlesey	d		21 58						22 24				22 58		23 24	
Cambridge	d	20 55			21 30	21 45				21 55	22 30	22 30				23 15
Foxton	d	21 05								22 05						23 24
Shepreth	d	21 07								22 07						23 27
Meldreth	d	21 10								22 10						23 30
Royston	d	21 15			21 44					22 15	22 44	22 44				23 34
Ashwell & Morden	d	21 20								22 20						23 39
Baldock	d	21 25			21 52					22 25	22 52	22 52				23 43
Letchworth Garden City	d	21 29			21 55					22 29	22 55	22 55				23 46
Hitchin ■	d	21 34	22 04		22 00		←		22 30	22 34	23 00	23 00	23 04		23 30	23 50
Stevenage ■	d	21 40	22 10	21 53	22 06		22 10	22 30	22 36	22 40	23 06	23 06	23 10	23 30	23 36	23 55
Hertford North	a		→					22 43						23 43		
Knebworth	d	21 44					22 14			22 44			23 14			23 59
Welwyn North	d	21 48					22 18			22 48			23 18			00 02
Welwyn Garden City ■	d	21 51					22 21			22 51			23 21			00 06
Hatfield	d	21 55					22 25			22 55			23 25			00 10
Potters Bar	d	22 01					22 31			23 01			23 31			00 15
Finsbury Park ⊖	d	22 10			22 24		22 40	23 18	22 54	23 10	23 24	23 24	23 40	00 18	00 04	00s32
London Kings Cross ■ ⊖	a	22 19		22 24	22 31	22 34	22 49	23 25	23 01	23 19	23 31	23 32	23 50	00 26	00 12	00 40

Sundays

until 9 September

		FC	FC ■	FC ■	FC ■	FC ■	FC	FC ■	FC ■	FC	FC ■	FC ■	FC ■	FC	FC ■	GR ■	FC ■	FC ■	FC ■	FC ■	FC ■	FC	FC ■
Peterborough ■	d		22p46		05 46			06 46			07 46				08 46	09 09			09 15				09 46
Huntingdon	d		23p00		06 00			07 00			08 00				09 00				09 30				10 00
St Neots	d		23p08		06 08			07 08			08 08				09 08				09 37				10 08
Sandy	d		23p15		06 15			07 15			08 15				09 15								10 15
Biggleswade	d		23p19		06 19			07 19			08 19				09 19				09 45				10 19
Arlesey	d		23p24		06 24			07 24			08 24				09 24								10 24
Cambridge	d			23p15		06 28			07 28			07 55	08 28				08 55	09 20		09 28			
Foxton	d			23p24								08 05					09 05						
Shepreth	d			23p27								08 07					09 07						
Meldreth	d			23p30								08 10					09 10						
Royston	d			23p34		06 43			07 43			08 15	08 42				09 15			09 42			
Ashwell & Morden	d			23p39								08 20					09 20						
Baldock	d			23p43		06 51			07 51			08 25	08 50				09 25			09 50			
Letchworth Garden City	d			23p46		06 54			07 54			08 29	08 53				09 29			09 53	09 59		
Hitchin ■	d		23p30	23p50	06 33	06 58		07 33	07 59		08 30	08 34	08 57		09 30		09 34			09 57	10 04		10 30
Stevenage ■	d	23p30	23p36	23p55	06 39	07 04	07 30	07 39	08 04	08 30	08 36	08 39	09 03	09 30	09 36	09 38	09 39			10 03	10 09	10 30	10 36
Hertford North	a	23p43					07 43			08 43				09 43								10 43	
Knebworth	d			23p59	06 43			07 43				08 43					09 43				10 13		
Welwyn North	d			00 02	06 47			07 47				08 47					09 47				10 17		
Welwyn Garden City ■	d			00 06	06 51			07 51				08 51					09 51				10 21		
Hatfield	d			00 10	06 54			07 54				08 54					09 54				10 24		
Potters Bar	d			00 15	07 00			08 00				09 00					10 00				10 30		
Finsbury Park ⊖	d	00 18	00 04	00s32	07 10	07 32	08 18	08 10	08 22	09 18	08 54	09 10	09 21	10 18	09 54		10 10			10 21	10 40	11 18	10 54
London Kings Cross ■ ⊖	a	00 26	00 12	00 40	07 20	07 39	08 26	08 20	08 30	09 25	09 01	09 19	09 28	10 25	10 01	10 07	10 19	10 09	10 15	10 28	10 49	11 25	11 01

A until 21 July, from 18 August, not 1 September, 8 September

B 28 July, 4 August, 11 August, 1 September, 8 September

C until 8 September, from 27 October

Table 25

Sundays
until 9 September

Peterborough, Cambridge and Stevenage - London

Network Diagram - see first Page of Table 24

		FC	FC	FC	FC	GR	FC	FC	FC	FC	FC	FC	FC	FC	FC	FC	FC	GR	FC	FC	FC
		1 A	1	1	1	R 1		1	1	1	1	1		1	1	1	1	R 1		1	1
Peterborough	d			10 15		10 33		10 46			11 20			11 46				12 35		12 46	
Huntingdon	d			10 30				11 00			11 35			12 00						13 00	
St Neots	d			10 37				11 08			11 42			12 08						13 08	
Sandy	d							11 15						12 15						13 15	
Biggleswade	d			10 45				11 19			11 50			12 19						13 19	
Arlesey	d							11 24						12 24						13 24	
Cambridge	d	09 55	10 20		10 28				10 55	11 20		11 28			11 55	12 20	12 28				12 55
Foxton	d	10 05							11 05						12 05						13 05
Shepreth	d	10 07							11 07						12 07						13 07
Meldreth	d	10 10							11 10						12 10						13 10
Royston	d	10 15			10 42				11 15			11 42			12 15		12 42				13 15
Ashwell & Morden	d	10 20							11 20						12 20						13 20
Baldock	d	10 25			10 50				11 25			11 50			12 25		12 50				13 25
Letchworth Garden City	d	10 29			10 53				11 29			11 53			12 29		12 53				13 29
Hitchin	d	10 34			10 57			11 30	11 34			11 57		12 30	12 34		12 57			13 30	13 34
Stevenage	d	10 39			11 03	11 04	11 30	11 36	11 39			12 03	12 30	12 36	12 39		13 03	13 05	13 30	13 36	13 39
Hertford North	a						11 43						12 43						13 43		
Knebworth	d	10 43							11 43						12 43						13 43
Welwyn North	d	10 47							11 47						12 47						13 47
Welwyn Garden City	d	10 51							11 51						12 51						13 51
Hatfield	d	10 54							11 54						12 54						13 54
Potters Bar	d	11 00							12 00						13 00						14 00
Finsbury Park	d	11 10			11 21		12 18	11 54	12 10			12 21	13 18	12 54	13 10		13 21		14 18	13 54	14 10
London Kings Cross	a	11 19	11 08	11 15	11 28	11 33	12 25	12 01	12 19	12 08	12 20	12 28	13 25	13 01	13 19	13 08	13 28	13 34	14 25	14 01	14 19

		FC	FC	FC	FC	FC	FC	FC	GR	FC	FC	FC	FC	FC	FC	FC	FC	FC
		1	1		1	1	1	1	R 1		1	1	1	1		1	1	1
Peterborough	d				13 46				14 33		14 46					15 46		
Huntingdon	d				14 00						15 00					16 00		
St Neots	d				14 08						15 08					16 08		
Sandy	d				14 15						15 15					16 15		
Biggleswade	d				14 19						15 19					16 19		
Arlesey	d				14 24						15 24					16 24		
Cambridge	d	13 20	13 28			13 55	14 20	14 28				14 55	15 20	15 28			15 55	16 20
Foxton	d					14 05						15 05					16 05	
Shepreth	d					14 07						15 07					16 07	
Meldreth	d					14 10						15 10					16 10	
Royston	d		13 42			14 15		14 42				15 15		15 42			16 15	
Ashwell & Morden	d					14 20						15 20					16 20	
Baldock	d		13 50			14 25		14 50				15 25		15 50			16 25	
Letchworth Garden City	d		13 53			14 29		14 53				15 29		15 53			16 29	
Hitchin	d		13 57		14 30	14 34		14 57			15 30	15 34		15 57		16 30	16 34	
Stevenage	d		14 03	14 30	14 36	14 39		15 03	15 06	15 30	15 36	15 39		16 03	16 30	16 36	16 39	
Hertford North	a			14 43						15 43					16 43			
Knebworth	d					14 43						15 43					16 43	
Welwyn North	d					14 47						15 47					16 47	
Welwyn Garden City	d					14 51						15 51					16 51	
Hatfield	d					14 54						15 54					16 54	
Potters Bar	d					15 00						16 00					17 00	
Finsbury Park	d		14 21	15 18	14 54	15 10		15 21		16 18	15 54	16 10		16 21	17 18	16 54	17 10	
London Kings Cross	a	14 08	14 28	15 25	15 01	15 19	15 08	15 28	15 33	16 25	16 01	16 19	16 08	16 28	17 25	17 01	17 19	17 08

		FC	GR	FC	FC	FC	FC	FC	GR	FC	FC	FC	FC	FC	FC	GR	FC	FC	FC
		1	R 1		1	1	1	1	R 1		1	1	1	1	1	R 1		1	1
Peterborough	d		16 33		16 46						17 46							18 46	
Huntingdon	d				17 00						18 00							19 00	
St Neots	d				17 08						18 08							19 08	
Sandy	d				17 15						18 15							19 15	
Biggleswade	d				17 19						18 19							19 19	
Arlesey	d				17 24						18 24							19 24	
Cambridge	d	16 28				16 55	17 20	17 28				17 55	18 20	18 28	18 45				18 55
Foxton	d					17 05						18 05							19 05
Shepreth	d					17 07						18 07							19 07
Meldreth	d					17 10						18 10							19 10
Royston	d	16 42				17 15		17 42				18 15		18 42					19 15
Ashwell & Morden	d					17 20						18 20							19 20
Baldock	d	16 50				17 25		17 50				18 25		18 50					19 25
Letchworth Garden City	d	16 53				17 29		17 53				18 29		18 53					19 29
Hitchin	d	16 57			17 30	17 34		17 57			18 30	18 34		18 57				19 30	19 34
Stevenage	d	17 03	17 05	17 30	17 36	17 39		18 03	18 04	18 30	18 36	18 39		19 03		19 07	19 30	19 36	19 39
Hertford North	a			17 43						18 43							19 43		
Knebworth	d					17 43						18 43							19 43
Welwyn North	d					17 47						18 47							19 47
Welwyn Garden City	d					17 51						18 51							19 51
Hatfield	d					17 54						18 54							19 54
Potters Bar	d					18 00						19 00							20 00
Finsbury Park	d	17 21		18 18	17 54	18 10		18 21		19 18	18 54	19 10		19 21			20 18	19 54	20 10
London Kings Cross	a	17 28	17 33	18 25	18 01	18 19	18 08	18 30	18 34	19 25	19 01	19 19	19 11	19 30	19 36	19 36	20 25	20 01	20 19

A until 22 July, 19 August, 26 August

Table 25

Sundays
until 9 September

Peterborough, Cambridge and Stevenage - London

Network Diagram - see first Page of Table 24

		FC	FC	GR	FC	FC	FC	FC	FC	GR	FC	FC	FC	FC	FC	FC	FC	FC
		1	1	R 1		1	1	1	1	R 1		1	1	1	1		1	1
Peterborough	d					19 46						20 46					21 46	
Huntingdon	d					20 00						21 00					22 00	
St Neots	d					20 08						21 08					22 08	
Sandy	d					20 15						21 15					22 15	
Biggleswade	d					20 19						21 19					22 19	
Arlesey	d					20 24						21 24					22 24	
Cambridge	d	19 20	19 28				19 55	20 20	20 28				20 55	21 20	21 28			21 55
Foxton	d						20 05						21 05					22 05
Shepreth	d						20 07						21 07					22 07
Meldreth	d						20 10						21 10					22 10
Royston	d		19 42				20 15		20 42				21 15		21 42			22 15
Ashwell & Morden	d						20 20						21 20					22 20
Baldock	d		19 50				20 25		20 50				21 25		21 50			22 25
Letchworth Garden City	d		19 53				20 29		20 53				21 29		21 53			22 29
Hitchin	d		19 57			20 30	20 34		20 57			21 30	21 34		21 57		22 30	22 34
Stevenage	d		20 03	20 07	20 30	20 36	20 39		21 03	21 08	21 30	21 36	21 39		22 03	22 30	22 36	22 39
Hertford North	a				20 43						21 43					22 43		
Knebworth	d						20 43						21 43					22 43
Welwyn North	d						20 47						21 47					22 47
Welwyn Garden City	d						20 51						21 51					22 51
Hatfield	d						20 54						21 54					22 54
Potters Bar	d						21 00						22 00					23 00
Finsbury Park	d		20 21		21 18	20 54	21 10		21 21		22 18	21 54	22 10		22 21	23 18	22 54	23 10
London Kings Cross	a	20 11	20 28	20 34	21 25	21 01	21 19	21 11	21 28	21 34	22 25	22 03	22 19	22 10	22 28	23 26	23 01	23 19

		FC	GR	GR	FC	GR	FC	FC	FC
		1	R 1	R 1	1	R 1		1	1
Peterborough	d		22 13	22 21		22 53		23 01	
Huntingdon	d							23 15	
St Neots	d							23 22	
Sandy	d							23 30	
Biggleswade	d							23 33	
Arlesey	d							23 38	
Cambridge	d	22 20			22 28				23 15
Foxton	d								23 24
Shepreth	d								23 26
Meldreth	d								23 29
Royston	d				22 42				23 34
Ashwell & Morden	d								23 38
Baldock	d				22 50				23 43
Letchworth Garden City	d				22 53				23 46
Hitchin	d				22 57			23 46	23 50
Stevenage	d		22 45	22 50	23 03	23s24	23 30	23 51	23 55
Hertford North	a						23 43		
Knebworth	d								23 58
Welwyn North	d								00 02
Welwyn Garden City	d								00 05
Hatfield	d								00 08
Potters Bar	d								00 14
Finsbury Park	d				23 21		00 18	00s13	00 27
London Kings Cross	a	23 08	23 15	23 21	23 28	00 01	00 27	00 24	00 39

Sundays
16 September to 21 October

		FC	FC	FC	FC	FC	FC	FC	FC	FC	FC	FC	FC	FC	FC	GR	FC	FC	FC	FC	FC	FC	FC
			1	bus	1	1	bus	1	1	bus	1	1	1	bus	1	R 1	1	1	1	1	1	bus	1
Peterborough	d		22p46		05 46			06 46			07 46				08 46	09 09			09 15				09 46
Huntingdon	d		23p00		06 00			07 00			08 00				09 00				09 30				10 00
St Neots	d		23p08		06 08			07 08			08 08				09 08				09 37				10 08
Sandy	d		23p15		06 15			07 15			08 15				09 15								10 15
Biggleswade	d		23p19		06 19			07 19			08 19				09 19				09 45				10 19
Arlesey	d		23p24		06 24			07 24			08 24				09 24								10 24
Cambridge	d					06 28			07 28			07 55	08 28				08 55	09 20		09 28			
Foxton	d											08 05					09 05						
Shepreth	d											08 07					09 07						
Meldreth	d											08 10					09 10						
Royston	d					06 43			07 43			08 15	08 42				09 15			09 42			
Ashwell & Morden	d											08 20					09 20						
Baldock	d					06 51			07 51			08 25	08 50				09 25			09 50			
Letchworth Garden City	d					06 54			07 54			08 29	08 53				09 29			09 53	10 04		
Hitchin	d		23p30		06 33	06 58		07 33	07 59		08 30	08 34	08 57		09 30		09 37			09 57	10 08		10 30
Stevenage	d	23p30	23p36	06 30	06 39	07 04	07 30	07 39	08 04	08 30	08 36	08 39	09 03	09 30	09 35	09 38	09 43			10 03	10 13	10 30	10 36
Hertford North	a	23p43		07 01			08 01			09 01				10 01								11 01	
Knebworth	d				06 43			07 43				08 43					09 46				10 17		
Welwyn North	d				06 47			07 47				08 47					09 50				10 21		
Welwyn Garden City	d				06 51			07 51				08 51					09 53				10 24		
Hatfield	d				06 54			07 54				08 54					09 57				10 27		
Potters Bar	d				07 00			08 00				09 00					10 03				10 33		
Finsbury Park	d	00 18	00 04		07 10	07 32		08 10	08 23		08 54	09 10	09 21		09 54		10 14			10 21	10 40		10 54
London Kings Cross	a	00 26	00 12		07 20	07 39		08 20	08 30		09 01	09 19	09 28		10 01	10 07	10 21	10 12	10 15	10 28	10 50		11 02

Peterborough, Cambridge and Stevenage - London

Network Diagram - see first Page of Table 24

		FC	FC	FC	FC	GR	FC	FC	FC	FC		FC	FC	FC	FC	FC	FC	FC	GR	FC	FC	FC
Peterborough	d			10 15		10 33		10 46				11 20			11 46				12 35		12 46	
Huntingdon	d			10 30				11 00				11 35			12 00						13 00	
St Neots	d			10 37				11 08				11 42			12 08						13 08	
Sandy	d							11 15							12 15						13 15	
Biggleswade	d			10 45				11 19				11 50			12 19						13 19	
Arlesey	d							11 24							12 24						13 24	
Cambridge	d	09 55	10 20		10 28				10 55	11 20			11 28			11 55	12 20	12 28				12 55
Foxton	d	10 05							11 05							12 05						13 05
Shepreth	d	10 07							11 07							12 07						13 07
Meldreth	d	10 10							11 10							12 10						13 10
Royston	d	10 15			10 42				11 15				11 42			12 15		12 42				13 15
Ashwell & Morden	d	10 20							11 20							12 20						13 20
Baldock	d	10 25			10 50				11 25				11 50			12 25		12 50				13 25
Letchworth Garden City	d	10 29			10 53				11 29				11 53			12 29		12 53				13 29
Hitchin	d	10 34			10 57			11 30	11 34				11 57		12 30	12 34		12 57			13 30	13 34
Stevenage	d	10 39			11 03	11 04	11 30	11 36	11 39				12 03	12 30	12 36	12 39		13 03	13 05	13 30	13 36	13 39
Hertford North	a						12 01							13 01						14 01		
Knebworth	d	10 43							11 43							12 43						13 43
Welwyn North	d	10 47							11 47							12 47						13 47
Welwyn Garden City	d	10 51							11 51							12 51						13 51
Hatfield	d	10 54							11 54							12 54						13 54
Potters Bar	d	11 00							12 02							13 00						14 00
Finsbury Park	d	11 12			11 21			11 54	12 10				12 21		12 54	13 10		13 21			13 54	14 10
London Kings Cross	a	11 19	11 09	11 16	11 28	11 33		12 01	12 19	12 08	12 15		12 28		13 01	13 19	13 08	13 28	13 34		14 01	14 19

		FC	FC	FC	FC	FC	FC	FC	GR	FC	FC	FC	FC	FC	FC	FC	FC	FC
Peterborough	d				13 46				14 33		14 46					15 46		
Huntingdon	d				14 00						15 00					16 00		
St Neots	d				14 08						15 08					16 08		
Sandy	d				14 15						15 15					16 15		
Biggleswade	d				14 19						15 19					16 19		
Arlesey	d				14 24						15 24					16 24		
Cambridge	d	13 20	13 28			13 55	14 20	14 28				14 55	15 20	15 28			15 55	16 20
Foxton	d					14 05						15 05					16 05	
Shepreth	d					14 07						15 07					16 07	
Meldreth	d					14 10						15 10					16 10	
Royston	d		13 42			14 15		14 42				15 15		15 42			16 15	
Ashwell & Morden	d					14 20						15 20					16 20	
Baldock	d		13 50			14 25		14 50				15 25		15 50			16 25	
Letchworth Garden City	d		13 53			14 29		14 53				15 29		15 53			16 29	
Hitchin	d		13 57		14 30	14 34		14 57			15 30	15 34		15 57		16 30	16 34	
Stevenage	d		14 03	14 30	14 36	14 39		15 03	15 06	15 30	15 36	15 39		16 03	16 30	16 36	16 39	
Hertford North	a			15 01						16 01					17 01			
Knebworth	d					14 43						15 43					16 43	
Welwyn North	d					14 47						15 47					16 47	
Welwyn Garden City	d					14 51						15 51					16 51	
Hatfield	d					14 54						15 54					16 54	
Potters Bar	d					15 00						16 00					17 00	
Finsbury Park	d		14 21		14 54	15 10		15 21			15 54	16 10		16 21		16 54	17 10	
London Kings Cross	a	14 08	14 28		15 01	15 19	15 08	15 28	15 33		16 02	16 19	16 08	16 28		17 01	17 19	17 08

		FC	GR	FC	FC	FC	FC	FC	GR	FC	FC	FC	FC	FC	FC	GR	FC	FC	FC
Peterborough	d		16 33		16 46						17 46							18 46	
Huntingdon	d				17 00						18 00							19 00	
St Neots	d				17 08						18 08							19 08	
Sandy	d				17 15						18 15							19 15	
Biggleswade	d				17 19						18 19							19 19	
Arlesey	d				17 24						18 24							19 24	
Cambridge	d	16 28				16 55	17 20	17 28				17 55	18 20	18 28	18 45				18 55
Foxton	d					17 05						18 05							19 05
Shepreth	d					17 07						18 07							19 07
Meldreth	d					17 10						18 10							19 10
Royston	d	16 42				17 15		17 42				18 15		18 42					19 15
Ashwell & Morden	d					17 20						18 20							19 20
Baldock	d	16 50				17 25		17 50				18 25		18 50					19 25
Letchworth Garden City	d	16 53				17 29		17 53				18 29		18 53					19 29
Hitchin	d	16 57			17 30	17 34		17 57			18 30	18 34		18 57				19 30	19 34
Stevenage	d	17 03	17 05	17 30	17 36	17 39		18 03	18 04	18 30	18 36	18 39		19 03		19 07	19 30	19 36	19 39
Hertford North	a			18 01						19 01							20 01		
Knebworth	d					17 43						18 43							19 43
Welwyn North	d					17 47						18 47							19 47
Welwyn Garden City	d					17 51						18 51							19 51
Hatfield	d					17 54						18 54							19 54
Potters Bar	d					18 00						19 00							20 00
Finsbury Park	d	17 21			17 54	18 10		18 21			18 54	19 10		19 21				19 54	20 10
London Kings Cross	a	17 28	17 33		18 01	18 19	18 08	18 30	18 34		19 01	19 19	19 11	19 30	19 36	19 36		20 01	20 19

Peterborough, Cambridge and Stevenage - London

Network Diagram - see first Page of Table 24

		FC	FC	GR	FC	FC	FC	FC	FC	GR	FC	FC	FC	FC	FC	FC	FC	FC
Peterborough	d					19 46						20 46					21 46	
Huntingdon	d					20 00						21 00					22 00	
St Neots	d					20 08						21 08					22 08	
Sandy	d					20 15						21 15					22 15	
Biggleswade	d					20 19						21 19					22 19	
Arlesey	d					20 24						21 24					22 24	
Cambridge	d	19 20	19 28				19 55	20 20	20 28				20 55	21 20	21 28			21 55
Foxton	d						20 05						21 05					22 05
Shepreth	d						20 07						21 07					22 07
Meldreth	d						20 10						21 10					22 10
Royston	d		19 42				20 15		20 42				21 15		21 42			22 15
Ashwell & Morden	d						20 20						21 20					22 20
Baldock	d		19 50				20 25		20 50				21 25		21 50			22 25
Letchworth Garden City	d		19 53				20 29		20 53				21 29		21 53			22 29
Hitchin	d		19 57			20 30	20 34		20 57			21 30	21 34		21 57		22 30	22 34
Stevenage	d		20 03	20 07	20 30	20 36	20 39		21 03	21 08	21 30	21 36	21 39		22 03	22 30	22 36	22 39
Hertford North	a				21 01						22 01					23 01		
Knebworth	d						20 43						21 43					22 43
Welwyn North	d						20 47						21 47					22 47
Welwyn Garden City	d						20 51						21 51					22 51
Hatfield	d						20 54						21 54					22 54
Potters Bar	d						21 00						22 00					23 00
Finsbury Park	d		20 21			20 54	21 10		21 21			21 54	22 10		22 21		22 54	23 10
London Kings Cross	a	20 11	20 28	20 34		21 01	21 19	21 11	21 28	21 34		22 03	22 19	22 10	22 28		23 01	23 19

		FC	GR	GR	FC	GR	FC	FC	FC
Peterborough	d		22 13	22 21		22 53		23 01	
Huntingdon	d							23 15	
St Neots	d							23 22	
Sandy	d							23 30	
Biggleswade	d							23 33	
Arlesey	d							23 38	
Cambridge	d	22 20			22 28				23 15
Foxton	d								23 24
Shepreth	d								23 26
Meldreth	d								23 29
Royston	d				22 42				23 34
Ashwell & Morden	d								23 38
Baldock	d				22 50				23 43
Letchworth Garden City	d				22 53				23 46
Hitchin	d				22 57			23 46	23 50
Stevenage	d		22 45	22 50	23 03	23s24	23 30	23 51	23 55
Hertford North	a						00 01		
Knebworth	d								23 58
Welwyn North	d								00 02
Welwyn Garden City	d								00 05
Hatfield	d								00 08
Potters Bar	d								00 14
Finsbury Park	d				23 21		01s59	00s13	00 27
London Kings Cross	a	23 08	23 15	23 21	23 28	00 01	02 14	00 24	00 39

Table 25

Sundays until 28 October

Peterborough, Cambridge and Stevenage - London

Network Diagram - see first Page of Table 24

		FC	FC	FC	FC	FC	FC	FC	FC	FC	FC	FC	FC	FC	FC	FC	FC	FC	FC	FC	FC	GR	FC
			1	1		1	1			1	1	1			1	1	1			1	1	1 ✕	1
				A	B 🚌			A	B 🚌		A	B	A	B 🚌				A	B 🚌	A	B		A
Peterborough	d		22p46			05 46				06 46					07 46					08 46	08 46	09 09	
Huntingdon	d		23p00			06 00				07 00					08 00					09 00	09 00		
St Neots	d		23p08			06 08				07 08					08 08					09 08	09 08		
Sandy	d		23p15			06 15				07 15					08 15					09 15	09 15		
Biggleswade	d		23p19			06 19				07 19					08 19					09 19	09 19		
Arlesey	d		23p24			06 24				07 24					08 24					09 24	09 24		
Cambridge	d			23p15			06 28				07 28	07 28				07 55	08 28						08 55
Foxton	d			23p24												08 05							09 05
Shepreth	d			23p27												08 07							09 07
Meldreth	d			23p30												08 10							09 10
Royston	d			23p34			06 43				07 43	07 43				08 15	08 42						09 15
Ashwell & Morden	d			23p39												08 20							09 20
Baldock	d			23p43			06 51				07 51	07 51				08 25	08 50						09 25
Letchworth Garden City	d			23p46			06 54				07 54	07 54				08 29	08 53						09 29
Hitchin	d		23p30	23p50		06 33	06 58			07 33	07 59	07 59			08 30	08 34	08 57			09 30	09 30		09 34
Stevenage	d	23p30	23p36	23p55	06 30	06 39	07 04	07 30	07 30	07 39	08 04	08 04	08 30	08 30	08 36	08 39	09 03	09 30	09 30	09 36	09 35	09 38	09 39
Hertford North	a	23p43			07 01			07 43	08 01				08 43	09 01				09 43	10 01				
Knebworth	d			23p59		06 43				07 43						08 43							09 43
Welwyn North	d			00 02		06 47				07 47						08 47							09 47
Welwyn Garden City	d			00 06		06 51				07 51						08 51							09 51
Hatfield	d			00 10		06 54				07 54						08 54							09 54
Potters Bar	d			00 15		07 00				08 00						09 00							10 00
Finsbury Park ⊖	d	00 18	00 04	00s32		07 10	07 32	08 18		08 10	08 22	08 23	09 18		08 54	09 10	09 21	10 18		09 54	09 54		10 10
London Kings Cross ⊖	a	00 26	00 12	00 40		07 20	07 39	08 26		08 20	08 30	08 30	09 25		09 01	09 19	09 28	10 25		10 01	10 01	10 07	10 19

		FC	FC	FC	FC	FC	FC	FC	FC	FC	FC	FC	FC	FC	FC	FC	FC	FC	FC	GR	FC	FC	FC
		1	1	1	1	1	1	1			1	1	1	1	1	1	1	1	1	1 ✕			1
		B	A	B			A	B	A	B 🚌	A	B	C	B	A	B	A	B			A	B 🚌	
Peterborough	d				09 15						09 46	09 46					10 15	10 15		10 33			10 46
Huntingdon	d				09 30						10 00	10 00					10 30	10 30					11 00
St Neots	d				09 37						10 08	10 08					10 37	10 37					11 08
Sandy	d										10 15	10 15											11 15
Biggleswade	d				09 45						10 19	10 19					10 45	10 45					11 19
Arlesey	d										10 24	10 24											11 24
Cambridge	d	08 55	09 20	09 20		09 28							09 55	09 55	10 20	10 20			10 28				
Foxton	d	09 05											10 05	10 05									
Shepreth	d	09 07											10 07	10 07									
Meldreth	d	09 10											10 10	10 10									
Royston	d	09 15				09 42							10 15	10 15					10 42				
Ashwell & Morden	d	09 20											10 20	10 20									
Baldock	d	09 25				09 50							10 25	10 25					10 50				
Letchworth Garden City	d	09 29				09 53	09 59	10 04					10 29	10 29					10 53				
Hitchin	d	09 37				09 57	10 04	10 08			10 30	10 30	10 34	10 34					10 57				11 30
Stevenage	d	09 43				10 03	10 09	10 13	10 30	10 30	10 36	10 36	10 39	10 39					11 03	11 04	11 30	11 30	11 36
Hertford North	a								10 43	11 01											11 43	12 01	
Knebworth	d	09 46					10 13	10 17					10 43	10 43									
Welwyn North	d	09 50					10 17	10 21					10 47	10 47									
Welwyn Garden City	d	09 53					10 21	10 24					10 51	10 51									
Hatfield	d	09 57					10 24	10 27					10 54	10 54									
Potters Bar	d	10 03					10 30	10 33					11 00	11 00									
Finsbury Park ⊖	d	10 14				10 21	10 40	10 40	11 18		10 54	10 54	11 10	11 12					11 21		12 18		11 54
London Kings Cross ⊖	a	10 21	10 09	10 12	10 15	10 28	10 49	10 50	11 25		11 01	11 02	11 19	11 19	11 08	11 09	11 15	11 16	11 28	11 33	12 25		12 01

A until 9 September, 28 October

B from 16 September until 21 October

C until 22 July, 19 August, 26 August, 28 October

Table 25

Sundays until 28 October

Peterborough, Cambridge and Stevenage - London

Network Diagram - see first Page of Table 24

		FC	FC	FC	FC	FC	FC	FC	FC	FC	FC	FC	GR	FC	FC	FC	FC	FC
		1	1	1	1	1			1	1	1	1	1 ✕			1	1	1
		A	B				A	B 🚌						A	B 🚌			
Peterborough	d				11 20				11 46				12 35			12 46		
Huntingdon	d				11 35				12 00							13 00		
St Neots	d				11 42				12 08							13 08		
Sandy	d								12 15							13 15		
Biggleswade	d				11 50				12 19							13 19		
Arlesey	d								12 24							13 24		
Cambridge	d	10 55	10 55	11 20		11 28				11 55	12 20	12 28					12 55	13 20
Foxton	d	11 05	11 05							12 05							13 05	
Shepreth	d	11 07	11 07							12 07							13 07	
Meldreth	d	11 10	11 10							12 10							13 10	
Royston	d	11 15	11 15			11 42				12 15		12 42					13 15	
Ashwell & Morden	d	11 20	11 20							12 20							13 20	
Baldock	d	11 25	11 25			11 50				12 25		12 50					13 25	
Letchworth Garden City	d	11 29	11 29			11 53				12 29		12 53					13 29	
Hitchin	d	11 34	11 34			11 57			12 30	12 34		12 57				13 30	13 34	
Stevenage	d	11 39	11 39			12 03	12 30	12 30	12 36	12 39		13 03	13 05	13 30	13 30	13 36	13 39	
Hertford North	a						12 43	13 01						13 43	14 01			
Knebworth	d	11 43	11 43							12 43							13 43	
Welwyn North	d	11 47	11 47							12 47							13 47	
Welwyn Garden City	d	11 51	11 51							12 51							13 51	
Hatfield	d	11 54	11 54							12 54							13 54	
Potters Bar	d	12 00	12 02							13 00							14 00	
Finsbury Park ⊖	d	12 10	12 10			12 21	13 18		12 54	13 10		13 21		14 18		13 54	14 10	
London Kings Cross ⊖	a	12 19	12 19	12 08	12 20	12 28	13 25		13 01	13 19	13 08	13 28	13 34	14 25		14 01	14 19	14 08

		FC	FC	FC	FC	FC	FC	FC	GR	FC	FC	FC	FC	FC	FC	FC	FC	FC	FC	FC
		1			1	1	1	1	1 ✕			1	1	1	1	1			1	1
			A	B 🚌						A	B 🚌	A	B				A	B 🚌		
Peterborough	d				13 46				14 33			14 46	14 46						15 46	
Huntingdon	d				14 00							15 00	15 00						16 00	
St Neots	d				14 08							15 08	15 08						16 08	
Sandy	d				14 15							15 15	15 15						16 15	
Biggleswade	d				14 19							15 19	15 19						16 19	
Arlesey	d				14 24							15 24	15 24						16 24	
Cambridge	d	13 28				13 55	14 20	14 28						14 55	15 20	15 28				15 55
Foxton	d					14 05								15 05						16 05
Shepreth	d					14 07								15 07						16 07
Meldreth	d					14 10								15 10						16 10
Royston	d	13 42				14 15		14 42						15 15		15 42				16 15
Ashwell & Morden	d					14 20								15 20						16 20
Baldock	d	13 50				14 25		14 50						15 25		15 50				16 25
Letchworth Garden City	d	13 53				14 29		14 53						15 29		15 53				16 29
Hitchin	d	13 57			14 30	14 34		14 57				15 30	15 30	15 34		15 57			16 30	16 34
Stevenage	d	14 03	14 30	14 30	14 36	14 39		15 03	15 06	15 30	15 30	15 36	15 36	15 39		16 03	16 30	16 30	16 36	16 39
Hertford North	a		14 43	15 01						15 43	16 01						16 43	17 01		
Knebworth	d					14 43								15 43						16 43
Welwyn North	d					14 47								15 47						16 47
Welwyn Garden City	d					14 51								15 51						16 51
Hatfield	d					14 54								15 54						16 54
Potters Bar	d					15 00								16 00						17 00
Finsbury Park ⊖	d	14 21	15 18		14 54	15 10		15 21		16 18		15 54	15 54	16 10		16 21	17 18		16 54	17 10
London Kings Cross ⊖	a	14 28	15 25		15 01	15 19	15 08	15 28	15 33	16 25		16 01	16 02	16 19	16 08	16 28	17 25		17 01	17 19

A until 9 September, 28 October

B from 16 September until 21 October

Peterborough, Cambridge and Stevenage - London

Network Diagram - see first Page of Table 24

		FC	FC	GR	FC	FC	FC	FC	FC	FC	GR	FC	FC	FC	FC	FC	FC
		1	1	1			1	1	1	1	1			1	1	1	1
					A	B						A	B				
Peterborough 8	d			16 33			16 46							17 46			
Huntingdon	d						17 00							18 00			
St Neots	d						17 08							18 08			
Sandy	d						17 15							18 15			
Biggleswade	d						17 19							18 19			
Arlesey	d						17 24							18 24			
Cambridge	d	16 20	16 28					16 55	17 20	17 28					17 55	18 20	18 28
Foxton	d							17 05							18 05		
Shepreth	d							17 07							18 07		
Meldreth	d							17 10							18 10		
Royston	d		16 42					17 15		17 42					18 15		18 42
Ashwell & Morden	d							17 20							18 20		
Baldock	d		16 50					17 25		17 50					18 25		18 50
Letchworth Garden City	d		16 53					17 29		17 53					18 29		18 53
Hitchin 4	d		16 57				17 30	17 34		17 57				18 30	18 34		18 57
Stevenage 4	d		17 03	17 05	17 30	17 30	17 36	17 39		18 03	18 04	18 30	18 30	18 36	18 39		19 03
Hertford North	a				17 43	18 01						18 43	19 01				
Knebworth	d							17 43							18 43		
Welwyn North	d							17 47							18 47		
Welwyn Garden City 4	d							17 51							18 51		
Hatfield	d							17 54							18 54		
Potters Bar	d							18 00							19 00		
Finsbury Park ⊖	d		17 21		18 18		17 54	18 10		18 21		19 18		18 54	19 10		19 21
London Kings Cross 15 ⊖	a	17 08	17 28	17 33	18 25		18 01	18 19	18 08	18 30	18 34	19 25		19 01	19 19	19 11	19 30

		FC	GR	FC	FC	FC	FC	FC	FC	GR	FC	FC	FC	FC	FC	FC	GR	FC	FC	FC
		1	1			1	1	1	1	1			1	1	1	1	1			1
				A	B						A	B						A	B	
Peterborough 8	d					18 46							19 46							20 46
Huntingdon	d					19 00							20 00							21 00
St Neots	d					19 08							20 08							21 08
Sandy	d					19 15							20 15							21 15
Biggleswade	d					19 19							20 19							21 19
Arlesey	d					19 24							20 24							21 24
Cambridge	d	18 45					18 55	19 20	19 28					19 55	20 20	20 28				
Foxton	d						19 05							20 05						
Shepreth	d						19 07							20 07						
Meldreth	d						19 10							20 10						
Royston	d						19 15		19 42					20 15		20 42				
Ashwell & Morden	d						19 20							20 20						
Baldock	d						19 25		19 50					20 25		20 50				
Letchworth Garden City	d						19 29		19 53					20 29		20 53				
Hitchin 4	d					19 30	19 34		19 57				20 30	20 34		20 57				21 30
Stevenage 4	d		19 07	19 30	19 30	19 36	19 39		20 03	20 07	20 30	20 30	20 36	20 39		21 03	21 08	21 30	21 30	21 36
Hertford North	a			19 43	20 01						20 43	21 01						21 43	22 01	
Knebworth	d						19 43							20 43						
Welwyn North	d						19 47							20 47						
Welwyn Garden City 4	d						19 51							20 51						
Hatfield	d						19 54							20 54						
Potters Bar	d						20 00							21 00						
Finsbury Park ⊖	d			20 18		19 54	20 10		20 21		21 18		20 54	21 10		21 21		22 18		21 54
London Kings Cross 15 ⊖	a	19 36	19 36	20 25		20 01	20 19	20 11	20 28	20 34	21 25		21 01	21 19	21 11	21 28	21 34	22 25		22 03

A until 9 September, 28 October

B from 16 September until 21 October

Peterborough, Cambridge and Stevenage - London

Network Diagram - see first Page of Table 24

		FC	FC	FC	FC	FC	FC	FC	FC	GR	GR	FC	GR	FC	FC	FC	FC
		1	1	1			1	1	1	1	1	1	1			1	1
					A	B								A	B		
Peterborough 8	d						21 46			22 13	22 21		22 53			23 01	
Huntingdon	d						22 00									23 15	
St Neots	d						22 08									23 22	
Sandy	d						22 15									23 30	
Biggleswade	d						22 19									23 33	
Arlesey	d						22 24									23 38	
Cambridge	d	20 55	21 20	21 28				21 55	22 20			22 28					23 15
Foxton	d	21 05						22 05									23 24
Shepreth	d	21 07						22 07									23 26
Meldreth	d	21 10						22 10									23 29
Royston	d	21 15		21 42				22 15				22 42					23 34
Ashwell & Morden	d	21 20						22 20									23 38
Baldock	d	21 25		21 50				22 25				22 50					23 43
Letchworth Garden City	d	21 29		21 53				22 29				22 53					23 46
Hitchin 4	d	21 34		21 57			22 30	22 34				22 57				23 46	23 50
Stevenage 4	d	21 39		22 03	22 30	22 30	22 36	22 39		22 45	22 50	23 03	23s24	23 30	23 30	23 51	23 55
Hertford North	a				22 43	23 01								23 43	00 01		
Knebworth	d	21 43						22 43									23 58
Welwyn North	d	21 47						22 47									00 02
Welwyn Garden City 4	d	21 51						22 51									00 05
Hatfield	d	21 54						22 54									00 08
Potters Bar	d	22 00						23 00									00 14
Finsbury Park ⊖	d	22 10		22 21	23 18		22 54	23 10				23 21		00 18	01s59	00s13	00 27
London Kings Cross 15 ⊖	a	22 19	22 10	22 28	23 26		23 01	23 19	23 08	23 15	23 21	23 28	00 01	00 27	02 14	00 24	00 39

A until 9 September, 28 October

B from 16 September until 21 October

Route Diagram for Table 26

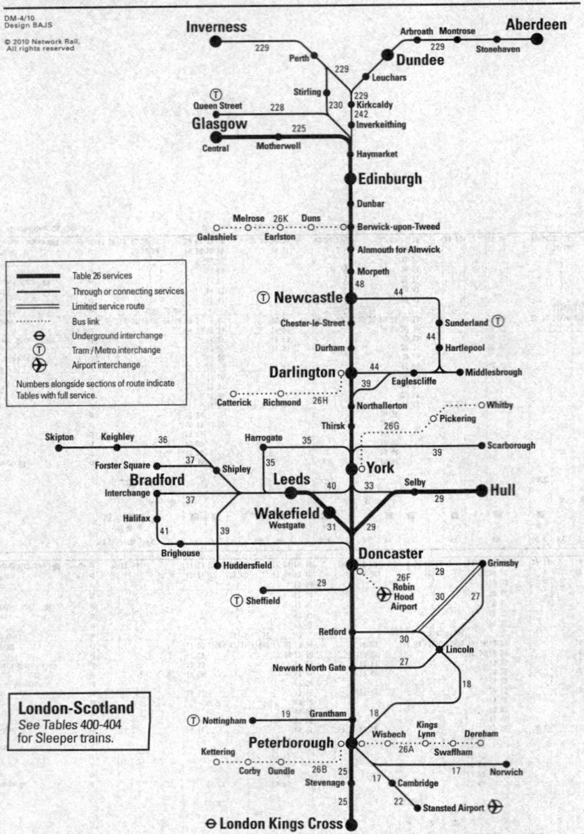

London - Humberside, Yorkshire, North East England and Scotland

Route Diagram - see first Page of Table 26

Miles	Miles	Miles			SR MX	TP MO	GR MO	GR MX	GR MO	GR MX	TP MX	GR	SR	NT	SR	GR	SR	XC	GR MO	GR MX	GR MO	GR	GR MO
						A	A		A			B							C	D	C	E	C
0	—	—	London Kings Cross ⊖	d			21p00	21p00	21p35	21p35		22p00							22p00	22p00		22p00	22p35
27½	—	—	Stevenage	d				21p20	21p55	21p55													
76¼	—	—	Peterborough	a			21p45	21p50	22p25	22p26		22p45							22p45	22p46		22p46	23b25
—	—	—	Norwich	d																			
—	—	—	Peterborough	d			21p45	21p51	22p26	22p26		22p45							22p45	22p46		22p46	
105¼	—	—	Grantham	a					22p47	22p47										23p07		23p07	23b48
—	—	—		d					22p47	22p48										23p07		23p07	
120	—	—	Newark North Gate	a				22p19	22p59	22p59										23p19		23p19	23b59
—	—	—		d				22p19	22p59	23p00										23p19		23p19	
—	—	—	Lincoln	a																			
138½	—	—	Retford	d					23p16	23p16													
156	0	—	Doncaster	a				22p45	23p35	23p31		23p42							23p42	23p48		23p48	00s29
—	—	—	Selby	a																			
—	—	—	Hull	a																			
—	—	—	Pontefract Monkhill	a																			
—	—	—	Wakefield Kirkgate	a																			
—	19¾	—	Wakefield Westgate	a					23p56	23p53													
—	29¾	—	Leeds	a					00 14	00 11													01 36
—	—	—	Mirfield	a																			
—	—	—	Brighouse	a																			
—	—	—	Halifax	a																			
—	—	—	Shipley	a																			
—	—	—	Bradford Forster Sqare	a																			
—	—	—	Bradford Interchange	a																			
—	—	—	Keighley	a																			
—	—	—	Skipton	a																			
—	—	—	Sheffield	d																			
—	—	—	Doncaster	d				22p45				23p42							23p43	23p49		23p49	
188½	—	—	York	a			22p58	23p10				00 10							00 33	00 17		00 39	
—	—	—	Scarborough	a																			
—	—	—	Harrogate	a																			
—	—	—	Leeds	d		22p12					22p42												
—	—	—	York	d		22p42	23p04	23p11			23p18	00 12							00 35	00 18	00 35	00 41	
210¼	—	—	Thirsk	d		23p06					23p31												
218½	—	—	Northallerton	d		23p16	23p39	23p40			23p49	00s44								00s45	01s07	01s11	
232½	—	—	Darlington	a		23p28	23p51	23p52			00 01	00s58								00s59	01s21	01s25	
—	—	—	Eaglescliffe	a																			
—	—	—	Middlesbrough	a																			
—	—	—	Darlington	d		23p28	23p52	23p53			00 02												
254½	—	—	Durham	d		23p45	00 09	00 11			00 20	01s16								01s17	01s39	01s43	
260¼	—	—	Chester-le-Street	d																			
—	—	—	Newcastle	a		00 15	00 43	00 45			00 51	01 49								01 53	02 12	02 18	
—	—	—	Hartlepool	a																			
—	—	—	Sunderland	a																			
268½	—	—	Newcastle	d										05 55		06 25		07 35					
285	—	—	Morpeth	d										06 15		06 40		07 48					
303¾	—	—	Alnmouth for Alnwick	d										06a32		06 54							
335½	—	—	Berwick-upon-Tweed	d												07 18		08 19					
363¾	—	—	Dunbar	d												07 42							
393	—	—	Edinburgh	a												08 10		09 04					
—	—	0	Edinburgh	d	21p40								05 30		07 28		08 28	09 11					
394¼	—	1¼	Haymarket	d	21p44								05 33		07 31		08 32	09 16					
437¼	—	—	Motherwell	a														10 04					
450¼	—	—	Glasgow Central	a														10 26					
—	—	—	Stirling	a																			
—	—	—	Perth	a																			
—	—	—	Inverness	a																			
—	—	13¼	Inverkeithing	a									05 46										
—	—	26	Kirkcaldy	a	22p12								06 02		08 02								
—	—	51	Leuchars	a	22p34								06 32		08 25		09 23						
—	—	59¼	Dundee	a	22p48								06 45		08 40		09 36						
—	—	76¼	Arbroath	a	23p05								07 10		08 57		09 56						
—	—	90	Montrose	a	23p18								07 23		09 12								
—	—	114¼	Stonehaven	a	23p40								07 48		09 34		10 31						
—	—	130½	Aberdeen	a	00 03								08 13		09 52		10 54						

A from 21 May
B from 2 July until 10 September
C from 21 May until 25 June, from 17 September
D from 26 June until 14 September
E until 22 June, from 18 September
b Previous night, stops to set down only

London - Humberside, Yorkshire, North East England and Scotland

Route Diagram - see first Page of Table 26

		GR MO A	GR C	GR MX B	GR MX B	GR MO C	GR MO C	GR MX B	GR MO C	GR MX B	GR MX	TP	NT	GR	NT	TP	XC MX J	TP
London Kings Cross	d	22p35	23p00		00 01	00 05	00 30	00 30	00 45	00 45	05 50							
Stevenage	d										06 11							
Peterborough	a	23b25	23b46		00s46	00s50			01s30	01s31	06 41							
Norwich	d																	
Peterborough	d										06 42							
Grantham	a	23b48			01s07	01s10			01s50	01s52	07 02							
	d										07 02							
Newark North Gate	a	23b59			01s19	01s22			02s02	02s04	07 14							
	d										07 14							
Lincoln	a																	
Retford	d		00 24								07 29							
Doncaster	a	00s36	00s39		01s44	01s47	01s58	02s06	02s27	02s29	07 43							
Selby	a																	
Hull	a																	
Pontefract Monkhill	a																	
Wakefield Kirkgate	a																	
Wakefield Westgate	a				02s02	02s06			02s46	02s47	08 01							
Leeds	a	01 10			02s20	02 23			03 03	03 05	08 20							
Mirfield	a																	
Brighouse	a																	
Halifax	a																	
Shipley	a																	
Bradford Forster Sqare	a																	
Bradford Interchange	a																	
Keighley	a																	
Skipton	a																	
Sheffield	d																06 33	
Doncaster	d													06 15			07 00	
York	a		01s02				02s21	02s32						06 36			07 26	
Scarborough	a																	
Harrogate	a																	
Leeds	d															06 35		
York	d											05 54		06 38		07 06	07 31	07 32
Thirsk	d											06 10				07 22		07 52
Nrthallerton	d											06 18				07 30		08 00
Darlington	a		01s31	01s42			02s50	03s01				06 29		07 05		07 41	07 56	
Eaglescliffe	a																	
Middlesbrough	a											07 03						08 32
Darlington	d												06 14	07 06	07 20	07 42	07 58	
Durham	d		01s49	02s00			03s08	03s19					06 35	07 23	07 41	07 59	08 16	
ChesterleStreet	d												06 42		07 48	08 05		
Newcastle	a		02 08	02 19			03 27	03 38					06 54	07 39	08 05	08 16	08 37	
Hartlepool	a																	
Sunderland	a																	
Newcastle	d													07 41				
Morpeth	d																	
Alnmouth for Alnwick	d													08 07				
Berwick-upon-Tweed	d													08 31				
Dnbar	d													08 54				
Edinburgh	a													09 24				
Edinburgh	d																	
Haymarket	d																	
Motherwell	a																	
Glasgow Central	a																	
Stirling	a																	
Perth	a																	
Inverness	a																	
Inverkeithing	a																	
Kirkcaldy	a																	
Leuchars	a																	
Dundee	a																	
Arbroath	a																	
Montrose	a																	
Stonehaven	a																	
Aberdeen	a																	

A from 2 Jly until 10 September
B from 31 Jly until 7 September, not from 14 August until 29 August
C 30 Jly to 13 August and 3 September, 10 September
J until 26 Octoberfrom 30 October
b Previous night, stops to set down only

London - Humberside, Yorkshire, North East England and Scotland

Route Diagram - see first Page of Table 26

		NT	SR	GR	NT	NT	TP	NT	NT	XC A	NT	GR	GR	TP B	XC	EM	GR	GR	GR	HT	TP	NT	NT
London Kings Cross	d											06 15	06 30				07 00	07 05	07 08	07 20			
Stevenage	d											06 34	06 49						07 27				
Peterborough	a											07 04	07 19				07 45	07 50	07 57				
Nrwich	d															05 50							
Peterborough	d											07 05	07 20			07 27	07 45	07 50	07 58				
Grantham	a											07 25	07 39			07 58			08 18	08 26			
	d											07 25	07 39						08 18	08 27			
Newark North Gate	a											07 37							08 30				
	d											07 37							08 30				
Lincoln	a																						
Retford	d											07 53							08 44	08 50			
Doncaster	a											08 08	08 12					08 40	08 59	09 04			
Selby	a																			09 22			
Hull	a																			10 04			
Pontefract Monkhill	a																						
Wakefield Kirkgate	a																						
Wakefield Westgate	a												08 31					09 00					
Leeds	a												08 49					09 18					
Mirfield	a																						
Brighouse	a																						
Halifax	a																						
Shipley	a																						
Bradford Forster Sqare	a																						
Bradford Interchange	a																						
Keighley	a																						
Skipton	a																						
Sheffield	d									07 12					07 54								
Doncaster	d											08 09			08 25				09 00				
York	a											08 32			08 45		08 51		09 29				
Scarborough	a																						
Harrogate	a																						
Leeds	d			07 10	07 29	07 41	07 50			07 57	07 13			08 12							08 28	07 43	08 41
York	d			07 37	08a06	08a16	08 23			08 28	08a32	08 34		08 42	08 49		08 53				08 58	08a59	09a21
Thirsk	d						08 39																
Nrthallerton	d						08 49					08 53									09 19		
Darlington	a			08 05						08 55		09 06		09 11	09 16		09 20				09 30		
Eaglescliffe	a																						
Middlesbrough	a						09 22																
Darlington	d			08 05				08 22		08 57		09 06		09 12	09 17		09 21				09 31		
Durham	d			08 23				08 43		09 12		09 24		09 29	09 34						09 47		
ChesterleStreet	d							08 50													09 53		
Newcastle	a			08 40				09 06		09 29		09 43		09 44	09 47		09 50				10 07		
Hartlepool	a																						
Sunderland	a																						
Newcastle	d	07 58		08 41					09 15	09 35							09 53						
Morpeth	d	08a18		08 56					09a36														
Alnmouth for Alnwick	d									09 59													
Berwick-upon-Tweed	d			09 31						10 20							10 38						
Dnbar	d			09 56																			
Edinburgh	a			10 20						11 05							11 25						
Edinburgh	d		09 28	10 27						11 11													
Haymarket	d		09 33	10 32						11 16													
Motherwell	a									11 52													
Glasgow Central	a									12 14													
Stirling	a																						
Perth	a																						
Inverness	a																						
Inverkeithing	a			10 47																			
Kirkcaldy	a			11 04																			
Leuchars	a			11 28																			
Dundee	a		10 32	11 43																			
Arbroath	a		10 49	12 00																			
Montrose	a		11 04	12 16																			
Stonehaven	a		11 25	12 39																			
Aberdeen	a		11 48	13 05																			

A to Edinburgh
B to Yrk

London - Humberside, Yorkshire, North East England and Scotland

Route Diagram - see first Page of Table 26

		TP	NT	SR	XC	GR	GR	NT	EM	XC	GC	GR	GR	TP	GC	NT	NT	TP	NT	SR	XC	GR
		◇1 ⊼		◇1 ⊼	◇1 ⊼	■ 1 ⊏⊐⊼	■ 1 ⊏⊐⊼			◇1 ⊼	■ 1 ⊏⊐	■ 1 ⊏⊐⊼	■ 1 ⊏⊐⊼	◇1 ⊼	■ 1 ⊏⊐			◇1 ⊼		◇1 ⊼	◇1 ⊼	■ 1 ⊏⊐⊼
London Kings Cross 15 ⊖	d					07 30	07 35				07 49	08 00	08 03									08 30
Stevenage 4	d						07 54															
Peterborough 8	a					08 16							08 51									09 15
Norwich	d																					
Peterborough 8	d					08 16			08 33				08 51									09 15
Grantham 7	a						08 39															
	d						08 39															
Newark North Gate 7	a					08 44																09 43
	d					08 44																09 43
Lincoln	a								09 59													
Retford 10	d																					
Doncaster 7	a					09 09	09 12						09 39									10 08
Selby	a																					
Hull	a																					
Pontefract Monkhill	a																					
Wakefield Kirkgate 4	a																					
Wakefield Westgate 7	a						09 31						09 59									
Leeds 10	a						09 49						10 18									
Mirfield	a																					
Brighouse	a																					
Halifax	a																					
Shipley	a																					
Bradford Forster Sqare	a																					
Bradford Interchange	a																					
Keighley	a																					
Skipton	a																					
Sheffield 7 ⇌	d				08 21					08 48											09 21	
Doncaster 7	d					09 09				09 20												10 09
York 8	a					09 33				09 44	09 47	09 50										10 32
Scarborough	a																					
Harrogate	a																					
Leeds 10	d	08 57			09 05			08 29						09 28	←	09 33	09 41	09 57			10 05	
York 8	d	09 26			09 32	09 35		09a45		09 48	10 01	09 53		09 58	10 01	10a06	10a21	10 26			10 32	10 34
Thirsk	d	09 46									→				10 18			10 46				
Northallerton	d	09 59												10 19	10 28			10 59				10 54
Darlington 7	a				09 57	10 02				10 13		10 20		10 30							11 00	11 06
Eaglescliffe	a														10 46							
Middlesbrough	a	10 30																11 30				
Darlington 7	d				09 59	10 03				10 15		10 21		10 31							11 02	11 07
Durham	d				10 17	10 21				10 31				10 47							11 20	11 24
Chester-le-Street	d																					
Newcastle 8 ⇌	a				10 30	10 39				10 44		10 50		11 05							11 34	11 43
Hartlepool	a														11 07							
Sunderland ⇌	a														11 40							
Newcastle 8 ⇌	d		10 15		10 35	10 41						10 53							11 15		11 40	
Morpeth	d		10a36																11a36			
Alnmouth for Alnwick	d					11 07																
Berwick-upon-Tweed	d											11 38									12 22	
Dunbar	d				11 37																	
Edinburgh 10	a				12 03	12 15						12 25									13 06	
Edinburgh	d			11 28																12 28	13 12	
Haymarket	d			11 32																12 32	13 16	
Motherwell	a																				13 52	
Glasgow Central 15	a																				14 12	
Stirling	a																					
Perth	a																					
Inverness	a																					
Inverkeithing	a																					
Kirkcaldy	a																					
Leuchars 3	a			12 25																13 23		
Dundee	a			12 38																13 35		
Arbroath	a			12 55																13 52		
Montrose	a																			14 07		
Stonehaven	a			13 28																14 28		
Aberdeen	a			13 48																14 48		

London - Humberside, Yorkshire, North East England and Scotland

Route Diagram - see first Page of Table 26

		GR	XC	EM	EM	GR	GR	GR	TP	NT	TP	NT	SR	XC	GR	GR	HT	NT	XC	GR	TP	NT	TP
		■ 1 ⊏⊐⊼	◇1 ⊼	◇		■ 1 ⊏⊐⊼	■ 1 ⊏⊐⊼	■ 1 ⊏⊐	◇1 ⊼		◇1 ⊼		◇1 ⊼	◇1 ⊼	■ 1 ⊏⊐⊼	■ 1 ⊏⊐⊼	◇1 ⊠		◇1 ⊼	■ 1 A ⊏⊐⊼	◇1 ⊼		◇1 ⊼
London Kings Cross 15 ⊖	d	08 35				09 00	09 03	09 08							09 30	09 35	09 48			10 00			
Stevenage 4	d	08 54						09 28								09 54							
Peterborough 8	a					09 45	09 51	10 00							10 15								
Norwich	d			07 57																			
Peterborough 8	d			09 27	09 35	09 45	09 51	10 00							10 15								
Grantham 7	a	09 39		09 57				10 20								10 40	10 49						
	d	09 39		09 58				10 20								10 40	10 50						
Newark North Gate 7	a							10 32							10 43								
	d							10 32							10 43								
Lincoln	a				10 59																		
Retford 10	d							10 48									11 11						
Doncaster 7	a	10 12					10 40	11 03							11 08	11 12	11 23						
Selby	a																11 39						
Hull	a																12 18						
Pontefract Monkhill	a																						
Wakefield Kirkgate 4	a																						
Wakefield Westgate 7	a	10 31					11 00									11 31							
Leeds 10	a	10 49					11 18									11 49							
Mirfield	a																						
Brighouse	a																						
Halifax	a																						
Shipley	a																						
Bradford Forster Sqare	a																						
Bradford Interchange	a																						
Keighley	a																						
Skipton	a																						
Sheffield 7 ⇌	d		09 47	11a38										10 21					10 47				
Doncaster 7	d		10 19					11 03							11 10				11 19				
York 8	a		10 45			10 51		11 31							11 32				11 46	11 51			
Scarborough	a																						
Harrogate	a																						
Leeds 10	d								10 28	10 41	10 57			11 05				10 29			11 28	11 41	11 57
York 8	d		10 48			10 53			10 58	11a19	11 26			11 32	11 35			11a46	11 48	11 53	11 58	12a21	12 26
Thirsk	d										11 46												12 46
Northallerton	d								11 19		11 59										12 19		12 59
Darlington 7	a		11 13			11 20			11 30					11 57	12 03				12 13	12 21	12 30		
Eaglescliffe	a																						
Middlesbrough	a										12 30												13 30
Darlington 7	d		11 15			11 21			11 31					12 00	12 05				12 15	12 21	12 31		
Durham	d		11 31						11 47					12 22	12 25				12 31		12 47		
Chester-le-Street	d								11 53														
Newcastle 8 ⇌	a		11 45			11 50			12 06					12 34	12 41				12 44	12 51	13 03		
Hartlepool	a																						
Sunderland ⇌	a																						
Newcastle 8 ⇌	d					11 52						12 15		12 38	12 44					12 52			
Morpeth	d											12a36											
Alnmouth for Alnwick	d														13 10								
Berwick-upon-Tweed	d					12 37														13 39			
Dunbar	d													13 41									
Edinburgh 10	a					13 25								14 10	14 15					14 22			
Edinburgh	d												13 28							14 27			
Haymarket	d												13 32							14 32			
Motherwell	a																						
Glasgow Central 15	a																						
Stirling	a																						
Perth	a																						
Inverness	a																						
Inverkeithing	a																			14 46			
Kirkcaldy	a																			15 03			
Leuchars 3	a												14 23							15 28			
Dundee	a												14 35							15 46			
Arbroath	a												14 52							16 04			
Montrose	a																			16 20			
Stonehaven	a												15 26							16 43			
Aberdeen	a												15 46							17 09			

A The Northern Lights

Table 26

Mondays to Fridays

London - Humberside, Yorkshire, North East England and Scotland

Route Diagram - see first Page of Table 26

Station		NT	XC	EM	EM	GR	GR	GR	GR	GC	NT	XC	EM	GR	EM	GR	GR	TP	NT	GC	TP	NT
			A																			
London Kings Cross ⊖	d					10 03	10 08	10 30	10 35	10 48				11 00		11 05	11 08			11 23		
Stevenage	d						10 28		10 54								11 27					
Peterborough	a					10 50	10 59	11 15								11 51	11 57					
Norwich	d			08 57									09 57									
Peterborough	d			10 28	10 38	10 50	10 59	11 15					11 28		11 48	11 51	11 58					
Grantham	a			10 58			11 20		11 39				11 58				12 18					
	d			11 00			11 20		11 39				12 00				12 18					
Newark North Gate	a						11 36	11 43									12 30					
	d							11 43									12 30					
Lincoln	a				12 04										13 14							
Retford	d																12 44					
Doncaster	a					11 40		12 08	12 12	12 23					14 06	12 41	13 03					
Selby	a																					
Hull	a																					
Pontefract Monkhill	a									12 47												
Wakefield Kirkgate	a									13 07												
Wakefield Westgate	a					12 00			12 31							13 00						
Leeds	a					12 18			12 49							13 18						
Mirfield	a																					
Brighouse	a									13 30												
Halifax	a									13 40												
Shipley	a																					
Bradford Forster Sqare	a																					
Bradford Interchange	a									13 55												
Keighley	a																					
Skipton	a																					
Sheffield	d		11 21	12a38								11 47	13a38									
Doncaster	d							12 08				12 19					13 04					
York	a							12 32				12 46		12 49			13 31			13 21		
Scarborough	a																					
Harrogate	a																					
Leeds	d		12 05								11 29							12 28	12 41		12 57	
York	d		12 32					12 34			12a45	12 48		12 52				12 58	13a19	13 22	13 29	
Thirsk	d																			13 39	13 49	
Northallerton	d							12 54										13 19		13 46	13 59	
Darlington	a		12 58					13 06				13 13		13 19				13 30				
Eaglescliffe	a																			14 04		
Middlesbrough	a																				14 30	
Darlington	d		13 00					13 07				13 15		13 20				13 31				
Durham	d		13 16					13 24				13 31						13 47				
ChesterleStreet	d																	13 53				
Newcastle	a		13 29					13 43				13 45		13 49				14 06				
Hartlepool	a																			14 23		
Sunderland	a																			14 50		
Newcastle	d	13 15	13 38											13 51								14 15
Morpeth	d	13a36																				14a36
Alnmouth for Alnwick	d		14 02																			
Berwick-upon-Tweed	d		14 23											14 36								
Dunbar	d																					
Edinburgh	a		15 06											15 24								
Edinburgh	d		15 11																			
Haymarket	d		15 16																			
Motherwell	a		15 52																			
Glasgow Central	a		16 23																			
Stirling	a																					
Perth	a																					
Inverness	a																					
Inverkeithing	a																					
Kirkcaldy	a																					
Leuchars	a																					
Dundee	a																					
Arbroath	a																					
Montrose	a																					
Stonehaven	a																					
Aberdeen	a																					

A ⚒ to Edinburgh

Table 26

Mondays to Fridays

London - Humberside, Yorkshire, North East England and Scotland

Route Diagram - see first Page of Table 26

Station		SR	XC	GR	GR	HT	XC	NT	SR	GR	TP	NT	TP	NT	XC	EM	EM	GR	GR	GR	GR	NT	XC
										A					B								
London Kings Cross ⊖	d			11 30	11 35	11 48				12 00								12 05	12 08	12 30	12 35		
Stevenage	d				11 54														12 28		12 54		
Peterborough	a			12 15														12 50	12 59	13 15			
Norwich	d															10 57							
Peterborough	d			12 15												12 26	12 41	12 50	12 59	13 15			
Grantham	a				12 39	12 48										12 58			13 20		13 39		
	d				12 39	12 49										12 59			13 21		13 39		
Newark North Gate	a			12 43															13 36	13 43			
	d			12 43																13 43			
Lincoln	a																14 06						
Retford	d					13 11																	
Doncaster	a			13 08	13 12	13 23												13 39		14 08	14 12		
Selby	a					13 39																	
Hull	a					14 19																	
Pontefract Monkhill	a																						
Wakefield Kirkgate	a																						
Wakefield Westgate	a				13 31													13 59			14 31		
Leeds	a				13 49													14 18			14 49		
Mirfield	a																						
Brighouse	a																						
Halifax	a																						
Shipley	a																						
Bradford Forster Sqare	a																						
Bradford Interchange	a																						
Keighley	a																						
Skipton	a																						
Sheffield	d		12 21				12 47								13 21	14a38							13 47
Doncaster	d			13 10			13 19													14 08			14 19
York	a			13 32			13 40			13 53										14 32			14 44
Scarborough	a																						
Harrogate	a																						
Leeds	d		13 05					12 29			13 28	13 42	13 57		14 05							13 29	
York	d		13 32	13 35			13 43	13a46		13 54	13 58	14a22	14 26		14 32					14 34		14a46	14 48
Thirsk	d												14 46										
Northallerton	d										14 19		14 59							14 54			
Darlington	a		13 59	14 04			14 12			14 22	14 30				14 58					15 06			15 13
Eaglescliffe	a																						
Middlesbrough	a												15 30										
Darlington	d		14 01	14 05			14 13			14 23	14 31				15 00					15 07			15 15
Durham	d		14 18	14 22			14 30				14 47				15 16					15 24			15 31
ChesterleStreet	d																						
Newcastle	a		14 30	14 39			14 42			14 52	15 05				15 30					15 43			15 45
Hartlepool	a																						
Sunderland	a																						
Newcastle	d		14 36	14 43						14 54				15 15	15 37								
Morpeth	d		14 50											15a36									
Alnmouth for Alnwick	d			15 09											16 01								
Berwick-upon-Tweed	d									15 40					16 22								
Dunbar	d		15 41																				
Edinburgh	a		16 05	16 17						16 23					17 06								
Edinburgh	d	15 28							16 29	16 33					17 11								
Haymarket	d	15 32							16u33	16 38					17 15								
Motherwell	a														17 52								
Glasgow Central	a														18 16								
Stirling	a									17 19													
Perth	a									17 59													
Inverness	a									20 11													
Inverkeithing	a																						
Kirkcaldy	a																						
Leuchars	a	16 24							17 24														
Dundee	a	16 37							17 38														
Arbroath	a	16 54							18 01														
Montrose	a	17 08							18 16														
Stonehaven	a	17 33							18 40														
Aberdeen	a	17 53							19 00														

A The Highland Chieftain

B ⚒ to Edinburgh

London - Humberside, Yorkshire, North East England and Scotland

Route Diagram - see first Page of Table 26

		EM	EM	GR	GR	GR	TP	TP	NT	SR	XC	GR	GR	HT	NT	XC	GR	NT	TP	NT	XC	EM	GR
		◇		■1 🍴	■1 🍴	■1 □	◇1 ✕	◇1 ✕		◇1 ✕	◇1 A ✕	■1 🍴	■1 🍴	◇1 ⊠		◇1 ✕	■1 🍴		◇1 ✕		◇1 A ✕	◇	■1 🍴
London Kings Cross ⊖	d			13 00	13 05	13 08						13 30	13 35	13 48			14 00						14 05
Stevenage	d					13 28							13 54										
Peterborough	a			13 45	13 50	13 59						14 15											14 50
Norwich	d	11 57																				12 57	
Peterborough	d	13 27	13 40	13 45	13 51	14 00						14 15										14 26	14 50
Grantham	a	13 56				14 20							14 39	14 48								14 57	
	d	13 58				14 20							14 39	14 49								14 58	
Newark North Gate	a					14 32						14 43											
	d					14 32						14 43											
Lincoln	a		15 05																				
Retford	d					14 48								15 11									
Doncaster	a				14 39	15 02						15 08	15 12	15 23									15 39
Selby	a													15 39									
Hull	a													16 18									
Pontefract Monkhill	a																						
Wakefield Kirkgate	a																						
Wakefield Westgate	a				14 59								15 31										15 59
Leeds	a				15 18								15 49										16 18
Mirfield	a																						
Brighouse	a																						
Halifax	a																						
Shipley	a																						
Bradford Forster Sqare	a																						
Bradford Interchange	a																						
Keighley	a																						
Skipton	a																						
Sheffield ⇌	d	15a38									14 21					14 47					15 21	16a38	
Doncaster	d					15 03						15 09				15 19							
York	a			14 50		15 31						15 32				15 45	15 51						
Scarborough	a																						
Harrogate	a																						
Leeds	d						14 28	14 57			15 05				14 29			15 41	15 57		16 05		
York	d			14 52			14 58	15 26			15 32	15 34			15a47	15 48	15 53	16a21	16 26		16 32		
Thirsk	d							15 46											16 46				
Northallerton	d						15 19	15 59				15 54							16 59				
Darlington	a			15 19			15 30				15 58	16 06				16 13	16 21				16 58		
Eaglescliffe	a																						
Middlesbrough	a							16 30											17 30				
Darlington	d			15 20			15 31				16 00	16 07				16 15	16 21				17 00		
Durham	d						15 47				16 17	16 24				16 31					17 16		
Chester-le-Street	d						15 53																
Newcastle ⇌	a			15 49			16 09				16 30	16 43				16 45	16 51				17 31		
Hartlepool	a																						
Sunderland ⇌	a																						
Newcastle ⇌	d			15 51					16 15		16 37						16 52			17 15	17 37		
Morpeth	d								16a36											17 36			
Alnmouth for Alnwick	d										17 02									18a20	18 02		
Berwick-upon-Tweed	d			16 36													17 39				18 23		
Dunbar	d										17 43												
Edinburgh	a			17 25							18 07						18 23				19 06		
Edinburgh	d									17 37	18 11						18 30				19 11		
Haymarket	d									17 41	18 15						18 34				19 16		
Motherwell	a																				19 54		
Glasgow Central	a																				20 15		
Stirling	a																						
Perth	a																						
Inverness	a																						
Inverkeithing	a										18 28						18 54						
Kirkcaldy	a										18 46						19 11						
Leuchars	a									18 33	19 22						19 39						
Dundee	a									18 48	19 35						19 53						
Arbroath	a									19 05	19 51						20 11						
Montrose	a									19 21	20 05						20 27						
Stonehaven	a									19 43	20 26						20 50						
Aberdeen	a									20 06	20 45						21 16						

A ✕ to Edinburgh

Table 26

Mondays to Fridays

London - Humberside, Yorkshire, North East England and Scotland

Route Diagram - see first Page of Table 26

		GR	EM	GR	GR	GC	NT	XC	NT	GR	TP	NT	NT	SR	XC	EM	GR	GR	GR	GR	HT	EM
		■1 □		■1 🍴	■1 🍴	■1 □		◇1 ✕		■1 🍴	◇1 ✕			◇1 ✕	◇1 A ✕	◇	■1 🍴	■1 □	■1 🍴	■1 🍴	◇1 ⊠	
London Kings Cross ⊖	d	14 08		14 30	14 35	14 48				15 00							15 05	15 08	15 30	15 35	15 48	
Stevenage	d	14 27			14 54													15 28		15 54		
Peterborough	a	14 58		15 16													15 50	15 59	16 15			
Norwich	d															13 57						
Peterborough	d	14 59	15 10	15 16												15 28	15 50	15 59	16 15			16 25
Grantham	a	15 19			15 39											15 59		16 20		16 40	16 48	
	d	15 19			15 39											16 01		16 20		16 40	16 49	
Newark North Gate	a	15 35		15 43														16 32	16 43			
	d			15 43														16 32	16 43			
Lincoln	a		16 47																			17 51
Retford	d																	16 48			17 11	
Doncaster	a			16 08	16 12	16 22											16 39	17 03	17 09	17 13	17 23	
Selby	a																				17 39	
Hull	a																				18 21	
Pontefract Monkhill	a					16 47																
Wakefield Kirkgate	a					17 04																
Wakefield Westgate	a				16 30												17 00			17 31		
Leeds	a				16 51												17 18			17 50		
Mirfield	a					17 20																
Brighouse	a					17 29																
Halifax	a					17 40																
Shipley	a																					
Bradford Forster Sqare	a																					
Bradford Interchange	a					17 55																
Keighley	a																					
Skipton	a																					
Sheffield ⇌	d							15 47							16 21	17a36						
Doncaster	d			16 08				16 19										17 04	17 10			
York	a			16 32				16 45		16 51								17 31	17 33			
Scarborough	a																					
Harrogate	a																					
Leeds	d						15 29				16 28	16 41			17 07							
York	d			16 34			16a46	16 48		16 52	16 56	17a20			17 32				17 35			
Thirsk	d										17 14											
Northallerton	d			16 54							17 22								17 55			
Darlington	a			17 06				17 13		17 20	17 33				17 58				18 07			
Eaglescliffe	a																					
Middlesbrough	a																					
Darlington	d			17 07				17 15		17 21	17 34				18 00				18 08			
Durham	d			17 24				17 31			17 51				18 16				18 25			
Chester-le-Street	d										17 57											
Newcastle ⇌	a			17 43				17 45		17 50	18 09				18 33				18 41			
Hartlepool	a																					
Sunderland ⇌	a																					
Newcastle ⇌	d								17 38	17 52			18 25		18 39				18 43			
Morpeth	d								18a00				18a47									
Alnmouth for Alnwick	d																		19 11			
Berwick-upon-Tweed	d									18 37					19 22							
Dunbar	d														19 45							
Edinburgh	a									19 26					20 09				20 14			
Edinburgh	d													19 28	20 14				20 16			
Haymarket	d													19 31	20 17				20 21			
Motherwell	a																		21 03			
Glasgow Central	a																		21 28			
Stirling	a																					
Perth	a																					
Inverness	a																					
Inverkeithing	a														20 30							
Kirkcaldy	a																					
Leuchars	a													20 28	21 25							
Dundee	a													20 40	21 41							
Arbroath	a													20 57								
Montrose	a													21 12								
Stonehaven	a													21 33								
Aberdeen	a													21 53								

A ✕ to Edinburgh

London - Humberside, Yorkshire, North East England and Scotland

Route Diagram - see first Page of Table 26

Station		TP	XC	NT	GR	NT	NT	TP	XC	EM	GR	GR	GR	GR	GC	NT	GR	TP FX	TP FO	XC	EM	GR	GR
									A														B
London Kings Cross	d				16 00						16 05	16 08	16 30	16 33	16 48		17 00					17 03	17 19
Stevenage	d											16 29		16 52									
Peterborough	a										16 51	16 59	17 15									17 49	18 06
Norwich	d									14 57											15 52		
Peterborough	d									16 28	16 51	17 00	17 15								17 27	17 50	18 06
Grantham	a									16 59		17 20		17 39							17 58		18 27
	d									17 00		17 20		17 39							17 58		18 27
Newark North Gate	a											17 36	17 43										18 39
	d												17 43										18 39
Lincoln	a																						
Retford	d													18 02									
Doncaster	a										17 42		18 08									18 39	19 05
Selby	a																						19 22
Hull	a																						20 06
Pontefract Monkhill	a																						
Wakefield Kirkgate	a																						
Wakefield Westgate	a										18 00			18 31								18 59	
Leeds	a										18 18			18 50								19 18	
Mirfield	a																						
Brighouse	a																						
Halifax	a																						
Shipley	a																						
Bradford Forster Sqare	a																						
Bradford Interchange	a																						
Keighley	a																						
Skipton	a																						
Sheffield	d		16 47						17 21	18a39										17 47	19a39		
Doncaster	d		17 19										18 09										
York	a		17 40		17 51								18 33		18 39		18 49						
Scarborough	a																						
Harrogate	a																						
Leeds	d	17 12		16 29		17 28	17 41	17 57	18 06							17 29		18 28		18 35			
York	d	17 41	17 47	17a50	17 53	18a10	18a18	18 25	18 33				18 35		18 44	18a46	18 51	18 57	18 57	19 04			
Thirsk	d	18 01													19 00			19 14	19 14				
Northallerton	d	18 09						18 46					18 56		19 15			19 24	19 24				
Darlington	a		18 13		18 21			18 57	19 01				19 08				19 19			19 29			
Eaglescliffe	a														19 33								
Middlesbrough	a	18 42																19 56	19 56				
Darlington	d		18 15		18 22			18 58	19 03				19 09				19 19			19 32			
Durham	d		18 32					19 14	19 20				19 26							19 48			
Chester-le-Street	d							19 20															
Newcastle	a		18 46		18 51			19 34	19 35				19 42				19 49			20 03			
Hartlepool	a														19 52								
Sunderland	a														20 21								
Newcastle	d				18 53				19 38				19 44				19 51			20 11			
Morpeth	d												20 00										
Alnmouth for Alnwick	d								20 06											20 35			
Berwick-upon-Tweed	d				19 39				20 27								20 39						
Dunbar	d																						
Edinburgh	a				20 22				21 11				21 20				21 27			21 35			
Edinburgh	d				20 29				21 14														
Haymarket	d				20 34				21 19														
Motherwell	a								22 01														
Glasgow Central	a								22 27														
Stirling	a																						
Perth	a																						
Inverness	a																						
Inverkeithing	a				20 51																		
Kirkcaldy	a				21 08																		
Leuchars	a				21 37																		
Dundee	a				21 52																		
Arbroath	a				22 09																		
Montrose	a				22 25																		
Stonehaven	a				22 48																		
Aberdeen	a				23 14																		

A to Edinburgh   B The Hull Executive

London - Humberside, Yorkshire, North East England and Scotland

Route Diagram - see first Page of Table 26

Station		NT	TP	GR	GR	SR	XC	NT FX	XC	EM	GR	GR	GR	GR	TP	XC	GR	GR	HT	EM	NT	XC
							A									B						C
London Kings Cross	d			17 30	17 33						17 49	18 00	18 03	18 19			18 30	18 33	18 50			
Stevenage	d				17 53													18 52				
Peterborough	a			18 15							18 36		18 54				19 17					
Norwich	d									16 57										17 54		
Peterborough	d			18 16						18 26	18 40		18 55				19 18			19 26		
Grantham	a				18 41					18 54	19 04			19 22				19 42	19 51	19 58		
	d				18 41					18 56	19 04			19 22				19 42	19 53			
Newark North Gate	a			18 43									19 22				19 45					
	d			18 43									19 22				19 45					
Lincoln	a																					
Retford	d										19 26							20 04	20 14			
Doncaster	a				19 14						19 41		19 47				20 10	20 20	20 27			
Selby	a																		20 48			
Hull	a																		21 27			
Pontefract Monkhill	a																					
Wakefield Kirkgate	a																					
Wakefield Westgate	a				19 35						20 01		20 07					20 38				
Leeds	a				19 52						20 21		20 23					20 54				
Mirfield	a																					
Brighouse	a																					
Halifax	a																					
Shipley	a																	21s12				
Bradford Forster Sqare	a																	21 24				
Bradford Interchange	a																					
Keighley	a												20s55									
Skipton	a												21 14									
Sheffield	d						18 21		18 47	20a28						19 26						19 54
Doncaster	d								19 16								20 10					20 17
York	a			19 26					19 38			19 48		20 12			20 33					20 46
Scarborough	a																					
Harrogate	a				20 27																	
Leeds	d	18 41	18 57				19 06	18 29							19 57	20 08					19 29	
York	d	19a21	19 26	19 28			19 35	19a45	19 45			19 49		20 14	20 29	20 33	20 36				20a47	20 48
Thirsk	d		19 46												20 49							
Northallerton	d		19 57											20 33	20 59							
Darlington	a			19 56			20 02		20 10			20 17		20 46		20 58	21 05					21 14
Eaglescliffe	a																					
Middlesbrough	a		20 31												21 30							
Darlington	d			19 56			20 04		20 12			20 17		20 46		21 00	21 05					21 15
Durham	d			20 14			20 21		20 28					21 04		21 18	21 23					21 32
Chester-le-Street	d																					
Newcastle	a			20 33			20 34		20 42			20 47		21 23		21 31	21 39					21 44
Hartlepool	a																					
Sunderland	a																					
Newcastle	d						20 39					20 48				21 36	21 40					
Morpeth	d						20 55										21 56					
Alnmouth for Alnwick	d															22 02	22 12					
Berwick-upon-Tweed	d						21 26					21 33										
Dunbar	d						21 51					21 57										
Edinburgh	a						22 16					22 25				23 04	23 20					
Edinburgh	d					21 40																
Haymarket	d					21 44																
Motherwell	a																					
Glasgow Central	a																					
Stirling	a																					
Perth	a																					
Inverness	a																					
Inverkeithing	a																					
Kirkcaldy	a					22 12																
Leuchars	a					22 34																
Dundee	a					22 48																
Arbroath	a					23 05																
Montrose	a					23 18																
Stonehaven	a					23 40																
Aberdeen	a					00 03																

A to Newcastle   B to Leeds   C to Doncaster

London - Humberside, Yorkshire, North East England and Scotland

Route Diagram - see first Page of Table 26

		GR	GR	GR	GR	TP	GC	GR	XC	NT	GR	GR	EM	GC	XC	NT	GR	GR	HT	GR	XC	EM	XC
				A	B			FX			FO			C									
London Kings Cross	d	19 00	19 03	19 06	19 06		19 18	19 30			19 30	19 33		19 48			20 00	20 05	20 30	20 35			
Stevenage	d			19 26	19 27							19 52								20 54			
Peterborough	a		19 50	19 57	19 57			20 15			20 15							20 50		21 24			
Norwich	d												18 57										
Peterborough	d		19 51	19 57	19 59			20 16			20 16		20 28					20 50		21 25			
Grantham	a			20 18	20 20							20 40	20 58						21 31	21 46			
	d			20 18	20 21							20 40							21 32	21 46			
Newark North Gate	a			20 31	20 33			20 43			20 43							21 18		21 58			
	d			20 31	20 35			20 43			20 43							21 18		21 58			
Lincoln	a			21 01	21 03														21 52				
Retford	d																						
Doncaster	a		20 39					21 08			21 08	21 13		21 22				21 43	22 06	22 22			
Selby	a																		22 21				
Hull	a																		23 06				
Pontefract Monkhill	a																						
Wakefield Kirkgate	a																						
Wakefield Westgate	a		21 00									21 31						22 06		22 40			
Leeds	a		21 19									21 50						22 24		22 59			
Mirfield	a													22 15									
Brighouse	a													22 23									
Halifax	a													22 33									
Shipley	a																						
Bradford Forster Square	a																						
Bradford Interchange	a													22 48									
Keighley	a																						
Skipton	a																						
Sheffield	d								20 21						20 53						21 21	21 25	21 54
Doncaster	d							21 09			21 09				21 20								22 31
York	a	20 50					21 17	21 31			21 31				21 45		21 50						22 53
Scarborough	a																						
Harrogate	a																						
Leeds	d					20 45			21a05							20 29					22a02	22a19	
York	d	20 52				21 14	21 19	21 33			21 33				21 49	21a50	21 52						
Thirsk	d					21 31	21 36																
Northallerton	d					21 39	21 47	21 52			21 52												
Darlington	a	21 19				21 51		22 05			22 05				22 15		22 20						
Eaglescliffe	a						22 04																
Middlesbrough	a																						
Darlington	d	21 20				21 52		22 05			22 05				22 16		22 20						
Durham	d					22 08		22 23			22 23				22 34		22 38						
Chester-le-Street	d					22 14																	
Newcastle	a	21 50				22 28		22 41			22 41				22 50		22 57						
Hartlepool	a						22 24																
Sunderland	a						22 51																
Newcastle	d	21 54								22 00	22 42												
Morpeth	d									22a21	22 56												
Alnmouth for Alnwick	d										23 12												
Berwick-upon-Tweed	d	22 39									23 38												
Dunbar	d																						
Edinburgh	a	23 34									00 31												
Edinburgh	d																						
Haymarket	d																						
Motherwell	a																						
Glasgow Central	a																						
Stirling	a																						
Perth	a																						
Inverness	a																						
Inverkeithing	a																						
Kirkcaldy	a																						
Leuchars	a																						
Dundee	a																						
Arbroath	a																						
Montrose	a																						
Stonehaven	a																						
Aberdeen	a																						

A until 22 June

B from 25 June

C to Doncaster

London - Humberside, Yorkshire, North East England and Scotland

Route Diagram - see first Page of Table 26

		GR	GR	TP	GR	GR	EM	XC	GR	EM	GR	GR
					A	B			C		A	B
London Kings Cross	d	21 00	21 35		22 00	22 00			22 50		23 30	23 30
Stevenage	d	21 20	21 55									
Peterborough	a	21 50	22 26		22 46	22 46			23s46		00s24	00s24
Norwich	d											
Peterborough	d	21 51	22 26		22 46	22 46						
Grantham	a		22 47		23 07	23 07					00s46	00s46
	d		22 48		23 07	23 07						
Newark North Gate	a	22 19	22 59		23 19	23 19					00s57	00s57
	d	22 19	23 00		23 19	23 19						
Lincoln	a											
Retford	d		23 16						00s26			
Doncaster	a	22 45	23 31		23 48	23 48			00s41		01s25	01s25
Selby	a											
Hull	a											
Pontefract Monkhill	a											
Wakefield Kirkgate	a											
Wakefield Westgate	a		23 53									
Leeds	a		00 11								02 15	02 37
Mirfield	a											
Brighouse	a											
Halifax	a											
Shipley	a											
Bradford Forster Square	a											
Bradford Interchange	a											
Keighley	a											
Skipton	a											
Sheffield	d						22 19	22 30		22 53		
Doncaster	d	22 45			23 49	23 49						
York	a	23 10			00 17	00 39			01s13			
Scarborough	a											
Harrogate	a											
Leeds	d			22 42			23a05	23a15		23a41		
York	d	23 11		23 18	00 18	00 41						
Thirsk	d			23 31								
Northallerton	d	23 40		23 49	00s45	01s11						
Darlington	a	23 52		00 01	00s59	01s25			01s42			
Eaglescliffe	a											
Middlesbrough	a											
Darlington	d	23 53		00 02								
Durham	d	00 11		00 20	01s17	01s43			02s00			
Chester-le-Street	d											
Newcastle	a	00 45		00 51	01 53	02 18			02 19			
Hartlepool	a											
Sunderland	a											
Newcastle	d											
Morpeth	d											
Alnmouth for Alnwick	d											
Berwick-upon-Tweed	d											
Dunbar	d											
Edinburgh	a											
Edinburgh	d											
Haymarket	d											
Motherwell	a											
Glasgow Central	a											
Stirling	a											
Perth	a											
Inverness	a											
Inverkeithing	a											
Kirkcaldy	a											
Leuchars	a											
Dundee	a											
Arbroath	a											
Montrose	a											
Stonehaven	a											
Aberdeen	a											

A from 25 June until 14 September

B until 22 June, from 17 September

C from 27 July until 7 September, not from 13 August until 28 August

London - Humberside, Yorkshire, North East England and Scotland

Route Diagram - see first Page of Table 26

		SR	GR	GR	GR	TP	GR	GR	GR	GR	GR	GR	GR	GR	SR	TP	NT	SR	GR	SR	XC	GR	NT
							A	B	C	A	B	C	C	C									
London Kings Cross ⊖	d		19p30	21p00	21p35		22p00	22p00	22p50	23p30	23p30	00 10	00 45	00 55									
Stevenage	d			21p20	21p55																		
Peterborough	a		20p15	21p50	22p26		22p46	22p46	23b46	00s24	00s24	00s55		01s46									
Norwich	d																						
Peterborough	d		20p16	21p51	22p26		22p46	22p46															
Grantham	a				22p47		23p07	23p07		00s46	00s46	01s15		02s07									
	d				22p48		23p07	23p07															
Newark North Gate	a		20p43	22p19	22p59		23p19	23p19		00s57	00s57	01s27		02s19									
	d		20p43	22p19	23p00		23p19	23p19															
Lincoln	a																						
Retford	d				23p16				00s26														
Doncaster	a		21p08	22p45	23p31		23p48	23p48	00s41	01s25	01s25	01s52	02s15	02s44									
Selby	a																						
Hull	a																						
Pontefract Monkhill	a																						
Wakefield Kirkgate	a																						
Wakefield Westgate	a				23p53							02s13		03s15									
Leeds	a				00 11					02 15	02 37	02 30		03 33									
Mirfield	a																						
Brighouse	a																						
Halifax	a																						
Shipley	a																						
Bradford Forster Sqare	a																						
Bradford Interchange	a																						
Keighley	a																						
Skipton	a																						
Sheffield	d																						
Doncaster	d		21p09	22p45			23p49	23p49														06 10	
York	a		21p31	23p10			00 17	00 39	01s13				02s38									06 30	
Scarborough	a																						
Harrogate	a																						
Leeds	d					22p42																	
York	d		21p33	23p11		23p18	00 18	00 41								05 54						06 32	
Thirsk	d					23p31										06 10							
Northallerton	d		21p52	23p40		23p49	00s45	01s11								06 18						06 51	
Darlington	a		22p05	23p52		00 01	00s59	01s25	01s42				03s07			06 29						07 05	
Eaglescliffe	a																						
Middlesbrough	a															07 03							
Darlington	d		22p05	23p53		00 02																07 05	07 21
Durham	d		22p23	00 11		00 20	01s17	01s43	02s00				03s25									07 23	07 42
Chester-le-Street	d																						07 49
Newcastle	a		22p41	00 45		00 51	01 53	02 18	02 19				03 43									07 39	08 05
Hartlepool	a																						
Sunderland	a																						
Newcastle	d		22p42														05 55		06 30		07 38	07 42	
Morpeth	d		22p56														06 17		06 43		07 51		
Alnmouth for Alnwick	d		23p12														06a34		06 57			08 08	
Berwick-upon-Tweed	d		23p38																07 21		08 24	08 32	
Dunbar	d																		07 48			08 55	
Edinburgh	a		00 31																08 17		09 07	09 24	
Edinburgh	d	21p40													05 30			07 28		08 28	09 11		
Haymarket	d	21p44													05 33			07 31		08 32	09 16		
Motherwell	a																				10 05		
Glasgow Central	a																				10 25		
Stirling	a																						
Perth	a																						
Inverness	a																						
Inverkeithing	a														05 46								
Kirkcaldy	a	22p12													06 02			08 02					
Leuchars	a	22p34													06 32			08 25		09 23			
Dundee	a	22p48													06 45			08 40		09 36			
Arbroath	a	23p05													07 10			08 57		09 56			
Montrose	a	23p18													07 23			09 12					
Stonehaven	a	23p40													07 48			09 34		10 31			
Aberdeen	a	00 03													08 13			09 52		10 54			

A from 30 June until 15 September
B until 23 June, from 22 September
C 28 July, 4 August, 11 August, 1 September, 8 September
b Previous night, stops to set down only

London - Humberside, Yorkshire, North East England and Scotland

Route Diagram - see first Page of Table 26

		TP	NT	TP	NT	SR	GR	NT	XC	NT	TP	NT	NT	NT	XC	GR	TP	XC	SR	GR	TP	NT	TP
															A		B						C
London Kings Cross ⊖	d															06 15				07 00			
Stevenage	d															06 34							
Peterborough	a															07 04							
Norwich	d																						
Peterborough	d															07 05							
Grantham	a															07 25							
	d															07 25							
Newark North Gate	a															07 37							
	d															07 37							
Lincoln	a																						
Retford	d															07 53							
Doncaster	a															08 08							
Selby	a																						
Hull	a																						
Pontefract Monkhill	a																						
Wakefield Kirkgate	a																						
Wakefield Westgate	a																						
Leeds	a																						
Mirfield	a																						
Brighouse	a																						
Halifax	a																						
Shipley	a																						
Bradford Forster Sqare	a																						
Bradford Interchange	a																						
Keighley	a																						
Skipton	a																						
Sheffield	d								06 49						07 12			07 54					
Doncaster	d								07 17							08 08		08 25					
York	a								07 43							08 31		08 48		08 52			
Scarborough	a																						
Harrogate	a																						
Leeds	d	06 35	06 38				07 10	06 36		07 41	07 50	07 13			07 57		08 12				08 28	07 39	08 28
York	d	07 06	07a15	07 32			07 35	07a46	07 48	08a20	08 23	08a26			08 27	08 35	08 42	08 50		08 53	08 58	08a59	09a03
Thirsk	d	07 22		07 52							08 39												
Northallerton	d	07 30		08 00							08 49					08 54					09 19		
Darlington	a	07 41					08 04		08 13						08 56	09 07	09 11	09 16		09 21	09 30		
Eaglescliffe	a																						
Middlesbrough	a			08 32							09 22												
Darlington	d	07 42					08 05		08 15				08 22		08 57	09 07	09 12	09 18		09 22	09 31		
Durham	d	07 59					08 23		08 31				08 43		09 14	09 25	09 29	09 35			09 47		
Chester-le-Street	d	08 05											08 50								09 53		
Newcastle	a	08 16					08 39		08 44				09 01		09 26	09 41	09 46	09 47		09 52	10 07		
Hartlepool	a																						
Sunderland	a																						
Newcastle	d				07 58		08 41							09 15	09 35	09 44				09 54			
Morpeth	d				08a19		08 56							09a36									
Alnmouth for Alnwick	d														09 59								
Berwick-upon-Tweed	d						09 31								10 20					10 39			
Dunbar	d						09 56																
Edinburgh	a						10 24								11 05	11 13				11 31			
Edinburgh	d					09 28	10 27								11 11				11 28				
Haymarket	d					09 33	10 32								11 16				11 32				
Motherwell	a														11 52								
Glasgow Central	a														12 13								
Stirling	a																						
Perth	a																						
Inverness	a																						
Inverkeithing	a						10 47																
Kirkcaldy	a						11 04																
Leuchars	a					10 23	11 28												12 25				
Dundee	a					10 32	11 43												12 38				
Arbroath	a					10 49	12 00												12 55				
Montrose	a					11 04	12 16																
Stonehaven	a					11 25	12 39												13 28				
Aberdeen	a					11 48	13 05												13 48				

A to Edinburgh
B to York
C until 23 June, from 15 September

London - Humberside, Yorkshire, North East England and Scotland

Route Diagram - see first Page of Table 26

Station		NT	TP	NT	XC	EM	GR	GR	GC	NT	EM	XC	SR	GR	GR	EM	EM	TP	NT	TP	NT	XC
																A	B					
London Kings Cross ⊖	d						07 03	07 30	07 48					08 00	08 03							
Stevenage	d						07 22															
Peterborough	a						07 52	08 15							08 50							
Norwich	d					05 52																
Peterborough	d					07 27	07 53	08 15			08 33				08 50							
Grantham	a					07 55	08 13								09 12							
	d					07 58	08 13								09 12							
Newark North Gate	a						08 25								09 24							
	d						08 25								09 24							
Lincoln	a										09 59											
Retford	d							08 54														
Doncaster	a						08 49	09 09							09 49							
Selby	a																					
Hull	a																					
Pontefract Monkhill	a																					
Wakefield Kirkgate	a																					
Wakefield Westgate	a						09 08								10 07							
Leeds	a						09 25								10 26							
Mirfield	a																					
Brighouse	a																					
Halifax	a																					
Shipley	a																					
Bradford Forster Sqare	a																					
Bradford Interchange	a																					
Keighley	a																					
Skipton	a																					
Sheffield	d				08 21	09a38						08 48				09 21	09 21					09 21
Doncaster	d							09 11				09 20				09 55	09 55					
York	a							09 33	09 39			09 44		09 49		10 16	10 16					
Scarborough	a																11 07					
Harrogate	a																					
Leeds	d	08 41	08 57		09 05					08 29								09 28	09 41	09 57		10 05
York	d	09a21	09 26		09 33			09 36	09 44	09a45		09 49		09 52				09 58	10a21	10 26		10 32
Thirsk	d		09 46						10 00											10 46		
Northallerton	d		09 59						10 16									10 19		10 59		
Darlington	a				09 58			10 03				10 15		10 20				10 30				10 58
Eaglescliffe	a								10 37													
Middlesbrough	a		10 30																	11 30		
Darlington	d				10 00			10 04				10 16		10 21				10 31				11 00
Durham	d				10 16			10 21				10 33						10 47				11 16
Chester-le-Street	d																					
Newcastle	a				10 31			10 37				10 45		10 50				11 05				11 29
Hartlepool	a								11 07													
Sunderland	a								11 40													
Newcastle	d			10 15	10 36			10 39						10 54							11 15	11 36
Morpeth	d			10a35																	11a36	
Alnmouth for Alnwick	d							11 05														
Berwick-upon-Tweed	d													11 39								12 20
Dunbar	d				11 38																	
Edinburgh	a				12 07			12 15						12 31								13 04
Edinburgh	d												12 28									13 11
Haymarket	d												12 32									13 16
Motherwell	a																					13 52
Glasgow Central	a																					14 13
Stirling	a																					
Perth	a																					
Inverness	a																					
Inverkeithing	a																					
Kirkcaldy	a																					
Leuchars	a												13 23									
Dundee	a												13 35									
Arbroath	a												13 52									
Montrose	a												14 07									
Stonehaven	a												14 28									
Aberdeen	a												14 48									

A from 15 September

B until 8 September

London - Humberside, Yorkshire, North East England and Scotland

Route Diagram - see first Page of Table 26

Station		GR	NT	XC	SR	GR	TP	NT	TP	NT	XC	EM	EM	GR	GR	HT	NT	XC	GR	TP	NT	TP	NT
																			A				
London Kings Cross ⊖	d	08 30				09 00								09 03	09 30	09 48			10 00				
Stevenage	d													09 22									
Peterborough	a	09 15												09 52	10 15								
Norwich	d											07 57											
Peterborough	d	09 15										09 30	09 33	09 53	10 15								
Grantham	a											09 58		10 14		10 48							
	d											09 58		10 14		10 49							
Newark North Gate	a	09 43												10 26									
	d	09 43												10 26									
Lincoln	a												10 59										
Retford	d														10 53	11 10							
Doncaster	a	10 08												10 50	11 08	11 24							
Selby	a															11 40							
Hull	a															12 20							
Pontefract Monkhill	a																						
Wakefield Kirkgate	a																						
Wakefield Westgate	a													11 07									
Leeds	a													11 26									
Mirfield	a																						
Brighouse	a																						
Halifax	a																						
Shipley	a																						
Bradford Forster Sqare	a																						
Bradford Interchange	a																						
Keighley	a																						
Skipton	a																						
Sheffield	d			09 47							10 21	11a38						10 47					
Doncaster	d	10 09		10 19											11 09			11 19					
York	a	10 33		10 40		10 52									11 33			11 40	11 51				
Scarborough	a																						
Harrogate	a																						
Leeds	d		09 29				10 28	10 41	10 57		11 05						10 29			11 28	11 41	11 57	
York	d	10 35	10a45	10 48		10 53	10 58	11a18	11 26		11 32				11 35		11a45	11 48	11 53	11 58	12a21	12 26	
Thirsk	d								11 46													12 46	
Northallerton	d	10 54					11 19		11 59											12 19		12 59	
Darlington	a	11 07		11 13		11 21	11 30				11 57				12 04			12 13	12 21	12 30			
Eaglescliffe	a																						
Middlesbrough	a								12 30													13 30	
Darlington	d	11 07		11 15		11 22	11 31				12 00				12 04			12 15	12 22	12 31			
Durham	d	11 25		11 31			11 47				12 16				12 22			12 31		12 47			
Chester-le-Street	d						11 53																
Newcastle	a	11 41		11 46		11 51	12 06				12 31				12 38			12 45	12 51	13 03			
Hartlepool	a																						
Sunderland	a																						
Newcastle	d	11 44				11 54				12 15	12 36				12 40				12 54				13 15
Morpeth	d									12a35													13a37
Alnmouth for Alnwick	d														13 06								
Berwick-upon-Tweed	d					12 39													13 40				
Dunbar	d										13 38												
Edinburgh	a	13 13				13 31					14 07				14 15				14 24				
Edinburgh	d				13 28														14 27				
Haymarket	d				13 32														14 32				
Motherwell	a																						
Glasgow Central	a																						
Stirling	a																						
Perth	a																						
Inverness	a																						
Inverkeithing	a																		14 46				
Kirkcaldy	a																		15 03				
Leuchars	a				14 23														15 28				
Dundee	a				14 35														15 46				
Arbroath	a				14 52														16 04				
Montrose	a																		16 20				
Stonehaven	a				15 26														16 43				
Aberdeen	a				15 46														17 09				

A The Northern Lights

London - Humberside, Yorkshire, North East England and Scotland

Route Diagram - see first Page of Table 26

		XC	EM	GR	GR	GC	NT	XC	EM	EM	SR	GR	GR	TP	GC	NT	TP	NT	XC	GR	GR	HT
		A				B																
London Kings Cross	d			10 03	10 30	10 48						11 00	11 03		11 20					11 30	11 35	11 48
Stevenage	d												11 22									
Peterborough	a			10 50	11 15								11 52							12 15	12 21	
Norwich	d		08 57						09 57													
Peterborough	d		10 26	10 51	11 15				11 25	11 48			11 53							12 15	12 22	
Grantham	a		10 57	11 10					11 57				12 13									12 48
	d		10 58	11 10					11 58				12 13									12 49
Newark North Gate	a			11 23	11 43								12 25									
	d			11 23	11 43								12 25									
Lincoln	a									13 14												
Retford	d																			12 53		13 10
Doncaster	a			11 50	12 08	12 18							12 50							13 09	13 12	13 24
Selby	a																					13 40
Hull	a																					14 20
Pontefract Monkhill	a																					
Wakefield Kirkgate	a					12 42																
Wakefield Westgate	a			12 07									13 07								13 30	
Leeds	a			12 26									13 26								13 49	
Mirfield	a					12 55																
Brighouse	a					13 05																
Halifax	a					13 21																
Shipley	a																					
Bradford Forster Sqare	a																					
Bradford Interchange	a					13 38																
Keighley	a																					
Skipton	a																					
Sheffield	d	11 21	12a38					11 47	13a38										12 21			
Doncaster	d				12 08			12 17												13 10		
York	a				12 33			12 39				12 48			13 14					13 33		
Scarborough	a																					
Harrogate	a																					
Leeds	d	12 05					11 29							12 28		12 41	12 57		13 05			
York	d	12 32			12 34		12a45	12 48				12 53		12 58	13 16	13a19	13 26		13 32	13 35		
Thirsk	d														13 33		13 46					
Northallerton	d				12 54									13 19	13 40		13 59					
Darlington	a	12 58			13 06			13 13				13 20		13 30					13 57	14 03		
Eaglescliffe	a														13 58							
Middlesbrough	a																14 30					
Darlington	d	13 00			13 07			13 15				13 21		13 31					13 59	14 04		
Durham	d	13 16			13 24			13 31						13 47					14 16	14 21		
Chester-le-Street	d													13 53								
Newcastle	a	13 29			13 40			13 44				13 50		14 06					14 28	14 38		
Hartlepool	a														14 20							
Sunderland	a														14 50							
Newcastle	d	13 35			13 44							13 54						14 15	14 35	14 40		
Morpeth	d																	14a37	14 48			
Alnmouth for Alnwick	d	14 00																		15 06		
Berwick-upon-Tweed	d	14 20										14 39										
Dunbar	d																		15 40			
Edinburgh	a	15 07			15 15							15 31							16 04	16 15		
Edinburgh	d	15 11									15 28											
Haymarket	d	15 16									15 32											
Motherwell	a	15 52																				
Glasgow Central	a	16 23																				
Stirling	a																					
Perth	a																					
Inverness	a																					
Inverkeithing	a																					
Kirkcaldy	a																					
Leuchars	a										16 24											
Dundee	a										16 37											
Arbroath	a										16 54											
Montrose	a										17 08											
Stonehaven	a										17 33											
Aberdeen	a										17 53											

A ✠ to Edinburgh
B ■ to Doncaster

London - Humberside, Yorkshire, North East England and Scotland

Route Diagram - see first Page of Table 26

		XC	NT	SR	GR	TP	NT	TP	NT	XC	EM	EM	GR	GR	NT	XC	EM	GR	GR	TP	NT	TP	NT
					A					B													
London Kings Cross	d				12 00								12 03	12 30				13 00	13 03				
Stevenage	d																		13 22				
Peterborough	a												12 51	13 15					13 52				
Norwich	d										10 57						11 57						
Peterborough	d										12 25	12 41	12 51	13 15			13 28		13 53				
Grantham	a										12 58		13 14				13 56	14 00	14 13				
	d										12 58		13 15				13 58	14 00	14 13				
Newark North Gate	a												13 26	13 43					14 25				
	d												13 27	13 43					14 25				
Lincoln	a											14 06											
Retford	d																						
Doncaster	a												13 52	14 09					14 50				
Selby	a																						
Hull	a																						
Pontefract Monkhill	a																						
Wakefield Kirkgate	a																						
Wakefield Westgate	a												14 11						15 07				
Leeds	a												14 30						15 26				
Mirfield	a																						
Brighouse	a																						
Halifax	a																						
Shipley	a																						
Bradford Forster Sqare	a																						
Bradford Interchange	a																						
Keighley	a																						
Skipton	a																						
Sheffield	d	12 47								13 21	14a38					13 47	15a38						
Doncaster	d	13 19												14 10		14 19							
York	a	13 40			13 52									14 33		14 40		14 51					
Scarborough	a																						
Harrogate	a																						
Leeds	d		12 29			13 28	13 42	13 57		14 05					13 29					14 28	14 41	14 57	
York	d	13 43	13a48		13 54	13 58	14a22	14 26		14 32				14 35	14a46	14 48		14 53		14 58	15a17	15 26	
Thirsk	d							14 46														15 46	
Northallerton	d					14 19		14 59						14 54						15 19		15 59	
Darlington	a	14 12			14 22	14 30				14 58				15 07		15 13		15 20		15 30			
Eaglescliffe	a																						
Middlesbrough	a							15 30														16 30	
Darlington	d	14 13			14 22	14 31				15 00				15 07		15 15		15 21		15 31			
Durham	d	14 30				14 47				15 16				15 25		15 31				15 47			
Chester-le-Street	d																			15 53			
Newcastle	a	14 42			14 52	15 05				15 29				15 41		15 45		15 50		16 09			
Hartlepool	a																						
Sunderland	a																						
Newcastle	d				14 53				15 15	15 34				15 44				15 54					16 15
Morpeth	d								15a35														16a36
Alnmouth for Alnwick	d									15 59													
Berwick-upon-Tweed	d				15 40					16 19								16 39					
Dunbar	d																						
Edinburgh	a				16 26					17 07				17 15				17 31					
Edinburgh	d			16 29	16 32					17 11													
Haymarket	d			16u33	16 38					17 16													
Motherwell	a									17 52													
Glasgow Central	a									18 11													
Stirling	a				17 18																		
Perth	a				17 59																		
Inverness	a				20 11																		
Inverkeithing	a																						
Kirkcaldy	a																						
Leuchars	a			17 24																			
Dundee	a			17 38																			
Arbroath	a			18 01																			
Montrose	a			18 16																			
Stonehaven	a			18 40																			
Aberdeen	a			19 00																			

A The Highland Chieftain
B ✠ to Edinburgh

London - Humberside, Yorkshire, North East England and Scotland

Route Diagram - see first Page of Table 26

		SR	XC	GR	NT	XC		GR	NT	TP	NT	NT	XC	EM	GR	EM		GR	HT	NT	XC	SR	GR	TP	NT
			A										A												
London Kings Cross	d			13 30				14 00							14 03			14 30	14 48				15 00		
Stevenage	d																								
Peterborough	a			14 15											14 50			15 15							
Norwich	d													12 57											
Peterborough	d			14 15										14 26	14 50	15 11		15 15							
Grantham	a													14 57	15 09				15 48						
	d													14 58	15 09				15 49						
Newark North Gate	a														15 22			15 43							
	d														15 22			15 43							
Lincoln	a															16 48									
Retford	d			14 54															16 10						
Doncaster	a			15 11											15 47			16 08	16 24						
Selby	a																		16 41						
Hull	a																		17 25						
Pontefract Monkhill	a																								
Wakefield Kirkgate	a																								
Wakefield Westgate	a														16 07										
Leeds	a														16 26										
Mirfield	a																								
Brighouse	a																								
Halifax	a																								
Shipley	a																								
Bradford Forster Sqare	a																								
Bradford Interchange	a																								
Keighley	a																								
Skipton	a																								
Sheffield	d		14 21			14 47							15 21	16a38							15 47				
Doncaster	d			15 12		15 19												16 08			16 19				
York	a			15 33		15 40		15 49										16 32			16 41		16 52		
Scarborough	a																								
Harrogate	a																								
Leeds	d		15 05		14 29				15 41	15 57			16 05							15 29				16 28	16 41
York	d		15 32	15 36	15a47	15 48		15 51	16a21	16 26			16 32					16 35		16a45	16 48		16 53	16 58	17a21
Thirsk	d									16 46														17 15	
Northallerton	d									16 59								16 54						17 23	
Darlington	a		15 58	16 03		16 13		16 19					16 58					17 07			17 13		17 21	17 34	
Eaglescliffe	a																								
Middlesbrough	a									17 30															
Darlington	d		16 00	16 04		16 15		16 20					17 00					17 07			17 15		17 22	17 35	
Durham	d		16 16	16 21		16 31							17 16					17 25			17 31			17 52	
Chester-le-Street	d																							17 58	
Newcastle	a		16 29	16 39		16 45		16 49					17 29					17 41			17 45		17 51	18 10	
Hartlepool	a																								
Sunderland	a																								
Newcastle	d		16 35	16 44				16 52			17 00	17 22	17 37					17 44					17 54		
Morpeth	d										17 22	17a42													
Alnmouth for Alnwick	d		17 00								17a45		18 01												
Berwick-upon-Tweed	d							17 40					18 21										18 40		
Dunbar	d		17 39																						
Edinburgh	a		18 05	18 13				18 27					19 08					19 15					19 31		
Edinburgh	d	17 37	18 11					18 30					19 11									19 28			
Haymarket	d	17 41	18 15					18 35					19 16									19 31			
Motherwell	a												19 52												
Glasgow Central	a												20 11												
Stirling	a																								
Perth	a																								
Inverness	a																								
Inverkeithing	a		18 28					18 54																	
Kirkcaldy	a		18 46					19 11																	
Leuchars	a	18 33	19 17					19 38														20 28			
Dundee	a	18 48	19 32					19 52														20 40			
Arbroath	a	19 05	19 49					20 10														20 57			
Montrose	a	19 21	20 03					20 26														21 12			
Stonehaven	a	19 43	20 23					20 49														21 33			
Aberdeen	a	20 06	20 43					21 15														21 53			

A to Edinburgh

London - Humberside, Yorkshire, North East England and Scotland

Route Diagram - see first Page of Table 26

		TP		NT	XC	XC	EM	GR	GR	GC	EM	XC		NT	GR	NT	TP	XC	XC	EM	GR	GR		GC	NT
					A	B				C								B	D						
London Kings Cross	d							15 03	15 30	15 48					16 00						16 03	16 30		16 48	
Stevenage	d							15 22																	
Peterborough	a							15 52	16 15												16 50	17 15			
Norwich	d						13 57													14 57					
Peterborough	d						15 25	15 53	16 15		16 25									16 27	16 51	17 15			
Grantham	a						15 57	16 13												16 55	17 11				
	d						15 58	16 13												16 56	17 11				
Newark North Gate	a							16 25													17 23	17 43			
	d							16 25													17 23	17 43			
Lincoln	a										17 51														
Retford	d								16 53																
Doncaster	a							16 50	17 08	17 20											17 49	18 08			
Selby	a																								
Hull	a																								
Pontefract Monkhill	a																								
Wakefield Kirkgate	a									17 44															
Wakefield Westgate	a							17 07													18 07				
Leeds	a							17 26													18 26				
Mirfield	a									17 57															
Brighouse	a									18 06															
Halifax	a									18 23															
Shipley	a																								
Bradford Forster Sqare	a																								
Bradford Interchange	a									18 39															
Keighley	a																								
Skipton	a																								
Sheffield	d				16 21	16 21	17a34					16 47						17 21	17 21	18a39					
Doncaster	d								17 09			17 19										18 08			
York	a								17 33			17 37			17 49							18 32		18 39	
Scarborough	a																								
Harrogate	a																								
Leeds	d	16 57			17 05	17 05								16 29		17 41	17 57	18 06	18 06						17 29
York	d	17 26			17 31	17 31			17 35			17 47		17a52	17 53	18a24	18 26	18 32	18 32			18 35		18 43	18a45
Thirsk	d	17 46															18 46							18 59	
Northallerton	d	17 58															18 59					18 55		19 10	
Darlington	a				17 56	17 56			18 02			18 12			18 21			18 59	18 59			19 07			
Eaglescliffe	a																							19 28	
Middlesbrough	a	18 30															19 31								
Darlington	d				17 58	17 58			18 03			18 14			18 22			19 00	19 00			19 08			
Durham	d				18 14	18 14			18 20			18 30						19 18	19 18			19 25			
Chester-le-Street	d																								
Newcastle	a				18 27	18 29			18 39			18 44			18 51			19 31	19 31			19 41			
Hartlepool	a																							19 47	
Sunderland	a																							20 21	
Newcastle	d			18 19	18 36	18 36			18 41						18 53			19 33	19 37			19 45			
Morpeth	d			18a40																		20 00			
Alnmouth for Alnwick	d								19 08									20 00	20 04						
Berwick-upon-Tweed	d				19 18	19 18									19 39			20 21	20 25						
Dunbar	d				19 41	19 41																			
Edinburgh	a				20 06	20 06			20 16						20 27			21 09	21 09			21 19			
Edinburgh	d				20 15	20 14												21 13	21 13						
Haymarket	d				20 20	20 18												21 18	21 18						
Motherwell	a																	22 00	22 00						
Glasgow Central	a																	22 22	22 22						
Stirling	a																								
Perth	a																								
Inverness	a																								
Inverkeithing	a				20 35	20 33																			
Kirkcaldy	a				20 52	20 50																			
Leuchars	a				21 27	21 25																			
Dundee	a				21 44	21 43																			
Arbroath	a																								
Montrose	a																								
Stonehaven	a																								
Aberdeen	a																								

A until 8 September
B from 15 September. to Edinburgh
C to Doncaster
D until 8 September. to Edinburgh

London - Humberside, Yorkshire, North East England and Scotland

Route Diagram - see first Page of Table 26

Station		GR	TP	XC	NT	TP	XC	NT	SR	XC	EM	GR	GR	GR	GR	HT	XC	NT	GR	TP	XC	XC	EM
							A			B											A	B	
London Kings Cross	d	17 00										17 03	17 10	17 30	17 35	17 48			18 00				
Stevenage	d											17 22											
Peterborough	a											17 52	17 58	18 16	18 22								
Nrwich	d										15 52												16 57
Peterborough	d										17 27	17 53	17 59	18 16	18 22								18 26
Grantham	a										17 58	18 13	18 20			18 48							18 55
	d										18 03	18 13	18 20			18 49							18 58
Newark North Gate	a											18 25		18 45									
	d											18 25		18 45									
Lincoln	a																						
Retford	d															19 12							
Doncaster	a											18 49	18 53	19 09	19 14	19 26							
Selby	a												19 09			19 42							
Hull	a												19 54			20 24							
Pontefract Monkhill	a																						
Wakefield Kirkgate	a																						
Wakefield Westgate	a											19 07			19 32								
Leeds	a											19 25			19 48								
Mirfield	a																						
Brighouse	a																						
Halifax	a																						
Shipley	a																						
Bradford Forster Sqare	a																						
Bradford Interchange	a																						
Keighley	a																						
Skipton	a																						
Sheffield	d			17 47			18 21			18 21	19a39						18 47				19 22	19 22	20a27
Doncaster	d													19 10			19 18						
York	a	18 50												19 33			19 39		19 53				
Scarborough	a																						
Harrogate	a														20 27								
Leeds	d		18 28	18 35	18 41	18 57	19 05			19 05								18 29		19 57	20 08	20 08	
York	d	18 53	18 58	19 05	19a21	19 26	19 32			19 32				19 36			19 44	19a45	19 55	20 29	20 33	20 33	
Thirsk	d					19 46														20 49			
Nrthallerton	d		19 19			19 57														20 59			
Darlington	a	19 23	19 30	19 35			19 57			19 57				20 04			20 11		20 22		20 58	20 58	
Eaglescliffe	a																						
Middlesbrough	a					20 30														21 30			
Darlington	d	19 24	19 31	19 37			19 59			19 59				20 04			20 13		20 23		21 00	21 00	
Durham	d		19 47	19 53			20 15			20 15				20 22			20 30				21 17	21 17	
ChesterleStreet	d		19 53																				
Newcastle	a	19 53	20 07	20 08			20 28			20 28				20 41			20 42		20 52		21 29	21 29	
Hartlepool	a																						
Sunderland	a																						
Newcastle	d	19 57						20 20		20 38									20 54			21 38	
Morpeth	d							20a41		20 53									21 09				
Alnmouth for Alnwick	d																		21 25				
Berwick-upon-Tweed	d	20 43								21 24									21 49			22 02	
Dnbar	d									21 50									22 13				
Edinburgh	a	21 33								22 14									22 41			23 10	
Edinburgh	d								21 40														
Haymarket	d								21 44														
Motherwell	a																						
Glasgow Central	a																						
Stirling	a																						
Perth	a																						
Inverness	a																						
Inverkeithing	a																						
Kirkcaldy	a								22 12														
Leuchars	a								22 34														
Dundee	a								22 48														
Arbroath	a								23 05														
Montrose	a								23 18														
Stonehaven	a								23 40														
Aberdeen	a								00 03														

A from 15 September until 20 October

B until 8 September, from 27 October

London - Humberside, Yorkshire, North East England and Scotland

Route Diagram - see first Page of Table 26

Station		GR	GR	GR	GR	EM	XC	GR	GC	GC	GC	GR	HT	EM	TP	NT	XC	XC	XC	GR	GR	GR
										A	B					C	C	D		E	F	
London Kings Cross	d	18 03	18 08	18 30	18 35			19 00	19 07	19 20	19 20	19 30	19 48							20 00	20 00	20 30
Stevenage	d		18 28									19 49										
Peterborough	a	18 51	18 58	19 15	19 21							20 19								20 46	20 46	21 15
Nrwich	d					17 54								18 57								
Peterborough	d	18 52	18 59	19 15	19 22	19 30						20 20		20 27						20 47	20 47	21 15
Grantham	a		19 19			19 59						20 40	20 49	20 58								21 35
	d		19 20									20 40	20 50									21 35
Newark North Gate	a	19 18	19 33	19 43								20 52								21 14	21 14	21 47
	d	19 18	19 33	19 43								20 52								21 14	21 14	21 47
Lincoln	a		20 03																			
Retford	d	19 34											21 14									22 02
Doncaster	a	19 49		20 08	20 12					20 51	20 51	21 16	21 28							21 39	21 39	22 17
Selby	a												21 44									
Hull	a												22 26									
Pontefract Monkhill	a										21 15											
Wakefield Kirkgate	a																					
Wakefield Westgate	a	20 07			20 32							21 34										22 35
Leeds	a	20 25			20 47							21 50										22 54
Mirfield	a									21 23	21 47											
Brighouse	a									21 31	21 57											
Halifax	a									21 42	22 08											
Shipley	a											22s11										
Bradford Forster Sqare	a											22 23										
Bradford Interchange	a									21 57	22 24											
Keighley	a				21s13																	
Skipton	a				21 28																	
Sheffield	d						19 54										20 53	20 53	20 24			
Doncaster	d			20 08			20 19										21 23	21 23		21 40	21 40	
York	a			20 32			20 40	20 49	20 54								21 44	21 45		22 02	22 03	
Scarborough	a																					
Harrogate	a																					
Leeds	d														20 45	20 48			21 15			
York	d			20 35			20 48	20 52	20 58						21 14	21a30	21 48	21 48	21a57	22 05	22 05	
Thirsk	d								21 15						21 31							
Nrthallerton	d			20 55					21 22						21 39							
Darlington	a			21 07			21 13	21 19							21 51		22 13	22 13		22 33	22 33	
Eaglescliffe	a								21 40													
Middlesbrough	a																					
Darlington	d			21 08			21 15	21 20							21 52		22 15	22 15		22 34	22 34	
Durham	d			21 25			21 31								22 08		22 31	22 31		22 52	22 52	
ChesterleStreet	d														22 14							
Newcastle	a			21 44			21 44	21 52							22 28		22 47	22 47		23 11	23 11	
Hartlepool	a								21 59													
Sunderland	a								22 36													
Newcastle	d																					
Morpeth	d																					
Alnmouth for Alnwick	d																					
Berwick-upon-Tweed	d																					
Dnbar	d																					
Edinburgh	a																					
Edinburgh	d																					
Haymarket	d																					
Motherwell	a																					
Glasgow Central	a																					
Stirling	a																					
Perth	a																					
Inverness	a																					
Inverkeithing	a																					
Kirkcaldy	a																					
Leuchars	a																					
Dundee	a																					
Arbroath	a																					
Montrose	a																					
Stonehaven	a																					
Aberdeen	a																					

A from 30 une until 8 September. [1] to Dncaster

B until 23 une, from 15 September. [1] to Dncaster

C until 8 September

D from 15 September

E until 30 une

F from 7 uly

Table 26

Saturdays

London - Humberside, Yorkshire, North East England and Scotland

Route Diagram - see first Page of Table 26

		EM	NT	GR	XC	EM	GR	XC	EM	XC	XC	GR	XC
										A	B	C	B
London Kings Cross ⊖	d			21 00			22 00					23 00	
Stevenage	d												
Peterborough	a			21 45			22 46					23s46	
Norwich	d												
Peterborough	d	21 27		21 46			22 47						
Grantham	a	22 00					23 06						
	d						23 06						
Newark North Gate	a						23 18						
	d						23 18						
Lincoln	a												
Retford	d						23 33					00s24	
Doncaster	a						23 48					00s39	
Selby	a												
Hull	a												
Pontefract Monkhill	a												
Wakefield Kirkgate	a												
Wakefield Westgate	a						00 05						
Leeds	a						00 24						
Mirfield	a												
Brighouse	a												
Halifax	a												
Shipley	a												
Bradford Forster Sqare	a												
Bradford Interchange	a												
Keighley	a												
Skipton	a												
Sheffield	d				21 21	21 25		22 09	22 19	22 27	22 27		23 12
Doncaster	d							22 34		22 53	22 53		
York	a			22 51				22 57				01s02	
Scarborough	a												
Harrogate	a												
Leeds	d		22 00		22a02	22a19			23a04	23a27	23a27		23a51
York	d		22a40	22 52									
Thirsk	d												
Northallerton	d			23 13									
Darlington	a			23 26								01s31	
Eaglescliffe	a												
Middlesbrough	a												
Darlington	d			23 26									
Durham	d			23 44								01s49	
Chester-le-Street	d												
Newcastle	a			00 04								02 08	
Hartlepool	a												
Sunderland	a												
Newcastle	d												
Morpeth	d												
Alnmouth for Alnwick	d												
Berwick-upon-Tweed	d												
Dunbar	d												
Edinburgh	a												
Edinburgh	d												
Haymarket	d												
Motherwell	a												
Glasgow Central	a												
Stirling	a												
Perth	a												
Inverness	a												
Inverkeithing	a												
Kirkcaldy	a												
Leuchars	a												
Dundee	a												
Arbroath	a												
Montrose	a												
Stonehaven	a												
Aberdeen	a												

A from 15 September
B until 8 September
C 28 July, 4 August, 11 August, 1 September, 8 September

Table 26

Sundays until 24 June

London - Humberside, Yorkshire, North East England and Scotland

Route Diagram - see first Page of Table 26

		GR	SR	GR	TP	XC	GR	SR	XC	GR	TP	NT	XC	NT	GR	TP	NT	SR	XC	TP	GR	GR	TP
													A						A				
London Kings Cross ⊖	d	21p00		22p00																	09 00	09 03	
Stevenage	d																					09 22	
Peterborough	a	21p45		22p46																		09 52	
Norwich	d																						
Peterborough	d	21p46		22p47																		09 53	
Grantham	a			23p06																		10 13	
	d			23p06																		10 13	
Newark North Gate	a			23p18																		10 25	
	d			23p18																		10 25	
Lincoln	a																						
Retford	d			23p33																			
Doncaster	a			23p48																		10 50	
Selby	a																						
Hull	a																						
Pontefract Monkhill	a																						
Wakefield Kirkgate	a																						
Wakefield Westgate	a			00 05																		11 08	
Leeds	a			00 24																		11 29	
Mirfield	a																						
Brighouse	a																						
Halifax	a																						
Shipley	a																						
Bradford Forster Sqare	a																						
Bradford Interchange	a																						
Keighley	a																						
Skipton	a																						
Sheffield	d																		09 21				
Doncaster	d														09 37								
York	a	22p51													09 58						10 46		
Scarborough	a																						
Harrogate	a																						
Leeds	d				07 59						08 40	08 54	09 08			09 40	09 50		10 08	10 17			10 40
York	d	22p52			08 28					09 00	09 10	09a35	09 37		10 00	10 06	10a28		10 33	10 42	10 53		11 10
Thirsk	d				08 44															10 59			
Northallerton	d	23p13			08 52					09 18	09 31					10 29				11 07			11 31
Darlington	a	23p26			09 03					09 31	09 42		10 02		10 27	10 40			10 58		11 20		11 42
Eaglescliffe	a																						
Middlesbrough	a				09 32															11 38			
Darlington	d	23p26								09 31	09 43		10 04	10 20	10 28	10 41			11 00		11 21		11 43
Durham	d	23p44								09 49	09 59		10 21		10 45	11 00			11 17				11 59
Chester-le-Street	d																						
Newcastle	a	00 04								10 05	10 18		10 34		11 01	11 17			11 29		11 50		12 15
Hartlepool	a													10 59									
Sunderland	a													11 26									
Newcastle	d								09 45	10 13			10 38	11a48	11 03				11 38		11 52		
Morpeth	d								09 58	10 29													
Alnmouth for Alnwick	d								10 12	10 45													
Berwick-upon-Tweed	d									11 09			11 20		11 48				12 20		12 37		
Dunbar	d									11 33													
Edinburgh	a								11 13	12 01			12 03		12 35				13 03		13 24		
Edinburgh	d		21p40			08 04	09 10	10 55					12 17					12 40	13 10				
Haymarket	d		21p44			08 08	09 14	10 59					12 21					12 44	13 15				
Motherwell	a												12 55						13 50				
Glasgow Central	a												13 12						14 14				
Stirling	a																						
Perth	a																						
Inverness	a																						
Inverkeithing	a					08 24	09 31	11 15										13 00					
Kirkcaldy	a		22p12			08 39	09 48	11 31										13 16					
Leuchars	a		22p34			09 05	10 13	11 54										13 39					
Dundee	a		22p48			09 18	10 27	12 07										13 52					
Arbroath	a		23p05			09 35	10 45	12 24										14 09					
Montrose	a		23p18			09 49	11 01	12 37										14 24					
Stonehaven	a		23p40			10 09	11 24	12 58										14 45					
Aberdeen	a		00 03			10 29	11 52	13 23										15 05					

A to Edinburgh

London - Humberside, Yorkshire, North East England and Scotland

Route Diagram - see first Page of Table 26

		XC	GR	GC	GR	GR	NT	NT	TP	XC	EM	EM	GR	HT	TP	GR	GR	NT	TP	XC	GR	EM	GC
		◇1	1	1	1 A	1			◇1	◇1 B	◇1	◇	1	◇1	◇1	1	1		◇1	◇1	1	◇	1 C
London Kings Cross	d		09 30	09 48	10 00	10 03							10 30	10 45		11 00	11 03				11 30		11 48
Stevenage	d													11u05			11 22						
Peterborough	a		10 15			10 50							11 15				11 52				12 15		
Norwich	d											09 33										10 47	
Peterborough	d		10 15			10 50						11 11	11 15				11 53				12 15	12 18	
Grantham	a					11 10						11 53		11 48			12 13					12 53	
	d					11 10						11 56		11 49			12 13					12 54	
Newark North Gate	a					11 22							11 43				12 25						
	d					11 22							11 43				12 25						
Lincoln	a																						
Retford	d		10 54											12 10							12 54		
Doncaster	a		11 09			11 47							12 08	12 23			12 50				13 09		13 16
Selby	a													12 43									
Hull	a													13 25									
Pontefract Monkhill	a																						
Wakefield Kirkgate	a																						13 45
Wakefield Westgate	a					12 06											13 08						
Leeds	a					12 28											13 29						
Mirfield	a																						14 00
Brighouse	a																						14 08
Halifax	a																						14 19
Shipley	a																						
Bradford Forster Sqare	a																						
Bradford Interchange	a																						14 37
Keighley	a																						
Skipton	a																						
Sheffield	d	10 21								11 21	11 31	13a33								12 21		14a35	
Doncaster	d		11 09								11 53		12 08								13 09		
York	a		11 33	11 36	11 49						12 15		12 31			12 46					13 33		
Scarborough	a																						
Harrogate	a																						
Leeds	d	11 08					11 25	10 54	11 40	12 08					12 12			12 25	12 40	13 08			
York	d	11 32	11 35	11 41	11 51		11a59	12a07	12 08	12 32			12 35		12 42	12 53		13a02	13 10	13 32	13 35		
Thirsk	d			11 58											13 00								
Northallerton	d			12 06					12 29				12 55		13 08				13 31				
Darlington	a	11 57	12 02		12 19				12 40	12 57			13 07			13 21			13 42	13 57	14 02		
Eaglescliffe	a			12 23																			
Middlesbrough	a														13 40								
Darlington	d	11 59	12 03		12 20				12 41	12 59			13 08			13 22			13 43	13 59	14 03		
Durham	d	12 16	12 20						12 57	13 15			13 25						13 59	14 15	14 20		
Chester-le-Street	d																		14 05				
Newcastle	a	12 29	12 36		12 49				13 12	13 32			13 41			13 51			14 17	14 28	14 36		
Hartlepool	a			12 50																			
Sunderland	a			13 21																			
Newcastle	d	12 38	12 44		12 54					13 36			13 45			13 54				14 36	14 42		
Morpeth	d																			14 49			
Alnmouth for Alnwick	d		13 10							14 00													
Berwick-upon-Tweed	d				13 41					14 21											15 08		
Dunbar	d	13 40	13 54													14 39				15 41			
Edinburgh	a	14 07	14 22		14 24					15 05			15 18			15 26				16 06	16 16		
Edinburgh	d				14 33					15 10													
Haymarket	d				14 38					15 15													
Motherwell	a									15 51													
Glasgow Central	a									16 13													
Stirling	a																						
Perth	a																						
Inverness	a																						
Inverkeithing	a				14 56																		
Kirkcaldy	a				15 13																		
Leuchars	a				15 37																		
Dundee	a				15 52																		
Arbroath	a				16 09																		
Montrose	a				16 25																		
Stonehaven	a				16 48																		
Aberdeen	a				17 14																		

A The Northern Lights
B to Edinburgh
C 1 to Doncaster

London - Humberside, Yorkshire, North East England and Scotland

Route Diagram - see first Page of Table 26

		GR	GR	NT	NT	TP	GR	SR	XC	GR	HT	XC	TP	GR	GR	NT	TP	XC	GR	NT	GC	XC
		1 A	1			◇1	1	◇1	◇1 B	1	◇1	◇1	◇1	1	1		◇1	◇1 B	1		1	◇1
London Kings Cross	d	12 00	12 03				12 20			12 30	12 45			13 00	13 03				13 30		13 48	
Stevenage	d										13u05				13 22							
Peterborough	a		12 50				13 08			13 15					13 52				14 15			
Norwich	d																					
Peterborough	d		12 50				13 08			13 15					13 53				14 15			
Grantham	a		13 10								13 48				14 13							
	d		13 10								13 49				14 13							
Newark North Gate	a		13 22							13 43					14 25							
	d		13 22							13 43					14 25							
Lincoln	a																					
Retford	d										14 10								14 54			
Doncaster	a		13 47				13 56			14 09	14 23				14 50				15 09			
Selby	a										14 39											
Hull	a										15 21											
Pontefract Monkhill	a																					
Wakefield Kirkgate	a																					
Wakefield Westgate	a		14 06												15 08							
Leeds	a		14 28												15 29							
Mirfield	a																					
Brighouse	a																					
Halifax	a																					
Shipley	a																					
Bradford Forster Sqare	a																					
Bradford Interchange	a																					
Keighley	a																					
Skipton	a																					
Sheffield	d								13 21			13 51						14 21				14 51
Doncaster	d						13 57			14 09		14 15							15 09			15 19
York	a	13 49					14 19			14 32		14 40		14 52					15 32		15 40	15 43
Scarborough	a																					
Harrogate	a																					
Leeds	d			13 25	12 54	13 40			14 08				14 12			14 25	14 40	15 08				
York	d	13 51		13a59	14a08	14 10	14 22		14 32	14 35		14 46	14 50	14 54		15a02	15 10	15 32	15 35		15 44	15 47
Thirsk	d												15 13								16 08	
Northallerton	d					14 31				14 54			15 21				15 31				16 15	
Darlington	a	14 19				14 42	14 49		14 57	15 07		15 13		15 22			15 42	15 57	16 02			16 13
Eaglescliffe	a																				16 33	
Middlesbrough	a												15 52									
Darlington	d	14 19				14 43	14 50		14 59	15 07		15 14		15 22			15 43	15 59	16 03	16 12		16 14
Durham	d					14 59	15 07		15 15	15 25		15 31					15 59	16 15	16 20			16 31
Chester-le-Street	d																16 05					
Newcastle	a	14 49				15 15	15 26		15 28	15 41		15 44		15 52			16 18	16 28	16 39			16 44
Hartlepool	a																			16 50	16 58	
Sunderland	a																			17 22	17 27	
Newcastle	d	14 52							15 37	15 45				15 54				16 34	16 42	17a48		
Morpeth	d																					
Alnmouth for Alnwick	d								16 02									16 59	17 09			
Berwick-upon-Tweed	d	15 39							16 22					16 39								
Dunbar	d																	17 40				
Edinburgh	a	16 22							17 06	17 15				17 27				18 07	18 18			
Edinburgh	d	16 30						17 05	17 11									18 13				
Haymarket	d	16 35						17 09	17 15									18 16				
Motherwell	a								17 52													
Glasgow Central	a								18 12													
Stirling	a	17 17																				
Perth	a	17 53																				
Inverness	a	20 19																				
Inverkeithing	a							17 22										18 28				
Kirkcaldy	a							17 38										18 44				
Leuchars	a							18 01										19 14				
Dundee	a							18 14										19 29				
Arbroath	a							18 31										19 46				
Montrose	a							18 46										20 00				
Stonehaven	a							19 07										20 23				
Aberdeen	a							19 30										20 43				

A The Highland Chieftain
B to Edinburgh

Table 26

London - Humberside, Yorkshire, North East England and Scotland

Route Diagram - see first Page of Table 26

		GR	GR	NT	NT	TP	XC	GR	HT	TP	XC	GR	NT	NT	TP	XC	EM	GR	GR	GC	XC	GR	NT
							A													B			
London Kings Cross	d	14 00	14 03					14 30	14 45			15 00						15 03	15 30	15 48		16 00	
Stevenage	d								15u05									15 22					
Peterborough	a		14 51					15 16										15 52	16 16				
Norwich	d																13 49						
Peterborough	d		14 52					15 16									15 26	15 53	16 16				
Grantham	a		15 12						15 48								15 56	16 13	16 37				
	d		15 12						15 49								15 59	16 13	16 37				
Newark North Gate	a		15 24					15 45										16 25					
	d		15 24					15 45										16 25					
Lincoln	a																						
Retford	d								16 10									16 40					
Doncaster	a		15 49					16 10	16 23									16 57	17 10	17 19			
Selby	a								16 44														
Hull	a								17 26														
Pontefract Monkhill	a																						
Wakefield Kirkgate	a																			17 47			
Wakefield Westgate	a		16 08															17 17					
Leeds	a		16 28															17 38					
Mirfield	a																			18 02			
Brighouse	a																			18 10			
Halifax	a																			18 20			
Shipley	a																						
Bradford Forster Sqare	a																						
Bradford Interchange	a																			18 37			
Keighley	a																						
Skipton	a																						
Sheffield	d						15 21				15 51					16 21	17a40				16 51		
Doncaster	d							16 10			16 17								17 10		17 17		
York	a	15 49						16 34			16 40	16 47							17 35		17 42	17 46	
Scarborough	a																						
Harrogate	a																						
Leeds	d			15 25	14 54	15 40	16 08			16 12			16 25	15 54	16 40	17 08							17 25
York	d	15 51		15a59	16a06	16 10	16 32	16 35		16 42	16 47	16 52	17a02	17a10	17 10	17 32			17 37		17 46	17 51	18a02
Thirsk	d									17 04													
Northallerton	d					16 31		16 57		17 16					17 31								
Darlington	a	16 19				16 42	16 57	17 09			17 15	17 20			17 42	17 57			18 05		18 11	18 18	
Eaglescliffe	a																						
Middlesbrough	a									17 50													
Darlington	d	16 19				16 43	16 59	17 10			17 17	17 21			17 43	17 59			18 06		18 13	18 19	
Durham	d					16 59	17 15	17 28			17 34				17 59	18 15			18 24		18 30		
Chester-le-Street	d														18 05								
Newcastle	a	16 49				17 14	17 30	17 44			17 47	17 51			18 18	18 28			18 40		18 43	18 48	
Hartlepool	a																						
Sunderland	a																						
Newcastle	d	16 53					17 38	17 47				17 54				18 36			18 42			18 54	
Morpeth	d																						
Alnmouth for Alnwick	d						18 02												19 10				
Berwick-upon-Tweed	d	17 40					18 23					18 39				19 18						19 39	
Dunbar	d															19 41							
Edinburgh	a	18 23					19 06	19 18				19 26				20 05			20 18			20 26	
Edinburgh	d	18 42					19 18																
Haymarket	d	18 47					19 23																
Motherwell	a						20 00																
Glasgow Central	a						20 20																
Stirling	a																						
Perth	a																						
Inverness	a																						
Inverkeithing	a	19 01																					
Kirkcaldy	a	19 18																					
Leuchars	a	19 43																					
Dundee	a	19 57																					
Arbroath	a	20 15																					
Montrose	a	20 31																					
Stonehaven	a	20 54																					
Aberdeen	a	21 20																					

A to Edinburgh
B to Doncaster

Table 26

London - Humberside, Yorkshire, North East England and Scotland

Route Diagram - see first Page of Table 26

		NT	TP	SR	XC	EM	EM	GR	EM	GR	GR	TP	GC	GR	GR	GR	NT	TP	NT	XC	XC	GR
					A																	
London Kings Cross	d							16 05		16 30	16 35		16 48	17 00	17 05	17 20						17 30
Stevenage	d										16 54											
Peterborough	a							16 50		17 15					17 50							18 15
Norwich	d						14 49		15 53													
Peterborough	d						16 24	16 50	17 11	17 15					17 50							18 15
Grantham	a						16 54	17 10	17 45		17 39					18 23						18 35
	d						16 56	17 10	17 55		17 39					18 23						18 35
Newark North Gate	a							17 22		17 43					18 18	18 36						
	d							17 22		17 43					18 18	18 36						
Lincoln	a																					
Retford	d										18 02											
Doncaster	a							17 48		18 08	18 17				18 48	19 03						19 09
Selby	a															19 23						
Hull	a															20 03						
Pontefract Monkhill	a																					
Wakefield Kirkgate	a																					
Wakefield Westgate	a							18 12			18 38				19 07							
Leeds	a							18 30			18 57				19 27							
Mirfield	a																					
Brighouse	a																					
Halifax	a																					
Shipley	a																					
Bradford Forster Sqare	a																					
Bradford Interchange	a																					
Keighley	a																					
Skipton	a																					
Sheffield	d				17 21	17 34	18a34		19a31											17 51	18 21	
Doncaster	d									18 09										18 15		19 11
York	a									18 31			18 40	18 46								19 35
Scarborough	a																					
Harrogate	a																					
Leeds	d	16 54	17 40		18 08	18a24						18 12					18 23	18 40	17 54	18 57	19 08	
York	d	18a10	18 10		18 32					18 35		18 42	18 47	18 52			19a01	19 10	19a12	19 21	19 32	19 37
Thirsk	d											18 59	19 04									
Northallerton	d		18 31							18 55		19 08	19 18					19 31				
Darlington	a		18 42		18 57					19 07				19 21				19 42		19 46	19 59	20 04
Eaglescliffe	a												19 35									
Middlesbrough	a											19 40										
Darlington	d		18 43		18 59					19 08				19 22				19 43		19 48	20 00	20 05
Durham	d		18 59		19 15					19 25								19 59		20 04	20 18	20 22
Chester-le-Street	d																	20 05				
Newcastle	a		19 16		19 30					19 41				19 51				20 18		20 19	20 31	20 38
Hartlepool	a												20 06									
Sunderland	a												20 39									
Newcastle	d				19 40					19 44				19 53							20 38	20 43
Morpeth	d									19 59											20 53	20 59
Alnmouth for Alnwick	d				20 05																	21 15
Berwick-upon-Tweed	d				20 25									20 39							21 26	
Dunbar	d									20 54											21 51	
Edinburgh	a				21 08					21 17				21 26							22 16	22 22
Edinburgh	d			21 00	21 13					21 21												
Haymarket	d			21 05	21 17					21 26												
Motherwell	a				21 53					22 06												
Glasgow Central	a				22 14					22 29												
Stirling	a																					
Perth	a																					
Inverness	a																					
Inverkeithing	a			21 18																		
Kirkcaldy	a			21 34																		
Leuchars	a			22 05																		
Dundee	a			22 18																		
Arbroath	a			22 37																		
Montrose	a			22 52																		
Stonehaven	a			23 13																		
Aberdeen	a			23 36																		

A to Edinburgh

London - Humberside, Yorkshire, North East England and Scotland

Sundays until 24 June

Route Diagram - see first Page of Table 26

		GR	HT	XC	EM	GR	GR	TP	NT	GC	XC	GR	GR	EM	XC	GR	GR	GR	GC	TP	NT	XC	GR
											A								B				
London Kings Cross ⊖	d	17 35	17 45			18 00	18 05			18 23		18 30	18 35			19 00	19 05	19 08	19 23				19 30
Stevenage	d	17 54	18u05										18 54					19 28					
Peterborough	a						18 53					19 16					19 50	19 58					20 17
Norwich	d				16 54									17 54									
Peterborough	d				18 26		18 53					19 17		19 26			19 51	19 59					20 17
Grantham	a	18 41	18 48		18 56								19 40	19 56				20 20					
	d	18 41	18 49		18 58								19 40					20 20					
Newark North Gate	a						19 22					19 44					20 18	20 33					20 46
	d						19 22					19 44					20 18	20 34					20 46
Lincoln	a																	21 03					
Retford	d		19 10										20 03										
Doncaster	a	19 14	19 23				19 50					20 09	20 19				20 47		20 58				21 13
Selby	a		19 45																				
Hull	a		20 26																				
Pontefract Monkhill	a																						
Wakefield Kirkgate	a																		21 22				
Wakefield Westgate	a	19 32					20 09						20 38				21 05						
Leeds	a	19 52					20 25						20 55				21 28						
Mirfield	a																		21 37				
Brighouse	a																		21 46				
Halifax	a																		21 57				
Shipley	a																						
Bradford Forster Sqare	a																						
Bradford Interchange	a																		22 11				
Keighley	a												21s22										
Skipton	a												21 41										
Sheffield	d			18 51	20a31						19 21				19 51							20 21	
Doncaster	d			19 17								20 10			20 18								21 14
York	a			19 43		19 46				20 14		20 32			20 45	20 49							21 36
Scarborough	a																						
Harrogate	a						21 05																
Leeds	d							19 40	18 54		20 08									20 40	19 54	21 08	
York	d			19 46		19 51		20 10	20a11	20 20	20 32	20 35			20 47	20 51				21 08	21a15	21a31	21 40
Thirsk	d							20 26		20 36										21 26			
Northallerton	d							20 36		20 44		20 55								21 34			
Darlington	a			20 11		20 18					20 59	21 07			21 12	21 19				21 45			22 17
Eaglescliffe	a									21 01													
Middlesbrough	a							21 07															
Darlington	d			20 13		20 19					21 00	21 08			21 14	21 20				21 46			22 18
Durham	d			20 29							21 18	21 25			21 32					22 03			22 36
Chester-le-Street	d																						
Newcastle	a			20 42		20 48					21 31	21 43			21 44	21 49				22 17			23 09
Hartlepool	a									21 21													
Sunderland	a									21 51													
Newcastle	d			20 51		21 00					21 38					21 51							
Morpeth	d															22 07							
Alnmouth for Alnwick	d										22 06					22 23							
Berwick-upon-Tweed	d					21 49										22 47							
Dunbar	d															23 12							
Edinburgh	a			22 23		22 36					23 08					23 41							
Edinburgh	d																						
Haymarket	d																						
Motherwell	a																						
Glasgow Central	a																						
Stirling	a																						
Perth	a																						
Inverness	a																						
Inverkeithing	a																						
Kirkcaldy	a																						
Leuchars	a																						
Dundee	a																						
Arbroath	a																						
Montrose	a																						
Stonehaven	a																						
Aberdeen	a																						

A to Leeds

B to Doncaster

London - Humberside, Yorkshire, North East England and Scotland

Sundays until 24 June

Route Diagram - see first Page of Table 26

		GR	HT	EM	XC	GR	GR	GR	EM	XC	TP	GR	EM	GR	GR	XC	GR	XC	EM
London Kings Cross ⊖	d	19 35	19 45			20 00	20 05	20 35				21 00		21 35	22 00		22 35		
Stevenage	d	19 54	20 05					20 54						21 55					
Peterborough	a	20 24				20 45	20 50	21 24				21 45		22 25	22 45		23s25		
Norwich	d			18 56									20 52						
Peterborough	d	20 25		20 31		20 45	20 51	21 25				21 45	22 22	22 26	22 45				
Grantham	a	20 45	20 50	21 01				21 45					22 52	22 47			23s48		
	d	20 45	20 51					21 45						22 47					
Newark North Gate	a							21 57						22 59			23s59		
	d							21 57						22 59					
Lincoln	a																		
Retford	d		21 11				21 29							23 16					
Doncaster	a	21 17	21 25				21 47	22 22						23 35	23 42		00s29		
Selby	a		21 43																
Hull	a		22 26																
Pontefract Monkhill	a																		
Wakefield Kirkgate	a																		
Wakefield Westgate	a	21 36					22 06	22 40						23 56					
Leeds	a	21 56					22 25	22 59						00 14			01 36		
Mirfield	a																		
Brighouse	a																		
Halifax	a																		
Shipley	a																		
Bradford Forster Sqare	a																		
Bradford Interchange	a																		
Keighley	a																		
Skipton	a																		
Sheffield	d				20 51				21 03	21 21						22 21		23 24	23 30
Doncaster	d				21 23										23 43				
York	a				21 44	21 52						22 58			00 33				
Scarborough	a																		
Harrogate	a																		
Leeds	d								21a44	22a04	22 12					23a01		00a16	00a18
York	d				21 47	21 58					22 42	23 04			00 35				
Thirsk	d										23 06								
Northallerton	d										23 16	23 39			01s07				
Darlington	a				22 22	22 38					23 28	23 51			01s21				
Eaglescliffe	a																		
Middlesbrough	a																		
Darlington	d				22 24	22 39					23 28	23 52							
Durham	d				22 41	22 56					23 45	00 09			01s39				
Chester-le-Street	d																		
Newcastle	a				23 10	23 30					00 15	00 43			02 12				
Hartlepool	a																		
Sunderland	a																		
Newcastle	d																		
Morpeth	d																		
Alnmouth for Alnwick	d																		
Berwick-upon-Tweed	d																		
Dunbar	d																		
Edinburgh	a																		
Edinburgh	d																		
Haymarket	d																		
Motherwell	a																		
Glasgow Central	a																		
Stirling	a																		
Perth	a																		
Inverness	a																		
Inverkeithing	a																		
Kirkcaldy	a																		
Leuchars	a																		
Dundee	a																		
Arbroath	a																		
Montrose	a																		
Stonehaven	a																		
Aberdeen	a																		

Sundays
1 July to 16 September

London - Humberside, Yorkshire, North East England and Scotland

Route Diagram - see first Page of Table 26

		GR	SR	GR	GR	GR	GR	GR	TP	TP	XC	GR	SR	XC	XC	GR	TP	NT	XC	XC	NT	XC
					A	A	A	A	D	E				D	E				F	E		E
London Kings Cross ⊖	d	21p00		22p00	23p00	00 05	00 20	00 50														
Stevenage	d																					
Peterborough	a	21p45		22p46	23b46	00s50		01s37														
Norwich	d																					
Peterborough	d	21p46		22p47																		
Grantham	a			23p06		01s10		01s57														
	d			23p06																		
Newark North Gate	a			23p18		01s22		02s09														
	d			23p18																		
Lincoln	a																					
Retford	d			23p33	00s24																	
Doncaster	a			23p48	00s39	01s47	01s52	02s34														
Selby	a																					
Hull	a																					
Pontefract Monkhill	a																					
Wakefield Kirkgate	a																					
Wakefield Westgate	a			00 05		02s06		02s53														
Leeds	a			00 24		02 23		03 10														
Mirfield	a																					
Brighouse	a																					
Halifax	a																					
Shipley	a																					
Bradford Forster Sqare	a																					
Bradford Interchange	a																					
Keighley	a																					
Skipton	a																					
Sheffield	d																					
Doncaster	d																					
York	a	22p51			01s02		02s15															
Scarborough	a																					
Harrogate	a																					
Leeds	d								07 40	07 59							08 40	08 54	09 08	09 15		
York	d	22p52							08 21	08 28						09 00	09 10	09a35	09 37	09 38		
Thirsk	d								08 37	08 44												
Northallerton	d	23p13							08 45	08 52						09 18	09 31					
Darlington	a	23p26			01s31		02s44		08 56	09 03						09 31	09 42		10 02	10 03		
Eaglescliffe	a																					
Middlesbrough	a								09 25	09 32												
Darlington	d	23p26														09 31	09 43		10 04	10 05	10 20	
Durham	d	23p44			01s49		03s02									09 49	09 59		10 21	10 21		
Chester-le-Street	d																					
Newcastle	a	00 04			02 08		03 21									10 05	10 18		10 34	10 34		
Hartlepool	a																				10 59	
Sunderland	a																				11 26	
Newcastle	d													09 45	09 45	10 13			10 38		11a48	10 45
Morpeth	d													09 58	10 15	10 29						
Alnmouth for Alnwick	d													10 12	10 50	10 45						
Berwick-upon-Tweed	d														11a45	11 09			11 20			12a20
Dunbar	d															11 33						
Edinburgh	a													11 13		12 01			12 03			
Edinburgh	d		21p40								08 04	09 10	10 55						12 17			
Haymarket	d		21p44								08 08	09 14	10 59						12 21			
Motherwell	a																		12 55			
Glasgow Central	a																		13 12			
Stirling	a																					
Perth	a																					
Inverness	a																					
Inverkeithing	a										08 24	09 31	11 15									
Kirkcaldy	a		22p12								08 39	09 48	11 31									
Leuchars	a		22p34								09 05	10 13	11 54									
Dundee	a		22p48								09 18	10 27	12 07									
Arbroath	a		23p05								09 35	10 45	12 24									
Montrose	a		23p18								09 49	11 01	12 37									
Stonehaven	a		23p40								10 09	11 24	12 58									
Aberdeen	a		00 03								10 29	11 52	13 23									

A 29 July, 5 August, 12 August, 2 September, 9 September
D not 16 September
E 16 September
F not 16 September. ⌶ to Edinburgh
b previous night, stops to set down only

Sundays
1 July to 16 September

London - Humberside, Yorkshire, North East England and Scotland

Route Diagram - see first Page of Table 26

		GR	TP	TP	NT	XC	SR	XC	TP	TP	XC	GR	GR	TP	TP	XC	GR	GC	XC	GR	GR	NT	NT
			A	B		B		C	B	A	B			A	B	B			B	D			
London Kings Cross ⊖	d											09 00	09 03				09 30	09 48		10 00	10 03		
Stevenage	d												09 22										
Peterborough	a												09 52				10 15				10 50		
Norwich	d																						
Peterborough	d												09 53				10 15				10 50		
Grantham	a												10 13								11 10		
	d												10 13								11 10		
Newark North Gate	a												10 25								11 22		
	d												10 25								11 22		
Lincoln	a																						
Retford	d																10 54						
Doncaster	a												10 50				11 09				11 47		
Selby	a																						
Hull	a																						
Pontefract Monkhill	a																						
Wakefield Kirkgate	a																						
Wakefield Westgate	a												11 08								12 06		
Leeds	a												11 29								12 28		
Mirfield	a																						
Brighouse	a																						
Halifax	a																						
Shipley	a																						
Bradford Forster Sqare	a																						
Bradford Interchange	a																						
Keighley	a																						
Skipton	a																						
Sheffield	d					09 21		09 21								10 21							
Doncaster	d	09 37															11 09						
York	a	09 58										10 48					11 33	11 36		11 49			
Scarborough	a																						
Harrogate	a																						
Leeds	d		09 40	09 45	09 50	10 05		10 08	10 17					10 40	10 40	11 05						11 25	10 54
York	d	10 00	10 13	10 13	10a28	10 29		10 33	10 42	10 42		10 53		11 10	11 11	11 29	11 35	11 41		11 51		11a59	12a07
Thirsk	d								10 59	10 59								11 58					
Northallerton	d		10 35	10 36					11 07	11 07				11 31	11 32			12 06					
Darlington	a	10 27	10 46	10 47		10 54		10 58				11 20		11 42	11 43	11 54	12 02			12 19			
Eaglescliffe	a																	12 23					
Middlesbrough	a								11 38	11 39													
Darlington	d	10 28	10 47	10 48		10 56		11 00				11 21		11 43	11 44	11 56	12 03			12 20			
Durham	d	10 45	11 08	11 03		11 12		11 17						11 59	12 00	12 13	12 20						
Chester-le-Street	d																						
Newcastle	a	11 01	11 24	11 19		11 24		11 29				11 50		12 15	12 16	12 25	12 36			12 49			
Hartlepool	a																	12 50					
Sunderland	a																	13 21					
Newcastle	d	11 03						11 38			11 45	11 52					12 44		12 45	12 54			
Morpeth	d																						
Alnmouth for Alnwick	d																13 10						
Berwick-upon-Tweed	d	11 48						12 20			13a20	12 37							14 20	13 41			
Dunbar	d																13 54		15a00				
Edinburgh	a	12 35						13 03				13 24					14 22			14 24			
Edinburgh	d						12 40	13 10												14 33			
Haymarket	d						12 44	13 15												14 38			
Motherwell	a							13 50															
Glasgow Central	a							14 14															
Stirling	a																						
Perth	a																						
Inverness	a																						
Inverkeithing	a						13 00													14 56			
Kirkcaldy	a						13 16													15 13			
Leuchars	a						13 39													15 37			
Dundee	a						13 52													15 52			
Arbroath	a						14 09													16 09			
Montrose	a						14 24													16 25			
Stonehaven	a						14 45													16 48			
Aberdeen	a						15 05													17 14			

A not 16 September
B 16 September
C not 16 September. ⌶ to Edinburgh
D The Northern Lights

1 July to 16 September

London - Humberside, Yorkshire, North East England and Scotland

Route Diagram - see first Page of Table 26

		TP	TP	XC	XC	EM	EM	GR	HT	TP	XC	GR	GR	NT	TP	XC	XC	GR	EM	GC	GC	XC
		A	B	B	C		A				B					A	B			D	E	B
London Kings Cross	d							10 30	10 45			11 00	11 03					11 30		11 48	11 48	
Stevenage	d								11u05				11 22									
Peterborough	a							11 15					11 52					12 15				
Norwich	d						09 33												10 47			
Peterborough	d						11 11	11 15					11 53					12 15	12 18			
Grantham	a						11 53		11 48				12 13						12 53			
	d						11 56		11 49				12 13						12 54			
Newark North Gate	a							11 43					12 25									
	d							11 43					12 25									
Lincoln	a																					
Retford	d								12 10									12 54				
Doncaster	a							12 08	12 23				12 50					13 09		13 16	13 16	
Selby	a								12 43													
Hull	a								13 25													
Pontefract Monkhill	a																					
Wakefield Kirkgate	a																			13 45	13 45	
Wakefield Westgate	a												13 08									
Leeds	a												13 29									
Mirfield	a																			14 00		
Brighouse	a																			14 08		
Halifax	a																			14 19		
Shipley	a																					
Bradford Forster Sqare	a																					
Bradford Interchange	a																			14 37	14 40	
Keighley	a																					
Skipton	a																					
Sheffield	d			11 21	11 21	11 31	13a33									12 21	12 21		14a35			
Doncaster	d					11 53		12 08										13 09				
York	a					12 15		12 31				12 46						13 33				
Scarborough	a																					
Harrogate	a																					
Leeds	d	11 40	11 40	12 08	12 08					12 12				12 25	12 40	13 08	13 08					
York	d	12 08	12 10	12 32	12 32			12 35		12 42		12 53		13a02	13 10	13 32	13 34	13 35				
Thirsk	d									13 00												
Northallerton	d	12 29	12 31					12 55		13 08					13 31							
Darlington	a	12 40	12 42	12 57	12 57			13 07				13 21			13 42	13 57	14 00	14 02				
Eaglescliffe	a																					
Middlesbrough	a									13 40												
Darlington	d	12 41	12 43	12 59	12 59			13 08				13 22			13 43	13 59	14 01	14 03				
Durham	d	12 57	12 59	13 15	13 15			13 25							13 59	14 15	14 18	14 20				
Chester-le-Street	d														14 05							
Newcastle	a	13 12	13 14	13 31	13 32			13 41				13 51			14 17	14 28	14 32	14 36				
Hartlepool	a																					
Sunderland	a																					
Newcastle	d				13 36			13 45			13 45	13 54				14 36		14 42				14 45
Morpeth	d															14 49						15 15
Alnmouth for Alnwick	d				14 00						14 45							15 08				
Berwick-upon-Tweed	d				14 21						15a40	14 39										16 25
Dunbar	d															15 41						17a05
Edinburgh	a				15 05			15 18				15 26				16 06		16 16				
Edinburgh	d				15 10																	
Haymarket	d				15 15																	
Motherwell	a				15 51																	
Glasgow Central	a				16 13																	
Stirling	a																					
Perth	a																					
Inverness	a																					
Inverkeithing	a																					
Kirkcaldy	a																					
Leuchars	a																					
Dundee	a																					
Arbroath	a																					
Montrose	a																					
Stonehaven	a																					
Aberdeen	a																					

A not 16 September
B 16 September
C not 16 September. to Edinburgh
D not 16 September. to Doncaster
E 16 September. to Doncaster

1 July to 16 September

London - Humberside, Yorkshire, North East England and Scotland

Route Diagram - see first Page of Table 26

		GR	GR	NT	NT	TP	GR	GR	TP	SR	XC	XC	GR	HT	XC	TP	XC	GR	GR	NT	TP	XC	XC
		A					B	C	B		D	B					B					D	B
London Kings Cross	d	12 00	12 03				12 15	12 20					12 30	12 45				13 00	13 03				
Stevenage	d													13u05					13 22				
Peterborough	a		12 50				13 01	13 08					13 15						13 52				
Norwich	d																						
Peterborough	d		12 50				13 08	13 08					13 15						13 53				
Grantham	a		13 10											13 48					14 13				
	d		13 10											13 49					14 13				
Newark North Gate	a		13 22										13 43						14 25				
	d		13 22										13 43						14 25				
Lincoln	a																						
Retford	d													14 10									
Doncaster	a		13 47				13 56	13 56					14 09	14 23					14 50				
Selby	a													14 39									
Hull	a													15 21									
Pontefract Monkhill	a																						
Wakefield Kirkgate	a																						
Wakefield Westgate	a		14 06																15 08				
Leeds	a		14 28																15 29				
Mirfield	a																						
Brighouse	a																						
Halifax	a																						
Shipley	a																						
Bradford Forster Sqare	a																						
Bradford Interchange	a																						
Keighley	a																						
Skipton	a																						
Sheffield	d										13 21	13 21			13 51							14 21	14 21
Doncaster	d						13 57	13 57					14 09		14 15								
York	a	13 49					14 19	14 19					14 32		14 40			14 52					
Scarborough	a																						
Harrogate	a																						
Leeds	d			13 25	12 54	13 40			13 57		14 08	14 08				14 12				14 25	14 40	15 08	15 08
York	d	13 51		13a59	14a08	14 10	14 22	14 22	14a24		14 32	14 34	14 35		14 46	14 50		14 54		15a02	15 10	15 32	15 32
Thirsk	d															15 13							
Northallerton	d					14 31							14 54			15 21					15 31		
Darlington	a	14 19				14 42	14 49	14 49			14 57	15 00	15 07		15 13			15 22			15 42	15 57	15 57
Eaglescliffe	a																						
Middlesbrough	a															15 52							
Darlington	d	14 19				14 43	14 50	14 50			14 59	15 02	15 07		15 14			15 22			15 43	15 59	15 59
Durham	d					14 59	15 07	15 07			15 15	15 20	15 25		15 31						15 59	16 15	16 15
Chester-le-Street	d																				16 05		
Newcastle	a	14 49				15 15	15 26	15 26			15 28	15 34	15 41		15 44			15 52			16 18	16 28	16 30
Hartlepool	a																						
Sunderland	a																						
Newcastle	d	14 52									15 37		15 45				15 45	15 54				16 34	
Morpeth	d																						
Alnmouth for Alnwick	d										16 02						16 40					16 59	
Berwick-upon-Tweed	d	15 39									16 22						17a35	16 39					
Dunbar	d																					17 40	
Edinburgh	a	16 22									17 06		17 15					17 27				18 07	
Edinburgh	d	16 30								17 05	17 11											18 13	
Haymarket	d	16 35								17 09	17 15											18 16	
Motherwell	a										17 52												
Glasgow Central	a										18 12												
Stirling	a	17 17																					
Perth	a	17 53																					
Inverness	a	20 19																					
Inverkeithing	a									17 22												18 28	
Kirkcaldy	a									17 38												18 44	
Leuchars	a									18 01												19 14	
Dundee	a									18 14												19 29	
Arbroath	a									18 31												19 46	
Montrose	a									18 46												20 00	
Stonehaven	a									19 07												20 23	
Aberdeen	a									19 30												20 43	

A The Highland Chieftain
B 16 September
C not 16 September
D not 16 September. to Edinburgh

Table 26

Sundays
1 July to 16 September

London - Humberside, Yorkshire, North East England and Scotland

Route Diagram - see first Page of Table 26

		XC	GR	NT	GC	XC	XC	GR	GR	NT	NT	TP	XC	GR	HT	TP	XC	GR	NT	NT	TP	XC
		◇■ A	■		■	◇■	A	■	■			◇■	◇■ B	■	◇■	◇■	◇■	■			◇■	◇■
London Kings Cross ⊖	d		13 30		13 48			14 00	14 03					14 30	14 45			15 00				
Stevenage	d														15u05							
Peterborough	a		14 15						14 51					15 16								
Norwich	d																					
Peterborough	d		14 15						14 52					15 16								
Grantham	a								15 12						15 48							
	d								15 12						15 49							
Newark North Gate	a								15 24					15 45								
	d								15 24					15 45								
Lincoln	a																					
Retford	d		14 54												16 10							
Doncaster	a		15 09						15 49					16 10	16 23							
Selby	a														16 44							
Hull	a														17 26							
Pontefract Monkhill	a																					
Wakefield Kirkgate	a																					
Wakefield Westgate	a								16 08													
Leeds	a								16 28													
Mirfield	a																					
Brighouse	a																					
Halifax	a																					
Shipley	a																					
Bradford Forster Sqare	a																					
Bradford Interchange	a																					
Keighley	a																					
Skipton	a																					
Sheffield	d					14 51							15 21				15 51					16 21
Doncaster	d		15 09			15 19								16 10			16 17					
York	a		15 32		15 40	15 43		15 49						16 34			16 40	16 47				
Scarborough	a																					
Harrogate	a																					
Leeds	d									15 25	14 54	15 40	16 08			16 12			16 25	15 54	16 40	17 08
York	d		15 35		15 44	15 47		15 51		15a59	16a06	16 10	16 32	16 35		16 42	16 47	16 52	17a02	17a10	17 10	17 32
Thirsk	d				16 08											17 04						
Northallerton	d				16 15							16 31		16 57		17 16					17 31	
Darlington	a		16 02			16 13		16 19				16 42	16 57	17 09			17 15	17 20			17 42	17 57
Eaglescliffe	a				16 33																	
Middlesbrough	a															17 50						
Darlington	d		16 03	16 12		16 14		16 19				16 43	16 59	17 10			17 17	17 21			17 43	17 59
Durham	d		16 20			16 31						16 59	17 15	17 28			17 34				17 59	18 15
Chester-le-Street	d																				18 05	
Newcastle	a		16 39			16 44		16 49				17 14	17 30	17 44			17 47	17 51			18 18	18 28
Hartlepool	a			16 50	16 58																	
Sunderland	a			17 22	17 27																	
Newcastle	d		16 42	17a48			16 45	16 53					17 38	17 47				17 54				18 36
Morpeth	d																					
Alnmouth for Alnwick	d		17 09				17a40						18 02									
Berwick-upon-Tweed	d							17 40					18 23					18 39				19 18
Dunbar	d																					19 41
Edinburgh	a		18 18					18 23					19 06	19 18				19 26				20 05
Edinburgh	d	18 13						18 42					19 18									
Haymarket	d	18 16						18 47					19 23									
Motherwell	a												20 00									
Glasgow Central	a												20 20									
Stirling	a																					
Perth	a																					
Inverness	a																					
Inverkeithing	a	18 28						19 01														
Kirkcaldy	a	18 44						19 18														
Leuchars	a	19 14						19 43														
Dundee	a	19 29						19 57														
Arbroath	a	19 46						20 15														
Montrose	a	20 01						20 31														
Stonehaven	a	20 23						20 54														
Aberdeen	a	20 43						21 20														

A 16 September
B to Edinburgh

Table 26

Sundays
1 July to 16 September

London - Humberside, Yorkshire, North East England and Scotland

Route Diagram - see first Page of Table 26

		EM	GR	GR	GC	GC	XC	NT	NT	TP	SR	XC	EM	EM	GR	EM	GR	GR	TP	TP	GC	GC	GR
		◇	■	■	■ A	■ B	◇■			◇■	◇■	◇■ C	◇■	◇	■	◇	■	■	◇■ D	◇■ E	■ E	■ D	■
London Kings Cross ⊖	d		15 03	15 30	15 48	15 48									16 05		16 30	16 35			16 48	16 48	17 00
Stevenage	d		15 22															16 54					
Peterborough	a		15 52	16 16											16 50		17 15						
Norwich	d	13 49												14 49		15 53							
Peterborough	d	15 26	15 53	16 16										16 24	16 50	17 11	17 15						
Grantham	a	15 56	16 13	16 37										16 54	17 10	17 45		17 39					
	d	15 59	16 13	16 37										16 56	17 10	17 55		17 39					
Newark North Gate	a		16 25												17 22		17 43						
	d		16 25												17 22		17 43						
Lincoln	a																						
Retford	d		16 40															18 02					
Doncaster	a		16 57	17 10	17 19	17 19									17 48		18 08	18 17					
Selby	a																						
Hull	a																						
Pontefract Monkhill	a																						
Wakefield Kirkgate	a				17 47	17 47																	
Wakefield Westgate	a		17 17												18 12			18 38					
Leeds	a		17 38												18 30			18 57					
Mirfield	a				18 02	18 02																	
Brighouse	a				18 10	18 10																	
Halifax	a				18 20	18 20																	
Shipley	a																						
Bradford Forster Sqare	a																						
Bradford Interchange	a					18 37																	
Keighley	a																						
Skipton	a																						
Sheffield	d	17a40					16 51					17 21	17 34	18a34		19a31							
Doncaster	d			17 10			17 17										18 09						
York	a			17 35			17 42										18 31				18 40	18 40	18 46
Scarborough	a																						
Harrogate	a																						
Leeds	d							17 25	16 54	17 40		18 08	18a24						18 12	18 12			
York	d			17 37			17 46	18a02	18a10	18 10		18 32					18 35		18 42	18 42	18 47	18 47	18 52
Thirsk	d																		18 59	19 00	19 04	19 04	
Northallerton	d									18 31							18 55		19 08	19 08	19 18	19 18	
Darlington	a			18 05			18 11			18 42		18 57					19 07						19 21
Eaglescliffe	a																				19 35	19 35	
Middlesbrough	a																		19 40	19 40			
Darlington	d			18 06			18 13			18 43		18 59					19 08						19 22
Durham	d			18 24			18 30			18 59		19 15					19 25						
Chester-le-Street	d																						
Newcastle	a			18 40			18 43			19 16		19 30					19 41						19 51
Hartlepool	a																				20 06	20 06	
Sunderland	a																				20 39	20 39	
Newcastle	d			18 42								19 40					19 44						19 53
Morpeth	d																19 59						
Alnmouth for Alnwick	d			19 10								20 05											
Berwick-upon-Tweed	d											20 25											20 39
Dunbar	d																20 54						
Edinburgh	a			20 18								21 08					21 17						21 26
Edinburgh	d										21 00	21 13					21 21						
Haymarket	d										21 05	21 17					21 26						
Motherwell	a											21 53					22 06						
Glasgow Central	a											22 14					22 29						
Stirling	a																						
Perth	a																						
Inverness	a																						
Inverkeithing	a										21 18												
Kirkcaldy	a										21 34												
Leuchars	a										22 05												
Dundee	a										22 18												
Arbroath	a										22 37												
Montrose	a										22 52												
Stonehaven	a										23 13												
Aberdeen	a										23 36												

A 16 September. ■ to Doncaster
B not 16 September. ■ to Doncaster
C to Edinburgh
D 16 September
E not 16 September

1 July to 16 September

London - Humberside, Yorkshire, North East England and Scotland

Route Diagram - see first Page of Table 26

		GR	GR	NT	TP	NT	XC	XC	GR	GR	HT	XC	EM	EM	GR	GR	NT	TP	NT	GC	XC	GR	GR
		■1	■1		◇1		◇1	◇1	■1	■1	◇1	◇1	◇	◇	■1	■1		◇1		■1	◇1	■1	■1
						A							B	A			B				C		
		⊡⇌	⊡⇌				⇌	⇌	⊡⇌	⊡⇌	⊠	⇌			⊡⇌	⊡⇌				⊡	⇌	⊡⇌	⊡⇌
London Kings Cross 15 ⊖	d	17 05	17 20						17 30	17 35	17 45				18 00	18 05				18 23		18 30	18 35
Stevenage 4	d									17 54	18u05												18 54
Peterborough 8	a	17 50							18 15							18 53						19 16	
Norwich	d												16§54	16§54									
Peterborough 8	d	17 50							18 15				18§26	18§26		18 53						19 17	
Grantham 7	a		18 23						18 35	18 41	18 48		18§55	18§56									19 40
	d		18 23						18 35	18 41	18 49		18§58	18§58									19 40
Newark North Gate 7	a	18 18	18 36													19 22						19 44	
	d	18 18	18 36													19 22						19 44	
Lincoln	a																						
Retford 10	d										19 10												20 03
Doncaster 7	a	18 48	19 03						19 09	19 14	19 23					19 50						20 09	20 19
Selby	a		19 23								19 45												
Hull	a		20 03								20 26												
Pontefract Monkhill	a																						
Wakefield Kirkgate 4	a																						
Wakefield Westgate 7	a	19 07								19 32						20 09							20 38
Leeds 10	a	19 27								19 52						20 25							20 55
Mirfield	a																						
Brighouse	a																						
Halifax	a																						
Shipley	a																						
Bradford Forster Sqare	a																						
Bradford Interchange	a																						
Keighley	a																						21s22
Skipton	a																						21 41
Sheffield 7 ⇌	d						17 51	18 21				18 51	20a31	20a31							19 21		
Doncaster 7	d						18 15		19 11			19 17										20 10	
York 8	a								19 35			19 43			19 46					20 14		20 32	
Scarborough	a																						
Harrogate	a															21 05							
Leeds 10	d			18 23	18 40	17§54	18 57	19 08									19§25	19 40	18 54		20 08		
York 8	d			19a01	19 10	19a12	19 21	19 32	19 37			19 46			19 51		19a59	20 10	20a11	20 20	20 32	20 35	
Thirsk	d																	20 26		20 36			
Northallerton	d				19 31													20 36		20 44		20 55	
Darlington 7	a				19 42		19 46	19 59	20 04			20 11			20 18						20 59	21 07	
Eaglescliffe	a																			21 01			
Middlesbrough	a																	21 07					
Darlington 7	d				19 43		19 48	20 00	20 05			20 13			20 19						21 00	21 08	
Durham	d				19 59		20 04	20 18	20 22			20 29									21 18	21 25	
Chester-le-Street	d				20 05																		
Newcastle 8 ⇌	a				20 18		20 19	20 31	20 38			20 42			20 48						21 31	21 43	
Hartlepool	a																			21 21			
Sunderland ⇌	a																			21 51			
Newcastle 8 ⇌	d							20 38	20 43			20 51			21 00						21 38		
Morpeth	d							20 53	20 59														
Alnmouth for Alnwick	d								21 15												22 06		
Berwick-upon-Tweed	d							21 26							21 49								
Dunbar	d							21 51															
Edinburgh 10	a							22 16	22 22			22 23			22 36						23 08		
Edinburgh	d																						
Haymarket	d																						
Motherwell	a																						
Glasgow Central 15	a																						
Stirling	a																						
Perth	a																						
Inverness	a																						
Inverkeithing	a																						
Kirkcaldy	a																						
Leuchars 8	a																						
Dundee	a																						
Arbroath	a																						
Montrose	a																						
Stonehaven	a																						
Aberdeen	a																						

A not 16 September

B 16 September

C ⇌ to Leeds

1 July to 16 September

London - Humberside, Yorkshire, North East England and Scotland

Route Diagram - see first Page of Table 26

		EM	XC	GR	GR	GR	GC	GC	TP	NT	XC	GR	GR	HT	EM	EM	XC	GR	GR	GR	EM	XC
		◇	◇1	■1	■1	■1	■1	■1	◇1		◇1	■1	■1	◇1	◇	◇1	◇1	■1	■1	■1	◇1	◇1
							A	B								C					D	
			⇌	⊡⇌	⊡⇌	⊡⇌	⊡	⊡			⇌	⊡⇌	⊡⇌	⊠		⇌		⊡⇌	⊡⇌	⊡⇌	⇌	
London Kings Cross 15 ⊖	d			19 00	19 05	19 08	19§23	19§23				19 30	19 35	19 45				20 00	20 05	20 35		
Stevenage 4	d					19 28							19 54	20 05						20 54		
Peterborough 8	a				19 50	19 58						20 17	20 24					20 45	20 50	21 24		
Norwich	d	17 54													18 56							
Peterborough 8	d	19 26			19 51	19 59						20 17	20 25		20 31			20 45	20 51	21 25		
Grantham 7	a	19 56				20 20							20 45	20 50	21 01					21 45		
	d					20 20							20 45	20 51						21 45		
Newark North Gate 7	a				20 18	20 33						20 46								21 57		
	d				20 18	20 34						20 46								21 57		
Lincoln	a					21 03																
Retford 10	d													21 11					21 29			
Doncaster 7	a				20 47		20§58	20§58				21 13	21 17	21 25					21 47	22 22		
Selby	a													21 43								
Hull	a													22 26								
Pontefract Monkhill	a																					
Wakefield Kirkgate 4	a						21§22	21§22														
Wakefield Westgate 7	a				21 05								21 36						22 06	22 40		
Leeds 10	a				21 28								21 56						22 25	22 59		
Mirfield	a						21§37	21§37														
Brighouse	a						21§46	21§46														
Halifax	a						21§57	21§57														
Shipley	a																					
Bradford Forster Sqare	a																					
Bradford Interchange	a							22§11														
Keighley	a																					
Skipton	a																					
Sheffield 7 ⇌	d		19 51								20 21					20§45	20 51				21§03	21 21
Doncaster 7	d		20 18									21 14					21 23					
York 8	a		20 45	20 49								21 36					21 44	21 52				
Scarborough	a																					
Harrogate	a																					
Leeds 10	d								20 40	19 54	21 08					21a30					21a44	22a04
York 8	d		20 47	20 51					21 08	21a15	21a31	21 40					21 47	21 58				
Thirsk	d								21 26													
Northallerton	d								21 34													
Darlington 7	a		21 12	21 19					21 45			22 17					22 22	22 38				
Eaglescliffe	a																					
Middlesbrough	a																					
Darlington 7	d		21 14	21 20					21 46			22 18					22 24	22 39				
Durham	d		21 32						22 03			22 36					22 41	22 56				
Chester-le-Street	d																					
Newcastle 8 ⇌	a		21 44	21 49					22 17			23 09					23 10	23 30				
Hartlepool	a																					
Sunderland ⇌	a																					
Newcastle 8 ⇌	d			21 51																		
Morpeth	d			22 07																		
Alnmouth for Alnwick	d			22 23																		
Berwick-upon-Tweed	d			22 47																		
Dunbar	d			23 12																		
Edinburgh 10	a			23 41																		
Edinburgh	d																					
Haymarket	d																					
Motherwell	a																					
Glasgow Central 15	a																					
Stirling	a																					
Perth	a																					
Inverness	a																					
Inverkeithing	a																					
Kirkcaldy	a																					
Leuchars 8	a																					
Dundee	a																					
Arbroath	a																					
Montrose	a																					
Stonehaven	a																					
Aberdeen	a																					

A 16 September. 1 ⊡ ■ to Doncaster

B not 16 September. 1 ⊡ ■ to Doncaster

C not 16 September

D 16 September

Table 26

Sundays
1 July to 16 September

London - Humberside, Yorkshire, North East England and Scotland

Route Diagram - see first Page of Table 26

		TP	GR	EM	GR	GR	GR	XC	GR	GR	GR	EM	EM	XC
		◇1	1	◇	1	1	1	◇1	1	1	1	◇1	◇1	◇1
						A	B		B	A	C	A	B	
London Kings Cross 15 ⊖	d		21 00		21 35	22 00	22 00		22 35	22 35	23 00			
Stevenage 4	d				21 55									
Peterborough 6	a		21 45		22 25	22 45	22 45		23s25	23s25	23s46			
Norwich	d			20 52										
Peterborough 6	d		21 45	22 22	22 26	22 45	22 45							
Grantham 7	a			22 52	22 47				23s48	23s48				
	d				22 47									
Newark North Gate 7	a				22 59				23s59	23s59				
	d				22 59									
Lincoln	a													
Retford 10	d				23 16						00s24			
Doncaster 7	a				23 35	23 42	23 42		00s29	00s36	00s39			
Selby	a													
Hull	a													
Pontefract Monkhill	a													
Wakefield Kirkgate 4	a													
Wakefield Westgate 7	a				23 56									
Leeds 10	a				00 14				01 36	01 10				
Mirfield	a													
Brighouse	a													
Halifax	a													
Shipley	a													
Bradford Forster Sqare	a													
Bradford Interchange	a													
Keighley	a													
Skipton	a													
Sheffield 7	d							22 21				23 12	23 16	23 24
Doncaster 7	d					23 42	23 43							
York 8	a		22 58			00 10	00 33				01s02			
Scarborough	a													
Harrogate	a													
Leeds 10	d	22 12						23a01				23a53	00a01	00a11
York 8	d	22 42	23 04			00 12	00 35							
Thirsk	d	23 06												
Northallerton	d	23 16	23 39			00s44	01s07							
Darlington 7	a	23 28	23 51			00s58	01s21				01s31			
Eaglescliffe	a													
Middlesbrough	a													
Darlington 7	d	23 28	23 52											
Durham	d	23 45	00 09			01s16	01s39				01s49			
Chester-le-Street	d													
Newcastle 8	a	00 15	00 43			01 49	02 12				02 08			
Hartlepool	a													
Sunderland	a													
Newcastle 8	d													
Morpeth	d													
Alnmouth for Alnwick	d													
Berwick-upon-Tweed	d													
Dunbar	d													
Edinburgh 10	a													
Edinburgh	d													
Haymarket	d													
Motherwell	a													
Glasgow Central 15	a													
Stirling	a													
Perth	a													
Inverness	a													
Inverkeithing	a													
Kirkcaldy	a													
Leuchars 8	a													
Dundee	a													
Arbroath	a													
Montrose	a													
Stonehaven	a													
Aberdeen	a													

A not 16 September
B 16 September
C 29 July, 5 August, 12 August, 2 September, 9 September

Table 26

Sundays
from 23 September

London - Humberside, Yorkshire, North East England and Scotland

Route Diagram - see first Page of Table 26

		GR	SR	GR	XC	TP	TP	GR	SR	XC		XC	GR	TP	NT	XC	XC	NT	XC	GR		TP	NT	XC	SR
		1	◇1	1	◇	◇1	◇1	1	◇1	◇1			1	◇1		◇1	◇1			1		◇1		◇1	◇1
						A	B			A		B				B	C		B					B	
London Kings Cross 15 ⊖	d	21p00		22p00																					
Stevenage 4	d																								
Peterborough 6	a	21p45		22p46																					
Norwich	d																								
Peterborough 6	d	21p46		22p47																					
Grantham 7	a			23p06																					
	d			23p06																					
Newark North Gate 7	a			23p18																					
	d			23p18																					
Lincoln	a																								
Retford 10	d			23p33																					
Doncaster 7	a			23p48																					
Selby	a																								
Hull	a																								
Pontefract Monkhill	a																								
Wakefield Kirkgate 4	a																								
Wakefield Westgate 7	a			00 05																					
Leeds 10	a			00 24																					
Mirfield	a																								
Brighouse	a																								
Halifax	a																								
Shipley	a																								
Bradford Forster Sqare	a																								
Bradford Interchange	a																								
Keighley	a																								
Skipton	a																								
Sheffield 7	d																							09 21	
Doncaster 7	d																			09 37					
York 8	a	22p51																		09 58					
Scarborough	a																								
Harrogate	a																								
Leeds 10	d						07 59							08 40	08 54	09 15	09 15					09 45	09 50	10 05	
York 8	d	22p52				08 21	08 28						09 00	09 10	09a35	09 38	09 38			10 00		10 13	10a28	10 29	
Thirsk	d					08 37	08 44																		
Northallerton	d	23p13				08 45	08 52						09 18	09 31								10 36			
Darlington 7	a	23p26				08 56	09 03						09 31	09 42		10 03	10 03			10 27		10 47		10 54	
Eaglescliffe	a																								
Middlesbrough	a					09 25	09 32																		
Darlington 7	d	23p26											09 31	09 43		10 05	10 05	10 20		10 28		10 48		10 56	
Durham	d	23p44											09 49	09 59		10 21	10 21			10 45		11 03		11 12	
Chester-le-Street	d																								
Newcastle 8	a	00 04											10 05	10 18		10 34	10 34			11 01		11 19		11 24	
Hartlepool	a																	10 59							
Sunderland	a																	11 26							
Newcastle 8	d									09 45		09 45	10 13				10 38	11a48	10 45	11 03					
Morpeth	d									09 58		10 15	10 29												
Alnmouth for Alnwick	d									10 12		10 50	10 45												
Berwick-upon-Tweed	d											11a45	11 09				11 20		12a20	11 48					
Dunbar	d												11 33												
Edinburgh 10	a									11 13			12 01				12 03			12 35					
Edinburgh	d		21p40		08 04			09 10	10 55								12 17								12 40
Haymarket	d		21p44		08 08			09 14	10 59								12 21								12 44
Motherwell	a																12 55								
Glasgow Central 15	a																13 12								
Stirling	a																								
Perth	a																								
Inverness	a																								
Inverkeithing	a				08 24			09 31	11 15																13 00
Kirkcaldy	a		22p12		08 39			09 48	11 31																13 16
Leuchars 8	a		22p34		09 05			10 13	11 54																13 39
Dundee	a		22p48		09 18			10 27	12 07																13 52
Arbroath	a		23p05		09 35			10 45	12 24																14 09
Montrose	a		23p18		09 49			11 01	12 37																14 24
Stonehaven	a		23p40		10 09			11 24	12 58																14 45
Aberdeen	a		00 03		10 29			11 52	13 23																15 05

A from 28 October
B from 23 September until 21 October
C from 28 October. Buffet to Edinburgh

Sundays
from 23 September

London - Humberside, Yorkshire, North East England and Scotland

Route Diagram - see first Page of Table 26

		XC	TP	XC	GR	GR	TP	XC	GR	GC	XC	GR	GR	NT	NT	TP	XC	EM	GR	HT	TP	XC	GR
		◇1 A	◇1	B	1	1	◇1	◇1 B	1	1	B	1 C	1			◇1	◇1 B	◇1	1	◇1	◇1	B	1
London Kings Cross 15 ⊖	d				09 00	09 03			09 30	09 48		10 00	10 03						10 30	10 45			11 00
Stevenage 4	d					09 22														11u05			
Peterborough 8	a					09 52			10 15				10 50						11 15				
Norwich	d																						
Peterborough 8	d					09 53			10 15				10 50						11 15				
Grantham 7	a					10 13							11 10							11 48			
	d					10 13							11 10							11 49			
Newark North Gate 7	a					10 25							11 22						11 43				
	d					10 25							11 22						11 43				
Lincoln	a																						
Retford 10	d								10 54											12 10			
Doncaster 7	a					10 50			11 09				11 47						12 08	12 23			
Selby	a																			12 43			
Hull	a																			13 25			
Pontefract Monkhill	a																						
Wakefield Kirkgate 4	a																						
Wakefield Westgate 7	a					11 08							12 06										
Leeds 10	a					11 29							12 28										
Mirfield	a																						
Brighouse	a																						
Halifax	a																						
Shipley	a																						
Bradford Forster Sqare	a																						
Bradford Interchange	a																						
Keighley	a																						
Skipton	a																						
Sheffield 7	d	09 21						10 21									11 21	11 31					
Doncaster 7	d								11 09									11 53	12 08				
York 8	a				10 48				11 33	11 36		11 49						12 15	12 31				12 46
Scarborough	a																						
Harrogate	a																						
Leeds 10	d	10 05	10 17				10 40	11 05						11 25	10 54	11 40	12 08				12 12		
York 8	d	10 29	10 42		10 53		11 11	11 29	11 35	11 41		11 51		11a59	12a07	12 10	12 32		12 35		12 42		12 53
Thirsk	d		10 59							11 58											13 00		
Northallerton	d		11 07				11 32			12 06						12 31			12 55		13 08		
Darlington 7	a	10 54			11 20		11 43	11 54	12 02			12 19				12 42	12 57		13 07				13 21
Eaglescliffe	a									12 23													
Middlesbrough	a		11 38																		13 40		
Darlington 7	d	10 56			11 21		11 44	11 56	12 03			12 20				12 43	12 59		13 08				13 22
Durham	d	11 12					12 00	12 13	12 20							12 59	13 15		13 25				
Chester-le-Street	d																						
Newcastle 8	a	11 25			11 50		12 16	12 25	12 36			12 49				13 14	13 31		13 41				13 51
Hartlepool	a									12 50													
Sunderland	a									13 21													
Newcastle 8	d	11 33		11 45	11 52				12 44		12 45	12 54							13 45			13 45	13 54
Morpeth	d																						
Alnmouth for Alnwick	d								13 10														
Berwick-upon-Tweed	d	12 15		13a20	12 37						14 20	13 41										14 45	14 39
Dunbar	d								13 54		15a00											15a40	
Edinburgh 10	a	12 59			13 24				14 22			14 24							15 18				15 26
Edinburgh	d	13 10										14 33											
Haymarket	d	13 15										14 38											
Motherwell	a	13 50																					
Glasgow Central 15	a	14 14																					
Stirling	a																						
Perth	a																						
Inverness	a																						
Inverkeithing	a											14 56											
Kirkcaldy	a											15 13											
Leuchars 3	a											15 37											
Dundee	a											15 52											
Arbroath	a											16 09											
Montrose	a											16 25											
Stonehaven	a											16 48											
Aberdeen	a											17 14											

A from 28 October. ⚒ to Edinburgh
B from 23 September until 21 October
C The Northern Lights

Sundays
from 23 September

London - Humberside, Yorkshire, North East England and Scotland

Route Diagram - see first Page of Table 26

		GR	NT	TP	XC	XC	GR	EM	EM	GC	GC	XC	GR	GR	NT	NT	TP	GR	GR	TP	SR	XC
		1		◇1	◇1 A	◇1 B	1	◇ A	◇ B	1 C	1 D	B	1 E	1			◇1	1 B	1 A	◇1	◇1	◇1 F
London Kings Cross 15 ⊖	d	11 03					11 30			11 48	11 48		12 00	12 03				12 15	12 20			
Stevenage 4	d	11 22																				
Peterborough 8	a	11 52					12 15							12 50				13 01	13 08			
Norwich	d							10 47	10 47													
Peterborough 8	d	11 53					12 15	12 18	12 18					12 50				13 08	13 08			
Grantham 7	a	12 13							12 53					13 10								
	d	12 13							12 54					13 10								
Newark North Gate 7	a	12 25												13 22								
	d	12 25												13 22								
Lincoln	a																					
Retford 10	d						12 54															
Doncaster 7	a	12 50					13 09			13 16	13 16			13 47				13 56	13 56			
Selby	a																					
Hull	a																					
Pontefract Monkhill	a																					
Wakefield Kirkgate 4	a									13 45	13 45											
Wakefield Westgate 7	a	13 08												14 06								
Leeds 10	a	13 29												14 28								
Mirfield	a									14 00												
Brighouse	a									14 08												
Halifax	a									14 19												
Shipley	a																					
Bradford Forster Sqare	a																					
Bradford Interchange	a									14 37	14 40											
Keighley	a																					
Skipton	a																					
Sheffield 7	d				12 21	12 21		14a35	14a35													13 21
Doncaster 7	d						13 09											13 57	13 57			
York 8	a						13 33						13 49					14 19	14 19			
Scarborough	a																					
Harrogate	a																					
Leeds 10	d		12 25	12 40	13 08	13 08									13 25	12 54	13 40			13 57		14 08
York 8	d		13a02	13 10	13 32	13 34	13 35						13 51		13a59	14a08	14 10	14 22	14 22	14a24		14 32
Thirsk	d																					
Northallerton	d			13 31													14 31					
Darlington 7	a			13 42	13 57	14 00	14 02						14 19				14 42	14 49	14 49			14 57
Eaglescliffe	a																					
Middlesbrough	a																					
Darlington 7	d			13 43	13 59	14 01	14 03						14 19				14 43	14 50	14 50			14 59
Durham	d			13 59	14 15	14 18	14 20										14 59	15 07	15 07			15 15
Chester-le-Street	d			14 05																		
Newcastle 8	a			14 17	14 28	14 32	14 36						14 49				15 15	15 26	15 26			15 28
Hartlepool	a																					
Sunderland	a																					
Newcastle 8	d				14 33		14 42					14 45	14 52									15 37
Morpeth	d				14 47							15 15										
Alnmouth for Alnwick	d						15 08															16 02
Berwick-upon-Tweed	d											16 25	15 39									16 22
Dunbar	d				15 38							17a05										
Edinburgh 10	a				16 04		16 16						16 22									17 06
Edinburgh	d												16 30								17 05	17 11
Haymarket	d												16 35								17 09	17 15
Motherwell	a																					17 52
Glasgow Central 15	a																					18 12
Stirling	a												17 17									
Perth	a												17 53									
Inverness	a												20 19									
Inverkeithing	a																				17 22	
Kirkcaldy	a																				17 38	
Leuchars 3	a																				18 01	
Dundee	a																				18 14	
Arbroath	a																				18 31	
Montrose	a																				18 46	
Stonehaven	a																				19 07	
Aberdeen	a																				19 30	

A from 28 October
B from 23 September until 21 October
C from 28 October. 1 to Doncaster
D from 23 September until 21 October. 1 to Doncaster
E The Highland Chieftain
F from 28 October. ⚒ to Edinburgh

Table 26

Sundays from 23 September

London - Humberside, Yorkshire, North East England and Scotland

Route Diagram - see first Page of Table 26

		XC	GR	HT	XC	TP	XC	GR	GR	NT	TP	XC	XC	XC	GR	NT	GC	XC	XC	GR	GR	NT	NT
		A					A					A	B	A					A				
London Kings Cross	d		12 30	12 45				13 00	13 03						13 30		13 48			14 00	14 03		
Stevenage	d			13u05					13 22														
Peterborough	a		13 15						13 52						14 15						14 51		
Norwich	d																						
Peterborough	d		13 15						13 53						14 15						14 52		
Grantham	a			13 48					14 13												15 12		
	d			13 49					14 13												15 12		
Newark North Gate	a		13 43						14 25												15 24		
	d		13 43						14 25												15 24		
Lincoln	a																						
Retford	d			14 10											14 54								
Doncaster	a		14 09	14 23					14 50						15 09						15 49		
Selby	a			14 39																			
Hull	a			15 21																			
Pontefract Monkhill	a																						
Wakefield Kirkgate	a																						
Wakefield Westgate	a								15 08												16 08		
Leeds	a								15 29												16 28		
Mirfield	a																						
Brighouse	a																						
Halifax	a																						
Shipley	a																						
Bradford Forster Sqare	a																						
Bradford Interchange	a																						
Keighley	a																						
Skipton	a																						
Sheffield	d	13 21			13 51								14 21	14 21				14 51					
Doncaster	d		14 09		14 15										15 09			15 19					
York	a		14 32		14 40			14 52							15 32		15 40	15 43		15 49			
Scarborough	a																						
Harrogate	a																						
Leeds	d	14 08				14 12				14 25	14 40		15 08	15 08								15 25	14 54
York	d	14 34	14 35		14 46	14 50		14 54		15a02	15 10		15 32	15 32	15 35		15 44	15 47		15 51		15a59	16a07
Thirsk	d					15 13											16 08						
Northallerton	d		14 54			15 21					15 31						16 15						
Darlington	a	15 00	15 07		15 13			15 22			15 42		15 57	15 57	16 02			16 13		16 19			
Eaglescliffe	a																16 33						
Middlesbrough	a					15 52																	
Darlington	d	15 02	15 07		15 14			15 22			15 43		15 59	15 59	16 03	16 12		16 14		16 19			
Durham	d	15 20	15 25		15 31						15 59		16 15	16 15	16 20			16 31					
Chester-le-Street	d										16 05												
Newcastle	a	15 34	15 41		15 44			15 52			16 18		16 28	16 30	16 39			16 44		16 49			
Hartlepool	a															16 50	16 58						
Sunderland	a															17 22	17 27						
Newcastle	d		15 45				15 45	15 54					16 34		16 42	17a48			16 45	16 53			
Morpeth	d																						
Alnmouth for Alnwick	d						16 40						16 59		17 09				17a40				
Berwick-upon-Tweed	d						17a35	16 39												17 40			
Dunbar	d												17 40										
Edinburgh	a		17 15					17 27					18 07		18 18					18 23			
Edinburgh	d											18 13	18 13							18 42			
Haymarket	d											18 16	18 18							18 47			
Motherwell	a																						
Glasgow Central	a																						
Stirling	a																						
Perth	a																						
Inverness	a																						
Inverkeithing	a											18 28	18 31							19 01			
Kirkcaldy	a											18 44	18 46							19 18			
Leuchars	a											19 14	19 16							19 43			
Dundee	a											19 29	19 31							19 57			
Arbroath	a											19 46	19 47							20 15			
Montrose	a											20 01	20 01							20 31			
Stonehaven	a											20 23	20 23							20 54			
Aberdeen	a											20 43	20 43							21 20			

A from 23 September until 21 October

B from 28 October. ✠ to Edinburgh

Table 26

Sundays from 23 September

London - Humberside, Yorkshire, North East England and Scotland

Route Diagram - see first Page of Table 26

		TP	XC	GR	HT	TP	XC	GR	NT	TP	NT	XC	EM	EM	GR	GR	GC	GC	XC	NT	TP	NT
			A										B	C			D	E				
London Kings Cross	d			14 30	14 45			15 00							15 03	15 30	15 48	15 48				
Stevenage	d				15u05										15 22							
Peterborough	a			15 16											15 52	16 16						
Norwich	d												13 49	13 49								
Peterborough	d			15 16									15 26	15 26	15 53	16 16						
Grantham	a				15 48								15 56		16 13	16 37						
	d				15 49								15 59		16 13	16 37						
Newark North Gate	a			15 45											16 25							
	d			15 45											16 25							
Lincoln	a																					
Retford	d				16 10										16 40							
Doncaster	a			16 10	16 23										16 57	17 10	17 19	17 19				
Selby	a				16 44																	
Hull	a				17 26																	
Pontefract Monkhill	a																					
Wakefield Kirkgate	a																17 47	17 47				
Wakefield Westgate	a														17 17							
Leeds	a														17 38							
Mirfield	a																18 02	18 02				
Brighouse	a																18 10	18 10				
Halifax	a																18 20	18 20				
Shipley	a																					
Bradford Forster Sqare	a																					
Bradford Interchange	a																	18 37				
Keighley	a																					
Skipton	a																					
Sheffield	d		15 21				15 51					16 21	17a40	17a40					16 51			
Doncaster	d			16 10			16 17									17 10			17 17			
York	a			16 34			16 40	16 47								17 35			17 42			
Scarborough	a																					
Harrogate	a																					
Leeds	d	15 40	16 08			16 12			16 25	16 40	15 54	17 08								17 25	17 40	16 54
York	d	16 10	16 32	16 35		16 42	16 47	16 52	17a02	17 10	17a12	17 32				17 37			17 46	18a02	18 10	18a12
Thirsk	d					17 04																
Northallerton	d	16 31		16 57		17 16				17 31											18 31	
Darlington	a	16 42	16 57	17 09			17 15	17 20		17 42		17 57				18 05			18 11		18 42	
Eaglescliffe	a																					
Middlesbrough	a					17 50																
Darlington	d	16 43	16 59	17 10			17 17	17 21		17 43		17 59				18 06			18 13		18 43	
Durham	d	16 59	17 15	17 28			17 34			17 59		18 15				18 24			18 30		18 59	
Chester-le-Street	d									18 05												
Newcastle	a	17 14	17 30	17 44			17 47	17 51		18 18		18 28				18 40			18 43		19 16	
Hartlepool	a																					
Sunderland	a																					
Newcastle	d		17 38	17 47				17 54				18 36				18 42						
Morpeth	d																					
Alnmouth for Alnwick	d		18 02													19 10						
Berwick-upon-Tweed	d		18 23					18 39				19 18										
Dunbar	d											19 41										
Edinburgh	a		19 06	19 18				19 26				20 05				20 18						
Edinburgh	d		19 18																			
Haymarket	d		19 23																			
Motherwell	a		20 00																			
Glasgow Central	a		20 20																			
Stirling	a																					
Perth	a																					
Inverness	a																					
Inverkeithing	a																					
Kirkcaldy	a																					
Leuchars	a																					
Dundee	a																					
Arbroath	a																					
Montrose	a																					
Stonehaven	a																					
Aberdeen	a																					

A ✠ to Edinburgh

B from 23 September until 21 October

C from 28 October

D from 23 September until 21 October. ■ to Doncaster

E from 28 October. ■ to Doncaster

London - Humberside, Yorkshire, North East England and Scotland

Sundays from 23 September

Route Diagram - see first Page of Table 26

		SR	XC	EM	EM	EM	GR	EM	EM	GR	GR	TP	GC	GR	GR	GR	NT	TP	NT	XC	XC	GR	GR
		◇1	◇1 A	◇1	◇ B	◇ C	1	◇ C	◇ B	1	1	◇1	1	1	1	1		◇1	C	◇1	◇1	1	1
London Kings Cross 15 ⊖	d						16 05			16 30	16 35		16 48	17 00	17 05	17 20						17 30	17 35
Stevenage 4	d										16 54												17 54
Peterborough 8	a						16 50			17 15					17 50							18 15	
Norwich	d				14 49	14 49		15 53	15 53														
Peterborough 8	d				16 24	16 24	16 50	17 11	17 11	17 15					17 50							18 15	
Grantham 7	a				16 54		17 10		17 45		17 39					18 23						18 35	18 41
	d				16 56		17 10		17 55		17 39					18 23						18 35	18 41
Newark North Gate 7	a						17 22			17 43					18 18	18 36							
	d						17 22			17 43					18 18	18 36							
Lincoln	a																						
Retford 10	d										18 02												
Doncaster 7	a						17 48			18 08	18 17				18 48	19 03						19 09	19 14
Selby	a															19 23							
Hull	a															20 03							
Pontefract Monkhill	a																						
Wakefield Kirkgate 4	a																						
Wakefield Westgate 7	a						18 12				18 38				19 07								19 32
Leeds 10	a						18 30				18 57				19 27								19 52
Mirfield	a																						
Brighouse	a																						
Halifax	a																						
Shipley	a																						
Bradford Forster Sqare	a																						
Bradford Interchange	a																						
Keighley	a																						
Skipton	a																						
Sheffield 7	d		17 21	17 34	18a34	18a34		19a31	19a31											17 51	18 21		
Doncaster 7	d									18 09										18 15		19 11	
York 8	a									18 31			18 40	18 46								19 35	
Scarborough	a																						
Harrogate	a																						
Leeds 10	d		18 08	18a24								18 12					18 23	18 40	17 54	18 57	19 08		
York 8	d		18 32							18 35		18 42	18 47	18 52			19a01	19 10	19a12	19 21	19 32	19 37	
Thirsk	d											18 59	19 04										
Northallerton	d									18 55		19 08	19 18					19 31					
Darlington 7	a		18 57							19 07				19 21				19 42		19 46	19 59	20 04	
Eaglescliffe	a												19 35										
Middlesbrough	a											19 40											
Darlington 7	d		18 59							19 08				19 22				19 43		19 48	20 00	20 05	
Durham	d		19 15							19 25								19 59		20 04	20 18	20 22	
Chester-le-Street	d																	20 05					
Newcastle 8	a		19 30							19 41				19 51				20 18		20 19	20 31	20 38	
Hartlepool	a												20 06										
Sunderland	a												20 39										
Newcastle 8	d		19 40							19 44				19 53							20 38	20 43	
Morpeth	d									19 59											20 53	20 59	
Alnmouth for Alnwick	d		20 05																			21 15	
Berwick-upon-Tweed	d		20 25											20 39							21 26		
Dunbar	d									20 54											21 51		
Edinburgh 10	a		21 08							21 17				21 26							22 16	22 22	
Edinburgh	d	21 00	21 13							21 21													
Haymarket	d	21 05	21 17							21 26													
Motherwell	a		21 53							22 06													
Glasgow Central 15	a		22 14							22 29													
Stirling	a																						
Perth	a																						
Inverness	a																						
Inverkeithing	a	21 18																					
Kirkcaldy	a	21 34																					
Leuchars 8	a	22 05																					
Dundee	a	22 18																					
Arbroath	a	22 37																					
Montrose	a	22 52																					
Stonehaven	a	23 13																					
Aberdeen	a	23 36																					

A to Edinburgh
B from 23 September until 21 October
C from 28 October

London - Humberside, Yorkshire, North East England and Scotland

Sundays from 23 September

Route Diagram - see first Page of Table 26

		HT	XC	EM	EM	EM	GR	GR	NT	TP	NT	GC	XC	GR	GR	EM	EM	XC	GR	GR	GR	GC	GC
		◇1	◇1	◇ A	◇ B	◇ B	1	1		◇1		1	◇1 C	1	1	◇ A	◇ B	◇1	1	1	1	1 D	1 E
London Kings Cross 15 ⊖	d	17 45					18 00	18 05				18 23		18 30	18 35				19 00	19 05	19 08	19 23	19 23
Stevenage 4	d	18u05													18 54						19 28		
Peterborough 8	a							18 53						19 16						19 50	19 58		
Norwich	d			16 54	16 54	17 54										17 54	18 56						
Peterborough 8	d			18 26	18 26	19a24		18 53						19 17		19 26	20a29			19 51	19 59		
Grantham 7	a	18 48		18 55											19 40	19 56					20 20		
	d	18 49		18 58											19 40						20 20		
Newark North Gate 7	a							19 22						19 44						20 18	20 33		
	d							19 22						19 44						20 18	20 34		
Lincoln	a																				21 03		
Retford 10	d	19 10													20 03								
Doncaster 7	a	19 23						19 50						20 09	20 19					20 47		20 58	20 58
Selby	a	19 45																					
Hull	a	20 26																					
Pontefract Monkhill	a																						
Wakefield Kirkgate 4	a																					21 22	21 22
Wakefield Westgate 7	a							20 09							20 38					21 05			
Leeds 10	a							20 25							20 55					21 28			
Mirfield	a																					21 37	21 37
Brighouse	a																					21 46	21 46
Halifax	a																					21 57	21 57
Shipley	a																						
Bradford Forster Sqare	a																						
Bradford Interchange	a																						22 11
Keighley	a														21s22								
Skipton	a														21 41								
Sheffield 7	d		18 51	20a31	20a31								19 21					19 51					
Doncaster 7	d		19 17											20 10				20 18					
York 8	a		19 43				19 46					20 14		20 32				20 45	20 49				
Scarborough	a																						
Harrogate	a							21 05															
Leeds 10	d								19 25	19 40	18 54		20 08										
York 8	d		19 46				19 51		19a59	20 10	20a12	20 20	20 32	20 35				20 47	20 51				
Thirsk	d									20 26		20 36											
Northallerton	d									20 36		20 44		20 55									
Darlington 7	a		20 11				20 18						20 59	21 07				21 12	21 19				
Eaglescliffe	a											21 01											
Middlesbrough	a									21 07													
Darlington 7	d		20 13				20 19						21 00	21 08				21 14	21 20				
Durham	d		20 29										21 18	21 25				21 32					
Chester-le-Street	d																						
Newcastle 8	a		20 42				20 48						21 31	21 43				21 44	21 49				
Hartlepool	a											21 21											
Sunderland	a											21 51											
Newcastle 8	d		20 51				21 00						21 38						21 51				
Morpeth	d																		22 07				
Alnmouth for Alnwick	d												22 06						22 23				
Berwick-upon-Tweed	d						21 49												22 47				
Dunbar	d																		23 12				
Edinburgh 10	a		22 23				22 36						23 08						23 41				
Edinburgh	d																						
Haymarket	d																						
Motherwell	a																						
Glasgow Central 15	a																						
Stirling	a																						
Perth	a																						
Inverness	a																						
Inverkeithing	a																						
Kirkcaldy	a																						
Leuchars 8	a																						
Dundee	a																						
Arbroath	a																						
Montrose	a																						
Stonehaven	a																						
Aberdeen	a																						

A from 23 September until 21 October
B from 28 October
C to Leeds
D from 23 September until 21 October. 1 to Doncaster
E from 28 October. 1 to Doncaster

London - Humberside, Yorkshire, North East England and Scotland

Route Diagram - see first Page of Table 26

		TP	NT	XC	GR	GR	HT	EM	XC	GR	GR	GR	EM	EM	XC	TP	GR	EM	GR	GR	XC	GR	EM	XC
		◇■		◇■	■	■	◇■	◇	◇■	■	■	■	◇	◇■	◇■	◇■	■	◇	■	■	◇■	■	◇■	◇■
								A					B					A						A
London Kings Cross ⊖	d				19 30	19 35	19 45			20 00	20 05	20 35					21 00		21 35	22 00		22 35		
Stevenage	d					19 54	20 05					20 54							21 55					
Peterborough	a				20 17	20 24				20 45	20 50	21 24					21 45		22 25	22 45		23s25		
Norwich	d							18 56					20 52					20 52						
Peterborough	d				20 17	20 25		20 31		20 45	20 51	21 25	22a20				21 45	22 22	22 26	22 45				
Grantham	a					20 45	20 50	21 01				21 45						22 52	22 47			23s48		
	d					20 45	20 51					21 45							22 47					
Newark North Gate	a				20 46							21 57							22 59			23s59		
	d				20 46							21 57							22 59					
Lincoln	a																							
Retford	d						21 11				21 29								23 16					
Doncaster	a				21 13	21 17	21 25				21 47	22 22							23 35	23 42		00s29		
Selby	a						21 43																	
Hull	a						22 26																	
Pontefract Monkhill	a																							
Wakefield Kirkgate	a																							
Wakefield Westgate	a					21 36					22 06	22 40							23 56					
Leeds	a					21 56					22 25	22 59							00 14			01 36		
Mirfield	a																							
Brighouse	a																							
Halifax	a																							
Shipley	a																							
Bradford Forster Sqare	a																							
Bradford Interchange	a																							
Keighley	a																							
Skipton	a																							
Sheffield	d			20 21					20 51					21 03	21 21						22 21		23 16	23 24
Doncaster	d				21 14				21 23											23 43				
York	a				21 36				21 44	21 52							22 58			00 33				
Scarborough	a																							
Harrogate	a																							
Leeds	d	20 40	19 54	21 08										21a44	22a04	22 12					23a01		00a01	00a11
York	d	21 08	21a15	21a31	21 40				21 47	21 58						22 42	23 04			00 35				
Thirsk	d	21 26														23 06								
Northallerton	d	21 34														23 16	23 39			01s07				
Darlington	a	21 45			22 17				22 22	22 38						23 28	23 51			01s21				
Eaglescliffe	a																							
Middlesbrough	a																							
Darlington	d	21 46			22 18				22 24	22 39						23 28	23 52							
Durham	d	22 03			22 36				22 41	22 56						23 45	00 09			01s39				
Chester-le-Street	d																							
Newcastle	a	22 17			23 09				23 10	23 30						00 15	00 43			02 12				
Hartlepool	a																							
Sunderland	a																							
Newcastle	d																							
Morpeth	d																							
Alnmouth for Alnwick	d																							
Berwick-upon-Tweed	d																							
Dunbar	d																							
Edinburgh	a																							
Edinburgh	d																							
Haymarket	d																							
Motherwell	a																							
Glasgow Central	a																							
Stirling	a																							
Perth	a																							
Inverness	a																							
Inverkeithing	a																							
Kirkcaldy	a																							
Leuchars	a																							
Dundee	a																							
Arbroath	a																							
Montrose	a																							
Stonehaven	a																							
Aberdeen	a																							

A from 23 September until 21 October

B from 28 October

London - Humberside, Yorkshire, North East England and Scotland

Route Diagram - see first Page of Table 26

London Kings Cross ⊖	d
Stevenage	d
Peterborough	a
Norwich	d
Peterborough	d
Grantham	a
	d
Newark North Gate	a
	d
Lincoln	a
Retford	d
Doncaster	a
Selby	a
Hull	a
Pontefract Monkhill	a
Wakefield Kirkgate	a
Wakefield Westgate	a
Leeds	a
Mirfield	a
Brighouse	a
Halifax	a
Shipley	a
Bradford Forster Sqare	a
Bradford Interchange	a
Keighley	a
Skipton	a
Sheffield	d
Doncaster	d
York	a
Scarborough	a
Harrogate	a
Leeds	d
York	d
Thirsk	d
Northallerton	d
Darlington	a
Eaglescliffe	a
Middlesbrough	a
Darlington	d
Durham	d
Chester-le-Street	d
Newcastle	a
Hartlepool	a
Sunderland	a
Newcastle	d
Morpeth	d
Alnmouth for Alnwick	d
Berwick-upon-Tweed	d
Dunbar	d
Edinburgh	a
Edinburgh	d
Haymarket	d
Motherwell	a
Glasgow Central	a
Stirling	a
Perth	a
Inverness	a
Inverkeithing	a
Kirkcaldy	a
Leuchars	a
Dundee	a
Arbroath	a
Montrose	a
Stonehaven	a
Aberdeen	a

Scotland, North East England, Yorkshire and Humberside - London

Route Diagram - see first Page of Table 26

Miles	Miles	Miles			GR MO A	SR A	SR MX	GR MX	GR MX	SR MO A	GR B	EM	GR	FC	GR	GR B	EM	GR	XC	NT	FC	GR	NT
—	—	0	Aberdeen	d					18p16	21p42													
—	—	16¼	Stonehaven	d					18p33	22c00													
—	—	40½	Montrose	d					18p56	22c25													
—	—	54¼	Arbroath	d					19p12	22c43													
—	—	71¼	Dundee	d					19p30	23c06													
—	—	79½	Leuchars	d					19p44	23c25													
—	—	104½	Kirkcaldy	d					20p08	23c53													
—	—	117¼	Inverkeithing	d					20p24	00u12													
—	—	—	Inverness	d		20p25	20p47																
—	—	—	Perth	d		23c00	23c21																
—	—	—	Stirling	d		23c45	00u06																
0	—	—	Glasgow Central	d																			
12¾	—	—	Motherwell	d																			
56	—	129¼	Haymarket	d					20p43														
57¼	—	130½	Edinburgh	a		00 47	01 00		20p48	00 36													
—	—	—	Edinburgh	d	19p00				21p00														
86½	—	—	Dunbar	d	19p20				21p21														
114¾	—	—	Berwick-upon-Tweed	d	19p45				21p47														
147	—	—	Alnmouth for Alnwick	d					22p10														
165¼	—	—	Morpeth	d					22p26														
181¾	—	—	Newcastle	a	20p30				22p43														
—	—	—	Sunderland	d																			
—	—	—	Hartlepool	d																06 20			
—	—	—	Newcastle	d	20p32			21p15	22p44											06a46			07 03
190	—	—	Chester-le-Street	d												04 15						04 45	07a51
195¾	—	—	Durham	d	20p45			21p27	22p58														
217¾	—	—	Darlington	a	21p03			21p45	23p19							04u27						04 59	
—	—	—	Middlesbrough	d																		05 16	
—	—	—	Eaglescliffe	d																			
—	—	—	Darlington	d	21p04			21p46	23p19														
231¾	—	—	Northallerton	d				21p57	23b46							04u46						05 17	
239½	—	—	Thirsk	d																		05 29	
261¾	—	—	York	a	21p31			22p17	00 13														
—	—	—	Leeds	a					00 50													05 57	
—	—	—	Harrogate	d																			
—	—	—	Scarborough	d																			
—	—	—	York	d	21p33			22p19															
294¼	—	—	Doncaster	a	21p55			22p42								05u15						06 00	
—	—	—	Skipton	d																		06 21	
—	—	—	Keighley	d																			
—	—	—	Bradford Interchange	d																			
—	—	—	Bradford Forster Sqare	d																			
—	—	—	Shipley	d																			
—	—	—	Halifax	d																			
—	—	—	Brighouse	d																			
—	—	—	Mirfield	d																			
—	0	—	Leeds	d							04 07				05 05		05 25	05 30	06 00				
—	10	—	Wakefield Westgate	d							04u18				05 16		05 37	05 42	06 12				
—	—	—	Wakefield Kirkgate	d																			
—	—	—	Pontefract Monkhill	d																			
—	—	—	Sheffield	a																			
—	—	—	Hull	d															06 41				
—	—	—	Selby	d																			
—	29¾	—	Doncaster	d	21p56			22p42			04u40				05 35	05u45	05a55	06 02				06 22	
311¾	—	—	Retford	d							04u54				05 50								
—	—	—	Lincoln	d																			
330¾	—	—	Newark North Gate	a	22p19			23p06							06 05			06 27				06 46	
—	—	—		d	22p19			23p06							06 05	06u09		06 27				06 46	
344¾	—	—	Grantham	a	22p32			23p18							06 17			06 40				06 59	
—	—	—		d	22p32			23p18							06 17			06 40				06 59	
374	—	—	Peterborough	a	22p53			23p39			05u26	05 51			06 38			07 00				07 20	
—	—	—	Norwich	a								06 25											
—	—	—	Peterborough	d	22p53			23p40			05u53		06 10	06 17	06 40			07 00			06 53	07 20	
422¾	—	—	Stevenage	a	23b24			00s21						06 58							07 35		
450¼	—	—	London Kings Cross ⊖	a	00 01			00 57			06 53		07 01	07 24	07 32	07 58		07 53			08 00	08 14	

A from 21 May

B from 30 July until 7 September, not from 13 August until 29 August

b Previous night, stops to set down only

c Previous night, stops to pick up only

Scotland, North East England, Yorkshire and Humberside - London

Route Diagram - see first Page of Table 26

		FC	FC	GR	NT	XC	GR	TP	NT	EM	GR	FC	GR A	XC	GR	HT	GR	GR	NT	TP	XC	TP	GR
Aberdeen	d																						
Stonehaven	d																						
Montrose	d																						
Arbroath	d																						
Dundee	d																						
Leuchars	d																						
Kirkcaldy	d																						
Inverkeithing	d																						
Inverness	d																						
Perth	d																						
Stirling	d																						
Glasgow Central	d																						
Motherwell	d																						
Haymarket	d																						
Edinburgh	a																						
Edinburgh	d																						
Dunbar	d																						
Berwick-upon-Tweed	d																						
Alnmouth for Alnwick	d																						
Morpeth	d																						
Newcastle	a																						
Sunderland	d																						
Hartlepool	d																						
Newcastle	d						05 25								05 56					06 11	06 25		06 30
Chester-le-Street	d																			06 21			
Durham	d						05 38								06 09					06 28	06 37		06 42
Darlington	a						05 56								06 27					06 44	06 53		07 00
Middlesbrough	d							05 55															
Eaglescliffe	d																						
Darlington	d						05 57								06 28					06 45	06 54		07 00
Northallerton	d						06 08	06 23												06 56			07 13
Thirsk	d							06 31												07 04		←	
York	a						06 28	06 49							06 56					07 30	07 20	07 30	07 33
Leeds	a							07 20												→		08 04	
Harrogate	d																						
Scarborough	d																						
York	d						06 30							06 32	06 58						07 23		07 35
Doncaster	a						06 52														07 48		
Skipton	d																						
Keighley	d																						
Bradford Interchange	d																						
Bradford Forster Sqare	d												06 30										
Shipley	d												06u35										
Halifax	d																						
Brighouse	d																						
Mirfield	d																						
Leeds	d			06 05		06 15				06 34	06 40		07 00	07 05				07 15					
Wakefield Westgate	d			06 17	06 24	06 27			06 41	06 46	06 51		07 12	07 18				07 26	07 41				
Wakefield Kirkgate	d				06 29				06a44										07a44				
Pontefract Monkhill	d				06a46																		
Sheffield	a									07 25				07 50							08 18		
Hull	d															06 25							
Selby	d															07 00							
Doncaster	d			06 35		06a43	06 53				07 09					07 19		07 45					
Retford	d			06 50												07 40							
Lincoln	d																07 20						
Newark North Gate	a			07 05							07 35						07 49						
	d			07 05							07 35						07 55						
Grantham	a			07 17			07 25									08 01		08 16					
	d			07 18			07 25									08 02		08 16					
Peterborough	a			07 38			07 46								08 09		08 26						08 41
Norwich	a																						
Peterborough	d	07 14	07 25	07 40			07 50					07 46			08 11		08 26						08 41
Stevenage	a	07 58										08 32					08 57	09 00					
London Kings Cross ⊖	a	08 23	08 30	08 35			08 44				08 52	08 58	08 59		09 08	09 18	09 26	09 29					09 39

A West Riding Limited

Scotland, North East England, Yorkshire and Humberside - London

Route Diagram - see first Page of Table 26

		EM	GR	GR	XC	GR	GR	GC	TP	EM	FC	GC	XC	GR	GR	NT	NT	NT	GR	NT	TP	XC	TP
			A				B																
Aberdeen	d																						
Stonehaven	d																						
Montrose	d																						
Arbroath	d																						
Dundee	d																						
Leuchars	d																						
Kirkcaldy	d																						
Inverkeithing	d																						
Inverness	d																						
Perth	d																						
Stirling	d																						
Glasgow Central	d																						
Motherwell	d																						
Haymarket	d																						
Edinburgh	a																						
Edinburgh	d						05 40								05 48							06 06	
Dunbar	d														06 08								
Berwick-upon-Tweed	d					06 00									06 33							06 46	
Alnmouth for Alnwick	d					06 19									06 53							07 08	
Morpeth	d					06 35									07 09								
Newcastle	a					06 52	07 02								07 26							07 38	
Sunderland	d											06 45				07 55	08 30						
Hartlepool	d											07 09								09 02			
Newcastle	d				06 44	06 55	07 03						07 25		07 28	08a16	08a52			09a51	07 33	07 41	
Chester-le-Street	d																				07 42		
Durham	d				06 56	07 07							07 37		07 41						07 49	07 55	
Darlington	a				07 12	07 25							07 53		07 58						08 05	08 10	
Middlesbrough	d								07 12														
Eaglescliffe	d											07 30											
Darlington	d				07 14	07 31							07 54		07 59						08 06	08 12	
Northallerton	d								07 43			07 50									08 17		
Thirsk	d								07 51			07 59									08 25		←
York	a				07 40	07 59			08 11			08 16	08 21		08 27						08 47	08 41	08 47
Leeds	a				08 08				08 52												→	09 08	09 22
Harrogate	d													07 28									
Scarborough	d																						
York	d					08 00						08 20	08 24		08 29								
Doncaster	a												08 48		08 52								
Skipton	d			06 55																			
Keighley	d			07u06																			
Bradford Interchange	d							06 51															
Bradford Forster Sqare	d																						
Shipley	d			07u14																			
Halifax	d							07 07															
Brighouse	d							07 18															
Mirfield	d							07 28															
Leeds	d			07 40	08 11									08 15					08 45			09 11	
Wakefield Westgate	d			07 51	08 23									08 27				08 39	08 56			09 24	
Wakefield Kirkgate	d							07 42										08a42					
Pontefract Monkhill	d							08 01															
Sheffield	a				08 51								09 17									09 51	
Hull	d		07 00																				
Selby	d		07 34																				
Doncaster	d		07 55	08 10				08 31						08 45	08 53				09 16				
Retford	d					08 33																	
Lincoln	d																						
Newark North Gate	a		08 20	08 37											09 16								
	d		08 21	08 37											09 16								
Grantham	a		08 33											09 18									
	d	08 27	08 34							09 10				09 19									
Peterborough	a	08 57	09 01	09 06						09 39					09 47				10 08				
Norwich	a	10 44								11 14													
Peterborough	d		09 02	09 06							09 16				09 48				10 08				
Stevenage	a										09 57			10 08									
London Kings Cross ⊖	a		09 56	10 01		10 04	09 40	10 13			10 22	10 25		10 37	10 45				11 01				

A The Hull Executive

B The Flying Scotsman

Scotland, North East England, Yorkshire and Humberside - London

Route Diagram - see first Page of Table 26

		GR	NT	HT	EM	GR	GR	XC	NT	GR	XC	GR	NT	TP	GR	EM	EM	GR	GC	TP	GR	XC
Aberdeen	d																					
Stonehaven	d																					
Montrose	d																					
Arbroath	d																					
Dundee	d																					
Leuchars	d																					
Kirkcaldy	d																					
Inverkeithing	d																					
Inverness	d																					
Perth	d																					
Stirling	d																					
Glasgow Central	d										06 01										06 50	
Motherwell	d										06 16										07 04	
Haymarket	d										06 57										07 45	
Edinburgh	a										07 02										07 52	
Edinburgh	d	06 25					06 55	07 00			07 07	07 30									08 00	
Dunbar	d										07 27											
Berwick-upon-Tweed	d	07 06						07 39				08 11										
Alnmouth for Alnwick	d		07 20					07 59													08 58	
Morpeth	d		07 54					08 13					08 49									
Newcastle	a	07 53	08 19				08 22	08 30			08 38	08 56	09 14								09 27	
Sunderland	d																		08 42			
Hartlepool	d																		09 07			
Newcastle	d	07 55					08 25	08 35			08 43	08 58								09 15	09 28	09 35
Chester-le-Street	d																			09 24		
Durham	d						08 37	08 47			08 56									09 31	09 41	09 47
Darlington	a	08 23					08 55	09 03			09 11	09 25								09 47	09 59	10 04
Middlesbrough	d													08 50								
Eaglescliffe	d																		09 27			
Darlington	d	08 24					08 56	09 04			09 13	09 26								09 48	09 59	10 05
Northallerton	d						09 07							09 18					09 46	09 59		
Thirsk	d													09 28					09 57			
York	a	08 53					09 27	09 31			09 41	09 53		09 47					10 16	10 21	10 28	10 32
Leeds	a										10 08			10 22						10 52		
Harrogate	d																					
Scarborough	d																					
York	d	08 55					09 29	09 35				09 55			10 01				10 25		10 29	10 34
Doncaster	a						09 52	09 57							10 24						10 53	10 57
Skipton	d																					
Keighley	d																					
Bradford Interchange	d																					
Bradford Forster Sqare	d																					
Shipley	d																					
Halifax	d																					
Brighouse	d																					
Mirfield	d																					
Leeds	d					09 15				09 45	10 11							10 15				
Wakefield Westgate	d					09 27			09 39	09 56	10 23							10 27				
Wakefield Kirkgate	d								09a42													
Pontefract Monkhill	d																					
Sheffield	a							10 20			10 51											11 20
Hull	d			08 25																		
Selby	d			09 00																		
Doncaster	d			09 25		09 45	09 53			10 16					10 24	10 24		10 45			10 53	
Retford	d			09 39											10 39							
Lincoln	d															11a17						
Newark North Gate	a						10 16								10 54						11 17	
	d						10 16								10 54						11 17	
Grantham	a			10 00		10 17									11 06			11 17				
	d			10 01	10 11	10 17									11 06		11 10	11 17				
Peterborough	a				10 40		10 47			11 06					11 26		11 39				11 47	
Norwich	a				12 13												13 13					
Peterborough	d						10 48			11 06					11 27						11 49	
Stevenage	a					11 00									11 56			12 00				
London Kings Cross ⊖	a	10 54		11 09		11 28	11 46			11 59		11 55			12 24			12 28	12 29		12 46	

Scotland, North East England, Yorkshire and Humberside - London

Route Diagram - see first Page of Table 26

Station		NT	NT	GR	XC	GR	NT	TP	TP	HT	NT	GR	NT	EM	GR	GR	GC	XC	NT	GR	XC	GR	NT
					A																A		
Aberdeen	d																						
Stonehaven	d																						
Montrose	d																						
Arbroath	d																						
Dundee	d				06 32																		
Leuchars	d				06 46																		
Kirkcaldy	d				07 21																		
Inverkeithing	d				07 43																		
Inverness	d																						
Perth	d																						
Stirling	d																						
Glasgow Central	d																				07 50		
Motherwell	d																				08 05		
Haymarket	d				08 01																08 50		
Edinburgh	a				08 06																08 55		
Edinburgh	d				08 10	08 30															09 08	09 30	
Dunbar	d																				09 28		
Berwick-upon-Tweed	d				08 50																09 51	10 11	
Alnmouth for Alnwick	d																						
Morpeth	d						09 49																10 49
Newcastle	a				09 39	09 55	10 14														10 38	10 56	11 13
Sunderland	d																						
Hartlepool	d	10 02									11 02		12 02										
Newcastle	d	10a51			09 41	09 56			10 17		11a51		12a52			10 25		10 35			10 44	10 58	
Chester-le-Street	d																						
Durham	d				09 55				10 31							10 37		10 47			10 56		
Darlington	a				10 10	10 25			10 46							10 55		11 03			11 12	11 25	
Middlesbrough	d							09 50															
Eaglescliffe	d																						
Darlington	d				10 12	10 25			10 48							10 56		11 04			11 13	11 26	
Northallerton	d							10 18	10 59							11 07							
Thirsk	d							10 28															
York	a				10 41	10 53		10 47	11 23							11 27		11 31			11 41	11 53	
Leeds	a				11 07			11 22	11 52												12 08		
Harrogate	d																						
Scarborough	d																						
York	d					10 55										11 29		11 34				11 55	
Doncaster	a															11 52		11 57					
Skipton	d																						
Keighley	d																						
Bradford Interchange	d																10 22						
Bradford Forster Sqare	d																						
Shipley	d																						
Halifax	d																10 37						
Brighouse	d																10 48						
Mirfield	d																10 56						
Leeds	d			10 45	11 11										11 15					11 45	12 12		
Wakefield Westgate	d		10 39	10 56	11 24										11 27				11 39	11 56	12 24		
Wakefield Kirkgate	d		10a42														11 11		11a42				
Pontefract Monkhill	d																11 34						
Sheffield	a				11 51													12 20			12 51		
Hull	d									10 30													
Selby	d									11 05													
Doncaster	d			11 16						11 25					11 45	11 53	12 08			12 16			
Retford	d									11 39													
Lincoln	d																						
Newark North Gate	a															12 16							
	d											11 54				12 16							
Grantham	a									12 00		12 05			12 16								
	d									12 01		12 05		12 11	12 16								
Peterborough	a			12 07								12 27		12 40		12 48				13 06			
Norwich	a													14 13									
Peterborough	d			12 08								12 27				12 49				13 07			
Stevenage	a											12 57			13 02								
London Kings Cross	a			13 01		12 54				13 10		13 26			13 29	13 43	13 45			13 59		13 55	

A from Edinburgh

Table 26 — Mondays to Fridays

Scotland, North East England, Yorkshire and Humberside - London

Route Diagram - see first Page of Table 26

Station		TP	TP	GR	EM	GR	GR	XC	NT	EM	GR	XC	SR	GR	NT	TP	TP	HT	GR	EM	GR	GR
												A										
Aberdeen	d													07 52								
Stonehaven	d													08 09								
Montrose	d													08 32								
Arbroath	d													08 48								
Dundee	d													09 06								
Leuchars	d													09 20								
Kirkcaldy	d													09 44								
Inverkeithing	d													10 01								
Inverness	d																					
Perth	d																					
Stirling	d																					
Glasgow Central	d											09 00										
Motherwell	d											09 15										
Haymarket	d											09 58		10 17								
Edinburgh	a											10 02		10 25								
Edinburgh	d						10 00					10 10	10 13	10 30								
Dunbar	d												10a38									
Berwick-upon-Tweed	d											10 49										
Alnmouth for Alnwick	d						10 58															
Morpeth	d											11 21			11 49							
Newcastle	a						11 27					11 39		11 55	12 13							
Sunderland	d																					
Hartlepool	d																					
Newcastle	d		11 15				11 28	11 35				11 44		11 57			12 17					12 25
Chester-le-Street	d		11 24																			
Durham	d		11 31				11 41	11 47				11 56					12 29					12 37
Darlington	a		11 46				11 59	12 04				12 12		12 25			12 45					12 55
Middlesbrough	d	10 50														11 50						
Eaglescliffe	d																					
Darlington	d		11 48				11 59	12 05				12 13		12 26			12 46					12 56
Northallerton	d	11 18	11 59													12 18	12 58					13 07
Thirsk	d	11 28														12 28						
York	a	11 47	12 21				12 28	12 31				12 41		12 54		12 47	13 21					13 27
Leeds	a	12 22	12 52									13 07				13 22	13 52					
Harrogate	d																					
Scarborough	d																					
York	d			12 01			12 29	12 34						12 55								13 29
Doncaster	a			12 24			12 53	12 57														13 52
Skipton	d																					
Keighley	d																					
Bradford Interchange	d																					
Bradford Forster Sqare	d																					
Shipley	d																					
Halifax	d																					
Brighouse	d																					
Mirfield	d																					
Leeds	d					12 15					12 45	13 11									13 15	
Wakefield Westgate	d					12 27			12 39		12 56	13 23									13 27	
Wakefield Kirkgate	d								12a42													
Pontefract Monkhill	d																					
Sheffield	a							13 20				13 51										
Hull	d																	12 30				
Selby	d																	13 05				
Doncaster	d			12 24		12 45	12 53			13 05	13 16							13 25			13 45	13 53
Retford	d			12 39														13 39				
Lincoln	d									13a55												
Newark North Gate	a			12 54			13 17															14 16
	d			12 55			13 17												13 54			14 16
Grantham	a			13 07		13 17												14 00	14 05		14 16	
	d			13 07	13 09	13 17												14 01	14 05	14 10	14 16	
Peterborough	a			13 27	13 39		13 47				14 07								14 26	14 39		14 51
Norwich	a				15 13															16 14		
Peterborough	d			13 28			13 49				14 07								14 26			14 52
Stevenage	a			13 58		14 02													14 56		15 00	
London Kings Cross	a			14 26		14 29	14 46				15 02			14 53				15 10	15 25		15 28	15 45

A from Edinburgh

Table 26

Mondays to Fridays

Scotland, North East England, Yorkshire and Humberside - London

Route Diagram - see first Page of Table 26

		XC	NT	GR	XC	GR	NT	TP	GR		GC	NT	TP	TP	NT	EM	NT	EM	GR		GR	XC	NT	GR	XC
					A	B							C	D											
Aberdeen	d				08 20																				
Stonehaven	d				08 38																				
Montrose	d				08 59																				
Arbroath	d				09 15																				
Dundee	d				09 32																				
Leuchars	d				09 47																				
Kirkcaldy	d				10 17																				
Inverkeithing	d				10 32																				
Inverness	d					07 55																			
Perth	d					09 56																			
Stirling	d					10 30																			
Glasgow Central	d																								10 59
Motherwell	d																								11 14
Haymarket	d				10 54	11 11																			11 57
Edinburgh	a				10 58	11 17																			12 02
Edinburgh	d				11 05	11 30															12 00				12 08
Dnbar	d				11 25																				
Berwick-upon-Tweed	d				11 48																12 41				12 47
Alnmouth for Alnwick	d				12 08																				
Morpeth	d						12 49																		
Newcastle	a				12 38	12 55	13 13														13 26				13 34
Sunderland	d										12 28														
Hartlepool	d										12 52	13 02			14 02		15 02								
Newcastle	d	12 35			12 41	12 56						13a51	13 15	13 15	14a51		15a51				13 28	13 35			13 42
ChesterleStreet	d												13 24	13 24											
Durham	d	12 47			12 53								13 31	13 31							13 41	13 47			13 54
Darlington	a	13 04			13 10	13 25							13 46	13 46							13 59	14 04			14 10
Middlesbrough	d							12 50																	
Eaglescliffe	d										13 12														
Darlington	d	13 04			13 11	13 25							13 48	13 48							13 59	14 05			14 11
Nrthallerton	d							13 18			13 31		13 58	13 58											
Thirsk	d							13 28			13 42														
York	a	13 31			13 41	13 53		13 47			14 00		14 22	14 23							14 28	14 31			14 41
Leeds	a				14 07			14 22					14 52	14 52											15 07
Harrogate	d																								
Scarborough	d																								
York	d	13 34				13 55			14 01		14 05										14 29	14 34			
Doncaster	a	13 57							14 22												14 53	14 57			
Skipton	d																								
Keighley	d																								
Bradford Interchange	d																								
Bradford Forster Sqare	d																								
Shipley	d																								
Halifax	d																								
Brighouse	d																								
Mirfield	d																								
Leeds	d			13 45	14 11														14 15					14 45	15 11
Wakefield Westgate	d		13 39	13 57	14 23														14 27				14 39	14 56	15 23
Wakefield Kirkgate	d		13a42																				14a42		
Pontefract Monkhill	d																								
Sheffield	a	14 20			14 51																	15 20			15 51
Hull	d																								
Selby	d																								
Doncaster	d			14 16					14 23							14 27			14 45		14 53			15 16	
Retford	d								14 39																
Lincoln	d															15a18									
Newark North Gate	a								14 54												15 17				
	d								14 54												15 18				
Grantham	a								15 06										15 16						
	d								15 06									15 11	15 16						
Peterborough	a			15 07					15 26									15 38			15 47			16 05	
Nrwich	a																	17 13							
Peterborough	d			15 08					15 27												15 49			16 06	
Stevenage	a								15 57										16 02						
London Kings Cross	a			16 02		15 54			16 25		16 09								16 28		16 46			16 59	

A from Edinburgh
B The Highland Chieftain
C from 21 May
D until 18 May

Table 26

Mondays to Fridays

Scotland, North East England, Yorkshire and Humberside - London

Route Diagram - see first Page of Table 26

		SR	GR	NT	TP		TP	GR	NT	EM	GR	GR	XC	HT	NT		GR	XC	GR	NT	TP FX	GR	NT	EM	GR
			A																						
Aberdeen	d		09 52																						
Stonehaven	d		10 09																						
Montrose	d		10 32																						
Arbroath	d		10 49																						
Dundee	d		11 06																						
Leuchars	d		11 20																						
Kirkcaldy	d		11 44																						
Inverkeithing	d		12 01																						
Inverness	d																								
Perth	d																								
Stirling	d																								
Glasgow Central	d																								
Motherwell	d																								
Haymarket	d		12 17																						
Edinburgh	a		12 25																						
Edinburgh	d	12 11	12 30															13 06	13 30						
Dnbar	d	12a36																13 28							
Berwick-upon-Tweed	d																		14 11						
Alnmouth for Alnwick	d																	14 08							
Morpeth	d			13 49																14 49					
Newcastle	a		13 55	14 13														14 38	14 56	15 14					
Sunderland	d																								
Hartlepool	d								16 02														17 02		
Newcastle	d		13 56				14 18		16a51			14 25	14 35					14 42	14 58				17a51		
ChesterleStreet	d																								
Durham	d						14 31					14 38	14 47					14 55							
Darlington	a		14 25				14 46					14 55	15 03					15 10	15 24						
Middlesbrough	d				13 50																14 50				
Eaglescliffe	d																								
Darlington	d		14 25				14 48					14 56	15 04					15 12	15 25						
Nrthallerton	d				14 18		14 59					15 07									15 18				
Thirsk	d				14 28																15 28				
York	a		14 53		14 47		15 22					15 27	15 31					15 41	15 53		15 47				
Leeds	a				15 23		15 52											16 07			16 22				
Harrogate	d																								
Scarborough	d																								
York	d		14 55									15 29	15 34						15 55			16 01			
Doncaster	a											15 52	15 57									16 24			
Skipton	d																								
Keighley	d																								
Bradford Interchange	d																								
Bradford Forster Sqare	d																								
Shipley	d																								
Halifax	d																								
Brighouse	d																								
Mirfield	d																								
Leeds	d										15 15						15 45	16 11							16 15
Wakefield Westgate	d										15 27				15 39		15 56	16 23							16 27
Wakefield Kirkgate	d														15a42										
Pontefract Monkhill	d																								
Sheffield	a												16 20					16 51							
Hull	d													15 10											
Selby	d													15 46											
Doncaster	d										15 45	15 53		16 05			16 16					16 24			16 45
Retford	d													16 19								16 39			
Lincoln	d																								
Newark North Gate	a											16 18										16 54			
	d							15 52				16 18										16 54			
Grantham	a							16 03			16 17			16 39								17 07			17 16
	d							16 03		16 10	16 17			16 40								17 07		17 11	17 16
Peterborough	a							16 24		16 39		16 48					17 06					17 27		17 40	
Nrwich	a									18 18														19 15	
Peterborough	d							16 25				16 49					17 07					17 28			
Stevenage	a							16 54			17 00											17 58			18 03
London Kings Cross	a		16 54					17 22			17 29	17 42		17 46			18 00		17 56			18 27			18 30

A The Nrthern Lights

Scotland, North East England, Yorkshire and Humberside - London

Route Diagram - see first Page of Table 26

		NT	XC	TP FO	TP	GR	GR	GC	NT	XC	SR	GR	NT	TP	TP	GR	EM	GR	GR	XC	HT	NT
				A						B												
Aberdeen	d																					
Stonehaven	d																					
Montrose	d																					
Arbroath	d																					
Dundee	d																					
Leuchars	d																					
Kirkcaldy	d																					
Inverkeithing	d																					
Inverness	d																					
Perth	d																					
Stirling	d																					
Glasgow Central	d									12 51												
Motherwell	d									13 06												
Haymarket	d																					
Edinburgh	a									13 54												
Edinburgh	d					14 00				14 08	14 11	14 30										
Dunbar	d										14a36											
Berwick-upon-Tweed	d									14 49		15 11										
Alnmouth for Alnwick	d					14 58																
Morpeth	d												15 49									
Newcastle	a					15 27				15 34		15 56	16 14									
Sunderland	d																					
Hartlepool	d																					
Newcastle	d		15 03		15 15	15 28				15 41		15 58			16 15				16 25	16 35		
Chester-le-Street	d				15 24										16 24							
Durham	d		15 16		15 31	15 41				15 53					16 31				16 37	16 47		
Darlington	a		15 32		15 46	16 00				16 09		16 25			16 46				16 55	17 03		
Middlesbrough	d			14 50										15 50								
Eaglescliffe	d																					
Darlington	d		15 33		15 48	16 00				16 10		16 26			16 48				16 56	17 04		
Northallerton	d			15 18	15 59									16 18	16 59				17 07			
Thirsk	d			15 28										16 28								
York	a		16 01	15 47	16 21	16 28				16 41		16 53		16 47	17 23				17 28	17 31		
Leeds	a		16 32	16 59	16 52					17 06				17 22	17 52							
Harrogate	d																					
Scarborough	d																					
York	d					16 29						16 55							17 30	17 34		
Doncaster	a					16 52													17 52	17 57		
Skipton	d																					
Keighley	d																					
Bradford Interchange	d							15 37														
Bradford Forster Sqare	d																					
Shipley	d																					
Halifax	d							15 52														
Brighouse	d							16 05														
Mirfield	d							16 13														
Leeds	d		16 40				16 45		16 57	17 11								17 15				
Wakefield Westgate	d	16 39	16 52				16 56		17 09	17 23								17 27				17 39
Wakefield Kirkgate	d	16a42						16 40														17a42
Pontefract Monkhill	d							16 56														
Sheffield	a		17 20							17 51										18 20		
Hull	d																				17 10	
Selby	d																				17 45	
Doncaster	d					16 52	17 16	17 25	17a45									17 45	17 54		18 03	
Retford	d																	17 59			18 17	
Lincoln	d																					
Newark North Gate	a					17 19													18 17			
	d					17 19										17 54			18 17			
Grantham	a															18 05		18 22			18 38	
	d															18 05	18 11	18 22			18 39	
Peterborough	a					17 49	18 06									18 26	18 38		18 48			
Norwich	a																20 22					
Peterborough	d					17 50	18 07									18 26			18 50			
Stevenage	a															18 56		19 07				
London Kings Cross ⊖	a					18 45	19 01	19 05				18 54				19 25		19 35	19 45		19 47	

A ■ to York ◇ to York   B ⌶ from Edinburgh

Scotland, North East England, Yorkshire and Humberside - London

Route Diagram - see first Page of Table 26

		GR	XC	GR	NT	TP	TP	GR	EM	GR	NT	NT	GR	XC	NT	GR	XC	TP FO	GR	SR	TP FX	GC	NT
											A	B					C						
Aberdeen	d																						
Stonehaven	d																						
Montrose	d																						
Arbroath	d																						
Dundee	d																						
Leuchars	d																						
Kirkcaldy	d																						
Inverkeithing	d																						
Inverness	d																						
Perth	d																						
Stirling	d																						
Glasgow Central	d																15 00						
Motherwell	d																15 14						
Haymarket	d																15 56						
Edinburgh	a																16 01						
Edinburgh	d		15 08	15 30													16 05		16 30	16 33			
Dunbar	d		15 28																	16a58			
Berwick-upon-Tweed	d			16 11															17 11				
Alnmouth for Alnwick	d																17 01						
Morpeth	d				16 49												17 16						
Newcastle	a		16 35	16 56	17 15												17 34		17 56				
Sunderland	d																					17 31	18 42
Hartlepool	d																					17 55	
Newcastle	d		16 42	16 58			17 02						17 25	17 32			17 41		17 58				19a05
Chester-le-Street	d						17 11							17 41									
Durham	d		16 52				17 18						17 37	17 48			17 53						
Darlington	a		17 10	17 25			17 34						17 55	18 03			18 09		18 24				
Middlesbrough	d					16 50												17 50			17 50		
Eaglescliffe	d																					18 20	
Darlington	d		17 10	17 26			17 35						17 56	18 05			18 10		18 25				
Northallerton	d					17 18	17 46						18 07					18 18			18 18	18 40	
Thirsk	d					17 28												18 28			18 28	18 49	
York	a		17 40	17 53		17 47	18 09						18 27	18 31			18 41	18 47	18 53		18 47	19 07	
Leeds	a		18 07			18 22	18 37										19 08				19 37		
Harrogate	d																						
Scarborough	d										16 21	16 23											
York	d			17 56				18 01					18 29	18 34					18 55			19 10	
Doncaster	a							18 22					18 52	18 57									
Skipton	d																						
Keighley	d																						
Bradford Interchange	d																						
Bradford Forster Sqare	d																						
Shipley	d																						
Halifax	d																						
Brighouse	d																						
Mirfield	d																						
Leeds	d	17 45	18 11							18 15						18 45	19 11						
Wakefield Westgate	d	17 56	18 23							18 27					18 39	18 56	19 23						
Wakefield Kirkgate	d														18a42								
Pontefract Monkhill	d																						
Sheffield	a		18 51											19 20			19 51						
Hull	d										17 52	17 52											
Selby	d										18 26	18 26											
Doncaster	d	18 16						18 23		18 45	18a47	18a47	18 53			19 15							
Retford	d							18 38															
Lincoln	d																						
Newark North Gate	a							18 53					19 17										
	d							18 53					19 17										
Grantham	a							19 05		19 16													
	d							19 05	19 08	19 16													
Peterborough	a	19 06						19 27	19 38				19 50			20 05							
Norwich	a								21 14														
Peterborough	d	19 07						19 27					19 50			20 06							
Stevenage	a							19 56		20 01			20 20						20 23				
London Kings Cross ⊖	a	19 59		19 53				20 26		20 29			20 48			21 00			20 55			21 05	

A from 1 October   B until 28 September   C ⌶ from Edinburgh

Scotland, North East England, Yorkshire and Humberside - London

Route Diagram - see first Page of Table 26

		NT	EM	GR	GR	XC	HT	NT	GR	XC	NT	TP	NT	SR	NT	NT	TP	GR	TP	NT	XC	EM
										A				B							B	
Aberdeen	d																	14 50				
Stonehaven	d																	15 07				
Montrose	d																	15 30				
Arbroath	d																	15 46				
Dundee	d																	16 04				
Leuchars	d																	16 18				
Kirkcaldy	d																	16 45				
Inverkeithing	d																	17 03				
Inverness	d													20 47								
Perth	d													23u21								
Stirling	d													00u06								
Glasgow Central	d																					
Motherwell	d																					
Haymarket	d																	17 19				
Edinburgh	a													01 00				17 27				
Edinburgh	d				17 00					17 08								17 30				
Dunbar	d									17 28								17 51				
Berwick-upon-Tweed	d									17 51								18 16				
Alnmouth for Alnwick	d				17 58															19 01		
Morpeth	d										18 26									19 25		
Newcastle	a				18 27					18 38	18 49							19 03				
Sunderland	d															21 58						
Hartlepool	d	19 02											20 10									
Newcastle	d	19a51			18 28	18 35				18 41			21a02			22a19	18 52	19 04			19 35	
Chester-le-Street	d																19 01					
Durham	d				18 41	18 47				18 53							19 08				19 50	
Darlington	a				19 00	19 04				19 09							19 24	19 33			20 05	
Middlesbrough	d											18 50										
Eaglescliffe	d																					
Darlington	d				19 00	19 05				19 10							19 25	19 33			20 07	
Northallerton	d											19 18					19 36					
Thirsk	d											19 26							←			
York	a				19 28	19 31				19 39		19 50					20 07	20 01	20 07		20 33	
Leeds	a									20 08							→		20 35			
Harrogate	d																					
Scarborough	d																					
York	d				19 29	19 34												20 03			20 35	
Doncaster	a				19 53	19 57												20 26			21 00	
Skipton	d																					
Keighley	d																					
Bradford Interchange	d																					
Bradford Forster Sqare	d																					
Shipley	d																					
Halifax	d																					
Brighouse	d																					
Mirfield	d																					
Leeds	d			19 15					19 45	20 11												
Wakefield Westgate	d			19 27				19 42	19 56	20 23					20 50							
Wakefield Kirkgate	d							19a44							20a54							
Pontefract Monkhill	d																					
Sheffield	a					20 20				20 51											21 26	
Hull	d						19 10															
Selby	d						19 45															
Doncaster	d		19 34	19 45	19 54		20 03		20 16									20 27				20 33
Retford	d						20 17															21a26
Lincoln	d		20a25																			
Newark North Gate	a				20 17																	
	d				20 17																	
Grantham	a			20 16			20 37															
	d			20 16			20 38															
Peterborough	a				20 46				21 03									21 16				
Norwich	a																					
Peterborough	d				20 46				21 04									21 16				
Stevenage	a			20 59	21 15													21 47				
London Kings Cross ⊖	a			21 28	21 45		21 46		21 57									22 20				

A to Leeds   B to York

Scotland, North East England, Yorkshire and Humberside - London

Route Diagram - see first Page of Table 26

		EM	GR	XC	TP FX	NT	TP	GR	XC	GR	NT	TP	TP	NT	NT	GR	SR FO	SR FX	NT	NT	SR FO	NT
				A													B					
Aberdeen	d															18 16	21 42					
Stonehaven	d															18 33	22u00					
Montrose	d															18 56	22u25					
Arbroath	d															19 12	22u43					
Dundee	d															19 30	23u06					
Leuchars	d															19 44	23u25					
Kirkcaldy	d															20 08	23u53					
Inverkeithing	d															20 24	00u12					
Inverness	d																					
Perth	d																					
Stirling	d																					
Glasgow Central	d			16 52					18 59													
Motherwell	d			17 14					19 15													
Haymarket	d			17 54					19 53							20 43						
Edinburgh	a			17 59					19 58							20 48	00 41					
Edinburgh	d			18 04				18 30	20 05							21 00		22 06			23 01	
Dunbar	d			18 25				18 51	20 25							21 21		22a41			23a33	
Berwick-upon-Tweed	d			18 48				19 14	20 48							21 47						
Alnmouth for Alnwick	d			19 08		19 22		19 36	21 08							22 10						
Morpeth	d					19 47		19 53								22 26			22 45			
Newcastle	a			19 39		20 07		20 12	21 38							22 43			23 07			
Sunderland	d																					
Hartlepool	d																					
Newcastle	d			19 42				20 14		21 15			21 55		22 21	22 44						
Chester-le-Street	d														22 31							
Durham	d			19 54				20 27		21 27			22 08		22 39	22 58						
Darlington	a			20 10				20 45		21 45			22 24		22 59	23 19						
Middlesbrough	d				18 50		20 04					21 50										
Eaglescliffe	d																					
Darlington	d			20 12			20 35	20 46		21 46		22 19	22 25			23 19						
Northallerton	d				19 18		20 46			21 57		22 30	22 37			23s46						
Thirsk	d				19 26		21 00					22 38										
York	a			20 41	19 50		21 24	21 14		22 17		22 56	23 01			00 13						
Leeds	a			21 08	21 37								23 33			00 50						
Harrogate	d																					
Scarborough	d																					
York	d							21 16		22 19												
Doncaster	a							21 38		22 42												
Skipton	d																					
Keighley	d																					
Bradford Interchange	d																					
Bradford Forster Sqare	d																					
Shipley	d																					
Halifax	d																					
Brighouse	d																					
Mirfield	d																					
Leeds	d		20 45	21 11																		
Wakefield Westgate	d		20 56	21 23							21 41			21 57						22 48		23 04
Wakefield Kirkgate	d										21a44			22 00						22a51		23 07
Pontefract Monkhill	d													22a18								23a25
Sheffield	a			21 51																		
Hull	d																					
Selby	d																					
Doncaster	d		21 16					21 39		22 42												
Retford	d		21 33																			
Lincoln	d																					
Newark North Gate	a							22 02		23 06												
	d							22 02		23 06												
Grantham	a		21 55					22 15		23 18												
	d	21 10	21 55					22 15		23 18												
Peterborough	a	21 37	22 15					22 35		23 39												
Norwich	a	23 18																				
Peterborough	d		22 16					22 35		23 40												
Stevenage	a		22 47					23 05		00s21												
London Kings Cross ⊖	a		23 13					23 36		00 57												

A to Leeds

Scotland, North East England, Yorkshire and Humberside - London

Route Diagram - see first Page of Table 26

		SR	GR	GR	SR	EM	GR	GR	GR	GR	XC	GR	NT	XC	NT	EM	NT	GR	GR	XC	GR	GR	TP
							A		A									A		B	A	A	
Aberdeen	d			18p16	21p42																		
Stonehaven	d			18p33	22b00																		
Montrose	d			18p56	22b25																		
Arbroath	d			19p12	22b43																		
Dundee	d			19p30	23b06																		
Leuchars	d			19p44	23b25																		
Kirkcaldy	d			20p08	23b53																		
Inverkeithing	d			20p24	00u12																		
Inverness	d	20p47																					
Perth	d	23b21																					
Stirling	d	00u06																					
Glasgow Central	d																						
Motherwell	d																						
Haymarket	d			20p43																			
Edinburgh	a	01 00		20p48	00 41																		
Edinburgh	d			21p00																			
Dunbar	d			21p21																			
Berwick-upon-Tweed	d			21p47																			
Alnmouth for Alnwick	d			22p10																			
Morpeth	d			22p26																			
Newcastle	a			22p43																			
Sunderland	d														06 28								
Hartlepool	d														06a54		07 03						
Newcastle	d		21p15	22p44					04 15	04 45													
Chesterle Street	d																07a51				05 28		
Durham	d		21p27	22p58					04u27	04 59													
Darlington	a		21p45	23p19						05 16											05u40		
Middlesbrough	d																						
Eaglescliffe	d																						05 55
Darlington	d		21p46	23p19					04u46	05 17													
Northallerton	d		21p57	23c46						05 29											06u00		
Thirsk	d																						06 23
York	a		22p17	00 13						05 57													06 31
Leeds	a			00 50																			06 49
Harrogate	d																						07 20
Scarborough	d																						
York	d		22p19						05u15	06 00													
Doncaster	a		22p42							06 22										06 17	06u34		
Skipton	d																						
Keighley	d																						
Bradford Interchange	d																						
Bradford Forster Sqare	d																						
Shipley	d																						
Halifax	d																						
Brighouse	d																						
Mirfield	d																						
Leeds	d						04 44	05 05			06 00	06 05		06 15		06 34		06 40	07 05	07 10			
Wakefield Westgate	d						04u56	05 16			06 12	06 17	06 24	06 29		06 46		06u51	07 16	07 23			
Wakefield Kirkgate	d												06 29										
Pontefract Monkhill	d												06a46										
Sheffield	a										06 45					07 22				07 51			
Hull	d																						
Selby	d																						
Doncaster	d		22p42				05u15	05 35	05u42	06 23		06 35		06a46				07u14	07 35		07u07	← 07 14	
Retford	d						05u29	05 49				06 49						→	→			0u28	
Lincoln	d																						
Newark North Gate	a		23p06					06 04				07 04											
	d		23p06					06 04	06u15			07 04											
Grantham	a		23p18					06 17				07 17										07u49	
	d		23p18			05 51	05u57	06 17				07 17											
Peterborough	a		23p39			06 25		06 37		07 11		07 37									07u46		
Norwich	a																						
Peterborough	d		23p40				06u21	06 37		07 13		07 37											
Stevenage	a		00s21					07 06				08 06										08u23	
London Kings Cross	a		00 57				07 14	07 36	07 44	08 08		08 36									08 53	09 25	

A 28 July, 4 August, 11 August, 1 September, 8 September
B from 15 September
b Previous night, stops to pick up only
c Previous night, stops to set down only

Scotland, North East England, Yorkshire and Humberside - London

Route Diagram - see first Page of Table 26

		XC	GR	NT	FC	GR	GR	TP	XC	TP	GR	EM	EM	GR	GR	XC	XC	GR	GC	GC	TP	NT	FC
		A														B	A		C	D			
Aberdeen	d																						
Stonehaven	d																						
Montrose	d																						
Arbroath	d																						
Dundee	d																						
Leuchars	d																						
Kirkcaldy	d																						
Inverkeithing	d																						
Inverness	d																						
Perth	d																						
Stirling	d																						
Glasgow Central	d																						
Motherwell	d																						
Haymarket	d																						
Edinburgh	a																						
Edinburgh	d																						
Dunbar	d																						
Berwick-upon-Tweed	d																						
Alnmouth for Alnwick	d																						
Morpeth	d																						
Newcastle	a																						
Sunderland	d																						
Hartlepool	d																						
Newcastle	d		06 00					06 11	06 22		06 30					06 45		06 55					
Chesterle Street	d							06 21															
Durham	d		06 12					06 28	06 37		06 42					06 57		07 07					
Darlington	a		06 30					06 44	06 52		07 00					07 13		07 25					
Middlesbrough	d																				07 12		
Eaglescliffe	d																						
Darlington	d		06 30					06 45	06 54		07 01					07 14		07 26					
Northallerton	d							06 56			07 12										07 43		
Thirsk	d							07 04		←											07 51		
York	a		06 58					07 30	07 21	07 30	07 32					07 40		07 53			08 11		
Leeds	a							→		08 04						08 08					08 52		
Harrogate	d																						
Scarborough	d																						
York	d	06 40	07 00						07 24		07 34						07 44	07 55					
Doncaster	a		07 23						07 48		07 56							08 17					
Skipton	d													06 55									
Keighley	d													07u08									
Bradford Interchange	d																		06 51	06 51			
Bradford Forster Sqare	d														07 33								
Shipley	d													07u18	07u39								
Halifax	d																		07 03	07 03			
Brighouse	d																		07 14	07 14			
Mirfield	d																		07 22	07 22			
Leeds	d	07 10										07 34		07 35	08 05	08 12	08 12						
Wakefield Westgate	d	07 23		07 29								07 46			08 16	08 24	08 24					08 29	
Wakefield Kirkgate	d			07a33															07 38	07 41		08a32	
Pontefract Monkhill	d																		07 58				
Sheffield	a	07 51							08 18			08 21				08 51	08 51						
Hull	d						06 50																
Selby	d					←	07 24																
Doncaster	d		07 24			07 35	07 43				07 57			08 09	08 35			08 18	08 31	08 31			
Retford	d														→								
Lincoln	d																						
Newark North Gate	a					07 59					08 21												
	d					07 59					08 21												
Grantham	a					08 11	08 16							08 41									
	d					08 11	08 16						08 20	08 42									
Peterborough	a		08 13			08 31	08 38				08 51		08 58										
Norwich	a												10 43										
Peterborough	d		08 14		08 09	08 32	08 39				08 51												09 09
Stevenage	a					09 01																	
London Kings Cross	a		09 10		09 13	09 29	09 36				09 46			09 51				09 54	10 09	10 09			10 11

A until 8 September
B from 15 September
C until 23 June, from 15 September. to Doncaster ✕ from Doncaster
D from 30 June until 8 September. to Doncaster ✕ from Doncaster

Scotland, North East England, Yorkshire and Humberside - London

Route Diagram - see first Page of Table 26

		GC		GR	NT	NT	EM	GR	XC	GR	HT	GR		EM	GR	XC	TP	GR	NT	NT	FC	GR		XC	EM
Aberdeen	d																								
Stonehaven	d																								
Montrose	d																								
Arbroath	d																								
Dundee	d																								
Leuchars	d																								
Kirkcaldy	d																								
Inverkeithing	d																								
Inverness	d																								
Perth	d																								
Stirling	d																								
Glasgow Central	d																								
Motherwell	d																								
Haymarket	d																								
Edinburgh	a																								
Edinburgh	d															06 06		06 20				06 55		07 00	
Dunbar	d																	06 40							
Berwick-upon-Tweed	d															06 48		07 05						07 40	
Alnmouth for Alnwick	d															07 08		07 25	07 22					08 00	
Morpeth	d																	07 41	07 55					08 14	
Newcastle	a															07 38		07 58	08 20			08 22		08 32	
Sunderland	d	06 43			07 55	08 30																			
Hartlepool	d	07 09																							
Newcastle	d				08a18	08a52		07 22	07 35							07 40	07 43	07 59				08 24		08 36	
Chester-le-Street	d																								
Durham	d							07 35	07 47							07 52	07 57					08 37		08 48	
Darlington	a							07 52	08 03							08 08	08 13	08 27				08 55		09 04	
Middlesbrough	d																								
Eaglescliffe	d	07 30																							
Darlington	d							07 53	08 04							08 10	08 14	08 27				08 56		09 05	
Northallerton	d	07 48						08 06									08 26					09 07			
Thirsk	d	07 57															08 34								
York	a	08 14						08 27	08 30							08 41	08 52	08 55				09 27		09 32	
Leeds	a															09 07	09 22								
Harrogate	d														08 13										
Scarborough	d																								
York	d	08 16						08 28	08 34									08 56				09 29		09 35	
Doncaster	a							08 53	08 57													09 52		09 57	
Skipton	d																								
Keighley	d																								
Bradford Interchange	d																								
Bradford Forster Sqare	d																								
Shipley	d																								
Halifax	d																								
Brighouse	d																								
Mirfield	d																								
Leeds	d									08 40					09 05	09 11									
Wakefield Westgate	d									08 51					09 17	09 24				09 29					
Wakefield Kirkgate	d																			09a32					
Pontefract Monkhill	d																								
Sheffield	a								09 20							09 52								10 20	
Hull	d										08 25														
Selby	d			⟵							09 00														
Doncaster	d			08 35				08 53		09 12	09 24				09 35							09 52			10 24
Retford	d			08 52							09 38											10 07			
Lincoln	d											09 30													11a16
Newark North Gate	a			09 08				09 19				09 52			09 59										
	d			09 08				09 19				09 52			09 59										
Grantham	a							09 32			09 59	10 06			10 12							10 29			
	d						09 03	09 32			10 00	10 06		10 09	10 12							10 29			
Peterborough	a			09 36			09 41			10 00		10 26		10 38	10 36			10 05				10 50			
Norwich	a						11 15							12 18											
Peterborough	d			09 37						10 00		10 27			10 36			10 06			10 10	10 51			
Stevenage	a											10 59			11 06										
London Kings Cross ⊖	a	10 15		10 30				10 44		10 54	11 09	11 27			11 37			11 02			11 14	11 46			

Scotland, North East England, Yorkshire and Humberside - London

Route Diagram - see first Page of Table 26

		EM	GR	XC A	XC B	SR	GR	NT		TP	GC	NT	TP	GR	XC	NT	NT	HT		NT	NT	EM	GR	XC	GR
Aberdeen	d																								
Stonehaven	d																								
Montrose	d																								
Arbroath	d																								
Dundee	d																							06 32	
Leuchars	d																							06 46	
Kirkcaldy	d																							07 21	
Inverkeithing	d																							07 38	
Inverness	d																								
Perth	d																								
Stirling	d																								
Glasgow Central	d			06 01	06 01									06 50											
Motherwell	d			06 16	06 16									07 04											
Haymarket	d			06 57	06 57	06 33								07 46										07 56	
Edinburgh	a			07 01	07 02	06 39								07 52										08 01	
Edinburgh	d			07 07	07 07	09a12	07 30							08 00										08 05	08 30
Dunbar	d			07 27	07 27																				
Berwick-upon-Tweed	d						08 12																	08 46	09 11
Alnmouth for Alnwick	d													08 58										09 08	
Morpeth	d							08 49																	
Newcastle	a			08 37	08 37		08 57	09 14						09 27										09 39	09 58
Sunderland	d										08 30														
Hartlepool	d										08 54	09 02				10 02				11 02	12 02				
Newcastle	d			08 43	08 43		08 59					09a51	09 15	09 28	09 35	10a51				11a51	12a52			09 41	09 59
Chester-le-Street	d												09 24												
Durham	d			08 56	08 56								09 31	09 41	09 47									09 55	
Darlington	a			09 12	09 12		09 25						09 47	09 59	10 04									10 10	10 28
Middlesbrough	d									08 50															
Eaglescliffe	d										09 17														
Darlington	d			09 13	09 13		09 26						09 48	09 59	10 05									10 12	10 28
Northallerton	d									09 18	09 40		09 59												
Thirsk	d									09 28	09 49														
York	a			09 43	09 43		09 54			09 47	10 06		10 21	10 28	10 31									10 41	10 56
Leeds	a			10 09	10 09					10 22			10 52											11 08	
Harrogate	d																								
Scarborough	d																								
York	d						09 56				10 09			10 29	10 34										10 58
Doncaster	a													10 52	10 57										
Skipton	d																								
Keighley	d																								
Bradford Interchange	d																								
Bradford Forster Sqare	d																								
Shipley	d																								
Halifax	d																								
Brighouse	d																								
Mirfield	d																								
Leeds	d		10 05	10 12	10 12																		11 05	11 11	
Wakefield Westgate	d		10 16	10 24	10 24												10 29						11 16	11 23	
Wakefield Kirkgate	d																10a32								
Pontefract Monkhill	d																								
Sheffield	a			10 51	10 51										11 20									11 51	
Hull	d																	10 30							
Selby	d																	11 05							
Doncaster	d		10 35											10 52				11 26					11 35		
Retford	d																	11 40							
Lincoln	d																								
Newark North Gate	a		10 59											11 18									11 59		
	d		10 59											11 18									11 59		
Grantham	a		11 11															12 00					12 11		
	d	11 10	11 13															12 01				12 07	12 11		
Peterborough	a	11 39	11 36											11 47								12 38	12 32		
Norwich	a	13 13																				14 13			
Peterborough	d		11 36											11 49									12 33		
Stevenage	a																						13 01		
London Kings Cross ⊖	a		12 30				11 56				12 07			12 46				13 09					13 30		12 55

A until 8 September. from Edinburgh

B from 15 September. from Edinburgh

Scotland, North East England, Yorkshire and Humberside - London

Route Diagram - see first Page of Table 26

		NT	TP	TP	GR	GC	GC	GC	XC	NT	EM	GR	XC	GR	NT	TP	TP	GR	XC	NT	EM	EM
						A	B	C														
Aberdeen	d																					
Stonehaven	d																					
Montrose	d																					
Arbroath	d																					
Dundee	d																					
Leuchars	d																					
Kirkcaldy	d																					
Inverkeithing	d																					
Inverness	d																					
Perth	d																					
Stirling	d																					
Glasgow Central	d											07 50										
Motherwell	d											08 05										
Haymarket	d											08 50										
Edinburgh	a											08 54										
Edinburgh	d				09 00								09 06	09 30				10 00				
Dunbar	d												09 26									
Berwick-upon-Tweed	d												09 49	10 11								
Alnmouth for Alnwick	d																	10 58				
Morpeth	d	09 49													10 49							
Newcastle	a	10 14			10 23								10 38	10 57	11 13			11 27				
Sunderland	d																					
Hartlepool	d																					
Newcastle	d			10 15	10 25				10 35				10 44	10 59			11 15	11 28	11 35			
Chester-le-Street	d			10 24													11 24					
Durham	d			10 31	10 38				10 47				10 56				11 31	11 41	11 47			
Darlington	a			10 47	10 55				11 03				11 12	11 27			11 46	11 59	12 04			
Middlesbrough	d		09 50													10 50						
Eaglescliffe	d																					
Darlington	d			10 48	10 56				11 04				11 13	11 28			11 48	11 59	12 05			
Northallerton	d		10 18	10 59	11 07											11 18	11 59					
Thirsk	d		10 28													11 28						
York	a		10 47	11 22	11 28				11 31				11 41	11 56		11 47	12 21	12 28	12 31			
Leeds	a		11 22	11 53									12 07			12 22	12 52					
Harrogate	d																					
Scarborough	d																					
York	d				11 30				11 34					11 57				12 29	12 34			
Doncaster	a				11 52				11 57									12 52	12 57			
Skipton	d																					
Keighley	d																					
Bradford Interchange	d					10 22	10 22	10 22														
Bradford Forster Sqare	d																					
Shipley	d																					
Halifax	d					10 38	10 38	10 38														
Brighouse	d					10 48	10 48	10 48														
Mirfield	d					10 56	10 56	10 56														
Leeds	d											12 05	12 11									
Wakefield Westgate	d									11 29		12 16	12 24							12 29		
Wakefield Kirkgate	d					11 11	11 11	11 13		11a32										12a32		
Pontefract Monkhill	d						11 35	11 37														
Sheffield	a								12 20				12 51						13 20			
Hull	d																					
Selby	d																					
Doncaster	d				11 53	12 05	12 05	12 07				12 35						12 52			13 05	
Retford	d				12 08																	
Lincoln	d																				13a55	
Newark North Gate	a											13 02						13 17				
	d											13 02						13 17				
Grantham	a											13 14										
	d										13 09	13 14										14 07
Peterborough	a				12 48						13 38	13 35						13 46				14 41
Norwich	a										15 13											16 15
Peterborough	d				12 50							13 37						13 49				
Stevenage	a																					
London Kings Cross	a				13 45	13 46	13 46	13 46				14 30		13 55				14 45				

A from 30 June until 8 September
B until 23 June
C from 15 September

Scotland, North East England, Yorkshire and Humberside - London

Route Diagram - see first Page of Table 26

		GR	XC	GR	NT	TP	TP	GR	XC	HT	NT	EM	GR	XC	TP	GC	GR	NT	NT	TP	GR	XC	NT
			A											A			B						
Aberdeen	d			07 52										08 20									
Stonehaven	d			08 09										08 38									
Montrose	d			08 32										08 59									
Arbroath	d			08 48										09 15									
Dundee	d			09 06										09 32									
Leuchars	d			09 20										09 47									
Kirkcaldy	d			09 44										10 17									
Inverkeithing	d			10 01										10 32									
Inverness	d																07 55						
Perth	d																09 56						
Stirling	d																10 30						
Glasgow Central	d		09 00																				
Motherwell	d		09 15																				
Haymarket	d		09 57	10 19										10 52			11 11						
Edinburgh	a		10 02	10 26										10 58			11 17						
Edinburgh	d		10 05	10 30				11 00						11 05			11 30				12 00		
Dunbar	d													11 25									
Berwick-upon-Tweed	d		10 48	11 11										11 48			12 11						
Alnmouth for Alnwick	d													12 08							12 58		
Morpeth	d		11 19		11 49													12 49					
Newcastle	a		11 38	11 58	12 13			12 23						12 38			12 58	13 13			13 27		
Sunderland	d															12 18							
Hartlepool	d															12 43			13 02				14 02
Newcastle	d		11 42	11 59			12 17	12 25	12 35					12 44			12 59		13a51	13 15	13 28	13 35	14a51
Chester-le-Street	d																			13 24			
Durham	d		11 55				12 29	12 38	12 47					12 56						13 31	13 41	13 47	
Darlington	a		12 11	12 28			12 45	12 55	13 03					13 12			13 28			13 46	13 59	14 04	
Middlesbrough	d					11 50									12 50								
Eaglescliffe	d															13 05							
Darlington	d		12 12	12 28			12 46	12 56	13 04					13 13			13 28			13 48	13 59	14 05	
Northallerton	d					12 18	12 58	13 07							13 18	13 27				13 58			
Thirsk	d					12 28									13 28	13 36							
York	a		12 42	12 56		12 47	13 21	13 27	13 31					13 41	13 47	13 53	13 56			14 22	14 28	14 31	
Leeds	a		13 08			13 22	13 52							14 08	14 22					14 52			
Harrogate	d																						
Scarborough	d																						
York	d			12 58				13 29	13 34							13 55	13 58				14 29	14 34	
Doncaster	a							13 51	13 57												14 53	14 57	
Skipton	d																						
Keighley	d																						
Bradford Interchange	d																						
Bradford Forster Sqare	d																						
Shipley	d																						
Halifax	d																						
Brighouse	d																						
Mirfield	d																						
Leeds	d	13 05	13 11										14 05	14 11									
Wakefield Westgate	d	13 16	13 23								13 39		14 16	14 24									
Wakefield Kirkgate	d										13a42												
Pontefract Monkhill	d																						
Sheffield	a		13 51						14 20					14 51								15 20	
Hull	d									13 30													
Selby	d									14 06													
Doncaster	d	13 35						13 52		14 26			14 35								14 53		
Retford	d							14 07		14 40													
Lincoln	d																						
Newark North Gate	a	13 59											15 03								15 17		
	d	13 59											15 03								15 18		
Grantham	a	14 12								15 01			15 16										
	d	14 12								15 02		15 10	15 16										
Peterborough	a	14 32						14 47				15 39	15 36								15 47		
Norwich	a											17 13											
Peterborough	d	14 32						14 49					15 36								15 49		
Stevenage	a	15 01																					
London Kings Cross	a	15 30		14 55				15 45		16 10			16 30			15 49	15 57				16 45		

A from Edinburgh
B The Highland Chieftain

Scotland, North East England, Yorkshire and Humberside - London

Route Diagram - see first Page of Table 26

	NT	NT	EM	GR	NT	EM	GR	XC	GR	NT	TP	TP	GR	XC	NT	HT	EM	NT	EM	GR	XC	GR
									A													
Aberdeen d									09 52													
Stonehaven d									10 09													
Montrose d									10 32													
Arbroath d									10 49													
Dundee d									11 06													
Leuchars d									11 20													
Kirkcaldy d									11 44													
Inverkeithing d									12 01													
Inverness d																						
Perth d																						
Stirling d																						
Glasgow Central d								10 59														
Motherwell d								11 14														
Haymarket d								11 56	12 17													
Edinburgh a								12 02	12 25													
Edinburgh d								12 09	12 30				13 00								13 08	13 30
Dunbar d																					13 29	
Berwick-upon-Tweed d								12 48	13 11													14 11
Alnmouth for Alnwick d																					14 09	
Morpeth d										13 49												
Newcastle a								13 35	13 58	14 15			14 23								14 39	14 56
Sunderland d																						
Hartlepool d		15 02			16 02													17 02				
Newcastle d		15a51			16a51			13 44	13 59			14 18	14 25	14 35				17a51			14 44	14 58
Chester-le-Street d																						
Durham d								13 56				14 31	14 38	14 47							14 56	
Darlington a								14 12	14 28			14 46	14 55	15 03							15 12	15 25
Middlesbrough d											13 50											
Eaglescliffe d																						
Darlington d								14 13	14 28			14 48	14 56	15 04							15 13	15 26
Northallerton d											14 18	14 59	15 07									
Thirsk d											14 28											
York a								14 41	14 56		14 47	15 22	15 28	15 31							15 41	15 53
Leeds a								15 06			15 22	15 53									16 07	
Harrogate d																						
Scarborough d																						
York d									14 58				15 30	15 34								15 55
Doncaster a													15 52	15 57								
Skipton d																						
Keighley d																						
Bradford Interchange d																						
Bradford Forster Sqare d																						
Shipley d																						
Halifax d																						
Brighouse d																						
Mirfield d																						
Leeds d				14 40			15 05	15 12												16 05	16 12	
Wakefield Westgate d	14 39			14 52			15 17	15 24							15 29					16 17	16 24	
Wakefield Kirkgate d	14a42														15a32							
Pontefract Monkhill d																						
Sheffield a								15 51						16 20							16 51	
Hull d																15 30						
Selby d																16 05						
Doncaster d			15 07	15 11			15 35						15 53			16 24	16 27			16 35		
Retford d													16 07			16 38						
Lincoln d			15a57														17a20					
Newark North Gate a							15 59													16 59		
Newark North Gate d							15 59													16 59		
Grantham a							16 12									16 59				17 11		
Grantham d						16 07	16 12									17 00			17 06	17 11		
Peterborough a				15 59		16 40	16 33						16 47						17 37	17 31		
Norwich a						18 18													19 19			
Peterborough d				16 00			16 33						16 49							17 32		
Stevenage a							17 03															
London Kings Cross a				16 55			17 32		17 00				17 46			18 08				18 26		17 55

A The Northern Lights

Table 26 Saturdays

Scotland, North East England, Yorkshire and Humberside - London

Route Diagram - see first Page of Table 26

	NT	TP	NT	XC	TP	GR	GC	GC	GR	XC	GR	NT	TP	TP	NT	EM	GR	XC	EM	EM	GR
							A	B		C									D		
Aberdeen d																					
Stonehaven d																					
Montrose d																					
Arbroath d																					
Dundee d																					
Leuchars d																					
Kirkcaldy d																					
Inverkeithing d																					
Inverness d																					
Perth d																					
Stirling d																					
Glasgow Central d										12 51											
Motherwell d										13 06											
Haymarket d																					
Edinburgh a										13 54											
Edinburgh d						14 00				14 08	14 30						15 00				
Dunbar d																					
Berwick-upon-Tweed d										14 49	15 11										
Alnmouth for Alnwick d						14 58															
Morpeth d	14 49											15 49									
Newcastle a	15 14					15 27				15 35	15 56	16 14					16 23				
Sunderland d																					
Hartlepool d																					
Newcastle d				15 07	15 15	15 28				15 41	15 58			16 15			16 25	16 35			
Chester-le-Street d					15 24									16 24							
Durham d				15 19	15 31	15 41				15 53				16 31			16 38	16 47			
Darlington a				15 35	15 46	15 59				16 10	16 25			16 46			16 55	17 03			
Middlesbrough d		14 50											15 50								
Eaglescliffe d																					
Darlington d				15 36	15 48	15 59				16 11	16 26			16 48			16 56	17 04			
Northallerton d		15 18			15 59								16 18	16 59			17 07				
Thirsk d		15 28											16 28								
York a		15 47		16 03	16 21	16 28				16 41	16 53		16 47	17 23			17 27	17 31			
Leeds a		16 22		16 32	16 52					17 07			17 22	17 52							
Harrogate d																					
Scarborough d																					
York d						16 29					16 55						17 29	17 34	17 50		
Doncaster a						16 55											17 52	17 57	18 11		
Skipton d																					
Keighley d																					
Bradford Interchange d							15 22	15 22													
Bradford Forster Sqare d																					
Shipley d																					
Halifax d							15 35	15 35													
Brighouse d							15 46	15 46													
Mirfield d																					
Leeds d				16 40					17 05	17 11											18 05
Wakefield Westgate d			16 29	16 52					17 17	17 23					17 29						18 16
Wakefield Kirkgate d			16a32				16 11	16 11							17a32						
Pontefract Monkhill d							16 29														
Sheffield a				17 20						17 51								18 20	18 44		
Hull d																					
Selby d																					
Doncaster d						16 56	17 03	17 03	17 35								17 53				18 39
Retford d																	18 07				
Lincoln d																					
Newark North Gate a						17 19			17 59												19 02
Newark North Gate d						17 19			17 59												19 02
Grantham a									18 11												19 15
Grantham d									18 11							18 15				19 08	19 15
Peterborough a						17 49			18 31							18 42	18 47			19 39	19 35
Norwich a																20 18				21 14	
Peterborough d						17 49			18 32								18 50				19 36
Stevenage a									19 01												
London Kings Cross a						18 44	18 45	18 45	19 29		18 55						19 45				20 30

A until 23 June, from 15 September
B from 30 June until 8 September
C from Edinburgh
D from 15 September

Scotland, North East England, Yorkshire and Humberside - London

Route Diagram - see first Page of Table 26

		NT	NT	EM	XC	GR	NT	TP	TP	GR	XC	NT	HT	GR	XC	GR	TP	GC	NT	GR	XC	NT	NT
						■				■				■		■		■		■			
				◇1	◇1	1		◇1	◇1	1	◇1		◇1	1	◇1	1	◇1	1		1	◇1		
		A	B	C																			
				⊤	⊤	⊡⊤				⊡⊤	⊤		⊠	⊡⊤	⊤	⊡⊤		⊡		⊡⊤	⊤		
Aberdeen	d																						
Stonehaven	d																						
Montrose	d																						
Arbroath	d																						
Dundee	d																						
Leuchars 3	d																						
Kirkcaldy	d																						
Inverkeithing	d																						
Inverness	d																						
Perth	d																						
Stirling	d																						
Glasgow Central 15	d														15 00								
Motherwell	d														15 14								
Haymarket	d														15 56								
Edinburgh 10	a														16 01								
Edinburgh	d				15 08	15 30				16 00					16 05	16 30				17 00			
Dnbar	d				15 28																		
Berwick-upon-Tweed	d					16 11										17 11							
Alnmouth for Alnwick	d														17 03					17 58			
Morpeth	d						16 49								17 17				17 52				
Newcastle 8	a				16 35	16 56	17 13			17 23					17 35	17 56			18 15	18 27			
Sunderland	d																	17 29				18 42	
Hartlepool	d																	17 53					19 02
Newcastle 8	d				16 41	16 58			17 02	17 25	17 32				17 44	17 58				18 28	18 35	19a04	19a51
ChesterleStreet	d								17 11		17 41												
Durham	d				16 52				17 18	17 38	17 48				17 56					18 41	18 48		
Darlington 7	a				17 09	17 25			17 34	17 55	18 03				18 12	18 25				18 59	19 04		
Middlesbrough	d							16 50									17 50						
Eaglescliffe	d																	18 12					
Darlington 7	d				17 10	17 26			17 35	17 56	18 05				18 13	18 26				18 59	19 05		
Nrthallerton	d							17 18	17 46	18 07							18 18	18 31					
Thirsk	d							17 28									18 28	18 41					
York 8	a				17 41	17 53		17 47	18 09	18 27	18 31				18 41	18 53	18 47	18 58		19 28	19 31		
Leeds 10	a				18 08			18 22	18 37						19 08		19 35						
Harrogate	d																						
Scarborough	d	16 21	16 23	17 03																			
York 8	d			17 50		17 55				18 29	18 34					18 55		19 01		19 29	19 34		
Doncaster 7	a			18 11						18 52	18 57									19 53	19 57		
Skipton	d																						
Keighley	d																						
Bradford Interchange	d																						
Bradford Forster Sqare	d																						
Shipley	d																						
Halifax	d																						
Brighouse	d																						
Mirfield	d																						
Leeds 10	d				18 11									19 05	19 11								
Wakefield Westgate 7	d				18 23							18 29		19 16	19 24								
Wakefield Kirkgate 4	d											18a36											
Pontefract Monkhill	d																						
Sheffield 7	a			18 44	18 51						19 21				19 51						20 20		
Hull	d	17 52	17 52										18 30										
Selby	d	18 26	18 26										19 05										
Doncaster 7	d	18a47	18a47							18 53			19 28	19 36						19 54			
Retford 10	d																						
Lincoln	d																						
Newark North Gate 7	a									19 17				20 00									
	d									19 17				20 00									
Grantham 7	a												19 57	20 12						20 26			
	d												19 58	20 12						20 26			
Peterborough 8	a									19 47				20 32						20 48			
Nrwich	a																						
Peterborough 8	d									19 49				20 33						20 49			
Stevenage 4	a													21 02									
London Kings Cross 15 ⊖	a					19 55				20 45			21 09	21 30		20 55		20 57		21 46			

A from 6 October B until 29 September C until 8 September

Scotland, North East England, Yorkshire and Humberside - London

Route Diagram - see first Page of Table 26

		NT	NT	NT	GR	XC	TP	NT	TP	GR	TP	NT	NT	XC	XC	GR	TP	GR	EM	GR	EM	NT
					■					■						■		■		■		
					1	◇1	◇1		◇1	1	◇1			◇1	◇1	1	◇1	1		1	◇	
						A								B	C							
					⊡⊤	⊤				⊡⊤				⊤	⊤	⊡⊤		⊡⊤		⊡⊤		
Aberdeen	d									14 50												
Stonehaven	d									15 07												
Montrose	d									15 30												
Arbroath	d									15 46												
Dundee	d									16 04												
Leuchars 3	d									16 18												
Kirkcaldy	d									16 45												
Inverkeithing	d									17 01												
Inverness	d																					
Perth	d																					
Stirling	d																					
Glasgow Central 15	d														16 52							
Motherwell	d														17 14							
Haymarket	d									17 18					17 56							
Edinburgh 10	a									17 26					18 01							
Edinburgh	d					17 08				17 30					18 05	18 30		19 00				
Dnbar	d					17 28				17 50					18 25			19 20				
Berwick-upon-Tweed	d					17 51				18 15					18 48	19 11		19 45				
Alnmouth for Alnwick	d												18 48		19 08			20 07				
Morpeth	d											18 50	19 13					20 24				21 15
Newcastle 8	a					18 38				19 01		19 13	19 34		19 41	20 01		20 41				21 39
Sunderland	d		20 38	21 43																		
Hartlepool	d																					
Newcastle 8	d		21a04	22a04		18 44			18 52	19 03				19 35	19 44			20 42				
ChesterleStreet	d								19 01													
Durham	d					18 56			19 08					19 49	19 56			20 55				
Darlington 7	a					19 12			19 24	19 31				20 05	20 12			21 14				
Middlesbrough	d						18 50										20 10					
Eaglescliffe	d																					
Darlington 7	d					19 13			19 25	19 32				20 06	20 13			21 14				
Nrthallerton	d						19 18		19 36								20 39	21 26				
Thirsk	d						19 26				←						20 47					
York 8	a					19 41	19 50		20 07	20 00	20 07			20 31	20 42		21 06	21 46				
Leeds 10	a					20 08			→		20 35				21 07		21 37					
Harrogate	d																					
Scarborough	d																					
York 8	d									20 01				20 34				21 48				
Doncaster 7	a									20 25				20 55				22 16				
Skipton	d																					
Keighley	d																					
Bradford Interchange	d																					
Bradford Forster Sqare	d																					
Shipley	d																					
Halifax	d																					
Brighouse	d																					
Mirfield	d																					
Leeds 10	d				20 05	20 11									21 11							
Wakefield Westgate 7	d	19 41			20 16	20 23		20 50							21 23							
Wakefield Kirkgate 4	d	19a44						20a54														
Pontefract Monkhill	d																					
Sheffield 7	a					20 52								21 20	21 51							
Hull	d																					
Selby	d																			←		
Doncaster 7	d				20 35					20 25									20 33	20 35		
Retford 10	d				→															20 50		
Lincoln	d																		21a26			
Newark North Gate 7	a																			21 05		
	d																			21 05		
Grantham 7	a									20 57												
	d									20 58											21 07	
Peterborough 8	a									21 19										21 34	21 36	
Nrwich	a																				23 20	
Peterborough 8	d									21 21										21 35		
Stevenage 4	a									21 52												
London Kings Cross 15 ⊖	a									22 24										22 29		

A ⊤ to Leeds B ⊤ to Yrk C ⊤ from Edinburgh to Leeds

Table 26

Saturdays

Scotland, North East England, Yorkshire and Humberside - London

Route Diagram - see first Page of Table 26

		NT	TP	NT	NT	SR	NT	NT
			◇1					
Aberdeen	d							
Stonehaven	d							
Montrose	d							
Arbroath	d							
Dundee	d							
Leuchars	d							
Kirkcaldy	d							
Inverkeithing	d							
Inverness	d							
Perth	d							
Stirling	d							
Glasgow Central	d							
Motherwell	d							
Haymarket	d							
Edinburgh	a							
Edinburgh	d					22 06		
Dunbar	d					22a31		
Berwick-upon-Tweed	d							
Alnmouth for Alnwick	d							
Morpeth	d							
Newcastle	a							
Sunderland	d							
Hartlepool	d							
Newcastle	d			21 50				
Chester-le-Street	d			22 00				
Durham	d			22 08				
Darlington	a			22 29				
Middlesbrough	d		21 50					
Eaglescliffe	d			22a48				
Darlington	d		22 19					
Northallerton	d		22 30					
Thirsk	d		22 38					
York	a		22 57					
Leeds	a		23 33					
Harrogate	d							
Scarborough	d							
York	d							
Doncaster	a							
Skipton	d							
Keighley	d							
Bradford Interchange	d							
Bradford Forster Square	d							
Shipley	d							
Halifax	d							
Brighouse	d							
Mirfield	d							
Leeds	d							
Wakefield Westgate	d	21 41			21 57		22 42	23 04
Wakefield Kirkgate	d	21a44			22 00		22a45	23 07
Pontefract Monkhill	d				22a18			23a29
Sheffield	a							
Hull	d							
Selby	d							
Doncaster	d							
Retford	d							
Lincoln	d							
Newark North Gate	a							
	d							
Grantham	a							
	d							
Peterborough	a							
Norwich	a							
Peterborough	d							
Stevenage	a							
London Kings Cross ⊖	a							

Table 26

Sundays
until 24 June

Scotland, North East England, Yorkshire and Humberside - London

Route Diagram - see first Page of Table 26

		GR	FC	GR	GC	GR	TP	XC	EM	XC		FC	GR	EM	EM	HT	XC	GR	FC	GR		XC	GR	TP	GC
					A																				
Aberdeen	d																								
Stonehaven	d																								
Montrose	d																								
Arbroath	d																								
Dundee	d																								
Leuchars	d																								
Kirkcaldy	d																								
Inverkeithing	d																								
Inverness	d																								
Perth	d																								
Stirling	d																								
Glasgow Central	d																								
Motherwell	d																								
Haymarket	d																								
Edinburgh	a																								
Edinburgh	d																								
Dunbar	d																								
Berwick-upon-Tweed	d																								
Alnmouth for Alnwick	d																								
Morpeth	d																								
Newcastle	a																								
Sunderland	d																								09 12
Hartlepool	d																								09 36
Newcastle	d					07 55	08 00											08 55				09 20	09 25	09 31	
Chester-le-Street	d																							09 40	
Durham	d					08 08	08 13											09 07				09 33	09 37	09 47	
Darlington	a					08 25	08 31											09 25				09 48	09 55	10 03	
Middlesbrough	d																								
Eaglescliffe	d																								09 59
Darlington	d					08 26	08 31											09 26				09 50	09 56	10 04	
Northallerton	d						08 43																10 07	10 15	10 20
Thirsk	d						08 51																		10 29
York	a					08 55	09 11											09 53				10 18	10 27	10 41	10 45
Leeds	a						09 38															10 51		11 08	
Harrogate	d																								
Scarborough	d																								
York	d	08 00				08 56											09 28	09 56					10 29		10 50
Doncaster	a	08 21																					10 51		
Skipton	d																								
Keighley	d																								
Bradford Interchange	d				07 55																				
Bradford Forster Square	d																								
Shipley	d																								
Halifax	d				08 07																				
Brighouse	d				08 18																				
Mirfield	d				08 26																				
Leeds	d			08 05				08 10	08 42	09 00			09 05	09 46			10 00			10 05		11 00			
Wakefield Westgate	d			08 16				08 23	08 59	09 11			09 17	09 59			10 12			10 17		11 12			
Wakefield Kirkgate	d				08 43																				
Pontefract Monkhill	d																								
Sheffield	a							08 51	09 30					10 26											
Hull	d															09 30									
Selby	d															10 05									
Doncaster	d	08 22		08 35	09 06					09a31			09 35			10 24	10a28			10 35		11a28	10 52		
Retford	d			08 49												10 38				10 51					
Lincoln	d																								
Newark North Gate	a			09 04									09 59							11 06			11 15		
	d			09 04									09 59							11 06			11 15		
Grantham	a			09 17									10 11			10 59				11 19					
	d			09 17									10 11		10 29	11 00				11 19					
Peterborough	a	09 09		09 38		10 03							10 32		11 06			11 01		11 41			11 47		
Norwich	a														13 06										
Peterborough	d	09 09	09 15	09 38		10 04						10 15	10 33					11 02	11 20	11 41			11 50		
Stevenage	a	09 38											11 04			11s48									
London Kings Cross ⊖	a	10 07	10 15	10 33	10 40	10 58						11 15	11 33			12 14		11 59	12 20	12 36			12 43		12 44

A ◇ from Doncaster ▮ to Doncaster

Scotland, North East England, Yorkshire and Humberside - London

Sundays until 24 June

Route Diagram - see first Page of Table 26

		NT	GR	NT	TP	NT		GR	XC	NT	EM	GR	GR	TP	HT	EM		GR	XC	GR	GC	GR	TP	GR	GR
Aberdeen	d																							
Stonehaven	d																							
Montrose	d																							
Arbroath	d																							
Dundee	d																							
Leuchars	d																							
Kirkcaldy	d																							
Inverkeithing	d																							
Inverness	d																							
Perth	d																							
Stirling	d																							
Glasgow Central	d																							
Motherwell	d																							
Haymarket	d																							
Edinburgh	a																							
Edinburgh	d							08 50			09 00	09 30						09 50	10 00		10 30			10 55
Dunbar	d																							
Berwick-upon-Tweed	d							09 33				10 11									11 11			
Alnmouth for Alnwick	d																	10 49	10 58					
Morpeth	d																	11 04						12 06
Newcastle	a							10 19			10 25	10 57						11 19	11 27		11 56			12 23
Sunderland	d	09 28																							
Hartlepool	d			10 01		11 00				12 01															
Newcastle	d	09a50	10 00	10a48		11a48			10 24	12a48		10 28	10 59	11 08					11 25	11 28		11 58	12 10		12 25
Chester-le-Street	d																							
Durham	d							10 37			10 42		11 20					11 37	11 41			12 22		12 38
Darlington	a		10 26						10 53			11 00	11 26	11 36					11 54	12 00		12 25	12 38		12 55
Middlesbrough	d				10 15																					
Eaglescliffe	d																							
Darlington	d		10 27						10 54			11 01	11 27	11 37					11 55	12 00		12 26	12 39		12 56
Northallerton	d				10 43							11 14		11 49												
Thirsk	d				10 51																			13 07
York	a		10 54		11 10				11 23			11 34	11 54	12 12					12 22	12 28		12 53	13 11		13 28
Leeds	a				11 38				11 51					12 38					12 51				13 37		
Harrogate	d																							
Scarborough	d																							
York	d		10 56									11 36	11 56							12 30		12 55			13 30
Doncaster	a											11 59								12 53					13 53
Skipton	d																							
Keighley	d																							
Bradford Interchange	d																				12 04				
Bradford Forster Sqare	d																							
Shipley	d																							
Halifax	d																				12 15				
Brighouse	d																				12 26				
Mirfield	d																				12 35				
Leeds	d							11 05	12 00									12 05	13 00					13 05	
Wakefield Westgate	d							11 17	12 12									12 17	13 12					13 16	
Wakefield Kirkgate	d																				12 51				
Pontefract Monkhill	d																							
Sheffield	a																							
Hull	d														11 30										
Selby	d														12 05										
Doncaster	d							11 35	12a28			12 00			12 26			12 37	13a28	12 54	13 23			13 35	13 54
Retford	d											12 15			12 40										14 08
Lincoln	d																							
Newark North Gate	a							11 59										13 00		13 17				13 59	
	d							12 00										13 00		13 17				13 59	
Grantham	a							12 12							13 01			13 13						14 11	
	d							12 13			12 18				13 02	13 12		13 15						14 11	
Peterborough	a		12 01					12 34			12 50	12 56				13 41		13 38		13 47				14 32	14 48
Norwich	a										14 35					15 30									
Peterborough	d		12 01					12 35				12 56						13 40		13 50				14 33	14 49
Stevenage	a							13 05							13s46									15 06	
London Kings Cross	a		12 54					13 34				13 53	13 56		14 14			14 33		14 45	14 55	14 57		15 33	15 43

Scotland, North East England, Yorkshire and Humberside - London

Sundays until 24 June

Route Diagram - see first Page of Table 26

		EM		EM	GR	XC	TP	GC	GR	TP	GR	GR		NT	XC	NT	EM	HT	GR	XC	GR	TP		GR	GR
																						A				
Aberdeen	d																					09 47				
Stonehaven	d																					10 04				
Montrose	d																					10 27				
Arbroath	d																					10 43				
Dundee	d																					11 02				
Leuchars	d																					11 16				
Kirkcaldy	d																					11 40				
Inverkeithing	d																					11 56				
Inverness	d																							
Perth	d																							
Stirling	d																							
Glasgow Central	d																				10 55					
Motherwell	d																				11 10					
Haymarket	d																				11 51	12 16				
Edinburgh	a																				11 55	12 23				
Edinburgh	d					11 05			11 30			12 00								12 08	12 30				13 00
Dunbar	d					11 25																		
Berwick-upon-Tweed	d					11 50			12 11											12 49	13 11				
Alnmouth for Alnwick	d					12 10						12 58													
Morpeth	d																							
Newcastle	a					12 37			12 57			13 27								13 34	13 58				14 23
Sunderland	d							12 12						13 28											
Hartlepool	d							12 36								14 01									
Newcastle	d					12 40			12 59	13 04	13 12	13 28		13a49	13 35	14a48				13 40	13 59	14 08		14 12	14 25
Chester-le-Street	d									13 13															
Durham	d					12 52				13 20	13 24	13 41			13 47					13 52		14 20		14 25	14 38
Darlington	a					13 08			13 27	13 36	13 41	13 59			14 04					14 09	14 28	14 36		14 42	14 56
Middlesbrough	d						12 45																	
Eaglescliffe	d							13 02																
Darlington	d					13 09			13 28	13 37	13 42	13 59			14 05					14 10	14 28	14 37		14 43	14 57
Northallerton	d						13 13	13 23			13 55											14 49		14 57	
Thirsk	d						13 23	13 32																
York	a					13 36	13 43	13 48	13 56	14 10	14 15	14 28			14 31					14 37	14 56	15 12		15 18	15 24
Leeds	a					14 03	14 08			14 38										15 05		15 38			
Harrogate	d																							
Scarborough	d																							
York	d							13 52	13 57		14 16	14 29			14 34						14 58			15 19	15 29
Doncaster	a										14 44	14 53			14 57									15 43	15 52
Skipton	d																							
Keighley	d																							
Bradford Interchange	d																							
Bradford Forster Sqare	d																							
Shipley	d																							
Halifax	d																							
Brighouse	d																							
Mirfield	d																							
Leeds	d	13 59			14 05	14 10													15 05	15 10					
Wakefield Westgate	d	14 12			14 17	14 23													15 16	15 23					
Wakefield Kirkgate	d																							
Pontefract Monkhill	d																							
Sheffield	a	14 39				14 52									15 21					15 51					
Hull	d																	14 30							
Selby	d																	15 05							
Doncaster	d				14 35						14 44	14 53						15 26	15 35					15 43	15 54
Retford	d																	15 40							16 08
Lincoln	d																							
Newark North Gate	a				14 59							15 17							15 59					16 07	
	d				14 59							15 17							15 59					16 08	
Grantham	a				15 11													16 01	16 11						
	d			14 22	15 11												15 20	16 02	16 11						
Peterborough	a			14 51	15 32						15 38	15 46					15 58		16 32					16 38	16 49
Norwich	a			16 35													17 35								
Peterborough	d				15 33						15 39	15 49							16 33					16 38	16 50
Stevenage	a																	16s46	17 05						
London Kings Cross	a				16 26			15 46	15 55		16 33	16 45						17 15	17 33		16 55			17 37	17 44

A The Northern Lights

Scotland, North East England, Yorkshire and Humberside - London

Route Diagram - see first Page of Table 26

Station		XC	XC	TP	GC	GR	TP	XC	NT	NT	EM	GR	GR	GC	NT	EM	GR	XC	GR	TP	HT	GR	EM
			A			B												A					
Aberdeen	d																	11 12	11 47				
Stonehaven	d																	11 29	12 04				
Montrose	d																	11 50	12 27				
Arbroath	d																	12 06	12 43				
Dundee	d																	12 25	13 01				
Leuchars	d																	12 38	13 15				
Kirkcaldy	d																	13 03	13 39				
Inverkeithing	d																	13 18	13 58				
Inverness	d					09 40																	
Perth	d					11 58																	
Stirling	d					12 34																	
Glasgow Central	d		11 51																				
Motherwell	d		12 07																				
Haymarket	d		12 49			13 14												13 37	14 18				
Edinburgh	a		12 54			13 19												13 42	14 25				
Edinburgh	d		13 06			13 30		13 50					14 00					14 08	14 30				
Dunbar	d		13 25																				
Berwick-upon-Tweed	d					14 12		14 33										14 49	15 11				
Alnmouth for Alnwick	d		14 08										14 58										
Morpeth	d																						
Newcastle	a		14 35			14 59		15 18					15 27					15 34	15 57				
Sunderland	d				14 12				15 28														
Hartlepool	d				14 36					16 01					16 51								
Newcastle	d	14 35	14 40			15 00	15 07	15 23	15a48	16a48			15 28		17a48			15 40	15 59	16 08		16 12	
Chester-le-Street	d						15 16																
Durham	d	14 47	14 52				15 23	15 36					15 41					15 52		16 20		16 24	
Darlington	a	15 03	15 08			15 29	15 39	15 52					16 00					16 08	16 27	16 36		16 41	
Middlesbrough	d			14 42																			
Eaglescliffe	d				14 59																		
Darlington	d	15 04	15 09			15 29	15 40	15 53					16 00					16 09	16 28	16 37		16 42	
Northallerton	d			15 10	15 22															16 49		16 54	
Thirsk	d			15 18	15 31																		
York	a	15 31	15 37	15 42	15 46	15 57	16 12	16 19					16 28					16 37	16 56	17 12		17 16	
Leeds	a		16 03	16 08			16 38											17 06		17 38			
Harrogate	d																						
Scarborough	d																						
York	d	15 34			15 50	15 59		16 23					16 29						16 57			17 17	
Doncaster	a	15 57						16 48					16 54										
Skipton	d																						
Keighley	d																						
Bradford Interchange	d													15 42									
Bradford Forster Sqare	d																						
Shipley	d																						
Halifax	d													15 54									
Brighouse	d													16 05									
Mirfield	d													16 14									
Leeds	d		16 10									16 15					16 45	17 10					
Wakefield Westgate	d		16 22									16 27					16 56	17 22					
Wakefield Kirkgate	d													16 30									
Pontefract Monkhill	d																						
Sheffield	a	16 21	16 51					17 19										17 51					
Hull	d																				16 30		
Selby	d																				17 05		
Doncaster	d											16 46	16 54	17 12			17 17				17 26		
Retford	d																				17 40		
Lincoln	d																						
Newark North Gate	a												17 18				17 44					17 59	
	d												17 18				17 44					17 59	
Grantham	a											17 17									18 01		
	d										16 22	17 17				17 21					18 02		18 17
Peterborough	a										16 55		17 47			17 50	18 14					18 28	18 46
Norwich	a										18 30					19 29							20 29
Peterborough	d												17 50				18 14					18 29	
Stevenage	a											18 04									18s49		
London Kings Cross ⊖	a				17 45	17 57						18 34	18 46	18 44			19 11		18 56		19 18	19 22	

A ⚮ from Edinburgh B The Highland Chieftain

Scotland, North East England, Yorkshire and Humberside - London

Route Diagram - see first Page of Table 26

Station		GR	GR	XC	GR	EM	XC	TP	GR	TP	GR	GR	XC	EM	GR	XC	SR	TP	GR	TP	XC	HT
							A									A	B					
Aberdeen	d																		13 50			
Stonehaven	d																		14 07			
Montrose	d																		14 30			
Arbroath	d																		14 46			
Dundee	d																		15 04			
Leuchars	d																		15 18			
Kirkcaldy	d																		15 42			
Inverkeithing	d																		15 58			
Inverness	d																20 25					
Perth	d																23u00					
Stirling	d																23u45					
Glasgow Central	d						13 49									14 55						
Motherwell	d						14 04									15 11						
Haymarket	d						14 42									15 51			16 18			
Edinburgh	a						14 47									15 56	00 47		16 25			
Edinburgh	d		15 00				15 07		15 30			16 00				16 05			16 30			
Dunbar	d						15 27															
Berwick-upon-Tweed	d								16 11										17 11			
Alnmouth for Alnwick	d											16 58				17 07						
Morpeth	d															17 22						
Newcastle	a		16 23				16 34		16 56			17 27				17 37			17 57			
Sunderland	d																					
Hartlepool	d																					
Newcastle	d		16 25	16 35			16 40		16 58	17 05		17 28	17 35			17 40		17 52	17 59		18 20	
Chester-le-Street	d									17 14												
Durham	d		16 38	16 47			16 52			17 21		17 41	17 47			17 52		18 04			18 32	
Darlington	a		16 56	17 03			17 08		17 25	17 37		18 00	18 04			18 08		18 20	18 26		18 49	
Middlesbrough	d							16 42														
Eaglescliffe	d																					
Darlington	d		16 57	17 04			17 09		17 26	17 38		18 00	18 05			18 09		18 21	18 27		18 51	
Northallerton	d							17 10		17 49								18 33				
Thirsk	d							17 18												←		
York	a		17 24	17 30			17 37	17 42	17 53	18 12		18 28	18 31			18 36		19 03	18 56	19 03	19 17	
Leeds	a						18 04	18 08		18 38						19 03		→		19 38		
Harrogate	d				17 05																	
Scarborough	d																					
York	d		17 29	17 34		17 42			17 55			18 29	18 34						18 57		19 24	
Doncaster	a		17 52	17 57		18 04						18 53	18 57								19 47	
Skipton	d																					
Keighley	d																					
Bradford Interchange	d																					
Bradford Forster Sqare	d																					
Shipley	d																					
Halifax	d																					
Brighouse	d																					
Mirfield	d																					
Leeds	d	17 15			17 45		18 10				18 15				18 45	19 10						
Wakefield Westgate	d	17 27			17 57		18 22				18 27				18 56	19 22						
Wakefield Kirkgate	d																					
Pontefract Monkhill	d																					
Sheffield	a			18 23		18 28	18 51						19 21			19 50					20 16	
Hull	d																					18 30
Selby	d																					19 05
Doncaster	d	17 46	17 54		18 17						18 46	18 53			19 17							19 26
Retford	d	18 00																				19 40
Lincoln	d																					
Newark North Gate	a				18 42							19 17			19 44							
	d				18 43							19 17			19 44							
Grantham	a	18 23	18 27								19 17											20 01
	d	18 23	18 27								19 17			19 27								20 02
Peterborough	a		18 50		19 13							19 47		19 56	20 14							
Norwich	a													21 35								
Peterborough	d		18 50		19 13							19 50			20 15							
Stevenage	a	19 07									20 07											20s50
London Kings Cross ⊖	a	19 36	19 45		20 11				19 53		20 34	20 45			21 11				20 56			21 18

A ⚮ from Edinburgh

Scotland, North East England, Yorkshire and Humberside - London

Route Diagram - see first Page of Table 26

		GR	GR	GR	XC	TP	GC	GR	NT	TP		XC	GR	NT	NT	EM	GR	XC	GR	TP		TP	GR	NT	GR
		■ 1	■ 1	■ 1	◇1	◇1	■ 1	■ 1		◇1		◇1	■ 1			◇	■ 1	◇1	■ 1	◇1		◇1	■ 1		■ 1
					A													A							
Aberdeen	d																								
Stonehaven	d																								
Montrose	d																								
Arbroath	d																								
Dundee	d																								
Leuchars	d																								
Kirkcaldy	d																								
Inverkeithing	d																								
Inverness	d																								
Perth	d																								
Stirling	d																								
Glasgow Central	d																	16 55							
Motherwell	d																	17 11							
Haymarket	d																	17 51							
Edinburgh	a																	17 56							
Edinburgh	d		17 00		17 07			17 30					18 00					18 07	18 30				19 00		20 00
Dunbar	d				17 27			17 50										18 26					19 20		20 21
Berwick-upon-Tweed	d				17 52			18 15										18 52	19 11				19 45		20 46
Alnmouth for Alnwick	d												18 58												21 09
Morpeth	d																								21 26
Newcastle	a		18 23		18 36			19 00					19 27					19 36	19 56				20 30		21 42
Sunderland	d						18 12		18 43					19 28	20 29										
Hartlepool	d						18 36																		
Newcastle	d		18 25		18 39			19 02	19a05	19 10		19 25	19 28	19a52	20a47			19 40	19 58			20 08	20 32	21 06	21 44
Chester-le-Street	d																							21 15	
Durham	d		18 38		18 51					19 22		19 37	19 41					19 52				20 20	20 45	21 24	21 58
Darlington	a		18 55		19 07			19 29		19 38		19 53	20 00					20 08	20 24			20 36	21 03	21 44	22 16
Middlesbrough	d					18 45														20 06					
Eaglescliffe	d						18 59																	22a00	
Darlington	d		18 56		19 08			19 30		19 39		19 54	20 00					20 09	20 25			20 37	21 04		22 17
Northallerton	d		19 07			19 13	19 21													20 38		20 49			22 30
Thirsk	d					19 21	19 30													20 46					
York	a		19 28		19 35	19 42	19 47	19 57		20 11		20 21	20 28					20 36	20 53	21 06		21 12	21 31		23 02
Leeds	a				20 05	20 08				20 38								21 02				21 38			23 34
Harrogate	d																								
Scarborough	d																								
York	d		19 30				19 51	19 59				20 24	20 29						20 55				21 33		
Doncaster	a		19 53									20 47	20 53						21 18				21 55		
Skipton	d																								
Keighley	d																								
Bradford Interchange	d																								
Bradford Forster Sqare	d																								
Shipley	d																								
Halifax	d																								
Brighouse	d																								
Mirfield	d																								
Leeds	d	19 15		19 45	20 10												20 45	21 10							
Wakefield Westgate	d	19 26		19 56	20 22												20 56	21 22							
Wakefield Kirkgate	d																								
Pontefract Monkhill	d																								
Sheffield	a				20 51							21 17						21 50							
Hull	d																								
Selby	d																								
Doncaster	d	19 45	19 54	20 19									20 53				21 15		21 19				21 56		
Retford	d	19 59															21 29								
Lincoln	d																								
Newark North Gate	a		20 17	20 43									21 17						21 47				22 19		
	d		20 17	20 43									21 17						21 47				22 19		
Grantham	a	20 22						20 47									21 52		22 00				22 32		
	d	20 22						20 48								21 19	21 52		22 00				22 32		
Peterborough	a		20 48	21 13				21 08					21 46			21 52	22 13		22 21				22 53		
Norwich	a															23 28									
Peterborough	d		20 50	21 13				21 08					21 48				22 13		22 21				22 53		
Stevenage	a	21 08															22 45		22 50				23s24		
London Kings Cross ⊖	a	21 34	21 44	22 09			21 45	22 03					22 46				23 15		23 21				00 01		

A to Leeds

Scotland, North East England, Yorkshire and Humberside - London

Route Diagram - see first Page of Table 26

		XC	GR	SR	TP
		◇1	■ 1		◇1
Aberdeen	d			21 42	
Stonehaven	d			22u00	
Montrose	d			22u25	
Arbroath	d			22u43	
Dundee	d			23u06	
Leuchars	d			23u25	
Kirkcaldy	d			23u53	
Inverkeithing	d			00u12	
Inverness	d				
Perth	d				
Stirling	d				
Glasgow Central	d	18 57			
Motherwell	d	19 11			
Haymarket	d	19 51			
Edinburgh	a	19 56		00 36	
Edinburgh	d	20 05	21 00		
Dunbar	d	20 29	21 21		
Berwick-upon-Tweed	d	20 55	21 46		
Alnmouth for Alnwick	d		22 08		
Morpeth	d				
Newcastle	a	21 48	22 42		
Sunderland	d				
Hartlepool	d				
Newcastle	d				
Chester-le-Street	d				
Durham	d				
Darlington	a				
Middlesbrough	d				22 06
Eaglescliffe	d				
Darlington	d				
Northallerton	d				22 34
Thirsk	d				22 42
York	a				23 09
Leeds	a				23 38
Harrogate	d				
Scarborough	d				
York	d				
Doncaster	a				
Skipton	d				
Keighley	d				
Bradford Interchange	d				
Bradford Forster Sqare	d				
Shipley	d				
Halifax	d				
Brighouse	d				
Mirfield	d				
Leeds	d				
Wakefield Westgate	d				
Wakefield Kirkgate	d				
Pontefract Monkhill	d				
Sheffield	a				
Hull	d				
Selby	d				
Doncaster	d				
Retford	d				
Lincoln	d				
Newark North Gate	a				
	d				
Grantham	a				
	d				
Peterborough	a				
Norwich	a				
Peterborough	d				
Stevenage	a				
London Kings Cross ⊖	a				

Table 26

Sundays

1 July to 16 September

Scotland, North East England, Yorkshire and Humberside - London

Route Diagram - see first Page of Table 26

		GR	GR	GR	GR	FC	GR	GR	GC	GC	GR	TP	XC	EM	XC	FC	FC	GR	EM	EM	EM	HT	HT
		■ 1	■ 1	■ 1	■ 1	1	■ 1	■ 1	■ ◇1	■ ◇1	■ 1	◇1	◇1	◇1	◇1	1	1	■ 1	◇1	◇1	◇	◇1	◇1
		A	A	A			A		B	C				D		E	D		E	D	E	E	D
Aberdeen	d																						
Stonehaven	d																						
Montrose	d																						
Arbroath	d																						
Dundee	d																						
Leuchars	d																						
Kirkcaldy	d																						
Inverkeithing	d																						
Inverness	d																						
Perth	d																						
Stirling	d																						
Glasgow Central	d																						
Motherwell	d																						
Haymarket	d																						
Edinburgh	a																						
Edinburgh	d																						
Dunbar	d																						
Berwick-upon-Tweed	d																						
Alnmouth for Alnwick	d																						
Morpeth	d																						
Newcastle	a																						
Sunderland	d																						
Hartlepool	d																						
Newcastle	d		06 00				07 05				07 55	08 00											
Chester-le-Street	d																						
Durham	d		06u12				07u17				08 08	08 13											
Darlington	a										08 25	08 31											
Middlesbrough	d																						
Eaglescliffe	d																						
Darlington	d		06u31				07u36				08 26	08 31											
Northallerton	d											08 43											
Thirsk	d											08 51											
York	a										08 55	09 11											
Leeds	a											09 38											
Harrogate	d																						
Scarborough	d																						
York	d		07u00		08 00		08u05				08 56												
Doncaster	a				08 21																		
Skipton	d																						
Keighley	d																						
Bradford Interchange	d								07 55	08 05													
Bradford Forster Sqare	d																						
Shipley	d																						
Halifax	d								08 07														
Brighouse	d								08 18														
Mirfield	d								08 26														
Leeds	d	06 30		07 00				08 05					08 10	08 42	09 00			09 05	09 44	09 46			
Wakefield Westgate	d	06u41		07u11				08 16					08 23	08 55	09 11			09 17	09 58	09 58			
Wakefield Kirkgate	d								08 43	08 43													
Pontefract Monkhill	d																						
Sheffield	a												08 51	09 23					10 25	10 26			
Hull	d																					09 30	09 30
Selby	d																					10 05	10 05
Doncaster	d	06u59	07u23	0u30	08 22		08u28	08 35	09 06	09 06					09a31			09 35				10 24	10 24
Retford	d		07u37	07u44				08 49														10 38	10 38
Lincoln	d																						
Newark North Gate	a							09 04										09 59					
	d	07u22					08u51	09 04										09 59					
Grantham	a							09 17										10 11				10 59	10 59
	d	07u35	08u00	08u07				09 17										10 11			10 29	11 00	11 00
Peterborough	a				09 09			09 38			10 03							10 32			11 06		
Norwich	a																				13 06		
Peterborough	d	07u56	08u21	08u28	09 09	09 15		09 38			10 04					10 15	10 15	10 33					
Stevenage	a				09 38													11 04				11s48	11s50
London Kings Cross	a	08 51	09 22	09 25	10 07	10 15	10 22	10 33	10 40	10 40	10 58					11 15	11 16	11 33				12 14	12 15

A 29 July, 5 August, 12 August, 2 September, 9 September

B not 16 September. ◇ from Doncaster ■ to Doncaster

C 16 September. ◇ from Doncaster ■ to Doncaster

D 16 September

E not 16 September

Table 26

Sundays

1 July to 16 September

Scotland, North East England, Yorkshire and Humberside - London

Route Diagram - see first Page of Table 26

		XC	XC	GR	FC	GR	EM	XC	GR	XC	TP	TP	GC	GC	NT	GR	NT	TP	NT	GR	XC	XC	XC
		◇1	◇1	■ 1	1	■ 1	◇1	◇1	■ 1	◇1	◇1	◇1	■ 1	■ 1		■ 1		◇1		■ 1	◇1		◇1
		A	B				A	A		B	A	B	A	B							A	B	B
Aberdeen	d																						
Stonehaven	d																						
Montrose	d																						
Arbroath	d																						
Dundee	d																						
Leuchars	d																						
Kirkcaldy	d																						
Inverkeithing	d																						
Inverness	d																						
Perth	d																						
Stirling	d																						
Glasgow Central	d																						
Motherwell	d																						
Haymarket	d																						
Edinburgh	a																						
Edinburgh	d																				08 50	08 50	
Dunbar	d																						
Berwick-upon-Tweed	d																				09 33	10a10	
Alnmouth for Alnwick	d																						
Morpeth	d																						
Newcastle	a																				10 19		
Sunderland	d												09 12	09 12	09 28								
Hartlepool	d												09 36	09 37			10 01		11 00				
Newcastle	d			08 55				09 20	09 25	09 30	09 31	09 33			09a50	10 00	10a48		11a48		10 24		10 24
Chester-le-Street	d										09 40	09 43											
Durham	d			09 07				09 33	09 37	09 44	09 47	09 49									10 37		10 37
Darlington	a			09 25				09 48	09 55	10 00	10 03	10 05				10 26					10 53		10 53
Middlesbrough	d																	10 15					
Eaglescliffe	d												09 59	09 59									
Darlington	d			09 26				09 50	09 56	10 02	10 04	10 06				10 27					10 54		10 54
Northallerton	d								10 07		10 15	10 18	10 20	10 22				10 43					
Thirsk	d												10 29	10 31				10 51					
York	a			09 53				10 18	10 27	10 31	10 41	10 41	10 45	10 48		10 54		11 10			11 23		11 23
Leeds	a							10 51		10 57	11 08	11 08						11 38			11 51		11 51
Harrogate	d																						
Scarborough	d																						
York	d	09 28	09 30	09 56					10 29				10 50	10 50		10 56							
Doncaster	a								10 51														
Skipton	d																						
Keighley	d																						
Bradford Interchange	d																						
Bradford Forster Sqare	d																						
Shipley	d																						
Halifax	d																						
Brighouse	d																						
Mirfield	d																						
Leeds	d	10 00	10 00			10 05	10 15	11 00		11 00										11 05	12 00		12 00
Wakefield Westgate	d	10 12	10 12			10 17	10 27	11 12		11 12										11 17	12 12		12 12
Wakefield Kirkgate	d																						
Pontefract Monkhill	d																						
Sheffield	a						10 57																
Hull	d																						
Selby	d																						
Doncaster	d	10a28	10a28			10 35		11a28	10 52	11a28										11 35	12a28		12a28
Retford	d					10 51																	
Lincoln	d																						
Newark North Gate	a					11 06			11 15											11 59			
	d					11 06			11 15											12 00			
Grantham	a					11 19														12 12			
	d					11 19														12 13			
Peterborough	a			11 01		11 41			11 47							12 01				12 34			
Norwich	a																						
Peterborough	d			11 02	11 20	11 41			11 50							12 01				12 35			
Stevenage	a																			13 05			
London Kings Cross	a			11 59	12 20	12 36			12 43				12 44	12 44		12 54				13 34			

A not 16 September

B 16 September

Scotland, North East England, Yorkshire and Humberside - London

Route Diagram - see first Page of Table 26

		NT		EM	GR	GR	XC	TP	HT	HT	EM	GR		XC	XC	XC	GR	GC	GC	GR	TP	TP		GR	GR
				◇ A	1	1	B	◇1	◇1 A	◇1 B	◇	1		◇1 A	B	◇1 B	1	1 A	1 B	1	◇1 B	◇1 A		1	1
Aberdeen	d																								
Stonehaven	d																								
Montrose	d																								
Arbroath	d																								
Dundee	d																								
Leuchars	d																								
Kirkcaldy	d																								
Inverkeithing	d																								
Inverness	d																								
Perth	d																								
Stirling	d																								
Glasgow Central	d																								
Motherwell	d																								
Haymarket	d																								
Edinburgh	a																								
Edinburgh	d				09 00	09 30								09 50	09 50		10 00			10 30					10 55
Dunbar	d																								
Berwick-upon-Tweed	d					10 11														11 11					
Alnmouth for Alnwick	d						10 05							10 49	11 55		10 58								
Morpeth	d						10 45							11 04	12a35										
Newcastle	a				10 25	10 57	11 15							11 19			11 27			11 56					12 06
Sunderland	d																								12 23
Hartlepool	d	12 01																							
Newcastle	d	12a48			10 28	10 59		11 08						11 25		11 25	11 28			11 58	12 10	12 10			12 25
Chester-le-Street	d																								
Durham	d				10 42			11 20						11 37		11 37	11 41				12 22	12 22			12 38
Darlington	a				11 00	11 26		11 36						11 54		11 54	12 00			12 25	12 38	12 38			12 55
Middlesbrough	d																								
Eaglescliffe	d																								
Darlington	d				11 01	11 27		11 37						11 55		11 55	12 00			12 26	12 39	12 39			12 56
Northallerton	d				11 14			11 49																	
Thirsk	d																								13 07
York	a				11 34	11 54		12 12						12 22		12 22	12 28			12 53	13 11	13 11			13 28
Leeds	a							12 38						12 51		12 51					13 37	13 38			
Harrogate	d																								
Scarborough	d																								
York	d				11 36	11 56											12 30			12 55					13 30
Doncaster	a				11 59												12 53								13 53
Skipton	d																								
Keighley	d																								
Bradford Interchange	d																	12 04							
Bradford Forster Sqare	d																								
Shipley	d																								
Halifax	d																	12 15	12 20						
Brighouse	d																	12 26	12 31						
Mirfield	d																	12 35	12 40						
Leeds	d											12 05		13 00		13 00								13 05	
Wakefield Westgate	d											12 17		13 12		13 12								13 16	
Wakefield Kirkgate	d																	12 51	13 01						
Pontefract Monkhill	d																								
Sheffield	a																								
Hull	d								11 30	11 30															
Selby	d								12 05	12 05															
Doncaster	d				12 00				12 26	12 26		12 37		13a28		13a28	12 54	13 23	13 23					13 35	13 54
Retford	d				12 15				12 40	12 40															14 08
Lincoln	d																								
Newark North Gate	a											13 00					13 17							13 59	
	d											13 00					13 17							13 59	
Grantham	a								13 01	13 01		13 13												14 11	
	d			12 18					13 02	13 02	13 12	13 15												14 11	
Peterborough	a			12 50	12 56						13 41	13 38					13 47							14 32	14 48
Norwich	a			14 35							15 30														
Peterborough	d				12 56							13 40					13 50							14 33	14 49
Stevenage	a								13s46	13s50														15 06	
London Kings Cross ⊖	a				13 53	13 56			14 14	14 15		14 33					14 45	14 55	14 55	14 57				15 33	15 43

A not 16 September

B 16 September

Scotland, North East England, Yorkshire and Humberside - London

Route Diagram - see first Page of Table 26

		EM	EM	GR	XC	XC	XC	TP		GC	GR	TP	TP	GR	GR	NT	XC	NT		EM	HT	GR	XC	XC	XC
		◇1	◇	1	◇1 A	B	◇1 B	◇1		1	1	◇1 A	◇1 B	1	1		◇1			◇	◇1	1	◇1 A	B	◇1 B
Aberdeen	d																								
Stonehaven	d																								
Montrose	d																								
Arbroath	d																								
Dundee	d																								
Leuchars	d																								
Kirkcaldy	d																								
Inverkeithing	d																								
Inverness	d																								
Perth	d																								
Stirling	d																								
Glasgow Central	d																						10 55		
Motherwell	d																						11 10		
Haymarket	d																						11 51		
Edinburgh	a																						11 55		
Edinburgh	d				11 05	11 05					11 30				12 00								12 08	12 08	
Dunbar	d				11 25																				
Berwick-upon-Tweed	d				11 50	12 40					12 11												12 49	13a28	
Alnmouth for Alnwick	d				12 10	13a35									12 58										
Morpeth	d																								
Newcastle	a				12 37						12 57				13 27								13 34		
Sunderland	d									12 12						13 28									
Hartlepool	d									12 36								14 01							
Newcastle	d				12 40		12 40				12 59	13 04	13 04	13 12	13 28	13a49	13 35	14a48					13 40		13 40
Chester-le-Street	d											13 13	13 13												
Durham	d				12 52		12 52					13 20	13 20	13 24	13 41		13 47						13 52		13 52
Darlington	a				13 08		13 08				13 27	13 36	13 36	13 41	13 59		14 04						14 09		14 09
Middlesbrough	d							12 45																	
Eaglescliffe	d									13 02															
Darlington	d				13 09		13 09				13 28	13 37	13 37	13 42	13 59		14 05						14 10		14 10
Northallerton	d							13 13		13 23				13 55											
Thirsk	d							13 23		13 32															
York	a				13 36		13 36	13 43		13 48	13 56	14 10	14 10	14 15	14 28		14 31						14 37		14 38
Leeds	a				14 03		14 03	14 08				14 38	14 39										15 05		15 04
Harrogate	d																								
Scarborough	d																								
York	d									13 52	13 57			14 16	14 29		14 34								
Doncaster	a													14 44	14 53		14 57								
Skipton	d																								
Keighley	d																								
Bradford Interchange	d																								
Bradford Forster Sqare	d																								
Shipley	d																								
Halifax	d																								
Brighouse	d																								
Mirfield	d																								
Leeds	d	13 59		14 05	14 10		14 10															15 05	15 10		15 10
Wakefield Westgate	d	14 12		14 17	14 23		14 23															15 16	15 23		15 23
Wakefield Kirkgate	d																								
Pontefract Monkhill	d																								
Sheffield	a	14 39			14 52		14 52										15 21						15 51		15 51
Hull	d																				14 30				
Selby	d																				15 05				
Doncaster	d			14 35										14 44	14 53						15 26	15 35			
Retford	d																				15 40				
Lincoln	d																								
Newark North Gate	a			14 59											15 17							15 59			
	d			14 59											15 17							15 59			
Grantham	a			15 11																	16 01	16 11			
	d		14 22	15 11																15 20	16 02	16 11			
Peterborough	a		14 51	15 32										15 38	15 46					15 58		16 32			
Norwich	a		16 35																	17 35					
Peterborough	d			15 33										15 39	15 49							16 33			
Stevenage	a																				16s46	17 05			
London Kings Cross ⊖	a			16 26						15 46	15 55			16 33	16 45						17 15	17 33			

A not 16 September

B 16 September

Table 26

Sundays

1 July to 16 September

Scotland, North East England, Yorkshire and Humberside - London

Route Diagram - see first Page of Table 26

		GR	TP	GR	GR	XC	XC	XC	XC	TP	GC	GR	TP	XC	XC	NT	NT	EM	GR	GR	GC	GC
		A					B	C	C			D		E	C						E	C
Aberdeen	d	09 47																				
Stonehaven	d	10 04																				
Montrose	d	10 27																				
Arbroath	d	10 43																				
Dundee	d	11 02																				
Leuchars	d	11 16																				
Kirkcaldy	d	11 40																				
Inverkeithing	d	11 56																				
Inverness	d											09 40										
Perth	d											11 58										
Stirling	d											12 34										
Glasgow Central	d						11 51															
Motherwell	d						12 07															
Haymarket	d	12 16					12 49					13 14										
Edinburgh	a	12 23					12 54					13 19										
Edinburgh	d	12 30			13 00		13 06	13 06				13 30		13 50						14 00		
Dunbar	d						13 25	14 01														
Berwick-upon-Tweed	d	13 11						14 41				14 12		14 33						14 58		
Alnmouth for Alnwick	d						14 08	15a36														
Morpeth	d																					
Newcastle	a	13 58			14 23		14 35					14 59		15 18						15 27		
Sunderland	d										14 12					15 28						
Hartlepool	d										14 36						16 01					
Newcastle	d	13 59	14 08	14 12	14 25	14 35	14 40		14 40			15 00	15 07	15 23	15 23	15a48	16a48			15 28		
Chester-le-Street	d												15 16									
Durham	d		14 20	14 25	14 38	14 47	14 52		14 52				15 23	15 36	15 36					15 41		
Darlington	a	14 28	14 36	14 42	14 56	15 03	15 08		15 08			15 29	15 39	15 52	15 52					16 00		
Middlesbrough	d									14 42												
Eaglescliffe	d										14 59											
Darlington	d	14 28	14 37	14 43	14 57	15 04	15 09		15 09			15 29	15 40	15 53	15 53					16 00		
Northallerton	d		14 49	14 57						15 10	15 22											
Thirsk	d									15 18	15 31											
York	a	14 56	15 12	15 18	15 24	15 31	15 37		15 37	15 42	15 46	15 57	16 12	16 19	16 19					16 28		
Leeds	a		15 38				16 03		16 05	16 08			16 38									
Harrogate	d																					
Scarborough	d																					
York	d	14 58		15 19	15 29	15 34					15 50	15 59		16 23	16 23					16 29		
Doncaster	a			15 43	15 52	15 57								16 48	16 48					16 54		
Skipton	d																					
Keighley	d																					
Bradford Interchange	d																				15 42	15 37
Bradford Forster Sqare	d																					
Shipley	d																					
Halifax	d																				15 54	
Brighouse	d																				16 05	
Mirfield	d																				16 14	
Leeds	d						16 10		16 10										16 15			
Wakefield Westgate	d						16 22		16 22										16 27			
Wakefield Kirkgate	d																				16 30	16 30
Pontefract Monkhill	d																					
Sheffield	a					16 21	16 51		16 51					17 19	17 19							
Hull	d																					
Selby	d																					
Doncaster	d			15 43	15 54														16 46	16 54	17 12	17 12
Retford	d				16 08																	
Lincoln	d																					
Newark North Gate	a			16 07																17 18		
	d			16 08																17 18		
Grantham	a																		17 17			
	d																	16 22	17 17			
Peterborough	a			16 38	16 49													16 55		17 47		
Norwich	a																	18 30				
Peterborough	d			16 38	16 50															17 50		
Stevenage	a																		18 04			
London Kings Cross ⊖	a	16 55		17 37	17 44						17 45	17 57							18 34	18 46	18 44	18 50

A The Northern Lights
B not 16 September. from Edinburgh
C 16 September
D The Highland Chieftain
E not 16 September

Table 26

Sundays

1 July to 16 September

Scotland, North East England, Yorkshire and Humberside - London

Route Diagram - see first Page of Table 26

		NT	EM	EM	GR	XC	XC	XC	GR	TP	HT	GR	EM	GR	GR	XC	GR	EM	EM	XC	XC	XC	TP
			A	B		C	B	B										A	B	C	B	B	
Aberdeen	d					11 12			11 47														
Stonehaven	d					11 29			12 04														
Montrose	d					11 50			12 27														
Arbroath	d					12 06			12 43														
Dundee	d					12 25			13 01														
Leuchars	d					12 38			13 15														
Kirkcaldy	d					13 03			13 39														
Inverkeithing	d					13 18			13 58														
Inverness	d																						
Perth	d																						
Stirling	d																						
Glasgow Central	d																			13 49			
Motherwell	d																			14 04			
Haymarket	d					13 37			14 18											14 42			
Edinburgh	a					13 42			14 25											14 47			
Edinburgh	d					14 08	14 08		14 30						15 00					15 07	15 07		
Dunbar	d																			15 27	16a02		
Berwick-upon-Tweed	d					14 49	15a28		15 11														
Alnmouth for Alnwick	d																						
Morpeth	d																						
Newcastle	a					15 34			15 57						16 23					16 34			
Sunderland	d																						
Hartlepool	d	16 51																					
Newcastle	d	17a48				15 40		15 40	15 59	16 08		16 12			16 25	16 35				16 40		16 40	
Chester-le-Street	d																						
Durham	d					15 52		15 52		16 20		16 24			16 38	16 47				16 52		16 52	
Darlington	a					16 08		16 08	16 27	16 36		16 41			16 56	17 03				17 08		17 08	
Middlesbrough	d																						16 42
Eaglescliffe	d																						
Darlington	d					16 09		16 09	16 28	16 37		16 42			16 57	17 04				17 09		17 09	
Northallerton	d									16 49		16 54											17 10
Thirsk	d																						17 18
York	a					16 37		16 38	16 56	17 12		17 16			17 24	17 30				17 37		17 37	17 42
Leeds	a					17 06		17 06		17 38										18 04		18 04	18 08
Harrogate	d																17 05						
Scarborough	d																						
York	d								16 57			17 17			17 29	17 34		17 42	17 42				
Doncaster	a														17 52	17 57		18 04	18 04				
Skipton	d																						
Keighley	d																						
Bradford Interchange	d																						
Bradford Forster Sqare	d																						
Shipley	d																						
Halifax	d																						
Brighouse	d																						
Mirfield	d																						
Leeds	d				16 45	17 10		17 10						17 15			17 45			18 10		18 10	
Wakefield Westgate	d				16 56	17 22		17 22						17 27			17 57			18 22		18 22	
Wakefield Kirkgate	d																						
Pontefract Monkhill	d																						
Sheffield	a					17 51		17 51								18 23		18 28	18 39	18 51		18 51	
Hull	d										16 30												
Selby	d										17 05												
Doncaster	d				17 17						17 26			17 46	17 54		18 17						
Retford	d										17 40			18 00									
Lincoln	d																						
Newark North Gate	a				17 44							17 59					18 42						
	d				17 44							17 59					18 43						
Grantham	a										18 01			18 23	18 27								
	d		17 21	17 22							18 02		18 17	18 23	18 27								
Peterborough	a		17 50	17 50	18 14							18 28	18 46		18 50		19 13						
Norwich	a		19 29	19 29									20 29										
Peterborough	d				18 14							18 29			18 50		19 13						
Stevenage	a										18s49			19 07									
London Kings Cross ⊖	a				19 11				18 56		19 18	19 22		19 36	19 45		20 11						

A not 16 September
B 16 September
C not 16 September. from Edinburgh

Scotland, North East England, Yorkshire and Humberside - London

Route Diagram - see first Page of Table 26

		GR	TP	GR	GR	XC	XC	EM	GR	XC	XC	XC	SR	TP	GR	TP	XC	HT	GR	GR	GR	XC	XC
						A				B	A	A										A	C
Aberdeen	d														13 50								
Stonehaven	d														14 07								
Montrose	d														14 30								
Arbroath	d														14 46								
Dundee	d														15 04								
Leuchars	d														15 18								
Kirkcaldy	d														15 42								
Inverkeithing	d														15 58								
Inverness	d												20 25										
Perth	d												23u00										
Stirling	d												23u45										
Glasgow Central	d									14 55													
Motherwell	d									15 11													
Haymarket	d									15 51					16 18								
Edinburgh	a									15 56			00 47		16 25								
Edinburgh	d	15 30			16 00					16 05	16 05				16 30					17 00		17 07	17 07
Dunbar	d																					17 27	17 27
Berwick-upon-Tweed	d	16 11													17 11							17 52	17 52
Alnmouth for Alnwick	d				16 58	16 20				17 07	18 10												
Morpeth	d					17 00				17 22	18a50												
Newcastle	a	16 56			17 27	17 30				17 37					17 57					18 23		18 36	18 36
Sunderland	d																						
Hartlepool	d																						
Newcastle	d	16 58	17 05		17 28		17 35			17 40		17 40		17 52	17 59		18 20			18 25		18 39	18 39
Chester-le-Street	d		17 14																				
Durham	d		17 21		17 41		17 47			17 52		17 52		18 04			18 32			18 38		18 51	18 51
Darlington	a	17 25	17 37		18 00		18 04			18 08		18 08		18 20	18 26		18 49			18 55		19 07	19 07
Middlesbrough	d																						
Eaglescliffe	d																						
Darlington	d	17 26	17 38		18 00		18 05			18 09		18 09		18 21	18 27		18 51			18 56		19 08	19 08
Northallerton	d		17 49											18 33						19 07			
Thirsk	d																						
York	a	17 53	18 12		18 28		18 31			18 36		18 36		19 03	18 56	← 19 03	19 17			19 28		19 35	19 35
Leeds	a		18 38							19 03		19 03		→		19 38						20 05	20 05
Harrogate	d																						
Scarborough	d																						
York	d	17 55			18 29		18 34								18 57		19 24			19 30			
Doncaster	a				18 53		18 57										19 47			19 53			
Skipton	d																						
Keighley	d																						
Bradford Interchange	d																						
Bradford Forster Square	d																						
Shipley	d																						
Halifax	d																						
Brighouse	d																						
Mirfield	d																						
Leeds	d			18 15					18 45	19 10		19 10							19 15		19 45	20 10	20 10
Wakefield Westgate	d			18 27					18 56	19 22		19 22							19 26		19 56	20 22	20 22
Wakefield Kirkgate	d																						
Pontefract Monkhill	d																						
Sheffield	a						19 21			19 50		19 50					20 16					20 51	20 51
Hull	d																	18 30					
Selby	d																	19 05					
Doncaster	d			18 46	18 53				19 17									19 26	19 45	19 54	20 19		
Retford	d																	19 40	19 59				
Lincoln	d																						
Newark North Gate	a				19 17				19 44											20 17	20 43		
	d				19 17				19 44											20 17	20 43		
Grantham	a			19 17														20 01	20 22				
	d			19 17				19 27										20 02	20 22				
Peterborough	a				19 47			19 56	20 14											20 48	21 13		
Norwich	a							21 35															
Peterborough	d				19 50				20 15											20 50	21 13		
Stevenage	a			20 07														20s50	21 08				
London Kings Cross	a	19 53		20 34	20 45				21 11						20 56			21 18	21 34	21 44	22 09		

A 16 September

B not 16 September. from Edinburgh

C not 16 September. to Leeds

Scotland, North East England, Yorkshire and Humberside - London

Route Diagram - see first Page of Table 26

		TP	GC	GR	NT	TP	XC	GR	NT	NT	EM	GR	XC	GR	TP	TP	GR	NT	GR	XC	GR	SR	TP	TP
													A										B	C
Aberdeen	d																					21 42		
Stonehaven	d																					22u00		
Montrose	d																					22u25		
Arbroath	d																					22u43		
Dundee	d																					23u06		
Leuchars	d																					23u25		
Kirkcaldy	d																					23u53		
Inverkeithing	d																					00u12		
Inverness	d																							
Perth	d																							
Stirling	d																							
Glasgow Central	d												16 55							18 57				
Motherwell	d												17 11							19 11				
Haymarket	d												17 51							19 51				
Edinburgh	a												17 56							19 56		00 36		
Edinburgh	d			17 30				18 00					18 07	18 30			19 00		20 00	20 05	21 00			
Dunbar	d			17 50									18 26				19 20		20 21	20 29	21 21			
Berwick-upon-Tweed	d			18 15									18 52	19 11			19 45		20 46	20 55	21 46			
Alnmouth for Alnwick	d							18 58											21 09		22 08			
Morpeth	d																		21 26					
Newcastle	a			19 00				19 27					19 36	19 56			20 30		21 42	21 48	22 42			
Sunderland	d		18 12		18 43				19 28	20 29														
Hartlepool	d		18 36																					
Newcastle	d			19 02	19a05	19 10	19 25	19 28	19a52	20a47			19 40	19 58		20 08	20 32	21 06	21 44					
Chester-le-Street	d																	21 15						
Durham	d					19 22	19 37	19 41					19 52			20 20	20 45	21 24	21 58					
Darlington	a			19 29		19 38	19 53	20 00					20 08	20 24		20 36	21 03	21 44	22 16					
Middlesbrough	d	18 45													20 06								22 06	22 06
Eaglescliffe	d		18 59															22a00						
Darlington	d			19 30		19 39	19 54	20 00					20 09	20 25		20 37	21 04		22 17					
Northallerton	d	19 13	19 21												20 38	20 49			22 30				22 34	22 35
Thirsk	d	19 21	19 30												20 46								22 42	22 43
York	a	19 42	19 47	19 57		20 11	20 21	20 28					20 36	20 53	21 06	21 12	21 31		23 02				23 09	23 09
Leeds	a	20 08				20 38							21 02			21 38			23 34				23 38	23 38
Harrogate	d																							
Scarborough	d																							
York	d		19 51	19 59			20 24	20 29						20 55			21 33							
Doncaster	a						20 47	20 53						21 18			21 55							
Skipton	d																							
Keighley	d																							
Bradford Interchange	d																							
Bradford Forster Square	d																							
Shipley	d																							
Halifax	d																							
Brighouse	d																							
Mirfield	d																							
Leeds	d											20 45	21 10											
Wakefield Westgate	d											20 56	21 22											
Wakefield Kirkgate	d																							
Pontefract Monkhill	d																							
Sheffield	a						21 17						21 50											
Hull	d																							
Selby	d																							
Doncaster	d							20 53				21 15		21 19			21 56							
Retford	d											21 29												
Lincoln	d																							
Newark North Gate	a							21 17						21 47			22 19							
	d							21 17						21 47			22 19							
Grantham	a			20 47								21 52		22 00			22 32							
	d			20 48							21 19	21 52		22 00			22 32							
Peterborough	a			21 08				21 46			21 52	22 13		22 21			22 53							
Norwich	a										23 28													
Peterborough	d			21 08				21 48				22 13		22 21			22 53							
Stevenage	a											22 45		22 50			23s24							
London Kings Cross	a		21 45	22 03				22 46				23 15		23 21			00 01							

A to Leeds

B 16 September

C not 16 September

Scotland, North East England, Yorkshire and Humberside - London

Route Diagram - see first Page of Table 26

Station		GR	FC	GR	GC	GR	TP	XC	EM	XC	FC	FC	GR	HT	HT	EM	EM	XC	GR	FC	GR	GR	EM
					A				B		C	B		C	B	C	B						C
Aberdeen	d																						
Stonehaven	d																						
Montrose	d																						
Arbroath	d																						
Dundee	d																						
Leuchars	d																						
Kirkcaldy	d																						
Inverkeithing	d																						
Inverness	d																						
Perth	d																						
Stirling	d																						
Glasgow Central	d																						
Motherwell	d																						
Haymarket	d																						
Edinburgh	a																						
Edinburgh	d																						
Dnbar	d																						
Berwick-upon-Tweed	d																						
Alnmouth for Alnwick	d																						
Morpeth	d																						
Newcastle	a																						
Sunderland	d																						
Hartlepool	d																						
Newcastle	d					07 55	08 00												08 55			09 25	
ChesterleStreet	d																						
Durham	d					08 08	08 13												09 07			09 37	
Darlington	a					08 25	08 31												09 25			09 55	
Middlesbrough	d																						
Eaglescliffe	d																						
Darlington	d					08 26	08 31												09 26			09 56	
Nrthallerton	d						08 43															10 07	
Thirsk	d						08 51																
York	a					08 55	09 11												09 53			10 27	
Leeds	a						09 38																
Harrogate	d																						
Scarborough	d																						
York	d	08 00				08 56												09 30	09 56			10 29	
Doncaster	a	08 21																				10 51	
Skipton	d																						
Keighley	d																						
Bradford Interchange	d				08 05																		
Bradford Forster Sqare	d																						
Shipley	d																						
Halifax	d																						
Brighouse	d																						
Mirfield	d																						
Leeds	d			08 05				08 10	08 42	09 00			09 05			09 44	09 46	10 00			10 05		10 15
Wakefield Westgate	d			08 16				08 23	08 55	09 11			09 17			09 58	09 58	10 12			10 17		10 27
Wakefield Kirkgate	d				08 43																		
Pontefract Monkhill	d																						
Sheffield	a							08 51	09 23							10 25	10 26						10 57
Hull	d													09 30	09 30								
Selby	d													10 05	10 05								
Doncaster	d	08 22		08 35	09 06					09a31			09 35	10 24	10 24			10a28			10 35	10 52	
Retford	d			08 49										10 38	10 38						10 51		
Lincoln	d																						
Newark North Gate	a			09 04									09 59								11 06	11 15	
	d			09 04									09 59								11 06	11 15	
Grantham	a			09 17									10 11	10 59	10 59						11 19		
	d			09 17									10 11	11 00	11 00						11 19		
Peterborough	a	09 09		09 38		10 03							10 32						11 01		11 41	11 47	
Nrwich	a																						
Peterborough	d	09 09	09 15	09 38		10 04					10 15	10 15	10 33						11 02	11 20	11 41	11 50	
Stevenage	a	09 38											11 04	11s48	11s50								
London Kings Cross ⊖	a	10 07	10 15	10 33	10 40	10 58					11 15	11 16	11 33	12 14	12 15				11 59	12 20	12 36	12 43	

A ◇ from Dncaster

B from 23 September until 21 October

C from 28 October

Scotland, North East England, Yorkshire and Humberside - London

Route Diagram - see first Page of Table 26

Station		XC	TP	GC	NT	GR	NT	TP	NT	GR	XC	XC	XC	GR	GR	XC	TP	HT	HT	NT	EM	GR	XC
											A	B	B			B		A	B		B		A
Aberdeen	d																						
Stonehaven	d																						
Montrose	d																						
Arbroath	d																						
Dundee	d																						
Leuchars	d																						
Kirkcaldy	d																						
Inverkeithing	d																						
Inverness	d																						
Perth	d																						
Stirling	d																						
Glasgow Central	d																						
Motherwell	d																						
Haymarket	d																						
Edinburgh	a																						
Edinburgh	d										08 50	08 50		09 00	09 30								09 50
Dnbar	d																						
Berwick-upon-Tweed	d										09 33	10a10			10 11								
Alnmouth for Alnwick	d															10 05							10 49
Morpeth	d															10 45							11 04
Newcastle	a										10 19			10 25	10 57	11 15							11 19
Sunderland	d			09 12	09 28																		
Hartlepool	d			09 37			10 01		11 00											12 01			
Newcastle	d	09 30	09 33		09a50	10 00	10a48		11a48		10 24		10 24	10 28	10 59		11 08			12a48			11 25
ChesterleStreet	d		09 43																				
Durham	d	09 44	09 49								10 37		10 37	10 42			11 20						11 37
Darlington	a	10 00	10 05			10 26					10 53		10 53	11 00	11 26		11 36						11 54
Middlesbrough	d							10 15															
Eaglescliffe	d			09 59																			
Darlington	d	10 02	10 06			10 27					10 54		10 54	11 01	11 27		11 37						11 55
Nrthallerton	d		10 18	10 22				10 43						11 14			11 49						
Thirsk	d			10 31				10 51															
York	a	10 31	10 41	10 48		10 54		11 10			11 23		11 23	11 34	11 54		12 12						12 22
Leeds	a	10 57	11 08					11 38			11 51		11 51				12 38						12 51
Harrogate	d																						
Scarborough	d																						
York	d			10 50		10 56								11 36	11 56								
Doncaster	a													11 59									
Skipton	d																						
Keighley	d																						
Bradford Interchange	d																						
Bradford Forster Sqare	d																						
Shipley	d																						
Halifax	d																						
Brighouse	d																						
Mirfield	d																						
Leeds	d	11 00								11 05	12 00		12 00									12 05	13 00
Wakefield Westgate	d	11 12								11 17	12 12		12 12									12 17	13 12
Wakefield Kirkgate	d																						
Pontefract Monkhill	d																						
Sheffield	a																						
Hull	d																	11 30	11 30				
Selby	d																	12 05	12 05				
Doncaster	d	11a28								11 35	12a28		12a28	12 00				12 26	12 26			12 37	13a28
Retford	d													12 15				12 40	12 40				
Lincoln	d																						
Newark North Gate	a									11 59												13 00	
	d									12 00												13 00	
Grantham	a									12 12								13 01	13 01			13 13	
	d									12 13								13 02	13 02		13 12	13 15	
Peterborough	a					12 01				12 34				12 56							13 41	13 38	
Nrwich	a																				15 30		
Peterborough	d					12 01				12 35				12 56								13 40	
Stevenage	a									13 05								13s46	13s50				
London Kings Cross ⊖	a			12 44		12 54				13 34				13 53	13 56			14 14	14 15			14 33	

A from 28 October

B from 23 September until 21 October

Scotland, North East England, Yorkshire and Humberside - London

Route Diagram - see first Page of Table 26

		XC	XC	GR	GC	GC	GR	TP	GR	GR	XC	EM	EM	EM	GR	XC	TP	GC	GR	TP	GR	GR
		A	A		B	A					A	A	B	A		A						
Aberdeen	d																					
Stonehaven	d																					
Montrose	d																					
Arbroath	d																					
Dundee	d																					
Leuchars	d																					
Kirkcaldy	d																					
Inverkeithing	d																					
Inverness	d																					
Perth	d																					
Stirling	d																					
Glasgow Central	d																					
Motherwell	d																					
Haymarket	d																					
Edinburgh	a																					
Edinburgh	d	09 50		10 00			10 30			10 55	11 05								11 30			12 00
Dunbar	d																					
Berwick-upon-Tweed	d						11 11				12 40								12 11			
Alnmouth for Alnwick	d	11 55		10 58							13a35											12 58
Morpeth	d	12a35								12 06												
Newcastle	a			11 27			11 56			12 23									12 57			13 27
Sunderland	d																	12 12				
Hartlepool	d																	12 36				
Newcastle	d		11 25	11 28			11 58	12 10		12 25						12 40			12 59	13 04	13 12	13 28
Chester-le-Street	d																			13 13		
Durham	d		11 37	11 41				12 22		12 38						12 52				13 20	13 24	13 41
Darlington	a		11 54	12 00			12 25	12 38		12 55						13 08			13 27	13 36	13 41	13 59
Middlesbrough	d																12 45					
Eaglescliffe	d																	13 02				
Darlington	d		11 55	12 00			12 26	12 39		12 56						13 09			13 28	13 37	13 42	13 59
Northallerton	d									13 07							13 13	13 23			13 55	
Thirsk	d																13 23	13 32				
York	a		12 22	12 28			12 53	13 11		13 28						13 36	13 43	13 48	13 56	14 10	14 15	14 28
Leeds	a		12 51					13 37								14 03	14 08			14 39		
Harrogate	d																					
Scarborough	d																					
York	d			12 30			12 55			13 30								13 52	13 57		14 16	14 29
Doncaster	a			12 53						13 53											14 44	14 53
Skipton	d																					
Keighley	d																					
Bradford Interchange	d				12 04																	
Bradford Forster Sqare	d																					
Shipley	d																					
Halifax	d				12 15	12 20																
Brighouse	d				12 26	12 31																
Mirfield	d				12 35	12 40																
Leeds	d		13 00						13 05			13 59	13 59		14 05	14 10						
Wakefield Westgate	d		13 12						13 16			14 12	14 12		14 17	14 23						
Wakefield Kirkgate	d				12 51	13 01																
Pontefract Monkhill	d																					
Sheffield	a											14 39	14 43			14 52						
Hull	d																					
Selby	d																					
Doncaster	d		13a28	12 54	13 23	13 23			13 35	13 54					14 35						14 44	14 53
Retford	d									14 08												
Lincoln	d																					
Newark North Gate	a			13 17					13 59						14 59							15 17
	d			13 17					13 59						14 59							15 17
Grantham	a								14 11						15 11							
	d								14 11					14 22	15 11							
Peterborough	a			13 47					14 32	14 48				14 51	15 32						15 38	15 46
Norwich	a													16 35								
Peterborough	d			13 50					14 33	14 49					15 33						15 39	15 49
Stevenage	a								15 06													
London Kings Cross	a			14 45	14 55	14 55	14 57		15 33	15 43					16 26			15 46	15 55		16 33	16 45

A from 23 September until 21 October

B from 28 October

Scotland, North East England, Yorkshire and Humberside - London

Route Diagram - see first Page of Table 26

		NT	XC	NT	EM	HT	GR	XC	XC	XC	GR	TP	GR	GR	XC	XC	XC	XC	TP	GC	GR	TP	XC
								A	B	B	C					D	B	B			E		A
Aberdeen	d										09 47												
Stonehaven	d										10 04												
Montrose	d										10 27												
Arbroath	d										10 43												
Dundee	d										11 02												
Leuchars	d										11 16												
Kirkcaldy	d										11 40												
Inverkeithing	d										11 56												
Inverness	d																				09 40		
Perth	d																				11 58		
Stirling	d																				12 34		
Glasgow Central	d							10 55								11 51							
Motherwell	d							11 10								12 07							
Haymarket	d							11 51			12 16					12 49					13 14		
Edinburgh	a							11 55			12 23					12 54					13 19		
Edinburgh	d							12 08	12 08		12 30			13 00		13 06	13 06				13 30		13 50
Dunbar	d															13 25	14 01						
Berwick-upon-Tweed	d							12 49	13a28		13 11						14 41				14 12		14 33
Alnmouth for Alnwick	d															14 08	15a36						
Morpeth	d																						
Newcastle	a							13 34			13 58			14 23		14 35					14 59		15 18
Sunderland	d	13 28																		14 12			
Hartlepool	d			14 01																14 36			
Newcastle	d	13a49	13 35	14a48				13 40		13 40	13 59	14 08	14 12	14 25	14 35	14 40		14 40			15 00	15 07	15 23
Chester-le-Street	d																					15 16	
Durham	d		13 47					13 52		13 52		14 20	14 25	14 38	14 47	14 52		14 52				15 23	15 36
Darlington	a		14 04					14 09		14 09	14 28	14 36	14 42	14 56	15 03	15 08		15 08			15 29	15 39	15 52
Middlesbrough	d																		14 42				
Eaglescliffe	d																			14 59			
Darlington	d		14 05					14 10		14 10	14 28	14 37	14 43	14 57	15 04	15 09		15 09			15 29	15 40	15 53
Northallerton	d											14 49	14 57						15 10	15 22			
Thirsk	d																		15 18	15 31			
York	a		14 31					14 37		14 38	14 56	15 12	15 18	15 24	15 31	15 37		15 37	15 42	15 46	15 57	16 12	16 19
Leeds	a							15 05		15 04		15 38				16 03		16 05	16 08			16 38	
Harrogate	d																						
Scarborough	d																						
York	d		14 34								14 58		15 19	15 29	15 34					15 50	15 59		16 23
Doncaster	a		14 57										15 43	15 52	15 57								16 48
Skipton	d																						
Keighley	d																						
Bradford Interchange	d																						
Bradford Forster Sqare	d																						
Shipley	d																						
Halifax	d																						
Brighouse	d																						
Mirfield	d																						
Leeds	d						15 05	15 10		15 10						16 10		16 10					
Wakefield Westgate	d						15 16	15 23		15 23						16 22		16 22					
Wakefield Kirkgate	d																						
Pontefract Monkhill	d																						
Sheffield	a		15 21					15 51		15 51					16 21	16 51		16 51					17 19
Hull	d					14 30																	
Selby	d					15 05																	
Doncaster	d					15 26	15 35						15 43	15 54									
Retford	d					15 40								16 08									
Lincoln	d																						
Newark North Gate	a						15 59						16 07										
	d						15 59						16 08										
Grantham	a					16 01	16 11																
	d				15 20	16 02	16 11																
Peterborough	a				15 58		16 32						16 38	16 49									
Norwich	a				17 35																		
Peterborough	d						16 33						16 38	16 50									
Stevenage	a					16s46	17 05																
London Kings Cross	a					17 15	17 33				16 55		17 37	17 44						17 45	17 57		

A from 28 October

B from 23 September until 21 October

C The Northern Lights

D from 28 October. from Edinburgh

E The Highland Chieftain

Sundays
from 23 September

Scotland, North East England, Yorkshire and Humberside - London

Route Diagram - see first Page of Table 26

		XC ◇■ A ⌶	NT	NT		EM ◇ A	GR ■ 🍴⌶	GR ■ 🍴⌶	GC ■ A 🍴	GC ■ B 🍴	NT	EM ◇ A	GR ■ 🍴⌶	XC ◇■ C ⌶		XC A 🚌	XC ◇■ A ⌶	GR ■ 🍴⌶	TP ◇■	HT ◇■ ⊠	GR ■ 🍴⌶	EM ◇ A	GR ■ 🍴⌶	GR ■ 🍴⌶
Aberdeen	d													11 12				11 47						
Stonehaven	d													11 29				12 04						
Montrose	d													11 50				12 27						
Arbroath	d													12 06				12 43						
Dundee	d													12 25				13 01						
Leuchars ■	d													12 38				13 15						
Kirkcaldy	d													13 03				13 39						
Inverkeithing	d													13 18				13 58						
Inverness	d																							
Perth	d																							
Stirling	d																							
Glasgow Central ■	d																							
Motherwell	d																							
Haymarket	d													13 37				14 18						
Edinburgh ■	a													13 42				14 25						
Edinburgh	d							14 00						14 08		14 08		14 30						15 00
Dunbar	d																							
Berwick-upon-Tweed	d													14 49		15a28		15 11						
Alnmouth for Alnwick	d							14 58																
Morpeth	d																							
Newcastle ■	a							15 27						15 34				15 57						16 23
Sunderland	d		15 28																					
Hartlepool	d			16 01							16 51													
Newcastle ■	d	15 23	15a48	16a48				15 28			17a48			15 40			15 40	15 59	16 08		16 12			16 25
Chester-le-Street	d																							
Durham	d	15 36						15 41						15 52			15 52		16 20		16 24			16 38
Darlington ■	a	15 52						16 00						16 08			16 08	16 27	16 36		16 41			16 56
Middlesbrough	d																							
Eaglescliffe	d																							
Darlington ■	d	15 53						16 00						16 09			16 09	16 28	16 37		16 42			16 57
Northallerton	d																		16 49		16 54			
Thirsk	d																							
York ■	a	16 19						16 28						16 37			16 38	16 56	17 12		17 16			17 24
Leeds ■	a													17 06			17 06		17 38					
Harrogate	d																							
Scarborough	d																							
York ■	d	16 23						16 29										16 57			17 17			17 29
Doncaster ■	a	16 48						16 54																17 52
Skipton	d																							
Keighley	d																							
Bradford Interchange	d								15 37	15 42														
Bradford Forster Sqare	d																							
Shipley	d																							
Halifax	d									15 54														
Brighouse	d									16 05														
Mirfield	d									16 14														
Leeds ■	d						16 15						16 45	17 10			17 10						17 15	
Wakefield Westgate ■	d						16 27						16 56	17 22			17 22						17 27	
Wakefield Kirkgate ■	d								16 30	16 30														
Pontefract Monkhill	d																							
Sheffield ■	a	17 19												17 51			17 51							
Hull	d																			16 30				
Selby	d																			17 05				
Doncaster ■	d						16 46	16 54	17 12	17 12			17 17							17 26			17 46	17 54
Retford ■	d																			17 40			18 00	
Lincoln	d																							
Newark North Gate ■	a							17 18					17 44								17 59			
	d							17 18					17 44								17 59			
Grantham ■	a						17 17													18 01			18 23	18 27
	d					16 22	17 17					17 22								18 02		18 17	18 23	18 27
Peterborough ■	a					16 55		17 47				17 50	18 14								18 28	18 46		18 50
Norwich	a					18 30						19 29										20 29		
Peterborough ■	d							17 50					18 14								18 29			18 50
Stevenage ■	a						18 04													18s49			19 07	
London Kings Cross ■ ⊖	a						18 34	18 46	18 50	18 51			19 11					18 56		19 18	19 22		19 36	19 45

A from 23 September until 21 October
B from 28 October
C from 28 October. ⌶ from Edinburgh

Sundays
from 23 September

Scotland, North East England, Yorkshire and Humberside - London

Route Diagram - see first Page of Table 26

		XC ◇■ ⌶	GR ■ 🍴⌶	EM ◇■ ⌶	XC ◇■ A ⌶	XC B 🚌	XC ◇■ B ⌶	TP ◇■	GR ■ 🍴⌶	TP ◇■		GR ■ 🍴⌶	GR ■ 🍴⌶	XC B 🚌	XC ◇■ ⌶	EM ◇ B	GR ■ 🍴⌶	XC ◇■ A ⌶	XC B 🚌	XC ◇■ B ⌶		SR ■ 🛏	TP ◇■	GR ■ 🍴⌶	TP ◇■
Aberdeen	d																							13 50	
Stonehaven	d																							14 07	
Montrose	d																							14 30	
Arbroath	d																							14 46	
Dundee	d																							15 04	
Leuchars ■	d																							15 18	
Kirkcaldy	d																							15 42	
Inverkeithing	d																							15 58	
Inverness	d																					20 25			
Perth	d																					23u00			
Stirling	d																					23u45			
Glasgow Central ■	d				13 49													14 55							
Motherwell	d				14 04													15 11							
Haymarket	d				14 42													15 51						16 18	
Edinburgh ■	a				14 47													15 56				00 47		16 25	
Edinburgh	d				15 07	15 07			15 30				16 00					16 05	16 05					16 30	
Dunbar	d				15 27	16a02																			
Berwick-upon-Tweed	d								16 11															17 11	
Alnmouth for Alnwick	d												16 58	16 20				17 07	18 10						
Morpeth	d													17 00				17 22	18a50						
Newcastle ■	a				16 34				16 56				17 27	17 30				17 37						17 57	
Sunderland	d																								
Hartlepool	d																								
Newcastle ■	d	16 35			16 40		16 40		16 58	17 05			17 28		17 35			17 40		17 40			17 52	17 59	
Chester-le-Street	d									17 14															
Durham	d	16 47			16 52		16 52			17 21			17 41		17 47			17 52		17 52			18 04		
Darlington ■	a	17 03			17 08		17 08		17 25	17 37			18 00		18 04			18 08		18 08			18 20	18 26	
Middlesbrough	d							16 42																	
Eaglescliffe	d																								
Darlington ■	d	17 04			17 09		17 09		17 26	17 38			18 00		18 05			18 09		18 09			18 21	18 27	
Northallerton	d							17 10		17 49													18 33		
Thirsk	d							17 18																	←
York ■	a	17 30			17 37		17 37	17 42	17 53	18 12			18 28		18 31			18 36		18 36			19 03	18 56	19 03
Leeds ■	a				18 04		18 04	18 08		18 38								19 03		19 03			→		19 38
Harrogate	d		17 05																						
Scarborough	d																								
York ■	d	17 34		17 42					17 55				18 29		18 34									18 57	
Doncaster ■	a	17 57		18 04									18 53		18 57										
Skipton	d																								
Keighley	d																								
Bradford Interchange	d																								
Bradford Forster Sqare	d																								
Shipley	d																								
Halifax	d																								
Brighouse	d																								
Mirfield	d																								
Leeds ■	d		17 45		18 10		18 10					18 15					18 45	19 10		19 10					
Wakefield Westgate ■	d		17 57		18 22		18 22					18 27					18 56	19 22		19 22					
Wakefield Kirkgate ■	d																								
Pontefract Monkhill	d																								
Sheffield ■	a	18 23		18 39	18 51		18 51								19 21			19 50		19 50					
Hull	d																								
Selby	d																								
Doncaster ■	d		18 17									18 46	18 53				19 17								
Retford ■	d																								
Lincoln	d																								
Newark North Gate ■	a		18 42										19 17				19 44								
	d		18 43										19 17				19 44								
Grantham ■	a											19 17													
	d											19 17				19 27									
Peterborough ■	a		19 13										19 47			19 56	20 14								
Norwich	a															21 35									
Peterborough ■	d		19 13										19 50				20 15								
Stevenage ■	a											20 07													
London Kings Cross ■ ⊖	a		20 11						19 53			20 34	20 45				21 11							20 56	

A from 28 October. ⌶ from Edinburgh
B from 23 September until 21 October

Scotland, North East England, Yorkshire and Humberside - London

Route Diagram - see first Page of Table 26

		XC	HT	GR	GR	GR	XC	XC	TP	GC	GR	NT	TP	XC	GR	NT	NT	EM	GR	XC	GR	TP	TP
							A	B										A		C			
Aberdeen	d																						
Stonehaven	d																						
Montrose	d																						
Arbroath	d																						
Dundee	d																						
Leuchars	d																						
Kirkcaldy	d																						
Inverkeithing	d																						
Inverness	d																						
Perth	d																						
Stirling	d																						
Glasgow Central	d																			16 55			
Motherwell	d																			17 11			
Haymarket	d																			17 51			
Edinburgh	a																			17 56			
Edinburgh	d				17 00		17 07	17 07			17 30				18 00					18 07	18 30		
Dunbar	d						17 27	17 27			17 50									18 26			
Berwick-upon-Tweed	d						17 52	17 52			18 15									18 52	19 11		
Alnmouth for Alnwick	d														18 58								
Morpeth	d																						
Newcastle	a				18 23		18 36	18 36			19 00				19 27					19 36	19 56		
Sunderland	d									18 12		18 43				19 28	20 29						
Hartlepool	d									18 36													
Newcastle	d	18 20			18 25		18 39	18 39			19 02	19a05	19 10	19 25	19 28	19a52	20a47			19 40	19 58		20 08
Chester-le-Street	d																						
Durham	d	18 32			18 38		18 51	18 51					19 22	19 37	19 41					19 52			20 20
Darlington	a	18 49			18 55		19 07	19 07			19 29		19 38	19 53	20 00					20 08	20 24		20 36
Middlesbrough	d								18 45														
Eaglescliffe	d									18 59												20 06	
Darlington	d	18 51			18 56		19 08	19 08			19 30		19 39	19 54	20 00					20 09	20 25		20 37
Northallerton	d				19 07				19 13	19 21												20 38	20 49
Thirsk	d								19 21	19 30												20 46	
York	a	19 17			19 28		19 35	19 35	19 42	19 47	19 57		20 11	20 21	20 28					20 36	20 53	21 06	21 12
Leeds	a						20 05	20 05	20 08				20 38							21 02			21 38
Harrogate	d																						
Scarborough	d																						
York	d	19 24			19 30					19 51	19 59			20 24	20 29						20 55		
Doncaster	a	19 47			19 53									20 47	20 53						21 18		
Skipton	d																						
Keighley	d																						
Bradford Interchange	d																						
Bradford Forster Sqare	d																						
Shipley	d																						
Halifax	d																						
Brighouse	d																						
Mirfield	d																						
Leeds	d			19 15		19 45	20 10	20 10											20 45	21 10			
Wakefield Westgate	d			19 26		19 56	20 22	20 22											20 56	21 22			
Wakefield Kirkgate	d																						
Pontefract Monkhill	d																						
Sheffield	a	20 16					20 51	20 51						21 17						21 50			
Hull	d		18 30																				
Selby	d		19 05																				
Doncaster	d		19 26	19 45	19 54	20 19									20 53				21 15		21 19		
Retford	d		19 40	19 59															21 29				
Lincoln	d																						
Newark North Gate	a				20 17	20 43									21 17						21 47		
	d				20 17	20 43									21 17						21 47		
Grantham	a		20 01	20 22							20 47								21 52		22 00		
	d		20 02	20 22							20 48							21 19	21 52		22 00		
Peterborough	a				20 48	21 13					21 08				21 46			21 52	22 13		22 21		
Norwich	a																	23 28					
Peterborough	d				20 50	21 13					21 08				21 48				22 13		22 21		
Stevenage	a		20s50	21 08															22 45		22 50		
London Kings Cross	a		21 18	21 34	21 44	22 09				21 45	22 03				22 46				23 15		23 21		

A from 23 September until 21 October
B from 28 October. ✕ to Leeds
C ✕ to Leeds

Table 26

Sundays
from 23 September

Scotland, North East England, Yorkshire and Humberside - London

Route Diagram - see first Page of Table 26

		GR	NT	GR	XC	GR	SR	TP
							B	
Aberdeen	d						21 42	
Stonehaven	d						22u00	
Montrose	d						22u25	
Arbroath	d						22u43	
Dundee	d						23u06	
Leuchars	d						23u25	
Kirkcaldy	d						23u53	
Inverkeithing	d						00u12	
Inverness	d							
Perth	d							
Stirling	d							
Glasgow Central	d				18 57			
Motherwell	d				19 11			
Haymarket	d				19 51			
Edinburgh	a				19 56		00 36	
Edinburgh	d	19 00		20 00	20 05	21 00		
Dunbar	d	19 20		20 21	20 29	21 21		
Berwick-upon-Tweed	d	19 45		20 46	20 55	21 46		
Alnmouth for Alnwick	d			21 09		22 08		
Morpeth	d			21 26				
Newcastle	a	20 30		21 42	21 48	22 42		
Sunderland	d							
Hartlepool	d							
Newcastle	d	20 32	21 06	21 44				
Chester-le-Street	d		21 15					
Durham	d	20 45	21 24	21 58				
Darlington	a	21 03	21 44	22 16				
Middlesbrough	d							22 06
Eaglescliffe	d		22a00					
Darlington	d	21 04		22 17				
Northallerton	d			22 30				22 34
Thirsk	d							22 42
York	a	21 31		23 02				23 09
Leeds	a			23 34				23 38
Harrogate	d							
Scarborough	d							
York	d	21 33						
Doncaster	a	21 55						
Skipton	d							
Keighley	d							
Bradford Interchange	d							
Bradford Forster Sqare	d							
Shipley	d							
Halifax	d							
Brighouse	d							
Mirfield	d							
Leeds	d							
Wakefield Westgate	d							
Wakefield Kirkgate	d							
Pontefract Monkhill	d							
Sheffield	a							
Hull	d							
Selby	d							
Doncaster	d	21 56						
Retford	d							
Lincoln	d							
Newark North Gate	a	22 19						
	d	22 19						
Grantham	a	22 32						
	d	22 32						
Peterborough	a	22 53						
Norwich	a							
Peterborough	d	22 53						
Stevenage	a	23s24						
London Kings Cross	a	00 01						

Table 26A

Mondays to Saturdays

Peterborough - Wisbech, Kings Lynn, Swaffham and Dereham
Bus Service

		GR SX	GR SX	GR SO	GR	GR	GR	GR	GR	GR	GR	GR	GR	GR	GR	GR	GR	GR	GR	GR	GR	GR	GR
Peterborough	d	07 00	07 30	07 35	08 05	08 35	09 05	09 35	10 05	10 35	11 05	11 35	12 05	12 35	13 05	13 35	14 05	14 35	15 05	15 35	16 05	16 35	17 10
Wisbech Bus Station	d	07 51	08 21	08 26	08 56	09 26	09 56	10 26	10 56	11 26	11 56	12 26	12 56	13 26	13 56	14 26	14 56	15 26	15 56	16 26	16 56	17 26	18 00
Kings Lynn Bus Station	d	08 32	09 02	09 02	09 32	10 02	10 32	11 02	11 32	12 02	12 32	13 02	13 32	14 02	14 32	15 02	15 32	16 02	16 32	17 02	17 32	18 02	18 35
Swaffham Market Place	d	09 04	09 34	09 34	10 04	10 34	11 04	11 34	12 04	12 34	13 04	13 34	14 04	14 34	15 04	15 34	16 04	16 34	17 04	17 34	18 04	18 34	19 06
Dereham Market Place	a	09 37	10 07	10 07	10 37	11 07	11 37	12 07	12 37	13 07	13 37	14 07	14 37	15 07	15 37	16 07	16 37	17 07	17 37	18 07	18 37	19 07	19 37

		GR	GR	GR	GR	GR	GR	GR
Peterborough	d	17 40	18 10	18 40	19 10	20 10	21 10	22 10
Wisbech Bus Station	d	18 30	19 00	19 30	20 00	21 00	22 00	23 00
Kings Lynn Bus Station	d	18a58	19 35	19a58	20 35	21 35	22a28	23a28
Swaffham Market Place	d		20 06		21 06	22 06		
Dereham Market Place	a		20 37		21 37	22 37		

Sundays

		GR	GR	GR	GR	GR	GR	GR	GR	GR	GR	GR	GR	GR	GR	GR
Peterborough	d	08 10	09 10	10 10	11 10	12 10	13 10	14 10	15 10	16 10	17 10	18 10	19 10	20 10	21 10	22 10
Wisbech Bus Station	d	09 00	10 00	11 00	12 00	13 00	14 00	15 00	16 00	17 00	18 00	19 00	20 00	21 00	22 00	23 00
Kings Lynn Bus Station	d	09 35	10 35	11 35	12 35	13 35	14 35	15 35	16 35	17 35	18 35	19 35	20 35	21 35	22a28	23a28
Swaffham Market Place	d	10 06	11 06	12 06	13 06	14 06	15 06	16 06	17 06	18 06	19 06	20 06	21 06	22 06		
Dereham Market Place	a	10 37	11 37	12 37	13 37	14 37	15 37	16 37	17 37	18 37	19 37	20 37	21 37	22 37		

Table 26A

Mondays to Saturdays

Dereham, Swaffham, Kings Lynn and Wisbech - Peterborough
Bus Service

		GR SX	GR SX	GR	GR	GR	GR SX	GR SO	GR SX	GR SO	GR SX	GR SO	GR SX	GR SO	GR	GR	GR	GR	GR	GR	GR	GR	GR
Dereham Market Place	d						07 05	07 09	07 30	07 39	08 00	08 09	08 35	08 36	09 05	09 35	10 05	10 35	11 05	11 35	12 05	12 35	13 05
Swaffham Market Place	d						07 35	07 39	08 02	08 09	08 32	08 39	09 07	09 07	09 37	10 07	10 37	11 07	11 35	12 07	12 37	13 07	13 37
Kings Lynn Bus Station	d	05 40	06 10	06 45	07 15	07 45	08 15	08 15	08 45	08 45	09 15	09 15	09 45	09 45	10 15	10 45	11 15	11 45	12 15	12 45	13 15	13 45	14 15
Wisbech Bus Station	d	06 13	06 43	07 18	07 48	08 18	08 48	08 48	09 18	09 18	09 48	09 48	10 18	10 18	10 48	11 18	11 48	12 18	12 48	13 18	13 48	14 18	14 48
Peterborough	a	06 54	07 24	07 59	08 29	08 59	09 29	09 29	09 59	09 59	10 29	10 29	10 59	10 59	11 29	11 59	12 29	12 59	13 29	13 59	14 29	14 59	15 29

		GR	GR	GR	GR	GR	GR	GR	GR SO	GR SX	GR SO	GR SX	GR	GR
Dereham Market Place	d	13 35	14 05	14 35	15 05	15 35	16 05	16 35	17 40	17 44	18 40	18 44	19 44	20 44
Swaffham Market Place	d	14 07	14 37	15 07	15 37	16 07	16 37	17 07	18 12	18 14	19 12	19 14	20 14	21 14
Kings Lynn Bus Station	d	14 45	15 15	15 45	16 15	16 45	17 15	17 45	18 50	18 50	19 50	19 50	20 50	21 50
Wisbech Bus Station	d	15 18	15 48	16 18	16 48	17 18	17 48	18 18	19 22	19 22	20 22	20 22	21 22	22 22
Peterborough	a	15 59	16 29	16 59	17 29	17 59	18 29	18 59	20 01	20 01	21 01	21 01	22 01	23 01

Sundays

		GR	GR	GR	GR	GR	GR	GR	GR	GR	GR	GR	GR	GR	GR	GR	GR
Dereham Market Place	d				08 44	09 44	10 44	11 44	12 44	13 44	14 44	15 44	16 44	17 44	18 44	19 44	20 44
Swaffham Market Place	d				09 14	10 14	11 14	12 14	13 14	14 14	15 14	16 14	17 14	18 14	19 14	20 14	21 14
Kings Lynn Bus Station	d	06 50	07 50	08 50	09 50	10 50	11 50	12 50	13 50	14 50	15 50	16 50	17 50	18 50	19 50	20 50	21 50
Wisbech Bus Station	d	07 22	08 22	09 22	10 22	11 22	12 22	13 22	14 22	15 22	16 22	17 22	18 22	19 22	20 22	21 22	22 22
Peterborough	a	08 01	09 01	10 01	11 01	12 01	13 01	14 01	15 01	16 01	17 01	18 01	19 01	20 01	21 01	22 01	23 01

Sunday service operates on Bank Holiday Monday

Table 26B

Mondays to Saturdays

Peterborough - Oundle, Corby and Kettering
Bus Service

		GR	GR	GR	GR	GR	GR	GR	GR	GR	GR	GR	GR	GR	GR
Peterborough Queensgate	d	07 05	07 40	09 10	10 10	11 10	12 10	13 10	14 10	15 10	16 10	17 10	18 30	19 30	20 30
Oundle Market Place	a	07 27	08 22	09 32	10 32	11 32	12 32	13 32	14 32	15 32	16 32	17 32	18 57	19 57	20 57
Corby George Street	a	08 05	09 05	10 05	11 05	12 05	13 05	14 05	15 05	16 05	17 05	18 05	19 25	20 25	21 25
Kettering Library	a	08 35	09 35	10 35	11 35	12 35	13 35	14 35	15 35	16 35	17 35	18 35	19 55	20 55	21 55

Sundays

		GR	GR	GR	GR	GR	GR
Peterborough Queensgate	d	10 10	12 10	14 10	16 10	18 10	20 10
Oundle Market Place	a	10 37	12 37	14 37	16 37	18 37	20 37
Corby George Street	a	11 05	13 05	15 05	17 05	19 05	21 05
Kettering Library	a	11 35	13 35	15 35	17 35	19 35	21 33

Table 26B

Mondays to Saturdays

Kettering and Corby, Oundle - Peterborough
Bus Service

		GR	GR	GR	GR	GR	GR	GR	GR	GR	GR	GR	GR	GR	GR	GR
Kettering Library	d	05 30	06 00	07 05		08 45	09 45	10 45	11 45	12 45	13 45	14 45	15 45	16 50	17 55	18 55
Corby George Street	d	05 55	06 25	07 30		09 10	10 10	11 10	12 10	13 10	14 10	15 10	16 10	17 15	18 20	19 20
Oundle Market Place	d	06 23	06 53	07 58	08 38	09 38	10 38	11 38	12 38	13 38	14 38	15 38	16 38	17 43	18 48	19 48
Peterborough Queensgate	a	06 40	07 25	08 30	09 00	10 00	11 00	12 00	13 00	14 00	15 00	16 00	17 00	18 05	19 10	20 20

Sundays

		GR	GR	GR	GR	GR	GR
Kettering Library	d	08 15	10 15	12 15	14 15	16 15	18 15
Corby George Street	d	08 40	10 40	12 40	14 40	16 40	18 40
Oundle Market Place	d	09 08	11 08	13 08	15 08	17 08	19 08
Peterborough Queensgate	a	09 40	11 40	13 40	15 40	17 40	19 40

Doncaster - Robin Hood Airport

Bus Service

		GR	GR	GR	GR	GR	GR	GR	GR	GR	GR	GR	GR	GR	GR	GR	GR	GR	GR
Doncaster Interchange	d	05 35	06 35	07 35	08 35	09 35	10 35	11 35	12 35	13 35	14 35	15 35	16 35	17 35	18 35	19 35	20 35	21 35	22 35
Robin Hood Airport	a	05 59	06 59	07 59	08 59	09 59	10 59	11 59	12 59	13 59	14 59	15 59	16 59	17 59	18 59	19 59	20 59	21 59	22 59

Sundays

		GR	GR	GR	GR	GR	GR	GR	GR	GR
Doncaster Interchange	d	08 35	09 35	10 35	11 35	12 35	13 35	15 35	16 35	17 35
Robin Hood Airport	a	08 59	09 59	10 59	11 59	12 59	13 59	15 59	16 59	17 59

Table 26F

Mondays to Saturdays

Robin Hood Airport - Doncaster

Bus Service

		GR	GR	GR	GR	GR	GR	GR	GR	GR	GR	GR	GR	GR	GR	GR	GR	GR	GR
Robin Hood Airport	d	06 05	07 05	08 05	09 05	10 05	11 05	12 05	13 05	14 05	15 05	16 05	17 05	18 05	19 05	20 05	21 05	22 05	23 05
Doncaster Interchange	a	06 30	07 30	08 30	09 30	10 30	11 30	12 30	13 30	14 30	15 30	16 30	17 30	18 30	19 30	20 30	21 30	22 30	23 30

Sundays

		GR	GR	GR	GR	GR	GR	GR	GR	GR	GR
Robin Hood Airport	d	09 05	10 05	11 05	12 05	13 05	14 05	15 05	16 05	17 05	18 05
Doncaster Interchange	a	09 30	10 30	11 30	12 30	13 30	14 30	15 30	16 30	17 30	18 30

York - Pickering and Whitby

Bus Service

		GR	GR	GR	GR	GR	GR	GR	GR	GR	GR
York	d	08 38	09 42	10 42	11 42	12 42	13 42	14 42	15 44	16 19	18 09
Eden Camp	a	09 42	10 42	11 42	12 42	13 42	14 42	15 42	16 52	17 27	19 07
Flamingo Land	a										
Pickering Eastgate	a	09 58	10 58	11 58	12 58	13 58	14 58	15 58	17 08	17 43	19 23
Whitby Bus Station	a	11 02		13 02				17 02			

Saturdays

		GR	GR	GR	GR	GR	GR	GR	GR
York	d	08 42	10 42	11 42	13 42	14 42	15 42	16 42	17 42
Eden Camp	a	09 42	11 42	12 42	14 42	15 42	16 42	17 42	18 42
Flamingo Land	a								
Pickering Eastgate	a	09 58	11 58	12 58	14 58	15 58	16 58	17 58	18 58
Whitby Bus Station	a	11 02	13 02			17 02			

Sundays

		GR	GR
York	d	12 52	14 52
Eden Camp	a	13 58	15 52
Flamingo Land	a		
Pickering Eastgate	a	14 14	16 08
Whitby Bus Station	a		

Table 26G

Mondays to Fridays

Whitby and Pickering - York

Bus Service

		GR	GR	GR	GR	GR	GR	GR	GR	GR	GR	GR
Whitby Bus Station	d					11 14		13 14			17 50	
Pickering Eastgate	d	06 47	08 47	09 17	11 17	12 17	13 17	14 17	15 37	17 25	18 53	19 35
Flamingo Land	d											
Eden Camp	d	07 03	09 03	09 33	11 33	12 33	13 27	14 33	16 09	17 41	19 09	19 45
York	a	08 10	10 05	10 35	12 35	13 35	14 35	15 35	17 37	19 08	20 08	20 50

Saturdays

		GR	GR	GR	GR	GR	GR	GR	GR
Whitby Bus Station	d				11 14		13 14	17 50	
Pickering Eastgate	d	07 07	09 17	11 17	12 17	13 17	14 17	18 53	19 13
Flamingo Land	d								
Eden Camp	d	07 23	09 33	11 33	12 33	13 27	14 33	19 09	19 29
York	a	08 25	10 35	12 35	13 35	14 35	15 35	20 08	20 50

Sundays

		GR	GR	GR
Whitby Bus Station	d			
Pickering Eastgate	d	08 52	14 27	16 27
Flamingo Land	d			
Eden Camp	d	09 08	14 43	16 43
York	a	10 25	15 45	18 05

Table 26H

Mondays to Saturdays

Darlington - Richmond and Catterick

Bus Service

		GR SX	GR SX	GR	GR	GR	GR	GR	GR	GR	GR	GR	GR	GR	GR	GR	GR	GR	GR	GR	GR	GR	GR
Darlington	d	06 23	06 53	07 33	08 03	08 33	09 03	09 33	10 03	10 33	11 03	11 33	12 03	12 33	13 03	13 33	14 03	14 33	15 03	15 33	16 03	16 33	17 03
Richmond (Market)	a	06 54	07 24	08 04	08 34	09 04	09 34	10 04	10 34	11 04	11 34	12 04	12 34	13 04	13 34	14 04	14 34	15 04	15 34	16 04	16 34	17 04	17 34
Catterick Garrison Tesco	a	07 05	07 35	08 15	08 45	09 15	09 45	10 15	10 45	11 15	11 45	12 15	12 45	13 15	13 45	14 15	14 45	15 15	15 45	16 15	16 45	17 15	17 45
Catterick Camp Centre	a	07 07	07 37	08 17	08 47	09 17	09 47	10 17	10 47	11 17	11 47	12 17	12 47	13 17	13 47	14 17	14 47	15 17	15 47	16 17	16 47	17 17	17 47
Catterick Garrison Kemmel	a	07 15	07 45	08 25	08 55	09 25	09 55	10 25	10 55	11 25	11 55	12 25	12 55	13 25	13 55	14 25	14 55	15 25	15 55	16 25	16 55	17 25	17 55

		GR	GR	GR	GR	GR
Darlington	d	17 33	18 03	19 03	20 03	21 03
Richmond (Market)	a	18 04	18 36	19 36	20 36	21 36
Catterick Garrison Tesco	a	18 15	18 47	19 47	20 47	21 47
Catterick Camp Centre	a	18 17	18 49	19 49	20 49	21 49
Catterick Garrison Kemmel	a	18 25	18 57	19 57	20 57	21 57

Sundays

		GR	GR	GR	GR	GR	GR	GR	GR	GR	GR	GR	GR	GR	GR	GR	GR	GR
Darlington	d	09 03	10 03	11 03	12 03	13 03	14 03	15 03	16 03	17 03	18 03	18 33	19 03	19 33	20 03	21 03	22 03	23 03
Richmond (Market)	a	09 34	10 34	11 34	12 34	13 34	14 34	15 34	16 34	17 34	18 36	19 06	19 36	20 06	20 36	21 36	22 36	23 36
Catterick Garrison Tesco	a	09 45	10 45	11 45	12 45	13 45	14 45	15 45	16 45	17 45	18 47	19 17	19 47	20 17	20 47	21 47	22 47	23 47
Catterick Camp Centre	a	09 47	10 47	11 47	12 47	13 47	14 47	15 47	16 47	17 47	18 49	19 19	19 49	20 19	20 49	21 49	22 49	23 49
Catterick Garrison Kemmel	a	09 55	10 55	11 55	12 55	13 55	14 55	15 55	16 55	17 55	18 57	19 27	19 57	20 27	20 57	21 57	22 57	23 57

Table 26H

Mondays to Saturdays

Catterick and Richmond - Darlington

Bus Service

		GR SX	GR SX	GR SO	GR SX	GR SO	GR	GR	GR	GR	GR	GR	GR	GR	GR	GR	GR	GR	GR	GR	GR	GR	GR
Catterick Garrison Kemmel	d	06 22	07 22	07 27	07 52	07 57	08 32	09 02	09 32	10 02	10 32	11 02	11 32	12 02	12 32	13 02	13 32	14 02	14 32	15 02	15 32	16 02	16 32
Catterick Camp Centre	d	06 30	07 30	07 35	08 00	08 05	08 40	09 10	09 40	10 10	10 40	11 10	11 40	12 10	12 40	13 10	13 40	14 10	14 40	15 10	15 40	16 10	16 40
Catterick Garrison Tesco	d	06 32	07 32	07 37	08 02	08 07	08 42	09 12	09 42	10 12	10 42	11 12	11 42	12 12	12 42	13 12	13 42	14 12	14 42	15 12	15 42	16 12	16 42
Richmond (Market)	d	06 44	07 44	07 49	08 14	08 19	08 54	09 24	09 54	10 24	10 54	11 24	11 54	12 24	12 54	13 24	13 54	14 24	14 54	15 24	15 54	16 24	16 54
Darlington	a	07 15	08 20	08 20	08 45	08 50	09 25	09 55	10 25	10 55	11 25	11 55	12 25	12 55	13 25	13 55	14 25	14 55	15 25	15 55	16 25	16 55	17 25

		GR	GR	GR	GR	GR	GR	GR	GR
Catterick Garrison Kemmel	d	17 02	17 32	18 02	18 32	19 02	20 02	21 02	22 02
Catterick Camp Centre	d	17 10	17 40	18 10	18 40	19 10	20 10	21 10	22 10
Catterick Garrison Tesco	d	17 12	17 42	18 12	18 42	19 12	20 12	21 12	22 12
Richmond (Market)	d	17 24	17 54	18 24	18 54	19 24	20 24	21 24	22 24
Darlington	a	17 55	18 25	18 55	19 25	19 57	20 57	21 57	22 57

Sundays

		GR	GR	GR	GR	GR	GR	GR	GR	GR	GR	GR	GR	GR	GR
Catterick Garrison Kemmel	d	09 02	10 02	11 02	12 02	13 02	14 02	15 02	16 02	17 02	18 02	19 02	20 02	21 02	22 02
Catterick Camp Centre	d	09 10	10 10	11 10	12 10	13 10	14 10	15 10	16 10	17 10	18 10	19 10	20 10	21 10	22 10
Catterick Garrison Tesco	d	09 12	10 12	11 12	12 12	13 12	14 12	15 12	16 12	17 12	18 12	19 12	20 12	21 12	22 12
Richmond (Market)	d	09 24	10 24	11 24	12 24	13 24	14 24	15 24	16 24	17 24	18 24	19 24	20 24	21 24	22 24
Darlington	a	09 55	10 55	11 55	12 55	13 55	14 55	15 55	16 55	17 55	18 55	19 57	20 57	21 57	22 57

Table 26K

Mondays to Fridays

Berwick-upon-Tweed - Scottish Border Towns

Bus Service

This service is operated by First Lowland under contract to Scottish Borders Council. Telephone 01835 824000

		XC	XC	XC	XC	XC	XC	XC	XC	XC
Berwick-upon-Tweed	d	06 57	08 12	09 52	10 52	12 52	15 07	17 47	18 47	20 22
Duns	a	07 30	08 45	10 25	11 25	13 25	15 40	18 20	19 20	20 55
Earlston	a	08 08	09 33	11 03	12 03	14 03	16 28	18 58	19 58	21 33
Melrose	a	08 22	09 47	11 15	12 15	14 15	16 40	19 10	20 10	21 45
Galashiels Bus Station	a	08 40	10 02	11 30	12 30	14 30	16 55	19 25	20 25	22 00

Saturdays

		XC	XC	XC	XC	XC	XC
Berwick-upon-Tweed	d	08 22	10 52	12 52	15 17	17 17	19 17
Duns	a	08 55	11 25	13 25	15 50	17 50	19 50
Earlston	a	09 33	12 03	14 03	16 28	18 28	20 28
Melrose	a	09 47	12 15	14 15	16 40	18 40	20 40
Galashiels Bus Station	a	10 02	12 30	14 30	16 55	18 55	20 55

No Sunday service

Table 26K

Mondays to Fridays

Scottish Border Towns - Berwick-upon-Tweed

Bus Service

This service is operated by First Lowland under contract to Scottish Borders Council. Telephone 01835 824000

		XC	XC	XC	XC	XC	XC	XC	XC
Galashiels Bus Station	d	06 25	07 40	08 10	10 50	12 50	14 40	16 32	17 20
Melrose	d	06 40	07 55	08 28	11 05	13 05	14 55	16 50	17 35
Earlston	d	06 52	08 07	08 40	11 17	13 17	15 07	17 02	17 47
Duns	d	07 30	08 50	09 20	11 55	13 55	15 55	17 40	18 30
Berwick-upon-Tweed	a	08 01	09 26	09 56	12 26	14 26	16 26	18 11	19 01

Saturdays

		XC	XC	XC	XC	XC	XC
Galashiels Bus Station	d	06 35	08 20	10 50	12 50	14 50	17 20
Melrose	d	06 50	08 35	11 05	13 05	15 05	17 35
Earlston	d	07 02	08 47	11 17	13 17	15 17	17 52
Duns	d	07 40	09 25	11 55	13 55	15 55	18 30
Berwick-upon-Tweed	a	08 11	09 56	12 26	14 26	16 26	19 01

No Sunday service

Cleethorpes - Lincoln - Newark - Nottingham

Network Diagram - see first Page of Table 18

Mondays to Fridays

until 28 September

Miles	Miles			EM	EM	EM ◇1 A	GR 1 B	EM C	EM	EM D	EM	EM D	EM	EM D	EM	EM D	EM	EM D	EM D	EM D	EM	EM D	EM
0	—	**Cleethorpes**	d		05 49																		
3¼	—	**Grimsby Town**	d		05 56				07 03				09 20				11 28				13 49		
11¼	—	Habrough	d		06 06				07 13				09 30				11 38				13 59		
17¾	—	Barnetby	d		06 15				07 22				09 39				11 47				14 08		
32¼	—	Market Rasen	d		06 32				07 39				09 55				12 03				14 24		
47	—	**Lincoln**	a		06 51				07 57				10 14				12 22				14 44		
—	—		d	05 26	06 53	07 04	07 20	07 26	07 59	08 35	09 11	09 32	10 15	10 36	11 35	11 42	12 23	12 30	13 40	14 33	14 46	15 30	15 45
51	—	Hykeham	d	05 34	07 01			07 34		08 43				10 44				12 38				15 37	
55¾	—	Swinderby	d	05 40	07 07			07 40		08 49				10 50				12 44				15 43	
58½	0	Collingham	d	05 45	07 12	07 19		07 45	08 15	08 54	09 26		10 32	10 55			12 40	12 48			15 02	15 48	
—	5	**Newark North Gate** 7	a	05 56	07 22		07 49		08 25		09 35		10 44		12 01		12 52				15 11		16 11
—	—		d	05 59																			
63½	—	**Newark Castle**	d	06 10		07 29		07 56		09 04		09 56		11 05		12 05		12 57	14 05	14 59		15 58	
67	—	Rolleston	d	06 16				08 02				10 02						13 04				16 04	
68	—	Fiskerton	d	06 18				08 04				10 04						13 06				16 06	
69¾	—	Bleasby	d	06 22				08 08				10 08						13 09				16 10	
70¾	—	Thurgarton	d	06 25				08 10				10 11						13 12				16 12	
71½	—	Lowdham	d	06 29		07 42		08 14		09 18		10 15		11 18		12 18		13 17	14 17	15 12		16 16	
75¾	—	Burton Joyce	d	06 34				08 18				10 19								15 16			
77¾	—	Carlton	d	06 38				08 22				10 23						13 23		15 20		16 23	
80¾	—	**Nottingham** 8	a	06 47		07 57		08 30		09 30		10 30		11 30		12 30		13 30	14 30	15 29		16 30	

		EM D	EM	EM D	EM	EM D	EM	EM	EM	EM	EM
Cleethorpes	d									21 15	
Grimsby Town	d		15 45				18 29			21 22	
Habrough	d		15 55				18 39			21 33	
Barnetby	d		16 04				18 48			21 42	
Market Rasen	d		16 19				19 03			21 57	
Lincoln	a		16 38				19 22			22 15	
	d	16 34	16 44	17 28	18 18	18 35	19 25	20 45	21 42		22 27
Hykeham	d	16 42		17 36			19 33				22 35
Swinderby	d	16 48		17 42			19 39				22 41
Collingham	d	16 53	16 59	17 47	18 34		19 44	21 00			22 46
Newark North Gate 7	a		17 12		18 44		19 54				
	d										
Newark Castle	d	17 04		17 58		19 03		21 13	22 09		22 57
Rolleston	d			18 04							
Fiskerton	d			18 06							23 04
Bleasby	d			18 10							23 07
Thurgarton	d			18 13							
Lowdham	d	17 16		18 17		19 16		21 26	22 22		23 12
Burton Joyce	d			18 21							23 16
Carlton	d	17 22		18 24							23 20
Nottingham 8	a	17 30		18 32		19 29		21 42	22 34		23 32

Mondays to Fridays

from 1 October

		EM	EM	EM ◇1 A	GR 1 B	EM C	EM	EM D	EM	EM D	EM	EM D	EM	EM D	EM	EM D	EM D	EM D	EM	EM D	EM	EM D	EM
Cleethorpes	d		05 49																				
Grimsby Town	d		05 56				07 03				09 20				11 28				13 49				15 45
Habrough	d		06 06				07 13				09 30				11 38				13 59				15 55
Barnetby	d		06 15				07 22				09 39				11 47				14 08				16 04
Market Rasen	d		06 32				07 39				09 55				12 03				14 24				16 19
Lincoln	a		06 51				07 57				10 14				12 22				14 44				16 38
	d	05 26	06 53	07 04	07 20	07 26	07 59	08 35	09 11	09 32	10 15	10 36	11 35	11 42	12 23	12 30	13 40	14 33	14 46	15 30	15 45	16 34	16 44
Hykeham	d	05 34	07 01			07 34		08 43				10 44				12 38				15 37		16 42	
Swinderby	d	05 40	07 07			07 40		08 49				10 50				12 44				15 43		16 48	
Collingham	d	05 45	07 12	07 19		07 45	08 15	08 54	09 26		10 32	10 55			12 40	12 48			15 02	15 48		16 53	16 59
Newark North Gate 7	a	05 56	07 22		07 49		08 25		09 35		10 44		12 01		12 52				15 11		16 11		17 12
	d	05 59																					
Newark Castle	d	06 10		07 29		07 56		09 04		09 56		11 05		12 05		12 57	14 05	14 59		15 58		17 04	
Rolleston	d	06 16				08 02				10 02						13 04				16 04			
Fiskerton	d	06 18				08 04				10 04						13 06				16 06			
Bleasby	d	06 22				08 08				10 08						13 09				16 10			
Thurgarton	d	06 25				08 10				10 11						13 12				16 12			
Lowdham	d	06 29		07 42		08 14		09 18		10 15		11 18		12 18		13 17	14 17	15 12		16 16		17 16	
Burton Joyce	d	06 34				08 18				10 19								15 16					
Carlton	d	06 38				08 22				10 23						13 23		15 20		16 23		17 22	
Nottingham 8	a	06 48		07 57		08 32		09 32		10 32		11 32		12 32		13 32	14 32	15 31		16 32		17 32	

A To St Pancras International
B To London Kings Cross
C From Sleaford to Leicester
D To Leicester

For connections to London Kings Cross please refer to Table 26

Cleethorpes - Lincoln - Newark - Nottingham

Network Diagram - see first Page of Table 18

Mondays to Fridays

from 1 October

		EM A	EM	EM A	EM	EM	EM	EM	EM
Cleethorpes	d							21 15	
Grimsby Town	d				18 29			21 22	
Habrough	d				18 39			21 33	
Barnetby	d				18 48			21 42	
Market Rasen	d				19 03			21 57	
Lincoln	a				19 22			22 15	
	d	17 26	18 18	18 35	19 25	20 45	21 42		22 27
Hykeham	d	17 34			19 33				22 35
Swinderby	d	17 40			19 39				22 41
Collingham	d	17 45	18 34		19 44	21 00			22 46
Newark North Gate 7	a		18 44		19 54				
	d								
Newark Castle	d	17 56		19 03		21 13	22 09		22 57
Rolleston	d	18 02							
Fiskerton	d	18 04							23 04
Bleasby	d	18 08							23 07
Thurgarton	d	18 11							
Lowdham	d	18 15		19 16		21 26	22 22		23 12
Burton Joyce	d	18 19							23 16
Carlton	d	18 23							23 20
Nottingham 8	a	18 33		19 31		21 42	22 34		23 32

Saturdays

until 29 September

		EM	EM ◇1 B	EM C	EM	EM A	EM	EM A	GR 1 D	EM	EM A	EM	EM A	EM	EM A	EM A	EM A	EM	EM A	EM A	EM	EM A	EM A
Cleethorpes	d																						
Grimsby Town	d				06 50					09 20				11 28				13 49			16 00		
Habrough	d				07 00					09 30				11 38				13 59			16 09		
Barnetby	d				07 09					09 39				11 47				14 08			16 18		
Market Rasen	d				07 26					09 55				12 03				14 24			16 33		
Lincoln	a				07 44					10 14				12 22				14 44			16 52		
	d	05 26	07 04	07 26	07 46	08 35	09 01	09 19	09 30	10 15	10 36	11 35	11 42	12 23	12 30	13 40	14 35	14 45	15 27	16 34	16 54	17 26	18 34
Hykeham	d	05 34		07 34		08 43					10 44				12 38				15 34	16 42		17 34	
Swinderby	d	05 40		07 40		08 49					10 50				12 44				15 40	16 48		17 40	
Collingham	d	05 45	07 19	07 45	08 02	08 54	09 16			10 32	10 55			12 40	12 48			15 01	15 45	16 53	17 09	17 45	
Newark North Gate 7	a	05 56			08 12		09 25		09 52	10 44		12 01		12 52				15 11			17 22		
	d	05 59																					
Newark Castle	d	06 10	07 29	07 55		09 04		09 48			11 04		12 05		12 57	14 05	15 01		15 58	17 03		17 57	19 02
Rolleston	d	06 16		08 02				09 55							13 04				16 04			18 03	
Fiskerton	d	06 18		08 04				09 57							13 06				16 06			18 05	
Bleasby	d	06 22		08 07				10 01							13 09				16 10			18 09	
Thurgarton	d	06 25		08 10				10 04							13 12				16 12			18 12	
Lowdham	d	06 29	07 42	08 14		09 18		10 08			11 17		12 18		13 17	14 17	15 14		16 16	17 16		18 16	19 16
Burton Joyce	d	06 34		08 18				10 13									15 19					18 20	
Carlton	d	06 38		08 22				10 17							13 23		15 23		16 23	17 22		18 23	
Nottingham 8	a	06 47	07 58	08 30		09 30		10 25			11 29		12 30		13 30	14 30	15 30		16 30	17 30		18 31	19 29

		EM	EM	EM	EM
Cleethorpes	d				
Grimsby Town	d	18 26		19 45	
Habrough	d	18 36		19 54	
Barnetby	d	18 47		20 03	
Market Rasen	d	19 02		20 18	
Lincoln	a	19 21		20 37	
	d	19 23	19 35		20 45
Hykeham	d	19 31			
Swinderby	d	19 37			
Collingham	d	19 42			21 00
Newark North Gate 7	a	19 52			
	d				
Newark Castle	d		20 03		21 10
Rolleston	d				
Fiskerton	d				
Bleasby	d				
Thurgarton	d				
Lowdham	d		20 16		21 23
Burton Joyce	d				
Carlton	d				
Nottingham 8	a		20 30		21 39

A To Leicester
B To St Pancras International
C From Sleaford to Leicester
D To London Kings Cross

For connections to London Kings Cross please refer to Table 26

Table 27

Saturdays from 6 October

Cleethorpes - Lincoln - Newark - Nottingham

Network Diagram - see first Page of Table 18

		EM	EM	EM	EM	EM	EM	EM	GR	EM	EM	EM	EM	EM	EM	EM	EM	EM	EM	EM	EM	EM	EM
			◇ A	B		C		C	D		C		C		C	C	C		C	C		C	C
Cleethorpes	d																						
Grimsby Town	d				06 50					09 20				11 28				13 49			16 00		
Habrough	d				07 00					09 30				11 38				13 59			16 09		
Barnetby	d				07 09					09 39				11 47				14 08			16 18		
Market Rasen	d				07 26					09 55				12 03				14 24			16 33		
Lincoln	a				07 44					10 14				12 22				14 44			16 52		
	d	05 26	07 04	07 26	07 46	08 35	09 01	09 19	09 30	10 15	10 36	11 35	11 42	12 23	12 30	13 40	14 35	14 45	15 27	16 34	16 54	17 26	18 34
Hykeham	d	05 34		07 34		08 43					10 44				12 38				15 34	16 42		17 34	
Swinderby	d	05 40		07 40		08 49					10 50				12 44				15 40	16 48		17 40	
Collingham	d	05 45	07 19	07 45	08 02	08 54	09 16			10 32	10 55			12 40	12 48			15 01	15 45	16 53	17 09	17 45	
Newark North Gate	a	05 56			08 12		09 25		09 52	10 44		12 01		12 52				15 11			17 22		
	d	05 59																					
Newark Castle	d	06 10	07 29	07 55		09 04		09 48			11 04		12 05		12 57	14 05	15 01		15 58	17 03		17 57	19 02
Rolleston	d	06 16		08 02				09 55							13 04				16 04			18 03	
Fiskerton	d	06 18		08 04				09 57							13 06				16 06			18 05	
Bleasby	d	06 22		08 07				10 01							13 09				16 10			18 09	
Thurgarton	d	06 25		08 10				10 04							13 12				16 12			18 12	
Lowdham	d	06 29	07 42	08 14		09 18		10 08			11 17		12 18		13 17	14 17	15 14		16 16	17 16		18 16	19 16
Burton Joyce	d	06 34		08 18				10 13									15 19					18 20	
Carlton	d	06 38		08 22				10 17							13 23		15 23		16 23	17 22		18 23	
Nottingham	a	06 48	07 58	08 32		09 32		10 27			11 31		12 30		13 32	14 32	15 32		16 32	17 30		18 33	19 31

		EM	EM	EM	EM
Cleethorpes	d				
Grimsby Town	d	18 26		19 45	
Habrough	d	18 36		19 54	
Barnetby	d	18 47		20 03	
Market Rasen	d	19 02		20 18	
Lincoln	a	19 21		20 37	
	d	19 23	19 35		20 45
Hykeham	d	19 31			
Swinderby	d	19 37			
Collingham	d	19 42			21 00
Newark North Gate	a	19 52			
	d				
Newark Castle	d		20 03		21 10
Rolleston	d				
Fiskerton	d				
Bleasby	d				
Thurgarton	d				
Lowdham	d		20 16		21 23
Burton Joyce	d				
Carlton	d				
Nottingham	a		20 30		21 39

Sundays until 9 September

		EM	EM	EM	EM	EM	EM	EM	EM	EM	EM	EM	EM	EM
Cleethorpes	d			13 56						18 18			20 15	
Grimsby Town	d			14 03						18 25			20 22	
Habrough	d			14 13						18 35			20 33	
Barnetby	d			14 22						18 44			20 42	
Market Rasen	d			14 37						18 59			20 57	
Lincoln	a			14 56						19 18			21 15	
	d	11 05	13 00	15 00	15 45	17 08	17 25	18 05	19 03	19 22	20 05	21 00	21 26	22 10
Hykeham	d			15 08		17 16		18 13	19 11		20 13	21 08	21 34	22 18
Swinderby	d			15 14		17 22		18 19	19 17		20 19	21 14	21 40	22 24
Collingham	d	11 20	13 15	15 18		17 26		18 23	19 22		20 23	21 18	21 45	22 28
Newark North Gate	a	11 30	13 25	15 28	16 09		17 49			19 46		21 27	21 55	
	d			15 32								21 31		
Newark Castle	d			15 42		17 36		18 34	19 33		20 35	21 40		22 39
Rolleston	d							18 40						22 45
Fiskerton	d							18 42						22 47
Bleasby	d							18 46						22 50
Thurgarton	d							18 49						22 53
Lowdham	d			15 55		17 49		18 53	19 45		20 47	21 53		22 58
Burton Joyce	d							18 57						23 02
Carlton	d							19 01						23 05
Nottingham	a			16 11		18 06		19 11	20 03		21 03	22 09		23 17

A To St Pancras International
B From Sleaford to Leicester
C To Leicester
D To London Kings Cross

For connections to London Kings Cross please refer to Table 26

Table 27

Sundays 16 September to 30 September

Cleethorpes - Lincoln - Newark - Nottingham

Network Diagram - see first Page of Table 18

		EM	EM	EM	EM	EM	EM	EM	EM	EM	EM
Cleethorpes	d										
Grimsby Town	d										
Habrough	d										
Barnetby	d										
Market Rasen	d										
Lincoln	a										
	d	11 05	13 00	15 00	17 25	18 05	19 03	20 05	21 00	21 26	22 10
Hykeham	d			15 08		18 13	19 11	20 13	21 08	21 34	22 18
Swinderby	d			15 14		18 19	19 17	20 19	21 14	21 40	22 24
Collingham	d	11 20	13 15	15 18		18 23	19 22	20 23	21 18	21 45	22 28
Newark North Gate	a	11 30	13 25	15 28	17 49				21 27	21 55	
	d			15 32					21 31		
Newark Castle	d			15 42		18 34	19 33	20 35	21 40		22 39
Rolleston	d					18 40					22 45
Fiskerton	d					18 42					22 47
Bleasby	d					18 46					22 50
Thurgarton	d					18 49					22 53
Lowdham	d			15 55		18 53	19 45	20 47	21 53		22 58
Burton Joyce	d					18 57					23 02
Carlton	d					19 01					23 05
Nottingham	a			16 11		19 11	20 05	21 03	22 09		23 17

Sundays from 7 October

		EM	EM	EM	EM	EM	EM	EM	EM	EM	EM
Cleethorpes	d										
Grimsby Town	d										
Habrough	d										
Barnetby	d										
Market Rasen	d										
Lincoln	a										
	d	11 05	13 00	15 00	17 25	18 05	19 03	20 05	21 00	21 26	22 10
Hykeham	d			15 08		18 13	19 11	20 13	21 08	21 34	22 18
Swinderby	d			15 14		18 19	19 17	20 19	21 14	21 40	22 24
Collingham	d	11 20	13 15	15 18		18 23	19 22	20 23	21 18	21 45	22 28
Newark North Gate	a	11 30	13 25	15 28	17 49				21 27	21 55	
	d			15 32					21 31		
Newark Castle	d			15 42		18 34	19 33	20 35	21 40		22 39
Rolleston	d					18 40					22 45
Fiskerton	d					18 42					22 47
Bleasby	d					18 46					22 50
Thurgarton	d					18 49					22 53
Lowdham	d			15 55		18 53	19 45	20 47	21 53		22 58
Burton Joyce	d					18 57					23 02
Carlton	d					19 01					23 05
Nottingham	a			16 11		19 11	20 05	21 03	22 09		23 17

For connections to London Kings Cross please refer to Table 26

Nottingham - Newark - Lincoln - Cleethorpes

Mondays to Fridays until 28 September

Network Diagram - see first Page of Table 18

Miles	Miles			EM	EM	EM A	EM	EM	EM B	EM C	EM	EM	EM C	EM C	EM	EM C	EM A	EM C	EM	EM C	EM A	EM C	EM D
0	—	**Nottingham**	d		05 55	06 53			08 05	09 21			10 29	11 17		12 27		13 17		14 29		15 27	16 14
3	—	Carlton	d		06 01	06 59			08 12	09 28				11 23				13 23				15 33	16 20
5	—	Burton Joyce	d		06 05	07 03			08 16					11 27				13 27					16 24
9¼	—	Lowdham	d		06 10	07 08			08 20	09 34			10 40	11 32		12 38		13 32		14 40		15 40	16 29
10	—	Thurgarton	d		06 14	07 12			08 24					11 36				13 36					16 33
11	—	Bleasby	d		06 17	07 15			08 27					11 39				13 39					16 36
12¾	—	Fiskerton	d		06 20	07 18			08 30					11 42				13 42					16 39
13¾	—	Rolleston	d		06 22	07 20			08 33					11 45				13 44					16 42
17¼	—	**Newark Castle**	d		06 30	07 28			08 40	09 51			10 59	11 52		12 54		13 53		14 53		15 54	16 54
—	0	**Newark North Gate**	a																				
—	—		d				07 40	08 31			09 57	10 50			12 06		13 02				15 28		
22¼	5	Collingham	d		06 40	07 36	07 49	08 40			10 05		11 09	12 01	12 15		13 11	14 01			15 37	16 03	17 03
25	—	Swinderby	d		06 44		07 54	08 45					11 13		12 19			14 05				16 07	
29¾	—	Hykeham	d		06 50		08 00	08 51					11 19		12 26			14 11				16 13	
33¾	—	**Lincoln**	a		07 04	07 56	08 10	09 02	09 07	10 17	10 23	11 14	11 31	12 21	12 36	13 20	13 30	14 23		15 22	15 55	16 25	17 18
—	—		d	05 57			08 14				10 25				12 37				14 37				
48½	—	Market Rasen	d	06 13			08 31				10 42				12 54				14 53				
63½	—	Barnetby	a	06 30			08 48				10 59				13 10				15 10				
69½	—	Habrough	a	06 41			09 01				11 08				13 19				15 19				
77½	—	**Grimsby Town**	a	06 56			09 15				11 23				13 35				15 34				
80¾	—	**Cleethorpes**	a																				

		EM	EM	EM C	EM	EM C	EM	EM C	EM	GR E	GR F	EM G	EM
Nottingham	d			17 17	17 50	18 15		19 20				20 29	22 25
Carlton	d			17 23		18 21		19 26					22 31
Burton Joyce	d			17 27		18 25		19 30					22 35
Lowdham	d			17 32	18 01	18 30		19 35				20 40	22 40
Thurgarton	d			17 36		18 34							
Bleasby	d			17 39		18 37		19 40					22 45
Fiskerton	d			17 42		18 40		19 43					22 48
Rolleston	d			17 45		18 43		19 46					
Newark Castle	d			17 53	18 18	18 53		19 55				20 54	22 57
Newark North Gate	a												23 06
	d	16 45	17 28				19 34		20 03	20 31	20 35		23 09
Collingham	d		17 36	18 02	18 27	19 02	19 43		20 12			21 03	23 18
Swinderby	d			18 07	18 31	19 06							23 23
Hykeham	d			18 13	18 37	19 12							23 29
Lincoln	a	17 13	18 00	18 26	18 50	19 23	20 01	20 17	20 27	21 01	21 03	21 22	23 41
	d	17 23					20 02						
Market Rasen	d	17 39					20 19						
Barnetby	a	17 54					20 35						
Habrough	a	18 03					20 44						
Grimsby Town	a	18 15					20 56						
Cleethorpes	a						21 03						

Mondays to Fridays from 1 October

		EM	EM	EM A	EM	EM	EM B	EM C	EM	EM	EM C	EM C	EM	EM C	EM A	EM C	EM	EM C	EM A	EM C	EM D	EM	EM
Nottingham	d		05 55	06 53			08 05	09 21			10 29	11 17		12 27		13 17		14 29		15 27	16 14		
Carlton	d		06 01	06 59			08 12	09 28				11 23				13 23				15 33	16 20		
Burton Joyce	d		06 05	07 03			08 16					11 27				13 27					16 24		
Lowdham	d		06 10	07 08			08 20	09 34			10 40	11 32		12 38		13 32		14 40		15 40	16 29		
Thurgarton	d		06 14	07 12			08 24					11 36				13 36					16 33		
Bleasby	d		06 17	07 15			08 27					11 39				13 39					16 36		
Fiskerton	d		06 20	07 18			08 30					11 42				13 42					16 39		
Rolleston	d		06 22	07 20			08 33					11 45				13 44					16 42		
Newark Castle	d		06 30	07 28			08 40	09 51			10 59	11 52		12 54		13 53		14 53		15 54	16 54		
Newark North Gate	a																						
	d				07 40	08 31			09 57	10 50			12 06		13 02				15 28			16 45	17 28
Collingham	d		06 41	07 36	07 49	08 40			10 05		11 09	12 01	12 15		13 11	14 01			15 37	16 03	17 03		17 36
Swinderby	d		06 45		07 54	08 45					11 13		12 19			14 05				16 07			
Hykeham	d		06 51		08 00	08 51					11 19		12 26			14 11				16 13			
Lincoln	a		07 07	07 58	08 10	09 02	09 09	10 18	10 23	11 14	11 33	12 23	12 36	13 22	13 30	14 26		15 24	15 55	16 27	17 19	17 13	18 00
	d	05 57			08 14				10 25				12 37				14 37					17 23	
Market Rasen	d	06 13			08 31				10 42				12 54				14 53					17 39	
Barnetby	a	06 30			08 48				10 59				13 10				15 10					17 54	
Habrough	a	06 41			09 01				11 08				13 19				15 19					18 03	
Grimsby Town	a	06 56			09 15				11 23				13 35				15 34					18 15	
Cleethorpes	a																						

A To Peterborough
B From Worksop
C From Leicester
D From Leicester to Sleaford
E until 22 June. From London Kings Cross
F from 25 June until 28 September. From London Kings Cross
G From St Pancras International

For connections from London Kings Cross please refer to Table 26

Nottingham - Newark - Lincoln - Cleethorpes

Mondays to Fridays from 1 October

Network Diagram - see first Page of Table 18

		EM A	EM	EM A	EM	EM A	EM	GR B	EM C	EM
Nottingham	d	17 17	17 50	18 15		19 20			20 29	22 25
Carlton	d	17 23		18 21		19 26				22 31
Burton Joyce	d	17 27		18 25		19 30				22 35
Lowdham	d	17 32	18 01	18 30		19 35			20 40	22 40
Thurgarton	d	17 36		18 34						
Bleasby	d	17 39		18 37		19 40				22 45
Fiskerton	d	17 42		18 40		19 43				22 48
Rolleston	d	17 45		18 43		19 46				
Newark Castle	d	17 53	18 18	18 53		19 55			20 54	22 57
Newark North Gate	a									23 06
	d				19 34		20 03	20 35		23 09
Collingham	d	18 02	18 27	19 02	19 43		20 12		21 03	23 18
Swinderby	d	18 07	18 31	19 06						23 23
Hykeham	d	18 13	18 37	19 12						23 29
Lincoln	a	18 28	18 52	19 23	20 01	20 17	20 27	21 03	21 22	23 41
	d				20 02					
Market Rasen	d				20 19					
Barnetby	a				20 35					
Habrough	a				20 44					
Grimsby Town	a				20 56					
Cleethorpes	a				21 03					

Saturdays until 29 September

		EM	EM	EM D	EM	EM	EM	EM	EM A	EM	EM A	EM A	EM	EM A	EM D	EM A	EM	EM A	EM D	EM A	EM A	EM	EM A
Nottingham	d		05 55	06 55			08 01		09 23		10 29	11 17		12 27		13 17		14 29		15 23	16 14		17 13
Carlton	d		06 01	07 01			08 08		09 29			11 23				13 23				15 29	16 20		17 19
Burton Joyce	d		06 05	07 05			08 12					11 27				13 27					16 24		17 23
Lowdham	d		06 10	07 10			08 17		09 36		10 40	11 32		12 38		13 32		14 40		15 36	16 29		17 28
Thurgarton	d		06 14	07 14			08 21					11 36				13 36					16 33		17 32
Bleasby	d		06 17	07 17			08 24					11 39				13 39					16 36		17 35
Fiskerton	d		06 20	07 20			08 27					11 42				13 42					16 39		17 38
Rolleston	d		06 22	07 22			08 30					11 45				13 44					16 42		17 41
Newark Castle	d		06 30	07 29			08 37		09 50		10 58	11 55		12 51		13 51		14 55		15 50	16 51		17 49
Newark North Gate	a																						
	d					08 20		09 35		10 52			12 06		13 02				15 29				
Collingham	d		06 40	07 39		08 29		09 43			11 08	12 08	12 15		13 11	14 00			15 38	15 59	17 00		17 58
Swinderby	d		06 44			08 34					11 12		12 19			14 05				16 03			18 03
Hykeham	d		06 50			08 41					11 18		12 26			14 11				16 09			18 09
Lincoln	a		07 02	07 58		08 55	09 09	09 59	10 17	11 20	11 30	12 27	12 36	13 18	13 30	14 23		15 22	15 56	16 21	17 16		18 22
	d	05 38			08 12			10 07					12 37				14 52					17 21	
Market Rasen	d	05 54			08 30			10 24					12 54				15 07					17 37	
Barnetby	a	06 11			08 47			10 40					13 10				15 23					17 53	
Habrough	a	06 22			09 01			10 50					13 20				15 33					18 02	
Grimsby Town	a	06 37			09 15			11 08					13 36				15 48					18 17	
Cleethorpes	a																						

		EM	EM A	GR B	EM C	EM	EM A	EM A
Nottingham	d		18 15		19 29		20 29	21 25
Carlton	d		18 21					
Burton Joyce	d		18 25					21 33
Lowdham	d		18 30		19 40		20 40	21 37
Thurgarton	d		18 34					
Bleasby	d		18 37					21 42
Fiskerton	d		18 40					21 46
Rolleston	d		18 43					
Newark Castle	d		18 53		19 53		20 56	21 57
Newark North Gate	a							22 06
	d	18 07		19 33		20 32		22 09
Collingham	d	18 16	19 02		20 08	20 41	21 04	22 18
Swinderby	d		19 07					22 22
Hykeham	d		19 13					22 28
Lincoln	a	18 35	19 25	20 03	20 26	20 56	21 23	22 40
	d	18 35				20 58		
Market Rasen	d	18 51				21a15		
Barnetby	a	19 07						
Habrough	a	19 16						
Grimsby Town	a	19 31						
Cleethorpes	a							

A From Leicester
B From London Kings Cross
C From St Pancras International
D To Peterborough

For connections from London Kings Cross please refer to Table 26

Table 27

Nottingham - Newark - Lincoln - Cleethorpes

Saturdays from 6 October

Network Diagram - see first Page of Table 18

		EM	EM	EM	EM	EM	EM	EM	EM	EM	EM	EM	EM	EM	EM	EM	EM	EM	EM	EM	EM	EM	EM
				A					B		B	B		B	A	B		B	A	B	B		B
Nottingham ■	d		05 55	06 53			08 01		09 23		10 29	11 17		12 27		13 17		14 29		15 23	16 14		17 13
Carlton	d		06 01	06 59			08 08		09 29			11 23				13 23				15 29	16 20		17 19
Burton Joyce	d		06 05	07 03			08 12					11 27				13 27					16 24		17 23
Lowdham	d		06 10	07 09			08 17		09 36		10 40	11 32		12 38		13 32		14 40		15 36	16 29		17 28
Thurgarton	d		06 14	07 13			08 21					11 36				13 36					16 33		17 32
Bleasby	d		06 17	07 16			08 24					11 39				13 39					16 36		17 35
Fiskerton	d		06 20	07 19			08 27					11 42				13 42					16 39		17 38
Rolleston	d		06 22	07 21			08 30					11 45				13 44					16 42		17 41
Newark Castle	d		06 30	07 29			08 37		09 50		10 58	11 55		12 51		13 51		14 55		15 50	16 51		17 49
Newark North Gate ■	a																						
	d					08 20		09 35		10 52			12 06		13 02				15 29				
Collingham	d		06 40	07 39		08 29		09 43			11 08	12 08	12 15		13 11	14 00			15 38	15 59	17 00		17 58
Swinderby	d		06 44			08 34					11 12		12 19			14 05				16 03			18 03
Hykeham	d		06 50			08 41					11 18		12 26			14 11				16 09			18 09
Lincoln	a		07 02	07 58		08 55	09 11	09 59	10 18	11 20	11 32	12 29	12 36	13 20	13 30	14 26		15 24	15 56	16 23	17 17		18 24
	d	05 38			08 12			10 07					12 37				14 52					17 21	
Market Rasen	d	05 54			08 30			10 24					12 54				15 07					17 37	
Barnetby	a	06 11			08 47			10 40					13 10				15 23					17 53	
Habrough	a	06 22			09 01			10 50					13 20				15 33					18 02	
Grimsby Town	a	06 37			09 15			11 08					13 36				15 48					18 17	
Cleethorpes	a																						

		EM	EM	GR	EM	EM	EM	EM
			B	■ 1 C	◇1 D		B	B
Nottingham ■	d		18 15		19 29		20 29	21 25
Carlton	d		18 21					
Burton Joyce	d		18 25					21 33
Lowdham	d		18 30		19 40		20 40	21 37
Thurgarton	d		18 34					
Bleasby	d		18 37					21 42
Fiskerton	d		18 40					21 46
Rolleston	d		18 43					
Newark Castle	d		18 53		19 53		20 56	21 57
Newark North Gate ■	a							22 06
	d	18 07		19 33		20 32		22 09
Collingham	d	18 16	19 02		20 08	20 41	21 04	22 18
Swinderby	d		19 07					22 22
Hykeham	d		19 13					22 28
Lincoln	a	18 35	19 27	20 03	20 26	20 56	21 23	22 40
	d	18 35				20 58		
Market Rasen	d	18 51				21a15		
Barnetby	a	19 07						
Habrough	a	19 16						
Grimsby Town	a	19 31						
Cleethorpes	a							

Sundays until 9 September

		EM	EM	EM	EM	EM	EM	EM	EM	EM	EM	GR	EM	EM	EM
												■ 1 C			
Nottingham ■	d			15 29		16 33		17 26	18 42		19 33		20 37		22 28
Carlton	d							17 32							22 34
Burton Joyce	d							17 35							22 37
Lowdham	d			15 39		16 44		17 39	18 52		19 43		20 47		22 42
Thurgarton	d							17 43							22 46
Bleasby	d							17 46							22 49
Fiskerton	d							17 50							22 52
Rolleston	d							17 52							22 54
Newark Castle	d			15 59		16 59		18 00	19 07		19 58		21 03		23 03
Newark North Gate ■	a								19 17						23 13
	d	11 35	13 35		16 37		17 56		19 22	19 53		20 34		22 10	23 17
Collingham	d	11 43	13 43	16 08	16 45	17 08		18 09	19 30		20 07		21 12	22 19	23 25
Swinderby	d				16 50	17 12		18 14	19 35		20 12		21 17		23 30
Hykeham	d				16 56	17 18		18 20	19 41		20 18		21 23		23 36
Lincoln	a	12 00	14 02	16 26	17 08	17 31	18 20	18 33	19 53	20 19	20 30	21 03	21 35	22 37	23 48
	d	12 02		16 27			18 22								
Market Rasen	d	12 18		16 43			18 38								
Barnetby	a	12 33		16 58			18 53								
Habrough	a	12 41		17 06			19 01								
Grimsby Town	a	12 53		17 18			19 13								
Cleethorpes	a	13 16		17 28			19 24								

A To Peterborough
B From Leicester
C From London Kings Cross
D From St Pancras International

For connections from London Kings Cross please refer to Table 26

Table 27

Nottingham - Newark - Lincoln - Cleethorpes

Sundays 16 September to 30 September

Network Diagram - see first Page of Table 18

		EM	EM	EM	EM	EM	EM	EM	GR	EM	EM	EM
									■ 1 A			
Nottingham ■	d			16 33		17 26	18 42	19 33		20 37		22 28
Carlton	d					17 32						22 34
Burton Joyce	d					17 35						22 37
Lowdham	d			16 44		17 39	18 52	19 43		20 47		22 42
Thurgarton	d					17 43						22 46
Bleasby	d					17 46						22 49
Fiskerton	d					17 50						22 52
Rolleston	d					17 52						22 54
Newark Castle	d			16 59		18 00	19 07	19 58		21 03		23 03
Newark North Gate ■	a						19 17					23 13
	d	11 35	13 35		17 56		19 22		20 34		22 10	23 17
Collingham	d	11 43	13 43	17 08		18 09	19 30	20 07		21 12	22 19	23 25
Swinderby	d			17 12		18 14	19 35	20 12		21 17		23 30
Hykeham	d			17 18		18 20	19 41	20 18		21 23		23 36
Lincoln	a	12 02	14 02	17 31	18 20	18 33	19 53	20 30	21 03	21 35	22 37	23 48
	d											
Market Rasen	d											
Barnetby	a											
Habrough	a											
Grimsby Town	a											
Cleethorpes	a											

Sundays from 7 October

		EM	EM	EM	EM	EM	EM	EM	GR	EM	EM	EM
									■ 1 A			
Nottingham ■	d			16 33		17 26	18 42	19 33		20 37		22 28
Carlton	d					17 32						22 34
Burton Joyce	d					17 35						22 37
Lowdham	d			16 44		17 39	18 52	19 43		20 47		22 42
Thurgarton	d					17 43						22 46
Bleasby	d					17 46						22 49
Fiskerton	d					17 50						22 52
Rolleston	d					17 52						22 54
Newark Castle	d			16 59		18 00	19 07	19 58		21 03		23 03
Newark North Gate ■	a						19 17					23 13
	d	11 35	13 35		17 56		19 22		20 34		22 10	23 17
Collingham	d	11 43	13 43	17 08		18 09	19 30	20 07		21 12	22 19	23 25
Swinderby	d			17 12		18 14	19 35	20 12		21 17		23 30
Hykeham	d			17 18		18 20	19 41	20 18		21 23		23 36
Lincoln	a	12 02	14 02	17 31	18 20	18 33	19 53	20 30	21 03	21 35	22 37	23 48
	d											
Market Rasen	d											
Barnetby	a											
Habrough	a											
Grimsby Town	a											
Cleethorpes	a											

A From London Kings Cross

For connections from London Kings Cross please refer to Table 26

Hull and Cleethorpes - Doncaster - Meadowhall, Sheffield, Manchester and Manchester Airport, Cleethorpes - Barton-on-Humber

Network Diagram - see first Page of Table 18

Miles	Miles	Miles	Miles	Miles			NT MX	NT MX	TP MX	TP MO	TP	TP	EM	TP	NT		NT	NT	NT	TP	TP	EM	TP	NT	NT
									◇1	◇1	◇1	◇1	◇1	◇1						◇1	◇1		◇1		
								A					B ☒✠				A			✠	✠	C	D ✠		
0	0	—	—	—	**Hull**	d	22p20											05 20					06 00		06 03
4¾	4¾	—	—	—	Hessle	d	22p27																		06 10
7½	7½	—	—	—	Ferriby	d	22p32																		06 15
10½	10½	—	—	—	Brough	d	22p37											05 32					06 12		06 20
14½	14½	—	—	—	Broomfleet	d																			
17	17	—	—	—	Gilberdyke	d																	06 19		06 27
—	19¼	—	—	—	Eastrington	d																			
—	22¼	—	—	—	Howden	d																	06 26		
—	25	—	—	—	Wressle	d																			
—	31	—	—	—	**Selby**	a																	06 36		
—	—	—	—	—		d													06 18				06 36		
—	—	—	—	—	York 8 33	a																			
20¾	—	—	—	—	Saltmarshe	d																			06 33
23¾	—	—	—	—	Goole	d	22p51											05 46							06 38
31	—	—	—	—	Thorne North	d	23p00											05 55							06 47
—	—	0	0	—	**Cleethorpes**	d															05 18	05 49		06 00	
—	—	1½	1½	—	New Clee	d																			
—	—	2¼	2¼	—	Grimsby Docks	d																			
—	—	3¼	3¼	—	**Grimsby Town**	a															05 25	05 55		06 08	
—	—	—	—	—		d															05 26	05 56		06 08	
—	—	5¼	5¼	—	Great Coates	d																			
—	—	6¼	6¼	—	Healing	d																		06 15	
—	—	7½	7½	—	Stallingborough	d																		06 18	
—	—	11¼	11¼	—	Habrough	d															05 36	06 06		06 24	
—	—	—	13	—	Ulceby	d																		06 28	
—	—	—	15¾	—	Thornton Abbey	d																			
—	—	—	17¼	—	Goxhill	d																		06 35	
—	—	—	19¼	—	New Holland	d																		06 40	
—	—	—	20¾	—	Barrow Haven	d																		06 43	
—	—	—	22¾	—	**Barton-on-Humber**	a																		06 48	
—	—	—	—	—	Barton-on-Humber	d																			
—	—	—	—	—	Hull Paragon Interchange	a																			
—	—	17¾	—	—	Barnetby	d															05 45	06a15			
—	—	29	—	—	**Scunthorpe**	a															06 00				
—	—	—	—	—		d															06 00				
—	—	32½	—	—	Althorpe	d															06 05				
—	—	36¼	—	—	Crowle	d															06 11				
—	—	42¼	—	—	Thorne South	d															06 20				
34¼	—	45¼	—	—	Hatfield & Stainforth	d	23p06											06 01			06 25				06 53
37	—	48	—	—	Kirk Sandall	d	23p10											06 06							06 57
—	—	—	—	0	Adwick 31	d																			
—	—	—	—	2¼	Bentley (S.Yorks) 31	d																			
41	49¼	52	—	4	**Doncaster 7** 31	a	23p21											06 15	06 38		06 38				07 08
—	—	—	—	—	London Kings Cross 15 ⊖26	a																			
—	—	—	—	—	York 8 26	d			04 00	04 23	05 26			05 57						06 28					
—	—	—	—	—	**Doncaster 7**	d	23p22					05 40	05 57		06 00			06 25			06 40				
45¾	—	—	—	—	Conisbrough	d	23p29								06 07			06 32							
48	—	—	—	—	Mexborough	d	23p33								06 11			06 36							
49¼	—	—	—	—	Swinton (S.Yorks)	d	23p36	23p56							06 14		06 23	06 39							
53¾	—	—	—	—	Rotherham Central	d	23p45	00 03							06 22		06 31	06 46							
56½	—	—	—	—	**Meadowhall** ⇌	d	23p54	00 09				05 58			06 27		06 38	06 52			06 58				
60	—	—	—	—	**Sheffield 7** ⇌	a	00 04	00 23				06 08	06 18		06 38		06 47	07 05			07 06				
—	—	—	—	—		d						06 11									07 09				
96¾	—	—	—	—	Stockport 78	a						06 53									07 53				
102¾	—	—	—	—	**Manchester Piccadilly 10** ⇌	a			06 02	06 02	06 50	07 02		07 19						07 51	08 02		08 05		
112½	—	—	—	—	**Manchester Airport** 85 ✈	a			06 24	06 24	07 12	07 29		07 42						08 12	08 26				

A From Leeds
B From Leeds to St Pancras International
C To Newark North Gate
D To Liverpool Lime Street

Hull and Cleethorpes - Doncaster - Meadowhall, Sheffield, Manchester and Manchester Airport, Cleethorpes - Barton-on-Humber

Network Diagram - see first Page of Table 18

		HT	TP	XC	NT BHX	NT	XC	NT	TP	EM		NT	NT BHX	NT	XC	NT	GR	NT	NT	TP	XC		NT	NT
		◇1	◇1	◇1			◇1		◇1						◇1		1			◇1	◇1			
		☒	✠	A ✠	🚌	B	C ✠	D	✠	E			🚌		F ✠		G ✠	H	I	✠	J ✠		D	
Hull	d	06 25	06 37													06 40	07 00	07 07		07 37				
Hessle	d															06 47								
Ferriby	d															06 52								
Brough	d	06 37	06 49													06 57	07 12	07 19		07 49				
Broomfleet	d																							
Gilberdyke	d															07 04		07 26						
Eastrington	d																	07 31						
Howden	d	06 49																07 35		08 01				
Wressle	d																	07 40						
Selby	a	06 59	07 08														07 33	07 48		08 10				
	d	07 00	07 08														07 34	07 48		08 11				
York 8 33	a																	08 21						
Saltmarshe	d															07 10								
Goole	d															07 15								
Thorne North	d															07 24								
Cleethorpes	d								06 18			07 00												
New Clee	d																							
Grimsby Docks	d											07 05												
Grimsby Town	a								06 25			07 08												
	d								06 26	07 03		07 08												
Great Coates	d											07 12												
Healing	d											07 15												
Stallingborough	d											07 18												
Habrough	d								06 36	07 13		07 24												
Ulceby	d											07 28												
Thornton Abbey	d											07 32												
Goxhill	d											07 35												
New Holland	d											07 40												
Barrow Haven	d											07 43												
Barton-on-Humber	a											07 48												
Barton-on-Humber	d				06 53								08 10											
Hull Paragon Interchange	a				07 20								08 37											
Barnetby	d								06 45	07a22														
Scunthorpe	a								07 00															
	d								07 00										07 22					
Althorpe	d																		07 27					
Crowle	d																		07 33					
Thorne South	d																		07 41					
Hatfield & Stainforth	d															07 30			07 47					
Kirk Sandall	d															07 34			07 51					
Adwick 31	d													07 29										08 15
Bentley (S.Yorks) 31	d													07 33										08 18
Doncaster 7 31	a	07 17							07 33					07 37		07 46	07 52		08 04					08 23
London Kings Cross 15 ⊖26	a	09 18															09 56							
York 8 26	d						06 32								07 23						07 44			
Doncaster 7	d			06 45		07 02			07 35					07 39	07 55	07 48								08 25
Conisbrough	d					07 09								07 46		07 55								08 32
Mexborough	d					07 13								07 50		07 59								08 36
Swinton (S.Yorks)	d					07 16		07 30						07 53		08 02							08 34	08 42
Rotherham Central	d					07 27		07 39						08 00		08 12							08 43	08 50
Meadowhall ⇌	d					07 33		07 45	07 53					08 06		08 23							08 51	08 57
Sheffield 7 ⇌	a			07 11		07 40	07 50	07 56	08 00					08 18	08 18	08 33					08 51		08 59	09 05
	d								08 05															
Stockport 78	a								08 53															
Manchester Piccadilly 10 ⇌	a		08 36						09 02											09 36				
Manchester Airport 85 ✈	a								09 33															

A From Leeds to Southampton Central
B To Worksop
C To Plymouth
D From Leeds
E To Newark North Gate
F From Newcastle to Reading
G The Hull Executive
H From Beverley to Hull
I To Adwick
J From Newcastle to Plymouth

Hull and Cleethorpes - Doncaster - Meadowhall, Sheffield, Manchester and Manchester Airport, Cleethorpes - Barton-on-Humber

Network Diagram - see first Page of Table 18

		TP	XC	NT	NT	NT	NT	HT	XC	NT	NT	NT	TP	TP	TP	NT	NT	NT	NT	EM	XC	NT	XC
		◇■	◇■					◇■	◇■				◇■	◇■	◇■						◇■		◇■
			A		B	B	C		D	E		F					bus	B		G	H	C	I
Hull	d				07 40	08 03		08 25				08 28	08 40					08 56	09 02				
Hessle	d				07 47							08 35											
Ferriby	d				07 52							08 40											
Brough	d				07 57	08 15		08 37				08 45	08 52					09 08	09 14				
Broomfleet	d				08 02																		
Gilberdyke	d				08 07							08 52							09 21				
Eastrington	d																						
Howden	d							08 49											09 28				
Wressle	d																						
Selby	a							08 59					09 11						09 38				
	d							09 00					09 11						09 38				
York ■ 33	a																		10 10				
Saltmarshe	d				08 12																		
Goole	d				08 17	08 29						09 01						09 23					
Thorne North	d				08 26							09 09											
Cleethorpes	d	07 26													08 26	08 55							
New Clee	d															08x58							
Grimsby Docks	d															09 00							
Grimsby Town	a	07 33													08 33	09 03							
	d	07 34													08 34	09 03				09 20			
Great Coates	d															09 07							
Healing	d															09 10							
Stallingborough	d															09 13							
Habrough	d	07 44													08 44	09 19				09 30			
Ulceby	d															09 23							
Thornton Abbey	d															09 27							
Goxhill	d															09 30							
New Holland	d															09 35							
Barrow Haven	d															09 38							
Barton-on-Humber	a															09 43							
Barton-on-Humber	d																10 00						
Hull Paragon Interchange	a																10 27						
Barnetby	d	07 53													08 53					09a39			
Scunthorpe	a	08 08													09 08								
	d	08 08					08 19								09 08							09 19	
Althorpe	d						08 24															09 24	
Crowle	d						08 30															09 30	
Thorne South	d						08 39															09 39	
Hatfield & Stainforth	d				08 33		08 45					09 16										09 44	
Kirk Sandall	d				08 36		08 50					09 20										09 49	
Adwick 31	d			08 33							09 15												
Bentley (S.Yorks) 31	d			08 37							09 19												
Doncaster ■ 31	a	08 38		08 41	08 46	08 54	09 01	09 24			09 24	09 31			09 38			09 49				10 01	
London Kings Cross ■ ⊖26	a							11 09															
York ■ 26	d		08 24						08 44					09 28							09 35		09 45
Doncaster ■	d	08 41	08 50			08 56	09 01				09 26				09 42			09 50			09 58	10 04	
Conisbrough	d						09 08				09 33											10 11	
Mexborough	d						09 12				09 35											10 15	
Swinton (S.Yorks)	d						09 16			09 35	09 42											10 18	
Rotherham Central	d						09 27			09 44	09 50											10 27	
Meadowhall	d	09 01				09 16	09 33			09 50	09 55				10 01			10 08				10 33	
Sheffield ■	a	09 08	09 17			09 26	09 41		09 51	10 00	10 05				10 08			10 19			10 20	10 41	10 51
	d	09 11													10 11								
Stockport 78	a	09 53													10 53								
Manchester Piccadilly ■	a	10 02											10 36	10 49	11 02								
Manchester Airport 85	a	10 26												11 12	11 26								

A From Newcastle to Southampton Central
B From Bridlington
C To Lincoln
D From Edinburgh to Plymouth
E From Leeds
F From Scarborough
G To Newark North Gate
H From Edinburgh to Reading
I From Glasgow Central to Plymouth

Hull and Cleethorpes - Doncaster - Meadowhall, Sheffield, Manchester and Manchester Airport, Cleethorpes - Barton-on-Humber

Network Diagram - see first Page of Table 18

		NT	NT	NT	TP	TP	NT	NT	XC	NT	XC	NT	NT	NT	HT	TP	TP	NT	NT	NT	NT	EM	XC
					◇■	◇■			◇■		◇■				◇■	◇■	◇■		BHX				◇■
		A		B			C	D	E	F	G	A							bus	H	I	J	K
Hull	d			09 25	09 40		09 56	10 08						10 18	10 30	10 40				10 57	10 57		
Hessle	d			09 32										10 25									
Ferriby	d			09 37										10 30									
Brough	d			09 42	09 52		10 08	10 20						10 35	10 42	10 52				11 09	11 09		
Broomfleet	d																						
Gilberdyke	d			09 49				10 26						10 42									
Eastrington	d																						
Howden	d							10 34							10 54								
Wressle	d																						
Selby	a				10 11			10 47							11 04	11 11							
	d				10 11			10 47							11 05	11 11							
York ■ 33	a							11 18															
Saltmarshe	d													10 48									
Goole	d			10 01			10 22							11 01						11 23	11 23		
Thorne North	d			10 09										11 08									
Cleethorpes	d					09 26											10 26	10 55					
New Clee	d																	10x58					
Grimsby Docks	d																	11 00					
Grimsby Town	a					09 33											10 33	11 03					
	d					09 34											10 34	11 03				11 28	
Great Coates	d																	11 07					
Healing	d																	11 10					
Stallingborough	d																	11 13					
Habrough	d																10 44	11 19				11 38	
Ulceby	d																	11 23					
Thornton Abbey	d																	11 27					
Goxhill	d																	11 30					
New Holland	d																	11 35					
Barrow Haven	d																	11 38					
Barton-on-Humber	a																	11 43					
Barton-on-Humber	d																		12 00				
Hull Paragon Interchange	a																		12 27				
Barnetby	d					09 53											10 53					11a47	
Scunthorpe	a					10 08											11 08						
	d					10 08				10 19							11 08						
Althorpe	d									10 24													
Crowle	d									10 30													
Thorne South	d									10 39													
Hatfield & Stainforth	d			10 15						10 44				11 14									
Kirk Sandall	d			10 20						10 49				11 19									
Adwick 31	d		10 15										11 15										
Bentley (S.Yorks) 31	d		10 19										11 19										
Doncaster ■ 31	a		10 24	10 30		10 38	10 47			11 00			11 24	11 30	11 24		11 38			11 47	11 48		
London Kings Cross ■ ⊖26	a														13 10								
York ■ 26	d								10 34		10 44												11 34
Doncaster ■	d		10 26			10 42	10 49		10 58	11 04			11 26				11 42			11 48	11 48		11 58
Conisbrough	d		10 33							11 11			11 33										
Mexborough	d		10 37							11 15			11 37										
Swinton (S.Yorks)	d	10 35	10 43							11 18		11 35	11 43										
Rotherham Central	d	10 44	10 52							11 27		11 44	11 52										
Meadowhall	d	10 50	10 58			11 01	11 08			11 33		11 51	11 56				12 01			12 08	12 08		
Sheffield ■	a	11 01	11 05			11 08	11 20		11 20	11 41	11 51	12 01	12 05				12 08			12 19	12 19		12 20
	d					11 11											12 11						
Stockport 78	a					11 53											12 53						
Manchester Piccadilly ■	a				11 36	12 02										12 36	13 02						
Manchester Airport 85	a					12 26											13 26						

A From Leeds
B From Beverley
C From Bridlington
D To Hull
E From Newcastle to Southampton Central
F To Lincoln
G From Dundee to Plymouth
H from 1 October. From Bridlington
I until 28 September. From Bridlington
J To Newark North Gate
K From Newcastle to Reading

Hull and Cleethorpes - Doncaster - Meadowhall, Sheffield, Manchester and Manchester Airport, Cleethorpes - Barton-on-Humber

Network Diagram - see first Page of Table 18

		NT	NT	XC	NT	NT	NT	TP	TP	NT	NT	XC	NT	NT	HT	TP	XC	NT	NT	TP	NT	NT BHX	NT
				◇1				◇1	◇1			◇1			◇1	◇1	◇1			◇1			
			A	B	C					D	E	F	A				G	C					H
				✠				✠	✠			✠			⊠	✠	✠			✠		🚌	
Hull	d						11 23	11 40		11 55	12 03			12 18	12 30	12 40							12 57
Hessle	d						11 30							12 25									
Ferriby	d						11 35							12 30									
Brough	d						11 40	11 52		12 07	12 15			12 35	12 42	12 52							13 09
Broomfleet	d						11 45																
Gilberdyke	d						11 50							12 43									
Eastrington	d																						
Howden	d										12 27				12 55								
Wressle	d																						
Selby	a							12 11			12 37				13 04	13 11							
	d							12 11			12 38				13 05	13 11							
York 8 33	a										13 04												
Saltmarshe	d													12 49									
Goole	d						12 01			12 22				13 01									13 23
Thorne North	d						12 09							13 09									
Cleethorpes	d								11 26											12 26	12 55		
New Clee	d																				12x58		
Grimsby Docks	d																				13 00		
Grimsby Town	a								11 33											12 33	13 03		
	d								11 34											12 34	13 03		
Great Coates	d																				13 07		
Healing	d																				13 10		
Stallingborough	d																				13 13		
Habrough	d																				13 19		
Ulceby	d																				13 23		
Thornton Abbey	d																				13 27		
Goxhill	d																				13 30		
New Holland	d																				13 35		
Barrow Haven	d																				13 38		
Barton-on-Humber	a																				13 43		
Barton-on-Humber	d																					14 00	
Hull Paragon Interchange	a																					14 27	
Barnetby	d								11 53											12 53			
Scunthorpe	a								12 08											13 08			
	d		11 19						12 08				12 19							13 08			
Althorpe	d		11 24										12 24										
Crowle	d		11 30										12 30										
Thorne South	d		11 39										12 39										
Hatfield & Stainforth	d		11 44				12 15						12 44	13 13									
Kirk Sandall	d		11 49				12 20						12 49	13 18									
Adwick 31	d					12 15													13 14				
Bentley (S.Yorks) 31	d					12 19													13 18				
Doncaster 7 31	a		12 00			12 25	12 30		12 38	12 47			13 01	13 30	13 24				13 26	13 38			13 47
London Kings Cross 15 ⊖26	a														15 10								
York 8 26	d	11 05		11 45								12 34					12 44						
Doncaster 7	d		12 03			12 26			12 42	12 48		12 59	13 02						13 26	13 42			13 48
Conisbrough	d		12 11			12 33							13 11						13 33				
Mexborough	d		12 15			12 37							13 15						13 37				
Swinton (S.Yorks)	d	12 10	12 18		12 35	12 43							13 18					13 35	13 42				
Rotherham Central	d	12 19	12 27		12 44	12 52							13 27					13 44	13 52				
Meadowhall ⇌	d	12 24	12 33		12 51	12 56			13 01	13 08			13 33					13 51	13 56	14 01			14 05
Sheffield 7 ⇌	a	12 36	12 41	12 51	13 01	13 05			13 08	13 20		13 20	13 41				13 51	14 01	14 05	14 08			14 20
	d								13 11											14 11			
Stockport 78	a								13 53											14 53			
Manchester Piccadilly 10 ⇌	a							13 36	14 02							14 36				15 02			
Manchester Airport 85 ✈	a								14 26											15 26			

A To Lincoln
B From Glasgow Central to Plymouth
C From Leeds
D From Bridlington
E To Hull
F From Newcastle to Southampton Central
G From Glasgow Central to Penzance
H from 1 October. From Scarborough

Hull and Cleethorpes - Doncaster - Meadowhall, Sheffield, Manchester and Manchester Airport, Cleethorpes - Barton-on-Humber

Network Diagram - see first Page of Table 18

		NT	NT	XC	NT	XC	NT	NT	NT	TP	TP	EM	NT	NT	XC	NT	XC	NT	NT	NT	TP	TP
				◇1		◇1				◇1	◇1				◇1		◇1				◇1	◇1
		A	B	C	D	E	F					G	H	B	I	D	J	F				
				✠		✠				✠	✠				✠		✠				✠	✠
Hull	d	12 57	13 12						13 25	13 40			13 57	14 19						14 25	14 40	
Hessle	d								13 32											14 32		
Ferriby	d								13 37											14 37		
Brough	d	13 09	13 24						13 42	13 52			14 09	14 31						14 42	14 52	
Broomfleet	d																					
Gilberdyke	d		13 32						13 49											14 49		
Eastrington	d		13 36																			
Howden	d		13 41											14 43								
Wressle	d		13 47																			
Selby	a		13 54							14 11				14 53							15 11	
	d		13 55							14 11				14 53							15 11	
York 8 33	a		14 27											15 25								
Saltmarshe	d																					
Goole	d	13 23							14 01				14 23							15 01		
Thorne North	d								14 09											15 09		
Cleethorpes	d										13 26											14 26
New Clee	d																					
Grimsby Docks	d																					
Grimsby Town	a										13 33											14 33
	d										13 34	13 49										14 34
Great Coates	d																					
Healing	d																					
Stallingborough	d																					
Habrough	d											13 59										14 44
Ulceby	d																					
Thornton Abbey	d																					
Goxhill	d																					
New Holland	d																					
Barrow Haven	d																					
Barton-on-Humber	a																					
Barton-on-Humber	d																					
Hull Paragon Interchange	a																					
Barnetby	d										13 53	14a08										14 53
Scunthorpe	a										14 08											15 08
	d				13 19						14 08					14 19						15 08
Althorpe	d				13 24											14 24						
Crowle	d				13 30											14 30						
Thorne South	d				13 39											14 39						
Hatfield & Stainforth	d				13 44				14 15							14 44				15 15		
Kirk Sandall	d				13 49				14 20							14 49				15 20		
Adwick 31	d							14 15											15 15			
Bentley (S.Yorks) 31	d							14 19											15 19			
Doncaster 7 31	a	13 47			13 59			14 24	14 31		14 38		14 46			14 59			15 24	15 30		15 38
London Kings Cross 15 ⊖26	a																					
York 8 26	d			13 34		13 44									14 34		14 44					
Doncaster 7	d	13 48		13 58	14 03			14 26			14 42		14 48		14 58	15 04			15 25			15 42
Conisbrough	d				14 12			14 31								15 11			15 32			
Mexborough	d				14 16			14 35								15 15			15 37			
Swinton (S.Yorks)	d				14 18		14 35	14 42								15 18		15 35	15 42			
Rotherham Central	d				14 29		14 44	14 52								15 27		15 44	15 50			
Meadowhall ⇌	d	14 08			14 34		14 50	14 56			15 01		15 07			15 33		15 50	15 57			16 01
Sheffield 7 ⇌	a	14 20		14 20	14 42	14 51	15 01	15 05			15 08		15 19		15 20	15 41	15 51	16 01	16 05			16 08
	d										15 11											16 11
Stockport 78	a										15 53											16 53
Manchester Piccadilly 10 ⇌	a									15 36	16 02										16 36	17 02
Manchester Airport 85 ✈	a										16 26											17 32

A until 28 September. From Scarborough
B To Hull
C From Newcastle to Reading
D To Lincoln
E From Aberdeen to Penzance
F From Leeds
G To Newark North Gate
H From Bridlington
I From Newcastle to Eastleigh
J From Glasgow Central to Penzance

Table 29

Mondays to Fridays

Hull and Cleethorpes - Doncaster - Meadowhall, Sheffield, Manchester and Manchester Airport, Cleethorpes - Barton-on-Humber

Network Diagram - see first Page of Table 18

		NT	NT	NT	NT	XC	NT	NT	HT	XC	TP			NT	NT	NT	TP	TP	EM	NT	XC		NT	NT	NT
			BHX								FO														
						◇■			◇■	◇■	◇■						◇■	◇■			◇■				
				A		B	C	D		E				F	G				H	I	B		J	D	A
			🚌			⊼			⊠	⊼	⊼						⊼	⊼			⊼				
Hull	d			14 57	15 02				15 10							15 24	15 40			15 57			16 10		16 26
Hessle	d															15 31									16 33
Ferriby	d															15 36									16 38
Brough	d			15 09	15 14				15 22							15 41	15 52			16 09			16 22		16 43
Broomfleet	d																								16 49
Gilberdyke	d															15 49							16 29		16 53
Eastrington	d																								
Howden	d				15 26				15 36														16 36		
Wressle	d																								
Selby	a				15 36				15 45								16 11						16 46		
	d				15 38				15 46								16 11						16 47		
York ■ 33	a				16 06																		17 13		
Saltmarshe	d																								16 59
Goole	d			15 23												16 00				16 23					17 04
Thorne North	d															16 09									17 12
Cleethorpes	d	14 55																15 26							
New Clee	d	14x58																							
Grimsby Docks	d	15 00																							
Grimsby Town	a	15 03																15 33							
	d	15 03																15 34	15 45						
Great Coates	d	15 07																							
Healing	d	15 10																							
Stallingborough	d	15 13																							
Habrough	d	15 19																	15 55						
Ulceby	d	15 23																							
Thornton Abbey	d	15 27																							
Goxhill	d	15 30																							
New Holland	d	15 35																							
Barrow Haven	d	15 38																							
Barton-on-Humber	a	15 43																							
Barton-on-Humber	d		16 00																						
Hull Paragon Interchange	a		16 27																						
Barnetby	d																	15 53	16a03						
Scunthorpe	a																	16 08							
	d							15 19										16 08						16 19	
Althorpe	d							15 24																16 24	
Crowle	d							15 30																16 30	
Thorne South	d							15 39																16 39	
Hatfield & Stainforth	d							15 44								16 14								16 44	17 18
Kirk Sandall	d							15 49								16 19								16 49	17 22
Adwick	31 d														16 15										
Bentley (S.Yorks)	31 d														16 19										
Doncaster ■	31 a			15 47				15 59	16 03						16 24	16 30		16 38		16 47				16 59	17 34
London Kings Cross ■ ⊖26	a								17 46																
York ■	26 d					15 34	15 01			15 44	15 57										16 04				
Doncaster ■	d			15 48		15 58		16 03							16 26			16 42		16 48				17 01	
Conisbrough	d							16 11							16 33									17 08	
Mexborough	d							16 15							16 37									17 12	
Swinton (S.Yorks)	d						16 00	16 16						16 35	16 42									17 16	
Rotherham Central	d						16 09	16 27						16 44	16 50									17 27	
Meadowhall	⇌ d			16 07			16 18	16 33						16 50	16 55			17 01		17 09				17 33	
Sheffield ■	⇌ a			16 20		16 20	16 27	16 41		16 51				17 00	17 05			17 08		17 20	17 20			17 41	
	d																	17 11							
Stockport	78 a																	17 53							
Manchester Piccadilly ■	⇌ a										17 21						17 36	18 02							
Manchester Airport	85 ✈ a																	18 26							

A From Scarborough
B From Newcastle to Reading
C From Sheffield
D To Lincoln
E From Edinburgh to Plymouth
F From Leeds
G To RetfordRetford
H To Newark North Gate
I From Bridlington
J To Hull

Table 29

Mondays to Fridays

Hull and Cleethorpes - Doncaster - Meadowhall, Sheffield, Manchester and Manchester Airport, Cleethorpes - Barton-on-Humber

Network Diagram - see first Page of Table 18

		TP	XC	NT	NT	TP	NT	NT	NT	TP	XC	NT	HT	NT	XC		NT		NT	NT	TP	EM	NT	NT	NT
									BHX														BHX		
		◇■	◇■			◇■				◇■	◇■		◇■		◇■						◇■				
			A	B			C			D	E			F	G		H		B			I			J
		⊼	⊼			⊼			🚌		⊼		⊠		⊼						⊼		🚌	🚌	
Hull	d	16 40					16 54			17 01			17 10	17 18											17 42
Hessle	d													17 25											17 49
Ferriby	d													17 30											17 54
Brough	d	16 52					17 06			17 13			17 22	17 35											17 59
Broomfleet	d													17 40											
Gilberdyke	d						17 13							17 45											18 06
Eastrington	d													17 49											
Howden	d												17 34	17 54											
Wressle	d													17 59											
Selby	a	17 11								17 31			17 44	18 06											
	d	17 11											17 45	18 07											
York ■ 33	a													18 33											
Saltmarshe	d																								18 12
Goole	d						17 22																		18 19
Thorne North	d																								18 28
Cleethorpes	d					16 26		16 55													17 26				
New Clee	d																								
Grimsby Docks	d							17 00																	
Grimsby Town	a					16 33		17 03													17 33				
	d					16 34		17 04													17 34	18 29			
Great Coates	d							17 08																	
Healing	d							17 11																	
Stallingborough	d							17 14																	
Habrough	d					16 44		17 20													17 44	18 39			
Ulceby	d							17 23																	
Thornton Abbey	d							17 28																	
Goxhill	d							17 31																	
New Holland	d							17 35																	
Barrow Haven	d							17 38																	
Barton-on-Humber	a							17 44																	
Barton-on-Humber	d								18 00														19 53	21 56	
Hull Paragon Interchange	a								18 27														20 20	22 23	
Barnetby	d					16 53															17 53	18a47			
Scunthorpe	a					17 08															18 08				
	d					17 08						17 19									18 08				
Althorpe	d											17 24													
Crowle	d											17 30													
Thorne South	d											17 39													
Hatfield & Stainforth	d											17 44													18 34
Kirk Sandall	d											17 49													18 39
Adwick	31 d																18 14								
Bentley (S.Yorks)	31 d																18 18								
Doncaster ■	31 a					17 38	17 46					17 58	18 02				18 25				18 38				18 51
London Kings Cross ■ ⊖26	a												19 47												⟶
York ■	26 d		16 44								17 34				17 44										
Doncaster ■	d				17 24	17 42	17 47				17 59	18 02								18 26	18 42				
Conisbrough	d				17 31							18 09								18 33					
Mexborough	d				17 35							18 13								18 37					
Swinton (S.Yorks)	d			17 35	17 42							18 16							18 35	18 42					
Rotherham Central	d			17 44	17 50							18 27							18 45	18 49					
Meadowhall	⇌ d			17 50	17 57	18 01	18 08					18 32							18 50	18 57	19 01				
Sheffield ■	⇌ a		17 51	18 01	18 05	18 08	18 19				18 20	18 42			18 51				19 00	19 06	19 08				
	d					18 11															19 11				
Stockport	78 a					18 53															19 53				
Manchester Piccadilly ■	⇌ a	18 37				19 02															20 02				
Manchester Airport	85 ✈ a					19 28															20 39				

A From Glasgow Central to Plymouth
B From Leeds
C From Bridlington
D To Huddersfield
E From Newcastle to Reading
F To Leeds
G From Edinburgh to Plymouth
H To Scunthorpe
I To Newark North Gate
J To Sheffield

Hull and Cleethorpes - Doncaster - Meadowhall, Sheffield, Manchester and Manchester Airport, Cleethorpes - Barton-on-Humber

Network Diagram - see first Page of Table 18

	NT	NT	TP	XC	NT	NT	NT	XC	TP	NT	NT	TP	TP	NT	TP	NT	NT	HT	NT	NT	XC
									FO												
			◇1	◇1				◇1	◇1			◇1	◇1		◇1			◇1			◇1
	A	B		C	D		E	F		G		H	I		J						K
			⌶	⌶				⌶										⊠			⌶
Hull d	17 52	17 52	17 58				18 23							18 53	18 59			19 10	19 15	19 25	
Hessle d							18 30													19 32	
Ferriby d							18 35													19 37	
Brough d	18 04	18 04	18 10				18 40							19 05	19 11			19 22	19 28	19 42	
Broomfleet d																					
Gilberdyke d							18 47												19 36	19 49	
Eastrington d																					
Howden d																		19 34	19 43		
Wressle d																					
Selby a	18 25	18 25	18 29												19 29			19 44	19 53		
d	18 26	18 26	18 29															19 45	19 53		
York 8 33 a																			20 21		
Saltmarshe d																					
Goole d							18 59							19 19						20 01	
Thorne North d							19 08													20 09	
Cleethorpes d												18 26	18 26			19 00					
New Clee d																					
Grimsby Docks d																19 05					
Grimsby Town a												18 33	18 33			19 08					
d												18 34	18 34			19 09					
Great Coates d																19 13					
Healing d																19 16					
Stallingborough d																19 19					
Habrough d																19 25					
Ulceby d																19 28					
Thornton Abbey d																19 33					
Goxhill d																19 36					
New Holland d																19 40					
Barrow Haven d																19 43					
Barton-on-Humber a																19 49					
Barton-on-Humber d																					
Hull Paragon Interchange a																					
Barnetby d												18 53	18 53								
Scunthorpe a												19 08	19 08								
d						18 19						19 08	19 08				19 15				
Althorpe d						18 24											19 20				
Crowle d						18 30											19 26				
Thorne South d						18 39											19 35				
Hatfield & Stainforth d						18 46	19 15										19 40			20 15	
Kirk Sandall d						18 50	19 19										19 45			20 20	
Adwick 31 d																					
Bentley (S.Yorks) 31 d																					
Doncaster 7 31 a	18 47	18 47			← 18 51	19 01	19 31					19 38	19 38	19 48			19 57	20 01		20 33	
London Kings Cross 15 ⊖26 a																		21 46			
York 8 26 d				18 34				18 45	19 08												19 34
Doncaster 7 d	18 49	18 49		18 58	19 01						19 28	19 42	19 42	19 49							19 58
Conisbrough d					19 08						19 35										
Mexborough d					19 12						19 39										
Swinton (S.Yorks) d					19 15					19 35	19 43										
Rotherham Central d					19 23					19 45	19 50										
Meadowhall d	19 08	19 08			19 28					19 51	19 57	20 01	20 01	20 08							
Sheffield 7 a	19 17	19 19		19 20	19 37			19 51		19 59	20 05	20 08	20 08	20 18							20 20
d												20 11	20 11								
Stockport 78 a												20 53	20 53								
Manchester Piccadilly 10 a			19 57						20 33			21 02	21 02								
Manchester Airport 85 ✈ a									20 57			21 36	21 38								

A from 1 October. From Scarborough
B until 28 September. From Scarborough
C From Newcastle to Guildford
D From Hull
E From Bridlington
F From Glasgow Central to Bristol Temple Meads
G From Leeds
H ThFO
I MTWO
J To Leeds
K From Newcastle to Birmingham New Street

Mondays to Fridays

Hull and Cleethorpes - Doncaster - Meadowhall, Sheffield, Manchester and Manchester Airport, Cleethorpes - Barton-on-Humber

Network Diagram - see first Page of Table 18

	NT	XC	NT	TP	NT	XC	NT	TP	XC	TP	TP	NT	NT	TP	NT	NT	EM	TP	NT	NT	NT	NT	NT	NT
								FO		FX	FX													
		◇1		◇1		◇1		◇1	◇1	◇1	◇1			◇1				◇1						
	A	B	C			D	E		F	G		C					H					C		C
Hull d							20 03	20 35		20 45					20 56			21 33					22 20	
Hessle d							20 10																22 27	
Ferriby d							20 15																22 32	
Brough d							20 20	20 47		20 57					21 08			21 45					22 37	
Broomfleet d																								
Gilberdyke d							20 27											21 52						
Eastrington d																								
Howden d																								
Wressle d																								
Selby a								21 06		21 16								22 07						
d								21 06										22 07						
York 8 33 a																								
Saltmarshe d																								
Goole d							20 36								21 22				21 35				22 51	
Thorne North d							20 44												21 44				23 00	
Cleethorpes d				19 26										20 26		21 03	21 15							
New Clee d																								
Grimsby Docks d																21 08								
Grimsby Town a				19 33										20 33		21 11	21 21							
d				19 34										20 34		21 11	21 22							
Great Coates d																21 15								
Healing d																21 18								
Stallingborough d																21 21								
Habrough d				19 44												21 27	21 33							
Ulceby d																21 31								
Thornton Abbey d																21 35								
Goxhill d																21 38								
New Holland d																21 43								
Barrow Haven d																21 46								
Barton-on-Humber a																21 51								
Barton-on-Humber d																								
Hull Paragon Interchange a																								
Barnetby d				19 53										20 53			21a42							
Scunthorpe a				20 08										21 08										
d				20 08	20 21									21 08						21 31	22 21			
Althorpe d					20 26															21 36	22 26			
Crowle d					20 32															21 42	22 32			
Thorne South d					20 41															21 51	22 41			
Hatfield & Stainforth d					20 46		20 51												21 50	21 56	22 46		23 06	
Kirk Sandall d					20 51		20 56												21 54	22 01	22 51		23 10	
Adwick 31 d																								
Bentley (S.Yorks) 31 d																								
Doncaster 7 31 a				20 40	21 01		21 05							21 40	21 47				22 08	22 11	23 03		23 21	
London Kings Cross 15 ⊖26 a																								
York 8 26 d		19 44				20 35			20 45		21 14													
Doncaster 7 d	20 03			20 42		21 02	21 07						21 30	21 42	21 48					22 13			23 22	
Conisbrough d	20 10			20 50			21 14						21 37							22 20			23 29	
Mexborough d	20 14			20 54			21 17						21 41							22 24			23 33	
Swinton (S.Yorks) d	20 17		20 35	20 57			21 20					21 35	21 44							22 29		22 35	23 36	23 56
Rotherham Central d	20 28		20 45	21 03			21 28					21 44	21 55							22 38		22 46	23 45	00 03
Meadowhall d	20 33		20 51	21 09			21 34					21 52	22 03	21 59	22 07					22 44		22 53	23 54	00 09
Sheffield 7 a	20 41	20 51	21 02	21 19		21 26	21 46		21 51			22 04	22 11	22 08	22 21					22 54		23 02	00 04	00 23
d														22 11										
Stockport 78 a														22 53										
Manchester Piccadilly 10 a								22 33			22 33			23 02				23 37						
Manchester Airport 85 ✈ a								22 57			22 57			23 26										

A To Worksop
B From Edinburgh to Bristol Temple Meads
C From Leeds
D From Newcastle to Birmingham New Street
E From Bridlington
F From Glasgow Central to Birmingham New Street
G To Leeds
H To Lincoln

Table 29

Saturdays

Hull and Cleethorpes - Doncaster - Meadowhall, Sheffield, Manchester and Manchester Airport, Cleethorpes - Barton-on-Humber

Network Diagram - see first Page of Table 18

		NT	NT	TP	TP	TP	TP	TP	NT	NT	TP	NT	NT	XC	NT	NT	XC	TP	TP	NT	TP	XC	NT
				◇1	◇1	◇1	◇1	◇1			◇1			◇1			◇1	◇1	◇1		◇1	◇1	
			A											B	bus		C		D			E	A
Hull	d	22p20								05 20									06 00	06 06	06 37		
Hessle	d	22p27																		06 13			
Ferriby	d	22p32																		06 18			
Brough	d	22p37								05 32									06 12	06 23	06 49		
Broomfleet	d																						
Gilberdyke	d																		06 19	06 31			
Eastrington	d																						
Howden	d																		06 26				
Wressle	d																						
Selby	a																		06 36		07 08		
	d												06 18						06 36		07 08		
York 8 33	a																						
Saltmarshe	d																			06 37			
Goole	d	22p51								05 46										06 42			
Thorne North	d	23p00								05 55										06 50			
Cleethorpes	d										05 18	06 00											
New Clee	d																						
Grimsby Docks	d																						
Grimsby Town	a										05 25	06 08											
	d										05 26	06 08											
Great Coates	d																						
Healing	d											06 15											
Stallingborough	d											06 18											
Habrough	d										05 36	06 24											
Ulceby	d											06 28											
Thornton Abbey	d																						
Goxhill	d											06 35											
New Holland	d											06 40											
Barrow Haven	d											06 43											
Barton-on-Humber	a											06 48											
Barton-on-Humber	d														06 53								
Hull Paragon Interchange	a														07 20								
Barnetby	d										05 45												
Scunthorpe	a										06 00												
	d										06 00												
Althorpe	d										06 05												
Crowle	d										06 11												
Thorne South	d										06 20												
Hatfield & Stainforth	d	23p06								06 01	06 25									06 56			
Kirk Sandall	d	23p10								06 06										07 01			
Adwick 31	d																						
Bentley (S.Yorks) 31	d																						
Doncaster 7 31	a	23p21								06 15	06 38		06 39							07 11			
London Kings Cross 15 ⊖26	a																						
York 8 26	d			02 40	03 52	05 26		05 57									06 17	06 28				06 40	
Doncaster 7	d	23p22					05 40		06 00	06 23	06 40			06 47		07 02							
Conisbrough	d	23p29							06 07	06 30						07 09							
Mexborough	d	23p33							06 11	06 34						07 13							
Swinton (S.Yorks)	d	23p36	23p56						06 14	06 37						07 16							07 30
Rotherham Central	d	23p45	00 03						06 25	06 49						07 26							07 38
Meadowhall	d	23p54	00 09				05 58		06 30	06 52	06 58					07 32							07 47
Sheffield 7	a	00 04	00 23				06 08		06 38	07 05	07 06			07 15		07 40	07 51					07 51	07 54
	d						06 11				07 09												
Stockport 78	a						06 53				07 53												
Manchester Piccadilly 10	a			04 52	06 02	06 50	07 02	07 19			08 02							07 51	08 05		08 36		
Manchester Airport 85	a			05 10	06 24	07 12	07 29	07 42			08 26							08 12					

A From Leeds
B From Leeds to Southampton Central
C from 15 September. To Plymouth
D To Liverpool Lime Street
E until 8 September. To Plymouth

Table 29

Saturdays

Hull and Cleethorpes - Doncaster - Meadowhall, Sheffield, Manchester and Manchester Airport, Cleethorpes - Barton-on-Humber

Network Diagram - see first Page of Table 18

		NT	NT	TP	NT	EM	GR	NT	NT	NT	XC	NT	NT	TP	XC	NT
				◇1			1				◇1			◇1	◇1	
		A	A		B	C			bus	D	E	F	G		H	I
Hull	d	06 40					06 50			07 07				07 37		
Hessle	d	06 47														
Ferriby	d	06 52														
Brough	d	06 57					07 02			07 19				07 49		
Broomfleet	d															
Gilberdyke	d	07 04								07 26						
Eastrington	d									07 31						
Howden	d									07 35				08 01		
Wressle	d									07 40						
Selby	a						07 23			07 48				08 10		
	d						07 24			07 48				08 11		
York 8 33	a									08 21						
Saltmarshe	d	07 10														
Goole	d	07 15														
Thorne North	d	07 24														
Cleethorpes	d			06 18				07 00								
New Clee	d															
Grimsby Docks	d							07 05								
Grimsby Town	a			06 25				07 08								
	d			06 26		06 50		07 08								
Great Coates	d							07 12								
Healing	d							07 15								
Stallingborough	d							07 18								
Habrough	d			06 36		07 00		07 24								
Ulceby	d							07 28								
Thornton Abbey	d							07 32								
Goxhill	d							07 35								
New Holland	d							07 40								
Barrow Haven	d							07 43								
Barton-on-Humber	a							07 48								
Barton-on-Humber	d								08 10							
Hull Paragon Interchange	a								08 37							
Barnetby	d			06 45		07a09										
Scunthorpe	a			07 00												
	d			07 00									07 30			
Althorpe	d												07 35			
Crowle	d												07 42			
Thorne South	d												07 51			
Hatfield & Stainforth	d	07 30											07 56			
Kirk Sandall	d	07 34											08 01			
Adwick 31	d		07 23													
Bentley (S.Yorks) 31	d		07 27									←				
Doncaster 7 31	a	07 46	07 31	07 33			07 43					07 46	08 12			
London Kings Cross 15 ⊖26	a	→					09 36									
York 8 26	d				←						07 24				07 44	
Doncaster 7	d		07 39	07 35	07 39						07 52	07 48				
Conisbrough	d		→		07 46							07 55				
Mexborough	d				07 50							07 59				
Swinton (S.Yorks)	d				07 53							08 02				08 35
Rotherham Central	d				08 01							08 14				08 44
Meadowhall	d			07 53	08 07							08 25				08 51
Sheffield 7	a			08 00	08 18						08 18	08 32			08 51	08 59
	d			08 05												
Stockport 78	a			08 53												
Manchester Piccadilly 10	a			09 02										09 36		
Manchester Airport 85	a			09 26												

A To Sheffield
B From Adwick
C To Newark North Gate
D From Beverley to Hull
E From Newcastle to Reading
F From Hull
G To Adwick
H From Newcastle to Plymouth
I From Leeds

Hull and Cleethorpes - Doncaster - Meadowhall, Sheffield, Manchester and Manchester Airport, Cleethorpes - Barton-on-Humber

Network Diagram - see first Page of Table 18

Station		NT		TP	NT	NT	XC	NT	NT	HT	XC	NT	NT	NT	TP	TP	TP	NT	NT	NT	NT	EM		XC	NT
				◇1 🍴			◇1 🍴			◇1 ☒	◇1 🍴				◇1 🍴	◇1 🍴	◇1 🍴			🚌				◇1 🍴	
							A	B	C		D	E		F		E		B			G	H		I	C
Hull	d					07 40		08 03		08 25				08 29	08 40			08 56			09 02				
Hessle	d					07 47								08 36											
Ferriby	d					07 52								08 41											
Brough	d					07 57		08 15		08 37				08 46	08 52			09 08			09 14				
Broomfleet	d					08 02																			
Gilberdyke	d					08 07								08 53							09 21				
Eastrington	d																								
Howden	d									08 49											09 28				
Wressle	d																								
Selby	a									08 59					09 11						09 38				
	d									09 00					09 11						09 38				
York 8	33 a																				10 14				
Saltmarshe	d					08 12																			
Goole	d					08 17		08 29						09 02				09 23							
Thorne North	d					08 26								09 10											
Cleethorpes	d			07 26													08 26		09 00						
New Clee	d																		09x03						
Grimsby Docks	d																		09 05						
Grimsby Town	a			07 33													08 33		09 08						
	d			07 34													08 34		09 08			09 20			
Great Coates	d																		09 12						
Healing	d																		09 15						
Stallingborough	d																		09 18						
Habrough	d			07 44													08 44		09 24			09 30			
Ulceby	d																		09 28						
Thornton Abbey	d																		09 32						
Goxhill	d																		09 35						
New Holland	d																		09 40						
Barrow Haven	d																		09 43						
Barton-on-Humber	a																		09 48						
Barton-on-Humber	d																			10 00					
Hull Paragon Interchange	a																			10 27					
Barnetby	d			07 53													08 53					09a39			
Scunthorpe	a			08 08													09 08								
	d			08 08					08 19								09 08								09 19
Althorpe	d								08 24																09 24
Crowle	d								08 30																09 30
Thorne South	d								08 39																09 39
Hatfield & Stainforth	d					08 33			08 46					09 17											09 44
Kirk Sandall	d					08 37			08 50					09 21											09 49
Adwick	31 d	08 15			08 33								09 15												
Bentley (S.Yorks)	31 d	08 19			08 37								09 19												
Doncaster 7	31 a	08 23		08 38	08 42	08 50		08 58	09 02	09 23			09 24	09 32			09 38	09 48							10 01
London Kings Cross 15 ⊖	26 a									11 09															
York 8	26 d						08 34				08 44					09 25								09 35	
Doncaster 7	d	08 26		08 41			08 58	09 01	09 03				09 26				09 42	09 49						09 58	10 04
Conisbrough	d	08 33							09 11				09 33												10 11
Mexborough	d	08 37							09 15				09 37												10 15
Swinton (S.Yorks)	d	08 43							09 18			09 35	09 42												10 18
Rotherham Central	d	08 50							09 27			09 46	09 51												10 27
Meadowhall	d	08 56		09 01				09 24	09 33			09 50	09 55				10 01	10 08							10 33
Sheffield 7	a	09 05		09 08			09 20	09 33	09 41		09 52	10 00	10 05				10 08	10 19						10 20	10 41
	d			09 11													10 11								
Stockport	78 a			09 53													10 53								
Manchester Piccadilly 10	a			10 02											10 36	10 49	11 02								
Manchester Airport	85 ✈ a			10 26												11 12	11 26								

A From Newcastle to Southampton Central
B From Bridlington
C To Lincoln
D From Edinburgh to Plymouth
E From Leeds
F From Scarborough
G To Hull
H To Newark North Gate
I From Edinburgh to Reading

Hull and Cleethorpes - Doncaster - Meadowhall, Sheffield, Manchester and Manchester Airport, Cleethorpes - Barton-on-Humber

Network Diagram - see first Page of Table 18

Station		XC	NT	NT	NT	TP	TP	NT		NT	XC	NT	XC	NT	NT	NT	HT	TP	TP	NT	NT	NT	NT	XC	NT
		◇1 🍴				◇1	◇1 🍴				◇1 🍴		◇1 🍴				◇1 ☒	◇1	◇1 🍴		🚌			◇1 🍴	
		A	B		C			D		E	F	G	H	B								D	E	I	J
Hull	d				09 25	09 40		09 56		10 08						10 18	10 30	10 40				10 57	11 05		
Hessle	d				09 32											10 25									
Ferriby	d				09 37											10 30									
Brough	d				09 42	09 52		10 08		10 20						10 35	10 42	10 52				11 09	11 17		
Broomfleet	d																								
Gilberdyke	d				09 49					10 27						10 43									
Eastrington	d																								
Howden	d									10 34							10 54						11 29		
Wressle	d																								
Selby	a					10 11				10 47							11 04	11 11					11 40		
	d					10 11				10 47							11 05	11 11					11 40		
York 8	33 a									11 18													12 08		
Saltmarshe	d															10 49									
Goole	d				09 58			10 22								10 58						11 23			
Thorne North	d				10 06											11 06									
Cleethorpes	d						09 26												10 26	10 55					
New Clee	d																			10x58					
Grimsby Docks	d																			11 00					
Grimsby Town	a						09 33												10 33	11 03					
	d						09 34												10 34	11 03					
Great Coates	d																			11 07					
Healing	d																			11 10					
Stallingborough	d																			11 13					
Habrough	d																		10 44	11 19					
Ulceby	d																			11 23					
Thornton Abbey	d																			11 27					
Goxhill	d																			11 30					
New Holland	d																			11 35					
Barrow Haven	d																			11 38					
Barton-on-Humber	a																			11 43					
Barton-on-Humber	d																				12 00				
Hull Paragon Interchange	a																				12 27				
Barnetby	d						09 53												10 53						
Scunthorpe	a						10 08												11 08						
	d						10 08					10 19							11 08						
Althorpe	d											10 24													
Crowle	d											10 30													
Thorne South	d											10 39													
Hatfield & Stainforth	d				10 12							10 44				11 11									
Kirk Sandall	d				10 17							10 49				11 17									
Adwick	31 d			10 15											11 15										
Bentley (S.Yorks)	31 d			10 19											11 19										
Doncaster 7	31 a			10 24	10 27		10 38	10 47				11 01			11 24	11 27	11 24		11 38			11 47			
London Kings Cross 15 ⊖	26 a																13 09								
York 8	26 d	09 46									10 34		10 45											11 34	11 05
Doncaster 7	d			10 26			10 42	10 49			10 58	11 04			11 26				11 42			11 49		11 58	
Conisbrough	d			10 33								11 11			11 33										
Mexborough	d			10 37								11 15			11 37										
Swinton (S.Yorks)	d		10 35	10 43								11 18		11 35	11 43										12 10
Rotherham Central	d		10 44	10 52								11 27		11 44	11 52										12 19
Meadowhall	d		10 50	10 58			11 01	11 08				11 33		11 50	11 58				12 01			12 08			12 24
Sheffield 7	a	10 51	11 00	11 06			11 08	11 20			11 20	11 41	11 51	12 00	12 05				12 08			12 20		12 20	12 36
	d						11 11												12 11						
Stockport	78 a						11 53												12 53						
Manchester Piccadilly 10	a					11 36	12 02											12 36	13 02						
Manchester Airport	85 ✈ a						12 26												13 26						

A From Glasgow Central to Paignton
B From Leeds
C From Beverley
D From Bridlington
E To Hull
F From Newcastle to Southampton Central
G To Lincoln
H From Dundee to Plymouth
I From Newcastle to Reading
J From Sheffield

Table 29

Saturdays

Hull and Cleethorpes - Doncaster - Meadowhall, Sheffield, Manchester and Manchester Airport, Cleethorpes - Barton-on-Humber

Network Diagram - see first Page of Table 18

		NT	XC	NT	NT	NT	NT	EM	TP	TP	NT	NT	XC	NT	XC	NT	NT	NT	TP	TP	NT	NT	NT
			◇1						◇1	◇1			◇1		◇1				◇1	◇1			
		A	B	C				D			E	F	G	A	H	C							I
			🍴						🍴	🍴			🍴		🍴				🍴	🍴		🚌	
Hull	d						11 23		11 40		11 55	12 03						12 18	12 40				12 57
Hessle	d						11 30											12 25					
Ferriby	d						11 35											12 30					
Brough	d						11 40		11 52		12 07	12 15						12 35	12 52				13 09
Broomfleet	d						11 45																
Gilberdyke	d						11 50											12 42					
Eastrington	d																						
Howden	d											12 27											
Wressle	d																						
Selby	a								12 11			12 37							13 11				
	d								12 11			12 38							13 11				
York 8 33	a											13 04											
Saltmarshe	d																	12 48					
Goole	d						11 58				12 22							12 58					13 23
Thorne North	d						12 07											13 06					
Cleethorpes	d					11 10				11 26										12 26	12 55		
New Clee	d																				12x58		
Grimsby Docks	d																				13 00		
Grimsby Town	a					11 16				11 33										12 33	13 03		
	d					11 17		11 28		11 34										12 34	13 03		
Great Coates	d																				13 07		
Healing	d																				13 10		
Stallingborough	d																				13 13		
Habrough	d					11 28		11 38													13 19		
Ulceby	d																				13 23		
Thornton Abbey	d																				13 27		
Goxhill	d																				13 30		
New Holland	d																				13 35		
Barrow Haven	d																				13 38		
Barton-on-Humber	a																				13 43		
Barton-on-Humber	d																					14 00	
Hull Paragon Interchange	a																					14 27	
Barnetby	d					11 38		11a47		11 53										12 53			
Scunthorpe	a									12 08										13 08			
	d	11 18								12 08				12 18						13 08			
Althorpe	d	11 23												12 23									
Crowle	d	11 29												12 29									
Thorne South	d	11 38												12 38									
Hatfield & Stainforth	d	11 43					12 13							12 43				13 12					
Kirk Sandall	d	11 48					12 17							12 48				13 17					
Adwick 31	d				12 14												13 15						
Bentley (S.Yorks) 31	d				12 18												13 19						
Doncaster 7 31	a	11 58			12 24		12 28			12 38	12 47			12 59			13 24	13 27		13 38			13 46
London Kings Cross 15 ⊖26	a																						
York 8 26	d		11 45										12 34		12 45								
Doncaster 7	d	12 03			12 26					12 42	12 48		12 58	13 04			13 24			13 42			13 48
Conisbrough	d	12 11			12 33									13 11			13 32						
Mexborough	d	12 15			12 37									13 15			13 36						
Swinton (S.Yorks)	d	12 18		12 35	12 43									13 18		13 35	13 42						
Rotherham Central	d	12 27		12 44	12 52									13 27		13 44	13 52						
Meadowhall ⇌	d	12 33		12 50	12 58					13 01	13 08			13 33		13 50	13 58			14 01			14 08
Sheffield 7 ⇌	a	12 41	12 51	13 00	13 05	13 23				13 08	13 20		13 20	13 41	13 51	14 00	14 05			14 08			14 20
	d									13 11										14 11			
Stockport 78	a									13 53										14 53			
Manchester Piccadilly 10 ⇌	a								13 36	14 02									14 36	15 02			
Manchester Airport 85 ✈	a									14 26										15 26			

A To Lincoln
B From Glasgow Central to Plymouth
C From Leeds
D To Newark North Gate
E From Bridlington
F To Hull
G From Newcastle to Southampton Central
H From Glasgow Central to Penzance
I From Scarborough

Table 29

Saturdays

Hull and Cleethorpes - Doncaster - Meadowhall, Sheffield, Manchester and Manchester Airport, Cleethorpes - Barton-on-Humber

Network Diagram - see first Page of Table 18

		NT	XC	NT	XC	NT	NT	NT	HT	TP	TP	EM	NT	NT	XC	NT	XC	NT	NT	NT	TP	TP	NT
			◇1		◇1				◇1	◇1	◇1				◇1		◇1				◇1	◇1	
		A	B	C	D	E						F	G	A	H	C	I	E					J
			🍴		🍴				☒		🍴				🍴		🍴					🍴	
Hull	d	13 12						13 18	13 30	13 40			13 57	14 19						14 25	14 40		14 56
Hessle	d							13 25												14 32			
Ferriby	d							13 30												14 37			
Brough	d	13 24						13 35	13 42	13 52			14 09	14 31						14 42	14 52		15 08
Broomfleet	d																						
Gilberdyke	d	13 32						13 43												14 49			
Eastrington	d	13 36																					
Howden	d	13 42							13 56					14 43									
Wressle	d	13 47																					
Selby	a	13 54							14 05	14 11				14 53							15 11		
	d	13 55							14 06	14 11				14 53							15 11		
York 8 33	a	14 27												15 25									
Saltmarshe	d																						
Goole	d							13 58					14 23							14 58			15 23
Thorne North	d							14 07												15 06			
Cleethorpes	d										13 26											14 26	
New Clee	d																						
Grimsby Docks	d																						
Grimsby Town	a										13 33											14 33	
	d										13 34	13 49										14 34	
Great Coates	d																						
Healing	d																						
Stallingborough	d																						
Habrough	d											13 59										14 44	
Ulceby	d																						
Thornton Abbey	d																						
Goxhill	d																						
New Holland	d																						
Barrow Haven	d																						
Barton-on-Humber	a																						
Barton-on-Humber	d																						
Hull Paragon Interchange	a																						
Barnetby	d										13 53	14a08										14 53	
Scunthorpe	a										14 08											15 08	
	d			13 19							14 08					14 19						15 08	
Althorpe	d			13 24												14 24							
Crowle	d			13 30												14 30							
Thorne South	d			13 39												14 39							
Hatfield & Stainforth	d			13 44				14 13								14 44				15 12			
Kirk Sandall	d			13 49				14 17								14 49				15 17			
Adwick 31	d						14 15												15 15				
Bentley (S.Yorks) 31	d						14 19												15 19				
Doncaster 7 31	a			13 57			14 24	14 30	14 25		14 38		14 47			14 59			15 24	15 27		15 38	15 47
London Kings Cross 15 ⊖26	a								16 10														
York 8 26	d		13 34		13 44										14 34		14 44						
Doncaster 7	d		13 58	14 01			14 26				14 42		14 48		14 58	15 04			15 26			15 42	15 49
Conisbrough	d			14 11			14 33									15 11			15 33				
Mexborough	d			14 15			14 37									15 15			15 37				
Swinton (S.Yorks)	d			14 18		14 35	14 43									15 18		15 35	15 42				
Rotherham Central	d			14 27		14 44	14 52									15 27		15 44	15 50				
Meadowhall ⇌	d			14 33		14 50	14 58				15 01		15 07			15 33		15 50	15 57			16 01	16 07
Sheffield 7 ⇌	a		14 20	14 40	14 51	15 00	15 05				15 08		15 20		15 20	15 41	15 51	16 00	16 05			16 08	16 22
	d										15 11											16 11	
Stockport 78	a										15 53											16 53	
Manchester Piccadilly 10 ⇌	a									15 36	16 02										16 36	17 02	
Manchester Airport 85 ✈	a										16 26											17 32	

A To Hull
B From Newcastle to Reading
C To Lincoln
D From Aberdeen to Penzance
E From Leeds
F To Newark North Gate
G From Bridlington
H From Newcastle to Southampton Central
I From Glasgow Central to Plymouth
J From Scarborough

Hull and Cleethorpes - Doncaster - Meadowhall, Sheffield, Manchester and Manchester Airport, Cleethorpes - Barton-on-Humber

Network Diagram - see first Page of Table 18

		NT	NT	NT	XC	NT	NT	NT	HT	TP	XC	NT	NT	NT	TP	NT	EM	XC	NT	NT	NT	TP	XC	NT
			🚌		◇1 A ⊤		B		◇1 ⊠	◇1 ⊤	◇1 C ⊤	D	E		◇1 ⊤	F	G	◇1 A ⊤	H	B		◇1	◇1 I ⊤	D
Hull	d			15 02				15 18	15 30	15 40						15 57			16 10		16 27	16 40		
Hessle	d							15 25													16 34			
Ferriby	d							15 30													16 39			
Brough	d			15 14				15 35	15 42	15 52						16 09			16 22		16 44	16 52		
Broomfleet	d																				16 49			
Gilberdyke	d							15 42											16 29		16 54			
Eastrington	d																							
Howden	d			15 26					15 54										16 36					
Wressle	d																							
Selby	a			15 36					16 04	16 11									16 46			17 11		
	d			15 38					16 05	16 11									16 47			17 11		
York 8 33	a			16 06															17 13					
Saltmarshe	d																				16 59			
Goole	d							15 58								16 23					17 04			
Thorne North	d							16 06													17 13			
Cleethorpes	d	15 00												15 20	15 26									
New Clee	d	15x03																						
Grimsby Docks	d	15 05																						
Grimsby Town	a	15 08												15 26	15 33									
	d	15 08												15 27	15 34		16 00							
Great Coates	d	15 12																						
Healing	d	15 15																						
Stallingborough	d	15 18																						
Habrough	d	15 24												15 37			16 09							
Ulceby	d	15 28																						
Thornton Abbey	d	15 32																						
Goxhill	d	15 35																						
New Holland	d	15 40																						
Barrow Haven	d	15 43																						
Barton-on-Humber	a	15 48																						
Barton-on-Humber	d		16 00																					
Hull Paragon Interchange	a		16 27																					
Barnetby	d													15 48	15 53		16a18							
Scunthorpe	a														16 08									
	d						15 18								16 08					16 19				
Althorpe	d						15 23													16 24				
Crowle	d						15 29													16 30				
Thorne South	d						15 38													16 39				
Hatfield & Stainforth	d						15 43	16 12												16 44	17 19			
Kirk Sandall	d						15 48	16 17												16 49	17 23			
Adwick 31	d												16 15											
Bentley (S.Yorks) 31	d												16 18											
Doncaster 7 31	a						15 58	16 27	16 23				16 25		16 38	16 47				16 57	17 35			
London Kings Cross 15 ⊖26	a								18 08															
York 8 26	d				15 34	15 01					15 45							16 06					16 44	
Doncaster 7	d				15 58		16 01						16 26		16 42	16 48				17 00				
Conisbrough	d						16 11						16 33							17 08				
Mexborough	d						16 15						16 37							17 12				
Swinton (S.Yorks)	d					16 01	16 18					16 35	16 41							17 16				17 35
Rotherham Central	d					16 10	16 27					16 44	16 50							17 27				17 44
Meadowhall 🚋	d					16 18	16 33					16 50	16 55		17 01	17 08				17 33				17 50
Sheffield 7 🚋	a				16 20	16 27	16 41				16 51	17 00	17 05	17 23	17 08	17 19		17 20		17 41			17 51	18 00
	d														17 11									
Stockport 78	a														17 53									
Manchester Piccadilly 10 🚋	a														18 02									
Manchester Airport 85 ✈	a									17 36					18 26							18 37		

A From Newcastle to Reading
B To Lincoln
C From Edinburgh to Plymouth
D From Leeds
E To Retford
F From Bridlington
G To Newark North Gate
H To Hull
I From Glasgow Central to Plymouth

Table 29 Saturdays

Hull and Cleethorpes - Doncaster - Meadowhall, Sheffield, Manchester and Manchester Airport, Cleethorpes - Barton-on-Humber

Network Diagram - see first Page of Table 18

		NT	TP	NT	NT	NT	NT	TP	NT	XC	NT	EM	XC	NT	NT	NT	TP	EM	NT	NT	NT	TP	XC
			◇1 ⊤	A	B		🚌	◇1 C	C	◇1 D ⊤	E	◇1 F ⊤	◇1 G ⊤	H	I		◇1 ⊤	J	K	L	M	◇1	◇1 N ⊤
Hull	d			16 54	16 54			17 01	17 18										17 42	17 52	17 52	17 58	
Hessle	d								17 25										17 49				
Ferriby	d								17 30										17 54				
Brough	d			17 06	17 06			17 13	17 35										17 59	18 04	18 04	18 10	
Broomfleet	d								17 40														
Gilberdyke	d			17 13	17 13				17 45										18 06				
Eastrington	d								17 49														
Howden	d								17 54														
Wressle	d								17 59														
Selby	a							17 32	18 06											18 26	18 26	18 29	
	d								18 07											18 26	18 26	18 29	
York 8 33	a								18 33														
Saltmarshe	d																		18 12				
Goole	d			17 22	17 22														18 19				
Thorne North	d																		18 28				
Cleethorpes	d		16 26			17 00											17 26						
New Clee	d																						
Grimsby Docks	d					17 05																	
Grimsby Town	a		16 33			17 08											17 33						
	d		16 34			17 09											17 34	18 26					
Great Coates	d					17 13																	
Healing	d					17 16																	
Stallingborough	d					17 19																	
Habrough	d					17 25											17 44	18 36					
Ulceby	d					17 28																	
Thornton Abbey	d					17 33																	
Goxhill	d					17 36																	
New Holland	d					17 40																	
Barrow Haven	d					17 43																	
Barton-on-Humber	a					17 49																	
Barton-on-Humber	d						18 00																
Hull Paragon Interchange	a						18 27																
Barnetby	d		16 53														17 53	18a44					
Scunthorpe	a		17 08														18 08						
	d		17 08								17 18						18 08						
Althorpe	d										17 23												
Crowle	d										17 29												
Thorne South	d										17 38												
Hatfield & Stainforth	d										17 43								18 34				
Kirk Sandall	d										17 48								18 39				
Adwick 31	d													18 16									
Bentley (S.Yorks) 31	d													18 20									
Doncaster 7 31	a		17 38	17 48	17 48						17 58			18 27			18 38		18 50	18 47	18 47		
London Kings Cross 15 ⊖26	a																		→				
York 8 26	d									17 34		17 50	17 44										18 34
Doncaster 7	d	17 24	17 42	17 49	17 49					17 58	18 02	18 18				18 26	18 42			18 48	18 48		18 58
Conisbrough	d	17 31									18 09					18 33							
Mexborough	d	17 35									18 13					18 37							
Swinton (S.Yorks)	d	17 42									18 16				18 35	18 42							
Rotherham Central	d	17 50									18 27				18 44	18 49							
Meadowhall 🚋	d	17 57	18 01	18 08	18 08						18 33				18 50	18 56	19 01			19 08	19 08		
Sheffield 7 🚋	a	18 05	18 08	18 19	18 21					18 20	18 41	18 44	18 51		19 00	19 06	19 08			19 17	19 19		19 21
	d		18 11														19 11						
Stockport 78	a		18 53														19 53						
Manchester Piccadilly 10 🚋	a		19 02														20 02						
Manchester Airport 85 ✈	a		19 28														20 36					19 57	

A until 29 September. From Bridlington
B from 6 October. From Bridlington
C To Leeds
D From Newcastle to Reading
E To Lincoln
F From Scarborough to St Pancras International
G From Edinburgh to Plymouth
H To Scunthorpe
I From Leeds
J To Newark North Gate
K To Sheffield
L from 6 October. From Scarborough
M until 29 September. From Scarborough
N From Newcastle to Guildford

Hull and Cleethorpes - Doncaster - Meadowhall, Sheffield, Manchester and Manchester Airport, Cleethorpes - Barton-on-Humber

Network Diagram - see first Page of Table 18

		NT	NT	HT	NT	XC	NT	NT	TP	NT	TP	XC	NT	NT	NT	NT	NT	XC		TP	NT	TP	EM	NT	XC
				◇1		◇1			◇1		◇1	◇1						◇1		◇1		◇1			◇1
		A		⊠	B	C ⌶	D				E	F ⌶			🚌	G		H		E	D		I		F
Hull	d			18 30	18 32					18 53	18 59						19 25			19 56					
Hessle	d				18 39												19 32								
Ferriby	d				18 44												19 37								
Brough	d			18 43	18 49					19 05	19 11						19 42			20 08					
Broomfleet	d																								
Gilberdyke	d				18 56												19 50								
Eastrington	d																								
Howden	d			18 55																					
Wressle	d																								
Selby	a			19 04							19 29									20 26					
	d			19 05																					
York 8 33	a																								
Saltmarshe	d																								
Goole	d				19 05					19 19							19 58								
Thorne North	d				19 14												20 07								
Cleethorpes	d								18 26				18 36	19 00								19 26			
New Clee	d																								
Grimsby Docks	d													19 05								19 33			
Grimsby Town	a								18 33				18 42	19 08								19 34	19 45		
	d								18 34				18 43	19 09											
Great Coates	d													19 13											
Healing	d													19 16											
Stallingborough	d													19 19											
Habrough	d												18 53	19 25								19 44	19 54		
Ulceby	d													19 28											
Thornton Abbey	d													19 33											
Goxhill	d													19 36											
New Holland	d													19 40											
Barrow Haven	d													19 43											
Barton-on-Humber	a													19 49											
Barton-on-Humber	d														19 53										
Hull Paragon Interchange	a														20 20										
Barnetby	d								18 53				19 02									19 53	20a03		
Scunthorpe	a								19 08													20 08			
	d		18 19						19 08							19 19						20 08		20 21	
Althorpe	d		18 24													19 24								20 26	
Crowle	d		18 30													19 30								20 32	
Thorne South	d		18 39													19 39								20 41	
Hatfield & Stainforth	d		18 46		19 21											19 44	20 16							20 46	
Kirk Sandall	d		18 50		19 25											19 49	20 20							20 51	
Adwick 31	d																								
Bentley (S.Yorks) 31	d	←																							
Doncaster 7 31	a	18 50	19 01	19 26	19 36				19 38	19 47						19 59	20 31					20 40		21 03	
London Kings Cross 15 ⊖26	a			21 09																					
York 8 26	d					18 44						19 34						19 44							20 34
Doncaster 7	d	19 01						19 28	19 42	19 50		19 58				20 03						20 42			21 00
Conisbrough	d	19 08						19 35								20 10						20 50			
Mexborough	d	19 12						19 39								20 14						20 54			
Swinton (S.Yorks)	d	19 15					19 35	19 43								20 17					20 35	20 57			
Rotherham Central	d	19 23					19 44	19 51								20 28					20 45	21 03			
Meadowhall 🚋	d	19 28					19 51	19 57	20 01	20 08						20 33					20 51	21 09			
Sheffield 7 🚋	a	19 37				19 51	20 00	20 06	20 08	20 18		20 20	20 34			20 41		20 52			21 00	21 19			21 20
	d								20 11																
Stockport 78	a								20 53																
Manchester Piccadilly 10 🚋	a								21 02																
Manchester Airport 85 ✈	a								21 36																

A From Hull
B From Bridlington
C From Glasgow Central to Bristol Temple Meads
D From Leeds
E To Leeds
F From Newcastle to Birmingham New Street
G To Worksop
H From Edinburgh to Birmingham New Street
I To Lincoln

Table 29

Saturdays

Hull and Cleethorpes - Doncaster - Meadowhall, Sheffield, Manchester and Manchester Airport, Cleethorpes - Barton-on-Humber

Network Diagram - see first Page of Table 18

		NT	XC	NT		NT	TP	NT	NT	NT	NT	TP	NT	NT	NT		NT	NT	NT
			◇1				◇1					◇1							
		A	B	C					D		🚌						C	C	A
Hull	d	20 03						20 55	21 01			21 33							22 17
Hessle	d	20 10																	22 24
Ferriby	d	20 15																	22 29
Brough	d	20 20						21 07	21 13			21 45							22 34
Broomfleet	d																		
Gilberdyke	d	20 27										21 52							
Eastrington	d																		
Howden	d								21 25										
Wressle	d																		
Selby	a								21 35			22 07							
	d								21 35			22 07							
York 8 33	a								21 57										
Saltmarshe	d																		
Goole	d	20 36						21 21					21 35						22 48
Thorne North	d	20 44											21 44						22 57
Cleethorpes	d						20 26			21 03									
New Clee	d																		
Grimsby Docks	d									21 08									
Grimsby Town	a						20 33			21 11									
	d						20 34			21 11									
Great Coates	d									21 15									
Healing	d									21 18									
Stallingborough	d									21 21									
Habrough	d									21 27									
Ulceby	d									21 31									
Thornton Abbey	d									21 35									
Goxhill	d									21 38									
New Holland	d									21 43									
Barrow Haven	d									21 46									
Barton-on-Humber	a									21 51									
Barton-on-Humber	d										21 56								
Hull Paragon Interchange	a										22 23								
Barnetby	d						20 53												
Scunthorpe	a						21 08												
	d						21 08							21 31	22 21				
Althorpe	d													21 36	22 26				
Crowle	d													21 42	22 32				
Thorne South	d													21 51	22 41				
Hatfield & Stainforth	d	20 51											21 50	21 56	22 46				23 03
Kirk Sandall	d	20 56											21 54	22 01	22 51				23 07
Adwick 31	d																		
Bentley (S.Yorks) 31	d																		
Doncaster 7 31	a	21 05					21 40	21 45					22 08	22 11	23 02				23 18
London Kings Cross 15 ⊖26	a																		
York 8 26	d		20 45																
Doncaster 7	d	21 07				21 30	21 42	21 47						22 13					23 19
Conisbrough	d	21 14				21 37								22 20					23 26
Mexborough	d	21 18				21 41								22 24					23 30
Swinton (S.Yorks)	d	21 21		21 34		21 44								22 29			22 37	23 30	23 33
Rotherham Central	d	21 28		21 42		21 55								22 37			22 46	23 38	23 43
Meadowhall 🚋	d	21 35		21 50		22 03	21 59	22 12						22 43			22 53	23 44	23 49
Sheffield 7 🚋	a	21 46	21 51	22 02		22 13	22 10	22 22						22 54			23 03	23 58	23 59
	d																		
Stockport 78	a																		
Manchester Piccadilly 10 🚋	a											23 37							
Manchester Airport 85 ✈	a																		

A From Bridlington
B From Glasgow Central to Birmingham New Street
C From Leeds
D To Hull

Table 27

Sundays until 24 June

Hull and Cleethorpes - Doncaster - Meadowhall, Sheffield, Manchester and Manchester Airport, Cleethorpes - Barton-on-Humber

Network Diagram - see first Page of Table 18

	TP	TP	NT	NT	XC	NT	NT	NT	TP	NT	XC	HT	NT	TP	NT	NT	NT	XC	TP	NT	TP	NT
	◇1	◇1			◇1 A	B		C	◇1 D		◇1 E	◇1		◇1		Bus		◇1 F	◇1	G	◇1 H	B
Hull d							08 40	08 54	09 00			09 30	09 33							10 50	10 58	
Hessle d													09 40									
Ferriby d													09 45									
Brough d							08 52	09 06	09 12			09 42	09 50							11 02	11 10	
Broomfleet d																						
Gilberdyke d							08 59						09 57							11 09		
Eastrington d																						
Howden d								09 18				09 54										
Wressle d																						
Selby a								09 27	09 32			10 04									11 28	
d								09 28				10 05										
York 8 33 a								09 52														
Saltmarshe d																						
Goole d							09 09			09 43			10 06							11 18		
Thorne North d										09 51			10 14							11 26		
Cleethorpes d														09 26	09 58				10 26			
New Clee d															10 01							
Grimsby Docks d															10 04							
Grimsby Town a														09 33	10 06				10 33			
d														09 34	10 07				10 34			
Great Coates d															10 11							
Healing d															10 14							
Stallingborough d															10 15							
Habrough d														09 44	10 21				10 44			
Ulceby d															10 25							
Thornton Abbey d															10 30							
Goxhill d															10 33							
New Holland d															10 38							
Barrow Haven d															10 41							
Barton-on-Humber a															10 48							
Barton-on-Humber d																10 55						
Hull Paragon Interchange a																11 19						
Barnetby d														09 53					10 53			
Scunthorpe a														10 08					11 08			
d														10 08					11 08			
Althorpe d																						
Crowle d																						
Thorne South d																						
Hatfield & Stainforth d										09 57			10 20									
Kirk Sandall d										10 02			10 25									
Adwick 31 d																						
Bentley (S.Yorks) 31 d																						
Doncaster 7 31 a							09 29			10 11		10 23	10 35	10 40					11 38	11 46		
London Kings Cross 15 ⊖26 a												12 14										
York 8 26 d	04 20	05 25									09 28							10 28				
Doncaster 7 d			08 03	09 13	09 32		09 39			10 13	10 30			10 42			11 13	11 30	11 42	11 48		
Conisbrough d			08 10	09 20						10 20							11 20					
Mexborough d			08 14	09 24						10 24							11 24					
Swinton (S.Yorks) d			08 17	09 28		09 35				10 27							11 27					12 05
Rotherham Central d			08 25	09 35		09 48				10 35							11 35					12 13
Meadowhall d			08 30	09 41		09 54	10 00			10 40				11 00			11 40		12 00	12 08		12 21
Sheffield 7 a			08 41	09 51	09 55	10 03	10 08			10 52	10 54			11 07			11 51	11 53	12 07	12 18		12 32
d														11 10					12 10			
Stockport 78 a														11 53					12 53			
Manchester Piccadilly 10 a	06 17	07 26												12 06					13 06			
Manchester Airport 85 ✈ a	06 35	07 46												12 27					13 27			

A From Leeds to Plymouth
B From Leeds
C To Hull
D To Leeds
E From LeedsLeeds to Plymouth
F From Newcastle to Plymouth
G From Bridlington
H To Huddersfield

Table 27

Sundays until 24 June

Hull and Cleethorpes - Doncaster - Meadowhall, Sheffield, Manchester and Manchester Airport, Cleethorpes - Barton-on-Humber

Network Diagram - see first Page of Table 18

	NT	XC	HT	TP	NT	NT	TP	NT	NT	NT	XC	NT	TP	TP	NT	TP	NT	XC	NT	NT	TP	TP
		◇1 A	◇1	◇1	B		◇1 C		Bus		◇1 D	E	◇1 C	◇1 F	B	◇1	G	◇1 A		E	◇1 F	◇1
Hull d			11 30		11 46	11 53	12 00					12 46	12 58		13 29					13 35		
Hessle d																				13 42		
Ferriby d																				13 47		
Brough d			11 42		11 58	12 05	12 12					12 58	13 10		13 41					13 52		
Broomfleet d																						
Gilberdyke d						12 12						13 05								14 00		
Eastrington d																						
Howden d			11 54		12 10										13 53							
Wressle d																						
Selby a			12 04		12 19		12 32						13 28		14 02							
d			12 05		12 20										14 03							
York 8 33 a					12 44										14 30							
Saltmarshe d																						
Goole d	11 43					12 21						13 14							13 43	14 08		
Thorne North d	11 51					12 29													13 51			
Cleethorpes d				11 26				12 58														13 26
New Clee d								13 01														
Grimsby Docks d								13 04														
Grimsby Town a				11 33				13 06														13 33
d				11 34				13 07														13 34
Great Coates d								13 11														
Healing d								13 14														
Stallingborough d								13 15														
Habrough d								13 21														
Ulceby d								13 25														
Thornton Abbey d								13 30														
Goxhill d								13 33														
New Holland d								13 38														
Barrow Haven d								13 41														
Barton-on-Humber a								13 48														
Barton-on-Humber d									13 55													
Hull Paragon Interchange a									14 19													
Barnetby d				11 53																		13 53
Scunthorpe a				12 08																		14 08
d				12 08																		14 08
Althorpe d																						
Crowle d																						
Thorne South d																						
Hatfield & Stainforth d	11 57																		13 57			
Kirk Sandall d	12 02																		14 02			
Adwick 31 d																						
Bentley (S.Yorks) 31 d																						
Doncaster 7 31 a	12 11		12 25	12 40		12 47						13 37							14 11	14 31		14 37
London Kings Cross 15 ⊖26 a			14 14																			
York 8 26 d		11 28									12 28			13 15				13 40			14 15	
Doncaster 7 d	12 13	12 30		12 42						13 13	13 30	13 38				13 42			14 13	14 33		14 42
Conisbrough d	12 20									13 20									14 20			
Mexborough d	12 24									13 24									14 24			
Swinton (S.Yorks) d	12 27									13 27							14 06		14 30			
Rotherham Central d	12 38									13 36							14 14		14 42			
Meadowhall d	12 43			13 00						13 44		13 56				14 00	14 21		14 48	14 52		15 00
Sheffield 7 a	12 55	12 54		13 07						13 52	13 54	14 06				14 07	14 32	14 52	14 55	15 03		15 07
d				13 10												14 11						15 11
Stockport 78 a				13 53												14 53						15 53
Manchester Piccadilly 10 a				14 06										15 08		15 06					16 08	16 06
Manchester Airport 85 ✈ a				14 27										15 24		15 28					16 25	16 34

A From Edinburgh to Plymouth
B To Hull
C To Huddersfield
D From Edinburgh to Penzance
E From Scarborough
F From Newcastle
G From Leeds

Table 29

Sundays until 24 June

Hull and Cleethorpes - Doncaster - Meadowhall, Sheffield, Manchester and Manchester Airport, Cleethorpes - Barton-on-Humber

Network Diagram - see first Page of Table 18

		EM	NT	HT	XC	XC	NT	NT	TP	NT	NT	TP	XC	NT	XC	NT	NT	NT	TP	TP	XC	HT
		A	B	◇1	◇1 C	◇1 D		E	◇1		🚌	◇1 F	◇1 C	G	◇1 H		I		◇1 J	◇1	◇1 K	◇1
				⊠	🛒	🛒							🛒		🛒						🛒	⊠
Hull	d		14 23	14 30				14 41				14 58					15 41	16 00				16 30
Hessle	d																					
Ferriby	d																					
Brough	d		14 35	14 42				14 53				15 10					15 53	16 12				16 42
Broomfleet	d																					
Gilberdyke	d							15 00									16 00					
Eastrington	d																					
Howden	d		14 47	14 54														16 24				16 54
Wressle	d																					
Selby	a		14 56	15 04								15 28						16 33				17 04
	d		14 57	15 05														16 34				17 05
York 8	33 a		15 25															16 59				
Saltmarshe	d																					
Goole	d							15 09								15 43	16 09					
Thorne North	d															15 51						
Cleethorpes	d	13 56							14 26	14 58										15 26		
New Clee	d									15 01												
Grimsby Docks	d									15 04												
Grimsby Town	a	14 02							14 33	15 06										15 33		
	d	14 03							14 34	15 07										15 34		
Great Coates	d									15 11												
Healing	d									15 14												
Stallingborough	d									15 15												
Habrough	d	14 13							14 44	15 21												
Ulceby	d									15 25												
Thornton Abbey	d									15 30												
Goxhill	d									15 33												
New Holland	d									15 38												
Barrow Haven	d									15 41												
Barton-on-Humber	a									15 48												
Barton-on-Humber	d										15 55											
Hull Paragon Interchange	a										16 19											
Barnetby	d	14a21							14 53											15 53		
Scunthorpe	a								15 08											16 08		
	d								15 08											16 08		
Althorpe	d																					
Crowle	d																					
Thorne South	d																					
Hatfield & Stainforth	d															15 57						
Kirk Sandall	d															16 02						
Adwick	31 d																					
Bentley (S.Yorks)	31 d																					
Doncaster 7	31 a			15 25				15 32	15 39							16 11	16 32			16 39		17 25
London Kings Cross 15	⊖26 a			17 15																		19 18
York 8	26 d				14 34	14 40							15 34		15 40				16 15		16 23	
Doncaster 7	d				14 59		15 13	15 33	15 42				15 59			16 13	16 33			16 42	16 51	
Conisbrough	d						15 20									16 20						
Mexborough	d						15 24									16 24						
Swinton (S.Yorks)	d						15 30							16 05		16 29						
Rotherham Central	d						15 41							16 13		16 41						
Meadowhall	⇌ d						15 48	15 52	16 00					16 19		16 47	16 53			17 00		
Sheffield 7	⇌ a				15 21	15 51	15 55	16 01	16 07				16 21	16 31	16 51	16 55	17 04			17 07	17 19	
	d								16 11											17 11		
Stockport	78 a								16 53											17 53		
Manchester Piccadilly 10	⇌ a								17 06										18 08	18 06		
Manchester Airport	85 ✈ a								17 27										18 24	18 27		

A To Nottingham
B To Hull
C From Newcastle to Reading
D From Glasgow Central to Penzance
E From Bridlington
F To Huddersfield
G From Leeds
H From Glasgow Central to Plymouth
I From Scarborough
J From Newcastle
K From Edinburgh to Reading

Table 29

Sundays until 24 June

Hull and Cleethorpes - Doncaster - Meadowhall, Sheffield, Manchester and Manchester Airport, Cleethorpes - Barton-on-Humber

Network Diagram - see first Page of Table 18

		XC	NT	NT	TP	TP	NT	XC	NT	EM	NT	XC	NT	NT	TP	NT	NT	EM	HT	XC	NT	XC	NT
		◇1 A		B	◇1	◇1 C	D	◇1 E		◇1 F	G	◇1 H		I	◇1		🚌	J	◇1	◇1 K	L	◇1 M	
		🛒						🛒		🛒		🛒							⊠	🛒		🛒	
Hull	d			16 41		16 58	17 23							17 41					18 30				
Hessle	d																						
Ferriby	d																						
Brough	d			16 53		17 10	17 35							17 53					18 42				
Broomfleet	d																						
Gilberdyke	d			17 00										18 00									
Eastrington	d																						
Howden	d						17 47												18 54				
Wressle	d																						
Selby	a					17 28	17 56												19 04				
	d						17 57												19 05				
York 8	33 a						18 25																
Saltmarshe	d																						
Goole	d			17 09					17 42					18 09									
Thorne North	d								17 50														
Cleethorpes	d				16 26										17 26	17 58		18 18					
New Clee	d															18 01							
Grimsby Docks	d															18 04							
Grimsby Town	a				16 33										17 33	18 06		18 24					
	d				16 34										17 34	18 07		18 25					
Great Coates	d															18 11							
Healing	d															18 14							
Stallingborough	d															18 15							
Habrough	d														17 44	18 21		18 35					
Ulceby	d															18 25							
Thornton Abbey	d															18 30							
Goxhill	d															18 33							
New Holland	d															18 38							
Barrow Haven	d															18 41							
Barton-on-Humber	a															18 48							
Barton-on-Humber	d																18 55						
Hull Paragon Interchange	a																19 19						
Barnetby	d				16 53										17 53			18a43					
Scunthorpe	a				17 08										18 08								
	d				17 08										18 08								
Althorpe	d																						
Crowle	d																						
Thorne South	d																						
Hatfield & Stainforth	d								17 56														
Kirk Sandall	d								18 01														
Adwick	31 d																						
Bentley (S.Yorks)	31 d																						
Doncaster 7	31 a			17 31	17 38				18 09					18 33	18 38				19 25				
London Kings Cross 15	⊖26 a																		21 18				
York 8	26 d	16 40						17 34		17 42		17 40								18 34	18 10	18 40	
Doncaster 7	d		17 13	17 32	17 42			17 59		18 06			18 19	18 34	18 42					18 59			19 18
Conisbrough	d		17 21										18 26										19 25
Mexborough	d		17 25										18 30										19 29
Swinton (S.Yorks)	d		17 30								18 10		18 33								19 01		19 33
Rotherham Central	d		17 41								18 19		18 42								19 13		19 41
Meadowhall	⇌ d		17 48	17 53	18 00						18 25		18 47	18 53	19 00						19 18		19 47
Sheffield 7	⇌ a	17 51	17 55	18 01	18 08			18 23		18 28	18 36	18 51	18 57	19 03	19 07					19 21	19 27	19 50	19 55
	d				18 11										19 11								
Stockport	78 a				18 53										19 53								
Manchester Piccadilly 10	⇌ a				19 06										20 09								
Manchester Airport	85 ✈ a				19 27										20 30								

A From Aberdeen to Plymouth
B From Bridlington
C To Huddersfield
D To Hull
E From Newcastle to Reading
F To St Pancras International
G From Leeds
H From Glasgow Central to Plymouth
I From Scarborough
J To Newark North Gate
K From Newcastle to Guildford
L From Sheffield
M From Glasgow Central to Bristol Temple Meads

Hull and Cleethorpes - Doncaster - Meadowhall, Sheffield, Manchester and Manchester Airport, Cleethorpes - Barton-on-Humber

Network Diagram - see first Page of Table 18

		NT A	TP ◇1	TP ◇1 B		XC ◇1 C ⊥	NT D	NT E	XC ◇1 F	NT	TP ◇1	TP ◇1 G	EM H	XC ◇1 C ⊥		NT I	NT J	XC ◇1 K	NT L	TP ◇1	TP ◇1 D	NT E	NT	
Hull	d	18 38		18 58			19 24									20 01	20 29				21 00		21 35	
Hessle	d															20 08								
Ferriby	d															20 13								
Brough	d	18 50		19 10			19 36									20 18	20 41				21 12		21 47	
Broomfleet	d																							
Gilberdyke	d	18 57														20 25							21 54	
Eastrington	d																							
Howden	d						19 48										20 53							
Wressle	d																							
Selby	a			19 28			19 57										21 02				21 30			
	d						19 58										21 03							
York 8 33	a						20 25										21 30							
Saltmarshe	d																							
Goole	d	19 06														20 34							22 03	
Thorne North	d	19 14														20 42							22 11	
Cleethorpes	d		18 26								19 26		20 15							20 26				
New Clee	d																							
Grimsby Docks	d																							
Grimsby Town	a		18 33								19 33		20 21							20 33				
	d		18 34								19 34		20 22							20 34				
Great Coates	d																							
Healing	d																							
Stallingborough	d																							
Habrough	d												20 33							20 44				
Ulceby	d																							
Thornton Abbey	d																							
Goxhill	d																							
New Holland	d																							
Barrow Haven	d																							
Barton-on-Humber	a																							
Barton-on-Humber	d																							
Hull Paragon Interchange	a																							
Barnetby	d		18 53								19 53		20a42							20 53				
Scunthorpe	a		19 08								20 08									21 08				
	d		19 08								20 08									21 08				
Althorpe	d																							
Crowle	d																							
Thorne South	d																							
Hatfield & Stainforth	d	19 20																					22 15	
Kirk Sandall	d	19 25																					22 20	
Adwick 31	d																							
Bentley (S.Yorks) 31	d																							
Doncaster 7 31	a	19 35	19 38								20 40					20 59				21 40			22 32	
London Kings Cross 15 ⊖ 26	a																							
York 8 26	d					19 24			19 40			20 15		20 24				20 40	20 50					
Doncaster 7	d	19 37	19 42			19 50				20 14	20 42			20 50		21 01				21 42			22 40	
Conisbrough	d									20 21						21 08							22 47	
Mexborough	d									20 25						21 12							22 51	
Swinton (S.Yorks)	d							20 09		20 29						21 15			21 45	21 52		22 32	22 53	
Rotherham Central	d							20 17		20 41						21 22			21 52	21 58		22 40	22 58	
Meadowhall	d	19 57	20 00					20 23		20 47	21 00					21 28			21 58	22 04		22 45	23 04	
Sheffield 7	a	20 06	20 07			20 16		20 34	20 51	20 55	21 07			21 17		21 38		21 50	22 09	22 13		22 54	23 15	
	d		20 11								21 11													
Stockport 78	a		20 53								21 53													
Manchester Piccadilly 10	a		21 06								22 06	22 13												
Manchester Airport 85	a		21 27								22 27													

A From Bridlington
B To Huddersfield
C From Newcastle to Birmingham New Street
D To Leeds
E From Leeds
F From Edinburgh to Bristol Temple Meads
G From Newcastle
H To Newark North Gate
I From Scarborough
J To Hull
K From Glasgow Central to Birmingham New Street
L From Sheffield

Hull and Cleethorpes - Doncaster - Meadowhall, Sheffield, Manchester and Manchester Airport, Cleethorpes - Barton-on-Humber

Network Diagram - see first Page of Table 18

		TP ◇1	TP ◇1	TP ◇1	TP ◇1	TP ◇1	NT	TP ◇1	TP ◇1 A	NT		XC ◇1 B ⊥	NT C	NT	NT D	TP ◇1	NT	XC ◇1 E ⊥	HT ◇1 ☒	NT		TP ◇1	NT	NT 🚌	NT
Hull	d													08 40	08 54	09 00			09 30	09 33					
Hessle	d																			09 40					
Ferriby	d																			09 45					
Brough	d													08 52	09 06	09 12			09 42	09 50					
Broomfleet	d																								
Gilberdyke	d													08 59						09 57					
Eastrington	d																								
Howden	d														09 18				09 54						
Wressle	d																								
Selby	a														09 27	09 32			10 04						
	d														09 28	09 33			10 05						
York 8 33	a														09 52										
Saltmarshe	d																								
Goole	d													09 09			09 43			10 06					
Thorne North	d																09 51			10 14					
Cleethorpes	d																					09 26	09 58		
New Clee	d																						10 01		
Grimsby Docks	d																						10 04		
Grimsby Town	a																					09 33	10 06		
	d																					09 34	10 07		
Great Coates	d																						10 11		
Healing	d																						10 14		
Stallingborough	d																						10 15		
Habrough	d																					09 44	10 21		
Ulceby	d																						10 25		
Thornton Abbey	d																						10 30		
Goxhill	d																						10 33		
New Holland	d																						10 38		
Barrow Haven	d																						10 41		
Barton-on-Humber	a																						10 48		
Barton-on-Humber	d																							10 55	
Hull Paragon Interchange	a																							11 19	
Barnetby	d																					09 53			
Scunthorpe	a																					10 08			
	d																					10 08			
Althorpe	d																								
Crowle	d																								
Thorne South	d																								
Hatfield & Stainforth	d																09 57			10 20					
Kirk Sandall	d																10 02			10 25					
Adwick 31	d																								
Bentley (S.Yorks) 31	d																								
Doncaster 7 31	a													09 29			10 11		10 23	10 35		10 40			
London Kings Cross 15 ⊖ 26	a																		12 14						
York 8 26	d	02 44	03 59	05 12	06 12	07 12		08 10	08 45									09 28							
Doncaster 7	d						08 03			09 13		09 32		09 39			10 13	10 30				10 42			11 13
Conisbrough	d						08 10			09 20							10 20								11 20
Mexborough	d						08 14			09 24							10 24								11 24
Swinton (S.Yorks)	d						08 17			09 28			09 35				10 27								11 27
Rotherham Central	d						08 25			09 35			09 48				10 35								11 35
Meadowhall	d						08 30			09 41			09 54	10 00			10 40					11 00			11 40
Sheffield 7	a						08 41			09 51		09 55	10 03	10 08			10 52	10 54				11 07			11 51
	d																					11 10			
Stockport 78	a																					11 53			
Manchester Piccadilly 10	a	04 02	05 17	06 34	07 34	08 34		09 34	10 05							11 03						12 06			
Manchester Airport 85	a	04 23	05 38	06 55	07 55	08 55		09 55														12 27			

A To Liverpool Lime Street
B From Leeds to Plymouth
C From Leeds
D To Hull
E To Plymouth

Table 29

Sundays

1 July to 9 September

Hull and Cleethorpes - Doncaster - Meadowhall, Sheffield, Manchester and Manchester Airport, Cleethorpes - Barton-on-Humber

Network Diagram - see first Page of Table 18

		XC	TP	NT	TP	NT	NT	XC	HT	TP	NT	NT	TP	NT	NT	NT	XC	NT	TP	TP	NT	TP	NT
		◇■ A ✠	◇■	B	◇■	C		◇■ D ✠	◇■ ⊠	◇■	E		◇■		(bus)		◇■ F ✠	G	◇■ H	◇■	E	◇■	C
Hull	d			10 50	10 58				11 30		11 46	11 53	12 00					12 46		12 58	13 29		
Hessle	d																						
Ferriby	d																						
Brough	d			11 02	11 10				11 42		11 58	12 05	12 12					12 58		13 10	13 41		
Broomfleet	d																						
Gilberdyke	d			11 09								12 12						13 05					
Eastrington	d																				13 53		
Howden	d								11 54		12 10												
Wressle	d																						
Selby	a				11 28				12 04		12 19		12 32							13 28	14 02		
	d				11 29				12 05		12 20		12 32							13 29	14 03		
York ■ 33	a										12 44										14 30		
Saltmarshe	d																						
Goole	d			11 18			11 43					12 21						13 14					
Thorne North	d			11 26			11 51					12 29											
Cleethorpes	d		10 26							11 26				12 58									
New Clee	d													13 01									
Grimsby Docks	d													13 04									
Grimsby Town	a		10 33							11 33				13 06									
	d		10 34							11 34				13 07									
Great Coates	d													13 11									
Healing	d													13 14									
Stallingborough	d													13 15									
Habrough	d		10 44											13 21									
Ulceby	d													13 25									
Thornton Abbey	d													13 30									
Goxhill	d													13 33									
New Holland	d													13 38									
Barrow Haven	d													13 41									
Barton-on-Humber	a													13 48									
Barton-on-Humber	d														13 55								
Hull Paragon Interchange	a														14 19								
Barnetby	d		10 53							11 53													
Scunthorpe	a		11 08							12 08													
	d		11 08							12 08													
Althorpe	d																						
Crowle	d																						
Thorne South	d																						
Hatfield & Stainforth	d						11 57																
Kirk Sandall	d						12 02																
Adwick 31	d																						
Bentley (S.Yorks) 31	d																						
Doncaster ■ 31	a		11 38	11 46			12 11		12 25	12 40		12 47						13 37					
London Kings Cross ■ ⊖26	a								14 14														
York ■ 26	d	10 28						11 28									12 28		13 15				
Doncaster ■	d	11 30	11 42	11 48			12 13	12 30		12 42						13 13	13 30	13 38				13 42	
Conisbrough	d						12 20									13 20							
Mexborough	d						12 24									13 24							
Swinton (S.Yorks)	d					12 05	12 27									13 27							14 06
Rotherham Central	d					12 13	12 38									13 36							14 14
Meadowhall	d		12 00	12 08		12 21	12 43			13 00						13 44		13 56				14 00	14 21
Sheffield ■	a	11 53	12 07	12 18		12 32	12 55	12 54		13 07						13 52	13 54	14 06				14 07	14 32
	d		12 10							13 10												14 11	
Stockport 78	a		12 53							13 53												14 53	
Manchester Piccadilly ■	a		13 06		12 54					14 06			13 54						14 34	14 54		15 06	
Manchester Airport 85	a		13 27							14 27									14 55			15 28	

A From Newcastle to Plymouth
B From Bridlington
C From Leeds
D From Edinburgh to Reading
E To Hull
F From Edinburgh to Penzance
G From Scarborough
H From Newcastle

Table 29

Sundays

1 July to 9 September

Hull and Cleethorpes - Doncaster - Meadowhall, Sheffield, Manchester and Manchester Airport, Cleethorpes - Barton-on-Humber

Network Diagram - see first Page of Table 18

		XC	NT	NT	TP	NT	TP	TP	EM	HT	XC	XC	NT	NT	TP	TP	NT	XC	NT	NT	XC	NT
		◇■ A ✠		B	◇■ C	D	◇■	◇■	E	◇■ ⊠	◇■ F ✠	◇■ G ✠		H	◇■	◇■		◇■ F ✠	(bus)	I	◇■ J ✠	
Hull	d			13 35		14 23				14 30				14 41	14 58							
Hessle	d			13 42																		
Ferriby	d			13 47																		
Brough	d			13 52		14 35				14 42				14 53	15 10							
Broomfleet	d																					
Gilberdyke	d			14 00										15 00								
Eastrington	d																					
Howden	d					14 47				14 54												
Wressle	d																					
Selby	a					14 56				15 04					15 28							
	d					14 57				15 05					15 29							
York ■ 33	a					15 25																
Saltmarshe	d																					
Goole	d		13 43	14 08										15 09								15 43
Thorne North	d		13 51																			15 51
Cleethorpes	d							13 26	13 56							14 26	14 58					
New Clee	d																15 01					
Grimsby Docks	d																15 04					
Grimsby Town	a							13 33	14 02							14 33	15 06					
	d							13 34	14 03							14 34	15 07					
Great Coates	d																15 11					
Healing	d																15 14					
Stallingborough	d																15 15					
Habrough	d								14 13							14 44	15 21					
Ulceby	d																15 25					
Thornton Abbey	d																15 30					
Goxhill	d																15 33					
New Holland	d																15 38					
Barrow Haven	d																15 41					
Barton-on-Humber	a																15 48					
Barton-on-Humber	d																		15 55			
Hull Paragon Interchange	a																		16 19			
Barnetby	d							13 53	14a21							14 53						
Scunthorpe	a							14 08								15 08						
	d							14 08								15 08						
Althorpe	d																					
Crowle	d																					
Thorne South	d																					
Hatfield & Stainforth	d		13 57																			15 57
Kirk Sandall	d		14 02																			16 02
Adwick 31	d																					
Bentley (S.Yorks) 31	d																					
Doncaster ■ 31	a		14 11	14 31				14 37		15 25				15 32		15 39						16 11
London Kings Cross ■ ⊖26	a									17 15												
York ■ 26	d	13 40			14 15		14 33				14 34	14 40						15 34			15 40	
Doncaster ■	d		14 13	14 33				14 42			14 59		15 13	15 33		15 42		15 59				16 13
Conisbrough	d		14 20										15 20									16 20
Mexborough	d		14 24										15 24									16 24
Swinton (S.Yorks)	d		14 30										15 30							16 05		16 29
Rotherham Central	d		14 42										15 41							16 13		16 41
Meadowhall	d		14 48	14 52				15 00					15 48	15 52		16 00				16 21		16 47
Sheffield ■	a	14 52	14 55	15 03				15 07			15 21	15 51	15 55	16 01		16 07		16 21		16 32	16 51	16 55
	d							15 11								16 11						
Stockport 78	a							15 53								16 53						
Manchester Piccadilly ■	a				15 34		15 54	16 06							16 54	17 06						
Manchester Airport 85	a				15 55			16 34								17 27						

A From Edinburgh to Plymouth
B From Scarborough
C From Newcastle
D To Hull
E To Nottingham
F From Newcastle to Reading
G From Glasgow Central to Penzance
H From Bridlington
I From Leeds
J From Glasgow Central to Plymouth

Hull and Cleethorpes - Doncaster - Meadowhall, Sheffield, Manchester and Manchester Airport, Cleethorpes - Barton-on-Humber

Network Diagram - see first Page of Table 18

		NT	NT	TP	TP	XC	HT	TP		XC	NT	NT	TP	TP	NT	XC	EM	NT	NT	XC	NT	NT	TP	NT	NT
		A		◇1 B	◇1	◇1 C ⊼	◇1 ⊠	◇1		◇1 D ⊼		E	◇1	◇1	F	◇1 G ⊼	◇1 H ⊼		I	◇1 J ⊼		A	◇1		🚌
Hull	d	15 41	16 00				16 30					16 41	16 58		17 23							17 41			
Hessle	d																								
Ferriby	d																								
Brough	d	15 53	16 12				16 42					16 53	17 10		17 35							17 53			
Broomfleet	d																								
Gilberdyke	d	16 00										17 00										18 00			
Eastrington	d																								
Howden	d		16 24				16 54								17 47										
Wressle	d																								
Selby	a		16 33				17 04						17 28		17 56										
	d		16 34				17 05						17 29		17 57										
York 8 33	a		16 59												18 25										
Saltmarshe	d																								
Goole	d	16 09										17 09						17 42				18 09			
Thorne North	d																	17 50							
Cleethorpes	d				15 26									16 26									17 26	17 58	
New Clee	d																							18 01	
Grimsby Docks	d																							18 04	
Grimsby Town	a				15 33									16 33									17 33	18 06	
	d				15 34									16 34									17 34	18 07	
Great Coates	d																							18 11	
Healing	d																							18 14	
Stallingborough	d																							18 15	
Habrough	d																						17 44	18 21	
Ulceby	d																							18 25	
Thornton Abbey	d																							18 30	
Goxhill	d																							18 33	
New Holland	d																							18 38	
Barrow Haven	d																							18 41	
Barton-on-Humber	a																							18 48	
Barton-on-Humber	d																								18 55
Hull Paragon Interchange	a																								19 19
Barnetby	d				15 53									16 53									17 53		
Scunthorpe	a				16 08									17 08									18 08		
	d				16 08									17 08									18 08		
Althorpe	d																								
Crowle	d																								
Thorne South	d																								
Hatfield & Stainforth	d																	17 56							
Kirk Sandall	d																	18 01							
Adwick 31	d																								
Bentley (S.Yorks) 31	d																								
Doncaster 7 31	a	16 32			16 39		17 25					17 31		17 38				18 09				18 33	18 38		
London Kings Cross 15 ⊖26	a						19 18																		
York 8 26	d			16 15		16 23		16 33		16 40						17 34	17 42			17 40					
Doncaster 7	d	16 33			16 42	16 51					17 13	17 32		17 42		17 59	18 06				18 19	18 34	18 42		
Conisbrough	d										17 21										18 26				
Mexborough	d										17 25										18 30				
Swinton (S.Yorks)	d										17 30								18 10		18 33				
Rotherham Central	d										17 41								18 19		18 42				
Meadowhall	d	16 53			17 00						17 48	17 53		18 00					18 25		18 47	18 53	19 00		
Sheffield 7	a	17 04			17 07	17 19				17 51	17 55	18 01		18 07		18 23	18 28		18 36	18 51	18 57	19 03	19 07		
	d				17 11									18 11									19 11		
Stockport 78	a				17 53									18 53									19 53		
Manchester Piccadilly 10	a			17 34	18 06			17 54					18 54	19 06									20 09		
Manchester Airport 85 ✈	a			17 55	18 27									19 27									20 30		

A From Scarborough
B From Newcastle
C From Edinburgh to Reading
D From Aberdeen to Plymouth
E From Bridlington
F To Hull
G From Newcastle to Reading
H From York Holgate Sidings to St Pancras International
I From Leeds
J From Glasgow Central to Plymouth

Hull and Cleethorpes - Doncaster - Meadowhall, Sheffield, Manchester and Manchester Airport, Cleethorpes - Barton-on-Humber

Network Diagram - see first Page of Table 18

		EM	HT	XC		NT	TP	XC		NT	NT	TP	TP	XC		NT	NT	XC	NT	TP	TP	EM	XC	NT
		A	◇1 ⊠	◇1 B ⊼		C	◇1	◇1 D ⊼			E	◇1	◇1	◇1 F ⊼		G	H	◇1 I		◇1 J	◇1	A	◇1 F ⊼	K
Hull	d		18 30								18 38	18 58				19 24								20 01
Hessle	d																							20 08
Ferriby	d																							20 13
Brough	d		18 42								18 50	19 10				19 36								20 18
Broomfleet	d																							
Gilberdyke	d										18 57													20 25
Eastrington	d																							
Howden	d		18 54													19 48								
Wressle	d																							
Selby	a		19 04									19 28				19 57								
	d		19 05									19 29				19 58								
York 8 33	a															20 25								
Saltmarshe	d																							
Goole	d										19 06													20 34
Thorne North	d										19 14													20 42
Cleethorpes	d	18 18											18 26								19 26	20 15		
New Clee	d																							
Grimsby Docks	d																							
Grimsby Town	a	18 24											18 33								19 33	20 21		
	d	18 25											18 34								19 34	20 22		
Great Coates	d																							
Healing	d																							
Stallingborough	d																							
Habrough	d	18 35																				20 33		
Ulceby	d																							
Thornton Abbey	d																							
Goxhill	d																							
New Holland	d																							
Barrow Haven	d																							
Barton-on-Humber	a																							
Barton-on-Humber	d																							
Hull Paragon Interchange	a																							
Barnetby	d	18a43											18 53								19 53	20a42		
Scunthorpe	a												19 08								20 08			
	d												19 08								20 08			
Althorpe	d																							
Crowle	d																							
Thorne South	d																							
Hatfield & Stainforth	d										19 20													
Kirk Sandall	d										19 25													
Adwick 31	d																							
Bentley (S.Yorks) 31	d																							
Doncaster 7 31	a		19 25								19 35		19 38								20 40			20 59
London Kings Cross 15 ⊖26	a		21 18																					
York 8 26	d			18 34		18 10	18 33	18 40						19 24				19 40		20 15			20 24	
Doncaster 7	d			18 59						19 18	19 37		19 42	19 50					20 14		20 42		20 50	21 01
Conisbrough	d									19 25									20 21					21 08
Mexborough	d									19 29									20 25					21 12
Swinton (S.Yorks)	d					19 01				19 33							20 07		20 29					21 15
Rotherham Central	d					19 13				19 41							20 15		20 41					21 22
Meadowhall	d					19 18				19 47	19 57		20 00				20 21		20 47		21 00			21 28
Sheffield 7	a			19 21		19 27		19 50		19 55	20 06		20 07	20 16			20 34	20 51	20 55		21 07		21 17	21 38
	d												20 11								21 11			
Stockport 78	a												20 53								21 53			
Manchester Piccadilly 10	a						19 54					20 54	21 06							21 36	22 06			
Manchester Airport 85 ✈	a												21 27								22 27			

A To Newark North Gate
B From Newcastle to Guildford
C From Sheffield
D From Glasgow Central to Bristol Temple Meads
E From Bridlington
F From Newcastle to Birmingham New Street
G To Leeds
H From Leeds
I From Edinburgh to Bristol Temple Meads
J From Newcastle
K From Scarborough

Table 29

Sundays
1 July to 9 September

Hull and Cleethorpes - Doncaster - Meadowhall, Sheffield, Manchester and Manchester Airport, Cleethorpes - Barton-on-Humber

Network Diagram - see first Page of Table 18

		NT	XC	NT	TP	TP	NT	NT
			◇1		◇1	◇1		
		A	B	C		D	E	
Hull	d	20 29				21 00		21 35
Hessle	d							
Ferriby	d							
Brough	d	20 41				21 12		21 47
Broomfleet	d							
Gilberdyke	d							21 54
Eastrington	d							
Howden	d	20 53						
Wressle	d							
Selby	a	21 02				21 30		
	d	21 03						
York 8 33	a	21 30						
Saltmarshe	d							
Goole	d							22 03
Thorne North	d							22 11
Cleethorpes	d				20 26			
New Clee	d							
Grimsby Docks	d							
Grimsby Town	a				20 33			
	d				20 34			
Great Coates	d							
Healing	d							
Stallingborough	d							
Habrough	d				20 44			
Ulceby	d							
Thornton Abbey	d							
Goxhill	d							
New Holland	d							
Barrow Haven	d							
Barton-on-Humber	a							
Barton-on-Humber	d							
Hull Paragon Interchange	a							
Barnetby	d				20 53			
Scunthorpe	a				21 08			
	d				21 08			
Althorpe	d							
Crowle	d							
Thorne South	d							
Hatfield & Stainforth	d							22 15
Kirk Sandall	d							22 20
Adwick 31	d							
Bentley (S.Yorks) 31	d							
Doncaster 7 31	a				21 40			22 32
London Kings Cross 15 ⊖26	a							
York 8 26	d		20 40	20 50				
Doncaster 7	d				21 42			22 40
Conisbrough	d							22 47
Mexborough	d							22 51
Swinton (S.Yorks)	d			21 45	21 52		22 32	22 53
Rotherham Central	d			21 52	21 58		22 40	22 58
Meadowhall	d			21 58	22 04		22 45	23 04
Sheffield 7	a		21 50	22 09	22 13		22 54	23 15
	d							
Stockport 78	a							
Manchester Piccadilly 10	a							
Manchester Airport 85	a							

A To Hull
B From Glasgow Central to Birmingham New Street
C From Sheffield
D To Leeds
E From Leeds

Table 29

Sundays
16 September to 21 October

Hull and Cleethorpes - Doncaster - Meadowhall, Sheffield, Manchester and Manchester Airport, Cleethorpes - Barton-on-Humber

Network Diagram - see first Page of Table 18

		TP	NT	TP	NT	XC	NT	NT	NT	TP		NT	XC	HT	NT	TP	NT	XC	TP	NT		TP	NT	NT	XC
		◇1		◇1		◇1				◇1			◇1	◇1		◇1		◇1	◇1			◇1			◇1
						A	B		C	D			E	☒				F		G		H	B		F
Hull	d							08 40	08 54	09 00				09 30	09 33					10 50		10 58			
Hessle	d														09 40										
Ferriby	d														09 45										
Brough	d							08 52	09 06	09 12				09 42	09 50					11 02		11 10			
Broomfleet	d																								
Gilberdyke	d							08 59							09 57					11 09					
Eastrington	d																								
Howden	d								09 18					09 54											
Wressle	d																								
Selby	a								09 27	09 32				10 04								11 28			
	d								09 28					10 05											
York 8 33	a								09 54																
Saltmarshe	d																								
Goole	d							09 09				09 43			10 06					11 18				11 43	
Thorne North	d											09 51			10 14					11 26				11 51	
Cleethorpes	d															09 26			10 26						
New Clee	d																								
Grimsby Docks	d																								
Grimsby Town	a															09 33			10 33						
	d															09 34			10 34						
Great Coates	d																								
Healing	d																								
Stallingborough	d																								
Habrough	d															09 44			10 44						
Ulceby	d																								
Thornton Abbey	d																								
Goxhill	d																								
New Holland	d																								
Barrow Haven	d																								
Barton-on-Humber	a																								
Barton-on-Humber	d																								
Hull Paragon Interchange	a																								
Barnetby	d															09 55			10 53						
Scunthorpe	a															10 10			11 08						
	d															10 10			11 08						
Althorpe	d																								
Crowle	d																								
Thorne South	d																								
Hatfield & Stainforth	d											09 57			10 20									11 57	
Kirk Sandall	d											10 02			10 25									12 02	
Adwick 31	d																								
Bentley (S.Yorks) 31	d																								
Doncaster 7 31	a							09 29				10 11		10 23	10 35	10 40			11 38	11 46				12 11	
London Kings Cross 15 ⊖26	a													12 15											
York 8 26	d	06 45		08 10									09 30					10 34							11 28
Doncaster 7	d		08 03		09 13	09 32		09 39				10 13	10 30			10 42	11 13	11 30	11 42	11 48				12 13	12 30
Conisbrough	d		08 10		09 20							10 20					11 20							12 20	
Mexborough	d		08 14		09 24							10 24					11 24							12 24	
Swinton (S.Yorks)	d		08 17		09 28		09 35					10 27					11 27						12 05	12 27	
Rotherham Central	d		08 25		09 35		09 48					10 35					11 35						12 13	12 38	
Meadowhall	d		08 30		09 41		09 54	10 00				10 40				11 00	11 40		12 00	12 08			12 21	12 43	
Sheffield 7	a		08 41		09 51	09 55	10 03	10 08				10 52	10 54			11 07	11 51	11 53	12 07	12 18			12 32	12 55	12 54
	d															11 10			12 10						
Stockport 78	a															11 53			12 50						
Manchester Piccadilly 10	a	08 36		10 25												12 06			13 03						
Manchester Airport 85	a	08 55		10 42												12 34			13 27						

A From Leeds to Plymouth
B From Leeds
C To Hull
D To Leeds
E From Leeds to Reading
F From Newcastle to Reading
G From Bridlington
H To Huddersfield

Hull and Cleethorpes - Doncaster - Meadowhall, Sheffield, Manchester and Manchester Airport, Cleethorpes - Barton-on-Humber

Network Diagram - see first Page of Table 18

		HT	TP	NT	NT	TP		NT	XC	NT	TP	TP	NT
		◇1	◇1			◇1			◇1		◇1	◇1	
		⊠		A		B			C ⊼	D	B	E	A
Hull	d	11 30		11 46	11 53	12 00				12 46	12 58		13 29
Hessle	d												
Ferriby	d												
Brough	d	11 42		11 58	12 05	12 12				12 58	13 10		13 41
Broomfleet	d												
Gilberdyke	d				12 12					13 05			
Eastrington	d												
Howden	d	11 54		12 10									13 53
Wressle	d												
Selby	a	12 04		12 19		12 32					13 28		14 02
	d	12 05		12 20									14 03
York	33 a			12 44									14 30
Saltmarshe	d												
Goole	d				12 21					13 14			
Thorne North	d				12 29								
Cleethorpes	d		11 26										
New Clee	d												
Grimsby Docks	d												
Grimsby Town	a		11 33										
	d		11 34										
Great Coates	d												
Healing	d												
Stallingborough	d												
Habrough	d												
Ulceby	d												
Thornton Abbey	d												
Goxhill	d												
New Holland	d												
Barrow Haven	d												
Barton-on-Humber	a												
Barton-on-Humber	d												
Hull Paragon Interchange	a												
Barnetby	d		11 53										
Scunthorpe	a		12 10										
	d		12 11										
Althorpe	d												
Crowle	d												
Thorne South	d												
Hatfield & Stainforth	d												
Kirk Sandall	d												
Adwick	31 d												
Bentley (S.Yorks)	31 d												
Doncaster	31 a	12 25	12 40		12 47					13 37			
London Kings Cross	⊖26 a	14 15											
York	26 d								12 28			13 15	
Doncaster	d		12 42					13 13	13 30	13 38			
Conisbrough	d							13 20					
Mexborough	d							13 24					
Swinton (S.Yorks)	d							13 27					
Rotherham Central	d							13 36					
Meadowhall	d		13 00					13 44		13 56			
Sheffield	a		13 07					13 52	13 54	14 06			
	d		13 10										
Stockport	78 a		13 53										
Manchester Piccadilly	a		14 06									15 08	
Manchester Airport	85 a		14 34									15 24	

		TP	NT	XC		NT	NT	TP	TP	NT	HT	XC	XC
		◇1		◇1				◇1	◇1		◇1	◇1	◇1
			F	G ⊼			D	E		A	⊠	H ⊼	C ⊼
Hull	d						13 35			14 23	14 30		
Hessle	d						13 42						
Ferriby	d						13 47						
Brough	d						13 52			14 35	14 42		
Broomfleet	d												
Gilberdyke	d						14 00						
Eastrington	d												
Howden	d									14 47	14 54		
Wressle	d												
Selby	a									14 56	15 04		
	d									14 57	15 05		
York	33 a									15 25			
Saltmarshe	d												
Goole	d					13 43	14 08						
Thorne North	d					13 51							
Cleethorpes	d								13 26				
New Clee	d												
Grimsby Docks	d												
Grimsby Town	a								13 33				
	d								13 34				
Great Coates	d												
Healing	d												
Stallingborough	d												
Habrough	d												
Ulceby	d												
Thornton Abbey	d												
Goxhill	d												
New Holland	d												
Barrow Haven	d												
Barton-on-Humber	a												
Barton-on-Humber	d												
Hull Paragon Interchange	a												
Barnetby	d								13 53				
Scunthorpe	a								14 08				
	d								14 08				
Althorpe	d												
Crowle	d												
Thorne South	d												
Hatfield & Stainforth	d					13 57							
Kirk Sandall	d					14 02							
Adwick	31 d												
Bentley (S.Yorks)	31 d												
Doncaster	31 a					14 11	14 31		14 37		15 25		
London Kings Cross	⊖26 a										17 15		
York	26 d			13 40				14 16				14 34	14 41
Doncaster	d	13 42				14 13	14 33		14 42			14 59	
Conisbrough	d					14 20							
Mexborough	d					14 24							
Swinton (S.Yorks)	d		14 06			14 30							
Rotherham Central	d		14 14			14 42							
Meadowhall	d	14 00	14 21			14 48	14 52		15 00				
Sheffield	a	14 07	14 32	14 52		14 55	15 03		15 07			15 21	15 51
	d	14 11							15 11				
Stockport	78 a	14 53							15 53				
Manchester Piccadilly	a	15 06						16 08	16 06				
Manchester Airport	85 a	15 34						16 24	16 34				

A To Hull
B To Huddersfield
C From Newcastle to Plymouth
D From Scarborough
E From Newcastle
F From Leeds
G From Newcastle to Penzance
H From Newcastle to Reading

Hull and Cleethorpes - Doncaster - Meadowhall, Sheffield, Manchester and Manchester Airport, Cleethorpes - Barton-on-Humber

Network Diagram - see first Page of Table 18

		NT		NT	TP	TP	XC	NT	XC	NT	NT	NT	
					◇1	◇1	◇1		◇1				
				A		B	C ⊼	D	E ⊼		F		
Hull	d			14 41		14 58					15 41	16 00	
Hessle	d												
Ferriby	d												
Brough	d			14 53		15 10					15 53	16 12	
Broomfleet	d												
Gilberdyke	d			15 00							16 00		
Eastrington	d												
Howden	d											16 24	
Wressle	d												
Selby	a					15 28						16 33	
	d											16 34	
York	33 a											16 59	
Saltmarshe	d												
Goole	d			15 09						15 43	16 09		
Thorne North	d									15 51			
Cleethorpes	d				14 26								
New Clee	d												
Grimsby Docks	d												
Grimsby Town	a				14 33								
	d				14 34								
Great Coates	d												
Healing	d												
Stallingborough	d												
Habrough	d				14 44								
Ulceby	d												
Thornton Abbey	d												
Goxhill	d												
New Holland	d												
Barrow Haven	d												
Barton-on-Humber	a												
Barton-on-Humber	d												
Hull Paragon Interchange	a												
Barnetby	d				14 53								
Scunthorpe	a				15 08								
	d				15 08								
Althorpe	d												
Crowle	d												
Thorne South	d												
Hatfield & Stainforth	d									15 57			
Kirk Sandall	d									16 02			
Adwick	31 d												
Bentley (S.Yorks)	31 d												
Doncaster	31 a			15 32	15 39					16 11	16 32		
London Kings Cross	⊖26 a												
York	26 d						15 34		15 40				
Doncaster	d	15 13		15 33	15 42		15 59			16 13	16 33		
Conisbrough	d	15 20								16 20			
Mexborough	d	15 24								16 24			
Swinton (S.Yorks)	d	15 30						16 05		16 29			
Rotherham Central	d	15 41						16 13		16 41			
Meadowhall	d	15 48		15 52	16 00			16 21		16 47	16 53		
Sheffield	a	15 55		16 01	16 07		16 21	16 32	16 51	16 55	17 04		
	d				16 11								
Stockport	78 a				16 53								
Manchester Piccadilly	a				17 06								
Manchester Airport	85 a				17 27								

		TP	TP	XC	HT	XC	NT	NT	TP	TP		NT	XC
		◇1	◇1	◇1	◇1	◇1			◇1	◇1			◇1
		G		C ⊼	⊠	E ⊼		A		B		H	C ⊼
Hull	d				16 30			16 41		16 58		17 23	
Hessle	d												
Ferriby	d												
Brough	d				16 42			16 53		17 10		17 35	
Broomfleet	d												
Gilberdyke	d							17 00					
Eastrington	d												
Howden	d				16 54							17 47	
Wressle	d												
Selby	a				17 04					17 28		17 56	
	d				17 05							17 57	
York	33 a											18 25	
Saltmarshe	d												
Goole	d							17 09					
Thorne North	d												
Cleethorpes	d		15 26						16 26				
New Clee	d												
Grimsby Docks	d												
Grimsby Town	a		15 33						16 33				
	d		15 34						16 34				
Great Coates	d												
Healing	d												
Stallingborough	d												
Habrough	d												
Ulceby	d												
Thornton Abbey	d												
Goxhill	d												
New Holland	d												
Barrow Haven	d												
Barton-on-Humber	a												
Barton-on-Humber	d												
Hull Paragon Interchange	a												
Barnetby	d		15 53						16 53				
Scunthorpe	a		16 08						17 08				
	d		16 08						17 08				
Althorpe	d												
Crowle	d												
Thorne South	d												
Hatfield & Stainforth	d												
Kirk Sandall	d												
Adwick	31 d												
Bentley (S.Yorks)	31 d												
Doncaster	31 a		16 39		17 25			17 31	17 38				
London Kings Cross	⊖26 a				19 18								
York	26 d	16 15		16 23		16 41							17 34
Doncaster	d		16 42	16 51			17 13	17 32	17 42				17 59
Conisbrough	d						17 21						
Mexborough	d						17 25						
Swinton (S.Yorks)	d						17 30						
Rotherham Central	d						17 41						
Meadowhall	d		17 00				17 48	17 53	18 00				
Sheffield	a		17 07	17 19		17 51	17 55	18 01	18 08				18 23
	d		17 11						18 11				
Stockport	78 a		17 53						18 53				
Manchester Piccadilly	a	18 08	18 06						19 06				
Manchester Airport	85 a	18 24	18 27						19 27				

A From Bridlington
B To Huddersfield
C From Newcastle to Reading
D From Leeds
E From Newcastle to Plymouth
F From Scarborough
G From Newcastle
H To Hull

Hull and Cleethorpes - Doncaster - Meadowhall, Sheffield, Manchester and Manchester Airport, Cleethorpes - Barton-on-Humber

Network Diagram - see first Page of Table 18

		NT	NT	EM	XC	NT	NT	TP		HT	XC	NT	XC	NT	NT	TP	TP	XC		NT	NT	XC	NT	TP	TP
				◇1	◇1			◇1		◇1	◇1		◇1			◇1	◇1	◇1				◇1		◇1	◇1
			A	B	C		D				E	F	C		G		H	I		J	A	K			L
				⊤	⊤					⊠	⊤		⊤					⊤				⊤			
Hull	d						17 41			18 30					18 38		18 58			19 24					
Hessle	d																								
Ferriby	d																								
Brough	d						17 53			18 42					18 50		19 10			19 36					
Broomfleet	d																								
Gilberdyke	d						18 00								18 57										
Eastrington	d																								
Howden	d									18 54										19 48					
Wressle	d																								
Selby	a									19 04							19 28			19 57					
	d									19 05										19 58					
York 8 33	a																			20 25					
Saltmarshe	d																								
Goole	d	17 42					18 09								19 06										
Thorne North	d	17 50													19 14										
Cleethorpes	d							17 26								18 26								19 26	
New Clee	d																								
Grimsby Docks	d																								
Grimsby Town	a							17 33								18 33								19 33	
	d							17 34								18 34								19 34	
Great Coates	d																								
Healing	d																								
Stallingborough	d																								
Habrough	d							17 44																	
Ulceby	d																								
Thornton Abbey	d																								
Goxhill	d																								
New Holland	d																								
Barrow Haven	d																								
Barton-on-Humber	a																								
Barton-on-Humber	d																								
Hull Paragon Interchange	a																								
Barnetby	d							17 53								18 53								19 53	
Scunthorpe	a							18 08								19 08								20 08	
	d							18 08								19 08								20 08	
Althorpe	d																								
Crowle	d																								
Thorne South	d																								
Hatfield & Stainforth	d	17 56													19 20										
Kirk Sandall	d	18 01													19 25										
Adwick 31	d																								
Bentley (S.Yorks) 31	d																								
Doncaster 7 31	a	18 09					18 33	18 38		19 25					19 35	19 38								20 40	
London Kings Cross 15 ⊖26	a									21 18															
York 8 26	d			17 42	17 40						18 34	18 10	18 41					19 24				19 40			20 15
Doncaster 7	d			18 08		18 19	18 34	18 42			18 59			19 18	19 37	19 42		19 50					20 14	20 42	
Conisbrough	d					18 26								19 25									20 21		
Mexborough	d					18 30								19 29									20 25		
Swinton (S.Yorks)	d		18 10			18 33						19 01		19 33							20 07		20 29		
Rotherham Central	d		18 19			18 42						19 13		19 41							20 17		20 41		
Meadowhall ⇌	d		18 25			18 47	18 53	19 00				19 18		19 47	19 57	20 00					20 23		20 47	21 00	
Sheffield 7 ⇌	a		18 36	18 39	18 51	18 57	19 03	19 07			19 21	19 27	19 50	19 55	20 06	20 07		20 16			20 34	20 51	20 55	21 07	
	d							19 11								20 11								21 11	
Stockport 78	a							19 53								20 53								21 53	
Manchester Piccadilly 10 ⇌	a							20 09								21 06								22 06	22 14
Manchester Airport 85 ✈	a							20 30								21 27								22 27	

A From Leeds
B From York Holgate Sidings to St Pancras International
C From Newcastle to Bristol Temple Meads
D From Scarborough
E From Newcastle to Guildford
F From Sheffield
G From Bridlington
H To Huddersfield
I From Newcastle to Birmingham New Street
J To Leeds
K From Edinburgh to Bristol Temple Meads
L From Newcastle

Table 29

Sundays

16 September to 21 October

Hull and Cleethorpes - Doncaster - Meadowhall, Sheffield, Manchester and Manchester Airport, Cleethorpes - Barton-on-Humber

Network Diagram - see first Page of Table 18

		XC	NT	NT		XC	NT	TP	TP	NT	NT
		◇1				◇1		◇1	◇1		
		A	B	C		D	E		F	G	
		⊤									
Hull	d		20 01	20 29					21 00		21 35
Hessle	d		20 08								
Ferriby	d		20 13								
Brough	d		20 18	20 41					21 12		21 47
Broomfleet	d										
Gilberdyke	d		20 25								21 54
Eastrington	d										
Howden	d			20 53							
Wressle	d										
Selby	a			21 02					21 30		
	d			21 03							
York 8 33	a			21 30							
Saltmarshe	d										
Goole	d		20 34								22 03
Thorne North	d		20 42								22 11
Cleethorpes	d							20 26			
New Clee	d										
Grimsby Docks	d										
Grimsby Town	a							20 33			
	d							20 34			
Great Coates	d										
Healing	d										
Stallingborough	d										
Habrough	d							20 44			
Ulceby	d										
Thornton Abbey	d										
Goxhill	d										
New Holland	d										
Barrow Haven	d										
Barton-on-Humber	a										
Barton-on-Humber	d										
Hull Paragon Interchange	a										
Barnetby	d							20 53			
Scunthorpe	a							21 08			
	d							21 08			
Althorpe	d										
Crowle	d										
Thorne South	d										
Hatfield & Stainforth	d										22 15
Kirk Sandall	d										22 20
Adwick 31	d										
Bentley (S.Yorks) 31	d										
Doncaster 7 31	a		20 59					21 40			22 32
London Kings Cross 15 ⊖26	a										
York 8 26	d	20 24				20 40	20 50				
Doncaster 7	d	20 50	21 01					21 42			22 40
Conisbrough	d		21 08								22 47
Mexborough	d		21 12								22 51
Swinton (S.Yorks)	d		21 15				21 45	21 52		22 32	22 53
Rotherham Central	d		21 22				21 52	21 58		22 40	22 58
Meadowhall ⇌	d		21 28				21 58	22 04		22 45	23 04
Sheffield 7 ⇌	a	21 17	21 38			21 50	22 09	22 13		22 54	23 15
	d										
Stockport 78	a										
Manchester Piccadilly 10 ⇌	a										
Manchester Airport 85 ✈	a										

A From Newcastle to Birmingham New Street
B From Scarborough
C To Hull
D From Glasgow Central to Birmingham New Street
E From Sheffield
F To Leeds
G From Leeds

Hull and Cleethorpes - Doncaster - Meadowhall, Sheffield, Manchester and Manchester Airport, Cleethorpes - Barton-on-Humber

Network Diagram - see first Page of Table 18

	TP	TP	TP	NT	TP	NT	XC	NT	NT		NT	TP	NT	HT	XC	NT	TP	NT	XC		TP	NT	TP	NT
					◇1		◇1					◇1		◇1	◇1		◇1		◇1		◇1		◇1	
							A	B			C	D			E				F			G	H	B
	🚌	🚌	🚌				🛒							⊠	🛒				🛒					
Hull d									08 40		08 54	09 00		09 30		09 33						10 50	10 58	
Hessle d																09 40								
Ferriby d																09 45								
Brough d									08 52		09 06	09 12		09 42		09 50						11 02	11 10	
Broomfleet d																								
Gilberdyke d									08 59							09 57						11 09		
Eastrington d																								
Howden d											09 18			09 54										
Wressle d																								
Selby a											09 27	09 32		10 04									11 28	
d											09 28			10 05										
York 33 a											09 54													
Saltmarshe d																								
Goole d									09 09				09 43			10 06						11 18		
Thorne North d													09 51			10 14						11 26		
Cleethorpes d																	09 26				10 26			
New Clee d																								
Grimsby Docks d																								
Grimsby Town a																	09 33				10 33			
d																	09 34				10 34			
Great Coates d																								
Healing d																								
Stallingborough d																								
Habrough d																	09 44				10 44			
Ulceby d																								
Thornton Abbey d																								
Goxhill d																								
New Holland d																								
Barrow Haven d																								
Barton-on-Humber a																								
Barton-on-Humber d																								
Hull Paragon Interchange a																								
Barnetby d																	09 55				10 53			
Scunthorpe a																	10 10				11 08			
d																	10 10				11 08			
Althorpe d																								
Crowle d																								
Thorne South d																								
Hatfield & Stainforth d													09 57			10 20								
Kirk Sandall d													10 02			10 25								
Adwick 31 d																								
Bentley (S.Yorks) 31 d																								
Doncaster 31 a									09 29				10 11	10 23		10 35	10 40				11 38	11 46		
London Kings Cross ⊖26 a														12 14										
York 26 d	03 30	04 55	05 55		08 30										09 30				10 34					
Doncaster d				08 03		09 13	09 32		09 39				10 13		10 30		10 42	11 13	11 30		11 42	11 48		
Conisbrough d				08 10		09 20							10 20					11 20						
Mexborough d				08 14		09 24							10 24					11 24						
Swinton (S.Yorks) d				08 17		09 28		09 35					10 27					11 27						12 05
Rotherham Central d				08 25		09 35		09 48					10 35					11 35						12 13
Meadowhall d				08 30		09 41		09 54	10 00				10 40				11 00	11 40			12 00	12 08		12 21
Sheffield a				08 41		09 51	09 55	10 03	10 08				10 52		10 54		11 07	11 51	11 53		12 07	12 18		12 32
d																	11 10				12 10			
Stockport 78 a																	11 53				12 50			
Manchester Piccadilly a	05 55	07 40	08 40		10 33												12 06				13 03			
Manchester Airport 85 a	06 20	08 05	09 05		10 54												12 34				13 27			

A From Leeds to Birmingham New Street
B From Leeds
C To Hull
D To Leeds
E To Birmingham New Street
F From Newcastle to Plymouth
G From Bridlington
H To Huddersfield

Hull and Cleethorpes - Doncaster - Meadowhall, Sheffield, Manchester and Manchester Airport, Cleethorpes - Barton-on-Humber

Network Diagram - see first Page of Table 18

	NT	XC	HT	TP	NT		NT	TP	NT	XC	NT	TP	TP	NT	TP		NT	NT	NT	TP	TP	NT	HT	XC
		◇1	◇1	◇1				◇1		◇1		◇1	◇1		◇1					◇1	◇1		◇1	◇1
		A			B			C		D	E	C	F	B			G		E	F		B		H
		🛒	⊠							🛒													⊠	🛒
Hull d			11 30		11 46		11 53	12 00			12 46	12 58		13 29					13 35			14 23	14 30	
Hessle d																			13 42					
Ferriby d																			13 47					
Brough d			11 42		11 58		12 05	12 12			12 58	13 10		13 41					13 52			14 35	14 42	
Broomfleet d																								
Gilberdyke d							12 12				13 05								14 00					
Eastrington d																								
Howden d			11 54		12 10									13 53								14 47	14 54	
Wressle d																								
Selby a			12 04		12 19			12 32				13 28		14 02								14 56	15 04	
d			12 05		12 20									14 03								14 57	15 05	
York 33 a					12 44									14 30								15 25		
Saltmarshe d																								
Goole d	11 43						12 21				13 14							13 43	14 08					
Thorne North d	11 51						12 29											13 51						
Cleethorpes d				11 26																	13 26			
New Clee d																								
Grimsby Docks d																								
Grimsby Town a				11 33																	13 33			
d				11 34																	13 34			
Great Coates d																								
Healing d																								
Stallingborough d																								
Habrough d																								
Ulceby d																								
Thornton Abbey d																								
Goxhill d																								
New Holland d																								
Barrow Haven d																								
Barton-on-Humber a																								
Barton-on-Humber d																								
Hull Paragon Interchange a																								
Barnetby d				11 53																	13 53			
Scunthorpe a				12 10																	14 08			
d				12 11																	14 08			
Althorpe d																								
Crowle d																								
Thorne South d																								
Hatfield & Stainforth d	11 57																	13 57						
Kirk Sandall d	12 02																	14 02						
Adwick 31 d																								
Bentley (S.Yorks) 31 d																								
Doncaster 31 a	12 11		12 25	12 40			12 47				13 37							14 11	14 31		14 37		15 25	
London Kings Cross ⊖26 a			14 14																				17 15	
York 26 d		11 28								12 28			13 15							14 16				14 34
Doncaster d	12 13	12 30		12 42					13 13	13 30	13 38				13 42			14 13	14 33		14 42			14 59
Conisbrough d	12 20								13 20									14 20						
Mexborough d	12 24								13 24									14 24						
Swinton (S.Yorks) d	12 27								13 27								14 06	14 30						
Rotherham Central d	12 38								13 36								14 14	14 42						
Meadowhall d	12 43			13 00					13 44		13 56				14 00		14 21	14 48	14 52		15 00			
Sheffield a	12 55	12 54		13 07					13 52	13 54	14 06				14 07		14 32	14 55	15 03		15 07			15 21
d				13 10											14 11						15 11			
Stockport 78 a				13 53											14 53						15 53			
Manchester Piccadilly a				14 06									15 08		15 06					16 08	16 06			
Manchester Airport 85 a				14 34									15 24		15 34					16 24	16 34			

A From Edinburgh to Birmingham New Street
B To Hull
C To Huddersfield
D From Edinburgh to Penzance
E From Scarborough
F From Newcastle
G From Leeds
H From Newcastle to Reading

Table 29

Sundays from 28 October

Hull and Cleethorpes - Doncaster - Meadowhall, Sheffield, Manchester and Manchester Airport, Cleethorpes - Barton-on-Humber

Network Diagram - see first Page of Table 18

		XC ◇■ A ✠		NT	NT B	TP ◇■	TP ◇■ C	XC ◇■ D ✠	NT E	XC ◇■ F ✠	NT	NT G		NT	TP ◇■ H	TP ◇■	XC ◇■ I ✠	HT ◇■ ⊠	XC ◇■ J ✠	NT	NT B	TP ◇■		TP ◇■ C	NT K
Hull	d				14 41		14 58					15 41		16 00				16 30			16 41			16 58	17 23
Hessle	d																								
Ferriby	d																								
Brough	d				14 53		15 10					15 53		16 12				16 42			16 53			17 10	17 35
Broomfleet	d																								
Gilberdyke	d				15 00							16 00									17 00				
Eastrington	d																								
Howden	d													16 24				16 54							17 47
Wressle	d																								
Selby	a						15 28							16 33				17 04						17 28	17 56
	d													16 34				17 05							17 57
York ■ 33	a													16 59											18 25
Saltmarshe	d																								
Goole	d				15 09						15 43	16 09									17 09				
Thorne North	d										15 51														
Cleethorpes	d					14 26										15 26						16 26			
New Clee	d																								
Grimsby Docks	d																								
Grimsby Town	a					14 33										15 33						16 33			
	d					14 34										15 34						16 34			
Great Coates	d																								
Healing	d																								
Stallingborough	d																								
Habrough	d					14 44																			
Ulceby	d																								
Thornton Abbey	d																								
Goxhill	d																								
New Holland	d																								
Barrow Haven	d																								
Barton-on-Humber	a																								
Barton-on-Humber	d																								
Hull Paragon Interchange	a																								
Barnetby	d					14 53										15 53						16 53			
Scunthorpe	a					15 08										16 08						17 08			
	d					15 08										16 08						17 08			
Althorpe	d																								
Crowle	d																								
Thorne South	d																								
Hatfield & Stainforth	d										15 57														
Kirk Sandall	d										16 02														
Adwick 31	d																								
Bentley (S.Yorks) 31	d																								
Doncaster ■ 31	a				15 32	15 39					16 11	16 32				16 39		17 25			17 31	17 38			
London Kings Cross ■ ⊖26	a																	19 18							
York ■ 26	d	14 40						15 34		15 40					16 15		16 23		16 40						
Doncaster ■	d			15 13	15 33	15 42		15 59			16 13	16 33				16 42	16 51			17 13	17 32	17 42			
Conisbrough	d			15 20							16 20									17 21					
Mexborough	d			15 24							16 24									17 25					
Swinton (S.Yorks)	d			15 30					16 05		16 29									17 30					
Rotherham Central	d			15 41					16 13		16 41									17 41					
Meadowhall ⇌	d			15 48	15 52	16 00			16 21		16 47	16 53				17 00				17 48	17 53	18 00			
Sheffield ■ ⇌	a	15 51		15 55	16 01	16 07		16 21	16 32	16 51	16 55	17 04				17 07	17 19		17 51	17 55	18 01	18 08			
	d					16 11										17 11						18 11			
Stockport 78	a					16 53										17 53						18 53			
Manchester Piccadilly ■ ⇌	a					17 06									18 08	18 06						19 06			
Manchester Airport 85 ✈	a					17 27									18 24	18 27						19 27			

A From Glasgow Central to Penance
B From Bridlington
C To Huddersfield
D From Newcastle to Reading
E From Leeds
F From Glasgow Central to Plymouth
G From Scarborough
H From Newcastle
I From Edinburgh to Reading
J From Aberdeen to Plymouth
K To Hull

Table 29

Sundays from 28 October

Hull and Cleethorpes - Doncaster - Meadowhall, Sheffield, Manchester and Manchester Airport, Cleethorpes - Barton-on-Humber

Network Diagram - see first Page of Table 18

		XC ◇■ A ✠	NT	NT B	EM ◇■ C ✠	XC ◇■ D ✠	NT	NT E		TP ◇■	HT ◇■ ⊠	XC ◇■ F ✠	NT G	XC ◇■ H ✠	NT	NT I	TP ◇■	TP ◇■ J		XC ◇■ K ✠	NT L	NT B	XC ◇■ M	NT	TP ◇■
Hull	d							17 41			18 30					18 38		18 58			19 24				
Hessle	d																								
Ferriby	d																								
Brough	d							17 53			18 42					18 50		19 10			19 36				
Broomfleet	d																								
Gilberdyke	d							18 00								18 57									
Eastrington	d																								
Howden	d										18 54										19 48				
Wressle	d																								
Selby	a										19 04							19 28			19 57				
	d										19 05										19 58				
York ■ 33	a																				20 25				
Saltmarshe	d																								
Goole	d		17 42					18 09								19 06									
Thorne North	d		17 50													19 14									
Cleethorpes	d									17 26							18 26								19 26
New Clee	d																								
Grimsby Docks	d																								
Grimsby Town	a									17 33							18 33								19 33
	d									17 34							18 34								19 34
Great Coates	d																								
Healing	d																								
Stallingborough	d																								
Habrough	d									17 44															
Ulceby	d																								
Thornton Abbey	d																								
Goxhill	d																								
New Holland	d																								
Barrow Haven	d																								
Barton-on-Humber	a																								
Barton-on-Humber	d																								
Hull Paragon Interchange	a																								
Barnetby	d									17 53							18 53								19 53
Scunthorpe	a									18 08							19 08								20 08
	d									18 08							19 08								20 08
Althorpe	d																								
Crowle	d																								
Thorne South	d																								
Hatfield & Stainforth	d		17 56													19 20									
Kirk Sandall	d		18 01													19 25									
Adwick 31	d																								
Bentley (S.Yorks) 31	d																								
Doncaster ■ 31	a		18 09					18 33		18 38	19 25					19 35	19 38								20 40
London Kings Cross ■ ⊖26	a										21 18														
York ■ 26	d	17 34			17 42	17 40						18 34		18 40						19 24			19 40		
Doncaster ■	d	17 59			18 08		18 19	18 34		18 42		18 59			19 18	19 37	19 42			19 50				20 14	20 42
Conisbrough	d						18 26								19 25									20 21	
Mexborough	d						18 30								19 29									20 25	
Swinton (S.Yorks)	d			18 10			18 33						19 01		19 33							20 07		20 29	
Rotherham Central	d			18 19			18 42						19 13		19 41							20 17		20 41	
Meadowhall ⇌	d			18 25			18 47	18 53		19 00			19 18		19 47	19 57	20 00					20 23		20 47	21 00
Sheffield ■ ⇌	a	18 23		18 36	18 39	18 51	18 57	19 03		19 07		19 21	19 27	19 50	19 55	20 06	20 07			20 16		20 34	20 51	20 55	21 07
	d									19 11							20 11								21 11
Stockport 78	a									19 53							20 53								21 53
Manchester Piccadilly ■ ⇌	a									20 09							21 06								22 06
Manchester Airport 85 ✈	a									20 30							21 27								22 27

A From Newcastle to Reading
B From Leeds
C To St Pancras International
D From Glasgow Central to Plymouth
E From Scarborough
F From Newcastle to Guildford
G From Moorthorpe
H From Glasgow Central to Bristol Temple Meads
I From Bridlington
J To Huddersfield
K From Newcastle to Birmingham New Street
L To Leeds
M From Edinburgh to Bristol Temple Meads

Sundays
from 28 October

Hull and Cleethorpes - Doncaster - Meadowhall, Sheffield, Manchester and Manchester Airport, Cleethorpes - Barton-on-Humber

Network Diagram - see first Page of Table 18

Station			TP	XC	NT	NT	XC	TP	NT	TP	NT	NT
			◇■	◇■			◇■	◇■		◇■		
			A	B	C	D	E	F	G		H	
				🍴								
Hull		d			20 01	20 29		21 00				21 35
Hessle		d			20 08							
Ferriby		d			20 13							
Brough		d			20 18	20 41		21 12				21 47
Broomfleet		d										
Gilberdyke		d			20 25							21 54
Eastrington		d										
Howden		d				20 53						
Wressle		d										
Selby		a				21 02		21 30				
		d				21 03						
York ■	33	a				21 30						
Saltmarshe		d										
Goole		d			20 34							22 03
Thorne North		d			20 42							22 11
Cleethorpes		d								20 26		
New Clee		d										
Grimsby Docks		d										
Grimsby Town		a								20 33		
		d								20 34		
Great Coates		d										
Healing		d										
Stallingborough		d										
Habrough		d								20 44		
Ulceby		d										
Thornton Abbey		d										
Goxhill		d										
New Holland		d										
Barrow Haven		d										
Barton-on-Humber		a										
BartonenHumber		d										
Hull Paragon Interchange		a										
Barnetby		d								20 53		
Scunthorpe		a								21 08		
		d								21 08		
Althorpe		d										
Crowle		d										
Thorne South		d										
Hatfield & Stainforth		d										22 15
Kirk Sandall		d										22 20
Adwick	31	d										
Bentley (S.Yorks)	31	d										
Doncaster ■	31	a			20 59					21 40		22 32
London Kings Cross ■	⊖26	a										
York ■	26	d	20 15	20 24			20 40					
Doncaster ■		d		20 50	21 01					21 42		22 40
Conisbrough		d			21 08							22 47
Mexborough		d			21 12							22 51
Swinton (S.Yorks)		d			21 15				21 33	21 52	22 32	22 53
Rotherham Central		d			21 22				21 48	21 58	22 40	22 58
Meadowhall	⇌	d			21 28				21 54	22 04	22 45	23 04
Sheffield ■	⇌	a		21 17	21 38		21 50		22 05	22 13	22 54	23 15
		d										
Stockport	78	a										
Manchester Piccadilly ■	⇌	a	22 14									
Manchester Airport	85 ✈	a										

A From Newcastle
B From Newcastle to Birmingham New Street
C From Scarborough
D To Hull
E From Glasgow Central to Birmingham New Street
F To Leeds
G From Moorthorpe
H From Leeds

Mondays to Fridays

Manchester Airport, Manchester, Sheffield and Meadowhall-Doncaster-Cleethorpes and Hull Barton-on-Humber - Cleethorpes

Network Diagram - see first Page of Table 18

Miles	Miles	Miles	Miles	Miles	Station			TP MX	TP MO	NT MX	NT MO	NT	NT	GR	NT	EM
								◇■	◇■					■		
									A		A	H	I	J	H	K
														🍴		
0	—	—	—	—	**Manchester Airport**	85 ✈	d	20p47								
9¾	—	—	—	—	**Manchester Piccadilly** ■	⇌	d	21p20								
15¾	—	—	—	—	Stockport	78	d	21p28								
52½	—	—	—	—	**Sheffield** ■	⇌	a	22p08								
—	—	—	—	—			d	22p11	22p30	23p27	23p34	05 22	05 29			
56	—	—	—	—	**Meadowhall**	⇌	d	22p16	22p35	23p33	23p40	05 28	05 35			
58¾	—	—	—	—	Rotherham Central		d			23p39	23p47	05 34	05 41			
63¼	—	—	—	—	Swinton (S.Yorks)		d			23p48	23p55	05a42	05 49			
64½	—	—	—	—	Mexborough		d			23p51	23p58		05 52			
66¾	—	—	—	—	Conisbrough		d			23p55	00 02		05 56			
—	—	—	—	—	London Kings Cross		d									
71½	—	—	—	—	**Doncaster** ■		a	22p42	22p56	00 07	00 13		06 06			
—	—	—	—	—	York ■	26	a									
—	0	0	—	0	**Doncaster**	31	d	22p44	22p58				06 12	06 15	06 26	
—	—	—	—	1¾	Bentley (S.Yorks)	31	a								06 29	
—	—	—	—	4	Adwick	31	a								06 33	
75½	—	4	—	—	Kirk Sandall		d	22p49					06 18			
78¼	—	6¾	—	—	Hatfield & Stainforth		d	22p54					06 23			
—	—	9¾	—	—	Thorne South		d	22p58								
—	—	15¾	—	—	Crowle		d	23p07								
—	—	19½	—	—	Althorpe		d	23p12								
—	—	23	—	—	**Scunthorpe**		a	23p17	23p23							
—	—	—	—	—			d	23p18	23p24							
—	—	34½	—	—	Barnetby		d	23p32	23p38							06 31
—	—	—	—	—	Hull Paragon Interchange		d									
—	—	—	—	—	BartonenHumber		a									
—	—	—	0	—	**Barton-on-Humber**		d									
—	—	—	2	—	Barrow Haven		d									
—	—	—	3½	—	New Holland		d									
—	—	—	5½	—	Goxhill		d									
—	—	—	7	—	Thornton Abbey		d									
—	—	—	9¾	—	Ulceby		d									
—	—	40¾	11½	—	Habrough		d	23p42								06 41
—	—	44½	15¼	—	Stallingborough		d									
—	—	45½	16¼	—	Healing		d									
—	—	46½	17¼	—	Great Coates		d									
—	—	48¾	19½	—	**Grimsby Town**		a	23p55	23p57							06 56
—	—	—	—	—			d	23p56	23p58							
—	—	49¾	20½	—	Grimsby Docks		d									
—	—	50½	21¼	—	New Clee		d									
—	—	52	22¾	—	**Cleethorpes**		a	00 09	00 09							
81¼	—	—	—	—	Thorne North		d						06 28			
88¾	—	—	—	—	Goole		d						06 37			
92¼	—	—	—	—	Saltmarshe		d						06 42			
—	—	—	—	—	York ■	33	d							06a36		
—	18¼	—	—	—	**Selby**		a									
—	24½	—	—	—	Wressle		d									
—	27	—	—	—	Howden		d									
—	30	—	—	—	Eastrington		d									
95½	32¼	—	—	—	Gilberdyke		d						06 51			
98	34¾	—	—	—	Broomfleet		d						06 55			
102	38¾	—	—	—	Brough		d						07 01			
105	41¾	—	—	—	Ferriby		d						07 05			
107¾	44½	—	—	—	Hessle		d						07 10			
112	49¼	—	—	—	**Hull**		a						07 21			

A from 21 May
H To Leeds
I To Beverley
J To Edinburgh
K From Lincoln

Table 29

Mondays to Fridays

Manchester Airport, Manchester, Sheffield and Meadowhall-Doncaster-Cleethorpes and Hull Barton-on-Humber - Cleethorpes

Network Diagram - see first Page of Table 18

		NT	NT	NT	XC	NT BHX	NT	NT	NT	TP		XC	NT	NT	NT	TP	NT	NT	NT	NT			NT BHX	NT	NT
				A	◇1 B ✕	🚌		A		◇1		◇1 C ✕	A	A	D	◇1 ✕	E		A				🚌		G
Manchester Airport 85 ✈	d									05 15															
Manchester Piccadilly 10	d									05 44						06 21									
Stockport 78	d									05 52															
Sheffield 7	a									06 49															
	d		06 18	06 28	06 33				06 52	06 55		07 12	07 14							07 24					
Meadowhall	d		06 24	06 34					06 58	07 01			07 21							07 30					
Rotherham Central	d		06 30	06 40					07 04				07 27							07 36					
Swinton (S.Yorks)	d		06 38	06a51					07 14				07a35							07 44					
Mexborough	d		06 41						07 17											07 47					
Conisbrough	d		06 45						07 21											07 51					
London Kings Cross	d																								
Doncaster 7	a		06 56		06 57				07 32	07 22										08 01					
York 8 26	a				07 26							08 22													
Doncaster 31	d	06 39	06 59					07 08	07 34	07 24				07 26			07 28		07 56	08 03					08 16
Bentley (S.Yorks) 31	a		07 02					07 11	07 37					07 29					07 59						08 18
Adwick 31	a		07 08					07 15	07 43					07 33					08 03						08 24
Kirk Sandall	d	06 45															07 34			08 09					
Hatfield & Stainforth	d	06 50															07 39			08 14					
Thorne South	d	06 55																		08 18					
Crowle	d	07 04																		08 27					
Althorpe	d	07 10																		08 33					
Scunthorpe	a	07 18								07 49										08 44					
	d									07 50															
Barnetby	d									08 04															
Hull Paragon Interchange	d					06 20																	06 55		
Barton-on-Humber	a					06 52																	07 30		
Barton-on-Humber	d						06 58																	07 58	
Barrow Haven	d						07 03																	08 03	
New Holland	d						07 07																	08 06	
Goxhill	d						07 11																	08 11	
Thornton Abbey	d																							08 14	
Ulceby	d						07 19																	08 18	
Habrough	d						07 23			08 12														08 23	
Stallingborough	d						07 28																	08 28	
Healing	d						07 31																	08 31	
Great Coates	d																							08 34	
Grimsby Town	a						07 38			08 26														08 39	
	d						07 39			08 33														08 39	
Grimsby Docks	d																							08 42	
New Clee	d																							08x44	
Cleethorpes	a						07 51			08 44														08 49	
Thorne North	d																07 44								
Goole	d																07 53								
Saltmarshe	d																07 58								
York 8 33	d																	07 29							
Selby	a															07 43		07 50							
Wressle	d																	07 58							
Howden	d															07 52		08 03							
Eastrington	d																	08 08							
Gilberdyke	d														07 39		08 04	08 12							
Broomfleet	d														07 43			08 16							
Brough	d														07 49	08 04	08 12	08 22							
Ferriby	d														07 53		08 16	08 27							
Hessle	d														07 58		08 21	08 31							
Hull	a														08 11	08 20	08 34	08 46							

A To Leeds
B until 26 October, MX from 30 October. From Derby to Newcastle
C From Birmingham New Street to Glasgow Central
D To Scarborough
E To Beverley
G From Scunthorpe

Table 29

Mondays to Fridays

Manchester Airport, Manchester, Sheffield and Meadowhall-Doncaster-Cleethorpes and Hull Barton-on-Humber - Cleethorpes

Network Diagram - see first Page of Table 18

		NT	XC	NT	EM	TP	TP		NT	XC		GR	NT	NT	NT	HT	NT			NT	XC	NT	NT	NT BHX	NT
		A	◇1 B ✕	C	D	◇1 ✕	◇1 ✕		C	◇1 E ✕		1 F ✕	G			◇1 ⊠				A	◇1 B ✕	C	I	🚌	
Manchester Airport 85 ✈	d					06 55																			
Manchester Piccadilly 10	d					07 20	07 36																		
Stockport 78	d					07 28																			
Sheffield 7	a					08 10																			
	d	07 41	07 54			08 11			08 14	08 21							08 24			08 41	08 48		08 53		
Meadowhall	d	07 47				08 16			08 21								08 31			08 47			09 00		
Rotherham Central	d	07 55							08 28								08 37						09 06		
Swinton (S.Yorks)	d	08 03							08a37								08 48						09 16		
Mexborough	d	08 06															08 51						09 19		
Conisbrough	d	08 10															08 55						09 23		
London Kings Cross	d											07 08				07 20									
Doncaster 7	a	08 19	08 24			08 38						08 59				09 04	09 06			09 15	09 18		09 31		
York 8 26	a		08 45							09 26		09 29									09 44				
Doncaster 31	d	08 21		08 26		08 41						10a24		08 49	08 55	09 06	09 06			09 18		09 26	09 34		
Bentley (S.Yorks) 31	a			08 29										08 52								09 29	09 37		
Adwick 31	a			08 33										08 58								09 33	09 43		
Kirk Sandall	d														09 01		09 14								
Hatfield & Stainforth	d														09 06		09 19								
Thorne South	d																09 24								
Crowle	d																09 32								
Althorpe	d																09 38								
Scunthorpe	a					09 06											09 46								
	d					09 07																			
Barnetby	d				08 49	09 21																			
Hull Paragon Interchange	d																							09 05	
Barton-on-Humber	a																							09 40	
Barton-on-Humber	d																								09 52
Barrow Haven	d																								09 57
New Holland	d																								10 00
Goxhill	d																								10 05
Thornton Abbey	d																								10 08
Ulceby	d																								10 12
Habrough	d				09 01	09 29																			10 17
Stallingborough	d																								10 22
Healing	d																								10 25
Great Coates	d																								10 28
Grimsby Town	a				09 15	09 43																			10 33
	d					09 44																			10 33
Grimsby Docks	d																								10 36
New Clee	d																								10x38
Cleethorpes	a					09 55																			10 43
Thorne North	d														09 11										
Goole	d	08 43													09 19					09 35					
Saltmarshe	d																								
York 8 33	d												08 43												
Selby	a						08 57						09 06			09 22									
Wressle	d																								
Howden	d												09 16			09 33									
Eastrington	d																								
Gilberdyke	d														09 28										
Broomfleet	d																								
Brough	d	08 57											09 28		09 35	09 45				09 52					
Ferriby	d														09 40										
Hessle	d														09 45										
Hull	a	09 13					09 31						09 47		09 58	10 04				10 09					

A To Bridlington
B From Birmingham New Street to Newcastle
C To Leeds
D From Newark North Gate
E From Birmingham New Street to Edinburgh
F not from 30 July until 10 August, from 30 August until 7 September. To London Kings Cross
G From Beverley
H To Edinburgh
I From Worksop

Manchester Airport, Manchester, Sheffield and Meadowhall-Doncaster-Cleethorpes and Hull Barton-on-Humber - Cleethorpes

Network Diagram - see first Page of Table 18

		TP	TP	NT	XC	NT	NT	NT	NT	XC	NT	NT	NT	EM	TP	TP	NT	XC	GR	NT	NT
		◇1	◇1		◇1					◇1					◇1	◇1		◇1	1		
				A	B				D	E	F	A	G	H			A	I	J		
		✠	✠		✠					✠					✠	✠		✠	✠		
Manchester Airport 85 ✈	d	07 53													08 55						
Manchester Piccadilly 10	d	08 20	08 42												09 20	09 42					
Stockport 78	d	08 28													09 28						
Sheffield 7	a	09 08													10 08						
	d	09 11		09 14	09 21		09 24	09 29	09 41	09 47			09 53		10 11		10 14	10 21			10 24
Meadowhall	d	09 16		09 21			09 30	09 35	09 47				09 59		10 16		10 21				10 30
Rotherham Central	d			09 27			09 37	09 42					10 06				10 27				10 36
Swinton (S.Yorks)	d			09a36			09 48	09 51					10 15				10a36				10 44
Mexborough	d						09 51						10 18								10 47
Conisbrough	d						09 55						10 22								10 51
London Kings Cross	d																		09 08		
Doncaster 7	a	09 35					10 05		10 15	10 18			10 32		10 35				11 03		11 04
York 8 26	a				10 26			10 56		10 45								11 26	11 31		
Doncaster 31	d	09 37				09 51	10 07		10 19			10 26	10 34		10 37				12a24	10 51	11 08
Bentley (S.Yorks) 31	a											10 29	10 37								
Adwick 31	a											10 33	10 43								
Kirk Sandall	d					09 57	10 13													10 57	11 14
Hatfield & Stainforth	d					10 02	10 18													11 02	11 19
Thorne South	d						10 23														11 24
Crowle	d						10 32														11 32
Althorpe	d						10 38														11 38
Scunthorpe	a	10 02					10 46								11 02						11 46
	d	10 03													11 03						
Barnetby	d	10 17												10 59	11 17						
Hull Paragon Interchange	d																				
Barton-on-Humber	a																				
Barton-on-Humber	d																				
Barrow Haven	d																				
New Holland	d																				
Goxhill	d																				
Thornton Abbey	d																				
Ulceby	d																				
Habrough	d													11 08							
Stallingborough	d																				
Healing	d																				
Great Coates	d																				
Grimsby Town	a	10 39												11 23	11 37						
	d	10 40													11 38						
Grimsby Docks	d																				
New Clee	d																				
Cleethorpes	a	10 51													11 50						
Thorne North	d					10 07														11 07	
Goole	d					10 16			10 38											11 16	
Saltmarshe	d																				
York 8 33	d										10 20										
Selby	a		09 57								10 40					10 57					
Wressle	d																				
Howden	d										10 50										
Eastrington	d																				
Gilberdyke	d					10 24					10 57									11 25	
Broomfleet	d																			11 30	
Brough	d		10 16			10 32			10 51		11 05					11 16				11 36	
Ferriby	d					10 37														11 40	
Hessle	d					10 41														11 45	
Hull	a		10 35			10 54			11 09		11 23					11 35				12 01	

A To Leeds
B From Bath Spa to Glasgow Central
D To Scarborough
E From Guildford to Newcastle
F From Leeds
G From Lincoln
H From Newark North Gate
I From Plymouth to Edinburgh
J To London Kings Cross. ✠ from York

Manchester Airport, Manchester, Sheffield and Meadowhall-Doncaster-Cleethorpes and Hull Barton-on-Humber - Cleethorpes

Network Diagram - see first Page of Table 18

		NT	XC	HT	NT	NT	NT BHX	NT	TP	TP	NT	XC	NT	NT	NT	NT	XC	NT	NT	NT BHX	EM
			◇1	◇1					◇1	◇1		◇1					◇1				
		B	C		D	E	🚌				D	F	G			I	J	D	E	🚌	K
			✠	☒					✠	✠		✠					✠				
Manchester Airport 85 ✈	d								09 55												
Manchester Piccadilly 10	d								10 20	10 42											
Stockport 78	d								10 28												
Sheffield 7	a								11 08												
	d	10 41	10 47			10 53			11 11		11 14	11 21			11 24	11 41	11 47		11 53		
Meadowhall	d	10 47				10 59			11 16		11 21				11 30	11 47			11 59		
Rotherham Central	d					11 05					11 27				11 37				12 05		
Swinton (S.Yorks)	d					11 16					11a36				11 48				12 16		
Mexborough	d					11 19									11 51				12 19		
Conisbrough	d					11 23									11 55				12 23		
London Kings Cross	d			09 48																	
Doncaster 7	a	11 14	11 18	11 23		11 32			11 35						12 04	12 15	12 18		12 32		
York 8 26	a		11 46									12 26					12 46				
Doncaster 31	d	11 19		11 25	11 26	11 34			11 37					11 51	12 08	12 19		12 26	12 34		
Bentley (S.Yorks) 31	a				11 29	11 37												12 29	12 38		
Adwick 31	a				11 33	11 43												12 33	12 43		
Kirk Sandall	d													11 57	12 14						
Hatfield & Stainforth	d													12 02	12 19						
Thorne South	d														12 24						
Crowle	d														12 32						
Althorpe	d														12 38						
Scunthorpe	a								12 02						12 46						
	d								12 03												
Barnetby	d								12 17												13 10
Hull Paragon Interchange	d						11 05													13 05	
Barton-on-Humber	a						11 40													13 40	
Barton-on-Humber	d							11 52													
Barrow Haven	d							11 57													
New Holland	d							12 00													
Goxhill	d							12 05													
Thornton Abbey	d							12 08													
Ulceby	d							12 12													
Habrough	d							12 17	12 26												13 19
Stallingborough	d							12 22													
Healing	d							12 25													
Great Coates	d							12 28													
Grimsby Town	a							12 33	12 39												13 35
	d							12 33	12 40												
Grimsby Docks	d							12 36													
New Clee	d							12x38													
Cleethorpes	a							12 43	12 52												
Thorne North	d													12 07							
Goole	d	11 37												12 16		12 35					
Saltmarshe	d																				
York 8 33	d												11 45								
Selby	a			11 39						11 57			12 04								
Wressle	d																				
Howden	d			11 50									12 14								
Eastrington	d																				
Gilberdyke	d												12 21	12 27							
Broomfleet	d																				
Brough	d	11 51		12 02						12 16			12 29	12 35		12 49					
Ferriby	d													12 40							
Hessle	d													12 44							
Hull	a	12 09		12 18						12 36			12 49	12 58		13 09					

B To Bridlington
C From Reading to Newcastle
D To Leeds
E From Lincoln
F From Plymouth to Glasgow Central
G From Hull
I To Scarborough
J From Winchester to Newcastle
K From Newark North Gate

Table 29

Mondays to Fridays

Manchester Airport, Manchester, Sheffield and Meadowhall-Doncaster-Cleethorpes and Hull Barton-on-Humber - Cleethorpes

Network Diagram - see first Page of Table 18

		TP	TP	NT	XC	GR	NT	NT	NT	NT	XC	HT	NT	NT	NT	TP	TP	NT	XC	NT	NT	NT
		◇1	◇1	A	◇1 B	1 C				E	◇1 F	◇1	A	G		◇1	◇1	A	◇1 H	I		
Manchester Airport 85	d	10 55														11 55						
Manchester Piccadilly	d	11 20	11 42													12 20	12 42					
Stockport 78	d	11 28														12 28						
Sheffield	a	12 08														13 08						
	d	12 11		12 14	12 21				12 24	12 41	12 47			12 53		13 11		13 14	13 21			13 24
Meadowhall	d	12 16		12 21					12 30	12 47				12 59		13 16		13 21				13 30
Rotherham Central	d			12 27					12 37					13 05				13 27				13 37
Swinton (S.Yorks)	d			12a36					12 48					13 16				13a36				13 47
Mexborough	d								12 51					13 19								13 50
Conisbrough	d								12 55					13 23								13 54
London Kings Cross	d					11 08						11 48										
Doncaster	a	12 35				13 03			13 04	13 15	13 18	13 23		13 33		13 35						14 04
York 26	a				13 26	13 31					13 40								14 26			
Doncaster 31	d	12 37				14a22		12 51	13 08	13 19		13 25	13 26	13 34		13 37					13 50	14 08
Bentley (S.Yorks) 31	a												13 29	13 37								
Adwick 31	a												13 33	13 43								
Kirk Sandall	d							12 57	13 14												13 56	14 14
Hatfield & Stainforth	d							13 02	13 19												14 01	14 19
Thorne South	d								13 24													14 26
Crowle	d								13 33													14 34
Althorpe	d								13 39													14 40
Scunthorpe	a	13 02							13 46							14 02						14 48
	d	13 03														14 03						
Barnetby	d	13 17														14 17						
Hull Paragon Interchange	d																					
Barton-on-Humber	a																					
Barton-on-Humber	d														13 52							
Barrow Haven	d														13 57							
New Holland	d														14 00							
Goxhill	d														14 05							
Thornton Abbey	d														14 08							
Ulceby	d														14 12							
Habrough	d														14 17	14 26						
Stallingborough	d														14 22							
Healing	d														14 25							
Great Coates	d														14 28							
Grimsby Town	a	13 37													14 33	14 39						
	d	13 38													14 33	14 40						
Grimsby Docks	d														14 36							
New Clee	d														14x38							
Cleethorpes	a	13 50													14 43	14 52						
Thorne North	d							13 07													14 06	
Goole	d							13 16		13 38											14 16	
Saltmarshe	d																				14 21	
York 33	d						12 47													13 44		
Selby	a		12 57				13 06					13 39					13 57			14 07		
Wressle	d																					
Howden	d						13 16					13 50								14 17		
Eastrington	d																					
Gilberdyke	d							13 27													14 27	
Broomfleet	d																					
Brough	d		13 16				13 28	13 35		13 52		14 02					14 16			14 30	14 36	
Ferriby	d							13 40													14 40	
Hessle	d							13 44													14 45	
Hull	a		13 35				13 48	14 00		14 09		14 19					14 35			14 52	14 56	

A To Leeds
B From Plymouth to Edinburgh
C To London Kings Cross. from York
E To Bridlington
F From Reading to Newcastle
G From Lincoln
H From Penzance to Glasgow Central
I From Hull

Table 29

Mondays to Fridays

Manchester Airport, Manchester, Sheffield and Meadowhall-Doncaster-Cleethorpes and Hull Barton-on-Humber - Cleethorpes

Network Diagram - see first Page of Table 18

		NT	NT	XC	NT	NT	NT BHX	EM	TP	TP	NT	XC	NT	NT	NT	NT	XC	HT	NT
		B	C	◇1 D	E			F	◇1	◇1	E	◇1 G	H	I		J	◇1 K	◇1	E
Manchester Airport 85	d								12 55										
Manchester Piccadilly	d								13 20	13 42									
Stockport 78	d								13 28										
Sheffield	a								14 08										
	d	13 29	13 41	13 47		13 53			14 11		14 14	14 21			14 24	14 41	14 47		
Meadowhall	d	13 35	13 46			13 59			14 16		14 21				14 30	14 47			
Rotherham Central	d	13 41				14 05					14 27				14 37				
Swinton (S.Yorks)	d	13 50				14 17					14a35				14 48				
Mexborough	d					14 20									14 51				
Conisbrough	d					14 24									14 55				
London Kings Cross	d																	13 48	
Doncaster	a		14 15	14 18		14 32			14 35						15 04	15 17	15 18	15 23	
York 26	a	14 55		14 44								15 26					15 45		
Doncaster 31	d		14 19		14 26	14 34			14 37					14 50	15 07	15 19		15 25	15 26
Bentley (S.Yorks) 31	a				14 29	14 37													15 29
Adwick 31	a				14 33	14 43													15 33
Kirk Sandall	d													14 57	15 14				
Hatfield & Stainforth	d													15 02	15 19				
Thorne South	d														15 24				
Crowle	d														15 32				
Althorpe	d														15 38				
Scunthorpe	a								15 02						15 47				
	d								15 03										
Barnetby	d							15 11	15 17										
Hull Paragon Interchange	d						15 05												
Barton-on-Humber	a						15 40												
Barton-on-Humber	d																		
Barrow Haven	d																		
New Holland	d																		
Goxhill	d																		
Thornton Abbey	d																		
Ulceby	d																		
Habrough	d							15 19											
Stallingborough	d																		
Healing	d																		
Great Coates	d																		
Grimsby Town	a							15 34	15 37										
	d								15 38										
Grimsby Docks	d																		
New Clee	d																		
Cleethorpes	a								15 50										
Thorne North	d													15 07					
Goole	d		14 37											15 16		15 37			
Saltmarshe	d																		
York 33	d												14 47						
Selby	a									14 57			15 06					15 39	
Wressle	d																		
Howden	d												15 16					15 50	
Eastrington	d																		
Gilberdyke	d													15 27					
Broomfleet	d																		
Brough	d		14 54							15 16			15 28	15 35		15 51		16 02	
Ferriby	d													15 40					
Hessle	d													15 44					
Hull	a		15 12							15 35			15 48	15 55		16 08		16 18	

B To Sheffield
C To Bridlington
D From Southampton Central to Newcastle
E To Leeds
F From Lincoln
G From Plymouth to Aberdeen
H From Hull
I To Beverley
J To Scarborough
K From Reading to Newcastle

Manchester Airport, Manchester, Sheffield and Meadowhall-Doncaster-Cleethorpes and Hull Barton-on-Humber - Cleethorpes

Network Diagram - see first Page of Table 18

Station	Table		NT A	NT	TP ◇1	TP ◇1	NT B	XC ◇1 C	NT	NT	NT B	NT E	XC ◇1 F	NT A	TP ◇1	NT G	TP ◇1	NT B	XC ◇1 H	GR ■ 1 I	NT
Manchester Airport	85	d			13 55										14 55						
Manchester Piccadilly 10		d			14 20	14 42									15 20		15 42				
Stockport	78	d			14 28										15 28						
Sheffield 7		a			15 08										16 08						
		d	14 53		15 11		15 14	15 21		15 24		15 41	15 47	15 53	16 11			16 14	16 21		16 23
Meadowhall		d	14 59		15 16		15 20			15 30		15 47		15 59	16 16			16 20			16 29
Rotherham Central		d	15 05				15 26			15 37				16 05				16 26			16 37
Swinton (S.Yorks)		d	15 16				15a34			15 48				16 16				16a36			16 47
Mexborough		d	15 19							15 51				16 19							16 50
Conisbrough		d	15 23							15 55				16 23							16 54
London Kings Cross		d																		15 08	
Doncaster 7		a	15 33		15 35					16 04		16 15	16 18	16 32	16 35					17 03	17 07
York 8	26	a						16 28					16 45						17 28	17 31	
Doncaster	31	d	15 34		15 37				15 51	16 08	16 16	16 19		16 34	16 37					18a22	
Bentley (S.Yorks)	31	a	15 37								16 19			16 37							
Adwick	31	a	15 42								16 23			16 43							
Kirk Sandall		d							15 57	16 14											
Hatfield & Stainforth		d							16 02	16 19											
Thorne South		d								16 24											
Crowle		d								16 33											
Althorpe		d								16 39											
Scunthorpe		a			16 02					16 46					17 02						
		d			16 03										17 03						
Barnetby		d			16 17										17 17						
Hull Paragon Interchange		d																			
Barton-on-Humber		a																			
Barton-on-Humber		d		15 52																	
Barrow Haven		d		15 57																	
New Holland		d		16 00																	
Goxhill		d		16 05																	
Thornton Abbey		d		16 08																	
Ulceby		d		16 12																	
Habrough		d		16 17	16 26																
Stallingborough		d		16 22																	
Healing		d		16 25																	
Great Coates		d		16 28																	
Grimsby Town		a		16 33	16 39										17 37						
		d		16 33	16 40										17 38						
Grimsby Docks		d		16 36																	
New Clee		d																			
Cleethorpes		a		16 42	16 52										17 50						
Thorne North		d							16 07												
Goole		d							16 16			16 38									
Saltmarshe		d							16 21												
York 8	33	d														16 12					
Selby		a				15 57										16 36	17 00				
Wressle		d														16 44					
Howden		d														16 49					
Eastrington		d																			
Gilberdyke		d							16 27							16 55					
Broomfleet		d																			
Brough		d				16 16			16 35			16 52				17 03	17 18				
Ferriby		d							16 39							17 08					
Hessle		d							16 44							17 12					
Hull		a				16 35			16 57			17 06				17 27	17 37				

A From Lincoln
B To Leeds
C From Penzance to Glasgow Central
E To Bridlington
F From Southampton Central to Newcastle
G From Hull
H From Plymouth to Dundee
I To London Kings Cross

Manchester Airport, Manchester, Sheffield and Meadowhall-Doncaster-Cleethorpes and Hull Barton-on-Humber - Cleethorpes

Network Diagram - see first Page of Table 18

Station	Table		NT A	NT B	XC ◇1 C	NT	HT ◇1	NT D	NT E	NT F	EM G	NT BHX	NT	TP ◇1	TP ◇1	NT E	XC ◇1 H	NT	NT	NT J	XC ◇1 K	NT L
Manchester Airport	85	d												15 55								
Manchester Piccadilly 10		d												16 20	16 42							
Stockport	78	d												16 28								
Sheffield 7		a												17 08								
		d		16 41	16 47					16 53				17 11		17 13	17 21	17 27		17 41	17 47	
Meadowhall		d		16 47						16 59				17 16		17 20		17 33		17 47		
Rotherham Central		d								17 05						17 26		17 39				
Swinton (S.Yorks)		d								17 16						17a36		17 48				
Mexborough		d								17 19								17 51				
Conisbrough		d								17 23								17 55				
London Kings Cross		d					15 48															
Doncaster 7		a		17 16	17 18		17 23			17 32				17 35				18 07		18 12		
York 8	26	a			17 40												18 29				19 01	
Doncaster	31	d	16 51	17 19		17 22	17 25		17 26	17 34				17 47					17 56	18 16		
Bentley (S.Yorks)	31	a							17 29	17 37												
Adwick	31	a							17 33	17 43												
Kirk Sandall		d	16 57			17 28													18 02			
Hatfield & Stainforth		d	17 02			17 33													18 07			
Thorne South		d				17 39																
Crowle		d				17 48																
Althorpe		d				17 54																
Scunthorpe		a				18 01								18 12								
		d												18 13								
Barnetby		d									17 55			18 27								
Hull Paragon Interchange		d										17 10										
Barton-on-Humber		a										17 45										
Barton-on-Humber		d											17 55									
Barrow Haven		d											18 00									
New Holland		d											18 03									
Goxhill		d											18 08									
Thornton Abbey		d											18 11									
Ulceby		d											18 15									
Habrough		d									18 03		18 20	18 36								
Stallingborough		d											18 25									
Healing		d											18 28									
Great Coates		d											18 31									
Grimsby Town		a									18 15		18 36	18 49								
		d											18 36	18 50								
Grimsby Docks		d											18 39									
New Clee		d																				
Cleethorpes		a											18 45	19 01								
Thorne North		d	17 07	17 33															18 12			
Goole		d	17 16	17 42															18 21	18 36		
Saltmarshe		d																	18 26			
York 8	33	d						17 19														18 18
Selby		a					17 39	17 45							17 59							18 42
Wressle		d																				18 50
Howden		d					17 50	17 56							18 08							18 54
Eastrington		d																				18 59
Gilberdyke		d	17 24					18 03											18 37			19 03
Broomfleet		d																	18 41			
Brough		d	17 32	17 55			18 02	18 11							18 20				18 47	18 53		19 10
Ferriby		d	17 37																18 51			
Hessle		d	17 41																18 56			
Hull		a	17 54	18 13			18 21	18 30							18 39				19 06	19 09		19 29

A To Beverley
B To Bridlington
C From Reading to Newcastle
D From Hull
E To Leeds
F From Lincoln
G From Newark North Gate
H From Plymouth to Glasgow Central
I To Edinburgh
J To Scarborough
K From Southampton Central to Edinburgh
L From Leeds

Manchester Airport, Manchester, Sheffield and Meadowhall-Doncaster-Cleethorpes and Hull Barton-on-Humber - Cleethorpes

Network Diagram - see first Page of Table 18

		TP	NT	NT	NT	NT	XC	TP	GR	NT	NT	XC	NT	NT	NT	NT	NT	TP	TP	NT	XC	NT
		◇1	A	B	C	A	◇1 D	◇1	1 E		F	◇1 G	H	A		BHX		◇1	◇1	A	◇1 D	
Manchester Airport 85	d							16 55										17 55				
Manchester Piccadilly 10	d	17 42						17 20										18 20	18 42			
Stockport 78	d							17 28										18 28				
Sheffield 7	a							18 10										19 09				
	d				17 53	18 13	18 21	18 24		18 29	18 41	18 47	19 00					19 11		19 18	19 26	19 30
Meadowhall	d				17 59	18 20		18 29		18 35	18 47		19 06					19 16		19 25		19 36
Rotherham Central	d				18 05	18 26				18 42			19 12							19 31		19 42
Swinton (S.Yorks)	d				18 16	18a36				18 50			19 20							19a40		19 51
Mexborough	d				18 20					18 53			19 23									19 55
Conisbrough	d				18 24					18 57			19 27									19 59
London Kings Cross	d								17 19													
Doncaster 7	a				18 35			18 53	19 05	19 09	19 12	19 14	19 36					19 41				20 08
York 8 26	a						19 29					19 38									20 29	
Doncaster 31	d		18 26	18 29	18 39			18 55	19 07		19 16			19 20	19 21			19 48				
Bentley (S.Yorks) 31	a		18 29											19 23								
Adwick 31	a		18 33											19 27								
Kirk Sandall	d			18 37	18 45										19 27							
Hatfield & Stainforth	d			18 42	18 50										19 32							
Thorne South	d			18 47											19 36							
Crowle	d			18 55											19 45							
Althorpe	d			19 01											19 51							
Scunthorpe	a			19 10				19 23							19 59			20 14				
	d							19 23										20 14				
Barnetby	d							19 37										20 28				
Hull Paragon Interchange	d															19 25						
Barton-on-Humber	a															19 52						
Barton-on-Humber	d																19 58					
Barrow Haven	d																20 03					
New Holland	d																20 06					
Goxhill	d																20 11					
Thornton Abbey	d																20 14					
Ulceby	d																20 18					
Habrough	d																20 23					
Stallingborough	d																20 28					
Healing	d																20 31					
Great Coates	d																20 34					
Grimsby Town	a							19 57									20 39	20 47				
	d							19 58									20 39	20 48				
Grimsby Docks	d																20 42					
New Clee	d																					
Cleethorpes	a							20 10									20 48	21 00				
Thorne North	d				18 55																	
Goole	d				19 12						19 37											
Saltmarshe	d																					
York 8 33	d																					
Selby	a	19 00							19 22										20 00			
Wressle	d																					
Howden	d																		20 10			
Eastrington	d																					
Gilberdyke	d				19 21																	
Broomfleet	d																					
Brough	d	19 19			19 29				19 45		19 54								20 22			
Ferriby	d				19 34																	
Hessle	d				19 38																	
Hull	a	19 38			19 50				20 06		20 10								20 43			

A To Leeds
B From Adwick
C From Lincoln
D From Plymouth to Edinburgh
E The Hull Executive
F To Bridlington
G From Reading to Newcastle
H From Retford

Manchester Airport, Manchester, Sheffield and Meadowhall-Doncaster-Cleethorpes and Hull Barton-on-Humber - Cleethorpes

Network Diagram - see first Page of Table 18

		NT	NT	XC	NT	NT	HT	NT	EM	TP	TP FO	TP FX	NT	NT	NT	XC	NT	NT	NT	TP FO	NT	NT
			A	◇1 B		C	◇1	D	E	◇1	◇1 F	◇1 F		C		◇1 H	C			◇1	A	C
Manchester Airport 85	d									18 55										19 55		
Manchester Piccadilly 10	d									19 18	20 11	20 11								20 20		
Stockport 78	d									19 26										20 28		
Sheffield 7	a									20 08										21 11		
	d		19 44	19 54				19 58		20 11			20 15	20 27	20 38	20 53				21 11	21 15	21 30
Meadowhall	d		19 50					20 04		20 16			20 21	20 35	20 45					21 16	21 21	21 36
Rotherham Central	d							20 11					20 27	20 41	20 52						21 27	21 42
Swinton (S.Yorks)	d							20 22					20 36	20a50	21 00						21 36	21a50
Mexborough	d							20 25					20 39		21 03						21 39	
Conisbrough	d							20 29					20 43		21 07						21 43	
London Kings Cross	d						18 50															
Doncaster 7	a		20 12	20 15			20 27	20 37		20 44			20 55		21 18	21 19				21 40	21 54	
York 8 26	a			20 46												21 45						
Doncaster 31	d	19 53	20 17		20 25	20 26	20 34	20 44		20 45			20 56		21 18		21 22			21 42	21 56	
Bentley (S.Yorks) 31	a					20 29											21 25					
Adwick 31	a					20 33											21 29					
Kirk Sandall	d	19 59			20 31								21 03		21 26						22 02	
Hatfield & Stainforth	d	20 04			20 36								21 08		21 31						22 07	
Thorne South	d				20 41										21 38							
Crowle	d				20 50										21 46							
Althorpe	d				20 56										21 52							
Scunthorpe	a				21 04					21 11					22 01					22 07		
	d									21 12										22 08		
Barnetby	d								20 35	21 26										22 22		
Hull Paragon Interchange	d																	21 25				
Barton-on-Humber	a																	21 52				
Barton-on-Humber	d																		21 58			
Barrow Haven	d																		22 03			
New Holland	d																		22 06			
Goxhill	d																		22 11			
Thornton Abbey	d																		22 14			
Ulceby	d																		22 18			
Habrough	d								20 44	21 35									22 23	22 31		
Stallingborough	d																		22 28			
Healing	d																		22 31			
Great Coates	d																		22 34			
Grimsby Town	a								20 56	21 48									22 39	22 44		
	d								20 56	21 49									22 39	22 45		
Grimsby Docks	d																		22 42			
New Clee	d																					
Cleethorpes	a								21 03	22 00									22 48	22 57		
Thorne North	d	20 09											21 14									22 13
Goole	d	20 18	20 36										21a23									22 22
Saltmarshe	d																					22 26
York 8 33	d																					
Selby	a						20 48	21 01			21 34	21 34										
Wressle	d																					
Howden	d						20 59				21 43	21 43										
Eastrington	d																					
Gilberdyke	d	20 26						21 15														22 32
Broomfleet	d																					
Brough	d	20 34	20 50				21 11	21 23			21 55	21 55										22 39
Ferriby	d	20 39						21 28														
Hessle	d	20 43						21 32														
Hull	a	20 56	21 07				21 27	21 45			22 12	22 13										22 58

A To Beverley
B From Southampton Central to Newcastle. to Doncaster
C To Leeds
D To Bridlington
E From Newark North Gate
F From Liverpool Lime Street
H From Reading to Newcastle

Manchester Airport, Manchester, Sheffield and Meadowhall-Doncaster-Cleethorpes and Hull Barton-on-Humber - Cleethorpes

Network Diagram - see first Page of Table 18

		TP	HT	XC	NT	NT	TP	NT	NT	TP	NT	NT
		FX										
		◇1	◇1	◇1			◇1			◇1		
				A		B		B		F	B	
			⊠									
Manchester Airport 85 ✈	d						20 47					
Manchester Piccadilly 10	d						21 20					
Stockport 78	d						21 28					
Sheffield 7	a						22 08					
	d	21 34		21 54			22 11	22 24	22 34		23 15	23 27
Meadowhall	d	21 40					22 16	22 30	22 40		23 21	23 33
Rotherham Central	d							22 36	22 46		23 27	23 39
Swinton (S.Yorks)	d							22a45	22 54		23a36	23 48
Mexborough	d								22 57			23 51
Conisbrough	d								23 01			23 55
London Kings Cross	d		20 30									
Doncaster 7	a	22 02	22 06	22 29			22 42		23 12			00 07
York 8 26	a			22 53								
Doncaster 31	d	22 05	22 07			22 26	22 44		23 15			
Bentley (S.Yorks) 31	a					22 29						
Adwick 31	a					22 33						
Kirk Sandall	d						22 49		23 21			
Hatfield & Stainforth	d						22 54		23 26			
Thorne South	d						22 58					
Crowle	d						23 07					
Althorpe	d						23 12					
Scunthorpe	a	22 30					23 17					
	d	22 31					23 18					
Barnetby	d	22 46					23 32					
Hull Paragon Interchange	d											
BartonenHumber	a											
Barton-on-Humber	d											
Barrow Haven	d											
New Holland	d											
Goxhill	d											
Thornton Abbey	d											
Ulceby	d											
Habrough	d	22 54					23 42					
Stallingborough	d											
Healing	d											
Great Coates	d											
Grimsby Town	a	23 09					23 55					
	d	23 10					23 56					
Grimsby Docks	d											
New Clee	d											
Cleethorpes	a	23 20					00 09					
Thorne North	d								23 32			
Goole	d								23a43			
Saltmarshe	d											
York 8 33	d				22 13							
Selby	a		22 21		22 32							
Wressle	d											
Howden	d		22 32		22 41							
Eastrington	d											
Gilberdyke	d				22 48							
Broomfleet	d											
Brough	d		22 47		22 55					23 06		
Ferriby	d				23 00							
Hessle	d				23 05							
Hull	a		23 06		23 18					23 25		

A From Southampton Central to Leeds
B To Leeds
F From Leeds

Manchester Airport, Manchester, Sheffield and Meadowhall-Doncaster-Cleethorpes and Hull Barton-on-Humber - Cleethorpes

Network Diagram - see first Page of Table 18

		TP	NT	NT	GR	NT	EM	NT	NT	NT	NT	XC	NT	NT	NT	TP	NT	XC	NT
		◇1			8 1							◇1				◇1		◇1	
					D	E	F	G			G	H						I	G
					🍴							🍴		🚌			🚌	🍴	
Manchester Airport 85 ✈	d	20p47														05 20			
Manchester Piccadilly 10	d	21p20														05 44			
Stockport 78	d	21p28														05 52			
Sheffield 7	a	22p08														06 49			
	d	22p11	23p27			05 29				06 12	06 28	06 49	06 52			06 55		07 12	07 14
Meadowhall	d	22p16	23p33			05 35				06 18	06 34		06 58			07 01			07 21
Rotherham Central	d		23p39			05 41				06 24	06 40		07 04						07 27
Swinton (S.Yorks)	d		23p48			05 49				06 35	06a51		07 15						07a33
Mexborough	d		23p51			05 52				06 38			07 18						
Conisbrough	d		23p55			05 56				06 42			07 22						
London Kings Cross	d																		
Doncaster 7	a	22p42	00 07			06 06				06 53		07 16	07 33			07 22			
York 8 26	a											07 43						08 23	
Doncaster 31	d	22p44		05 52	06 10	06 12		06 26	06 47	06 55			07 34			07 24			
Bentley (S.Yorks) 31	a							06 29		06 58			07 37						
Adwick 31	a							06 33		07 05			07 43						
Kirk Sandall	d	22p49				06 18			06 53										
Hatfield & Stainforth	d	22p54				06 23			06 58										
Thorne South	d	22p58							07 03										
Crowle	d	23p07							07 11										
Althorpe	d	23p12							07 17										
Scunthorpe	a	23p17							07 27							07 49			
	d	23p18														07 50			
Barnetby	d	23p32					06 12									08 04			
Hull Paragon Interchange	d													06 20			06 55		
BartonenHumber	a													06 52			07 30		
Barton-on-Humber	d														06 58				
Barrow Haven	d														07 03				
New Holland	d														07 07				
Goxhill	d														07 11				
Thornton Abbey	d																		
Ulceby	d														07 19				
Habrough	d	23p42					06 22								07 23				
Stallingborough	d														07 28				
Healing	d														07 31				
Great Coates	d																		
Grimsby Town	a	23p55					06 37								07 38	08 24			
	d	23p56													07 39	08 33			
Grimsby Docks	d																		
New Clee	d																		
Cleethorpes	a	00 09													07 51	08 44			
Thorne North	d					06 28													
Goole	d					06 37													
Saltmarshe	d					06 42													
York 8 33	d				06a30														
Selby	a			06 11															
Wressle	d																		
Howden	d																		
Eastrington	d																		
Gilberdyke	d					06 51													
Broomfleet	d					06 55													
Brough	d					07 01													
Ferriby	d					07 05													
Hessle	d					07 10													
Hull	a					07 22													

D To Edinburgh
E To Beverley
F From Lincoln
G To Leeds
H From Derby to Newcastle
I From Birmingham New Street to Glasgow Central

Manchester Airport, Manchester, Sheffield and Meadowhall-Doncaster-Cleethorpes and Hull Barton-on-Humber - Cleethorpes

Network Diagram - see first Page of Table 18

		NT	NT	TP	NT	NT	NT	NT	NT	NT	NT	XC	NT	EM	NT	TP	TP	NT	XC	NT	NT	NT
				◇1								◇1				◇1	◇1		◇1			
		A	B		C				E	F	G	H	A	I				A	J	K		
												(trolley)				(trolley)	(trolley)		(trolley)			
Manchester Airport 85 ✈	d															06 55						
Manchester Piccadilly 10 ⇌	d			06 21												07 20	07 36					
Stockport 78	d															07 28						
Sheffield 7 ⇌	a															08 10						
	d					07 24				07 41	07 41	07 54			08 03	08 11		08 14	08 21			
Meadowhall ⇌	d					07 30				07 47	07 47					08 16		08 22				
Rotherham Central	d					07 36				07 55	07 55							08 28				
Swinton (S.Yorks)	d					07 46				08 03	08 03							08a37				
Mexborough	d					07 49				08 06	08 06											
Conisbrough	d					07 53				08 10	08 10											
London Kings Cross	d																					
Doncaster 7	a					08 01				08 19	08 21	08 23				08 38						
York 8 26	a											08 48							09 27			
Doncaster 31	d	07 26			07 28	08 03			08 16	08 21	08 22		08 26			08 41					08 53	08 54
Bentley (S.Yorks) 31	a	07 29							08 19				08 29									08 57
Adwick 31	a	07 33							08 23				08 33									09 04
Kirk Sandall	d				07 34	08 09															09 00	
Hatfield & Stainforth	d				07 39	08 14															09 05	
Thorne South	d					08 18																
Crowle	d					08 27																
Althorpe	d					08 33																
Scunthorpe	a					08 44										09 06						
	d															09 07						
Barnetby	d													08 52	09 39	09 21						
Hull Paragon Interchange	d																					
Barton-on-Humber	a																					
Barton-on-Humber	d							08 00														
Barrow Haven	d							08 05														
New Holland	d							08 08														
Goxhill	d							08 13														
Thornton Abbey	d							08 16														
Ulceby	d							08 20														
Habrough	d							08 25						09 01	09 48	09 29						
Stallingborough	d							08 30														
Healing	d							08 33														
Great Coates	d							08 36														
Grimsby Town	a							08 41						09 15	10 00	09 43						
	d							08 43							10 01	09 44						
Grimsby Docks	d							08 45														
New Clee	d							08x48														
Cleethorpes	a							08 52							10 13	09 55						
Thorne North	d				07 44																09 10	
Goole	d				07 53					08 43	08 43										09 19	
Saltmarshe	d				07 58																	
York 8 33	d						07 38													08 43		
Selby	a			07 43			07 57										08 57			09 06		
Wressle	d						08 05															
Howden	d			07 52			08 10													09 16		
Eastrington	d						08 15															
Gilberdyke	d		07 39		08 04		08 17														09 28	
Broomfleet	d		07 43				08 21															
Brough	d		07 49	08 04	08 12		08 27			08 57	08 57									09 28	09 36	
Ferriby	d		07 53		08 16		08 32														09 40	
Hessle	d		07 58		08 21		08 36														09 45	
Hull	a		08 11	08 20	08 37		08 50			09 13	09 13						09 31			09 47	09 58	

A To Leeds
B To Scarborough
C To Beverley
E From Scunthorpe
F until 29 September. To Bridlington
G from 6 October. To Bridlington
H From Birmingham New Street to Newcastle
I From Lincoln
J From Birmingham New Street to Edinburgh
K From Beverley

Manchester Airport, Manchester, Sheffield and Meadowhall-Doncaster-Cleethorpes and Hull Barton-on-Humber - Cleethorpes

Network Diagram - see first Page of Table 18

		NT	NT	XC	NT	NT	NT	NT	TP	TP	NT	EM	XC	NT	NT	NT	NT	NT	XC	NT
				◇1					◇1	◇1		◇1	◇1						◇1	
			B	C	D		🚌				D	E	F			G	H	I	J	D
				(trolley)					(trolley)			(trolley)	(trolley)						(trolley)	
Manchester Airport 85 ✈	d								07 53											
Manchester Piccadilly 10 ⇌	d								08 20	08 42										
Stockport 78	d								08 28											
Sheffield 7 ⇌	a								09 08											
	d	08 25	08 41	08 48		08 53			09 11		09 14	09 21	09 21		09 25	09 29		09 41	09 47	
Meadowhall ⇌	d	08 31	08 47			09 00			09 16		09 21				09 34	09 35		09 47		
Rotherham Central	d	08 35				09 06					09 27				09 41	09 42				
Swinton (S.Yorks)	d	08 47				09 16					09a36				09 49	09 51				
Mexborough	d	08 51				09 19									09 52					
Conisbrough	d	08 55				09 23									09 56					
London Kings Cross	d																			
Doncaster 7	a	09 05	09 14	09 18		09 33			09 35			09 53			10 07			10 14	10 17	
York 8 26	a			09 44								10 16	10 26			10 55			10 40	
Doncaster 31	d	09 07	09 18		09 26	09 34			09 37					09 41	10 08			10 19		10 26
Bentley (S.Yorks) 31	a				09 29	09 37														10 29
Adwick 31	a				09 33	09 43														10 33
Kirk Sandall	d	09 14												09 48	10 15					
Hatfield & Stainforth	d	09 19												09 53	10 20					
Thorne South	d	09 24													10 25					
Crowle	d	09 32													10 33					
Althorpe	d	09 38													10 39					
Scunthorpe	a	09 47							10 02						10 48					
	d								10 03											
Barnetby	d								10 17											
Hull Paragon Interchange	d						09 05													
Barton-on-Humber	a						09 40													
Barton-on-Humber	d							09 52												
Barrow Haven	d							09 57												
New Holland	d							10 00												
Goxhill	d							10 05												
Thornton Abbey	d							10 08												
Ulceby	d							10 12												
Habrough	d							10 17												
Stallingborough	d							10 22												
Healing	d							10 25												
Great Coates	d							10 28												
Grimsby Town	a							10 33	10 39											
	d							10 33	10 40											
Grimsby Docks	d							10 36												
New Clee	d							10x38												
Cleethorpes	a							10 43	10 51											
Thorne North	d													09 58						
Goole	d		09 38											10 07				10 38		
Saltmarshe	d																			
York 8 33	d																09 50			
Selby	a									09 57							10 09			
Wressle	d																			
Howden	d																10 19			
Eastrington	d																			
Gilberdyke	d													10 15			10 26			
Broomfleet	d																			
Brough	d		09 55							10 16				10 23			10 34	10 51		
Ferriby	d													10 28						
Hessle	d													10 32						
Hull	a		10 12							10 35				10 45			10 53	11 09		

B To Bridlington
C From Birmingham New Street to Newcastle
D To Leeds
E From St Pancras International
F From Bristol Temple Meads to Glasgow Central
G To Sheffield
H From Beverley
I To Scarborough
J From Guildford to Newcastle

Manchester Airport, Manchester, Sheffield and Meadowhall-Doncaster-Cleethorpes and Hull Barton-on-Humber - Cleethorpes

Network Diagram - see first Page of Table 18

		NT	EM	TP	TP	NT	XC	NT	NT	NT	NT	XC	HT	NT	NT	NT	NT	TP	TP	NT	XC	NT
		A	B	◇1	◇1	C	◇1 D			F	G	◇1 H	◇1	C	A	bus		◇1	◇1	C	◇1 I	
Manchester Airport 85 ✈	d			08 55														09 55				
Manchester Piccadilly 10	d			09 20	09 42													10 20	10 42			
Stockport 78	d			09 28														10 28				
Sheffield 7	a			10 08														11 08				
	d	09 53		10 11		10 14	10 21		10 24		10 41	10 47			10 53			11 11		11 14	11 21	
Meadowhall	d	09 59		10 16		10 21			10 30		10 47				10 59			11 16		11 21		
Rotherham Central	d	10 05				10 27			10 36						11 05					11 27		
Swinton (S.Yorks)	d	10 15				10a36			10 44						11 16					11a36		
Mexborough	d	10 18							10 50						11 19							
Conisbrough	d	10 22							10 54						11 23							
London Kings Cross	d												09 48									
Doncaster 7	a	10 32		10 35					11 04		11 13	11 15	11 24		11 32			11 35				
York 8 26	a						11 26					11 40									12 26	
Doncaster 31	d	10 34		10 37				10 41	11 08		11 18		11 26	11 26	11 34			11 37				11 41
Bentley (S.Yorks) 31	a	10 37												11 29	11 37							
Adwick 31	a	10 43												11 33	11 43							
Kirk Sandall	d							10 47	11 14													11 47
Hatfield & Stainforth	d							10 52	11 19													11 52
Thorne South	d								11 24													
Crowle	d								11 32													
Althorpe	d								11 38													
Scunthorpe	a			11 02					11 46									12 02				
	d			11 03														12 03				
Barnetby	d		10 41	11 17														12 17				
Hull Paragon Interchange	d															11 05						
Barton-on-Humber	a															11 40						
Barton-on-Humber	d																11 52					
Barrow Haven	d																11 57					
New Holland	d																12 00					
Goxhill	d																12 05					
Thornton Abbey	d																12 08					
Ulceby	d																12 12					
Habrough	d		10 50														12 17	12 26				
Stallingborough	d																12 22					
Healing	d																12 25					
Great Coates	d																12 28					
Grimsby Town	a		11 08	11 37													12 33	12 39				
	d			11 38													12 33	12 40				
Grimsby Docks	d																12 36					
New Clee	d																12x38					
Cleethorpes	a			11 50													12 43	12 52				
Thorne North	d							10 57														11 57
Goole	d							11 07			11 38											12 07
Saltmarshe	d																					
York 8 33	d									10 43												
Selby	a				10 57					11 03			11 40						11 57			
Wressle	d																					
Howden	d									11 15			11 51									
Eastrington	d																					
Gilberdyke	d							11 17		11 21												12 16
Broomfleet	d							11 21														
Brough	d				11 16			11 27		11 31	11 52		12 03						12 16			12 24
Ferriby	d							11 32														12 29
Hessle	d							11 36														12 33
Hull	a				11 35			11 51		11 51	12 10		12 20						12 36			12 45

A From Lincoln
B From Newark North Gate
C To Leeds
D From Plymouth to Edinburgh
F From Hull
G To Bridlington
H From Bournemouth to Newcastle
I From Plymouth to Glasgow Central

Table 29
Saturdays

Manchester Airport, Manchester, Sheffield and Meadowhall-Doncaster-Cleethorpes and Hull Barton-on-Humber - Cleethorpes

Network Diagram - see first Page of Table 18

		NT	NT	NT	XC	NT	NT	EM	NT	TP	TP	NT	XC	NT	NT	NT	NT	NT	XC
			B	C	◇1 D	E	F	G		◇1	◇1	E	◇1 H			B	I	J	◇1 K
Manchester Airport 85 ✈	d									10 55									
Manchester Piccadilly 10	d									11 20	11 42								
Stockport 78	d									11 28									
Sheffield 7	a									12 08									
	d	11 24		11 41	11 47		11 53		12 00	12 11		12 14	12 21		12 24		12 41	12 41	12 47
Meadowhall	d	11 30		11 47			11 59			12 16		12 21			12 30		12 47	12 47	
Rotherham Central	d	11 37					12 05					12 27			12 37				
Swinton (S.Yorks)	d	11 47					12 16					12a36			12 47				
Mexborough	d	11 50					12 19								12 50				
Conisbrough	d	11 54					12 23								12 54				
London Kings Cross	d																		
Doncaster 7	a	12 04		12 14	12 15		12 33			12 35					13 04		13 14	13 14	13 17
York 8 26	a				12 39								13 26						13 40
Doncaster 31	d	12 08		12 17		12 26	12 34			12 37				12 42	13 08		13 17	13 19	
Bentley (S.Yorks) 31	a					12 29	12 37												
Adwick 31	a					12 33	12 43												
Kirk Sandall	d	12 14												12 48	13 14				
Hatfield & Stainforth	d	12 19												12 53	13 19				
Thorne South	d	12 24													13 24				
Crowle	d	12 32													13 33				
Althorpe	d	12 38													13 39				
Scunthorpe	a	12 46								13 02					13 46				
	d									13 03									
Barnetby	d							13 11	13 38	13 17									
Hull Paragon Interchange	d																		
Barton-on-Humber	a																		
Barton-on-Humber	d																		
Barrow Haven	d																		
New Holland	d																		
Goxhill	d																		
Thornton Abbey	d																		
Ulceby	d																		
Habrough	d							13 20	13 47										
Stallingborough	d																		
Healing	d																		
Great Coates	d																		
Grimsby Town	a							13 36	14 00	13 37									
	d								14 00	13 38									
Grimsby Docks	d																		
New Clee	d																		
Cleethorpes	a								14 11	13 50									
Thorne North	d													12 58					
Goole	d			12 38										13 07			13 37	13 38	
Saltmarshe	d																		
York 8 33	d		11 45													12 47			
Selby	a		12 04								12 57					13 06			
Wressle	d																		
Howden	d		12 14													13 16			
Eastrington	d																		
Gilberdyke	d		12 21											13 15					
Broomfleet	d																		
Brough	d		12 29	12 51							13 16			13 23		13 28	13 51	13 52	
Ferriby	d													13 28					
Hessle	d													13 32					
Hull	a		12 49	13 11							13 35			13 45		13 48	14 08	14 09	

B From Hull
C To Scarborough
D From Southampton Central to Newcastle
E To Leeds
F From Lincoln
G From Newark North Gate
H From Plymouth to Edinburgh
I until 29 September. To Bridlington
J from 6 October. To Bridlington
K From Reading to Newcastle

Manchester Airport, Manchester, Sheffield and Meadowhall-Doncaster-Cleethorpes and Hull Barton-on-Humber - Cleethorpes

Network Diagram - see first Page of Table 18

		HT	NT	NT	NT	NT	TP	TP	NT	XC	NT	NT	NT	NT	NT	XC	NT	NT	TP	TP	NT	XC	NT
		◇1 ☒	A	B	🚌		◇1 ✠	◇1	A	◇1 C ✠				E	F	◇1 G ✠	A	B	◇1 ✠	◇1 ✠	A	◇1 H ✠	
Manchester Airport 85 ✈	d						11 55												12 55				
Manchester Piccadilly 10	d						12 20	12 42											13 20	13 42			
Stockport 78	d						12 28												13 28				
Sheffield 7	a						13 08												14 08				
	d			12 53			13 11		13 14	13 21		13 24	13 29		13 41	13 47		13 53	14 11		14 14	14 21	
Meadowhall	d			12 59			13 16		13 21			13 30	13 35		13 47			13 59	14 16		14 21		
Rotherham Central	d			13 05					13 27			13 37	13 41					14 05			14 27		
Swinton (S.Yorks)	d			13 16					13a36			13 47	13 50					14 17			14a36		
Mexborough	d			13 19								13 50						14 20					
Conisbrough	d			13 23								13 54						14 24					
London Kings Cross	d	11 48																					
Doncaster 7	a	13 24		13 32			13 35					14 03			14 16	14 18		14 32	14 35				
York 8 26	a									14 26			14 55			14 40						15 28	
Doncaster 31	d	13 26	13 26	13 34			13 37				13 41	14 07			14 17		14 26	14 34	14 37				14 40
Bentley (S.Yorks) 31	a		13 29	13 37													14 29	14 37					
Adwick 31	a		13 33	13 43													14 33	14 43					
Kirk Sandall	d										13 47	14 13											14 46
Hatfield & Stainforth	d										13 52	14 18											14 51
Thorne South	d											14 25											
Crowle	d											14 33											
Althorpe	d											14 39											
Scunthorpe	a						14 02					14 48							15 02				
	d						14 03												15 03				
Barnetby	d						14 18												15 17				
Hull Paragon Interchange	d				13 05																		
Barton-on-Humber	a				13 40																		
Barton-on-Humber	d					13 52																	
Barrow Haven	d					13 57																	
New Holland	d					14 00																	
Goxhill	d					14 05																	
Thornton Abbey	d					14 08																	
Ulceby	d					14 12																	
Habrough	d					14 17	14 26																
Stallingborough	d					14 22																	
Healing	d					14 25																	
Great Coates	d					14 28																	
Grimsby Town	a					14 33	14 39												15 37				
	d					14 33	14 40												15 38				
Grimsby Docks	d					14 36																	
New Clee	d					14x38																	
Cleethorpes	a					14 43	14 52												15 50				
Thorne North	d										13 57												14 56
Goole	d										14 07				14 38								15 07
Saltmarshe	d										14 12												
York 8 33	d													13 44									
Selby	a	13 40						13 57						14 07						14 57			
Wressle	d																						
Howden	d	13 51												14 17									
Eastrington	d																						
Gilberdyke	d										14 16												15 15
Broomfleet	d																						
Brough	d	14 03						14 16			14 24			14 30	14 52					15 16			15 23
Ferriby	d										14 29												15 28
Hessle	d										14 33												15 32
Hull	a	14 20						14 35			14 48			14 52	15 09					15 35			15 45

A To Leeds
B From Lincoln
C From Penzance to Glasgow Central
E From Hull
F To Bridlington
G From Southampton Central to Newcastle
H From Plymouth to Aberdeen

Manchester Airport, Manchester, Sheffield and Meadowhall-Doncaster-Cleethorpes and Hull Barton-on-Humber - Cleethorpes

Network Diagram - see first Page of Table 18

		NT	NT	NT	XC	EM	NT	NT	NT	NT	TP	TP	NT	XC	NT	NT	NT	XC	NT	HT	NT
			B	C	◇1 D ✠	E	F	E	🚌		◇1 ✠	◇1	F	◇1 G ✠			H	◇1 I ✠	F	◇1 ☒	E
Manchester Airport 85 ✈	d										13 55										
Manchester Piccadilly 10	d										14 20	14 42									
Stockport 78	d										14 28										
Sheffield 7	a										15 08										
	d	14 24		14 41	14 47			14 53			15 11		15 14	15 21		15 24	15 41	15 47			15 53
Meadowhall	d	14 30		14 47				14 59			15 16		15 21			15 30	15 47				15 59
Rotherham Central	d	14 37						15 05					15 27			15 36					16 05
Swinton (S.Yorks)	d	14 48						15 17					15a36			15 47					16 16
Mexborough	d	14 51						15 20								15 50					16 19
Conisbrough	d	14 55						15 24								15 54					16 23
London Kings Cross	d																			14 48	
Doncaster 7	a	15 04		15 16	15 17			15 34			15 35					16 04	16 14	16 18		16 24	16 32
York 8 26	a				15 40									16 26				16 41			
Doncaster 31	d	15 07		15 17			15 26	15 34			15 37				15 41	16 08	16 19		16 25	16 26	16 34
Bentley (S.Yorks) 31	a						15 29	15 37											16 28		16 37
Adwick 31	a						15 33	15 43											16 32		16 43
Kirk Sandall	d	15 13													15 47	16 14					
Hatfield & Stainforth	d	15 18													15 52	16 19					
Thorne South	d	15 23														16 24					
Crowle	d	15 31														16 33					
Althorpe	d	15 37														16 39					
Scunthorpe	a	15 46									16 02					16 46					
	d										16 03										
Barnetby	d					15 25					16 17										
Hull Paragon Interchange	d								15 05												
Barton-on-Humber	a								15 40												
Barton-on-Humber	d									15 54											
Barrow Haven	d									15 59											
New Holland	d									16 02											
Goxhill	d									16 07											
Thornton Abbey	d									16 10											
Ulceby	d									16 14											
Habrough	d					15 33				16 19	16 26										
Stallingborough	d									16 24											
Healing	d									16 27											
Great Coates	d									16 30											
Grimsby Town	a					15 48				16 35	16 39										
	d									16 35	16 40										
Grimsby Docks	d									16 38											
New Clee	d																				
Cleethorpes	a									16 44	16 52										
Thorne North	d														15 57						
Goole	d			15 37											16 07		16 38				
Saltmarshe	d																				
York 8 33	d		14 47																		
Selby	a		15 06									15 57								16 41	
Wressle	d																				
Howden	d		15 16																	16 54	
Eastrington	d																				
Gilberdyke	d														16 18						
Broomfleet	d																				
Brough	d		15 28	15 51								16 16			16 26		16 52			17 10	
Ferriby	d														16 30						
Hessle	d														16 35						
Hull	a		15 48	16 08								16 35			16 48		17 06			17 25	

B From Hull
C To Scarborough
D From Reading to Newcastle
E From Lincoln
F To Leeds
G From Penzance to Glasgow Central
H To Bridlington
I From Southampton Central to Newcastle

Manchester Airport, Manchester, Sheffield and Meadowhall-Doncaster-Cleethorpes and Hull Barton-on-Humber - Cleethorpes

Network Diagram - see first Page of Table 18

		NT	TP	NT	TP	NT	XC	NT	NT	NT	XC	NT	NT	NT	NT	EM	NT	NT	TP	TP	NT
			◇1	A	◇1	B	◇1 C		E	F	◇1 G	A		B	H	H	bus		◇1	◇1	B
Manchester Airport 85	d		14 55																15 55		
Manchester Piccadilly 10	d		15 20		15 42														16 20	16 42	
Stockport 78	d		15 28																16 28		
Sheffield 7	a		16 08																17 08		
	d	16 00	16 11			16 14	16 21	16 24		16 41	16 47				16 53				17 11		17 14
Meadowhall	d		16 16			16 21		16 30		16 47					16 59				17 16		17 21
Rotherham Central	d					16 27		16 37							17 05						17 27
Swinton (S.Yorks)	d					16a36		16 46							17 16						17a37
Mexborough	d							16 49							17 19						
Conisbrough	d							16 53							17 23						
London Kings Cross	d																				
Doncaster 7	a		16 35					17 06		17 12	17 16				17 32				17 35		
York 8 26	a						17 26				17 37										
Doncaster 31	d		16 37						16 42	17 19			17 22	17 26	17 34				17 43		
Bentley (S.Yorks) 31	a													17 29	17 37						
Adwick 31	a													17 33	17 43						
Kirk Sandall	d								16 48				17 29								
Hatfield & Stainforth	d								16 53				17 34								
Thorne South	d												17 39								
Crowle	d												17 48								
Althorpe	d												17 54								
Scunthorpe	a		17 02										18 02						18 08		
	d		17 03																18 09		
Barnetby	d	17 38	17 17													17 54			18 23		
Hull Paragon Interchange	d																17 10				
Barton-on-Humber	a																17 45				
Barton-on-Humber	d																	17 55			
Barrow Haven	d																	18 00			
New Holland	d																	18 03			
Goxhill	d																	18 08			
Thornton Abbey	d																	18 11			
Ulceby	d																	18 15			
Habrough	d	17 47														18 02		18 20	18 32		
Stallingborough	d																	18 25			
Healing	d																	18 28			
Great Coates	d																	18 31			
Grimsby Town	a	18 01	17 37													18 17		18 36	18 45		
	d	18 02	17 38															18 36	18 46		
Grimsby Docks	d																	18 42			
New Clee	d																				
Cleethorpes	a	18 11	17 50															18 49	18 58		
Thorne North	d								16 58	17 33											
Goole	d								17 07	17 42											
Saltmarshe	d																				
York 8 33	d			16 12								17 19									
Selby	a			16 36	17 00							17 45								17 59	
Wressle	d			16 44																	
Howden	d			16 49								17 56								18 08	
Eastrington	d																				
Gilberdyke	d			16 55					17 14			18 03									
Broomfleet	d																				
Brough	d			17 03	17 18				17 22	17 55		18 11								18 20	
Ferriby	d			17 08					17 27												
Hessle	d			17 12					17 31												
Hull	a			17 27	17 37				17 47	18 13		18 30								18 39	

A From Hull
B To Leeds
C From Newquay to Dundee
E To Beverley
F To Bridlington
G From Reading to Newcastle
H From Lincoln

Manchester Airport, Manchester, Sheffield and Meadowhall-Doncaster-Cleethorpes and Hull Barton-on-Humber - Cleethorpes

Network Diagram - see first Page of Table 18

		XC	NT	NT	NT	XC	NT	TP	NT	NT	NT	GR	NT	XC	EM	TP	NT	NT	XC	NT	NT
		◇1 A			C	◇1 D		◇1	E	F	G	1	E	◇1 H	I	◇1		K	◇1 L		E
Manchester Airport 85	d															16 55					
Manchester Piccadilly 10	d							17 42								17 20					
Stockport 78	d															17 28					
Sheffield 7	a															18 10					
	d	17 21	17 25		17 41	17 47					17 53		18 13	18 21		18 24	18 29	18 41	18 47		
Meadowhall	d		17 31		17 47						17 58		18 21			18 30	18 35	18 47			
Rotherham Central	d		17 37								18 05		18 27				18 42				
Swinton (S.Yorks)	d		17 45								18 16		18a37				18 50				
Mexborough	d		17 48								18 20						18 53				
Conisbrough	d		17 52								18 24						18 57				
London Kings Cross	d											17 10									
Doncaster 7	a		18 11		18 13						18 38	18 53				18 58	19 08	19 13	19 16		
York 8 26	a	18 28				18 58								19 26					19 39		
Doncaster 31	d			17 47	18 16				18 26	18 29	18 40	18 53				19 00		19 16		19 20	19 22
Bentley (S.Yorks) 31	a								18 29												19 25
Adwick 31	a								18 33												19 29
Kirk Sandall	d			17 53						18 36	18 47									19 27	
Hatfield & Stainforth	d			17 58						18 41	18 52									19 32	
Thorne South	d									18 46										19 37	
Crowle	d									18 54										19 46	
Althorpe	d									19 00										19 52	
Scunthorpe	a									19 10						19 25				20 01	
	d															19 26					
Barnetby	d														19 08	19 40					
Hull Paragon Interchange	d																				
Barton-on-Humber	a																				
Barton-on-Humber	d																				
Barrow Haven	d																				
New Holland	d																				
Goxhill	d																				
Thornton Abbey	d																				
Ulceby	d																				
Habrough	d														19 16						
Stallingborough	d																				
Healing	d																				
Great Coates	d																				
Grimsby Town	a														19 31	20 00					
	d															20 01					
Grimsby Docks	d																				
New Clee	d																				
Cleethorpes	a															20 12					
Thorne North	d			18 03							18 57										
Goole	d			18 12	18 36						19 12							19 37			
Saltmarshe	d			18 17																	
York 8 33	d						18 18														
Selby	a						18 42	19 00				19 09									
Wressle	d						18 50														
Howden	d						18 54														
Eastrington	d						18 59														
Gilberdyke	d			18 23			19 03				19 21										
Broomfleet	d			18 27																	
Brough	d			18 33	18 53		19 10	19 19			19 29	19 36						19 54			
Ferriby	d			18 38							19 34										
Hessle	d			18 42							19 38										
Hull	a			18 55	19 09		19 29	19 38			19 50	19 54						20 10			

A From Plymouth to Glasgow Central
C To Scarborough
D From Southampton Central to Newcastle
E To Leeds
F From Adwick
G From Lincoln
H From Plymouth to Newcastle
I From Newark North Gate
K To Bridlington
L From Reading to Newcastle

Manchester Airport, Manchester, Sheffield and Meadowhall-Doncaster-Cleethorpes and Hull
Barton-on-Humber - Cleethorpes

Network Diagram - see first Page of Table 18

	HT	NT	NT	NT	TP	TP	NT	XC	NT	NT	NT	NT	XC	NT	NT	TP	NT	XC	NT	NT
	◇1 ⊠	A	🚌		◇1 ✠	◇1	B	◇1 C ✠	D			F	◇1 G ✠	B	H	◇1		◇1 I ✠	B	
Manchester Airport 85 ✈ d					17 55											18 55				
Manchester Piccadilly 10 d					18 20	18 42										19 18				
Stockport 78 d					18 28											19 26				
Sheffield 7 a					19 09											20 08				
Sheffield d		19 00			19 11		19 18	19 22			19 25	19 44	19 54		19 58	20 11	20 15	20 24	20 27	20 38
Meadowhall d		19 06			19 16		19 25				19 31	19 50			20 04	20 16	20 21		20 35	20 45
Rotherham Central d		19 12					19 31				19 37				20 11		20 27		20 41	20 53
Swinton (S.Yorks) d		19 18					19a40				19 47				20 21		20 40		20a50	21 01
Mexborough d		19 23									19 50				20 24		20 43			21 04
Conisbrough d		19 25									19 54				20 28		20 47			21 08
London Kings Cross d	17 48																			
Doncaster 7 a	19 26	19 39			19 41						20 02	20 14	20 17		20 36	20 44	20 55			21 18
York 8 26 a								20 29					20 40					21 57		
Doncaster 31 d	19 28				19 48					19 55	20 07	20 16		20 26	20 43	20 45	20 56			21 20
Bentley (S.Yorks) 31 a														20 29						
Adwick 31 a														20 33						
Kirk Sandall d										20 01	20 13						21 03			21 26
Hatfield & Stainforth d										20 06	20 18						21 08			21 31
Thorne South d											20 22									21 38
Crowle d											20 31									21 46
Althorpe d											20 37									21 52
Scunthorpe a					20 14						20 45					21 11				22 01
Scunthorpe d					20 14											21 12				
Barnetby d					20 28											21 26				
Hull Paragon Interchange d			19 25																	
Barton-on-Humber a			19 52																	
Barton-on-Humber d				19 58																
Barrow Haven d				20 03																
New Holland d				20 06																
Goxhill d				20 11																
Thornton Abbey d				20 14																
Ulceby d				20 18																
Habrough d				20 23												21 35				
Stallingborough d				20 28																
Healing d				20 31																
Great Coates d				20 34																
Grimsby Town a				20 39	20 47											21 48				
Grimsby Town d				20 39	20 48											21 49				
Grimsby Docks d				20 42																
New Clee d																				
Cleethorpes a				20 48	21 00											22 00				
Thorne North d										20 11							21 14			
Goole d										20 20		20 36					21a23			
Saltmarshe d																				
York 8 33 d									19 47											
Selby a	19 42					20 00			20 06						21 01					
Wressle d																				
Howden d	19 53					20 10			20 16											
Eastrington d																				
Gilberdyke d										20 28					21 15					
Broomfleet d																				
Brough d	20 05					20 22			20 30	20 36		20 49			21 23					
Ferriby d										20 41					21 28					
Hessle d										20 45					21 32					
Hull a	20 24					20 43			20 48	21 00		21 07			21 47					

A From Retford
B To Leeds
C From Plymouth to Newcastle
D From Blackpool North
F To Beverley
G From Southampton Central to Newcastle
H To Bridlington
I From Plymouth

Manchester Airport, Manchester, Sheffield and Meadowhall-Doncaster-Cleethorpes and Hull
Barton-on-Humber - Cleethorpes

Network Diagram - see first Page of Table 18

	XC	XC	NT	NT	TP	HT	NT	NT	NT	NT	TP	XC	NT	NT	NT	TP	NT	XC	XC	NT	TP	NT
	◇1 A	◇1 B	C	🚌	◇1 D	◇1 ⊠	G	H	C		◇1	◇1 I	J	K	C	◇1	C	◇1 L	◇1 M ✠		◇1 D	
Manchester Airport 85 ✈ d																20 47						
Manchester Piccadilly 10 d																21 20						
Stockport 78 d																21 28						
Sheffield 7 a																22 08						
Sheffield d	20 53	20 53					21 14	21 14	21 30		21 34	22 09				22 11	22 24	22 27	22 27	22 30		23 27
Meadowhall d							21 21	21 21	21 36		21 40					22 16	22 30			22 36		23 33
Rotherham Central d							21 27	21 27	21 42								22 36			22 45		23 39
Swinton (S.Yorks) d							21 32	21 36	21a50								22a45			22 53		23 48
Mexborough d							21 35	21 39												22 56		23 51
Conisbrough d							21 39	21 43												23 00		23 55
London Kings Cross d						19 48																
Doncaster 7 a	21 21	21 21				21 28	21 54	21 54			22 03	22 30				22 36		22 51	22 51	23 09		00 08
York 8 26 a	21 44	21 45										22 57										
Doncaster 31 d			21 22			21 30	21 56	21 56			22 05				22 26	22 37				23 10		
Bentley (S.Yorks) 31 a			21 25												22 29							
Adwick 31 a			21 29												22 33							
Kirk Sandall d							22 02	22 02								22 43				23 17		
Hatfield & Stainforth d							22 07	22 07								22 47				23 22		
Thorne South d																22 52						
Crowle d																23 00						
Althorpe d																23 06						
Scunthorpe a											22 30					23 11						
Scunthorpe d											22 31					23 11						
Barnetby d											22 46					23 26						
Hull Paragon Interchange d				21 25																		
Barton-on-Humber a				21 52																		
Barton-on-Humber d										21 58												
Barrow Haven d										22 03												
New Holland d										22 06												
Goxhill d										22 11												
Thornton Abbey d										22 14												
Ulceby d										22 18												
Habrough d										22 23	22 54					23 34						
Stallingborough d										22 28												
Healing d										22 31												
Great Coates d										22 34												
Grimsby Town a										22 39	23 09					23 47						
Grimsby Town d										22 39	23 10					23 48						
Grimsby Docks d										22 42												
New Clee d																						
Cleethorpes a										22 48	23 20					23 59						
Thorne North d							22 13	22 13												23 27		
Goole d							22 22	22 22												23a38		
Saltmarshe d							22 26	22 26														
York 8 33 d													22 10	22 11								
Selby a						21 44							22 28	22 29								
Wressle d																						
Howden d					21 39	21 55							22 39	22 39								
Eastrington d																						
Gilberdyke d							22 32	22 32					22 45	22 45								
Broomfleet d																						
Brough d					21 51	22 07	22 40	22 40					22 53	22 53							23 06	
Ferriby d													22 58	22 58								
Hessle d													23 02	23 02								
Hull a					22 10	22 26	22 58	22 58					23 14	23 14							23 25	

A until 8 September. From Reading to Newcastle
B from 15 September. From Reading to Newcastle
C To Leeds
D From Leeds
G until 29 September. To Beverley
H from 6 October. To Beverley
I From Southampton Central
J from 15 September. From Hull
K until 8 September. From Hull
L from 15 September. From Plymouth to Leeds
M until 8 September. From Bournemouth to Leeds

Manchester Airport, Manchester, Sheffield and Meadowhall-Doncaster-Cleethorpes and Hull Barton-on-Humber - Cleethorpes

Network Diagram - see first Page of Table 18

Station		NT	NT	NT	NT	NT	XC	NT	GR	NT		TP	XC	NT	NT	TP	NT	NT		NT		NT	NT	XC	EM
							◇1		1			◇1	◇1			◇1								◇1	◇1
					A	B	C	A	D	E			F			G	H	B					A	I	J
Manchester Airport 85	d																								
Manchester Piccadilly	d																								
Stockport 78	d																								
Sheffield	a																								
	d	23p27	08 00			08 45	09 21	09 36				09 52	10 21					10 26		11 05				11 21	11 31
Meadowhall	d	23p33	08 06			08 51		09 42				09 57						10 32		11 11					
Rotherham Central	d	23p39	08 12			08 57		09 48				10 03								11 17					
Swinton (S.Yorks)	d	23p48	08 20			09 05		09a58				10 09								11 25					
Mexborough	d	23p51	08 23			09 08						10 13								11 28					
Conisbrough	d	23p55	08 27			09 12						10 17								11 32					
London Kings Cross	d																								
Doncaster	a	00 08	08 38			09 22						10 26						10 51		11 43					11 52
York 26	a						10 29						11 29											12 29	12 15
Doncaster 31	d			09 07	09 12	09 26			09 37	10 19		10 28						10 55				11 07	11 12		
Bentley (S.Yorks) 31	a				09 15																		11 15		
Adwick 31	a				09 19																		11 19		
Kirk Sandall	d			09 13																		11 13			
Hatfield & Stainforth	d			09 18																		11 18			
Thorne South	d																								
Crowle	d																								
Althorpe	d																								
Scunthorpe	a											10 54													
	d											10 55													
Barnetby	d											11 09													
Hull Paragon Interchange	d													10 25											
Barton-on-Humber	a													10 50											
Barton-on-Humber	d														11 00										
Barrow Haven	d														11 05										
New Holland	d														11 08										
Goxhill	d														11 13										
Thornton Abbey	d														11 16										
Ulceby	d														11 20										
Habrough	d														11 25										
Stallingborough	d														11 30										
Healing	d														11 33										
Great Coates	d														11 36										
Grimsby Town	a											11 29			11 41										
	d											11 33			11 41										
Grimsby Docks	d														11 44										
New Clee	d														11 47										
Cleethorpes	a											11 40			11 55										
Thorne North	d			09 24		09 38				10 31												11 25			
Goole	d			09a35		09 47				10 40								11 14				11a36			
Saltmarshe	d																								
York 33	d								09a58								10 40								
Selby	a																10 58								
Wressle	d																								
Howden	d																11 08								
Eastrington	d																								
Gilberdyke	d					09 55				10 48								11 24							
Broomfleet	d																								
Brough	d					10 03				10 56						11 04	11 19	11 32							
Ferriby	d									11 00															
Hessle	d									11 05															
Hull	a					10 21				11 17						11 21	11 41	11 47							

A To Leeds
B To Scarborough
C To Glasgow Central
D To Edinburgh
E To Bridlington
F From Birmingham New Street to Edinburgh
G From Leeds
H From Hull
I From Birmingham New Street to Glasgow Central
J From Leicester

Manchester Airport, Manchester, Sheffield and Meadowhall-Doncaster-Cleethorpes and Hull Barton-on-Humber - Cleethorpes

Network Diagram - see first Page of Table 18

Station		NT	NT	HT	EM		TP	XC	NT	NT		TP		EM	NT		XC		TP	NT	NT		NT	XC
				◇1			◇1	◇1				◇1		◇			◇1		◇1					◇1
		B			C			D		E				G	B		H		I	J	K		B	L
Manchester Airport 85	d						10 44																	
Manchester Piccadilly	d						11 18					12 20		12 44										
Stockport 78	d						11 27					12 28		12 55										
Sheffield	a						12 09					13 08		13 37										
	d	11 36					12 11	12 21	12 24	12 28		13 11					13 21				13 24		13 36	13 51
Meadowhall	d	11 42					12 16		12 30	12 34		13 16									13 30		13 42	
Rotherham Central	d	11 49							12 36												13 36		13 49	
Swinton (S.Yorks)	d	12a00							12 49												13 47		13a57	
Mexborough	d								12 52												13 50			
Conisbrough	d								12 56												13 54			
London Kings Cross	d			10 45																				
Doncaster	a			12 23			12 35		13 04	12 56		13 34									14 02			14 13
York 26	a							13 29									14 29							14 40
Doncaster 31	d			12 29			12 37		13 05	12 58					13 12						14 05			
Bentley (S.Yorks) 31	a														13 15									
Adwick 31	a														13 19									
Kirk Sandall	d								13 11															
Hatfield & Stainforth	d								13 16															
Thorne South	d																							
Crowle	d																							
Althorpe	d																							
Scunthorpe	a						13 06																	
	d						13 06																	
Barnetby	d				12 33		13 21																	
Hull Paragon Interchange	d																							
Barton-on-Humber	a																							
Barton-on-Humber	d																							
Barrow Haven	d																							
New Holland	d																							
Goxhill	d																							
Thornton Abbey	d																							
Ulceby	d																							
Habrough	d				12 41		13 29																	
Stallingborough	d																							
Healing	d																							
Great Coates	d																							
Grimsby Town	a				12 53		13 42																	
	d				13 05		13 43																	
Grimsby Docks	d																							
New Clee	d																							
Cleethorpes	a				13 16		13 53																	
Thorne North	d								13 22															
Goole	d								13a32	13 17											14 25			
Saltmarshe	d																							
York 33	d		12 05																	13 40				
Selby	a		12 24	12 43																13 59				
Wressle	d																							
Howden	d		12 34	12 54																14 09				
Eastrington	d																							
Gilberdyke	d									13 25											14 33			
Broomfleet	d																							
Brough	d		12 46	13 07						13 33									13 41	14 21	14 41			
Ferriby	d									13 38														
Hessle	d									13 42														
Hull	a		13 06	13 25						13 57									13 59	14 40	15 01			

B To Leeds
C From Newark North Gate
D From Bristol Temple Meads to Edinburgh
E To Scarborough
G To Norwich
H From Bristol Temple Meads to Glasgow Central
I From Huddersfield
J From Hull
K To Bridlington
L From Birmingham New Street to Newcastle

Table 29

Sundays
until 24 June

Manchester Airport, Manchester, Sheffield and Meadowhall-Doncaster-Cleethorpes and Hull
Barton-on-Humber - Cleethorpes

Network Diagram - see first Page of Table 18

	HT	NT	NT	TP	XC	NT	NT	NT	XC	NT	TP	XC	NT	NT	TP	NT	NT	XC	NT	HT
	◇■ ⊠	bus		◇■	◇■ A 🍴		B	C	◇■ E 🍴	F	◇■	◇■ G 🍴		bus	◇■ H	I	F	◇■ J 🍴	B	◇■ ⊠
Manchester Airport 85 ✈ d				12 55							13 55									
Manchester Piccadilly 10 ⇌ d				13 20							14 20									
Stockport 78 d				13 29							14 28									
Sheffield 7 ⇌ a				14 08							15 08									
d				14 10	14 21	14 22		14 28	14 51		15 11	15 21	15 24			15 28	15 36	15 51		
Meadowhall ⇌ d				14 16		14 28		14 34			15 16		15 30			15 34	15 42			
Rotherham Central d						14 35							15 37				15 50			
Swinton (S.Yorks) d						14 46							15 47				15a58			
Mexborough d						14 49							15 50							
Conisbrough d						14 53							15 54							
London Kings Cross d	12 45																			14 45
Doncaster 7 a	14 23			14 35		15 03		14 56	15 13		15 35		16 04			15 56		16 15		16 23
York 8 26 a					15 29				15 43			16 29						16 40		
Doncaster 31 d	14 25			14 37		15 05		14 59		15 12	15 37					15 56				16 30
Bentley (S.Yorks) 31 a										15 15										
Adwick 31 a										15 19										
Kirk Sandall d						15 11														
Hatfield & Stainforth d						15 16														
Thorne South d																				
Crowle d																				
Althorpe d																				
Scunthorpe a				15 02							16 02									
d				15 03							16 03									
Barnetby d				15 17							16 17									
Hull Paragon Interchange d		13 25												15 30						
Barton-on-Humber a		13 50												15 55						
Barton-on-Humber d			14 00																	
Barrow Haven d			14 05																	
New Holland d			14 08																	
Goxhill d			14 13																	
Thornton Abbey d			14 16																	
Ulceby d			14 20																	
Habrough d			14 25								16 26									
Stallingborough d			14 30																	
Healing d			14 33																	
Great Coates d			14 36																	
Grimsby Town a			14 41	15 37							16 39									
d			14 41	15 38							16 40									
Grimsby Docks d			14 44																	
New Clee d			14 47																	
Cleethorpes a			14 55	15 49							16 50									
Thorne North d						15 24										16 10				
Goole d						15a33		15 19								16 19				
Saltmarshe d																				
York 8 33 d							14 49												16 06	
Selby a	14 39						15 08												16 24	16 44
Wressle d																				
Howden d	14 50						15 18												16 34	16 55
Eastrington d																				
Gilberdyke d								15 29								16 27				
Broomfleet d																				
Brough d	15 03						15 30	15 37							15 41	16 35			16 46	17 07
Ferriby d																				
Hessle d																				
Hull a	15 21						15 49	15 56							15 59	16 53			17 07	17 26

A From Plymouth to Aberdeen
B From Hull
C To Scarborough
E From Birmingham New Street to Newcastle
F To Leeds
G From Plymouth to Glasgow Central
H From Huddersfield
I To Bridlington
J From Guildford to Newcastle

Table 29

Sundays
until 24 June

Manchester Airport, Manchester, Sheffield and Meadowhall-Doncaster-Cleethorpes and Hull
Barton-on-Humber - Cleethorpes

Network Diagram - see first Page of Table 18

	NT	EM	TP	XC	NT	NT	NT	XC	NT	TP	XC	NT	TP	NT	NT	NT	XC	EM	TP
		A	◇■	◇■ B 🍴		C	E	◇■ F 🍴	G	◇■	◇■ H 🍴		◇■ I		J	G	◇■ F 🍴	L	◇■
Manchester Airport 85 ✈ d			14 55							15 55									16 55
Manchester Piccadilly 10 ⇌ d			15 20							16 20									17 20
Stockport 78 d			15 28							16 28									17 28
Sheffield 7 ⇌ a			16 09							17 08									18 08
d			16 11	16 21	16 24	16 28	16 36	16 51		17 11	17 21	17 25			17 28	17 36	17 51		18 11
Meadowhall ⇌ d			16 16		16 30	16 34	16 42			17 16		17 31			17 34	17 44			18 16
Rotherham Central d					16 37		16 49					17 37				17 50			
Swinton (S.Yorks) d					16 47		16 58					17 47				17a58			
Mexborough d					16 50							17 50							
Conisbrough d					16 54							17 54							
London Kings Cross d																			
Doncaster 7 a			16 35		17 03	16 56		17 13		17 35		18 05			17 55		18 13		18 35
York 8 26 a				17 29			17 59	17 42			18 29						19 18		
Doncaster 31 d			16 37		17 04	16 58			17 14	17 37					17 57				18 37
Bentley (S.Yorks) 31 a									17 17										
Adwick 31 a									17 21										
Kirk Sandall d					17 10														
Hatfield & Stainforth d					17 15														
Thorne South d																			
Crowle d																			
Althorpe d																			
Scunthorpe a			17 02							18 02									19 02
d			17 03							18 03									19 03
Barnetby d		16 58	17 17							18 17								18 53	19 17
Hull Paragon Interchange d																			
Barton-on-Humber a																			
Barton-on-Humber d	16 15																		
Barrow Haven d	16 20																		
New Holland d	16 23																		
Goxhill d	16 28																		
Thornton Abbey d	16 31																		
Ulceby d	16 35																		
Habrough d	16 40	17 06																19 01	19 26
Stallingborough d	16 45																		
Healing d	16 48																		
Great Coates d	16 51																		
Grimsby Town a	16 56	17 18	17 37							18 37								19 13	19 39
d	16 56	17 19	17 38							18 38								19 13	19 40
Grimsby Docks d	16 59																		
New Clee d	17 02																		
Cleethorpes a	17 10	17 28	17 48							18 48								19 24	19 48
Thorne North d					17 24														
Goole d					17a33	17 17									18 16				
Saltmarshe d																			
York 8 33 d														17 11					
Selby a														17 30					
Wressle d																			
Howden d														17 41					
Eastrington d																			
Gilberdyke d						17 25									18 24				
Broomfleet d																			
Brough d						17 33							17 41	17 53	18 32				
Ferriby d																			
Hessle d																			
Hull a						17 51							17 59	18 12	18 48				

A From Nottingham
B From Penzance to Edinburgh
C To Scarborough
E To Sheffield
F From Reading to Newcastle
G To Leeds
H From Plymouth to Glasgow Central
I From Huddersfield
J To Bridlington
L From Newark North Gate

Manchester Airport, Manchester, Sheffield and Meadowhall-Doncaster-Cleethorpes and Hull Barton-on-Humber - Cleethorpes

Network Diagram - see first Page of Table 18

		XC	NT	NT	GR	XC	NT	NT	NT	NT	TP	NT	HT	TP	XC	NT	NT	XC	TP	NT	TP
		◇1 A		B	1	◇1 D	E	bus		F	◇1 G	H	◇1 ⊠	◇1	◇1 I		F	◇1 K	◇1 G		◇1
Manchester Airport 85 ✈	d													17 55							18 55
Manchester Piccadilly 10 ⇌	d													18 20							19 20
Stockport 78	d													18 28							19 28
Sheffield 7 ⇌	a													19 08							20 08
	d	18 21	18 25	18 28		18 51	18 57							19 11	19 21	19 29	19 36	19 51		20 02	20 11
Meadowhall ⇌	d		18 31	18 35			19 05							19 16		19 35	19 42			20 09	20 16
Rotherham Central	d		18 37				19 11									19 41	19 49				
Swinton (S.Yorks)	d		18 48				19 19									19 49	19a57				
Mexborough	d		18 51													19 52					
Conisbrough	d		18 55													19 56					
London Kings Cross	d				17 20								17 45								
Doncaster 7	a		19 06	18 54	19 03	19 15							19 23	19 35		20 07		20 16		20 30	20 35
York 8 26	a	19 29				19 43	20 18								20 29			20 45			
Doncaster 31	d			18 55	19 04					19 27			19 30	19 37						20 30	20 37
Bentley (S.Yorks) 31	a									19 30											
Adwick 31	a									19 34											
Kirk Sandall	d			19 01																	
Hatfield & Stainforth	d			19 06																	
Thorne South	d																				
Crowle	d																				
Althorpe	d																				
Scunthorpe	a													20 02							21 02
	d													20 03							21 03
Barnetby	d													20 17							21 17
Hull Paragon Interchange	d							18 30													
Barton-on-Humber	a							18 55													
Barton-on-Humber	d								19 15												
Barrow Haven	d								19 20												
New Holland	d								19 23												
Goxhill	d								19 28												
Thornton Abbey	d								19 31												
Ulceby	d								19 35												
Habrough	d								19 40												21 26
Stallingborough	d								19 45												
Healing	d								19 48												
Great Coates	d								19 51												
Grimsby Town	a								19 56					20 37							21 39
	d								19 56					20 38							21 40
Grimsby Docks	d								19 59												
New Clee	d								20 02												
Cleethorpes	a								20 10					20 48							21 50
Thorne North	d			19 12																	
Goole	d			19 21																20 49	
Saltmarshe	d																				
York 8 33	d											19 10									
Selby	a				19 23							19 35	19 45								
Wressle	d																				
Howden	d											19 46	19 56								
Eastrington	d																				
Gilberdyke	d			19 29																20 57	
Broomfleet	d																				
Brough	d			19 37	19 45						19 51	19 58	20 08						20 36	21 05	
Ferriby	d																				
Hessle	d																				
Hull	a			19 55	20 03						20 05	20 17	20 26						20 54	21 23	

A From Newquay to Edinburgh
B To Beverley
D From Reading to Edinburgh
E To Sheffield
F To Leeds
G From Huddersfield
H From Hull
I From Plymouth to Edinburgh
K From Reading to Newcastle

Manchester Airport, Manchester, Sheffield and Meadowhall-Doncaster-Cleethorpes and Hull Barton-on-Humber - Cleethorpes

Network Diagram - see first Page of Table 18

		XC	NT	XC	TP	HT	TP	NT	NT	NT	NT	TP	NT	NT	TP	NT
		◇1 A		◇1 C	◇1 D	◇1 ⊠	◇1	E	F		F	◇1 G			◇1	
Manchester Airport 85 ✈	d						19 55									
Manchester Piccadilly 10 ⇌	d						20 18									
Stockport 78	d						20 27									
Sheffield 7 ⇌	a						21 08									
	d	20 21	20 28	20 51			21 11			21 24	21 36		22 13	22 26	22 30	23 34
Meadowhall ⇌	d		20 34				21 16			21 30	21 42		22 19	22 32	22 35	23 40
Rotherham Central	d		20 40							21 37	21 48			22 38		23 47
Swinton (S.Yorks)	d		20 48							21 47	21a56			22 48		23 55
Mexborough	d		20 51							21 50				22 51		23 58
Conisbrough	d		20 55							21 54				22 55		00 02
London Kings Cross	d					19 45										
Doncaster 7	a		21 05	21 19		21 25	21 35			22 03			22 38	23 05	22 56	00 13
York 8 26	a	21 31		21 44												
Doncaster 31	d		21 07			21 27	21 37		21 52	22 04			22 41		22 58	
Bentley (S.Yorks) 31	a								21 55							
Adwick 31	a								21 59							
Kirk Sandall	d		21 13													
Hatfield & Stainforth	d		21 18													
Thorne South	d															
Crowle	d															
Althorpe	d															
Scunthorpe	a						22 02								23 23	
	d						22 03								23 24	
Barnetby	d						22 17								23 38	
Hull Paragon Interchange	d															
Barton-on-Humber	a															
Barton-on-Humber	d															
Barrow Haven	d															
New Holland	d															
Goxhill	d															
Thornton Abbey	d															
Ulceby	d															
Habrough	d						22 26									
Stallingborough	d															
Healing	d															
Great Coates	d															
Grimsby Town	a						22 39								23 57	
	d						22 40								23 58	
Grimsby Docks	d															
New Clee	d															
Cleethorpes	a						22 50								00 09	
Thorne North	d		21 24										22 53			
Goole	d		21a34							22 23			23 02			
Saltmarshe	d															
York 8 33	d							21 41								
Selby	a					21 43		22 00								
Wressle	d															
Howden	d					21 55		22 10								
Eastrington	d															
Gilberdyke	d									22 31			23 10			
Broomfleet	d															
Brough	d				21 58	22 07		22 22		22 39		23 02	23 18			
Ferriby	d															
Hessle	d															
Hull	a				22 12	22 26		22 36		22 56		23 19	23 39			

A From Plymouth to Leeds
C From Reading to Newcastle
D From Huddersfield
E From Hull
F To Leeds
G From Leeds

Table 29

Sundays
1 July to 9 September

Manchester Airport, Manchester, Sheffield and Meadowhall-Doncaster-Cleethorpes and Hull Barton-on-Humber - Cleethorpes

Network Diagram - see first Page of Table 18

		NT	NT	NT	NT	NT	XC	NT	GR	NT	TP	TP	NT	NT	NT	NT	NT	NT	NT	XC
					B	C	◇■ D	B	■ E	F	◇■ G	◇■	H	C					B	◇■ I
Manchester Airport 85 ✈	d																			
Manchester Piccadilly	d										09 11									
Stockport 78	d																			
Sheffield	a																			
	d	23p27	08 00			08 45	09 21	09 36				09 52		10 26			11 05			11 21
Meadowhall	d	23p33	08 06			08 51		09 42				09 57		10 32			11 11			
Rotherham Central	d	23p39	08 12			08 57		09 48				10 03					11 17			
Swinton (S.Yorks)	d	23p48	08 20			09 05		09a58				10 09					11 25			
Mexborough	d	23p51	08 23			09 08						10 13					11 28			
Conisbrough	d	23p55	08 27			09 12						10 17					11 32			
London Kings Cross	d																			
Doncaster	a	00 08	08 38			09 22						10 26		10 51			11 43			
York 26	a						10 29													12 29
Doncaster 31	d			09 07	09 12	09 26			09 37	10 19		10 28		10 55				11 07	11 12	
Bentley (S.Yorks) 31	a				09 15														11 15	
Adwick 31	a				09 19														11 19	
Kirk Sandall	d			09 13														11 13		
Hatfield & Stainforth	d			09 18														11 18		
Thorne South	d																			
Crowle	d																			
Althorpe	d																			
Scunthorpe	a											10 54								
	d											10 55								
Barnetby	d											11 09								
Hull Paragon Interchange	d														10 25					
Barton-on-Humber	a														10 50					
Barton-on-Humber	d															11 00				
Barrow Haven	d															11 05				
New Holland	d															11 08				
Goxhill	d															11 13				
Thornton Abbey	d															11 16				
Ulceby	d															11 20				
Habrough	d															11 25				
Stallingborough	d															11 30				
Healing	d															11 33				
Great Coates	d															11 36				
Grimsby Town	a											11 29				11 41				
	d											11 33				11 41				
Grimsby Docks	d															11 44				
New Clee	d															11 47				
Cleethorpes	a											11 40				11 55				
Thorne North	d			09 24		09 38				10 31								11 25		
Goole	d			09a35		09 47				10 40				11 14				11a36		
Saltmarshe	d																			
York 33	d								09a58				10 40							
Selby	a										10 44		10 58							
Wressle	d																			
Howden	d												11 08							
Eastrington	d																			
Gilberdyke	d					09 55				10 48				11 24						
Broomfleet	d																			
Brough	d					10 03				10 56	11 04		11 19	11 32						
Ferriby	d									11 00										
Hessle	d									11 05										
Hull	a					10 21				11 17	11 18		11 41	11 47						

B To Leeds
C To Scarborough
D To Glasgow Central
E To Edinburgh
F To Bridlington
G From Liverpool Lime Street
H From Hull
I From Birmingham New Street to Glasgow Central

Table 29

Sundays
1 July to 9 September

Manchester Airport, Manchester, Sheffield and Meadowhall-Doncaster-Cleethorpes and Hull Barton-on-Humber - Cleethorpes

Network Diagram - see first Page of Table 18

		EM	NT	NT	HT	EM	TP	XC	NT	NT	TP	TP	EM	NT	XC	NT	NT	NT
		◇■ A	C		◇■	D	◇■	◇■ E		F	◇■	◇■	◇ H	C	◇■ I	J	K	C
Manchester Airport 85 ✈	d						10 44											
Manchester Piccadilly	d						11 18				12 01	12 20	12 44					
Stockport 78	d						11 27					12 28	12 55					
Sheffield	a						12 09					13 08	13 37					
	d	11 31	11 36				12 11	12 21	12 24	12 28		13 11			13 21		13 24	13 36
Meadowhall	d		11 42				12 16		12 30	12 34		13 16					13 30	13 42
Rotherham Central	d		11 49						12 36								13 36	13 49
Swinton (S.Yorks)	d		12a00						12 49								13 47	13a57
Mexborough	d								12 52								13 50	
Conisbrough	d								12 56								13 54	
London Kings Cross	d				10 45													
Doncaster	a	11 52			12 23		12 35		13 04	12 56		13 34					14 02	
York 26	a	12 15						13 29							14 29			
Doncaster 31	d				12 29		12 37		13 05	12 58				13 12			14 05	
Bentley (S.Yorks) 31	a													13 15				
Adwick 31	a													13 19				
Kirk Sandall	d								13 11									
Hatfield & Stainforth	d								13 16									
Thorne South	d																	
Crowle	d																	
Althorpe	d																	
Scunthorpe	a						13 06											
	d						13 06											
Barnetby	d					12 33	13 21											
Hull Paragon Interchange	d																	
Barton-on-Humber	a																	
Barton-on-Humber	d																	
Barrow Haven	d																	
New Holland	d																	
Goxhill	d																	
Thornton Abbey	d																	
Ulceby	d																	
Habrough	d					12 41	13 29											
Stallingborough	d																	
Healing	d																	
Great Coates	d																	
Grimsby Town	a					12 53	13 42											
	d					13 05	13 43											
Grimsby Docks	d																	
New Clee	d																	
Cleethorpes	a					13 16	13 53											
Thorne North	d								13 22									
Goole	d								13a32	13 17							14 25	
Saltmarshe	d																	
York 33	d			12 05												13 40		
Selby	a			12 24	12 43						13 23					13 59		
Wressle	d																	
Howden	d			12 34	12 54											14 09		
Eastrington	d																	
Gilberdyke	d									13 25							14 33	
Broomfleet	d																	
Brough	d			12 46	13 07					13 33	13 41					14 21	14 41	
Ferriby	d									13 38								
Hessle	d									13 42								
Hull	a			13 06	13 25					13 57	13 59					14 40	15 01	

A From Leicester
C To Leeds
D From Newark North Gate
E From Bristol Temple Meads to Edinburgh
F To Scarborough
H To Norwich
I From Bristol Temple Meads to Glasgow Central
J From Hull
K To Bridlington

1 July to 9 September

Manchester Airport, Manchester, Sheffield and Meadowhall-Doncaster-Cleethorpes and Hull Barton-on-Humber - Cleethorpes

Network Diagram - see first Page of Table 18

		XC	HT	NT	NT	TP	XC	NT	NT	NT		TP		XC	NT	TP	XC	NT	NT			NT		XC	NT
		◇1 A	◇1	bus		◇1	◇1 B		C	D		◇1		◇1 A	F	◇1	◇1 G		H			F		◇1 I	C
Manchester Airport 85 ✈	d					12 55										13 55									
Manchester Piccadilly 10	d					13 20						14 02				14 20									
Stockport 78	d					13 28										14 28									
Sheffield 7	a					14 08										15 08									
	d	13 51				14 11	14 21	14 22		14 28				14 51		15 11	15 21	15 24	15 28			15 36		15 51	
Meadowhall	d					14 16		14 28		14 34						15 16		15 30	15 34			15 42			
Rotherham Central	d							14 35										15 37				15 50			
Swinton (S.Yorks)	d							14 46										15 47				15a58			
Mexborough	d							14 49										15 50							
Conisbrough	d							14 53										15 54							
London Kings Cross	d		12 45																						
Doncaster 7	a	14 13	14 23			14 35		15 03		14 56				15 13		15 35		16 04	15 56					16 15	
York 8 26	a	14 40					15 29							15 43			16 29							16 40	
Doncaster 31	d		14 25			14 37		15 05		14 59					15 12	15 37			15 56						
Bentley (S.Yorks) 31	a														15 15										
Adwick 31	a														15 19										
Kirk Sandall	d							15 11																	
Hatfield & Stainforth	d							15 16																	
Thorne South	d																								
Crowle	d																								
Althorpe	d																								
Scunthorpe	a					15 02										16 02									
	d					15 03										16 03									
Barnetby	d					15 17										16 17									
Hull Paragon Interchange	d			13 25																					
Barton-on-Humber	a			13 50																					
Barton-on-Humber	d				14 00																				
Barrow Haven	d				14 05																				
New Holland	d				14 08																				
Goxhill	d				14 13																				
Thornton Abbey	d				14 16																				
Ulceby	d				14 20																				
Habrough	d				14 25											16 26									
Stallingborough	d				14 30																				
Healing	d				14 33																				
Great Coates	d				14 36																				
Grimsby Town	a				14 41	15 37										16 39									
	d				14 41	15 38										16 40									
Grimsby Docks	d				14 44																				
New Clee	d				14 47																				
Cleethorpes	a				14 55	15 49										16 50									
Thorne North	d							15 24											16 10						
Goole	d							15a33		15 19									16 19						
Saltmarshe	d																								
York 8 33	d								14 49																16 06
Selby	a		14 39						15 08			15 23													16 24
Wressle	d																								
Howden	d		14 50						15 18																16 34
Eastrington	d																								
Gilberdyke	d									15 29									16 27						
Broomfleet	d																								
Brough	d		15 03						15 30	15 37		15 41							16 35						16 46
Ferriby	d																								
Hessle	d																								
Hull	a		15 21						15 49	15 56		15 59							16 53						17 07

A From Birmingham New Street to Newcastle
B From Plymouth to Aberdeen
C From Hull
D To Scarborough
F To Leeds
G From Plymouth to Glasgow Central
H To Bridlington
I From Guildford to Newcastle

1 July to 9 September

Manchester Airport, Manchester, Sheffield and Meadowhall-Doncaster-Cleethorpes and Hull Barton-on-Humber - Cleethorpes

Network Diagram - see first Page of Table 18

		HT	NT	NT	EM	TP	XC	NT	NT		TP	NT	XC	NT	NT	TP	XC	NT		NT		NT	XC	NT	EM
		◇1	bus		A	◇1	◇1 B		C		◇1	E	◇1 F		G	◇1	◇1 H			I		G	◇1 F	bus	K
Manchester Airport 85 ✈	d					14 55										15 55									
Manchester Piccadilly 10	d					15 20					16 02					16 20									
Stockport 78	d					15 28										16 28									
Sheffield 7	a					16 09										17 08									
	d					16 11	16 21	16 24	16 28			16 36	16 51			17 11	17 21	17 25		17 28		17 36	17 51		
Meadowhall	d					16 16		16 30	16 34			16 42				17 16		17 31		17 34		17 44			
Rotherham Central	d							16 37				16 49						17 37				17 50			
Swinton (S.Yorks)	d							16 47				16 58						17 47				17a58			
Mexborough	d							16 50										17 50							
Conisbrough	d							16 54										17 54							
London Kings Cross	d	14 45																							
Doncaster 7	a	16 23				16 35		17 03	16 56				17 13			17 35		18 05		17 55			18 13		
York 8 26	a						17 29					17 59	17 42				18 29						19 18		
Doncaster 31	d	16 30				16 37		17 04	16 58						17 14	17 37				17 57					
Bentley (S.Yorks) 31	a														17 17										
Adwick 31	a														17 21										
Kirk Sandall	d							17 10																	
Hatfield & Stainforth	d							17 15																	
Thorne South	d																								
Crowle	d																								
Althorpe	d																								
Scunthorpe	a					17 02										18 02									
	d					17 03										18 03									
Barnetby	d				16 58	17 17										18 17									18 53
Hull Paragon Interchange	d		15 30																					18 30	
Barton-on-Humber	a		15 55																					18 55	
Barton-on-Humber	d			16 15																					
Barrow Haven	d			16 20																					
New Holland	d			16 23																					
Goxhill	d			16 28																					
Thornton Abbey	d			16 31																					
Ulceby	d			16 35																					
Habrough	d			16 40	17 06																				19 01
Stallingborough	d			16 45																					
Healing	d			16 48																					
Great Coates	d			16 51																					
Grimsby Town	a			16 56	17 18	17 37										18 37									19 13
	d			16 56	17 19	17 38										18 38									19 13
Grimsby Docks	d			16 59																					
New Clee	d			17 02																					
Cleethorpes	a			17 10	17 28	17 48										18 48									19 24
Thorne North	d							17 24																	
Goole	d							17a33	17 17											18 16					
Saltmarshe	d																								
York 8 33	d													17 11											
Selby	a	16 44									17 23			17 30											
Wressle	d																								
Howden	d	16 55												17 41											
Eastrington	d																								
Gilberdyke	d								17 25											18 24					
Broomfleet	d																								
Brough	d	17 07							17 33		17 41			17 53						18 32					
Ferriby	d																								
Hessle	d																								
Hull	a	17 26							17 51		17 59			18 12						18 48					

A From Nottingham
B From Penzance to Edinburgh
C To Scarborough
D To Edinburgh
E To Sheffield
F From Reading to Newcastle
G To Leeds
H From Plymouth to Glasgow Central
I To Bridlington
J To Glasgow Central
K From Newark North Gate

Table 29

Sundays
1 July to 9 September

Manchester Airport, Manchester, Sheffield and Meadowhall-Doncaster-Cleethorpes and Hull
Barton-on-Humber - Cleethorpes

Network Diagram - see first Page of Table 18

		TP	XC	NT	NT	GR	TP	XC	NT	NT	NT	NT	HT	TP	TP	XC	NT	NT	XC	NT
		◇1	◇1 A 🍴		B	1 🍴	◇1	◇1 D 🍴	E	F		G	◇1 ☒	◇1	◇1	◇1 H		G	◇1 J 🍴	
Manchester Airport 85 ✈	d	16 55												17 55						
Manchester Piccadilly 10 ⇌	d	17 20					18 02							18 20	19 02					
Stockport 78	d	17 28												18 28						
Sheffield 7 ⇌	a	18 08												19 08						
	d	18 11	18 21	18 25	18 28			18 51	18 57					19 11		19 21	19 29	19 36	19 51	20 02
Meadowhall ⇌	d	18 16		18 31	18 35				19 05					19 16			19 35	19 42		20 09
Rotherham Central	d			18 37					19 11								19 41	19 49		
Swinton (S.Yorks)	d			18 48					19 19								19 49	19a57		
Mexborough	d			18 51													19 52			
Conisbrough	d			18 55													19 56			
London Kings Cross	d					17 20							17 45							
Doncaster 7	a	18 35		19 06	18 54	19 03		19 15					19 23	19 35			20 07		20 16	20 30
York 8 26	a		19 29					19 43	20 18							20 29			20 45	
Doncaster 31	d	18 37			18 55	19 04						19 27	19 30	19 37						20 30
Bentley (S.Yorks) 31	a											19 30								
Adwick 31	a											19 34								
Kirk Sandall	d				19 01															
Hatfield & Stainforth	d				19 06															
Thorne South	d																			
Crowle	d																			
Althorpe	d																			
Scunthorpe	a	19 02												20 02						
	d	19 03												20 03						
Barnetby	d	19 17												20 17						
Hull Paragon Interchange	d																			
Barton-on-Humber	a																			
Barton-on-Humber	d										19 15									
Barrow Haven	d										19 20									
New Holland	d										19 23									
Goxhill	d										19 28									
Thornton Abbey	d										19 31									
Ulceby	d										19 35									
Habrough	d	19 26									19 40									
Stallingborough	d										19 45									
Healing	d										19 48									
Great Coates	d										19 51									
Grimsby Town	a	19 39									19 56			20 37						
	d	19 40									19 56			20 38						
Grimsby Docks	d										19 59									
New Clee	d										20 02									
Cleethorpes	a	19 48									20 10			20 48						
Thorne North	d				19 12															20 49
Goole	d				19 21															
Saltmarshe	d																			
York 8 33	d									19 10										
Selby	a					19 23	19 28			19 35			19 45		20 17					
Wressle	d																			
Howden	d									19 46			19 56							
Eastrington	d																			20 57
Gilberdyke	d				19 29															
Broomfleet	d																			
Brough	d				19 37	19 45	19 48			19 58			20 08		20 36					21 05
Ferriby	d																			
Hessle	d																			
Hull	a				19 55	20 03	20 05			20 17			20 26		20 54					21 23

A From Newquay to Edinburgh
B To Beverley
D From Reading to Edinburgh
E To Sheffield
F From Hull
G To Leeds
H From Plymouth to Edinburgh
J From Reading to Newcastle

Table 29

Sundays
1 July to 9 September

Manchester Airport, Manchester, Sheffield and Meadowhall-Doncaster-Cleethorpes and Hull
Barton-on-Humber - Cleethorpes

Network Diagram - see first Page of Table 18

		TP	TP	XC	NT	XC	HT	TP	NT	NT	NT	NT	TP	NT	NT	TP	NT
		◇1	◇1	◇1 A 🍴		◇1 C	◇1 ☒	◇1	D	E		E	◇1 F			◇1	
Manchester Airport 85 ✈	d	18 55						19 55									
Manchester Piccadilly 10 ⇌	d	19 20	20 06					20 18									
Stockport 78	d	19 28						20 27									
Sheffield 7 ⇌	a	20 08						21 08									
	d	20 11		20 21	20 28	20 51		21 11			21 24	21 36		22 13	22 26	22 30	23 34
Meadowhall ⇌	d	20 16			20 34			21 16			21 30	21 42		22 19	22 32	22 35	23 40
Rotherham Central	d				20 40						21 37	21 48			22 38		23 47
Swinton (S.Yorks)	d				20 48						21 47	21a56			22 48		23 55
Mexborough	d				20 51						21 50				22 51		23 58
Conisbrough	d				20 55						21 54				22 55		00 02
London Kings Cross	d						19 45										
Doncaster 7	a	20 35			21 05	21 19	21 25	21 35			22 03			22 38	23 05	22 56	00 13
York 8 26	a			21 31		21 44											
Doncaster 31	d	20 37			21 07		21 27	21 37		21 52	22 04			22 41		22 58	
Bentley (S.Yorks) 31	a									21 55							
Adwick 31	a									21 59							
Kirk Sandall	d				21 13												
Hatfield & Stainforth	d				21 18												
Thorne South	d																
Crowle	d																
Althorpe	d																
Scunthorpe	a	21 02						22 02								23 23	
	d	21 03						22 03								23 24	
Barnetby	d	21 17						22 17								23 38	
Hull Paragon Interchange	d																
Barton-on-Humber	a																
Barton-on-Humber	d																
Barrow Haven	d																
New Holland	d																
Goxhill	d																
Thornton Abbey	d																
Ulceby	d																
Habrough	d	21 26						22 26									
Stallingborough	d																
Healing	d																
Great Coates	d																
Grimsby Town	a	21 39						22 39								23 57	
	d	21 40						22 40								23 58	
Grimsby Docks	d																
New Clee	d																
Cleethorpes	a	21 50						22 50								00 09	
Thorne North	d				21 24									22 53			
Goole	d				21a34						22 23			23 02			
Saltmarshe	d																
York 8 33	d								21 41								
Selby	a		21 38				21 43		22 00								
Wressle	d																
Howden	d						21 55		22 10								
Eastrington	d																
Gilberdyke	d										22 31			23 10			
Broomfleet	d																
Brough	d		21 58				22 07		22 22		22 39		23 02	23 18			
Ferriby	d																
Hessle	d																
Hull	a		22 12				22 26		22 36		22 56		23 19	23 39			

A From Plymouth to Leeds
C From Reading to Newcastle
D From Hull
E To Leeds
F From Leeds

Manchester Airport, Manchester, Sheffield and Meadowhall-Doncaster-Cleethorpes and Hull Barton-on-Humber - Cleethorpes

Network Diagram - see first Page of Table 18

		NT	NT	NT	NT	NT	XC	NT	GR	NT	TP	XC	TP	NT	NT	NT	NT	NT	XC	EM	NT
					A	B	◇■ C	A	■ D	E	◇■	◇■ F	◇■ G	H	B			A	◇■ I	◇■ J	A
Manchester Airport 85 ✈	d																				
Manchester Piccadilly ■	d																				
Stockport 78	d																				
Sheffield ■	a																				
	d	23p27	08 00			08 45	09 21	09 36			09 52	10 21			10 26	11 05			11 21	11 31	11 36
Meadowhall	d	23p33	08 06			08 51		09 42			09 57				10 32	11 11					11 42
Rotherham Central	d	23p39	08 12			08 57		09 48			10 03					11 17					11 49
Swinton (S.Yorks)	d	23p48	08 20			09 05		09a58			10 09					11 25					12a00
Mexborough	d	23p51	08 23			09 08					10 13					11 28					
Conisbrough	d	23p55	08 27			09 12					10 17					11 32					
London Kings Cross	d																				
Doncaster ■	a	00 08	08 38			09 22					10 26				10 51	11 43				11 52	
York ■ 26	a						10 27					11 26							12 29	12 15	
Doncaster 31	d			09 07	09 12	09 26			09 37	10 19	10 28				10 55		11 07	11 12			
Bentley (S.Yorks) 31	a				09 15													11 15			
Adwick 31	a				09 19													11 19			
Kirk Sandall	d			09 13													11 13				
Hatfield & Stainforth	d			09 18													11 18				
Thorne South	d																				
Crowle	d																				
Althorpe	d																				
Scunthorpe	a										10 54										
	d										10 55										
Barnetby	d										11 09										
Hull Paragon Interchange	d																				
BartonenHumber	a																				
Barton-on-Humber	d																				
Barrow Haven	d																				
New Holland	d																				
Goxhill	d																				
Thornton Abbey	d																				
Ulceby	d																				
Habrough	d																				
Stallingborough	d																				
Healing	d																				
Great Coates	d																				
Grimsby Town	a										11 29										
	d										11 33										
Grimsby Docks	d																				
New Clee	d																				
Cleethorpes	a										11 40										
Thorne North	d			09 24		09 38				10 31							11 25				
Goole	d			09a35		09 47				10 40					11 14		11a36				
Saltmarshe	d																				
York ■ 33	d								09a58					10 40							
Selby	a													10 58							
Wressle	d																				
Howden	d													11 08							
Eastrington	d																				
Gilberdyke	d					09 55				10 48					11 24						
Broomfleet	d																				
Brough	d					10 03				10 56			11 04	11 19	11 32						
Ferriby	d									11 00											
Hessle	d									11 05											
Hull	a					10 21				11 17			11 21	11 41	11 47						

A To Leeds
B To Scarborough
C To Newcastle
E To Bridlington
F From Derby to Newcastle
G From Leeds
H From Hull
I From Birmingham New Street to Newcastle
J From Leicester

Manchester Airport, Manchester, Sheffield and Meadowhall-Doncaster-Cleethorpes and Hull Barton-on-Humber - Cleethorpes

Network Diagram - see first Page of Table 18

		NT	HT	TP	XC	NT	NT	TP	EM	NT	XC	TP	NT	NT	NT	XC	HT	TP	XC	NT
			◇■ ⊠	◇■	◇■ A		B	◇■	◇ E	F	◇■ G	◇■ H	I	J	F	◇■ A	◇■ ⊠	◇■	◇■ G	
Manchester Airport 85 ✈	d			10 44														12 55		
Manchester Piccadilly ■	d			11 18				12 18	12 44									13 20		
Stockport 78	d			11 27				12 28	12 55									13 28		
Sheffield ■	a			12 09				13 08	13 37									14 08		
	d			12 11	12 21	12 24	12 28	13 11			13 21			13 24	13 36	13 51		14 11	14 21	14 22
Meadowhall	d			12 16		12 30	12 34	13 16						13 30	13 42			14 16		14 28
Rotherham Central	d					12 36								13 36	13 49					14 35
Swinton (S.Yorks)	d					12 49								13 47	13a57					14 46
Mexborough	d					12 52								13 50						14 49
Conisbrough	d					12 56								13 54						14 53
London Kings Cross	d		10 45														12 45			
Doncaster ■	a		12 23	12 35		13 04	12 56	13 34						14 02		14 13	14 23	14 35		15 03
York ■ 26	a				13 31						14 31					14 40			15 29	
Doncaster 31	d		12 29	12 37		13 05	12 58			13 12				14 05			14 25	14 37		15 05
Bentley (S.Yorks) 31	a									13 15										
Adwick 31	a									13 19										
Kirk Sandall	d					13 11														15 11
Hatfield & Stainforth	d					13 16														15 16
Thorne South	d																			
Crowle	d																			
Althorpe	d																			
Scunthorpe	a			13 06														15 02		
	d			13 06														15 03		
Barnetby	d			13 21														15 17		
Hull Paragon Interchange	d																			
BartonenHumber	a																			
Barton-on-Humber	d																			
Barrow Haven	d																			
New Holland	d																			
Goxhill	d																			
Thornton Abbey	d																			
Ulceby	d																			
Habrough	d			13 29																
Stallingborough	d																			
Healing	d																			
Great Coates	d																			
Grimsby Town	a			13 42														15 37		
	d			13 43														15 38		
Grimsby Docks	d																			
New Clee	d																			
Cleethorpes	a			13 53														15 49		
Thorne North	d					13 22														15 24
Goole	d					13a32	13 17							14 25						15a33
Saltmarshe	d																			
York ■ 33	d	12 05											13 40							
Selby	a	12 24	12 43										13 59				14 39			
Wressle	d																			
Howden	d	12 34	12 54										14 09				14 50			
Eastrington	d																			
Gilberdyke	d						13 25							14 33						
Broomfleet	d																			
Brough	d	12 46	13 07				13 33					13 41	14 21	14 41			15 03			
Ferriby	d						13 38													
Hessle	d						13 42													
Hull	a	13 06	13 25				13 57					13 59	14 40	15 01			15 21			

A From Birmingham New Street to Newcastle
B To Scarborough
E To Norwich
F To Leeds
G From Bristol Temple Meads to Newcastle
H From Huddersfield
I From Hull
J To Bridlington

Sundays

16 September to 21 October

Manchester Airport, Manchester, Sheffield and Meadowhall-Doncaster-Cleethorpes and Hull Barton-on-Humber - Cleethorpes

Network Diagram - see first Page of Table 18

	NT	NT	XC	NT	TP	XC	NT	TP	NT	NT	XC	NT	HT	TP	XC	NT	NT	NT
	A	B	◇1 D 🍴	E	◇1	◇1 F 🍴		◇1 G	H	E	◇1 I 🍴	A	◇1 ⊠	◇1	◇1 J 🍴		B	K
Manchester Airport 85 ✈ d					13 55									14 55				
Manchester Piccadilly 10 ⇌ d					14 20									15 20				
Stockport 78 d					14 28									15 28				
Sheffield 7 ⇌ a					15 08									16 09				
d		14 28	14 51		15 11	15 21	15 24		15 28	15 36	15 51			16 11	16 21	16 24	16 28	16 36
Meadowhall ⇌ d		14 34			15 16		15 30		15 34	15 42				16 16		16 30	16 34	16 42
Rotherham Central d							15 37			15 50						16 37		16 49
Swinton (S.Yorks) d							15 47			15a58						16 47		16 58
Mexborough d							15 50									16 50		
Conisbrough d							15 54									16 54		
London Kings Cross d													14 45					
Doncaster 7 a		14 56	15 13		15 35		16 04		15 56		16 15		16 23	16 35		17 03	16 56	
York 8 26 a			15 43			16 29					16 40				17 29			17 59
Doncaster 31 d		14 59		15 12	15 37				15 56				16 30	16 37		17 04	16 58	
Bentley (S.Yorks) 31 a				15 15														
Adwick 31 a				15 19														
Kirk Sandall d																17 10		
Hatfield & Stainforth d																17 15		
Thorne South d																		
Crowle d																		
Althorpe d																		
Scunthorpe a					16 02									17 02				
d					16 03									17 03				
Barnetby d					16 17									17 17				
Hull Paragon Interchange d																		
Barton-on-Humber a																		
Barton-on-Humber d																		
Barrow Haven d																		
New Holland d																		
Goxhill d																		
Thornton Abbey d																		
Ulceby d																		
Habrough d					16 26													
Stallingborough d																		
Healing d																		
Great Coates d																		
Grimsby Town a					16 39									17 37				
d					16 40									17 38				
Grimsby Docks d																		
New Clee d																		
Cleethorpes a					16 50									17 48				
Thorne North d									16 10							17 24		
Goole d		15 19							16 19							17a33	17 17	
Saltmarshe d																		
York 8 33 d	14 49											16 06						
Selby a	15 08											16 24	16 44					
Wressle d																		
Howden d	15 18											16 34	16 55					
Eastrington d																		
Gilberdyke d		15 29							16 27								17 25	
Broomfleet d																		
Brough d	15 30	15 37						15 41	16 35			16 46	17 07				17 33	
Ferriby d																		
Hessle d																		
Hull a	15 49	15 56						15 59	16 53			17 07	17 26				17 51	

A From Hull
B To Scarborough
D From Birmingham New Street to Newcastle
E To Leeds
F From Plymouth to Glasgow Central
G From Huddersfield
H To Bridlington
I From Guildford to Newcastle
J From Plymouth to Edinburgh
K To Sheffield

Table 29

Sundays

16 September to 21 October

Manchester Airport, Manchester, Sheffield and Meadowhall-Doncaster-Cleethorpes and Hull Barton-on-Humber - Cleethorpes

Network Diagram - see first Page of Table 18

	XC	NT	TP	XC	NT	TP	NT	NT	NT	XC	TP	XC	NT	NT	GR	XC	NT	NT	TP	NT
	◇1 A 🍴	B	◇1	◇1 C 🍴		◇1 D		E	B	◇1 A 🍴	◇1	◇1 G 🍴		H	■ 1 🍴	◇1 J 🍴	K	B	◇1 D	L
Manchester Airport 85 ✈ d			15 55								16 55									
Manchester Piccadilly 10 ⇌ d			16 20								17 20									
Stockport 78 d			16 28								17 28									
Sheffield 7 ⇌ a			17 08								18 08									
d	16 51		17 11	17 21	17 25			17 28	17 36	17 51	18 11	18 21	18 25	18 28		18 51	18 57			
Meadowhall ⇌ d			17 16		17 31			17 34	17 44		18 16		18 31	18 35			19 05			
Rotherham Central d					17 37				17 50				18 37				19 11			
Swinton (S.Yorks) d					17 47				17a58				18 48				19 19			
Mexborough d					17 50								18 51							
Conisbrough d					17 54								18 55							
London Kings Cross d															17 20					
Doncaster 7 a	17 13		17 35		18 05			17 55		18 13	18 35		19 06	18 54	19 03	19 15				
York 8 26 a	17 42			18 29						19 18		19 28				19 43	20 18			
Doncaster 31 d		17 14	17 37					17 57			18 37			18 55	19 04			19 27		
Bentley (S.Yorks) 31 a		17 17																19 30		
Adwick 31 a		17 21																19 34		
Kirk Sandall d														19 01						
Hatfield & Stainforth d														19 06						
Thorne South d																				
Crowle d																				
Althorpe d																				
Scunthorpe a			18 02								19 02									
d			18 03								19 03									
Barnetby d			18 17								19 17									
Hull Paragon Interchange d																				
Barton-on-Humber a																				
Barton-on-Humber d																				
Barrow Haven d																				
New Holland d																				
Goxhill d																				
Thornton Abbey d																				
Ulceby d																				
Habrough d											19 26									
Stallingborough d																				
Healing d																				
Great Coates d																				
Grimsby Town a			18 37								19 39									
d			18 38								19 40									
Grimsby Docks d																				
New Clee d																				
Cleethorpes a			18 48								19 48									
Thorne North d														19 12						
Goole d								18 16						19 21						
Saltmarshe d																				
York 8 33 d							17 11													19 10
Selby a							17 30								19 23					19 35
Wressle d																				
Howden d							17 41													19 46
Eastrington d																				
Gilberdyke d								18 24						19 29						
Broomfleet d																				
Brough d						17 41	17 53	18 32						19 37	19 45				19 51	19 58
Ferriby d																				
Hessle d																				
Hull a						17 59	18 12	18 48						19 55	20 03				20 05	20 17

A From Reading to Newcastle
B To Leeds
C From Penzance to Glasgow Central
D From Huddersfield
E To Bridlington
G From Plymouth to Edinburgh
H To Beverley
J From Reading to Edinburgh
K To Sheffield
L From Hull

Manchester Airport, Manchester, Sheffield and Meadowhall-Doncaster-Cleethorpes and Hull Barton-on-Humber - Cleethorpes

Network Diagram - see first Page of Table 18

		HT	TP	XC	NT	NT	XC	TP	NT	TP	XC	NT	XC	TP	HT	TP	NT	NT	NT	NT
		◇1 ⊠	◇1	◇1 A		C	◇1 D ✠	◇1 E		◇1	◇1 F ✠		◇1 D	◇1 E	◇1 ⊠	◇1	G	C		C
Manchester Airport 85 ✈	d		17 55							18 55						19 55				
Manchester Piccadilly 10	d		18 20							19 20						20 18				
Stockport 78	d		18 28							19 28						20 27				
Sheffield 7	a		19 08							20 08						21 08				
	d		19 11	19 21	19 29	19 36	19 51		20 02	20 11	20 21	20 28	20 51			21 11			21 24	21 36
Meadowhall	d		19 16		19 35	19 42			20 09	20 16		20 34				21 16			21 30	21 42
Rotherham Central	d				19 41	19 49						20 40							21 37	21 48
Swinton (S.Yorks)	d				19 49	19a57						20 48							21 47	21a56
Mexborough	d				19 52							20 51							21 50	
Conisbrough	d				19 56							20 55							21 54	
London Kings Cross	d	17 45													19 45					
Doncaster 7	a	19 23	19 35		20 07		20 16		20 30	20 35		21 05	21 19		21 25	21 35			22 03	
York 8 26	a			20 29			20 45				21 31		21 44							
Doncaster 31	d	19 30	19 37						20 30	20 37		21 07			21 27	21 37		21 52	22 04	
Bentley (S.Yorks) 31	a																	21 55		
Adwick 31	a																	21 59		
Kirk Sandall	d											21 13								
Hatfield & Stainforth	d											21 18								
Thorne South	d																			
Crowle	d																			
Althorpe	d																			
Scunthorpe	a		20 02							21 02						22 02				
	d		20 03							21 03						22 03				
Barnetby	d		20 17							21 17						22 17				
Hull Paragon Interchange	d																			
Barton-on-Humber	a																			
Barton-on-Humber	d																			
Barrow Haven	d																			
New Holland	d																			
Goxhill	d																			
Thornton Abbey	d																			
Ulceby	d																			
Habrough	d									21 26						22 26				
Stallingborough	d																			
Healing	d																			
Great Coates	d																			
Grimsby Town	a		20 37							21 39						22 39				
	d		20 38							21 40						22 40				
Grimsby Docks	d																			
New Clee	d																			
Cleethorpes	a		20 48							21 50						22 50				
Thorne North	d											21 24								
Goole	d								20 49			21a34							22 23	
Saltmarshe	d																			
York 8 33	d																21 41			
Selby	a	19 45													21 43		22 00			
Wressle	d																			
Howden	d	19 56													21 55		22 10			
Eastrington	d																			
Gilberdyke	d								20 57											
Broomfleet	d																		22 31	
Brough	d	20 08						20 36	21 05					21 58	22 07		22 22		22 39	
Ferriby	d																			
Hessle	d																			
Hull	a	20 26						20 54	21 23					22 12	22 26		22 36		22 56	

A From Plymouth to Edinburgh
C To Leeds
D From Reading to Newcastle
E From Huddersfield
F From Plymouth to Leeds
G From Hull

Table 29

Sundays

16 September to 21 October

Manchester Airport, Manchester, Sheffield and Meadowhall-Doncaster-Cleethorpes and Hull Barton-on-Humber - Cleethorpes

Network Diagram - see first Page of Table 18

		TP	NT	NT	TP	NT
		◇1 A			◇1	
Manchester Airport 85 ✈	d					
Manchester Piccadilly 10	d					
Stockport 78	d					
Sheffield 7	a					
	d		22 13	22 26	22 30	23 34
Meadowhall	d		22 19	22 32	22 35	23 40
Rotherham Central	d			22 38		23 47
Swinton (S.Yorks)	d			22 48		23 55
Mexborough	d			22 51		23 58
Conisbrough	d			22 55		00 02
London Kings Cross	d					
Doncaster 7	a		22 38	23 05	22 56	00 13
York 8 26	a					
Doncaster 31	d		22 41		22 58	
Bentley (S.Yorks) 31	a					
Adwick 31	a					
Kirk Sandall	d					
Hatfield & Stainforth	d					
Thorne South	d					
Crowle	d					
Althorpe	d					
Scunthorpe	a				23 23	
	d				23 24	
Barnetby	d				23 38	
Hull Paragon Interchange	d					
Barton-on-Humber	a					
Barton-on-Humber	d					
Barrow Haven	d					
New Holland	d					
Goxhill	d					
Thornton Abbey	d					
Ulceby	d					
Habrough	d					
Stallingborough	d					
Healing	d					
Great Coates	d					
Grimsby Town	a				23 57	
	d				23 58	
Grimsby Docks	d					
New Clee	d					
Cleethorpes	a				00 09	
Thorne North	d		22 53			
Goole	d		23 02			
Saltmarshe	d					
York 8 33	d					
Selby	a					
Wressle	d					
Howden	d					
Eastrington	d					
Gilberdyke	d		23 10			
Broomfleet	d					
Brough	d	23 02	23 18			
Ferriby	d					
Hessle	d					
Hull	a	23 19	23 39			

A From Leeds

Sundays from 28 October

Manchester Airport, Manchester, Sheffield and Meadowhall-Doncaster-Cleethorpes and Hull Barton-on-Humber - Cleethorpes

Network Diagram - see first Page of Table 18

		NT	NT	NT	NT	NT	XC	NT	GR	NT		TP	TP	NT	NT		NT	NT	NT	EM			NT	NT	HT
					A	B	◇■ C 🍴	A	■ ■ D 🍴	E		◇■	◇■ F	G	B				A	◇■ H 🍴			A		◇■ ⊠
Manchester Airport 85 ✈	d																								
Manchester Piccadilly 10	d																								
Stockport 78	d																								
Sheffield 7	a																								
	d	23p27	08 00			08 45	09 21	09 36				09 52			10 26		11 05			11 31			11 36		
Meadowhall	d	23p33	08 06			08 51		09 42				09 57			10 32		11 11						11 42		
Rotherham Central	d	23p39	08 12			08 57		09 48				10 03					11 17						11 49		
Swinton (S.Yorks)	d	23p48	08 20			09 05		09a58				10 09					11 25						12a00		
Mexborough	d	23p51	08 23			09 08						10 13					11 28								
Conisbrough	d	23p55	08 27			09 12						10 17					11 32								
London Kings Cross	d																								10 45
Doncaster 7	a	00 08	08 38			09 22						10 26			10 51		11 43			11 52					12 23
York 8 26	a						10 27													12 15					
Doncaster 31	d			09 07	09 12	09 26			09 37	10 19		10 28			10 55			11 07	11 12						12 29
Bentley (S.Yorks) 31	a				09 15														11 15						
Adwick 31	a				09 19														11 19						
Kirk Sandall	d			09 13														11 13							
Hatfield & Stainforth	d			09 18														11 18							
Thorne South	d																								
Crowle	d																								
Althorpe	d																								
Scunthorpe	a											10 54													
	d											10 55													
Barnetby	d											11 09													
Hull Paragon Interchange	d																								
BartonenHumber	a																								
Barton-on-Humber	d																								
Barrow Haven	d																								
New Holland	d																								
Goxhill	d																								
Thornton Abbey	d																								
Ulceby	d																								
Habrough	d																								
Stallingborough	d																								
Healing	d																								
Great Coates	d																								
Grimsby Town	a											11 29													
	d											11 33													
Grimsby Docks	d																								
New Clee	d																								
Cleethorpes	a											11 40													
Thorne North	d			09 24		09 38				10 31								11 25							
Goole	d			09a35		09 47				10 40					11 14			11a36							
Saltmarshe	d																								
York 8 33	d								09a58					10 40										12 05	
Selby	a													10 58										12 24	12 43
Wressle	d																								
Howden	d													11 08										12 34	12 54
Eastrington	d																								
Gilberdyke	d					09 55				10 48					11 24										
Broomfleet	d																								
Brough	d					10 03				10 56			11 04	11 19	11 32									12 46	13 07
Ferriby	d									11 00															
Hessle	d									11 05															
Hull	a					10 21				11 17			11 21	11 41	11 47									13 06	13 25

A To Leeds
B To Scarborough
C To Glasgow Central
E To Bridlington
F From Leeds
G From Hull
H From Leicester

Sundays from 28 October

Manchester Airport, Manchester, Sheffield and Meadowhall-Doncaster-Cleethorpes and Hull Barton-on-Humber - Cleethorpes

Network Diagram - see first Page of Table 18

		TP	XC	NT	NT			TP		EM	NT	XC	TP	NT	NT			NT	XC	HT	TP	XC	NT	NT	NT
		◇■	◇■ A 🍴		B			◇■		◇ E	F	◇■ G 🍴	◇■ H	I	J			F	◇■ K 🍴	◇■ ⊠	◇■	◇■ L 🍴		I	B
Manchester Airport 85 ✈	d	10 44																			12 55				
Manchester Piccadilly 10	d	11 18						12 18		12 44											13 20				
Stockport 78	d	11 27						12 28		12 55											13 28				
Sheffield 7	a	12 09						13 08		13 37											14 08				
	d	12 11	12 21	12 24	12 28			13 11				13 21			13 24			13 36	13 51		14 11	14 21	14 22		14 28
Meadowhall	d	12 16		12 30	12 34			13 16							13 30			13 42			14 16		14 28		14 34
Rotherham Central	d			12 36											13 36			13 49					14 35		
Swinton (S.Yorks)	d			12 49											13 47			13a57					14 46		
Mexborough	d			12 52											13 50								14 49		
Conisbrough	d			12 56											13 54								14 53		
London Kings Cross	d																			12 45					
Doncaster 7	a	12 35		13 04	12 56			13 34							14 02				14 13	14 23	14 35		15 03		14 56
York 8 26	a		13 29									14 29							14 40			15 29			
Doncaster 31	d	12 37		13 05	12 58						13 12				14 05					14 25	14 37		15 05		14 59
Bentley (S.Yorks) 31	a										13 15														
Adwick 31	a										13 19														
Kirk Sandall	d			13 11																			15 11		
Hatfield & Stainforth	d			13 16																			15 16		
Thorne South	d																								
Crowle	d																								
Althorpe	d																								
Scunthorpe	a	13 06																			15 02				
	d	13 06																			15 03				
Barnetby	d	13 21																			15 17				
Hull Paragon Interchange	d																								
BartonenHumber	a																								
Barton-on-Humber	d																								
Barrow Haven	d																								
New Holland	d																								
Goxhill	d																								
Thornton Abbey	d																								
Ulceby	d																								
Habrough	d	13 29																							
Stallingborough	d																								
Healing	d																								
Great Coates	d																								
Grimsby Town	a	13 42																			15 37				
	d	13 43																			15 38				
Grimsby Docks	d																								
New Clee	d																								
Cleethorpes	a	13 53																			15 49				
Thorne North	d			13 22																			15 24		
Goole	d			13a32	13 17										14 25								15a33		15 19
Saltmarshe	d																								
York 8 33	d													13 40										14 49	
Selby	a													13 59						14 39				15 08	
Wressle	d																								
Howden	d													14 09						14 50				15 18	
Eastrington	d																								
Gilberdyke	d				13 25										14 33										15 29
Broomfleet	d																								
Brough	d				13 33								13 41	14 21	14 41					15 03				15 30	15 37
Ferriby	d				13 38																				
Hessle	d				13 42																				
Hull	a				13 57								13 59	14 40	15 01					15 21				15 49	15 56

A From Birmingham New Street to Edinburgh
B To Scarborough
E To Norwich
F To Leeds
G From Birmingham New Street to Glasgow Central
H From Huddersfield
I From Hull
J To Bridlington
K From Birmingham New Street to Newcastle
L From Birmingham New Street to Aberdeen

Manchester Airport, Manchester, Sheffield and Meadowhall-Doncaster-Cleethorpes and Hull Barton-on-Humber - Cleethorpes

Network Diagram - see first Page of Table 18

		XC ◇1 B	NT C	TP ◇1	XC ◇1 D	NT	TP ◇1 E	NT F	NT C	XC ◇1 G	NT H	HT ◇1	TP ◇1	XC ◇1 I	NT	NT J	NT K	XC ◇1 L	NT C
Manchester Airport 85	d			13 55									14 55						
Manchester Piccadilly 10	d			14 20									15 20						
Stockport 78	d			14 28									15 28						
Sheffield 7	a			15 08									16 09						
	d	14 51		15 11	15 21	15 24		15 28	15 36	15 51			16 11	16 21	16 24	16 28	16 36	16 51	
Meadowhall	d			15 16		15 30		15 34	15 42				16 16		16 30	16 34	16 42		
Rotherham Central	d					15 37			15 50						16 37		16 49		
Swinton (S.Yorks)	d					15 47			15a58						16 47		16a58		
Mexborough	d					15 50									16 50				
Conisbrough	d					15 54									16 54				
London Kings Cross	d											14 45							
Doncaster 7	a	15 13		15 35		16 04		15 56		16 15		16 23	16 35		17 03	16 56		17 13	
York 8 26	a	15 43			16 29					16 40				17 29				17 42	
Doncaster 31	d		15 12	15 37				15 56				16 30	16 37		17 04	16 58			17 14
Bentley (S.Yorks) 31	a		15 15																17 17
Adwick 31	a		15 19																17 21
Kirk Sandall	d														17 10				
Hatfield & Stainforth	d														17 15				
Thorne South	d																		
Crowle	d																		
Althorpe	d																		
Scunthorpe	a			16 02									17 02						
	d			16 03									17 03						
Barnetby	d			16 17									17 17						
Hull Paragon Interchange	d																		
BartonenHumber	a																		
Barton-on-Humber	d																		
Barrow Haven	d																		
New Holland	d																		
Goxhill	d																		
Thornton Abbey	d																		
Ulceby	d																		
Habrough	d			16 26															
Stallingborough	d																		
Healing	d																		
Great Coates	d																		
Grimsby Town	a			16 39									17 37						
	d			16 40									17 38						
Grimsby Docks	d																		
New Clee	d																		
Cleethorpes	a			16 50									17 48						
Thorne North	d							16 10							17 24				
Goole	d							16 19							17a33	17 17			
Saltmarshe	d																		
York 8 33	d										16 06								
Selby	a										16 24	16 44							
Wressle	d																		
Howden	d										16 34	16 55							
Eastrington	d																		
Gilberdyke	d							16 27								17 25			
Broomfleet	d																		
Brough	d						15 41	16 35			16 46	17 07				17 33			
Ferriby	d																		
Hessle	d																		
Hull	a						15 59	16 53			17 07	17 26				17 51			

B From Birmingham New Street to Newcastle
C To Leeds
D From Plymouth to Glasgow Central
E From Huddersfield
F To Bridlington
G From Guildford to Newcastle
H From Hull
I From Birmingham New Street to Edinburgh
J To Scarborough
K To Moorthorpe
L From Reading to Newcastle

Manchester Airport, Manchester, Sheffield and Meadowhall-Doncaster-Cleethorpes and Hull Barton-on-Humber - Cleethorpes

Network Diagram - see first Page of Table 18

		TP ◇1	XC ◇1 A	NT	TP ◇1 B	NT	NT C	NT E	XC ◇1 F	TP ◇1	XC ◇1 G	NT	NT H	GR 1	XC ◇1 J	NT K	NT E	TP ◇1 B	NT L	HT ◇1	TP ◇1
Manchester Airport 85	d	15 55								16 55											17 55
Manchester Piccadilly 10	d	16 20								17 20											18 20
Stockport 78	d	16 28								17 28											18 28
Sheffield 7	a	17 08								18 08											19 08
	d	17 11	17 21	17 25			17 28	17 36	17 51	18 11	18 21	18 25	18 28		18 51	18 57					19 11
Meadowhall	d	17 16		17 31			17 34	17 44		18 16		18 31	18 35			19 05					19 16
Rotherham Central	d			17 37				17 50				18 37				19 11					
Swinton (S.Yorks)	d			17 47				17a58				18 48				19a19					
Mexborough	d			17 50								18 51									
Conisbrough	d			17 54								18 55									
London Kings Cross	d													17 20						17 45	
Doncaster 7	a	17 35		18 05			17 55		18 13	18 35		19 06	18 54	19 03	19 15					19 23	19 35
York 8 26	a		18 29						19 18		19 29				19 43						
Doncaster 31	d	17 37					17 57			18 37			18 55	19 04			19 27			19 30	19 37
Bentley (S.Yorks) 31	a																19 30				
Adwick 31	a																19 34				
Kirk Sandall	d												19 01								
Hatfield & Stainforth	d												19 06								
Thorne South	d																				
Crowle	d																				
Althorpe	d																				
Scunthorpe	a	18 02								19 02											20 02
	d	18 03								19 03											20 03
Barnetby	d	18 17								19 17											20 17
Hull Paragon Interchange	d																				
BartonenHumber	a																				
Barton-on-Humber	d																				
Barrow Haven	d																				
New Holland	d																				
Goxhill	d																				
Thornton Abbey	d																				
Ulceby	d																				
Habrough	d									19 26											
Stallingborough	d																				
Healing	d																				
Great Coates	d																				
Grimsby Town	a	18 37								19 39											20 37
	d	18 38								19 40											20 38
Grimsby Docks	d																				
New Clee	d																				
Cleethorpes	a	18 48								19 48											20 48
Thorne North	d												19 12								
Goole	d						18 16						19 21								
Saltmarshe	d																				
York 8 33	d					17 11													19 10		
Selby	a					17 30								19 23					19 35	19 45	
Wressle	d																				
Howden	d					17 41													19 46	19 56	
Eastrington	d																				
Gilberdyke	d						18 24						19 29								
Broomfleet	d																				
Brough	d				17 41	17 53	18 32						19 37	19 45				19 51	19 58	20 08	
Ferriby	d																				
Hessle	d																				
Hull	a				17 59	18 12	18 48						19 55	20 03				20 05	20 17	20 26	

A From Plymouth to Glasgow Central
B From Huddersfield
C To Bridlington
E To Leeds
F From Reading to Newcastle
G From Plymouth to Edinburgh
H To Beverley
J From Reading to Edinburgh
K To Moorthorpe
L From Hull

Table 29

Sundays
from 28 October

Manchester Airport, Manchester, Sheffield and Meadowhall-Doncaster-Cleethorpes and Hull Barton-on-Humber - Cleethorpes

Network Diagram - see first Page of Table 18

	XC	NT	NT	XC	TP	NT	TP	XC	NT	XC	TP	HT	TP	NT	NT	NT	NT	TP	NT
	◇1 A		C	◇1 D ✠	◇1 E		◇1	◇1 F ✠		◇1 D	◇1 E	◇1 ⊠	◇1	G	C		C	◇1 H	
Manchester Airport 85 ✈ d							18 55						19 55						
Manchester Piccadilly 10 ⇌ d							19 20						20 18						
Stockport 78 d							19 28						20 27						
Sheffield 7 ⇌ a							20 08						21 08						
d	19 21	19 29	19 36	19 51		20 02	20 11	20 21	20 28	20 51			21 11			21 24	21 36		22 13
Meadowhall ⇌ d		19 35	19 42			20 09	20 16		20 34				21 16			21 30	21 42		22 19
Rotherham Central d		19 41	19 49						20 40							21 37	21 48		
Swinton (S.Yorks) d		19 49	19a57						20 48							21 47	21a56		
Mexborough d		19 52							20 51							21 50			
Conisbrough d		19 56							20 55							21 54			
London Kings Cross d												19 45							
Doncaster 7 a		20 07		20 16		20 30	20 35		21 05	21 19		21 25	21 35			22 03			22 38
York 8 26 a	20 29			20 45				21 31		21 44									
Doncaster 31 d						20 30	20 37		21 07			21 27	21 37		21 52	22 04			22 41
Bentley (S.Yorks) 31 a															21 55				
Adwick 31 a															21 59				
Kirk Sandall d									21 13										
Hatfield & Stainforth d									21 18										
Thorne South d																			
Crowle d																			
Althorpe d																			
Scunthorpe a							21 02						22 02						
d							21 03						22 03						
Barnetby d							21 17						22 17						
Hull Paragon Interchange d																			
Barton-on-Humber a																			
Barton-on-Humber d																			
Barrow Haven d																			
New Holland d																			
Goxhill d																			
Thornton Abbey d																			
Ulceby d																			
Habrough d							21 26						22 26						
Stallingborough d																			
Healing d																			
Great Coates d																			
Grimsby Town a							21 39						22 39						
d							21 40						22 40						
Grimsby Docks d																			
New Clee d																			
Cleethorpes a							21 50						22 50						
Thorne North d									21 24										22 53
Goole d						20 49			21a34							22 23			23 02
Saltmarshe d																			
York 8 33 d														21 41					
Selby a												21 43		22 00					
Wressle d																			
Howden d												21 55		22 10					
Eastrington d																			
Gilberdyke d						20 57										22 31			23 10
Broomfleet d																			
Brough d					20 36	21 05					21 58	22 07		22 22		22 39		23 02	23 18
Ferriby d																			
Hessle d																			
Hull a					20 54	21 23					22 12	22 26		22 36		22 56		23 19	23 39

A From Plymouth to Edinburgh
C To Leeds
D From Reading to Newcastle
E From Huddersfield
F From Plymouth to Leeds
G From Hull
H From Leeds

Table 29

Sundays
from 28 October

Manchester Airport, Manchester, Sheffield and Meadowhall-Doncaster-Cleethorpes and Hull Barton-on-Humber - Cleethorpes

Network Diagram - see first Page of Table 18

	NT	TP	NT
		◇1	
Manchester Airport 85 ✈ d			
Manchester Piccadilly 10 ⇌ d			
Stockport 78 d			
Sheffield 7 ⇌ a			
d	22 26	22 30	23 34
Meadowhall ⇌ d	22 32	22 35	23 40
Rotherham Central d	22 38		23 47
Swinton (S.Yorks) d	22 48		23 55
Mexborough d	22 51		23 58
Conisbrough d	22 55		00 02
London Kings Cross d			
Doncaster 7 a	23 05	22 56	00 13
York 8 26 a			
Doncaster 31 d		22 58	
Bentley (S.Yorks) 31 a			
Adwick 31 a			
Kirk Sandall d			
Hatfield & Stainforth d			
Thorne South d			
Crowle d			
Althorpe d			
Scunthorpe a		23 23	
d		23 24	
Barnetby d		23 38	
Hull Paragon Interchange d			
Barton-on-Humber a			
Barton-on-Humber d			
Barrow Haven d			
New Holland d			
Goxhill d			
Thornton Abbey d			
Ulceby d			
Habrough d			
Stallingborough d			
Healing d			
Great Coates d			
Grimsby Town a		23 57	
d		23 58	
Grimsby Docks d			
New Clee d			
Cleethorpes a		00 09	
Thorne North d			
Goole d			
Saltmarshe d			
York 8 33 d			
Selby a			
Wressle d			
Howden d			
Eastrington d			
Gilberdyke d			
Broomfleet d			
Brough d			
Ferriby d			
Hessle d			
Hull a			

Sheffield - Retford and Lincoln

until 28 September

Network Diagram - see first Page of Table 18

Miles		NT	NT	NT	NT	NT	NT	NT	NT	NT	NT	NT
						B		C	C	C	C	C
—	Huddersfield 34 d											
—	Barnsley 34 d											
—	Meadowhall 34 d					07 33		09 33	10 33	11 33	12 33	13 33
0	**Sheffield** 7 d	05 39	05 46	06 43	07 30	07 44	08 44	09 44	10 44	11 44	12 44	13 44
2¼	Darnall d		05 51	06 48	07 35		08 49	09 49	10 49	11 49	12 49	13 49
5¼	Woodhouse d		05 56	06 53	07 40		08 54	09 54	10 54	11 54	12 54	13 54
9½	Kiveton Bridge d		06 03	07 00	07 47		09 01	10 01	11 01	12 01	13 01	14 01
10¾	Kiveton Park d	05 54	06 06	07 03	07 50	07 59	09 04	10 04	11 04	12 04	13 04	14 04
13¾	Shireoaks d		06 11	07 08	07 55		09 09	10 09	11 09	12 09	13 09	14 09
15¾	Worksop d	06 01	06 23	07 14	07 59	08a10	09 13	10 13	11 13	12 13	13 13	14 13
23½	**Retford** 10 a	06 10	06 37	07 23	08 09		09 23	10 23	11 23	12 23	13 23	14 23
—	d	06 10		07 24	08 09		09 23	10 24	11 23	12 23	13 23	14 23
33	Gainsborough Lea Road 18 d	06 25		07 38	08 24		09 38	10 38	11 38	12 38	13 39	14 38
42½	Saxilby 18 d	06 37		07 51	08 37		09 51	10 51	11 51	12 51	13 52	14 51
48½	**Lincoln** 18 a	06 53		08 06	08 52		10 06	11 06	12 06	13 06	14 06	15 06

Miles		NT	NT	NT	NT	NT	NT	NT	NT	NT	NT
		C	C	C	D	C			B		
—	Huddersfield 34 d									20 18	
—	Barnsley 34 d									21 12	
—	Meadowhall 34 d	14 34	15 33	16 33	16 55	17 33			20 33	21 30	
0	**Sheffield** 7 d	14 44	15 44	16 44	17 24	17 44	18 45	19 48	20 44	21 44	22 44
2¼	Darnall d	14 50	15 49	16 49	17 29	17 49	18 50	19 53	20 49	21 49	22 49
5¼	Woodhouse d	14 55	15 54	16 54	17 34	17 54	18 55	19 58	20 54	21 54	22 54
9½	Kiveton Bridge d	15 02	16 01	17 01	17 41	18 01	19 02	20 05	21 01	22 01	23 01
10¾	Kiveton Park d	15 05	16 04	17 04	17 44	18 04	19 05	20 08	21 04	22 04	23 04
13¾	Shireoaks d	15 09	16 09	17 09	17 48	18 09	19 10	20 13	21 09	22 07	23 09
15¾	Worksop d	15 14	16 13	17 13	17 52	18 13	19 14	20 17	21a21	22 14	23a22
23½	**Retford** 10 a	15 23	16 23	17 23	18 06	18 23	19 24	20 27		22 28	
—	d	15 24	16 23	17 23		18 23	19 24	20 27			
33	Gainsborough Lea Road 18 d	15 38	16 38	17 38		18 38	19 39	20 42			
42½	Saxilby 18 d	15 51	16 51	17 51		18 51	19 52	20 55			
48½	**Lincoln** 18 a	16 10	17 06	18 06		19 07	20 06	21 10			

Mondays to Fridays

from 1 October

	NT	NT	NT	NT	NT	NT	NT	NT	NT	NT	NT
					B		C	C	C	C	C
Huddersfield 34 d											
Barnsley 34 d											
Meadowhall 34 d					07 33		09 33	10 33	11 33	12 33	13 33
Sheffield 7 d	05 39	05 46	06 43	07 30	07 44	08 44	09 44	10 44	11 44	12 44	13 44
Darnall d		05 51	06 48	07 35		08 49	09 49	10 49	11 49	12 49	13 49
Woodhouse d		05 56	06 53	07 40		08 54	09 54	10 54	11 54	12 54	13 54
Kiveton Bridge d		06 03	07 00	07 47		09 01	10 01	11 01	12 01	13 01	14 01
Kiveton Park d	05 54	06 06	07 03	07 50	07 59	09 04	10 04	11 04	12 04	13 04	14 04
Shireoaks d		06 11	07 08	07 55		09 09	10 09	11 09	12 09	13 09	14 09
Worksop d	06 01	06 23	07 14	07 59	08a10	09 13	10 13	11 13	12 13	13 13	14 13
Retford 10 a	06 10	06 37	07 23	08 09		09 23	10 23	11 23	12 23	13 23	14 23
d	06 10		07 24	08 09		09 23	10 24	11 23	12 23	13 23	14 23
Gainsborough Lea Road 18 d	06 25		07 38	08 24		09 38	10 38	11 38	12 38	13 39	14 38
Saxilby 18 d	06 37		07 51	08 37		09 51	10 51	11 51	12 51	13 52	14 51
Lincoln 18 a	06 53		08 06	08 52		10 06	11 06	12 06	13 06	14 06	15 06

	NT	NT	NT	NT	NT	NT	NT	NT	NT	NT
	C	C	C	D	C			B		
Huddersfield 34 d									20 15	
Barnsley 34 d									21 12	
Meadowhall 34 d	14 34	15 33	16 33	16 55	17 33			20 33	21 30	
Sheffield 7 d	14 44	15 44	16 44	17 24	17 44	18 45	19 48	20 44	21 44	22 44
Darnall d	14 50	15 49	16 49	17 29	17 49	18 50	19 53	20 49	21 49	22 49
Woodhouse d	14 55	15 54	16 54	17 34	17 54	18 55	19 58	20 54	21 54	22 54
Kiveton Bridge d	15 02	16 01	17 01	17 41	18 01	19 02	20 05	21 01	22 01	23 01
Kiveton Park d	15 05	16 04	17 04	17 44	18 04	19 05	20 08	21 04	22 04	23 04
Shireoaks d	15 09	16 09	17 09	17 48	18 09	19 10	20 13	21 09	22 07	23 09
Worksop d	15 14	16 13	17 13	17 52	18 13	19 14	20 17	21a21	22 14	23a22
Retford 10 a	15 23	16 23	17 23	18 06	18 23	19 24	20 27		22 28	
d	15 24	16 23	17 23		18 23	19 24	20 27			
Gainsborough Lea Road 18 d	15 38	16 38	17 38		18 38	19 39	20 42			
Saxilby 18 d	15 51	16 51	17 51		18 51	19 52	20 55			
Lincoln 18 a	16 10	17 06	18 06		19 07	20 06	21 10			

Sundays

	NT	NT	NT	NT	NT	NT
Huddersfield 34 d						
Barnsley 34 d						
Meadowhall 34 d						
Sheffield 7 d	13 42	13 57	15 43	17 43	19 32	21 06
Darnall d		14 03	15 48	17 48	19 37	21 11
Woodhouse d		14 08	15 53	17 53	19 42	21 16
Kiveton Bridge d		14 14	16 00	18 00	19 49	21 23
Kiveton Park d		14 17	16 03	18 03	19 52	21 26
Shireoaks d		14 22	16 07	18 07	19 56	21 30
Worksop d	14 02	14 26	16 11	18 11	20 00	21 39
Retford 10 a	14 11	14 39	16 20	18 20	20 09	21 48
d	14 12		16 21	18 21	20 10	
Gainsborough Lea Road 18 d	14 26		16 35	18 35	20 24	
Saxilby 18 d	14 39		16 48	18 48	20 37	
Lincoln 18 a	14 54		17 02	19 03	20 51	

B From Doncaster
C From Scunthorpe
D From Adwick

For connections to London Kings Cross please refer to Table 26

Sheffield - Retford and Lincoln

Saturdays

Network Diagram - see first Page of Table 18

	NT	NT	NT A	NT	NT	NT	NT	NT B	NT B	NT B	NT
Huddersfield 34 d											
Barnsley 34 d			06 21								
Meadowhall 34 d			06 42					09 33	10 33	11 33	
Sheffield 7 d	05 39	05 46	06a55	06 43	07 30	08 03	08 44	09 44	10 44	11 44	12 00
Darnall d		05 51		06 48	07 35	08 08	08 49	09 49	10 49	11 49	12 05
Woodhouse d		05 56		06 53	07 40	08 13	08 54	09 54	10 54	11 54	12 10
Kiveton Bridge d		06 03		07 00	07 47	08 20	09 01	10 01	11 01	12 01	12 17
Kiveton Park d	05 54	06 06		07 03	07 50	08 23	09 04	10 04	11 04	12 04	12 20
Shireoaks d		06 11		07 08	07 55	08 28	09 09	10 09	11 09	12 09	12 25
Worksop d	06 01	06 23		07 14	07 59	08 32	09 13	10 13	11 13	12 13	12 35
Retford 10 a	06 10	06 38		07 23	08 09	08 42	09 23	10 23	11 23	12 23	12 44
d	06 10			07 24	08 09	08 42	09 23	10 23	11 23	12 23	12 45
Gainsborough Lea Road 18 d	06 25			07 38	08 24		09 38	10 38	11 38	12 38	
Saxilby 18 d	06 37			07 51	08 37		09 51	10 51	11 51	12 51	
Lincoln 18 a	06 53			08 06	08 52		10 06	11 06	12 06	13 06	
Gainsborough Central d						08 57					13 00
Kirton Lindsey d						09 11					13 13
Brigg d						09 24					13 22
Barnetby 29 a						09 38					13 37
Habrough 29 a						09 48					13 47
Grimsby Town 29 a						10 00					14 00
Cleethorpes 29 a						10 13					14 11

	NT B	NT B	NT B	NT B	NT	NT B	NT C	NT B	NT B	NT	NT B
Huddersfield 34 d											
Barnsley 34 d											
Meadowhall 34 d	12 33	13 33	14 33	15 33		16 33	16 55	17 33	18 33		20 33
Sheffield 7 d	12 44	13 44	14 44	15 44	16 00	16 44	17 23	17 44	18 45	19 48	20 44
Darnall d	12 49	13 49	14 49	15 49	16 05	16 49	17 29	17 49	18 50	19 53	20 48
Woodhouse d	12 54	13 54	14 54	15 54	16 10	16 54	17 34	17 54	18 55	19 58	20 54
Kiveton Bridge d	13 01	14 01	15 01	16 01	16 17	17 01	17 40	18 01	19 02	20 05	21 00
Kiveton Park d	13 04	14 04	15 04	16 04	16 20	17 04	17 43	18 04	19 05	20 08	21 04
Shireoaks d	13 09	14 09	15 09	16 09	16 25	17 09	17 48	18 09	19 10	20 13	21 09
Worksop d	13 13	14 13	15 13	16 13	16 36	17 13	17 52	18 13	19 14	20 17	21a24
Retford 10 a	13 23	14 23	15 23	16 23	16 46	17 23	18 06	18 23	19 24	20 27	
d	13 23	14 23	15 23	16 23	16 46	17 23		18 24	19 24	20 27	
Gainsborough Lea Road 18 d	13 37	14 36	15 40	16 38		17 38		18 38	19 39	20 42	
Saxilby 18 d	13 50	14 49	15 53	16 51		17 51		18 51	19 52	20 55	
Lincoln 18 a	14 07	15 06	16 10	17 06		18 06		19 07	20 06	21 10	
Gainsborough Central d					17 01						
Kirton Lindsey d					17 15						
Brigg d					17 27						
Barnetby 29 a					17 37						
Habrough 29 a					17 47						
Grimsby Town 29 a					18 01						
Cleethorpes 29 a					18 11						

	NT D	NT E	NT
Huddersfield 34 d	20 15	20 18	
Barnsley 34 d	21 12	21 12	
Meadowhall 34 d	21 29	21 29	
Sheffield 7 d	21 44	21 44	22 44
Darnall d	21 49	21 49	22 49
Woodhouse d	21 54	21 54	22 54
Kiveton Bridge d	22 01	22 01	23 01
Kiveton Park d	22 04	22 04	23 04
Shireoaks d	22 08	22 08	23 09
Worksop d	22 14	22 14	23a22
Retford 10 a	22 28	22 28	
d			
Gainsborough Lea Road 18 d			
Saxilby 18 d			
Lincoln 18 a			
Gainsborough Central d			
Kirton Lindsey d			
Brigg d			
Barnetby 29 a			
Habrough 29 a			
Grimsby Town 29 a			
Cleethorpes 29 a			

A To Nottingham
B From Scunthorpe
C From Adwick
D from 6 October
E until 29 September

For connections to London Kings Cross please refer to Table 26

Lincoln and Retford - Sheffield

Network Diagram - see first Page of Table 18

Miles			NT MX	NT	NT A	NT A	NT A	NT A	NT A	NT	NT A	NT A	NT A	NT B	NT	NT C	NT	NT	NT	NT	NT	NT	NT
0	Lincoln	18 d		07 00		08 25	09 25	10 25	11 25	12 27	13 26	14 25	15 24	16 25	17 22		18 24	19 43	20 27		21 27		
6	Saxilby	18 d		07 10		08 34	09 34	10 34	11 34	12 36	13 35	14 34	15 33	16 35	17 31		18 33	19 52	20 36		21 36		
15½	Gainsborough Lea Road	18 d		07 22		08 48	09 48	10 48	11 48	12 49	13 48	14 48	15 48	16 48	17 44		18 46	20 05	20 49		21 49		
25	**Retford**	a		07 36		09 02	10 02	11 02	12 02	13 03	14 02	15 02	16 02	17 02	17 58		19 04	20 18	21 03		22 03		
—		d		07 40		09 02	10 02	11 02	12 02	13 03	14 02	15 02	16 02	17 02	17 58	18 14	19 04	20 19	21 03		22 03	22 45	
32¾	Worksop	d	23p28	07 52	08 14	09 14	10 14	11 14	12 14	13 15	14 14	15 14	16 14	17 14	18 10	18 25	19 16	20 31	21 15	21 26	22 15	22 58	23 28
34¾	Shireoaks	d	23p32	07 55	08 19	09 18	10 18	11 18	12 18	13 19	14 18	15 18	16 18	17 18		18 29	19 20	20 35		21 30	22 19	23 02	23 32
37¾	Kiveton Park	d	23p38	08 01	08 25	09 24	10 24	11 24	12 24	13 25	14 24	15 24	16 24	17 24		18 34	19 26	20 41	21 23	21 36	22 25	23 08	23 38
39	Kiveton Bridge	d	23p41	08 04	08 28	09 27	10 27	11 27	12 27	13 28	14 27	15 27	16 27	17 27		18 37	19 29	20 44		21 39	22 28	23 11	23 41
43¼	Woodhouse	d	23p52	08 10	08 34	09 33	10 33	11 33	12 33	13 34	14 33	15 33	16 33	17 33		18 43	19 35	20 50		21 46	22 34	23 17	23 52
46¼	Darnall	d	23p57	08 15	08 39	09 38	10 38	11 38	12 38	13 39	14 38	15 38	16 38	17 38		18 48	19 40	20 55		21 51	22 39	23 22	23 57
48½	**Sheffield**	a	00 04	08 26	08 48	09 47	10 47	11 47	12 48	13 48	14 48	15 48	16 48	17 49	18 35	18 57	19 54	21 05	21 44	22 03	22 50	23 33	00 04
—	Meadowhall	34 a			08 59	09 58	10 58	11 58	12 58		14 58	15 58	16 58	17 58		19 06							
—	Barnsley	34 a																					
—	Huddersfield	34 a																					

Sundays

until 30 September

		NT	NT	NT	NT	NT	NT	NT
Lincoln	18 d			15 15	17 15	19 15	21 10	
Saxilby	18 d			15 25	17 25	19 25	21 20	
Gainsborough Lea Road	18 d			15 37	17 37	19 37	21 32	
Retford	a			15 51	17 51	19 51	21 46	
	d		14 50	15 51	17 51	19 51	21 46	22 24
Worksop	d	23p28	15 01	16 03	18 03	20 03	21 58	22 35
Shireoaks	d	23p32	15 05	16 06	18 06	20 06	22 01	22 39
Kiveton Park	d	23p38	15 10	16 12	18 12	20 12	22 07	22 44
Kiveton Bridge	d	23p41	15 13	16 15	18 15	20 15	22 10	22 47
Woodhouse	d	23p47	15 19	16 21	18 21	20 21	22 16	22 53
Darnall	d	23p52	15 24	16 26	18 26	20 26	22 21	22 58
Sheffield	a	00 01	15 33	16 36	18 35	20 35	22 29	23 07
Meadowhall	34 a		15 42	16 44				
Barnsley	34 a		16 03	17 05				
Huddersfield	34 a		16 53					

Sundays

from 7 October

		NT	NT	NT	NT	NT	NT	NT
Lincoln	18 d			15 15	17 15	19 15	21 10	
Saxilby	18 d			15 25	17 25	19 25	21 20	
Gainsborough Lea Road	18 d			15 37	17 37	19 37	21 32	
Retford	a			15 51	17 51	19 51	21 46	
	d		14 50	15 51	17 51	19 51	21 46	22 24
Worksop	d	23p28	15 01	16 03	18 03	20 03	21 58	22 35
Shireoaks	d	23p32	15 05	16 06	18 06	20 06	22 01	22 39
Kiveton Park	d	23p38	15 10	16 12	18 12	20 12	22 07	22 44
Kiveton Bridge	d	23p41	15 13	16 15	18 15	20 15	22 10	22 47
Woodhouse	d	23p47	15 19	16 21	18 21	20 21	22 16	22 53
Darnall	d	23p52	15 24	16 26	18 26	20 26	22 21	22 58
Sheffield	a	00 01	15 33	16 36	18 35	20 35	22 29	23 07
Meadowhall	34 a		15 42	16 44				
Barnsley	34 a		16 03	17 05				
Huddersfield	34 a		16 57					

A To Adwick B To Hull C To Doncaster

For connections from London Kings Cross please refer to Table 26

Lincoln and Retford - Sheffield

Network Diagram - see first Page of Table 18

		NT	NT	NT	NT A	NT A	NT A	NT A	NT	NT A	NT A	NT A	NT A	NT	NT B	NT	NT C	NT	NT	NT	NT	NT	NT
Cleethorpes	29 d								11 10					15 20					18 36				
Grimsby Town	29 d								11 17					15 27					18 43				
Habrough	29 d								11 28					15 37					18 53				
Barnetby	29 d								11 38					15 48					19 02				
Brigg	d								11 44					15 53					19 08				
Kirton Lindsey	d								11 53					16 02					19 17				
Gainsborough Central	d								12 20					16 20					19 35				
Lincoln	18 d			07 00	08 25	09 25	10 25	11 25		12 27	13 25	14 25	15 24		16 25	17 22		18 24		19 43	20 27		21 27
Saxilby	18 d			07 10	08 34	09 34	10 34	11 34		12 36	13 34	14 34	15 33		16 35	17 31		18 33		19 52	20 36		21 36
Gainsborough Lea Road	18 d			07 22	08 48	09 48	10 48	11 48		12 49	13 48	14 48	15 48		16 48	17 44		18 46		20 05	20 49		21 49
Retford	a			07 36	09 02	10 02	11 02	12 02	12 35	13 03	14 02	15 02	16 02	16 35	17 02	17 58		19 04	19 49	20 16	21 03		22 03
	d			07 40	09 02	10 02	11 02	12 02	12 35	13 03	14 02	15 02	16 02	16 35	17 02	17 58	18 14	19 04	19 50	20 18	21 03		22 03
Worksop	d	23p28	06 30	07 52	09 14	10 14	11 14	12 14	12 47	13 15	14 14	15 14	16 14	16 47	17 14	18 10	18 25	19 16	20 01	20 31	21 15	21 26	22 15
Shireoaks	d	23p32	06 33	07 55	09 18	10 18	11 18	12 18	12 51	13 19	14 18	15 18	16 18	16 51	17 18		18 29	19 20	20 05	20 35		21 30	22 19
Kiveton Park	d	23p38	06 39	08 01	09 24	10 24	11 24	12 24	12 57	13 25	14 24	15 24	16 24	16 57	17 24		18 34	19 26	20 09	20 41	21 23	21 36	22 25
Kiveton Bridge	d	23p41	06 42	08 04	09 27	10 27	11 27	12 27	13 00	13 28	14 27	15 27	16 27	17 00	17 27		18 37	19 29	20 14	20 44		21 39	22 28
Woodhouse	d	23p52	06 48	08 10	09 33	10 33	11 33	12 33	13 06	13 34	14 33	15 33	16 33	17 06	17 33		18 43	19 35	20 21	20 50		21 44	22 34
Darnall	d	23p57	06 53	08 15	09 38	10 38	11 38	12 38	13 11	13 39	14 38	15 38	16 38	17 11	17 38		18 48	19 40	20 26	20 55		21 49	22 39
Sheffield	a	00 04	07 02	08 26	09 48	10 48	11 48	12 48	13 23	13 48	14 48	15 48	16 48	17 23	17 49	18 35	18 57	19 54	20 34	21 05	21 46	22 00	22 50
Meadowhall	34 a				09 58	10 58	11 58	12 58		13 58	14 58	15 58	16 58		17 57		19 06						
Barnsley	34 a																						
Huddersfield	34 a																						

		NT	NT
Cleethorpes	29 d		
Grimsby Town	29 d		
Habrough	29 d		
Barnetby	29 d		
Brigg	d		
Kirton Lindsey	d		
Gainsborough Central	d		
Lincoln	18 d		
Saxilby	18 d		
Gainsborough Lea Road	18 d		
Retford	a		
	d	22 45	
Worksop	d	22 58	23 28
Shireoaks	d	23 02	23 32
Kiveton Park	d	23 08	23 38
Kiveton Bridge	d	23 11	23 41
Woodhouse	d	23 17	23 47
Darnall	d	23 22	23 52
Sheffield	a	23 32	00 01
Meadowhall	34 a		
Barnsley	34 a		
Huddersfield	34 a		

A To Adwick B To Hull C To Doncaster

For connections from London Kings Cross please refer to Table 26

Network Diagram for Tables 31, 32, 33, 34

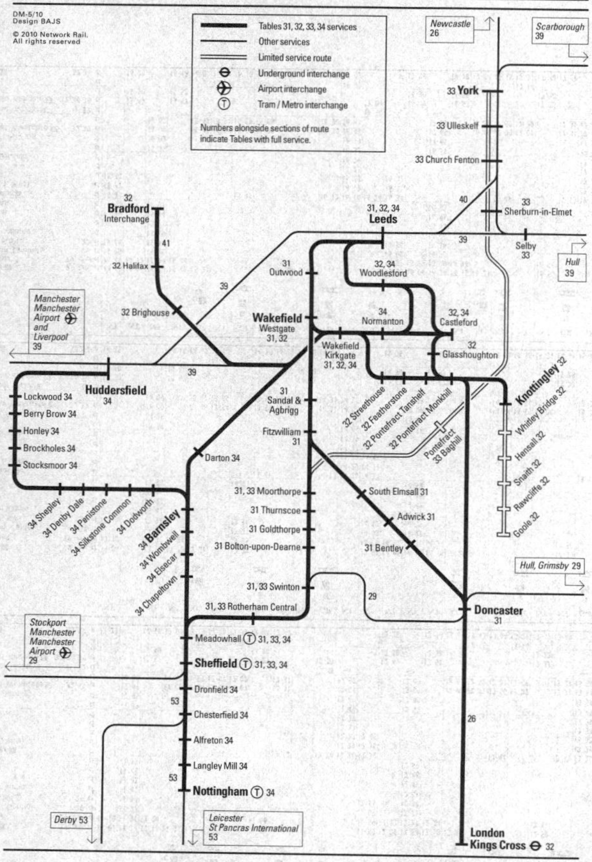

Sheffield, Doncaster and Wakefield - Leeds

Network Diagram - see first page of Table 31

Miles	Miles				NT	GR	GR	NT	NT	EM	NT	GR	GR	NT	NT	NT	NT	NT	NT		NT	NT	NT	NT	NT	NT
					MO	MX	MO	MX	MX	MO	MX															
					A		A			B		C	C													
—	0	**Sheffield**	29	d	22p39			23p15	23p24	23p30				05 22	05 50			06 06	06 18		06 28	06 49			06 52	07 06
—	3½	Meadowhall	29	d	22p45			23p21	23p30					05 28	05 56			06 12	06 24		06 34	06 55			06 58	07 12
—	6¾	Rotherham Central	29	d				23p27						05 34					06 30		06 40				07 04	
—	10¾	Swinton (S.Yorks)	29	d				23p36						05 42					06 38		06 51				07 14	
—	13	Bolton-upon-Dearne		d				23p41						05 46							06 56					
—	14¾	Goldthorpe		d				23p44						05 49							06 58					
—	15	Thurnscoe		d				23p47						05 52							07 01					
—	18½	Moorthorpe		d				23p52						05 57							07 06					
0	—	**Doncaster**		d		23p32	23p36						02 28				06 26		06 59				07 08	07 26	07 34	
1¾	—	Bentley (S.Yorks)		d													06 29		07 02				07 11	07 29	07 37	
4	—	Adwick		a													06 33		07 08				07 15	07 33	07 43	
—	—			d													06 33						07 15	07 33		
8¾	—	South Elmsall		d													06 39						07 21	07 39		
13¼	22¼	Fitzwilliam		d										06 02			06 44				07 12		07 34	07 44		
18	27	Sandal & Agbrigg		d							←			06 08			06 50				07 18		07 40	07 50		
19¾	28¾	**Wakefield Westgate**	32,39	a		23p53	23p56	00 09		00 01	00 09	02s06	02s46	06 12			06 54				07 22		07 44	07 54		
—	—			d		23p53	23p56	00 10		00 02	00 10			06 13		06 24	06 54				07 23		07 44	07 54		
—	—	Pontefract Monkhill	32	d				→															→	→		
—	—	Wakefield Kirkgate	32,34,39	a	23p26				00s10						06 27	06 29		06 49				07 27				07 49
—	—			d	23p27										06 28			06 50				07 28				07 50
22¼	31¼	Outwood		d										06 18			06 59				07 28					
29¾	38¾	**Leeds**	32,34	a	00 05	00 11	00 14			00 18	00 29	02 23	03 03	06 33	06 50		07 14	07 28			07 44	07 51				08 25

			XC	NT	NT	GR	NT	NT	NT	NT	GR		NT	NT	NT	NT	XC	NT	GR	NT	NT	NT	GR	NT	NT	NT
Sheffield	29	d	07 12				07 14	07 20		07 51			08 06		08 14	08 18	08 21					08 51			08 53	09 06
Meadowhall	29	d					07 21	07 26		07 57			08 12		08 21	08 25						08 57			09 00	09 12
Rotherham Central	29	d					07 27								08 28										09 06	
Swinton (S.Yorks)	29	d					07 35								08 37										09 16	
Bolton-upon-Dearne		d					07 39								08 41											
Goldthorpe		d					07 42								08 44											
Thurnscoe		d					07 45								08 47											
Moorthorpe		d					07 54								08 52											
Doncaster		d				07 44			07 56		08 12			08 16				08 26	08 41		08 49		09 12	09 26	09 34	
Bentley (S.Yorks)		d							07 59					08 18				08 29			08 52			09 29	09 37	
Adwick		a							08 03					08 24				08 33			08 58			09 33	09 43	
		d							08 03									08 33						09 33		
South Elmsall		d							08 09									08 39						09 39		
Fitzwilliam		d					08 00		08 14						08 58			08 45						09 44		
Sandal & Agbrigg		d		←	←		08 06		08 20						09 04			08 50		←				09 50		
Wakefield Westgate	32,39	a	07 36	07 44	07 54	08 01	08 10		08 24		08 31				09 08		08 46	08 54	09 00	09 08			09 31	09 54		
		d	07 37	07 44	07 54	08 01	08 11		08 25		08 31				09 08		08 47	08 55	09 00	09 08			09 31	09 54		
Pontefract Monkhill	32	d													→									→		
Wakefield Kirkgate	32,34,39	a						07 57		08 27			08 49			08 57						09 27				09 49
		d						07 58		08 28			08 50			08 58						09 28				09 50
Outwood		d		07 49	07 59		08 16		08 29									08 59		09 13						
Leeds	32,34	a	07 52	08 02	08 13	08 20	08 36	08 21	08 42	08 49	08 49		09 25			09 20	09 03	09 14	09 18	09 31		09 49	09 49			10 25

			NT		NT	XC	NT	NT	GR	NT	NT	GR	NT	NT	NT	NT	NT	XC	NT		GR	NT	NT	GR	NT	NT
Sheffield	29	d	09 14		09 18	09 21		09 29			09 50			09 53	10 06	10 14	10 18	10 21					10 50			10 53
Meadowhall	29	d	09 21		09 24			09 35			09 56			09 59	10 12	10 21	10 24						10 56			10 59
Rotherham Central	29	d	09 27					09 42						10 06		10 27										11 05
Swinton (S.Yorks)	29	d	09 36					09 51						10 15		10 36										11 16
Bolton-upon-Dearne		d	09 41													10 41										
Goldthorpe		d	09 43													10 43										
Thurnscoe		d	09 46													10 46										
Moorthorpe		d	09 51					10a01								10 53										
Doncaster		d							09 41			10 12	10 26	10 34							10 42			11 13	11 26	11 34
Bentley (S.Yorks)		d											10 29	10 37											11 29	11 37
Adwick		a											10 33	10 43											11 33	11 43
		d											10 33												11 33	
South Elmsall		d											10 39												11 39	
Fitzwilliam		d	09 56										10 44			10 59									11 45	
Sandal & Agbrigg		d	10 02				←			←			10 50			11 05			←			←			11 50	
Wakefield Westgate	32,39	a	10 06			09 46	09 54		09 59	10 06		10 31	10 54			11 09		10 46	10 54		11 00	11 09		11 31	11 54	
		d	10 06			09 47	09 54		09 59	10 06		10 31	10 54			11 09		10 47	10 54		11 00	11 09		11 31	11 55	
Pontefract Monkhill	32	d	→										→			→									→	
Wakefield Kirkgate	32,34,39	a			09 57						10 27				10 49		10 57						11 27			
		d			09 58						10 28				10 50		10 58						11 28			
Outwood		d					09 59			10 11									10 59			11 14				
Leeds	32,34	a			10 18	10 02	10 14		10 18	10 31	10 48	10 49			11 25		11 18	11 02	11 15		11 18	11 31	11 48	11 49		

A from 21 May until 30 July
B from 21 May until 25 June
C 30 July

Sheffield, Doncaster and Wakefield - Leeds

Network Diagram - see first page of Table 31

			NT	NT	NT	XC	NT	GR	NT	NT	GR		GC	NT	NT	NT	NT	NT	XC	NT	GR	NT	NT	GR	NT	NT
					◇	◇1		1			1		1					◇	◇1		1			1		
Sheffield 7	29 ⇌	d	11 06	11 14	11 18	11 21				11 50					11 53	12 06	12 14	12 18	12 21				12 50			12 53
Meadowhall	29 ⇌	d	11 12	11 21	11 24					11 56					11 59	12 12	12 21	12 24					12 56			12 59
Rotherham Central	29	d		11 27											12 05		12 27									13 05
Swinton (S.Yorks)	29	d		11 36											12 16		12 36									13 16
Bolton-upon-Dearne		d		11 41													12 41									
Goldthorpe		d		11 43													12 43									
Thurnscoe		d		11 46													12 46									
Moorthorpe		d		11 53													12 52									
Doncaster 7		d						11 41			12 12		12 24	12 26	12 34						12 41			13 12	13 26	13 34
Bentley (S.Yorks)		d												12 29	12 38										13 29	13 37
Adwick		a												12 33	12 43										13 33	13 43
		d												12 33											13 33	
South Elmsall		d												12 39											13 39	
Fitzwilliam		d		11 59										12 44			12 58								13 45	
Sandal & Agbrigg		d		12 05			←		←					12 49			13 05			←		←			13 50	
Wakefield Westgate 7	32,39	a		12 09		11 46	11 54	12 00	12 09		12 31			12 51			13 09		12 46	12 51	13 00	13 09		13 31	13 54	
		d		12 09		11 47	11 55	12 01	12 09		12 31			12 52			13 09		12 47	12 52	13 01	13 09		13 31	13 55	
Pontefract Monkhill	32	d		→									12 49	→			→								→	
Wakefield Kirkgate 4	32,34,39	a	11 49		11 57					12 27			13 07			12 49		12 57					13 27			
		d	11 50		11 58					12 28						12 50		12 58					13 28			
Outwood		d					11 59		12 14											12 56		13 14				
Leeds 10	32,34	a	12 25		12 18	12 01	12 15	12 18	12 31	12 48	12 49					13 25		13 18	13 03	13 13	13 18	13 29	13 49	13 49		

			NT		NT	NT	XC	NT	NT	GR	NT	NT	GR	NT	NT	NT	NT	NT	XC		NT	GR	NT	NT	GR	NT
						◇	◇1			1			1					◇	◇1			1			1	
Sheffield 7	29 ⇌	d	13 06		13 14	13 18	13 21		13 29			13 50			13 53	14 06	14 14	14 18	14 21					14 50		
Meadowhall	29 ⇌	d	13 12		13 21	13 24			13 35			13 56			13 59	14 12	14 21	14 24						14 56		
Rotherham Central	29	d			13 27				13 41						14 05		14 27									
Swinton (S.Yorks)	29	d			13 36				13 50						14 17		14 35									
Bolton-upon-Dearne		d			13 41												14 40									
Goldthorpe		d			13 43												14 42									
Thurnscoe		d			13 46												14 45									
Moorthorpe		d			13 53				14a01								14 52									
Doncaster 7		d								13 41			14 12	14 26	14 34							14 41			15 12	15 26
Bentley (S.Yorks)		d												14 29	14 37											15 29
Adwick		a												14 33	14 43											15 33
		d												14 33												15 33
South Elmsall		d												14 39												15 39
Fitzwilliam		d			13 59									14 45			14 58									15 44
Sandal & Agbrigg		d			14 05			←			←			14 50			15 04				←		←			15 50
Wakefield Westgate 7	32,39	a			14 09		13 46	13 54		13 59	14 09		14 31	14 54			15 08		14 46		14 54	14 59	15 08		15 31	15 54
		d			14 09		13 47	13 55		13 59	14 09		14 31	14 55			15 08		14 47		14 55	14 59	15 08		15 31	15 54
Pontefract Monkhill	32	d			→									→			→									→
Wakefield Kirkgate 4	32,34,39	a	13 50			13 57						14 27				14 49		14 57						15 27		
		d	13 50			13 58						14 28				14 50		14 58						15 28		
Outwood		d						13 59			14 14										14 59		15 13			
Leeds 10	32,34	a	14 25			14 18	14 02	14 14		14 18	14 31	14 48	14 49			15 25		15 18	15 01		15 13	15 18	15 31	15 49	15 49	

			NT	NT	NT	NT	XC	NT	GR	NT	NT		GR	NT	GC	NT	NT	NT	NT	XC	GR	NT	NT	GR	NT	NT
						◇	◇1		1				1		1				◇	◇1	1			1		
Sheffield 7	29 ⇌	d	14 53	15 06	15 14	15 18	15 21				15 50					15 53	16 06	16 14	16 18	16 21			16 50			16 53
Meadowhall	29 ⇌	d	14 59	15 12	15 20	15 24					15 56					15 59	16 12	16 20	16 24				16 56			16 59
Rotherham Central	29	d	15 05		15 26											16 05		16 26								17 05
Swinton (S.Yorks)	29	d	15 16		15 34											16 16		16 36								17 16
Bolton-upon-Dearne		d			15 39													16 40								
Goldthorpe		d			15 41													16 43								
Thurnscoe		d			15 44													16 46								
Moorthorpe		d			15 51													16 53								
Doncaster 7		d	15 34						15 41				16 12	16 16	16 24	16 34					16 41			17 13	17 26	17 34
Bentley (S.Yorks)		d	15 37											16 19		16 37									17 29	17 37
Adwick		a	15 42											16 23		16 43									17 33	17 43
		d												16 23											17 33	
South Elmsall		d												16 29											17 39	
Fitzwilliam		d			15 57									16 33				16 59							17 45	
Sandal & Agbrigg		d			16 03			←		←				16 39				17 05				←			17 51	
Wakefield Westgate 7	32,39	a			16 08		15 46	15 54	15 59	16 08			16 30	16 43				17 09		16 49	17 00	17 09		17 31	17 55	
		d			16 08		15 47	15 54	15 59	16 08			16 30	16 43				17 09		16 50	17 00	17 09		17 31	17 55	
Pontefract Monkhill	32	d			→										16 48			→							→	
Wakefield Kirkgate 4	32,34,39	a		15 49		15 57					16 27				17 04		16 49		16 57				17 28			
		d		15 50		15 58					16 28						16 50		16 58				17 28			
Outwood		d						15 59		16 13				16 49								17 14				
Leeds 10	32,34	a		16 25		16 18	16 02	16 14	16 18	16 31	16 49		16 51	17 03			17 25		17 18	17 04	17 18	17 31	17 48	17 50		

Table 31

Mondays to Fridays

until 30 July

Sheffield, Doncaster and Wakefield - Leeds

Network Diagram - see first page of Table 31

			NT		NT	NT	XC	NT	GR	NT	XC	GR	NT	NT	NT	NT	XC	NT	GR		NT	GR	NT	NT	NT	NT
						◇	◇1		1		◇1	1				◇	◇1		1			1				◇
Sheffield 7	29 ⇌	d	17 06		17 13	17 18	17 21				17 47		17 50	18 06	18 13	18 18	18 21						18 50	19 06	19 18	19 22
Meadowhall	29 ⇌	d	17 12		17 20	17 24							17 56	18 12	18 20	18 24							18 56	19 12	19 25	19 28
Rotherham Central	29	d			17 26										18 26										19 31	
Swinton (S.Yorks)	29	d			17 36										18 36										19 40	
Bolton-upon-Dearne		d			17 40										18 41										19 44	
Goldthorpe		d			17 43										18 43										19 47	
Thurnscoe		d			17 46										18 46										19 50	
Moorthorpe		d			17 52										18 53										20 00	
Doncaster 7		d							17 42									18 26	18 40			19 17				
Bentley (S.Yorks)		d																18 29								
Adwick		a																18 33								
		d																18 33								
South Elmsall		d																18 39								
Fitzwilliam		d			17 58										18 59			18 45							20 05	
Sandal & Agbrigg		d			18 05			←		←					19 05			18 50			←				20 11	
Wakefield Westgate 7	32,39	a			18 09		17 47	17 55	18 00	18 09	18 13				19 10		18 47	18 54	18 59		19 10	19 35			20 15	
		d			18 09		17 48	17 55	18 00	18 09	18 14	18 31			19 10		18 48	18 55	18 59		19 10	19 35			20 16	
Pontefract Monkhill	32	d			→										→										→	
Wakefield Kirkgate 4	32,34,39	a	17 49			17 57							18 28	18 50		18 59							19 29	19 50		19 58
		d	17 50			17 58							18 32	18 50		18 59							19 32	19 50		19 58
Outwood		d						18 00		18 14								18 59			19 15					
Leeds 10	32,34	a	18 25			18 18	18 03	18 14	18 18	18 32	18 31	18 50	18 51	19 27		19 23	19 03	19 14	19 18		19 31	19 52	19 55	20 26		20 19

			XC	NT	GR	GR	NT	NT	GR	NT	NT		XC	NT	GR	NT	GR	NT	XC	NT FX	NT FO	NT	EM	GR	NT	GR
			◇1		1	1			1		◇		◇1		1		1		◇1				◇1	1		1
Sheffield 7	29 ⇌	d	19 26					19 51		20 06	20 18		20 21			20 27		21 06	21 21				21 25		21 30	
Meadowhall	29 ⇌	d						19 57		20 12	20 24					20 35		21 12							21 36	
Rotherham Central	29	d														20 41									21 42	
Swinton (S.Yorks)	29	d														20 50									21 50	
Bolton-upon-Dearne		d														20 55									21 55	
Goldthorpe		d														20 57									21 57	
Thurnscoe		d														21 00									22 00	
Moorthorpe		d														21 05									22 05	
Doncaster 7		d		19 20	19 42	19 49			20 20					20 26	20 40		21 13			21 22	21 22			21 43		22 22
Bentley (S.Yorks)		d		19 23										20 29						21 25	21 25					
Adwick		a		19 27										20 33						21 29	21 29					
		d		19 27										20 33						21 29	21 29					
South Elmsall		d		19 33										20 39						21 35	21 35					
Fitzwilliam		d		19 46										20 45		21 11				21 45	21 46				22 11	
Sandal & Agbrigg		d		19 51			←							20 51		21 17				21 51	21 52				22 17	
Wakefield Westgate 7	32,39	a	19 50	19 55	20 01	20 07	20 15		20 38				20 46	20 55	21 00	21 22	21 31		21 46	21 56	21 56		21 59	22 06	22 21	22 40
		d	19 51	19 56	20 01	20 07	20 16		20 38				20 47	20 55	21 00	21 22	21 31		21 47	21 56	21 57	21 57	22 00	22 06	22 21	22 40
Pontefract Monkhill	32	d																								
Wakefield Kirkgate 4	32,34,39	a						20 28		20 49	20 57							21 52				22 00				
		d						20 28		20 50	20 58							21 52								
Outwood		d		20 00			20 21							21 00		21 27				22 01	22 02				22 26	
Leeds 10	32,34	a	20 05	20 17	20 21	20 23	20 34	20 48	20 54	21 26	21 20		21 05	21 14	21 19	21 47	21 50	22 29	22 02	22 15	22 15		22 19	22 24	22 46	22 59

			NT FX		EM	NT	NT	XC	NT FO	NT	NT	EM	GR	NT FX	NT FO	NT FX
					◇1			◇1				◇1	1			
Sheffield 7	29 ⇌	d	22 06		22 19		22 24	22 30				22 53		23 15	23 15	23 24
Meadowhall	29 ⇌	d	22 12				22 30							23 21	23 21	23 30
Rotherham Central	29	d					22 36							23 27	23 27	
Swinton (S.Yorks)	29	d					22 45							23 36	23 36	
Bolton-upon-Dearne		d					22 49							23 41	23 41	
Goldthorpe		d					22 52							23 44	23 44	
Thurnscoe		d					22 55							23 47	23 47	
Moorthorpe		d					23 00							23 52	23 52	
Doncaster 7		d				22 26							23 32			
Bentley (S.Yorks)		d				22 29										
Adwick		a				22 33										
		d				22 33										
South Elmsall		d				22 39										
Fitzwilliam		d				22 45	23 07									
Sandal & Agbrigg		d				22 51	23 13				←					
Wakefield Westgate 7	32,39	a			22 46	22 55	23 17	22 59			23 17	23 21	23 53	00 09		
		d			22 47	22 55	23 18	23 00		23 04	23 18	23 22	23 53	00 10		
Pontefract Monkhill	32	d					→									
Wakefield Kirkgate 4	32,34,39	a	22 51							23 07						00s10
		d	22 51						22 51							
Outwood		d				23 00					23 23					
Leeds 10	32,34	a	23 30		23 05	23 14		23 15	23 30		23 41	23 41	00 11	00 29	00 30	

Sheffield, Doncaster and Wakefield - Leeds

Network Diagram - see first page of Table 31

Station			NT MO	GR MX	GR MO	NT MX	NT MX	GR	GR	GR MX	GR MO	GR MX	NT	NT	NT	NT	NT	NT	NT	NT	NT	NT	NT	NT	XC
								A	B	C	D	C													
Sheffield	29	d	22p39			23p15	23p24						05 22	05 50			06 06	06 18	06 28	06 49			06 52	07 06	07 12
Meadowhall	29	d	22p45			23p21	23p30						05 28	05 56			06 12	06 24	06 34	06 55			06 58	07 12	
Rotherham Central	29	d				23p27							05 34					06 30	06 40				07 04		
Swinton (S.Yorks)	29	d				23p36							05 42					06 38	06 51				07 14		
Bolton-upon-Dearne		d				23p41							05 46						06 56						
Goldthorpe		d				23p44							05 49						06 58						
Thurnscoe		d				23p47							05 52						07 01						
Moorthorpe		d				23p52							05 57						07 06						
Doncaster		d		23p32	23p36			01 48			02 28					06 26		06 59			07 08	07 26	07 34		
Bentley (S.Yorks)		d														06 29		07 02			07 11	07 29	07 37		
Adwick		a														06 33		07 08			07 15	07 33	07 43		
		d														06 33					07 15	07 33			
South Elmsall		d														06 39					07 21	07 39			
Fitzwilliam		d											06 02			06 44			07 12		07 34	07 44			
Sandal & Agbrigg		d											06 08			06 50			07 18		07 40	07 50			
Wakefield Westgate	32,39	a		23p53	23p56	00 09		02 06	02s06	02s12	02s46	02s47	06 12			06 54			07 22		07 44	07 54			07 36
		d		23p53	23p56	00 10		02 06					06 13		06 24	06 54			07 23		07 44	07 54			07 37
Pontefract Monkhill	32	d																			→	→			
Wakefield Kirkgate	32,34,39	a	23p26				00s10							06 27	06 29		06 49			07 27				07 49	
		d	23p27											06 28			06 50			07 28				07 50	
Outwood		d											06 18			06 59			07 28						
Leeds	32,34	a	00 05	00 11	00 14	00 29		02 23	02 23	02 30	03 03	03 05	06 33	06 50		07 14	07 28		07 44	07 51				08 25	07 52

Station			NT	NT	GR	NT	NT	NT	NT	GR	NT	NT	NT	NT	XC	NT	GR	NT	NT	NT	GR	NT	NT	NT
Sheffield	29	d				07 14	07 20		07 51		08 06		08 14	08 18	08 21					08 51			08 53	09 06
Meadowhall	29	d				07 21	07 26		07 57		08 12		08 21	08 25						08 57			09 00	09 12
Rotherham Central	29	d				07 27							08 28										09 06	
Swinton (S.Yorks)	29	d				07 35							08 37										09 16	
Bolton-upon-Dearne		d				07 39							08 41											
Goldthorpe		d				07 42							08 44											
Thurnscoe		d				07 45							08 47											
Moorthorpe		d				07 54							08 52											
Doncaster		d			07 44			07 56		08 12		08 16				08 26	08 41		08 49		09 12	09 26	09 34	
Bentley (S.Yorks)		d						07 59				08 18				08 29			08 52			09 29	09 37	
Adwick		a						08 03				08 24				08 33			08 58			09 33	09 43	
		d						08 03								08 33						09 33		
South Elmsall		d						08 09								08 39						09 39		
Fitzwilliam		d				08 00		08 14					08 58			08 45						09 44		
Sandal & Agbrigg		d	←	←		08 06		08 20					09 04			08 50		←				09 50		
Wakefield Westgate	32,39	a	07 44	07 54	08 01	08 10		08 24		08 31			09 08		08 46	08 54	09 00	09 08			09 31	09 54		
		d	07 44	07 54	08 01	08 11		08 25		08 31			09 08		08 47	08 55	09 00	09 08			09 31	09 54		
Pontefract Monkhill	32	d											→									→		
Wakefield Kirkgate	32,34,39	a					07 57		08 27		08 49			08 57						09 27				09 49
		d					07 58		08 28		08 50			08 58						09 28				09 50
Outwood		d	07 49	07 59		08 16		08 29								08 59		09 13						
Leeds	32,34	a	08 02	08 13	08 20	08 36	08 21	08 42	08 49	08 49	09 25			09 20	09 03	09 14	09 18	09 31		09 49	09 49			10 25

Station			NT	NT	XC	NT	NT	GR	NT	NT	GR	NT	NT	NT	NT	NT	XC	NT	GR	NT	NT	GR	NT	NT	NT
Sheffield	29	d	09 14	09 18	09 21		09 29			09 50			09 53	10 06	10 14	10 18	10 21				10 50			10 53	11 06
Meadowhall	29	d	09 21	09 24			09 35			09 56			09 59	10 12	10 21	10 24					10 56			10 59	11 12
Rotherham Central	29	d	09 27				09 42						10 06		10 27									11 05	
Swinton (S.Yorks)	29	d	09 36				09 51						10 15		10 36									11 16	
Bolton-upon-Dearne		d	09 41												10 41										
Goldthorpe		d	09 43												10 43										
Thurnscoe		d	09 46												10 46										
Moorthorpe		d	09 51				10a01								10 53										
Doncaster		d						09 41			10 12	10 26	10 34						10 42			11 13	11 26	11 34	
Bentley (S.Yorks)		d										10 29	10 37										11 29	11 37	
Adwick		a										10 33	10 43										11 33	11 43	
		d										10 33											11 33		
South Elmsall		d										10 39											11 39		
Fitzwilliam		d	09 56									10 44			10 59								11 45		
Sandal & Agbrigg		d	10 02			←			←			10 50			11 05			←		←			11 50		
Wakefield Westgate	32,39	a	10 06		09 46	09 54		09 59	10 06		10 31	10 54			11 09		10 46	10 54	11 00	11 09		11 31	11 54		
		d	10 06		09 47	09 54		09 59	10 06		10 31	10 54			11 09		10 47	10 54	11 00	11 09		11 31	11 55		
Pontefract Monkhill	32	d	→									→			→								→		
Wakefield Kirkgate	32,34,39	a		09 57						10 27				10 49		10 57					11 27				11 49
		d		09 58						10 28				10 50		10 58					11 28				11 50
Outwood		d				09 59			10 11									10 59		11 14					
Leeds	32,34	a		10 18	10 02	10 14		10 18	10 31	10 48	10 49			11 25		11 18	11 02	11 15	11 18	11 31	11 48	11 49			12 25

A 13 August, 3 September
B 6 August
C not from 14 August until 29 August
D not 20 August, 27 August

Sheffield, Doncaster and Wakefield - Leeds

Network Diagram - see first page of Table 31

Station			NT	NT	XC	NT	GR	NT	NT	GR	GC	NT	NT	NT	NT	NT	XC	NT	GR	NT	NT	GR	NT	NT
Sheffield	29	d	11 14	11 18	11 21				11 50				11 53	12 06	12 14	12 18	12 21				12 50			12 53
Meadowhall	29	d	11 21	11 24					11 56				11 59	12 12	12 21	12 24					12 56			12 59
Rotherham Central	29	d	11 27										12 05		12 27									13 05
Swinton (S.Yorks)	29	d	11 36										12 16		12 36									13 16
Bolton-upon-Dearne		d	11 41												12 41									
Goldthorpe		d	11 43												12 43									
Thurnscoe		d	11 46												12 46									
Moorthorpe		d	11 53												12 52									
Doncaster		d					11 41			12 12	12 24	12 26	12 34						12 41			13 12	13 26	13 34
Bentley (S.Yorks)		d										12 29	12 38										13 29	13 37
Adwick		a										12 33	12 43										13 33	13 43
		d										12 33											13 33	
South Elmsall		d										12 39											13 39	
Fitzwilliam		d	11 59									12 44			12 58								13 45	
Sandal & Agbrigg		d	12 05			←		←				12 49			13 05			←		←			13 50	
Wakefield Westgate	32,39	a	12 09		11 46	11 54	12 00	12 09		12 31		12 51			13 09		12 46	12 51	13 00	13 09		13 31	13 54	
		d	12 09		11 47	11 55	12 01	12 09		12 31		12 52			13 09		12 47	12 52	13 01	13 09		13 31	13 55	
Pontefract Monkhill	32	d	→								12 49	→			→								→	
Wakefield Kirkgate	32,34,39	a		11 57					12 27		13 07			12 49		12 57					13 27			
		d		11 58					12 28					12 50		12 58					13 28			
Outwood		d				11 59		12 14										12 56		13 14				
Leeds	32,34	a		12 18	12 01	12 15	12 18	12 31	12 48	12 49				13 25		13 18	13 03	13 13	13 18	13 29	13 49	13 49		

Station			NT	NT	NT	XC	NT	NT	GR	NT	NT	GR	NT	NT	NT	NT	NT	XC	NT	GR	NT	NT	GR	NT	NT
Sheffield	29	d	13 06	13 14	13 18	13 21		13 29			13 50			13 53	14 06	14 14	14 18	14 21				14 50			14 53
Meadowhall	29	d	13 12	13 21	13 24			13 35			13 56			13 59	14 12	14 21	14 24					14 56			14 59
Rotherham Central	29	d		13 27				13 41						14 05		14 27									15 05
Swinton (S.Yorks)	29	d		13 36				13 50						14 17		14 35									15 16
Bolton-upon-Dearne		d		13 41												14 40									
Goldthorpe		d		13 43												14 42									
Thurnscoe		d		13 46												14 45									
Moorthorpe		d		13 53				14a01								14 52									
Doncaster		d							13 41			14 12	14 26	14 34						14 41			15 12	15 26	15 34
Bentley (S.Yorks)		d											14 29	14 37										15 29	15 37
Adwick		a											14 33	14 43										15 33	15 42
		d											14 33											15 33	
South Elmsall		d											14 39											15 39	
Fitzwilliam		d		13 59									14 45			14 58								15 44	
Sandal & Agbrigg		d		14 05			←			←			14 50			15 04			←		←			15 50	
Wakefield Westgate	32,39	a		14 09		13 46	13 54		13 59	14 09		14 31	14 54			15 08		14 46	14 54	14 59	15 08		15 31	15 54	
		d		14 09		13 47	13 55		13 59	14 09		14 31	14 55			15 08		14 47	14 55	14 59	15 08		15 31	15 54	
Pontefract Monkhill	32	d		→									→			→								→	
Wakefield Kirkgate	32,34,39	a	13 50		13 57						14 27				14 49		14 57					15 27			
		d	13 50		13 58						14 28				14 50		14 58					15 28			
Outwood		d					13 59			14 14									14 59		15 13				
Leeds	32,34	a	14 25		14 18	14 02	14 14		14 18	14 31	14 48	14 49			15 25		15 18	15 01	15 13	15 18	15 31	15 49	15 49		

Station			NT	NT	NT	XC	NT	GR	NT	NT	GR	NT	GC	NT	NT	NT	NT	XC	GR	NT	NT	GR	NT	NT
Sheffield	29	d	15 06	15 14	15 18	15 21				15 50				15 53	16 06	16 14	16 18	16 21			16 50			16 53
Meadowhall	29	d	15 12	15 20	15 24					15 56				15 59	16 12	16 20	16 24				16 56			16 59
Rotherham Central	29	d		15 26										16 05		16 26								17 05
Swinton (S.Yorks)	29	d		15 34										16 16		16 36								17 16
Bolton-upon-Dearne		d		15 39												16 40								
Goldthorpe		d		15 41												16 43								
Thurnscoe		d		15 44												16 46								
Moorthorpe		d		15 51												16 53								
Doncaster		d						15 41			16 12	16 16	16 24	16 34					16 41			17 13	17 26	17 34
Bentley (S.Yorks)		d										16 19		16 37									17 29	17 37
Adwick		a										16 23		16 43									17 33	17 43
		d										16 23											17 33	
South Elmsall		d										16 29											17 39	
Fitzwilliam		d		15 57								16 33				16 59							17 45	
Sandal & Agbrigg		d		16 03			←		←			16 39				17 05				←			17 51	
Wakefield Westgate	32,39	a		16 08		15 46	15 54	15 59	16 08		16 30	16 43				17 09		16 49	17 00	17 09		17 31	17 55	
		d		16 08		15 47	15 54	15 59	16 08		16 30	16 43				17 09		16 50	17 00	17 09		17 31	17 55	
Pontefract Monkhill	32	d		→									16 48			→							→	
Wakefield Kirkgate	32,34,39	a	15 49		15 57					16 27			17 04		16 49		16 57				17 28			
		d	15 50		15 58					16 28					16 50		16 58				17 28			
Outwood		d					15 59		16 13			16 49								17 14				
Leeds	32,34	a	16 25		16 18	16 02	16 14	16 18	16 31	16 49	16 51	17 03			17 25		17 18	17 04	17 18	17 31	17 48	17 50		

Table 31

Mondays to Fridays

6 August to 7 September

Sheffield, Doncaster and Wakefield - Leeds

Network Diagram - see first page of Table 31

Station		NT	NT	NT	XC	NT	GR	NT	XC	GR	NT	NT	NT	NT	XC	NT		GR	NT	GR	NT	NT	NT	NT	XC
				◇	◇1 ✕		1 ✕		◇1 ✕	1 ✕				◇	◇1 ✕			1 ✕		1 ✕				◇	◇1 ✕
Sheffield 7	29 ⇌ d	17 06	17 13	17 18	17 21				17 47		17 50	18 06	18 13	18 18	18 21						18 50	19 06	19 18	19 22	19 26
Meadowhall	29 ⇌ d	17 12	17 20	17 24							17 56	18 12	18 20	18 24							18 56	19 12	19 25	19 28	
Rotherham Central	29 d		17 26										18 26										19 31		
Swinton (S.Yorks)	29 d		17 36										18 36										19 40		
Bolton-upon-Dearne	d		17 40										18 41										19 44		
Goldthorpe	d		17 43										18 43										19 47		
Thurnscoe	d		17 46										18 46										19 50		
Moorthorpe	d		17 52										18 53										20 00		
Doncaster 7	d						17 42									18 26		18 40		19 17					
Bentley (S.Yorks)	d															18 29									
Adwick	a															18 33									
	d															18 33									
South Elmsall	d															18 39									
Fitzwilliam	d		17 58										18 59			18 45							20 05		
Sandal & Agbrigg	d		18 05			←		←					19 05			18 50			←				20 11		
Wakefield Westgate 7	32,39 a		18 09		17 47	17 55	18 00	18 09	18 13				19 10		18 47	18 54		18 59	19 10	19 35			20 15		19 50
	d		18 09		17 48	17 55	18 00	18 09	18 14	18 31			19 10		18 48	18 55		18 59	19 10	19 35			20 16		19 51
Pontefract Monkhill	32 d		→										→										→		
Wakefield Kirkgate 4	32,34,39 a	17 49		17 57							18 28	18 50		18 59							19 29	19 50		19 58	
	d	17 50		17 58							18 32	18 50		18 59							19 32	19 50		19 58	
Outwood	d					18 00		18 14								18 59			19 15						
Leeds 10	32,34 a	18 25		18 18	18 03	18 14	18 18	18 32	18 31	18 50	18 51	19 27		19 23	19 03	19 14		19 18	19 31	19 52	19 55	20 26		20 19	20 05

Station		NT	GR	GR	NT	NT	GR	NT		NT	XC	NT	GR	NT	GR	NT	XC	NT FX	NT FO	NT	EM	GR	NT	GR
			1 ✕	1 ✕			1 ✕			◇	◇1 ✕		1 ✕		1 ✕		◇1				◇1 ✕	1 ✕		1
Sheffield 7	29 ⇌ d					19 51		20 06		20 18	20 21			20 27		21 06	21 21				21 25		21 30	
Meadowhall	29 ⇌ d					19 57		20 12		20 24				20 35		21 12							21 36	
Rotherham Central	29 d													20 41									21 42	
Swinton (S.Yorks)	29 d													20 50									21 50	
Bolton-upon-Dearne	d													20 55									21 55	
Goldthorpe	d													20 57									21 57	
Thurnscoe	d													21 00									22 00	
Moorthorpe	d													21 05									22 05	
Doncaster 7	d	19 20	19 42	19 49			20 20					20 26	20 40		21 13			21 22	21 22			21 43		22 22
Bentley (S.Yorks)	d	19 23										20 29						21 25	21 25					
Adwick	a	19 27										20 33						21 29	21 29					
	d	19 27										20 33						21 29	21 29					
South Elmsall	d	19 33										20 39						21 35	21 35					
Fitzwilliam	d	19 46										20 45		21 11				21 45	21 46				22 11	
Sandal & Agbrigg	d	19 51			←							20 51		21 17				21 51	21 52				22 17	
Wakefield Westgate 7	32,39 a	19 55	20 01	20 07	20 15		20 38				20 46	20 55	21 00	21 22	21 31		21 46	21 56	21 56		21 59	22 06	22 21	22 40
	d	19 56	20 01	20 07	20 16		20 38				20 47	20 55	21 00	21 22	21 31		21 47	21 56	21 57	21 57	22 00	22 06	22 21	22 40
Pontefract Monkhill	32 d																							
Wakefield Kirkgate 4	32,34,39 a					20 28		20 49		20 57						21 52				22 00				
	d					20 28		20 50		20 58						21 52								
Outwood	d	20 00			20 21							21 00		21 27				22 01	22 02				22 26	
Leeds 10	32,34 a	20 17	20 21	20 23	20 34	20 48	20 54	21 26		21 20	21 05	21 14	21 19	21 47	21 50	22 29	22 02	22 15	22 15		22 19	22 24	22 46	22 59

Station		NT FX	EM	NT	NT	XC	NT FO	NT	NT	EM	GR	NT FX	NT FO	NT FX
			◇1 ✕			◇1				◇1	1			
Sheffield 7	29 ⇌ d	22 06	22 19		22 24	22 30				22 53		23 15	23 15	23 24
Meadowhall	29 ⇌ d	22 12			22 30							23 21	23 21	23 30
Rotherham Central	29 d				22 36							23 27	23 27	
Swinton (S.Yorks)	29 d				22 45							23 36	23 36	
Bolton-upon-Dearne	d				22 49							23 41	23 41	
Goldthorpe	d				22 52							23 44	23 44	
Thurnscoe	d				22 55							23 47	23 47	
Moorthorpe	d				23 00							23 52	23 52	
Doncaster 7	d			22 26							23 32			
Bentley (S.Yorks)	d			22 29										
Adwick	a			22 33										
	d			22 33										
South Elmsall	d			22 39										
Fitzwilliam	d			22 45	23 07									
Sandal & Agbrigg	d			22 51	23 13				←					
Wakefield Westgate 7	32,39 a		22 46	22 55	23 17	22 59			23 17	23 21	23 53	00 09		
	d		22 47	22 55	23 18	23 00		23 04	23 18	23 22	23 53	00 10		
Pontefract Monkhill	32 d				→									
Wakefield Kirkgate 4	32,34,39 a	22 51						23 07						00s10
	d	22 51					22 51							
Outwood	d			23 00					23 23					
Leeds 10	32,34 a	23 30	23 05	23 14		23 15	23 30		23 41	23 41	00 11	00 29	00 30	

Table 31

Mondays to Fridays

from 10 September

Sheffield, Doncaster and Wakefield - Leeds

Network Diagram - see first page of Table 31

Station		NT MO	NT MX	EM MO	NT MX	GR MX	GR MO	NT MX	GR	GR	NT	NT	NT	NT	NT	NT		NT	NT	NT	NT	NT	NT	XC	NT
				◇1 A ✕		1	1 ✕		1 B	1 B														◇1 ✕	
Sheffield 7	29 ⇌ d	22p39	23p15	23p16	23p24						05 22	05 50			06 06	06 18		06 28	06 49			06 52	07 06	07 12	
Meadowhall	29 ⇌ d	22p45	23p21		23p30						05 28	05 56			06 12	06 24		06 34	06 55			06 58	07 12		
Rotherham Central	29 d		23p27								05 34					06 30		06 40				07 04			
Swinton (S.Yorks)	29 d		23p36								05 42					06 38		06 51				07 14			
Bolton-upon-Dearne	d		23p41								05 46							06 56							
Goldthorpe	d		23p44								05 49							06 58							
Thurnscoe	d		23p47								05 52							07 01							
Moorthorpe	d		23p52								05 57							07 06							
Doncaster 7	d					23p32	23p36		01 48	02 28				06 26		06 59				07 08	07 26	07 34			
Bentley (S.Yorks)	d													06 29		07 02				07 11	07 29	07 37			
Adwick	a													06 33		07 08				07 15	07 33	07 43			
	d													06 33						07 15	07 33				
South Elmsall	d													06 39						07 21	07 39				
Fitzwilliam	d										06 02			06 44				07 12		07 34	07 44				
Sandal & Agbrigg	d							←			06 08			06 50				07 18		07 40	07 50				←
Wakefield Westgate 7	32,39 a		00 09	23p40		23p53	23p56	00 09	02 06	02s46	06 12			06 54				07 22		07 44	07 54			07 36	07 44
	d		00 10	23p41		23p53	23p56	00 10	02 06		06 13		06 24	06 54				07 23		07 44	07 54			07 37	07 44
Pontefract Monkhill	32 d		→																	→	→				
Wakefield Kirkgate 4	32,34,39 a	23p26			00s10							06 27	06 29		06 49				07 27				07 49		
	d	23p27										06 28			06 50				07 28				07 50		
Outwood	d										06 18			06 59				07 28							07 49
Leeds 10	32,34 a	00 05		00 01		00 11	00 14	00 29	02 23	03 03	06 33	06 50		07 14	07 28			07 44	07 51				08 25	07 52	08 02

Station		NT	GR	NT	NT	NT	NT	GR		NT	NT	NT	NT	XC	NT	GR	NT	NT	NT	GR	NT	NT	NT	NT
			1					1						◇1 ✕		1 ✕				1 ✕				
Sheffield 7	29 ⇌ d			07 14	07 20		07 51			08 06		08 14	08 18	08 21					08 51			08 53	09 06	09 14
Meadowhall	29 ⇌ d			07 21	07 26		07 57			08 12		08 21	08 25						08 57			09 00	09 12	09 21
Rotherham Central	29 d			07 27								08 28										09 06		09 27
Swinton (S.Yorks)	29 d			07 35								08 37										09 16		09 36
Bolton-upon-Dearne	d			07 39								08 41												09 41
Goldthorpe	d			07 42								08 44												09 43
Thurnscoe	d			07 45								08 47												09 46
Moorthorpe	d			07 54								08 52												09 51
Doncaster 7	d		07 44			07 56		08 12			08 16				08 26	08 41		08 49		09 12	09 26	09 34		
Bentley (S.Yorks)	d					07 59					08 18				08 29			08 52			09 29	09 37		
Adwick	a					08 03					08 24				08 33			08 58			09 33	09 43		
	d					08 03									08 33						09 33			
South Elmsall	d					08 09									08 39						09 39			
Fitzwilliam	d			08 00		08 14						08 58			08 45						09 44			09 56
Sandal & Agbrigg	d	←		08 06		08 20						09 04			08 50		←				09 50			10 02
Wakefield Westgate 7	32,39 a	07 54	08 01	08 10		08 24		08 31				09 08		08 46	08 54	09 00	09 08			09 31	09 54			10 06
	d	07 54	08 01	08 11		08 25		08 31				09 08		08 47	08 55	09 00	09 08			09 31	09 54			10 06
Pontefract Monkhill	32 d											→									→			→
Wakefield Kirkgate 4	32,34,39 a				07 57		08 27			08 49			08 57						09 27				09 49	
	d				07 58		08 28			08 50			08 58						09 28				09 50	
Outwood	d	07 59		08 16		08 29									08 59		09 13							
Leeds 10	32,34 a	08 13	08 20	08 36	08 21	08 42	08 49	08 49		09 25			09 20	09 03	09 14	09 18	09 31		09 49	09 49			10 25	

Station		NT	XC	NT	NT	GR	NT	NT	GR	NT	NT	NT	NT	NT	XC	NT		GR	NT	NT	GR	NT	NT	NT	NT
			◇1 ✕			1 ✕			1 ✕						◇1 ✕			1 ✕			1 ✕				
Sheffield 7	29 ⇌ d	09 18	09 21		09 29			09 50			09 53	10 06	10 14	10 18	10 21					10 50			10 53	11 06	11 14
Meadowhall	29 ⇌ d	09 24			09 35			09 56			09 59	10 12	10 21	10 24						10 56			10 59	11 12	11 21
Rotherham Central	29 d				09 42						10 06		10 27										11 05		11 27
Swinton (S.Yorks)	29 d				09 51						10 15		10 36										11 16		11 36
Bolton-upon-Dearne	d												10 41												11 41
Goldthorpe	d												10 43												11 43
Thurnscoe	d												10 46												11 46
Moorthorpe	d				10a01								10 53												11 53
Doncaster 7	d					09 41			10 12	10 26	10 34							10 42			11 13	11 26	11 34		
Bentley (S.Yorks)	d									10 29	10 37											11 29	11 37		
Adwick	a									10 33	10 43											11 33	11 43		
	d									10 33												11 33			
South Elmsall	d									10 39												11 39			
Fitzwilliam	d									10 44			10 59									11 45			11 59
Sandal & Agbrigg	d			←			←			10 50			11 05			←			←			11 50			12 05
Wakefield Westgate 7	32,39 a		09 46	09 54		09 59	10 06		10 31	10 54			11 09		10 46	10 54		11 00	11 09		11 31	11 54			12 09
	d		09 47	09 54		09 59	10 06		10 31	10 54			11 09		10 47	10 54		11 00	11 09		11 31	11 55			12 09
Pontefract Monkhill	32 d									→			→									→			→
Wakefield Kirkgate 4	32,34,39 a	09 57						10 27				10 49		10 57						11 27				11 49	
	d	09 58						10 28				10 50		10 58						11 28				11 50	
Outwood	d			09 59			10 11									10 59			11 14						
Leeds 10	32,34 a	10 18	10 02	10 14		10 18	10 31	10 48	10 49			11 25		11 18	11 02	11 15		11 18	11 31	11 48	11 49			12 25	

A from 17 September

B 10 September

Sheffield, Doncaster and Wakefield - Leeds

Network Diagram - see first page of Table 31

		NT	XC	NT	GR	NT	NT	GR	GC	NT	NT	NT	NT	NT	XC	NT	GR	NT	NT	GR	NT	NT	NT
		◇	◇1		1			1	1					◇	◇1		1			1			
Sheffield 7 29	d	11 18	11 21				11 50				11 53	12 06	12 14	12 18	12 21				12 50			12 53	13 06
Meadowhall 29	d	11 24					11 56				11 59	12 12	12 21	12 24					12 56			12 59	13 12
Rotherham Central 29	d										12 05		12 27									13 05	
Swinton (S.Yorks) 29	d										12 16		12 36									13 16	
Bolton-upon-Dearne	d												12 41										
Goldthorpe	d												12 43										
Thurnscoe	d												12 46										
Moorthorpe	d												12 52										
Doncaster 7	d				11 41			12 12	12 24	12 26	12 34						12 41			13 12	13 26	13 34	
Bentley (S.Yorks)	d									12 29	12 38										13 29	13 37	
Adwick	a									12 33	12 43										13 33	13 43	
	d									12 33											13 33		
South Elmsall	d									12 39											13 39		
Fitzwilliam	d									12 44			12 58								13 45		
Sandal & Agbrigg	d			←		←				12 49			13 05			←		←			13 50		
Wakefield Westgate 7 32,39	a		11 46	11 54	12 00	12 09		12 31		12 51			13 09		12 46	12 51	13 00	13 09		13 31	13 54		
	d		11 47	11 55	12 01	12 09		12 31		12 52			13 09		12 47	12 52	13 01	13 09		13 31	13 55		
Pontefract Monkhill 32	d								12 49	→			→								→		
Wakefield Kirkgate 4 32,34,39	a	11 57					12 27		13 07			12 49		12 57					13 27				13 50
	d	11 58					12 28					12 50		12 58					13 28				13 50
Outwood	d			11 59		12 14										12 56		13 14					
Leeds 10 32,34	a	12 18	12 01	12 15	12 18	12 31	12 48	12 49				13 25		13 18	13 03	13 13	13 18	13 29	13 49	13 49			14 25

		NT	NT	XC	NT	NT	GR	NT	NT	GR	NT	NT	NT	NT	NT	XC	NT	GR	NT	NT	GR	NT	NT	NT
			◇	◇1			1			1					◇	◇1		1			1			
Sheffield 7 29	d	13 14	13 18	13 21		13 29			13 50			13 53	14 06	14 14	14 18	14 21				14 50			14 53	15 06
Meadowhall 29	d	13 21	13 24			13 35			13 56			13 59	14 12	14 21	14 24					14 56			14 59	15 12
Rotherham Central 29	d	13 27				13 41						14 05		14 27									15 05	
Swinton (S.Yorks) 29	d	13 36				13 50						14 17		14 35									15 16	
Bolton-upon-Dearne	d	13 41												14 40										
Goldthorpe	d	13 43												14 42										
Thurnscoe	d	13 46												14 45										
Moorthorpe	d	13 53				14a01								14 52										
Doncaster 7	d						13 41			14 12	14 26	14 34						14 41			15 12	15 26	15 34	
Bentley (S.Yorks)	d										14 29	14 37										15 29	15 37	
Adwick	a										14 33	14 43										15 33	15 42	
	d										14 33											15 33		
South Elmsall	d										14 39											15 39		
Fitzwilliam	d	13 59									14 45			14 58								15 44		
Sandal & Agbrigg	d	14 05			←			←			14 50			15 04			←		←			15 50		
Wakefield Westgate 7 32,39	a	14 09		13 46	13 54		13 59	14 09		14 31	14 54			15 08		14 46	14 54	14 59	15 08		15 31	15 54		
	d	14 09		13 47	13 55		13 59	14 09		14 31	14 55			15 08		14 47	14 55	14 59	15 08		15 31	15 54		
Pontefract Monkhill 32	d	→									→			→								→		
Wakefield Kirkgate 4 32,34,39	a		13 57						14 27				14 49		14 57					15 27				15 49
	d		13 58						14 28				14 50		14 58					15 28				15 50
Outwood	d				13 59			14 14									14 59		15 13					
Leeds 10 32,34	a		14 18	14 02	14 14		14 18	14 31	14 48	14 49			15 25		15 18	15 01	15 13	15 18	15 31	15 49	15 49			16 25

		NT	NT	XC	NT	GR	NT	NT	GR	NT	GC	NT	NT	NT	NT	XC	GR	NT	NT	GR	NT	NT	NT
			◇	◇1		1			1		1				◇	◇1	1			1			
Sheffield 7 29	d	15 14	15 18	15 21				15 50				15 53	16 06	16 14	16 18	16 21			16 50			16 53	17 06
Meadowhall 29	d	15 20	15 24					15 56				15 59	16 12	16 20	16 24				16 56			16 59	17 12
Rotherham Central 29	d	15 26										16 05		16 26								17 05	
Swinton (S.Yorks) 29	d	15 34										16 16		16 36								17 16	
Bolton-upon-Dearne	d	15 39												16 40									
Goldthorpe	d	15 41												16 43									
Thurnscoe	d	15 44												16 46									
Moorthorpe	d	15 51												16 53									
Doncaster 7	d					15 41			16 12	16 16	16 24	16 34					16 41			17 13	17 26	17 34	
Bentley (S.Yorks)	d									16 19		16 37									17 29	17 37	
Adwick	a									16 23		16 43									17 33	17 43	
	d									16 23											17 33		
South Elmsall	d									16 29											17 39		
Fitzwilliam	d	15 57								16 33				16 59							17 45		
Sandal & Agbrigg	d	16 03			←		←			16 39				17 05				←			17 51		
Wakefield Westgate 7 32,39	a	16 08		15 46	15 54	15 59	16 08		16 30	16 43				17 09		16 49	17 00	17 09		17 31	17 55		
	d	16 08		15 47	15 54	15 59	16 08		16 30	16 43				17 09		16 50	17 00	17 09		17 31	17 55		
Pontefract Monkhill 32	d	→									16 48			→							→		
Wakefield Kirkgate 4 32,34,39	a		15 57					16 27			17 04		16 49		16 57				17 28				17 49
	d		15 58					16 28					16 50		16 58				17 28				17 50
Outwood	d				15 59		16 13			16 49								17 14					
Leeds 10 32,34	a		16 18	16 02	16 14	16 18	16 31	16 49	16 51	17 03			17 25		17 18	17 04	17 18	17 31	17 48	17 50			18 25

		NT	NT	XC	NT	GR	NT	XC	GR	NT	NT	NT	NT	XC	NT	GR	NT	GR	NT	NT	NT	NT	XC	NT
			◇	◇1		1		◇1	1				◇	◇1		1		1				◇	◇1	
Sheffield 7 29	d	17 13	17 18	17 21				17 47		17 50	18 06	18 13	18 18	18 21					18 50	19 06	19 18	19 22	19 26	
Meadowhall 29	d	17 20	17 24							17 56	18 12	18 20	18 24						18 56	19 12	19 25	19 28		
Rotherham Central 29	d	17 26										18 26									19 31			
Swinton (S.Yorks) 29	d	17 36										18 36									19 40			
Bolton-upon-Dearne	d	17 40										18 41									19 44			
Goldthorpe	d	17 43										18 43									19 47			
Thurnscoe	d	17 46										18 46									19 50			
Moorthorpe	d	17 52										18 53									20 00			
Doncaster 7	d					17 42									18 26	18 40		19 17						19 20
Bentley (S.Yorks)	d														18 29									19 23
Adwick	a														18 33									19 27
	d														18 33									19 27
South Elmsall	d														18 39									19 33
Fitzwilliam	d	17 58										18 59			18 45						20 05			19 46
Sandal & Agbrigg	d	18 05			←		←					19 05			18 50		←				20 11			19 51
Wakefield Westgate 7 32,39	a	18 09		17 47	17 55	18 00	18 09	18 13				19 10		18 47	18 54	18 59	19 10	19 35			20 15		19 50	19 55
	d	18 09		17 48	17 55	18 00	18 09	18 14	18 31			19 10		18 48	18 55	18 59	19 10	19 35			20 16		19 51	19 56
Pontefract Monkhill 32	d	→										→									→			
Wakefield Kirkgate 4 32,34,39	a		17 57							18 28	18 50		18 59						19 29	19 50		19 58		
	d		17 58							18 32	18 50		18 59						19 32	19 50		19 58		
Outwood	d				18 00		18 14								18 59		19 15							20 00
Leeds 10 32,34	a		18 18	18 03	18 14	18 18	18 32	18 31	18 50	18 51	19 27		19 23	19 03	19 14	19 18	19 31	19 52	19 55	20 26		20 19	20 05	20 17

		GR	GR	NT	NT	GR	NT	NT	XC	NT	GR	NT	GR	NT	XC	NT FX	NT FO	NT	EM	GR	NT	GR	NT FX
		1	1			1		◇	◇1		1		1		◇1				◇1	1		1	
Sheffield 7 29	d				19 51		20 06	20 18	20 21			20 27		21 06	21 21				21 25		21 30		22 06
Meadowhall 29	d				19 57		20 12	20 24				20 35		21 12							21 36		22 12
Rotherham Central 29	d											20 41									21 42		
Swinton (S.Yorks) 29	d											20 50									21 50		
Bolton-upon-Dearne	d											20 55									21 55		
Goldthorpe	d											20 57									21 57		
Thurnscoe	d											21 00									22 00		
Moorthorpe	d											21 05									22 05		
Doncaster 7	d	19 42	19 49			20 20				20 26	20 40		21 13			21 22	21 22			21 43		22 22	
Bentley (S.Yorks)	d									20 29						21 25	21 25						
Adwick	a									20 33						21 29	21 29						
	d									20 33						21 29	21 29						
South Elmsall	d									20 39						21 35	21 35						
Fitzwilliam	d									20 45		21 11				21 45	21 46				22 11		
Sandal & Agbrigg	d			←						20 51		21 17				21 51	21 52				22 17		
Wakefield Westgate 7 32,39	a	20 01	20 07	20 15		20 38			20 46	20 55	21 00	21 22	21 31		21 46	21 56	21 56		21 59	22 06	22 21	22 40	
	d	20 01	20 07	20 16		20 38			20 47	20 55	21 00	21 22	21 31		21 47	21 56	21 57	21 57	22 00	22 06	22 21	22 40	
Pontefract Monkhill 32	d																						
Wakefield Kirkgate 4 32,34,39	a				20 28		20 49	20 57						21 52				22 00					22 51
	d				20 28		20 50	20 58						21 52									22 51
Outwood	d			20 21						21 00		21 27				22 01	22 02				22 26		
Leeds 10 32,34	a	20 21	20 23	20 34	20 48	20 54	21 26	21 20	21 05	21 14	21 19	21 47	21 50	22 29	22 02	22 15	22 15		22 19	22 24	22 46	22 59	23 30

		EM	NT	NT	XC	NT FO	NT	NT	EM	GR	NT FX	NT FO	NT FX
		◇1			◇1				◇1	1			
Sheffield 7 29	d	22 19		22 24	22 30				22 53		23 15	23 15	23 24
Meadowhall 29	d			22 30							23 21	23 21	23 30
Rotherham Central 29	d			22 36							23 27	23 27	
Swinton (S.Yorks) 29	d			22 45							23 36	23 36	
Bolton-upon-Dearne	d			22 49							23 41	23 41	
Goldthorpe	d			22 52							23 44	23 44	
Thurnscoe	d			22 55							23 47	23 47	
Moorthorpe	d			23 00							23 52	23 52	
Doncaster 7	d		22 26							23 32			
Bentley (S.Yorks)	d		22 29										
Adwick	a		22 33										
	d		22 33										
South Elmsall	d		22 39										
Fitzwilliam	d		22 45	23 07									
Sandal & Agbrigg	d		22 51	23 13				←					
Wakefield Westgate 7 32,39	a	22 46	22 55	23 17	22 59			23 17	23 21	23 53	00 09		
	d	22 47	22 55	23 18	23 00		23 04	23 18	23 22	23 53	00 10		
Pontefract Monkhill 32	d			→									
Wakefield Kirkgate 4 32,34,39	a						23 07						00s10
	d					22 51							
Outwood	d		23 00					23 23					
Leeds 10 32,34	a	23 05	23 14		23 15	23 30		23 41	23 41	00 11	00 29	00 30	

Table 31

Sheffield, Doncaster and Wakefield - Leeds

Saturdays until 23 June

Network Diagram - see first page of Table 31

	GR	NT	NT	NT	NT	NT	NT	NT	NT	NT	XC	NT	NT	NT	NT	NT	NT	NT	XC	NT	GR	NT	NT
	■										◇■								◇■		■		
Sheffield 29 d		23p15			06 06	06 12	06 28		06 52	07 06	07 12		07 14	07 51	08 06		08 14	08 18	08 21				08 51
Meadowhall 29 d		23p21			06 12	06 18	06 34		06 58	07 12			07 21	07 57	08 12		08 22	08 25					08 57
Rotherham Central 29 d		23p27				06 24	06 40		07 04				07 27				08 28						
Swinton (S.Yorks) 29 d		23p36				06 35	06 51		07 15				07 33				08 37						
Bolton-upon-Dearne d		23p41					06 56						07 38				08 42						
Goldthorpe d		23p44					06 58						07 40				08 44						
Thurnscoe d		23p47					07 01						07 43				08 47						
Moorthorpe d		23p52					07 06						07 52				08 53						
Doncaster d	23p32			06 26		06 55		07 26	07 34							08 16				08 26	08 50		
Bentley (S.Yorks) d				06 29		06 58		07 29	07 37							08 19				08 29			
Adwick a				06 33		07 05		07 33	07 43							08 23				08 33			
d				06 33				07 33												08 33			
South Elmsall d				06 39				07 39												08 39			
Fitzwilliam d				06 44			07 12	07 44					07 58				09 09			08 45			
Sandal & Agbrigg d				06 50			07 18	07 50				←	08 04				09 15			08 49		←	
Wakefield Westgate 32,39 a	23p53			06 54			07 22	07 54			07 36	07 54	08 10				09 19		08 45	08 54	09 08	09 19	
d	23p53		06 24	06 54			07 23	07 54			07 37	07 54	08 11				09 19		08 46	08 55	09 08	09 19	
Pontefract Monkhill 32 d								→									→						
Wakefield Kirkgate 32,34,39 a			06 29		06 49					07 49				08 27	08 49			08 57					09 27
d					06 50					07 50				08 28	08 50			08 58					09 28
Outwood d				06 59			07 28					07 59	08 16							08 58		09 24	
Leeds 32,34 a	00 11	00 30		07 13	07 28		07 44			08 25	07 52	08 14	08 32	08 49	09 25			09 20	09 03	09 14	09 25	09 40	09 49

	NT	NT	NT	NT	NT	NT	XC	NT	NT	GR	NT	NT	NT	NT	NT	NT	NT	XC	NT	GR	NT	NT
							◇■			■								◇■		■		
Sheffield 29 d			08 53	09 06	09 14	09 18	09 21		09 29			09 50		09 53	10 06	10 14	10 18	10 21				10 50
Meadowhall 29 d			09 00	09 12	09 21	09 24			09 35			09 56		09 59	10 12	10 21	10 24					10 56
Rotherham Central 29 d			09 06		09 27				09 42					10 05		10 27						
Swinton (S.Yorks) 29 d			09 16		09 36				09 51					10 15		10 36						
Bolton-upon-Dearne d					09 41											10 41						
Goldthorpe d					09 43											10 43						
Thurnscoe d					09 46											10 46						
Moorthorpe d					09 53				10a01							10 53						
Doncaster d	08 54	09 26	09 34							09 50			10 26	10 34						10 50		
Bentley (S.Yorks) d	08 57	09 29	09 37										10 29	10 37								
Adwick a	09 04	09 33	09 43										10 33	10 43								
d		09 33											10 33									
South Elmsall d		09 39											10 39									
Fitzwilliam d		09 45			10 09								10 45			11 09						
Sandal & Agbrigg d		09 49			10 15			←			←		10 49			11 15			←		←	
Wakefield Westgate 32,39 a		09 54			10 19		09 46	09 54		10 07	10 19		10 54			11 19		10 46	10 54	11 07	11 19	
d		09 55			10 19		09 47	09 55		10 07	10 19		10 55			11 19		10 47	10 55	11 07	11 19	
Pontefract Monkhill 32 d		→			→								→			→						
Wakefield Kirkgate 32,34,39 a				09 49		09 57						10 27			10 49		10 57					11 27
d				09 50		09 58						10 28			10 50		10 58					11 28
Outwood d								09 58			10 24								10 58		11 24	
Leeds 32,34 a				10 25		10 18	10 02	10 14		10 26	10 40	10 48			11 25		11 18	11 02	11 14	11 26	11 40	11 48

	NT	NT	NT	NT	NT	XC	NT	GR	NT	NT	GC	NT	NT	NT	NT	NT	XC	NT	GR	NT	NT	GR	NT
						◇■		■			■						◇■		■			■	
Sheffield 29 d		10 53	11 06	11 14	11 18	11 21				11 50			11 53	12 06	12 14	12 18	12 21				12 50		
Meadowhall 29 d		10 59	11 12	11 21	11 24					11 56			11 59	12 12	12 21	12 24					12 56		
Rotherham Central 29 d		11 05		11 27									12 05		12 27								
Swinton (S.Yorks) 29 d		11 16		11 36									12 16		12 36								
Bolton-upon-Dearne d				11 41											12 41								
Goldthorpe d				11 43											12 43								
Thurnscoe d				11 46											12 46								
Moorthorpe d				11 53											12 53								
Doncaster d	11 26	11 34						11 50			12 20	12 26	12 34						12 50			13 13	13 26
Bentley (S.Yorks) d	11 29	11 37										12 29	12 37										13 29
Adwick a	11 33	11 43										12 33	12 43										13 33
d	11 33											12 33											13 33
South Elmsall d	11 39											12 39											13 39
Fitzwilliam d	11 45			12 09								12 45			13 09								13 45
Sandal & Agbrigg d	11 49			12 15			←		←			12 49			13 15			←		←			13 49
Wakefield Westgate 32,39 a	11 54			12 19		11 46	11 54	12 07	12 19			12 54			13 19		12 46	12 54	13 07	13 19		13 30	13 54
d	11 55			12 19		11 47	11 55	12 07	12 19			12 55			13 19		12 47	12 55	13 07	13 19		13 31	13 55
Pontefract Monkhill 32 d	→			→								→			→								→
Wakefield Kirkgate 32,34,39 a			11 49		11 57					12 27	12 42			12 49		12 57					13 27		
d			11 50		11 58					12 28				12 50		12 58					13 28		
Outwood d							11 58		12 24									12 58		13 24			
Leeds 32,34 a			12 25		12 18	12 02	12 14	12 26	12 40	12 48				13 25		13 18	13 02	13 13	13 26	13 43	13 49	13 49	

Table 31

Sheffield, Doncaster and Wakefield - Leeds

Saturdays until 23 June

Network Diagram - see first page of Table 31

	NT	NT	NT	NT	XC	NT	NT	GR	NT	NT	NT	NT	NT	NT	NT	XC	NT	GR	NT	NT	NT	NT
					◇■			■								◇■		■				
Sheffield 29 d	12 53	13 06	13 14	13 18	13 21		13 29			13 50		13 53	14 06	14 14	14 18	14 21				14 50		14 53
Meadowhall 29 d	12 59	13 12	13 21	13 24			13 35			13 56		13 59	14 12	14 21	14 24					14 56		14 59
Rotherham Central 29 d	13 05		13 27				13 41					14 05		14 27								15 05
Swinton (S.Yorks) 29 d	13 16		13 36				13 50					14 17		14 36								15 17
Bolton-upon-Dearne d			13 41											14 41								
Goldthorpe d			13 43											14 43								
Thurnscoe d			13 46											14 46								
Moorthorpe d			13 53				14a01							14 53								
Doncaster d	13 34							13 53			14 26	14 34						14 50			15 26	15 34
Bentley (S.Yorks) d	13 37										14 29	14 37									15 29	15 37
Adwick a	13 43										14 33	14 43									15 33	15 43
d											14 33										15 33	
South Elmsall d											14 39										15 39	
Fitzwilliam d			14 09								14 45			15 09							15 45	
Sandal & Agbrigg d			14 15			←			←		14 49			15 15			←		←		15 49	
Wakefield Westgate 32,39 a			14 19		13 46	13 54		14 11	14 19		14 54			15 19		14 46	14 54	15 07	15 19		15 54	
d			14 19		13 47	13 55		14 12	14 19		14 55			15 19		14 47	14 55	15 07	15 19		15 55	
Pontefract Monkhill 32 d			→								→			→							→	
Wakefield Kirkgate 32,34,39 a		13 50		13 57						14 27			14 49		14 57					15 27		
d		13 50		13 58						14 28			14 50		14 58					15 28		
Outwood d						13 58			14 24								14 58		15 24			
Leeds 32,34 a		14 25		14 18	14 02	14 14		14 30	14 40	14 48			15 25		15 18	15 02	15 14	15 26	15 40	15 49		

	NT	NT	NT	XC	NT	GR	NT	NT	NT	NT	NT	NT	NT	XC	NT	GR	NT	NT	GC	NT	NT	NT	NT
				◇■		■								◇■		■			■				
Sheffield 29 d	15 06	15 14	15 18	15 21				15 50		15 53	16 06	16 14	16 18	16 21				16 50			16 53	17 06	17 14
Meadowhall 29 d	15 12	15 21	15 24					15 56		15 59	16 12	16 21	16 24					16 56			16 59	17 12	17 21
Rotherham Central 29 d		15 27								16 05		16 27									17 05		17 27
Swinton (S.Yorks) 29 d		15 36								16 16		16 36									17 16		17 37
Bolton-upon-Dearne d		15 41										16 41											17 41
Goldthorpe d		15 43										16 43											17 44
Thurnscoe d		15 46										16 46											17 47
Moorthorpe d		15 53										16 53											17 52
Doncaster d						15 50			16 25	16 34						16 50			17 21	17 26	17 34		
Bentley (S.Yorks) d									16 28	16 37										17 29	17 37		
Adwick a									16 32	16 43										17 33	17 43		
d									16 32											17 33			
South Elmsall d									16 38											17 39			
Fitzwilliam d		16 09							16 42			17 09								17 45			18 13
Sandal & Agbrigg d		16 15			←		←		16 48			17 15			←		←			17 51			18 19
Wakefield Westgate 32,39 a		16 19		15 46	15 54	16 07	16 19		16 52			17 19		16 46	16 52	17 07	17 19			17 55			18 23
d		16 19		15 47	15 55	16 07	16 19		16 52			17 19		16 47	16 52	17 07	17 19			17 55			18 23
Pontefract Monkhill 32 d		→							→			→								→			→
Wakefield Kirkgate 32,34,39 a	15 49		15 57					16 27			16 49		16 57					17 28	17 44			17 49	
d	15 50		15 58					16 28			16 50		16 58					17 28				17 50	
Outwood d					15 58		16 24								16 59		17 24						
Leeds 32,34 a	16 25		16 18	16 02	16 13	16 26	16 40	16 49			17 25		17 18	17 02	17 13	17 26	17 41	17 48				18 25	

	NT	XC	NT	GR	XC	NT	NT	NT	NT	NT	XC	NT	GR	NT	GR	NT	NT	NT	NT	XC	NT	GR
		◇■		■	◇■						◇■		■		■					◇■		■
Sheffield 29 d	17 18	17 21			17 47		17 50	18 06	18 13	18 18	18 21					18 50	19 06	19 16	19 18	19 22		
Meadowhall 29 d	17 24						17 56	18 12	18 21	18 24						18 56	19 12	19 22	19 25			
Rotherham Central 29 d									18 27										19 31			
Swinton (S.Yorks) 29 d									18 37										19 40			
Bolton-upon-Dearne d									18 41										19 44			
Goldthorpe d									18 44										19 47			
Thurnscoe d									18 47										19 50			
Moorthorpe d									18 53										20 01			
Doncaster d				17 50								18 26	18 50		19 14						19 22	19 50
Bentley (S.Yorks) d												18 29									19 25	
Adwick a												18 33									19 29	
d												18 33									19 29	
South Elmsall d												18 39									19 35	
Fitzwilliam d									19 09			18 44							20 07		19 48	
Sandal & Agbrigg d			←			←			19 15			18 50		←					20 13		19 53	
Wakefield Westgate 32,39 a		17 47	17 55	18 07	18 12	18 23			19 19		18 46	18 53	19 07	19 19	19 32				20 17	19 49	19 57	20 07
d		17 47	17 55	18 07	18 13	18 23			19 19		18 47	18 54	19 07	19 19	19 33				20 17	19 50	19 58	20 07
Pontefract Monkhill 32 d									→										→			
Wakefield Kirkgate 32,34,39 a	17 57						18 28	18 50		18 59						19 29	19 50	19 58				
d	17 58						18 32	18 50		18 59						19 32	19 50	19 58				
Outwood d			18 00			18 28						18 57		19 24							20 02	
Leeds 32,34 a	18 18	18 02	18 14	18 26	18 31	18 44	18 51	19 27		19 23	19 01	19 14	19 25	19 43	19 48	19 55	20 26	20 20		20 05	20 16	20 25

Sheffield, Doncaster and Wakefield - Leeds

Saturdays until 23 June

Network Diagram - see first page of Table 31

		NT	GR	NT	NT	NT	XC	NT	GC	NT	GR	NT	XC	NT	NT	EM	NT	GR	EM	NT	NT	NT	XC	NT	NT
Sheffield 7	29 ⇌ d			19 51	20 06	20 18	20 24			20 27		21 06	21 21			21 25	21 30		22 19			22 24	22 27		
Meadowhall	29 ⇌ d			19 57	20 12	20 24				20 35		21 12					21 36					22 30			
Rotherham Central	29 d									20 41							21 42					22 36			
Swinton (S.Yorks)	29 d									20 50							21 50					22 45			
Bolton-upon-Dearne	d									20 55							21 54					22 49			
Goldthorpe	d									20 57							21 57					22 52			
Thurnscoe	d									21 00							22 00					22 55			
Moorthorpe	d									21 05							22 05					23 00			
Doncaster 7	d		20 12					20 26	20 53		21 17			21 22				22 18		22 26			22 53		
Bentley (S.Yorks)	d							20 29						21 25						22 29					
Adwick	a							20 33						21 29						22 33					
	d							20 33						21 29						22 33					
South Elmsall	d							20 39						21 35						22 39					
Fitzwilliam	d							20 44		21 11				21 42			22 11			22 44		23 07			
Sandal & Agbrigg	d	←						20 50		21 17				21 48			22 17			22 50		23 13			←
Wakefield Westgate 7	32,39 a	20 17	20 32				20 48	20 54		21 22	21 34		21 49	21 52		21 59	22 21	22 35	22 44	22 54		23 18	23 10		23 18
	d	20 17	20 33				20 49	20 54		21 22	21 34		21 50	21 53	21 57	22 00	22 21	22 35	22 45	22 54	23 04	23 18	23 11		23 18
Pontefract Monkhill	32 d								21 16																
Wakefield Kirkgate 4	32,34,39 a			20 28	20 49	20 57						21 52			22 00						23 07	→			
	d			20 28	20 50	20 58						21 52												22 51	
Outwood	d	20 22						20 59		21 27				21 58			22 26			22 59					23 23
Leeds 10	32,34 a	20 38	20 47	20 48	21 26	21 20	21 03	21 18		21 47	21 50	22 29	22 02	22 17		22 19	22 45	22 54	23 04	23 14			23 27	23 30	23 40

		GR
Sheffield 7	29 ⇌ d	
Meadowhall	29 ⇌ d	
Rotherham Central	29 d	
Swinton (S.Yorks)	29 d	
Bolton-upon-Dearne	d	
Goldthorpe	d	
Thurnscoe	d	
Moorthorpe	d	
Doncaster 7	d	23 48
Bentley (S.Yorks)	d	
Adwick	a	
	d	
South Elmsall	d	
Fitzwilliam	d	
Sandal & Agbrigg	d	
Wakefield Westgate 7	32,39 a	00 05
	d	00 05
Pontefract Monkhill	32 d	
Wakefield Kirkgate 4	32,34,39 a	
	d	
Outwood	d	
Leeds 10	32,34 a	00 24

Saturdays 30 June to 8 September

		GR	NT	GR	GR	NT	NT	NT	NT	NT	GC	NT	NT	NT	XC	NT		NT	NT	NT	NT	NT	NT	XC	NT
				A	A																				
Sheffield 7	29 ⇌ d		23p15					06 06	06 12	06 28			06 52	07 06	07 12			07 14	07 51	08 06		08 14	08 18	08 21	
Meadowhall	29 ⇌ d		23p21					06 12	06 18	06 34			06 58	07 12				07 21	07 57	08 12		08 22	08 25		
Rotherham Central	29 d		23p27						06 24	06 40			07 04					07 27				08 28			
Swinton (S.Yorks)	29 d		23p36						06 35	06 51			07 15					07 33				08 37			
Bolton-upon-Dearne	d		23p41							06 56								07 38				08 42			
Goldthorpe	d		23p44							06 58								07 40				08 44			
Thurnscoe	d		23p47							07 01								07 43				08 47			
Moorthorpe	d		23p52							07 06								07 52				08 53			
Doncaster 7	d	23p32		01 55	02 46		06 26		06 55			07 26	07 34								08 16				08 26
Bentley (S.Yorks)	d						06 29		06 58			07 29	07 37								08 19				08 29
Adwick	a						06 33		07 05			07 33	07 43								08 23				08 33
	d						06 33					07 33													08 33
South Elmsall	d						06 39					07 39													08 39
Fitzwilliam	d						06 44			07 12		07 44						07 58				09 09			08 45
Sandal & Agbrigg	d						06 50			07 18		07 50				←		08 04				09 15			08 49
Wakefield Westgate 7	32,39 a	23p53		02s13	03s15		06 54			07 22		07 54			07 36	07 54		08 10				09 19		08 45	08 54
	d	23p53				06 24	06 54			07 23		07 54			07 37	07 54		08 11				09 19		08 46	08 55
Pontefract Monkhill	32 d										07 05	→										→			
Wakefield Kirkgate 4	32,34,39 a					06 29		06 49			07 30			07 49					08 27	08 49			08 57		
	d							06 50						07 50					08 28	08 50			08 58		
Outwood	d						06 59			07 28						07 59		08 16							08 58
Leeds 10	32,34 a	00 11	00 30	02 30	03 33		07 13	07 28		07 44				08 25	07 52	08 14		08 32	08 49	09 25			09 20	09 03	09 14

A 28 July, 4 August, 11 August, 1 September, 8 September

Sheffield, Doncaster and Wakefield - Leeds

Saturdays 30 June to 8 September

Network Diagram - see first page of Table 31

		GR	NT	NT	NT	NT	NT	NT		NT	NT	XC	NT	NT	GR	NT	NT	NT	NT	NT	NT	NT	XC	NT	
Sheffield 7	29 ⇌ d			08 51			08 53	09 06		09 14	09 18	09 21		09 29			09 50		09 53	10 06	10 14	10 18	10 21		
Meadowhall	29 ⇌ d			08 57			09 00	09 12		09 21	09 24			09 35			09 56		09 59	10 12	10 21	10 24			
Rotherham Central	29 d						09 06			09 27				09 42					10 05		10 27				
Swinton (S.Yorks)	29 d						09 16			09 36				09 51					10 15		10 36				
Bolton-upon-Dearne	d									09 41											10 41				
Goldthorpe	d									09 43											10 43				
Thurnscoe	d									09 46											10 46				
Moorthorpe	d									09 53				10a01							10 53				
Doncaster 7	d	08 50			08 54	09 26	09 34								09 50			10 26	10 34						
Bentley (S.Yorks)	d				08 57	09 29	09 37											10 29	10 37						
Adwick	a				09 04	09 33	09 43											10 33	10 43						
	d					09 33												10 33							
South Elmsall	d					09 39												10 39							
Fitzwilliam	d					09 45				10 09								10 45			11 09				
Sandal & Agbrigg	d		←			09 49				10 15			←			←		10 49			11 15			←	
Wakefield Westgate 7	32,39 a	09 08	09 19			09 54				10 19		09 46	09 54		10 07	10 19		10 54			11 19		10 46	10 54	
	d	09 08	09 19			09 55				10 19		09 47	09 55		10 07	10 19		10 55			11 19		10 47	10 55	
Pontefract Monkhill	32 d					→				→								→			→				
Wakefield Kirkgate 4	32,34,39 a			09 27				09 49			09 57						10 27			10 49		10 57			
	d			09 28				09 50			09 58						10 28			10 50		10 58			
Outwood	d		09 24										09 58			10 24								10 58	
Leeds 10	32,34 a	09 25	09 40	09 49				10 25			10 18	10 02	10 14		10 26	10 40	10 48			11 25		11 18	11 02	11 14	

		GC	GR	NT	NT	NT	NT	NT	NT	NT	XC	NT	GR	NT	NT	GC		NT	NT	NT	NT	NT	XC	NT	GR
Sheffield 7	29 ⇌ d				10 50		10 53	11 06	11 14	11 18	11 21				11 50				11 53	12 06	12 14	12 18	12 21		
Meadowhall	29 ⇌ d				10 56		10 59	11 12	11 21	11 24					11 56				11 59	12 12	12 21	12 24			
Rotherham Central	29 d						11 05		11 27										12 05		12 27				
Swinton (S.Yorks)	29 d						11 16		11 36										12 16		12 36				
Bolton-upon-Dearne	d								11 41												12 41				
Goldthorpe	d								11 43												12 43				
Thurnscoe	d								11 46												12 46				
Moorthorpe	d								11 53												12 53				
Doncaster 7	d		10 50			11 26	11 34						11 50			12 20		12 26	12 34						12 50
Bentley (S.Yorks)	d					11 29	11 37											12 29	12 37						
Adwick	a					11 33	11 43											12 33	12 43						
	d					11 33												12 33							
South Elmsall	d					11 39												12 39							
Fitzwilliam	d					11 45			12 09									12 45			13 09				
Sandal & Agbrigg	d			←		11 49			12 15			←		←				12 49			13 15			←	
Wakefield Westgate 7	32,39 a		11 07	11 19		11 54			12 19		11 46	11 54	12 07	12 19				12 54			13 19		12 46	12 54	13 07
	d		11 07	11 19		11 55			12 19		11 47	11 55	12 07	12 19				12 55			13 19		12 47	12 55	13 07
Pontefract Monkhill	32 d	10 35				→			→									→			→				
Wakefield Kirkgate 4	32,34,39 a	11 00			11 27			11 49		11 57					12 27	12 42				12 49		12 57			
	d				11 28			11 50		11 58					12 28					12 50		12 58			
Outwood	d			11 24								11 58		12 24										12 58	
Leeds 10	32,34 a		11 26	11 40	11 48			12 25		12 18	12 02	12 14	12 26	12 40	12 48					13 25		13 18	13 02	13 13	13 26

		NT	NT	GR	NT	NT	NT	NT		NT	XC	NT	NT	GR	NT	NT	NT	NT	NT	NT	NT	XC	NT	GR	
Sheffield 7	29 ⇌ d		12 50			12 53	13 06	13 14		13 18	13 21		13 29			13 50		13 53	14 06	14 14	14 18	14 21			
Meadowhall	29 ⇌ d		12 56			12 59	13 12	13 21		13 24			13 35			13 56		13 59	14 12	14 21	14 24				
Rotherham Central	29 d					13 05		13 27					13 41					14 05		14 27					
Swinton (S.Yorks)	29 d					13 16		13 36					13 50					14 17		14 36					
Bolton-upon-Dearne	d							13 41												14 41					
Goldthorpe	d							13 43												14 43					
Thurnscoe	d							13 46												14 46					
Moorthorpe	d							13 53					14a01							14 53					
Doncaster 7	d			13 13	13 26	13 34								13 53			14 26	14 34						14 50	
Bentley (S.Yorks)	d				13 29	13 37											14 29	14 37							
Adwick	a				13 33	13 43											14 33	14 43							
	d				13 33												14 33								
South Elmsall	d				13 39												14 39								
Fitzwilliam	d				13 45			14 09									14 45			15 09					
Sandal & Agbrigg	d	←			13 49			14 15				←			←		14 49			15 15			←		
Wakefield Westgate 7	32,39 a	13 19		13 30	13 54			14 19			13 46	13 54		14 11	14 19		14 54			15 19		14 46	14 54	15 07	
	d	13 19		13 31	13 55			14 19			13 47	13 55		14 12	14 19		14 55			15 19		14 47	14 55	15 07	
Pontefract Monkhill	32 d				→			→									→			→					
Wakefield Kirkgate 4	32,34,39 a		13 27				13 50			13 57						14 27			14 49		14 57				
	d		13 28				13 50			13 58						14 28			14 50		14 58				
Outwood	d	13 24										13 58			14 24								14 58		
Leeds 10	32,34 a	13 43	13 49	13 49			14 25			14 18	14 02	14 14		14 30	14 40	14 48			15 25		15 18	15 02	15 14	15 26	

Table 31

Saturdays
30 June to 8 September

Sheffield, Doncaster and Wakefield - Leeds

Network Diagram - see first page of Table 31

Station			NT	NT	NT	NT	NT	NT	NT	XC	NT	GC	GR	NT	NT	NT	NT		NT	NT	NT	XC	NT	GR	NT	NT
Sheffield	29 ⇌	d		14 50		14 53	15 06	15 14	15 18	15 21					15 50		15 53		16 06	16 14	16 18	16 21				16 50
Meadowhall	29 ⇌	d		14 56		14 59	15 12	15 21	15 24						15 56		15 59		16 12	16 21	16 24					16 56
Rotherham Central	29	d				15 05		15 27									16 05			16 27						
Swinton (S.Yorks)	29	d				15 17		15 36									16 16			16 36						
Bolton-upon-Dearne		d						15 41												16 41						
Goldthorpe		d						15 43												16 43						
Thurnscoe		d						15 46												16 46						
Moorthorpe		d						15 53												16 53						
Doncaster		d			15 26	15 34							15 50			16 25	16 34							16 50		
Bentley (S.Yorks)		d			15 29	15 37										16 28	16 37									
Adwick		a			15 33	15 43										16 32	16 43									
		d			15 33											16 32										
South Elmsall		d			15 39											16 38										
Fitzwilliam		d			15 45			16 09								16 42				17 09						
Sandal & Agbrigg		d	←		15 49			16 15			←			←		16 48				17 15			←		←	
Wakefield Westgate	32,39	a	15 19		15 54			16 19		15 46	15 54		16 07	16 19		16 52				17 19		16 46	16 52	17 07	17 19	
		d	15 19		15 55			16 19		15 47	15 55		16 07	16 19		16 52				17 19		16 47	16 52	17 07	17 19	
Pontefract Monkhill	32	d			→			→				15 35				→				→						
Wakefield Kirkgate	32,34,39	a		15 27			15 49		15 57			16 00			16 27				16 49		16 57					17 28
		d		15 28			15 50		15 58						16 28				16 50		16 58					17 28
Outwood		d	15 24								15 58			16 24									16 59		17 24	
Leeds	32,34	a	15 40	15 49			16 25		16 18	16 02	16 13		16 26	16 40	16 49				17 25		17 18	17 02	17 13	17 26	17 41	17 48

Station			GC	NT	NT	NT	NT	NT	XC		NT	GR	XC	NT	NT	NT	NT	NT	XC	NT	GR	NT	GR	NT	NT	
Sheffield	29 ⇌	d			16 53	17 06	17 14	17 18	17 21				17 47		17 50	18 06	18 13	18 18	18 21					18 50	19 06	
Meadowhall	29 ⇌	d			16 59	17 12	17 21	17 24							17 56	18 12	18 21	18 24						18 56	19 12	
Rotherham Central	29	d			17 05		17 27										18 27									
Swinton (S.Yorks)	29	d			17 16		17 37										18 37									
Bolton-upon-Dearne		d					17 41										18 41									
Goldthorpe		d					17 44										18 44									
Thurnscoe		d					17 47										18 47									
Moorthorpe		d					17 52										18 53									
Doncaster		d	17 21	17 26	17 34							17 50								18 26	18 50		19 14			
Bentley (S.Yorks)		d		17 29	17 37															18 29						
Adwick		a		17 33	17 43															18 33						
		d		17 33																18 33						
South Elmsall		d		17 39																18 39						
Fitzwilliam		d		17 45			18 13										19 09			18 44						
Sandal & Agbrigg		d		17 51			18 19				←			←			19 15			18 50		←				
Wakefield Westgate	32,39	a		17 55			18 23		17 47		17 55	18 07	18 12	18 23			19 19		18 46	18 53	19 07	19 19	19 32			
		d		17 55			18 23		17 47		17 55	18 07	18 13	18 23			19 19		18 47	18 54	19 07	19 19	19 33			
Pontefract Monkhill	32	d		→			→										→									
Wakefield Kirkgate	32,34,39	a	17 44			17 49		17 57							18 28	18 50		18 59						19 29	19 50	
		d				17 50		17 58							18 32	18 50		18 59						19 32	19 50	
Outwood		d									18 00			18 28						18 57		19 24				
Leeds	32,34	a				18 25		18 18	18 02		18 14	18 26	18 31	18 44	18 51	19 27		19 23	19 01	19 14	19 25	19 43	19 48	19 55	20 26	

Station			NT	NT	XC	NT	GR	NT	GR	NT	NT	NT	XC	NT	NT	GC	GR		NT	XC	NT	NT	EM	NT	GR	EM
Sheffield	29 ⇌	d	19 16	19 18	19 22					19 51	20 06	20 18	20 24		20 27				21 06	21 21			21 25	21 30		22 19
Meadowhall	29 ⇌	d	19 22	19 25						19 57	20 12	20 24			20 35				21 12					21 36		
Rotherham Central	29	d		19 31											20 41									21 42		
Swinton (S.Yorks)	29	d		19 40											20 50									21 50		
Bolton-upon-Dearne		d		19 44											20 55									21 54		
Goldthorpe		d		19 47											20 57									21 57		
Thurnscoe		d		19 50											21 00									22 00		
Moorthorpe		d		20 01											21 05									22 05		
Doncaster		d				19 22	19 50		20 12					20 26			21 17				21 22				22 18	
Bentley (S.Yorks)		d				19 25								20 29							21 25					
Adwick		a				19 29								20 33							21 29					
		d				19 29								20 33							21 29					
South Elmsall		d				19 35								20 39							21 35					
Fitzwilliam		d		20 07		19 48								20 44	21 11						21 42			22 11		
Sandal & Agbrigg		d		20 13		19 53		←						20 50	21 17						21 48			22 17		
Wakefield Westgate	32,39	a		20 17	19 49	19 57	20 07	20 17	20 32				20 48	20 54	21 22		21 34			21 49	21 52		21 59	22 21	22 35	22 44
		d		20 17	19 50	19 58	20 07	20 17	20 33				20 49	20 54	21 22		21 34			21 50	21 53	21 57	22 00	22 21	22 35	22 45
Pontefract Monkhill	32	d		→												21 05										
Wakefield Kirkgate	32,34,39	a	19 58							20 28	20 49	20 57				21 30			21 52			22 00				
		d	19 58							20 28	20 50	20 58							21 52							
Outwood		d				20 02		20 22						20 59	21 27						21 58			22 26		
Leeds	32,34	a	20 20		20 05	20 16	20 25	20 38	20 47	20 48	21 26	21 20	21 03	21 18	21 47		21 50		22 29	22 02	22 17		22 19	22 45	22 54	23 04

Table 31

Saturdays
30 June to 8 September

Sheffield, Doncaster and Wakefield - Leeds

Network Diagram - see first page of Table 31

Station			NT	NT	NT	XC	NT	NT	GR
Sheffield	29 ⇌	d			22 24	22 27			
Meadowhall	29 ⇌	d			22 30				
Rotherham Central	29	d			22 36				
Swinton (S.Yorks)	29	d			22 45				
Bolton-upon-Dearne		d			22 49				
Goldthorpe		d			22 52				
Thurnscoe		d			22 55				
Moorthorpe		d			23 00				
Doncaster		d	22 26			22 53			23 48
Bentley (S.Yorks)		d	22 29						
Adwick		a	22 33						
		d	22 33						
South Elmsall		d	22 39						
Fitzwilliam		d	22 44		23 07				
Sandal & Agbrigg		d	22 50		23 13			←	
Wakefield Westgate	32,39	a	22 54		23 18	23 10		23 18	00 05
		d	22 54	23 04	23 18	23 11		23 18	00 05
Pontefract Monkhill	32	d			→				
Wakefield Kirkgate	32,34,39	a		23 07					
		d					22 51		
Outwood		d	22 59					23 23	
Leeds	32,34	a	23 14			23 27	23 30	23 40	00 24

Saturdays
from 15 September

Station			GR	NT	NT	NT	NT	NT	NT	NT	NT	NT	XC	NT	NT	NT	NT		NT	NT	NT	XC	NT	GR	NT	NT
Sheffield	29 ⇌	d		23p15			06 06	06 12	06 28		06 52	07 06	07 12		07 14	07 51	08 06			08 14	08 18	08 21				08 51
Meadowhall	29 ⇌	d		23p21			06 12	06 18	06 34		06 58	07 12			07 21	07 57	08 12			08 22	08 25					08 57
Rotherham Central	29	d		23p27				06 24	06 40		07 04				07 27					08 28						
Swinton (S.Yorks)	29	d		23p36				06 35	06 51		07 15				07 33					08 37						
Bolton-upon-Dearne		d		23p41					06 56						07 38					08 42						
Goldthorpe		d		23p44					06 58						07 40					08 44						
Thurnscoe		d		23p47					07 01						07 43					08 47						
Moorthorpe		d		23p52					07 06						07 52					08 53						
Doncaster		d	23p32			06 26		06 55		07 26	07 34								08 16				08 26	08 50		
Bentley (S.Yorks)		d				06 29		06 58		07 29	07 37								08 19				08 29			
Adwick		a				06 33		07 05		07 33	07 43								08 23				08 33			
		d				06 33				07 33													08 33			
South Elmsall		d				06 39				07 39													08 39			
Fitzwilliam		d				06 44			07 12	07 44					07 58					09 09			08 45			
Sandal & Agbrigg		d				06 50			07 18	07 50				←	08 04					09 15			08 49		←	
Wakefield Westgate	32,39	a	23p53			06 54			07 22	07 54			07 36	07 54	08 10					09 19		08 45	08 54	09 08	09 19	
		d	23p53		06 24	06 54			07 23	07 54			07 37	07 54	08 11					09 19		08 46	08 55	09 08	09 19	
Pontefract Monkhill	32	d								→										→						
Wakefield Kirkgate	32,34,39	a			06 29		06 49					07 49				08 27	08 49				08 57					09 27
		d					06 50					07 50				08 28	08 50				08 58					09 28
Outwood		d				06 59			07 28					07 59	08 16								08 58		09 24	
Leeds	32,34	a	00 11	00 30		07 13	07 28		07 44			08 25	07 52	08 14	08 32	08 49	09 25				09 20	09 03	09 14	09 25	09 40	09 49

Station			NT	NT	NT	NT	NT	NT	XC		NT	NT	GR	NT	NT	NT	NT	NT	NT	NT	XC	NT	GR	NT	NT	
Sheffield	29 ⇌	d			08 53	09 06	09 14	09 18	09 21			09 29			09 50		09 53	10 06	10 14	10 18	10 21				10 50	
Meadowhall	29 ⇌	d			09 00	09 12	09 21	09 24				09 35			09 56		09 59	10 12	10 21	10 24					10 56	
Rotherham Central	29	d			09 06		09 27					09 42					10 05		10 27							
Swinton (S.Yorks)	29	d			09 16		09 36					09 51					10 15		10 36							
Bolton-upon-Dearne		d					09 41												10 41							
Goldthorpe		d					09 43												10 43							
Thurnscoe		d					09 46												10 46							
Moorthorpe		d					09 53					10a01							10 53							
Doncaster		d	08 54	09 26	09 34								09 50			10 26	10 34						10 50			
Bentley (S.Yorks)		d	08 57	09 29	09 37											10 29	10 37									
Adwick		a	09 04	09 33	09 43											10 33	10 43									
		d		09 33												10 33										
South Elmsall		d		09 39												10 39										
Fitzwilliam		d		09 45			10 09									10 45			11 09							
Sandal & Agbrigg		d		09 49			10 15				←			←		10 49			11 15			←		←		
Wakefield Westgate	32,39	a		09 54			10 19		09 46		09 54		10 07	10 19		10 54			11 19		10 46	10 54	11 07	11 19		
		d		09 55			10 19		09 47		09 55		10 07	10 19		10 55			11 19		10 47	10 55	11 07	11 19		
Pontefract Monkhill	32	d		→			→									→			→							
Wakefield Kirkgate	32,34,39	a				09 49		09 57							10 27			10 49		10 57					11 27	
		d				09 50		09 58							10 28			10 50		10 58					11 28	
Outwood		d									09 58			10 24								10 58		11 24		
Leeds	32,34	a				10 25		10 18	10 02		10 14		10 26	10 40	10 48			11 25		11 18	11 02	11 14	11 26	11 40	11 48	

Sheffield, Doncaster and Wakefield - Leeds

Network Diagram - see first page of Table 31

			NT	NT	NT	NT	NT	XC	NT	GR	NT	NT	GC	NT
								◇1		R 1			R 1	
Sheffield 7	29	d		10 53	11 06	11 14	11 18	11 21				11 50		
Meadowhall	29	d		10 59	11 12	11 21	11 24					11 56		
Rotherham Central	29	d		11 05		11 27								
Swinton (S.Yorks)	29	d		11 16		11 36								
Bolton-upon-Dearne		d				11 41								
Goldthorpe		d				11 43								
Thurnscoe		d				11 46								
Moorthorpe		d				11 53								
Doncaster 7		d	11 26	11 34						11 50			12 20	12 26
Bentley (S.Yorks)		d	11 29	11 37										12 29
Adwick		a	11 33	11 43										12 33
		d	11 33											12 33
South Elmsall		d	11 39											12 39
Fitzwilliam		d	11 45			12 09								12 45
Sandal & Agbrigg		d	11 49			12 15			←		←			12 49
Wakefield Westgate 7	32,39	a	11 54			12 19		11 46	11 54	12 07	12 19			12 54
		d	11 55			12 19		11 47	11 55	12 07	12 19			12 55
Pontefract Monkhill	32	d	→			→								→
Wakefield Kirkgate 4	32,34,39	a			11 49		11 57					12 27	12 42	
		d			11 50		11 58					12 28		
Outwood		d							11 58		12 24			
Leeds 10	32,34	a			12 25		12 18	12 02	12 14	12 26	12 40	12 48		

			NT	NT	NT		NT	XC	NT	GR	NT	NT	GR	NT
								◇1		R 1			R 1	
Sheffield 7	29	d	11 53	12 06	12 14		12 18	12 21				12 50		
Meadowhall	29	d	11 59	12 12	12 21		12 24					12 56		
Rotherham Central	29	d	12 05		12 27									
Swinton (S.Yorks)	29	d	12 16		12 36									
Bolton-upon-Dearne		d			12 41									
Goldthorpe		d			12 43									
Thurnscoe		d			12 46									
Moorthorpe		d			12 53									
Doncaster 7		d	12 34							12 50			13 13	13 26
Bentley (S.Yorks)		d	12 37											13 29
Adwick		a	12 43											13 33
		d												13 33
South Elmsall		d												13 39
Fitzwilliam		d			13 09									13 45
Sandal & Agbrigg		d			13 15				←		←			13 49
Wakefield Westgate 7	32,39	a			13 19			12 46	12 54	13 07	13 19		13 30	13 54
		d			13 19			12 47	12 55	13 07	13 19		13 31	13 55
Pontefract Monkhill	32	d			→									→
Wakefield Kirkgate 4	32,34,39	a		12 49			12 57					13 27		
		d		12 50			12 58					13 28		
Outwood		d							12 58		13 24			
Leeds 10	32,34	a		13 25			13 18	13 02	13 13	13 26	13 43	13 49	13 49	

			NT	NT	NT	NT	XC	NT	NT		GR	NT	NT	NT
							◇1				R 1			
Sheffield 7	29	d	12 53	13 06	13 14	13 18	13 21		13 29				13 50	
Meadowhall	29	d	12 59	13 12	13 21	13 24			13 35				13 56	
Rotherham Central	29	d	13 05		13 27				13 41					
Swinton (S.Yorks)	29	d	13 16		13 36				13 50					
Bolton-upon-Dearne		d			13 41									
Goldthorpe		d			13 43									
Thurnscoe		d			13 46									
Moorthorpe		d			13 53				14a01					
Doncaster 7		d	13 34								13 53			14 26
Bentley (S.Yorks)		d	13 37											14 29
Adwick		a	13 43											14 33
		d												14 33
South Elmsall		d												14 39
Fitzwilliam		d			14 09									14 45
Sandal & Agbrigg		d			14 15			←				←		14 49
Wakefield Westgate 7	32,39	a			14 19		13 46	13 54			14 11	14 19		14 54
		d			14 19		13 47	13 55			14 12	14 19		14 55
Pontefract Monkhill	32	d			→									→
Wakefield Kirkgate 4	32,34,39	a		13 50		13 57							14 27	
		d		13 50		13 58							14 28	
Outwood		d						13 58				14 24		
Leeds 10	32,34	a		14 25		14 18	14 02	14 14			14 30	14 40	14 48	

			NT	NT	NT	NT	XC	NT	GR	NT	NT	NT	NT	
							◇1		R 1					
Sheffield 7	29	d	13 53	14 06	14 14	14 18	14 21				14 50		14 53	
Meadowhall	29	d	13 59	14 12	14 21	14 24					14 56		14 59	
Rotherham Central	29	d	14 05		14 27								15 05	
Swinton (S.Yorks)	29	d	14 17		14 36								15 17	
Bolton-upon-Dearne		d			14 41									
Goldthorpe		d			14 43									
Thurnscoe		d			14 46									
Moorthorpe		d			14 53									
Doncaster 7		d	14 34						14 50			15 26	15 34	
Bentley (S.Yorks)		d	14 37									15 29	15 37	
Adwick		a	14 43									15 33	15 43	
		d										15 33		
South Elmsall		d										15 39		
Fitzwilliam		d			15 09							15 45		
Sandal & Agbrigg		d			15 15			←		←		15 49		
Wakefield Westgate 7	32,39	a			15 19		14 46	14 54	15 07	15 19		15 54		
		d			15 19		14 47	14 55	15 07	15 19		15 55		
Pontefract Monkhill	32	d			→							→		
Wakefield Kirkgate 4	32,34,39	a		14 49		14 57					15 27			
		d		14 50		14 58					15 28			
Outwood		d						14 58		15 24				
Leeds 10	32,34	a		15 25		15 18	15 02	15 14	15 26	15 40	15 49			

			NT	NT	NT	XC	NT	GR	NT	NT	NT	NT	NT	NT
						◇1		R 1						
Sheffield 7	29	d	15 06	15 14	15 18	15 21				15 50		15 53	16 06	16 14
Meadowhall	29	d	15 12	15 21	15 24					15 56		15 59	16 12	16 21
Rotherham Central	29	d		15 27								16 05		16 27
Swinton (S.Yorks)	29	d		15 36								16 16		16 36
Bolton-upon-Dearne		d		15 41										16 41
Goldthorpe		d		15 43										16 43
Thurnscoe		d		15 46										16 46
Moorthorpe		d		15 53										16 53
Doncaster 7		d						15 50			16 25	16 34		
Bentley (S.Yorks)		d									16 28	16 37		
Adwick		a									16 32	16 43		
		d									16 32			
South Elmsall		d									16 38			
Fitzwilliam		d		16 09							16 42			17 09
Sandal & Agbrigg		d		16 15			←		←		16 48			17 15
Wakefield Westgate 7	32,39	a		16 19		15 46	15 54	16 07	16 19		16 52			17 19
		d		16 19		15 47	15 55	16 07	16 19		16 52			17 19
Pontefract Monkhill	32	d		→							→			→
Wakefield Kirkgate 4	32,34,39	a	15 49		15 57					16 27			16 49	
		d	15 50		15 58					16 28			16 50	
Outwood		d					15 58		16 24					
Leeds 10	32,34	a	16 25		16 18	16 02	16 13	16 26	16 40	16 49			17 25	

			NT	XC	NT		GR	NT	NT	GC	NT	NT	NT	NT
				◇1			R 1			R 1				
Sheffield 7	29	d	16 18	16 21					16 50			16 53	17 06	17 14
Meadowhall	29	d	16 24						16 56			16 59	17 12	17 21
Rotherham Central	29	d										17 05		17 27
Swinton (S.Yorks)	29	d										17 16		17 37
Bolton-upon-Dearne		d												17 41
Goldthorpe		d												17 44
Thurnscoe		d												17 47
Moorthorpe		d												17 52
Doncaster 7		d					16 50			17 21	17 26	17 34		
Bentley (S.Yorks)		d									17 29	17 37		
Adwick		a									17 33	17 43		
		d									17 33			
South Elmsall		d									17 39			
Fitzwilliam		d									17 45			18 13
Sandal & Agbrigg		d			←			←			17 51			18 19
Wakefield Westgate 7	32,39	a		16 46	16 52		17 07	17 19			17 55			18 23
		d		16 47	16 52		17 07	17 19			17 55			18 23
Pontefract Monkhill	32	d									→			→
Wakefield Kirkgate 4	32,34,39	a	16 57						17 28	17 44			17 49	
		d	16 58						17 28				17 50	
Outwood		d			16 59			17 24						
Leeds 10	32,34	a	17 18	17 02	17 13		17 26	17 41	17 48				18 25	

Sheffield, Doncaster and Wakefield - Leeds

Network Diagram - see first page of Table 31

			NT	XC	NT	GR	XC	NT	NT		NT	NT	NT	XC
				◇1		R 1	◇1							◇1
Sheffield 7	29	d	17 18	17 21			17 47		17 50		18 06	18 13	18 18	18 21
Meadowhall	29	d	17 24						17 56		18 12	18 21	18 24	
Rotherham Central	29	d										18 27		
Swinton (S.Yorks)	29	d										18 37		
Bolton-upon-Dearne		d										18 41		
Goldthorpe		d										18 44		
Thurnscoe		d										18 47		
Moorthorpe		d										18 53		
Doncaster 7		d				17 50								
Bentley (S.Yorks)		d												
Adwick		a												
		d												
South Elmsall		d												
Fitzwilliam		d										19 09		
Sandal & Agbrigg		d			←			←				19 15		
Wakefield Westgate 7	32,39	a		17 47	17 55	18 07	18 12	18 23				19 19		18 46
		d		17 47	17 55	18 07	18 13	18 23				19 19		18 47
Pontefract Monkhill	32	d										→		
Wakefield Kirkgate 4	32,34,39	a	17 57						18 28		18 50		18 59	
		d	17 58						18 32		18 50		18 59	
Outwood		d			18 00			18 28						
Leeds 10	32,34	a	18 18	18 02	18 14	18 26	18 31	18 44	18 51		19 27		19 23	19 01

			NT	GR	NT	GR	NT	NT	NT	NT	XC	NT	GR	
				R 1		R 1					◇1		R 1	
Sheffield 7	29	d					18 50	19 06	19 16	19 18	19 22			
Meadowhall	29	d					18 56	19 12	19 22	19 25				
Rotherham Central	29	d								19 31				
Swinton (S.Yorks)	29	d								19 40				
Bolton-upon-Dearne		d								19 44				
Goldthorpe		d								19 47				
Thurnscoe		d								19 50				
Moorthorpe		d								20 01				
Doncaster 7		d	18 26	18 50		19 14						19 22	19 50	
Bentley (S.Yorks)		d	18 29									19 25		
Adwick		a	18 33									19 29		
		d	18 33									19 29		
South Elmsall		d	18 39									19 35		
Fitzwilliam		d	18 44							20 07		19 48		
Sandal & Agbrigg		d	18 50		←					20 13		19 53		
Wakefield Westgate 7	32,39	a	18 53	19 07	19 19	19 32				20 17	19 49	19 57	20 07	
		d	18 54	19 07	19 19	19 33				20 17	19 50	19 58	20 07	
Pontefract Monkhill	32	d								→				
Wakefield Kirkgate 4	32,34,39	a					19 29	19 50	19 58					
		d					19 32	19 50	19 58					
Outwood		d	18 57		19 24							20 02		
Leeds 10	32,34	a	19 14	19 25	19 43	19 48	19 55	20 26	20 20		20 05	20 16	20 25	

			NT	GR	NT	NT	NT	XC	NT	NT	GR	NT	XC	NT
				R 1				◇1			R 1		◇1	
Sheffield 7	29	d			19 51	20 06	20 18	20 24		20 27		21 06	21 21	
Meadowhall	29	d			19 57	20 12	20 24			20 35		21 12		
Rotherham Central	29	d								20 41				
Swinton (S.Yorks)	29	d								20 50				
Bolton-upon-Dearne		d								20 55				
Goldthorpe		d								20 57				
Thurnscoe		d								21 00				
Moorthorpe		d								21 05				
Doncaster 7		d		20 12					20 26		21 17			21 22
Bentley (S.Yorks)		d							20 29					21 25
Adwick		a							20 33					21 29
		d							20 33					21 29
South Elmsall		d							20 39					21 35
Fitzwilliam		d							20 44	21 11				21 42
Sandal & Agbrigg		d	←						20 50	21 17				21 48
Wakefield Westgate 7	32,39	a	20 17	20 32				20 48	20 54	21 22	21 34		21 48	21 52
		d	20 17	20 33				20 49	20 54	21 22	21 34		21 49	21 53
Pontefract Monkhill	32	d												
Wakefield Kirkgate 4	32,34,39	a			20 28	20 49	20 57					21 52		
		d			20 28	20 50	20 58					21 52		
Outwood		d	20 22						20 59	21 27				21 58
Leeds 10	32,34	a	20 38	20 47	20 48	21 26	21 20	21 03	21 18	21 47	21 50	22 29	22 02	22 17

			NT	EM	NT		GR	EM	NT	NT	NT	XC	NT	NT
				◇1			R 1	◇1				◇1		
Sheffield 7	29	d		21 25	21 30			22 19			22 24	22 27		
Meadowhall	29	d			21 36						22 30			
Rotherham Central	29	d			21 42						22 36			
Swinton (S.Yorks)	29	d			21 50						22 45			
Bolton-upon-Dearne		d			21 54						22 49			
Goldthorpe		d			21 57						22 52			
Thurnscoe		d			22 00						22 55			
Moorthorpe		d			22 05						23 00			
Doncaster 7		d					22 18		22 26			22 53		
Bentley (S.Yorks)		d							22 29					
Adwick		a							22 33					
		d							22 33					
South Elmsall		d							22 39					
Fitzwilliam		d			22 11				22 44		23 07			
Sandal & Agbrigg		d			22 17				22 50		23 13			←
Wakefield Westgate 7	32,39	a		21 59	22 21		22 35	22 44	22 54		23 18	23 10		23 18
		d	21 57	22 00	22 21		22 35	22 45	22 54	23 04	23 18	23 11		23 18
Pontefract Monkhill	32	d									→			
Wakefield Kirkgate 4	32,34,39	a	22 00							23 07				
		d											22 51	
Outwood		d			22 26				22 59					23 23
Leeds 10	32,34	a		22 19	22 45		22 54	23 04	23 14			23 27	23 30	23 40

			GR
			R 1
Sheffield 7	29	d	
Meadowhall	29	d	
Rotherham Central	29	d	
Swinton (S.Yorks)	29	d	
Bolton-upon-Dearne		d	
Goldthorpe		d	
Thurnscoe		d	
Moorthorpe		d	
Doncaster 7		d	23 48
Bentley (S.Yorks)		d	
Adwick		a	
		d	
South Elmsall		d	
Fitzwilliam		d	
Sandal & Agbrigg		d	
Wakefield Westgate 7	32,39	a	00 05
		d	00 05
Pontefract Monkhill	32	d	
Wakefield Kirkgate 4	32,34,39	a	
		d	
Outwood		d	
Leeds 10	32,34	a	00 24

Sheffield, Doncaster and Wakefield - Leeds

Sundays until 24 June

Network Diagram - see first page of Table 31

	GR	NT	NT	NT	XC	NT	XC	GR	NT	NT	NT	XC	GR	NT	NT		XC	GR	NT	NT	GC	NT	XC	GR
Sheffield 29 d			08 39	09 17	09 21	09 36	10 21			10 39	11 17	11 21		11 36	12 16		12 21			12 39		13 17	13 21	
Meadowhall 29 d			08 45	09 23		09 42				10 45	11 23			11 42	12 23					12 45		13 23		
Rotherham Central 29 d						09 48								11 49										
Swinton (S.Yorks) 29 d						09 58								12 00										
Bolton-upon-Dearne d						10 03								12 04										
Goldthorpe d						10 05								12 07										
Thurnscoe d						10 08								12 10										
Moorthorpe d						10 13								12 15										
Doncaster d	23p48	09 12						10 50	11 12				11 48					12 50	13 12		13 17			13 48
Bentley (S.Yorks) d		09 15							11 15										13 15					
Adwick a		09 19							11 19										13 19					
Adwick d		09 19							11 19										13 19					
South Elmsall d		09 25							11 25										13 25					
Fitzwilliam d		09 30				10 19			11 30					12 21					13 30					
Sandal & Agbrigg d		09 36				10 25			11 36					12 27					13 36					
Wakefield Westgate 32,39 a	00 05	09 40			09 44	10 29	10 44	11 08	11 40			11 44	12 06	12 31			12 44	13 08	13 40				13 45	14 06
Wakefield Westgate d	00 05	09 40			09 45	10 30	10 45	11 08	11 40			11 45	12 06	12 31			12 45	13 08	13 40				13 46	14 06
Pontefract Monkhill 32 d																								
Wakefield Kirkgate 32,34,39 a			09 29	09 55						11 29	11 53				12 52					13 29	13 45	13 52		
Wakefield Kirkgate d			09 30	09 55						11 30	11 53				12 53					13 30		13 53		
Outwood d		09 45				10 35			11 45					12 36					13 45					
Leeds 32,34 a	00 24	09 59	10 04	10 15	10 02	10 52	11 02	11 29	11 59	12 05	12 19	12 01	12 28	12 53	13 18		13 02	13 29	13 59	14 04		14 18	14 02	14 28

	NT	NT	XC	GR	NT	NT	NT		XC	GR	NT	NT	XC	NT	GR	NT	NT	GC	NT	XC	EM	GR	NT
Sheffield 29 d	13 36	14 17	14 21			14 39	15 17		15 21		15 36	16 17	16 21	16 36			16 39		17 17	17 21	17 34		17 36
Meadowhall 29 d	13 42	14 23				14 45	15 23				15 42	16 23		16 42			16 45		17 23				17 44
Rotherham Central 29 d	13 49										15 50			16 49									17 50
Swinton (S.Yorks) 29 d	13 57										15 58			16 58									17 58
Bolton-upon-Dearne d	14 01										16 03			17 02									18 03
Goldthorpe d	14 04										16 05			17 05									18 05
Thurnscoe d	14 07										16 08			17 08									18 08
Moorthorpe d	14 12										16 13			17a13									18 13
Doncaster d				14 50	15 12					15 50					16 59	17 14		17 20				17 49	
Bentley (S.Yorks) d					15 15											17 17							
Adwick a					15 19											17 21							
Adwick d					15 19											17 21							
South Elmsall d					15 25											17 27							
Fitzwilliam d	14 17				15 30						16 19					17 32							18 19
Sandal & Agbrigg d	14 23				15 36						16 25					17 38							18 25
Wakefield Westgate 32,39 a	14 27		14 44	15 08	15 40				15 44	16 08	16 29		16 44		17 17	17 42				17 47	18 06	18 12	18 29
Wakefield Westgate d	14 28		14 45	15 08	15 40				15 45	16 08	16 29		16 45		17 17	17 42				17 47	18 07	18 12	18 30
Pontefract Monkhill 32 d																							
Wakefield Kirkgate 32,34,39 a		14 52				15 29	15 52					16 52					17 29	17 47	17 52				
Wakefield Kirkgate d		14 53				15 30	15 53					16 53					17 30		17 53				
Outwood d	14 33				15 45						16 34					17 47							18 35
Leeds 32,34 a	14 47	15 18	15 02	15 29	15 59	16 04	16 18		16 02	16 28	16 54	17 18	17 02		17 38	18 01	18 05		18 18	18 02	18 24	18 30	18 50

	XC	GR	NT	XC	GR	GR	NT	NT	NT	XC	NT	GR	NT	GR	NT		XC	GR	GC	NT	EM	GR	XC	GR
Sheffield 29 d	17 51		18 17	18 21			18 39	18 57	19 16	19 21			19 36		20 17		20 21			20 39	21 03		21 21	
Meadowhall 29 d			18 23				18 45	19 05	19 23				19 42		20 23					20 45				
Rotherham Central 29 d								19 11					19 49											
Swinton (S.Yorks) 29 d								19 19					19 57											
Bolton-upon-Dearne d													20 02											
Goldthorpe d													20 04											
Thurnscoe d													20 07											
Moorthorpe d								19a29					20 12											
Doncaster d	18 15	18 19			18 49	19 14					19 27	19 50		20 19				20 47	21 01			21 18		21 48
Bentley (S.Yorks) d											19 30													
Adwick a											19 34													
Adwick d											19 34													
South Elmsall d											19 41													
Fitzwilliam d											19 47		20 18											
Sandal & Agbrigg d											19 53		20 24											
Wakefield Westgate 32,39 a	18 33	18 38		18 47	19 07	19 32				19 48	19 57	20 09	20 28	20 38			20 46	21 05			21 27	21 36	21 47	22 06
Wakefield Westgate d	18 34	18 38		18 48	19 07	19 32				19 49	19 57	20 09	20 28	20 38			20 47	21 05			21 28	21 36	21 48	22 06
Pontefract Monkhill 32 d																								
Wakefield Kirkgate 32,34,39 a			18 52				19 29		19 52						20 52				21 22	21 29				
Wakefield Kirkgate d			18 53				19 30		19 53						20 53					21 30				
Outwood d											20 02		20 33											
Leeds 32,34 a	18 51	18 57	19 18	19 04	19 27	19 52	20 05		20 18	20 05	20 16	20 25	20 52	20 55	21 16		21 03	21 28		22 04	21 44	21 56	22 04	22 25

Sheffield, Doncaster and Wakefield - Leeds

Sundays until 24 June

Network Diagram - see first page of Table 31

	NT	NT	GR	XC	NT	GR	EM
Sheffield 29 d		21 36		22 21	22 39		23 30
Meadowhall 29 d		21 42			22 45		
Rotherham Central 29 d		21 48					
Swinton (S.Yorks) 29 d		21 56					
Bolton-upon-Dearne d		22 00					
Goldthorpe d		22 03					
Thurnscoe d		22 06					
Moorthorpe d		22 11					
Doncaster d	21 52		22 23			23 36	
Bentley (S.Yorks) d	21 55						
Adwick a	21 59						
Adwick d	21 59						
South Elmsall d	22 05						
Fitzwilliam d	22 12	22 17					
Sandal & Agbrigg d	22 18	22 23					
Wakefield Westgate 32,39 a	22 22	22 27	22 40	22 43		23 56	00 01
Wakefield Westgate d	22 23	22 28	22 40	22 43		23 56	00 02
Pontefract Monkhill 32 d							
Wakefield Kirkgate 32,34,39 a					23 26		
Wakefield Kirkgate d					23 27		
Outwood d	22 28	22 33					
Leeds 32,34 a	22 41	22 52	22 59	23 01	00 05	00 14	00 18

Sundays 1 July to 9 September

	GR	GR	GR	NT	NT	NT	XC	NT	GR	NT	NT	NT	XC	GR	NT		NT	XC	GR	NT	NT	GC	NT	XC
		A	A																					
Sheffield 29 d					08 39	09 17	09 21	09 36			10 39	11 17	11 21		11 36		12 16	12 21			12 39		13 17	13 21
Meadowhall 29 d					08 45	09 23		09 42			10 45	11 23			11 42		12 23				12 45		13 23	
Rotherham Central 29 d								09 48							11 49									
Swinton (S.Yorks) 29 d								09 58							12 00									
Bolton-upon-Dearne d								10 03							12 04									
Goldthorpe d								10 05							12 07									
Thurnscoe d								10 08							12 10									
Moorthorpe d								10 13							12 15									
Doncaster d	23p48	01 48	02 35	09 12					10 50	11 12				11 48					12 50	13 12		13 17		
Bentley (S.Yorks) d				09 15						11 15										13 15				
Adwick a				09 19						11 19										13 19				
Adwick d				09 19						11 19										13 19				
South Elmsall d				09 25						11 25										13 25				
Fitzwilliam d				09 30				10 19		11 30					12 21					13 30				
Sandal & Agbrigg d				09 36				10 25		11 36					12 27					13 36				
Wakefield Westgate 32,39 a	00 05	02s06	02s53	09 40			09 44	10 29	11 08	11 40			11 44	12 06	12 31			12 44	13 08	13 40				13 45
Wakefield Westgate d	00 05			09 40			09 45	10 30	11 08	11 40			11 45	12 06	12 31			12 45	13 08	13 40				13 46
Pontefract Monkhill 32 d																								
Wakefield Kirkgate 32,34,39 a					09 29	09 55					11 29	11 53					12 52				13 29	13 45	13 52	
Wakefield Kirkgate d					09 30	09 55					11 30	11 53					12 53				13 30		13 53	
Outwood d				09 45				10 35		11 45					12 36					13 45				
Leeds 32,34 a	00 24	02 23	03 10	09 59	10 04	10 15	10 02	10 52	11 29	11 59	12 05	12 19	12 01	12 28	12 53		13 18	13 02	13 29	13 59	14 04		14 18	14 02

	GR	NT	NT	XC	GR	NT	NT		NT	XC	GR	NT	NT	XC	NT	GR	NT	NT	GC	NT	XC	EM	GR
Sheffield 29 d		13 36	14 17	14 21			14 39		15 17	15 21		15 36	16 17	16 21	16 36			16 39		17 17	17 21	17 34	
Meadowhall 29 d		13 42	14 23				14 45		15 23			15 42	16 23		16 42			16 45		17 23			
Rotherham Central 29 d		13 49										15 50			16 49								
Swinton (S.Yorks) 29 d		13 57										15 58			16 58								
Bolton-upon-Dearne d		14 01										16 02			17 02								
Goldthorpe d		14 04										16 05			17 05								
Thurnscoe d		14 07										16 08			17 08								
Moorthorpe d		14 12										16 13			17a13								
Doncaster d	13 48				14 50	15 12					15 50					16 59	17 14		17 20				17 49
Bentley (S.Yorks) d						15 15											17 17						
Adwick a						15 19											17 21						
Adwick d						15 19											17 21						
South Elmsall d						15 25											17 27						
Fitzwilliam d		14 17				15 30						16 19					17 32						
Sandal & Agbrigg d		14 23				15 36						16 25					17 38						
Wakefield Westgate 32,39 a	14 06	14 27		14 44	15 08	15 40				15 44	16 08	16 29		16 44		17 17	17 42				17 47	18 05	18 12
Wakefield Westgate d	14 06	14 28		14 45	15 08	15 40				15 45	16 08	16 29		16 45		17 17	17 42				17 47	18 06	18 12
Pontefract Monkhill 32 d																							
Wakefield Kirkgate 32,34,39 a			14 52				15 29		15 52				16 52					17 29	17 47	17 52			
Wakefield Kirkgate d			14 53				15 30		15 53				16 53					17 30		17 53			
Outwood d		14 33				15 45						16 34					17 47						
Leeds 32,34 a	14 28	14 47	15 18	15 02	15 29	15 59	16 04		16 18	16 02	16 28	16 54	17 18	17 02		17 38	18 01	18 05		18 18	18 02	18 24	18 30

A 29 July, 5 August, 12 August, 2 September, 9 September

Sheffield, Doncaster and Wakefield - Leeds

Network Diagram - see first page of Table 31

1 July to 9 September

			NT	XC	GR	NT	XC	GR	GR	NT	NT	NT	XC	NT	GR	NT	GR		NT	XC	GR	GC	NT	EM	GR	XC
Sheffield 7	29	d	17 36	17 51		18 17	18 21			18 39	18 57	19 16	19 21			19 36			20 17	20 21			20 39	20 45		21 21
Meadowhall	29	d	17 44			18 23				18 45	19 05	19 23				19 42			20 23				20 45			
Rotherham Central	29	d	17 50								19 11					19 49										
Swinton (S.Yorks)	29	d	17 58								19 19					19 57										
Bolton-upon-Dearne		d	18 03													20 02										
Goldthorpe		d	18 05													20 04										
Thurnscoe		d	18 08													20 07										
Moorthorpe		d	18 13								19a29					20 12										
Doncaster 7		d		18 15	18 19			18 49	19 14					19 27	19 50		20 19				20 47	21 01			21 18	
Bentley (S.Yorks)		d												19 30												
Adwick		a												19 34												
		d												19 34												
South Elmsall		d												19 41												
Fitzwilliam		d	18 19											19 47		20 18										
Sandal & Agbrigg		d	18 25											19 53		20 24										
Wakefield Westgate 7	32,39	a	18 29	18 33	18 38		18 47	19 07	19 32				19 48	19 57	20 09	20 28	20 38			20 46	21 05			21 10	21 36	21 47
		d	18 30	18 34	18 38		18 48	19 07	19 32				19 49	19 57	20 09	20 28	20 38			20 47	21 05			21 11	21 36	21 48
Pontefract Monkhill	32	d																								
Wakefield Kirkgate 4	32,34,39	a				18 52				19 29		19 52							20 52			21 22	21 29			
		d				18 53				19 30		19 53							20 53				21 30			
Outwood		d	18 35											20 02		20 33										
Leeds 10	32,34	a	18 50	18 51	18 57	19 18	19 04	19 27	19 52	20 05		20 18	20 05	20 16	20 25	20 52	20 55		21 16	21 03	21 28		22 04	21 30	21 56	22 04

			GR	NT	NT	GR	XC	NT	EM		GR
Sheffield 7	29	d			21 36		22 21	22 39	23 12		
Meadowhall	29	d			21 42			22 45			
Rotherham Central	29	d			21 48						
Swinton (S.Yorks)	29	d			21 56						
Bolton-upon-Dearne		d			22 00						
Goldthorpe		d			22 03						
Thurnscoe		d			22 06						
Moorthorpe		d			22 11						
Doncaster 7		d	21 48	21 52		22 23					23 36
Bentley (S.Yorks)		d		21 55							
Adwick		a		21 59							
		d		21 59							
South Elmsall		d		22 05							
Fitzwilliam		d		22 12	22 17						
Sandal & Agbrigg		d		22 18	22 23						
Wakefield Westgate 7	32,39	a	22 06	22 22	22 27	22 40	22 43		23 36		23 56
		d	22 06	22 23	22 28	22 40	22 43		23 37		23 56
Pontefract Monkhill	32	d									
Wakefield Kirkgate 4	32,34,39	a						23 26			
		d						23 27			
Outwood		d		22 28	22 33						
Leeds 10	32,34	a	22 25	22 41	22 52	22 59	23 01	00 05	23 53		00 14

Sundays

16 September to 21 October

			GR	NT	NT	NT	XC	NT	XC	GR	NT	NT	NT	XC	GR	NT	NT		XC	GR	NT	NT	GC	NT	XC	GR
Sheffield 7	29	d			08 39	09 17	09 21	09 36	10 21			10 39	11 17	11 21		11 36	12 16		12 21			12 39		13 17	13 21	
Meadowhall	29	d			08 45	09 23		09 42				10 45	11 23			11 42	12 23					12 45		13 23		
Rotherham Central	29	d						09 48								11 49										
Swinton (S.Yorks)	29	d						09 58								12 00										
Bolton-upon-Dearne		d						10 03								12 04										
Goldthorpe		d						10 05								12 07										
Thurnscoe		d						10 08								12 10										
Moorthorpe		d						10 13								12 15										
Doncaster 7		d	23p48	09 12						10 50	11 12				11 48					12 50	13 12		13 17			13 48
Bentley (S.Yorks)		d		09 15							11 15										13 15					
Adwick		a		09 19							11 19										13 19					
		d		09 19							11 19										13 19					
South Elmsall		d		09 25							11 25										13 25					
Fitzwilliam		d		09 30				10 19			11 30					12 21					13 30					
Sandal & Agbrigg		d		09 36				10 25			11 36					12 27					13 36					
Wakefield Westgate 7	32,39	a	00 05	09 40			09 44	10 29	10 44	11 08	11 40			11 44	12 06	12 31			12 44	13 08	13 40				13 45	14 06
		d	00 05	09 40			09 45	10 30	10 45	11 08	11 40			11 45	12 06	12 31			12 45	13 08	13 40				13 46	14 06
Pontefract Monkhill	32	d																								
Wakefield Kirkgate 4	32,34,39	a			09 29	09 55						11 29	11 53				12 52					13 29	13 45	13 52		
		d			09 30	09 55						11 30	11 53				12 53					13 30		13 53		
Outwood		d		09 45				10 35			11 45					12 36					13 45					
Leeds 10	32,34	a	00 24	09 59	10 04	10 15	10 02	10 52	11 02	11 29	11 59	12 05	12 19	12 01	12 28	12 53	13 18		13 02	13 29	13 59	14 04		14 18	14 02	14 28

Sheffield, Doncaster and Wakefield - Leeds

Network Diagram - see first page of Table 31

16 September to 21 October

			NT	NT	XC	GR	NT	NT	NT		XC	GR	NT	NT	XC	NT	GR	NT	NT	GC	NT	XC	EM	GR	NT
Sheffield 7	29	d	13 36	14 17	14 21			14 39	15 17		15 21		15 36	16 17	16 21	16 36			16 39		17 17	17 21	17 34		17 36
Meadowhall	29	d	13 42	14 23				14 45	15 23				15 42	16 23		16 42			16 45		17 23				17 44
Rotherham Central	29	d	13 49										15 50			16 49									17 50
Swinton (S.Yorks)	29	d	13 57										15 58			16 58									17 58
Bolton-upon-Dearne		d	14 01										16 03			17 02									18 03
Goldthorpe		d	14 04										16 05			17 05									18 05
Thurnscoe		d	14 07										16 08			17 08									18 08
Moorthorpe		d	14 12										16 13			17a13									18 13
Doncaster 7		d				14 50	15 12					15 50					16 59	17 14		17 20				17 49	
Bentley (S.Yorks)		d					15 15											17 17							
Adwick		a					15 19											17 21							
		d					15 19											17 21							
South Elmsall		d					15 25											17 27							
Fitzwilliam		d	14 17				15 30						16 19					17 32							18 19
Sandal & Agbrigg		d	14 23				15 36						16 25					17 38							18 25
Wakefield Westgate 7	32,39	a	14 27		14 44	15 08	15 40				15 44	16 08	16 29		16 44		17 17	17 42				17 47	18 06	18 12	18 29
		d	14 28		14 45	15 08	15 40				15 45	16 08	16 29		16 45		17 17	17 42				17 47	18 07	18 12	18 30
Pontefract Monkhill	32	d																							
Wakefield Kirkgate 4	32,34,39	a		14 52				15 29	15 52					16 52					17 29	17 47	17 52				
		d		14 53				15 30	15 53					16 53					17 30		17 53				
Outwood		d	14 33				15 45						16 34					17 47							18 35
Leeds 10	32,34	a	14 47	15 18	15 02	15 29	15 59	16 04	16 18		16 02	16 28	16 54	17 18	17 02		17 38	18 01	18 05		18 18	18 02	18 24	18 30	18 50

			XC	GR	NT	XC	GR	GR	NT	NT	NT	XC	NT	GR	NT	GR	NT		XC	GR	GC	NT	EM	GR	XC	GR
Sheffield 7	29	d	17 51		18 17	18 21			18 39	18 57	19 16	19 21			19 36		20 17		20 21			20 39	21 03		21 21	
Meadowhall	29	d			18 23				18 45	19 05	19 23				19 42		20 23					20 45				
Rotherham Central	29	d								19 11					19 49											
Swinton (S.Yorks)	29	d								19 19					19 57											
Bolton-upon-Dearne		d													20 02											
Goldthorpe		d													20 04											
Thurnscoe		d													20 07											
Moorthorpe		d								19a29					20 12											
Doncaster 7		d	18 15	18 19			18 49	19 14					19 27	19 50		20 19				20 47	21 01			21 18		21 48
Bentley (S.Yorks)		d											19 30													
Adwick		a											19 34													
		d											19 34													
South Elmsall		d											19 41													
Fitzwilliam		d											19 47		20 18											
Sandal & Agbrigg		d											19 53		20 24											
Wakefield Westgate 7	32,39	a	18 33	18 38		18 47	19 07	19 32				19 48	19 57	20 09	20 28	20 38			20 46	21 05			21 30	21 36	21 47	22 06
		d	18 34	18 38		18 48	19 07	19 32				19 49	19 57	20 09	20 28	20 38			20 47	21 05			21 31	21 36	21 48	22 06
Pontefract Monkhill	32	d																								
Wakefield Kirkgate 4	32,34,39	a			18 52				19 29		19 52						20 52				21 22	21 29				
		d			18 53				19 30		19 53						20 53					21 30				
Outwood		d											20 02		20 33											
Leeds 10	32,34	a	18 51	18 57	19 18	19 04	19 27	19 52	20 05		20 18	20 05	20 16	20 25	20 52	20 55	21 16		21 03	21 28		22 04	21 44	21 56	22 04	22 25

			NT	NT	GR	XC	NT	EM	GR
Sheffield 7	29	d		21 36		22 21	22 39	23 16	
Meadowhall	29	d		21 42			22 45		
Rotherham Central	29	d		21 48					
Swinton (S.Yorks)	29	d		21 56					
Bolton-upon-Dearne		d		22 00					
Goldthorpe		d		22 03					
Thurnscoe		d		22 06					
Moorthorpe		d		22 11					
Doncaster 7		d	21 52		22 23				23 36
Bentley (S.Yorks)		d	21 55						
Adwick		a	21 59						
		d	21 59						
South Elmsall		d	22 05						
Fitzwilliam		d	22 12	22 17					
Sandal & Agbrigg		d	22 18	22 23					
Wakefield Westgate 7	32,39	a	22 22	22 27	22 40	22 45		23 40	23 56
		d	22 23	22 28	22 40	22 45		23 41	23 56
Pontefract Monkhill	32	d							
Wakefield Kirkgate 4	32,34,39	a					23 26		
		d					23 27		
Outwood		d	22 28	22 33					
Leeds 10	32,34	a	22 41	22 52	22 59	23 03	00 05	00 01	00 14

Sundays
from 28 October

Sheffield, Doncaster and Wakefield - Leeds

Network Diagram - see first page of Table 31

Station			GR	NT	NT	NT	XC	NT	GR	NT	NT	NT	GR	NT	NT	XC	GR		NT	NT	GC	NT	XC	GR	NT	NT
			1			◇	◇1		1				1			◇1	1				1		◇1	1		
Sheffield	29	d			08 39	09 17	09 21	09 36			10 39	11 17		11 36	12 16	12 21				12 39		13 17	13 21		13 36	14 17
Meadowhall	29	d			08 45	09 23		09 42			10 45	11 23		11 42	12 23					12 45		13 23			13 42	14 23
Rotherham Central	29	d						09 48						11 49											13 49	
Swinton (S.Yorks)	29	d						09 58						12 00											13 57	
Bolton-upon-Dearne		d						10 03						12 04											14 01	
Goldthorpe		d						10 05						12 07											14 04	
Thurnscoe		d						10 08						12 10											14 07	
Moorthorpe		d						10 13						12 15											14 12	
Doncaster		d	23p48	09 12					10 50	11 12			11 48				12 50		13 12		13 17			13 48		
Bentley (S.Yorks)		d		09 15						11 15									13 15							
Adwick		a		09 19						11 19									13 19							
		d		09 19						11 19									13 19							
South Elmsall		d		09 25						11 25									13 25							
Fitzwilliam		d		09 30				10 19		11 30				12 21					13 30						14 17	
Sandal & Agbrigg		d		09 36				10 25		11 36				12 27					13 36						14 23	
Wakefield Westgate	32,39	a	00 05	09 40			09 44	10 29	11 08	11 40			12 06	12 31		12 44	13 08		13 40				13 45	14 06	14 27	
		d	00 05	09 40			09 45	10 30	11 08	11 40			12 06	12 31		12 45	13 08		13 40				13 46	14 06	14 28	
Pontefract Monkhill	32	d																								
Wakefield Kirkgate	32,34,39	a			09 29	09 55					11 29	11 53			12 52					13 29	13 45	13 52				14 52
		d			09 30	09 55					11 30	11 53			12 53					13 30		13 53				14 53
Outwood		d		09 45				10 35		11 45				12 36					13 45						14 33	
Leeds	32,34	a	00 24	09 59	10 04	10 15	10 02	10 52	11 29	11 59	12 05	12 19	12 28	12 53	13 18	13 02	13 29		13 59	14 04		14 18	14 02	14 28	14 47	15 18

Station			XC	GR	NT	NT	NT	XC	GR		NT	NT	XC	GR	NT	NT	GC	NT	XC	EM	GR	NT	XC	GR	NT
			◇1	1				◇1	1				◇1	1			1		◇1	◇1	1		◇1	1	
Sheffield	29	d	14 21			14 39	15 17	15 21			15 36	16 17	16 21			16 39		17 17	17 21	17 34		17 36	17 51		18 17
Meadowhall	29	d				14 45	15 23				15 42	16 23				16 45		17 23				17 44			18 23
Rotherham Central	29	d									15 50											17 50			
Swinton (S.Yorks)	29	d									15 58											17 58			
Bolton-upon-Dearne		d									16 03											18 03			
Goldthorpe		d									16 05											18 05			
Thurnscoe		d									16 08											18 08			
Moorthorpe		d									16 13											18 13			
Doncaster		d		14 50	15 12				15 50					16 59	17 14		17 20				17 49		18 15	18 19	
Bentley (S.Yorks)		d			15 15										17 17										
Adwick		a			15 19										17 21										
		d			15 19										17 21										
South Elmsall		d			15 25										17 27										
Fitzwilliam		d			15 30						16 19				17 32							18 19			
Sandal & Agbrigg		d			15 36						16 25				17 38							18 25			
Wakefield Westgate	32,39	a	14 44	15 08	15 40			15 44	16 08		16 29		16 44	17 17	17 42				17 47	18 06	18 12	18 29	18 33	18 38	
		d	14 45	15 08	15 40			15 45	16 08		16 29		16 45	17 17	17 42				17 47	18 07	18 12	18 30	18 34	18 38	
Pontefract Monkhill	32	d																							
Wakefield Kirkgate	32,34,39	a				15 29	15 52					16 52				17 29	17 47	17 52							18 52
		d				15 30	15 53					16 53				17 30		17 53							18 53
Outwood		d			15 45						16 34				17 47							18 35			
Leeds	32,34	a	15 02	15 29	15 59	16 04	16 18	16 02	16 28		16 54	17 18	17 02	17 38	18 01	18 05		18 18	18 02	18 24	18 30	18 50	18 51	18 57	19 18

Station			XC	GR	GR	NT	NT	XC	NT	GR	NT	GR	NT	XC	GR	GC	NT		EM	GR	XC	GR	NT	NT	GR	XC
			◇1	1	1			◇1		1		1		◇1	1	1			◇1	1	◇1	1			1	◇1
Sheffield	29	d	18 21			18 39	19 16	19 21			19 36		20 17	20 21			20 39		21 03		21 21			21 36		22 21
Meadowhall	29	d				18 45	19 23				19 42		20 23				20 45							21 42		
Rotherham Central	29	d									19 49													21 48		
Swinton (S.Yorks)	29	d									19 57													21 56		
Bolton-upon-Dearne		d									20 02													22 00		
Goldthorpe		d									20 04													22 03		
Thurnscoe		d									20 07													22 06		
Moorthorpe		d									20 12													22 11		
Doncaster		d		18 49	19 14				19 27	19 50		20 19			20 47	21 01				21 18		21 48	21 52		22 23	
Bentley (S.Yorks)		d							19 30														21 55			
Adwick		a							19 34														21 59			
		d							19 34														21 59			
South Elmsall		d							19 41														22 05			
Fitzwilliam		d							19 47		20 18												22 12	22 17		
Sandal & Agbrigg		d							19 53		20 24												22 18	22 23		
Wakefield Westgate	32,39	a	18 47	19 07	19 32			19 48	19 57	20 09	20 28	20 38		20 46	21 05				21 27	21 36	21 47	22 06	22 22	22 27	22 40	22 43
		d	18 48	19 07	19 32			19 49	19 57	20 09	20 28	20 38		20 47	21 05				21 28	21 36	21 48	22 06	22 23	22 28	22 40	22 43
Pontefract Monkhill	32	d																								
Wakefield Kirkgate	32,34,39	a				19 29	19 52						20 52			21 22	21 29									
		d				19 30	19 53						20 53				21 30									
Outwood		d							20 02		20 33												22 28	22 33		
Leeds	32,34	a	19 04	19 27	19 52	20 05	20 18	20 05	20 16	20 25	20 52	20 55	21 16	21 03	21 28		22 04		21 44	21 56	22 04	22 25	22 41	22 51	22 59	23 01

Table 31

Sundays
from 28 October

Sheffield, Doncaster and Wakefield - Leeds

Network Diagram - see first page of Table 31

Station			NT	EM	GR
				◇1	1
Sheffield	29	d	22 39	23 16	
Meadowhall	29	d	22 45		
Rotherham Central	29	d			
Swinton (S.Yorks)	29	d			
Bolton-upon-Dearne		d			
Goldthorpe		d			
Thurnscoe		d			
Moorthorpe		d			
Doncaster		d			23 36
Bentley (S.Yorks)		d			
Adwick		a			
		d			
South Elmsall		d			
Fitzwilliam		d			
Sandal & Agbrigg		d			
Wakefield Westgate	32,39	a		23 40	23 56
		d		23 41	23 56
Pontefract Monkhill	32	d			
Wakefield Kirkgate	32,34,39	a	23 26		
		d	23 27		
Outwood		d			
Leeds	32,34	a	00 05	00 01	00 14

Leeds - Wakefield, Doncaster and Sheffield

Network Diagram - see first page of Table 31

Miles	Miles		NT MX	NT MX	NT MX	GR A	GR	EM	GR	NT	XC	NT	NT	GR	XC	NT	EM		NT	GR	NT	GR B	XC	NT
0	0	Leeds 10 32,34 d	22p37	23p09		04 07	05 05	05 25	05 30	05 33	06 00		06 05	06 05	06 15	06 19	06 34		06 38	06 40	06 43	07 00	07 05	
7½	7½	Outwood d		23p20						05 44						06 28					06 54			
—	—	Wakefield Kirkgate 4 32,34,39 a	23p10										06 21						07 07					
—	—	d	23p10									06 04	06 21						07 08					
—	—	Pontefract Monkhill d																						
10	10	Wakefield Westgate 7 32,39 a		23p24	00 17		05 16	05 36	05 42	05 49	06 11			06 16	06 26	06 32	06 45			06 51	06 58	07 12	07 17	
—	—	d		23p24		04u18	05 16	05 37	05 42	05 49	06 12			06 17	06 27	06 33	06 46			06 51	06 58		07 18	
11¾	11¾	Sandal & Agbrigg d		23p28						05 53						06 36					07 02			
16½	16½	Fitzwilliam d		23p35						06 00						06 43					07 09			
21	—	South Elmsall d														06 48								
25¾	—	Adwick a														06 53								
—	—	d														06 54								
28	—	Bentley (S.Yorks) d														06 58								
29¾	—	Doncaster 7 a					05 35	05 55	06 01					06 34	06 43	07 08				07 09				
—	20¼	Moorthorpe d		23p41						06 06											07 15			
—	23¾	Thurnscoe d		23p47						06 12											07 21			
—	24½	Goldthorpe d		23p49						06 15											07 23			
—	25¾	Bolton-upon-Dearne d		23p52						06 18											07 26			
—	28	Swinton (S.Yorks) 29 a		23p56						06 23											07 30			
—	32½	Rotherham Central 29 a		00 03						06 31											07 37			←
—	35¼	Meadowhall 29 a	23p51	00 08						06 37		06 41	06 49						07 48		07 44			07 48
—	38¾	Sheffield 7 29 a	00 02	00 23				06 18		06 47	06 41	06 55	07 00		07 11		07 25		→		07 56		07 50	07 58

	NT	NT	GR	NT	GC	NT	NT	NT	GR		NT	NT	XC	NT	NT	GR	NT	NT	NT	NT	GR	NT	NT	XC
Leeds 10 32,34 d	07 05		07 15	07 18		07 29	07 35		07 40		07 48	08 02	08 11			08 15	08 19	08 32	08 37		08 45	08 48	09 05	09 11
Outwood d				07 28				←			07 59						08 28			←		08 59		
Wakefield Kirkgate 4 32,34,39 a	07 25					08 00	07 54	08 00				08 23						09 03	08 54	09 03			09 23	
d	07 25				07 42	08 04	07 55	08 04				08 23						09 05	08 55	09 05			09 23	
Pontefract Monkhill d					08 01	→												→						
Wakefield Westgate 7 32,39 a			07 26	07 34					07 51		08 03		08 22			08 27	08 31				08 56	09 03		09 23
d			07 26	07 34					07 51		08 03		08 23			08 27	08 32				08 56	09 03		09 24
Sandal & Agbrigg d				07 36							08 07						08 36					09 07		
Fitzwilliam d				07 43							08 14						08 41					09 14		
South Elmsall d				07 49													08 46							
Adwick a				07 52													08 52							
d		07 29		07 52										08 15	08 33		08 52							
Bentley (S.Yorks) d		07 33		07 56										08 18	08 37		08 56							
Doncaster 7 a		07 37	07 45	08 07	08 29				08 09					08 23	08 41	08 45	09 06				09 15			
Moorthorpe d											08 20											09 20		
Thurnscoe d											08 26											09 26		
Goldthorpe d											08 28											09 28		
Bolton-upon-Dearne d											08 31											09 31		
Swinton (S.Yorks) 29 a		07 53									08 34			08 42								09 35		
Rotherham Central 29 a		08 00									08 43			08 50								09 44		
Meadowhall 29 a	07 53	08 05					08 31	08 45			08 50	08 52		08 56					09 27	09 46		09 50	09 52	
Sheffield 7 29 a	08 05	08 18					08 39	08 56			08 59	09 02	08 51	09 05					09 37	09 56		10 00	10 02	09 51

	NT		GR	NT	NT	NT	NT	GR	NT	NT	XC	NT	GR	NT	NT	NT	NT		GR	NT	GC	NT	XC	NT
Leeds 10 32,34 d			09 15	09 20	09 32	09 37		09 45	09 48	10 05	10 11		10 15	10 20	10 32	10 37			10 45	10 48		11 05	11 11	
Outwood d				09 29			←		09 59					10 29			←			10 59				
Wakefield Kirkgate 4 32,34,39 a					10 01	09 55	10 01			10 23					11 01	10 54	11 01					11 23		
d					10 04	09 56	10 04			10 23					11 04	10 55	11 04				11 11	11 23		
Pontefract Monkhill d					→										→						11 34			
Wakefield Westgate 7 32,39 a			09 27	09 33				09 56	10 03		10 22		10 27	10 33					10 56	11 03			11 23	
d			09 27	09 33				09 56	10 03		10 23		10 27	10 33					10 56	11 03			11 24	
Sandal & Agbrigg d				09 35					10 07					10 36						11 07				
Fitzwilliam d				09 44					10 14					10 44						11 14				
South Elmsall d				09 47										10 49										
Adwick a				09 52										10 54										
d	09 15			09 53								10 15		10 55										11 15
Bentley (S.Yorks) d	09 19			09 57								10 19		10 59										11 19
Doncaster 7 a	09 24		09 45	10 08				10 15				10 24	10 44	11 09					11 15		12 07			11 24
Moorthorpe d									10 20											11 20				
Thurnscoe d									10 26											11 26				
Goldthorpe d									10 28											11 28				
Bolton-upon-Dearne d									10 31											11 31				
Swinton (S.Yorks) 29 a	09 42								10 35			10 42								11 35				11 43
Rotherham Central 29 a	09 50								10 44			10 52								11 44				11 52
Meadowhall 29 a	09 55					10 27	10 46		10 50	10 52		10 57				11 27	11 46			11 51		11 52		11 55
Sheffield 7 29 a	10 05					10 37	10 56		11 01	11 02	10 51	11 05				11 37	11 57			12 01		12 02	11 51	12 05

A 30 July

B West Riding Limited

Leeds - Wakefield, Doncaster and Sheffield

Network Diagram - see first page of Table 31

	GR	NT	NT	NT	NT	NT	GR	NT	NT		XC	NT	GR	NT	NT	NT	NT	GR	NT	NT	XC	NT	GR	NT
Leeds 10 32,34 d	11 15	11 20		11 32	11 37		11 45	11 48	12 05		12 12		12 15	12 20	12 32	12 37		12 45	12 48	13 05	13 11		13 15	13 20
Outwood d		11 29				←		11 59						12 29			←		12 59					13 29
Wakefield Kirkgate 4 32,34,39 a				12 01	11 54	12 01			12 23						13 02	12 54	13 02			13 23				
d				12 04	11 55	12 04			12 23						13 04	12 55	13 04			13 23				
Pontefract Monkhill d				→											→									
Wakefield Westgate 7 32,39 a	11 27	11 33					11 56	12 03			12 23		12 27	12 33				12 56	13 03		13 22		13 27	13 33
d	11 27	11 33					11 56	12 03			12 24		12 27	12 33				12 56	13 03		13 23		13 27	13 33
Sandal & Agbrigg d		11 36						12 07						12 36					13 07					13 36
Fitzwilliam d		11 44						12 14						12 44					13 14					13 44
South Elmsall d		11 49												12 49										13 49
Adwick a		11 54												12 52										13 54
d		11 55										12 15		12 53								13 14		13 55
Bentley (S.Yorks) d		11 59										12 19		12 57								13 18		13 59
Doncaster 7 a	11 45	12 08					12 15					12 25	12 45	13 07				13 15				13 26	13 44	14 08
Moorthorpe d			11 59					12 20											13 20					
Thurnscoe d								12 26											13 26					
Goldthorpe d								12 28											13 28					
Bolton-upon-Dearne d								12 31											13 31					
Swinton (S.Yorks) 29 a			12 08					12 35				12 42							13 35			13 42		
Rotherham Central 29 a			12 18					12 44				12 52							13 44			13 51		
Meadowhall 29 a			12 24		12 27	12 46		12 51	12 52			12 55				13 27	13 46		13 51	13 52		13 55		
Sheffield 7 29 a			12 36		12 37	12 56		13 01	13 02		12 51	13 05				13 37	13 56		14 01	14 02	13 51	14 05		

	NT		NT	NT	GR	NT	NT	XC	NT	GR	NT	NT	NT	NT	GR	NT	NT		XC	NT	GR	NT	NT	NT
Leeds 10 32,34 d	13 32		13 37		13 45	13 48	14 05	14 11		14 15	14 20	14 32	14 37		14 45	14 48	15 05		15 11		15 15	15 20		15 32
Outwood d				←		13 59					14 29			←		14 59						15 29		
Wakefield Kirkgate 4 32,34,39 a	14 01		13 54	14 01			14 23					15 01	14 54	15 01			15 23							16 01
d	14 04		13 55	14 04			14 23					15 04	14 55	15 04			15 23							16 04
Pontefract Monkhill d	→											→												→
Wakefield Westgate 7 32,39 a					13 56	14 03		14 22		14 27	14 33				14 56	15 03			15 22		15 27	15 33		
d					13 57	14 03		14 23		14 27	14 33				14 56	15 03			15 23		15 27	15 33		
Sandal & Agbrigg d						14 07					14 36					15 07						15 36		
Fitzwilliam d						14 14					14 44					15 14						15 44		
South Elmsall d											14 49											15 49		
Adwick a											14 52											15 54		
d									14 15		14 53									15 15		15 55		
Bentley (S.Yorks) d									14 19		14 57									15 19		15 59		
Doncaster 7 a					14 15				14 24	14 44	15 08				15 15					15 24	15 44	16 08		
Moorthorpe d						14 20										15 20							15 50	
Thurnscoe d						14 26										15 26								
Goldthorpe d						14 28										15 28								
Bolton-upon-Dearne d						14 31										15 31								
Swinton (S.Yorks) 29 a						14 35			14 41							15 35				15 42			16 00	
Rotherham Central 29 a						14 44			14 52							15 44				15 50			16 09	
Meadowhall 29 a			14 27	14 46		14 50	14 52		14 55				15 27	15 46		15 50	15 51			15 55			16 17	
Sheffield 7 29 a			14 37	14 56		15 01	15 02	14 51	15 05				15 37	15 56		16 01	16 03		15 51	16 05			16 27	

	NT	NT	GR	NT	NT	XC	NT	GR	NT		GC	NT	NT	XC	NT	GR	NT	NT	NT	XC	GR	NT	NT	NT
Leeds 10 32,34 d	15 37		15 45	15 48	16 05	16 11		16 15	16 20			16 32	16 37	16 40		16 45	16 48	16 57	17 05	17 11	17 15	17 20	17 32	17 37
Outwood d		←		15 59					16 29						←		16 59					17 29		
Wakefield Kirkgate 4 32,34,39 a	15 54	16 01			16 23							17 01	16 54		17 01				17 22				18 01	17 54
d	15 55	16 04			16 23						16 40	17 04	16 55		17 04				17 23				18 04	17 55
Pontefract Monkhill d											16 56	→											→	
Wakefield Westgate 7 32,39 a			15 56	16 03		16 22		16 27	16 32					16 51		16 56	17 03	17 08		17 22	17 27	17 33		
d			15 56	16 03		16 23		16 27	16 32					16 52		16 56	17 03	17 09		17 23	17 27	17 33		
Sandal & Agbrigg d				16 07					16 35								17 07					17 36		
Fitzwilliam d				16 14					16 43								17 14	17 18				17 44		
South Elmsall d									16 48									17 25				17 49		
Adwick a									16 53									17 29				17 54		
d							16 15		16 54									17 30				17 55		
Bentley (S.Yorks) d							16 19		16 58									17 35				17 59		
Doncaster 7 a			16 15				16 24	16 45	17 07		17 24					17 16		17 45			17 44	18 08		
Moorthorpe d				16 20													17 20							
Thurnscoe d				16 26													17 26							
Goldthorpe d				16 28													17 28							
Bolton-upon-Dearne d				16 31													17 31							
Swinton (S.Yorks) 29 a				16 35			16 42										17 35							
Rotherham Central 29 a				16 44			16 50										17 44							
Meadowhall 29 a	16 27	16 46		16 50	16 52		16 55						17 27		17 46		17 50		17 51					18 27
Sheffield 7 29 a	16 37	16 56		17 00	17 02	16 51	17 05						17 37	17 20	17 56		18 01		18 03	17 51				18 38

until 30 July

Leeds - Wakefield, Doncaster and Sheffield

Network Diagram - see first page of Table 31

	NT		GR	NT	NT	XC	NT	GR	NT	NT	NT	NT	GR	NT	NT	XC	GR		NT	NT	NT	NT	GR	NT
			1		◇	◇1		1					1		◇	◇1	1						1	
Leeds 10 32,34 d			17 45	17 46	18 05	18 11		18 15	18 20	18 32	18 43		18 45	18 48	19 05	19 11	19 15		19 19	19 37	19 43		19 45	19 48
Outwood d	←			17 57					18 29			←		18 59					19 28			←		19 59
Wakefield Kirkgate 4 32,34,39 a	18 01				18 23					19 04	18 59	19 04			19 24					20 06	19 59	20 06		
d	18 04				18 23					19 05	18 59	19 05			19 24					20 07	20 00	20 07		
Pontefract Monkhill d										→										→				
Wakefield Westgate 7 32,39 a			17 56	18 01		18 22		18 27	18 33				18 56	19 03		19 22	19 27		19 32				19 56	20 03
d			17 56	18 01		18 23		18 27	18 33				18 56	19 03		19 23	19 27		19 32				19 56	20 03
Sandal & Agbrigg d				18 07					18 36					19 07					19 35					20 07
Fitzwilliam d				18 14					18 44					19 14					19 42					20 14
South Elmsall d									18 50										19 47					
Adwick a									18 55										19 52					
d							18 14		18 56										19 53					
Bentley (S.Yorks) d							18 18		19 00										19 59					
Doncaster 7 a			18 15				18 25	18 44	19 08				19 13				19 44		20 07				20 16	
Moorthorpe d				18 20										19 20										20 20
Thurnscoe d				18 26										19 26										20 26
Goldthorpe d				18 28										19 28										20 28
Bolton-upon-Dearne d				18 31										19 31										20 31
Swinton (S.Yorks) 29 a				18 35										19 35										20 35
Rotherham Central 29 a				18 44										19 45										20 44
Meadowhall 29 ⇌ a	18 46			18 50	18 52						19 33	19 47		19 50	19 52						20 33	20 45		20 51
Sheffield 7 29 ⇌ a	18 56			19 00	19 03	18 51					19 43	19 56		19 59	20 04	19 51					20 44	20 58		21 02

	XC	NT	NT	NT	GR	NT	XC	NT	NT		NT	NT	NT	NT	NT	NT
	◇1				1		◇1									
Leeds 10 32,34 d	20 11	20 20	20 30	20 37	20 45	20 48	21 11	21 21			21 37	21 48		22 37	22 40	23 09
Outwood d		20 29				20 59		21 30				21 59			22 49	23 20
Wakefield Kirkgate 4 32,34,39 a			20 46	21 06							22 06			23 10		
d			20 46	21 07					21 47		22 07		22 55	23 10		
Pontefract Monkhill d																
Wakefield Westgate 7 32,39 a	20 22	20 33			20 56	21 03	21 22	21 34	21 53			22 03	23 01		22 53	23 24
d	20 23	20 33			20 56	21 03	21 23	21 34				22 03			22 53	23 24
Sandal & Agbrigg d		20 36				21 07		21 37				22 07			22 56	23 28
Fitzwilliam d		20 44				21 13		21 44				22 14			23 03	23 35
South Elmsall d		20 49						21 49							23 08	
Adwick a		20 54						21 54							23 13	
d		20 55						21 55							23 14	
Bentley (S.Yorks) d		20 59						21 59							23 18	
Doncaster 7 a		21 10			21 15			22 08							23 28	
Moorthorpe d						21 20						22 20				23 41
Thurnscoe d						21 27						22 26				23 47
Goldthorpe d						21 29						22 28				23 49
Bolton-upon-Dearne d						21 32						22 31				23 52
Swinton (S.Yorks) 29 a						21 35						22 35				23 56
Rotherham Central 29 a						21 44						22 46				00 03
Meadowhall 29 ⇌ a			21 19	21 45		21 51					22 47	22 52		23 51		00 08
Sheffield 7 29 ⇌ a	20 51		21 30	21 57		22 04	21 51				22 58	23 02		00 02		00 23

Mondays to Fridays

6 August to 7 September

	NT MX	NT MX	NT MX	GR	GR	EM	GR	NT	XC	NT	NT	GR	XC	NT	EM		NT	GR	NT	GR	XC	NT	NT	NT
				1 A	1	◇1	1		◇1			1	◇1		◇1			1		1 B	◇1			
Leeds 10 32,34 d	22p37	23p09		04 07	05 05	05 25	05 30	05 33	06 00		06 05	06 05	06 15	06 19	06 34		06 38	06 40	06 43	07 00	07 05		07 05	
Outwood d		23p20						05 44						06 28					06 54					
Wakefield Kirkgate 4 32,34,39 a	23p10										06 21						07 07						07 25	
d	23p10									06 04	06 21						07 08						07 25	
Pontefract Monkhill d																								
Wakefield Westgate 7 32,39 a		23p24	00 17		05 16	05 36	05 42	05 49	06 11			06 16	06 26	06 32	06 45			06 51	06 58	07 12	07 17			
d		23p24		04u18	05 16	05 37	05 42	05 49	06 12			06 17	06 27	06 33	06 46			06 51	06 58		07 18			
Sandal & Agbrigg d		23p28						05 53						06 36					07 02					
Fitzwilliam d		23p35						06 00						06 43					07 09					
South Elmsall d														06 48										
Adwick a														06 53										
d														06 54										07 29
Bentley (S.Yorks) d														06 58										07 33
Doncaster 7 a					05 35	05 55	06 01					06 34	06 43	07 08				07 09						07 37
Moorthorpe d		23p41						06 06											07 15					
Thurnscoe d		23p47						06 12											07 21					
Goldthorpe d		23p49						06 15											07 23					
Bolton-upon-Dearne d		23p52						06 18											07 26					
Swinton (S.Yorks) 29 a		23p56						06 23											07 30					07 53
Rotherham Central 29 a		00 03						06 31											07 37			←		08 00
Meadowhall 29 ⇌ a	23p51	00 08						06 37		06 41	06 49						07 48		07 44			07 48	07 53	08 05
Sheffield 7 29 ⇌ a	00 02	00 23				06 18		06 47	06 41	06 55	07 00		07 11		07 25		→		07 56		07 50	07 58	08 05	08 18

A not from 13 August until 29 August

B West Riding Limited

6 August to 7 September

Leeds - Wakefield, Doncaster and Sheffield

Network Diagram - see first page of Table 31

	GR	NT	GC	NT	NT	NT	GR		NT	NT	XC	NT	NT	GR	NT	NT	NT	NT	GR	NT	NT	XC	NT
	1		1				1				◇1			1					1			◇1	
Leeds 10 32,34 d	07 15	07 18		07 29	07 35		07 40		07 48	08 02	08 11			08 15	08 19	08 32	08 37		08 45	08 48	09 05	09 11	
Outwood d		07 28				←			07 59						08 28			←		08 59			
Wakefield Kirkgate 4 32,34,39 a				08 00	07 54	08 00				08 23						09 03	08 54	09 03			09 23		
d			07 42	08 04	07 55	08 04				08 23						09 05	08 55	09 05			09 23		
Pontefract Monkhill d			08 01	→												→							
Wakefield Westgate 7 32,39 a	07 26	07 34					07 51		08 03		08 22			08 27	08 31				08 56	09 03		09 23	
d	07 26	07 34					07 51		08 03		08 23			08 27	08 32				08 56	09 03		09 24	
Sandal & Agbrigg d		07 36							08 07						08 36					09 07			
Fitzwilliam d		07 43							08 14						08 41					09 14			
South Elmsall d		07 49													08 46								
Adwick a		07 52													08 52								
d		07 52										08 15	08 33		08 52								09 15
Bentley (S.Yorks) d		07 56										08 18	08 37		08 56								09 19
Doncaster 7 a	07 45	08 07	08 29				08 09					08 23	08 41	08 45	09 06				09 15				09 24
Moorthorpe d									08 20											09 20			
Thurnscoe d									08 26											09 26			
Goldthorpe d									08 28											09 28			
Bolton-upon-Dearne d									08 31											09 31			
Swinton (S.Yorks) 29 a									08 34			08 42								09 35			09 42
Rotherham Central 29 a									08 43			08 50								09 44			09 50
Meadowhall 29 ⇌ a					08 31	08 45			08 50	08 52		08 56					09 27	09 46		09 50	09 52		09 55
Sheffield 7 29 ⇌ a					08 39	08 56			08 59	09 02	08 51	09 05					09 37	09 56		10 00	10 02	09 51	10 05

	GR	NT	NT	NT	NT	GR	NT	NT	XC	NT	GR	NT	NT	NT	NT		GR	NT	GC	NT	XC	NT	GR	NT
	1					1		◇	◇1		1						1		1	◇	◇1		1	
Leeds 10 32,34 d	09 15	09 20	09 32	09 37		09 45	09 48	10 05	10 11		10 15	10 20	10 32	10 37			10 45	10 48		11 05	11 11		11 15	11 20
Outwood d		09 29			←		09 59					10 29			←			10 59						11 29
Wakefield Kirkgate 4 32,34,39 a			10 01	09 55	10 01			10 23					11 01	10 54	11 01					11 23				
d			10 04	09 56	10 04			10 23					11 04	10 55	11 04				11 11	11 23				
Pontefract Monkhill d			→										→						11 34					
Wakefield Westgate 7 32,39 a	09 27	09 33				09 56	10 03		10 22		10 27	10 33					10 56	11 03			11 23		11 27	11 33
d	09 27	09 33				09 56	10 03		10 23		10 27	10 33					10 56	11 03			11 24		11 27	11 33
Sandal & Agbrigg d		09 35					10 07					10 36						11 07						11 36
Fitzwilliam d		09 44					10 14					10 44						11 14						11 44
South Elmsall d		09 47										10 49												11 49
Adwick a		09 52										10 54												11 54
d		09 53								10 15		10 55										11 15		11 55
Bentley (S.Yorks) d		09 57								10 19		10 59										11 19		11 59
Doncaster 7 a	09 45	10 08				10 15				10 24	10 44	11 09					11 15		12 07			11 24	11 45	12 08
Moorthorpe d							10 20											11 20						
Thurnscoe d							10 26											11 26						
Goldthorpe d							10 28											11 28						
Bolton-upon-Dearne d							10 31											11 31						
Swinton (S.Yorks) 29 a							10 35			10 42								11 35				11 43		
Rotherham Central 29 a							10 44			10 52								11 44				11 52		
Meadowhall 29 ⇌ a				10 27	10 46		10 50	10 52		10 57				11 27	11 46			11 51		11 52		11 55		
Sheffield 7 29 ⇌ a				10 37	10 56		11 01	11 02	10 51	11 05				11 37	11 57			12 01		12 02	11 51	12 05		

	NT	NT	NT	NT	GR	NT	NT		XC	NT	GR	NT	NT	NT	NT	GR	NT	NT	XC	NT	GR	NT	NT
					1		◇		◇1		1					1		◇	◇1		1		
Leeds 10 32,34 d		11 32	11 37		11 45	11 48	12 05		12 12		12 15	12 20	12 32	12 37		12 45	12 48	13 05	13 11		13 15	13 20	13 32
Outwood d				←		11 59						12 29			←		12 59					13 29	
Wakefield Kirkgate 4 32,34,39 a		12 01	11 54	12 01			12 23						13 02	12 54	13 02			13 23					14 01
d		12 04	11 55	12 04			12 23						13 04	12 55	13 04			13 23					14 04
Pontefract Monkhill d		→											→										→
Wakefield Westgate 7 32,39 a					11 56	12 03			12 23		12 27	12 33				12 56	13 03		13 22		13 27	13 33	
d					11 56	12 03			12 24		12 27	12 33				12 56	13 03		13 23		13 27	13 33	
Sandal & Agbrigg d						12 07						12 36					13 07					13 36	
Fitzwilliam d						12 14						12 44					13 14					13 44	
South Elmsall d												12 49										13 49	
Adwick a												12 52										13 54	
d										12 15		12 53								13 14		13 55	
Bentley (S.Yorks) d										12 19		12 57								13 18		13 59	
Doncaster 7 a					12 15					12 25	12 45	13 07				13 15				13 26	13 44	14 08	
Moorthorpe d	11 59					12 20											13 20						
Thurnscoe d						12 26											13 26						
Goldthorpe d						12 28											13 28						
Bolton-upon-Dearne d						12 31											13 31						
Swinton (S.Yorks) 29 a	12 08					12 35				12 42							13 35			13 42			
Rotherham Central 29 a	12 18					12 44				12 52							13 44			13 51			
Meadowhall 29 ⇌ a	12 24		12 27	12 46		12 51	12 52			12 55				13 27	13 46		13 51	13 52		13 55			
Sheffield 7 29 ⇌ a	12 36		12 37	12 56		13 01	13 02		12 51	13 05				13 37	13 56		14 01	14 02	13 51	14 05			

Leeds - Wakefield, Doncaster and Sheffield

Station			NT	NT	GR	NT	NT	XC	NT	GR	NT	NT	NT	NT	GR	NT	NT		XC	NT	GR	NT	NT	NT	NT	NT
Leeds 10	32,34	d	13 37		13 45	13 48	14 05	14 11		14 15	14 20	14 32	14 37		14 45	14 48	15 05		15 11		15 15	15 20		15 32	15 37	
Outwood		d		←		13 59					14 29			←		14 59						15 29				←
Wakefield Kirkgate 4	32,34,39	a	13 54	14 01			14 23					15 01	14 54	15 01			15 23							16 01	15 54	16 01
		d	13 55	14 04			14 23					15 04	14 55	15 04			15 23							16 04	15 55	16 04
Pontefract Monkhill		d										→												→		
Wakefield Westgate 7	32,39	a			13 56	14 03		14 22		14 27	14 33				14 56	15 03			15 22		15 27	15 33				
		d			13 57	14 03		14 23		14 27	14 33				14 56	15 03			15 23		15 27	15 33				
Sandal & Agbrigg		d				14 07					14 36					15 07						15 36				
Fitzwilliam		d				14 14					14 44					15 14						15 44				
South Elmsall		d									14 49											15 49				
Adwick		a									14 52											15 54				
		d							14 15		14 53									15 15		15 55				
Bentley (S.Yorks)		d							14 19		14 57									15 19		15 59				
Doncaster 7		a			14 15				14 24	14 44	15 08				15 15					15 24	15 44	16 08				
Moorthorpe		d				14 20										15 20							15 50			
Thurnscoe		d				14 26										15 26										
Goldthorpe		d				14 28										15 28										
Bolton-upon-Dearne		d				14 31										15 31										
Swinton (S.Yorks)	29	a				14 35			14 41							15 35				15 42			16 00			
Rotherham Central	29	a				14 44			14 52							15 44				15 50			16 09			
Meadowhall	29	a	14 27	14 46		14 50	14 52		14 55				15 27	15 46		15 50	15 51			15 55			16 17		16 27	16 46
Sheffield 7	29	a	14 37	14 56		15 01	15 02	14 51	15 05				15 37	15 56		16 01	16 03		15 51	16 05			16 27		16 37	16 56

Station			GR	NT	NT	XC	NT	GR	NT		GC	NT	NT	XC	NT	GR	NT	NT	NT	XC	GR	NT	NT	NT	NT	
Leeds 10	32,34	d	15 45	15 48	16 05	16 11		16 15	16 20			16 32	16 37	16 40		16 45	16 48	16 57	17 05	17 11	17 15	17 20	17 32	17 37		
Outwood		d		15 59					16 29						←		16 59					17 29			←	
Wakefield Kirkgate 4	32,34,39	a			16 23							17 01	16 54		17 01				17 22				18 01	17 54	18 01	
		d			16 23						16 40	17 04	16 55		17 04				17 23				18 04	17 55	18 04	
Pontefract Monkhill		d									16 56	→											→			
Wakefield Westgate 7	32,39	a	15 56	16 03		16 22		16 27	16 32					16 51		16 56	17 03	17 08		17 22	17 27	17 33				
		d	15 56	16 03		16 23		16 27	16 32					16 52		16 56	17 03	17 09		17 23	17 27	17 33				
Sandal & Agbrigg		d		16 07					16 35								17 07					17 36				
Fitzwilliam		d		16 14					16 43								17 14	17 18				17 44				
South Elmsall		d							16 48									17 25				17 49				
Adwick		a							16 53									17 29				17 54				
		d					16 15		16 54									17 30				17 55				
Bentley (S.Yorks)		d					16 19		16 58									17 35				17 59				
Doncaster 7		a	16 15				16 24	16 45	17 07		17 24					17 16		17 45			17 44	18 08				
Moorthorpe		d		16 20													17 20									
Thurnscoe		d		16 26													17 26									
Goldthorpe		d		16 28													17 28									
Bolton-upon-Dearne		d		16 31													17 31									
Swinton (S.Yorks)	29	a		16 35			16 42										17 35									
Rotherham Central	29	a		16 44			16 50										17 44									
Meadowhall	29	a		16 50	16 52		16 55						17 27		17 46		17 50		17 51					18 27	18 46	
Sheffield 7	29	a		17 00	17 02	16 51	17 05						17 37	17 20	17 56		18 01		18 03	17 51				18 38	18 56	

Station			GR	NT	NT	XC	NT	GR	NT	NT	NT	NT	GR	NT	NT	XC	GR		NT	NT	NT	NT	GR	NT	XC	NT
Leeds 10	32,34	d	17 45	17 46	18 05	18 11		18 15	18 20	18 32	18 43		18 45	18 48	19 05	19 11	19 15		19 19	19 37	19 43		19 45	19 48	20 11	20 20
Outwood		d		17 57					18 29			←		18 59					19 28			←		19 59		20 29
Wakefield Kirkgate 4	32,34,39	a			18 23					19 04	18 59	19 04			19 24					20 06	19 59	20 06				
		d			18 23					19 05	18 59	19 05			19 24					20 07	20 00	20 07				
Pontefract Monkhill		d								→										→						
Wakefield Westgate 7	32,39	a	17 56	18 01		18 22		18 27	18 33				18 56	19 03		19 22	19 27		19 32				19 56	20 03	20 22	20 33
		d	17 56	18 01		18 23		18 27	18 33				18 56	19 03		19 23	19 27		19 32				19 56	20 03	20 23	20 33
Sandal & Agbrigg		d		18 07					18 36					19 07					19 35					20 07		20 36
Fitzwilliam		d		18 14					18 44					19 14					19 42					20 14		20 44
South Elmsall		d							18 50										19 47							20 49
Adwick		a							18 55										19 52							20 54
		d					18 14		18 56										19 53							20 55
Bentley (S.Yorks)		d					18 18		19 00										19 59							20 59
Doncaster 7		a	18 15				18 25	18 44	19 08				19 13				19 44		20 07				20 16			21 10
Moorthorpe		d		18 20										19 20										20 20		
Thurnscoe		d		18 26										19 26										20 26		
Goldthorpe		d		18 28										19 28										20 28		
Bolton-upon-Dearne		d		18 31										19 31										20 31		
Swinton (S.Yorks)	29	a		18 35										19 35										20 35		
Rotherham Central	29	a		18 44										19 45										20 44		
Meadowhall	29	a		18 50	18 52						19 33	19 47		19 50	19 52						20 33	20 45		20 51		
Sheffield 7	29	a		19 00	19 03	18 51					19 43	19 56		19 59	20 04	19 51					20 44	20 58		21 02	20 51	

Leeds - Wakefield, Doncaster and Sheffield

Station			NT	NT	GR	NT	XC	NT	NT		NT	NT	NT	NT	NT	NT
Leeds 10	32,34	d	20 30	20 37	20 45	20 48	21 11	21 21			21 37	21 48		22 37	22 40	23 09
Outwood		d				20 59		21 30				21 59			22 49	23 20
Wakefield Kirkgate 4	32,34,39	a	20 46	21 06							22 06			23 10		
		d	20 46	21 07					21 47		22 07		22 55	23 10		
Pontefract Monkhill		d														
Wakefield Westgate 7	32,39	a			20 56	21 03	21 22	21 34	21 53			22 03	23 01		22 53	23 24
		d			20 56	21 03	21 23	21 34				22 03			22 53	23 24
Sandal & Agbrigg		d				21 07		21 37				22 07			22 56	23 28
Fitzwilliam		d				21 13		21 44				22 14			23 03	23 35
South Elmsall		d						21 49							23 08	
Adwick		a						21 54							23 13	
		d						21 55							23 14	
Bentley (S.Yorks)		d						21 59							23 18	
Doncaster 7		a			21 15			22 08							23 28	
Moorthorpe		d				21 20						22 20				23 41
Thurnscoe		d				21 27						22 26				23 47
Goldthorpe		d				21 29						22 28				23 49
Bolton-upon-Dearne		d				21 32						22 31				23 52
Swinton (S.Yorks)	29	a				21 35						22 35				23 56
Rotherham Central	29	a				21 44						22 46				00 03
Meadowhall	29	a	21 19	21 45		21 51					22 47	22 52		23 51		00 08
Sheffield 7	29	a	21 30	21 57		22 04	21 51				22 58	23 02		00 02		00 23

Mondays to Fridays

from 10 September

Station			NT MX	NT MX	NT MX	GR	EM	GR	NT	XC	NT	NT	GR	XC	NT	EM	NT		GR	NT	GR A	XC	NT	NT	NT	GR
Leeds 10	32,34	d	22p37	23p09		05 05	05 25	05 30	05 33	06 00		06 05	06 05	06 15	06 19	06 34	06 38		06 40	06 43	07 00	07 05		07 05		07 15
Outwood		d		23p20					05 44						06 28					06 54						
Wakefield Kirkgate 4	32,34,39	a	23p10									06 21					07 07							07 25		
		d	23p10								06 04	06 21					07 08							07 25		
Pontefract Monkhill		d																								
Wakefield Westgate 7	32,39	a		23p24	00 17	05 16	05 36	05 42	05 49	06 11			06 16	06 26	06 32	06 45			06 51	06 58	07 12	07 17				07 26
		d		23p24		05 16	05 37	05 42	05 49	06 12			06 17	06 27	06 33	06 46			06 51	06 58		07 18				07 26
Sandal & Agbrigg		d		23p28					05 53						06 36					07 02						
Fitzwilliam		d		23p35					06 00						06 43					07 09						
South Elmsall		d													06 48											
Adwick		a													06 53											
		d													06 54										07 29	
Bentley (S.Yorks)		d													06 58										07 33	
Doncaster 7		a				05 35	05 55	06 01					06 34	06 43	07 08				07 09						07 37	07 45
Moorthorpe		d		23p41					06 06											07 15						
Thurnscoe		d		23p47					06 12											07 21						
Goldthorpe		d		23p49					06 15											07 23						
Bolton-upon-Dearne		d		23p52					06 18											07 26						
Swinton (S.Yorks)	29	a		23p56					06 23											07 30					07 53	
Rotherham Central	29	a		00 03					06 31											07 37			←		08 00	
Meadowhall	29	a	23p51	00 08					06 37		06 41	06 49					07 48			07 44			07 48	07 53	08 05	
Sheffield 7	29	a	00 02	00 23			06 18		06 47	06 41	06 55	07 00		07 11		07 25	→			07 56		07 50	07 58	08 05	08 18	

Station			NT	GC	NT	NT	NT	GR	NT		NT	XC	NT	NT	GR	NT	NT	NT	NT	GR	NT	NT	XC	NT	GR	
Leeds 10	32,34	d	07 18		07 29	07 35		07 40	07 48		08 02	08 11			08 15	08 19	08 32	08 37		08 45	08 48	09 05	09 11		09 15	
Outwood		d	07 28				←		07 59							08 28			←		08 59					
Wakefield Kirkgate 4	32,34,39	a			08 00	07 54	08 00				08 23						09 03	08 54	09 03			09 23				
		d		07 42	08 04	07 55	08 04				08 23						09 05	08 55	09 05			09 23				
Pontefract Monkhill		d		08 01	→												→									
Wakefield Westgate 7	32,39	a	07 34					07 51	08 03			08 22			08 27	08 31				08 56	09 03		09 23		09 27	
		d	07 34					07 51	08 03			08 23			08 27	08 32				08 56	09 03		09 24		09 27	
Sandal & Agbrigg		d	07 36						08 07							08 36					09 07					
Fitzwilliam		d	07 43						08 14							08 41					09 14					
South Elmsall		d	07 49													08 46										
Adwick		a	07 52													08 52										
		d	07 52										08 15	08 33		08 52								09 15		
Bentley (S.Yorks)		d	07 56										08 18	08 37		08 56								09 19		
Doncaster 7		a	08 07	08 29				08 09					08 23	08 41	08 45	09 06				09 15				09 24	09 45	
Moorthorpe		d							08 20												09 20					
Thurnscoe		d							08 26												09 26					
Goldthorpe		d							08 28												09 28					
Bolton-upon-Dearne		d							08 31												09 31					
Swinton (S.Yorks)	29	a							08 34				08 42								09 35			09 42		
Rotherham Central	29	a							08 43				08 50								09 44			09 50		
Meadowhall	29	a				08 31	08 45		08 50		08 52		08 56					09 27	09 46		09 50	09 52		09 55		
Sheffield 7	29	a				08 39	08 56		08 59		09 02	08 51	09 05					09 37	09 56		10 00	10 02	09 51	10 05		

A West Riding Limited

Leeds - Wakefield, Doncaster and Sheffield

Network Diagram - see first page of Table 31

			NT	NT	NT	NT	GR	NT	NT	XC	NT	GR	NT	NT	NT	NT	GR		NT	GC	NT	XC	NT	GR	NT	NT
							■ 1		◇	◇ 1		■ 1					■ 1			■ 1	◇	◇ 1		■ 1		
Leeds	32,34	d	09 20	09 32	09 37		09 45	09 48	10 05	10 11		10 15	10 20	10 32	10 37		10 45		10 48		11 05	11 11		11 15	11 20	
Outwood		d	09 29			←		09 59					10 29			←			10 59						11 29	
Wakefield Kirkgate	32,34,39	a		10 01	09 55	10 01			10 23					11 01	10 54	11 01					11 23					
		d		10 04	09 56	10 04			10 23					11 04	10 55	11 04				11 11	11 23					
Pontefract Monkhill		d		→										→						11 34						
Wakefield Westgate	32,39	a	09 33				09 56	10 03		10 22		10 27	10 33				10 56		11 03			11 23		11 27	11 33	
		d	09 33				09 56	10 03		10 23		10 27	10 33				10 56		11 03			11 24		11 27	11 33	
Sandal & Agbrigg		d	09 35					10 07					10 36						11 07						11 36	
Fitzwilliam		d	09 44					10 14					10 44						11 14						11 44	
South Elmsall		d	09 47										10 49												11 49	
Adwick		a	09 52										10 54												11 54	
		d	09 53								10 15		10 55										11 15		11 55	
Bentley (S.Yorks)		d	09 57								10 19		10 59										11 19		11 59	
Doncaster		a	10 08				10 15				10 24	10 44	11 09				11 15			12 07			11 24	11 45	12 08	
Moorthorpe		d						10 20											11 20							11 59
Thurnscoe		d						10 26											11 26							
Goldthorpe		d						10 28											11 28							
Bolton-upon-Dearne		d						10 31											11 31							
Swinton (S.Yorks)	29	a						10 35			10 42								11 35				11 43			12 08
Rotherham Central	29	a						10 44			10 52								11 44				11 52			12 18
Meadowhall	29	a			10 27	10 46		10 50	10 52		10 57				11 27	11 46			11 51		11 52		11 55			12 24
Sheffield	29	a			10 37	10 56		11 01	11 02	10 51	11 05				11 37	11 57			12 01		12 02	11 51	12 05			12 36

			NT	NT	NT	GR	NT	NT	XC		NT	GR	NT	NT	NT	NT	GR	NT	NT	XC	NT	GR	NT	NT	NT	
						■ 1		◇	◇ 1			■ 1					■ 1		◇	◇ 1		■ 1				
Leeds	32,34	d	11 32	11 37		11 45	11 48	12 05	12 12			12 15	12 20	12 32	12 37		12 45	12 48	13 05	13 11		13 15	13 20	13 32	13 37	
Outwood		d			←		11 59						12 29			←		12 59					13 29			
Wakefield Kirkgate	32,34,39	a	12 01	11 54	12 01			12 23						13 02	12 54	13 02			13 23					14 01	13 54	
		d	12 04	11 55	12 04			12 23						13 04	12 55	13 04			13 23					14 04	13 55	
Pontefract Monkhill		d	→											→										→		
Wakefield Westgate	32,39	a				11 56	12 03		12 23			12 27	12 33				12 56	13 03		13 22		13 27	13 33			
		d				11 56	12 03		12 24			12 27	12 33				12 56	13 03		13 23		13 27	13 33			
Sandal & Agbrigg		d					12 07						12 36					13 07					13 36			
Fitzwilliam		d					12 14						12 44					13 14					13 44			
South Elmsall		d											12 49										13 49			
Adwick		a											12 52										13 54			
		d									12 15		12 53								13 14		13 55			
Bentley (S.Yorks)		d									12 19		12 57								13 18		13 59			
Doncaster		a				12 15					12 25	12 45	13 07				13 15				13 26	13 44	14 08			
Moorthorpe		d					12 20											13 20								
Thurnscoe		d					12 26											13 26								
Goldthorpe		d					12 28											13 28								
Bolton-upon-Dearne		d					12 31											13 31								
Swinton (S.Yorks)	29	a					12 35				12 42							13 35			13 42					
Rotherham Central	29	a					12 44				12 52							13 44			13 51					
Meadowhall	29	a		12 27	12 46		12 51	12 52			12 55				13 27	13 46		13 51	13 52		13 55				14 27	
Sheffield	29	a		12 37	12 56		13 01	13 02	12 51		13 05				13 37	13 56		14 01	14 02	13 51	14 05				14 37	

			NT	GR	NT	NT	XC	NT	GR	NT	NT	NT	NT	GR	NT	NT	XC		NT	GR	NT	NT	NT	NT	NT	GR
				■ 1		◇	◇ 1		■ 1					■ 1		◇	◇ 1			■ 1						■ 1
Leeds	32,34	d		13 45	13 48	14 05	14 11		14 15	14 20	14 32	14 37		14 45	14 48	15 05	15 11			15 15	15 20		15 32	15 37		15 45
Outwood		d	←		13 59					14 29			←		14 59						15 29				←	
Wakefield Kirkgate	32,34,39	a	14 01			14 23					15 01	14 54	15 01			15 23							16 01	15 54	16 01	
		d	14 04			14 23					15 04	14 55	15 04			15 23							16 04	15 55	16 04	
Pontefract Monkhill		d									→												→			
Wakefield Westgate	32,39	a		13 56	14 03		14 22		14 27	14 33				14 56	15 03		15 22			15 27	15 33					15 56
		d		13 57	14 03		14 23		14 27	14 33				14 56	15 03		15 23			15 27	15 33					15 56
Sandal & Agbrigg		d			14 07					14 36					15 07						15 36					
Fitzwilliam		d			14 14					14 44					15 14						15 44					
South Elmsall		d								14 49											15 49					
Adwick		a								14 52											15 54					
		d						14 15		14 53									15 15		15 55					
Bentley (S.Yorks)		d						14 19		14 57									15 19		15 59					
Doncaster		a		14 15				14 24	14 44	15 08				15 15					15 24	15 44	16 08					16 15
Moorthorpe		d			14 20										15 20							15 50				
Thurnscoe		d			14 26										15 26											
Goldthorpe		d			14 28										15 28											
Bolton-upon-Dearne		d			14 31										15 31											
Swinton (S.Yorks)	29	a			14 35			14 41							15 35				15 42			16 00				
Rotherham Central	29	a			14 44			14 52							15 44				15 50			16 09				
Meadowhall	29	a	14 46		14 50	14 52		14 55				15 27	15 46		15 50	15 51			15 55			16 17		16 27	16 46	
Sheffield	29	a	14 56		15 01	15 02	14 51	15 05				15 37	15 56		16 01	16 03	15 51		16 05			16 27		16 37	16 56	

Leeds - Wakefield, Doncaster and Sheffield

Network Diagram - see first page of Table 31

			NT	NT	XC	NT	GR	NT	GC		NT	NT	XC	NT	GR	NT	NT	NT	XC	GR	NT	NT	NT	NT	GR	
				◇	◇ 1		■ 1		■ 1				◇ 1		■ 1			◇	◇ 1	■ 1					■ 1	
Leeds	32,34	d	15 48	16 05	16 11		16 15	16 20			16 32	16 37	16 40		16 45	16 48	16 57	17 05	17 11	17 15	17 20	17 32	17 37		17 45	
Outwood		d	15 59					16 29						←		16 59					17 29			←		
Wakefield Kirkgate	32,34,39	a		16 23							17 01	16 54		17 01				17 22				18 01	17 54	18 01		
		d		16 23					16 40		17 04	16 55		17 04				17 23				18 04	17 55	18 04		
Pontefract Monkhill		d							16 56		→											→				
Wakefield Westgate	32,39	a	16 03		16 22		16 27	16 32					16 51		16 56	17 03	17 08		17 22	17 27	17 33				17 56	
		d	16 03		16 23		16 27	16 32					16 52		16 56	17 03	17 09		17 23	17 27	17 33				17 56	
Sandal & Agbrigg		d	16 07					16 35								17 07					17 36					
Fitzwilliam		d	16 14					16 43								17 14	17 18				17 44					
South Elmsall		d						16 48									17 25				17 49					
Adwick		a						16 53									17 29				17 54					
		d				16 15		16 54									17 30				17 55					
Bentley (S.Yorks)		d				16 19		16 58									17 35				17 59					
Doncaster		a				16 24	16 45	17 07	17 24						17 16		17 45			17 44	18 08				18 15	
Moorthorpe		d	16 20													17 20										
Thurnscoe		d	16 26													17 26										
Goldthorpe		d	16 28													17 28										
Bolton-upon-Dearne		d	16 31													17 31										
Swinton (S.Yorks)	29	a	16 35			16 42										17 35										
Rotherham Central	29	a	16 44			16 50										17 44										
Meadowhall	29	a	16 50	16 52		16 55						17 27		17 46		17 50		17 51					18 27	18 46		
Sheffield	29	a	17 00	17 02	16 51	17 05						17 37	17 20	17 56		18 01		18 03	17 51				18 38	18 56		

			NT	NT	XC	NT	GR	NT	NT	NT	NT	GR	NT	NT	XC	GR	NT		NT	NT	NT	GR	NT	XC	NT	NT
				◇	◇ 1		■ 1					■ 1		◇	◇ 1	■ 1						■ 1		◇ 1		
Leeds	32,34	d	17 46	18 05	18 11		18 15	18 20	18 32	18 43		18 45	18 48	19 05	19 11	19 15	19 19		19 37	19 43		19 45	19 48	20 11	20 20	20 30
Outwood		d	17 57					18 29			←		18 59				19 28				←		19 59		20 29	
Wakefield Kirkgate	32,34,39	a		18 23					19 04	18 59	19 04			19 24					20 06	19 59	20 06					20 46
		d		18 23					19 05	18 59	19 05			19 24					20 07	20 00	20 07					20 46
Pontefract Monkhill		d							→										→							
Wakefield Westgate	32,39	a	18 01		18 22		18 27	18 33				18 56	19 03		19 22	19 27	19 32					19 56	20 03	20 22	20 33	
		d	18 01		18 23		18 27	18 33				18 56	19 03		19 23	19 27	19 32					19 56	20 03	20 23	20 33	
Sandal & Agbrigg		d	18 07					18 36					19 07				19 35						20 07		20 36	
Fitzwilliam		d	18 14					18 44					19 14				19 42						20 14		20 44	
South Elmsall		d						18 50									19 47								20 49	
Adwick		a						18 55									19 52								20 54	
		d				18 14		18 56									19 53								20 55	
Bentley (S.Yorks)		d				18 18		19 00									19 59								20 59	
Doncaster		a				18 25	18 44	19 08				19 13				19 44	20 07					20 16			21 10	
Moorthorpe		d	18 20										19 20										20 20			
Thurnscoe		d	18 26										19 26										20 26			
Goldthorpe		d	18 28										19 28										20 28			
Bolton-upon-Dearne		d	18 31										19 31										20 31			
Swinton (S.Yorks)	29	a	18 35										19 35										20 35			
Rotherham Central	29	a	18 44										19 45										20 44			
Meadowhall	29	a	18 50	18 52						19 33	19 47		19 50	19 52						20 33	20 45		20 51			21 19
Sheffield	29	a	19 00	19 03	18 51					19 43	19 56		19 59	20 04	19 51					20 44	20 58		21 02	20 51		21 30

			NT	GR	NT	XC	NT	NT	NT		NT	NT	NT	NT	NT
				■ 1		◇ 1									
Leeds	32,34	d	20 37	20 45	20 48	21 11	21 21		21 37		21 48		22 37	22 40	23 09
Outwood		d			20 59		21 30				21 59			22 49	23 20
Wakefield Kirkgate	32,34,39	a	21 06						22 06				23 10		
		d	21 07					21 47	22 07			22 55	23 10		
Pontefract Monkhill		d													
Wakefield Westgate	32,39	a		20 56	21 03	21 22	21 34	21 53			22 03	23 01		22 53	23 24
		d		20 56	21 03	21 23	21 34				22 03			22 53	23 24
Sandal & Agbrigg		d			21 07		21 37				22 07			22 56	23 28
Fitzwilliam		d			21 13		21 44				22 14			23 03	23 35
South Elmsall		d					21 49							23 08	
Adwick		a					21 54							23 13	
		d					21 55							23 14	
Bentley (S.Yorks)		d					21 59							23 18	
Doncaster		a		21 15			22 08							23 28	
Moorthorpe		d			21 20						22 20				23 41
Thurnscoe		d			21 27						22 26				23 47
Goldthorpe		d			21 29						22 28				23 49
Bolton-upon-Dearne		d			21 32						22 31				23 52
Swinton (S.Yorks)	29	a			21 35						22 35				23 56
Rotherham Central	29	a			21 44						22 46				00 03
Meadowhall	29	a	21 45		21 51				22 47		22 52		23 51		00 08
Sheffield	29	a	21 57		22 04	21 51			22 58		23 02		00 02		00 23

Leeds - Wakefield, Doncaster and Sheffield

Network Diagram - see first page of Table 31

	NT	NT	GR	XC	GR	XC	NT	EM	NT	NT	NT	NT	GR	XC	NT		NT	GC	NT	EM	NT	NT	NT	GR
Leeds [10] 32,34 d	22p37	23p09	05 05	06 00	06 05	06 15	06 20	06 34	06 38	06 43		07 05	07 05	07 10			07 20		07 29	07 34	07 35		07 48	08 05
Outwood d		23p20					06 29			06 54							07 29					←	07 59	
Wakefield Kirkgate [4] 32,34,39 a	23p10								07 07			07 25							08 00		07 54	08 00		
d	23p10								07 08			07 25						07 38	08 04		07 55	08 04		
Pontefract Monkhill d																		07 58	→					
Wakefield Westgate [7] 32,39 a		23p24	05 16	06 11	06 17	06 28	06 33	06 45		06 58			07 16	07 22			07 34			07 45			08 03	08 16
d		23p24	05 16	06 12	06 17	06 29	06 33	06 46		06 58			07 16	07 23			07 34			07 46			08 03	08 16
Sandal & Agbrigg d		23p28					06 36			07 02							07 37						08 07	
Fitzwilliam d		23p35					06 44			07 09							07 44						08 14	
South Elmsall d							06 49										07 49							
Adwick a							06 54										07 54							
d							06 55								07 23		07 55							
Bentley (S.Yorks) d							06 59								07 27		07 59							
Doncaster [7] a			05 34		06 34	06 46	07 07						07 35		07 31		08 07	08 27						08 34
Moorthorpe d		23p41								07 15													08 20	
Thurnscoe d		23p47								07 21													08 26	
Goldthorpe d		23p49								07 23													08 28	
Bolton-upon-Dearne d		23p52								07 26													08 31	
Swinton (S.Yorks) 29 a		23p56								07 30					07 53								08 35	
Rotherham Central 29 a		00 03								07 37	←				08 01								08 44	
Meadowhall 29 a	23p51	00 08							07 48	07 46	07 48	07 53			08 06						08 31	08 45	08 49	
Sheffield [7] 29 a	00 02	00 23		06 45		07 15		07 22	→	07 54	07 58	08 05		07 51	08 18					08 21	08 39	08 56	08 59	

	NT	XC	NT	NT	NT	NT	NT		NT	GR	NT	GR	NT	XC	NT	NT	NT	NT	NT	NT	NT	GR	XC
Leeds [10] 32,34 d	08 05	08 12			08 20	08 32	08 37			08 40	08 48	09 05	09 05	09 11		09 20	09 32	09 37		09 48	10 05	10 05	10 12
Outwood d					08 29				←		08 59					09 29			←	09 59			
Wakefield Kirkgate [4] 32,34,39 a	08 23					09 03	08 54		09 03				09 23				10 01	09 55	10 01		10 23		
d	08 23					09 05	08 55		09 05				09 23				10 04	09 56	10 04		10 23		
Pontefract Monkhill d						→											→						
Wakefield Westgate [7] 32,39 a		08 23			08 33					08 51	09 03	09 17		09 23		09 33				10 03		10 16	10 23
d		08 24			08 33					08 51	09 03	09 17		09 24		09 33				10 03		10 16	10 24
Sandal & Agbrigg d					08 36						09 07					09 35				10 07			
Fitzwilliam d					08 44						09 14					09 44				10 14			
South Elmsall d					08 49											09 47							
Adwick a					08 54											09 53							
d			08 15	08 33	08 55										09 15	09 53							
Bentley (S.Yorks) d			08 19	08 37	08 59										09 19	09 57							
Doncaster [7] a			08 23	08 42	09 07					09 12		09 34			09 24	10 08						10 35	
Moorthorpe d											09 20									10 20			
Thurnscoe d											09 26									10 26			
Goldthorpe d											09 28									10 28			
Bolton-upon-Dearne d											09 31									10 31			
Swinton (S.Yorks) 29 a			08 43								09 35				09 42					10 35			
Rotherham Central 29 a			08 50								09 45				09 50					10 44			
Meadowhall 29 a	08 52		08 56				09 27		09 46		09 50		09 52		09 54			10 27	10 46	10 50	10 52		
Sheffield [7] 29 a	09 02	08 51	09 05				09 37		09 56		10 00		10 02	09 52	10 05			10 37	10 56	11 00	11 02		10 51

	NT	NT	NT	NT	NT	NT	GR	GC	NT	XC	NT	NT	NT	NT	NT		NT	NT	NT	GR	XC	NT	NT	NT
Leeds [10] 32,34 d		10 20	10 32	10 37		10 48	11 05		11 05	11 11		11 20		11 32	11 37			11 48	12 05	12 05	12 11		12 20	12 32
Outwood d		10 29			←	10 59						11 29					←	11 59					12 29	
Wakefield Kirkgate [4] 32,34,39 a			11 01	10 54	11 01				11 23					12 01	11 54		12 01		12 23					13 02
d			11 04	10 55	11 04			11 11	11 23					12 04	11 55		12 04		12 23					13 04
Pontefract Monkhill d			→					11 35						→										→
Wakefield Westgate [7] 32,39 a		10 33				11 03	11 16			11 22		11 33						12 03		12 16	12 23		12 33	
d		10 33				11 03	11 16			11 23		11 33						12 03		12 16	12 24		12 33	
Sandal & Agbrigg d		10 36				11 07						11 36						12 07					12 36	
Fitzwilliam d		10 44				11 14						11 44						12 14					12 44	
South Elmsall d		10 49										11 49											12 49	
Adwick a		10 54										11 54											12 54	
d	10 15	10 55									11 15	11 55										12 14	12 55	
Bentley (S.Yorks) d	10 19	10 59									11 19	11 59										12 18	12 59	
Doncaster [7] a	10 24	11 07					11 35	12 03			11 24	12 07								12 35		12 24	13 07	
Moorthorpe d						11 20							11 59					12 20						
Thurnscoe d						11 26												12 26						
Goldthorpe d						11 28												12 28						
Bolton-upon-Dearne d						11 31												12 31						
Swinton (S.Yorks) 29 a	10 42					11 35					11 42		12 08					12 35				12 42		
Rotherham Central 29 a	10 52					11 44					11 52		12 18					12 43				12 52		
Meadowhall 29 a	10 57			11 27	11 46	11 50			11 52		11 57		12 24		12 27		12 46	12 49	12 52			12 57		
Sheffield [7] 29 a	11 06			11 37	11 57	12 00			12 02	11 51	12 05		12 36		12 37		12 56	13 00	13 02		12 51	13 05		

until 23 June

Leeds - Wakefield, Doncaster and Sheffield

Network Diagram - see first page of Table 31

	NT	NT	NT	NT	GR	XC	NT		NT	NT	NT	NT	NT	NT	GR	XC	NT	NT	NT	NT	NT	GR	NT
Leeds [10] 32,34 d	12 37		12 48	13 05	13 05	13 11			13 20	13 32	13 37		13 48	14 05	14 05	14 11		14 20	14 32	14 37		14 40	14 48
Outwood d		←	12 59						13 29			←	13 59					14 29			←		14 59
Wakefield Kirkgate [4] 32,34,39 a	12 54	13 02		13 23						14 01	13 54	14 01		14 23					15 01	14 54	15 01		
d	12 55	13 04		13 23						14 04	13 55	14 04		14 23					15 04	14 55	15 04		
Pontefract Monkhill d										→									→				
Wakefield Westgate [7] 32,39 a			13 03		13 16	13 22			13 33				14 03		14 16	14 23		14 33				14 52	15 03
d			13 03		13 16	13 23			13 33				14 03		14 16	14 24		14 33				14 52	15 03
Sandal & Agbrigg d			13 07						13 36				14 07					14 36					15 07
Fitzwilliam d			13 14						13 44				14 14					14 44					15 14
South Elmsall d									13 49									14 49					
Adwick a									13 54									14 54					
d							13 15		13 55								14 15	14 55					
Bentley (S.Yorks) d							13 19		13 59								14 19	14 59					
Doncaster [7] a					13 35		13 24		14 07						14 35		14 24	15 07				15 10	
Moorthorpe d			13 20										14 20										15 20
Thurnscoe d			13 26										14 26										15 26
Goldthorpe d			13 28										14 28										15 28
Bolton-upon-Dearne d			13 31										14 31										15 31
Swinton (S.Yorks) 29 a			13 35				13 42						14 35				14 43						15 35
Rotherham Central 29 a			13 43				13 52						14 43				14 52						15 43
Meadowhall 29 a	13 27	13 46	13 49	13 52			13 57				14 27	14 46	14 49	14 52			14 57			15 27	15 46		15 49
Sheffield [7] 29 a	13 37	13 56	14 00	14 02		13 51	14 05				14 37	14 56	15 00	15 02		14 51	15 05			15 37	15 56		16 00

	NT	GR	XC	NT	NT	NT	NT	NT	NT	NT	GR	GC	NT	XC	NT		NT	NT	NT	XC	NT	NT	NT	GR
Leeds [10] 32,34 d	15 05	15 05	15 12		15 20		15 32	15 37		15 48	16 05		16 05	16 12			16 20	16 32	16 37	16 40		16 48	17 05	17 05
Outwood d					15 29				←	15 59							16 29				←	16 59		
Wakefield Kirkgate [4] 32,34,39 a	15 23						16 01	15 54	16 01				16 23					17 01	16 54		17 01		17 22	
d	15 23						16 04	15 55	16 04			16 11	16 23					17 04	16 55		17 04		17 23	
Pontefract Monkhill d							→					16 29						→						
Wakefield Westgate [7] 32,39 a		15 16	15 23		15 33					16 03	16 17			16 23			16 33			16 51		17 03		17 17
d		15 17	15 24		15 33					16 03	16 17			16 24			16 33			16 52		17 03		17 17
Sandal & Agbrigg d					15 36					16 07							16 36					17 07		
Fitzwilliam d					15 44					16 14							16 44					17 14		
South Elmsall d					15 49												16 49							
Adwick a					15 54												16 54							
d				15 15	15 55										16 15		16 55							
Bentley (S.Yorks) d				15 19	15 59										16 18		16 59							
Doncaster [7] a		15 34		15 24	16 07						16 35	17 02			16 25		17 07							17 35
Moorthorpe d						15 50				16 20												17 20		
Thurnscoe d										16 26												17 26		
Goldthorpe d										16 28												17 28		
Bolton-upon-Dearne d										16 31												17 31		
Swinton (S.Yorks) 29 a				15 42		16 01				16 35					16 41							17 35		
Rotherham Central 29 a				15 50		16 09				16 43					16 50							17 43		
Meadowhall 29 a	15 51			15 56		16 17		16 27	16 46	16 49			16 52		16 55				17 27		17 46	17 49	17 51	
Sheffield [7] 29 a	16 03		15 51	16 05		16 27		16 37	16 56	17 00			17 02	16 51	17 05				17 37	17 20	17 56	18 00	18 03	

	XC	NT	NT	NT	NT	NT	NT		NT	GR	XC	NT	NT	NT	NT	NT	NT	GR	XC	NT	NT	NT	NT
Leeds [10] 32,34 d	17 11	17 20		17 32	17 37		17 48		18 05	18 05	18 11	18 20	18 32	18 37		18 48	19 05	19 05	19 11	19 20	19 37	19 43	
Outwood d		17 29				←	17 59					18 29			←	18 59				19 29			←
Wakefield Kirkgate [4] 32,34,39 a				18 01	17 54	18 01			18 23				19 04	18 54	19 04		19 24				20 06	19 59	20 06
d				18 04	17 55	18 04			18 23				19 05	18 55	19 05		19 24				20 07	20 00	20 07
Pontefract Monkhill d				→									→								→		
Wakefield Westgate [7] 32,39 a	17 22	17 33					18 03			18 16	18 22	18 33				19 03		19 16	19 23	19 33			
d	17 23	17 33					18 03			18 16	18 23	18 33				19 03		19 16	19 24	19 33			
Sandal & Agbrigg d		17 36					18 07					18 36				19 07				19 36			
Fitzwilliam d		17 44					18 14					18 44				19 14				19 44			
South Elmsall d		17 49										18 49								19 49			
Adwick a		17 54										18 54								19 54			
d		17 55	18 16									18 55								19 55			
Bentley (S.Yorks) d		17 59	18 20									18 59								19 59			
Doncaster [7] a		18 07	18 27							18 35		19 07						19 36		20 07			
Moorthorpe d							18 20									19 20							
Thurnscoe d							18 26									19 26							
Goldthorpe d							18 28									19 28							
Bolton-upon-Dearne d							18 31									19 31							
Swinton (S.Yorks) 29 a							18 35									19 35							
Rotherham Central 29 a							18 44									19 44							
Meadowhall 29 a					18 27	18 46	18 50		18 52					19 28	19 47	19 50	19 52					20 33	20 45
Sheffield [7] 29 a	17 51				18 38	18 56	19 00		19 03		18 51			19 39	19 56	20 00	20 04		19 51			20 44	20 58

Leeds - Wakefield, Doncaster and Sheffield

Saturdays until 23 June

Network Diagram - see first page of Table 31

Station		NT	GR	XC	NT	NT	NT	NT	XC	NT	NT	NT	NT	NT	NT	NT		NT	NT
			■ 1	◇1					◇1										
Leeds 10	32,34 d	19 48	20 05	20 11	20 20	20 30	20 37	20 48	21 11	21 20		21 37	21 48	22 16				22 37	22 44
Outwood	d	19 59			20 29			20 59		21 29			21 59	22 25					22 55
Wakefield Kirkgate 4	32,34,39 a					20 46	21 06					22 06						23 10	
	d					20 46	21 07				21 48	22 07			22 55	23 07			
Pontefract Monkhill	d															23a29			
Wakefield Westgate 7	32,39 a	20 03	20 16	20 22	20 33			21 03	21 22	21 33	21 53		22 03	22 29	23 01				22 59
	d	20 03	20 16	20 23	20 33			21 03	21 23	21 33			22 03	22 30					22 59
Sandal & Agbrigg	d	20 07			20 36			21 07		21 36			22 07	22 33					23 03
Fitzwilliam	d	20 14			20 44			21 13		21 44			22 14	22 39					23 10
South Elmsall	d				20 49					21 49				22 44					
Adwick	a				20 54					21 54				22 50					
	d				20 55					21 55				22 50					
Bentley (S.Yorks)	d				20 59					21 59				22 54					
Doncaster 7	a		20 35		21 07					22 07				23 04					
Moorthorpe	d	20 20						21 19					22 20						23 15
Thurnscoe	d	20 26						21 25					22 26						23 21
Goldthorpe	d	20 28						21 27					22 28						23 23
Bolton-upon-Dearne	d	20 31						21 30					22 31						23 26
Swinton (S.Yorks)	29 a	20 35						21 34					22 37						23 30
Rotherham Central	29 a	20 45						21 41					22 44						23 37
Meadowhall	29 a	20 50				21 19	21 45	21 49				22 47	22 52						23 43
Sheffield 7	29 a	21 00		20 52		21 30	21 57	22 02	21 51			22 58	23 03						23 58

Saturdays 30 June to 8 September

Station		NT	NT	GR	GR	GR	XC	GR	XC	NT	EM	NT	GR	NT	NT	NT		GR	XC	NT	NT	GC	GC	NT	EM
				■ 1 A	■ 1 B	■ 1	◇1	■ 1	◇1		◇1		■ 1 C					■ 1	◇1			■ 1			◇1
Leeds 10	32,34 d	22p37	23p09	04 44	04 44	05 05	06 00	06 05	06 15	06 20	06 34	06 38	06 40	06 43		07 05		07 05	07 10		07 20			07 29	07 34
Outwood	d		23p20							06 29				06 54							07 29				
Wakefield Kirkgate 4	32,34,39 a	23p10										07 07				07 25								08 00	
	d	23p10										07 08				07 25						07 41	07 45	08 04	
Pontefract Monkhill	d																						08a10	→	
Wakefield Westgate 7	32,39 a		23p24	04 56		05 16	06 11	06 17	06 28	06 33	06 45		06 51	06 58				07 16	07 22		07 34				07 45
	d		23p24	04 56	04u56	05 16	06 12	06 17	06 29	06 33	06 46		06 51	06 58				07 16	07 23		07 34				07 46
Sandal & Agbrigg	d		23p28							06 36				07 02							07 37				
Fitzwilliam	d		23p35							06 44				07 09							07 44				
South Elmsall	d									06 49											07 49				
Adwick	a									06 54											07 54				
	d									06 55										07 23	07 55				
Bentley (S.Yorks)	d									06 59										07 27	07 59				
Doncaster 7	a			05 14	05 14	05 34		06 34	06 46	07 07			07 13					07 35		07 31	08 07	08 27			
Moorthorpe	d		23p41											07 15											
Thurnscoe	d		23p47											07 21											
Goldthorpe	d		23p49											07 23											
Bolton-upon-Dearne	d		23p52											07 26											
Swinton (S.Yorks)	29 a		23p56											07 30						07 53					
Rotherham Central	29 a		00 03											07 37	←					08 01					
Meadowhall	29 a	23p51	00 08									07 48		07 46	07 48	07 53				08 06					
Sheffield 7	29 a	00 02	00 23				06 45		07 15		07 22	→		07 54	07 58	08 05			07 51	08 18					08 21

Station		NT	NT	NT	GR	NT	XC	NT		NT	NT	NT	NT	NT	GR	NT	GR	NT	XC	NT	NT	NT	NT	NT
					■ 1		◇1								■ 1		■ 1		◇1					
Leeds 10	32,34 d	07 35		07 48	08 05	08 05	08 12				08 20	08 32	08 37		08 40	08 48	09 05	09 05	09 11		09 20	09 32	09 37	
Outwood	d		←	07 59							08 29			←		08 59					09 29			←
Wakefield Kirkgate 4	32,34,39 a	07 54	08 00			08 23						09 03	08 54	09 03				09 23				10 01	09 55	10 01
	d	07 55	08 04			08 23						09 05	08 55	09 05				09 23				10 04	09 56	10 04
Pontefract Monkhill	d											→										→		
Wakefield Westgate 7	32,39 a			08 03	08 16		08 23				08 33				08 51	09 03	09 17		09 23		09 33			
	d			08 03	08 16		08 24				08 33				08 51	09 03	09 17		09 24		09 33			
Sandal & Agbrigg	d			08 07							08 36					09 07					09 35			
Fitzwilliam	d			08 14							08 44					09 14					09 44			
South Elmsall	d										08 49										09 47			
Adwick	a										08 54										09 53			
	d							08 15		08 33	08 55									09 15	09 53			
Bentley (S.Yorks)	d							08 19		08 37	08 59									09 19	09 57			
Doncaster 7	a				08 34			08 23		08 42	09 07				09 12		09 34			09 24	10 08			
Moorthorpe	d			08 20												09 20								
Thurnscoe	d			08 26												09 26								
Goldthorpe	d			08 28												09 28								
Bolton-upon-Dearne	d			08 31												09 31								
Swinton (S.Yorks)	29 a			08 35				08 43								09 35				09 42				
Rotherham Central	29 a			08 44				08 50								09 45				09 50				
Meadowhall	29 a	08 31	08 45	08 49		08 52		08 56					09 27	09 46		09 50		09 52		09 54			10 27	10 46
Sheffield 7	29 a	08 39	08 56	08 59		09 02	08 51	09 05					09 37	09 56		10 00		10 02	09 52	10 05			10 37	10 56

A 28 July, 4 August, 11 August
B 1 September, 8 September
C 28 July, 4 August, 11 August, 1 September, 8 September

Leeds - Wakefield, Doncaster and Sheffield

Saturdays 30 June to 8 September

Network Diagram - see first page of Table 31

Station		NT	NT	GR	XC	NT	NT	NT	NT	NT	NT	GR	GC	GC	NT	XC		NT	NT	NT	NT	NT	NT	NT	NT
				■ 1	◇1							■ 1	■ 1			◇1									
Leeds 10	32,34 d	09 48	10 05	10 05	10 12		10 20	10 32	10 37		10 48	11 05			11 05	11 11			11 20		11 32	11 37		11 48	12 05
Outwood	d	09 59					10 29			←	10 59								11 29				←	11 59	
Wakefield Kirkgate 4	32,34,39 a		10 23					11 01	10 54	11 01					11 23						12 01	11 54	12 01		12 23
	d		10 23					11 04	10 55	11 04			11 11	11 15	11 23						12 04	11 55	12 04		12 23
Pontefract Monkhill	d							→						11a40							→				
Wakefield Westgate 7	32,39 a	10 03		10 16	10 23		10 33				11 03	11 16				11 22			11 33					12 03	
	d	10 03		10 16	10 24		10 33				11 03	11 16				11 23			11 33					12 03	
Sandal & Agbrigg	d	10 07					10 36				11 07								11 36					12 07	
Fitzwilliam	d	10 14					10 44				11 14								11 44					12 14	
South Elmsall	d						10 49												11 49						
Adwick	a						10 54												11 54						
	d					10 15	10 55											11 15	11 55						
Bentley (S.Yorks)	d					10 19	10 59											11 19	11 59						
Doncaster 7	a			10 35		10 24	11 07					11 35	12 03					11 24	12 07						
Moorthorpe	d	10 20									11 20									11 59				12 20	
Thurnscoe	d	10 26									11 26													12 26	
Goldthorpe	d	10 28									11 28													12 28	
Bolton-upon-Dearne	d	10 31									11 31													12 31	
Swinton (S.Yorks)	29 a	10 35				10 42					11 35							11 42		12 08				12 35	
Rotherham Central	29 a	10 44				10 52					11 44							11 52		12 18				12 43	
Meadowhall	29 a	10 50	10 52			10 57			11 27	11 46	11 50				11 52			11 57		12 24		12 27	12 46	12 49	12 52
Sheffield 7	29 a	11 00	11 02		10 51	11 06			11 37	11 57	12 00				12 02	11 51		12 05		12 36		12 37	12 56	13 00	13 02

Station		GR	XC	NT	NT	NT	NT	NT		NT	NT	GR	XC	NT	NT	NT	NT	NT	NT	NT	GR	XC	NT	NT
		■ 1	◇1									■ 1	◇1								■ 1	◇1		
Leeds 10	32,34 d	12 05	12 11		12 20	12 32	12 37			12 48	13 05	13 05	13 11		13 20	13 32	13 37		13 48	14 05	14 05	14 11		14 20
Outwood	d				12 29			←		12 59					13 29			←	13 59					14 29
Wakefield Kirkgate 4	32,34,39 a					13 02	12 54	13 02			13 23					14 01	13 54	14 01		14 23				
	d					13 04	12 55	13 04			13 23					14 04	13 55	14 04		14 23				
Pontefract Monkhill	d					→										→								
Wakefield Westgate 7	32,39 a	12 16	12 23		12 33					13 03		13 16	13 22		13 33				14 03		14 16	14 23		14 33
	d	12 16	12 24		12 33					13 03		13 16	13 23		13 33				14 03		14 16	14 24		14 33
Sandal & Agbrigg	d				12 36					13 07					13 36				14 07					14 36
Fitzwilliam	d				12 44					13 14					13 44				14 14					14 44
South Elmsall	d				12 49										13 49									14 49
Adwick	a				12 54										13 54									14 54
	d			12 14	12 55									13 15	13 55								14 15	14 55
Bentley (S.Yorks)	d			12 18	12 59									13 19	13 59								14 19	14 59
Doncaster 7	a	12 35		12 24	13 07							13 35		13 24	14 07						14 35		14 24	15 07
Moorthorpe	d									13 20									14 20					
Thurnscoe	d									13 26									14 26					
Goldthorpe	d									13 28									14 28					
Bolton-upon-Dearne	d									13 31									14 31					
Swinton (S.Yorks)	29 a			12 42						13 35				13 42					14 35				14 43	
Rotherham Central	29 a			12 52						13 43				13 52					14 43				14 52	
Meadowhall	29 a			12 57			13 27	13 46		13 49	13 52			13 57			14 27	14 46	14 49	14 52			14 57	
Sheffield 7	29 a		12 51	13 05			13 37	13 56		14 00	14 02		13 51	14 05			14 37	14 56	15 00	15 02		14 51	15 05	

Station		NT	NT	NT	GR	NT	NT	GR	XC	NT	NT	NT	NT	NT	NT	NT		GR	GC	GC	NT	XC	NT	NT	NT
					■ 1			■ 1	◇1									■ 1	■ 1			◇1			
Leeds 10	32,34 d	14 32	14 37		14 40	14 48	15 05	15 05	15 12		15 20		15 32	15 37		15 48		16 05			16 05	16 12		16 20	16 32
Outwood	d			←		14 59					15 29				←	15 59								16 29	
Wakefield Kirkgate 4	32,34,39 a	15 01	14 54	15 01			15 23						16 01	15 54	16 01						16 23				17 01
	d	15 04	14 55	15 04			15 23						16 04	15 55	16 04				16 11	16 15	16 23				17 04
Pontefract Monkhill	d	→											→							16a40					→
Wakefield Westgate 7	32,39 a				14 52	15 03		15 16	15 23		15 33					16 03		16 17				16 23		16 33	
	d				14 52	15 03		15 17	15 24		15 33					16 03		16 17				16 24		16 33	
Sandal & Agbrigg	d					15 07					15 36					16 07								16 36	
Fitzwilliam	d					15 14					15 44					16 14								16 44	
South Elmsall	d										15 49													16 49	
Adwick	a										15 54													16 54	
	d									15 15	15 55												16 15	16 55	
Bentley (S.Yorks)	d									15 19	15 59												16 18	16 59	
Doncaster 7	a				15 10			15 34		15 24	16 07							16 35	17 02				16 25	17 07	
Moorthorpe	d					15 20						15 50				16 20									
Thurnscoe	d					15 26										16 26									
Goldthorpe	d					15 28										16 28									
Bolton-upon-Dearne	d					15 31										16 31									
Swinton (S.Yorks)	29 a					15 35				15 42		16 01				16 35							16 41		
Rotherham Central	29 a					15 43				15 50		16 09				16 43							16 50		
Meadowhall	29 a		15 27	15 46		15 49	15 51			15 56		16 17		16 27	16 46	16 49					16 52		16 55		
Sheffield 7	29 a		15 37	15 56		16 00	16 03		15 51	16 05		16 27		16 37	16 56	17 00					17 02	16 51	17 05		

Leeds - Wakefield, Doncaster and Sheffield

30 June to 8 September

Network Diagram - see first page of Table 31

	NT	XC	NT	NT	NT	GR	XC	NT	NT	NT	NT	NT	NT	NT	GR	XC	NT	NT	NT	NT	NT	NT
		◇1				1	◇1								1	◇1						
Leeds 10 32,34 d	16 37	16 40		16 48	17 05	17 05	17 11	17 20		17 32	17 37		17 48	18 05	18 05	18 11	18 20	18 32	18 37		18 48	19 05
Outwood d			←	16 59				17 29				←	17 59				18 29			←	18 59	
Wakefield Kirkgate 4 32,34,39 a	16 54		17 01		17 22					18 01	17 54	18 01		18 23				19 04	18 54	19 04		19 24
d	16 55		17 04		17 23					18 04	17 55	18 04		18 23				19 05	18 55	19 05		19 24
Pontefract Monkhill d										→								→				
Wakefield Westgate 7 32,39 a		16 51		17 03		17 17	17 22	17 33					18 03		18 16	18 22	18 33				19 03	
d		16 52		17 03		17 17	17 23	17 33					18 03		18 16	18 23	18 33				19 03	
Sandal & Agbrigg d				17 07				17 36					18 07				18 36				19 07	
Fitzwilliam d				17 14				17 44					18 14				18 44				19 14	
South Elmsall d								17 49									18 49					
Adwick a								17 54									18 54					
d								17 55	18 16								18 55					
Bentley (S.Yorks) d								17 59	18 20								18 59					
Doncaster 7 a						17 35		18 07	18 27						18 35		19 07					
Moorthorpe d				17 20									18 20								19 20	
Thurnscoe d				17 26									18 26								19 26	
Goldthorpe d				17 28									18 28								19 28	
Bolton-upon-Dearne d				17 31									18 31								19 31	
Swinton (S.Yorks) 29 a				17 35									18 35								19 35	
Rotherham Central 29 a				17 43									18 44								19 44	
Meadowhall 29 a	17 27		17 46	17 49	17 51						18 27	18 46	18 50	18 52					19 28	19 47	19 50	19 52
Sheffield 7 29 a	17 37	17 20	17 56	18 00	18 03		17 51				18 38	18 56	19 00	19 03		18 51			19 39	19 56	20 00	20 04

	GR	XC	NT	NT	NT	NT	NT	GR	XC	NT	NT	NT	NT	XC	NT	GC	NT	NT	NT	NT	NT	NT	NT
	1	◇1						1	◇1					◇1									
Leeds 10 32,34 d	19 05	19 11	19 20	19 37	19 43		19 48	20 05	20 11	20 20	20 30	20 37	20 48	21 11	21 20			21 37	21 48	22 16			22 37
Outwood d			19 29			←	19 59			20 29			20 59		21 29				21 59	22 25			
Wakefield Kirkgate 4 32,34,39 a				20 06	19 59	20 06					20 46	21 06						22 06					23 10
d				20 07	20 00	20 07					20 46	21 07				21 45	21 48	22 07			22 55	23 07	
Pontefract Monkhill d				→												22a10						23a29	
Wakefield Westgate 7 32,39 a	19 16	19 23	19 33				20 03	20 16	20 22	20 33			21 03	21 22	21 33		21 53		22 03	22 29	23 01		
d	19 16	19 24	19 33				20 03	20 16	20 23	20 33			21 03	21 23	21 33				22 03	22 30			
Sandal & Agbrigg d			19 36				20 07			20 36			21 07		21 36				22 07	22 33			
Fitzwilliam d			19 44				20 14			20 44			21 13		21 44				22 14	22 39			
South Elmsall d			19 49							20 49					21 49					22 44			
Adwick a			19 54							20 54					21 54					22 50			
d			19 55							20 55					21 55					22 50			
Bentley (S.Yorks) d			19 59							20 59					21 59					22 54			
Doncaster 7 a	19 36		20 07					20 35		21 07					22 07					23 04			
Moorthorpe d							20 20						21 19						22 20				
Thurnscoe d							20 26						21 25						22 26				
Goldthorpe d							20 28						21 27						22 28				
Bolton-upon-Dearne d							20 31						21 30						22 31				
Swinton (S.Yorks) 29 a							20 35						21 34						22 37				
Rotherham Central 29 a							20 45						21 41						22 44				
Meadowhall 29 a					20 33	20 45	20 50				21 19	21 45	21 49					22 47	22 52				
Sheffield 7 29 a		19 51			20 44	20 58	21 00		20 52		21 30	21 57	22 02	21 51				22 58	23 03				

	NT
Leeds 10 32,34 d	22 44
Outwood d	22 55
Wakefield Kirkgate 4 32,34,39 a	
d	
Pontefract Monkhill d	
Wakefield Westgate 7 32,39 a	22 59
d	22 59
Sandal & Agbrigg d	23 03
Fitzwilliam d	23 10
South Elmsall d	
Adwick a	
d	
Bentley (S.Yorks) d	
Doncaster 7 a	
Moorthorpe d	23 15
Thurnscoe d	23 21
Goldthorpe d	23 23
Bolton-upon-Dearne d	23 26
Swinton (S.Yorks) 29 a	23 30
Rotherham Central 29 a	23 37
Meadowhall 29 a	23 43
Sheffield 7 29 a	23 58

Leeds - Wakefield, Doncaster and Sheffield

Saturdays

from 15 September

Network Diagram - see first page of Table 31

	NT	NT	GR	XC	GR	XC	NT	EM	NT	NT	NT	NT	GR	XC	NT	NT	GC	NT	EM	NT	NT	NT	GR
			1	◇1	1	◇1		◇1					1	◇1			1		◇1				1
Leeds 10 32,34 d	22p37	23p09	05 05	06 00	06 05	06 15	06 20	06 34	06 38	06 43		07 05	07 05	07 10		07 20		07 29	07 34	07 35		07 48	08 05
Outwood d		23p20					06 29			06 54						07 29					←	07 59	
Wakefield Kirkgate 4 32,34,39 a	23p10								07 07			07 25						08 00		07 54	08 00		
d	23p10								07 08			07 25					07 38	08 04		07 55	08 04		
Pontefract Monkhill d																	07 58	→					
Wakefield Westgate 7 32,39 a		23p24	05 16	06 11	06 17	06 28	06 33	06 45		06 58			07 16	07 22		07 34			07 45			08 03	08 16
d		23p24	05 16	06 12	06 17	06 29	06 33	06 46		06 58			07 16	07 23		07 34			07 46			08 03	08 16
Sandal & Agbrigg d		23p28					06 36			07 02						07 37						08 07	
Fitzwilliam d		23p35					06 44			07 09						07 44						08 14	
South Elmsall d							06 49									07 49							
Adwick a							06 54									07 54							
d							06 55								07 23	07 55							
Bentley (S.Yorks) d							06 59								07 27	07 59							
Doncaster 7 a			05 34		06 34	06 46	07 07						07 35		07 31	08 07	08 27						08 34
Moorthorpe d		23p41								07 15												08 20	
Thurnscoe d		23p47								07 21												08 26	
Goldthorpe d		23p49								07 23												08 28	
Bolton-upon-Dearne d		23p52								07 26												08 31	
Swinton (S.Yorks) 29 a		23p56								07 30					07 53							08 35	
Rotherham Central 29 a		00 03								07 37	←				08 01							08 44	
Meadowhall 29 a	23p51	00 08							07 48	07 46	07 48	07 53			08 06					08 31	08 45	08 49	
Sheffield 7 29 a	00 02	00 23		06 45		07 15		07 22	→	07 54	07 58	08 05		07 51	08 18				08 21	08 39	08 56	08 59	

	NT	XC	NT	NT	NT	NT	NT	NT	GR	NT	GR	NT	XC	NT	NT	NT	NT	NT	NT	NT	GR	XC
		◇1							1		1		◇1								1	◇1
Leeds 10 32,34 d	08 05	08 12			08 20	08 32	08 37		08 40	08 48	09 05	09 05	09 11		09 20	09 32	09 37		09 48	10 05	10 05	10 12
Outwood d					08 29			←		08 59					09 29			←	09 59			
Wakefield Kirkgate 4 32,34,39 a	08 23					09 03	08 54	09 03				09 23				10 01	09 55	10 01		10 23		
d	08 23					09 05	08 55	09 05				09 23				10 04	09 56	10 04		10 23		
Pontefract Monkhill d						→										→						
Wakefield Westgate 7 32,39 a		08 23			08 33				08 51	09 03	09 17		09 23		09 33				10 03		10 16	10 23
d		08 24			08 33				08 51	09 03	09 17		09 24		09 33				10 03		10 16	10 24
Sandal & Agbrigg d					08 36					09 07					09 35				10 07			
Fitzwilliam d					08 44					09 14					09 44				10 14			
South Elmsall d					08 49										09 47							
Adwick a					08 54										09 53							
d			08 15	08 33	08 55									09 15	09 53							
Bentley (S.Yorks) d			08 19	08 37	08 59									09 19	09 57							
Doncaster 7 a			08 23	08 42	09 07				09 12		09 34			09 24	10 08						10 35	
Moorthorpe d										09 20									10 20			
Thurnscoe d										09 26									10 26			
Goldthorpe d										09 28									10 28			
Bolton-upon-Dearne d										09 31									10 31			
Swinton (S.Yorks) 29 a			08 43							09 35				09 42					10 35			
Rotherham Central 29 a			08 50							09 45				09 50					10 44			
Meadowhall 29 a	08 52		08 56				09 27	09 46		09 50		09 52		09 54			10 27	10 46	10 50	10 52		
Sheffield 7 29 a	09 02	08 51	09 05				09 37	09 56		10 00		10 02	09 52	10 05			10 37	10 56	11 00	11 02		10 51

	NT	NT	NT	NT	NT	NT	GR	GC	NT	XC	NT	NT	NT	NT	NT	NT	NT	NT	GR	XC	NT	NT	NT
							1	1		◇1									1	◇1			
Leeds 10 32,34 d		10 20	10 32	10 37		10 48	11 05		11 05	11 11		11 20		11 32	11 37		11 48	12 05	12 05	12 11		12 20	12 32
Outwood d		10 29			←	10 59						11 29				←	11 59					12 29	
Wakefield Kirkgate 4 32,34,39 a			11 01	10 54	11 01				11 23					12 01	11 54	12 01		12 23					13 02
d			11 04	10 55	11 04			11 13	11 23					12 04	11 55	12 04		12 23					13 04
Pontefract Monkhill d			→					11 37						→									→
Wakefield Westgate 7 32,39 a		10 33				11 03	11 16			11 22		11 33					12 03		12 16	12 23		12 33	
d		10 33				11 03	11 16			11 23		11 33					12 03		12 16	12 24		12 33	
Sandal & Agbrigg d		10 36				11 07						11 36					12 07					12 36	
Fitzwilliam d		10 44				11 14						11 44					12 14					12 44	
South Elmsall d		10 49										11 49										12 49	
Adwick a		10 54										11 54										12 54	
d	10 15	10 55									11 15	11 55									12 14	12 55	
Bentley (S.Yorks) d	10 19	10 59									11 19	11 59									12 18	12 59	
Doncaster 7 a	10 24	11 07					11 35	12 04			11 24	12 07							12 35		12 24	13 07	
Moorthorpe d						11 20							11 59				12 20						
Thurnscoe d						11 26											12 26						
Goldthorpe d						11 28											12 28						
Bolton-upon-Dearne d						11 31											12 31						
Swinton (S.Yorks) 29 a	10 42					11 35					11 42		12 08				12 35				12 42		
Rotherham Central 29 a	10 52					11 44					11 52		12 18				12 43				12 52		
Meadowhall 29 a	10 57			11 27	11 46	11 50			11 52		11 57		12 24		12 27	12 46	12 49	12 52			12 57		
Sheffield 7 29 a	11 06			11 37	11 57	12 00			12 02	11 51	12 05		12 36		12 37	12 56	13 00	13 02		12 51	13 05		

Leeds - Wakefield, Doncaster and Sheffield

Saturdays from 15 September

Network Diagram - see first page of Table 31

	NT	NT	NT	NT	GR	XC	NT	NT	NT	NT	NT	NT	NT	GR	XC	NT	NT	NT	NT	NT	GR	NT
					1	◇1								1	◇1						1	
Leeds 10 32,34 d	12 37		12 48	13 05	13 05	13 11		13 20	13 32	13 37		13 48	14 05	14 05	14 11		14 20	14 32	14 37		14 40	14 48
Outwood d		←	12 59					13 29			←	13 59					14 29			←		14 59
Wakefield Kirkgate 4 32,34,39 a	12 54	13 02		13 23					14 01	13 54	14 01		14 23					15 01	14 54	15 01		
d	12 55	13 04		13 23					14 04	13 55	14 04		14 23					15 04	14 55	15 04		
Pontefract Monkhill d									→									→				
Wakefield Westgate 7 32,39 a			13 03		13 16	13 22		13 33				14 03		14 16	14 23		14 33				14 52	15 03
d			13 03		13 16	13 23		13 33				14 03		14 16	14 24		14 33				14 52	15 03
Sandal & Agbrigg d			13 07					13 36				14 07					14 36					15 07
Fitzwilliam d			13 14					13 44				14 14					14 44					15 14
South Elmsall d								13 49									14 49					
Adwick a								13 54									14 54					
d							13 15	13 55								14 15	14 55					
Bentley (S.Yorks) d							13 19	13 59								14 19	14 59					
Doncaster 7 a					13 35		13 24	14 07						14 35		14 24	15 07				15 10	
Moorthorpe d			13 20									14 20										15 20
Thurnscoe d			13 26									14 26										15 26
Goldthorpe d			13 28									14 28										15 28
Bolton-upon-Dearne d			13 31									14 31										15 31
Swinton (S.Yorks) 29 a			13 35				13 42					14 35				14 43						15 35
Rotherham Central 29 a			13 43				13 52					14 43				14 52						15 43
Meadowhall 29 a	13 27	13 46	13 49	13 52			13 57			14 27	14 46	14 49	14 52			14 57			15 27	15 46		15 49
Sheffield 7 29 a	13 37	13 56	14 00	14 02		13 51	14 05			14 37	14 56	15 00	15 02		14 51	15 05			15 37	15 56		16 00

	NT	GR	XC	NT	NT	NT	NT	NT	NT	NT	GR	GC	NT	XC	NT	NT	NT	NT	XC	NT	NT	NT	GR
		1	◇1								1	1		◇1					◇1				1
Leeds 10 32,34 d	15 05	15 05	15 12		15 20		15 32	15 37		15 48	16 05		16 05	16 12		16 20	16 32	16 37	16 40		16 48	17 05	17 05
Outwood d					15 29				←	15 59						16 29				←	16 59		
Wakefield Kirkgate 4 32,34,39 a	15 23						16 01	15 54	16 01				16 23				17 01	16 54		17 01		17 22	
d	15 23						16 04	15 55	16 04			16 11	16 23				17 04	16 55		17 04		17 23	
Pontefract Monkhill d							→					16 29					→						
Wakefield Westgate 7 32,39 a		15 16	15 23		15 33					16 03	16 17			16 23		16 33			16 51		17 03		17 17
d		15 17	15 24		15 33					16 03	16 17			16 24		16 33			16 52		17 03		17 17
Sandal & Agbrigg d					15 36					16 07						16 36					17 07		
Fitzwilliam d					15 44					16 14						16 44					17 14		
South Elmsall d					15 49											16 49							
Adwick a					15 54											16 54							
d				15 15	15 55										16 15	16 55							
Bentley (S.Yorks) d				15 19	15 59										16 18	16 59							
Doncaster 7 a		15 34		15 24	16 07						16 35	17 02			16 25	17 07							17 35
Moorthorpe d						15 50				16 20											17 20		
Thurnscoe d										16 26											17 26		
Goldthorpe d										16 28											17 28		
Bolton-upon-Dearne d										16 31											17 31		
Swinton (S.Yorks) 29 a				15 42		16 01				16 35					16 41						17 35		
Rotherham Central 29 a				15 50		16 09				16 43					16 50						17 43		
Meadowhall 29 a	15 51			15 56		16 17		16 27	16 46	16 49			16 52		16 55			17 27		17 46	17 49	17 51	
Sheffield 7 29 a	16 03		15 51	16 05		16 27		16 37	16 56	17 00			17 02	16 51	17 05			17 37	17 20	17 56	18 00	18 03	

	XC	NT	NT	NT	NT	NT	NT	NT	GR	XC	NT	NT	NT	NT	NT	NT	GR	XC	NT	NT	NT	NT
	◇1								1	◇1							1	◇1				
Leeds 10 32,34 d	17 11	17 20		17 32	17 37		17 48	18 05	18 05	18 11	18 20	18 32	18 37		18 48	19 05	19 05	19 11	19 20	19 37	19 43	
Outwood d		17 29				←	17 59				18 29			←	18 59				19 29			←
Wakefield Kirkgate 4 32,34,39 a				18 01	17 54	18 01		18 23				19 04	18 54	19 04		19 24				20 06	19 59	20 06
d				18 04	17 55	18 04		18 23				19 05	18 55	19 05		19 24				20 07	20 00	20 07
Pontefract Monkhill d				→								→								→		
Wakefield Westgate 7 32,39 a	17 22	17 33					18 03		18 16	18 22	18 33				19 03		19 16	19 23	19 33			
d	17 23	17 33					18 03		18 16	18 23	18 33				19 03		19 16	19 24	19 33			
Sandal & Agbrigg d		17 36					18 07				18 36				19 07				19 36			
Fitzwilliam d		17 44					18 14				18 44				19 14				19 44			
South Elmsall d		17 49									18 49								19 49			
Adwick a		17 54									18 54								19 54			
d		17 55	18 16								18 55								19 55			
Bentley (S.Yorks) d		17 59	18 20								18 59								19 59			
Doncaster 7 a		18 07	18 27						18 35		19 07						19 36		20 07			
Moorthorpe d							18 20								19 20							
Thurnscoe d							18 26								19 26							
Goldthorpe d							18 28								19 28							
Bolton-upon-Dearne d							18 31								19 31							
Swinton (S.Yorks) 29 a							18 35								19 35							
Rotherham Central 29 a							18 44								19 44							
Meadowhall 29 a					18 27	18 46	18 50	18 52					19 28	19 47	19 50	19 52					20 33	20 45
Sheffield 7 29 a	17 51				18 38	18 56	19 00	19 03		18 51			19 39	19 56	20 00	20 04		19 51			20 44	20 58

Leeds - Wakefield, Doncaster and Sheffield

Saturdays from 15 September

Network Diagram - see first page of Table 31

	NT	GR	XC	NT	NT	NT	NT	XC	NT	NT	NT	NT	NT	NT	NT	NT	NT
		1	◇1					◇1									
Leeds 10 32,34 d	19 48	20 05	20 11	20 20	20 30	20 37	20 48	21 11	21 20		21 37	21 48	22 16			22 37	22 44
Outwood d	19 59			20 29			20 59		21 29			21 59	22 25				22 55
Wakefield Kirkgate 4 32,34,39 a					20 46	21 06					22 06					23 10	
d					20 46	21 07				21 48	22 07			22 55	23 07		
Pontefract Monkhill d															23a29		
Wakefield Westgate 7 32,39 a	20 03	20 16	20 22	20 33			21 03	21 22	21 33	21 53		22 03	22 29	23 01			22 59
d	20 03	20 16	20 23	20 33			21 03	21 23	21 33			22 03	22 30				22 59
Sandal & Agbrigg d	20 07			20 36			21 07		21 36			22 07	22 33				23 03
Fitzwilliam d	20 14			20 44			21 13		21 44			22 14	22 39				23 10
South Elmsall d				20 49					21 49				22 44				
Adwick a				20 54					21 54				22 50				
d				20 55					21 55				22 50				
Bentley (S.Yorks) d				20 59					21 59				22 54				
Doncaster 7 a		20 35		21 07					22 07				23 04				
Moorthorpe d	20 20						21 19					22 20					23 15
Thurnscoe d	20 26						21 25					22 26					23 21
Goldthorpe d	20 28						21 27					22 28					23 23
Bolton-upon-Dearne d	20 31						21 30					22 31					23 26
Swinton (S.Yorks) 29 a	20 35						21 34					22 37					23 30
Rotherham Central 29 a	20 45						21 41					22 44					23 37
Meadowhall 29 a	20 50				21 19	21 45	21 49				22 47	22 52					23 43
Sheffield 7 29 a	21 00		20 52		21 30	21 57	22 02	21 51			22 58	23 03					23 58

Sundays until 24 June

	GR	XC	GC	NT	EM	NT	XC	NT	GR	EM	XC	NT	GR	NT	NT	NT	XC	GR	NT	NT	NT	XC	GR
	1	◇1	1		◇1		◇1		1	◇1	◇1		1				◇1	1				◇1	1
Leeds 10 32,34 d	08 05	08 10		08 34	08 42	08 48	09 00	09 05	09 05	09 46	10 00	10 02	10 05	10 17	10 18	10 57	11 00	11 05	11 18	11 29		12 00	12 05
Outwood d						08 59									10 27				11 29				
Wakefield Kirkgate 4 32,34,39 a				09 03				09 21				10 18		10 46		11 13				11 46			
d			08 43	09 03				09 21				10 18		10 46		11 13				11 46			
Pontefract Monkhill d																							
Wakefield Westgate 7 32,39 a	08 16	08 22			08 58	09 03	09 11		09 17	09 58	10 11		10 16		10 32		11 11	11 16	11 33			12 11	12 17
d	08 16	08 23			08 59	09 03	09 11		09 17	09 59	10 12		10 17		10 32		11 12	11 17	11 33			12 12	12 17
Sandal & Agbrigg d						09 07									10 35				11 37				
Fitzwilliam d						09 14									10 42				11 44				
South Elmsall d															10 47								
Adwick a															10 52								
d															10 53								
Bentley (S.Yorks) d															10 57								
Doncaster 7 a	08 34		09 04				09 31		09 35		10 28		10 35		11 05		11 28	11 35				12 28	12 36
Moorthorpe d						09 20													11 50				
Thurnscoe d						09 26													11 56				
Goldthorpe d						09 28													11 58				
Bolton-upon-Dearne d						09 31													12 01				
Swinton (S.Yorks) 29 a						09 35													12 05				
Rotherham Central 29 a						09 44													12 12		←		
Meadowhall 29 a				09 44		09 53		09 57				10 51		11 32		11 46			12 20	12 17	12 20		
Sheffield 7 29 a		08 51		09 55	09 30	10 03	09 55	10 04		10 26	10 54	11 02		11 44		11 56	11 53		→	12 29	12 32	12 54	

	NT	NT	GC	NT	XC	GR	NT	EM	GR	NT	XC	NT	NT	GR	NT	XC	NT	NT	XC	GR	GC	NT
			1		◇1	1		◇1	1		◇1			1		◇1			◇1	1	1	
Leeds 10 32,34 d	12 18	12 29		12 34	13 00	13 05	13 18	13 59	14 05	14 06	14 10	14 17	14 18	15 05	15 06	15 10	15 18	16 06	16 10	16 15		16 17
Outwood d	12 27						13 29						14 27				15 29					
Wakefield Kirkgate 4 32,34,39 a		12 46		13 04						14 22		14 46			15 22			16 22				16 46
d		12 46	12 51	13 04						14 22		14 46			15 22			16 22			16 30	16 46
Pontefract Monkhill d																						
Wakefield Westgate 7 32,39 a	12 31				13 11	13 16	13 33	14 11	14 17		14 22		14 31	15 16		15 22	15 33		16 21	16 27		
d	12 32				13 12	13 16	13 33	14 12	14 17		14 23		14 32	15 16		15 23	15 33		16 22	16 27		
Sandal & Agbrigg d	12 35						13 37						14 35				15 37					
Fitzwilliam d	12 41						13 45						14 41				15 44					
South Elmsall d	12 46												14 46									
Adwick a	12 52												14 52									
d	12 52												14 52									
Bentley (S.Yorks) d	12 56												14 56									
Doncaster 7 a	13 04		13 22		13 28	13 35			14 35				15 05	15 35						16 45	17 10	
Moorthorpe d							13 51										15 50					
Thurnscoe d							13 57										15 56					
Goldthorpe d							13 59										15 58					
Bolton-upon-Dearne d							14 02										16 01					
Swinton (S.Yorks) 29 a							14 06										16 05					
Rotherham Central 29 a							14 13										16 12					
Meadowhall 29 a		13 18		13 48			14 20			14 55		15 35			15 55		16 19	16 56				17 34
Sheffield 7 29 a		13 29		13 58	13 54		14 32	14 39		15 06	14 52	15 44			16 05	15 51	16 31	17 05	16 51			17 44

Leeds - Wakefield, Doncaster and Sheffield

Network Diagram - see first page of Table 31

		NT	GR	NT	XC	GR	NT	GR	NT	XC	GR	NT	NT	NT	GR	NT		XC	GR	NT	GR	XC	NT	NT	GR
			1		◇1	1		1		◇1	1				1			◇1	1		1	◇1			1
Leeds 10 32,34	d	16 18	16 45	17 06	17 10	17 15	17 18	17 45	18 06	18 10	18 15		18 17	18 18	18 45	19 06		19 10	19 15	19 18	19 45	20 10	20 17	20 18	20 45
Outwood	d	16 27					17 29							18 27						19 29				20 27	
Wakefield Kirkgate 4 32,34,39	a			17 22					18 22				18 45			19 22							20 46		
	d			17 22					18 22				18 45			19 22							20 46		
Pontefract Monkhill	d																								
Wakefield Westgate 7 32,39	a	16 32	16 56		17 21	17 27	17 33	17 56		18 21	18 27			18 32	18 56			19 21	19 26	19 33	19 56	20 21		20 31	20 56
	d	16 32	16 56		17 22	17 27	17 33	17 57		18 22	18 27			18 32	18 56			19 22	19 26	19 33	19 56	20 22		20 32	20 56
Sandal & Agbrigg	d	16 35					17 37							18 35						19 37				20 35	
Fitzwilliam	d	16 42					17 47							18 42						19 44				20 41	
South Elmsall	d	16 47												18 47										20 46	
Adwick	a	16 52												18 52										20 52	
	d	16 53												18 53										20 52	
Bentley (S.Yorks)	d	16 57												18 57										20 56	
Doncaster 7	a	17 06	17 17			17 45		18 16			18 45			19 06	19 17				19 44		20 16			21 05	21 14
Moorthorpe	d						17 54					18 52								19 50					
Thurnscoe	d						18 00													19 56					
Goldthorpe	d						18 02													19 58					
Bolton-upon-Dearne	d						18 05													20 01					
Swinton (S.Yorks) 29	a						18 10					19 01								20 09					
Rotherham Central 29	a						18 17					19 12								20 16					
Meadowhall 29	a			17 55			18 25		18 56			19 18	19 32			19 54				20 22			21 33		
Sheffield 7 29	a			18 05	17 51		18 36		19 05	18 51		19 27	19 43			20 04		19 50		20 34		20 51	21 42		

		XC	NT	NT	NT	NT
		◇1				
Leeds 10 32,34	d	21 10	21 18		21 40	22 17
Outwood	d		21 27		21 51	
Wakefield Kirkgate 4 32,34,39	a					22 46
	d					22 46
Pontefract Monkhill	d					
Wakefield Westgate 7 32,39	a	21 21	21 31		21 55	
	d	21 22	21 31		21 55	
Sandal & Agbrigg	d		21 34		21 59	
Fitzwilliam	d		21 41		22 06	
South Elmsall	d		21 46			
Adwick	a		21 51			
	d		21 52			
Bentley (S.Yorks)	d		21 56			
Doncaster 7	a		22 05			
Moorthorpe	d			21 36	22 13	
Thurnscoe	d				22 19	
Goldthorpe	d				22 21	
Bolton-upon-Dearne	d				22 24	
Swinton (S.Yorks) 29	a			21 45	22 32	
Rotherham Central 29	a			21 52	22 39	
Meadowhall 29	a			21 57	22 45	23 30
Sheffield 7 29	a	21 50		22 09	22 54	23 43

Sundays
1 July to 9 September

		GR	GR	GR	XC	GC	NT	NT	XC	NT	GR	EM	XC	NT	GR	EM		NT	NT	NT	XC	GR	NT	NT	NT
		1 A	1 A	1	◇1	1			◇1		1	◇1	◇1		1	◇1					◇1	1			
Leeds 10 32,34	d	06 30	07 00	08 05	08 10		08 34	08 48	09 00	09 05	09 05	09 44	10 00	10 02	10 05	10 15		10 17	10 18	10 57	11 00	11 05	11 18	11 29	
Outwood	d							08 59											10 27				11 29		
Wakefield Kirkgate 4 32,34,39	a						09 03			09 21				10 18				10 46		11 13				11 46	
	d					08 43	09 03			09 21				10 18				10 46		11 13				11 46	
Pontefract Monkhill	d																								
Wakefield Westgate 7 32,39	a		07 11	08 16	08 22			09 03	09 11		09 17	09 57	10 11		10 16	10 26			10 32		11 11	11 16	11 33		
	d	06u41	07 11	08 16	08 23			09 03	09 11		09 17	09 58	10 12		10 17	10 27			10 32		11 12	11 17	11 33		
Sandal & Agbrigg	d							09 07											10 35				11 37		
Fitzwilliam	d							09 14											10 42				11 44		
South Elmsall	d																		10 47						
Adwick	a																		10 52						
	d																		10 53						
Bentley (S.Yorks)	d																		10 57						
Doncaster 7	a	06 58	07 29	08 34		09 04			09 31		09 35		10 28		10 35				11 05		11 28	11 35			
Moorthorpe	d							09 20															11 50		
Thurnscoe	d							09 26															11 56		
Goldthorpe	d							09 28															11 58		
Bolton-upon-Dearne	d							09 31															12 01		
Swinton (S.Yorks) 29	a							09 35															12 05		
Rotherham Central 29	a							09 44															12 12		←
Meadowhall 29	a						09 44	09 53		09 57				10 51				11 32		11 46			12 20	12 17	12 20
Sheffield 7 29	a				08 51		09 55	10 03	09 55	10 04		10 25	10 54	11 02		10 57		11 44		11 56	11 53		→	12 29	12 32

A 29 July, 5 August, 12 August, 2 September, 9 September

Leeds - Wakefield, Doncaster and Sheffield

Network Diagram - see first page of Table 31

		XC	GR	NT	NT	GC	NT	XC		GR	NT	EM	GR	NT	XC	NT	NT	GR	NT	XC	NT	NT	XC	GR
		◇1	1			1		◇1		1		◇1	1		◇1			1		◇1			◇1	1
Leeds 10 32,34	d	12 00	12 05	12 18	12 29		12 34	13 00		13 05	13 18	13 59	14 05	14 06	14 10	14 17	14 18	15 05	15 06	15 10	15 18	16 06	16 10	16 15
Outwood	d			12 27							13 29						14 27				15 29			
Wakefield Kirkgate 4 32,34,39	a				12 46		13 04							14 22		14 46			15 22			16 22		
	d				12 46	12 51	13 04							14 22		14 46			15 22			16 22		
Pontefract Monkhill	d																							
Wakefield Westgate 7 32,39	a	12 11	12 17	12 31				13 11		13 16	13 33	14 11	14 17		14 22		14 31	15 16		15 22	15 33		16 21	16 27
	d	12 12	12 17	12 32				13 12		13 16	13 33	14 12	14 17		14 23		14 32	15 16		15 23	15 33		16 22	16 27
Sandal & Agbrigg	d			12 35							13 37						14 35				15 37			
Fitzwilliam	d			12 41							13 45						14 41				15 44			
South Elmsall	d			12 46													14 46							
Adwick	a			12 52													14 52							
	d			12 52													14 52							
Bentley (S.Yorks)	d			12 56													14 56							
Doncaster 7	a	12 28	12 36	13 04		13 22		13 28		13 35			14 35				15 05	15 35						16 45
Moorthorpe	d										13 51										15 50			
Thurnscoe	d										13 57										15 56			
Goldthorpe	d										13 59										15 58			
Bolton-upon-Dearne	d										14 02										16 01			
Swinton (S.Yorks) 29	a										14 06										16 05			
Rotherham Central 29	a										14 13										16 12			
Meadowhall 29	a				13 18		13 48				14 20			14 55		15 35			15 55		16 20	16 56		
Sheffield 7 29	a	12 54			13 29		13 58	13 54			14 32	14 39		15 06	14 52	15 44			16 05	15 51	16 32	17 05	16 51	

		GC	NT	NT	GR	NT	XC	GR	NT	GR	NT	XC	GR	NT	NT	NT		GR	NT	XC	GR	NT	GR	XC	NT
		1			1		◇1	1		1		◇1	1					1		◇1	1		1	◇1	
Leeds 10 32,34	d		16 17	16 18	16 45	17 06	17 10	17 15	17 18	17 45	18 06	18 10	18 15		18 17	18 18		18 45	19 06	19 10	19 15	19 18	19 45	20 10	20 17
Outwood	d			16 27					17 29							18 27						19 29			
Wakefield Kirkgate 4 32,34,39	a		16 46			17 22					18 22				18 45				19 22						20 46
	d	16 30	16 46			17 22					18 22				18 45				19 22						20 46
Pontefract Monkhill	d																								
Wakefield Westgate 7 32,39	a			16 32	16 56		17 21	17 27	17 33	17 56		18 21	18 27			18 32		18 56		19 21	19 26	19 33	19 56	20 21	
	d			16 32	16 56		17 22	17 27	17 33	17 57		18 22	18 27			18 32		18 56		19 22	19 26	19 33	19 56	20 22	
Sandal & Agbrigg	d			16 35					17 37							18 35						19 37			
Fitzwilliam	d			16 42					17 47							18 42						19 44			
South Elmsall	d			16 47												18 47									
Adwick	a			16 52												18 52									
	d			16 53												18 53									
Bentley (S.Yorks)	d			16 57												18 57									
Doncaster 7	a	17 10		17 06	17 17			17 45		18 16			18 45			19 06		19 17			19 44		20 16		
Moorthorpe	d								17 54					18 52								19 50			
Thurnscoe	d								18 00													19 56			
Goldthorpe	d								18 02													19 58			
Bolton-upon-Dearne	d								18 05													20 01			
Swinton (S.Yorks) 29	a								18 10					19 01								20 07			
Rotherham Central 29	a								18 17					19 12								20 14			
Meadowhall 29	a		17 34			17 55			18 25		18 56			19 18	19 32				19 54			20 20			21 33
Sheffield 7 29	a		17 44			18 05	17 51		18 36		19 05	18 51		19 27	19 43				20 04	19 50		20 34		20 51	21 42

		NT	GR	XC	NT	NT	NT	NT
			1	◇1				
Leeds 10 32,34	d	20 18	20 45	21 10	21 18		21 40	22 17
Outwood	d	20 27			21 27		21 51	
Wakefield Kirkgate 4 32,34,39	a							22 46
	d							22 46
Pontefract Monkhill	d							
Wakefield Westgate 7 32,39	a	20 31	20 56	21 21	21 31		21 55	
	d	20 32	20 56	21 22	21 31		21 55	
Sandal & Agbrigg	d	20 35			21 34		21 59	
Fitzwilliam	d	20 41			21 41		22 06	
South Elmsall	d	20 46			21 46			
Adwick	a	20 52			21 51			
	d	20 52			21 52			
Bentley (S.Yorks)	d	20 56			21 56			
Doncaster 7	a	21 05	21 14		22 05			
Moorthorpe	d					21 36	22 13	
Thurnscoe	d						22 19	
Goldthorpe	d						22 21	
Bolton-upon-Dearne	d						22 24	
Swinton (S.Yorks) 29	a					21 45	22 32	
Rotherham Central 29	a					21 52	22 39	
Meadowhall 29	a					21 57	22 45	23 30
Sheffield 7 29	a			21 50		22 09	22 54	23 43

Table 31

Leeds - Wakefield, Doncaster and Sheffield

Sundays

16 September to 21 October

Network Diagram - see first page of Table 31

		GR	XC	GC	NT	EM	NT	XC	NT	GR	EM	XC	NT	GR	NT	NT		NT	XC	GR	NT	NT	NT	XC	GR
Leeds 10	32,34 d	08 05	08 10		08 34	08 42	08 48	09 00	09 05	09 05	09 46	10 00	10 02	10 05	10 17	10 18		10 57	11 00	11 05	11 18	11 29		12 00	12 05
Outwood	d						08 59									10 27					11 29				
Wakefield Kirkgate 4	32,34,39 a				09 03				09 21				10 18		10 46			11 13				11 46			
	d			08 43	09 03				09 21				10 18		10 46			11 13				11 46			
Pontefract Monkhill	d																								
Wakefield Westgate 7	32,39 a	08 16	08 22			08 54	09 03	09 11		09 17	09 57	10 11		10 16		10 32			11 11	11 16	11 33			12 11	12 17
	d	08 16	08 23			08 55	09 03	09 11		09 17	09 58	10 12		10 17		10 32			11 12	11 17	11 33			12 12	12 17
Sandal & Agbrigg	d						09 07									10 35					11 37				
Fitzwilliam	d						09 14									10 42					11 44				
South Elmsall	d															10 47									
Adwick	a															10 52									
	d															10 53									
Bentley (S.Yorks)	d															10 57									
Doncaster 7	a	08 34		09 04				09 31		09 35		10 28		10 35		11 05			11 28	11 35				12 28	12 36
Moorthorpe	d						09 20														11 50				
Thurnscoe	d						09 26														11 56				
Goldthorpe	d						09 28														11 58				
Bolton-upon-Dearne	d						09 31														12 01				
Swinton (S.Yorks)	29 a						09 35														12 05				
Rotherham Central	29 a						09 44														12 12		←		
Meadowhall	29 a				09 44		09 53		09 57				10 51		11 32			11 46			12 20	12 17	12 20		
Sheffield 7	29 a		08 51		09 55	09 23	10 03	09 55	10 04		10 26	10 54	11 02		11 44			11 56	11 53		→	12 29	12 32	12 54	

		NT	NT	GC	NT	XC	GR	NT		EM	GR	NT	XC	NT	NT	GR	NT	XC	NT	NT	XC	GR	GC	NT	
Leeds 10	32,34 d	12 18	12 29		12 34	13 00	13 05	13 18		13 59	14 05	14 06	14 10	14 17	14 18	15 05	15 06	15 10	15 18	16 06	16 10	16 15		16 17	
Outwood	d	12 27						13 29							14 27				15 29						
Wakefield Kirkgate 4	32,34,39 a		12 46		13 04							14 22		14 46			15 22			16 22				16 46	
	d		12 46	13 01	13 04							14 22		14 46			15 22			16 22			16 30	16 46	
Pontefract Monkhill	d																								
Wakefield Westgate 7	32,39 a	12 31				13 11	13 16	13 33		14 11	14 17		14 22		14 31	15 16		15 22	15 33		16 21	16 27			
	d	12 32				13 12	13 16	13 33		14 12	14 17		14 23		14 32	15 16		15 23	15 33		16 22	16 27			
Sandal & Agbrigg	d	12 35						13 37							14 35				15 37						
Fitzwilliam	d	12 41						13 45							14 41				15 44						
South Elmsall	d	12 46													14 46										
Adwick	a	12 52													14 52										
	d	12 52													14 52										
Bentley (S.Yorks)	d	12 56													14 56										
Doncaster 7	a	13 04		13 22		13 28	13 35				14 35				15 05	15 35						16 45	17 10		
Moorthorpe	d							13 51											15 50						
Thurnscoe	d							13 57											15 56						
Goldthorpe	d							13 59											15 58						
Bolton-upon-Dearne	d							14 02											16 01						
Swinton (S.Yorks)	29 a							14 06											16 05						
Rotherham Central	29 a							14 13											16 12						
Meadowhall	29 a		13 18		13 48			14 20				14 55		15 35			15 55		16 20	16 56				17 34	
Sheffield 7	29 a		13 29		13 58	13 54		14 32		14 39		15 06	14 52	15 44			16 05	15 51	16 32	17 05	16 51			17 44	

		NT	GR	NT	XC	GR	NT	GR	NT	XC	GR	NT	NT	NT	GR	NT		XC	GR	NT	GR	XC	NT	NT	GR
Leeds 10	32,34 d	16 18	16 45	17 06	17 10	17 15	17 18	17 45	18 06	18 10	18 15		18 17	18 18	18 45	19 06		19 10	19 15	19 18	19 45	20 10	20 17	20 18	20 45
Outwood	d	16 27					17 29							18 27						19 29				20 27	
Wakefield Kirkgate 4	32,34,39 a			17 22					18 22				18 45			19 22							20 46		
	d			17 22					18 22				18 45			19 22							20 46		
Pontefract Monkhill	d																								
Wakefield Westgate 7	32,39 a	16 32	16 56		17 21	17 27	17 33	17 56		18 21	18 27			18 32	18 56			19 21	19 26	19 33	19 56	20 21		20 31	20 56
	d	16 32	16 56		17 22	17 27	17 33	17 57		18 22	18 27			18 32	18 56			19 22	19 26	19 33	19 56	20 22		20 32	20 56
Sandal & Agbrigg	d	16 35					17 37							18 35						19 37				20 35	
Fitzwilliam	d	16 42					17 47							18 42						19 44				20 41	
South Elmsall	d	16 47												18 47										20 46	
Adwick	a	16 52												18 52										20 52	
	d	16 53												18 53										20 52	
Bentley (S.Yorks)	d	16 57												18 57										20 56	
Doncaster 7	a	17 06	17 17			17 45		18 16			18 45			19 06	19 17				19 44		20 16			21 05	21 14
Moorthorpe	d						17 54					18 52								19 50					
Thurnscoe	d						18 00													19 56					
Goldthorpe	d						18 02													19 58					
Bolton-upon-Dearne	d						18 05													20 01					
Swinton (S.Yorks)	29 a						18 10					19 01								20 07					
Rotherham Central	29 a						18 17					19 12								20 16					
Meadowhall	29 a			17 55			18 25		18 56			19 18	19 32			19 54				20 22			21 33		
Sheffield 7	29 a			18 05	17 51		18 36		19 05	18 51		19 27	19 43			20 04		19 50		20 34		20 51	21 42		

Table 31

Leeds - Wakefield, Doncaster and Sheffield

Sundays

16 September to 21 October

Network Diagram - see first page of Table 31

		XC	NT	NT	NT	NT
Leeds 10	32,34 d	21 10	21 18		21 40	22 17
Outwood	d		21 27		21 51	
Wakefield Kirkgate 4	32,34,39 a					22 46
	d					22 46
Pontefract Monkhill	d					
Wakefield Westgate 7	32,39 a	21 21	21 31		21 55	
	d	21 22	21 31		21 55	
Sandal & Agbrigg	d		21 34		21 59	
Fitzwilliam	d		21 41		22 06	
South Elmsall	d		21 46			
Adwick	a		21 51			
	d		21 52			
Bentley (S.Yorks)	d		21 56			
Doncaster 7	a		22 05			
Moorthorpe	d			21 36	22 13	
Thurnscoe	d				22 19	
Goldthorpe	d				22 21	
Bolton-upon-Dearne	d				22 24	
Swinton (S.Yorks)	29 a			21 45	22 32	
Rotherham Central	29 a			21 52	22 39	
Meadowhall	29 a			21 57	22 45	23 30
Sheffield 7	29 a	21 50		22 09	22 54	23 43

Sundays

from 28 October

		GR	XC	GC	NT	NT	XC	NT	GR	EM	XC	NT	GR	EM	NT	NT		NT	XC	GR	NT	NT	NT	XC	GR
Leeds 10	32,34 d	08 05	08 10		08 34	08 48	09 00	09 05	09 05	09 44	10 00	10 02	10 05	10 15	10 17	10 18		10 57	11 00	11 05	11 18	11 29		12 00	12 05
Outwood	d					08 59										10 27					11 29				
Wakefield Kirkgate 4	32,34,39 a				09 03			09 21				10 18			10 46			11 13				11 46			
	d			08 43	09 03			09 21				10 18			10 46			11 13				11 46			
Pontefract Monkhill	d																								
Wakefield Westgate 7	32,39 a	08 16	08 22			09 03	09 11		09 17	09 57	10 11		10 16	10 26		10 32			11 11	11 16	11 33			12 11	12 17
	d	08 16	08 23			09 03	09 11		09 17	09 58	10 12		10 17	10 27		10 32			11 12	11 17	11 33			12 12	12 17
Sandal & Agbrigg	d					09 07										10 35					11 37				
Fitzwilliam	d					09 14										10 42					11 44				
South Elmsall	d															10 47									
Adwick	a															10 52									
	d															10 53									
Bentley (S.Yorks)	d															10 57									
Doncaster 7	a	08 34		09 04			09 31		09 35		10 28		10 35			11 05			11 28	11 35				12 28	12 36
Moorthorpe	d					09 20															11 50				
Thurnscoe	d					09 26															11 56				
Goldthorpe	d					09 28															11 58				
Bolton-upon-Dearne	d					09 31															12 01				
Swinton (S.Yorks)	29 a					09 35															12 05				
Rotherham Central	29 a					09 44															12 12		←		
Meadowhall	29 a				09 44	09 53		09 57				10 51			11 32			11 46			12 20	12 17	12 20		
Sheffield 7	29 a		08 51		09 55	10 03	09 55	10 04		10 25	10 54	11 02		10 57	11 44			11 56	11 53		→	12 29	12 32	12 54	

		NT	NT	GC	NT	XC	GR	NT		EM	GR	NT	NT	NT	GR	NT	XC	NT	NT	XC	GR	GC	NT	NT	
Leeds 10	32,34 d	12 18	12 29		12 34	13 00	13 05	13 18		13 59	14 05	14 06	14 17	14 18	15 05	15 06	15 10	15 18	16 06	16 10	16 15		16 17	16 18	
Outwood	d	12 27						13 29						14 27				15 29						16 27	
Wakefield Kirkgate 4	32,34,39 a		12 46		13 04							14 22	14 46			15 22			16 22				16 46		
	d		12 46	12 51	13 04							14 22	14 46			15 22			16 22			16 30	16 46		
Pontefract Monkhill	d																								
Wakefield Westgate 7	32,39 a	12 31				13 11	13 16	13 33		14 11	14 17			14 31	15 16		15 22	15 33		16 21	16 27			16 32	
	d	12 32				13 12	13 16	13 33		14 12	14 17			14 32	15 16		15 23	15 33		16 22	16 27			16 32	
Sandal & Agbrigg	d	12 35						13 37						14 35				15 37						16 35	
Fitzwilliam	d	12 41						13 45						14 41				15 44						16 42	
South Elmsall	d	12 46												14 46										16 47	
Adwick	a	12 52												14 52										16 52	
	d	12 52												14 52										16 53	
Bentley (S.Yorks)	d	12 56												14 56										16 57	
Doncaster 7	a	13 04		13 12		13 28	13 35				14 35			15 05	15 35						16 45	17 10		17 06	
Moorthorpe	d							13 51										15 50							
Thurnscoe	d							13 57										15 56							
Goldthorpe	d							13 59										15 58							
Bolton-upon-Dearne	d							14 02										16 01							
Swinton (S.Yorks)	29 a							14 06										16 05							
Rotherham Central	29 a							14 13										16 12							
Meadowhall	29 a		13 18		13 48			14 20				14 55	15 35			15 55		16 20	16 56				17 34		
Sheffield 7	29 a		13 29		13 58	13 54		14 32		14 43		15 06	15 44			16 05	15 51	16 32	17 05	16 51			17 44		

Leeds - Wakefield, Doncaster and Sheffield

Sundays
from 28 October

Network Diagram - see first page of Table 31

		GR	NT	XC	GR	NT	GR	NT	XC	GR	NT	NT	NT	GR	NT	XC		GR	NT	GR	XC	NT	NT	GR	XC
		■ 1		◇1	■ 1		■ 1		◇1	■ 1				■ 1		◇1		■ 1		■ 1	◇1			■ 1	◇1
Leeds 10 ... 32,34	d	16 45	17 06	17 10	17 15	17 18	17 45	18 06	18 10	18 15		18 17	18 18	18 45	19 06	19 10		19 15	19 18	19 45	20 10	20 17	20 18	20 45	21 10
Outwood	d					17 29							18 27						19 29				20 27		
Wakefield Kirkgate 4 ... 32,34,39	a		17 22					18 22				18 45			19 22							20 46			
	d		17 22					18 22				18 45			19 22							20 46			
Pontefract Monkhill	d																								
Wakefield Westgate 7 ... 32,39	a	16 56		17 21	17 27	17 33	17 56		18 21	18 27			18 32	18 56		19 21		19 26	19 33	19 56	20 21		20 31	20 56	21 21
	d	16 56		17 22	17 27	17 33	17 57		18 22	18 27			18 32	18 56		19 22		19 26	19 33	19 56	20 22		20 32	20 56	21 22
Sandal & Agbrigg	d					17 37							18 35						19 37				20 35		
Fitzwilliam	d					17 47							18 42						19 44				20 41		
South Elmsall	d												18 47										20 46		
Adwick	a												18 52										20 52		
	d												18 53										20 52		
Bentley (S.Yorks)	d												18 57										20 56		
Doncaster 7	a	17 17			17 45		18 16			18 45			19 06	19 17				19 44		20 16			21 05	21 14	
Moorthorpe	d					17 54					18 52								19 50						
Thurnscoe	d					18 00													19 56						
Goldthorpe	d					18 02													19 58						
Bolton-upon-Dearne	d					18 05													20 01						
Swinton (S.Yorks) ... 29	a					18 10					19 01								20 07						
Rotherham Central ... 29	a					18 17					19 12								20 16						
Meadowhall ... 29	a		17 55			18 25		18 56			19 18	19 32			19 54				20 22			21 33			
Sheffield 7 ... 29	a		18 05	17 51		18 36		19 05	18 51		19 27	19 43			20 04	19 50			20 34		20 51	21 42			21 50

		NT	NT	NT	NT
Leeds 10 ... 32,34	d	21 18		21 40	22 17
Outwood	d	21 27		21 51	
Wakefield Kirkgate 4 ... 32,34,39	a				22 46
	d				22 46
Pontefract Monkhill	d				
Wakefield Westgate 7 ... 32,39	a	21 31		21 55	
	d	21 31		21 55	
Sandal & Agbrigg	d	21 34		21 59	
Fitzwilliam	d	21 41		22 06	
South Elmsall	d	21 46			
Adwick	a	21 51			
	d	21 52			
Bentley (S.Yorks)	d	21 56			
Doncaster 7	a	22 05			
Moorthorpe	d		21 24	22 13	
Thurnscoe	d			22 19	
Goldthorpe	d			22 21	
Bolton-upon-Dearne	d			22 24	
Swinton (S.Yorks) ... 29	a		21 33	22 32	
Rotherham Central ... 29	a		21 40	22 39	
Meadowhall ... 29	a		21 53	22 45	23 30
Sheffield 7 ... 29	a		22 05	22 54	23 43

Bradford, Leeds and Wakefield - Pontefract, Knottingley and Goole

Network Diagram - see first page of Table 31

Miles	Miles			NT SX	NT	NT	NT SO	NT SX	NT	GC SO	GC SX	GC SO		NT	NT SO	NT SX	NT	NT	NT	NT	NT	NT SO		NT SX	NT
										■ 1 A	■ 1	■ 1 B													
—	—	Bradford Interchange ... 41	d							06 51	06 51														
—	—	Halifax ... 41	d							07 03	07 07														
—	—	Brighouse ... 41	d							07 14	07 18														
—	—	Mirfield	d							07 22	07 28														
0	—	**Leeds** 10 ... 31,34	d	05 46		06 38	07 00	07 00						07 29	08 00	08 05		08 32	09 00		09 32	10 00		10 00	
6	—	Woodlesford ... 34	d	05 54		06 46	07 08	07 08						07 37	08 08	08 15		08 40	09 08		09 40	10 08		10 08	
10¾	—	Castleford ... 34	a	06 03		06 54	07 19	07 17						07 45	08 17	08 24		08 48	09 17		09 48	10 17		10 17	
—	—		d	06 05		06 57	07 19	07 19						07 48	08 19	08 26		08 51	09 19		09 51	10 18		10 19	
12¼	—	Glasshoughton	d	06 09			07 24	07 24							08 24	08 31			09 24			10 24		10 24	
—	0	**Wakefield Westgate** 7 ... 31,39	d		06 24																				
—	1	Wakefield Kirkgate 4 ... 31,34,39	a		06 29	07 07				07 36	07 40			08 00				09 03			10 01				
—	—		d		06 29				07 31	07 38	07 42	07 45					08 31			09 31					10 31
—	5¼	Streethouse	d		06 36				07 39								08 39			09 39					10 39
—	7	Featherstone	d		06 40				07 43								08 43			09 43					10 43
—	9	Pontefract Tanshelf	d		06 44				07 46								08 46			09 46					10 46
14	9¾	Pontefract Monkhill	a	06 14	06 46		07 28	07 28	07 50	07 56	07 58	08 10			08 28	08 35	08 49		09 28	09 49		10 28		10 28	10 49
—	—		d	06 14	06 47		07 28	07 28	07 50	07 58	08 01				08 28	08 35	08 49		09 28	09 49		10 28		10 28	10 49
—	—	London Kings Cross 15 ⊖26	a							10 09	10 13														
16	—	**Knottingley**	a	06 20	06 55		07 36	07 36	07 56						08 36	08 44	08 56		09 37	09 56		10 36		10 36	10 56
—	—		d																						
20¾	—	Whitley Bridge	d																						
22	—	Hensall	d																						
25¾	—	Snaith	d																						
28½	—	Rawcliffe	d																						
32½	—	**Goole**	a																						

		NT	NT	GC SX	GC SO	GC SO	GC SO	NT		NT	NT	NT	NT	NT	NT	NT	NT	NT		NT	NT	NT	NT	GC SO	NT
				■ 1	■ 1 C	■ 1 D	■ 1 B																	■ 1 E	
Bradford Interchange ... 41	d			10 22	10 22	10 22																		15 22	
Halifax ... 41	d			10 37	10 38	10 38																		15 35	
Brighouse ... 41	d			10 48	10 48	10 48																		15 46	
Mirfield	d			10 56	10 56	10 56																			
Leeds 10 ... 31,34	d	10 32	11 00							11 32	12 00		12 32	13 00		13 32	14 00			14 32	15 00		15 32		16 00
Woodlesford ... 34	d	10 40	11 08							11 40	12 08		12 40	13 08		13 40	14 08			14 40	15 08		15 40		16 08
Castleford ... 34	a	10 48	11 17							11 48	12 17		12 48	13 17		13 48	14 17			14 48	15 17		15 48		16 17
	d	10 51	11 19							11 51	12 19		12 51	13 19		13 51	14 19			14 51	15 19		15 51		16 19
Glasshoughton	d		11 24								12 24			13 24			14 24				15 24				16 24
Wakefield Westgate 7 ... 31,39	d																								
Wakefield Kirkgate 4 ... 31,34,39	a	11 01		11 10	11 11	11 11				12 01			13 02			14 01				15 01			16 01	16 09	
	d			11 11	11 11	11 13	11 15	11 31				12 31			13 31			14 31				15 31		16 11	
Streethouse	d							11 39				12 39			13 39			14 39				15 39			
Featherstone	d							11 43				12 43			13 43			14 43				15 43			
Pontefract Tanshelf	d							11 46				12 46			13 46			14 46				15 46			
Pontefract Monkhill	a		11 29	11 33	11 34	11 35	11 40	11 49			12 28	12 49		13 28	13 49		14 28	14 49			15 28	15 49		16 27	16 28
	d		11 29	11 34	11 35	11 37		11 49			12 28	12 49		13 28	13 49		14 28	14 49			15 28	15 49		16 29	16 28
London Kings Cross 15 ⊖26	a			13 45	13 46	13 46																		18 45	
Knottingley	a		11 35					11 56			12 35	12 56		13 35	13 56		14 35	14 56			15 36	15 56			16 36
	d																								
Whitley Bridge	d																								
Hensall	d																								
Snaith	d																								
Rawcliffe	d																								
Goole	a																								

A until 23 June, from 15 September. ⊡ to Pontefract Monkhill
B from 30 June until 8 September
C until 23 June
D from 15 September
E until 23 June, from 15 September

Bradford, Leeds and Wakefield - Pontefract, Knottingley and Goole

Network Diagram - see first page of Table 31

Station		GC SO A	NT	GC SX		NT	NT SO	NT SX	NT	NT	NT	NT	NT	NT SO		NT SX	NT	NT	NT	NT	NT	NT	GC SO A	NT
Bradford Interchange 41	d			15 37																				
Halifax 41	d			15 52																				
Brighouse 41	d			16 05																				
Mirfield	d			16 13																				
Leeds 31,34	d					16 32	17 16	17 16		17 32	18 00		18 32	18 59		18 59		19 37	20 05		20 37	21 05		
Woodlesford 34	d					16 40	17 24	17 24		17 40	18 08		18 40	19 08		19 08		19 45	20 13		20 45	21 13		
Castleford 34	a					16 48	17 33	17 34		17 48	18 17		18 48	19 17		19 18		19 53	20 22		20 53	21 22		
	d					16 51	17 36	17 36		17 51	18 19		18 51	19 19		19 19		19 56	20 24		20 56	21 24		
Glasshoughton	d						17 40	17 40			18 24			19 24		19 24			20 29			21 29		21 57
Wakefield Westgate 31,39	d																							22 00
Wakefield Kirkgate 31,34,39	a			16 36		17 01				18 01			19 04					20 06			21 06			22 00
	d	16 15	16 31	16 40					17 31			18 33					19 33			20 54			21 45	22 00
Streethouse	d		16 39						17 39			18 41					19 41			21 02				22 08
Featherstone	d		16 43						17 43			18 45					19 45			21 06				22 12
Pontefract Tanshelf	d		16 46						17 46			18 48					19 48			21 09				22 16
Pontefract Monkhill	a	16 40	16 49	16 55			17 44	17 44	17 49		18 28	18 51		19 28		19 28	19 51		20 33	21 12		21 33	22 10	22 18
	d		16 49	16 56			17 44	17 44	17 49		18 28	18 51		19 28		19 28	19 51		20 33	21 12		21 33		22 19
London Kings Cross ⊖26	a			19 05																				
Knottingley	a		16 56				17 51	17 51	17 57		18 35	18 58		19 35		19 35	19 58		20 40	21 19		21 40		22 25
	d						17 53	17 53																
Whitley Bridge	d						17 59	17 59																
Hensall	d						18 03	18 03																
Snaith	d						18 10	18 10																
Rawcliffe	d						18 15	18 15																
Goole	a						18 26	18 26																

Station		NT	NT	NT SX	NT SO	NT
Bradford Interchange 41	d					
Halifax 41	d					
Brighouse 41	d					
Mirfield	d					
Leeds 31,34	d	21 37	22 08			22 37
Woodlesford 34	d	21 45	22 16			22 45
Castleford 34	a	21 53	22 27			22 53
	d	21 56	22 27			22 56
Glasshoughton	d		22 32			
Wakefield Westgate 31,39	d			23 04	23 04	
Wakefield Kirkgate 31,34,39	a	22 06		23 07	23 07	23 10
	d			23 07	23 07	
Streethouse	d			23 15	23 15	
Featherstone	d			23 19	23 19	
Pontefract Tanshelf	d			23 23	23 23	
Pontefract Monkhill	a		22 36	23 25	23 29	
	d		22 36	23 26		
London Kings Cross ⊖26	a					
Knottingley	a		22 44	23 32		
	d					
Whitley Bridge	d					
Hensall	d					
Snaith	d					
Rawcliffe	d					
Goole	a					

Sundays

Station		GC B	GC C	NT	NT	NT	NT	NT	NT	NT	NT	NT		NT	NT	NT	NT	NT	NT
Bradford Interchange 41	d	07 55	08 05																
Halifax 41	d	08 07																	
Brighouse 41	d	08 18																	
Mirfield	d																		
Leeds 31,34	d			08 34	09 34	10 17	11 17	12 34	13 17	14 17	15 17	16 17		17 17	18 17	19 17	20 17	21 17	22 17
Woodlesford 34	d			08 42	09 42	10 25	11 25	12 42	13 25	14 25	15 25	16 25		17 25	18 25	19 25	20 25	21 25	22 25
Castleford 34	a			08 50	09 50	10 33	11 33	12 50	13 33	14 33	15 33	16 33		17 33	18 33	19 35	20 33	21 33	22 33
	d			08 53	09 53	10 36	11 36	12 53	13 36	14 36	15 36	16 36		17 36	18 36	19 36	20 36	21 36	22 36
Glasshoughton	d				09 57		11 40		13 40		15 40			17 40		19 40		21 40	
Wakefield Westgate 31,39	d																		
Wakefield Kirkgate 31,34,39	a	08 42	08 42	09 03		10 46		13 04		14 46		16 46			18 45		20 46		22 46
	d																		
Streethouse	d																		
Featherstone	d																		
Pontefract Tanshelf	d																		
Pontefract Monkhill	a				10 02		11 45		13 45		15 45			17 45		19 45		21 45	
	d				10 02		11 45		13 45		15 45			17 45		19 45		21 45	
London Kings Cross ⊖26	a	10 40	10 40																
Knottingley	a				10 08		11 52		13 52		15 52			17 52		19 52		21 52	
	d																		
Whitley Bridge	d																		
Hensall	d																		
Snaith	d																		
Rawcliffe	d																		
Goole	a																		

A from 30 June until 8 September B until 09 September C from 16 September

Goole, Knottingley and Pontefract - Wakefield and Leeds, Bradford

Network Diagram - see first page of Table 31

Miles	Miles	Station		NT SX	NT SO	NT SX	NT	GC SO A	NT SX	NT SX	NT SO	NT		NT	NT	NT	NT	NT	NT	NT	NT	NT		GC SO A	NT
0	—	**Goole**	d							07 04	07 04														
4	—	Rawcliffe	d							07 11	07 11														
6¾	—	Snaith	d							07 16	07 16														
10½	—	Hensall	d							07 23	07 23														
12¼	—	Whitley Bridge	d							07 30	07 30														
16½	—	**Knottingley**	a							07 38	07 37														
—	—		d	06 25			06 56			07 38	07 38			07 53	08 16		08 53	09 16		09 53	10 16				10 53
—	—	London Kings Cross ⊖26	d																						
18½	0	Pontefract Monkhill	a	06 29			07 00			07 42	07 42			07 57	08 20		08 57	09 20		09 57	10 20				10 57
—	—		d	06 29			07 00	07 05		07 42	07 42			07 57	08 20		08 57	09 20		09 57	10 20			10 35	10 57
—	0¾	Pontefract Tanshelf	d				07 03							08 00			09 00			10 00					11 00
—	2¾	Featherstone	d				07 06							08 03			09 03			10 03					11 03
—	4½	Streethouse	d				07 10							08 07			09 07			10 07					11 07
—	8¾	Wakefield Kirkgate 31,34,39	a				07 21	07 30						08 18			09 18			10 20				11 00	11 18
—	—		d		06 50	06 50						07 50				08 50			09 50			10 50			
—	9¾	**Wakefield Westgate** 31,39	a																						
20	—	Glasshoughton 34	d	06 34						07 48	07 48				08 25			09 25			10 25				
21½	—	Castleford	a	06 38	07 00	06 59				07 52	07 52	07 59			08 30	09 00		09 29	10 00		10 29	11 00			
—	—		d	06 41	07 02	07 02			07 38	07 55	07 55	08 01			08 32	09 02		09 32	10 02		10 32	11 02			
26½	—	Woodlesford 34	d	06 50	07 12	07 12			07 47	08 04	08 04	08 11			08 41	09 12		09 41	10 12		10 41	11 12			
32½	—	**Leeds** 31,34	a	07 04	07 28	07 28			08 01	08 18	08 18	08 25			08 54	09 25		09 53	10 25		10 55	11 25			
—	—	Mirfield	a																						
—	—	Brighouse 41	a																						
—	—	Halifax 41	a																						
—	—	Bradford Interchange 41	a																						

Station		NT	NT	NT	NT	NT	GC SX	NT		NT	NT	NT	NT SO	NT SX	NT	NT	NT	NT		GC SO A	NT	NT	NT	GC SX	NT
Goole	d																								
Rawcliffe	d																								
Snaith	d																								
Hensall	d																								
Whitley Bridge	d																								
Knottingley	a																								
	d	11 16		11 53	12 16			12 53		13 16		13 53	14 16	14 16		14 53	15 16				15 53	16 16			16 53
London Kings Cross ⊖26	d						10 48																	14 48	
Pontefract Monkhill	a	11 20		11 57	12 20		12 47	12 57		13 20		13 57	14 20	14 20		14 57	15 20				15 57	16 20		16 47	16 57
	d	11 20		11 57	12 20		12 49	12 57		13 20		13 57	14 20	14 20		14 57	15 20			15 35	15 57	16 20		16 48	16 57
Pontefract Tanshelf	d			12 00				13 00				14 00				15 00					16 00				17 00
Featherstone	d			12 03				13 03				14 03				15 03					16 03				17 03
Streethouse	d			12 07				13 07				14 07				15 07					16 07				17 07
Wakefield Kirkgate 31,34,39	a			12 18			13 07	13 18				14 18				15 18				16 00	16 19			17 04	17 18
	d		11 50			12 50	13 09				13 50				14 50			15 50					16 50	17 08	
Wakefield Westgate 31,39	a																								
Glasshoughton 34	d	11 25			12 25					13 25			14 25	14 25			15 25					16 25			
Castleford	a	11 29	12 00		12 29	13 00				13 29	14 00		14 28	14 29	15 00		15 29	16 00				16 29	17 00		
	d	11 32	12 02		12 32	13 02				13 32	14 02		14 32	14 32	15 02		15 32	16 02				16 32	17 02		
Woodlesford 34	d	11 41	12 12		12 41	13 12				13 41	14 12		14 41	14 41	15 12		15 41	16 12				16 41	17 12		
Leeds 31,34	a	11 54	12 25		12 54	13 25				13 53	14 25		14 53	14 53	15 25		15 54	16 25				16 54	17 25		
Mirfield	a																							17 20	
Brighouse 41	a						13 30																	17 29	
Halifax 41	a						13 40																	17 40	
Bradford Interchange 41	a						13 55																	17 55	

Station		NT	NT	NT		NT	NT	NT	NT	NT	NT	NT	NT	GC SO A		GC SO B	NT	NT SX	NT SO	NT	NT	NT SX	NT SO	NT	NT
Goole	d								18 49																
Rawcliffe	d								18 56																
Snaith	d								19 01																
Hensall	d								19 08																
Whitley Bridge	d								19 12																
Knottingley	a								19 20																
	d	17 15		18 02		18 39		19 02	19 21		19 55	20 16					21 16	21 23	21 23		22 16			22 30	23 05
London Kings Cross ⊖26	d															19 20									
Pontefract Monkhill	a	17 19		18 06		18 43		19 06	19 25		19 59	20 20				21 15	21 20	21 27	21 27		22 22			22 34	23 09
	d	17 19		18 06		18 43		19 06	19 25		19 59	20 20		21 05		21 16	21 20	21 27	21 27		22 22			22 34	23 09
Pontefract Tanshelf	d			18 09				19 09			20 02							21 30	21 30					22 37	
Featherstone	d			18 12				19 12			20 05							21 33	21 33					22 40	
Streethouse	d			18 16				19 16			20 09							21 37	21 37					22 44	
Wakefield Kirkgate 31,34,39	a			18 27				19 28			20 20			21 30				21 47	21 47					22 55	
	d		17 50				18 50			19 50			20 50					21 47	21 48	21 52		22 51	22 51	22 55	
Wakefield Westgate 31,39	a																	21 53	21 53					23 01	
Glasshoughton 34	d	17 24				18 48			19 30			20 25					21 25				22 27				23 14
Castleford	a	17 28	18 00			18 54	19 00		19 34	20 00		20 29	21 00				21 29			22 04	22 31	23 01	23 02		23 18
	d	17 31	18 02			18 57	19 03		19 37	20 02		20 32	21 02				21 32			22 05	22 34	23 04	23 04		23 21
Woodlesford 34	d	17 41	18 12			19 06	19 13		19 46	20 12		20 44	21 12				21 41			22 15	22 43	23 14	23 14		23 30
Leeds 31,34	a	17 54	18 25			19 20	19 27		20 00	20 26		20 57	21 26				21 53			22 29	22 57	23 30	23 30		23 44
Mirfield	a															21 47									
Brighouse 41	a															21 57									
Halifax 41	a															22 08									
Bradford Interchange 41	a															22 24									

A from 30 June until 8 September B until 23 June, from 15 September

Sundays

Goole, Knottingley and Pontefract - Wakefield and Leeds, Bradford

Network Diagram - see first page of Table 31

	NT	NT	NT	GC ◇1 ⊡ A	NT	NT	NT	NT	GC ◇1 ⊡ A
Goole d									
Rawcliffe d									
Snaith d									
Hensall d									
Whitley Bridge d									
Knottingley a									
d		10 26			12 26		14 26		
London Kings Cross 15 ⊖26 d				11 48					15 48
Pontefract Monkhill a		10 30			12 30		14 30		
d		10 30			12 30		14 30		
Pontefract Tanshelf d									
Featherstone d									
Streethouse d									
Wakefield Kirkgate 4 31,34,39 a				13 45					17 47
d	09 30		11 30	13 46		13 30		15 30	17 48
Wakefield Westgate 7 31,39 a									
Glasshoughton 34 d		10 35			12 35		14 35		
Castleford a	09 40	10 39	11 40		12 39	13 40	14 39	15 40	
d	09 42	10 42	11 41		12 42	13 42	14 42	15 41	
Woodlesford 34 d	09 52	10 51	11 51		12 52	13 51	14 51	15 51	
Leeds 10 31,34 a	10 04	11 04	12 05		13 05	14 04	15 04	16 04	
Mirfield a									
Brighouse 41 a				14 08					18 10
Halifax 41 a				14 19					18 20
Bradford Interchange 41 a				14 37					18 37

	NT	NT	NT	GC ◇1 ⊡ A	NT	NT	NT	NT
Goole d								
Rawcliffe d								
Snaith d								
Hensall d								
Whitley Bridge d								
Knottingley a								
d	16 26		18 26			20 26		22 26
London Kings Cross 15 ⊖26 d				19 23				
Pontefract Monkhill a	16 30		18 30			20 30		22 30
d	16 30		18 30			20 30		22 30
Pontefract Tanshelf d								
Featherstone d								
Streethouse d								
Wakefield Kirkgate 4 31,34,39 a				21 22				
d		17 30		21 23	19 30		21 30	
Wakefield Westgate 7 31,39 a								
Glasshoughton 34 d	16 35		18 35			20 35		22 35
Castleford a	16 39	17 40	18 39		19 41	20 39	21 40	22 39
d	16 42	17 42	18 42		19 44	20 42	21 42	22 42
Woodlesford 34 d	16 51	17 51	18 51		19 53	20 51	21 51	22 51
Leeds 10 31,34 a	17 04	18 05	19 04		20 05	21 03	22 04	23 04
Mirfield a								
Brighouse 41 a				21 46				
Halifax 41 a				21 57				
Bradford Interchange 41 a				22 11				

A until 9 September

Mondays to Fridays

Sheffield and Selby - York

Local services only

Network Diagram - see first page of Table 31

Miles	Miles		NT	NT A	NT B	NT A	NT	NT A	NT	NT	NT	NT A
0	—	**Sheffield 7** 29,31 ⇌ d							09 29			
3½	—	Meadowhall 29,31 ⇌ d							09 35			
6¼	—	Rotherham Central 29,31 d							09 42			
10¾	—	Swinton (S.Yorks) 29,31 d							09 51			
18½	—	Moorthorpe 31 d							10 01			
25½	—	Pontefract Baghill d							10 10			
—	—	Hull 29 d			07 07		09 02			10 08		
—	0	**Selby** d	06 48		07 48		09 38			10 47	11 40	
33¾	8¼	Sherburn-in-Elmet d	07 00		08 03		09 53		10 27	11 00	11 52	
36	10½	Church Fenton d	07 04	08 00		09 05		10 05	10 32			12 05
38	12½	Ulleskelf d			08 09				10 36			
46¾	21	**York 8** 29 a	07 20	08 16	08 21	09 21	10 10	10 21	10 56	11 18	12 14	12 21

Miles	Miles		NT	NT A	NT	NT	NT	NT	NT A	NT	NT E	NT
0	—	**Sheffield 7** 29,31 ⇌ d				13 29						
3½	—	Meadowhall 29,31 ⇌ d				13 35						
6¼	—	Rotherham Central 29,31 d				13 41						
10¾	—	Swinton (S.Yorks) 29,31 d				13 50						
18½	—	Moorthorpe 31 d				14 01						
25½	—	Pontefract Baghill d				14 10						
—	—	Hull 29 d	12 03		13 12		14 19	15 02		16 10		17 18
—	0	**Selby** d	12 38		13 55		14 53	15 38		16 47		18 07
33¾	8¼	Sherburn-in-Elmet d			14 09	14 28	15 05					
36	10½	Church Fenton d		14 06		14 32			16 05		17 53	
38	12½	Ulleskelf d				14 36					17 58	
46¾	21	**York 8** 29 a	13 04	14 22	14 27	14 55	15 25	16 06	16 21	17 13	18 10	18 33

	TP ◇1	NT A	NT	NT A	NT	NT A
Sheffield 7 29,31 ⇌ d						
Meadowhall 29,31 ⇌ d						
Rotherham Central 29,31 d						
Swinton (S.Yorks) 29,31 d						
Moorthorpe 31 d						
Pontefract Baghill d						
Hull 29 d	18 59		19 15			
Selby d	19a29		19 53		21 21	
Sherburn-in-Elmet d						
Church Fenton d		19 05		21 12		23 26
Ulleskelf d				21 16		
York 8 29 a		19 21	20 21	21 30	21 43	23 42

Saturdays

	NT	NT A	NT B	NT A	NT	NT A	NT	NT	NT	NT A	NT
Sheffield 7 29,31 ⇌ d							09 29				
Meadowhall 29,31 ⇌ d							09 35				
Rotherham Central 29,31 d							09 42				
Swinton (S.Yorks) 29,31 d							09 51				
Moorthorpe 31 d							10 02				
Pontefract Baghill d							10 10				
Hull 29 d			07 07		09 02			10 08	11 05		12 03
Selby d	06 48		07 48		09 38			10 47	11 40		12 38
Sherburn-in-Elmet d	07 00		08 03		09 53		10 27	11 00			
Church Fenton d	07 04	08 05		09 05		10 05	10 32			12 05	
Ulleskelf d			08 09				10 36				
York 8 29 a	07 20	08 20	08 21	09 21	10 14	10 21	10 55	11 18	12 08	12 21	13 04

	NT A	NT	NT	NT	NT	NT A	NT	TP ◇1	NT A	NT	TP ◇1
Sheffield 7 29,31 ⇌ d			13 29								
Meadowhall 29,31 ⇌ d			13 35								
Rotherham Central 29,31 d			13 41								
Swinton (S.Yorks) 29,31 d			13 50								
Moorthorpe 31 d			14 01								
Pontefract Baghill d			14 10								
Hull 29 d		13 12		14 19	15 02		16 10	17 01		17 18	18 59
Selby d		13 55		14 53	15 38		16 47	17a32		18 07	19a29
Sherburn-in-Elmet d		14 09	14 28	15 05							
Church Fenton d	14 06		14 32			16 05			18 05		
Ulleskelf d			14 36						18 10		
York 8 29 a	14 22	14 27	14 55	15 25	16 06	16 21	17 13		18 24	18 33	

	NT A	NT A	NT	NT J	NT K
Sheffield 7 29,31 ⇌ d					
Meadowhall 29,31 ⇌ d					
Rotherham Central 29,31 d					
Swinton (S.Yorks) 29,31 d					
Moorthorpe 31 d					
Pontefract Baghill d					
Hull 29 d			21 01		
Selby d			21 35		
Sherburn-in-Elmet d					
Church Fenton d	19 05	21 12		23 20	23 20
Ulleskelf d		21 16			
York 8 29 a	19 21	21 30	21 57	23 38	23 40

Sundays

	NT L	NT M	NT N	NT O	NT P	NT	NT A	NT	NT A	NT
Sheffield 7 29,31 ⇌ d										
Meadowhall 29,31 ⇌ d										
Rotherham Central 29,31 d										
Swinton (S.Yorks) 29,31 d										
Moorthorpe 31 d										
Pontefract Baghill d										
Hull 29 d		08 54	08 54			11 46		13 29		14 23
Selby d		09 28	09 28			12 20		14 03		14 57
Sherburn-in-Elmet d										
Church Fenton d	09 18			10 52	10 52		12 49		14 49	
Ulleskelf d										
York 8 29 a	09 35	09 52	09 54	11 07	11 08	12 44	13 02	14 30	15 02	15 25

	NT	NT A	NT Q	NT	NT A	NT Q	NT	NT A	NT	NT E
Sheffield 7 29,31 ⇌ d			16 36			18 57				
Meadowhall 29,31 ⇌ d			16 42			19 05				
Rotherham Central 29,31 d			16 49			19 11				
Swinton (S.Yorks) 29,31 d			16 58			19 19				
Moorthorpe 31 d			17 13			19 29				
Pontefract Baghill d			17 21			19 38				
Hull 29 d	16 00			17 23			19 24		20 29	
Selby d	16 34			17 57			19 58		21 03	
Sherburn-in-Elmet d			17 38			19 56				
Church Fenton d		16 49	17 43		18 47	20 00		20 49		23 07
Ulleskelf d										
York 8 29 a	16 59	17 02	17 59	18 25	19 01	20 18	20 25	21 03	21 30	23 23

A From Blackpool North
B From Beverley
E From Leeds
J until 8 September. From Blackpool North
K from 15 September. From Blackpool North
L From Bradford Interchange
M until 9 September
N from 16 September
O from 16 September. From Huddersfield
P until 9 September. From Huddersfield
Q until 21 October

York - Selby and Sheffield

Local services only

Network Diagram - see first page of Table 31

Miles	Miles	Station			NT	NT A	NT	NT B	NT	NT A	NT	NT	NT	NT A	NT	NT	NT A	NT	NT	NT	NT A	NT A	NT	TP FO B
0	0	York 8	29	d	05 44	07 06	07 29	07 48	08 43	09 11	10 20	11 00	11 05	11 09	11 45	12 47	13 09	13 44	14 47	15 01	15 08	16 08	16 12	16 13
8¾	8¾	Ulleskelf		d		07 15							11 15							15 11				
10¾	10¾	Church Fenton		a		07 20		08 00		09 22			11 19	11 20			13 20			15 15	15 20	16 20		16 25
—	—			d									11 19							15 15				
12¾	12¾	Sherburn-in-Elmet		d					08 55			11 12	11 23					13 56		15 19			16 25	
—	21	Selby		a	06 08		07 50		09 06		10 40	11 24			12 04	13 06		14 07	15 06				16 36	
—	—	Hull	29	a			08 46		09 47		11 23				12 49	13 48		14 52	15 48				17 27	
21¼	—	Pontefract Baghill		d									11 43							15 38				
28¼	—	Moorthorpe	31	a									11 59							15 50				
36	—	Swinton (S.Yorks)	29,31	a									12 08							16 00				
40½	—	Rotherham Central	29,31	a									12 18							16 09				
43¼	—	Meadowhall	29,31	a									12 24							16 17				
46¾	—	Sheffield 7	29,31	a									12 36							16 27				

Station			NT	NT A	NT	NT B	NT	NT B	NT B	NT	NT B
York 8	29	d	17 19	18 05	18 18	19 04	20 17	21 22	22 09	22 13	23 13
Ulleskelf		d		18 15				21 31			
Church Fenton		a	17 30	18 21		19 17		21 33	22 21		23 28
		d	17 30								
Sherburn-in-Elmet		d	17 34		18 31		20 29				
Selby		a	17 45		18 42		20 42			22 32	
Hull	29	a	18 30		19 29					23 18	
Pontefract Baghill		d									
Moorthorpe	31	a									
Swinton (S.Yorks)	29,31	a									
Rotherham Central	29,31	a									
Meadowhall	29,31	a									
Sheffield 7	29,31	a									

Saturdays

Station			NT	NT A	NT	NT A	NT	NT A	NT	NT	NT	NT A	NT	NT	NT A	NT	NT	NT	NT A	NT A	NT	NT	NT A	NT
York 8	29	d	06 09	07 06	07 38	08 09	08 43	09 11	09 50	10 43	11 05	11 09	11 45	12 47	13 09	13 44	14 47	15 01	15 09	16 08	16 12	17 19	18 05	18 18
Ulleskelf		d		07 15							11 15							15 11					18 15	
Church Fenton		a		07 20		08 20		09 22			11 19	11 20			13 20			15 15	15 21	16 20		17 30	18 21	
		d									11 19							15 15				17 30		
Sherburn-in-Elmet		d					08 55				11 23					13 56		15 19			16 25	17 34		18 31
Selby		a	06 30		07 57		09 06		10 09	11 03			12 04	13 06		14 07	15 06				16 36	17 45		18 42
Hull	29	a			08 50		09 47		10 53	11 51			12 49	13 48		14 52	15 48				17 27	18 30		19 29
Pontefract Baghill		d									11 43							15 38						
Moorthorpe	31	a									11 59							15 50						
Swinton (S.Yorks)	29,31	a									12 08							16 01						
Rotherham Central	29,31	a									12 18							16 09						
Meadowhall	29,31	a									12 24							16 17						
Sheffield 7	29,31	a									12 36							16 27						

Station			NT B	NT	NT B	NT L	NT M	NT B
York 8	29	d	19 04	19 47	21 18	22 10	22 11	23 13
Ulleskelf		d			21 27			
Church Fenton		a	19 17		21 33			23 28
		d						
Sherburn-in-Elmet		d						
Selby		a		20 06		22 28	22 29	
Hull	29	a		20 48		23 14	23 14	
Pontefract Baghill		d						
Moorthorpe	31	a						
Swinton (S.Yorks)	29,31	a						
Rotherham Central	29,31	a						
Meadowhall	29,31	a						
Sheffield 7	29,31	a						

Sundays

Station			NT A	NT A	NT	NT A	NT	NT	NT A	NT	NT A	NT	NT	NT A	NT P	NT	NT A	NT P	NT	NT B
York 8	29	d	08 50	09 52	10 40	11 52	12 05	13 40	13 52	14 49	15 52	16 06	17 11	17 52	18 10	19 10	19 52	20 50	21 41	21 52
Ulleskelf		d																		
Church Fenton		a	09 01	10 03		12 03			14 03		16 03			18 03	18 21		20 03	21 01		22 04
		d													18 21			21 01		
Sherburn-in-Elmet		d													18 25			21 05		
Selby		a			10 58		12 24	13 59		15 08		16 24	17 30			19 35			22 00	
Hull	29	a			11 41		13 06	14 40		15 49		17 07	18 12			20 17			22 36	
Pontefract Baghill		d													18 40			21 20		
Moorthorpe	31	a													18 51			21 35		
Swinton (S.Yorks)	29,31	a													19 01			21 45		
Rotherham Central	29,31	a													19 12			21 52		
Meadowhall	29,31	a													19 18			21 57		
Sheffield 7	29,31	a													19 27			22 09		

A To Blackpool North
B To Leeds
L from 15 September
M until 8 September
P until 21 October

Nottingham, Sheffield - Barnsley - Huddersfield and Leeds

Network Diagram - see first page of Table 31

Miles	Miles	Station			NT MO A	NT MX	NT MX B	NT	NT	NT C	NT	NT	NT	NT D	NT	NT	NT	NT D	TP ◇1 E	NT F	NT	NT	NT G	EM ◇ H
0	—	Nottingham 8		d	21p30																	06 23		06 40
12	—	Langley Mill		d	21p52																	06 38		
18¼	—	Alfreton		d	22p00																	06 46		07 02
28¼	—	Chesterfield		d	22p13												06 26					06 58		07 13
33½	—	Dronfield		d	22p20												06 33					07 05		07 20
40½	—	Sheffield 7	29,31	a	22p36												06 46					07 18		07 31
—	—			d	22p39	23p15	23p24	05 16	05 22	05 29	05 36	05 50	06 06	06 18	06 28	06 36	06 49	06 52	06 55	07 06	07 14	07 20	07 24	
44	3½	Meadowhall 4	29,31	a	22p44	23p20	23p29	05 22	05 27	05 34	05 41	05 55	06 11	06 23	06 33	06 41	06 54	06 57	07 00	07 11	07 20	07 25	07 30	
—	—			d	22p45	23p21	23p30	05 22	05 28		05 42	05 56	06 12		06 34	06 42	06 55			07 12	07 21	07 26		
47¾	7¼	Chapeltown		d	22p51		23p36	05 28			05 48		06 18			06 48				07 18				
51	10½	Elsecar		d	22p56		23p41	05 33					06 23							07 23				
52½	12	Wombwell		d	23p00		23p45	05 37			05 55		06 27			06 55				07 27				
56½	16	Barnsley		a	23p05		23p50	05 44			06 00	06 10	06 32			07 00	07 09			07 32		07 41		
—	—			d	23p10		23p51				06 01	06 10	06 33			07 01	07 12			07 33		07 42		
—	19	Dodworth		d							06 07					07 07								
—	20¼	Silkstone Common		d							06 11					07 11								
—	23½	Penistone		d							06 18					07 18								
—	27½	Denby Dale		d							06 24					07 24								
—	29¾	Shepley		d							06 29					07 29								
—	30¾	Stocksmoor		d							06 32					07 32								
—	32¾	Brockholes		d							06 36					07 36								
—	33¾	Honley		d							06 38					07 38								
—	34¾	Berry Brow		d							06 41					07 41								
—	35¾	Lockwood		d							06 44					07 44								
—	37	Huddersfield		a							06 50					07 49								
60	—	Darton		d	23p15		23p56						06 38							07 38				
67½	—	Wakefield Kirkgate 4	31	a	23p26		00s10					06 27	06 49				07 27			07 49		07 57		
—	—			d	23p27							06 28	06 50				07 28			07 50		07 58		
70½	—	Normanton		d	23p34							06 33	06 54				07 33			07 54				
74	—	Castleford		a	23p40								06 59							07 59				
78¾	—	Woodlesford		a	23p53								07 12							08 11				
84¾	—	Leeds 10	31	a	00 05	00 29			06 33			06 50	07 28		07 44		07 51			08 25	08 36	08 21		

Station			NT	NT I	NT J	EM ◇1 K	NT	TP ◇1 E	NT	NT	NT G	NT	EM ◇ H	NT I	NT	NT L	NT	TP ◇1 E	NT	NT	NT G	NT M	NT	NT N
Nottingham 8		d								07 13			07 45							08 11				
Langley Mill		d								07 29										08 31				
Alfreton		d								07 37			08 07							08 39				
Chesterfield		d				07 42				07 50			08 18							08 51				
Dronfield		d				07 49							08 25							08 58				
Sheffield 7	29,31	a				08 00				08 08			08 38							09 16				
		d	07 36	07 41	07 51		08 06	08 11	08 14	08 18	08 24	08 36		08 41	08 51	08 53	09 06	09 11	09 14	09 18	09 24	09 29	09 36	09 41
Meadowhall 4	29,31	a	07 41	07 46	07 57		08 11	08 16	08 21	08 24	08 30	08 41		08 46	08 56	08 59	09 11	09 16	09 20	09 23	09 29	09 34	09 41	09 46
		d	07 42		07 57		08 12		08 21	08 25		08 42			08 57		09 12		09 21	09 24			09 42	
Chapeltown		d	07 48				08 18					08 48					09 18						09 48	
Elsecar		d					08 23										09 23							
Wombwell		d	07 55				08 27					08 55					09 27						09 55	
Barnsley		a	08 00		08 11		08 32			08 40		09 00			09 11		09 32			09 40			10 00	
		d	08 01		08 12		08 33			08 42		09 01			09 12		09 33			09 42			10 01	
Dodworth		d	08 07									09 07											10 07	
Silkstone Common		d	08 11									09 11											10 11	
Penistone		d	08 18									09 18											10 18	
Denby Dale		d	08 24									09 24											10 24	
Shepley		d	08 29									09 29											10 29	
Stocksmoor		d	08 32									09 32											10 32	
Brockholes		d	08 36									09 36											10 36	
Honley		d	08 38									09 38											10 38	
Berry Brow		d	08 41									09 41											10 41	
Lockwood		d	08 44									09 44											10 44	
Huddersfield		a	08 49									09 49											10 49	
Darton		d					08 38										09 38							
Wakefield Kirkgate 4	31	a			08 27		08 49			08 57					09 27		09 49			09 57				
		d			08 28		08 50			08 58					09 28		09 50			09 58				
Normanton		d					08 54										09 54							
Castleford		a					09 00										10 00							
Woodlesford		a					09 12										10 12							
Leeds 10	31	a			08 49		09 25		09 31	09 20					09 49		10 25		10 31	10 18				

A from 21 May until 24 September
B To Wakefield Westgate
C To Beverley
D To Adwick
E From Manchester Airport to Cleethorpes
F From Worksop
G To Scunthorpe
H To Liverpool Lime Street
I To Bridlington
J From Retford
K From Derby
L From Worksop to Adwick
M To York
N To Scarborough

Table 34

Mondays to Fridays

until 28 September

Nottingham, Sheffield - Barnsley - Huddersfield and Leeds

Network Diagram - see first page of Table 31

	NT	NT A	NT	TP ◇1 B ⊼	NT	NT	NT C	NT	NT D	NT	NT A	NT	TP ◇1 B ⊼	NT	NT ◇	NT C	NT	NT E	NT	NT A	NT
Nottingham 8 ⇌ d						09 15									10 15						
Langley Mill d						09 32									10 32						
Alfreton d						09 40									10 40						
Chesterfield d						09 52									10 52						
Dronfield d						09 59									10 59						
Sheffield 7 29,31 ⇌ a						10 16									11 17						
d	09 50	09 53	10 06	10 11	10 14	10 18	10 24	10 36	10 41	10 50	10 53	11 06	11 11	11 14	11 18	11 24	11 36	11 41	11 50	11 53	12 06
Meadowhall 4 29,31 ⇌ a	09 55	09 58	10 11	10 16	10 20	10 23	10 29	10 41	10 46	10 55	10 58	11 11	11 16	11 20	11 23	11 29	11 41	11 46	11 55	11 58	12 11
d	09 56		10 12		10 21	10 24		10 42		10 56		11 12		11 21	11 24		11 42		11 56		12 12
Chapeltown d			10 18					10 48				11 18					11 48				12 18
Elsecar d			10 23									11 23									12 23
Wombwell d			10 27					10 55				11 27					11 55				12 27
Barnsley a	10 11		10 32			10 40		11 00		11 11		11 32			11 40		12 00		12 10		12 32
d	10 12		10 33			10 42		11 01		11 12		11 33			11 41		12 01		12 11		12 33
Dodworth d								11 07									12 07				
Silkstone Common d								11 11									12 11				
Penistone d								11 18									12 18				
Denby Dale d								11 24									12 24				
Shepley d								11 29									12 29				
Stocksmoor d								11 32									12 32				
Brockholes d								11 36									12 36				
Honley d								11 38									12 38				
Berry Brow d								11 41									12 41				
Lockwood d								11 44									12 44				
Huddersfield a								11 49									12 49				
Darton d			10 38									11 38									12 38
Wakefield Kirkgate 4 31 a	10 27		10 49			10 57				11 27		11 49			11 57				12 27		12 49
d	10 28		10 50			10 58				11 28		11 50			11 58				12 28		12 50
Normanton d			10 54									11 54									12 54
Castleford a			11 00									12 00									13 00
Woodlesford a			11 12									12 12									13 12
Leeds 10 31 a	10 48		11 25		11 31	11 18				11 48		12 25		12 31	12 18				12 48		13 25

	TP ◇1 B ⊼	NT	NT ◇	NT C	NT	NT D	NT	NT A	NT	TP ◇1 B ⊼	NT	NT ◇	NT C	NT F	NT	NT D	NT	NT G	NT	TP ◇1 B ⊼	NT	NT ◇
Nottingham 8 ⇌ d			11 15									12 15										13 15
Langley Mill d			11 31									12 32										13 32
Alfreton d			11 39									12 40										13 40
Chesterfield d			11 52									12 52										13 52
Dronfield d			11 59									12 59										13 59
Sheffield 7 29,31 ⇌ a			12 16									13 16										14 16
d	12 11	12 14	12 18	12 24	12 36	12 41	12 50	12 53	13 06	13 11	13 14	13 18	13 24	13 29	13 36	13 41	13 50	13 53	14 06	14 11	14 14	14 18
Meadowhall 4 29,31 ⇌ a	12 16	12 20	12 23	12 29	12 41	12 46	12 55	12 58	13 11	13 16	13 20	13 23	13 29	13 34	13 41	13 46	13 55	13 58	14 11	14 16	14 20	14 23
d		12 21	12 24		12 42		12 56		13 12		13 21	13 24			13 42		13 56		14 12		14 21	14 24
Chapeltown d					12 48				13 18						13 48				14 18			
Elsecar d									13 23										14 23			
Wombwell d					12 55				13 27						13 55				14 27			
Barnsley a			12 40		13 00		13 11		13 32			13 40			14 00		14 11		14 32			14 40
d			12 42		13 01		13 12		13 33			13 42			14 01		14 12		14 33			14 42
Dodworth d					13 07										14 07							
Silkstone Common d					13 11										14 11							
Penistone d					13 18										14 18							
Denby Dale d					13 24										14 24							
Shepley d					13 29										14 29							
Stocksmoor d					13 32										14 32							
Brockholes d					13 36										14 36							
Honley d					13 38										14 38							
Berry Brow d					13 41										14 41							
Lockwood d					13 44										14 44							
Huddersfield a					13 49										14 49							
Darton d									13 38										14 38			
Wakefield Kirkgate 4 31 a			12 57				13 27		13 50			13 57					14 27		14 49			14 57
d			12 58				13 28		13 50			13 58					14 28		14 50			14 58
Normanton d									13 54										14 54			
Castleford a									14 00										15 00			
Woodlesford a									14 12										15 12			
Leeds 10 31 a		13 29	13 18				13 49		14 25		14 31	14 18					14 48		15 25		15 31	15 18

A From Lincoln to Adwick
B From Manchester Airport to Cleethorpes
C To Scunthorpe
D To Bridlington
E To Scarborough
F To Sheffield
G To Adwick

Table 34

Mondays to Fridays

until 28 September

Nottingham, Sheffield - Barnsley - Huddersfield and Leeds

Network Diagram - see first page of Table 31

	NT A	NT	NT B	NT	NT C	NT	TP ◇1 D ⊼	NT	NT ◇	NT A	NT	NT E	NT	NT C	NT	TP ◇1 D ⊼	NT	NT ◇	NT F	NT	NT E	NT
Nottingham 8 ⇌ d									14 15									15 15				
Langley Mill d									14 30									15 32				
Alfreton d									14 38									15 40				
Chesterfield d									14 52									15 53				
Dronfield d									14 59									16 00				
Sheffield 7 29,31 ⇌ a									15 16									16 16				
d	14 24	14 36	14 41	14 50	14 53	15 06	15 11	15 14	15 18	15 24	15 36	15 41	15 50	15 53	16 06	16 11	16 14	16 18	16 23	16 36	16 41	16 50
Meadowhall 4 29,31 ⇌ a	14 29	14 41	14 46	14 55	14 58	15 11	15 16	15 20	15 23	15 29	15 41	15 46	15 55	15 58	16 11	16 16	16 20	16 23	16 29	16 41	16 46	16 55
d		14 42		14 56		15 12		15 20	15 24		15 42		15 56		16 12		16 20	16 24		16 42		16 56
Chapeltown d		14 48				15 18					15 48				16 18					16 48		
Elsecar d						15 23									16 23					16 53		
Wombwell d		14 55				15 27					15 55				16 27					16 57		
Barnsley a		15 00		15 11		15 32			15 40		16 00		16 11		16 32			16 40		17 02		17 11
d		15 01		15 12		15 33			15 42		16 01		16 12		16 33			16 42		17 03		17 12
Dodworth d		15 07									16 07									17 09		
Silkstone Common d		15 11									16 11									17 13		
Penistone d		15 18									16 18									17 20		
Denby Dale d		15 24									16 24									17 26		
Shepley d		15 29									16 29									17 31		
Stocksmoor d		15 32									16 32									17 34		
Brockholes d		15 36									16 36									17 38		
Honley d		15 38									16 38									17 40		
Berry Brow d		15 41									16 41									17 43		
Lockwood d		15 44									16 44									17 46		
Huddersfield a		15 49									16 49									17 50		
Darton d						15 38									16 38							
Wakefield Kirkgate 4 31 a				15 27		15 49			15 57				16 27		16 49			16 57				17 28
d				15 28		15 50			15 58				16 28		16 50			16 58				17 28
Normanton d						15 54									16 54							
Castleford a						16 00									17 00							
Woodlesford a						16 12									17 12							
Leeds 10 31 a				15 49		16 25		16 31	16 18				16 49		17 25		17 31	17 18				17 48

	NT C	NT	TP ◇1 D ⊼	NT	NT ◇	NT F	NT	NT B	NT	NT G	NT	NT	NT ◇	TP ◇1 D ⊼	NT F	NT	NT E	NT	NT H	NT	TP ◇1 D ⊼
Nottingham 8 ⇌ d					16 15								17 15								
Langley Mill d					16 32								17 32								
Alfreton d					16 40								17 40								
Chesterfield d					16 55								17 52								
Dronfield d					17 02								17 59								
Sheffield 7 29,31 ⇌ a					17 17								18 14								
d	16 53	17 06	17 11	17 13	17 18	17 27	17 36	17 41	17 50	17 53	18 06	18 13	18 18	18 24	18 29	18 36	18 41	18 50	19 00	19 06	19 11
Meadowhall 4 29,31 ⇌ a	16 58	17 11	17 16	17 20	17 23	17 32	17 41	17 46	17 55	17 58	18 12	18 20	18 23	18 29	18 34	18 41	18 46	18 55	19 06	19 12	19 16
d		17 12		17 20	17 24		17 42		17 56		18 12	18 20	18 24			18 42		18 56		19 12	
Chapeltown d		17 18					17 48				18 18					18 48				19 18	
Elsecar d		17 23					17 53				18 23					18 53				19 23	
Wombwell d		17 27					17 57				18 27					18 57				19 27	
Barnsley a		17 32			17 40		18 02		18 11		18 33		18 42			19 02		19 14		19 33	
d		17 33			17 42		18 03		18 12		18 33		18 42			19 08		19 14		19 33	
Dodworth d							18 09									19 14					
Silkstone Common d							18 13									19 18					
Penistone d							18 27									19 25					
Denby Dale d							18 33									19 31					
Shepley d							18 38									19 36					
Stocksmoor d							18 41									19 39					
Brockholes d							18 45									19 43					
Honley d							18 47									19 45					
Berry Brow d							18 50									19 48					
Lockwood d							18 53									19 51					
Huddersfield a							18 57									19 56					
Darton d		17 38									18 38									19 38	
Wakefield Kirkgate 4 31 a		17 49			17 57				18 28		18 50		18 59					19 29		19 50	
d		17 50			17 58				18 32		18 50		18 59					19 32		19 50	
Normanton d		17 54									18 54									19 54	
Castleford a		18 00									19 00									20 00	
Woodlesford a		18 12									19 13									20 12	
Leeds 10 31 a		18 25		18 32	18 18				18 51		19 27	19 31	19 23					19 55		20 26	

A To Scunthorpe
B To Scarborough
C From Lincoln to Adwick
D From Manchester Airport to Cleethorpes
E To Bridlington
F To Doncaster
G From Lincoln to Hull
H From Retford to Doncaster

Table 34

Mondays to Fridays

until 28 September

Nottingham, Sheffield - Barnsley - Huddersfield and Leeds

Network Diagram - see first page of Table 31

Station		NT	NT ◇	NT A	NT	NT B	NT	NT C	NT	TP ◇■ D	NT E	NT ◇	NT	NT F	NT	NT	TP FO ◇■ D	NT B	NT	TP FX ◇■ G	NT	NT FO	NT FX
Nottingham	d		18 15									19 15											
Langley Mill	d		18 32									19 32											
Alfreton	d		18 40									19 40											
Chesterfield	d		18 52									19 52											
Dronfield	d		18 59									19 59											
Sheffield 29,31	a		19 17									20 15											
	d	19 18	19 22	19 30	19 36	19 44	19 51	19 58	20 06	20 11	20 15	20 18	20 27	20 38	20 41	21 06	21 11	21 15	21 30	21 34	21 41	22 06	22 06
Meadowhall 29,31	a	19 24	19 27	19 35	19 41	19 49	19 56	20 03	20 11	20 16	20 20	20 24	20 34	20 44	20 47	21 11	21 16	21 21	21 35	21 39	21 46	22 11	22 11
	d	19 25	19 28		19 42		19 57		20 12			20 24	20 35		20 47	21 12			21 36		21 47	22 12	22 12
Chapeltown	d				19 48				20 18						20 53	21 18					21 53	22 18	22 18
Elsecar	d				19 53				20 23							21 23						22 23	22 23
Wombwell	d				19 57				20 27						21 00	21 27					22 00	22 27	22 27
Barnsley	a		19 42		20 02		20 12		20 32			20 40			21 07	21 33					22 05	22 32	22 32
	d		19 42		20 08		20 12		20 33			20 42			21 08	21 34					22 08		22 33
Dodworth	d				20 14										21 14						22 14		
Silkstone Common	d				20 18										21 18						22 18		
Penistone	d				20 25										21 25						22 25		
Denby Dale	d				20 31										21 31						22 31		
Shepley	d				20 36										21 36						22 36		
Stocksmoor	d				20 39										21 39						22 39		
Brockholes	d				20 43										21 43						22 43		
Honley	d				20 45										21 45						22 45		
Berry Brow	d				20 48										21 48						22 48		
Lockwood	d				20 51										21 51						22 51		
Huddersfield	a				20 55										21 56						22 57		
Darton	d								20 38							21 38							22 38
Wakefield Kirkgate 31	a		19 58				20 28		20 49			20 57				21 52							22 51
	d		19 58				20 28		20 50			20 58				21 52							22 51
Normanton	d								20 54							21 57							22 56
Castleford	a								21 00							22 04							23 01
Woodlesford	a								21 12							22 14							23 14
Leeds 31	a	20 34	20 19				20 48		21 26			21 20	21 47			22 29			22 46				23 30

Station		TP ◇■ D	NT	NT FO	NT	NT E	NT	NT FX	NT FO	NT FX H	NT A
Nottingham	d		21 11								
Langley Mill	d		21 38								
Alfreton	d		21 46								
Chesterfield	d		22 00								
Dronfield	d		22 07								
Sheffield 29,31	a		22 19								
	d	22 11			22 24	22 34	22 41	23 15	23 15	23 24	23 27
Meadowhall 29,31	a	22 16			22 30	22 39	22 46	23 20	23 20	23 29	23 32
	d				22 30		22 47	23 21	23 21	23 30	
Chapeltown	d						22 53			23 36	
Elsecar	d						22 58			23 41	
Wombwell	d						23 02			23 45	
Barnsley	a						23 07			23 50	
	d						23 08			23 51	
Dodworth	d						23 14				
Silkstone Common	d						23 18				
Penistone	d						23 25				
Denby Dale	d						23 31				
Shepley	d						23 36				
Stocksmoor	d						23 39				
Brockholes	d						23 43				
Honley	d						23 45				
Berry Brow	d						23 48				
Lockwood	d						23 51				
Huddersfield	a						23 55				
Darton	d									23 56	
Wakefield Kirkgate 31	a									00s10	
	d			22 51							
Normanton	d			22 56							
Castleford	a			23 01							
Woodlesford	a			23 14							
Leeds 31	a			23 30	23 41			00 29	00 30		

A To Doncaster
B To Beverley
C To Bridlington
D From Manchester Airport to Cleethorpes
E To Goole
F To Scunthorpe
G To Cleethorpes
H To Wakefield Westgate

Table 34

Mondays to Fridays

from 1 October

Nottingham, Sheffield - Barnsley - Huddersfield and Leeds

Network Diagram - see first page of Table 31

Station		NT MO	NT MX	NT MX A	NT	NT	NT B	NT	NT	NT	NT C	NT	NT	NT	NT C	TP ◇■ D	NT E	NT	NT	NT F	EM ◇ G	NT	NT H
Nottingham	d	21p30																	06 23		06 40		
Langley Mill	d	21p52																	06 38				
Alfreton	d	22p00																	06 46		07 02		
Chesterfield	d	22p13												06 26					06 58		07 13		
Dronfield	d	22p20												06 33					07 05		07 20		
Sheffield 29,31	a	22p36												06 46					07 18		07 31		
	d	22p39	23p15	23p24	05 16	05 22	05 29	05 36	05 50	06 06	06 18	06 28	06 36	06 49	06 52	06 55	07 06	07 14	07 20	07 24		07 36	07 41
Meadowhall 29,31	a	22p44	23p20	23p29	05 22	05 27	05 34	05 41	05 55	06 11	06 23	06 33	06 41	06 54	06 57	07 00	07 11	07 20	07 25	07 30		07 41	07 46
	d	22p45	23p21	23p30	05 22	05 28		05 42	05 56	06 12		06 34	06 42	06 55			07 12	07 21	07 26			07 42	
Chapeltown	d	22p51		23p36	05 28			05 48		06 18			06 48				07 18					07 48	
Elsecar	d	22p56		23p41	05 33					06 23							07 23						
Wombwell	d	23p00		23p45	05 37			05 55		06 27			06 55				07 27					07 55	
Barnsley	a	23p05		23p50	05 44			06 00	06 10	06 32			07 00	07 09			07 32		07 41			08 00	
	d	23p10		23p51				06 01	06 10	06 33			07 01	07 12			07 33		07 42			08 01	
Dodworth	d							06 07					07 07									08 07	
Silkstone Common	d							06 11					07 11									08 11	
Penistone	d							06 18					07 18									08 18	
Denby Dale	d							06 24					07 24									08 24	
Shepley	d							06 29					07 29									08 29	
Stocksmoor	d							06 32					07 32									08 32	
Brockholes	d							06 36					07 36									08 36	
Honley	d							06 38					07 38									08 38	
Berry Brow	d							06 41					07 41									08 41	
Lockwood	d							06 44					07 44									08 44	
Huddersfield	a							06 55					07 54									08 53	
Darton	d	23p15		23p56						06 38							07 38						
Wakefield Kirkgate 31	a	23p26		00s10					06 27	06 49				07 27			07 49		07 57				
	d	23p27							06 28	06 50				07 28			07 50		07 58				
Normanton	d	23p34							06 33	06 54				07 33			07 54						
Castleford	a	23p40								06 59							07 59						
Woodlesford	a	23p53								07 12							08 11						
Leeds 31	a	00 05	00 29			06 33			06 50	07 28		07 44		07 51			08 25	08 36	08 21				

Station		NT I	EM ◇■ J	NT	TP ◇■ D	NT	NT	NT F	NT	EM ◇ G	NT H	NT	NT K	NT	TP ◇■ D	NT	NT	NT F	NT L	NT	NT M	NT	NT N
Nottingham	d						07 13			07 45							08 11						
Langley Mill	d						07 29										08 31						
Alfreton	d						07 37			08 07							08 39						
Chesterfield	d		07 42				07 50			08 18							08 51						
Dronfield	d		07 49							08 25							08 58						
Sheffield 29,31	a		08 00				08 08			08 38							09 16						
	d	07 51		08 06	08 11	08 14	08 18	08 24	08 36		08 41	08 51	08 53	09 06	09 11	09 14	09 18	09 24	09 29	09 36	09 41	09 50	09 53
Meadowhall 29,31	a	07 57		08 11	08 16	08 21	08 24	08 30	08 41		08 46	08 56	08 59	09 11	09 16	09 20	09 23	09 29	09 34	09 41	09 46	09 55	09 58
	d	07 57		08 12		08 21	08 25		08 42			08 57		09 12		09 21	09 24			09 42		09 56	
Chapeltown	d			08 18					08 48					09 18						09 48			
Elsecar	d			08 23										09 23									
Wombwell	d			08 27					08 55					09 27						09 55			
Barnsley	a	08 11		08 32			08 40		09 00			09 11		09 32			09 40			10 00		10 11	
	d	08 12		08 33			08 42		09 01			09 12		09 33			09 42			10 01		10 12	
Dodworth	d								09 07											10 07			
Silkstone Common	d								09 11											10 11			
Penistone	d								09 18											10 18			
Denby Dale	d								09 24											10 24			
Shepley	d								09 29											10 29			
Stocksmoor	d								09 32											10 32			
Brockholes	d								09 36											10 36			
Honley	d								09 38											10 38			
Berry Brow	d								09 41											10 41			
Lockwood	d								09 44											10 44			
Huddersfield	a								09 50											10 53			
Darton	d			08 38										09 38									
Wakefield Kirkgate 31	a	08 27		08 49			08 57					09 27		09 49			09 57					10 27	
	d	08 28		08 50			08 58					09 28		09 50			09 58					10 28	
Normanton	d			08 54										09 54									
Castleford	a			09 00										10 00									
Woodlesford	a			09 12										10 12									
Leeds 31	a	08 49		09 25		09 31	09 20					09 49		10 25		10 31	10 18					10 48	

A To Wakefield Westgate
B To Beverley
C To Adwick
D From Manchester Airport to Cleethorpes
E From Worksop
F To Scunthorpe
G To Liverpool Lime Street
H To Bridlington
I From Retford
J From Derby
K From Worksop to Adwick
L To York
M To Scarborough
N From Lincoln to Adwick

Nottingham, Sheffield - Barnsley - Huddersfield and Leeds

Network Diagram - see first page of Table 31

		NT	TP ◇1 A	NT	NT	NT B	NT	NT C	NT	NT D	NT	TP ◇1 A	NT	NT ◇	NT B	NT	NT E	NT	NT D	NT	TP ◇1 A	NT
Nottingham 8	d				09 15									10 15								
Langley Mill	d				09 32									10 32								
Alfreton	d				09 40									10 40								
Chesterfield	d				09 52									10 52								
Dronfield	d				09 59									10 59								
Sheffield 7 29,31	a				10 16									11 17								
	d	10 06	10 11	10 14	10 18	10 24	10 36	10 41	10 50	10 53	11 06	11 11	11 14	11 18	11 24	11 36	11 41	11 50	11 53	12 06	12 11	12 14
Meadowhall 4 29,31	a	10 11	10 16	10 20	10 23	10 29	10 41	10 46	10 55	10 58	11 11	11 16	11 20	11 23	11 29	11 41	11 46	11 55	11 58	12 11	12 16	12 20
	d	10 12		10 21	10 24		10 42		10 56		11 12		11 21	11 24		11 42		11 56		12 12		12 21
Chapeltown	d	10 18					10 48				11 18					11 48				12 18		
Elsecar	d	10 23									11 23									12 23		
Wombwell	d	10 27					10 55				11 27					11 55				12 27		
Barnsley	a	10 32			10 40		11 00		11 11		11 32			11 40		12 00		12 10		12 32		
	d	10 33			10 42		11 01		11 12		11 33			11 41		12 01		12 11		12 33		
Dodworth	d						11 07									12 07						
Silkstone Common	d						11 11									12 11						
Penistone	d						11 18									12 18						
Denby Dale	d						11 24									12 24						
Shepley	d						11 29									12 29						
Stocksmoor	d						11 32									12 32						
Brockholes	d						11 36									12 36						
Honley	d						11 38									12 38						
Berry Brow	d						11 41									12 41						
Lockwood	d						11 44									12 44						
Huddersfield	a						11 53									12 52						
Darton	d	10 38									11 38									12 38		
Wakefield Kirkgate 4 31	a	10 49			10 57				11 27		11 49			11 57				12 27		12 49		
	d	10 50			10 58				11 28		11 50			11 58				12 28		12 50		
Normanton	d	10 54									11 54									12 54		
Castleford	a	11 00									12 00									13 00		
Woodlesford	a	11 12									12 12									13 12		
Leeds 10 31	a	11 25		11 31	11 18				11 48		12 25		12 31	12 18				12 48		13 25		13 29

		NT ◇	NT B	NT	NT C	NT	NT D	NT	TP ◇1 A	NT	NT ◇	NT B	NT F	NT	NT C	NT	NT G	NT	TP ◇1 A	NT	NT ◇	NT B	NT
Nottingham 8	d	11 15									12 15										13 15		
Langley Mill	d	11 31									12 32										13 32		
Alfreton	d	11 39									12 40										13 40		
Chesterfield	d	11 52									12 52										13 52		
Dronfield	d	11 59									12 59										13 59		
Sheffield 7 29,31	a	12 16									13 16										14 16		
	d	12 18	12 24	12 36	12 41	12 50	12 53	13 06	13 11	13 14	13 18	13 24	13 29	13 36	13 41	13 50	13 53	14 06	14 11	14 14	14 18	14 24	14 36
Meadowhall 4 29,31	a	12 23	12 29	12 41	12 46	12 55	12 58	13 11	13 16	13 20	13 23	13 29	13 34	13 41	13 46	13 55	13 58	14 11	14 16	14 20	14 23	14 29	14 41
	d	12 24		12 42		12 56		13 12		13 21	13 24			13 42		13 56		14 12		14 21	14 24		14 42
Chapeltown	d			12 48				13 18						13 48				14 18					14 48
Elsecar	d							13 23										14 23					
Wombwell	d			12 55				13 27						13 55				14 27					14 55
Barnsley	a	12 40		13 00		13 11		13 32			13 40			14 00		14 11		14 32			14 40		15 00
	d	12 42		13 01		13 12		13 33			13 42			14 01		14 12		14 33			14 42		15 01
Dodworth	d			13 07										14 07									15 07
Silkstone Common	d			13 11										14 11									15 11
Penistone	d			13 18										14 18									15 18
Denby Dale	d			13 24										14 24									15 24
Shepley	d			13 29										14 29									15 29
Stocksmoor	d			13 32										14 32									15 32
Brockholes	d			13 36										14 36									15 36
Honley	d			13 38										14 38									15 38
Berry Brow	d			13 41										14 41									15 41
Lockwood	d			13 44										14 44									15 44
Huddersfield	a			13 53										14 53									15 53
Darton	d							13 38										14 38					
Wakefield Kirkgate 4 31	a	12 57				13 27		13 50			13 57					14 27		14 49			14 57		
	d	12 58				13 28		13 50			13 58					14 28		14 50			14 58		
Normanton	d							13 54										14 54					
Castleford	a							14 00										15 00					
Woodlesford	a							14 12										15 12					
Leeds 10 31	a	13 18				13 49		14 25		14 31	14 18					14 48		15 25		15 31	15 18		

A From Manchester Airport to Cleethorpes
B To Scunthorpe
C To Bridlington
D From Lincoln to Adwick
E To Scarborough
F To Sheffield
G To Adwick

Nottingham, Sheffield - Barnsley - Huddersfield and Leeds

Network Diagram - see first page of Table 31

		NT A	NT	NT B	NT	TP ◇1 C	NT	NT ◇	NT D	NT	NT E	NT	NT B	NT	TP ◇1 C	NT	NT ◇	NT F	NT	NT E	NT	NT B
Nottingham 8	d							14 15									15 15					
Langley Mill	d							14 30									15 32					
Alfreton	d							14 38									15 40					
Chesterfield	d							14 52									15 53					
Dronfield	d							14 59									16 00					
Sheffield 7 29,31	a							15 16									16 16					
	d	14 41	14 50	14 53	15 06	15 11	15 14	15 18	15 24	15 36	15 41	15 50	15 53	16 06	16 11	16 14	16 18	16 23	16 36	16 41	16 50	16 53
Meadowhall 4 29,31	a	14 46	14 55	14 58	15 11	15 16	15 20	15 23	15 29	15 41	15 46	15 55	15 58	16 11	16 16	16 20	16 23	16 29	16 41	16 46	16 55	16 58
	d		14 56		15 12		15 20	15 24		15 42		15 56		16 12		16 20	16 24		16 42		16 56	
Chapeltown	d				15 18					15 48				16 18					16 48			
Elsecar	d				15 23									16 23					16 53			
Wombwell	d				15 27					15 55				16 27					16 57			
Barnsley	a		15 11		15 32			15 40		16 00		16 11		16 32			16 40		17 02		17 11	
	d		15 12		15 33			15 42		16 01		16 12		16 33			16 42		17 03		17 12	
Dodworth	d									16 07									17 09			
Silkstone Common	d									16 11									17 13			
Penistone	d									16 18									17 20			
Denby Dale	d									16 24									17 26			
Shepley	d									16 29									17 31			
Stocksmoor	d									16 32									17 34			
Brockholes	d									16 36									17 38			
Honley	d									16 38									17 40			
Berry Brow	d									16 41									17 43			
Lockwood	d									16 44									17 46			
Huddersfield	a									16 52									17 51			
Darton	d				15 38									16 38								
Wakefield Kirkgate 4 31	a		15 27		15 49			15 57				16 27		16 49			16 57				17 28	
	d		15 28		15 50			15 58				16 28		16 50			16 58				17 28	
Normanton	d				15 54									16 54								
Castleford	a				16 00									17 00								
Woodlesford	a				16 12									17 12								
Leeds 10 31	a		15 49		16 25		16 31	16 18				16 49		17 25		17 31	17 18				17 48	

		NT	TP ◇1 C	NT	NT ◇	NT F	NT	NT A	NT	NT G	NT	NT	NT ◇	TP ◇1 C	NT F	NT	NT E	NT	NT H	NT	TP ◇1 C	NT	NT ◇
Nottingham 8	d				16 15								17 15										18 15
Langley Mill	d				16 32								17 32										18 32
Alfreton	d				16 40								17 40										18 40
Chesterfield	d				16 55								17 52										18 52
Dronfield	d				17 02								17 59										18 59
Sheffield 7 29,31	a				17 17								18 14										19 17
	d	17 06	17 11	17 13	17 18	17 27	17 36	17 41	17 50	17 53	18 06	18 13	18 18	18 24	18 29	18 36	18 41	18 50	19 00	19 06	19 11	19 18	19 22
Meadowhall 4 29,31	a	17 11	17 16	17 20	17 23	17 32	17 41	17 46	17 55	17 58	18 12	18 20	18 23	18 29	18 34	18 41	18 46	18 55	19 06	19 12	19 16	19 24	19 27
	d	17 12		17 20	17 24		17 42		17 56		18 12	18 20	18 24			18 42		18 56		19 12		19 25	19 28
Chapeltown	d	17 18					17 48				18 18					18 48				19 18			
Elsecar	d	17 23					17 53				18 23					18 53				19 23			
Wombwell	d	17 27					17 57				18 27					18 57				19 27			
Barnsley	a	17 32			17 40		18 02		18 11		18 33		18 42			19 02		19 14		19 33			19 42
	d	17 33			17 42		18 03		18 12		18 33		18 42			19 08		19 14		19 33			19 42
Dodworth	d						18 09									19 14							
Silkstone Common	d						18 13									19 18							
Penistone	d						18 27									19 25							
Denby Dale	d						18 33									19 31							
Shepley	d						18 38									19 36							
Stocksmoor	d						18 41									19 39							
Brockholes	d						18 45									19 43							
Honley	d						18 47									19 45							
Berry Brow	d						18 50									19 48							
Lockwood	d						18 53									19 51							
Huddersfield	a						19 02									20 01							
Darton	d	17 38									18 38									19 38			
Wakefield Kirkgate 4 31	a	17 49			17 57				18 28		18 50		18 59					19 29		19 50			19 58
	d	17 50			17 58				18 32		18 50		18 59					19 32		19 50			19 58
Normanton	d	17 54									18 54									19 54			
Castleford	a	18 00									19 00									20 00			
Woodlesford	a	18 12									19 13									20 12			
Leeds 10 31	a	18 25		18 32	18 18				18 51		19 27	19 31	19 23					19 55		20 26		20 34	20 19

A To Scarborough
B From Lincoln to Adwick
C From Manchester Airport to Cleethorpes
D To Scunthorpe
E To Bridlington
F To Doncaster
G From Lincoln to Hull
H From Retford to Doncaster

Table 34

Mondays to Fridays
from 1 October

Nottingham, Sheffield - Barnsley - Huddersfield and Leeds

Network Diagram - see first page of Table 31

		NT A	NT	NT B	NT	NT C	NT	TP ◇1 D	NT E	NT ◇	NT	NT F	NT	NT	TP FO ◇1 D	NT B	NT	TP FX ◇1 G	NT	NT FO	NT FX	TP ◇1 D	NT
Nottingham 8	d									19 15													21 11
Langley Mill	d									19 32													21 38
Alfreton	d									19 40													21 46
Chesterfield	d									19 52													22 00
Dronfield	d									19 59													22 07
Sheffield 7 29,31	a									20 15													22 19
	d	19 30	19 36	19 44	19 51	19 58	20 06	20 11	20 15	20 18	20 27	20 38	20 41	21 06	21 11	21 15	21 30	21 34	21 41	22 06	22 06	22 11	
Meadowhall 4 29,31	a	19 35	19 41	19 49	19 56	20 03	20 11	20 16	20 20	20 24	20 34	20 44	20 47	21 11	21 16	21 21	21 35	21 39	21 46	22 11	22 11	22 16	
	d		19 42		19 57		20 12			20 24	20 35		20 47	21 12			21 36		21 47	22 12	22 12		
Chapeltown	d		19 48				20 18						20 53	21 18					21 53	22 18	22 18		
Elsecar	d		19 53				20 23							21 23						22 23	22 23		
Wombwell	d		19 57				20 27						21 00	21 27					22 00	22 27	22 27		
Barnsley	a		20 02		20 12		20 32			20 40			21 07	21 33					22 05	22 32	22 32		
	d		20 08		20 12		20 33			20 42			21 08	21 34					22 08		22 33		
Dodworth	d		20 14										21 14						22 14				
Silkstone Common	d		20 18										21 18						22 18				
Penistone	d		20 25										21 25						22 25				
Denby Dale	d		20 31										21 31						22 31				
Shepley	d		20 36										21 36						22 36				
Stocksmoor	d		20 39										21 39						22 39				
Brockholes	d		20 43										21 43						22 43				
Honley	d		20 45										21 45						22 45				
Berry Brow	d		20 48										21 48						22 48				
Lockwood	d		20 51										21 51						22 51				
Huddersfield	a		21 00										21 59						23 00				
Darton	d						20 38							21 38							22 38		
Wakefield Kirkgate 4 31	a				20 28		20 49			20 57				21 52							22 51		
	d				20 28		20 50			20 58				21 52							22 51		
Normanton	d						20 54							21 57							22 56		
Castleford	a						21 00							22 04							23 01		
Woodlesford	a						21 12							22 14							23 14		
Leeds 10 31	a				20 48		21 26			21 20	21 47			22 29			22 46				23 30		

		NT FO	NT	NT E	NT	NT FX	NT FO	NT FX H	NT A
Nottingham 8	d								
Langley Mill	d								
Alfreton	d								
Chesterfield	d								
Dronfield	d								
Sheffield 7 29,31	a								
	d		22 24	22 34	22 41	23 15	23 15	23 24	23 27
Meadowhall 4 29,31	a		22 30	22 39	22 46	23 20	23 20	23 29	23 32
	d		22 30		22 47	23 21	23 21	23 30	
Chapeltown	d				22 53			23 36	
Elsecar	d				22 58			23 41	
Wombwell	d				23 02			23 45	
Barnsley	a				23 07			23 50	
	d				23 08			23 51	
Dodworth	d				23 14				
Silkstone Common	d				23 18				
Penistone	d				23 25				
Denby Dale	d				23 31				
Shepley	d				23 36				
Stocksmoor	d				23 39				
Brockholes	d				23 43				
Honley	d				23 45				
Berry Brow	d				23 48				
Lockwood	d				23 51				
Huddersfield	a				23 55				
Darton	d							23 56	
Wakefield Kirkgate 4 31	a							00s10	
	d	22 51							
Normanton	d	22 56							
Castleford	a	23 01							
Woodlesford	a	23 14							
Leeds 10 31	a	23 30	23 41			00 29	00 30		

A To Doncaster
B To Beverley
C To Bridlington
D From Manchester Airport to Cleethorpes
E To Goole
F To Scunthorpe
G To Cleethorpes
H To Wakefield Westgate

Table 34

Saturdays
until 29 September

Nottingham, Sheffield - Barnsley - Huddersfield and Leeds

Network Diagram - see first page of Table 31

		NT	NT A	NT	NT	NT B	NT	NT	NT B	TP ◇1 C	NT	NT	NT D	EM ◇ E	NT	NT F	NT G	EM ◇1 H	NT	TP ◇1 C	NT	NT	NT D
Nottingham 8	d													06 40								07 11	
Langley Mill	d																					07 27	
Alfreton	d													07 02								07 35	
Chesterfield	d													07 13				07 42				07 50	
Dronfield	d													07 20				07 49					
Sheffield 7 29,31	a													07 31				07 59				08 08	
	d	23p15	05 29	05 43	06 06	06 12	06 28	06 36	06 52	06 55	07 06	07 14	07 24		07 36	07 41	07 51		08 06	08 11	08 14	08 18	08 25
Meadowhall 4 29,31	a	23p20	05 34	05 48	06 11	06 17	06 33	06 41	06 57	07 00	07 11	07 20	07 29		07 41	07 46	07 57		08 11	08 16	08 21	08 25	08 30
	d	23p21		05 49	06 12		06 34	06 42			07 12	07 21			07 42		07 57		08 12		08 22	08 25	
Chapeltown	d			05 55	06 18			06 48			07 18				07 48				08 18				
Elsecar	d			06 01	06 23						07 23								08 23				
Wombwell	d			06 05	06 27			06 55			07 27				07 55				08 27				
Barnsley	a			06 11	06 32			07 00			07 32				08 00		08 11		08 32			08 40	
	d				06 33			07 01			07 33				08 01		08 12		08 33			08 42	
Dodworth	d							07 07							08 07								
Silkstone Common	d							07 11							08 11								
Penistone	d							07 18							08 18								
Denby Dale	d							07 24							08 24								
Shepley	d							07 29							08 29								
Stocksmoor	d							07 32							08 32								
Brockholes	d							07 36							08 36								
Honley	d							07 38							08 38								
Berry Brow	d							07 41							08 41								
Lockwood	d							07 44							08 44								
Huddersfield	a							07 49							08 49								
Darton	d				06 38						07 38								08 38				
Wakefield Kirkgate 4 31	a				06 49						07 49						08 27		08 49			08 57	
	d				06 50						07 50						08 28		08 50			08 58	
Normanton	d				06 54						07 54								08 54				
Castleford	a				07 00						07 59								09 00				
Woodlesford	a				07 12						08 11								09 12				
Leeds 10 31	a	00 30			07 28		07 44				08 25	08 32					08 49		09 25		09 40	09 20	

		NT	EM ◇ E	NT F	NT	NT B	NT	TP ◇1 C	NT	NT	NT D	NT I	NT	NT J	NT	NT K	NT	TP ◇1 C	NT	NT	NT D	NT	NT F
Nottingham 8	d		07 45							08 11										09 15			
Langley Mill	d									08 31										09 32			
Alfreton	d		08 07							08 39										09 40			
Chesterfield	d		08 18							08 51										09 52			
Dronfield	d		08 25							08 58										09 59			
Sheffield 7 29,31	a		08 38							09 16										10 15			
	d	08 36		08 41	08 51	08 53	09 06	09 11	09 14	09 18	09 25	09 29	09 36	09 41	09 50	09 53	10 06	10 11	10 14	10 18	10 24	10 36	10 41
Meadowhall 4 29,31	a	08 41		08 46	08 56	08 59	09 11	09 15	09 20	09 23	09 33	09 35	09 41	09 46	09 55	09 58	10 11	10 16	10 20	10 23	10 29	10 41	10 46
	d	08 42			08 57		09 12		09 21	09 24			09 42		09 56		10 12		10 21	10 24		10 42	
Chapeltown	d	08 48					09 18						09 48				10 18					10 48	
Elsecar	d						09 23										10 23						
Wombwell	d	08 55					09 27						09 55				10 27					10 55	
Barnsley	a	09 00			09 11		09 32			09 40			10 00		10 11		10 32			10 40		11 00	
	d	09 01			09 12		09 33			09 42			10 01		10 12		10 33			10 42		11 01	
Dodworth	d	09 07											10 07									11 07	
Silkstone Common	d	09 11											10 11									11 11	
Penistone	d	09 18											10 18									11 18	
Denby Dale	d	09 24											10 24									11 24	
Shepley	d	09 29											10 29									11 29	
Stocksmoor	d	09 32											10 32									11 32	
Brockholes	d	09 36											10 36									11 36	
Honley	d	09 38											10 38									11 38	
Berry Brow	d	09 41											10 41									11 41	
Lockwood	d	09 44											10 44									11 44	
Huddersfield	a	09 49											10 49									11 49	
Darton	d						09 38										10 38						
Wakefield Kirkgate 4 31	a				09 27		09 49			09 57					10 27		10 49			10 57			
	d				09 28		09 50			09 58					10 28		10 50			10 58			
Normanton	d						09 54										10 54						
Castleford	a						10 00										11 00						
Woodlesford	a						10 12										11 12						
Leeds 10 31	a				09 49		10 25		10 40	10 18					10 48		11 25		11 40	11 18			

A To Beverley
B To Adwick
C From Manchester Airport to Cleethorpes
D To Scunthorpe
E To Liverpool Lime Street
F To Bridlington
G From Retford
H From Derby
I To Sheffield
J To Scarborough
K From Lincoln to Adwick

Nottingham, Sheffield - Barnsley - Huddersfield and Leeds

Network Diagram - see first page of Table 31

Station		NT	NT A	NT	TP ◇1 B	NT	NT	NT C	NT	NT D	NT	NT A	NT	TP ◇1 B	NT	NT	NT C	NT	NT E	NT	NT A	NT
Nottingham 8	d						10 15									11 15						
Langley Mill	d						10 32									11 31						
Alfreton	d						10 40									11 39						
Chesterfield	d						10 52									11 52						
Dronfield	d						10 59															
Sheffield 7 29,31	a						11 15									12 16						
	d	10 50	10 53	11 06	11 11	11 14	11 18	11 24	11 36	11 41	11 50	11 53	12 06	12 11	12 14	12 18	12 24	12 36	12 41	12 50	12 53	13 06
Meadowhall 4 29,31	a	10 55	10 58	11 11	11 16	11 20	11 23	11 29	11 41	11 46	11 55	11 58	12 11	12 16	12 20	12 23	12 29	12 41	12 46	12 55	12 58	13 11
	d	10 56		11 12		11 21	11 24		11 42		11 56		12 12		12 21	12 24		12 42		12 56		13 12
Chapeltown	d			11 18					11 48				12 18					12 48				13 18
Elsecar	d			11 23									12 23									13 23
Wombwell	d			11 27					11 55				12 27					12 55				13 27
Barnsley	a	11 11		11 32			11 40		12 00		12 10		12 32			12 40		13 00		13 11		13 32
	d	11 12		11 33			11 41		12 01		12 11		12 33			12 42		13 01		13 12		13 33
Dodworth	d								12 07									13 07				
Silkstone Common	d								12 11									13 11				
Penistone	d								12 18									13 18				
Denby Dale	d								12 24									13 24				
Shepley	d								12 29									13 29				
Stocksmoor	d								12 32									13 32				
Brockholes	d								12 36									13 36				
Honley	d								12 38									13 38				
Berry Brow	d								12 41									13 41				
Lockwood	d								12 44									13 44				
Huddersfield	a								12 49									13 49				
Darton	d			11 38									12 38									13 38
Wakefield Kirkgate 4 31	a	11 27		11 49			11 57				12 27		12 49			12 57				13 27		13 50
	d	11 28		11 50			11 58				12 28		12 50			12 58				13 28		13 50
Normanton	d			11 54									12 54									13 54
Castleford	a			12 00									13 00									14 00
Woodlesford	a			12 12									13 12									14 12
Leeds 10 31	a	11 48		12 25		12 40	12 18				12 48		13 25		13 43	13 18				13 49		14 25

Station		TP ◇1 B	NT	NT	NT C	NT F	NT	NT E	NT	NT A	NT	TP ◇1 B	NT	NT	NT C	NT	NT D	NT	NT A	NT	TP ◇1 B	NT	NT
Nottingham 8	d			12 15										13 15									14 15
Langley Mill	d			12 32										13 32									14 30
Alfreton	d			12 40										13 40									14 38
Chesterfield	d			12 52										13 52									14 52
Dronfield	d			12 59										13 59									14 59
Sheffield 7 29,31	a			13 15										14 15									15 15
	d	13 11	13 14	13 18	13 24	13 29	13 36	13 41	13 50	13 53	14 06	14 11	14 14	14 18	14 24	14 36	14 41	14 50	14 53	15 06	15 11	15 14	15 18
Meadowhall 4 29,31	a	13 16	13 20	13 23	13 29	13 34	13 41	13 46	13 55	13 58	14 11	14 16	14 20	14 23	14 29	14 41	14 46	14 55	14 58	15 11	15 16	15 20	15 23
	d		13 21	13 24			13 42		13 56		14 12		14 21	14 24		14 42		14 56		15 12		15 21	15 24
Chapeltown	d						13 48				14 18					14 48				15 18			
Elsecar	d										14 23									15 23			
Wombwell	d						13 55				14 27					14 55				15 27			
Barnsley	a			13 40			14 00		14 11		14 32			14 40		15 00		15 11		15 32			15 40
	d			13 42			14 01		14 12		14 33			14 42		15 01		15 12		15 33			15 42
Dodworth	d						14 07									15 07							
Silkstone Common	d						14 11									15 11							
Penistone	d						14 18									15 18							
Denby Dale	d						14 24									15 24							
Shepley	d						14 29									15 29							
Stocksmoor	d						14 32									15 32							
Brockholes	d						14 36									15 36							
Honley	d						14 38									15 38							
Berry Brow	d						14 41									15 41							
Lockwood	d						14 44									15 44							
Huddersfield	a						14 49									15 49							
Darton	d										14 38									15 38			
Wakefield Kirkgate 4 31	a			13 57					14 27		14 49			14 57				15 27		15 49			15 57
	d			13 58					14 28		14 50			14 58				15 28		15 50			15 58
Normanton	d										14 54									15 54			
Castleford	a										15 00									16 00			
Woodlesford	a										15 12									16 12			
Leeds 10 31	a		14 40	14 18					14 48		15 25		15 40	15 18				15 49		16 25		16 40	16 18

A From Lincoln to Adwick
B From Manchester Airport to Cleethorpes
C To Scunthorpe
D To Scarborough
E To Bridlington
F To York

Nottingham, Sheffield - Barnsley - Huddersfield and Leeds

Network Diagram - see first page of Table 31

Station		NT A	NT	NT B	NT	NT C	NT	TP ◇1 D	NT	NT	NT E	NT	NT B	NT	NT C	NT	TP ◇1 D	NT	NT	NT E	NT	NT F
Nottingham 8	d									15 15									16 15			
Langley Mill	d									15 32									16 32			
Alfreton	d									15 40									16 40			
Chesterfield	d									15 53									16 55			
Dronfield	d									16 00									17 02			
Sheffield 7 29,31	a									16 14									17 17			
	d	15 24	15 36	15 41	15 50	15 53	16 06	16 11	16 14	16 18	16 24	16 36	16 41	16 50	16 53	17 06	17 11	17 14	17 18	17 25	17 36	17 41
Meadowhall 4 29,31	a	15 29	15 41	15 46	15 55	15 58	16 11	16 16	16 20	16 23	16 29	16 41	16 46	16 55	16 58	17 11	17 16	17 21	17 23	17 30	17 41	17 46
	d		15 42		15 56		16 12		16 21	16 24		16 42		16 56		17 12		17 21	17 24		17 42	
Chapeltown	d		15 48				16 18					16 48				17 18					17 48	
Elsecar	d						16 23					16 53				17 23					17 53	
Wombwell	d		15 55				16 27					16 57				17 27					17 57	
Barnsley	a		16 00		16 11		16 32			16 40		17 02		17 11		17 32			17 40		18 02	
	d		16 01		16 12		16 33			16 42		17 03		17 12		17 33			17 42		18 03	
Dodworth	d		16 07									17 09									18 09	
Silkstone Common	d		16 11									17 13									18 13	
Penistone	d		16 18									17 20									18 20	
Denby Dale	d		16 24									17 26									18 26	
Shepley	d		16 29									17 31									18 31	
Stocksmoor	d		16 32									17 34									18 34	
Brockholes	d		16 36									17 38									18 38	
Honley	d		16 38									17 40									18 40	
Berry Brow	d		16 41									17 43									18 43	
Lockwood	d		16 44									17 46									18 46	
Huddersfield	a		16 49									17 50									18 51	
Darton	d						16 38									17 38						
Wakefield Kirkgate 4 31	a				16 27		16 49			16 57				17 28		17 49			17 57			
	d				16 28		16 50			16 58				17 28		17 50			17 58			
Normanton	d						16 54									17 54						
Castleford	a						17 00									18 00						
Woodlesford	a						17 12									18 12						
Leeds 10 31	a				16 49		17 25		17 41	17 18				17 48		18 25		18 44	18 18			

Station		NT	NT G	NT	NT	NT	TP ◇1 D	NT E	NT	NT B	NT	NT H	NT	TP ◇1 D	NT	NT	NT A	NT	NT I	NT	NT B	NT	TP ◇1 D
Nottingham 8	d					17 15									18 15								
Langley Mill	d					17 32									18 32								
Alfreton	d					17 40									18 40								
Chesterfield	d					17 52									18 55								
Dronfield	d					17 59									19 02								
Sheffield 7 29,31	a					18 14									19 15								
	d	17 50	17 53	18 06	18 13	18 18	18 24	18 29	18 36	18 41	18 50	19 00	19 06	19 11	19 16	19 18	19 25	19 36	19 44	19 51	19 58	20 06	20 11
Meadowhall 4 29,31	a	17 55	17 57	18 12	18 20	18 23	18 29	18 34	18 41	18 46	18 55	19 06	19 11	19 16	19 22	19 24	19 30	19 41	19 49	19 56	20 03	20 11	20 16
	d	17 56		18 12	18 21	18 24			18 42		18 56		19 12		19 22	19 25		19 42		19 57		20 12	
Chapeltown	d			18 18					18 48				19 18					19 48				20 18	
Elsecar	d			18 23					18 53				19 23					19 53				20 23	
Wombwell	d			18 27					18 57				19 27					19 57				20 27	
Barnsley	a	18 11		18 33		18 42			19 02		19 14		19 33		19 40			20 02		20 12		20 32	
	d	18 12		18 33		18 42			19 03		19 14		19 33		19 42			20 08		20 12		20 33	
Dodworth	d								19 09									20 14					
Silkstone Common	d								19 13									20 18					
Penistone	d								19 20									20 25					
Denby Dale	d								19 26									20 31					
Shepley	d								19 31									20 36					
Stocksmoor	d								19 34									20 39					
Brockholes	d								19 38									20 43					
Honley	d								19 41									20 45					
Berry Brow	d								19 44									20 48					
Lockwood	d								19 46									20 51					
Huddersfield	a								19 51									20 55					
Darton	d			18 38									19 38									20 38	
Wakefield Kirkgate 4 31	a	18 28		18 50		18 59					19 29		19 50		19 58					20 28		20 49	
	d	18 32		18 50		18 59					19 32		19 50		19 58					20 28		20 50	
Normanton	d			18 54									19 54									20 54	
Castleford	a			19 00									20 00									21 00	
Woodlesford	a			19 13									20 12									21 12	
Leeds 10 31	a	18 51		19 27	19 43	19 23					19 55		20 26		20 20	20 38				20 48		21 26	

A To Scunthorpe
B To Bridlington
C From Lincoln to Adwick
D From Manchester Airport to Cleethorpes
E To Doncaster
F To Scarborough
G From Lincoln to Hull
H From Retford to Doncaster
I To Beverley

Table 34

Saturdays until 29 September

Nottingham, Sheffield - Barnsley - Huddersfield and Leeds

Network Diagram - see first page of Table 31

		NT A	NT	NT	NT B	NT	NT	NT C	NT	TP ◇■ D	NT	TP ◇■ E	NT	NT	NT	NT A	NT	NT F
Nottingham ■	d		19 15										21 15					
Langley Mill	d		19 32										21 31					
Alfreton	d		19 40										21 39					
Chesterfield	d		19 52										21 50					
Dronfield	d		19 59										21 57					
Sheffield ■ 29,31	a		20 15										22 13					
	d	20 15	20 18	20 27	20 38	20 41	21 06	21 14	21 30	21 34	22 06	22 11			22 24	22 30	22 41	23 27
Meadowhall ■ 29,31	a	20 20	20 24	20 34	20 44	20 47	21 11	21 21	21 36	21 39	22 11	22 16			22 30	22 35	22 46	23 32
	d		20 24	20 35		20 47	21 12		21 36		22 12				22 30		22 47	
Chapeltown	d					20 53	21 18				22 18						22 53	
Elsecar	d						21 23				22 23						22 58	
Wombwell	d					21 00	21 27				22 27						23 02	
Barnsley	a		20 40			21 07	21 33				22 32						23 07	
	d		20 42			21 08	21 33										23 08	
Dodworth	d					21 14											23 14	
Silkstone Common	d					21 18											23 18	
Penistone	d					21 25											23 25	
Denby Dale	d					21 31											23 31	
Shepley	d					21 36											23 36	
Stocksmoor	d					21 39											23 39	
Brockholes	d					21 43											23 43	
Honley	d					21 45											23 45	
Berry Brow	d					21 48											23 48	
Lockwood	d					21 51											23 51	
Huddersfield	a					21 56											23 59	
Darton	d						21 38											
Wakefield Kirkgate ■ 31	a		20 57				21 52											
	d		20 58				21 52							22 51				
Normanton	d						21 57							22 56				
Castleford	a						22 04							23 02				
Woodlesford	a						22 14							23 14				
Leeds ■ 31	a		21 20	21 47			22 29		22 45					23 30	23 40			

Saturdays from 6 October

		NT	NT C	NT	NT	NT G	NT	NT	NT G	TP ◇■ E	NT	NT	NT B	EM ◇ H	NT	NT I	NT J	EM ◇■ K	NT	TP ◇■ E	NT	NT	NT B
Nottingham ■	d													06 40								07 11	
Langley Mill	d																					07 27	
Alfreton	d													07 02								07 35	
Chesterfield	d													07 13				07 42				07 50	
Dronfield	d													07 20				07 49					
Sheffield ■ 29,31	a													07 31				07 59				08 08	
	d	23p15	05 29	05 43	06 06	06 12	06 28	06 36	06 52	06 55	07 06	07 14	07 24		07 36	07 41	07 51		08 06	08 11	08 14	08 18	08 25
Meadowhall ■ 29,31	a	23p20	05 34	05 48	06 11	06 17	06 33	06 41	06 57	07 00	07 11	07 20	07 29		07 41	07 46	07 57		08 11	08 16	08 21	08 25	08 30
	d	23p21		05 49	06 12		06 34	06 42			07 12	07 21			07 42		07 57		08 12		08 22	08 25	
Chapeltown	d			05 55	06 18			06 48			07 18				07 48				08 18				
Elsecar	d			06 01	06 23						07 23								08 23				
Wombwell	d			06 05	06 27			06 55			07 27				07 55				08 27				
Barnsley	a			06 11	06 32			07 00			07 32				08 00		08 11		08 32			08 40	
	d				06 33			07 01			07 33				08 01		08 12		08 33			08 42	
Dodworth	d							07 07							08 07								
Silkstone Common	d							07 11							08 11								
Penistone	d							07 18							08 18								
Denby Dale	d							07 24							08 24								
Shepley	d							07 29							08 29								
Stocksmoor	d							07 32							08 32								
Brockholes	d							07 36							08 36								
Honley	d							07 38							08 38								
Berry Brow	d							07 41							08 41								
Lockwood	d							07 44							08 44								
Huddersfield	a							07 54							08 53								
Darton	d				06 38						07 38								08 38				
Wakefield Kirkgate ■ 31	a				06 49						07 49						08 27		08 49			08 57	
	d				06 50						07 50						08 28		08 50			08 58	
Normanton	d				06 54						07 54								08 54				
Castleford	a				07 00						07 59								09 00				
Woodlesford	a				07 12						08 11								09 12				
Leeds ■ 31	a	00 30			07 28		07 44				08 25	08 32					08 49		09 25		09 40	09 20	

A To Goole
B To Scunthorpe
C To Beverley
D To Cleethorpes
E From Manchester Airport to Cleethorpes
F To Doncaster
G To Adwick
H To Liverpool Lime Street
I To Bridlington
J From Retford
K From Derby

Table 34

Saturdays from 6 October

Nottingham, Sheffield - Barnsley - Huddersfield and Leeds

Network Diagram - see first page of Table 31

		NT	EM ◇ A	NT B	NT	NT C	NT	TP ◇■ D	NT	NT	NT E	NT F	NT	NT G	NT	NT H	NT	TP ◇■ D	NT	NT	NT E	NT	NT B
Nottingham ■	d		07 45							08 11										09 15			
Langley Mill	d									08 31										09 32			
Alfreton	d		08 07							08 39										09 40			
Chesterfield	d		08 18							08 51										09 52			
Dronfield	d		08 25							08 58										09 59			
Sheffield ■ 29,31	a		08 38							09 16										10 15			
	d	08 36		08 41	08 51	08 53	09 06	09 11	09 14	09 18	09 25	09 29	09 36	09 41	09 50	09 53	10 06	10 11	10 14	10 18	10 24	10 36	10 41
Meadowhall ■ 29,31	a	08 41		08 46	08 56	08 59	09 11	09 15	09 20	09 23	09 33	09 35	09 41	09 46	09 55	09 58	10 11	10 16	10 20	10 23	10 29	10 41	10 46
	d	08 42			08 57		09 12		09 21	09 24			09 42		09 56		10 12		10 21	10 24		10 42	
Chapeltown	d	08 48					09 18						09 48				10 18					10 48	
Elsecar	d						09 23										10 23						
Wombwell	d	08 55					09 27						09 55				10 27					10 55	
Barnsley	a	09 00			09 11		09 32			09 40			10 00		10 11		10 32			10 40		11 00	
	d	09 01			09 12		09 33			09 42			10 01		10 12		10 33			10 42		11 01	
Dodworth	d	09 07											10 07									11 07	
Silkstone Common	d	09 11											10 11									11 11	
Penistone	d	09 18											10 18									11 18	
Denby Dale	d	09 24											10 24									11 24	
Shepley	d	09 29											10 29									11 29	
Stocksmoor	d	09 32											10 32									11 32	
Brockholes	d	09 36											10 36									11 36	
Honley	d	09 38											10 38									11 38	
Berry Brow	d	09 41											10 41									11 41	
Lockwood	d	09 44											10 44									11 44	
Huddersfield	a	09 50											10 53									11 53	
Darton	d						09 38										10 38						
Wakefield Kirkgate ■ 31	a				09 27		09 49			09 57					10 27		10 49			10 57			
	d				09 28		09 50			09 58					10 28		10 50			10 58			
Normanton	d						09 54										10 54						
Castleford	a						10 00										11 00						
Woodlesford	a						10 12										11 12						
Leeds ■ 31	a				09 49		10 25		10 40	10 18					10 48		11 25		11 40	11 18			

		NT	NT H	NT	TP ◇■ D	NT	NT	NT E	NT	NT G	NT	NT H	NT	TP ◇■ D	NT	NT	NT E	NT	NT B	NT	NT H	NT
Nottingham ■	d						10 15									11 15						
Langley Mill	d						10 32									11 31						
Alfreton	d						10 40									11 39						
Chesterfield	d						10 52									11 52						
Dronfield	d						10 59															
Sheffield ■ 29,31	a						11 15									12 16						
	d	10 50	10 53	11 06	11 11	11 14	11 18	11 24	11 36	11 41	11 50	11 53	12 06	12 11	12 14	12 18	12 24	12 36	12 41	12 50	12 53	13 06
Meadowhall ■ 29,31	a	10 55	10 58	11 11	11 16	11 20	11 23	11 29	11 41	11 46	11 55	11 58	12 11	12 16	12 20	12 23	12 29	12 41	12 46	12 55	12 58	13 11
	d	10 56		11 12		11 21	11 24		11 42		11 56		12 12		12 21	12 24		12 42		12 56		13 12
Chapeltown	d			11 18					11 48				12 18					12 48				13 18
Elsecar	d			11 23									12 23									13 23
Wombwell	d			11 27					11 55				12 27					12 55				13 27
Barnsley	a	11 11		11 32			11 40		12 00		12 10		12 32			12 40		13 00		13 11		13 32
	d	11 12		11 33			11 41		12 01		12 11		12 33			12 42		13 01		13 12		13 33
Dodworth	d								12 07									13 07				
Silkstone Common	d								12 11									13 11				
Penistone	d								12 18									13 18				
Denby Dale	d								12 24									13 24				
Shepley	d								12 29									13 29				
Stocksmoor	d								12 32									13 32				
Brockholes	d								12 36									13 36				
Honley	d								12 38									13 38				
Berry Brow	d								12 41									13 41				
Lockwood	d								12 44									13 44				
Huddersfield	a								12 52									13 53				
Darton	d			11 38									12 38									13 38
Wakefield Kirkgate ■ 31	a	11 27		11 49			11 57				12 27		12 49			12 57				13 27		13 50
	d	11 28		11 50			11 58				12 28		12 50			12 58				13 28		13 50
Normanton	d			11 54									12 54									13 54
Castleford	a			12 00									13 00									14 00
Woodlesford	a			12 12									13 12									14 12
Leeds ■ 31	a	11 48		12 25		12 40	12 18				12 48		13 25		13 43	13 18				13 49		14 25

A To Liverpool Lime Street
B To Bridlington
C To Adwick
D From Manchester Airport to Cleethorpes
E To Scunthorpe
F To Sheffield
G To Scarborough
H From Lincoln to Adwick

Nottingham, Sheffield - Barnsley - Huddersfield and Leeds

Saturdays from 6 October

Network Diagram - see first page of Table 31

		TP ◇1 A	NT	NT	NT B	NT C	NT	NT D	NT	NT E	NT	TP ◇1 A	NT	NT	NT B	NT	NT F	NT	NT E	NT	TP ◇1 A	NT	NT
Nottingham 8 ⇌	d			12 15										13 15									14 15
Langley Mill	d			12 32										13 32									14 30
Alfreton	d			12 40										13 40									14 38
Chesterfield	d			12 52										13 52									14 52
Dronfield	d			12 59										13 59									14 59
Sheffield 7 29,31 ⇌	a			13 15										14 15									15 15
	d	13 11	13 14	13 18	13 24	13 29	13 36	13 41	13 50	13 53	14 06	14 11	14 14	14 18	14 24	14 36	14 41	14 50	14 53	15 06	15 11	15 14	15 18
Meadowhall 4 29,31 ⇌	a	13 16	13 20	13 23	13 29	13 34	13 41	13 46	13 55	13 58	14 11	14 16	14 20	14 23	14 29	14 41	14 46	14 55	14 58	15 11	15 16	15 20	15 23
	d		13 21	13 24			13 42		13 56		14 12		14 21	14 24		14 42		14 56		15 12		15 21	15 24
Chapeltown	d						13 48				14 18					14 48				15 18			
Elsecar	d										14 23									15 23			
Wombwell	d						13 55				14 27					14 55				15 27			
Barnsley	a			13 40			14 00		14 11		14 32			14 40		15 00		15 11		15 32			15 40
	d			13 42			14 01		14 12		14 33			14 42		15 01		15 12		15 33			15 42
Dodworth	d						14 07									15 07							
Silkstone Common	d						14 11									15 11							
Penistone	d						14 18									15 18							
Denby Dale	d						14 24									15 24							
Shepley	d						14 29									15 29							
Stocksmoor	d						14 32									15 32							
Brockholes	d						14 36									15 36							
Honley	d						14 38									15 38							
Berry Brow	d						14 41									15 41							
Lockwood	d						14 44									15 44							
Huddersfield	a						14 53									15 53							
Darton	d										14 38									15 38			
Wakefield Kirkgate 4 31	a			13 57					14 27		14 49			14 57				15 27		15 49			15 57
	d			13 58					14 28		14 50			14 58				15 28		15 50			15 58
Normanton	d										14 54									15 54			
Castleford	a										15 00									16 00			
Woodlesford	a										15 12									16 12			
Leeds 10 31	a		14 40	14 18					14 48		15 25		15 40	15 18				15 49		16 25		16 40	16 18

		NT B	NT	NT D	NT	NT E	NT	TP ◇1 A	NT	NT	NT G	NT	NT D	NT	NT E	NT	TP ◇1 A	NT	NT	NT G	NT	NT F
Nottingham 8 ⇌	d									15 15									16 15			
Langley Mill	d									15 32									16 32			
Alfreton	d									15 40									16 40			
Chesterfield	d									15 53									16 55			
Dronfield	d									16 00									17 02			
Sheffield 7 29,31 ⇌	a									16 14									17 17			
	d	15 24	15 36	15 41	15 50	15 53	16 06	16 11	16 14	16 18	16 24	16 36	16 41	16 50	16 53	17 06	17 11	17 14	17 18	17 25	17 36	17 41
Meadowhall 4 29,31 ⇌	a	15 29	15 41	15 46	15 55	15 58	16 11	16 16	16 20	16 23	16 29	16 41	16 46	16 55	16 58	17 11	17 16	17 21	17 23	17 30	17 41	17 46
	d		15 42		15 56		16 12		16 21	16 24		16 42		16 56		17 12		17 21	17 24		17 42	
Chapeltown	d		15 48				16 18					16 48				17 18					17 48	
Elsecar	d						16 23					16 53				17 23					17 53	
Wombwell	d		15 55				16 27					16 57				17 27					17 57	
Barnsley	a		16 00		16 11		16 32			16 40		17 02		17 11		17 32			17 40		18 02	
	d		16 01		16 12		16 33			16 42		17 03		17 12		17 33			17 42		18 03	
Dodworth	d		16 07									17 09									18 09	
Silkstone Common	d		16 11									17 13									18 13	
Penistone	d		16 18									17 20									18 20	
Denby Dale	d		16 24									17 26									18 26	
Shepley	d		16 29									17 31									18 31	
Stocksmoor	d		16 32									17 34									18 34	
Brockholes	d		16 36									17 38									18 38	
Honley	d		16 38									17 40									18 40	
Berry Brow	d		16 41									17 43									18 43	
Lockwood	d		16 44									17 46									18 46	
Huddersfield	a		16 52									17 54									18 53	
Darton	d						16 38									17 38						
Wakefield Kirkgate 4 31	a				16 27		16 49			16 57				17 28		17 49			17 57			
	d				16 28		16 50			16 58				17 28		17 50			17 58			
Normanton	d						16 54									17 54						
Castleford	a						17 00									18 00						
Woodlesford	a						17 12									18 12						
Leeds 10 31	a				16 49		17 25		17 41	17 18				17 48		18 25		18 44	18 18			

A From Manchester Airport to Cleethorpes
B To Scunthorpe
C To York
D To Bridlington
E From Lincoln to Adwick
F To Scarborough
G To Doncaster

Table 34

Nottingham, Sheffield - Barnsley - Huddersfield and Leeds

Saturdays from 6 October

Network Diagram - see first page of Table 31

		NT	NT A	NT	NT	NT	TP ◇1 B	NT C	NT	NT D	NT	NT E	NT	TP ◇1 B	NT	NT	NT F	NT	NT G	NT	NT D	NT	TP ◇1 B
Nottingham 8 ⇌	d					17 15									18 15								
Langley Mill	d					17 32									18 32								
Alfreton	d					17 40									18 40								
Chesterfield	d					17 52									18 55								
Dronfield	d					17 59									19 02								
Sheffield 7 29,31 ⇌	a					18 14									19 15								
	d	17 50	17 53	18 06	18 13	18 18	18 24	18 29	18 36	18 41	18 50	19 00	19 06	19 11	19 16	19 18	19 25	19 36	19 44	19 51	19 58	20 06	20 11
Meadowhall 4 29,31 ⇌	a	17 55	17 57	18 12	18 20	18 23	18 29	18 34	18 41	18 46	18 55	19 06	19 11	19 16	19 22	19 24	19 30	19 41	19 49	19 56	20 03	20 11	20 16
	d	17 56		18 12	18 21	18 24			18 42		18 56		19 12		19 22	19 25		19 42		19 57		20 12	
Chapeltown	d			18 18					18 48				19 18					19 48				20 18	
Elsecar	d			18 23					18 53				19 23					19 53				20 23	
Wombwell	d			18 27					18 57				19 27					19 57				20 27	
Barnsley	a	18 11		18 33		18 42			19 02		19 14		19 33		19 40			20 02		20 12		20 32	
	d	18 12		18 33		18 42			19 03		19 14		19 33		19 42			20 08		20 12		20 33	
Dodworth	d								19 09									20 14					
Silkstone Common	d								19 13									20 18					
Penistone	d								19 20									20 25					
Denby Dale	d								19 26									20 31					
Shepley	d								19 31									20 36					
Stocksmoor	d								19 34									20 39					
Brockholes	d								19 38									20 43					
Honley	d								19 41									20 45					
Berry Brow	d								19 44									20 48					
Lockwood	d								19 46									20 51					
Huddersfield	a								19 54									21 00					
Darton	d			18 38									19 38									20 38	
Wakefield Kirkgate 4 31	a	18 28		18 50		18 59					19 29		19 50		19 58					20 28		20 49	
	d	18 32		18 50		18 59					19 32		19 50		19 58					20 28		20 50	
Normanton	d			18 54									19 54									20 54	
Castleford	a			19 00									20 00									21 00	
Woodlesford	a			19 13									20 12									21 12	
Leeds 10 31	a	18 51		19 27	19 43	19 23					19 55		20 26		20 20	20 38				20 48		21 26	

		NT H	NT	NT	NT F	NT	NT	NT G	NT	TP ◇1 I	NT	NT	TP ◇1 B	NT	NT	NT	NT H	NT	NT C
Nottingham 8 ⇌	d		19 15											21 15					
Langley Mill	d		19 32											21 31					
Alfreton	d		19 40											21 39					
Chesterfield	d		19 52											21 50					
Dronfield	d		19 59											21 57					
Sheffield 7 29,31 ⇌	a		20 15											22 13					
	d	20 15	20 18	20 27	20 38	20 41	21 06	21 14	21 30	21 34	21 41	22 06	22 11			22 24	22 30	22 41	23 27
Meadowhall 4 29,31 ⇌	a	20 20	20 24	20 34	20 44	20 47	21 11	21 21	21 36	21 39	21 46	22 11	22 16			22 30	22 35	22 46	23 32
	d		20 24	20 35		20 47	21 12		21 36		21 47	22 12				22 30		22 47	
Chapeltown	d					20 53	21 18				21 53	22 18						22 53	
Elsecar	d						21 23					22 23						22 58	
Wombwell	d					21 00	21 27				22 00	22 27						23 02	
Barnsley	a		20 40			21 07	21 33				22 05	22 32						23 07	
	d		20 42			21 08	21 33				22 08							23 08	
Dodworth	d					21 14					22 14							23 14	
Silkstone Common	d					21 18					22 18							23 18	
Penistone	d					21 25					22 25							23 25	
Denby Dale	d					21 31					22 31							23 31	
Shepley	d					21 36					22 36							23 36	
Stocksmoor	d					21 39					22 39							23 39	
Brockholes	d					21 43					22 43							23 43	
Honley	d					21 45					22 45							23 45	
Berry Brow	d					21 48					22 48							23 48	
Lockwood	d					21 51					22 51							23 51	
Huddersfield	a					22 01					23 01							00 03	
Darton	d						21 38												
Wakefield Kirkgate 4 31	a		20 57				21 52												
	d		20 58				21 52								22 51				
Normanton	d						21 57								22 56				
Castleford	a						22 04								23 02				
Woodlesford	a						22 14								23 14				
Leeds 10 31	a		21 20	21 47			22 29		22 45						23 30	23 40			

A From Lincoln to Hull
B From Manchester Airport to Cleethorpes
C To Doncaster
D To Bridlington
E From Retford to Doncaster
F To Scunthorpe
G To Beverley
H To Goole
I To Cleethorpes

Table 34

Sundays until 24 June

Nottingham, Sheffield - Barnsley - Huddersfield and Leeds

Network Diagram - see first page of Table 31

	NT	NT	NT	NT	NT	NT	TP	NT	EM	NT	NT	NT	NT	NT	TP	NT	NT	NT	NT	NT	TP	NT
	A		B	◇			◇1 C	B	◇ D		A				◇1 E		F	B			◇1 G	
Nottingham d									09 31			10 06				11 15						12 19
Langley Mill d												10 27				11 31						12 35
Alfreton d									09 53			10 35				11 39						12 43
Chesterfield d									10 08			10 55				11 51						12 54
Dronfield d									10 15			11 02				11 58						13 01
Sheffield 29,31 a									10 33			11 15				12 15						13 16
d	08 00	08 39	08 45	09 17	09 36	09 39	09 52	10 26		10 39	11 05	11 17	11 36	11 49	12 11	12 16	12 24	12 28	12 35	12 39	13 11	13 17
Meadowhall 29,31 a	08 05	08 44	08 50	09 22	09 41	09 44	09 57	10 31		10 44	11 10	11 23	11 41	11 54	12 16	12 22	12 29	12 33	12 40	12 44	13 16	13 22
d		08 45		09 23	09 42	09 45				10 45		11 23	11 42	11 55		12 23			12 41	12 45		13 23
Chapeltown d		08 51				09 51				10 51				12 01						12 55		
Elsecar d		08 56				09 56				10 56				12 06						13 00		
Wombwell d		09 00				10 00				11 00				12 10						13 04		
Barnsley a		09 05		09 37		10 05				11 05		11 37		12 15		12 37			12 55	13 09		13 37
d		09 10		09 37		10 06				11 10		11 38		12 16		12 37			13 06	13 10		13 37
Dodworth d						10 12								12 22					13 12			
Silkstone Common d						10 16								12 26					13 16			
Penistone d						10 23								12 33					13 23			
Denby Dale d						10 29								12 39					13 29			
Shepley d						10 34								12 44					13 34			
Stocksmoor d						10 37								12 47					13 37			
Brockholes d						10 41								12 51					13 41			
Honley d						10 43								12 53					13 43			
Berry Brow d						10 46								12 56					13 46			
Lockwood d						10 49								12 59					13 49			
Huddersfield a						10 53								13 08					13 53			
Darton d		09 15								11 15										13 15		
Wakefield Kirkgate 31 a		09 29		09 55						11 29		11 53				12 52				13 29		13 52
d		09 30		09 55						11 30		11 53				12 53				13 30		13 53
Normanton d		09 34								11 34										13 34		
Castleford a		09 40								11 40										13 40		
Woodlesford a		09 52								11 51										13 51		
Leeds 31 a		10 04		10 15	10 52					12 05		12 19	12 53			13 18				14 04		14 18

	NT	NT	NT	TP	NT	NT	NT	NT	TP	NT	NT	NT	NT	NT	TP	NT	NT	NT	NT	NT	NT	TP
	H			◇1 E		F	B		◇1 E		A	H		I	◇1 E		F	B	J	K		◇1 E
Nottingham d					13 09					14 19						15 12						
Langley Mill d					13 27					14 35						15 34						
Alfreton d					13 35					14 43						15 44						
Chesterfield d					13 46					14 54						15 53						
Dronfield d					13 53					15 01						16 00						
Sheffield 29,31 a					14 07					15 15						16 15						
d	13 24	13 36	13 39	14 10	14 17	14 22	14 28	14 39	15 11	15 17	15 24	15 28	15 36	15 39	16 11	16 17	16 24	16 28	16 36	16 39	16 54	17 11
Meadowhall 29,31 a	13 29	13 41	13 44	14 15	14 22	14 27	14 33	14 44	15 16	15 22	15 29	15 33	15 41	15 42	16 16	16 22	16 29	16 33	16 41	16 44	16 59	17 16
d		13 42	13 45		14 23			14 45		15 23			15 42	15 43		16 23				16 45	17 00	
Chapeltown d			13 51					14 51						15 49						16 51		
Elsecar d			13 56					14 56						15 54						16 56		
Wombwell d			14 00					15 00						15 58						17 00		
Barnsley a			14 05		14 37			15 05		15 37				16 03		16 37				17 05	17 14	
d			14 06		14 37			15 10		15 37				16 04		16 37				17 10	17 15	
Dodworth d			14 12											16 10							17 21	
Silkstone Common d			14 16											16 14							17 25	
Penistone d			14 23											16 21							17 32	
Denby Dale d			14 29											16 27							17 38	
Shepley d			14 34											16 32							17 43	
Stocksmoor d			14 37											16 35							17 46	
Brockholes d			14 41											16 39							17 50	
Honley d			14 43											16 41							17 52	
Berry Brow d			14 46											16 44							17 55	
Lockwood d			14 49											16 47							17 58	
Huddersfield a			14 53											16 53							18 05	
Darton d								15 15												17 15		
Wakefield Kirkgate 31 a					14 52			15 29		15 52						16 52				17 29		
d					14 53			15 30		15 53						16 53				17 30		
Normanton d								15 34												17 34		
Castleford a								15 40												17 40		
Woodlesford a								15 51												17 51		
Leeds 31 a		14 47			15 18			16 04		16 18			16 54			17 18				18 05		

A To Doncaster
B To Scarborough
C To Cleethorpes
D To Liverpool Lime Street
E From Manchester Airport to Cleethorpes
F To Goole
G From Manchester Piccadilly to Doncaster
H To Bridlington
I From Retford
J To Sheffield
K From Lincoln

Table 34

Sundays until 24 June

Nottingham, Sheffield - Barnsley - Huddersfield and Leeds

Network Diagram - see first page of Table 31

	NT	NT	NT	NT	NT	TP	NT	NT	NT	NT	NT	TP	NT	NT	NT	NT	NT	TP	NT	NT	NT	NT
		A	B			◇1 C		A	D		E	◇1 C		A			F	◇1 C			G	
Nottingham d	16 14						17 14						18 14						19 19	20 15		
Langley Mill d	16 30						17 30						18 30						19 35	20 33		
Alfreton d	16 38						17 38						18 38						19 43	20 41		
Chesterfield d	16 50						17 51						18 52						19 54	20 53		
Dronfield d	16 57						17 58						18 58						20 01			
Sheffield 29,31 a	17 15						18 14						19 16						20 15	21 14		
d	17 17	17 25	17 28	17 36	17 39	18 11	18 17	18 25	18 28	18 39	18 57	19 11	19 16	19 29	19 36	19 39	20 02	20 11	20 17		20 28	20 39
Meadowhall 29,31 a	17 22	17 30	17 33	17 44	17 46	18 16	18 22	18 30	18 34	18 44	19 04	19 16	19 22	19 34	19 41	19 44	20 08	20 16	20 22		20 33	20 44
d	17 23			17 44	17 46		18 23			18 45			19 23		19 42	19 45			20 23			20 45
Chapeltown d					17 52					18 51						19 51						20 51
Elsecar d					17 58					18 56						19 56						20 56
Wombwell d					18 01					19 00						20 00						21 00
Barnsley a	17 37				18 08		18 37			19 05			19 37			20 05			20 37			21 06
d	17 37				18 10		18 37			19 10			19 37			20 06			20 37			21 10
Dodworth d					18 16											20 12						
Silkstone Common d					18 20											20 16						
Penistone d					18 27											20 23						
Denby Dale d					18 34											20 29						
Shepley d					18 39											20 34						
Stocksmoor d					18 41											20 37						
Brockholes d					18 45											20 41						
Honley d					18 48											20 43						
Berry Brow d					18 51											20 46						
Lockwood d					18 53											20 49						
Huddersfield a					18 58											20 53						
Darton d										19 15												21 15
Wakefield Kirkgate 31 a	17 52						18 52			19 29			19 52						20 52			21 29
d	17 53						18 53			19 30			19 53						20 53			21 30
Normanton d										19 34												21 34
Castleford a										19 41												21 40
Woodlesford a										19 53												21 51
Leeds 31 a	18 18			18 50			19 18			20 05			20 18		20 52				21 16			22 04

	TP	NT	NT	NT	NT	NT	TP	NT	NT
	◇1 C	F			F	A	◇1 H		A
Nottingham d								21 30	
Langley Mill d								21 52	
Alfreton d								22 00	
Chesterfield d								22 13	
Dronfield d								22 20	
Sheffield 29,31 a								22 36	
d	21 11	21 24	21 36	21 43	22 13	22 26	22 30	22 39	23 34
Meadowhall 29,31 a	21 16	21 29	21 41	21 48	22 18	22 31	22 35	22 44	23 39
d			21 42	21 49				22 45	
Chapeltown d				21 55				22 51	
Elsecar d				22 00				22 56	
Wombwell d				22 04				23 00	
Barnsley a				22 09				23 05	
d								23 10	
Dodworth d									
Silkstone Common d									
Penistone d									
Denby Dale d									
Shepley d									
Stocksmoor d									
Brockholes d									
Honley d									
Berry Brow d									
Lockwood d									
Huddersfield a									
Darton d								23 15	
Wakefield Kirkgate 31 a								23 26	
d								23 27	
Normanton d								23 34	
Castleford a								23 40	
Woodlesford a								23 53	
Leeds 31 a			22 52					00 05	

A To Doncaster
B To Bridlington
C From Manchester Airport to Cleethorpes
D To Beverley
E To Sheffield
F To Hull
G To Goole
H To Cleethorpes

Sundays

1 July to 9 September

Nottingham, Sheffield - Barnsley - Huddersfield and Leeds

Network Diagram - see first page of Table 31

		NT	NT	NT	NT	NT	NT	TP	NT	EM	NT	NT	NT	NT	NT	TP	NT	NT	NT	NT	NT	TP	NT
					◇			◇■		◇						◇■						◇■	
		A		B				C	B	D		A				E		F	B			G	
Nottingham	d									09 31			10 06				11 15						12 19
Langley Mill	d												10 27				11 31						12 35
Alfreton	d									09 53			10 35				11 39						12 43
Chesterfield	d									10 08			10 55				11 51						12 54
Dronfield	d									10 15			11 02				11 58						13 01
Sheffield 29,31	a									10 33			11 15				12 15						13 16
	d	08 00	08 39	08 45	09 17	09 36	09 39	09 52	10 26		10 39	11 05	11 17	11 36	11 49	12 11	12 16	12 24	12 28	12 35	12 39	13 11	13 17
Meadowhall 29,31	a	08 05	08 44	08 50	09 22	09 41	09 44	09 57	10 31		10 44	11 10	11 23	11 41	11 54	12 16	12 22	12 29	12 33	12 40	12 44	13 16	13 22
	d		08 45		09 23	09 42	09 45				10 45		11 23	11 42	11 55		12 23			12 41	12 45		13 23
Chapeltown	d		08 51				09 51				10 51				12 01						12 55		
Elsecar	d		08 56				09 56				10 56				12 06						13 00		
Wombwell	d		09 00				10 00				11 00				12 10						13 04		
Barnsley	a		09 05		09 37		10 05				11 05		11 37		12 15		12 37			12 55	13 09		13 37
	d		09 10		09 37		10 06				11 10		11 38		12 16		12 37			13 06	13 10		13 37
Dodworth	d						10 12								12 22					13 12			
Silkstone Common	d						10 16								12 26					13 16			
Penistone	d						10 23								12 33					13 23			
Denby Dale	d						10 29								12 39					13 29			
Shepley	d						10 34								12 44					13 34			
Stocksmoor	d						10 37								12 47					13 37			
Brockholes	d						10 41								12 51					13 41			
Honley	d						10 43								12 53					13 43			
Berry Brow	d						10 46								12 56					13 46			
Lockwood	d						10 49								12 59					13 49			
Huddersfield	a						10 53								13 08					13 53			
Darton	d		09 15								11 15										13 15		
Wakefield Kirkgate 31	a		09 29		09 55						11 29		11 53				12 52				13 29		13 52
	d		09 30		09 55						11 30		11 53				12 53				13 30		13 53
Normanton	d		09 34								11 34										13 34		
Castleford	a		09 40								11 40										13 40		
Woodlesford	a		09 52								11 51										13 51		
Leeds 31	a		10 04		10 15	10 52					12 05		12 19	12 53			13 18				14 04		14 18

		NT	NT	NT	TP	NT	NT	NT	NT	TP	NT	NT	NT	NT	NT	TP	NT	NT	NT	NT	NT	NT	TP
					◇■					◇■						◇■							◇■
		H			E		F	B		E		A	H		I	E		F	B	J	K		E
Nottingham	d					13 09					14 19						15 12						
Langley Mill	d					13 27					14 35						15 34						
Alfreton	d					13 35					14 43						15 44						
Chesterfield	d					13 46					14 54						15 53						
Dronfield	d					13 53					15 01						16 00						
Sheffield 29,31	a					14 07					15 15						16 15						
	d	13 24	13 36	13 39	14 11	14 17	14 22	14 28	14 39	15 11	15 17	15 24	15 28	15 36	15 39	16 11	16 17	16 24	16 28	16 36	16 39	16 54	17 11
Meadowhall 29,31	a	13 29	13 41	13 44	14 16	14 22	14 27	14 33	14 44	15 16	15 22	15 29	15 33	15 41	15 42	16 16	16 22	16 29	16 33	16 41	16 44	16 59	17 16
	d		13 42	13 45		14 23			14 45		15 23			15 42	15 43		16 23				16 45	17 00	
Chapeltown	d			13 51					14 51						15 49						16 51		
Elsecar	d			13 56					14 56						15 54						16 56		
Wombwell	d			14 00					15 00						15 58						17 00		
Barnsley	a			14 05		14 37			15 05		15 37				16 03		16 37				17 05	17 14	
	d			14 06		14 37			15 10		15 37				16 04		16 37				17 10	17 15	
Dodworth	d			14 12											16 10							17 21	
Silkstone Common	d			14 16											16 14							17 25	
Penistone	d			14 23											16 21							17 32	
Denby Dale	d			14 29											16 27							17 38	
Shepley	d			14 34											16 32							17 43	
Stocksmoor	d			14 37											16 35							17 46	
Brockholes	d			14 41											16 39							17 50	
Honley	d			14 43											16 41							17 52	
Berry Brow	d			14 46											16 44							17 55	
Lockwood	d			14 49											16 47							17 58	
Huddersfield	a			14 53											16 53							18 05	
Darton	d								15 15												17 15		
Wakefield Kirkgate 31	a					14 52			15 29		15 52						16 52				17 29		
	d					14 53			15 30		15 53						16 53				17 30		
Normanton	d								15 34												17 34		
Castleford	a								15 40												17 40		
Woodlesford	a								15 51												17 51		
Leeds 31	a		14 47			15 18			16 04		16 18			16 54			17 18				18 05		

A To Doncaster
B To Scarborough
C To Cleethorpes
D To Liverpool Lime Street
E From Manchester Airport to Cleethorpes
F To Goole
G From Manchester Piccadilly to Doncaster
H To Bridlington
I From Retford
J To Sheffield
K From Lincoln

Sundays

1 July to 9 September

Nottingham, Sheffield - Barnsley - Huddersfield and Leeds

Network Diagram - see first page of Table 31

		NT	NT	NT	NT	NT	TP	NT	NT	NT	NT	NT	TP	NT	NT	NT	NT	NT	TP	NT	NT	NT	NT
							◇■						◇■						◇■				
			A	B			C		A	D		E	C		A			F	C			G	
Nottingham	d	16 14						17 14						18 14						19 19	20 15		
Langley Mill	d	16 30						17 30						18 30						19 35	20 33		
Alfreton	d	16 38						17 38						18 38						19 43	20 41		
Chesterfield	d	16 50						17 51						18 52						19 54	20 53		
Dronfield	d	16 57						17 58						18 58						20 01			
Sheffield 29,31	a	17 15						18 14						19 16						20 15	21 14		
	d	17 17	17 25	17 28	17 36	17 39	18 11	18 17	18 25	18 28	18 39	18 57	19 11	19 16	19 29	19 36	19 39	20 02	20 11	20 17		20 28	20 39
Meadowhall 29,31	a	17 22	17 30	17 33	17 44	17 46	18 16	18 22	18 30	18 34	18 44	19 04	19 16	19 22	19 34	19 41	19 44	20 08	20 16	20 22		20 33	20 44
	d	17 23			17 44	17 46		18 23			18 45			19 23		19 42	19 45			20 23			20 45
Chapeltown	d					17 52					18 51						19 51						20 51
Elsecar	d					17 58					18 56						19 56						20 56
Wombwell	d					18 01					19 00						20 00						21 00
Barnsley	a	17 37				18 08		18 37			19 05			19 37			20 05			20 37			21 06
	d	17 37				18 10		18 37			19 10			19 37			20 06			20 37			21 10
Dodworth	d					18 16											20 12						
Silkstone Common	d					18 20											20 16						
Penistone	d					18 27											20 23						
Denby Dale	d					18 34											20 29						
Shepley	d					18 39											20 34						
Stocksmoor	d					18 41											20 37						
Brockholes	d					18 45											20 41						
Honley	d					18 48											20 43						
Berry Brow	d					18 51											20 46						
Lockwood	d					18 53											20 49						
Huddersfield	a					18 58											20 53						
Darton	d										19 15												21 15
Wakefield Kirkgate 31	a	17 52						18 52			19 29			19 52						20 52			21 29
	d	17 53						18 53			19 30			19 53						20 53			21 30
Normanton	d										19 34												21 34
Castleford	a										19 41												21 40
Woodlesford	a										19 53												21 51
Leeds 31	a	18 18			18 50			19 18			20 05			20 18		20 52				21 16			22 04

		TP	NT	NT	NT	NT	NT	TP	NT	NT
		◇■						◇■		
		C	F			F	A	H		A
Nottingham	d								21 30	
Langley Mill	d								21 52	
Alfreton	d								22 00	
Chesterfield	d								22 13	
Dronfield	d								22 20	
Sheffield 29,31	a								22 36	
	d	21 11	21 24	21 36	21 43	22 13	22 26	22 30	22 39	23 34
Meadowhall 29,31	a	21 16	21 29	21 41	21 48	22 18	22 31	22 35	22 44	23 39
	d			21 42	21 49				22 45	
Chapeltown	d				21 55				22 51	
Elsecar	d				22 00				22 56	
Wombwell	d				22 04				23 00	
Barnsley	a				22 09				23 05	
	d								23 10	
Dodworth	d									
Silkstone Common	d									
Penistone	d									
Denby Dale	d									
Shepley	d									
Stocksmoor	d									
Brockholes	d									
Honley	d									
Berry Brow	d									
Lockwood	d									
Huddersfield	a									
Darton	d								23 15	
Wakefield Kirkgate 31	a								23 26	
	d								23 27	
Normanton	d								23 34	
Castleford	a								23 40	
Woodlesford	a								23 53	
Leeds 31	a			22 52					00 05	

A To Doncaster
B To Bridlington
C From Manchester Airport to Cleethorpes
D To Beverley
E To Sheffield
F To Hull
G To Goole
H To Cleethorpes

Table 34

16 September to 30 September

Nottingham, Sheffield - Barnsley - Huddersfield and Leeds

Network Diagram - see first page of Table 31

Station			NT A	NT	NT B	NT ◇	NT	NT	TP ◇1 C	NT B	EM ◇ D	NT	NT A	NT	NT	NT	TP ◇1 E	NT	NT F	NT B	NT	NT	TP ◇1 G	NT
Nottingham 8	⇌	d									09 31			10 06				11 15						12 19
Langley Mill		d												10 27				11 30						12 35
Alfreton		d									09 53			10 35				11 39						12 43
Chesterfield		d									10 08			10 55				11 51						12 54
Dronfield		d									10 15			11 02				11 58						13 01
Sheffield 7	29,31 ⇌	a									10 33			11 15				12 15						13 16
		d	08 00	08 39	08 45	09 17	09 36	09 39	09 52	10 26		10 39	11 05	11 17	11 36	11 49	12 11	12 16	12 24	12 28	12 35	12 39	13 11	13 17
Meadowhall 4	29,31 ⇌	a	08 05	08 44	08 50	09 22	09 41	09 44	09 57	10 31		10 44	11 10	11 23	11 41	11 54	12 16	12 22	12 29	12 33	12 40	12 44	13 16	13 22
		d		08 45		09 23	09 42	09 45				10 45		11 23	11 42	11 55		12 23			12 41	12 45		13 23
Chapeltown		d		08 51				09 51				10 51				12 01						12 55		
Elsecar		d		08 56				09 56				10 56				12 06						13 00		
Wombwell		d		09 00				10 00				11 00				12 10						13 04		
Barnsley		a		09 05		09 37		10 05				11 05		11 37		12 15		12 37			12 55	13 09		13 37
		d		09 10		09 37		10 06				11 10		11 38		12 16		12 37			13 06	13 10		13 37
Dodworth		d						10 12								12 22					13 12			
Silkstone Common		d						10 16								12 26					13 16			
Penistone		d						10 23								12 33					13 23			
Denby Dale		d						10 29								12 39					13 29			
Shepley		d						10 34								12 44					13 34			
Stocksmoor		d						10 37								12 47					13 37			
Brockholes		d						10 41								12 51					13 41			
Honley		d						10 43								12 53					13 43			
Berry Brow		d						10 46								12 56					13 46			
Lockwood		d						10 49								12 59					13 49			
Huddersfield		a						10 53								13 08					13 53			
Darton		d		09 15								11 15										13 15		
Wakefield Kirkgate 4	31	a		09 29		09 55						11 29		11 53				12 52				13 29		13 52
		d		09 30		09 55						11 30		11 53				12 53				13 30		13 53
Normanton		d		09 34								11 34										13 34		
Castleford		a		09 40								11 40										13 40		
Woodlesford		a		09 52								11 51										13 51		
Leeds 10	31	a		10 04		10 15	10 52					12 05		12 19	12 53			13 18				14 04		14 18

Station			NT H	NT	NT	TP ◇1 E	NT	NT F	NT B	NT	TP ◇1 E	NT	NT A	NT H	NT	NT I	TP ◇1 E	NT	NT F	NT B	NT J	NT K	NT	TP ◇1 E
Nottingham 8	⇌	d					13 09					14 19						15 12						
Langley Mill		d					13 27					14 35						15 34						
Alfreton		d					13 35					14 43						15 44						
Chesterfield		d					13 46					14 54						15 53						
Dronfield		d					13 53					15 01						16 00						
Sheffield 7	29,31 ⇌	a					14 07					15 15						16 15						
		d	13 24	13 36	13 39	14 11	14 17	14 22	14 28	14 39	15 11	15 17	15 24	15 28	15 36	15 39	16 11	16 17	16 24	16 28	16 36	16 39	16 54	17 11
Meadowhall 4	29,31 ⇌	a	13 29	13 41	13 44	14 16	14 22	14 27	14 33	14 44	15 16	15 22	15 29	15 33	15 41	15 42	16 16	16 22	16 29	16 33	16 41	16 44	16 59	17 16
		d		13 42	13 45		14 23			14 45		15 23			15 42	15 43		16 23				16 45	17 00	
Chapeltown		d			13 51					14 51						15 49						16 51		
Elsecar		d			13 56					14 56						15 54						16 56		
Wombwell		d			14 00					15 00						15 58						17 00		
Barnsley		a			14 05		14 37			15 05		15 37				16 03		16 37				17 05	17 14	
		d			14 06		14 37			15 10		15 37				16 04		16 37				17 10	17 15	
Dodworth		d			14 12											16 10							17 21	
Silkstone Common		d			14 16											16 14							17 25	
Penistone		d			14 23											16 21							17 32	
Denby Dale		d			14 29											16 27							17 38	
Shepley		d			14 34											16 32							17 43	
Stocksmoor		d			14 37											16 35							17 46	
Brockholes		d			14 41											16 39							17 50	
Honley		d			14 43											16 41							17 52	
Berry Brow		d			14 46											16 44							17 55	
Lockwood		d			14 49											16 47							17 58	
Huddersfield		a			14 53											16 53							18 07	
Darton		d								15 15												17 15		
Wakefield Kirkgate 4	31	a					14 52			15 29		15 52						16 52				17 29		
		d					14 53			15 30		15 53						16 53				17 30		
Normanton		d								15 34												17 34		
Castleford		a								15 40												17 40		
Woodlesford		a								15 51												17 51		
Leeds 10	31	a		14 47			15 18			16 04		16 18			16 54			17 18				18 05		

A To Doncaster
B To Scarborough
C To Cleethorpes
D To Liverpool Lime Street
E From Manchester Airport to Cleethorpes
F To Goole
G From Manchester Piccadilly to Doncaster
H To Bridlington
I From Retford
J To Sheffield
K From Lincoln

Table 34

16 September to 30 September

Nottingham, Sheffield - Barnsley - Huddersfield and Leeds

Network Diagram - see first page of Table 31

Station			NT	NT A	NT B	NT	NT	TP ◇1 C	NT	NT A	NT D	NT	NT E	TP ◇1 C	NT	NT A	NT	NT	NT F	TP ◇1 C	NT	NT	NT G	NT
Nottingham 8	⇌	d	16 14						17 14						18 14						19 19	20 15		
Langley Mill		d	16 30						17 30						18 30						19 35	20 33		
Alfreton		d	16 38						17 38						18 38						19 43	20 41		
Chesterfield		d	16 50						17 51						18 52						19 54	20 53		
Dronfield		d	16 57						17 58						18 58						20 01			
Sheffield 7	29,31 ⇌	a	17 15						18 14						19 16						20 15	21 14		
		d	17 17	17 25	17 28	17 36	17 39	18 11	18 17	18 25	18 28	18 39	18 57	19 11	19 16	19 29	19 36	19 39	20 02	20 11	20 17		20 28	20 39
Meadowhall 4	29,31 ⇌	a	17 22	17 30	17 33	17 44	17 46	18 16	18 22	18 30	18 34	18 44	19 04	19 16	19 22	19 34	19 41	19 44	20 08	20 16	20 22		20 33	20 44
		d	17 23			17 44	17 46		18 23			18 45			19 23		19 42	19 45			20 23			20 45
Chapeltown		d					17 52					18 51						19 51						20 51
Elsecar		d					17 58					18 56						19 56						20 56
Wombwell		d					18 01					19 00						20 00						21 00
Barnsley		a	17 37				18 08		18 37			19 05			19 37			20 05			20 37			21 06
		d	17 37				18 10		18 37			19 10			19 37			20 06			20 37			21 10
Dodworth		d					18 16											20 12						
Silkstone Common		d					18 20											20 16						
Penistone		d					18 27											20 23						
Denby Dale		d					18 34											20 29						
Shepley		d					18 39											20 34						
Stocksmoor		d					18 41											20 37						
Brockholes		d					18 45											20 41						
Honley		d					18 48											20 43						
Berry Brow		d					18 51											20 46						
Lockwood		d					18 53											20 49						
Huddersfield		a					18 58											20 53						
Darton		d										19 15												21 15
Wakefield Kirkgate 4	31	a	17 52						18 52			19 29			19 52						20 52			21 29
		d	17 53						18 53			19 30			19 53						20 53			21 30
Normanton		d										19 34												21 34
Castleford		a										19 41												21 40
Woodlesford		a										19 53												21 51
Leeds 10	31	a	18 18			18 50			19 18			20 05			20 18		20 52				21 16			22 04

Station			TP ◇1 C	NT F	NT	NT	NT F	NT A	TP ◇1 H	NT	NT A
Nottingham 8	⇌	d								21 30	
Langley Mill		d								21 52	
Alfreton		d								22 00	
Chesterfield		d								22 13	
Dronfield		d								22 20	
Sheffield 7	29,31 ⇌	a								22 36	
		d	21 11	21 24	21 36	21 43	22 13	22 26	22 30	22 39	23 34
Meadowhall 4	29,31 ⇌	a	21 16	21 29	21 41	21 48	22 18	22 31	22 35	22 44	23 39
		d			21 42	21 49				22 45	
Chapeltown		d				21 55				22 51	
Elsecar		d				22 00				22 56	
Wombwell		d				22 04				23 00	
Barnsley		a				22 09				23 05	
		d								23 10	
Dodworth		d									
Silkstone Common		d									
Penistone		d									
Denby Dale		d									
Shepley		d									
Stocksmoor		d									
Brockholes		d									
Honley		d									
Berry Brow		d									
Lockwood		d									
Huddersfield		a									
Darton		d								23 15	
Wakefield Kirkgate 4	31	a								23 26	
		d								23 27	
Normanton		d								23 34	
Castleford		a								23 40	
Woodlesford		a								23 53	
Leeds 10	31	a			22 52					00 05	

A To Doncaster
B To Bridlington
C From Manchester Airport to Cleethorpes
D To Beverley
E To Sheffield
F To Hull
G To Goole
H To Cleethorpes

Nottingham, Sheffield - Barnsley - Huddersfield and Leeds

Network Diagram - see first page of Table 31

		NT	NT	NT	NT	NT	NT	NT	TP	NT		EM	NT	NT	NT	NT	NT	TP	NT	NT		NT	NT	NT	TP
						◇			◇1			◇						◇1							◇1
			A		B				C	B		D		A				E		F		B			G
Nottingham 8	d											09 31			10 06				11 15						
Langley Mill	d														10 27				11 30						
Alfreton	d											09 53			10 35				11 39						
Chesterfield	d											10 08			10 55				11 51						
Dronfield	d											10 15			11 02				11 58						
Sheffield 7 29,31	a											10 33			11 15				12 15						
	d	22p41	08 00	08 39	08 45	09 17	09 36	09 39	09 52	10 26			10 39	11 05	11 17	11 36	11 49	12 11	12 16	12 24		12 28	12 35	12 39	13 11
Meadowhall 4 29,31	a	22p46	08 05	08 44	08 50	09 22	09 41	09 44	09 57	10 31			10 44	11 10	11 23	11 41	11 54	12 16	12 22	12 29		12 33	12 40	12 44	13 16
	d	22p47		08 45		09 23	09 42	09 45					10 45		11 23	11 42	11 55		12 23				12 41	12 45	
Chapeltown	d	22p53		08 51				09 51					10 51				12 01							12 55	
Elsecar	d	22p58		08 56				09 56					10 56				12 06							13 00	
Wombwell	d	23p02		09 00				10 00					11 00				12 10							13 04	
Barnsley	a	23p07		09 05		09 37		10 05					11 05		11 37		12 15		12 37				12 55	13 09	
	d	23p08		09 10		09 37		10 06					11 10		11 38		12 16		12 37				13 06	13 10	
Dodworth	d	23p14						10 12									12 22						13 12		
Silkstone Common	d	23p18						10 16									12 26						13 16		
Penistone	d	23p25						10 23									12 33						13 23		
Denby Dale	d	23p31						10 29									12 39						13 29		
Shepley	d	23p36						10 34									12 44						13 34		
Stocksmoor	d	23p39						10 37									12 47						13 37		
Brockholes	d	23p43						10 41									12 51						13 41		
Honley	d	23p45						10 43									12 53						13 43		
Berry Brow	d	23p48						10 46									12 56						13 46		
Lockwood	d	23p51						10 49									12 59						13 49		
Huddersfield	a	00 03						10 58									13 08						13 56		
Darton	d			09 15									11 15											13 15	
Wakefield Kirkgate 4 31	a			09 29		09 55							11 29		11 53				12 52					13 29	
	d			09 30		09 55							11 30		11 53				12 53					13 30	
Normanton	d			09 34									11 34											13 34	
Castleford	a			09 40									11 40											13 40	
Woodlesford	a			09 52									11 51											13 51	
Leeds 10 31	a			10 04		10 15	10 52						12 05		12 19	12 53			13 18					14 04	

		NT	NT	NT	NT	TP		NT	NT	NT	NT	TP	NT	NT	NT	NT		NT	TP	NT	NT	NT	NT	NT	NT
						◇1						◇1							◇1						
			H			E			F	B		E		A	H			I	E		F	B	J	K	
Nottingham 8	d	12 19						13 09					14 19							15 12					
Langley Mill	d	12 35						13 27					14 35							15 34					
Alfreton	d	12 43						13 35					14 43							15 44					
Chesterfield	d	12 54						13 46					14 54							15 53					
Dronfield	d	13 01						13 53					15 01							16 00					
Sheffield 7 29,31	a	13 16						14 07					15 15							16 15					
	d	13 17	13 24	13 36	13 39	14 11		14 17	14 22	14 28	14 39	15 11	15 17	15 24	15 28	15 36		15 39	16 11	16 17	16 24	16 28	16 36	16 39	16 54
Meadowhall 4 29,31	a	13 22	13 29	13 41	13 44	14 16		14 22	14 27	14 33	14 44	15 16	15 22	15 29	15 33	15 41		15 42	16 16	16 22	16 29	16 33	16 41	16 44	16 59
	d	13 23		13 42	13 45			14 23			14 45		15 23			15 42		15 43		16 23				16 45	17 00
Chapeltown	d				13 51						14 51							15 49						16 51	
Elsecar	d				13 56						14 56							15 54						16 56	
Wombwell	d				14 00						15 00							15 58						17 00	
Barnsley	a	13 37			14 05			14 37			15 05		15 37					16 03		16 37				17 05	17 14
	d	13 37			14 06			14 37			15 10		15 37					16 04		16 37				17 10	17 15
Dodworth	d				14 12													16 10							17 21
Silkstone Common	d				14 16													16 14							17 25
Penistone	d				14 23													16 21							17 32
Denby Dale	d				14 29													16 27							17 38
Shepley	d				14 34													16 32							17 43
Stocksmoor	d				14 37													16 35							17 46
Brockholes	d				14 41													16 39							17 50
Honley	d				14 43													16 41							17 52
Berry Brow	d				14 46													16 44							17 55
Lockwood	d				14 49													16 47							17 58
Huddersfield	a				14 58													16 57							18 07
Darton	d										15 15													17 15	
Wakefield Kirkgate 4 31	a	13 52						14 52			15 29		15 52							16 52				17 29	
	d	13 53						14 53			15 30		15 53							16 53				17 30	
Normanton	d										15 34													17 34	
Castleford	a										15 40													17 40	
Woodlesford	a										15 51													17 51	
Leeds 10 31	a	14 18		14 47				15 18			16 04		16 18			16 54				17 18				18 05	

A To Doncaster
B To Scarborough
C To Cleethorpes
D To Liverpool Lime Street
E From Manchester Airport to Cleethorpes
F To Goole
G From Manchester Piccadilly to Doncaster
H To Bridlington
I From Retford
J To Sheffield
K From Lincoln

Nottingham, Sheffield - Barnsley - Huddersfield and Leeds

Network Diagram - see first page of Table 31

		TP		NT	NT	NT	NT	NT	TP	NT	NT	NT		NT	NT	TP	NT	NT	NT	NT	NT	TP	NT	NT	NT
		◇1							◇1							◇1						◇1			
		A			B	C			A		B	D			E	A		B			F	A			G
Nottingham 8	d			16 14						17 14							18 14						19 19	20 15	
Langley Mill	d			16 30						17 30							18 30						19 35	20 33	
Alfreton	d			16 38						17 38							18 38						19 43	20 41	
Chesterfield	d			16 50						17 51							18 52						19 54	20 53	
Dronfield	d			16 57						17 58							18 58						20 01		
Sheffield 7 29,31	a			17 15						18 14							19 16						20 15	21 14	
	d	17 11		17 17	17 25	17 28	17 36	17 39	18 11	18 17	18 25	18 28		18 39	18 57	19 11	19 16	19 29	19 36	19 39	20 02	20 11	20 17		20 28
Meadowhall 4 29,31	a	17 16		17 22	17 30	17 33	17 44	17 46	18 16	18 22	18 30	18 34		18 44	19 04	19 16	19 22	19 34	19 41	19 44	20 08	20 16	20 22		20 33
	d			17 23			17 44	17 46		18 23				18 45			19 23		19 42	19 45			20 23		
Chapeltown	d							17 52						18 51						19 51					
Elsecar	d							17 58						18 56						19 56					
Wombwell	d							18 01						19 00						20 00					
Barnsley	a			17 37				18 08		18 37				19 05			19 37			20 05			20 37		
	d			17 37				18 10		18 37				19 10			19 37			20 06			20 37		
Dodworth	d							18 16												20 12					
Silkstone Common	d							18 20												20 16					
Penistone	d							18 27												20 23					
Denby Dale	d							18 34												20 29					
Shepley	d							18 39												20 34					
Stocksmoor	d							18 41												20 37					
Brockholes	d							18 45												20 41					
Honley	d							18 48												20 44					
Berry Brow	d							18 51												20 47					
Lockwood	d							18 53												20 49					
Huddersfield	a							19 00												20 57					
Darton	d													19 15											
Wakefield Kirkgate 4 31	a			17 52						18 52				19 29			19 52						20 52		
	d			17 53						18 53				19 30			19 53						20 53		
Normanton	d													19 34											
Castleford	a													19 41											
Woodlesford	a													19 53											
Leeds 10 31	a			18 18			18 50			19 18				20 05			20 18		20 52				21 16		

		NT	TP	NT	NT	NT	NT	NT		TP	NT	NT
			◇1							◇1		
			A	F			F	B		H		B
Nottingham 8	d										21 30	
Langley Mill	d										21 52	
Alfreton	d										22 00	
Chesterfield	d										22 13	
Dronfield	d										22 20	
Sheffield 7 29,31	a										22 36	
	d	20 39	21 11	21 24	21 36	21 43	22 13	22 26		22 30	22 39	23 34
Meadowhall 4 29,31	a	20 44	21 16	21 29	21 41	21 48	22 18	22 31		22 35	22 44	23 39
	d	20 45			21 42	21 49					22 45	
Chapeltown	d	20 51				21 55					22 51	
Elsecar	d	20 56				22 00					22 56	
Wombwell	d	21 00				22 04					23 00	
Barnsley	a	21 06				22 09					23 05	
	d	21 10									23 10	
Dodworth	d											
Silkstone Common	d											
Penistone	d											
Denby Dale	d											
Shepley	d											
Stocksmoor	d											
Brockholes	d											
Honley	d											
Berry Brow	d											
Lockwood	d											
Huddersfield	a											
Darton	d	21 15									23 15	
Wakefield Kirkgate 4 31	a	21 29									23 26	
	d	21 30									23 27	
Normanton	d	21 34									23 34	
Castleford	a	21 40									23 40	
Woodlesford	a	21 51									23 53	
Leeds 10 31	a	22 04			22 52						00 05	

A From Manchester Airport to Cleethorpes
B To Doncaster
C To Bridlington
D To Beverley
E To Sheffield
F To Hull
G To Goole
H To Cleethorpes

Nottingham, Sheffield - Barnsley - Huddersfield and Leeds

Network Diagram - see first page of Table 31

Station		NT	NT A	NT	NT B	NT ◇	NT	NT	TP ◇1 C	NT B	EM ◇ D	NT	NT A	NT	NT	NT	TP ◇1 E	NT	NT F	NT B	NT	NT	TP ◇1 G
Nottingham	d										09 31			10 06				11 15					
Langley Mill	d													10 27				11 31					
Alfreton	d										09 53			10 35				11 39					
Chesterfield	d										10 08			10 55				11 51					
Dronfield	d										10 15			11 02				11 58					
Sheffield 29,31	a										10 33			11 15				12 15					
	d	22p41	08 00	08 39	08 45	09 17	09 36	09 39	09 52	10 26		10 39	11 05	11 17	11 36	11 49	12 11	12 16	12 24	12 28	12 35	12 39	13 11
Meadowhall 29,31	a	22p46	08 05	08 44	08 50	09 22	09 41	09 44	09 57	10 31		10 44	11 10	11 23	11 41	11 54	12 16	12 22	12 29	12 33	12 40	12 44	13 16
	d	22p47		08 45		09 23	09 42	09 45				10 45		11 23	11 42	11 55		12 23			12 41	12 45	
Chapeltown	d	22p53		08 51				09 51				10 51				12 01						12 55	
Elsecar	d	22p58		08 56				09 56				10 56				12 06						13 00	
Wombwell	d	23p02		09 00				10 00				11 00				12 10						13 04	
Barnsley	a	23p07		09 05		09 37		10 05				11 05		11 37		12 15		12 37			12 55	13 09	
	d	23p08		09 10		09 37		10 06				11 10		11 38		12 16		12 37			13 06	13 10	
Dodworth	d	23p14						10 12								12 22					13 12		
Silkstone Common	d	23p18						10 16								12 26					13 16		
Penistone	d	23p25						10 23								12 33					13 23		
Denby Dale	d	23p31						10 29								12 39					13 29		
Shepley	d	23p36						10 34								12 44					13 34		
Stocksmoor	d	23p39						10 37								12 47					13 37		
Brockholes	d	23p43						10 41								12 51					13 41		
Honley	d	23p45						10 43								12 53					13 43		
Berry Brow	d	23p48						10 46								12 56					13 46		
Lockwood	d	23p51						10 49								12 59					13 49		
Huddersfield	a	00 03						10 58								13 08					13 56		
Darton	d			09 15								11 15										13 15	
Wakefield Kirkgate 31	a			09 29		09 55						11 29		11 53				12 52				13 29	
	d			09 30		09 55						11 30		11 53				12 53				13 30	
Normanton	d			09 34								11 34										13 34	
Castleford	a			09 40								11 40										13 40	
Woodlesford	a			09 52								11 51										13 51	
Leeds 31	a			10 04		10 15	10 52					12 05		12 19	12 53			13 18				14 04	

Station		NT	NT H	NT	NT	TP ◇1 E	NT	NT F	NT B	NT	TP ◇1 E	NT	NT A	NT H	NT	NT I	TP ◇1 E	NT	NT F	NT B	NT J	NT K	NT
Nottingham	d	12 19					13 09					14 19						15 12					
Langley Mill	d	12 35					13 27					14 35						15 34					
Alfreton	d	12 43					13 35					14 43						15 44					
Chesterfield	d	12 54					13 46					14 54						15 53					
Dronfield	d	13 01					13 53					15 01						16 00					
Sheffield 29,31	a	13 16					14 07					15 15						16 15					
	d	13 17	13 24	13 36	13 39	14 11	14 17	14 22	14 28	14 39	15 11	15 17	15 24	15 28	15 36	15 39	16 11	16 17	16 24	16 28	16 36	16 39	16 54
Meadowhall 29,31	a	13 22	13 29	13 41	13 44	14 16	14 22	14 27	14 33	14 44	15 16	15 22	15 29	15 33	15 41	15 42	16 16	16 22	16 29	16 33	16 41	16 44	16 59
	d	13 23		13 42	13 45		14 23			14 45		15 23			15 42	15 43		16 23				16 45	17 00
Chapeltown	d				13 51					14 51						15 49						16 51	
Elsecar	d				13 56					14 56						15 54						16 56	
Wombwell	d				14 00					15 00						15 58						17 00	
Barnsley	a	13 37			14 05		14 37			15 05		15 37				16 03		16 37				17 05	17 14
	d	13 37			14 06		14 37			15 10		15 37				16 04		16 37				17 10	17 15
Dodworth	d				14 12											16 10							17 21
Silkstone Common	d				14 16											16 14							17 25
Penistone	d				14 23											16 21							17 32
Denby Dale	d				14 29											16 27							17 38
Shepley	d				14 34											16 32							17 43
Stocksmoor	d				14 37											16 35							17 46
Brockholes	d				14 41											16 39							17 50
Honley	d				14 43											16 41							17 52
Berry Brow	d				14 46											16 44							17 55
Lockwood	d				14 49											16 47							17 58
Huddersfield	a				14 58											16 57							18 07
Darton	d									15 15												17 15	
Wakefield Kirkgate 31	a	13 52					14 52			15 29		15 52						16 52				17 29	
	d	13 53					14 53			15 30		15 53						16 53				17 30	
Normanton	d									15 34												17 34	
Castleford	a									15 40												17 40	
Woodlesford	a									15 51												17 51	
Leeds 31	a	14 18		14 47			15 18			16 04		16 18			16 54			17 18				18 05	

A To Doncaster
B To Scarborough
C To Cleethorpes
D To Liverpool Lime Street
E From Manchester Airport to Cleethorpes
F To Goole
G From Manchester Piccadilly to Doncaster
H To Bridlington
I From Retford
J To Moorthorpe
K From Lincoln

Table 34

Sundays
from 28 October

Nottingham, Sheffield - Barnsley - Huddersfield and Leeds

Network Diagram - see first page of Table 31

Station		TP ◇1 A	NT	NT B	NT C	NT	NT	TP ◇1 A	NT	NT B	NT D	NT	NT E	TP ◇1 A	NT	NT B	NT	NT	NT F	TP ◇1 A	NT	NT	NT G
Nottingham	d		16 14						17 14						18 14						19 19	20 15	
Langley Mill	d		16 30						17 30						18 30						19 35	20 33	
Alfreton	d		16 38						17 38						18 38						19 43	20 41	
Chesterfield	d		16 50						17 51						18 52						19 54	20 53	
Dronfield	d		16 57						17 58						18 58						20 01		
Sheffield 29,31	a		17 15						18 14						19 16						20 15	21 14	
	d	17 11	17 17	17 25	17 28	17 36	17 39	18 11	18 17	18 25	18 28	18 39	18 57	19 11	19 16	19 29	19 36	19 39	20 02	20 11	20 17		20 28
Meadowhall 29,31	a	17 16	17 22	17 30	17 33	17 44	17 46	18 16	18 22	18 30	18 34	18 44	19 04	19 16	19 22	19 34	19 41	19 44	20 08	20 16	20 22		20 33
	d		17 23			17 44	17 46		18 23			18 45			19 23		19 42	19 45			20 23		
Chapeltown	d						17 52					18 51						19 51					
Elsecar	d						17 58					18 56						19 56					
Wombwell	d						18 01					19 00						20 00					
Barnsley	a		17 37				18 08		18 37			19 05			19 37			20 05			20 37		
	d		17 37				18 10		18 37			19 10			19 37			20 06			20 37		
Dodworth	d						18 16											20 12					
Silkstone Common	d						18 20											20 16					
Penistone	d						18 27											20 23					
Denby Dale	d						18 34											20 29					
Shepley	d						18 39											20 34					
Stocksmoor	d						18 41											20 37					
Brockholes	d						18 45											20 41					
Honley	d						18 48											20 44					
Berry Brow	d						18 51											20 47					
Lockwood	d						18 53											20 49					
Huddersfield	a						19 00											20 57					
Darton	d											19 15											
Wakefield Kirkgate 31	a		17 52						18 52			19 29			19 52						20 52		
	d		17 53						18 53			19 30			19 53						20 53		
Normanton	d											19 34											
Castleford	a											19 41											
Woodlesford	a											19 53											
Leeds 31	a		18 18			18 50			19 18			20 05			20 18		20 52				21 16		

Station		NT	TP ◇1 A	NT F	NT	NT	NT F	NT B	TP ◇1 H	NT	NT B
Nottingham	d									21 30	
Langley Mill	d									21 52	
Alfreton	d									22 00	
Chesterfield	d									22 13	
Dronfield	d									22 20	
Sheffield 29,31	a									22 36	
	d	20 39	21 11	21 24	21 36	21 43	22 13	22 26	22 30	22 39	23 34
Meadowhall 29,31	a	20 44	21 16	21 29	21 41	21 48	22 18	22 31	22 35	22 44	23 39
	d	20 45			21 42	21 49				22 45	
Chapeltown	d	20 51				21 55				22 51	
Elsecar	d	20 56				22 00				22 56	
Wombwell	d	21 00				22 04				23 00	
Barnsley	a	21 06				22 09				23 05	
	d	21 10								23 10	
Dodworth	d										
Silkstone Common	d										
Penistone	d										
Denby Dale	d										
Shepley	d										
Stocksmoor	d										
Brockholes	d										
Honley	d										
Berry Brow	d										
Lockwood	d										
Huddersfield	a										
Darton	d	21 15								23 15	
Wakefield Kirkgate 31	a	21 29								23 26	
	d	21 30								23 27	
Normanton	d	21 34								23 34	
Castleford	a	21 40								23 40	
Woodlesford	a	21 51								23 53	
Leeds 31	a	22 04			22 51					00 05	

A From Manchester Airport to Cleethorpes
B To Doncaster
C To Bridlington
D To Beverley
E To Moorthorpe
F To Hull
G To Goole
H To Cleethorpes

Leeds and Huddersfield - Barnsley - Sheffield, Nottingham

Network Diagram - see first page of Table 31

Miles	Miles	Station			NT MX	NT MX A	NT MX	NT	NT	TP ◇1 B	NT	NT C	NT	NT	NT	NT A	TP ◇1 D 🛒	NT	NT E	NT	NT	TP ◇1 D 🛒	NT	NT F
0	—	**Leeds** [10]	31	d	22p37		23p09						05 33		06 05					06 38	06 43		07 05	
6	—	Woodlesford		d	22p45															06 46				
10¾	—	Castleford		d	22p56															06 57				
14¾	—	Normanton		d	23p01															07 03				
17¼	—	Wakefield Kirkgate [4]	31	a	23p10										06 21					07 07			07 25	
—	—			d	23p10									06 04	06 21					07 08			07 25	
24¾	—	Darton		d	23p24									06 15						07 19				
—	0	**Huddersfield**		d														06 10						
—	1¼	Lockwood		d														06 13						
—	2¼	Berry Brow		d														06 16						
—	3¼	Honley		d														06 19						
—	4¼	Brockholes		d														06 22						
—	6¼	Stocksmoor		d														06 26						
—	7¼	Shepley		d														06 28						
—	9½	Denby Dale		d														06 34						
—	13½	Penistone		d														06 42						
—	16¾	Silkstone Common		d														06 47						
—	18	Dodworth		d														06 51						
28¼	21	**Barnsley**		a	23p31									06 20	06 37			06 57		07 25			07 40	
—	—			d	23p31			05 23			05 50			06 21	06 38			06 58		07 25			07 40	
32¼	25	Wombwell		d	23p36			05 28			05 55			06 26				07 03		07 30				
33¾	26½	Elsecar		d	23p40			05 32			05 59			06 30				07 07		07 34				
37	29¾	Chapeltown		d	23p45			05 37			06 04			06 35				07 12		07 39				
40¾	33½	**Meadowhall**	29,31 🚋	a	23p51		00 08	05 43			06 15		06 37	06 41	06 49			07 21		07 48	07 44		07 53	
—	—			d	23p51	23p54	00 09	05 43		05 58	06 15	06 27	06 38	06 42	06 49	06 52	06 58	07 21	07 33	07 49	07 45	07 53	07 54	08 06
44¼	37	**Sheffield** [7]	29,31 🚋	a	00 02	00 04	00 23	05 54		06 08	06 25	06 38	06 47	06 55	07 00	07 05	07 06	07 29	07 40	07 58	07 56	08 00	08 05	08 18
—	—			d					06 00						07 03								08 05	
51¼	—	Dronfield		d					06 10						07 13								08 15	
56½	—	Chesterfield		d					06 16						07 20								08 24	
66½	—	Alfreton		d					06 30						07 33								08 35	
72¾	—	Langley Mill		d					06 37						07 40								08 42	
84¾	—	**Nottingham**		a					07 02						08 02								09 02	

Station			NT	NT A	NT G	NT	NT H	NT	NT	NT F	TP ◇1 D 🛒	NT I	NT	NT G	NT	NT J	NT H	NT	NT	NT F	TP ◇1 D 🛒	NT I	NT	NT G
Leeds [10]	31	d			07 29	07 35		07 48	08 02					08 32	08 37			08 48	09 05					09 32
Woodlesford		d			07 37									08 40										09 40
Castleford		d			07 48									08 51										09 51
Normanton		d			07 54		←							08 57			←							09 57
Wakefield Kirkgate [4]	31	a			08 00	07 54	08 00		08 23					09 03	08 54		09 03		09 23					10 01
		d			08 04	07 55	08 04		08 23					09 05	08 55		09 05		09 23					10 04
Darton		d			→		08 15							→			09 17							→
Huddersfield		d	07 10										08 10										09 13	
Lockwood		d	07 13										08 13										09 16	
Berry Brow		d	07 16										08 16										09 19	
Honley		d	07 19										08 19										09 22	
Brockholes		d	07 22										08 22										09 25	
Stocksmoor		d	07 26										08 26										09 29	
Shepley		d	07 28										08 28										09 31	
Denby Dale		d	07 34										08 34										09 36	
Penistone		d	07 42										08 42										09 44	
Silkstone Common		d	07 47										08 47										09 49	
Dodworth		d	07 51										08 51										09 53	
Barnsley		a	07 57			08 11	08 21		08 39				08 57		09 11		09 23		09 39				10 00	
		d	07 58			08 14	08 24		08 40				08 58		09 14		09 24		09 40				10 01	
Wombwell		d	08 03				08 29						09 03				09 29						10 06	
Elsecar		d	08 07				08 33						09 07				09 33							
Chapeltown		d	08 12				08 38						09 12				09 38						10 13	
Meadowhall	29,31 🚋	a	08 20			08 31	08 45	08 50	08 52				09 19		09 27		09 46	09 50	09 52				10 20	
		d	08 21	08 23		08 31	08 45	08 51	08 52	08 57	09 01	09 16	09 21		09 28	09 33	09 46	09 50	09 52	09 55	10 01	10 08	10 21	
Sheffield [7]	29,31 🚋	a	08 29	08 33		08 39	08 56	08 59	09 02	09 05	09 08	09 26	09 28		09 37	09 41	09 56	10 00	10 02	10 05	10 08	10 19	10 30	
		d							09 05										10 05					
Dronfield		d							09 15										10 15					
Chesterfield		d							09 22										10 22					
Alfreton		d							09 32										10 33					
Langley Mill		d							09 40										10 40					
Nottingham		a							10 00										11 00					

A From Hull
B From Doncaster to Manchester Airport
C From Doncaster
D From Cleethorpes to Manchester Airport
E From Doncaster to Worksop
F From Adwick
G To Sheffield
H From Leeds
I From Bridlington
J From Scunthorpe to Lincoln

Leeds and Huddersfield - Barnsley - Sheffield, Nottingham

Network Diagram - see first page of Table 31

Station			NT	NT A	NT B	NT	NT ◇	NT C	TP ◇1 D 🛒	NT E	NT	NT F	NT	NT A	NT B	NT	NT ◇	NT C	TP ◇1 D 🛒	NT E	NT	NT G	NT F
Leeds [10]	31	d	09 37			09 48	10 05					10 32	10 37			10 48	11 05						11 32
Woodlesford		d										10 40											11 40
Castleford		d										10 51											11 51
Normanton		d			←							10 57			←								11 57
Wakefield Kirkgate [4]	31	a	09 55		10 01		10 23					11 01	10 54		11 01		11 23						12 01
		d	09 56		10 04		10 23					11 04	10 55		11 04		11 23						12 04
Darton		d			10 15							→			11 15								→
Huddersfield		d									10 13										11 13		
Lockwood		d									10 16										11 16		
Berry Brow		d									10 19										11 19		
Honley		d									10 22										11 22		
Brockholes		d									10 25										11 25		
Stocksmoor		d									10 29										11 29		
Shepley		d									10 31										11 31		
Denby Dale		d									10 36										11 36		
Penistone		d									10 44										11 44		
Silkstone Common		d									10 49										11 49		
Dodworth		d									10 53										11 53		
Barnsley		a	10 12		10 21		10 39				11 00		11 11		11 21		11 39				12 00		
		d	10 14		10 24		10 40				11 01		11 14		11 24		11 40				12 01		
Wombwell		d			10 29						11 06				11 29						12 06		
Elsecar		d			10 33										11 33								
Chapeltown		d			10 38						11 13				11 38						12 13		
Meadowhall	29,31 🚋	a	10 27		10 46	10 50	10 52				11 20		11 27		11 46	11 51	11 52				12 20		
		d	10 28	10 33	10 47	10 50	10 52	10 58	11 01	11 08	11 21		11 28	11 33	11 46	11 51	11 52	11 56	12 01	12 08	12 21	12 24	
Sheffield [7]	29,31 🚋	a	10 37	10 41	10 56	11 01	11 02	11 05	11 08	11 20	11 30		11 37	11 41	11 57	12 01	12 02	12 05	12 08	12 19	12 30	12 36	
		d					11 05										12 05						
Dronfield		d					11 15										12 15						
Chesterfield		d					11 22										12 22						
Alfreton		d					11 33										12 33						
Langley Mill		d					11 40										12 40						
Nottingham		a					12 00										13 01						

Station			NT	NT A	NT B	NT	NT ◇	NT C	TP ◇1 D 🛒	NT E	NT	NT F	NT	NT A	NT B	NT	NT ◇	NT C	TP ◇1 D 🛒	NT H	NT	NT F	NT	NT A
Leeds [10]	31	d	11 37			11 48	12 05					12 32	12 37			12 48	13 05					13 32	13 37	
Woodlesford		d										12 40										13 40		
Castleford		d										12 51										13 51		
Normanton		d			←							12 57			←							13 57		
Wakefield Kirkgate [4]	31	a	11 54		12 01		12 23					13 02	12 54		13 02		13 23					14 01	13 54	
		d	11 55		12 04		12 23					13 04	12 55		13 04		13 23					14 04	13 55	
Darton		d			12 15							→			13 17							→		
Huddersfield		d									12 13										13 13			
Lockwood		d									12 16										13 16			
Berry Brow		d									12 19										13 19			
Honley		d									12 22										13 22			
Brockholes		d									12 25										13 25			
Stocksmoor		d									12 29										13 29			
Shepley		d									12 31										13 31			
Denby Dale		d									12 36										13 36			
Penistone		d									12 44										13 44			
Silkstone Common		d									12 49										13 49			
Dodworth		d									12 53										13 53			
Barnsley		a	12 11		12 21		12 39				13 00		13 11		13 22		13 39				14 00		14 11	
		d	12 14		12 24		12 40				13 01		13 14		13 24		13 40				14 01		14 14	
Wombwell		d			12 29						13 06				13 29						14 06			
Elsecar		d			12 33										13 33									
Chapeltown		d			12 38						13 13				13 38						14 13			
Meadowhall	29,31 🚋	a	12 27		12 46	12 51	12 52				13 20		13 27		13 46	13 51	13 52				14 20		14 27	
		d	12 28	12 33	12 46	12 51	12 52	12 56	13 01	13 08	13 21		13 28	13 33	13 46	13 51	13 52	13 56	14 01	14 08	14 21		14 28	14 34
Sheffield [7]	29,31 🚋	a	12 37	12 41	12 56	13 01	13 02	13 05	13 08	13 20	13 29		13 37	13 41	13 56	14 01	14 02	14 05	14 08	14 20	14 29		14 37	14 42
		d					13 05										14 05							
Dronfield		d					13 15										14 15							
Chesterfield		d					13 22										14 22							
Alfreton		d					13 33										14 33							
Langley Mill		d					13 40										14 40							
Nottingham		a					14 00										15 00							

A From Scunthorpe to Lincoln
B From Leeds
C From Adwick
D From Cleethorpes to Manchester Airport
E From Bridlington
F To Sheffield
G From York
H From Scarborough

Leeds and Huddersfield - Barnsley - Sheffield, Nottingham

Network Diagram - see first page of Table 31

		NT A	NT	NT ◇	NT B	TP ◇1 C ✠		NT D	NT	NT E	NT	NT F	NT A	NT	NT ◇	NT B		TP ◇1 C ✠	NT G	NT H	NT	NT E	NT	EM ◇ I	NT F
Leeds 10 (31)	d		13 48	14 05						14 32	14 37			14 48	15 05							15 32	15 37		
Woodlesford	d									14 40												15 40			
Castleford	d									14 51												15 51			
Normanton	d	←								14 57			←									15 57			
Wakefield Kirkgate 4 (31)	a	14 01		14 23						15 01	14 54		15 01		15 23							16 01	15 54		
	d	14 04		14 23						15 04	14 55		15 04		15 23							16 04	15 55		
Darton	d	14 15								→			15 15									→			
Huddersfield	d								14 13												15 13				
Lockwood	d								14 16												15 16				
Berry Brow	d								14 19												15 19				
Honley	d								14 22												15 22				
Brockholes	d								14 25												15 25				
Stocksmoor	d								14 29												15 29				
Shepley	d								14 31												15 31				
Denby Dale	d								14 36												15 36				
Penistone	d								14 44												15 44				
Silkstone Common	d								14 49												15 49				
Dodworth	d								14 53												15 53				
Barnsley	a	14 21		14 39					15 00		15 13		15 21		15 39						16 00		16 11		
	d	14 24		14 40					15 01		15 14		15 24		15 40						16 01		16 14		
Wombwell	d	14 29							15 06				15 29								16 06				
Elsecar	d	14 33											15 33												
Chapeltown	d	14 38							15 13				15 38								16 13				
Meadowhall (29,31)	a	14 46	14 50	14 52					15 20		15 27		15 46	15 50	15 51						16 20		16 27		
	d	14 46	14 50	14 52	14 56	15 01		15 07	15 21		15 28	15 33	15 46	15 50	15 52	15 57		16 01	16 07	16 18	16 21		16 28		16 33
Sheffield 7 (29,31)	a	14 56	15 01	15 02	15 05	15 08		15 19	15 29		15 37	15 41	15 56	16 01	16 03	16 05		16 08	16 20	16 27	16 29		16 37		16 41
	d			15 05											16 04									16 38	
Dronfield	d			15 15											16 14									16 48	
Chesterfield	d			15 22											16 21									16 56	
Alfreton	d			15 33											16 32									17 07	
Langley Mill	d			15 40											16 40										
Nottingham	a			16 00											17 00									17 31	

		NT A		NT	NT ◇	NT J	TP ◇1 C ✠	NT D	NT	NT E	NT	NT F		EM ◇ I	NT A	NT	NT ◇	NT K	TP ◇1 C ✠	NT D	NT	NT E		NT	NT L
Leeds 10 (31)	d			15 48	16 05					16 32	16 37					16 48	17 05					17 32		17 37	
Woodlesford	d									16 40												17 40			
Castleford	d									16 51												17 51			
Normanton	d	←								16 57					←		17 18					17 57			
Wakefield Kirkgate 4 (31)	a	16 01			16 23					17 01	16 54				17 01		17 22					18 01		17 54	
	d	16 04			16 23					17 04	16 55				17 04		17 23					18 04		17 55	
Darton	d	16 15								→					17 15							→			
Huddersfield	d								16 13												17 13				
Lockwood	d								16 16												17 16				
Berry Brow	d								16 19												17 19				
Honley	d								16 22												17 22				
Brockholes	d								16 25												17 25				
Stocksmoor	d								16 29												17 29				
Shepley	d								16 31												17 31				
Denby Dale	d								16 36												17 36				
Penistone	d								16 44												17 44				
Silkstone Common	d								16 49												17 49				
Dodworth	d								16 53												17 53				
Barnsley	a	16 21			16 39				17 00		17 11				17 21		17 39				18 00			18 11	
	d	16 24			16 40				17 01		17 14				17 24		17 40				18 01			18 14	
Wombwell	d	16 29							17 06						17 29						18 06				
Elsecar	d	16 33													17 33										
Chapeltown	d	16 38							17 13						17 38						18 13				
Meadowhall (29,31)	a	16 46		16 50	16 52				17 20		17 27				17 46	17 50	17 51				18 20			18 27	
	d	16 46		16 50	16 52	16 55	17 01	17 09	17 21		17 28	17 33			17 46	17 50	17 52	17 57	18 01	18 08	18 21			18 28	18 32
Sheffield 7 (29,31)	a	16 56		17 00	17 02	17 05	17 08	17 20	17 32		17 37	17 41			17 56	18 01	18 03	18 05	18 08	18 19	18 29			18 38	18 42
	d				17 05									17 44			18 05								
Dronfield	d				17 15									17 56			18 15								
Chesterfield	d				17 22									18 02			18 22								
Alfreton	d				17 33									18 12			18 33								
Langley Mill	d				17 40												18 40								
Nottingham	a				18 00									18 34			19 00								

A From Leeds
B From Adwick
C From Cleethorpes to Manchester Airport
D From Bridlington
E To Sheffield
F From Scunthorpe to Lincoln
G From Scarborough
H From Sheffield
I From Liverpool Lime Street to Norwich
J From Adwick to RetfordRetford
K From Doncaster
L From Scunthorpe

Table 34 — Mondays to Fridays until 28 September

Leeds and Huddersfield - Barnsley - Sheffield, Nottingham

Network Diagram - see first page of Table 31

		NT A	NT B	NT B	NT	NT ◇	NT C	TP ◇1 D ✠		NT E	NT F	NT G	NT A	NT B	NT	NT A	NT	NT ◇		NT C	TP ◇1 D	NT G	NT	NT H	NT B
Leeds 10 (31)	d			17 43	17 46	18 05								18 32	18 43		18 48	19 05							19 37
Woodlesford	d													18 40											19 45
Castleford	d													18 51											19 56
Normanton	d	←												19 00		←									20 02
Wakefield Kirkgate 4 (31)	a	18 01				18 23								19 04	18 59	19 04		19 24							20 06
	d	18 04				18 23								19 05	18 59	19 05		19 24							20 07
Darton	d	18 15												→		19 19									→
Huddersfield	d		17 56	18 22																			19 18		
Lockwood	d		17 59	18 25																			19 21		
Berry Brow	d		18 02	18 28																			19 24		
Honley	d		18 05	18 31																			19 27		
Brockholes	d		18 08	18 34																			19 30		
Stocksmoor	d		18 12	18 38																			19 34		
Shepley	d		18 14	18 40																			19 36		
Denby Dale	d		18 19	18 45																			19 41		
Penistone	d		18 31	18 53																			19 49		
Silkstone Common	d		18 36	18 58																			19 54		
Dodworth	d		18 40	19 02							←		←										19 58		
Barnsley	a	18 21	18 47	19 08		18 39					18 47		19 08		19 15	19 26		19 40					20 05		
	d	18 24	18 55	19 10		18 40					18 55		19 10		19 18	19 26		19 40					20 06		
Wombwell	d	18 29	→	→							19 00		19 15			19 31							20 11		
Elsecar	d	18 33									19 04					19 35									
Chapeltown	d	18 38									19 09		19 22			19 40							20 18		
Meadowhall (29,31)	a	18 46			18 50	18 52					19 17		19 27		19 33	19 47	19 50	19 52					20 24		
	d	18 46			18 50	18 52	18 57	19 01		19 08	19 17	19 28	19 30		19 34	19 47	19 51	19 52		19 57	20 01	20 08	20 26	20 33	
Sheffield 7 (29,31)	a	18 56			19 00	19 03	19 06	19 08		19 19	19 27	19 37	19 42		19 43	19 56	19 59	20 04		20 05	20 08	20 18	20 36	20 41	
	d					19 05												20 05							
Dronfield	d					19 15												20 15							
Chesterfield	d					19 22												20 22							
Alfreton	d					19 33												20 33							
Langley Mill	d					19 40												20 40							
Nottingham	a					20 00												21 00							

		NT	NT A	NT		TP ◇1 I	NT	EM ◇ J	NT K	NT L	NT	NT	TP ◇1 D	NT C		NT G	NT	NT M	NT	NT	NT	NT	NT G	NT
Leeds 10 (31)	d	19 43		19 48			20 30				20 37	20 48							21 37	21 48		22 37		23 09
Woodlesford	d										20 45								21 45			22 45		
Castleford	d										20 56								21 56			22 56		
Normanton	d		←								21 02								22 02			23 01		
Wakefield Kirkgate 4 (31)	a	19 59	20 06				20 46				21 06								22 06			23 10		
	d	20 00	20 07				20 46				21 07								22 07			23 10		
Darton	d		20 19								21 18								22 21			23 24		
Huddersfield	d								20 18								21 18				22 18			
Lockwood	d								20 21								21 21				22 21			
Berry Brow	d								20 24								21 24				22 24			
Honley	d								20 27								21 27				22 27			
Brockholes	d								20 30								21 30				22 30			
Stocksmoor	d								20 34								21 34				22 34			
Shepley	d								20 36								21 36				22 36			
Denby Dale	d								20 41								21 41				22 41			
Penistone	d								20 52								21 49				22 49			
Silkstone Common	d								20 57								21 54				22 54			
Dodworth	d								21 01								21 58				22 58			
Barnsley	a	20 16	20 24				21 02		21 08		21 24						22 05		22 27		23 05	23 31		
	d	20 16	20 24				21 03		21 12		21 24						22 06		22 28		23 06	23 31		
Wombwell	d		20 29						21 17		21 29						22 11		22 33		23 11	23 36		
Elsecar	d		20 33								21 33								22 37		23 15	23 40		
Chapeltown	d		20 38						21 24		21 38						22 18		22 42		23 20	23 45		
Meadowhall (29,31)	a	20 33	20 45	20 51			21 19		21 28		21 45	21 51					22 24		22 47	22 52	23 25	23 51		00 08
	d	20 35	20 46	20 51		21 09	21 20		21 30	21 34	21 46	21 52	21 59	22 03		22 07	22 25	22 44	22 47	22 53	23 26	23 51	23 54	00 09
Sheffield 7 (29,31)	a	20 44	20 58	21 02		21 19	21 30		21 40	21 46	21 57	22 04	22 08	22 11		22 21	22 36	22 54	22 58	23 02	23 36	00 02	00 04	00 23
	d							21 39																
Dronfield	d							21 49																
Chesterfield	d							21 55																
Alfreton	d							22 05																
Langley Mill	d							22 12																
Nottingham	a							22 38																

A From Leeds
B To Sheffield
C From Doncaster
D From Cleethorpes to Manchester Airport
E From Scarborough
F From Huddersfield
G From Hull
H From Doncaster to Worksop
I From Cleethorpes
J From Liverpool Lime Street
K To Retford
L From Bridlington
M From Scunthorpe

Leeds and Huddersfield - Barnsley - Sheffield, Nottingham

Network Diagram - see first page of Table 31

		NT MX	NT MX A	NT MX	NT	NT	TP ◇1 B	NT	NT C	NT	NT	NT	NT A	TP ◇1 D	NT	NT E	NT	NT	TP ◇1 D	NT	NT F	NT	NT A
Leeds 10	31 d	22p37		23p09						05 33		06 05					06 38	06 43		07 05			
Woodlesford	d	22p45															06 46						
Castleford	d	22p56															06 57						
Normanton	d	23p01															07 03						
Wakefield Kirkgate 4	31 a	23p10										06 21					07 07			07 25			
	d	23p10									06 04	06 21					07 08			07 25			
Darton	d	23p24									06 15						07 19						
Huddersfield	d														06 05							07 05	
Lockwood	d														06 08							07 08	
Berry Brow	d														06 11							07 11	
Honley	d														06 14							07 14	
Brockholes	d														06 17							07 17	
Stocksmoor	d														06 21							07 21	
Shepley	d														06 23							07 23	
Denby Dale	d														06 34							07 34	
Penistone	d														06 42							07 42	
Silkstone Common	d														06 47							07 47	
Dodworth	d														06 51							07 51	
Barnsley	a	23p31									06 20	06 37			06 57		07 25			07 40		07 57	
	d	23p31			05 23			05 50			06 21	06 38			06 58		07 25			07 40		07 58	
Wombwell	d	23p36			05 28			05 55			06 26				07 03		07 30					08 03	
Elsecar	d	23p40			05 32			05 59			06 30				07 07		07 34					08 07	
Chapeltown	d	23p45			05 37			06 04			06 35				07 12		07 39					08 12	
Meadowhall	29,31 ⇌ a	23p51		00 08	05 43			06 15		06 37	06 41	06 49			07 21		07 48	07 44		07 53		08 20	
	d	23p51	23p54	00 09	05 43		05 58	06 15	06 27	06 38	06 42	06 49	06 52	06 58	07 21	07 33	07 49	07 45	07 53	07 54	08 06	08 21	08 23
Sheffield 7	29,31 ⇌ a	00 02	00 04	00 23	05 54		06 08	06 25	06 38	06 47	06 55	07 00	07 05	07 06	07 29	07 40	07 58	07 56	08 00	08 05	08 18	08 29	08 33
	d					06 00						07 03								08 05			
Dronfield	d					06 10						07 13								08 15			
Chesterfield	d					06 16						07 20								08 24			
Alfreton	d					06 30						07 33								08 35			
Langley Mill	d					06 37						07 40								08 42			
Nottingham	a					07 02						08 02								09 02			

		NT G	NT	NT H	NT	NT	NT F	TP ◇1 D	NT I	NT	NT G	NT	NT J	NT H	NT	NT	NT F	TP ◇1 D	NT I	NT	NT G	NT	NT J
Leeds 10	31 d	07 29	07 35		07 48	08 02					08 32	08 37			08 48	09 05					09 32	09 37	
Woodlesford	d	07 37									08 40										09 40		
Castleford	d	07 48									08 51										09 51		
Normanton	d	07 54		←							08 57			←							09 57		
Wakefield Kirkgate 4	31 a	08 00	07 54	08 00		08 23					09 03	08 54		09 03		09 23					10 01	09 55	
	d	08 04	07 55	08 04		08 23					09 05	08 55		09 05		09 23					10 04	09 56	
Darton	d	→		08 15							→			09 17							→		
Huddersfield	d									08 07										09 08			
Lockwood	d									08 10										09 11			
Berry Brow	d									08 13										09 14			
Honley	d									08 16										09 17			
Brockholes	d									08 19										09 20			
Stocksmoor	d									08 23										09 24			
Shepley	d									08 25										09 26			
Denby Dale	d									08 34										09 36			
Penistone	d									08 42										09 44			
Silkstone Common	d									08 47										09 49			
Dodworth	d									08 51										09 53			
Barnsley	a		08 11	08 21		08 39				08 57		09 11		09 23		09 39				10 00		10 12	
	d		08 14	08 24		08 40				08 58		09 14		09 24		09 40				10 01		10 14	
Wombwell	d			08 29						09 03				09 29						10 06			
Elsecar	d			08 33						09 07				09 33									
Chapeltown	d			08 38						09 12				09 38						10 13			
Meadowhall	29,31 ⇌ a		08 31	08 45	08 50	08 52				09 19		09 27		09 46	09 50	09 52				10 20		10 27	
	d		08 31	08 45	08 51	08 52	08 57	09 01	09 16	09 20		09 28	09 33	09 46	09 50	09 52	09 55	10 01	10 08	10 21		10 28	10 33
Sheffield 7	29,31 ⇌ a		08 39	08 56	08 59	09 02	09 05	09 08	09 26	09 28		09 37	09 41	09 56	10 00	10 02	10 05	10 08	10 19	10 30		10 37	10 41
	d					09 05										10 05							
Dronfield	d					09 15										10 15							
Chesterfield	d					09 22										10 22							
Alfreton	d					09 32										10 33							
Langley Mill	d					09 40										10 40							
Nottingham	a					10 00										11 00							

A From Hull
B From Doncaster to Manchester Airport
C From Doncaster
D From Cleethorpes to Manchester Airport
E From Doncaster to Worksop
F From Adwick
G To Sheffield
H From Leeds
I From Bridlington
J From Scunthorpe to Lincoln

Leeds and Huddersfield - Barnsley - Sheffield, Nottingham

Network Diagram - see first page of Table 31

		NT A	NT	NT ◇	NT B	TP ◇1 C	NT D	NT	NT E	NT	NT F	NT A	NT	NT ◇	NT B	TP ◇1 C	NT D	NT	NT G	NT E	NT	NT F
Leeds 10	31 d		09 48	10 05					10 32	10 37			10 48	11 05						11 32	11 37	
Woodlesford	d								10 40											11 40		
Castleford	d								10 51											11 51		
Normanton	d	←							10 57			←								11 57		
Wakefield Kirkgate 4	31 a	10 01		10 23					11 01	10 54		11 01		11 23						12 01	11 54	
	d	10 04		10 23					11 04	10 55		11 04		11 23						12 04	11 55	
Darton	d	10 15							→			11 15								→		
Huddersfield	d							10 08										11 08				
Lockwood	d							10 11										11 11				
Berry Brow	d							10 14										11 14				
Honley	d							10 17										11 17				
Brockholes	d							10 20										11 20				
Stocksmoor	d							10 24										11 24				
Shepley	d							10 26										11 26				
Denby Dale	d							10 36										11 36				
Penistone	d							10 44										11 44				
Silkstone Common	d							10 49										11 49				
Dodworth	d							10 53										11 53				
Barnsley	a	10 21		10 39				11 00		11 11		11 21		11 39				12 00			12 11	
	d	10 24		10 40				11 01		11 14		11 24		11 40				12 01			12 14	
Wombwell	d	10 29						11 06				11 29						12 06				
Elsecar	d	10 33										11 33										
Chapeltown	d	10 38						11 13				11 38						12 13				
Meadowhall	29,31 ⇌ a	10 46	10 50	10 52				11 20		11 27		11 46	11 51	11 52				12 20			12 27	
	d	10 47	10 50	10 52	10 58	11 01	11 08	11 21		11 28	11 33	11 46	11 51	11 52	11 56	12 01	12 08	12 21	12 24		12 28	12 33
Sheffield 7	29,31 ⇌ a	10 56	11 01	11 02	11 05	11 08	11 20	11 30		11 37	11 41	11 57	12 01	12 02	12 05	12 08	12 19	12 30	12 36		12 37	12 41
	d			11 05										12 05								
Dronfield	d			11 15										12 15								
Chesterfield	d			11 22										12 22								
Alfreton	d			11 33										12 33								
Langley Mill	d			11 40										12 40								
Nottingham	a			12 00										13 01								

		NT A	NT	NT ◇	NT B	TP ◇1 C	NT D	NT	NT E	NT	NT F	NT A	NT	NT ◇	NT B	TP ◇1 C	NT H	NT	NT E	NT	NT F	NT A	NT
Leeds 10	31 d		11 48	12 05					12 32	12 37			12 48	13 05					13 32	13 37			13 48
Woodlesford	d								12 40										13 40				
Castleford	d								12 51										13 51				
Normanton	d	←							12 57			←							13 57			←	
Wakefield Kirkgate 4	31 a	12 01		12 23					13 02	12 54		13 02		13 23					14 01	13 54		14 01	
	d	12 04		12 23					13 04	12 55		13 04		13 23					14 04	13 55		14 04	
Darton	d	12 15							→			13 17							→			14 15	
Huddersfield	d							12 08										13 08					
Lockwood	d							12 11										13 11					
Berry Brow	d							12 14										13 14					
Honley	d							12 17										13 17					
Brockholes	d							12 20										13 20					
Stocksmoor	d							12 24										13 24					
Shepley	d							12 26										13 26					
Denby Dale	d							12 36										13 36					
Penistone	d							12 44										13 44					
Silkstone Common	d							12 49										13 49					
Dodworth	d							12 53										13 53					
Barnsley	a	12 21		12 39				13 00		13 11		13 22		13 39				14 00		14 11		14 21	
	d	12 24		12 40				13 01		13 14		13 24		13 40				14 01		14 14		14 24	
Wombwell	d	12 29						13 06				13 29						14 06				14 29	
Elsecar	d	12 33										13 33										14 33	
Chapeltown	d	12 38						13 13				13 38						14 13				14 38	
Meadowhall	29,31 ⇌ a	12 46	12 51	12 52				13 20		13 27		13 46	13 51	13 52				14 20		14 27		14 46	14 50
	d	12 46	12 51	12 52	12 56	13 01	13 08	13 21		13 28	13 33	13 46	13 51	13 52	13 56	14 01	14 05	14 21		14 28	14 34	14 46	14 50
Sheffield 7	29,31 ⇌ a	12 56	13 01	13 02	13 05	13 08	13 20	13 29		13 37	13 41	13 56	14 01	14 02	14 05	14 08	14 20	14 29		14 37	14 42	14 56	15 01
	d			13 05										14 05									
Dronfield	d			13 15										14 15									
Chesterfield	d			13 22										14 22									
Alfreton	d			13 33										14 33									
Langley Mill	d			13 40										14 40									
Nottingham	a			14 00										15 00									

A From Leeds
B From Adwick
C From Cleethorpes to Manchester Airport
D From Bridlington
E To Sheffield
F From Scunthorpe to Lincoln
G From York
H From Scarborough

Table 34

Mondays to Fridays

from 1 October

Leeds and Huddersfield - Barnsley - Sheffield, Nottingham

Network Diagram - see first page of Table 31

			NT ◇	NT A	TP ◇1 B ⚒	NT C	NT	NT D	NT	NT E	NT F	NT	NT ◇	NT A	TP ◇1 B ⚒	NT G	NT H	NT	NT D	NT	EM ◇ I	NT E	NT F
Leeds 10	31	d	14 05					14 32	14 37			14 48	15 05						15 32	15 37			
Woodlesford		d						14 40											15 40				
Castleford		d						14 51											15 51				
Normanton		d						14 57			←								15 57				←
Wakefield Kirkgate 4	31	a	14 23					15 01	14 54		15 01		15 23						16 01	15 54			16 01
		d	14 23					15 04	14 55		15 04		15 23						16 04	15 55			16 04
Darton		d						→			15 15								→				16 15
Huddersfield		d					14 08											15 08					
Lockwood		d					14 11											15 11					
Berry Brow		d					14 14											15 14					
Honley		d					14 17											15 17					
Brockholes		d					14 20											15 20					
Stocksmoor		d					14 24											15 24					
Shepley		d					14 26											15 26					
Denby Dale		d					14 36											15 36					
Penistone		d					14 44											15 44					
Silkstone Common		d					14 49											15 49					
Dodworth		d					14 53											15 53					
Barnsley		a	14 39				15 00		15 13		15 21		15 39					16 00		16 11			16 21
		d	14 40				15 01		15 14		15 24		15 40					16 01		16 14			16 24
Wombwell		d					15 06				15 29							16 06					16 29
Elsecar		d									15 33												16 33
Chapeltown		d					15 13				15 38							16 13					16 38
Meadowhall	29,31	a	14 52				15 20		15 27		15 46	15 50	15 51					16 20		16 27			16 46
		d	14 52	14 56	15 01	15 07	15 21		15 28	15 33	15 46	15 50	15 52	15 57	16 01	16 07	16 18	16 21		16 28		16 33	16 46
Sheffield 7	29,31	a	15 02	15 05	15 08	15 19	15 29		15 37	15 41	15 56	16 01	16 03	16 05	16 08	16 20	16 27	16 29		16 37		16 41	16 56
		d	15 05										16 04								16 38		
Dronfield		d	15 15										16 14								16 48		
Chesterfield		d	15 22										16 21								16 56		
Alfreton		d	15 33										16 32								17 07		
Langley Mill		d	15 40										16 40										
Nottingham		a	16 00										17 00								17 31		

			NT	NT ◇	NT J	TP ◇1 B ⚒	NT C	NT	NT D	NT	NT E	EM ◇ I	NT F	NT	NT ◇	NT K	TP ◇1 B ⚒	NT C	NT	NT D	NT	NT L	NT F	NT D
Leeds 10	31	d	15 48	16 05					16 32	16 37				16 48	17 05					17 32	17 37			
Woodlesford		d							16 40											17 40				
Castleford		d							16 51											17 51				
Normanton		d							16 57				←		17 18					17 57			←	
Wakefield Kirkgate 4	31	a		16 23					17 01	16 54			17 01		17 22					18 01	17 54		18 01	
		d		16 23					17 04	16 55			17 04		17 23					18 04	17 55		18 04	
Darton		d							→				17 15							→			18 15	
Huddersfield		d						16 08											17 08					17 56
Lockwood		d						16 11											17 11					17 59
Berry Brow		d						16 14											17 14					18 02
Honley		d						16 17											17 17					18 05
Brockholes		d						16 20											17 20					18 08
Stocksmoor		d						16 24											17 24					18 12
Shepley		d						16 26											17 26					18 14
Denby Dale		d						16 36											17 36					18 19
Penistone		d						16 44											17 44					18 31
Silkstone Common		d						16 49											17 49					18 36
Dodworth		d						16 53											17 53					18 40
Barnsley		a		16 39				17 00		17 11			17 21		17 39				18 00		18 11		18 21	18 47
		d		16 40				17 01		17 14			17 24		17 40				18 01		18 14		18 24	18 55
Wombwell		d						17 06					17 29						18 06				18 29	→
Elsecar		d											17 33										18 33	
Chapeltown		d						17 13					17 38						18 13				18 38	
Meadowhall	29,31	a	16 50	16 52				17 20		17 27			17 46	17 50	17 51				18 20		18 27		18 46	
		d	16 50	16 52	16 55	17 01	17 09	17 21		17 28	17 33		17 46	17 50	17 52	17 57	18 01	18 08	18 21		18 28	18 32	18 46	
Sheffield 7	29,31	a	17 00	17 02	17 05	17 08	17 20	17 32		17 37	17 41		17 56	18 01	18 03	18 05	18 08	18 19	18 29		18 38	18 42	18 56	
		d		17 05								17 44			18 05									
Dronfield		d		17 15								17 56			18 15									
Chesterfield		d		17 22								18 02			18 22									
Alfreton		d		17 33								18 12			18 33									
Langley Mill		d		17 40											18 40									
Nottingham		a		18 00								18 34			19 00									

A From Adwick
B From Cleethorpes to Manchester Airport
C From Bridlington
D To Sheffield
E From Scunthorpe to Lincoln
F From Leeds
G From Scarborough
H From Sheffield
I From Liverpool Lime Street to Norwich
J From Adwick to Retford
K From Doncaster
L From Scunthorpe

Table 34

Mondays to Fridays

from 1 October

Leeds and Huddersfield - Barnsley - Sheffield, Nottingham

Network Diagram - see first page of Table 31

			NT A	NT	NT ◇	NT B	TP ◇1 C ⚒	NT D	NT E	NT F	NT G	NT A	NT	NT G	NT	NT ◇	NT B	TP ◇1 C	NT F	NT	NT H	NT A	NT	NT G
Leeds 10	31	d	17 43	17 46	18 05							18 32	18 43		18 48	19 05						19 37	19 43	
Woodlesford		d										18 40										19 45		
Castleford		d										18 51										19 56		
Normanton		d										19 00		←								20 02		←
Wakefield Kirkgate 4	31	a			18 23							19 04	18 59	19 04		19 24						20 06	19 59	20 06
		d			18 23							19 05	18 59	19 05		19 24						20 07	20 00	20 07
Darton		d										→		19 19								→		20 19
Huddersfield		d	18 22																	19 15				
Lockwood		d	18 25																	19 18				
Berry Brow		d	18 28																	19 21				
Honley		d	18 31																	19 24				
Brockholes		d	18 34																	19 27				
Stocksmoor		d	18 38																	19 31				
Shepley		d	18 40																	19 33				
Denby Dale		d	18 45																	19 43				
Penistone		d	18 53																	19 49				
Silkstone Common		d	18 58																	19 54				
Dodworth		d	19 02						←		←									19 58				
Barnsley		a	19 08		18 39				18 47		19 08		19 15	19 26		19 40				20 05			20 16	20 24
		d	19 10		18 40				18 55		19 10		19 18	19 26		19 40				20 06			20 16	20 24
Wombwell		d	→						19 00		19 15			19 31						20 11				20 29
Elsecar		d							19 04					19 35										20 33
Chapeltown		d							19 09		19 22			19 40						20 18				20 38
Meadowhall	29,31	a		18 50	18 52				19 17		19 27		19 33	19 47	19 50	19 52				20 24			20 33	20 45
		d		18 50	18 52	18 57	19 01	19 08	19 17	19 28	19 30		19 34	19 47	19 51	19 52	19 57	20 01	20 08	20 26	20 33		20 35	20 46
Sheffield 7	29,31	a		19 00	19 03	19 06	19 08	19 17	19 27	19 37	19 42		19 43	19 56	19 59	20 04	20 05	20 08	20 18	20 36	20 41		20 44	20 58
		d			19 05											20 05								
Dronfield		d			19 15											20 15								
Chesterfield		d			19 22											20 22								
Alfreton		d			19 33											20 33								
Langley Mill		d			19 40											20 40								
Nottingham		a			20 00											21 00								

			NT	TP ◇1 I	NT	EM ◇ J	NT K	NT L	NT	NT	TP ◇1 C	NT B	NT F	NT	NT M	NT	NT	NT	NT	NT F	NT
Leeds 10	31	d	19 48		20 30				20 37	20 48						21 37	21 48		22 37		23 09
Woodlesford		d							20 45							21 45			22 45		
Castleford		d							20 56							21 56			22 56		
Normanton		d							21 02							22 02			23 01		
Wakefield Kirkgate 4	31	a			20 46				21 06							22 06			23 10		
		d			20 46				21 07							22 07			23 10		
Darton		d							21 18							22 21			23 24		
Huddersfield		d					20 15							21 15				22 15			
Lockwood		d					20 18							21 18				22 18			
Berry Brow		d					20 21							21 21				22 21			
Honley		d					20 24							21 24				22 24			
Brockholes		d					20 27							21 27				22 27			
Stocksmoor		d					20 31							21 31				22 31			
Shepley		d					20 33							21 33				22 36			
Denby Dale		d					20 41							21 41				22 41			
Penistone		d					20 49							21 49				22 49			
Silkstone Common		d					20 54							21 54				22 54			
Dodworth		d					20 58							21 58				22 58			
Barnsley		a			21 02		21 09		21 24					22 05		22 27		23 05	23 31		
		d			21 03		21 12		21 24					22 06		22 28		23 06	23 31		
Wombwell		d					21 17		21 29					22 11		22 33		23 11	23 36		
Elsecar		d							21 33							22 37		23 15	23 40		
Chapeltown		d					21 24		21 38					22 18		22 42		23 20	23 45		
Meadowhall	29,31	a	20 51		21 19		21 28		21 45	21 51				22 24		22 47	22 52	23 25	23 51		00 08
		d	20 51	21 09	21 20		21 30	21 34	21 46	21 52	21 59	22 03	22 07	22 25	22 44	22 47	22 53	23 26	23 51	23 54	00 09
Sheffield 7	29,31	a	21 02	21 19	21 30		21 40	21 46	21 57	22 04	22 08	22 11	22 21	22 36	22 54	22 58	23 02	23 36	00 02	00 04	00 23
		d				21 39															
Dronfield		d				21 49															
Chesterfield		d				21 55															
Alfreton		d				22 05															
Langley Mill		d				22 12															
Nottingham		a				22 38															

A To Sheffield
B From Doncaster
C From Cleethorpes to Manchester Airport
D From Scarborough
E From Huddersfield
F From Hull
G From Leeds
H From Doncaster to Worksop
I From Cleethorpes
J From Liverpool Lime Street
K To Retford
L From Bridlington
M From Scunthorpe

Leeds and Huddersfield - Barnsley - Sheffield, Nottingham

Network Diagram - see first page of Table 31

Station			NT	NT A	NT	NT	TP ◇1 B	NT	NT C	NT	NT A	TP ◇1 D	NT	NT C	NT	NT	TP ◇1 D	NT	NT E	NT	NT A	NT F	NT	NT G
Leeds 10	31	d	22p37		23p09										06 38	06 43		07 05				07 29	07 35	
Woodlesford		d	22p45												06 46							07 37		
Castleford		d	22p56												06 57							07 48		
Normanton		d	23p01												07 03							07 54		←
Wakefield Kirkgate 4	31	a	23p10												07 07			07 25				08 00	07 54	08 00
		d	23p10												07 08			07 25				08 04	07 55	08 04
Darton		d	23p24												07 19							→		08 15
Huddersfield		d											06 10							07 10				
Lockwood		d											06 13							07 13				
Berry Brow		d											06 16							07 16				
Honley		d											06 19							07 19				
Brockholes		d											06 22							07 22				
Stocksmoor		d											06 26							07 26				
Shepley		d											06 28							07 28				
Denby Dale		d											06 34							07 34				
Penistone		d											06 42							07 42				
Silkstone Common		d											06 47							07 47				
Dodworth		d											06 51							07 51				
Barnsley		a	23p31										06 57		07 25			07 40		07 57			08 11	08 21
		d	23p31			05 23		05 50		06 21			06 58		07 25			07 40		07 58			08 14	08 24
Wombwell		d	23p36			05 28		05 55		06 26			07 03		07 30					08 03				08 29
Elsecar		d	23p40			05 32		05 59		06 30			07 07		07 34					08 07				08 33
Chapeltown		d	23p45			05 37		06 04		06 35			07 12		07 39					08 12				08 38
Meadowhall	29,31 ⇌	a	23p51		00 08	05 43		06 10		06 41			07 21		07 48	07 46		07 53		08 20			08 31	08 45
		d	23p51	23p54	00 09	05 43	05 58	06 10	06 30	06 42	06 52	06 58	07 21	07 32	07 49	07 47	07 53	07 54	08 07	08 21	08 25		08 31	08 46
Sheffield 7	29,31 ⇌	a	00 02	00 04	00 23	05 54	06 08	06 25	06 38	06 55	07 05	07 06	07 29	07 40	07 58	07 54	08 00	08 05	08 18	08 29	08 32		08 39	08 56
		d								07 03								08 05						
Dronfield		d								07 13								08 15						
Chesterfield		d								07 20								08 24						
Alfreton		d								07 33								08 35						
Langley Mill		d								07 40								08 42						
Nottingham		a								08 02								09 02						

Station			NT	NT	NT E	TP ◇1 D	NT	NT H	NT F	NT	NT I	NT G	NT	NT	NT E	TP ◇1 D	NT H	NT	NT F	NT	NT I	NT G	NT	NT
Leeds 10	31	d	07 48	08 05					08 32	08 37			08 48	09 05					09 32	09 37			09 48	10 05
Woodlesford		d							08 40										09 40					
Castleford		d							08 51										09 51					
Normanton		d							08 57			←							09 57			←		
Wakefield Kirkgate 4	31	a		08 23					09 03	08 54		09 03		09 23					10 01	09 55		10 01		10 23
		d		08 23					09 05	08 55		09 05		09 23					10 04	09 56		10 04		10 23
Darton		d							→			09 17							→			10 15		
Huddersfield		d					08 10											09 13						
Lockwood		d					08 13											09 16						
Berry Brow		d					08 16											09 19						
Honley		d					08 19											09 22						
Brockholes		d					08 22											09 25						
Stocksmoor		d					08 26											09 29						
Shepley		d					08 28											09 31						
Denby Dale		d					08 34											09 36						
Penistone		d					08 42											09 44						
Silkstone Common		d					08 47											09 49						
Dodworth		d					08 51											09 53						
Barnsley		a		08 39			08 57			09 11		09 23		09 39				10 00		10 12		10 21		10 39
		d		08 40			08 58			09 14		09 24		09 40				10 01		10 14		10 24		10 40
Wombwell		d					09 03					09 29						10 06				10 29		
Elsecar		d					09 07					09 33										10 33		
Chapeltown		d					09 12					09 38						10 13				10 38		
Meadowhall	29,31 ⇌	a	08 49	08 52			09 19			09 27		09 46	09 50	09 52				10 20		10 27		10 46	10 50	10 52
		d	08 51	08 52	08 56	09 01	09 20	09 24		09 29	09 33	09 46	09 50	09 52	09 55	10 01	10 08	10 21		10 28	10 33	10 47	10 50	10 52
Sheffield 7	29,31 ⇌	a	08 59	09 02	09 05	09 08	09 28	09 33		09 37	09 41	09 56	10 00	10 02	10 05	10 08	10 19	10 30		10 37	10 41	10 56	11 00	11 02
		d		09 05										10 04										11 05
Dronfield		d		09 16										10 14										11 15
Chesterfield		d		09 23										10 21										11 22
Alfreton		d		09 32										10 32										11 35
Langley Mill		d		09 41										10 40										11 40
Nottingham		a		10 00										11 00										12 00

A From Hull
B From Doncaster to Manchester Airport
C From Doncaster
D From Cleethorpes to Manchester Airport
E From Adwick
F To Sheffield
G From Leeds
H From Bridlington
I From Scunthorpe to Lincoln

Leeds and Huddersfield - Barnsley - Sheffield, Nottingham

Network Diagram - see first page of Table 31

Station			NT A	TP ◇1 B	NT C	NT	NT D	NT	NT E	NT F	NT	NT	NT A	TP ◇1 B	NT C	NT	NT G	NT D	NT	NT E	NT F	NT	NT
Leeds 10	31	d					10 32	10 37			10 48	11 05						11 32	11 37			11 48	12 05
Woodlesford		d					10 40											11 40					
Castleford		d					10 51											11 51					
Normanton		d					10 57			←								11 57			←		
Wakefield Kirkgate 4	31	a					11 01	10 54		11 01		11 23						12 01	11 54		12 01		12 23
		d					11 04	10 55		11 04		11 23						12 04	11 55		12 04		12 23
Darton		d					→			11 15								→			12 15		
Huddersfield		d				10 13										11 13							
Lockwood		d				10 16										11 16							
Berry Brow		d				10 19										11 19							
Honley		d				10 22										11 22							
Brockholes		d				10 25										11 25							
Stocksmoor		d				10 29										11 29							
Shepley		d				10 31										11 31							
Denby Dale		d				10 36										11 36							
Penistone		d				10 44										11 44							
Silkstone Common		d				10 49										11 49							
Dodworth		d				10 53										11 53							
Barnsley		a				11 00		11 11		11 21		11 39				12 00			12 11		12 21		12 39
		d				11 01		11 14		11 24		11 40				12 01			12 14		12 24		12 40
Wombwell		d				11 06				11 29						12 06					12 29		
Elsecar		d								11 33											12 33		
Chapeltown		d				11 13				11 38						12 13					12 38		
Meadowhall	29,31 ⇌	a				11 20		11 27		11 46	11 50	11 52				12 20			12 27		12 46	12 49	12 52
		d	10 58	11 01	11 08	11 21		11 28	11 33	11 46	11 50	11 52	11 58	12 01	12 08	12 21	12 24		12 28	12 33	12 46	12 50	12 52
Sheffield 7	29,31 ⇌	a	11 06	11 08	11 20	11 30		11 37	11 41	11 57	12 00	12 02	12 05	12 08	12 20	12 30	12 36		12 37	12 41	12 56	13 00	13 02
		d										12 05											13 05
Dronfield		d										12 15											13 15
Chesterfield		d										12 22											13 22
Alfreton		d										12 33											13 33
Langley Mill		d										12 40											13 40
Nottingham		a										13 01											14 00

Station			NT A	TP ◇1 B	NT C	NT	NT D	NT	NT E	NT F	NT	NT	NT A	TP ◇1 B	NT H	NT	NT D	NT	NT E	NT F	NT	NT	NT A	TP ◇1 B
Leeds 10	31	d					12 32	12 37			12 48	13 05					13 32	13 37			13 48	14 05		
Woodlesford		d					12 40										13 40							
Castleford		d					12 51										13 51							
Normanton		d					12 57			←							13 57			←				
Wakefield Kirkgate 4	31	a					13 02	12 54		13 02		13 23					14 01	13 54		14 01		14 23		
		d					13 04	12 55		13 04		13 23					14 04	13 55		14 04		14 23		
Darton		d					→			13 17							→			14 15				
Huddersfield		d				12 08										13 13								
Lockwood		d				12 11										13 16								
Berry Brow		d				12 14										13 19								
Honley		d				12 17										13 22								
Brockholes		d				12 20										13 25								
Stocksmoor		d				12 24										13 29								
Shepley		d				12 26										13 31								
Denby Dale		d				12 36										13 36								
Penistone		d				12 44										13 44								
Silkstone Common		d				12 49										13 49								
Dodworth		d				12 53										13 53								
Barnsley		a				13 00		13 11		13 22		13 38				14 00		14 11		14 21		14 39		
		d				13 01		13 14		13 24		13 40				14 01		14 14		14 24		14 40		
Wombwell		d				13 06				13 29						14 06				14 29				
Elsecar		d								13 33										14 33				
Chapeltown		d				13 13				13 38						14 13				14 38				
Meadowhall	29,31 ⇌	a				13 20		13 27		13 46	13 49	13 52				14 20		14 27		14 46	14 49	14 52		
		d	12 58	13 01	13 08	13 21		13 28	13 33	13 46	13 50	13 52	13 58	14 01	14 08	14 21		14 28	14 33	14 46	14 50	14 52	14 58	15 01
Sheffield 7	29,31 ⇌	a	13 05	13 08	13 20	13 29		13 37	13 41	13 56	14 00	14 02	14 05	14 08	14 20	14 29		14 37	14 40	14 56	15 00	15 02	15 05	15 08
		d										14 05										15 05		
Dronfield		d										14 15										15 15		
Chesterfield		d										14 22										15 22		
Alfreton		d										14 33										15 33		
Langley Mill		d										14 40										15 40		
Nottingham		a										15 00										16 00		

A From Adwick
B From Cleethorpes to Manchester Airport
C From Bridlington
D To Sheffield
E From Scunthorpe to Lincoln
F From Leeds
G From Sheffield
H From Scarborough

Table 34

Saturdays until 29 September

Leeds and Huddersfield - Barnsley - Sheffield, Nottingham

Network Diagram - see first page of Table 31

	NT A	NT	NT B	NT	NT C	NT D	NT	NT	NT E	TP ◇1 F	NT G	NT H	NT	NT B	NT	EM ◇ I	NT C	NT D	NT	NT	NT J
Leeds 10 31 d			14 32	14 37			14 48	15 05						15 32	15 37				15 48	16 05	
Woodlesford d			14 40											15 40							
Castleford d			14 51											15 51							
Normanton d			14 57			←								15 57				←			
Wakefield Kirkgate 4 31 a			15 01	14 54		15 01		15 23						16 01	15 54			16 01		16 23	
d			15 04	14 55		15 04		15 23						16 04	15 55			16 04		16 23	
Darton d			→			15 15								→				16 15			
Huddersfield d		14 13											15 13								
Lockwood d		14 16											15 16								
Berry Brow d		14 19											15 19								
Honley d		14 22											15 22								
Brockholes d		14 25											15 25								
Stocksmoor d		14 29											15 29								
Shepley d		14 31											15 31								
Denby Dale d		14 36											15 36								
Penistone d		14 44											15 44								
Silkstone Common d		14 49											15 49								
Dodworth d		14 53											15 53								
Barnsley a		15 00		15 13		15 21		15 39					16 00		16 11			16 21		16 39	
d		15 01		15 14		15 24		15 40					16 01		16 14			16 24		16 40	
Wombwell d		15 06				15 29							16 06					16 29			
Elsecar d						15 33												16 33			
Chapeltown d		15 13				15 38							16 13					16 38			
Meadowhall 29,31 a		15 20		15 27		15 46	15 49	15 51					16 20		16 27			16 46	16 49	16 52	
d	15 07	15 21		15 28	15 33	15 46	15 50	15 52	15 57	16 01	16 07	16 18	16 21		16 28		16 33	16 46	16 50	16 52	16 55
Sheffield 7 29,31 a	15 20	15 29		15 37	15 41	15 56	16 00	16 03	16 05	16 08	16 22	16 27	16 29		16 37		16 41	16 56	17 00	17 02	17 05
d								16 04								16 38				17 05	
Dronfield d								16 14								16 48				17 15	
Chesterfield d								16 21								16 53				17 22	
Alfreton d								16 32								17 04				17 33	
Langley Mill d								16 40												17 40	
Nottingham a								17 00								17 29				18 00	

	TP ◇1 F	NT A	NT	NT B	NT	NT C	EM ◇ I	NT D	NT	NT	NT K	TP ◇1 F	NT A	NT	NT B	NT	NT C	NT D	NT	NT	NT K	TP ◇1 F
Leeds 10 31 d				16 32	16 37				16 48	17 05					17 32	17 37			17 48	18 05		
Woodlesford d				16 40											17 40							
Castleford d				16 51											17 51							
Normanton d				16 57				←		17 18					17 57			←				
Wakefield Kirkgate 4 31 a				17 01	16 54			17 01		17 22					18 01	17 54		18 01		18 23		
d				17 04	16 55			17 04		17 23					18 04	17 55		18 04		18 23		
Darton d				→				17 15							→			18 15				
Huddersfield d			16 13											17 13								
Lockwood d			16 16											17 16								
Berry Brow d			16 19											17 19								
Honley d			16 22											17 22								
Brockholes d			16 25											17 25								
Stocksmoor d			16 29											17 29								
Shepley d			16 31											17 31								
Denby Dale d			16 36											17 36								
Penistone d			16 44											17 44								
Silkstone Common d			16 49											17 49								
Dodworth d			16 53											17 53								
Barnsley a			17 00		17 11			17 21		17 39				18 00		18 11		18 21		18 39		
d			17 01		17 14			17 24		17 40				18 01		18 14		18 24		18 40		
Wombwell d			17 06					17 29						18 06				18 29				
Elsecar d								17 33										18 33				
Chapeltown d			17 13					17 38						18 13				18 38				
Meadowhall 29,31 a			17 20		17 27			17 46	17 49	17 51				18 20		18 27		18 46	18 50	18 52		
d	17 01	17 08	17 21		17 28	17 33		17 46	17 50	17 52	17 57	18 01	18 08	18 21		18 28	18 33	18 46	18 50	18 52	18 56	19 01
Sheffield 7 29,31 a	17 08	17 19	17 32		17 37	17 41		17 56	18 00	18 03	18 05	18 08	18 19	18 29		18 38	18 41	18 56	19 00	19 03	19 06	19 08
d							17 44			18 06										19 05		
Dronfield d							17 55			18 15										19 15		
Chesterfield d							18 01			18 22										19 22		
Alfreton d							18 11			18 33										19 33		
Langley Mill d										18 40										19 40		
Nottingham a							18 33			19 00										20 00		

A From Bridlington
B To Sheffield
C From Scunthorpe to Lincoln
D From Leeds
E From Adwick
F From Cleethorpes to Manchester Airport
G From Scarborough
H From York
I From Liverpool Lime Street to Norwich
J From Adwick to Retford
K From Doncaster

Table 34

Saturdays until 29 September

Leeds and Huddersfield - Barnsley - Sheffield, Nottingham

Network Diagram - see first page of Table 31

	NT A	NT	NT B	NT C	NT	NT D	NT	NT	NT E	TP ◇1 F	NT B	NT	NT G	NT C	NT	NT D	NT	TP ◇1 H	NT	EM ◇ I	NT J	NT K
Leeds 10 31 d				18 32	18 37		18 48	19 05						19 37	19 43		19 48		20 30			
Woodlesford d				18 40										19 45								
Castleford d				18 51										19 56								
Normanton d				19 00		←								20 02		←						
Wakefield Kirkgate 4 31 a				19 04	18 54	19 04		19 24						20 06	19 59	20 06			20 46			
d				19 05	18 55	19 05		19 24						20 07	20 00	20 07			20 46			
Darton d				→		19 19								→		20 19						
Huddersfield d		18 13										19 18									20 18	
Lockwood d		18 16										19 21									20 21	
Berry Brow d		18 19										19 24									20 24	
Honley d		18 22										19 27									20 27	
Brockholes d		18 25										19 30									20 30	
Stocksmoor d		18 29										19 34									20 34	
Shepley d		18 31										19 36									20 36	
Denby Dale d		18 36										19 41									20 41	
Penistone d		18 44										19 49									20 52	
Silkstone Common d		18 49										19 54									20 57	
Dodworth d		18 53										19 58									21 01	
Barnsley a		19 01			19 11	19 26		19 40				20 05			20 16	20 24			21 02		21 09	
d		19 01			19 14	19 26		19 40				20 06			20 16	20 24			21 03		21 12	
Wombwell d		19 06				19 31						20 11				20 29					21 17	
Elsecar d						19 35										20 33						
Chapeltown d		19 13				19 40						20 18				20 38					21 24	
Meadowhall 29,31 a		19 20			19 28	19 47	19 50	19 52				20 24			20 33	20 45	20 50		21 19		21 28	
d	19 08	19 20	19 28		19 30	19 47	19 51	19 52	19 57	20 01	20 08	20 24	20 33		20 35	20 46	20 51	21 09	21 20		21 29	21 35
Sheffield 7 29,31 a	19 19	19 30	19 37		19 39	19 56	20 00	20 04	20 06	20 08	20 18	20 36	20 41		20 44	20 58	21 00	21 19	21 30		21 41	21 46
d								20 05												21 38		
Dronfield d								20 15												21 48		
Chesterfield d								20 22												21 54		
Alfreton d								20 33												22 05		
Langley Mill d								20 40												22 12		
Nottingham a								21 00												22 33		

	NT	NT	TP ◇1 H	NT E	NT B	NT	NT L	NT	NT	NT	NT	NT K
Leeds 10 31 d	20 37	20 48						21 37	21 48		22 44	
Woodlesford d	20 45							21 45				
Castleford d	20 56							21 56				
Normanton d	21 02							22 02				
Wakefield Kirkgate 4 31 a	21 06							22 06				
d	21 07							22 07				
Darton d	21 18							22 21				
Huddersfield d						21 18				22 18		
Lockwood d						21 21				22 21		
Berry Brow d						21 24				22 24		
Honley d						21 27				22 27		
Brockholes d						21 30				22 30		
Stocksmoor d						21 34				22 34		
Shepley d						21 36				22 36		
Denby Dale d						21 41				22 41		
Penistone d						21 49				22 49		
Silkstone Common d						21 54				22 54		
Dodworth d						21 58				22 58		
Barnsley a	21 24					22 05		22 27		23 05		
d	21 24					22 06		22 28		23 06		
Wombwell d	21 29					22 11		22 33		23 11		
Elsecar d	21 33							22 37		23 15		
Chapeltown d	21 38					22 18		22 42		23 20		
Meadowhall 29,31 a	21 45	21 49				22 24		22 47	22 52	23 25	23 43	
d	21 46	21 50	21 59	22 03	22 12	22 25	22 43	22 48	22 53	23 26	23 44	23 49
Sheffield 7 29,31 a	21 57	22 02	22 10	22 13	22 22	22 36	22 54	22 58	23 03	23 36	23 58	23 59
d												
Dronfield d												
Chesterfield d												
Alfreton d												
Langley Mill d												
Nottingham a												

A From Scarborough
B From Hull
C To Sheffield
D From Leeds
E From Doncaster
F From Cleethorpes to Manchester Airport
G From Scunthorpe to Worksop
H From Cleethorpes
I From Liverpool Lime Street
J To Retford
K From Bridlington
L From Scunthorpe

Leeds and Huddersfield - Barnsley - Sheffield, Nottingham

Network Diagram - see first page of Table 31

		NT	NT A	NT	NT	TP ◇1 B	NT	NT C	NT	NT A		TP ◇1 D	NT	NT C	NT	NT	TP ◇1 D	NT	NT E	NT		NT A	NT F	NT	NT G
Leeds 10 31	d	22p37		23p09											06 38	06 43		07 05					07 29	07 35	
Woodlesford	d	22p45													06 46								07 37		
Castleford	d	22p56													06 57								07 48		
Normanton	d	23p01													07 03								07 54		←
Wakefield Kirkgate 4 31	a	23p10													07 07			07 25					08 00	07 54	08 00
	d	23p10													07 08			07 25					08 04	07 55	08 04
Darton	d	23p24													07 19								→		08 15
Huddersfield	d												06 05							07 05					
Lockwood	d												06 08							07 08					
Berry Brow	d												06 11							07 11					
Honley	d												06 14							07 14					
Brockholes	d												06 17							07 17					
Stocksmoor	d												06 21							07 21					
Shepley	d												06 23							07 23					
Denby Dale	d												06 34							07 34					
Penistone	d												06 42							07 42					
Silkstone Common	d												06 47							07 47					
Dodworth	d												06 51							07 51					
Barnsley	a	23p31											06 57		07 25			07 40		07 57				08 11	08 21
	d	23p31			05 23		05 50		06 21				06 58		07 25			07 40		07 58				08 14	08 24
Wombwell	d	23p36			05 28		05 55		06 26				07 03		07 30					08 03					08 29
Elsecar	d	23p40			05 32		05 59		06 30				07 07		07 34					08 07					08 33
Chapeltown	d	23p45			05 37		06 04		06 35				07 12		07 39					08 12					08 38
Meadowhall 29,31 ⇌	a	23p51		00 08	05 43		06 10		06 41				07 21		07 48	07 46		07 53		08 20				08 31	08 45
	d	23p51	23p54	00 09	05 43	05 58	06 10	06 30	06 42	06 52		06 58	07 21	07 32	07 49	07 47	07 53	07 54	08 07	08 21		08 25		08 31	08 46
Sheffield 7 29,31 ⇌	a	00 02	00 04	00 23	05 54	06 08	06 25	06 38	06 55	07 05		07 06	07 29	07 40	07 58	07 54	08 00	08 05	08 18	08 29		08 32		08 39	08 56
	d								07 03									08 05							
Dronfield	d								07 13									08 15							
Chesterfield	d								07 20									08 24							
Alfreton	d								07 33									08 35							
Langley Mill	d								07 40									08 42							
Nottingham	a								08 02									09 02							

		NT	NT	NT E	TP ◇1 D	NT		NT H	NT F	NT	NT I	NT G	NT	NT	NT E	TP ◇1 D		NT H	NT	NT F	NT	NT I	NT G	NT	NT
Leeds 10 31	d	07 48	08 05						08 32	08 37			08 48	09 05						09 32	09 37			09 48	10 05
Woodlesford	d								08 40											09 40					
Castleford	d								08 51											09 51					
Normanton	d								08 57			←								09 57			←		
Wakefield Kirkgate 4 31	a		08 23						09 03	08 54		09 03		09 23						10 01	09 55		10 01		10 23
	d		08 23						09 05	08 55		09 05		09 23						10 04	09 56		10 04		10 23
Darton	d								→			09 17								→			10 15		
Huddersfield	d					08 07													09 08						
Lockwood	d					08 10													09 11						
Berry Brow	d					08 13													09 14						
Honley	d					08 16													09 17						
Brockholes	d					08 19													09 20						
Stocksmoor	d					08 23													09 24						
Shepley	d					08 25													09 26						
Denby Dale	d					08 34													09 36						
Penistone	d					08 42													09 44						
Silkstone Common	d					08 47													09 49						
Dodworth	d					08 51													09 53						
Barnsley	a		08 39			08 57				09 11		09 23		09 39					10 00		10 12		10 21		10 39
	d		08 40			08 58				09 14		09 24		09 40					10 01		10 14		10 24		10 40
Wombwell	d					09 03						09 29							10 06				10 29		
Elsecar	d					09 07						09 33											10 33		
Chapeltown	d					09 12						09 38							10 13				10 38		
Meadowhall 29,31 ⇌	a	08 49	08 52			09 19				09 27		09 46	09 50	09 52					10 20		10 27		10 46	10 50	10 52
	d	08 51	08 52	08 56	09 01	09 20		09 24		09 29	09 33	09 46	09 50	09 52	09 55	10 01		10 08	10 21		10 28	10 33	10 47	10 50	10 52
Sheffield 7 29,31 ⇌	a	08 59	09 02	09 05	09 08	09 28		09 33		09 37	09 41	09 56	10 00	10 02	10 05	10 08		10 19	10 30		10 37	10 41	10 56	11 00	11 02
	d		09 05											10 04											11 05
Dronfield	d		09 16											10 14											11 15
Chesterfield	d		09 23											10 21											11 22
Alfreton	d		09 32											10 32											11 35
Langley Mill	d		09 41											10 40											11 40
Nottingham	a		10 00											11 00											12 00

A From Hull
B From Doncaster to Manchester Airport
C From Doncaster
D From Cleethorpes to Manchester Airport
E From Adwick
F To Sheffield
G From Leeds
H From Bridlington
I From Scunthorpe to Lincoln

Leeds and Huddersfield - Barnsley - Sheffield, Nottingham

Network Diagram - see first page of Table 31

		NT A		TP ◇1 B	NT C	NT	NT D	NT	NT E	NT F	NT	NT		NT A	TP ◇1 B	NT C	NT	NT G	NT D	NT	NT E	NT F		NT	NT
Leeds 10 31	d						10 32	10 37			10 48	11 05							11 32	11 37				11 48	12 05
Woodlesford	d						10 40												11 40						
Castleford	d						10 51												11 51						
Normanton	d						10 57			←									11 57			←			
Wakefield Kirkgate 4 31	a						11 01	10 54		11 01		11 23							12 01	11 54		12 01			12 23
	d						11 04	10 55		11 04		11 23							12 04	11 55		12 04			12 23
Darton	d						→			11 15									→			12 15			
Huddersfield	d					10 08											11 08								
Lockwood	d					10 11											11 11								
Berry Brow	d					10 14											11 14								
Honley	d					10 17											11 17								
Brockholes	d					10 20											11 20								
Stocksmoor	d					10 24											11 24								
Shepley	d					10 26											11 26								
Denby Dale	d					10 36											11 36								
Penistone	d					10 44											11 44								
Silkstone Common	d					10 49											11 49								
Dodworth	d					10 53											11 53								
Barnsley	a					11 00		11 11		11 21		11 39					12 00			12 11		12 21			12 39
	d					11 01		11 14		11 24		11 40					12 01			12 14		12 24			12 40
Wombwell	d					11 06				11 29							12 06					12 29			
Elsecar	d									11 33												12 33			
Chapeltown	d					11 13				11 38							12 13					12 38			
Meadowhall 29,31 ⇌	a					11 18		11 27		11 46	11 50	11 52					12 20			12 27		12 46		12 49	12 52
	d	10 58		11 01	11 08	11 19		11 28	11 33	11 46	11 50	11 52		11 58	12 01	12 08	12 21	12 24		12 28	12 33	12 46		12 50	12 52
Sheffield 7 29,31 ⇌	a	11 06		11 08	11 20	11 30		11 37	11 41	11 57	12 00	12 02		12 05	12 08	12 20	12 30	12 36		12 37	12 41	12 56		13 00	13 02
	d											12 05													13 05
Dronfield	d											12 15													13 15
Chesterfield	d											12 22													13 22
Alfreton	d											12 33													13 33
Langley Mill	d											12 40													13 40
Nottingham	a											13 01													14 00

		NT A	TP ◇1 B	NT C	NT	NT D	NT	NT E		NT F	NT	NT	NT A	TP ◇1 B	NT H	NT	NT D	NT		NT E	NT F	NT	NT	NT A	TP ◇1 B
Leeds 10 31	d					12 32	12 37				12 48	13 05					13 32	13 37				13 48	14 05		
Woodlesford	d					12 40											13 40								
Castleford	d					12 51											13 51								
Normanton	d					12 57				←							13 57				←				
Wakefield Kirkgate 4 31	a					13 02	12 54			13 02		13 23					14 01	13 54			14 01		14 23		
	d					13 04	12 55			13 04		13 23					14 04	13 55			14 04		14 23		
Darton	d					→				13 17							→				14 15				
Huddersfield	d				12 08											13 08									
Lockwood	d				12 11											13 11									
Berry Brow	d				12 14											13 14									
Honley	d				12 17											13 17									
Brockholes	d				12 20											13 20									
Stocksmoor	d				12 24											13 24									
Shepley	d				12 26											13 26									
Denby Dale	d				12 36											13 36									
Penistone	d				12 44											13 44									
Silkstone Common	d				12 49											13 49									
Dodworth	d				12 53											13 53									
Barnsley	a				13 00		13 11			13 22		13 38				14 00		14 11			14 21		14 39		
	d				13 01		13 14			13 24		13 40				14 01		14 14			14 24		14 40		
Wombwell	d				13 06					13 29						14 06					14 29				
Elsecar	d									13 33											14 33				
Chapeltown	d				13 13					13 38						14 13					14 38				
Meadowhall 29,31 ⇌	a				13 20		13 27			13 46	13 49	13 52				14 20		14 27			14 46	14 49	14 52		
	d	12 58	13 01	13 08	13 21		13 28	13 33		13 46	13 50	13 52	13 58	14 01	14 08	14 21		14 28		14 33	14 46	14 50	14 52	14 58	15 01
Sheffield 7 29,31 ⇌	a	13 05	13 08	13 20	13 29		13 37	13 41		13 56	14 00	14 02	14 05	14 08	14 20	14 29		14 37		14 40	14 56	15 00	15 02	15 05	15 08
	d											14 05											15 05		
Dronfield	d											14 15											15 15		
Chesterfield	d											14 22											15 22		
Alfreton	d											14 33											15 33		
Langley Mill	d											14 40											15 40		
Nottingham	a											15 00											16 00		

A From Adwick
B From Cleethorpes to Manchester Airport
C From Bridlington
D To Sheffield
E From Scunthorpe to Lincoln
F From Leeds
G From Sheffield
H From Scarborough

Table 34

Saturdays
from 6 October

Leeds and Huddersfield - Barnsley - Sheffield, Nottingham

Network Diagram - see first page of Table 31

		NT A	NT	NT B	NT	NT C	NT D	NT	NT	NT E	TP ◇1 F	NT G	NT H	NT	NT B	NT	EM ◇ I	NT C	NT D	NT	NT	NT J
Leeds 10	31 d			14 32	14 37			14 48	15 05						15 32	15 37				15 48	16 05	
Woodlesford	d			14 40											15 40							
Castleford	d			14 51											15 51							
Normanton	d			14 57			←								15 57				←			
Wakefield Kirkgate 4	31 a			15 01	14 54		15 01		15 23						16 01	15 54			16 01		16 23	
	d			15 04	14 55		15 04		15 23						16 04	15 55			16 04		16 23	
Darton	d			→			15 15								→				16 15			
Huddersfield	d		14 08											15 08								
Lockwood	d		14 11											15 11								
Berry Brow	d		14 14											15 14								
Honley	d		14 17											15 17								
Brockholes	d		14 20											15 20								
Stocksmoor	d		14 24											15 24								
Shepley	d		14 26											15 26								
Denby Dale	d		14 36											15 36								
Penistone	d		14 44											15 44								
Silkstone Common	d		14 49											15 49								
Dodworth	d		14 53											15 53								
Barnsley	a		15 00		15 13		15 21		15 39					16 00		16 11			16 21		16 39	
	d		15 01		15 14		15 24		15 40					16 01		16 14			16 24		16 40	
Wombwell	d		15 06				15 29							16 06					16 29			
Elsecar	d						15 33												16 33			
Chapeltown	d		15 13				15 38							16 13					16 38			
Meadowhall	29,31 ⇌ a		15 20		15 27		15 46	15 49	15 51					16 20		16 27			16 46	16 49	16 52	
	d	15 07	15 21		15 28	15 33	15 46	15 50	15 52	15 57	16 01	16 07	16 18	16 21		16 28		16 33	16 46	16 50	16 52	16 55
Sheffield 7	29,31 ⇌ a	15 20	15 29		15 37	15 41	15 56	16 00	16 03	16 05	16 08	16 22	16 27	16 29		16 37		16 41	16 56	17 00	17 02	17 05
	d								16 04								16 38				17 05	
Dronfield	d								16 14								16 48				17 15	
Chesterfield	d								16 21								16 53				17 22	
Alfreton	d								16 32								17 04				17 33	
Langley Mill	d								16 40												17 40	
Nottingham	a								17 00								17 29				18 00	

		TP ◇1 F	NT A	NT	NT B	NT	NT C	EM ◇ I	NT D	NT	NT	NT K	TP ◇1 F	NT A	NT	NT B	NT	NT C	NT D	NT	NT	NT K	TP ◇1 F
Leeds 10	31 d				16 32	16 37				16 48	17 05					17 32	17 37			17 48	18 05		
Woodlesford	d				16 40											17 40							
Castleford	d				16 51											17 51							
Normanton	d				16 57				←		17 18					17 57			←				
Wakefield Kirkgate 4	31 a				17 01	16 54			17 01		17 22					18 01	17 54		18 01		18 23		
	d				17 04	16 55			17 04		17 23					18 04	17 55		18 04		18 23		
Darton	d				→				17 15							→			18 15				
Huddersfield	d			16 08											17 13								
Lockwood	d			16 11											17 16								
Berry Brow	d			16 14											17 19								
Honley	d			16 17											17 22								
Brockholes	d			16 20											17 25								
Stocksmoor	d			16 24											17 29								
Shepley	d			16 26											17 31								
Denby Dale	d			16 36											17 36								
Penistone	d			16 44											17 44								
Silkstone Common	d			16 49											17 49								
Dodworth	d			16 53											17 53								
Barnsley	a			17 00		17 11			17 21		17 39				18 00		18 11		18 21		18 39		
	d			17 01		17 14			17 24		17 40				18 01		18 14		18 24		18 40		
Wombwell	d			17 06					17 29						18 06				18 29				
Elsecar	d								17 33										18 33				
Chapeltown	d			17 13					17 38						18 13				18 38				
Meadowhall	29,31 ⇌ a			17 20		17 27			17 46	17 49	17 51				18 20		18 27		18 46	18 50	18 52		
	d	17 01	17 08	17 21		17 28	17 33		17 46	17 50	17 52	17 57	18 01	18 08	18 21		18 28	18 33	18 46	18 50	18 52	18 56	19 01
Sheffield 7	29,31 ⇌ a	17 08	17 19	17 32		17 37	17 41		17 56	18 00	18 03	18 05	18 08	18 21	18 29		18 38	18 41	18 56	19 00	19 03	19 06	19 08
	d							17 44			18 06										19 05		
Dronfield	d							17 55			18 15										19 15		
Chesterfield	d							18 01			18 22										19 22		
Alfreton	d							18 11			18 33										19 33		
Langley Mill	d										18 40										19 40		
Nottingham	a							18 33			19 00										20 00		

A From Bridlington
B To Sheffield
C From Scunthorpe to Lincoln
D From Leeds
E From Adwick
F From Cleethorpes to Manchester Airport
G From Scarborough
H From York
I From Liverpool Lime Street to Norwich
J From Adwick to Retford
K From Doncaster

Table 34

Saturdays
from 6 October

Leeds and Huddersfield - Barnsley - Sheffield, Nottingham

Network Diagram - see first page of Table 31

		NT A	NT	NT B	NT C	NT	NT D	NT	NT	NT E	TP ◇1 F	NT B	NT	NT G	NT C	NT	NT D	NT	TP ◇1 H	NT	EM ◇ I	NT J	NT K
Leeds 10	31 d				18 32	18 37		18 48	19 05						19 37	19 43		19 48		20 30			
Woodlesford	d				18 40										19 45								
Castleford	d				18 51										19 56								
Normanton	d				19 00		←								20 02		←						
Wakefield Kirkgate 4	31 a				19 04	18 54	19 04		19 24						20 06	19 59	20 06			20 46			
	d				19 05	18 55	19 05		19 24						20 07	20 00	20 07			20 46			
Darton	d				→		19 19								→		20 19						
Huddersfield	d		18 08										19 15									20 15	
Lockwood	d		18 11										19 18									20 18	
Berry Brow	d		18 14										19 21									20 21	
Honley	d		18 17										19 24									20 24	
Brockholes	d		18 20										19 27									20 27	
Stocksmoor	d		18 24										19 31									20 31	
Shepley	d		18 26										19 33									20 33	
Denby Dale	d		18 36										19 41									20 41	
Penistone	d		18 44										19 49									20 52	
Silkstone Common	d		18 49										19 54									20 57	
Dodworth	d		18 53										19 58									21 01	
Barnsley	a		19 01			19 11	19 26		19 40				20 05			20 16	20 24			21 02		21 09	
	d		19 01			19 14	19 26		19 40				20 06			20 16	20 24			21 03		21 12	
Wombwell	d		19 06				19 31						20 11				20 29					21 17	
Elsecar	d						19 35										20 33						
Chapeltown	d		19 13				19 40						20 18				20 38					21 24	
Meadowhall	29,31 ⇌ a		19 20			19 28	19 47	19 50	19 52				20 24			20 33	20 45	20 50		21 19		21 28	
	d	19 08	19 20	19 28		19 30	19 47	19 51	19 52	19 57	20 01	20 08	20 24	20 33		20 35	20 46	20 51	21 09	21 20		21 29	21 35
Sheffield 7	29,31 ⇌ a	19 17	19 30	19 37		19 39	19 56	20 00	20 04	20 06	20 08	20 18	20 36	20 41		20 44	20 58	21 00	21 19	21 30		21 41	21 46
	d								20 05												21 38		
Dronfield	d								20 15												21 48		
Chesterfield	d								20 22												21 54		
Alfreton	d								20 33												22 05		
Langley Mill	d								20 40												22 12		
Nottingham	a								21 00												22 33		

		NT	NT	TP ◇1 H	NT E	NT B	NT	NT L	NT	NT	NT	NT	NT K
Leeds 10	31 d	20 37	20 48						21 37	21 48		22 44	
Woodlesford	d	20 45							21 45				
Castleford	d	20 56							21 56				
Normanton	d	21 02							22 02				
Wakefield Kirkgate 4	31 a	21 06							22 06				
	d	21 07							22 07				
Darton	d	21 18							22 21				
Huddersfield	d						21 15				22 15		
Lockwood	d						21 18				22 18		
Berry Brow	d						21 21				22 21		
Honley	d						21 24				22 24		
Brockholes	d						21 27				22 27		
Stocksmoor	d						21 31				22 31		
Shepley	d						21 33				22 33		
Denby Dale	d						21 41				22 41		
Penistone	d						21 49				22 49		
Silkstone Common	d						21 54				22 54		
Dodworth	d						21 58				22 58		
Barnsley	a	21 24					22 05		22 27		23 05		
	d	21 24					22 06		22 28		23 06		
Wombwell	d	21 29					22 11		22 33		23 11		
Elsecar	d	21 33							22 37		23 15		
Chapeltown	d	21 38					22 18		22 42		23 20		
Meadowhall	29,31 ⇌ a	21 45	21 49				22 24		22 47	22 52	23 25	23 43	
	d	21 46	21 50	21 59	22 03	22 12	22 25	22 43	22 48	22 53	23 26	23 44	23 49
Sheffield 7	29,31 ⇌ a	21 57	22 02	22 10	22 13	22 22	22 36	22 54	22 58	23 03	23 36	23 58	23 59
	d												
Dronfield	d												
Chesterfield	d												
Alfreton	d												
Langley Mill	d												
Nottingham	a												

A From Scarborough
B From Hull
C To Sheffield
D From Leeds
E From Doncaster
F From Cleethorpes to Manchester Airport
G From Scunthorpe to Worksop
H From Cleethorpes
I From Liverpool Lime Street
J To Retford
K From Bridlington
L From Scunthorpe

Leeds and Huddersfield - Barnsley - Sheffield, Nottingham

Network Diagram - see first page of Table 31

			NT	NT	TP	NT	NT	NT	NT	NT	NT	NT	NT	TP	NT	NT	NT	NT	TP	NT	NT	NT	NT	NT
			A		◇1 B	A				C		D		◇1 E			A		◇1 E	F				D
Leeds 10	31	d					08 34	08 48	09 05				10 02			10 17		10 57			11 18	11 29		
Woodlesford		d					08 42									10 25								
Castleford		d					08 53									10 36								
Normanton		d					08 58									10 41								
Wakefield Kirkgate 4	31	a					09 03		09 21				10 18			10 46		11 13				11 46		
		d					09 03		09 21				10 18			10 46		11 13				11 46		
Darton		d					09 17									11 00								
Huddersfield		d									09 19				10 15								11 29	
Lockwood		d									09 22				10 18								11 32	
Berry Brow		d									09 25				10 21								11 35	
Honley		d									09 28				10 24								11 38	
Brockholes		d									09 31				10 27								11 41	
Stocksmoor		d									09 35				10 31								11 45	
Shepley		d									09 37				10 33								11 47	
Denby Dale		d									09 42				10 39								11 52	
Penistone		d									09 50				10 46								12 00	
Silkstone Common		d									09 55				10 52								12 05	
Dodworth		d									09 59				10 55								12 09	
Barnsley		a					09 24		09 40		10 06		10 37		11 03	11 08		11 32				12 05	12 16	
		d					09 24		09 41		10 12		10 38		11 03	11 12		11 33				12 06	12 17	
Wombwell		d					09 29				10 17					11 17							12 22	
Elsecar		d					09 33				10 21					11 21							12 26	
Chapeltown		d					09 38				10 26					11 26							12 31	
Meadowhall	29,31 ⇌	a					09 44	09 53	09 57		10 32		10 51		11 20	11 32		11 46			12 20	12 17	12 34	
		d	08 30		09 00	09 41	09 44	09 54	09 57	10 00	10 33	10 40	10 51	11 00	11 20	11 35	11 40	11 46	12 00	12 08	12 21	12 17	12 35	12 43
Sheffield 7	29,31 ⇌	a	08 41		09 07	09 51	09 55	10 03	10 04	10 08	10 43	10 52	11 02	11 07	11 28	11 44	11 51	11 56	12 07	12 18	12 32	12 29	12 47	12 55
		d		09 00					10 07				11 03					12 00				12 31		
Dronfield		d		09 10					10 17				11 13					12 10				12 42		
Chesterfield		d		09 17					10 23				11 20					12 18				12 49		
Alfreton		d		09 28					10 33				11 30					12 28				12 59		
Langley Mill		d		09 35					10 41				11 38					12 36				13 07		
Nottingham		a		09 53					10 57				11 54					12 52				13 24		

			TP	NT	NT	NT	NT	TP	NT	NT	NT	NT	NT	TP	NT	NT	NT	NT	NT	TP	NT	NT	NT	NT
			◇1 E		A		G	◇1 H			D	G		◇1 E			A	F		◇1 E			D	G
Leeds 10	31	d		12 29		12 34			13 18				14 06			14 17			15 06		15 18			
Woodlesford		d				12 42										14 25								
Castleford		d				12 53										14 36								
Normanton		d				12 58										14 41								
Wakefield Kirkgate 4	31	a		12 46		13 04							14 22			14 46			15 22					
		d		12 46		13 04							14 22			14 46			15 22					
Darton		d				13 18										15 00								
Huddersfield		d								13 19					14 15							15 19		
Lockwood		d								13 22					14 18							15 22		
Berry Brow		d								13 25					14 21							15 25		
Honley		d								13 28					14 24							15 28		
Brockholes		d								13 31					14 27							15 31		
Stocksmoor		d								13 35					14 31							15 35		
Shepley		d								13 37					14 33							15 37		
Denby Dale		d								13 42					14 39							15 42		
Penistone		d								13 50					14 46							15 50		
Silkstone Common		d								13 55					14 52							15 55		
Dodworth		d								13 59					14 55							15 59		
Barnsley		a		13 05		13 24				14 06			14 41		15 03	15 07			15 41			16 06		
		d		13 06		13 24				14 12			14 42		15 03	15 12			15 42			16 12		
Wombwell		d				13 29				14 17						15 17						16 17		
Elsecar		d				13 33				14 21						15 21						16 21		
Chapeltown		d				13 38				14 26						15 26						16 26		
Meadowhall	29,31 ⇌	a		13 18		13 48			14 20	14 32			14 55		15 20	15 35			15 55		16 19	16 32		
		d	13 00	13 18	13 44	13 51	13 56	14 00	14 21	14 33	14 48	14 52	14 56	15 00	15 21	15 35	15 48	15 52	15 56	16 00	16 19	16 34	16 47	16 53
Sheffield 7	29,31 ⇌	a	13 07	13 29	13 52	13 58	14 06	14 07	14 32	14 48	14 55	15 03	15 06	15 07	15 28	15 44	15 55	16 01	16 05	16 07	16 31	16 44	16 55	17 04
		d		13 31									15 07						16 07					
Dronfield		d		13 42									15 17						16 17					
Chesterfield		d		13 48									15 24						16 23					
Alfreton		d		13 59									15 34						16 33					
Langley Mill		d		14 06									15 42						16 41					
Nottingham		a		14 22									15 59						16 56					

A From Doncaster
B To Manchester Piccadilly
C From Hull
D From Goole
E From Cleethorpes to Manchester Airport
F From Bridlington
G From Scarborough
H From Doncaster to Manchester Airport

Leeds and Huddersfield - Barnsley - Sheffield, Nottingham

Network Diagram - see first page of Table 31

			NT	TP	NT	NT	NT	NT	TP	NT	NT	NT	NT	NT	TP	NT	NT	NT	NT	NT	TP	NT	NT
				◇1 A		B	C		◇1 A			B	D		◇1 A	E		B		C	◇1 A		
Leeds 10	31	d	16 06		16 17			17 06		17 18				18 06			18 17		19 06			19 18	
Woodlesford		d			16 25												18 25						
Castleford		d			16 36												18 36						
Normanton		d			16 41												18 40						
Wakefield Kirkgate 4	31	a	16 22		16 46			17 22						18 22			18 45		19 22				
		d	16 22		16 46			17 22						18 22			18 45		19 22				
Darton		d			17 00												18 59						
Huddersfield		d									17 19												19 19
Lockwood		d									17 22												19 22
Berry Brow		d									17 25												19 25
Honley		d									17 28												19 28
Brockholes		d									17 31												19 31
Stocksmoor		d									17 35												19 35
Shepley		d									17 37												19 37
Denby Dale		d									17 47												19 42
Penistone		d									17 54												19 50
Silkstone Common		d									18 00												19 55
Dodworth		d									18 03												19 59
Barnsley		a	16 41		17 07			17 41			18 11			18 41			19 05		19 40				20 06
		d	16 42		17 12			17 42			18 12			18 42			19 11		19 41				20 12
Wombwell		d			17 17						18 17						19 17						20 17
Elsecar		d			17 21						18 21						19 21						20 21
Chapeltown		d			17 26						18 26						19 26						20 26
Meadowhall	29,31 ⇌	a	16 56		17 34			17 55		18 25	18 32			18 56			19 32		19 54			20 22	20 34
		d	16 56	17 00	17 35	17 48	17 53	17 56	18 00	18 25	18 33	18 47	18 53	18 56	19 00	19 18	19 33	19 47	19 54	19 57	20 00	20 23	20 34
Sheffield 7	29,31 ⇌	a	17 05	17 07	17 44	17 55	18 01	18 05	18 08	18 36	18 44	18 57	19 03	19 05	19 07	19 27	19 43	19 55	20 04	20 06	20 07	20 34	20 43
		d	17 07					18 07						19 07					20 06				
Dronfield		d	17 17					18 17						19 17					20 16				
Chesterfield		d	17 23					18 25						19 25					20 23				
Alfreton		d	17 33					18 36						19 36					20 34				
Langley Mill		d	17 41					18 43						19 43					20 41				
Nottingham		a	17 58					19 00						20 00					20 57				

			NT	TP	NT	EM	NT	NT	TP	NT	NT	NT	NT
			B	◇1 A	D	◇ F		E	◇1 G			H	
Leeds 10	31	d					20 17				21 40		22 17
Woodlesford		d					20 25						22 25
Castleford		d					20 36						22 36
Normanton		d					20 41						22 41
Wakefield Kirkgate 4	31	a					20 46						22 46
		d					20 46						22 46
Darton		d					21 00						23 00
Huddersfield		d											
Lockwood		d											
Berry Brow		d											
Honley		d											
Brockholes		d											
Stocksmoor		d											
Shepley		d											
Denby Dale		d											
Penistone		d											
Silkstone Common		d											
Dodworth		d											
Barnsley		a					21 07						23 07
		d					21 12			22 21			23 12
Wombwell		d					21 17			22 26			23 17
Elsecar		d					21 21			22 30			23 21
Chapeltown		d					21 26			22 35			23 26
Meadowhall	29,31 ⇌	a					21 33			22 40	22 45		23 30
		d	20 47	21 00	21 28		21 33	21 58	22 04	22 41	22 45	23 04	23 32
Sheffield 7	29,31 ⇌	a	20 55	21 07	21 38		21 42	22 09	22 13	22 51	22 54	23 15	23 43
		d				21 40							
Dronfield		d				21 50							
Chesterfield		d				21 56							
Alfreton		d				22 07							
Langley Mill		d				22 14							
Nottingham		a				22 35							

A From Cleethorpes to Manchester Airport
B From Doncaster
C From Bridlington
D From Scarborough
E From Sheffield
F From Liverpool Lime Street
G From Cleethorpes
H From Hull

Table 34

Sundays
24 June to 9 September

Leeds and Huddersfield - Barnsley - Sheffield, Nottingham

Network Diagram - see first page of Table 31

		NT	NT	TP	NT	NT	NT	NT	NT	NT	NT	NT	TP	NT	NT	NT	NT	TP	NT	NT	NT	NT	NT
		A		◇1 B	A				C		D		◇1 E			A		◇1 E	F				D
Leeds 10 (31)	d					08 34	08 48	09 05				10 02			10 17		10 57			11 18	11 29		
Woodlesford	d					08 42									10 25								
Castleford	d					08 53									10 36								
Normanton	d					08 58									10 41								
Wakefield Kirkgate 4 (31)	a					09 03		09 21				10 18			10 46		11 13				11 46		
	d					09 03		09 21				10 18			10 46		11 13				11 46		
Darton	d					09 17									11 00								
Huddersfield	d									09 19				10 15								11 29	
Lockwood	d									09 22				10 18								11 32	
Berry Brow	d									09 25				10 21								11 35	
Honley	d									09 28				10 24								11 38	
Brockholes	d									09 31				10 27								11 41	
Stocksmoor	d									09 35				10 31								11 45	
Shepley	d									09 37				10 33								11 47	
Denby Dale	d									09 42				10 39								11 52	
Penistone	d									09 50				10 46								12 00	
Silkstone Common	d									09 55				10 52								12 05	
Dodworth	d									09 59				10 55								12 09	
Barnsley	a					09 24		09 40		10 06		10 37		11 03	11 08		11 32				12 05	12 16	
	d					09 24		09 41		10 12		10 38		11 03	11 12		11 33				12 06	12 17	
Wombwell	d					09 29				10 17					11 17							12 22	
Elsecar	d					09 33				10 21					11 21							12 26	
Chapeltown	d					09 38				10 26					11 26							12 31	
Meadowhall (29,31) ⇌	a					09 44	09 53	09 57		10 32		10 51		11 20	11 32		11 46			12 20	12 17	12 34	
	d	08 30		09 00	09 41	09 44	09 54	09 57	10 00	10 33	10 40	10 51	11 00	11 20	11 35	11 40	11 46	12 00	12 08	12 21	12 17	12 35	12 43
Sheffield 7 (29,31) ⇌	a	08 41		09 07	09 51	09 55	10 03	10 04	10 08	10 43	10 52	11 02	11 07	11 28	11 44	11 51	11 56	12 07	12 18	12 32	12 29	12 47	12 55
	d		09 00					10 07				11 03					12 00				12 31		
Dronfield	d		09 10					10 17				11 13					12 10				12 42		
Chesterfield	d		09 17					10 23				11 20					12 18				12 49		
Alfreton	d		09 28					10 33				11 30					12 28				12 59		
Langley Mill	d		09 35					10 41				11 38					12 36				13 07		
Nottingham	a		09 53					10 57				11 54					12 52				13 24		

		TP	NT	NT	NT	NT	TP	NT	NT	NT	NT	NT	TP	NT	NT	NT	NT	NT	TP	NT	NT	NT	NT
		◇1 E		A		G	◇1 H			D	G		◇1 E			A	F		◇1 E	I	J		D
Leeds 10 (31)	d		12 29		12 34			13 18				14 06			14 17			15 06		15 18	15 18		
Woodlesford	d				12 42										14 25								
Castleford	d				12 53										14 36								
Normanton	d				12 58										14 41								
Wakefield Kirkgate 4 (31)	a		12 46		13 04							14 22			14 46			15 22					
	d		12 46		13 04							14 22			14 46			15 22					
Darton	d				13 18										15 00								
Huddersfield	d								13 19					14 15								15 19	
Lockwood	d								13 22					14 18								15 22	
Berry Brow	d								13 25					14 21								15 25	
Honley	d								13 28					14 24								15 28	
Brockholes	d								13 31					14 27								15 31	
Stocksmoor	d								13 35					14 31								15 35	
Shepley	d								13 37					14 33								15 37	
Denby Dale	d								13 42					14 39								15 42	
Penistone	d								13 50					14 46								15 50	
Silkstone Common	d								13 55					14 52								15 55	
Dodworth	d								13 59					14 55								15 59	
Barnsley	a		13 05		13 24				14 06			14 41		15 03	15 07			15 41				16 06	
	d		13 06		13 24				14 12			14 42		15 03	15 12			15 42				16 12	
Wombwell	d				13 29				14 17						15 17							16 17	
Elsecar	d				13 33				14 21						15 21							16 21	
Chapeltown	d				13 38				14 26						15 26							16 26	
Meadowhall (29,31) ⇌	a		13 18		13 48			14 20	14 32			14 55		15 20	15 35			15 55		16 19	16 20	16 32	
	d	13 00	13 18	13 44	13 51	13 56	14 00	14 21	14 33	14 48	14 52	14 56	15 00	15 21	15 35	15 48	15 52	15 56	16 00	16 19	16 21	16 34	16 47
Sheffield 7 (29,31) ⇌	a	13 07	13 29	13 52	13 58	14 06	14 07	14 32	14 48	14 55	15 03	15 06	15 07	15 28	15 44	15 55	16 01	16 05	16 07	16 31	16 32	16 44	16 55
	d		13 31									15 07						16 07					
Dronfield	d		13 42									15 17						16 17					
Chesterfield	d		13 48									15 24						16 23					
Alfreton	d		13 59									15 34						16 33					
Langley Mill	d		14 06									15 42						16 41					
Nottingham	a		14 22									15 59						16 56					

A From Doncaster
B To Manchester Piccadilly
C From Hull
D From Goole
E From Cleethorpes to Manchester Airport
F From Bridlington
G From Scarborough
H From Doncaster to Manchester Airport
I 24 June
J not 24 June

Table 34

Sundays
24 June to 9 September

Leeds and Huddersfield - Barnsley - Sheffield, Nottingham

Network Diagram - see first page of Table 31

		NT	NT	TP	NT	NT	NT	NT	TP	TP	NT	NT	NT	NT	NT	TP	NT	NT	NT	NT	NT	TP
		A		◇1 B		C	D		◇1 E	◇1 F			C	A		◇1 B	G		C		D	◇1 B
Leeds 10 (31)	d		16 06		16 17			17 06			17 18				18 06			18 17		19 06		
Woodlesford	d				16 25													18 25				
Castleford	d				16 36													18 36				
Normanton	d				16 41													18 40				
Wakefield Kirkgate 4 (31)	a		16 22		16 46			17 22							18 22			18 45		19 22		
	d		16 22		16 46			17 22							18 22			18 45		19 22		
Darton	d				17 00													18 59				
Huddersfield	d											17 19										
Lockwood	d											17 22										
Berry Brow	d											17 25										
Honley	d											17 28										
Brockholes	d											17 31										
Stocksmoor	d											17 35										
Shepley	d											17 37										
Denby Dale	d											17 47										
Penistone	d											17 54										
Silkstone Common	d											18 00										
Dodworth	d											18 03										
Barnsley	a		16 41		17 07			17 41				18 11			18 41			19 05		19 40		
	d		16 42		17 12			17 42				18 12			18 42			19 11		19 41		
Wombwell	d				17 17							18 17						19 17				
Elsecar	d				17 21							18 21						19 21				
Chapeltown	d				17 26							18 26						19 26				
Meadowhall (29,31) ⇌	a		16 56		17 34			17 55			18 25	18 32			18 56			19 32		19 54		
	d	16 53	16 56	17 00	17 35	17 48	17 53	17 56	18 00	18 00	18 25	18 33	18 47	18 53	18 56	19 00	19 18	19 33	19 47	19 54	19 57	20 00
Sheffield 7 (29,31) ⇌	a	17 04	17 05	17 07	17 44	17 55	18 01	18 05	18 07	18 08	18 36	18 44	18 57	19 03	19 05	19 07	19 27	19 43	19 55	20 04	20 06	20 07
	d		17 07					18 07							19 07					20 06		
Dronfield	d		17 17					18 17							19 17					20 16		
Chesterfield	d		17 23					18 25							19 25					20 23		
Alfreton	d		17 33					18 36							19 36					20 34		
Langley Mill	d		17 41					18 43							19 43					20 41		
Nottingham	a		17 58					19 00							20 00					20 57		

		NT	NT	NT	NT	TP	NT	EM	NT	NT	TP	NT	NT	NT	NT
		H	I		C	◇1 B	A	◇ J		G	◇1 K			L	
Leeds 10 (31)	d	19 18	19 18						20 17				21 40		22 17
Woodlesford	d								20 25						22 25
Castleford	d								20 36						22 36
Normanton	d								20 41						22 41
Wakefield Kirkgate 4 (31)	a								20 46						22 46
	d								20 46						22 46
Darton	d								21 00						23 00
Huddersfield	d			19 19											
Lockwood	d			19 22											
Berry Brow	d			19 25											
Honley	d			19 28											
Brockholes	d			19 31											
Stocksmoor	d			19 35											
Shepley	d			19 37											
Denby Dale	d			19 42											
Penistone	d			19 50											
Silkstone Common	d			19 55											
Dodworth	d			19 59											
Barnsley	a			20 06					21 07						23 07
	d			20 12					21 12			22 21			23 12
Wombwell	d			20 17					21 17			22 26			23 17
Elsecar	d			20 21					21 21			22 30			23 21
Chapeltown	d			20 26					21 26			22 35			23 26
Meadowhall (29,31) ⇌	a	20 20	20 22	20 34					21 33			22 40	22 45		23 30
	d	20 21	20 23	20 34	20 47	21 00	21 28		21 33	21 58	22 04	22 41	22 45	23 04	23 32
Sheffield 7 (29,31) ⇌	a	20 34	20 34	20 43	20 55	21 07	21 38		21 42	22 09	22 13	22 51	22 54	23 15	23 43
	d							21 40							
Dronfield	d							21 50							
Chesterfield	d							21 56							
Alfreton	d							22 07							
Langley Mill	d							22 14							
Nottingham	a							22 35							

A From Scarborough
B From Cleethorpes to Manchester Airport
C From Doncaster
D From Bridlington
E not 24 June. From Cleethorpes to Manchester Airport
F 24 June. From Cleethorpes to Manchester Airport
G From Sheffield
H not 24 June
I 24 June
J From Liverpool Lime Street
K From Cleethorpes
L From Hull

Sundays

16 September to 30 September

Leeds and Huddersfield - Barnsley - Sheffield, Nottingham

Network Diagram - see first page of Table 31

		NT A	NT	TP ◇1 B	NT A	NT	NT	NT	NT C	NT	NT D	NT	TP ◇1 E	NT	NT	NT A	NT	TP ◇1 E	NT F	NT	NT	NT	NT D
Leeds 10 31	d					08 34	08 48	09 05				10 02			10 17		10 57			11 18	11 29		
Woodlesford	d					08 42									10 25								
Castleford	d					08 53									10 36								
Normanton	d					08 58									10 41								
Wakefield Kirkgate 4 31	a					09 03		09 21				10 18			10 46		11 13				11 46		
	d					09 03		09 21				10 18			10 46		11 13				11 46		
Darton	d					09 17									11 00								
Huddersfield	d									09 19				10 15								11 29	
Lockwood	d									09 22				10 18								11 32	
Berry Brow	d									09 25				10 21								11 35	
Honley	d									09 28				10 24								11 38	
Brockholes	d									09 31				10 27								11 41	
Stocksmoor	d									09 35				10 31								11 45	
Shepley	d									09 37				10 33								11 47	
Denby Dale	d									09 42				10 39								11 52	
Penistone	d									09 50				10 46								12 00	
Silkstone Common	d									09 55				10 52								12 05	
Dodworth	d									09 59				10 55								12 09	
Barnsley	a					09 24		09 40		10 06		10 37		11 03	11 08		11 32				12 05	12 16	
	d					09 24		09 41		10 12		10 38		11 03	11 12		11 33				12 06	12 17	
Wombwell	d					09 29				10 17					11 17							12 22	
Elsecar	d					09 33				10 21					11 21							12 26	
Chapeltown	d					09 38				10 26					11 26							12 31	
Meadowhall 29,31	a					09 44	09 53	09 57		10 32		10 51		11 20	11 32		11 46			12 20	12 17	12 34	
	d	08 30		09 00	09 41	09 44	09 54	09 57	10 00	10 33	10 40	10 51	11 00	11 20	11 35	11 40	11 46	12 00	12 08	12 21	12 17	12 35	12 43
Sheffield 7 29,31	a	08 41		09 07	09 51	09 55	10 03	10 04	10 08	10 43	10 52	11 02	11 07	11 28	11 44	11 51	11 56	12 07	12 18	12 32	12 29	12 47	12 55
	d		09 00					10 07				11 03					12 00				12 31		
Dronfield	d		09 10					10 17				11 13					12 10				12 42		
Chesterfield	d		09 17					10 23				11 20					12 18				12 49		
Alfreton	d		09 28					10 33				11 30					12 28				12 59		
Langley Mill	d		09 35					10 41				11 38					12 36				13 07		
Nottingham	a		09 53					10 57				11 54					12 52				13 24		

		TP ◇1 E	NT	NT A	NT	NT G	TP ◇1 H	NT	NT	NT D	NT G	NT	TP ◇1 E	NT	NT	NT A	NT F	NT	TP ◇1 E	NT	NT	NT D	NT G
Leeds 10 31	d		12 29		12 34			13 18				14 06			14 17			15 06		15 18			
Woodlesford	d				12 42										14 25								
Castleford	d				12 53										14 36								
Normanton	d				12 58										14 41								
Wakefield Kirkgate 4 31	a		12 46		13 04							14 22			14 46			15 22					
	d		12 46		13 04							14 22			14 46			15 22					
Darton	d				13 18										15 00								
Huddersfield	d								13 19					14 15							15 19		
Lockwood	d								13 22					14 18							15 22		
Berry Brow	d								13 25					14 21							15 25		
Honley	d								13 28					14 24							15 28		
Brockholes	d								13 31					14 27							15 31		
Stocksmoor	d								13 35					14 31							15 35		
Shepley	d								13 37					14 33							15 37		
Denby Dale	d								13 42					14 39							15 42		
Penistone	d								13 50					14 46							15 50		
Silkstone Common	d								13 55					14 52							15 55		
Dodworth	d								13 59					14 55							15 59		
Barnsley	a		13 05		13 24				14 06			14 41		15 03	15 07			15 41			16 06		
	d		13 06		13 24				14 12			14 42		15 03	15 12			15 42			16 12		
Wombwell	d				13 29				14 17						15 17						16 17		
Elsecar	d				13 33				14 21						15 21						16 21		
Chapeltown	d				13 38				14 26						15 26						16 26		
Meadowhall 29,31	a		13 18		13 48			14 20	14 32			14 55		15 20	15 35			15 55		16 20	16 32		
	d	13 00	13 18	13 44	13 51	13 56	14 00	14 21	14 33	14 48	14 52	14 56	15 00	15 21	15 35	15 48	15 52	15 56	16 00	16 21	16 34	16 47	16 53
Sheffield 7 29,31	a	13 07	13 29	13 52	13 58	14 06	14 07	14 32	14 48	14 55	15 03	15 06	15 07	15 28	15 44	15 55	16 01	16 05	16 07	16 32	16 44	16 55	17 04
	d		13 31									15 07						16 07					
Dronfield	d		13 42									15 17						16 17					
Chesterfield	d		13 48									15 24						16 23					
Alfreton	d		13 59									15 34						16 33					
Langley Mill	d		14 06									15 42						16 41					
Nottingham	a		14 22									15 59						16 56					

A From Doncaster
B To Manchester Piccadilly
C From Hull
D From Goole
E From Cleethorpes to Manchester Airport
F From Bridlington
G From Scarborough
H From Doncaster to Manchester Airport

Sundays

16 September to 30 September

Leeds and Huddersfield - Barnsley - Sheffield, Nottingham

Network Diagram - see first page of Table 31

		NT	TP ◇1 A	NT	NT B	NT C	NT	TP ◇1 A	NT	NT	NT B	NT D	NT	TP ◇1 A	NT E	NT	NT B	NT	NT C	TP ◇1 A	NT	NT
Leeds 10 31	d	16 06		16 17			17 06		17 18				18 06			18 17		19 06			19 18	
Woodlesford	d			16 25												18 25						
Castleford	d			16 36												18 36						
Normanton	d			16 41												18 40						
Wakefield Kirkgate 4 31	a	16 22		16 46			17 22						18 22			18 45		19 22				
	d	16 22		16 46			17 22						18 22			18 45		19 22				
Darton	d			17 00												18 59						
Huddersfield	d									17 19												19 19
Lockwood	d									17 22												19 22
Berry Brow	d									17 25												19 25
Honley	d									17 28												19 28
Brockholes	d									17 31												19 31
Stocksmoor	d									17 35												19 35
Shepley	d									17 37												19 37
Denby Dale	d									17 47												19 42
Penistone	d									17 54												19 50
Silkstone Common	d									18 00												19 55
Dodworth	d									18 03												19 59
Barnsley	a	16 41		17 07			17 41			18 11			18 41			19 05		19 40				20 06
	d	16 42		17 12			17 42			18 12			18 42			19 11		19 41				20 12
Wombwell	d			17 17						18 17						19 17						20 17
Elsecar	d			17 21						18 21						19 21						20 21
Chapeltown	d			17 26						18 26						19 26						20 26
Meadowhall 29,31	a	16 56		17 34			17 55		18 25	18 32			18 56			19 32		19 54			20 22	20 34
	d	16 56	17 00	17 35	17 48	17 53	17 56	18 00	18 25	18 33	18 47	18 53	18 56	19 00	19 18	19 33	19 47	19 54	19 57	20 00	20 23	20 34
Sheffield 7 29,31	a	17 05	17 07	17 44	17 55	18 01	18 05	18 08	18 36	18 44	18 57	19 03	19 05	19 07	19 27	19 43	19 55	20 04	20 06	20 07	20 34	20 43
	d	17 07					18 07						19 07					20 06				
Dronfield	d	17 17					18 17						19 17					20 16				
Chesterfield	d	17 23					18 25						19 25					20 23				
Alfreton	d	17 33					18 36						19 36					20 34				
Langley Mill	d	17 41					18 43						19 43					20 41				
Nottingham	a	17 58					19 00						20 00					20 57				

		NT B	TP ◇1 A	NT D	EM ◇ F	NT	NT E	TP ◇1 G	NT	NT	NT H	NT
Leeds 10 31	d					20 17				21 40		22 17
Woodlesford	d					20 25						22 25
Castleford	d					20 36						22 36
Normanton	d					20 41						22 41
Wakefield Kirkgate 4 31	a					20 46						22 46
	d					20 46						22 46
Darton	d					21 00						23 00
Huddersfield	d											
Lockwood	d											
Berry Brow	d											
Honley	d											
Brockholes	d											
Stocksmoor	d											
Shepley	d											
Denby Dale	d											
Penistone	d											
Silkstone Common	d											
Dodworth	d											
Barnsley	a					21 07						23 07
	d					21 12			22 21			23 12
Wombwell	d					21 17			22 26			23 17
Elsecar	d					21 21			22 30			23 21
Chapeltown	d					21 26			22 35			23 26
Meadowhall 29,31	a					21 33			22 40	22 45		23 30
	d	20 47	21 00	21 28		21 33	21 58	22 04	22 41	22 45	23 04	23 32
Sheffield 7 29,31	a	20 55	21 07	21 38		21 42	22 09	22 13	22 51	22 54	23 15	23 43
	d				21 40							
Dronfield	d				21 50							
Chesterfield	d				21 56							
Alfreton	d				22 07							
Langley Mill	d				22 14							
Nottingham	a				22 35							

A From Cleethorpes to Manchester Airport
B From Doncaster
C From Bridlington
D From Scarborough
E From Sheffield
F From Liverpool Lime Street
G From Cleethorpes
H From Hull

7 October to 21 October

Leeds and Huddersfield - Barnsley - Sheffield, Nottingham

Network Diagram - see first page of Table 31

		NT	NT	TP	NT	NT	NT	NT	NT	NT		NT	NT	TP	NT	NT	NT	NT	TP	NT		NT	NT	NT	NT
				◇1										◇1					◇1						
		A		B	A				C			D		E			A		E	F					D
Leeds 10 31	d					08 34	08 48	09 05					10 02			10 17		10 57				11 18	11 29		
Woodlesford	d					08 42										10 25									
Castleford	d					08 53										10 36									
Normanton	d					08 58										10 41									
Wakefield Kirkgate 4 31	a					09 03		09 21					10 18			10 46		11 13					11 46		
	d					09 03		09 21					10 18			10 46		11 13					11 46		
Darton	d					09 17										11 00									
Huddersfield	d									09 16					10 11									11 24	
Lockwood	d									09 19					10 14									11 27	
Berry Brow	d									09 22					10 17									11 30	
Honley	d									09 25					10 20									11 33	
Brockholes	d									09 28					10 23									11 36	
Stocksmoor	d									09 32					10 27									11 40	
Shepley	d									09 34					10 29									11 42	
Denby Dale	d									09 42					10 39									11 52	
Penistone	d									09 50					10 46									12 00	
Silkstone Common	d									09 55					10 52									12 05	
Dodworth	d									09 59					10 55									12 09	
Barnsley	a					09 24		09 40		10 06			10 37		11 03	11 08		11 32					12 05	12 16	
	d					09 24		09 41		10 12			10 38		11 03	11 12		11 33					12 06	12 17	
Wombwell	d					09 29				10 17						11 17								12 22	
Elsecar	d					09 33				10 21						11 21								12 26	
Chapeltown	d					09 38				10 26						11 26								12 31	
Meadowhall 29,31 ⇌	a					09 44	09 53	09 57		10 32			10 51		11 20	11 32		11 46				12 20	12 17	12 34	
	d	08 30		09 00	09 41	09 44	09 54	09 57	10 00	10 33		10 40	10 51	11 00	11 20	11 35	11 40	11 46	12 00	12 08		12 21	12 17	12 35	12 43
Sheffield 7 29,31 ⇌	a	08 41		09 07	09 51	09 55	10 03	10 04	10 08	10 43		10 52	11 02	11 07	11 28	11 44	11 51	11 56	12 07	12 18		12 32	12 29	12 47	12 55
	d		09 00					10 07					11 03					12 00					12 31		
Dronfield	d		09 10					10 17					11 13					12 10					12 42		
Chesterfield	d		09 17					10 23					11 20					12 18					12 49		
Alfreton	d		09 28					10 33					11 30					12 28					12 59		
Langley Mill	d		09 35					10 41					11 38					12 36					13 07		
Nottingham	a		09 53					10 57					11 54					12 52					13 24		

		TP	NT	NT	NT	NT		TP	NT	NT	NT	NT	NT	TP	NT	NT		NT	NT	NT	TP	NT	NT	NT	NT
		◇1						◇1						◇1							◇1				
		E		A		G		H			D	G		E				A	F		E			D	G
Leeds 10 31	d		12 29		12 34				13 18				14 06			14 17				15 06		15 18			
Woodlesford	d				12 42											14 25									
Castleford	d				12 53											14 36									
Normanton	d				12 58											14 41									
Wakefield Kirkgate 4 31	a		12 46		13 04								14 22			14 46				15 22					
	d		12 46		13 04								14 22			14 46				15 22					
Darton	d				13 18											15 00									
Huddersfield	d									13 14					14 11								15 14		
Lockwood	d									13 17					14 14								15 17		
Berry Brow	d									13 20					14 17								15 20		
Honley	d									13 23					14 20								15 23		
Brockholes	d									13 26					14 23								15 26		
Stocksmoor	d									13 30					14 27								15 30		
Shepley	d									13 32					14 29								15 32		
Denby Dale	d									13 42					14 39								15 42		
Penistone	d									13 50					14 46								15 50		
Silkstone Common	d									13 55					14 52								15 55		
Dodworth	d									13 59					14 55								15 59		
Barnsley	a		13 05		13 24					14 06			14 41		15 03	15 07				15 41			16 06		
	d		13 06		13 24					14 12			14 42		15 03	15 12				15 42			16 12		
Wombwell	d				13 29					14 17						15 17							16 17		
Elsecar	d				13 33					14 21						15 21							16 21		
Chapeltown	d				13 38					14 26						15 26							16 26		
Meadowhall 29,31 ⇌	a		13 18		13 48				14 20	14 32			14 55		15 20	15 35				15 55		16 20	16 32		
	d	13 00	13 18	13 44	13 51	13 56		14 00	14 21	14 33	14 48	14 52	14 56	15 00	15 21	15 35		15 48	15 52	15 56	16 00	16 21	16 34	16 47	16 53
Sheffield 7 29,31 ⇌	a	13 07	13 29	13 52	13 58	14 06		14 07	14 32	14 48	14 55	15 03	15 06	15 07	15 28	15 44		15 55	16 01	16 05	16 07	16 32	16 44	16 55	17 04
	d		13 31										15 07							16 07					
Dronfield	d		13 42										15 17							16 17					
Chesterfield	d		13 48										15 24							16 23					
Alfreton	d		13 59										15 34							16 33					
Langley Mill	d		14 06										15 42							16 41					
Nottingham	a		14 22										15 59							16 56					

A From Doncaster
B To Manchester Piccadilly
C From Hull
D From Goole
E From Cleethorpes to Manchester Airport
F From Bridlington
G From Scarborough
H From Doncaster to Manchester Airport

7 October to 21 October

Leeds and Huddersfield - Barnsley - Sheffield, Nottingham

Network Diagram - see first page of Table 31

		NT		TP	NT	NT	NT	NT	TP	NT	NT	NT		NT	NT	TP	NT	NT	NT	NT	NT	TP		NT	NT
				◇1					◇1							◇1						◇1			
				A		B	C		A			B		D		A	E		B		C	A			
Leeds 10 31	d	16 06			16 17			17 06		17 18					18 06			18 17		19 06				19 18	
Woodlesford	d				16 25													18 25							
Castleford	d				16 36													18 36							
Normanton	d				16 41													18 40							
Wakefield Kirkgate 4 31	a	16 22			16 46			17 22							18 22			18 45		19 22					
	d	16 22			16 46			17 22							18 22			18 45		19 22					
Darton	d				17 00													18 59							
Huddersfield	d										17 19														19 14
Lockwood	d										17 22														19 17
Berry Brow	d										17 25														19 20
Honley	d										17 28														19 23
Brockholes	d										17 31														19 26
Stocksmoor	d										17 35														19 30
Shepley	d										17 37														19 32
Denby Dale	d										17 47														19 42
Penistone	d										17 54														19 50
Silkstone Common	d										18 00														19 55
Dodworth	d										18 03														19 59
Barnsley	a	16 41			17 07			17 41			18 11				18 41			19 05		19 40					20 06
	d	16 42			17 12			17 42			18 12				18 42			19 11		19 41					20 12
Wombwell	d				17 17						18 17							19 17							20 17
Elsecar	d				17 21						18 21							19 21							20 21
Chapeltown	d				17 26						18 26							19 26							20 26
Meadowhall 29,31 ⇌	a	16 56			17 34			17 55		18 25	18 32				18 56			19 32		19 54				20 22	20 34
	d	16 56		17 00	17 35	17 48	17 53	17 56	18 00	18 25	18 33	18 47		18 53	18 56	19 00	19 18	19 33	19 47	19 54	19 57	20 00		20 23	20 34
Sheffield 7 29,31 ⇌	a	17 05		17 07	17 44	17 55	18 01	18 05	18 08	18 36	18 44	18 57		19 03	19 05	19 07	19 27	19 43	19 55	20 04	20 06	20 07		20 34	20 43
	d	17 07						18 07							19 07					20 06					
Dronfield	d	17 17						18 17							19 17					20 16					
Chesterfield	d	17 23						18 25							19 25					20 23					
Alfreton	d	17 33						18 36							19 36					20 34					
Langley Mill	d	17 41						18 43							19 43					20 41					
Nottingham	a	17 58						19 00							20 00					20 57					

		NT	TP	NT	EM	NT	NT	TP		NT	NT	NT	NT
			◇1		◇			◇1					
		B	A	D	F		E	G				H	
Leeds 10 31	d					20 17					21 40		22 17
Woodlesford	d					20 25							22 25
Castleford	d					20 36							22 36
Normanton	d					20 41							22 41
Wakefield Kirkgate 4 31	a					20 46							22 46
	d					20 46							22 46
Darton	d					21 00							23 00
Huddersfield	d												
Lockwood	d												
Berry Brow	d												
Honley	d												
Brockholes	d												
Stocksmoor	d												
Shepley	d												
Denby Dale	d												
Penistone	d												
Silkstone Common	d												
Dodworth	d												
Barnsley	a					21 07							23 07
	d					21 12				22 21			23 12
Wombwell	d					21 17				22 26			23 17
Elsecar	d					21 21				22 30			23 21
Chapeltown	d					21 26				22 35			23 26
Meadowhall 29,31 ⇌	a					21 33				22 40	22 45		23 30
	d	20 47	21 00	21 28		21 33	21 58	22 04		22 41	22 45	23 04	23 32
Sheffield 7 29,31 ⇌	a	20 55	21 07	21 38		21 42	22 09	22 13		22 51	22 54	23 15	23 43
	d				21 40								
Dronfield	d				21 50								
Chesterfield	d				21 56								
Alfreton	d				22 07								
Langley Mill	d				22 14								
Nottingham	a				22 35								

A From Cleethorpes to Manchester Airport
B From Doncaster
C From Bridlington
D From Scarborough
E From Sheffield
F From Liverpool Lime Street
G From Cleethorpes
H From Hull

Leeds and Huddersfield - Barnsley - Sheffield, Nottingham

Network Diagram - see first page of Table 31

		NT A	NT	TP ◇1 B	NT A	NT	NT	NT	NT C	NT	NT D	NT	TP ◇1 E	NT	NT	NT A	NT	TP ◇1 E	NT F	NT	NT	NT	NT D
Leeds 10	31 d					08 34	08 48	09 05				10 02			10 17		10 57			11 18	11 29		
Woodlesford	d					08 42									10 25								
Castleford	d					08 53									10 36								
Normanton	d					08 58									10 41								
Wakefield Kirkgate 4	31 a					09 03		09 21				10 18			10 46		11 13				11 46		
	d					09 03		09 21				10 18			10 46		11 13				11 46		
Darton	d					09 17									11 00								
Huddersfield	d									09 16				10 11								11 24	
Lockwood	d									09 19				10 14								11 27	
Berry Brow	d									09 22				10 17								11 30	
Honley	d									09 25				10 20								11 33	
Brockholes	d									09 28				10 23								11 36	
Stocksmoor	d									09 32				10 27								11 40	
Shepley	d									09 34				10 29								11 42	
Denby Dale	d									09 42				10 39								11 52	
Penistone	d									09 50				10 46								12 00	
Silkstone Common	d									09 55				10 52								12 05	
Dodworth	d									09 59				10 55								12 09	
Barnsley	a					09 24		09 40		10 06		10 37		11 03	11 08		11 32				12 05	12 16	
	d					09 24		09 41		10 12		10 38		11 03	11 12		11 33				12 06	12 17	
Wombwell	d					09 29				10 17					11 17							12 22	
Elsecar	d					09 33				10 21					11 21							12 26	
Chapeltown	d					09 38				10 26					11 26							12 31	
Meadowhall	29,31 a					09 44	09 53	09 57		10 32		10 51		11 20	11 32		11 46			12 20	12 17	12 34	
	d	08 30		09 00	09 41	09 44	09 54	09 57	10 00	10 33	10 40	10 51	11 00	11 20	11 35	11 40	11 46	12 00	12 08	12 21	12 17	12 35	12 43
Sheffield 7	29,31 a	08 41		09 07	09 51	09 55	10 03	10 04	10 08	10 43	10 52	11 02	11 07	11 28	11 44	11 51	11 56	12 07	12 18	12 32	12 29	12 47	12 55
	d		09 00					10 07				11 03					12 00				12 31		
Dronfield	d		09 10					10 17				11 13					12 10				12 42		
Chesterfield	d		09 17					10 23				11 20					12 18				12 49		
Alfreton	d		09 28					10 33				11 30					12 28				12 59		
Langley Mill	d		09 35					10 41				11 38					12 36				13 07		
Nottingham	a		09 53					10 57				11 54					12 52				13 24		

		TP ◇1 E	NT	NT A	NT	NT G	TP ◇1 H	NT	NT	NT D	NT G	NT	TP ◇1 E	NT	NT	NT A	NT F	NT	TP ◇1 E	NT	NT	NT D	NT G
Leeds 10	31 d		12 29		12 34			13 18				14 06			14 17			15 06		15 18			
Woodlesford	d				12 42										14 25								
Castleford	d				12 53										14 36								
Normanton	d				12 58										14 41								
Wakefield Kirkgate 4	31 a		12 46		13 04							14 22			14 46			15 22					
	d		12 46		13 04							14 22			14 46			15 22					
Darton	d				13 18										15 00								
Huddersfield	d								13 14					14 11							15 14		
Lockwood	d								13 17					14 14							15 17		
Berry Brow	d								13 20					14 17							15 20		
Honley	d								13 23					14 20							15 23		
Brockholes	d								13 26					14 23							15 26		
Stocksmoor	d								13 30					14 27							15 30		
Shepley	d								13 32					14 29							15 32		
Denby Dale	d								13 42					14 39							15 42		
Penistone	d								13 50					14 46							15 50		
Silkstone Common	d								13 55					14 52							15 55		
Dodworth	d								13 59					14 55							15 59		
Barnsley	a		13 05		13 24				14 06			14 41		15 03	15 07			15 41			16 06		
	d		13 06		13 24				14 12			14 42		15 03	15 12			15 42			16 12		
Wombwell	d				13 29				14 17						15 17						16 17		
Elsecar	d				13 33				14 21						15 21						16 21		
Chapeltown	d				13 38				14 26						15 26						16 26		
Meadowhall	29,31 a		13 18		13 48			14 20	14 32			14 55		15 20	15 35			15 55		16 20	16 32		
	d	13 00	13 18	13 44	13 51	13 56	14 00	14 21	14 33	14 48	14 52	14 56	15 00	15 21	15 35	15 48	15 52	15 56	16 00	16 21	16 34	16 47	16 53
Sheffield 7	29,31 a	13 07	13 29	13 52	13 58	14 06	14 07	14 32	14 48	14 55	15 03	15 06	15 07	15 28	15 44	15 55	16 01	16 05	16 07	16 32	16 44	16 55	17 04
	d		13 31									15 07						16 07					
Dronfield	d		13 42									15 17						16 17					
Chesterfield	d		13 48									15 24						16 23					
Alfreton	d		13 59									15 34						16 33					
Langley Mill	d		14 06									15 42						16 41					
Nottingham	a		14 22									15 59						16 56					

A From Doncaster
B To Manchester Piccadilly
C From Hull
D From Goole
E From Cleethorpes to Manchester Airport
F From Bridlington
G From Scarborough
H From Doncaster to Manchester Airport

Table 34

Sundays

from 28 October

Leeds and Huddersfield - Barnsley - Sheffield, Nottingham

Network Diagram - see first page of Table 31

		NT	TP ◇1 A	NT	NT B	NT C	NT	TP ◇1 A	NT	NT	NT B	NT D	NT	TP ◇1 A	NT E	NT	NT B	NT	NT C	TP ◇1 A	NT	NT
Leeds 10	31 d	16 06		16 17			17 06		17 18				18 06			18 17		19 06			19 18	
Woodlesford	d			16 25												18 25						
Castleford	d			16 36												18 36						
Normanton	d			16 41												18 40						
Wakefield Kirkgate 4	31 a	16 22		16 46			17 22						18 22			18 45		19 22				
	d	16 22		16 46			17 22						18 22			18 45		19 22				
Darton	d			17 00												18 59						
Huddersfield	d									17 19												19 14
Lockwood	d									17 22												19 17
Berry Brow	d									17 25												19 20
Honley	d									17 28												19 23
Brockholes	d									17 31												19 26
Stocksmoor	d									17 35												19 30
Shepley	d									17 37												19 32
Denby Dale	d									17 47												19 42
Penistone	d									17 54												19 50
Silkstone Common	d									18 00												19 55
Dodworth	d									18 03												19 59
Barnsley	a	16 41		17 07			17 41			18 11			18 41			19 05		19 40				20 06
	d	16 42		17 12			17 42			18 12			18 42			19 11		19 41				20 12
Wombwell	d			17 17						18 17						19 17						20 17
Elsecar	d			17 21						18 21						19 21						20 21
Chapeltown	d			17 26						18 26						19 26						20 26
Meadowhall	29,31 a	16 56		17 34			17 55		18 25	18 32			18 56			19 32		19 54			20 22	20 34
	d	16 56	17 00	17 35	17 48	17 53	17 56	18 00	18 25	18 33	18 47	18 53	18 56	19 00	19 18	19 33	19 47	19 54	19 57	20 00	20 23	20 34
Sheffield 7	29,31 a	17 05	17 07	17 44	17 55	18 01	18 05	18 08	18 36	18 44	18 57	19 03	19 05	19 07	19 27	19 43	19 55	20 04	20 06	20 07	20 34	20 43
	d	17 07					18 07						19 07					20 06				
Dronfield	d	17 17					18 17						19 17					20 16				
Chesterfield	d	17 23					18 25						19 25					20 23				
Alfreton	d	17 33					18 36						19 36					20 34				
Langley Mill	d	17 41					18 43						19 43					20 41				
Nottingham	a	17 58					19 00						20 00					20 57				

		NT B	TP ◇1 A	NT D	EM ◇ F	NT	NT E	TP ◇1 G	NT	NT	NT H	NT
Leeds 10	31 d					20 17				21 40		22 17
Woodlesford	d					20 25						22 25
Castleford	d					20 36						22 36
Normanton	d					20 41						22 41
Wakefield Kirkgate 4	31 a					20 46						22 46
	d					20 46						22 46
Darton	d					21 00						23 00
Huddersfield	d											
Lockwood	d											
Berry Brow	d											
Honley	d											
Brockholes	d											
Stocksmoor	d											
Shepley	d											
Denby Dale	d											
Penistone	d											
Silkstone Common	d											
Dodworth	d											
Barnsley	a					21 07						23 07
	d					21 12			22 21			23 12
Wombwell	d					21 17			22 26			23 17
Elsecar	d					21 21			22 30			23 21
Chapeltown	d					21 26			22 35			23 26
Meadowhall	29,31 a					21 33			22 40	22 45		23 30
	d	20 47	21 00	21 28		21 33	21 54	22 04	22 41	22 45	23 04	23 32
Sheffield 7	29,31 a	20 55	21 07	21 38		21 42	22 05	22 13	22 51	22 54	23 15	23 43
	d				21 40							
Dronfield	d				21 50							
Chesterfield	d				21 56							
Alfreton	d				22 07							
Langley Mill	d				22 14							
Nottingham	a				22 35							

A From Cleethorpes to Manchester Airport
B From Doncaster
C From Bridlington
D From Scarborough
E From Moorthorpe
F From Liverpool Lime Street
G From Cleethorpes
H From Hull

Network Diagram for Tables 35, 36, 37, 38

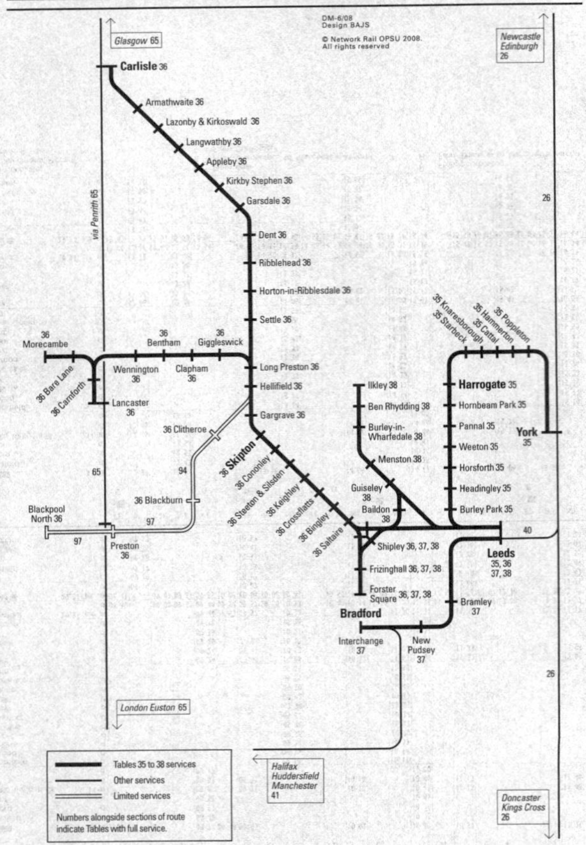

Table 35

York - Harrogate - Leeds

Mondays to Fridays

until 28 September

Network Diagram - see first page of Table 35

Miles			NT	NT	NT	GR ■ 1 A	NT	NT	NT	NT	NT		NT	NT	NT	NT	NT	NT	NT	NT	NT		NT	NT	NT
0	**York** ■	40 d					06 52				07 57			08 45	09 10		10 11		11 11		12 11			13 11	
3	Poppleton	d					06 56				08 01			08 50	09 14		10 15		11 15		12 15			13 15	
8¾	Hammerton	d					07 04				08 09			08 58	09 22		10 23		11 23		12 23			13 23	
10¼	Cattal	d					07 07				08 12			09 01	09 26		10 26		11 26		12 26			13 26	
16¾	**Knaresborough**	a					07 15				08 21			09 09	09 34		10 34		11 34		12 34			13 34	
—		d			07 00		07 24	07 42	07 56		08 21		08 55	09 10	09 35	10 05	10 35	11 05	11 35	12 05	12 35		13 05	13 35	14 05
18¼	Starbeck	d			07 03		07 27	07 45	07 59		08 24		08 58	09 13	09 38	10 08	10 38	11 08	11 38	12 08	12 38		13 08	13 38	14 08
20½	**Harrogate**	a			07 08		07 32	07 50	08 04		08 29		09 03	09 18	09 43	10 13	10 43	11 13	11 43	12 13	12 43		13 13	13 43	14 13
—		d	06 05	06 28	07 11	07 28	07 40	07 51	08 06	08 14	08 30		09 04	09 19	09 44	10 14	10 44	11 14	11 44	12 14	12 44		13 14	13 44	14 14
21½	Hornbeam Park	d	06 08	06 30	07 14		07 42	07 54		08 17	08 33		09 07	09 22	09 47	10 17	10 47	11 17	11 47	12 17	12 47		13 17	13 47	14 17
23¾	Pannal	d	06 13	06 35	07 19		07 47	07 59		08 22	08 38			09 27	09 52	10 22	10 52	11 22	11 52	12 22	12 52		13 22	13 52	14 22
27	Weeton	d	06 18	06 40	07 23		07 51	08 03		08 26	08 42			09 31	09 56	10 26	10 56	11 26	11 56	12 26	12 56		13 26	13 56	14 26
33	Horsforth	d	06 27	06 48	07 32	07u45	08 00	08 12	08 23	08 35	08 51		09 22	09 40	10 05	10 35	11 05	11 35	12 05	12 35	13 05		13 35	14 05	14 35
35¾	Headingley	d	06 31	06 52	07 36		08 04	08 16	08 27	08 39	08 55		09 26	09 44	10 09	10 39	11 09	11 39	12 09	12 39	13 09		13 39	14 09	14 39
36½	Burley Park	d	06 34	06 54	07 38		08 06	08 18	08 29	08 41	08 57		09 27	09 47	10 11	10 41	11 11	11 41	12 11	12 41	13 11		13 41	14 11	14 41
38¾	**Leeds** 10	40 a	06 44	07 06	07 49	07 57	08 16	08 32	08 40	08 52	09 08		09 37	09 56	10 22	10 52	11 22	11 52	12 22	12 52	13 22		13 52	14 22	14 52

		NT	NT	NT	NT	NT	NT		NT	NT	NT	NT	NT	NT	NT	NT	NT
York ■	40 d	14 11		15 11		16 11			17 09	17 29		18 11		19 11	20 11	21 11	22 11
Poppleton	d	14 15		15 15		16 15			17 13	17 35		18 15		19 15	20 15	21 16	22 15
Hammerton	d	14 23		15 23		16 23			17 21	17 43		18 23		19 23	20 23	21 23	22 23
Cattal	d	14 26		15 26		16 26			17 25	17 46		18 26		19 26	20 26	21 27	22 27
Knaresborough	a	14 34		15 34		16 34			17 33	17 54		18 34		19 34	20 34	21 34	22 35
	d	14 35	15 05	15 35	16 05	16 35	17 05		17 33	17 55	18 05	18 35	19 05	19 35	20 35	21 35	22 36
Starbeck	d	14 38	15 08	15 38	16 08	16 38	17 08		17 37	17 58	18 12	18 38	19 08	19 38	20 38	21 39	22 40
Harrogate	a	14 43	15 13	15 43	16 13	16 43	17 13		17 41	18 03	18 17	18 43	19 13	19 43	20 43	21 43	22 45
	d	14 44	15 14	15 44	16 14	16 44	17 14		17 43	18 04	18 18	18 44	19 14	19 44	20 44	21 45	22 47
Hornbeam Park	d	14 47	15 17	15 47	16 17	16 47	17 17		17 45	18 07	18 21	18 47	19 17	19 47	20 47	21 48	22 49
Pannal	d	14 52	15 22	15 52	16 22	16 52	17 22		17 50	18 12	18 26	18 52	19 22	19 52	20 52	21 53	22 54
Weeton	d	14 56	15 26	15 56	16 26	16 56	17 26		17 55	18 16	18 30	18 56	19 26	19 56	20 56	21 58	22 59
Horsforth	d	15 05	15 35	16 05	16 35	17 05	17 38		18 03	18 25	18 39	19 05	19 35	20 05	21 05	22 06	23 08
Headingley	d	15 09	15 39	16 09	16 39	17 09	17 42		18 07	18 29	18 43	19 09	19 39	20 09	21 09	22 10	23 12
Burley Park	d	15 11	15 41	16 11	16 41	17 11	17 44		18 09	18 31	18 45	19 11	19 41	20 11	21 11	22 13	23 15
Leeds 10	40 a	15 22	15 52	16 22	16 52	17 22	17 55		18 20	18 43	18 55	19 24	19 52	20 22	21 23	22 23	23 24

Mondays to Fridays

from 1 October

		NT	NT	NT	GR ■ 1 A	NT	NT	NT	NT	NT		NT	NT	NT	NT	NT	NT	NT	NT	NT		NT	NT	NT	NT
York ■	40 d					06 52				07 57			08 45	09 10		10 11		11 11		12 11			13 11		14 11
Poppleton	d					06 56				08 01			08 50	09 14		10 15		11 15		12 15			13 15		14 15
Hammerton	d					07 04				08 09			08 58	09 22		10 23		11 23		12 23			13 23		14 23
Cattal	d					07 07				08 12			09 01	09 26		10 26		11 26		12 26			13 26		14 26
Knaresborough	a					07 15				08 21			09 09	09 34		10 34		11 34		12 34			13 34		14 34
	d			07 00		07 24	07 42	07 56		08 21		08 55	09 10	09 35	10 05	10 35	11 05	11 35	12 05	12 35		13 05	13 35	14 05	14 35
Starbeck	d			07 03		07 27	07 45	07 59		08 24		08 58	09 13	09 38	10 08	10 38	11 08	11 38	12 08	12 38		13 08	13 38	14 08	14 38
Harrogate	a			07 08		07 32	07 50	08 04		08 29		09 03	09 18	09 43	10 13	10 43	11 13	11 43	12 13	12 43		13 13	13 43	14 13	14 43
	d	06 05	06 28	07 11	07 28	07 40	07 51	08 06	08 14	08 30		09 04	09 19	09 44	10 14	10 44	11 14	11 44	12 14	12 44		13 14	13 44	14 14	14 44
Hornbeam Park	d	06 08	06 30	07 14		07 42	07 54		08 17	08 33		09 07	09 22	09 47	10 17	10 47	11 17	11 47	12 17	12 47		13 17	13 47	14 17	14 47
Pannal	d	06 13	06 35	07 19		07 47	07 59		08 22	08 38			09 27	09 52	10 22	10 52	11 22	11 52	12 22	12 52		13 22	13 52	14 22	14 52
Weeton	d	06 18	06 40	07 23		07 51	08 03		08 26	08 42			09 31	09 56	10 26	10 56	11 26	11 56	12 26	12 56		13 26	13 56	14 26	14 56
Horsforth	d	06 27	06 48	07 32	07u45	08 00	08 12	08 23	08 35	08 51		09 22	09 40	10 05	10 35	11 05	11 35	12 05	12 35	13 05		13 35	14 05	14 35	15 05
Headingley	d	06 31	06 52	07 36		08 04	08 16	08 27	08 39	08 55		09 26	09 44	10 09	10 39	11 09	11 39	12 09	12 39	13 09		13 39	14 09	14 39	15 09
Burley Park	d	06 34	06 54	07 38		08 06	08 18	08 29	08 41	08 57		09 27	09 47	10 11	10 41	11 11	11 41	12 11	12 41	13 11		13 41	14 11	14 41	15 11
Leeds 10	40 a	06 44	07 06	07 49	07 57	08 16	08 32	08 40	08 52	09 08		09 37	09 56	10 22	10 52	11 22	11 52	12 22	12 52	13 22		13 52	14 22	14 52	15 22

		NT	NT	NT	NT	NT		NT	NT	NT	NT	NT	NT	NT	NT	NT
York ■	40 d		15 11		16 11			17 09	17 29		18 11		19 11	20 11	21 11	22 11
Poppleton	d		15 15		16 15			17 13	17 35		18 15		19 15	20 15	21 16	22 15
Hammerton	d		15 23		16 23			17 21	17 43		18 23		19 23	20 23	21 23	22 23
Cattal	d		15 26		16 26			17 25	17 46		18 26		19 26	20 26	21 27	22 27
Knaresborough	a		15 34		16 34			17 33	17 54		18 34		19 34	20 34	21 34	22 35
	d	15 05	15 35	16 05	16 35	17 05		17 33	17 55	18 05	18 35	19 05	19 35	20 35	21 35	22 36
Starbeck	d	15 08	15 38	16 08	16 38	17 08		17 37	17 58	18 12	18 38	19 08	19 38	20 38	21 39	22 40
Harrogate	a	15 13	15 43	16 13	16 43	17 13		17 41	18 03	18 17	18 43	19 13	19 43	20 43	21 43	22 45
	d	15 14	15 44	16 14	16 44	17 14		17 43	18 04	18 18	18 44	19 14	19 44	20 44	21 45	22 47
Hornbeam Park	d	15 17	15 47	16 17	16 47	17 17		17 45	18 07	18 21	18 47	19 17	19 47	20 47	21 48	22 49
Pannal	d	15 22	15 52	16 22	16 52	17 22		17 50	18 12	18 26	18 52	19 22	19 52	20 52	21 53	22 54
Weeton	d	15 26	15 56	16 26	16 56	17 26		17 55	18 16	18 30	18 56	19 26	19 56	20 56	21 58	22 59
Horsforth	d	15 35	16 05	16 35	17 05	17 38		18 03	18 25	18 39	19 05	19 35	20 05	21 05	22 06	23 08
Headingley	d	15 39	16 09	16 39	17 09	17 42		18 07	18 29	18 43	19 09	19 39	20 09	21 09	22 10	23 12
Burley Park	d	15 41	16 11	16 41	17 11	17 44		18 09	18 31	18 45	19 11	19 41	20 11	21 11	22 13	23 15
Leeds 10	40 a	15 52	16 22	16 52	17 22	17 55		18 20	18 43	18 55	19 24	19 52	20 22	21 23	22 23	23 24

A To London Kings Cross

York - Harrogate - Leeds

until 29 September

Network Diagram - see first page of Table 35

	NT	NT	NT	NT	GR A	NT	NT	NT	NT	NT	NT
York [8] 40 d			06 53			07 57		08 45	09 10		10 11
Poppleton d			06 57			08 01		08 49	09 14		10 15
Hammerton d			07 05			08 09		08 57	09 22		10 23
Cattal d			07 08			08 12		09 00	09 26		10 26
Knaresborough a			07 16			08 20		09 08	09 34		10 34
d		06 47	07 21	07 51		08 21	08 51	09 09	09 35	10 05	10 35
Starbeck d		06 50	07 24	07 54		08 24	08 54	09 12	09 38	10 08	10 38
Harrogate a		06 55	07 29	07 59		08 29	08 59	09 17	09 43	10 13	10 43
d	06 06	06 56	07 31	08 00	08 13	08 30	09 00	09 18	09 44	10 14	10 44
Hornbeam Park d	06 08	06 59	07 33	08 03		08 33	09 03	09 21	09 47	10 17	10 47
Pannal d	06 13	07 04	07 38	08 08		08 38	09 08	09 26	09 52	10 22	10 52
Weeton d	06 18	07 08	07 42	08 12		08 42	09 12	09 30	09 56	10 26	10 56
Horsforth d	06 28	07 17	07 51	08 21		08 51	09 21	09 39	10 05	10 35	11 05
Headingley d	06 32	07 21	07 55	08 25		08 55	09 25	09 43	10 09	10 39	11 09
Burley Park d	06 34	07 23	07 57	08 27		08 57	09 27	09 47	10 11	10 41	11 11
Leeds [10] 40 a	06 45	07 34	08 08	08 38	08 45	09 08	09 37	09 55	10 22	10 52	11 22

	NT	NT	NT	NT	NT	NT	NT	NT	NT	NT	NT
York [8] 40 d		11 11		12 11		13 11		14 11		15 11	
Poppleton d		11 15		12 15		13 15		14 15		15 15	
Hammerton d		11 23		12 23		13 23		14 23		15 23	
Cattal d		11 26		12 26		13 26		14 26		15 26	
Knaresborough a		11 34		12 34		13 34		14 34		15 34	
d	11 05	11 35	12 05	12 35	13 05	13 35	14 05	14 35	15 05	15 35	16 05
Starbeck d	11 08	11 38	12 08	12 38	13 08	13 38	14 08	14 38	15 08	15 38	16 08
Harrogate a	11 13	11 43	12 13	12 43	13 13	13 43	14 13	14 43	15 13	15 43	16 13
d	11 14	11 44	12 14	12 44	13 14	13 44	14 14	14 44	15 14	15 44	16 14
Hornbeam Park d	11 17	11 47	12 17	12 47	13 17	13 47	14 17	14 47	15 17	15 47	16 17
Pannal d	11 22	11 52	12 22	12 52	13 22	13 52	14 22	14 52	15 22	15 52	16 22
Weeton d	11 26	11 56	12 26	12 56	13 26	13 56	14 26	14 56	15 26	15 56	16 26
Horsforth d	11 35	12 05	12 35	13 05	13 35	14 05	14 35	15 05	15 35	16 05	16 35
Headingley d	11 39	12 09	12 39	13 09	13 39	14 09	14 39	15 09	15 39	16 09	16 39
Burley Park d	11 41	12 11	12 41	13 11	13 41	14 11	14 41	15 11	15 41	16 11	16 41
Leeds [10] 40 a	11 52	12 22	12 52	13 20	13 52	14 22	14 52	15 22	15 52	16 22	16 52

	NT	NT	NT	NT	NT	NT	NT	NT	NT	NT
York [8] 40 d	16 11		16 51	17 20		18 11	19 11	20 11	21 11	21 57
Poppleton d	16 15		16 55	17 24		18 15	19 15	20 15	21 16	22 01
Hammerton d	16 23		17 03	17 32		18 23	19 23	20 23	21 23	22 09
Cattal d	16 26		17 06	17 35		18 26	19 26	20 26	21 27	22 12
Knaresborough a	16 34		17 14	17 43		18 34	19 34	20 34	21 35	22 20
d	16 35	17 05	17 15	17 44	18 05	18 35	19 35	20 36	21 36	22 21
Starbeck d	16 38	17 08	17 18	17 47	18 12	18 38	19 38	20 39	21 40	22 24
Harrogate a	16 43	17 13	17 23	17 52	18 17	18 43	19 43	20 44	21 44	22 29
d	16 44	17 14	17 37	17 59	18 18	18 44	19 44	20 45	21 46	22 37
Hornbeam Park d	16 47	17 17	17 39	18 01	18 21	18 47	19 47	20 48	21 49	22 39
Pannal d	16 52	17 22	17 44	18 06	18 26	18 52	19 52	20 53	21 54	22 44
Weeton d	16 56	17 26	17 49	18 11	18 30	18 56	19 56	20 57	21 59	22 49
Horsforth d	17 05	17 38	17 57	18 19	18 39	19 05	20 05	21 06	22 07	22 57
Headingley d	17 09	17 42	18 01	18 23	18 43	19 09	20 09	21 10	22 12	23 01
Burley Park d	17 11	17 44	18 04	18 26	18 45	19 11	20 11	21 12	22 14	23 04
Leeds [10] 40 a	17 22	17 55	18 16	18 39	18 55	19 22	20 22	21 23	22 25	23 14

Saturdays

from 6 October

	NT	NT	NT	NT	GR A	NT	NT	NT	NT	NT	NT
York [8] 40 d			06 53			07 57		08 45	09 10		10 11
Poppleton d			06 57			08 01		08 49	09 14		10 15
Hammerton d			07 05			08 09		08 57	09 22		10 23
Cattal d			07 08			08 12		09 00	09 26		10 26
Knaresborough a			07 16			08 20		09 08	09 34		10 34
d		06 47	07 21	07 51		08 21	08 51	09 09	09 35	10 05	10 35
Starbeck d		06 50	07 24	07 54		08 24	08 54	09 12	09 38	10 08	10 38
Harrogate a		06 55	07 29	07 59		08 29	08 59	09 17	09 43	10 13	10 43
d	06 06	06 56	07 31	08 00	08 13	08 30	09 00	09 18	09 44	10 14	10 44
Hornbeam Park d	06 08	06 59	07 33	08 03		08 33	09 03	09 21	09 47	10 17	10 47
Pannal d	06 13	07 04	07 38	08 08		08 38	09 08	09 26	09 52	10 22	10 52
Weeton d	06 18	07 08	07 42	08 12		08 42	09 12	09 30	09 56	10 26	10 56
Horsforth d	06 28	07 17	07 51	08 21		08 51	09 21	09 39	10 05	10 35	11 05
Headingley d	06 32	07 21	07 55	08 25		08 55	09 25	09 43	10 09	10 39	11 09
Burley Park d	06 34	07 23	07 57	08 27		08 57	09 27	09 47	10 11	10 41	11 11
Leeds [10] 40 a	06 45	07 34	08 08	08 38	08 45	09 08	09 37	09 55	10 22	10 52	11 22

	NT	NT	NT	NT	NT	NT	NT	NT	NT	NT	NT
York [8] 40 d		11 11		12 11		13 11		14 11		15 11	
Poppleton d		11 15		12 15		13 15		14 15		15 15	
Hammerton d		11 23		12 23		13 23		14 23		15 23	
Cattal d		11 26		12 26		13 26		14 26		15 26	
Knaresborough a		11 34		12 34		13 34		14 34		15 34	
d	11 05	11 35	12 05	12 35	13 05	13 35	14 05	14 35	15 05	15 35	16 05
Starbeck d	11 08	11 38	12 08	12 38	13 08	13 38	14 08	14 38	15 08	15 38	16 08
Harrogate a	11 13	11 43	12 13	12 43	13 13	13 43	14 13	14 43	15 13	15 43	16 13
d	11 14	11 44	12 14	12 44	13 14	13 44	14 14	14 44	15 14	15 44	16 14
Hornbeam Park d	11 17	11 47	12 17	12 47	13 17	13 47	14 17	14 47	15 17	15 47	16 17
Pannal d	11 22	11 52	12 22	12 52	13 22	13 52	14 22	14 52	15 22	15 52	16 22
Weeton d	11 26	11 56	12 26	12 56	13 26	13 56	14 26	14 56	15 26	15 56	16 26
Horsforth d	11 35	12 05	12 35	13 05	13 35	14 05	14 35	15 05	15 35	16 05	16 35
Headingley d	11 39	12 09	12 39	13 09	13 39	14 09	14 39	15 09	15 39	16 09	16 39
Burley Park d	11 41	12 11	12 41	13 11	13 41	14 11	14 41	15 11	15 41	16 11	16 41
Leeds [10] 40 a	11 52	12 22	12 52	13 20	13 52	14 22	14 52	15 22	15 52	16 22	16 52

	NT	NT	NT	NT	NT	NT	NT	NT	NT	NT
York [8] 40 d	16 11		16 51	17 20		18 11	19 11	20 11	21 11	21 57
Poppleton d	16 15		16 55	17 24		18 15	19 15	20 15	21 16	22 01
Hammerton d	16 23		17 03	17 32		18 23	19 23	20 23	21 23	22 09
Cattal d	16 26		17 06	17 35		18 26	19 26	20 26	21 27	22 12
Knaresborough a	16 34		17 14	17 43		18 34	19 34	20 34	21 35	22 20
d	16 35	17 05	17 15	17 44	18 05	18 35	19 35	20 36	21 36	22 21
Starbeck d	16 38	17 08	17 18	17 47	18 12	18 38	19 38	20 39	21 40	22 24
Harrogate a	16 43	17 13	17 23	17 52	18 17	18 43	19 43	20 44	21 44	22 29
d	16 44	17 14	17 37	17 59	18 18	18 44	19 44	20 45	21 46	22 37
Hornbeam Park d	16 47	17 17	17 39	18 01	18 21	18 47	19 47	20 48	21 49	22 39
Pannal d	16 52	17 22	17 44	18 06	18 26	18 52	19 52	20 53	21 54	22 44
Weeton d	16 56	17 26	17 49	18 11	18 30	18 56	19 56	20 57	21 59	22 49
Horsforth d	17 05	17 38	17 57	18 19	18 39	19 05	20 05	21 06	22 07	22 57
Headingley d	17 09	17 42	18 01	18 23	18 43	19 09	20 09	21 10	22 12	23 01
Burley Park d	17 11	17 44	18 04	18 26	18 45	19 11	20 11	21 12	22 14	23 04
Leeds [10] 40 a	17 22	17 55	18 16	18 39	18 55	19 22	20 22	21 23	22 25	23 14

A To London Kings Cross

York - Harrogate - Leeds

Sundays

until 30 September

Network Diagram - see first page of Table 35

	NT	NT	NT	NT	NT	NT	GR A	NT	NT	NT	NT	NT	NT
York [8] 40 d				12 18	14 20	16 18		17 17	18 17	19 17	20 17	21 26	
Poppleton d				12 22	14 24	16 22		17 21	18 21	19 21	20 21	21 30	
Hammerton d				12 30	14 32	16 30		17 29	18 29	19 29	20 29	21 38	
Cattal d				12 33	14 35	16 33		17 32	18 32	19 32	20 32	21 41	
Knaresborough a				12 41	14 43	16 41		17 40	18 40	19 40	20 40	21 49	
d			11 42	12 42	14 44	16 42		17 42	18 42	19 42	20 42	21 50	
Starbeck d			11 45	12 45	14 47	16 45		17 45	18 45	19 45	20 45	21 53	
Harrogate a			11 50	12 50	14 52	16 50		17 50	18 50	19 50	20 50	21 58	
d	09 53	10 53	11 53	12 53	14 53	16 53	17 05	17 53	18 53	19 53	20 53	22 02	23 12
Hornbeam Park d	09 56	10 56	11 56	12 56	14 56	16 56		17 56	18 56	19 56	20 56	22 04	23 15
Pannal d	10 01	11 01	12 01	13 01	15 01	17 01		18 01	19 01	20 01	21 01	22 09	23 20
Weeton d	10 05	11 05	12 05	13 05	15 05	17 05		18 05	19 05	20 05	21 05	22 14	23 24
Horsforth d	10 14	11 14	12 14	13 14	15 14	17 14		18 14	19 14	20 14	21 14	22 23	23 33
Headingley d	10 18	11 18	12 18	13 18	15 18	17 18		18 18	19 18	20 18	21 18	22 27	23 37
Burley Park d	10 20	11 20	12 20	13 20	15 20	17 20		18 20	19 20	20 20	21 20	22 30	23 39
Leeds [10] 40 a	10 30	11 30	12 30	13 30	15 30	17 30	17 32	18 30	19 30	20 30	21 30	22 38	23 54

Sundays

from 7 October

	NT	NT	NT	NT	NT	NT	GR A	NT	NT	NT	NT	NT	NT
York [8] 40 d				12 18	14 20	16 18		17 17	18 17	19 17	20 17	21 26	
Poppleton d				12 22	14 24	16 22		17 21	18 21	19 21	20 21	21 30	
Hammerton d				12 30	14 32	16 30		17 29	18 29	19 29	20 29	21 38	
Cattal d				12 33	14 35	16 33		17 32	18 32	19 32	20 32	21 41	
Knaresborough a				12 41	14 43	16 41		17 40	18 40	19 40	20 40	21 49	
d			11 42	12 42	14 44	16 42		17 42	18 42	19 42	20 42	21 50	
Starbeck d			11 45	12 45	14 47	16 45		17 45	18 45	19 45	20 45	21 53	
Harrogate a			11 50	12 50	14 52	16 50		17 50	18 50	19 50	20 50	21 58	
d	09 53	10 53	11 53	12 53	14 53	16 53	17 05	17 53	18 53	19 53	20 53	22 02	23 12
Hornbeam Park d	09 56	10 56	11 56	12 56	14 56	16 56		17 56	18 56	19 56	20 56	22 04	23 15
Pannal d	10 01	11 01	12 01	13 01	15 01	17 01		18 01	19 01	20 01	21 01	22 09	23 20
Weeton d	10 05	11 05	12 05	13 05	15 05	17 05		18 05	19 05	20 05	21 05	22 14	23 24
Horsforth d	10 14	11 14	12 14	13 14	15 14	17 14		18 14	19 14	20 14	21 14	22 23	23 33
Headingley d	10 18	11 18	12 18	13 18	15 18	17 18		18 18	19 18	20 18	21 18	22 27	23 37
Burley Park d	10 20	11 20	12 20	13 20	15 20	17 20		18 20	19 20	20 20	21 20	22 30	23 39
Leeds [10] 40 a	10 30	11 30	12 30	13 30	15 30	17 30	17 32	18 30	19 30	20 30	21 30	22 38	23 54

A To London Kings Cross

Table 35

Leeds - Harrogate - York

Mondays to Fridays
until 28 September

Network Diagram - see first page of Table 35

Miles				NT MX	NT	NT	NT	NT	NT	NT	NT	NT	NT	NT	NT	NT	NT	NT	NT	NT	NT	NT	NT	NT
0	**Leeds** 10	40	d	23p29	06 09	06 29	07 13	07 43	07 59	08 29	08 59	09 29	09 59	10 29	10 59	11 29	11 59	12 29	12 59	13 29	13 59	14 29	14 59	15 29
2¼	Burley Park		d	23p33	06 13	06 33	07 17	07 47	08 03	08 33	09 03	09 33	10 03	10 33	11 03	11 33	12 03	12 33	13 03	13 33	14 03	14 33	15 03	15 33
3	Headingley		d	23p36	06 16	06 36	07 20	07 50	08 06	08 36	09 06	09 36	10 06	10 36	11 06	11 36	12 06	12 36	13 06	13 36	14 06	14 36	15 06	15 36
5¾	Horsforth		d	23p41	06 21	06 41	07 25	07 55	08 11	08 41	09 11	09 41	10 11	10 41	11 11	11 41	12 11	12 41	13 11	13 41	14 11	14 41	15 11	15 41
11¾	Weeton		d	23p49	06 29	06 49	07 33		08 19	08 49	09 19	09 49	10 19	10 49	11 19	11 49	12 19	12 49	13 19	13 49	14 19	14 49	15 19	15 49
15	Pannal		d	23p55	06 35	06 55	07 39		08 25	08 55	09 25	09 55	10 25	10 55	11 25	11 55	12 25	12 55	13 25	13 55	14 25	14 55	15 25	15 55
17¼	Hornbeam Park		d	23p58	06 40	07 00	07 44	08 10	08 30	09 00	09 30	10 00	10 30	11 00	11 30	12 00	12 30	13 00	13 30	14 00	14 30	15 00	15 30	16 00
18¼	**Harrogate**		a	00 06	06 43	07 05	07 49	08 13	08 33	09 03	09 33	10 03	10 33	11 03	11 33	12 03	12 33	13 05	13 33	14 03	14 33	15 03	15 33	16 03
—			d		06 45	07 05	07 49	08 16	08 34	09 05	09 35	10 05	10 35	11 05	11 35	12 05	12 35	13 07	13 35	14 05	14 35	15 05	15 35	16 05
20½	Starbeck		d		06 49	07 08	07 52	08 19	08 38	09 08	09 38	10 08	10 38	11 08	11 38	12 08	12 38	13 10	13 38	14 08	14 38	15 08	15 38	16 08
22	**Knaresborough**		a		06 54	07 16	07 59	08 25	08 45	09 14	09 45	10 14	10 45	11 14	11 45	12 14	12 45	13 16	13 45	14 14	14 45	15 14	15 45	16 14
—			d		06 55	07 19	07 59	08 28		09 15		10 14		11 14		12 14		13 16		14 14		15 14		16 14
28½	Cattal		d		07 03	07 27	08 07	08 36		09 23		10 22		11 22		12 22		13 24		14 22		15 22		16 22
30	Hammerton		d		07 06	07 30	08 11	08 39		09 27		10 26		11 26		12 26		13 28		14 26		15 26		16 26
35¾	Poppleton		d		07 13	07 37	08 18	08 46		09 34		10 33		11 33		12 33		13 35		14 33		15 33		16 33
38¾	**York** 8	40	a		07 21	07 48	08 32	08 58		09 45		10 45		11 44		12 45		13 44		14 44		15 46		16 45

			NT	NT	NT	NT	NT	NT	NT	NT	NT	NT	NT	GR 1st class, Reservations, A, Restaurant	NT	NT	NT	NT
Leeds 10	40	d	15 59	16 29	16 42	16 59	17 13	17 29	17 44	17 59	18 29	18 59	19 29	19 59	20 29	21 29	22 31	23 29
Burley Park		d	16 03	16 33	16 46	17 03	17 17	17 33	17 48	18 03	18 33	19 03	19 33		20 33	21 33	22 35	23 33
Headingley		d	16 06	16 36	16 49	17 06	17 20	17 36	17 51	18 06	18 36	19 06	19 36		20 36	21 36	22 38	23 36
Horsforth		d	16 11	16 41	16a55	17 11	17 25	17 41	17 56	18 11	18 41	19 11	19 41		20 41	21 41	22 43	23 41
Weeton		d	16 19	16 49		17 19	17 33	17 49		18 19	18 49	19 19	19 49		20 49	21 49	22 52	23 49
Pannal		d	16 25	16 55		17 25	17 39	17 55		18 25	18 55	19 25	19 55		20 55	21 55	22 57	23 55
Hornbeam Park		d	16 30	17 00		17 30	17 44	18 00		18 30	19 00	19 30	20 00		21 00	22 00	23 03	23 58
Harrogate		a	16 33	17 03		17 33	17 47	18 03	18 15	18 33	19 03	19 33	20 03	20 27	21 03	22 03	23 09	00 06
		d	16 35	17 05		17 35	17 49	18 05	18 16	18 35	19 05	19 35	20 05		21 05	22 05		
Starbeck		d	16 38	17 08		17 38	17 52	18 08	18 20	18 39	19 08	19 38	20 08		21 08	22 08		
Knaresborough		a	16 45	17 13		17 45	18 01	18 14	18 26	18 45	19 14	19 45	20 14		21 14	22 16		
		d		17 13				18 14			19 14		20 14		21 14			
Cattal		d		17 21				18 22			19 22		20 22		21 22			
Hammerton		d		17 25				18 26			19 26		20 26		21 26			
Poppleton		d		17 32				18 33			19 33		20 33		21 33			
York 8	40	a		17 50				18 46			19 43		20 45		21 47			

Mondays to Fridays
from 1 October

			NT MX	NT	NT	NT	NT	NT	NT	NT	NT	NT	NT	NT	NT	NT	NT	NT	NT	NT	NT	NT	NT	NT
Leeds 10	40	d	23p29	06 09	06 29	07 13	07 43	07 59	08 29	08 59	09 29	09 59	10 29	10 59	11 29	11 59	12 29	12 59	13 29	13 59	14 29	14 59	15 29	15 59
Burley Park		d	23p33	06 13	06 33	07 17	07 47	08 03	08 33	09 03	09 33	10 03	10 33	11 03	11 33	12 03	12 33	13 03	13 33	14 03	14 33	15 03	15 33	16 03
Headingley		d	23p36	06 16	06 36	07 20	07 50	08 06	08 36	09 06	09 36	10 06	10 36	11 06	11 36	12 06	12 36	13 06	13 36	14 06	14 36	15 06	15 36	16 06
Horsforth		d	23p41	06 21	06 41	07 25	07 55	08 11	08 41	09 11	09 41	10 11	10 41	11 11	11 41	12 11	12 41	13 11	13 41	14 11	14 41	15 11	15 41	16 11
Weeton		d	23p49	06 29	06 49	07 33		08 19	08 49	09 19	09 49	10 19	10 49	11 19	11 49	12 19	12 49	13 19	13 49	14 19	14 49	15 19	15 49	16 19
Pannal		d	23p55	06 35	06 55	07 39		08 25	08 55	09 25	09 55	10 25	10 55	11 25	11 55	12 25	12 55	13 25	13 55	14 25	14 55	15 25	15 55	16 25
Hornbeam Park		d	23p58	06 40	07 00	07 44	08 10	08 30	09 00	09 30	10 00	10 30	11 00	11 30	12 00	12 30	13 00	13 30	14 00	14 30	15 00	15 30	16 00	16 30
Harrogate		a	00 06	06 43	07 05	07 49	08 13	08 33	09 03	09 33	10 03	10 33	11 03	11 33	12 03	12 33	13 05	13 33	14 03	14 33	15 03	15 33	16 03	16 33
		d		06 45	07 05	07 49	08 16	08 34	09 05	09 35	10 05	10 35	11 05	11 35	12 05	12 35	13 07	13 35	14 05	14 35	15 05	15 35	16 05	16 35
Starbeck		d		06 49	07 08	07 52	08 19	08 38	09 08	09 38	10 08	10 38	11 08	11 38	12 08	12 38	13 10	13 38	14 08	14 38	15 08	15 38	16 08	16 38
Knaresborough		a		06 54	07 16	07 59	08 25	08 47	09 14	09 47	10 14	10 47	11 14	11 47	12 14	12 47	13 16	13 47	14 14	14 47	15 14	15 47	16 14	16 47
		d		06 55	07 19	07 59	08 28		09 15		10 14		11 14		12 14		13 16		14 14		15 14		16 14	
Cattal		d		07 03	07 27	08 07	08 36		09 23		10 22		11 22		12 22		13 24		14 22		15 22		16 22	
Hammerton		d		07 06	07 30	08 11	08 39		09 27		10 26		11 26		12 26		13 28		14 26		15 26		16 26	
Poppleton		d		07 13	07 37	08 18	08 46		09 34		10 33		11 33		12 33		13 35		14 33		15 33		16 33	
York 8	40	a		07 21	07 47	08 32	08 59		09 45		10 45		11 46		12 45		13 46		14 46		15 47		16 46	

			NT	NT	NT	NT	NT	NT	NT	NT	NT	NT	GR 1st class, Reservations, A, Restaurant	NT	NT	NT	NT
Leeds 10	40	d	16 29	16 42	16 59	17 13	17 29	17 44	17 59	18 29	18 59	19 29	19 59	20 29	21 29	22 31	23 29
Burley Park		d	16 33	16 46	17 03	17 17	17 33	17 48	18 03	18 33	19 03	19 33		20 33	21 33	22 35	23 33
Headingley		d	16 36	16 49	17 06	17 20	17 36	17 51	18 06	18 36	19 06	19 36		20 36	21 36	22 38	23 36
Horsforth		d	16 41	16a55	17 11	17 25	17 41	17 56	18 11	18 41	19 11	19 41		20 41	21 41	22 43	23 41
Weeton		d	16 49		17 19	17 33	17 49		18 19	18 49	19 19	19 49		20 49	21 49	22 52	23 49
Pannal		d	16 55		17 25	17 39	17 55		18 25	18 55	19 25	19 55		20 55	21 55	22 57	23 55
Hornbeam Park		d	17 00		17 30	17 44	18 00		18 30	19 00	19 30	20 00		21 00	22 00	23 03	23 58
Harrogate		a	17 03		17 33	17 47	18 03	18 15	18 33	19 03	19 33	20 03	20 27	21 03	22 03	23 09	00 06
		d	17 05		17 35	17 49	18 05	18 16	18 35	19 05	19 35	20 05		21 05	22 05		
Starbeck		d	17 08		17 38	17 52	18 08	18 20	18 39	19 08	19 38	20 08		21 08	22 08		
Knaresborough		a	17 13		17 47	18 03	18 14	18 28	18 47	19 14	19 47	20 14		21 14	22 18		
		d	17 13				18 14			19 14		20 14		21 14			
Cattal		d	17 21				18 22			19 22		20 22		21 22			
Hammerton		d	17 25				18 26			19 26		20 26		21 26			
Poppleton		d	17 32				18 33			19 33		20 33		21 33			
York 8	40	a	17 50				18 46			19 45		20 47		21 50			

A From London Kings Cross

Table 35

Leeds - Harrogate - York

Saturdays
until 29 September

Network Diagram - see first page of Table 35

			NT	NT	NT	NT	NT	NT	NT	NT	NT	NT	NT	NT	NT	NT	NT	NT	NT	NT	NT	NT	NT	NT
Leeds 10	40	d	23p29	06 09	06 36	07 13	07 39	07 54	08 29	08 59	09 29	09 59	10 29	10 59	11 29	11 59	12 29	12 59	13 29	13 59	14 29	14 59	15 29	15 59
Burley Park		d	23p33	06 13	06 40	07 17	07 43	07 58	08 33	09 03	09 33	10 03	10 33	11 03	11 33	12 03	12 33	13 03	13 33	14 03	14 33	15 03	15 33	16 03
Headingley		d	23p36	06 16	06 43	07 20	07 46	08 01	08 36	09 06	09 36	10 06	10 36	11 06	11 36	12 06	12 36	13 06	13 36	14 06	14 36	15 06	15 36	16 06
Horsforth		d	23p41	06 21	06 48	07 25	07 51	08 06	08 41	09 11	09 41	10 11	10 41	11 11	11 41	12 11	12 41	13 11	13 41	14 11	14 41	15 11	15 41	16 11
Weeton		d	23p49	06 29	06 56	07 33	07 59	08 14	08 49	09 19	09 49	10 19	10 49	11 19	11 49	12 19	12 49	13 19	13 49	14 19	14 49	15 19	15 49	16 19
Pannal		d	23p55	06 35	07 02	07 39	08 09	08 22	08 55	09 25	09 55	10 25	10 55	11 25	11 55	12 25	12 55	13 25	13 55	14 25	14 55	15 25	15 55	16 25
Hornbeam Park		d	23p58	06 40	07 07	07 44	08 14	08 28	09 00	09 30	10 00	10 30	11 00	11 30	12 00	12 30	13 00	13 30	14 00	14 30	15 00	15 30	16 00	16 30
Harrogate		a	00 06	06 43	07 10	07 47	08 17	08 31	09 03	09 33	10 03	10 33	11 03	11 33	12 03	12 33	13 03	13 33	14 03	14 33	15 03	15 33	16 03	16 33
		d		06 45	07 12	07 49	08 19	08 31	09 05	09 35	10 05	10 35	11 05	11 35	12 05	12 35	13 05	13 35	14 05	14 35	15 05	15 35	16 05	16 35
Starbeck		d		06 49	07 15	07 52	08 22	08 36	09 08	09 38	10 08	10 38	11 08	11 38	12 08	12 38	13 08	13 38	14 08	14 38	15 08	15 38	16 08	16 38
Knaresborough		a		06 54	07 21	07 59	08 28	08 42	09 14	09 45	10 14	10 45	11 14	11 45	12 14	12 45	13 14	13 45	14 14	14 45	15 14	15 45	16 14	16 45
		d		06 55	07 21	07 59	08 28		09 15		10 14		11 14		12 14		13 14		14 14		15 14		16 14	
Cattal		d		07 03	07 29	08 07	08 36		09 23		10 22		11 22		12 22		13 22		14 22		15 22		16 22	
Hammerton		d		07 06	07 33	08 11	08 40		09 27		10 26		11 26		12 26		13 26		14 26		15 26		16 26	
Poppleton		d		07 13	07 40	08 19	08 47		09 34		10 33		11 33		12 33		13 33		14 33		15 33		16 33	
York 8	40	a		07 21	07 46	08 26	08 59		09 45		10 45		11 45		12 45		13 45		14 44		15 46		16 44	

			NT	NT	NT	NT	NT	NT	NT	GR 1st class, Reservations, A, Restaurant	NT	NT	NT	NT
Leeds 10	40	d	16 29	16 59	17 13	17 29	17 59	18 29	19 29	19 59	20 29	21 20	22 33	23 21
Burley Park		d	16 33	17 03	17 17	17 33	18 03	18 33	19 33		20 33	21 24	22 37	23 25
Headingley		d	16 36	17 06	17 20	17 36	18 06	18 36	19 36		20 36	21 27	22 40	23 28
Horsforth		d	16 41	17 11	17 25	17 41	18 11	18 41	19 41		20 41	21 32	22 45	23 33
Weeton		d	16 49	17 19	17 33	17 49	18 19	18 49	19 49		20 49	21 40	22 53	23 41
Pannal		d	16 55	17 25	17 39	17 55	18 25	18 55	19 55		20 55	21 46	22 59	23 47
Hornbeam Park		d	17 00	17 30	17 44	18 00	18 30	19 00	20 00		21 00	21 51	23 04	23 52
Harrogate		a	17 03	17 33	17 47	18 03	18 33	19 03	20 04	20 27	21 03	21 54	23 10	23 58
		d	17 08	17 35	17 49	18 05	18 35	19 05	20 04		21 05	21 56		
Starbeck		d	17 11	17 38	17 52	18 08	18 38	19 08	20 08		21 08	21 59		
Knaresborough		a	17 17	17 45	18 00	18 14	18 45	19 14	20 14		21 14	22 06		
		d	17 21			18 14		19 14	20 14		21 14			
Cattal		d	17 29			18 22		19 22	20 22		21 22			
Hammerton		d	17 34			18 26		19 26	20 26		21 27			
Poppleton		d	17 41			18 33		19 33	20 33		21 34			
York 8	40	a	17 52			18 44		19 45	20 47		21 48			

Saturdays
from 6 October

			NT	NT	NT	NT	NT	NT	NT	NT	NT	NT	NT	NT	NT	NT	NT	NT	NT	NT	NT	NT	NT	NT
Leeds 10	40	d	23p29	06 09	06 36	07 13	07 39	07 54	08 29	08 59	09 29	09 59	10 29	10 59	11 29	11 59	12 29	12 59	13 29	13 59	14 29	14 59	15 29	15 59
Burley Park		d	23p33	06 13	06 40	07 17	07 43	07 58	08 33	09 03	09 33	10 03	10 33	11 03	11 33	12 03	12 33	13 03	13 33	14 03	14 33	15 03	15 33	16 03
Headingley		d	23p36	06 16	06 43	07 20	07 46	08 01	08 36	09 06	09 36	10 06	10 36	11 06	11 36	12 06	12 36	13 06	13 36	14 06	14 36	15 06	15 36	16 06
Horsforth		d	23p41	06 21	06 48	07 25	07 51	08 06	08 41	09 11	09 41	10 11	10 41	11 11	11 41	12 11	12 41	13 11	13 41	14 11	14 41	15 11	15 41	16 11
Weeton		d	23p49	06 29	06 56	07 33	07 59	08 14	08 49	09 19	09 49	10 19	10 49	11 19	11 49	12 19	12 49	13 19	13 49	14 19	14 49	15 19	15 49	16 19
Pannal		d	23p55	06 35	07 02	07 39	08 09	08 22	08 55	09 25	09 55	10 25	10 55	11 25	11 55	12 25	12 55	13 25	13 55	14 25	14 55	15 25	15 55	16 25
Hornbeam Park		d	23p58	06 40	07 07	07 44	08 14	08 28	09 00	09 30	10 00	10 30	11 00	11 30	12 00	12 30	13 00	13 30	14 00	14 30	15 00	15 30	16 00	16 30
Harrogate		a	00 06	06 43	07 10	07 47	08 17	08 31	09 03	09 33	10 03	10 33	11 03	11 33	12 03	12 33	13 03	13 33	14 03	14 33	15 03	15 33	16 03	16 33
		d		06 45	07 12	07 49	08 19	08 31	09 05	09 35	10 05	10 35	11 05	11 35	12 05	12 35	13 05	13 35	14 05	14 35	15 05	15 35	16 05	16 35
Starbeck		d		06 49	07 15	07 52	08 22	08 36	09 08	09 38	10 08	10 38	11 08	11 38	12 08	12 38	13 08	13 38	14 08	14 38	15 08	15 38	16 08	16 38
Knaresborough		a		06 54	07 21	07 59	08 28	08 45	09 14	09 46	10 14	10 47	11 14	11 47	12 14	12 47	13 14	13 47	14 14	14 47	15 14	15 47	16 14	16 47
		d		06 55	07 21	07 59	08 28		09 15		10 14		11 14		12 14		13 14		14 14		15 14		16 14	
Cattal		d		07 03	07 29	08 07	08 36		09 23		10 22		11 22		12 22		13 22		14 22		15 22		16 22	
Hammerton		d		07 06	07 33	08 11	08 40		09 27		10 26		11 26		12 26		13 26		14 26		15 26		16 26	
Poppleton		d		07 13	07 40	08 19	08 47		09 34		10 33		11 33		12 33		13 33		14 33		15 33		16 33	
York 8	40	a		07 21	07 47	08 26	08 59		09 45		10 45		11 45		12 45		13 48		14 46		15 47		16 45	

			NT	NT	NT	NT	NT	NT	NT	GR 1st class, Reservations, A, Restaurant	NT	NT	NT	NT
Leeds 10	40	d	16 29	16 59	17 13	17 29	17 59	18 29	19 29	19 59	20 29	21 20	22 33	23 21
Burley Park		d	16 33	17 03	17 17	17 33	18 03	18 33	19 33		20 33	21 24	22 37	23 25
Headingley		d	16 36	17 06	17 20	17 36	18 06	18 36	19 36		20 36	21 27	22 40	23 28
Horsforth		d	16 41	17 11	17 25	17 41	18 11	18 41	19 41		20 41	21 32	22 45	23 33
Weeton		d	16 49	17 19	17 33	17 49	18 19	18 49	19 49		20 49	21 40	22 53	23 41
Pannal		d	16 55	17 25	17 39	17 55	18 25	18 55	19 55		20 55	21 46	22 59	23 47
Hornbeam Park		d	17 00	17 30	17 44	18 00	18 30	19 00	20 00		21 00	21 51	23 04	23 52
Harrogate		a	17 03	17 33	17 47	18 03	18 33	19 03	20 04	20 27	21 03	21 54	23 10	23 58
		d	17 08	17 35	17 49	18 05	18 35	19 05	20 04		21 05	21 56		
Starbeck		d	17 11	17 38	17 52	18 08	18 38	19 08	20 08		21 08	21 59		
Knaresborough		a	17 17	17 47	18 03	18 14	18 47	19 14	20 14		21 14	22 08		
		d	17 21			18 14		19 14	20 14		21 14			
Cattal		d	17 29			18 22		19 22	20 22		21 22			
Hammerton		d	17 34			18 26		19 26	20 26		21 27			
Poppleton		d	17 41			18 33		19 33	20 33		21 34			
York 8	40	a	17 52			18 45		19 45	20 47		21 48			

A From London Kings Cross

Leeds - Harrogate - York

Sundays until 30 September

Network Diagram - see first page of Table 35

			NT	NT	NT	NT	NT	NT	NT	NT	NT		GR A	NT	NT	NT
Leeds	40	d	09 54	10 54	12 54	14 54	15 54	16 54	17 54	18 54	19 54		20 37	21 16	22 26	23 23
Burley Park		d	09 59	10 59	12 59	14 59	15 59	16 59	17 59	18 59	19 59			21 21	22 31	23 28
Headingley		d	10 01	11 01	13 01	15 01	16 01	17 01	18 01	19 01	20 01			21 23	22 33	23 30
Horsforth		d	10 07	11 07	13 07	15 07	16 07	17 07	18 07	19 07	20 07			21 29	22 39	23 36
Weeton		d	10 14	11 14	13 14	15 14	16 14	17 14	18 14	19 14	20 14			21 37	22 46	23 43
Pannal		d	10 20	11 20	13 20	15 20	16 20	17 20	18 20	19 20	20 20			21 43	22 52	23 49
Hornbeam Park		d	10 25	11 25	13 25	15 25	16 25	17 25	18 25	19 25	20 25			21 48	22 57	23 54
Harrogate		a	10 31	11 28	13 28	15 28	16 28	17 28	18 28	19 28	20 28		21 05	21 51	23 03	23 59
		d		11 30	13 30	15 30	16 30	17 33	18 30	19 30	20 30			21 53		
Starbeck		d		11 34	13 34	15 34	16 34	17 36	18 34	19 34	20 34			21 57		
Knaresborough		a		11 39	13 39	15 39	16 39	17 42	18 39	19 39	20 39			22 03		
		d		11 40	13 40	15 40	16 45	17 44	18 44	19 44	20 45					
Cattal		d		11 48	13 48	15 48	16 53	17 52	18 52	19 52	20 53					
Hammerton		d		11 51	13 51	15 51	16 56	17 55	18 55	19 55	20 56					
Poppleton		d		11 58	13 58	15 58	17 03	18 02	19 02	20 02	21 03					
York	40	a		12 07	14 08	16 06	17 10	18 10	19 12	20 11	21 15					

Sundays from 7 October

			NT	NT	NT	NT	NT	NT	NT	NT	NT		GR A	NT	NT	NT
Leeds	40	d	09 54	10 54	12 54	14 54	15 54	16 54	17 54	18 54	19 54		20 37	21 16	22 26	23 23
Burley Park		d	09 59	10 59	12 59	14 59	15 59	16 59	17 59	18 59	19 59			21 21	22 31	23 28
Headingley		d	10 01	11 01	13 01	15 01	16 01	17 01	18 01	19 01	20 01			21 23	22 33	23 30
Horsforth		d	10 07	11 07	13 07	15 07	16 07	17 07	18 07	19 07	20 07			21 29	22 39	23 36
Weeton		d	10 14	11 14	13 14	15 14	16 14	17 14	18 14	19 14	20 14			21 37	22 46	23 43
Pannal		d	10 20	11 20	13 20	15 20	16 20	17 20	18 20	19 20	20 20			21 43	22 52	23 49
Hornbeam Park		d	10 25	11 25	13 25	15 25	16 25	17 25	18 25	19 25	20 25			21 48	22 57	23 54
Harrogate		a	10 31	11 28	13 28	15 28	16 28	17 28	18 28	19 28	20 28		21 05	21 51	23 03	23 59
		d		11 30	13 30	15 30	16 30	17 33	18 30	19 30	20 30			21 53		
Starbeck		d		11 34	13 34	15 34	16 34	17 36	18 34	19 34	20 34			21 57		
Knaresborough		a		11 39	13 39	15 39	16 39	17 42	18 39	19 39	20 39			22 06		
		d		11 40	13 40	15 40	16 45	17 44	18 44	19 44	20 45					
Cattal		d		11 48	13 48	15 48	16 53	17 52	18 52	19 52	20 53					
Hammerton		d		11 51	13 51	15 51	16 56	17 55	18 55	19 55	20 56					
Poppleton		d		11 58	13 58	15 58	17 03	18 02	19 02	20 02	21 03					
York	40	a		12 07	14 08	16 07	17 12	18 12	19 12	20 12	21 15					

A From London Kings Cross

Leeds and Bradford - Skipton, Lancaster, Morecambe and Carlisle

Mondays to Fridays

Network Diagram - see first page of Table 35

Miles	Miles	Miles				NT MX	NT	NT	NT	NT	NT	NT	NT	NT		NT	NT	NT	NT	NT	NT	NT	NT	NT		NT
—	—	—	London Kings Cross	⊖26	d																					
0	0	—	**Leeds**	37	d	23p18		05 29		06 16		06 56		07 25			07 51		08 19	08 25		08 49	08 56			09 26
—	—	0	**Bradford Forster Square**	37	d				06 04		06 39		07 15			07 42		08 09			08 41			09 11		
—	—	1¾	Frizinghall	37	d				06 07		06 43		07 18			07 45		08 12			08 44			09 14		
10¼	10¼	2¾	Shipley	37	a	23p31		05 41	06 11	06 27	06 47	07 08	07 22	07 36		07 49	08 02	08 16	08 31	08 37	08 48	09 01	09 07	09 18		09 37
—	—	—			d	23p32		05 42	06 12	06 28	06 48	07 08	07 23	07 37		07 50	08 03	08 17	08 32	08 37	08 49	09 02	09 09	09 19		09 38
11½	11½	—	Saltaire		d	23p34		05 44	06 14	06 30	06 50	07 10	07 25	07 39		07 52	08 05	08 20		08 40	08 52		09 11	09 22		09 40
13¾	13¾	—	Bingley		d	23p38		05 49	06 18	06 34	06 54	07 14	07 29	07 43		07 56	08 09	08 24	08 37	08 44	08 56	09 06	09 14	09 26		09 44
14½	14½	—	Crossflatts		d	23p40		05 51	06 20	06 36	06 56	07 17	07 31	07 46		07 58	08 11	08 26		08 46	08 58		09 17	09 28		09 47
17	17	—	Keighley		d	23p44		05 56	06 25	06 41	07 01	07 21	07 36	07 50		08 03	08 15	08 31	08 43	08 50	09 03	09 12	09 21	09 33		09 51
20	20	—	Steeton & Silsden		d	23p48		06 00	06 29	06 45	07 05	07 26	07 40	07 55		08 07	08 19	08 35		08 54	09 07		09 26	09 37		09 56
23¼	23¼	—	Cononley		d	23p52		06 05	06 33	06 49	07 09	07 30	07 44	07 59		08 11	08 23	08 40		08 59	09 12		09 30	09 42		10 00
26¼	26¼	—	**Skipton**		a	00 02		06 12	06 42	06 59	07 18	07 39	07 52	08 08		08 20	08 32	08 48	08 55	09 09	09 20	09 24	09 40	09 50		10 11
—	—	—			d		05 40	06 15											09 00			09 26				
30	30	—	Gargrave		d		05 45												09 05			09 32				
—	—	—	Blackpool North	94	d																					
—	—	—	Preston		d																					
—	—	—	Blackburn	97	d																					
—	—	—	Clitheroe	94	d																					
36¼	36¼	—	Hellifield		d		05 54	06 26											09 14			09 40				
37½	37½	—	Long Preston		d		05 57												09 17			09 43				
—	41¼	—	Giggleswick		d		06 07												09 24							
—	48	—	Clapham (N Yorkshire)		d		06 15												09 33							
—	51¼	—	Bentham		d		06 21												09 39							
—	54½	—	Wennington		d		06 26												09 44							
—	64	—	Carnforth	82	a		06 42												10 00							
—	70¼	—	**Lancaster**	65,82,98	a		06 52												10 12							
—	72¾	—	Bare Lane	98	a														10 26							
—	75½	—	**Morecambe**	98	a														10 31							
41¼	—	—	Settle		d			06 34														09 50				
47½	—	—	Horton-in-Ribblesdale		d																	09 58				
52¼	—	—	Ribblehead		d			06 49														10 06				
58¾	—	—	Dent		d																	10 16				
61¾	—	—	Garsdale		d			07 04														10 21				
71½	—	—	Kirkby Stephen		d			07 16														10 34				
82¼	—	—	Appleby		d			07 30														10 47				
93¼	—	—	Langwathby		d			07 44														11 01				
97½	—	—	Lazonby & Kirkoswald		d			07 49														11 07				
103	—	—	Armathwaite		d			07 57														11 15				
113	—	—	**Carlisle**	65	a			08 17														11 34				

			NT	NT	NT	NT	NT A	NT	NT	NT		NT	NT	NT	NT	NT	NT	NT	NT	NT		NT	NT	NT	NT	NT
London Kings Cross	⊖26	d																								
Leeds	37	d		09 47	09 56		10 19	10 26		10 49		10 56		11 26		11 56		12 26		12 49		12 56		13 26		13 49
Bradford Forster Square	37	d	09 41			10 11			10 41				11 11		11 41		12 11		12 41				13 11		13 41	
Frizinghall	37	d	09 44			10 14			10 44				11 14		11 44		12 14		12 44				13 14		13 44	
Shipley	37	a	09 48	10 01	10 07	10 18	10 31	10 37	10 48	11 01		11 07	11 18	11 38	11 48	12 07	12 18	12 37	12 48	13 01		13 07	13 18	13 37	13 48	14 03
		d	09 49	10 02	10 08	10 19	10 32	10 38	10 49	11 02		11 08	11 19	11 39	11 49	12 08	12 19	12 38	12 49	13 02		13 08	13 19	13 38	13 49	14 03
Saltaire		d	09 52		10 10	10 22		10 40	10 52			11 10	11 21	11 40	11 51	12 10	12 22	12 40	12 52			13 10	13 22	13 40	13 52	
Bingley		d	09 56	10 06	10 14	10 26	10 37	10 44	10 56	11 06		11 14	11 25	11 44	11 55	12 14	12 26	12 44	12 56	13 06		13 14	13 26	13 44	13 56	14 08
Crossflatts		d	09 58		10 17	10 28		10 47	10 58			11 17	11 27	11 47	11 57	12 17	12 28	12 47	12 58			13 17	13 28	13 47	13 58	
Keighley		d	10 03	10 12	10 21	10 33	10 42	10 51	11 03	11 12		11 21	11 32	11 51	12 02	12 21	12 33	12 51	13 03	13 12		13 21	13 33	13 51	14 03	14 14
Steeton & Silsden		d	10 07		10 26	10 37		10 56	11 07			11 26	11 36	11 56	12 06	12 26	12 37	12 56	13 07			13 26	13 37	13 56	14 07	
Cononley		d	10 12		10 30	10 42		11 00	11 12			11 30	11 40	12 00	12 10	12 30	12 42	13 00	13 12			13 30	13 42	14 00	14 11	
Skipton		a	10 20	10 24	10 39	10 50	10 55	11 11	11 20	11 24		11 40	11 50	12 11	12 20	12 40	12 50	13 10	13 20	13 24		13 38	13 50	14 10	14 20	14 26
		d		10 26			11 00			11 26										13 26						14 34
Gargrave		d					11 05													13 31						14 39
Blackpool North	94	d																								
Preston		d																								
Blackburn	97	d																								
Clitheroe	94	d																								
Hellifield		d					11 14			11 37										13 40						14 48
Long Preston		d					11 17													13 42						14 51
Giggleswick		d					11 24																			14 58
Clapham (N Yorkshire)		d					11 33																			15 07
Bentham		d					11 39																			15 13
Wennington		d					11 44																			15 18
Carnforth	82	a					12 00																			15 34
Lancaster	65,82,98	a					12 11																			15 47
Bare Lane	98	a					12 34																			16 09
Morecambe	98	a					12 39																			16 13
Settle		d		10 44						11 46										13 48						
Horton-in-Ribblesdale		d								11 54										13 57						
Ribblehead		d								12 02										14 05						
Dent		d								12 12										14 14						
Garsdale		d								12 17										14 20						
Kirkby Stephen		d		11 22						12 30										14 32						
Appleby		d		11 36						12 43										14 45						
Langwathby		d								12 57										14 59						
Lazonby & Kirkoswald		d								13 03										15 04						
Armathwaite		d								13 11										15 12						
Carlisle	65	a		12 17						13 29										15 32						

A To Heysham Port

Table 36

Mondays to Fridays

Leeds and Bradford - Skipton, Lancaster, Morecambe and Carlisle

Network Diagram - see first page of Table 35

			NT	NT	NT	NT	NT	NT	NT	NT	NT	NT	NT	NT	NT	NT	NT	NT	NT	NT	NT	NT	NT	NT
London Kings Cross 15	⊖26	d																						
Leeds 10	37	d	13 56		14 26		14 49	14 56		15 26		15 56		16 26		16 39	16 56		17 26		17 39	17 56	18 06	
Bradford Forster Square	37	d		14 11		14 41			15 11		15 41		16 11		16 40			17 11		17 38				18 16
Frizinghall	37	d		14 14		14 44			15 14		15 44		16 14		16 43			17 14		17 41				18 19
Shipley	37	a	14 07	14 18	14 37	14 48	15 01	15 07	15 18	15 37	15 48	16 07	16 18	16 37	16 48	16 53	17 07	17 18	17 37	17 45	17 53	18 07	18 18	18 23
		d	14 08	14 19	14 38	14 49	15 02	15 08	15 19	15 38	15 49	16 08	16 19	16 38	16 49	16 55	17 08	17 19	17 38	17 46	17 54	18 08	18 18	18 23
Saltaire		d	14 10	14 22	14 40	14 52		15 10	15 22	15 40	15 52	16 10	16 22	16 40	16 52		17 10	17 22	17 40	17 49	17 56	18 10		18 27
Bingley		d	14 14	14 26	14 44	14 56	15 06	15 14	15 26	15 44	15 56	16 14	16 26	16 44	16 56	17 03	17 14	17 26	17 44	17 53	18 00	18 14	18 24	18 31
Crossflatts		d	14 17	14 28	14 47	14 58		15 17	15 28	15 47	15 58	16 17	16 28	16 47	16 58		17 17	17 28	17 47	17 55	18 03	18 17		18 33
Keighley		d	14 21	14 33	14 51	15 03	15 12	15 21	15 33	15 51	16 03	16 21	16 33	16 51	17 03	17 10	17 21	17 33	17 51	18 00	18 07	18 21	18 29	18 38
Steeton & Silsden		d	14 26	14 37	14 56	15 07		15 26	15 37	15 56	16 07	16 26	16 37	16 56	17 07		17 26	17 37	17 56	18 04	18 12	18 26	18 34	18 42
Cononley		d	14 30	14 41	15 00	15 12		15 30	15 42	16 00	16 11	16 30	16 41	17 00	17 11		17 30	17 42	18 00	18 09	18 16	18 30		18 47
Skipton		a	14 40	14 50	15 10	15 20	15 24	15 40	15 50	16 10	16 20	16 40	16 50	17 10	17 19	17 24	17 40	17 50	18 10	18 17	18 24	18 40	18 45	18 55
		d					15 26									17 24							18 46	
Gargrave		d														17 30							18 51	
Blackpool North	94	d																						
Preston		d																						
Blackburn	97	d																						
Clitheroe	94	d																						
Hellifield		d					15 37									17 39							19 00	
Long Preston		d														17 42							19 02	
Giggleswick		d														17 49								
Clapham (N Yorkshire)		d														17 57								
Bentham		d														18 04								
Wennington		d														18 09								
Carnforth	82	a														18 29								
Lancaster 6	65,82,98	a														18 42								
Bare Lane	98	a														18 55								
Morecambe	98	a														19 01								
Settle		d					15 45																19 08	
Horton-in-Ribblesdale		d					15 53																19 17	
Ribblehead		d					16 01																19 25	
Dent		d					16 11																19 34	
Garsdale		d					16 16																19 40	
Kirkby Stephen		d					16 29																19 52	
Appleby		d					16 41																20 05	
Langwathby		d					16 55																20 19	
Lazonby & Kirkoswald		d					17 01																20 24	
Armathwaite		d					17 09																20 32	
Carlisle 8	65	a					17 28																20 52	

			NT	NT	NT	NT	NT	NT	NT	NT	NT	NT	GR	NT	NT	NT	NT	NT	NT	NT	NT	NT
													R 1									
London Kings Cross 15	⊖26	d											18 03									
Leeds 10	37	d	18 26		18 54		19 19	19 26		19 56		20 26	20 33	20 56		21 26	21 56		22 26	22 56		23 18
Bradford Forster Square	37	d		18 41		19 07			19 36		20 07				21 05			22 05			23 09	
Frizinghall	37	d		18 44		19 10			19 39		20 10				21 08			22 08			23 12	
Shipley	37	a	18 38	18 48	19 05	19 14	19 31	19 37	19 43	20 07	20 15	20 37		21 07	21 12	21 38	22 07	22 12	22 37	23 08	23 16	23 31
		d	18 38	18 49	19 06	19 15	19 32	19 38	19 44	20 08	20 15	20 38		21 08	21 14	21 38	22 08	22 14	22 38	23 09	23 17	23 32
Saltaire		d	18 40	18 51	19 08	19 18		19 40	19 47	20 10	20 17	20 40		21 10	21 17	21 40	22 10	22 16	22 40	23 11	23 20	23 34
Bingley		d	18 44	18 55	19 12	19 22	19 36	19 44	19 51	20 14	20 21	20 44		21 14	21 21	21 44	22 14	22 20	22 44	23 16	23 24	23 38
Crossflatts		d	18 47	18 57	19 15	19 24		19 47	19 53	20 17	20 23	20 47		21 17	21 23	21 47	22 17	22 22	22 47	23 18	23 26	23 40
Keighley		d	18 51	19 02	19 19	19 29	19 42	19 51	19 58	20 21	20 28	20 51	20s55	21 21	21 28	21 51	22 21	22 27	22 51	23 23	23 31	23 44
Steeton & Silsden		d	18 56	19 06	19 24	19 33		19 56	20 02	20 26	20 32	20 56		21 26	21 32	21 56	22 26	22 31	22 56	23 27	23 35	23 48
Cononley		d	19 00	19 10	19 28	19 38		20 00	20 07	20 30	20 36	21 00		21 30	21 37	22 00	22 30	22 35	23 00	23 32	23 40	23 52
Skipton		a	19 10	19 19	19 35	19 46	19 57	20 10	20 15	20 37	20 47	21 10	21 14	21 40	21 44	22 10	22 40	22 42	23 11	23 38	23 48	00 02
		d					20 00															
Gargrave		d					20 06															
Blackpool North	94	d																				
Preston		d																				
Blackburn	97	d																				
Clitheroe	94	d																				
Hellifield		d					20 15															
Long Preston		d					20 18															
Giggleswick		d																				
Clapham (N Yorkshire)		d																				
Bentham		d																				
Wennington		d																				
Carnforth	82	a																				
Lancaster 6	65,82,98	a																				
Bare Lane	98	a																				
Morecambe	98	a																				
Settle		d					20 24															
Horton-in-Ribblesdale		d					20 32															
Ribblehead		d					20a42															
Dent		d																				
Garsdale		d																				
Kirkby Stephen		d																				
Appleby		d																				
Langwathby		d																				
Lazonby & Kirkoswald		d																				
Armathwaite		d																				
Carlisle 8	65	a																				

Table 36

Saturdays

Leeds and Bradford - Skipton, Lancaster, Morecambe and Carlisle

Network Diagram - see first page of Table 35

			NT	NT	NT	NT	NT	NT	NT	NT	NT A	NT	NT	NT	NT	NT	NT	NT	NT	NT	NT	NT B	NT	NT
London Kings Cross 15	⊖26	d																						
Leeds 10	37	d	23p18	05 55		06 19	06 56		07 56		08 19	08 25		08 49	08 56		09 26		09 47	09 56		10 19	10 26	
Bradford Forster Square	37	d			06 10			07 11		08 11			08 41			09 11		09 41			10 11			10 41
Frizinghall	37	d			06 13			07 14		08 14			08 44			09 14		09 44			10 14			10 44
Shipley	37	a	23p31	06 07	06 17	06 31	07 08	07 18	08 08	08 18	08 31	08 37	08 48	09 01	09 07	09 18	09 37	09 48	10 01	10 07	10 18	10 31	10 37	10 48
		d	23p32	06 08	06 19	06 32	07 08	07 19	08 08	08 19	08 32	08 37	08 49	09 02	09 09	09 19	09 38	09 49	10 02	10 08	10 19	10 32	10 38	10 49
Saltaire		d	23p34	06 10	06 22		07 10	07 22	08 10	08 22		08 40	08 52		09 11	09 22	09 40	09 52		10 10	10 22		10 40	10 52
Bingley		d	23p38	06 15	06 26	06 36	07 14	07 26	08 14	08 26	08 37	08 44	08 56	09 06	09 14	09 26	09 44	09 56	10 06	10 14	10 26	10 37	10 44	10 56
Crossflatts		d	23p40	06 17	06 28		07 17	07 28	08 16	08 28		08 46	08 58		09 17	09 28	09 47	09 58		10 17	10 28		10 47	10 58
Keighley		d	23p44	06 22	06 33	06 42	07 21	07 33	08 20	08 33	08 43	08 50	09 03	09 12	09 21	09 33	09 51	10 03	10 12	10 21	10 33	10 42	10 51	11 03
Steeton & Silsden		d	23p48	06 26	06 37		07 26	07 37	08 24	08 37		08 54	09 07		09 26	09 37	09 56	10 07		10 26	10 37		10 56	11 07
Cononley		d	23p52	06 31	06 42		07 30	07 42	08 28	08 42		08 59	09 12		09 30	09 42	10 00	10 12		10 30	10 42		11 00	11 12
Skipton		a	00 02	06 38	06 49	06 55	07 39	07 50	08 39	08 50	08 55	09 09	09 20	09 24	09 40	09 50	10 11	10 20	10 24	10 39	10 50	10 55	11 11	11 20
		d		06 40		06 56					09 00			09 26					10 26			11 00		
Gargrave		d		06 45							09 05			09 32								11 05		
Blackpool North	94	d																						
Preston		d																						
Blackburn	97	d																						
Clitheroe	94	d																						
Hellifield		d		06 54		07 08					09 14			09 40								11 14		
Long Preston		d		06 57							09 17			09 43								11 17		
Giggleswick		d		07 07							09 24											11 25		
Clapham (N Yorkshire)		d		07 15							09 33											11 33		
Bentham		d		07 21							09 39											11 39		
Wennington		d		07 26							09 44											11 44		
Carnforth	82	a		07 42							10 00											12 00		
Lancaster 6	65,82,98	a		07 52							10 12											12 12		
Bare Lane	98	a									10 25											12 31		
Morecambe	98	a									10 32											12 36		
Settle		d				07 15								09 50					10 44					
Horton-in-Ribblesdale		d				07 24								09 58										
Ribblehead		d				07 32								10 06										
Dent		d				07 41								10 16										
Garsdale		d				07 47								10 21										
Kirkby Stephen		d				07 59								10 34					11 22					
Appleby		d				08 12								10 47					11 36					
Langwathby		d				08 26								11 01										
Lazonby & Kirkoswald		d				08 31								11 07										
Armathwaite		d				08 39								11 15										
Carlisle 8	65	a				08 58								11 34					12 17					

			NT	NT	NT	NT	NT	NT	NT	NT	NT	NT	NT	NT	NT	NT	NT	NT	NT	NT	NT	NT	NT	NT
London Kings Cross 15	⊖26	d																						
Leeds 10	37	d	10 49	10 56		11 26		11 56		12 26		12 49	12 56		13 26		13 49	13 56		14 26		14 49	14 56	
Bradford Forster Square	37	d			11 11		11 41		12 11		12 41			13 11		13 41			14 11		14 41			15 11
Frizinghall	37	d			11 14		11 44		12 14		12 44			13 14		13 44			14 14		14 44			15 14
Shipley	37	a	11 01	11 07	11 18	11 38	11 48	12 07	12 18	12 37	12 48	13 01	13 07	13 18	13 37	13 48	14 03	14 07	14 18	14 37	14 48	15 01	15 07	15 18
		d	11 02	11 08	11 19	11 38	11 49	12 08	12 19	12 38	12 49	13 02	13 08	13 19	13 38	13 49	14 03	14 08	14 19	14 38	14 49	15 02	15 08	15 19
Saltaire		d		11 10	11 21	11 40	11 51	12 10	12 22	12 40	12 52		13 10	13 22	13 40	13 52		14 10	14 22	14 40	14 52		15 10	15 22
Bingley		d	11 06	11 14	11 25	11 44	11 55	12 14	12 26	12 44	12 56	13 06	13 14	13 26	13 44	13 56	14 08	14 14	14 26	14 44	14 56	15 06	15 14	15 26
Crossflatts		d		11 17	11 27	11 47	11 57	12 17	12 28	12 47	12 58		13 17	13 28	13 47	13 58		14 17	14 28	14 47	14 58		15 17	15 28
Keighley		d	11 12	11 21	11 32	11 51	12 02	12 21	12 33	12 51	13 03	13 12	13 21	13 33	13 51	14 03	14 14	14 21	14 33	14 51	15 03	15 12	15 21	15 33
Steeton & Silsden		d		11 26	11 36	11 56	12 06	12 26	12 37	12 56	13 07		13 26	13 37	13 56	14 07		14 26	14 37	14 56	15 07		15 26	15 37
Cononley		d		11 30	11 40	12 00	12 10	12 30	12 42	13 00	13 12		13 30	13 42	14 00	14 11		14 30	14 41	15 00	15 12		15 30	15 42
Skipton		a	11 24	11 40	11 50	12 11	12 20	12 40	12 50	13 10	13 20	13 24	13 38	13 50	14 10	14 20	14 26	14 40	14 50	15 10	15 20	15 24	15 40	15 50
		d	11 26									13 26					14 34					15 26		
Gargrave		d										13 31					14 39							
Blackpool North	94	d																						
Preston		d																						
Blackburn	97	d																						
Clitheroe	94	d																						
Hellifield		d	11 37									13 40					14 48					15 37		
Long Preston		d										13 42					14 51							
Giggleswick		d															14 59							
Clapham (N Yorkshire)		d															15 07							
Bentham		d															15 13							
Wennington		d															15 18							
Carnforth	82	a															15 34							
Lancaster 6	65,82,98	a															15 45							
Bare Lane	98	a															15 55							
Morecambe	98	a															16 02							
Settle		d	11 46									13 48										15 45		
Horton-in-Ribblesdale		d	11 54									13 57										15 53		
Ribblehead		d	12 02									14 05										16 01		
Dent		d	12 12									14 14										16 11		
Garsdale		d	12 17									14 20										16 16		
Kirkby Stephen		d	12 30									14 32										16 29		
Appleby		d	12 43									14 45										16 41		
Langwathby		d	12 57									14 59										16 55		
Lazonby & Kirkoswald		d	13 03									15 04										17 01		
Armathwaite		d	13 11									15 12										17 09		
Carlisle 8	65	a	13 29									15 27										17 28		

B To Heysham Port

Leeds and Bradford - Skipton, Lancaster, Morecambe and Carlisle

Network Diagram - see first page of Table 35

Station			NT		NT	NT	NT	NT	NT	NT	NT	NT	NT		NT	NT	NT	NT	NT	NT	NT	NT	NT		NT	NT
London Kings Cross	⊖26	d																								
Leeds	37	d	15 26			15 56		16 26		16 39	16 56		17 26			17 50	17 56		18 26		18 56		19 19		19 26	
Bradford Forster Square	37	d			15 41		16 11		16 40			17 11			17 41			18 11		18 41		19 07				19 36
Frizinghall	37	d			15 44		16 14		16 43			17 14			17 44			18 14		18 44		19 10				19 39
Shipley	37	a	15 37		15 48	16 07	16 18	16 37	16 48	16 53	17 07	17 18	17 37		17 48	18 02	18 07	18 18	18 38	18 48	19 07	19 14	19 31		19 37	19 43
		d	15 38		15 49	16 08	16 19	16 38	16 49	16 55	17 08	17 19	17 38		17 49	18 03	18 08	18 19	18 38	18 49	19 08	19 15	19 32		19 38	19 44
Saltaire		d	15 40		15 52	16 10	16 22	16 40	16 52		17 10	17 22	17 40		17 51		18 10	18 22	18 40	18 51	19 10	19 18			19 40	19 47
Bingley		d	15 44		15 56	16 14	16 26	16 44	16 56	17 03	17 14	17 26	17 44		17 55	18 08	18 14	18 26	18 44	18 55	19 14	19 22	19 36		19 44	19 51
Crossflatts		d	15 47		15 58	16 17	16 28	16 47	16 58		17 17	17 28	17 47		17 57		18 17	18 28	18 47	18 57	19 17	19 24			19 47	19 53
Keighley		d	15 51		16 03	16 21	16 33	16 51	17 03	17 10	17 21	17 33	17 51		18 02	18 14	18 21	18 33	18 51	19 02	19 21	19 29	19 42		19 51	19 58
Steeton & Silsden		d	15 56		16 07	16 26	16 37	16 56	17 07		17 26	17 37	17 56		18 06	18 19	18 26	18 37	18 56	19 06	19 26	19 33			19 56	20 02
Cononley		d	16 00		16 11	16 30	16 41	17 00	17 11		17 30	17 42	18 00		18 10		18 30	18 42	19 00	19 10	19 30	19 38			20 00	20 07
Skipton		a	16 10		16 20	16 40	16 50	17 10	17 19	17 24	17 40	17 50	18 10		18 17	18 29	18 40	18 50	19 10	19 19	19 40	19 46	19 57		20 10	20 15
		d								17 24						18 35							20 00			
Gargrave		d								17 30						18 40							20 06			
Blackpool North	94	d																								
Preston		d																								
Blackburn	97	d																								
Clitheroe	94	d																								
Hellifield		d								17 39						18 49							20 15			
Long Preston		d								17 42						18 51							20 18			
Giggleswick		d								17 49																
Clapham (N. Yorkshire)		d								17 57																
Bentham		d								18 04																
Wennington		d								18 09																
Carnforth	82	a								18 26																
Lancaster	65,82,98	a								18 38																
Bare Lane	98	a								18 53																
Morecambe	98	a								18 59																
Settle		d														18 57							20 24			
Horton in Ribblesdale		d														19 06							20 32			
Ribblehead		d														19 14							20a42			
Dent		d														19 23										
Garsdale		d														19 29										
Kirkby Stephen		d														19 41										
Appleby		d														19 54										
Langwathby		d														20 08										
Lazonby & Kirkoswald		d														20 13										
Armathwaite		d														20 21										
Carlisle	65	a														20 41										

Station			NT	NT	NT	GR	NT	NT	NT		NT	NT	NT	NT	NT	NT
London Kings Cross	⊖26	d				18 35										
Leeds	37	d	19 56		20 26	20 54	20 56		21 26			22 03	22 26	22 56		23 18
Bradford Forster Square	37	d		20 07				21 05			22 01				23 05	
Frizinghall	37	d		20 10				21 08			22 04				23 08	
Shipley	37	a	20 07	20 15	20 37		21 07	21 12	21 38		22 08	22 15	22 37	23 08	23 12	23 31
		d	20 08	20 15	20 38		21 08	21 17	21 38		22 09	22 16	22 38	23 09	23 14	23 32
Saltaire		d	20 10	20 17	20 40		21 10	21 20	21 40		22 12	22 18	22 40	23 11	23 17	23 34
Bingley		d	20 14	20 21	20 44		21 14	21 24	21 44		22 16	22 22	22 44	23 15	23 21	23 38
Crossflatts		d	20 17	20 23	20 47		21 17	21 26	21 47		22 18	22 25	22 47	23 18	23 23	23 40
Keighley		d	20 21	20 28	20 51	21s13	21 21	21 31	21 51		22 23	22 29	22 51	23 22	23 28	23 44
Steeton & Silsden		d	20 26	20 32	20 56		21 26	21 35	21 56		22 27	22 34	22 56	23 27	23 32	23 48
Cononley		d	20 30	20 36	21 00		21 30	21 40	22 00		22 31	22 38	23 00	23 31	23 37	23 52
Skipton		a	20 37	20 47	21 10	21 28	21 40	21 47	22 10		22 39	22 47	23 11	23 40	23 44	00 02
		d														
Gargrave		d														
Blackpool North	94	d														
Preston		d														
Blackburn	97	d														
Clitheroe	94	d														
Hellifield		d														
Long Preston		d														
Giggleswick		d														
Clapham (N. Yorkshire)		d														
Bentham		d														
Wennington		d														
Carnforth	82	a														
Lancaster	65,82,98	a														
Bare Lane	98	a														
Morecambe	98	a														
Settle		d														
Horton in Ribblesdale		d														
Ribblehead		d														
Dent		d														
Garsdale		d														
Kirkby Stephen		d														
Appleby		d														
Langwathby		d														
Lazonby & Kirkoswald		d														
Armathwaite		d														
Carlisle	65	a														

Leeds and Bradford - Skipton, Lancaster, Morecambe and Carlisle

Network Diagram - see first page of Table 35

Station			NT	NT	NT	NT	NT	NT	NT	NT	NT		NT	NT	NT	NT	NT	NT	NT	NT	NT		NT	NT	NT	NT
London Kings Cross	⊖26	d																								
Leeds	37	d	23p18	08 40	09 00			10 08		10 51	11 08		12 08		13 08	13 15	14 08		14 57	15 08	16 08			17 08	17 21	17 33
Bradford Forster Square	37	d							10 48					12 48				14 48					16 48			
Frizinghall	37	d							10 51					12 51				14 51					16 51			
Shipley	37	a	23p31	08 52	09 15			10 19	10 54	11 03	11 19		12 19	12 54	13 19	13 28	14 19	14 54	15 09	15 19	16 19		16 54	17 19	17 33	17 45
		d	23p32	08 53	09 16			10 20	10 55	11 04	11 20		12 20	12 55	13 20	13 29	14 20	14 55	15 10	15 20	16 20		16 55	17 20	17 34	17 46
Saltaire		d	23p34	08 55	09 18			10 22	10 57		11 22		12 22	12 57	13 22		14 22	14 57		15 22	16 22		16 57	17 22		
Bingley		d	23p38	09 00	09 23			10 26	11 01	11 09	11 26		12 26	13 01	13 26	13 34	14 26	15 01	15 15	15 26	16 26		17 01	17 26	17 39	17 50
Crossflatts		d	23p40	09 02	09 25			10 28	11 03		11 28		12 28	13 03	13 28		14 28	15 03		15 28	16 28		17 03	17 28		
Keighley		d	23p44	09 07	09 30			10 32	11 08	11 15	11 32		12 32	13 08	13 32	13 39	14 32	15 08	15 20	15 32	16 32		17 08	17 32	17 44	17 56
Steeton & Silsden		d	23p48	09 11	09 34			10 36	11 12		11 36		12 36	13 12	13 36		14 36	15 12		15 36	16 36		17 12	17 36		
Cononley		d	23p52	09 16	09 39			10 40	11 16		11 40		12 40	13 16	13 40		14 40	15 16		15 40	16 40		17 16	17 40		
Skipton		a	00 02	09 23	09 46			10 48	11 23	11 28	11 48		12 48	13 23	13 48	13 53	14 48	15 23	15 33	15 48	16 48		17 23	17 48	17 57	18 08
		d		09 26	09 48					11 30						13 54			15 36						18 00	18 11
Gargrave		d		09 31	09 53					11 35						14 00			15 41						18 05	
Blackpool North	94	d				08 36																				
Preston		d				09 05	10 00																			
Blackburn	97	d				09 27	10 21																			
Clitheroe	94	d				09 51	10 45																			
Hellifield		d		09 40	10 02	10 15	11 08			11 44						14 08			15 50						18 14	18 22
Long Preston		d		09 43						11 46						14 11			15 53						18 18	
Giggleswick		d		09 52						11 54									16 00						18 25	
Clapham (N. Yorkshire)		d		10 00						12 02									16 08						18 33	
Bentham		d		10 06						12 08									16 15						18 39	
Wennington		d		10 11						12 13									16 20						18 44	
Carnforth	82	a		10 30						12 30									16 36						19 00	
Lancaster	65,82,98	a		10 40						12 44									16 46						19 13	
Bare Lane	98	a		10 51						13 07									16 56						19 31	
Morecambe	98	a		10 57						13 13									17 03						19 37	
Settle		d			10 10	10 35	11 17									14 17										18 30
Horton in Ribblesdale		d			10 19	10 44	11 26									14 26										18 39
Ribblehead		d			10 27	10 52	11 33									14 34										18 47
Dent		d			10 37	11 02	11 43									14 44										18 57
Garsdale		d			10 43	11 07	11 49									14 50										19 02
Kirkby Stephen		d			10 56	11 20	12 01									15 03										19 15
Appleby		d			11 09	11 34	12 14									15 15										19 28
Langwathby		d			11 23	11 48	12 28									15 29										19 42
Lazonby & Kirkoswald		d			11 29	11 54	12 34									15 35										19 48
Armathwaite		d			11 37	12 02	12 42									15 43										19 56
Carlisle	65	a			11 56	12 17	12 57									16 00										20 13

Station			NT	NT	NT	NT	NT		GR	NT	NT	NT	NT
London Kings Cross	⊖26	d							18 35				
Leeds	37	d	18 08		19 08	20 08			21 03	21 08	22 08		23 20
Bradford Forster Square	37	d		18 48			20 48					22 48	
Frizinghall	37	d		18 51			20 51					22 51	
Shipley	37	a	18 19	18 54	19 19	20 19	20 54			21 19	22 19	22 54	23 31
		d	18 20	18 55	19 20	20 20	20 55			21 20	22 20	22 55	23 32
Saltaire		d	18 22	18 57	19 22	20 22	20 57			21 22	22 22	22 57	23 34
Bingley		d	18 26	19 01	19 26	20 26	21 01			21 26	22 26	23 01	23 38
Crossflatts		d	18 28	19 03	19 28	20 28	21 03			21 28	22 28	23 03	23 40
Keighley		d	18 32	19 08	19 32	20 32	21 08		21s22	21 32	22 32	23 08	23 44
Steeton & Silsden		d	18 36	19 12	19 36	20 36	21 12			21 36	22 36	23 12	23 48
Cononley		d	18 40	19 16	19 40	20 40	21 16			21 40	22 40	23 16	23 52
Skipton		a	18 48	19 23	19 48	20 48	21 23		21 41	21 48	22 48	23 23	23 59
		d											
Gargrave		d											
Blackpool North	94	d											
Preston		d											
Blackburn	97	d											
Clitheroe	94	d											
Hellifield		d											
Long Preston		d											
Giggleswick		d											
Clapham (N. Yorkshire)		d											
Bentham		d											
Wennington		d											
Carnforth	82	a											
Lancaster	65,82,98	a											
Bare Lane	98	a											
Morecambe	98	a											
Settle		d											
Horton in Ribblesdale		d											
Ribblehead		d											
Dent		d											
Garsdale		d											
Kirkby Stephen		d											
Appleby		d											
Langwathby		d											
Lazonby & Kirkoswald		d											
Armathwaite		d											
Carlisle	65	a											

Table 36

Sundays 16 September to 21 October

Leeds and Bradford - Skipton, Lancaster, Morecambe and Carlisle

Network Diagram - see first page of Table 35

			NT	NT	NT	NT 🚌	NT	NT	NT	NT	NT	NT	NT	NT	NT	NT	NT	NT	NT	NT	NT	NT	NT	NT
London Kings Cross	⊖26	d																						
Leeds	37	d	23p18	08 40	09 00		10 08		10 51	11 08	12 08		13 08	13 15	14 08		14 57	15 08	16 08		17 08	17 21	17 33	18 08
Bradford Forster Square	37	d						10 48				12 48				14 48				16 48				
Frizinghall	37	d						10 51				12 51				14 51				16 51				
Shipley	37	a	23p31	08 52	09 15		10 19	10 54	11 03	11 19	12 19	12 54	13 19	13 28	14 19	14 54	15 09	15 19	16 19	16 54	17 19	17 33	17 45	18 19
		d	23p32	08 53	09 16		10 20	10 55	11 04	11 20	12 20	12 55	13 20	13 29	14 20	14 55	15 10	15 20	16 20	16 55	17 20	17 34	17 46	18 20
Saltaire		d	23p34	08 55	09 18		10 22	10 57		11 22	12 22	12 57	13 22		14 22	14 57		15 22	16 22	16 57	17 22			18 22
Bingley		d	23p38	09 00	09 23		10 26	11 01	11 09	11 26	12 26	13 01	13 26	13 34	14 26	15 01	15 15	15 26	16 26	17 01	17 26	17 39	17 50	18 26
Crossflatts		d	23p40	09 02	09 25		10 28	11 03		11 28	12 28	13 03	13 28		14 28	15 03		15 28	16 28	17 03	17 28			18 28
Keighley		d	23p44	09 07	09 30		10 32	11 08	11 15	11 32	12 32	13 08	13 32	13 39	14 32	15 08	15 20	15 32	16 32	17 08	17 32	17 44	17 56	18 32
Steeton & Silsden		d	23p48	09 11	09 34		10 36	11 12		11 36	12 36	13 12	13 36		14 36	15 12		15 36	16 36	17 12	17 36			18 36
Cononley		d	23p52	09 16	09 39		10 40	11 16		11 40	12 40	13 16	13 40		14 40	15 16		15 40	16 40	17 16	17 40			18 40
Skipton		a	00 02	09 23	09 46		10 48	11 23	11 28	11 48	12 48	13 23	13 48	13 53	14 48	15 23	15 33	15 48	16 48	17 23	17 48	17 57	18 08	18 48
		d		09 26	09 48				11 30					13 54			15 36					18 00	18 11	
Gargrave		d		09 31	09 53				11 35					14 00			15 41					18 05		
Blackpool North	94	d				08 36																		
Preston		d				09 05																		
Blackburn	97	d				09 27																		
Clitheroe	94	d				09 51																		
Hellifield		d		09 40	10 02	10 15			11 44					14 08			15 50					18 14	18 22	
Long Preston		d		09 43					11 46					14 11			15 53					18 18		
Giggleswick		d		09 52					11 54								16 00					18 25		
Clapham (N Yorkshire)		d		10 00					12 02								16 08					18 33		
Bentham		d		10 06					12 08								16 15					18 39		
Wennington		d		10 11					12 13								16 20					18 44		
Carnforth	82	a		10 30					12 30								16 36					19 00		
Lancaster	65,82,98	a		10 40					12 44								16 46					19 13		
Bare Lane	98	a		10 51					13 07								16 56					19 31		
Morecambe	98	a		10 57					13 13								17 03					19 37		
Settle		d			10 10	10 35								14 17									18 30	
Horton-in-Ribblesdale		d			10 19	10 44								14 26									18 39	
Ribblehead		d			10 27	10 52								14 34									18 47	
Dent		d			10 37	11 02								14 44									18 57	
Garsdale		d			10 43	11 07								14 50									19 02	
Kirkby Stephen		d			10 56	11 20								15 03									19 15	
Appleby		d			11 09	11 34								15 15									19 28	
Langwathby		d			11 23	11 48								15 29									19 42	
Lazonby & Kirkoswald		d			11 29	11 54								15 35									19 48	
Armathwaite		d			11 37	12 02								15 43									19 56	
Carlisle	65	a			11 56	12 17								16 00									20 13	

			NT	NT	NT	NT	GR 1	NT	NT	NT	NT
London Kings Cross	⊖26	d					18 35				
Leeds	37	d		19 08	20 08		21 03	21 08	22 08		23 20
Bradford Forster Square	37	d	18 48			20 48				22 48	
Frizinghall	37	d	18 51			20 51				22 51	
Shipley	37	a	18 54	19 19	20 19	20 54		21 19	22 19	22 54	23 31
		d	18 55	19 20	20 20	20 55		21 20	22 20	22 55	23 32
Saltaire		d	18 57	19 22	20 22	20 57		21 22	22 22	22 57	23 34
Bingley		d	19 01	19 26	20 26	21 01		21 26	22 26	23 01	23 38
Crossflatts		d	19 03	19 28	20 28	21 03		21 28	22 28	23 03	23 40
Keighley		d	19 08	19 32	20 32	21 08	21s22	21 32	22 32	23 08	23 44
Steeton & Silsden		d	19 12	19 36	20 36	21 12		21 36	22 36	23 12	23 48
Cononley		d	19 16	19 40	20 40	21 16		21 40	22 40	23 16	23 52
Skipton		a	19 23	19 48	20 48	21 23	21 41	21 48	22 48	23 23	23 59
		d									
Gargrave		d									
Blackpool North	94	d									
Preston		d									
Blackburn	97	d									
Clitheroe	94	d									
Hellifield		d									
Long Preston		d									
Giggleswick		d									
Clapham (N Yorkshire)		d									
Bentham		d									
Wennington		d									
Carnforth	82	a									
Lancaster	65,82,98	a									
Bare Lane	98	a									
Morecambe	98	a									
Settle		d									
Horton-in-Ribblesdale		d									
Ribblehead		d									
Dent		d									
Garsdale		d									
Kirkby Stephen		d									
Appleby		d									
Langwathby		d									
Lazonby & Kirkoswald		d									
Armathwaite		d									
Carlisle	65	a									

Table 36

Sundays from 28 October

Leeds and Bradford - Skipton, Lancaster, Morecambe and Carlisle

Network Diagram - see first page of Table 35

			NT	NT	NT	NT	NT	NT	NT	NT	NT	NT	NT	NT	NT	NT	NT	NT	NT	NT	NT	NT	NT	NT
London Kings Cross	⊖26	d																						
Leeds	37	d	23p18	08 40	09 00	10 08		10 51	11 08	12 08		13 08	13 15	14 08		14 57	15 08	16 08		17 08	17 21	17 33	18 08	
Bradford Forster Square	37	d					10 48				12 48				14 48				16 48					18 48
Frizinghall	37	d					10 51				12 51				14 51				16 51					18 51
Shipley	37	a	23p31	08 52	09 15	10 19	10 54	11 03	11 19	12 19	12 54	13 19	13 28	14 19	14 54	15 09	15 19	16 19	16 54	17 19	17 33	17 45	18 19	18 54
		d	23p32	08 53	09 16	10 20	10 55	11 04	11 20	12 20	12 55	13 20	13 29	14 20	14 55	15 10	15 20	16 20	16 55	17 20	17 34	17 46	18 20	18 55
Saltaire		d	23p34	08 55	09 18	10 22	10 57		11 22	12 22	12 57	13 22		14 22	14 57		15 22	16 22	16 57	17 22			18 22	18 57
Bingley		d	23p38	09 00	09 23	10 26	11 01	11 09	11 26	12 26	13 01	13 26	13 34	14 26	15 01	15 15	15 26	16 26	17 01	17 26	17 39	17 50	18 26	19 01
Crossflatts		d	23p40	09 02	09 25	10 28	11 03		11 28	12 28	13 03	13 28		14 28	15 03		15 28	16 28	17 03	17 28			18 28	19 03
Keighley		d	23p44	09 07	09 30	10 32	11 08	11 15	11 32	12 32	13 08	13 32	13 39	14 32	15 08	15 20	15 32	16 32	17 08	17 32	17 44	17 56	18 32	19 08
Steeton & Silsden		d	23p48	09 11	09 34	10 36	11 12		11 36	12 36	13 12	13 36		14 36	15 12		15 36	16 36	17 12	17 36			18 36	19 12
Cononley		d	23p52	09 16	09 39	10 40	11 16		11 40	12 40	13 16	13 40		14 40	15 16		15 40	16 40	17 16	17 40			18 40	19 16
Skipton		a	00 02	09 23	09 46	10 48	11 23	11 28	11 48	12 48	13 23	13 48	13 53	14 48	15 23	15 33	15 48	16 48	17 23	17 48	17 57	18 08	18 48	19 23
		d		09 26	09 48			11 30					13 54			15 36					18 00	18 11		
Gargrave		d		09 31	09 53			11 35					14 00			15 41					18 05			
Blackpool North	94	d																						
Preston		d																						
Blackburn	97	d																						
Clitheroe	94	d																						
Hellifield		d		09 40	10 02			11 44					14 08			15 50					18 14	18 22		
Long Preston		d		09 43				11 46					14 11			15 53					18 18			
Giggleswick		d		09 52				11 54								16 00					18 25			
Clapham (N Yorkshire)		d		10 00				12 02								16 08					18 33			
Bentham		d		10 06				12 08								16 15					18 39			
Wennington		d		10 11				12 13								16 20					18 44			
Carnforth	82	a		10 30				12 30								16 36					19 00			
Lancaster	65,82,98	a		10 40				12 44								16 46					19 13			
Bare Lane	98	a		10 51				13 07								16 56					19 31			
Morecambe	98	a		10 57				13 13								17 03					19 37			
Settle		d			10 10								14 17									18 30		
Horton-in-Ribblesdale		d			10 19								14 26									18 39		
Ribblehead		d			10 27								14 34									18 47		
Dent		d			10 37								14 44									18 57		
Garsdale		d			10 43								14 50									19 02		
Kirkby Stephen		d			10 56								15 03									19 15		
Appleby		d			11 09								15 15									19 28		
Langwathby		d			11 23								15 29									19 42		
Lazonby & Kirkoswald		d			11 29								15 35									19 48		
Armathwaite		d			11 37								15 43									19 56		
Carlisle	65	a			11 56								16 00									20 13		

			NT	NT	NT	GR 1	NT	NT	NT	NT
London Kings Cross	⊖26	d				18 35				
Leeds	37	d	19 08	20 08		21 03	21 08	22 08		23 20
Bradford Forster Square	37	d			20 48				22 48	
Frizinghall	37	d			20 51				22 51	
Shipley	37	a	19 19	20 19	20 54		21 19	22 19	22 54	23 31
		d	19 20	20 20	20 55		21 20	22 20	22 55	23 32
Saltaire		d	19 22	20 22	20 57		21 22	22 22	22 57	23 34
Bingley		d	19 26	20 26	21 01		21 26	22 26	23 01	23 38
Crossflatts		d	19 28	20 28	21 03		21 28	22 28	23 03	23 40
Keighley		d	19 32	20 32	21 08	21s22	21 32	22 32	23 08	23 44
Steeton & Silsden		d	19 36	20 36	21 12		21 36	22 36	23 12	23 48
Cononley		d	19 40	20 40	21 16		21 40	22 40	23 16	23 52
Skipton		a	19 48	20 48	21 23	21 41	21 48	22 48	23 23	23 59
		d								
Gargrave		d								
Blackpool North	94	d								
Preston		d								
Blackburn	97	d								
Clitheroe	94	d								
Hellifield		d								
Long Preston		d								
Giggleswick		d								
Clapham (N Yorkshire)		d								
Bentham		d								
Wennington		d								
Carnforth	82	a								
Lancaster	65,82,98	a								
Bare Lane	98	a								
Morecambe	98	a								
Settle		d								
Horton-in-Ribblesdale		d								
Ribblehead		d								
Dent		d								
Garsdale		d								
Kirkby Stephen		d								
Appleby		d								
Langwathby		d								
Lazonby & Kirkoswald		d								
Armathwaite		d								
Carlisle	65	a								

Carlisle, Morecambe, Lancaster and Skipton - Bradford and Leeds

Network Diagram - see first page of Table 35

Miles	Miles	Miles	Station		NT	NT	NT	NT	NT	GR	NT	NT	NT		NT	NT	NT	NT	NT	NT	NT	NT	NT		NT
0	—	—	Carlisle	65 d														05 53							
10	—	—	Armathwaite	d														06 07							
15½	—	—	Lazonby & Kirkoswald	d														06 14							
19¾	—	—	Langwathby	d														06 20							
30¾	—	—	Appleby	d														06 35							
41½	—	—	Kirkby Stephen	d														06 48							
51¼	—	—	Garsdale	d														07 01							
54¾	—	—	Dent	d																					
60¾	—	—	Ribblehead	d														07 16							
65½	—	—	Horton-in-Ribblesdale	d														07 22							
71¾	—	—	Settle	d														07 30							
—	0	—	**Morecambe**	98 d																					
—	1¾	—	Bare Lane	98 d																					
—	4¼	—	**Lancaster**	65,82,98 d																	07 10				
—	11½	—	Carnforth	82 d																	07 20				
—	21	—	Wennington	d																	07 33				
—	24¼	—	Bentham	d																	07 39				
—	27½	—	Clapham (N Yorkshire)	d																	07 45				
—	34¼	—	Giggleswick	d																	07 54				
75½	38	—	Long Preston	d														07 36			08 02				
76¾	39¼	—	Hellifield	d														07 39			08 06				
—	—	—	Clitheroe	94 a																					
—	—	—	Blackburn	94,97 a																					
—	—	—	Preston	97 a																					
—	—	—	Blackpool North	97 a																					
83	45½	—	Gargrave	d														07 47			08 14				
86¾	49¼	—	**Skipton**	a														07 55			08 23				
—	—	—		d	05 48	06 02	06 16	06 27	06 42	06 55	07 01	07 08	07 24		07 30	07 39	07 47	07 57	08 01	08 15	08 27	08 32	08 43		09 02
89¾	52¼	—	Cononley	d	05 52	06 06	06 20	06 31	06 46		07 05	07 12	07 28		07 34		07 51		08 05	08 19		08 36	08 47		09 06
93	55½	—	Steeton & Silsden	d	05 56	06 10	06 25	06 35	06 51		07 10	07 17	07 33		07 39	07 47	07 56	08 04	08 10	08 24		08 40	08 51		09 10
96	58½	—	Keighley	d	06 01	06 15	06 29	06 40	06 56	07u06	07 15	07 21	07 37		07 43	07 51	08 00	08 09	08 14	08 28	08 37	08 45	08 56		09 15
98½	61	—	Crossflatts	d	06 04	06 18	06 33	06 43	07 00		07 19	07 26	07 41		07 47		08 04		08 18	08 32		08 48	08 59		09 18
99¼	61¾	—	Bingley	d	06 07	06 21	06 35	06 46	07 02		07 22	07 28	07 44		07 50	07 56	08 07	08 14	08 21	08 35	08 42	08 51	09 02		09 21
101½	64	—	Saltaire	d	06 10	06 24	06 39	06 49	07 06		07 25	07 32	07 48		07 54		08 11		08 25	08 39		08 54	09 05		09 24
102¼	64¾	0	Shipley	a	06 12	06 27	06 41	06 53	07 08		07 28	07 34	07 50		07 56	08 01	08 13	08 19	08 27	08 41	08 46	08 57	09 07		09 27
—	—	—		d	06 13	06 28	06 42	06 53	07 09	07u14	07 28	07 35	07 50		08 00	08 01	08 13	08 19	08 28	08 41	08 47	08 58	09 08		09 28
—	—	1	Frizinghall	37 a		06 32		06 57			07 32				08 03				08 31			09 02			09 32
—	—	2¾	**Bradford Forster Square**	37 a		06 38		07 03			07 39				08 09				08 38			09 09			09 38
113	75½	—	**Leeds**	37 a	06 27		06 57		07 23	07 29		07 49	08 05			08 18	08 28	08 37		08 56	09 04		09 22		
—	—	—	London Kings Cross	⊖26 a						10 01															

Station		NT	NT	NT	NT	NT	NT	NT	NT		NT	NT	NT	NT	NT	NT	NT	NT	NT		NT	NT	NT	NT	NT
Carlisle	65 d								08 53																11 55
Armathwaite	d								09 07																12 09
Lazonby & Kirkoswald	d								09 14																12 16
Langwathby	d								09 20																12 22
Appleby	d								09 35																12 37
Kirkby Stephen	d								09 48																12 50
Garsdale	d								10 02																13 03
Dent	d								10 07																13 08
Ribblehead	d								10 17																13 18
Horton-in-Ribblesdale	d								10 24																13 24
Settle	d								10 32																13 32
Morecambe	98 d															10 34									
Bare Lane	98 d															10 38									
Lancaster	65,82,98 d															10 49									
Carnforth	82 d															11 09									
Wennington	d															11 23									
Bentham	d															11 29									
Clapham (N Yorkshire)	d															11 35									
Giggleswick	d															11 44									
Long Preston	d															11 52									13 38
Hellifield	d								10 39							11 56									13 41
Clitheroe	94 a																								
Blackburn	94,97 a																								
Preston	97 a																								
Blackpool North	97 a																								
Gargrave	d															12 04									13 49
Skipton	a								10 54							12 13									13 57
	d	09 18	09 32	09 48	10 02	10 18	10 32	10 48	10 59		11 02	11 18	11 33	11 48	12 02	12 13	12 18	12 32	12 48		13 02	13 18	13 32	13 48	13 58
Cononley	d	09 22	09 36	09 52	10 06	10 22	10 36	10 52			11 06	11 22	11 37	11 52	12 06		12 22	12 36	12 52		13 06	13 22	13 36	13 52	
Steeton & Silsden	d	09 26	09 40	09 56	10 10	10 26	10 40	10 56			11 10	11 26	11 41	11 56	12 10		12 26	12 40	12 56		13 10	13 26	13 40	13 56	
Keighley	d	09 31	09 45	10 01	10 15	10 31	10 45	11 01	11 09		11 15	11 31	11 46	12 01	12 15	12 23	12 31	12 45	13 01		13 15	13 31	13 45	14 01	14 09
Crossflatts	d	09 34	09 48	10 04	10 18	10 34	10 48	11 04			11 18	11 34	11 49	12 04	12 18		12 34	12 48	13 04		13 18	13 34	13 48	14 04	
Bingley	d	09 37	09 51	10 07	10 21	10 37	10 51	11 07	11 13		11 21	11 37	11 52	12 07	12 21		12 37	12 51	13 07		13 21	13 37	13 51	14 07	14 13
Saltaire	d	09 40	09 54	10 10	10 24	10 40	10 54	11 10			11 24	11 40	11 55	12 10	12 24		12 40	12 54	13 10		13 24	13 40	13 54	14 10	
Shipley	a	09 43	09 58	10 12	10 27	10 42	10 57	11 12	11 18		11 27	11 43	11 58	12 14	12 27	12 33	12 42	12 57	13 12		13 27	13 42	13 57	14 12	14 18
	d	09 44	09 58	10 14	10 28	10 44	10 58	11 14	11 18		11 28	11 44	11 58	12 14	12 28	12 33	12 44	12 58	13 14		13 28	13 44	13 58	14 14	14 18
Frizinghall	37 a		10 02		10 32		11 02				11 32		12 02		12 32			13 02			13 32		14 02		
Bradford Forster Square	37 a		10 08		10 38		11 08				11 38		12 10		12 38			13 08			13 38		14 08		
Leeds	37 a	09 59		10 28		10 58		11 28	11 36			11 58		12 29		12 55	12 58		13 28			13 58		14 28	14 37
London Kings Cross	⊖26 a																								

Carlisle, Morecambe, Lancaster and Skipton - Bradford and Leeds

Network Diagram - see first page of Table 35

Station		NT	NT	NT	NT		NT	NT A	NT	NT	NT	NT	NT	NT	NT		NT	NT	NT	NT	NT	NT	NT	NT	NT
Carlisle	65 d												14 04					15 05							
Armathwaite	d												14 18												
Lazonby & Kirkoswald	d												14 25												
Langwathby	d												14 31												
Appleby	d												14 47					15 42							
Kirkby Stephen	d												15 00					15 55							
Garsdale	d												15 13												
Dent	d												15 18												
Ribblehead	d												15 27												
Horton-in-Ribblesdale	d												15 34												
Settle	d												15 43					16 35							
Morecambe	98 d							13 29														16 19			
Bare Lane	98 d							13 36														16 23			
Lancaster	65,82,98 d							13 48																	
Carnforth	82 d							13 58														16 32			
Wennington	d							14 12														16 46			
Bentham	d							14 18														16 52			
Clapham (N Yorkshire)	d							14 24														16 59			
Giggleswick	d							14 33														17 10			
Long Preston	d							14 40														17 18			
Hellifield	d							14 44					15 50									17 22			
Clitheroe	94 a																								
Blackburn	94,97 a																								
Preston	97 a																								
Blackpool North	97 a																								
Gargrave	d							14 52														17 30			
Skipton	a							15 03					16 05					16 55				17 39			
	d	14 02	14 18	14 32	14 48		15 00	15 10	15 18	15 32	15 48	16 02	16 10	16 18	16 36		16 49	16 58	17 02	17 19	17 28	17 40	17 49	18 02	18 16
Cononley	d	14 06	14 22	14 36	14 52		15 04		15 22	15 36	15 52	16 06		16 22	16 40		16 53		17 06	17 23	17 32		17 53	18 06	18 20
Steeton & Silsden	d	14 10	14 27	14 40	14 56		15 08		15 26	15 40	15 56	16 10		16 26	16 44		16 57		17 10	17 27	17 36		17 57	18 10	18 25
Keighley	d	14 15	14 31	14 45	15 01		15 13	15 20	15 31	15 45	16 01	16 15	16 21	16 31	16 49		17 02	17 08	17 15	17 32	17 41	17 50	18 02	18 15	18 29
Crossflatts	d	14 18	14 35	14 48	15 04		15 16		15 34	15 48	16 04	16 18		16 34	16 52		17 05		17 18	17 35	17 44		18 05	18 18	18 33
Bingley	d	14 21	14 38	14 51	15 07		15 19	15 25	15 37	15 51	16 07	16 21	16 26	16 37	16 55		17 08	17 15	17 21	17 38	17 47		18 08	18 21	18 35
Saltaire	d	14 24	14 42	14 54	15 10		15 22		15 40	15 54	16 10	16 24		16 40	16 58		17 11		17 24	17 41	17 50		18 11	18 24	18 39
Shipley	a	14 28	14 44	14 57	15 12		15 26	15 30	15 43	15 57	16 12	16 27	16 31	16 42	17 02		17 13	17 20	17 27	17 43	17 55	17 58	18 13	18 28	18 42
	d	14 28	14 45	14 58	15 14		15 28	15 30	15 44	15 58	16 14	16 28	16 31	16 44	17 02		17 15	17 23	17 28	17 45	17 56	17 58	18 14	18 28	18 44
Frizinghall	37 a	14 32		15 02			15 32			16 02		16 31			17 06				17 32		17 59			18 32	
Bradford Forster Square	37 a	14 38		15 08			15 38			16 08		16 38			17 12				17 38		18 05			18 38	
Leeds	37 a		15 00		15 28			15 47	15 58		16 28		16 51	16 58			17 29	17 40		18 00		18 15	18 29		18 59
London Kings Cross	⊖26 a																								

Station		NT	NT	NT	NT	NT	NT	NT	NT	NT		NT	NT	NT	NT	NT	NT	NT	NT
Carlisle	65 d	16 18								18 18									
Armathwaite	d	16 32								18 32									
Lazonby & Kirkoswald	d	16 39								18 39									
Langwathby	d	16 45								18 45									
Appleby	d	17 01								19 00									
Kirkby Stephen	d	17 14								19 13									
Garsdale	d	17 27								19 26									
Dent	d	17 32								19 31									
Ribblehead	d	17 42								19 41							21 00		
Horton-in-Ribblesdale	d	17 48								19 47							21 06		
Settle	d	17 57								19 55							21 14		
Morecambe	98 d												19 08						
Bare Lane	98 d												19 12						
Lancaster	65,82,98 d												19 24						
Carnforth	82 d												19 34						
Wennington	d												19 48						
Bentham	d												19 54						
Clapham (N Yorkshire)	d												20 00						
Giggleswick	d												20 09						
Long Preston	d	18 03											20 17				21 20		
Hellifield	d	18 06								20 03			20 21				21 23		
Clitheroe	94 a																		
Blackburn	94,97 a																		
Preston	97 a																		
Blackpool North	97 a																		
Gargrave	d	18 14											20 29				21 31		
Skipton	a	18 23								20 18			20 38				21 38		
	d	18 28	18 32	18 48	19 00	19 18	19 32	19 48	19 54	20 20		20 23	20 42	20 48	20 54	21 18	21 48	21 54	22 18
Cononley	d		18 36	18 52	19 04	19 22	19 36	19 52	19 58			20 29		20 52	20 58	21 22	21 52	21 58	22 22
Steeton & Silsden	d		18 40	18 56	19 08	19 26	19 40	19 56	20 02			20 33		20 56	21 02	21 26	21 56	22 02	22 26
Keighley	d	18 38	18 45	19 01	19 13	19 31	19 45	20 01	20 07	20 30		20 38	20 52	21 01	21 07	21 31	22 01	22 07	22 31
Crossflatts	d		18 48	19 04	19 16	19 34	19 48	20 04	20 10			20 41		21 04	21 10	21 34	22 04	22 10	22 34
Bingley	d	18 42	18 51	19 07	19 19	19 37	19 51	20 07	20 13	20 34		20 44		21 07	21 13	21 37	22 07	22 13	22 37
Saltaire	d		18 54	19 10	19 22	19 40	19 54	20 10	20 17			20 47		21 10	21 16	21 40	22 10	22 16	22 40
Shipley	a	18 48	18 58	19 12	19 25	19 42	19 58	20 12	20 19	20 39		20 49	20 59	21 12	21 19	21 42	22 13	22 21	22 42
	d	18 48	18 58	19 14	19 26	19 44	19 58	20 14	20 20	20 41		20 50	20 59	21 14	21 19	21 43	22 14	22 21	22 43
Frizinghall	37 a		19 02		19 29		20 01		20 24						21 23			22 24	
Bradford Forster Square	37 a		19 08		19 35		20 08		20 32						21 29			22 31	
Leeds	37 a	19 07		19 31		19 59		20 28		21 01		21 05	21 17	21 30		21 59	22 33		23 01
London Kings Cross	⊖26 a																		

A From Heysham Port

Carlisle, Morecambe, Lancaster and Skipton - Bradford and Leeds

Network Diagram - see first page of Table 35

	NT	NT	NT	GR	NT	NT	NT	NT	NT	NT	NT	NT	NT	NT	NT	NT	NT	NT	NT	NT	NT	NT
Carlisle ■ 65 d																		07 52				
Armathwaite d																		08 06				
Lazonby & Kirkoswald d																		08 13				
Langwathby d																		08 19				
Appleby d																		08 34				
Kirkby Stephen d																		08 47				
Garsdale d																		09 00				
Dent d																		09 05				
Ribblehead d								07 16										09 15				
Horton-in-Ribblesdale d								07 22										09 21				
Settle d								07 30										09 29				
Morecambe 98 d																						
Bare Lane 98 d																						
Lancaster ■ 65,82,98 d																08 24						
Carnforth 82 d																08 34						
Wennington d																08 48						
Bentham d																08 53						
Clapham (N Yorkshire) d																09 00						
Giggleswick d																09 08						
Long Preston d								07 36								09 16						
Hellifield d								07 39								09 20		09 37				
Clitheroe 94 a																						
Blackburn 94,97 a																						
Preston ■ 97 a																						
Blackpool North 97 a																						
Gargrave d								07 47								09 28						
Skipton a								07 55								09 37		09 53				
d	05 48	06 02	06 47	06 55	07 05	07 30	07 47	07 57	08 01	08 18	08 32	08 48	09 02	09 18	09 32	09 42	09 48	09 57	10 02	10 18	10 32	10 48
Cononley d	05 52	06 06	06 51		07 09	07 34	07 51		08 05	08 22	08 36	08 52	09 06	09 22	09 36		09 52		10 06	10 22	10 36	10 52
Steeton & Silsden d	05 56	06 10	06 56		07 14	07 39	07 56	08 04	08 10	08 27	08 40	08 56	09 10	09 26	09 40		09 56		10 10	10 26	10 40	10 56
Keighley d	06 01	06 15	07 00	07u08	07 19	07 43	08 00	08 09	08 14	08 31	08 45	09 01	09 15	09 31	09 45	09 52	10 01	10 08	10 15	10 31	10 45	11 01
Crossflatts d	06 04	06 18	07 04		07 23	07 47	08 04		08 18	08 35	08 48	09 04	09 18	09 34	09 48		10 04		10 18	10 34	10 48	11 04
Bingley d	06 07	06 21	07 07		07 26	07 50	08 07	08 14	08 21	08 38	08 51	09 07	09 21	09 37	09 51	09 58	10 07	10 12	10 21	10 37	10 51	11 07
Saltaire d	06 10	06 24	07 11		07 29	07 54	08 11		08 25	08 42	08 54	09 10	09 24	09 40	09 54		10 10		10 24	10 40	10 54	11 10
Shipley a	06 12	06 27	07 13		07 32	07 56	08 13	08 19	08 27	08 44	08 57	09 12	09 27	09 43	09 58	10 02	10 12	10 19	10 27	10 42	10 57	11 12
d	06 13	06 28	07 13	07u18	07 32	08 00	08 13	08 19	08 28	08 44	08 58	09 14	09 28	09 44	09 58	10 02	10 14	10 19	10 28	10 44	10 58	11 14
Frizinghall 37 a		06 32			07 36	08 03			08 31		09 02		09 32		10 02				10 32		11 02	
Bradford Forster Square 37 a		06 38			07 42	08 09			08 38		09 09		09 38		10 08				10 38		11 08	
Leeds ■ 37 a	06 27		07 27	07 33			08 28	08 37		08 58		09 28		09 59		10 20	10 28	10 34		10 58		11 28
London Kings Cross ■ ⊖26 a				09 51																		

	NT	NT	NT	NT	NT	NT	NT	NT	NT	NT	NT	NT	NT	NT	NT	NT	NT	NT	NT	NT	NT A	NT
Carlisle ■ 65 d			09 26												11 51							
Armathwaite d			09 40												12 05							
Lazonby & Kirkoswald d			09 47												12 12							
Langwathby d			09 53												12 18							
Appleby d			10 08												12 33							
Kirkby Stephen d			10 21												12 46							
Garsdale d			10 35												12 59							
Dent d			10 40												13 04							
Ribblehead d			10 49												13 14							
Horton-in-Ribblesdale d			10 56												13 20							
Settle d			11 04												13 28							
Morecambe 98 d							10 34														13 29	
Bare Lane 98 d							10 38														13 36	
Lancaster ■ 65,82,98 d							10 49														13 48	
Carnforth 82 d							11 09														13 58	
Wennington d							11 23														14 12	
Bentham d							11 29														14 18	
Clapham (N Yorkshire) d							11 36														14 25	
Giggleswick d							11 44														14 33	
Long Preston d							11 52								13 34						14 40	
Hellifield d			11 11				11 56								13 37						14 44	
Clitheroe 94 a																						
Blackburn 94,97 a																						
Preston ■ 97 a																						
Blackpool North 97 a																						
Gargrave d							12 04								13 45						14 52	
Skipton a			11 26				12 13								13 55						15 03	
d	11 02	11 18	11 28	11 33	11 48	12 02	12 13	12 18	12 32	12 48	13 02	13 18	13 32	13 48	13 58	14 02	14 18	14 32	14 48	15 00	15 10	15 18
Cononley d	11 06	11 22		11 37	11 52	12 06		12 22	12 36	12 52	13 06	13 22	13 36	13 52		14 06	14 22	14 36	14 52	15 04		15 22
Steeton & Silsden d	11 10	11 26		11 41	11 56	12 10		12 26	12 40	12 56	13 10	13 26	13 40	13 56		14 10	14 27	14 40	14 56	15 08		15 26
Keighley d	11 15	11 31	11 38	11 46	12 01	12 15	12 23	12 31	12 45	13 01	13 15	13 31	13 45	14 01	14 09	14 15	14 31	14 45	15 01	15 13	15 20	15 31
Crossflatts d	11 18	11 34		11 49	12 04	12 18		12 34	12 48	13 04	13 18	13 34	13 48	14 04		14 18	14 35	14 48	15 04	15 16		15 34
Bingley d	11 21	11 37	11 42	11 52	12 07	12 21		12 37	12 51	13 07	13 21	13 37	13 51	14 07	14 13	14 21	14 38	14 51	15 07	15 19	15 25	15 37
Saltaire d	11 24	11 40		11 55	12 10	12 24		12 40	12 54	13 10	13 24	13 40	13 54	14 10		14 24	14 42	14 54	15 10	15 22		15 40
Shipley a	11 27	11 43	11 49	11 58	12 14	12 27	12 33	12 42	12 57	13 12	13 27	13 42	13 57	14 12	14 18	14 28	14 44	14 57	15 12	15 26	15 30	15 43
d	11 28	11 44	11 49	11 58	12 14	12 28	12 33	12 44	12 58	13 14	13 28	13 44	13 58	14 14	14 18	14 28	14 45	14 58	15 14	15 28	15 30	15 44
Frizinghall 37 a	11 32			12 02		12 32			13 02		13 32		14 02			14 32		15 02		15 32		
Bradford Forster Square 37 a	11 38			12 10		12 38			13 08		13 38		14 08			14 38		15 08		15 38		
Leeds ■ 37 a		11 58	12 07		12 29		12 55	12 58		13 28		13 58		14 28	14 37		15 00		15 28		15 47	15 58
London Kings Cross ■ ⊖26 a																						

A From Heysham Port

Table 36 — Saturdays

Carlisle, Morecambe, Lancaster and Skipton - Bradford and Leeds

Network Diagram - see first page of Table 35

	NT	NT	NT	NT	NT	NT	NT	NT	NT	NT	NT	NT	NT	NT	NT	NT	NT	NT	NT	NT	NT
Carlisle ■ 65 d					14 26						15 49					16 18					
Armathwaite d					14 40											16 32					
Lazonby & Kirkoswald d					14 47											16 39					
Langwathby d					14 53											16 45					
Appleby d					15 09						16 26					17 01					
Kirkby Stephen d					15 22						16 39					17 14					
Garsdale d					15 35											17 27					
Dent d					15 40											17 32					
Ribblehead d					15 49											17 42					
Horton-in-Ribblesdale d					15 56											17 48					
Settle d					16 04						17 16					17 57					
Morecambe 98 d													16 19								
Bare Lane 98 d													16 24								
Lancaster ■ 65,82,98 d													16 40								
Carnforth 82 d													16 50								
Wennington d													17 04								
Bentham d													17 09								
Clapham (N Yorkshire) d													17 16								
Giggleswick d													17 25								
Long Preston d													17 33			18 03					
Hellifield d					16 11								17 36			18 06					
Clitheroe 94 a																					
Blackburn 94,97 a																					
Preston ■ 97 a																					
Blackpool North 97 a																					
Gargrave d													17 44			18 14					
Skipton a					16 26						17 38		17 54			18 23					
d	15 32	15 48	16 02	16 18	16 28	16 33	16 49	17 02	17 19	17 28	17 41	17 49	17 58	18 02	18 16	18 28	18 32	18 48	19 00	19 18	19 32
Cononley d	15 36	15 52	16 06	16 22		16 37	16 53	17 06	17 23	17 32		17 53		18 06	18 20		18 36	18 52	19 04	19 22	19 36
Steeton & Silsden d	15 40	15 56	16 10	16 26		16 41	16 57	17 10	17 27	17 36		17 57		18 10	18 25		18 40	18 56	19 08	19 26	19 40
Keighley d	15 45	16 01	16 15	16 31	16 38	16 46	17 02	17 15	17 32	17 41	17 51	18 02	18 08	18 15	18 29	18 38	18 45	19 01	19 13	19 31	19 45
Crossflatts d	15 48	16 04	16 18	16 34		16 49	17 05	17 18	17 35	17 44		18 05		18 18	18 33		18 48	19 04	19 16	19 34	19 48
Bingley d	15 51	16 07	16 21	16 37	16 42	16 52	17 08	17 21	17 38	17 47	17 55	18 08	18 14	18 21	18 35	18 42	18 51	19 07	19 19	19 37	19 51
Saltaire d	15 54	16 10	16 24	16 40		16 55	17 11	17 24	17 41	17 50		18 11		18 24	18 39		18 54	19 10	19 22	19 40	19 54
Shipley a	15 57	16 12	16 27	16 42	16 49	16 59	17 13	17 27	17 43	17 55	18 00	18 13	18 19	18 28	18 42	18 48	18 58	19 12	19 25	19 42	19 57
d	15 58	16 14	16 28	16 44	16 49	16 59	17 15	17 28	17 45	17 56	18 00	18 14	18 19	18 28	18 44	18 48	18 58	19 14	19 26	19 44	19 58
Frizinghall 37 a	16 02		16 31			17 03		17 32		17 59				18 32			19 02		19 29		20 01
Bradford Forster Square 37 a	16 08		16 38			17 08		17 38		18 05				18 38			19 08		19 35		20 08
Leeds ■ 37 a		16 28		16 58	17 07		17 29		18 00		18 17	18 29	18 42		18 59	19 07		19 29		19 59	
London Kings Cross ■ ⊖26 a																					

	NT	NT	NT	NT	NT	NT	NT	NT	NT	NT	NT	NT
Carlisle ■ 65 d			18 07									
Armathwaite d			18 21									
Lazonby & Kirkoswald d			18 28									
Langwathby d			18 34									
Appleby d			18 49									
Kirkby Stephen d			19 02									
Garsdale d			19 15									
Dent d			19 20									
Ribblehead d			19 30						21 00			
Horton-in-Ribblesdale d			19 36						21 06			
Settle d			19 44						21 14			
Morecambe 98 d					19 09							
Bare Lane 98 d					19 13							
Lancaster ■ 65,82,98 d					19 24							
Carnforth 82 d					19 35							
Wennington d					19 49							
Bentham d					19 54							
Clapham (N Yorkshire) d					20 01							
Giggleswick d					20 10							
Long Preston d					20 18				21 20			
Hellifield d			19 52		20 21				21 23			
Clitheroe 94 a												
Blackburn 94,97 a												
Preston ■ 97 a												
Blackpool North 97 a												
Gargrave d					20 29				21 31			
Skipton a			20 07		20 38				21 38			
d	19 48	19 54	20 07	20 18	20 38	20 48	20 54	21 18		21 48	21 54	22 18
Cononley d	19 52	19 58		20 22		20 52	20 58	21 22		21 52	21 58	22 22
Steeton & Silsden d	19 56	20 02		20 26		20 56	21 02	21 26		21 56	22 02	22 26
Keighley d	20 01	20 07	20 17	20 31	20 48	21 01	21 07	21 31		22 01	22 07	22 31
Crossflatts d	20 04	20 10		20 33		21 04	21 10	21 34		22 04	22 10	22 34
Bingley d	20 07	20 13	20 22	20 37	20 53	21 07	21 13	21 37		22 07	22 13	22 37
Saltaire d	20 10	20 17		20 39		21 10	21 16	21 40		22 10	22 16	22 40
Shipley a	20 12	20 20	20 27	20 42	20 57	21 12	21 22	21 42		22 13	22 20	22 42
d	20 14	20 20	20 28	20 43	20 57	21 14	21 22	21 43		22 14	22 21	22 43
Frizinghall 37 a		20 24					21 26				22 24	
Bradford Forster Square 37 a		20 32					21 32				22 31	
Leeds ■ 37 a	20 28		20 46	21 00	21 16	21 30		21 59		22 33		23 01
London Kings Cross ■ ⊖26 a												

Carlisle, Morecambe, Lancaster and Skipton - Bradford and Leeds

Network Diagram - see first page of Table 35

Station		NT	NT	NT	NT	NT	NT	NT	NT	NT	NT	NT	NT	NT	NT	NT	NT A	NT	NT	NT	NT	NT	NT
Carlisle 8	65 d						09 25									13 51		15 35					16 37
Armathwaite	d						09 39									14 05		15 49					16 51
Lazonby & Kirkoswald	d						09 46									14 12		15 56					16 58
Langwathby	d						09 53									14 19		16 03					17 05
Appleby	d						10 07									14 33		16 18					17 20
Kirkby Stephen	d						10 21									14 47		16 32					17 34
Garsdale	d						10 34									15 00		16 45					17 47
Dent	d						10 40									15 06		16 51					17 53
Ribblehead	d						10 49									15 15		17 00					18 02
Horton-in-Ribblesdale	d						10 56									15 22		17 07					18 09
Settle	d						11 04									15 30		17 15					18 19
Morecambe	98 d											12 20					14 46						
Bare Lane	98 d											12 24					14 50						
Lancaster 6	65,82,98 d											12 48											
Carnforth	82 d											12 58					15 00						
Wennington	d											13 12					15 14						
Bentham	d											13 17					15 20						
Clapham (N Yorkshire)	d											13 24					15 26						
Giggleswick	d											13 32					15 35						
Long Preston	d						11 10					13 40				15 36	15 45						
Hellifield	d						11 13					13 44				15 39	15 49	17 26					18 26
Clitheroe	94 a																	17 49					
Blackburn	94,97 a																	18 21					
Preston 8	97 a																	18 48					
Blackpool North	97 a																						
Gargrave	d						11 21					13 52				15 47	15 57						
Skipton	a						11 30					14 01				15 54	16 06						18 41
	d	08 35	09 15	09 36	10 15	11 15	11 30	11 37	12 15	13 15	13 37	14 02	14 15	15 15	15 37	15 57	16 08		16 15	17 15	17 37	18 15	18 43
Cononley	d	08 39	09 19	09 40	10 19	11 19		11 41	12 19	13 19	13 41		14 19	15 19	15 41				16 19	17 19	17 41	18 19	
Steeton & Silsden	d	08 44	09 23	09 44	10 23	11 23		11 45	12 23	13 23	13 45		14 23	15 23	15 45				16 23	17 23	17 45	18 23	
Keighley	d	08 48	09 28	09 49	10 28	11 28	11 40	11 50	12 28	13 28	13 50	14 12	14 28	15 28	15 50	16 07	16 18		16 28	17 28	17 50	18 28	18 53
Crossflatts	d	08 52	09 31	09 52	10 31	11 31		11 53	12 31	13 31	13 53		14 31	15 31	15 53				16 31	17 31	17 53	18 31	
Bingley	d	08 54	09 34	09 55	10 34	11 34	11 44	11 56	12 34	13 34	13 56	14 16	14 34	15 34	15 56	16 11	16 23		16 34	17 34	17 56	18 34	18 57
Saltaire	d	08 58	09 37	09 58	10 37	11 37		11 59	12 37	13 37	13 59		14 37	15 37	15 59				16 37	17 37	17 59	18 37	
Shipley	a	09 00	09 39	10 01	10 39	11 39	11 49	12 02	12 39	13 39	14 02	14 21	14 39	15 39	16 02	16 16	16 27		16 39	17 39	18 02	18 39	19 02
	d	09 00	09 40	10 01	10 40	11 40	11 49	12 02	12 40	13 40	14 02	14 21	14 40	15 40	16 02	16 16	16 29		16 40	17 40	18 02	18 40	19 03
Frizinghall	37 a			10 05				12 06			14 06				16 06						18 06		
Bradford Forster Square	37 a			10 12				12 12			14 12				16 12						18 12		
Leeds 10	37 a	09 14	09 54		10 54	11 54	12 06		12 54	13 54		14 39	14 54	15 54		16 34	16 47		16 54	17 54		18 54	19 21
London Kings Cross 15	⊖26 a																						

Station		NT	NT	NT	NT	NT	NT	NT B	NT C	NT	NT	NT
Carlisle 8	65 d		17 41									
Armathwaite	d		17 55									
Lazonby & Kirkoswald	d		18 03									
Langwathby	d		18 09									
Appleby	d		18 25									
Kirkby Stephen	d		18 38									
Garsdale	d		18 52									
Dent	d		18 57									
Ribblehead	d		19 07									
Horton-in-Ribblesdale	d		19 14									
Settle	d		19 22									
Morecambe	98 d	17 45						20 00	20 00			
Bare Lane	98 d	17 49						20 04	20 04			
Lancaster 6	65,82,98 d	18 04						20 18	20 18			
Carnforth	82 d	18 14						20 28	20 28			
Wennington	d	18 28						20 42	20 42			
Bentham	d	18 33						20 47	20 47			
Clapham (N Yorkshire)	d	18 40						20 54	20 54			
Giggleswick	d	18 49						21 03	21 03			
Long Preston	d	18 57						21 11	21 11			
Hellifield	d	19 00	19 32					21 14	21 14			
Clitheroe	94 a		19 56									
Blackburn	94,97 a		20 22									
Preston 8	97 a		20 47									
Blackpool North	97 a		21 16									
Gargrave	d	19 09						21 22	21 22			
Skipton	a	19 17						21 30	21 31			
	d	19 18		19 24	19 37	20 15	21 15	21 33	21 33	21 39	22 15	23 15
Cononley	d			19 28	19 41	20 19	21 19			21 43	22 19	23 19
Steeton & Silsden	d			19 32	19 45	20 23	21 23			21 47	22 23	23 23
Keighley	d	19 28		19 37	19 50	20 28	21 28	21 43	21 43	21 52	22 28	23 29
Crossflatts	d			19 40	19 53	20 31	21 31			21 55	22 31	23 31
Bingley	d	19 32		19 43	19 56	20 34	21 34	21 48	21 48	21 58	22 34	23 34
Saltaire	d			19 46	19 59	20 37	21 37			22 01	22 37	23 37
Shipley	a	19 37		19 48	20 02	20 39	21 39	21 53	21 53	22 04	22 39	23 41
	d	19 38		19 49	20 02	20 40	21 40	21 54	21 54	22 04	22 40	23 41
Frizinghall	37 a				20 06					22 08		
Bradford Forster Square	37 a				20 12					22 14		
Leeds 10	37 a	19 56		20 03		20 54	21 54	22 10	22 10		22 54	23 58
London Kings Cross 15	⊖26 a											

A From Lancaster
B from 1 July until 9 September
C until 24 June

Carlisle, Morecambe, Lancaster and Skipton - Bradford and Leeds

Network Diagram - see first page of Table 35

Station		NT	NT	NT	NT	NT	NT	NT	NT	NT	NT	NT	NT	NT	NT	NT	NT A	NT	NT	NT	NT	NT	NT
Carlisle 8	65 d						09 25									13 51						16 37	
Armathwaite	d						09 39									14 05						16 51	
Lazonby & Kirkoswald	d						09 46									14 12						16 58	
Langwathby	d						09 53									14 19						17 05	
Appleby	d						10 07									14 33						17 20	
Kirkby Stephen	d						10 21									14 47						17 34	
Garsdale	d						10 34									15 00						17 47	
Dent	d						10 40									15 06						17 53	
Ribblehead	d						10 49									15 15						18 02	
Horton-in-Ribblesdale	d						10 56									15 22						18 09	
Settle	d						11 04									15 30						18 19	
Morecambe	98 d											12 20					14 46						17 45
Bare Lane	98 d											12 24					14 50						17 49
Lancaster 6	65,82,98 d											12 48											18 04
Carnforth	82 d											12 58					15 00						18 14
Wennington	d											13 12					15 14						18 28
Bentham	d											13 17					15 20						18 33
Clapham (N Yorkshire)	d											13 24					15 26						18 40
Giggleswick	d											13 32					15 35						18 49
Long Preston	d						11 10					13 40				15 36	15 45						18 57
Hellifield	d						11 13					13 44				15 39	15 49					18 26	19 00
Clitheroe	94 a																						
Blackburn	94,97 a																						
Preston 8	97 a																						
Blackpool North	97 a																						
Gargrave	d						11 21					13 52				15 47	15 57						19 09
Skipton	a						11 30					14 01				15 54	16 06					18 41	19 17
	d	08 35	09 15	09 36	10 15	11 15	11 30	11 37	12 15	13 15	13 37	14 02	14 15	15 15	15 37	15 57	16 08	16 15	17 15	17 37	18 15	18 43	19 18
Cononley	d	08 39	09 19	09 40	10 19	11 19		11 41	12 19	13 19	13 41		14 19	15 19	15 41			16 19	17 19	17 41	18 19		
Steeton & Silsden	d	08 44	09 23	09 44	10 23	11 23		11 45	12 23	13 23	13 45		14 23	15 23	15 45			16 23	17 23	17 45	18 23		
Keighley	d	08 48	09 28	09 49	10 28	11 28	11 40	11 50	12 28	13 28	13 50	14 12	14 28	15 28	15 50	16 07	16 18	16 28	17 28	17 50	18 28	18 53	19 28
Crossflatts	d	08 52	09 31	09 52	10 31	11 31		11 53	12 31	13 31	13 53		14 31	15 31	15 53			16 31	17 31	17 53	18 31		
Bingley	d	08 54	09 34	09 55	10 34	11 34	11 44	11 56	12 34	13 34	13 56	14 16	14 34	15 34	15 56	16 11	16 23	16 34	17 34	17 56	18 34	18 57	19 32
Saltaire	d	08 58	09 37	09 58	10 37	11 37		11 59	12 37	13 37	13 59		14 37	15 37	15 59			16 37	17 37	17 59	18 37		
Shipley	a	09 00	09 39	10 01	10 39	11 39	11 49	12 02	12 39	13 39	14 02	14 21	14 39	15 39	16 02	16 16	16 27	16 39	17 39	18 02	18 39	19 02	19 37
	d	09 00	09 40	10 01	10 40	11 40	11 49	12 02	12 40	13 40	14 02	14 21	14 40	15 40	16 02	16 16	16 29	16 40	17 40	18 02	18 40	19 03	19 38
Frizinghall	37 a			10 05				12 06			14 06				16 06					18 06			
Bradford Forster Square	37 a			10 12				12 12			14 12				16 12					18 12			
Leeds 10	37 a	09 14	09 54		10 54	11 54	12 06		12 54	13 54		14 39	14 54	15 54		16 34	16 47	16 54	17 54		18 54	19 21	19 56
London Kings Cross 15	⊖26 a																						

Station		NT	NT	NT	NT	NT	NT	NT	NT	NT
Carlisle 8	65 d	17 41								
Armathwaite	d	17 55								
Lazonby & Kirkoswald	d	18 03								
Langwathby	d	18 09								
Appleby	d	18 25								
Kirkby Stephen	d	18 38								
Garsdale	d	18 52								
Dent	d	18 57								
Ribblehead	d	19 07								
Horton-in-Ribblesdale	d	19 14								
Settle	d	19 22								
Morecambe	98 d						20 00			
Bare Lane	98 d						20 04			
Lancaster 6	65,82,98 d						20 18			
Carnforth	82 d						20 28			
Wennington	d						20 42			
Bentham	d						20 47			
Clapham (N Yorkshire)	d						20 54			
Giggleswick	d						21 03			
Long Preston	d						21 11			
Hellifield	d	19 32					21 14			
Clitheroe	94 a	19 56								
Blackburn	94,97 a	20 22								
Preston 8	97 a	20 47								
Blackpool North	97 a	21 16								
Gargrave	d						21 22			
Skipton	a						21 31			
	d		19 24	19 37	20 15	21 15	21 33	21 39	22 15	23 15
Cononley	d		19 28	19 41	20 19	21 19		21 43	22 19	23 19
Steeton & Silsden	d		19 32	19 45	20 23	21 23		21 47	22 23	23 23
Keighley	d		19 37	19 50	20 28	21 28	21 43	21 52	22 28	23 29
Crossflatts	d		19 40	19 53	20 31	21 31		21 55	22 31	23 31
Bingley	d		19 43	19 56	20 34	21 34	21 48	21 58	22 34	23 34
Saltaire	d		19 46	19 59	20 37	21 37		22 01	22 37	23 37
Shipley	a		19 48	20 02	20 39	21 39	21 53	22 04	22 39	23 41
	d		19 49	20 02	20 40	21 40	21 54	22 04	22 40	23 41
Frizinghall	37 a			20 06				22 08		
Bradford Forster Square	37 a			20 12				22 14		
Leeds 10	37 a		20 03		20 54	21 54	22 10		22 54	23 58
London Kings Cross 15	⊖26 a									

A From Lancaster

Table 36

Sundays from 28 October

Carlisle, Morecambe, Lancaster and Skipton - Bradford and Leeds

Network Diagram - see first page of Table 35

	NT	NT	NT	NT	NT	NT	NT	NT	NT	NT	NT	NT	NT	NT	NT	NT A	NT	NT	NT	NT	NT	NT
Carlisle 65 d						09 25									13 51						16 37	
Armathwaite d						09 39									14 05						16 51	
Lazonby & Kirkoswald d						09 46									14 12						16 58	
Langwathby d						09 53									14 19						17 05	
Appleby d						10 07									14 33						17 20	
Kirkby Stephen d						10 21									14 47						17 34	
Garsdale d						10 34									15 00						17 47	
Dent d						10 40									15 06						17 53	
Ribblehead d						10 49									15 15						18 02	
Horton-in-Ribblesdale d						10 56									15 22						18 09	
Settle d						11 04									15 30						18 19	
Morecambe 98 d											12 20					14 46						17 45
Bare Lane 98 d											12 24					14 50						17 49
Lancaster 65,82,98 d											12 48											18 04
Carnforth 82 d											12 58					15 00						18 14
Wennington d											13 12					15 14						18 28
Bentham d											13 17					15 20						18 33
Clapham (N Yorkshire) d											13 24					15 26						18 40
Giggleswick d											13 32					15 35						18 49
Long Preston d						11 10					13 40				15 36	15 45						18 57
Hellifield d						11 13					13 44				15 39	15 49					18 26	19 00
Clitheroe 94 a																						
Blackburn 94,97 a																						
Preston 97 a																						
Blackpool North 97 a																						
Gargrave d						11 21					13 52				15 47	15 57						19 09
Skipton a						11 30					14 01				15 54	16 06					18 41	19 17
d	08 35	09 15	09 36	10 15	11 15	11 30	11 37	12 15	13 15	13 37	14 02	14 15	15 15	15 37	15 57	16 08	16 15	17 15	17 37	18 15	18 43	19 18
Cononley d	08 39	09 19	09 40	10 19	11 19		11 41	12 19	13 19	13 41		14 19	15 19	15 41			16 19	17 19	17 41	18 19		
Steeton & Silsden d	08 44	09 23	09 44	10 23	11 23		11 45	12 23	13 23	13 45		14 23	15 23	15 45			16 23	17 23	17 45	18 23		
Keighley d	08 48	09 28	09 49	10 28	11 28	11 40	11 50	12 28	13 28	13 50	14 12	14 28	15 28	15 50	16 07	16 18	16 28	17 28	17 50	18 28	18 53	19 28
Crossflatts d	08 52	09 31	09 52	10 31	11 31		11 53	12 31	13 31	13 53		14 31	15 31	15 53			16 31	17 31	17 53	18 31		
Bingley d	08 54	09 34	09 55	10 34	11 34	11 44	11 56	12 34	13 34	13 56	14 16	14 34	15 34	15 56	16 11	16 23	16 34	17 34	17 56	18 34	18 57	19 32
Saltaire d	08 58	09 37	09 58	10 37	11 37		11 59	12 37	13 37	13 59		14 37	15 37	15 59			16 37	17 37	17 59	18 37		
Shipley a	09 00	09 39	10 01	10 39	11 39	11 49	12 02	12 39	13 39	14 02	14 21	14 39	15 39	16 02	16 16	16 27	16 39	17 39	18 02	18 39	19 02	19 37
d	09 00	09 40	10 01	10 40	11 40	11 49	12 02	12 40	13 40	14 02	14 21	14 40	15 40	16 02	16 16	16 29	16 40	17 40	18 02	18 40	19 03	19 38
Frizinghall 37 a			10 05				12 06			14 06				16 06					18 06			
Bradford Forster Square 37 a			10 12				12 12			14 12				16 12					18 12			
Leeds 37 a	09 14	09 54		10 54	11 54	12 06		12 54	13 54		14 39	14 54	15 54		16 34	16 47	16 54	17 54		18 54	19 21	19 56
London Kings Cross ⊖26 a																						

	NT	NT	NT	NT	NT	NT	NT	NT
Carlisle 65 d								
Armathwaite d								
Lazonby & Kirkoswald d								
Langwathby d								
Appleby d								
Kirkby Stephen d								
Garsdale d								
Dent d								
Ribblehead d								
Horton-in-Ribblesdale d								
Settle d								
Morecambe 98 d					20 00			
Bare Lane 98 d					20 04			
Lancaster 65,82,98 d					20 18			
Carnforth 82 d					20 28			
Wennington d					20 42			
Bentham d					20 47			
Clapham (N Yorkshire) d					20 54			
Giggleswick d					21 03			
Long Preston d					21 11			
Hellifield d					21 14			
Clitheroe 94 a								
Blackburn 94,97 a								
Preston 97 a								
Blackpool North 97 a								
Gargrave d					21 22			
Skipton a					21 31			
d	19 24	19 37	20 15	21 15	21 33	21 39	22 15	23 15
Cononley d	19 28	19 41	20 19	21 19		21 43	22 19	23 19
Steeton & Silsden d	19 32	19 45	20 23	21 23		21 47	22 23	23 23
Keighley d	19 37	19 50	20 28	21 28	21 43	21 52	22 28	23 29
Crossflatts d	19 40	19 53	20 31	21 31		21 55	22 31	23 31
Bingley d	19 43	19 56	20 34	21 34	21 48	21 58	22 34	23 34
Saltaire d	19 46	19 59	20 37	21 37		22 01	22 37	23 37
Shipley a	19 48	20 02	20 39	21 39	21 53	22 04	22 39	23 41
d	19 49	20 02	20 40	21 40	21 54	22 04	22 40	23 41
Frizinghall 37 a		20 06				22 08		
Bradford Forster Square 37 a		20 12				22 14		
Leeds 37 a	20 03		20 54	21 54	22 10		22 54	23 58
London Kings Cross ⊖26 a								

A From Lancaster

Table 37

Mondays to Fridays

Leeds - Shipley and Bradford

Network Diagram - see first page of Table 35

Miles	Miles		NT	NT	NT	NT	NT	NT	NT	NT	NT	NT	NT	NT	NT	NT	NT	NT	NT	NT	NT	NT
0	0	**Leeds** d	05 08	05 29	05 51	06 03	06 16	06 22		06 37			06 49	06 51	06 56	07 08		07 23		07 25	07 37	
10¾	—	**Shipley** a		05 41			06 27						07 01		07 08					07 36		
—	—	d							06 28		06 41	06 53	07 02				07 15		07 28			07 47
11¾	—	Frizinghall d							06 32		06 44	06 57	07 04				07 17		07 32			07 49
—	4	Bramley d	05 15		05 58			06 29		06 44						07 15		07 30			07 44	
—	5¾	New Pudsey d	05 20		06 02	06 13		06 34		06 49				07 01		07 20		07 35			07 49	
—	9½	**Bradford Interchange** a	05 28		06 13	06 21		06 42		06 57				07 11		07 28		07 43			07 57	
13½	—	**Bradford Forster Square** a							06 38		06 50	07 03	07 10				07 22		07 39			07 56

	NT	NT	NT	NT	NT	NT	NT	NT	NT	NT	NT	NT	NT	NT	NT	NT	NT	NT	NT	NT	NT	NT
Leeds d	07 39	07 51		07 51	08 08		08 10		08 19	08 23	08 25	08 37		08 40		08 49	08 51	08 56	09 07		09 10	09 23
Shipley a	07 50			08 02			08 22		08 31		08 37			08 51		09 01		09 07			09 21	
d	07 51		08 00			08 13	08 23	08 28					08 48	08 52	08 58					09 18	09 22	
Frizinghall d	07 53		08 03			08 16	08 25	08 31					08 50	08 54	09 02					09 21	09 24	
Bramley d					08 15					08 30		08 44							09 14			09 30
New Pudsey d		08 01			08 20					08 35		08 49					09 00		09 19			09 35
Bradford Interchange a		08 09			08 28					08 43		08 57					09 12		09 28			09 43
Bradford Forster Square a	07 59		08 09			08 22	08 31	08 38					08 56	09 00	09 09					09 27	09 31	

	NT	NT	NT	NT	NT	NT	NT	NT	NT	NT	NT	NT	NT	NT	NT	NT	NT	NT	NT	NT	NT
Leeds d		09 26	09 37		09 40		09 47	09 53	09 56	10 07		10 10		10 19	10 23	10 26	10 37		10 40		10 49
Shipley a		09 37			09 52		10 01		10 07			10 21		10 31		10 37			10 51		11 01
d	09 28			09 44	09 52	09 58					10 14	10 22	10 28					10 44	10 52	10 58	
Frizinghall d	09 32			09 47	09 54	10 02					10 17	10 24	10 32					10 47	10 54	11 02	
Bramley d			09 44							10 14					10 30		10 44				
New Pudsey d			09 49					10 02		10 20					10 35		10 49				
Bradford Interchange a			09 57					10 12		10 28					10 43		10 57				
Bradford Forster Square a	09 38			09 53	10 02	10 08					10 23	10 30	10 38					10 53	11 00	11 08	

	NT	NT	NT	NT	NT	NT	NT	NT	NT	NT	NT	NT	NT	NT	NT	NT	NT	NT	NT	NT	NT	NT
Leeds d	10 53	10 56	11 07		11 10	11 23		11 26	11 37		11 40	11 53		11 56	12 07		12 10	12 23		12 26	12 37	
Shipley a		11 07			11 21			11 38			11 51			12 07			12 21			12 37		
d				11 14	11 22		11 28			11 44	11 52		11 58			12 14	12 22		12 28			12 44
Frizinghall d				11 17	11 24		11 32			11 47	11 54		12 02			12 17	12 24		12 32			12 47
Bramley d			11 14			11 30			11 44						12 14			12 30			12 44	
New Pudsey d	11 02		11 19			11 35			11 49			12 02			12 19			12 35			12 49	
Bradford Interchange a	11 11		11 28			11 43			11 57			12 11			12 28			12 43			12 57	
Bradford Forster Square a				11 23	11 30		11 38			11 53	12 00		12 10			12 24	12 31		12 38			12 53

	NT	NT	NT	NT	NT	NT	NT	NT	NT	NT	NT	NT	NT	NT	NT	NT	NT	NT	NT	NT	NT	NT
Leeds d	12 40		12 49	12 53	12 56	13 07		13 10	13 23		13 26	13 37		13 40		13 49	13 53	13 56	14 07		14 10	14 23
Shipley a	12 51		13 01		13 07			13 21			13 37			13 51		14 03		14 07			14 21	
d	12 52	12 58					13 14	13 22		13 28			13 44	13 52	13 58					14 14	14 22	
Frizinghall d	12 54	13 02					13 17	13 24		13 32			13 47	13 54	14 02					14 17	14 24	
Bramley d						13 14			13 30			13 44							14 14			14 30
New Pudsey d				13 02		13 19			13 35			13 49					14 02		14 19			14 35
Bradford Interchange a				13 12		13 28			13 43			13 58					14 12		14 28			14 43
Bradford Forster Square a	13 00	13 08					13 23	13 30		13 38			13 53	14 00	14 08					14 23	14 30	

	NT	NT	NT	NT	NT	NT	NT	NT	NT	NT	NT	NT	NT	NT	NT	NT	NT	NT	NT	NT	NT
Leeds d		14 26	14 37		14 40		14 49	14 53	14 56	15 07		15 10	15 23		15 26	15 37		15 40	15 52		15 56
Shipley a		14 37			14 51		15 01		15 07			15 21			15 37			15 52			16 07
d	14 28			14 44	14 52	14 58					15 14	15 22		15 28			15 44	15 52		15 58	
Frizinghall d	14 32			14 47	14 54	15 02					15 17	15 24		15 32			15 47	15 55		16 02	
Bramley d			14 44							15 14			15 30			15 44					
New Pudsey d			14 49					15 02		15 19			15 35			15 49			16 01		
Bradford Interchange a			14 57					15 12		15 28			15 43			15 57			16 10		
Bradford Forster Square a	14 38			14 53	15 00	15 08					15 23	15 30		15 38			15 53	16 01		16 08	

	NT	NT	NT	NT	NT	NT	NT	NT	NT	NT	NT	NT	NT	NT	NT	NT	NT	NT	NT	NT	NT	NT
Leeds d	16 07		16 10	16 23		16 26		16 35	16 37	16 39	16 51		16 56	17 07		17 10	17 23		17 26		17 36	17 37
Shipley a			16 21			16 37		16 49		16 53			17 07			17 21			17 37		17 49	
d		16 14	16 22		16 28		16 44	16 49				17 02			17 15	17 22		17 28		17 44	17 50	
Frizinghall d		16 17	16 24		16 31		16 47	16 52				17 06			17 17	17 24		17 32		17 46	17 52	
Bramley d	16 14			16 30					16 44					17 14			17 30					17 44
New Pudsey d	16 19			16 35					16 49		17 00			17 19			17 35					17 49
Bradford Interchange a	16 28			16 43					16 57		17 10			17 28			17 43					17 57
Bradford Forster Square a		16 23	16 30		16 38		16 53	16 58				17 12			17 23	17 30		17 38		17 53	17 58	

	NT	NT	NT	NT	NT	NT	NT	NT	NT	NT	NT	NT	NT	NT	NT	NT	NT	NT	NT	NT	NT
Leeds d	17 39	17 51		17 56		18 06	18 08	18 10	18 23		18 26	18 37		18 40	18 51		18 54	19 08		19 10	
Shipley a	17 53			18 07		18 18		18 22			18 38			18 52			19 05			19 21	
d			17 56		18 14			18 22		18 28			18 44	18 52		18 58			19 14	19 22	19 26
Frizinghall d			17 59		18 17			18 24		18 32			18 46	18 55		19 02			19 17	19 24	19 29
Bramley d							18 15		18 30			18 44						19 15			
New Pudsey d		18 01					18 20		18 35			18 49			19 01			19 20			
Bradford Interchange a		18 10					18 28		18 43			18 58			19 10			19 28			
Bradford Forster Square a			18 05		18 23			18 31		18 38			18 52	19 01		19 08			19 23	19 30	19 35

Leeds - Shipley and Bradford

Network Diagram - see first page of Table 35

Mondays to Fridays

		NT	NT	NT	NT	NT	NT	NT	NT	NT		NT	NT	NT	NT	NT	NT	NT	GR	NT		NT	NT	NT	NT
Leeds	d	19 19	19 23	19 26	19 37			19 56	20 08				20 26	20 37		20 51		20 56	21 00	21 08			21 26	21 37	
Shipley	a	19 31		19 37				20 07					20 37					21 07	21s12				21 38		
	d					19 44	19 58			20 20		20 28			20 48		21 03					21 19			21 48
Frizinghall	d					19 47	20 01			20 24		20 30			20 51		21 05					21 23			21 51
Bramley	d		19 30		19 44				20 15					20 44						21 15				21 44	
New Pudsey	d		19 35		19 49				20 20					20 49		21 01				21 20				21 49	
Bradford Interchange	a		19 44		19 57				20 28					20 57		21 10				21 28				21 57	
Bradford Forster Square	a					19 53	20 08			20 32		20 36			20 57		21 12		21 24			21 29			21 57

		NT	NT	NT	NT	NT		NT	NT	NT	NT	NT	NT
Leeds	d		21 56	22 08		22 26		22 37			22 56	23 08	23 18
Shipley	a		22 07			22 37					23 08		23 31
	d	22 03			22 21				22 48	23 03			
Frizinghall	d	22 05			22 24				22 51	23 05			
Bramley	d			22 15				22 44				23 15	
New Pudsey	d			22 20				22 49				23 20	
Bradford Interchange	a			22 28				22 57				23 29	
Bradford Forster Square	a	22 11			22 31				22 57	23 13			

Saturdays

		NT	NT	NT	NT	NT	NT	NT	NT	NT		NT	NT	NT	NT	NT	NT	NT	NT	NT		NT	NT	NT	NT
Leeds	d	05 37	05 51	05 55	06 16		06 19	06 37		06 51		06 56	07 08	07 10	07 23		07 37		07 51			07 56	08 08	08 10	
Shipley	a			06 07			06 31					07 08		07 21								08 08		08 22	
	d					06 28			06 44					07 22		07 32		07 47		08 00				08 23	08 28
Frizinghall	d					06 32			06 47					07 24		07 36		07 49		08 03				08 25	08 31
Bramley	d	05 44	05 58		06 23			06 44					07 15		07 30		07 44						08 15		
New Pudsey	d	05 49	06 02		06 28			06 49		07 01			07 20		07 35		07 49		08 01				08 20		
Bradford Interchange	a	05 57	06 13		06 36			06 57		07 11			07 28		07 43		07 57		08 09				08 28		
Bradford Forster Square	a					06 38			06 55					07 30		07 42		07 56		08 09				08 31	08 38

		NT A	NT	NT	NT	NT		NT	NT	NT	NT	NT	NT	NT	NT	NT		NT	NT	NT	NT	NT	NT	NT	NT
Leeds	d	08 19	08 23	08 25	08 37			08 40		08 49	08 51	08 56	09 07		09 10	09 23			09 26	09 37		09 40		09 47	09 53
Shipley	a	08 31		08 37				08 51		09 01		09 07			09 21				09 37			09 52		10 01	
	d					08 44		08 52	08 58					09 14	09 22			09 28			09 44	09 52	09 58		
Frizinghall	d					08 46		08 54	09 02					09 17	09 24			09 32			09 47	09 54	10 02		
Bramley	d		08 30		08 44								09 14			09 30				09 44					
New Pudsey	d		08 35		08 49						09 00		09 19			09 35				09 49					10 02
Bradford Interchange	a		08 43		08 57						09 12		09 28			09 43				09 57					10 11
Bradford Forster Square	a					08 53		09 00	09 09					09 24	09 31			09 38			09 53	10 02	10 08		

		NT		NT	NT	NT	NT	NT	NT	NT	NT	NT		NT	NT	NT	NT	NT	NT	NT	NT	NT		NT	NT
Leeds	d	09 56		10 07		10 10		10 19	10 23	10 26	10 37			10 40		10 49	10 53	10 56	11 07		11 10	11 23			11 26
Shipley	a	10 07				10 21		10 31		10 37				10 51		11 01		11 07			11 21				11 38
	d				10 14	10 22	10 28					10 44		10 52	10 58					11 14	11 22			11 28	
Frizinghall	d				10 17	10 24	10 32					10 47		10 54	11 02					11 17	11 24			11 32	
Bramley	d			10 14					10 30		10 44								11 14			11 30			
New Pudsey	d			10 19					10 35		10 49						11 02		11 19			11 35			
Bradford Interchange	a			10 28					10 43		10 57						11 12		11 28			11 43			
Bradford Forster Square	a				10 23	10 30	10 38					10 53		11 00	11 08					11 23	11 30			11 38	

		NT	NT	NT	NT	NT	NT	NT		NT	NT	NT	NT	NT	NT	NT	NT	NT		NT	NT	NT	NT	NT	NT
Leeds	d	11 37		11 40	11 53		11 56	12 07			12 10	12 23		12 26	12 37		12 40			12 49	12 53	12 56	13 07		13 10
Shipley	a			11 51			12 07				12 21			12 37			12 51			13 01		13 07			13 21
	d		11 44	11 52		11 58				12 14	12 22		12 28			12 44	12 52	12 58						13 14	13 22
Frizinghall	d		11 47	11 54		12 02				12 17	12 24		12 32			12 47	12 54	13 02						13 17	13 24
Bramley	d	11 44						12 14				12 30			12 44								13 14		
New Pudsey	d	11 49			12 02			12 19				12 35			12 49						13 02		13 19		
Bradford Interchange	a	11 57			12 12			12 28				12 43			12 57						13 12		13 28		
Bradford Forster Square	a		11 53	12 00		12 10				12 24	12 31		12 38			12 53	13 00	13 08						13 23	13 30

		NT	NT	NT		NT	NT	NT	NT	NT	NT	NT	NT	NT		NT	NT	NT	NT	NT	NT	NT	NT	NT	
Leeds	d	13 23		13 26		13 37		13 40		13 49	13 53	13 56	14 07			14 10	14 23		14 26	14 37		14 40		14 49	
Shipley	a			13 37				13 51		14 03		14 07				14 21			14 37			14 51		15 01	
	d		13 28				13 44	13 52	13 58					14 14		14 22		14 28			14 44	14 52	14 58		
Frizinghall	d		13 32				13 47	13 54	14 02					14 17		14 24		14 32			14 47	14 54	15 02		
Bramley	d	13 30				13 44							14 14				14 30			14 44					
New Pudsey	d	13 35				13 49					14 02		14 19				14 35			14 49					
Bradford Interchange	a	13 43				13 58					14 12		14 28				14 43			14 58					
Bradford Forster Square	a		13 38				13 53	14 00	14 08					14 23		14 30		14 38			14 53	15 00	15 08		

		NT	NT	NT	NT	NT	NT	NT	NT	NT		NT	NT	NT	NT	NT	NT	NT	NT	NT		NT	NT	NT	NT
Leeds	d	14 53	14 56	15 07		15 10	15 23		15 26	15 37			15 40	15 52		15 56	16 07		16 10	16 23			16 26		16 35
Shipley	a		15 07			15 21			15 37				15 52			16 07			16 21				16 37		16 49
	d				15 14	15 22		15 28				15 44	15 52		15 58			16 14	16 22			16 28		16 44	16 49
Frizinghall	d				15 17	15 24		15 32				15 47	15 55		16 02			16 17	16 24			16 31		16 47	16 52
Bramley	d			15 14			15 30			15 44							16 14			16 30					
New Pudsey	d	15 02		15 19			15 35			15 49				16 01			16 19			16 35					
Bradford Interchange	a	15 12		15 28			15 43			15 57				16 10			16 28			16 43					
Bradford Forster Square	a				15 23	15 30		15 38				15 53	16 01		16 08			16 23	16 30			16 38		16 53	16 58

Leeds - Shipley and Bradford

Network Diagram - see first page of Table 35

		NT	NT	NT	NT	NT		NT	NT	NT	NT	NT	NT	NT	NT	NT		NT	NT	NT	NT	NT	NT	NT	NT
Leeds	d	16 37	16 39	16 51		16 56		17 07		17 10	17 23		17 26	17 37		17 40			17 50	17 51	17 56	18 08		18 10	18 23
Shipley	a		16 53			17 07				17 21			17 37			17 51			18 02		18 07			18 22	
	d				16 59				17 15	17 22		17 28			17 44	17 52		17 56					18 14	18 22	
Frizinghall	d				17 03				17 17	17 24		17 32			17 46	17 54		17 59					18 17	18 24	
Bramley	d	16 44						17 14			17 30			17 44								18 15			18 30
New Pudsey	d	16 49		17 00				17 19			17 35			17 49						18 01		18 20			18 35
Bradford Interchange	a	16 57		17 10				17 28			17 43			17 57						18 09		18 28			18 43
Bradford Forster Square	a				17 08				17 23	17 30		17 38			17 53	18 00		18 05					18 23	18 31	

		NT		NT	NT	NT	NT	NT	NT	NT	NT	NT		NT	NT	NT	NT	NT	NT	NT	NT	NT		NT	NT
Leeds	d			18 26	18 37		18 40	18 51		18 56	19 08			19 10		19 19	19 23	19 26	19 37			19 56		20 08	
Shipley	a			18 38			18 52			19 07				19 21		19 31		19 37				20 07			
	d	18 28				18 44	18 52		18 58			19 14		19 22	19 26					19 44	19 58				20 20
Frizinghall	d	18 32				18 46	18 55		19 02			19 17		19 24	19 29					19 47	20 01				20 24
Bramley	d				18 44						19 15						19 30		19 44					20 15	
New Pudsey	d				18 49			19 01			19 20						19 35		19 49					20 20	
Bradford Interchange	a				18 58			19 10			19 28						19 44		19 57					20 28	
Bradford Forster Square	a	18 38				18 52	19 01		19 08			19 23		19 30	19 35					19 53	20 08				20 32

		NT	NT	NT	NT	NT	NT	NT		NT	NT	NT	NT	NT	NT	GR	NT	NT		NT	NT	NT	NT	NT	NT
Leeds	d		20 26	20 37		20 51		20 56		21 08		21 26	21 37			21 59	22 03	22 08			22 26			22 56	23 00
Shipley	a		20 37					21 07				21 38				22s11	22 15				22 37			23 08	
	d	20 28			20 48		21 03				21 22			21 48	22 03					22 21		22 48	23 03		
Frizinghall	d	20 30			20 51		21 05				21 26			21 51	22 05					22 24		22 51	23 05		
Bramley	d			20 44						21 15			21 44					22 15							23 07
New Pudsey	d			20 49		21 01				21 20			21 49					22 20							23 12
Bradford Interchange	a			20 57		21 10				21 28			21 57					22 28							23 21
Bradford Forster Square	a	20 36			20 57		21 12				21 32			21 57	22 11	22 23				22 31		22 57	23 13		

		NT
Leeds	d	23 18
Shipley	a	23 31
	d	
Frizinghall	d	
Bramley	d	
New Pudsey	d	
Bradford Interchange	a	
Bradford Forster Square	a	

Sundays

until 9 September

		NT	NT A	NT	NT	NT	NT	NT	NT	NT		NT	NT	NT	NT	NT	NT	NT	NT	NT		NT	NT	NT	NT
Leeds	d	08 02	08 21	08 34	08 40	08 45	09 00	09 02	09 18	09 34		09 35	09 54			10 08	10 12	10 34	10 35	10 51		10 54	11 08	11 12	11 34
Shipley	a			08 45	08 52		09 15			09 45						10 19		10 45		11 03			11 19		11 45
	d			08 46						09 46				10 01	10 15			10 46							11 46
Frizinghall	d			08 48						09 48				10 05	10 18			10 48							11 48
Bramley	d	08 09	08 28					09 09	09 25				10 01				10 19					11 01		11 19	
New Pudsey	d	08 14	08 33			08 54		09 14	09 30			09 44	10 06				10 24		10 44			11 06		11 24	
Bradford Interchange	a	08 22	08 41			09 03		09 22	09 38			09 53	10 14				10 32		10 53			11 14		11 32	
Bradford Forster Square	a			08 54						09 54				10 12	10 24			10 54							11 54

		NT	NT	NT	NT	NT		NT	NT	NT	NT	NT	NT	NT	NT	NT		NT	NT	NT	NT	NT	NT	NT	NT
Leeds	d	11 35	11 54			12 08		12 12	12 34	12 35	12 54	13 08	13 12	13 15	13 34	13 35		13 54			14 08	14 12	14 34	14 35	14 54
Shipley	a					12 19			12 45			13 19		13 28	13 45						14 19		14 45		
	d			12 02	12 15				12 46						13 46				14 02	14 15			14 46		
Frizinghall	d			12 06	12 18				12 48						13 48				14 06	14 18			14 48		
Bramley	d		12 01					12 19			13 01		13 19					14 01				14 19			15 01
New Pudsey	d	11 44	12 06					12 24		12 44	13 06		13 24			13 44		14 06				14 24		14 44	15 06
Bradford Interchange	a	11 53	12 14					12 32		12 53	13 14		13 32			13 53		14 14				14 32		14 53	15 14
Bradford Forster Square	a			12 12	12 24				12 54						13 54				14 12	14 24			14 54		

		NT		NT	NT	NT	NT	NT	NT	NT	NT	NT		NT	NT	NT	NT	NT	NT	NT	NT	NT		NT	NT
Leeds	d	14 57		15 08	15 12	15 34	15 35	15 54			16 08	16 13		16 35	16 35	16 54	17 08	17 12	17 21	17 33	17 35	17 37		17 54	
Shipley	a	15 09		15 19		15 45					16 19				16 46		17 19		17 33	17 45		17 48			
	d					15 46			16 02	16 15					16 46							17 49			18 02
Frizinghall	d					15 48			16 06	16 18					16 48							17 51			18 06
Bramley	d				15 19			16 01				16 20				17 01		17 19						18 01	
New Pudsey	d				15 24		15 44	16 06				16 25		16 44		17 06		17 24			17 44			18 06	
Bradford Interchange	a				15 32		15 53	16 14				16 33		16 53		17 14		17 32			17 53			18 14	
Bradford Forster Square	a					15 54			16 12	16 24					16 55							17 58			18 12

		NT	NT	NT	NT	NT	NT	NT		NT	NT	NT	NT	NT	NT	NT	NT	NT		NT	NT	NT	NT	NT	NT
Leeds	d		18 08	18 13	18 34	18 35	19 03	19 08		19 34	19 35	19 54			20 08	20 12	20 34	20 35		21 04	21 08	21 34	21 35		22 05
Shipley	a		18 19		18 45			19 19		19 45					20 19		20 45				21 19	21 45			
	d	18 15			18 46					19 46			20 02	20 15			20 46					21 46		22 04	
Frizinghall	d	18 18			18 48					19 48			20 06	20 18			20 48					21 48		22 08	
Bramley	d			18 20			19 10					20 01				20 19				21 12			21 43		22 12
New Pudsey	d			18 25		18 44	19 15				19 44	20 06				20 24		20 44		21 17			21 47		22 17
Bradford Interchange	a			18 33		18 53	19 24				19 53	20 14				20 34		20 53		21 25			21 56		22 27
Bradford Forster Square	a	18 24			18 54					19 54			20 12	20 24			20 54					21 54		22 14	

A until 24 June

Table 37

Sundays until 9 September

Leeds - Shipley and Bradford

Network Diagram - see first page of Table 35

		NT	NT	NT		NT	NT	NT
Leeds 10	d		22 08	22 34		22 38	23 20	23 22
Shipley	a		22 19	22 46			23 31	
	d	22 15		22 47				
Frizinghall	d	22 18		22 49				
Bramley	d					22 45		23 29
New Pudsey	d					22 50		23 34
Bradford Interchange	a					22 58		23 43
Bradford Forster Square	a	22 24		22 56				

Sundays 16 September to 21 October

		NT (bus)	NT	NT	NT	NT	NT	NT	NT (bus)	NT		NT	NT	NT	NT	NT	NT (bus)	NT	NT	NT		NT	NT	NT (bus)	NT
Leeds 10	d	07 50	08 02	08 30	08 34	08 40	09 00	09 18	09 25	09 34		09 40			10 08	10 12	10 25	10 34	10 40	10 51		11 08	11 12	11 25	11 34
Shipley	a				08 45	08 52	09 15			09 45					10 19			10 45		11 03		11 19			11 45
	d				08 46					09 46			10 01	10 15				10 46							11 46
Frizinghall	d				08 48					09 48			10 05	10 18				10 48							11 48
Bramley	d	08 05	08 09	08 37				09 25				09 47				10 19			10 47				11 19		
New Pudsey	d	08 15	08 14	08 42				09 30				09 52				10 24			10 52				11 24		
Bradford Interchange	a	08 25	08 22	08 50				09 38	09 50			10 00				10 32	10 50		11 00				11 32	11 50	
Bradford Forster Square	a				08 54					09 54			10 12	10 24				10 54							11 54

		NT	NT	NT	NT	NT		NT (bus)	NT	NT	NT	NT	NT	NT (bus)	NT	NT		NT	NT	NT	NT	NT (bus)	NT	NT	NT
Leeds 10	d	11 40			12 08	12 12		12 25	12 34	12 40	13 08	13 12	13 15	13 25	13 34	13 40				14 08	14 12	14 25	14 34	14 40	14 57
Shipley	a				12 19				12 45		13 19		13 28		13 45					14 19			14 45		15 09
	d		12 02	12 15					12 46						13 46			14 02	14 15				14 46		
Frizinghall	d		12 06	12 18					12 48						13 48			14 06	14 18				14 48		
Bramley	d	11 47				12 19				12 47		13 19				13 47					14 19			14 47	
New Pudsey	d	11 52				12 24				12 52		13 24				13 52					14 24			14 52	
Bradford Interchange	a	12 00				12 32		12 50		13 00		13 32		13 50		14 00					14 32	14 50		15 00	
Bradford Forster Square	a		12 12	12 24					12 54						13 54			14 12	14 24				14 54		

		NT		NT	NT (bus)	NT	NT	NT	NT	NT	NT	NT (bus)		NT	NT	NT	NT	NT	NT (bus)	NT	NT	NT		NT	NT
Leeds 10	d	15 08		15 12	15 25	15 34	15 40			16 08	16 13	16 25		16 35	16 40	17 08	17 12	17 21	17 25	17 33	17 37	17 40			
Shipley	a	15 19				15 45				16 19				16 46		17 19		17 33		17 45	17 48				
	d					15 46		16 02	16 15					16 46							17 49			18 02	18 15
Frizinghall	d					15 48		16 06	16 18					16 48							17 51			18 06	18 18
Bramley	d			15 19			15 47				16 20				16 47		17 19					17 47			
New Pudsey	d			15 24			15 52				16 25				16 52		17 24					17 52			
Bradford Interchange	a			15 32	15 50		16 00				16 33	16 50			17 00		17 32		17 50			18 00			
Bradford Forster Square	a					15 54		16 12	16 24					16 55							17 58			18 12	18 24

		NT	NT	NT (bus)	NT	NT	NT	NT		NT (bus)	NT	NT	NT	NT	NT	NT	NT	NT		NT	NT	NT	NT	NT	NT
Leeds 10	d	18 08	18 13	18 25	18 34	18 40	19 08	19 12		19 25	19 34	19 40			20 08	20 12	20 34	20 40		21 04	21 08	21 34	21 43		22 05
Shipley	a	18 19			18 45		19 19				19 45				20 19		20 45				21 19	21 45			
	d				18 46						19 46		20 02	20 15			20 46					21 46		22 04	
Frizinghall	d				18 48						19 48		20 06	20 18			20 48					21 48		22 08	
Bramley	d		18 20			18 47		19 19				19 47				20 19		20 47		21 12			21 50		22 12
New Pudsey	d		18 25			18 52		19 24				19 52				20 24		20 52		21 17			21 55		22 17
Bradford Interchange	a		18 33	18 50		19 00		19 32		19 50		20 00				20 34		21 00		21 25			22 03		22 27
Bradford Forster Square	a				18 54						19 54		20 12	20 24			20 54					21 54		22 14	

		NT	NT	NT		NT	NT	NT
Leeds 10	d		22 08	22 34		22 38	23 20	23 22
Shipley	a		22 19	22 46			23 31	
	d	22 15		22 47				
Frizinghall	d	22 18		22 49				
Bramley	d					22 45		23 29
New Pudsey	d					22 50		23 34
Bradford Interchange	a					22 58		23 43
Bradford Forster Square	a	22 24		22 56				

Sundays from 28 October

		NT	NT	NT	NT	NT	NT	NT	NT	NT		NT	NT	NT	NT	NT	NT	NT	NT	NT		NT	NT	NT	NT
Leeds 10	d	08 02	08 21	08 34	08 40	08 45	09 00	09 02	09 18	09 34		09 35	09 54			10 08	10 12	10 34	10 35	10 51		10 54	11 08	11 12	11 34
Shipley	a			08 45	08 52		09 15			09 45						10 19		10 45		11 03			11 19		11 45
	d			08 46						09 46				10 01	10 15			10 46							11 46
Frizinghall	d			08 48						09 48				10 05	10 18			10 48							11 48
Bramley	d	08 09	08 28					09 09	09 25				10 01				10 19					11 01		11 19	
New Pudsey	d	08 14	08 33			08 54		09 14	09 30			09 44	10 06				10 24		10 44			11 06		11 24	
Bradford Interchange	a	08 22	08 41			09 03		09 22	09 38			09 53	10 14				10 32		10 53			11 14		11 32	
Bradford Forster Square	a			08 54						09 54				10 12	10 24			10 54							11 54

Table 37

Sundays from 28 October

Leeds - Shipley and Bradford

Network Diagram - see first page of Table 35

		NT	NT	NT	NT	NT		NT	NT	NT	NT	NT	NT	NT	NT	NT		NT	NT	NT	NT	NT	NT	NT	NT
Leeds 10	d	11 35	11 54			12 08		12 12	12 34	12 35	12 54	13 08	13 12	13 15	13 34	13 35		13 54			14 08	14 12	14 34	14 35	14 54
Shipley	a					12 19			12 45			13 19		13 28	13 45						14 19		14 45		
	d			12 02	12 15				12 46						13 46				14 02	14 15			14 46		
Frizinghall	d			12 06	12 18				12 48						13 48				14 06	14 18			14 48		
Bramley	d		12 01					12 19			13 01		13 19					14 01				14 19			15 01
New Pudsey	d	11 44	12 06					12 24		12 44	13 06		13 24			13 44		14 06				14 24		14 44	15 06
Bradford Interchange	a	11 53	12 14					12 32		12 53	13 14		13 32			13 53		14 14				14 32		14 53	15 14
Bradford Forster Square	a			12 12	12 24				12 54						13 54				14 12	14 24			14 54		

		NT		NT	NT	NT	NT	NT	NT	NT	NT	NT		NT	NT	NT	NT	NT	NT	NT	NT	NT		NT	NT
Leeds 10	d	14 57		15 08	15 12	15 34	15 35	15 54			16 08	16 13		16 35	16 35	16 54	17 08	17 12	17 21	17 33	17 35	17 37		17 54	
Shipley	a	15 09		15 19		15 45					16 19				16 46		17 19		17 33	17 45		17 48			
	d					15 46			16 02	16 15					16 46							17 49			18 02
Frizinghall	d					15 48			16 06	16 18					16 48							17 51			18 06
Bramley	d				15 19			16 01				16 20				17 01		17 19						18 01	
New Pudsey	d				15 24		15 44	16 06				16 25		16 44		17 06		17 24			17 44			18 06	
Bradford Interchange	a				15 32		15 53	16 14				16 33		16 53		17 14		17 32			17 53			18 14	
Bradford Forster Square	a					15 54			16 12	16 24					16 55							17 58			18 12

		NT	NT	NT	NT	NT	NT	NT		NT	NT	NT	NT	NT	NT	NT	NT	NT		NT	NT	NT	NT	NT	NT
Leeds 10	d		18 08	18 13	18 34	18 35	19 03	19 08		19 34	19 35	19 54			20 08	20 12	20 34	20 35		21 04	21 08	21 34	21 35		22 05
Shipley	a		18 19		18 45			19 19		19 45					20 19		20 45				21 19	21 45			
	d	18 15			18 46					19 46			20 02	20 15			20 46					21 46		22 04	
Frizinghall	d	18 18			18 48					19 48			20 06	20 18			20 48					21 48		22 08	
Bramley	d			18 20			19 10					20 01				20 19				21 12			21 43		22 12
New Pudsey	d			18 25		18 44	19 15				19 44	20 06				20 24		20 44		21 17			21 47		22 17
Bradford Interchange	a			18 33		18 53	19 24				19 53	20 14				20 34		20 53		21 25			21 56		22 27
Bradford Forster Square	a	18 24			18 54					19 54			20 12	20 24			20 54					21 54		22 14	

		NT	NT	NT		NT	NT	NT
Leeds 10	d		22 08	22 34		22 38	23 20	23 22
Shipley	a		22 19	22 46			23 31	
	d	22 15		22 47				
Frizinghall	d	22 18		22 49				
Bramley	d					22 45		23 29
New Pudsey	d					22 50		23 34
Bradford Interchange	a					22 58		23 43
Bradford Forster Square	a	22 24		22 56				

Bradford and Shipley - Leeds

Network Diagram - see first page of Table 35

Miles	Miles			NT MX	NT MO A	NT MO B	NT MX	NT	NT	NT	NT	NT		GR C	NT	NT	NT	NT	NT	NT	NT	NT		GR	NT
0	—	Bradford Forster Square	d					05 59	06 04		06 15			06 30	06 39		06 44		06 55			07 11			07 15
—	0	Bradford Interchange	d	23p46	23p47		00 37					06 18						06 48			07 02				
—	3½	New Pudsey	d	23p54	23p55	23b55						06 27						06 57			07 11				
—	5½	Bramley	d	23p58	23p59	00s05						06 31						07 01			07 15				
1¾	—	Frizinghall	d					06 02	06 07		06 18				06 43		06 47		06 58			07 14			07 18
2¾	—	Shipley	a					06 06	06 11		06 22				06 47		06 51		07 02			07 18			07 22
—	—		d					06 07		06 13				06u35		06 42			07 02	07 09				07u14	
13½	9½	Leeds 10	a	00 08	00 08	00 25	00 55	06 22		06 27		06 41		06 52		06 57		07 09	07 16	07 23	07 27			07 29	

		NT	NT	NT	NT	NT	NT	NT		NT	NT	NT	NT	NT	NT	NT	NT	NT		NT	NT	NT	NT	NT	NT
Bradford Forster Square	d				07 42	07 46					07 59	08 09			08 16			08 26				08 41	08 46		
Bradford Interchange	d	07 20		07 34				07 50						08 05			08 20				08 34				08 50
New Pudsey	d	07 28		07 42				07 58						08 13			08 28				08 42				08 58
Bramley	d			07 46				08 02						08 18							08 46				09 02
Frizinghall	d				07 45	07 49					08 02	08 12			08 19			08 29				08 44	08 49		
Shipley	a				07 49	07 53					08 06	08 16			08 23			08 33				08 48	08 53		
	d		07 35				07 50			08 01	08 07		08 13			08 19		08 33		08 41				08 47	
Leeds 10	a	07 39	07 49	07 57			08 05	08 12		08 18	08 24		08 28	08 29		08 37	08 39	08 49		08 56	08 57			09 04	09 12

		NT	NT	NT		NT	NT	NT	NT	NT	NT	NT	NT	NT		NT	NT	NT	NT	NT	NT	NT	NT	NT	
Bradford Forster Square	d		09 01			09 11	09 16		09 31		09 41		09 46			10 01		10 11		10 16		10 31	10 41		
Bradford Interchange	d			09 04				09 20		09 34				09 50			10 05				10 18				
New Pudsey	d			09 12				09 27		09 42				09 58			10 13				10 28				
Bramley	d			09 16						09 46				10 02			10 17								
Frizinghall	d		09 04			09 14	09 19		09 34		09 44		09 49			10 04		10 14		10 19		10 34	10 44		
Shipley	a		09 08			09 18	09 23		09 38		09 48		09 53			10 08		10 18		10 23		10 38	10 48		
	d	09 08	09 09						09 39			09 44				10 09			10 14			10 39		10 44	
Leeds 10	a	09 22	09 25	09 27				09 39	09 53	09 57		09 59		10 12		10 25	10 27		10 28		10 38	10 53		10 58	

		NT	NT	NT	NT	NT	NT	NT	NT	NT		NT	NT	NT	NT	NT	NT	NT	NT	NT		NT	NT	NT	NT
Bradford Forster Square	d		10 46		11 01		11 11		11 16				11 31	11 41			11 46		12 01			12 11		12 16	
Bradford Interchange	d	10 34		10 50		11 05						11 20				11 34		11 50		12 05					12 19
New Pudsey	d	10 42		10 58		11 13						11 28				11 42		11 58		12 13					12 28
Bramley	d	10 46		11 02		11 17										11 46		12 02		12 17					
Frizinghall	d		10 49		11 04		11 14		11 19				11 34	11 44			11 49		12 04			12 14		12 19	
Shipley	a		10 53		11 08		11 18		11 23				11 38	11 48			11 53		12 08			12 18		12 23	
	d				11 09			11 14		11 18			11 39		11 44				12 09				12 14		
Leeds 10	a	10 59		11 13	11 24	11 27		11 28		11 36		11 39	11 55		11 58	12 00		12 12	12 24	12 27			12 29		12 39

		NT	NT	NT	NT	NT		NT	NT	NT	NT	NT	NT	NT	NT	NT		NT	NT	NT	NT	NT	NT	NT	NT
Bradford Forster Square	d		12 31	12 41				12 46		13 01		13 11		13 16		13 31		13 41			13 46		14 01		14 11
Bradford Interchange	d					12 34			12 50		13 05				13 19					13 34		13 50		14 05	
New Pudsey	d					12 42			12 58		13 13				13 28					13 42		13 58		14 13	
Bramley	d					12 46			13 02		13 17									13 46		14 02		14 17	
Frizinghall	d		12 34	12 44				12 49		13 04		13 14		13 19		13 34		13 44			13 49		14 04		14 14
Shipley	a		12 38	12 48				12 53		13 08		13 18		13 23		13 38		13 48			13 53		14 08		14 18
	d	12 33	12 39		12 44					13 09			13 14			13 39			13 44				14 09		
Leeds 10	a	12 55	12 55		12 58	12 59			13 12	13 24	13 27		13 28		13 40	13 54			13 58	14 00		14 13	14 24	14 27	

		NT		NT	NT	NT	NT	NT	NT	NT	NT	NT		NT	NT	NT	NT	NT	NT	NT	NT	NT		NT	NT
Bradford Forster Square	d			14 16			14 31		14 41		14 46			15 01		15 11		15 16			15 31	15 41			
Bradford Interchange	d					14 19		14 34				14 50			15 05				15 19						15 34
New Pudsey	d					14 28		14 42				14 58			15 13				15 28						15 42
Bramley	d							14 46				15 02			15 17										15 46
Frizinghall	d			14 19			14 34		14 44		14 49			15 04		15 14		15 19			15 34	15 44			
Shipley	a			14 23			14 38		14 48		14 53			15 08		15 18		15 23			15 38	15 48			
	d	14 14			14 18		14 39			14 45				15 09			15 14			15 30	15 39			15 44	
Leeds 10	a	14 28			14 37	14 39	14 52	15 00		15 00		15 12		15 24	15 27		15 28		15 39	15 47	15 54			15 58	16 00

		NT	NT	NT	NT	NT	NT	NT		NT	NT	NT	NT	NT	NT	NT	NT	NT		NT	NT	NT	NT	NT	NT
Bradford Forster Square	d	15 46		16 01		16 11		16 16				16 31		16 40		16 44		17 01			17 11		17 16		
Bradford Interchange	d		15 50		16 05					16 19			16 34				16 50			17 04				17 19	
New Pudsey	d		15 58		16 13					16 28			16 42				16 58			17 13				17 28	
Bramley	d		16 02		16 17								16 46				17 02			17 17					
Frizinghall	d	15 49		16 04		16 14		16 19				16 34		16 43		16 48		17 04			17 14		17 19		
Shipley	a	15 53		16 08		16 18		16 23				16 38		16 48		16 52		17 08			17 18		17 23		
	d			16 09			16 14				16 31	16 39			16 44			17 09				17 15			17 23
Leeds 10	a		16 12	16 24	16 27		16 28			16 39	16 51	16 53	16 58		16 58		17 12	17 24		17 27		17 29		17 39	17 40

		NT	NT	NT		NT	NT	NT	NT	NT	NT	NT	NT	NT		NT	NT	NT	NT	NT	NT	NT	NT	NT	
Bradford Forster Square	d	17 31		17 38			17 46			18 01		18 11		18 16			18 27		18 41		18 46			19 01	
Bradford Interchange	d		17 34					17 50			18 04					18 19		18 34					18 52		
New Pudsey	d		17 42					17 58			18 13					18 28		18 40					19 00		
Bramley	d		17 46					18 02			18 17							18 45					19 04		
Frizinghall	d	17 34		17 41			17 49			18 04		18 14		18 19			18 30		18 44		18 49			19 04	
Shipley	a	17 38		17 45			17 53			18 08		18 18		18 23			18 34		18 48		18 53			19 08	
	d	17 39				17 45			17 58	18 09			18 14				18 34			18 44		18 48		19 09	
Leeds 10	a	17 55	17 57			18 00		18 12	18 15	18 24	18 29		18 29			18 39	18 48	18 56		18 59		19 07	19 13	19 26	

A from 21 May
B from 17 September until 22 October
C West Riding Limited
b Previous night, stops to set down only

Bradford and Shipley - Leeds

Network Diagram - see first page of Table 35

		NT	NT	NT	NT	NT	NT	NT	NT	NT		NT	NT	NT	NT	NT	NT	NT	NT	NT		NT	NT	NT	NT
Bradford Forster Square	d		19 07			19 31		19 36	19 41				20 07				20 25		20 38						21 05
Bradford Interchange	d	19 05			19 19		19 34					19 50			20 04	20 19		20 37						21 04	
New Pudsey	d	19 13			19 27		19 42					19 59			20 13	20 28		20 46						21 13	
Bramley	d	19 17					19 46					20 03			20 17			20 50						21 17	
Frizinghall	d		19 10			19 34		19 39	19 44				20 10				20 28		20 41						21 08
Shipley	a		19 14			19 38		19 43	19 48				20 15				20 32		20 45						21 12
	d			19 14		19 39				19 44				20 14						20 41		20 50	20 59		
Leeds 10	a	19 28		19 31	19 39	19 55	19 56			19 59		20 13		20 28	20 29	20 38		20 59		21 01		21 05	21 17	21 25	

		NT	NT	NT	NT	NT		NT	NT	NT	NT	NT	NT	NT	NT	NT FX		NT FO	NT	NT	NT
Bradford Forster Square	d		21 25	21 38					22 05			22 25		22 38					23 09	23 20	
Bradford Interchange	d					21 37		22 04			22 17		22 37			23 04		23 04			23 46
New Pudsey	d					21 46		22 13			22 25		22 46			23 13		23 13			23 54
Bramley	d					21 50		22 17					22 50			23 17		23 17			23 58
Frizinghall	d		21 28	21 41					22 08			22 28		22 41					23 12	23 23	
Shipley	a		21 32	21 45					22 12			22 32		22 45					23 16	23 27	
	d	21 14			21 43					22 14					22 43						
Leeds 10	a	21 30			21 59	22 01		22 25		22 33	22 38		23 00		23 01	23 26		23 27			00 08

Saturdays

		NT	NT	NT	NT	NT	NT	NT	NT	NT		NT	NT	NT	GR	NT	GR	NT	NT	NT		NT	NT	NT	NT
Bradford Forster Square	d			06 01	06 10		06 15		07 01			07 11		07 15			07 33			07 59		08 11			08 16
Bradford Interchange	d	23p46	00 37					06 26		07 05						07 20		07 34	07 50					08 05	
New Pudsey	d	23p54						06 35		07 14						07 28		07 42	07 58					08 14	
Bramley	d	23p58						06 39		07 18								07 46	08 02					08 18	
Frizinghall	d			06 04	06 13		06 18		07 04			07 14		07 18						08 02		08 14			08 19
Shipley	a			06 08	06 17		06 22		07 08			07 18		07 23						08 06		08 18			08 23
	d			06 08		06 13			07 09				07 13		07u18		07u39			08 07			08 13		
Leeds 10	a	00 08	00 55	06 22		06 27		06 49	07 23	07 27			07 27		07 33	07 39	07 54	07 57	08 11	08 24			08 28	08 30	

		NT	NT	NT	NT	NT		NT	NT	NT	NT	NT	NT	NT	NT	NT		NT	NT	NT	NT	NT	NT	NT	NT
Bradford Forster Square	d			08 31		08 41			08 46		09 01		09 11		09 16			09 31		09 41		09 46			10 01
Bradford Interchange	d		08 20		08 34					08 50		09 04				09 20			09 34				09 50		
New Pudsey	d		08 28		08 42					08 58		09 12				09 27			09 42				09 58		
Bramley	d				08 46					09 02		09 16							09 46				10 02		
Frizinghall	d			08 34		08 44			08 49		09 04		09 14		09 19			09 34		09 44		09 49			10 04
Shipley	a			08 38		08 48			08 53		09 08		09 18		09 23			09 38		09 48		09 53			10 08
	d	08 19		08 38				08 44			09 09			09 14				09 39			09 44			10 02	10 09
Leeds 10	a	08 37	08 39	08 54	08 56			08 58		09 12	09 25	09 27		09 28		09 39		09 53	09 58		09 59		10 12	10 20	10 25

		NT		NT	NT	NT	NT	NT	NT	NT	NT	NT		NT	NT	NT	NT	NT	NT	NT	NT	NT		NT	NT
Bradford Forster Square	d			10 11		10 16			10 31	10 41				10 46		11 01		11 11		11 16		11 31		11 41	
Bradford Interchange	d	10 05						10 18				10 34			10 50		11 05				11 20				
New Pudsey	d	10 13						10 28				10 42			10 58		11 13				11 28				
Bramley	d	10 17										10 46			11 02		11 17								
Frizinghall	d			10 14		10 19			10 34	10 44				10 49		11 04		11 14		11 19		11 34		11 44	
Shipley	a			10 18		10 23			10 38	10 48				10 53		11 08		11 18		11 23		11 38		11 48	
	d				10 14		10 19		10 39		10 44					11 09			11 14			11 39			11 44
Leeds 10	a	10 27			10 28		10 34	10 38	10 53		10 58	11 00			11 13	11 24	11 27		11 28		11 39	11 55			11 58

		NT	NT	NT	NT	NT	NT	NT		NT	NT	NT	NT	NT	NT	NT	NT	NT		NT	NT	NT	NT	NT	NT
Bradford Forster Square	d		11 46			12 01		12 11			12 16			12 31		12 41		12 46			13 01		13 11		13 16
Bradford Interchange	d	11 34			11 50		12 05					12 19			12 34					12 50		13 05			
New Pudsey	d	11 42			11 58		12 13					12 28			12 42					12 58		13 13			
Bramley	d	11 46			12 02		12 17								12 46					13 02		13 17			
Frizinghall	d		11 49			12 04		12 14			12 19			12 34		12 44		12 49			13 04		13 14		13 19
Shipley	a		11 53			12 08		12 18			12 23			12 38		12 48		12 53			13 08		13 18		13 23
	d			11 49		12 09				12 14			12 33	12 39			12 44				13 09			13 14	
Leeds 10	a	12 00		12 07	12 12	12 24	12 27			12 29		12 39	12 55	12 55	12 58		12 58			13 12	13 24	13 27		13 28	

		NT	NT	NT		NT	NT	NT	NT	NT	NT	NT	NT	NT		NT	NT	NT	NT	NT	NT	NT	NT	NT	
Bradford Forster Square	d		13 31			13 41		13 46		14 01		14 11		14 16				14 31		14 41		14 46		15 01	
Bradford Interchange	d	13 19		13 34					13 50		14 05						14 19		14 34				14 50		
New Pudsey	d	13 28		13 42					13 58		14 13						14 28		14 42				14 58		
Bramley	d			13 46					14 02		14 17								14 46				15 02		
Frizinghall	d		13 34			13 44		13 49		14 04		14 14		14 19				14 34		14 44		14 49		15 04	
Shipley	a		13 38			13 48		13 53		14 08		14 18		14 23				14 38		14 48		14 53		15 08	
	d		13 39				13 44			14 09			14 14			14 18		14 39			14 45			15 09	
Leeds 10	a	13 39	13 54	13 58			13 58		14 14	14 24	14 27		14 28			14 37	14 39	14 53	14 58		15 00		15 10	15 24	

		NT	NT	NT	NT	NT	NT	NT	NT	NT		NT	NT	NT	NT	NT	NT	NT	NT	NT		NT	NT	NT	NT
Bradford Forster Square	d		15 11		15 16			15 31	15 41				15 46		16 01		16 11		16 16			16 31	16 40		
Bradford Interchange	d	15 05				15 19						15 34		15 50		16 05				16 19					16 34
New Pudsey	d	15 13				15 28						15 42		15 58		16 13				16 28					16 42
Bramley	d	15 17										15 46		16 02		16 17									16 46
Frizinghall	d		15 14		15 19			15 34	15 44				15 49		16 04		16 14		16 19			16 34	16 43		
Shipley	a		15 18		15 23			15 38	15 48				15 53		16 08		16 18		16 23			16 38	16 48		
	d			15 14			15 30	15 39		15 44					16 09			16 14				16 39		16 44	
Leeds 10	a	15 27		15 28		15 39	15 47	15 54		15 58		16 00		16 12	16 24	16 27		16 28		16 39		16 53		16 58	16 59

Table 37

Bradford and Shipley - Leeds

Saturdays

Network Diagram - see first page of Table 35

		NT	NT	NT	NT	NT		NT	NT	NT	NT	NT	NT	NT	NT	NT		NT	NT	NT	NT	NT	NT	NT	NT
Bradford Forster Square	d	16 44			17 01			17 11		17 16		17 31		17 41		17 46				18 01		18 11		18 16	
Bradford Interchange	d			16 50		17 04					17 19		17 34					17 50			18 04				18 19
New Pudsey	d			16 58		17 13					17 28		17 42					17 58			18 13				18 28
Bramley	d			17 02		17 17							17 46					18 02			18 17				
Frizinghall	d	16 48			17 04			17 14		17 19		17 34		17 44		17 49				18 04		18 14		18 19	
Shipley	a	16 52			17 08			17 18		17 23		17 38		17 48		17 53				18 08		18 18		18 23	
	d		16 49		17 09				17 15			17 39			17 45				18 00	18 09			18 14		
Leeds	a		17 07	17 12	17 24	17 27			17 29		17 39	17 55	17 57		18 00			18 12	18 17	18 24	18 29		18 29		18 39

		NT		NT	NT	NT	NT	NT	NT	NT	NT	NT		NT	NT	NT	NT	NT	NT	NT	NT	NT		NT	NT
Bradford Forster Square	d			18 31		18 41		18 46			19 01			19 07			19 31		19 36	19 41				20 07	
Bradford Interchange	d				18 34					18 52		19 05				19 18		19 34				19 50			
New Pudsey	d				18 43					19 00		19 13				19 28		19 42				19 58			
Bramley	d				18 47					19 04		19 17						19 46				20 02			
Frizinghall	d			18 34		18 44		18 49			19 04			19 10			19 34		19 39	19 44				20 10	
Shipley	a			18 38		18 48		18 53			19 08			19 14			19 38		19 43	19 48				20 15	
	d	18 19		18 38			18 44		18 48		19 09				19 14		19 39				19 44				20 14
Leeds	a	18 42		18 52	18 56		18 59		19 07	19 13	19 26	19 28			19 29	19 39	19 55	19 58			19 59	20 12			20 28

		NT	NT	NT	NT	NT	NT	NT		NT	NT	NT	NT	NT	NT	NT	NT	NT		NT	NT	NT	NT	NT	NT
Bradford Forster Square	d			20 25			20 38					21 05		21 25		21 38		22 01					22 25		22 38
Bradford Interchange	d	20 04	20 19			20 37					21 04				21 37					22 04		22 17		22 37	
New Pudsey	d	20 13	20 28			20 46					21 13				21 46					22 13		22 25		22 46	
Bramley	d	20 17				20 50					21 17				21 50					22 17				22 50	
Frizinghall	d			20 28			20 41					21 08		21 28		21 41		22 04					22 28		22 41
Shipley	a			20 32			20 45					21 12		21 32		21 45		22 08					22 32		22 45
	d				20 28			20 43		20 57			21 14				21 43				22 14				
Leeds	a	20 30	20 38		20 46	20 59		21 00		21 16	21 25		21 30		21 59		21 59			22 24	22 33	22 35		23 01	

		NT	NT	NT		NT
Bradford Forster Square	d			23 05		23 20
Bradford Interchange	d		23 04			
New Pudsey	d		23 13			
Bramley	d		23 17			
Frizinghall	d			23 08		23 23
Shipley	a			23 12		23 27
	d	22 43				
Leeds	a	23 01	23 26			

Sundays

until 9 September

		NT	NT	NT	NT	NT	NT	NT	NT	NT		NT	NT	NT	NT	NT	NT	NT	NT	NT		NT	NT	NT	NT
Bradford Forster Square	d				09 02			10 02				10 38		10 48		11 02							12 02		12 38
Bradford Interchange	d	00 04	08 31			09 20			10 04	10 25					11 02		11 25		11 44			12 02		12 25	
New Pudsey	d	00 12	08 39			09 29			10 12	10 33					11 10		11 33		11 53			12 10		12 33	
Bramley	d	00 16	08 43			09 33			10 16	10 37							11 37		11 57					12 37	
Frizinghall	d				09 05			10 05				10 41		10 51		11 05							12 05		12 41
Shipley	a				09 08			10 08				10 44		10 54		11 09							12 08		12 44
	d			09 00	09 10		09 40	10 08					10 40			11 10		11 40		11 49			12 08		
Leeds	a	00 27	08 51	09 14	09 24	09 42	09 54	10 22	10 25	10 46			10 54		11 21	11 24	11 48	11 54	12 05	12 06		12 22	12 22	12 46	

		NT	NT	NT	NT	NT		NT	NT	NT	NT	NT	NT	NT	NT	NT		NT	NT	NT	NT	NT	NT	NT	NT
Bradford Forster Square	d			12 48		13 02						14 02			14 38				14 48		15 02				16 02
Bradford Interchange	d		12 44		13 02			13 25		13 44	14 02			14 25				14 44		15 02		15 25		15 44	
New Pudsey	d		12 53		13 10			13 33		13 53	14 11			14 33				14 53		15 10		15 33		15 53	
Bramley	d		12 57					13 37		13 57				14 37				14 57				15 37		15 57	
Frizinghall	d			12 51		13 05						14 05			14 41				14 51		15 05				16 05
Shipley	a			12 54		13 08						14 08			14 44				14 54		15 08				16 08
	d	12 40				13 08			13 40			14 08	14 21			14 40					15 08		15 40		16 08
Leeds	a	12 54	13 06		13 22	13 22		13 46	13 54	14 06	14 22	14 22	14 39	14 48		14 54		15 06		15 22	15 24	15 46	15 54	16 06	16 22

		NT		NT	NT	NT	NT	NT	NT	NT	NT	NT		NT	NT	NT	NT	NT	NT	NT	NT	NT		NT	NT
Bradford Forster Square	d						16 38			16 48		17 02						18 02		18 38				18 48	
Bradford Interchange	d	16 03			16 25				16 44		17 02			17 25		17 44	18 02		18 25			18 44			
New Pudsey	d	16 11			16 33				16 53		17 10			17 33		17 53	18 10		18 33			18 53			
Bramley	d				16 37				16 57					17 37		17 57			18 37			18 57			
Frizinghall	d						16 41			16 51		17 05						18 05		18 41				18 51	
Shipley	a						16 44			16 54		17 08						18 08		18 44				18 54	
	d			16 16		16 29		16 40				17 09			17 40			18 08			18 40				19 03
Leeds	a	16 22		16 34	16 46	16 47		16 54	17 05		17 21	17 23		17 46	17 54	18 05	18 21	18 23	18 46		18 54	19 07			19 21

		NT	NT	NT	NT	NT	NT	NT		NT	NT	NT	NT	NT	NT	NT	NT	NT		NT	NT	NT	NT	NT	NT
Bradford Forster Square	d		19 02							20 02		20 38		20 48		21 02							22 02		22 38
Bradford Interchange	d	19 02		19 25			19 44	20 02			20 25				21 02		21 26			21 44		22 02		22 26	
New Pudsey	d	19 10		19 33			19 53	20 10			20 33				21 10		21 34			21 53		22 10		22 35	
Bramley	d			19 37			19 57				20 37						21 38			21 57				22 39	
Frizinghall	d		19 05							20 05		20 41		20 51		21 05							22 05		22 41
Shipley	a		19 08							20 08		20 44		20 54		21 08							22 09		22 44
	d		19 08		19 38	19 49				20 08			20 40			21 08		21 40			21 54		22 09		
Leeds	a	19 22	19 22	19 47	19 56	20 03	20 08	20 22		20 22	20 47		20 54		21 22	21 24	21 48	21 54		22 05	22 10	22 21	22 23	22 47	

Table 37

Bradford and Shipley - Leeds

Sundays

until 9 September

Network Diagram - see first page of Table 35

		NT	NT	NT		NT	NT	NT	NT
Bradford Forster Square	d		22 48			23 05			
Bradford Interchange	d			23 04			23 25		23 47
New Pudsey	d			23 12			23 33		23 55
Bramley	d						23 37		23 59
Frizinghall	d		22 51			23 08			
Shipley	a		22 54			23 11			
	d	22 40				23 11		23 41	
Leeds	a	22 54		23 23		23 29	23 46	23 58	00 08

Sundays

16 September to 21 October

		NT 🚌	NT	NT	NT	NT	NT	NT	NT	NT		NT	NT	NT	NT	NT	NT 🚌	NT	NT 🚌	NT		NT	NT	NT 🚌	NT
Bradford Forster Square	d				09 02			10 02				10 38			10 48	11 02									12 02
Bradford Interchange	d		08 31			09 20			10 04	10 10				10 44			10 45	11 10	11 10			11 44		11 45	
New Pudsey	d	00s36	08 39			09 29			10 12	10 19				10 53			10 55	11 19	11a20			11 53			
Bramley	d	00s46	08 43			09 33			10 16	10 22				10 57			11 05	11 22				11 57			
Frizinghall	d				09 05			10 05				10 41			10 51	11 05									12 05
Shipley	a				09 08			10 08				10 44			10 54	11 09									12 08
	d			09 00	09 10		09 40	10 08					10 40			11 10				11 40			11 49		12 08
Leeds	a	01 06	08 51	09 14	09 24	09 42	09 54	10 22	10 25	10 32			10 54	11 07		11 24	11 25	11 35		11 54		12 05	12 06	12 10	12 22

		NT	NT	NT	NT	NT 🚌		NT	NT	NT	NT	NT	NT 🚌	NT	NT	NT		NT	NT	NT	NT 🚌	NT	NT	NT	NT
Bradford Forster Square	d		12 38					12 48	13 02					14 02				14 38				14 48	15 02		
Bradford Interchange	d	12 10			12 44	12 45				13 10		13 44	13 45		14 10					14 44	14 45			15 10	
New Pudsey	d	12 19			12 53					13 19		13 53			14 19					14 53				15 19	
Bramley	d	12 22			12 57					13 22		13 57			14 22					14 57				15 22	
Frizinghall	d		12 41					12 51	13 05					14 05				14 41				14 51	15 05		
Shipley	a		12 44					12 54	13 08					14 08				14 44				14 54	15 08		
	d			12 40					13 08		13 40			14 08		14 21			14 40				15 08		15 40
Leeds	a	12 32		12 54	13 06	13 10			13 22	13 32	13 54	14 06	14 10	14 22	14 32	14 39			14 54	15 06	15 10		15 24	15 32	15 54

		NT		NT 🚌	NT	NT	NT	NT	NT	NT	NT	NT 🚌		NT	NT	NT	NT	NT	NT 🚌	NT	NT	NT		NT	NT
Bradford Forster Square	d				16 02				16 38					16 48	17 02					18 02		18 38			
Bradford Interchange	d	15 44		15 45		16 10					16 44	16 45				17 10		17 44	17 45		18 10				18 44
New Pudsey	d	15 53				16 19					16 53					17 19		17 53			18 19				18 53
Bramley	d	15 57				16 22					16 57					17 22		17 57			18 22				18 57
Frizinghall	d				16 05				16 41					16 51	17 05					18 05		18 41			
Shipley	a				16 08				16 44					16 54	17 08					18 08		18 44			
	d				16 08		16 16	16 29		16 40					17 09		17 40			18 08				18 40	
Leeds	a	16 06		16 10	16 22	16 32	16 34	16 47		16 54	17 05	17 10			17 23	17 32	17 54	18 05	18 10	18 23	18 32			18 54	19 07

		NT 🚌	NT	NT	NT	NT	NT	NT		NT	NT 🚌	NT	NT	NT	NT	NT	NT 🚌	NT		NT	NT	NT	NT	NT	NT
Bradford Forster Square	d		18 48		19 02							20 02		20 38				20 48		21 02					22 02
Bradford Interchange	d	18 45				19 10				19 44	19 45		20 10			20 44	20 45				21 10		21 44		
New Pudsey	d					19 19				19 53			20 19			20 53					21 19		21 53		
Bramley	d					19 22				19 57			20 22			20 57					21 22		21 57		
Frizinghall	d		18 51		19 05							20 05		20 41				20 51		21 05					22 05
Shipley	a		18 54		19 08							20 08		20 44				20 54		21 08					22 09
	d			19 03	19 08		19 38	19 49				20 08			20 40					21 08		21 40		21 54	22 09
Leeds	a	19 10		19 21	19 22	19 32	19 56	20 03		20 08	20 10	20 22	20 34		20 54	21 09	21 10			21 24	21 33	21 54	22 05	22 10	22 23

		NT	NT	NT		NT	NT 🚌	NT	NT	NT	NT	NT
Bradford Forster Square	d		22 38					22 48	23 05			
Bradford Interchange	d	22 10				22 44	22 45			23 11		23 47
New Pudsey	d	22 19				22 53				23 20		23 55
Bramley	d	22 22				22 57				23 23		23 59
Frizinghall	d		22 41					22 51	23 08			
Shipley	a		22 44					22 54	23 11			
	d			22 40					23 11		23 41	
Leeds	a	22 30		22 54		23 07	23 10		23 29	23 31	23 58	00 08

Sundays

from 28 October

		NT	NT	NT	NT	NT	NT	NT	NT	NT		NT	NT	NT	NT	NT	NT	NT	NT	NT		NT	NT	NT	NT
Bradford Forster Square	d				09 02			10 02				10 38		10 48		11 02							12 02		12 38
Bradford Interchange	d	00 04	08 31			09 20			10 04	10 25					11 02		11 25		11 44			12 02		12 25	
New Pudsey	d	00 12	08 39			09 29			10 12	10 33					11 10		11 33		11 53			12 10		12 33	
Bramley	d	00 16	08 43			09 33			10 16	10 37							11 37		11 57					12 37	
Frizinghall	d				09 05			10 05				10 41		10 51		11 05							12 05		12 41
Shipley	a				09 08			10 08				10 44		10 54		11 09							12 08		12 44
	d			09 00	09 10		09 40	10 08					10 40			11 10		11 40		11 49			12 08		
Leeds	a	00 27	08 51	09 14	09 24	09 42	09 54	10 22	10 25	10 46			10 54		11 21	11 24	11 48	11 54	12 05	12 06		12 22	12 22	12 46	

from 28 October

Bradford and Shipley - Leeds

Network Diagram - see first page of Table 35

		NT	NT	NT	NT	NT	NT	NT	NT	NT	NT	NT	NT	NT	NT	NT	NT	NT	NT	NT	NT	NT	NT
Bradford Forster Square	d			12 48		13 02					14 02			14 38			14 48		15 02				16 02
Bradford Interchange	d		12 44		13 02		13 25		13 44	14 02			14 25			14 44		15 02		15 25		15 44	
New Pudsey	d		12 53		13 10		13 33		13 53	14 11			14 33			14 53		15 10		15 33		15 53	
Bramley	d		12 57				13 37		13 57				14 37			14 57				15 37		15 57	
Frizinghall	d			12 51		13 05					14 05			14 41			14 51		15 05				16 05
Shipley	a			12 54		13 08					14 08			14 44			14 54		15 08				16 08
	d	12 40				13 08		13 40			14 08	14 21			14 40				15 08		15 40		16 08
Leeds 10	a	12 54	13 06		13 22	13 22	13 46	13 54	14 06	14 22	14 22	14 39	14 48		14 54	15 06		15 22	15 24	15 46	15 54	16 06	16 22

		NT	NT	NT	NT	NT	NT	NT	NT	NT	NT	NT	NT	NT	NT	NT	NT	NT	NT	NT	NT	NT
Bradford Forster Square	d					16 38			16 48		17 02					18 02		18 38			18 48	
Bradford Interchange	d	16 03		16 25				16 44		17 02		17 25		17 44	18 02		18 25			18 44		
New Pudsey	d	16 11		16 33				16 53		17 10		17 33		17 53	18 10		18 33			18 53		
Bramley	d			16 37				16 57				17 37		17 57			18 37			18 57		
Frizinghall	d					16 41			16 51		17 05					18 05		18 41			18 51	
Shipley	a					16 44			16 54		17 08					18 08		18 44			18 54	
	d		16 16		16 29		16 40				17 09		17 40			18 08			18 40			19 03
Leeds 10	a	16 22	16 34	16 46	16 47		16 54	17 05		17 21	17 23	17 46	17 54	18 05	18 21	18 23	18 46		18 54	19 07		19 21

		NT	NT	NT	NT	NT	NT	NT	NT	NT	NT	NT	NT	NT	NT	NT	NT	NT	NT	NT	NT	NT	NT
Bradford Forster Square	d		19 02						20 02		20 38		20 48		21 02						22 02		22 38
Bradford Interchange	d	19 02		19 25			19 44	20 02		20 25				21 02		21 26		21 44		22 02		22 26	
New Pudsey	d	19 10		19 33			19 53	20 10		20 33				21 10		21 34		21 53		22 10		22 35	
Bramley	d			19 37			19 57			20 37						21 38		21 57				22 39	
Frizinghall	d		19 05						20 05		20 41		20 51		21 05						22 05		22 41
Shipley	a		19 08						20 08		20 44		20 54		21 08						22 09		22 44
	d		19 08		19 38	19 49			20 08			20 40			21 08		21 40		21 54		22 09		
Leeds 10	a	19 22	19 22	19 47	19 56	20 03	20 08	20 22	20 22	20 47		20 54		21 22	21 24	21 48	21 54	22 05	22 10	22 21	22 23	22 47	

		NT	NT	NT	NT	NT	NT	NT
Bradford Forster Square	d		22 48		23 05			
Bradford Interchange	d			23 04		23 25		23 47
New Pudsey	d			23 12		23 33		23 55
Bramley	d					23 37		23 59
Frizinghall	d		22 51		23 08			
Shipley	a		22 54		23 11			
	d	22 40			23 11		23 41	
Leeds 10	a	22 54		23 23	23 29	23 46	23 58	00 08

Mondays to Saturdays

Leeds and Bradford - Ilkley

Network Diagram - see first page of Table 35

Miles	Miles			NT	NT	NT SX	NT SX	NT SO	NT SX	NT SX	NT SO	NT SX	NT SX	NT SX	NT	NT	NT SO	NT SX	NT	NT	NT	NT	NT
0	—	Leeds 10	d	06 02		06 34		07 02	07 03			07 29	07 35		08 02		08 32	08 35		09 02		09 32	
—	0	Bradford Forster Square 37	d		06 15		06 44			07 11	07 15			07 46		08 16			08 46		09 16		09 46
—	1¾	Frizinghall 37	d		06 18		06 47			07 14	07 18			07 49		08 19			08 49		09 19		09 49
—	2¾	Shipley 37	d		06 22		06 51			07 18	07 23			07 53		08 23			08 53		09 23		09 53
—	4¼	Baildon	d		06 25		06 54			07 21	07 26			07 56		08 26			08 56		09 26		09 56
10¼	7½	Guiseley	d	06 14	06 31	06 48	07 00	07 14	07 15	07 27	07 32	07 42	07 50	08 02	08 14	08 32	08 44	08 48	09 02	09 14	09 32	09 45	10 02
11½	8¾	Menston	d	06 17	06 34	06 51	07 03	07 17	07 18	07 30	07 35	07 45	07 53	08 05	08 17	08 35	08 47	08 51	09 05	09 17	09 35	09 48	10 05
13	10¼	Burley-in-Wharfedale	d	06 20	06 37	06 54	07 06	07 20	07 21	07 33	07 38	07 48	07 56	08 09	08 20	08 38	08 50	08 54	09 08	09 20	09 38	09 52	10 08
15¼	12½	Ben Rhydding	d	06 23	06 40	06 57	07 09	07 24	07 24	07 36	07 41	07 52	07 59	08 12	08 23	08 41	08 53	08 57	09 11	09 24	09 41	09 55	10 11
16¼	13½	Ilkley	a	06 29	06 46	07 03	07 15	07 29	07 30	07 41	07 47	07 57	08 05	08 18	08 29	08 49	09 02	09 03	09 17	09 33	09 47	10 01	10 17

		NT	NT	NT	NT	NT	NT	NT	NT	NT	NT	NT	NT	NT	NT SO	NT SX	NT	NT	NT	NT	NT	NT	NT
Leeds 10	d	10 02		10 32		11 02		11 32		12 02		12 32		13 02			13 32		14 02		14 32		15 02
Bradford Forster Square 37	d		10 16		10 46		11 16		11 46		12 16		12 46		13 16	13 16		13 46		14 16		14 46	
Frizinghall 37	d		10 19		10 49		11 19		11 49		12 19		12 49		13 19	13 19		13 49		14 19		14 49	
Shipley 37	d		10 23		10 53		11 23		11 53		12 23		12 53		13 23	13 23		13 53		14 23		14 53	
Baildon	d		10 26		10 56		11 26		11 56		12 26		12 56		13 26	13 26		13 56		14 26		14 56	
Guiseley	d	10 14	10 32	10 44	11 02	11 14	11 32	11 44	12 02	12 14	12 32	12 44	13 02	13 14	13 32	13 32	13 44	14 02	14 14	14 32	14 44	15 02	15 14
Menston	d	10 17	10 35	10 47	11 05	11 17	11 35	11 47	12 05	12 17	12 35	12 47	13 05	13 17	13 35	13 35	13 47	14 05	14 17	14 35	14 47	15 05	15 17
Burley-in-Wharfedale	d	10 20	10 38	10 50	11 08	11 20	11 38	11 50	12 08	12 20	12 38	12 50	13 08	13 20	13 38	13 38	13 50	14 08	14 20	14 38	14 50	15 08	15 20
Ben Rhydding	d	10 23	10 41	10 53	11 11	11 23	11 41	11 53	12 11	12 23	12 41	12 53	13 11	13 23	13 41	13 42	13 53	14 11	14 23	14 41	14 53	15 11	15 23
Ilkley	a	10 30	10 47	10 59	11 17	11 30	11 47	12 00	12 17	12 29	12 47	13 01	13 17	13 29	13 47	13 47	13 59	14 17	14 29	14 47	14 59	15 17	15 31

		NT	NT	NT	NT	NT	NT	NT	NT	NT SX	NT SO	NT SX	NT	NT SX	NT SO	NT SX	NT SO	NT SX	NT SX	NT SO	NT	NT
Leeds 10	d		15 32		16 02		16 32		17 02	17 15			17 32	17 47			18 02	18 02			18 32	
Bradford Forster Square 37	d	15 16		15 46		16 16		16 44			17 16	17 16			17 46	17 46			18 11	18 16		18 46
Frizinghall 37	d	15 19		15 49		16 19		16 48			17 19	17 19			17 49	17 49			18 14	18 19		18 49
Shipley 37	d	15 23		15 53		16 23		16 52			17 23	17 25			17 53	17 53			18 19	18 23		18 53
Baildon	d	15 26		15 56		16 26		16 55			17 26	17 28			17 57	17 57			18 22	18 26		18 56
Guiseley	d	15 32	15 44	16 02	16 14	16 32	16 44	17 01	17 14	17 28	17 32	17 35	17 44	17 59	18 02	18 07	18 14	18 19	18 27	18 32	18 44	19 02
Menston	d	15 35	15 47	16 05	16 17	16 35	16 47	17 04	17 17	17 31	17 35	17 38	17 47	18 02	18 05	18 10	18 17	18 22	18 30	18 35	18 47	19 05
Burley-in-Wharfedale	d	15 38	15 50	16 08	16 20	16 38	16 50	17 07	17 20	17 34	17 38	17 42	17 51	18 05	18 08	18 17	18 20	18 26	18 35	18 38	18 50	19 08
Ben Rhydding	d	15 41	15 53	16 11	16 23	16 41	16 53	17 10	17 23	17 37	17 41	17 46	17 54	18 09	18 12	18 20	18 23	18 29	18 39	18 41	18 53	19 11
Ilkley	a	15 47	15 59	16 17	16 29	16 47	17 00	17 17	17 29	17 43	17 47	17 51	18 00	18 16	18 17	18 26	18 30	18 35	18 44	18 47	19 01	19 17

		NT	NT	NT	NT	NT	NT	NT	NT	NT	NT	NT
Leeds 10	d	19 02	19 32		20 02		21 06		22 06		23 15	
Bradford Forster Square 37	d			19 41		20 38		21 38		22 38		23 20
Frizinghall 37	d			19 44		20 41		21 41		22 41		23 23
Shipley 37	d			19 48		20 46		21 45		22 45		23 27
Baildon	d			19 51		20 49		21 48		22 48		23 30
Guiseley	d	19 14	19 44	19 56	20 14	20 54	21 18	21 54	22 18	22 54	23 27	23 36
Menston	d	19 17	19 47	19 59	20 17	20 57	21 21	21 57	22 21	22 57	23 30	23 39
Burley-in-Wharfedale	d	19 20	19 50	20 02	20 20	21 00	21 24	22 00	22 24	23 00	23 33	23 42
Ben Rhydding	d	19 24	19 53	20 06	20 23	21 04	21 27	22 03	22 27	23 03	23 36	23 45
Ilkley	a	19 29	20 00	20 12	20 30	21 10	21 33	22 09	22 34	23 09	23 42	23 51

Sundays

		NT	NT	NT	NT	NT	NT	NT	NT	NT	NT	NT	NT	NT	NT	NT	NT	NT	NT	NT	NT	NT	NT
Leeds 10	d	09 12	10 12		11 12	12 12		13 12	14 12		15 12	16 12		17 12	18 12		19 12	20 12		21 12	22 12		23 16
Bradford Forster Square 37	d			10 38			12 38			14 38			16 38			18 38			20 38			22 38	
Frizinghall 37	d			10 41			12 41			14 41			16 41			18 41			20 41			22 41	
Shipley 37	d			10 44			12 44			14 44			16 44			18 44			20 44			22 44	
Baildon	d			10 47			12 47			14 47			16 47			18 47			20 47			22 47	
Guiseley	d	09 23	10 23	10 52	11 23	12 23	12 52	13 23	14 23	14 52	15 23	16 23	16 52	17 23	18 23	18 52	19 23	20 23	20 52	21 23	22 23	22 52	23 27
Menston	d	09 26	10 26	10 55	11 26	12 26	12 55	13 26	14 26	14 55	15 26	16 26	16 55	17 26	18 26	18 55	19 26	20 26	20 55	21 26	22 26	22 55	23 30
Burley-in-Wharfedale	d	09 29	10 29	10 58	11 29	12 29	12 58	13 29	14 29	14 58	15 29	16 29	16 58	17 29	18 29	18 58	19 29	20 29	20 58	21 29	22 29	22 58	23 33
Ben Rhydding	d	09 33	10 33	11 02	11 33	12 33	13 02	13 33	14 33	15 02	15 33	16 33	17 02	17 33	18 33	19 02	19 33	20 33	21 02	21 33	22 33	23 02	23 37
Ilkley	a	09 38	10 38	11 07	11 38	12 38	13 07	13 38	14 38	15 07	15 38	16 38	17 07	17 38	18 38	19 07	19 38	20 38	21 07	21 38	22 38	23 07	23 42

Ilkley - Bradford and Leeds

Network Diagram - see first page of Table 35

Miles	Miles		NT SX	NT SO	NT SX	NT SO	NT SX	NT SX	NT	NT	NT SX	NT SX	NT SX	NT SX	NT SO	NT SX	NT SO	NT SX	NT	NT SO	NT SX
0	0	**Ilkley** d	06 04	06 09	06 17	06 19	06 34	06 50	07 10	07 22	07 40	07 50	07 57	08 05	08 10	08 17	08 21	08 24	08 40	08 51	08 54
1	1	Ben Rhydding d	06 06	06 11	06 19	06 21	06 36	06 52	07 12	07 24	07 42	07 52	07 59	08 07	08 12	08 19	08 23	08 26	08 42	08 53	08 56
3¼	3¼	Burley-in-Wharfedale d	06 12	06 17	06 25	06 27	06 42	06 58	07 18	07 30	07 48	07 58	08 04	08 13	08 18	08 25	08 29	08 32	08 48	08 59	09 02
4¾	4¾	Menston d	06 15	06 20	06 28	06 30	06 45	07 01	07 21	07 33	07 51	08 01	08 07	08 16	08 21	08 28	08 32	08 35	08 51	09 02	09 05
6	6	Guiseley d	06 18	06 23	06 31	06 34	06 48	07 04	07 24	07 36	07 54	08 04	08 11	08 19	08 24	08 31	08 35	08 39	08 54	09 05	09 08
—	9¼	Baildon d			06 36	06 39		07 09		07 41		08 09					08 40	08 44		09 10	09 13
—	10¾	Shipley 37 a			06 41	06 43		07 14		07 47		08 12					08 43	08 47		09 14	09 18
—	11¾	Frizinghall 37 a			06 44	06 47		07 17		07 49		08 16					08 46	08 50		09 17	09 21
—	13½	**Bradford Forster Square** 37 a			06 50	06 55		07 22		07 56		08 22					08 53	08 56		09 24	09 27
16¼	—	**Leeds** 10 a	06 32	06 39			07 02		07 38		08 09		08 25	08 35	08 39	08 46			09 11		

	NT	NT	NT	NT	NT	NT	NT	NT	NT	NT	NT	NT	NT	NT	NT	NT	NT	NT	NT	NT	NT	NT
Ilkley d	09 10	09 21	09 40	09 51	10 10	10 21	10 40	10 51	11 10	11 21	11 40	11 51	12 10	12 21	12 40	12 51	13 10	13 21	13 40	13 51	14 10	14 21
Ben Rhydding d	09 12	09 23	09 42	09 53	10 12	10 23	10 42	10 53	11 12	11 23	11 42	11 53	12 12	12 23	12 42	12 53	13 12	13 23	13 42	13 53	14 12	14 23
Burley-in-Wharfedale d	09 18	09 29	09 48	09 59	10 18	10 29	10 48	10 59	11 18	11 29	11 48	11 59	12 18	12 29	12 48	12 59	13 18	13 29	13 48	13 58	14 18	14 29
Menston d	09 21	09 32	09 51	10 02	10 21	10 32	10 51	11 02	11 21	11 32	11 51	12 02	12 21	12 32	12 51	13 02	13 21	13 32	13 51	14 01	14 21	14 32
Guiseley d	09 24	09 35	09 54	10 05	10 25	10 35	10 54	11 05	11 24	11 35	11 54	12 05	12 24	12 35	12 54	13 05	13 24	13 35	13 54	14 05	14 24	14 35
Baildon d		09 40		10 10		10 40		11 10		11 40		12 10		12 40		13 10		13 40		14 10		14 40
Shipley 37 a		09 44		10 14		10 44		11 14		11 44		12 14		12 44		13 14		13 44		14 14		14 44
Frizinghall 37 a		09 47		10 17		10 47		11 17		11 47		12 17		12 47		13 17		13 47		14 17		14 47
Bradford Forster Square 37 a		09 53		10 23		10 53		11 23		11 53		12 24		12 53		13 23		13 53		14 23		14 53
Leeds 10 a	09 39		10 11		10 41		11 08		11 39		12 08		12 39		13 08		13 38		14 09		14 39	

	NT	NT	NT	NT	NT	NT	NT SO	NT SX	NT	NT	NT	NT SO	NT SX	NT	NT SO	NT SX	NT	NT SX	NT SO	NT SX	NT
Ilkley d	14 40	14 51	15 10	15 21	15 40	15 51	16 10	16 12	16 21	16 40	16 51	17 10	17 14	17 21	17 40	17 42	17 51	18 04	18 10	18 10	18 21
Ben Rhydding d	14 42	14 53	15 12	15 23	15 42	15 53	16 12	16 14	16 23	16 42	16 53	17 12	17 16	17 23	17 42	17 44	17 53	18 06	18 12	18 12	18 23
Burley-in-Wharfedale d	14 48	14 59	15 18	15 29	15 48	15 59	16 18	16 20	16 29	16 48	16 59	17 18	17 22	17 29	17 48	17 50	17 59	18 12	18 18	18 18	18 29
Menston d	14 51	15 02	15 21	15 32	15 51	16 02	16 21	16 23	16 32	16 51	17 02	17 21	17 25	17 32	17 51	17 53	18 02	18 15	18 21	18 21	18 32
Guiseley d	14 54	15 05	15 24	15 35	15 54	16 05	16 24	16 27	16 35	16 54	17 05	17 24	17 29	17 35	17 54	17 56	18 05	18 18	18 24	18 24	18 35
Baildon d		15 10		15 40		16 10			16 40		17 10			17 40			18 10				18 40
Shipley 37 a		15 14		15 44		16 14			16 44		17 14			17 43			18 14				18 43
Frizinghall 37 a		15 17		15 47		16 17			16 47		17 17			17 46			18 17				18 46
Bradford Forster Square 37 a		15 23		15 53		16 23			16 53		17 23			17 53			18 23				18 52
Leeds 10 a	15 10		15 40		16 10		16 38	16 46		17 09		17 38	17 44		18 09	18 16		18 35	18 40	18 45	

	NT	NT	NT	NT	NT	NT	NT	NT	NT	NT	NT	NT	NT
Ilkley d	18 40	18 51	19 10	19 21	19 41	20 05	20 21	20 40	21 21	21 40	22 21	22 40	23 20
Ben Rhydding d	18 42	18 53	19 12	19 23	19 43	20 07	20 23	20 42	21 23	21 42	22 23	22 42	23 23
Burley-in-Wharfedale d	18 48	18 59	19 18	19 29	19 49	20 13	20 29	20 48	21 29	21 48	22 29	22 48	23 28
Menston d	18 51	19 02	19 21	19 32	19 52	20 16	20 32	20 51	21 32	21 51	22 32	22 51	23 31
Guiseley d	18 54	19 05	19 24	19 35	19 55	20 19	20 35	20 54	21 35	21 54	22 35	22 54	23 35
Baildon d		19 10		19 40		20 24		20 59		21 59		22 59	
Shipley 37 a		19 14		19 44		20 27		21 03		22 02		23 02	
Frizinghall 37 a		19 17		19 47		20 30		21 05		22 05		23 05	
Bradford Forster Square 37 a		19 23		19 53		20 36		21 12		22 11		23 13	
Leeds 10 a	19 09		19 40		20 12		20 53		21 49		22 49		23 49

Sundays

	NT	NT	NT	NT	NT	NT	NT	NT	NT	NT	NT	NT	NT	NT	NT	NT	NT	NT	NT	NT	NT	NT
Ilkley d	09 21	09 53	10 21	11 21	11 53	12 21	13 21	13 53	14 21	15 21	15 53	16 21	17 21	17 53	18 21	19 21	19 53	20 21	21 21	21 53	22 21	23 21
Ben Rhydding d	09 23	09 55	10 23	11 23	11 55	12 23	13 23	13 55	14 23	15 23	15 55	16 23	17 23	17 55	18 23	19 23	19 55	20 23	21 23	21 55	22 23	23 23
Burley-in-Wharfedale d	09 29	10 01	10 29	11 29	12 01	12 29	13 29	14 01	14 29	15 29	16 01	16 29	17 29	18 01	18 29	19 29	20 01	20 29	21 29	22 01	22 29	23 29
Menston d	09 32	10 04	10 32	11 32	12 04	12 32	13 32	14 04	14 32	15 32	16 04	16 32	17 32	18 04	18 32	19 32	20 04	20 32	21 32	22 04	22 32	23 32
Guiseley d	09 35	10 07	10 35	11 35	12 07	12 35	13 35	14 07	14 35	15 35	16 07	16 35	17 35	18 07	18 35	19 35	20 07	20 35	21 35	22 07	22 35	23 35
Baildon d		10 12			12 12			14 12			16 12			18 12			20 12			22 12		
Shipley 37 a		10 15			12 15			14 15			16 15			18 15			20 15			22 15		
Frizinghall 37 a		10 18			12 18			14 18			16 18			18 18			20 18			22 18		
Bradford Forster Square 37 a		10 24			12 24			14 24			16 24			18 24			20 24			22 24		
Leeds 10 a	09 50		10 49	11 49		12 49	13 49		14 49	15 49		16 49	17 49		18 49	19 49		20 49	21 49		22 49	23 50

Network Diagram for Tables 39, 40, 41, 43

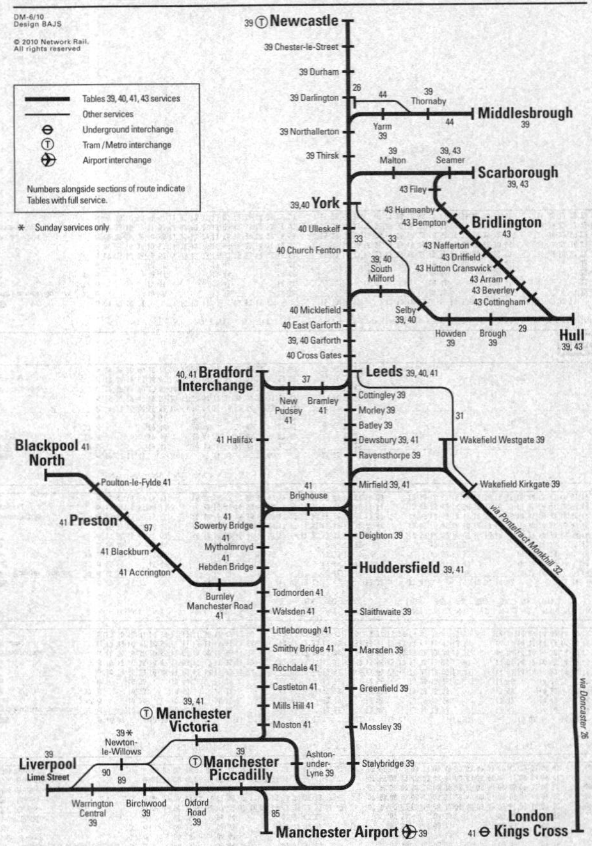

Newcastle, Middlesbrough, Scarborough, York, Hull, Leeds and Wakefield - Huddersfield - Manchester, Manchester Airport and Liverpool

Network Diagram - see first Page of Table 39

Miles	Miles	Miles	Miles	Miles			TP	TP	TP	TP	TP	TP	TP	TP	TP	TP	TP	NT	NT	TP	NT	NT	NT	TP
							MO	MX	MO	MO	MO	MX	MO	MX	MX	MO								
							◇1	◇1	◇1	◇1	◇1	◇1	◇1	◇1	◇1	◇1	◇1			◇1				◇1
							A		B	A														
																								🛒
0	—	—	—	—	Newcastle ■8	d		21p55																
8¼	—	—	—	—	Chester-le-Street	d																		
14	—	—	—	—	Durham	d		22p08																
—	—	0	—	—	Middlesbrough	d			22p06	22p06														
—	—	3¼	—	—	Thornaby	d			22p11	22p11														
—	—	8½	—	—	Yarm	d			22p19	22p19														
36	—	—	—	—	Darlington ■7	d		22p25																
50	—	20¾	—	—	Northallerton	d		22p37	22p35	22p34														
57¾	—	28½	—	—	Thirsk	d			22p43	22p42														
—	—	—	0	—	Scarborough	d	21p20																	
—	—	—	2¾	—	Seamer	d	21p25																	
—	—	—	21	—	Malton	d	21p43																	
80	—	50¾	42	—	York ■8	a	22p09	23p01	23p09	23p09														
—	—	—	—	—		d	22p12	23p07	23p12	23p12	01 38	01 38	02 47	02 52	04 00	04 23	05 26			05 57				06 28
—	—	—	—	0	Wakefield Westgate	d																06 41		
—	—	—	—	1	Wakefield Kirkgate	d																06 46		
—	0	—	—	—	Hull	d																		
—	10½	—	—	—	Brough	d																		
—	22¼	—	—	—	Howden	d																		
—	31	—	—	—	Selby	d																		
—	38¾	—	—	—	South Milford	d																		
98¼	44½	—	60¼	—	Garforth	d														06 12				
105½	51¾	—	67½	—	Leeds ■10	a	22p36	23p33	23p38	23p38	02 04	02 19	03 13	03 33	04 42	04 49	05 52			06 22				06 52
—	—	—	—	—		d	22p40	23p35	23p40	23p40	02 05	02 20	03 15	03 35	04 50	04 50	05 55		06 13	06 25			06 43	06 55
108½	—	—	—	—	Cottingley	d																	06 48	
110	—	—	—	—	Morley	d													06 21				06 52	
113½	—	—	—	—	Batley	d													06 26				06 57	
114¾	—	—	—	—	Dewsbury	a	22p50	23p45	23p51	23p51							06 06		06 29	06 36			07 00	07 06
—	—	—	—	—		d	22p51	23p46	23p51	23p51							06 06		06 29	06 36			07 01	07 06
116	—	—	—	—	Ravensthorpe	d																	07 04	
117¾	—	—	—	10½	Mirfield	d													06 35			06 59	07 08	
120¾	—	—	—	13½	Deighton	d																07 06	07 16	
122¾	—	—	—	15½	Huddersfield	a	23p02	23p54	23p59	00 02	02 42	02 42	03 56	03 56	05 27	05 27	06 14			06 44		07 12	07 20	07 15
—	—	—	—	—		d	23p04	23p55	00 01	00 04	02 45	02 45	03 59	03 59	05 28	05 28	06 15	06 29		06 45	06 57			07 16
127¼	—	—	—	20	Slaithwaite	d												06 36			07 04			
129¾	—	—	—	22½	Marsden	d												06 42			07 12			
135¾	—	—	—	28½	Greenfield	d												06 50			07 20			
138	—	—	—	30¾	Mossley (Gr Manchester)	d												06 54			07 24			
140¾	—	—	—	33½	Stalybridge	a											06 33	06 59		07 03	07 29			07 34
—	—	—	—	—		d											06 33	07 00		07 04	07 30			07 34
—	—	—	—	34¾	Ashton-under-Lyne	d												07 04			07 34			
—	—	—	—	41¼	Manchester Victoria	a	23b53			00s53								07 17	07 53		07 47			
148¼	—	—	—	—	Manchester Piccadilly ■10	a	00 08	00 53	00 43	01 08	03 44	03 44	04 58	04 58	06 02	06 02	06 50			07 19				07 51
—	—	—	—	—		d		00 54	00 44	01 10	03 44	03 44	05 00	05 00	06 08	06 08	06 54			07 23				07 54
—	—	—	—	—	Manchester Airport ✈	a		01 10	00 57	01 24	04 00	04 00	05 19	05 19	06 24	06 24	07 12			07 42				08 12
148¾	—	—	—	—	Manchester Oxford Road	a																		
161¼	—	—	—	—	Birchwood	a																		
164½	—	—	—	—	Warrington Central	a																		
177½	—	—	—	—	Liverpool South Parkway ■7 ✈	a																		
183	—	—	—	—	Liverpool Lime Street ■10	a																		

A from 21 May until 25 June, from 17 September
B from 2 July until 10 September
b Previous night, stops to set down only

Newcastle, Middlesbrough, Scarborough, York, Hull, Leeds and Wakefield - Huddersfield - Manchester, Manchester Airport and Liverpool

Network Diagram - see first Page of Table 39

		TP	NT	NT	TP	NT	TP	NT	NT	NT	NT	NT	TP	NT	TP	NT	NT	TP	TP	NT	NT	TP
		◇1			◇1		◇1						◇1		◇1			◇1	◇1			◇1
															A							
		🛒			🛒		🛒						🛒		🛒			🛒	🛒			🛒
Newcastle ■8	d														06 11							
Chester-le-Street	d														06 21							
Durham	d														06 28							
Middlesbrough	d				05 55			06 51														07 12
Thornaby	d				06 00			06a56														07 17
Yarm	d				06 08																	07 27
Darlington ■7	d														06 45							
Northallerton	d				06 23										06 56							07 43
Thirsk	d				06 31										07 04							07 51
Scarborough	d												06 30					07 00				
Seamer	d												06 35					07 05				
Malton	d												06 53					07 23				
York ■8	a				06 49								07 23		07 30			07 50				08 11
	d				06 55								07 26		07 40			07 55				08 25
Wakefield Westgate	d										07 41									08 39		
Wakefield Kirkgate	d										07 46									08 45		
Hull	d	06 00					06 37		07 07										07 37			
Brough	d	06 12					06 49		07 19										07 49			
Howden	d	06 26							07 35										08 01			
Selby	d	06 36					07 08		07a48										08 11			
South Milford	d																					
Garforth	d				07 10		07 24											08 12				08 40
Leeds ■10	a	07 00			07 20		07 35						07 52		08 04			08 22	08 36			08 52
	d	07 08	07 13		07 23		07 38					07 43	07 55		08 08		08 13	08 25	08 40		08 43	08 55
Cottingley	d											07 48					08 18				08 48	
Morley	d		07 21									07 52					08 22				08 52	
Batley	d		07 26									07 57					08 27				08 57	
Dewsbury	a		07 29		07 34							08 00	08 06				08 30	08 36			09 00	09 06
	d		07 29		07 34							08 01	08 06				08 31	08 36			09 01	09 06
Ravensthorpe	d											08 04					08 34				09 04	
Mirfield	d		07 36								07 59	08 08					08 38			08 58	09 08	
Deighton	d										08 04	08 13								09 05	09 16	
Huddersfield	a	07 25			07 43		07 56				08 11	08 20	08 15		08 25			08 44	08 58	09 11	09 20	09 15
	d	07 26		07 33	07 44		07 57			08 02			08 16		08 26	08 30		08 45	08 59			09 16
Slaithwaite	d			07 40						08 09						08 37						
Marsden	d			07 55						08 15						08 43						
Greenfield	d			08 03						08 23						08 51						
Mossley (Gr Manchester)	d			08 07		←				08 27						08 55						
Stalybridge	a	07 43		08 12	08 01	08 12	08 17			08 32					08 44	09 00						
	d	07 46		08 13	08 02	08 13	08 17			08 33				08 40	08 46	09 01						
Ashton-under-Lyne	d			→		08 17				08 37				08 44		09 05						
Manchester Victoria	a		08 53			08 31				08 52				08 54		09 20	09 53					
Manchester Piccadilly ■10	a	08 05			08 19		08 36						08 51		09 05			09 19	09 36			09 49
	d	08 07			08 24								08 54		09 07			09 24				09 54
Manchester Airport ✈	a				08 42								09 12					09 42				10 12
Manchester Oxford Road	a	08 09													09 09							
Birchwood	a	08 25													09 25							
Warrington Central	a	08 30													09 30							
Liverpool South Parkway ■7 ✈	a	08 47													09 47							
Liverpool Lime Street ■10	a	08 58													09 58							

A 🛒 from York

Newcastle, Middlesbrough, Scarborough, York, Hull, Leeds and Wakefield - Huddersfield - Manchester, Manchester Airport and Liverpool

Network Diagram - see first Page of Table 39

		NT	NT	NT	TP ◇■ ✕	NT	NT		TP ◇■ ✕	TP ◇■ ✕	NT	NT	NT	TP ◇■ ✕	NT	TP ◇■ ✕	NT		NT	TP ◇■ ✕	NT	TP ◇■ ✕	NT	NT	NT
Newcastle [8] ⇌	d								07 33																
Chester-le-Street	d								07 42																
Durham	d								07 49																
Middlesbrough	d	07 32	08 32																	08 50	09 32				
Thornaby	d	07a37	08a37																	08 55	09a37				
Yarm	d																			09 03					
Darlington [7]	d								08 06											09 18					
Northallerton	d								08 17											09 28					
Thirsk	d								08 25																
Scarborough	d				07 40											08 48									
Seamer	d				07 45											08 53									
Malton	d				08 03											09 11									
York [8]	a				08 30				08 47							09 38				09 47					
	d				08 40				08 57					09 28		09 40				09 57					
Wakefield Westgate	d											09 39												10 39	
Wakefield Kirkgate	d											09 45												10 45	
Hull	d									08 40	09 02											09 40	10 08		
Brough	d									08 52	09 14											09 52	10 20		
Howden	d										09 28												10 34		
Selby	d									09 11	09a38											10 11	10a47		
South Milford	d																								
Garforth	d								09 12											10 12					
Leeds [10]	a				09 04				09 22	09 36				09 52		10 04				10 22		10 36			
	d				09 08		09 13		09 25	09 40			09 43	09 55		10 08			10 13	10 25		10 40			10 43
Cottingley	d						09 18						09 48												10 48
Morley	d						09 22						09 52						10 21						10 52
Batley	d						09 27						09 57						10 26						10 57
Dewsbury	a						09 30		09 36				10 00	10 06					10 29	10 36					11 00
	d						09 31		09 36				10 01	10 06					10 29	10 36					11 01
Ravensthorpe	d												10 04												11 04
Mirfield	d						09 37					09 58	10 08						10 35					10 58	11 08
Deighton	d											10 05	10 14											11 05	11 14
Huddersfield	a				09 25				09 45	09 58		10 11	10 21	10 15		10 25				10 45		10 58		11 11	11 22
	d				09 26	09 30			09 46	09 59				10 16		10 26	10 30			10 46		10 59			
Slaithwaite	d					09 37											10 37								
Marsden	d					09 43											10 43								
Greenfield	d					09 51											10 51								
Mossley (Gr Manchester)	d					09 55											10 55								
Stalybridge	a				09 43	10 00										10 43	11 00								
	d			09 40	09 46	10 01									10 40	10 46	11 01								
Ashton-under-Lyne	d			09 44		10 05									10 44		11 05								
Manchester Victoria ⇌	a			09 55		10 20	10 53								10 55		11 20		11 53						
Manchester Piccadilly [10] ⇌	a				10 05				10 19	10 36				10 49		11 05				11 19		11 36			
	d				10 07				10 24					10 54		11 07				11 24					
Manchester Airport ✈	a								10 42					11 12						11 45					
Manchester Oxford Road	a				10 09											11 09									
Birchwood	a				10 25											11 25									
Warrington Central	a				10 30											11 30									
Liverpool South Parkway [7] ✈	a				10 47											11 47									
Liverpool Lime Street [10]	a				10 58											11 58									

Newcastle, Middlesbrough, Scarborough, York, Hull, Leeds and Wakefield - Huddersfield - Manchester, Manchester Airport and Liverpool

Network Diagram - see first Page of Table 39

		TP ◇■ ✕	TP ◇■ ✕		NT	NT	TP ◇■ ✕	NT	TP ◇■ ✕	NT	NT	TP FO ◇■ ✕	TP FX ◇■ ✕		NT	TP ◇■ ✕	NT	NT	TP ◇■ ✕	NT	TP ◇■ ✕	NT	NT		NT
Newcastle [8] ⇌	d	09 15										10 17	10 17												
Chester-le-Street	d	09 24																							
Durham	d	09 31										10 31	10 31												
Middlesbrough	d						09 50	10 32											10 50	11 32					
Thornaby	d						09 55	10a37											10 55	11a36					
Yarm	d						10 03												11 03						
Darlington [7]	d	09 48										10 48	10 48												
Northallerton	d	09 59					10 18					10 59	10 59						11 18						
Thirsk	d						10 28												11 28						
Scarborough	d		09 48													10 48									
Seamer	d		09 53													10 53									
Malton	d		10 11													11 11									
York [8]	a	10 21	10 38				10 47					11 23	11 23			11 38			11 47						
	d	10 27	10 40				10 57					11 26	11 26			11 40			11 57						
Wakefield Westgate	d									11 39													12 39		
Wakefield Kirkgate	d									11 45													12 45		
Hull	d								10 40												11 40	12 03			
Brough	d								10 52												11 52	12 15			
Howden	d																					12 27			
Selby	d								11 11												12 11	12a37			
South Milford	d																								
Garforth	d						11 12												12 12						
Leeds [10]	a	10 52	11 04				11 22		11 36			11 52	11 52			12 04			12 22		12 36				
	d	10 55	11 08			11 13	11 25		11 40		11 43	11 55	11 55			12 08		12 13	12 25		12 40				12 43
Cottingley	d										11 48														12 48
Morley	d					11 21					11 52							12 21							12 52
Batley	d					11 26					11 57							12 26							12 57
Dewsbury	a	11 06				11 29	11 36				12 00	12 06	12 06					12 29	12 36						13 00
	d	11 06				11 29	11 36				12 01	12 06	12 06					12 29	12 36						13 01
Ravensthorpe	d										12 04														13 04
Mirfield	d					11 35				11 58	12 08							12 35					12 58		13 08
Deighton	d									12 05	12 17												13 05		13 14
Huddersfield	a	11 15	11 25				11 45		11 58	12 11	12 21	12 15	12 15			12 25			12 45		12 58		13 11		13 21
	d	11 16	11 26		11 30		11 46		11 59			12 16	12 16			12 26	12 30		12 46		12 59				
Slaithwaite	d				11 37												12 37								
Marsden	d				11 43												12 43								
Greenfield	d				11 51												12 51								
Mossley (Gr Manchester)	d				11 55												12 55								
Stalybridge	a		11 43		12 00											12 43	13 00								
	d		11 46		12 01										12 40	12 46	13 01								
Ashton-under-Lyne	d				12 05										12 44		13 05								
Manchester Victoria ⇌	a				12 20	12 53									12 55		13 20	13 53							
Manchester Piccadilly [10] ⇌	a	11 49	12 05				12 19		12 36			12 49	12 49			13 05			13 19		13 36				
	d	11 54	12 07				12 24					12 54	12 54			13 07			13 24						
Manchester Airport ✈	a	12 12					12 42					13 11	13 12						13 42						
Manchester Oxford Road	a		12 09													13 09									
Birchwood	a		12 25													13 25									
Warrington Central	a		12 30													13 30									
Liverpool South Parkway [7] ✈	a		12 47													13 47									
Liverpool Lime Street [10]	a		12 58													13 58									

Newcastle, Middlesbrough, Scarborough, York, Hull, Leeds and Wakefield - Huddersfield - Manchester, Manchester Airport and Liverpool

Network Diagram - see first Page of Table 39

		TP	NT	TP	NT	NT	TP	NT	TP		NT	NT	NT	TP	NT	TP	NT	NT	TP		NT	TP	NT	NT	NT
		◇■ ⊥		◇■ ⊥			◇■ ⊥		◇■ ⊥					◇■ ⊥		◇■ ⊥			◇■ ⊥			◇■ ⊥			
Newcastle ■	d	11 15												12 17											
Chester-le-Street	d	11 24																							
Durham	d	11 31												12 29											
Middlesbrough	d						11 50	12 32											12 50		13 32				
Thornaby	d						11 55	12a37											12 55		13a37				
Yarm	d						12 03												13 03						
Darlington ■	d	11 48												12 46											
Northallerton	d	11 59					12 18							12 58					13 18						
Thirsk	d						12 28												13 28						
Scarborough	d			11 48												12 48									
Seamer	d			11 53												12 53									
Malton	d			12 11												13 11									
York ■	a	12 21		12 38			12 47							13 21		13 38			13 47						
	d	12 26		12 40			12 57							13 24		13 40			13 57						
Wakefield Westgate	d											13 39												14 39	
Wakefield Kirkgate	d											13 45												14 45	
Hull	d								12 40		13 12											13 40	14 19		
Brough	d								12 52		13 24											13 52	14 31		
Howden	d										13 41												14 43		
Selby	d								13 11		13a54											14 11	14a53		
South Milford	d																								
Garforth	d						13 12												14 12						
Leeds ■	a	12 52		13 04			13 22		13 35					13 52		14 04			14 22			14 36			
	d	12 55		13 08		13 13	13 25		13 40				13 43	13 55		14 08		14 13	14 25			14 40			14 43
Cottingley	d												13 48												14 48
Morley	d					13 21							13 52					14 21							14 52
Batley	d					13 26							13 57					14 26							14 57
Dewsbury	a	13 06				13 29	13 36						14 00	14 06				14 29	14 36						15 00
	d	13 06				13 29	13 36						14 01	14 06				14 29	14 36						15 01
Ravensthorpe	d												14 04												15 04
Mirfield	d					13 35						13 58	14 08					14 35						14 58	15 08
Deighton	d											14 05	14 14											15 05	15 16
Huddersfield	a	13 15		13 25			13 45		13 58			14 11	14 21	14 15		14 25			14 45			14 58		15 11	15 21
	d	13 16		13 26	13 30		13 46		13 59					14 16		14 26	14 30		14 46			14 59			
Slaithwaite	d				13 37												14 37								
Marsden	d				13 43												14 43								
Greenfield	d				13 51												14 51								
Mossley (Gr Manchester)	d				13 55												14 55								
Stalybridge	a			13 43	14 00											14 43	15 00								
	d		13 40	13 46	14 01										14 40	14 46	15 01								
Ashton-under-Lyne	d		13 44		14 05										14 44		15 05								
Manchester Victoria	a		13 55		14 20	14 52									14 58		15 20	15 53							
Manchester Piccadilly ■	a	13 49		14 05			14 19		14 36					14 49		15 05			15 19			15 36			
	d	13 54		14 07			14 24							14 54		15 07			15 24						
Manchester Airport	a	14 12					14 42							15 12					15 42						
Manchester Oxford Road	a			14 09												15 09									
Birchwood	a			14 25												15 25									
Warrington Central	a			14 30												15 30									
Liverpool South Parkway ■	a			14 47												15 47									
Liverpool Lime Street ■	a			14 58												15 58									

Newcastle, Middlesbrough, Scarborough, York, Hull, Leeds and Wakefield - Huddersfield - Manchester, Manchester Airport and Liverpool

Network Diagram - see first Page of Table 39

		TP	TP	NT	TP		NT	NT	TP	NT	TP	NT	NT	NT	TP		NT	TP	NT	NT	TP FX	TP FO	TP FO	TP FX	NT
		◇■ A ⊥	◇■ B ⊥		◇■ ⊥				◇■ ⊥		◇■ ⊥				◇■ ⊥		C	◇■ ⊥			◇■ ⊥	◇■ ⊥	◇■ ⊥	◇■ ⊥	
Newcastle ■	d	13 15	13 15												14 18										
Chester-le-Street	d	13 24	13 24																						
Durham	d	13 31	13 31												14 31										
Middlesbrough	d								13 50	14 32											14 50				
Thornaby	d								13 55	14a37											14 55				
Yarm	d								14 03												15 03				
Darlington ■	d	13 48	13 48												14 48										
Northallerton	d	13 58	13 58						14 18						14 59						15 18				
Thirsk	d								14 28												15 28				
Scarborough	d				13 48													14 48							
Seamer	d				13 53													14 53							
Malton	d				14 11													15 11							
York ■	a	14 22	14 23		14 38				14 47						15 22			15 38			15 47				
	d	14 26	14 26		14 40				14 57						15 26			15 40			15 57	15 57			
Wakefield Westgate	d												15 39												
Wakefield Kirkgate	d												15 45												
Hull	d										14 40	15 02											15 40	15 40	16 10
Brough	d										14 52	15 14											15 52	15 52	16 22
Howden	d											15 26													16 36
Selby	d										15 11	15a36											16 11	16 11	16a46
South Milford	d																								
Garforth	d								15 12												16 12		16 22		
Leeds ■	a	14 52	14 52		15 04				15 23		15 36				15 52			16 04			16 22	16 22	16 36	16 36	
	d	14 55	14 55		15 08			15 13	15 25		15 40			15 43	15 55			16 08		16 13	16 25	16 25	16 40	16 40	
Cottingley	d													15 48						16 18					
Morley	d							15 21						15 52						16 22					
Batley	d							15 26						15 57						16 27					
Dewsbury	a	15 06	15 06					15 29	15 36					16 00	16 06					16 30	16 36	16 36			
	d	15 06	15 06					15 29	15 36					16 01	16 06					16 31	16 36	16 36			
Ravensthorpe	d													16 04						16 34					
Mirfield	d							15 35					15 58	16 08						16 38					
Deighton	d												16 05	16 14											
Huddersfield	a	15 15	15 15		15 25				15 45		15 58		16 11	16 21	16 15			16 25			16 45	16 45	16 58	16 58	
	d	15 16	15 16		15 26		15 30		15 46		15 59				16 16			16 26	16 30		16 46	16 46	16 59	16 59	
Slaithwaite	d						15 37												16 37						
Marsden	d						15 43												16 43						
Greenfield	d						15 51												16 51						
Mossley (Gr Manchester)	d						15 55												16 55						
Stalybridge	a				15 43		16 00											16 43	17 00				17 18	17 18	
	d			15 40	15 46		16 01										16 42	16 46	17 01				17 18	17 18	
Ashton-under-Lyne	d			15 44			16 05										16 46		17 05						
Manchester Victoria	a			15 55			16 21	16 52									16 58		17 24	17 53					
Manchester Piccadilly ■	a	15 49	15 49		16 05				16 19		16 36				16 49			17 05			17 25	17 21	17 36	17 36	
	d	15 54	15 54		16 07				16 24						16 54			17 07							
Manchester Airport	a	16 12	16 12						16 42						17 12										
Manchester Oxford Road	a				16 09													17 09							
Birchwood	a				16 25													17 25							
Warrington Central	a				16 30													17 30							
Liverpool South Parkway ■	a				16 47													17 47							
Liverpool Lime Street ■	a				16 58													18 01							

A from 21 May B until 18 May C until 19 October

Newcastle, Middlesbrough, Scarborough, York, Hull, Leeds and Wakefield - Huddersfield - Manchester, Manchester Airport and Liverpool

Network Diagram - see first Page of Table 39

		NT	NT	TP ◇1 🛒	TP FO ◇1 A	NT	TP ◇1 🛒	GC 1 🍽	NT	NT	TP FO ◇1 🛒	TP FX ◇1 🛒	NT	TP ◇1 🛒	NT	NT	NT	TP ◇1 🛒	TP ◇1	TP ◇1 🛒	NT	NT
Newcastle 8 ⇌	d			15 15														16 15				
Chester-le-Street	d			15 24														16 24				
Durham	d			15 31														16 31				
Middlesbrough	d				14 50	15 32					15 50	15 50	16 32									
Thornaby	d				14 55	15a37					15 55	15 55	16a37									
Yarm	d				15 03						16 03	16 03										
Darlington 7	d			15 48														16 48				
Northallerton	d			15 59	15 18						16 18	16 18						16 59				
Thirsk	d				15 28						16 28	16 28										
Scarborough	d						15 48													16 48		
Seamer	d						15 53													16 53		
Malton	d						16 11													17 11		
York 8	a			16 21	15 47		16 38				16 47	16 47						17 23		17 38		
	d			16 26	16 13		16 40				16 57	16 57						17 26		17 40		
Wakefield Westgate	d	16 39														17 39						
Wakefield Kirkgate	d	16 45						17 08								17 45						
Hull	d													16 40					17 01			
Brough	d													16 52					17 13			
Howden	d																					
Selby	d													17 11					17 32			
South Milford	d																					
Garforth	d										17 12	17 12										
Leeds 10	a			16 52	16 59		17 04				17 22	17 22		17 36				17 52	17 58	18 04		
	d		16 43	16 55			17 08			17 13	17 26	17 26		17 40			17 43	17 55	18 02	18 08		18 13
Cottingley	d		16 48							17 18							17 48					18 18
Morley	d		16 52							17 22							17 52					18 22
Batley	d		16 57							17 27							17 57					18 27
Dewsbury	a		17 00	17 06						17 30	17 37	17 37					18 00	18 06	18 13			18 30
	d		17 01	17 06						17 31	17 37	17 37					18 01	18 06	18 13			18 31
Ravensthorpe	d		17 04							17 34							18 04					18 34
Mirfield	d	16 58	17 08					17a20		17 38						17 58	18 08					18 38
Deighton	d	17 05	17 14													18 05	18 13					
Huddersfield	a	17 11	17 21	17 15			17 25				17 46	17 46		17 58		18 11	18 20	18 15	18 23	18 25		
	d			17 16			17 26		17 30		17 46	17 46		17 59	18 04			18 16		18 26	18 30	
Slaithwaite	d								17 37						18 11						18 37	
Marsden	d								17 43						18 17						18 43	
Greenfield	d								17 51												18 51	
Mossley (Gr Manchester)	d								17 55												18 55	
Stalybridge	a						17 43		18 00					18 18	18 30					18 43	19 01	
	d						17 46		18 01					18 18	18 31					18 46	19 01	
Ashton-under-Lyne	d								18 05						18 35						19 05	
Manchester Victoria ⇌	a								18 20	18 54					18 48						19 20	19 54
Manchester Piccadilly 10 ⇌	a			17 49			18 05				18 19	18 19		18 37				18 49		19 05		
	d			17 54			18 07					18 24						18 54		19 07		
Manchester Airport ✈	a			18 12								18 42						19 13				
Manchester Oxford Road	a						18 09													19 09		
Birchwood	a						18 25													19 25		
Warrington Central	a						18 30													19 30		
Liverpool South Parkway 7 ✈	a						18 47													19 47		
Liverpool Lime Street 10	a						19 01													20 01		

A ◇1 to York

Table 39 — Mondays to Fridays

Newcastle, Middlesbrough, Scarborough, York, Hull, Leeds and Wakefield - Huddersfield - Manchester, Manchester Airport and Liverpool

Network Diagram - see first Page of Table 39

		TP ◇1 🛒	TP ◇1 🛒	NT	NT	NT	TP ◇1 🛒	TP ◇1	TP FO ◇1	NT	NT	TP FX ◇1	NT	NT	TP FO ◇1	TP ◇1	NT	NT	TP ◇1	TP ◇1	NT	NT	TP ◇1
Newcastle 8 ⇌	d		17 02																				18 52
Chester-le-Street	d		17 11																				19 01
Durham	d		17 18																				19 08
Middlesbrough	d	16 50		17 39					17 50			17 50	18 32	18 45						18 50			
Thornaby	d	16 55		17a44					17 55			17 55	18a37	18 50						18 55			
Yarm	d	17 03							18 03			18 03								19 03			
Darlington 7	d		17 35											19a12									19 25
Northallerton	d	17 18	17 46						18 18			18 18								19 18			19 36
Thirsk	d	17 28							18 28			18 28								19 26			
Scarborough	d							17 48											18 48				
Seamer	d							17 53											18 53				
Malton	d							18 11											19 11				
York 8	a	17 47	18 09					18 38	18 47			18 47							19 38	19 50			20 07
	d	17 57	18 12					18 40				19 08			19 08				19 40				20 10
Wakefield Westgate	d				18 39													19 42					
Wakefield Kirkgate	d				18 45													19 45					
Hull	d						17 58									18 59	19 15						
Brough	d						18 10									19 11	19 28						
Howden	d																19 43						
Selby	d						18 29									19 30	19a53						
South Milford	d																						
Garforth	d	18 12										19 22			19 22								
Leeds 10	a	18 22	18 37				18 52	19 04				19 37			19 37	19 56			20 04				20 35
	d	18 25	18 40			18 43	18 55	19 08			19 13	19 40			19 40				20 08			20 13	20 40
Cottingley	d					18 48					19 18											20 18	
Morley	d					18 52					19 22											20 22	
Batley	d					18 57					19 27											20 27	
Dewsbury	a	18 36				19 00	19 06				19 30	19 51			19 51							20 30	20 51
	d	18 36				19 01	19 06				19 31	19 51			19 51							20 31	20 51
Ravensthorpe	d					19 04					19 34											20 34	
Mirfield	d				18 58	19 08					19 38							19 59				20 37	
Deighton	d				19 05	19 13					19 45							20 08				20 44	
Huddersfield	a	18 45	18 58		19 11	19 20	19 15	19 25			19 49	19 59			19 59			20 13	20 25			20 51	20 59
	d	18 46	18 59				19 16	19 26		19 30		20 00			20 00				20 26		20 30		21 00
Slaithwaite	d									19 37											20 37		
Marsden	d									19 43											20 43		
Greenfield	d									19 51											20 51		
Mossley (Gr Manchester)	d									19 55											20 55		
Stalybridge	a							19 43		20 00									20 43		21 00		
	d							19 46		20 01									20 46		21 01		
Ashton-under-Lyne	d									20 05											21 05		
Manchester Victoria ⇌	a									20 20											21 20		
Manchester Piccadilly 10 ⇌	a	19 21	19 33				19 57	20 05				20 33			20 33				21 05				21 33
	d		19 40					20 07				20 40			20 40				21 07				21 40
Manchester Airport ✈	a		19 59									20 57			20 57								21 57
Manchester Oxford Road	a							20 09											21 09				
Birchwood	a							20 25											21 25				
Warrington Central	a							20 30											21 30				
Liverpool South Parkway 7 ✈	a							20 47											21 47				
Liverpool Lime Street 10	a							21 01											22 01				

Newcastle, Middlesbrough, Scarborough, York, Hull, Leeds and Wakefield - Huddersfield - Manchester, Manchester Airport and Liverpool

Network Diagram - see first Page of Table 39

		NT	TP		NT	NT	TP FX	NT	TP FO	TP FX	TP	TP FX	TP		NT	TP	NT	TP	TP	NT	NT	TP	NT		NT
			◇1				◇1		◇1	◇1	◇1	◇1	◇1			◇1		◇1	◇1			◇1			
Newcastle 8 ⇌	d																								
Chester-le-Street	d																								
Durham	d																								
Middlesbrough	d						18 50	19 40			20 04					20 50	21 01		21 50						
Thornaby	d						18 55	19a45			20 09					20 55	21a06		21 55						
Yarm	d						19 03									21 03									
Darlington 7	d										20 35								22 19						
Northallerton	d						19 18				20 46					21 18			22 30						
Thirsk	d						19 26				21 00								22 38						
Scarborough	d		19 48										20 48					22 03							
Seamer	d		19 53										20 53					22 08							
Malton	d		20 11										21 11					22 26							
York 8	a		20 38				19 50				21 24		21 38			21 43		22 55	22 56						
	d		20 40				21 14			21 14						21 46									
Wakefield Westgate	d	20 50													21 41										22 48
Wakefield Kirkgate	d	20 56													21 50										22 53
Hull	d								20 35			20 45										21 33			
Brough	d								20 47			20 57										21 45			
Howden	d																								
Selby	d								21 06			21 16										22 07			
South Milford	d								21 16			21 26										22 16			
Garforth	d																								
Leeds 10	a		21 04				21 37		21 35	21 37		21 44				22 07						22 35			
	d		21 08			21 13	21 40		21 40	21 40						22 10					22 18	22 40			
Cottingley	d					21 18															22 23				
Morley	d					21 22															22 27				
Batley	d					21 27															22 32				
Dewsbury	a					21 30	21 51		21 51	21 51											22 35	22 51			
	d					21 31	21 51		21 51	21 51											22 36	22 51			
Ravensthorpe	d					21 34															22 39				
Mirfield	d	21 09				21 38									22 03						22 44				23 06
Deighton	d	21 16				21 45									22 10						22 49				23 14
Huddersfield	a	21 21	21 25			21 49	21 59		21 59	21 59					22 14	22 27					22 54	22 59			23 21
	d		21 26		21 30		22 00		22 00	22 00						22 28				22 34		23 00	23 05		
Slaithwaite	d				21 37															22 41			23 12		
Marsden	d				21 43															22 47			23 18		
Greenfield	d				21 51															22 55			23 26		
Mossley (Gr Manchester)	d				21 55															22 59			23 30		
Stalybridge	a		21 43		22 00											22 45				23 04			23 35		
	d		21 46		22 01											22 46				23 05			23 36		
Ashton-under-Lyne	d				22 05															23 09			23 40		
Manchester Victoria ⇌	a				22 20															23 24			23 53		
Manchester Piccadilly 10 ⇌	a		22 05				22 33		22 33	22 33						23 05						23 37			
	d		22 07				22 40		22 40	22 40															
Manchester Airport ✈	a						22 57		22 57	22 57															
Manchester Oxford Road	a		22 09																						
Birchwood	a		22 25																						
Warrington Central	a		22 30																						
Liverpool South Parkway 7 ✈	a		22 47																						
Liverpool Lime Street 10	a		23 01																						

Newcastle, Middlesbrough, Scarborough, York, Hull, Leeds and Wakefield - Huddersfield - Manchester, Manchester Airport and Liverpool

Network Diagram - see first Page of Table 39

		NT	TP	NT
			◇1	
Newcastle 8 ⇌	d		21 55	22 21
Chester-le-Street	d			22 31
Durham	d		22 08	22 39
Middlesbrough	d			
Thornaby	d			
Yarm	d			
Darlington 7	d		22 25	22a59
Northallerton	d		22 37	
Thirsk	d			
Scarborough	d			
Seamer	d			
Malton	d			
York 8	a		23 01	
	d		23 07	
Wakefield Westgate	d			
Wakefield Kirkgate	d			
Hull	d			
Brough	d			
Howden	d			
Selby	d			
South Milford	d			
Garforth	d			
Leeds 10	a		23 33	
	d	23 13	23 35	
Cottingley	d	23 18		
Morley	d	23 22		
Batley	d	23 27		
Dewsbury	a	23 30	23 45	
	d	23 31	23 46	
Ravensthorpe	d	23 34		
Mirfield	d	23 38		
Deighton	d	23 45		
Huddersfield	a	23 49	23 54	
	d		23 55	
Slaithwaite	d			
Marsden	d			
Greenfield	d			
Mossley (Gr Manchester)	d			
Stalybridge	a			
	d			
Ashton-under-Lyne	d			
Manchester Victoria ⇌	a			
Manchester Piccadilly 10 ⇌	a		00 53	
	d		00 54	
Manchester Airport ✈	a		01 10	
Manchester Oxford Road	a			
Birchwood	a			
Warrington Central	a			
Liverpool South Parkway 7 ✈	a			
Liverpool Lime Street 10	a			

Newcastle, Middlesbrough, Scarborough, York, Hull, Leeds and Wakefield - Huddersfield - Manchester, Manchester Airport and Liverpool

Network Diagram - see first Page of Table 39

		TP	TP	TP	TP	TP	TP	TP	TP	TP	TP	TP	NT	NT	TP	NT	NT	NT	TP	TP	NT	NT	TP
		MO	MX	MO	MO	MO	MX	MO	MX	MX	MO												
		◇1	◇1	◇1	◇1	◇1	◇1	◇1	◇1	◇1	◇1	◇1			◇1				◇1	◇1			◇1
		A		B	A																		
																			⊼	⊼			⊼
Newcastle	d		21p55																				
Chester-le-Street	d																						
Durham	d		22p08																				
Middlesbrough	d			22p06	22p06																		05 55
Thornaby	d			22p11	22p11																		06 00
Yarm	d			22p19	22p19																		06 08
Darlington	d		22p25																				
Northallerton	d		22p37	22p35	22p34																		06 23
Thirsk	d			22p43	22p42																		06 31
Scarborough	d	21p20																					
Seamer	d	21p25																					
Malton	d	21p43																					
York	a	22p09	23p01	23p09	23p09																		06 49
	d	22p12	23p07	23p12	23p12	01 38	01 38	02 47	02 52	04 00	04 23	05 26			05 57				06 28				06 55
Wakefield Westgate	d																06 41						
Wakefield Kirkgate	d																06 46						
Hull	d																			06 00			
Brough	d																			06 12			
Howden	d																			06 26			
Selby	d																			06 36			
South Milford	d																						
Garforth	d														06 12								07 10
Leeds	a	22p36	23p33	23p38	23p38	02 04	02 19	03 13	03 33	04 42	04 49	05 52			06 22				06 52	07 00			07 20
	d	22p40	23p35	23p40	23p40	02 05	02 20	03 15	03 35	04 50	04 50	05 55		06 13	06 25			06 43	06 55	07 08	07 13		07 23
Cottingley	d																	06 48					
Morley	d													06 21				06 52			07 21		
Batley	d													06 26				06 57			07 26		
Dewsbury	a	22p50	23p45	23p51	23p51							06 06		06 29	06 36			07 00	07 06		07 29		07 34
	d	22p51	23p46	23p51	23p51							06 06		06 29	06 36			07 01	07 06		07 29		07 34
Ravensthorpe	d																	07 04					
Mirfield	d													06 35			06 59	07 08			07 36		
Deighton	d																07 06	07 16					
Huddersfield	a	23p02	23p54	23p59	00 02	02 42	02 42	03 56	03 56	05 27	05 27	06 14			06 44		07 12	07 20	07 15	07 25			07 43
	d	23p04	23p55	00 01	00 04	02 45	02 45	03 59	03 59	05 28	05 28	06 15	06 29		06 45	06 57			07 16	07 26		07 33	07 44
Slaithwaite	d												06 36			07 04						07 40	
Marsden	d												06 42			07 12						07 55	
Greenfield	d												06 50			07 20						08 03	
Mossley (Gr Manchester)	d												06 54			07 24						08 07	
Stalybridge	a											06 33	06 59		07 03	07 29			07 34	07 43		08 12	08 01
	d											06 33	07 00		07 04	07 30			07 34	07 46		08 13	08 02
Ashton-under-Lyne	d												07 04			07 34						→	
Manchester Victoria	a	23b53			00s53								07 17	07 53		07 47					08 53		
Manchester Piccadilly	a	00 08	00 53	00 43	01 08	03 44	03 44	04 58	04 58	06 02	06 02	06 50			07 19				07 51	08 05			08 19
	d		00 54	00 44	01 10	03 44	03 44	05 00	05 00	06 08	06 08	06 54			07 23				07 54	08 07			08 24
Manchester Airport	a		01 10	00 57	01 24	04 00	04 00	05 19	05 19	06 24	06 24	07 12			07 42				08 12				08 42
Manchester Oxford Road	a																			08 09			
Birchwood	a																			08 25			
Warrington Central	a																			08 30			
Liverpool South Parkway	a																			08 47			
Liverpool Lime Street	a																			08 58			

A from 21 May until 25 June, from 17 September

B from 2 July until 10 September

b Previous night, stops to set down only

Newcastle, Middlesbrough, Scarborough, York, Hull, Leeds and Wakefield - Huddersfield - Manchester, Manchester Airport and Liverpool

Network Diagram - see first Page of Table 39

		NT	TP	NT	NT	NT	NT	NT	TP	NT	TP	NT	NT	TP	TP	NT	NT	TP	NT	NT	NT	TP	NT
			◇1						◇1		◇1			◇1	◇1			◇1				◇1	
											A												
			⊼						⊼		⊼			⊼	⊼			⊼				⊼	
Newcastle	d										06 11												
Chester-le-Street	d										06 21												
Durham	d										06 28												
Middlesbrough	d			06 51														07 12	07 32	08 32			
Thornaby	d			06a56														07 17	07a37	08a37			
Yarm	d																	07 27					
Darlington	d										06 45												
Northallerton	d										06 56							07 43					
Thirsk	d										07 04							07 51					
Scarborough	d								06 30					07 00								07 40	
Seamer	d								06 35					07 05								07 45	
Malton	d								06 53					07 23								08 03	
York	a								07 23		07 30			07 50				08 11				08 30	
	d								07 26		07 40			07 55				08 25				08 40	
Wakefield Westgate	d						07 41									08 39							
Wakefield Kirkgate	d						07 46									08 45							
Hull	d		06 37		07 07										07 37								
Brough	d		06 49		07 19										07 49								
Howden	d				07 35										08 01								
Selby	d		07 08		07a48										08 11								
South Milford	d																						
Garforth	d		07 24											08 12				08 40					
Leeds	a		07 35						07 52		08 04			08 22	08 36			08 52				09 04	
	d		07 38					07 43	07 55		08 08		08 13	08 25	08 40		08 43	08 55				09 08	
Cottingley	d							07 48					08 18				08 48						
Morley	d							07 52					08 22				08 52						
Batley	d							07 57					08 27				08 57						
Dewsbury	a							08 00	08 06				08 30	08 36			09 00	09 06					
	d							08 01	08 06				08 31	08 36			09 01	09 06					
Ravensthorpe	d							08 04					08 34				09 04						
Mirfield	d						07 59	08 08					08 38			08 58	09 08						
Deighton	d						08 04	08 13								09 05	09 16						
Huddersfield	a		07 56				08 11	08 20	08 15		08 25			08 44	08 58	09 11	09 20	09 15				09 25	
	d		07 57			08 02			08 16		08 26	08 30		08 45	08 59			09 16				09 26	09 30
Slaithwaite	d					08 09						08 37											09 37
Marsden	d					08 15						08 43											09 43
Greenfield	d					08 23						08 51											09 51
Mossley (Gr Manchester)	d	←				08 27						08 55											09 55
Stalybridge	a	08 12	08 17			08 32					08 44	09 00										09 43	10 00
	d	08 13	08 17			08 33				08 40	08 46	09 01									09 40	09 46	10 01
Ashton-under-Lyne	d	08 17				08 37				08 44		09 05									09 44		10 05
Manchester Victoria	a	08 31				08 52				08 54		09 20	09 53								09 55		10 20
Manchester Piccadilly	a		08 36						08 51		09 05			09 19	09 36			09 49				10 05	
	d								08 54		09 07			09 24				09 54				10 07	
Manchester Airport	a								09 12					09 42				10 12					
Manchester Oxford Road	a										09 09											10 09	
Birchwood	a										09 25											10 25	
Warrington Central	a										09 30											10 30	
Liverpool South Parkway	a										09 47											10 47	
Liverpool Lime Street	a										09 58											10 58	

A ⊼ from York

Newcastle, Middlesbrough, Scarborough, York, Hull, Leeds and Wakefield - Huddersfield - Manchester, Manchester Airport and Liverpool

Network Diagram - see first Page of Table 39

		NT	TP	TP	NT	NT	NT	TP	NT	TP	NT	NT	TP	NT	TP	NT	NT	NT	TP	TP	NT	NT
			◇1 ⊼	◇1 ⊼				◇1 ⊼		◇1 ⊼			◇1 ⊼		◇1 ⊼				◇1 ⊼	◇1 ⊼		
Newcastle 8	d		07 33																09 15			
Chester-le-Street	d		07 42																09 24			
Durham	d		07 49																09 31			
Middlesbrough	d												08 50	09 32								
Thornaby	d												08 55	09a37								
Yarm	d												09 03									
Darlington 7	d		08 06																09 48			
Northallerton	d		08 17										09 18						09 59			
Thirsk	d		08 25										09 28									
Scarborough	d									08 48										09 48		
Seamer	d									08 53										09 53		
Malton	d									09 11										10 11		
York 8	a		08 47							09 38			09 47						10 21	10 38		
	d		08 57					09 28		09 40			09 57						10 27	10 40		
Wakefield Westgate	d					09 39											10 39					
Wakefield Kirkgate	d					09 45											10 45					
Hull	d			08 40	09 02										09 40	10 08						
Brough	d			08 52	09 14										09 52	10 20						
Howden	d				09 28											10 34						
Selby	d			09 11	09a38										10 11	10a47						
South Milford	d																					
Garforth	d		09 12										10 12									
Leeds 10	a		09 22	09 36				09 52		10 04			10 22		10 36				10 52	11 04		
	d	09 13	09 25	09 40			09 43	09 55		10 08		10 13	10 25		10 40			10 43	10 55	11 08		11 13
Cottingley	d	09 18					09 48											10 48				
Morley	d	09 22					09 52					10 21						10 52				11 21
Batley	d	09 27					09 57					10 26						10 57				11 26
Dewsbury	a	09 30	09 36				10 00	10 06				10 29	10 36					11 00	11 06			11 29
	d	09 31	09 36				10 01	10 06				10 29	10 36					11 01	11 06			11 29
Ravensthorpe	d						10 04											11 04				
Mirfield	d	09 37				09 58	10 08					10 35					10 58	11 08				11 35
Brighouse	d					10 05	10 14										11 05	11 14				
Huddersfield	a		09 45	09 58		10 11	10 21	10 15		10 25			10 45		10 58		11 11	11 22	11 15	11 25		
	d		09 46	09 59				10 16		10 26	10 30		10 46		10 59				11 16	11 26	11 30	
Slaithwaite	d										10 37										11 37	
Marsden	d										10 43										11 43	
Greenfield	d										10 51										11 51	
Mossley (Gr Manchester)	d										10 55										11 55	
Stalybridge	a									10 43	11 00									11 43	12 00	
	d								10 40	10 46	11 01									11 46	12 01	
Ashton-under-Lyne	d								10 44		11 05										12 05	
Manchester Victoria	a	10 53							10 55		11 20	11 53									12 20	12 53
Manchester Piccadilly 10	a		10 19	10 36				10 49		11 05			11 19		11 36				11 49	12 05		
	d		10 24					10 54		11 07			11 24						11 54	12 07		
Manchester Airport	a		10 42					11 12					11 45						12 12			
Manchester Oxford Road	a									11 09										12 09		
Birchwood	a									11 25										12 25		
Warrington Central	a									11 30										12 30		
Liverpool South Parkway 7	a									11 47										12 47		
Liverpool Lime Street 10	a									11 58										12 58		

Newcastle, Middlesbrough, Scarborough, York, Hull, Leeds and Wakefield - Huddersfield - Manchester, Manchester Airport and Liverpool

Network Diagram - see first Page of Table 39

		TP	NT	TP	NT	NT	TP	TP	NT	TP	NT	NT	TP	NT	TP	NT	NT	NT	TP	NT	TP	NT	NT
							FO	FX															
		◇1 ⊼		◇1 ⊼			◇1 ⊼	◇1 ⊼		◇1 ⊼			◇1 ⊼		◇1 ⊼				◇1 ⊼		◇1 ⊼		
Newcastle 8	d						10 17	10 17											11 15				
Chester-le-Street	d																		11 24				
Durham	d						10 31	10 31											11 31				
Middlesbrough	d	09 50	10 32										10 50	11 32									
Thornaby	d	09 55	10a37										10 55	11a36									
Yarm	d	10 03											11 03										
Darlington 7	d						10 48	10 48											11 48				
Northallerton	d	10 18					10 59	10 59					11 18						11 59				
Thirsk	d	10 28											11 28										
Scarborough	d									10 48											11 48		
Seamer	d									10 53											11 53		
Malton	d									11 11											12 11		
York 8	a	10 47					11 23	11 23		11 38			11 47						12 21		12 38		
	d	10 57					11 26	11 26		11 40			11 57						12 26		12 40		
Wakefield Westgate	d				11 39												12 39						
Wakefield Kirkgate	d				11 45												12 45						
Hull	d			10 40											11 40	12 03							
Brough	d			10 52											11 52	12 15							
Howden	d															12 27							
Selby	d			11 11											12 11	12a37							
South Milford	d																						
Garforth	d	11 12											12 12										
Leeds 10	a	11 22		11 36			11 52	11 52		12 04			12 22		12 36				12 52		13 04		
	d	11 25		11 40		11 43	11 55	11 55		12 08		12 13	12 25		12 40			12 43	12 55		13 08		13 13
Cottingley	d					11 48												12 48					
Morley	d					11 52						12 21						12 52					13 21
Batley	d					11 57						12 26						12 57					13 26
Dewsbury	a	11 36				12 00	12 06	12 06				12 29	12 36					13 00	13 06				13 29
	d	11 36				12 01	12 06	12 06				12 29	12 36					13 01	13 06				13 29
Ravensthorpe	d					12 04												13 04					
Mirfield	d				11 58	12 08						12 35					12 58	13 08					13 35
Brighouse	d				12 05	12 17											13 05	13 14					
Huddersfield	a	11 45		11 58	12 11	12 21	12 15	12 15		12 25			12 45		12 58		13 11	13 21	13 15		13 25		
	d	11 46		11 59			12 16	12 16		12 26	12 30		12 46		12 59				13 16		13 26	13 30	
Slaithwaite	d										12 37											13 37	
Marsden	d										12 43											13 43	
Greenfield	d										12 51											13 51	
Mossley (Gr Manchester)	d										12 55											13 55	
Stalybridge	a									12 43	13 00										13 43	14 00	
	d								12 40	12 46	13 01									13 40	13 46	14 01	
Ashton-under-Lyne	d								12 44		13 05									13 44		14 05	
Manchester Victoria	a								12 55		13 20	13 53								13 55		14 20	14 52
Manchester Piccadilly 10	a	12 19		12 36			12 49	12 49		13 05			13 19		13 36				13 49		14 05		
	d	12 24					12 54	12 54		13 07			13 24						13 54		14 07		
Manchester Airport	a	12 42					13 11	13 12					13 42						14 12				
Manchester Oxford Road	a									13 09											14 09		
Birchwood	a									13 25											14 25		
Warrington Central	a									13 30											14 30		
Liverpool South Parkway 7	a									13 47											14 47		
Liverpool Lime Street 10	a									13 58											14 58		

Newcastle, Middlesbrough, Scarborough, York, Hull, Leeds and Wakefield - Huddersfield - Manchester, Manchester Airport and Liverpool

Network Diagram - see first Page of Table 39

		TP ◇1 ⌶	NT	TP ◇1 ⌶		NT	NT	NT	TP ◇1 ⌶	NT	TP ◇1 ⌶	NT	NT	TP ◇1 ⌶		NT	TP ◇1 ⌶	NT	NT	NT	TP ◇1 A ⌶	TP ◇1 B ⌶	NT	TP ◇1 ⌶
Newcastle 8	d								12 17												13 15	13 15		
Chester-le-Street	d																				13 24	13 24		
Durham	d								12 29												13 31	13 31		
Middlesbrough	d	11 50	12 32											12 50		13 32								
Thornaby	d	11 55	12a37											12 55		13a37								
Yarm	d	12 03												13 03										
Darlington 7	d								12 46												13 48	13 48		
Northallerton	d	12 18							12 58					13 18							13 58	13 58		
Thirsk	d	12 28												13 28										
Scarborough	d										12 48													13 48
Seamer	d										12 53													13 53
Malton	d										13 11													14 11
York 8	a	12 47							13 21		13 38			13 47							14 22	14 23		14 38
	d	12 57							13 24		13 40			13 57							14 26	14 26		14 40
Wakefield Westgate	d						13 39												14 39					
Wakefield Kirkgate	d						13 45												14 45					
Hull	d			12 40		13 12											13 40	14 19						
Brough	d			12 52		13 24											13 52	14 31						
Howden	d					13 41												14 43						
Selby	d			13 11		13a54											14 11	14a53						
South Milford	d																							
Garforth	d	13 12												14 12										
Leeds 10	a	13 22		13 35					13 52		14 04			14 22			14 36				14 52	14 52		15 04
	d	13 25		13 40				13 43	13 55		14 08		14 13	14 25			14 40			14 43	14 55	14 55		15 08
Cottingley	d							13 48												14 48				
Morley	d							13 52					14 21							14 52				
Batley	d							13 57					14 26							14 57				
Dewsbury	a	13 36						14 00	14 06				14 29	14 36						15 00	15 06	15 06		
	d	13 36						14 01	14 06				14 29	14 36						15 01	15 06	15 06		
Ravensthorpe	d							14 04												15 04				
Mirfield	d						13 58	14 08					14 35						14 58	15 08				
Deighton	d						14 05	14 14											15 05	15 16				
Huddersfield	a	13 45		13 58			14 11	14 21	14 15		14 25			14 45			14 58		15 11	15 21	15 15	15 15		15 25
	d	13 46		13 59					14 16		14 26	14 30		14 46			14 59				15 16	15 16		15 26
Slaithwaite	d											14 37												
Marsden	d											14 43												
Greenfield	d											14 51												
Mossley (Gr Manchester)	d											14 55												
Stalybridge	a										14 43	15 00												15 43
	d									14 40	14 46	15 01											15 40	15 46
Ashton-under-Lyne	d									14 44		15 05											15 44	
Manchester Victoria	a									14 58		15 20	15 53										15 55	
Manchester Piccadilly 10	a	14 19		14 36					14 49		15 05			15 19			15 36				15 49	15 49		16 05
	d	14 24							14 54		15 07			15 24							15 54	15 54		16 07
Manchester Airport	a	14 42							15 12					15 42							16 12	16 12		
Manchester Oxford Road	a										15 09													16 09
Birchwood	a										15 25													16 25
Warrington Central	a										15 30													16 30
Liverpool South Parkway 7	a										15 47													16 47
Liverpool Lime Street 10	a										15 58													16 58

A from 21 May

B until 18 May

Newcastle, Middlesbrough, Scarborough, York, Hull, Leeds and Wakefield - Huddersfield - Manchester, Manchester Airport and Liverpool

Network Diagram - see first Page of Table 39

		NT	NT	TP ◇1 ⌶	NT	TP ◇1 ⌶	NT	NT	NT	TP ◇1 ⌶		NT A	TP ◇1 ⌶	NT	NT	TP FX ◇1 ⌶	TP FO ◇1 ⌶	TP FO ◇1 ⌶	TP FX ◇1 ⌶	NT		NT	NT	TP ◇1 ⌶	TP FO ◇1 B
Newcastle 8	d									14 18														15 15	
Chester-le-Street	d																							15 24	
Durham	d									14 31														15 31	
Middlesbrough	d			13 50	14 32											14 50									14 50
Thornaby	d			13 55	14a37											14 55									14 55
Yarm	d			14 03												15 03									15 03
Darlington 7	d									14 48														15 48	
Northallerton	d			14 18						14 59						15 18								15 59	15 18
Thirsk	d			14 28												15 28									15 28
Scarborough	d												14 48												
Seamer	d												14 53												
Malton	d												15 11												
York 8	a			14 47						15 22			15 38			15 47								16 21	15 47
	d			14 57						15 26			15 40			15 57	15 57							16 26	16 13
Wakefield Westgate	d							15 39														16 39			
Wakefield Kirkgate	d							15 45														16 45			
Hull	d					14 40	15 02											15 40	15 40	16 10					
Brough	d					14 52	15 14											15 52	15 52	16 22					
Howden	d						15 26													16 36					
Selby	d					15 11	15a36											16 11	16 11	16a46					
South Milford	d																								
Garforth	d			15 12												16 12		16 22							
Leeds 10	a			15 23		15 36				15 52			16 04			16 22	16 22	16 36	16 36					16 52	16 59
	d		15 13	15 25		15 40			15 43	15 55			16 08		16 13	16 25	16 25	16 40	16 40				16 43	16 55	
Cottingley	d								15 48						16 18								16 48		
Morley	d		15 21						15 52						16 22								16 52		
Batley	d		15 26						15 57						16 27								16 57		
Dewsbury	a		15 29	15 36					16 00	16 06					16 30	16 36	16 36						17 00	17 06	
	d		15 29	15 36					16 01	16 06					16 31	16 36	16 36						17 01	17 06	
Ravensthorpe	d								16 04						16 34								17 04		
Mirfield	d		15 35					15 58	16 08						16 38							16 58	17 08		
Deighton	d							16 05	16 14													17 05	17 14		
Huddersfield	a			15 45		15 58		16 11	16 21	16 15			16 25			16 45	16 45	16 58	16 58			17 11	17 21	17 15	
	d	15 30		15 46		15 59				16 16			16 26	16 30		16 46	16 46	16 59	16 59					17 16	
Slaithwaite	d	15 37												16 37											
Marsden	d	15 43												16 43											
Greenfield	d	15 51												16 51											
Mossley (Gr Manchester)	d	15 55												16 55											
Stalybridge	a	16 00											16 43	17 00				17 18	17 18						
	d	16 01										16 42	16 46	17 01				17 18	17 18						
Ashton-under-Lyne	d	16 05										16 46		17 05											
Manchester Victoria	a	16 21	16 52									16 58		17 24	17 53										
Manchester Piccadilly 10	a			16 19		16 36				16 49			17 05			17 25	17 21	17 36	17 36					17 49	
	d			16 24						16 54			17 07											17 54	
Manchester Airport	a			16 42						17 12														18 12	
Manchester Oxford Road	a												17 09												
Birchwood	a												17 25												
Warrington Central	a												17 30												
Liverpool South Parkway 7	a												17 47												
Liverpool Lime Street 10	a												18 01												

A until 19 October

B 1 ◇ to York

Newcastle, Middlesbrough, Scarborough, York, Hull, Leeds and Wakefield - Huddersfield - Manchester, Manchester Airport and Liverpool

Network Diagram - see first Page of Table 39

		NT	TP	GC	NT	NT	TP	TP	NT	TP	NT	NT	NT	TP	TP	TP	NT	NT	TP	TP	NT	NT	NT
							FO	FX															
			◇1 ✠	1			◇1 ✠	◇1 ✠		◇1 ✠				◇1 ✠	◇1	◇1 ✠			◇1 ✠	◇1 ✠			
Newcastle 8	d													16 15						17 02			
Chester-le-Street	d													16 24						17 11			
Durham	d													16 31						17 18			
Middlesbrough	d	15 32					15 50	15 50	16 32										16 50		17 39		
Thornaby	d	15a37					15 55	15 55	16a37										16 55		17a44		
Yarm	d						16 03	16 03											17 03				
Darlington 7	d													16 48						17 35			
Northallerton	d						16 18	16 18						16 59					17 18	17 46			
Thirsk	d						16 28	16 28											17 28				
Scarborough	d		15 48													16 48							
Seamer	d		15 53													16 53							
Malton	d		16 11													17 11							
York 8	a		16 38				16 47	16 47						17 23		17 38			17 47	18 09			
	d		16 40				16 57	16 57						17 26		17 40			17 57	18 12			
Wakefield Westgate	d											17 39										18 39	
Wakefield Kirkgate	d			17 08								17 45										18 45	
Hull	d									16 40					17 01								
Brough	d									16 52					17 13								
Howden	d																						
Selby	d									17 11					17 32								
South Milford	d																						
Garforth	d						17 12	17 12											18 12				
Leeds 10	a		17 04				17 22	17 22		17 36				17 52	17 58	18 04			18 22	18 37			
	d		17 08			17 13	17 26	17 26		17 40			17 43	17 55	18 02	18 08		18 13	18 25	18 40			18 43
Cottingley	d					17 18							17 48					18 18					18 48
Morley	d					17 22							17 52					18 22					18 52
Batley	d					17 27							17 57					18 27					18 57
Dewsbury	a					17 30	17 37	17 37					18 00	18 06	18 13			18 30	18 36				19 00
	d					17 31	17 37	17 37					18 01	18 06	18 13			18 31	18 36				19 01
Ravensthorpe	d					17 34							18 04					18 34					19 04
Mirfield	d			17a20		17 38						17 58	18 08					18 38				18 58	19 08
Deighton	d											18 05	18 13									19 05	19 13
Huddersfield	a		17 25				17 46	17 46		17 58		18 11	18 20	18 15	18 23	18 25			18 45	18 58		19 11	19 20
	d		17 26		17 30		17 46	17 46		17 59	18 04			18 16		18 26	18 30		18 46	18 59			
Slaithwaite	d				17 37						18 11						18 37						
Marsden	d				17 43						18 17						18 43						
Greenfield	d				17 51												18 51						
Mossley (Gtr Manchester)	d				17 55												18 55						
Stalybridge	a		17 43		18 00					18 18	18 30					18 43	19 01						
	d		17 46		18 01					18 18	18 31					18 46	19 01						
Ashton-under-Lyne	d				18 05						18 35						19 05						
Manchester Victoria	a				18 20	18 54					18 48						19 20	19 54					
Manchester Piccadilly 10	a		18 05				18 19	18 19		18 37				18 49		19 05			19 21	19 33			
	d		18 07					18 24						18 54		19 07				19 40			
Manchester Airport	a							18 42						19 13						19 59			
Manchester Oxford Road	a		18 09													19 09							
Birchwood	a		18 25													19 25							
Warrington Central	a		18 30													19 30							
Liverpool South Parkway 7	a		18 47													19 47							
Liverpool Lime Street 10	a		19 01													20 01							

Newcastle, Middlesbrough, Scarborough, York, Hull, Leeds and Wakefield - Huddersfield - Manchester, Manchester Airport and Liverpool

Network Diagram - see first Page of Table 39

		TP	TP	TP	NT	NT	TP	NT	NT	TP	TP	NT	NT	TP	TP	NT	NT	TP	NT	TP	NT	NT
				FO			FX			FO												
		◇1 ✠	◇1	◇1			◇1			◇1	◇1			◇1	◇1			◇1		◇1		
Newcastle 8	d																	18 52				
Chester-le-Street	d																	19 01				
Durham	d																	19 08				
Middlesbrough	d			17 50			17 50	18 32	18 45						18 50							
Thornaby	d			17 55			17 55	18a37	18 50						18 55							
Yarm	d			18 03			18 03								19 03							
Darlington 7	d								19a12									19 25				
Northallerton	d			18 18			18 18								19 18			19 36				
Thirsk	d			18 28			18 28								19 26							
Scarborough	d		17 48											18 48						19 48		
Seamer	d		17 53											18 53						19 53		
Malton	d		18 11											19 11						20 11		
York 8	a		18 38	18 47			18 47							19 38	19 50			20 07		20 38		
	d		18 40				19 08			19 08				19 40				20 10		20 40		
Wakefield Westgate	d												19 42						20 50			
Wakefield Kirkgate	d												19 45						20 56			
Hull	d	17 58									18 59	19 15										
Brough	d	18 10									19 11	19 28										
Howden	d											19 43										
Selby	d	18 29									19 30	19a53										
South Milford	d																					
Garforth	d						19 22			19 22												
Leeds 10	a	18 52	19 04				19 37			19 37	19 56			20 04				20 35		21 04		
	d	18 55	19 08			19 13	19 40			19 40				20 08			20 13	20 40		21 08		21 13
Cottingley	d					19 18											20 18					21 18
Morley	d					19 22											20 22					21 22
Batley	d					19 27											20 27					21 27
Dewsbury	a	19 06				19 30	19 51			19 51							20 30	20 51				21 30
	d	19 06				19 31	19 51			19 51							20 31	20 51				21 31
Ravensthorpe	d					19 34											20 34					21 34
Mirfield	d					19 38							19 59				20 37		21 09			21 38
Deighton	d					19 45							20 08				20 44		21 16			21 45
Huddersfield	a	19 15	19 25			19 49	19 59			19 59			20 13	20 25			20 51	20 59	21 21	21 25		21 49
	d	19 16	19 26		19 30		20 00			20 00				20 26		20 30		21 00		21 26	21 30	
Slaithwaite	d				19 37											20 37					21 37	
Marsden	d				19 43											20 43					21 43	
Greenfield	d				19 51											20 51					21 51	
Mossley (Gtr Manchester)	d				19 55											20 55					21 55	
Stalybridge	a		19 43		20 00									20 43		21 00				21 43	22 00	
	d		19 46		20 01									20 46		21 01				21 46	22 01	
Ashton-under-Lyne	d				20 05											21 05					22 05	
Manchester Victoria	a				20 20											21 20					22 20	
Manchester Piccadilly 10	a	19 57	20 05				20 33			20 33				21 05				21 33		22 05		
	d		20 07				20 40			20 40				21 07				21 40		22 07		
Manchester Airport	a						20 57			20 57								21 57				
Manchester Oxford Road	a		20 09											21 09						22 09		
Birchwood	a		20 25											21 25						22 25		
Warrington Central	a		20 30											21 30						22 30		
Liverpool South Parkway 7	a		20 47											21 47						22 47		
Liverpool Lime Street 10	a		21 01											22 01						23 01		

Table 39

Mondays to Fridays

Newcastle, Middlesbrough, Scarborough, York, Hull, Leeds and Wakefield - Huddersfield - Manchester, Manchester Airport and Liverpool

Network Diagram - see first Page of Table 39

		TP FX ◇■	NT	TP FO ◇■	TP FX ◇■	TP ◇■	TP FX ◇■	TP ◇■	NT	TP ◇■	NT	TP ◇■	TP ◇■	NT	NT	TP ◇■	NT	NT	NT	TP ◇■	NT
Newcastle ■	d																			21 55	22 21
Chester-le-Street	d																				22 31
Durham	d																			22 08	22 39
Middlesbrough	d	18 50	19 40			20 04				20 50	21 01		21 50								
Thornaby	d	18 55	19a45			20 09				20 55	21a06		21 55								
Yarm	d	19 03								21 03											
Darlington ■	d					20 35							22 19							22 25	22a59
Northallerton	d	19 18				20 46				21 18			22 30							22 37	
Thirsk	d	19 26				21 00							22 38								
Scarborough	d							20 48				22 03									
Seamer	d							20 53				22 08									
Malton	d							21 11				22 26									
York ■	a	19 50				21 24		21 38		21 43		22 55	22 56							23 01	
	d	21 14			21 14					21 46										23 07	
Wakefield Westgate	d								21 41									22 48			
Wakefield Kirkgate	d								21 50									22 53			
Hull	d			20 35			20 45									21 33					
Brough	d			20 47			20 57									21 45					
Howden	d																				
Selby	d			21 06			21 16									22 07					
South Milford	d			21 16			21 26									22 16					
Garforth	d																				
Leeds ■	a	21 37		21 35	21 37		21 44			22 07						22 35				23 33	
	d	21 40		21 40	21 40					22 10					22 18	22 40			23 13	23 35	
Cottingley	d														22 23				23 18		
Morley	d														22 27				23 22		
Batley	d														22 32				23 27		
Dewsbury	a	21 51		21 51	21 51										22 35	22 51			23 30	23 45	
	d	21 51		21 51	21 51										22 36	22 51			23 31	23 46	
Ravensthorpe	d														22 39				23 34		
Mirfield	d								22 03						22 44			23 06	23 38		
Deighton	d								22 10						22 49			23 14	23 45		
Huddersfield	a	21 59		21 59	21 59				22 14	22 27					22 54	22 59		23 21	23 49	23 54	
	d	22 00		22 00	22 00					22 28				22 34		23 00	23 05			23 55	
Slaithwaite	d													22 41			23 12				
Marsden	d													22 47			23 18				
Greenfield	d													22 55			23 26				
Mossley (Gr Manchester)	d													22 59			23 30				
Stalybridge	a									22 45				23 04			23 35				
	d									22 46				23 05			23 36				
Ashton-under-Lyne	d													23 09			23 40				
Manchester Victoria	a													23 24			23 53				
Manchester Piccadilly ■	a	22 33		22 33	22 33					23 05						23 37				00 53	
	d	22 40		22 40	22 40															00 54	
Manchester Airport	a	22 57		22 57	22 57															01 10	
Manchester Oxford Road	a																				
Birchwood	a																				
Warrington Central	a																				
Liverpool South Parkway ■	a																				
Liverpool Lime Street ■	a																				

Table 39

Saturdays

Newcastle, Middlesbrough, Scarborough, York, Hull, Leeds and Wakefield - Huddersfield - Manchester, Manchester Airport and Liverpool

Network Diagram - see first Page of Table 39

		TP ◇■	TP ◇■	TP ◇■	TP ◇■	TP ◇■	TP ◇■	TP ◇■	TP ◇■ ⌶	NT	NT	TP ◇■	NT	TP ◇■	NT	NT	NT	NT	NT	TP ◇■	NT A	NT	TP ◇■ ⌶	NT
Newcastle ■	d	21p55																					06 11	
Chester-le-Street	d																						06 21	
Durham	d	22p08																					06 28	
Middlesbrough	d											05 55			06 51									
Thornaby	d											06 00			06a56									
Yarm	d											06 08												
Darlington ■	d	22p25																					06 45	
Northallerton	d	22p37										06 23											06 56	
Thirsk	d											06 31											07 04	
Scarborough	d																			06 30				
Seamer	d																			06 35				
Malton	d																			06 53				
York ■	a	23p01										06 49								07 23			07 30	
	d	23p07	01 52	02 40	03 52	05 26	05 57	06 28				06 55								07 26			07 40	
Wakefield Westgate	d																	07 29						
Wakefield Kirkgate	d																	07 35						
Hull	d								06 00					06 37		07 07								
Brough	d								06 12					06 49		07 19								
Howden	d								06 26							07 35								
Selby	d								06 36					07 08		07a48								
South Milford	d																							
Garforth	d						06 12					07 10		07 24										
Leeds ■	a	23p33	02 18	03 06	04 34	05 52	06 22	06 52	07 00			07 20		07 35						07 52			08 04	
	d	23p35	02 20	03 10	04 45	05 55	06 25	06 55	07 08	07 13		07 23		07 38					07 43	07 55			08 08	
Cottingley	d																		07 48					
Morley	d									07 21									07 52					
Batley	d									07 26									07 57					
Dewsbury	a	23p45				06 06	06 36	07 06		07 29		07 34							08 00	08 06				
	d	23p46				06 06	06 36	07 06		07 29		07 34							08 01	08 06				
Ravensthorpe	d																		08 04					
Mirfield	d									07 35								07 50	08 08					
Deighton	d																	07 56	08 13					
Huddersfield	a	23p54	02 56	03 49	05 27	06 14	06 44	07 15	07 25			07 43		07 56				08 03	08 20	08 15			08 25	
	d	23p55	02 56	03 59	05 28	06 15	06 45	07 16	07 26		07 33	07 44		07 57			08 02			08 16			08 26	08 30
Slaithwaite	d										07 40						08 09							08 37
Marsden	d										07 55						08 15							08 43
Greenfield	d										08 03						08 23							08 51
Mossley (Gr Manchester)	d										08 07		←				08 27							08 55
Stalybridge	a					06 33	07 03	07 34	07 43		08 12	08 01	08 12	08 17			08 32						08 44	09 00
	d					06 33	07 04	07 34	07 46		08 13	08 02	08 13	08 17			08 33				08 40		08 46	09 01
Ashton-under-Lyne	d										→		08 17				08 37				08 44			09 05
Manchester Victoria	a									08 53			08 31				08 52				08 55	09d39		09 20
Manchester Piccadilly ■	a	00 53	03 44	04 52	06 02	06 50	07 19	07 51	08 05			08 19		08 36						08 51			09 05	
	d	00 54	03 44	04 54	06 08	06 54	07 23	07 54	08 07			08 24								08 54			09 07	
Manchester Airport	a	01 10	04 00	05 10	06 24	07 12	07 42	08 12				08 42								09 12				
Manchester Oxford Road	a								08 09														09 09	
Birchwood	a								08 25														09 25	
Warrington Central	a								08 30														09 30	
Liverpool South Parkway ■	a								08 47														09 47	
Liverpool Lime Street ■	a								08 58													10 41	09 58	

A until 20 October

Newcastle, Middlesbrough, Scarborough, York, Hull, Leeds and Wakefield - Huddersfield - Manchester, Manchester Airport and Liverpool

Network Diagram - see first Page of Table 39

		NT	TP	TP	NT	NT	TP	NT	NT	NT	NT	TP	NT	NT	TP	TP	NT	NT	NT	TP	NT	NT	TP	NT	NT
			◇1	◇1			◇1			A		◇1			◇1	◇1				◇1	A		◇1		
			🍴	🍴			🍴					🍴			🍴	🍴				🍴					
Newcastle 8	d														07 43										
Chester-le-Street	d																								
Durham	d														07 57										
Middlesbrough	d						07 12	07 32	08 32																
Thornaby	d						07 17	07a37	08a37																
Yarm	d						07 27																		
Darlington 7	d														08 14										
Northallerton	d						07 43								08 26										
Thirsk	d						07 51								08 34										
Scarborough	d		06 58									07 48											08 48		
Seamer	d		07 03									07 53											08 53		
Malton	d		07 21									08 11											09 11		
York 8	a		07 47				08 11					08 38			08 52								09 38		
	d		07 53				08 25					08 40			08 57					09 25			09 40		
Wakefield Westgate	d				08 29													09 29							
Wakefield Kirkgate	d				08 35													09 35							
Hull	d			07 37												08 40	09 02								
Brough	d			07 49												08 52	09 14								
Howden	d			08 01													09 28								
Selby	d			08 11												09 11	09a38								
South Milford	d																								
Garforth	d		08 12				08 40								09 12										
Leeds 10	a		08 22	08 36			08 52					09 04			09 22	09 36				09 53			10 04		
	d	08 13	08 25	08 40		08 43	08 55					09 08		09 13	09 25	09 40			09 43	09 55			10 08		10 13
Cottingley	d	08 18				08 48								09 18					09 48						
Morley	d	08 22				08 52								09 22					09 52						10 21
Batley	d	08 27				08 57								09 27					09 57						10 26
Dewsbury	a	08 30	08 36			09 00	09 06							09 30	09 36				10 00	10 06					10 29
	d	08 31	08 36			09 01	09 06							09 31	09 36				10 01	10 06					10 29
Ravensthorpe	d	08 34				09 04													10 04						
Mirfield	d	08 38			08 51	09 08								09 37				09 51	10 08						10 35
Deighton	d				08 58	09 17												09 58	10 14						
Huddersfield	a		08 44	08 58	09 05	09 21	09 15					09 25			09 45	09 58		10 05	10 21	10 15			10 25		
	d		08 45	08 59			09 16					09 26	09 30		09 46	09 59				10 16			10 26	10 30	
Slaithwaite	d												09 37											10 37	
Marsden	d												09 43											10 43	
Greenfield	d												09 51											10 51	
Mossley (Gr Manchester)	d												09 55											10 55	
Stalybridge	a											09 43	10 00										10 43	11 00	
	d									09 40		09 46	10 01								10 40		10 46	11 01	
Ashton-under-Lyne	d									09 44			10 05								10 44			11 05	
Manchester Victoria	a	09 53								09 55	10d39		10 20	10 53							10 55	11d39		11 20	11 53
Manchester Piccadilly 10	a		09 19	09 36			09 49					10 05			10 19	10 36				10 49			11 05		
	d		09 24				09 54					10 07			10 24					10 54			11 07		
Manchester Airport	a		09 42				10 12								10 42					11 12					
Manchester Oxford Road	a											10 09											11 09		
Birchwood	a											10 25											11 25		
Warrington Central	a											10 30											11 30		
Liverpool South Parkway 7	a											10 47											11 47		
Liverpool Lime Street 10	a										11 41	10 58										12 41	11 58		

A until 20 October

Newcastle, Middlesbrough, Scarborough, York, Hull, Leeds and Wakefield - Huddersfield - Manchester, Manchester Airport and Liverpool

Network Diagram - see first Page of Table 39

		TP	NT	TP	NT	NT	NT	TP	NT	NT	TP	NT		NT	TP	TP	NT	TP	NT	NT	NT	TP	NT	NT	TP
		◇1		◇1				◇1	A		◇1				◇1	◇1		◇1				◇1	A		◇1
		🍴						🍴			🍴				🍴	B						🍴			🍴
Newcastle 8	d							09 15														10 15			
Chester-le-Street	d							09 24														10 24			
Durham	d							09 31														10 31			
Middlesbrough	d	08 50	09 32												09 50		10 32								
Thornaby	d	08 55	09a37												09 55		10a37								
Yarm	d	09 03													10 03										
Darlington 7	d							09 48														10 48			
Northallerton	d	09 18						09 59							10 18							10 59			
Thirsk	d	09 28													10 28										
Scarborough	d										09 48					10 30									10 48
Seamer	d										09 53														10 53
Malton	d										10 11					10 51									11 11
York 8	a	09 47						10 21			10 38				10 47	11 18						11 22			11 38
	d	09 57						10 27			10 40				10 57							11 26			11 40
Wakefield Westgate	d					10 29														11 29					
Wakefield Kirkgate	d					10 35														11 35					
Hull	d			09 40	10 08													10 40	11 05						
Brough	d			09 52	10 20													10 52	11 17						
Howden	d				10 34														11 29						
Selby	d			10 11	10a47													11 11	11a40						
South Milford	d																								
Garforth	d	10 12													11 12										
Leeds 10	a	10 22		10 36				10 52			11 04				11 22			11 36				11 53			12 04
	d	10 25		10 40			10 43	10 55			11 08			11 13	11 25			11 40			11 43	11 55			12 08
Cottingley	d						10 48														11 48				
Morley	d						10 52							11 21							11 52				
Batley	d						10 57							11 26							11 57				
Dewsbury	a	10 36					11 00	11 06						11 29	11 36						12 00	12 06			
	d	10 36					11 01	11 06						11 29	11 36						12 01	12 06			
Ravensthorpe	d						11 04														12 04				
Mirfield	d					10 51	11 08							11 35						11 49	12 08				
Deighton	d					10 58	11 14													11 58	12 14				
Huddersfield	a	10 45		10 58		11 05	11 21	11 15			11 25				11 45			11 58		12 05	12 21	12 15			12 25
	d	10 46		10 59				11 16			11 26	11 30			11 46			11 59				12 16			12 26
Slaithwaite	d											11 37													
Marsden	d											11 43													
Greenfield	d											11 51													
Mossley (Gr Manchester)	d											11 55													
Stalybridge	a										11 43	12 00													12 43
	d								11 40		11 46	12 01											12 40		12 46
Ashton-under-Lyne	d								11 44			12 05											12 44		
Manchester Victoria	a								11 55	12d39		12 20		12 53									12 55	13d39	
Manchester Piccadilly 10	a	11 19		11 36				11 49			12 05				12 19			12 36				12 49			13 05
	d	11 24						11 54			12 07				12 24							12 54			13 07
Manchester Airport	a	11 42						12 12							12 42							13 12			
Manchester Oxford Road	a										12 09														13 09
Birchwood	a										12 25														13 25
Warrington Central	a										12 30														13 30
Liverpool South Parkway 7	a										12 47														13 47
Liverpool Lime Street 10	a									13 43	12 58													14 41	13 58

A until 20 October

B from 30 June until 8 September

Newcastle, Middlesbrough, Scarborough, York, Hull, Leeds and Wakefield - Huddersfield - Manchester, Manchester Airport and Liverpool

Network Diagram - see first Page of Table 39

		NT	NT	TP	NT	TP	NT	NT	GC	NT	TP	NT	NT	TP	NT	NT	TP	NT	TP	NT	NT	NT	TP	NT	NT
				◇1		◇1					◇1			◇1			◇1		◇1				◇1		
												A												A	
				⊼		⊼					⊼						⊼		⊼				⊼		
Newcastle ■	d										11 15												12 17		
Chester-le-Street	d										11 24														
Durham	d										11 31												12 29		
Middlesbrough	d			10 50	11 32												11 50	12 32							
Thornaby	d			10 55	11a36												11 55	12a37							
Yarm	d			11 03													12 03								
Darlington ■	d										11 48												12 46		
Northallerton	d			11 18							11 59						12 18						12 58		
Thirsk	d			11 28													12 28								
Scarborough	d													11 48											
Seamer	d													11 53											
Malton	d													12 11											
York ■	a			11 47							12 21			12 38			12 47						13 21		
	d			11 57							12 26			12 40			12 57						13 24		
Wakefield Westgate	d							12 29													13 39				
Wakefield Kirkgate	d							12 35	12 43												13 45				
Hull	d					11 40	12 03												12 40	13 12					
Brough	d					11 52	12 15												12 52	13 24					
Howden	d						12 27													13 42					
Selby	d					12 11	12a37												13 11	13a54					
South Milford	d																								
Garforth	d			12 12													13 12								
Leeds ■	a			12 22		12 36					12 52			13 04			13 22		13 36				13 52		
	d		12 13	12 25		12 40				12 43	12 55			13 08		13 13	13 25		13 40			13 43	13 55		
Cottingley	d									12 48												13 48			
Morley	d		12 21							12 52						13 21						13 52			
Batley	d		12 26							12 57						13 26						13 57			
Dewsbury	a		12 29	12 36						13 00	13 06					13 29	13 36					14 00	14 06		
	d		12 29	12 36						13 01	13 06					13 29	13 36					14 01	14 06		
Ravensthorpe	d									13 04												14 04			
Mirfield	d		12 35					12 49	12a55	13 08						13 35					13 58	14 08			
Deighton	d							12 58		13 14											14 05	14 14			
Huddersfield	a			12 45		12 58		13 05		13 21	13 15			13 25			13 45		13 58		14 11	14 21	14 15		
	d	12 30		12 46		12 59					13 16			13 26	13 30		13 46		13 59				14 16		
Slaithwaite	d	12 37													13 37										
Marsden	d	12 43													13 43										
Greenfield	d	12 51													13 51										
Mossley (Gtr Manchester)	d	12 55													13 55										
Stalybridge	a	13 00												13 43	14 00										
	d	13 01										13 40		13 46	14 01									14 40	
Ashton-under-Lyne	d	13 05										13 44			14 05									14 44	
Manchester Victoria	a	13 20	13 53									13 55	14d39		14 20	14 53								14 55	15d39
Manchester Piccadilly ■	a			13 19		13 36					13 49			14 05			14 19		14 36				14 49		
	d			13 24							13 54			14 07			14 24						14 54		
Manchester Airport	a			13 42							14 12						14 42						15 12		
Manchester Oxford Road	a													14 09											
Birchwood	a													14 25											
Warrington Central	a													14 30											
Liverpool South Parkway ■	a													14 47											
Liverpool Lime Street ■	a												15 41	14 58											16 41

A until 20 October

Newcastle, Middlesbrough, Scarborough, York, Hull, Leeds and Wakefield - Huddersfield - Manchester, Manchester Airport and Liverpool

Network Diagram - see first Page of Table 39

		TP	NT	NT	TP	NT	TP	NT	NT	NT	TP	NT	NT	TP		NT	NT	TP	NT	TP	NT	NT	NT	TP	
		◇1			◇1		◇1				◇1			◇1				◇1		◇1				◇1	
												A													
		⊼			⊼						⊼			⊼				⊼						⊼	
Newcastle ■	d										13 15													14 18	
Chester-le-Street	d										13 24														
Durham	d										13 31													14 31	
Middlesbrough	d				12 50	13 32												13 50	14 32						
Thornaby	d				12 55	13a37												13 55	14a37						
Yarm	d				13 03													14 03							
Darlington ■	d										13 48													14 48	
Northallerton	d				13 18						13 58							14 18						14 59	
Thirsk	d				13 28													14 28							
Scarborough	d	12 48												13 48											
Seamer	d	12 53												13 53											
Malton	d	13 11												14 11											
York ■	a	13 38			13 47						14 22			14 38				14 47						15 22	
	d	13 40			13 57						14 27			14 40				14 57						15 26	
Wakefield Westgate	d								14 39													15 29			
Wakefield Kirkgate	d								14 45													15 35			
Hull	d						13 40	14 19												14 40	15 02				
Brough	d						13 52	14 31												14 52	15 14				
Howden	d							14 43													15 26				
Selby	d						14 11	14a53												15 11	15a36				
South Milford	d																								
Garforth	d				14 12													15 12							
Leeds ■	a	14 04			14 22		14 35				14 52			15 04				15 22		15 36				15 53	
	d	14 08		14 13	14 25		14 37			14 43	14 55			15 08			15 13	15 25		15 40			15 43	15 55	
Cottingley	d									14 48													15 48		
Morley	d			14 21						14 52							15 21						15 52		
Batley	d			14 26						14 57							15 26						15 57		
Dewsbury	a			14 29	14 36					15 00	15 06						15 29	15 36					16 00	16 06	
	d			14 29	14 36					15 01	15 06						15 29	15 36					16 01	16 06	
Ravensthorpe	d									15 04													16 04		
Mirfield	d			14 35					14 58	15 08							15 35					15 51	16 08		
Deighton	d								15 05	15 14												15 58	16 15		
Huddersfield	a	14 25			14 45		14 55		15 11	15 21	15 15			15 25				15 45		15 58		16 05	16 21	16 15	
	d	14 26	14 30		14 46		14 56				15 16			15 26		15 30		15 46		15 59				16 16	
Slaithwaite	d		14 37													15 37									
Marsden	d		14 43													15 43									
Greenfield	d		14 51													15 51									
Mossley (Gtr Manchester)	d		14 55													15 55									
Stalybridge	a	14 43	15 00											15 43		16 00									
	d	14 46	15 01									15 40		15 46		16 01									
Ashton-under-Lyne	d		15 05									15 44				16 05									
Manchester Victoria	a		15 20	15 53								15 55	16d39			16 20	16 53								
Manchester Piccadilly ■	a	15 05			15 19		15 36				15 49			16 05				16 19		16 36				16 49	
	d	15 07			15 24						15 54			16 07				16 24						16 54	
Manchester Airport	a				15 42						16 12							16 42						17 12	
Manchester Oxford Road	a	15 09												16 09											
Birchwood	a	15 25												16 25											
Warrington Central	a	15 30												16 30											
Liverpool South Parkway ■	a	15 47												16 47											
Liverpool Lime Street ■	a	15 58											17 41	16 58											

A until 20 October

Newcastle, Middlesbrough, Scarborough, York, Hull, Leeds and Wakefield - Huddersfield - Manchester, Manchester Airport and Liverpool

Network Diagram - see first Page of Table 39

		NT	TP	NT	NT	TP	NT	TP	NT	NT	NT	NT	TP	NT	NT	TP	NT	NT	TP	NT	TP	NT	GC	NT
			◇1			◇1		◇1					◇1	A		◇1			◇1		◇1			
			✠			✠		✠					✠			✠			✠					
Newcastle 8 ⇌	d												15 15											
Chester-le-Street	d												15 24											
Durham	d												15 31											
Middlesbrough	d					14 50	15 32												15 50	16 32				
Thornaby	d					14 55	15a37												15 55	16a37				
Yarm	d					15 03													16 03					
Darlington 7	d												15 48											
Northallerton	d					15 18							15 59						16 18					
Thirsk	d					15 28													16 28					
Scarborough	d		14 48													15 48								
Seamer	d		14 53													15 53								
Malton	d		15 11													16 11								
York 8	a		15 38			15 47							16 21			16 38			16 47					
	d		15 40			15 57							16 26			16 40			16 57					
Wakefield Westgate	d										16 29											17 29		
Wakefield Kirkgate	d										16 35											17 35	17 45	
Hull	d							15 40	16 10												16 40			
Brough	d							15 52	16 22												16 52			
Howden	d								16 36															
Selby	d							16 11	16a46												17 11			
South Milford	d																							
Garforth	d					16 12													17 12					
Leeds 10	a		16 04			16 22		16 36					16 52			17 04			17 22		17 36			
	d		16 08		16 13	16 25		16 40				16 43	16 55			17 08		17 13	17 26		17 40			17 43
Cottingley	d				16 18							16 48						17 18						17 48
Morley	d				16 22							16 52						17 22						17 52
Batley	d				16 27							16 57						17 27						17 57
Dewsbury	a				16 30	16 36						17 00	17 06					17 30	17 37					18 00
	d				16 31	16 36						17 01	17 06					17 31	17 37					18 01
Ravensthorpe	d				16 34							17 04						17 34						18 04
Mirfield	d				16 38						16 51	17 08						17 38				17 51	17a57	18 08
Deighton	d										16 58	17 14										17 58		18 13
Huddersfield	a		16 25			16 45		16 58			17 05	17 21	17 15			17 25			17 46		17 58	18 05		18 21
	d		16 26	16 30		16 46		16 59		17 04			17 16			17 26	17 30		17 46		17 59			
Slaithwaite	d			16 37						17 11							17 37							
Marsden	d			16 43						17a17							17 43							
Greenfield	d			16 51													17 51							
Mossley (Gr Manchester)	d			16 55													17 55							
Stalybridge	a		16 43	17 00				17 18								17 43	18 00				18 18			
	d	16 40	16 46	17 01				17 18						17 40		17 46	18 01				18 18			
Ashton-under-Lyne	d	16 44		17 05										17 44			18 05							
Manchester Victoria ⇌	a	16 55		17 20	17 53									17 55	18d39		18 20	18 54						
Manchester Piccadilly 10 ⇌	a		17 05			17 21		17 36					17 49			18 05			18 19		18 37			
	d		17 07										17 54			18 07			18 24					
Manchester Airport ✈	a												18 12						18 42					
Manchester Oxford Road	a		17 09													18 09								
Birchwood	a		17 25													18 25								
Warrington Central	a		17 30													18 30								
Liverpool South Parkway 7 ✈	a		17 47													18 47								
Liverpool Lime Street 10	a		18 01												19 41	19 01								

A until 20 October

Newcastle, Middlesbrough, Scarborough, York, Hull, Leeds and Wakefield - Huddersfield - Manchester, Manchester Airport and Liverpool

Network Diagram - see first Page of Table 39

		TP	TP	TP	NT	NT	TP	TP	NT	NT	NT	TP	TP	NT	NT	TP	NT	TP	NT	TP	TP	NT	NT
		◇1	◇1	◇1			◇1	◇1				◇1	◇1			◇1		◇1		◇1	◇1		
		✠																					
Newcastle 8 ⇌	d	16 15						17 02															
Chester-le-Street	d	16 24						17 11															
Durham	d	16 31						17 18															
Middlesbrough	d						16 50		17 39							17 50	18 32				18 50	19 40	
Thornaby	d						16 55		17a44							17 55	18a37				18 55	19a45	
Yarm	d						17 03									18 03					19 03		
Darlington 7	d	16 48						17 35															
Northallerton	d	16 59					17 18	17 46								18 18					19 18		
Thirsk	d						17 28									18 28					19 26		
Scarborough	d			16 48									17 48							18 48			
Seamer	d			16 53									17 53							18 53			
Malton	d			17 11									18 11							19 11			
York 8	a	17 23		17 38			17 47	18 09					18 38			18 47				19 38	19 50		
	d	17 26		17 40			17 57	18 12					18 40			19 08				19 40			
Wakefield Westgate	d									18 29									19 41				
Wakefield Kirkgate	d									18 37									19 45				
Hull	d		17 01									17 58						18 59					
Brough	d		17 13									18 10						19 11					
Howden	d																						
Selby	d		17 32									18 29						19 30					
South Milford	d																						
Garforth	d						18 12									19 22							
Leeds 10	a	17 52	17 58	18 04			18 22	18 37				18 52	19 04			19 35		19 56		20 04			
	d	17 55		18 08		18 13	18 25	18 40			18 43	18 55	19 08		19 13	19 40				20 08			
Cottingley	d					18 18					18 48				19 18								
Morley	d					18 22					18 52				19 22								
Batley	d					18 27					18 57				19 27								
Dewsbury	a	18 06				18 30	18 36				19 00	19 06			19 30	19 51							
	d	18 06				18 31	18 36				19 01	19 06			19 31	19 51							
Ravensthorpe	d					18 34					19 04				19 34								
Mirfield	d					18 38				18 51	19 08				19 38				19 59				
Deighton	d									19 00	19 13				19 45				20 08				
Huddersfield	a	18 15		18 25			18 45	18 58		19 06	19 20	19 15	19 25		19 49	19 59			20 13	20 25			
	d	18 16		18 26	18 30		18 46	18 59				19 16	19 26	19 30		20 00				20 26			20 30
Slaithwaite	d				18 37									19 37									20 37
Marsden	d				18 43									19 43									20 43
Greenfield	d				18 51									19 51									20 51
Mossley (Gr Manchester)	d				18 55									19 55									20 55
Stalybridge	a			18 43	19 00								19 43	20 00						20 43			21 00
	d			18 46	19 01								19 46	20 01						20 46			21 01
Ashton-under-Lyne	d				19 05									20 05									21 05
Manchester Victoria ⇌	a				19 20	19 54								20 20									21 20
Manchester Piccadilly 10 ⇌	a	18 49		19 05			19 21	19 33				19 57	20 05			20 33				21 05			
	d	18 54		19 07				19 40					20 07			20 40				21 07			
Manchester Airport ✈	a	19 13						19 59								20 57							
Manchester Oxford Road	a			19 09									20 09							21 09			
Birchwood	a			19 25									20 25							21 25			
Warrington Central	a			19 30									20 30							21 30			
Liverpool South Parkway 7 ✈	a			19 47									20 47							21 47			
Liverpool Lime Street 10	a			20 01									21 01							22 01			

Table 39

Saturdays

Newcastle, Middlesbrough, Scarborough, York, Hull, Leeds and Wakefield - Huddersfield - Manchester, Manchester Airport and Liverpool

Network Diagram - see first Page of Table 39

		NT	TP ◇1	TP ◇1	NT	TP ◇1	NT	NT	NT	TP ◇1 A	TP ◇1 B	NT	NT	TP ◇1 A	TP ◇1 B	TP ◇1	NT	NT	TP ◇1	NT	NT	NT
Newcastle 8	d		18 52																			
Chester-le-Street	d		19 01																			
Durham	d		19 08																			
Middlesbrough	d									20 10	20 10	20 45		20 50	20 50							
Thornaby	d									20 15	20 15	20a50		20 55	20 55							
Yarm	d									20 23	20 23			21 03	21 03							
Darlington 7	d		19 25																			
Northallerton	d		19 36							20 39	20 39			21 18	21 18							
Thirsk	d									20 47	20 47											
Scarborough	d					19 48										22 03						
Seamer	d					19 53										22 08						
Malton	d					20 11										22 26						
York 8	a		20 07			20 38				21 06	21 06			21 44	21 44	22 55						
	d		20 10			20 40				21 13	21 14			21 45	21 46							
Wakefield Westgate	d				20 50								21 41								22 42	
Wakefield Kirkgate	d				20 56								21 50								22 47	
Hull	d			19 56			21 01												21 33			
Brough	d			20 08			21 13												21 45			
Howden	d						21 25															
Selby	d			20 27			21a35												22 07			
South Milford	d			20 36															22 16			
Garforth	d																					
Leeds 10	a		20 35	20 56		21 04				21 37	21 37			22 07	22 07				22 35			
	d	20 13	20 40			21 08			21 13	21 40	21 40			22 10	22 10			22 17	22 40			23 05
Cottingley	d	20 18							21 18									22 22				23 10
Morley	d	20 22							21 22									22 26				23 14
Batley	d	20 27							21 27									22 31				23 19
Dewsbury	a	20 30	20 51						21 30	21 51	21 51							22 34	22 51			23 22
	d	20 31	20 51						21 31	21 51	21 51							22 35	22 51			23 23
Ravensthorpe	d	20 34							21 34									22 38				23 26
Mirfield	d	20 38			21 09				21 38				22 03					22 42			23 00	23 30
Deighton	d	20 44			21 16				21 45				22 10					22 48			23 08	23 37
Huddersfield	a	20 48	20 59		21 21	21 25			21 49	21 59	21 59		22 14	22 27	22 27			22 53	22 59		23 15	23 41
	d	20 48	21 00			21 26		21 30		22 00	22 00			22 28	22 28		22 34		23 00	23 05		
Slaithwaite	d	20 55						21 37									22 41			23 12		
Marsden	d	21a02						21 43									22 47			23 18		
Greenfield	d							21 51									22 55			23 26		
Mossley (Gr Manchester)	d							21 55									22 59			23 30		
Stalybridge	a					21 43		22 01						22 45	22 45		23 04			23 35		
	d					21 46		22 01						22 46	22 46		23 05			23 36		
Ashton-under-Lyne	d							22 06									23 09			23 40		
Manchester Victoria	a							22 20									23 24			23 53		
Manchester Piccadilly 10	a		21 33			22 05				22 33	22 33			23 05	23 05				23 37			
	d		21 40			22 07				22 40	22 40											
Manchester Airport	a		21 57							22 57	22 57											
Manchester Oxford Road	a					22 09																
Birchwood	a					22 25																
Warrington Central	a					22 30																
Liverpool South Parkway 7	a					22 47																
Liverpool Lime Street 10	a					23 01																

A from 15 September

B until 8 September

Table 39

Saturdays

Newcastle, Middlesbrough, Scarborough, York, Hull, Leeds and Wakefield - Huddersfield - Manchester, Manchester Airport and Liverpool

Network Diagram - see first Page of Table 39

		TP ◇1 A	TP ◇1 B	NT
Newcastle 8	d			21 50
Chester-le-Street	d			22 00
Durham	d			22 08
Middlesbrough	d	21 50	21 50	
Thornaby	d	21 55	21 55	
Yarm	d			
Darlington 7	d	22 19	22 19	22a29
Northallerton	d	22 30	22 30	
Thirsk	d	22 38	22 38	
Scarborough	d			
Seamer	d			
Malton	d			
York 8	a	22 57	22 57	
	d	23 07	23 07	
Wakefield Westgate	d			
Wakefield Kirkgate	d			
Hull	d			
Brough	d			
Howden	d			
Selby	d			
South Milford	d			
Garforth	d			
Leeds 10	a	23 33	23 33	
	d	23 35	23 35	
Cottingley	d			
Morley	d			
Batley	d			
Dewsbury	a	23 46	23 46	
	d	23 46	23 46	
Ravensthorpe	d			
Mirfield	d			
Deighton	d			
Huddersfield	a	23 55	23 55	
	d	23 56	23 56	
Slaithwaite	d			
Marsden	d			
Greenfield	d			
Mossley (Gr Manchester)	d			
Stalybridge	a			
	d			
Ashton-under-Lyne	d			
Manchester Victoria	a			
Manchester Piccadilly 10	a	00 27	00 27	
	d		00 31	
Manchester Airport	a		00 46	
Manchester Oxford Road	a			
Birchwood	a			
Warrington Central	a			
Liverpool South Parkway 7	a			
Liverpool Lime Street 10	a			

A from 27 October

B until 20 October

Newcastle, Middlesbrough, Scarborough, York, Hull and Leeds - Huddersfield - Manchester, Manchester Airport and Liverpool

Network Diagram - see first Page of Table 39

		TP	TP	TP	TP	TP	TP	NT	TP	TP	NT	NT	NT	NT	TP	TP	TP	TP	NT	TP	NT	NT	TP
		◇1	◇1	bus	◇1	◇1	◇1		◇1	◇1		bus	bus		◇1	◇1	◇1	◇1	bus	◇1	bus		◇1
Newcastle 8	d															08 00							09 31
Chester-le-Street	d																						09 40
Durham	d															08 13							09 47
Middlesbrough	d	21p50									09 31												
Thornaby	d	21p55									09a36												
Yarm	d																						
Darlington 7	d	22p19														08 31							10 04
Northallerton	d	22p30														08 43							10 15
Thirsk	d	22p38														08 51							
Scarborough	d																			09 20			
Seamer	d																			09 25			
Malton	d																			09 43			
York 8	a	22p57														09 11				10 09			10 41
	d	23p07	02 00		04 20	05 25	06 45			08 10					08 30	09 15		09 45		10 15			10 45
Hull	d							08 54									09 00						
Brough	d							09 06									09 12						
Howden	d							09 18															
Selby	d							09a27									09 33						
South Milford	d																09 42						
Garforth	d																						
Leeds 10	a	23p33	02 26		04 46	05 51	07 11			08 37					08 53	09 38	10 00	10 08		10 38			11 08
	d	23p35	02 26		04 48	05 53	07 13			08 40				08 47	08 58	09 40		10 10		10 40		10 44	11 10
Cottingley	d													08 52								10 49	
Morley	d													08 56								10 53	
Batley	d													09 01								10 58	
Dewsbury	a	23p46				06 03	07 24			08 51				09 04	09 09	09 51				10 51		11 01	
	d	23p46				06 04	07 24			08 51				09 05	09 09	09 51				10 51		11 02	
Ravensthorpe	d													09 08								11 05	
Mirfield	d													09 12								11 09	
Deighton	d													09 19								11 15	
Huddersfield	a	23p55	02 45		05 05	06 12	07 33			09 00				09 23	09 18	10 02				11 02		11 20	
	d	23p56		02 55	05 09	06 16	07 36			09 09			09 10		09 24	10 03			10 10	11 04	11 10		
Slaithwaite	d												09 26						10 26		11 26		
Marsden	d												09 31						10 31		11 31		
Greenfield	d												09 51						10 51		11 51		
Mossley (Gr Manchester)	d												09 57						10 57		11 57		
Stalybridge	a												10 05						11 05		12 05		
	d											10 02	10 05						11 05		12 05		
Ashton-under-Lyne	d											10 12	10 15						11 15		12 15		
Manchester Victoria	a									10 04		10 26	10 38		10 10	10 53		11 04	11 38	11 53	12 38		12 04
	d								09 15	10 06					10 15	10 54		11 09		11 54			12 09
Manchester Piccadilly 10	a	00 27		03 55	06 17	07 26	08 36			10 25						11 08				12 08			
	d	00 31		03 55	06 18	07 30	08 38			10 27						11 10				12 10			
Manchester Airport	a	00 46		04 20	06 35	07 46	08 55			10 41						11 24				12 24			
Manchester Oxford Road	a																						
Newton-le-Willows	a								09 33						10 33			11 26					12 26
Birchwood	a																						
Warrington Central	a																						
Liverpool South Parkway 7	a																						
Liverpool Lime Street 10	a								09 56						10 57			11 56					12 56

Newcastle, Middlesbrough, Scarborough, York, Hull and Leeds - Huddersfield - Manchester, Manchester Airport and Liverpool

Network Diagram - see first Page of Table 39

		TP	NT	NT	TP	TP	TP	NT	NT	NT	TP	TP	TP	NT	TP	TP	TP	NT	NT	NT	NT	NT	TP
		◇1		bus	◇1	◇1	◇1		bus		◇1	◇1	◇1	bus	◇1	◇1	◇1				bus		◇1
Newcastle 8	d						11 08						12 10				13 04						
Chester-le-Street	d																13 13						
Durham	d						11 20						12 22				13 20						
Middlesbrough	d	10 15	11 31													12 45			13 31				
Thornaby	d	10 20	11a36													12 50			13a36				
Yarm	d	10 28														12 58							
Darlington 7	d						11 37						12 39				13 37						
Northallerton	d	10 43					11 49									13 13							
Thirsk	d	10 51														13 23							
Scarborough	d					10 51						11 51											
Seamer	d					10 56						11 56											
Malton	d					11 14						12 14											
York 8	a	11 10				11 40	12 12					12 40	13 11			13 43	14 10						
	d	11 15				11 45	12 15					12 45	13 15			13 45	14 15						14 33
Hull	d				10 58			11 46			12 00				12 58			13 29		14 23			
Brough	d				11 10			11 58			12 12				13 10			13 41		14 35			
Howden	d							12 10										13 53		14 47			
Selby	d				11 29			12a19			12 32				13 29			14a02		14a56			
South Milford	d				11 38										13 38								
Garforth	d																						
Leeds 10	a	11 38			11 56	12 09	12 38				12 56	13 08	13 37		13 56	14 08	14 38						14 56
	d	11 40			11 59	12 10	12 40			12 44	12 59	13 10	13 40		13 59	14 10	14 40					14 44	14 59
Cottingley	d									12 49												14 49	
Morley	d									12 53												14 53	
Batley	d									12 58												14 58	
Dewsbury	a	11 51			12 10		12 51			13 01	13 10		13 51		14 10		14 51					15 01	15 10
	d	11 51			12 10		12 51			13 02	13 10		13 51		14 10		14 51					15 02	15 10
Ravensthorpe	d									13 05												15 05	
Mirfield	d									13 09												15 09	
Deighton	d									13 20												15 20	
Huddersfield	a	12 02			12 24		13 02			13 24	13 20		14 02		14 20		15 02					15 24	15 20
	d	12 04		12 10			13 04		13 10				14 04	14 10			15 04				15 10		
Slaithwaite	d			12 26					13 26					14 26							15 26		
Marsden	d			12 31					13 31					14 31							15 31		
Greenfield	d			12 51					13 51					14 51							15 51		
Mossley (Gr Manchester)	d			12 57					13 57					14 57							15 56		
Stalybridge	a			13 05					14 05					15 05							16 05		
	d			13 05					14 05					15 05							16 05		
Ashton-under-Lyne	d			13 15					14 15					15 15							16 15		
Manchester Victoria	a	12 53		13 38		13 04	13 53		14 38			14 04	14 53	15 38		15 09	15 53				16 38		
	d	12 54				13 09	13 54					14 09	14 53			15 09	15 54						
Manchester Piccadilly 10	a	13 08					14 08						15 08				16 08						
	d	13 10					14 10						15 10				16 10						
Manchester Airport	a	13 24					14 24						15 24				16 25						
Manchester Oxford Road	a																						
Newton-le-Willows	a					13 26						14 26				15 26							
Birchwood	a																						
Warrington Central	a																						
Liverpool South Parkway 7	a																						
Liverpool Lime Street 10	a					13 56						14 56				15 56							

Table 39

Sundays until 24 June

Newcastle, Middlesbrough, Scarborough, York, Hull and Leeds - Huddersfield - Manchester, Manchester Airport and Liverpool

Network Diagram - see first Page of Table 39

		TP ◇1	TP ◇1	NT (bus)	TP ◇1	TP ◇1	TP ◇1	NT	NT	NT (bus)	NT	TP ◇1	TP ◇1	TP ◇1	NT (bus)	TP ◇1	TP ◇1	TP ◇1	NT	NT	NT (bus)	NT	TP ◇1
Newcastle 8	d		14 08				15 07							16 08				17 05					
Chester-le-Street	d						15 16											17 14					
Durham	d		14 20				15 23							16 20				17 21					
Middlesbrough	d					14 42		15 31									16 42			17 45			
Thornaby	d					14 47		15a36									16 47			17a50			
Yarm	d					14 55											16 55						
Darlington 7	d		14 37				15 40							16 37				17 38					
Northallerton	d		14 49			15 10								16 49			17 10	17 49					
Thirsk	d					15 18											17 18						
Scarborough	d	13 51											15 51										
Seamer	d	13 56											15 56										
Malton	d	14 14											16 14										
York 8	a	14 40	15 12			15 42	16 12						16 40	17 12			17 42	18 12					
	d	14 45	15 15			15 45	16 15					16 33	16 45	17 15			17 45	18 15					18 33
Hull	d				14 58				16 00							16 58			17 23				
Brough	d				15 10				16 12							17 10			17 35				
Howden	d								16 24										17 47				
Selby	d				15 29				16a33							17 29			17a56				
South Milford	d				15 38											17 38							
Garforth	d																						
Leeds 10	a	15 07	15 38		15 56	16 08	16 38					16 56	17 08	17 38		17 56	18 08	18 38					18 57
	d	15 10	15 40		15 59	16 10	16 40				16 44	16 59	17 10	17 40		17 59	18 10	18 40				18 44	18 59
Cottingley	d										16 49											18 49	
Morley	d										16 53											18 53	
Batley	d										16 58											18 58	
Dewsbury	a		15 51		16 10		16 51				17 01	17 10		17 51		18 10		18 51				19 01	19 10
	d		15 51		16 10		16 51				17 02	17 10		17 51		18 10		18 51				19 02	19 10
Ravensthorpe	d										17 05											19 05	
Mirfield	d										17 09											19 09	
Deighton	d										17 20											19 20	
Huddersfield	a		16 02		16 22		17 02				17 24	17 20		18 02		18 20		19 02				19 24	19 20
	d		16 04	16 10			17 04			17 10				18 04	18 10			19 04			19 10		
Slaithwaite	d			16 26						17 26					18 26						19 26		
Marsden	d			16 31						17 31					18 31						19 31		
Greenfield	d			16 51						17 51					18 51						19 51		
Mossley (Gr Manchester)	d			16 57						17 57					18 57						19 57		
Stalybridge	a			17 05						18 05					19 05						20 05		
	d			17 05						18 05					19 05						20 05		
Ashton-under-Lyne	d			17 15						18 15					19 15						20 15		
Manchester Victoria	a	16 05	16 53	17 38		17 04	17 53			18 38			18 04	18 54	19 38		19 09	19 53			20 38		
	d	16 09	16 54			17 09	17 54						18 09	18 54			19 09	19 54					
Manchester Piccadilly 10	a		17 08				18 08							19 10				20 08					
	d		17 10				18 10							19 10				20 10					
Manchester Airport	a		17 24				18 24							19 26				20 24					
Manchester Oxford Road	a																						
Newton-le-Willows	a	16 26				17 26							18 26				19 26						
Birchwood	a																						
Warrington Central	a																						
Liverpool South Parkway 7	a																						
Liverpool Lime Street 10	a	16 56				17 56							18 56				19 56						

Table 39

Sundays until 24 June

Newcastle, Middlesbrough, Scarborough, York, Hull and Leeds - Huddersfield - Manchester, Manchester Airport and Liverpool

Network Diagram - see first Page of Table 39

		TP ◇1	TP ◇1	NT (bus)	TP ◇1	TP ◇1	TP ◇1	NT	NT	NT (bus)	NT	TP ◇1	TP ◇1	TP ◇1	TP ◇1	NT	NT (bus)	NT (bus)	TP ◇1	NT	TP ◇1
Newcastle 8	d		17 52				19 10							20 08		21 06					
Chester-le-Street	d															21 15					
Durham	d		18 04				19 22							20 20		21 24					
Middlesbrough	d					18 45		19 31					20 06								22 06
Thornaby	d					18 50		19a36					20 11								22 11
Yarm	d					18 58							20 19								22 19
Darlington 7	d		18 21				19 39							20 37		21a44					
Northallerton	d		18 33			19 13							20 38	20 49							22 34
Thirsk	d					19 21							20 46								22 42
Scarborough	d	17 51										19 51							21 20		
Seamer	d	17 56										19 56							21 25		
Malton	d	18 14										20 14							21 43		
York 8	a	18 40	19 03			19 42	20 11					20 40	21 06	21 12					22 09		23 09
	d	18 45	19 15			19 45	20 15					20 45		21 15					22 12		23 12
Hull	d				18 58				20 29						21 00						
Brough	d				19 10				20 41						21 12						
Howden	d								20 53												
Selby	d				19 29				21a02						21 31						
South Milford	d				19 38										21 40						
Garforth	d																				
Leeds 10	a	19 08	19 38		19 56	20 08	20 38					21 08		21 38	21 59				22 36		23 38
	d	19 10	19 40		19 59	20 10	20 40				20 44	21 10		21 40					22 40	22 44	23 40
Cottingley	d										20 49									22 49	
Morley	d										20 53									22 53	
Batley	d										20 58									22 58	
Dewsbury	a		19 51		20 10		20 51				21 01			21 51					22 50	23 01	23 51
	d		19 51		20 10		20 51				21 02			21 51					22 51	23 02	23 51
Ravensthorpe	d										21 05									23 05	
Mirfield	d										21 09									23 09	
Deighton	d										21 15									23 16	
Huddersfield	a		20 02		20 20		21 02				21 19			22 02					23 02	23 20	00 02
	d		20 04	20 10			21 04			21 10	21 19			22 04				22 10	23 04		00 04
Slaithwaite	d			20 26						21 26	21 26							22 26			
Marsden	d			20 31						21 31	21a33							22 31			
Greenfield	d			20 51						21 51								22 51			
Mossley (Gr Manchester)	d			20 57						21 57								22 57			
Stalybridge	a			21 05						22 05								23 05			
	d			21 05						22 05							22 52	23 05			
Ashton-under-Lyne	d			21 15						22 15							23 02	23 15			
Manchester Victoria	a	20 04	20 53	21 38		21 04	21 52			22 38		22 04		22 52			23 26	23 38	23s53		00s53
	d	20 09	20 54			21 09	21 54					22 09		22 53							
Manchester Piccadilly 10	a		21 08				22 13							23 07					00 08		01 08
	d		21 09											23 09							01 10
Manchester Airport	a		21 24											23 24							01 24
Manchester Oxford Road	a																				
Newton-le-Willows	a	20 26				21 26						22 26									
Birchwood	a																				
Warrington Central	a																				
Liverpool South Parkway 7	a																				
Liverpool Lime Street 10	a	20 56				21 56						22 56									

1 July to 9 September

Newcastle, Middlesbrough, Scarborough, York, Hull and Leeds - Huddersfield - Manchester, Manchester Airport and Liverpool

Network Diagram - see first Page of Table 39

		TP ◇1	TP (bus)	TP ◇1	TP ◇1	TP ◇1	TP ◇1	TP ◇1	NT	TP ◇1	TP ◇1		NT	TP ◇1	NT	NT	TP ◇1	TP ◇1	NT	TP ◇1	TP ◇1	NT		TP ◇1	NT
Newcastle 8	d																08 00							09 31	
Chester-le-Street	d																							09 40	
Durham	d																08 13							09 47	
Middlesbrough	d	21p50													09 31										
Thornaby	d	21p55													09a36										
Yarm	d																								
Darlington 7	d	22p19															08 31							10 04	
Northallerton	d	22p30															08 43							10 15	
Thirsk	d	22p38															08 51								
Scarborough	d																				09 20				
Seamer	d																				09 25				
Malton	d																				09 43				
York 8	a	22p57															09 11				10 09			10 41	
	d	23p07		02 44	03 59	05 12	06 12	07 12			08 10			08 45			09 15				10 15			10 45	
Hull	d								08 54									09 00							
Brough	d								09 06									09 12							
Howden	d								09 18																
Selby	d								09a27									09 33							
South Milford	d																	09 42							
Garforth	d																								
Leeds 10	a	23p33		03 10	04 25	05 38	06 38	07 38			08 37			09 08			09 38	10 00			10 38			11 08	
	d	23p35		03 10	04 25	05 40	06 40	07 40			08 40		08 47	09 10			09 40	10 08			10 40	10 44		11 10	
Cottingley	d												08 52									10 49			
Morley	d												08 56									10 53			
Batley	d												09 01									10 58			
Dewsbury	a	23p46				05 51	06 51	07 51			08 51		09 04				09 51				10 51	11 01			
	d	23p46				05 51	06 51	07 51			08 51		09 05				09 51				10 51	11 02			
Ravensthorpe	d												09 08									11 05			
Mirfield	d												09 12									11 09			
Deighton	d												09 19									11 15			
Huddersfield	a	23p55		03 29	04 44	06 00	07 00	08 00			09 00		09 23	09 27			10 00	10 25			11 00	11 20		11 27	
	d	23p56	02 55	03 30	04 45	06 01	07 01	08 01			09 01			09 28		09 37	10 01	10 26	10 37		11 01			11 28	11 37
Slaithwaite	d															09 44			10 44						11 44
Marsden	d															09 50			10 50						11 50
Greenfield	d															09 58			10 58						11 58
Mossley (Gr Manchester)	d															10 02			11 02						12 02
Stalybridge	a						07 18	08 18			09 18			09 45		10 07		10 45	11 07					11 45	12 07
	d						07 19	08 19			09 19			09 46		10 08		10 46	11 08					11 46	12 08
Ashton-under-Lyne	d															10 12			11 12						12 12
Manchester Victoria	a															10 26			11 26						12 26
	d																								
Manchester Piccadilly 10	a	00 27	03 55	04 02	05 17	06 34	07 34	08 34			09 34			10 05			10 34	11 03			11 34			12 05	
	d	00 31	03 55	04 06	05 21	06 38	07 38	08 38		09 07	09 38			10 07			10 38			11 07	11 38			12 07	
Manchester Airport	a	00 46	04 20	04 23	05 38	06 55	07 55	08 55			09 55						10 55				11 55				
Manchester Oxford Road	a									09 09				10 09						11 09				12 09	
Newton-le-Willows	a																								
Birchwood	a									09 25				10 24						11 25				12 25	
Warrington Central	a									09 30				10 29						11 30				12 30	
Liverpool South Parkway 7	a									09 47				10 45						11 47				12 47	
Liverpool Lime Street 10	a									10 00				10 57						11 59				12 58	

Table 39

Sundays

1 July to 9 September

Newcastle, Middlesbrough, Scarborough, York, Hull and Leeds - Huddersfield - Manchester, Manchester Airport and Liverpool

Network Diagram - see first Page of Table 39

		TP ◇1	TP ◇1	TP ◇1	NT	NT	NT	TP ◇1	NT		TP ◇1	TP ◇1	NT	TP ◇1	TP ◇1	TP ◇1	NT	NT	NT	NT		TP ◇1	NT	TP ◇1	TP ◇1
Newcastle 8	d							11 08						12 10								13 04			
Chester-le-Street	d																					13 13			
Durham	d							11 20						12 22								13 20			
Middlesbrough	d	10 15			11 31											12 45		13 31							
Thornaby	d	10 20			11a36											12 50		13a36							
Yarm	d	10 28														12 58									
Darlington 7	d							11 37						12 39								13 37			
Northallerton	d	10 43						11 49								13 13									
Thirsk	d	10 51														13 23									
Scarborough	d			10 51								11 51													13 51
Seamer	d			10 56								11 56													13 56
Malton	d			11 14								12 14													14 14
York 8	a	11 10		11 40				12 12				12 40		13 11		13 43						14 10			14 40
	d	11 15		11 45				12 15				12 45		13 15		13 45						14 15		14 33	14 45
Hull	d		10 58			11 46					12 00				12 58		13 29		14 23						
Brough	d		11 10			11 58					12 12				13 10		13 41		14 35						
Howden	d					12 10											13 53		14 47						
Selby	d		11 29			12a19					12 32				13 29		14a02		14a56						
South Milford	d		11 38												13 38										
Garforth	d																								
Leeds 10	a	11 38	11 56	12 09				12 38			12 56	13 08		13 38	13 56	14 08						14 38		14 56	15 08
	d	11 40	11 59	12 10				12 40	12 44		12 59	13 10		13 40	13 59	14 10						14 40	14 44	14 59	15 10
Cottingley	d								12 49														14 49		
Morley	d								12 53														14 53		
Batley	d								12 58														14 58		
Dewsbury	a	11 51						12 51	13 01					13 51								14 51	15 01		
	d	11 51						12 51	13 02					13 51								14 51	15 02		
Ravensthorpe	d								13 05														15 05		
Mirfield	d								13 09														15 09		
Deighton	d								13 20														15 20		
Huddersfield	a	12 00	12 16	12 27				13 00	13 24		13 16	13 27		14 00	14 16	14 27						15 00	15 24	15 16	15 27
	d	12 01	12 17	12 28			12 37	13 01			13 17	13 28	13 37	14 01	14 17	14 28				14 37		15 01		15 17	15 28
Slaithwaite	d						12 44						13 44							14 44					
Marsden	d						12 50						13 50							14 50					
Greenfield	d						12 58						13 58							14 58					
Mossley (Gr Manchester)	d						13 02						14 02							15 02					
Stalybridge	a			12 45			13 07					13 45	14 07			14 45				15 07					15 45
	d			12 46			13 08					13 46	14 08			14 46				15 08					15 46
Ashton-under-Lyne	d						13 12						14 12							15 12					
Manchester Victoria	a						13 26						14 26							15 26					
	d																								
Manchester Piccadilly 10	a	12 34	12 54	13 05				13 34			13 54	14 05		14 34	14 54	15 05						15 34		15 54	16 05
	d	12 38		13 07				13 38				14 07		14 38		15 07						15 38			16 07
Manchester Airport	a	12 55						13 55						14 55								15 55			
Manchester Oxford Road	a			13 09								14 09				15 09									16 09
Newton-le-Willows	a																								
Birchwood	a			13 25								14 25				15 25									16 25
Warrington Central	a			13 30								14 30				15 30									16 30
Liverpool South Parkway 7	a			13 47								14 47				15 47									16 47
Liverpool Lime Street 10	a			13 58								14 58				15 58									16 58

Table 39

Sundays

1 July to 9 September

Newcastle, Middlesbrough, Scarborough, York, Hull and Leeds - Huddersfield - Manchester, Manchester Airport and Liverpool

Network Diagram - see first Page of Table 39

		NT	TP	TP	TP	NT	NT		NT	TP	NT	TP	TP	NT	TP	TP	TP	NT		NT	NT	TP	NT	TP	TP
			◇1	◇1	◇1					◇1		◇1	◇1		◇1	◇1	◇1					◇1		◇1	◇1
Newcastle 8	d		14 08							15 07					16 08							17 05			
Chester-le-Street	d									15 16												17 14			
Durham	d		14 20							15 23					16 20							17 21			
Middlesbrough	d				14 42	15 31											16 42			17 45					
Thornaby	d				14 47	15a36											16 47			17a50					
Yarm	d				14 55												16 55								
Darlington 7	d		14 37							15 40					16 37							17 38			
Northallerton	d		14 49		15 10										16 49		17 10					17 49			
Thirsk	d				15 18												17 18								
Scarborough	d												15 51												17 51
Seamer	d												15 56												17 56
Malton	d												16 14												18 14
York 8	a		15 12		15 42					16 12			16 40		17 12		17 42					18 12			18 40
	d		15 15		15 45					16 15		16 33	16 45		17 15		17 45					18 15		18 33	18 45
Hull	d			14 58			16 00									16 58		17 23							
Brough	d			15 10			16 12									17 10		17 35							
Howden	d						16 24											17 47							
Selby	d			15 29			16a33									17 29		17a56							
South Milford	d			15 38												17 38									
Garforth	d																								
Leeds 10	a		15 38	15 56	16 08					16 38		16 56	17 08		17 38	17 56	18 08					18 38		18 57	19 08
	d		15 40	15 59	16 10					16 40	16 44	16 59	17 10		17 40	17 59	18 10					18 40	18 44	18 59	19 10
Cottingley	d										16 49												18 49		
Morley	d										16 53												18 53		
Batley	d										16 58												18 58		
Dewsbury	a		15 51							16 51	17 01				17 51							18 51	19 01		
	d		15 51							16 51	17 02				17 51							18 51	19 02		
Ravensthorpe	d										17 05												19 05		
Mirfield	d										17 09												19 09		
Deighton	d										17 20												19 20		
Huddersfield	a		16 00	16 16	16 27					17 00	17 24	17 16	17 27		18 00	18 16	18 27					19 00	19 24	19 16	19 27
	d	15 37	16 01	16 17	16 28				16 37	17 01		17 17	17 28	17 37	18 01	18 17	18 28				18 37	19 01		19 17	19 28
Slaithwaite	d	15 44							16 44					17 44							18 44				
Marsden	d	15 50							16 50					17 50							18 50				
Greenfield	d	15 58							16 58					17 58							18 58				
Mossley (Gtr Manchester)	d	16 02							17 02					18 02							19 02				
Stalybridge	a	16 07			16 45				17 07				17 45	18 07			18 45				19 07				19 45
	d	16 08			16 46				17 08				17 46	18 08			18 46				19 08				19 46
Ashton-under-Lyne	d	16 12							17 12					18 12							19 12				
Manchester Victoria	a	16 26							17 26					18 26							19 26				
	d																								
Manchester Piccadilly 10	a		16 34	16 54	17 05					17 34		17 54	18 05		18 34	18 54	19 05					19 34		19 54	20 05
	d		16 38		17 07					17 38			18 07		18 38		19 07					19 38			20 07
Manchester Airport	a		16 55							17 55					18 55							19 55			
Manchester Oxford Road	a				17 09								18 09				19 09								20 09
Newton-le-Willows	a																								
Birchwood	a				17 25								18 25				19 25								20 25
Warrington Central	a				17 30								18 30				19 30								20 30
Liverpool South Parkway 7	a				17 47								18 47				19 47								20 47
Liverpool Lime Street 10	a				17 58								18 58				19 58								20 58

Table 39

Sundays

1 July to 9 September

Newcastle, Middlesbrough, Scarborough, York, Hull and Leeds - Huddersfield - Manchester, Manchester Airport and Liverpool

Network Diagram - see first Page of Table 39

		NT	TP	TP	TP		NT	NT	NT	TP	NT	TP	TP	NT	TP	TP		NT	TP	NT	TP				
			◇1	◇1	◇1					◇1		◇1	◇1		◇1	◇1			◇1		◇1				
Newcastle 8	d		17 52							19 10					20 08			21 06							
Chester-le-Street	d																	21 15							
Durham	d		18 04							19 22					20 20			21 24							
Middlesbrough	d				18 45		19 31						20 06								22 06				
Thornaby	d				18 50		19a36						20 11								22 11				
Yarm	d				18 58								20 19								22 19				
Darlington 7	d		18 21							19 39					20 37			21a44							
Northallerton	d		18 33		19 13								20 38		20 49						22 35				
Thirsk	d				19 21								20 46								22 43				
Scarborough	d											19 51							21 20						
Seamer	d											19 56							21 25						
Malton	d											20 14							21 43						
York 8	a		19 03		19 42					20 11		20 40	21 06		21 12				22 09		23 09				
	d		19 15		19 45					20 15		20 45			21 15				22 12		23 12				
Hull	d			18 58				20 29								21 00									
Brough	d			19 10				20 41								21 12									
Howden	d							20 53																	
Selby	d			19 29				21a02								21 31									
South Milford	d			19 38												21 40									
Garforth	d																								
Leeds 10	a		19 38	19 54	20 08					20 38		21 08			21 38	21 59			22 36		23 38				
	d		19 40	19 59	20 10					20 40	20 44	21 10			21 40				22 40	22 44	23 40				
Cottingley	d										20 49									22 49					
Morley	d										20 53									22 53					
Batley	d										20 58									22 58					
Dewsbury	a		19 51							20 50	21 01				21 51					23 01	23 51				
	d		19 51							20 51	21 02				21 51					23 02	23 51				
Ravensthorpe	d										21 05									23 05					
Mirfield	d										21 09									23 09					
Deighton	d										21 15									23 16					
Huddersfield	a		20 00	20 16	20 27					21 00	21 19	21 27			22 00				22 57	23 20	23 59				
	d	19 37	20 01	20 17	20 28				20 37	21 01	21 19	21 28		21 37	22 01				22 58		00 01				
Slaithwaite	d	19 44							20 44		21 26			21 44											
Marsden	d	19 50							20 50		21a33			21 50											
Greenfield	d	19 58							20 58					21 58											
Mossley (Gtr Manchester)	d	20 02							21 02					22 02											
Stalybridge	a	20 07			20 45				21 07	21 18				22 07	22 18				23 18						
	d	20 08			20 46				21 08	21 19				22 08	22 19				23 19						
Ashton-under-Lyne	d	20 12							21 12					22 12											
Manchester Victoria	a	20 26							21 26					22 26											
	d																								
Manchester Piccadilly 10	a		20 34	20 54	21 05					21 36		22 05			22 36				23 36		00 43				
	d		20 38		21 07							22 07			22 38						00 44				
Manchester Airport	a		20 55												22 55						00 57				
Manchester Oxford Road	a				21 09							22 09													
Newton-le-Willows	a																								
Birchwood	a				21 25							22 25													
Warrington Central	a				21 30							22 30													
Liverpool South Parkway 7	a				21 47							22 47													
Liverpool Lime Street 10	a				21 58							22 58													

Newcastle, Middlesbrough, Scarborough, York, Hull and Leeds - Huddersfield - Manchester, Manchester Airport and Liverpool

Network Diagram - see first Page of Table 39

		TP ◇1	TP ◇1	TP (bus)	TP ◇1	TP ◇1	TP ◇1	NT	TP ◇1	TP ◇1	NT		NT (bus)	NT (bus)	NT	TP ◇1	TP ◇1	TP ◇1	TP ◇1	NT (bus)	TP ◇1	NT (bus)		NT	TP ◇1
Newcastle 8	d																08 00								09 33
Chester-le-Street	d																								09 43
Durham	d																08 13								09 49
Middlesbrough	d	21p50									09 31														
Thornaby	d	21p55									09a36														
Yarm	d																								
Darlington 7	d	22p19															08 31								10 06
Northallerton	d	22p30															08 43								10 18
Thirsk	d	22p38															08 51								
Scarborough	d																				09 20				
Seamer	d																				09 25				
Malton	d																				09 43				
York 8	a	22p57															09 11				10 09				10 41
	d	23p07	02 00		04 20	05 25	06 45			08 10						08 30	09 15		09 45		10 15				10 45
Hull	d							08 54										09 00							
Brough	d							09 06										09 12							
Howden	d							09 18																	
Selby	d							09a27										09 33							
South Milford	d																	09 42							
Garforth	d																								
Leeds 10	a	23p33	02 26		04 46	05 51	07 11			08 37						08 53	09 38	10 00	10 08		10 38				11 08
	d	23p35	02 26		04 48	05 53	07 13			08 40					08 47	08 58	09 40		10 10		10 40			10 44	11 10
Cottingley	d														08 52									10 49	
Morley	d														08 56									10 53	
Batley	d														09 01									10 58	
Dewsbury	a	23p46				06 03	07 24			08 49					09 04	09 09	09 51				10 51			11 01	
	d	23p46				06 04	07 24			08 49					09 05	09 09	09 51				10 51			11 02	
Ravensthorpe	d														09 08									11 05	
Mirfield	d														09 12									11 09	
Deighton	d														09 19									11 15	
Huddersfield	a	23p55	02 45		05 05	06 12	07 33			09 00					09 23	09 18	10 02				11 02			11 20	
	d	23p56		02 55	05 09	06 16	07 36			09 09				09 10		09 24	10 03			10 10	11 04	11 10			
Slaithwaite	d													09 26						10 26		11 26			
Marsden	d													09 31						10 31		11 31			
Greenfield	d													09 51						10 51		11 51			
Mossley (Gr Manchester)	d													09 57						10 57		11 57			
Stalybridge	a													10 05						11 05		12 05			
	d												10 02	10 05						11 05		12 05			
Ashton-under-Lyne	d												10 12	10 15						11 15		12 15			
Manchester Victoria	a				05 55					10 03			10 26	10 38		10 10	10 53		11 04	11 38	11 53	12 38			12 04
	d				06 03				09 15	10 04						10 15	10 54		11 09		11 54				12 09
Manchester Piccadilly 10	a	00 27		03 55	06 17	07 15	08 36			10 25							11 08				12 08				
	d	00 31		03 55	06 18	07 17	08 39			10 28							11 10				12 10				
Manchester Airport	a	00 46		04 20	06 35	07 34	08 55			10 42							11 24				12 24				
Manchester Oxford Road	a																								
Newton-le-Willows	a								09 33							10 33			11 26						12 26
Birchwood	a																								
Warrington Central	a																								
Liverpool South Parkway 7	a																								
Liverpool Lime Street 10	a								09 56							10 57			11 56						12 56

Newcastle, Middlesbrough, Scarborough, York, Hull and Leeds - Huddersfield - Manchester, Manchester Airport and Liverpool

Network Diagram - see first Page of Table 39

		TP ◇1	NT	NT (bus)	TP ◇1	TP ◇1	TP ◇1	NT	NT (bus)		NT	TP ◇1	TP ◇1	TP ◇1	NT (bus)	TP ◇1	TP ◇1	TP ◇1	NT	NT		NT	NT (bus)	NT	TP ◇1
Newcastle 8	d						11 08							12 10				13 04							
Chester-le-Street	d																	13 13							
Durham	d						11 20							12 22				13 20							
Middlesbrough	d	10 15	11 31														12 45			13 31					
Thornaby	d	10 20	11a36														12 50			13a36					
Yarm	d	10 28															12 58								
Darlington 7	d						11 37							12 39				13 37							
Northallerton	d	10 43					11 49										13 13								
Thirsk	d	10 51															13 23								
Scarborough	d					10 51							11 51												
Seamer	d					10 56							11 56												
Malton	d					11 14							12 14												
York 8	a	11 10				11 40	12 12						12 40	13 11			13 43	14 10							
	d	11 15				11 45	12 15						12 45	13 15			13 45	14 16							14 33
Hull	d				10 58			11 46				12 00				12 58			13 29			14 23			
Brough	d				11 10			11 58				12 12				13 10			13 41			14 35			
Howden	d							12 10											13 53			14 47			
Selby	d				11 29			12a19				12 32				13 29			14a02			14a56			
South Milford	d				11 38											13 38									
Garforth	d																								
Leeds 10	a	11 38			11 56	12 09	12 38					12 56	13 08	13 37		13 56	14 08	14 39							14 56
	d	11 40			11 59	12 10	12 40				12 44	12 59	13 10	13 40		13 59	14 10	14 40						14 44	14 59
Cottingley	d										12 49													14 49	
Morley	d										12 53													14 53	
Batley	d										12 58													14 58	
Dewsbury	a	11 51			12 10		12 51				13 01	13 10		13 51		14 10		14 51						15 01	15 10
	d	11 51			12 10		12 51				13 02	13 10		13 51		14 10		14 51						15 02	15 10
Ravensthorpe	d										13 05													15 05	
Mirfield	d										13 09													15 09	
Deighton	d										13 20													15 20	
Huddersfield	a	12 02			12 24		13 02				13 24	13 20		14 02		14 20		15 02						15 24	15 20
	d	12 04		12 10			13 04		13 10					14 04	14 10			15 04					15 10		
Slaithwaite	d			12 26					13 26						14 26								15 26		
Marsden	d			12 31					13 31						14 31								15 31		
Greenfield	d			12 51					13 51						14 51								15 51		
Mossley (Gr Manchester)	d			12 57					13 57						14 57								15 56		
Stalybridge	a			13 05					14 05						15 05								16 05		
	d			13 05					14 05						15 05								16 05		
Ashton-under-Lyne	d			13 15					14 15						15 15								16 15		
Manchester Victoria	a	12 53		13 38		13 04	13 53		14 38				14 04	14 53	15 38		15 09	15 53					16 38		
	d	12 54				13 09	13 54						14 09	14 53			15 09	15 54							
Manchester Piccadilly 10	a	13 08					14 08							15 08				16 08							
	d	13 10					14 10							15 10				16 10							
Manchester Airport	a	13 24					14 24							15 24				16 24							
Manchester Oxford Road	a																								
Newton-le-Willows	a					13 26							14 26				15 26								
Birchwood	a																								
Warrington Central	a																								
Liverpool South Parkway 7	a																								
Liverpool Lime Street 10	a					13 56							14 56				15 56								

Table 39

Sundays

16 September to 21 October

Newcastle, Middlesbrough, Scarborough, York, Hull and Leeds - Huddersfield - Manchester, Manchester Airport and Liverpool

Network Diagram - see first Page of Table 39

		TP	TP	NT	TP	TP	TP		NT	NT	NT	NT	TP	TP	TP	NT	TP	TP		TP	NT	NT	NT	NT	TP
		◇1	◇1	bus	◇1	◇1	◇1				bus		◇1	◇1	◇1	bus	◇1	◇1		◇1			bus		◇1
Newcastle 8	d		14 08				15 07								16 08					17 05					
Chester-le-Street	d						15 16													17 14					
Durham	d		14 20				15 23								16 20					17 21					
Middlesbrough	d					14 42			15 31									16 42				17 45			
Thornaby	d					14 47			15a36									16 47				17a50			
Yarm	d					14 55												16 55							
Darlington 7	d		14 37				15 40								16 37					17 38					
Northallerton	d		14 49			15 10									16 49			17 10		17 49					
Thirsk	d					15 18												17 18							
Scarborough	d	13 51												15 51											
Seamer	d	13 56												15 56											
Malton	d	14 14												16 14											
York 8	a	14 40	15 12			15 42	16 12							16 40	17 12			17 42		18 12					
	d	14 45	15 15			15 45	16 15						16 33	16 45	17 15			17 45		18 15					18 33
Hull	d				14 58					16 00							16 58				17 23				
Brough	d				15 10					16 12							17 10				17 35				
Howden	d									16 24											17 47				
Selby	d				15 29					16a33							17 29				17a56				
South Milford	d				15 38												17 38								
Garforth	d																								
Leeds 10	a	15 07	15 38		15 56	16 08	16 38						16 56	17 08	17 38		17 56	18 08		18 38					18 57
	d	15 10	15 40		15 59	16 10	16 40					16 44	16 59	17 10	17 40		17 59	18 10		18 40				18 44	18 59
Cottingley	d											16 49												18 49	
Morley	d											16 53												18 53	
Batley	d											16 58												18 58	
Dewsbury	a		15 51		16 10		16 51					17 01	17 10		17 51		18 10			18 51				19 01	19 10
	d		15 51		16 10		16 51					17 02	17 10		17 51		18 10			18 51				19 02	19 10
Ravensthorpe	d											17 05												19 05	
Mirfield	d											17 09												19 09	
Brighouse	d											17 20												19 20	
Huddersfield	a		16 02		16 22		17 02					17 24	17 20		18 02		18 20			19 02				19 24	19 20
	d		16 04	16 10			17 04				17 10				18 04	18 10				19 04			19 10		
Slaithwaite	d			16 26							17 26					18 26							19 26		
Marsden	d			16 31							17 31					18 31							19 31		
Greenfield	d			16 51							17 51					18 51							19 51		
Mossley (Gr Manchester)	d			16 57							17 57					18 57							19 57		
Stalybridge	a			17 05							18 05					19 05							20 05		
	d			17 05							18 05					19 05							20 05		
Ashton-under-Lyne	d			17 15							18 15					19 15							20 15		
Manchester Victoria	a	16 05	16 53	17 38		17 04	17 53				18 38			18 04	18 54	19 38		19 09		19 53			20 38		
	d	16 09	16 54			17 09	17 54							18 09	18 54			19 09		19 54					
Manchester Piccadilly 10	a		17 08				18 08								19 10					20 08					
	d		17 10				18 10								19 10					20 10					
Manchester Airport	a		17 24				18 24								19 26					20 24					
Manchester Oxford Road	a																								
Newton-le-Willows	a	16 26				17 26								18 26				19 26							
Birchwood	a																								
Warrington Central	a																								
Liverpool South Parkway 7	a																								
Liverpool Lime Street 10	a	16 56				17 56								18 56				19 56							

Table 39

Sundays

16 September to 21 October

Newcastle, Middlesbrough, Scarborough, York, Hull and Leeds - Huddersfield - Manchester, Manchester Airport and Liverpool

Network Diagram - see first Page of Table 39

		TP	TP	NT	TP		TP	TP	NT	NT	NT	NT	TP	TP	TP	TP		NT	NT	NT	TP	NT	TP		
		◇1	◇1	bus	◇1		◇1	◇1			bus		◇1	◇1	◇1	◇1			bus	bus	◇1		◇1		
Newcastle 8	d		17 52					19 10							20 08			21 06							
Chester-le-Street	d																	21 15							
Durham	d		18 04					19 22							20 20			21 24							
Middlesbrough	d						18 45		19 31					20 06									22 06		
Thornaby	d						18 50		19a36					20 11									22 11		
Yarm	d						18 58							20 19									22 19		
Darlington 7	d		18 21					19 39							20 37			21a44							
Northallerton	d		18 33				19 13							20 38	20 49								22 34		
Thirsk	d						19 21							20 46									22 42		
Scarborough	d	17 51											19 51								21 20				
Seamer	d	17 56											19 56								21 25				
Malton	d	18 14											20 14								21 43				
York 8	a	18 40	19 03				19 42	20 11					20 40	21 06	21 12						22 09		23 09		
	d	18 45	19 15				19 45	20 15					20 45		21 15						22 12		23 12		
Hull	d				18 58					20 29						21 00									
Brough	d				19 10					20 41						21 12									
Howden	d									20 53															
Selby	d				19 29					21a02						21 31									
South Milford	d				19 38											21 40									
Garforth	d																								
Leeds 10	a	19 08	19 38		19 56		20 08	20 38					21 08		21 38	21 59					22 36		23 38		
	d	19 10	19 40		19 59		20 10	20 40				20 44	21 10		21 40						22 40	22 44	23 40		
Cottingley	d											20 49										22 49			
Morley	d											20 53										22 53			
Batley	d											20 58										22 58			
Dewsbury	a		19 51		20 10			20 51				21 01			21 51						22 50	23 01	23 51		
	d		19 51		20 10			20 51				21 02			21 51						22 51	23 02	23 51		
Ravensthorpe	d											21 05										23 05			
Mirfield	d											21 09										23 09			
Brighouse	d											21 15										23 16			
Huddersfield	a		20 02		20 20			21 02				21 19			22 02						23 02	23 20	00 02		
	d		20 04	20 10				21 04			21 10	21 19			22 04					22 10	23 04		00 04		
Slaithwaite	d			20 26							21 26	21 26								22 26					
Marsden	d			20 31							21 31	21a33								22 31					
Greenfield	d			20 51							21 51									22 51					
Mossley (Gr Manchester)	d			20 57							21 57									22 57					
Stalybridge	a			21 05							22 05									23 05					
	d			21 05							22 05								22 52	23 05					
Ashton-under-Lyne	d			21 15							22 15								23 02	23 15					
Manchester Victoria	a	20 04	20 53	21 38			21 04	21 52			22 38		22 04		22 53				23 26	23 38	23s53		00s53		
	d	20 09	20 54				21 09	21 54					22 09		22 54										
Manchester Piccadilly 10	a		21 08					22 14							23 08						00 08		01 08		
	d		21 09												23 10								01 10		
Manchester Airport	a		21 24												23 24								01 24		
Manchester Oxford Road	a																								
Newton-le-Willows	a	20 26					21 26						22 26												
Birchwood	a																								
Warrington Central	a																								
Liverpool South Parkway 7	a																								
Liverpool Lime Street 10	a	20 56					21 56						22 56												

Newcastle, Middlesbrough, Scarborough, York, Hull and Leeds - Huddersfield - Manchester, Manchester Airport and Liverpool

Network Diagram - see first Page of Table 39

		TP	TP	TP	TP	NT	TP	NT	NT	NT	TP			NT	TP	TP	TP	NT	TP	NT	NT	TP	TP		NT
		◇1	🚌	🚌	🚌		◇1	🚌		🚌	◇1			🚌	◇1	◇1	◇1	🚌	◇1	🚌		◇1	◇1		
Newcastle 8 ⇌	d														08 00							09 33			
Chester-le-Street	d																					09 43			
Durham	d														08 13							09 49			
Middlesbrough	d	21p50							09 31														10 15		11 31
Thornaby	d	21p55							09a36														10 20		11a36
Yarm	d																						10 28		
Darlington 7	d	22p19													08 31							10 06			
Northallerton	d	22p30													08 43							10 18	10 43		
Thirsk	d	22p38													08 51								10 51		
Scarborough	d																		09 20						
Seamer	d																		09 25						
Malton	d																		09 43						
York 8	a	22p57													09 11				10 09			10 41	11 10		
	d	23p07	03 30	04 55	05 55						08 30				09 15		09 45		10 15			10 45	11 15		
Hull	d					08 54										09 00									
Brough	d					09 06										09 12									
Howden	d					09 18																			
Selby	d					09a27										09 33									
South Milford	d															09 42									
Garforth	d																								
Leeds 10	a	23p33	04 20	05 45	06 45						08 53				09 38	10 00	10 08		10 38			11 08	11 38		
	d	23p35	04 20	05 45	06 45					08 45	08 58				09 40		10 10		10 40		10 44	11 10	11 40		
Cottingley	d									09 00											10 49				
Morley	d									09 10											10 53				
Batley	d									09 20				←							10 58				
Dewsbury	a	23p46		06 10	07 10					09 28	09 09			09 28	09 51				10 51		11 01		11 51		
	d	23p46		06 10	07 10					09 28	09 09			09 28	09 51				10 51		11 02		11 51		
Ravensthorpe	d									→				09 35							11 05				
Mirfield	d													09 40							11 09				
Deighton	d													09 50							11 15				
Huddersfield	a	23p55	04 55	06 35	07 35						09 18			09 59	10 02				11 02		11 20		12 02		
	d	23p56	04 55	06 35	07 35			09 10			09 24				10 03			10 10	11 04	11 10			12 04		
Slaithwaite	d							09 26										10 26		11 26					
Marsden	d							09 31										10 31		11 31					
Greenfield	d							09 51										10 51		11 51					
Mossley (Gr Manchester)	d							09 57										10 57		11 57					
Stalybridge	a			07 20	08 20			10 05										11 05		12 05					
	d			07 20	08 20			10 05										11 05		12 05					
Ashton-under-Lyne	d							10 15										11 15		12 15					
Manchester Victoria ⇌	a							10 38			10 10				10 53		11 04	11 38	11 53	12 38		12 04	12 53		
	d										10 18	10 15			10 54		11 09		11 54			12 09	12 54		
Manchester Piccadilly 10 ⇌	a	00 27	05 55	07 40	08 40						10 33				11 08				12 08				13 08		
	d		05 55	07 40	08 40		09 07				10 37				11 10				12 10				13 10		
Manchester Airport ✈	a		06 20	08 05	09 05						10 54				11 24				12 24				13 24		
Manchester Oxford Road	a						09 09																		
Newton-le-Willows	a											10 33					11 26					12 26			
Birchwood	a						09 24																		
Warrington Central	a						09 29																		
Liverpool South Parkway 7 ✈	a						09 46																		
Liverpool Lime Street 10	a						09 59					10 57					11 56					12 56			

Newcastle, Middlesbrough, Scarborough, York, Hull and Leeds - Huddersfield - Manchester, Manchester Airport and Liverpool

Network Diagram - see first Page of Table 39

		NT	TP	TP	TP	NT	NT	NT	TP	TP		TP	NT	TP	TP	TP	NT	NT	NT	NT	NT		TP	TP	TP
		🚌	◇1	◇1	◇1		🚌		◇1	◇1		◇1	🚌	◇1	◇1	◇1				🚌			◇1	◇1	◇1
Newcastle 8 ⇌	d				11 08							12 10				13 04									14 08
Chester-le-Street	d															13 13									
Durham	d				11 20							12 22				13 20									14 20
Middlesbrough	d														12 45			13 31							
Thornaby	d														12 50			13a36							
Yarm	d														12 58										
Darlington 7	d				11 37							12 39				13 37									14 37
Northallerton	d				11 49										13 13										14 49
Thirsk	d														13 23										
Scarborough	d			10 51						11 51														13 51	
Seamer	d			10 56						11 56														13 56	
Malton	d			11 14						12 14														14 14	
York 8	a			11 40	12 12					12 40		13 11			13 43	14 10								14 40	15 12
	d			11 45	12 15					12 45		13 15			13 45	14 16							14 33	14 45	15 15
Hull	d		10 58			11 46			12 00					12 58			13 29		14 23						
Brough	d		11 10			11 58			12 12					13 10			13 41		14 35						
Howden	d					12 10											13 53		14 47						
Selby	d		11 29			12a19			12 32					13 29			14a02		14a56						
South Milford	d		11 38											13 38											
Garforth	d																								
Leeds 10	a		11 56	12 09	12 38				12 56	13 08		13 37		13 56	14 08	14 39							14 56	15 07	15 38
	d		11 59	12 10	12 40			12 44	12 59	13 10		13 40		13 59	14 10	14 40					14 44		14 59	15 10	15 40
Cottingley	d							12 49													14 49				
Morley	d							12 53													14 53				
Batley	d							12 58													14 58				
Dewsbury	a		12 10		12 51			13 01	13 10			13 51		14 10		14 51					15 01		15 10		15 51
	d		12 10		12 51			13 02	13 10			13 51		14 10		14 51					15 02		15 10		15 51
Ravensthorpe	d							13 05													15 05				
Mirfield	d							13 09													15 09				
Deighton	d							13 20													15 20				
Huddersfield	a		12 24		13 02			13 24	13 20			14 02		14 20		15 02					15 24		15 20		16 02
	d	12 10			13 04		13 10					14 04	14 10			15 04				15 10					16 04
Slaithwaite	d	12 26					13 26						14 26							15 26					
Marsden	d	12 31					13 31						14 31							15 31					
Greenfield	d	12 51					13 51						14 51							15 51					
Mossley (Gr Manchester)	d	12 57					13 57						14 57							15 56					
Stalybridge	a	13 05					14 05						15 05							16 05					
	d	13 05					14 05						15 05							16 05					
Ashton-under-Lyne	d	13 15					14 15						15 15							16 15					
Manchester Victoria ⇌	a	13 38		13 04	13 53		14 38			14 04		14 53	15 38		15 09	15 53				16 38				16 05	16 53
	d			13 09	13 54					14 09		14 53			15 09	15 54								16 09	16 54
Manchester Piccadilly 10 ⇌	a				14 08							15 08				16 08									17 08
	d				14 10							15 10				16 10									17 10
Manchester Airport ✈	a				14 24							15 24				16 24									17 24
Manchester Oxford Road	a																								
Newton-le-Willows	a			13 26						14 26					15 26									16 26	
Birchwood	a																								
Warrington Central	a																								
Liverpool South Parkway 7 ✈	a																								
Liverpool Lime Street 10	a			13 56						14 56					15 56									16 56	

Newcastle, Middlesbrough, Scarborough, York, Hull and Leeds - Huddersfield - Manchester, Manchester Airport and Liverpool

Network Diagram - see first Page of Table 39

		NT	TP	TP	TP	NT	NT	NT		NT	TP	TP	TP	NT	TP	TP	TP	NT	NT		NT	NT	TP	TP	TP
			◇1	◇1	◇1						◇1	◇1	◇1		◇1	◇1	◇1						◇1	◇1	◇1
		🚌						🚌						🚌							🚌				
Newcastle 8	d				15 07								16 08				17 05								17 52
Chester-le-Street	d				15 16												17 14								
Durham	d				15 23								16 20				17 21								18 04
Middlesbrough	d			14 42		15 31										16 42			17 45						
Thornaby	d			14 47		15a36										16 47			17a50						
Yarm	d			14 55												16 55									
Darlington 7	d				15 40								16 37				17 38								18 21
Northallerton	d			15 10									16 49			17 10	17 49								18 33
Thirsk	d			15 18												17 18									
Scarborough	d											15 51												17 51	
Seamer	d											15 56												17 56	
Malton	d											16 14												18 14	
York 8	a			15 42	16 12							16 40	17 12			17 42	18 12							18 40	19 03
	d			15 45	16 15						16 33	16 45	17 15			17 45	18 15						18 33	18 45	19 15
Hull	d		14 58				16 00								16 58			17 23							
Brough	d		15 10				16 12								17 10			17 35							
Howden	d						16 24											17 47							
Selby	d		15 29				16a33								17 29			17a56							
South Milford	d		15 38												17 38										
Garforth	d																								
Leeds 10	a		15 56	16 08	16 38						16 56	17 08	17 38		17 56	18 08	18 38						18 57	19 08	19 38
	d		15 59	16 10	16 40					16 44	16 59	17 10	17 40		17 59	18 10	18 40					18 44	18 59	19 10	19 40
Cottingley	d									16 49												18 49			
Morley	d									16 53												18 53			
Batley	d									16 58												18 58			
Dewsbury	a		16 10		16 51					17 01	17 10		17 51		18 10		18 51					19 01	19 10		19 51
	d		16 10		16 51					17 02	17 10		17 51		18 10		18 51					19 02	19 10		19 51
Ravensthorpe	d									17 05												19 05			
Mirfield	d									17 09												19 09			
Deighton	d									17 20												19 20			
Huddersfield	a		16 22		17 02					17 24	17 20		18 02		18 20		19 02					19 24	19 20		20 02
	d	16 10			17 04			17 10					18 04	18 10			19 04				19 10				20 04
Slaithwaite	d	16 26						17 26						18 26							19 26				
Marsden	d	16 31						17 31						18 31							19 31				
Greenfield	d	16 51						17 51						18 51							19 51				
Mossley (Gr Manchester)	d	16 57						17 57						18 57							19 57				
Stalybridge	a	17 05						18 05						19 05							20 05				
	d	17 05						18 05						19 05							20 05				
Ashton-under-Lyne	d	17 15						18 15						19 15							20 15				
Manchester Victoria ⇌	a	17 38		17 04	17 53			18 38				18 04	18 54	19 38		19 09	19 53				20 38			20 04	20 53
	d			17 09	17 54							18 09	18 54			19 09	19 54							20 09	20 54
Manchester Piccadilly 10 ⇌	a				18 08								19 10				20 08								21 08
	d				18 10								19 10				20 10								21 09
Manchester Airport ✈	a				18 24								19 26				20 24								21 24
Manchester Oxford Road	a																								
Newton-le-Willows	a			17 26								18 26				19 26								20 26	
Birchwood	a																								
Warrington Central	a																								
Liverpool South Parkway 7 ✈	a																								
Liverpool Lime Street 10	a			17 56								18 56				19 56								20 56	

Newcastle, Middlesbrough, Scarborough, York, Hull and Leeds - Huddersfield - Manchester, Manchester Airport and Liverpool

Network Diagram - see first Page of Table 39

		NT	TP	TP	TP	NT		NT	NT	NT	TP	TP	TP	TP	NT	NT	TP		NT	TP					
			◇1	◇1	◇1						◇1	◇1	◇1	◇1			◇1			◇1					
		🚌							🚌							🚌									
Newcastle 8	d				19 10								20 08		21 06										
Chester-le-Street	d														21 15										
Durham	d				19 22								20 20		21 24										
Middlesbrough	d			18 45		19 31						20 06								22 06					
Thornaby	d			18 50		19a36						20 11								22 11					
Yarm	d			18 58								20 19								22 19					
Darlington 7	d				19 39								20 37		21a44										
Northallerton	d			19 13								20 38	20 49							22 34					
Thirsk	d			19 21								20 46								22 42					
Scarborough	d										19 51						21 20								
Seamer	d										19 56						21 25								
Malton	d										20 14						21 43								
York 8	a			19 42	20 11						20 40	21 06	21 12				22 09			23 09					
	d			19 45	20 15						20 45		21 15				22 12			23 12					
Hull	d		18 58					20 29						21 00											
Brough	d		19 10					20 41						21 12											
Howden	d							20 53																	
Selby	d		19 29					21a02						21 31											
South Milford	d		19 38											21 40											
Garforth	d																								
Leeds 10	a		19 56	20 08	20 38						21 08		21 38	21 59			22 36			23 38					
	d		19 59	20 10	20 40					20 44	21 10		21 40				22 40		22 44	23 40					
Cottingley	d									20 49									22 49						
Morley	d									20 53									22 53						
Batley	d									20 58									22 58						
Dewsbury	a		20 10		20 51					21 01			21 51				22 50		23 01	23 51					
	d		20 10		20 51					21 02			21 51				22 51		23 02	23 51					
Ravensthorpe	d									21 05									23 05						
Mirfield	d									21 09									23 09						
Deighton	d									21 15									23 16						
Huddersfield	a		20 20		21 02					21 19			22 02				23 02		23 20	00 02					
	d	20 10			21 04				21 10	21 19			22 04			22 10	23 04			00 04					
Slaithwaite	d	20 26							21 26	21 26						22 26									
Marsden	d	20 31							21 31	21a33						22 31									
Greenfield	d	20 51							21 51							22 51									
Mossley (Gr Manchester)	d	20 57							21 57							22 57									
Stalybridge	a	21 05							22 05							23 05									
	d	21 05							22 05							23 05									
Ashton-under-Lyne	d	21 15							22 15							23 15									
Manchester Victoria ⇌	a	21 38		21 04	21 52				22 38		22 04		22 53			23 38	23s53			00s53					
	d			21 09	21 54						22 09		22 54												
Manchester Piccadilly 10 ⇌	a				22 14								23 08				00 08			01 08					
	d												23 10							01 10					
Manchester Airport ✈	a												23 24							01 24					
Manchester Oxford Road	a																								
Newton-le-Willows	a			21 26							22 26														
Birchwood	a																								
Warrington Central	a																								
Liverpool South Parkway 7 ✈	a																								
Liverpool Lime Street 10	a			21 56							22 56														

Liverpool, Manchester Airport and Manchester - Huddersfield - Wakefield, Leeds, Hull, York, Scarborough, Middlesbrough and Newcastle

Network Diagram - see first Page of Table 39

Miles	Miles	Miles	Miles	Miles			TP	TP	TP	TP	TP	TP	TP	TP	TP		TP	TP	TP	TP	NT	TP	TP	TP	NT
							MO	MO	MX	MO	MX	MO	MX	MX	MO		MO	MO	MX	MO					
							◇1	◇1	◇1	◇1	◇1	◇1	◇1	◇1	◇1		◇1	◇1	◇1	◇1		◇1	◇1	◇1	
							A	B		A		B			C		D	A							
0	—	—	—	—	**Liverpool Lime Street** 10	d	20p22	20p22		21p52		21p52	22p30												
5½	—	—	—	—	Liverpool South Parkway 7 ✈	d	20p32			22p02			22p40												
18½	—	—	—	—	Warrington Central	d	20p45			22p15			22p53												
21¾	—	—	—	—	Birchwood	d	20p50			22p20			22p58												
34¼	—	—	—	—	Manchester Oxford Road	d	21p07			22p37			23p17												
—	—	—	—	—	**Manchester Airport** ✈	d			21p20		22p22			23p18	23p22		23p22	23p20	00 38	00 48			04 12		
34¾	—	—	—	—	**Manchester Piccadilly** 10	a	21p09		21p36	22p39	22p36		23p19	23p34	23p35		23p35	23p37	00 51	01 01			04 27		
—	—	—	—	—		d	21p11		21p42	22p42	22p42		23p21	23p38	23p39		23p40	23p42	00 53	01 03			04 30	05 39	
—	—	—	—	0	**Manchester Victoria**	d		21p05				22p38		23p56	23p55		23p55								
—	—	—	—	6½	Ashton-under-Lyne	d																			
42¼	—	—	—	7¾	**Stalybridge**	a	21p24		21p55	22p54	22p55		23p34											05 52	
—	—	—	—	—		d	21p24		21p55	22p54	22p55		23p34											05 52	
45	—	—	—	10½	Mossley (Gr Manchester)	d																			
47½	—	—	—	12¾	Greenfield	d																			
53¼	—	—	—	18¾	Marsden	d																			
55¾	—	—	—	21¼	Slaithwaite	d																			
60¼	—	—	—	25¾	**Huddersfield**	a	21p42		22p15	23p12	23p15	23p23	23p52	00 25	00 40		00 40	00 11					05 31	06 10	
—	—	—	—	—		d	21p43		22p16	23p12	23p16	23p26	23p53	00 26	00 43		00 43	00 12			05 32		05 38	06 11	
62¼	—	—	—	27¾	Deighton	d															05 36				
65¼	—	—	—	30¼	Mirfield	d															05 41				
66¼	—	—	—	—	Ravensthorpe	d																			
68¼	—	—	—	—	**Dewsbury**	a		21p58	22p25	23p22	23p25	23p35		00s35											
—	—	—	—	—		d		21p59	22p26	23p22	23p26	23p35													
69¾	—	—	—	—	Batley	d																			
73	—	—	—	—	Morley	d																			
74½	—	—	—	—	Cottingley	d																			
77½	0	—	0	—	**Leeds** 10	a	22p04	22p12	22p41	23p39	23p41	23p50	00 30	00 50	01 04		01 04	00 51	02 01	02 32			06 01	06 32	
—	—	—	—	—		d	22p12	22p12	22p42	23p42	23p42	23p53	00 32	00 54	01 06		01 06	00 54	02 08	02 34			06 04	06 35	06 38
84¾	7¼	—	7¼	—	Garforth	d																			06 50
—	12¾	—	—	—	South Milford	a																			
—	20¾	—	—	—	Selby	a																			
—	29½	—	—	—	Howden	a																			
—	41¼	—	—	—	Brough	a																			
—	51¾	—	—	—	**Hull**	a																			
—	—	—	—	—	Wakefield Kirkgate	a															05 57				
—	—	—	—	—	**Wakefield Westgate**	a															06 05				
103	—	0	25½	—	**York** 8	a	22p40	22p40	23p07	00 26	00 09	00 22	01 11	01 43	01 34		01 34	01 22	02 45	03 04			06 28	07 01	07 15
—	—	—	—	—		d	22p42	22p42	23p18													05 54	06 40	07 06	
—	—	—	46½	—	Malton	d																	07 04		
—	—	—	64¾	—	Seamer	a																	07 21		
—	—	—	67½	—	**Scarborough**	a																	07 30		
125½	—	22¼	—	—	Thirsk	a	23p06	23p05	23p31													06 10		07 22	
133	—	30½	—	—	Northallerton	a	23p16	23p15	23p49													06 18		07 30	
147	—	—	—	—	**Darlington** 7	a	23p28	23p28	00 01													06 29		07 41	
—	—	42¼	—	—	Yarm	d																			
—	—	47½	—	—	Thornaby	a																06 53			
—	—	50¾	—	—	**Middlesbrough**	a																07 03			
169	—	—	—	—	Durham	a	23p45	23p45	00 19															07 58	
174¾	—	—	—	—	Chester-le-Street	a																		08 04	
183	—	—	—	—	**Newcastle** 8	a	00 15	00 15	00 51															08 16	

A from 2 July until 10 September

B from 21 May until 25 June, MO from 17 September

C from 21 May until 25 June

D from 17 September

Liverpool, Manchester Airport and Manchester - Huddersfield - Wakefield, Leeds, Hull, York, Scarborough, Middlesbrough and Newcastle

Network Diagram - see first Page of Table 39

			NT	TP	NT	NT	NT	TP	NT	NT	NT		TP	TP	NT	NT	NT	NT	TP	TP	NT		NT	TP	NT
				◇1				◇1					◇1	◇1					◇1	◇1				◇1	
								⊼						⊼					⊼	⊼				⊼	
Liverpool Lime Street 10	d																		06 15						
Liverpool South Parkway 7 ✈	d																		06 25						
Warrington Central	d																		06 38						
Birchwood	d																		06 43						
Manchester Oxford Road	d																		07 07						
Manchester Airport ✈	d			05 37										06 23										07 05	
Manchester Piccadilly 10	a			05 51										06 39					07 09					07 22	
	d			05 57				06 21						06 54					07 11					07 27	
Manchester Victoria	d								05 51							06 17	06 55				06 43				06 58
Ashton-under-Lyne	d																07 05								
Stalybridge	a													07 07			07 10		07 23						
	d										06 41			07 07			07 11		07 23						
Mossley (Gr Manchester)	d										06 45						07 15								
Greenfield	d										06 49						07 19								
Marsden	d									06 48	06 58						07 28								
Slaithwaite	d									06 52	07 02						07 32								
Huddersfield	a			06 26				06 54		07 00	07 10			07 25			07 41		07 44					07 56	
	d			06 27		06 31	06 41	06 56		07 00				07 26				07 29	07 45				07 49	07 57	
Deighton	d					06 34	06 45			07 03													07 53		
Mirfield	d					06 39	06 50			07 08					07 20								07 58		08 06
Ravensthorpe	d					06 42				07 11					07 23										
Dewsbury	a			06 36		06 46		07 05		07 15					07 27				07 54					08 06	08 11
	d			06 37		06 46		07 06		07 15					07 35				07 55					08 07	08 12
Batley	d					06 49				07 18					07 38										08 15
Morley	d					06 55				07 24					07 44										08 21
Cottingley	d					06 59				07 28					07 47										08 24
Leeds 10	a			06 52		07 09		07 19	07 27	07 38				07 47	07 56	07 57		08 29	08 10		08 12			08 24	08 33
	d		06 48	06 55	06 58			07 23	07 29					07 50		08 00			08 12		08 15			08 28	
Garforth	d		06 58		07 10				07 41					08 00		08 12					08 27				
South Milford	a				07 20											08 22					08 38				
Selby	a		07 20		07 31			07 43								08 36					08 53				
Howden	a							07 52																	
Brough	a							08 04																	
Hull	a							08 20																	
Wakefield Kirkgate	a						07 03																08 13		
Wakefield Westgate	a						07 10																08 20		
York 8	a			07 22					08 06					08 21					08 35					08 52	
	d			07 25									07 32	08 23					08 40	08 42				08 58	
Malton	d			07 49															09 04						
Seamer	a			08 06															09 21						
Scarborough	a			08 15															09 30						
Thirsk	a												07 52	08 39											
Northallerton	a												08 00	08 49										09 18	
Darlington 7	a																			09 11				09 30	
Yarm	d												08 14	09 03											
Thornaby	a												08 24	09 11											
Middlesbrough	a												08 32	09 22											
Durham	a																			09 28				09 47	
Chester-le-Street	a																							09 53	
Newcastle 8	a																			09 44				10 07	

Table 39

Mondays to Fridays

Liverpool, Manchester Airport and Manchester - Huddersfield - Wakefield, Leeds, Hull, York, Scarborough, Middlesbrough and Newcastle

Network Diagram - see first Page of Table 39

		TP ◇1	NT	NT	NT	TP ◇1	NT	NT	TP ◇1	NT	TP ◇1	NT	NT A	NT	NT	TP ◇1	NT	TP ◇1	NT	NT	TP ◇1	NT	NT
Liverpool Lime Street	d								07 15					07 16							08 22		
Liverpool South Parkway	d								07 25												08 32		
Warrington Central	d								07 40												08 45		
Birchwood	d								07 45												08 50		
Manchester Oxford Road	d								08 06												09 07		
Manchester Airport	d					07 35					08 05							08 35					
Manchester Piccadilly	a					07 49			08 08		08 22							08 49			09 09		
	d	07 36				07 56			08 10		08 26					08 42		08 55			09 11		
Manchester Victoria	d		07 40							07 48		08 00	08 02	08 27								08 48	08 57
Ashton-under-Lyne	d		07 49										08 12	08 37									09 07
Stalybridge	a	07 49	07 54			08 09			08 26				08 18	08 41							09 26		09 13
	d	07 49	07 54			08 09			08 26					08 42							09 26		
Mossley (Gr Manchester)	d		07 59											08 46									
Greenfield	d		08 03											08 50									
Marsden	d		08 11											08 59									
Slaithwaite	d		08 16											09 03									
Huddersfield	a	08 09	08 24			08 28			08 44		08 56			09 13		09 15		09 26			09 44		
	d	08 10		08 13	08 21	08 30	08 33	08 37	08 45		08 57					09 16	09 23	09 27	09 31	09 35	09 45		
Deighton	d			08 16			08 36	08 40											09 34	09 38			
Mirfield	d			08 21			08 41	08 45				09 07							09 39	09 43			
Ravensthorpe	d			08 24			08 44												09 42				
Dewsbury	a	08 19		08 27		08 39	08 48				09 06	09 12						09 36	09 46				
	d	08 20		08 27		08 39	08 53				09 07	09 12						09 37	09 46				
Batley	d			08 30			08 56					09 15							09 49				
Morley	d			08 36			09 02					09 21							09 55				
Cottingley	d			08 39			09 06												09 59				
Leeds	a	08 36		08 52	09 27	08 54	09 17		09 09	09 12	09 22	09 32				09 36	10 27	09 52	10 07		10 09	10 12	
	d	08 38				08 57			09 12	09 15	09 28				09 33	09 38		09 57			10 12	10 15	
Garforth	d					09 05				09 27								10 05				10 27	
South Milford	a									09 38												10 38	
Selby	a	08 57								09 53					10 40	09 57						10 53	
Howden	a														10 50								
Brough	a														11 04	10 15							
Hull	a	09 31													11 23	10 35							
Wakefield Kirkgate	a							09 02												10 02			
Wakefield Westgate	a							09 08												10 10			
York	a					09 23			09 36		09 52							10 23			10 36		
	d					09 26			09 41		09 58							10 26			10 41		
Malton	d								10 04												11 04		
Seamer	a								10 21												11 21		
Scarborough	a								10 30												11 30		
Thirsk	a					09 45												10 45					
Northallerton	a					09 58					10 18							10 58					
Darlington	a										10 30												
Yarm	d					10 13												11 13					
Thornaby	a					10 21												11 21					
Middlesbrough	a					10 30												11 30					
Durham	a										10 47												
Chester-le-Street	a																						
Newcastle	a										11 05												

A until 19 October

Table 39

Mondays to Fridays

Liverpool, Manchester Airport and Manchester - Huddersfield - Wakefield, Leeds, Hull, York, Scarborough, Middlesbrough and Newcastle

Network Diagram - see first Page of Table 39

		TP ◇1	NT	NT	NT	TP ◇1	NT	NT	TP ◇1	NT	NT	TP ◇1	NT	TP ◇1	NT	NT	TP ◇1	NT	TP ◇1	NT	NT	TP ◇1
Liverpool Lime Street	d				08 44							09 22										10 22
Liverpool South Parkway	d											09 32										10 32
Warrington Central	d											09 45										10 45
Birchwood	d											09 50										10 50
Manchester Oxford Road	d											10 07										11 07
Manchester Airport	d	09 05							09 35					10 05					10 35			
Manchester Piccadilly	a	09 22							09 52			10 09		10 22					10 52			11 09
	d	09 27				09 42			09 57			10 11		10 27			10 42		10 57			11 11
Manchester Victoria	d		09 00	09 27	09 57								09 48		10 00	10 27						
Ashton-under-Lyne	d			09 37	10 07											10 37						
Stalybridge	a			09 42	10 13							10 26				10 42						11 26
	d			09 42								10 26				10 42						11 26
Mossley (Gr Manchester)	d			09 47												10 47						
Greenfield	d			09 51												10 51						
Marsden	d			09 59												10 59						
Slaithwaite	d			10 04												11 04						
Huddersfield	a	09 56		10 12		10 15			10 26			10 44		10 56		11 12	11 15		11 26			11 44
	d	09 57				10 16		10 23	10 27	10 31	10 35	10 45		10 57			11 16	11 23	11 27	11 31	11 35	11 45
Deighton	d									10 34	10 38									11 34	11 38	
Mirfield	d		10 07							10 39	10 43				11 07					11 39	11 43	
Ravensthorpe	d									10 42										11 42		
Dewsbury	a	10 06	10 12						10 36	10 46				11 06	11 12				11 36	11 46		
	d	10 07	10 12						10 37	10 46				11 07	11 12				11 37	11 46		
Batley	d		10 15							10 49					11 15					11 49		
Morley	d		10 21							10 55					11 21					11 55		
Cottingley	d									10 59										11 59		
Leeds	a	10 22	10 32			10 36		11 27	10 52	11 07		11 09	11 13	11 22	11 33		11 36	12 27	11 52	12 07		12 09
	d	10 28				10 38	10 41		10 57			11 12	11 15	11 28			11 38		11 57			12 12
Garforth	d						10 53		11 05				11 27						12 05			
South Milford	a												11 38									
Selby	a					10 57							11 54				11 57					
Howden	a																					
Brough	a					11 15											12 15					
Hull	a					11 35											12 36					
Wakefield Kirkgate	a										11 02										12 02	
Wakefield Westgate	a										11 08										12 08	
York	a	10 52					11 19		11 23			11 36		11 52					12 23			12 36
	d	10 58							11 26			11 41		11 58					12 26			12 41
Malton	d											12 04										13 04
Seamer	a											12 21										13 21
Scarborough	a											12 30										13 30
Thirsk	a								11 45										12 45			
Northallerton	a	11 18							11 58					12 18					12 58			
Darlington	a	11 30												12 30								
Yarm	d								12 13										13 13			
Thornaby	a								12 21										13 21			
Middlesbrough	a								12 30										13 30			
Durham	a	11 47												12 47								
Chester-le-Street	a	11 53																				
Newcastle	a	12 06												13 03								

Liverpool, Manchester Airport and Manchester - Huddersfield - Wakefield, Leeds, Hull, York, Scarborough, Middlesbrough and Newcastle

Network Diagram - see first Page of Table 39

		NT	TP ◇1	NT	NT	NT	TP ◇1	NT	NT	TP ◇1	NT	NT	TP ◇1	NT	TP ◇1	NT	NT	NT	TP ◇1	NT	TP ◇1	NT	NT
Liverpool Lime Street 10	d					10 46							11 22					11 46					
Liverpool South Parkway 7 ✈	d												11 32										
Warrington Central	d												11 45										
Birchwood	d												11 50										
Manchester Oxford Road	d												12 07										
Manchester Airport ✈	d		11 05							11 35					12 05						12 35		
Manchester Piccadilly 10	a		11 22							11 52			12 09		12 22						12 52		
	d		11 27				11 42			11 57			12 11		12 27				12 42		12 57		
Manchester Victoria	d	10 48		11 00	11 27	11 57								11 48		12 00	12 27	12 57					
Ashton-under-Lyne	d				11 37	12 07											12 37	13 07					
Stalybridge	a				11 42	12 13							12 26				12 42	13 13					
	d				11 42								12 26				12 42						
Mossley (Gr Manchester)	d				11 47												12 47						
Greenfield	d				11 51												12 51						
Marsden	d				11 59												12 59						
Slaithwaite	d				12 04												13 04						
Huddersfield	a		11 56		12 12		12 15			12 26			12 44		12 56		13 12		13 15		13 26		
	d		11 57				12 16		12 23	12 27	12 31	12 35	12 45		12 57				13 16	13 23	13 27	13 31	13 35
Deighton	d										12 34	12 38										13 34	13 38
Mirfield	d			12 07							12 39	12 43				13 07						13 39	13 43
Ravensthorpe	d										12 42											13 42	
Dewsbury	a		12 06	12 12						12 36	12 46				13 06	13 12					13 36	13 46	
	d		12 07	12 12						12 37	12 46				13 07	13 12					13 37	13 46	
Batley	d			12 15							12 49					13 15						13 49	
Morley	d			12 21							12 55					13 21						13 55	
Cottingley	d										12 59											13 59	
Leeds 10	a	12 12	12 22	12 31			12 36		13 27	12 52	13 07		13 09	13 12	13 22	13 32			13 36	14 27	13 51	14 07	
	d	12 15	12 28				12 38	12 41		12 57			13 12	13 15	13 28				13 38		13 57		
Garforth	d	12 27						12 53		13 05				13 27							14 05		
South Milford	a	12 38												13 38									
Selby	a	12 50					12 57							13 51					13 57				
Howden	a																						
Brough	a						13 15												14 15				
Hull	a						13 35												14 35				
Wakefield Kirkgate	a											13 02											14 02
Wakefield Westgate	a											13 08											14 08
York 8	a		12 52					13 19		13 23			13 36		13 52						14 23		
	d		12 58							13 29			13 41		13 58						14 26		
Malton	d												14 04										
Seamer	a												14 21										
Scarborough	a												14 30										
Thirsk	a									13 48											14 45		
Northallerton	a		13 18							13 58					14 18						14 58		
Darlington 7	a		13 30												14 30								
Yarm	d									14 13											15 13		
Thornaby	a									14 21											15 21		
Middlesbrough	a									14 30											15 30		
Durham	a		13 47												14 47								
Chester-le-Street	a		13 53																				
Newcastle 8	a		14 06												15 05								

Liverpool, Manchester Airport and Manchester - Huddersfield - Wakefield, Leeds, Hull, York, Scarborough, Middlesbrough and Newcastle

Network Diagram - see first Page of Table 39

		TP ◇1	NT	TP ◇1	NT	NT	NT	TP ◇1	NT	NT	TP ◇1	NT	NT	TP ◇1	NT	TP ◇1	NT	NT	NT	TP ◇1	NT	TP ◇1	NT
Liverpool Lime Street 10	d	12 22					12 46							13 22					13 46				
Liverpool South Parkway 7 ✈	d	12 32												13 32									
Warrington Central	d	12 45												13 45									
Birchwood	d	12 50												13 50									
Manchester Oxford Road	d	13 07												14 07									
Manchester Airport ✈	d			13 05							13 35					14 05						14 35	
Manchester Piccadilly 10	a	13 09		13 22							13 52			14 09		14 22						14 52	
	d	13 11		13 27				13 42			13 57			14 11		14 27				14 42		14 57	
Manchester Victoria	d		12 48		13 00	13 27	13 57								13 48		14 00	14 27	14 57				
Ashton-under-Lyne	d					13 37	14 07											14 37	15 07				
Stalybridge	a	13 26				13 42	14 13							14 26				14 42	15 13				
	d	13 26				13 42								14 26				14 42					
Mossley (Gr Manchester)	d					13 47												14 47					
Greenfield	d					13 51												14 51					
Marsden	d					13 59												14 59					
Slaithwaite	d					14 04												15 04					
Huddersfield	a	13 44		13 56		14 12		14 15			14 26			14 44		14 56		15 12		15 15		15 26	
	d	13 45		13 57				14 16		14 23	14 27	14 31	14 35	14 45		14 57				15 16	15 23	15 27	15 31
Deighton	d											14 34	14 38										15 34
Mirfield	d				14 07							14 39	14 43				15 07						15 39
Ravensthorpe	d											14 42											15 42
Dewsbury	a			14 06	14 12						14 36	14 46				15 06	15 12					15 36	15 46
	d			14 07	14 12						14 37	14 46				15 07	15 12					15 37	15 46
Batley	d				14 15							14 49					15 15						15 49
Morley	d				14 21							14 55					15 21						15 55
Cottingley	d											14 59											15 59
Leeds 10	a	14 09	14 13	14 22	14 32			14 36		15 27	14 52	15 07		15 09	15 12	15 22	15 32			15 36	16 27	15 52	16 07
	d	14 12	14 15	14 28				14 38	14 41		14 57			15 12	15 15	15 28				15 38		15 57	
Garforth	d		14 27						14 53		15 05				15 27							16 05	
South Milford	a		14 38												15 38								
Selby	a		14 51					14 57							15 53					15 57			
Howden	a																						
Brough	a							15 15												16 15			
Hull	a							15 35												16 35			
Wakefield Kirkgate	a												15 02										
Wakefield Westgate	a												15 08										
York 8	a	14 36		14 52					15 18		15 23			15 36		15 52						16 23	
	d	14 41		14 58							15 26			15 41								16 26	
Malton	d	15 04												16 04									
Seamer	a	15 21												16 21									
Scarborough	a	15 30												16 30									
Thirsk	a										15 45											16 45	
Northallerton	a			15 18							15 58											16 58	
Darlington 7	a			15 30																			
Yarm	d										16 13											17 13	
Thornaby	a										16 21											17 21	
Middlesbrough	a										16 30											17 30	
Durham	a			15 47																			
Chester-le-Street	a			15 53																			
Newcastle 8	a			16 09																			

Liverpool, Manchester Airport and Manchester - Huddersfield - Wakefield, Leeds, Hull, York, Scarborough, Middlesbrough and Newcastle

Network Diagram - see first Page of Table 39

		NT	TP	NT	TP	NT	NT	NT	TP	NT	NT	TP	NT	NT	TP	NT	TP	NT	NT	NT	TP	NT
			◇1 ⊼		◇1 ⊼				◇1 ⊼			◇1 ⊼			◇1 ⊼		◇1 ⊼				◇1 ⊼	
Liverpool Lime Street 10	d		14 22					14 46							15 22							
Liverpool South Parkway 7 ✈	d		14 32												15 32							
Warrington Central	d		14 45												15 45							
Birchwood	d		14 50												15 50							
Manchester Oxford Road	d		15 07												16 07							
Manchester Airport ✈	d				15 05							15 35					16 05					
Manchester Piccadilly 10	a		15 09		15 22							15 52			16 09		16 22					
	d		15 11		15 27				15 42			15 57			16 11		16 27				16 42	
Manchester Victoria	d			14 48		15 00	15 27	15 57								15 48		16 00	16 17	16 27		
Ashton-under-Lyne	d						15 37	16 07											16 27	16 37		
Stalybridge	a		15 26				15 42	16 13							16 26				16 31	16 42		
	d		15 26				15 42								16 26					16 42		
Mossley (Gr Manchester)	d						15 47													16 47		
Greenfield	d						15 51													16 51		
Marsden	d						15 59													16 59		
Slaithwaite	d						16 04													17 04		
Huddersfield	a		15 44		15 56		16 12		16 15			16 26			16 44		16 56			17 12	17 15	
	d	15 35	15 45		15 57				16 16		16 23	16 27	16 31	16 35	16 45		16 57				17 16	
Deighton	d	15 38											16 34	16 38								
Mirfield	d	15 43				16 07							16 39	16 43				17 07				
Ravensthorpe	d												16 42									
Dewsbury	a				16 06	16 12						16 36	16 46				17 06	17 12				
	d				16 07	16 12						16 37	16 46				17 07	17 12				
Batley	d					16 15							16 49					17 15				
Morley	d					16 21							16 55					17 21				
Cottingley	d												16 59									
Leeds 10	a		16 09	16 12	16 22	16 32			16 36		17 27	16 52	17 07		17 09	17 12	17 22	17 31			17 36	
	d		16 12	16 15	16 28				16 38	16 57		16 57			17 12	17 15	17 24				17 38	17 41
Garforth	d			16 27								17 05				17 28	17 34					17 53
South Milford	a			16 39												17 39						
Selby	a			16 54					17 00							17 51					17 59	
Howden	a																				18 08	
Brough	a								17 18												18 20	
Hull	a								17 37												18 39	
Wakefield Kirkgate	a	16 02												17 02								
Wakefield Westgate	a	16 08								17 08				17 12								
York 8	a		16 36		16 52							17 21			17 37		17 55					18 18
	d		16 41		16 56							17 24			17 41		18 00					
Malton	d		17 04									17 47					18 24					
Seamer	a		17 21									18 04					18 41					
Scarborough	a		17 30									18 15					18 50					
Thirsk	a				17 14										18 00							
Northallerton	a				17 22										18 08							
Darlington 7	a				17 33																	
Yarm	d														18 23							
Thornaby	a														18 32							
Middlesbrough	a														18 42							
Durham	a				17 50																	
Chester-le-Street	a				17 56																	
Newcastle 8	a				18 09																	

Liverpool, Manchester Airport and Manchester - Huddersfield - Wakefield, Leeds, Hull, York, Scarborough, Middlesbrough and Newcastle

Network Diagram - see first Page of Table 39

		NT	NT	TP	NT	NT	NT	TP	NT	NT	TP FX	TP FO	NT	NT	TP	NT	TP FO	TP	NT	NT	NT	TP	NT
				◇1 ⊼				◇1 ⊼			◇1 ⊼	◇1 ⊼			◇1 ⊼		◇1 ⊼	◇1 ⊼				◇1 ⊼	
Liverpool Lime Street 10	d				15 46			16 22											16 46			17 22	
Liverpool South Parkway 7 ✈	d							16 32														17 32	
Warrington Central	d							16 45														17 45	
Birchwood	d							16 50														17 50	
Manchester Oxford Road	d							17 07														18 07	
Manchester Airport ✈	d			16 35							17 05							17 35					
Manchester Piccadilly 10	a			16 52				17 09			17 22							17 52				18 09	
	d			16 56				17 11			17 26	17 26			17 42			17 56				18 11	
Manchester Victoria	d				16 57				16 48	17 15			17 00	17 27					17 57				17 43
Ashton-under-Lyne	d				17 07					17 24				17 38					18 07				
Stalybridge	a			17 08	17 12			17 26		17 29	17 38	17 38		17 43				18 08	18 12			18 26	
	d			17 08	17 12			17 26		17 29	17 38	17 38		17 43				18 08	18 12			18 26	
Mossley (Gr Manchester)	d				17 17					17 34				17 48					18 17				
Greenfield	d				17 21					17 38				17 52					18 21				
Marsden	d				17 29									18 01					18 29				
Slaithwaite	d				17 34														18 34				
Huddersfield	a			17 26	17 42			17 44		17 54	17 56	17 57		18 12	18 15			18 26	18 43			18 44	
	d		17 23	17 27		17 31	17 35	17 45			17 57	17 57			18 16	18 23		18 27		18 36	18 40	18 45	
Deighton	d					17 34	17 38													18 39	18 43		
Mirfield	d					17 39	17 43						18 07							18 44	18 48		
Ravensthorpe	d					17 42														18 47			
Dewsbury	a			17 36		17 46					18 06	18 07	18 13					18 36		18 51			
	d			17 37		17 46					18 07	18 07	18 13					18 37		18 56			
Batley	d					17 49							18 16							18 59			
Morley	d					17 55							18 22							19 05			
Cottingley	d					17 59														19 09			
Leeds 10	a		18 29	17 52		18 06		18 09	18 12		18 22	18 22	18 34		18 36	19 28		18 52		19 19		19 09	19 13
	d	17 46		17 57				18 12	18 15		18 28	18 28			18 38			18 57				19 12	19 15
Garforth	d	17 57		18 05					18 27									19 05					19 27
South Milford	a	18 09							18 38						18 51								
Selby	a	18 21							18 49						19 00								
Howden	a																						
Brough	a														19 18								
Hull	a														19 38								
Wakefield Kirkgate	a						18 02														19 02		
Wakefield Westgate	a						18 08														19 08		
York 8	a			18 23				18 36			18 53	18 53						19 23				19 36	19 53
	d			18 25				18 41			18 57						18 57	19 26				19 41	
Malton	d							19 04														20 04	
Seamer	a							19 21														20 21	
Scarborough	a							19 30														20 30	
Thirsk	a										19 13						19 13	19 45					
Northallerton	a			18 45							19 24						19 24	19 57					
Darlington 7	a			18 57																			
Yarm	d										19 38						19 38	20 11					
Thornaby	a										19 46						19 46	20 21					
Middlesbrough	a										19 56						19 56	20 31					
Durham	a			19 14																			
Chester-le-Street	a			19 20																			
Newcastle 8	a			19 34																			

Liverpool, Manchester Airport and Manchester - Huddersfield - Wakefield, Leeds, Hull, York, Scarborough, Middlesbrough and Newcastle

Network Diagram - see first Page of Table 39

		TP	NT		NT	TP FO	TP FX	NT	NT	TP	NT	NT	TP		NT	TP	NT	NT	NT	NT	TP FO	TP FX	TP		NT
		◇1 🍴				◇1 🍴	◇1 🍴			◇1			◇1			◇1					◇1	◇1	◇1		
Liverpool Lime Street 10	d												18 22								19 22	19 22			
Liverpool South Parkway 7 ✈	d												18 32								19 32	19 32			
Warrington Central	d												18 45								19 45	19 45			
Birchwood	d												18 50								19 50	19 50			
Manchester Oxford Road	d												19 07								20 07	20 07			
Manchester Airport ✈	d									18 35						19 20							20 20		
Manchester Piccadilly 10	a									18 52			19 09			19 36					20 09	20 09	20 36		
	d	18 27				18 42	18 42			18 57			19 11			19 42					20 11	20 11	20 42		
Manchester Victoria	d		18 00		18 27										19 00		19 27								20 27
Ashton-under-Lyne	d				18 37												19 37								20 37
Stalybridge	a				18 42								19 26				19 42				20 26	20 26			20 42
	d				18 42								19 26				19 42				20 26	20 26			20 42
Mossley (Gr Manchester)	d				18 47												19 47								20 47
Greenfield	d				18 51												19 51								20 51
Marsden	d				18 59												19 59								20 59
Slaithwaite	d				19 04												20 04								21 04
Huddersfield	a	18 56			19 12	19 15	19 15			19 26			19 44			20 15	20 12				20 44	20 44	21 15		21 12
	d	18 57				19 16	19 16		19 23	19 27	19 31	19 35	19 45			20 16		20 25	20 31	20 35	20 45	20 45	21 16		
Deighton	d										19 34	19 38							20 34	20 38					
Mirfield	d		19 08								19 39	19 43			20 07				20 39	20 43					
Ravensthorpe	d										19 42								20 42						
Dewsbury	a	19 06	19 13							19 36	19 46				20 12	20 25			20 46				21 25		
	d	19 07	19 13							19 37	19 46				20 12	20 26			20 46				21 26		
Batley	d		19 16								19 49				20 15				20 49						
Morley	d		19 22								19 55				20 21				20 55						
Cottingley	d										19 59								20 59						
Leeds 10	a	19 23	19 33			19 36	19 36		20 29	19 52	20 07		20 09		20 34	20 41		21 25	21 07		21 09	21 09	21 41		
	d	19 28				19 38	19 38	19 41		19 57			20 12			20 45					21 12	21 12	21 42		
Garforth	d							19 53		20 05															
South Milford	a					19 51	19 50														21 24	21 23			
Selby	a					20 00	20 00														21 34	21 34			
Howden	a					20 09	20 09														21 43	21 42			
Brough	a					20 21	20 21														21 55	21 54			
Hull	a					20 43	20 43														22 12	22 13			
Wakefield Kirkgate	a											20 02								21 02					
Wakefield Westgate	a											20 09								21 09					
York 8	a	19 53						20 22		20 23			20 36			21 09							22 06		
	d									20 29			20 41			21 14							22 09		
Malton	d												21 04										22 32		
Seamer	a												21 21										22 49		
Scarborough	a												21 30										22 58		
Thirsk	a									20 48						21 30									
Northallerton	a									20 58						21 38									
Darlington 7	a															21 51									
Yarm	d									21 13															
Thornaby	a									21 21															
Middlesbrough	a									21 30															
Durham	a															22 08									
Chester-le-Street	a															22 14									
Newcastle 8	a															22 28									

Liverpool, Manchester Airport and Manchester - Huddersfield - Wakefield, Leeds, Hull, York, Scarborough, Middlesbrough and Newcastle

Network Diagram - see first Page of Table 39

		NT	NT	NT	NT	TP	NT	TP	TP		NT	NT FX	NT FO	NT	TP	NT	TP FX	TP FO	TP FO		TP FX
						◇1		◇1	◇1						◇1		◇1	◇1	◇1		◇1
Liverpool Lime Street 10	d					20 22											22 30	22 30			
Liverpool South Parkway 7 ✈	d					20 32											22 40	22 40			
Warrington Central	d					20 45											22 53	22 53			
Birchwood	d					20 50											22 58	22 58			
Manchester Oxford Road	d					21 07											23 17	23 17			
Manchester Airport ✈	d								21 20						22 22				23 18		23 18
Manchester Piccadilly 10	a					21 09			21 36						22 36		23 19	23 19	23 34		23 34
	d					21 11			21 42						22 42		23 21	23 21	23 38		23 38
Manchester Victoria	d						21 27				22 08					23 00					23 56
Ashton-under-Lyne	d						21 37				22 18					23 10					
Stalybridge	a					21 26	21 42		21 55		22 22				22 55	23 14	23 34	23 34			
	d					21 26	21 42		21 55		22 23				22 55	23 15	23 34	23 34			
Mossley (Gr Manchester)	d						21 47				22 27					23 19					
Greenfield	d						21 51				22 31					23 23					
Marsden	d						21 59				22 40					23 32					
Slaithwaite	d						22 04				22 44					23 36					
Huddersfield	a					21 44	22 12		22 15		22 53				23 15	23 44	23 52	23 52	00 09		00 25
	d		21 27	21 31	21 35	21 45			22 16			22 25	22 25	22 31	23 16		23 53	23 53	00 09		00 26
Deighton	d			21 34	21 38									22 34							
Mirfield	d			21 39	21 43									22 39							
Ravensthorpe	d			21 42										22 42							
Dewsbury	a			21 46					22 25					22 46	23 25				00s18		00s35
	d			21 46					22 26					22 46	23 26						
Batley	d			21 49										22 49							
Morley	d			21 55										22 55							
Cottingley	d			21 59										22 59							
Leeds 10	a		22 25	22 08		22 09			22 41			23 26	23 27	23 07	23 41		00 30	00 31	00 35		00 50
	d	21 55				22 12		22 22	22 42						23 42		00 32	00 34	00 37		00 54
Garforth	d	22 07																			
South Milford	a							22 36													
Selby	a							22 46													
Howden	a																				
Brough	a							23 05													
Hull	a							23 25													
Wakefield Kirkgate	a				22 02																
Wakefield Westgate	a				22 10																
York 8	a	22 32				22 38			23 07						00 09		01 11	01 16	01 20		01 43
	d								23 18												
Malton	d																				
Seamer	a																				
Scarborough	a																				
Thirsk	a								23 31												
Northallerton	a								23 49												
Darlington 7	a								00 01												
Yarm	d																				
Thornaby	a																				
Middlesbrough	a																				
Durham	a								00 19												
Chester-le-Street	a																				
Newcastle 8	a								00 51												

Table 39

Liverpool, Manchester Airport and Manchester - Huddersfield - Wakefield, Leeds, Hull, York, Scarborough, Middlesbrough and Newcastle

Network Diagram - see first Page of Table 39

		TP ◇■	TP ◇■	TP ◇■	TP ◇■	TP ◇■	TP ◇■	TP ◇■	TP ◇■	TP ◇■		TP ◇■	NT	NT	NT	NT	TP ◇■	TP ◇■	TP ◇■ 🚲	NT		NT	NT	NT	NT
Liverpool Lime Street	d			22p30																					
Liverpool South Parkway	d			22p40																					
Warrington Central	d			22p53																					
Birchwood	d			22p58																					
Manchester Oxford Road	d			23p17																					
Manchester Airport	d	21p20	22p22		23p18	00 38	04 15		04 15			05 37							06 23						
Manchester Piccadilly	a	21p36	22p36	23p19	23p34	00 51	04 29		04 29			05 51							06 39						
	d	21p42	22p42	23p21	23p38	00 53	04 30		04 30	05 39		05 57					06 21		06 54						
Manchester Victoria	d																			06 17		06 55			
Ashton-under-Lyne	d																					07 05			
Stalybridge	a	21p55	22p55	23p34						05 52									07 07			07 10			
	d	21p55	22p55	23p34						05 52									07 07			07 11			
Mossley (Gr Manchester)	d																					07 15			
Greenfield	d																					07 19			
Marsden	d														07 00							07 28			
Slaithwaite	d														07 04							07 32			
Huddersfield	a	22p15	23p15	23p52	00 09	01 34	05 10		05 10	06 10		06 26			07 12		06 54		07 25			07 41			
	d	22p16	23p16	23p53	00 09	01 35	05 11		05 11	06 11		06 27	06 31	06 41			06 56		07 26					07 29	07 32
Deighton	d												06 34	06 45											07 36
Mirfield	d												06 39	06 50											07 41
Ravensthorpe	d												06 42												
Dewsbury	a	22p25	23p25		00s18							06 36	06 46				07 05								
	d	22p26	23p26									06 37	06 46				07 06								
Batley	d												06 49												
Morley	d												06 55												
Cottingley	d												06 59												
Leeds	a	22p41	23p41	00 31	00 35	02 13	05 32		05 32	06 32		06 52	07 07				07 19		07 47	07 57				08 30	
	d	22p42	23p42	00 34	00 37	02 16	05 34		05 34	06 35		06 55				07 14	07 23		07 50	08 00			08 12		
Garforth	d																		08 00	08 12			08 24		
South Milford	a																			08 22			08 36		
Selby	a															07 37	07 43			08 36			08 54		
Howden	a																07 52								
Brough	a																08 04								
Hull	a																08 20								
Wakefield Kirkgate	a													07 03											07 57
Wakefield Westgate	a													07 10											08 08
York	a	23p07	00 09	01 16	01 20	02 45	06 00		06 00	07 01		07 22							08 21						
	d	23p18						05 54	06 40	07 06		07 25						07 32	08 23						
Malton	d								07 04			07 49													
Seamer	a								07 21			08 06													
Scarborough	a								07 30			08 15													
Thirsk	a	23p31						06 10		07 22								07 52	08 39						
Northallerton	a	23p49						06 18		07 30								08 00	08 49						
Darlington	a	00 01						06 29		07 41															
Yarm	d																	08 14	09 03						
Thornaby	a							06 53										08 24	09 11						
Middlesbrough	a							07 03										08 32	09 22						
Durham	a	00 19								07 58															
Chester-le-Street	a									08 04															
Newcastle	a	00 51								08 16															

Table 39

Liverpool, Manchester Airport and Manchester - Huddersfield - Wakefield, Leeds, Hull, York, Scarborough, Middlesbrough and Newcastle

Network Diagram - see first Page of Table 39

		TP ◇■ 🚲		TP ◇■ 🚲	TP A	NT		TP ◇■ 🚲	NT	NT	NT	NT	TP ◇■ 🚲	NT	NT	TP ◇■ B		TP ◇■ 🚲	NT	TP ◇■ 🚲	NT	NT	TP ◇■	NT	TP ◇■ 🚲
Liverpool Lime Street	d	06 15								06 46								07 15				07 16			
Liverpool South Parkway	d	06 25																07 25							
Warrington Central	d	06 38																07 40							
Birchwood	d	06 43																07 45							
Manchester Oxford Road	d	07 07																08 06							
Manchester Airport	d			07 05									07 33							08 05					08 35
Manchester Piccadilly	a	07 09		07 22									07 48					08 08		08 22					08 49
	d	07 11		07 27				07 36					07 56					08 10		08 26			08 42		08 57
Manchester Victoria	d					06 58			07 40	07 57									07 48		08 00	08 27			
Ashton-under-Lyne	d								07 49	08 07												08 37			
Stalybridge	a	07 23						07 49	07 54	08 13			08 09					08 26				08 41			
	d	07 23						07 49	07 54				08 09					08 26				08 42			
Mossley (Gr Manchester)	d								07 59													08 46			
Greenfield	d								08 03													08 50			
Marsden	d								08 11													08 59			
Slaithwaite	d								08 16													09 03			
Huddersfield	a	07 44		07 56				08 09	08 24				08 28					08 44		08 56		09 12	09 15		09 26
	d	07 45		07 57				08 10			08 14	08 21	08 30	08 33	08 37			08 45		08 57			09 16	09 23	09 27
Deighton	d										08 17			08 36	08 40										
Mirfield	d					08 06					08 22			08 41	08 45						09 07				
Ravensthorpe	d										08 25			08 44											
Dewsbury	a	07 54		08 06		08 11		08 19			08 29		08 39	08 48						09 06	09 12				09 36
	d	07 55		08 07		08 12		08 20			08 29		08 39	08 53						09 07	09 12				09 37
Batley	d					08 15					08 32			08 56							09 15				
Morley	d					08 21					08 38			09 02							09 21				
Cottingley	d					08 24					08 42			09 06											
Leeds	a	08 10		08 24		08 31		08 36			08 52	09 27	08 54	09 16				09 09	09 12	09 22	09 32		09 36	10 27	09 52
	d	08 12		08 28	08 28			08 38					08 57					09 12	09 15	09 28			09 38		09 57
Garforth	d												09 05						09 27						10 05
South Milford	a																		09 38						
Selby	a							08 57											09 53				09 57		
Howden	a																								
Brough	a																						10 15		
Hull	a							09 31															10 35		
Wakefield Kirkgate	a														09 02										
Wakefield Westgate	a														09 08										
York	a	08 35		08 52	09 03								09 23					09 36		09 52					10 23
	d	08 40	08 42	08 58									09 26			09 31		09 41		09 58					10 26
Malton	d	09 04																10 04							
Seamer	a	09 21																10 21							
Scarborough	a	09 30														10 17		10 30							
Thirsk	a												09 45												10 45
Northallerton	a			09 18									09 58							10 18					10 58
Darlington	a		09 11	09 30																10 30					
Yarm	d												10 13												11 13
Thornaby	a												10 21												11 21
Middlesbrough	a												10 30												11 30
Durham	a		09 27	09 47																10 47					
Chester-le-Street	a			09 53																					
Newcastle	a		09 46	10 07																11 05					

A until 23 June, from 15 September

B from 30 June until 8 September

Liverpool, Manchester Airport and Manchester - Huddersfield - Wakefield, Leeds, Hull, York, Scarborough, Middlesbrough and Newcastle

Network Diagram - see first Page of Table 39

		NT		NT	TP ◇1	NT	NT	TP ◇1	NT	NT	NT	TP ◇1		NT	NT	TP ◇1	NT	NT	TP ◇1 A	TP ◇1	NT	TP ◇1		NT	NT
Liverpool Lime Street 10	d				08 22						08 44									09 22					
Liverpool South Parkway 7 ✈	d				08 32															09 32					
Warrington Central	d				08 45															09 45					
Birchwood	d				08 50															09 50					
Manchester Oxford Road	d				09 07															10 07					
Manchester Airport ✈	d							09 05								09 35						10 05			
Manchester Piccadilly 10	a				09 09			09 22								09 52				10 09		10 22			
	d				09 11			09 27				09 42				09 57				10 11		10 27			
Manchester Victoria	d					08 48	08 57		09 00	09 27	09 57										09 48			10 00	10 27
Ashton-under-Lyne	d						09 07			09 37	10 07														10 37
Stalybridge	a				09 26		09 13			09 42	10 13									10 26					10 42
	d				09 26					09 42										10 26					10 42
Mossley (Gr Manchester)	d									09 47															10 47
Greenfield	d									09 51															10 51
Marsden	d									09 59															10 59
Slaithwaite	d									10 04															11 04
Huddersfield	a				09 44			09 56		10 12		10 15				10 26				10 44		10 56			11 12
	d	09 31		09 35	09 45			09 57				10 16			10 23	10 27	10 31	10 35		10 45		10 57			
Deighton	d	09 34		09 38													10 34	10 38							
Mirfield	d	09 39		09 43					10 07								10 39	10 43							
Ravensthorpe	d	09 42															10 42							11 07	
Dewsbury	a	09 46						10 06	10 12							10 36	10 46					11 06		11 12	
	d	09 46						10 07	10 12							10 37	10 46					11 07		11 12	
Batley	d	09 49							10 15								10 49							11 15	
Morley	d	09 55							10 21								10 55							11 21	
Cottingley	d	09 59															10 59								
Leeds 10	a	10 07			10 09	10 12		10 22	10 32			10 36			11 27	10 52	11 07			11 09	11 13	11 22		11 35	
	d				10 12	10 15		10 28				10 38		10 41		10 57				11 12	11 15	11 28			
Garforth	d					10 27								10 53		11 05					11 27				
South Milford	a					10 38															11 38				
Selby	a					10 53						10 57									11 55				
Howden	a																								
Brough	a											11 15													
Hull	a											11 35													
Wakefield Kirkgate	a			10 02														11 02							
Wakefield Westgate	a			10 10														11 08							
York 8	a				10 36			10 52						11 18		11 23				11 36		11 52			
	d				10 41			10 58								11 26			11 31	11 41		11 58			
Malton	d				11 04															12 04					
Seamer	a				11 21															12 21					
Scarborough	a				11 30														12 17	12 30					
Thirsk	a															11 45									
Northallerton	a							11 18								11 58						12 18			
Darlington 7	a							11 30														12 30			
Yarm	d															12 13									
Thornaby	a															12 21									
Middlesbrough	a															12 30									
Durham	a							11 47														12 47			
Chester-le-Street	a							11 53																	
Newcastle 8	a							12 06														13 03			

A from 30 June until 8 September

Liverpool, Manchester Airport and Manchester - Huddersfield - Wakefield, Leeds, Hull, York, Scarborough, Middlesbrough and Newcastle

Network Diagram - see first Page of Table 39

		NT	TP ◇1	NT	TP ◇1	NT	NT	TP ◇1		NT	TP ◇1	NT	NT	NT	TP ◇1	NT	NT	TP ◇1		NT	NT	TP ◇1 A	TP ◇1	NT	TP ◇1
Liverpool Lime Street 10	d	09 46						10 22						10 46									11 22		
Liverpool South Parkway 7 ✈	d							10 32															11 32		
Warrington Central	d							10 45															11 45		
Birchwood	d							10 50															11 50		
Manchester Oxford Road	d							11 07															12 07		
Manchester Airport ✈	d				10 35						11 05							11 35							12 05
Manchester Piccadilly 10	a				10 52			11 09			11 22							11 52					12 09		12 22
	d		10 42		10 57			11 11			11 27				11 42			11 57					12 11		12 27
Manchester Victoria	d	10 57								10 48		11 00	11 27	11 57										11 48	
Ashton-under-Lyne	d	11 07											11 37	12 07											
Stalybridge	a	11 13						11 26					11 42	12 13									12 26		
	d							11 26					11 42										12 26		
Mossley (Gr Manchester)	d												11 47												
Greenfield	d												11 51												
Marsden	d												11 59												
Slaithwaite	d												12 04												
Huddersfield	a		11 15		11 26			11 44			11 56		12 12		12 15			12 26					12 44		12 56
	d		11 16	11 23	11 27	11 31	11 35	11 45			11 57				12 16		12 23	12 27		12 31	12 35		12 45		12 57
Deighton	d					11 34	11 38													12 34	12 38				
Mirfield	d					11 39	11 43					12 07								12 39	12 43				
Ravensthorpe	d					11 42														12 42					
Dewsbury	a				11 36	11 46					12 06	12 12						12 36		12 46					13 06
	d				11 37	11 46					12 07	12 12						12 37		12 46					13 07
Batley	d					11 49						12 15								12 49					
Morley	d					11 55						12 21								12 55					
Cottingley	d					11 59														12 59					
Leeds 10	a		11 36	12 27	11 52	12 07		12 09		12 12	12 22	12 32			12 36		13 27	12 52		13 07			13 09	13 12	13 22
	d		11 38		11 57			12 12		12 15	12 28				12 38	12 41		12 57					13 12	13 15	13 28
Garforth	d				12 05					12 27						12 53		13 05						13 27	
South Milford	a									12 38														13 38	
Selby	a		11 57							12 50					12 57									13 52	
Howden	a																								
Brough	a		12 15												13 15										
Hull	a		12 36												13 35										
Wakefield Kirkgate	a						12 02														13 02				
Wakefield Westgate	a						12 08														13 08				
York 8	a				12 23			12 36			12 52					13 19		13 23					13 36		13 52
	d				12 26			12 41			12 58							13 26				13 31	13 41		13 58
Malton	d							13 04															14 04		
Seamer	a							13 21															14 21		
Scarborough	a							13 30														14 17	14 30		
Thirsk	a				12 45													13 45							
Northallerton	a				12 59						13 18							13 58							14 18
Darlington 7	a										13 30														14 30
Yarm	d				13 13													14 13							
Thornaby	a				13 21													14 21							
Middlesbrough	a				13 30													14 30							
Durham	a										13 47														14 47
Chester-le-Street	a										13 53														
Newcastle 8	a										14 06														15 05

A from 30 June until 8 September

Table 39

Saturdays

Liverpool, Manchester Airport and Manchester - Huddersfield - Wakefield, Leeds, Hull, York, Scarborough, Middlesbrough and Newcastle

Network Diagram - see first Page of Table 39

		NT	NT	NT		TP	NT	TP	NT	NT	TP	NT	TP	NT		NT	NT	TP	NT	NT	TP	NT	NT	TP
						◇1		◇1 H			◇1 H		◇1 H					◇1 H			◇1 H			◇1 H
Liverpool Lime Street 10	d			11 46							12 22						12 46							13 22
Liverpool South Parkway 7 ✈	d										12 32													13 32
Warrington Central	d										12 45													13 45
Birchwood	d										12 50													13 50
Manchester Oxford Road	d										13 07													14 07
Manchester Airport ✈	d							12 35					13 05								13 35			
Manchester Piccadilly 10 ⛴	a							12 52			13 09		13 22								13 52			14 09
	d					12 42		12 57			13 11		13 27					13 42			13 57			14 11
Manchester Victoria ⛴	d	12 00	12 27	12 57								12 48		13 00		13 27	13 57							
Ashton-under-Lyne	d		12 37	13 07												13 37	14 07							
Stalybridge	a		12 42	13 13							13 26					13 42	14 13							14 26
	d		12 42								13 26					13 42								14 26
Mossley (Gr Manchester)	d		12 47													13 47								
Greenfield	d		12 51													13 51								
Marsden	d		12 59													13 59								
Slaithwaite	d		13 04													14 04								
Huddersfield	a		13 12			13 15		13 26			13 44		13 56			14 12		14 15			14 26			14 44
	d					13 16	13 23	13 27	13 31	13 35	13 45		13 57					14 16		14 23	14 27	14 31	14 35	14 45
Deighton	d								13 34	13 38												14 34	14 38	
Mirfield	d	13 07							13 39	13 43				14 07								14 39	14 43	
Ravensthorpe	d								13 42													14 42		
Dewsbury	a	13 12						13 36	13 46				14 06	14 12							14 36	14 46		
	d	13 12						13 37	13 46				14 07	14 12							14 37	14 46		
Batley	d	13 15							13 49					14 15								14 49		
Morley	d	13 21							13 55					14 21								14 55		
Cottingley	d								13 59													14 59		
Leeds 10	a	13 32				13 36	14 27	13 52	14 07		14 09	14 14	14 22	14 32				14 36		15 27	14 52	15 07		15 09
	d					13 38		13 57			14 12	14 15	14 28					14 38	14 41		14 57			15 12
Garforth	d							14 05				14 27							14 53		15 05			
South Milford	a											14 38												
Selby	a					13 57						14 51						14 57						
Howden	a																							
Brough	a					14 15												15 15						
Hull	a					14 35												15 35						
Wakefield Kirkgate	a									14 02													15 02	
Wakefield Westgate	a									14 08													15 08	
York 8	a							14 23			14 36		14 52						15 17		15 23			15 36
	d							14 26			14 41		14 58								15 26			15 41
Malton	d										15 04													16 04
Seamer	a										15 21													16 21
Scarborough	a										15 30													16 30
Thirsk	a							14 45													15 45			
Northallerton	a							14 58					15 18								15 58			
Darlington 7	a												15 30											
Yarm	d							15 13													16 13			
Thornaby	a							15 21													16 21			
Middlesbrough	a							15 30													16 30			
Durham	a												15 47											
Chester-le-Street	a												15 53											
Newcastle 8 ⛴	a												16 09											

Table 39

Saturdays

Liverpool, Manchester Airport and Manchester - Huddersfield - Wakefield, Leeds, Hull, York, Scarborough, Middlesbrough and Newcastle

Network Diagram - see first Page of Table 39

		NT	TP	NT	NT	NT	TP	NT	TP	NT		NT	TP	NT	TP	NT	NT	NT	TP	NT		TP	NT	NT	TP
			◇1 H				◇1		◇1				◇1 H		◇1 H				◇1			◇1 H			◇1
Liverpool Lime Street 10	d					13 46							14 22					14 46							15 22
Liverpool South Parkway 7 ✈	d												14 32												15 32
Warrington Central	d												14 45												15 45
Birchwood	d												14 50												15 50
Manchester Oxford Road	d												15 07												16 07
Manchester Airport ✈	d		14 05						14 35						15 05							15 35			
Manchester Piccadilly 10 ⛴	a		14 22						14 52				15 09		15 22							15 52			16 09
	d		14 27				14 42		14 57				15 11		15 27				15 42			15 57			16 11
Manchester Victoria ⛴	d	13 48		14 00	14 27	14 57								14 48		15 00	15 27	15 57							
Ashton-under-Lyne	d				14 37	15 07											15 37	16 07							
Stalybridge	a				14 42	15 13							15 26				15 42	16 13							16 26
	d				14 42								15 26				15 42								16 26
Mossley (Gr Manchester)	d				14 47												15 47								
Greenfield	d				14 51												15 51								
Marsden	d				14 59												15 59								
Slaithwaite	d				15 04												16 04								
Huddersfield	a		14 56		15 12		15 15		15 26				15 44		15 56		16 12		16 15			16 26			16 44
	d		14 57				15 16	15 23	15 27	15 31		15 35	15 45		15 57				16 16	16 23		16 27	16 31	16 35	16 45
Deighton	d									15 34		15 38											16 34	16 38	
Mirfield	d			15 07						15 39		15 43				16 07							16 39	16 43	
Ravensthorpe	d									15 42													16 42		
Dewsbury	a		15 06	15 12					15 36	15 46					16 06	16 12						16 36	16 46		
	d		15 07	15 12					15 37	15 46					16 07	16 12						16 37	16 46		
Batley	d			15 15						15 49						16 15							16 49		
Morley	d			15 21						15 55						16 21							16 55		
Cottingley	d									15 59													16 59		
Leeds 10	a	15 10	15 22	15 32			15 36	16 27	15 52	16 08			16 09	16 12	16 22	16 31			16 36	17 27		16 52	17 08		17 09
	d	15 15	15 28				15 38		15 57				16 12	16 15	16 28				16 38			16 57			17 12
Garforth	d	15 27							16 05					16 27								17 05			
South Milford	a	15 38												16 39											
Selby	a	15 53					15 57							16 54					17 00						
Howden	a																								
Brough	a						16 15												17 18						
Hull	a						16 35												17 37						
Wakefield Kirkgate	a											16 02												17 02	
Wakefield Westgate	a											16 08												17 12	
York 8	a		15 52						16 23				16 36		16 52							17 23			17 36
	d								16 26				16 41		16 58							17 26			17 41
Malton	d												17 04												18 04
Seamer	a												17 21												18 21
Scarborough	a												17 30												18 30
Thirsk	a								16 45						17 15							17 45			
Northallerton	a								16 58						17 23							17 58			
Darlington 7	a														17 34										
Yarm	d								17 13													18 13			
Thornaby	a								17 21													18 21			
Middlesbrough	a								17 30													18 30			
Durham	a														17 51										
Chester-le-Street	a														17 57										
Newcastle 8 ⛴	a														18 10										

Liverpool, Manchester Airport and Manchester - Huddersfield - Wakefield, Leeds, Hull, York, Scarborough, Middlesbrough and Newcastle

Network Diagram - see first Page of Table 39

Station		NT	TP ◇1	NT	NT	NT		TP ◇1	NT	TP ◇1	NT	NT	NT
Liverpool Lime Street	d					15 46							
Liverpool South Parkway	d												
Warrington Central	d												
Birchwood	d												
Manchester Oxford Road	d												
Manchester Airport	d		16 05							16 35			
Manchester Piccadilly	a		16 22							16 52			
	d		16 27					16 42		16 56			
Manchester Victoria	d	15 48		16 00	16 27	16 57							
Ashton-under-Lyne	d				16 37	17 07							
Stalybridge	a				16 42	17 13				17 08			
	d				16 42					17 08			
Mossley (Gr Manchester)	d				16 47								
Greenfield	d				16 51								
Marsden	d				16 59						17 29		
Slaithwaite	d				17 04						17 33		
Huddersfield	a		16 56		17 12			17 15		17 26	17 41		
	d		16 57					17 16	17 23	17 27		17 31	17 35
Deighton	d											17 34	17 38
Mirfield	d			17 07								17 39	17 43
Ravensthorpe	d											17 42	
Dewsbury	a		17 06	17 12						17 36		17 46	
	d		17 07	17 12						17 37		17 46	
Batley	d			17 15								17 49	
Morley	d			17 21								17 55	
Cottingley	d											17 59	
Leeds	a	17 12	17 22	17 31				17 36	18 29	17 52		18 06	
	d	17 15	17 24					17 38		17 57			
Garforth	d	17 30	17 34							18 05			
South Milford	a	17 41											
Selby	a	17 55						17 59					
Howden	a							18 08					
Brough	a							18 20					
Hull	a							18 39					
Wakefield Kirkgate	a												18 02
Wakefield Westgate	a												18 08
York	a		17 55							18 22			
	d									18 26			
Malton	d												
Seamer	a												
Scarborough	a												
Thirsk	a									18 45			
Northallerton	a									18 58			
Darlington	a												
Yarm	d									19 13			
Thornaby	a									19 21			
Middlesbrough	a									19 31			
Durham	a												
Chester-le-Street	a												
Newcastle	a												

Station		TP ◇1	NT	TP ◇1		NT	NT	XC ◇1	TP ◇1	NT	TP ◇1	XC ◇1 A	NT
Liverpool Lime Street	d	16 22											
Liverpool South Parkway	d	16 32											
Warrington Central	d	16 45											
Birchwood	d	16 50											
Manchester Oxford Road	d	17 07											
Manchester Airport	d			17 05							17 35		
Manchester Piccadilly	a	17 09		17 22							17 52		
	d	17 11		17 26					17 42		17 56		
Manchester Victoria	d		16 48			17 00	17 27						
Ashton-under-Lyne	d						17 37						
Stalybridge	a	17 26		17 38			17 42				18 08		
	d	17 26		17 38			17 42				18 08		
Mossley (Gr Manchester)	d						17 47						
Greenfield	d						17 51						
Marsden	d						17 59						
Slaithwaite	d						18 04						
Huddersfield	a	17 44		17 56			18 12		18 15		18 26		
	d	17 45		17 57					18 16	18 23	18 27		18 31
Deighton	d												18 34
Mirfield	d					18 07							18 39
Ravensthorpe	d												18 42
Dewsbury	a			18 06		18 12					18 36		18 46
	d			18 07		18 13					18 37		18 46
Batley	d					18 16							18 49
Morley	d					18 22							18 55
Cottingley	d												18 59
Leeds	a	18 09	18 12	18 21		18 31			18 36	19 28	18 52		19 07
	d	18 12	18 15	18 28				18 35	18 38		18 57	19 05	
Garforth	d		18 27								19 05		
South Milford	a		18 38						18 51				
Selby	a		18 50						19 00				
Howden	a												
Brough	a								19 18				
Hull	a								19 38				
Wakefield Kirkgate	a												
Wakefield Westgate	a												
York	a	18 36		18 52				18 58			19 23	19 26	
	d	18 41		18 58				19 05			19 26	19 32	
Malton	d	19 04											
Seamer	a	19 21											
Scarborough	a	19 30											
Thirsk	a										19 45		
Northallerton	a			19 17							19 57		
Darlington	a			19 30				19 35				19 57	
Yarm	d										20 11		
Thornaby	a										20 21		
Middlesbrough	a										20 30		
Durham	a			19 47				19 52				20 14	
Chester-le-Street	a			19 53									
Newcastle	a			20 07				20 08				20 28	

A from 15 September until 20 October

Liverpool, Manchester Airport and Manchester - Huddersfield - Wakefield, Leeds, Hull, York, Scarborough, Middlesbrough and Newcastle

Network Diagram - see first Page of Table 39

Station		NT		TP ◇1	NT	NT	NT	TP ◇1	NT	NT	TP ◇1	NT	
Liverpool Lime Street	d			17 22									
Liverpool South Parkway	d			17 32									
Warrington Central	d			17 45									
Birchwood	d			17 50									
Manchester Oxford Road	d			18 07									
Manchester Airport	d										18 35		
Manchester Piccadilly	a			18 09							18 52		
	d			18 11				18 42			18 57		
Manchester Victoria	d				17 43	18 00	18 27						
Ashton-under-Lyne	d						18 37						
Stalybridge	a			18 26			18 42						
	d			18 26			18 42						
Mossley (Gr Manchester)	d						18 47						
Greenfield	d						18 51						
Marsden	d						18 59						
Slaithwaite	d						19 04						
Huddersfield	a			18 44			19 12	19 15			19 26		
	d	18 35		18 45				19 16		19 23	19 27	19 31	
Deighton	d	18 39										19 34	
Mirfield	d	18 44				19 08						19 39	
Ravensthorpe	d											19 42	
Dewsbury	a			18 55		19 13					19 36	19 46	
	d			18 55		19 13					19 37	19 46	
Batley	d					19 16						19 49	
Morley	d					19 22						19 55	
Cottingley	d											19 59	
Leeds	a			19 10	19 13	19 33		19 36		20 30	19 52	20 07	
	d			19 12	19 16			19 38	19 41		19 57		
Garforth	d				19 28				19 53		20 05		
South Milford	a							19 51					
Selby	a							20 00					
Howden	a							20 09					
Brough	a							20 21					
Hull	a							20 43					
Wakefield Kirkgate	a	19 02											
Wakefield Westgate	a	19 08											
York	a			19 36	19 53				20 18		20 23		
	d			19 41							20 29		
Malton	d			20 04									
Seamer	a			20 21									
Scarborough	a			20 30									
Thirsk	a										20 48		
Northallerton	a										20 58		
Darlington	a												
Yarm	d										21 13		
Thornaby	a										21 21		
Middlesbrough	a										21 30		
Durham	a												
Chester-le-Street	a												
Newcastle	a												

Station		NT	XC ◇1 A	TP ◇1	NT	TP ◇1	NT	NT	NT	NT		TP ◇1	TP ◇1
Liverpool Lime Street	d			18 22									19 22
Liverpool South Parkway	d			18 32									19 32
Warrington Central	d			18 45									19 45
Birchwood	d			18 50									19 50
Manchester Oxford Road	d			19 07									20 07
Manchester Airport	d					19 20							
Manchester Piccadilly	a			19 09		19 36							20 09
	d			19 11		19 42							20 11
Manchester Victoria	d				19 00		19 27						
Ashton-under-Lyne	d						19 37						
Stalybridge	a			19 26			19 42						20 26
	d			19 26			19 42						20 26
Mossley (Gr Manchester)	d						19 47						
Greenfield	d						19 51						
Marsden	d						19 59						
Slaithwaite	d						20 04						
Huddersfield	a			19 44		20 15	20 12						20 44
	d	19 35		19 45		20 16		20 25	20 31	20 35			20 45
Deighton	d	19 38							20 34	20 38			
Mirfield	d	19 43			20 07				20 39	20 43			
Ravensthorpe	d								20 42				
Dewsbury	a				20 12	20 25			20 46				
	d				20 12	20 26			20 46				
Batley	d				20 15				20 49				
Morley	d				20 21				20 55				
Cottingley	d								20 59				
Leeds	a			20 09	20 33	20 41		21 25	21 07				21 09
	d		20 08	20 12		20 45						21 08	21 12
Garforth	d												
South Milford	a											21 20	
Selby	a											21 30	
Howden	a											21 39	
Brough	a											21 51	
Hull	a											22 10	
Wakefield Kirkgate	a	20 02								21 02			
Wakefield Westgate	a	20 09								21 09			
York	a		20 29	20 36		21 09							21 41
	d		20 33	20 41		21 14							
Malton	d			21 04									
Seamer	a			21 21									
Scarborough	a			21 30									
Thirsk	a					21 30							
Northallerton	a					21 38							
Darlington	a		20 58			21 51							
Yarm	d												
Thornaby	a												
Middlesbrough	a												
Durham	a		21 15			22 08							
Chester-le-Street	a					22 14							
Newcastle	a		21 29			22 28							

A from 15 September until 20 October

Table 39 — Saturdays

Liverpool, Manchester Airport and Manchester - Huddersfield - Wakefield, Leeds, Hull, York, Scarborough, Middlesbrough and Newcastle

Network Diagram - see first Page of Table 39

		NT	XC ◇1	TP ◇1 A	TP ◇1 B	NT	NT	NT	TP ◇1 A	TP ◇1 B	NT	TP ◇1	NT	TP ◇1	NT	NT	NT		TP ◇1	NT	TP ◇1 C	TP ◇1 D	TP ◇1 E	TP ◇1 F	TP E 🚌
Liverpool Lime Street 10	d								20 22	20 22											22 30	22 30	22 30		
Liverpool South Parkway 7 ✈	d								20 32	20 32											22 40	22 40	22 40		
Warrington Central	d								20 45	20 45											22 53	22 53	22 53		
Birchwood	d								20 50	20 50											22 58	22 58	22 58		
Manchester Oxford Road	d								21 07	21 07											23 15	23 17	23 17		
Manchester Airport ✈	d			20 20	20 20									21 20					22 22					23 24	23 25
Manchester Piccadilly 10 ⛴	a			20 36	20 36				21 09	21 09				21 36					22 36		23 17	23 19	23 19	23 39	23 50
	d			20 42	20 42				21 11	21 11				21 42					22 42		23 19	23 21	23 21	23 43	23 50
Manchester Victoria ⛴	d	20 27									21 27				22 08					23 00					
Ashton-under-Lyne	d	20 37									21 37				22 18					23 10					
Stalybridge	a	20 42							21 26	21 26	21 41			21 55	22 22				22 55	23 14	23 31	23 34	23 34		
	d	20 42							21 26	21 26	21 42			21 55	22 23				22 55	23 15	23 31	23 34	23 34		
Mossley (Gr Manchester)	d	20 47									21 46				22 27					23 19					
Greenfield	d	20 51									21 50				22 31					23 23					
Marsden	d	20 59					21 19				21 59				22 40					23 32					
Slaithwaite	d	21 04					21 23				22 03				22 44					23 36					
Huddersfield	a	21 12		21 15	21 15		21 30		21 44	21 44	22 12			22 15	22 53				23 15	23 43	23 52	23 52	23 52	00 11	00 50
	d			21 16	21 16	21 27	21 31	21 35	21 45	21 45				22 16		22 20	22 25		23 16		23 53	23 53		00 12	00 50
Deighton	d						21 34	21 38								22 23									
Mirfield	d						21 39	21 43								22 28									
Ravensthorpe	d						21 42									22 31									
Dewsbury	a			21 25	21 25		21 46							22 25		22 35			23 25					00s21	
	d			21 26	21 26		21 46							22 26		22 35			23 26						
Batley	d						21 49									22 38									
Morley	d						21 55									22 44									
Cottingley	d						21 59									22 48									
Leeds 10	a			21 41	21 41	22 24	22 07		22 09	22 09				22 41		22 56	23 26		23 41		00 14	00 14		00 37	01 25
	d		21 15	21 42	21 42				22 12	22 12		22 22	22 37	22 42					23 42		00 15	00 15		00 40	01 25
Garforth	d																								
South Milford	a											22 36													
Selby	a											22 46													
Howden	a																								
Brough	a											23 05													
Hull	a											23 25													
Wakefield Kirkgate	a							22 02					23 10												
Wakefield Westgate	a							22 10																	
York 8	a		21 57	22 06	22 10				22 38	22 41				23 07					00 09		00 42	00 42		01 09	02 15
	d			22 14	22 14																				
Malton	d			22 37	22 37																				
Seamer	a			22 54	22 54																				
Scarborough	a			23 03	23 03																				
Thirsk	a																								
Northallerton	a																								
Darlington 7	a																								
Yarm	d																								
Thornaby	a																								
Middlesbrough	a																								
Durham	a																								
Chester-le-Street	a																								
Newcastle 8 ⛴	a																								

A until 8 September
B from 15 September
C until 23 June, from 15 September until 20 October
D from 30 June until 8 September
E from 27 October
F until 20 October

Table 39 — Sundays until 24 June

Liverpool, Manchester Airport and Manchester - Huddersfield, Leeds, Hull, York, Scarborough, Middlesbrough and Newcastle

Network Diagram - see first Page of Table 39

		TP ◇1	TP ◇1	TP ◇1	TP 🚌	TP ◇1	TP ◇1	NT 🚌	NT 🚌	TP ◇1	NT 🚌		NT	TP ◇1	TP ◇1	TP ◇1	TP ◇1	NT	TP ◇1	NT 🚌	TP ◇1	TP ◇1		TP ◇1	TP ◇1
Liverpool Lime Street 10	d		22p30																08 22					09 22	
Liverpool South Parkway 7 ✈	d		22p40																						
Warrington Central	d		22p53																						
Birchwood	d		22p58																						
Newton-le-Willows	d																		08 40					09 40	
Manchester Oxford Road	d		23p15																						
Manchester Airport ✈	d	22p22		23p24	01 20					06 11						07 50						09 03			10 03
Manchester Piccadilly 10 ⛴	a	22p36	23p17	23p39	01 45					06 24						08 03						09 19			10 18
	d	22p42	23p19	23p43	01 45					06 26						08 05						09 20			10 21
Manchester Victoria ⛴	a															08 20			09 03			09 35		10 03	10 35
	d						05 50	08 17								08 23			09 05	09 17		09 38		10 05	10 38
Ashton-under-Lyne	d							08 40												09 40					
Stalybridge	a	22p55	23p31					08 50												09 50					
	d	22p55	23p31					08 50												09 50					
Mossley (Gr Manchester)	d							08 58												09 58					
Greenfield	d							09 04												10 04					
Marsden	d							09 24												10 24					
Slaithwaite	d							09 29												10 29					
Huddersfield	a	23p15	23p52	00 11	02 45		06 35	09 45		07 23						09 08			09 51	10 45				10 54	
	d	23p16	23p53	00 12		02 55	06 39		07 23	07 27			07 51			09 12		09 44	09 53					10 56	
Deighton	d								07 32				07 54					09 47							
Mirfield	d								07 42				07 59					09 52							
Ravensthorpe	d								07 47		←		08 02					09 55							
Dewsbury	a	23p25		00s21					07 55	07 36	07 55		08 06			09 22		09 59				10 21			11 21
	d	23p26							07 55	07 36	07 55		08 06			09 22		10 03				10 23			11 22
Batley	d								→		08 03		08 09					10 06							
Morley	d										08 15		08 15					10 12							
Cottingley	d										08 25		08 19					10 15							
Leeds 10	a	23p41	00 14	00 37		03 16	07 00			07 56	08 40		08 27			09 37		10 23	10 14			10 38		11 15	11 37
	d	23p42	00 15	00 40		03 18	07 01			07 59				08 40	09 12	09 40	10 04		10 17		10 24	10 40		11 18	11 40
Garforth	d																								
South Milford	a																				10 36				
Selby	a																				10 46				
Howden	a																								
Brough	a																				11 04				
Hull	a																				11 21				
York 8	a	00 09	00 42	01 09		03 44	07 29			08 26				09 08	09 37	10 04	10 29		10 41			11 08		11 39	12 05
	d									08 28				09 10	09 40	10 06	10 32		10 42			11 10		11 44	12 08
Malton	d														10 04		10 56							12 08	
Seamer	a														10 20		11 13							12 25	
Scarborough	a														10 30		11 22							12 34	
Thirsk	a									08 44									10 59						
Northallerton	a									08 52				09 30		10 28			11 07			11 30			12 28
Darlington 7	a									09 03				09 42		10 40						11 42			12 40
Yarm	d																		11 21						
Thornaby	a									09 23									11 29						
Middlesbrough	a									09 32									11 38						
Durham	a													09 59		11 00						11 59			12 57
Chester-le-Street	a																								
Newcastle 8 ⛴	a													10 18		11 17						12 15			13 12

Liverpool, Manchester Airport and Manchester - Huddersfield, Leeds, Hull, York, Scarborough, Middlesbrough and Newcastle

Network Diagram - see first Page of Table 39

		NT	TP	NT	TP	TP	NT	TP	TP	TP	NT	TP	TP	NT	TP	NT	TP	TP	TP	NT	TP	TP	NT
		🚌	◇1		◇1	◇1	🚌	◇1	◇1	◇1	🚌	◇1	◇1		◇1	🚌	◇1	◇1	◇1	🚌	◇1	◇1	
Liverpool Lime Street 10	d		10 22						11 22				12 22					13 22				14 22	
Liverpool South Parkway 7 ✈	d																						
Warrington Central	d																						
Birchwood	d																						
Newton-le-Willows	d		10 40						11 40				12 40					13 40				14 40	
Manchester Oxford Road	d																						
Manchester Airport ✈	d					11 03				12 03					13 03				14 03				
Manchester Piccadilly 10	a					11 18				12 18					13 18				14 18				
	d					11 21				12 21					13 21				14 21				
Manchester Victoria	a		11 03			11 35			12 03	12 35			13 03		13 35			14 03	14 35			15 03	
	d	10 43	11 05			11 38	11 43		12 05	12 38	12 43		13 05		13 38	13 43		14 05	14 38	14 43		15 05	
Ashton-under-Lyne	d	11 06					12 06				13 06					14 06				15 06			
Stalybridge	a	11 16					12 16				13 16					14 16				15 16			
	d	11 16					12 16				13 16					14 16				15 16			
Mossley (Gr Manchester)	d	11 24					12 24				13 24					14 24				15 24			
Greenfield	d	11 30					12 30				13 30					14 30				15 30			
Marsden	d	11 50					12 50				13 50					14 50				15 50			
Slaithwaite	d	11 55					12 55				13 55					14 55				15 55			
Huddersfield	a	12 11					13 11				14 11					15 11				16 11			
	d			11 58				12 30				13 30		13 58			14 30				15 30		15 58
Deighton	d			12 01										14 01									16 01
Mirfield	d			12 06										14 06									16 06
Ravensthorpe	d			12 09										14 09									16 09
Dewsbury	a		11 58	12 13		12 21		12 42	12 58	13 21		13 39	13 58	14 13	14 21		14 39	14 58	15 21		15 39	15 58	16 13
	d		11 59	12 13		12 22		12 43	12 59	13 22		13 40	13 59	14 13	14 22		14 40	14 59	15 22		15 40	15 59	16 13
Batley	d			12 16										14 16									16 16
Morley	d			12 22										14 22									16 22
Cottingley	d			12 26										14 26									16 26
Leeds 10	a		12 12	12 34		12 37		12 57	13 12	13 37		13 54	14 11	14 34	14 37		14 54	15 12	15 37		15 54	16 12	16 34
	d		12 12			12 40		13 01	13 12	13 40		13 57	14 12		14 40		15 01	15 12	15 40		15 57	16 12	
Garforth	d																						
South Milford	a							13 13									15 13						
Selby	a							13 23									15 23						
Howden	a																						
Brough	a							13 41									15 41						
Hull	a							13 59									15 59						
York 8	a		12 39			13 07			13 39	14 04		14 24	14 38		15 07			15 37	16 05		16 24	16 38	
	d		12 42		12 49	13 10			13 43	14 10			14 50		15 10			15 43	16 10			16 42	
Malton	d								14 07									16 07					
Seamer	a								14 24									16 24					
Scarborough	a				13 36				14 33									16 33					
Thirsk	a		12 59										15 12									17 04	
Northallerton	a		13 07			13 30				14 30			15 20		15 30				16 30			17 16	
Darlington 7	a					13 42				14 42					15 42				16 42				
Yarm	d		13 22										15 35									17 32	
Thornaby	a		13 30										15 44									17 40	
Middlesbrough	a		13 40										15 52									17 50	
Durham	a					13 59				14 59					15 59				16 59				
Chester-le-Street	a					14 05									16 05								
Newcastle 8	a					14 17				15 15					16 18				17 14				

Liverpool, Manchester Airport and Manchester - Huddersfield, Leeds, Hull, York, Scarborough, Middlesbrough and Newcastle

Network Diagram - see first Page of Table 39

		TP	NT	TP	TP	TP	NT	TP	TP	NT	TP	TP	NT	TP	TP	TP	NT	TP	TP	NT	TP	NT	TP
		◇1	🚌	◇1	◇1	◇1	🚌	◇1	◇1		◇1	◇1	🚌	◇1	◇1	◇1	🚌	◇1	◇1		◇1	🚌	◇1
Liverpool Lime Street 10	d				15 22				16 22						17 22				18 22				
Liverpool South Parkway 7 ✈	d																						
Warrington Central	d																						
Birchwood	d																						
Newton-le-Willows	d				15 40				16 40						17 40				18 40				
Manchester Oxford Road	d																						
Manchester Airport ✈	d	15 03				16 03						17 03				18 03					19 03		
Manchester Piccadilly 10	a	15 18				16 18						17 18				18 18					19 18		
	d	15 21				16 21						17 21				18 21					19 21		
Manchester Victoria	a	15 35			16 03	16 35			17 03			17 35			18 03	18 35			19 03		19 35		
	d	15 38	15 43		16 05	16 38	16 43		17 05			17 38	17 43		18 05	18 38	18 43		19 05		19 38	19 43	
Ashton-under-Lyne	d		16 06				17 06						18 06				19 06					20 06	
Stalybridge	a		16 16				17 16						18 16				19 16					20 16	
	d		16 16				17 16						18 16				19 16					20 16	
Mossley (Gr Manchester)	d		16 24				17 24						18 24				19 24					20 24	
Greenfield	d		16 30				17 30						18 30				19 30					20 30	
Marsden	d		16 50				17 50						18 50				19 50					20 50	
Slaithwaite	d		16 55				17 55						18 55				19 55					20 55	
Huddersfield	a		17 11				18 11						19 11				20 11					21 11	
	d			16 30				17 30		17 58				18 30				19 30		19 58			20 33
Deighton	d									18 01										20 01			
Mirfield	d									18 06										20 06			
Ravensthorpe	d									18 09										20 09			
Dewsbury	a	16 21		16 39	16 58	17 21		17 39	17 58	18 13		18 21		18 39	18 58	19 21		19 39	19 58	20 13	20 21		20 42
	d	16 22		16 40	16 59	17 22		17 40	17 59	18 13		18 22		18 40	18 59	19 22		19 40	19 59	20 13	20 22		20 43
Batley	d									18 16										20 16			
Morley	d									18 22										20 22			
Cottingley	d									18 26										20 26			
Leeds 10	a	16 37		16 55	17 12	17 37		17 54	18 12	18 34		18 37		18 55	19 12	19 37		19 55	20 12	20 34	20 37		20 58
	d	16 40		17 01	17 12	17 40		17 57	18 12			18 40		19 01	19 12	19 40		19 57	20 12		20 40		21 04
Garforth	d																						
South Milford	a			17 14										19 16									
Selby	a			17 23										19 29				20 17					21 38
Howden	a																						
Brough	a			17 41										19 51				20 36					21 58
Hull	a			17 59										20 05				20 54					22 12
York 8	a	17 07			17 40	18 07		18 24	18 38			19 05			19 36	20 04			20 38		21 05		
	d	17 10			17 43	18 10			18 42		18 46	19 10			19 46	20 10			20 44		21 08		
Malton	d				18 07										20 10				21 08				
Seamer	a				18 24										20 27				21 25				
Scarborough	a				18 33						19 33				20 36				21 34				
Thirsk	a								18 58							20 26					21 26		
Northallerton	a	17 30				18 30			19 07			19 30				20 34					21 34		
Darlington 7	a	17 42				18 42						19 42									21 45		
Yarm	d								19 22							20 50							
Thornaby	a								19 30							20 58							
Middlesbrough	a								19 40							21 07							
Durham	a	17 59				18 59						19 59									22 02		
Chester-le-Street	a	18 05										20 05											
Newcastle 8	a	18 18				19 16						20 18									22 17		

Table 39

Sundays until 24 June

Liverpool, Manchester Airport and Manchester - Huddersfield, Leeds, Hull, York, Scarborough, Middlesbrough and Newcastle

Network Diagram - see first Page of Table 39

		TP ◇1	TP ◇1	NT	TP ◇1	TP ◇1	NT	TP ◇1	NT	TP ◇1	TP ◇1
Liverpool Lime Street 10	d	19 22			20 22					21 52	
Liverpool South Parkway 7 ✈	d										
Warrington Central	d										
Birchwood	d										
Newton-le-Willows	d	19 40			20 40					22 09	
Manchester Oxford Road	d										
Manchester Airport ✈	d		20 03					21 03			23 22
Manchester Piccadilly 10	a		20 18					21 18			23 35
	d		20 21					21 21			23 39
Manchester Victoria	a	20 03	20 35		21 03			21 35		22 29	23 52
	d	20 05	20 38	20 43	21 05			21 38	21 43	22 38	23 55
Ashton-under-Lyne	d			21 06					22 06		
Stalybridge	a			21 16					22 16		
	d			21 16							
Mossley (Gr Manchester)	d			21 24							
Greenfield	d			21 30							
Marsden	d			21 50			21 47				
Slaithwaite	d			21 55			21 51				
Huddersfield	a			22 11			21 57	22 23		23 23	00 40
	d						21 57	22 26		23 26	00 43
Deighton	d						22 01				
Mirfield	d						22 06				
Ravensthorpe	d						22 09				
Dewsbury	a	20 56	21 22		21 58		22 13	22 35		23 35	
	d	20 57	21 22		21 59		22 13	22 35		23 35	
Batley	d						22 16				
Morley	d						22 22				
Cottingley	d						22 26				
Leeds 10	a	21 12	21 37		22 12		22 33	22 50		23 50	01 04
	d	21 12	21 40		22 12	22 22		22 53		23 53	01 06
Garforth	d										
South Milford	a					22 34					
Selby	a					22 44					
Howden	a										
Brough	a					23 02					
Hull	a					23 19					
York 8	a	21 38	22 08		22 40			23 28		00 22	01 34
	d		22 10		22 42						
Malton	d		22 35								
Seamer	a		22 51								
Scarborough	a		22 59								
Thirsk	a				23 05						
Northallerton	a				23 15						
Darlington 7	a				23 28						
Yarm	d										
Thornaby	a										
Middlesbrough	a										
Durham	a				23 45						
Chester-le-Street	a										
Newcastle 8	a				00 15						

Table 39

Sundays 1 July to 9 September

Liverpool, Manchester Airport and Manchester - Huddersfield, Leeds, Hull, York, Scarborough, Middlesbrough and Newcastle

Network Diagram - see first Page of Table 39

		TP ◇1	TP ◇1	TP ◇1	TP ◇1	TP ◇1	TP ◇1	NT	NT	TP ◇1	TP ◇1	TP ◇1	NT	TP ◇1	TP ◇1	NT	NT	TP ◇1	TP ◇1	TP ◇1	TP ◇1	NT	TP ◇1
Liverpool Lime Street 10	d		22p30												08 22					09 22			10 22
Liverpool South Parkway 7 ✈	d		22p40												08 32					09 32			10 32
Warrington Central	d		22p53												08 45					09 45			10 45
Birchwood	d		22p58												08 50					09 50			10 50
Newton-le-Willows	d																						
Manchester Oxford Road	d		23p17												09 07					10 07			11 07
Manchester Airport ✈	d	22p22		23p24	01 22	04 43	06 24			07 24		08 06							09 22		10 20		
Manchester Piccadilly 10	a	22p36	23p19	23p39	01 36	04 57	06 38			07 37		08 24			09 09				09 37	10 09	10 37		11 09
	d	22p42	23p21	23p43	01 42	05 02	06 42			07 42		08 28			09 11				09 42	10 11	10 42		11 11
Manchester Victoria	a																						
	d												08 43			09 43						10 43	
Ashton-under-Lyne	d												08 53			09 53						10 53	
Stalybridge	a	22p55	23p34				06 53			07 54		08 41	08 57		09 24	09 57				10 24		10 57	11 24
	d	22p55	23p34				06 54			07 54		08 41	08 58		09 24	09 58				10 24		10 58	11 24
Mossley (Gr Manchester)	d												09 03			10 02						11 02	
Greenfield	d												09 07			10 06						11 06	
Marsden	d												09 16			10 15						11 15	
Slaithwaite	d												09 20			10 19						11 19	
Huddersfield	a	23p15	23p52	00 11	02 11	05 31	07 11			08 11		08 59	09 27		09 42	10 27			10 11	10 42	11 11	11 27	11 42
	d	23p16	23p53	00 12	02 12	05 32	07 12	07 23	07 51	08 12		09 02			09 43		09 51		10 12	10 43	11 12		11 43
Deighton	d							07 32	07 54								09 54						
Mirfield	d							07 42	07 59								09 59						
Ravensthorpe	d							07 47	08 02								10 02						
Dewsbury	a	23p25		00s21			07 21	07 55	08 06	08 21		09 11					10 06		10 22		11 21		
	d	23p26					07 22	07 55	08 06	08 22		09 11					10 06		10 22		11 22		
Batley	d							08 03	08 09								10 09						
Morley	d							08 15	08 15								10 15						
Cottingley	d							08 25	08 19								10 19						
Leeds 10	a	23p41	00 14	00 37	02 33	05 53	07 37	08 40	08 27	08 37		09 27			10 07		10 27		10 37	11 04	11 37		12 04
	d	23p42	00 15	00 40	02 35	05 55	07 40			08 40	09 12	09 40		10 04	10 22				10 40	11 12	11 40		12 12
Garforth	d																						
South Milford	a														10 34								
Selby	a														10 44								
Howden	a																						
Brough	a														11 03								
Hull	a														11 18								
York 8	a	00 09	00 42	01 09	03 03	06 23	08 08			09 07	09 37	10 07		10 29					11 07	11 39	12 05		12 39
	d						08 21			09 10	09 40	10 13		10 32				10 42	11 10	11 44	12 08		12 42
Malton	d										10 04			10 56						12 08			
Seamer	a										10 20			11 13						12 25			
Scarborough	a										10 30			11 22						12 34			
Thirsk	a						08 37											10 59					12 59
Northallerton	a						08 45			09 30		10 35						11 07	11 30		12 28		13 07
Darlington 7	a						08 56			09 42		10 46							11 42		12 40		
Yarm	d																	11 21					13 22
Thornaby	a						09 16											11 29					13 30
Middlesbrough	a						09 25											11 39					13 40
Durham	a									09 59		11 08							11 59		12 57		
Chester-le-Street	a																						
Newcastle 8	a									10 18		11 24							12 15		13 12		

Liverpool, Manchester Airport and Manchester - Huddersfield, Leeds, Hull, York, Scarborough, Middlesbrough and Newcastle

Network Diagram - see first Page of Table 39

		NT	NT	TP	TP	TP	TP	TP	NT		TP	TP	NT	NT	TP	TP	TP	TP	NT	TP		TP	NT	NT	TP
				◇1	◇1	◇1	◇1	◇1			◇1	◇1			◇1	◇1	◇1	◇1		◇1		◇1			◇1
Liverpool Lime Street 10	d						11 22					12 22					13 22					14 22			
Liverpool South Parkway 7 ✈	d						11 32					12 32					13 32					14 32			
Warrington Central	d						11 45					12 45					13 45					14 45			
Birchwood	d						11 50					12 50					13 50					14 50			
Newton-le-Willows	d																								
Manchester Oxford Road	d						12 07					13 07					14 07					15 07			
Manchester Airport ✈	d				11 20			12 20							13 20			14 20							15 20
Manchester Piccadilly 10 ⇌	a				11 35		12 09	12 37				13 09			13 37		14 09	14 37				15 09			15 37
	d				11 42	12 01	12 11	12 42			13 02	13 11			13 42	14 02	14 11	14 42		15 02		15 11			15 42
Manchester Victoria ⇌	a																								
	d	11 43							12 43				13 43						14 43				15 43		
Ashton-under-Lyne	d	11 53							12 53				13 53						14 53				15 53		
Stalybridge	a	11 57					12 24		12 57			13 24	13 57				14 24		14 57			15 24	15 57		
	d	11 58					12 24		12 58			13 24	13 58				14 24		14 58			15 24	15 58		
Mossley (Gr Manchester)	d	12 02							13 02				14 02						15 02				16 02		
Greenfield	d	12 06							13 06				14 06						15 06				16 06		
Marsden	d	12 15							13 15				14 15						15 15				16 15		
Slaithwaite	d	12 19							13 19				14 19						15 19				16 19		
Huddersfield	a	12 27			12 11	12 32	12 42	13 11	13 27		13 32	13 42	14 27		14 11	14 32	14 42	15 11	15 27	15 32		15 42	16 27		16 11
	d		11 58		12 12	12 33	12 43	13 12			13 33	13 43		13 58	14 12	14 33	14 43	15 12		15 33		15 43		15 58	16 12
Deighton	d		12 01											14 01										16 01	
Mirfield	d		12 06											14 06										16 06	
Ravensthorpe	d		12 09											14 09										16 09	
Dewsbury	a		12 13		12 21			13 21						14 13	14 21			15 21						16 13	16 22
	d		12 13		12 22			13 22						14 13	14 22			15 22						16 13	16 22
Batley	d		12 16											14 16										16 16	
Morley	d		12 22											14 22										16 22	
Cottingley	d		12 26											14 26										16 26	
Leeds 10	a		12 34		12 37	12 54	13 04	13 37			13 54	14 04		14 34	14 37	14 53	15 04	15 37		15 54		16 04		16 34	16 37
	d				12 40	13 01	13 12	13 40			13 57	14 12			14 40	15 01	15 12	15 40		15 57		16 12			16 40
Garforth	d																								
South Milford	a					13 13										15 13									
Selby	a					13 23										15 23									
Howden	a																								
Brough	a					13 41										15 41									
Hull	a					13 59										15 59									
York 8	a				13 07		13 39	14 05			14 24	14 38			15 07		15 35	16 05		16 22		16 38			17 09
	d			12 49	13 10		13 43	14 10				14 50			15 10		15 43	16 10				16 42			17 10
Malton	d						14 07										16 07								
Seamer	a						14 24										16 24								
Scarborough	a			13 36			14 33										16 33								
Thirsk	a											15 12										17 04			
Northallerton	a				13 30			14 30				15 20			15 30			16 30				17 16			17 30
Darlington 7	a				13 42			14 42							15 42			16 42							17 42
Yarm	d											15 35										17 32			
Thornaby	a											15 44										17 41			
Middlesbrough	a											15 52										17 50			
Durham	a				13 59			14 59							15 59			16 59							17 59
Chester-le-Street	a				14 05										16 05										18 05
Newcastle 8 ⇌	a				14 17			15 15							16 18			17 14							18 18

Liverpool, Manchester Airport and Manchester - Huddersfield, Leeds, Hull, York, Scarborough, Middlesbrough and Newcastle

Network Diagram - see first Page of Table 39

		TP	TP	TP	NT	TP	TP		NT	NT	TP	TP	TP	TP	TP	NT	TP	TP		NT	NT	TP	TP	TP	TP
		◇1	◇1	◇1		◇1	◇1				◇1	◇1	◇1	◇1	◇1		◇1	◇1				◇1	◇1	◇1	◇1
Liverpool Lime Street 10	d		15 22				16 22						17 22					18 22						19 22	
Liverpool South Parkway 7 ✈	d		15 32				16 32						17 32					18 32						19 32	
Warrington Central	d		15 45				16 45						17 45					18 45						19 45	
Birchwood	d		15 50				16 50						17 50					18 50						19 50	
Newton-le-Willows	d																								
Manchester Oxford Road	d		16 07				17 07						18 07					19 07						20 07	
Manchester Airport ✈	d			16 20								17 20			18 20							19 20			20 20
Manchester Piccadilly 10 ⇌	a		16 09	16 37			17 09					17 37		18 09	18 37			19 09				19 37		20 09	20 37
	d	16 02	16 11	16 42		17 02	17 11					17 42	18 02	18 11	18 42		19 02	19 11				19 42	20 06	20 11	20 42
Manchester Victoria ⇌	a																								
	d				16 43				17 43							18 43				19 43					
Ashton-under-Lyne	d				16 53				17 53							18 53				19 53					
Stalybridge	a		16 24		16 57		17 24		17 57					18 24		18 57		19 24		19 57				20 24	
	d		16 24		16 58		17 24		17 58					18 24		18 58		19 24		19 58				20 24	
Mossley (Gr Manchester)	d				17 02				18 02							19 02				20 02					
Greenfield	d				17 06				18 06							19 06				20 06					
Marsden	d				17 15				18 15							19 15				20 15					
Slaithwaite	d				17 19				18 19							19 19				20 19					
Huddersfield	a	16 32	16 42	17 11	17 27	17 32	17 42		18 27			18 11	18 32	18 42	19 11	19 27	19 32	19 42		20 27		20 11	20 36	20 42	21 11
	d	16 33	16 43	17 12		17 33	17 43			17 58		18 12	18 33	18 43	19 12		19 33	19 43			19 58	20 12	20 37	20 43	21 12
Deighton	d									18 01											20 01				
Mirfield	d									18 06											20 06				
Ravensthorpe	d									18 09											20 09				
Dewsbury	a			17 21						18 13		18 21			19 21						20 13	20 21			21 21
	d			17 22						18 13		18 22			19 22						20 13	20 22			21 22
Batley	d									18 16											20 16				
Morley	d									18 22											20 22				
Cottingley	d									18 26											20 26				
Leeds 10	a	16 54	17 04	17 37		17 54	18 04			18 34		18 37	18 54	19 04	19 37		19 54	20 04			20 34	20 37	20 58	21 04	21 37
	d	17 01	17 12	17 40		17 57	18 12					18 40	19 01	19 12	19 40		19 57	20 12				20 40	21 04	21 12	21 40
Garforth	d																								
South Milford	a	17 14											19 16												
Selby	a	17 23											19 28				20 17						21 38		
Howden	a																								
Brough	a	17 41											19 48				20 36						21 58		
Hull	a	17 59											20 05				20 54						22 12		
York 8	a		17 39	18 07		18 24	18 38					19 05		19 38	20 04			20 38				21 05		21 38	22 08
	d		17 43	18 10			18 42				18 46	19 10		19 46	20 10			20 44				21 08			22 10
Malton	d		18 07											20 10				21 08							22 35
Seamer	a		18 24											20 27				21 25							22 51
Scarborough	a		18 33								19 33			20 36				21 34							22 59
Thirsk	a						18 59								20 26							21 26			
Northallerton	a			18 30			19 07					19 30			20 34							21 34			
Darlington 7	a			18 42								19 42										21 45			
Yarm	d						19 22								20 50										
Thornaby	a						19 30								20 58										
Middlesbrough	a						19 40								21 07										
Durham	a			18 59								19 59										22 02			
Chester-le-Street	a											20 05													
Newcastle 8 ⇌	a			19 16								20 18										22 17			

Sundays

1 July to 9 September

Liverpool, Manchester Airport and Manchester - Huddersfield, Leeds, Hull, York, Scarborough, Middlesbrough and Newcastle

Network Diagram - see first Page of Table 39

		NT	TP ◇1	NT	TP ◇1	NT	TP ◇1	TP ◇1	TP ◇1
Liverpool Lime Street 10	d		20 22					21 52	
Liverpool South Parkway 7 ✈	d		20 32					22 02	
Warrington Central	d		20 45					22 15	
Birchwood	d		20 50					22 20	
Newton-le-Willows	d								
Manchester Oxford Road	d		21 07					22 37	
Manchester Airport ✈	d						21 20		23 20
Manchester Piccadilly 10	a		21 09				21 37	22 39	23 37
	d		21 11				21 42	22 42	23 42
Manchester Victoria	a								
	d	20 43		21 43					
Ashton-under-Lyne	d	20 53		21 53					
Stalybridge	a	20 57	21 24	21 57				22 54	
	d	20 58	21 24					22 54	
Mossley (Gr Manchester)	d	21 02							
Greenfield	d	21 06							
Marsden	d	21 15				21 47			
Slaithwaite	d	21 19				21 51			
Huddersfield	a	21 27	21 42			21 57	22 11	23 12	00 11
	d		21 43			21 57	22 12	23 12	00 12
Deighton	d					22 01			
Mirfield	d					22 06			
Ravensthorpe	d					22 09			
Dewsbury	a					22 13	22 21	23 22	
	d					22 13	22 22	23 22	
Batley	d					22 16			
Morley	d					22 22			
Cottingley	d					22 26			
Leeds 10	a		22 04			22 33	22 37	23 39	00 51
	d		22 12		22 22		22 40	23 42	00 54
Garforth	d								
South Milford	a				22 34				
Selby	a				22 44				
Howden	a								
Brough	a				23 02				
Hull	a				23 19				
York 8	a		22 40				23 11	00 26	01 22
	d		22 42						
Malton	d								
Seamer	a								
Scarborough	a								
Thirsk	a		23 06						
Northallerton	a		23 16						
Darlington 7	a		23 28						
Yarm	d								
Thornaby	a								
Middlesbrough	a								
Durham	a		23 45						
Chester-le-Street	a								
Newcastle 8	a		00 15						

Sundays

16 September to 21 October

Liverpool, Manchester Airport and Manchester - Huddersfield, Leeds, Hull, York, Scarborough, Middlesbrough and Newcastle

Network Diagram - see first Page of Table 39

		TP ◇1	TP ◇1	TP ◇1	TP bus	TP ◇1	TP ◇1	NT bus	NT bus	TP ◇1	NT bus	NT	TP ◇1	XC ◇1	TP ◇1	TP ◇1	NT	NT	TP ◇1	NT bus	TP ◇1	TP ◇1	TP ◇1
Liverpool Lime Street 10	d		22p30																08 22				09 22
Liverpool South Parkway 7 ✈	d		22p40																				
Warrington Central	d		22p53																				
Birchwood	d		22p58																				
Newton-le-Willows	d																		08 41				09 40
Manchester Oxford Road	d		23p15																				
Manchester Airport ✈	d	22p22		23p24	01 20					06 11						07 50						09 03	
Manchester Piccadilly 10	a	22p36	23p17	23p39	01 45					06 24						08 04						09 19	
	d	22p42	23p19	23p43	01 45					06 26						08 08						09 20	
Manchester Victoria	a															08 25			09 03			09 35	10 03
	d						05 35	08 17								08 28			09 05	09 17		09 38	10 05
Ashton-under-Lyne	d							08 40												09 40			
Stalybridge	a	22p55	23p31					08 50												09 50			
	d	22p55	23p31					08 50												09 50			
Mossley (Gr Manchester)	d							08 58												09 58			
Greenfield	d							09 04												10 04			
Marsden	d							09 24												10 24			
Slaithwaite	d							09 29												10 29			
Huddersfield	a	23p15	23p52	00 11	02 45		06 20	09 45		07 23						09 15			09 51	10 45			10 54
	d	23p16	23p53	00 12		02 55	06 24		07 23	07 27		07 51				09 16		09 44	09 53				10 56
Deighton	d								07 32			07 54						09 47					
Mirfield	d								07 42			07 59						09 52					
Ravensthorpe	d								07 47		←	08 02						09 55					
Dewsbury	a	23p25		00s21					07 55	07 36	07 55	08 06				09 25		09 59				10 21	
	d	23p26							07 55	07 36	07 55	08 06				09 26		10 03				10 23	
Batley	d								→		08 03	08 09						10 06					
Morley	d										08 15	08 15						10 12					
Cottingley	d										08 25	08 19						10 15					
Leeds 10	a	23p41	00 14	00 37		03 16	06 45			07 56	08 40	08 27				09 42		10 23	10 14			10 38	11 15
	d	23p42	00 15	00 40		03 18	06 46			07 59			08 40	09 15	09 19	09 45	09 50		10 17		10 24	10 40	11 18
Garforth	d																10 02						
South Milford	a																				10 36		
Selby	a																				10 46		
Howden	a																						
Brough	a																				11 04		
Hull	a																				11 21		
York 8	a	00 09	00 42	01 09		03 44	07 14			08 26			09 08	09 36	09 42	10 10	10 28		10 42			11 10	11 39
	d									08 28			09 10	09 38	09 45	10 13			10 42			11 11	11 44
Malton	d														10 08								12 08
Seamer	a														10 25								12 25
Scarborough	a														10 34								12 34
Thirsk	a									08 44									10 59				
Northallerton	a									08 52			09 30			10 35			11 07			11 31	
Darlington 7	a									09 03			09 42	10 03		10 47						11 43	
Yarm	d																		11 21				
Thornaby	a									09 23									11 29				
Middlesbrough	a									09 32									11 38				
Durham	a												09 59	10 20		11 03						12 00	
Chester-le-Street	a																						
Newcastle 8	a												10 18	10 34		11 19						12 16	

16 September to 21 October

Liverpool, Manchester Airport and Manchester - Huddersfield, Leeds, Hull, York, Scarborough, Middlesbrough and Newcastle

Network Diagram - see first Page of Table 39

		TP	NT	TP	NT	TP	NT	TP	TP	TP	NT	TP	TP	NT	TP	NT	TP	TP	TP	NT	TP	TP	NT
		◇1		◇1		◇1		◇1	◇1	◇1		◇1	◇1		◇1		◇1	◇1	◇1		◇1	◇1	
Liverpool Lime Street 10	d			10 22					11 22				12 22					13 22				14 22	
Liverpool South Parkway 7 ✈	d																						
Warrington Central	d																						
Birchwood	d																						
Newton-le-Willows	d			10 41					11 40				12 41					13 40				14 41	
Manchester Oxford Road	d																						
Manchester Airport ✈	d	10 03				11 03				12 03					13 03				14 03				
Manchester Piccadilly 10	a	10 17				11 18				12 18					13 18				14 18				
	d	10 20				11 21				12 21					13 21				14 21				
Manchester Victoria	a	10 35		11 03		11 35			12 03	12 35			13 03		13 35			14 03	14 35			15 03	
	d	10 38	10 43	11 05		11 38	11 43		12 05	12 38	12 43		13 05		13 38	13 43		14 05	14 38	14 43		15 05	
Ashton-under-Lyne	d		11 06				12 06				13 06					14 06				15 06			
Stalybridge	a		11 16				12 16				13 16					14 16				15 16			
	d		11 16				12 16				13 16					14 16				15 16			
Mossley (Gtr Manchester)	d		11 24				12 24				13 24					14 24				15 24			
Greenfield	d		11 30				12 30				13 30					14 30				15 30			
Marsden	d		11 50				12 50				13 50					14 50				15 50			
Slaithwaite	d		11 55				12 55				13 55					14 55				15 55			
Huddersfield	a		12 11				13 11				14 11					15 11				16 11			
	d				11 58			12 30				13 30		13 58			14 30				15 30		15 58
Deighton	d				12 01									14 01									16 01
Mirfield	d				12 06									14 06									16 06
Ravensthorpe	d				12 09									14 09									16 09
Dewsbury	a	11 21		11 58	12 13	12 21		12 42	12 58	13 21		13 39	13 58	14 13	14 21		14 39	14 58	15 21		15 39	15 58	16 13
	d	11 22		11 59	12 13	12 22		12 43	12 59	13 22		13 40	13 59	14 13	14 22		14 40	14 59	15 22		15 40	15 59	16 13
Batley	d				12 16									14 16									16 16
Morley	d				12 22									14 22									16 22
Cottingley	d				12 26									14 26									16 26
Leeds 10	a	11 37		12 12	12 34	12 37		12 57	13 12	13 37		13 54	14 11	14 34	14 37		14 54	15 12	15 37		15 54	16 12	16 34
	d	11 40		12 12		12 40		13 01	13 12	13 40		13 57	14 12		14 40		15 01	15 12	15 40		15 57	16 12	
Garforth	d																						
South Milford	a							13 13									15 13						
Selby	a							13 23									15 23						
Howden	a																						
Brough	a							13 41									15 41						
Hull	a							13 59									15 59						
York 8	a	12 08		12 39		13 08			13 39	14 04		14 24	14 38		15 07			15 37	16 05		16 24	16 38	
	d	12 10		12 42		13 10			13 43	14 10			14 50		15 10			15 43	16 10			16 42	
Malton	d								14 07									16 07					
Seamer	a								14 24									16 24					
Scarborough	a								14 33									16 33					
Thirsk	a			12 59									15 12									17 04	
Northallerton	a	12 30		13 07		13 30				14 30			15 20		15 30				16 30			17 16	
Darlington 7	a	12 42				13 42				14 42					15 42				16 42				
Yarm	d			13 22									15 35									17 32	
Thornaby	a			13 30									15 44									17 40	
Middlesbrough	a			13 40									15 52									17 50	
Durham	a	12 59				13 59				14 59					15 59				16 59				
Chester-le-Street	a					14 05									16 05								
Newcastle 8	a	13 14				14 17				15 15					16 18				17 14				

16 September to 21 October

Liverpool, Manchester Airport and Manchester - Huddersfield, Leeds, Hull, York, Scarborough, Middlesbrough and Newcastle

Network Diagram - see first Page of Table 39

		TP	NT	TP	TP	TP	NT	TP	TP	NT	TP	NT	TP	TP	TP	NT	TP	TP	NT	TP	NT	TP	TP
		◇1		◇1	◇1	◇1		◇1	◇1		◇1		◇1	◇1	◇1		◇1	◇1		◇1		◇1	◇1
Liverpool Lime Street 10	d				15 22				16 22					17 22				18 22					19 22
Liverpool South Parkway 7 ✈	d																						
Warrington Central	d																						
Birchwood	d																						
Newton-le-Willows	d				15 40				16 41					17 41				18 40					19 40
Manchester Oxford Road	d																						
Manchester Airport ✈	d	15 03				16 03					17 03				18 03					19 03			
Manchester Piccadilly 10	a	15 18				16 18					17 18				18 18					19 18			
	d	15 21				16 21					17 21				18 21					19 21			
Manchester Victoria	a	15 35			16 03	16 35			17 03		17 35			18 03	18 35			19 03		19 35			20 03
	d	15 38	15 43		16 05	16 38	16 43		17 05		17 38	17 43		18 05	18 38	18 43		19 05		19 38	19 43		20 05
Ashton-under-Lyne	d		16 06				17 06					18 06				19 06					20 06		
Stalybridge	a		16 16				17 16					18 16				19 16					20 16		
	d		16 16				17 16					18 16				19 16					20 16		
Mossley (Gtr Manchester)	d		16 24				17 24					18 24				19 24					20 24		
Greenfield	d		16 30				17 30					18 30				19 30					20 30		
Marsden	d		16 50				17 50					18 50				19 50					20 50		
Slaithwaite	d		16 55				17 55					18 55				19 55					20 55		
Huddersfield	a		17 11				18 11					19 11				20 11					21 11		
	d			16 30				17 30		17 58			18 30				19 30		19 58			20 33	
Deighton	d									18 01									20 01				
Mirfield	d									18 06									20 06				
Ravensthorpe	d									18 09									20 09				
Dewsbury	a	16 21		16 39	16 58	17 21		17 39	17 58	18 13	18 21		18 39	18 58	19 21		19 39	19 58	20 13	20 21		20 42	20 56
	d	16 22		16 40	16 59	17 22		17 40	17 59	18 13	18 22		18 40	18 59	19 22		19 40	19 59	20 13	20 22		20 43	20 57
Batley	d									18 16									20 16				
Morley	d									18 22									20 22				
Cottingley	d									18 26									20 26				
Leeds 10	a	16 37		16 55	17 12	17 37		17 54	18 12	18 34	18 37		18 55	19 12	19 37		19 55	20 12	20 34	20 37		20 58	21 12
	d	16 40		17 01	17 12	17 40		17 57	18 12		18 40		19 01	19 12	19 40		19 57	20 12		20 40		21 04	21 12
Garforth	d																						
South Milford	a			17 14									19 16										
Selby	a			17 23									19 29				20 17					21 38	
Howden	a																						
Brough	a			17 41									19 51				20 36					21 58	
Hull	a			17 59									20 05				20 54					22 12	
York 8	a	17 07			17 39	18 07		18 24	18 38		19 05			19 36	20 04			20 38		21 05			21 38
	d	17 10			17 43	18 10			18 42		19 10			19 46	20 10			20 44		21 08			
Malton	d				18 07									20 10				21 08					
Seamer	a				18 24									20 27				21 25					
Scarborough	a				18 33									20 36				21 34					
Thirsk	a								18 58						20 26					21 26			
Northallerton	a	17 30				18 30			19 07		19 30				20 34					21 34			
Darlington 7	a	17 42				18 42					19 42									21 45			
Yarm	d								19 22						20 50								
Thornaby	a								19 30						20 58								
Middlesbrough	a								19 40						21 07								
Durham	a	17 59				18 59					19 59									22 02			
Chester-le-Street	a	18 05									20 05												
Newcastle 8	a	18 18				19 16					20 18									22 17			

Table 39

Sundays
16 September to 21 October

Liverpool, Manchester Airport and Manchester - Huddersfield, Leeds, Hull, York, Scarborough, Middlesbrough and Newcastle

Network Diagram - see first Page of Table 39

		TP	NT	TP	TP		NT	TP	NT	TP	TP
		◇1	bus	◇1	◇1			◇1	bus	◇1	◇1
Liverpool Lime Street 10	d			20 22						21 52	
Liverpool South Parkway 7 ✈	d										
Warrington Central	d										
Birchwood	d										
Newton-le-Willows	d			20 40						22 09	
Manchester Oxford Road	d										
Manchester Airport ✈	d	20 03						21 03			23 22
Manchester Piccadilly 10	a	20 18						21 18			23 35
	d	20 21						21 21			23 40
Manchester Victoria	a	20 35		21 03				21 35		22 29	23 53
	d	20 38	20 43	21 05				21 38	21 43	22 38	23 55
Ashton-under-Lyne	d		21 06						22 06		
Stalybridge	a		21 16						22 16		
	d		21 16								
Mossley (Gr Manchester)	d		21 24								
Greenfield	d		21 30								
Marsden	d		21 50				21 47				
Slaithwaite	d		21 55				21 51				
Huddersfield	a		22 11				21 57	22 23		23 23	00 40
	d						21 57	22 26		23 26	00 43
Deighton	d						22 01				
Mirfield	d						22 06				
Ravensthorpe	d						22 09				
Dewsbury	a	21 22		21 58			22 13	22 35		23 35	
	d	21 22		21 59			22 13	22 35		23 35	
Batley	d						22 16				
Morley	d						22 22				
Cottingley	d						22 26				
Leeds 10	a	21 37		22 12			22 33	22 50		23 50	01 04
	d	21 40		22 12	22 22			22 53		23 53	01 06
Garforth	d										
South Milford	a				22 34						
Selby	a				22 44						
Howden	a										
Brough	a				23 02						
Hull	a				23 19						
York 8	a	22 08		22 40				23 28		00 22	01 34
	d	22 10		22 42							
Malton	d	22 35									
Seamer	a	22 51									
Scarborough	a	22 59									
Thirsk	a			23 05							
Northallerton	a			23 15							
Darlington 7	a			23 28							
Yarm	d										
Thornaby	a										
Middlesbrough	a										
Durham	a			23 45							
Chester-le-Street	a										
Newcastle 8	a			00 15							

Table 39

Sundays
from 28 October

Liverpool, Manchester Airport and Manchester - Huddersfield, Leeds, Hull, York, Scarborough, Middlesbrough and Newcastle

Network Diagram - see first Page of Table 39

		TP	TP	TP	TP	NT	TP	NT	TP	TP	TP		TP	NT	TP	NT	TP	TP	TP	TP	NT	TP		NT	TP
		◇1	bus	bus	bus	bus	bus	bus	◇1	◇1	◇1		◇1		◇1	bus	◇1	◇1	◇1	◇1	bus	◇1			◇1
Liverpool Lime Street 10	d														08 22				09 22			10 22			
Liverpool South Parkway 7 ✈	d																								
Warrington Central	d																								
Birchwood	d																								
Newton-le-Willows	d														08 41				09 40			10 41			
Manchester Oxford Road	d																								
Manchester Airport ✈	d	22p22	23p25	01 20	05 05		06 05											09 03		10 03					11 03
Manchester Piccadilly 10	a	22p36	23p50	01 45	05 30		06 30											09 19		10 18					11 18
	d	22p42	23p50	01 45	05 30		06 30						08 08					09 20		10 21					11 21
Manchester Victoria	a												08 25		09 03			09 35	10 03	10 35		11 03			11 35
	d							08 17					08 28		09 05	09 17		09 38	10 05	10 38	10 43	11 05			11 38
Ashton-under-Lyne	d							08 40								09 40					11 06				
Stalybridge	a	22p55					06 55	08 50								09 50					11 16				
	d	22p55					06 55	08 50								09 50					11 16				
Mossley (Gr Manchester)	d							08 58								09 58					11 24				
Greenfield	d							09 04								10 04					11 30				
Marsden	d							09 24								10 24					11 50				
Slaithwaite	d							09 29								10 29					11 55				
Huddersfield	a	23p15	00 50	02 45	06 30		07 40	09 45					09 15		09 51	10 45			10 54		12 11				
	d	23p16	00 50	02 45	06 30	07 23	07 40						09 18	09 44	09 53				10 56					11 58	
Deighton	d					07 32								09 47										12 01	
Mirfield	d					07 42								09 52										12 06	
Ravensthorpe	d					07 47								09 55										12 09	
Dewsbury	a	23p25			06 55	07 55	08 05						09 27	09 59				10 21		11 21		11 58		12 13	12 21
	d	23p26			06 55	07 55	08 05						09 27	10 03				10 23		11 22		11 59		12 13	12 22
Batley	d					08 03								10 06										12 16	
Morley	d					08 15								10 12										12 22	
Cottingley	d					08 25								10 15										12 26	
Leeds 10	a	23p41	01 25	03 20	07 20	08 40	08 30						09 43	10 23	10 14			10 38	11 15	11 37		12 12		12 34	12 37
	d	23p42	01 25	03 20	07 20					08 40	09 19		09 45		10 17		10 24	10 40	11 18	11 40		12 12			12 40
Garforth	d																								
South Milford	a																10 36								
Selby	a																10 46								
Howden	a																								
Brough	a																11 04								
Hull	a																11 21								
York 8	a	00 09	02 15	04 10	08 10					09 08	09 42		10 10		10 42			11 10	11 39	12 08		12 39			13 08
	d								08 21	09 10	09 45		10 13		10 42			11 11	11 44	12 10		12 42			13 10
Malton	d										10 08								12 08						
Seamer	a										10 25								12 25						
Scarborough	a										10 34								12 34						
Thirsk	a								08 37						10 59							12 59			
Northallerton	a								08 45	09 30			10 35		11 07			11 31		12 30		13 07			13 30
Darlington 7	a								08 56	09 42			10 47					11 43		12 42					13 42
Yarm	d														11 21							13 22			
Thornaby	a								09 16						11 29							13 30			
Middlesbrough	a								09 25						11 38							13 40			
Durham	a									09 59			11 03					12 00		12 59					13 59
Chester-le-Street	a																								14 05
Newcastle 8	a									10 18			11 19					12 16		13 14					14 17

Liverpool, Manchester Airport and Manchester - Huddersfield, Leeds, Hull, York, Scarborough, Middlesbrough and Newcastle

Network Diagram - see first Page of Table 39

		NT	TP	TP	TP	NT	TP	TP	NT		TP	NT	TP	TP	TP	NT	TP	TP	NT	TP		NT	TP	TP	TP
		🚌	◇1	◇1	◇1	🚌	◇1	◇1			◇1	🚌	◇1	◇1	◇1	🚌	◇1	◇1		◇1		🚌	◇1	◇1	◇1
Liverpool Lime Street 10	d			11 22				12 22						13 22				14 22						15 22	
Liverpool South Parkway 7 ✈	d																								
Warrington Central	d																								
Birchwood	d																								
Newton-le-Willows	d			11 40				12 41						13 40				14 41						15 40	
Manchester Oxford Road	d																								
Manchester Airport ✈	d				12 03						13 03				14 03					15 03					16 03
Manchester Piccadilly 10	a				12 18						13 18				14 18					15 18					16 18
	d				12 21						13 21				14 21					15 21					16 21
Manchester Victoria	a			12 03	12 35			13 03			13 35			14 03	14 35			15 03		15 35				16 03	16 35
	d	11 43		12 05	12 38	12 43		13 05			13 38	13 43		14 05	14 38	14 43		15 05		15 38		15 43		16 05	16 38
Ashton-under-Lyne	d	12 06				13 06						14 06				15 06						16 06			
Stalybridge	a	12 16				13 16						14 16				15 16						16 16			
	d	12 16				13 16						14 16				15 16						16 16			
Mossley (Gr Manchester)	d	12 24				13 24						14 24				15 24						16 24			
Greenfield	d	12 30				13 30						14 30				15 30						16 30			
Marsden	d	12 50				13 50						14 50				15 50						16 50			
Slaithwaite	d	12 55				13 55						14 55				15 55						16 55			
Huddersfield	a	13 11				14 11						15 11				16 11						17 11			
	d		12 30				13 30		13 58				14 30				15 30		15 58				16 30		
Deighton	d								14 01										16 01						
Mirfield	d								14 06										16 06						
Ravensthorpe	d								14 09										16 09						
Dewsbury	a		12 42	12 58	13 21		13 39	13 58	14 13		14 21		14 39	14 58	15 21		15 39	15 58	16 13	16 21			16 39	16 58	17 21
	d		12 43	12 59	13 22		13 40	13 59	14 13		14 22		14 40	14 59	15 22		15 40	15 59	16 13	16 22			16 40	16 59	17 22
Batley	d								14 16										16 16						
Morley	d								14 22										16 22						
Cottingley	d								14 26										16 26						
Leeds 10	a		12 57	13 12	13 37		13 54	14 11	14 34		14 37		14 54	15 12	15 37		15 54	16 12	16 34	16 37			16 55	17 12	17 37
	d		13 01	13 12	13 40		13 57	14 12			14 40		15 01	15 12	15 40		15 57	16 12		16 40			17 01	17 12	17 40
Garforth	d																								
South Milford	a		13 13										15 13										17 14		
Selby	a		13 23										15 23										17 23		
Howden	a																								
Brough	a		13 41										15 41										17 41		
Hull	a		13 59										15 59										17 59		
York 8	a			13 39	14 04		14 24	14 38			15 07			15 37	16 05		16 24	16 38		17 07				17 39	18 07
	d			13 43	14 10			14 50			15 10			15 43	16 10			16 42		17 10				17 43	18 10
Malton	d			14 07										16 07										18 07	
Seamer	a			14 24										16 24										18 24	
Scarborough	a			14 33										16 33										18 33	
Thirsk	a							15 12										17 04							
Northallerton	a				14 30			15 20			15 30				16 30			17 16		17 30					18 30
Darlington 7	a				14 42						15 42				16 42					17 42					18 42
Yarm	d							15 35										17 32							
Thornaby	a							15 44										17 40							
Middlesbrough	a							15 52										17 50							
Durham	a				14 59						15 59				16 59					17 59					18 59
Chester-le-Street	a										16 05									18 05					
Newcastle 8	a				15 15						16 18				17 14					18 18					19 16

Liverpool, Manchester Airport and Manchester - Huddersfield, Leeds, Hull, York, Scarborough, Middlesbrough and Newcastle

Network Diagram - see first Page of Table 39

		NT	TP	TP	NT	TP	NT		TP	TP	TP	NT	TP	TP	NT	TP	NT	TP		TP	TP	NT	TP	TP	NT
		🚌	◇1	◇1		◇1	🚌		◇1	◇1	◇1	🚌	◇1	◇1		◇1	🚌	◇1		◇1	◇1	🚌	◇1	◇1	
Liverpool Lime Street 10	d			16 22						17 22				18 22						19 22			20 22		
Liverpool South Parkway 7 ✈	d																								
Warrington Central	d																								
Birchwood	d																								
Newton-le-Willows	d			16 41						17 41				18 40						19 40			20 40		
Manchester Oxford Road	d																								
Manchester Airport ✈	d					17 03					18 03					19 03					20 03				
Manchester Piccadilly 10	a					17 18					18 18					19 18					20 18				
	d					17 21					18 21					19 21					20 21				
Manchester Victoria	a			17 03		17 35				18 03	18 35			19 03		19 35				20 03	20 35		21 03		
	d	16 43		17 05		17 38	17 43			18 05	18 38	18 43		19 05		19 38	19 43			20 05	20 38	20 43	21 05		
Ashton-under-Lyne	d	17 06					18 06					19 06					20 06					21 06			
Stalybridge	a	17 16					18 16					19 16					20 16					21 16			
	d	17 16					18 16					19 16					20 16					21 16			
Mossley (Gr Manchester)	d	17 24					18 24					19 24					20 24					21 24			
Greenfield	d	17 30					18 30					19 30					20 30					21 30			
Marsden	d	17 50					18 50					19 50					20 50					21 50			21 47
Slaithwaite	d	17 55					18 55					19 55					20 55					21 55			21 51
Huddersfield	a	18 11					19 11					20 11					21 11					22 11			21 57
	d		17 30		17 58				18 30				19 30		19 58			20 33							21 57
Deighton	d				18 01										20 01										22 01
Mirfield	d				18 06										20 06										22 06
Ravensthorpe	d				18 09										20 09										22 09
Dewsbury	a		17 39	17 58	18 13	18 21			18 39	18 58	19 21		19 39	19 58	20 13	20 21		20 42		20 56	21 22		21 58		22 13
	d		17 40	17 59	18 13	18 22			18 40	18 59	19 22		19 40	19 59	20 13	20 22		20 43		20 57	21 22		21 59		22 13
Batley	d				18 16										20 16										22 16
Morley	d				18 22										20 22										22 22
Cottingley	d				18 26										20 26										22 26
Leeds 10	a		17 54	18 12	18 34	18 37			18 55	19 12	19 37		19 55	20 12	20 34	20 37		20 58		21 12	21 37		22 12		22 33
	d		17 57	18 12		18 40			19 01	19 12	19 40		19 57	20 12		20 40		21 04		21 12	21 40		22 12	22 22	
Garforth	d																								
South Milford	a								19 16															22 34	
Selby	a								19 29				20 17					21 38						22 44	
Howden	a																								
Brough	a								19 51				20 36					21 58						23 02	
Hull	a								20 05				20 54					22 12						23 19	
York 8	a		18 24	18 38		19 05				19 36	20 04			20 38		21 05				21 38	22 08		22 40		
	d			18 42		19 10				19 46	20 10			20 44		21 08					22 10		22 42		
Malton	d									20 10				21 08							22 35				
Seamer	a									20 27				21 25							22 51				
Scarborough	a									20 36				21 34							22 59				
Thirsk	a			18 58							20 26					21 26							23 05		
Northallerton	a			19 07		19 30					20 34					21 34							23 15		
Darlington 7	a					19 42										21 45							23 28		
Yarm	d			19 22							20 50														
Thornaby	a			19 30							20 58														
Middlesbrough	a			19 40							21 07														
Durham	a					19 59										22 02							23 45		
Chester-le-Street	a					20 05																			
Newcastle 8	a					20 18										22 17							00 15		

Table 39

Liverpool, Manchester Airport and Manchester - Huddersfield, Leeds, Hull, York, Scarborough, Middlesbrough and Newcastle

Network Diagram - see first Page of Table 39

		TP	NT	TP	TP
		◇1	🚌	◇1	◇1
Liverpool Lime Street 10	d			21 52	
Liverpool South Parkway 7 ✈	d				
Warrington Central	d				
Birchwood	d				
Newton-le-Willows	d			22 09	
Manchester Oxford Road	d				
Manchester Airport ✈	d	21 03			23 22
Manchester Piccadilly 10 🚊	a	21 18			23 35
	d	21 21			23 40
Manchester Victoria 🚊	a	21 35		22 29	23 53
	d	21 38	21 43	22 38	23 55
Ashton-under-Lyne	d		22 06		
Stalybridge	a		22 16		
	d				
Mossley (Gr Manchester)	d				
Greenfield	d				
Marsden	d				
Slaithwaite	d				
Huddersfield	a	22 23		23 23	00 40
	d	22 26		23 26	00 43
Deighton	d				
Mirfield	d				
Ravensthorpe	d				
Dewsbury	a	22 35		23 35	
	d	22 35		23 35	
Batley	d				
Morley	d				
Cottingley	d				
Leeds 10	a	22 50		23 50	01 04
	d	22 53		23 53	01 06
Garforth	d				
South Milford	a				
Selby	a				
Howden	a				
Brough	a				
Hull	a				
York 8	a	23 28		00 22	01 34
	d				
Malton	d				
Seamer	a				
Scarborough	a				
Thirsk	a				
Northallerton	a				
Darlington 7	a				
Yarm	d				
Thornaby	a				
Middlesbrough	a				
Durham	a				
Chester-le-Street	a				
Newcastle 8 🚊	a				

Table 40

York and Selby - Leeds

Miles	Miles			GR MX	TP MO	TP MX	TP MO	TP MX	TP MX	TP MO	TP	NT		TP	NT		TP	XC	TP	NT	TP	TP	NT	TP	NT
				1	◇1	◇1	◇1	◇1	◇1	◇1	◇1			◇1			◇1 ⊼	◇1 ⊼	◇1 ⊼		◇1 ⊼	◇1 ⊼		◇1 ⊼	
0	—	**York** 8	33 d	00 17	01 38	01 38	02 47	02 52	04 00	04 23	05 26	05 40		05 57	06 13		06 28	06 32			06 55		07 06	07 26	
8¾	—	Ulleskelf	33 d																				07 15		
10¾	—	Church Fenton	33 d																				07 21		
—	0	**Selby**	d																06 36	06 42		07 08			07 23
—	7¾	South Milford	d																	06 51					07 32
15¾	11	Micklefield	d									05 59			06 28					06 58			07 28		07 41
17½	12¾	East Garforth	d									06 03			06 32					07 02			07 32		07 46
18	13¼	Garforth	d									06 05		06 12	06 35					07 04	07 10	07 24	07 35		07 48
21	16¼	Cross Gates	d									06 10			06 40					07 09			07 40	07 44	07 53
25½	20¾	**Leeds** 10	a	00 50	02 04	02 19	03 13	03 33	04 42	04 49	05 52	06 21		06 22	06 49		06 52	06 55	07 00	07 19	07 20	07 35	07 49	07 52	08 01
—	—	Bradford Interchange	37 a												07 11					07 43			08 09		08 28

			TP	XC		NT	NT	TP	TP	NT	TP	NT	TP		XC	NT	TP		TP	NT	TP	TP	XC	NT	TP
			◇1 ⊼	◇1 ⊼				◇1 ⊼	◇1 ⊼		◇1 ⊼		◇1 ⊼		◇1 ⊼		◇1 ⊼		◇1 ⊼		◇1 ⊼	◇1 ⊼	◇1 ⊼		◇1 ⊼
York 8	33 d		07 40	07 44			07 48	07 55		08 12	08 25		08 40		08 44		08 57			09 11	09 28	09 40	09 45		09 57
Ulleskelf	33 d																								
Church Fenton	33 d						08 05													09 23					
Selby	d					07 43			08 11			08 24				08 43			09 11					09 43	
South Milford	d					07 52						08 34				08 53								09 52	
Micklefield	d					07 57	08 13			08 27		08 41				08 56				09 30				09 58	
East Garforth	d					08 01	08 17			08 31		08 45				09 01				09 34				10 02	
Garforth	d					08 04	08 20	08 12		08 33	08 40	08 48				09 04	09 12			09 37				10 05	10 12
Cross Gates	d					08 10	08 25			08 38		08 52				09 08				09 42				10 10	
Leeds 10	a		08 04	08 08		08 19	08 35	08 22	08 36	08 49	08 52	09 02	09 04		09 08	09 19	09 22		09 36	09 51	09 52	10 04	10 08	10 19	10 22
Bradford Interchange	37 a					08 43				09 12						09 43				10 12				10 43	

		TP	NT		TP	TP		XC	NT	TP		NT	TP	NT	TP	TP	XC	NT			TP	TP	NT	TP	TP
		◇1 ⊼			◇1 ⊼	◇1 ⊼		◇1 ⊼		◇1 ⊼			◇1 ⊼		◇1 ⊼	◇1 ⊼	◇1 ⊼				◇1 ⊼	◇1 ⊼		◇1 ⊼	◇1 ⊼
York 8	33 d		10 11		10 27	10 40		10 44		10 57		11 05		11 09	11 26	11 40	11 45				11 57		12 13	12 26	12 40
Ulleskelf	33 d											11 15													
Church Fenton	33 d											11a19		11 21											
Selby	d	10 11							10 42				11 11					11 43				12 11			
South Milford	d								10 52									11 52							
Micklefield	d		10 29						10 57					11 29				11 57					12 28		
East Garforth	d		10 33						11 02					11 33				12 02					12 32		
Garforth	d		10 35						11 05	11 12				11 35				12 05			12 12		12 35		
Cross Gates	d		10 40						11 09					11 40				12 09					12 40		
Leeds 10	a	10 36	10 49		10 52	11 04		11 07	11 19	11 22			11 36	11 49	11 52	12 04	12 08	12 19			12 22	12 36	12 49	12 52	13 04
Bradford Interchange	37 a		11 11						11 43					12 11				12 43					13 12		

		XC	NT	NT	TP	TP	NT	TP		TP	XC	NT		TP	TP	NT	TP	TP	XC	NT			TP	NT	TP
		◇1 ⊼			◇1 ⊼	◇1 ⊼		◇1 ⊼		◇1 ⊼	◇1 ⊼			◇1 ⊼	◇1 ⊼		◇1 ⊼	◇1 ⊼	◇1 ⊼				◇1 ⊼		◇1 ⊼
York 8	33 d	12 44		12 47	12 57		13 09	13 24		13 40	13 44			13 57		14 13	14 26	14 40	14 44				14 57	15 01	
Ulleskelf	33 d																							15 11	
Church Fenton	33 d						13 21																	15a15	
Selby	d		12 43	13a06		13 11						13 43			14 11					14 43					15 11
South Milford	d		12 53									13 52								14 52					
Micklefield	d		12 58				13 29					13 57				14 29				14 56					
East Garforth	d		13 02				13 33					14 02				14 33				15 00					
Garforth	d		13 05		13 12		13 35					14 05		14 12		14 35				15 03			15 12		
Cross Gates	d		13 10				13 40					14 09				14 40				15 08					
Leeds 10	a	13 07	13 19		13 22	13 35	13 49	13 52		14 04	14 07	14 20		14 22	14 36	14 49	14 52	15 04	15 07	15 19			15 23		15 36
Bradford Interchange	37 a		13 43				14 12					14 43				15 12				15 43					

		NT	TP	TP	XC	NT	TP FX	TP FO	XC	TP FO		TP FX	NT		TP FO	TP	TP	XC	NT	TP	TP	NT	NT		TP
			◇1 ⊼	◇1 ⊼	◇1 ⊼		◇1 ⊼	◇1 ⊼	◇1 ⊼	◇1 ⊼		◇1 ⊼				◇1 ⊼	◇1 ⊼	◇1 ⊼		◇1 ⊼	◇1 ⊼				◇1 ⊼
York 8	33 d	15 08	15 26	15 40	15 44		15 57	15 57	16 04				16 08		16 13	16 26	16 40	16 44		16 57		17 13	17 19		17 26
Ulleskelf	33 d																								
Church Fenton	33 d	15 20											16 20		16 38								17 30		
Selby	d					15 41				16 11		16 11							16 43		17 11		17a45		
South Milford	d					15 52													16 53						
Micklefield	d	15 29				15 55							16 28						16 58			17 28			
East Garforth	d	15 33				15 59							16 32						17 02			17 32			
Garforth	d	15 35				16 02	16 12			16 22			16 35						17 05	17 12		17 35			
Cross Gates	d	15 40				16 07							16 40						17 10			17 40			
Leeds 10	a	15 49	15 52	16 04	16 07	16 19	16 22	16 22	16 32	16 36		16 36	16 49		16 59	16 52	17 04	17 06	17 19	17 22	17 36	17 49			17 52
Bradford Interchange	37 a	16 10				16 43							17 10									18 10			

York and Selby - Leeds

	TP	TP	XC	NT	TP	NT	NT	TP	TP	TP	XC	NT	NT	NT	TP	TP	TP	XC	TP	NT	TP
	◇1	◇1 🍴	◇1 🍴		◇1 🍴			◇1 🍴	◇1 🍴	◇1	◇1 🍴				◇1	◇1	◇1	◇1 🍴	◇1		◇1
York 8 33 d		17 40	17 44		17 57		18 05	18 12		18 40	18 45			19 04	19 08		19 40	19 44	20 10	20 13	20 40
Ulleskelf 33 d							18 15														
Church Fenton 33 d							18 22							19 20							
Selby d	17 32			17 38		18 00			18 29			18 46	19 00			19 30					
South Milford d				17 49								18 52									
Micklefield d				17 56			18 30					18 58		19 28						20 27	
East Garforth d				18 01			18 34					19 02		19 32						20 31	
Garforth d				18 03	18 12	18 18	18 36					19 04	19 15	19 34	19 22					20 34	
Cross Gates d				18 08			18 41					19 10		19 39						20 39	
Leeds 10 a	17 58	18 04	18 07	18 19	18 22	18 32	18 49	18 37	18 52	19 04	19 08	19 20	19 27	19 48	19 37	19 56	20 04	20 08	20 35	20 48	21 04
Bradford Interchange 37 a				18 43		18 58	19 10					19 44								21 10	

	XC	TP	TP	TP	NT	TP	TP	NT	TP	NT
		FO	FX	FX						
	◇1 🍴	◇1	◇1	◇1		◇1	◇1		◇1	
York 8 33 d	20 45		21 14		21 22	21 46		22 09	23 07	23 13
Ulleskelf 33 d					21 31					
Church Fenton 33 d					21 33			22 22		23 28
Selby d		21 06		21 16			22 07			
South Milford d		21 16		21 26			22 16			
Micklefield d					21 41			22 28		23 35
East Garforth d					21 45			22 32		23 39
Garforth d					21 47			22 34		23 42
Cross Gates d					21 52			22 39		23 47
Leeds 10 a	21 08	21 35	21 37	21 44	22 01	22 07	22 35	22 50	23 33	23 56
Bradford Interchange 37 a										

Saturdays
until 8 September

	GR	TP	TP	TP	TP	TP	NT	TP	TP	XC	NT	TP	TP	NT	TP	TP	XC	NT	TP	TP
	1	◇1	◇1	◇1	◇1	◇1		◇1	◇1 🍴	◇1 🍴		◇1	◇1		◇1	◇1 🍴	◇1 🍴		◇1 🍴	◇1 🍴
York 8 33 d	00 17	01 52	02 40	03 52	05 26	05 57	06 13	06 28		06 40		06 55		07 06	07 26	07 40	07 44		07 53	
Ulleskelf 33 d														07 15						
Church Fenton 33 d														07 21						
Selby d									06 36		06 42		07 08					07 42		08 11
South Milford d											06 51							07 52		
Micklefield d							06 28				06 58			07 28				07 57		
East Garforth d							06 32				07 02			07 32				08 02		
Garforth d						06 12	06 35				07 04	07 10	07 24	07 35				08 07	08 12	
Cross Gates d							06 40				07 09			07 40	07 44			08 10		
Leeds 10 a	00 50	02 18	03 06	04 34	05 52	06 22	06 49	06 52	07 00	07 03	07 19	07 20	07 35	07 49	07 52	08 04	08 08	08 19	08 22	08 36
Bradford Interchange 37 a							07 11				07 43			08 09				08 43		

	NT	TP	TP	XC	NT	TP	TP	NT	TP	TP	XC	NT	TP	TP	NT	TP	TP	XC	NT
		◇1 🍴	◇1 🍴	◇1 🍴		◇1 🍴	◇1 🍴		◇1 🍴	◇1 🍴	◇1 🍴		◇1 🍴	◇1		◇1 🍴	◇1 🍴	◇1 🍴	
York 8 33 d	08 09	08 25	08 40	08 44		08 57		09 11	09 25	09 40	09 46		09 57		10 11	10 27	10 40	10 45	
Ulleskelf 33 d																			
Church Fenton 33 d	08 21							09 23											
Selby d					08 43		09 11					09 43		10 11					10 42
South Milford d					08 53							09 53							10 52
Micklefield d	08 26				08 58			09 30				09 58			10 29				10 56
East Garforth d	08 30				09 02			09 34				10 02			10 33				11 00
Garforth d	08 34	08 40			09 05	09 12		09 37				10 05	10 12		10 35				11 03
Cross Gates d	08 39				09 10			09 42				10 10			10 41				11 08
Leeds 10 a	08 49	08 52	09 04	09 07	09 19	09 22	09 36	09 51	09 53	10 04	10 09	10 19	10 22	10 36	10 49	10 52	11 04	11 08	11 19
Bradford Interchange 37 a	09 12				09 43			10 11				10 43			11 12				11 43

	TP	NT	TP	NT	TP	TP	XC	NT	TP	TP	NT	TP	TP	XC	NT	TP	TP	NT	TP	TP
	◇1 🍴		◇1		◇1 🍴	◇1 🍴	◇1 🍴		◇1 🍴	◇1 🍴		◇1 🍴	◇1	◇1 🍴		◇1 🍴	◇1 🍴		◇1 🍴	◇1 🍴
York 8 33 d	10 57	11 05		11 09	11 26	11 40	11 45		11 57		12 13	12 26	12 40	12 45		12 57		13 09	13 24	13 40
Ulleskelf 33 d		11 15																		
Church Fenton 33 d		11a19		11 21														13 21		
Selby d			11 11					11 43		12 11					12 44		13 11			
South Milford d								11 53							12 56					
Micklefield d				11 29				11 58			12 28				12 58			13 29		
East Garforth d				11 33				12 02			12 32				13 03			13 33		
Garforth d	11 12			11 35				12 05	12 12		12 35				13 06	13 12		13 35		
Cross Gates d				11 40				12 10			12 40				13 10			13 40		
Leeds 10 a	11 22		11 36	11 49	11 53	12 04	12 07	12 19	12 22	12 36	12 49	12 52	13 04	13 08	13 20	13 22	13 36	13 49	13 52	14 04
Bradford Interchange 37 a				12 12				12 43			13 12				13 43			14 12		

Saturdays
until 8 September

York and Selby - Leeds

	XC	NT	TP	TP	NT	TP	TP	XC	NT	TP	NT	TP	NT	TP	TP	XC	NT	TP	XC	TP
	◇1 🍴		◇1 🍴	◇1		◇1 🍴	◇1 🍴	◇1 🍴		◇1 🍴		◇1		◇1 🍴	◇1 🍴	◇1 🍴		◇1 🍴	◇1 🍴	◇1 🍴
York 8 33 d	13 44		13 57		14 13	14 27	14 40	14 44		14 57	15 01		15 09	15 26	15 40	15 45		15 57	16 06	
Ulleskelf 33 d											15 11									
Church Fenton 33 d											15a15		15 21							
Selby d		13 43		14 11					14 43			15 11					15 41			16 11
South Milford d		13 53							14 54								15 52			
Micklefield d		13 58			14 29				14 57				15 29				15 56			
East Garforth d		14 02			14 33				15 02				15 33				16 01			
Garforth d		14 05	14 12		14 35				15 05	15 12			15 35				16 03	16 12		
Cross Gates d		14 10			14 40				15 09				15 40				16 08			
Leeds 10 a	14 08	14 19	14 22	14 35	14 49	14 52	15 04	15 06	15 19	15 22		15 36	15 49	15 53	16 04	16 07	16 18	16 22	16 32	16 36
Bradford Interchange 37 a		14 43			15 12				15 43				16 10				16 43			

	NT	TP	TP	XC	NT	TP	TP	NT	NT	TP	TP	TP	XC	NT	TP	NT	TP	TP	TP	XC
		◇1 🍴	◇1 🍴	◇1 🍴		◇1 🍴	◇1			◇1 🍴	◇1	◇1	◇1 🍴		◇1		◇1	◇1	◇1	◇1 🍴
York 8 33 d	16 08	16 26	16 40	16 44		16 57		17 12	17 19	17 26		17 40	17 44		17 57	18 05	18 12		18 40	18 44
Ulleskelf 33 d																18 15				
Church Fenton 33 d	16 20								17 30							18 22				
Selby d					16 43		17 11		17a45		17 32			17 39				18 29		
South Milford d					16 53									17 49						
Micklefield d	16 28				16 58			17 29						17 56		18 30				
East Garforth d	16 32				17 02			17 33						18 01		18 34				
Garforth d	16 35				17 05	17 12		17 36						18 04	18 12	18 36				
Cross Gates d	16 40				17 10			17 41						18 08		18 41				
Leeds 10 a	16 49	16 52	17 04	17 07	17 19	17 22	17 36	17 49		17 52	17 58	18 04	18 08	18 18	18 22	18 49	18 37	18 52	19 04	19 08
Bradford Interchange 37 a	17 10				17 43			18 09						18 43		19 10				

	NT	NT	NT	TP	TP	TP	XC	TP	NT	TP	TP	XC	TP	NT	TP	TP	NT	TP	NT
				◇1	◇1	◇1	◇1 🍴	◇1		◇1	◇1	◇1 🍴	◇1		◇1	◇1		◇1	
York 8 33 d			19 04	19 08		19 40	19 44	20 10	20 13		20 40	20 45	21 14	21 18	21 46		22 13	23 07	23 13
Ulleskelf 33 d														21 27					
Church Fenton 33 d			19 20											21 33					23 28
Selby d	18 46	18 55			19 30					20 27						22 07			
South Milford d	18 55									20 36						22 16			
Micklefield d	18 58		19 28						20 27					21 41			22 28		23 35
East Garforth d	19 02		19 32						20 31					21 45			22 32		23 39
Garforth d	19 05	19 12	19 34	19 22					20 34					21 47			22 34		23 42
Cross Gates d	19 10		19 39						20 39					21 52			22 39		23 47
Leeds 10 a	19 21	19 25	19 48	19 35	19 56	20 04	20 08	20 35	20 48	20 56	21 04	21 07	21 37	22 01	22 07	22 35	22 50	23 33	23 56
Bradford Interchange 37 a	19 44								21 10										

Saturdays
from 15 September

	GR	TP	TP	TP	TP	TP	NT	XC	TP	TP	NT	TP	TP	NT	TP	TP	XC	NT	TP	TP
	1	◇1	◇1	◇1	◇1	◇1		◇1 🍴	◇1	◇1 🍴		◇1	◇1		◇1	◇1 🍴	◇1 🍴		◇1 🍴	◇1 🍴
York 8 33 d	00 17	01 52	02 40	03 52	05 26	05 57	06 13	06 17	06 28			06 55		07 06	07 26	07 40	07 44		07 53	
Ulleskelf 33 d														07 15						
Church Fenton 33 d														07 21						
Selby d										06 36	06 42		07 08					07 42		08 11
South Milford d											06 51							07 52		
Micklefield d							06 28				06 58			07 28				07 57		
East Garforth d							06 32				07 02			07 32				08 02		
Garforth d						06 12	06 35				07 04	07 10	07 24	07 35				08 07	08 12	
Cross Gates d							06 40				07 09			07 40	07 44			08 10		
Leeds 10 a	00 50	02 18	03 06	04 34	05 52	06 22	06 49	06 57	06 52	07 00	07 19	07 20	07 35	07 49	07 52	08 04	08 08	08 19	08 22	08 36
Bradford Interchange 37 a							07 11				07 43			08 09				08 43		

	NT	TP	TP	XC	NT	TP	TP	NT	TP	TP	XC	NT	TP	TP	NT	TP	TP	XC	NT
		◇1 🍴	◇1 🍴	◇1 🍴		◇1 🍴	◇1 🍴		◇1 🍴	◇1 🍴	◇1 🍴		◇1 🍴	◇1		◇1 🍴	◇1 🍴	◇1 🍴	
York 8 33 d	08 09	08 25	08 40	08 44		08 57		09 11	09 25	09 40	09 46		09 57		10 11	10 27	10 40	10 45	
Ulleskelf 33 d																			
Church Fenton 33 d	08 21							09 23											
Selby d					08 43		09 11					09 43		10 11					10 42
South Milford d					08 53							09 53							10 52
Micklefield d	08 26				08 58			09 30				09 58			10 29				10 56
East Garforth d	08 30				09 02			09 34				10 02			10 33				11 00
Garforth d	08 34	08 40			09 05	09 12		09 37				10 05	10 12		10 35				11 03
Cross Gates d	08 39				09 10			09 42				10 10			10 41				11 08
Leeds 10 a	08 49	08 52	09 04	09 07	09 19	09 22	09 36	09 51	09 53	10 04	10 09	10 19	10 22	10 36	10 49	10 52	11 04	11 08	11 19
Bradford Interchange 37 a	09 12				09 43			10 11				10 43			11 12				11 43

Table 40

York and Selby - Leeds

Saturdays from 15 September

		TP	NT	TP	NT	TP	TP	XC	NT	TP	TP	NT	TP	TP	XC	NT	TP	TP	NT	TP	TP
		◇1 🍴		◇1		◇1 🍴	◇1 🍴	◇1 🍴		◇1 🍴	◇1 🍴		◇1 🍴	◇1	◇1 🍴		◇1 🍴	◇1 🍴		◇1 🍴	◇1 🍴
York 8	33 d	10 57	11 05		11 09	11 26	11 40	11 45		11 57		12 13	12 26	12 40	12 45		12 57		13 09	13 24	13 40
Ulleskelf	33 d		11 15																		
Church Fenton	33 d		11a19		11 21														13 21		
Selby	d			11 11					11 43		12 11					12 44		13 11			
South Milford	d								11 53							12 56					
Micklefield	d				11 29				11 58			12 28				12 58			13 29		
East Garforth	d				11 33				12 02			12 32				13 03			13 33		
Garforth	d	11 12			11 35				12 05	12 12		12 35				13 06	13 12		13 35		
Cross Gates	d				11 40				12 10			12 40				13 10			13 40		
Leeds 10	a	11 22		11 36	11 49	11 53	12 04	12 07	12 19	12 22	12 36	12 49	12 52	13 04	13 08	13 20	13 22	13 36	13 49	13 52	14 04
Bradford Interchange	37 a				12 12				12 43			13 12				13 43			14 12		

		XC	NT	TP	TP	NT	TP	TP	XC	NT	TP	NT	TP	NT	TP	TP	XC	NT	TP	XC	TP
		◇1 🍴		◇1 🍴	◇1		◇1 🍴	◇1 🍴	◇1 🍴		◇1 🍴		◇1		◇1 🍴	◇1 🍴	◇1 🍴		◇1 🍴	◇1 🍴	◇1 🍴
York 8	33 d	13 44		13 57		14 13	14 27	14 40	14 44		14 57	15 01		15 09	15 26	15 40	15 45		15 57	16 06	
Ulleskelf	33 d											15 11									
Church Fenton	33 d											15a15		15 21							
Selby	d		13 43		14 11					14 43			15 11					15 41			16 11
South Milford	d		13 53							14 54								15 52			
Micklefield	d		13 58			14 29				14 57				15 29				15 56			
East Garforth	d		14 02			14 33				15 02				15 33				16 01			
Garforth	d		14 05	14 12		14 35				15 05	15 12			15 35				16 03	16 12		
Cross Gates	d		14 10			14 40				15 09				15 40				16 08			
Leeds 10	a	14 08	14 19	14 22	14 35	14 49	14 52	15 04	15 06	15 19	15 22		15 36	15 49	15 53	16 04	16 07	16 18	16 22	16 32	16 36
Bradford Interchange	37 a		14 43			15 12				15 43				16 10				16 43			

		NT	TP	TP	XC	NT	TP	TP	NT	NT	TP	TP	TP	XC	NT	TP	NT	TP	TP	TP	XC
			◇1 🍴	◇1 🍴	◇1 🍴		◇1 🍴	◇1			◇1 🍴	◇1	◇1	◇1 🍴		◇1		◇1	◇1	◇1	◇1 🍴
York 8	33 d	16 08	16 26	16 40	16 44		16 57		17 12	17 19	17 26		17 40	17 44		17 57	18 05	18 12		18 40	18 44
Ulleskelf	33 d																18 15				
Church Fenton	33 d	16 20								17 30							18 22				
Selby	d					16 43		17 11		17a45		17 32			17 39				18 29		
South Milford	d					16 53									17 49						
Micklefield	d	16 28				16 58			17 29						17 56		18 30				
East Garforth	d	16 32				17 02			17 33						18 01		18 34				
Garforth	d	16 35				17 05	17 12		17 36						18 04	18 12	18 36				
Cross Gates	d	16 40				17 10			17 41						18 08		18 41				
Leeds 10	a	16 49	16 52	17 04	17 07	17 19	17 22	17 36	17 49		17 52	17 58	18 04	18 08	18 18	18 22	18 49	18 37	18 52	19 04	19 08
Bradford Interchange	37 a	17 10				17 43			18 09						18 43		19 10				

		NT	NT	NT	TP	TP	TP	XC	TP	NT	TP	TP	XC	TP	NT	TP	TP	NT	TP	NT
					◇1	◇1	◇1	◇1 🍴	◇1		◇1	◇1	◇1 🍴	◇1		◇1	◇1		◇1	
York 8	33 d			19 04	19 08		19 40	19 44	20 10	20 13		20 40	20 45	21 13	21 18	21 45		22 13	23 07	23 13
Ulleskelf	33 d														21 27					
Church Fenton	33 d			19 20											21 33					23 28
Selby	d	18 46	18 55			19 30					20 27						22 07			
South Milford	d	18 55									20 36						22 16			
Micklefield	d	18 58		19 28						20 27					21 41			22 28		23 35
East Garforth	d	19 02		19 32						20 31					21 45			22 32		23 39
Garforth	d	19 05	19 12	19 34	19 22					20 34					21 47			22 34		23 42
Cross Gates	d	19 10		19 39						20 39					21 52			22 39		23 47
Leeds 10	a	19 21	19 25	19 48	19 35	19 56	20 04	20 08	20 35	20 48	20 56	21 04	21 07	21 37	21 57	22 07	22 35	22 50	23 33	23 56
Bradford Interchange	37 a	19 44								21 10										

Sundays until 24 June

		TP	TP	TP	TP	TP	TP	NT	TP	XC	TP	TP	NT	TP	XC	TP	NT	TP	XC	TP	TP	NT
		◇1	◇1	◇1	◇1	◇1	◇1		◇1	◇1 🍴	◇1	◇1		◇1	◇1 🍴	◇1		◇1	◇1 🍴	◇1	◇1	
York 8	33 d	02 00	04 20	05 25	06 45	08 10	08 30	08 50	09 15	09 28		09 45	09 52	10 15	10 28	10 45	10 57	11 15	11 28		11 45	11 52
Ulleskelf	33 d																					
Church Fenton	33 d							09 02					10 04									12 04
Selby	d										09 33									11 29		
South Milford	d										09 42									11 38		
Micklefield	d							09 09					10 12				11 12					12 11
East Garforth	d							09 13					10 16				11 16					12 15
Garforth	d							09 16					10 18				11 18					12 18
Cross Gates	d							09 21					10 23				11 23					12 23
Leeds 10	a	02 26	04 46	05 51	07 11	08 37	08 53	09 30	09 38	09 54	10 00	10 08	10 32	10 38	10 51	11 08	11 32	11 38	11 51	11 56	12 09	12 32
Bradford Interchange	37 a							09 53					10 53				11 53					12 53

Table 40

York and Selby - Leeds

Sundays until 24 June

		TP	XC	TP	TP	NT	TP	TP	XC	TP	NT	TP	TP	XC	TP	NT	TP	TP	XC	TP	NT
		◇1	◇1 🍴	◇1	◇1		◇1	◇1	◇1 🍴	◇1		◇1	◇1	◇1 🍴	◇1		◇1	◇1	◇1 🍴	◇1	
York 8	33 d	12 15	12 28		12 45	12 52	13 15		13 40	13 45	13 52	14 15	14 33	14 40	14 45	14 52	15 15		15 40	15 45	15 52
Ulleskelf	33 d																				
Church Fenton	33 d										14 04										16 04
Selby	d			12 32				13 29										15 29			
South Milford	d							13 38										15 38			
Micklefield	d					13 07					14 11					15 07					16 11
East Garforth	d					13 11					14 15					15 11					16 15
Garforth	d					13 13					14 18					15 13					16 18
Cross Gates	d					13 18					14 23					15 18					16 23
Leeds 10	a	12 38	12 51	12 56	13 08	13 27	13 37	13 56	14 03	14 08	14 32	14 38	14 56	15 05	15 07	15 27	15 38	15 56	16 03	16 08	16 32
Bradford Interchange	37 a					13 53					14 53					15 53					16 53

		TP	TP	XC	TP	NT	TP	TP	XC	TP	NT	NT	TP	TP	XC	TP	NT	TP	TP	XC
		◇1	◇1	◇1 🍴	◇1		◇1	◇1	◇1 🍴	◇1			◇1	◇1	◇1 🍴	◇1		◇1	◇1	◇1 🍴
York 8	33 d	16 15	16 33	16 40	16 45	16 52	17 15		17 40	17 45	17 52	18 10	18 15	18 33	18 40	18 45	18 52	19 15		19 40
Ulleskelf	33 d																			
Church Fenton	33 d										18 04	18a21								
Selby	d							17 29											19 29	
South Milford	d							17 38											19 38	
Micklefield	d					17 07					18 11						19 07			
East Garforth	d					17 11					18 15						19 11			
Garforth	d					17 13					18 18						19 13			
Cross Gates	d					17 18					18 23						19 18			
Leeds 10	a	16 38	16 56	17 06	17 08	17 27	17 38	17 56	18 04	18 08	18 32		18 38	18 57	19 03	19 08	19 27	19 38	19 56	20 05
Bradford Interchange	37 a					17 53					18 53						19 53			

		TP	NT	TP	XC	TP	NT	NT	TP	TP	XC	NT	TP	GR	TP
		◇1		◇1	◇1 🍴	◇1			◇1	◇1			◇1	■ 1 🍴	◇1
York 8	33 d	19 45	19 52	20 15	20 40	20 45	20 50	20 57	21 15		21 45	21 52	22 12	23 03	23 12
Ulleskelf	33 d														
Church Fenton	33 d		20 04				21a01					22 04			
Selby	d									21 31					
South Milford	d									21 40					
Micklefield	d		20 12					21 12				22 12			
East Garforth	d		20 16					21 17				22 16			
Garforth	d		20 18					21 19				22 19			
Cross Gates	d		20 23					21 24				22 23			
Leeds 10	a	20 08	20 32	20 38	21 02	21 08		21 33	21 38	21 59	22 11	22 32	22 36	23 34	23 38
Bradford Interchange	37 a		20 53					21 56							

Sundays 1 July to 9 September

		TP	TP	TP	TP	TP	TP	TP	NT	TP	XC	TP	NT	TP	XC	NT	TP	NT	TP	XC	TP	TP	NT
		◇1	◇1	◇1	◇1	◇1	◇1	◇1		◇1	◇1 🍴	◇1		◇1	◇1 🍴		◇1		◇1	◇1 🍴	◇1	◇1	
York 8	33 d	02 44	03 59	05 12	06 12	07 12	08 10	08 45	08 50	09 15	09 28		09 52	10 15	10 28	10 40	10 45	10 57	11 15	11 28		11 45	11 52
Ulleskelf	33 d																						
Church Fenton	33 d								09 02				10 04										12 04
Selby	d											09 33				10a58					11 29		
South Milford	d											09 42									11 38		
Micklefield	d								09 09				10 12					11 12					12 11
East Garforth	d								09 13				10 16					11 16					12 15
Garforth	d								09 16				10 18					11 18					12 18
Cross Gates	d								09 21				10 23					11 23					12 23
Leeds 10	a	03 10	04 25	05 38	06 38	07 38	08 37	09 08	09 30	09 38	09 54	10 00	10 32	10 38	10 51		11 08	11 32	11 38	11 51	11 56	12 09	12 32
Bradford Interchange	37 a								09 53				10 53					11 53					12 53

		TP	XC	TP	TP	NT	TP	TP	XC	TP	NT	TP	TP	XC	TP	NT	TP	TP	XC	TP	NT
		◇1	◇1 🍴	◇1	◇1		◇1	◇1	◇1 🍴	◇1		◇1	◇1	◇1 🍴	◇1		◇1	◇1	◇1 🍴	◇1	
York 8	33 d	12 15	12 28		12 45	12 52	13 15		13 40	13 45	13 52	14 15	14 33	14 40	14 45	14 52	15 15		15 40	15 45	15 52
Ulleskelf	33 d																				
Church Fenton	33 d										14 04										16 04
Selby	d			12 32				13 29										15 29			
South Milford	d							13 38										15 38			
Micklefield	d					13 07					14 11					15 07					16 11
East Garforth	d					13 11					14 15					15 11					16 15
Garforth	d					13 13					14 18					15 13					16 18
Cross Gates	d					13 18					14 23					15 18					16 23
Leeds 10	a	12 38	12 51	12 56	13 08	13 27	13 38	13 56	14 03	14 08	14 32	14 38	14 56	15 05	15 08	15 27	15 38	15 56	16 03	16 08	16 32
Bradford Interchange	37 a					13 53					14 53					15 53					16 53

York and Selby - Leeds

Sundays
1 July to 9 September

	TP	TP	XC	TP	NT	TP	TP	XC	TP	NT	NT	TP	TP	XC	TP	NT	TP	TP	XC
	◇■	◇■	◇■ ⊼	◇■		◇■	◇■	◇■ ⊼	◇■			◇■	◇■	◇■ ⊼	◇■		◇■	◇■	◇■ ⊼
York ■ 33 d	16 15	16 33	16 40	16 45	16 52	17 15		17 40	17 45	17 52	18 10	18 15	18 33	18 40	18 45	18 52	19 15		19 40
Ulleskelf 33 d																			
Church Fenton 33 d										18 04	18a21								
Selby d							17 29											19 29	
South Milford d							17 38											19 38	
Micklefield d					17 07					18 11						19 07			
East Garforth d					17 11					18 15						19 11			
Garforth d					17 13					18 18						19 13			
Cross Gates d					17 18					18 23						19 18			
Leeds ■ a	16 38	16 56	17 06	17 08	17 27	17 38	17 56	18 04	18 08	18 32		18 38	18 57	19 03	19 08	19 27	19 38	19 54	20 05
Bradford Interchange 37 a					17 53					18 53						19 53			

	TP	NT	TP	XC	TP	NT	NT	TP	TP	XC	NT	TP	GR	TP
	◇■		◇■	◇■ ⊼	◇■			◇■	◇■			◇■	■ ■ ⊼	◇■
York ■ 33 d	19 45	19 52	20 15	20 40	20 45	20 50	20 57	21 15		21 45	21 52	22 12	23 03	23 12
Ulleskelf 33 d														
Church Fenton 33 d		20 04				21a01					22 04			
Selby d									21 31					
South Milford d									21 40					
Micklefield d		20 12					21 12				22 12			
East Garforth d		20 16					21 17				22 16			
Garforth d		20 18					21 19				22 19			
Cross Gates d		20 23					21 24				22 23			
Leeds ■ a	20 08	20 32	20 38	21 02	21 08		21 33	21 38	21 59	22 11	22 32	22 36	23 34	23 38
Bradford Interchange 37 a		20 53					21 56							

Sundays
16 September to 21 October

	TP	TP	TP	TP	TP	TP	NT	TP	XC	TP	TP	NT	TP	XC	TP	NT	TP	XC	TP	TP	NT
	◇■	◇■	◇■	◇■	◇■	◇■		◇■	◇■ ⊼	◇■	◇■		◇■	◇■ ⊼	◇■		◇■	◇■ ⊼	◇■	◇■	
York ■ 33 d	02 00	04 20	05 25	06 45	08 10	08 30	08 50	09 15	09 30		09 45	09 52	10 15	10 34	10 45	10 53	11 15	11 28		11 45	11 52
Ulleskelf 33 d																					
Church Fenton 33 d							09 02					10 04									12 04
Selby d										09 33									11 29		
South Milford d										09 42									11 38		
Micklefield d							09 09					10 12				11 08					12 11
East Garforth d							09 13					10 16				11 12					12 15
Garforth d							09 16					10 18				11 14					12 18
Cross Gates d							09 21					10 23				11 19					12 23
Leeds ■ a	02 26	04 46	05 51	07 11	08 37	08 53	09 30	09 38	09 54	10 00	10 08	10 32	10 38	10 57	11 08	11 28	11 38	11 51	11 56	12 09	12 32
Bradford Interchange 37 a																					

	TP	XC	TP	TP	NT	TP	TP	XC	TP	NT	TP	TP	XC	TP	NT	TP	TP	XC	TP	NT
	◇■	◇■ ⊼	◇■	◇■		◇■	◇■	◇■ ⊼	◇■		◇■	◇■	◇■ ⊼	◇■		◇■	◇■	◇■ ⊼	◇■	
York ■ 33 d	12 15	12 28		12 45	12 52	13 15		13 40	13 45	13 52	14 16	14 33	14 41	14 45	14 52	15 15		15 40	15 45	15 52
Ulleskelf 33 d																				
Church Fenton 33 d										14 04										16 04
Selby d			12 32				13 29										15 29			
South Milford d							13 38										15 38			
Micklefield d					13 14					14 11					15 07					16 11
East Garforth d					13 18					14 15					15 11					16 15
Garforth d					13 20					14 18					15 13					16 18
Cross Gates d					13 25					14 23					15 18					16 23
Leeds ■ a	12 38	12 51	12 56	13 08	13 32	13 37	13 56	14 03	14 08	14 32	14 39	14 56	15 04	15 07	15 27	15 38	15 56	16 05	16 08	16 32
Bradford Interchange 37 a																				

	TP	TP	XC	TP	NT	TP	TP	XC	TP	NT	NT	TP	TP	XC	TP	NT	TP	TP	XC
	◇■	◇■	◇■ ⊼	◇■		◇■	◇■	◇■ ⊼	◇■			◇■	◇■	◇■ ⊼	◇■		◇■	◇■	◇■ ⊼
York ■ 33 d	16 15	16 33	16 41	16 45	16 52	17 15		17 40	17 45	17 52	18 10	18 15	18 33	18 41	18 45	18 52	19 15		19 40
Ulleskelf 33 d																			
Church Fenton 33 d										18 04	18a21								
Selby d							17 29											19 29	
South Milford d							17 38											19 38	
Micklefield d					17 07					18 11						19 07			
East Garforth d					17 11					18 15						19 11			
Garforth d					17 13					18 18						19 13			
Cross Gates d					17 18					18 23						19 18			
Leeds ■ a	16 38	16 56	17 06	17 08	17 27	17 38	17 56	18 04	18 08	18 32		18 38	18 57	19 03	19 08	19 27	19 38	19 56	20 05
Bradford Interchange 37 a																			

York and Selby - Leeds

Sundays
16 September to 21 October

	TP	NT	TP	XC	TP	NT	NT	TP	TP	NT	TP	GR	TP
	◇■		◇■	◇■ ⊼	◇■			◇■	◇■		◇■	■ ■ ⊼	◇■
York ■ 33 d	19 45	19 52	20 15	20 40	20 45	20 50	20 57	21 15		21 52	22 12	23 03	23 12
Ulleskelf 33 d													
Church Fenton 33 d		20 04				21a01				22 04			
Selby d									21 31				
South Milford d									21 40				
Micklefield d		20 12					21 12			22 12			
East Garforth d		20 16					21 17			22 16			
Garforth d		20 18					21 19			22 19			
Cross Gates d		20 23					21 24			22 23			
Leeds ■ a	20 08	20 32	20 38	21 02	21 08		21 33	21 38	21 59	22 32	22 36	23 34	23 38
Bradford Interchange 37 a													

Sundays
from 28 October

	TP	TP	TP	TP	NT	TP	XC	TP	TP	NT	TP	XC	TP	NT	TP	XC	TP	TP	NT	TP	XC
	🚌	🚌	🚌	◇■		◇■	◇■ ⊼	◇■	◇■		◇■	◇■ ⊼	◇■		◇■	◇■ ⊼	◇■	◇■		◇■	◇■ ⊼
York ■ 33 d	03 30	04 55	05 55	08 30	08 50	09 15	09 30		09 45	09 52	10 15	10 34	10 45	10 53	11 15	11 28		11 45	11 52	12 15	12 28
Ulleskelf 33 d																					
Church Fenton 33 d					09 02					10 04									12 04		
Selby d								09 33									11 29				
South Milford d								09 42									11 38				
Micklefield d					09 09					10 12				11 08					12 11		
East Garforth d					09 13					10 16				11 12					12 15		
Garforth d					09 16					10 18				11 14					12 18		
Cross Gates d					09 21					10 23				11 19					12 23		
Leeds ■ a	04 20	05 45	06 45	08 53	09 30	09 38	09 54	10 00	10 08	10 32	10 38	10 57	11 08	11 28	11 38	11 51	11 56	12 09	12 32	12 38	12 51
Bradford Interchange 37 a					09 53					10 53				11 53					12 53		

	TP	TP	NT	TP	TP	TP	NT	TP	TP	XC	TP	NT	TP	TP	XC	TP	NT	TP	TP
	◇■	◇■		◇■	◇■	◇■		◇■	◇■	◇■ ⊼	◇■		◇■	◇■	◇■ ⊼	◇■		◇■	◇■
York ■ 33 d		12 45	12 52	13 15		13 45	13 52	14 16	14 33	14 40	14 45	14 52	15 15		15 40	15 45	15 52	16 15	16 33
Ulleskelf 33 d																			
Church Fenton 33 d							14 04										16 04		
Selby d	12 32				13 29									15 29					
South Milford d					13 38									15 38					
Micklefield d			13 14				14 11					15 07					16 11		
East Garforth d			13 18				14 15					15 11					16 15		
Garforth d			13 20				14 18					15 13					16 18		
Cross Gates d			13 25				14 23					15 18					16 23		
Leeds ■ a	12 56	13 08	13 32	13 37	13 56	14 08	14 32	14 39	14 56	15 05	15 07	15 27	15 38	15 56	16 03	16 08	16 32	16 38	16 56
Bradford Interchange 37 a			13 53				14 53					15 53					16 53		

	XC	TP	NT	TP	TP	XC	TP	NT	TP	TP	XC	TP	NT	TP	TP	XC	TP	NT	TP	XC
	◇■ ⊼	◇■		◇■	◇■	◇■ ⊼	◇■		◇■	◇■	◇■ ⊼	◇■		◇■	◇■	◇■ ⊼	◇■		◇■	◇■ ⊼
York ■ 33 d	16 40	16 45	16 52	17 15		17 40	17 45	17 52	18 15	18 33	18 40	18 45	18 52	19 15		19 40	19 45	19 52	20 15	20 40
Ulleskelf 33 d																				
Church Fenton 33 d								18 04										20 04		
Selby d					17 29										19 29					
South Milford d					17 38										19 38					
Micklefield d			17 07					18 11					19 07					20 12		
East Garforth d			17 11					18 15					19 11					20 16		
Garforth d			17 13					18 18					19 13					20 18		
Cross Gates d			17 18					18 23					19 18					20 23		
Leeds ■ a	17 06	17 08	17 27	17 38	17 56	18 04	18 08	18 32	18 38	18 57	19 03	19 08	19 27	19 38	19 56	20 05	20 08	20 32	20 38	21 02
Bradford Interchange 37 a			17 53					18 53					19 53					20 53		

	TP	NT	TP	TP	NT	TP	GR	TP
	◇■		◇■	◇■		◇■	■ ■ ⊼	◇■
York ■ 33 d	20 45	20 57	21 15		21 52	22 12	23 03	23 12
Ulleskelf 33 d								
Church Fenton 33 d					22 04			
Selby d				21 31				
South Milford d				21 40				
Micklefield d		21 12			22 12			
East Garforth d		21 17			22 16			
Garforth d		21 19			22 19			
Cross Gates d		21 24			22 23			
Leeds ■ a	21 08	21 33	21 38	21 59	22 32	22 36	23 34	23 38
Bradford Interchange 37 a		21 56						

Leeds - Selby and York

Mondays to Fridays

Miles	Miles	Station	TP MX	TP MO A	TP MO B	TP MX	TP MO A	TP MX	TP MO B	TP MX	TP MO	TP	TP	NT		NT	TP	NT	GR	TP	NT	NT	TP	XC
—	—	Bradford Interchange 37 d																			07 02	07 20		
0	0	**Leeds** d	23p42	23p42	23p53	00 32	00 54	00 54	01 06	02 08	02 34	06 04	06 35	06 38		06 48	06 55	06 58	07 10	07 23	07 29	07 41	07 50	07 57
4¼	4¼	Cross Gates d												06 44				07 05			07 36			
7¼	7¼	Garforth d												06 50		06 58		07 10			07 41	07 51	08 00	
8	8	East Garforth d												06 52				07 12			07 43			
9	9	Micklefield d												06 56				07 16			07 47			
—	12¾	South Milford d																07 20						
—	20¾	**Selby** a														07 20		07 31		07 43				
14¾	—	Church Fenton 33 a																				07 59		
16½	—	Ulleskelf 33 a																						
25½	—	**York** 33 a	00 09	00 26	00 22	01 11	01 22	01 43	01 34	02 45	03 04	06 28	07 01	07 15			07 22		07 34		08 06	08 16	08 21	08 22

Station	NT	TP	NT		TP	TP	NT	TP	XC	TP	NT	TP	NT	TP	NT	TP		XC	TP	NT	TP	TP	NT	TP
Bradford Interchange 37 d	07 34		07 50				08 20				08 50				09 20					09 50			10 18	
Leeds d	08 00	08 12	08 15		08 28	08 38	08 41	08 57	09 05	09 12	09 15	09 28	09 33	09 38	09 41	09 57		10 05	10 12	10 15	10 28	10 38	10 41	10 57
Cross Gates d	08 06		08 22				08 48				09 22				09 48					10 22			10 48	
Garforth d	08 12		08 27				08 53	09 05			09 27				09 53	10 05				10 27			10 53	11 05
East Garforth d	08 14		08 29				08 56				09 29				09 56					10 29			10 56	
Micklefield d	08 18		08 33				08 59				09 33				09 59					10 33			10 59	
South Milford d	08 22		08 38								09 38									10 38				
Selby a	08 36		08 53			08 57					09 53			09 57						10 53		10 57		
Church Fenton 33 a							09 05								10 05									
Ulleskelf 33 a																								
York 33 a		08 35			08 52		09 21	09 23	09 26	09 36		09 52	10 06		10 21	10 23		10 26	10 36		10 52		11 19	11 23

Station	XC	TP	NT	TP	TP		NT	TP	XC	TP	NT	TP	TP	NT	TP	XC	TP	NT		TP	TP	NT	TP	XC
Bradford Interchange 37 d			10 50				11 20				11 50			12 19				12 50				13 19		
Leeds d	11 05	11 12	11 15	11 28	11 38		11 41	11 57	12 05	12 12	12 15	12 28	12 38	12 41	12 57	13 05	13 12	13 15		13 28	13 38	13 42	13 57	14 05
Cross Gates d			11 22				11 48				12 22			12 48				13 22				13 49		
Garforth d			11 27				11 53	12 05			12 27			12 53	13 05			13 27				13 54	14 05	
East Garforth d			11 29				11 56				12 29			12 56				13 29				13 57		
Micklefield d			11 33				11 59				12 33			12 59				13 33				14 00		
South Milford d			11 38								12 38							13 38						
Selby a			11 54		11 57						12 50		12 57					13 51			13 57			
Church Fenton 33 a							12 05															14 06		
Ulleskelf 33 a																								
York 33 a	11 26	11 36		11 52			12 21	12 23	12 26	12 36		12 52		13 19	13 23	13 26	13 36			13 52		14 22	14 23	14 26

Station	TP	NT	TP	TP	NT	TP	XC		TP	NT	TP	TP	NT	TP	XC	TP	NT	TP	TP	NT		TP	XC	TP
Bradford Interchange 37 d		13 50			14 19					14 50			15 19				15 50			16 19				
Leeds d	14 12	14 15	14 28	14 38	14 41	14 57	15 05		15 12	15 15	15 28	15 38	15 41	15 57	16 05	16 12	16 15	16 28	16 38	16 41		16 57	17 07	17 12
Cross Gates d		14 22			14 48					15 22			15 48				16 22			16 48				17 18
Garforth d		14 27			14 53	15 05				15 27			15 53	16 05			16 27			16 53		17 05		
East Garforth d		14 29			14 56					15 29			15 56				16 30			16 56				
Micklefield d		14 33			14 59					15 33			15 59				16 34			16 59				
South Milford d		14 38								15 38							16 39							
Selby a		14 51		14 57						15 53		15 57					16 54		17 00					
Church Fenton 33 a													16 05											
Ulleskelf 33 a																								
York 33 a	14 36		14 52		15 18	15 23	15 26		15 36		15 52		16 21	16 23	16 28	16 36		16 52		17 20		17 21	17 28	17 37

Station	NT	TP	NT	TP	NT	NT	TP	XC	TP		NT	TP	XC	TP	NT	TP	XC	TP	NT	TP	TP	NT		TP
Bradford Interchange 37 d	16 50				17 19						17 50				18 19				18 52			19 19		
Leeds d	17 15	17 24	17 28	17 38	17 41	17 46	17 57	18 06	18 12		18 15	18 28	18 35	18 38	18 41	18 57	19 06	19 12	19 15	19 28	19 38	19 41		19 57
Cross Gates d	17 22		17 35		17 48	17 52					18 22				18 48				19 22			19 48		
Garforth d	17 28	17 34	17 40		17 53	17 57	18 05				18 27				18 53	19 05			19 27			19 53		20 05
East Garforth d	17 30		17 42		17 56	18 00					18 29				18 56				19 29			19 55		
Micklefield d	17 34		17 46		17 59	18 04					18 33				18 59				19 33			19 59		
South Milford d	17 39					18 09					18 38			18 51							19 51			
Selby a	17 51			17 59		18 21					18 49			19 00							20 00			
Church Fenton 33 a			17 51												19 05									
Ulleskelf 33 a			17 57																					
York 33 a		17 55	18 10		18 18		18 23	18 29	18 36			18 53	19 01		19 21	19 23	19 29	19 36	19 53	19 53		20 22		20 23

A from 2 July until 10 September

B from 21 May until 25 June, MO from 17 September

Leeds - Selby and York

Mondays to Fridays

Station	XC	TP	TP	NT	TP	TP	NT	TP	TP	TP	NT		TP
Bradford Interchange 37 d				20 19							22 17		
Leeds d	20 08	20 12	20 45	20 48	21 12	21 42	21 55	22 12	22 22	22 42	23 02		23 42
Cross Gates d				20 55			22 02				23 09		
Garforth d				21 00			22 07				23 14		
East Garforth d				21 02			22 10				23 16		
Micklefield d				21 06			22 14				23 20		
South Milford d					21 24				22 36				
Selby a					21 34				22 46				
Church Fenton 33 a				21 11							23 25		
Ulleskelf 33 a				21 15									
York 33 a	20 29	20 36	21 09	21 30		22 06	22 32	22 38		23 07	23 42		00 09

Saturdays

until 8 September

Station	TP	TP	TP	TP	TP	TP	NT	TP	GR	NT	TP	NT		TP	XC	NT	TP	NT	TP	TP A	TP	NT	TP	XC
Bradford Interchange 37 d												07 20				07 34						08 20		
Leeds d	23p42	00 34	00 37	02 16	05 34	06 35	06 38	06 55	07 10	07 14	07 23	07 41		07 50	07 57	08 00	08 12	08 12	08 28	08 28	08 38	08 41	08 57	09 05
Cross Gates d							06 44					07 48				08 06		08 20				08 48		
Garforth d							06 50					07 53		08 00		08 12		08 24				08 53	09 05	
East Garforth d							06 52					07 56				08 14		08 26				08 56		
Micklefield d							06 56					07 59				08 18		08 30				08 59		
South Milford d																08 22		08 36						
Selby a										07 37	07 43					08 36		08 54			08 57			
Church Fenton 33 a												08 05										09 05		
Ulleskelf 33 a																								
York 33 a	00 09	01 16	01 20	02 45	06 00	07 01	07 15	07 22	07 34			08 20		08 21	08 23		08 35		08 52	09 03		09 21	09 23	09 27

Station	TP		NT	TP	TP	NT	TP	XC	TP	NT	TP	TP	NT	TP		XC	TP	NT	TP	TP	NT	TP	XC	TP
Bradford Interchange 37 d			08 50			09 20				09 50			10 18					10 50			11 20			
Leeds d	09 12		09 15	09 28	09 38	09 41	09 57	10 05	10 12	10 15	10 28	10 38	10 41	10 57		11 05	11 12	11 15	11 28	11 38	11 41	11 57	12 05	12 12
Cross Gates d			09 22			09 48				10 22			10 48					11 22			11 48			
Garforth d			09 27			09 53	10 05			10 27			10 53	11 05				11 27			11 53	12 05		
East Garforth d			09 29			09 56				10 29			10 56					11 29			11 56			
Micklefield d			09 33			09 59				10 33			10 59					11 33			11 59			
South Milford d			09 38							10 38								11 38						
Selby a			09 53		09 57					10 53		10 57						11 55		11 57				
Church Fenton 33 a						10 05															12 05			
Ulleskelf 33 a																								
York 33 a	09 36			09 52		10 21	10 23	10 26	10 36		10 52		11 18	11 23		11 26	11 36		11 52		12 21	12 23	12 26	12 36

Station	NT	TP	TP		NT	TP	XC	TP	NT	TP	TP	NT	TP	XC	TP	NT		TP	TP	NT	TP	XC	TP	NT
Bradford Interchange 37 d	11 50				12 19				12 50			13 19				13 50				14 19				14 50
Leeds d	12 15	12 28	12 38		12 41	12 57	13 05	13 12	13 15	13 28	13 38	13 42	13 57	14 05	14 12	14 15		14 28	14 38	14 41	14 57	15 05	15 12	15 15
Cross Gates d	12 22				12 48				13 22			13 49				14 22				14 48				15 22
Garforth d	12 27				12 53	13 05			13 27			13 54	14 05			14 27				14 53	15 05			15 27
East Garforth d	12 29				12 56				13 29			13 57				14 29				14 56				15 29
Micklefield d	12 33				12 59				13 33			14 00				14 33				14 59				15 33
South Milford d	12 38								13 38							14 38								15 38
Selby a	12 50		12 57						13 52		13 57					14 51			14 57					15 53
Church Fenton 33 a												14 06												
Ulleskelf 33 a																								
York 33 a		12 52			13 19	13 23	13 26	13 36		13 52		14 22	14 23	14 26	14 36			14 52		15 17	15 23	15 28	15 36	

Station	TP	TP	NT	TP	XC		TP	NT	TP	TP	NT	TP	XC	TP	NT	TP	TP	NT		TP	XC	TP	NT	TP
Bradford Interchange 37 d			15 19					15 50			16 19				16 50			17 19					17 50	
Leeds d	15 28	15 38	15 41	15 57	16 05		16 12	16 15	16 28	16 38	16 41	16 57	17 05	17 12	17 15	17 24	17 38	17 41		17 57	18 06	18 12	18 15	18 28
Cross Gates d			15 48					16 22			16 48				17 23			17 48					18 22	
Garforth d			15 53	16 05				16 27			16 53	17 05			17 30	17 34		17 53		18 05			18 27	
East Garforth d			15 56					16 30			16 56				17 32			17 56					18 29	
Micklefield d			15 59					16 34			16 59				17 36			17 59					18 33	
South Milford d								16 39							17 41								18 38	
Selby a		15 57						16 54		17 00					17 55		17 59						18 50	
Church Fenton 33 a			16 05															18 05						
Ulleskelf 33 a																		18 09						
York 33 a	15 52		16 21	16 23	16 26		16 36		16 52		17 21	17 23	17 26	17 36		17 55		18 24		18 22	18 28	18 36		18 52

A until 23 June

Leeds - Selby and York

until 8 September

	XC	TP	NT	TP	XC	TP	NT		TP	NT	TP	XC	TP	TP	NT	TP	TP	XC	TP	NT		TP	TP	TP
	◇1 ⊼	◇1		◇1	◇1 ⊼	◇1			◇1		◇1	◇1 ⊼	◇1	◇1		◇1	◇1	◇1 ⊼	◇1			◇1	◇1	◇1
Bradford Interchange 37 d			18 19				18 52			19 18					20 19									
Leeds 10 d	18 35	18 38	18 41	18 57	19 05	19 12	19 16		19 38	19 41	19 57	20 08	20 12	20 45	20 48	21 08	21 12	21 15	21 42	22 00		22 12	22 22	22 42
Cross Gates d			18 48				19 22			19 48					20 55					22 07				
Garforth d			18 53	19 05			19 28			19 53	20 05				21 00					22 12				
East Garforth d			18 56				19 30			19 56					21 02					22 14				
Micklefield d			18 59				19 34			19 59					21 06					22 18				
South Milford d		18 51							19 51							21 21							22 36	
Selby a		19 00							20 00							21 30							22 46	
Church Fenton 33 a			19 05												21 11									
Ulleskelf 33 a															21 16									
York 8 33 a	18 58		19 21	19 23	19 26	19 36	19 53			20 18	20 23	20 29	20 36	21 09	21 30		21 41	21 57	22 06	22 36		22 38		23 07

	NT	TP
		◇1
Bradford Interchange 37 d	22 17	
Leeds 10 d	22 56	23 42
Cross Gates d	23 03	
Garforth d	23 08	
East Garforth d	23 10	
Micklefield d	23 14	
South Milford d		
Selby a		
Church Fenton 33 a	23 19	
Ulleskelf 33 a		
York 8 33 a	23 38	00 09

Saturdays

from 15 September

	TP	TP	TP	TP	TP	TP	NT	TP	GR	NT	TP	NT		TP	XC	NT	TP	NT	TP	TP	TP	NT	TP	XC
	◇1	◇1	◇1	◇1	◇1	◇1		◇1	■ 1 ⊼		◇1			◇1 ⊼	◇1 ⊼		◇1 ⊼		◇1 ⊼		◇1 ⊼		◇1 ⊼	◇1 ⊼
Bradford Interchange 37 d												07 20				07 34						08 20		
Leeds 10 d	23p42	00 34	00 37	02 16	05 34	06 35	06 38	06 55	07 10	07 14	07 23	07 41		07 50	07 57	08 00	08 12	08 12	08 28	08 28	08 38	08 41	08 57	09 05
Cross Gates d							06 44					07 48				08 06		08 20				08 48		
Garforth d							06 50					07 53		08 00		08 12		08 24				08 53	09 05	
East Garforth d							06 52					07 56				08 14		08 26				08 56		
Micklefield d							06 56					07 59				08 18		08 30				08 59		
South Milford d																08 22		08 36						
Selby a										07 37	07 43					08 36		08 54			08 57			
Church Fenton 33 a												08 05										09 05		
Ulleskelf 33 a																								
York 8 33 a	00 09	01 16	01 20	02 45	06 00	07 01	07 15	07 22	07 34			08 20		08 21	08 23		08 35		08 52	09 03		09 21	09 23	09 27

	TP		NT	TP	TP	NT	TP	XC	TP	NT	TP	TP	NT	TP		XC	TP	NT	TP	TP	NT	TP	XC	TP
	◇1 ⊼			◇1 ⊼	◇1		◇1 ⊼	◇1 ⊼	◇1 ⊼		◇1 ⊼	◇1 ⊼		◇1 ⊼		◇1 ⊼	◇1 ⊼		◇1	◇1 ⊼		◇1 ⊼	◇1 ⊼	◇1 ⊼
Bradford Interchange 37 d			08 50			09 20				09 50			10 18					10 50			11 20			
Leeds 10 d	09 12		09 15	09 28	09 38	09 41	09 57	10 05	10 12	10 15	10 28	10 38	10 41	10 57		11 05	11 12	11 15	11 28	11 38	11 41	11 57	12 05	12 12
Cross Gates d			09 22			09 48				10 22			10 48					11 22			11 48			
Garforth d			09 27			09 53	10 05			10 27			10 53	11 05				11 27			11 53	12 05		
East Garforth d			09 29			09 56				10 29			10 56					11 29			11 56			
Micklefield d			09 33			09 59				10 33			10 59					11 33			11 59			
South Milford d			09 38							10 38								11 38						
Selby a			09 53		09 57					10 53		10 57						11 55		11 57				
Church Fenton 33 a						10 05															12 05			
Ulleskelf 33 a																								
York 8 33 a	09 36			09 52		10 21	10 23	10 26	10 36		10 52		11 18	11 23		11 26	11 36		11 52		12 21	12 23	12 26	12 36

	NT	TP	TP		NT	TP	XC	TP	NT	TP	TP	NT	TP	XC	TP	NT		TP	TP	NT	TP	XC	TP	NT
		◇1 ⊼	◇1			◇1 ⊼	◇1 ⊼	◇1 ⊼		◇1 ⊼	◇1		◇1 ⊼	◇1 ⊼	◇1 ⊼			◇1 ⊼	◇1 ⊼		◇1 ⊼	◇1 ⊼	◇1 ⊼	
Bradford Interchange 37 d	11 50				12 19				12 50			13 19				13 50				14 19				14 50
Leeds 10 d	12 15	12 28	12 38		12 41	12 57	13 05	13 12	13 15	13 28	13 38	13 42	13 57	14 05	14 12	14 15		14 28	14 38	14 41	14 57	15 05	15 12	15 15
Cross Gates d	12 22				12 48				13 22			13 49				14 22				14 48				15 22
Garforth d	12 27				12 53	13 05			13 27			13 54	14 05			14 27				14 53	15 05			15 27
East Garforth d	12 29				12 56				13 29			13 57				14 29				14 56				15 29
Micklefield d	12 33				12 59				13 33			14 00				14 33				14 59				15 33
South Milford d	12 38								13 38							14 38								15 38
Selby a	12 50		12 57						13 52		13 57					14 51			14 57					15 53
Church Fenton 33 a												14 06												
Ulleskelf 33 a																								
York 8 33 a		12 52			13 19	13 23	13 26	13 36		13 52		14 22	14 23	14 26	14 36			14 52		15 17	15 23	15 28	15 36	

Leeds - Selby and York

from 15 September

	TP	TP	NT	TP	XC		TP	NT	TP	TP	NT	TP	XC	TP	NT	TP	TP	NT		TP	XC	TP	NT	TP
	◇1 ⊼	◇1		◇1	◇1 ⊼		◇1 ⊼		◇1 ⊼	◇1		◇1 ⊼	◇1 ⊼	◇1		◇1	◇1			◇1	◇1 ⊼	◇1		◇1
Bradford Interchange 37 d			15 19					15 50			16 19				16 50			17 19					17 50	
Leeds 10 d	15 28	15 38	15 41	15 57	16 05		16 12	16 15	16 28	16 38	16 41	16 57	17 05	17 12	17 15	17 24	17 38	17 41		17 57	18 06	18 12	18 15	18 28
Cross Gates d			15 48					16 22			16 48				17 23			17 48					18 22	
Garforth d			15 53	16 05				16 27			16 53	17 05			17 30	17 34		17 53		18 05			18 27	
East Garforth d			15 56					16 30			16 56				17 32			17 56					18 29	
Micklefield d			15 59					16 34			16 59				17 36			17 59					18 33	
South Milford d								16 39							17 41								18 38	
Selby a		15 57						16 54		17 00					17 55		17 59						18 50	
Church Fenton 33 a			16 05															18 05						
Ulleskelf 33 a																		18 09						
York 8 33 a	15 52		16 21	16 23	16 26		16 36		16 52		17 21	17 23	17 26	17 36		17 55		18 24		18 22	18 28	18 36		18 52

	XC	TP	NT	TP	XC	TP	NT		TP	NT	TP	XC	TP	TP	NT	TP	TP	XC	TP	NT		TP	TP	TP
	◇1 ⊼	◇1		◇1	◇1 ⊼	◇1			◇1		◇1	◇1 ⊼	◇1	◇1		◇1	◇1	◇1 ⊼	◇1			◇1	◇1	◇1
Bradford Interchange 37 d			18 19				18 52			19 18					20 19									
Leeds 10 d	18 35	18 38	18 41	18 57	19 05	19 12	19 16		19 38	19 41	19 57	20 08	20 12	20 45	20 48	21 08	21 12	21 15	21 42	22 00		22 12	22 22	22 42
Cross Gates d			18 48				19 22			19 48					20 55					22 07				
Garforth d			18 53	19 05			19 28			19 53	20 05				21 00					22 12				
East Garforth d			18 56				19 30			19 56					21 02					22 14				
Micklefield d			18 59				19 34			19 59					21 06					22 18				
South Milford d		18 51							19 51							21 21							22 36	
Selby a		19 00							20 00							21 30							22 46	
Church Fenton 33 a			19 05												21 11									
Ulleskelf 33 a															21 16									
York 8 33 a	18 58		19 21	19 23	19 26	19 36	19 53			20 18	20 23	20 29	20 36	21 09	21 30		21 41	21 57	22 10	22 40		22 41		23 07

	NT	TP
		◇1
Bradford Interchange 37 d	22 17	
Leeds 10 d	22 56	23 42
Cross Gates d	23 03	
Garforth d	23 08	
East Garforth d	23 10	
Micklefield d	23 14	
South Milford d		
Selby a		
Church Fenton 33 a	23 20	
Ulleskelf 33 a		
York 8 33 a	23 40	00 09

Sundays

until 24 June

	TP	TP	TP	TP	TP	TP	TP	NT	XC	TP	TP	NT		TP	XC	TP	TP	NT	TP	XC	TP	NT	TP	XC
	◇1	◇1	◇1	◇1	◇1	◇1	◇1		◇1 ⊼	◇1	◇1			◇1	◇1 ⊼	◇1	◇1		◇1	◇1 ⊼	◇1		◇1	◇1 ⊼
Bradford Interchange 37 d								08 31				09 20						10 04				11 02		
Leeds 10 d	23p42	00 15	00 40	03 18	07 01	07 59	08 40	08 54	09 08	09 12	09 40	09 50		10 04	10 08	10 17	10 24	10 28	10 40	11 08	11 18	11 25	11 40	12 08
Cross Gates d								09 00				09 56						10 34				11 32		
Garforth d								09 06				10 02						10 40				11 37		
East Garforth d								09 08				10 04						10 42				11 39		
Micklefield d								09 12				10 08						10 46				11 43		
South Milford d																	10 37							
Selby a																	10 46							
Church Fenton 33 a								09 18										10 52						
Ulleskelf 33 a																								
York 8 33 a	00 09	00 42	01 09	03 44	07 29	08 26	09 08	09 35	09 34	09 37	10 04	10 28		10 29	10 29	10 41		11 08	11 08	11 29	11 39	11 59	12 05	12 29

	TP		NT	TP	TP	XC	TP	NT	TP	TP	XC	TP	NT	TP		TP	XC	TP	NT	TP	TP	XC	TP	NT
	◇1			◇1	◇1	◇1 ⊼	◇1		◇1	◇1	◇1 ⊼	◇1		◇1		◇1	◇1 ⊼	◇1		◇1	◇1	◇1 ⊼	◇1	
Bradford Interchange 37 d			12 02					13 02					14 02						15 02					16 03
Leeds 10 d	12 12		12 25	12 40	13 01	13 08	13 12	13 25	13 40	13 57	14 08	14 12	14 25	14 40		15 01	15 08	15 12	15 25	15 40	15 57	16 08	16 12	16 25
Cross Gates d			12 32					13 32					14 32						15 32					16 32
Garforth d			12 37					13 37					14 37						15 37					16 37
East Garforth d			12 39					13 39					14 39						15 39					16 39
Micklefield d			12 43					13 43					14 43						15 43					16 43
South Milford d					13 14											15 14								
Selby a					13 23											15 23								
Church Fenton 33 a			12 48										14 48											16 48
Ulleskelf 33 a																								
York 8 33 a	12 39		13 02	13 07		13 29	13 39	13 59	14 04	14 24	14 29	14 38	15 02	15 07			15 29	15 37	15 59	16 05	16 24	16 29	16 38	17 02

Table 40

Leeds - Selby and York

Sundays until 24 June

	TP	TP	XC	TP	NT	TP	TP	XC	TP	NT	TP	XC	TP	XC	TP	NT	TP	TP	XC	TP	NT	TP
Bradford Interchange 37 d					17 02					18 02						19 02					20 02	
Leeds d	16 40	17 01	17 08	17 12	17 25	17 40	17 57	18 08	18 12	18 23	18 40	18 57	19 01	19 08	19 12	19 25	19 40	19 57	20 08	20 12	20 25	20 40
Cross Gates d					17 32					18 30						19 32					20 32	
Garforth d					17 37					18 35						19 37					20 37	
East Garforth d					17 39					18 38						19 39					20 39	
Micklefield d					17 43					18 41						19 43					20 43	
South Milford d		17 14											19 16									
Selby a		17 23											19 29					20 17				
Church Fenton 33 a										18 47											20 48	
Ulleskelf 33 a																						
York 33 a	17 07		17 29	17 40	18 02	18 07	18 24	18 29	18 38	19 01	19 05	19 18		19 29	19 36	19 59	20 04		20 29	20 38	21 03	21 05

	TP	XC	TP	NT	TP	TP	TP	NT	TP	TP
Bradford Interchange 37 d				21 02						
Leeds d	21 04	21 08	21 12	21 26	21 40	22 12	22 22	22 43	22 53	23 53
Cross Gates d				21 33				22 49		
Garforth d				21 38				22 55		
East Garforth d				21 40				22 57		
Micklefield d				21 44				23 01		
South Milford d							22 35			
Selby a	21 38						22 44			
Church Fenton 33 a								23 07		
Ulleskelf 33 a										
York 33 a		21 31	21 38	22 00	22 08	22 40		23 23	23 28	00 22

Sundays 1 July to 9 September

	TP	TP	TP	TP	TP	TP	TP	NT	XC	TP	TP	NT	TP	XC	TP	NT	TP	TP	NT	TP	XC	TP	NT
Bradford Interchange 37 d								08 31				09 20				10 04			11 02				12 02
Leeds d	23p42	00 15	00 40	02 35	05 55	07 40	08 40	08 54	09 08	09 12	09 40	09 50	10 04	10 08	10 22	10 28	10 40	11 12	11 25	11 40	12 08	12 12	12 25
Cross Gates d								09 00				09 56				10 34			11 32				12 32
Garforth d								09 06				10 02				10 40			11 37				12 37
East Garforth d								09 08				10 04				10 42			11 39				12 39
Micklefield d								09 12				10 08				10 46			11 43				12 43
South Milford d															10 35								
Selby a															10 44								
Church Fenton 33 a								09 18								10 52							12 48
Ulleskelf 33 a																							
York 33 a	00 09	00 42	01 09	03 03	06 23	08 08	09 07	09 35	09 34	09 37	10 07	10 28	10 29	10 29		11 08	11 07	11 39	11 59	12 05	12 29	12 39	13 02

	TP	TP	XC	TP	NT	TP	TP	XC	TP	NT	TP	TP	XC	TP	NT	TP	TP	XC	TP	NT	TP	TP
Bradford Interchange 37 d					13 02					14 02					15 02					16 03		
Leeds d	12 40	13 01	13 08	13 12	13 25	13 40	13 57	14 08	14 12	14 25	14 40	15 01	15 08	15 12	15 25	15 40	15 57	16 08	16 12	16 25	16 40	17 01
Cross Gates d					13 32					14 32					15 32					16 32		
Garforth d					13 37					14 37					15 37					16 37		
East Garforth d					13 39					14 39					15 39					16 39		
Micklefield d					13 43					14 43					15 43					16 43		
South Milford d		13 14										15 14										17 14
Selby a		13 23										15 23										17 23
Church Fenton 33 a										14 48										16 48		
Ulleskelf 33 a																						
York 33 a	13 07		13 29	13 39	13 59	14 05	14 24	14 29	14 38	15 02	15 07		15 29	15 35	15 59	16 05	16 22	16 29	16 38	17 02	17 09	

	XC	TP	NT	TP	TP	XC	TP	NT	TP	XC	TP	XC	TP	NT	TP	TP	XC	TP	NT	TP	TP	XC
Bradford Interchange 37 d			17 02					18 02						19 02					20 02			
Leeds d	17 08	17 12	17 25	17 40	17 57	18 08	18 12	18 23	18 40	18 57	19 01	19 08	19 12	19 25	19 40	19 57	20 08	20 12	20 25	20 40	21 04	21 08
Cross Gates d			17 32					18 30						19 32					20 32			
Garforth d			17 37					18 35						19 37					20 37			
East Garforth d			17 39					18 38						19 39					20 39			
Micklefield d			17 43					18 41						19 43					20 43			
South Milford d											19 16											
Selby a											19 28					20 17					21 38	
Church Fenton 33 a								18 47											20 48			
Ulleskelf 33 a																						
York 33 a	17 29	17 39	18 02	18 07	18 24	18 29	18 38	19 01	19 05	19 18		19 29	19 38	19 59	20 04		20 29	20 38	21 03	21 05		21 31

Table 40

Leeds - Selby and York

Sundays 1 July to 9 September

	TP	NT	TP	TP	TP	TP	NT	TP
Bradford Interchange 37 d		21 02						
Leeds d	21 12	21 26	21 40	22 12	22 22	22 40	22 43	23 42
Cross Gates d		21 33					22 49	
Garforth d		21 38					22 55	
East Garforth d		21 40					22 57	
Micklefield d		21 44					23 01	
South Milford d					22 35			
Selby a					22 44			
Church Fenton 33 a							23 07	
Ulleskelf 33 a								
York 33 a	21 38	22 00	22 08	22 40		23 11	23 23	00 26

Sundays 16 September to 21 October

	TP	TP	TP	TP	TP	TP	TP	NT	XC	TP	TP	NT	XC	TP	TP	NT	TP	XC	TP	NT	TP	XC	TP
Bradford Interchange 37 d								08 31				09 20				10 04							
Leeds d	23p42	00 15	00 40	03 18	06 46	07 59	08 40	08 54	09 15	09 19	09 45	09 50	10 05	10 17	10 24	10 28	10 40	11 05	11 18	11 25	11 40	12 08	12 12
Cross Gates d								09 00				09 56				10 34				11 32			
Garforth d								09 06				10 02				10 40				11 37			
East Garforth d								09 08				10 04				10 42				11 39			
Micklefield d								09 12				10 08				10 46				11 43			
South Milford d															10 37								
Selby a															10 46								
Church Fenton 33 a								09 18								10 52							
Ulleskelf 33 a																							
York 33 a	00 09	00 42	01 09	03 44	07 14	08 26	09 08	09 34	09 36	09 42	10 10	10 28	10 27	10 42		11 07	11 10	11 26	11 39	11 59	12 08	12 29	12 39

	NT	TP	TP	XC	TP	NT	TP	TP	XC	TP	NT	TP	TP	XC	TP	NT	TP	TP	XC	TP	NT	TP
Bradford Interchange 37 d																						
Leeds d	12 25	12 40	13 01	13 08	13 12	13 25	13 40	13 57	14 08	14 12	14 25	14 40	15 01	15 08	15 12	15 25	15 40	15 57	16 08	16 12	16 25	16 40
Cross Gates d	12 32					13 32					14 32					15 32					16 32	
Garforth d	12 37					13 37					14 37					15 37					16 37	
East Garforth d	12 39					13 39					14 39					15 39					16 39	
Micklefield d	12 43					13 43					14 43					15 43					16 43	
South Milford d			13 14										15 14									
Selby a			13 23										15 23									
Church Fenton 33 a	12 48										14 48										16 48	
Ulleskelf 33 a																						
York 33 a	13 02	13 08		13 31	13 39	13 59	14 04	14 24	14 31	14 38	15 02	15 07		15 29	15 37	15 59	16 05	16 24	16 29	16 38	17 02	17 07

	TP	XC	TP	NT	TP	TP	XC	TP	NT	TP	XC	TP	XC	TP	NT	TP	TP	XC	TP	NT	TP	TP
Bradford Interchange 37 d																						
Leeds d	17 01	17 08	17 12	17 25	17 40	17 57	18 08	18 12	18 23	18 40	18 57	19 01	19 08	19 12	19 25	19 40	19 57	20 08	20 12	20 25	20 40	21 04
Cross Gates d				17 32					18 30						19 32					20 32		
Garforth d				17 37					18 35						19 37					20 37		
East Garforth d				17 39					18 38						19 39					20 39		
Micklefield d				17 43					18 41						19 43					20 43		
South Milford d	17 14											19 16										
Selby a	17 23											19 29					20 17					21 38
Church Fenton 33 a									18 47											20 48		
Ulleskelf 33 a																						
York 33 a		17 29	17 39	18 02	18 07	18 24	18 29	18 38	19 01	19 05	19 18		19 28	19 36	19 59	20 04		20 29	20 38	21 03	21 05	

	XC	TP	NT	TP	TP	TP	NT	TP	TP
Bradford Interchange 37 d									
Leeds d	21 08	21 12	21 26	21 40	22 12	22 22	22 43	22 53	23 53
Cross Gates d			21 33				22 49		
Garforth d			21 38				22 55		
East Garforth d			21 40				22 57		
Micklefield d			21 44				23 01		
South Milford d						22 35			
Selby a						22 44			
Church Fenton 33 a							23 07		
Ulleskelf 33 a									
York 33 a	21 31	21 38	22 00	22 08	22 40		23 23	23 28	00 22

Leeds - Selby and York

Station			TP ◇1	TP 🚌	TP 🚌	TP 🚌	TP ◇1	NT	XC ◇1 🍴	TP ◇1	TP ◇1	NT	XC ◇1 🍴	TP ◇1		TP ◇1	NT	TP ◇1	TP ◇1	NT	TP ◇1	TP ◇1	NT	TP ◇1	TP ◇1	XC ◇1 🍴
Bradford Interchange	37	d						08 31				09 20					10 04			11 02			12 02			
Leeds 10		d	23p42	01 25	03 20	07 20	08 40	08 54	09 15	09 19	09 45	09 50	10 05	10 17		10 24	10 28	10 40	11 18	11 25	11 40	12 12	12 25	12 40	13 01	13 08
Cross Gates		d						09 00				09 56					10 34			11 32			12 32			
Garforth		d						09 06				10 02					10 40			11 37			12 37			
East Garforth		d						09 08				10 04					10 42			11 39			12 39			
Micklefield		d						09 12				10 08					10 46			11 43			12 43			
South Milford		d														10 37									13 14	
Selby		a														10 46									13 23	
Church Fenton	33	a						09 18									10 52						12 48			
Ulleskelf	33	a																								
York 8	33	a	00 09	02 15	04 10	08 10	09 08	09 35	09 36	09 42	10 10	10 28	10 27	10 42			11 07	11 10	11 39	11 59	12 08	12 39	13 02	13 08		13 29

Station			TP ◇1		NT	TP ◇1	TP ◇1	XC ◇1 🍴	TP ◇1	NT	TP ◇1	TP ◇1	XC ◇1 🍴	TP ◇1	NT	TP ◇1		TP ◇1	XC ◇1 🍴	TP ◇1	NT	TP ◇1	TP ◇1	XC ◇1 🍴	TP ◇1	NT
Bradford Interchange	37	d			13 02					14 02					15 02						16 03					17 02
Leeds 10		d	13 12		13 25	13 40	13 57	14 08	14 12	14 25	14 40	15 01	15 08	15 12	15 25	15 40		15 57	16 08	16 12	16 25	16 40	17 01	17 08	17 12	17 25
Cross Gates		d			13 32					14 32					15 32						16 32					17 32
Garforth		d			13 37					14 37					15 37						16 37					17 37
East Garforth		d			13 39					14 39					15 39						16 39					17 39
Micklefield		d			13 43					14 43					15 43						16 43					17 43
South Milford		d										15 14											17 14			
Selby		a										15 23											17 23			
Church Fenton	33	a								14 48											16 48					
Ulleskelf	33	a																								
York 8	33	a	13 39		13 59	14 04	14 24	14 29	14 38	15 02	15 07		15 29	15 37	15 59	16 05		16 24	16 29	16 38	17 02	17 07		17 29	17 39	18 02

Station			TP ◇1	TP ◇1	XC ◇1 🍴		TP ◇1	NT	TP ◇1	XC ◇1 🍴	TP ◇1	XC ◇1 🍴	TP ◇1	NT	TP ◇1	TP ◇1	XC ◇1	TP ◇1		NT	TP ◇1	TP ◇1	XC ◇1 🍴	TP ◇1	NT	TP ◇1
Bradford Interchange	37	d						18 02						19 02						20 02					21 02	
Leeds 10		d	17 40	17 57	18 08		18 12	18 23	18 40	18 57	19 01	19 08	19 12	19 25	19 40	19 57	20 08	20 12		20 25	20 40	21 04	21 08	21 12	21 26	21 40
Cross Gates		d						18 30						19 32						20 32					21 33	
Garforth		d						18 35						19 37						20 37					21 38	
East Garforth		d						18 38						19 39						20 39					21 40	
Micklefield		d						18 41						19 43						20 43					21 44	
South Milford		d									19 16															
Selby		a									19 29					20 17						21 38				
Church Fenton	33	a						18 47												20 48						
Ulleskelf	33	a																								
York 8	33	a	18 07	18 24	18 29		18 38	19 01	19 05	19 18		19 29	19 36	19 59	20 04		20 29	20 38		21 03	21 05		21 31	21 38	22 00	22 08

Station			TP ◇1	TP ◇1	NT	TP ◇1	TP ◇1
Bradford Interchange	37	d					
Leeds 10		d	22 12	22 22	22 43	22 53	23 53
Cross Gates		d			22 49		
Garforth		d			22 55		
East Garforth		d			22 57		
Micklefield		d			23 01		
South Milford		d		22 35			
Selby		a		22 44			
Church Fenton	33	a			23 07		
Ulleskelf	33	a					
York 8	33	a	22 40		23 23	23 28	00 22

Leeds and Bradford - Huddersfield, Blackpool North, Rochdale and Manchester Victoria via Halifax and Brighouse

Network Diagram - see first Page of Table 39

Miles	Miles	Miles	Miles	Miles	Station			NT MX	NT MX	NT	NT	NT	NT	NT A	GC 1	NT		NT	NT B	NT	NT	NT C	NT	NT	NT B	NT
—	—	—	—	—	York 8	40	d											06 13						07 06		
—	—	—	—	—	Selby	40	d															06 42				07 23
0	0	—	—	0	**Leeds** 10	37,39	d	22p37	23p08	05 08	05 51	06 03	06 13			06 37		06 51		07 08	07 13	07 23	07 37	07 51		08 08
4	4	—	—	—	Bramley	37	d	22p44	23p15	05 15	05 58					06 44				07 15		07 30	07 44			08 15
5¾	5¾	—	—	—	New Pudsey	37	d	22p49	23p20	05 20	06 02	06 13				06 49		07 01		07 20		07 35	07 49	08 01		08 20
9½	9½	—	—	—	**Bradford Interchange**	37	a	22p57	23p29	05 28	06 13	06 21				06 57		07 11		07 28		07 43	07 57	08 09		08 28
—	—	—	—	—			d	23p00	23p31	05 32	06 14	06 24			06 51	07 00		07 14		07 31		07 46	08 00	08 12		08 32
17½	17½	0	—	—	**Halifax**		a	23p12	23p44	05 44	06 25	06 36			07 06	07 12		07 25		07 43		07 59	08 12	08 23		08 44
—	—	—	—	—			d	23p12	23p44	05 44	06 26	06 36		07 02	07 07	07 12		07 26		07 44		08 06	08 12	08 24		08 44
—	—	—	9¼	—	Dewsbury	39	d						06 29								07 29					
—	—	—	12¼	—	Mirfield	39	a						06 35								07 35					
—	—	—	—	—			d						06 35								07 36					
—	—	5¾	16¼	—	Brighouse		d		23p55				06 49	07a12	07 18						07 49	08 16				
—	—	—	—	—	London Kings Cross 15 ⊖	26	a								10 13											
—	—	10½	—	—	**Huddersfield**	39	a		00 08													08 30				
21	21	—	22	—	Sowerby Bridge		d	23p19		05 51		06 43	06 59			07 19					07 59		08 19			
25	25	—	26	—	Mytholmroyd		d	23p25		05 57		06 49	07 05			07 25					08 05		08 25			
26¼	26¼	—	27¼	—	**Hebden Bridge**		a	23p28		06 00	06 37	06 52	07 08			07 28		07 37		07 55	08 08		08 28	08 35		08 56
—	—	—	—	—			d	23p28		06 00	06 38	06 52	07 08			07 28		07 38		07 56	08 08		08 28	08 36		08 56
—	39	—	—	—	Burnley Manchester Road	97	a				06 57							07 57						08 57		
—	45¼	—	—	—	Accrington	97	a				07 06							08 06						09 06		
—	51½	—	—	—	Blackburn	97	a				07 16							08 14						09 14		
—	63½	—	—	—	**Preston** 8	97	a				07 36							08 38						09 32		
—	78	—	—	—	Poulton-le-Fylde	97	a				07 54							08 56						09 50		
—	81	—	—	—	**Blackpool North**	97	a				08 05							09 05						10 01		
30½	—	—	—	—	Todmorden		d	23p36		06 08		06 59	07 15			07 36			07 44	08 04	08 15		08 36			09 04
32	—	—	—	—	Walsden		d	23p39		06 11		07 02				07 39			07 47				08 39			
36	—	—	—	—	Littleborough		d	23p45		06 17		07 09	07 23			07 45			07 53		08 23		08 45			
37	—	—	—	—	Smithy Bridge		d	23p48		06 20		07 11	07 25			07 48			07 56		08 25		08 48			
39¼	—	—	—	—	**Rochdale**		a	23p52		06 24		07 15	07 29			07 51			08 00	08 14	08 29		08 51			09 14
—	—	—	—	—			d	23p52		06 24		07 16	07 30			07 51			08 00	08 14	08 30		08 51		09 04	09 14
41	—	—	—	—	Castleton		d			06 27		07 19	07 33			07 54			08 03	08 17	08 33				09 07	
43¾	—	—	—	—	Mills Hill		d			06 32		07 24	07 38			07 59			08 08	08 22	08 37				09 12	
45¾	—	—	—	—	Moston		d			06 35		07 27	07 41			08 02			08 11	08 25	08 40				09 15	
49¼	—	—	—	—	**Manchester Victoria** ⇌		a	00 10		06 48		07 39	07 53			08 14			08 22	08 37	08 53		09 08		09 26	09 30

Station			NT	NT C	NT	NT	NT	NT B	NT	NT	NT C		NT	NT	GC 1	NT B	NT	NT	NT C	NT	NT		NT B	NT	NT
York 8	40	d				08 12								09 11							10 11				
Selby	40	d		07 43							08 43								09 43						
Leeds 10	37,39	d	08 13	08 23	08 37	08 51			09 07	09 13	09 23		09 37	09 53			10 07	10 13	10 23	10 37	10 53			11 07	11 13
Bramley	37	d		08 30	08 44				09 14		09 30		09 44				10 14		10 30	10 44				11 14	
New Pudsey	37	d		08 35	08 49	09 00			09 19		09 35		09 49	10 02			10 20		10 35	10 49	11 02			11 19	
Bradford Interchange	37	a		08 43	08 57	09 12			09 28		09 43		09 57	10 12			10 28		10 43	10 57	11 11			11 28	
		d		08 46	09 00	09 13			09 32		09 46		10 00	10 14	10 22		10 32		10 46	11 00	11 12			11 31	
Halifax		a		08 59	09 12	09 25			09 44		09 59		10 12	10 25	10 33		10 44		10 59	11 12	11 25			11 43	
		d		09 06	09 12	09 25			09 44		10 06		10 12	10 26	10 37		10 44		11 06	11 12	11 25			11 44	
Dewsbury	39	d	08 31							09 31								10 29							11 29
Mirfield	39	a	08 37							09 36								10 35							11 35
		d	08 38							09 37								10 35							11 35
Brighouse		d	08 49	09 16						09 49	10 16				10 48			10 49	11 16						11 49
London Kings Cross 15 ⊖	26	a													13 45										
Huddersfield	39	a		09 29							10 29								11 30						
Sowerby Bridge		d	08 59		09 19					09 59			10 19					10 59		11 19					11 59
Mytholmroyd		d	09 05		09 25					10 05			10 25					11 05		11 25					12 05
Hebden Bridge		a	09 08		09 28	09 37			09 56	10 08			10 28	10 37			10 56	11 08		11 28	11 37			11 55	12 08
		d	09 08		09 28	09 37			09 56	10 08			10 28	10 38			10 56	11 08		11 28	11 38			11 56	12 08
Burnley Manchester Road	97	a				09 56								10 57							11 57				
Accrington	97	a				10 06								11 06							12 06				
Blackburn	97	a				10 14								11 14							12 14				
Preston 8	97	a				10 32								11 32							12 32				
Poulton-le-Fylde	97	a				10 50								11 50							12 50				
Blackpool North	97	a				11 01								12 00							13 00				
Todmorden		d	09 15		09 36				10 04	10 15			10 36				11 04	11 15		11 36				12 03	12 15
Walsden		d			09 39								10 39							11 39					
Littleborough		d	09 23		09 45					10 23			10 45					11 23		11 45					12 23
Smithy Bridge		d	09 25		09 48					10 25			10 48					11 25		11 48					12 25
Rochdale		a	09 29		09 51				10 14	10 29			10 51				11 14	11 29		11 51				12 13	12 29
		d	09 30		09 51			10 05	10 14	10 30			10 51			11 04	11 14	11 30		11 51			12 04	12 14	12 30
Castleton		d	09 33					10 08		10 33						11 07		11 33					12 07		12 33
Mills Hill		d	09 37					10 13		10 38						11 12		11 38					12 12		12 38
Moston		d	09 40					10 16		10 41						11 15		11 41					12 15		12 41
Manchester Victoria ⇌		a	09 53		10 08			10 26	10 32	10 53			11 08			11 26	11 32	11 53		12 08			12 25	12 30	12 53

A To Leeds
B To Wigan Wallgate
C To Wakefield Westgate

For connections to Liverpool Lime Street please refer to Table 90

Leeds and Bradford - Huddersfield, Blackpool North, Rochdale and Manchester Victoria via Halifax and Brighouse

Network Diagram - see first Page of Table 39

	NT	NT	NT	NT	NT	NT	NT	NT	NT	NT	NT	NT	NT	NT	NT	NT	NT	NT	NT	NT	NT	NT
	A			C			A			C			A				C			A		
York 40 d			11 09						12 13						13 09							14 13
Selby 40 d	10 42						11 43						12 43							13 43		
Leeds 37,39 d	11 23	11 37	11 53		12 07	12 13	12 23	12 37	12 53		13 07	13 13	13 23	13 37	13 53			14 07	14 13	14 23	14 37	14 53
Bramley 37 d	11 30	11 44			12 14		12 30	12 44			13 14		13 30	13 44				14 14		14 30	14 44	
New Pudsey 37 d	11 35	11 49	12 02		12 19		12 35	12 49	13 02		13 19		13 35	13 49	14 02			14 19		14 35	14 49	15 02
Bradford Interchange 37 a	11 43	11 57	12 11		12 28		12 43	12 57	13 12		13 28		13 43	13 58	14 12			14 28		14 43	14 57	15 12
d	11 46	12 00	12 14		12 32		12 46	13 00	13 14		13 32		13 46	14 00	14 14			14 32		14 46	15 00	15 14
Halifax a	11 59	12 12	12 25		12 44		12 59	13 12	13 25		13 44		13 59	14 12	14 25			14 44		14 59	15 12	15 25
d	12 06	12 12	12 26		12 44		13 06	13 12	13 26		13 44		14 06	14 13	14 26			14 44		15 06	15 12	15 26
Dewsbury 39 d						12 29						13 29							14 29			
Mirfield 39 a						12 35						13 35							14 35			
d						12 35						13 35							14 35			
Brighouse d	12 16					12 49	13 16					13 49	14 16						14 49	15 16		
London Kings Cross ⊖26 a																						
Huddersfield 39 a	12 30						13 29						14 29							15 29		
Sowerby Bridge d		12 19				12 59		13 19				13 59		14 19					14 59		15 19	
Mytholmroyd d		12 25				13 05		13 25				14 05		14 25					15 05		15 25	
Hebden Bridge a		12 28	12 37		12 56	13 08		13 28	13 37		13 56	14 08		14 28	14 37			14 56	15 08		15 28	15 37
d		12 28	12 38		12 56	13 08		13 28	13 38		13 56	14 08		14 29	14 38			14 56	15 08		15 28	15 38
Burnley Manchester Road 97 a			12 57						13 57						14 57							15 57
Accrington 97 a			13 06						14 06						15 06							16 06
Blackburn 97 a			13 14						14 14						15 14							16 14
Preston 97 a			13 32						14 32						15 32							16 32
Poulton-le-Fylde 97 a			13 50						14 50						15 50							16 50
Blackpool North 97 a			14 00						15 00						16 00							17 00
Todmorden d		12 36			13 04	13 15		13 36			14 04	14 15		14 36				15 04	15 15		15 36	
Walsden d		12 39						13 39						14 39							15 39	
Littleborough d		12 45				13 23		13 45				14 23		14 46					15 23		15 45	
Smithy Bridge d		12 48				13 25		13 48				14 25		14 48					15 25		15 48	
Rochdale a		12 51			13 14	13 29		13 51			14 14	14 29		14 51				15 14	15 29		15 51	
d		12 51		13 04	13 14	13 30		13 51		14 04	14 14	14 30		14 52			15 04	15 14	15 30		15 51	
Castleton d				13 07		13 33				14 07		14 33					15 07		15 33			
Mills Hill d				13 12		13 38				14 12		14 38					15 12		15 38			
Moston d				13 15		13 41				14 15		14 41					15 15		15 41			
Manchester Victoria a		13 08		13 25	13 32	13 53		14 08		14 25	14 32	14 52		15 08			15 26	15 31	15 53		16 08	

	NT	NT	NT	GC	NT	NT	NT	NT	NT	NT	NT	NT	NT	NT	NT	NT	NT	NT	NT	NT	NT
	C			■ 1 🚌	A			F			A			F			A				
York 40 d							15 08						16 08						17 13		
Selby 40 d					14 43						15 41										
Leeds 37,39 d		15 07	15 13		15 23	15 37	15 52		16 07	16 13	16 23	16 37	16 51		17 07	17 13	17 23	17 37	17 51		18 08
Bramley 37 d		15 14			15 30	15 44			16 14		16 30	16 44			17 14		17 30	17 44			18 15
New Pudsey 37 d		15 19			15 35	15 49	16 01		16 19		16 35	16 49	17 00		17 19		17 35	17 49	18 01		18 20
Bradford Interchange 37 a		15 28			15 43	15 57	16 10		16 28		16 43	16 57	17 10		17 28		17 43	17 57	18 10		18 28
d		15 32		15 37	15 46	16 00	16 13		16 32		16 46	17 00	17 12		17 31		17 46	18 00	18 12		18 32
Halifax a		15 44		15 50	15 59	16 12	16 24		16 44		16 59	17 12	17 23		17 43		17 59	18 12	18 24		18 44
d		15 44		15 52	16 06	16 12	16 25		16 44		17 06	17 12	17 24		17 44		18 06	18 12	18 24		18 44
Dewsbury 39 d			15 29							16 31						17 31					
Mirfield 39 a			15 35							16 37						17 37					
d			15 35							16 38						17 38					
Brighouse d			15 49	16 05	16 16					16 49	17 16					17 49	18 16				
London Kings Cross ⊖26 a				19 05																	
Huddersfield 39 a					16 29						17 29						18 30				
Sowerby Bridge d			15 59			16 19	16 32			16 59		17 19	17 31			17 59		18 19	18 31		
Mytholmroyd d			16 05			16 25				17 05		17 25				18 05		18 25			
Hebden Bridge a		15 56	16 08			16 28	16 38		16 56	17 08		17 28	17 37		17 56	18 08		18 28	18 37		18 56
d		15 56	16 08			16 28	16 39		16 56	17 08		17 28	17 38		17 56	18 08		18 28	18 38		18 56
Burnley Manchester Road 97 a							16 57						17 57						18 57		
Accrington 97 a							17 06						18 06						19 06		
Blackburn 97 a							17 14						18 14						19 14		
Preston 97 a							17 32						18 33						19 32		
Poulton-le-Fylde 97 a							17 56						18 50						19 50		
Blackpool North 97 a							18 06						19 00						20 00		
Todmorden d		16 04	16 15			16 36			17 04	17 15		17 36			18 04	18 15		18 36			19 04
Walsden d						16 39						17 39				18 19		18 39			
Littleborough d			16 23			16 45				17 23		17 45				18 25		18 45			
Smithy Bridge d			16 25			16 48				17 25		17 48				18 28		18 48			
Rochdale a		16 14	16 29			16 51			17 14	17 29		17 51			18 14	18 32		18 51			19 15
d	16 04	16 14	16 30			16 51		17 03	17 14	17 30		17 51		18 02	18 14	18 32		18 51		19 00	19 15
Castleton d	16 07		16 33					17 06		17 33				18 05		18 35				19 03	
Mills Hill d	16 12		16 38					17 11		17 38				18 10		18 40				19 08	
Moston d	16 15		16 41					17 14		17 41				18 13		18 43				19 11	
Manchester Victoria a	16 27	16 32	16 52			17 08		17 23	17 32	17 53		18 08		18 21	18 32	18 54		19 10		19 21	19 32

A To Wakefield Westgate C To Wigan Wallgate F To Blackburn

For connections to Liverpool Lime Street please refer to Table 90

Leeds and Bradford - Huddersfield, Blackpool North, Rochdale and Manchester Victoria via Halifax and Brighouse

Network Diagram - see first Page of Table 39

	NT	NT	NT	NT	NT	NT	NT	NT	NT	NT	NT	NT	NT	NT	NT	NT	NT
		A				A											
York 40 d				18 05								20 13					
Selby 40 d		17 38	18 00			18 46											
Leeds 37,39 d	18 13	18 23	18 37	18 51	19 08	19 23		19 37	20 08		20 37	20 51	21 08	21 37	22 08	22 37	23 08
Bramley 37 d		18 30	18 44		19 15	19 30		19 44	20 15		20 44		21 15	21 44	22 15	22 44	23 15
New Pudsey 37 d		18 35	18 49	19 01	19 20	19 35		19 49	20 20		20 49	21 01	21 20	21 49	22 20	22 49	23 20
Bradford Interchange 37 a		18 43	18 58	19 10	19 28	19 44		19 57	20 28		20 57	21 10	21 28	21 57	22 28	22 57	23 29
d		18 46	19 00	19 12	19 32	19 46		20 00	20 31		21 00	21 13	21 31	22 00	22 31	23 00	23 31
Halifax a		18 59	19 12	19 24	19 44	19 59		20 12	20 44		21 12	21 24	21 44	22 12	22 44	23 12	23 44
d		19 06	19 12	19 24	19 44	20 06		20 12	20 44		21 12	21 25	21 44	22 12	22 44	23 12	23 44
Dewsbury 39 d	18 31																
Mirfield 39 a	18 37																
d	18 38																
Brighouse d	18 49	19 16				20 16			20 55				21 55		22 55		23 55
London Kings Cross ⊖26 a																	
Huddersfield 39 a		19 29				20 29			21 08				22 08		23 08		00 08
Sowerby Bridge d	18 59		19 19					20 19			21 19			22 19		23 19	
Mytholmroyd d	19 05		19 25					20 25			21 25			22 25		23 25	
Hebden Bridge a	19 08		19 28	19 36	19 56			20 28			21 28	21 36		22 28		23 28	
d	19 08		19 28	19 36	19 56			20 28			21 28	21 37		22 28		23 28	
Burnley Manchester Road 97 a				19 56								21 56					
Accrington 97 a				20 05								22 05					
Blackburn 97 a				20 14								22 13					
Preston 97 a				20 32								22 31					
Poulton-le-Fylde 97 a				20 50								22 49					
Blackpool North 97 a				21 00								22 59					
Todmorden d	19 15		19 36		20 04			20 36			21 36			22 36		23 36	
Walsden d	19 19		19 39					20 39			21 39			22 39		23 39	
Littleborough d	19 25		19 45					20 45			21 45			22 45		23 45	
Smithy Bridge d	19 28		19 48					20 48			21 48			22 48		23 48	
Rochdale a	19 32		19 52		20 14			20 52			21 52			22 52		23 52	
d	19 32		19 52		20 14		20 25	20 52		21 25	21 52			22 52		23 52	
Castleton d	19 35		19 55				20 28	20 55		21 28	21 55			22 55			
Mills Hill d	19 40		20 00				20 33	21 00		21 33	22 00			23 00			
Moston d	19 43		20 03				20 36	21 03		21 36	22 03			23 03			
Manchester Victoria a	19 54		20 15		20 32		20 46	21 13		21 46	22 15			23 15		00 10	

Saturdays

	NT	NT	NT	NT	NT	GC	NT	NT	NT	NT	NT	NT	NT	NT	NT	NT	NT	NT	NT	NT	NT	NT
						■ 1 C 🚌			E				A				E			A		
York 40 d										06 13					07 06							08 09
Selby 40 d													06 42							07 42		
Leeds 37,39 d	22p37	23p08	05 37	05 51	06 16		06 37			06 51	07 08	07 13	07 23	07 37	07 51			08 08	08 13	08 23	08 37	08 51
Bramley 37 d	22p44	23p15	05 44	05 58	06 23		06 44				07 15		07 30	07 44				08 15		08 30	08 44	
New Pudsey 37 d	22p49	23p20	05 49	06 02	06 28		06 49			07 01	07 20		07 35	07 49	08 01			08 20		08 35	08 49	09 00
Bradford Interchange 37 a	22p57	23p29	05 57	06 13	06 36		06 57			07 11	07 28		07 43	07 57	08 09			08 28		08 43	08 57	09 12
d	23p00	23p31	06 00	06 14	06 40	06 51	07 00			07 14	07 31		07 46	08 00	08 12			08 32		08 46	09 00	09 13
Halifax a	23p12	23p44	06 12	06 25	06 52	07 02	07 12			07 25	07 43		07 59	08 12	08 23			08 44		08 59	09 12	09 24
d	23p12	23p44	06 12	06 26	06 52	07 03	07 12			07 26	07 44		08 06	08 12	08 24			08 44		09 06	09 12	09 24
Dewsbury 39 d												07 29							08 31			
Mirfield 39 a												07 35							08 37			
d												07 35							08 38			
Brighouse d		23p55				07 14						07 49	08 16						08 49	09 16		
London Kings Cross ⊖26 a						10 09																
Huddersfield 39 a		00 08											08 30							09 29		
Sowerby Bridge d	23p19		06 19		06 59		07 19					07 59		08 19					08 59		09 19	
Mytholmroyd d	23p25		06 25		07 05		07 25					08 05		08 25					09 05		09 25	
Hebden Bridge a	23p28		06 28	06 37	07 08		07 28			07 37	07 55	08 08		08 28	08 35			08 56	09 08		09 28	09 37
d	23p28		06 28	06 38	07 08		07 28		07 33	07 38	07 56	08 08		08 28	08 36			08 56	09 08		09 28	09 37
Burnley Manchester Road 97 a				06 57						07 57					08 57							09 56
Accrington 97 a				07 06						08 06					09 06							10 06
Blackburn 97 a				07 16						08 14					09 14							10 14
Preston 97 a				07 36						08 38					09 32							10 32
Poulton-le-Fylde 97 a				07 54						08 56					09 50							10 50
Blackpool North 97 a				08 05						09 05					10 01							11 01
Todmorden d	23p36		06 35		07 15		07 36		07 44		08 04	08 15		08 36				09 04	09 15		09 36	
Walsden d	23p39		06 38				07 39		07 47					08 39							09 39	
Littleborough d	23p45		06 45		07 23		07 45		07 53			08 23		08 45					09 23		09 45	
Smithy Bridge d	23p48		06 47		07 25		07 48		07 56			08 25		08 48					09 25		09 48	
Rochdale a	23p52		06 54		07 29		07 52		08 00		08 14	08 29		08 51				09 14	09 29		09 51	
d	23p52		06 55		07 30		07 52		08 00		08 14	08 30		08 51			09 04	09 14	09 30		09 51	
Castleton d			06 58		07 33		07 55		08 03		08 17	08 33					09 07		09 33			
Mills Hill d			07 03		07 38		08 00		08 08		08 22	08 37					09 12		09 37			
Moston d			07 06		07 41		08 03		08 11		08 25	08 40					09 15		09 40			
Manchester Victoria a	00 10		07 17		07 53		08 14		08 22		08 37	08 53		09 08			09 26	09 32	09 53		10 07	

A To Wakefield Westgate C 🚌 to Brighouse E To Wigan Wallgate

For connections to Liverpool Lime Street please refer to Table 90

Leeds and Bradford - Huddersfield, Blackpool North, Rochdale and Manchester Victoria via Halifax and Brighouse

Network Diagram - see first Page of Table 39

	NT	NT	NT	NT	NT	NT	NT	GC	NT	NT	NT	NT	NT	NT	NT	NT	NT	NT	NT	NT	NT	NT
		B			C				E			C			E			C			B	
York 40 d							09 11							10 11						11 09		
Selby 40 d					08 43							09 43						10 42				
Leeds 37,39 d			09 07	09 13	09 23	09 37	09 53			10 07	10 13	10 23	10 37	10 53		11 07	11 13	11 23	11 37	11 53		12 07
Bramley 37 d			09 14		09 30	09 44				10 14		10 30	10 44			11 14		11 30	11 44			12 14
New Pudsey 37 d			09 19		09 35	09 49	10 02			10 19		10 35	10 49	11 02		11 19		11 35	11 49	12 02		12 19
Bradford Interchange 37 a			09 28		09 43	09 57	10 11			10 28		10 43	10 57	11 12		11 28		11 43	11 57	12 12		12 28
d			09 32		09 46	10 00	10 14	10 22		10 32		10 46	11 00	11 14		11 31		11 46	12 00	12 14		12 32
Halifax a			09 44		10 01	10 12	10 25	10 34		10 44		10 59	11 12	11 24		11 43		11 59	12 12	12 25		12 44
d			09 44		10 06	10 12	10 26	10 38		10 44		11 06	11 12	11 26		11 44		12 06	12 12	12 26		12 44
Dewsbury 39 d				09 31							10 29						11 29					
Mirfield 39 a				09 36							10 35						11 35					
d				09 37							10 35						11 35					
Brighouse d				09 49	10 16			10 48			10 49	11 16					11 49	12 16				
London Kings Cross ⊖26 a								13 46														
Huddersfield 39 a					10 29							11 30						12 30				
Sowerby Bridge d				09 59		10 19					10 59		11 19				11 59		12 19			
Mytholmroyd d				10 05		10 25					11 05		11 25				12 05		12 25			
Hebden Bridge a			09 56	10 08		10 28	10 37			10 56	11 08		11 28	11 36		11 55	12 08		12 28	12 37		12 56
d			09 56	10 08		10 28	10 38			10 56	11 08		11 28	11 38		11 56	12 08		12 28	12 38		12 56
Burnley Manchester Road 97 a							10 57							11 57						12 57		
Accrington 97 a							11 06							12 06						13 06		
Blackburn 97 a							11 14							12 14						13 14		
Preston 97 a							11 32							12 32						13 32		
Poulton-le-Fylde 97 a							11 50							12 50						13 50		
Blackpool North 97 a							12 00							13 00						14 00		
Todmorden d			10 04	10 15		10 36				11 04	11 15		11 36			12 03	12 15		12 36			13 04
Walsden d						10 39							11 39						12 39			
Littleborough d				10 23		10 45					11 23		11 45				12 23		12 45			
Smithy Bridge d				10 25		10 48					11 25		11 48				12 25		12 48			
Rochdale a			10 14	10 29		10 51				11 14	11 29		11 51			12 13	12 29		12 51			13 14
d		10 05	10 14	10 30		10 51			11 04	11 14	11 30		11 51		12 04	12 14	12 30		12 51		13 04	13 14
Castleton d		10 08		10 33					11 07		11 33				12 07		12 33				13 07	
Mills Hill d		10 13		10 38					11 12		11 38				12 12		12 38				13 12	
Moston d		10 16		10 41					11 15		11 41				12 15		12 41				13 15	
Manchester Victoria a		10 26	10 32	10 53		11 07			11 26	11 32	11 53		12 07		12 25	12 32	12 53		13 07		13 25	13 32

	NT	NT	NT	NT	NT	NT	NT	NT	NT	NT	NT	NT	NT	NT	NT	NT	NT	GC	NT	NT	NT
		C			E			C				B			C				F	A	
York 40 d				12 13						13 09							14 13				
Selby 40 d		11 43						12 44							13 43						
Leeds 37,39 d	12 13	12 23	12 37	12 53		13 07	13 13	13 23	13 37	13 53			14 07	14 13	14 23	14 37	14 53				15 07
Bramley 37 d		12 30	12 44			13 14		13 30	13 44				14 14		14 30	14 44					15 14
New Pudsey 37 d		12 35	12 49	13 02		13 19		13 35	13 49	14 02			14 19		14 35	14 49	15 02				15 19
Bradford Interchange 37 a		12 43	12 57	13 12		13 28		13 43	13 58	14 12			14 28		14 43	14 58	15 12				15 28
d		12 46	13 00	13 14		13 32		13 46	14 00	14 14			14 32		14 46	15 01	15 14	15 22			15 32
Halifax a		12 59	13 12	13 25		13 44		13 59	14 12	14 25			14 44		14 59	15 13	15 25	15 33			15 44
d		13 06	13 12	13 26		13 44		14 06	14 13	14 26			14 44		15 06	15 13	15 26	15 35			15 44
Dewsbury 39 d	12 29						13 29							14 29							
Mirfield 39 a	12 35						13 35							14 35							
d	12 35						13 35							14 35							
Brighouse d	12 49	13 16					13 49	14 16						14 49	15 16			15 46			
London Kings Cross ⊖26 a																		18 45			
Huddersfield 39 a		13 29						14 29							15 29						
Sowerby Bridge d	12 59		13 19				13 59		14 19					14 59		15 20					
Mytholmroyd d	13 05		13 25				14 05		14 25					15 05		15 26					
Hebden Bridge a	13 08		13 28	13 37		13 56	14 08		14 28	14 37			14 56	15 08		15 29	15 37				15 56
d	13 08		13 28	13 38		13 56	14 08		14 29	14 38			14 56	15 08		15 29	15 38				15 56
Burnley Manchester Road 97 a				13 57						14 57							15 57				
Accrington 97 a				14 06						15 06							16 06				
Blackburn 97 a				14 14						15 14							16 14				
Preston 97 a				14 32						15 32							16 32				
Poulton-le-Fylde 97 a				14 50						15 50							16 50				
Blackpool North 97 a				15 00						16 00							17 00				
Todmorden d	13 15		13 36			14 04	14 15		14 36				15 04	15 15		15 37					16 04
Walsden d			13 39						14 39							15 40					
Littleborough d	13 23		13 45				14 23		14 46					15 23		15 46					
Smithy Bridge d	13 25		13 48				14 25		14 48					15 25		15 49					
Rochdale a	13 29		13 51			14 14	14 29		14 51				15 14	15 29		15 52					16 14
d	13 30		13 51		14 04	14 14	14 30		14 52			15 04	15 14	15 30		15 52			16 04	16 04	16 14
Castleton d	13 33				14 07		14 33					15 07		15 33					16 07	16 07	
Mills Hill d	13 38				14 12		14 38					15 12		15 38					16 12	16 12	
Moston d	13 41				14 15		14 41					15 15		15 41					16 15	16 15	
Manchester Victoria a	13 53		14 07		14 25	14 32	14 53		15 08			15 26	15 32	15 53		16 08			16 25	16 26	16 32

C To Wakefield Westgate

F To Wigan Wallgate

For connections to Liverpool Lime Street please refer to Table 90

Leeds and Bradford - Huddersfield, Blackpool North, Rochdale and Manchester Victoria via Halifax and Brighouse

Network Diagram - see first Page of Table 39

	NT	NT	NT	NT	NT	NT	NT	NT	NT	NT	NT	NT	NT	NT	NT	NT	NT	NT	NT	NT	NT	NT
		A			C			A			C			A						A		
York 40 d				15 09						16 08						17 12						18 05
Selby 40 d		14 43						15 41						16 43						17 39		
Leeds 37,39 d	15 13	15 23	15 37	15 52		16 07	16 13	16 23	16 37	16 51		17 07	17 13	17 23	17 37	17 51		18 08	18 13	18 23	18 37	18 51
Bramley 37 d		15 30	15 44			16 14		16 30	16 44			17 14		17 30	17 44			18 15		18 30	18 44	
New Pudsey 37 d		15 35	15 49	16 01		16 19		16 35	16 49	17 00		17 19		17 35	17 49	18 01		18 20		18 35	18 49	19 01
Bradford Interchange 37 a		15 43	15 57	16 10		16 28		16 43	16 57	17 10		17 28		17 43	17 57	18 09		18 28		18 43	18 58	19 10
d		15 46	16 00	16 13		16 32		16 46	17 00	17 12		17 32		17 46	18 00	18 12		18 32		18 46	19 00	19 12
Halifax a		15 59	16 12	16 24		16 44		16 59	17 12	17 23		17 44		17 59	18 12	18 23		18 44		18 59	19 12	19 24
d		16 06	16 12	16 25		16 44		17 06	17 12	17 24		17 44		18 06	18 12	18 24		18 44		19 06	19 13	19 24
Dewsbury 39 d	15 29						16 31						17 31						18 31			
Mirfield 39 a	15 35						16 37						17 37						18 37			
d	15 35						16 38						17 38						18 38			
Brighouse d	15 49	16 16					16 49	17 16					17 49	18 16					18 49	19 16		
London Kings Cross ⊖26 a																						
Huddersfield 39 a		16 29						17 29						18 30						19 29		
Sowerby Bridge d	15 59		16 19	16 31			16 59		17 19	17 31			17 59		18 19	18 31			18 59		19 19	
Mytholmroyd d	16 05		16 25				17 05		17 25				18 05		18 25				19 05		19 25	
Hebden Bridge a	16 08		16 28	16 37		16 56	17 08		17 28	17 37		17 56	18 08		18 28	18 37		18 56	19 08		19 28	19 36
d	16 08		16 28	16 38		16 56	17 08		17 28	17 38		17 56	18 08		18 28	18 38		18 56	19 08		19 28	19 36
Burnley Manchester Road 97 a				16 57						17 57						18 57						19 56
Accrington 97 a				17 06						18 06						19 06						20 05
Blackburn 97 a				17 14						18 14						19 14						20 14
Preston 97 a				17 32						18 33						19 32						20 32
Poulton-le-Fylde 97 a				17 56						18 50						19 50						20 50
Blackpool North 97 a				18 06						19 00						20 00						21 00
Todmorden d	16 15		16 36			17 04	17 15		17 36			18 04	18 15		18 36			19 04	19 15		19 36	
Walsden d			16 39						17 39				18 19		18 39				19 19		19 39	
Littleborough d	16 23		16 45				17 23		17 45				18 25		18 45				19 25		19 45	
Smithy Bridge d	16 25		16 48				17 25		17 48				18 28		18 48				19 28		19 48	
Rochdale a	16 29		16 51			17 14	17 29		17 51			18 14	18 32		18 51			19 15	19 32		19 52	
d	16 30		16 51		17 03	17 14	17 30		17 51		18 02	18 14	18 32		18 51		19 02	19 15	19 32		19 52	
Castleton d	16 33				17 06		17 33				18 05		18 35				19 05		19 35		19 55	
Mills Hill d	16 38				17 11		17 38				18 10		18 40				19 10		19 40		20 00	
Moston d	16 41				17 14		17 41				18 13		18 43				19 13		19 43		20 03	
Manchester Victoria a	16 53		17 07		17 23	17 33	17 53		18 07		18 22	18 32	18 54		19 10		19 22	19 32	19 54		20 15	

	NT	NT	NT	NT	NT	NT	NT	NT	NT	NT	NT	NT	NT
		A											
York 40 d								20 13					
Selby 40 d		18 46											
Leeds 37,39 d	19 08	19 23		19 37	20 08		20 37	20 51	21 08	21 37	22 08	23 00	
Bramley 37 d	19 15	19 30		19 44	20 15		20 44		21 15	21 44	22 15	23 07	
New Pudsey 37 d	19 20	19 35		19 49	20 20		20 49	21 01	21 20	21 49	22 20	23 12	
Bradford Interchange 37 a	19 28	19 44		19 57	20 28		20 57	21 10	21 28	21 57	22 28	23 21	
d	19 32	19 46		20 00	20 31		21 00	21 13	21 31	22 00	22 31	23 23	
Halifax a	19 44	19 59		20 12	20 44		21 12	21 24	21 44	22 12	22 44	23 36	
d	19 44	20 06		20 12	20 44		21 12	21 25	21 44	22 12	22 44	23 36	
Dewsbury 39 d													
Mirfield 39 a													
d													
Brighouse d		20 16			20 55				21 55		22 55	23 47	
London Kings Cross ⊖26 a													
Huddersfield 39 a		20 29			21 08				22 08		23 08	23 59	
Sowerby Bridge d				20 19			21 19			22 19			
Mytholmroyd d				20 25			21 25			22 25			
Hebden Bridge a	19 56			20 28			21 28	21 36		22 28			
d	19 56			20 28			21 28	21 37		22 28			
Burnley Manchester Road 97 a								21 56					
Accrington 97 a								22 05					
Blackburn 97 a								22 13					
Preston 97 a								22 31					
Poulton-le-Fylde 97 a								22 49					
Blackpool North 97 a								22 59					
Todmorden d	20 04			20 36			21 36			22 36			
Walsden d				20 39			21 39			22 39			
Littleborough d				20 45			21 45			22 45			
Smithy Bridge d				20 48			21 48			22 48			
Rochdale a	20 14			20 52			21 52			22 52			
d	20 14		20 25	20 52		21 25	21 52			22 52			23 04
Castleton d			20 28	20 55		21 28	21 55			22 55			23 07
Mills Hill d			20 33	21 00		21 33	22 00			23 00			23 12
Moston d			20 36	21 03		21 36	22 03			23 03			23 15
Manchester Victoria a	20 32		20 46	21 14		21 46	22 14			23 14			23 27

A To Wakefield Westgate

C To Blackburn

For connections to Liverpool Lime Street please refer to Table 90

Sundays until 24 June

Leeds and Bradford - Huddersfield, Blackpool North, Rochdale and Manchester Victoria via Halifax and Brighouse

Network Diagram - see first Page of Table 39

	GC A	NT	NT	NT	NT	NT	NT	NT	NT	NT	NT	NT	NT	NT	NT	NT	GC	NT	NT	NT	NT	NT	NT	NT
York 40 d								08 50				09 52				10 57					11 52			
Selby 40 d																								
Leeds 37,39 d		08 02		08 21	08 45	09 02	09 18	09 35		09 54	10 12	10 35		10 54	11 12	11 35			11 54	12 12	12 35		12 54	13 12
Bramley 37 d		08 09		08 28		09 09	09 25			10 01	10 19			11 01	11 19				12 01	12 19			13 01	13 19
New Pudsey 37 d		08 14		08 33	08 54	09 14	09 30	09 44		10 06	10 24	10 44		11 06	11 24	11 44			12 06	12 24	12 44		13 06	13 24
Bradford Interchange 37 a		08 22		08 41	09 03	09 22	09 38	09 53		10 14	10 32	10 53		11 14	11 32	11 53			12 14	12 32	12 53		13 14	13 32
d	07 55			08 45	09 05	09 25	09 44	09 55		10 17	10 35	10 55		11 17	11 35	11 55	12 04		12 17	12 35	12 55		13 17	13 35
Halifax a	08 06			08 57	09 17	09 37	09 57	10 07		10 29	10 48	11 07		11 29	11 48	12 07	12 15		12 29	12 48	13 07		13 29	13 48
d	08 07			09 01	09 17	09 37	09 59	10 07		10 29	10 48	11 07		11 29		12 07	12 15		12 29	12 48	13 07		13 29	
Dewsbury 39 d																								
Mirfield 39 a																								
d																								
Brighouse d	08 18						10 09				10 58						12 26			12 58				
London Kings Cross ⊖26 a	10 40																14 55							
Huddersfield 39 a							10 22				11 12									13 12				
Sowerby Bridge d				09 06		09 44				10 36				11 36					12 36				13 36	
Mytholmroyd d				09 12		09 50				10 42				11 42					12 42				13 42	
Hebden Bridge a				09 17	09 29	09 53		10 19		10 45		11 19		11 45		12 19			12 45		13 19		13 45	
d				09 17	09 29	09 53		10 19		10 45		11 19		11 45		12 19			12 45		13 19		13 45	
Burnley Manchester Road 97 a					09 50			10 38				11 38				12 38					13 38			
Accrington 97 a					09 59			10 47				11 47				12 47					13 47			
Blackburn 97 a					10 07			10 56				11 55				12 55					13 55			
Preston 97 a					10 27			11 13				12 13				13 13					14 13			
Poulton-le-Fylde 97 a					10 45			11 31				12 31				13 31					14 30			
Blackpool North 97 a					10 53			11 39				12 38				13 38					14 38			
Todmorden d				09 24		10 00				10 52				11 52					12 52				13 52	
Walsden d				09 27		10 03				10 55				11 55					12 55				13 55	
Littleborough d				09 34		10 10				11 02				12 02					13 02				14 02	
Smithy Bridge d				09 36		10 12				11 04				12 04					13 04				14 04	
Rochdale a				09 41		10 16				11 08				12 08					13 08				14 08	
d			08 58	09 41		10 17			10 22	11 09			11 22	12 09				12 22	13 09			13 22	14 09	
Castleton d			09 01						10 25				11 25					12 25				13 25		
Mills Hill d			09 06						10 30				11 30					12 30				13 30		
Moston d			09 09						10 33				11 33					12 33				13 33		
Manchester Victoria a			09 19	09 56		10 32			10 43	11 24			11 43	12 24				12 43	13 24			13 43	14 24	

	NT	NT	NT	NT	NT	NT	NT	NT	GC	NT	NT	NT	NT	NT	NT	NT	NT	NT	NT	NT	NT	NT	NT	NT
York 40 d	12 52				13 52					14 52				15 52				16 52				17 52		18 52
Selby 40 d																								
Leeds 37,39 d	13 35		13 54	14 12	14 35		14 54	15 12		15 35		15 54	16 13	16 35		16 54	17 12	17 35		17 54	18 13	18 35	19 03	19 35
Bramley 37 d			14 01	14 19			15 01	15 19				16 01	16 20			17 01	17 19			18 01	18 20		19 10	
New Pudsey 37 d	13 44		14 06	14 24	14 44		15 06	15 24		15 44		16 06	16 25	16 44		17 06	17 24	17 44		18 06	18 25	18 44	19 15	19 44
Bradford Interchange 37 a	13 53		14 14	14 32	14 53		15 14	15 32		15 53		16 14	16 33	16 53		17 14	17 32	17 53		18 14	18 33	18 53	19 24	19 53
d	13 55		14 17	14 35	14 55		15 17	15 35	15 42	15 55		16 17	16 36	16 55		17 17	17 35	17 55		18 17	18 36	18 55	19 27	19 55
Halifax a	14 07		14 29	14 48	15 07		15 29	15 48	15 54	16 07		16 29	16 49	17 07		17 29	17 48	18 07		18 29	18 49	19 07	19 39	20 07
d	14 07		14 29	14 48	15 07		15 29		15 54	16 07		16 29	16 49	17 07		17 29		18 07		18 29	18 49	19 07	19 39	20 07
Dewsbury 39 d																								
Mirfield 39 a																								
d																								
Brighouse d				14 58					16 05				16 59								18 59			
London Kings Cross ⊖26 a									18 44															
Huddersfield 39 a				15 12									17 12								19 12			
Sowerby Bridge d			14 40				15 36					16 36				17 36				18 40			19 46	
Mytholmroyd d			14 46				15 42					16 42				17 42				18 46			19 52	
Hebden Bridge a	14 19		14 49		15 19		15 45			16 19		16 45		17 19		17 45		18 19		18 49		19 19	19 55	20 19
d	14 19		14 49		15 19		15 45			16 19		16 45		17 19		17 45		18 19		18 49		19 19	19 55	20 19
Burnley Manchester Road 97 a	14 38				15 38					16 38				17 38				18 38				19 38		20 38
Accrington 97 a	14 47				15 47					16 47				17 47				18 47				19 47		20 47
Blackburn 97 a	14 55				15 55					16 55				17 55				18 55				19 56		20 55
Preston 97 a	15 13				16 13					17 13				18 13				19 13				20 14		21 13
Poulton-le-Fylde 97 a	15 32				16 31					17 31				18 31				19 31				20 32		21 31
Blackpool North 97 a	15 39				16 38					17 38				18 38				19 38				20 39		21 38
Todmorden d			14 57				15 52					16 53				17 52				18 57			20 02	
Walsden d			15 00				15 55					16 56				17 55				19 00			20 05	
Littleborough d			15 06				16 02					17 02				18 02				19 06			20 11	
Smithy Bridge d			15 09				16 04					17 05				18 04				19 09			20 14	
Rochdale a			15 13				16 08					17 09				18 08				19 13			20 18	
d		14 22	15 13			15 22	16 09				16 22	17 09			17 22	18 09			18 22	19 13			20 19	
Castleton d		14 25				15 25					16 25				17 25				18 25	19 16			20 22	
Mills Hill d		14 30				15 30					16 30				17 30				18 30	19 21			20 27	
Moston d		14 33				15 33					16 33				17 33				18 33	19 24			20 30	
Manchester Victoria a		14 43	15 29			15 43	16 25				16 43	17 24			17 43	18 24			18 43	19 37			20 41	

A ■ to Brighouse

For connections to Liverpool Lime Street please refer to Table 90

Sundays until 24 June

Leeds and Bradford - Huddersfield, Blackpool North, Rochdale and Manchester Victoria via Halifax and Brighouse

Network Diagram - see first Page of Table 39

	NT	NT		NT	NT	NT	NT	NT
York 40 d				19 52		20 57		
Selby 40 d								
Leeds 37,39 d	19 54	20 12		20 35	21 04	21 35	22 05	22 38
Bramley 37 d	20 01	20 19			21 12	21 43	22 12	22 45
New Pudsey 37 d	20 06	20 24		20 44	21 17	21 47	22 17	22 50
Bradford Interchange 37 a	20 14	20 34		20 53	21 25	21 56	22 27	22 58
d	20 19	20 35		20 55	21 28	22 00	22 29	23 01
Halifax a	20 31	20 47		21 07	21 40	22 12	22 42	23 14
d	20 31	20 48		21 07	21 40	22 17	22 42	23 14
Dewsbury 39 d								
Mirfield 39 a								
d								
Brighouse d		20 58					22 52	23a25
London Kings Cross ⊖26 a								
Huddersfield 39 a		21 12					23 04	
Sowerby Bridge d	20 38				21 47	22 24		
Mytholmroyd d	20 44				21 53	22 30		
Hebden Bridge a	20 47			21 19	21 57	22 33		
d	20 47			21 19		22 33		
Burnley Manchester Road 97 a				21 38				
Accrington 97 a				21 47				
Blackburn 97 a				21 55				
Preston 97 a				22 13				
Poulton-le-Fylde 97 a				22 31				
Blackpool North 97 a				22 38				
Todmorden d	20 54					22 40		
Walsden d	20 57					22 43		
Littleborough d	21 03					22 50		
Smithy Bridge d	21 06					22 52		
Rochdale a	21 10					22 56		
d	21 11					22 57		
Castleton d	21 14					23 00		
Mills Hill d	21 19					23 05		
Moston d	21 22					23 08		
Manchester Victoria a	21 33					23 17		

Sundays 1 July to 9 September

	GC	NT	NT	NT	NT	NT	NT	NT	NT	NT	NT	NT	NT	NT	NT	GC	NT	NT	NT	NT	NT	NT	NT	NT A
York 40 d							08 50				09 52				10 57					11 52				12 52
Selby 40 d																								
Leeds 37,39 d		08 02	08 45		09 02	09 18	09 35		09 54	10 12	10 35		10 54	11 12	11 35			11 54	12 12	12 35		12 54	13 12	13 35
Bramley 37 d		08 09			09 09	09 25			10 01	10 19			11 01	11 19				12 01	12 19			13 01	13 19	
New Pudsey 37 d		08 14	08 54		09 14	09 30	09 44		10 06	10 24	10 44		11 06	11 24	11 44			12 06	12 24	12 44		13 06	13 24	13 44
Bradford Interchange 37 a		08 22	09 03		09 22	09 38	09 53		10 14	10 32	10 53		11 14	11 32	11 53			12 14	12 32	12 53		13 14	13 32	13 53
d	07 55		09 05		09 25	09 44	09 55		10 17	10 35	10 55		11 17	11 35	11 55	12 04		12 17	12 35	12 55		13 17	13 35	13 55
Halifax a	08 06		09 17		09 37	09 57	10 07		10 29	10 48	11 07		11 29	11 48	12 07	12 15		12 29	12 48	13 07		13 29	13 48	14 07
d	08 07		09 17		09 37	09 59	10 07		10 29	10 48	11 07		11 29		12 07	12 15		12 29	12 48	13 07		13 29		14 07
Dewsbury 39 d																								
Mirfield 39 a																								
d																								
Brighouse d	08 18					10 09				10 58						12 26			12 58					
London Kings Cross ⊖26 a	10 40															14 55								
Huddersfield 39 a						10 22				11 12									13 12					
Sowerby Bridge d					09 44				10 36				11 36					12 36				13 36		
Mytholmroyd d					09 50				10 42				11 42					12 42				13 42		
Hebden Bridge a			09 29		09 53		10 19		10 45		11 19		11 45		12 19			12 45		13 19		13 45		14 19
d			09 29		09 53		10 19		10 45		11 19		11 45		12 19			12 45		13 19		13 45		14 19
Burnley Manchester Road 97 a			09 50				10 38				11 38				12 38					13 38				14 38
Accrington 97 a			09 59				10 47				11 47				12 47					13 47				14 47
Blackburn 97 a			10 07				10 56				11 55				12 55					13 55				14 55
Preston 97 a			10 27				11 13				12 13				13 13					14 13				15 13
Poulton-le-Fylde 97 a			10 45				11 31				12 31				13 31					14 30				15 32
Blackpool North 97 a			10 53				11 39				12 38				13 38					14 38				15 39
Todmorden d					10 00				10 52				11 52					12 52				13 52		
Walsden d					10 03				10 55				11 55					12 55				13 55		
Littleborough d					10 10				11 02				12 02					13 02				14 02		
Smithy Bridge d					10 12				11 04				12 04					13 04				14 04		
Rochdale a					10 16				11 08				12 08					13 08				14 08		
d				08 58	10 17			10 22	11 09			11 22	12 09				12 22	13 09			13 22	14 09		
Castleton d				09 01				10 25				11 25					12 25				13 25			
Mills Hill d				09 06				10 30				11 30					12 30				13 30			
Moston d				09 09				10 33				11 33					12 33				13 33			
Manchester Victoria a				09 19	10 32			10 43	11 24			11 43	12 24				12 43	13 24			13 43	14 24		

For connections to Liverpool Lime Street please refer to Table 90

Leeds and Bradford - Huddersfield, Blackpool North, Rochdale and Manchester Victoria via Halifax and Brighouse

Network Diagram - see first Page of Table 39

Station		NT	NT	NT	NT	NT	NT	GC	NT	NT	NT	NT	NT	NT	NT	NT	NT	NT	NT	NT	NT	NT	NT	NT	NT
York	40 d				13 52					14 52				15 52				16 52				17 52		18 52	
Selby	40 d																								
Leeds	37,39 d		13 54	14 12	14 35		14 54		15 12	15 35		15 54	16 13	16 35		16 54	17 12	17 35		17 54	18 13	18 35	19 03	19 35	19 54
Bramley	37 d		14 01	14 19			15 01		15 19			16 01	16 20			17 01	17 19			18 01	18 20		19 10		20 01
New Pudsey	37 d		14 06	14 24	14 44		15 06		15 24	15 44		16 06	16 25	16 44		17 06	17 24	17 44		18 06	18 25	18 44	19 15	19 44	20 06
Bradford Interchange	37 a		14 14	14 32	14 53		15 14		15 32	15 53		16 14	16 33	16 53		17 14	17 32	17 53		18 14	18 33	18 53	19 24	19 53	20 14
	d		14 17	14 35	14 55		15 17	15 42	15 35	15 55		16 17	16 36	16 55		17 17	17 35	17 55		18 17	18 36	18 55	19 27	19 55	20 19
Halifax	a		14 29	14 48	15 07		15 29	15 54	15 48	16 07		16 29	16 49	17 07		17 29	17 48	18 07		18 29	18 49	19 07	19 39	20 07	20 31
	d		14 29	14 48	15 07		15 29	15 54		16 07		16 29	16 49	17 07		17 29		18 07		18 29	18 49	19 07	19 39	20 07	20 31
Dewsbury	39 d																								
Mirfield	39 a																								
	d																								
Brighouse	d			14 58				16 05					16 59								18 59				
London Kings Cross ⊖	26 a							18 44																	
Huddersfield	39 a			15 12									17 12								19 12				
Sowerby Bridge	d		14 40				15 36					16 36				17 36				18 40			19 46		20 38
Mytholmroyd	d		14 46				15 42					16 42				17 42				18 46			19 52		20 44
Hebden Bridge	a		14 49		15 19		15 45			16 19		16 45		17 19		17 45		18 19		18 49		19 19	19 55	20 19	20 47
	d		14 49		15 19		15 45			16 19		16 45		17 19		17 45		18 19		18 49		19 19	19 55	20 19	20 47
Burnley Manchester Road	97 a				15 38					16 38				17 38				18 38				19 38		20 38	
Accrington	97 a				15 47					16 47				17 47				18 47				19 47		20 47	
Blackburn	97 a				15 55					16 55				17 55				18 55				19 56		20 55	
Preston	97 a				16 13					17 13				18 13				19 13				20 14		21 13	
Poulton-le-Fylde	97 a				16 31					17 31				18 31				19 31				20 32		21 31	
Blackpool North	97 a				16 38					17 38				18 38				19 38				20 39		21 38	
Todmorden	d		14 57				15 52					16 53				17 52				18 57			20 02		20 54
Walsden	d		15 00				15 55					16 56				17 55				19 00			20 05		20 57
Littleborough	d		15 06				16 02					17 02				18 02				19 06			20 11		21 03
Smithy Bridge	d		15 09				16 04					17 05				18 04				19 09			20 14		21 06
Rochdale	a		15 13				16 08					17 09				18 08				19 13			20 18		21 10
	d	14 22	15 13			15 22	16 09				16 22	17 09			17 22	18 09			18 22	19 13			20 19		21 11
Castleton	d	14 25				15 25					16 25				17 25				18 25	19 16			20 22		21 14
Mills Hill	d	14 30				15 30					16 30				17 30				18 30	19 21			20 27		21 19
Moston	d	14 33				15 33					16 33				17 33				18 33	19 24			20 30		21 22
Manchester Victoria	a	14 43	15 29			15 43	16 25				16 43	17 24			17 43	18 24			18 43	19 37			20 41		21 33

Station		NT	NT	NT	NT	NT	NT
York	40 d		19 52		20 57		
Selby	40 d						
Leeds	37,39 d	20 12	20 35	21 04	21 35	22 05	22 38
Bramley	37 d	20 19		21 12	21 43	22 12	22 45
New Pudsey	37 d	20 24	20 44	21 17	21 47	22 17	22 50
Bradford Interchange	37 a	20 34	20 53	21 25	21 56	22 27	22 58
	d	20 35	20 55	21 28	22 00	22 29	23 01
Halifax	a	20 47	21 07	21 40	22 12	22 42	23 14
	d	20 48	21 07	21 40	22 12	22 42	23 14
Dewsbury	39 d						
Mirfield	39 a						
	d						
Brighouse	d	20 58				22 52	23a25
London Kings Cross ⊖	26 a						
Huddersfield	39 a	21 12				23 04	
Sowerby Bridge	d			21 47	22 19		
Mytholmroyd	d			21 53	22 25		
Hebden Bridge	a		21 19	21 57	22 28		
	d		21 19		22 28		
Burnley Manchester Road	97 a		21 38				
Accrington	97 a		21 47				
Blackburn	97 a		21 55				
Preston	97 a		22 13				
Poulton-le-Fylde	97 a		22 31				
Blackpool North	97 a		22 38				
Todmorden	d				22 40		
Walsden	d				22 43		
Littleborough	d				22 50		
Smithy Bridge	d				22 52		
Rochdale	a				22 56		
	d				22 57		
Castleton	d				23 00		
Mills Hill	d				23 05		
Moston	d				23 08		
Manchester Victoria	a				23 17		

For connections to Liverpool Lime Street please refer to Table 90

Leeds and Bradford - Huddersfield, Blackpool North, Rochdale and Manchester Victoria via Halifax and Brighouse

Network Diagram - see first Page of Table 39

Station		GC	NT	NT	NT	NT	NT	NT	NT	NT	NT	NT	NT	NT	NT	GC	NT	GC	NT	NT	NT	NT	NT	NT	NT
		A																							
York	40 d								08 50				09 52				10 53					11 52			12 52
Selby	40 d																								
Leeds	37,39 d		08 02		08 21	08 36	09 08		09 35				10 35				11 35					12 35			13 35
Bramley	37 d		08 09																						
New Pudsey	37 d		08 14																						
Bradford Interchange	37 a		08 22																						
	d							09 20				10 15				11 45					12 15				
Halifax	a				08 47	09 08	09 33	09 45	10 00			10 40	11 00				12 00				12 40	13 00			14 00
	d	07 30			09 01	09 17	09 37	09 45	10 07		10 29	10 40	11 07		11 29	12 11	12 07	12 20		12 29	12 40	13 07		13 29	14 07
Dewsbury	39 d																								
Mirfield	39 a																								
	d																								
Brighouse	d	07a50						10 00				10 55						12 31			12 55				
London Kings Cross ⊖	26 a																	14 55							
Huddersfield	39 a							10 15				11 10									13 10				
Sowerby Bridge	d				09 06		09 44				10 36				11 36					12 36				13 36	
Mytholmroyd	d				09 12		09 50				10 42				11 42					12 42				13 42	
Hebden Bridge	a				09 17	09 29	09 53		10 19		10 45		11 19		11 45		12 19			12 45		13 19		13 45	14 19
	d				09 17	09 29	09 53		10 19		10 45		11 19		11 45		12 19			12 45		13 19		13 45	14 19
Burnley Manchester Road	97 a					09 50			10 38				11 38				12 38					13 38			14 38
Accrington	97 a					09 59			10 47				11 47				12 47					13 47			14 47
Blackburn	97 a					10 07			10 56				11 55				12 55					13 55			14 55
Preston	97 a					10 27			11 13				12 13				13 13					14 13			15 13
Poulton-le-Fylde	97 a					10 45			11 31				12 31				13 31					14 30			15 32
Blackpool North	97 a					10 53			11 39				12 38				13 38					14 38			15 39
Todmorden	d				09 24		10 00				10 52				11 52					12 52				13 52	
Walsden	d				09 27		10 03				10 55				11 55					12 55				13 55	
Littleborough	d				09 34		10 10				11 02				12 02					13 02				14 02	
Smithy Bridge	d				09 36		10 12				11 04				12 04					13 04				14 04	
Rochdale	a				09 41		10 16				11 08				12 08					13 08				14 08	
	d			08 58	09 41		10 17			10 22	11 09			11 22	12 09				12 22	13 09			13 22	14 09	
Castleton	d			09 01	09 44		10 20			10 25				11 25					12 25				13 25		
Mills Hill	d			09 06	09 49		10 25			10 30				11 30					12 30				13 30		
Moston	d			09 09	09 52		10 28			10 33				11 33					12 33				13 33		
Manchester Victoria	a			09 19	10 02		10 38			10 43	11 24			11 43	12 24				12 43	13 24			13 43	14 24	

Station		NT	NT	NT	NT	GC		NT	NT	NT	NT	NT	NT	NT	NT	NT		NT	NT	NT	NT	NT	NT	NT	NT
						A																			
York	40 d				13 52					14 52				15 52				16 52				17 52		18 52	
Selby	40 d																								
Leeds	37,39 d				14 35					15 35				16 35				17 35				18 35		19 35	
Bramley	37 d																								
New Pudsey	37 d																								
Bradford Interchange	37 a																								
	d			14 15									16 15								18 15				
Halifax	a			14 40	15 00					16 00			16 40	17 00				18 00			18 40	19 00		20 00	
	d		14 29	14 40	15 07	15 20			15 29	16 07		16 29	16 40	17 07		17 29		18 07		18 29	18 40	19 07	19 39	20 07	20 31
Dewsbury	39 d																								
Mirfield	39 a																								
	d																								
Brighouse	d			14 55		15a40							16 55								18 55				
London Kings Cross ⊖	26 a																								
Huddersfield	39 a			15 10									17 10								19 10				
Sowerby Bridge	d		14 40						15 36			16 36				17 36				18 40			19 46		20 38
Mytholmroyd	d		14 46						15 42			16 42				17 42				18 46			19 52		20 44
Hebden Bridge	a		14 49		15 19				15 45	16 19		16 45		17 19		17 45		18 19		18 49		19 19	19 55	20 19	20 47
	d		14 49		15 19				15 45	16 19		16 45		17 19		17 45		18 19		18 49		19 19	19 55	20 19	20 47
Burnley Manchester Road	97 a				15 38					16 38				17 38				18 38				19 38		20 38	
Accrington	97 a				15 47					16 47				17 47				18 47				19 47		20 47	
Blackburn	97 a				15 55					16 55				17 55				18 55				19 56		20 55	
Preston	97 a				16 13					17 13				18 13				19 13				20 14		21 13	
Poulton-le-Fylde	97 a				16 31					17 31				18 31				19 31				20 32		21 31	
Blackpool North	97 a				16 38					17 38				18 38				19 38				20 39		21 38	
Todmorden	d		14 57						15 52			16 52				17 52				18 57			20 02		20 54
Walsden	d		15 00						15 55			16 55				17 55				19 00			20 05		20 57
Littleborough	d		15 06						16 02			17 02				18 02				19 06			20 11		21 03
Smithy Bridge	d		15 09						16 04			17 04				18 04				19 09			20 14		21 06
Rochdale	a		15 13						16 08			17 08				18 08				19 13			20 18		21 10
	d	14 22	15 13					15 22	16 09		16 22	17 09			17 22	18 09			18 22	19 13			20 19		21 11
Castleton	d	14 25						15 25			16 25				17 25	18 12			18 25	19 16			20 22		21 14
Mills Hill	d	14 30						15 30			16 30				17 30	18 17			18 30	19 21			20 27		21 19
Moston	d	14 33						15 33			16 33				17 33	18 20			18 33	19 24			20 30		21 22
Manchester Victoria	a	14 43	15 29					15 43	16 25		16 43	17 24			17 43	18 30			18 43	19 37			20 41		21 33

A To Wakefield Kirkgate

For connections to Liverpool Lime Street please refer to Table 90

Table 41

Sundays 16 September to 21 October

Leeds and Bradford - Huddersfield, Blackpool North, Rochdale and Manchester Victoria via Halifax and Brighouse

Network Diagram - see first Page of Table 39

	NT	NT	NT	NT	NT
	🚌			🚌	🚌
York 40 d		19 52	20 57		
Selby 40 d					
Leeds 37,39 d		20 35	21 35		
Bramley 37 d					
New Pudsey 37 d					
Bradford Interchange 37 a					
d	20 15			22 15	23 05
Halifax a	20 40	21 00	22 11	22 40	23 30
d	20 40	21 07	22 17	22 40	23 30
Dewsbury 39 d					
Mirfield 39 a					
d					
Brighouse d	20 55			22 55	23a45
London Kings Cross ⊖26 a					
Huddersfield 39 a	21 10			23 10	
Sowerby Bridge d			22 24		
Mytholmroyd d			22 30		
Hebden Bridge a		21 19	22 33		
d		21 19	22 33		
Burnley Manchester Road 97 a		21 38			
Accrington 97 a		21 47			
Blackburn 97 a		21 55			
Preston 97 a		22 13			
Poulton-le-Fylde 97 a		22 31			
Blackpool North 97 a		22 38			
Todmorden d			22 40		
Walsden d			22 43		
Littleborough d			22 50		
Smithy Bridge d			22 52		
Rochdale a			22 56		
d			22 57		
Castleton d			23 00		
Mills Hill d			23 05		
Moston d			23 08		
Manchester Victoria a			23 17		

Sundays from 28 October

	GC	NT	NT	NT	NT	NT	NT	NT	NT	NT	NT	NT
	🚌											
York 40 d								08 50				09 52
Selby 40 d												
Leeds 37,39 d		08 02		08 21	08 45	09 02	09 18	09 35		09 54	10 12	10 35
Bramley 37 d		08 09		08 28		09 09	09 25			10 01	10 19	
New Pudsey 37 d		08 14		08 33	08 54	09 14	09 30	09 44		10 06	10 24	10 44
Bradford Interchange 37 a		08 22		08 41	09 03	09 22	09 38	09 53		10 14	10 32	10 53
d				08 45	09 05	09 25	09 44	09 55		10 17	10 35	10 55
Halifax a				08 57	09 17	09 37	09 57	10 07		10 29	10 48	11 07
d	07 30			09 01	09 17	09 37	09 59	10 07		10 29	10 48	11 07
Dewsbury 39 d												
Mirfield 39 a												
d												
Brighouse d	07a50						10 09				10 58	
London Kings Cross ⊖26 a												
Huddersfield 39 a							10 22				11 12	
Sowerby Bridge d				09 06		09 44				10 36		
Mytholmroyd d				09 12		09 50				10 42		
Hebden Bridge a				09 17	09 29	09 53		10 19		10 45		11 19
d				09 17	09 29	09 53		10 19		10 45		11 19
Burnley Manchester Road 97 a					09 50			10 38				11 38
Accrington 97 a					09 59			10 47				11 47
Blackburn 97 a					10 07			10 56				11 55
Preston 97 a					10 27			11 13				12 13
Poulton-le-Fylde 97 a					10 45			11 31				12 31
Blackpool North 97 a					10 53			11 39				12 38
Todmorden d				09 24		10 00				10 52		
Walsden d				09 27		10 03				10 55		
Littleborough d				09 34		10 10				11 02		
Smithy Bridge d				09 36		10 12				11 04		
Rochdale a				09 41		10 16				11 08		
d			08 58	09 41		10 17			10 22	11 09		
Castleton d			09 01	09 44		10 20			10 25			
Mills Hill d			09 06	09 49		10 25			10 30			
Moston d			09 09	09 52		10 28			10 33			
Manchester Victoria a			09 19	10 02		10 38			10 43	11 24		

	NT	NT	NT	NT	GC	NT	NT	NT	NT	NT	NT	NT
York 40 d				10 53					11 52			
Selby 40 d												
Leeds 37,39 d		10 54	11 12	11 35			11 54	12 12	12 35		12 54	13 12
Bramley 37 d		11 01	11 19				12 01	12 19			13 01	13 19
New Pudsey 37 d		11 06	11 24	11 44			12 06	12 24	12 44		13 06	13 24
Bradford Interchange 37 a		11 14	11 32	11 53			12 14	12 32	12 53		13 14	13 32
d		11 17	11 35	11 55	12 04		12 17	12 35	12 55		13 17	13 35
Halifax a		11 29	11 48	12 07	12 15		12 29	12 48	13 07		13 29	13 48
d		11 29		12 07	12 15		12 29	12 48	13 07		13 29	
Dewsbury 39 d												
Mirfield 39 a												
d												
Brighouse d					12 26			12 58				
London Kings Cross ⊖26 a					14 55							
Huddersfield 39 a								13 12				
Sowerby Bridge d		11 36					12 36				13 36	
Mytholmroyd d		11 42					12 42				13 42	
Hebden Bridge a		11 45		12 19			12 45		13 19		13 45	
d		11 45		12 19			12 45		13 19		13 45	
Burnley Manchester Road 97 a				12 38					13 38			
Accrington 97 a				12 47					13 47			
Blackburn 97 a				12 55					13 55			
Preston 97 a				13 13					14 13			
Poulton-le-Fylde 97 a				13 31					14 30			
Blackpool North 97 a				13 38					14 38			
Todmorden d		11 52					12 52				13 52	
Walsden d		11 55					12 55				13 55	
Littleborough d		12 02					13 02				14 02	
Smithy Bridge d		12 04					13 04				14 04	
Rochdale a		12 08					13 08				14 08	
d	11 22	12 09				12 22	13 09			13 22	14 09	
Castleton d	11 25					12 25				13 25		
Mills Hill d	11 30					12 30				13 30		
Moston d	11 33					12 33				13 33		
Manchester Victoria a	11 43	12 24				12 43	13 24			13 43	14 24	

For connections to Liverpool Lime Street please refer to Table 90

Table 41

Sundays from 28 October

Leeds and Bradford - Huddersfield, Blackpool North, Rochdale and Manchester Victoria via Halifax and Brighouse

Network Diagram - see first Page of Table 39

	NT	NT	NT	NT	NT	NT	NT	NT	GC	NT	NT	NT
York 40 d	12 52				13 52					14 52		
Selby 40 d												
Leeds 37,39 d	13 35		13 54	14 12	14 35		14 54	15 12		15 35		15 54
Bramley 37 d			14 01	14 19			15 01	15 19				16 01
New Pudsey 37 d	13 44		14 06	14 24	14 44		15 06	15 24		15 44		16 06
Bradford Interchange 37 a	13 53		14 14	14 32	14 53		15 14	15 32		15 53		16 14
d	13 55		14 17	14 35	14 55		15 17	15 35	15 42	15 55		16 17
Halifax a	14 07		14 29	14 48	15 07		15 29	15 48	15 54	16 07		16 29
d	14 07		14 29	14 48	15 07		15 29		15 54	16 07		16 29
Dewsbury 39 d												
Mirfield 39 a												
d												
Brighouse d				14 58					16 05			
London Kings Cross ⊖26 a									18 51			
Huddersfield 39 a				15 12								
Sowerby Bridge d			14 40				15 36					16 36
Mytholmroyd d			14 46				15 42					16 42
Hebden Bridge a	14 19		14 49		15 19		15 45			16 19		16 45
d	14 19		14 49		15 19		15 45			16 19		16 45
Burnley Manchester Road 97 a	14 38				15 38					16 38		
Accrington 97 a	14 47				15 47					16 47		
Blackburn 97 a	14 55				15 55					16 55		
Preston 97 a	15 13				16 13					17 13		
Poulton-le-Fylde 97 a	15 32				16 31					17 31		
Blackpool North 97 a	15 39				16 38					17 38		
Todmorden d			14 57				15 52					16 52
Walsden d			15 00				15 55					16 55
Littleborough d			15 06				16 02					17 02
Smithy Bridge d			15 09				16 04					17 04
Rochdale a			15 13				16 08					17 08
d		14 22	15 13			15 22	16 09				16 22	17 09
Castleton d		14 25				15 25					16 25	
Mills Hill d		14 30				15 30					16 30	
Moston d		14 33				15 33					16 33	
Manchester Victoria a		14 43	15 29			15 43	16 25				16 43	17 24

	NT	NT	NT	NT	NT	NT	NT	NT	NT	NT	NT
York 40 d		15 52				16 52				17 52	
Selby 40 d											
Leeds 37,39 d	16 13	16 35		16 54	17 12	17 35		17 54	18 13	18 35	19 03
Bramley 37 d	16 20			17 01	17 19			18 01	18 20		19 10
New Pudsey 37 d	16 25	16 44		17 06	17 24	17 44		18 06	18 25	18 44	19 15
Bradford Interchange 37 a	16 33	16 53		17 14	17 32	17 53		18 14	18 33	18 53	19 24
d	16 36	16 55		17 17	17 35	17 55		18 17	18 36	18 55	19 27
Halifax a	16 49	17 07		17 29	17 48	18 07		18 29	18 49	19 07	19 39
d	16 49	17 07		17 29		18 07		18 29	18 49	19 07	19 39
Dewsbury 39 d											
Mirfield 39 a											
d											
Brighouse d	16 59								18 59		
London Kings Cross ⊖26 a											
Huddersfield 39 a	17 12								19 12		
Sowerby Bridge d				17 36				18 40			19 46
Mytholmroyd d				17 42				18 46			19 52
Hebden Bridge a		17 19		17 45		18 19		18 49		19 19	19 55
d		17 19		17 45		18 19		18 49		19 19	19 55
Burnley Manchester Road 97 a		17 38				18 38				19 38	
Accrington 97 a		17 47				18 47				19 47	
Blackburn 97 a		17 55				18 55				19 56	
Preston 97 a		18 13				19 13				20 14	
Poulton-le-Fylde 97 a		18 31				19 31				20 32	
Blackpool North 97 a		18 38				19 38				20 39	
Todmorden d				17 52				18 57			20 02
Walsden d				17 55				19 00			20 05
Littleborough d				18 02				19 06			20 11
Smithy Bridge d				18 04				19 09			20 14
Rochdale a				18 08				19 13			20 18
d			17 22	18 09			18 22	19 13			20 19
Castleton d			17 25	18 12			18 25	19 16			20 22
Mills Hill d			17 30	18 17			18 30	19 21			20 27
Moston d			17 33	18 20			18 33	19 24			20 30
Manchester Victoria a			17 43	18 30			18 43	19 37			20 41

	NT	NT	NT	NT	NT	NT	NT	NT
York 40 d	18 52			19 52		20 57		
Selby 40 d								
Leeds 37,39 d	19 35	19 54	20 12	20 35	21 04	21 35	22 05	22 38
Bramley 37 d		20 01	20 19		21 12	21 43	22 12	22 45
New Pudsey 37 d	19 44	20 06	20 24	20 44	21 17	21 47	22 17	22 50
Bradford Interchange 37 a	19 53	20 14	20 34	20 53	21 25	21 56	22 27	22 58
d	19 55	20 19	20 35	20 55	21 28	22 00	22 29	23 01
Halifax a	20 07	20 31	20 47	21 07	21 40	22 12	22 42	23 14
d	20 07	20 31	20 48	21 07	21 40	22 17	22 42	23 14
Dewsbury 39 d								
Mirfield 39 a								
d								
Brighouse d			20 58				22 52	23a25
London Kings Cross ⊖26 a								
Huddersfield 39 a			21 12				23 04	
Sowerby Bridge d		20 38			21 47	22 24		
Mytholmroyd d		20 44			21 53	22 30		
Hebden Bridge a	20 19	20 47		21 19	21 57	22 33		
d	20 19	20 47		21 19		22 33		
Burnley Manchester Road 97 a	20 38			21 38				
Accrington 97 a	20 47			21 47				
Blackburn 97 a	20 55			21 55				
Preston 97 a	21 13			22 13				
Poulton-le-Fylde 97 a	21 31			22 31				
Blackpool North 97 a	21 38			22 38				
Todmorden d		20 54				22 40		
Walsden d		20 57				22 43		
Littleborough d		21 03				22 50		
Smithy Bridge d		21 06				22 52		
Rochdale a		21 10				22 56		
d		21 11				22 57		
Castleton d		21 14				23 00		
Mills Hill d		21 19				23 05		
Moston d		21 22				23 08		
Manchester Victoria a		21 33				23 17		

For connections to Liverpool Lime Street please refer to Table 90

Manchester Victoria, Rochdale, Blackpool North and Huddersfield - Bradford and Leeds via Brighouse and Halifax

Network Diagram - see first Page of Table 39

Miles	Miles	Miles	Miles		NT MO A ⇌	NT MX	NT MX	NT	NT	NT B	NT	NT B	NT		NT	NT	NT	NT B	NT	NT	NT	NT	NT B
0	—	—	—	Manchester Victoria ⇌ d		22p28	23p20			05 51			06 17		06 43		06 58		07 17	07 48		08 00	
4	—	—	—	Moston d		22p34	23p27						06 23				07 04		07 23			08 06	
6	—	—	—	Mills Hill d		22p39	23p32						06 28				07 09		07 28			08 11	
8¾	—	—	—	Castleton d		22p44	23p37						06 33				07 14		07 33			08 16	
10½	—	—	—	Rochdale a		22p47	23p40			06 05			06 36		06 56		07 17		07 36	08 01		08 19	
—	—	—	—	d		22p48	23p41			06 05			06 37		06 56		07 18		07 37	08 01		08 20	
12¾	—	—	—	Smithy Bridge d		22p52	23p45			06 09			06 41				07 22		07 41			08 24	
13¾	—	—	—	Littleborough d		22p55	23p48			06 13			06 44				07 25		07 44			08 27	
17¾	—	—	—	Walsden d		23p01	23p54			06 19			06 50				07 31		07 50				
19¾	—	—	—	Todmorden d		23p05	23p58			06 22			06 54		07 08		07 35		07 54	08 13		08 34	
—	0	—	—	Blackpool North 97 d								05 29						06 28					07 29
—	3	—	—	PoultonleFylde 97 d								05 35						06 34					07 35
—	17½	—	—	Preston ■ 97 d								05 54						06 54					07 54
—	29½	—	—	Blackburn 97 d								06 10						07 10					08 10
—	35¾	—	—	Accrington 97 d								06 17						07 17					08 17
—	42	—	—	Burnley Manchester Road 97 d								06 26						07 26					08 26
23½	54¾	—	0	Hebden Bridge a		23p11	00 04			06 29		06 49	07 00		07 14		07 41	07 49	08 00	08 19		08 41	08 49
—	—	—	—	d		23p11	00 04	05 47	06 17	06 29		06 50	07 00		07 16		07 41	07 50	08 00	08 21		08 41	08 50
24¾	56	—	1¼	Mytholmroyd d		23p15	00 08	05 50	06 20	06 32			07 03		07 19		07 45		08 04			08 44	
28¾	60	—	5¼	Sowerby Bridge d		23p20	00 13	05 56	06 26	06 38		06 57	07 09		07 25		07 50	07 57	08 09			08 50	08 57
—	—	0	—	Huddersfield 39 d												07 29					08 21		
—	—	—	—	London Kings Cross ■ ⊖26 d																			
—	—	5¾	11	Brighouse d												07 39	07 59				08 33	08 58	
—	—	—	15	Mirfield 39 a													08 06					09 06	
—	—	—	—	d													08 06					09 07	
—	—	—	18	Dewsbury 39 a													08 11					09 12	
32¼	63½	10½	—	Halifax a		23p29	00 20	06 02	06 32	06 45		07 03	07 16		07 32	07 50		08 03	08 16	08 33	08 43		09 03
—	—	—	—	d	23p20	23p29	00 20	06 03	06 33	06 45	07 02	07 03	07 16		07 33	07 50		08 03	08 16	08 33	08 48		09 03
40¼	71½	—	—	Bradford Interchange a	23b45	23p43	00 34	06 16	06 46	07 00		07 17	07 31		07 47	08 03		08 17	08 31	08 47	09 02		09 17
—	—	—	—	d	⟆	23p46	00 37	06 18	06 48	07 02		07 20	07 34		07 50	08 05		08 20	08 34	08 50	09 04		09 20
43¾	75	—	—	New Pudsey 37 a	23b55	23p54		06 27	06 57	07 11		07 28	07 42		07 58	08 13		08 28	08 42	08 58	09 12		09 27
45¾	77	—	—	Bramley 37 a	00s05	23p58		06 30	07 00	07 14			07 46		08 02	08 18			08 46	09 02	09 16		
49¾	81	—	27¼	Leeds ■ 37,39 a	00s25	00 08	00 55	06 41	07 09	07 27	07 56	07 39	07 57		08 12	08 29	08 33	08 39	08 57	09 12	09 27	09 32	09 39
—	—	—	—	Selby 40 a									08 36		08 53					09 53			
—	—	—	—	York ■ 40 a						08 06		08 16						09 21					10 21

	NT	NT D	NT	NT	NT	NT	NT	NT	NT		NT	NT	NT	NT	NT E	NT	NT	NT	NT		NT	NT E	NT	NT
Manchester Victoria ⇌ d	08 22	08 30	08 48		09 00		09 22	09 33	09 48			10 00		10 21	10 30	10 48		11 00			11 21	11 30	11 48	
Moston d		08 36			09 06			09 39				10 06			10 36			11 06				11 36		
Mills Hill d		08 40			09 11			09 44				10 11			10 40			11 11				11 40		
Castleton d		08 45			09 16			09 49				10 16			10 45			11 16				11 45		
Rochdale a	08 34	08 51	09 02		09 19		09 35	09 54	10 02			10 19		10 34	10 51	11 02		11 19			11 34	11 51	12 02	
d	08 35		09 02		09 20		09 36		10 02			10 20		10 35		11 02		11 20			11 35		12 02	
Smithy Bridge d	08 39				09 24		09 40					10 24		10 39				11 24			11 39			
Littleborough d	08 42				09 27		09 43					10 27		10 42				11 27			11 42			
Walsden d	08 48						09 49							10 48							11 48			
Todmorden d	08 52		09 14		09 34		09 53		10 14			10 34		10 52		11 14		11 34			11 52		12 14	
Blackpool North 97 d						08 29							09 29						10 29					
PoultonleFylde 97 d						08 35							09 35						10 35					
Preston ■ 97 d						08 54							09 54						10 54					
Blackburn 97 d						09 10							10 10						11 10					
Accrington 97 d						09 17							10 17						11 17					
Burnley Manchester Road 97 d						09 26							10 26						11 28					
Hebden Bridge a	08 58		09 20		09 41	09 49	09 59		10 20			10 41	10 49	10 58		11 20		11 41	11 49		11 58		12 20	
d	09 00		09 21		09 41	09 50	10 00		10 21			10 41	10 50	11 00		11 21		11 41	11 50		12 00		12 21	
Mytholmroyd d	09 03				09 44		10 03					10 44		11 03				11 44			12 03			
Sowerby Bridge d	09 09				09 50		10 09					10 50		11 09				11 50			12 09			
Huddersfield 39 d				09 23							10 23						11 23							12 23
London Kings Cross ■ ⊖26 d																								
Brighouse d				09 33	09 58						10 33	10 58					11 33	11 58						12 33
Mirfield 39 a					10 06							11 06						12 06						
d					10 07							11 07						12 07						
Dewsbury 39 a					10 12							11 12						12 12						
Halifax a	09 15		09 33	09 44		10 02	10 15		10 33		10 43		11 02	11 15		11 33	11 43		12 02		12 15		12 33	12 43
d	09 16		09 33	09 49		10 03	10 16		10 33		10 49		11 03	11 16		11 33	11 49		12 03		12 16		12 33	12 49
Bradford Interchange a	09 31		09 47	10 02		10 17	10 31		10 47		11 02		11 17	11 31		11 47	12 02		12 17		12 31		12 47	13 02
d	09 34		09 50	10 05		10 18	10 34		10 50		11 05		11 20	11 34		11 50	12 05		12 19		12 34		12 50	13 05
New Pudsey 37 a	09 42		09 58	10 13		10 27	10 42		10 58		11 13		11 28	11 42		11 58	12 13		12 27		12 42		12 58	13 13
Bramley 37 a	09 46		10 02	10 17			10 46		11 02		11 17			11 46		12 02	12 17				12 46		13 02	13 17
Leeds ■ 37,39 a	09 57		10 12	10 27	10 32	10 38	10 59		11 13		11 27	11 33	11 39	12 00		12 12	12 27	12 31	12 39		12 59		13 12	13 27
Selby 40 a			10 53						11 54							12 50							13 51	
York ■ 40 a						11 19							12 21						13 19					

A from 17 September until 22 October
D From Kirkby
E From Wigan Wallgate
b Previous night, stops to set down only

For connections from Liverpool Lime Street please refer to Table 90

Manchester Victoria, Rochdale, Blackpool North and Huddersfield - Bradford and Leeds via Brighouse and Halifax

Network Diagram - see first Page of Table 39

	NT	NT	NT	NT B	NT		GC ■ 1	NT	NT	NT	NT	NT B	NT	NT	NT		NT	NT	NT B	NT	NT	NT	NT	NT
Manchester Victoria ⇌ d	12 00		12 21	12 30	12 48				13 00		13 21	13 30	13 48		14 00			14 21	14 30	14 48		15 00		15 21
Moston d	12 06			12 36					13 06			13 36			14 06				14 36			15 06		
Mills Hill d	12 11			12 40					13 11			13 40			14 11				14 40			15 11		
Castleton d	12 16			12 45					13 16			13 45			14 16				14 45			15 16		
Rochdale a	12 19		12 34	12 51	13 02				13 19		13 34	13 51	14 02		14 19			14 34	14 51	15 02		15 19		15 34
d	12 20		12 35		13 02				13 20		13 35		14 02		14 20			14 35		15 02		15 20		15 35
Smithy Bridge d	12 24		12 39						13 24		13 39				14 24			14 39				15 24		15 39
Littleborough d	12 27		12 42						13 27		13 42				14 27			14 42				15 27		15 42
Walsden d			12 48								13 48							14 48						15 48
Todmorden d	12 34		12 52		13 14				13 34		13 52		14 14		14 34			14 52		15 14		15 34		15 52
Blackpool North 97 d		11 29								12 29							13 29						14 29	
PoultonleFylde 97 d		11 35								12 35							13 35						14 35	
Preston ■ 97 d		11 54								12 54							13 54						14 54	
Blackburn 97 d		12 10								13 10							14 10						15 10	
Accrington 97 d		12 17								13 17							14 17						15 17	
Burnley Manchester Road 97 d		12 26								13 26							14 26						15 26	
Hebden Bridge a	12 41	12 49	12 58		13 20				13 41	13 49	13 58		14 20		14 41		14 49	14 58		15 20		15 41	15 49	16 00
d	12 41	12 50	13 00		13 21				13 41	13 50	14 00		14 21		14 41		14 50	15 00		15 21		15 41	15 50	16 01
Mytholmroyd d	12 44		13 03						13 44		14 03				14 44			15 03				15 44		16 04
Sowerby Bridge d	12 50		13 09						13 50		14 09				14 50			15 09				15 50		16 10
Huddersfield 39 d								13 23						14 23							15 23			
London Kings Cross ■ ⊖26 d							10 48																	
Brighouse d	12 58						13 31	13 33	13 58					14 33	14 58						15 33	15 58		
Mirfield 39 a	13 06								14 06						15 06							16 06		
d	13 07								14 07						15 07							16 07		
Dewsbury 39 a	13 12								14 12						15 12							16 12		
Halifax a		13 02	13 15		13 33		13 40	13 45		14 02	14 15		14 33	14 43			15 02	15 15		15 33	15 43		16 02	16 16
d		13 03	13 16		13 33		13 42	13 49		14 03	14 16		14 33	14 49			15 03	15 16		15 33	15 49		16 03	16 17
Bradford Interchange a		13 17	13 31		13 47		13 55	14 02		14 17	14 31		14 47	15 02			15 17	15 31		15 47	16 02		16 17	16 31
d		13 19	13 34		13 50			14 05		14 19	14 34		14 50	15 05			15 19	15 34		15 50	16 05		16 19	16 34
New Pudsey 37 a		13 27	13 42		13 58			14 13		14 28	14 42		14 58	15 13			15 27	15 42		15 58	16 13		16 27	16 42
Bramley 37 a			13 46		14 02			14 17			14 46		15 02	15 17				15 46		16 02	16 17			16 46
Leeds ■ 37,39 a	13 32	13 40	14 00		14 13			14 27	14 32	14 39	15 00		15 12	15 27	15 32		15 39	16 00		16 12	16 27	16 32	16 39	16 58
Selby 40 a					14 51								15 53							16 54				
York ■ 40 a		14 22								15 18							16 21						17 20	

	NT B		NT	NT	NT	NT	NT	NT B	NT	GC ■ 1	NT		NT	NT	NT	NT	NT B	NT	NT	NT C	NT		NT	NT
Manchester Victoria ⇌ d	15 30		15 48		16 00		16 24	16 30	16 48					17 00		17 17	17 30	17 43			18 00			18 21
Moston d	15 36				16 06			16 36						17 06		17 24	17 36	17 49						
Mills Hill d	15 40				16 11			16 40						17 11		17 28	17 40	17 54			18 09			
Castleton d	15 45				16 16			16 45						17 16		17 33	17 45	17 59			18 14			
Rochdale a	15 51		16 02		16 19		16 37	16 51	17 02					17 19		17 37	17 51	18 02			18 18			18 35
d			16 02		16 20		16 37		17 02					17 20		17 38		18 03			18 18			18 36
Smithy Bridge d					16 24		16 41							17 24		17 42					18 22			18 40
Littleborough d					16 27		16 45							17 27		17 45		18 08			18 26			18 43
Walsden d							16 51									17 51					18 32			18 49
Todmorden d			16 14		16 34		16 54		17 14					17 34		17 55		18 16			18 35			18 53
Blackpool North 97 d						15 29									16 29								17 14	
PoultonleFylde 97 d						15 35									16 35								17 20	
Preston ■ 97 d						15 54									16 54								17 44	
Blackburn 97 d						16 10									17 10								18 11	
Accrington 97 d						16 17									17 17								18 19	
Burnley Manchester Road 97 d						16 26									17 26								18 28	
Hebden Bridge a			16 20		16 41	16 49	17 01		17 20					17 41	17 49	17 59		18 22			18 42		18 49	18 59
d			16 21		16 41	16 50	17 01		17 21					17 41	17 50	17 59		18 23			18 42		18 50	19 00
Mytholmroyd d					16 44		17 04							17 44		18 05					18 45			19 03
Sowerby Bridge d					16 50		17 10							17 50		18 10					18 51			19 09
Huddersfield 39 d				16 23									17 23							18 23				
London Kings Cross ■ ⊖26 d										14 48														
Brighouse d				16 33	16 58					17 30			17 33	17 58						18 33	18 59			
Mirfield 39 a					17 06									18 07							19 07			
d					17 07									18 07							19 08			
Dewsbury 39 a					17 12									18 13							19 13			
Halifax a			16 33	16 46		17 02	17 17		17 33	17 40			17 49		18 02	18 15		18 35		18 46			19 03	19 15
d			16 33	16 49		17 03	17 17		17 33	17 41			17 49		18 03	18 15		18 35		18 49			19 03	19 16
Bradford Interchange a			16 47	17 02		17 17	17 31		17 47	17 55			18 04		18 17	18 31		18 49		19 02			19 17	19 31
d			16 50	17 04		17 19	17 34		17 50				18 04		18 19	18 34		18 52		19 05			19 19	19 34
New Pudsey 37 a			16 58	17 13		17 28	17 42		17 58				18 13		18 28	18 40		19 00		19 13			19 27	19 42
Bramley 37 a			17 02	17 17			17 46		18 02				18 17			18 45		19 04		19 17				19 46
Leeds ■ 37,39 a			17 12	17 27	17 31	17 39	17 57		18 12				18 29	18 34	18 39	18 56		19 13		19 28	19 33		19 39	19 56
Selby 40 a			17 51						18 49						20 42									
York ■ 40 a						18 18												19 53					20 22	

B From Wigan Wallgate

For connections from Liverpool Lime Street please refer to Table 90

Manchester Victoria, Rochdale, Blackpool North and Huddersfield - Bradford and Leeds via Brighouse and Halifax

Network Diagram - see first Page of Table 39

	NT	NT	NT	NT	NT	NT	NT	NT	NT	NT	NT	NT	NT	GC	NT FX	NT FO	NT	NT
	A													◇1 B ⊠				
Manchester Victoria d	18 26	18 48		19 00		19 21	19 55		20 21	20 55			21 21				22 28	23 20
Moston d	18 32			19 06		19 27	20 01		20 27	21 01			21 27				22 34	23 27
Mills Hill d	18 36			19 11		19 32	20 05		20 32	21 06			21 32				22 39	23 32
Castleton d	18 41			19 16		19 37	20 10		20 37	21 11			21 37				22 44	23 37
Rochdale a	18 47	19 01		19 19		19 40	20 14		20 40	21 16			21 40				22 47	23 40
Rochdale d		19 01		19 19		19 41			20 41				21 41				22 48	23 41
Smithy Bridge d				19 23		19 45			20 45				21 45				22 52	23 45
Littleborough d				19 27		19 48			20 48				21 48				22 55	23 48
Walsden d						19 54			20 54				21 54				23 01	23 54
Todmorden d		19 13		19 34		19 58			20 58				21 58				23 05	23 58
Blackpool North 97 d					18 29							20 29						
Poulton-le-Fylde 97 d					18 35							20 35						
Preston 97 d					18 54							20 54						
Blackburn 97 d					19 10							21 10						
Accrington 97 d					19 17							21 18						
Burnley Manchester Road 97 d					19 26							21 27						
Hebden Bridge a		19 20		19 41	19 49	20 04			21 04			21 49	22 04				23 11	00 04
Hebden Bridge d		19 20		19 41	19 50	20 05			21 05			21 49	22 05				23 11	00 04
Mytholmroyd d				19 44		20 08			21 08				22 08				23 15	00 08
Sowerby Bridge d				19 50		20 14			21 14				22 14				23 20	00 13
Huddersfield 39 d			19 23					20 25			21 27				22 25	22 25		
London Kings Cross ⊖26 d														19 48				
Brighouse d			19 33	19 58				20 35			21 37			22 24	22 35	22 35		
Mirfield 39 a				20 07														
Mirfield d				20 07														
Dewsbury 39 a				20 12														
Halifax a		19 32	19 43		20 03	20 20		20 45	21 20		21 47	22 01	22 20	22 33	22 45	22 45	23 29	00 20
Halifax d		19 32	19 49		20 03	20 21		20 49	21 21		21 49	22 01	22 21	22 34	22 49	22 49	23 29	00 20
Bradford Interchange a		19 48	20 02		20 17	20 35		21 02	21 35		22 02	22 15	22 35	22 48	23 02	23 02	23 43	00 34
Bradford Interchange d		19 50	20 04		20 19	20 37		21 04	21 37		22 04	22 17	22 37		23 04	23 04	23 46	00 37
New Pudsey 37 a		19 59	20 13		20 28	20 46		21 13	21 46		22 13	22 25	22 46		23 13	23 13	23 54	
Bramley 37 a		20 03	20 16			20 49		21 16	21 49		22 16		22 49		23 16	23 16	23 58	
Leeds 37,39 a		20 13	20 29	20 34	20 38	20 59		21 25	22 01		22 25	22 38	23 00		23 26	23 27	00 08	00 55
Selby 40 a																		
York 40 a					21 30							23 42						

Saturdays

	NT	NT	NT	NT	NT	NT	NT	NT	NT	NT	NT	NT	NT D	NT	NT	NT	NT E	NT	NT D	NT	NT	NT
Manchester Victoria d	22p28	23p20		05 54		06 17	06 43		06 58		07 17	07 48		08 00		08 22	08 30	08 48		09 00		09 22
Moston d	22p34	23p27				06 23			07 04		07 23			08 06			08 36			09 06		
Mills Hill d	22p39	23p32				06 28			07 09		07 28			08 11			08 40			09 11		
Castleton d	22p44	23p37				06 33			07 14		07 33			08 16			08 45			09 16		
Rochdale a	22p47	23p40		06 08		06 36	06 56		07 17		07 36	08 01		08 19		08 35	08 51	09 02		09 19		09 35
Rochdale d	22p48	23p41		06 09		06 37	06 56		07 18		07 37	08 01		08 20		08 35		09 02		09 20		09 36
Smithy Bridge d	22p52	23p45		06 13		06 41			07 22		07 41			08 24		08 39				09 24		09 40
Littleborough d	22p55	23p48		06 16		06 44			07 25		07 44			08 27		08 42				09 27		09 43
Walsden d	23p01	23p54		06 22		06 50			07 31		07 50					08 48						09 49
Todmorden d	23p05	23p58		06 26		06 54	07 08		07 35		07 54	08 13		08 34		08 52		09 14		09 34		09 53
Blackpool North 97 d					05 29					06 28					07 29						08 29	
Poulton-le-Fylde 97 d					05 35					06 34					07 35						08 35	
Preston 97 d					05 54					06 54					07 54						08 54	
Blackburn 97 d					06 10					07 10					08 10						09 10	
Accrington 97 d					06 17					07 17					08 17						09 17	
Burnley Manchester Road 97 d					06 26					07 26					08 26						09 26	
Hebden Bridge a	23p11	00 04		06 32	06 49	07 00	07 14		07 41	07 49	08 00	08 19		08 41	08 49	09 00		09 20		09 41	09 49	09 59
Hebden Bridge d	23p11	00 04	05 55	06 33	06 50	07 00	07 16		07 41	07 50	08 00	08 21		08 41	08 50	09 00		09 21		09 41	09 50	10 00
Mytholmroyd d	23p15	00 08	05 58	06 36		07 04	07 19		07 45		08 04			08 44		09 03				09 44		10 03
Sowerby Bridge d	23p20	00 13	06 04	06 42	06 57	07 09	07 25		07 50	07 57	08 09			08 50	08 57	09 09				09 50		10 09
Huddersfield 39 d								07 29					08 21						09 23			
London Kings Cross ⊖26 d																						
Brighouse d								07 39	07 59				08 33	08 58					09 33	09 58		
Mirfield 39 a									08 06					09 06						10 06		
Mirfield d									08 06					09 07						10 07		
Dewsbury 39 a									08 11					09 12						10 12		
Halifax a	23p29	00 20	06 10	06 48	07 03	07 16	07 32	07 50		08 03	08 16	08 33	08 43		09 03	09 16		09 33	09 44		10 02	10 15
Halifax d	23p29	00 20	06 11	06 49	07 03	07 16	07 33	07 50		08 03	08 16	08 33	08 48		09 03	09 16		09 33	09 49		10 03	10 16
Bradford Interchange a	23p43	00 34	06 24	07 03	07 17	07 31	07 47	08 03		08 17	08 31	08 47	09 02		09 17	09 31		09 47	10 02		10 17	10 31
Bradford Interchange d	23p46	00 37	06 26	07 05	07 20	07 34	07 50	08 05		08 20	08 34	08 50	09 04		09 20	09 34		09 50	10 05		10 18	10 34
New Pudsey 37 a	23p54		06 35	07 14	07 28	07 42	07 58	08 14		08 28	08 42	08 58	09 12		09 27	09 42		09 58	10 13		10 27	10 42
Bramley 37 a	23p58		06 38	07 17		07 46	08 02	08 18			08 46	09 02	09 16			09 46		10 02	10 17			10 46
Leeds 37,39 a	00 08	00 55	06 49	07 27	07 39	07 57	08 11	08 30	08 31	08 39	08 56	09 12	09 27	09 32	09 39	09 58		10 12	10 27	10 32	10 38	11 00
Selby 40 a						08 36						09 53						10 53				
York 40 a					08 20					09 21					10 21						11 18	

A From Clitheroe
B ⊠ ◇ from Brighouse
D From Wakefield Westgate
E From Kirkby

For connections from Liverpool Lime Street please refer to Table 90

Manchester Victoria, Rochdale, Blackpool North and Huddersfield - Bradford and Leeds via Brighouse and Halifax

Network Diagram - see first Page of Table 39

	NT	NT	NT B	NT	NT	NT	NT D	NT	NT B	NT	NT	NT	NT D	NT	NT B	NT	NT	NT	GC	NT D	NT	NT B
Manchester Victoria d	09 33	09 48		10 00		10 21	10 30	10 48		11 00		11 21	11 30	11 48		12 00		12 21		12 30	12 48	
Moston d	09 39			10 06			10 36			11 06			11 36			12 06				12 36		
Mills Hill d	09 44			10 11			10 40			11 11			11 40			12 11				12 40		
Castleton d	09 49			10 16			10 45			11 16			11 45			12 16				12 45		
Rochdale a	09 54	10 02		10 19		10 34	10 51	11 02		11 19		11 34	11 51	12 02		12 19		12 34		12 51	13 02	
Rochdale d		10 02		10 20		10 35		11 02		11 20		11 35		12 02		12 20		12 35			13 02	
Smithy Bridge d				10 24		10 39				11 24		11 39				12 24		12 39				
Littleborough d				10 27		10 42				11 27		11 42				12 27		12 42				
Walsden d						10 48						11 48						12 48				
Todmorden d		10 14		10 34		10 52		11 14		11 34		11 52		12 14		12 34		12 52			13 14	
Blackpool North 97 d					09 29						10 29						11 29					
Poulton-le-Fylde 97 d					09 35						10 35						11 35					
Preston 97 d					09 54						10 54						11 54					
Blackburn 97 d					10 10						11 10						12 10					
Accrington 97 d					10 18						11 17						12 17					
Burnley Manchester Road 97 d					10 26						11 28						12 26					
Hebden Bridge a		10 20		10 41	10 50	10 58		11 20		11 41	11 49	11 58		12 20		12 41	12 49	12 58			13 20	
Hebden Bridge d		10 21		10 41	10 50	11 00		11 21		11 41	11 50	12 00		12 21		12 41	12 50	13 00			13 21	
Mytholmroyd d				10 44		11 03				11 44		12 03				12 44		13 03				
Sowerby Bridge d				10 50		11 09				11 50		12 09				12 50		13 09				
Huddersfield 39 d			10 23						11 23						12 23							13 23
London Kings Cross ⊖26 d																			10 48			
Brighouse d			10 33	10 58					11 33	11 58					12 33	12 58			13 06			13 33
Mirfield 39 a				11 06						12 06						13 06						
Mirfield d				11 07						12 07						13 07						
Dewsbury 39 a				11 12						12 12						13 12						
Halifax a		10 33	10 43		11 02	11 15		11 33	11 43		12 02	12 15		12 33	12 43		13 02	13 15	13 21		13 33	13 45
Halifax d		10 33	10 49		11 03	11 16		11 33	11 49		12 03	12 16		12 33	12 49		13 03	13 16	13 22		13 33	13 49
Bradford Interchange a		10 47	11 02		11 17	11 31		11 47	12 02		12 17	12 31		12 47	13 02		13 17	13 31	13 38		13 47	14 02
Bradford Interchange d		10 50	11 05		11 20	11 34		11 50	12 05		12 19	12 34		12 50	13 05		13 19	13 34			13 50	14 05
New Pudsey 37 a		10 58	11 13		11 28	11 42		11 58	12 13		12 27	12 42		12 58	13 13		13 27	13 42			13 58	14 13
Bramley 37 a		11 02	11 17			11 46		12 02	12 17			12 46		13 02	13 17			13 46			14 02	14 17
Leeds 37,39 a		11 13	11 27	11 35	11 39	12 00		12 12	12 27	12 32	12 39	12 58		13 12	13 27	13 32	13 39	13 58			14 14	14 27
Selby 40 a		11 55						12 50						13 52							14 51	
York 40 a					12 21						13 19						14 22					

	NT	NT	NT	NT D	NT	NT B	NT	NT	NT	NT D	NT	NT B	NT	NT	NT	NT D	NT	NT B	NT	NT	NT
Manchester Victoria d	13 00		13 21	13 30	13 48		14 00		14 21	14 30	14 48		15 00		15 21	15 30	15 48		16 00		16 24
Moston d	13 06			13 36			14 06			14 36			15 06			15 36			16 06		
Mills Hill d	13 11			13 40			14 11			14 40			15 11			15 40			16 11		
Castleton d	13 16			13 45			14 16			14 45			15 16			15 45			16 16		
Rochdale a	13 19		13 34	13 51	14 02		14 19		14 34	14 51	15 02		15 19		15 34	15 51	16 02		16 19		16 37
Rochdale d	13 20		13 35		14 02		14 20		14 35		15 02		15 20		15 35		16 02		16 20		16 37
Smithy Bridge d	13 24		13 39				14 24		14 39				15 24		15 39				16 24		16 41
Littleborough d	13 27		13 42				14 27		14 42				15 27		15 42				16 27		16 45
Walsden d			13 48						14 48						15 48						16 51
Todmorden d	13 34		13 52		14 14		14 34		14 52		15 14		15 34		15 52		16 14		16 34		16 54
Blackpool North 97 d		12 29						13 29						14 29						15 29	
Poulton-le-Fylde 97 d		12 35						13 35						14 35						15 35	
Preston 97 d		12 53						13 54						14 54						15 54	
Blackburn 97 d		13 09						14 10						15 10						16 10	
Accrington 97 d		13 16						14 17						15 17						16 17	
Burnley Manchester Road 97 d		13 25						14 26						15 26						16 26	
Hebden Bridge a	13 41	13 49	13 58		14 20		14 41	14 49	14 58		15 20		15 41	15 49	16 00		16 20		16 41	16 49	17 01
Hebden Bridge d	13 41	13 50	14 00		14 21		14 41	14 50	15 00		15 21		15 41	15 50	16 01		16 21		16 41	16 50	17 01
Mytholmroyd d	13 44		14 03				14 44		15 03				15 44		16 04				16 44		17 04
Sowerby Bridge d	13 50		14 09				14 50		15 09				15 50		16 10				16 50		17 10
Huddersfield 39 d						14 23						15 23						16 23			
London Kings Cross ⊖26 d																					
Brighouse d	13 58					14 33	14 58					15 33	15 58					16 33	16 58		
Mirfield 39 a	14 06						15 06						16 06						17 06		
Mirfield d	14 07						15 07						16 07						17 07		
Dewsbury 39 a	14 12						15 12						16 12						17 12		
Halifax a		14 02	14 15		14 33	14 43		15 02	15 15		15 33	15 43		16 02	16 16		16 33	16 46		17 02	17 17
Halifax d		14 03	14 16		14 33	14 49		15 03	15 16		15 33	15 49		16 03	16 17		16 33	16 49		17 03	17 17
Bradford Interchange a		14 17	14 31		14 47	15 02		15 17	15 31		15 47	16 02		16 17	16 31		16 47	17 02		17 17	17 31
Bradford Interchange d		14 19	14 34		14 50	15 05		15 19	15 34		15 50	16 05		16 19	16 34		16 50	17 04		17 19	17 34
New Pudsey 37 a		14 28	14 42		14 58	15 13		15 27	15 42		15 58	16 13		16 27	16 42		16 58	17 13		17 28	17 42
Bramley 37 a			14 46		15 02	15 17			15 46		16 02	16 17			16 46		17 02	17 17			17 46
Leeds 37,39 a	14 32	14 39	14 58		15 10	15 27	15 32	15 39	16 00		16 12	16 27	16 31	16 39	16 59		17 12	17 27	17 31	17 39	17 57
Selby 40 a					15 53						16 54						17 55				
York 40 a		15 17						16 21						17 21						18 24	

B From Wakefield Westgate
D From Wigan Wallgate

For connections from Liverpool Lime Street please refer to Table 90

Table 41

Saturdays

Manchester Victoria, Rochdale, Blackpool North and Huddersfield - Bradford and Leeds via Brighouse and Halifax

Network Diagram - see first Page of Table 39

		NT	NT	NT	NT B	NT	NT	NT	GC	NT A	NT	NT	NT B	NT	NT	NT	NT D	NT E	NT	NT	NT	NT	NT
Manchester Victoria	d	16 30	16 48			17 00		17 18		17 30	17 43			18 00		18 21	18 28	18 28	18 48		19 00		19 21
Moston	d	16 36				17 06		17 24		17 36	17 49						18 34	18 34			19 06		19 27
Mills Hill	d	16 40				17 11		17 29		17 40	17 54			18 09			18 39	18 38			19 10		19 32
Castleton	d	16 45				17 16		17 34		17 45	17 59			18 14			18 44	18 43			19 15		19 37
Rochdale	a	16 51	17 02			17 19		17 37		17 51	18 02			18 18		18 35	18 47	18 49	19 01		19 19		19 40
	d		17 02	17 03		17 20		17 38			18 03	18 02		18 18		18 36			19 01		19 19		19 41
Smithy Bridge	d					17 24		17 42						18 22		18 40					19 23		19 45
Littleborough	d					17 27		17 46			18 08			18 26		18 43					19 27		19 48
Walsden	d							17 52						18 32		18 49							19 54
Todmorden	d		17 14			17 34		17 55			18 16			18 35		18 53			19 13		19 34		19 58
Blackpool North	97 d						16 29								17 14							18 29	
Poulton le Fylde	97 d						16 35								17 20							18 35	
Preston 8	97 d						16 54								17 44							18 54	
Blackburn	97 d			18a21			17 10					19a21			18 11							19 10	
Accrington	97 d						17 17								18 19							19 17	
Burnley Manchester Road	97 d						17 26								18 28							19 26	
Hebden Bridge	a		17 20			17 41	17 49	18 02			18 22			18 42	18 49	18 59			19 19		19 41	19 49	20 04
	d		17 21			17 41	17 50	18 02			18 23			18 42	18 50	19 00			19 20		19 41	19 50	20 05
Mytholmroyd	d					17 44		18 05						18 45		19 03					19 44		20 08
Sowerby Bridge	d					17 50		18 11						18 51		19 09					19 50		20 14
Huddersfield	39 d				17 23								18 23							19 23			
London Kings Cross 15 ⊖	26 d								15 48														
Brighouse	d				17 33	17 58			18 07				18 33	18 59						19 33	19 58		
Mirfield	39 a					18 07								19 07							20 07		
	d					18 07								19 08							20 07		
Dewsbury	39 a					18 12								19 13							20 12		
Halifax	a		17 33		17 49		18 02	18 17	18 23		18 35		18 46		19 02	19 15			19 32	19 43		20 03	20 20
	d		17 33		17 49		18 03	18 18	18 24		18 35		18 49		19 03	19 16			19 32	19 49		20 03	20 21
Bradford Interchange	a		17 47		18 04		18 17	18 32	18 39		18 49		19 02		19 17	19 31			19 48	20 02		20 17	20 35
	d		17 50		18 04		18 19	18 34			18 52		19 05		19 18	19 34			19 50	20 04		20 19	20 37
New Pudsey	37 a		17 58		18 13		18 28	18 43			19 00		19 13		19 27	19 42			19 58	20 13		20 28	20 46
Bramley	37 a		18 02		18 17			18 46			19 04		19 17			19 46			20 02	20 16			20 49
Leeds 10	37,39 a		18 12		18 29	18 31	18 39	18 56			19 13		19 28	19 33	19 39	19 58			20 12	20 30	20 33	20 38	20 59
Selby	40 a		18 50				20 06																
York 8	40 a										19 53				20 18							21 30	

		NT	NT	NT	GC F	NT	NT	NT	GC I	NT	NT	NT	NT J	NT K	NT
Manchester Victoria	d	19 55		20 21		20 55				21 21	22 21		22 54	22 54	23 20
Moston	d	20 01		20 27		21 01				21 27	22 27				23 26
Mills Hill	d	20 05		20 32		21 06				21 32	22 32				23 31
Castleton	d	20 10		20 37		21 11				21 37	22 37				23 36
Rochdale	a	20 14		20 40		21 16				21 40	22 42		23 07	23 07	23 41
	d			20 41						21 41			23 07	23 07	
Smithy Bridge	d			20 45						21 45			23 11	23 11	
Littleborough	d			20 48						21 48			23 15	23 15	
Walsden	d			20 54						21 54			23 21	23 21	
Todmorden	d			20 58						21 58			23 24	23 24	
Blackpool North	97 d							20 29							
Poulton le Fylde	97 d							20 35							
Preston 8	97 d							20 54							
Blackburn	97 d							21 10							
Accrington	97 d							21 18							
Burnley Manchester Road	97 d							21 27							
Hebden Bridge	a			21 04				21 49		22 04			23 31	23 31	
	d			21 05				21 49		22 05			23 31	23 31	
Mytholmroyd	d			21 08						22 08			23 34	23 34	
Sowerby Bridge	d			21 14						22 14			23 40	23 40	
Huddersfield	39 d		20 25				21 27					22 25			
London Kings Cross 15 ⊖	26 d				19 20				19 20						
Brighouse	d		20 35		21 32		21 38		21 59			22 35			
Mirfield	39 a														
	d														
Dewsbury	39 a														
Halifax	a		20 45	21 20	21 42		21 47	22 01	22 08	22 20		22 45	23 46	23 46	
	d		20 49	21 21	21 43		21 48	22 01	22 10	22 21		22 49	23 47	23 49	
Bradford Interchange	a		21 02	21 35	21 57		22 02	22 15	22 24	22 35		23 02	00 02		
	d		21 04	21 37			22 04	22 17		22 37		23 04	00 04		
New Pudsey	37 a		21 13	21 46			22 13	22 25		22 46		23 13	00 12		
Bramley	37 a		21 16	21 49			22 16			22 49		23 16	00 15		
Leeds 10	37,39 a		21 25	21 59			22 24	22 35		23 01		23 26	00 27	00 20	
Selby	40 a														
York 8	40 a							23 38							

B From Wakefield Westgate
D until 29 September. From Clitheroe
E from 6 October. From Clitheroe
F from 30 June until 8 September
I until 23 June, from 15 September
J until 8 September, from 27 October
K from 15 September until 20 October

For connections from Liverpool Lime Street please refer to Table 90

Table 41

Sundays
until 24 June

Manchester Victoria, Rochdale, Blackpool North and Huddersfield - Bradford and Leeds via Brighouse and Halifax

Network Diagram - see first Page of Table 39

		NT	NT	NT	NT	NT	NT	NT	NT	NT	NT	NT	NT	NT	NT	NT	NT	NT	NT	NT	NT	NT	GC ■	NT
Manchester Victoria	d	22p54		08 32			09 14		09 48	10 14	10 48			11 14	11 48			12 14	12 48			13 14		13 48
Moston	d								09 54		10 54				11 54				12 54					13 54
Mills Hill	d								09 58		10 58				11 58				12 58					13 58
Castleton	d								10 03		11 03				12 03				13 03					14 03
Rochdale	a	23p07		08 48			09 27		10 09	10 27	11 09			11 27	12 09			12 28	13 09			13 27		14 09
	d	23p07					09 28			10 28				11 28				12 28				13 28		
Smithy Bridge	d	23p11					09 32			10 32				11 32				12 32				13 32		
Littleborough	d	23p15					09 36			10 36				11 36				12 36				13 36		
Walsden	d	23p21					09 42			10 42				11 42				12 42				13 42		
Todmorden	d	23p24					09 45			10 45				11 45				12 45				13 45		
Blackpool North	97 d							09 01					10 11				11 13				12 11			
Poulton le Fylde	97 d							09 07					10 17				11 19				12 17			
Preston 8	97 d							09 27					10 37				11 37				12 37			
Blackburn	97 d							09 44					10 54				11 54				12 54			
Accrington	97 d							09 51					11 01				12 01				13 01			
Burnley Manchester Road	97 d							10 00					11 10				12 10				13 10			
Hebden Bridge	a	23p31					09 52	10 22		10 52			11 32	11 52			12 32	12 52			13 32	13 52		
	d	23p31					09 52	10 22		10 52			11 32	11 52			12 32	12 52			13 32	13 52		
Mytholmroyd	d	23p34					09 55			10 55				11 55				12 55				13 55		
Sowerby Bridge	d	23p40					10 01			11 01				12 01				13 01				14 01		
Huddersfield	39 d					09 27						11 08								13 08				
London Kings Cross 15 ⊖	26 d																						11 48	
Brighouse	d					09 37						11 18								13 18			14 09	
Mirfield	39 a																							
	d																							
Dewsbury	39 a																							
Halifax	a	23p46				09 48	10 08	10 34		11 08		11 28	11 44	12 08			12 44	13 08		13 28	13 44	14 08	14 19	
	d	23p47			09 05	09 48	10 08	10 45		11 08		11 29	11 45	12 08		12 29	12 45	13 08		13 29	13 46	14 08	14 20	
Bradford Interchange	a	00 02			09 18	10 01	10 22	11 00		11 22		11 42	11 59	12 22		12 42	12 59	13 22		13 42	14 00	14 22	14 37	
	d	00 04	08 31		09 20	10 04	10 25	11 02		11 25		11 44	12 02	12 25		12 44	13 02	13 25		13 44	14 02	14 25		
New Pudsey	37 a	00 12	08 39		09 29	10 12	10 33	11 10		11 33		11 53	12 10	12 33		12 53	13 10	13 33		13 53	14 10	14 33		
Bramley	37 a	00 15	08 43		09 32	10 16	10 37			11 37		11 56		12 37		12 56		13 37		13 56		14 37		
Leeds 10	37,39 a	00 27	08 51		09 42	10 25	10 46	11 21		11 48		12 05	12 22	12 46		13 06	13 22	13 46		14 06	14 22	14 48		
Selby	40 a																							
York 8	40 a		09 35		10 28	11 08		11 59					13 02				13 59				15 02			

		NT	NT	NT	NT	NT	NT	NT	NT	NT	NT	NT	NT	NT	NT	NT	GC ■	NT	NT	NT	NT	NT	NT
Manchester Victoria	d			14 14	14 48			15 14	15 48			16 14	16 48			17 14		17 48			18 08		
Moston	d				14 54				15 54				16 54					17 54			18 15		
Mills Hill	d				14 58				15 58				16 58					17 58			18 19		
Castleton	d				15 03				16 03				17 03					18 03			18 24		
Rochdale	a			14 27	15 09			15 27	16 09			16 27	17 09			17 27		18 09			18 28		
	d			14 28				15 28				16 28				17 28					18 28		
Smithy Bridge	d			14 32				15 32				16 32				17 32					18 32		
Littleborough	d			14 36				15 36				16 36				17 36					18 36		
Walsden	d			14 42				15 42				16 42				17 42					18 42		
Todmorden	d			14 45				15 45				16 45				17 45					18 45		
Blackpool North	97 d		13 13				14 11				15 13				16 11					17 11			18 11
Poulton le Fylde	97 d		13 19				14 17				15 19				16 17					17 17			18 17
Preston 8	97 d		13 37				14 37				15 37				16 37					17 37			18 37
Blackburn	97 d		13 54				14 54				15 54				16 54					17 54			18 54
Accrington	97 d		14 01				15 01				16 01				17 01					18 01			19 01
Burnley Manchester Road	97 d		14 10				15 10				16 10				17 10					18 10			19 10
Hebden Bridge	a		14 32	14 52			15 32	15 52			16 32	16 52			17 32	17 52				18 32	18 52		19 32
	d		14 32	14 52			15 32	15 52			16 32	16 52			17 32	17 52				18 32	18 52		19 32
Mytholmroyd	d			14 55				15 55				16 55				17 55					18 55		
Sowerby Bridge	d			15 01				16 01				17 01				18 01					19 01		
Huddersfield	39 d					15 08								17 08								19 08	
London Kings Cross 15 ⊖	26 d																15 48						
Brighouse	d					15 18								17 17			18 11					19 18	
Mirfield	39 a																						
	d																						
Dewsbury	39 a																						
Halifax	a		14 44	15 08		15 28	15 44	16 08			16 44	17 08		17 27	17 44	18 08	18 20			18 44	19 08	19 28	19 44
	d	14 29	14 45	15 08		15 29	15 46	16 08		16 29	16 45	17 08		17 29	17 45	18 08	18 21		18 29	18 45	19 08	19 29	19 45
Bradford Interchange	a	14 42	14 59	15 22		15 42	16 00	16 22		16 42	16 59	17 22		17 42	17 59	18 22	18 37		18 42	18 59	19 22	19 42	19 59
	d	14 44	15 02	15 25		15 44	16 03	16 25		16 44	17 02	17 25		17 44	18 02	18 25			18 44	19 02	19 25	19 44	20 02
New Pudsey	37 a	14 53	15 10	15 33		15 53	16 11	16 33		16 53	17 10	17 33		17 53	18 10	18 33			18 53	19 10	19 33	19 53	20 10
Bramley	37 a	14 56		15 37		15 56		16 37		16 56		17 37		17 56		18 37			18 56		19 37	19 56	
Leeds 10	37,39 a	15 06	15 22	15 46		16 06	16 22	16 46		17 05	17 21	17 46		18 05	18 21	18 46			19 07	19 22	19 47	20 08	20 22
Selby	40 a																						
York 8	40 a		15 59				17 02				18 02				19 01					19 59			21 03

For connections from Liverpool Lime Street please refer to Table 90

Table 41

Sundays until 24 June

Manchester Victoria, Rochdale, Blackpool North and Huddersfield - Bradford and Leeds via Brighouse and Halifax

Network Diagram - see first Page of Table 39

		NT	NT	NT	NT	NT	GC	NT	NT	NT
Manchester Victoria	d	19 08		20 08				21 08		22 08
Moston	d	19 15		20 15				21 15		22 15
Mills Hill	d	19 19		20 19				21 19		22 19
Castleton	d	19 24		20 24				21 24		22 24
Rochdale	a	19 28		20 28				21 28		22 28
	d	19 28		20 28				21 28		22 28
Smithy Bridge	d	19 32		20 32				21 32		22 32
Littleborough	d	19 36		20 36				21 36		22 36
Walsden	d	19 42		20 42				21 42		22 42
Todmorden	d	19 45		20 45				21 45		22 45
Blackpool North	97 d		19 13			20 11			21 13	
Poulton-le-Fylde	97 d		19 19			20 17			21 19	
Preston [8]	97 d		19 37			20 37			21 39	
Blackburn	97 d		19 54			20 54			21 55	
Accrington	97 d		20 01			21 01			22 02	
Burnley Manchester Road	97 d		20 10			21 10			22 12	
Hebden Bridge	a	19 52	20 32	20 52		21 32		21 52	22 34	22 52
	d	19 52	20 32	20 52		21 32		21 52	22 34	22 52
Mytholmroyd	d	19 55		20 55				21 55		22 55
Sowerby Bridge	d	20 01		21 01				22 01		23 01
Huddersfield	39 d				21 08					
London Kings Cross [15] ⊖26	d						19 23			
Brighouse	d				21 18		21 47			
Mirfield	39 a									
	d									
Dewsbury	39 a									
Halifax	a	20 08	20 44	21 08	21 28	21 44	21 57	22 08	22 46	23 08
	d	20 08	20 45	21 08	21 30	21 45	21 58	22 09	22 47	23 08
Bradford Interchange	a	20 22	20 59	21 22	21 42	21 59	22 11	22 23	23 01	23 22
	d	20 25	21 02	21 26	21 44	22 02		22 26	23 04	23 25
New Pudsey	37 a	20 33	21 10	21 34	21 53	22 10		22 34	23 12	23 33
Bramley	37 a	20 37		21 38	21 56			22 38		23 37
Leeds [10]	37,39 a	20 47	21 22	21 48	22 05	22 21		22 47	23 23	23 46
Selby	40 a									
York [8]	40 a		22 00							

Sundays 1 July to 9 September

		NT	NT	NT	NT	NT	NT	NT	NT	NT	NT	NT	NT
Manchester Victoria	d	22p54		08 32			09 14		09 48	10 14	10 48		
Moston	d								09 54		10 54		
Mills Hill	d								09 58		10 58		
Castleton	d								10 03		11 03		
Rochdale	a	23p07		08 48			09 27		10 09	10 27	11 09		
	d	23p07					09 28			10 28			
Smithy Bridge	d	23p11					09 32			10 32			
Littleborough	d	23p15					09 36			10 36			
Walsden	d	23p21					09 42			10 42			
Todmorden	d	23p24					09 45			10 45			
Blackpool North	97 d							09 01					10 11
Poulton-le-Fylde	97 d							09 07					10 17
Preston [8]	97 d							09 27					10 37
Blackburn	97 d							09 44					10 54
Accrington	97 d							09 51					11 01
Burnley Manchester Road	97 d							10 00					11 10
Hebden Bridge	a	23p31					09 52	10 22		10 52			11 32
	d	23p31					09 52	10 22		10 52			11 32
Mytholmroyd	d	23p34					09 55			10 55			
Sowerby Bridge	d	23p40					10 01			11 01			
Huddersfield	39 d					09 27						11 08	
London Kings Cross [15] ⊖26	d												
Brighouse	d					09 37						11 18	
Mirfield	39 a												
	d												
Dewsbury	39 a												
Halifax	a	23p46				09 48	10 08	10 34		11 08		11 28	11 44
	d	23p47			09 05	09 48	10 08	10 45		11 08		11 29	11 45
Bradford Interchange	a	00 02			09 18	10 01	10 22	11 00		11 22		11 42	11 59
	d	00 04	08 31		09 20	10 04	10 25	11 02		11 25		11 44	12 02
New Pudsey	37 a	00 12	08 39		09 29	10 12	10 33	11 10		11 33		11 53	12 10
Bramley	37 a	00 15	08 43		09 32	10 16	10 37			11 37		11 56	
Leeds [10]	37,39 a	00 27	08 51		09 42	10 25	10 46	11 21		11 48		12 05	12 22
Selby	40 a												
York [8]	40 a		09 35		10 28	11 08		11 59					13 02

		NT	NT	NT	NT	NT	NT	NT	NT	NT	GC	NT
Manchester Victoria	d	11 14	11 48			12 14	12 48			13 14		13 48
Moston	d		11 54				12 54					13 54
Mills Hill	d		11 58				12 58					13 58
Castleton	d		12 03				13 03					14 03
Rochdale	a	11 27	12 09			12 28	13 09			13 27		14 09
	d	11 28				12 28				13 28		
Smithy Bridge	d	11 32				12 32				13 32		
Littleborough	d	11 36				12 36				13 36		
Walsden	d	11 42				12 42				13 42		
Todmorden	d	11 45				12 45				13 45		
Blackpool North	97 d				11 13				12 11			
Poulton-le-Fylde	97 d				11 19				12 17			
Preston [8]	97 d				11 37				12 37			
Blackburn	97 d				11 54				12 54			
Accrington	97 d				12 01				13 01			
Burnley Manchester Road	97 d				12 10				13 10			
Hebden Bridge	a	11 52			12 32	12 52			13 32	13 52		
	d	11 52			12 32	12 52			13 32	13 52		
Mytholmroyd	d	11 55				12 55				13 55		
Sowerby Bridge	d	12 01				13 01				14 01		
Huddersfield	39 d							13 08				
London Kings Cross [15] ⊖26	d										11 48	
Brighouse	d							13 18			14 09	
Mirfield	39 a											
	d											
Dewsbury	39 a											
Halifax	a	12 08			12 44	13 08		13 28	13 44	14 08	14 19	
	d	12 08		12 29	12 45	13 08		13 29	13 46	14 08	14 20	
Bradford Interchange	a	12 22		12 42	12 59	13 22		13 42	14 00	14 22	14 37	
	d	12 25		12 44	13 02	13 25		13 44	14 02	14 25		
New Pudsey	37 a	12 33		12 53	13 10	13 33		13 53	14 10	14 33		
Bramley	37 a	12 37		12 56		13 37		13 56		14 37		
Leeds [10]	37,39 a	12 46		13 06	13 22	13 46		14 06	14 22	14 48		
Selby	40 a											
York [8]	40 a				13 59				15 02			

For connections from Liverpool Lime Street please refer to Table 90

Table 41

Sundays 1 July to 9 September

Manchester Victoria, Rochdale, Blackpool North and Huddersfield - Bradford and Leeds via Brighouse and Halifax

Network Diagram - see first Page of Table 39

		NT	NT	NT	NT	NT	NT	NT	NT	NT	NT	NT	NT
Manchester Victoria	d			14 14	14 48			15 14	15 48			16 14	16 48
Moston	d				14 54				15 54				16 54
Mills Hill	d				14 58				15 58				16 58
Castleton	d				15 03				16 03				17 03
Rochdale	a			14 27	15 09			15 27	16 09			16 27	17 09
	d			14 28				15 28				16 28	
Smithy Bridge	d			14 32				15 32				16 32	
Littleborough	d			14 36				15 36				16 36	
Walsden	d			14 42				15 42				16 42	
Todmorden	d			14 45				15 45				16 45	
Blackpool North	97 d		13 13				14 11				15 13		
Poulton-le-Fylde	97 d		13 19				14 17				15 19		
Preston [8]	97 d		13 37				14 37				15 37		
Blackburn	97 d		13 54				14 54				15 54		
Accrington	97 d		14 01				15 01				16 01		
Burnley Manchester Road	97 d		14 10				15 10				16 10		
Hebden Bridge	a		14 32	14 52			15 32	15 52			16 32	16 52	
	d		14 32	14 52			15 32	15 52			16 32	16 52	
Mytholmroyd	d			14 55				15 55				16 55	
Sowerby Bridge	d			15 01				16 01				17 01	
Huddersfield	39 d					15 08							
London Kings Cross [15] ⊖26	d												
Brighouse	d					15 18							
Mirfield	39 a												
	d												
Dewsbury	39 a												
Halifax	a		14 44	15 08		15 28	15 44	16 08			16 44	17 08	
	d	14 29	14 45	15 08		15 29	15 46	16 08		16 29	16 45	17 08	
Bradford Interchange	a	14 42	14 59	15 22		15 42	16 00	16 22		16 42	16 59	17 22	
	d	14 44	15 02	15 25		15 44	16 03	16 25		16 44	17 02	17 25	
New Pudsey	37 a	14 53	15 10	15 33		15 53	16 11	16 33		16 53	17 10	17 33	
Bramley	37 a	14 56		15 37		15 56		16 37		16 56		17 37	
Leeds [10]	37,39 a	15 06	15 22	15 46		16 06	16 22	16 46		17 05	17 21	17 46	
Selby	40 a												
York [8]	40 a		15 59				17 02				18 02		

		NT	NT	NT	GC	NT	NT	NT	NT	NT	NT
Manchester Victoria	d			17 14		17 48			18 08		
Moston	d					17 54			18 15		
Mills Hill	d					17 58			18 19		
Castleton	d					18 03			18 24		
Rochdale	a			17 27		18 09			18 28		
	d			17 28					18 28		
Smithy Bridge	d			17 32					18 32		
Littleborough	d			17 36					18 36		
Walsden	d			17 42					18 42		
Todmorden	d			17 45					18 45		
Blackpool North	97 d		16 11					17 11			18 11
Poulton-le-Fylde	97 d		16 17					17 17			18 17
Preston [8]	97 d		16 37					17 37			18 37
Blackburn	97 d		16 54					17 54			18 54
Accrington	97 d		17 01					18 01			19 01
Burnley Manchester Road	97 d		17 10					18 10			19 10
Hebden Bridge	a		17 32	17 52				18 32	18 52		19 32
	d		17 32	17 52				18 32	18 52		19 32
Mytholmroyd	d			17 55					18 55		
Sowerby Bridge	d			18 01					19 01		
Huddersfield	39 d	17 08								19 08	
London Kings Cross [15] ⊖26	d				15 48						
Brighouse	d	17 17			18 11					19 18	
Mirfield	39 a										
	d										
Dewsbury	39 a										
Halifax	a	17 27	17 44	18 08	18 20			18 44	19 08	19 28	19 44
	d	17 29	17 45	18 08	18 21		18 29	18 45	19 08	19 29	19 45
Bradford Interchange	a	17 42	17 59	18 22	18 37		18 42	18 59	19 22	19 42	19 59
	d	17 44	18 02	18 25			18 44	19 02	19 25	19 44	20 02
New Pudsey	37 a	17 53	18 10	18 33			18 53	19 10	19 33	19 53	20 10
Bramley	37 a	17 56		18 37			18 56		19 37	19 56	
Leeds [10]	37,39 a	18 05	18 21	18 46			19 07	19 22	19 47	20 08	20 22
Selby	40 a										
York [8]	40 a		19 01					19 59			21 03

		NT	NT	NT	NT	NT	GC	NT	NT	NT
Manchester Victoria	d	19 08		20 08				21 08		22 08
Moston	d	19 15		20 15				21 15		22 15
Mills Hill	d	19 19		20 19				21 19		22 19
Castleton	d	19 24		20 24				21 24		22 24
Rochdale	a	19 28		20 28				21 28		22 28
	d	19 28		20 28				21 28		22 28
Smithy Bridge	d	19 32		20 32				21 32		22 32
Littleborough	d	19 36		20 36				21 36		22 36
Walsden	d	19 42		20 42				21 42		22 42
Todmorden	d	19 45		20 45				21 45		22 45
Blackpool North	97 d		19 13			20 11			21 13	
Poulton-le-Fylde	97 d		19 19			20 17			21 19	
Preston [8]	97 d		19 37			20 37			21 39	
Blackburn	97 d		19 54			20 54			21 55	
Accrington	97 d		20 01			21 01			22 02	
Burnley Manchester Road	97 d		20 10			21 10			22 12	
Hebden Bridge	a	19 52	20 32	20 52		21 32		21 52	22 34	22 52
	d	19 52	20 32	20 52		21 32		21 52	22 34	22 52
Mytholmroyd	d	19 55		20 55				21 55		22 55
Sowerby Bridge	d	20 01		21 01				22 01		23 01
Huddersfield	39 d				21 08					
London Kings Cross [15] ⊖26	d						19 23			
Brighouse	d				21 18		21 47			
Mirfield	39 a									
	d									
Dewsbury	39 a									
Halifax	a	20 08	20 44	21 08	21 28	21 44	21 57	22 08	22 46	23 08
	d	20 08	20 45	21 08	21 30	21 45	21 58	22 09	22 47	23 08
Bradford Interchange	a	20 22	20 59	21 22	21 42	21 59	22 11	22 23	23 01	23 22
	d	20 25	21 02	21 26	21 44	22 02		22 26	23 04	23 25
New Pudsey	37 a	20 33	21 10	21 34	21 53	22 10		22 34	23 12	23 33
Bramley	37 a	20 37		21 38	21 56			22 38		23 37
Leeds [10]	37,39 a	20 47	21 22	21 48	22 05	22 21		22 47	23 23	23 46
Selby	40 a									
York [8]	40 a		22 00							

For connections from Liverpool Lime Street please refer to Table 90

16 September to 21 October

Manchester Victoria, Rochdale, Blackpool North and Huddersfield - Bradford and Leeds via Brighouse and Halifax

Network Diagram - see first Page of Table 39

			NT	NT	NT	NT	NT	NT	NT	NT	NT	NT	NT	NT	NT	NT	NT	NT	NT	NT	NT	NT	NT	NT
				🚌		🚌	🚌			🚌			🚌		🚌	🚌	🚌	🚌				🚌	🚌	🚌
Manchester Victoria		d	22p54		08 32			09 14	09 48			10 14		10 48						11 14	11 48			
Moston		d							09 54					10 54							11 54			
Mills Hill		d							09 58					10 58							11 58			
Castleton		d							10 03					11 03							12 03			
Rochdale		a	23p07		08 48			09 27	10 09			10 27		11 09						11 27	12 09			
		d	23p07					09 28				10 28								11 28				
Smithy Bridge		d	23p11					09 32				10 32								11 32				
Littleborough		d	23p15					09 36				10 36								11 36				
Walsden		d	23p21					09 42				10 42								11 42				
Todmorden		d	23p24					09 45				10 45								11 45				
Blackpool North	97	d									09 01								10 11					
Poulton-le-Fylde	97	d									09 07								10 17					
Preston	97	d									09 27								10 37					
Blackburn	97	d									09 44								10 54					
Accrington	97	d									09 51								11 01					
Burnley Manchester Road	97	d									10 00								11 10					
Hebden Bridge		a	23p31					09 52			10 22	10 52							11 32	11 52				
		d	23p31					09 52			10 22	10 52							11 32	11 52				
Mytholmroyd		d	23p34					09 55				10 55								11 55				
Sowerby Bridge		d	23p40					10 01				11 01								12 01				
Huddersfield	39	d					09 05									10 35							11 35	
London Kings Cross	⊖26	d																						
Brighouse		d					09 20									10 50							11 50	
Mirfield	39	a																						
		d																						
Dewsbury	39	a																						
Halifax		a	23p46				09 35	10 08			10 34	11 08				11 05			11 44	12 08			12 05	
		d	23p49	00 01		08 45	09 35			10 20	10 45		10 45		11 00	11 05	11 20	11 35	11 47			12 00	12 05	12 20
Bradford Interchange		a		00s26		09 05	10 00			10 45			11 10		11 25	11 30	11 45	12 00				12 25	12 30	12 45
		d								10 45			11 10				11 45							12 45
New Pudsey	37	a		00s36						10 55			11 20											
Bramley	37	a		00s46						11 05														
Leeds	37,39	a	00 20	01 06						11 25	11 20						12 10		12 17					13 10
Selby	40	a																						
York	40	a									11 59								13 02					

			NT	NT	NT	NT	NT	NT	NT	NT	NT	NT	NT	NT	NT	NT	GC B	NT	NT	NT	NT	NT	NT	NT	NT
			🚌				🚌	🚌	🚌				🚌	🚌	🚌	🚌	🚌				🚌	🚌	🚌		
Manchester Victoria		d			12 14	12 48					13 14	13 48							14 14	14 48					15 14
Moston		d				12 54						13 54								14 54					
Mills Hill		d				12 58						13 58								14 58					
Castleton		d				13 03						14 03								15 03					
Rochdale		a			12 28	13 09					13 27	14 09							14 27	15 09					15 27
		d			12 28						13 28								14 28						15 28
Smithy Bridge		d			12 32						13 32								14 32						15 32
Littleborough		d			12 36						13 36								14 36						15 36
Walsden		d			12 42						13 42								14 42						15 42
Todmorden		d			12 45						13 45								14 45						15 45
Blackpool North	97	d		11 13						12 11								13 13						14 11	
Poulton-le-Fylde	97	d		11 19						12 17								13 19						14 17	
Preston	97	d		11 37						12 37								13 37						14 37	
Blackburn	97	d		11 54						12 54								13 54						14 54	
Accrington	97	d		12 01						13 01								14 01						15 01	
Burnley Manchester Road	97	d		12 10						13 10								14 10						15 10	
Hebden Bridge		a		12 32	12 52					13 32	13 52							14 32	14 52					15 32	15 52
		d		12 32	12 52					13 32	13 52							14 32	14 52					15 32	15 52
Mytholmroyd		d			12 55						13 55								14 55						15 55
Sowerby Bridge		d			13 01						14 01								15 01						16 01
Huddersfield	39	d												13 35											
London Kings Cross	⊖26	d																							
Brighouse		d												13 50			14 35								
Mirfield	39	a																							
		d																							
Dewsbury	39	a																							
Halifax		a		12 44	13 08					13 44	14 08			14 05			14 55	14 44	15 08					15 44	16 08
		d	12 35	12 47			13 00	13 20	13 35	13 47			14 00	14 05	14 20	14 35		14 47			15 00	15 20	15 35	15 47	
Bradford Interchange		a	13 00				13 25	13 45	14 00				14 25	14 30	14 45	15 00					15 25	15 45	16 00		
		d						13 45							14 45							15 45			
New Pudsey	37	a																							
Bramley	37	a																							
Leeds	37,39	a		13 16				14 10		14 16					15 10			15 16				16 10		16 16	
Selby	40	a																							
York	40	a		13 59						15 02								15 59						17 02	

B From Wakefield Kirkgate

For connections from Liverpool Lime Street please refer to Table 90

16 September to 21 October

Manchester Victoria, Rochdale, Blackpool North and Huddersfield - Bradford and Leeds via Brighouse and Halifax

Network Diagram - see first Page of Table 39

			NT	NT	NT	NT	NT	NT	NT	NT	NT	NT	NT	NT	NT	NT	NT	NT	NT	GC	NT	NT	NT
				🚌	🚌	🚌	🚌				🚌	🚌	🚌				🚌	🚌	🚌	🚌	🚌		
Manchester Victoria		d	15 48						16 14	16 48					17 14	17 48							18 08
Moston		d	15 54							16 54						17 54							18 15
Mills Hill		d	15 58							16 58						17 58							18 19
Castleton		d	16 03							17 03						18 03							18 24
Rochdale		a	16 09						16 27	17 09					17 27	18 09							18 28
		d							16 28						17 28								18 28
Smithy Bridge		d							16 32						17 32								18 32
Littleborough		d							16 36						17 36								18 36
Walsden		d							16 42						17 42								18 42
Todmorden		d							16 45						17 45								18 45
Blackpool North	97	d						15 13						16 11								17 11	
Poulton-le-Fylde	97	d						15 19						16 17								17 17	
Preston	97	d						15 37						16 37								17 37	
Blackburn	97	d						15 54						16 54								17 54	
Accrington	97	d						16 01						17 01								18 01	
Burnley Manchester Road	97	d						16 10						17 10								18 10	
Hebden Bridge		a						16 32	16 52					17 32	17 52							18 32	18 52
		d						16 32	16 52					17 32	17 52							18 32	18 52
Mytholmroyd		d							16 55						17 55								18 55
Sowerby Bridge		d							17 01						18 01								19 01
Huddersfield	39	d			15 35													17 35					
London Kings Cross	⊖26	d																					
Brighouse		d			15 50													17 50					
Mirfield	39	a																					
		d																					
Dewsbury	39	a																					
Halifax		a			16 05			16 44	17 08					17 44	18 08			18 05				18 44	19 08
		d		16 00	16 05	16 20	16 35	16 47			17 00	17 20	17 35	17 47			18 00	18 05	18 20	18 30	18 35	18 47	
Bradford Interchange		a		16 25	16 30	16 45	17 00				17 25	17 45	18 00				18 25	18 30	18 45	18 55	19 00		
		d				16 45						17 45							18 45				
New Pudsey	37	a																					
Bramley	37	a																					
Leeds	37,39	a				17 10		17 16				18 10		18 16					19 10			19 16	
Selby	40	a																					
York	40	a						18 02						19 01								19 59	

			NT	NT	NT	NT	NT	NT	NT	NT	NT	NT	NT	NT	NT	NT	NT	NT	NT	NT	GC	NT	NT	NT
			🚌	🚌	🚌			🚌	🚌	🚌	🚌		🚌		🚌	🚌	🚌			🚌	🚌	🚌		🚌
Manchester Victoria		d					19 08							20 08					21 08					
Moston		d					19 15							20 15					21 15					
Mills Hill		d					19 19							20 19					21 19					
Castleton		d					19 24							20 24					21 24					
Rochdale		a					19 28							20 28					21 28					
		d					19 28							20 28					21 28					
Smithy Bridge		d					19 32							20 32					21 32					
Littleborough		d					19 36							20 36					21 36					
Walsden		d					19 42							20 42					21 42					
Todmorden		d					19 45							20 45					21 45					
Blackpool North	97	d				18 11						19 13						20 11					21 13	
Poulton-le-Fylde	97	d				18 17						19 19						20 17					21 19	
Preston	97	d				18 37						19 37						20 37					21 39	
Blackburn	97	d				18 54						19 54						20 54					21 55	
Accrington	97	d				19 01						20 01						21 01					22 02	
Burnley Manchester Road	97	d				19 10						20 10						21 10					22 12	
Hebden Bridge		a				19 32	19 52					20 32		20 52				21 32	21 52				22 34	
		d				19 32	19 52					20 32		20 52				21 32	21 52				22 34	
Mytholmroyd		d					19 55							20 55					21 55					
Sowerby Bridge		d					20 01							21 01					22 01					
Huddersfield	39	d							19 35								21 15							
London Kings Cross	⊖26	d																						
Brighouse		d							19 50								21 30							
Mirfield	39	a																						
		d																						
Dewsbury	39	a																						
Halifax		a				19 44	20 08		20 05			20 44		21 08			21 45	21 44	22 08				22 46	
		d	19 00	19 20	19 35	19 47		20 00	20 05	20 20	20 35	20 47	21 00	21 12	21 20	21 35	21 45	21 47		22 00	22 05	22 20	22 49	23 00
Bradford Interchange		a	19 25	19 45	20 00			20 25	20 30	20 45	21 00		21 25		21 45	22 00	22 11			22 25	22 30	22 45		23 25
		d		19 45						20 45												22 45		
New Pudsey	37	a																						
Bramley	37	a																						
Leeds	37,39	a		20 10		20 19				21 10		21 16		21 41				22 20				23 10	23 18	
Selby	40	a																						
York	40	a				21 03						22 00												

For connections from Liverpool Lime Street please refer to Table 90

Sundays
16 September to 21 October

Manchester Victoria, Rochdale, Blackpool North and Huddersfield - Bradford and Leeds via Brighouse and Halifax

Network Diagram - see first Page of Table 39

	NT	NT ═
Manchester Victoria ⇌ d	22 08	
Moston d	22 15	
Mills Hill d	22 19	
Castleton d	22 24	
Rochdale a	22 28	
d	22 28	
Smithy Bridge d	22 32	
Littleborough d	22 36	
Walsden d	22 42	
Todmorden d	22 45	
Blackpool North 97 d		
Poulton-le-Fylde 97 d		
Preston 8 97 d		
Blackburn 97 d		
Accrington 97 d		
Burnley Manchester Road 97 d		
Hebden Bridge a	22 52	
d	22 52	
Mytholmroyd d	22 55	
Sowerby Bridge d	23 01	
Huddersfield 39 d		
London Kings Cross 15 ⊖26 d		
Brighouse d		
Mirfield 39 a		
d		
Dewsbury 39 a		
Halifax a	23 08	
d	23 11	23 20
Bradford Interchange a		23s45
d		
New Pudsey 37 a		23s55
Bramley 37 a		00s05
Leeds 10 37,39 a	23 38	00 25
Selby 40 a		
York 8 40 a		

Sundays
from 28 October

	NT	NT	NT	NT	NT	NT	NT	NT	NT	NT	NT	NT	NT	NT	NT	NT	NT	NT	NT	NT	NT	GC ■ ✈	NT
Manchester Victoria ⇌ d	22p54		08 32			09 14		09 48	10 14	10 48			11 14	11 48			12 14	12 48			13 14		13 48
Moston d								09 54		10 54				11 54				12 54					13 54
Mills Hill d								09 58		10 58				11 58				12 58					13 58
Castleton d								10 03		11 03				12 03				13 03					14 03
Rochdale a	23p07		08 48			09 27		10 09	10 27	11 09			11 27	12 09			12 28	13 09			13 27		14 09
d	23p07					09 28			10 28				11 28				12 28				13 28		
Smithy Bridge d	23p11					09 32			10 32				11 32				12 32				13 32		
Littleborough d	23p15					09 36			10 36				11 36				12 36				13 36		
Walsden d	23p21					09 42			10 42				11 42				12 42				13 42		
Todmorden d	23p24					09 45			10 45				11 45				12 45				13 45		
Blackpool North 97 d							09 01					10 11				11 13				12 11			
Poulton-le-Fylde 97 d							09 07					10 17				11 19				12 17			
Preston 8 97 d							09 27					10 37				11 37				12 37			
Blackburn 97 d							09 44					10 54				11 54				12 54			
Accrington 97 d							09 51					11 01				12 01				13 01			
Burnley Manchester Road 97 d							10 00					11 10				12 10				13 10			
Hebden Bridge a	23p31					09 52	10 22		10 52			11 32	11 52			12 32	12 52			13 32	13 52		
d	23p31					09 52	10 22		10 52			11 32	11 52			12 32	12 52			13 32	13 52		
Mytholmroyd d	23p34					09 55			10 55				11 55				12 55				13 55		
Sowerby Bridge d	23p40					10 01			11 01				12 01				13 01				14 01		
Huddersfield 39 d					09 27						11 08								13 08				
London Kings Cross 15 ⊖26 d																						11 48	
Brighouse d					09 37						11 18								13 18			14 09	
Mirfield 39 a																							
d																							
Dewsbury 39 a																							
Halifax a	23p46				09 48	10 08	10 34		11 08		11 28	11 44	12 08			12 44	13 08		13 28	13 44	14 08	14 19	
d	23p47			09 05	09 48	10 08	10 45		11 08		11 29	11 45	12 08		12 29	12 45	13 08		13 29	13 46	14 08	14 20	
Bradford Interchange a	00 02			09 18	10 01	10 22	11 00		11 22		11 42	11 59	12 22		12 42	12 59	13 22		13 42	14 00	14 22	14 37	
d	00 04	08 31		09 20	10 04	10 25	11 02		11 25		11 44	12 02	12 25		12 44	13 02	13 25		13 44	14 02	14 25		
New Pudsey 37 a	00 12	08 39		09 29	10 12	10 33	11 10		11 33		11 53	12 10	12 33		12 53	13 10	13 33		13 53	14 10	14 33		
Bramley 37 a	00 15	08 43		09 32	10 16	10 37			11 37		11 56		12 37		12 56		13 37		13 56		14 37		
Leeds 10 37,39 a	00 27	08 51		09 42	10 25	10 46	11 21		11 48		12 05	12 22	12 46		13 06	13 22	13 46		14 06	14 22	14 48		
Selby 40 a																							
York 8 40 a		09 35		10 28	11 07		11 59					13 02				13 59				15 02			

For connections from Liverpool Lime Street please refer to Table 90

Sundays
from 28 October

Manchester Victoria, Rochdale, Blackpool North and Huddersfield - Bradford and Leeds via Brighouse and Halifax

Network Diagram - see first Page of Table 39

	NT	NT	NT	NT	NT	NT	NT	NT	NT	NT	NT	NT	NT	NT	NT	GC ■ ✈	NT	NT	NT	NT	NT
Manchester Victoria ⇌ d			14 14	14 48			15 14	15 48			16 14	16 48			17 14		17 48			18 08	
Moston d				14 54				15 54				16 54					17 54			18 15	
Mills Hill d				14 58				15 58				16 58					17 58			18 19	
Castleton d				15 03				16 03				17 03					18 03			18 24	
Rochdale a			14 27	15 09			15 27	16 09			16 27	17 09			17 27		18 09			18 28	
d			14 28				15 28				16 28				17 28					18 28	
Smithy Bridge d			14 32				15 32				16 32				17 32					18 32	
Littleborough d			14 36				15 36				16 36				17 36					18 36	
Walsden d			14 42				15 42				16 42				17 42					18 42	
Todmorden d			14 45				15 45				16 45				17 45					18 45	
Blackpool North 97 d		13 13				14 11				15 13				16 11					17 11		
Poulton-le-Fylde 97 d		13 19				14 17				15 19				16 17					17 17		
Preston 8 97 d		13 37				14 37				15 37				16 37					17 37		
Blackburn 97 d		13 54				14 54				15 54				16 54					17 54		
Accrington 97 d		14 01				15 01				16 01				17 01					18 01		
Burnley Manchester Road 97 d		14 10				15 10				16 10				17 10					18 10		
Hebden Bridge a		14 32	14 52			15 32	15 52			16 32	16 52			17 32	17 52				18 32	18 52	
d		14 32	14 52			15 32	15 52			16 32	16 52			17 32	17 52				18 32	18 52	
Mytholmroyd d			14 55				15 55				16 55				17 55					18 55	
Sowerby Bridge d			15 01				16 01				17 01				18 01					19 01	
Huddersfield 39 d					15 08								17 08								19 08
London Kings Cross 15 ⊖26 d																15 48					
Brighouse d					15 18								17 17			18 11					19 18
Mirfield 39 a																					
d																					
Dewsbury 39 a																					
Halifax a		14 44	15 08		15 28	15 44	16 08			16 44	17 08		17 27	17 44	18 08	18 20			18 44	19 08	19 28
d	14 29	14 45	15 08		15 29	15 46	16 08		16 29	16 45	17 08		17 29	17 45	18 08	18 21		18 29	18 45	19 08	19 29
Bradford Interchange a	14 42	14 59	15 22		15 42	16 00	16 22		16 42	16 59	17 22		17 42	17 59	18 22	18 37		18 42	18 59	19 22	19 42
d	14 44	15 02	15 25		15 44	16 03	16 25		16 44	17 02	17 25		17 44	18 02	18 25			18 44	19 02	19 25	19 44
New Pudsey 37 a	14 53	15 10	15 33		15 53	16 11	16 33		16 53	17 10	17 33		17 53	18 10	18 33			18 53	19 10	19 33	19 53
Bramley 37 a	14 56		15 37		15 56		16 37		16 56		17 37		17 56		18 37			18 56		19 37	19 56
Leeds 10 37,39 a	15 06	15 22	15 46		16 06	16 22	16 46		17 05	17 21	17 46		18 05	18 21	18 46			19 07	19 22	19 47	20 08
Selby 40 a																					
York 8 40 a		15 59				17 02				18 02				19 01					19 59		

	NT	NT	NT	NT	NT	NT	GC	NT	NT	NT
Manchester Victoria ⇌ d		19 08		20 08				21 08		22 08
Moston d		19 15		20 15				21 15		22 15
Mills Hill d		19 19		20 19				21 19		22 19
Castleton d		19 24		20 24				21 24		22 24
Rochdale a		19 28		20 28				21 28		22 28
d		19 28		20 28				21 28		22 28
Smithy Bridge d		19 32		20 32				21 32		22 32
Littleborough d		19 36		20 36				21 36		22 36
Walsden d		19 42		20 42				21 42		22 42
Todmorden d		19 45		20 45				21 45		22 45
Blackpool North 97 d	18 11		19 13			20 11			21 13	
Poulton-le-Fylde 97 d	18 17		19 19			20 17			21 19	
Preston 8 97 d	18 37		19 37			20 37			21 39	
Blackburn 97 d	18 54		19 54			20 54			21 55	
Accrington 97 d	19 01		20 01			21 01			22 02	
Burnley Manchester Road 97 d	19 10		20 10			21 10			22 12	
Hebden Bridge a	19 32	19 52	20 32	20 52		21 32		21 52	22 34	22 52
d	19 32	19 52	20 32	20 52		21 32		21 52	22 34	22 52
Mytholmroyd d		19 55		20 55				21 55		22 55
Sowerby Bridge d		20 01		21 01				22 01		23 01
Huddersfield 39 d					21 08					
London Kings Cross 15 ⊖26 d							19 23			
Brighouse d					21 18		21 47			
Mirfield 39 a										
d										
Dewsbury 39 a										
Halifax a	19 44	20 08	20 44	21 08	21 28	21 44	21 57	22 08	22 46	23 08
d	19 45	20 08	20 45	21 08	21 30	21 45	21 58	22 09	22 47	23 08
Bradford Interchange a	19 59	20 22	20 59	21 22	21 42	21 59	22 11	22 23	23 01	23 22
d	20 02	20 25	21 02	21 26	21 44	22 02		22 26	23 04	23 25
New Pudsey 37 a	20 10	20 33	21 10	21 34	21 53	22 10		22 34	23 12	23 33
Bramley 37 a		20 37		21 38	21 56			22 38		23 37
Leeds 10 37,39 a	20 22	20 47	21 22	21 48	22 05	22 21		22 47	23 23	23 46
Selby 40 a										
York 8 40 a	21 03		22 00							

For connections from Liverpool Lime Street please refer to Table 90

Hull - Beverley, Bridlington and Scarborough

Network Diagram - see first Page of Table 39

Mondays to Saturdays
until 28 September

Miles			NT	TP	TP	NT	NT	NT	NT	TP	NT	NT	NT	TP	NT	NT	NT	NT	TP	TP	NT	NT	NT
															SX	SO					SX	SO	
				◇■	◇■					◇■ 🛒				◇■ 🛒					◇■ 🛒	◇■ 🛒			
0	**Hull**	d	06 23			06 54	07 14	07 36	07 52		08 14	08 37	09 17		09 47	09 47	10 14	10 44			11 14	11 14	11 44
4	Cottingham	d	06 30			07 01	07 21	07 43	07 59		08 21	08 44	09 24		09 54	09 54	10 21	10 51			11 21	11 21	11 51
8¼	**Beverley**	d	06 36			07 07	07 27	07a51	08 05		08 27	08a53	09 30		10 00	10 01	10 27	10 57			11 28	11 28	11 57
11¼	Arram	d				07 12			08 10														
16¾	Hutton Cranswick	d				07 19	07 36		08 17		08 36		09 39		10 09	10 10		11 06					12 06
19½	Driffield	d	06 48			07 24	07 42		08 22		08 42		09 45		10 15	10 15	10 39	11 12			11 40	11 40	12 12
21½	Nafferton	d				07 28	07 46		08 26		08 46		09 49		10 19	10 19		11 16					12 16
31	**Bridlington**	a	07 06			07 40	07 59		08 40		08 57		10 02		10 31	10 32	10 56	11 29			11 55	11 55	12 29
—		d				07 49					09 00				10 37	10 36					12 05	12 05	
34½	Bempton	d				07 56					09 07				10 44	10 43					12 12	12 12	
41¾	Hunmanby	d				08 06					09 17				10 54	10 53					12 22	12 22	
44½	Filey	d				08 11					09 22				10 59	10 58					12 27	12 27	
51	Seamer	d		07 21	08 06	08 22				09 21	09 34			10 21	11 10	11 10			11 21	12 21	12 38	12 39	
53¾	**Scarborough**	a		07 30	08 15	08 30				09 30	09 41			10 30	11 17	11 17			11 30	12 30	12 44	12 45	

		NT	NT	TP	TP	NT	NT	NT	NT	TP	NT	NT	NT	NT	TP	TP	NT	NT	NT	NT	NT	TP	TP
								SO	SX					SX			SO	SX		SO	SX	SX	SO
				◇■ 🛒	◇■ 🛒					◇■ 🛒					◇■ 🛒	◇■ 🛒						◇■ 🛒	◇■
Hull	d	12 14	12 44			13 14	13 44	14 14	14 14		14 44	15 14	15 44	16 00			16 14	16 19	16 44	17 14	17 14		
Cottingham	d	12 21	12 51			13 21	13 51	14 21	14 21		14 51	15 21	15 51	16 07			16 21	16 26	16 51	17 21	17 21		
Beverley	d	12 27	12 57			13 28	13 57	14 27	14 27		14 57	15 27	15 57	16a14			16 27	16 32	16 57	17 27	17 27		
Arram	d		13 02										16 02										
Hutton Cranswick	d		13 09				14 06				15 06		16 09				16 36	16 41		17 36	17 36		
Driffield	d	12 39	13 14			13 40	14 12	14 39	14 39		15 12	15 39	16 14				16 41	16 46	17 09	17 42	17 42		
Nafferton	d		13 18				14 16				15 16		16 18				16 45	16 50		17 46	17 46		
Bridlington	a	12 56	13 33			13 55	14 29	14 55	14 56		15 27	15 56	16 33				16 56	17 01	17 26	18 00	18 01		
	d					14 05					15 31						17 04	17 04					
Bempton	d					14 12					15 38						17 10	17 10					
Hunmanby	d					14 22					15 48						17 20	17 20					
Filey	d					14 27					15 53						17 25	17 25					
Seamer	d			13 21	14 21	14 38				15 21	16 05				16 21	17 21	17 36	17 36				18 04	18 21
Scarborough	a			13 30	14 30	14 45				15 30	16 10				16 30	17 30	17 43	17 43				18 15	18 30

		TP	NT	NT	NT	NT	TP	TP	TP	TP	NT	NT	NT	NT	TP	NT	TP	TP	NT
		SX					SO	SX	SO	SX	SX	SO					SX	SO	
		◇■ 🛒					◇■	◇■ 🛒	◇■	◇■ 🛒					◇■		◇■	◇■	
Hull	d		17 38	17 57	18 15	18 44					19 17	19 20	20 14	21 10		21 48			23 00
Cottingham	d		17 45	18 04	18 22	18 51					19 24	19 27	20 21	21 17		21 55			23 07
Beverley	d		17 51	18a12	18 29	18a58					19 30	19 33	20 27	21a24		22 01			23a15
Arram	d		17 56										20 32						
Hutton Cranswick	d		18 03		18 38						19 39	19 42	20 39			22 10			
Driffield	d		18 08		18 43						19 44	19 47	20 44			22 16			
Nafferton	d		18 12		18 47						19 49	19 52	20 48			22 20			
Bridlington	a		18 24		19 02						20 00	20 03	21 04			22 33			
	d		18 30								20 03	20 20							
Bempton	d		18 37								20 10	20 27							
Hunmanby	d		18 47								20 20	20 37							
Filey	d		18 52								20 25	20 42							
Seamer	d	18 41	19 03				19 21	19 21	20 21	20 21	20 36	20 54			21 21		22 49	22 54	
Scarborough	a	18 50	19 09				19 30	19 30	20 30	20 30	20 45	21 04			21 30		22 58	23 03	

Mondays to Saturdays
from 1 October

		NT	TP	TP	NT	NT	NT	NT	TP	NT	NT	NT	TP	NT	NT	NT	TP	TP	NT	NT	NT	NT	TP
			◇■	◇■					◇■ 🛒				◇■ 🛒				◇■ 🛒	◇■ 🛒					◇■ 🛒
Hull	d	06 23			06 54	07 14	07 36	07 52		08 14	08 37	09 17		09 47	10 14	10 44			11 14	11 44	12 14	12 44	
Cottingham	d	06 30			07 01	07 21	07 43	07 59		08 21	08 44	09 24		09 54	10 21	10 51			11 21	11 51	12 21	12 51	
Beverley	d	06 37			07 08	07 28	07a52	08 06		08 28	08a53	09 31		10 00	10 28	10 58			11 28	11 58	12 28	12 58	
Arram	d				07 12			08 10														13 02	
Hutton Cranswick	d				07 19	07 37		08 17		08 37		09 40		10 09		11 07				12 07		13 09	
Driffield	d	06 49			07 25	07 42		08 23		08 42		09 45		10 15	10 40	11 12			11 40	12 12	12 40	13 15	
Nafferton	d				07 29	07 46		08 27		08 46		09 49		10 19		11 16				12 16		13 19	
Bridlington	a	07 07			07 41	08 01		08 42		08 59		10 04		10 32	10 58	11 31			11 55	12 31	12 58	13 34	
	d				07 47					09 02				10 36					12 05				
Bempton	d				07 54					09 09				10 43					12 12				
Hunmanby	d				08 04					09 19				10 53					12 22				
Filey	d				08 09					09 24				10 58					12 27				
Seamer	d		07 21	08 06	08 22				09 21	09 36			10 21	11 10			11 21	12 21	12 39				13 21
Scarborough	a		07 30	08 15	08 30				09 30	09 44			10 30	11 17			11 30	12 30	12 45				13 30

Table 43

Hull - Beverley, Bridlington and Scarborough

Network Diagram - see first Page of Table 39

Mondays to Saturdays
from 1 October

		TP	NT	NT	NT	TP	NT	NT	NT	NT	TP	TP	NT	NT	NT	NT	TP	TP	TP	NT	NT	NT	NT
										SX			SO	SX			SX	SO	SX			SX	SO
		◇■ 🛒				◇■ 🛒					◇■ 🛒	◇■ 🛒					◇■ 🛒	◇■	◇■ 🛒				
Hull	d		13 14	13 44	14 14		14 44	15 14	15 44	16 00			16 14	16 19	16 44	17 14				17 38	17 57	18 14	18 15
Cottingham	d		13 21	13 51	14 21		14 51	15 21	15 51	16 07			16 21	16 26	16 51	17 21				17 45	18 04	18 21	18 22
Beverley	d		13 28	13 58	14 28		14 58	15 28	15 58	16a15			16 27	16 32	16 58	17 28				17 51	18a13	18 27	18 29
Arram	d								16 02											17 56			
Hutton Cranswick	d			14 07			15 07		16 09				16 36	16 41		17 37				18 03		18 36	18 38
Driffield	d		13 40	14 12	14 40		15 12	15 40	16 15				16 42	16 47	17 10	17 42				18 08		18 43	18 44
Nafferton	d			14 16			15 16		16 19				16 46	16 51		17 46				18 12		18 47	18 48
Bridlington	a		13 55	14 31	14 58		15 28	15 58	16 34				16 59	17 02	17 28	18 01				18 24		19 03	19 03
	d		14 05				15 31						17 04	17 04						18 30			
Bempton	d		14 12				15 38						17 10	17 11						18 37			
Hunmanby	d		14 22				15 48						17 20	17 21						18 47			
Filey	d		14 27				15 53						17 25	17 26						18 52			
Seamer	d	14 21	14 39			15 21	16 05				16 21	17 21	17 36	17 38			18 04	18 21	18 41	19 03			
Scarborough	a	14 30	14 46			15 30	16 10				16 30	17 30	17 43	17 43			18 15	18 30	18 50	19 09			

		NT	TP	TP	TP	TP	NT	NT	NT	NT	TP	NT	TP	TP	NT
			SO	SX	SO	SX	SX	SO					SX	SO	
			◇■	◇■ 🛒	◇■	◇■ 🛒					◇■		◇■	◇■	
Hull	d	18 44					19 17	19 20	20 14	21 10		21 48			23 00
Cottingham	d	18 51					19 24	19 27	20 21	21 17		21 55			23 07
Beverley	d	18a58					19 30	19 34	20 28	21a26		22 01			23a15
Arram	d								20 32						
Hutton Cranswick	d						19 39	19 43	20 39			22 11			
Driffield	d						19 44	19 48	20 45			22 17			
Nafferton	d						19 49	19 52	20 49			22 21			
Bridlington	a						20 00	20 03	21 04			22 35			
	d						20 03	20 20							
Bempton	d						20 10	20 27							
Hunmanby	d						20 20	20 37							
Filey	d						20 26	20 42							
Seamer	d		19 21	19 21	20 21	20 21	20 38	20 54			21 21		22 49	22 54	
Scarborough	a		19 30	19 30	20 30	20 30	20 46	21 04			21 30		22 58	23 03	

Sundays
until 9 September

		NT	TP	NT	TP	NT	NT	TP	NT	NT	TP	NT	NT	TP	NT	NT	NT	TP	NT	NT	NT	TP	TP	TP
			◇■		◇■			◇■			◇■			◇■				◇■				◇■	◇■	◇■
Hull	d	09 00		09 25		10 25	11 25		12 00	13 00		14 05	15 05		16 05	16 55	17 15		18 00	19 00	20 00			
Cottingham	d	09 07		09 32		10 32	11 32		12 07	13 07		14 12	15 12		16 12	17 02	17 22		18 07	19 07	20 06			
Beverley	d	09 13		09 38		10 38	11 38		12 13	13 13		14 18	15 18		16 18	17 08	17 28		18 13	19 13	20a13			
Arram	d			09 43																				
Hutton Cranswick	d			09 50		10 47			12 22			14 27			16 27		17 37			19 22				
Driffield	d	09 25		09 55		10 53	11 50		12 28	13 25		14 33	15 30		16 33	17 20	17 43		18 25	19 28				
Nafferton	d			09 59		10 57			12 32			14 37			16 37		17 47			19 32				
Bridlington	a	09 41		10 11		11 08	12 06		12 43	13 42		14 48	15 46		16 48	17 37	18 00		18 39	19 45				
	d			10 13		11 11			12 46			14 51			16 53				18 45					
Bempton	d			10 20		11 18			12 53			14 58			17 00				18 52					
Hunmanby	d			10 30		11 28			13 03			15 08			17 10				19 02					
Filey	d			10 35		11 33			13 08			15 13			17 15				19 07					
Seamer	d		10 20	10 46	11 13	11 44		12 25	13 20		14 24	15 24		16 24	17 26			18 24	19 19			20 27	21 25	22 51
Scarborough	a		10 30	10 54	11 22	11 50		12 34	13 25		14 33	15 30		16 33	17 32			18 33	19 24			20 36	21 34	22 59

Sundays
16 September to 30 September

		NT	TP	NT	NT	NT	TP	NT	NT	TP	NT	NT	TP	NT	NT	NT	TP	NT	NT	NT	TP	TP	TP
			◇■				◇■			◇■			◇■				◇■				◇■	◇■	◇■
Hull	d	09 00		09 25	10 25	11 25		12 00	13 00		14 05	15 05		16 05	16 55	17 15		18 00	19 00	20 00			
Cottingham	d	09 07		09 32	10 32	11 32		12 07	13 07		14 12	15 12		16 12	17 02	17 22		18 07	19 07	20 06			
Beverley	d	09 13		09 38	10 38	11 38		12 13	13 13		14 18	15 18		16 18	17 08	17 28		18 13	19 13	20a13			
Arram	d			09 43																			
Hutton Cranswick	d			09 50	10 47			12 22			14 27			16 27		17 37			19 22				
Driffield	d	09 25		09 55	10 53	11 50		12 28	13 25		14 33	15 30		16 33	17 20	17 43		18 25	19 28				
Nafferton	d			09 59	10 57			12 32			14 37			16 37		17 47			19 32				
Bridlington	a	09 41		10 11	11 08	12 06		12 43	13 42		14 48	15 46		16 48	17 37	18 00		18 39	19 45				
	d			10 13	11 11			12 46			14 51			16 53				18 45					
Bempton	d			10 20	11 18			12 53			14 58			17 00				18 52					
Hunmanby	d			10 30	11 28			13 03			15 08			17 10				19 02					
Filey	d			10 35	11 33			13 08			15 13			17 15				19 07					
Seamer	d		10 25	10 46	11 44		12 25	13 20		14 24	15 24		16 24	17 26			18 24	19 19			20 27	21 25	22 51
Scarborough	a		10 34	10 54	11 50		12 34	13 25		14 33	15 30		16 33	17 32			18 33	19 24			20 36	21 34	22 59

Sundays
from 7 October

		NT	TP	NT	NT	NT	TP	NT	NT	TP	NT	NT	TP	NT	NT	NT	TP	NT	NT	NT	TP	TP	TP
			◇■				◇■			◇■			◇■				◇■				◇■	◇■	◇■
Hull	d	09 00		09 25	10 25	11 25		12 00	13 00		14 05	15 05		16 05	16 55	17 15		18 00	19 00	20 00			
Cottingham	d	09 07		09 32	10 32	11 32		12 07	13 07		14 12	15 12		16 12	17 02	17 22		18 07	19 07	20 06			
Beverley	d	09 14		09 39	10 38	11 39		12 14	13 14		14 18	15 19		16 19	17 09	17 29		18 14	19 14	20a13			
Arram	d			09 43																			
Hutton Cranswick	d			09 50	10 47			12 23			14 27			16 28		17 38			19 23				
Driffield	d	09 26		09 56	10 53	11 51		12 28	13 26		14 33	15 31		16 33	17 21	17 43		18 26	19 28				
Nafferton	d			10 00	10 57			12 32			14 37			16 37		17 47			19 32				
Bridlington	a	09 41		10 12	11 08	12 07		12 45	13 44		14 50	15 47		16 49	17 39	18 01		18 40	19 46				
	d			10 15	11 11			12 47			14 52			16 53				18 45					
Bempton	d			10 22	11 18			12 54			14 59			17 00				18 52					
Hunmanby	d			10 32	11 28			13 04			15 09			17 10				19 02					
Filey	d			10 37	11 33			13 09			15 14			17 15				19 07					
Seamer	d		10 25	10 49	11 45		12 25	13 21		14 24	15 26		16 24	17 27			18 24	19 19			20 27	21 25	22 51
Scarborough	a		10 34	10 57	11 52		12 34	13 27		14 33	15 33		16 33	17 34			18 33	19 24			20 36	21 34	22 59

Table 43

Scarborough, Bridlington and Beverley - Hull

Mondays to Saturdays

until 28 September

Network Diagram - see first Page of Table 39

Miles			TP	TP	NT	NT	NT	NT	NT	NT	NT	TP	TP	TP	TP	NT	TP	TP	NT	NT	NT	TP	NT
			SX	SO	SO	SX	SX					SO	SX	SX	SO		SX	SO					
			◇1 🛒	◇1								◇1 🛒	◇1 🛒	◇1 🛒	◇1 🛒		◇1 🛒	◇1				◇1 🛒	
0	**Scarborough**	d	06 30	06 30							06 50	06 58	07 00	07 40	07 48		08 48	08 48			09 02	09 48	
2¾	Seamer	d	06a35	06a35							06 55	07a03	07a05	07a45	07a53		08a53	08a53			09 07	09a53	
9¼	Filey	d									07 04										09 16		
12	Hunmanby	d									07 09										09 21		
19¼	Bempton	d									07 19										09 31		
22¾	**Bridlington**	a									07 25										09 38		
—		d						06 46	07 14		07 32					08 08				09 05	09 41		10 11
32¼	Nafferton	d						06 56	07 24		07 43					08 19				09 16	09 52		
24¼	Driffield	d						07 01	07 29		07 47					08 23				09 20	09 56		10 24
37½	Hutton Cranswick	d						07 05	07 33		07 52					08 28				09 25	10 01		
42½	Arram	d									07 59									09 32			
45½	**Beverley**	d			06 30	06 38	06 58	07 15	07 43	07 57	08 06					08 38			09 00	09 37	10 11		10 37
49¾	Cottingham	d			06 36	06 44	07 03	07 21	07 49	08 03	08 12					08 44			09 06	09 43	10 17		10 43
53¾	**Hull**	a			06 44	06 53	07 13	07 33	07 59	08 13	08 23					08 54			09 15	09 53	10 27		10 53

		NT	TP	NT	NT	NT	TP	TP	NT	TP	NT	NT	NT	TP	NT	TP	NT	NT	NT	TP	NT	NT	NT
							SX	SO										SX	SO				
			◇1 🛒				◇1 🛒	◇1		◇1 🛒				◇1 🛒		◇1 🛒				◇1 🛒			
Scarborough	d	10 00	10 48			11 28	11 48	11 48		12 48			13 28	13 48		14 48		14 54	14 54	15 48			16 23
Seamer	d	10 05	10a53			11 33	11a53	11a53		12a53			13 33	13a53		14a53		14 59	14 59	15a53			16 28
Filey	d	10 14				11 42							13 42					15 08	15 08				16 37
Hunmanby	d	10 19				11 47							13 47					15 13	15 12				16 42
Bempton	d	10 29				11 57							13 57					15 23	15 22				16 52
Bridlington	a	10 36				12 04							14 04					15 30	15 30				16 59
	d	10 41		11 11	11 41	12 09			12 41		13 11	13 41	14 11		14 41		15 11	15 36	15 38		16 09	16 41	17 04
Nafferton	d	10 52			11 52				12 52			13 52			14 52			15 47	15 49			16 52	
Driffield	d	10 56		11 24	11 56	12 22			12 56		13 24	13 56	14 24		14 56		15 24	15 51	15 53		16 22	16 56	17 16
Hutton Cranswick	d	11 01			12 01				13 01			14 01			15 01			15 56	15 58			17 01	
Arram	d				12 08																	17 08	
Beverley	d	11 11		11 37	12 13	12 36			13 11		13 37	14 11	14 37		15 11		15 37	16 06	16 08		16 35	17 13	17 30
Cottingham	d	11 17		11 43	12 19	12 42			13 17		13 43	14 17	14 43		15 17		15 43	16 12	16 14		16 41	17 19	17 36
Hull	a	11 27		11 54	12 29	12 54			13 27		13 53	14 27	14 53		15 29		15 53	16 24	16 25		16 51	17 30	17 49

		TP	TP	NT	NT	TP	NT	NT	NT	TP	NT	NT	TP	NT	TP	NT	NT	NT	TP	NT
		SO	SX	SO	SX							SO		SX	SX		SO	SX		
		◇1	◇1 🛒			◇1				◇1			◇1		◇1				◇1	
Scarborough	d	16 48	16 48			17 48			17 53	18 48		19 40	19 48	20 03	20 48				22 03	
Seamer	d	16a53	16a53			17a53			17 58	18a53		19 45	19a53	20 08	20a53				22a08	
Filey	d								18 07			19 54		20 17						
Hunmanby	d								18 12			19 59		20 25						
Bempton	d								18 22			20 09		20 34						
Bridlington	a								18 29			20 17		20 42						
	d			17 34	17 34			18 15	18 41		19 10	20 27		20 44			21 28	21 28		22 41
Nafferton	d			17 45	17 45				18 52		19 21	20 38		20 55			21 39	21 39		22 52
Driffield	d			17 49	17 49			18 28	18 56		19 25	20 42		21 00			21 43	21 43		22 57
Hutton Cranswick	d			17 54	17 54				19 01		19 30	20 47		21 05			21 48	21 48		23 02
Arram	d																			
Beverley	d			18 04	18 04		18 20	18 41	19 11		19 40	20 57		21 14		21 40	21 58	21 59		23 13
Cottingham	d			18 10	18 10		18 26	18 47	19 17		19 46	21 03		21 20		21 46	22 04	22 05		23 19
Hull	a			18 20	18 21		18 36	18 58	19 27		19 58	21 15		21 30		21 57	22 14	22 14		23 28

Mondays to Saturdays

from 1 October

		TP	TP	NT	NT	NT	NT	NT	NT	NT	NT	TP	TP	TP	TP	NT	NT	TP	TP	NT	NT	NT	TP
		SX	SO	SO	SX	SX	SO	SX				SO	SX	SX	SO	SX	SO	SX	SO				
		◇1 🛒	◇1									◇1 🛒	◇1 🛒	◇1 🛒	◇1 🛒			◇1 🛒	◇1				◇1 🛒
Scarborough	d	06 30	06 30								06 50	06 58	07 00	07 40	07 48			08 48	08 48			09 00	09 48
Seamer	d	06a35	06a35								06 55	07a03	07a05	07a45	07a53			08a53	08a53			09 05	09a53
Filey	d										07 04											09 14	
Hunmanby	d										07 09											09 20	
Bempton	d										07 19											09 30	
Bridlington	a										07 27											09 37	
	d						06 44	06 44	07 12		07 32					08 06	08 06				09 03	09 40	
Nafferton	d						06 54	06 55	07 23		07 43					08 17	08 17				09 14	09 51	
Driffield	d						06 59	06 59	07 27		07 47					08 21	08 21				09 18	09 55	
Hutton Cranswick	d						07 03	07 04	07 32		07 52					08 26	08 26				09 23	10 00	
Arram	d										07 59										09 30		
Beverley	d			06 30	06 38	06 58	07 14	07 15	07 42	07 57	08 06					08 36	08 36			09 00	09 36	10 10	
Cottingham	d			06 36	06 44	07 03	07 20	07 21	07 48	08 03	08 12					08 42	08 42			09 06	09 42	10 16	
Hull	a			06 45	06 53	07 15	07 33	07 33	07 59	08 13	08 23					08 53	08 54			09 15	09 53	10 27	

Table 43

Scarborough, Bridlington and Beverley - Hull

Mondays to Saturdays

from 1 October

Network Diagram - see first Page of Table 39

		NT	NT	TP	NT	NT	NT	TP	TP	NT	TP	NT	NT	NT	NT	TP	NT	TP	NT	NT	NT	TP	NT
								SX	SO			SX	SO							SO	SX		SO
				◇1 🛒				◇1 🛒	◇1		◇1 🛒					◇1 🛒		◇1 🛒				◇1 🛒	
Scarborough	d		09 58	10 48			11 27	11 48	11 48		12 48				13 28	13 48		14 48		14 54	14 54	15 48	
Seamer	d		10 03	10a53			11 32	11a53	11a53		12a53				13 33	13a53		14a53		14 59	14 59	15a53	
Filey	d		10 12				11 41								13 42					15 08	15 08		
Hunmanby	d		10 17				11 46								13 47					15 13	15 13		
Bempton	d		10 27				11 56								13 57					15 23	15 23		
Bridlington	a		10 35				12 03								14 04					15 30	15 30		
	d	10 09	10 40		11 09	11 40	12 09			12 40		13 09	13 09	13 40	14 09		14 40		15 09	15 36	15 36		16 09
Nafferton	d		10 51			11 51				12 51				13 51			14 51			15 47	15 47		
Driffield	d	10 22	10 55		11 22	11 55	12 22			12 55		13 22	13 22	13 55	14 22		14 55		15 22	15 51	15 51		16 22
Hutton Cranswick	d		11 00			12 00				13 00				14 00			15 00			15 56	15 56		
Arram	d					12 07																	
Beverley	d	10 36	11 10		11 36	12 12	12 36			13 10		13 36	13 36	14 10	14 36		15 10		15 36	16 06	16 07		16 35
Cottingham	d	10 42	11 16		11 42	12 18	12 42			13 16		13 42	13 43	14 16	14 42		15 16		15 42	16 12	16 13		16 41
Hull	a	10 53	11 27		11 54	12 29	12 54			13 27		13 53	13 53	14 27	14 53		15 29		15 53	16 25	16 25		16 50

		NT	NT	NT	NT	TP	TP	NT	TP	NT	NT	NT	TP	NT	NT	TP	NT	TP	NT	NT	TP	NT
		SX		SO	SX	SO	SX								SO		SX	SX				
						◇1	◇1 🛒		◇1				◇1			◇1		◇1			◇1	
Scarborough	d			16 21	16 21	16 48	16 48		17 48			17 53	18 48		19 40	19 48	20 01	20 48			22 03	
Seamer	d			16 26	16 26	16a53	16a53		17a53			17 58	18a53		19 45	19a53	20 06	20a53			22a08	
Filey	d			16 35	16 35							18 07			19 54		20 15					
Hunmanby	d			16 40	16 40							18 12			19 59		20 23					
Bempton	d			16 50	16 50							18 22			20 09		20 32					
Bridlington	a			16 59	16 59							18 29			20 16		20 40					
	d	16 09	16 40	17 04	17 04			17 32			18 13	18 40		19 09	20 28		20 42			21 26		22 40
Nafferton	d		16 51					17 43				18 51		19 20	20 39		20 53			21 37		22 51
Driffield	d	16 22	16 55	17 16	17 16			17 47			18 26	18 55		19 24	20 43		20 58			21 41		22 56
Hutton Cranswick	d		17 00					17 52				19 00		19 29	20 48		21 03			21 46		23 01
Arram	d		17 07																			
Beverley	d	16 35	17 12	17 30	17 30			18 03		18 20	18 40	19 10		19 39	20 58		21 12		21 40	21 57		23 11
Cottingham	d	16 41	17 18	17 36	17 36			18 09		18 26	18 46	19 16		19 45	21 04		21 18		21 46	22 03		23 17
Hull	a	16 51	17 30	17 48	17 49			18 21		18 36	18 58	19 27		19 58	21 15		21 28		21 57	22 14		23 28

Sundays

until 9 September

		TP	NT	TP	NT	TP	NT	NT	TP	NT	NT	TP	NT	NT	NT	TP	NT	NT	NT	NT	TP	TP
		◇1		◇1		◇1			◇1			◇1				◇1					◇1	◇1
Scarborough	d	09 20		10 51	11 12	11 51	12 08		13 51	14 08		15 51	16 08			17 51		18 08		19 40	19 51	21 20
Seamer	d	09a25		10a56	11 17	11a56	12 13		13a56	14 13		15a56	16 13			17a56		18 13		19 45	19a56	21a25
Filey	d				11 26		12 22			14 22			16 22					18 22		19 54		
Hunmanby	d				11 30		12 27			14 27			16 27					18 27		19 59		
Bempton	d				11 40		12 37			14 37			16 37					18 37		20 09		
Bridlington	a				11 48		12 44			14 44			16 44					18 44		20 16		
	d		09 51		11 51		12 51	13 51		14 51	15 51		16 51	17 21	17 51		18 11	18 57	19 57	20 19		
Nafferton	d		10 02		12 01			14 02			16 02			17 32				19 08	20 08			
Driffield	d		10 06		12 06		13 04	14 06		15 04	16 06		17 04	17 36	18 04		18 24	19 12	20 12	20 32		
Hutton Cranswick	d		10 11		12 10			14 11			16 11			17 41				19 17	20 17			
Arram	d																	19 24				
Beverley	d		10 21		12 20		13 17	14 21		15 17	16 21		17 17	17 51	18 17		18 37	19 29	20 27	20 45		
Cottingham	d		10 27		12 25		13 23	14 27		15 23	16 27		17 23	17 57	18 23		18 43	19 35	20 33	20 51		
Hull	a		10 37		12 35		13 33	14 37		15 33	16 37		17 34	18 07	18 33		18 53	19 45	20 43	21 00		

Sundays

16 September to 30 September

		TP	NT	TP	NT	TP	NT	NT	TP	NT	NT	TP	NT	NT	NT	TP	NT	NT	NT	NT	TP	TP
		◇1		◇1		◇1			◇1			◇1				◇1					◇1	◇1
Scarborough	d	09 20		10 51	11 12	11 51	12 08		13 51	14 08		15 51	16 08			17 51		18 08		19 40	19 51	21 20
Seamer	d	09a25		10a56	11 17	11a56	12 13		13a56	14 13		15a56	16 13			17a56		18 13		19 45	19a56	21a25
Filey	d				11 26		12 22			14 22			16 22					18 22		19 54		
Hunmanby	d				11 30		12 27			14 27			16 27					18 27		19 59		
Bempton	d				11 40		12 37			14 37			16 37					18 37		20 09		
Bridlington	a				11 48		12 44			14 44			16 44					18 44		20 16		
	d		09 51		11 51		12 51	13 51		14 51	15 51		16 51	17 21	17 51		18 11	18 57	19 57	20 19		
Nafferton	d		10 02		12 01			14 02			16 02			17 32				19 08	20 08			
Driffield	d		10 06		12 06		13 04	14 06		15 04	16 06		17 04	17 36	18 04		18 24	19 12	20 12	20 32		
Hutton Cranswick	d		10 11		12 10			14 11			16 11			17 41				19 17	20 17			
Arram	d																	19 24				
Beverley	d		10 21		12 20		13 17	14 21		15 17	16 21		17 17	17 51	18 17		18 37	19 29	20 27	20 45		
Cottingham	d		10 27		12 25		13 23	14 27		15 23	16 27		17 23	17 57	18 23		18 43	19 35	20 33	20 51		
Hull	a		10 37		12 35		13 33	14 37		15 33	16 37		17 34	18 07	18 33		18 53	19 45	20 43	21 00		

Sundays

from 7 October

		TP	NT	TP	NT	TP	NT	NT	TP	NT	NT	TP	NT	NT	NT	TP	NT	NT	NT	NT	TP	TP
		◇1		◇1		◇1			◇1			◇1				◇1					◇1	◇1
Scarborough	d	09 20		10 51	11 11	11 51	12 08		13 51	14 08		15 51	16 08			17 51		18 07		19 37	19 51	21 20
Seamer	d	09a25		10a56	11 16	11a56	12 13		13a56	14 13		15a56	16 13			17a56		18 12		19 43	19a56	21a25
Filey	d				11 26		12 22			14 22			16 22					18 21		19 52		
Hunmanby	d				11 30		12 27			14 27			16 27					18 26		19 57		
Bempton	d				11 40		12 37			14 37			16 37					18 36		20 07		
Bridlington	a				11 48		12 45			14 44			16 45					18 44		20 14		
	d		09 49		11 51		12 49	13 49		14 51	15 49		16 49	17 19	17 49		18 09	18 55	19 55	20 17		
Nafferton	d		10 00		12 01			14 00			16 00			17 30				19 06	20 06			
Driffield	d		10 04		12 06		13 02	14 04		15 04	16 04		17 02	17 34	18 02		18 22	19 10	20 10	20 30		
Hutton Cranswick	d		10 10		12 10			14 09			16 09			17 39				19 15	20 15			
Arram	d																	19 22				
Beverley	d		10 20		12 20		13 16	14 20		15 17	16 20		17 15	17 50	18 15		18 36	19 28	20 26	20 44		
Cottingham	d		10 26		12 25		13 22	14 26		15 23	16 26		17 22	17 56	18 22		18 42	19 34	20 32	20 50		
Hull	a		10 37		12 35		13 33	14 37		15 33	16 37		17 32	18 07	18 33		18 53	19 45	20 43	21 00		

Network Diagram for Tables 44, 45, 48

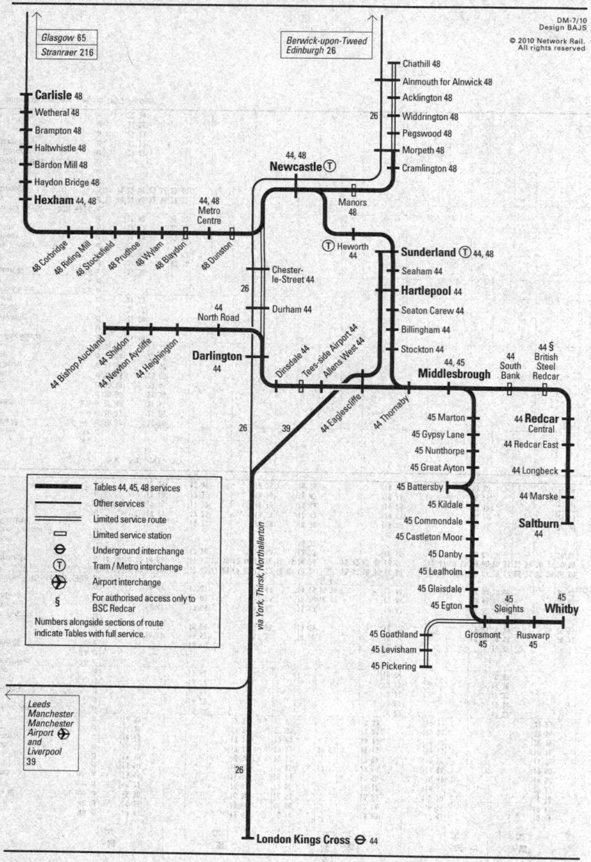

Table 44

Mondays to Fridays
until 28 September

Newcastle, Sunderland, Bishop Auckland and Darlington - Middlesbrough and Saltburn

Network Diagram - see first Page of Table 44

Miles	Miles			NT	NT	NT	TP	NT	GC	NT	NT	NT		TP	NT	NT	TP	NT	GC	NT	NT	NT		TP	NT
							◇1		R 1					◇1			◇1		R 1					◇1	
—	—	Hexham	48 d									06 16								07 42					08 43
—	—	Metrocentre	48 d																	08 16					09 16
—	0	**Newcastle**	26 d	06 00								07 00			07 30					08 30					09 30
—	2¾	Heworth	d	06 07								07 07			07 37					08 37					09 37
—	12	**Sunderland**	a	06 19								07 18			07 49					08 50					09 49
—	—		d	06 20					06 45			07 19			07 50				08 42	08 51					09 50
—	17¼	Seaham	d	06 28								07 27			07 58					08 58					09 58
—	30	**Hartlepool**	d	06a46					07 09			07 45			08 15				09 07	09 15					10 15
—	32¼	Seaton Carew	d									07 49			08 19					09 19					10 19
—	37¼	Billingham	d									07 56			08 26					09 26					10 26
—	41¾	Stockton	d									08 04			08 33					09 34					10 33
0	—	**Bishop Auckland**	d								07 20							08 21				09 26			
2¾	—	Shildon	d								07 25							08 26				09 31			
5	—	Newton Aycliffe	d								07 30							08 31				09 36			
6¼	—	Heighington	d								07 33							08 34				09 39			
10¾	—	North Road	d								07 42							08 43				09 48			
—	—	Chester-le-Street	26 d																						
—	—	Durham	26 d																						
12	—	**Darlington**	26 a								07 46							08 47				09 51			
—	—		d			06 30	06 36	06 58		07 25	07 48					08 30		08 59			09 30	09 53			
15¾	—	Dinsdale	d			06 37		07 03		07 30	07 53					08 35		09 04				09 59			
17½	—	Teesside Airport	d																						
20	—	Allens West	d			06 43		07 10		07 37	08 00					08 42		09 11			09 40	10 05			
20¾	—	Eaglescliffe	a			06 45		07 12	07 29	07 39	08 02					08 44		09 13	09 26		09 42	10 07			
—	—		d			06 46		07 12	07 30	07 39	08 02					08 44		09 13	09 27		09 43	10 08			
—	—	London Kings Cross 15 ⊖	26 a						10 25										12 29						
23¾	44	Thornaby	d			06 51	06 54	07 17		07 46	08 08	08 12		08 24	08 39	08 50	09 12	09 20		09 39	09 48	10 13		10 22	10 39
27	47¼	**Middlesbrough**	a			06 57	07 03	07 23		07 52	08 14	08 22		08 32	08 47	08 56	09 22	09 26		09 50	09 58	10 19		10 30	10 48
—	—		d		06 34	06 59		07 24		07 54						08 57		09 27			09 58	10 20			
29½	—	South Bank	d							07 58						09 01									
32¾	—	British Steel Redcar §	d							08 04															
34½	—	**Redcar Central**	d		06 44	07 09		07 34		08 07						09 09		09 37			10 09	10 31			
35½	—	Redcar East	d		06 47			07 37		08 10						09 11		09 40			10 11	10 33			
37	—	Longbeck	d		06 51			07 41		08 14						09 15		09 44			10 15	10 37			
37½	—	Marske	d		06 52			07 42		08 15						09 17		09 45			10 17	10 39			
39½	—	**Saltburn**	a		07 01	07 21		07 50		08 23						09 26		09 53			10 25	10 51			

		NT	NT	TP	NT	NT	TP	NT		NT	NT	GC	TP	NT	NT	NT	TP	NT		NT	NT	TP	NT	NT	NT
				◇1			◇1					R 1	◇1				◇1					◇1			
Hexham	48 d							10 44						11 43				12 45					13 43		
Metrocentre	48 d							11 16						12 16				13 16					14 15		
Newcastle	26 d							11 30						12 30				13 30					14 30		
Heworth	d							11 37						12 37				13 37					14 37		
Sunderland	a							11 49						12 49				13 49					14 49		
	d							11 50				12 28		12 50				13 50					14 50		
Seaham	d							11 58						12 58				13 58					14 58		
Hartlepool	d							12 15				12 52		13 15				14 15					15 15		
Seaton Carew	d							12 19						13 19				14 19					15 19		
Billingham	d							12 26						13 26				14 26					15 26		
Stockton	d							12 33						13 33				14 33					15 33		
Bishop Auckland	d					11 25										13 25									15 25
Shildon	d					11 30										13 30									15 30
Newton Aycliffe	d					11 35										13 35									15 35
Heighington	d					11 38										13 38									15 38
North Road	d					11 47										13 47									15 47
Chester-le-Street	26 d																								
Durham	26 d																								
Darlington	26 a					11 51										13 51									15 51
	d	10 30	10 53		11 30	11 53				12 30	12 53				13 30	13 53				14 30	14 53			15 30	15 53
Dinsdale	d		10 58			11 59					12 58					13 58					14 58				15 58
Teesside Airport	d																								
Allens West	d	10 40	11 05		11 40	12 05				12 40	13 05				13 40	14 05				14 40	15 05			15 40	16 05
Eaglescliffe	a	10 42	11 07		11 42	12 07				12 42	13 07	13 11			13 42	14 09				14 42	15 07			15 42	16 07
	d	10 43	11 07		11 43	12 08				12 43	13 07	13 12			13 43	14 09				14 43	15 07			15 43	16 07
London Kings Cross 15 ⊖	26 a											16 09													
Thornaby	d	10 49	11 13	11 22	11 48	12 13	12 22	12 39		12 48	13 13		13 22	13 39	13 48	14 14	14 22	14 39		14 49	15 13	15 22	15 39	15 48	16 13
Middlesbrough	a	10 55	11 19	11 30	11 56	12 19	12 30	12 46		12 54	13 19		13 30	13 48	13 54	14 20	14 30	14 45		14 54	15 19	15 30	15 48	15 54	16 19
	d	10 56	11 20		11 56	12 20				12 56	13 20				13 56	14 21				14 56	15 20			15 56	16 20
South Bank	d																								16 25
British Steel Redcar §	d																								
Redcar Central	d	11 06	11 31		12 06	12 31				13 06	13 31				14 06	14 31				15 06	15 31			16 06	16 32
Redcar East	d	11 09	11 33		12 09	12 33				13 09	13 33				14 09	14 34				15 09	15 33			16 09	16 35
Longbeck	d	11 13	11 37		12 13	12 37				13 13	13 37				14 13	14 38				15 13	15 37			16 13	16 39
Marske	d	11 14	11 39		12 14	12 39				13 14	13 39				14 14	14 39				15 14	15 39			16 14	16 40
Saltburn	a	11 23	11 49		12 24	12 47				13 23	13 49				14 24	14 50				15 23	15 49			16 23	16 49

§ For authorised access only to BSC Redcar

Table 44

Mondays to Fridays

until 28 September

Newcastle, Sunderland, Bishop Auckland and Darlington - Middlesbrough and Saltburn

Network Diagram - see first Page of Table 44

	TP	NT	NT		NT	TP	NT	NT	NT	NT	GC	TP	NT	NT		NT	TP	NT	NT	TP	NT	NT		TP
	◇1 🍴					◇1 🍴					■ 1 ☕	◇1 🍴					◇1 🍴			◇1 🍴				◇1
Hexham 48 d		14 43					15 42		16 14				16 43			17 45					18 45			
Metrocentre 48 d		15 16					16 16		16 38				17 16			18 16					19 18			
Newcastle 8 26 ⛴ d		15 30					16 30		16 53				17 30			18 30					19 30			
Heworth ⛴ d		15 37					16 37		17 00				17 37			18 37					19 37			
Sunderland ⛴ a		15 49					16 49		17 14				17 50			18 49					19 50			
d		15 50					16 50		17 15		17 31		17 50			18 50					19 50			
Seaham d		15 58					16 58		17 22				17 58			18 58					19 58			
Hartlepool d		16 15					17 15		17 39		17 55		18 15			19 15					20 15			
Seaton Carew d		16 19					17 19		17 43				18 19			19 19					20 19			
Billingham d		16 26					17 26		17 50				18 26			19 26					20 26			
Stockton d		16 33					17 33		17 57				18 33			19 33					20 33			
Bishop Auckland d					16 24									18 02					19 25					
Shildon d					16 29									18 07					19 30					
Newton Aycliffe d					16 34									18 12					19 35					
Heighington d					16 37									18 15					19 38					
North Road d					16 46									18 24					19 47					
Chester-le-Street 26 d																								
Durham 26 d																								
Darlington 7 26 a					16 50									18 28					19 51					
d			16 29		16 53			17 30		18 00				18 30				19 30	19 53			20 32		
Dinsdale d			16 35		16 58			17 35		18 06				18 35				19 35	19 59			20 35		
Teesside Airport d																								
Allens West d			16 42		17 05			17 42		18 12				18 42				19 42	20 05			20 42		
Eaglescliffe a			16 44		17 07			17 44		18 14	18 17			18 44				19 44	20 07			20 45		
d			16 44		17 07			17 44		18 15	18 20			18 44				19 44	20 08			20 45		
London Kings Cross 15 ⊖26 a											21 05													
Thornaby d	16 22	16 39	16 50		17 13	17 22	17 39	17 52	18 03	18 21		18 32	18 39	18 50		19 36	19 47	19 54	20 14	20 22	20 38	20 50		21 22
Middlesbrough a	16 30	16 47	16 56		17 19	17 30	17 48	17 56	18 15	18 26		18 42	18 48	18 56		19 47	19 56	20 00	20 21	20 31	20 48	20 58		21 30
d			16 58		17 20			17 58		18 27				18 58				20 00				20 59		
South Bank d										18 32														
British Steel Redcar § d																								
Redcar Central d			17 08		17 31			18 08		18 39				19 08				20 11				21 08		
Redcar East d			17 11		17 33			18 11		18 42				19 11				20 14				21 11		
Longbeck d			17 15		17 37			18 15		18 46				19 15				20 18				21 15		
Marske d			17 16		17 39			18 16		18 47				19 16				20 19				21 16		
Saltburn a			17 25		17 49			18 25		18 56				19 25				20 28				21 25		

	NT	NT	NT	NT
Hexham 48 d				
Metrocentre 48 d				
Newcastle 8 26 ⛴ d	20 30		21 18	
Heworth ⛴ d	20 37		21 25	
Sunderland ⛴ a	20 49		21 37	
d	20 50		21 38	
Seaham d	20 58		21 46	
Hartlepool d	21 15		22 03	
Seaton Carew d	21 19		22 07	
Billingham d	21 26		22 14	
Stockton d	21 33		22 21	
Bishop Auckland d		21 10		
Shildon d		21 15		
Newton Aycliffe d		21 20		
Heighington d		21 23		
North Road d		21 32		
Chester-le-Street 26 d				
Durham 26 d				
Darlington 7 26 a		21 36		
d		21 38		22 38
Dinsdale d		21 43		22 43
Teesside Airport d				
Allens West d		21 50		22 50
Eaglescliffe a		21 52		22 52
d		21 52		22 52
London Kings Cross 15 ⊖26 a				
Thornaby d	21 40	21 58	22 30	22 58
Middlesbrough a	21 48	22 05	22 36	23 04
d		22 06		
South Bank d				
British Steel Redcar § d				
Redcar Central d		22 17		
Redcar East d		22 19		
Longbeck d		22 23		
Marske d		22 25		
Saltburn a		22 34		

§ For authorised access only to BSC Redcar

Table 44

Mondays to Fridays

from 1 October

Newcastle, Sunderland, Bishop Auckland and Darlington - Middlesbrough and Saltburn

Network Diagram - see first Page of Table 44

	NT	NT	NT	TP	NT	GC	NT	NT	NT		TP	NT	NT	TP	NT	GC	NT	NT	NT		TP	NT	NT	NT
				◇1		■ 1 ☕					◇1			◇1 🍴		■ 1 ☕					◇1 🍴			
Hexham 48 d									06 14								07 40					08 43		
Metrocentre 48 d																	08 16					09 16		
Newcastle 8 26 ⛴ d	06 00								07 00			07 30					08 30					09 30		
Heworth ⛴ d	06 07								07 07			07 37					08 37					09 37		
Sunderland ⛴ a	06 19								07 18			07 49					08 50					09 49		
d	06 20					06 45			07 19			07 50				08 42	08 51					09 50		
Seaham d	06 28								07 27			07 58					08 58					09 58		
Hartlepool d	06a46					07 09			07 45			08 15				09 07	09 15					10 15		
Seaton Carew d									07 49			08 19					09 19					10 19		
Billingham d									07 56			08 26					09 26					10 26		
Stockton d									08 04			08 33					09 34					10 33		
Bishop Auckland d								07 20							08 21				09 26					
Shildon d								07 25							08 26				09 31					
Newton Aycliffe d								07 30							08 31				09 36					
Heighington d								07 33							08 34				09 39					
North Road d								07 42							08 43				09 48					
Chester-le-Street 26 d																								
Durham 26 d																								
Darlington 7 26 a								07 46							08 47				09 51					
d			06 30	06 36	06 58		07 25	07 48					08 30		08 59			09 30	09 53				10 30	10 53
Dinsdale d			06 37		07 03		07 30	07 53					08 35		09 04				09 59					10 58
Teesside Airport d																								
Allens West d			06 43		07 10		07 37	08 00					08 42		09 11			09 40	10 05				10 40	11 05
Eaglescliffe a			06 45		07 12	07 29	07 39	08 02					08 44		09 13	09 26		09 42	10 07				10 42	11 07
d			06 46		07 12	07 30	07 39	08 02					08 44		09 13	09 27		09 43	10 08				10 43	11 07
London Kings Cross 15 ⊖26 a						10 25										12 29								
Thornaby d			06 51	06 54	07 17		07 46	08 08	08 12		08 24	08 39	08 50	09 12	09 20		09 39	09 48	10 13		10 22	10 39	10 49	11 13
Middlesbrough a			06 57	07 03	07 23		07 52	08 14	08 22		08 32	08 47	08 56	09 22	09 26		09 50	09 58	10 19		10 30	10 48	10 55	11 19
d		06 34	06 59		07 24		07 54						08 57		09 27			09 58	10 20				10 56	11 20
South Bank d							07 58						09 01											
British Steel Redcar § d							08 04																	
Redcar Central d		06 44	07 09		07 34		08 07						09 09		09 37			10 09	10 31				11 06	11 31
Redcar East d		06 47			07 37		08 10						09 11		09 40			10 11	10 33				11 09	11 33
Longbeck d		06 51			07 41		08 14						09 15		09 44			10 15	10 37				11 13	11 37
Marske d		06 52			07 42		08 15						09 17		09 45			10 17	10 39				11 14	11 39
Saltburn a		07 01	07 21		07 50		08 23						09 26		09 53			10 25	10 51				11 23	11 49

	TP	NT	NT	NT	TP		NT	NT	NT	GC	TP	NT	NT	NT	TP		NT	NT	NT	TP	NT	NT	NT	TP
	◇1 🍴				◇1 🍴					■ 1 ☕	◇1 🍴				◇1 🍴					◇1 🍴				◇1 🍴
Hexham 48 d		09 44					10 42					11 43					12 43				13 43			
Metrocentre 48 d		10 16					11 16					12 16					13 16				14 15			
Newcastle 8 26 ⛴ d		10 30					11 30					12 30					13 30				14 30			
Heworth ⛴ d		10 37					11 37					12 37					13 37				14 37			
Sunderland ⛴ a		10 49					11 49					12 49					13 49				14 49			
d		10 50					11 50			12 28		12 50					13 50				14 50			
Seaham d		10 58					11 58					12 58					13 58				14 58			
Hartlepool d		11 16					12 15			12 52		13 15					14 15				15 15			
Seaton Carew d		11 20					12 19					13 19					14 19				15 19			
Billingham d		11 27					12 26					13 26					14 26				15 26			
Stockton d		11 34					12 33					13 33					14 33				15 33			
Bishop Auckland d				11 25										13 25									15 25	
Shildon d				11 30										13 30									15 30	
Newton Aycliffe d				11 35										13 35									15 35	
Heighington d				11 38										13 38									15 38	
North Road d				11 47										13 47									15 47	
Chester-le-Street 26 d																								
Durham 26 d																								
Darlington 7 26 a				11 51										13 51									15 51	
d			11 30	11 53				12 30	12 53				13 30	13 53				14 30	14 53			15 30	15 53	
Dinsdale d				11 59					12 58					13 58					14 58				15 58	
Teesside Airport d																								
Allens West d			11 40	12 05				12 40	13 05				13 40	14 05				14 40	15 05			15 40	16 05	
Eaglescliffe a			11 42	12 07				12 42	13 07	13 11			13 42	14 09				14 42	15 07			15 42	16 07	
d			11 43	12 08				12 43	13 07	13 12			13 43	14 09				14 43	15 07			15 43	16 07	
London Kings Cross 15 ⊖26 a										16 09														
Thornaby d	11 22	11 40	11 48	12 13	12 22		12 39	12 48	13 13		13 22	13 39	13 48	14 14	14 22		14 39	14 49	15 13	15 22	15 39	15 48	16 13	16 22
Middlesbrough a	11 30	11 50	11 56	12 19	12 30		12 50	12 54	13 19		13 30	13 48	13 54	14 20	14 30		14 45	14 54	15 19	15 30	15 48	15 54	16 19	16 30
d			11 56	12 20				12 56	13 20				13 56	14 21				14 56	15 20			15 56	16 20	
South Bank d																							16 25	
British Steel Redcar § d																								
Redcar Central d			12 06	12 31				13 06	13 31				14 06	14 31				15 06	15 31			16 06	16 32	
Redcar East d			12 09	12 33				13 09	13 33				14 09	14 34				15 09	15 33			16 09	16 35	
Longbeck d			12 13	12 37				13 13	13 37				14 13	14 38				15 13	15 37			16 13	16 39	
Marske d			12 14	12 39				13 14	13 39				14 14	14 39				15 14	15 39			16 14	16 40	
Saltburn a			12 24	12 47				13 23	13 49				14 24	14 50				15 23	15 49			16 23	16 49	

§ For authorised access only to BSC Redcar

from 1 October

Newcastle, Sunderland, Bishop Auckland and Darlington - Middlesbrough and Saltburn

Network Diagram - see first Page of Table 44

	NT	NT	NT	TP	NT	NT	NT	NT	GC	TP	NT	NT	NT	TP	NT	NT	TP	NT	NT	TP	NT
				◇1 ⊼					■ 1 ⊡	◇1 ⊼				◇1 ⊼			◇1 ⊼			◇1	
Hexham 48 d	14 43				15 42		16 12				16 43		17 43					18 43			
Metrocentre 48 d	15 16				16 16		16 38				17 16		18 16					19 18			
Newcastle 8 26 ⇌ d	15 30				16 30		16 53				17 30		18 30					19 30			20 30
Heworth ⇌ d	15 37				16 37		17 00				17 37		18 37					19 37			20 37
Sunderland ⇌ a	15 49				16 49		17 14				17 50		18 49					19 50			20 49
d	15 50				16 50		17 15		17 31		17 50		18 50					19 50			20 50
Seaham d	15 58				16 58		17 22				17 58		18 58					19 58			20 58
Hartlepool d	16 15				17 15		17 39		17 55		18 15		19 15					20 15			21 15
Seaton Carew d	16 19				17 19		17 43				18 19		19 19					20 19			21 19
Billingham d	16 26				17 26		17 50				18 26		19 26					20 26			21 26
Stockton d	16 33				17 33		17 57				18 33		19 33					20 33			21 33
Bishop Auckland d			16 24									18 02				19 25					
Shildon d			16 29									18 07				19 30					
Newton Aycliffe d			16 34									18 12				19 35					
Heighington d			16 37									18 15				19 38					
North Road d			16 46									18 24				19 47					
Chester-le-Street 26 d																					
Durham 26 d																					
Darlington 7 26 a			16 50									18 28				19 51					
d		16 29	16 53			17 30		18 00				18 30			19 30	19 53			20 32		
Dinsdale d		16 35	16 58			17 35		18 06				18 35			19 35	19 59			20 35		
Teesside Airport d																					
Allens West d		16 42	17 05			17 42		18 12				18 42			19 42	20 05			20 42		
Eaglescliffe a		16 44	17 07			17 44		18 14	18 17			18 44			19 44	20 07			20 45		
d		16 44	17 07			17 44		18 15	18 20			18 44			19 44	20 08			20 45		
London Kings Cross 15 ⊖26 a									21 05												
Thornaby d	16 39	16 50	17 13	17 22	17 39	17 52	18 03	18 21		18 32	18 39	18 50	19 39	19 47	19 54	20 14	20 22	20 38	20 50	21 22	21 40
Middlesbrough a	16 47	16 56	17 19	17 30	17 48	17 56	18 15	18 26		18 42	18 48	18 56	19 48	19 56	20 00	20 21	20 31	20 48	20 58	21 30	21 48
d		16 58	17 20			17 58		18 27				18 58			20 00				20 59		
South Bank d								18 32													
British Steel Redcar § d																					
Redcar Central d		17 08	17 31			18 08		18 39				19 08			20 11				21 08		
Redcar East d		17 11	17 33			18 11		18 42				19 11			20 14				21 11		
Longbeck d		17 15	17 37			18 15		18 46				19 15			20 18				21 15		
Marske d		17 16	17 39			18 16		18 47				19 16			20 19				21 16		
Saltburn a		17 25	17 49			18 25		18 56				19 25			20 28				21 25		

	NT	NT	NT
Hexham 48 d			
Metrocentre 48 d			
Newcastle 8 26 ⇌ d		21 18	
Heworth ⇌ d		21 25	
Sunderland ⇌ a		21 37	
d		21 38	
Seaham d		21 46	
Hartlepool d		22 03	
Seaton Carew d		22 07	
Billingham d		22 14	
Stockton d		22 21	
Bishop Auckland d	21 10		
Shildon d	21 15		
Newton Aycliffe d	21 20		
Heighington d	21 23		
North Road d	21 32		
Chester-le-Street 26 d			
Durham 26 d			
Darlington 7 26 a	21 36		
d	21 38		22 38
Dinsdale d	21 43		22 43
Teesside Airport d			
Allens West d	21 50		22 50
Eaglescliffe a	21 52		22 52
d	21 52		22 52
London Kings Cross 15 ⊖26 a			
Thornaby d	21 58	22 30	22 58
Middlesbrough a	22 05	22 36	23 04
d	22 06		
South Bank d			
British Steel Redcar § d			
Redcar Central d	22 17		
Redcar East d	22 19		
Longbeck d	22 23		
Marske d	22 25		
Saltburn a	22 34		

§ For authorised access only to BSC Redcar

until 29 September

Newcastle, Sunderland, Bishop Auckland and Darlington - Middlesbrough and Saltburn

Network Diagram - see first Page of Table 44

	NT	NT	NT	TP	NT	GC	NT	NT	NT	TP	NT	NT	TP	NT	GC	NT	NT	NT	TP	NT	NT	NT
				◇1		■ 1 ⊡				◇1			◇1 ⊼		■ 1 ⊡				◇1 ⊼			
Hexham 48 d									06 16							07 42				08 43		
Metrocentre 48 d																08 16				09 16		
Newcastle 8 26 ⇌ d	06 00								07 00		07 30					08 30				09 30		
Heworth ⇌ d	06 07								07 07		07 37					08 37				09 37		
Sunderland ⇌ a	06 27								07 18		07 49					08 50				09 49		
d	06 28					06 43			07 19		07 50				08 30	08 51				09 50		
Seaham d	06 35								07 27		07 58					08 58				09 58		
Hartlepool d	06a54					07 09			07 45		08 15				08 54	09 15				10 15		
Seaton Carew d									07 49		08 19					09 19				10 19		
Billingham d									07 56		08 26					09 26				10 26		
Stockton d									08 04		08 33					09 34				10 33		
Bishop Auckland d								07 20						08 21				09 26				
Shildon d								07 25						08 26				09 31				
Newton Aycliffe d								07 30						08 31				09 36				
Heighington d								07 33						08 34				09 40				
North Road d								07 42						08 43				09 48				
Chester-le-Street 26 d																						
Durham 26 d																						
Darlington 7 26 a								07 46						08 47				09 54				
d			06 28	06 36	06 58		07 30	07 48				08 23		08 59			09 30	09 55			10 30	10 53
Dinsdale d			06 34		07 03		07 35	07 53				08 28		09 04				09 59				10 58
Teesside Airport d																						
Allens West d			06 40		07 10		07 42	08 00				08 35		09 11			09 40	10 05			10 40	11 05
Eaglescliffe a			06 42		07 12	07 29	07 43	08 02				08 37		09 13	09 15		09 42	10 07			10 42	11 07
d			06 43		07 12	07 30	07 43	08 02				08 37		09 13	09 17		09 43	10 08			10 43	11 07
London Kings Cross 15 ⊖26 a						10 15									12 07							
Thornaby d			06 48	06 53	07 17		07 49	08 08	08 12	08 24	08 39	08 45	09 12	09 19		09 39	09 48	10 13	10 22	10 39	10 48	11 13
Middlesbrough a			06 54	07 03	07 23		07 55	08 14	08 22	08 32	08 47	08 51	09 22	09 26		09 50	09 54	10 17	10 30	10 48	10 54	11 19
d		06 34	06 59		07 25		07 56					08 53		09 27			09 56	10 20			10 56	11 20
South Bank d							08 00					08 57										
British Steel Redcar § d																						
Redcar Central d		06 44	07 09		07 35		08 08					09 05		09 38			10 06	10 31			11 06	11 31
Redcar East d		06 47			07 38		08 10					09 07		09 40			10 09	10 33			11 09	11 33
Longbeck d		06 51			07 42		08 14					09 11		09 44			10 13	10 37			11 13	11 37
Marske d		06 52			07 43		08 16					09 13		09 46			10 14	10 39			11 14	11 39
Saltburn a		07 00	07 21		07 51		08 24					09 23		09 55			10 23	10 49			11 23	11 49

	TP	NT	NT	NT	TP	NT	NT	GC	NT	TP	NT	NT	NT	TP	NT	NT	NT	TP	NT	NT	NT	TP
	◇1 ⊼				◇1 ⊼			■ 1 ⊡		◇1 ⊼				◇1 ⊼				◇1 ⊼				◇1 ⊼
Hexham 48 d		09 45				10 44					11 43				12 45				13 43			
Metrocentre 48 d		10 16				11 16					12 16				13 16				14 15			
Newcastle 8 26 ⇌ d		10 30				11 30					12 30				13 30				14 30			
Heworth ⇌ d		10 37				11 37					12 37				13 37				14 37			
Sunderland ⇌ a		10 49				11 49					12 49				13 49				14 49			
d		10 50				11 50		12 18			12 50				13 50				14 50			
Seaham d		10 58				11 58					12 58				13 58				14 58			
Hartlepool d		11 16				12 15		12 43			13 15				14 15				15 15			
Seaton Carew d		11 20				12 19					13 19				14 19				15 19			
Billingham d		11 27				12 26					13 26				14 26				15 26			
Stockton d		11 34				12 33					13 33				14 33				15 33			
Bishop Auckland d				11 25									13 25								15 25	
Shildon d				11 30									13 30								15 30	
Newton Aycliffe d				11 35									13 35								15 35	
Heighington d				11 38									13 38								15 38	
North Road d				11 47									13 47								15 47	
Chester-le-Street 26 d																						
Durham 26 d																						
Darlington 7 26 a				11 51									13 51								15 51	
d			11 32	11 53			12 32		12 53			13 30	13 53			14 30	14 53			15 30	15 53	
Dinsdale d				11 59					12 58				13 58				14 58				15 58	
Teesside Airport d																						
Allens West d			11 42	12 05			12 42		13 05			13 40	14 05			14 40	15 05			15 40	16 05	
Eaglescliffe a			11 44	12 07			12 44	13 04	13 07			13 42	14 07			14 42	15 07			15 42	16 07	
d			11 45	12 08			12 45	13 05	13 07			13 43	14 07			14 43	15 07			15 43	16 07	
London Kings Cross 15 ⊖26 a								15 49														
Thornaby d	11 22	11 40	11 50	12 13	12 22	12 39	12 50		13 13	13 22	13 39	13 48	14 13	14 22	14 39	14 49	15 13	15 22	15 39	15 48	16 13	16 22
Middlesbrough a	11 30	11 50	11 56	12 19	12 30	12 49	12 56		13 19	13 30	13 48	13 55	14 19	14 30	14 45	14 54	15 19	15 30	15 48	15 54	16 19	16 30
d			11 56	12 20			12 56		13 20			13 56	14 20			14 56	15 20			15 56	16 20	
South Bank d																					16 25	
British Steel Redcar § d																						
Redcar Central d			12 06	12 31			13 07		13 31			14 06	14 31			15 06	15 31			16 06	16 32	
Redcar East d			12 08	12 33			13 09		13 33			14 09	14 33			15 09	15 33			16 09	16 35	
Longbeck d			12 12	12 37			13 13		13 37			14 13	14 37			15 13	15 37			16 13	16 39	
Marske d			12 14	12 39			13 15		13 39			14 14	14 39			15 14	15 39			16 14	16 40	
Saltburn a			12 24	12 48			13 23		13 49			14 23	14 50			15 23	15 49			16 23	16 49	

§ For authorised access only to BSC Redcar

Table 44

Saturdays until 29 September

Newcastle, Sunderland, Bishop Auckland and Darlington - Middlesbrough and Saltburn

Network Diagram - see first Page of Table 44

		NT	NT	NT	TP	NT	NT	NT	GC	NT	TP	NT	NT	TP	NT	NT	NT	TP	NT	NT	TP	NT	NT	NT
					◇1				1		◇1 ⌶			◇1				◇1			◇1			
Hexham	48 d	14 43				15 42		16 14				16 43			17 43				18 45					
Metrocentre	48 d	15 16				16 16		16 38				17 16			18 16				19 18				20 47	
Newcastle 8	26 ⇌ d	15 30				16 30		16 53				17 30			18 30				19 30				21 00	21 50
Heworth	⇌ d	15 37				16 37		17 00				17 37			18 37				19 37				21 08	
Sunderland	⇌ a	15 49				16 49		17 14				17 50			18 49				19 50				21 20	
	d	15 50				16 50		17 15	17 29			17 50			18 50				19 50				21 20	
Seaham	d	15 58				16 58		17 22				17 58			18 58				19 58				21 28	
Hartlepool	d	16 15				17 15		17 39	17 53			18 15			19 15				20 15				21 45	
Seaton Carew	d	16 19				17 19		17 43				18 19			19 19				20 19				21 49	
Billingham	d	16 26				17 26		17 50				18 26			19 26				20 26				21 56	
Stockton	d	16 33				17 33		17 57				18 33			19 33				20 33				22 03	
Bishop Auckland	d			16 23									18 02				19 25					21 10		
Shildon	d			16 28									18 07				19 30					21 15		
Newton Aycliffe	d			16 33									18 12				19 35					21 20		
Heighington	d			16 36									18 15				19 38					21 23		
North Road	d			16 45									18 24				19 47					21 32		
Chester-le-Street	26 d																							22 00
Durham	26 d																							22 08
Darlington 7	26 a			16 49									18 28				19 51					21 36		22 29
	d		16 29	16 53			17 30			18 00			18 30			19 36	19 53			20 30		21 38		22 34
Dinsdale	d		16 35	16 58			17 35			18 06			18 35			19 41	19 59			20 35		21 43		22 39
Teesside Airport	d																							
Allens West	d		16 42	17 05			17 42			18 12			18 42			19 48	20 05			20 42		21 50		22 46
Eaglescliffe	a		16 44	17 07			17 44		18 11	18 14			18 44			19 50	20 07			20 44		21 52		22 48
	d		16 44	17 07			17 44		18 12	18 15			18 44			19 50	20 08			20 44		21 52		22 48
London Kings Cross 15 ⊖26	a								20 57															
Thornaby	d	16 39	16 50	17 13	17 22	17 39	17 52	18 04		18 20	18 22	18 39	18 50	19 22	19 39	19 56	20 13	20 21	20 38	20 50	21 22	21 59	22 10	22 54
Middlesbrough	a	16 47	16 56	17 19	17 30	17 48	17 56	18 15		18 26	18 30	18 48	18 56	19 31	19 48	20 02	20 20	20 30	20 48	20 57	21 30	22 06	22 18	23 02
	d		16 58	17 20			17 58			18 27			18 58			20 02				20 58		22 06		
South Bank	d									18 32														
British Steel Redcar §	d																							
Redcar Central	d		17 08	17 31			18 08			18 39			19 08			20 13				21 08		22 17		
Redcar East	d		17 11	17 33			18 11			18 42			19 11			20 15				21 11		22 19		
Longbeck	d		17 15	17 37			18 15			18 46			19 15			20 19				21 15		22 23		
Marske	d		17 16	17 39			18 16			18 47			19 16			20 21				21 16		22 25		
Saltburn	a		17 25	17 48			18 25			18 56			19 25			20 30				21 25		22 34		

Saturdays from 6 October

		NT	NT	NT	TP	NT	GC	NT	NT	NT	TP	NT	NT	TP	NT	GC	NT	NT	NT	TP	NT	NT	NT
					◇1		1				◇1			◇1 ⌶		1				◇1 ⌶			
Hexham	48 d									06 14							07 40				08 45		
Metrocentre	48 d																08 16				09 16		
Newcastle 8	26 ⇌ d	06 00								07 00		07 30					08 30				09 30		
Heworth	⇌ d	06 07								07 07		07 37					08 37				09 37		
Sunderland	⇌ a	06 27								07 18		07 49					08 50				09 49		
	d	06 28					06 43			07 19		07 50				08 30	08 51				09 50		
Seaham	d	06 35								07 27		07 58					08 58				09 58		
Hartlepool	d	06a54					07 09			07 45		08 15				08 54	09 15				10 15		
Seaton Carew	d									07 49		08 19					09 19				10 19		
Billingham	d									07 56		08 26					09 26				10 26		
Stockton	d									08 04		08 33					09 34				10 33		
Bishop Auckland	d								07 20						08 21				09 26				
Shildon	d								07 25						08 26				09 31				
Newton Aycliffe	d								07 30						08 31				09 36				
Heighington	d								07 33						08 34				09 40				
North Road	d								07 42						08 43				09 48				
Chester-le-Street	26 d																						
Durham	26 d																						
Darlington 7	26 a								07 46						08 47				09 54				
	d			06 28	06 36	06 58		07 30	07 48				08 23		08 59			09 30	09 55			10 30	10 53
Dinsdale	d			06 34		07 03		07 35	07 53				08 28		09 04				09 59				10 58
Teesside Airport	d																						
Allens West	d			06 40		07 10		07 42	08 00				08 35		09 11			09 40	10 05			10 40	11 05
Eaglescliffe	a			06 42		07 12	07 29	07 43	08 02				08 37		09 13	09 15		09 42	10 07			10 42	11 07
	d			06 43		07 12	07 30	07 43	08 02				08 37		09 13	09 17		09 43	10 08			10 43	11 07
London Kings Cross 15 ⊖26	a						10 15									12 07							
Thornaby	d			06 48	06 53	07 17		07 49	08 08	08 12	08 24	08 39	08 45	09 12	09 19		09 39	09 48	10 13	10 22	10 39	10 48	11 13
Middlesbrough	a			06 54	07 03	07 23		07 55	08 14	08 22	08 32	08 47	08 51	09 22	09 26		09 50	09 54	10 17	10 30	10 48	10 54	11 19
	d		06 34	06 59		07 25		07 56					08 53		09 27			09 56	10 20			10 56	11 20
South Bank	d							08 00					08 57										
British Steel Redcar §	d																						
Redcar Central	d		06 44	07 09		07 35		08 08					09 05		09 38			10 06	10 31			11 06	11 31
Redcar East	d		06 47			07 38		08 10					09 07		09 40			10 09	10 33			11 09	11 33
Longbeck	d		06 51			07 42		08 14					09 11		09 44			10 13	10 37			11 13	11 37
Marske	d		06 52			07 43		08 16					09 13		09 46			10 14	10 39			11 14	11 39
Saltburn	a		07 00	07 21		07 51		08 24					09 23		09 55			10 23	10 49			11 23	11 49

Table 44

Saturdays from 6 October

Newcastle, Sunderland, Bishop Auckland and Darlington - Middlesbrough and Saltburn

Network Diagram - see first Page of Table 44

		TP	NT	NT	NT	TP	NT	NT	GC	NT	TP	NT	NT	NT	TP	NT	NT	NT	TP	NT	NT	NT	TP
		◇1 ⌶				◇1 ⌶			1		◇1 ⌶				◇1 ⌶				◇1 ⌶				◇1 ⌶
Hexham	48 d		09 44				10 42					11 43				12 43				13 43			
Metrocentre	48 d		10 16				11 16					12 16				13 16				14 15			
Newcastle 8	26 ⇌ d		10 30				11 30					12 30				13 30				14 30			
Heworth	⇌ d		10 37				11 37					12 37				13 37				14 37			
Sunderland	⇌ a		10 49				11 49					12 49				13 49				14 49			
	d		10 50				11 50		12 18			12 50				13 50				14 50			
Seaham	d		10 58				11 58					12 58				13 58				14 58			
Hartlepool	d		11 16				12 15		12 43			13 15				14 15				15 15			
Seaton Carew	d		11 20				12 19					13 19				14 19				15 19			
Billingham	d		11 27				12 26					13 26				14 26				15 26			
Stockton	d		11 34				12 33					13 33				14 33				15 33			
Bishop Auckland	d				11 25									13 25								15 25	
Shildon	d				11 30									13 30								15 30	
Newton Aycliffe	d				11 35									13 35								15 35	
Heighington	d				11 38									13 38								15 38	
North Road	d				11 47									13 47								15 47	
Chester-le-Street	26 d																						
Durham	26 d																						
Darlington 7	26 a				11 51									13 51								15 51	
	d			11 32	11 53			12 32		12 53			13 30	13 53			14 30	14 53			15 30	15 53	
Dinsdale	d				11 59					12 58				13 58				14 58				15 58	
Teesside Airport	d																						
Allens West	d			11 42	12 05			12 42		13 05			13 40	14 05			14 40	15 05			15 40	16 05	
Eaglescliffe	a			11 44	12 07			12 44	13 04	13 07			13 42	14 07			14 42	15 07			15 42	16 07	
	d			11 45	12 08			12 45	13 05	13 07			13 43	14 07			14 43	15 07			15 43	16 07	
London Kings Cross 15 ⊖26	a								15 49														
Thornaby	d	11 22	11 40	11 50	12 13	12 22	12 39	12 50		13 13	13 22	13 39	13 48	14 13	14 22	14 39	14 49	15 13	15 22	15 39	15 48	16 13	16 22
Middlesbrough	a	11 30	11 50	11 56	12 19	12 30	12 50	12 56		13 19	13 30	13 48	13 55	14 19	14 30	14 45	14 54	15 19	15 30	15 48	15 54	16 19	16 30
	d			11 56	12 20			12 56		13 20			13 56	14 20			14 56	15 20			15 56	16 20	
South Bank	d																					16 25	
British Steel Redcar §	d																						
Redcar Central	d			12 06	12 31			13 07		13 31			14 06	14 31			15 06	15 31			16 06	16 32	
Redcar East	d			12 08	12 33			13 09		13 33			14 09	14 33			15 09	15 33			16 09	16 35	
Longbeck	d			12 12	12 37			13 13		13 37			14 13	14 37			15 13	15 37			16 13	16 39	
Marske	d			12 14	12 39			13 15		13 39			14 14	14 39			15 14	15 39			16 14	16 40	
Saltburn	a			12 24	12 48			13 23		13 49			14 23	14 50			15 23	15 49			16 23	16 49	

		NT	NT	NT	TP	NT	NT	NT	GC	NT	TP	NT	NT	TP	NT	NT	NT	TP	NT	NT	TP	NT	NT	NT
					◇1				1		◇1 ⌶			◇1				◇1			◇1			
Hexham	48 d	14 43				15 42		16 12				16 43			17 43				18 43					
Metrocentre	48 d	15 16				16 16		16 38				17 16			18 16				19 18				20 47	
Newcastle 8	26 ⇌ d	15 30				16 30		16 53				17 30			18 30				19 30				21 00	21 50
Heworth	⇌ d	15 37				16 37		17 00				17 37			18 37				19 37				21 08	
Sunderland	⇌ a	15 49				16 49		17 14				17 50			18 49				19 50				21 20	
	d	15 50				16 50		17 15	17 29			17 50			18 50				19 50				21 20	
Seaham	d	15 58				16 58		17 22				17 58			18 58				19 58				21 28	
Hartlepool	d	16 15				17 15		17 39	17 53			18 15			19 15				20 15				21 45	
Seaton Carew	d	16 19				17 19		17 43				18 19			19 19				20 19				21 49	
Billingham	d	16 26				17 26		17 50				18 26			19 26				20 26				21 56	
Stockton	d	16 33				17 33		17 57				18 33			19 33				20 33				22 03	
Bishop Auckland	d			16 23									18 02				19 25					21 10		
Shildon	d			16 28									18 07				19 30					21 15		
Newton Aycliffe	d			16 33									18 12				19 35					21 20		
Heighington	d			16 36									18 15				19 38					21 23		
North Road	d			16 45									18 24				19 47					21 32		
Chester-le-Street	26 d																							22 00
Durham	26 d																							22 08
Darlington 7	26 a			16 49									18 28				19 51					21 36		22 29
	d		16 29	16 53			17 30			18 00			18 30			19 36	19 53			20 30		21 38		22 34
Dinsdale	d		16 35	16 58			17 35			18 06			18 35			19 41	19 59			20 35		21 43		22 39
Teesside Airport	d																							
Allens West	d		16 42	17 05			17 42			18 12			18 42			19 48	20 05			20 42		21 50		22 46
Eaglescliffe	a		16 44	17 07			17 44		18 11	18 14			18 44			19 50	20 07			20 44		21 52		22 48
	d		16 44	17 07			17 44		18 12	18 15			18 44			19 50	20 08			20 44		21 52		22 48
London Kings Cross 15 ⊖26	a								20 57															
Thornaby	d	16 39	16 50	17 13	17 22	17 39	17 52	18 04		18 20	18 22	18 39	18 50	19 22	19 39	19 56	20 13	20 21	20 38	20 50	21 22	21 59	22 10	22 54
Middlesbrough	a	16 47	16 56	17 19	17 30	17 50	17 56	18 15		18 26	18 30	18 48	18 56	19 31	19 48	20 02	20 20	20 30	20 48	20 57	21 30	22 06	22 18	23 02
	d		16 58	17 20			17 58			18 27			18 58			20 02				20 58		22 06		
South Bank	d									18 32														
British Steel Redcar §	d																							
Redcar Central	d		17 08	17 31			18 08			18 39			19 08			20 13				21 08		22 17		
Redcar East	d		17 11	17 33			18 11			18 42			19 11			20 15				21 11		22 19		
Longbeck	d		17 15	17 37			18 15			18 46			19 15			20 19				21 15		22 23		
Marske	d		17 16	17 39			18 16			18 47			19 16			20 21				21 16		22 25		
Saltburn	a		17 25	17 48			18 25			18 56			19 25			20 30				21 25		22 34		

§ For authorised access only to BSC Redcar

Newcastle, Sunderland, Bishop Auckland and Darlington - Middlesbrough and Saltburn

Network Diagram - see first Page of Table 44

	NT	NT	TP	NT	GC	NT	NT	NT	NT		TP	NT	NT	GC	NT	NT	NT	TP	NT		GC	NT	NT	NT
			◇1		1						◇1			1				◇1			1			
Hexham 48 d																								
Metrocentre 48 d													10 48			11 48	12 48						13 48	14 48
Newcastle 26 d						09 00		09 45					11 00			12 00	13 00						14 00	15 00
Heworth d						09 07		09 52					11 06			12 06	13 06						14 06	15 06
Sunderland a						09 22		10 05					11 22			12 21	13 22						14 21	15 22
d					09 12			10 06					11 22	12 12		12 21					14 12		14 21	
Seaham d								10 14					11 30			12 29							14 29	
Hartlepool d					09 36			10 31					11 46	12 36		12 45					14 36		14 45	
Seaton Carew d								10 35					11 51			12 50							14 50	
Billingham d								10 42					11 58			12 57							14 57	
Stockton d								10 49					12 05			13 04							15 04	
Bishop Auckland d				08 39					10 17						12 17									
Shildon d				08 44					10 22						12 22									
Newton Aycliffe d				08 49					10 27						12 27									
Heighington d				08 53					10 30						12 30									
North Road d				09 01					10 39						12 39									
Chester-le-Street 26 d																								
Durham 26 d																								
Darlington 26 a				09 09					10 43						12 44									
d	08 17	08 45	09 07	09 11			09 45		10 45			11 45			12 46				13 45			14 45		
Dinsdale d	08 23	08 50		09 16			09 50		10 50			11 50			12 51				13 50			14 50		
Teesside Airport d																								
Allens West d	08 30	08 57		09 23			09 57		10 57			11 57			12 58				13 57			14 57		
Eaglescliffe a	08 32	08 59		09 25	09 58		09 59		10 59			11 59	12 11	12 59	13 00				13 59		14 58	14 59		
d	08 32	08 59		09 25	09 59		09 59		10 59			11 59		13 02	13 00				13 59		14 59	14 59		
London Kings Cross 26 a					12 44									15 46							17 45			
Thornaby d	08 38	09 05	09 24	09 31			10 05	10 55	11 05		11 30	12 05			13 06	13 11		13 30	14 05			15 05	15 10	
Middlesbrough a	08 44	09 10	09 32	09 40			10 10	11 04	11 13		11 38	12 10			13 11	13 20		13 40	14 11			15 11	15 18	
d		09 12					10 12		11 14			12 12			13 13				14 12			15 12		
South Bank d																								
British Steel Redcar § d																								
Redcar Central d		09 22					10 22		11 23			12 22			13 23				14 22			15 22		
Redcar East d		09 25					10 25		11 26			12 25			13 26				14 25			15 25		
Longbeck d		09 29					10 29		11 30			12 29			13 30				14 29			15 29		
Marske d		09 30					10 30		11 31			12 30			13 31				14 30			15 30		
Saltburn a		09 37					10 37		11 39			12 37			13 38				14 37			15 37		

	NT	TP	NT	NT	NT		TP	NT	NT	GC	NT	NT	NT	NT	TP		NT	NT	TP	NT	NT	NT
		◇1					◇1			1					◇1				◇1			
Hexham 48 d																						
Metrocentre 48 d					15 48				16 48			17 48		18 48								
Newcastle 26 d					16 00				17 00			18 00		19 00						20 00	21 06	
Heworth d					16 06				17 06			18 07		19 06						20 07		
Sunderland a					16 21				17 22			18 21		19 22						20 21		
d					16 21				17 22	18 12		18 21								20 21		
Seaham d					16 29				17 30			18 29								20 29		
Hartlepool d					16 45				17 46	18 36		18 45								20 45		
Seaton Carew d					16 50				17 51			18 50								20 50		
Billingham d					16 57				17 58			18 57								20 57		
Stockton d					17 04				18 05			19 04								21 04		
Bishop Auckland d			15 17					17 16					18 24					20 04				
Shildon d			15 22					17 21					18 29					20 09				
Newton Aycliffe d			15 27					17 26					18 34					20 14				
Heighington d			15 30					17 29					18 37					20 17				
North Road d			15 39					17 38					18 46					20 26				
Chester-le-Street 26 d																					21 15	
Durham 26 d																					21 24	
Darlington 26 a			15 43					17 42					18 52					20 30			21 44	
d	15 01		15 45	16 45				17 45			18 45						19 45	20 32			21 45	22 45
Dinsdale d			15 50	16 50				17 50			18 50						19 50	20 37			21 51	
Teesside Airport d																						
Allens West d			15 57	16 57				17 57			18 57						19 57	20 44			21 58	
Eaglescliffe a			15 59	16 59				17 59	18 11	18 58	18 59						19 59	20 46			22 00	22 56
d			15 59	16 59				17 59		18 59	18 59						19 59	20 46			22 00	22 56
London Kings Cross 26 a										21 45												
Thornaby d	15 17	15 45	16 05	17 05	17 10		17 41	18 05			19 05	19 09			19 30		20 05	20 52	20 58	21 08	22 05	23 02
Middlesbrough a	15 23	15 52	16 10	17 11	17 18		17 50	18 10			19 10	19 18			19 40		20 10	20 57	21 07	21 20	22 10	23 10
d			16 12	17 12				18 12			19 12						20 12	20 58			22 11	
South Bank d																						
British Steel Redcar § d																						
Redcar Central d			16 22	17 22				18 22			19 22						20 22	21 08			22 21	
Redcar East d			16 25	17 25				18 25			19 25						20 25	21 11			22 24	
Longbeck d			16 29	17 29				18 29			19 29						20 29	21 15			22 28	
Marske d			16 30	17 30				18 30			19 30						20 30	21 16			22 29	
Saltburn a			16 37	17 37				18 37			19 37						20 37	21 24			22 37	

§ For authorised access only to BSC Redcar

Newcastle, Sunderland, Bishop Auckland and Darlington - Middlesbrough and Saltburn

Network Diagram - see first Page of Table 44

	NT	NT	TP	NT	GC	NT	NT	NT	NT		TP	NT	NT	GC	NT	NT	NT	TP	NT		GC	NT	NT	NT
			◇1		1						◇1			1				◇1			1			
Hexham 48 d																								
Metrocentre 48 d													10 48			11 48	12 48						13 48	14 48
Newcastle 26 d						09 00		09 45					11 00			12 00	13 00						14 00	15 00
Heworth d						09 07		09 52					11 06			12 06	13 06						14 06	15 06
Sunderland a						09 22		10 05					11 22			12 21	13 22						14 21	15 22
d					09 12			10 06					11 22	12 12		12 21					14 12		14 21	
Seaham d								10 14					11 30			12 29							14 29	
Hartlepool d					09 36			10 31					11 46	12 36		12 45					14 36		14 45	
Seaton Carew d								10 35					11 51			12 50							14 50	
Billingham d								10 42					11 58			12 57							14 57	
Stockton d								10 49					12 05			13 04							15 04	
Bishop Auckland d				08 39					10 17						12 17									
Shildon d				08 44					10 22						12 22									
Newton Aycliffe d				08 49					10 27						12 27									
Heighington d				08 53					10 30						12 30									
North Road d				09 01					10 39						12 39									
Chester-le-Street 26 d																								
Durham 26 d																								
Darlington 26 a				09 09					10 43						12 44									
d	08 17	08 45	09 00	09 11			09 45		10 45			11 45			12 46				13 45			14 45		
Dinsdale d	08 23	08 50		09 16			09 50		10 50			11 50			12 51				13 50			14 50		
Teesside Airport d																								
Allens West d	08 30	08 57		09 23			09 57		10 57			11 57			12 58				13 57			14 57		
Eaglescliffe a	08 32	08 59		09 25	09 58		09 59		10 59			11 59	12 11	12 59	13 00				13 59		14 58	14 59		
d	08 32	08 59		09 25	09 59		09 59		10 59			11 59		13 02	13 00				13 59		14 59	14 59		
London Kings Cross 26 a					12 44									15 46							17 45			
Thornaby d	08 38	09 05	09 16	09 31			10 05	10 55	11 05		11 30	12 05			13 06	13 11		13 30	14 05			15 05	15 10	
Middlesbrough a	08 44	09 10	09 25	09 40			10 10	11 04	11 13		11 39	12 10			13 11	13 20		13 40	14 11			15 11	15 18	
d		09 12					10 12		11 14			12 12			13 13				14 12			15 12		
South Bank d																								
British Steel Redcar § d																								
Redcar Central d		09 22					10 22		11 23			12 22			13 23				14 22			15 22		
Redcar East d		09 25					10 25		11 26			12 25			13 26				14 25			15 25		
Longbeck d		09 29					10 29		11 30			12 29			13 30				14 29			15 29		
Marske d		09 30					10 30		11 31			12 30			13 31				14 30			15 30		
Saltburn a		09 37					10 37		11 39			12 37			13 38				14 37			15 37		

	NT	TP	NT	NT	NT		TP	NT	NT	GC	NT	NT	NT	NT	TP		NT	NT	TP	NT	NT	NT
		◇1					◇1			1					◇1				◇1			
Hexham 48 d																						
Metrocentre 48 d					15 48				16 48			17 48		18 48								
Newcastle 26 d					16 00				17 00			18 00		19 00						20 00	21 06	
Heworth d					16 06				17 06			18 07		19 06						20 07		
Sunderland a					16 21				17 22			18 21		19 22						20 21		
d					16 21				17 22	18 12		18 21								20 21		
Seaham d					16 29				17 30			18 29								20 29		
Hartlepool d					16 45				17 46	18 36		18 45								20 45		
Seaton Carew d					16 50				17 51			18 50								20 50		
Billingham d					16 57				17 58			18 57								20 57		
Stockton d					17 04				18 05			19 04								21 04		
Bishop Auckland d			15 17					17 16					18 24					20 04				
Shildon d			15 22					17 21					18 29					20 09				
Newton Aycliffe d			15 27					17 26					18 34					20 14				
Heighington d			15 30					17 29					18 37					20 17				
North Road d			15 39					17 38					18 46					20 26				
Chester-le-Street 26 d																					21 15	
Durham 26 d																					21 24	
Darlington 26 a			15 43					17 42					18 52					20 30			21 44	
d	15 01		15 45	16 45				17 45			18 45						19 45	20 32			21 45	22 45
Dinsdale d			15 50	16 50				17 50			18 50						19 50	20 37			21 51	
Teesside Airport d																						
Allens West d			15 57	16 57				17 57			18 57						19 57	20 44			21 58	
Eaglescliffe a			15 59	16 59				17 59	18 11	18 58	18 59						19 59	20 46			22 00	22 56
d			15 59	16 59				17 59		18 59	18 59						19 59	20 46			22 00	22 56
London Kings Cross 26 a										21 45												
Thornaby d	15 17	15 45	16 05	17 05	17 10		17 41	18 05			19 05	19 09			19 30		20 05	20 52	20 58	21 08	22 05	23 02
Middlesbrough a	15 23	15 52	16 10	17 11	17 18		17 50	18 10			19 10	19 18			19 40		20 10	20 57	21 07	21 20	22 10	23 10
d			16 12	17 12				18 12			19 12						20 12	20 58			22 11	
South Bank d																						
British Steel Redcar § d																						
Redcar Central d			16 22	17 22				18 22			19 22						20 22	21 08			22 21	
Redcar East d			16 25	17 25				18 25			19 25						20 25	21 11			22 24	
Longbeck d			16 29	17 29				18 29			19 29						20 29	21 15			22 28	
Marske d			16 30	17 30				18 30			19 30						20 30	21 16			22 29	
Saltburn a			16 37	17 37				18 37			19 37						20 37	21 24			22 37	

§ For authorised access only to BSC Redcar

Table 44

Sundays

16 September to 21 October

Newcastle, Sunderland, Bishop Auckland and Darlington - Middlesbrough and Saltburn

Network Diagram - see first Page of Table 44

	NT	TP	GC	NT	NT	NT	NT	TP	NT	NT	GC	NT	NT	NT	TP	NT	GC	NT	NT	NT	TP	NT
		◇■	■ ■					◇■			■ ■				◇■		■ ■				◇■	
Hexham 48 d																						
Metrocentre 48 d										10 48			11 48	12 48					13 48	14 48		
Newcastle 26 d				09 00		09 45				11 00			12 00	13 00					14 00	15 00		
Heworth d				09 07		09 52				11 06			12 06	13 06					14 06	15 06		
Sunderland a				09 22		10 05				11 22			12 21	13 22					14 21	15 22		
d			09 12			10 06				11 22	12 12		12 21				14 12		14 21			
Seaham d						10 14				11 30			12 29						14 29			
Hartlepool d			09 37			10 31				11 46	12 36		12 45				14 36		14 45			
Seaton Carew d						10 35				11 51			12 50						14 50			
Billingham d						10 42				11 58			12 57						14 57			
Stockton d						10 49				12 05			13 04						15 04			
Bishop Auckland d							10 17					12 17										15 17
Shildon d							10 22					12 22										15 22
Newton Aycliffe d							10 27					12 27										15 27
Heighington d							10 30					12 30										15 30
North Road d							10 39					12 39										15 39
Chester-le-Street 26 d																						
Durham 26 d																						
Darlington 26 a							10 43					12 44										15 43
d	08 45	09 07			09 45		10 45		11 45			12 46				13 45		14 45				15 45
Dinsdale d	08 50				09 50		10 50		11 50			12 51				13 50		14 50				15 50
Teesside Airport d																						
Allens West d	08 57				09 57		10 57		11 57			12 58				13 57		14 57				15 57
Eaglescliffe a	08 59		09 58		09 59		10 59		11 59	12 11	12 59	13 00				13 59	14 58	14 59				15 59
d	08 59		09 59		09 59		10 59		11 59		13 02	13 00				13 59	14 59	14 59				15 59
London Kings Cross ⊖26 a			12 44								15 46						17 45					
Thornaby d	09 05	09 24			10 05	10 55	11 05	11 30	12 05			13 06	13 11		13 30	14 05		15 05	15 10		15 45	16 05
Middlesbrough a	09 10	09 32			10 10	11 05	11 13	11 38	12 10			13 11	13 20		13 40	14 11		15 11	15 18		15 52	16 10
d	09 12				10 12		11 14		12 12			13 13				14 12		15 12				16 12
South Bank d																						
British Steel Redcar § d																						
Redcar Central d	09 22				10 22		11 23		12 22			13 23				14 22		15 22				16 22
Redcar East d	09 25				10 25		11 26		12 25			13 26				14 25		15 25				16 25
Longbeck d	09 29				10 29		11 30		12 29			13 30				14 29		15 29				16 29
Marske d	09 30				10 30		11 31		12 30			13 31				14 30		15 30				16 30
Saltburn a	09 37				10 37		11 39		12 37			13 38				14 37		15 37				16 37

	NT	NT	TP	NT	NT	GC	NT	NT	NT	TP	NT	NT	TP	NT	NT	NT
			◇■			■ ■				◇■			◇■			
Hexham 48 d																
Metrocentre 48 d		15 48			16 48			17 48	18 48							
Newcastle 26 d		16 00			17 00			18 00	19 00					20 00	21 06	
Heworth d		16 06			17 06			18 07	19 06					20 07		
Sunderland a		16 21			17 22			18 21	19 22					20 21		
d		16 21			17 22	18 12		18 21						20 21		
Seaham d		16 29			17 30			18 29						20 29		
Hartlepool d		16 45			17 46	18 36		18 45						20 45		
Seaton Carew d		16 50			17 51			18 50						20 50		
Billingham d		16 57			17 58			18 57						20 57		
Stockton d		17 04			18 05			19 04						21 04		
Bishop Auckland d				17 16							19 17					
Shildon d				17 21							19 22					
Newton Aycliffe d				17 26							19 27					
Heighington d				17 29							19 30					
North Road d				17 38							19 39					
Chester-le-Street 26 d															21 15	
Durham 26 d															21 24	
Darlington 26 a				17 42							19 43				21 44	
d	16 45			17 45			18 45				19 45	20 32			21 45	22 45
Dinsdale d	16 50			17 50			18 50				19 50	20 37			21 51	
Teesside Airport d																
Allens West d	16 57			17 57			18 57				19 57	20 44			21 58	
Eaglescliffe a	16 59			17 59	18 11	18 58	18 59				19 59	20 46			22 00	22 56
d	16 59			17 59		18 59	18 59				19 59	20 46			22 00	22 56
London Kings Cross ⊖26 a						21 45										
Thornaby d	17 05	17 10	17 41	18 05			19 05	19 09		19 30	20 05	20 52	20 58	21 08	22 05	23 02
Middlesbrough a	17 11	17 18	17 50	18 10			19 10	19 18		19 40	20 10	20 57	21 07	21 20	22 10	23 10
d	17 12			18 12			19 12				20 12	20 58			22 11	
South Bank d																
British Steel Redcar § d																
Redcar Central d	17 22			18 22			19 22				20 22	21 08			22 21	
Redcar East d	17 25			18 25			19 25				20 25	21 11			22 24	
Longbeck d	17 29			18 29			19 29				20 29	21 15			22 28	
Marske d	17 30			18 30			19 30				20 30	21 16			22 29	
Saltburn a	17 37			18 37			19 37				20 37	21 24			22 37	

§ For authorised access only to BSC Redcar

Table 44

Sundays

from 28 October

Newcastle, Sunderland, Bishop Auckland and Darlington - Middlesbrough and Saltburn

Network Diagram - see first Page of Table 44

	NT	TP	GC	NT	NT	NT	NT	TP	NT	NT	GC	NT	NT	NT	TP	NT	GC	NT	NT	NT	TP	NT
		◇■	■ ■					◇■			■ ■				◇■		■ ■				◇■	
Hexham 48 d																						
Metrocentre 48 d										10 48			11 48	12 48					13 48	14 48		
Newcastle 26 d				09 00		09 45				11 00			12 00	13 00					14 00	15 00		
Heworth d				09 07		09 52				11 06			12 06	13 06					14 06	15 06		
Sunderland a				09 22		10 05				11 22			12 21	13 22					14 21	15 22		
d			09 12			10 06				11 22	12 12		12 21				14 12		14 21			
Seaham d						10 14				11 30			12 29						14 29			
Hartlepool d			09 37			10 31				11 46	12 36		12 45				14 36		14 45			
Seaton Carew d						10 35				11 51			12 50						14 50			
Billingham d						10 42				11 58			12 57						14 57			
Stockton d						10 49				12 05			13 04						15 04			
Bishop Auckland d							10 17					12 17										15 17
Shildon d							10 22					12 22										15 22
Newton Aycliffe d							10 27					12 27										15 27
Heighington d							10 30					12 30										15 30
North Road d							10 39					12 39										15 39
Chester-le-Street 26 d																						
Durham 26 d																						
Darlington 26 a							10 43					12 44										15 43
d	08 45	09 00			09 45		10 45		11 45			12 46				13 45		14 45				15 45
Dinsdale d	08 50				09 50		10 50		11 50			12 51				13 50		14 50				15 50
Teesside Airport d																						
Allens West d	08 57				09 57		10 57		11 57			12 58				13 57		14 57				15 57
Eaglescliffe a	08 59		09 58		09 59		10 59		11 59	12 11	12 59	13 00				13 59	14 58	14 59				15 59
d	08 59		09 59		09 59		10 59		11 59		13 02	13 00				13 59	14 59	14 59				15 59
London Kings Cross ⊖26 a			12 44								15 46						17 45					
Thornaby d	09 05	09 16			10 05	10 55	11 05	11 30	12 05			13 06	13 11		13 30	14 05		15 05	15 10		15 45	16 05
Middlesbrough a	09 10	09 25			10 10	11 05	11 13	11 38	12 10			13 11	13 20		13 40	14 11		15 11	15 18		15 52	16 10
d	09 12				10 12		11 14		12 12			13 13				14 12		15 12				16 12
South Bank d																						
British Steel Redcar § d																						
Redcar Central d	09 22				10 22		11 23		12 22			13 23				14 22		15 22				16 22
Redcar East d	09 25				10 25		11 26		12 25			13 26				14 25		15 25				16 25
Longbeck d	09 29				10 29		11 30		12 29			13 30				14 29		15 29				16 29
Marske d	09 30				10 30		11 31		12 30			13 31				14 30		15 30				16 30
Saltburn a	09 37				10 37		11 39		12 37			13 38				14 37		15 37				16 37

	NT	NT	TP	NT	NT	GC	NT	NT	NT	TP	NT	NT	TP	NT	NT	NT
			◇■			■ ■				◇■			◇■			
Hexham 48 d																
Metrocentre 48 d		15 48			16 48			17 48	18 48							
Newcastle 26 d		16 00			17 00			18 00	19 00					20 00	21 06	
Heworth d		16 06			17 06			18 07	19 06					20 07		
Sunderland a		16 21			17 22			18 21	19 22					20 21		
d		16 21			17 22	18 12		18 21						20 21		
Seaham d		16 29			17 30			18 29						20 29		
Hartlepool d		16 45			17 46	18 36		18 45						20 45		
Seaton Carew d		16 50			17 51			18 50						20 50		
Billingham d		16 57			17 58			18 57						20 57		
Stockton d		17 04			18 05			19 04						21 04		
Bishop Auckland d				17 16							19 17					
Shildon d				17 21							19 22					
Newton Aycliffe d				17 26							19 27					
Heighington d				17 29							19 30					
North Road d				17 38							19 39					
Chester-le-Street 26 d															21 15	
Durham 26 d															21 24	
Darlington 26 a				17 42							19 43				21 44	
d	16 45			17 45			18 45				19 45	20 32			21 45	22 45
Dinsdale d	16 50			17 50			18 50				19 50	20 37			21 51	
Teesside Airport d																
Allens West d	16 57			17 57			18 57				19 57	20 44			21 58	
Eaglescliffe a	16 59			17 59	18 11	18 58	18 59				19 59	20 46			22 00	22 56
d	16 59			17 59		18 59	18 59				19 59	20 46			22 00	22 56
London Kings Cross ⊖26 a						21 45										
Thornaby d	17 05	17 10	17 41	18 05			19 05	19 09		19 30	20 05	20 52	20 58	21 08	22 05	23 02
Middlesbrough a	17 11	17 18	17 50	18 10			19 10	19 18		19 40	20 10	20 57	21 07	21 20	22 10	23 10
d	17 12			18 12			19 12				20 12	20 58			22 11	
South Bank d																
British Steel Redcar § d																
Redcar Central d	17 22			18 22			19 22				20 22	21 08			22 21	
Redcar East d	17 25			18 25			19 25				20 25	21 11			22 24	
Longbeck d	17 29			18 29			19 29				20 29	21 15			22 28	
Marske d	17 30			18 30			19 30				20 30	21 16			22 29	
Saltburn a	17 37			18 37			19 37				20 37	21 24			22 37	

§ For authorised access only to BSC Redcar

Saltburn and Middlesbrough - Darlington, Bishop Auckland, Sunderland and Newcastle

Network Diagram - see first Page of Table 44

Miles	Miles			NT	TP	NT	NT	NT	NT	TP	NT	NT	NT	NT	NT	NT	NT	TP	NT	NT	TP	NT	NT
					◇1 ✠					◇1 ✠								◇1 ✠			◇1 ✠		
0	—	**Saltburn**	d					06 22					07 11	07 25	07 54				08 31			09 31	09 58
2	—	Marske	d					06 26					07 15	07 29	07 58				08 35			09 35	10 02
2½	—	Longbeck	d					06 29					07 18	07 32	08 01				08 38			09 38	10 05
4	—	Redcar East	d					06 32					07 21	07 35	08 04				08 41			09 41	10 08
5	—	**Redcar Central**	d					06 35					07 24	07 38	08 07				08 44			09 44	10 11
6¾	—	British Steel Redcar §	d																				
10	—	South Bank	d										07 31						08 51				
12½	0	**Middlesbrough**	a					06 45					07 37	07 49	08 19				08 56			09 55	10 22
—	—		d	05 45	05 55			06 47	06 51	07 12	07 32		07 37	07 49	08 20	08 32	08 44	08 50	09 08	09 32	09 50	09 56	10 22
15¾	3¼	Thornaby	d	05 50	06a00			06 52	06 56	07a17	07 37		07 42	07 54	08 25	08 37	08 50	08a55	09 13	09 37	09a55	10 01	10 27
—	—	London Kings Cross 15 ⊖26	d																				
18¾	—	Eaglescliffe	a	05 55				06 57					07 47	07 59	08 30		08 55		09 18			10 06	10 32
—	—		d	05 55				06 57					07 48	08 00	08 31		08 55		09 18			10 07	10 33
19½	—	Allens West	d	05 58				07 00					07 50	08 02	08 33		08 58		09 21			10 09	10 35
22	—	Teesside Airport	d																				
23¾	—	Dinsdale	d	06 04				07 06					07 57	08 09	08 40		09 04		09 27				10 42
27½	—	**Darlington** 7	26 a	06 14				07 19					08 07	08 19	08 50		09 13		09 39			10 23	10 52
—	—		d	06 14		06 47		07 20				07 48		08 22	08 52								10 54
28¾	—	North Road	d			06 50						07 51			08 55								10 57
33¼	—	Heighington	d			06 58						07 59			09 03								11 05
34½	—	Newton Aycliffe	d			07 02						08 03			09 07								11 08
36¾	—	Shildon	d			07 06						08 07			09 11								11 13
39½	—	**Bishop Auckland**	a			07 14						08 15			09 18								11 20
—	5½	Stockton	d						07 02		07 43					08 43				09 43			
—	10	Billingham	d						07 09		07 50					08 50				09 50			
—	15	Seaton Carew	d						07 15		07 56					08 56				09 56			
—	17¼	**Hartlepool**	d				07 03		07 21		08 02					09 02				10 02			
—	30	Seaham	d				07 18		07 36		08 17					09 17				10 17			
—	35¼	**Sunderland**	a				07 28		07 50		08 28					09 27				10 28			
—	—		d				07 30		07 55		08 30					09 30				10 30			
—	44½	Heworth	d				07 41		08 07		08 42					09 42				10 42			
—	47¼	**Newcastle** 8	26 a	06 54			07 51	08 05	08 16		08 52			09 06		09 51				10 51			
—	—	Metrocentre	48 a				08 00									10 02				11 01			
—	—	Hexham	48 a				08 38									10 36				11 38			

		NT	GC	TP	NT	NT	NT	TP	NT	NT	NT	TP	NT	NT	NT	GC	TP	NT	NT	NT	TP FO	TP FX	NT
			1	◇1 ✠				◇1 ✠				◇1 ✠				1	◇1 ✠				◇1	◇1 ✠	
Saltburn	d				10 31	10 58			11 31	11 57			12 30	12 58				13 31	13 57				14 31
Marske	d				10 35	11 02			11 35	12 01			12 34	13 02				13 35	14 02				14 35
Longbeck	d				10 38	11 05			11 38	12 04			12 37	13 05				13 38	14 05				14 38
Redcar East	d				10 41	11 08			11 41	12 07			12 40	13 08				13 41	14 08				14 41
Redcar Central	d				10 44	11 11			11 45	12 10			12 43	13 11				13 44	14 11				14 44
British Steel Redcar §	d																						
South Bank	d																						
Middlesbrough	a				10 54	11 21			11 55	12 21			12 54	13 21				13 54	14 21				14 54
	d	10 32		10 50	10 55	11 22	11 32	11 50	11 56	12 22	12 32	12 50	12 55	13 22	13 32		13 50	13 55	14 22	14 32	14 50	14 50	14 55
Thornaby	d	10 37		10a55	11 00	11 27	11 36	11a55	12 01	12 27	12 37	12a55	13 00	13 27	13 37		13a55	14 00	14 27	14 37	14a55	14a55	15 00
London Kings Cross 15 ⊖26	d		07 49													11 23							
Eaglescliffe	a		10 46		11 05	11 32			12 06	12 32			13 05	13 32		14 04		14 05	14 32				15 05
	d		10 47		11 06	11 33			12 06	12 33			13 06	13 33		14 05		14 06	14 33				15 06
Allens West	d				11 08	11 35			12 09	12 35			13 08	13 35				14 08	14 35				15 08
Teesside Airport	d																						
Dinsdale	d					11 42				12 42				13 42					14 42				
Darlington 7	26 a				11 23	11 52			12 24	12 54			13 23	13 52				14 23	14 52				15 23
	d									12 54									14 54				
North Road	d									12 57									14 57				
Heighington	d									13 05									15 05				
Newton Aycliffe	d									13 08									15 08				
Shildon	d									13 13									15 13				
Bishop Auckland	a									13 20									15 20				
Stockton	d	10 43					11 42				12 42				13 43					14 43			
Billingham	d	10 50					11 50				12 50				13 50					14 50			
Seaton Carew	d	10 56					11 56				12 56				13 56					14 56			
Hartlepool	d	11 02	11 13				12 02				13 02				14 02	14 24				15 02			
Seaham	d	11 17					12 17				13 17				14 17					15 17			
Sunderland	a	11 27	11 40				12 27				13 28				14 27	14 50				15 27			
	d	11 30					12 30				13 30				14 30					15 30			
Heworth	d	11 42					12 42				13 42				14 42					15 42			
Newcastle 8	26 a	11 51					12 52				13 51				14 51					15 51			
Metrocentre	48 a	12 01					13 01				14 01				15 02					16 01			
Hexham	48 a	12 38					13 38				14 38				15 39					16 38			

§ For authorised access only to BSC Redcar

Saltburn and Middlesbrough - Darlington, Bishop Auckland, Sunderland and Newcastle

Network Diagram - see first Page of Table 44

		NT	NT	TP	NT	NT	NT	TP	NT	NT	NT	TP	NT	NT	NT	NT	TP	NT	NT	GC	NT	NT
				◇1 ✠				◇1 ✠				◇1					◇1			1		
Saltburn	d	14 58			15 31	15 58			16 27	16 58			17 31	17 58				18 31	18 58			19 31
Marske	d	15 02			15 35	16 02			16 31	17 02			17 35	18 02				18 35	19 02			19 35
Longbeck	d	15 05			15 38	16 05			16 34	17 05			17 38	18 05				18 38	19 05			19 38
Redcar East	d	15 08			15 41	16 08			16 37	17 08			17 41	18 08				18 41	19 08			19 41
Redcar Central	d	15 11			15 44	16 11			16 40	17 11			17 44	18 11				18 44	19 11			19 44
British Steel Redcar §	d								16 43													
South Bank	d								16 49	17 18												
Middlesbrough	a	15 21			15 54	16 21			16 54	17 23			17 54	18 21				18 54	19 21			19 54
	d	15 22	15 32	15 50	15 55	16 22	16 32	16 50	16 58	17 24	17 39	17 50	17 55	18 22	18 32	18 45	18 50	18 55	19 22		19 40	19 55
Thornaby	d	15 27	15 37	15a55	16 00	16 28	16 37	16a55	17 03	17 29	17 44	17a55	18 00	18 27	18 37	18 50	18a55	19 00	19 27		19 45	20 00
London Kings Cross 15 ⊖26	d																			16 48		
Eaglescliffe	a	15 32			16 05	16 35			17 08	17 34			18 05	18 32				19 05	19 32	19 33		20 05
	d	15 33			16 06	16 35			17 08	17 35			18 06	18 33				19 06	19 33	19 34		20 06
Allens West	d	15 35			16 08	16 38			17 11	17 37			18 08	18 35				19 08	19 35			20 08
Teesside Airport	d																					
Dinsdale	d	15 42			16 15	16 44			17 17	17 44			18 15					19 15				20 15
Darlington 7	26 a	15 54			16 23	16 52			17 26	17 53			18 23	18 50		19 12		19 23	19 50			20 23
	d	15 54							17 28					18 54								20 32
North Road	d	15 57							17 31					18 57								20 35
Heighington	d	16 05							17 39					19 05								20 43
Newton Aycliffe	d	16 08							17 42					19 08								20 46
Shildon	d	16 13							17 47					19 13								20 51
Bishop Auckland	a	16 20							17 54					19 20								20 58
Stockton	d		15 43				16 43				17 50				18 43						19 51	
Billingham	d		15 50				16 50				17 57				18 50						19 58	
Seaton Carew	d		15 56				16 56				18 03				18 56						20 04	
Hartlepool	d		16 02				17 02				18 09				19 02					19 53	20 10	
Seaham	d		16 17				17 17				18 24				19 17						20 27	
Sunderland	a		16 27				17 28				18 38				19 27					20 21	20 37	
	d		16 30				17 30				18 42				19 29						20 38	
Heworth	d		16 42				17 42				18 55				19 42						20 53	
Newcastle 8	26 a		16 51				17 51				19 05				19 51						21 02	
Metrocentre	48 a		17 01				18 01								20 01						21 11	
Hexham	48 a		17 39				18 32															

		TP	TP	NT	NT	GC	TP	NT	NT
		◇1	◇1			1	◇1		
Saltburn	d			20 32				21 30	22 36
Marske	d			20 36				21 34	22 40
Longbeck	d			20 39				21 37	22 43
Redcar East	d			20 42				21 40	22 46
Redcar Central	d			20 45				21 43	22 49
British Steel Redcar §	d								
South Bank	d								
Middlesbrough	a			20 55				21 53	22 59
	d	20 04	20 50	20 56	21 01		21 50	21 54	23 00
Thornaby	d	20 09	20a55	21 01	21 06		21 55	21 59	23 05
London Kings Cross 15 ⊖26	d					19 18			
Eaglescliffe	a			21 06		22 04		22 04	23 10
	d			21 07		22 05		22 05	23 11
Allens West	d			21 09				22 07	23 13
Teesside Airport	d								
Dinsdale	d			21 16				22 14	23 20
Darlington 7	26 a	20 29		21 24			22 15	22 25	23 30
	d								
North Road	d								
Heighington	d								
Newton Aycliffe	d								
Shildon	d								
Bishop Auckland	a								
Stockton	d				21 12				
Billingham	d				21 19				
Seaton Carew	d				21 25				
Hartlepool	d				21 31	22 25			
Seaham	d				21 46				
Sunderland	a				21 57	22 51			
	d				21 58				
Heworth	d				22 09				
Newcastle 8	26 a				22 19				
Metrocentre	48 a								
Hexham	48 a								

§ For authorised access only to BSC Redcar

Saltburn and Middlesbrough - Darlington, Bishop Auckland, Sunderland and Newcastle

Network Diagram - see first Page of Table 44

		NT	TP	NT	NT	NT	NT	TP	NT	NT	NT	NT	NT	NT	NT	TP	NT	NT	TP	NT	NT	NT	GC
			◇1 ✠					◇1 ✠								◇1 ✠			◇1 ✠				■ 1 ⊏
Saltburn	d					06 22					07 11	07 25	07 54				08 31			09 31	09 58		
Marske	d					06 26					07 15	07 29	07 58				08 35			09 35	10 02		
Longbeck	d					06 29					07 18	07 32	08 01				08 38			09 38	10 05		
Redcar East	d					06 32					07 21	07 35	08 04				08 41			09 41	10 08		
Redcar Central	d					06 35					07 24	07 38	08 07				08 44			09 44	10 11		
British Steel Redcar §	d																						
South Bank	d										07 31						08 51						
Middlesbrough	a					06 45					07 37	07 49	08 19				08 56			09 55	10 22		
	d	05 45	05 55			06 47	06 51	07 12	07 32		07 37	07 49	08 20	08 32	08 44	08 50	09 08	09 32	09 50	09 56	10 22	10 32	
Thornaby	d	05 50	06a00			06 52	06 56	07a17	07 37		07 42	07 54	08 25	08 37	08 50	08a55	09 13	09 37	09a55	10 01	10 27	10 37	
London Kings Cross 15 ⊖26	d																						07 49
Eaglescliffe	a	05 55				06 57					07 47	07 59	08 30		08 55		09 18			10 06	10 32		10 46
	d	05 55				06 57					07 48	08 00	08 31		08 55		09 18			10 07	10 33		10 47
Allens West	d	05 58				07 00					07 50	08 02	08 33		08 58		09 21			10 09	10 35		
Teesside Airport	d																						
Dinsdale	d	06 04				07 06					07 57	08 09	08 40		09 04		09 27				10 42		
Darlington 7	26 a	06 14				07 19					08 07	08 19	08 50		09 13		09 39			10 23	10 52		
	d	06 14		06 47		07 20				07 48		08 22	08 52								10 54		
North Road	d			06 50						07 51			08 55								10 57		
Heighington	d			06 58						07 59			09 03								11 05		
Newton Aycliffe	d			07 02						08 03			09 07								11 08		
Shildon	d			07 06						08 07			09 11								11 13		
Bishop Auckland	a			07 14						08 15			09 18								11 20		
Stockton	d						07 02		07 43					08 43				09 43				10 43	
Billingham	d						07 09		07 50					08 50				09 50				10 50	
Seaton Carew	d						07 15		07 56					08 56				09 56				10 56	
Hartlepool	d				07 03		07 21		08 02					09 02				10 02				11 02	11 13
Seaham	d				07 18		07 36		08 17					09 15				10 17				11 17	
Sunderland ⇌	a				07 28		07 50		08 28					09 27				10 28				11 27	11 40
	d				07 30		07 55		08 30					09 30				10 30				11 30	
Heworth ⇌	d				07 41		08 07		08 42					09 42				10 42				11 42	
Newcastle 8	26 ⇌ a	06 54			07 51	08 05	08 16		08 52			09 06		09 51				10 51				11 51	
Metrocentre	48 a				08 00									10 02				11 01				12 01	
Hexham	48 a				08 38									10 36				11 38				12 38	

		TP	NT	NT	NT	TP	NT	NT	NT	TP	NT	NT	NT	GC	TP	NT	NT	NT	TP FO	TP FX	NT	NT	NT
		◇1 ✠				◇1 ✠				◇1 ✠				■ 1 ⊏	◇1 ✠				◇1	◇1 ✠			
Saltburn	d		10 31	10 58			11 31	11 57			12 30	12 58				13 31	13 57				14 31	14 58	
Marske	d		10 35	11 02			11 35	12 01			12 34	13 02				13 35	14 02				14 35	15 02	
Longbeck	d		10 38	11 05			11 38	12 04			12 37	13 05				13 38	14 05				14 38	15 05	
Redcar East	d		10 41	11 08			11 41	12 07			12 40	13 08				13 41	14 08				14 41	15 08	
Redcar Central	d		10 44	11 11			11 45	12 10			12 43	13 11				13 44	14 11				14 44	15 11	
British Steel Redcar §	d																						
South Bank	d																						
Middlesbrough	a		10 54	11 21			11 55	12 21			12 54	13 21				13 54	14 21				14 54	15 21	
	d	10 50	10 55	11 22	11 32	11 50	11 56	12 22	12 32	12 50	12 55	13 22	13 32		13 50	13 55	14 22	14 32	14 50	14 50	14 55	15 22	15 32
Thornaby	d	10a55	11 00	11 27	11 36	11a55	12 01	12 27	12 37	12a55	13 00	13 27	13 37		13a55	14 00	14 27	14 37	14a55	14a55	15 00	15 27	15 37
London Kings Cross 15 ⊖26	d													11 23									
Eaglescliffe	a		11 05	11 32			12 06	12 32			13 05	13 32		14 04		14 05	14 32				15 05	15 32	
	d		11 06	11 33			12 06	12 33			13 06	13 33		14 05		14 06	14 33				15 06	15 33	
Allens West	d		11 08	11 35			12 09	12 35			13 08	13 35				14 08	14 35				15 08	15 35	
Teesside Airport	d																						
Dinsdale	d			11 42				12 42				13 42					14 42					15 42	
Darlington 7	26 a		11 23	11 52			12 24	12 54			13 23	13 52				14 23	14 52				15 23	15 54	
	d							12 54									14 54					15 54	
North Road	d							12 57									14 57					15 57	
Heighington	d							13 05									15 05					16 05	
Newton Aycliffe	d							13 08									15 08					16 08	
Shildon	d							13 13									15 13					16 13	
Bishop Auckland	a							13 20									15 20					16 20	
Stockton	d				11 42				12 42				13 43					14 43					15 43
Billingham	d				11 50				12 50				13 50					14 50					15 50
Seaton Carew	d				11 56				12 56				13 56					14 56					15 56
Hartlepool	d				12 02				13 02				14 02	14 24				15 02					16 02
Seaham	d				12 17				13 17				14 17					15 17					16 17
Sunderland ⇌	a				12 27				13 28				14 27	14 50				15 27					16 27
	d				12 30				13 30				14 30					15 30					16 30
Heworth ⇌	d				12 42				13 42				14 42					15 42					16 42
Newcastle 8	26 ⇌ a				12 52				13 51				14 51					15 51					16 51
Metrocentre	48 a				13 01				14 01				15 01					16 01					17 01
Hexham	48 a				13 38				14 38				15 39					16 38					17 39

§ For authorised access only to BSC Redcar

Table 44

Mondays to Fridays
from 1 October

Saltburn and Middlesbrough - Darlington, Bishop Auckland, Sunderland and Newcastle

Network Diagram - see first Page of Table 44

		TP	NT	NT	NT	TP	NT	NT	NT	TP	NT	NT	NT	NT	TP	NT	NT	GC	NT	NT	TP	TP
		◇1 ✠				◇1 ✠				◇1					◇1			■ 1 ⊏			◇1	◇1
Saltburn	d		15 31	15 58			16 27	16 58			17 31	17 58				18 31	18 58			19 31		
Marske	d		15 35	16 02			16 31	17 02			17 35	18 02				18 35	19 02			19 35		
Longbeck	d		15 38	16 05			16 34	17 05			17 38	18 05				18 38	19 05			19 38		
Redcar East	d		15 41	16 08			16 37	17 08			17 41	18 08				18 41	19 08			19 41		
Redcar Central	d		15 44	16 11			16 40	17 11			17 44	18 11				18 44	19 11			19 44		
British Steel Redcar §	d						16 43															
South Bank	d						16 49	17 18														
Middlesbrough	a		15 54	16 21			16 54	17 23			17 54	18 21				18 54	19 21			19 54		
	d	15 50	15 55	16 22	16 32	16 50	16 58	17 24	17 39	17 50	17 55	18 22	18 32	18 45	18 50	18 55	19 22		19 40	19 55	20 04	20 50
Thornaby	d	15a55	16 00	16 28	16 37	16a55	17 03	17 29	17 44	17a55	18 00	18 27	18 37	18 50	18a55	19 00	19 27		19 45	20 00	20 09	20a55
London Kings Cross 15 ⊖26	d																	16 48				
Eaglescliffe	a		16 05	16 35			17 08	17 34			18 05	18 32				19 05	19 32	19 33		20 05		
	d		16 06	16 35			17 08	17 35			18 06	18 33				19 06	19 33	19 34		20 06		
Allens West	d		16 08	16 38			17 11	17 37			18 08	18 35				19 08	19 35			20 08		
Teesside Airport	d																					
Dinsdale	d		16 15	16 44			17 17	17 44			18 15					19 15				20 15		
Darlington 7	26 a		16 23	16 52			17 26	17 53			18 23	18 50		19 12		19 23	19 50			20 23	20 29	
	d						17 28					18 54								20 32		
North Road	d						17 31					18 57								20 35		
Heighington	d						17 39					19 05								20 43		
Newton Aycliffe	d						17 42					19 08								20 46		
Shildon	d						17 47					19 13								20 51		
Bishop Auckland	a						17 54					19 20								20 58		
Stockton	d				16 43				17 50				18 43						19 51			
Billingham	d				16 50				17 57				18 50						19 58			
Seaton Carew	d				16 56				18 03				18 56						20 04			
Hartlepool	d				17 02				18 09				19 02					19 53	20 10			
Seaham	d				17 17				18 24				19 17						20 27			
Sunderland ⇌	a				17 28				18 38				19 27					20 21	20 37			
	d				17 30				18 42				19 29						20 38			
Heworth ⇌	d				17 42				18 55				19 42						20 53			
Newcastle 8	26 ⇌ a				17 51				19 05				19 51						21 02			
Metrocentre	48 a				18 01								20 01						21 11			
Hexham	48 a				18 32																	

		NT	NT	GC	TP	NT	NT
				■ 1 ⊏	◇1		
Saltburn	d	20 32				21 30	22 36
Marske	d	20 36				21 34	22 40
Longbeck	d	20 39				21 37	22 43
Redcar East	d	20 42				21 40	22 46
Redcar Central	d	20 45				21 43	22 49
British Steel Redcar §	d						
South Bank	d						
Middlesbrough	a	20 55				21 53	22 59
	d	20 56	21 01		21 50	21 54	23 00
Thornaby	d	21 01	21 06		21 55	21 59	23 05
London Kings Cross 15 ⊖26	d			19 18			
Eaglescliffe	a	21 06		22 04		22 04	23 10
	d	21 07		22 05		22 05	23 11
Allens West	d	21 09				22 07	23 13
Teesside Airport	d						
Dinsdale	d	21 16				22 14	23 20
Darlington 7	26 a	21 24			22 15	22 25	23 30
	d						
North Road	d						
Heighington	d						
Newton Aycliffe	d						
Shildon	d						
Bishop Auckland	a						
Stockton	d		21 12				
Billingham	d		21 19				
Seaton Carew	d		21 25				
Hartlepool	d		21 31	22 25			
Seaham	d		21 46				
Sunderland ⇌	a		21 57	22 51			
	d		21 58				
Heworth ⇌	d		22 09				
Newcastle 8	26 ⇌ a		22 19				
Metrocentre	48 a						
Hexham	48 a						

§ For authorised access only to BSC Redcar

Saltburn and Middlesbrough - Darlington, Bishop Auckland, Sunderland and Newcastle

Network Diagram - see first Page of Table 44

		NT	TP	NT	NT	NT	NT	TP	NT	NT	NT	NT	NT	NT	NT	TP	NT	NT	TP	NT	NT	NT	GC
			◇1					◇1								◇1			◇1				1
Saltburn	d					06 22					07 12	07 26	07 55				08 31			09 31	09 58		
Marske	d					06 26					07 16	07 30	07 59				08 35			09 35	10 02		
Longbeck	d					06 29					07 19	07 33	08 02				08 38			09 38	10 05		
Redcar East	d					06 32					07 22	07 36	08 05				08 41			09 41	10 08		
Redcar Central	d					06 35					07 25	07 39	08 08				08 44			09 44	10 11		
British Steel Redcar §	d																						
South Bank	d											07 46					08 51						
Middlesbrough	a					06 45					07 36	07 51	08 18				08 56			09 55	10 22		
	d	05 45	05 55			06 47	06 51	07 12	07 32		07 37	07 52	08 19	08 32	08 44	08 50	09 08	09 32	09 50	09 56	10 22	10 32	
Thornaby	d	05 50	06a00			06 52	06 56	07a17	07 37		07 42	07 57	08 24	08 37	08 50	08a55	09 13	09 37	09a55	10 01	10 27	10 37	
London Kings Cross ⊖26	d																						07 48
Eaglescliffe	a	05 55				06 57					07 47	08 02	08 29		08 55		09 21			10 06	10 32		10 37
	d	05 55				06 57					07 47	08 03	08 30		08 55		09 21			10 07	10 33		10 38
Allens West	d	05 58				07 00					07 50	08 05	08 32		08 58		09 24			10 09	10 35		
Teesside Airport	d																						
Dinsdale	d	06 04				07 06					07 56	08 12	08 39		09 04		09 30				10 42		
Darlington 7 26	a	06 13				07 20					08 05	08 22	08 50		09 13		09 42			10 23	10 52		
	d			06 47		07 21				07 48		08 22	08 52								10 54		
North Road	d			06 50						07 51			08 55								10 57		
Heighington	d			06 58						07 59			09 03								11 05		
Newton Aycliffe	d			07 01						08 03			09 07								11 08		
Shildon	d			07 06						08 07			09 11								11 13		
Bishop Auckland	a			07 14						08 15			09 18								11 20		
Stockton	d						07 02		07 43					08 43				09 43				10 43	
Billingham	d						07 09		07 50					08 50				09 50				10 50	
Seaton Carew	d						07 15		07 56					08 56				09 56				10 56	
Hartlepool	d				07 03		07 21		08 02					09 02				10 02				11 02	11 14
Seaham	d				07 18		07 36		08 17					09 17				10 17				11 17	
Sunderland ⇌	a				07 28		07 50		08 28					09 27				10 28				11 27	11 40
	d				07 30		07 55		08 30					09 30				10 30				11 30	
Heworth ⇌	d				07 41		08 07		08 42					09 42				10 42				11 42	
Newcastle 8 26 ⇌	a				07 51	08 05	08 18		08 52			09 01		09 51				10 51				11 51	
Metrocentre 48	a				08 00									10 02				11 01				12 01	
Hexham 48	a				08 38									10 36				11 38				12 38	

		TP	NT	NT	NT	TP	NT	NT	NT	TP	NT	NT	NT	GC	TP	NT	NT	NT	TP	NT	NT	NT	TP
		◇1				◇1				◇1				1	◇1				◇1				◇1
Saltburn	d		10 31	10 58			11 31	11 57			12 30	12 58				13 31	13 57			14 31	14 58		
Marske	d		10 35	11 02			11 35	12 01			12 34	13 02				13 35	14 02			14 35	15 02		
Longbeck	d		10 38	11 05			11 38	12 04			12 37	13 05				13 38	14 05			14 38	15 05		
Redcar East	d		10 41	11 08			11 41	12 07			12 40	13 08				13 41	14 08			14 41	15 08		
Redcar Central	d		10 44	11 11			11 44	12 10			12 43	13 11				13 44	14 11			14 44	15 11		
British Steel Redcar §	d																						
South Bank	d																						
Middlesbrough	a		10 54	11 21			11 54	12 21			12 54	13 21				13 54	14 21			14 54	15 21		
	d	10 50	10 55	11 22	11 32	11 50	11 55	12 22	12 32	12 50	12 55	13 22	13 32		13 50	13 55	14 22	14 32	14 50	14 55	15 22	15 32	15 50
Thornaby	d	10a55	11 00	11 27	11 36	11a55	12 00	12 27	12 37	12a55	13 00	13 27	13 37		13a55	14 00	14 27	14 37	14a55	15 00	15 27	15 37	15a55
London Kings Cross ⊖26	d													11 20									
Eaglescliffe	a		11 05	11 32			12 05	12 32			13 08	13 32		13 58		14 05	14 32			15 05	15 32		
	d		11 06	11 33			12 06	12 33			13 09	13 33		13 59		14 06	14 33			15 06	15 33		
Allens West	d		11 08	11 35			12 08	12 35			13 11	13 35				14 08	14 35			15 08	15 35		
Teesside Airport	d																						
Dinsdale	d			11 42				12 42				13 42					14 42				15 42		
Darlington 7 26	a		11 23	11 52			12 23	12 54			13 26	13 52				14 23	14 52			15 23	15 54		
	d							12 54									14 54				15 54		
North Road	d							12 57									14 57				15 57		
Heighington	d							13 05									15 05				16 05		
Newton Aycliffe	d							13 08									15 08				16 08		
Shildon	d							13 13									15 13				16 13		
Bishop Auckland	a							13 20									15 20				16 20		
Stockton	d				11 42				12 42				13 43					14 43				15 43	
Billingham	d				11 50				12 50				13 50					14 50				15 50	
Seaton Carew	d				11 56				12 56				13 56					14 56				15 56	
Hartlepool	d				12 02				13 02				14 02	14 22				15 02				16 02	
Seaham	d				12 17				13 17				14 17					15 17				16 17	
Sunderland ⇌	a				12 27				13 28				14 27	14 50				15 27				16 27	
	d				12 30				13 30				14 30					15 30				16 30	
Heworth ⇌	d				12 42				13 42				14 42					15 42				16 42	
Newcastle 8 26 ⇌	a				12 52				13 51				14 51					15 51				16 51	
Metrocentre 48	a				13 01				14 01				15 02					16 01				17 01	
Hexham 48	a				13 38				14 38				15 39					16 38				17 39	

§ For authorised access only to BSC Redcar

Saltburn and Middlesbrough - Darlington, Bishop Auckland, Sunderland and Newcastle

Network Diagram - see first Page of Table 44

		NT	NT	NT	TP	NT	NT	NT	TP	NT	NT	NT	TP	NT	GC	NT	NT	NT	TP	NT	TP	NT
					◇1				◇1				◇1		1				◇1		◇1	
Saltburn	d	15 31	15 58			16 27	16 58			17 31	17 58			18 31		18 58		19 31				20 32
Marske	d	15 35	16 02			16 31	17 02			17 35	18 02			18 35		19 02		19 35				20 36
Longbeck	d	15 38	16 05			16 34	17 05			17 38	18 05			18 38		19 05		19 38				20 39
Redcar East	d	15 41	16 08			16 37	17 08			17 41	18 08			18 41		19 08		19 41				20 42
Redcar Central	d	15 44	16 11			16 40	17 11			17 44	18 11			18 44		19 11		19 44				20 45
British Steel Redcar §	d					16 43																
South Bank	d					16 49	17 18															
Middlesbrough	a	15 54	16 21			16 54	17 23			17 54	18 21			18 54		19 21		19 54				20 55
	d	15 55	16 22	16 32	16 50	16 57	17 24	17 39	17 50	17 55	18 22	18 32	18 50	18 55		19 22	19 40	19 57	20 10	20 45	20 50	20 56
Thornaby	d	16 00	16 27	16 37	16a55	17 02	17 29	17 44	17a55	18 00	18 27	18 37	18a55	19 00		19 27	19 45	20 02	20a15	20 50	20a55	21 01
London Kings Cross ⊖26	d														16 48							
Eaglescliffe	a	16 05	16 32			17 07	17 34			18 05	18 32			19 05	19 28	19 32		20 07				21 06
	d	16 06	16 33			17 07	17 35			18 06	18 33			19 06	19 29	19 33		20 07				21 07
Allens West	d	16 08	16 35			17 10	17 37			18 08	18 35			19 08		19 35		20 10				21 09
Teesside Airport	d																					
Dinsdale	d	16 15	16 42			17 16	17 44			18 15				19 15				20 16				21 16
Darlington 7 26	a	16 23	16 52			17 26	17 53			18 24	18 50			19 23		19 52		20 27				21 24
	d					17 28					18 54							20 32				
North Road	d					17 31					18 57							20 35				
Heighington	d					17 39					19 05							20 43				
Newton Aycliffe	d					17 42					19 08							20 46				
Shildon	d					17 47					19 13							20 51				
Bishop Auckland	a					17 54					19 21							20 58				
Stockton	d			16 43				17 50				18 43					19 51			20 56		
Billingham	d			16 50				17 57				18 50					19 58			21 03		
Seaton Carew	d			16 56				18 03				18 56					20 04			21 09		
Hartlepool	d			17 02				18 09				19 02			19 49		20 10			21 15		
Seaham	d			17 17				18 24				19 17					20 27			21 30		
Sunderland ⇌	a			17 27				18 38				19 27			20 21		20 37			21 40		
	d			17 30				18 42				19 29					20 38			21 43		
Heworth ⇌	d			17 42				18 55				19 42					20 53			21 54		
Newcastle 8 26 ⇌	a			17 51				19 04				19 51					21 04			22 04		
Metrocentre 48	a			18 01								20 01										
Hexham 48	a			18 32																		

		GC	TP	NT	NT
		1	◇1		
Saltburn	d			21 30	22 36
Marske	d			21 34	22 40
Longbeck	d			21 37	22 43
Redcar East	d			21 40	22 46
Redcar Central	d			21 43	22 49
British Steel Redcar §	d				
South Bank	d				
Middlesbrough	a			21 53	22 59
	d		21 50	21 54	23 00
Thornaby	d		21 55	21 59	23 05
London Kings Cross ⊖26	d	19 07			
Eaglescliffe	a	21 40		22 04	23 10
	d	21 41		22 05	23 11
Allens West	d			22 07	23 13
Teesside Airport	d				
Dinsdale	d			22 14	23 20
Darlington 7 26	a		22 15	22 24	23 30
	d				
North Road	d				
Heighington	d				
Newton Aycliffe	d				
Shildon	d				
Bishop Auckland	a				
Stockton	d				
Billingham	d				
Seaton Carew	d				
Hartlepool	d	22 01			
Seaham	d				
Sunderland ⇌	a	22 36			
	d				
Heworth ⇌	d				
Newcastle 8 26 ⇌	a				
Metrocentre 48	a				
Hexham 48	a				

§ For authorised access only to BSC Redcar

Saltburn and Middlesbrough - Darlington, Bishop Auckland, Sunderland and Newcastle

Network Diagram - see first Page of Table 44

	NT	TP	NT	NT	NT	NT	TP	NT	NT	NT	NT	NT	NT	NT	TP	NT	NT	TP	NT	NT	NT	GC
		◇1					◇1 🛒								◇1 🛒			◇1 🛒				■ 1 ☕
Saltburn d					06 22					07 12	07 26	07 55				08 31			09 31	09 58		
Marske d					06 26					07 16	07 30	07 59				08 35			09 35	10 02		
Longbeck d					06 29					07 19	07 33	08 02				08 38			09 38	10 05		
Redcar East d					06 32					07 22	07 36	08 05				08 41			09 41	10 08		
Redcar Central d					06 35					07 25	07 39	08 08				08 44			09 44	10 11		
British Steel Redcar § d																						
South Bank d											07 46					08 51						
Middlesbrough a					06 45					07 36	07 51	08 18				08 56			09 55	10 22		
d	05 45	05 55			06 47	06 51	07 12	07 32		07 37	07 52	08 19	08 32	08 44	08 50	09 08	09 32	09 50	09 56	10 22	10 32	
Thornaby d	05 50	06a00			06 52	06 56	07a17	07 37		07 42	07 57	08 24	08 37	08 50	08a55	09 13	09 37	09a55	10 01	10 27	10 37	
London Kings Cross 15 ⊖26 d																						07 48
Eaglescliffe a	05 55				06 57					07 47	08 02	08 29		08 55		09 21			10 06	10 32		10 37
d	05 55				06 57					07 47	08 03	08 30		08 55		09 21			10 07	10 33		10 38
Allens West d	05 58				07 00					07 50	08 05	08 32		08 58		09 24			10 09	10 35		
Teesside Airport d																						
Dinsdale d	06 04				07 06					07 56	08 12	08 39		09 04		09 30				10 42		
Darlington 7 26 a	06 13				07 20					08 05	08 22	08 50		09 13		09 42			10 23	10 52		
d			06 47		07 21				07 48		08 22	08 52								10 54		
North Road d			06 50						07 51			08 55								10 57		
Heighington d			06 58						07 59			09 03								11 05		
Newton Aycliffe d			07 01						08 03			09 07								11 08		
Shildon d			07 06						08 07			09 11								11 13		
Bishop Auckland a			07 14						08 15			09 18								11 20		
Stockton d						07 02		07 43					08 43				09 43				10 43	
Billingham d						07 09		07 50					08 50				09 50				10 50	
Seaton Carew d						07 15		07 56					08 56				09 56				10 56	
Hartlepool d				07 03		07 21		08 02					09 02				10 02				11 02	11 14
Seaham d				07 18		07 36		08 17					09 16				10 17				11 17	
Sunderland a				07 28		07 50		08 28					09 27				10 28				11 27	11 40
d				07 30		07 55		08 30					09 30				10 30				11 30	
Heworth d				07 41		08 07		08 42					09 42				10 42				11 42	
Newcastle 8 26 a				07 51	08 05	08 18		08 52			09 01		09 51				10 51				11 51	
Metrocentre 48 a				08 00									10 02				11 01				12 01	
Hexham 48 a				08 38									10 36				11 38				12 38	

	TP	NT	NT	NT	TP	NT	NT	NT	TP	NT	NT	NT	GC	TP	NT	NT	NT	TP	NT	NT	NT	TP
	◇1 🛒				◇1 🛒				◇1 🛒				■ 1 ☕	◇1 🛒				◇1 🛒				◇1 🛒
Saltburn d		10 31	10 58			11 31	11 57			12 30	12 58				13 31	13 57			14 31	14 58		
Marske d		10 35	11 02			11 35	12 01			12 34	13 02				13 35	14 02			14 35	15 02		
Longbeck d		10 38	11 05			11 38	12 04			12 37	13 05				13 38	14 05			14 38	15 05		
Redcar East d		10 41	11 08			11 41	12 07			12 40	13 08				13 41	14 08			14 41	15 08		
Redcar Central d		10 44	11 11			11 44	12 10			12 43	13 11				13 44	14 11			14 44	15 11		
British Steel Redcar § d																						
South Bank d																						
Middlesbrough a		10 54	11 21			11 54	12 21			12 54	13 21				13 54	14 21			14 54	15 21		
d	10 50	10 55	11 22	11 32	11 50	11 55	12 22	12 32	12 50	12 55	13 22	13 32		13 50	13 55	14 22	14 32	14 50	14 55	15 22	15 32	15 50
Thornaby d	10a55	11 00	11 27	11 36	11a55	12 00	12 27	12 37	12a55	13 00	13 27	13 37		13a55	14 00	14 27	14 37	14a55	15 00	15 27	15 37	15a55
London Kings Cross 15 ⊖26 d													11 20									
Eaglescliffe a		11 05	11 32			12 05	12 32			13 08	13 32		13 58		14 05	14 32			15 05	15 32		
d		11 06	11 33			12 06	12 33			13 09	13 33		13 59		14 06	14 33			15 06	15 33		
Allens West d		11 08	11 35			12 08	12 35			13 11	13 35				14 08	14 35			15 08	15 35		
Teesside Airport d																						
Dinsdale d			11 42				12 42				13 42					14 42				15 42		
Darlington 7 26 a		11 23	11 52			12 23	12 54			13 26	13 52				14 23	14 52			15 23	15 54		
d							12 54									14 54				15 54		
North Road d							12 57									14 57				15 57		
Heighington d							13 05									15 05				16 05		
Newton Aycliffe d							13 08									15 08				16 08		
Shildon d							13 13									15 13				16 13		
Bishop Auckland a							13 20									15 20				16 20		
Stockton d				11 42				12 42				13 43					14 43				15 43	
Billingham d				11 50				12 50				13 50					14 50				15 50	
Seaton Carew d				11 56				12 56				13 56					14 56				15 56	
Hartlepool d				12 02				13 02				14 02	14 22				15 02				16 02	
Seaham d				12 17				13 17				14 17					15 17				16 17	
Sunderland a				12 27				13 28				14 27	14 50				15 27				16 27	
d				12 30				13 30				14 30					15 30				16 30	
Heworth d				12 42				13 42				14 42					15 42				16 42	
Newcastle 8 26 a				12 52				13 51				14 51					15 51				16 51	
Metrocentre 48 a				13 01				14 01				15 02					16 01				17 01	
Hexham 48 a				13 38				14 38				15 37					16 38				17 39	

§ For authorised access only to BSC Redcar

Table 44

Saturdays from 6 October

Saltburn and Middlesbrough - Darlington, Bishop Auckland, Sunderland and Newcastle

Network Diagram - see first Page of Table 44

	NT	NT	NT	TP	NT	NT	NT	TP	NT	NT	NT	TP	NT	GC	NT	NT	NT	TP	NT	TP	NT
				◇1				◇1				◇1		■ 1 ☕				◇1		◇1	
Saltburn d	15 31	15 58			16 27	16 58			17 31	17 58			18 31		18 58		19 31				20 32
Marske d	15 35	16 02			16 31	17 02			17 35	18 02			18 35		19 02		19 35				20 36
Longbeck d	15 38	16 05			16 34	17 05			17 38	18 05			18 38		19 05		19 38				20 39
Redcar East d	15 41	16 08			16 37	17 08			17 41	18 08			18 41		19 08		19 41				20 42
Redcar Central d	15 44	16 11			16 40	17 11			17 44	18 11			18 44		19 11		19 44				20 45
British Steel Redcar § d					16 43																
South Bank d					16 49	17 18															
Middlesbrough a	15 54	16 21			16 54	17 23			17 54	18 21			18 54		19 21		19 54				20 55
d	15 55	16 22	16 32	16 50	16 57	17 24	17 39	17 50	17 55	18 22	18 32	18 50	18 55		19 22	19 40	19 57	20 10	20 45	20 50	20 56
Thornaby d	16 00	16 27	16 37	16a55	17 02	17 29	17 44	17a55	18 00	18 27	18 37	18a55	19 00		19 27	19 45	20 02	20a15	20 50	20a55	21 01
London Kings Cross 15 ⊖26 d														16 48							
Eaglescliffe a	16 05	16 32			17 07	17 34			18 05	18 32			19 05	19 28	19 32		20 07				21 06
d	16 06	16 33			17 07	17 35			18 06	18 33			19 06	19 29	19 33		20 07				21 07
Allens West d	16 08	16 35			17 10	17 37			18 08	18 35			19 08		19 35		20 10				21 09
Teesside Airport d																					
Dinsdale d	16 15	16 42			17 16	17 44			18 15				19 15				20 16				21 16
Darlington 7 26 a	16 23	16 52			17 26	17 53			18 24	18 50			19 23		19 52		20 27				21 24
d					17 28					18 54							20 32				
North Road d					17 31					18 57							20 35				
Heighington d					17 39					19 05							20 43				
Newton Aycliffe d					17 42					19 08							20 46				
Shildon d					17 47					19 13							20 51				
Bishop Auckland a					17 54					19 21							20 58				
Stockton d			16 43				17 50				18 43					19 51			20 56		
Billingham d			16 50				17 57				18 50					19 58			21 03		
Seaton Carew d			16 56				18 03				18 56					20 04			21 09		
Hartlepool d			17 02				18 09				19 02			19 49		20 10			21 15		
Seaham d			17 17				18 24				19 17					20 27			21 30		
Sunderland a			17 28				18 38				19 27			20 21		20 37			21 40		
d			17 30				18 42				19 29					20 38			21 43		
Heworth d			17 42				18 55				19 42					20 53			21 54		
Newcastle 8 26 a			17 51				19 04				19 51					21 04			22 04		
Metrocentre 48 a			18 01								20 01										
Hexham 48 a			18 32																		

	GC	TP	NT	NT
	■ 1 ☕	◇1		
Saltburn d			21 30	22 36
Marske d			21 34	22 40
Longbeck d			21 37	22 43
Redcar East d			21 40	22 46
Redcar Central d			21 43	22 49
British Steel Redcar § d				
South Bank d				
Middlesbrough a			21 53	22 59
d		21 50	21 54	23 00
Thornaby d		21 55	21 59	23 05
London Kings Cross 15 ⊖26 d	19 07			
Eaglescliffe a	21 40		22 04	23 10
d	21 41		22 05	23 11
Allens West d			22 07	23 13
Teesside Airport d				
Dinsdale d			22 14	23 20
Darlington 7 26 a		22 15	22 24	23 30
d				
North Road d				
Heighington d				
Newton Aycliffe d				
Shildon d				
Bishop Auckland a				
Stockton d				
Billingham d				
Seaton Carew d				
Hartlepool d	22 01			
Seaham d				
Sunderland a	22 36			
d				
Heworth d				
Newcastle 8 26 a				
Metrocentre 48 a				
Hexham 48 a				

§ For authorised access only to BSC Redcar

Sundays
until 24 June

Saltburn and Middlesbrough - Darlington, Bishop Auckland, Sunderland and Newcastle

Network Diagram - see first Page of Table 44

	NT	NT	NT	NT	NT	NT	TP	NT	NT	NT	NT	GC	TP	NT	NT	NT	NT	TP	NT	NT	NT	NT
							◇1					1	◇1					◇1				
Saltburn d						09 44			10 44		11 44			12 44			13 44		14 44			15 44
Marske d						09 48			10 48		11 48			12 48			13 48		14 48			15 48
Longbeck d						09 51			10 51		11 51			12 51			13 51		14 51			15 51
Redcar East d						09 54			10 54		11 54			12 54			13 54		14 54			15 54
Redcar Central d						09 57			10 57		11 57			12 57			13 57		14 57			15 57
British Steel Redcar § d																						
South Bank d																						
Middlesbrough a						10 07			11 07		12 07			13 07			14 07		15 07			16 07
d		08 38	09 08		09 31	10 08	10 15		11 08	11 31	12 08		12 45	13 08		13 31	14 08	14 42	15 08		15 31	16 08
Thornaby d		08 43	09 13		09 36	10 13	10a20		11 13	11 36	12 13		12a50	13 13		13 36	14 13	14a47	15 13		15 36	16 13
London Kings Cross 15 ⊖26 d												09 48										
Eaglescliffe a		08 48	09 18			10 18			11 18		12 18	12 23		13 18			14 18		15 18			16 18
d		08 49	09 19			10 19		10 36	11 19		12 19	12 25		13 19			14 19		15 19			16 19
Allens West d		08 51	09 21			10 21			11 21		12 21			13 21			14 21		15 21			16 21
Teesside Airport d																						
Dinsdale d		08 58	09 28			10 28			11 28		12 28			13 28			14 28		15 28			16 28
Darlington 7 26 a		09 07	09 37			10 37			11 37		12 36			13 37			14 37		15 39			16 37
d	08 05		09 38						11 38								14 38					16 38
North Road d	08 08		09 41						11 41								14 41					16 41
Heighington d	08 16		09 49						11 49								14 49					16 49
Newton Aycliffe d	08 19		09 52						11 52								14 52					16 52
Shildon d	08 24		09 57						11 57								14 57					16 57
Bishop Auckland a	08 31		10 02						12 02								15 04					17 02
Stockton d					09 42			10 41		11 42						13 42					15 42	
Billingham d					09 49			10 49		11 49						13 49					15 49	
Seaton Carew d					09 55			10 55		11 55						13 55					15 55	
Hartlepool d					10 01			11 00		12 01		12 52				14 01					16 01	
Seaham d					10 16			11 16		12 16						14 16					16 16	
Sunderland a					10 26			11 26		12 26		13 21				14 26					16 26	
d				09 28	10 28			11 28		12 28					13 28	14 28				15 28	16 28	
Heworth d				09 39	10 38			11 38		12 38					13 39	14 39				15 39	16 39	
Newcastle 8 26 a				09 50	10 48			11 48		12 48					13 49	14 48				15 48	16 48	
Metrocentre 48 a				10 01	10 59			11 57		12 59					13 59	14 59				15 59	16 57	
Hexham 48 a																						

	NT	GC	TP	NT	NT	NT	NT	NT	TP	NT	NT	NT	GC	TP	NT	GC	NT	NT	TP	NT
		1	◇1						◇1				1	◇1		1			◇1	
Saltburn d				16 44			17 44			18 44					19 44		20 44	21 37		22 44
Marske d				16 48			17 48			18 48					19 48		20 48	21 41		22 48
Longbeck d				16 51			17 51			18 51					19 51		20 51	21 44		22 51
Redcar East d				16 54			17 54			18 54					19 54		20 54	21 47		22 54
Redcar Central d				16 57			17 57			18 57					19 57		20 57	21 50		22 57
British Steel Redcar § d																				
South Bank d																				
Middlesbrough a				17 07			18 07			19 07					20 11		21 07	22 00		23 07
d			16 42	17 08	17 22	17 45	18 08	18 40	18 45	19 08		19 31		20 06	20 12		21 08	22 02	22 06	23 08
Thornaby d			16a47	17 13	17 27	17 50	18 13	18 45	18a50	19 13		19 36		20a11	20 17		21 13	22 07	22a11	23 13
London Kings Cross 15 ⊖26 d		13 48											16 48			18 23				
Eaglescliffe a		16 33		17 18	17 32		18 18	18 50		19 18			19 35		20 22	21 01	21 18	22 12		23 18
d	16 26	16 34		17 19	17 32		18 19	18 50		19 19			19 39		20 22	21 03	21 19	22 12		23 18
Allens West d				17 21	17 35		18 21	18 53		19 21					20 25		21 21	22 15		23 21
Teesside Airport d																				
Dinsdale d				17 28	17 41		18 28	19 01		19 28					20 31		21 28	22 21		23 27
Darlington 7 26 a				17 37	17 52		18 37	19 14		19 37					20 43		21 38	22 32		23 38
d					17 54			19 15												
North Road d					17 57			19 18												
Heighington d					18 05			19 27												
Newton Aycliffe d					18 08			19 30												
Shildon d					18 13			19 34												
Bishop Auckland a					18 19			19 42												
Stockton d	16 32					17 56						19 42								
Billingham d	16 39					18 03						19 49								
Seaton Carew d	16 45					18 09						19 55								
Hartlepool d	16 51	17 01				18 15						20 01	20 13			21 23				
Seaham d	17 07					18 30						20 16								
Sunderland a	17 22	17 27				18 41						20 26	20 39			21 51				
d	17 26					18 43					19 28	20 29								
Heworth d	17 39					18 54					19 39	20 40								
Newcastle 8 26 a	17 48					19 05					19 52	20 47								
Metrocentre 48 a	17 59																			
Hexham 48 a																				

§ For authorised access only to BSC Redcar

Sundays
1 July to 9 September

Saltburn and Middlesbrough - Darlington, Bishop Auckland, Sunderland and Newcastle

Network Diagram - see first Page of Table 44

	NT	NT	NT	NT	NT	NT	TP	NT	NT	NT	NT	GC	TP	NT	NT	NT	NT	TP	NT	NT	NT	NT
							◇1					1	◇1					◇1				
Saltburn d						09 44			10 44		11 44			12 44			13 44		14 44			15 44
Marske d						09 48			10 48		11 48			12 48			13 48		14 48			15 48
Longbeck d						09 51			10 51		11 51			12 51			13 51		14 51			15 51
Redcar East d						09 54			10 54		11 54			12 54			13 54		14 54			15 54
Redcar Central d						09 57			10 57		11 57			12 57			13 57		14 57			15 57
British Steel Redcar § d																						
South Bank d																						
Middlesbrough a						10 07			11 07		12 07			13 07			14 07		15 07			16 07
d		08 38	09 08		09 31	10 08	10 15		11 08	11 31	12 08		12 45	13 08		13 31	14 08	14 42	15 08		15 31	16 08
Thornaby d		08 43	09 13		09 36	10 13	10a20		11 13	11 36	12 13		12a50	13 13		13 36	14 13	14a47	15 13		15 36	16 13
London Kings Cross 15 ⊖26 d												09 48										
Eaglescliffe a		08 48	09 18			10 18			11 18		12 18	12 23		13 18			14 18		15 18			16 18
d		08 49	09 19			10 19		10 36	11 19		12 19	12 25		13 19			14 19		15 19			16 19
Allens West d		08 51	09 21			10 21			11 21		12 21			13 21			14 21		15 21			16 21
Teesside Airport d																						
Dinsdale d		08 58	09 28			10 28			11 28		12 28			13 28			14 28		15 28			16 28
Darlington 7 26 a		09 07	09 37			10 37			11 37		12 36			13 37			14 37		15 39			16 37
d	08 05		09 38						11 38								14 38					16 38
North Road d	08 08		09 41						11 41								14 41					16 41
Heighington d	08 16		09 49						11 49								14 49					16 49
Newton Aycliffe d	08 19		09 52						11 52								14 52					16 52
Shildon d	08 24		09 57						11 57								14 57					16 57
Bishop Auckland a	08 31		10 02						12 02								15 04					17 02
Stockton d					09 42			10 41		11 42						13 42					15 42	
Billingham d					09 49			10 49		11 49						13 49					15 49	
Seaton Carew d					09 55			10 55		11 55						13 55					15 55	
Hartlepool d					10 01			11 00		12 01		12 52				14 01					16 01	
Seaham d					10 16			11 16		12 16						14 16					16 16	
Sunderland a					10 26			11 26		12 26		13 21				14 26					16 26	
d				09 28	10 28			11 28		12 28					13 28	14 28				15 28	16 28	
Heworth d				09 39	10 38			11 38		12 38					13 39	14 39				15 39	16 39	
Newcastle 8 26 a				09 50	10 48			11 48		12 48					13 49	14 48				15 48	16 48	
Metrocentre 48 a				10 01	10 59			11 57		12 59					13 59	14 59				15 59	16 57	
Hexham 48 a																						

	NT	GC	TP	NT	NT	NT	NT	NT	TP	NT	NT	NT	GC	TP	NT	GC	NT	NT	TP	NT
		1	◇1						◇1				1	◇1		1			◇1	
Saltburn d				16 44			17 44			18 44					19 44		20 44	21 37		22 44
Marske d				16 48			17 48			18 48					19 48		20 48	21 41		22 48
Longbeck d				16 51			17 51			18 51					19 51		20 51	21 44		22 51
Redcar East d				16 54			17 54			18 54					19 54		20 54	21 47		22 54
Redcar Central d				16 57			17 57			18 57					19 57		20 57	21 50		22 57
British Steel Redcar § d																				
South Bank d																				
Middlesbrough a				17 07			18 07			19 07					20 11		21 07	22 00		23 07
d			16 42	17 08	17 22	17 45	18 08	18 40	18 45	19 08		19 31		20 06	20 12		21 08	22 02	22 06	23 08
Thornaby d			16a47	17 13	17 27	17 50	18 13	18 45	18a50	19 13		19 36		20a11	20 17		21 13	22 07	22a11	23 13
London Kings Cross 15 ⊖26 d		13 48											16 48			18 23				
Eaglescliffe a		16 33		17 18	17 32		18 18	18 50		19 18			19 35		20 22	21 01	21 18	22 12		23 18
d	16 26	16 34		17 19	17 32		18 19	18 50		19 19			19 39		20 22	21 03	21 19	22 12		23 18
Allens West d				17 21	17 35		18 21	18 53		19 21					20 25		21 21	22 15		23 21
Teesside Airport d																				
Dinsdale d				17 28	17 41		18 28	19 01		19 28					20 31		21 28	22 21		23 27
Darlington 7 26 a				17 37	17 52		18 37	19 14		19 37					20 43		21 38	22 32		23 38
d					17 54			19 15												
North Road d					17 57			19 18												
Heighington d					18 05			19 27												
Newton Aycliffe d					18 08			19 30												
Shildon d					18 13			19 34												
Bishop Auckland a					18 19			19 42												
Stockton d	16 32					17 56						19 42								
Billingham d	16 39					18 03						19 49								
Seaton Carew d	16 45					18 09						19 55								
Hartlepool d	16 51	17 01				18 15						20 01	20 13			21 23				
Seaham d	17 07					18 30						20 16								
Sunderland a	17 22	17 27				18 41						20 26	20 39			21 51				
d	17 26					18 43					19 28	20 29								
Heworth d	17 39					18 54					19 39	20 40								
Newcastle 8 26 a	17 48					19 05					19 52	20 47								
Metrocentre 48 a	17 59																			
Hexham 48 a																				

§ For authorised access only to BSC Redcar

Table 44

Sundays
16 September to 21 October

Saltburn and Middlesbrough - Darlington, Bishop Auckland, Sunderland and Newcastle

Network Diagram - see first Page of Table 44

	NT	NT	NT	NT	NT	TP	NT	NT	NT		NT	GC	TP	NT	NT	NT	NT	TP	NT		NT	NT	NT	NT
						◇1						■ 1 ⊡	◇1					◇1						
Saltburn d					09 44			10 44			11 44			12 44			13 44		14 44				15 44	
Marske d					09 48			10 48			11 48			12 48			13 48		14 48				15 48	
Longbeck d					09 51			10 51			11 51			12 51			13 51		14 51				15 51	
Redcar East d					09 54			10 54			11 54			12 54			13 54		14 54				15 54	
Redcar Central d					09 57			10 57			11 57			12 57			13 57		14 57				15 57	
British Steel Redcar § d																								
South Bank d																								
Middlesbrough a					10 07			11 07			12 07			13 07			14 07		15 07				16 07	
d	08 38	09 08		09 31	10 08	10 15		11 08	11 31		12 08		12 45	13 08		13 31	14 08	14 42	15 08			15 31	16 08	
Thornaby d	08 43	09 13		09 36	10 13	10a20		11 13	11 36		12 13		12a50	13 13		13 36	14 13	14a47	15 13			15 36	16 13	
London Kings Cross 15 ⊖26 d												09 48												
Eaglescliffe a	08 48	09 18			10 18			11 18			12 18	12 23		13 18			14 18		15 18				16 18	
d	08 49	09 19			10 19		10 36	11 19			12 19	12 25		13 19			14 19		15 19				16 19	16 26
Allens West d	08 51	09 21			10 21			11 21			12 21			13 21			14 21		15 21				16 21	
Teesside Airport d																								
Dinsdale d	08 58	09 28			10 28			11 28			12 28			13 28			14 28		15 28				16 28	
Darlington 7 26 a	09 07	09 37			10 37			11 37			12 36			13 37			14 37		15 39				16 37	
d		09 38						11 38									14 38						16 38	
North Road d		09 41						11 41									14 41						16 41	
Heighington d		09 49						11 49									14 49						16 49	
Newton Aycliffe d		09 52						11 52									14 52						16 52	
Shildon d		09 57						11 57									14 57						16 57	
Bishop Auckland a		10 02						12 02									15 04						17 02	
Stockton d				09 42			10 41		11 42							13 42						15 42		16 32
Billingham d				09 49			10 49		11 49							13 49						15 49		16 39
Seaton Carew d				09 55			10 55		11 55							13 55						15 55		16 45
Hartlepool d				10 01			11 00		12 01			12 52				14 01						16 01		16 51
Seaham d				10 16			11 16		12 16							14 16						16 16		17 07
Sunderland ⇌ a				10 26			11 26		12 26			13 21				14 26						16 26		17 22
d			09 28	10 28			11 28		12 28						13 28	14 28					15 28	16 28		17 26
Heworth ⇌ d			09 39	10 38			11 38		12 38						13 39	14 39					15 39	16 39		17 39
Newcastle 8 26 ⇌ a			09 50	10 48			11 48		12 48						13 49	14 48					15 48	16 48		17 48
Metrocentre 48 a			10 01	10 59			11 57		12 59						13 59	14 59					15 59	16 57		17 59
Hexham 48 a																								

	GC	TP	NT	NT	NT		TP	NT	NT	NT	GC	TP	NT	GC	NT		NT	TP	NT
	■ 1 ⊡	◇1					◇1				■ 1	◇1		■ 1 ⊡				◇1	
Saltburn d			16 44		17 44			18 44					19 44		20 44		21 37		22 44
Marske d			16 48		17 48			18 48					19 48		20 48		21 41		22 48
Longbeck d			16 51		17 51			18 51					19 51		20 51		21 44		22 51
Redcar East d			16 54		17 54			18 54					19 54		20 54		21 47		22 54
Redcar Central d			16 57		17 57			18 57					19 57		20 57		21 50		22 57
British Steel Redcar § d																			
South Bank d																			
Middlesbrough a			17 07		18 07			19 07					20 11		21 07		22 00		23 07
d		16 42	17 08	17 45	18 08		18 45	19 08		19 31		20 06	20 12		21 08		22 02	22 06	23 08
Thornaby d		16a47	17 13	17 50	18 13		18a50	19 13		19 36		20a11	20 17		21 13		22 07	22a11	23 13
London Kings Cross 15 ⊖26 d	13 48										16 48			18 23					
Eaglescliffe a	16 33		17 18		18 18			19 18			19 35		20 22	21 01	21 18		22 12		23 18
d	16 34		17 19		18 19			19 19			19 39		20 22	21 03	21 19		22 12		23 18
Allens West d			17 21		18 21			19 21					20 25		21 21		22 15		23 21
Teesside Airport d																			
Dinsdale d			17 28		18 28			19 28					20 31		21 28		22 21		23 27
Darlington 7 26 a			17 37		18 37			19 37					20 43		21 38		22 32		23 38
d					18 38														
North Road d					18 41														
Heighington d					18 49														
Newton Aycliffe d					18 52														
Shildon d					18 57														
Bishop Auckland a					19 02														
Stockton d				17 56						19 42									
Billingham d				18 03						19 49									
Seaton Carew d				18 09						19 55									
Hartlepool d	17 01			18 15						20 01	20 13			21 23					
Seaham d				18 30						20 16									
Sunderland ⇌ a	17 27			18 41						20 26	20 39			21 51					
d				18 43					19 28	20 29									
Heworth ⇌ d				18 54					19 39	20 40									
Newcastle 8 26 ⇌ a				19 05					19 52	20 47									
Metrocentre 48 a																			
Hexham 48 a																			

§ For authorised access only to BSC Redcar

Table 44

Sundays
from 28 October

Saltburn and Middlesbrough - Darlington, Bishop Auckland, Sunderland and Newcastle

Network Diagram - see first Page of Table 44

	NT	NT	NT	NT	NT	TP	NT	NT	NT		NT	GC	TP	NT	NT	NT	NT	TP	NT		NT	NT	NT	NT
						◇1						■ 1 ⊡	◇1					◇1						
Saltburn d					09 44			10 44			11 44			12 44			13 44		14 44				15 44	
Marske d					09 48			10 48			11 48			12 48			13 48		14 48				15 48	
Longbeck d					09 51			10 51			11 51			12 51			13 51		14 51				15 51	
Redcar East d					09 54			10 54			11 54			12 54			13 54		14 54				15 54	
Redcar Central d					09 57			10 57			11 57			12 57			13 57		14 57				15 57	
British Steel Redcar § d																								
South Bank d																								
Middlesbrough a					10 07			11 07			12 07			13 07			14 07		15 07				16 07	
d	08 38	09 08		09 31	10 08	10 15		11 08	11 31		12 08		12 45	13 08		13 31	14 08	14 42	15 08			15 31	16 08	
Thornaby d	08 43	09 13		09 36	10 13	10a20		11 13	11 36		12 13		12a50	13 13		13 36	14 13	14a47	15 13			15 36	16 13	
London Kings Cross 15 ⊖26 d												09 48												
Eaglescliffe a	08 48	09 18			10 18			11 18			12 18	12 23		13 18			14 18		15 18				16 18	
d	08 49	09 19			10 19		10 36	11 19			12 19	12 25		13 19			14 19		15 19				16 19	16 26
Allens West d	08 51	09 21			10 21			11 21			12 21			13 21			14 21		15 21				16 21	
Teesside Airport d																								
Dinsdale d	08 58	09 28			10 28			11 28			12 28			13 28			14 28		15 28				16 28	
Darlington 7 26 a	09 07	09 37			10 37			11 37			12 36			13 37			14 37		15 39				16 37	
d		09 38						11 38									14 38						16 38	
North Road d		09 41						11 41									14 41						16 41	
Heighington d		09 49						11 49									14 49						16 49	
Newton Aycliffe d		09 52						11 52									14 52						16 52	
Shildon d		09 57						11 57									14 57						16 57	
Bishop Auckland a		10 02						12 02									15 04						17 02	
Stockton d				09 42			10 41		11 42							13 42						15 42		16 32
Billingham d				09 49			10 49		11 49							13 49						15 49		16 39
Seaton Carew d				09 55			10 55		11 55							13 55						15 55		16 45
Hartlepool d				10 01			11 00		12 01			12 52				14 01						16 01		16 51
Seaham d				10 16			11 16		12 16							14 16						16 16		17 07
Sunderland ⇌ a				10 26			11 26		12 26			13 21				14 26						16 26		17 22
d			09 28	10 28			11 28		12 28						13 28	14 28					15 28	16 28		17 26
Heworth ⇌ d			09 39	10 38			11 38		12 38						13 39	14 39					15 39	16 39		17 39
Newcastle 8 26 ⇌ a			09 50	10 48			11 48		12 48						13 49	14 48					15 48	16 48		17 48
Metrocentre 48 a			10 01	10 59			11 57		12 59						13 59	14 59					15 59	16 57		17 59
Hexham 48 a																								

	GC	TP	NT	NT	NT		TP	NT	NT	NT	GC	TP	NT	GC	NT		NT	TP	NT
	■ 1 ⊡	◇1					◇1				■ 1	◇1		■ 1 ⊡				◇1	
Saltburn d			16 44		17 44			18 44					19 44		20 44		21 37		22 44
Marske d			16 48		17 48			18 48					19 48		20 48		21 41		22 48
Longbeck d			16 51		17 51			18 51					19 51		20 51		21 44		22 51
Redcar East d			16 54		17 54			18 54					19 54		20 54		21 47		22 54
Redcar Central d			16 57		17 57			18 57					19 57		20 57		21 50		22 57
British Steel Redcar § d																			
South Bank d																			
Middlesbrough a			17 07		18 07			19 07					20 11		21 07		22 00		23 07
d		16 42	17 08	17 45	18 08		18 45	19 08		19 31		20 06	20 12		21 08		22 02	22 06	23 08
Thornaby d		16a47	17 13	17 50	18 13		18a50	19 13		19 36		20a11	20 17		21 13		22 07	22a11	23 13
London Kings Cross 15 ⊖26 d	13 48										16 48			18 23					
Eaglescliffe a	16 33		17 18		18 18			19 18			19 35		20 22	21 01	21 18		22 12		23 18
d	16 34		17 19		18 19			19 19			19 39		20 22	21 03	21 19		22 12		23 18
Allens West d			17 21		18 21			19 21					20 25		21 21		22 15		23 21
Teesside Airport d																			
Dinsdale d			17 28		18 28			19 28					20 31		21 28		22 21		23 27
Darlington 7 26 a			17 37		18 37			19 37					20 43		21 38		22 32		23 38
d					18 38														
North Road d					18 41														
Heighington d					18 49														
Newton Aycliffe d					18 52														
Shildon d					18 57														
Bishop Auckland a					19 02														
Stockton d				17 56						19 42									
Billingham d				18 03						19 49									
Seaton Carew d				18 09						19 55									
Hartlepool d	17 01			18 15						20 01	20 13			21 23					
Seaham d				18 30						20 16									
Sunderland ⇌ a	17 27			18 41						20 26	20 39			21 51					
d				18 43					19 28	20 29									
Heworth ⇌ d				18 54					19 39	20 40									
Newcastle 8 26 ⇌ a				19 05					19 52	20 47									
Metrocentre 48 a																			
Hexham 48 a																			

§ For authorised access only to BSC Redcar

Middlesbrough and Pickering - Whitby

Network Diagram - see first Page of Table 44

Miles	Station		NT	NT	NT	NY A	NT	NT	NY A G	NT	NT	NT	NY B H	NY C H	NT	NT	NT
—	Newcastle 8 44	d			07 30			10 30			13 30	15 30				16 30	18 30
0	**Middlesbrough**	d	07 04	08 14	08 47		10 38	11 50		14 16	14 46	16 47			17 40	17b54	19 49
3	Marton	d	07 09	08 19	08 52		10 43	11 56		14 21	14 52	16 52			17 45	17 59	19 54
4	Gypsy Lane	d	07 12	08 23	08 55		10 46	12 00		14 24	14 55	16 55			17 48	18 02	19 57
4½	Nunthorpe	d	07 17	08a29	09a01		10 49	12a04		14 27	15a00	17a00			17 51	18a07	20a03
8½	Great Ayton	d	07 23				10 55			14 33					17 57		
11	Battersby	a	07 29				11 01			14 39					18 03		
—		d	07 36				11 05			14 43					18 07		
12¾	Kildale	d	07 41				11 10			14 48					18 12		
16¾	Commondale	d	07 48				11 17			14 55					18 19		
18½	Castleton Moor	d	07 52				11 20			14 58					18 22		
20	Danby	d	07 55				11 23			15 01					18 25		
23½	Lealholm	d	08 02				11 30			15 08					18 32		
25½	Glaisdale	a	08 07				11 34			15 12					18 36		
—		d	08 09				11 37			15 15					18 39		
27¼	Egton	d	08 13				11 40			15 18					18 42		
—	**Pickering** §	d				09 00			12 00				15c00	16 00			
—	Levisham §	d				09 19			12 20				15c20	16 20			
—	Goathland §	d				09 45			12 50				16 10	16 50			
28¾	Grosmont	d	08 17			10 10	11 44		13 10	15 22			16 35	17 10	18 46		
32	Sleights	d	08 26				11 53			15 31					18 55		
33½	Ruswarp	d	08 31				11 58			15 36					19 00		
35	**Whitby**	a	08 38			10 35	12 05		13 35	15 43			17 00	17 35	19 07		

Saturdays

Station		NT	NT	NT	NY D	NT	NT	NY D G	NT	NT	NT	NY E H	NY F H	NT	NT	NT
Newcastle 8 44	d			07 30			10 30			13 30	15 30				16 30	18 30
Middlesbrough	d	07 04	08 14	08 47		10 38	11 50		14 16	14 46	16 47			17 40	17 54	19 49
Marton	d	07 09	08 19	08 52		10 43	11 56		14 21	14 52	16 52			17 45	17 59	19 54
Gypsy Lane	d	07 12	08 23	08 55		10 46	12 00		14 24	14 55	16 55			17 48	18 02	19 57
Nunthorpe	d	07 17	08a27	08a59		10 49	12a04		14 27	15a00	16a59			17 51	18a05	20a03
Great Ayton	d	07 23				10 55			14 33					17 57		
Battersby	a	07 29				11 01			14 39					18 03		
	d	07 36				11 05			14 43					18 07		
Kildale	d	07 41				11 10			14 48					18 12		
Commondale	d	07 48				11 17			14 55					18 19		
Castleton Moor	d	07 52				11 20			14 58					18 22		
Danby	d	07 55				11 23			15 01					18 25		
Lealholm	d	08 02				11 30			15 08					18 32		
Glaisdale	a	08 07				11 34			15 12					18 36		
	d	08 09				11 37			15 15					18 39		
Egton	d	08 13				11 40			15 18					18 42		
Pickering §	d				09 00			12 00				15c00	16 00			
Levisham §	d				09 19			12 20				15c20	16 20			
Goathland §	d				09 45			12 50				16 10	16 50			
Grosmont	d	08 17			10 10	11 44		13 10	15 22			16 35	17 10	18 46		
Sleights	d	08 26				11 53			15 31					18 55		
Ruswarp	d	08 31				11 58			15 36					19 00		
Whitby	a	08 38			10 35	12 05		13 35	15 43			17 00	17 35	19 07		

Sundays
until 9 September

Station		NT	NT	NT	NT	NT
Newcastle 8 44	d			09 45		
Middlesbrough	d	08 47	09 48	11 06	14 17	15 25
Marton	d	08 52	09 53	11 12	14 23	15 30
Gypsy Lane	d	08 55	09 56	11 15	14 26	15 33
Nunthorpe	d	08 58	09 59	11 18	14 29	15 36
Great Ayton	d	09 04	10 05	11 24	14 35	15 42
Battersby	a	09 10	10 11	11 30	14 41	15 48
	d	09 14	10 15	11 34	14 45	15 52
Kildale	d	09 19	10 20	11 39	14 50	15 57
Commondale	d	09 26	10 27	11 46	14 57	16 04
Castleton Moor	d	09 29	10 30	11 49	15 00	16 07
Danby	d	09 32	10 33	11 52	15 03	16 10
Lealholm	d	09 39	10 40	11 59	15 10	16 17
Glaisdale	a	09 43	10 44	12 03	15 14	16 21
	d	09 46	10 50	12 06	15 17	16 26
Egton	d	09 49	10 53	12 09	15 20	16 29
Pickering §	d					
Levisham §	d					
Goathland §	d					
Grosmont	d	09 53	10 57	12 13	15 24	16 33
Sleights	d	10 02	11 06	12 22	15 33	16 42
Ruswarp	d	10 07	11 11	12 27	15 38	16 47
Whitby	a	10 17	11 21	12 37	15 48	16 56

§ North Yorkshire Moors Railway. For full service between Grosmont and Pickering please refer to separate publicity
A until 2 November
B until 20 July except 4 June until 8 June, and from 3 September until 2 November
C from 4 June until 8 June, and from 23 July until 31 August
D until 3 November
E until 21 July except 2 June and 9 June, and from 8 September until 3 Novemeber except 15 September, 29 September and 13 October
F 2 June, 9 June, 28 July until 1 September
G The Yorkshire Coast Express
H The Moors Explorer

For connections to Darlington please refer to Table 44

Sundays
from 16 September

Middlesbrough and Pickering - Whitby

Network Diagram - see first Page of Table 44

Station		NY A	NY A G	NY B H	NY C H
Newcastle 8 44	d				
Middlesbrough	d				
Marton	d				
Gypsy Lane	d				
Nunthorpe	d				
Great Ayton	d				
Battersby	a				
	d				
Kildale	d				
Commondale	d				
Castleton Moor	d				
Danby	d				
Lealholm	d				
Glaisdale	a				
	d				
Egton	d				
Pickering §	d	09 00	12 00	15c00	16 00
Levisham §	d	09 19	12 20	15c20	16 20
Goathland §	d	09 48	12 50	16 10	16 50
Grosmont	d	10 10	13 10	16 35	17 10
Sleights	d				
Ruswarp	d				
Whitby	a	10 35	13 35	17 00	17 35

§ North Yorkshire Moors Railway. For full service between Grosmont and Pickering please refer to separate publicity
A until 4 November
B from 23 September until 4 November except 30 September and 14 October
C 16 September, 30 September, 14 October
G The Yorkshire Coast Express
H The Moors Explorer

No Sunday Service operated by Northern Rail

For connections to Darlington please refer to Table 44

Table 45

Mondays to Fridays

Whitby - Pickering and Middlesbrough

Network Diagram - see first Page of Table 44

Miles			NT	NT	NT	NT	NY	NT	NT	NY	NT	NT	NT	NY	NY	NT	NT
							A			A				B	C	FX	
							H			G					G		
0	**Whitby**	d				08 50	11 00		12 41	14 00			16 00	17 30	18 00		19 15
1½	Ruswarp	d				08 54			12 45				16 04				19 19
3	Sleights	d				08 59			12 50				16 09				19 24
6¼	Grosmont	d				09 07	11a22		12 58	14a22			16 17	17a50	18a22		19 32
—	Goathland §	a					11 50			14 50				18 15	18 45		
—	Levisham §	a					12 20			15 20				18 40	19 10		
—	**Pickering §**	a					12 40			15 40				19 00	19 30		
7¾	Egton	d				09 10			13 01				16 21				19 35
9½	Glaisdale	a				09 14			13 05				16 25				19 39
—		d				09 17			13 08				16 28				19 42
11½	Lealholm	d				09 22			13 13				16 33				19 47
15	Danby	d				09 28			13 19				16 40				19 53
16½	Castleton Moor	d				09 31			13 22				16 44				19 56
18¾	Commondale	d				09 35			13 26				16 47				20 00
22¼	Kildale	d				09 42			13 33				16 54				20 07
24	Battersby	a				09 47			13 38				16 59				20 12
—		d				09 51			13 42				17 04				20 16
26½	Great Ayton	d				09 56			13 47				17 09				20 21
30½	Nunthorpe	d	07 21	08 31	09 16	10 03		12 16	13 54		15 16	17 02	17 16			18 24	20 28
31	Gypsy Lane	d	07 23	08 33	09 18	10 05		12 18	13 56		15 18	17 04	17 18			18 26	20 30
32	Marton	d	07 25	08 36	09 21	10 08		12 21	13 59		15 21	17 06	17 20			18 29	20 33
35	**Middlesbrough**	a	07 31	08 43	09 29	10 17		12 28	14 07		15 28	17 15	17 30			18 35	20 41
—	Newcastle 8 44	a	08 52		10 51			13 51			16 51						

Saturdays

		NT	NT	NT	NT	NY	NT	NT	NY	NT	NT	NT	NY	NY	NT	NT
						D			D				E	F		
						H			G					G		
Whitby	d				08 50	11 00		12 41	14 00			16 00	17 30	18 00		19 15
Ruswarp	d				08 54			12 45				16 04				19 19
Sleights	d				08 59			12 50				16 09				19 24
Grosmont	d				09 07	11a22		12 58	14a22			16 17	17a50	18a22		19 32
Goathland §	a					11 50			14 50				18 15	18 45		
Levisham §	a					12 20			15 20				18 40	19 10		
Pickering §	a					12 40			15 40				19 00	19 30		
Egton	d				09 10			13 01				16 21				19 35
Glaisdale	a				09 14			13 05				16 25				19 39
	d				09 17			13 08				16 28				19 42
Lealholm	d				09 22			13 13				16 33				19 47
Danby	d				09 28			13 19				16 40				19 53
Castleton Moor	d				09 31			13 22				16 44				19 56
Commondale	d				09 35			13 26				16 47				20 00
Kildale	d				09 42			13 33				16 54				20 07
Battersby	a				09 47			13 38				16 59				20 12
	d				09 51			13 42				17 04				20 16
Great Ayton	d				09 56			13 47				17 09				20 21
Nunthorpe	d	07 21	08 31	09 16	10 03		12 16	13 54		15 16	17 02	17 16			18 24	20 28
Gypsy Lane	d	07 23	08 33	09 18	10 05		12 18	13 56		15 18	17 04	17 18			18 26	20 30
Marton	d	07 25	08 36	09 21	10 08		12 21	13 59		15 21	17 06	17 20			18 29	20 33
Middlesbrough	a	07 31	08 43	09 29	10 17		12 27	14 07		15 28	17 15	17 30			18 35	20 41
Newcastle 8 44	a	08 52		10 51			13 51			16 51						22 04

Sundays
until 9 September

		NT	NT	NT	NT	NT
Whitby	d	10 24	12 44	15 55	17 10	18 00
Ruswarp	d	10 28	12 48	15 59	17 14	18 04
Sleights	d	10 33	12 53	16 04	17 19	18 09
Grosmont	d	10 41	13 01	16 12	17 27	18 17
Goathland §	a					
Levisham §	a					
Pickering §	a					
Egton	d	10 44	13 04	16 15	17 30	18 20
Glaisdale	a	10 48	13 08	16 19	17 34	18 24
	d	10 53	13 11	16 24	17 37	18 27
Lealholm	d	10 58	13 16	16 29	17 42	18 32
Danby	d	11 04	13 22	16 35	17 48	18 38
Castleton Moor	d	11 07	13 25	16 38	17 51	18 41
Commondale	d	11 11	13 29	16 42	17 55	18 45
Kildale	d	11 18	13 36	16 49	18 02	18 52
Battersby	a	11 23	13 41	16 54	18 07	18 57
	d	11 39	13 45	16 58	18 11	19 01
Great Ayton	d	11 44	13 50	17 03	18 16	19 06
Nunthorpe	d	11 51	13 57	17 10	18 23	19 13
Gypsy Lane	d	11 53	13 59	17 12	18 25	19 15
Marton	d	11 56	14 02	17 15	18 28	19 18
Middlesbrough	a	12 02	14 12	17 22	18 39	19 30
Newcastle 8 44	a					20 47

§ North Yorkshire Moors Railway. For full service between Grosmont and Pickering please refer to separate publicity
A until 2 November
B until 20 July except 4 June until 8 June, and from 3 September until 2 November
C from 4 June until 8 June, and from 23 July until 31 August
D until 3 November
E until 14 July except 2 June and 9 June, and from 8 September until 3 November except 15 September, 29 September and 13 October
F 2 June, 9 June, 21 July until 1 September, 15 September, 29 September and 13 October
G The Yorkshire Coast Express
H The Moors Explorer

For connections to Darlington please refer to Table 44

Table 45

Sundays
from 16 September

Whitby - Pickering and Middlesbrough

Network Diagram - see first Page of Table 44

		NY	NY	NY	NY
		A	A	B	C
		H	G		
Whitby	d	11 00	14 00	17 30	18 02
Ruswarp	d				
Sleights	d				
Grosmont	d	11a22	14a22	17a50	18a22
Goathland §	a	11 50	14 50	18 15	18 45
Levisham §	a	12 20	15 20	18 40	19 10
Pickering §	a	12 40	15 40	19 00	19 30
Egton	d				
Glaisdale	a				
	d				
Lealholm	d				
Danby	d				
Castleton Moor	d				
Commondale	d				
Kildale	d				
Battersby	a				
	d				
Great Ayton	d				
Nunthorpe	d				
Gypsy Lane	d				
Marton	d				
Middlesbrough	a				
Newcastle 8 44	a				

§ North Yorkshire Moors Railway. For full service between Grosmont and Pickering please refer to separate publicity
A until 4 November
B from 23 September until 4 November except 30 September and 14 October
C 16 September, 30 September, 14 October
G The Yorkshire Coast Express
H The Moors Explorer

No Sunday Service operated by Northern Rail

For connections to Darlington please refer to Table 44

Chathill and Morpeth - Newcastle - Metrocentre, Hexham and Carlisle

Network Diagram - see first Page of Table 44

Miles	Miles			GR	NT	NT	GR	XC	NT	NT	XC	NT	NT	NT	GR	NT	NT	NT	NT	NT	NT	NT	GR
0	—	**Chathill**	d						07 08														
11¼	—	Alnmouth for Alnwick 26	d	06 19			06 53	07 08	07 20		07 59				08 58								10 58
17½	—	Acklington	d						07 36														
22¾	—	Widdrington	d						07 44														
27½	—	Pegswood	d						07 50														
39½	—	**Morpeth** 26	d	06 35			07 09		07 54		08 13		08 49						09 49			10 49	
36¼	—	Cramlington	d						08 02				08 57						09 57			10 57	
45½	—	Manors	d						08 15				09 10						10 10			11 10	
46	—	**Newcastle** 26	a	06 52			07 26	07 38	08 19		08 30		09 14		09 27				10 14			11 13	11 27
—	—	Sunderland 26,44	d							07 30								09 30			10 30		
—	—	**Newcastle**	d		06 30	06 47				07 53		08 24		08 54		09 26	09 44	09 54	10 15	10 22	10 54	11 15	
48¼	2¼	Dunston	d															09 59					
49½	3½	**Metrocentre**	a							08 00		08 31		09 01		09 33	09 52	10 02	10 22	10 30	11 01	11 22	
—	—		d							08 01		08 32		09 02		09 34		10 02		10 32	11 02		
—	5½	Blaydon	d							08 05				09 06									
—	9¾	Wylam	d		06 44					08 11		08 40		09 12				10 10			11 10		
—	12	Prudhoe	d		06 48	07 03				08 15		08 44		09 16		09 43		10 14		10 42	11 14		
—	14½	Stocksfield	d		06 53					08 20		08 48		09 21				10 18			11 18		
—	16¾	Riding Mill	d		06 57					08 24				09 25				10 23			11 23		
—	19¼	Corbridge	d		07 01					08 28				09 29				10 26			11 26		
—	22¼	**Hexham**	a		07 10	07 16				08 38		08 58		09 39		09 57		10 36		10 55	11 38		
—	—		d			07 16						08 59				09 57				10 55			
—	30	Haydon Bridge	d			07 25						09 08								11 04			
—	33¾	Bardon Mill	d			07 32						09 14								11 11			
—	38½	Haltwhistle	d			07 39						09 21				10 15				11 18			
—	50¾	Brampton (Cumbria)	d			07 54						09 37								11 33			
—	57½	Wetheral	d			08 03						09 46								11 42			
—	61¾	**Carlisle**	a			08 13						09 57				10 48				11 57			

		XC	NT	NT	NT	NT	XC	NT	NT	NT	NT	NT	NT	NT	NT	XC	NT	NT	NT	NT	GR	NT	NT
Chathill	d																						
Alnmouth for Alnwick 26	d						12 08									14 08					14 58		
Acklington	d																						
Widdrington	d																						
Pegswood	d																						
Morpeth 26	d	11 21				11 49					12 49				13 49					14 49			
Cramlington	d					11 57					12 57				13 57					14 57			
Manors	d					12 10					13 10				14 10					15 10			
Newcastle 26	a	11 39				12 13	12 38				13 13				14 13	14 38				15 14	15 27		
Sunderland 26,44	d				11 30					12 30				13 30					14 30				
Newcastle	d		11 22	11 44	11 54	12 15		12 22	12 44	12 54	13 15	13 22	13 44	13 54	14 15		14 24	14 44	14 56	15 15		15 24	15 44
Dunston	d																						
Metrocentre	a		11 31	11 52	12 01	12 23		12 31	12 52	13 01	13 22	13 31	13 51	14 01	14 22		14 31	14 51	15 02	15 22		15 31	15 51
	d		11 32		12 02			12 32		13 02		13 32		14 02			14 32		15 02			15 32	
Blaydon	d																						
Wylam	d				12 10					13 10				14 10					15 10				
Prudhoe	d		11 42		12 14			12 42		13 14		13 43		14 14			14 42		15 16			15 42	
Stocksfield	d				12 18					13 18				14 18					15 18				
Riding Mill	d				12 23					13 23				14 23					15 23				
Corbridge	d				12 26					13 26				14 26					15 26				
Hexham	a		11 55		12 38			12 55		13 38		13 55		14 38			14 55		15 39			15 56	
	d		11 55					12 55				13 56					14 55					15 56	
Haydon Bridge	d							13 04									15 04					16 05	
Bardon Mill	d							13 11									15 11						
Haltwhistle	d		12 14					13 18				14 15					15 18					16 18	
Brampton (Cumbria)	d							13 33									15 33						
Wetheral	d							13 42									15 42						
Carlisle	a		12 47					13 54				14 49					15 57					16 51	

For connections from London Kings Cross please refer to Table 26

Chathill and Morpeth - Newcastle - Metrocentre, Hexham and Carlisle

Network Diagram - see first Page of Table 44

		NT	NT	NT	NT	NT	NT	XC	NT	NT	NT	NT	GR	NT	NT	NT	XC	NT	NT	NT	GR	NT
Chathill	d																	19 10				
Alnmouth for Alnwick 26	d							17 01					17 58				19 08	19 22			19 36	
Acklington	d																	19 30				
Widdrington	d																	19 37				
Pegswood	d																	19 43				
Morpeth 26	d		15 49				16 49	17 16							18 26	19 01		19 47			19 53	
Cramlington	d		15 57				16 57								18 34	19 09		19 56				
Manors	d		16 10				17 10															
Newcastle 26	a		16 14				17 15	17 34					18 27		18 49	19 25	19 39	20 07			20 12	
Sunderland 26,44	d	15 30				16 30						17 30								19 29		
Newcastle	d	15 54	16 15	16 22	16 44	16 54			17 16	17 24	17 44	17 54		18 24					19 25	19 54		20 15
Dunston	d										17 50											
Metrocentre	a	16 01	16 22	16 31	16 53	17 01			17 23	17 31	17 53	18 01		18 31					19 28	20 01		20 22
	d	16 02		16 31		17 02			17 24	17 32		18 02		18 32					19 32			20 23
Blaydon	d									17 36												
Wylam	d	16 10		16 40		17 10			17 32	17 42		18 10		18 40					19 40			20 31
Prudhoe	d	16 14		16 44		17 14			17 36	17 46		18 14		18 44					19 44			20 35
Stocksfield	d	16 18		16 48		17 18				17 51		18 18		18 48					19 48			20 39
Riding Mill	d	16 23		16 53		17 23				17 55		18 23		18 53					19 53			20 44
Corbridge	d	16 26		16 56		17 26				17 59		18 26		18 56					19 56			20 47
Hexham	a	16 38		17 03		17 39			17 51	18 09		18 32		19 02					20 00			20 57
	d			17 03					17 52			18 33		19 03					20 03			
Haydon Bridge	d			17 12					18 01			18 42							20 12			
Bardon Mill	d			17 18					18 07			18 48							20 18			
Haltwhistle	d			17 25					18 14			18 55		19 22					20 25			
Brampton (Cumbria)	d			17 41					18 30			19 11							20 41			
Wetheral	d			17 50					18 39			19 20							20 50			
Carlisle	a			17 59					18 54			19 35		19 55					21 03			

		NT	XC	NT	NT	GR	NT	NT
Chathill	d							
Alnmouth for Alnwick 26	d		21 08			22 10		
Acklington	d							
Widdrington	d							
Pegswood	d							
Morpeth 26	d					22 26		22 45
Cramlington	d							22 53
Manors	d							
Newcastle 26	a		21 38			22 43		23 07
Sunderland 26,44	d	20 38						
Newcastle	d	21 04		21 18	21 52		22 35	
Dunston	d							
Metrocentre	a	21 11		21 25	22 01		22 42	
	d			21 26			22 43	
Blaydon	d							
Wylam	d			21 34			22 51	
Prudhoe	d			21 38			22 55	
Stocksfield	d			21 42			22 59	
Riding Mill	d			21 47			23 04	
Corbridge	d			21 50			23 07	
Hexham	a			21 56			23 18	
	d			21 57				
Haydon Bridge	d			22 06				
Bardon Mill	d			22 12				
Haltwhistle	d			22 19				
Brampton (Cumbria)	d			22 35				
Wetheral	d			22 43				
Carlisle	a			22 56				

For connections from London Kings Cross please refer to Table 26

Chathill and Morpeth - Newcastle - Metrocentre, Hexham and Carlisle

Network Diagram - see first Page of Table 44

		GR	NT	NT	GR	XC	NT	NT	XC	NT		NT	NT	GR	NT	NT	NT	NT	NT	NT		NT	GR	XC	NT
		■ 1 🍴			■ 1 🍴	◇1 ☕			◇1 ☕					■ 1 🍴									■ 1 🍴	◇1 ☕	
Chathill	d						07 08																		
Alnmouth for Alnwick 26	d	06 19			06 53	07 08	07 20		07 59					08 58									10 58		
Acklington	d						07 36																		
Widdrington	d						07 44																		
Pegswood	d						07 50																		
Morpeth 26	d	06 35			07 09		07 54		08 13			08 49						09 49				10 49		11 21	
Cramlington	d						08 02					08 57						09 57				10 57			
Manors	d						08 15					09 10						10 10				11 10			
Newcastle 8 26	a	06 52			07 26	07 38	08 19		08 30			09 14		09 27				10 14				11 13	11 27	11 39	
Sunderland 26,44	d							07 30									09 30			10 30					
Newcastle 8	d		06 30	06 47				07 53		08 24			08 54		09 26	09 44	09 54	10 15	10 22	10 54		11 15			11 22
Dunston	d																09 59								
Metrocentre	a							08 00		08 31			09 01		09 33	09 52	10 02	10 22	10 30	11 01		11 22			11 31
	d							08 01		08 32			09 02		09 34		10 02		10 32	11 02					11 32
Blaydon	d							08 05					09 06												
Wylam	d		06 44					08 11		08 40			09 12				10 10			11 10					
Prudhoe	d		06 48	07 03				08 15		08 44			09 16		09 43		10 14		10 42	11 14					11 42
Stocksfield	d		06 53					08 20		08 48			09 21				10 18			11 18					
Riding Mill	d		06 57					08 24					09 25				10 23			11 23					
Corbridge	d		07 01					08 28					09 29				10 26			11 26					
Hexham	a		07 10	07 16				08 38		09 00			09 39		09 58		10 36		10 56	11 38					11 57
	d			07 16						09 01					09 58				10 56						11 57
Haydon Bridge	d			07 25						09 10									11 05						
Bardon Mill	d			07 32						09 16									11 12						
Haltwhistle	d			07 39						09 23					10 16				11 19						12 16
Brampton (Cumbria)	d			07 54						09 39									11 34						
Wetheral	d			08 03						09 48									11 43						
Carlisle 8	a			08 13						09 59					10 50				11 58						12 49

		NT	NT	NT	XC	NT		NT	NT	NT	NT	NT	NT	NT	XC	NT		NT	NT	NT	GR	NT	NT	NT	NT
					◇1 ☕										◇1 ☕						■ 1 🍴				
Chathill	d																								
Alnmouth for Alnwick 26	d				12 08										14 08						14 58				
Acklington	d																								
Widdrington	d																								
Pegswood	d																								
Morpeth 26	d			11 49						12 49				13 49						14 49					15 49
Cramlington	d			11 57						12 57				13 57						14 57					15 57
Manors	d			12 10						13 10				14 10						15 10					16 10
Newcastle 8 26	a			12 13	12 38					13 13				14 13	14 38					15 14	15 27				16 14
Sunderland 26,44	d		11 30						12 30				13 30						14 30					15 30	
Newcastle 8	d	11 44	11 54	12 15		12 22		12 44	12 54	13 15	13 22	13 44	13 54	14 15		14 24		14 44	14 54	15 15		15 24	15 44	15 54	16 15
Dunston	d																								
Metrocentre	a	11 52	12 01	12 23		12 31		12 52	13 01	13 22	13 31	13 51	14 01	14 22		14 31		14 51	15 01	15 22		15 31	15 51	16 01	16 22
	d		12 02			12 32			13 02		13 32		14 02			14 32			15 02			15 32		16 02	
Blaydon	d																								
Wylam	d		12 10						13 10				14 10						15 10					16 10	
Prudhoe	d		12 14			12 42			13 14		13 43		14 14			14 42			15 16			15 42		16 14	
Stocksfield	d		12 18						13 18				14 18						15 18					16 18	
Riding Mill	d		12 23						13 23				14 23						15 23					16 23	
Corbridge	d		12 26						13 26				14 26						15 26					16 26	
Hexham	a		12 38			12 57			13 38		13 55		14 38			14 55			15 39			15 57		16 38	
	d					12 57					13 56					14 55						15 57			
Haydon Bridge	d					13 06										15 04						16 06			
Bardon Mill	d					13 13										15 11									
Haltwhistle	d					13 20					14 15					15 18						16 18			
Brampton (Cumbria)	d					13 35										15 33									
Wetheral	d					13 44										15 42									
Carlisle 8	a					13 59					14 49					15 57						16 52			

For connections from London Kings Cross please refer to Table 26

Chathill and Morpeth - Newcastle - Metrocentre, Hexham and Carlisle

Network Diagram - see first Page of Table 44

		NT		NT	NT	NT	XC	NT	NT	NT	NT	GR		NT	NT	NT	XC	NT	NT	NT	GR	NT		NT	XC
							◇1 ☕					■ 1 🍴					◇1 ☕				■ 1 🍴				◇1
Chathill	d																	19 10							
Alnmouth for Alnwick 26	d						17 01					17 58					19 08	19 22			19 36				21 08
Acklington	d																	19 30							
Widdrington	d																	19 37							
Pegswood	d																	19 43							
Morpeth 26	d					16 49	17 16								18 26	19 01		19 47			19 53				
Cramlington	d					16 57									18 34	19 09		19 56							
Manors	d					17 10																			
Newcastle 8 26	a					17 15	17 34					18 27			18 49	19 25	19 39	20 07			20 12				21 38
Sunderland 26,44	d				16 30						17 30									19 29				20 38	
Newcastle 8	d	16 22		16 44	16 54			17 16	17 24	17 44	17 54			18 24					19 25	19 54		20 15		21 04	
Dunston	d									17 50															
Metrocentre	a	16 31		16 53	17 01			17 23	17 31	17 53	18 01			18 31					19 31	20 01		20 22		21 11	
	d	16 31			17 02			17 24	17 32		18 02			18 32					19 32			20 23			
Blaydon	d								17 36																
Wylam	d	16 40			17 10			17 32	17 42		18 10			18 40					19 42			20 31			
Prudhoe	d	16 44			17 14			17 36	17 46		18 14			18 44					19 46			20 35			
Stocksfield	d	16 48			17 18				17 51		18 18			18 48					19 50			20 39			
Riding Mill	d	16 53			17 23				17 55		18 23			18 53					19 55			20 44			
Corbridge	d	16 56			17 26				17 59		18 26			18 56					19 58			20 47			
Hexham	a	17 03			17 39			17 51	18 10		18 32			19 04					20 06			20 59			
	d	17 03						17 52			18 33			19 05					20 07						
Haydon Bridge	d	17 12						18 01			18 42								20 16						
Bardon Mill	d	17 18						18 07			18 48								20 22						
Haltwhistle	d	17 25						18 14			18 55			19 24					20 29						
Brampton (Cumbria)	d	17 41						18 30			19 11								20 45						
Wetheral	d	17 50						18 39			19 20								20 54						
Carlisle 8	a	17 59						18 54			19 35			20 00					21 08						

		NT	NT	GR	NT	NT
				■ 1		
Chathill	d					
Alnmouth for Alnwick 26	d			22 10		
Acklington	d					
Widdrington	d					
Pegswood	d					
Morpeth 26	d			22 26	22 45	
Cramlington	d				22 53	
Manors	d					
Newcastle 8 26	a			22 43	23 07	
Sunderland 26,44	d					
Newcastle 8	d	21 18	21 52			22 35
Dunston	d					
Metrocentre	a	21 25	22 01			22 42
	d	21 26				22 43
Blaydon	d					
Wylam	d	21 34				22 51
Prudhoe	d	21 38				22 55
Stocksfield	d	21 42				22 59
Riding Mill	d	21 47				23 04
Corbridge	d	21 50				23 07
Hexham	a	21 56				23 18
	d	21 57				
Haydon Bridge	d	22 06				
Bardon Mill	d	22 12				
Haltwhistle	d	22 19				
Brampton (Cumbria)	d	22 35				
Wetheral	d	22 43				
Carlisle 8	a	22 59				

For connections from London Kings Cross please refer to Table 26

Chathill and Morpeth - Newcastle - Metrocentre, Hexham and Carlisle

Network Diagram - see first Page of Table 44

Station			NT	XC	NT	GR	NT	XC	NT	NT	NT		GR	XC	NT	NT	NT	NT	NT	NT	NT		NT	GR	XC	NT
				◇1		1		◇1					1	◇1										1	◇1	
Chathill		d			07 10																					
Alnmouth for Alnwick	26	d		07 08	07 22	07 25		08 00					08 58	09 08										10 58		
Acklington		d			07 37																					
Widdrington		d			07 45																					
Pegswood		d			07 51																					
Morpeth	26	d			07 55	07 41		08 14		08 49								09 49					10 49		11 19	
Cramlington		d			08 03					08 57								09 57					10 57			
Manors		d			08 16					09 10								10 10					11 10			
Newcastle	26	a		07 38	08 20	07 58		08 32		09 14			09 27	09 39				10 14					11 13	11 27	11 38	
Sunderland	26,44	d					07 30										09 30				10 30					
Newcastle		d	06 30				07 53		08 24		08 54				09 26	09 44	09 54	10 15	10 22	10 44	10 54		11 15			11 22
Dunston		d															09 59									
Metrocentre		a					08 00		08 31		09 01				09 33	09 52	10 02	10 22	10 30	10 54	11 01		11 22			11 31
		d					08 01		08 32		09 02				09 34		10 02		10 32		11 02					11 32
Blaydon		d					08 05				09 06															
Wylam		d	06 44				08 11		08 40		09 12						10 10				11 10					
Prudhoe		d	06 48				08 15		08 44		09 16				09 43		10 14		10 42		11 14					11 42
Stocksfield		d	06 53				08 20		08 48		09 21						10 18				11 18					
Riding Mill		d	06 57				08 24				09 25						10 23				11 23					
Corbridge		d	07 01				08 28				09 29						10 26				11 26					
Hexham		a	07 07				08 38		08 58		09 39				09 57		10 36		10 55		11 38					11 55
		d	07 07						08 59						09 57				10 55							11 55
Haydon Bridge		d	07 16						09 08										11 04							
Bardon Mill		d	07 23						09 14										11 11							
Haltwhistle		d	07 30						09 21						10 15				11 18							12 14
Brampton (Cumbria)		d	07 45						09 37										11 33							
Wetheral		d	07 54						09 46										11 42							
Carlisle		a	08 04						09 57						10 48				11 57							12 47

Station			NT	NT	NT	XC	NT		NT	NT	NT	GR	NT	NT	NT	NT	XC		NT	NT	NT	NT	GR	NT	NT	NT
						◇1						1					◇1						1			
Chathill		d																								
Alnmouth for Alnwick	26	d				12 08						12 58					14 09						14 58			
Acklington		d																								
Widdrington		d																								
Pegswood		d																								
Morpeth	26	d			11 49						12 49					13 49						14 49				
Cramlington		d			11 57						12 57					13 57						14 57				
Manors		d			12 11						13 10					14 10						15 11				
Newcastle	26	a			12 13	12 38					13 13	13 27				14 15	14 39					15 14	15 27			
Sunderland	26,44	d		11 30						12 30					13 30						14 30					15 30
Newcastle		d	11 44	11 54	12 15		12 22		12 44	12 54	13 14		13 22	13 44	13 54	14 15			14 24	14 44	14 56	15 15		15 24	15 44	15 54
Dunston		d																								
Metrocentre		a	11 52	12 01	12 23		12 31		12 52	13 01	13 22		13 31	13 51	14 01	14 22			14 31	14 51	15 02	15 22		15 31	15 51	16 01
		d		12 02			12 32			13 02			13 32		14 02				14 32		15 02			15 32		16 02
Blaydon		d																								
Wylam		d		12 10						13 10					14 10						15 10					16 10
Prudhoe		d		12 14			12 43			13 14			13 43		14 14				14 42		15 16			15 42		16 14
Stocksfield		d		12 18						13 18					14 18						15 18					16 18
Riding Mill		d		12 23						13 23					14 23						15 23					16 23
Corbridge		d		12 26						13 26					14 26						15 26					16 26
Hexham		a		12 38			12 55			13 38			13 55		14 38				14 55		15 39			15 56		16 38
		d					12 56						13 56						14 55					15 56		
Haydon Bridge		d					13 05												15 04					16 05		
Bardon Mill		d					13 11												15 11							
Haltwhistle		d					13 18						14 15						15 18					16 18		
Brampton (Cumbria)		d					13 33												15 33							
Wetheral		d					13 42												15 42							
Carlisle		a					13 54						14 49						15 57					16 53		

For connections from London Kings Cross please refer to Table 26

Chathill and Morpeth - Newcastle - Metrocentre, Hexham and Carlisle

Network Diagram - see first Page of Table 44

Station			NT		NT	NT	NT	NT	XC	NT	NT	NT	NT		NT	GR	NT	NT	NT	XC	NT	NT	GR		NT	NT
									◇1							1				◇1			1			
Chathill		d																	18 36							
Alnmouth for Alnwick	26	d							17 03							17 58			18 48	19 08			20 07			
Acklington		d																	18 56							
Widdrington		d																	19 03							
Pegswood		d																	19 09							
Morpeth	26	d	15 49					16 49	17 17						17 52			18 50	19 13				20 24			
Cramlington		d	15 57					16 57							18 00			18 58	19 22							
Manors		d	16 11					17 10																		
Newcastle	26	a	16 14					17 13	17 35						18 15	18 27		19 13	19 34	19 41			20 41			
Sunderland	26,44	d					16 30						17 30									19 29				
Newcastle		d	16 15		16 22	16 46	16 54			17 16	17 24	17 44	17 54				18 24				19 25	19 54			20 15	20 30
Dunston		d										17 50														
Metrocentre		a	16 22		16 31	16 53	17 01			17 23	17 31	17 53	18 01				18 31				19 28	20 01			20 22	20 39
		d			16 31		17 02			17 24	17 32		18 02				18 32				19 32				20 23	
Blaydon		d									17 36															
Wylam		d			16 40		17 10			17 32	17 42		18 10				18 40				19 40				20 31	
Prudhoe		d			16 44		17 14			17 36	17 46		18 14				18 44				19 44				20 35	
Stocksfield		d			16 48		17 18				17 51		18 18				18 48				19 48				20 39	
Riding Mill		d			16 53		17 23				17 55		18 23				18 53				19 53				20 44	
Corbridge		d			16 56		17 26				17 59		18 26				18 56				19 56				20 47	
Hexham		a			17 02		17 39			17 51	18 09		18 32				19 02				20 00				20 58	
		d			17 03					17 52			18 33				19 03				20 03					
Haydon Bridge		d			17 12					18 01			18 42								20 12					
Bardon Mill		d			17 18					18 07			18 48								20 18					
Haltwhistle		d			17 25					18 14			18 55				19 22				20 25					
Brampton (Cumbria)		d			17 41					18 30			19 11								20 41					
Wetheral		d			17 50					18 39			19 20								20 50					
Carlisle		a			18 03					18 54			19 35				19 53				21 03					

Station			NT	NT	NT
Chathill		d			
Alnmouth for Alnwick	26	d			
Acklington		d			
Widdrington		d			
Pegswood		d			
Morpeth	26	d	21 15		
Cramlington		d	21 23		
Manors		d			
Newcastle	26	a	21 39		
Sunderland	26,44	d			
Newcastle		d		21 18	21 52
Dunston		d			
Metrocentre		a		21 25	22 01
		d		21 26	22 02
Blaydon		d			
Wylam		d		21 34	22 10
Prudhoe		d		21 38	22a13
Stocksfield		d		21 42	
Riding Mill		d		21 47	
Corbridge		d		21 50	
Hexham		a		21 56	
		d		21 57	
Haydon Bridge		d		22 06	
Bardon Mill		d		22 12	
Haltwhistle		d		22 19	
Brampton (Cumbria)		d		22 35	
Wetheral		d		22 43	
Carlisle		a		22 56	

For connections from London Kings Cross please refer to Table 26

Table 48

Saturdays
15 September to 29 September

Chathill and Morpeth - Newcastle - Metrocentre, Hexham and Carlisle

Network Diagram - see first Page of Table 44

Station			NT	XC	NT	GR	NT	XC	NT	NT	NT	GR	XC	NT	NT	NT	NT	NT	NT	NT	NT	GR	XC	NT
				◇1 ✠		■ 1 ✠		◇1 ✠				■ 1 ✠	◇1 ✠									■ 1 ✠	◇1 ✠	
Chathill		d			07 10																			
Alnmouth for Alnwick	26	d		07 08	07 22	07 25		08 00				08 58	09 08									10 58		
Acklington		d			07 37																			
Widdrington		d			07 45																			
Pegswood		d			07 51																			
Morpeth	26	d			07 55	07 41		08 14		08 49							09 49				10 49		11 19	
Cramlington		d			08 03					08 57							09 57				10 57			
Manors		d			08 16					09 10							10 10				11 10			
Newcastle ■	26 ⇌	a		07 38	08 20	07 58		08 32		09 14		09 27	09 39				10 14				11 13	11 27	11 38	
Sunderland	26,44 ⇌	d					07 30									09 30				10 30				
Newcastle ■	⇌	d	06 30				07 53		08 24		08 54			09 26	09 44	09 54	10 15	10 22	10 44	10 54	11 15			11 22
Dunston		d														09 59								
Metrocentre		a					08 00		08 31		09 01			09 33	09 52	10 02	10 22	10 30	10 54	11 01	11 22			11 31
		d					08 01		08 32		09 02			09 34		10 02		10 32		11 02				11 32
Blaydon		d					08 05				09 06													
Wylam		d	06 44				08 11		08 40		09 12					10 10				11 10				
Prudhoe		d	06 48				08 15		08 44		09 16			09 43		10 14		10 42		11 14				11 42
Stocksfield		d	06 53				08 20		08 48		09 21					10 18				11 18				
Riding Mill		d	06 57				08 24				09 25					10 23				11 23				
Corbridge		d	07 01				08 28				09 29					10 26				11 26				
Hexham		a	07 07				08 38		08 58		09 39			09 57		10 36		10 55		11 38				11 55
		d	07 07						08 59					09 57				10 55						11 55
Haydon Bridge		d	07 16						09 08									11 04						
Bardon Mill		d	07 23						09 14									11 11						
Haltwhistle		d	07 30						09 21					10 15				11 18						12 14
Brampton (Cumbria)		d	07 45						09 37									11 33						
Wetheral		d	07 54						09 46									11 42						
Carlisle ■		a	08 04						09 57					10 48				11 57						12 47

Station			NT	NT	NT	XC	NT	NT	NT	NT	GR	NT	NT	NT	NT	XC	NT	NT	NT	NT	GR	NT	NT	NT
						◇1 ✠					■ 1 ✠					◇1 ✠					■ 1 ✠			
Chathill		d																						
Alnmouth for Alnwick	26	d				12 08					12 58					14 09					14 58			
Acklington		d																						
Widdrington		d																						
Pegswood		d																						
Morpeth	26	d			11 49					12 49					13 49					14 49				
Cramlington		d			11 57					12 57					13 57					14 57				
Manors		d			12 11					13 10					14 10					15 11				
Newcastle ■	26 ⇌	a			12 13	12 38				13 13	13 27				14 15	14 39				15 14	15 27			
Sunderland	26,44 ⇌	d		11 30					12 30					13 30					14 30					15 30
Newcastle ■	⇌	d	11 44	11 54	12 15		12 22	12 44	12 54	13 14		13 22	13 44	13 54	14 15		14 24	14 44	14 56	15 15		15 24	15 44	15 54
Dunston		d																						
Metrocentre		a	11 52	12 01	12 23		12 31	12 52	13 01	13 22		13 31	13 51	14 01	14 22		14 31	14 51	15 02	15 22		15 31	15 51	16 01
		d		12 02			12 32		13 02			13 32		14 02			14 32		15 02			15 32		16 02
Blaydon		d																						
Wylam		d		12 10					13 10					14 10					15 10					16 10
Prudhoe		d		12 14			12 43		13 14			13 43		14 14			14 42		15 16			15 42		16 14
Stocksfield		d		12 18					13 18					14 18					15 18					16 18
Riding Mill		d		12 23					13 23					14 23					15 23					16 23
Corbridge		d		12 26					13 26					14 26					15 26					16 26
Hexham		a		12 38			12 55		13 38			13 55		14 38			14 55		15 39			15 56		16 38
		d					12 56					13 56					14 55					15 56		
Haydon Bridge		d					13 05										15 04					16 05		
Bardon Mill		d					13 11										15 11							
Haltwhistle		d					13 18					14 15					15 18					16 18		
Brampton (Cumbria)		d					13 33										15 33							
Wetheral		d					13 42										15 42							
Carlisle ■		a					13 54					14 49					15 57					16 53		

For connections from London Kings Cross please refer to Table 26

Table 48

Saturdays
15 September to 29 September

Chathill and Morpeth - Newcastle - Metrocentre, Hexham and Carlisle

Network Diagram - see first Page of Table 44

Station			NT	NT	NT	NT	NT	XC	NT	NT	NT	NT	NT	GR	NT	NT	NT	XC	NT	NT	GR	NT	NT
								◇1 ✠						■ 1 ✠				◇1 ✠			■ 1 ✠		
Chathill		d															18 36						
Alnmouth for Alnwick	26	d						17 03						17 58			18 48	19 08			20 07		
Acklington		d															18 56						
Widdrington		d															19 03						
Pegswood		d															19 09						
Morpeth	26	d	15 49				16 49	17 17					17 52			18 50	19 13				20 24		
Cramlington		d	15 57				16 57						18 00			18 58	19 22						
Manors		d	16 11				17 10																
Newcastle ■	26 ⇌	a	16 14				17 13	17 35					18 15	18 27		19 13	19 34	19 41			20 41		
Sunderland	26,44 ⇌	d				16 30						17 30								19 29			
Newcastle ■	⇌	d	16 15	16 22	16 46	16 54			17 16	17 24	17 44	17 54			18 24				19 25	19 54		20 15	20 30
Dunston		d									17 50												
Metrocentre		a	16 22	16 31	16 53	17 01			17 23	17 31	17 53	18 01			18 31				19 28	20 01		20 22	20 39
		d		16 31		17 02			17 24	17 32		18 02			18 32				19 32			20 23	
Blaydon		d								17 36													
Wylam		d		16 40		17 10			17 32	17 42		18 10			18 40				19 40			20 31	
Prudhoe		d		16 44		17 14			17 36	17 46		18 14			18 44				19 44			20 35	
Stocksfield		d		16 48		17 18				17 51		18 18			18 48				19 48			20 39	
Riding Mill		d		16 53		17 23				17 55		18 23			18 53				19 53			20 44	
Corbridge		d		16 56		17 26				17 59		18 26			18 56				19 56			20 47	
Hexham		a		17 02		17 39			17 51	18 09		18 32			19 02				20 00			20 58	
		d		17 03					17 52			18 33			19 03				20 03				
Haydon Bridge		d		17 12					18 01			18 42							20 12				
Bardon Mill		d		17 18					18 07			18 48							20 18				
Haltwhistle		d		17 25					18 14			18 55			19 22				20 25				
Brampton (Cumbria)		d		17 41					18 30			19 11							20 41				
Wetheral		d		17 50					18 39			19 20							20 50				
Carlisle ■		a		18 03					18 54			19 35			19 53				21 03				

Station			NT	NT	NT
Chathill		d			
Alnmouth for Alnwick	26	d			
Acklington		d			
Widdrington		d			
Pegswood		d			
Morpeth	26	d	21 15		
Cramlington		d	21 23		
Manors		d			
Newcastle ■	26 ⇌	a	21 39		
Sunderland	26,44 ⇌	d			
Newcastle ■	⇌	d		21 18	21 52
Dunston		d			
Metrocentre		a		21 25	22 01
		d		21 26	22 02
Blaydon		d			
Wylam		d		21 34	22 10
Prudhoe		d		21 38	22a13
Stocksfield		d		21 42	
Riding Mill		d		21 47	
Corbridge		d		21 50	
Hexham		a		21 56	
		d		21 57	
Haydon Bridge		d		22 06	
Bardon Mill		d		22 12	
Haltwhistle		d		22 19	
Brampton (Cumbria)		d		22 35	
Wetheral		d		22 43	
Carlisle ■		a		22 56	

For connections from London Kings Cross please refer to Table 26

Chathill and Morpeth - Newcastle - Metrocentre, Hexham and Carlisle

Network Diagram - see first Page of Table 44

			NT	XC	NT	GR	NT	XC	NT	NT	NT		GR	XC	NT	NT	NT	NT	NT	NT	NT		NT	GR	XC	NT
				◇1		1		◇1					1	◇1										1	◇1	
Chathill		d			07 10																					
Alnmouth for Alnwick	26	d		07 08	07 22	07 25		08 00					08 58	09 08										10 58		
Acklington		d			07 37																					
Widdrington		d			07 45																					
Pegswood		d			07 51																					
Morpeth	26	d			07 55	07 41		08 14		08 49								09 49					10 49		11 19	
Cramlington		d			08 03					08 57								09 57					10 57			
Manors		d			08 16					09 10								10 10					11 10			
Newcastle 8	26 ⇌	a		07 38	08 20	07 58		08 32		09 14			09 27	09 39				10 14					11 13	11 27	11 38	
Sunderland	26,44 ⇌	d					07 30										09 30				10 30					
Newcastle 8	⇌	d	06 30				07 53		08 24		08 54				09 26	09 44	09 54	10 15	10 22	10 44	10 54		11 15			11 22
Dunston		d															09 59									
Metrocentre		a					08 00		08 31		09 01				09 33	09 52	10 02	10 22	10 29	10 54	11 01		11 22			11 31
		d					08 01		08 32		09 02				09 34		10 02		10 32		11 02					11 32
Blaydon		d					08 05				09 06															
Wylam		d	06 44				08 11		08 40		09 12						10 10				11 10					
Prudhoe		d	06 48				08 15		08 44		09 16				09 43		10 14		10 42		11 14					11 42
Stocksfield		d	06 53				08 20		08 48		09 21						10 18				11 18					
Riding Mill		d	06 57				08 24				09 25						10 23				11 23					
Corbridge		d	07 01				08 28				09 29						10 26				11 26					
Hexham		a	07 07				08 38		09 00		09 39				09 58		10 36		10 57		11 38					11 57
		d	07 07						09 01						09 58				10 57							11 57
Haydon Bridge		d	07 16						09 10										11 06							
Bardon Mill		d	07 23						09 16										11 13							
Haltwhistle		d	07 30						09 23						10 17				11 20							12 16
Brampton (Cumbria)		d	07 45						09 39										11 35							
Wetheral		d	07 54						09 48										11 44							
Carlisle 8		a	08 04						10 02						10 53				11 58							12 52

			NT	NT	NT	XC	NT		NT	NT	NT	GR	NT	NT	NT	NT	XC		NT	NT	NT	NT	GR	NT	NT	NT
						◇1						1					◇1						1			
Chathill		d																								
Alnmouth for Alnwick	26	d				12 08						12 58					14 09						14 58			
Acklington		d																								
Widdrington		d																								
Pegswood		d																								
Morpeth	26	d			11 49						12 49					13 49						14 49				
Cramlington		d			11 57						12 57					13 57						14 57				
Manors		d			12 11						13 10					14 10						15 11				
Newcastle 8	26 ⇌	a			12 13	12 38					13 13	13 27				14 15	14 39					15 14	15 27			
Sunderland	26,44 ⇌	d		11 30						12 30					13 30						14 30					15 30
Newcastle 8	⇌	d	11 44	11 54	12 15		12 22		12 44	12 54	13 14		13 22	13 44	13 54	14 15			14 24	14 44	14 56	15 15		15 24	15 44	15 54
Dunston		d																								
Metrocentre		a	11 52	12 01	12 23		12 31		12 52	13 01	13 22		13 31	13 51	14 01	14 22			14 31	14 51	15 02	15 22		15 31	15 51	16 01
		d		12 02			12 32			13 02			13 32		14 02				14 32		15 02			15 32		16 02
Blaydon		d																								
Wylam		d		12 10						13 10					14 10						15 10					16 10
Prudhoe		d		12 14			12 42			13 14			13 43		14 14				14 42		15 16			15 42		16 14
Stocksfield		d		12 18						13 18					14 18						15 18					16 18
Riding Mill		d		12 23						13 23					14 23						15 23					16 23
Corbridge		d		12 26						13 26					14 26						15 26					16 26
Hexham		a		12 38			12 57			13 38			13 55		14 38				14 55		15 37			15 57		16 38
		d					12 57						13 56						14 55					15 57		
Haydon Bridge		d					13 06												15 04					16 06		
Bardon Mill		d					13 13												15 11							
Haltwhistle		d					13 20						14 15						15 18					16 18		
Brampton (Cumbria)		d					13 35												15 33							
Wetheral		d					13 44												15 42							
Carlisle 8		a					13 59						14 49						15 57					16 53		

For connections from London Kings Cross please refer to Table 26

Table 48

Saturdays

6 October to 20 October

Chathill and Morpeth - Newcastle - Metrocentre, Hexham and Carlisle

Network Diagram - see first Page of Table 44

			NT		NT	NT	NT	NT	XC	NT	NT	NT	NT		NT	GR	NT	NT	NT	XC	NT	NT	GR		NT	NT
									◇1							1				◇1			1			
Chathill		d																	18 36							
Alnmouth for Alnwick	26	d							17 03							17 58			18 48	19 08			20 07			
Acklington		d																	18 56							
Widdrington		d																	19 03							
Pegswood		d																	19 09							
Morpeth	26	d	15 49					16 49	17 17						17 52			18 50	19 13				20 24			
Cramlington		d	15 57					16 57							18 00			18 58	19 22							
Manors		d	16 11					17 10																		
Newcastle 8	26 ⇌	a	16 14					17 13	17 35						18 15	18 27		19 13	19 34	19 41			20 41			
Sunderland	26,44 ⇌	d					16 30						17 30									19 29				
Newcastle 8	⇌	d	16 15		16 22	16 46	16 54			17 16	17 24	17 44	17 54				18 24				19 25	19 54			20 15	20 30
Dunston		d										17 50														
Metrocentre		a	16 22		16 31	16 53	17 01			17 23	17 31	17 53	18 01				18 31				19 31	20 01			20 22	20 39
		d			16 31		17 02			17 24	17 32		18 02				18 32				19 32				20 23	
Blaydon		d									17 36															
Wylam		d			16 40		17 10			17 32	17 42		18 10				18 40				19 42				20 31	
Prudhoe		d			16 44		17 14			17 36	17 46		18 14				18 44				19 46				20 35	
Stocksfield		d			16 48		17 18				17 51		18 18				18 48				19 50				20 39	
Riding Mill		d			16 53		17 23				17 55		18 23				18 53				19 55				20 44	
Corbridge		d			16 56		17 26				17 59		18 26				18 56				19 58				20 47	
Hexham		a			17 02		17 39			17 51	18 09		18 32				19 02				20 06				20 58	
		d			17 03					17 52			18 33				19 03				20 07					
Haydon Bridge		d			17 12					18 01			18 42								20 16					
Bardon Mill		d			17 18					18 07			18 48								20 22					
Haltwhistle		d			17 25					18 14			18 55				19 22				20 29					
Brampton (Cumbria)		d			17 41					18 30			19 11								20 45					
Wetheral		d			17 50					18 39			19 20								20 54					
Carlisle 8		a			18 03					18 54			19 35				19 53				21 08					

			NT	NT	NT
Chathill		d			
Alnmouth for Alnwick	26	d			
Acklington		d			
Widdrington		d			
Pegswood		d			
Morpeth	26	d	21 15		
Cramlington		d	21 23		
Manors		d			
Newcastle 8	26 ⇌	a	21 39		
Sunderland	26,44 ⇌	d			
Newcastle 8	⇌	d		21 18	21 52
Dunston		d			
Metrocentre		a		21 25	22 01
		d		21 26	22 02
Blaydon		d			
Wylam		d		21 34	22 10
Prudhoe		d		21 38	22a13
Stocksfield		d		21 42	
Riding Mill		d		21 47	
Corbridge		d		21 50	
Hexham		a		21 56	
		d		21 57	
Haydon Bridge		d		22 06	
Bardon Mill		d		22 12	
Haltwhistle		d		22 19	
Brampton (Cumbria)		d		22 35	
Wetheral		d		22 43	
Carlisle 8		a		23 00	

For connections from London Kings Cross please refer to Table 26

Chathill and Morpeth - Newcastle - Metrocentre, Hexham and Carlisle

Network Diagram - see first Page of Table 44

	NT	XC	NT	GR	NT	XC	NT	NT	NT	GR	XC	NT	NT	NT	NT	NT	NT	NT	NT	GR	XC	NT
Chathill d			07 10																			
Alnmouth for Alnwick 26 d		07 08	07 22	07 25		08 00				08 58	09 08									10 58		
Acklington d			07 37																			
Widdrington d			07 45																			
Pegswood d			07 51																			
Morpeth 26 d			07 55	07 41		08 14		08 49							09 49				10 49		11 19	
Cramlington d			08 03					08 57							09 57				10 57			
Manors d			08 16					09 10							10 10				11 10			
Newcastle 26 ⇌ a		07 38	08 20	07 58		08 32		09 14		09 27	09 39				10 14				11 13	11 27	11 38	
Sunderland 26,44 ⇌ d					07 30									09 30				10 30				
Newcastle ⇌ d	06 30				07 53		08 24		08 54			09 26	09 44	09 54	10 15	10 22	10 44	10 54	11 15			11 22
Dunston d														09 59								
Metrocentre a					08 00		08 31		09 01			09 33	09 52	10 02	10 22	10 29	10 54	11 01	11 22			11 31
d					08 01		08 32		09 02			09 34		10 02		10 32		11 02				11 32
Blaydon d					08 05				09 06													
Wylam d	06 44				08 11		08 40		09 12					10 10				11 10				
Prudhoe d	06 48				08 15		08 44		09 16			09 43		10 14		10 42		11 14				11 42
Stocksfield d	06 53				08 20		08 48		09 21					10 18				11 18				
Riding Mill d	06 57				08 24				09 25					10 23				11 23				
Corbridge d	07 01				08 28				09 29					10 26				11 26				
Hexham a	07 07				08 38		09 00		09 39			09 58		10 36		10 57		11 38				11 57
d	07 07						09 01					09 58				10 57						11 57
Haydon Bridge d	07 16						09 10									11 06						
Bardon Mill d	07 23						09 16									11 13						
Haltwhistle d	07 30						09 23					10 17				11 20						12 16
Brampton (Cumbria) d	07 45						09 39									11 35						
Wetheral d	07 54						09 48									11 44						
Carlisle a	08 04						10 02					10 53				11 58						12 52

	NT	NT	NT	XC	NT	NT	NT	NT	GR	NT	NT	NT	NT	XC	NT	NT	NT	NT	GR	NT	NT	NT
Chathill d																						
Alnmouth for Alnwick 26 d				12 08					12 58					14 09					14 58			
Acklington d																						
Widdrington d																						
Pegswood d																						
Morpeth 26 d			11 49					12 49					13 49					14 49				
Cramlington d			11 57					12 57					13 57					14 57				
Manors d			12 11					13 10					14 10					15 11				
Newcastle 26 ⇌ a			12 13	12 38				13 13	13 27				14 15	14 39				15 14	15 27			
Sunderland 26,44 ⇌ d		11 30					12 30					13 30					14 30					15 30
Newcastle ⇌ d	11 44	11 54	12 15		12 22	12 44	12 54	13 14		13 22	13 44	13 54	14 15		14 24	14 44	14 56	15 15		15 24	15 44	15 54
Dunston d																						
Metrocentre a	11 52	12 01	12 23		12 31	12 52	13 01	13 22		13 31	13 51	14 01	14 22		14 31	14 51	15 02	15 22		15 31	15 51	16 01
d		12 02			12 32		13 02			13 32		14 02			14 32		15 02			15 32		16 02
Blaydon d																						
Wylam d		12 10					13 10					14 10					15 10					16 10
Prudhoe d		12 14			12 42		13 14			13 43		14 14			14 42		15 16			15 42		16 14
Stocksfield d		12 18					13 18					14 18					15 18					16 18
Riding Mill d		12 23					13 23					14 23					15 23					16 23
Corbridge d		12 26					13 26					14 26					15 26					16 26
Hexham a		12 38			12 57		13 38			13 55		14 38			14 55		15 37			15 57		16 38
d					12 57					13 56					14 55					15 57		
Haydon Bridge d					13 06										15 04					16 06		
Bardon Mill d					13 13										15 11							
Haltwhistle d					13 20					14 15					15 18					16 18		
Brampton (Cumbria) d					13 35										15 33							
Wetheral d					13 44										15 42							
Carlisle a					13 59					14 49					15 57					16 53		

For connections from London Kings Cross please refer to Table 26

Chathill and Morpeth - Newcastle - Metrocentre, Hexham and Carlisle

Network Diagram - see first Page of Table 44

	NT	NT	NT	NT	NT	XC	NT	NT	NT	NT	NT	GR	NT	NT	NT	XC	NT	NT	GR	NT	NT
Chathill d															18 36						
Alnmouth for Alnwick 26 d						17 03						17 58			18 48	19 08			20 07		
Acklington d															18 56						
Widdrington d															19 03						
Pegswood d															19 09						
Morpeth 26 d	15 49				16 49	17 17					17 52			18 50	19 13				20 24		
Cramlington d	15 57				16 57						18 00			18 58	19 22						
Manors d	16 11				17 10																
Newcastle 26 ⇌ a	16 14				17 13	17 35					18 15	18 27		19 13	19 34	19 41			20 41		
Sunderland 26,44 ⇌ d				16 30						17 30								19 29			
Newcastle ⇌ d	16 15	16 22	16 46	16 54			17 16	17 24	17 44	17 54			18 24				19 25	19 54		20 15	20 30
Dunston d									17 50												
Metrocentre a	16 22	16 31	16 53	17 01			17 23	17 31	17 53	18 01			18 31				19 31	20 01		20 22	20 39
d		16 31		17 02			17 24	17 32		18 02			18 32				19 32			20 23	
Blaydon d								17 36													
Wylam d		16 40		17 10			17 32	17 42		18 10			18 40				19 42			20 31	
Prudhoe d		16 44		17 14			17 36	17 46		18 14			18 44				19 46			20 35	
Stocksfield d		16 48		17 18				17 51		18 18			18 48				19 50			20 39	
Riding Mill d		16 53		17 23				17 55		18 23			18 53				19 55			20 44	
Corbridge d		16 56		17 26				17 59		18 26			18 56				19 58			20 47	
Hexham a		17 02		17 39			17 51	18 09		18 32			19 02				20 06			20 58	
d		17 03					17 52			18 33			19 03				20 07				
Haydon Bridge d		17 12					18 01			18 42							20 16				
Bardon Mill d		17 18					18 07			18 48							20 22				
Haltwhistle d		17 25					18 14			18 55			19 22				20 29				
Brampton (Cumbria) d		17 41					18 30			19 11							20 45				
Wetheral d		17 50					18 39			19 20							20 54				
Carlisle a		18 03					18 54			19 35			19 53				21 08				

	NT	NT	NT
Chathill d			
Alnmouth for Alnwick 26 d			
Acklington d			
Widdrington d			
Pegswood d			
Morpeth 26 d	21 15		
Cramlington d	21 23		
Manors d			
Newcastle 26 ⇌ a	21 39		
Sunderland 26,44 ⇌ d			
Newcastle ⇌ d		21 18	21 52
Dunston d			
Metrocentre a		21 25	22 01
d		21 26	22 02
Blaydon d			
Wylam d		21 34	22 10
Prudhoe d		21 38	22a13
Stocksfield d		21 42	
Riding Mill d		21 47	
Corbridge d		21 50	
Hexham a		21 56	
d		21 57	
Haydon Bridge d		22 06	
Bardon Mill d		22 12	
Haltwhistle d		22 19	
Brampton (Cumbria) d		22 35	
Wetheral d		22 43	
Carlisle a		23 00	

For connections from London Kings Cross please refer to Table 26

Chathill and Morpeth - Newcastle - Metrocentre, Hexham and Carlisle

Network Diagram - see first Page of Table 44

	NT	NT	NT	NT	NT	XC	GR	NT	NT	NT	GR	XC	NT	NT	NT	GR	NT	NT	NT	XC	NT	NT
Chathill d																						
Alnmouth for Alnwick 26 d						10 49	10 58					12 10				12 58				14 08		
Acklington d																						
Widdrington d																						
Pegswood d																						
Morpeth 26 d						11 04					12 06											
Cramlington d																						
Manors d																						
Newcastle 26 a						11 19	11 27				12 23	12 37				13 27				14 35		
Sunderland 26,44 d		09 28			10 28					11 28					12 28				13 28			
Newcastle d	09 10	09 53	10 10	10 30	10 50			11 10	11 30	11 50			12 10	12 30	12 50		13 10	13 30	13 50		14 10	14 30
Dunston d																						
Metrocentre a	09 17	10 01	10 17	10 37	10 59			11 17	11 37	11 57			12 17	12 37	12 59		13 17	13 37	13 59		14 17	14 37
d	09 18		10 18					11 18					12 18				13 18				14 18	
Blaydon d																						
Wylam d	09 26		10 26					11 26					12 26				13 26				14 26	
Prudhoe d	09 30		10 30					11 30					12 30				13 30				14 30	
Stocksfield d	09 34		10 34					11 34					12 34				13 34				14 34	
Riding Mill d	09 39		10 39					11 39					12 39				13 39				14 39	
Corbridge d	09 42		10 42					11 42					12 42				13 42				14 42	
Hexham a	09 48		10 48					11 48					12 48				13 48				14 48	
d	09 49		10 49					11 49					12 49				13 49				14 49	
Haydon Bridge d	09 58		10 58										12 58									
Bardon Mill d	10 04		11 04										13 04									
Haltwhistle d	10 11		11 11					12 08					13 11				14 08				15 08	
Brampton (Cumbria) d	10 27		11 27										13 27									
Wetheral d	10 35		11 35										13 35									
Carlisle a	10 44		11 49					12 38					13 45				14 38				15 40	

	NT	GR	NT	NT	NT	NT	NT	NT	GR	XC	NT	NT	NT	NT	NT	NT	GR	NT	GR	GR
Chathill d																				
Alnmouth for Alnwick 26 d		14 58							16 58	17 07							18 58		21 09	22 08
Acklington d																				
Widdrington d																				
Pegswood d																				
Morpeth 26 d										17 22									21 26	
Cramlington d																				
Manors d																				
Newcastle 26 a		15 27							17 27	17 37							19 27		21 42	22 42
Sunderland 26,44 d	14 28				15 28			16 28					17 26							
Newcastle d	14 50		15 10	15 30	15 50	16 10	16 30	16 50			17 10	17 30	17 50	18 10	18 30	18 50		20 15		
Dunston d																				
Metrocentre a	14 59		15 17	15 37	15 59	16 19	16 37	16 57			17 17	17 37	17 59	18 17	18 37	18 59		20 22		
d			15 18			16 20					17 18			18 18				20 23		
Blaydon d																				
Wylam d			15 26			16 28					17 26			18 26				20 31		
Prudhoe d			15 30			16 32					17 30			18 30				20 35		
Stocksfield d			15 34			16 37					17 34			18 34				20 39		
Riding Mill d			15 39			16 41					17 39			18 39				20 44		
Corbridge d			15 42			16 45					17 42			18 42				20 47		
Hexham a			15 48			16 51					17 48			18 48				20 53		
d			15 49			16 51					17 49			18 49				20 54		
Haydon Bridge d			15 58											18 58				21 03		
Bardon Mill d			16 04											19 04				21 09		
Haltwhistle d			16 11			17 10					18 08			19 11				21 16		
Brampton (Cumbria) d			16 27											19 27				21 32		
Wetheral d			16 35											19 35				21 40		
Carlisle a			16 45			17 44					18 38			19 45				21 51		

For connections from London Kings Cross please refer to Table 26

Chathill and Morpeth - Newcastle - Metrocentre, Hexham and Carlisle

Network Diagram - see first Page of Table 44

	NT	NT	XC	NT	NT	NT	GR	NT	NT	NT	GR	XC	XC	NT	NT	NT	GR	NT	NT	NT	XC	NT
Chathill d																						
Alnmouth for Alnwick 26 d			10 05				10 58					11 35	11 55				12 58				13 35	
Acklington d																						
Widdrington d																						
Pegswood d																						
Morpeth 26 d			10 45								12 06		12a35									
Cramlington d																						
Manors d																						
Newcastle 26 a			11 15				11 27				12 23	12 30					13 27				14 30	
Sunderland 26,44 d		09 28				10 28				11 28						12 28				13 28		
Newcastle d	09 10	09 53		10 10	10 30	10 50		11 10	11 30	11 50				12 10	12 30	12 50		13 10	13 30	13 50		14 10
Dunston d																						
Metrocentre a	09 17	10 01		10 17	10 37	10 59		11 17	11 37	11 57				12 17	12 37	12 59		13 17	13 37	13 59		14 17
d	09 18			10 18				11 18						12 18				13 18				14 18
Blaydon d																						
Wylam d	09 26			10 26				11 26						12 26				13 26				14 26
Prudhoe d	09 30			10 30				11 30						12 30				13 30				14 30
Stocksfield d	09 34			10 34				11 34						12 34				13 34				14 34
Riding Mill d	09 39			10 39				11 39						12 39				13 39				14 39
Corbridge d	09 42			10 42				11 42						12 42				13 42				14 42
Hexham a	09 48			10 48				11 48						12 48				13 48				14 48
d	09 49			10 49				11 49						12 49				13 49				14 49
Haydon Bridge d	09 58			10 58										12 58								
Bardon Mill d	10 04			11 04										13 04								
Haltwhistle d	10 11			11 11				12 08						13 11				14 08				15 08
Brampton (Cumbria) d	10 27			11 27										13 27								
Wetheral d	10 35			11 35										13 35								
Carlisle a	10 44			11 49				12 38						13 45				14 38				15 40

	NT	NT	GR	NT	NT	NT	NT	XC	NT	NT	GR	NT	NT	NT	XC	NT	NT	NT	GR	NT	GR	GR
Chathill d																						
Alnmouth for Alnwick 26 d			14 58					16 20			16 58				18 10				18 58		21 09	22 08
Acklington d																						
Widdrington d																						
Pegswood d																						
Morpeth 26 d								17 00							18a50						21 26	
Cramlington d																						
Manors d																						
Newcastle 26 a			15 27					17 30			17 27								19 27		21 42	22 42
Sunderland 26,44 d		14 28				15 28				16 28				17 26								
Newcastle d	14 30	14 50		15 10	15 30	15 50	16 10		16 30	16 50		17 10	17 30	17 50		18 10	18 30	18 50		20 15		
Dunston d																						
Metrocentre a	14 37	14 59		15 17	15 37	15 59	16 19		16 37	16 57		17 17	17 37	17 59		18 17	18 37	18 59		20 22		
d				15 18			16 20					17 18				18 18				20 23		
Blaydon d																						
Wylam d				15 26			16 28					17 26				18 26				20 31		
Prudhoe d				15 30			16 32					17 30				18 30				20 35		
Stocksfield d				15 34			16 37					17 34				18 34				20 39		
Riding Mill d				15 39			16 41					17 39				18 39				20 44		
Corbridge d				15 42			16 45					17 42				18 42				20 47		
Hexham a				15 48			16 51					17 48				18 48				20 53		
d				15 49			16 51					17 49				18 49				20 54		
Haydon Bridge d				15 58												18 58				21 03		
Bardon Mill d				16 04												19 04				21 09		
Haltwhistle d				16 11			17 10					18 08				19 11				21 16		
Brampton (Cumbria) d				16 27												19 27				21 32		
Wetheral d				16 35												19 35				21 40		
Carlisle a				16 45			17 44					18 38				19 45				21 51		

For connections from London Kings Cross please refer to Table 26

Table 48

Sundays
7 October to 21 October

Chathill and Morpeth - Newcastle - Metrocentre, Hexham and Carlisle

Network Diagram - see first Page of Table 44

	NT	NT	XC	NT	NT	NT	GR	NT	NT	NT	GR	XC	XC	NT	NT	NT	GR	NT	NT	NT	XC	NT
Chathill d																						
Alnmouth for Alnwick 26 d			10 05				10 58					11 35	11 55				12 58				13 35	
Acklington d																						
Widdrington d																						
Pegswood d																						
Morpeth 26 d			10 45								12 06		12a35									
Cramlington d																						
Manors d																						
Newcastle 26 a			11 15				11 27				12 23	12 30					13 27				14 30	
Sunderland 26,44 d		09 28				10 28				11 28						12 28				13 28		
Newcastle d	09 10	09 53		10 10	10 30	10 50		11 06	11 30	11 50				12 06	12 30	12 50		13 07	13 30	13 50		14 10
Dunston d																						
Metrocentre a	09 17	10 01		10 17	10 37	10 59		11 13	11 37	11 57				12 13	12 37	12 59		13 14	13 37	13 59		14 17
d	09 18			10 18				11 14						12 14				13 15				14 18
Blaydon d																						
Wylam d	09 26			10 26				11 22						12 22				13 23				14 26
Prudhoe d	09 30			10 30				11 26						12 26				13 27				14 30
Stocksfield d	09 34			10 34				11 30						12 30				13 31				14 34
Riding Mill d	09 39			10 39				11 35						12 35				13 36				14 39
Corbridge d	09 42			10 42				11 38						12 38				13 39				14 42
Hexham a	09 48			10 48				11 44						12 44				13 45				14 48
d	09 49			10 49				11 45						12 45				13 46				14 49
Haydon Bridge d	09 58			10 58										12 54								
Bardon Mill d	10 04			11 04										13 00								
Haltwhistle d	10 11			11 11				12 04						13 07				14 05				15 08
Brampton (Cumbria) d	10 27			11 27										13 23								
Wetheral d	10 35			11 35										13 31								
Carlisle a	10 46			11 50				12 38						13 45				14 39				15 40

	NT	NT	GR	NT	NT	NT	NT	XC	NT	NT	GR	NT	NT	NT	XC	NT	NT	NT	GR	NT	GR	GR
Chathill d																						
Alnmouth for Alnwick 26 d			14 58					16 20			16 58				18 10				18 58		21 09	22 08
Acklington d																						
Widdrington d																						
Pegswood d																						
Morpeth 26 d								17 00							18a50						21 26	
Cramlington d																						
Manors d																						
Newcastle 26 a			15 27					17 30			17 27								19 27		21 42	22 42
Sunderland 26,44 d		14 28				15 28				16 28				17 26								
Newcastle d	14 30	14 50		15 07	15 30	15 50	16 10		16 30	16 50		17 10	17 30	17 50		18 10	18 30	18 50		20 15		
Dunston d																						
Metrocentre a	14 37	14 59		15 14	15 37	15 59	16 19		16 37	16 57		17 17	17 37	17 59		18 17	18 37	18 59		20 22		
d				15 15			16 20					17 18				18 18				20 23		
Blaydon d																						
Wylam d				15 23			16 28					17 26				18 26				20 31		
Prudhoe d				15 27			16 32					17 30				18 30				20 35		
Stocksfield d				15 31			16 36					17 34				18 34				20 39		
Riding Mill d				15 36			16 41					17 39				18 39				20 44		
Corbridge d				15 39			16 44					17 42				18 42				20 47		
Hexham a				15 45			16 50					17 48				18 48				20 53		
d				15 46			16 51					17 49				18 49				20 54		
Haydon Bridge d				15 55												18 58				21 03		
Bardon Mill d				16 01												19 04				21 09		
Haltwhistle d				16 08			17 10					18 08				19 11				21 16		
Brampton (Cumbria) d				16 24												19 27				21 32		
Wetheral d				16 32												19 35				21 40		
Carlisle a				16 45			17 43					18 38				19 46				21 52		

For connections from London Kings Cross please refer to Table 26

Table 48

Sundays
from 28 October

Chathill and Morpeth - Newcastle - Metrocentre, Hexham and Carlisle

Network Diagram - see first Page of Table 44

	NT	NT	NT	NT	NT	XC	GR	NT	NT	NT	GR	NT	NT	NT	GR	NT	NT	NT	XC	NT	NT	NT
Chathill d																						
Alnmouth for Alnwick 26 d						10 49	10 58								12 58				14 08			
Acklington d																						
Widdrington d																						
Pegswood d																						
Morpeth 26 d						11 04					12 06											
Cramlington d																						
Manors d																						
Newcastle 26 a						11 19	11 27				12 23				13 27				14 35			
Sunderland 26,44 d		09 28			10 28					11 28				12 28				13 28				14 28
Newcastle d	09 10	09 53	10 10	10 30	10 50			11 06	11 30	11 50		12 06	12 30	12 50		13 07	13 30	13 50		14 10	14 30	14 50
Dunston d																						
Metrocentre a	09 17	10 01	10 17	10 37	10 59			11 13	11 37	11 57		12 13	12 37	12 59		13 14	13 37	13 59		14 17	14 37	14 59
d	09 18		10 18					11 14				12 14				13 15				14 18		
Blaydon d																						
Wylam d	09 26		10 26					11 22				12 22				13 23				14 26		
Prudhoe d	09 30		10 30					11 26				12 26				13 27				14 30		
Stocksfield d	09 34		10 34					11 30				12 30				13 31				14 34		
Riding Mill d	09 39		10 39					11 35				12 35				13 36				14 39		
Corbridge d	09 42		10 42					11 38				12 38				13 39				14 42		
Hexham a	09 48		10 48					11 44				12 44				13 45				14 48		
d	09 49		10 49					11 45				12 45				13 46				14 49		
Haydon Bridge d	09 58		10 58									12 54										
Bardon Mill d	10 04		11 04									13 00										
Haltwhistle d	10 11		11 11					12 04				13 07				14 05				15 08		
Brampton (Cumbria) d	10 27		11 27									13 23										
Wetheral d	10 35		11 35									13 31										
Carlisle a	10 46		11 50					12 38				13 45				14 39				15 40		

	GR	NT	NT	NT	NT	NT	NT	GR	XC	NT	NT	NT	NT	NT	NT	GR	NT	GR	GR
Chathill d																			
Alnmouth for Alnwick 26 d	14 58							16 58	17 07							18 58		21 09	22 08
Acklington d																			
Widdrington d																			
Pegswood d																			
Morpeth 26 d									17 22									21 26	
Cramlington d																			
Manors d																			
Newcastle 26 a	15 27							17 27	17 37							19 27		21 42	22 42
Sunderland 26,44 d				15 28			16 28					17 26							
Newcastle d		15 07	15 30	15 50	16 10	16 30	16 50			17 10	17 30	17 50	18 10	18 30	18 50		20 15		
Dunston d																			
Metrocentre a		15 14	15 37	15 59	16 19	16 37	16 57			17 17	17 37	17 59	18 17	18 37	18 59		20 22		
d		15 15			16 20					17 18			18 18				20 23		
Blaydon d																			
Wylam d		15 23			16 28					17 26			18 26				20 31		
Prudhoe d		15 27			16 32					17 30			18 30				20 35		
Stocksfield d		15 31			16 36					17 34			18 34				20 39		
Riding Mill d		15 36			16 41					17 39			18 39				20 44		
Corbridge d		15 39			16 44					17 42			18 42				20 47		
Hexham a		15 45			16 50					17 48			18 48				20 53		
d		15 46			16 51					17 49			18 49				20 54		
Haydon Bridge d		15 55											18 58				21 03		
Bardon Mill d		16 01											19 04				21 09		
Haltwhistle d		16 08			17 10					18 08			19 11				21 16		
Brampton (Cumbria) d		16 24											19 27				21 32		
Wetheral d		16 32											19 35				21 40		
Carlisle a		16 45			17 43					18 38			19 46				21 52		

For connections from London Kings Cross please refer to Table 26

until 28 September

Carlisle, Hexham and Metrocentre - Newcastle - Morpeth and Chathill

Network Diagram - see first Page of Table 44

Miles	Miles				NT MX	NT	NT	NT	GR	XC	GR	NT	NT		NT	GR	NT	NT	NT	XC	NT	NT	NT		GR	NT
									1	◇ 1	1					1				◇ 1					1	
0	—	**Carlisle**		d				06 25					07 17					08 28					09 37			
4¼	—	Wetheral		d				06 33					07 25					08 36								
11	—	Brampton (Cumbria)		d				06 43					07 35					08 46								
23¼	—	Haltwhistle		d				06 57					07 49					09 00					10 08			
28	—	Bardon Mill		d				07 05					07 57					09 08								
31¾	—	Haydon Bridge		d				07 10					08 02					09 13								
39½	—	**Hexham**		a				07 19					08 11					09 22					10 26			
—	—			d	23p20		06 16	07 19				07 42	08 11				08 43	09 22					10 26			
42½	—	Corbridge		d	23p24		06 20	07 24				07 46	08 16				08 47									
45	—	Riding Mill		d	23p29		06 25	07 27				07 51	08 20				08 52									
47¼	—	Stocksfield		d	23p33		06 29	07 31				07 55	08 24				08 56									
49¾	—	Prudhoe		d	23p37		06 33	07 37				07 59	08 29				09 00	09 34					10 38			
52	—	Wylam		d	23p41		06 37	07 41				08 03	08 33				09 04									
56¼	—	Blaydon		d								08 09	08 39													
58¼	—	**Metrocentre**		a	23p50			07 49				08 14	08 44				09 15	09 45					10 49			
—	—			d	23p50			07 50				08 16	08 44				09 16	09 46			10 01	10 31	10 50			11 00
59½	1¼	Dunston		d									08 47													
61¾	3½	**Newcastle**		a	00 05		06 55	08 03				08 27	08 57				09 26	10 00			10 10	10 39	11 07			11 10
—	—	Sunderland	26,44	a			07 18					08 50					09 49									
—	—	**Newcastle**	26	d		05 55			06 25	07 35	07 41				07 58	08 41			09 15	09 35	10 15				10 41	11 15
—	4	Manors		d															09 17		10 17					11 17
—	13¼	Cramlington		d		06 07									08 07				09 28		10 28					11 28
—	20	**Morpeth**	26	d		06 15			06 40	07a47					08a18	08a56			09a36		10a36					11a36
—	22	Pegswood		d																						
—	26¾	Widdrington		d																						
—	32	Acklington		d																						
—	38¼	Alnmouth for Alnwick	26	d		06 32			06a54		08a07									09a58					11a07	
—	49½	**Chathill**		a		06 46																				

			NT	NT	NT	NT	NT	NT	NT		GR	NT	NT	NT	NT	XC	NT	NT	NT		NT	XC	GR	NT	NT	NT
											1					◇ 1						◇ 1	1			
Carlisle		d			10 28				11 34						12 28						13 28					
Wetheral		d			10 36										12 36						13 36					
Brampton (Cumbria)		d			10 46										12 46						13 46					
Haltwhistle		d			11 00				12 03						13 00						14 00					
Bardon Mill		d			11 08										13 08						14 09					
Haydon Bridge		d			11 13										13 13						14 15					
Hexham		a			11 22				12 21						13 22						14 24					
		d	10 44		11 22		11 43		12 22				12 45		13 22			13 43			14 24				14 43	
Corbridge		d	10 48				11 47						12 49					13 47							14 47	
Riding Mill		d	10 53				11 52						12 54					13 52							14 52	
Stocksfield		d	10 57				11 56						12 58					13 56							14 56	
Prudhoe		d	11 01		11 33		12 00		12 33				13 02		13 34			14 00			14 33				15 00	
Wylam		d	11 05				12 04						13 06					14 04							15 04	
Blaydon		d																								
Metrocentre		a	11 15		11 45		12 15		12 44				13 15		13 45			14 14			14 45				15 15	
		d	11 16	11 31	11 46	12 01	12 16	12 31	12 45			13 00	13 16	13 31	13 46		14 01	14 15	14 31		14 46			15 01	15 16	15 31
Dunston		d																								
Newcastle		a	11 26	11 39	11 59	12 10	12 27	12 39	12 57			13 10	13 26	13 39	14 00		14 10	14 27	14 39		15 03			15 10	15 27	15 39
Sunderland	26,44	a	11 49				12 49						13 49					14 49							15 49	
Newcastle	26	d				12 15					12 44	13 15				13 38	14 15					14 36	14 43	15 15		
Manors		d				12 17						13 17					14 17							15 17		
Cramlington		d				12 28						13 28					14 28							15 28		
Morpeth	26	d				12a36						13a36					14a36					14a49		15a36		
Pegswood		d																								
Widdrington		d																								
Acklington		d																								
Alnmouth for Alnwick	26	d									13a10					14a01							15a09			
Chathill		a																								

For connections to London Kings Cross please refer to Table 26

until 28 September

Carlisle, Hexham and Metrocentre - Newcastle - Morpeth and Chathill

Network Diagram - see first Page of Table 44

			NT	XC	NT		NT	NT	NT	XC	NT	NT	XC	NT	NT		NT	NT	NT	GR	NT	NT	XC	GR	XC
				◇ 1						◇ 1			◇ 1							1			◇ 1	1	◇ 1
Carlisle		d	14 33						15 26						16 28				17 28			18 37			
Wetheral		d													16 36				17 36			18 45			
Brampton (Cumbria)		d													16 46				17 46			18 54			
Haltwhistle		d	15 03						15 55						17 00				18 01			19 09			
Bardon Mill		d													17 08				18 08			19 16			
Haydon Bridge		d													17 13				18 13			19 21			
Hexham		a	15 21						16 13						17 22				18 27			19 30			
		d	15 21				15 42		16 14			16 43			17 22			17 45	18 28		18 45	19 31			
Corbridge		d					15 46					16 47						17 49	18 32		18 49	19 35			
Riding Mill		d					15 51					16 52						17 54	18 37		18 54	19 40			
Stocksfield		d					15 55					16 56						17 58	18 41		18 58	19 44			
Prudhoe		d	15 32				16 00		16 25			17 00			17 34			18 02	18 45		19 02	19 48			
Wylam		d					16 04					17 04						18 06	18 49		19 06	19 52			
Blaydon		d																			19 12				
Metrocentre		a	15 44				16 15		16 38			17 15			17 44			18 15	19 00		19 17	20 00			
		d	15 45		16 01		16 16	16 30	16 38		17 01	17 16		17 29	17 45		18 06	18 16	19 00		19 18	20 01			
Dunston		d															18 08								
Newcastle		a	15 54		16 10		16 26	16 39	16 49		17 09	17 27		17 37	17 59		18 14	18 28	19 12		19 28	20 15			
Sunderland	26,44	a					16 49		17 14			17 50						18 49			19 50				
Newcastle	26	d		15 37	16 15					16 37	17 15		17 37	17 38			18 25			18 43			19 38	19 44	20 11
Manors		d			16 17						17 17			17 41			18 27								
Cramlington		d			16 28						17 28			17 52			18 38								
Morpeth	26	d			16a36						17 36			18a00			18a47							19a58	
Pegswood		d									17 40														
Widdrington		d									17 46														
Acklington		d									18 02														
Alnmouth for Alnwick	26	d		16a00						17a00	18 21		18a01							19a09			20a04		20a34
Chathill		a									18 35														

			NT	NT	XC	NT	NT	XC	GR	NT	NT		NT	GR FO	NT
					◇ 1			◇ 1	1					1	
Carlisle		d		19 41									21 28		
Wetheral		d											21 36		
Brampton (Cumbria)		d											21 46		
Haltwhistle		d		20 10									22 01		
Bardon Mill		d											22 08		
Haydon Bridge		d											22 13		
Hexham		a		20 28									22 22		
		d		20 28			21 12						22 23		23 20
Corbridge		d		20 33			21 16						22 27		23 24
Riding Mill		d		20 37			21 21						22 32		23 29
Stocksfield		d		20 41			21 25						22 36		23 33
Prudhoe		d		20 46			21 29						22 40		23 37
Wylam		d		20 49			21 33						22 44		23 41
Blaydon		d													
Metrocentre		a		20 58			21 44						22 53		23 50
		d	20 31	20 59		21 22	21 45				22 15		22 53		23 50
Dunston		d													
Newcastle		a	20 39	21 11		21 30	21 56				22 25		23 07		00 05
Sunderland	26,44	a													
Newcastle	26	d			20 39			21 36	21 40	22 00				22 42	
Manors		d													
Cramlington		d								22 12					
Morpeth	26	d			20a54				21 56	22a21				22 56	
Pegswood		d													
Widdrington		d													
Acklington		d													
Alnmouth for Alnwick	26	d						21a59	22a10					23a11	
Chathill		a													

For connections to London Kings Cross please refer to Table 26

Table 48

Mondays to Fridays
from 1 October

Carlisle, Hexham and Metrocentre - Newcastle - Morpeth and Chathill

Network Diagram - see first Page of Table 44

		NT MX	NT	NT	NT	GR	XC	NT	NT	GR		NT	GR	NT	NT	NT	XC	NT	NT	NT		NT	GR	NT	NT
Carlisle	d				06 25				07 17						08 28							09 37			
Wetheral	d				06 33				07 25						08 36										
Brampton (Cumbria)	d				06 43				07 35						08 46										
Haltwhistle	d				06 57				07 49						09 00							10 08			
Bardon Mill	d				07 05				07 57						09 08										
Haydon Bridge	d				07 10				08 02						09 13										
Hexham	a				07 19				08 11						09 22							10 26			
	d	23p20		06 14	07 19			07 40	08 11					08 43	09 22				09 44			10 26			10 42
Corbridge	d	23p24		06 18	07 24			07 44	08 16					08 47					09 48						10 46
Riding Mill	d	23p29		06 23	07 28			07 49	08 20					08 52					09 53						10 51
Stocksfield	d	23p33		06 27	07 32			07 53	08 24					08 56					09 57						10 55
Prudhoe	d	23p37		06 31	07 37			07 57	08 29					09 00	09 34				10 01			10 38			10 59
Wylam	d	23p41		06 35	07 41			08 01	08 33					09 04					10 05						11 03
Blaydon	d							08 07	08 39																
Metrocentre	a	23p50			07 50			08 14	08 44					09 15	09 45				10 16			10 49			11 15
	d	23p50			07 51			08 16	08 44					09 16	09 46			10 01	10 16	10 31		10 50		11 00	11 16
Dunston	d								08 47																
Newcastle	a	00 05		06 55	08 08			08 27	08 57					09 26	10 00			10 10	10 27	10 39		11 07		11 10	11 26
Sunderland 26,44	a			07 18				08 50						09 49					10 49						11 49
Newcastle 26	d		05 55			06 25	07 35			07 41		07 58	08 41			09 15	09 35	10 15					10 41	11 15	
Manors	d															09 17		10 17						11 17	
Cramlington	d		06 07									08 07				09 28		10 28						11 28	
Morpeth 26	d		06 15			06 40	07a47					08a18	08a56			09a36		10a36						11a36	
Pegswood	d																								
Widdrington	d																								
Acklington	d																								
Alnmouth for Alnwick 26	d		06 32			06a54				08a07							09a58						11a07		
Chathill	a		06 46																						

		NT	NT	NT	NT	NT		NT	GR	NT	NT	NT	NT	XC	NT	NT		NT	NT	XC	GR	NT	NT	NT	NT
Carlisle	d		10 23					11 27					12 23						13 28						14 33
Wetheral	d		10 31										12 31						13 38						
Brampton (Cumbria)	d		10 41										12 41						13 48						
Haltwhistle	d		10 55					11 56					12 55						14 02						15 03
Bardon Mill	d		11 03										13 03						14 10						
Haydon Bridge	d		11 08										13 08						14 15						
Hexham	a		11 20					12 18					13 20						14 24						15 21
	d		11 20		11 43			12 19			12 43		13 20			13 43			14 24				14 43		15 21
Corbridge	d				11 47						12 47					13 47							14 47		
Riding Mill	d				11 52						12 52					13 52							14 52		
Stocksfield	d				11 56						12 56					13 56							14 56		
Prudhoe	d		11 31		12 00			12 30			13 00		13 32			14 00			14 36				15 00		15 32
Wylam	d				12 04						13 04					14 04							15 04		
Blaydon	d																								
Metrocentre	a		11 45		12 15			12 45			13 15		13 45			14 14			14 47				15 15		15 44
	d	11 31	11 46	12 01	12 16	12 31		12 45		13 00	13 16	13 31	13 46		14 01	14 15		14 31	14 48			15 01	15 16	15 31	15 45
Dunston	d																								
Newcastle	a	11 39	11 59	12 10	12 27	12 39		12 57		13 10	13 26	13 39	14 00		14 10	14 27		14 39	15 03			15 10	15 27	15 39	15 54
Sunderland 26,44	a				12 49						13 49					14 49							15 49		
Newcastle 26	d			12 15					12 44	13 15				13 38	14 15					14 36	14 43	15 15			
Manors	d			12 17						13 17					14 17							15 17			
Cramlington	d			12 28						13 28					14 28							15 28			
Morpeth 26	d			12a36						13a36					14a36					14a49		15a36			
Pegswood	d																								
Widdrington	d																								
Acklington	d																								
Alnmouth for Alnwick 26	d								13a10					14a01							15a09				
Chathill	a																								

For connections to London Kings Cross please refer to Table 26

Table 48

Mondays to Fridays
from 1 October

Carlisle, Hexham and Metrocentre - Newcastle - Morpeth and Chathill

Network Diagram - see first Page of Table 44

		XC		NT	NT	NT	NT	XC	NT	NT	XC	NT		NT	NT	NT	NT	GR	NT	NT	XC	GR		XC	NT
Carlisle	d						15 21							16 23			17 21			18 37					
Wetheral	d													16 31			17 29			18 45					
Brampton (Cumbria)	d													16 41			17 39			18 54					
Haltwhistle	d						15 50							16 55			17 54			19 09					
Bardon Mill	d													17 03			18 01			19 16					
Haydon Bridge	d													17 08			18 06			19 21					
Hexham	a						16 11							17 20			18 20			19 30					
	d				15 42		16 12			16 43				17 20		17 43	18 21		18 43	19 31					
Corbridge	d				15 46					16 47						17 47	18 25		18 47	19 35					
Riding Mill	d				15 51					16 52						17 52	18 30		18 52	19 40					
Stocksfield	d				15 55					16 56						17 56	18 34		18 56	19 44					
Prudhoe	d				16 00		16 23			17 00				17 32		18 00	18 38		19 00	19 48					
Wylam	d				16 04					17 04						18 04	18 42		19 04	19 52					
Blaydon	d																		19 10						
Metrocentre	a				16 15		16 38			17 15				17 45		18 15	18 53		19 17	20 00					
	d			16 01	16 16	16 30	16 38		17 01	17 16		17 29		17 46	18 06	18 16	18 53		19 18	20 01					20 31
Dunston	d														18 08										
Newcastle	a			16 10	16 26	16 39	16 49		17 09	17 27		17 37		17 59	18 14	18 28	19 05		19 28	20 15					20 39
Sunderland 26,44	a				16 49		17 14			17 50						18 49			19 50						
Newcastle 26	d	15 37		16 15				16 37	17 15		17 37	17 38			18 25			18 43			19 38	19 44		20 11	
Manors	d			16 17					17 17			17 41			18 27										
Cramlington	d			16 28					17 28			17 52			18 38										
Morpeth 26	d			16a36					17 36			18a00			18a47							19a58			
Pegswood	d								17 40																
Widdrington	d								17 46																
Acklington	d								18 02																
Alnmouth for Alnwick 26	d	16a00						17a00	18 21		18a01							19a09			20a04			20a34	
Chathill	a								18 35																

		NT	XC	NT	NT	XC	GR	NT		NT	NT	GR FO	NT
Carlisle	d	19 34									21 23		
Wetheral	d										21 31		
Brampton (Cumbria)	d										21 41		
Haltwhistle	d	20 03									21 56		
Bardon Mill	d										22 03		
Haydon Bridge	d										22 08		
Hexham	a	20 25									22 20		
	d	20 25			21 12						22 21		23 20
Corbridge	d	20 31			21 16						22 25		23 24
Riding Mill	d	20 35			21 21						22 30		23 29
Stocksfield	d	20 39			21 25						22 34		23 33
Prudhoe	d	20 43			21 29						22 38		23 37
Wylam	d	20 47			21 33						22 42		23 41
Blaydon	d												
Metrocentre	a	20 57			21 44						22 53		23 50
	d	20 58		21 22	21 45					22 15	22 53		23 50
Dunston	d												
Newcastle	a	21 10		21 30	21 57					22 25	23 07		00 05
Sunderland 26,44	a												
Newcastle 26	d		20 39			21 36	21 40	22 00				22 42	
Manors	d												
Cramlington	d							22 12					
Morpeth 26	d		20a54				21 56	22a21				22 56	
Pegswood	d												
Widdrington	d												
Acklington	d												
Alnmouth for Alnwick 26	d					21a59	22a10					23a11	
Chathill	a												

For connections to London Kings Cross please refer to Table 26

Carlisle, Hexham and Metrocentre - Newcastle - Morpeth and Chathill

Network Diagram - see first Page of Table 44

	NT	NT	NT	NT	GR	XC	GR	NT	NT	NT	GR	NT	NT	NT	XC	NT	NT	NT	NT	GR	NT	NT
Carlisle d				06 25					07 17				08 28						09 37			
Wetheral d				06 33					07 25				08 36									
Brampton (Cumbria) d				06 43					07 35				08 46									
Haltwhistle d				06 57					07 49				09 00						10 08			
Bardon Mill d				07 05					07 57				09 08									
Haydon Bridge d				07 10					08 02				09 13									
Hexham a				07 19					08 11				09 22						10 26			
d	23p20		06 16	07 19				07 42	08 11			08 43	09 22				09 45		10 26			10 44
Corbridge d	23p24		06 20	07 24				07 46	08 16			08 47					09 49					10 48
Riding Mill d	23p29		06 25	07 27				07 51	08 20			08 52					09 54					10 53
Stocksfield d	23p33		06 29	07 31				07 55	08 24			08 56					09 58					10 57
Prudhoe d	23p37		06 33	07 37				07 59	08 29			09 00	09 34				10 02		10 38			11 01
Wylam d	23p41		06 37	07 41				08 03	08 33			09 04					10 06					11 05
Blaydon d								08 09	08 39													
Metrocentre a	23p50			07 49				08 14	08 44			09 15	09 45				10 16		10 49			11 15
d	23p50			07 50				08 16	08 44			09 16	09 46			10 01	10 16	10 31	10 50		11 00	11 16
Dunston d									08 47													
Newcastle a	00 05		06 55	08 08				08 27	08 57			09 26	10 03			10 10	10 27	10 39	11 07		11 10	11 26
Sunderland 26,44 a			07 18					08 50				09 49					10 49					11 49
Newcastle 26 d		05 55			06 30	07 38	07 42			07 58	08 41			09 15	09 35	10 15				10 39	11 15	
Manors d														09 17		10 17					11 17	
Cramlington d		06 07								08 09				09 28		10 28					11 28	
Morpeth 26 d		06 17			06 43	07a50				08a19	08a55			09a36		10a35					11a36	
Pegswood d																						
Widdrington d																						
Acklington d																						
Alnmouth for Alnwick 26 d		06 35			06a57		08a08								09a58					11a05		
Chathill a		06 50																				

	NT	NT	NT	NT	NT	NT	GR	NT	NT	NT	NT	XC	NT	NT	NT	NT	XC	GR	NT	NT	NT	NT
Carlisle d		10 28				11 34					12 28					13 29						14 33
Wetheral d		10 36									12 36					13 38						
Brampton (Cumbria) d		10 46									12 46					13 48						
Haltwhistle d		11 00				12 03					13 00					14 02						15 03
Bardon Mill d		11 08									13 08					14 10						
Haydon Bridge d		11 13									13 13					14 15						
Hexham a		11 22				12 21					13 22					14 24						15 21
d		11 22		11 43		12 22			12 45		13 22			13 43		14 24				14 43		15 21
Corbridge d				11 47					12 49					13 47						14 47		
Riding Mill d				11 52					12 54					13 52						14 52		
Stocksfield d				11 56					12 58					13 56						14 56		
Prudhoe d		11 33		12 00		12 33			13 02		13 34			14 00		14 36				15 00		15 32
Wylam d				12 04					13 06					14 04						15 04		
Blaydon d																						
Metrocentre a		11 45		12 15		12 45			13 15		13 45			14 14		14 47				15 15		15 44
d	11 31	11 46	12 01	12 16	12 31	12 45		13 01	13 16	13 31	13 46		14 01	14 15	14 31	14 48			15 01	15 16	15 31	15 45
Dunston d																						
Newcastle a	11 39	11 59	12 10	12 27	12 39	12 57		13 10	13 26	13 39	14 00		14 10	14 27	14 39	15 03			15 11	15 27	15 39	15 54
Sunderland 26,44 a				12 49					13 49					14 49						15 49		
Newcastle 26 d			12 15				12 40	13 15				13 35	14 15				14 35	14 40	15 15			
Manors d			12 17					13 17					14 17						15 17			
Cramlington d			12 28					13 28					14 28						15 28			
Morpeth 26 d			12a35					13a37					14a37				14a47		15a35			
Pegswood d																						
Widdrington d																						
Acklington d																						
Alnmouth for Alnwick 26 d							13a06					13a59						15a06				
Chathill a																						

For connections to London Kings Cross please refer to Table 26

Carlisle, Hexham and Metrocentre - Newcastle - Morpeth and Chathill

Network Diagram - see first Page of Table 44

	XC	NT	NT	NT	NT	XC	NT	NT	NT	NT	XC	NT	NT	NT	GR	NT	NT	XC	GR	NT	NT
Carlisle d					15 26					16 28				17 28			18 37				
Wetheral d										16 36				17 36			18 45				
Brampton (Cumbria) d										16 46				17 46			18 54				
Haltwhistle d					15 55					17 00				18 01			19 09				
Bardon Mill d										17 08				18 08			19 16				
Haydon Bridge d										17 13				18 13			19 21				
Hexham a					16 13					17 22				18 22			19 30				
d			15 42		16 14				16 43	17 22			17 43	18 23		18 45	19 31				
Corbridge d			15 46						16 47				17 47	18 27		18 49	19 35				
Riding Mill d			15 51						16 52				17 52	18 32		18 54	19 40				
Stocksfield d			15 55						16 56				17 56	18 36		18 58	19 44				
Prudhoe d			16 00		16 25				17 00	17 34			18 00	18 40		19 02	19 48				
Wylam d			16 04						17 04				18 04	18 44		19 06	19 52				
Blaydon d																19 12					
Metrocentre a			16 15		16 38				17 15	17 44			18 15	18 54		19 17	20 00				
d		16 01	16 16	16 30	16 38		16 50	17 07	17 16	17 45		18 06	18 16	18 54		19 18	20 01			20 15	
Dunston d												18 08									
Newcastle a		16 10	16 26	16 38	16 49		16 58	17 15	17 27	17 59		18 14	18 28	19 07		19 28	20 15			20 23	
Sunderland 26,44 a			16 49		17 14				17 50				18 49			19 50					
Newcastle 26 d	15 34	16 15				16 35	17 00	17 22			17 37	18 19			18 41			19 37	19 45		20 20
Manors d		16 17					17 03	17 24				18 21									
Cramlington d		16 28					17 14	17 35				18 32									20 32
Morpeth 26 d		16a36					17 22	17a42				18a40							19a59		20a41
Pegswood d							17 25														
Widdrington d							17 31														
Acklington d							17 38														
Alnmouth for Alnwick 26 d	15a58					16a58	17 46				18a00				19a07			20a03			
Chathill a							17 59														

	XC	NT	NT	GR	NT	XC	NT	NT
Carlisle d			19 41					21 20
Wetheral d								21 27
Brampton (Cumbria) d								21 37
Haltwhistle d			20 10					21 52
Bardon Mill d								21 59
Haydon Bridge d								22 04
Hexham a			20 28					22 13
d			20 28		21 12			22 14
Corbridge d			20 33		21 16			22 18
Riding Mill d			20 37		21 21			22 23
Stocksfield d			20 41		21 25			22 27
Prudhoe d			20 46		21 29			22 31
Wylam d			20 49		21 33			22 35
Blaydon d								
Metrocentre a			20 58		21 44			22 44
d		20 47	20 59		21 45		22 30	22 45
Dunston d								
Newcastle a		20 55	21 11		21 56		22 39	23 00
Sunderland 26,44 a		21 20						
Newcastle 26 d	20 38			20 54		21 38		
Manors d								
Cramlington d								
Morpeth 26 d	20a50			21 09				
Pegswood d								
Widdrington d								
Acklington d								
Alnmouth for Alnwick 26 d				21a24		22a01		
Chathill a								

For connections to London Kings Cross please refer to Table 26

Table 48

Saturdays

15 September to 29 September

Carlisle, Hexham and Metrocentre - Newcastle - Morpeth and Chathill

Network Diagram - see first Page of Table 44

		NT	NT	NT	NT	GR	XC	GR	NT	NT	NT	GR	NT	NT	NT	XC	NT	NT	NT	NT	GR	NT	NT
						■ 1	◇1	■ 1				■ 1				◇1					■ 1		
Carlisle	d				06 25					07 17				08 28						09 37			
Wetheral	d				06 33					07 25				08 36									
Brampton (Cumbria)	d				06 43					07 35				08 46									
Haltwhistle	d				06 57					07 49				09 00						10 08			
Bardon Mill	d				07 05					07 57				09 08									
Haydon Bridge	d				07 10					08 02				09 13									
Hexham	a				07 19					08 11				09 22						10 26			
	d	23p20		06 16	07 19				07 42	08 11			08 43	09 22				09 45		10 26			10 44
Corbridge	d	23p24		06 20	07 24				07 46	08 16			08 47					09 49					10 48
Riding Mill	d	23p29		06 25	07 27				07 51	08 20			08 52					09 54					10 53
Stocksfield	d	23p33		06 29	07 31				07 55	08 24			08 56					09 58					10 57
Prudhoe	d	23p37		06 33	07 37				07 59	08 29			09 00	09 34				10 02		10 38			11 01
Wylam	d	23p41		06 37	07 41				08 03	08 33			09 04					10 06					11 05
Blaydon	d								08 09	08 39													
Metrocentre	a	23p50			07 49				08 14	08 44			09 15	09 45				10 16		10 49			11 15
	d	23p50			07 50				08 16	08 44			09 16	09 46			10 01	10 16	10 31	10 50		11 00	11 16
Dunston	d									08 47													
Newcastle	a	00 05		06 55	08 08				08 27	08 57			09 26	10 03			10 10	10 27	10 39	11 07		11 10	11 26
Sunderland 26,44	a			07 18					08 50				09 49					10 49					11 49
Newcastle 26	d		05 55			06 30	07 38	07 42			07 58	08 41			09 15	09 35	10 15				10 39	11 15	
Manors	d														09 17		10 17					11 17	
Cramlington	d		06 07								08 09				09 28		10 28					11 28	
Morpeth 26	d		06 17			06 43	07a50				08a19	08a55			09a36		10a35					11a36	
Pegswood	d																						
Widdrington	d																						
Acklington	d																						
Alnmouth for Alnwick 26	d		06 35			06a57		08a08								09a58					11a05		
Chathill	a		06 50																				

		NT	NT	NT	NT	NT	NT	GR	NT	NT	NT	NT	XC	NT	NT	NT	NT	XC	GR	NT	NT	NT	NT
								■ 1					◇1					◇1	■ 1				
Carlisle	d		10 28				11 34					12 28					13 29						14 33
Wetheral	d		10 36									12 36					13 38						
Brampton (Cumbria)	d		10 46									12 46					13 48						
Haltwhistle	d		11 00				12 03					13 00					14 02						15 03
Bardon Mill	d		11 08									13 08					14 10						
Haydon Bridge	d		11 13									13 13					14 15						
Hexham	a		11 22				12 21					13 22					14 24						15 21
	d		11 22		11 43		12 22			12 45		13 22			13 43		14 24				14 43		15 21
Corbridge	d				11 47					12 49					13 47						14 47		
Riding Mill	d				11 52					12 54					13 52						14 52		
Stocksfield	d				11 56					12 58					13 56						14 56		
Prudhoe	d		11 33		12 00		12 33			13 02		13 34			14 00		14 36				15 00		15 32
Wylam	d				12 04					13 06					14 04						15 04		
Blaydon	d																						
Metrocentre	a		11 45		12 15		12 45			13 15		13 45			14 14		14 47				15 15		15 44
	d	11 31	11 46	12 01	12 16	12 31	12 45		13 01	13 16	13 31	13 46		14 01	14 15	14 31	14 48			15 01	15 16	15 31	15 45
Dunston	d																						
Newcastle	a	11 39	11 59	12 10	12 27	12 39	12 57		13 10	13 26	13 39	14 00		14 10	14 27	14 39	15 03			15 11	15 27	15 39	15 54
Sunderland 26,44	a				12 49					13 49					14 49						15 49		
Newcastle 26	d			12 15				12 40	13 15				13 35	14 15				14 35	14 40	15 15			
Manors	d			12 17					13 17					14 17						15 17			
Cramlington	d			12 28					13 28					14 28						15 28			
Morpeth 26	d			12a35					13a37					14a37				14a47		15a35			
Pegswood	d																						
Widdrington	d																						
Acklington	d																						
Alnmouth for Alnwick 26	d							13a06					13a59						15a06				
Chathill	a																						

For connections to London Kings Cross please refer to Table 26

Table 48

Saturdays

15 September to 29 September

Carlisle, Hexham and Metrocentre - Newcastle - Morpeth and Chathill

Network Diagram - see first Page of Table 44

		XC	NT	NT	NT	NT	XC	NT	NT	NT	NT	XC	NT	NT	NT	GR	NT	NT	XC	GR	NT	NT
		◇1					◇1					◇1				■ 1			◇1	■ 1		
Carlisle	d					15 26					16 28				17 28			18 37				
Wetheral	d										16 36				17 36			18 45				
Brampton (Cumbria)	d										16 46				17 46			18 54				
Haltwhistle	d					15 55					17 00				18 01			19 09				
Bardon Mill	d										17 08				18 08			19 16				
Haydon Bridge	d										17 13				18 13			19 21				
Hexham	a					16 13					17 22				18 22			19 30				
	d			15 42		16 14				16 43	17 22			17 43	18 23		18 45	19 31				
Corbridge	d			15 46						16 47				17 47	18 27		18 49	19 35				
Riding Mill	d			15 51						16 52				17 52	18 32		18 54	19 40				
Stocksfield	d			15 55						16 56				17 56	18 36		18 58	19 44				
Prudhoe	d			16 00		16 25				17 00	17 34			18 00	18 40		19 02	19 48				
Wylam	d			16 04						17 04				18 04	18 44		19 06	19 52				
Blaydon	d																19 12					
Metrocentre	a			16 15		16 38				17 15	17 44			18 15	18 54		19 17	20 00				
	d		16 01	16 16	16 30	16 38		16 50	17 07	17 16	17 45		18 06	18 16	18 54		19 18	20 01			20 15	
Dunston	d												18 08									
Newcastle	a		16 10	16 26	16 38	16 49		16 58	17 15	17 27	17 59		18 14	18 28	19 07		19 28	20 15			20 23	
Sunderland 26,44	a			16 49		17 14				17 50				18 49			19 50					
Newcastle 26	d	15 34	16 15				16 35	17 00	17 22			17 37	18 19			18 41			19 33	19 45		20 20
Manors	d		16 17					17 03	17 24				18 21									
Cramlington	d		16 28					17 14	17 35				18 32									20 32
Morpeth 26	d		16a36					17 22	17a42				18a40							19a59		20a41
Pegswood	d							17 25														
Widdrington	d							17 31														
Acklington	d							17 38														
Alnmouth for Alnwick 26	d	15a58					16a58	17 46				18a00				19a07			19a59			
Chathill	a							17 59														

		NT	NT	GR	NT	NT	NT
				■ 1			
Carlisle	d		19 41				21 20
Wetheral	d						21 27
Brampton (Cumbria)	d						21 37
Haltwhistle	d		20 10				21 52
Bardon Mill	d						21 59
Haydon Bridge	d						22 04
Hexham	a		20 28				22 13
	d		20 28		21 12		22 14
Corbridge	d		20 33		21 16		22 18
Riding Mill	d		20 37		21 21		22 23
Stocksfield	d		20 41		21 25		22 27
Prudhoe	d		20 46		21 29		22 31
Wylam	d		20 49		21 33		22 35
Blaydon	d						
Metrocentre	a		20 58		21 44		22 44
	d	20 47	20 59		21 45	22 30	22 45
Dunston	d						
Newcastle	a	20 55	21 11		21 56	22 39	23 00
Sunderland 26,44	a	21 20					
Newcastle 26	d			20 54			
Manors	d						
Cramlington	d						
Morpeth 26	d			21 09			
Pegswood	d						
Widdrington	d						
Acklington	d						
Alnmouth for Alnwick 26	d			21a24			
Chathill	a						

For connections to London Kings Cross please refer to Table 26

Carlisle, Hexham and Metrocentre - Newcastle - Morpeth and Chathill

Network Diagram - see first Page of Table 44

		NT	NT	NT	NT	GR	XC	NT	NT	GR		NT	GR	NT	NT	NT	XC	NT	NT	NT		NT	GR	NT	NT
						■ 1 🍴	◇1 🍴			■ 1 🍴			■ 1 🍴				◇1 🍴						■ 1 🍴		
Carlisle ■	d				06 25				07 17						08 28							09 37			
Wetheral	d				06 33				07 25						08 36										
Brampton (Cumbria)	d				06 43				07 35						08 46										
Haltwhistle	d				06 57				07 49						09 00							10 08			
Bardon Mill	d				07 05				07 57						09 08										
Haydon Bridge	d				07 10				08 02						09 13										
Hexham	a				07 19				08 11						09 22							10 26			
	d	23p20		06 14	07 19			07 40	08 11					08 45	09 22				09 44			10 26			10 42
Corbridge	d	23p24		06 18	07 24			07 44	08 16					08 49					09 48						10 46
Riding Mill	d	23p29		06 23	07 28			07 49	08 20					08 54					09 53						10 51
Stocksfield	d	23p33		06 27	07 32			07 53	08 24					08 58					09 57						10 55
Prudhoe	d	23p37		06 31	07 37			07 57	08 29					09 02	09 34				10 01			10 38			10 59
Wylam	d	23p41		06 35	07 41			08 01	08 33					09 06					10 05						11 03
Blaydon	d							08 07	08 39																
Metrocentre	a	23p50			07 50			08 14	08 44					09 15	09 45				10 16			10 49			11 15
	d	23p50			07 51			08 16	08 44					09 16	09 46			10 01	10 16	10 31		10 50		11 00	11 16
Dunston	d								08 47																
Newcastle ■ ⇌	a	00 05		06 56	08 08			08 27	08 57					09 26	10 03			10 10	10 27	10 39		11 07		11 10	11 26
Sunderland 26,44 ⇌	a			07 18				08 50						09 49					10 49						11 49
Newcastle ■ 26 ⇌	d		05 55			06 30	07 38			07 42		07 58	08 41			09 15	09 35	10 15					10 39	11 15	
Manors	d															09 17		10 17						11 17	
Cramlington	d		06 07									08 09				09 28		10 28						11 28	
Morpeth 26	d		06 17			06 43	07a50					08a19	08a55			09a36		10a35						11a36	
Pegswood	d																								
Widdrington	d																								
Acklington	d																								
Alnmouth for Alnwick 26	d		06 35			06a57				08a08							09a58						11a05		
Chathill	a		06 50																						

		NT	NT	NT	NT	NT		NT	GR	NT	NT	NT	NT	XC	NT	NT		NT	NT	XC	GR	NT	NT	NT	NT
									■ 1 🍴					◇1 🍴						◇1 🍴	■ 1 🍴				
Carlisle ■	d		10 23					11 27					12 23						13 29						14 33
Wetheral	d		10 31										12 31						13 38						
Brampton (Cumbria)	d		10 41										12 41						13 48						
Haltwhistle	d		10 55					11 56					12 55						14 02						15 03
Bardon Mill	d		11 03										13 03						14 10						
Haydon Bridge	d		11 08										13 08						14 15						
Hexham	a		11 20					12 18					13 20						14 23						15 21
	d		11 20		11 43			12 19			12 43		13 20			13 43			14 24				14 43		15 21
Corbridge	d				11 47						12 47					13 47							14 47		
Riding Mill	d				11 52						12 52					13 52							14 52		
Stocksfield	d				11 56						12 56					13 56							14 56		
Prudhoe	d		11 31		12 00			12 30			13 00		13 32			14 00			14 36				15 00		15 32
Wylam	d				12 04						13 04					14 06							15 04		
Blaydon	d																								
Metrocentre	a		11 45		12 15			12 45			13 15		13 45			14 14			14 47				15 15		15 44
	d	11 31	11 46	12 01	12 16	12 31		12 45		13 01	13 16	13 31	13 46		14 01	14 15		14 31	14 48			15 01	15 16	15 31	15 45
Dunston	d																								
Newcastle ■ ⇌	a	11 39	11 59	12 10	12 27	12 39		12 57		13 10	13 26	13 39	14 00		14 10	14 27		14 39	15 03			15 11	15 27	15 39	15 54
Sunderland 26,44 ⇌	a				12 49						13 49					14 49							15 49		
Newcastle ■ 26 ⇌	d			12 15					12 40	13 15				13 35	14 15					14 35	14 40	15 15			
Manors	d			12 17						13 17					14 17							15 17			
Cramlington	d			12 28						13 28					14 28							15 28			
Morpeth 26	d			12a35						13a37					14a37					14a47		15a35			
Pegswood	d																								
Widdrington	d																								
Acklington	d																								
Alnmouth for Alnwick 26	d								13a06					13a59							15a06				
Chathill	a																								

For connections to London Kings Cross please refer to Table 26

Carlisle, Hexham and Metrocentre - Newcastle - Morpeth and Chathill

Network Diagram - see first Page of Table 44

		XC		NT	NT	NT	NT	XC	NT	NT	NT	NT		XC	NT	NT	NT	GR	NT	NT	XC	GR		NT	NT
		◇1 🍴						◇1 🍴						◇1 🍴				■ 1			◇1 🍴	■ 1 🍴			
Carlisle ■	d						15 21					16 23					17 21			18 37					
Wetheral	d											16 31					17 29			18 45					
Brampton (Cumbria)	d											16 41					17 39			18 54					
Haltwhistle	d						15 50					16 55					17 54			19 09					
Bardon Mill	d											17 03					18 01			19 16					
Haydon Bridge	d											17 08					18 06			19 21					
Hexham	a						16 11					17 20					18 20			19 30					
	d				15 42		16 12				16 43	17 20				17 43	18 21		18 43	19 31					
Corbridge	d				15 46						16 47					17 47	18 25		18 47	19 35					
Riding Mill	d				15 51						16 52					17 52	18 30		18 52	19 40					
Stocksfield	d				15 55						16 56					17 56	18 34		18 56	19 44					
Prudhoe	d				16 00		16 23				17 00	17 32				18 00	18 38		19 00	19 48					
Wylam	d				16 04						17 04					18 04	18 42		19 04	19 52					
Blaydon	d																		19 10						
Metrocentre	a				16 15		16 38				17 15	17 45				18 15	18 53		19 17	20 00					
	d			16 01	16 16	16 30	16 38		16 50	17 07	17 16	17 45			18 06	18 16	18 53		19 18	20 01				20 15	
Dunston	d														18 08										
Newcastle ■ ⇌	a			16 10	16 26	16 38	16 49		16 58	17 15	17 27	17 59			18 14	18 28	19 05		19 28	20 15				20 23	
Sunderland 26,44 ⇌	a				16 49		17 14				17 50					18 49			19 50						
Newcastle ■ 26 ⇌	d	15 34		16 15				16 35	17 00	17 22				17 37	18 19			18 41			19 33	19 45			20 20
Manors	d			16 17					17 03	17 24					18 21										
Cramlington	d			16 28					17 14	17 35					18 32										20 32
Morpeth 26	d			16a36					17 22	17a42					18a40							19a59			20a41
Pegswood	d								17 25																
Widdrington	d								17 31																
Acklington	d								17 38																
Alnmouth for Alnwick 26	d	15a58						16a58	17 46					18a00				19a07			19a59				
Chathill	a								17 59																

		NT	NT	GR	NT	NT	NT
				■ 1 🍴			
Carlisle ■	d		19 34				21 15
Wetheral	d						21 23
Brampton (Cumbria)	d						21 33
Haltwhistle	d		20 03				21 48
Bardon Mill	d						21 55
Haydon Bridge	d						22 00
Hexham	a		20 25				22 12
	d		20 26		21 12		22 13
Corbridge	d		20 30		21 16		22 17
Riding Mill	d		20 35		21 21		22 22
Stocksfield	d		20 39		21 25		22 26
Prudhoe	d		20 43		21 29		22 30
Wylam	d		20 47		21 33		22 34
Blaydon	d						
Metrocentre	a		20 58		21 44		22 45
	d	20 47	20 58		21 45	22 30	22 45
Dunston	d						
Newcastle ■ ⇌	a	20 55	21 10		21 57	22 39	23 00
Sunderland 26,44 ⇌	a	21 20					
Newcastle ■ 26 ⇌	d			20 54			
Manors	d						
Cramlington	d						
Morpeth 26	d			21 09			
Pegswood	d						
Widdrington	d						
Acklington	d						
Alnmouth for Alnwick 26	d			21a24			
Chathill	a						

For connections to London Kings Cross please refer to Table 26

Table 48

Saturdays
from 27 October

Carlisle, Hexham and Metrocentre - Newcastle - Morpeth and Chathill

Network Diagram - see first Page of Table 44

		NT	NT	NT	NT	GR	XC	NT	NT	GR		NT	GR	NT	NT	NT	XC	NT	NT	NT		NT	GR	NT	NT
						■ 1 ✕	◇1 ✕			■ 1 ✕			■ 1 ✕				◇1 ✕						■ 1 ✕		
Carlisle ■	d				06 25				07 17						08 28							09 37			
Wetheral	d				06 33				07 25						08 36										
Brampton (Cumbria)	d				06 43				07 35						08 46										
Haltwhistle	d				06 57				07 49						09 00							10 08			
Bardon Mill	d				07 05				07 57						09 08										
Haydon Bridge	d				07 10				08 02						09 13										
Hexham	a				07 19				08 11						09 22							10 26			
	d	23p20		06 14	07 19			07 40	08 11					08 45	09 22				09 44			10 26			10 42
Corbridge	d	23p24		06 18	07 24			07 44	08 16					08 49					09 48						10 46
Riding Mill	d	23p29		06 23	07 28			07 49	08 20					08 54					09 53						10 51
Stocksfield	d	23p33		06 27	07 32			07 53	08 24					08 58					09 57						10 55
Prudhoe	d	23p37		06 31	07 37			07 57	08 29					09 02	09 34				10 01			10 38			10 59
Wylam	d	23p41		06 35	07 41			08 01	08 33					09 06					10 05						11 03
Blaydon	d							08 07	08 39																
Metrocentre	a	23p50			07 50			08 14	08 44					09 15	09 45				10 16			10 49			11 15
	d	23p50			07 51			08 16	08 44					09 16	09 46			10 01	10 16	10 31		10 50		11 00	11 16
Dunston	d								08 47																
Newcastle ■ ⇌	a	00 05		06 56	08 08			08 27	08 57					09 26	10 03			10 10	10 27	10 39		11 07		11 10	11 26
Sunderland 26,44 ⇌	a			07 18				08 50						09 49					10 49						11 49
Newcastle ■ 26 ⇌	d		05 55			06 30	07 38			07 42		07 58	08 41			09 15	09 35	10 15					10 39	11 15	
Manors	d															09 17		10 17						11 17	
Cramlington	d		06 07									08 09				09 28		10 28						11 28	
Morpeth 26	d		06 17			06 43	07a50					08a19	08a55			09a36		10a35						11a36	
Pegswood	d																								
Widdrington	d																								
Acklington	d																								
Alnmouth for Alnwick 26	d		06 35			06a57				08a08							09a58						11a05		
Chathill	a		06 50																						

		NT	NT	NT	NT	NT		NT	GR	NT	NT	NT	NT	XC	NT	NT		NT	NT	XC	GR	NT	NT	NT	NT
									■ 1 ✕					◇1 ✕						◇1 ✕	■ 1 ✕				
Carlisle ■	d		10 23					11 27					12 23						13 29						14 33
Wetheral	d		10 31										12 31						13 38						
Brampton (Cumbria)	d		10 41										12 41						13 48						
Haltwhistle	d		10 55					11 56					12 55						14 02						15 03
Bardon Mill	d		11 03										13 03						14 10						
Haydon Bridge	d		11 08										13 08						14 15						
Hexham	a		11 20					12 18					13 20						14 23						15 21
	d		11 20		11 43			12 19			12 43		13 20			13 43			14 24				14 43		15 21
Corbridge	d				11 47						12 47					13 47							14 47		
Riding Mill	d				11 52						12 52					13 52							14 52		
Stocksfield	d				11 56						12 56					13 56							14 56		
Prudhoe	d		11 31		12 00			12 30			13 00		13 32			14 00			14 36				15 00		15 32
Wylam	d				12 04						13 04					14 06							15 04		
Blaydon	d																								
Metrocentre	a		11 45		12 15			12 45			13 15		13 45			14 14			14 47				15 15		15 44
	d	11 31	11 46	12 01	12 16	12 31		12 45		13 01	13 16	13 31	13 46		14 01	14 15		14 31	14 48			15 01	15 16	15 31	15 45
Dunston	d																								
Newcastle ■ ⇌	a	11 39	11 59	12 10	12 27	12 39		12 57		13 10	13 26	13 39	14 00		14 10	14 27		14 39	15 03			15 11	15 27	15 39	15 54
Sunderland 26,44 ⇌	a				12 49						13 49					14 49							15 49		
Newcastle ■ 26 ⇌	d			12 15					12 40	13 15				13 35	14 15					14 35	14 40	15 15			
Manors	d			12 17						13 17					14 17							15 17			
Cramlington	d			12 28						13 28					14 28							15 28			
Morpeth 26	d			12a35						13a37					14a37					14a47		15a35			
Pegswood	d																								
Widdrington	d																								
Acklington	d																								
Alnmouth for Alnwick 26	d								13a06					13a59							15a06				
Chathill	a																								

For connections to London Kings Cross please refer to Table 26

Table 48

Saturdays
from 27 October

Carlisle, Hexham and Metrocentre - Newcastle - Morpeth and Chathill

Network Diagram - see first Page of Table 44

		XC		NT	NT	NT	NT	XC	NT	NT	NT	NT		XC	NT	NT	NT	GR	NT	NT	XC	GR		NT	NT
		◇1 ✕						◇1 ✕						◇1 ✕				■ 1			◇1 ✕	■ 1 ✕			
Carlisle ■	d						15 21					16 23					17 21			18 37					
Wetheral	d											16 31					17 29			18 45					
Brampton (Cumbria)	d											16 41					17 39			18 54					
Haltwhistle	d						15 50					16 55					17 54			19 09					
Bardon Mill	d											17 03					18 01			19 16					
Haydon Bridge	d											17 08					18 06			19 21					
Hexham	a						16 11					17 20					18 20			19 30					
	d				15 42		16 12				16 43	17 20				17 43	18 21		18 43	19 31					
Corbridge	d				15 46						16 47					17 47	18 25		18 47	19 35					
Riding Mill	d				15 51						16 52					17 52	18 30		18 52	19 40					
Stocksfield	d				15 55						16 56					17 56	18 34		18 56	19 44					
Prudhoe	d				16 00		16 23				17 00	17 32				18 00	18 38		19 00	19 48					
Wylam	d				16 04						17 04					18 04	18 42		19 04	19 52					
Blaydon	d																		19 10						
Metrocentre	a				16 15		16 38				17 15	17 45				18 15	18 53		19 17	20 00					
	d			16 01	16 16	16 30	16 38		16 50	17 07	17 16	17 45			18 06	18 16	18 53		19 18	20 01				20 15	
Dunston	d														18 08										
Newcastle ■ ⇌	a			16 10	16 26	16 38	16 49		16 58	17 15	17 27	17 59			18 14	18 28	19 05		19 28	20 15				20 23	
Sunderland 26,44 ⇌	a				16 49		17 14				17 50					18 49			19 50						
Newcastle ■ 26 ⇌	d	15 34		16 15				16 35	17 00	17 22				17 37	18 19			18 41			19 33	19 45			20 20
Manors	d			16 17					17 03	17 24					18 21										
Cramlington	d			16 28					17 14	17 35					18 32										20 32
Morpeth 26	d			16a36					17 22	17a42					18a40							19a59			20a41
Pegswood	d								17 25																
Widdrington	d								17 31																
Acklington	d								17 38																
Alnmouth for Alnwick 26	d	15a58						16a58	17 46					18a00				19a07			19a59				
Chathill	a								17 59																

		XC	NT	NT	GR	NT	XC	NT		NT
		◇1 ✕			■ 1 ✕		◇1 ✕			
Carlisle ■	d			19 34						21 15
Wetheral	d									21 23
Brampton (Cumbria)	d									21 33
Haltwhistle	d			20 03						21 48
Bardon Mill	d									21 55
Haydon Bridge	d									22 00
Hexham	a			20 25						22 12
	d			20 26		21 12				22 13
Corbridge	d			20 30		21 16				22 17
Riding Mill	d			20 35		21 21				22 22
Stocksfield	d			20 39		21 25				22 26
Prudhoe	d			20 43		21 29				22 30
Wylam	d			20 47		21 33				22 34
Blaydon	d									
Metrocentre	a			20 58		21 44				22 45
	d		20 47	20 58		21 45		22 30		22 45
Dunston	d									
Newcastle ■ ⇌	a		20 55	21 10		21 57		22 39		23 00
Sunderland 26,44 ⇌	a		21 20							
Newcastle ■ 26 ⇌	d	20 38			20 54		21 38			
Manors	d									
Cramlington	d									
Morpeth 26	d	20a50			21 09					
Pegswood	d									
Widdrington	d									
Acklington	d									
Alnmouth for Alnwick 26	d				21a24		22a01			
Chathill	a									

For connections to London Kings Cross please refer to Table 26

Carlisle, Hexham and Metrocentre - Newcastle - Morpeth and Chathill

Network Diagram - see first Page of Table 44

			XC	NT	NT	GR	NT	NT	NT	NT	NT	NT	GR	NT	NT	NT	XC	NT	NT	NT	XC	GR	NT	NT
Carlisle		d			09 05				10 05			11 12				12 05				13 12				
Wetheral		d			09 12				10 12							12 12								
Brampton (Cumbria)		d			09 22				10 22							12 22								
Haltwhistle		d			09 36				10 36			11 40				12 36				13 40				
Bardon Mill		d			09 44				10 44							12 44								
Haydon Bridge		d			09 49				10 49							12 49								
Hexham		a			09 58				10 58			11 58				12 58				13 58				
		d			09 59				10 59			11 59				12 59				13 59				
Corbridge		d			10 03				11 03			12 03				13 03				14 03				
Riding Mill		d			10 08				11 08			12 08				13 08				14 08				
Stocksfield		d			10 12				11 12			12 12				13 12				14 12				
Prudhoe		d			10 16				11 16			12 16				13 16				14 16				
Wylam		d			10 20				11 20			12 20				13 20				14 20				
Blaydon		d																						
Metrocentre		a			10 29				11 29			12 29				13 29				14 29				
		d		10 10	10 30		10 48	11 10	11 30	11 48	12 10	12 30		12 48	13 15	13 30		13 48	14 10	14 30			14 48	15 10
Dunston		d																						
Newcastle		a		10 18	10 40		10 56	11 18	11 40	11 56	12 18	12 40		12 56	13 23	13 40		13 56	14 18	14 40			14 56	15 18
Sunderland	26,44	a					11 22			12 21				13 22				14 21					15 22	
Newcastle	26	d	09 45			10 13							12 44				13 36				14 36	14 42		
Manors		d																						
Cramlington		d																						
Morpeth	26	d	09 58			10 29															14a48			
Pegswood		d																						
Widdrington		d																						
Acklington		d																						
Alnmouth for Alnwick	26	d	10a11			10a43							13a10				13a59					15a08		
Chathill		a																						

			NT	XC	NT	NT	NT	XC	GR	NT	NT	NT	XC	NT	NT	NT	GR	NT	NT	NT	XC	GR	NT	XC
Carlisle		d	14 12				15 05					16 12				17 12				18 05			20 15	
Wetheral		d					15 12													18 12				
Brampton (Cumbria)		d					15 22													18 22				
Haltwhistle		d	14 40				15 36					16 40				17 40				18 36			20 43	
Bardon Mill		d					15 44													18 44				
Haydon Bridge		d					15 49													18 49				
Hexham		a	14 58				15 58					16 58				17 58				18 58			21 01	
		d	14 59				15 59					16 59				17 59				18 59			21 01	
Corbridge		d	15 03				16 03					17 03				18 03				19 03			21 05	
Riding Mill		d	15 08				16 08					17 08				18 08				19 08			21 10	
Stocksfield		d	15 12				16 12					17 12				18 12				19 12			21 14	
Prudhoe		d	15 16				16 16					17 16				18 16				19 16			21 18	
Wylam		d	15 20				16 20					17 20				18 20				19 20			21 22	
Blaydon		d																						
Metrocentre		a	15 29				16 29					17 29				18 29				19 29			21 31	
		d	15 30		15 48	16 10	16 30			16 48	17 10	17 30		17 48	18 10	18 30		18 48	19 10	19 30			21 31	
Dunston		d																						
Newcastle		a	15 40		15 58	16 18	16 40			16 56	17 18	17 40		17 58	18 18	18 40		18 56	19 18	19 40			21 43	
Sunderland	26,44	a			16 21					17 22				18 21				19 22						
Newcastle	26	d		15 37				16 34	16 42				17 38				18 42				19 40	19 44		20 38
Manors		d																						
Cramlington		d																						
Morpeth	26	d																				19a58		20a52
Pegswood		d																						
Widdrington		d																						
Acklington		d																						
Alnmouth for Alnwick	26	d		16a01				16a58	17a08				18a01				19a08				20a04			
Chathill		a																						

For connections to London Kings Cross please refer to Table 26

Carlisle, Hexham and Metrocentre - Newcastle - Morpeth and Chathill

Network Diagram - see first Page of Table 44

			GR	XC	GR
Carlisle		d			
Wetheral		d			
Brampton (Cumbria)		d			
Haltwhistle		d			
Bardon Mill		d			
Haydon Bridge		d			
Hexham		a			
		d			
Corbridge		d			
Riding Mill		d			
Stocksfield		d			
Prudhoe		d			
Wylam		d			
Blaydon		d			
Metrocentre		a			
		d			
Dunston		d			
Newcastle		a			
Sunderland	26,44	a			
Newcastle	26	d	20 43	21 38	21 51
Manors		d			
Cramlington		d			
Morpeth	26	d	20 59		22 07
Pegswood		d			
Widdrington		d			
Acklington		d			
Alnmouth for Alnwick	26	d	21a13	22a04	22a22
Chathill		a			

Sundays
16 September to 30 September

			XC	NT	NT	GR	NT	NT	NT	NT	NT	NT	GR	NT	NT	NT	XC	NT	NT	NT	GR	XC	NT	NT
Carlisle		d			09 05				10 05			11 12				12 05				13 12				
Wetheral		d			09 12				10 12							12 12								
Brampton (Cumbria)		d			09 22				10 22							12 22								
Haltwhistle		d			09 36				10 36			11 40				12 36				13 40				
Bardon Mill		d			09 44				10 44							12 44								
Haydon Bridge		d			09 49				10 49							12 49								
Hexham		a			09 58				10 58			11 58				12 58				13 58				
		d			09 59				10 59			11 59				12 59				13 59				
Corbridge		d			10 03				11 03			12 03				13 03				14 03				
Riding Mill		d			10 08				11 08			12 08				13 08				14 08				
Stocksfield		d			10 12				11 12			12 12				13 12				14 12				
Prudhoe		d			10 16				11 16			12 16				13 16				14 16				
Wylam		d			10 20				11 20			12 20				13 20				14 20				
Blaydon		d																						
Metrocentre		a			10 29				11 29			12 29				13 29				14 29				
		d		10 10	10 30		10 48	11 10	11 30	11 48	12 10	12 30		12 48	13 15	13 30		13 48	14 10	14 30			14 48	15 10
Dunston		d																						
Newcastle		a		10 18	10 40		10 56	11 18	11 40	11 56	12 18	12 40		12 56	13 23	13 40		13 56	14 18	14 40			14 56	15 18
Sunderland	26,44	a					11 22			12 21				13 22				14 21					15 22	
Newcastle	26	d	09 45			10 13							12 44				13 45				14 42	14 45		
Manors		d																						
Cramlington		d																						
Morpeth	26	d	10 15			10 29																15a15		
Pegswood		d																						
Widdrington		d																						
Acklington		d																						
Alnmouth for Alnwick	26	d	10a50			10a43							13a10				14a45				15a08			
Chathill		a																						

For connections to London Kings Cross please refer to Table 26

Sundays

16 September to 30 September

Carlisle, Hexham and Metrocentre - Newcastle - Morpeth and Chathill

Network Diagram - see first Page of Table 44

		NT	XC	NT	NT	NT	GR	XC	NT	NT	NT	XC	NT	NT	NT	GR	NT	NT	NT	XC	GR	NT	XC
Carlisle	d	14 12				15 05					16 12				17 12				18 05			20 15	
Wetheral	d					15 12													18 12				
Brampton (Cumbria)	d					15 22													18 22				
Haltwhistle	d	14 40				15 36					16 40				17 40				18 36			20 43	
Bardon Mill	d					15 44													18 44				
Haydon Bridge	d					15 49													18 49				
Hexham	a	14 58				15 58					16 58				17 58				18 58			21 01	
	d	14 59				15 59					16 59				17 59				18 59			21 01	
Corbridge	d	15 03				16 03					17 03				18 03				19 03			21 05	
Riding Mill	d	15 08				16 08					17 08				18 08				19 08			21 10	
Stocksfield	d	15 12				16 12					17 12				18 12				19 12			21 14	
Prudhoe	d	15 16				16 16					17 16				18 16				19 16			21 18	
Wylam	d	15 20				16 20					17 20				18 20				19 20			21 22	
Blaydon	d																						
Metrocentre	a	15 29				16 29					17 29				18 29				19 29			21 31	
	d	15 30		15 48	16 10	16 30			16 48	17 10	17 30		17 48	18 10	18 30		18 48	19 10	19 30			21 31	
Dunston	d																						
Newcastle	a	15 40		15 58	16 18	16 40			16 56	17 18	17 40		17 58	18 18	18 40		18 56	19 18	19 40			21 43	
Sunderland 26,44	a			16 21					17 22				18 21				19 22						
Newcastle 26	d		15 45				16 42	16 45				17 38				18 42				19 40	19 44		20 38
Manors	d																						
Cramlington	d																						
Morpeth 26	d																				19a58		20a52
Pegswood	d																						
Widdrington	d																						
Acklington	d																						
Alnmouth for Alnwick 26	d		16a40				17a08	17a40				18a01				19a08				20a04			
Chathill	a																						

		GR	XC	GR
Carlisle	d			
Wetheral	d			
Brampton (Cumbria)	d			
Haltwhistle	d			
Bardon Mill	d			
Haydon Bridge	d			
Hexham	a			
	d			
Corbridge	d			
Riding Mill	d			
Stocksfield	d			
Prudhoe	d			
Wylam	d			
Blaydon	d			
Metrocentre	a			
	d			
Dunston	d			
Newcastle	a			
Sunderland 26,44	a			
Newcastle 26	d	20 43	21 38	21 51
Manors	d			
Cramlington	d			
Morpeth 26	d	20 59		22 07
Pegswood	d			
Widdrington	d			
Acklington	d			
Alnmouth for Alnwick 26	d	21a13	22a04	22a22
Chathill	a			

For connections to London Kings Cross please refer to Table 26

Sundays

7 October to 21 October

Carlisle, Hexham and Metrocentre - Newcastle - Morpeth and Chathill

Network Diagram - see first Page of Table 44

		XC	NT	NT	GR	NT	NT	NT	NT	NT	NT	GR	NT	NT	NT	XC	NT	NT	NT	GR	XC	NT	NT
Carlisle	d			09 05				10 05			11 08				12 05				13 09				
Wetheral	d			09 12				10 12							12 12								
Brampton (Cumbria)	d			09 22				10 22							12 22								
Haltwhistle	d			09 36				10 36			11 36				12 36				13 37				
Bardon Mill	d			09 44				10 44							12 44								
Haydon Bridge	d			09 49				10 49							12 49								
Hexham	a			09 58				10 58			11 54				12 58				13 55				
	d			09 59				10 59			11 55				12 59				13 56				
Corbridge	d			10 03				11 03			11 59				13 03				14 00				
Riding Mill	d			10 08				11 08			12 04				13 08				14 05				
Stocksfield	d			10 12				11 12			12 08				13 12				14 09				
Prudhoe	d			10 16				11 16			12 12				13 16				14 13				
Wylam	d			10 20				11 20			12 16				13 20				14 17				
Blaydon	d																						
Metrocentre	a			10 33				11 33			12 29				13 33				14 29				
	d		10 10	10 33		10 48	11 10	11 33	11 48	12 10	12 30		12 48	13 15	13 33		13 48	14 10	14 30			14 48	15 10
Dunston	d																						
Newcastle	a		10 18	10 43		10 56	11 18	11 43	11 56	12 18	12 40		12 56	13 23	13 43		13 56	14 18	14 40			14 56	15 18
Sunderland 26,44	a					11 22			12 21				13 22				14 21					15 22	
Newcastle 26	d	09 45			10 13							12 44				13 45				14 42	14 45		
Manors	d																						
Cramlington	d																						
Morpeth 26	d	10 15			10 29																15a15		
Pegswood	d																						
Widdrington	d																						
Acklington	d																						
Alnmouth for Alnwick 26	d	10a50			10a43							13a10				14a45				15a08			
Chathill	a																						

		NT	XC	NT	NT	NT	GR	XC	NT	NT	NT	XC	NT	NT	NT	GR	NT	NT	NT	XC	GR	NT	XC
Carlisle	d	14 09				15 05					16 11				17 10				18 01			20 15	
Wetheral	d					15 12													18 08				
Brampton (Cumbria)	d					15 22													18 18				
Haltwhistle	d	14 37				15 36					16 39				17 38				18 32			20 43	
Bardon Mill	d					15 44													18 40				
Haydon Bridge	d					15 49													18 45				
Hexham	a	14 55				15 58					16 57				17 56				18 54			21 01	
	d	14 56				15 59					16 58				17 57				18 55			21 01	
Corbridge	d	15 00				16 03					17 02				18 01				18 59			21 05	
Riding Mill	d	15 05				16 08					17 07				18 06				19 04			21 10	
Stocksfield	d	15 09				16 12					17 11				18 10				19 08			21 14	
Prudhoe	d	15 13				16 16					17 15				18 14				19 12			21 18	
Wylam	d	15 17				16 20					17 19				18 18				19 16			21 22	
Blaydon	d																						
Metrocentre	a	15 29				16 33					17 32				18 31				19 29			21 34	
	d	15 30		15 48	16 10	16 33			16 48	17 10	17 33		17 48	18 10	18 32		18 48	19 10	19 29			21 34	
Dunston	d																						
Newcastle	a	15 40		15 58	16 18	16 43			16 56	17 18	17 43		17 58	18 18	18 42		18 56	19 18	19 39			21 46	
Sunderland 26,44	a			16 21					17 22				18 21				19 22						
Newcastle 26	d		15 45				16 42	16 45				17 38				18 42				19 40	19 44		20 38
Manors	d																						
Cramlington	d																						
Morpeth 26	d																				19a58		20a52
Pegswood	d																						
Widdrington	d																						
Acklington	d																						
Alnmouth for Alnwick 26	d		16a40				17a08	17a40				18a01				19a08				20a04			
Chathill	a																						

For connections to London Kings Cross please refer to Table 26

Carlisle, Hexham and Metrocentre - Newcastle - Morpeth and Chathill

Sundays
7 October to 21 October

Network Diagram - see first Page of Table 44

Station			GR	XC	GR
Carlisle		d			
Wetheral		d			
Brampton (Cumbria)		d			
Haltwhistle		d			
Bardon Mill		d			
Haydon Bridge		d			
Hexham		a			
		d			
Corbridge		d			
Riding Mill		d			
Stocksfield		d			
Prudhoe		d			
Wylam		d			
Blaydon		d			
Metrocentre		a			
		d			
Dunston		d			
Newcastle		a			
Sunderland	26,44	a			
Newcastle	26	d	20 43	21 38	21 51
Manors		d			
Cramlington		d			
Morpeth	26	d	20 59		22 07
Pegswood		d			
Widdrington		d			
Acklington		d			
Alnmouth for Alnwick	26	d	21a13	22a04	22a22
Chathill		a			

Sundays
from 28 October

Station			XC	NT	NT	GR	NT	NT	NT	NT	NT	NT	GR	NT	NT	NT	NT	NT	NT	XC	GR	NT	NT	NT
Carlisle		d			09 05				10 05			11 08				12 05			13 09					14 09
Wetheral		d			09 12				10 12							12 12								
Brampton (Cumbria)		d			09 22				10 22							12 22								
Haltwhistle		d			09 36				10 36			11 36				12 36			13 37					14 37
Bardon Mill		d			09 44				10 44							12 44								
Haydon Bridge		d			09 49				10 49							12 49								
Hexham		a			09 58				10 58			11 54				12 58			13 55					14 55
		d			09 59				10 59			11 55				12 59			13 56					14 56
Corbridge		d			10 03				11 03			11 59				13 03			14 00					15 00
Riding Mill		d			10 08				11 08			12 04				13 08			14 05					15 05
Stocksfield		d			10 12				11 12			12 08				13 12			14 09					15 09
Prudhoe		d			10 16				11 16			12 12				13 16			14 13					15 13
Wylam		d			10 20				11 20			12 16				13 20			14 17					15 17
Blaydon		d																						
Metrocentre		a			10 33				11 33			12 29				13 33			14 29					15 29
		d		10 10	10 33		10 48	11 10	11 33	11 48	12 10	12 30		12 48	13 15	13 33	13 48	14 10	14 30			14 48	15 10	15 30
Dunston		d																						
Newcastle		a		10 18	10 43		10 56	11 18	11 43	11 56	12 18	12 40		12 56	13 23	13 43	13 56	14 18	14 40			14 56	15 18	15 40
Sunderland	26,44	a					11 22			12 21				13 22			14 21					15 22		
Newcastle	26	d	09 45			10 13							12 44							14 33	14 42			
Manors		d																						
Cramlington		d																						
Morpeth	26	d	09 58			10 29														14a46				
Pegswood		d																						
Widdrington		d																						
Acklington		d																						
Alnmouth for Alnwick	26	d	10a11			10a43							13a10								15a08			
Chathill		a																						

For connections to London Kings Cross please refer to Table 26

Carlisle, Hexham and Metrocentre - Newcastle - Morpeth and Chathill

Sundays
from 28 October

Network Diagram - see first Page of Table 44

Station			XC	NT	NT	NT	XC	GR	NT	NT	NT	XC	NT	NT	NT	GR	NT	NT	NT	XC	GR	NT	XC	GR
Carlisle		d				15 05					16 11				17 10				18 01			20 15		
Wetheral		d				15 12													18 08					
Brampton (Cumbria)		d				15 22													18 18					
Haltwhistle		d				15 36					16 39				17 38				18 32			20 43		
Bardon Mill		d				15 44													18 40					
Haydon Bridge		d				15 49													18 45					
Hexham		a				15 58					16 57				17 56				18 54			21 01		
		d				15 59					16 58				17 57				18 55			21 01		
Corbridge		d				16 03					17 02				18 01				18 59			21 05		
Riding Mill		d				16 08					17 07				18 06				19 04			21 10		
Stocksfield		d				16 12					17 11				18 10				19 08			21 14		
Prudhoe		d				16 16					17 15				18 14				19 12			21 18		
Wylam		d				16 20					17 19				18 18				19 16			21 22		
Blaydon		d																						
Metrocentre		a				16 33					17 32				18 31				19 29			21 34		
		d		15 48	16 10	16 33			16 48	17 10	17 33		17 48	18 10	18 32		18 48	19 10	19 29			21 34		
Dunston		d																						
Newcastle		a		15 58	16 18	16 43			16 56	17 18	17 43		17 58	18 18	18 42		18 56	19 18	19 39			21 46		
Sunderland	26,44	a		16 21					17 22				18 21				19 22							
Newcastle	26	d	15 37				16 34	16 42				17 38				18 42				19 40	19 44		20 38	20 43
Manors		d																						
Cramlington		d																						
Morpeth	26	d																			19a58		20a52	20 59
Pegswood		d																						
Widdrington		d																						
Acklington		d																						
Alnmouth for Alnwick	26	d	16a01				16a58	17a08				18a01				19a08				20a04				21a13
Chathill		a																						

Station			XC	GR
Carlisle		d		
Wetheral		d		
Brampton (Cumbria)		d		
Haltwhistle		d		
Bardon Mill		d		
Haydon Bridge		d		
Hexham		a		
		d		
Corbridge		d		
Riding Mill		d		
Stocksfield		d		
Prudhoe		d		
Wylam		d		
Blaydon		d		
Metrocentre		a		
		d		
Dunston		d		
Newcastle		a		
Sunderland	26,44	a		
Newcastle	26	d	21 38	21 51
Manors		d		
Cramlington		d		
Morpeth	26	d		22 07
Pegswood		d		
Widdrington		d		
Acklington		d		
Alnmouth for Alnwick	26	d	22a04	22a22
Chathill		a		

For connections to London Kings Cross please refer to Table 26

Route Diagram for Table 49

DM-4/09(2)
Design BAJS

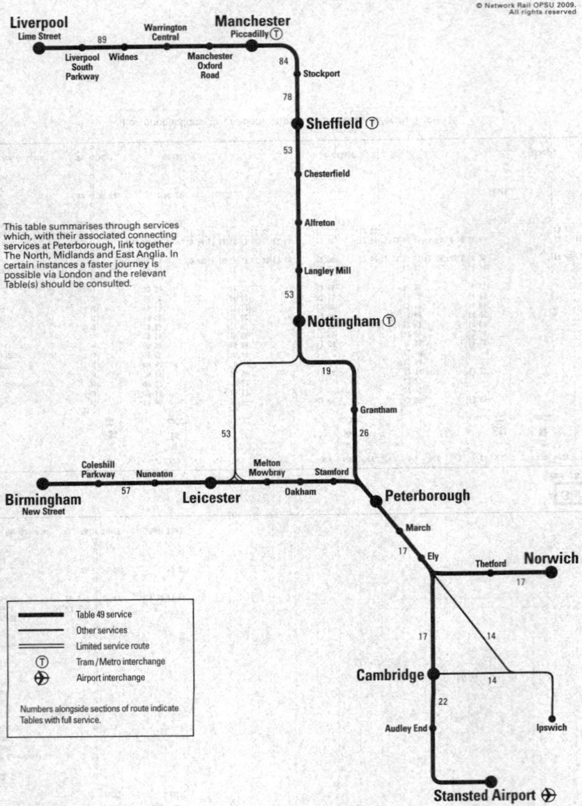

This table summarises through services which, with their associated connecting services at Peterborough, link together The North, Midlands and East Anglia. In certain instances a faster journey is possible via London and the relevant Table(s) should be consulted.

Stansted Airport - East Anglia - East Midlands - Birmingham and North West England

Route Diagram - see first Page of Table 49

Miles	Miles	Miles	Miles			XC	XC	EM	EM	EM	EM	XC	EM	XC		EM	EM	XC	EM	XC	EM	XC	EM	XC
						◇■1	◇■1	◇	◇	◇	◇	◇■1	◇	◇■1		◇	◇	◇■1	◇	◇■1	◇	◇■1	◇	◇■1
							A ✕					A ✕		A ✕			B ✕	A ✕		A ✕		A ✕		A ✕
0	0	—	0	**Norwich**	d						05 50		06 52			07 57			08 57		09 57		10 57	
30½	30½	—	30½	Thetford	d						06 23		07 20			08 24			09 24		10 24		11 24	
—	—	0	—	**Stansted Airport** ✈	d		05 16					06 06		07 21				08 21		09 21		10 27		11 27
—	—	10¾	—	Audley End	d		05 37					06 23		07 37				08 37		09 39		10 40		11 40
—	—	24¾	—	**Cambridge**	d	05 15	05 55					06 55		08 00				09 00		10 00		11 00		12 00
53¾	53¾	39½	53¾	Ely	d	05 30	06 10				06 51	07 12	07 45	08 15		08 50		09 15	09 49	10 15	10 54	11 15	11 53	12 15
69	69	—	69	March	d	05 46	06 28				07 07	07 28	08 01	08 31		09 07		09 31		10 31		11 31		12 31
82¾	82¾	—	82¾	**Peterborough**	a	06 08	06 50				07 25	07 51	08 24	08 50		09 25		09 50	10 26	10 50	11 27	11 50	12 24	12 50
—	—	—	—		d	06 10	06 52				07 27	07 52	08 26	08 52		09 27		09 52	10 28	10 52	11 28	11 52	12 26	12 52
95¼	—	—	—	Stamford	d	06 23	07 05					08 05		09 05				10 05		11 05		12 05		13 05
108¾	—	—	—	Oakham	d	06 39	07 21					08 21		09 21			09 49	10 21		11 21		12 21		13 21
120¼	—	—	—	Melton Mowbray	d	06 50	07 33					08 33		09 33			10a00	10 33		11 33		12 33		13 33
135¼	—	—	—	**Leicester**	d	07 10	07 49					08 49		09 49				10 49		11 49		12 49		13 49
154	—	—	—	Nuneaton	a	07 29	08 15					09 08		10 08				11 07		12 08		13 07		14 08
165½	—	—	—	Coleshill Parkway	a	07 45	08 32					09 25		10 25				11 24		12 25		13 24		14 25
175	—	—	—	**Birmingham New Street**	a	07 58	08 45					09 38		10 38				11 38		12 39		13 38		14 38
—	112	—	—	Grantham	d						07 58		08 55			09 58			11 00		12 00		12 59	
—	134¾	—	152½	**Nottingham**	a						08 40		09 36			10 36			11 35		12 36		13 36	
—	—	—	—		d			05 20	06 40	07 45	08 45		09 45			10 45			11 45		12 45		13 45	
—	146¾	—	164½	Langley Mill	d																			
—	153	—	170¾	Alfreton	d				07 02	08 07	09 07		10 07			11 07			12 07		13 07		14 07	
—	162¾	—	180¾	Chesterfield	d			05 49	07 13	08 18	09 18		10 18			11 18			12 18		13 18		14 19	
—	174¾	—	193	**Sheffield**	a			06 15	07 31	08 38	09 38		10 38			11 38			12 38		13 38		14 38	
—	—	—	—		d			06 20	07 35	08 42	09 42		10 42			11 42			12 42		13 42		14 42	
—	212	—	229¾	Stockport	a			07 22	08 24	09 25	10 25		11 25			12 25			13 25		14 25		15 25	
—	218	—	232¾	**Manchester Piccadilly**	a			07 34	08 36	09 36	10 36		11 36			12 36			13 36		14 36		15 36	
—	218½	—	236¼	Manchester Oxford Road	a			07 37	08 40	09 40	10 40		11 40			12 40			13 40		14 40		15 40	
—	234¼	—	252	Warrington Central	a			07 53	08 57	09 57	10 57		11 57			12 57			13 57		14 57		15 57	
—	240½	—	258¼	Widnes	a			08 01	09 05	10 05	11 05		12 05			13 05			14 05		15 05		16 05	
—	247¼	—	265	Liverpool South Parkway ✈	a			08 18	09 15	10 15	11 15		12 15			13 15			14 15		15 15		16 15	
—	252¾	—	270½	**Liverpool Lime Street**	a			08 31	09 31	10 31	11 31		12 31			13 31			14 31		15 31		16 31	

		EM	XC	EM	XC	EM	XC	EM	XC	EM		XC	EM	XC	EM	EM	XC	EM	XC				EM	XC
		◇	◇■1	◇	◇■1	◇	◇■1	◇	◇■1	◇		◇■1	◇	◇■1	◇	◇■1	◇■1	◇	◇■1					◇■1
			A ✕		A ✕		A ✕							A ✕		C ✕							D	
Norwich	d	11 57		12 57		13 57		14 57		15 52			16 57		17 54			18 57						
Thetford	d	12 24		13 24		14 24		15 24		16 27			17 27		18 27			19 24						
Stansted Airport ✈	d		12 27		13 27		14 27		15 27			16 27		17 27			18 21		19 21					20 21
Audley End	d		12 40		13 40		14 40		15 40			16 40		17 40			18 38		19 38					20 39
Cambridge	d		13 00		14 00		15 00		16 00			17 00		18 00			19 00		20 00					21 00
Ely	d	12 52	13 15	13 52	14 15	14 53	15 15	15 52	16 15	16 51		17 15	17 52	18 15	18 52		19 15	19 52	20 15					21 15
March	d		13 31		14 31		15 31		16 31			17 31		18 33	19 08		19 31		20 31					21 31
Peterborough	a	13 25	13 50	14 25	14 50	15 27	15 50	16 27	16 50	17 26		17 51	18 25	18 50	19 26		19 50	20 26	20 50					21 51
	d	13 27	13 52	14 26	14 52	15 28	15 52	16 28	16 52	17 27		17 52	18 26	18 52	19 26		19 52	20 28	20 52				21 30	21 52
Stamford	d		14 05		15 05		16 05		17 05			18 06		19 05			20 05		21 05				21 43	22 05
Oakham	d		14 21		15 21		16 21		17 21			18 21		19 21		19 40	20 21		21 21				21 58	22 21
Melton Mowbray	d		14 33		15 33		16 33		17 33			18 33		19 33		19a52	20 33		21 33				22 11	22 33
Leicester	d		14 49		15 49		16 49		17 49			18 49		19 49			20 49		21 49					22 49
Nuneaton	a		15 08		16 07		17 08		18 15			19 08		20 07			21 07		22 08					23 08
Coleshill Parkway	a		15 25		16 24		17 25		18 31			19 25		20 24			21 24		22 25					23 25
Birmingham New Street	a		15 38		16 38		17 38		18 45			19 38		20 38			21 37		22 38					23 41
Grantham	d	13 58		14 58		16 01		17 00		17 58			18 56		19 59			20 59						
Nottingham	a	14 36		15 36		16 36		17 36		18 36			19 36		20 31			21 35					22 50	
	d	14 45		15 45		16 45		17 45		18 45			19 40											
Langley Mill	d							18 02																
Alfreton	d	15 07		16 07		17 07		18 09		19 07			20 01											
Chesterfield	d	15 22		16 18		17 18		18 21		19 18			20 12											
Sheffield	a	15 38		16 38		17 36		18 39		19 39			20 28											
	d	15 42		16 42		17 40		18 43		19 42			20 32											
Stockport	a	16 25		17 25		18 25		19 25		20 25			21 20											
Manchester Piccadilly	a	16 36		17 37		18 36		19 36		20 36			21 32											
Manchester Oxford Road	a	16 40		17 40		18 40		19 40		20 40														
Warrington Central	a	16 57		18 03		18 57		19 57		20 57														
Widnes	a	17 05		18 11		19 05		20 05		21 05														
Liverpool South Parkway ✈	a	17 15		18 21		19 18		20 16		21 19														
Liverpool Lime Street	a	17 31		18 35		19 35		20 35		21 35														

A ✕ from Peterborough
B From Corby. to Derby
C From St Pancras International
D From Spalding

For connections from Ipswich please refer to Table 14

Stansted Airport - East Anglia - East Midlands - Birmingham and North West England

Route Diagram - see first Page of Table 49

		XC ◇1	EM ◇	XC ◇1 A 🛒	EM ◇	EM ◇	EM ◇	XC ◇1 A 🛒	EM ◇	XC ◇1 A 🛒	EM ◇	XC ◇1 A 🛒
Norwich	d						05 52		06 53		07 57	
Thetford	d						06 25		07 22		08 24	
Stansted Airport ✈	d			05 25				06 27		07 27		08 27
Audley End	d			05 37				06 40		07 40		08 40
Cambridge	d	05 15		05 55				06 57		08 00		09 00
Ely 4	d	05 30		06 10			06 51	07 12	07 53	08 15	08 54	09 15
March	d	05 46		06 28			07 07	07 29	08 08	08 31	09 11	09 31
Peterborough 8	a	06 08		06 50			07 25	07 50	08 31	08 50	09 28	09 50
	d	06 10		06 52			07 27	07 52	08 33	08 52	09 30	09 52
Stamford	d	06 23		07 05				08 05		09 05		10 05
Oakham	d	06 39		07 21				08 21		09 21		10 21
Melton Mowbray	d	06 50		07 33				08 33		09 33		10 33
Leicester	d	07 16		07 49				08 49		09 49		10 49
Nuneaton	a	07 34		08 07				09 07		10 07		11 07
Coleshill Parkway	a	07 50		08 23				09 24		10 24		11 24
Birmingham New Street 12	a	08 04		08 38				09 38		10 38		11 38
Grantham 7	d						07 58		09 09		09 58	
Nottingham 8 🚌	a						08 39		09 40		10 40	
	d		05 20		06 40	07 45	08 45		09 45		10 45	
Langley Mill	d											
Alfreton	d				07 02	08 07	09 07		10 07		11 07	
Chesterfield	d		05 49		07 13	08 18	09 18		10 18		11 18	
Sheffield 7 🚌	a		06 15		07 31	08 38	09 38		10 38		11 38	
	d		06 20		07 35	08 42	09 42		10 42		11 42	
Stockport	a		07 22		08 24	09 25	10 25		11 25		12 25	
Manchester Piccadilly 10 🚌	a		07 34		08 36	09 36	10 36		11 36		12 36	
Manchester Oxford Road	a		07 37		08 40	09 40	10 40		11 40		12 40	
Warrington Central	a		07 53		08 57	09 57	10 57		11 57		12 57	
Widnes	a		08 01		09 05	10 05	11 05		12 05		13 05	
Liverpool South Parkway 7 ✈	a		08 18		09 15	10 15	11 15		12 15		13 15	
Liverpool Lime Street 10	a		08 31		09 31	10 31	11 31		12 31		13 31	

		EM ◇	XC ◇1 A 🛒	EM ◇	XC ◇1 A 🛒	EM ◇	XC ◇1 A 🛒	EM ◇	XC ◇1 A 🛒	EM ◇	XC ◇1 A 🛒	EM ◇
Norwich	d	08 57		09 57		10 57		11 57		12 57		13 57
Thetford	d	09 24		10 24		11 24		12 24		13 24		14 24
Stansted Airport ✈	d		09 27		10 27		11 27		12 27		13 27	
Audley End	d		09 40		10 40		11 40		12 40		13 40	
Cambridge	d		10 00		11 00		12 00		13 00		14 00	
Ely 4	d	09 51	10 15	10 53	11 15	11 53	12 15	12 54	13 15	13 53	14 15	14 53
March	d		10 31		11 31		12 31		13 31		14 31	
Peterborough 8	a	10 25	10 50	11 24	11 50	12 24	12 50	13 26	13 50	14 25	14 50	15 25
	d	10 26	10 52	11 25	11 52	12 25	12 52	13 28	13 52	14 26	14 52	15 25
Stamford	d		11 05		12 05		13 05		14 05		15 05	
Oakham	d		11 21		12 21		13 21		14 21		15 21	
Melton Mowbray	d		11 33		12 33		13 33		14 33		15 33	
Leicester	d		11 49		12 49		13 49		14 49		15 49	
Nuneaton	a		12 07		13 07		14 07		15 07		16 07	
Coleshill Parkway	a		12 24		13 24		14 24		15 24		16 24	
Birmingham New Street 12	a		12 38		13 38		14 38		15 38		16 38	
Grantham 7	d	10 58		11 58		12 58		13 58		14 58		15 58
Nottingham 8 🚌	a	11 35		12 36		13 36		14 36		15 36		16 36
	d	11 45		12 45		13 45		14 45		15 45		16 45
Langley Mill	d											
Alfreton	d	12 07		13 07		14 07		15 07		16 07		17 07
Chesterfield	d	12 18		13 18		14 18		15 18		16 18		17 18
Sheffield 7 🚌	a	12 38		13 38		14 38		15 38		16 38		17 34
	d	12 42		13 42		14 42		15 42		16 42		17 40
Stockport	a	13 25		14 25		15 25		16 25		17 25		18 25
Manchester Piccadilly 10 🚌	a	13 36		14 36		15 36		16 36		17 37		18 36
Manchester Oxford Road	a	13 40		14 40		15 40		16 40		17 40		18 40
Warrington Central	a	13 57		14 57		15 57		16 57		18 03		18 57
Widnes	a	14 05		15 05		16 05		17 05		18 11		19 05
Liverpool South Parkway 7 ✈	a	14 15		15 15		16 15		17 15		18 21		19 18
Liverpool Lime Street 10	a	14 31		15 31		16 31		17 31		18 35		19 35

		XC ◇1 A 🛒	EM ◇	XC ◇1	EM ◇	XC ◇1	EM ◇	XC ◇1 A 🛒	EM ◇	XC ◇1	EM ◇	XC ◇1	EM B
Norwich	d		14 57		15 52		16 57		17 54		18 57		
Thetford	d		15 24		16 23		17 27		18 27		19 24		
Stansted Airport ✈	d	14 27		15 27		16 27		17 27		18 27		19 27	
Audley End	d	14 40		15 40		16 40		17 40		18 40		19 40	
Cambridge	d	15 00		16 00		17 00		18 00		19 00		20 00	
Ely 4	d	15 15	15 52	16 15	16 52	17 15	17 52	18 15	18 53	19 15	19 51	20 15	
March	d	15 31		16 31		17 31		18 33	19 09	19 31		20 31	
Peterborough 8	a	15 50	16 25	16 50	17 26	17 50	18 25	18 50	19 29	19 50	20 25	20 50	
	d	15 52	16 27	16 52	17 27	17 52	18 26	18 52	19 30	19 52	20 27	20 52	21 27
Stamford	d	16 05		17 05		18 05		19 05		20 05		21 05	
Oakham	d	16 21		17 21		18 21		19 21		20 21		21 21	
Melton Mowbray	d	16 33		17 33		18 33		19 33		20 33		21 33	
Leicester	d	16 49		17 49		18 49		19 49		20 49		21 49	
Nuneaton	a	17 07		18 07		19 07		20 07		21 07		22 07	
Coleshill Parkway	a	17 24		18 24		19 24		20 24		21 24		22 24	
Birmingham New Street 12	a	17 38		18 38		19 38		20 38		21 38		22 38	
Grantham 7	d		16 56		18 03		18 58		20 03		20 58		22 02
Nottingham 8 🚌	a		17 36		18 36		19 36		20 37		21 32		22 32
	d		17 45		18 45		19 40						
Langley Mill	d		18 03										
Alfreton	d		18 10		19 07		20 01						
Chesterfield	d		18 22		19 18		20 11						
Sheffield 7 🚌	a		18 39		19 39		20 27						
	d		18 42		19 42		20 31						
Stockport	a		19 25		20 25		21 20						
Manchester Piccadilly 10 🚌	a		19 36		20 36		21 32						
Manchester Oxford Road	a		19 40		20 40								
Warrington Central	a		19 57		20 57								
Widnes	a		20 05		21 05								
Liverpool South Parkway 7 ✈	a		20 15		21 19								
Liverpool Lime Street 10	a		20 30		21 35								

A 🛒 from Peterborough

B From Spalding

For connections from Ipswich please refer to Table 14

Stansted Airport - East Anglia - East Midlands - Birmingham and North West England

Route Diagram - see first Page of Table 49

		EM ◇	EM ◇	EM ◇	EM ◇	XC ◇1 A 🛒	EM ◇	XC ◇1 A 🛒	XC ◇1 A 🛒	XC ◇1 A 🛒	EM ◇	EM ◇
Norwich	d				09 33		10 47					
Thetford	d				10 00		11 14					
Stansted Airport ✈	d					10 25		11 25	12 25	13 25		
Audley End	d					10 39		11 39	12 39	13 39		
Cambridge	d					11 00		12 00	13 00	14 00		
Ely 4	d				10 32	11 15	11 39	12 15	13 15	14 15		
March	d					11 31		12 31	13 31	14 31		
Peterborough 8	a				11 09	11 50	12 16	12 50	13 50	14 50		
	d				11 11	11 52	12 18	12 52	13 52	14 52		
Stamford	d					12 05		13 05	14 05	15 05		
Oakham	d					12 19		13 19	14 19	15 19		
Melton Mowbray	d					12 30		13 30	14 30	15 30		
Leicester	d					12 49		13 49	14 49	15 49		
Nuneaton	a					13 07		14 07	15 07	16 05		
Coleshill Parkway	a					13 23		14 23	15 23	16 22		
Birmingham New Street 12	a					13 36		14 36	15 36	16 36		
Grantham 7	d				11 56		12 54					
Nottingham 8 🚌	a				12 29		13 33					
	d	09 31	10 41	11 46	12 39		13 38				14 37	15 44
Langley Mill	d				12 56		13 55				14 54	
Alfreton	d	09 53	11 03	12 08	13 04		14 03				15 02	16 06
Chesterfield	d	10 08	11 16	12 18	13 17		14 17				15 13	16 23
Sheffield 7 🚌	a	10 33	11 35	12 36	13 33		14 35				15 34	16 39
	d	10 41	11 38	12 41	13 38		14 39				15 38	16 44
Stockport	a	11 25	12 25	13 25	14 25		15 25				16 25	17 28
Manchester Piccadilly 10 🚌	a	11 37	12 35	13 37	14 37		15 37				16 37	17 37
Manchester Oxford Road	a	11 41	12 41	13 41	14 41		15 41				16 41	17 41
Warrington Central	a	11 58	12 58	13 58	14 58		15 58				16 58	17 58
Widnes	a	12 06	13 06	14 06	15 06		16 06				17 06	18 06
Liverpool South Parkway 7 ✈	a	12 16	13 16	14 16	15 16		16 16				17 16	18 16
Liverpool Lime Street 10	a	12 30	13 30	14 30	15 30		16 30				17 30	18 30

		EM ◇	XC ◇1 A 🛒	EM ◇	XC ◇1	EM ◇	XC ◇1	EM ◇	XC ◇1	EM B	EM ◇	XC ◇1
Norwich	d	13 49		14 49		15 53		16 54			17 54	
Thetford	d	14 16		15 16		16 20		17 21			18 21	
Stansted Airport ✈	d		14 25		15 25		16 25		17 25			18 25
Audley End	d		14 39		15 39		16 39		17 39			18 39
Cambridge	d		15 00		16 00		17 00		18 00			19 00
Ely 4	d	14 45	15 15	15 48	16 15		17 15	17 48	18 15		18 48	19 15
March	d		15 31		16 31		17 31		18 31			19 31
Peterborough 8	a	15 24	15 50	16 22	16 50	17 10	17 50	18 23	18 50		19 24	19 50
	d	15 26	15 52	16 24	16 52	17 11	17 52	18 26	18 52		19 26	19 52
Stamford	d		16 05		17 05		18 05		19 05			20 05
Oakham	d		16 19		17 19		18 19		19 19			20 19
Melton Mowbray	d		16 30		17 30		18 30		19 31			20 30
Leicester	d		16 49		17 49		18 49		19 49			20 49
Nuneaton	a		17 07		18 07		19 07		20 07			21 07
Coleshill Parkway	a		17 23		18 23		19 23		20 23			21 23
Birmingham New Street 12	a		17 36		18 36		19 36		20 36			21 36
Grantham 7	d	15 59		16 56		17 55		18 58		19 37	19 57	
Nottingham 8 🚌	a	16 28		17 25		18 29		19 33		20 14	20 31	
	d	16 40		17 35		18 37		19 38				
Langley Mill	d	17 00		17 54		18 54						
Alfreton	d	17 08		18 02		19 02		20 00				
Chesterfield	d	17 22		18 17		19 13		20 12				
Sheffield 7 🚌	a	17 40		18 34		19 31		20 31				
	d	17 44		18 37		19 35		20 35				
Stockport	a	18 25		19 25		20 25		21 24				
Manchester Piccadilly 10 🚌	a	18 37		19 37		20 38		21 36				
Manchester Oxford Road	a	18 41		19 41								
Warrington Central	a	18 58		19 58								
Widnes	a	19 06		20 06								
Liverpool South Parkway 7 ✈	a	19 16		20 16								
Liverpool Lime Street 10	a	19 30		20 30								

		EM ◇	XC ◇1	EM ◇
Norwich	d	18 56		20 52
Thetford	d	19 23		21 19
Stansted Airport ✈	d		19 25	
Audley End	d		19 39	
Cambridge	d		20 00	
Ely 4	d	19 48	20 15	21 44
March	d		20 31	
Peterborough 8	a	20 29	20 50	22 20
	d	20 31	20 52	22 22
Stamford	d		21 05	
Oakham	d		21 19	
Melton Mowbray	d		21 30	
Leicester	d		21 49	
Nuneaton	a		22 07	
Coleshill Parkway	a		22 23	
Birmingham New Street 12	a		22 36	
Grantham 7	d	21 03		22 54
Nottingham 8 🚌	a	21 35		23 28
	d			
Langley Mill	d			
Alfreton	d			
Chesterfield	d			
Sheffield 7 🚌	a			
	d			
Stockport	a			
Manchester Piccadilly 10 🚌	a			
Manchester Oxford Road	a			
Warrington Central	a			
Widnes	a			
Liverpool South Parkway 7 ✈	a			
Liverpool Lime Street 10	a			

A 🛒 from Peterborough

B From Skegness to Mansfield Woodhouse

For connections from Ipswich please refer to Table 14

Table 49

Sundays
1 July to 9 September

Stansted Airport - East Anglia - East Midlands - Birmingham and North West England

Route Diagram - see first Page of Table 49

		EM	EM	EM	EM	EM	XC	XC	XC	EM		EM	EM	XC	EM	XC	EM	XC	EM	XC		EM	EM	EM	EM
		◇	◇	◇	◇	◇	◇1	◇1	◇1	◇		◇	◇	◇1	◇	◇1	◇	◇1	◇	◇1			◇	◇	◇
							A	A	A					A								B			
Norwich	d				09 33	10 47							13 49		14 49		15 53		16 54				17 54	18 56	20 52
Thetford	d				10 00	11 14							14 16		15 16		16 20		17 21				18 21	19 23	21 19
Stansted Airport ✈	d						11 25	12 25	13 25					14 25		15 25		16 25		17 25					
Audley End	d						11 39	12 39	13 39					14 39		15 39		16 39		17 39					
Cambridge	d						12 00	13 00	14 00					15 00		16 00		17 00		18 00					
Ely 4	d				10 32	11 39	12 15	13 15	14 15				14 45	15 15	15 48	16 15		17 15	17 48	18 15			18 48	19 48	21 44
March	d						12 31	13 31	14 31					15 31		16 31		17 31		18 31					
Peterborough 8	a				11 09	12 16	12 50	13 50	14 50				15 24	15 50	16 22	16 50	17 10	17 50	18 23	18 50			19 24	20 29	22 20
	d				11 11	12 18	12 52	13 52	14 52				15 26	15 52	16 24	16 52	17 11	17 52	18 26	18 52			19 26	20 31	22 22
Stamford	d						13 05	14 05	15 05					16 05		17 05		18 05		19 05					
Oakham	d						13 19	14 19	15 19					16 19		17 19		18 19		19 19					
Melton Mowbray	d						13 30	14 30	15 30					16 30		17 30		18 30		19 31					
Leicester	d						13 49	14 49	15 49					16 49		17 49		18 49		19 49					
Nuneaton	a						14 07	15 07	16 05					17 07		18 07		19 07		20 07					
Coleshill Parkway	a						14 23	15 23	16 22					17 23		18 23		19 23		20 23					
Birmingham New Street 12	a						14 36	15 36	16 36					17 36		18 36		19 36		20 36					
Grantham 7	d				11 56	12 54							15 59		16 56		17 55		18 58			19 37	19 57	21 03	22 54
Nottingham 8	a				12 29	13 33							16 28		17 25		18 29		19 33			20 14	20 31	21 35	23 28
	d	09 31	10 41	11 46	12 39	13 38				14 37		15 44	16 40		17 35		18 37		19 38						
Langley Mill	d				12 56	13 55				14 54			17 00		17 54		18 54								
Alfreton	d	09 53	11 03	12 08	13 04	14 03				15 02		16 06	17 08		18 02		19 02		20 00						
Chesterfield	d	10 08	11 16	12 18	13 17	14 17				15 13		16 23	17 22		18 17		19 13		20 12						
Sheffield 7	a	10 33	11 35	12 36	13 33	14 35				15 31		16 39	17 40		18 34		19 31		20 31						
	d	10 41	11 38	12 41	13 38	14 39				15 38		16 44	17 44		18 37		19 35		20 35						
Stockport	a	11 25	12 25	13 25	14 25	15 25				16 25		17 28	18 25		19 25		20 25		21 24						
Manchester Piccadilly 10	a	11 37	12 35	13 37	14 37	15 37				16 37		17 37	18 37		19 37		20 38		21 36						
Manchester Oxford Road	a	11 41	12 41	13 41	14 41	15 41				16 41		17 41	18 41		19 41										
Warrington Central	a	11 58	12 58	13 58	14 58	15 58				16 58		17 58	18 58		19 58										
Widnes	a	12 06	13 06	14 06	15 06	16 06				17 06		18 06	19 06		20 06										
Liverpool South Parkway 7 ✈	a	12 16	13 16	14 16	15 16	16 16				17 16		18 16	19 16		20 16										
Liverpool Lime Street 10	a	12 30	13 30	14 30	15 30	16 30				17 30		18 30	19 30		20 30										

A from Peterborough

B From Skegness to Mansfield Woodhouse

For connections from Ipswich please refer to Table 14

Table 49

Sundays
16 September to 21 October

Stansted Airport - East Anglia - East Midlands - Birmingham and North West England

Route Diagram - see first Page of Table 49

		EM	EM	EM	EM	EM	XC	XC	XC	EM		EM	EM	XC	EM	XC	EM	XC	EM	XC		EM	EM		EM
		◇	◇	◇	◇	◇	◇1	◇1	◇1	◇		◇	◇	◇1	◇	◇1	◇	◇1	◇	◇1		◇	◇		◇
							A	A	A					A											
Norwich	d					10 47							13 49		14 49		15 53		16 54			17 54	18 56		20 52
Thetford	d					11 14							14 16		15 16		16 20		17 21			18 21	19 23		21 19
Stansted Airport ✈	d						11 25	12 25	13 25					14 25		15 25		16 25		17 25					
Audley End	d						11 39	12 39	13 39					14 39		15 39		16 39		17 39					
Cambridge	d						12 00	13 00	14 00					15 00		16 00		17 00		18 00					
Ely 4	d					11 39	12 15	13 15	14 15				14 45	15 15	15 48	16 15		17 15	17 48	18 15		18 48	19 48		21 44
March	d						12 31	13 31	14 31					15 31		16 31		17 31		18 31					
Peterborough 8	a					12 16	12 50	13 50	14 50				15 24	15 50	16 22	16 50	17 10	17 50	18 23	18 50		19 24	20 29		22 20
	d					12 18	12 52	13 52	14 52				15 26	15 52	16 24	16 52	17 11	17 52	18 26	18 52		19 26	20 31		22 22
Stamford	d						13 05	14 05	15 05					16 05		17 05		18 05		19 05					
Oakham	d						13 19	14 19	15 19					16 19		17 19		18 19		19 19					
Melton Mowbray	d						13 30	14 30	15 30					16 30		17 30		18 30		19 31					
Leicester	d						13 49	14 49	15 49					16 49		17 49		18 49		19 49					
Nuneaton	a						14 07	15 07	16 05					17 07		18 07		19 07		20 07					
Coleshill Parkway	a						14 23	15 23	16 22					17 23		18 23		19 23		20 23					
Birmingham New Street 12	a						14 36	15 36	16 36					17 36		18 36		19 36		20 36					
Grantham 7	d					12 54							15 59		16 56		17 55		18 58			19 57	21 03		22 54
Nottingham 8	a					13 33							16 28		17 25		18 29		19 33			20 31	21 35		23 28
	d	09 31	10 41	11 46	12 39	13 38				14 37		15 44	16 40		17 35		18 37		19 38						
Langley Mill	d				12 56	13 55				14 54			17 00		17 54		18 54								
Alfreton	d	09 53	11 03	12 08	13 04	14 03				15 02		16 06	17 08		18 02		19 02		20 00						
Chesterfield	d	10 08	11 16	12 18	13 17	14 17				15 13		16 23	17 22		18 17		19 13		20 12						
Sheffield 7	a	10 33	11 35	12 36	13 33	14 35				15 34		16 39	17 40		18 34		19 31		20 31						
	d	10 41	11 38	12 41	13 38	14 39				15 38		16 44	17 44		18 37		19 35		20 35						
Stockport	a	11 25	12 25	13 25	14 25	15 25				16 25		17 28	18 25		19 25		20 25		21 24						
Manchester Piccadilly 10	a	11 37	12 37	13 37	14 37	15 37				16 37		17 37	18 37		19 37		20 38		21 36						
Manchester Oxford Road	a	11 41	12 41	13 41	14 41	15 41				16 41		17 41	18 41		19 41										
Warrington Central	a	11 58	12 58	13 58	14 58	15 58				16 58		17 58	18 58		19 58										
Widnes	a	12 06	13 06	14 06	15 06	16 06				17 06		18 06	19 06		20 06										
Liverpool South Parkway 7 ✈	a	12 16	13 16	14 16	15 16	16 16				17 16		18 16	19 16		20 16										
Liverpool Lime Street 10	a	12 30	13 30	14 30	15 30	16 30				17 30		18 30	19 30		20 30										

Sundays
from 28 October

		EM	EM	EM	EM	EM	XC	XC	XC	EM		EM	EM	EM	XC	EM	XC	EM	EM	XC	EM	XC	EM	EM	EM
		◇	◇	◇	◇	◇	◇1	◇1	◇1			◇	◇	◇	◇1	◇	◇1	◇		◇1	◇	◇1	◇	◇	◇
							A	A	A	B					A				B						
Norwich	d					10 47								13 49		14 49		15 53			16 54		17 54	18 56	20 52
Thetford	d					11 14								14 16		15 16		16 20			17 21		18 21	19 23	21 19
Stansted Airport ✈	d						11 25	12 25	13 25						14 25		15 25			16 25		17 25			
Audley End	d						11 39	12 39	13 39						14 39		15 39			16 39		17 39			
Cambridge	d						12 00	13 00	14 00						15 00		16 00			17 00		18 00			
Ely 4	d					11 39	12 15	13 15	14 15					14 45	15 15	15 48	16 15			17 15	17 48	18 15	18 48	19 48	21 44
March	d						12 31	13 31	14 31						15 31		16 31			17 31		18 31			
Peterborough 8	a					12 16	12 50	13 50	14 50					15 24	15 50	16 22	16 50	17 10		17 50	18 23	18 50	19 24	20 29	22 20
	d					12 18	12 52	13 52	14 52					15 26	15 52	16 24	16 52	17 11		17 52	18 26	18 52	19 26	20 31	22 22
Stamford	d						13 05	14 05	15 05						16 05		17 05			18 05		19 05			
Oakham	d						13 19	14 19	15 19						16 19		17 19			18 19		19 19			
Melton Mowbray	d						13 30	14 30	15 30						16 30		17 30			18 30		19 31			
Leicester	d						13 49	14 49	15 49						16 49		17 49			18 49		19 49			
Nuneaton	a						14 07	15 07	16 05						17 07		18 07			19 07		20 07			
Coleshill Parkway	a						14 23	15 23	16 22						17 23		18 23			19 23		20 23			
Birmingham New Street 12	a						14 36	15 36	16 36						17 36		18 36			19 36		20 36			
Grantham 7	d									13 26									15 58						
Nottingham 8	a					13 28				14 30				16 37		17 35		18 17	16 54		19 37		20 44	21 45	23 39
	d	09 31	10 41	11 46	12 39	13 38						14 37	15 46	16 49		17 38		18 37			19 38				
Langley Mill	d				12 56	13 55						14 54		17 05		17 54		18 54							
Alfreton	d	09 53	11 03	12 08	13 04	14 03						15 02	16 08	17 13		18 02		19 02			20 00				
Chesterfield	d	10 08	11 16	12 18	13 17	14 17						15 13	16 23	17 23		18 17		19 13			20 12				
Sheffield 7	a	10 33	11 35	12 36	13 33	14 35						15 31	16 39	17 40		18 34		19 31			20 31				
	d	10 41	11 38	12 41	13 38	14 39						15 38	16 44	17 44		18 37		19 35			20 35				
Stockport	a	11 25	12 25	13 25	14 25	15 25						16 25	17 28	18 25		19 25		20 25			21 24				
Manchester Piccadilly 10	a	11 37	12 37	13 37	14 37	15 37						16 37	17 37	18 37		19 37		20 38			21 36				
Manchester Oxford Road	a	11 41	12 41	13 41	14 41	15 41						16 41	17 41	18 41		19 41									
Warrington Central	a	11 58	12 58	13 58	14 58	15 58						16 58	17 58	18 58		19 58									
Widnes	a	12 06	13 06	14 06	15 06	16 06						17 06	18 06	19 06		20 06									
Liverpool South Parkway 7 ✈	a	12 16	13 16	14 16	15 16	16 16						17 16	18 16	19 16		20 16									
Liverpool Lime Street 10	a	12 30	13 30	14 30	15 30	16 30						17 30	18 30	19 30		20 30									

A from Peterborough

B From Sleaford to Netherfield

For connections from Ipswich please refer to Table 14

North West England and Birmingham - East Midlands - East Anglia - Stansted Airport

Route Diagram - see first Page of Table 49

Miles	Miles	Miles	Miles	Station		EM MO ◇ A	EM MO ◇ B	EM MX ◇	EM ◇	EM C	EM ◇■ D 🍴	XC ◇■	EM ◇	XC ◇■ E 🍴	EM	EM ◇ F	XC ◇■ E 🍴	EM ◇	XC ◇■ G 🍴	EM ◇	XC ◇■ E 🍴
—	0	—	0	**Liverpool Lime Street** 10	d	21p21	21p21	21p37												06 47	
—	5½	—	5½	Liverpool South Parkway 7 ✈	d	21p31	21p31	21p47												06 57	
—	12¼	—	12¼	Widnes	d	21p39	21p39	21p55												07 07	
—	18½	—	18½	Warrington Central	d	21p47	21p47	22p03												07 15	
—	34¼	—	34¼	Manchester Oxford Road	d	22p07	22p07	22p24												07 38	
—	34¾	—	34¾	**Manchester Piccadilly** 10 ⇌	d	22p11	22p11	22p28												07 42	
—	40¾	—	40¾	Stockport	d	22p28	22p28	22p37												07 54	
—	77½	—	77½	**Sheffield** 7 ⇌	a	23p25	23p25	23p35												08 34	
—	—	—	—		d	23p29	23p29	23p37												08 38	
—	89¾	—	89¾	Chesterfield	d	23p43	23p43	00 02												08 53	
—	99¾	—	99¾	Alfreton	d	23p54	23p54													09 03	
—	106	—	106	Langley Mill	d	00 02	00 02														
—	118	—	118	**Nottingham** 8 ⇌	a	00 25	00 32	00 40												09 30	
—	—	—	—		d				05 03	05 10			05 56		06 53	07 52		08 34		09 34	
—	140¾	—	—	Grantham 7	d					05 51						08 27		09 10		10 11	
0	—	—	—	**Birmingham New Street** 12	d							05 22		06 22			07 22		08 22		09 22
9½	—	—	—	Coleshill Parkway	d							05 35		06 35			07 35		08 35		09 35
21	—	—	—	Nuneaton	d							05 52		06 52			07 51		08 52		09 52
39¾	—	—	—	**Leicester**	d							06 15		07 18			08 18		09 18		10 18
54¾	—	—	—	Melton Mowbray	d				05 36		06 01	06 31	06 52	07 34			08 33		09 34		10 34
66¼	—	—	—	Oakham	d				05 48		06a12	06 42	07 05	07 45			08 45		09 45		10 44
79¾	—	—	—	Stamford	d				06 03			06 57	07 18	08 01			09 01		10 01		11 00
92¼	170	—	187¾	**Peterborough** 8	a				06 19	06 25		07 10	07 33	08 16	09 27	08 57	09 16	09 39	10 16	10 40	11 17
—	—	—	—		d				06 27			07 12	07 35	08 18		08 59	09 18	09 40	10 18	10 44	11 17
106¼	184	—	201¾	March	a				06 42			07 30	07 50	08 33			09 34		10 33		11 33
121½	206¾	0	217	Ely 4	a				07 01			07 51	08 11	08 52		09 41	09 52	10 13	10 52	11 16	11 52
—	—	14¾	—	**Cambridge**	a							08 07		09 08			10 08		11 08		12 08
—	—	28¾	—	Audley End	a							08 24		09 23			10 24		11 23		12 23
—	—	39½	—	**Stansted Airport** ✈	a							08 39		09 39			10 40		11 40		12 40
144½	222¼	—	240¼	Thetford	a				07 28				08 36			10 06		10 41		11 41	
152	252¾	—	270½	**Norwich**	a				08 13				09 13			10 44		11 14		12 13	

Station		EM ◇	XC ◇■ E 🍴	EM ◇	XC ◇■ E 🍴	EM ◇	XC ◇■ E 🍴	EM ◇	XC ◇■ E 🍴	EM ◇	XC ◇■ E 🍴	EM ◇	XC ◇■ E 🍴	EM ◇	EM ◇■ H 🍴	XC ◇■ E 🍴	EM ◇	XC ◇■	XC ◇■	EM ◇	EM ◇	XC ◇■	XC ◇■
Liverpool Lime Street 10	d	07 42		08 52		09 52		10 52		11 52		12 52		13 52			14 52			15 52	16 52		
Liverpool South Parkway 7 ✈	d	07 53		09 03		10 03		11 03		12 03		13 03		14 03			15 03			16 03	17 03		
Widnes	d	08 05		09 11		10 11		11 11		12 11		13 11		14 11			15 11			16 11	17 11		
Warrington Central	d	08 13		09 19		10 19		11 19		12 19		13 19		14 19			15 19			16 19	17 19		
Manchester Oxford Road	d	08 39		09 39		10 39		11 39		12 39		13 39		14 39			15 39			16 39	17 39		
Manchester Piccadilly 10 ⇌	d	08 43		09 43		10 43		11 43		12 43		13 43		14 43			15 43			16 43	17 43		
Stockport	d	08 54		09 54		10 54		11 54		12 54		13 54		14 54			15 54			16 54	17 54		
Sheffield 7 ⇌	a	09 35		10 35		11 34		12 35		13 35		14 35		15 35			16 34			17 40	18 41		
	d	09 38		10 38		11 38		12 38		13 38		14 38		15 38			16 38			17 44	18 45		
Chesterfield	d	09 53		10 52		11 53		12 53		13 52		14 53		15 53			16 56			18 02	19 01		
Alfreton	d	10 04		11 03		12 03		13 03		14 03		15 04		16 04			17 07			18 12	19 11		
Langley Mill	d																						
Nottingham 8 ⇌	a	10 30		11 30		12 30		13 30		14 30		15 28		16 33			17 31			18 34	19 38		
	d	10 34		11 34		12 34		13 34		14 34		15 34		16 34			17 34			18 37			
Grantham 7	d	11 10		12 11		13 09		14 10		15 11		16 10		17 11			18 11			19 08			
Birmingham New Street 12	d		10 22		11 22		12 22		13 22		14 22		15 22			16 22		16 52	17 22			18 22	19 22
Coleshill Parkway	d		10 35		11 35		12 35		13 35		14 35		15 35			16 35		17 05	17 35			18 35	19 35
Nuneaton	d		10 52		11 52		12 52		13 52		14 52		15 52			16 52		17 22	17 52			18 52	19 52
Leicester	d		11 18		12 18		13 18		14 18		15 18		16 18			17 18		17 51	18 18			19 18	20 18
Melton Mowbray	d		11 34		12 34		13 34		14 34		15 34		16 33		17 12	17 34		18 07	18 34			19 34	20 33
Oakham	d		11 45		12 45		13 45		14 45		15 45		16 45		17a23	17 45		18 19	18 45			19 45	20 44
Stamford	d		12 01		13 01		14 01		15 01		16 01		17 01			18 01		18 40	19 00			20 01	21 00
Peterborough 8	a	11 39	12 16	12 40	13 16	13 39	14 16	14 39	15 16	15 38	16 16	16 39	17 16	17 40		18 16	18 38	18 57	19 16	19 38		20 16	21 16
	d	11 41	12 18	12 43	13 18	13 41	14 18	14 41	15 18	15 40	16 18	16 41	17 18	17 42		18 18	18 45	18 59	19 18	19 40		20 18	21 18
March	a		12 33		13 33		14 33		15 34		16 33		17 36			18 33	19 00	19 14	19 34			20 34	21 34
Ely 4	a	12 14	12 52	13 16	13 52	14 14	14 52	15 14	15 52	16 13	16 52	17 14	17 58	18 16		18 52	19 24	19 33	19 53	20 13		20 53	21 52
Cambridge	a		13 08		14 08		15 08		16 08		17 08		18 16			19 08		19 50	20 08			21 08	22 08
Audley End	a		13 23		14 23		15 23		16 23		17 23		18 31			19 23			20 24			21 23	22 23
Stansted Airport ✈	a		13 40		14 40		15 40		16 40		17 40		18 54			19 39			20 39			21 40	22 52
Thetford	a	12 39		13 40		14 38		15 38		16 37		17 38		18 40			19 50			20 36			
Norwich	a	13 13		14 13		15 13		16 14		17 13		18 18		19 15			20 22			21 14			

A from 21 May until 25 June, from 17 September
B from 2 July until 10 September
C To Spalding
D To St Pancras International
E 🍴 to Peterborough
F From Mansfield Woodhouse
G From Gloucester. 🍴 to Peterborough
H From Derby to St Pancras International

For connections to Ipswich please refer to Table 14

North West England and Birmingham - East Midlands - East Anglia - Stansted Airport

Route Diagram - see first Page of Table 49

Station		EM ◇	EM ◇	EM ◇	XC ◇■	EM ◇
Liverpool Lime Street 10	d	17 52	18 52	19 52		21 37
Liverpool South Parkway 7 ✈	d	18 03	19 03	20 03		21 47
Widnes	d	18 11	19 11	20 11		21 55
Warrington Central	d	18 19	19 19	20 19		22 03
Manchester Oxford Road	d	18 39	19 39	20 39		22 24
Manchester Piccadilly 10 ⇌	d	18 43	19 43	20 43		22 28
Stockport	d	18 54	19 54	20 54		22 37
Sheffield 7 ⇌	a	19 33	20 36	21 35		23 35
	d	19 38	20 41	21 39		23 37
Chesterfield	d	19 53	20 58	21 55		00 02
Alfreton	d	20 04	21 09	22 05		
Langley Mill	d			22 12		
Nottingham 8 ⇌	a	20 31	21 38	22 38		00 40
	d	20 34				
Grantham 7	d	21 10				
Birmingham New Street 12	d				20 22	
Coleshill Parkway	d				20 35	
Nuneaton	d				20 52	
Leicester	d				21 18	
Melton Mowbray	d				21 34	
Oakham	d				21 45	
Stamford	d				22 01	
Peterborough 8	a	21 37			22 16	
	d	21 38			22 18	
March	a				22 35	
Ely 4	a	22 11			22 53	
Cambridge	a				23 10	
Audley End	a					
Stansted Airport ✈	a					
Thetford	a	22 35				
Norwich	a	23 18				

Saturdays

Station		EM ◇	EM ◇	EM A	XC ◇■	EM ◇	XC ◇■ B 🍴	EM C	EM D	EM ◇	XC ◇■ B 🍴	EM ◇	XC ◇■ E 🍴	EM ◇	XC ◇■ B 🍴	EM ◇	XC ◇■ B 🍴	EM ◇	XC ◇■ B 🍴	EM ◇	XC ◇■ B 🍴	EM ◇
Liverpool Lime Street 10	d	21p37												06 49		07 42		08 52		09 52		10 52
Liverpool South Parkway 7 ✈	d	21p47												06 59		07 52		09 03		10 03		11 03
Widnes	d	21p55												07 07		08 05		09 11		10 11		11 11
Warrington Central	d	22p03												07 15		08 13		09 19		10 19		11 19
Manchester Oxford Road	d	22p24												07 38		08 39		09 39		10 39		11 39
Manchester Piccadilly 10 ⇌	d	22p28												07 42		08 43		09 43		10 43		11 43
Stockport	d	22p37												07 54		08 54		09 54		10 54		11 54
Sheffield 7 ⇌	a	23p35												08 34		09 35		10 35		11 35		12 35
	d	23p37												08 38		09 38		10 38		11 38		12 38
Chesterfield	d	00 02												08 53		09 53		10 53		11 53		12 53
Alfreton	d													09 03		10 03		11 03		12 03		13 03
Langley Mill	d																					
Nottingham 8 ⇌	a	00 40												09 30		10 30		11 29		12 29		13 30
	d		05 04	05 10		05 54		06 53	06 55	07 45		08 32		09 34		10 34		11 34		12 34		13 34
Grantham 7	d			05 51						08 20		09 03		10 09		11 10		12 07		13 09		14 07
Birmingham New Street 12	d				05 22		06 22				07 22		08 22		09 22		10 22		11 22		12 22	
Coleshill Parkway	d				05 35		06 35				07 35		08 35		09 35		10 35		11 35		12 35	
Nuneaton	d				05 52		06 52				07 52		08 52		09 52		10 52		11 52		12 52	
Leicester	d				06 15		07 15				08 15		09 15		10 15		11 15		12 15		13 15	
Melton Mowbray	d		05 37		06 32	06 46	07 32				08 31		09 31		10 32		11 32		12 32		13 32	
Oakham	d		05 49		06 43	06 58	07 44				08 43		09 43		10 44		11 44		12 44		13 44	
Stamford	d		06 06		06 58	07 12	08 00				08 59		09 59		11 00		12 00		13 00		14 00	
Peterborough 8	a		06 19	06 25	07 12	07 29	08 16	09 27	09 27	08 58	09 16	09 41	10 14	10 38	11 16	11 39	12 14	12 38	13 16	13 38	14 16	14 41
	d		06 27		07 13	07 35	08 18			09 00	09 18	09 43	10 18	10 41	11 18	11 41	12 18	12 40	13 18	13 41	14 18	14 43
March	a		06 42		07 31	07 50	08 33				09 33		10 33		11 33		12 33		13 33		14 33	
Ely 4	a		07 01		07 52	08 11	08 52			09 35	09 52	10 14	10 52	11 17	11 52	12 14	12 52	13 13	13 52	14 14	14 52	15 14
Cambridge	a				08 08		09 07				10 07		11 07		12 07		13 07		14 07		15 07	
Audley End	a				08 23		09 23				10 23		11 23		12 23		13 23		14 23		15 23	
Stansted Airport ✈	a				08 39		09 40				10 40		11 40		12 40		13 40		14 40		15 40	
Thetford	a		07 30			08 36				10 04		10 40		11 44		12 38		13 39		14 38		15 40
Norwich	a		08 13			09 15				10 43		11 15		12 18		13 13		14 13		15 13		16 15

A To Spalding
B 🍴 to Peterborough
C from 6 October
D until 29 September
E From Gloucester. 🍴 to Peterborough

For connections to Ipswich please refer to Table 14

Saturdays

North West England and Birmingham - East Midlands - East Anglia - Stansted Airport

Route Diagram - see first Page of Table 49

		XC	EM	XC	EM	XC	EM	XC	EM	XC	EM
		◇■ A ⌶	◇	◇■ A ⌶	◇	◇■ A ⌶	◇	◇■ A ⌶	◇	◇■	◇
Liverpool Lime Street ■	d		11 52		12 52		13 52		14 52		15 52
Liverpool South Parkway ■ ✈	d		12 03		13 03		14 03		15 03		16 03
Widnes	d		12 11		13 11		14 11		15 11		16 11
Warrington Central	d		12 19		13 19		14 19		15 19		16 19
Manchester Oxford Road	d		12 39		13 39		14 39		15 39		16 39
Manchester Piccadilly ■ ⇌	d		12 43		13 43		14 43		15 43		16 43
Stockport	d		12 54		13 54		14 54		15 54		16 54
Sheffield ■ ⇌	a		13 35		14 35		15 36		16 35		17 37
	d		13 38		14 38		15 38		16 38		17 44
Chesterfield	d		13 53		14 53		15 53		16 53		18 01
Alfreton	d		14 03		15 04		16 04		17 04		18 11
Langley Mill	d										
Nottingham ■ ⇌	a		14 29		15 29		16 30		17 29		18 33
	d		14 34		15 34		16 34		17 34		18 34
Grantham ■	d		15 10		16 07		17 06		18 15		19 08
Birmingham New Street ■	d	13 22		14 22		15 22		16 22		17 22	
Coleshill Parkway	d	13 35		14 35		15 35		16 35		17 35	
Nuneaton	d	13 52		14 52		15 52		16 52		17 52	
Leicester	d	14 15		15 15		16 15		17 15		18 15	
Melton Mowbray	d	14 32		15 32		16 31		17 32		18 32	
Oakham	d	14 44		15 44		16 43		17 44		18 44	
Stamford	d	15 00		16 00		16 59		18 00		19 00	
Peterborough ■	a	15 16	15 39	16 16	16 40	17 16	17 37	18 15	18 42	19 17	19 39
	d	15 18	15 41	16 18	16 41	17 19	17 39	18 18	18 44	19 18	19 41
March	a	15 33		16 33		17 38		18 34	19 01	19 34	
Ely ■	a	15 52	16 14	16 52	17 13	17 59	18 12	18 52	19 19	19 51	20 14
Cambridge	a	16 07		17 07		18 17		19 09		20 08	
Audley End	a	16 23		17 23		18 34		19 25		20 24	
Stansted Airport ✈	a	16 40		17 40		18 53		19 40		20 40	
Thetford	a		16 38		17 39		18 36		19 43		20 36
Norwich	a		17 13		18 18		19 19		20 18		21 14

		EM	XC	XC	XC	EM	EM	EM	XC	EM	EM
		◇	◇■	◇■ B	◇■ C	◇	◇	◇	◇■	◇	◇
Liverpool Lime Street ■	d	16 52				17 52	18 52	19 52		20 52	21 37
Liverpool South Parkway ■ ✈	d	17 03				18 03	19 03	20 03		21 03	21 47
Widnes	d	17 11				18 11	19 11	20 11		21 11	21 55
Warrington Central	d	17 19				18 19	19 19	20 19		21 19	22 03
Manchester Oxford Road	d	17 39				18 39	19 39	20 39		21 39	22 27
Manchester Piccadilly ■ ⇌	d	17 43				18 43	19 43	20 43		21 43	22 31
Stockport	d	17 54				18 54	19 54	20 54		21 52	22 42
Sheffield ■ ⇌	a	18 35				19 35	20 35	21 34		22 31	23 39
	d	18 38				19 38	20 41	21 38		22 35	23 42
Chesterfield	d	18 53				19 53	20 59	21 54		22 51	23 57
Alfreton	d	19 03				20 04	21 09	22 05		23 02	
Langley Mill	d							22 12			
Nottingham ■ ⇌	a	19 33				20 31	21 33	22 33		23 32	00 34
	d					20 34					
Grantham ■	d					21 07					
Birmingham New Street ■	d		18 22	19 22	19 22				20 22		
Coleshill Parkway	d		18 35	19 35	19 35				20 35		
Nuneaton	d		18 52	19 52	19 52				20 52		
Leicester	d		19 15	20 15	20 15				21 15		
Melton Mowbray	d		19 31	20 32	20 32				21 31		
Oakham	d		19 43	20 44	20 44				21 43		
Stamford	d		19 59	21 00	21 00				21 59		
Peterborough ■	a		20 14	21 16	21 16	21 36			22 16		
	d		20 18	21 18	21 18	21 38			22 18		
March	a		20 33	21 33	21 33				22 33		
Ely ■	a		20 51	21 51	21 51	22 12			22 53		
Cambridge	a		21 07	22 07	22 07				23 10		
Audley End	a		21 23	22 23	22 23						
Stansted Airport ✈	a		21 40	22 40	22 42						
Thetford	a					22 36					
Norwich	a					23 20					

Sundays
until 24 June

		EM	EM	EM	EM	XC	EM	XC	EM	XC	EM	XC
		◇	D	◇	◇	◇■ A ⌶	◇	◇■ A ⌶	◇	◇■ A ⌶	◇	◇■ A ⌶
Liverpool Lime Street ■	d	21p37										
Liverpool South Parkway ■ ✈	d	21p47										
Widnes	d	21p55										
Warrington Central	d	22p03										
Manchester Oxford Road	d	22p27										
Manchester Piccadilly ■ ⇌	d	22p31									12 44	
Stockport	d	22p42									12 55	
Sheffield ■ ⇌	a	23p39									13 37	
	d	23p42			10 49				12 49		13 49	
Chesterfield	d	23p57			11 04				13 03		14 03	
Alfreton	d				11 14				13 14		14 14	
Langley Mill	d											
Nottingham ■ ⇌	a	00 34			11 39				13 39		14 39	
	d		09 41	09 52	11 45		12 37		13 49		14 45	
Grantham ■	d		10a15	10 29	12 18		13 12		14 22		15 20	
Birmingham New Street ■	d					11 22		12 22		13 22		14 22
Coleshill Parkway	d					11 35		12 35		13 35		14 35
Nuneaton	d					11 52		12 52		13 51		14 52
Leicester	d					12 15		13 15		14 15		15 15
Melton Mowbray	d					12 33		13 33		14 34		15 34
Oakham	d					12 45		13 45		14 45		15 45
Stamford	d					13 00		14 00		15 00		16 00
Peterborough ■	a			11 06	12 50	13 16	13 41	14 16	14 51	15 16	15 58	16 16
	d			11 09	12 53	13 18	13 43	14 18	14 53	15 18	16 03	16 18
March	a			11 25		13 33		14 33		15 33		16 33
Ely ■	a			11 48	13 32	13 52	14 16	14 52	15 29	15 52	16 38	16 52
Cambridge	a					14 08		15 08		16 08		17 07
Audley End	a					14 23		15 23		16 23		17 23
Stansted Airport ✈	a					14 45		15 45		16 45		17 45
Thetford	a			12 23	13 57		14 50		15 53		17 02	
Norwich	a			13 06	14 35		15 30		16 35		17 35	

		EM	XC	EM	XC	EM	XC	EM	EM	XC	XC
		◇	◇■ A ⌶	◇	◇■	◇	◇■	◇	◇	◇■	◇■
Liverpool Lime Street ■	d	12 52		13 52		14 52		15 52	16 52		
Liverpool South Parkway ■ ✈	d	13 03		14 03		15 03		16 03	17 03		
Widnes	d	13 11		14 11		15 11		16 11	17 11		
Warrington Central	d	13 19		14 19		15 19		16 19	17 19		
Manchester Oxford Road	d	13 39		14 39		15 39		16 39	17 39		
Manchester Piccadilly ■ ⇌	d	13 44		14 44		15 44		16 44	17 44		
Stockport	d	13 54		14 54		15 54		16 54	17 54		
Sheffield ■ ⇌	a	14 39		15 37		16 36		17 36	18 37		
	d	14 46		15 43		16 40		17 39	18 41		
Chesterfield	d	15 00		15 57		16 56		17 55	18 56		
Alfreton	d	15 11		16 08		17 07		18 05	19 06		
Langley Mill	d	15 18		16 15		17 14		18 13	19 14		
Nottingham ■ ⇌	a	15 40		16 32		17 30		18 29	19 34		
	d	15 49		16 45		17 36		18 47			
Grantham ■	d	16 22		17 21		18 17		19 27			
Birmingham New Street ■	d		15 22		16 22		17 22			18 22	19 22
Coleshill Parkway	d		15 35		16 35		17 35			18 35	19 35
Nuneaton	d		15 52		16 52		17 52			18 52	19 52
Leicester	d		16 15		17 15		18 15			19 15	20 15
Melton Mowbray	d		16 34		17 31		18 31			19 31	20 31
Oakham	d		16 45		17 43		18 42			19 42	20 42
Stamford	d		17 00		17 58		18 57			19 57	20 57
Peterborough ■	a	16 55	17 16	17 50	18 16	18 46	19 14	19 56		20 14	21 13
	d	16 59	17 18	17 56	18 18	18 48	19 18	19 58		20 18	21 18
March	a		17 33	18 11	18 33		19 33			20 33	21 33
Ely ■	a	17 32	17 52	18 32	18 52	19 21	19 52	20 31		20 52	21 52
Cambridge	a		18 07		19 07		20 07			21 07	22 07
Audley End	a		18 23		19 23		20 23			21 23	22 23
Stansted Airport ✈	a		18 45		19 45		20 45			21 45	22 45
Thetford	a	17 56		18 56		19 49		20 55			
Norwich	a	18 30		19 29		20 29		21 35			

A ⌶ to Peterborough
B until 21 July, from 18 August, not 1 September, 8 September
C 28 July, 4 August, 11 August, 1 September, 8 September
D From Mansfield Woodhouse to Skegness

For connections to Ipswich please refer to Table 14

Sundays
until 24 June

North West England and Birmingham - East Midlands - East Anglia - Stansted Airport

Route Diagram - see first Page of Table 49

		EM	EM	EM	XC	EM
		◇	◇	◇	◇■	◇
Liverpool Lime Street ■	d	17 52	18 52	19 52		21 21
Liverpool South Parkway ■ ✈	d	18 03	19 03	20 03		21 31
Widnes	d	18 11	19 11	20 11		21 39
Warrington Central	d	18 19	19 19	20 19		21 47
Manchester Oxford Road	d	18 39	19 39	20 39		22 07
Manchester Piccadilly ■ ⇌	d	18 44	19 44	20 44		22 11
Stockport	d	18 54	19 54	20 54		22 28
Sheffield ■ ⇌	a	19 34	20 34	21 36		23 25
	d	19 40	20 40	21 40		23 29
Chesterfield	d	19 55	20 55	21 56		23 43
Alfreton	d	20 06	21 06	22 07		23 54
Langley Mill	d	20 13	21 13	22 14		00 02
Nottingham ■ ⇌	a	20 30	21 34	22 35		00 25
	d	20 44				
Grantham ■	d	21 19				
Birmingham New Street ■	d				20 22	
Coleshill Parkway	d				20 35	
Nuneaton	d				20 52	
Leicester	d				21 15	
Melton Mowbray	d				21 31	
Oakham	d				21 43	
Stamford	d				21 59	
Peterborough ■	a	21 52			22 14	
	d	21 53			22 18	
March	a				22 33	
Ely ■	a	22 28			22 52	
Cambridge	a				23 07	
Audley End	a					
Stansted Airport ✈	a					
Thetford	a	22 52				
Norwich	a	23 28				

Sundays
1 July to 9 September

		EM	EM	EM	EM	XC	EM	XC	EM	XC	EM	XC
		◇	A	◇	◇	◇■ B ⌶	◇	◇■ B ⌶	◇	◇■ B ⌶	◇	◇■ B ⌶
Liverpool Lime Street ■	d	21p37										
Liverpool South Parkway ■ ✈	d	21p47										
Widnes	d	21p55										
Warrington Central	d	22p03										
Manchester Oxford Road	d	22p27										
Manchester Piccadilly ■ ⇌	d	22p31									12 44	
Stockport	d	22p42									12 55	
Sheffield ■ ⇌	a	23p39									13 37	
	d	23p42			10 49				12 49		13 49	
Chesterfield	d	23p57			11 04				13 03		14 03	
Alfreton	d				11 14				13 14		14 14	
Langley Mill	d											
Nottingham ■ ⇌	a	00 34			11 39				13 39		14 39	
	d		09 41	09 52	11 45		12 37		13 49		14 45	
Grantham ■	d		10a15	10 29	12 18		13 12		14 22		15 20	
Birmingham New Street ■	d					11 22		12 22		13 22		14 22
Coleshill Parkway	d					11 35		12 35		13 35		14 35
Nuneaton	d					11 52		12 52		13 51		14 52
Leicester	d					12 15		13 15		14 15		15 15
Melton Mowbray	d					12 33		13 33		14 34		15 34
Oakham	d					12 45		13 45		14 45		15 45
Stamford	d					13 00		14 00		15 00		16 00
Peterborough ■	a			11 06	12 50	13 16	13 41	14 16	14 51	15 16	15 58	16 16
	d			11 09	12 53	13 18	13 43	14 18	14 53	15 18	16 03	16 18
March	a			11 25		13 33		14 33		15 33		16 33
Ely ■	a			11 48	13 32	13 52	14 16	14 52	15 29	15 52	16 38	16 52
Cambridge	a					14 08		15 08		16 08		17 07
Audley End	a					14 23		15 23		16 23		17 23
Stansted Airport ✈	a					14 45		15 45		16 45		17 45
Thetford	a			12 23	13 57		14 50		15 53		17 02	
Norwich	a			13 06	14 35		15 30		16 35		17 35	

		EM	XC	EM	XC	EM	XC	EM	EM	XC	XC
		◇	◇■ B ⌶	◇	◇■	◇	◇■	◇	◇	◇■	◇■
Liverpool Lime Street ■	d	12 52		13 52		14 52		15 52	16 52		
Liverpool South Parkway ■ ✈	d	13 03		14 03		15 03		16 03	17 03		
Widnes	d	13 11		14 11		15 11		16 11	17 11		
Warrington Central	d	13 19		14 19		15 19		16 19	17 19		
Manchester Oxford Road	d	13 39		14 39		15 39		16 39	17 39		
Manchester Piccadilly ■ ⇌	d	13 44		14 44		15 44		16 44	17 44		
Stockport	d	13 54		14 54		15 54		16 54	17 54		
Sheffield ■ ⇌	a	14 39		15 37		16 36		17 36	18 37		
	d	14 46		15 43		16 40		17 39	18 41		
Chesterfield	d	15 00		15 57		16 56		17 55	18 56		
Alfreton	d	15 11		16 08		17 07		18 05	19 06		
Langley Mill	d	15 18		16 15		17 14		18 13	19 14		
Nottingham ■ ⇌	a	15 38		16 32		17 30		18 29	19 34		
	d	15 49		16 45		17 36		18 47			
Grantham ■	d	16 22		17 21		18 17		19 27			
Birmingham New Street ■	d		15 22		16 22		17 22			18 22	19 22
Coleshill Parkway	d		15 35		16 35		17 35			18 35	19 35
Nuneaton	d		15 52		16 52		17 52			18 52	19 52
Leicester	d		16 15		17 15		18 15			19 15	20 15
Melton Mowbray	d		16 34		17 31		18 31			19 31	20 31
Oakham	d		16 45		17 43		18 42			19 42	20 42
Stamford	d		17 00		17 58		18 57			19 57	20 57
Peterborough ■	a	16 55	17 16	17 50	18 16	18 46	19 14	19 56		20 14	21 13
	d	16 59	17 18	17 56	18 18	18 48	19 18	19 58		20 18	21 18
March	a		17 33	18 11	18 33		19 33			20 33	21 33
Ely ■	a	17 32	17 52	18 32	18 52	19 21	19 52	20 31		20 52	21 52
Cambridge	a		18 07		19 07		20 07			21 07	22 07
Audley End	a		18 23		19 23		20 23			21 23	22 23
Stansted Airport ✈	a		18 45		19 45		20 45			21 45	22 45
Thetford	a	17 56		18 56		19 49		20 55			
Norwich	a	18 30		19 29		20 29		21 35			

A From Mansfield Woodhouse to Skegness
B ⌶ to Peterborough

For connections to Ipswich please refer to Table 14

North West England and Birmingham - East Midlands - East Anglia - Stansted Airport

Route Diagram - see first Page of Table 49

		EM	EM	EM	EM
		◇	◇	◇	◇
Liverpool Lime Street 10	d	17 52	18 52	19 52	21 21
Liverpool South Parkway 7 ✈	d	18 03	19 03	20 03	21 31
Widnes	d	18 11	19 11	20 11	21 39
Warrington Central	d	18 19	19 19	20 19	21 47
Manchester Oxford Road	d	18 39	19 39	20 39	22 07
Manchester Piccadilly 10	d	18 44	19 44	20 44	22 11
Stockport	d	18 54	19 54	20 54	22 28
Sheffield 7	a	19 34	20 34	21 36	23 25
	d	19 40	20 40	21 40	23 29
Chesterfield	d	19 55	20 55	21 56	23 43
Alfreton	d	20 06	21 06	22 07	23 54
Langley Mill	d	20 13	21 13	22 14	00 02
Nottingham 8	a	20 30	21 34	22 35	00 32
	d	20 44			
Grantham 7	d	21 19			
Birmingham New Street 12	d				
Coleshill Parkway	d				
Nuneaton	d				
Leicester	d				
Melton Mowbray	d				
Oakham	d				
Stamford	d				
Peterborough 8	a	21 52			
	d	21 53			
March	a				
Ely 4	a	22 28			
Cambridge	a				
Audley End	a				
Stansted Airport ✈	a				
Thetford	a	22 52			
Norwich	a	23 28			

Sundays
16 September to 21 October

		EM		XC	EM	XC	EM	XC	EM	XC	EM	XC	EM	XC	EM	XC	EM	EM	XC	XC	EM	EM	EM	XC	EM
		◇		◇1	◇	◇1	◇	◇1	◇	◇1	◇	◇1	◇	◇1	◇	◇1	◇	◇	◇1	◇1	◇	◇	◇	◇1	◇
				A 🛒		A 🛒		A 🛒		A 🛒		A 🛒													
Liverpool Lime Street 10	d	21p37									12 52		13 52		14 52		15 52	16 52			17 52	18 52	19 52		21 21
Liverpool South Parkway 7 ✈	d	21p47									13 03		14 03		15 03		16 03	17 03			18 03	19 03	20 03		21 31
Widnes	d	21p55									13 11		14 11		15 11		16 11	17 11			18 11	19 11	20 11		21 39
Warrington Central	d	22p03									13 19		14 19		15 19		16 19	17 19			18 19	19 19	20 19		21 47
Manchester Oxford Road	d	22p27									13 39		14 39		15 39		16 39	17 39			18 39	19 39	20 39		22 07
Manchester Piccadilly 10	d	22p31							12 44		13 44		14 44		15 44		16 44	17 44			18 44	19 44	20 44		22 11
Stockport	d	22p42							12 55		13 54		14 54		15 54		16 54	17 54			18 54	19 54	20 54		22 28
Sheffield 7	a	23p39							13 37		14 39		15 37		16 36		17 36	18 37			19 34	20 34	21 36		23 25
	d	23p42					12 49		13 49		14 46		15 43		16 40		17 39	18 41			19 40	20 40	21 40		23 29
Chesterfield	d	23p57					13 03		14 03		15 00		15 57		16 56		17 55	18 56			19 55	20 55	21 56		23 43
Alfreton	d						13 14		14 14		15 11		16 08		17 07		18 05	19 06			20 06	21 06	22 07		23 54
Langley Mill	d										15 18		16 15		17 14		18 13	19 14			20 13	21 13	22 14		00 02
Nottingham 8	a	00 34					13 39		14 39		15 38		16 32		17 30		18 29	19 34			20 30	21 34	22 35		00 25
	d				12 37		13 49		14 45		15 49		16 45		17 36		18 47				20 44				
Grantham 7	d				13 12		14 22		15 20		16 22		17 22		18 17		19 27				21 19				
Birmingham New Street 12	d			11 22		12 22		13 22		14 22		15 22		16 22		17 22			18 22	19 22				20 22	
Coleshill Parkway	d			11 35		12 35		13 35		14 35		15 35		16 35		17 35			18 35	19 35				20 35	
Nuneaton	d			11 52		12 52		13 51		14 52		15 52		16 52		17 52			18 52	19 52				20 52	
Leicester	d			12 15		13 15		14 15		15 15		16 15		17 15		18 15			19 15	20 15				21 15	
Melton Mowbray	d			12 33		13 33		14 34		15 34		16 34		17 31		18 31			19 31	20 31				21 31	
Oakham	d			12 45		13 45		14 45		15 45		16 45		17 43		18 42			19 42	20 42				21 43	
Stamford	d			13 00		14 00		15 00		16 00		17 00		17 58		18 57			19 57	20 57				21 59	
Peterborough 8	a			13 16	13 41	14 16	14 51	15 16	15 58	16 16	16 55	17 16	17 50	18 16	18 46	19 14	19 56		20 14	21 13	21 52			22 14	
	d			13 18	13 43	14 18	14 53	15 18	16 03	16 18	16 59	17 18	17 56	18 18	18 48	19 18	19 58		20 18	21 18	21 53			22 18	
March	a			13 33		14 33		15 33		16 33		17 33	18 11	18 33		19 33			20 33	21 33				22 33	
Ely 4	a			13 52	14 16	14 52	15 29	15 52	16 38	16 52	17 32	17 52	18 32	18 52	19 21	19 52	20 31		20 52	21 52	22 28			22 52	
Cambridge	a			14 08		15 08		16 08		17 07		18 07		19 07		20 07			21 07	22 07				23 07	
Audley End	a			14 23		15 23		16 23		17 23		18 23		19 23		20 23			21 23	22 23					
Stansted Airport ✈	a			14 45		15 45		16 45		17 45		18 45		19 45		20 45			21 45	22 45					
Thetford	a				14 50		15 53		17 02		17 56		18 56		19 49		20 55				22 52				
Norwich	a				15 30		16 35		17 35		18 30		19 29		20 29		21 35				23 28				

A 🛒 to Peterborough

For connections to Ipswich please refer to Table 14

North West England and Birmingham - East Midlands - East Anglia - Stansted Airport

Route Diagram - see first Page of Table 49

		EM		XC	EM	EM	XC	EM	XC	EM		XC	EM	XC	EM	EM	XC	EM	XC	EM		EM	XC	XC	EM
		◇		◇1		◇	◇1	◇	◇1	◇		◇1	◇	◇1		◇	◇1	◇	◇1	◇		◇	◇1	◇1	◇
				A 🛒	B 🚌		A 🛒		A 🛒			A 🛒		A 🛒	B 🚌										
Liverpool Lime Street 10	d	21p37											12 52			13 52		14 52		15 52		16 52			17 52
Liverpool South Parkway 7 ✈	d	21p47											13 03			14 03		15 03		16 03		17 03			18 03
Widnes	d	21p55											13 11			14 11		15 11		16 11		17 11			18 11
Warrington Central	d	22p03											13 19			14 19		15 19		16 19		17 19			18 19
Manchester Oxford Road	d	22p27											13 39			14 39		15 39		16 39		17 39			18 39
Manchester Piccadilly 10	d	22p31							12 44				13 44			14 44		15 44		16 44		17 44			18 44
Stockport	d	22p42							12 55				13 54			14 54		15 54		16 54		17 54			18 54
Sheffield 7	a	23p39							13 37				14 39			15 37		16 36		17 36		18 37			19 34
	d	23p42					12 49		13 49				14 46			15 43		16 40		17 39		18 41			19 40
Chesterfield	d	23p57					13 03		14 03				15 00			15 57		16 56		17 55		18 56			19 55
Alfreton	d						13 14		14 14				15 11			16 08		17 07		18 05		19 06			20 06
Langley Mill	d												15 18			16 15		17 14		18 13		19 14			20 13
Nottingham 8	a	00 34					13 39		14 39				15 38			16 32		17 30		18 33		19 34			20 30
	d				12 28	12 34		13 42		14 45			15 44		15 41	16 36		17 35		18 41					20 37
Grantham 7	d				13a24					15 20					16a45										
Birmingham New Street 12	d			11 22			12 22		13 22			14 22		15 22			16 22		17 22				18 22	19 22	
Coleshill Parkway	d			11 35			12 35		13 35			14 35		15 35			16 35		17 35				18 35	19 35	
Nuneaton	d			11 52			12 52		13 51			14 52		15 52			16 52		17 52				18 52	19 52	
Leicester	d			12 15			13 15		14 15			15 15		16 15			17 15		18 15				19 15	20 15	
Melton Mowbray	d			12 33			13 33		14 34			15 34		16 34			17 31		18 31				19 31	20 31	
Oakham	d			12 45			13 45		14 45			15 45		16 45			17 43		18 42				19 42	20 42	
Stamford	d			13 00			14 00		15 00			16 00		17 00			17 58		18 57				19 57	20 57	
Peterborough 8	a			13 16		13 41	14 16	14 52	15 16	15 58		16 16	16 57	17 16		17 50	18 16	18 46	19 14	19 56			20 14	21 13	21 47
	d			13 18		13 43	14 18	14 53	15 18	16 03		16 18	16 59	17 18		17 56	18 18	18 48	19 18	19 58			20 18	21 18	21 53
March	a			13 33			14 33		15 33			16 33		17 33		18 11	18 33		19 33				20 33	21 33	
Ely 4	a			13 52		14 16	14 52	15 29	15 52	16 38		16 52	17 32	17 52		18 32	18 52	19 21	19 52	20 31			20 52	21 52	22 28
Cambridge	a			14 08			15 08		16 08			17 07		18 07			19 07		20 07				21 07	22 07	
Audley End	a			14 23			15 23		16 23			17 23		18 23			19 23		20 23				21 23	22 23	
Stansted Airport ✈	a			14 45			15 45		16 45			17 45		18 45			19 45		20 45				21 45	22 45	
Thetford	a					14 50		15 53		17 02			17 56			18 56		19 49		20 55					22 52
Norwich	a					15 30		16 35		17 35			18 30			19 29		20 29		21 35					23 28

Sundays
from 28 October

		EM	EM	XC	EM
		◇	◇	◇1	◇
Liverpool Lime Street 10	d	18 52	19 52		21 21
Liverpool South Parkway 7 ✈	d	19 03	20 03		21 31
Widnes	d	19 11	20 11		21 39
Warrington Central	d	19 19	20 19		21 47
Manchester Oxford Road	d	19 39	20 39		22 07
Manchester Piccadilly 10	d	19 44	20 44		22 11
Stockport	d	19 54	20 54		22 28
Sheffield 7	a	20 34	21 36		23 25
	d	20 40	21 40		23 29
Chesterfield	d	20 55	21 56		23 43
Alfreton	d	21 06	22 07		23 54
Langley Mill	d	21 13	22 14		00 02
Nottingham 8	a	21 34	22 35		00 25
	d				
Grantham 7	d				
Birmingham New Street 12	d			20 22	
Coleshill Parkway	d			20 35	
Nuneaton	d			20 52	
Leicester	d			21 15	
Melton Mowbray	d			21 31	
Oakham	d			21 43	
Stamford	d			21 59	
Peterborough 8	a			22 14	
	d			22 18	
March	a			22 33	
Ely 4	a			22 52	
Cambridge	a			23 07	
Audley End	a				
Stansted Airport ✈	a				
Thetford	a				
Norwich	a				

A 🛒 to Peterborough

B From Netherfield to Sleaford

For connections to Ipswich please refer to Table 14

Network Diagram for Tables 50, 55, 56, 57

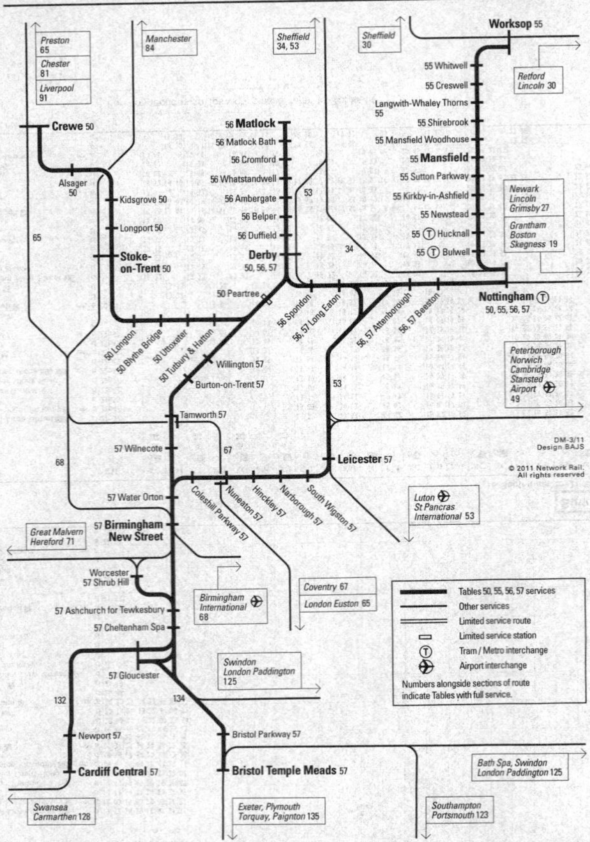

Derby - Stoke-on-Trent and Crewe

Mondays to Fridays

until 14 September

Network Diagram - see first Page of Table 50

Miles			NT	NT	LM	EM	NT	LM	EM	NT	LM		EM	NT	LM	EM	NT	LM	EM	NT	LM		EM	NT	LM
					◇1			◇1			◇1				◇1			◇1			◇1				◇1
			A	A	B		A	C		A	D			A	D		A	D		A	D			A	D
0	**Derby** 6	d				06 40			07 40				08 40			09 40			10 40				11 40		
1¼	Peartree	d							07 44																
11¼	Tutbury & Hatton	d				06 54			07 56				08 56			09 56			10 56				11 56		
19	Uttoxeter	d				07 05			08 07				09 07			10 07			11 07				12 07		
30	Blythe Bridge	d				07 19			08 21				09 21			10 21			11 21				12 21		
33½	Longton	d				07 25			08 27				09 27			10 27			11 27				12 27		
36	**Stoke-on-Trent**	a				07 31			08 32				09 33			10 33			11 33				12 33		
—		d	06 30	07 17	07 26	07 33	07 57	08 13	08 34	08 58	09 13		09 34	09 58	10 13	10 34	10 58	11 13	11 34	11 58	12 13		12 34	12 58	13 13
38¾	Longport	d	06 34	07 21		07 38			08 39				09 39			10 39			11 39				12 39		
42¼	Kidsgrove	d	06a38	07a25	07 34	07 44	08a04	08 21	08 45	09a05	09 21		09 45	10a05	10 21	10 45	11a05	11 21	11 45	12a05	12 21		12 45	13a05	13 21
44½	Alsager	d			07 39	07 48		08 26	08 49		09 26		09 49		10 26	10 49		11 26	11 49		12 26		12 49		13 26
51	**Crewe** 10	a			07 49	07 59		08 38	08 59		09 38		09 59		10 38	10 59		11 38	11 59		12 38		12 59		13 38

		EM	NT	LM	EM	NT	LM		EM	NT	LM	EM	NT	LM	EM	NT	EM		LM	NT	EM	LM	NT	LM	EM
				◇1			◇1				◇1								◇1			1		1	
			A	D		A	D			A	D		A	D		A			D	A		E	A	E	
Derby 6	d	12 40			13 40				14 40			15 40			16 40		17 40				18 40				19 40
Peartree	d														16 45		17 44								
Tutbury & Hatton	d	12 56			13 56				14 56			15 56			16 56		17 56				18 56				19 56
Uttoxeter	d	13 07			14 07				15 07			16 07			17 07		18 07				19 07				20 07
Blythe Bridge	d	13 21			14 21				15 21			16 21			17 21		18 21				19 21				20 21
Longton	d	13 27			14 27				15 27			16 27			17 27		18 27				19 27				20 27
Stoke-on-Trent	a	13 33			14 33				15 33			16 33			17 33		18 32				19 33				20 33
	d	13 34	13 58	14 13	14 34	14 58	15 13		15 34	15 58	16 13	16 34	16 58	17 13	17 34	17 58	18 34		18 43	18 58	19 34	19 43	19 58	20 13	20 34
Longport	d	13 39			14 39				15 39			16 39			17 39		18 39				19 39				20 39
Kidsgrove	d	13 45	14a05	14 21	14 45	15a05	15 21		15 45	16a05	16 21	16 45	17a05	17 21	17 46	18a05	18 45		18 51	19a05	19 45	19 51	20a05	20 21	20 45
Alsager	d	13 49		14 26	14 49		15 26		15 49		16 26	16 49		17 26	17 50		18 49		18 56		19 49	19 56		20 25	20 49
Crewe 10	a	13 59		14 38	14 59		15 38		15 59		16 38	16 59		17 38	17 59		18 59		19 05		19 59	20 05		20 37	20 59

		NT	LM		LM	EM	NT
			◇1		◇1		
		A	F		E		A
Derby 6	d					20 40	
Peartree	d						
Tutbury & Hatton	d					20 56	
Uttoxeter	d					21 07	
Blythe Bridge	d					21 21	
Longton	d					21 27	
Stoke-on-Trent	a					21 33	
	d	20 58	21 05		21 13	21 34	22 18
Longport	d					21 39	
Kidsgrove	d	21a05	21 14		21 21	21 45	22a25
Alsager	d		21 18		21 26	21 49	
Crewe 10	a		21 27		21 36	21 59	

Mondays to Fridays

17 September to 28 September

		NT	NT	LM	EM	NT	LM	EM	NT	LM		EM	NT	LM	EM	NT	LM	EM	NT	LM		EM	NT	LM	EM
				◇1			◇1			◇1				◇1			◇1			◇1				◇1	
		A	A	B		A	C		A	D			A	D		A	D		A	D			A	D	
Derby 6	d				06 40			07 40				08 42			09 42			10 42				11 42			12 42
Peartree	d							07 44																	
Tutbury & Hatton	d				06 54			07 56				08 56			09 56			10 56				11 56			12 56
Uttoxeter	d				07 05			08 07				09 07			10 07			11 07				12 07			13 07
Blythe Bridge	d				07 19			08 21				09 21			10 21			11 21				12 21			13 21
Longton	d				07 25			08 27				09 27			10 27			11 27				12 27			13 27
Stoke-on-Trent	a				07 31			08 32				09 33			10 33			11 33				12 33			13 33
	d	06 30	07 17	07 26	07 33	07 57	08 13	08 34	08 58	09 13		09 34	09 58	10 13	10 34	10 58	11 13	11 34	11 58	12 13		12 34	12 58	13 13	13 34
Longport	d	06 34	07 21		07 38			08 39				09 39			10 39			11 39				12 39			13 39
Kidsgrove	d	06a38	07a25	07 34	07 44	08a04	08 21	08 45	09a05	09 21		09 45	10a05	10 21	10 45	11a05	11 21	11 45	12a05	12 21		12 45	13a05	13 21	13 45
Alsager	d			07 39	07 48		08 26	08 49		09 26		09 49		10 26	10 49		11 26	11 49		12 26		12 49		13 26	13 49
Crewe 10	a			07 49	07 59		08 38	08 59		09 38		10 01		10 38	11 01		11 38	12 01		12 38		13 01		13 38	14 01

		NT	LM	EM	NT	LM		EM	NT	LM	EM	NT	LM	EM	NT	EM		LM	NT	EM	LM	NT	LM	EM	NT
			◇1			◇1				◇1			◇1					◇1			1		1		
		A	D		A	D			A	D		A	D		A			D	A		D	A	D		A
Derby 6	d			13 42				14 42			15 42			16 42		17 42				18 42				19 42	
Peartree	d													16 45		17 44									
Tutbury & Hatton	d			13 56				14 56			15 56			16 56		17 56				18 56				19 56	
Uttoxeter	d			14 07				15 07			16 07			17 07		18 07				19 07				20 07	
Blythe Bridge	d			14 21				15 21			16 21			17 21		18 21				19 21				20 21	
Longton	d			14 27				15 27			16 27			17 27		18 27				19 27				20 27	
Stoke-on-Trent	a			14 33				15 33			16 33			17 33		18 32				19 33				20 33	
	d	13 58	14 13	14 34	14 58	15 13		15 34	15 58	16 13	16 34	16 58	17 13	17 34	17 58	18 34		18 43	18 58	19 34	19 43	19 58	20 13	20 34	20 58
Longport	d			14 39				15 39			16 39			17 39		18 39				19 39				20 39	
Kidsgrove	d	14a05	14 21	14 45	15a05	15 21		15 45	16a05	16 21	16 45	17a05	17 21	17 46	18a05	18 45		18 51	19a05	19 45	19 51	20a05	20 21	20 45	21a05
Alsager	d		14 26	14 49		15 26		15 49		16 26	16 49		17 26	17 50		18 49		18 56		19 49	19 56		20 25	20 49	
Crewe 10	a		14 38	15 01		15 38		16 01		16 38	17 01		17 38	18 01		19 01		19 05		20 01	20 05		20 37	21 01	

A To Manchester Piccadilly
B From Bletchley
C From Northampton
D From London Euston
E from 10 September until 14 September. From London Euston
F until 7 September. From London Euston

Derby - Stoke-on-Trent and Crewe

Mondays to Fridays

17 September to 28 September

Network Diagram - see first Page of Table 50

		LM ◇1 A	EM	NT B
Derby 6	d		20 42	
Peartree	d			
Tutbury & Hatton	d		20 56	
Uttoxeter	d		21 07	
Blythe Bridge	d		21 21	
Longton	d		21 27	
Stoke-on-Trent	a		21 33	
	d	21 13	21 34	22 18
Longport	d		21 39	
Kidsgrove	d	21 21	21 45	22a25
Alsager	d	21 26	21 49	
Crewe 10	a	21 36	22 01	

Mondays to Fridays

from 1 October

		NT B	NT B	LM ◇1 C	EM	NT B	LM ◇1 D	EM	NT B	LM ◇1 A	EM	NT B	LM ◇1 A	EM	NT B	LM ◇1 A	EM	NT B	LM ◇1 A	EM	NT B	LM ◇1 A	EM
Derby 6	d				06 40			07 40			08 42			09 42			10 42			11 42			12 42
Peartree	d							07 44															
Tutbury & Hatton	d				06 54			07 56			08 56			09 56			10 56			11 56			12 56
Uttoxeter	d				07 05			08 07			09 07			10 07			11 07			12 07			13 07
Blythe Bridge	d				07 19			08 21			09 21			10 21			11 21			12 21			13 21
Longton	d				07 25			08 27			09 27			10 27			11 27			12 27			13 27
Stoke-on-Trent	a				07 31			08 32			09 33			10 33			11 33			12 33			13 33
	d	06 30	07 17	07 26	07 33	07 57	08 13	08 34	08 58	09 13	09 34	09 58	10 13	10 34	10 58	11 13	11 34	11 58	12 13	12 34	12 58	13 13	13 34
Longport	d	06 34	07 21		07 38			08 39			09 39			10 39			11 39			12 39			13 39
Kidsgrove	d	06a38	07a25	07 34	07 44	08a04	08 21	08 45	09a05	09 21	09 45	10a05	10 21	10 45	11a05	11 21	11 45	12a05	12 21	12 45	13a05	13 21	13 45
Alsager	d			07 39	07 48		08 26	08 49		09 26	09 49		10 26	10 49		11 26	11 49		12 26	12 49		13 26	13 49
Crewe 10	a			07 49	08 04		08 38	08 59		09 38	10 01		10 38	11 01		11 38	12 01		12 38	13 01		13 38	14 01

		NT B	LM ◇1 A	EM	NT B	LM ◇1 A	EM	NT B	LM ◇1 A	EM	NT B	LM ◇1 A	EM	NT B	EM	LM ◇1 A	NT B	EM	LM 1 A	NT B	LM 1 A	EM	NT B
Derby 6	d			13 42			14 42			15 42			16 42		17 42			18 42				19 42	
Peartree	d												16 45		17 44								
Tutbury & Hatton	d			13 56			14 56			15 56			16 56		17 56			18 56				19 56	
Uttoxeter	d			14 07			15 07			16 07			17 07		18 07			19 07				20 07	
Blythe Bridge	d			14 21			15 21			16 21			17 21		18 21			19 21				20 21	
Longton	d			14 27			15 27			16 27			17 27		18 27			19 27				20 27	
Stoke-on-Trent	a			14 33			15 33			16 33			17 33		18 32			19 33				20 33	
	d	13 58	14 13	14 34	14 58	15 13	15 34	15 58	16 13	16 34	16 58	17 13	17 34	17 58	18 34	18 43	18 58	19 34	19 43	19 58	20 13	20 34	20 58
Longport	d			14 39			15 39			16 39			17 39		18 39			19 39				20 39	
Kidsgrove	d	14a05	14 21	14 45	15a05	15 21	15 45	16a05	16 21	16 45	17a05	17 21	17 46	18a05	18 45	18 51	19a05	19 45	19 51	20a05	20 21	20 45	21a05
Alsager	d		14 26	14 49		15 26	15 49		16 26	16 49		17 26	17 50		18 49	18 56		19 49	19 56		20 25	20 49	
Crewe 10	a		14 38	15 01		15 38	16 01		16 38	17 01		17 38	18 01		19 01	19 05		20 01	20 05		20 37	21 06	

		LM ◇1 A	EM	NT B
Derby 6	d		20 42	
Peartree	d			
Tutbury & Hatton	d		20 56	
Uttoxeter	d		21 07	
Blythe Bridge	d		21 21	
Longton	d		21 27	
Stoke-on-Trent	a		21 33	
	d	21 13	21 34	22 18
Longport	d		21 39	
Kidsgrove	d	21 21	21 45	22a25
Alsager	d	21 26	21 49	
Crewe 10	a	21 36	22 06	

Saturdays

until 29 September

		NT B	LM ◇1 C	EM	NT B	LM ◇1 D	EM	NT B	LM ◇1 A	EM E	EM F	NT B	LM ◇1 A	EM E	EM F	NT B	LM ◇1 A	EM E	EM F	NT B	LM ◇1 A	EM E	EM F
Derby 6	d			06 40			07 40			08 40	08 42			09 40	09 42			10 40	10 42			11 40	11 42
Peartree	d						07 44																
Tutbury & Hatton	d			06 56			07 56			08 56	08 56			09 56	09 56			10 56	10 56			11 56	11 56
Uttoxeter	d			07 07			08 07			09 07	09 07			10 07	10 07			11 07	11 07			12 07	12 07
Blythe Bridge	d			07 21			08 21			09 21	09 21			10 21	10 21			11 21	11 21			12 21	12 21
Longton	d			07 28			08 27			09 27	09 27			10 27	10 27			11 27	11 27			12 27	12 27
Stoke-on-Trent	a			07 34			08 32			09 33	09 33			10 33	10 33			11 33	11 33			12 33	12 33
	d	06 57	07 13	07 34	07 57	08 13	08 34	08 58	09 13	09 34	09 34	09 58	10 13	10 34	10 34	10 58	11 13	11 34	11 34	11 58	12 13	12 34	12 34
Longport	d			07 39			08 39			09 39	09 39			10 39	10 39			11 39	11 39			12 39	12 39
Kidsgrove	d	07a04	07 21	07 46	08a04	08 21	08 45	09a05	09 21	09 45	09 45	10a05	10 21	10 45	10 45	11a05	11 21	11 45	11 45	12a05	12 21	12 45	12 45
Alsager	d		07 26	07 50		08 26	08 49		09 26	09 49	09 49		10 26	10 49	10 49		11 26	11 49	11 49		12 26	12 49	12 49
Crewe 10	a		07 36	07 59		08 37	08 59		09 38	09 59	10 01		10 38	10 59	11 01		11 38	11 59	12 01		12 38	12 59	13 01

A From London Euston
B To Manchester Piccadilly
C From Bletchley
D From Northampton
E until 8 September
F 15 September, 22 September, 29 September

Derby - Stoke-on-Trent and Crewe

Saturdays

until 29 September

Network Diagram - see first Page of Table 50

		NT A	LM ◇1 B	EM C	EM D	NT A	LM ◇1 B	EM C	EM D	NT A	LM ◇1 B	EM C	EM D	NT A	LM ◇1 B	EM C	EM D	NT A	LM ◇1 B	EM C	EM D	NT A	EM C
Derby 6	d			12 40	12 42			13 40	13 42			14 40	14 42			15 40	15 42			16 40	16 42		17 40
Peartree	d																						17 45
Tutbury & Hatton	d			12 56	12 56			13 56	13 56			14 56	14 56			15 56	15 56			16 56	16 56		17 57
Uttoxeter	d			13 07	13 07			14 07	14 07			15 07	15 07			16 07	16 07			17 07	17 07		18 07
Blythe Bridge	d			13 21	13 21			14 21	14 21			15 21	15 21			16 21	16 21			17 21	17 21		18 21
Longton	d			13 27	13 27			14 27	14 27			15 27	15 27			16 27	16 27			17 27	17 27		18 27
Stoke-on-Trent	a			13 33	13 33			14 33	14 33			15 33	15 33			16 33	16 33			17 32	17 32		18 32
	d	12 58	13 13	13 34	13 34	13 58	14 13	14 34	14 34	14 58	15 13	15 34	15 34	15 58	16 13	16 34	16 34	16 58	17 13	17 34	17 34	17 58	18 34
Longport	d			13 39	13 39			14 39	14 39			15 39	15 39			16 39	16 39			17 39	17 39		18 39
Kidsgrove	d	13a05	13 21	13 45	13 45	14a05	14 21	14 45	14 45	15a05	15 21	15 45	15 45	16a05	16 21	16 45	16 45	17a05	17 21	17 45	17 45	18a05	18 45
Alsager	d		13 26	13 49	13 49		14 26	14 49	14 49		15 26	15 49	15 49		16 26	16 49	16 49		17 26	17 49	17 49		18 49
Crewe 10	a		13 38	13 59	14 01		14 38	14 59	15 01		15 38	15 59	16 01		16 38	16 59	17 01		17 38	17 59	18 01		18 59

		EM D	LM ◇1 B	NT A	LM ◇1 B	EM C	EM D	NT A	LM 1 B	EM C	EM D	NT A	LM 1 B	EM C	EM D	NT A
Derby 6	d	17 42				18 40	18 42			19 40	19 42			20 40	20 42	
Peartree	d	17 45														
Tutbury & Hatton	d	17 57				18 56	18 56			19 56	19 56			20 56	20 56	
Uttoxeter	d	18 07				19 07	19 07			20 07	20 07			21 07	21 07	
Blythe Bridge	d	18 21				19 21	19 21			20 21	20 21			21 21	21 21	
Longton	d	18 27				19 27	19 27			20 27	20 27			21 27	21 27	
Stoke-on-Trent	a	18 32				19 33	19 33			20 33	20 33			21 33	21 33	
	d	18 34	18 41	18 58	19 13	19 34	19 34	19 58	20 13	20 34	20 34	20 58	21 15	21 34	21 34	22 18
Longport	d	18 39				19 39	19 39			20 39	20 39			21 39	21 39	
Kidsgrove	d	18 45	18 49	19a05	19 21	19 45	19 45	20a05	20 21	20 45	20 45	21a05	21 23	21 45	21 45	22a25
Alsager	d	18 49	18 54		19 26	19 49	19 49		20 26	20 49	20 49		21 28	21 49	21 49	
Crewe 10	a	19 01	19 05		19 36	19 59	20 01		20 36	20 59	21 01		21 38	21 59	22 01	

Saturdays

from 6 October

		NT A	LM ◇1 E	EM	NT A	LM ◇1 F	EM	NT A	LM ◇1 B	EM	NT A	LM ◇1 B	EM	NT A	LM ◇1 B	EM	NT A	LM ◇1 B	EM	NT A	LM ◇1 B	EM	NT A
Derby 6	d			06 40			07 40			08 42			09 42			10 42			11 42			12 42	
Peartree	d						07 44																
Tutbury & Hatton	d			06 56			07 56			08 56			09 56			10 56			11 56			12 56	
Uttoxeter	d			07 07			08 07			09 07			10 07			11 07			12 07			13 07	
Blythe Bridge	d			07 21			08 21			09 21			10 21			11 21			12 21			13 21	
Longton	d			07 28			08 27			09 27			10 27			11 27			12 27			13 27	
Stoke-on-Trent	a			07 34			08 32			09 33			10 33			11 33			12 33			13 33	
	d	06 57	07 13	07 34	07 57	08 13	08 34	08 58	09 13	09 34	09 58	10 13	10 34	10 58	11 13	11 34	11 58	12 13	12 34	12 58	13 13	13 34	13 58
Longport	d			07 39			08 39			09 39			10 39			11 39			12 39			13 39	
Kidsgrove	d	07a04	07 21	07 46	08a04	08 21	08 45	09a05	09 21	09 45	10a05	10 21	10 45	11a05	11 21	11 45	12a05	12 21	12 45	13a05	13 21	13 45	14a05
Alsager	d		07 26	07 50		08 26	08 49		09 26	09 49		10 26	10 49		11 26	11 49		12 26	12 49		13 26	13 49	
Crewe 10	a		07 36	08 04		08 37	08 59		09 38	10 01		10 38	11 01		11 38	12 01		12 38	13 01		13 38	14 01	

		LM ◇1 B	EM	NT A	LM ◇1 B	EM	NT A	LM ◇1 B	EM	NT A	LM ◇1 B	EM	NT A	EM	LM ◇1 B	NT A	LM ◇1 B	EM	NT A	LM 1 B	EM	NT A	LM 1 B
Derby 6	d		13 42			14 42			15 42			16 42		17 42				18 42			19 42		
Peartree	d													17 45									
Tutbury & Hatton	d		13 56			14 56			15 56			16 56		17 57				18 56			19 56		
Uttoxeter	d		14 07			15 07			16 07			17 07		18 07				19 07			20 07		
Blythe Bridge	d		14 21			15 21			16 21			17 21		18 21				19 21			20 21		
Longton	d		14 27			15 27			16 27			17 27		18 27				19 27			20 27		
Stoke-on-Trent	a		14 33			15 33			16 33			17 32		18 32				19 33			20 33		
	d	14 13	14 34	14 58	15 13	15 34	15 58	16 13	16 34	16 58	17 13	17 34	17 58	18 34	18 41	18 58	19 13	19 34	19 58	20 13	20 34	20 58	21 15
Longport	d		14 39			15 39			16 39			17 39		18 39				19 39			20 39		
Kidsgrove	d	14 21	14 45	15a05	15 21	15 45	16a05	16 21	16 45	17a05	17 21	17 45	18a05	18 45	18 49	19a05	19 21	19 45	20a05	20 21	20 45	21a05	21 23
Alsager	d	14 26	14 49		15 26	15 49		16 26	16 49		17 26	17 49		18 49	18 54		19 26	19 49		20 26	20 49		21 28
Crewe 10	a	14 38	15 01		15 38	16 01		16 38	17 01		17 38	18 01		19 01	19 05		19 36	20 01		20 36	21 06		21 38

		EM	NT A
Derby 6	d	20 42	
Peartree	d		
Tutbury & Hatton	d	20 56	
Uttoxeter	d	21 07	
Blythe Bridge	d	21 21	
Longton	d	21 27	
Stoke-on-Trent	a	21 33	
	d	21 34	22 18
Longport	d	21 39	
Kidsgrove	d	21 45	22a25
Alsager	d	21 49	
Crewe 10	a	22 06	

A To Manchester Piccadilly
B From London Euston
C until 8 September
D 15 September, 22 September, 29 September
E From Bletchley
F From Northampton

Table 50

Derby - Stoke-on-Trent and Crewe

Sundays

until 30 September

Network Diagram - see first Page of Table 50

		LM	LM	LM	NT	LM	EM	EM	LM	NT	EM	EM	LM	EM	LM	EM	LM	EM	LM	NT	EM	LM	EM
		■	■	◇■		◇■			◇■				◇■		◇■		◇■		◇■			◇■	
		A	B	B	C	A	D	E	B	C	D	E	B		F		B		B	C		B	G
Derby	d						14 34	14 38			15 30	15 38		16 38		17 40		18 41			19 38		20 40
Peartree	d																						
Tutbury & Hatton	d						14 48	14 52			15 44	15 52		16 52		17 53		18 52			19 52		20 54
Uttoxeter	d						14 59	15 03			15 55	16 03		17 03		18 03		19 03			20 03		21 05
Blythe Bridge	d						15 13	15 17			16 09	16 17		17 17		18 17		19 17			20 17		21 19
Longton	d						15 19	15 23			16 15	16 23		17 23		18 24		19 23			20 23		21 25
Stoke-on-Trent	a						15 29	15 29			16 29	16 29		17 29		18 30		19 29			20 30		21 34
	d	11 16	12 40	13 20	13 25	14 37	15 30	15 30	15 41	16 01	16 30	16 30	16 40	17 30	17 40	18 31	18 43	19 30	19 44	20 01	20 30	20 41	21 36
Longport	d						15 35	15 35			16 35	16 35		17 35		18 36		19 35			20 35		21 41
Kidsgrove	d	11 24	12 48	13 28	13a32	14 45	15 41	15 41	15 50	16a08	16 40	16 41	16 48	17 41	17 48	18 41	18 51	19 41	19 52	20a08	20 41	20 50	21 47
Alsager	d	11 28	12 53	13 32		14 50	15 46	15 46	15 54		16 44	16 45	16 53	17 45	17 53	18 46	18 55	19 46	19 56		20 46	20 54	21 52
Crewe	a	11 43	13 03	13 43		15 00	16 01	16 01	16 04		16 55	17 02	17 03	18 01	18 03	19 01	19 05	20 02	20 06		21 01	21 05	22 05

		EM	LM	NT	LM
			◇■		◇■
		H	B	C	B
Derby	d	20 40			
Peartree	d				
Tutbury & Hatton	d	20 54			
Uttoxeter	d	21 05			
Blythe Bridge	d	21 19			
Longton	d	21 25			
Stoke-on-Trent	a	21 35			
	d	21 36	21 43	22 39	22 43
Longport	d	21 41			
Kidsgrove	d	21 47	21 52	22a46	22 51
Alsager	d	21 51	21 57		22 55
Crewe	a	22 05	22 08		23 05

Sundays

from 7 October

		LM	LM	LM	NT	LM	EM	LM	NT	EM	LM	EM	EM	LM	EM	LM	NT	EM	LM	EM	LM	NT	LM
		■	■	◇■		◇■		◇■			◇■			◇■		◇■			◇■		◇■		◇■
		A	B	B	C	A		B	C		B			B		B	C		B		B	C	B
Derby	d						14 38			15 38		16 38	17 40		18 41			19 38		20 40			
Peartree	d																						
Tutbury & Hatton	d						14 52			15 52		16 52	17 53		18 52			19 52		20 54			
Uttoxeter	d						15 03			16 03		17 03	18 03		19 03			20 03		21 05			
Blythe Bridge	d						15 17			16 17		17 17	18 17		19 17			20 17		21 19			
Longton	d						15 23			16 23		17 23	18 24		19 23			20 23		21 25			
Stoke-on-Trent	a						15 29			16 29		17 29	18 30		19 29			20 30		21 34			
	d	11 16	12 40	13 20	13 25	14 37	15 30	15 41	16 01	16 30	16 40	17 30	18 31	18 43	19 30	19 44	20 01	20 30	20 41	21 36	21 43	22 39	22 43
Longport	d						15 35			16 35		17 35	18 36		19 35			20 35		21 41			
Kidsgrove	d	11 24	12 48	13 28	13a32	14 45	15 41	15 50	16a08	16 41	16 48	17 41	18 41	18 51	19 41	19 52	20a08	20 41	20 50	21 47	21 52	22a46	22 51
Alsager	d	11 28	12 53	13 32		14 50	15 46	15 54		16 45	16 53	17 45	18 46	18 55	19 46	19 56		20 46	20 54	21 52	21 57		22 55
Crewe	a	11 43	13 03	13 43		15 00	16 01	16 04		17 02	17 03	18 01	19 01	19 05	20 02	20 06		21 01	21 05	22 05	22 08		23 05

A From Northampton
B From London Euston
C To Manchester Piccadilly
D from 1 July until 9 September
E until 24 June, 16 September, 23 September, 30 September
F until 24 June. From London Euston
G from 1 July until 30 September
H until 24 June

Table 50

Crewe and Stoke-on-Trent - Derby

Mondays to Fridays

until 28 September

Network Diagram - see first Page of Table 50

Miles			XC	NT	EM	LM	EM	LM	EM	NT	LM	EM	NT	LM	EM	NT	LM	EM	NT	LM	EM	NT	LM
			◇■			◇■		◇■			◇■			◇■			◇■			◇■			◇■
			A ✠	B		C		C		D	C		D	C		D	C		D	C		D	C
0	**Crewe**	d	05 47		06 07	06 35	06 58	07 33	08 07		08 33	09 07		09 33	10 07		10 33	11 07		11 33	12 07		12 33
6¼	Alsager	d			06 16	06 44	07 07	07 41	08 16		08 41	09 16		09 41	10 16		10 41	11 16		11 41	12 16		12 41
8½	Kidsgrove	d		06 16	06 21	06 48	07 12	07 46	08 21	08 32	08 46	09 21	09 32	09 46	10 21	10 32	10 46	11 21	11 32	11 46	12 21	12 32	12 46
12	Longport	d			06 27		07 18		08 27			09 27			10 27			11 27			12 27		
15	**Stoke-on-Trent**	a	06 06	06 26	06 31	06 57	07 23	07 54	08 31	08 42	08 54	09 31	09 42	09 54	10 31	10 42	10 54	11 31	11 42	11 54	12 31	12 42	12 54
—		d			06 33		07 24		08 33			09 33			10 33			11 33			12 33		
17½	Longton	d			06 39		07 30		08 39			09 39			10 39			11 39			12 39		
20¾	Blythe Bridge	d			06 45		07 37		08 45			09 45			10 45			11 45			12 45		
31¾	Uttoxeter	d			06 58		07 49		08 58			09 58			10 58			11 58			12 58		
39½	Tutbury & Hatton	d			07 07		07 58		09 07			10 07			11 07			12 07			13 07		
49½	Peartree	d			07 20																		
51	**Derby**	a			07 24		08 16		09 24			10 24			11 24			12 24			13 24		

		EM	NT	LM	EM	NT	LM	EM	NT	LM	EM	NT	LM	EM	NT	LM	EM	NT	LM	EM	NT	LM	NT
				◇■			◇■			◇■			◇■			◇■			◇■			■	
			D	C		D	C		D	C		D	C		D	C		D	E		D	E	D
Crewe	d	13 07		13 33	14 07		14 33	15 07		15 33	16 07		16 33	17 07		17 33	18 07		18 33	19 07		19 33	
Alsager	d	13 16		13 41	14 16		14 41	15 16		15 41	16 16		16 41	17 16		17 41	18 16		18 41	19 16		19 41	
Kidsgrove	d	13 21	13 32	13 46	14 21	14 32	14 46	15 21	15 32	15 46	16 21	16 32	16 46	17 21	17 32	17 46	18 21	18 32	18 46	19 21	19 32	19 46	20 32
Longport	d	13 27			14 27			15 27			16 27			17 27			18 27			19 27			
Stoke-on-Trent	a	13 31	13 42	13 54	14 31	14 42	14 54	15 31	15 42	15 54	16 31	16 42	16 54	17 31	17 42	17 54	18 31	18 42	18 54	19 31	19 42	19 54	20 42
	d	13 33			14 33			15 33			16 33			17 33			18 33			19 33			
Longton	d	13 39			14 39			15 39			16 39			17 39			18 39			19 39			
Blythe Bridge	d	13 45			14 45			15 45			16 45			17 45			18 45			19 45			
Uttoxeter	d	13 58			14 58			15 58			16 58			17 58			18 58			19 58			
Tutbury & Hatton	d	14 07			15 07			16 07			17 07			18 07			19 07			20 07			
Peartree	d							16 18															
Derby	a	14 24			15 24			16 24			17 24			18 24			19 24			20 24			

		LM	EM	NT	NT
		■			
		F		D	D
Crewe	d	20 39	20 45		
Alsager	d	20 48	20 58		
Kidsgrove	d	20 52	21 07	21 32	22 32
Longport	d		21 12		
Stoke-on-Trent	a	21 00	21 16	21 42	22 42
	d		21 18		
Longton	d		21 24		
Blythe Bridge	d		21 29		
Uttoxeter	d		21 42		
Tutbury & Hatton	d		21 51		
Peartree	d				
Derby	a		22 09		

Mondays to Fridays

from 1 October

		XC	NT	EM	LM	EM	LM	EM	NT	LM	EM	NT	LM	EM	NT	LM	EM	NT	LM	EM	NT	LM	EM
		◇■			◇■		◇■			◇■			◇■			◇■			◇■			◇■	
		A ✠	B		C		C		D	C		D	C		D	C		D	C		D	C	
Crewe	d	05 47		06 07	06 35	06 58	07 33	08 07		08 33	09 07		09 33	10 07		10 33	11 07		11 33	12 07		12 33	13 07
Alsager	d			06 16	06 44	07 07	07 41	08 16		08 41	09 16		09 41	10 16		10 41	11 16		11 41	12 16		12 41	13 16
Kidsgrove	d		06 16	06 21	06 48	07 12	07 46	08 21	08 32	08 46	09 21	09 32	09 46	10 21	10 32	10 46	11 21	11 32	11 46	12 21	12 32	12 46	13 21
Longport	d			06 27		07 18		08 27			09 27			10 27			11 27			12 27			13 27
Stoke-on-Trent	a	06 06	06 26	06 31	06 57	07 23	07 54	08 31	08 42	08 54	09 31	09 42	09 54	10 31	10 42	10 54	11 31	11 42	11 54	12 31	12 42	12 54	13 31
	d			06 33		07 24		08 33			09 33			10 33			11 33			12 33			13 33
Longton	d			06 39		07 30		08 39			09 39			10 39			11 39			12 39			13 39
Blythe Bridge	d			06 45		07 37		08 45			09 45			10 45			11 45			12 45			13 45
Uttoxeter	d			06 58		07 49		08 58			09 58			10 58			11 58			12 58			13 58
Tutbury & Hatton	d			07 07		07 58		09 07			10 07			11 07			12 07			13 07			14 07
Peartree	d			07 20																			
Derby	a			07 27		08 17		09 26			10 26			11 26			12 26			13 26			14 26

		NT	LM	EM	NT	LM	EM	NT	LM	EM	NT	LM	EM	NT	LM	EM	NT	LM	EM	NT	LM	NT	LM
			◇■			◇■			◇■			◇■			◇■			◇■			■		■
		D	C		D	C		D	C		D	C		D	C		D	E		D	E	D	E
Crewe	d		13 33	14 07		14 33	15 07		15 33	16 07		16 33	17 07		17 33	18 07		18 33	19 07		19 33		20 39
Alsager	d		13 41	14 16		14 41	15 16		15 41	16 16		16 41	17 16		17 41	18 16		18 41	19 16		19 41		20 48
Kidsgrove	d	13 32	13 46	14 21	14 32	14 46	15 21	15 32	15 46	16 21	16 32	16 46	17 21	17 32	17 46	18 21	18 32	18 46	19 21	19 32	19 46	20 32	20 52
Longport	d			14 27			15 27			16 27			17 27			18 27			19 27				
Stoke-on-Trent	a	13 42	13 54	14 31	14 42	14 54	15 31	15 42	15 54	16 31	16 42	16 54	17 31	17 42	17 54	18 31	18 42	18 54	19 31	19 42	19 54	20 42	21 00
	d			14 33			15 33			16 33			17 33			18 33			19 33				
Longton	d			14 39			15 39			16 39			17 39			18 39			19 39				
Blythe Bridge	d			14 45			15 45			16 45			17 45			18 45			19 45				
Uttoxeter	d			14 58			15 58			16 58			17 58			18 58			19 58				
Tutbury & Hatton	d			15 07			16 07			17 07			18 07			19 07			20 07				
Peartree	d						16 18																
Derby	a			15 26			16 26			17 26			18 26			19 26			20 26				

A From Manchester Piccadilly to Bournemouth
B From Macclesfield
C To London Euston
D From Manchester Piccadilly
E To Northampton
F from 10 September until 28 September. To Northampton

Crewe and Stoke-on-Trent - Derby

Mondays to Fridays from 1 October

Network Diagram - see first Page of Table 50

		EM		NT A	NT A
Crewe 10	d	20 45			
Alsager	d	20 58			
Kidsgrove	d	21 07		21 32	22 32
Longport	d	21 12			
Stoke-on-Trent	a	21 16		21 42	22 42
	d	21 18			
Longton	d	21 24			
Blythe Bridge	d	21 29			
Uttoxeter	d	21 42			
Tutbury & Hatton	d	21 51			
Peartree	d				
Derby 6	a	22 09			

Saturdays until 29 September

		XC ◇1 B ✠	NT C	EM	LM ◇1 D	EM	NT A	LM ◇1 D	EM	NT A	LM ◇1 D	EM	NT A	LM ◇1 D	EM	NT A	LM ◇1 D	EM	NT A	LM ◇1 D	EM	NT A	LM ◇1 D
Crewe 10	d	05 47		06 07	06 38	07 07		07 38	08 07		08 33	09 07		09 33	10 07		10 33	11 07		11 33	12 07		12 33
Alsager	d			06 16	06 47	07 16		07 47	08 16		08 41	09 16		09 41	10 16		10 41	11 16		11 41	12 16		12 41
Kidsgrove	d		06 16	06 21	06 51	07 21	07 28	07 51	08 21	08 32	08 46	09 21	09 32	09 46	10 21	10 32	10 46	11 21	11 32	11 46	12 21	12 32	12 46
Longport	d			06 27		07 27			08 27			09 27			10 27			11 27			12 27		
Stoke-on-Trent	a	06 07	06 26	06 31	06 59	07 31	07 40	07 59	08 31	08 42	08 54	09 31	09 42	09 54	10 31	10 42	10 54	11 31	11 42	11 54	12 31	12 42	12 54
	d			06 33		07 33			08 33			09 33			10 33			11 33			12 33		
Longton	d			06 39		07 39			08 39			09 39			10 39			11 39			12 39		
Blythe Bridge	d			06 45		07 45			08 45			09 45			10 45			11 45			12 45		
Uttoxeter	d			06 58		07 58			08 58			09 58			10 58			11 58			12 58		
Tutbury & Hatton	d			07 07		08 07			09 07			10 07			11 07			12 07			13 07		
Peartree	d			07 19																			
Derby 6	a			07 23		08 22			09 23			10 23			11 23			12 23			13 23		

		EM	NT A	LM ◇1 D	EM	NT A	LM ◇1 D	EM	NT A	LM ◇1 D	EM	NT A	LM ◇1 D	EM	NT A	LM ◇1 E	EM	NT A	LM ◇1 E	EM	NT A	LM 1 F	NT A
Crewe 10	d	13 07		13 33	14 07		14 33	15 07		15 33	16 07		16 33	17 07		17 33	18 07		18 33	19 07		19 33	
Alsager	d	13 16		13 41	14 16		14 41	15 16		15 41	16 16		16 41	17 16		17 41	18 16		18 41	19 16		19 41	
Kidsgrove	d	13 21	13 32	13 46	14 21	14 32	14 46	15 21	15 32	15 46	16 21	16 32	16 46	17 21	17 32	17 46	18 21	18 32	18 46	19 21	19 32	19 46	20 32
Longport	d	13 27			14 27			15 27			16 27			17 27			18 27			19 27			
Stoke-on-Trent	a	13 31	13 42	13 54	14 31	14 42	14 54	15 31	15 42	15 54	16 31	16 42	16 54	17 31	17 42	17 54	18 31	18 42	18 54	19 31	19 42	19 54	20 42
	d	13 33			14 33			15 33			16 33			17 33			18 33			19 33			
Longton	d	13 39			14 39			15 39			16 39			17 39			18 39			19 39			
Blythe Bridge	d	13 45			14 45			15 45			16 45			17 45			18 45			19 45			
Uttoxeter	d	13 58			14 58			15 58			16 58			17 58			18 58			19 58			
Tutbury & Hatton	d	14 07			15 07			16 07			17 07			18 07			19 07			20 07			
Peartree	d							16 19															
Derby 6	a	14 23			15 23			16 23			17 23			18 23			19 23			20 23			

		EM	NT A	NT A
Crewe 10	d	20 45		
Alsager	d	20 54		
Kidsgrove	d	21 08	21 32	22 32
Longport	d	21 14		
Stoke-on-Trent	a	21 18	21 42	22 42
	d	21 19		
Longton	d	21 25		
Blythe Bridge	d	21 31		
Uttoxeter	d	21 44		
Tutbury & Hatton	d	21 53		
Peartree	d			
Derby 6	a	22 10		

Saturdays from 6 October

		XC ◇1 B ✠	NT C	EM	LM ◇1 D	EM	NT A	LM ◇1 D	EM	NT A	LM ◇1 D	EM	NT A	LM ◇1 D	EM	NT A	LM ◇1 D	EM	NT A	LM ◇1 D	EM	NT A	LM ◇1 D
Crewe 10	d	05 47		06 07	06 38	07 07		07 38	08 07		08 33	09 07		09 33	10 07		10 33	11 07		11 33	12 07		12 33
Alsager	d			06 16	06 47	07 16		07 47	08 16		08 41	09 16		09 41	10 16		10 41	11 16		11 41	12 16		12 41
Kidsgrove	d		06 16	06 21	06 51	07 21	07 28	07 51	08 21	08 32	08 46	09 21	09 32	09 46	10 21	10 32	10 46	11 21	11 32	11 46	12 21	12 32	12 46
Longport	d			06 27		07 27			08 27			09 27			10 27			11 27			12 27		
Stoke-on-Trent	a	06 07	06 26	06 31	06 59	07 31	07 40	07 59	08 31	08 42	08 54	09 31	09 42	09 54	10 31	10 42	10 54	11 31	11 42	11 54	12 31	12 42	12 54
	d			06 33		07 33			08 33			09 33			10 33			11 33			12 33		
Longton	d			06 39		07 39			08 39			09 39			10 39			11 39			12 39		
Blythe Bridge	d			06 45		07 45			08 45			09 45			10 45			11 45			12 45		
Uttoxeter	d			06 58		07 58			08 58			09 58			10 58			11 58			12 58		
Tutbury & Hatton	d			07 07		08 07			09 07			10 07			11 07			12 07			13 07		
Peartree	d			07 19																			
Derby 6	a			07 28		08 24			09 26			10 26			11 26			12 26			13 26		

A From Manchester Piccadilly
B From Manchester Piccadilly to Bournemouth
C From Macclesfield
D To London Euston
E To Northampton
F 15 September, 22 September, 29 September. To Northampton

Crewe and Stoke-on-Trent - Derby

Saturdays from 6 October

Network Diagram - see first Page of Table 50

		EM	NT A	LM ◇1 B	EM	NT A	LM ◇1 B	EM	NT A	LM ◇1 B	EM	NT A	LM ◇1 B	EM	NT A	LM ◇1 C	EM	NT A	LM ◇1 C	EM	NT A	LM 1 C	NT A
Crewe 10	d	13 07		13 33	14 07		14 33	15 07		15 33	16 07		16 33	17 07		17 33	18 07		18 33	19 07		19 33	
Alsager	d	13 16		13 41	14 16		14 41	15 16		15 41	16 16		16 41	17 16		17 41	18 16		18 41	19 16		19 41	
Kidsgrove	d	13 21	13 32	13 46	14 21	14 32	14 46	15 21	15 32	15 46	16 21	16 32	16 46	17 21	17 32	17 46	18 21	18 32	18 46	19 21	19 32	19 46	20 32
Longport	d	13 27			14 27			15 27			16 27			17 27			18 27			19 27			
Stoke-on-Trent	a	13 31	13 42	13 54	14 31	14 42	14 54	15 31	15 42	15 54	16 31	16 42	16 54	17 31	17 42	17 54	18 31	18 42	18 54	19 31	19 42	19 54	20 42
	d	13 33			14 33			15 33			16 33			17 33			18 33			19 33			
Longton	d	13 39			14 39			15 39			16 39			17 39			18 39			19 39			
Blythe Bridge	d	13 45			14 45			15 45			16 45			17 45			18 45			19 45			
Uttoxeter	d	13 58			14 58			15 58			16 58			17 58			18 58			19 58			
Tutbury & Hatton	d	14 07			15 07			16 07			17 07			18 07			19 07			20 07			
Peartree	d							16 19															
Derby 6	a	14 26			15 26			16 26			17 26			18 26			19 25			20 26			

		EM	NT A	NT A
Crewe 10	d	20 45		
Alsager	d	20 54		
Kidsgrove	d	21 08	21 32	22 32
Longport	d	21 14		
Stoke-on-Trent	a	21 18	21 42	22 42
	d	21 19		
Longton	d	21 25		
Blythe Bridge	d	21 31		
Uttoxeter	d	21 44		
Tutbury & Hatton	d	21 53		
Peartree	d			
Derby 6	a	22 10		

Sundays until 30 September

		LM ◇1 B	LM ◇1 B	LM ◇1 B	NT D	NT E	LM ◇1 B	LM ◇1 B	EM	LM ◇1 B	EM	NT A	LM ◇1 B	EM	LM ◇1 B	EM	LM ◇1 B	EM	LM ◇1 B	EM	NT A	LM ◇1 B	EM
Crewe 10	d	09 30	10 38	11 38			12 38	13 38	14 04	14 33	15 05		15 38	16 08	16 33	17 08	17 38	18 08	18 37	19 08		19 38	20 08
Alsager	d	09 38	10 46	11 46			12 46	13 47	14 13	14 41	15 14		15 46	16 17	16 41	17 17	17 46	18 17	18 45	19 17		19 46	20 20
Kidsgrove	d	09 43	10 50	11 50	12 25	12 26	12 50	13 51	14 18	14 45	15 21	15 25	15 50	16 22	16 45	17 22	17 50	18 22	18 49	19 22	19 28	19 50	20 25
Longport	d								14 24		15 26			16 29		17 29		18 29		19 29			20 33
Stoke-on-Trent	a	09 51	10 58	11 58	12 37	12 37	12 58	13 59	14 29	14 54	15 30	15 37	15 58	16 35	16 53	17 33	17 58	18 34	18 57	19 33	19 40	19 58	20 37
	d								14 29		15 32			16 35		17 35		18 35		19 35			20 39
Longton	d								14 35		15 38			16 41		17 41		18 41		19 41			20 46
Blythe Bridge	d								14 41		15 44			16 47		17 47		18 47		19 47			20 52
Uttoxeter	d								14 53		15 56			16 59		17 59		18 59		19 59			21 04
Tutbury & Hatton	d								15 02		16 06			17 08		18 08		19 08		20 08			21 13
Peartree	d																						
Derby 6	a								15 17		16 25			17 27		18 27		19 27		20 27			21 33

		LM ◇1 C	EM	NT A
Crewe 10	d	20 41	21 16	
Alsager	d	20 49	21 25	
Kidsgrove	d	20 53	21 30	22 26
Longport	d		21 36	
Stoke-on-Trent	a	21 03	21 40	22 36
	d		21 42	
Longton	d		21 53	
Blythe Bridge	d		21 59	
Uttoxeter	d		22 12	
Tutbury & Hatton	d		22 21	
Peartree	d			
Derby 6	a		22 40	

Sundays from 7 October

		LM ◇1 B	LM ◇1 B	LM ◇1 B	NT A	LM ◇1 B	LM ◇1 B	EM	LM ◇1 B	EM	NT A	LM ◇1 B	EM	LM ◇1 B	EM	LM ◇1 B	EM	LM ◇1 B	EM	NT A	LM ◇1 B	EM	LM ◇1 C	EM	NT A
Crewe 10	d	09 30	10 38	11 38		12 38	13 38	14 04	14 33	15 05		15 38	16 08	16 33	17 08	17 38	18 08	18 37	19 08		19 38	20 08	20 41	21 16	
Alsager	d	09 38	10 46	11 46		12 46	13 47	14 13	14 41	15 14		15 46	16 17	16 41	17 17	17 46	18 17	18 45	19 17		19 46	20 20	20 49	21 25	
Kidsgrove	d	09 43	10 50	11 50	12 26	12 50	13 51	14 18	14 45	15 21	15 25	15 50	16 22	16 45	17 22	17 50	18 22	18 49	19 22	19 28	19 50	20 25	20 53	21 30	22 26
Longport	d							14 24		15 26			16 29		17 29		18 29		19 29			20 33		21 36	
Stoke-on-Trent	a	09 51	10 58	11 58	12 37	12 58	13 59	14 29	14 54	15 30	15 37	15 58	16 35	16 53	17 33	17 58	18 34	18 57	19 33	19 40	19 58	20 37	21 03	21 40	22 36
	d							14 29		15 32			16 35		17 35		18 35		19 35			20 39		21 42	
Longton	d							14 35		15 38			16 41		17 41		18 41		19 41			20 46		21 53	
Blythe Bridge	d							14 41		15 44			16 47		17 47		18 47		19 47			20 52		21 59	
Uttoxeter	d							14 53		15 56			16 59		17 59		18 59		19 59			21 04		22 12	
Tutbury & Hatton	d							15 02		16 06			17 08		18 08		19 08		20 08			21 13		22 21	
Peartree	d																								
Derby 6	a							15 17		16 25			17 27		18 27		19 27		20 27			21 33		22 40	

A From Manchester Piccadilly
B To London Euston
C To Northampton
D until 9 September. From Manchester Piccadilly
E 16 September, 23 September, 30 September. From Manchester Piccadilly

Route Diagram for Table 51

DM-5/10
Design BAJS

This Table summarises through services which, with their associated connecting services at Birmingham New Street, link centres in the North and South of the country. In certain instances a faster journey is possible via London and the relevant Table(s) should be consulted.

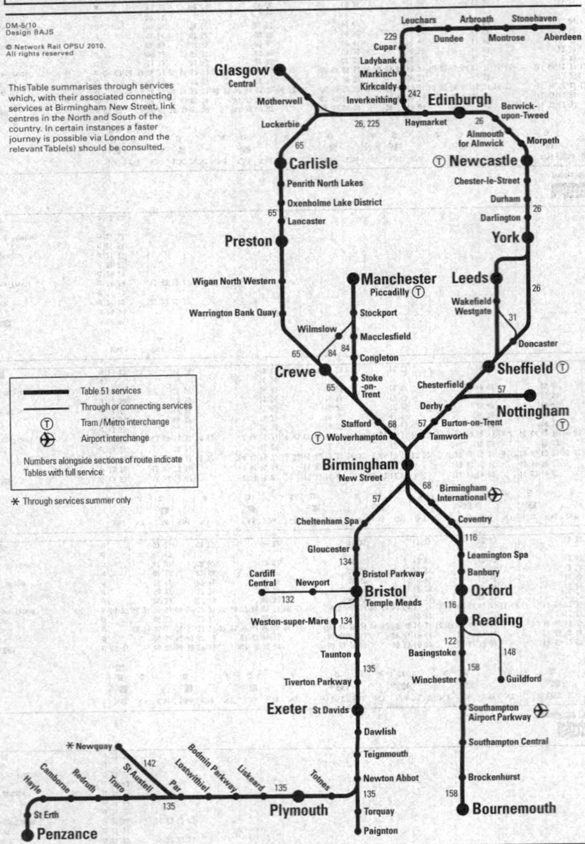

Scotland, The North East, North West England - The South West and South Coast

Route Diagram - see first Page of Table 51

		XC	XC	XC	XC	XC	XC	XC	XC	XC	XC	XC	XC	XC	VT	XC	XC	XC	XC	XC	XC	VT	XC
		MX	MO	MX							D	E				D		E					
		◇1	◇1	◇1	◇1	◇1	◇1	◇1	◇1	◇1	◇1	◇1	◇1	◇1	◇1	◇1	◇1	◇1	◇1	◇1	1	◇1	◇1
		A	B	C							D	E				D		E					
			🛒	🛒			🛒		🛒	🛒	🛒	🛒		🛒	⊠	🛒	🛒	🛒	🛒	🛒		⊠	🛒
Aberdeen	d																						
Stonehaven	d																						
Montrose	d																						
Arbroath	d																						
Dundee	d																						
Leuchars 3	d																						
Cupar	d																						
Ladybank	d																						
Markinch	d																						
Kirkcaldy	d																						
Inverkeithing	d																						
Glasgow Central 15	d																						
Motherwell	d																						
Haymarket	d																						
Edinburgh 10	d		17p07	17p08																			
Haymarket	d																						
Lockerbie	d																						
Carlisle 8	d																						
Penrith North Lakes	d																						
Oxenholme Lake District	d																					06 58	
Lancaster 6	d																					07 17	
Preston 8	d														06 16							07 28	
Wigan North Western	d														06 27							07 39	
Warrington Bank Quay	d														06 38								
M'chester Piccadilly 10	d									05 11				06 00						07 07			07 26
Stockport	d													06 08						07 16			07 35
Wilmslow	d																						
Crewe 10	d									05 47				06 38	07 01							08 01	
Macclesfield	d																						07 49
Congleton	d																						
Stoke-on-Trent	d									06 07										07 44			08 07
Stafford	d									06 25				06 58						08 02			08 25
Wolverhampton 7	d									06 41				07 15	07 32					08 16		08 32	08 41
Dunbar	d		17p27	17p28																			
Berwick-upon-Tweed	d		17p52	17p51																			
Alnmouth for Alnwick	d																						
Morpeth	d																						
Newcastle 8	d		18p39	18p41																			
Chester-le-Street	d																						
Durham	d		18p51	18p53																			
Darlington 7	d		19p08	19p10																			
York 8	d		19p40	19p44																			
Leeds 10	d		20p10	20p11													06 00		06 15				
Wakefield Westgate 7	d		20p22	20p23													06 12		06 27				
Doncaster 7	d																		06 45				
Sheffield 7	d		20p54	20p54									06 01				06 50		07 18				
Chesterfield	d		21p06	21p06									06 27				07 04		07 30				
Nottingham 8	d											06 00				06 37		06 56			07 37		
Derby 6	d		21p27	21p29							06 10	06 36	06 48			07 06	07 27	07 36	07 50		08 06		
Burton-on-Trent	d		21p37	21p40							06 20	06 48	06 58			07 18	07 38	07 50	08 00		08 18		
Tamworth	d		21p48	21p50							06 31	07 01	07 09			07 30	07 50	08 03	08 11		08 30		
Birmingham New Street 12	a		22p05	22p07						06 58	06 52	07 25	07 27	07 31	07 55	07 52	08 08	08 24	08 27	08 32	08 54	08 55	08 58
Birmingham New Street 12	d	22p04	22p12	22p12	05 00	05 42	06 04	06 33	06 42	07 04	07 12	07 30	07 33	07 42		08 04	08 12	08 30	08 33	08 42			09 04
Cheltenham Spa	a		22p50	23p30	06 01	06 43			07 21		07 51	08 14		08 23			08 51	09 11		09 23			
Gloucester 7	a		23p03		06 16	06 53						08 27						09 22					
Bristol Parkway 7	a		00 01	00 01					07 57		08 25			08 54			09 24			09 54			
Bristol Temple Meads 10	a		00 14	00 13					08 08		08 40			09 14			09 38			10 08			
Newport (South Wales)	a				07 09	07 52						09 12						10 09					
Cardiff Central 7	a				07 26	08 08						09 30						10 25					
Weston-super-Mare	a																						
Taunton	a								08 41		09 15						10 16						
Tiverton Parkway	a								08 54		09 28						10 29						
Exeter St Davids 6	a								09 08		09 42						10 45						
Dawlish	a																						
Teignmouth	a																						
Newton Abbot	a								09 29		10 02						11 06						
Torquay	a								09 40														
Paignton	a								09 47														
Totnes	a										10 16						11 20						
Plymouth	a										10 46						11 48						
Liskeard 8	a																						
Bodmin Parkway	a																						
Lostwithiel	a																						
Par	a																						
Newquay (Summer Only)	a																						
St Austell	a																						
Truro	a																						
Redruth	a																						
Camborne	a																						
Hayle	a																						
St Erth	a																						
Penzance	a																						
Birmingham International ✈	d						06 14			07 14						08 14							09 14
Coventry	d						06 25			07 25						08 25							09 25
Leamington Spa 8	d	22p53					06 38	07 00		07 38			08 04			08 38			09 00				09 38
Banbury	a	23p15					06 56	07 21		07 54			08 20			08 54			09 18				09 54
Oxford	a	23p35					07 14	07 41		08 14			08 41			09 14			09 41				10 14
Reading 7	a	00 07					07 39	08 10		08 39			09 11			09 39			10 10				10 39
Guildford	a																						
Basingstoke	a						08 08	08 40		09 08						10 08			10 39				11 08
Winchester	a						08 24	08 56		09 23						10 24			10 54				11 24
Southampton Airport Pkway ✈	a						08 32	09 08		09 32						10 32			11 08				11 32
Southampton Central ⛴	a						08 44	09 17		09 41						10 43			11 16				11 43
Brockenhurst 3	a						08 59			09 56						10 58							11 58
Bournemouth	a						09 14			10 12						11 12							12 12

A From 26 June until 14 September
B from 17 September until 22 October. 🛒 to Birmingham New Street
C until 22 June. 🛒 to Leeds
D 🛒 from Birmingham New Street
E 🛒 from Birmingham New Street to Newport (South Wales)

Scotland, The North East, North West England - The South West and South Coast

Route Diagram - see first Page of Table 51

		XC	XC	XC	XC	XC	VT	XC	XC	XC	XC	XC	XC	VT	XC	XC	XC	XC	XC	XC	VT	XC	XC
		◇■	◇■	◇■	◇■	■	◇■	◇■	◇■	◇■	◇■	◇■	■	◇■	◇■	◇■	◇■	◇■	◇■	■	◇■	◇■	◇■
			A							A				B			A						
		⊼	⊼	⊼	⊼		⊠	⊼	⊼	⊼	⊼	⊼		⊠	⊼	⊼	⊼	⊼	⊼		⊠	⊼	⊼
Aberdeen	d																						
Stonehaven	d																						
Montrose	d																						
Arbroath	d																						
Dundee	d																						
Leuchars ■	d																						
Cupar	d																						
Ladybank	d																						
Markinch	d																						
Kirkcaldy	d																						
Inverkeithing	d																						
Glasgow Central ■	d						05 50														08 00		06 01
Motherwell	d						06 04																06 16
Haymarket	d																						06 57
Edinburgh ■	d													06 52		06 06		07 00					07 07
Haymarket	d													06 56									
Lockerbie	d																						
Carlisle ■	d						07 04							08 07							09 10		
Penrith North Lakes	d						07 19							08 22									
Oxenholme Lake District	d						07 42																
Lancaster ■	d						07 57							08 57							09 57		
Preston ■	d						08 17							09 17							10 17		
Wigan North Western	d						08 28							09 28							10 28		
Warrington Bank Quay	d						08 39							09 39							10 39		
M'chester Piccadilly ■	d				08 07			08 27				09 07			09 27				10 07			10 27	
Stockport	d				08 16			08 35				09 16			09 35				10 16			10 35	
Wilmslow	d																						
Crewe ■	d						09 01							10 01							11 01		
Macclesfield	d							08 49							09 49							10 49	
Congleton	d																						
Stoke-on-Trent	d				08 44			09 07				09 44			10 07				10 44			11 07	
Stafford	d				09 03			09 25				10 03			10 25				11 02			11 25	
Wolverhampton ■	d				09 16		09 32	09 41				10 17		10 32	10 41				11 16		11 32	11 41	
Dunbar	d																						07 27
Berwick-upon-Tweed	d															06 46		07 39					
Alnmouth for Alnwick	d															07 08		07 59					
Morpeth	d																	08 13					
Newcastle ■	d			06 25					06 44		07 25					07 41		08 35					08 43
Chester-le-Street	d																						
Durham	d			06 37					06 56		07 37					07 55		08 47					08 56
Darlington ■	d			06 54					07 14		07 54					08 12		09 04					09 13
York ■	d	06 32		07 23					07 44		08 24					08 44		09 35					09 45
Leeds ■	d	07 05							08 11							09 11							10 11
Wakefield Westgate ■	d	07 18							08 23							09 24							10 23
Doncaster ■	d			07 55							08 50							09 58					
Sheffield ■	d	07 53		08 20					08 54		09 23					09 54		10 23					10 54
Chesterfield	d	08 06		08 32					09 06							10 06							11 06
Nottingham ■	d		08 08			08 37				09 11			09 37				10 11			10 37			
Derby ■	d	08 28	08 36	08 53		09 10			09 28	09 36	09 53		10 10			10 28	10 37	10 53		11 10			11 28
Burton-on-Trent	d	08 38	08 49			09 21			09 38	09 49			10 21				10 49			11 21			
Tamworth	d	08 50	09 02			09 33				10 02			10 33			10 48	11 02			11 33			
Birmingham New Street ■	a	09 09	09 24	09 27	09 32	09 54	09 55	09 58	10 07	10 24	10 27	10 39	10 54	10 55	10 58	11 08	11 24	11 27	11 32	11 54	11 55	11 58	12 07
Birmingham New Street ■	d	09 12	09 30	09 33	09 42			10 04	10 12	10 30	10 33	10 42			11 04	11 12	11 30	11 33	11 42			12 04	12 12
Cheltenham Spa	a	09 51	10 10		10 23				10 50	11 10		11 23				11 51	12 10		12 23				12 50
Gloucester ■	a		10 22							11 22							12 22						
Bristol Parkway ■	a	10 25			10 54				11 26			11 54				12 28			12 55				13 25
Bristol Temple Meads ■	a	10 41			11 12				11 37			12 08				12 40			13 10				13 38
Newport (South Wales)	a		11 11							12 10							13 11						
Cardiff Central ■	a		11 27							12 28							13 29						
Weston-super-Mare	a				11 32																		
Taunton	a	11 16			12 00				12 15							13 16							14 15
Tiverton Parkway	a	11 29			12 13				12 28							13 29							14 28
Exeter St Davids ■	a	11 45			12 30				12 42							13 45							14 42
Dawlish	a				12 43																		
Teignmouth	a				12 48																		
Newton Abbot	a	12 06			12 55				13 02							14 06							15 02
Torquay	a				13 06																		
Paignton	a				13 14																		
Totnes	a	12 20							13 15							14 20							15 15
Plymouth	a	12 49							13 41							14 48							15 41
Liskeard ■	a																						
Bodmin Parkway	a																						
Lostwithiel	a																						
Par	a																						
Newquay (Summer Only)	a																						
St Austell	a																						
Truro	a																						
Redruth	a																						
Camborne	a																						
Hayle	a																						
St Erth	a																						
Penzance	a																						
Birmingham International ✈	d							10 14							11 14							12 14	
Coventry	d							10 25							11 25							12 25	
Leamington Spa ■	d			10 00				10 38			11 00				11 38			12 00				12 38	
Banbury	a			10 17				10 54			11 17				11 54			12 17				12 54	
Oxford	a			10 41				11 14			11 40				12 14			12 40				13 14	
Reading ■	a			11 07				11 39			12 10				12 39			13 07				13 39	
Guildford	a																						
Basingstoke	a							12 08			12 39				13 08							14 08	
Winchester	a							12 24			12 54				13 24							14 24	
Southampton Airport Pkway ✈	a							12 32			13 08				13 32							14 34	
Southampton Central	a							12 41			13 17				13 41							14 42	
Brockenhurst ■	a							12 56							13 56							14 56	
Bournemouth	a							13 10							14 10							15 11	

A ⊼ to Newport (South Wales)
B from 2 July

Table 51

Mondays to Fridays

Scotland, The North East, North West England - The South West and South Coast

Route Diagram - see first Page of Table 51

		XC	XC	XC	XC	VT	XC	XC	XC	XC	XC	XC	VT	XC	XC	XC	XC	XC	XC	VT	XC	XC
		◇■	◇■	◇■	■	◇■	◇■	◇■	◇■	◇■	◇■	■	◇■	◇■	◇■	◇■	◇■	◇■	■	◇■	◇■	◇■
		A						B	C						B	C				D		E
		⊼	⊼	⊼	⊼	⊠	⊼	⊼	⊼	⊼	⊼	⊼	⊡	⊼	⊼	⊼	⊼	⊼	⊼	⊠	⊼	⊼
Aberdeen	d																					
Stonehaven	d																					
Montrose	d																					
Arbroath	d																					
Dundee	d							06 32														
Leuchars ■	d							06 46														
Cupar	d							06 54														
Ladybank	d							07 03														
Markinch	d							07 11														
Kirkcaldy	d							07 21														
Inverkeithing	d							07 43														
Glasgow Central ■	d												10 00		07 50							09 00
Motherwell	d														08 05							09 15
Haymarket	d							08 01							08 50							09 58
Edinburgh ■	d					08 52		08 10							09 08					10 51		10 10
Haymarket	d					08 57														10 57		
Lockerbie	d																					
Carlisle ■	d					10 07							11 11							12 07		
Penrith North Lakes	d												11 26									
Oxenholme Lake District	d					10 42														12 43		
Lancaster ■	d					10 57														12 57		
Preston ■	d					11 17							12 17							13 17		
Wigan North Western	d					11 28							12 28							13 28		
Warrington Bank Quay	d					11 39							12 39							13 39		
M'chester Piccadilly ■	d			11 07			11 27				12 07			12 27				13 07			13 27	
Stockport	d			11 16			11 35				12 16			12 35				13 16			13 35	
Wilmslow	d																					
Crewe ■	d					12 01							13 01							14 01		
Macclesfield	d						11 49							12 49							13 49	
Congleton	d																					
Stoke-on-Trent	d			11 44			12 07				12 44			13 07				13 44			14 07	
Stafford	d			12 03			12 25				13 02			13 25				14 02			14 25	
Wolverhampton ■	d			12 17		12 32	12 41				13 16		13 32	13 41				14 16		14 32	14 41	
Dunbar	d														09 28							
Berwick-upon-Tweed	d							08 50							09 51							10 49
Alnmouth for Alnwick	d																					
Morpeth	d																					11 21
Newcastle ■	d		09 35					09 41		10 35					10 44		11 35					11 44
Chester-le-Street	d																					
Durham	d		09 47					09 55		10 47					10 56		11 47					11 56
Darlington ■	d		10 05					10 12		11 04					11 13		12 05					12 13
York ■	d		10 34					10 44		11 34					11 45		12 34					12 44
Leeds ■	d							11 11							12 12							13 11
Wakefield Westgate ■	d							11 24							12 24							13 23
Doncaster ■	d		10 58							11 58							12 59					
Sheffield ■	d		11 23					11 54		12 23					12 54		13 23					13 54
Chesterfield	d							12 06							13 06							14 07
Nottingham ■	d	11 08			11 37				12 08			12 37				13 11			13 37			
Derby ■	d	11 36	11 53		12 10			12 28	12 36	12 53		13 06			13 28	13 36	13 53		14 10			14 28
Burton-on-Trent	d	11 49			12 21				12 49			13 21			13 38	13 49			14 21			
Tamworth	d	12 02			12 33			12 48	13 02			13 33				14 02			14 33			14 47
Birmingham New Street ■	a	12 24	12 27	12 39	12 54	12 55	12 58	13 07	13 24	13 27	13 39	13 54	13 55	13 58	14 06	14 24	14 27	14 32	14 54	14 55	14 58	15 07
Birmingham New Street ■	d	12 30	12 33	12 42			13 04	13 12	13 30	13 33	13 42			14 04	14 12	14 30	14 33	14 42			15 04	15 12
Cheltenham Spa	a	13 10		13 23				13 53	14 10		14 23				14 50	15 10		15 23				15 50
Gloucester ■	a	13 22							14 22							15 22						
Bristol Parkway ■	a			13 57				14 27			14 57				15 25			15 56				16 27
Bristol Temple Meads ■	a			14 09				14 41			15 10				15 39			16 08				16 40
Newport (South Wales)	a	14 09							15 11							16 10						
Cardiff Central ■	a	14 29							15 29							16 29						
Weston-super-Mare	a																					
Taunton	a							15 16			15 44				16 15							17 15
Tiverton Parkway	a							15 29			15 57				16 28							17 28
Exeter St Davids ■	a							15 46			16 13				16 42							17 42
Dawlish	a																					
Teignmouth	a																					
Newton Abbot	a							16 07							17 02							18 10
Torquay	a																					
Paignton	a																					
Totnes	a							16 21							17 15							18 23
Plymouth	a							16 49							17 42							18 50
Liskeard ■	a																					19 23
Bodmin Parkway	a																					19 35
Lostwithiel	a																					
Par	a																					19 46
Newquay (Summer Only)	a																					
St Austell	a																					19 53
Truro	a																					20 10
Redruth	a																					20 25
Camborne	a																					20 31
Hayle	a																					
St Erth	a																					20 42
Penzance	a																					20 52
Birmingham International ✈	d						13 14							14 14							15 14	
Coventry	d						13 25							14 25							15 25	
Leamington Spa ■	d		13 00				13 38			14 00				14 38			15 00				15 38	
Banbury	a		13 20				13 54			14 17				14 54			15 17				15 54	
Oxford	a		13 40				14 14			14 40				15 14			15 41				16 14	
Reading ■	a		14 10				14 39			15 07				15 39			16 10				16 39	
Guildford	a																					
Basingstoke	a		14 39				15 08							16 08			16 39				17 08	
Winchester	a		14 54				15 24							16 24			16 59				17 24	
Southampton Airport Pkway ✈	a		15 08				15 32							16 32							17 32	
Southampton Central	a		15 17				15 41							16 41			17 17				17 41	
Brockenhurst ■	a						15 56							16 56							17 56	
Bournemouth	a						16 10							17 10							18 15	

A ⊼ to Newport (South Wales)
B ⊼ from Edinburgh
C ⊼ from Birmingham New Street to Newport (South Wales)
D until 29 June, from 17 September
E ⊼ from Edinburgh to Plymouth

Scotland, The North East, North West England - The South West and South Coast

Route Diagram - see first Page of Table 51

		XC	XC	XC	XC	VT	XC	XC	XC	XC	XC	XC	VT	XC	XC	XC	XC	XC	XC	VT	XC	XC	XC
		A				B		C							D								
Aberdeen	d							08 20															
Stonehaven	d							08 38															
Montrose	d							08 59															
Arbroath	d							09 15															
Dundee	d							09 32															
Leuchars	d							09 47															
Cupar	d							09 54															
Ladybank	d							10 01															
Markinch	d							10 09															
Kirkcaldy	d							10 17															
Inverkeithing	d							10 32															
Glasgow Central	d					12 00									10 59					14 00			
Motherwell	d														11 14								
Haymarket	d							10 54							11 57								
Edinburgh	d							11 05					12 51		12 08							13 06	
Haymarket	d												12 57										
Lockerbie	d																						
Carlisle	d					13 09							14 07							15 09			
Penrith North Lakes	d												14 22							15 44			
Oxenholme Lake District	d																						
Lancaster	d					13 58							14 57										
Preston	d					14 17							15 17							16 17			
Wigan North Western	d					14 28							15 28							16 28			
Warrington Bank Quay	d					14 39							15 39							16 39			
M'chester Piccadilly	d			14 07			14 27				15 07			15 27				16 07			16 27		
Stockport	d			14 16			14 35				15 16			15 35				16 16			16 35		
Wilmslow	d																						
Crewe	d					15 01							16 01							17 01			
Macclesfield	d						14 49							15 49							16 49		
Congleton	d																						
Stoke-on-Trent	d			14 44			15 07				15 44			16 07				16 44			17 07		
Stafford	d			15 03			15 25				16 03			16 25				17 03			17 25		
Wolverhampton	d			15 17		15 32	15 41				16 17		16 32	16 41				17 16		17 32	17 41		
Dunbar	d							11 25														13 28	
Berwick-upon-Tweed	d							11 48							12 47							14 08	
Alnmouth for Alnwick	d							12 08															
Morpeth	d																						
Newcastle	d		12 35					12 41		13 35					13 42		14 35					14 42	
Chester-le-Street	d																						
Durham	d		12 47					12 53		13 47					13 54		14 47					14 55	
Darlington	d		13 04					13 11		14 05					14 11		15 04					15 12	
York	d		13 34					13 44		14 34					14 44		15 34					15 44	
Leeds	d							14 11							15 11							16 11	
Wakefield Westgate	d							14 23							15 23							16 23	
Doncaster	d		13 58							14 58							15 58						
Sheffield	d		14 23					14 54		15 23					15 54		16 23					16 54	
Chesterfield	d							15 06							16 06							17 06	
Nottingham	d	14 11			14 37				15 11			15 37				16 08			16 37				17 08
Derby	d	14 36	14 53		15 10			15 28	15 36	15 53		16 10			16 28	16 36	16 53		17 06			17 28	17 36
Burton-on-Trent	d	14 49			15 24			15 38	15 49			16 21				16 49			17 21			17 38	17 49
Tamworth	d	15 02			15 35				16 02			16 33			16 47	17 02			17 33				18 02
Birmingham New Street	a	15 24	15 27	15 39	15 54	15 55	15 58	16 04	16 24	16 27	16 39	16 54	16 55	16 58	17 09	17 24	17 27	17 32	17 52	17 55	17 58	18 07	18 24
Birmingham New Street	d	15 30	15 33	15 42			16 04	16 12	16 30	16 33	16 42			17 04	17 12	17 30	17 33	17 42			18 04	18 12	18 30
Cheltenham Spa	a	16 10		16 23				16 50	17 13		17 23				17 50	18 18		18 23				18 51	19 13
Gloucester	a	16 22							17 26							18 29							19 27
Bristol Parkway	a			16 56				17 25			17 58				18 28			18 55				19 27	
Bristol Temple Meads	a			17 10				17 39			18 10				18 41			19 06				19 38	
Newport (South Wales)	a	17 11							18 10							19 16							20 11
Cardiff Central	a	17 28							18 27							19 33							20 27
Weston-super-Mare	a																						
Taunton	a			17 44				18 15							19 15							20 16	
Tiverton Parkway	a			17 56				18 28							19 28							20 29	
Exeter St Davids	a			18 11				18 42							19 42							20 44	
Dawlish	a			18 23																			
Teignmouth	a			18 28																			
Newton Abbot	a			18 35				19 07							20 03							21 03	
Torquay	a			18 47																			
Paignton	a			18 55																			
Totnes	a							19 20							20 16							21 17	
Plymouth	a							19 46							20 43							21 48	
Liskeard	a							20 11							21 12								
Bodmin Parkway	a							20 23							21 24								
Lostwithiel	a														21 30								
Par	a							20 35							21 38								
Newquay (Summer Only)	a																						
St Austell	a							20 41							21 44								
Truro	a							21 00							22 03								
Redruth	a							21 15							22 14								
Camborne	a							21 22							22 21								
Hayle	a														22 29								
St Erth	a							21 33							22 34								
Penzance	a							21 42							22 43								
Birmingham International	d						16 14							17 14							18 14		
Coventry	d						16 25							17 25							18 25		
Leamington Spa	d		16 00				16 38			17 00				17 38			18 00				18 38		
Banbury	a		16 17				16 54			17 17				17 54			18 18				18 54		
Oxford	a		16 40				17 14			17 39				18 14			18 40				19 14		
Reading	a		17 07				17 39			18 09				18 39			19 07				19 39		
Guildford	a																						
Basingstoke	a						18 08			18 47				19 08							20 09		
Winchester	a						18 24			19 08				19 24							20 24		
Southampton Airport Pkway	a						18 32							19 32							20 32		
Southampton Central	a						18 44							19 41							20 41		
Brockenhurst	a						18 58							19 56							20 58		
Bournemouth	a						19 13							20 12							21 15		

A to Newport (South Wales)
B from 2 July
C from Edinburgh to Plymouth
D to Plymouth

Table 51 Mondays to Fridays

Scotland, The North East, North West England - The South West and South Coast

Route Diagram - see first Page of Table 51

		XC	XC	XC	VT	XC	XC	XC	XC	XC	XC	VT	VT	XC	XC	XC	XC	XC	XC	LM	XC	VT
			A		B	C	D			A		E	F	G	A	FO	FX	G	G			
Aberdeen	d																					
Stonehaven	d																					
Montrose	d																					
Arbroath	d																					
Dundee	d																					
Leuchars	d																					
Cupar	d																					
Ladybank	d																					
Markinch	d																					
Kirkcaldy	d																					
Inverkeithing	d																					
Glasgow Central	d						12 51					16 00	16 00									
Motherwell	d						13 06															
Haymarket	d																					
Edinburgh	d				14 51		14 08								15 08							16 52
Haymarket	d				14 57																	16 57
Lockerbie	d																					
Carlisle	d				16 07							17 09	17 09									18 07
Penrith North Lakes	d				16 21																	
Oxenholme Lake District	d											17 44	17 44									18 42
Lancaster	d				16 57																	18 57
Preston	d				17 17							18 17	18 17									19 16
Wigan North Western	d				17 28							18 28	18 28									19 29
Warrington Bank Quay	d				17 39							18 39	18 39									19 39
M'chester Piccadilly	d		17 05			17 27				18 05				18 27					19 07			
Stockport	d		17 13			17 35				18 13				18 35					19 16			
Wilmslow	d					17 44																
Crewe	d				18 01	18 07						19 01	19 01							19 55		20 01
Macclesfield	d		17 27							18 26												
Congleton	d													18 54								
Stoke-on-Trent	d		17 44							18 44				19 07					19 44			
Stafford	d		18 04			18 28				19 02				19 25					20 04	20 16		
Wolverhampton	d		18 16		18 32	18 41				19 16		19 32	19 33	19 41					20 17	20 29		20 34
Dunbar	d														15 28							
Berwick-upon-Tweed	d						14 49															
Alnmouth for Alnwick	d																					
Morpeth	d																					
Newcastle	d	15 03					15 41		16 35						16 42			17 32				
Chester-le-Street	d																	17 41				
Durham	d	15 16					15 53		16 47						16 52			17 48				
Darlington	d	15 33					16 10		17 04						17 10			18 05				
York	d	16 04					16 44		17 34						17 44			18 34				
Leeds	d	16 40					17 11								18 11							
Wakefield Westgate	d	16 52					17 23								18 23							
Doncaster	d								17 59									18 58				
Sheffield	d	17 23					17 54		18 23						18 54			19 23				
Chesterfield	d						18 07								19 06							
Nottingham	d			17 37				18 08			18 37					19 08	19 08				19 37	
Derby	d	17 53		18 10			18 28	18 37	18 53		19 10				19 28	19 36	19 36	19 54			20 10	
Burton-on-Trent	d			18 22				18 49			19 21				19 38	19 49	19 49				20 21	
Tamworth	d			18 34			18 47	19 02			19 33					20 02	20 02				20 33	
Birmingham New Street	a	18 27	18 38	18 54	18 55	18 58	19 08	19 24	19 27	19 32	19 54	19 55	19 55	19 58	20 09	20 24	20 24	20 27	20 33	20 47	20 54	20 55
Birmingham New Street	d	18 33	18 42			19 04	19 12	19 30	19 33	19 42				20 04	20 12	20 30	20 30	20 33	20 42			
Cheltenham Spa	a		19 23				19 50	20 10		20 23					20 51	21 10	21 10		21 25			
Gloucester	a							20 22								21 22	21 22					
Bristol Parkway	a		19 56				20 27			20 55					21 25				22 01			
Bristol Temple Meads	a		20 09				20 40			21 07					21 36				22 13			
Newport (South Wales)	a		20 47					21 11								22 15	22 15					
Cardiff Central	a		21 02					21 27								22 31	22 35					
Weston-super-Mare	a																					
Taunton	a						21 16			21 43					22 15							
Tiverton Parkway	a						21 29			21 56					22 28							
Exeter St Davids	a						21 43			22 11					22 43							
Dawlish	a																					
Teignmouth	a																					
Newton Abbot	a						22 04			22 30					23 05							
Torquay	a																					
Paignton	a																					
Totnes	a						22 16			22 43					23 18							
Plymouth	a						22 43			23 14					23 45							
Liskeard	a																					
Bodmin Parkway	a																					
Lostwithiel	a																					
Par	a																					
Newquay (Summer Only)	a																					
St Austell	a																					
Truro	a																					
Redruth	a																					
Camborne	a																					
Hayle	a																					
St Erth	a																					
Penzance	a																					
Birmingham International	d					19 14								20 14								
Coventry	d					19 25								20 25								
Leamington Spa	d	19 00				19 38			20 05					20 38				21 00				
Banbury	a	19 17				19 54			20 22					20 54				21 17				
Oxford	a	19 39				20 14			20 40					21 14				21 40				
Reading	a	20 10				20 39			21 07					21 40				22 17				
Guildford	a																	22 59				
Basingstoke	a					21 09								22 09								
Winchester	a					21 24								22 24								
Southampton Airport Pkway	a					21 32								22 32								
Southampton Central	a					21 41								22 42								
Brockenhurst	a					21 56								22 56								
Bournemouth	a					22 16								23 21								

A to Bristol Temple Meads
B until 29 June, from 17 September
C to Reading
D from Edinburgh to Bristol Temple Meads
E from 2 July
F until 29 June
G to Birmingham New Street

Scotland, The North East, North West England - The South West and South Coast

Route Diagram - see first Page of Table 51

		XC	XC	XC	XC	VT	XC	XC	XC	XC	XC	XC	XC	XC	VT	XC	XC	XC	XC
		◇1 A ⚲	◇1 B ⚲	◇1 ⚲	◇1	◇1 ☐	1	◇1	◇1 C	◇1 D	🚌	◇1 E ⚲	◇1 F ⚲	◇1 G ⚲	◇1 ☐	◇1	1	◇1 H ⚲	◇1 I
Aberdeen	d																		
Stonehaven	d																		
Montrose	d																		
Arbroath	d																		
Dundee	d																		
Leuchars	d																		
Cupar	d																		
Ladybank	d																		
Markinch	d																		
Kirkcaldy	d																		
Inverkeithing	d																		
Glasgow Central	d		15 00			17 40												16 52	
Motherwell	d		15 14															17 14	
Haymarket	d		15 56															17 54	
Edinburgh	d		16 05									17 08	17 08		18 52			18 04	
Haymarket	d														18 57				
Lockerbie	d					18 35													
Carlisle	d					18 54									20 08				
Penrith North Lakes	d					19 09													
Oxenholme Lake District	d					19 32									20 42				
Lancaster	d					19 47									20 57				
Preston	d					20 08									21 17				
Wigan North Western	d					20 19									21 28				
Warrington Bank Quay	d					20 31									21 39				
M'chester Piccadilly	d	19 27			20 07			20 27								21 27			22 07
Stockport	d	19 35			20 16			20 35								21 35			22 16
Wilmslow	d																		
Crewe	d					20 53									22 01				
Macclesfield	d	19 49						20 49								21 49			22 29
Congleton	d																		
Stoke-on-Trent	d	20 07			20 44			21 07								22 08			22 47
Stafford	d	20 26			21 03	21 13		21 25								22 26			23 07
Wolverhampton	d	20 43			21 16	21 32		21 41							22 32	22 41			23 23
Dunbar	d											17 28	17 28					18 25	
Berwick-upon-Tweed	d											17 51	17 51					18 48	
Alnmouth for Alnwick	d		17 01															19 08	
Morpeth	d		17 16																
Newcastle	d		17 41	18 35								18 41	18 41	19 35				19 42	
Chester-le-Street	d																		
Durham	d		17 53	18 47								18 53	18 53	19 50				19 54	
Darlington	d		18 10	19 05								19 10	19 10	20 07				20 12	
York	d		18 45	19 34								19 44	19 44	20 35				20 45	
Leeds	d		19 11									20 11	20 11					21 11	
Wakefield Westgate	d		19 23									20 23	20 23					21 23	
Doncaster	d			19 58										21 02					
Sheffield	d		19 54	20 23								20 54	20 54	21 28				22 00	
Chesterfield	d		20 06									21 06	21 06	21 41				22 24	
Nottingham	d						20 37										21 37		
Derby	d		20 28	20 54			21 06					21 29	21 29	22 02			22 10	22 45	
Burton-on-Trent	d						21 21					21 40	21 40				22 21	22 56	
Tamworth	d		20 47				21 33					21 50	21 50				22 33	23 06	
Birmingham New Street	a	21 00	21 07	21 29	21 33	21 48	21 54	22 00				22 09	22 07	22 51	22 55	22 58	23 00	23 25	2339
Birmingham New Street	d	21 04	21 12						22 04	22 04		22 12	22 12						
Cheltenham Spa	a		21 51									22 51	23 30						
Gloucester	a		22 01																
Bristol Parkway	a		22 32									23 21	00 01						
Bristol Temple Meads	a		22 44									23 40	00 13						
Newport (South Wales)	a																		
Cardiff Central	a																		
Weston-super-Mare	a																		
Taunton	a																		
Tiverton Parkway	a																		
Exeter St Davids	a																		
Dawlish	a																		
Teignmouth	a																		
Newton Abbot	a																		
Torquay	a																		
Paignton	a																		
Totnes	a																		
Plymouth	a																		
Liskeard	a																		
Bodmin Parkway	a																		
Lostwithiel	a																		
Par	a																		
Newquay (Summer Only)	a																		
St Austell	a																		
Truro	a																		
Redruth	a																		
Camborne	a																		
Hayle	a																		
St Erth	a																		
Penzance	a																		
Birmingham International	d	21 14							22 14										
Coventry	d	21 25							22 25		22 25								
Leamington Spa	d	21 38							22 38	22 53	22 38								
Banbury	a	21 54							22 54	23 15									
Oxford	a	22 14							23 14	23 35									
Reading	a	22 41							23 52	00 07									
Guildford	a																		
Basingstoke	a	23 06																	
Winchester	a	23 24																	
Southampton Airport Pkway	a	23 36																	
Southampton Central	a	23 43																	
Brockenhurst	a																		
Bournemouth	a																		

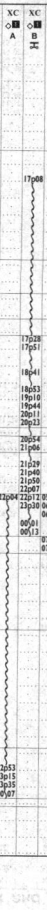

A ⚲ to Birmingham New Street
B ⚲ from Edinburgh to Birmingham New Street
C until 22 June, from 17 September
D from 25 June until 14 September
E from 25 June. ⚲ to Leeds
F until 22 June. ⚲ to Leeds
G ⚲ to York
H ⚲ to Leeds
I FO until 15 June and then from 22 June

Scotland, The North East, North West England - The South West and South Coast

Route Diagram - see first Page of Table 51

		XC	XC	XC	XC	XC	XC	XC	XC	XC		XC	XC	XC	VT	XC	XC	XC	XC	XC		XC	VT	XC	XC
		◇1 A	◇1 B ⚲	◇1	◇1	◇1 ⚲	◇1	◇1 ⚲	◇1 ⚲	◇1 C ⚲		◇1 D ⚲	◇1 C ⚲	◇1 ⚲	◇1 ☐	◇1 E ⚲	◇1 ⚲	◇1 D ⚲	◇1 ⚲	◇1 ⚲		1	◇1 ☐	◇1 ⚲	◇1 ⚲
Aberdeen	d																								
Stonehaven	d																								
Montrose	d																								
Arbroath	d																								
Dundee	d																								
Leuchars	d																								
Cupar	d																								
Ladybank	d																								
Markinch	d																								
Kirkcaldy	d																								
Inverkeithing	d																								
Glasgow Central	d																								
Motherwell	d																								
Haymarket	d																								
Edinburgh	d		17p08																						
Haymarket	d																								
Lockerbie	d																								
Carlisle	d																								
Penrith North Lakes	d																								
Oxenholme Lake District	d																								
Lancaster	d																						06 58		
Preston	d														06 17								07 17		
Wigan North Western	d														06 28								07 28		
Warrington Bank Quay	d														06 39								07 39		
M'chester Piccadilly	d								05 11					06 00						07 07				07 27	
Stockport	d													06 08						07 16				07 35	
Wilmslow	d																								
Crewe	d								05 47						07 01								08 01		
Macclesfield	d													06 21										07 49	
Congleton	d																								
Stoke-on-Trent	d								06 08					06 39						07 44				08 07	
Stafford	d								06 26					06 58						08 03				08 26	
Wolverhampton	d								06 41					07 15	07 32					08 18			08 32	08 41	
Dunbar	d		17p28																						
Berwick-upon-Tweed	d		17p51																						
Alnmouth for Alnwick	d																								
Morpeth	d																								
Newcastle	d		18p41																						
Chester-le-Street	d																								
Durham	d		18p53																						
Darlington	d		19p10																						
York	d		19p44																						06 40
Leeds	d		20p11														06 00		06 15						07 10
Wakefield Westgate	d		20p23														06 12		06 29						07 23
Doncaster	d																		06 47						
Sheffield	d		20p54										05 45				06 50		07 18						07 56
Chesterfield	d		21p06										05 57				07 03		07 30						08 08
Nottingham	d											05 57				06 37		06 56				07 37			
Derby	d		21p29							06 10		06 36	06 48			07 06	07 26	07 36	07 50			08 06			08 28
Burton-on-Trent	d		21p40							06 20		06 48	06 59			07 18	07 37	07 50	08 00			08 18			08 39
Tamworth	d		21p50							06 31		07 01	07 09			07 30	07 48	08 02	08 11			08 30			08 49
Birmingham New Street	a		22p07						06 57	06 50		07 24	07 27	07 31	07 55	07 52	08 08	08 24	08 27	08 39		08 54	08 55	08 58	09 09
Birmingham New Street	d	22p04	22p12	05 00	05 42	06 04	06 33	06 42	07 04	07 12		07 30	07 33	07 42		08 04	08 12	08 30	08 33	08 42				09 04	09 12
Cheltenham Spa	a		23p30	06 02	06 41			07 23		07 50		08 10		08 23			08 51	09 10		09 23					09 50
Gloucester	a			06 13	06 54							08 22						09 22							
Bristol Parkway	a		00 01					07 54		08 24				08 54			09 24			09 55					10 29
Bristol Temple Meads	a		00 13					08 05		08 38				09 08			09 38			10 06					10 42
Newport (South Wales)	a			07 06	07 52							09 07						10 07							
Cardiff Central	a			07 22	08 08							09 23						10 23							
Weston-super-Mare	a																								
Taunton	a							08 42		09 14							10 17			10 59					11 15
Tiverton Parkway	a							08 54		09 28							10 30			11 12					11 28
Exeter St Davids	a							09 09		09 41							10 46			11 26					11 42
Dawlish	a																10 59								
Teignmouth	a																11 06								
Newton Abbot	a							09 28		10 02							11 14			11 47					12 03
Torquay	a							09 40									11 25								
Paignton	a							09 47									11 35								
Totnes	a									10 15										12 02					12 16
Plymouth	a									10 41										12 31					12 43
Liskeard	a																			13 03					
Bodmin Parkway	a																			13 16					
Lostwithiel	a																								
Par	a																			13 30					
Newquay (Summer Only)	a																			14 41					
St Austell	a																								
Truro	a																								
Redruth	a																								
Camborne	a																								
Hayle	a																								
St Erth	a																								
Penzance	a																								
Birmingham International	d					06 14			07 14							08 14								09 14	
Coventry	d					06 25			07 25							08 25								09 25	
Leamington Spa	d	22p53				06 38	07 00		07 38				08 00			08 38			09 00					09 38	
Banbury	a	23p15				06 54	07 17		07 54				08 17			08 54			09 17					09 54	
Oxford	a	23p35				07 14	07 40		08 14				08 40			09 14			09 40					10 14	
Reading	a	00 07				07 39	08 06		08 39				09 11			09 39			10 07					10 39	
Guildford	a																								
Basingstoke	a					08 08	08 40		09 08							10 08			10 39					11 08	
Winchester	a					08 24	08 55		09 24							10 24			10 54					11 24	
Southampton Airport Pkway	a					08 32	09 08		09 32							10 32			11 08					11 32	
Southampton Central	a					08 41	09 17		09 40							10 43			11 17					11 41	
Brockenhurst	a					08 56			09 57							10 58								11 57	
Bournemouth	a					09 14			10 11							11 12								12 11	

A 30 June
B not 30 June. ⚲ to Leeds
C ⚲ from Birmingham New Street
D ⚲ from Birmingham New Street to Newport (South Wales)
E ⚲ from Derby

Saturdays
until 30 June

Scotland, The North East, North West England - The South West and South Coast

Route Diagram - see first Page of Table 51

		XC	XC	XC	XC	VT	XC	XC	XC	XC	XC	XC	VT	XC	XC	XC	XC	XC	XC	VT	XC	XC	XC
		A						B	A							A						C	A
Aberdeen	d																						
Stonehaven	d																						
Montrose	d																						
Arbroath	d																						
Dundee	d																						
Leuchars	d																						
Cupar	d																						
Ladybank	d																						
Markinch	d																						
Kirkcaldy	d																						
Inverkeithing	d																						
Glasgow Central	d					05 50														08 00		06 01	
Motherwell	d					06 04																06 16	
Haymarket	d																					06 57	
Edinburgh	d												06 52		06 06		07 00					07 07	
Haymarket	d												06 56										
Lockerbie	d																						
Carlisle	d					07 03							08 07							09 09			
Penrith North Lakes	d					07 18							08 22										
Oxenholme Lake District	d					07 42																	
Lancaster	d					07 57							08 57							09 57			
Preston	d					08 17							09 17							10 17			
Wigan North Western	d					08 28							09 28							10 28			
Warrington Bank Quay	d					08 39							09 39							10 39			
M'chester Piccadilly	d			08 07			08 27				09 07			09 27				10 07			10 27		
Stockport	d			08 16			08 35				09 16			09 35				10 16			10 35		
Wilmslow	d																						
Crewe	d					09 01							10 01							11 01			
Macclesfield	d						08 49							09 49							10 49		
Congleton	d																						
Stoke-on-Trent	d			08 44			09 07				09 44			10 07				10 44			11 07		
Stafford	d			09 03			09 26				10 03			10 26				11 03			11 26		
Wolverhampton	d			09 17		09 32	09 41				10 17		10 32	10 41				11 17		11 33	11 41		
Dunbar	d																					07 27	
Berwick-upon-Tweed	d														06 48		07 40						
Alnmouth for Alnwick	d														07 08		08 00						
Morpeth	d																08 14						
Newcastle	d		06 22							07 35					07 40		08 36					08 43	
Chester-le-Street	d																						
Durham	d		06 37							07 47					07 52		08 48					08 56	
Darlington	d		06 54							08 04					08 10		09 05					09 13	
York	d		07 24					07 44		08 34					08 44		09 35					09 46	
Leeds	d							08 12							09 11							10 12	
Wakefield Westgate	d							08 24							09 24							10 24	
Doncaster	d		07 52							08 58							09 58						
Sheffield	d		08 20					08 54		09 23					09 54		10 23					10 54	
Chesterfield	d		08 32					09 06							10 06							11 06	
Nottingham	d	08 08			08 37				09 08			09 37				10 08			10 37				11 11
Derby	d	08 36	08 53		09 10			09 27	09 36	09 53		10 10			10 28	10 37	10 53		11 10			11 27	11 36
Burton-on-Trent	d	08 49			09 21			09 41	09 49			10 21				10 49			11 21			11 39	11 49
Tamworth	d	09 02			09 33				10 02			10 33			10 48	11 02			11 33				12 02
Birmingham New Street	a	09 24	09 27	09 39	09 54	09 55	09 58	10 04	10 24	10 27	10 39	10 54	10 55	10 58	11 04	11 24	11 27	11 39	11 54	11 55	11 58	12 07	12 24
Birmingham New Street	d	09 30	09 33	09 42			10 04	10 12	10 30	10 33	10 42			11 04	11 12	11 30	11 33	11 42			12 04	12 12	12 30
Cheltenham Spa	a	10 10		10 23				10 51	11 10		11 23				11 50	12 10		12 23				12 50	13 10
Gloucester	a	10 22							11 22							12 22							13 22
Bristol Parkway	a			10 57				11 24			11 54				12 29			12 55				13 24	
Bristol Temple Meads	a			11 09				11 38			12 08				12 42			13 07				13 38	
Newport (South Wales)	a	11 08							12 07							13 11							14 08
Cardiff Central	a	11 24							12 23							13 27							14 24
Weston-super-Mare	a			11 29																			
Taunton	a			11 59				12 15							13 15							14 15	
Tiverton Parkway	a			12 12				12 28							13 28							14 28	
Exeter St Davids	a			12 26				12 42							13 42							14 45	
Dawlish	a			12 40																		15 06	
Teignmouth	a			12 45																		15 12	
Newton Abbot	a			12 52				13 08							14 02							15 20	
Torquay	a			13 03																		15 32	
Paignton	a			13 11																		15 42	
Totnes	a							13 21							14 15								
Plymouth	a							13 48							14 42								
Liskeard	a							14 12															
Bodmin Parkway	a							14 24															
Lostwithiel	a							14 31															
Par	a							14 39															
Newquay (Summer Only)	a																						
St Austell	a							14 47															
Truro	a							15 05															
Redruth	a							15 18															
Camborne	a							15 25															
Hayle	a							15 33															
St Erth	a							15 39															
Penzance	a							15 49															
Birmingham International	d						10 14							11 14							12 14		
Coventry	d						10 25							11 25							12 25		
Leamington Spa	d		10 00				10 38			11 00				11 38			12 00				12 38		
Banbury	a		10 17				10 54			11 17				11 54			12 17				12 54		
Oxford	a		10 40				11 14			11 40				12 14			12 40				13 14		
Reading	a		11 09				11 39			12 07				12 39			13 06				13 39		
Guildford	a																						
Basingstoke	a						12 08			12 40				13 08							14 08		
Winchester	a						12 24			12 55				13 24							14 24		
Southampton Airport Pkway	a						12 32			13 08				13 32							14 32		
Southampton Central	a						12 41			13 17				13 41							14 41		
Brockenhurst	a						12 57							13 57							14 57		
Bournemouth	a						13 11							14 11							15 11		

A to Newport (South Wales)
B to Plymouth
C from Edinburgh

Saturdays
until 30 June

Scotland, The North East, North West England - The South West and South Coast

Route Diagram - see first Page of Table 51

		XC	XC	XC	VT	XC	XC	XC	XC	XC	XC	VT	XC	XC	XC	XC	XC	XC	VT	XC	XC	XC
								A						B	A						C	D
Aberdeen	d																					
Stonehaven	d																					
Montrose	d																					
Arbroath	d																					
Dundee	d						06 32															
Leuchars	d						06 46															
Cupar	d						06 54															
Ladybank	d						07 03															
Markinch	d						07 11															
Kirkcaldy	d						07 21															
Inverkeithing	d						07 38															
Glasgow Central	d											10 00		07 50							09 00	
Motherwell	d													08 05							09 15	
Haymarket	d						07 56							08 50							09 57	
Edinburgh	d				08 52		08 05							09 06					10 52		10 05	
Haymarket	d				08 57														10 57			
Lockerbie	d																					
Carlisle	d				10 07							11 09							12 07			
Penrith North Lakes	d											11 24										
Oxenholme Lake District	d				10 42														12 43			
Lancaster	d				10 57														12 57			
Preston	d				11 17							12 17							13 17			
Wigan North Western	d				11 28							12 28							13 28			
Warrington Bank Quay	d				11 39							12 39							13 39			
M'chester Piccadilly	d		11 07			11 27				12 07			12 27				13 07			13 27		
Stockport	d		11 16			11 35				12 16			12 35				13 16			13 35		
Wilmslow	d																					
Crewe	d				12 01							13 01							14 01			
Macclesfield	d					11 49							12 49							13 49		
Congleton	d																					
Stoke-on-Trent	d		11 44			12 07				12 44			13 07				13 44			14 07		
Stafford	d		12 03			12 25				13 03			13 26				14 03			14 26		
Wolverhampton	d		12 17		12 32	12 41				13 16		13 32	13 41				14 17		14 32	14 41		
Dunbar	d													09 26								
Berwick-upon-Tweed	d						08 46							09 49							10 48	
Alnmouth for Alnwick	d						09 08															
Morpeth	d																				11 19	
Newcastle	d	09 35					09 41		10 35					10 44		11 35					11 42	
Chester-le-Street	d																					
Durham	d	09 47					09 55		10 47					10 56		11 47					11 55	
Darlington	d	10 05					10 12		11 04					11 13		12 05					12 12	
York	d	10 34					10 45		11 34					11 45		12 34					12 45	
Leeds	d						11 11							12 11							13 11	
Wakefield Westgate	d						11 23							12 24							13 23	
Doncaster	d	10 58							11 58							12 58						
Sheffield	d	11 23					11 54		12 23					12 54		13 23					13 54	
Chesterfield	d						12 07							13 06							14 07	
Nottingham	d			11 37				12 08			12 37				13 08			13 37				14 08
Derby	d	11 54		12 10			12 29	12 36	12 53		13 06			13 28	13 36	13 53		14 06			14 30	14 36
Burton-on-Trent	d			12 21				12 49			13 21			13 38	13 49			14 18				14 49
Tamworth	d			12 33			12 49	13 02			13 33				14 02			14 30			14 49	15 02
Birmingham New Street	a	12 27	12 39	12 54	12 55	12 58	13 09	13 24	13 27	13 39	13 54	13 55	13 58	14 07	14 24	14 27	14 39	14 54	14 55	14 58	15 08	15 24
Birmingham New Street	d	12 33	12 42			13 04	13 12	13 30	13 33	13 42			14 04	14 12	14 30	14 33	14 42			15 04	15 12	15 30
Cheltenham Spa	a		13 25				13 51	14 10		14 23				14 50	15 10		15 23				15 50	16 10
Gloucester	a							14 22							15 22							16 22
Bristol Parkway	a		13 57				14 26			14 57				15 23			15 55				16 29	
Bristol Temple Meads	a		14 08				14 41			15 09				15 37			16 08				16 42	
Newport (South Wales)	a							15 11							16 08							17 10
Cardiff Central	a							15 27							16 25							17 26
Weston-super-Mare	a																					
Taunton	a						15 16			15 43				16 15							17 17	
Tiverton Parkway	a						15 29			15 55				16 28							17 30	
Exeter St Davids	a						15 45			16 10				16 42							17 46	
Dawlish	a									16 34												
Teignmouth	a									16 40												
Newton Abbot	a						16 06			16 47											18 10	
Torquay	a									16 59												
Paignton	a									17 08												
Totnes	a						16 20							17 12							18 24	
Plymouth	a						16 48							17 39							18 52	
Liskeard	a						17 14							18 04							19 18	
Bodmin Parkway	a						17 27							18 16							19 32	
Lostwithiel	a																					
Par	a						17 40							18 27							19 44	
Newquay (Summer Only)	a						18 45															
St Austell	a													18 34							19 52	
Truro	a													18 51							20 10	
Redruth	a													19 08							20 26	
Camborne	a													19 14							20 33	
Hayle	a																					
St Erth	a													19 26							20 45	
Penzance	a													19 35							20 56	
Birmingham International	d					13 14							14 14							15 14		
Coventry	d					13 25							14 25							15 25		
Leamington Spa	d	13 02				13 38			14 00				14 38			15 00				15 38		
Banbury	a	13 19				13 54			14 17				14 54			15 19				15 54		
Oxford	a	13 40				14 14			14 40				15 14			15 41				16 14		
Reading	a	14 07				14 39			15 07				15 39			16 08				16 39		
Guildford	a																					
Basingstoke	a	14 40				15 08							16 08			16 40				17 08		
Winchester	a	14 55				15 24							16 24			16 55				17 24		
Southampton Airport Pkway	a	15 08				15 32							16 32			17 08				17 32		
Southampton Central	a	15 17				15 41							16 41			17 17				17 41		
Brockenhurst	a					15 57							16 57							17 57		
Bournemouth	a					16 11							17 11							18 11		

A from Birmingham New Street to Newport (South Wales)
B to Plymouth
C from Edinburgh to Plymouth
D to Newport (South Wales)

Scotland, The North East, North West England - The South West and South Coast

Route Diagram - see first Page of Table 51

		XC	XC	XC	VT	XC	XC	XC	XC	XC	XC	VT	XC	XC	XC	XC	XC	XC	VT	XC	XC	XC	XC
		◇■	◇■	■	◇■	◇■	◇■	◇■	◇■	◇■	■	◇■	◇■	◇■	◇■	◇■	◇■	■	◇■	◇■	◇■	◇■	◇■
							A																
		✠	✠	✠	🅿	✠	✠	✠	✠	✠	✠	🅿	✠	✠		✠	✠	✠	🅿	✠	✠		✠
Aberdeen	d						08 20																
Stonehaven	d						08 38																
Montrose	d						08 59																
Arbroath	d						09 15																
Dundee	d						09 32																
Leuchars ■	d						09 47																
Cupar	d						09 54																
Ladybank	d						10 01																
Markinch	d						10 08																
Kirkcaldy	d						10 17																
Inverkeithing	d						10 32																
Glasgow Central ■	d				12 00									10 59					14 00				
Motherwell	d													11 14									
Haymarket	d						10 52							11 56									
Edinburgh ■	d						11 05					12 52		12 09							13 08		
Haymarket	d											12 57											
Lockerbie	d																						
Carlisle ■	d				13 09							14 07							15 11				
Penrith North Lakes	d											14 22											
Oxenholme Lake District	d																		15 46				
Lancaster ■	d				13 58							14 57											
Preston ■	d				14 17							15 17							16 17				
Wigan North Western	d				14 28							15 28							16 28				
Warrington Bank Quay	d				14 39							15 39							16 39				
M'chester Piccadilly ■	d		14 07			14 27				15 07			15 27				16 07			16 27			
Stockport	d		14 16			14 35				15 16			15 35				16 16			16 35			
Wilmslow	d																						
Crewe ■	d				15 01							16 01							17 01				
Macclesfield	d					14 49							15 49							16 49			
Congleton	d																						
Stoke-on-Trent	d		14 44			15 07				15 44			16 07				16 44			17 07			
Stafford	d		15 03			15 26				16 03			16 25				17 03			17 26			
Wolverhampton ■	d		15 17		15 32	15 41				16 17		16 32	16 41				17 17		17 32	17 41			
Dunbar	d						11 25														13 29		
Berwick-upon-Tweed	d						11 48							12 48									
Alnmouth for Alnwick	d						12 08														14 09		
Morpeth	d																						
Newcastle ■	d	12 35					12 44		13 35					13 44		14 35					14 44		15 07
Chester-le-Street	d																						
Durham	d	12 47					12 56		13 47					13 56		14 47					14 56		15 19
Darlington ■	d	13 04					13 13		14 05					14 13		15 04					15 13		15 36
York ■	d	13 34					13 44		14 34					14 44		15 34					15 45		16 06
Leeds ■	d						14 11							15 12							16 12		16 40
Wakefield Westgate ■	d						14 24							15 24							16 24		16 52
Doncaster ■	d	13 58							14 58							15 58							
Sheffield ■	d	14 23					14 54		15 23					15 54		16 23					16 54		17 23
Chesterfield	d						15 06							16 07							17 06		
Nottingham ■	d			14 37				15 08			15 37				16 08			16 37				17 11	
Derby ■	d	14 53		15 10			15 28	15 36	15 53		16 10			16 28	16 36	16 53		17 06			17 28	17 36	17 53
Burton-on-Trent	d			15 24			15 38	15 49			16 21				16 49			17 21			17 38	17 49	
Tamworth	d			15 33				16 02			16 33			16 48	17 02			17 33				18 02	
Birmingham New Street ■	a	15 27	15 39	15 54	15 55	15 58	16 04	16 24	16 27	16 39	16 54	16 55	16 58	17 07	17 24	17 27	17 39	17 54	17 55	17 58	18 07	18 24	18 27
Birmingham New Street ■	d	15 33	15 42			16 04	16 12	16 30	16 33	16 42			17 04	17 12	17 30	17 33	17 42			18 04	18 12	18 30	18 33
Cheltenham Spa	a		16 23				16 50	17 10		17 23				17 50	18 17		18 23				18 50	19 10	
Gloucester ■	a							17 22							18 29							19 22	
Bristol Parkway ■	a		16 54				17 24			17 54				18 29			18 54				19 25		
Bristol Temple Meads ■	a		17 07				17 38			18 07				18 42			19 05				19 39		
Newport (South Wales)	a							18 05							19 12							20 05	
Cardiff Central ■	a							18 21							19 29							20 21	
Weston-super-Mare	a																						
Taunton	a						18 15							19 15							20 15		
Tiverton Parkway	a						18 28							19 28							20 28		
Exeter St Davids ■	a						18 42							19 43							20 42		
Dawlish	a																						
Teignmouth	a																						
Newton Abbot	a						19 04							20 03							21 03		
Torquay	a																						
Paignton	a																						
Totnes	a						19 17							20 16							21 16		
Plymouth	a						19 43							20 43							21 43		
Liskeard ■	a						20 10																
Bodmin Parkway	a						20 22																
Lostwithiel	a						20 28																
Par	a						20 35																
Newquay (Summer Only)	a																						
St Austell	a						20 42																
Truro	a						21 00																
Redruth	a						21 12																
Camborne	a						21 18																
Hayle	a						21 26																
St Erth	a						21 31																
Penzance	a						21 43																
Birmingham International	d					16 14							17 14							18 14			
Coventry	d					16 25							17 25							18 25			
Leamington Spa ■	d	16 02				16 38			17 00				17 38			18 02				18 38			19 00
Banbury	a	16 18				16 54			17 17				17 54			18 18				18 54			19 17
Oxford	a	16 40				17 14			17 41				18 14			18 40				19 14			19 40
Reading ■	a	17 07				17 39			18 07				18 39			19 07				19 39			20 10
Guildford	a																						
Basingstoke	a					18 08			18 40				19 08							20 08			
Winchester	a					18 24			18 55				19 24							20 24			
Southampton Airport Pkway	a					18 32			19 08				19 32							20 32			
Southampton Central	a					18 40			19 17				19 41							20 41			
Brockenhurst ■	a					18 57							19 57							20 57			
Bournemouth	a					19 11							20 11							21 11			

A ✠ from Edinburgh to Plymouth

Scotland, The North East, North West England - The South West and South Coast

Route Diagram - see first Page of Table 51

		XC	XC	VT	XC	XC	XC	XC	XC	XC	VT	XC	XC	XC	XC	XC	LM	XC	VT	XC	XC	XC
		◇■	■	◇■	◇■	◇■	◇■	◇■	◇■	■	◇■	◇■	◇■	◇■	◇■	◇■	◇■	■	◇■	◇■	◇■	◇■
					A	B						A	C		A					D	D	
		✠	✠	🅿	✠	✠		✠	✠	✠	🅿	✠	✠		✠	✠			🅿	✠	✠	✠
Aberdeen	d																					
Stonehaven	d																					
Montrose	d																					
Arbroath	d																					
Dundee	d																					
Leuchars ■	d																					
Cupar	d																					
Ladybank	d																					
Markinch	d																					
Kirkcaldy	d																					
Inverkeithing	d																					
Glasgow Central ■	d					12 51					16 00										15 00	
Motherwell	d					13 06															15 14	
Haymarket	d																				15 56	
Edinburgh ■	d			14 52		14 08							15 08						16 52		16 05	
Haymarket	d			14 57															16 57			
Lockerbie	d																					
Carlisle ■	d			16 07							17 09								18 08			
Penrith North Lakes	d			16 22																		
Oxenholme Lake District	d										17 44								18 42			
Lancaster ■	d			16 57															18 57			
Preston ■	d			17 17							18 17								19 17			
Wigan North Western	d			17 28							18 28								19 28			
Warrington Bank Quay	d			17 39							18 39								19 39			
M'chester Piccadilly ■	d	17 06			17 27				18 05			18 27				19 07				19 27		
Stockport	d				17 36				18 13			18 35				19 16				19 35		
Wilmslow	d																					
Crewe ■	d			18 01							19 01						19 51		20 01			
Macclesfield	d	17 26							18 26											19 49		
Congleton	d				17 54							18 54										
Stoke-on-Trent	d	17 44			18 08				18 44			19 07				19 44				20 07		
Stafford	d	18 04			18 27				19 03			19 25				20 03	20 12			20 26		
Wolverhampton ■	d	18 17		18 32	18 41				19 17		19 32	19 41				20 17	20 28		20 33	20 41		
Dunbar	d												15 28									
Berwick-upon-Tweed	d					14 49																
Alnmouth for Alnwick	d																				17 03	
Morpeth	d																				17 17	
Newcastle ■	d					15 41		16 35					16 41		17 32						17 44	18 35
Chester-le-Street	d														17 41							
Durham	d					15 53		16 47					16 52		17 48						17 56	18 48
Darlington ■	d					16 11		17 04					17 10		18 05						18 13	19 05
York ■	d					16 44		17 34					17 44		18 34						18 44	19 34
Leeds ■	d					17 11							18 11								19 11	
Wakefield Westgate ■	d					17 23							18 23								19 24	
Doncaster ■	d							17 58							18 58							19 58
Sheffield ■	d					17 54		18 23					18 54		19 24						19 54	20 23
Chesterfield	d					18 07							19 06								20 06	
Nottingham ■	d		17 37				18 08			18 37				19 08				19 37				
Derby ■	d		18 10			18 28	18 36	18 53		19 10			19 27	19 36	19 54			20 10			20 28	20 53
Burton-on-Trent	d		18 22				18 49			19 21			19 37	19 49				20 21				
Tamworth	d		18 34			18 46	19 02			19 33				20 02				20 33			20 46	
Birmingham New Street ■	a	18 38	18 54	18 55	18 58	19 06	19 24	19 27	19 33	19 54	19 55	19 58	20 06	20 24	20 27	20 33	20 47	20 54	20 55	20 58	21 03	21 25
Birmingham New Street ■	d	18 42			19 04	19 12	19 30	19 33	19 42			20 04	20 12	20 30	20 33	20 42				21 04	21 12	
Cheltenham Spa	a	19 23				19 50	20 10		20 23				20 49	21 10		21 23					21 49	
Gloucester ■	a						20 22							21 22							21 59	
Bristol Parkway ■	a	19 55				20 29			20 54				21 22			21 58					22 30	
Bristol Temple Meads ■	a	20 06				20 42			21 05				21 35			22 12					22 41	
Newport (South Wales)	a	20 55					21 11							22 21								
Cardiff Central ■	a	21 11					21 29							22 43								
Weston-super-Mare	a																					
Taunton	a					21 15							22 15									
Tiverton Parkway	a					21 28							22 28									
Exeter St Davids ■	a					21 42							22 43									
Dawlish	a																					
Teignmouth	a																					
Newton Abbot	a					22 04							23 10									
Torquay	a																					
Paignton	a																					
Totnes	a					22 20							23 24									
Plymouth	a					22 47							23 53									
Liskeard ■	a																					
Bodmin Parkway	a																					
Lostwithiel	a																					
Par	a																					
Newquay (Summer Only)	a																					
St Austell	a																					
Truro	a																					
Redruth	a																					
Camborne	a																					
Hayle	a																					
St Erth	a																					
Penzance	a																					
Birmingham International	d				19 14							20 14								21 14		
Coventry	d				19 25							20 25								21 25		
Leamington Spa ■	d				19 38			20 03				20 38			21 00					21 38		
Banbury	a				19 54			20 19				20 54			21 19					21 54		
Oxford	a				20 14			20 40				21 14			21 41					22 16		
Reading ■	a				20 39			21 10				21 40			22 10					22 41		
Guildford	a														22 59							
Basingstoke	a				21 08							22 09								23 07		
Winchester	a				21 24							22 24								23 24		
Southampton Airport Pkway	a				21 32							22 33								23 32		
Southampton Central	a				21 41							22 41								23 41		
Brockenhurst ■	a				21 57							22 56										
Bournemouth	a				22 15							23 21										

A ✠ to Reading
B ✠ from Edinburgh to Bristol Temple Meads
C ✠ to Bristol Temple Meads
D ✠ to Birmingham New Street

Scotland, The North East, North West England - The South West and South Coast

Route Diagram - see first Page of Table 51

		XC	VT	XC	XC	XC	XC	XC	VT	VT		XC	XC	XC	XC	XC
		◇■	◇■	■	◇■	◇■	◇■	◇■	◇■	◇■		◇■	■	◇■	◇■	◇■
						A		B					C	D	E	F
			R			✠		✠	R	R				✠		✠
Aberdeen	d															
Stonehaven	d															
Montrose	d															
Arbroath	d															
Dundee	d															
Leuchars ■	d															
Cupar	d															
Ladybank	d															
Markinch	d															
Kirkcaldy	d															
Inverkeithing	d															
Glasgow Central ■	d		18 00						18 40					16 52		16 52
Motherwell	d													17 14		17 14
Haymarket	d													17 56		17 56
Edinburgh ■	d					17 08				18 52				18 05		18 05
Haymarket	d									18 57						
Lockerbie	d															
Carlisle ■	d		19 09						19 48	20 08						
Penrith North Lakes	d								20 02	20 23						
Oxenholme Lake District	d								20 25	20 46						
Lancaster ■	d		19 56						20 40	21 01						
Preston ■	d		20 17						21 00	21 21						
Wigan North Western	d		20 28						21 11	21 32						
Warrington Bank Quay	d		20 39						21 22	21 43						
M'chester Piccadilly ■	d	20 07			20 27		21 07					21 27				
Stockport	d	20 16			20 35							21 36				
Wilmslow	d															
Crewe ■	d		21 01						21 43	22 05						
Macclesfield	d				20 49							21 50				
Congleton	d															
Stoke-on-Trent	d	20 44			21 07		21 45					22 08				
Stafford	d	21 03			21 27		22 03		22 08	22 25		22 33				
Wolverhampton ■	d	21 16	21 33		21 41		22 16		22 23	22 40		22 46				
Dunbar	d					17 28								18 25		18 25
Berwick-upon-Tweed	d					17 51								18 48		18 48
Alnmouth for Alnwick	d													19 08		19 08
Morpeth	d															
Newcastle ■	d					18 44		19 35						19 44		19 44
Chester-le-Street	d															
Durham	d					18 56		19 49						19 56		19 56
Darlington ■	d					19 13		20 06						20 13		20 13
York ■	d					19 44		20 34						20 45		20 45
Leeds ■	d					20 11								21 11		21 11
Wakefield Westgate ■	d					20 23								21 23		21 23
Doncaster ■	d							21 00								
Sheffield ■	d					20 54		21 23						21 54		21 54
Chesterfield	d					21 06		21 35						22 06		22 06
Nottingham ■	d			20 37									21 37			
Derby ■	d			21 06		21 28		21 53					22 10	22 26		22 26
Burton-on-Trent	d			21 21		21 38							22 21	22 38		
Tamworth	d			21 33		21 49							22 33	22 48	23 00	
Birmingham New Street ■	a	21 32	21 54	21 54	21 58	22 05	22 32	22 43	22 46	22 59		23 02	23 02	23 05	23 21	23 38
Birmingham New Street ■	d															
Cheltenham Spa	a															
Gloucester ■	a															
Bristol Parkway ■	a															
Bristol Temple Meads ■	a															
Newport (South Wales)	a															
Cardiff Central ■	a															
Weston-super-Mare	a															
Taunton	a															
Tiverton Parkway	a															
Exeter St Davids ■	a															
Dawlish	a															
Teignmouth	a															
Newton Abbot	a															
Torquay	a															
Paignton	a															
Totnes	a															
Plymouth	a															
Liskeard ■	a															
Bodmin Parkway	a															
Lostwithiel	a															
Par	a															
Newquay (Summer Only)	a															
St Austell	a															
Truro	a															
Redruth	a															
Camborne	a															
Hayle	a															
St Erth	a															
Penzance	a															
Birmingham International	d															
Coventry	d															
Leamington Spa ■	d															
Banbury	a															
Oxford	a															
Reading ■	a															
Guildford	a															
Basingstoke	a															
Winchester	a															
Southampton Airport Pkwy	a															
Southampton Central	a															
Brockenhurst ■	a															
Bournemouth	a															

A ✠ to Leeds
B ✠ to York
C not 30 June
D not 30 June. ✠ from Edinburgh to Leeds
E 30 June
F 30 June. ✠ from Edinburgh to Leeds

Scotland, The North East, North West England - The South West and South Coast

Route Diagram - see first Page of Table 51

		XC	XC	XC	XC	XC	XC	XC	XC	XC		XC	XC	VT	XC	XC	XC	XC	XC	XC		VT	XC	XC	XC
		◇■	◇■	◇■	◇■	◇■	◇■	◇■	◇■	◇■		◇■	◇■	◇■	◇■	◇■	◇■	◇■	◇■	■		◇■	◇■	◇■	◇■
									A	B		A			C		B								D
					✠		✠	✠	✠	✠		✠	✠	R	✠	✠	✠	✠	✠			R	✠	✠	✠
Aberdeen	d																								
Stonehaven	d																								
Montrose	d																								
Arbroath	d																								
Dundee	d																								
Leuchars ■	d																								
Cupar	d																								
Ladybank	d																								
Markinch	d																								
Kirkcaldy	d																								
Inverkeithing	d																								
Glasgow Central ■	d																								
Motherwell	d																								
Haymarket	d																								
Edinburgh ■	d																								
Haymarket	d																								
Lockerbie	d																								
Carlisle ■	d																								
Penrith North Lakes	d																								
Oxenholme Lake District	d																								
Lancaster ■	d																					06 58			
Preston ■	d													06 17								07 17			
Wigan North Western	d													06 28								07 28			
Warrington Bank Quay	d													06 39								07 39			
M'chester Piccadilly ■	d							05 11					06 00						07 07				07 27		
Stockport	d												06 08						07 16				07 35		
Wilmslow	d																								
Crewe ■	d							05 47						07 01								08 01			
Macclesfield	d												06 21										07 49		
Congleton	d																								
Stoke-on-Trent	d							06 08					06 39						07 44				08 07		
Stafford	d							06 26					06 58						08 03				08 26		
Wolverhampton ■	d							06 41					07 15	07 32					08 18			08 32	08 41		
Dunbar	d																								
Berwick-upon-Tweed	d																								
Alnmouth for Alnwick	d																								
Morpeth	d																								
Newcastle ■	d																								
Chester-le-Street	d																								
Durham	d																								
Darlington ■	d																								
York ■	d																							06 40	
Leeds ■	d															06 00		06 15						07 10	
Wakefield Westgate ■	d															06 12		06 29						07 23	
Doncaster ■	d																	06 47							
Sheffield ■	d											05 45				06 50		07 18						07 56	
Chesterfield	d											05 57				07 03		07 30						08 08	
Nottingham ■	d									05 57					06 37		06 56			07 37					08 08
Derby ■	d								06 10	06 36		06 48			07 06	07 26	07 36	07 50		08 06				08 28	08 36
Burton-on-Trent	d								06 20	06 48		06 59			07 18	07 37	07 50	08 00		08 18				08 39	08 49
Tamworth	d								06 31	07 01		07 09			07 30	07 48	08 02	08 11		08 30				08 49	09 02
Birmingham New Street ■	a							06 57	06 50	07 24		07 27	07 31	07 55	07 52	08 08	08 24	08 27	08 39	08 54		08 55	08 58	09 09	09 24
Birmingham New Street ■	d	22p04	05 00	05 42	06 04	06 33	06 42	07 04	07 12	07 30		07 33	07 42		08 04	08 12	08 30	08 33	08 42				09 04	09 12	09 30
Cheltenham Spa	a		06 02	06 41			07 23		07 50	08 10			08 23			08 51	09 10		09 23					09 50	10 10
Gloucester ■	a		06 13	06 54						08 22							09 22								10 22
Bristol Parkway ■	a						07 54		08 24				08 54			09 24			09 55					10 29	
Bristol Temple Meads ■	a						08 05		08 38				09 08			09 38			10 06					10 42	
Newport (South Wales)	a		07 06	07 52						09 07							10 07								11 08
Cardiff Central ■	a		07 22	08 08						09 23							10 23								11 24
Weston-super-Mare	a																								
Taunton	a						08 42		09 14							10 17			10 59					11 15	
Tiverton Parkway	a						08 54		09 28							10 30			11 12					11 28	
Exeter St Davids ■	a						09 09		09 41							10 46			11 26					11 42	
Dawlish	a															10 59									
Teignmouth	a															11 06									
Newton Abbot	a						09 28		10 02							11 14			11 47					12 03	
Torquay	a						09 40									11 25									
Paignton	a						09 47									11 35									
Totnes	a								10 15										12 02					12 16	
Plymouth	a								10 41										12 31					12 43	
Liskeard ■	a																		13 03						
Bodmin Parkway	a																		13 16						
Lostwithiel	a																								
Par	a																		13 30						
Newquay (Summer Only)	a																		14 41						
St Austell	a																								
Truro	a																								
Redruth	a																								
Camborne	a																								
Hayle	a																								
St Erth	a																								
Penzance	a																								
Birmingham International	d				06 14			07 14							08 14								09 14		
Coventry	d				06 25			07 25							08 25								09 25		
Leamington Spa ■	d	22p53			06 38	07 00		07 38				08 00			08 38			09 00					09 38		
Banbury	a	23p15			06 54	07 17		07 54				08 17			08 54			09 17					09 54		
Oxford	a	23p35			07 14	07 40		08 14				08 40			09 14			09 40					10 14		
Reading ■	a	00 07			07 39	08 06		08 39				09 11			09 39			10 07					10 39		
Guildford	a																								
Basingstoke	a				08 08	08 40		09 08							10 08			10 39					11 08		
Winchester	a				08 24	08 55		09 24							10 24			10 54					11 24		
Southampton Airport Pkwy	a				08 32	09 08		09 32							10 32			11 08					11 32		
Southampton Central	a				08 41	09 17		09 40							10 43			11 17					11 41		
Brockenhurst ■	a				08 56			09 57							10 58								11 57		
Bournemouth	a				09 14			10 11							11 12								12 11		

A ✠ from Birmingham New Street
B ✠ from Birmingham New Street to Newport (South Wales)
C ✠ from Derby
D ✠ to Newport (South Wales)

Scotland, The North East, North West England - The South West and South Coast

Route Diagram - see first Page of Table 51

		XC	XC	XC	VT	XC	XC	XC	XC	XC	XC	VT
		◇1	◇1	1	◇1	◇1	◇1	◇1	◇1	◇1	1	◇1
							A	B				
		✠	✠		🍴	✠	✠	✠	✠	✠		🍴
Aberdeen	d											
Stonehaven	d											
Montrose	d											
Arbroath	d											
Dundee	d											
Leuchars	d											
Cupar	d											
Ladybank	d											
Markinch	d											
Kirkcaldy	d											
Inverkeithing	d											
Glasgow Central	d				05 50							
Motherwell	d				06 04							
Haymarket	d											
Edinburgh	d											06 52
Haymarket	d											06 56
Lockerbie	d											
Carlisle	d				07 03							08 07
Penrith North Lakes	d				07 18							08 22
Oxenholme Lake District	d				07 42							
Lancaster	d				07 57							08 57
Preston	d				08 17							09 17
Wigan North Western	d				08 28							09 28
Warrington Bank Quay	d				08 39							09 39
M'chester Piccadilly	d		08 07			08 27				09 07		
Stockport	d		08 16			08 35				09 16		
Wilmslow	d											
Crewe	d				09 01							10 01
Macclesfield	d					08 49						
Congleton	d											
Stoke-on-Trent	d		08 44			09 07				09 44		
Stafford	d		09 03			09 26				10 03		
Wolverhampton	d		09 17		09 32	09 41				10 17		10 32
Dunbar	d											
Berwick-upon-Tweed	d											
Alnmouth for Alnwick	d											
Morpeth	d											
Newcastle	d	06 22							07 35			
Chester-le-Street	d											
Durham	d	06 37							07 47			
Darlington	d	06 54							08 04			
York	d	07 24					07 44		08 34			
Leeds	d						08 12					
Wakefield Westgate	d						08 24					
Doncaster	d	07 52							08 58			
Sheffield	d	08 20					08 54		09 23			
Chesterfield	d	08 32					09 06					
Nottingham	d			08 37				09 08			09 37	
Derby	d	08 53		09 10			09 27	09 36	09 53		10 10	
Burton-on-Trent	d			09 21			09 41	09 49			10 21	
Tamworth	d			09 33				10 02			10 33	
Birmingham New Street	a	09 27	09 39	09 54	09 55	09 58	10 04	10 24	10 27	10 39	10 54	10 55
Birmingham New Street	d	09 33	09 42			10 04	10 12	10 30	10 33	10 42		
Cheltenham Spa	a		10 23				10 51	11 10		11 23		
Gloucester	a							11 22				
Bristol Parkway	a		10 57				11 24			11 54		
Bristol Temple Meads	a		11 09				11 38			12 08		
Newport (South Wales)	a							12 07				
Cardiff Central	a							12 23				
Weston-super-Mare	a		11 29									
Taunton	a		11 59				12 15					
Tiverton Parkway	a		12 12				12 28					
Exeter St Davids	a		12 26				12 42					
Dawlish	a		12 40									
Teignmouth	a		12 45									
Newton Abbot	a		12 52				13 08					
Torquay	a		13 03									
Paignton	a		13 11									
Totnes	a						13 21					
Plymouth	a						13 48					
Liskeard	a						14 12					
Bodmin Parkway	a						14 24					
Lostwithiel	a						14 31					
Par	a						14 39					
Newquay (Summer Only)	a											
St Austell	a						14 47					
Truro	a						15 05					
Redruth	a						15 18					
Camborne	a						15 25					
Hayle	a						15 33					
St Erth	a						15 39					
Penzance	a						15 49					
Birmingham International	d					10 14						
Coventry	d					10 25						
Leamington Spa	d	10 00				10 38			11 00			
Banbury	a	10 17				10 54			11 17			
Oxford	a	10 40				11 14			11 40			
Reading	a	11 09				11 39			12 07			
Guildford	a											
Basingstoke	a					12 08			12 40			
Winchester	a					12 24			12 55			
Southampton Airport Pkwy	a					12 32			13 08			
Southampton Central	a					12 41			13 17			
Brockenhurst	a					12 57						
Bournemouth	a					13 11						

		XC	XC	XC	XC	XC	XC	VT	XC	XC	XC	XC
		◇1	◇1	◇1	◇1	◇1	1	◇1	◇1	◇1	◇1	◇1
				B						C	B	
		✠	✠	✠	✠	✠		🍴	✠	✠	✠	✠
Aberdeen	d											
Stonehaven	d											
Montrose	d											
Arbroath	d											
Dundee	d											
Leuchars	d											
Cupar	d											
Ladybank	d											
Markinch	d											
Kirkcaldy	d											
Inverkeithing	d											
Glasgow Central	d							08 00		06 01		
Motherwell	d									06 16		
Haymarket	d									06 57		
Edinburgh	d		06 06		07 00					07 07		
Haymarket	d											
Lockerbie	d											
Carlisle	d							09 09				
Penrith North Lakes	d											
Oxenholme Lake District	d											
Lancaster	d							09 57				
Preston	d							10 17				
Wigan North Western	d							10 28				
Warrington Bank Quay	d							10 39				
M'chester Piccadilly	d	09 27				10 07			10 27			
Stockport	d	09 35				10 16			10 35			
Wilmslow	d											
Crewe	d							11 01				
Macclesfield	d	09 49							10 49			
Congleton	d											
Stoke-on-Trent	d	10 07				10 44			11 07			
Stafford	d	10 26				11 03			11 26			
Wolverhampton	d	10 41				11 17		11 32	11 41			
Dunbar	d									07 27		
Berwick-upon-Tweed	d		06 48		07 40							
Alnmouth for Alnwick	d		07 08		08 00							
Morpeth	d				08 14							
Newcastle	d		07 40		08 36					08 43		09 35
Chester-le-Street	d											
Durham	d		07 52		08 48					08 56		09 47
Darlington	d		08 10		09 05					09 13		10 05
York	d		08 44		09 35					09 46		10 34
Leeds	d		09 11							10 12		
Wakefield Westgate	d		09 24							10 24		
Doncaster	d				09 58							10 58
Sheffield	d		09 54		10 23					10 54		11 23
Chesterfield	d		10 06							11 06		
Nottingham	d			10 08			10 37				11 11	
Derby	d		10 28	10 37	10 53		11 10			11 27	11 36	11 54
Burton-on-Trent	d			10 49			11 21			11 39	11 49	
Tamworth	d		10 48	11 02			11 33				12 02	
Birmingham New Street	a	10 58	11 04	11 24	11 27	11 39	11 54	11 55	11 58	12 07	12 24	12 27
Birmingham New Street	d	11 04	11 12	11 30	11 33	11 42			12 04	12 12	12 30	12 33
Cheltenham Spa	a		11 50	12 10		12 23				12 50	13 10	
Gloucester	a			12 22							13 22	
Bristol Parkway	a		12 29			12 55				13 24		
Bristol Temple Meads	a		12 42			13 07				13 38		
Newport (South Wales)	a			13 11							14 08	
Cardiff Central	a			13 27							14 24	
Weston-super-Mare	a											
Taunton	a		13 15							14 15		
Tiverton Parkway	a		13 28							14 28		
Exeter St Davids	a		13 42							14 45		
Dawlish	a									15 06		
Teignmouth	a									15 12		
Newton Abbot	a		14 02							15 20		
Torquay	a									15 32		
Paignton	a									15 42		
Totnes	a		14 15									
Plymouth	a		14 42									
Liskeard	a											
Bodmin Parkway	a											
Lostwithiel	a											
Par	a											
Newquay (Summer Only)	a											
St Austell	a											
Truro	a											
Redruth	a											
Camborne	a											
Hayle	a											
St Erth	a											
Penzance	a											
Birmingham International	d	11 14							12 14			
Coventry	d	11 25							12 25			
Leamington Spa	d	11 38			12 00				12 38			13 02
Banbury	a	11 54			12 17				12 54			13 19
Oxford	a	12 14			12 40				13 14			13 40
Reading	a	12 39			13 06				13 39			14 07
Guildford	a											
Basingstoke	a	13 08							14 08			14 40
Winchester	a	13 24							14 24			14 55
Southampton Airport Pkwy	a	13 32							14 32			15 08
Southampton Central	a	13 41							14 41			15 17
Brockenhurst	a	13 57							14 57			
Bournemouth	a	14 11							15 11			

A ✠ to Plymouth
B ✠ to Newport (South Wales)
C ✠ from Edinburgh

Scotland, The North East, North West England - The South West and South Coast

Route Diagram - see first Page of Table 51

		XC	XC	VT	XC	XC	XC	XC	XC	XC	VT
		◇1	1	◇1	◇1	◇1	◇1	◇1	◇1	1	◇1
							A				
		✠	✠	🍴	✠	✠	✠	✠	✠	✠	🍴
Aberdeen	d										
Stonehaven	d										
Montrose	d										
Arbroath	d										
Dundee	d					06 32					
Leuchars	d					06 46					
Cupar	d					06 54					
Ladybank	d					07 03					
Markinch	d					07 11					
Kirkcaldy	d					07 21					
Inverkeithing	d					07 38					
Glasgow Central	d										10 00
Motherwell	d										
Haymarket	d					07 56					
Edinburgh	d			08 52		08 05					
Haymarket	d			08 57							
Lockerbie	d										
Carlisle	d			10 07							11 09
Penrith North Lakes	d										11 24
Oxenholme Lake District	d			10 42							
Lancaster	d			10 57							
Preston	d			11 17							12 17
Wigan North Western	d			11 28							12 28
Warrington Bank Quay	d			11 39							12 39
M'chester Piccadilly	d	11 07			11 27				12 07		
Stockport	d	11 16			11 35				12 16		
Wilmslow	d										
Crewe	d			12 01							13 01
Macclesfield	d				11 49						
Congleton	d										
Stoke-on-Trent	d	11 44			12 07				12 44		
Stafford	d	12 03			12 25				13 03		
Wolverhampton	d	12 17		12 32	12 41				13 16		13 32
Dunbar	d										
Berwick-upon-Tweed	d					08 46					
Alnmouth for Alnwick	d					09 08					
Morpeth	d										
Newcastle	d					09 41		10 35			
Chester-le-Street	d										
Durham	d					09 55		10 47			
Darlington	d					10 12		11 04			
York	d					10 45		11 34			
Leeds	d					11 11					
Wakefield Westgate	d					11 23					
Doncaster	d							11 58			
Sheffield	d					11 54		12 23			
Chesterfield	d					12 07					
Nottingham	d		11 37				12 08			12 37	
Derby	d		12 10			12 29	12 36	12 53		13 06	
Burton-on-Trent	d		12 21				12 49			13 21	
Tamworth	d		12 33			12 49	13 02			13 33	
Birmingham New Street	a	12 39	12 54	12 55	12 58	13 09	13 24	13 27	13 39	13 54	13 55
Birmingham New Street	d	12 42			13 04	13 12	13 30	13 33	13 42		
Cheltenham Spa	a	13 25				13 51	14 10		14 23		
Gloucester	a						14 22				
Bristol Parkway	a	13 57				14 26			14 57		
Bristol Temple Meads	a	14 08				14 41			15 09		
Newport (South Wales)	a						15 11				
Cardiff Central	a						15 27				
Weston-super-Mare	a										
Taunton	a					15 16			15 43		
Tiverton Parkway	a					15 29			15 55		
Exeter St Davids	a					15 45			16 10		
Dawlish	a								16 34		
Teignmouth	a								16 40		
Newton Abbot	a					16 06			16 47		
Torquay	a								16 59		
Paignton	a								17 08		
Totnes	a					16 20					
Plymouth	a					16 48					
Liskeard	a					17 14					
Bodmin Parkway	a					17 27					
Lostwithiel	a										
Par	a					17 40					
Newquay (Summer Only)	a					18 45					
St Austell	a										
Truro	a										
Redruth	a										
Camborne	a										
Hayle	a										
St Erth	a										
Penzance	a										
Birmingham International	d				13 14						
Coventry	d				13 25						
Leamington Spa	d				13 38			14 00			
Banbury	a				13 54			14 17			
Oxford	a				14 14			14 40			
Reading	a				14 39			15 07			
Guildford	a										
Basingstoke	a				15 08						
Winchester	a				15 24						
Southampton Airport Pkwy	a				15 32						
Southampton Central	a				15 41						
Brockenhurst	a				15 57						
Bournemouth	a				16 11						

		XC	XC	XC	XC	XC	XC	XC	XC	XC	XC	XC
		◇1	◇1	◇1	◇1	◇1	1	◇1	◇1	◇1	◇1	◇1
			B	A					C	D		
		✠	✠	✠	✠	✠	✠	✠	✠	✠	✠	✠
Aberdeen	d											
Stonehaven	d											
Montrose	d											
Arbroath	d											
Dundee	d											
Leuchars	d											
Cupar	d											
Ladybank	d											
Markinch	d											
Kirkcaldy	d											
Inverkeithing	d											
Glasgow Central	d		07 50						09 00			
Motherwell	d		08 05						09 15			
Haymarket	d		08 50						09 57			
Edinburgh	d		09 06						10 05			
Haymarket	d											
Lockerbie	d											
Carlisle	d											
Penrith North Lakes	d											
Oxenholme Lake District	d											
Lancaster	d											
Preston	d											
Wigan North Western	d											
Warrington Bank Quay	d											
M'chester Piccadilly	d	12 27				13 07		13 27				14 07
Stockport	d	12 35				13 16		13 35				14 16
Wilmslow	d											
Crewe	d											
Macclesfield	d	12 49						13 49				
Congleton	d											
Stoke-on-Trent	d	13 07				13 44		14 07				14 44
Stafford	d	13 26				14 03		14 26				15 03
Wolverhampton	d	13 41				14 17		14 41				15 17
Dunbar	d		09 26									
Berwick-upon-Tweed	d		09 49						10 48			
Alnmouth for Alnwick	d											
Morpeth	d								11 19			
Newcastle	d		10 44		11 35				11 42		12 35	
Chester-le-Street	d											
Durham	d		10 56		11 47				11 55		12 47	
Darlington	d		11 13		12 05				12 12		13 04	
York	d		11 45		12 34				12 45		13 34	
Leeds	d		12 11						13 11			
Wakefield Westgate	d		12 24						13 23			
Doncaster	d				12 58						13 58	
Sheffield	d		12 54		13 23				13 54		14 23	
Chesterfield	d		13 06						14 07			
Nottingham	d			13 08			13 37			14 08		
Derby	d		13 28	13 36	13 53		14 06		14 30	14 36	14 53	
Burton-on-Trent	d		13 38	13 49			14 18			14 49		
Tamworth	d			14 02			14 30		14 49	15 02		
Birmingham New Street	a	13 58	14 07	14 24	14 27	14 39	14 54	14 58	15 08	15 24	15 27	15 39
Birmingham New Street	d	14 04	14 12	14 30	14 33	14 42		15 04	15 12	15 30	15 33	15 42
Cheltenham Spa	a		14 50	15 10		15 23			15 50	16 10		16 23
Gloucester	a			15 22						16 22		
Bristol Parkway	a		15 23			15 55			16 29			16 54
Bristol Temple Meads	a		15 37			16 08			16 42			17 07
Newport (South Wales)	a			16 08						17 10		
Cardiff Central	a			16 25						17 26		
Weston-super-Mare	a											
Taunton	a		16 15						17 17			
Tiverton Parkway	a		16 28						17 30			
Exeter St Davids	a		16 42						17 46			
Dawlish	a											
Teignmouth	a											
Newton Abbot	a								18 10			
Torquay	a											
Paignton	a											
Totnes	a		17 12						18 24			
Plymouth	a		17 39						18 52			
Liskeard	a		18 04						19 18			
Bodmin Parkway	a		18 16						19 32			
Lostwithiel	a											
Par	a		18 27						19 44			
Newquay (Summer Only)	a											
St Austell	a		18 34						19 52			
Truro	a		18 51						20 10			
Redruth	a		19 08						20 26			
Camborne	a		19 14						20 33			
Hayle	a											
St Erth	a		19 26						20 45			
Penzance	a		19 35						20 56			
Birmingham International	d	14 14						15 14				
Coventry	d	14 25						15 25				
Leamington Spa	d	14 38			15 00			15 38			16 02	
Banbury	a	14 54			15 19			15 54			16 18	
Oxford	a	15 14			15 41			16 14			16 40	
Reading	a	15 39			16 08			16 39			17 07	
Guildford	a											
Basingstoke	a	16 08			16 40			17 08				
Winchester	a	16 24			16 55			17 24				
Southampton Airport Pkwy	a	16 32			17 08			17 32				
Southampton Central	a	16 41			17 17			17 41				
Brockenhurst	a	16 57						17 57				
Bournemouth	a	17 11						18 11				

A ✠ from Birmingham New Street to Newport (South Wales)
B ✠ to Plymouth
C ✠ from Edinburgh to Plymouth
D ✠ to Newport (South Wales)

Table 51

Saturdays

7 July to 8 September

Scotland, The North East, North West England - The South West and South Coast

Route Diagram - see first Page of Table 51

		XC	VT	XC	XC	XC	XC	XC	XC	VT	XC	XC	XC	XC	XC	XC	VT	XC	XC	XC	XC	XC	XC
					A																		
Aberdeen	d				08 20																		
Stonehaven	d				08 38																		
Montrose	d				08 59																		
Arbroath	d				09 15																		
Dundee	d				09 32																		
Leuchars	d				09 47																		
Cupar	d				09 54																		
Ladybank	d				10 01																		
Markinch	d				10 08																		
Kirkcaldy	d				10 17																		
Inverkeithing	d				10 32																		
Glasgow Central	d		12 00									10 59					14 00						
Motherwell	d											11 14											
Haymarket	d				10 52							11 56											
Edinburgh	d				11 05					12 52		12 09							13 08				
Haymarket	d									12 57													
Lockerbie	d																						
Carlisle	d		13 09							14 07							15 11						
Penrith North Lakes	d									14 22													
Oxenholme Lake District	d																15 46						
Lancaster	d		13 58							14 57													
Preston	d		14 17							15 17							16 17						
Wigan North Western	d		14 28							15 28							16 28						
Warrington Bank Quay	d		14 39							15 39							16 39						
M'chester Piccadilly	d			14 27				15 07			15 27				16 07			16 27				17 06	
Stockport	d			14 35				15 16			15 35				16 16			16 35					
Wilmslow	d																						
Crewe	d		15 01							16 01							17 01						
Macclesfield	d			14 49							15 49							16 49				17 26	
Congleton	d																						
Stoke-on-Trent	d			15 07				15 44			16 07				16 44			17 07				17 44	
Stafford	d			15 26				16 03			16 25				17 03			17 26				18 04	
Wolverhampton	d		15 32	15 41				16 17		16 32	16 41				17 17		17 32	17 41				18 17	
Dunbar	d				11 25														13 29				
Berwick-upon-Tweed	d				11 48							12 48							14 09				
Alnmouth for Alnwick	d				12 08																		
Morpeth	d																						
Newcastle	d				12 44		13 35					13 44		14 35					14 44		15 07		
Chester-le-Street	d																						
Durham	d				12 56		13 47					13 56		14 47					14 56		15 19		
Darlington	d				13 13		14 05					14 13		15 04					15 13		15 36		
York	d				13 44		14 34					14 44		15 34					15 45		16 06		
Leeds	d				14 11							15 12							16 12		16 40		
Wakefield Westgate	d				14 24							15 24							16 24		16 52		
Doncaster	d						14 58							15 58									
Sheffield	d				14 54		15 23					15 54		16 23					16 54		17 23		
Chesterfield	d				15 06							16 07							17 06				
Nottingham	d	14 37				15 08			15 37				16 08			16 37				17 11			17 37
Derby	d	15 10			15 28	15 36	15 53		16 10			16 28	16 36	16 53		17 06			17 28	17 36	17 53		18 10
Burton-on-Trent	d	15 24			15 38	15 49			16 21				16 49			17 21			17 38	17 49			18 22
Tamworth	d	15 33				16 02			16 33			16 48	17 02			17 33				18 02			18 34
Birmingham New Street	a	15 54	15 55	15 58	16 04	16 24	16 27	16 39	16 54	16 55	16 58	17 07	17 24	17 27	17 39	17 54	17 55	17 58	18 07	18 24	18 27	18 38	18 54
Birmingham New Street	d			16 04	16 12	16 30	16 33	16 42			17 04	17 12	17 30	17 33	17 42			18 04	18 12	18 30	18 33	18 42	
Cheltenham Spa	a				16 50	17 10		17 23				17 50	18 17		18 23				18 50	19 10		19 23	
Gloucester	a					17 22							18 29							19 22			
Bristol Parkway	a				17 24			17 54				18 29			18 54				19 25			19 55	
Bristol Temple Meads	a				17 38			18 07				18 42			19 05				19 39			20 06	
Newport (South Wales)	a					18 05							19 12							20 05		20 55	
Cardiff Central	a					18 21							19 29							20 21		21 11	
Weston-super-Mare	a																						
Taunton	a				18 15							19 15							20 15				
Tiverton Parkway	a				18 28							19 28							20 28				
Exeter St Davids	a				18 42							19 43							20 42				
Dawlish	a																						
Teignmouth	a																						
Newton Abbot	a				19 04							20 03							21 03				
Torquay	a																						
Paignton	a																						
Totnes	a				19 17							20 16							21 16				
Plymouth	a				19 43							20 43							21 43				
Liskeard	a				20 10																		
Bodmin Parkway	a				20 22																		
Lostwithiel	a				20 28																		
Par	a				20 35																		
Newquay (Summer Only)	a																						
St Austell	a				20 42																		
Truro	a				21 00																		
Redruth	a				21 12																		
Camborne	a				21 18																		
Hayle	a				21 26																		
St Erth	a				21 31																		
Penzance	a				21 43																		
Birmingham International	d			16 14							17 14							18 14					
Coventry	d			16 25							17 25							18 25					
Leamington Spa	d			16 38			17 00				17 38			18 02				18 38			19 00		
Banbury	a			16 54			17 17				17 54			18 18				18 54			19 17		
Oxford	a			17 14			17 41				18 14			18 40				19 14			19 40		
Reading	a			17 39			18 07				18 39			19 07				19 39			20 10		
Guildford	a																						
Basingstoke	a			18 08			18 40				19 08							20 08					
Winchester	a			18 24			18 55				19 24							20 24					
Southampton Airport Pkway	a			18 32			19 08				19 32							20 32					
Southampton Central	a			18 40			19 17				19 41							20 41					
Brockenhurst	a			18 57							19 57							20 57					
Bournemouth	a			19 11							20 11							21 11					

A from Edinburgh to Plymouth

Table 51

Saturdays

7 July to 8 September

Scotland, The North East, North West England - The South West and South Coast

Route Diagram - see first Page of Table 51

		XC	XC	XC	XC	XC	XC	VT	XC	XC	XC	XC	XC	LM	XC	VT	XC	XC	XC	XC	VT	XC
		A	B						A	C		A					D	D				
Aberdeen	d																					
Stonehaven	d																					
Montrose	d																					
Arbroath	d																					
Dundee	d																					
Leuchars	d																					
Cupar	d																					
Ladybank	d																					
Markinch	d																					
Kirkcaldy	d																					
Inverkeithing	d																					
Glasgow Central	d		12 51					16 00										15 00			18 00	
Motherwell	d		13 06															15 14				
Haymarket	d																	15 56				
Edinburgh	d		14 08							15 08						16 52		16 05				
Haymarket	d															16 57						
Lockerbie	d																					
Carlisle	d							17 09								18 07					19 09	
Penrith North Lakes	d																					
Oxenholme Lake District	d							17 44								18 42						
Lancaster	d															18 57					19 56	
Preston	d							18 17								19 17					20 17	
Wigan North Western	d							18 28								19 28					20 28	
Warrington Bank Quay	d							18 39								19 39					20 39	
M'chester Piccadilly	d	17 27				18 05			18 27				19 07				19 27			20 07		
Stockport	d	17 36				18 13			18 35				19 16				19 35			20 16		
Wilmslow	d																					
Crewe	d							19 01						19 51		20 01					21 01	
Macclesfield	d					18 26											19 49					
Congleton	d	17 54							18 54													
Stoke-on-Trent	d	18 08				18 44			19 07				19 44				20 07			20 44		
Stafford	d	18 27				19 03			19 25				20 03	20 12			20 26			21 03		
Wolverhampton	d	18 41				19 17		19 32	19 41				20 17	20 28		20 32	20 41			21 16	21 33	
Dunbar	d									15 28												
Berwick-upon-Tweed	d		14 49																			
Alnmouth for Alnwick	d																	17 03				
Morpeth	d																	17 17				
Newcastle	d		15 41		16 35					16 41		17 32						17 44	18 35			
Chester-le-Street	d											17 41										
Durham	d		15 53		16 47					16 52		17 48						17 56	18 48			
Darlington	d		16 11		17 04					17 10		18 05						18 13	19 05			
York	d		16 44		17 34					17 44		18 34						18 44	19 34			
Leeds	d		17 11							18 11								19 11				
Wakefield Westgate	d		17 23							18 23								19 24				
Doncaster	d				17 58							18 58							19 58			
Sheffield	d		17 54		18 23					18 54		19 24						19 54	20 23			
Chesterfield	d		18 07							19 06								20 06				
Nottingham	d			18 08			18 37				19 08				19 37							20 37
Derby	d		18 28	18 36	18 53		19 10			19 27	19 36	19 54			20 10			20 28	20 53			21 06
Burton-on-Trent	d			18 49			19 21			19 37	19 49				20 21							21 21
Tamworth	d		18 46	19 02			19 33				20 02				20 33			20 46				21 33
Birmingham New Street	a	18 58	19 06	19 24	19 27	19 33	19 54	19 55	19 58	20 06	20 24	20 27	20 33	20 47	20 54	20 55	20 58	21 03	21 25	21 32	21 54	21 54
Birmingham New Street	d	19 04	19 12	19 30	19 33	19 42			20 04	20 12	20 30	20 33	20 42				21 04	21 12				
Cheltenham Spa	a		19 50	20 10		20 23				20 49	21 10		21 23					21 49				
Gloucester	a			20 22							21 22							21 59				
Bristol Parkway	a		20 29			20 54				21 22			21 58					22 30				
Bristol Temple Meads	a		20 42			21 05				21 35			22 12					22 41				
Newport (South Wales)	a			21 11							22 21											
Cardiff Central	a			21 29							22 43											
Weston-super-Mare	a																					
Taunton	a		21 15							22 15												
Tiverton Parkway	a		21 28							22 28												
Exeter St Davids	a		21 42							22 43												
Dawlish	a																					
Teignmouth	a																					
Newton Abbot	a		22 04							23 10												
Torquay	a																					
Paignton	a																					
Totnes	a		22 20							23 24												
Plymouth	a		22 47							23 53												
Liskeard	a																					
Bodmin Parkway	a																					
Lostwithiel	a																					
Par	a																					
Newquay (Summer Only)	a																					
St Austell	a																					
Truro	a																					
Redruth	a																					
Camborne	a																					
Hayle	a																					
St Erth	a																					
Penzance	a																					
Birmingham International	d	19 14							20 14								21 14					
Coventry	d	19 25							20 25								21 25					
Leamington Spa	d	19 38			20 03				20 38			21 00					21 38					
Banbury	a	19 54			20 19				20 54			21 19					21 54					
Oxford	a	20 14			20 40				21 14			21 41					22 16					
Reading	a	20 39			21 10				21 40			22 10					22 41					
Guildford	a											22 59										
Basingstoke	a	21 08							22 09								23 07					
Winchester	a	21 24							22 24								23 24					
Southampton Airport Pkway	a	21 32							22 33								23 32					
Southampton Central	a	21 41							22 41								23 41					
Brockenhurst	a	21 57							22 56													
Bournemouth	a	22 15							23 21													

A to Reading
B from Edinburgh to Bristol Temple Meads
C to Bristol Temple Meads
D to Birmingham New Street

Scotland, The North East, North West England - The South West and South Coast

Saturdays
7 July to 8 September

Route Diagram - see first Page of Table 51

		XC	XC	XC	XC	VT	VT	XC	XC	XC
		◇1	◇1	◇1	◇1	◇1	◇1	◇1	◇1	◇1
			A		B					C
			✠		✠	⊡	⊡			✠
Aberdeen	d									
Stonehaven	d									
Montrose	d									
Arbroath	d									
Dundee	d									
Leuchars	d									
Cupar	d									
Ladybank	d									
Markinch	d									
Kirkcaldy	d									
Inverkeithing	d									
Glasgow Central	d					18 40				16 52
Motherwell	d									17 14
Haymarket	d									17 56
Edinburgh	d		17 08				18 52			18 05
Haymarket	d						18 57			
Lockerbie	d									
Carlisle	d					19 48	20 08			
Penrith North Lakes	d					20 02	20 23			
Oxenholme Lake District	d					20 25	20 46			
Lancaster	d					20 40	21 01			
Preston	d					21 00	21 21			
Wigan North Western	d					21 11	21 32			
Warrington Bank Quay	d					21 22	21 43			
M'chester Piccadilly	d	20 27		21 07				21 27		
Stockport	d	20 35						21 36		
Wilmslow	d									
Crewe	d					21 43	22 05			
Macclesfield	d	20 49						21 50		
Congleton	d									
Stoke-on-Trent	d	21 07		21 45				22 08		
Stafford	d	21 27		22 03		22 08	22 25	22 33		
Wolverhampton	d	21 41		22 16		22 23	22 40	22 46		
Dunbar	d		17 28							18 25
Berwick-upon-Tweed	d		17 51							18 48
Alnmouth for Alnwick	d									19 08
Morpeth	d									
Newcastle	d		18 44		19 35					19 44
Chester-le-Street	d									
Durham	d		18 56		19 49					19 56
Darlington	d		19 13		20 06					20 13
York	d		19 44		20 34					20 45
Leeds	d		20 11							21 11
Wakefield Westgate	d		20 23							21 23
Doncaster	d				21 00					
Sheffield	d		20 54		21 23					21 54
Chesterfield	d		21 06		21 35					22 06
Nottingham	d									
Derby	d		21 28		21 53					22 26
Burton-on-Trent	d		21 38							
Tamworth	d		21 49						23 00	
Birmingham New Street	a	21 58	22 05	22 32	22 43	22 46	22 59	23 02	23 21	23 38
Birmingham New Street	d									
Cheltenham Spa	a									
Gloucester	a									
Bristol Parkway	a									
Bristol Temple Meads	a									
Newport (South Wales)	a									
Cardiff Central	a									
Weston-super-Mare	a									
Taunton	a									
Tiverton Parkway	a									
Exeter St Davids	a									
Dawlish	a									
Teignmouth	a									
Newton Abbot	a									
Torquay	a									
Paignton	a									
Totnes	a									
Plymouth	a									
Liskeard	a									
Bodmin Parkway	a									
Lostwithiel	a									
Par	a									
Newquay (Summer Only)	a									
St Austell	a									
Truro	a									
Redruth	a									
Camborne	a									
Hayle	a									
St Erth	a									
Penzance	a									
Birmingham International	d									
Coventry	d									
Leamington Spa	d									
Banbury	a									
Oxford	a									
Reading	a									
Guildford	a									
Basingstoke	a									
Winchester	a									
Southampton Airport Pkwy	a									
Southampton Central	a									
Brockenhurst	a									
Bournemouth	a									

A ✠ to Leeds
B ✠ to York
C ✠ from Edinburgh to Leeds

Scotland, The North East, North West England - The South West and South Coast

Saturdays
from 15 September

Route Diagram - see first Page of Table 51

		XC	XC	XC	XC	XC	XC	XC	XC	XC	XC	XC	VT	XC	XC	XC	XC	XC	XC	VT	XC	XC	XC
		◇1	◇1	◇1	◇1	◇1	◇1	◇1	◇1	◇1	◇1	◇1	◇1	◇1	◇1	◇1	◇1	◇1	1	◇1	◇1	◇1	◇1
		A							B	C	B			D		C							E
					✠		✠	✠	✠	✠	✠	✠	⊡	✠	✠	✠	✠	✠		⊡	✠	✠	✠
Aberdeen	d																						
Stonehaven	d																						
Montrose	d																						
Arbroath	d																						
Dundee	d																						
Leuchars	d																						
Cupar	d																						
Ladybank	d																						
Markinch	d																						
Kirkcaldy	d																						
Inverkeithing	d																						
Glasgow Central	d																						
Motherwell	d																						
Haymarket	d																						
Edinburgh	d																						
Haymarket	d																						
Lockerbie	d																						
Carlisle	d																						
Penrith North Lakes	d																						
Oxenholme Lake District	d																						
Lancaster	d																			06 58			
Preston	d												06 17							07 17			
Wigan North Western	d												06 28							07 28			
Warrington Bank Quay	d												06 39							07 39			
M'chester Piccadilly	d							05 11				06 00						07 07			07 27		
Stockport	d											06 08						07 16			07 35		
Wilmslow	d																						
Crewe	d							05 47					07 01							08 01			
Macclesfield	d											06 21									07 49		
Congleton	d																						
Stoke-on-Trent	d							06 08				06 39						07 44			08 07		
Stafford	d							06 26				06 58						08 03			08 26		
Wolverhampton	d							06 41				07 15	07 32					08 18		08 32	08 41		
Dunbar	d																						
Berwick-upon-Tweed	d																						
Alnmouth for Alnwick	d																						
Morpeth	d																						
Newcastle	d																						
Chester-le-Street	d																						
Durham	d																						
Darlington	d																						
York	d																					06 17	
Leeds	d														06 00		06 15					07 10	
Wakefield Westgate	d														06 12		06 29					07 23	
Doncaster	d																06 47						
Sheffield	d														06 50		07 18					07 56	
Chesterfield	d														07 03		07 30					08 08	
Nottingham	d									05 57				06 37		06 56			07 37				08 08
Derby	d								06 10	06 36	06 48			07 06	07 26	07 36	07 50		08 06			08 28	08 36
Burton-on-Trent	d								06 20	06 48	06 59			07 18	07 37	07 50	08 00		08 18			08 39	08 49
Tamworth	d								06 31	07 01	07 09			07 30	07 48	08 02	08 11		08 30			08 49	09 02
Birmingham New Street	a							06 57	06 50	07 24	07 27	07 31	07 55	07 52	08 08	08 24	08 27	08 38	08 54	08 55	08 58	09 08	09 24
Birmingham New Street	d	22p04	05 00	05 42	06 04	06 33	06 42	07 04	07 12	07 30	07 33	07 42		08 04	08 12	08 30	08 33	08 42			09 04	09 12	09 30
Cheltenham Spa	a		06 02	06 41			07 23		07 50	08 10		08 23			08 51	09 10		09 23				09 50	10 10
Gloucester	a		06 13	06 54						08 22						09 22							10 22
Bristol Parkway	a						07 54		08 24			08 54			09 24			09 55				10 29	
Bristol Temple Meads	a						08 05		08 38			09 08			09 38			10 06				10 42	
Newport (South Wales)	a		07 06	07 52						09 07						10 07							11 08
Cardiff Central	a		07 22	08 08						09 23						10 23							11 24
Weston-super-Mare	a																						
Taunton	a						08 42		09 14						10 17							11 15	
Tiverton Parkway	a						08 54		09 28						10 30							11 28	
Exeter St Davids	a						09 09		09 41						10 46							11 42	
Dawlish	a																						
Teignmouth	a																						
Newton Abbot	a						09 28		10 02						11 09							12 03	
Torquay	a						09 40																
Paignton	a						09 47																
Totnes	a								10 15						11 23							12 16	
Plymouth	a								10 41						11 51							12 43	
Liskeard	a																						
Bodmin Parkway	a																						
Lostwithiel	a																						
Par	a																						
Newquay (Summer Only)	a																						
St Austell	a																						
Truro	a																						
Redruth	a																						
Camborne	a																						
Hayle	a																						
St Erth	a																						
Penzance	a																						
Birmingham International	d				06 14			07 14						08 14							09 14		
Coventry	d				06 25			07 25						08 25							09 25		
Leamington Spa	d	22p53			06 38	07 00		07 38			08 00			08 38			09 00				09 38		
Banbury	a	23p15			06 54	07 17		07 54			08 17			08 54			09 17				09 54		
Oxford	a	23p35			07 14	07 40		08 14			08 40			09 14			09 40				10 14		
Reading	a	00 07			07 39	08 06		08 39			09 11			09 39			10 07				10 39		
Guildford	a																						
Basingstoke	a				08 08	08 40		09 08						10 08			10 39				11 08		
Winchester	a				08 24	08 55		09 24						10 24			10 54				11 24		
Southampton Airport Pkwy	a				08 32	09 08		09 32						10 32			11 08				11 32		
Southampton Central	a				08 41	09 17		09 40						10 43			11 17				11 41		
Brockenhurst	a				08 56			09 57						10 58							11 57		
Bournemouth	a				09 14			10 11						11 12							12 11		

A 15 September
B ✠ from Birmingham New Street
C ✠ from Birmingham New Street to Newport (South Wales)
D ✠ from Derby
E ✠ to Newport (South Wales)

Scotland, The North East, North West England - The South West and South Coast

Route Diagram - see first Page of Table 51

		XC	XC	XC	VT	XC	XC	XC	XC	XC	XC	VT	XC	XC	XC	XC	XC	XC	VT	XC	XC	XC	XC
		◇■	◇■	■	◇■	◇■	◇■	◇■	◇■	◇■	■	◇■	◇■	◇■	◇■	◇■	◇■	■	◇■	◇■	◇■	◇■	◇■
								A							A						B	A	
		⌶	⌶		⊏	⌶	⌶	⌶	⌶	⌶		⊏	⌶	⌶	⌶	⌶	⌶		⊏	⌶	⌶	⌶	⌶
Aberdeen	d																						
Stonehaven	d																						
Montrose	d																						
Arbroath	d																						
Dundee	d																						
Leuchars ■	d																						
Cupar	d																						
Ladybank	d																						
Markinch	d																						
Kirkcaldy	d																						
Inverkeithing	d																						
Glasgow Central ■	d				05 50														08 00		06 01		
Motherwell	d				06 04																06 16		
Haymarket	d																				06 57		
Edinburgh ■	d											06 52		06 06		07 00					07 07		
Haymarket	d											06 56											
Lockerbie	d																						
Carlisle ■	d				07 03							08 07							09 09				
Penrith North Lakes	d				07 18							08 22											
Oxenholme Lake District	d				07 42																		
Lancaster ■	d				07 57							08 57							09 57				
Preston ■	d				08 17							09 17							10 17				
Wigan North Western	d				08 28							09 28							10 28				
Warrington Bank Quay	d				08 39							09 39							10 39				
M'chester Piccadilly ■	d		08 07			08 27				09 07			09 27				10 07			10 27			
Stockport	d		08 16			08 35				09 16			09 35				10 16			10 35			
Wilmslow	d																						
Crewe ■	d				09 01							10 01							11 01				
Macclesfield	d					08 49							09 49							10 49			
Congleton	d																						
Stoke-on-Trent	d		08 44			09 07				09 44			10 07				10 44			11 07			
Stafford	d		09 03			09 26				10 03			10 26				11 03			11 26			
Wolverhampton ■	d		09 17		09 32	09 41				10 17		10 32	10 41				11 17		11 33	11 41			
Dunbar	d																				07 27		
Berwick-upon-Tweed	d													06 48		07 40							
Alnmouth for Alnwick	d													07 08		08 00							
Morpeth	d															08 14							
Newcastle ■	d	06 22					06 45		07 35					07 40		08 36					08 43		09 35
Chester-le-Street	d																						
Durham	d	06 37					06 57		07 47					07 52		08 48					08 56		09 47
Darlington ■	d	06 54					07 14		08 04					08 10		09 05					09 13		10 05
York ■	d	07 24					07 44		08 34					08 44		09 35					09 46		10 34
Leeds ■	d						08 12							09 11							10 12		
Wakefield Westgate ■	d						08 24							09 24							10 24		
Doncaster ■	d	07 52							08 58							09 58							10 58
Sheffield ■	d	08 20					08 54		09 23					09 54		10 23					10 54		11 23
Chesterfield	d	08 32					09 06							10 06							11 06		
Nottingham ■	d			08 37				09 08			09 37				10 08			10 37				11 11	
Derby ■	d	08 53		09 10			09 27	09 36	09 53		10 10			10 28	10 37	10 53		11 10			11 27	11 36	11 54
Burton-on-Trent	d			09 21			09 38	09 49			10 21				10 49			11 21			11 39	11 49	
Tamworth	d			09 33				10 02			10 33			10 48	11 02			11 33				12 02	
Birmingham New Street ■	a	09 27	09 39	09 54	09 55	09 58	10 04	10 24	10 27	10 39	10 54	10 55	10 58	11 04	11 24	11 27	11 39	11 54	11 55	11 58	12 07	12 24	12 27
Birmingham New Street ■	d	09 33	09 42			10 04	10 12	10 30	10 33	10 42			11 04	11 12	11 30	11 33	11 42			12 04	12 12	12 30	12 33
Cheltenham Spa	a		10 23				10 50	11 10		11 23				11 50	12 10		12 23				12 50	13 10	
Gloucester ■	a							11 22							12 22							13 22	
Bristol Parkway ■	a		10 57				11 24			11 54				12 29			12 55				13 24		
Bristol Temple Meads ■	a		11 09				11 37			12 08				12 42			13 07				13 38		
Newport (South Wales)	a							12 07							13 11							14 08	
Cardiff Central ■	a							12 23							13 27							14 24	
Weston-super-Mare	a		11 29																				
Taunton	a		11 59				12 15							13 15							14 15		
Tiverton Parkway	a		12 12				12 28							13 28							14 28		
Exeter St Davids ■	a		12 26				12 42							13 42							14 42		
Dawlish	a		12 40																				
Teignmouth	a		12 45																				
Newton Abbot	a		12 52				13 03							14 02							15 02		
Torquay	a		13 03																				
Paignton	a		13 11																				
Totnes	a						13 16							14 15							15 15		
Plymouth	a						13 43							14 42							15 42		
Liskeard ■	a																						
Bodmin Parkway	a																						
Lostwithiel	a																						
Par	a																						
Newquay (Summer Only)	a																						
St Austell	a																						
Truro	a																						
Redruth	a																						
Camborne	a																						
Hayle	a																						
St Erth	a																						
Penzance	a																						
Birmingham International ✈	d					10 14							11 14							12 14			
Coventry	d					10 25							11 25							12 25			
Leamington Spa ■	d	10 00				10 38			11 00				11 38			12 00				12 38			13 02
Banbury	a	10 17				10 54			11 17				11 54			12 17				12 54			13 19
Oxford	a	10 40				11 14			11 40				12 14			12 40				13 14			13 40
Reading ■	a	11 09				11 39			12 07				12 39			13 06				13 39			14 07
Guildford	a																						
Basingstoke	a					12 08			12 40				13 08							14 08			14 40
Winchester	a					12 24			12 55				13 24							14 24			14 55
Southampton Airport Pkway ✈	a					12 32			13 08				13 32							14 32			15 08
Southampton Central	a					12 41			13 17				13 41							14 41			15 17
Brockenhurst ■	a					12 57							13 57							14 57			
Bournemouth	a					13 11							14 11							15 11			

A ⌶ to Newport (South Wales)

B ⌶ from Edinburgh

Table 51

Saturdays
from 15 September

Scotland, The North East, North West England - The South West and South Coast

Route Diagram - see first Page of Table 51

		XC	XC	VT	XC	XC	XC	XC	XC	XC	VT	XC	XC	XC	XC	XC	XC	VT	XC	XC	XC	XC
		◇■	■	◇■	◇■	◇■	◇■	◇■	◇■	■	◇■	◇■	◇■	◇■	◇■	◇■	■	◇■	◇■	◇■	◇■	◇■
							A							A						B	C	
		⌶	⌶	⊏	⌶	⌶	⌶	⌶	⌶	⌶	⊏	⌶	⌶	⌶	⌶	⌶	⌶	⊏	⌶	⌶	⌶	⌶
Aberdeen	d																					
Stonehaven	d																					
Montrose	d																					
Arbroath	d																					
Dundee	d					06 32																
Leuchars ■	d					06 46																
Cupar	d					06 54																
Ladybank	d					07 03																
Markinch	d					07 11																
Kirkcaldy	d					07 21																
Inverkeithing	d					07 38																
Glasgow Central ■	d										10 00		07 50							09 00		
Motherwell	d												08 05							09 15		
Haymarket	d					07 56							08 50							09 57		
Edinburgh ■	d			08 52		08 05							09 06					10 52		10 05		
Haymarket	d			08 57														10 57				
Lockerbie	d																					
Carlisle ■	d			10 07							11 09							12 07				
Penrith North Lakes	d										11 24											
Oxenholme Lake District	d			10 42														12 43				
Lancaster ■	d			10 57														12 57				
Preston ■	d			11 17							12 17							13 17				
Wigan North Western	d			11 28							12 28							13 28				
Warrington Bank Quay	d			11 39							12 39							13 39				
M'chester Piccadilly ■	d	11 07			11 27				12 07			12 27				13 07			13 27			
Stockport	d	11 16			11 35				12 16			12 35				13 16			13 35			
Wilmslow	d																					
Crewe ■	d			12 01							13 01							14 01				
Macclesfield	d				11 49							12 49							13 49			
Congleton	d																					
Stoke-on-Trent	d	11 44			12 07				12 44			13 07				13 44			14 07			
Stafford	d	12 03			12 25				13 03			13 26				14 03			14 26			
Wolverhampton ■	d	12 17		12 32	12 41				13 16		13 32	13 41				14 17		14 32	14 41			
Dunbar	d												09 26									
Berwick-upon-Tweed	d					08 46							09 49							10 48		
Alnmouth for Alnwick	d					09 08																
Morpeth	d																			11 19		
Newcastle ■	d					09 41		10 35					10 44		11 35					11 42		12 35
Chester-le-Street	d																					
Durham	d					09 55		10 47					10 56		11 47					11 55		12 47
Darlington ■	d					10 12		11 04					11 13		12 05					12 12		13 04
York ■	d					10 45		11 34					11 45		12 34					12 45		13 34
Leeds ■	d					11 11							12 11							13 11		
Wakefield Westgate ■	d					11 23							12 24							13 23		
Doncaster ■	d							11 58							12 58							13 58
Sheffield ■	d					11 54		12 23					12 54		13 23					13 54		14 23
Chesterfield	d					12 07							13 06							14 07		
Nottingham ■	d		11 37				12 08			12 37				13 08			13 37				14 08	
Derby ■	d		12 10			12 29	12 36	12 53		13 06			13 28	13 36	13 53		14 06			14 30	14 36	14 53
Burton-on-Trent	d		12 21				12 49			13 21			13 38	13 49			14 18				14 49	
Tamworth	d		12 33			12 49	13 02			13 33				14 02			14 30			14 49	15 02	
Birmingham New Street ■	a	12 39	12 54	12 55	12 58	13 09	13 24	13 27	13 39	13 54	13 55	13 58	14 07	14 24	14 27	14 39	14 54	14 55	14 58	15 08	15 24	15 27
Birmingham New Street ■	d	12 42			13 04	13 12	13 30	13 33	13 42			14 04	14 12	14 30	14 33	14 42			15 04	15 12	15 30	15 33
Cheltenham Spa	a	13 25				13 51	14 10		14 23				14 50	15 10		15 23				15 50	16 10	
Gloucester ■	a						14 22							15 22							16 22	
Bristol Parkway ■	a	13 57				14 26			14 57				15 23			15 55				16 29		
Bristol Temple Meads ■	a	14 08				14 41			15 09				15 37			16 08				16 42		
Newport (South Wales)	a						15 11							16 08							17 10	
Cardiff Central ■	a						15 27							16 25							17 26	
Weston-super-Mare	a																					
Taunton	a					15 16			15 43				16 15							17 17		
Tiverton Parkway	a					15 29			15 55				16 28							17 30		
Exeter St Davids ■	a					15 45			16 10				16 42							17 46		
Dawlish	a																					
Teignmouth	a																					
Newton Abbot	a					16 06							17 02							18 10		
Torquay	a																					
Paignton	a																					
Totnes	a					16 20							17 15							18 24		
Plymouth	a					16 48							17 42							18 52		
Liskeard ■	a																			19 18		
Bodmin Parkway	a																			19 32		
Lostwithiel	a																					
Par	a																			19 44		
Newquay (Summer Only)	a																					
St Austell	a																			19 52		
Truro	a																			20 10		
Redruth	a																			20 26		
Camborne	a																			20 33		
Hayle	a																					
St Erth	a																			20 45		
Penzance	a																			20 56		
Birmingham International ✈	d				13 14							14 14							15 14			
Coventry	d				13 25							14 25							15 25			
Leamington Spa ■	d				13 38			14 00				14 38			15 00				15 38			16 02
Banbury	a				13 54			14 17				14 54			15 19				15 54			16 18
Oxford	a				14 14			14 40				15 14			15 41				16 14			16 40
Reading ■	a				14 39			15 07				15 39			16 08				16 39			17 07
Guildford	a																					
Basingstoke	a				15 08							16 08			16 40				17 08			
Winchester	a				15 24							16 24			16 55				17 24			
Southampton Airport Pkway ✈	a				15 32							16 32			17 08				17 32			
Southampton Central	a				15 41							16 41			17 17				17 41			
Brockenhurst ■	a				15 57							16 57							17 57			
Bournemouth	a				16 11							17 11							18 11			

A ⌶ from Birmingham New Street to Newport (South Wales)

B ⌶ from Edinburgh to Plymouth

C ⌶ to Newport (South Wales)

Scotland, The North East, North West England - The South West and South Coast

Route Diagram - see first Page of Table 51

		XC ◇■ H	XC ■ H	VT ◇■ ꟼ	XC ◇■ H	XC ◇■ A H	XC ◇■ H	XC ◇■ H	XC ◇■ H	XC ■ H	VT ◇■ ꟼ	XC ◇■ H	XC ◇■ B H	XC ◇■	XC ◇■ H	XC ◇■ H	XC ■ H	VT ◇■ ꟼ	XC ◇■ H	XC ◇■ H	XC ◇■	XC ◇■ H	XC ◇■ H
Aberdeen	d					08 20																	
Stonehaven	d					08 38																	
Montrose	d					08 59																	
Arbroath	d					09 15																	
Dundee	d					09 32																	
Leuchars ■	d					09 47																	
Cupar	d					09 54																	
Ladybank	d					10 01																	
Markinch	d					10 08																	
Kirkcaldy	d					10 17																	
Inverkeithing	d					10 32																	
Glasgow Central ■	d			12 00									10 59					14 00					
Motherwell	d												11 14										
Haymarket	d					10 52							11 56										
Edinburgh ■	d					11 05					12 52		12 09							13 08			
Haymarket	d										12 57												
Lockerbie	d																						
Carlisle ■	d			13 09							14 07							15 11					
Penrith North Lakes	d										14 22												
Oxenholme Lake District	d																	15 46					
Lancaster ■	d			13 58							14 57												
Preston ■	d			14 17							15 17							16 17					
Wigan North Western	d			14 28							15 28							16 28					
Warrington Bank Quay	d			14 39							15 39							16 39					
M'chester Piccadilly ■	d	14 07			14 27				15 07			15 27				16 07			16 27				17 06
Stockport	d	14 16			14 35				15 16			15 35				16 16			16 35				
Wilmslow	d																						
Crewe ■	d			15 01							16 01							17 01					
Macclesfield	d				14 49							15 49							16 49				17 26
Congleton	d																						
Stoke-on-Trent	d	14 44			15 07				15 44			16 07				16 44			17 07				17 44
Stafford	d	15 03			15 26				16 03			16 25				17 03			17 26				18 04
Wolverhampton ■	d	15 17		15 32	15 41				16 17		16 32	16 41				17 17		17 32	17 41				18 17
Dunbar	d					11 25																	
Berwick-upon-Tweed	d					11 48							12 48							13 29			
Alnmouth for Alnwick	d					12 08																	
Morpeth	d																			14 09			
Newcastle ■	d					12 44		13 35					13 44		14 35					14 44		15 07	
Chester-le-Street	d																						
Durham	d					12 56		13 47					13 56		14 47					14 56		15 19	
Darlington ■	d					13 13		14 05					14 13		15 04					15 13		15 36	
York ■	d					13 44		14 34					14 44		15 34					15 45		16 06	
Leeds ■	d					14 11							15 12							16 12		16 40	
Wakefield Westgate ■	d					14 24							15 24							16 24		16 52	
Doncaster ■	d							14 58							15 58								
Sheffield ■	d					14 54		15 23					15 54		16 23					16 54		17 23	
Chesterfield	d					15 06							16 07							17 06			
Nottingham ■	d		14 37				15 08			15 37				16 08			16 37				17 11		
Derby ■	d		15 10			15 28	15 36	15 53		16 10			16 28	16 36	16 53		17 06			17 28	17 36	17 53	
Burton-on-Trent	d		15 24			15 38	15 49			16 21				16 49			17 21			17 38	17 49		
Tamworth	d		15 33				16 02			16 33			16 48	17 02			17 33				18 02		
Birmingham New Street ■	a	15 39	15 54	15 55	15 58	16 04	16 24	16 27	16 39	16 54	16 55	16 58	17 07	17 24	17 27	17 39	17 54	17 55	17 58	18 07	18 24	18 27	18 38
Birmingham New Street ■	d	15 42			16 04	16 12	16 30	16 33	16 42			17 04	17 12	17 30	17 33	17 42			18 04	18 12	18 30	18 33	18 42
Cheltenham Spa	a	16 23				16 50	17 10		17 23				17 50	18 17		18 23				18 50	19 10		19 23
Gloucester ■	a						17 22							18 29							19 22		
Bristol Parkway ■	a	16 54				17 24			17 54				18 29			18 54				19 25			19 55
Bristol Temple Meads ■	a	17 07				17 38			18 07				18 42			19 05				19 39			20 06
Newport (South Wales)	a						18 05							19 12							20 05		20 55
Cardiff Central ■	a						18 21							19 29							20 21		21 11
Weston-super-Mare	a																						
Taunton	a	17 41				18 15							19 15							20 15			
Tiverton Parkway	a	17 53				18 28							19 28							20 28			
Exeter St Davids ■	a	18 08				18 42							19 43							20 42			
Dawlish	a	18 21																					
Teignmouth	a	18 26																					
Newton Abbot	a	18 33				19 04							20 03							21 03			
Torquay	a	18 45																					
Paignton	a	18 53																					
Totnes	a					19 17							20 16							21 16			
Plymouth	a					19 43							20 43							21 43			
Liskeard ■	a					20 10							21 24										
Bodmin Parkway	a					20 22							21 36										
Lostwithiel	a					20 28																	
Par	a					20 35							21 48										
Newquay (Summer Only)	a																						
St Austell	a					20 42							21 54										
Truro	a					21 00							22 12										
Redruth	a					21 12							22 27										
Camborne	a					21 18							22 34										
Hayle	a					21 26																	
St Erth	a					21 31							22 45										
Penzance	a					21 43							22 54										
Birmingham International	d				16 14							17 14							18 14				
Coventry	d				16 25							17 25							18 25				
Leamington Spa ■	d				16 38			17 00				17 38			18 02				18 38			19 00	
Banbury	a				16 54			17 17				17 54			18 18				18 54			19 17	
Oxford	a				17 14			17 41				18 14			18 40				19 14			19 40	
Reading ■	a				17 39			18 07				18 39			19 07				19 39			20 10	
Guildford	a																						
Basingstoke	a				18 08			18 40				19 08							20 08				
Winchester	a				18 24			18 55				19 24							20 24				
Southampton Airport Pkway	a				18 32			19 08				19 32							20 32				
Southampton Central	a				18 40			19 17				19 41							20 41				
Brockenhurst ■	a				18 57							19 57							20 57				
Bournemouth	a				19 11							20 11							21 11				

A H from Edinburgh to Plymouth

B H to Plymouth

Scotland, The North East, North West England - The South West and South Coast

Route Diagram - see first Page of Table 51

		XC ■ H	VT ◇■ ꟼ	XC ◇■ A H	XC ◇■ B H	XC ◇■	XC ◇■ H	XC ◇■ H	XC ■ H	VT ◇■ ꟼ	XC ◇■ A H	XC ◇■ C H	XC ◇■	XC ◇■ A H	XC ◇■ H	LM ◇■	XC ■	VT ◇■ ꟼ	XC ◇■ D H	XC ◇■ D H	XC ◇■ H	XC ◇■
Aberdeen	d																					
Stonehaven	d																					
Montrose	d																					
Arbroath	d																					
Dundee	d																					
Leuchars ■	d																					
Cupar	d																					
Ladybank	d																					
Markinch	d																					
Kirkcaldy	d																					
Inverkeithing	d																					
Glasgow Central ■	d				12 51					16 00										15 00		
Motherwell	d				13 06															15 14		
Haymarket	d																			15 56		
Edinburgh ■	d		14 52		14 08							15 08						16 52		16 05		
Haymarket	d		14 57															16 57				
Lockerbie	d																					
Carlisle ■	d		16 07							17 09								18 08				
Penrith North Lakes	d		16 22																			
Oxenholme Lake District	d									17 44								18 42				
Lancaster ■	d		16 57															18 57				
Preston ■	d		17 17							18 17								19 17				
Wigan North Western	d		17 28							18 28								19 28				
Warrington Bank Quay	d		17 39							18 39								19 39				
M'chester Piccadilly ■	d			17 27				18 05			18 27				19 07				19 27			20 07
Stockport	d			17 36				18 13			18 35				19 16				19 35			20 16
Wilmslow	d																					
Crewe ■	d		18 01							19 01						19 51		20 01				
Macclesfield	d							18 26											19 49			
Congleton	d			17 54							18 54											
Stoke-on-Trent	d			18 08				18 44			19 07				19 44				20 07			20 44
Stafford	d			18 27				19 03			19 25				20 03	20 12			20 26			21 03
Wolverhampton ■	d		18 32	18 41				19 17		19 32	19 41				20 17	20 28		20 33	20 41			21 16
Dunbar	d											15 28										
Berwick-upon-Tweed	d				14 49																	
Alnmouth for Alnwick	d																			17 03		
Morpeth	d																			17 17		
Newcastle ■	d				15 41		16 35					16 41		17 32						17 44	18 35	
Chester-le-Street	d													17 41								
Durham	d				15 53		16 47					16 52		17 48						17 56	18 48	
Darlington ■	d				16 11		17 04					17 10		18 05						18 13	19 05	
York ■	d				16 44		17 34					17 44		18 34						18 44	19 34	
Leeds ■	d				17 11							18 11								19 11		
Wakefield Westgate ■	d				17 23							18 23								19 24		
Doncaster ■	d						17 58							18 58							19 58	
Sheffield ■	d				17 54		18 23					18 54		19 24						19 54	20 23	
Chesterfield	d				18 07							19 06								20 06		
Nottingham ■	d	17 37				18 08			18 37				19 08				19 37					
Derby ■	d	18 10			18 28	18 36	18 53		19 10			19 27	19 36	19 54			20 10			20 28	20 53	
Burton-on-Trent	d	18 22				18 49			19 21			19 37	19 49				20 21					
Tamworth	d	18 34			18 46	19 02			19 33				20 02				20 33			20 46		
Birmingham New Street ■	a	18 54	18 55	18 58	19 06	19 24	19 27	19 33	19 54	19 55	19 58	20 06	20 24	20 27	20 33	20 47	20 54	20 55	20 58	21 03	21 25	21 32
Birmingham New Street ■	d			19 04	19 12	19 30	19 33	19 42			20 04	20 12	20 30	20 33	20 42				21 04	21 12		
Cheltenham Spa	a				19 50	20 10		20 23				20 49	21 10		21 23					21 49		
Gloucester ■	a					20 22							21 22							21 59		
Bristol Parkway ■	a				20 29			20 54				21 22			21 58					22 30		
Bristol Temple Meads ■	a				20 42			21 05				21 35			22 12					22 41		
Newport (South Wales)	a					21 11							22 21									
Cardiff Central ■	a					21 29							22 43									
Weston-super-Mare	a																					
Taunton	a				21 15							22 15										
Tiverton Parkway	a				21 28							22 28										
Exeter St Davids ■	a				21 42							22 43										
Dawlish	a																					
Teignmouth	a																					
Newton Abbot	a				22 04							23 10										
Torquay	a																					
Paignton	a																					
Totnes	a				22 20							23 24										
Plymouth	a				22 47							23 53										
Liskeard ■	a																					
Bodmin Parkway	a																					
Lostwithiel	a																					
Par	a																					
Newquay (Summer Only)	a																					
St Austell	a																					
Truro	a																					
Redruth	a																					
Camborne	a																					
Hayle	a																					
St Erth	a																					
Penzance	a																					
Birmingham International	d			19 14							20 14								21 14			
Coventry	d			19 25							20 25								21 25			
Leamington Spa ■	d			19 38			20 03				20 38			21 00					21 38			
Banbury	a			19 54			20 19				20 54			21 19					21 54			
Oxford	a			20 14			20 40				21 14			21 41					22 16			
Reading ■	a			20 39			21 18				21 40			22 10					22 41			
Guildford	a													22 59								
Basingstoke	a			21 08							22 08								23 07			
Winchester	a			21 24							22 23								23 24			
Southampton Airport Pkway	a			21 32							22 32								23 32			
Southampton Central	a			21 41							22 41								23 41			
Brockenhurst ■	a			21 57							22 56											
Bournemouth	a			22 15							23 20											

A H to Reading

B H from Edinburgh to Bristol Temple Meads

C H to Bristol Temple Meads

D H to Birmingham New Street

Saturdays from 15 September

Scotland, The North East, North West England - The South West and South Coast

Route Diagram - see first Page of Table 51

Station		VT ◇1	XC 1	XC ◇1	XC ◇1 A	XC ◇1	XC ◇1 B	VT ◇1	VT ◇1	XC ◇1	XC ◇1 C	XC ◇1 D	XC ◇1 E	XC F
Aberdeen	d													
Stonehaven	d													
Montrose	d													
Arbroath	d													
Dundee	d													
Leuchars	d													
Cupar	d													
Ladybank	d													
Markinch	d													
Kirkcaldy	d													
Inverkeithing	d													
Glasgow Central	d	18 00						18 40			16 52		16 52	
Motherwell	d										17 14		17 14	
Haymarket	d										17 56		17 56	
Edinburgh	d				17 08				18 52		18 05		18 05	
Haymarket	d								18 57					
Lockerbie	d													
Carlisle	d	19 09						19 48	20 08					
Penrith North Lakes	d							20 02	20 23					
Oxenholme Lake District	d							20 25	20 46					
Lancaster	d	19 56						20 40	21 01					
Preston	d	20 17						21 00	21 21					
Wigan North Western	d	20 28						21 11	21 32					
Warrington Bank Quay	d	20 39						21 22	21 43					
M'chester Piccadilly	d			20 27		21 07				21 27				
Stockport	d			20 35						21 36				
Wilmslow	d													
Crewe	d	21 01						21 43	22 05					
Macclesfield	d			20 49						21 50				
Congleton	d													
Stoke-on-Trent	d			21 07		21 45				22 08				
Stafford	d			21 27		22 03		22 08	22 25	22 33				
Wolverhampton	d	21 33		21 41		22 16		22 23	22 40	22 46				
Dunbar	d				17 28						18 25		18 25	
Berwick-upon-Tweed	d				17 51						18 48		18 48	
Alnmouth for Alnwick	d										19 08		19 08	
Morpeth	d													
Newcastle	d				18 44		19 35				19 44		19 44	
Chester-le-Street	d													
Durham	d				18 56		19 49				19 56		19 56	
Darlington	d				19 13		20 06				20 13		20 13	
York	d				19 44		20 34				20 45		20 45	
Leeds	d				20 11						21 11		21 11	
Wakefield Westgate	d				20 23						21 23		21 23	
Doncaster	d						21 00							
Sheffield	d				20 54		21 23				21 54		21 54	
Chesterfield	d				21 06		21 35				22 06		22 06	
Nottingham	d		20 37											
Derby	d		21 06		21 28		21 53				22 26		22 26	
Burton-on-Trent	d		21 21		21 38						22 38			22 45
Tamworth	d		21 33		21 49							23 00		23 05
Birmingham New Street	a	21 54	21 54	21 58	22 05	22 32	22 43	22 46	22 59	23 02	23 15	23 21	23 34	23 40
Birmingham New Street	d													
Cheltenham Spa	a													
Gloucester	a													
Bristol Parkway	a													
Bristol Temple Meads	a													
Newport (South Wales)	a													
Cardiff Central	a													
Weston-super-Mare	a													
Taunton	a													
Tiverton Parkway	a													
Exeter St Davids	a													
Dawlish	a													
Teignmouth	a													
Newton Abbot	a													
Torquay	a													
Paignton	a													
Totnes	a													
Plymouth	a													
Liskeard	a													
Bodmin Parkway	a													
Lostwithiel	a													
Par	a													
Newquay (Summer Only)	a													
St Austell	a													
Truro	a													
Redruth	a													
Camborne	a													
Hayle	a													
St Erth	a													
Penzance	a													
Birmingham International	d													
Coventry	d													
Leamington Spa	d													
Banbury	a													
Oxford	a													
Reading	a													
Guildford	a													
Basingstoke	a													
Winchester	a													
Southampton Airport Pkway	a													
Southampton Central	a													
Brockenhurst	a													
Bournemouth	a													

A to Leeds
B to York
C from 15 September until 20 October. from Edinburgh to Leeds
D from 27 October
E from 27 October. from Edinburgh to Leeds
F from 15 September until 20 October

Sundays until 24 June

Scotland, The North East, North West England - The South West and South Coast

Route Diagram - see first Page of Table 51

Station		XC ◇1	XC ◇1 A	XC ◇1 B	XC ◇1	XC ◇1	XC ◇1 B	XC ◇1	XC ◇1	XC ◇1	XC ◇1 B	XC ◇1	VT ◇1	XC ◇1 C	XC ◇1	XC ◇1 B	XC ◇1	VT ◇1	XC ◇1 C	XC ◇1	XC ◇1	XC ◇1 B	VT ◇1
Aberdeen	d																						
Stonehaven	d																						
Montrose	d																						
Arbroath	d																						
Dundee	d																						
Leuchars	d																						
Cupar	d																						
Ladybank	d																						
Markinch	d																						
Kirkcaldy	d																						
Inverkeithing	d																						
Glasgow Central	d																						
Motherwell	d																						
Haymarket	d																						
Edinburgh	d																						
Haymarket	d																						
Lockerbie	d																						
Carlisle	d																						
Penrith North Lakes	d																						
Oxenholme Lake District	d																						
Lancaster	d																						12 00
Preston	d												10 17					11 17					12 17
Wigan North Western	d												10 28					11 28					12 28
Warrington Bank Quay	d												10 39					11 39					12 39
M'chester Piccadilly	d			08 10			09 07				10 06					11 05						12 06	
Stockport	d			08 19			09 16				10 16					11 14						12 15	
Wilmslow	d			08 26																			
Crewe	d			08 47									11 01					12 01					13 01
Macclesfield	d						09 29				10 29					11 27						12 29	
Congleton	d																						
Stoke-on-Trent	d						09 46				10 47					11 45						12 47	
Stafford	d			09 07			10 10				11 05					12 03						13 07	
Wolverhampton	d			09 27			10 26				11 25		11 32			12 24		12 32				13 22	13 32
Dunbar	d																						
Berwick-upon-Tweed	d																						
Alnmouth for Alnwick	d																						
Morpeth	d																						
Newcastle	d																09 20						
Chester-le-Street	d																						
Durham	d																09 33						
Darlington	d																09 50						
York	d											09 28					10 28						
Leeds	d					08 10			09 00			10 00					11 00						
Wakefield Westgate	d					08 23			09 11			10 12					11 12						
Doncaster	d								09 32			10 30					11 30						
Sheffield	d					08 54			09 57			10 57					11 57						
Chesterfield	d					09 07			10 09			11 09					12 09						
Nottingham	d													11 11					12 10				
Derby	d					09 28			10 34			11 30		11 36			12 30		12 36				
Burton-on-Trent	d											11 41		11 48					12 48				
Tamworth	d								10 53					12 00			12 48		13 00				
Birmingham New Street	a			09 58		10 19	10 56		11 20		11 56	12 04	12 04	12 24		12 52	13 05	13 06	13 24			13 56	14 04
Birmingham New Street	d	09 04	09 12	10 04	10 12	10 30	11 04	11 12	11 30	11 33	12 04	12 12		12 30	12 33	13 04	13 12		13 30	13 33	13 42	14 04	
Cheltenham Spa	a		09 49		10 52	11 09		11 52	12 08			12 50		13 10			13 50		14 12		14 23		
Gloucester	a				11 03			12 03						13 21					14 22				
Bristol Parkway	a		10 21			11 39			12 39			13 21					14 21				14 54		
Bristol Temple Meads	a		10 32			11 52			12 51			13 32					14 32				15 07		
Newport (South Wales)	a				11 48			12 52						14 06					15 08				
Cardiff Central	a				12 08			13 12						14 26					15 31				
Weston-super-Mare	a																						
Taunton	a		11 15			12 26			13 26			14 15					15 15						
Tiverton Parkway	a		11 28			12 38			13 38			14 28					15 28						
Exeter St Davids	a		11 42			12 56			13 55			14 44					15 43						
Dawlish	a																						
Teignmouth	a																						
Newton Abbot	a		12 02			13 17			14 16			15 04					16 02						
Torquay	a																						
Paignton	a																						
Totnes	a		12 15			13 31			14 30			15 17					16 15						
Plymouth	a		12 42			13 59			14 57			15 43					16 42						
Liskeard	a		13 17																				
Bodmin Parkway	a		13 29																				
Lostwithiel	a																						
Par	a		13 40																				
Newquay (Summer Only)	a																						
St Austell	a		13 47																				
Truro	a		14 04																				
Redruth	a		14 18																				
Camborne	a		14 24																				
Hayle	a																						
St Erth	a		14 35																				
Penzance	a		14 49																				
Birmingham International	d	09 14		10 14			11 14				12 14					13 14						14 14	
Coventry	d	09 25		10 25			11 25				12 25					13 25						14 25	
Leamington Spa	d	09 38		10 38			11 38			12 00	12 38				13 00	13 38				14 00		14 38	
Banbury	a	09 54		10 54			11 54			12 17	12 54				13 17	13 54				14 17		14 54	
Oxford	a	10 14		11 14			12 14			12 38	13 14				13 41	14 14				14 38		15 14	
Reading	a	10 38		11 42			12 42			13 09	13 42				14 13	14 42				15 09		15 42	
Guildford	a																						
Basingstoke	a	11 09		12 09			13 09				14 09					15 09						16 09	
Winchester	a	11 24		12 24			13 24				14 24					15 24						16 24	
Southampton Airport Pkway	a	11 33		12 33			13 33				14 33					15 33						16 33	
Southampton Central	a	11 42		12 42			13 42				14 42					15 42						16 42	
Brockenhurst	a	12 02		13 02			14 01				15 02					16 02						17 02	
Bournemouth	a	12 26		13 26			14 26				15 26					16 26						17 26	

A to Plymouth
B from Birmingham New Street to Birmingham New Street
C to Newport (South Wales)

Scotland, The North East, North West England - The South West and South Coast

Route Diagram - see first Page of Table 51

		XC ◇■ ⊼	XC ◇■ A ⊼	XC ◇■ ⊼	XC ◇■ ⊼	XC ◇■ B ⊡⊼	VT ◇■ ⊡	XC ◇■ C ⊼	XC ◇■ A ⊼	XC ◇■ ⊼	XC ◇■ ⊼	XC ◇■ B ⊡⊼	XC ◇■ ⊼	VT ◇■ ⊡	XC ◇■ ⊼	XC ◇■ ⊼	XC ◇■ ⊼	XC ◇■ B ⊡⊼	XC ◇■ C ⊼	VT ◇■ ⊡	XC ◇■ A ⊼	XC ◇■ ⊼	XC ◇■ ⊼
Aberdeen	d																						
Stonehaven	d																						
Montrose	d																						
Arbroath	d																						
Dundee	d																						
Leuchars ■	d																						
Cupar	d																						
Ladybank	d																						
Markinch	d																						
Kirkcaldy	d																						
Inverkeithing	d																						
Glasgow Central ■	d													11 58					10 55				
Motherwell	d																		11 10				
Haymarket	d																		11 51				
Edinburgh ■	d	08 50					10 52	09 50					11 05						12 08	12 52			
Haymarket	d						10 57													12 56			
Lockerbie	d																						
Carlisle ■	d						12 07							13 10						14 07			
Penrith North Lakes	d																			14 22			
Oxenholme Lake District	d						12 43																
Lancaster ■	d						12 57							13 58						14 57			
Preston ■	d						13 17							14 17						15 17			
Wigan North Western	d						13 28							14 28						15 28			
Warrington Bank Quay	d						13 39							14 39						15 39			
M'chester Piccadilly ■ ⛴	d			12 41		13 03				13 42		14 05					14 42	15 02					15 42
Stockport	d			12 50		13 13				13 51		14 14					14 51	15 11					15 51
Wilmslow	d																						
Crewe ■	d						14 01							15 01						16 01			
Macclesfield	d			13 04		13 26				14 04		14 27					15 04	15 24					16 04
Congleton	d																						
Stoke-on-Trent	d			13 22		13 44				14 22		14 45					15 22	15 45					16 23
Stafford	d					14 02						15 06						16 06					
Wolverhampton ■ ⛴	d			13 53		14 21	14 33			14 54		15 20		15 32			15 54	16 22		16 32			16 54
Dunbar	d												11 25										
Berwick-upon-Tweed	d	09 33											11 50						12 49				
Alnmouth for Alnwick	d							10 49					12 10										
Morpeth	d							11 04															
Newcastle ■	d	10 24						11 25					12 40			13 35			13 40			14 35	
Chester-le-Street	d																						
Durham	d	10 37						11 37					12 52			13 47			13 52			14 47	
Darlington ■	d	10 54						11 55					13 09			14 05			14 10			15 04	
York ■	d	11 28						12 28					13 40			14 34			14 40			15 34	
Leeds ■	d	12 00						13 00					14 10						15 10				
Wakefield Westgate ■	d	12 12						13 12					14 23						15 23				
Doncaster ■	d	12 30						13 30								14 59						15 59	
Sheffield ■ ⛴	d	12 57						13 57			14 22		14 54			15 23			15 54			16 24	
Chesterfield	d	13 09						14 09			14 32		15 06						16 07				
Nottingham ■ ⛴	d		13 06						14 10						15 10						16 10		
Derby ■	d	13 32	13 36		13 54			14 31	14 35		14 53		15 26		15 35	15 54			16 29		16 35	16 55	
Burton-on-Trent	d	13 43	13 48						14 48				15 39		15 48						16 48		
Tamworth	d		14 00					14 50	15 00						16 00				16 48		17 00		
Birmingham New Street ■	a	14 08	14 24	14 27	14 27	14 56	15 05	15 06	15 21	15 27	15 27	15 56	16 02	16 07	16 24	16 27	16 27	16 52	17 04	17 07	17 19	17 27	17 28
Birmingham New Street ■	d	14 12	14 30	14 42	14 33	15 04		15 12	15 30	15 42	15 33	16 04	16 12		16 30	16 33	16 42	17 04	17 12		17 30	17 33	17 42
Cheltenham Spa	a	14 51	15 10	15 24				15 50	16 10	16 24			16 49		17 10		17 24		17 50		18 10		18 24
Gloucester ■	a		15 21						16 21						17 21						18 22		
Bristol Parkway ■	a	15 24		15 59				16 21		16 55			17 20				18 02		18 22				18 56
Bristol Temple Meads ■	a	15 36		16 11				16 35		17 08			17 35				18 13		18 40				19 08
Newport (South Wales)	a		16 06						17 06						18 07						19 07		
Cardiff Central ■	a		16 26						17 27						18 29						19 27		
Weston-super-Mare	a																						
Taunton	a	16 14		16 45				17 15					18 18						19 15				
Tiverton Parkway	a	16 26		16 57				17 28					18 31						19 28				
Exeter St Davids ■	a	16 44		17 12				17 43					18 46						19 47				
Dawlish	a			17 25																			
Teignmouth	a			17 30																			
Newton Abbot	a	17 04		17 37				18 02					19 05						20 07				
Torquay	a			17 48																			
Paignton	a			17 56																			
Totnes	a	17 18						18 15					19 18						20 20				
Plymouth	a	17 46						18 42					19 45						20 46				
Liskeard ■	a							19 17											21 12				
Bodmin Parkway	a							19 29											21 24				
Lostwithiel	a																						
Par	a							19 40											21 35				
Newquay (Summer Only)	a																						
St Austell	a							19 47											21 42				
Truro	a							20 08											21 59				
Redruth	a							20 19											22 11				
Camborne	a							20 26											22 17				
Hayle	a																						
St Erth	a							20 38											22 29				
Penzance	a							20 47											22 38				
Birmingham International ✈	d					15 14						16 14						17 14					
Coventry	d					15 25						16 25						17 25					
Leamington Spa ■	d				15 00	15 38					16 00	16 38				17 00		17 38				18 01	
Banbury	a				15 18	15 54					16 17	16 54				17 17		17 54				18 19	
Oxford	a				15 41	16 14					16 41	17 14				17 38		18 14				18 41	
Reading ■	a				16 09	16 42					17 13	17 41				18 16		18 41				19 13	
Guildford	a																						
Basingstoke	a					17 09						18 09						19 09					
Winchester	a					17 24						18 24						19 24					
Southampton Airport Pkway ✈	a					17 33						18 33						19 33					
Southampton Central ⛴	a					17 40						18 42						19 40					
Brockenhurst ■	a					18 02						19 01						20 02					
Bournemouth	a					18 26						19 26						20 26					

A ⊼ to Newport (South Wales)

B ⊡ from Birmingham New Street ⊼ to Birmingham New Street

C ⊼ to Plymouth

Scotland, The North East, North West England - The South West and South Coast

Route Diagram - see first Page of Table 51

		XC ◇■ A ⊡⊼	XC ◇■ B ⊼	VT ◇■ ⊡	XC ◇■ C ⊼	XC ◇■ ⊼	XC ◇■ ⊼	XC ◇■ D ⊡⊼	XC ◇■ E ⊼	VT ◇■ ⊡	XC ◇■ F ⊼	XC ◇■ ⊼	XC ◇■ ⊼	XC ◇■ D ⊡⊼	XC ◇■ E ⊼	VT ◇■ ⊡	XC ◇■ ⊼	XC ◇■ G ⊼	XC ◇■ F ⊼	XC ◇■ F ⊼	XC ◇■ H ⊼	VT ◇■ ⊡
Aberdeen	d								11 12													
Stonehaven	d								11 29													
Montrose	d								11 50													
Arbroath	d								12 06													
Dundee	d								12 25													
Leuchars ■	d								12 38													
Cupar	d								12 45													
Ladybank	d																					
Markinch	d																					
Kirkcaldy	d								13 03													
Inverkeithing	d								13 18													
Glasgow Central ■	d		11 51	13 55											13 49	15 57					14 55	
Motherwell	d		12 07												14 04						15 11	
Haymarket	d		12 49						13 37						14 42						15 51	
Edinburgh ■	d		13 06			13 50			14 08	14 52					15 07						16 05	16 52
Haymarket	d									14 57												16 56
Lockerbie	d																					
Carlisle ■	d			15 11						16 07						17 09						18 07
Penrith North Lakes	d									16 22												
Oxenholme Lake District	d			15 46												17 44						18 42
Lancaster ■	d									16 57												18 57
Preston ■	d			16 17						17 17						18 16						19 17
Wigan North Western	d			16 28						17 28						18 27						19 28
Warrington Bank Quay	d			16 39						17 39						18 38						19 39
M'chester Piccadilly ■ ⛴	d	16 02					16 42	17 02					17 42	18 02					18 42	19 02		
Stockport	d	16 11					16 51	17 11					17 51	18 11					18 51	19 11		
Wilmslow	d																					
Crewe ■	d			17 01						18 01						19 00						20 01
Macclesfield	d	16 24					17 04	17 24					18 04	18 24					19 04	19 24		
Congleton	d																					
Stoke-on-Trent	d	16 45					17 22	17 45					18 22	18 45					19 22	19 45		
Stafford	d	17 06						18 06						19 03						20 05		
Wolverhampton ■ ⛴	d	17 24		17 33			17 54	18 21		18 33			18 54	19 21		19 32			19 54	20 21		20 33
Dunbar	d		13 25												15 27							
Berwick-upon-Tweed	d					14 33			14 49													
Alnmouth for Alnwick	d		14 08																		17 07	
Morpeth	d																				17 22	
Newcastle ■	d		14 40			15 23			15 40			16 35			16 40			17 35			17 40	
Chester-le-Street	d																					
Durham	d		14 52			15 36			15 52			16 47			16 52			17 47			17 52	
Darlington ■	d		15 09			15 53			16 09			17 04			17 09			18 05			18 09	
York ■	d		15 40			16 23			16 40			17 34			17 40			18 34			18 40	
Leeds ■	d		16 10						17 10						18 10						19 10	
Wakefield Westgate ■	d		16 22						17 22						18 22						19 22	
Doncaster ■	d					16 51						17 59						18 59				
Sheffield ■ ⛴	d		16 54			17 24			17 54			18 24			18 54			19 24			19 54	
Chesterfield	d		17 06						18 06						19 06						20 06	
Nottingham ■ ⛴	d				17 10						18 10						19 10					
Derby ■	d		17 27		17 36	17 54			18 26		18 35	18 55			19 27		19 36	19 55			20 27	
Burton-on-Trent	d		17 38		17 48						18 48				19 38		19 48					
Tamworth	d				18 00				18 45		19 00						20 00				20 45	
Birmingham New Street ■	a	17 56	18 01	18 06	18 19	18 24	18 27	18 56	19 04	19 06	19 20	19 27	19 27	19 50	20 05	20 06	20 24	20 27	20 27	20 50	21 03	21 06
Birmingham New Street ■	d	18 04	18 12		18 30	18 33	18 42	19 04	19 12		19 30	19 33	19 42	20 04	20 12			20 33	20 42	21 04	21 12	
Cheltenham Spa	a		18 50		19 11		19 24		19 50		20 10		20 24		20 50				21 24		21 50	
Gloucester ■	a				19 26						20 21										22 02	
Bristol Parkway ■	a		19 21				20 03		20 21				20 57		21 21				21 59		22 34	
Bristol Temple Meads ■	a		19 35				20 14		20 35				21 08		21 32				22 10		22 45	
Newport (South Wales)	a				20 11						21 06											
Cardiff Central ■	a				20 31						21 26											
Weston-super-Mare	a						20 36															
Taunton	a		20 18				20 58		21 15						22 15							
Tiverton Parkway	a		20 31				21 11		21 28						22 28							
Exeter St Davids ■	a		20 46				21 25		21 43						22 46							
Dawlish	a						21 38															
Teignmouth	a						21 43															
Newton Abbot	a		21 05				21 50		22 07						23 05							
Torquay	a						22 01															
Paignton	a						22 09															
Totnes	a		21 18						22 24						23 20							
Plymouth	a		21 45						22 50						23 47							
Liskeard ■	a																					
Bodmin Parkway	a																					
Lostwithiel	a																					
Par	a																					
Newquay (Summer Only)	a																					
St Austell	a																					
Truro	a																					
Redruth	a																					
Camborne	a																					
Hayle	a																					
St Erth	a																					
Penzance	a																					
Birmingham International ✈	d	18 14						19 14						20 14						21 14		
Coventry	d	18 25						19 25						20 25						21 24		
Leamington Spa ■	d	18 38				19 00		19 38				20 00		20 38				21 00		21 35		
Banbury	a	18 54				19 17		19 54				20 18		20 54				21 17				
Oxford	a	19 14				19 38		20 14				20 40		21 14				21 38		22 08		
Reading ■	a	19 42				20 10		20 43				21 13		21 43				22 07		22 35		
Guildford	a																	22 42				
Basingstoke	a	20 09						21 09						22 09								
Winchester	a	20 24						21 24						22 24								
Southampton Airport Pkway ✈	a	20 33						21 33						22 33								
Southampton Central ⛴	a	20 42						21 43						22 42								
Brockenhurst ■	a	21 02						22 02														
Bournemouth	a	21 26						22 26														

A ⊡ from Birmingham New Street ⊼ to Birmingham New Street

B ⊼ from Edinburgh

C ⊼ to Newport (South Wales)

D ⊡ from Birmingham New Street to Reading ⊼ to Birmingham New Street

E ⊼ from Edinburgh to Bristol Temple Meads

F ⊼ to Birmingham New Street

G ⊼ to Reading

H ⊼ from Edinburgh to Birmingham New Street

Sundays
until 24 June

Scotland, The North East, North West England - The South West and South Coast

Route Diagram - see first Page of Table 51

		XC ◇1	XC ◇1 ⌶	XC ◇1	XC ◇1	XC ◇1 A ⌶	XC ◇1	XC ◇1 ⌶	VT ◇1 🛒	XC ◇1	XC ◇1 A ⌶	VT ◇1 🛒	XC ◇1
Aberdeen	d												
Stonehaven	d												
Montrose	d												
Arbroath	d												
Dundee	d												
Leuchars 3	d												
Cupar	d												
Ladybank	d												
Markinch	d												
Kirkcaldy	d												
Inverkeithing	d												
Glasgow Central 15	d								18 30		16 55		
Motherwell	d										17 11		
Haymarket	d										17 51		
Edinburgh 10	d					17 07					18 07	18 52	
Haymarket	d											18 57	
Lockerbie	d								19 44			20 07	
Carlisle 8	d											20 22	
Penrith North Lakes	d								20 19				
Oxenholme Lake District	d								20 34			20 57	
Lancaster 6	d								20 55			21 17	
Preston 8	d								21 07			21 28	
Wigan North Western	d								21 18			21 39	
Warrington Bank Quay	d												
M'chester Piccadilly 10	d			19 42	20 07					21 07			22 07
Stockport	d			19 51	20 16					21 16			22 16
Wilmslow	d												
Crewe 10	d								21 40			22 01	
Macclesfield	d			20 05	20 29					21 29			22 29
Congleton	d												
Stoke-on-Trent	d			20 23	20 47					21 47			22 47
Stafford	d			20 45	21 08				22 02	22 06			23 05
Wolverhampton 7	d			20 58	21 22				22 16	22 22		22 35	23 20
Dunbar	d					17 27					18 26		
Berwick-upon-Tweed	d					17 52					18 52		
Alnmouth for Alnwick	d												
Morpeth	d												
Newcastle 8	d		18 20			18 39		19 25			19 40		
Chester-le-Street	d												
Durham	d		18 32			18 51		19 37			19 52		
Darlington 7	d		18 51			19 08		19 54			20 09		
York 8	d		19 24			19 40		20 24			20 40		
Leeds 10	d					20 10					21 10		
Wakefield Westgate 7	d					20 22					21 22		
Doncaster 7	d		19 50					20 50					
Sheffield 7	d		20 20			20 54		21 20			21 54		
Chesterfield	d					21 06		21 32			22 06		
Nottingham 8	d	20 10					21 08						
Derby 6	d	20 36	20 54			21 27	21 36	21 53			22 26		
Burton-on-Trent	d	20 48				21 37	21 48	22 03			22 37		
Tamworth	d	21 00				21 47	22 00	22 14			22 47		
Birmingham New Street 12	a	21 19	21 28	21 27	21 50	22 04	22 23	22 30	22 52	22 52	23 04	23 06	23 49
Birmingham New Street 12	d			21 43		22 12							
Cheltenham Spa	a			22 23		22 50							
Gloucester 7	a												
Bristol Parkway 7	a			22 53		23 22							
Bristol Temple Meads 10	a			23 07		23 33							
Newport (South Wales)	a												
Cardiff Central 7	a												
Weston-super-Mare	a												
Taunton	a												
Tiverton Parkway	a												
Exeter St Davids 6	a												
Dawlish	a												
Teignmouth	a												
Newton Abbot	a												
Torquay	a												
Paignton	a												
Totnes	a												
Plymouth	a												
Liskeard 6	a												
Bodmin Parkway	a												
Lostwithiel	a												
Par	a												
Newquay (Summer Only)	a												
St Austell	a												
Truro	a												
Redruth	a												
Camborne	a												
Hayle	a												
St Erth	a												
Penzance	a												
Birmingham International ✈	d												
Coventry	d												
Leamington Spa 8	d												
Banbury	a												
Oxford	a												
Reading 7	a												
Guildford	a												
Basingstoke	a												
Winchester	a												
Southampton Airport Pkway ✈	a												
Southampton Central	a												
Brockenhurst 3	a												
Bournemouth	a												

A ⌶ to Leeds

Sundays
1 July to 9 September

Scotland, The North East, North West England - The South West and South Coast

Route Diagram - see first Page of Table 51

		XC 🚌	XC ◇1 ⌶	XC ◇1 A ⌶	XC 🚌	XC ◇1 ⌶	XC ◇1 ⌶	XC ◇1 ⌶	XC 🚌	XC ◇1 ⌶	XC ◇1 ⌶	XC ◇1 ⌶	XC ◇1 ⌶	VT ◇1 🛒	XC 🚌	XC ◇1 ⌶	XC ◇1 ⌶	XC ◇1 B ⌶	XC ◇1 ⌶	VT ◇1 🛒	XC 🚌	XC ◇1 ⌶	XC ◇1 ⌶	XC ◇1 B ⌶	XC ◇1 ⌶
Aberdeen	d																								
Stonehaven	d																								
Montrose	d																								
Arbroath	d																								
Dundee	d																								
Leuchars 3	d																								
Cupar	d																								
Ladybank	d																								
Markinch	d																								
Kirkcaldy	d																								
Inverkeithing	d																								
Glasgow Central 15	d																								
Motherwell	d																								
Haymarket	d																								
Edinburgh 10	d																								
Haymarket	d																								
Lockerbie	d																								
Carlisle 8	d																								
Penrith North Lakes	d																								
Oxenholme Lake District	d																								
Lancaster 6	d																								
Preston 8	d													10 17						11 17					
Wigan North Western	d													10 28						11 28					
Warrington Bank Quay	d													10 39						11 39					
M'chester Piccadilly 10	d					08 27				09 27						10 27						11 27			
Stockport	d					08 36				09 36						10 36						11 36			
Wilmslow	d					08 43																			
Crewe 10	d					09 05								11 01						12 01					
Macclesfield	d									09 49						10 49						11 49			
Congleton	d																								
Stoke-on-Trent	d									10 07						11 07						12 07			
Stafford	d					09 26				10 27						11 28						12 25			
Wolverhampton 7	d					09 41				10 43				11 32		11 42				12 32		12 41			
Dunbar	d																								
Berwick-upon-Tweed	d																								
Alnmouth for Alnwick	d																								
Morpeth	d																								
Newcastle 8	d																								
Chester-le-Street	d																								
Durham	d																								
Darlington 7	d																								
York 8	d																					09 28			
Leeds 10	d										08 10						09 00						10 00		
Wakefield Westgate 7	d										08 23						09 11						10 12		
Doncaster 7	d																09 32						10 30		
Sheffield 7	d										08 54						09 57						10 57		
Chesterfield	d										09 07						10 09						11 09		
Nottingham 8	d																								
Derby 6	d										09 37						10 32						11 34		
Burton-on-Trent	d																								
Tamworth	d																								
Birmingham New Street 12	a					09 58				10 59	10 48			11 55		12 00	11 48			12 55		12 58	12 48		
Birmingham New Street 12	d		09 04	09 12		10 04	10 12	10 30		11 04	11 12	11 30	11 33			12 04	12 12	12 30	12 33			13 04	13 12	13 30	13 33
Cheltenham Spa	a			09 49			10 52	11 09			11 50	12 10					12 52	13 10					13 50	14 12	
Gloucester 7	a						11 03					12 21						13 21						14 22	
Bristol Parkway 7	a			10 21				11 39			12 21						13 23						14 21		
Bristol Temple Meads 10	a			10 32				11 52			12 33						13 35						14 32		
Newport (South Wales)	a						11 48					13 06						14 06						15 08	
Cardiff Central 7	a						12 08					13 26						14 26						15 31	
Weston-super-Mare	a																								
Taunton	a			11 15				12 26			13 16						14 16						15 15		
Tiverton Parkway	a			11 28				12 40			13 28						14 29						15 28		
Exeter St Davids 6	a			11 42				12 56			13 45						14 45						15 43		
Dawlish	a																								
Teignmouth	a																								
Newton Abbot	a			12 02				13 16			14 06						15 06						16 02		
Torquay	a																								
Paignton	a																								
Totnes	a			12 15				13 31			14 20						15 20						16 15		
Plymouth	a			12 42				13 59			14 48						15 48						16 42		
Liskeard 6	a			13 17																					
Bodmin Parkway	a			13 29																					
Lostwithiel	a																								
Par	a			13 40																					
Newquay (Summer Only)	a																								
St Austell	a			13 47																					
Truro	a			14 04																					
Redruth	a			14 18																					
Camborne	a			14 24																					
Hayle	a																								
St Erth	a			14 35																					
Penzance	a			14 49																					
Birmingham International ✈	d																								
Coventry	d	09 05			10 05				11 05						12 05						13 05				
Leamington Spa 8	d	09a30	09 38		10a30	10 38			11a30	11 38			12 00		12a30	12 38			13 00		13a30	13 38			14 00
Banbury	a		09 54			10 54				11 54			12 17			12 54			13 17			13 54			14 17
Oxford	a		10 14			11 14				12 14			12 38			13 14			13 41			14 14			14 38
Reading 7	a		10 42			11 42				12 39			13 09			13 42			14 09			14 43			15 07
Guildford	a																								
Basingstoke	a		11 09			12 09				13 09						14 09						15 09			
Winchester	a		11 24			12 24				13 24						14 24						15 24			
Southampton Airport Pkway ✈	a		11 33			12 33				13 33						14 33						15 33			
Southampton Central	a		11 42			12 42				13 42						14 42						15 42			
Brockenhurst 3	a		12 02			13 02				14 01						15 02						16 02			
Bournemouth	a		12 26			13 26				14 26						15 26						16 26			

A ⌶ to Plymouth

B ⌶ to Newport (South Wales)

Scotland, The North East, North West England - The South West and South Coast

Sundays 1 July to 9 September

Route Diagram - see first Page of Table 51

		XC	VT	XC	XC	XC	XC	XC	VT	XC	XC	XC	XC	XC	VT	XC	XC	XC	XC	XC	VT	XC	XC	XC	XC
		◇1	◇1	◇1	◇1	◇1	◇1	◇1	◇1	◇1	◇1	◇1	◇1	◇1	◇1	◇1	◇1	◇1	◇1	◇1	◇1	◇1	◇1	◇1	◇1
						A				B	C	A				B						B	C	A	
		⊤	⊡	⊤	⊤	⊤	⊤	⊤	⊡	⊡⊤	⊤	⊤	⊤	⊤	⊡	⊡⊤	⊤	⊤	⊤	⊤	⊡	⊡⊤	⊤	⊤	⊤
Aberdeen	d																								
Stonehaven	d																								
Montrose	d																								
Arbroath	d																								
Dundee	d																								
Leuchars 8	d																								
Cupar	d																								
Ladybank	d																								
Markinch	d																								
Kirkcaldy	d																								
Inverkeithing	d																								
Glasgow Central 15	d														11 58								10 55		
Motherwell	d																						11 10		
Haymarket	d																						11 51		
Edinburgh 10	d							08 50	10 52		09 50						11 05				12 52		12 08		
Haymarket	d								10 57												12 56				
Lockerbie	d																								
Carlisle 8	d								12 07						13 10						14 07				
Penrith North Lakes	d																				14 22				
Oxenholme Lake District	d								12 43																
Lancaster 6	d		12 00						12 57						13 58						14 57				
Preston 8	d		12 17						13 17						14 17						15 17				
Wigan North Western	d		12 28						13 28						14 28						15 28				
Warrington Bank Quay	d		12 39						13 39						14 39						15 39				
M'chester Piccadilly 10	d			12 26			13 07			13 27				14 07		14 27				15 07		15 27			
Stockport	d			12 35						13 36						14 36						15 36			
Wilmslow	d																								
Crewe 10	d		13 01						14 01						15 01						16 01				
Macclesfield	d			12 49						13 49						14 49						15 49			
Congleton	d																								
Stoke-on-Trent	d			13 07			13 43			14 07				14 43		15 07				15 43		16 07			
Stafford	d			13 25						14 25						15 25						16 25			
Wolverhampton 7	d		13 32	13 41			14 15		14 33	14 41				15 15	15 32	15 41				16 15	16 32	16 41			
Dunbar	d																11 25								
Berwick-upon-Tweed	d							09 33									11 50						12 49		
Alnmouth for Alnwick	d										10 49						12 10								
Morpeth	d										11 04														
Newcastle 8	d				09 20			10 24			11 25						12 40		13 35				13 40		14 35
Chester-le-Street	d																								
Durham	d				09 33			10 37			11 37						12 52		13 47				13 52		14 47
Darlington 7	d				09 50			10 54			11 55						13 09		14 05				14 10		15 04
York 8	d				10 28			11 28			12 28						13 40		14 34				14 40		15 34
Leeds 10	d				11 00			12 00			13 00						14 10						15 10		
Wakefield Westgate 7	d				11 12			12 12			13 12						14 23						15 23		
Doncaster 7	d				11 30			12 30			13 30								14 59						15 59
Sheffield 7	d				11 57			12 57			13 57		14 22				14 54		15 23				15 54		16 24
Chesterfield	d				12 09			13 09			14 09		14 32				15 06						16 07		
Nottingham 8	d											14 10						15 10						16 10	
Derby 6	d				12 32			13 32			14 31	14 35	14 53				15 26	15 35	15 54				16 29	16 35	16 55
Burton-on-Trent	d											14 48					15 38	15 48						16 48	
Tamworth	d										14 50	15 00						16 00					16 48	17 00	
Birmingham New Street 12	a		13 55	13 58	13 47		14 31	14 48	14 55	14 58	15 06	15 21	15 27	15 31	15 55	15 58	16 01	16 24	16 27	16 31	16 55	16 58	17 04	17 19	17 27
Birmingham New Street 12	d	13 42		14 04	14 12	14 30	14 42	14 55		15 04	15 12	15 30	15 33	15 42		16 04	16 12	16 30	16 33	16 42		17 04	17 12	17 30	17 33
Cheltenham Spa	a	14 23			14 51	15 10	15 24				15 50	16 10		16 24			16 49	17 10		17 24			17 50	18 10	
Gloucester 7	a					15 21						16 21						17 21						18 22	
Bristol Parkway 7	a	14 54			15 24		15 59				16 21			16 55			17 20			18 02			18 22		
Bristol Temple Meads 10	a	15 07			15 36		16 11				16 35			17 08			17 35			18 13			18 40		
Newport (South Wales)	a					16 06						17 06						18 07						19 07	
Cardiff Central 7	a					16 26						17 27						18 29						19 27	
Weston-super-Mare	a																								
Taunton	a				16 14		16 45				17 15						18 18						19 15		
Tiverton Parkway	a				16 26		16 57				17 28						18 31						19 28		
Exeter St Davids 6	a				16 44		17 12				17 43						18 46						19 47		
Dawlish	a						17 25																		
Teignmouth	a						17 30																		
Newton Abbot	a				17 04		17 37				18 02						19 05						20 07		
Torquay	a						17 48																		
Paignton	a						17 56																		
Totnes	a				17 18						18 15						19 18						20 20		
Plymouth	a				17 46						18 42						19 45						20 46		
Liskeard 6	a										19 17												21 12		
Bodmin Parkway	a										19 29												21 24		
Lostwithiel	a																								
Par	a										19 40												21 35		
Newquay (Summer Only)	a																								
St Austell	a										19 47												21 42		
Truro	a										20 08												21 59		
Redruth	a										20 19												22 11		
Camborne	a										20 26												22 17		
Hayle	a																								
St Erth	a										20 38												22 29		
Penzance	a										20 47												22 38		
Birmingham International ✈	d			14 14						15 14						16 14						17 14			
Coventry	d			14 25						15 25						16 25						17 25			
Leamington Spa 8	d			14 38						15 38			16 00			16 38			17 00			17 38			18 01
Banbury	a			14 54						15 54			16 17			16 54			17 17			17 54			18 19
Oxford	a			15 14						16 14			16 41			17 14			17 38			18 14			18 41
Reading 7	a			15 42				16 25		16 43			17 11			17 38			18 13			18 40			19 07
Guildford	a																								
Basingstoke	a			16 09						17 09						18 09						19 09			
Winchester	a			16 24						17 24						18 24						19 24			
Southampton Airport Pkway ✈	a			16 33						17 33						18 33						19 33			
Southampton Central	a			16 42						17 40						18 42						19 40			
Brockenhurst 3	a			17 02						18 02						19 01						20 02			
Bournemouth	a			17 26						18 26						19 26						20 26			

A ⊤ to Newport (South Wales)
B ⊡ from Birmingham New Street ⊤ to Birmingham New Street
C ⊤ to Plymouth

Scotland, The North East, North West England - The South West and South Coast

Sundays 1 July to 9 September

Route Diagram - see first Page of Table 51

		XC	VT	XC	XC	XC	XC	XC	VT	XC	XC	XC	XC	VT	XC	XC	XC	XC	XC	VT	XC	XC	XC
		◇1	◇1	◇1	◇1	◇1	◇1	◇1	◇1	◇1	◇1	◇1	◇1	◇1	◇1	◇1	◇1	◇1	◇1	◇1	◇1	◇1	◇1
				A	B	C				D	E				D	E		F	G		G	H	
		⊤	⊡	⊡⊤	⊤	⊤	⊤	⊤	⊡	⊡⊤	⊤	⊤	⊤	⊡	⊡⊤	⊤	⊤	⊤	⊤	⊡	⊤	⊤	
Aberdeen	d										11 12												
Stonehaven	d										11 29												
Montrose	d										11 50												
Arbroath	d										12 06												
Dundee	d										12 25												
Leuchars 8	d										12 38												
Cupar	d										12 45												
Ladybank	d																						
Markinch	d																						
Kirkcaldy	d										13 03												
Inverkeithing	d										13 18												
Glasgow Central 15	d		13 55		11 51									15 57		13 49						14 55	
Motherwell	d				12 07											14 04						15 11	
Haymarket	d				12 49						13 37					14 42						15 51	
Edinburgh 10	d				13 06		13 50		14 52		14 08					15 07				16 52		16 05	
Haymarket	d								14 57											16 56			
Lockerbie	d																						
Carlisle 8	d		15 11						16 07					17 09						18 07			
Penrith North Lakes	d								16 22														
Oxenholme Lake District	d		15 46											17 44						18 42			
Lancaster 6	d								16 57											18 57			
Preston 8	d		16 17						17 17					18 17						19 17			
Wigan North Western	d		16 28						17 28					18 28						19 28			
Warrington Bank Quay	d		16 39						17 39					18 39						19 39			
M'chester Piccadilly 10	d	16 07		16 27				17 07		17 27			18 07		18 27				19 07		19 27		
Stockport	d			16 36						17 36					18 36						19 36		
Wilmslow	d																						
Crewe 10	d		17 01						18 01					19 01						20 01			
Macclesfield	d			16 49						17 49					18 49						19 49		
Congleton	d																						
Stoke-on-Trent	d	16 43		17 08				17 43		18 08			18 43		19 07				19 43		20 07		
Stafford	d			17 26						18 26					19 25						20 27		
Wolverhampton 7	d	17 15	17 32	17 41				18 15	18 33	18 41			19 15	19 32	19 41				20 15	20 33	20 41		
Dunbar	d				13 25											15 27							
Berwick-upon-Tweed	d						14 33				14 49												
Alnmouth for Alnwick	d				14 08																	17 07	
Morpeth	d																					17 22	
Newcastle 8	d				14 40		15 23				15 40	16 35				16 40		17 35				17 40	
Chester-le-Street	d																						
Durham	d				14 52		15 36				15 52	16 47				16 52		17 47				17 52	
Darlington 7	d				15 09		15 53				16 09	17 04				17 09		18 05				18 09	
York 8	d				15 40		16 23				16 40	17 34				17 40		18 34				18 40	
Leeds 10	d				16 10						17 10					18 10						19 10	
Wakefield Westgate 7	d				16 22						17 22					18 22						19 22	
Doncaster 7	d						16 51					17 59						18 59					
Sheffield 7	d				16 54		17 24				17 54	18 24				18 54		19 24				19 54	
Chesterfield	d				17 06						18 06					19 06						20 06	
Nottingham 8	d					17 10											19 10						20 10
Derby 6	d				17 27	17 36	17 54				18 26	18 55				19 27	19 36	19 56				20 27	20 36
Burton-on-Trent	d				17 38	17 48										19 38	19 48						20 48
Tamworth	d					18 00					18 45						20 00					20 45	21 00
Birmingham New Street 12	a	17 31	17 55	17 58	18 01	18 19	18 24	18 31	18 55	18 58	19 04	19 27	19 31	19 55	19 58	20 05	20 24	20 27	20 31	20 50	20 58	21 03	21 19
Birmingham New Street 12	d	17 42		18 04	18 12	18 30	18 33	18 42		19 04	19 12	19 33	19 42		20 04	20 12		20 33	20 42		21 04	21 12	
Cheltenham Spa	a	18 24			18 50	19 11		19 24			19 50		20 24			20 50			21 24			21 50	
Gloucester 7	a					19 26																22 02	
Bristol Parkway 7	a	18 56			19 21			20 03			20 21		20 57			21 21			21 59			22 34	
Bristol Temple Meads 10	a	19 08			19 35			20 14			20 35		21 08			21 32			22 10			22 45	
Newport (South Wales)	a					20 11																	
Cardiff Central 7	a					20 31																	
Weston-super-Mare	a							20 36															
Taunton	a				20 18			20 58			21 15					22 15							
Tiverton Parkway	a				20 31			21 11			21 28					22 28							
Exeter St Davids 6	a				20 46			21 27			21 43					22 46							
Dawlish	a							21 40															
Teignmouth	a							21 46															
Newton Abbot	a				21 05			21 53			22 02					23 05							
Torquay	a							22 05															
Paignton	a							22 13															
Totnes	a				21 18						22 19					23 20							
Plymouth	a				21 45						22 45					23 47							
Liskeard 6	a																						
Bodmin Parkway	a																						
Lostwithiel	a																						
Par	a																						
Newquay (Summer Only)	a																						
St Austell	a																						
Truro	a																						
Redruth	a																						
Camborne	a																						
Hayle	a																						
St Erth	a																						
Penzance	a																						
Birmingham International ✈	d			18 14						19 14					20 14						21 14		
Coventry	d			18 25						19 25					20 25						21 24		
Leamington Spa 8	d			18 38			19 00			19 38		20 00			20 38			21 00			21 35		
Banbury	a			18 54			19 17			19 54		20 18			20 54			21 17					
Oxford	a			19 14			19 38			20 14		20 40			21 14			21 38			22 08		
Reading 7	a			19 40			20 13			20 42		21 11			21 43			22 07			22 33		
Guildford	a																	22 42					
Basingstoke	a			20 09						21 09					22 09								
Winchester	a			20 24						21 24					22 24								
Southampton Airport Pkway ✈	a			20 33						21 33					22 33								
Southampton Central	a			20 42						21 43					22 42								
Brockenhurst 3	a			21 02						22 02													
Bournemouth	a			21 26						22 26													

A ⊡ from Birmingham New Street ⊤ to Birmingham New Street
B ⊤ from Edinburgh
C ⊤ to Newport (South Wales)
D ⊡ from Birmingham New Street to Reading ⊤ to Birmingham New Street
E ⊤ from Edinburgh to Bristol Temple Meads
F ⊤ to Reading
G ⊤ to Birmingham New Street
H ⊤ from Edinburgh to Birmingham New Street

Scotland, The North East, North West England - The South West and South Coast

Sundays

1 July to 9 September

Route Diagram - see first Page of Table 51

		XC	XC	XC	XC	XC	VT	XC		VT	XC	XC
		◇■	◇■	◇■	◇■	◇■	◇■	◇■		◇■	◇■	◇■
				A							A	
		✠		✠		✠	⊡			⊡	✠	
Aberdeen	d											
Stonehaven	d											
Montrose	d											
Arbroath	d											
Dundee	d											
Leuchars 3	d											
Cupar	d											
Ladybank	d											
Markinch	d											
Kirkcaldy	d											
Inverkeithing	d											
Glasgow Central 15	d						18 30				16 55	
Motherwell	d										17 11	
Haymarket	d										17 51	
Edinburgh 10	d			17 07						18 52	18 07	
Haymarket	d									18 57		
Lockerbie	d											
Carlisle 8	d						19 44			20 07		
Penrith North Lakes	d									20 22		
Oxenholme Lake District	d						20 19					
Lancaster 6	d						20 34			20 57		
Preston 8	d						20 55			21 17		
Wigan North Western	d						21 07			21 28		
Warrington Bank Quay	d						21 18			21 39		
M'chester Piccadilly 10 ⇌	d		20 07					21 07				22 07
Stockport	d		20 16					21 16				22 16
Wilmslow	d											
Crewe 10	d						21 40			22 01		
Macclesfield	d		20 29					21 29				22 29
Congleton	d											
Stoke-on-Trent	d		20 47					21 47				22 47
Stafford	d		21 09				22 02	22 06				23 05
Wolverhampton 7 ⇌	d		21 22				22 18	22 22		22 32		23 19
Dunbar	d			17 27							18 26	
Berwick-upon-Tweed	d			17 52							18 52	
Alnmouth for Alnwick	d											
Morpeth	d											
Newcastle 8	d	18 20		18 39		19 25					19 40	
Chester-le-Street	d											
Durham	d	18 32		18 51		19 37					19 52	
Darlington 7	d	18 51		19 08		19 54					20 09	
York 8	d	19 24		19 40		20 24					20 40	
Leeds 10	d			20 10							21 10	
Wakefield Westgate 7	d			20 22							21 22	
Doncaster 7	d	19 50				20 50						
Sheffield 7 ⇌	d	20 20		20 54		21 20					21 54	
Chesterfield	d			21 06		21 32					22 06	
Nottingham 8 ⇌	d				21 08							
Derby 6	d	20 54		21 27	21 36	21 53					22 26	
Burton-on-Trent	d			21 37	21 48	22 03					22 37	
Tamworth	d			21 47	22 00	22 14					22 47	
Birmingham New Street 12	a	21 28	21 39	22 04	22 23	22 30	22 38	22 39		22 55	23 04	23 36
Birmingham New Street 12	d		21 43	22 12								
Cheltenham Spa	a		22 23	22 50								
Gloucester 7	a											
Bristol Parkway 7	a		22 53	23 22								
Bristol Temple Meads 10	a		23 07	23 33								
Newport (South Wales)	a											
Cardiff Central 7	a											
Weston-super-Mare	a											
Taunton	a											
Tiverton Parkway	a											
Exeter St Davids 6	a											
Dawlish	a											
Teignmouth	a											
Newton Abbot	a											
Torquay	a											
Paignton	a											
Totnes	a											
Plymouth	a											
Liskeard 3	a											
Bodmin Parkway	a											
Lostwithiel	a											
Par	a											
Newquay (Summer Only)	a											
St Austell	a											
Truro	a											
Redruth	a											
Camborne	a											
Hayle	a											
St Erth	a											
Penzance	a											
Birmingham International ✈	d											
Coventry	d											
Leamington Spa 3	d											
Banbury	a											
Oxford	a											
Reading 7	a											
Guildford	a											
Basingstoke	a											
Winchester	a											
Southampton Airport Pkway ✈	a											
Southampton Central ⛴	a											
Brockenhurst 3	a											
Bournemouth	a											

A ✠ to Leeds

Scotland, The North East, North West England - The South West and South Coast

Sundays

16 September to 21 October

Route Diagram - see first Page of Table 51

		XC	XC	XC	XC	XC	XC	XC	XC	VT		XC	XC	XC	XC	VT	XC	XC	XC	XC		XC	VT	XC	XC
		◇■	◇■	◇■	◇■	◇■	◇■	◇■	◇■	◇■		◇■	◇■	◇■	◇■	◇■	◇■	◇■	◇■	◇■		◇■	◇■	◇■	◇■
				A			A					A			B		A		B					A	C
		✠	✠	⊡✠	✠	✠	⊡✠	✠	✠	⊡		⊡✠	✠	✠	✠	⊡	⊡✠	✠	✠	✠		✠	⊡	⊡✠	✠
Aberdeen	d																								
Stonehaven	d																								
Montrose	d																								
Arbroath	d																								
Dundee	d																								
Leuchars 3	d																								
Cupar	d																								
Ladybank	d																								
Markinch	d																								
Kirkcaldy	d																								
Inverkeithing	d																								
Glasgow Central 15	d																								
Motherwell	d																								
Haymarket	d																								
Edinburgh 10	d																								
Haymarket	d																								
Lockerbie	d																								
Carlisle 8	d																								
Penrith North Lakes	d																								
Oxenholme Lake District	d																								
Lancaster 6	d																						12 00		
Preston 8	d									10 17						11 17							12 17		
Wigan North Western	d									10 28						11 28							12 28		
Warrington Bank Quay	d									10 39						11 39							12 39		
M'chester Piccadilly 10 ⇌	d			08 27			09 27					10 27					11 27							12 26	
Stockport	d			08 36			09 36					10 36					11 36							12 35	
Wilmslow	d			08 43																					
Crewe 10	d			09 05						11 01						12 01							13 01		
Macclesfield	d						09 49					10 49					11 49							12 49	
Congleton	d																								
Stoke-on-Trent	d						10 07					11 07					12 07							13 07	
Stafford	d			09 26			10 27					11 28					12 25							13 25	
Wolverhampton 7 ⇌	d			09 41			10 43			11 32		11 42				12 32	12 41						13 32	13 41	
Dunbar	d																								
Berwick-upon-Tweed	d																								
Alnmouth for Alnwick	d																								
Morpeth	d																								
Newcastle 8	d																					09 30			
Chester-le-Street	d																								
Durham	d																					09 44			
Darlington 7	d																					10 02			
York 8	d													09 30								10 34			
Leeds 10	d					08 10			09 00					10 00								11 00			
Wakefield Westgate 7	d					08 23			09 11					10 12								11 12			
Doncaster 7	d								09 32					10 30								11 30			
Sheffield 7 ⇌	d					08 54			09 57					10 57								11 57			
Chesterfield	d					09 07			10 09					11 09								12 09			
Nottingham 8 ⇌	d																								
Derby 6	d					09 28			10 34					11 30								12 31			
Burton-on-Trent	d													11 41								12 42			
Tamworth	d																								
Birmingham New Street 12	a			09 58		10 16	10 59		11 25	11 55		12 00		12 21		12 55	12 58					13 20	13 55	13 58	
Birmingham New Street 12	d	09 04	09 12	10 04	10 12	10 30	11 04	11 12	11 30			12 04	12 12	12 33	12 30		13 04	13 12	13 30	13 33		13 33		14 04	14 12
Cheltenham Spa	a		09 49		10 52	11 09		11 52	12 08				12 49		13 10			13 49	14 12						14 50
Gloucester 7	a		10 01		11 03	11 20		12 03	12 19				13 02		13 21			14 02	14 22						15 09
Bristol Parkway 7	a		11 11			12 17			13 17				14 03					15 08							16 11
Bristol Temple Meads 10	a		11 35			12 35			13 35				14 32					15 32							16 32
Newport (South Wales)	a				11 48			12 52							14 06				15 08						
Cardiff Central 7	a				12 08			13 12							14 26				15 31						
Weston-super-Mare	a																								
Taunton	a		12 15			13 26			14 16				15 15					16 16							17 15
Tiverton Parkway	a		12 28			13 39			14 29				15 28					16 30							17 28
Exeter St Davids 6	a		12 42			13 55			14 45				15 43					16 46							17 43
Dawlish	a																								
Teignmouth	a																								
Newton Abbot	a		13 02			14 16			15 06				16 02					17 06							18 02
Torquay	a																								
Paignton	a																								
Totnes	a		13 15			14 30			15 20				16 15					17 20							18 15
Plymouth	a		13 42			14 58			15 48				16 42					17 48							18 42
Liskeard 3	a																								19 17
Bodmin Parkway	a																								19 29
Lostwithiel	a																								
Par	a																								19 40
Newquay (Summer Only)	a																								
St Austell	a																								19 47
Truro	a																								20 08
Redruth	a																								20 19
Camborne	a																								20 26
Hayle	a																								
St Erth	a																								20 38
Penzance	a																								20 47
Birmingham International ✈	d	09 14		10 14			11 14					12 14					13 14							14 14	
Coventry	d	09 25		10 25			11 25					12 25					13 25							14 25	
Leamington Spa 3	d	09 38		10 38			11 38					12 38		13 00			13 38			14 00		14 00		14 38	
Banbury	a	09 54		10 54			11 54					12 54		13 17			13 54			14 17		14 17		14 54	
Oxford	a	10 14		11 14			12 14					13 14		13 38			14 14			14 38		14 38		15 14	
Reading 7	a	10 38		11 42			12 42					13 42		14 13			14 43			15 07		15 13		15 45	
Guildford	a																								
Basingstoke	a	11 09		12 09			13 09					14 09					15 09							16 09	
Winchester	a	11 24		12 24			13 24					14 24					15 24							16 24	
Southampton Airport Pkway ✈	a	11 33		12 33			13 33					14 33					15 33							16 33	
Southampton Central ⛴	a	11 42		12 42			13 42					14 42					15 42							16 42	
Brockenhurst 3	a	12 02		13 02			14 01					15 02					16 02							17 02	
Bournemouth	a	12 26		13 26			14 26					15 26					16 26							17 26	

A ⊡ from Birmingham New Street ✠ to Birmingham New Street

B ✠ to Newport (South Wales)

C ✠ to Plymouth

Scotland, The North East, North West England - The South West and South Coast

Route Diagram - see first Page of Table 51

		XC	XC	XC	XC	VT	XC	XC	XC	XC	XC	VT	XC	XC	XC	XC	XC	VT	XC	XC	XC	XC	XC
		◇1	◇1	◇1	◇1	◇1	◇1	◇1	◇1	◇1	◇1	◇1	◇1	◇1	◇1	◇1	◇1	◇1	◇1	◇1	◇1	◇1	◇1
				A			B		A				B	C					B		A		
		⊥	⊥	⊥	⊥	⊏	⊏⊥	⊥	⊥	⊥	⊥	⊏	⊏⊥	⊥	⊥	⊥	⊥	⊏	⊏⊥	⊥	⊥	⊥	⊥
Aberdeen	d																						
Stonehaven	d																						
Montrose	d																						
Arbroath	d																						
Dundee	d																						
Leuchars [3]	d																						
Cupar	d																						
Ladybank	d																						
Markinch	d																						
Kirkcaldy	d																						
Inverkeithing	d																						
Glasgow Central [15]	d											11 58											
Motherwell	d																						
Haymarket	d																						
Edinburgh [10]	d					10 52												12 52					
Haymarket	d					10 57												12 56					
Lockerbie	d																						
Carlisle [8]	d					12 07						13 10						14 07					
Penrith North Lakes	d																	14 22					
Oxenholme Lake District	d					12 43																	
Lancaster [6]	d					12 57						13 58						14 57					
Preston [8]	d					13 17						14 17						15 17					
Wigan North Western	d					13 28						14 28						15 28					
Warrington Bank Quay	d					13 39						14 39						15 39					
M'chester Piccadilly [10]	d				13 07		13 27			14 07			14 27				15 07		15 27				16 07
Stockport	d						13 36						14 36						15 36				
Wilmslow	d																						
Crewe [10]	d					14 01						15 01						16 01					
Macclesfield	d						13 49						14 49						15 49				
Congleton	d																						
Stoke-on-Trent	d				13 43		14 07			14 43			15 07				15 43		16 07				16 43
Stafford	d						14 25						15 25						16 25				
Wolverhampton [7]	d				14 15	14 33	14 41			15 15		15 32	15 41				16 15	16 32	16 41				17 15
Dunbar	d																						
Berwick-upon-Tweed	d																						
Alnmouth for Alnwick	d																						
Morpeth	d																						
Newcastle [8]	d	10 24						11 25						12 40		13 35				13 40		14 35	
Chester-le-Street	d																						
Durham	d	10 37						11 37						12 52		13 47				13 52		14 47	
Darlington [7]	d	10 54						11 55						13 09		14 05				14 10		15 04	
York [8]	d	11 28						12 28						13 40		14 34				14 41		15 34	
Leeds [10]	d	12 00						13 00						14 10						15 10			
Wakefield Westgate [7]	d	12 12						13 12						14 23						15 23			
Doncaster [7]	d	12 30						13 30								14 59						15 59	
Sheffield [7]	d	12 57						13 57			14 22			14 54		15 23				15 54		16 24	
Chesterfield	d	13 09						14 09			14 32			15 06						16 07			
Nottingham [8]	d								14 10						15 10						16 10		
Derby [6]	d	13 32	13 54					14 31	14 35		14 53			15 27	15 35	15 54				16 28	16 35	16 55	
Burton-on-Trent	d	13 43							14 48					15 38	15 48						16 48		
Tamworth	d							14 50	15 00						16 00					16 48	17 00		
Birmingham New Street [12]	a	14 26	14 27		14 31	14 50	14 58	15 06	15 21	15 31	15 27	15 55	15 58	16 01	16 24	16 27	16 31	16 55	16 58	17 04	17 19	17 27	17 31
Birmingham New Street [12]	d	14 33	14 33	14 30			15 04	15 12	15 30		15 33		16 04	16 12	16 30	16 33			17 04	17 12	17 30	17 33	
Cheltenham Spa	a			15 10				15 50	16 10					16 51	17 10					17 50	18 10		
Gloucester [7]	a			15 21				16 02	16 21					17 01	17 21					18 01	18 22		
Bristol Parkway [7]	a							17 09						18 07						19 13			
Bristol Temple Meads [10]	a							17 35						18 40						19 35			
Newport (South Wales)	a			16 06					17 06						18 07						19 07		
Cardiff Central [7]	a			16 26					17 27						18 29						19 27		
Weston-super-Mare	a																						
Taunton	a							18 18						19 15						20 17			
Tiverton Parkway	a							18 31						19 28						20 30			
Exeter St Davids [6]	a							18 46						19 47						20 45			
Dawlish	a																						
Teignmouth	a																						
Newton Abbot	a							19 05						20 07						21 04			
Torquay	a																						
Paignton	a																						
Totnes	a							19 18						20 20						21 17			
Plymouth	a							19 45						20 46						21 44			
Liskeard [6]	a													21 12									
Bodmin Parkway	a													21 24									
Lostwithiel	a																						
Par	a													21 35									
Newquay (Summer Only)	a																						
St Austell	a													21 42									
Truro	a													21 59									
Redruth	a													22 11									
Camborne	a													22 17									
Hayle	a																						
St Erth	a													22 29									
Penzance	a													22 38									
Birmingham International	d						15 14						16 14						17 14				
Coventry	d						15 25						16 25						17 25				
Leamington Spa [8]	d	15 00	15 00				15 38				16 00		16 38			17 00			17 38			18 01	
Banbury	a	15 18	15 18				15 54				16 17		16 54			17 17			17 54			18 19	
Oxford	a	15 41	15 41				16 14				16 41		17 14			17 38			18 14			18 39	
Reading [7]	a	16 13	16 07				16 43				17 13		17 43			18 15			18 45			19 13	
Guildford	a																						
Basingstoke	a						17 09						18 09						19 09				
Winchester	a						17 24						18 24						19 24				
Southampton Airport Pkway	a						17 33						18 33						19 33				
Southampton Central	a						17 40						18 42						19 40				
Brockenhurst [3]	a						18 02						19 01						20 02				
Bournemouth	a						18 26						19 26						20 26				

A ⊥ to Newport (South Wales)
B ⊏ from Birmingham New Street ⊥ to Birmingham New Street
C ⊥ to Plymouth

Scotland, The North East, North West England - The South West and South Coast

Route Diagram - see first Page of Table 51

		VT	XC	XC	XC	XC	VT	XC	XC	XC	XC	XC	VT	XC	XC	XC	XC	XC	VT	XC	XC	XC
		◇1	◇1	◇1	◇1	◇1	◇1	◇1	◇1	◇1	◇1	◇1	◇1	◇1	◇1	◇1	◇1	◇1	◇1	◇1	◇1	◇1
			A	B				C	B	D				C			E			D	D	
		⊏	⊏⊥	⊥	⊥	⊥	⊏	⊏⊥	⊥	⊥	⊥	⊥	⊏	⊏⊥	⊥	⊥	⊥	⊥	⊏	⊥	⊥	
Aberdeen	d																					
Stonehaven	d																					
Montrose	d																					
Arbroath	d																					
Dundee	d																					
Leuchars [3]	d																					
Cupar	d																					
Ladybank	d																					
Markinch	d																					
Kirkcaldy	d																					
Inverkeithing	d																					
Glasgow Central [15]	d	13 55											15 57									
Motherwell	d																					
Haymarket	d																					
Edinburgh [10]	d						14 52												16 52			
Haymarket	d						14 57												16 56			
Lockerbie	d																					
Carlisle [8]	d	15 11					16 07						17 09						18 07			
Penrith North Lakes	d						16 22															
Oxenholme Lake District	d	15 46											17 44						18 42			
Lancaster [6]	d						16 57												18 57			
Preston [8]	d	16 17					17 17						18 17						19 17			
Wigan North Western	d	16 28					17 28						18 28						19 28			
Warrington Bank Quay	d	16 39					17 39						18 39						19 39			
M'chester Piccadilly [10]	d		16 27			17 07		17 27				18 07		18 27				19 07		19 27		
Stockport	d		16 36					17 36						18 36						19 36		
Wilmslow	d																					
Crewe [10]	d	17 01					18 01						19 01						20 01			
Macclesfield	d		16 49					17 49						18 49						19 49		
Congleton	d																					
Stoke-on-Trent	d		17 08			17 43		18 08				18 43		19 07				19 43		20 07		
Stafford	d		17 26					18 26						19 25						20 27		
Wolverhampton [7]	d	17 33	17 41			18 15	18 33	18 41				19 15	19 32	19 41				20 15	20 33	20 41		
Dunbar	d																					
Berwick-upon-Tweed	d																					
Alnmouth for Alnwick	d																					
Morpeth	d																					
Newcastle [8]	d			14 40	15 23				15 40		16 35				16 40		17 35				17 40	
Chester-le-Street	d																					
Durham	d			14 52	15 36				15 52		16 47				16 52		17 47				17 52	
Darlington [7]	d			15 09	15 53				16 09		17 04				17 09		18 05				18 09	
York [8]	d			15 40	16 23				16 41		17 34				17 40		18 34				18 41	
Leeds [10]	d			16 10					17 10						18 10						19 10	
Wakefield Westgate [7]	d			16 22					17 22						18 22						19 22	
Doncaster [7]	d				16 51						17 59						18 59					
Sheffield [7]	d			16 54	17 24				17 54		18 24				18 54		19 24				19 54	
Chesterfield	d			17 06					18 06						19 06						20 06	
Nottingham [8]	d									18 10						19 10						20 10
Derby [6]	d			17 27	17 54				18 26	18 35	18 55				19 27	19 36	19 56				20 27	20 36
Burton-on-Trent	d			17 38						18 48					19 38	19 48						20 48
Tamworth	d								18 45	19 00						19 59					20 45	21 00
Birmingham New Street [12]	a	17 55	17 58	18 01	18 25	18 31	18 55	18 58	19 04	19 20	19 27	19 31	19 55	19 58	20 05	20 24	20 27	20 31	20 50	20 58	21 03	21 19
Birmingham New Street [12]	d		18 04	18 12	18 33			19 04	19 12	19 30	19 33			20 04	20 12		20 33			21 04	21 12	
Cheltenham Spa	a			18 50					19 50	20 10					20 50						21 50	
Gloucester [7]	a			19 01					20 01	20 21					21 01						22 05	
Bristol Parkway [7]	a			20 03					21 13						22 06						23 12	
Bristol Temple Meads [10]	a			20 35					21 32						22 22						23 30	
Newport (South Wales)	a									21 06												
Cardiff Central [7]	a									21 26												
Weston-super-Mare	a																					
Taunton	a			21 15					22 15													
Tiverton Parkway	a			21 28					22 28													
Exeter St Davids [6]	a			21 43					22 46													
Dawlish	a																					
Teignmouth	a																					
Newton Abbot	a			22 02					23 05													
Torquay	a																					
Paignton	a																					
Totnes	a			22 19					23 20													
Plymouth	a			22 45					23 47													
Liskeard [6]	a																					
Bodmin Parkway	a																					
Lostwithiel	a																					
Par	a																					
Newquay (Summer Only)	a																					
St Austell	a																					
Truro	a																					
Redruth	a																					
Camborne	a																					
Hayle	a																					
St Erth	a																					
Penzance	a																					
Birmingham International	d		18 14					19 14						20 14						21 14		
Coventry	d		18 25					19 25						20 25						21 24		
Leamington Spa [8]	d		18 38		19 00			19 38			20 00			20 38			21 00			21 35		
Banbury	a		18 54		19 17			19 54			20 18			20 54			21 17					
Oxford	a		19 14		19 38			20 14			20 40			21 14			21 38			22 08		
Reading [7]	a		19 45		20 15			20 43			21 15			21 43			22 08			22 38		
Guildford	a																22 42					
Basingstoke	a		20 09					21 09						22 09								
Winchester	a		20 24					21 24						22 24								
Southampton Airport Pkway	a		20 33					21 33						22 33								
Southampton Central	a		20 42					21 43						22 42								
Brockenhurst [3]	a		21 02					22 02														
Bournemouth	a		21 26					22 26														

A ⊏ from Birmingham New Street ⊥ to Birmingham New Street
B ⊥ to Bristol Temple Meads
C ⊏ from Birmingham New Street to Reading ⊥ to Birmingham New Street
D ⊥ to Birmingham New Street
E ⊥ to Reading

Table 51

Sundays

16 September to 21 October

Scotland, The North East, North West England - The South West and South Coast

Route Diagram - see first Page of Table 51

		XC	XC	XC	XC	XC	VT	XC	VT	XC	XC
		◇1	◇1	◇1	◇1	◇1	◇1	◇1	◇1	◇1	◇1
				A						B	
		✠		✠		✠	⊟		⊟	✠	
Aberdeen	d										
Stonehaven	d										
Montrose	d										
Arbroath	d										
Dundee	d										
Leuchars	d										
Cupar	d										
Ladybank	d										
Markinch	d										
Kirkcaldy	d										
Inverkeithing	d										
Glasgow Central	d						18 30			16 55	
Motherwell	d									17 11	
Haymarket	d									17 51	
Edinburgh	d			17 07					18 52	18 07	
Haymarket	d								18 57		
Lockerbie	d										
Carlisle	d						19 44		20 07		
Penrith North Lakes	d								20 22		
Oxenholme Lake District	d						20 19				
Lancaster	d						20 34		20 57		
Preston	d						20 55		21 17		
Wigan North Western	d						21 07		21 28		
Warrington Bank Quay	d						21 18		21 39		
M'chester Piccadilly ⇌	d		20 07					21 07			22 07
Stockport	d		20 16					21 16			22 16
Wilmslow	d										
Crewe	d						21 40		22 01		
Macclesfield	d		20 29					21 29			22 29
Congleton	d										
Stoke-on-Trent	d		20 47					21 47			22 47
Stafford	d		21 09				22 02	22 06			23 05
Wolverhampton ⇌	d		21 22				22 18	22 22	22 32		23 19
Dunbar	d			17 27						18 26	
Berwick-upon-Tweed	d			17 52						18 52	
Alnmouth for Alnwick	d										
Morpeth	d										
Newcastle	d	18 20		18 39		19 25				19 40	
Chester-le-Street	d										
Durham	d	18 32		18 51		19 37				19 52	
Darlington	d	18 51		19 08		19 54				20 09	
York	d	19 24		19 40		20 24				20 40	
Leeds	d			20 10						21 10	
Wakefield Westgate	d			20 22						21 22	
Doncaster	d	19 50				20 50					
Sheffield ⇌	d	20 20		20 54		21 20				21 54	
Chesterfield	d			21 06		21 32				22 06	
Nottingham ⇌	d				21 08						
Derby	d	20 54		21 27	21 36	21 53				22 26	
Burton-on-Trent	d			21 37	21 48	22 03				22 37	
Tamworth	d			21 48	22 00	22 14				22 47	
Birmingham New Street	a	21 28	21 39	22 05	22 23	22 30	22 38	22 39	22 55	23 04	23 36
Birmingham New Street	d			22 12							
Cheltenham Spa	a			22 50							
Gloucester	a			23 03							
Bristol Parkway	a			00 01							
Bristol Temple Meads	a			00 14							
Newport (South Wales)	a										
Cardiff Central	a										
Weston-super-Mare	a										
Taunton	a										
Tiverton Parkway	a										
Exeter St Davids	a										
Dawlish	a										
Teignmouth	a										
Newton Abbot	a										
Torquay	a										
Paignton	a										
Totnes	a										
Plymouth	a										
Liskeard	a										
Bodmin Parkway	a										
Lostwithiel	a										
Par	a										
Newquay (Summer Only)	a										
St Austell	a										
Truro	a										
Redruth	a										
Camborne	a										
Hayle	a										
St Erth	a										
Penzance	a										
Birmingham International ✈	d										
Coventry	d										
Leamington Spa	d										
Banbury	a										
Oxford	a										
Reading	a										
Guildford	a										
Basingstoke	a										
Winchester	a										
Southampton Airport Pkwy ✈	a										
Southampton Central ⇌	a										
Brockenhurst	a										
Bournemouth	a										

A ✠ to Birmingham New Street

B ✠ to Leeds

Table 51

Sundays

from 28 October

Scotland, The North East, North West England - The South West and South Coast

Route Diagram - see first Page of Table 51

		XC	XC	XC	XC	XC	XC	XC	XC	XC	XC	VT	XC	XC	XC	VT	XC	XC	XC	XC	XC	VT	XC
		◇1			◇1	◇1	◇1	◇1	◇1	◇1	◇1	◇1	◇1	◇1	◇1	◇1	◇1	◇1	◇1	◇1	◇1	◇1	◇1
					A		A		A				A				A		B				A
		✠	🚌	🚌	⊟✠	✠	⊟✠	✠	⊟✠	✠	✠	⊟	⊟✠	✠	✠	⊟	⊟✠	✠	✠	✠	✠	⊟	⊟✠
Aberdeen	d																						
Stonehaven	d																						
Montrose	d																						
Arbroath	d																						
Dundee	d																						
Leuchars	d																						
Cupar	d																						
Ladybank	d																						
Markinch	d																						
Kirkcaldy	d																						
Inverkeithing	d																						
Glasgow Central	d																						
Motherwell	d																						
Haymarket	d																						
Edinburgh	d																	08 50					
Haymarket	d																						
Lockerbie	d																						
Carlisle	d																						
Penrith North Lakes	d																						
Oxenholme Lake District	d																						
Lancaster	d																					12 10	
Preston	d											10 30				11 30						12 42	
Wigan North Western	d																						
Warrington Bank Quay	d																						
M'chester Piccadilly ⇌	d				08 27		09 27		10 27			11s17	11 27			12s17	12 26			13 07		13s17	13 27
Stockport	d				08 36		09 36		10 36				11 36				12 35						13 36
Wilmslow	d				08 43																		
Crewe	d				09 05							12 01				13 01						14 01	
Macclesfield	d						09 49		10 49				11 49				12 49						13 49
Congleton	d																						
Stoke-on-Trent	d						10 07		11 07				12 07				13 07			13 43			14 07
Stafford	d				09 26		10 27		11 28				12 25				13 25						14 25
Wolverhampton ⇌	d				09 41		10 43		11 42			12 32	12 41			13 32	13 41			14 15		14 33	14 41
Dunbar	d																						
Berwick-upon-Tweed	d																	09 33					
Alnmouth for Alnwick	d																						
Morpeth	d																						
Newcastle	d													09 30				10 24					
Chester-le-Street	d																						
Durham	d													09 44				10 37					
Darlington	d													10 02				10 54					
York	d									09 30				10 34				11 28					
Leeds	d					08 10		09 00		10 00				11 00				12 00					
Wakefield Westgate	d					08 23		09 11		10 12				11 12				12 12					
Doncaster	d							09 32		10 30				11 30				12 30					
Sheffield ⇌	d					08 54		09 57		10 57				11 57				12 57					
Chesterfield	d					09 07		10 09		11 09				12 09				13 09					
Nottingham ⇌	d																						
Derby	d					09 45		10 34		11 30				12 31				13 32					
Burton-on-Trent	d									11 41				12 42				13 44					
Tamworth	d							10 56		11 54				12 51				13 59					
Birmingham New Street	a				09 58	10 56	10 59	11 16	12 00	12 17		12 55	12 58	13 09		13 55	13 58	14 19		14 31		14 50	14 58
Birmingham New Street	d	09 04	09 35	09 35	10 04	11 03	11 04		12 04		12 33		13 04	13 29	13 33		14 04		14 30	14 42	14 33		15 04
Cheltenham Spa	a		10 55			12 01								14 25					15 10	15 24			
Gloucester	a			11 00										14 43					15 21				
Bristol Parkway	a					12 34								15 18						15 59			
Bristol Temple Meads	a					12 46								15 29						16 11			
Newport (South Wales)	a																		16 06				
Cardiff Central	a																		16 26				
Weston-super-Mare	a																						
Taunton	a					13 26								16 16						16 45			
Tiverton Parkway	a					13 39								16 30						16 57			
Exeter St Davids	a					13 55								16 46						17 12			
Dawlish	a																			17 25			
Teignmouth	a																			17 30			
Newton Abbot	a					14 16								17 06						17 37			
Torquay	a																			17 48			
Paignton	a																			17 56			
Totnes	a					14 30								17 20									
Plymouth	a					14 57								17 48									
Liskeard	a																						
Bodmin Parkway	a																						
Lostwithiel	a																						
Par	a																						
Newquay (Summer Only)	a																						
St Austell	a																						
Truro	a																						
Redruth	a																						
Camborne	a																						
Hayle	a																						
St Erth	a																						
Penzance	a																						
Birmingham International ✈	d	09 14			10 14		11 14		12 14				13 14				14 14						15 14
Coventry	d	09 25			10 25		11 25		12 25				13 25				14 25						15 25
Leamington Spa	d	09 38			10 38		11 38		12 38		13 00		13 38		14 00		14 38				15 00		15 38
Banbury	a	09 54			10 54		11 54		12 54		13 17		13 54		14 17		14 54				15 18		15 54
Oxford	a	10 14			11 14		12 14		13 14		13 41		14 14		14 38		15 14				15 41		16 14
Reading	a	10 38			11 43		12 42		13 42		14 13		14 43		15 13		15 45				16 13		16 43
Guildford	a																						
Basingstoke	a	11 09			12 09		13 09		14 09				15 09				16 09						17 09
Winchester	a	11 24			12 24		13 24		14 24				15 24				16 24						17 24
Southampton Airport Pkwy ✈	a	11 33			12 33		13 33		14 33				15 33				16 33						17 33
Southampton Central ⇌	a	11 42			12 42		13 42		14 42				15 42				16 42						17 40
Brockenhurst	a	12 02			13 02		14 01		15 02				16 02				17 02						18 02
Bournemouth	a	12 26			13 26		14 26		15 26				16 26				17 26						18 26

A ⊟ from Birmingham New Street ✠ to Birmingham New Street

B ✠ to Newport (South Wales)

Scotland, The North East, North West England - The South West and South Coast

Route Diagram - see first Page of Table 51

Station		XC ◇■ A	XC ◇■ B	XC ◇■	XC ◇■	VT ◇■	XC ◇■ C	XC ◇■	XC ◇■	XC ◇■	VT ◇■	XC ◇■ C	XC ◇■ A	XC ◇■ B	XC ◇■	XC ◇■	VT ◇■	XC ◇■ C	XC ◇■ D	XC ◇■	XC ◇■	VT ◇■	XC ◇■ E
Aberdeen	d																						
Stonehaven	d																						
Montrose	d																						
Arbroath	d																						
Dundee	d																						
Leuchars	d																						
Cupar	d																						
Ladybank	d																						
Markinch	d																						
Kirkcaldy	d																						
Inverkeithing	d																						
Glasgow Central	d												10 55				13 55		11 51				
Motherwell	d												11 10						12 07				
Haymarket	d												11 51						12 49				
Edinburgh	d	09 50				10 52					12 52		12 08						13 06	13 50		14 52	
Haymarket	d					10 57					12 56											14 57	
Lockerbie	d																						
Carlisle	d					12 07					14 07						15 11					16 07	
Penrith North Lakes	d										14 22											16 22	
Oxenholme Lake District	d					12 43											15 46						
Lancaster	d					12 57					14 57											16 57	
Preston	d					13 30					15 17						16 17					17 17	
Wigan North Western	d										15 28						16 28					17 28	
Warrington Bank Quay	d										15 39						16 39					17 39	
M'chester Piccadilly	d			14 07		14s17	14 27			15 07		15 27				16 07		16 27			17 07		17 27
Stockport	d						14 36					15 36						16 36					17 36
Wilmslow	d																						
Crewe	d					15 01					16 01						17 01					18 01	
Macclesfield	d						14 49					15 49						16 49					17 49
Congleton	d																						
Stoke-on-Trent	d			14 43			15 07			15 43		16 07				16 43		17 08			17 43		18 08
Stafford	d						15 25					16 25						17 26					18 26
Wolverhampton	d			15 15		15 32	15 41			16 15	16 32	16 41				17 15	17 33	17 41			18 15	18 33	18 41
Dunbar	d																		13 25				
Berwick-upon-Tweed	d												12 49							14 33			
Alnmouth for Alnwick	d	10 49																	14 08				
Morpeth	d	11 04																					
Newcastle	d	11 25							13 35				13 40		14 35				14 40	15 23			
Chester-le-Street	d																						
Durham	d	11 37							13 47				13 52		14 47				14 52	15 36			
Darlington	d	11 55							14 05				14 10		15 04				15 09	15 53			
York	d	12 28							14 34				14 40		15 34				15 40	16 23			
Leeds	d	13 00											15 10						16 10				
Wakefield Westgate	d	13 12											15 23						16 22				
Doncaster	d	13 30							14 59						15 59					16 51			
Sheffield	d	13 57							15 23				15 54		16 24				16 54	17 24			
Chesterfield	d	14 09											16 07						17 06				
Nottingham	d		14 10					15 10						16 10									
Derby	d	14 31	14 35					15 35	15 54				16 29	16 35	16 55				17 27	17 54			
Burton-on-Trent	d		14 48					15 48						16 48					17 38				
Tamworth	d	14 50	15 00					16 00					16 47	17 00									
Birmingham New Street	a	15 06	15 21	15 31		15 50	15 58	16 24	16 27	16 31	16 55	16 58	17 03	17 19	17 27	17 31	17 55	17 58	18 01	18 24	18 31	18 55	18 58
Birmingham New Street	d	15 12	15 30	15 42	15 33		16 04	16 30	16 33	16 42		17 04	17 12	17 30	17 33	17 42		18 04	18 12	18 33	18 42		19 04
Cheltenham Spa	a	15 50	16 10	16 24				17 10		17 24			17 50	18 10		18 24			18 50		19 24		
Gloucester	a		16 21					17 21						18 22									
Bristol Parkway	a	16 21		17 00						18 02			18 22			18 56			19 21		20 03		
Bristol Temple Meads	a	16 35		17 11						18 13			18 40			19 08			19 35		20 14		
Newport (South Wales)	a		17 06					18 07						19 07									
Cardiff Central	a		17 27					18 29						19 27									
Weston-super-Mare	a																				20 36		
Taunton	a	17 15											19 15						20 17		20 58		
Tiverton Parkway	a	17 28											19 28						20 30		21 11		
Exeter St Davids	a	17 43											19 47						20 45		21 27		
Dawlish	a																				21 41		
Teignmouth	a																				21 46		
Newton Abbot	a	18 02											20 07						21 04		21 54		
Torquay	a																						
Paignton	a																						
Totnes	a	18 15											20 20						21 17				
Plymouth	a	18 42											20 46						21 44		22 37		
Liskeard	a	19 17											21 12										
Bodmin Parkway	a	19 29											21 24										
Lostwithiel	a																						
Par	a	19 40											21 35										
Newquay (Summer Only)	a																						
St Austell	a	19 47											21 42										
Truro	a	20 08											21 59										
Redruth	a	20 19											22 11										
Camborne	a	20 26											22 17										
Hayle	a																						
St Erth	a	20 38											22 29										
Penzance	a	20 47											22 38										
Birmingham International	d						16 14					17 14						18 14					19 14
Coventry	d						16 25					17 25						18 25					19 25
Leamington Spa	d				16 00		16 38		17 00			17 38			18 01			18 38		19 00			19 38
Banbury	a				16 17		16 54		17 17			17 54			18 19			18 54		19 17			19 54
Oxford	a				16 41		17 14		17 38			18 14			18 41			19 14		19 38			20 14
Reading	a				17 13		17 43		18 15			18 45			19 13			19 45		20 15			20 43
Guildford	a																						
Basingstoke	a						18 09					19 09						20 09					21 09
Winchester	a						18 24					19 24						20 24					21 24
Southampton Airport Pkway	a						18 33					19 33						20 33					21 33
Southampton Central	a						18 42					19 40						20 42					21 43
Brockenhurst	a						19 01					20 02						21 02					22 02
Bournemouth	a						19 26					20 26						21 26					22 26

A ⊼ to Plymouth
B ⊼ to Newport (South Wales)
C ⊏ from Birmingham New Street ⊼ to Birmingham New Street
D ⊼ from Edinburgh
E ⊏ from Birmingham New Street to Reading ⊼ to Birmingham New Street

Sundays
from 28 October

Scotland, The North East, North West England - The South West and South Coast

Route Diagram - see first Page of Table 51

Station		XC ◇■ A	XC ◇■ B	XC ◇■	XC ◇■	VT ◇■	XC ◇■ C	XC ◇■ A	XC ◇■	XC ◇■ D	XC ◇■ B	VT ◇■	XC ◇■ B	XC ◇■ E	XC ◇■	XC ◇■	XC ◇■	XC ◇■ F	XC ◇■	XC ◇■	VT ◇■	XC ◇■
Aberdeen	d	11 12																				
Stonehaven	d	11 29																				
Montrose	d	11 50																				
Arbroath	d	12 06																				
Dundee	d	12 25																				
Leuchars	d	12 38																				
Cupar	d	12 45																				
Ladybank	d																					
Markinch	d																					
Kirkcaldy	d	13 03																				
Inverkeithing	d	13 18																				
Glasgow Central	d					15 57		13 49						14 55							18 30	
Motherwell	d							14 04						15 11								
Haymarket	d	13 37						14 42						15 51								
Edinburgh	d	14 08						15 07				16 52		16 05				17 07				
Haymarket	d											16 56										
Lockerbie	d																					
Carlisle	d					17 09						18 07									19 44	
Penrith North Lakes	d																					
Oxenholme Lake District	d					17 44						18 42									20 19	
Lancaster	d											18 57									20 34	
Preston	d					18 17						19 17									20 55	
Wigan North Western	d					18 28						19 28									21 07	
Warrington Bank Quay	d					18 39						19 39									21 18	
M'chester Piccadilly	d				18 07		18 27				19 07		19 27				20 07					21 07
Stockport	d						18 36						19 36				20 16					21 16
Wilmslow	d																					
Crewe	d					19 01						20 01									21 40	
Macclesfield	d						18 49						19 49				20 29					21 29
Congleton	d																					
Stoke-on-Trent	d				18 43		19 07				19 43		20 07				20 47					21 47
Stafford	d						19 25						20 27				21 09				22 02	22 06
Wolverhampton	d				19 15	19 32	19 41				20 15	20 33	20 41				21 22				22 18	22 22
Dunbar	d							15 27										17 27				
Berwick-upon-Tweed	d	14 49																17 52				
Alnmouth for Alnwick	d													17 07								
Morpeth	d													17 22								
Newcastle	d	15 40		16 35				16 40		17 35				17 40		18 20		18 39		19 25		
Chester-le-Street	d																					
Durham	d	15 52		16 47				16 52		17 47				17 52		18 32		18 51		19 37		
Darlington	d	16 09		17 04				17 09		18 05				18 09		18 51		19 08		19 54		
York	d	16 40		17 34				17 40		18 34				18 40		19 24		19 40		20 24		
Leeds	d	17 10						18 10						19 10				20 10				
Wakefield Westgate	d	17 22						18 22						19 22				20 22				
Doncaster	d			17 59						18 59						19 50				20 50		
Sheffield	d	17 54		18 24				18 54		19 24				19 54		20 20		20 54		21 20		
Chesterfield	d	18 06						19 06						20 06				21 06		21 32		
Nottingham	d		18 10						19 10						20 10				21 08			
Derby	d	18 26	18 35	18 55				19 27	19 36	19 56				20 27	20 36	20 54		21 27	21 36	21 53		
Burton-on-Trent	d		18 48					19 38	19 48						20 48			21 37	21 48	22 03		
Tamworth	d	18 45	19 00						19 59					20 45	21 00			21 47	22 00	22 14		
Birmingham New Street	a	19 04	19 20	19 27	19 31	19 55	19 58	20 05	20 24	20 27	20 31	20 50	20 58	21 03	21 19	21 28	21 39	22 04	22 23	22 30	22 38	22 39
Birmingham New Street	d	19 12	19 30	19 33	19 42		20 04	20 12		20 33	20 42		21 04	21 12			21 43	22 12				
Cheltenham Spa	a	19 50	20 10		20 24			20 50			21 24			21 50			22 23	22 50				
Gloucester	a		20 21											22 02								
Bristol Parkway	a	20 21			20 57			21 21			21 59			22 34			22 53	23 22				
Bristol Temple Meads	a	20 35			21 08			21 32			22 10			22 45			23 07	23 33				
Newport (South Wales)	a		21 06																			
Cardiff Central	a		21 26																			
Weston-super-Mare	a																					
Taunton	a	21 15						22 15														
Tiverton Parkway	a	21 28						22 28														
Exeter St Davids	a	21 43						22 46														
Dawlish	a																					
Teignmouth	a																					
Newton Abbot	a	22 02						23 05														
Torquay	a																					
Paignton	a																					
Totnes	a	22 19						23 20														
Plymouth	a	22 45						23 47														
Liskeard	a																					
Bodmin Parkway	a																					
Lostwithiel	a																					
Par	a																					
Newquay (Summer Only)	a																					
St Austell	a																					
Truro	a																					
Redruth	a																					
Camborne	a																					
Hayle	a																					
St Erth	a																					
Penzance	a																					
Birmingham International	d						20 14						21 14									
Coventry	d						20 25						21 24									
Leamington Spa	d			20 00			20 38			21 00			21 35									
Banbury	a			20 18			20 54			21 17												
Oxford	a			20 40			21 14			21 38			22 08									
Reading	a			21 13			21 43			22 07			22 44									
Guildford	a									22 42												
Basingstoke	a						22 09															
Winchester	a						22 24															
Southampton Airport Pkway	a						22 33															
Southampton Central	a						22 42															
Brockenhurst	a																					
Bournemouth	a																					

A ⊼ from Edinburgh to Bristol Temple Meads
B ⊼ to Birmingham New Street
C ⊏ from Birmingham New Street to Reading ⊼ to Birmingham New Street
D ⊼ to Reading
E ⊼ from Edinburgh to Birmingham New Street
F ⊼ to Leeds

Sundays
from 28 October

Scotland, The North East, North West England - The South West and South Coast

Route Diagram - see first Page of Table 51

		VT	XC	XC
		◇■	◇■	◇■
			A	
			⌶	
Aberdeen	d			
Stonehaven	d			
Montrose	d			
Arbroath	d			
Dundee	d			
Leuchars	d			
Cupar	d			
Ladybank	d			
Markinch	d			
Kirkcaldy	d			
Inverkeithing	d			
Glasgow Central	d		16 55	
Motherwell	d		17 11	
Haymarket	d		17 51	
Edinburgh	d	18 52	18 07	
Haymarket	d	18 57		
Lockerbie	d			
Carlisle	d	20 07		
Penrith North Lakes	d	20 22		
Oxenholme Lake District	d			
Lancaster	d	20 57		
Preston	d	21 17		
Wigan North Western	d	21 28		
Warrington Bank Quay	d	21 39		
M'chester Piccadilly	d			22 07
Stockport	d			22 16
Wilmslow	d			
Crewe	d	22 01		
Macclesfield	d			22 29
Congleton	d			
Stoke-on-Trent	d			22 47
Stafford	d			23 05
Wolverhampton	d	22 32		23 19
Dunbar	d		18 26	
Berwick-upon-Tweed	d		18 52	
Alnmouth for Alnwick	d			
Morpeth	d			
Newcastle	d		19 40	
Chester-le-Street	d			
Durham	d		19 52	
Darlington	d		20 09	
York	d		20 40	
Leeds	d		21 10	
Wakefield Westgate	d		21 22	
Doncaster	d			
Sheffield	d		21 54	
Chesterfield	d		22 06	
Nottingham	d			
Derby	d		22 26	
Burton-on-Trent	d		22 37	
Tamworth	d		22 47	
Birmingham New Street	a	22 55	23 04	23 36
Birmingham New Street	d			
Cheltenham Spa	a			
Gloucester	a			
Bristol Parkway	a			
Bristol Temple Meads	a			
Newport (South Wales)	a			
Cardiff Central	a			
Weston-super-Mare	a			
Taunton	a			
Tiverton Parkway	a			
Exeter St Davids	a			
Dawlish	a			
Teignmouth	a			
Newton Abbot	a			
Torquay	a			
Paignton	a			
Totnes	a			
Plymouth	a			
Liskeard	a			
Bodmin Parkway	a			
Lostwithiel	a			
Par	a			
Newquay (Summer Only)	a			
St Austell	a			
Truro	a			
Redruth	a			
Camborne	a			
Hayle	a			
St Erth	a			
Penzance	a			
Birmingham International	d			
Coventry	d			
Leamington Spa	d			
Banbury	a			
Oxford	a			
Reading	a			
Guildford	a			
Basingstoke	a			
Winchester	a			
Southampton Airport Pkwy	a			
Southampton Central	a			
Brockenhurst	a			
Bournemouth	a			

A ⌶ to Leeds

South Coast and the South West - North West England, The North East and Scotland

Route Diagram - see first Page of Table 51

		XC	XC	XC	XC	XC MX	XC MX	XC	XC	XC		XC	VT	XC	XC	XC	XC	XC	XC	VT		XC	XC	XC	XC
		◇■	◇■	◇■	◇■	■	◇■	◇■	◇■	◇■		■	◇■	◇■	◇■	■	◇■	◇■	■	◇■		◇■	◇■	◇■	■
		A	B	C	D			E		F														G	
		⌶	⌶							⌶		⌶	⊠	⌶	⌶		⌶	⌶	⌶	⊠		⌶	⌶	⌶	
Bournemouth	d																								
Brockenhurst	d																								
Southampton Central	d																							05 15	
Southampton Airport Pkwy	d																							05 22	
Winchester	d																							05 31	
Basingstoke	d																							05 47	
Guildford	d																								
Reading	d																							06 11	
Oxford	d																							06 36	
Banbury	d																							06 54	
Leamington Spa	d																							07 12	
Coventry	d																							07 27	
Birmingham International	d																							07 38	
Penzance	d	15p30																							
St Erth	d	15p38																							
Hayle	d																								
Camborne	d	15p51																							
Redruth	d	15p57																							
Truro	d	16p09																							
St Austell	d	16p25																							
Newquay (Summer Only)	d																								
Par	d	16p33																							
Lostwithiel	d																								
Bodmin Parkway	d	16p44																							
Liskeard	d	16p56																							
Plymouth	d	17p26	18p23																						
Totnes	d	17p52	18p49																						
Paignton	d																								
Torquay	d																								
Newton Abbot	d	18p04	19p03																						
Teignmouth	d																								
Dawlish	d																								
Exeter St Davids	d	18p23	19p25																						
Tiverton Parkway	d	18p38	19p38																						
Taunton	d	18p52	19p54																						
Weston-super-Mare	d																								
Cardiff Central	d						21p50																		
Newport (South Wales)	d						22p05																		
Bristol Temple Meads	d	19p30	20p30					22p10																	
Bristol Parkway	d	19p45	20p40					22p24																	
Gloucester	d	21p00					22p47	23p21																	
Cheltenham Spa	d	21p12	21p12				22p58	23p33																	
London Paddington	d																								
Birmingham New Street	a	21p51	21p51				00 01	00 11																07 48	
Birmingham New Street	d	22p03	22p03	22p30	22p30	23p09			05 57	06 00		06 19	06 19	06 22	06 30	06 49	06 57	07 03	07 19	07 20		07 30	07 31	07 57	07 49
Tamworth	d	22p18	22p18			23p28						06 39				07 07		07 19	07 38						08 07
Burton-on-Trent	d					23p40						06 51				07 19		07 29	07 50						08 19
Derby	a	22p40	22p40			23p55				06 32		07 05			07 11	07 34		07 42	08 05			08 11			08 34
Nottingham	a					00 18						07 41				08 08			08 33						09 05
Chesterfield	a	23p04	23p04							06 53					07 31			08 02				08 32			
Sheffield	a	23p20	23p20							07 07					07 48			08 17				08 45			
Doncaster	a														08 24							09 18			
Wakefield Westgate	a									07 36								08 46							
Leeds	a	00 11	00 16							07 52								09 03							
York	a									08 22					08 45			09 26				09 44			
Darlington	a									08 55					09 16			09 57				10 13			
Durham	a									09 12					09 33			10 16				10 30			
Chester-le-Street	a																								
Newcastle	a									09 29					09 47			10 30				10 44			
Morpeth	a																								
Alnmouth for Alnwick	a									09 58															
Berwick-upon-Tweed	a									10 19															
Dunbar	a																	11 36							
Wolverhampton	d			22p48	22p48				06 16				06 36	06 40			07 15			07 37			07 49	08 15	
Stafford	a			23p00	23p00				06 29					06 53			07 29						08 00	08 29	
Stoke-on-Trent	a			23p21	23p20				06 50					07 13									08 19	08 54	
Congleton	a								07 02																
Macclesfield	a								07 11					07 30									08 36	09 11	
Crewe	a												07 07				07 50			08 07					
Wilmslow	a																08 08								
Stockport	a								07 27					07 45			08 20						08 50	09 27	
M'chester Piccadilly	a			00 12	00 12				07 37					07 59			08 34						08 59	09 39	
Warrington Bank Quay	a												07 26							08 26					
Wigan North Western	a												07 37							08 37					
Preston	a												07 51							08 51					
Lancaster	a												08 08							09 08					
Oxenholme Lake District	a												08 21												
Penrith North Lakes	a																			09 44					
Carlisle	a												09 01							09 59					
Lockerbie	a																								
Haymarket	a												10 16												
Edinburgh	a									11 05			10 21					12 03							
Haymarket	a									11 14															
Motherwell	a									11 52															
Glasgow Central	a									12 14										11 16					
Inverkeithing	a																								
Kirkcaldy	a																								
Markinch	a																								
Ladybank	a																								
Cupar	a																								
Leuchars	a																								
Dundee	a																								
Arbroath	a																								
Montrose	a																								
Stonehaven	a																								
Aberdeen	a																								

A MO from 17 September until 22 October. ⌶ from Plymouth to Birmingham New Street
B MO from 21 May until 10 September. ⌶ to Birmingham New Street
C MX until 22 June
D MX from 26 June
E MO from 17 September until 22 October
F ⌶ to Edinburgh
G ⌶ from Reading

South Coast and the South West - North West England, The North East and Scotland

Route Diagram - see first Page of Table 51

		XC	XC	XC	XC	VT	XC	XC	XC	XC	XC	VT	XC	XC	XC	XC	XC	XC	VT	XC	XC	XC	XC
		◇1	◇1	1	◇1	◇1	◇1	◇1	◇1	1	◇1	◇1	◇1	◇1	◇1	◇1	◇1	◇1	◇1	◇1	◇1	◇1	◇1
					A								B	C		D			E		C		
		✠		✠	✠	⊠	✠	✠	✠	✠	✠	⊠	✠	✠	✠	✠		✠	⊠	✠	✠	✠	✠
Bournemouth	d														06 30							07 30	
Brockenhurst	d														06 49							07 49	
Southampton Central	d							06 15							07 15							08 15	
Southampton Airport Pkway	d							06 22							07 22							08 22	
Winchester	d							06 31							07 31			08 01				08 31	
Basingstoke	d							06 47							07 47			08 18				08 47	
Guildford	d				06 02																		
Reading	d				06 41			07 09			07 40				08 11			08 41				09 11	
Oxford	d				07 07			07 36			08 07				08 36			09 07				09 36	
Banbury	d				07 26			07 54			08 27				08 54			09 26				09 54	
Leamington Spa	d				07 43			08 12			08 44				09 12			09 43				10 12	
Coventry	d							08 27							09 27							10 27	
Birmingham International	d							08 38							09 38							10 38	
Penzance	d																						
St Erth	d																						
Hayle	d																						
Camborne	d																						
Redruth	d																						
Truro	d																						
St Austell	d																						
Newquay (Summer Only)	d																						
Par	d																						
Lostwithiel	d																						
Bodmin Parkway	d																						
Liskeard	d																						
Plymouth	d								05 20							06 25							07 25
Totnes	d								05 45							06 50							07 50
Paignton	d																			07 02			
Torquay	d																			07 08			
Newton Abbot	d								06 02							07 03				07 19			08 03
Teignmouth	d																			07 26			
Dawlish	d																			07 31			
Exeter St Davids	d								06 22							07 23				07 45			08 23
Tiverton Parkway	d								06 36							07 37				07 58			08 37
Taunton	d								06 50							07 51				08 13			08 51
Weston-super-Mare	d																			08 34			
Cardiff Central	d												07 00	07 45							08 45		
Newport (South Wales)	d												07 15	08 02							09 02		
Bristol Temple Meads	d	06 27					07 00		07 30				08 00			08 30				09 00			09 30
Bristol Parkway	d	06 40					07 10		07 40				08 10			08 40				09 10			09 40
Gloucester	d		07 10											08 46							09 46		
Cheltenham Spa	d	07 12	07 21				07 42		08 12				08 42	08 57		09 12				09 42	09 57		10 12
London Paddington	d																						
Birmingham New Street	a	07 56	08 16		08 15		08 26	08 48	08 56		09 18		09 26	09 45	09 48	09 56		10 18		10 26	10 45	10 48	10 56
Birmingham New Street	d	08 03		08 19	08 30	08 20	08 31	08 57	09 03	09 19	09 30	09 20	09 31	09 49	09 57	10 03	10 19	10 30	10 20	10 31	10 49	10 57	11 03
Tamworth	d	08 19		08 36						09 36				10 07		10 19	10 36				11 09		
Burton-on-Trent	d	08 29		08 48					09 26	09 48				10 19			10 48				11 21		11 26
Derby	a	08 42		08 59	09 05				09 39	09 59	10 05			10 34		10 40	10 59	11 05			11 33		11 39
Nottingham	a			09 33						10 32				11 05			11 32				12 05		
Chesterfield	a	09 02							10 02							11 02							12 03
Sheffield	a	09 17			09 43				10 17		10 41					11 17		11 43					12 17
Doncaster	a				10 18						11 18							12 18					
Wakefield Westgate	a	09 46							10 46							11 46							12 46
Leeds	a	10 02							11 02							12 01							13 03
York	a	10 26			10 45				11 26		11 46					12 26		12 46					13 26
Darlington	a	11 00			11 13				11 57		12 13					12 58		13 13					13 59
Durham	a	11 19			11 30				12 21		12 30					13 15		13 30					14 17
Chester-le-Street	a																						
Newcastle	a	11 34			11 45				12 34		12 44					13 29		13 45					14 30
Morpeth	a																						14 49
Alnmouth for Alnwick	a															14 01							
Berwick-upon-Tweed	a	12 21														14 22							
Dunbar	a								13 39														15 40
Wolverhampton	d					08 37	08 49	09 15				09 37	09 49		10 15				10 37	10 49		11 15	
Stafford	a						09 00	09 29					10 00		10 29					11 00		11 28	
Stoke-on-Trent	a						09 19	09 54					10 19		10 54					11 19		11 54	
Congleton	a																						
Macclesfield	a							10 11							11 11							12 11	
Crewe	a					09 07						10 07							11 07				
Wilmslow	a																						
Stockport	a						09 49	10 27					10 49		11 27					11 49		12 27	
M'chester Piccadilly	a						09 59	10 39					10 59		11 39					11 59		12 39	
Warrington Bank Quay	a					09 26						10 26							11 26				
Wigan North Western	a					09 37						10 37							11 37				
Preston	a					09 51						10 51							11 51				
Lancaster	a					10 08						11 08							12 08				
Oxenholme Lake District	a					10 22													12 22				
Penrith North Lakes	a											11 44											
Carlisle	a					11 02						12 00							13 01				
Lockerbie	a																						
Haymarket	a					12 14													14 15				
Edinburgh	a	13 06				12 21			14 10							15 06			14 21				16 05
Haymarket	a	13 15														15 14							
Motherwell	a	13 52														15 52							
Glasgow Central	a	14 12										13 17				16 23							
Inverkeithing	a																						
Kirkcaldy	a																						
Markinch	a																						
Ladybank	a																						
Cupar	a																						
Leuchars	a																						
Dundee	a																						
Arbroath	a																						
Montrose	a																						
Stonehaven	a																						
Aberdeen	a																						

A ✠ from Reading
B ✠ from Bristol Temple Meads
C ✠ from Newport (South Wales)
D ✠ to Edinburgh
E until 29 June, from 17 September

South Coast and the South West - North West England, The North East and Scotland

Route Diagram - see first Page of Table 51

		XC	XC	VT	XC	XC	XC	XC	XC	VT	XC	XC	XC	XC	XC	XC	VT	XC	XC	XC	XC	XC
		◇1	◇1	◇1	◇1	◇1	◇1	◇1	◇1	◇1	◇1	◇1	◇1	◇1	1	◇1	◇1	◇1	◇1	◇1	1	◇1
				A			B					C		D						B		
			✠	⊡	✠	✠	✠	✠	✠	⊡	✠	✠	✠	✠		✠	⊡	✠	✠	✠		✠
Bournemouth	d					08 45							09 45						10 45			
Brockenhurst	d					09 00							10 00						11 00			
Southampton Central	d					09 15			09 46				10 15						11 15			11 46
Southampton Airport Pkway	d					09 22			09 53				10 22						11 22			11 53
Winchester	d					09 31			10 03				10 31						11 31			12 02
Basingstoke	d					09 47			10 19				10 47						11 47			12 18
Guildford	d																					
Reading	d		09 40			10 11			10 41				11 11			11 40			12 11			12 41
Oxford	d		10 07			10 36			11 07				11 36			12 07			12 36			13 07
Banbury	d		10 25			10 54			11 25				11 54			12 25			12 54			13 25
Leamington Spa	d		10 42			11 12			11 43				12 12			12 43			13 12			13 43
Coventry	d					11 27							12 27						13 27			
Birmingham International	d					11 38							12 38						13 38			
Penzance	d						06 28													08 28		
St Erth	d						06 36													08 36		
Hayle	d																					
Camborne	d						06 46													08 46		
Redruth	d						06 52													08 52		
Truro	d						07 04													09 04		
St Austell	d						07 20													09 20		
Newquay (Summer Only)	d																					
Par	d						07 28													09 28		
Lostwithiel	d																					
Bodmin Parkway	d						07 39													09 39		
Liskeard	d						07 53													09 51		
Plymouth	d						08 25							09 25						10 25		
Totnes	d						08 50							09 50						10 50		
Paignton	d																	10 07				
Torquay	d																	10 13				
Newton Abbot	d						09 03							10 03				10 24		11 03		
Teignmouth	d																	10 31				
Dawlish	d																	10 36				
Exeter St Davids	d						09 23							10 23				10 50		11 23		
Tiverton Parkway	d						09 37							10 37				11 03		11 37		
Taunton	d						09 51							10 51				11 18		11 51		
Weston-super-Mare	d																					
Cardiff Central	d											10 45										
Newport (South Wales)	d											11 00										
Bristol Temple Meads	d				10 00		10 30				11 00			11 30				12 00		12 30		
Bristol Parkway	d				10 10		10 40				11 10			11 40				12 10		12 40		
Gloucester	d											11 46										
Cheltenham Spa	d				10 42		11 12				11 42	11 57		12 12				12 42		13 12		
London Paddington	d																					
Birmingham New Street	a		11 18		11 26	11 48	11 58		12 18		12 26	12 45	12 48	12 56		13 18		13 26	13 48	13 56		14 18
Birmingham New Street	d	11 19	11 30	11 20	11 31	11 57	12 03	12 19	12 30	12 20	12 31	12 49	12 57	13 03	13 19	13 30	13 20	13 31	13 57	14 03	14 19	14 30
Tamworth	d	11 36					12 19	12 37				13 09			13 36					14 19	14 36	
Burton-on-Trent	d	11 48						12 50				13 20		13 28	13 48						14 48	
Derby	a	11 59	12 05				12 41	13 05	13 08			13 34		13 40	13 59	14 05				14 40	15 00	15 06
Nottingham	a	12 32						13 33				14 05			14 32						15 32	
Chesterfield	a						13 02							14 02						15 02		
Sheffield	a		12 41				13 17		13 41					14 17		14 41				15 17		15 41
Doncaster	a		13 18						14 18							15 18						16 18
Wakefield Westgate	a						13 46							14 46						15 46		
Leeds	a						14 02							15 01						16 02		
York	a		13 40				14 26		14 44					15 26		15 45				16 28		16 45
Darlington	a		14 12				14 58		15 13					15 58		16 13				16 58		17 13
Durham	a		14 29				15 15		15 30					16 16		16 30				17 15		17 30
Chester-le-Street	a																					
Newcastle	a		14 42				15 30		15 45					16 30		16 45				17 31		17 45
Morpeth	a																					
Alnmouth for Alnwick	a						16 00							17 00						18 01		
Berwick-upon-Tweed	a						16 21													18 22		
Dunbar	a													17 42								
Wolverhampton	d			11 37	11 49	12 15				12 37	12 49		13 15				13 37	13 49	14 15			
Stafford	a				12 00	12 29					13 00		13 29					14 00	14 29			
Stoke-on-Trent	a				12 19	12 54					13 19		13 54					14 19	14 54			
Congleton	a																					
Macclesfield	a					13 11							14 11						15 11			
Crewe	a			12 07						13 07							14 07					
Wilmslow	a																					
Stockport	a				12 49	13 27					13 49		14 27					14 49	15 27			
M'chester Piccadilly	a				12 59	13 39					13 59		14 39					14 59	15 39			
Warrington Bank Quay	a			12 26						13 26							14 26					
Wigan North Western	a			12 37						13 37							14 37					
Preston	a			12 51						13 51							14 51					
Lancaster	a			13 08						14 08							15 08					
Oxenholme Lake District	a			13 22													15 22					
Penrith North Lakes	a									14 44												
Carlisle	a			14 01						15 00							16 01					
Lockerbie	a																					
Haymarket	a									16 17												
Edinburgh	a						17 06			16 21				18 07						19 06		
Haymarket	a						17 14							18 14						19 14		
Motherwell	a						17 52													19 54		
Glasgow Central	a			15 17			18 16										17 14			20 15		
Inverkeithing	a													18 28								
Kirkcaldy	a													18 46								
Markinch	a													18 56								
Ladybank	a													19 03								
Cupar	a													19 15								
Leuchars	a													19 22								
Dundee	a													19 35								
Arbroath	a													19 51								
Montrose	a													20 05								
Stonehaven	a													20 26								
Aberdeen	a													20 45								

A from 2 July
B ✠ from Plymouth to Edinburgh
C ✠ from Newport (South Wales)
D ✠ to Edinburgh

South Coast and the South West - North West England, The North East and Scotland

Route Diagram - see first Page of Table 51

		VT	XC	XC	XC	XC	XC	VT	XC	XC	XC	XC	XC	VT	XC	XC	XC	XC MX	XC MO	XC	XC	VT	XC
		◇■ 🍴	◇■ ⊼	◇■ ⊼	◇■ A ⊼	■	◇■ ⊼	◇■ B 🍴	◇■ C ⊼	◇■ D ⊼	◇■ ⊼	◇■ A ⊼	■	■ E 🍴	◇■ F ⊼	◇■ ⊼	◇■ ⊼	◇■ G ⊼	◇■ G ⊼	■	◇■ ⊼	■ 🍴	◇■ ⊼
Bournemouth	d			11 45							12 45						13 45						
Brockenhurst	d			12 00							13 00						14 00						
Southampton Central	d			12 15							13 15				13 46		14 15						
Southampton Airport Pkway	d			12 22							13 22				13 53		14 22						
Winchester	d			12 31							13 31				14 03		14 31						
Basingstoke	d			12 47							13 47				14 19		14 47						
Guildford	d																						
Reading	d			13 11			13 40				14 11				14 41		15 11				15 40		
Oxford	d			13 36			14 07				14 36				15 07		15 36				16 07		
Banbury	d			13 54			14 26				14 54				15 25		15 54				16 26		
Leamington Spa	d			14 12			14 42				15 12				15 43		16 12				16 44		
Coventry	d			14 27							15 27						16 27						
Birmingham International	d			14 38							15 38						16 38						
Penzance	d								09 40														
St Erth	d								09 48														
Hayle	d								09 52														
Camborne	d								10 01														
Redruth	d								10 08														
Truro	d								10 19														
St Austell	d								10 35														
Newquay (Summer Only)	d																						
Par	d								10 43														
Lostwithiel	d								10 50														
Bodmin Parkway	d								10 57														
Liskeard	d								11 09														
Plymouth	d				11 25				11 50			12 23						13 23	13 23				
Totnes	d				11 50				12 15			12 49						13 49	13 49				
Paignton	d																						14 01
Torquay	d																						14 07
Newton Abbot	d				12 03				12 28			13 03						14 03	14 03				14 18
Teignmouth	d																						14 25
Dawlish	d																						14 30
Exeter St Davids	d				12 23				12 48			13 25						14 25	14 25				14 44
Tiverton Parkway	d				12 37				13 02			13 39						14 39	14 39				14 57
Taunton	d				12 51				13 16			13 54						14 54	14 54				15 12
Weston-super-Mare	d																						15 38
Cardiff Central	d									13 45													
Newport (South Wales)	d									14 00													
Bristol Temple Meads	d		13 00		13 30				14 00			14 30				15 00		15 30	15 30				16 00
Bristol Parkway	d		13 10		13 40				14 10			14 40				15 10		15 40	15 40				16 10
Gloucester	d									14 46													
Cheltenham Spa	d		13 42		14 12				14 42	14 57		15 12				15 42		16 11	16 12				16 42
London Paddington	d																						
Birmingham New Street	a		14 26	14 48	14 56		15 18		15 26	15 45	15 48	15 56			16 18	16 26	16 48	16 56	16 56		17 18		17 26
Birmingham New Street	d	14 20	14 31	14 57	15 03	15 19	15 30	15 20	15 31	15 49	15 57	16 03	16 19	16 20	16 30	16 31	16 57	17 03	17 03	17 19	17 30	17 20	17 31
Tamworth	d					15 36				16 09		16 19	16 39							17 36			
Burton-on-Trent	d				15 26	15 48				16 21			16 51					17 26	17 26	17 48			
Derby	a				15 39	16 00	16 06			16 34		16 40	17 05		17 08			17 38	17 38	17 59	18 05		
Nottingham	a					16 32				17 05			17 33							18 32			
Chesterfield	a				16 02							17 03						18 01	18 01				
Sheffield	a				16 17		16 41					17 19			17 44			18 18	18 18		18 44		
Doncaster	a						17 18														19 14		
Wakefield Westgate	a				16 49							17 47			18 13			18 47	18 47				
Leeds	a				17 04							18 03			18 31			19 03	19 03				
York	a				17 28		17 40					18 29			19 01			19 29	19 29		19 38		
Darlington	a				17 58		18 13					19 01			19 29			20 02	20 02		20 10		
Durham	a				18 15		18 31					19 19			19 47			20 20	20 20		20 27		
Chester-le-Street	a																						
Newcastle	a				18 33		18 46					19 35			20 03			20 34	20 34		20 42		
Morpeth	a																	20 54	20 54				
Alnmouth for Alnwick	a											20 04			20 34								
Berwick-upon-Tweed	a				19 21							20 26						21 25	21 25				
Dunbar	a				19 44													21 50	21 50				
Wolverhampton	d	14 37	14 49	15 15				15 37	15 50		16 15			16 37		16 49	17 15					17 37	17 50
Stafford	a		15 00	15 29					16 01		16 30					17 00	17 29						18 01
Stoke-on-Trent	a		15 19	15 54					16 20		16 54					17 19	17 54						18 20
Congleton	a																						
Macclesfield	a			16 11							17 11						18 11						
Crewe	a	15 07						16 07						17 07								18 07	
Wilmslow	a																						
Stockport	a		15 49	16 27					16 49		17 27					17 49	18 27						18 49
M'chester Piccadilly	a		15 59	16 39					16 59		17 39					17 59	18 39						18 59
Warrington Bank Quay	a	15 26						16 26						17 26								18 26	
Wigan North Western	a	15 37						16 37						17 37								18 37	
Preston	a	15 51						16 51						17 51								18 51	
Lancaster	a	16 08						17 08						18 08								19 08	
Oxenholme Lake District	a							17 22						18 22								19 22	
Penrith North Lakes	a	16 44						17 48						18 48									
Carlisle	a	17 00						18 05						19 04								20 01	
Lockerbie	a																						
Haymarket	a	18 12												20 16									
Edinburgh	a	18 22			20 09							21 11		20 22	21 35			22 16	22 16				
Haymarket	a				20 16							21 17											
Motherwell	a											22 01											
Glasgow Central	a							19 19				22 27										21 17	
Inverkeithing	a				20 30																		
Kirkcaldy	a																						
Markinch	a				21 01																		
Ladybank	a				21 09																		
Cupar	a				21 17																		
Leuchars	a				21 25																		
Dundee	a				21 41																		
Arbroath	a																						
Montrose	a																						
Stonehaven	a																						
Aberdeen	a																						

A ⊼ to Edinburgh
B until 29 June, from 17 September
C ⊼ from Plymouth
D ⊼ from Newport (South Wales)
E from 2 July
F ⊼ from Reading
G ⊼ to Newcastle

South Coast and the South West - North West England, The North East and Scotland

Route Diagram - see first Page of Table 51

		XC	XC	XC	XC	XC	VT	XC	XC	XC	XC	XC	XC	VT	XC	XC	XC	XC	XC	XC	XC	VT
		■	◇■ ⊼	◇■ A ⊼	■	◇■ B ⊼	◇■ 🍴	◇■ ⊼	◇■	◇■ ⊼	◇■ ⊼	■	◇■ C ⊼	◇■ 🍴	◇■ ⊼	◇■ D ⊼	◇■ D ⊼	◇■ D ⊼	◇■ D ⊼	◇■ D ⊼	◇■ D ⊼	◇■ 🍴
Bournemouth	d		14 45							15 45						16 45				17 45		
Brockenhurst	d		15 00							16 00						17 00				18 00		
Southampton Central	d		15 15			15 47				16 15						17 15		17 46		18 15		
Southampton Airport Pkway	d		15 22							16 22						17 22		17 53		18 22		
Winchester	d		15 31							16 31						17 31		18 02		18 31		
Basingstoke	d		15 47			16 18				16 47						17 47		18 18		18 47		
Guildford	d																					
Reading	d		16 11			16 40				17 11			17 41			18 11		18 41		19 11		
Oxford	d		16 36			17 07				17 36			18 07			18 36		19 12		19 36		
Banbury	d		16 54			17 28				17 54			18 26			18 54		19 31		19 54		
Leamington Spa	d		17 12			17 48				18 12			18 46			19 12		19 50		20 12		
Coventry	d		17 27							18 27						19 27				20 27		
Birmingham International	d		17 38							18 38						19 38				20 38		
Penzance	d																					
St Erth	d																					
Hayle	d																					
Camborne	d																					
Redruth	d																					
Truro	d																					
St Austell	d																					
Newquay (Summer Only)	d																					
Par	d																					
Lostwithiel	d																					
Bodmin Parkway	d																					
Liskeard	d																					
Plymouth	d			14 25							15 23						16 25				17 23	
Totnes	d			14 50							15 49						16 50				17 49	
Paignton	d																					
Torquay	d																					
Newton Abbot	d			15 03							16 03						17 03				18 03	
Teignmouth	d																					
Dawlish	d																					
Exeter St Davids	d			15 23							16 25				16 54		17 23				18 25	
Tiverton Parkway	d			15 37							16 39				17 08		17 37				18 39	
Taunton	d			15 51							16 54				17 22		17 51				18 54	
Weston-super-Mare	d																					
Cardiff Central	d								16 45													
Newport (South Wales)	d								17 00													
Bristol Temple Meads	d			16 30				17 00			17 30				18 00		18 30		19 00		19 30	
Bristol Parkway	d			16 40				17 10			17 40				18 10		18 40		19 10		19 40	
Gloucester	d								17 46													
Cheltenham Spa	d			17 12				17 42	17 58		18 12				18 42		19 12		19 42		20 12	
London Paddington	d																					
Birmingham New Street	a		17 48	17 56		18 18		18 26	18 45	18 48	18 55		19 18		19 26	19 48	19 56	20 18	20 28	20 48	20 52	
Birmingham New Street	d	17 39	17 57	18 03	18 19	18 30	18 20	18 31	18 49	18 57	19 03	19 19	19 30	19 20	19 31	19 57	20 03	20 30	20 31	20 57	21 03	21 20
Tamworth	d	18 02		18 19	18 36				19 09			19 36					20 19				21 19	
Burton-on-Trent	d	18 13			18 48				19 22		19 26	19 48									21 30	
Derby	a	18 31		18 40	18 59	19 05			19 34		19 39	19 59	20 05				20 42	21 11			21 43	
Nottingham	a				19 32				20 03			20 32										
Chesterfield	a			19 00		19 29					20 01						21 02	21 33			22 06	
Sheffield	a			19 19		19 47					20 18		20 48				21 18	21 51			22 24	
Doncaster	a					20 15							21 19					22 29				
Wakefield Westgate	a			19 50							20 46						21 46				22 59	
Leeds	a			20 05							21 05						22 02				23 15	
York	a			20 29		20 46							21 45					22 53				
Darlington	a			20 58		21 14							22 15									
Durham	a			21 17		21 31							22 33									
Chester-le-Street	a																					
Newcastle	a			21 31		21 44							22 50									
Morpeth	a																					
Alnmouth for Alnwick	a			21 59																		
Berwick-upon-Tweed	a																					
Dunbar	a																					
Wolverhampton	d		18 15				18 37	18 49		19 15				19 37	19 49	20 16			20 49	21 16		21 41
Stafford	a		18 29					19 00		19 27					20 00	20 29				21 31		21 53
Stoke-on-Trent	a		18 54					19 19		19 54					20 19	20 54			21 17	21 54		
Congleton	a																					
Macclesfield	a		19 11							20 11						21 11				22 11		
Crewe	a						19 07							20 07								22 17
Wilmslow	a																					
Stockport	a		19 27					19 48		20 27					20 48	21 27			21 46	22 25		
M'chester Piccadilly	a		19 39					19 59		20 39					20 58	21 39			21 59	22 35		
Warrington Bank Quay	a						19 26							20 26								22 36
Wigan North Western	a						19 37							20 37								22 46
Preston	a						19 51							20 51								23 01
Lancaster	a						20 08							21 08								
Oxenholme Lake District	a													21 22								
Penrith North Lakes	a						20 44															
Carlisle	a						21 00							22 01								
Lockerbie	a																					
Haymarket	a						22 14															
Edinburgh	a			23 04			22 22															
Haymarket	a																					
Motherwell	a																					
Glasgow Central	a													23 18								
Inverkeithing	a																					
Kirkcaldy	a																					
Markinch	a																					
Ladybank	a																					
Cupar	a																					
Leuchars	a																					
Dundee	a																					
Arbroath	a																					
Montrose	a																					
Stonehaven	a																					
Aberdeen	a																					

A ⊼ to Leeds
B ⊼ to Doncaster
C ⊼ to Sheffield
D ⊼ to Birmingham New Street

Table 51

South Coast and the South West - North West England, The North East and Scotland

Mondays to Fridays

Route Diagram - see first Page of Table 51

Station		XC ◇1	XC ◇1	XC ◇1 A ⊼	XC bus	XC 1	XC ◇1 B ⊼	XC ◇1	XC ◇1 C FX	XC ◇1 D	XC ◇1 E FO	XC ◇1 F	XC ◇1 G	XC 1	XC ◇1	XC ◇1	XC bus	XC ◇1 G	XC ◇1 F	XC ◇1
Bournemouth	d			18 45								19 45	19 45							
Brockenhurst 3	d			19 00								20 00	20 00							
Southampton Central	d			19 15								20 15	20 15							
Southampton Airport Pkway	d			19 22								20 22	20 22							
Winchester	d			19 31								20 31	20 31							
Basingstoke	d			19 47								20 47	20 47							
Guildford	d																			
Reading 7	d	19 40		20 11				20 40				21 11	21 11					21 46	21 46	
Oxford	d	20 07		20 36				21 08				21 36	21 36					22 30	22 30	
Banbury	d	20 28		20 54				21 33				21 54	21 54					22 54	22 54	
Leamington Spa 8	d	20 46		21 12	22 20			21 52				22 12	22 12				23 20	23 13	23 13	
Coventry	d			21 27	22 40							22 24					23 40		23 27	
Birmingham International	d			21 38								22 34					00 10		23 37	
Penzance	d																			
St Erth	d																			
Hayle	d																			
Camborne	d																			
Redruth	d																			
Truro	d																			
St Austell	d																			
Newquay (Summer Only)	d																			
Par	d																			
Lostwithiel	d																			
Bodmin Parkway	d																			
Liskeard 6	d																			
Plymouth	d						18 25													
Totnes	d						18 50													
Paignton	d																			
Torquay	d															20 14				
Newton Abbot	d						19 03									20 20				
Teignmouth	d															20 31				
Dawlish	d																			
Exeter St Davids 6	d						19 23													
Tiverton Parkway	d						19 37									20 52				
Taunton	d						19 51									21 04				
Weston-super-Mare	d															21 19				
Cardiff Central 7	d														21 05					21 50
Newport (South Wales)	d														21 21					22 05
Bristol Temple Meads 10	d		20 00				20 30									22 00				
Bristol Parkway 7	d		20 10				20 40									22 10				
Gloucester 7	d		20 46												22 04					22 47
Cheltenham Spa	d		20 56				21 17								22 15	22 42				22 58
London Paddington	d																			
Birmingham New Street 12	a	21 22	21 46	21 48			22 06	22 17				22 45	22 45		23 36	23 44		23 49	23 57	00 01
Birmingham New Street 12	d			21 57		22 03			22 30	22 30	22 30			23 09						
Tamworth	d					22 28								23 28						
Burton-on-Trent	d					22 40								23 40						
Derby 6	a					22 54								23 55						
Nottingham 8	a					23 27								00 18						
Chesterfield	a																			
Sheffield 7	a																			
Doncaster 7	a																			
Wakefield Westgate 7	a																			
Leeds 10	a																			
York 8	a																			
Darlington 7	a																			
Durham	a																			
Chester-le-Street	a																			
Newcastle 8	a																			
Morpeth	a																			
Alnmouth for Alnwick	a																			
Berwick-upon-Tweed	a																			
Dunbar	a																			
Wolverhampton 7	d			22 16					22 48	22 48	22 48									
Stafford	a			22 29					23 00	23 00	23 00									
Stoke-on-Trent	a			22 53					23 21	23 20	23 21									
Congleton	a																			
Macclesfield	a			23 11																
Crewe 10	a																			
Wilmslow	a																			
Stockport	a			23 25																
M'chester Piccadilly 10	a			23 37					00 12	00 12	00 13									
Warrington Bank Quay	a																			
Wigan North Western	a																			
Preston 8	a																			
Lancaster 6	a																			
Oxenholme Lake District	a																			
Penrith North Lakes	a																			
Carlisle 8	a																			
Lockerbie	a																			
Haymarket	a																			
Edinburgh 10	a																			
Haymarket	a																			
Motherwell	a																			
Glasgow Central 15	a																			
Inverkeithing	a																			
Kirkcaldy	a																			
Markinch	a																			
Ladybank	a																			
Cupar	a																			
Leuchars 3	a																			
Dundee	a																			
Arbroath	a																			
Montrose	a																			
Stonehaven	a																			
Aberdeen	a																			

A ⊼ to Reading
B ⊼ to Bristol Temple Meads
C until 21 June
D from 25 June
E until 22 June
F until 22 June, from 17 September
G from 25 June until 14 September

Table 51

South Coast and the South West - North West England, The North East and Scotland

Saturdays until 30 June

Route Diagram - see first Page of Table 51

Station		XC ◇1 A	XC ◇1 B	XC 1	XC ◇1	XC ◇1	XC ◇1 C ⊼	XC 1 ⊼	VT ◇1 ⊡	XC ◇1 ⊼	XC ◇1 ⊼	XC 1	XC ◇1 ⊼	XC ◇1 ⊼	XC 1 ⊼	VT ◇1 ⊡	XC ◇1 ⊼	XC ◇1 ⊼	XC ◇1 D ⊼	XC 1	XC ◇1 ⊼	XC ◇1	XC 1 ⊼
Bournemouth	d																						
Brockenhurst 3	d																						
Southampton Central	d																		05 09				
Southampton Airport Pkway	d																		05 16				
Winchester	d																		05 25				
Basingstoke	d																		05 41				
Guildford	d																						
Reading 7	d																		06 11				
Oxford	d																		06 38				
Banbury	d																		06 56				
Leamington Spa 8	d																		07 14				
Coventry	d																		07 27				
Birmingham International	d																		07 38				
Penzance	d																						
St Erth	d																						
Hayle	d																						
Camborne	d																						
Redruth	d																						
Truro	d																						
St Austell	d																						
Newquay (Summer Only)	d																						
Par	d																						
Lostwithiel	d																						
Bodmin Parkway	d																						
Liskeard 6	d																						
Plymouth	d																						
Totnes	d																						
Paignton	d																						
Torquay	d																						
Newton Abbot	d																						
Teignmouth	d																						
Dawlish	d																						
Exeter St Davids 6	d																						
Tiverton Parkway	d																						
Taunton	d																						
Weston-super-Mare	d																						
Cardiff Central 7	d				21p50																		
Newport (South Wales)	d				22p05																		
Bristol Temple Meads 10	d																				06 15		
Bristol Parkway 7	d																				06 25		
Gloucester 7	d				22p47																07 01	07 07	
Cheltenham Spa	d				22p58																07 12	07 18	
London Paddington	d																						
Birmingham New Street 12	a				00 01														07 48		07 56	08 08	
Birmingham New Street 12	d	22p30	22p30	23p09		05 57	05 57	06 19	06 20	06 30	06 31	06 49	06 57	07 03	07 19	07 20	07 30	07 31	07 57	07 49	08 03		08 19
Tamworth	d			23p28			06 13	06 39		06 46		07 07		07 19	07 38		07 46			08 07	08 19		08 36
Burton-on-Trent	d			23p40			06 24	06 51		06 56		07 19		07 29	07 50		07 56			08 17	08 29		08 48
Derby 6	a			23p55			06 35	07 05		07 09		07 34		07 42	08 05		08 09			08 34	08 42		08 59
Nottingham 8	a			00 18				07 38				08 08			08 34					09 05			09 33
Chesterfield	a						06 55			07 29				08 02			08 29				09 02		
Sheffield 7	a						07 09			07 48				08 17			08 45				09 17		
Doncaster 7	a									08 23							09 18						
Wakefield Westgate 7	a						07 36							08 45							09 46		
Leeds 10	a						07 52							09 03							10 02		
York 8	a						08 23			08 48				09 27			09 44				10 26		
Darlington 7	a						08 56			09 16				09 58			10 15				10 58		
Durham	a						09 13			09 34				10 15			10 32				11 15		
Chester-le-Street	a																						
Newcastle 8	a						09 26			09 47				10 31			10 45				11 29		
Morpeth	a																						
Alnmouth for Alnwick	a						09 58																
Berwick-upon-Tweed	a						10 19														12 19		
Dunbar	a													11 37									
Wolverhampton 7	d	22p48	22p48			06 16			06 37		06 49		07 15			07 37		07 49	08 15				
Stafford	a	23p00	23p00			06 29					07 00		07 29					08 00	08 29				
Stoke-on-Trent	a	23p20	23p21			06 50					07 18							08 19	08 54				
Congleton	a					07 02																	
Macclesfield	a					07 11					07 36							08 36	09 11				
Crewe 10	a								07 07				07 50			08 07							
Wilmslow	a												08 09										
Stockport	a					07 27					07 49		08 20					08 49	09 27				
M'chester Piccadilly 10	a	00 12	00 13			07 38					07 59		08 35					08 59	09 39				
Warrington Bank Quay	a								07 26							08 27							
Wigan North Western	a								07 37							08 38							
Preston 8	a								07 51							08 51							
Lancaster 6	a								08 08							09 08							
Oxenholme Lake District	a								08 21														
Penrith North Lakes	a															09 44							
Carlisle 8	a								09 00							10 02							
Lockerbie	a																						
Haymarket	a								10 16														
Edinburgh 10	a						11 05		10 22					12 07							13 04		
Haymarket	a						11 15														13 15		
Motherwell	a						11 52														13 52		
Glasgow Central 15	a						12 13									11 17					14 13		
Inverkeithing	a																						
Kirkcaldy	a																						
Markinch	a																						
Ladybank	a																						
Cupar	a																						
Leuchars 3	a																						
Dundee	a																						
Arbroath	a																						
Montrose	a																						
Stonehaven	a																						
Aberdeen	a																						

A 30 June
B not 30 June
C ⊼ to Edinburgh
D ⊼ from Reading

Saturdays
until 30 June

South Coast and the South West - North West England, The North East and Scotland

Route Diagram - see first Page of Table 51

		XC	VT	XC	XC	XC	XC	XC	VT	XC	XC	XC	XC	XC	XC	VT	XC	XC	XC	XC	XC	XC	VT
		◇1	◇1	◇1	◇1	◇1	1	◇1	◇1	◇1	◇1	◇1	◇1	1	◇1	◇1	◇1	◇1	◇1	◇1	1	◇1	◇1
		A		B						B	C		D				B	C					
		✕	⊡	⊡✕	✕	✕	✕	✕	⊡	⊡✕	✕	✕	✕		✕	⊡	⊡✕	✕	✕	✕		✕	⊡
Bournemouth	d							06 25				06 37							07 45				
Brockenhurst	d							06 39				06 55							08 00				
Southampton Central	d				06 15			06 53				07 15			07 47				08 15				
Southampton Airport Pkway	d				06 22			07 01				07 22			07 54				08 22				
Winchester	d				06 31			07 09				07 31			08 03				08 31				
Basingstoke	d				06 47			07 25				07 47			08 19				08 47				
Guildford	d	06 09																					
Reading	d	06 46			07 11			07 47				08 11			08 40				09 11			09 40	
Oxford	d	07 12			07 36			08 15				08 36			09 07				09 36			10 07	
Banbury	d	07 33			07 54			08 33				08 54			09 24				09 54			10 24	
Leamington Spa	d	07 51			08 12			08 50				09 12			09 42				10 13			10 42	
Coventry	d				08 27							09 27							10 27				
Birmingham International	d				08 38							09 38							10 38				
Penzance	d																						
St Erth	d																						
Hayle	d																						
Camborne	d																						
Redruth	d																						
Truro	d																						
St Austell	d																						
Newquay (Summer Only)	d																						
Par	d																						
Lostwithiel	d																						
Bodmin Parkway	d																						
Liskeard	d																						
Plymouth	d					05 25							06 25							07 25			
Totnes	d					05 50							06 50							07 50			
Paignton	d																07 02						
Torquay	d																07 08						
Newton Abbot	d					06 03							07 03				07 19			08 03			
Teignmouth	d																07 26						
Dawlish	d																07 31						
Exeter St Davids	d					06 23							07 23				07 45			08 23			
Tiverton Parkway	d					06 37							07 37				07 58			08 37			
Taunton	d					06 51							07 51				08 13			08 51			
Weston-super-Mare	d																						
Cardiff Central	d									07 00	07 45							08 45					
Newport (South Wales)	d									07 15	08 00							09 00					
Bristol Temple Meads	d			07 00		07 30				08 00			08 30				09 00			09 30			
Bristol Parkway	d			07 10		07 40				08 10			08 40				09 10			09 40			
Gloucester	d										08 47							09 46					
Cheltenham Spa	d			07 42		08 12				08 42	08 58		09 12				09 42	09 57		10 12			
London Paddington	d																						
Birmingham New Street	a	08 17		08 26	08 48	08 56		09 18		09 26	09 45	09 48	09 56		10 18		10 26	10 45	10 48	10 56		11 18	
Birmingham New Street	d	08 30	08 20	08 31	08 57	09 03	09 19	09 30	09 20	09 31	09 49	09 57	10 03	10 19	10 30	10 20	10 31	10 49	10 57	11 03	11 19	11 30	11 20
Tamworth	d						09 36				10 07		10 19	10 36				11 09			11 36		
Burton-on-Trent	d					09 28	09 48				10 19			10 48				11 21		11 28	11 48		
Derby	a	09 06				09 41	09 59	10 05			10 34		10 41	10 59	11 05			11 34		11 41	11 59	12 05	
Nottingham	a						10 33				11 05			11 33				12 05			12 33		
Chesterfield	a					10 02							11 02							12 02			
Sheffield	a	09 44				10 17		10 42					11 17		11 41					12 16		12 41	
Doncaster	a	10 17						11 15							12 15							13 17	
Wakefield Westgate	a					10 46							11 46							12 46			
Leeds	a					11 02							12 02							13 02			
York	a	10 40				11 26		11 40					12 26		12 39					13 26		13 40	
Darlington	a	11 13				11 57		12 13					12 58		13 13					13 57		14 12	
Durham	a	11 30				12 15		12 30					13 15		13 30					14 14		14 29	
Chester-le-Street	a																						
Newcastle	a	11 46				12 31		12 45					13 29		13 44					14 28		14 42	
Morpeth	a																			14 47			
Alnmouth for Alnwick	a												13 59										
Berwick-upon-Tweed	a												14 19										
Dunbar	a					13 37														15 39			
Wolverhampton	d		08 37	08 49	09 15				09 37	09 49		10 15				10 37	10 49		11 15				11 37
Stafford	a			09 00	09 29					10 00		10 29					11 00		11 29				
Stoke-on-Trent	a			09 19	09 54					10 19		10 54					11 19		11 54				
Congleton	a																						
Macclesfield	a				10 11							11 11							12 11				
Crewe	a		09 07						10 07							11 07							12 07
Wilmslow	a																						
Stockport	a			09 49	10 27					10 49		11 27					11 49		12 27				
M'chester Piccadilly	a			09 59	10 39					10 59		11 39					11 59		12 39				
Warrington Bank Quay	a		09 26						10 26							11 26							12 26
Wigan North Western	a		09 37						10 37							11 37							12 37
Preston	a		09 51						10 51							11 51							12 51
Lancaster	a		10 08						11 08							12 08							13 08
Oxenholme Lake District	a		10 22													12 22							13 22
Penrith North Lakes	a								11 44														
Carlisle	a		11 01						12 00							13 01							14 01
Lockerbie	a																						
Haymarket	a		12 16													14 15							
Edinburgh	a		12 22			14 07							15 07			14 22				16 04			
Haymarket	a												15 15										
Motherwell	a												15 52										
Glasgow Central	a								13 17				16 23										15 17
Inverkeithing	a																						
Kirkcaldy	a																						
Markinch	a																						
Ladybank	a																						
Cupar	a																						
Leuchars	a																						
Dundee	a																						
Arbroath	a																						
Montrose	a																						
Stonehaven	a																						
Aberdeen	a																						

A ✕ from Reading
B ⊡ from Birmingham New Street ✕ to Birmingham New Street
C ✕ from Newport (South Wales)
D ✕ to Edinburgh

Saturdays
until 30 June

South Coast and the South West - North West England, The North East and Scotland

Route Diagram - see first Page of Table 51

		XC	XC	XC	XC	XC	VT	XC	XC	XC	XC	XC	XC	VT	XC	XC	XC	XC	XC	VT	XC	XC
		◇1	◇1	◇1	1	◇1	◇1	◇1	◇1	◇1	◇1	1	◇1	◇1	◇1	◇1	◇1	1	◇1	◇1	◇1	◇1
		A		B				A	C		D				A		B				A	
		⊡✕	✕	✕	✕	✕	⊡	⊡✕	✕	✕	✕		✕	⊡	⊡✕	✕	✕		✕	⊡	⊡✕	✕
Bournemouth	d		08 45							09 45						10 45						11 45
Brockenhurst	d		09 00							10 00						11 00						12 00
Southampton Central	d		09 15			09 47				10 15						11 15			11 47			12 15
Southampton Airport Pkway	d		09 22			09 54				10 22						11 22			11 54			12 22
Winchester	d		09 31			10 03				10 31						11 31			12 03			12 31
Basingstoke	d		09 47			10 19				10 47						11 47			12 19			12 47
Guildford	d																					
Reading	d		10 11			10 40				11 11			11 40			12 11			12 40			13 11
Oxford	d		10 36			11 07				11 36			12 07			12 36			13 07			13 36
Banbury	d		10 54			11 24				11 54			12 24			12 54			13 24			13 54
Leamington Spa	d		11 12			11 42				12 12			12 42			13 12			13 42			14 12
Coventry	d		11 27							12 27						13 27						14 27
Birmingham International	d		11 38							12 38						13 38						14 38
Penzance	d			06 30													08 28					
St Erth	d			06 38													08 36					
Hayle	d			06 41																		
Camborne	d			06 51													08 46					
Redruth	d			06 57													08 52					
Truro	d			07 09													09 04					
St Austell	d			07 25													09 20					
Newquay (Summer Only)	d																					
Par	d			07 32													09 28					
Lostwithiel	d			07 39																		
Bodmin Parkway	d			07 46													09 39					
Liskeard	d			07 58													09 51					
Plymouth	d			08 25				08 38			09 18						10 25					
Totnes	d			08 50				09 03			09 43						10 50					
Paignton	d														10 07							
Torquay	d														10 13							
Newton Abbot	d			09 03				09 16			09 56				10 24		11 03					
Teignmouth	d										10 03				10 31							
Dawlish	d										10 09				10 36							
Exeter St Davids	d			09 23				09 41			10 26				10 50		11 23					
Tiverton Parkway	d			09 37				09 54			10 40				11 03		11 37					
Taunton	d			09 51				10 09			10 54				11 18		11 51					
Weston-super-Mare	d							10 33														
Cardiff Central	d								10 45													
Newport (South Wales)	d								11 00													
Bristol Temple Meads	d	10 00		10 30				11 00			11 30				12 00		12 30				13 00	
Bristol Parkway	d	10 10		10 40				11 10			11 40				12 10		12 40				13 10	
Gloucester	d								11 46													
Cheltenham Spa	d	10 42		11 12				11 42	11 57		12 12				12 42		13 12				13 42	
London Paddington	d																					
Birmingham New Street	a	11 26	11 48	11 56		12 18		12 26	12 45	12 48	12 56		13 18		13 26	13 48	13 56		14 18		14 26	14 48
Birmingham New Street	d	11 31	11 57	12 03	12 19	12 30	12 20	12 31	12 49	12 57	13 03	13 19	13 30	13 20	13 31	13 57	14 03	14 19	14 30	14 20	14 31	14 57
Tamworth	d			12 19	12 36				13 09			13 36					14 19	14 36				
Burton-on-Trent	d				12 48				13 21		13 27	13 50						14 47				
Derby	a			12 41	13 05	13 08			13 34		13 41	14 05	14 08				14 41	14 59	15 05			
Nottingham	a				13 33				14 05			14 33						15 33				
Chesterfield	a			13 02							14 02						15 02					
Sheffield	a			13 17		13 41					14 17		14 41				15 17		15 41			
Doncaster	a					14 18							15 17						16 18			
Wakefield Westgate	a			13 46							14 46						15 46					
Leeds	a			14 02							15 02						16 02					
York	a			14 26		14 40					15 28		15 40				16 26		16 41			
Darlington	a			14 58		15 13					15 58		16 13				16 58		17 13			
Durham	a			15 15		15 30					16 15		16 30				17 15		17 30			
Chester-le-Street	a																					
Newcastle	a			15 29		15 45					16 29		16 45				17 29		17 45			
Morpeth	a																					
Alnmouth for Alnwick	a			15 58							16 58						18 00					
Berwick-upon-Tweed	a			16 18													18 20					
Dunbar	a										17 38											
Wolverhampton	d	11 49	12 15				12 37	12 49		13 15				13 37	13 49	14 15				14 37	14 49	15 15
Stafford	a	12 00	12 29					13 00		13 29					14 00	14 29					15 00	15 29
Stoke-on-Trent	a	12 19	12 54					13 18		13 54					14 19	14 54					15 19	15 54
Congleton	a																					
Macclesfield	a		13 11							14 11						15 11						16 11
Crewe	a						13 07							14 07						15 07		
Wilmslow	a																					
Stockport	a	12 49	13 27					13 49		14 27					14 49	15 27					15 49	16 27
M'chester Piccadilly	a	12 59	13 39					13 59		14 39					14 59	15 39					15 59	16 39
Warrington Bank Quay	a						13 27							14 26						15 26		
Wigan North Western	a						13 38							14 37						15 37		
Preston	a						13 51							14 51						15 51		
Lancaster	a						14 08							15 08						16 08		
Oxenholme Lake District	a													15 22								
Penrith North Lakes	a						14 44													16 45		
Carlisle	a						15 00							16 01						17 00		
Lockerbie	a																					
Haymarket	a						16 16													18 14		
Edinburgh	a			17 07			16 22				18 05						19 08			18 22		
Haymarket	a			17 15							18 14						19 15					
Motherwell	a			17 52													19 52					
Glasgow Central	a			18 11										17 17			20 11					
Inverkeithing	a										18 28											
Kirkcaldy	a										18 46											
Markinch	a										18 56											
Ladybank	a										19 03											
Cupar	a										19 10											
Leuchars	a										19 17											
Dundee	a										19 32											
Arbroath	a										19 49											
Montrose	a										20 03											
Stonehaven	a										20 23											
Aberdeen	a										20 43											

A ⊡ from Birmingham New Street ✕ to Birmingham New Street
B ✕ from Plymouth to Edinburgh
C ✕ from Newport (South Wales)
D ✕ to Edinburgh

South Coast and the South West - North West England, The North East and Scotland

Route Diagram - see first Page of Table 51

Station		XC ◇1 A ✕	XC 1	XC ◇1 ✕	VT ◇1 ⊡	XC ◇1 B ⊡✕	XC ◇1 C ✕	XC ◇1 ✕	XC ◇1 D ✕	XC 1	XC ◇1 ✕	VT ◇1 ⊡	XC ◇1 B ⊡✕	XC ◇1 ✕	XC ◇1 ✕	XC 1	XC ◇1 ✕	VT ◇1 ⊡	XC ◇1 ✕	XC ◇1 ✕	XC ◇1 ✕	XC 1	XC ◇1 ✕
Bournemouth	d							12 45						13 45						14 45			
Brockenhurst	d							13 00						14 00						15 00			
Southampton Central	d							13 15			13 47			14 15						15 15			15 47
Southampton Airport Pkway	d							13 22			13 54			14 22						15 22			15 54
Winchester	d							13 31			14 03			14 31						15 31			16 03
Basingstoke	d							13 47			14 19			14 47						15 47			16 19
Guildford	d																						
Reading	d			13 40				14 11			14 40			15 11			15 40			16 11			16 40
Oxford	d			14 07				14 36			15 07			15 36			16 07			16 36			17 07
Banbury	d			14 24				14 54			15 24			15 54			16 24			16 54			17 24
Leamington Spa	d			14 42				15 12			15 42			16 12			16 42			17 12			17 42
Coventry	d							15 27						16 27						17 27			
Birmingham International	d							15 38						16 38						17 38			
Penzance	d																						
St Erth	d																						
Hayle	d																						
Camborne	d																						
Redruth	d																						
Truro	d																						
St Austell	d																						
Newquay (Summer Only)	d	09 27																					
Par	d	10 26																					
Lostwithiel	d																						
Bodmin Parkway	d	10 43																					
Liskeard	d	10 55																					
Plymouth	d	11 25													13 25						14 25		
Totnes	d	11 50													13 50						14 50		
Paignton	d								12 34										13 53				
Torquay	d								12 41										13 59				
Newton Abbot	d	12 03							12 53						14 03				14 10		15 03		
Teignmouth	d								13 02										14 17				
Dawlish	d								13 09										14 22				
Exeter St Davids	d	12 23							13 24						14 23				14 36		15 23		
Tiverton Parkway	d	12 37							13 39						14 37				14 49		15 37		
Taunton	d	12 51							13 53						14 52				15 04		15 51		
Weston-super-Mare	d																		15 30				
Cardiff Central	d						13 45																
Newport (South Wales)	d						14 00																
Bristol Temple Meads	d	13 30				14 00			14 30				15 00		15 30				16 00		16 30		
Bristol Parkway	d	13 40				14 10			14 40				15 10		15 40				16 10		16 40		
Gloucester	d						14 46																
Cheltenham Spa	d	14 12				14 42	14 57		15 12				15 42		16 12				16 42		17 12		
London Paddington	d																						
Birmingham New Street	a	14 56		15 18		15 26	15 45	15 48	15 55		16 18		16 26	16 48	16 56		17 18		17 26	17 48	17 56		18 18
Birmingham New Street	d	15 03	15 19	15 30	15 20	15 31	15 49	15 57	16 03	16 19	16 30	16 20	16 31	16 57	17 03	17 19	17 30	17 20	17 31	17 57	18 03	18 19	18 30
Tamworth	d		15 36				16 09		16 19	16 38						17 36					18 19	18 36	
Burton-on-Trent	d	15 27	15 48				16 21			16 50					17 26	17 48						18 47	
Derby	a	15 38	15 59	16 05			16 34		16 40	17 05	17 08				17 41	17 59	18 05				18 41	18 59	19 05
Nottingham	a		16 33				17 05			17 33						18 32						19 33	
Chesterfield	a	16 02							17 01						18 02						19 02		19 29
Sheffield	a	16 18		16 41					17 19		17 44				18 18		18 42				19 18		19 51
Doncaster	a			17 16													19 16						20 17
Wakefield Westgate	a	16 46							17 47		18 12				18 46						19 49		
Leeds	a	17 02							18 02		18 31				19 01						20 05		
York	a	17 26		17 37					18 28		18 58				19 26		19 39				20 29		20 40
Darlington	a	17 56		18 12					18 59		19 35				19 57		20 11				20 58		21 13
Durham	a	18 13		18 29					19 17		19 52				20 14		20 28				21 15		21 30
Chester-le-Street	a																						
Newcastle	a	18 27		18 44					19 31		20 08				20 28		20 42				21 29		21 44
Morpeth	a														20 50								
Alnmouth for Alnwick	a								20 03												22 01		
Berwick-upon-Tweed	a	19 17							20 24						21 23								
Dunbar	a	19 40													21 47								
Wolverhampton	d				15 37	15 49		16 15				16 37	16 49	17 15				17 37	17 49	18 15			
Stafford	a					16 00		16 29					17 00	17 29					18 00	18 29			
Stoke-on-Trent	a					16 18		16 54					17 19	17 54					18 19	18 54			
Congleton	a																						
Macclesfield	a							17 11						18 11						19 11			
Crewe	a				16 08							17 07						18 07					
Wilmslow	a																						
Stockport	a					16 48		17 27					17 49	18 27					18 49	19 27			
M'chester Piccadilly	a					16 59		17 39					17 59	18 39					18 59	19 39			
Warrington Bank Quay	a				16 26							17 26						18 26					
Wigan North Western	a				16 37							17 37						18 37					
Preston	a				16 51							17 51						18 51					
Lancaster	a				17 09							18 08						19 08					
Oxenholme Lake District	a				17 24							18 22						19 22					
Penrith North Lakes	a											18 48											
Carlisle	a				18 03							19 04						20 01					
Lockerbie	a																						
Haymarket	a											20 16											
Edinburgh	a	20 06							21 09			20 22			22 14						23 10		
Haymarket	a	20 19							21 16														
Motherwell	a								22 00														
Glasgow Central	a				19 17				22 22									21 17					
Inverkeithing	a	20 35																					
Kirkcaldy	a	20 52																					
Markinch	a	21 02																					
Ladybank	a	21 10																					
Cupar	a	21 18																					
Leuchars	a	21 27																					
Dundee	a	21 44																					
Arbroath	a																						
Montrose	a																						
Stonehaven	a																						
Aberdeen	a																						

A ✕ from Plymouth
B ⊡ from Birmingham New Street ✕ to Birmingham New Street
C ✕ from Newport (South Wales)
D ✕ to Edinburgh

South Coast and the South West - North West England, The North East and Scotland

Route Diagram - see first Page of Table 51

Station		VT ◇1 ⊡	XC ◇1 A ⊡✕	XC ◇1	XC ◇1 ✕	XC ◇1 ✕	XC 1	XC ◇1 B ✕	VT ◇1 ⊡	XC ◇1 A ⊡✕	XC ◇1 C ✕	XC ◇1 C ✕	XC ◇1 C ✕	VT ◇1 ⊡	XC ◇1 A ⊡✕	XC ◇1 ✕	XC ◇1 ✕	XC ◇1	XC ◇1	XC ◇1 D ✕	XC ◇1 E ✕	XC ◇1 F ✕
Bournemouth	d				15 45						16 45						17 45					18 45
Brockenhurst	d				16 00						17 00						18 00					19 00
Southampton Central	d				16 15						17 15		17 47				18 15					19 15
Southampton Airport Pkway	d				16 22						17 22		17 54				18 22					19 22
Winchester	d				16 31						17 31		18 03				18 31					19 31
Basingstoke	d				16 47						17 47		18 19				18 47					19 47
Guildford	d																					
Reading	d				17 11			17 40			18 11		18 40				19 11	19 40				20 11
Oxford	d				17 36			18 07			18 36		19 07				19 36	20 07				20 36
Banbury	d				17 54			18 24			18 54		19 24				19 54	20 29				20 54
Leamington Spa	d				18 12			18 42			19 12		19 42				20 12	20 46				21 12
Coventry	d				18 27						19 27						20 27					21 27
Birmingham International	d				18 38						19 38						20 38					21 38
Penzance	d																			16 25	16 25	
St Erth	d																			16 35	16 35	
Hayle	d																					
Camborne	d																			16 46	16 46	
Redruth	d																			16 53	16 53	
Truro	d																			17 06	17 06	
St Austell	d																			17 23	17 23	
Newquay (Summer Only)	d															15 25						
Par	d																					
Lostwithiel	d																					
Bodmin Parkway	d															16 37				17 40	17 40	
Liskeard	d															16 51				17 53	17 53	
Plymouth	d					15 25										17 25				18 23	18 23	
Totnes	d					15 50										17 50				18 49	18 49	
Paignton	d											16 36							18 05			
Torquay	d											16 43							18 12			
Newton Abbot	d					16 03						16 55				18 03			18 23	19 03	19 03	
Teignmouth	d											17 03										
Dawlish	d											17 10										
Exeter St Davids	d					16 23						17 25				18 23			18 50	19 25	19 25	
Tiverton Parkway	d					16 37						17 39				18 37			19 04	19 39	19 39	
Taunton	d					16 51						17 54				18 51			19 18	19 54	19 54	
Weston-super-Mare	d																					
Cardiff Central	d			16 45																		
Newport (South Wales)	d			17 00																		
Bristol Temple Meads	d		17 00			17 30				18 00		18 30			19 00	19 30			20 00	20 30	20 30	
Bristol Parkway	d		17 10			17 40				18 10		18 40			19 10	19 40			20 10	20 40	20 40	
Gloucester	d			17 46																		
Cheltenham Spa	d		17 42	17 58		18 12				18 42		19 12			19 42	20 12			20 42	21 12	21 12	
London Paddington	d																					
Birmingham New Street	a		18 26	18 45	18 48	18 56		19 18		19 26	19 48	19 58	20 18		20 26	20 54	20 48	21 18	21 38	21 52	21 52	21 48
Birmingham New Street	d	18 20	18 31	18 49	18 57	19 03	19 19	19 30	19 20	19 31	19 57	20 03	20 30	20 20	20 31	20 57	21 03			21 56	21 57	21 57
Tamworth	d			19 09			19 36					20 19					21 20					
Burton-on-Trent	d			19 21		19 27	19 48										21 30					
Derby	a			19 35		19 39	19 59	20 05				20 42	21 24				21 41			22 31	22 32	
Nottingham	a			20 05			20 32															
Chesterfield	a					20 04		20 29				21 04	21 45				22 07			22 53	22 53	
Sheffield	a					20 19		20 49				21 19	22 05				22 23			23 09	23 09	
Doncaster	a							21 21					22 30				22 51					
Wakefield Westgate	a					20 48						21 49					23 10					
Leeds	a					21 03						22 02					23 27			23 51	23 51	
York	a					21 57		21 44					22 57									
Darlington	a							22 13														
Durham	a							22 30														
Chester-le-Street	a																					
Newcastle	a							22 47														
Morpeth	a																					
Alnmouth for Alnwick	a																					
Berwick-upon-Tweed	a																					
Dunbar	a																					
Wolverhampton	d	18 37	18 49		19 15				19 37	19 49	20 15			20 37	20 49	21 15						22 16
Stafford	a		19 00		19 29					20 00	20 29			20 49	21 00	21 29						22 29
Stoke-on-Trent	a		19 19		19 54					20 19	20 54				21 20	21 52						22 50
Congleton	a																					
Macclesfield	a				20 11					20 36	21 11				21 38	22 10						23 07
Crewe	a	19 07							20 07					21 10								
Wilmslow	a																					
Stockport	a		19 49		20 27					20 49	21 27				21 53	22 26						23 21
M'chester Piccadilly	a		19 59		20 39					20 59	21 39				22 04	22 39						23 32
Warrington Bank Quay	a	19 26							20 26													
Wigan North Western	a	19 37							20 37													
Preston	a	19 54							20 59													
Lancaster	a																					
Oxenholme Lake District	a																					
Penrith North Lakes	a																					
Carlisle	a																					
Lockerbie	a																					
Haymarket	a																					
Edinburgh	a																					
Haymarket	a																					
Motherwell	a																					
Glasgow Central	a																					
Inverkeithing	a																					
Kirkcaldy	a																					
Markinch	a																					
Ladybank	a																					
Cupar	a																					
Leuchars	a																					
Dundee	a																					
Arbroath	a																					
Montrose	a																					
Stonehaven	a																					
Aberdeen	a																					

A ⊡ from Birmingham New Street ✕ to Birmingham New Street
B ✕ to Sheffield
C ✕ to Birmingham New Street
D not 30 June. ✕ to Birmingham New Street
E 30 June. ✕ to Birmingham New Street
F ✕ to Reading

Table 51

Saturdays
until 30 June

South Coast and the South West - North West England, The North East and Scotland

Route Diagram - see first Page of Table 51

		XC	XC	XC	XC	XC	XC	XC
		◇1	◇1	◇1	◇1	1		◇1
						A	B	
							🚌	✠
Bournemouth	d				19 45			
Brockenhurst	d				20 00			
Southampton Central	d				20 15			
Southampton Airport Pkway	d				20 22			
Winchester	d				20 31			
Basingstoke	d				20 47			
Guildford	d							
Reading	d	20 40			21 11			21 40
Oxford	d	21 07			21 36			22 07
Banbury	d	21 25			21 54			22 29
Leamington Spa	d	21 45			22 12			22 46
Coventry	d	21 56			22 27			
Birmingham International	d	22 11			22 38			
Penzance	d							
St Erth	d							
Hayle	d							
Camborne	d							
Redruth	d							
Truro	d							
St Austell	d							
Newquay (Summer Only)	d							
Par	d							
Lostwithiel	d							
Bodmin Parkway	d							
Liskeard	d							
Plymouth	d							
Totnes	d							
Paignton	d							
Torquay	d							
Newton Abbot	d							
Teignmouth	d							
Dawlish	d							
Exeter St Davids	d							
Tiverton Parkway	d							
Taunton	d							
Weston-super-Mare	d							
Cardiff Central	d			20 50				
Newport (South Wales)	d			21 05				
Bristol Temple Meads	d							
Bristol Parkway	d							
Gloucester	d			21 49				
Cheltenham Spa	d			22 00				
London Paddington	d							
Birmingham New Street	a	22 21		22 42	22 48			23 16
Birmingham New Street	d		22 31			22 49	22 49	
Tamworth	d					23 08	23 24	
Burton-on-Trent	d					23 20	23s44	
Derby	a					23 33	00 04	
Nottingham	a							
Chesterfield	a							
Sheffield	a							
Doncaster	a							
Wakefield Westgate	a							
Leeds	a							
York	a							
Darlington	a							
Durham	a							
Chester-le-Street	a							
Newcastle	a							
Morpeth	a							
Alnmouth for Alnwick	a							
Berwick-upon-Tweed	a							
Dunbar	a							
Wolverhampton	d		22 49					
Stafford	a		23 01					
Stoke-on-Trent	a		23 20					
Congleton	a							
Macclesfield	a		23 38					
Crewe	a							
Wilmslow	a							
Stockport	a		23 53					
M'chester Piccadilly	a		00 10					
Warrington Bank Quay	a							
Wigan North Western	a							
Preston	a							
Lancaster	a							
Oxenholme Lake District	a							
Penrith North Lakes	a							
Carlisle	a							
Lockerbie	a							
Haymarket	a							
Edinburgh	a							
Haymarket	a							
Motherwell	a							
Glasgow Central	a							
Inverkeithing	a							
Kirkcaldy	a							
Markinch	a							
Ladybank	a							
Cupar	a							
Leuchars	a							
Dundee	a							
Arbroath	a							
Montrose	a							
Stonehaven	a							
Aberdeen	a							

A not 30 June B 30 June

Table 51

Saturdays
7 July to 8 September

South Coast and the South West - North West England, The North East and Scotland

Route Diagram - see first Page of Table 51

		XC	XC	XC	XC	XC	XC	VT	XC	XC		XC	XC	XC	XC	VT	XC	XC	XC	XC		XC	XC	XC	XC
		◇1	1	◇1	◇1	◇1	1	◇1	◇1	◇1		1	◇1	◇1	1	◇1	◇1	◇1	◇1	1		◇1	◇1	1	◇1
						A													B						B
						✠	✠	⊡	✠	✠			✠	✠	✠	⊡	✠	✠	✠			✠		✠	✠
Bournemouth	d																								
Brockenhurst	d																								
Southampton Central	d																		05 09						
Southampton Airport Pkway	d																		05 16						
Winchester	d																		05 25						
Basingstoke	d																		05 41						
Guildford	d																								06 09
Reading	d																		06 11						06 46
Oxford	d																		06 38						07 12
Banbury	d																		06 56						07 33
Leamington Spa	d																		07 14						07 51
Coventry	d																		07 27						
Birmingham International	d																		07 38						
Penzance	d																								
St Erth	d																								
Hayle	d																								
Camborne	d																								
Redruth	d																								
Truro	d																								
St Austell	d																								
Newquay (Summer Only)	d																								
Par	d																								
Lostwithiel	d																								
Bodmin Parkway	d																								
Liskeard	d																								
Plymouth	d																								
Totnes	d																								
Paignton	d																								
Torquay	d																								
Newton Abbot	d																								
Teignmouth	d																								
Dawlish	d																								
Exeter St Davids	d																								
Tiverton Parkway	d																								
Taunton	d																								
Weston-super-Mare	d																								
Cardiff Central	d			21p50																					
Newport (South Wales)	d			22p05																					
Bristol Temple Meads	d																					06 15			
Bristol Parkway	d																					06 25			
Gloucester	d			22p47																		07 01	07 07		
Cheltenham Spa	d			22p58																		07 12	07 18		
London Paddington	d																								
Birmingham New Street	a			00 01															07 48			07 56	08 08		08 17
Birmingham New Street	d	22p30	23p09		05 57	05 57	06 19	06 20	06 30	06 31		06 49	06 57	07 03	07 19	07 20	07 30	07 31	07 57	07 49		08 03		08 19	08 30
Tamworth	d		23p28			06 13	06 39		06 46			07 07		07 19	07 38		07 46			08 07		08 19		08 36	
Burton-on-Trent	d		23p40			06 24	06 51		06 56			07 19		07 29	07 50		07 56			08 17		08 29		08 48	
Derby	a		23p55			06 35	07 05		07 09			07 34		07 42	08 05		08 09			08 34		08 42		08 59	09 06
Nottingham	a		00 18				07 38					08 08			08 34					09 05				09 33	
Chesterfield	a					06 55			07 29					08 02			08 29					09 02			
Sheffield	a					07 09			07 48					08 17			08 45					09 17			09 44
Doncaster	a								08 23								09 18								10 17
Wakefield Westgate	a					07 36								08 45								09 46			
Leeds	a					07 52								09 03								10 02			
York	a					08 23			08 48					09 27			09 44					10 26			10 40
Darlington	a					08 56			09 16					09 58			10 15					10 58			11 13
Durham	a					09 13			09 34					10 15			10 32					11 15			11 30
Chester-le-Street	a																								
Newcastle	a					09 26			09 47					10 31			10 45					11 29			11 46
Morpeth	a																								
Alnmouth for Alnwick	a					09 58																			
Berwick-upon-Tweed	a					10 19																12 19			
Dunbar	a													11 37											
Wolverhampton	d	22p48			06 16			06 37		06 49			07 15			07 37		07 49	08 15						
Stafford	a	23p00			06 29					07 00			07 29					08 00	08 29						
Stoke-on-Trent	a	23p20			06 50					07 18								08 19	08 54						
Congleton	a				07 02																				
Macclesfield	a				07 11					07 36								08 36	09 11						
Crewe	a							07 07					07 50			08 07									
Wilmslow	a												08 09												
Stockport	a				07 27					07 49			08 20					08 49	09 27						
M'chester Piccadilly	a	00 12			07 38					07 59			08 35					08 59	09 39						
Warrington Bank Quay	a							07 26								08 27									
Wigan North Western	a							07 37								08 38									
Preston	a							07 51								08 51									
Lancaster	a							08 08								09 08									
Oxenholme Lake District	a							08 21																	
Penrith North Lakes	a															09 44									
Carlisle	a							09 00								10 02									
Lockerbie	a																								
Haymarket	a							10 16																	
Edinburgh	a					11 05		10 22						12 07								13 04			
Haymarket	a					11 15																13 15			
Motherwell	a					11 52																13 52			
Glasgow Central	a					12 13										11 17						14 13			
Inverkeithing	a																								
Kirkcaldy	a																								
Markinch	a																								
Ladybank	a																								
Cupar	a																								
Leuchars	a																								
Dundee	a																								
Arbroath	a																								
Montrose	a																								
Stonehaven	a																								
Aberdeen	a																								

A ✠ to Edinburgh B ✠ from Reading

South Coast and the South West - North West England, The North East and Scotland

Route Diagram - see first Page of Table 51

		VT	XC	XC	XC	XC	XC	VT	XC	XC	XC	XC	XC	XC	XC	XC	XC	XC	XC	XC	VT	XC	XC
		◇■	◇■	◇■	◇■	■	◇■	◇■	◇■	◇■	◇■	◇■	■	◇■	◇■	◇■	◇■	◇■	■	◇■	◇■	◇■	◇■
			A						A	B		C			A	B						A	
		at-seat	at-seat trolley	trolley	trolley	trolley	trolley	at-seat	at-seat trolley	trolley	trolley	trolley		trolley	at-seat trolley	trolley	trolley	trolley		trolley	at-seat	at-seat trolley	trolley
Bournemouth	d						06 25				06 37						07 45						08 45
Brockenhurst	d						06 39				06 55						08 00						09 00
Southampton Central	d			06 15			06 53				07 15			07 47			08 15						09 15
Southampton Airport Pkway	d			06 22			07 01				07 22			07 54			08 22						09 22
Winchester	d			06 31			07 09				07 31			08 03			08 31						09 31
Basingstoke	d			06 47			07 25				07 47			08 19			08 47						09 47
Guildford	d																						
Reading	d			07 11			07 47				08 11			08 40			09 11			09 40			10 11
Oxford	d			07 36			08 15				08 36			09 07			09 36			10 07			10 36
Banbury	d			07 54			08 33				08 54			09 24			09 54			10 24			10 54
Leamington Spa	d			08 12			08 50				09 12			09 42			10 13			10 42			11 12
Coventry	d			08 27							09 27						10 27						11 27
Birmingham International	d			08 38							09 38						10 38						11 38
Penzance	d																						
St Erth	d																						
Hayle	d																						
Camborne	d																						
Redruth	d																						
Truro	d																						
St Austell	d																						
Newquay (Summer Only)	d																						
Par	d																						
Lostwithiel	d																						
Bodmin Parkway	d																						
Liskeard	d																						
Plymouth	d				05 25							06 25						07 25					
Totnes	d				05 50							06 50						07 50					
Paignton	d														07 02								
Torquay	d														07 08								
Newton Abbot	d				06 03							07 03			07 19			08 03					
Teignmouth	d														07 26								
Dawlish	d														07 31								
Exeter St Davids	d				06 23							07 23			07 45			08 23					
Tiverton Parkway	d				06 37							07 37			07 58			08 37					
Taunton	d				06 51							07 51			08 13			08 51					
Weston-super-Mare	d																						
Cardiff Central	d								07 00	07 45						08 45							
Newport (South Wales)	d								07 15	08 00						09 00							
Bristol Temple Meads	d		07 00		07 30				08 00			08 30			09 00			09 30				10 00	
Bristol Parkway	d		07 10		07 40				08 10			08 40			09 10			09 40				10 10	
Gloucester	d									08 47						09 46							
Cheltenham Spa	d		07 42		08 12				08 42	08 58		09 12			09 42	09 57		10 12				10 42	
London Paddington	d																						
Birmingham New Street	a		08 26	08 48	08 56		09 18		09 26	09 45	09 48	09 56		10 18	10 26	10 45	10 48	10 56		11 18		11 26	11 48
Birmingham New Street	d	08 20	08 31	08 57	09 03	09 19	09 30	09 20	09 31	09 49	09 57	10 03	10 19	10 30	10 31	10 49	10 57	11 03	11 19	11 30	11 20	11 31	11 57
Tamworth	d					09 36				10 07		10 19	10 36			11 09			11 36				
Burton-on-Trent	d				09 28	09 48				10 19			10 48			11 21		11 28	11 48				
Derby	a				09 41	09 59	10 05			10 34		10 41	10 59	11 05		11 34		11 41	11 59	12 05			
Nottingham	a					10 33				11 05			11 33			12 05			12 33				
Chesterfield	a				10 02							11 02						12 02					
Sheffield	a				10 17		10 42					11 17		11 41				12 16		12 41			
Doncaster	a						11 15							12 15						13 17			
Wakefield Westgate	a				10 46							11 46						12 46					
Leeds	a				11 02							12 02						13 02					
York	a				11 26		11 40					12 26		12 39				13 26		13 40			
Darlington	a				11 57		12 13					12 58		13 13				13 57		14 12			
Durham	a				12 15		12 30					13 15		13 30				14 14		14 29			
Chester-le-Street	a																						
Newcastle	a				12 31		12 45					13 29		13 44				14 28		14 42			
Morpeth	a																	14 47					
Alnmouth for Alnwick	a											13 59											
Berwick-upon-Tweed	a											14 19											
Dunbar	a				13 37													15 39					
Wolverhampton	d	08 37	08 49	09 15				09 37	09 49		10 15				10 49		11 15				11 37	11 49	12 15
Stafford	a		09 00	09 29					10 00		10 29				11 00		11 29					12 00	12 29
Stoke-on-Trent	a		09 19	09 54					10 19		10 54				11 19		11 54					12 19	12 54
Congleton	a																						
Macclesfield	a			10 11							11 11						12 11						13 11
Crewe	a	09 07						10 07													12 07		
Wilmslow	a																						
Stockport	a		09 49	10 27					10 49		11 27				11 49		12 27					12 49	13 27
M'chester Piccadilly	a		09 59	10 39					10 59		11 39				11 59		12 39					12 59	13 39
Warrington Bank Quay	a	09 26						10 26													12 26		
Wigan North Western	a	09 37						10 37													12 37		
Preston	a	09 51						10 51													12 51		
Lancaster	a	10 08						11 08													13 08		
Oxenholme Lake District	a	10 22																			13 22		
Penrith North Lakes	a							11 44															
Carlisle	a	11 01						12 00													14 01		
Lockerbie	a																						
Haymarket	a	12 16																					
Edinburgh	a	12 22			14 07							15 07						16 04					
Haymarket	a											15 15											
Motherwell	a											15 52											
Glasgow Central	a							13 17				16 23									15 17		
Inverkeithing	a																						
Kirkcaldy	a																						
Markinch	a																						
Ladybank	a																						
Cupar	a																						
Leuchars	a																						
Dundee	a																						
Arbroath	a																						
Montrose	a																						
Stonehaven	a																						
Aberdeen	a																						

A at-seat from Birmingham New Street, trolley to Birmingham New Street
B trolley from Newport (South Wales)
C trolley to Edinburgh

South Coast and the South West - North West England, The North East and Scotland

Route Diagram - see first Page of Table 51

		XC	XC	XC	VT	XC	XC	XC	XC	XC	XC	VT	XC	XC	XC	XC	XC	VT	XC	XC	XC	XC
		◇■	■	◇■	◇■	◇■	◇■	◇■	◇■	■	◇■	◇■	◇■	◇■	◇■	■	◇■	◇■	◇■	◇■	◇■	■
		A				B	C		D				B		A				B		E	
		trolley	trolley	trolley	at-seat	at-seat trolley	trolley	trolley	trolley		trolley	at-seat	at-seat trolley	trolley	trolley		trolley	at-seat	at-seat trolley	trolley	trolley	
Bournemouth	d							09 45						10 45						11 45		
Brockenhurst	d							10 00						11 00						12 00		
Southampton Central	d			09 47				10 15						11 15			11 47			12 15		
Southampton Airport Pkway	d			09 54				10 22						11 22			11 54			12 22		
Winchester	d			10 03				10 31						11 31			12 03			12 31		
Basingstoke	d			10 19				10 47						11 47			12 19			12 47		
Guildford	d																					
Reading	d			10 40				11 11			11 40			12 11			12 40			13 11		
Oxford	d			11 07				11 36			12 07			12 36			13 07			13 36		
Banbury	d			11 24				11 54			12 24			12 54			13 24			13 54		
Leamington Spa	d			11 42				12 12			12 42			13 12			13 42			14 12		
Coventry	d							12 27						13 27						14 27		
Birmingham International	d							12 38						13 38						14 38		
Penzance	d	06 30													08 28							
St Erth	d	06 38													08 36							
Hayle	d	06 41																				
Camborne	d	06 51													08 46							
Redruth	d	06 57													08 52							
Truro	d	07 09													09 04							
St Austell	d	07 25													09 20							
Newquay (Summer Only)	d																				09 27	
Par	d	07 32													09 28						10 26	
Lostwithiel	d	07 39																				
Bodmin Parkway	d	07 46													09 39						10 43	
Liskeard	d	07 58													09 51						10 55	
Plymouth	d	08 25				08 38			09 18						10 25						11 25	
Totnes	d	08 50				09 03			09 43						10 50						11 50	
Paignton	d												10 07									
Torquay	d												10 13									
Newton Abbot	d	09 03				09 16			09 56				10 24		11 03						12 03	
Teignmouth	d								10 03				10 31									
Dawlish	d								10 09				10 36									
Exeter St Davids	d	09 23				09 41			10 26				10 50		11 23						12 23	
Tiverton Parkway	d	09 37				09 54			10 40				11 03		11 37						12 37	
Taunton	d	09 51				10 09			10 54				11 18		11 51						12 51	
Weston-super-Mare	d					10 33																
Cardiff Central	d						10 45															
Newport (South Wales)	d						11 00															
Bristol Temple Meads	d	10 30				11 00			11 30				12 00		12 30				13 00		13 30	
Bristol Parkway	d	10 40				11 10			11 40				12 10		12 40				13 10		13 40	
Gloucester	d						11 46															
Cheltenham Spa	d	11 12				11 42	11 57		12 12				12 42		13 12				13 42		14 12	
London Paddington	d																					
Birmingham New Street	a	11 56		12 18		12 26	12 45	12 48	12 56		13 18		13 26	13 48	13 56		14 18		14 26	14 48	14 56	
Birmingham New Street	d	12 03	12 19	12 30	12 20	12 31	12 49	12 57	13 03	13 19	13 30	13 20	13 31	13 57	14 03	14 19	14 30	14 20	14 31	14 57	15 03	15 19
Tamworth	d	12 19	12 36				13 09			13 36					14 19	14 36						15 36
Burton-on-Trent	d		12 48				13 21		13 27	13 50						14 47					15 27	15 48
Derby	a	12 41	13 05	13 08			13 34		13 41	14 05	14 08				14 41	14 59	15 05				15 38	15 59
Nottingham	a		13 33				14 05			14 33						15 33						16 33
Chesterfield	a	13 02							14 02						15 02						16 02	
Sheffield	a	13 17		13 41					14 17		14 41				15 17		15 41				16 18	
Doncaster	a			14 18							15 17						16 18					
Wakefield Westgate	a	13 46							14 46						15 46						16 46	
Leeds	a	14 02							15 02						16 02						17 02	
York	a	14 26		14 40					15 28		15 40				16 26		16 41				17 26	
Darlington	a	14 58		15 13					15 58		16 13				16 58		17 13				17 56	
Durham	a	15 15		15 30					16 15		16 30				17 15		17 30				18 13	
Chester-le-Street	a																					
Newcastle	a	15 29		15 45					16 29		16 45				17 29		17 45				18 27	
Morpeth	a																					
Alnmouth for Alnwick	a	15 58							16 58						18 00							
Berwick-upon-Tweed	a	16 18													18 20						19 17	
Dunbar	a								17 38												19 40	
Wolverhampton	d				12 37	12 49		13 15				13 37	13 49	14 15				14 37	14 49	15 15		
Stafford	a					13 00		13 29					14 00	14 29					15 00	15 29		
Stoke-on-Trent	a					13 18		13 54					14 19	14 54					15 19	15 54		
Congleton	a																					
Macclesfield	a							14 11						15 11						16 11		
Crewe	a				13 07							14 07						15 07				
Wilmslow	a																					
Stockport	a					13 49		14 27					14 49	15 27					15 49	16 27		
M'chester Piccadilly	a					13 59		14 39					14 59	15 39					15 59	16 39		
Warrington Bank Quay	a				13 26							14 26						15 26				
Wigan North Western	a				13 37							14 37						15 37				
Preston	a				13 51							14 51						15 51				
Lancaster	a				14 08							15 08						16 08				
Oxenholme Lake District	a											15 22										
Penrith North Lakes	a				14 44													16 45				
Carlisle	a				15 00							16 01						17 00				
Lockerbie	a																					
Haymarket	a				16 16													18 14				
Edinburgh	a	17 07			16 22				18 05						19 08			18 22			20 06	
Haymarket	a	17 15							18 14						19 15						20 19	
Motherwell	a	17 52													19 52							
Glasgow Central	a	18 11										17 17			20 11							
Inverkeithing	a								18 28												20 35	
Kirkcaldy	a								18 46												20 52	
Markinch	a								18 56												21 02	
Ladybank	a								19 03												21 10	
Cupar	a								19 10												21 18	
Leuchars	a								19 17												21 27	
Dundee	a								19 32												21 44	
Arbroath	a								19 49													
Montrose	a								20 03													
Stonehaven	a								20 23													
Aberdeen	a								20 43													

A trolley from Plymouth to Edinburgh
B at-seat from Birmingham New Street, trolley to Birmingham New Street
C trolley from Newport (South Wales)
D trolley to Edinburgh
E trolley from Plymouth

South Coast and the South West - North West England, The North East and Scotland

Route Diagram - see first Page of Table 51

	XC ◇1 ⊼	XC ◇1 A ⊡⊼	XC ◇1 B ⊼	XC ◇1 ⊼	XC ◇1 C ⊼	XC 1	XC ◇1 ⊼	VT ◇1 ⊡	XC ◇1 A ⊡⊼	XC ◇1 ⊼	XC ◇1 ⊼	XC 1	XC ◇1 ⊼	VT ◇1 ⊡	XC ◇1 ⊼	XC ◇1 ⊼	XC ◇1 ⊼	XC 1	XC ◇1 ⊼	VT ◇1 ⊡	XC ◇1 A ⊡⊼	XC ◇1
Bournemouth d				12 45						13 45						14 45						
Brockenhurst d				13 00						14 00						15 00						
Southampton Central d				13 15			13 47			14 15						15 15			15 47			
Southampton Airport Pkway d				13 22			13 54			14 22						15 22			15 54			
Winchester d				13 31			14 03			14 31						15 31			16 03			
Basingstoke d				13 47			14 19			14 47						15 47			16 19			
Guildford d																						
Reading d	13 40			14 11			14 40			15 11			15 40			16 11			16 40			
Oxford d	14 07			14 36			15 07			15 36			16 07			16 36			17 07			
Banbury d	14 24			14 54			15 24			15 54			16 24			16 54			17 24			
Leamington Spa d	14 42			15 12			15 42			16 12			16 42			17 12			17 42			
Coventry d				15 27						16 27						17 27						
Birmingham International d				15 38						16 38						17 38						
Penzance d																						
St Erth d																						
Hayle d																						
Camborne d																						
Redruth d																						
Truro d																						
St Austell d																						
Newquay (Summer Only) d																						
Par d																						
Lostwithiel d																						
Bodmin Parkway d																						
Liskeard d																						
Plymouth d											13 25						14 25					
Totnes d											13 50						14 50					
Paignton d					12 34										13 53							
Torquay d					12 41										13 59							
Newton Abbot d					12 53						14 03				14 10		15 03					
Teignmouth d					13 02										14 17							
Dawlish d					13 09										14 22							
Exeter St Davids d					13 24						14 23				14 36		15 23					
Tiverton Parkway d					13 39						14 37				14 49		15 37					
Taunton d					13 53						14 52				15 04		15 51					
Weston-super-Mare d															15 30							
Cardiff Central d			13 45																			16 45
Newport (South Wales) d			14 00																			17 00
Bristol Temple Meads d		14 00			14 30				15 00		15 30				16 00		16 30				17 00	
Bristol Parkway d		14 10			14 40				15 10		15 40				16 10		16 40				17 10	
Gloucester d			14 46																			17 46
Cheltenham Spa d		14 42	14 57		15 12				15 42		16 12				16 42		17 12				17 42	17 58
London Paddington d																						
Birmingham New Street a	15 18	15 26	15 45	15 48	15 55		16 18		16 26	16 48	16 56		17 18		17 26	17 48	17 56		18 18		18 26	18 45
Birmingham New Street d	15 30	15 31	15 49	15 57	16 03	16 19	16 30	16 20	16 31	16 57	17 03	17 19	17 30	17 20	17 31	17 57	18 03	18 19	18 30	18 20	18 31	18 49
Tamworth d			16 09		16 19	16 38						17 36					18 19	18 36				19 09
Burton-on-Trent d			16 21			16 50					17 26	17 48						18 47				19 21
Derby a	16 05		16 34		16 40	17 05	17 08				17 41	17 59	18 05				18 41	18 59	19 05			19 35
Nottingham a			17 05			17 33						18 32						19 33				20 05
Chesterfield a					17 01						18 02						19 02		19 29			
Sheffield a	16 41				17 19		17 44				18 18		18 42				19 18		19 51			
Doncaster a	17 16												19 16						20 17			
Wakefield Westgate a					17 47		18 12				18 46						19 49					
Leeds a					18 02		18 31				19 01						20 05					
York a	17 37				18 28		18 58				19 26		19 39				20 29		20 40			
Darlington a	18 12				18 59		19 35				19 57		20 11				20 58		21 13			
Durham a	18 29				19 17		19 52				20 14		20 28				21 15		21 30			
Chester-le-Street a																						
Newcastle a	18 44				19 31		20 08				20 28		20 42				21 29		21 44			
Morpeth a											20 50											
Alnmouth for Alnwick a					20 03												22 01					
Berwick-upon-Tweed a					20 24						21 23											
Dunbar a											21 47											
Wolverhampton d		15 49		16 15				16 37	16 49	17 15				17 37	17 49	18 15				18 37	18 49	
Stafford a		16 00		16 29					17 00	17 29					18 00	18 29					19 00	
Stoke-on-Trent a		16 18		16 54					17 19	17 54					18 19	18 54					19 19	
Congleton a																						
Macclesfield a				17 11						18 11						19 11						
Crewe a								17 07						18 07						19 07		
Wilmslow a																						
Stockport a		16 48		17 27					17 49	18 27					18 49	19 27					19 49	
M'chester Piccadilly a		16 59		17 39					17 59	18 39					18 59	19 39					19 59	
Warrington Bank Quay a								17 26						18 26						19 26		
Wigan North Western a								17 37						18 37						19 37		
Preston a								17 51						18 51						19 54		
Lancaster a								18 08						19 08								
Oxenholme Lake District a								18 22						19 22								
Penrith North Lakes a								18 48														
Carlisle a								19 04						20 01								
Lockerbie a																						
Haymarket a								20 16														
Edinburgh a					21 09			20 22			22 14						23 10					
Haymarket a					21 16																	
Motherwell a					22 00																	
Glasgow Central a					22 22									21 17								
Inverkeithing a																						
Kirkcaldy a																						
Markinch a																						
Ladybank a																						
Cupar a																						
Leuchars a																						
Dundee a																						
Arbroath a																						
Montrose a																						
Stonehaven a																						
Aberdeen a																						

A ⊡ from Birmingham New Street ⊼ to Birmingham New Street
B ⊼ from Newport (South Wales)
C ⊼ to Edinburgh

South Coast and the South West - North West England, The North East and Scotland

Route Diagram - see first Page of Table 51

	XC ◇1 ⊼	XC ◇1 ⊼	XC 1	XC ◇1 A ⊼	XC ◇1 B ⊡⊼	XC ◇1 C ⊼	XC ◇1 C ⊼	XC ◇1 C ⊼	VT ◇1 ⊡	XC ◇1 B ⊡⊼	XC ◇1 ⊼	XC ◇1 ⊼	XC ◇1	XC ◇1	XC ◇1 C ⊼	XC ◇1 D ⊼	XC ◇1	XC ◇1	XC ◇1	XC ◇1	XC 🚌
Bournemouth d	15 45					16 45						17 45				18 45				19 45	
Brockenhurst d	16 00					17 00						18 00				19 00				20 00	
Southampton Central d	16 15					17 15		17 47				18 15				19 15				20 15	
Southampton Airport Pkway d	16 22					17 22		17 54				18 22				19 22				20 22	
Winchester d	16 31					17 31		18 03				18 31				19 31				20 31	
Basingstoke d	16 47					17 47		18 19				18 47				19 47				20 47	
Guildford d																					
Reading d	17 11			17 40		18 11		18 40				19 11	19 40			20 11	20 40			21 11	
Oxford d	17 36			18 07		18 36		19 07				19 36	20 07			20 36	21 07			21 36	
Banbury d	17 54			18 24		18 54		19 24				19 54	20 29			20 54	21 25			21 54	
Leamington Spa d	18 12			18 42		19 12		19 42				20 12	20 46			21 12	21 45			22 12	
Coventry d	18 27					19 27						20 27				21 27	21 56			22 27	
Birmingham International d	18 38					19 38						20 38				21 38	22 11			22 38	
Penzance d															16 25						
St Erth d															16 35						
Hayle d																					
Camborne d															16 46						
Redruth d															16 53						
Truro d															17 06						
St Austell d															17 23						
Newquay (Summer Only) d											15 25										
Par d																					
Lostwithiel d																					
Bodmin Parkway d											16 37				17 40						
Liskeard d											16 51				17 53						
Plymouth d		15 25									17 25				18 23						
Totnes d		15 50									17 50				18 49						
Paignton d							16 36							18 05							
Torquay d							16 43							18 12							
Newton Abbot d		16 03					16 55				18 03			18 23	19 03						
Teignmouth d							17 03														
Dawlish d							17 10														
Exeter St Davids d		16 23					17 25				18 23			18 50	19 25						
Tiverton Parkway d		16 37					17 39				18 37			19 04	19 39						
Taunton d		16 51					17 54				18 51			19 18	19 54						
Weston-super-Mare d																					
Cardiff Central d																			20 50		
Newport (South Wales) d																			21 05		
Bristol Temple Meads d		17 30			18 00		18 30			19 00	19 30			20 00	20 30						
Bristol Parkway d		17 40			18 10		18 40			19 10	19 40			20 10	20 40						
Gloucester d																			21 49		
Cheltenham Spa d		18 12			18 42		19 12			19 42	20 12			20 42	21 12				22 00		
London Paddington d																					
Birmingham New Street a	18 48	18 56		19 18	19 26	19 48	19 58	20 18		20 26	20 54	20 48	21 18	21 38	21 52	21 48	22 21		22 42	22 48	
Birmingham New Street d	18 57	19 03	19 19	19 30	19 31	19 57	20 03	20 30	20 20	20 31	20 57	21 03			21 57	21 57		22 31			22 49
Tamworth d			19 36				20 19					21 20									23 24
Burton-on-Trent d		19 27	19 48									21 30									23s44
Derby a		19 39	19 59	20 05			20 42	21 24				21 41			22 32						00 04
Nottingham a			20 32																		
Chesterfield a		20 04		20 29			21 04	21 45				22 07			22 53						
Sheffield a		20 19		20 49			21 19	22 05				22 23			23 09						
Doncaster a				21 21				22 30				22 51									
Wakefield Westgate a		20 48					21 49					23 10									
Leeds a		21 03					22 02					23 27			23 51						
York a		21 57		21 44				22 57													
Darlington a				22 13																	
Durham a				22 30																	
Chester-le-Street a																					
Newcastle a				22 47																	
Morpeth a																					
Alnmouth for Alnwick a																					
Berwick-upon-Tweed a																					
Dunbar a																					
Wolverhampton d	19 15				19 49	20 15			20 37	20 49	21 15					22 16		22 49			
Stafford a	19 29				20 00	20 29			20 49	21 00	21 29					22 29		23 01			
Stoke-on-Trent a	19 54				20 19	20 54				21 20	21 52					22 50		23 20			
Congleton a																					
Macclesfield a	20 11				20 36	21 11				21 38	22 10					23 07		23 38			
Crewe a									21 10												
Wilmslow a																					
Stockport a	20 27				20 49	21 27				21 53	22 26					23 21		23 53			
M'chester Piccadilly a	20 39				20 59	21 39				22 04	22 39					23 32		00 10			
Warrington Bank Quay a																					
Wigan North Western a																					
Preston a																					
Lancaster a																					
Oxenholme Lake District a																					
Penrith North Lakes a																					
Carlisle a																					
Lockerbie a																					
Haymarket a																					
Edinburgh a																					
Haymarket a																					
Motherwell a																					
Glasgow Central a																					
Inverkeithing a																					
Kirkcaldy a																					
Markinch a																					
Ladybank a																					
Cupar a																					
Leuchars a																					
Dundee a																					
Arbroath a																					
Montrose a																					
Stonehaven a																					
Aberdeen a																					

A ⊼ to Sheffield
B ⊡ from Birmingham New Street ⊼ to Birmingham New Street
C ⊼ to Birmingham New Street
D ⊼ to Reading

Saturdays
7 July to 8 September

South Coast and the South West - North West England, The North East and Scotland

Route Diagram - see first Page of Table 51

		XC
		◇1 ⊼
Bournemouth	d	
Brockenhurst	d	
Southampton Central ⛴	d	
Southampton Airport Pkway ✈	d	
Winchester	d	
Basingstoke	d	
Guildford	d	
Reading	d	21 40
Oxford	d	22 07
Banbury	d	22 29
Leamington Spa	d	22 46
Coventry	d	
Birmingham International ✈	d	
Penzance	d	
St Erth	d	
Hayle	d	
Camborne	d	
Redruth	d	
Truro	d	
St Austell	d	
Newquay (Summer Only)	d	
Par	d	
Lostwithiel	d	
Bodmin Parkway	d	
Liskeard	d	
Plymouth	d	
Totnes	d	
Paignton	d	
Torquay	d	
Newton Abbot	d	
Teignmouth	d	
Dawlish	d	
Exeter St Davids	d	
Tiverton Parkway	d	
Taunton	d	
WestonsuperMare	d	
Cardiff Central	d	
Newport (South Wales)	d	
Bristol Temple Meads	d	
Bristol Parkway	d	
Gloucester	d	
Cheltenham Spa	d	
London Paddington	d	
Birmingham New Street	a	23 16
Birmingham New Street	d	
Tamworth	d	
Burton-on-Trent	d	
Derby	a	
Nottingham	a	
Chesterfield	a	
Sheffield	a	
Doncaster	a	
Wakefield Westgate	a	
Leeds	a	
York	a	
Darlington	a	
Durham	a	
ChesterleStreet	a	
Newcastle	a	
Morpeth	a	
Alnmouth for Alnwick	a	
BerwickuponTweed	a	
Dunbar	a	
Wolverhampton	d	
Stafford	a	
StokeonTrent	a	
Congleton	a	
Macclesfield	a	
Crewe	a	
Wilmslow	a	
Stockport	a	
M'chester Piccadilly	a	
Warrington Bank Quay	a	
Wigan North Western	a	
Preston	a	
Lancaster	a	
Oxenholme Lake District	a	
Penrith North Lakes	a	
Carlisle	a	
Lockerbie	a	
Haymarket	a	
Edinburgh	a	
Haymarket	a	
Motherwell	a	
Glasgow Central	a	
Inverkeithing	a	
Kirkcaldy	a	
Markinch	a	
Ladybank	a	
Cupar	a	
Leuchars	a	
Dundee	a	
Arbroath	a	
Montrose	a	
Stonehaven	a	
Aberdeen	a	

Saturdays
from 15 September

South Coast and the South West - North West England, The North East and Scotland

Route Diagram - see first Page of Table 51

		XC	XC	XC	XC	XC	XC	VT	XC	XC		XC	XC	XC	XC	VT	XC	XC	XC	XC		XC	XC	XC	XC
		◇1	1	◇1	◇1	◇1 A ⊼	1 ⊼	◇1 ⊡	◇1 ⊼	◇1 ⊼		1	◇1 ⊼	◇1 ⊼	1 ⊼	◇1 ⊡	◇1 ⊼	◇1 ⊼	◇1 B ⊼	1		◇1 ⊼	◇1	1 ⊼	◇1 B ⊼
Bournemouth	d																								
Brockenhurst	d																								
Southampton Central ⛴	d																		05 09						
Southampton Airport Pkway ✈	d																		05 16						
Winchester	d																		05 25						
Basingstoke	d																		05 41						
Guildford	d																								
Reading	d																		06 11						06 09
Oxford	d																		06 38						06 46
Banbury	d																		06 56						07 12
Leamington Spa	d																		07 14						07 33
Coventry	d																		07 27						07 51
Birmingham International ✈	d																		07 38						
Penzance	d																								
St Erth	d																								
Hayle	d																								
Camborne	d																								
Redruth	d																								
Truro	d																								
St Austell	d																								
Newquay (Summer Only)	d																								
Par	d																								
Lostwithiel	d																								
Bodmin Parkway	d																								
Liskeard	d																								
Plymouth	d																								
Totnes	d																								
Paignton	d																								
Torquay	d																								
Newton Abbot	d																								
Teignmouth	d																								
Dawlish	d																								
Exeter St Davids	d																								
Tiverton Parkway	d																								
Taunton	d																								
WestonsuperMare	d																								
Cardiff Central	d			21p50																					
Newport (South Wales)	d			22p05																					
Bristol Temple Meads	d																					06 15			
Bristol Parkway	d																					06 25			
Gloucester	d			22p47																		07 01	07 07		
Cheltenham Spa	d			22p58																		07 12	07 18		
London Paddington	d																								
Birmingham New Street	a			00 01															07 48			07 56	08 08		08 17
Birmingham New Street	d	22p30	23p09		05 57	05 57	06 19	06 20	06 30	06 31		06 49	06 57	07 03	07 19	07 20	07 30	07 31	07 57	07 49		08 03		08 19	08 30
Tamworth	d		23p28			06 13	06 39		06 46			07 07		07 19	07 38		07 46			08 07		08 19		08 36	
Burton-on-Trent	d		23p40			06 24	06 51		06 56			07 19		07 29	07 50		07 56			08 17		08 29		08 48	
Derby	a		23p55			06 35	07 05		07 09			07 34		07 42	08 05		08 09			08 34		08 42		08 59	09 06
Nottingham	a		00 18				07 38					08 08			08 34					09 05				09 33	
Chesterfield	a					06 55			07 29					08 02			08 29					09 02			
Sheffield	a					07 09			07 48					08 17			08 45					09 17			09 44
Doncaster	a								08 23								09 18								10 17
Wakefield Westgate	a					07 36								08 45								09 46			
Leeds	a					07 52								09 03								10 02			
York	a					08 23			08 48					09 27			09 44					10 26			10 40
Darlington	a					08 56			09 16					09 58			10 15					10 58			11 13
Durham	a					09 13			09 34					10 15			10 32					11 15			11 30
ChesterleStreet	a																								
Newcastle	a					09 26			09 47					10 31			10 45					11 29			11 46
Morpeth	a																								
Alnmouth for Alnwick	a					09 58																			
BerwickuponTweed	a					10 19																12 19			
Dunbar	a													11 37											
Wolverhampton	d	22p48			06 16			06 37		06 49			07 15			07 37		07 49	08 15						
Stafford	a	23p00			06 29					07 00			07 29					08 00	08 29						
StokeonTrent	a	23p20			06 50					07 18								08 19	08 54						
Congleton	a				07 02																				
Macclesfield	a				07 11					07 36								08 36	09 11						
Crewe	a							07 07					07 50			08 07									
Wilmslow	a												08 09												
Stockport	a				07 27					07 49			08 20					08 49	09 27						
M'chester Piccadilly	a	00 12			07 38					07 59			08 35					08 59	09 39						
Warrington Bank Quay	a							07 26								08 27									
Wigan North Western	a							07 37								08 38									
Preston	a							07 51								08 51									
Lancaster	a							08 08								09 08									
Oxenholme Lake District	a							08 21																	
Penrith North Lakes	a															09 44									
Carlisle	a							09 00								10 02									
Lockerbie	a																								
Haymarket	a							10 16																	
Edinburgh	a					11 05		10 22						12 07								13 04			
Haymarket	a					11 15																13 15			
Motherwell	a					11 52																13 52			
Glasgow Central	a					12 13										11 17						14 13			
Inverkeithing	a																								
Kirkcaldy	a																								
Markinch	a																								
Ladybank	a																								
Cupar	a																								
Leuchars	a																								
Dundee	a																								
Arbroath	a																								
Montrose	a																								
Stonehaven	a																								
Aberdeen	a																								

A ⊼ to Edinburgh

B ⊼ from Reading

Table 51

Saturdays from 15 September

South Coast and the South West - North West England, The North East and Scotland

Route Diagram - see first Page of Table 51

Station		VT ◇■ ▭	XC ◇■ A ▭⌶	XC ◇■ ⌶	XC ◇■ ⌶	XC ■ ⌶	XC ◇■ ⌶	VT ◇■ ▭	XC ◇■ A ▭⌶	XC ◇■ B ⌶	XC ◇■ ⌶	XC ◇■ C ⌶	XC ■	XC ◇■ ⌶	VT ◇■ ▭	XC ◇■ A ▭⌶	XC ◇■ B ⌶	XC ◇■ ⌶	XC ◇■ ⌶	XC ■	XC ◇■ ⌶	VT ◇■ ▭	XC ◇■ A ▭⌶
Bournemouth	d						06 25				06 37							07 45					
Brockenhurst ■	d						06 39				06 55							08 00					
Southampton Central	d			06 15			06 53				07 15			07 47				08 15					
Southampton Airport Pkway	d			06 22			07 01				07 22			07 54				08 22					
Winchester	d			06 31			07 09				07 31			08 03				08 31					
Basingstoke	d			06 47			07 25				07 47			08 19				08 47					
Guildford	d																						
Reading ■	d			07 11			07 47				08 11			08 40				09 11			09 40		
Oxford	d			07 36			08 15				08 36			09 07				09 36			10 07		
Banbury	d			07 54			08 33				08 54			09 24				09 54			10 24		
Leamington Spa ■	d			08 12			08 50				09 12			09 42				10 13			10 42		
Coventry	d			08 27							09 27							10 27					
Birmingham International	d			08 38							09 38							10 38					
Penzance	d																						
St Erth	d																						
Hayle	d																						
Camborne	d																						
Redruth	d																						
Truro	d																						
St Austell	d																						
Newquay (Summer Only)	d																						
Par	d																						
Lostwithiel	d																						
Bodmin Parkway	d																						
Liskeard ■	d																						
Plymouth	d				05 25							06 25							07 25				
Totnes	d				05 50							06 50							07 50				
Paignton	d															07 02							
Torquay	d															07 08							
Newton Abbot	d				06 03							07 03				07 19			08 03				
Teignmouth	d															07 26							
Dawlish	d															07 31							
Exeter St Davids ■	d				06 23							07 23				07 45			08 23				
Tiverton Parkway	d				06 37							07 37				07 58			08 37				
Taunton	d				06 51							07 51				08 13			08 51				
Weston-super-Mare	d																						
Cardiff Central ■	d								07 00	07 45							08 45						
Newport (South Wales)	d								07 15	08 00							09 00						
Bristol Temple Meads ■	d		07 00		07 30				08 00			08 30				09 00			09 30				10 00
Bristol Parkway ■	d		07 10		07 40				08 10			08 40				09 10			09 40				10 10
Gloucester ■	d									08 47							09 46						
Cheltenham Spa	d		07 42		08 12				08 42	08 58		09 12				09 42	09 57		10 12				10 42
London Paddington	d																						
Birmingham New Street ■	a		08 26	08 48	08 56		09 18		09 26	09 45	09 48	09 56		10 18		10 26	10 45	10 48	10 56		11 18		11 26
Birmingham New Street ■	d	08 20	08 31	08 57	09 03	09 19	09 30	09 20	09 31	09 49	09 57	10 03	10 19	10 30	10 20	10 31	10 49	10 57	11 03	11 19	11 30	11 20	11 31
Tamworth	d					09 36				10 07		10 19	10 36				11 09			11 36			
Burton-on-Trent	d				09 28	09 48				10 19			10 48				11 21		11 28	11 48			
Derby ■	a				09 41	09 59	10 05			10 34		10 41	10 59	11 05			11 34		11 41	11 59	12 05		
Nottingham ■	a					10 33				11 05			11 33				12 05			12 33			
Chesterfield	a				10 02							11 02							12 02				
Sheffield ■	a				10 17		10 42					11 17		11 41					12 16		12 41		
Doncaster ■	a						11 15							12 15							13 17		
Wakefield Westgate ■	a				10 46							11 46							12 46				
Leeds ■	a				11 02							12 02							13 02				
York ■	a				11 26		11 40					12 26		12 39					13 26		13 40		
Darlington ■	a				11 57		12 13					12 58		13 13					13 57		14 12		
Durham	a				12 15		12 30					13 15		13 30					14 14		14 29		
Chester-le-Street	a																						
Newcastle ■	a				12 31		12 45					13 29		13 44					14 28		14 42		
Morpeth	a																		14 47				
Alnmouth for Alnwick	a											13 59											
Berwick-upon-Tweed	a											14 19											
Dunbar	a				13 37														15 39				
Wolverhampton ■	d	08 37	08 49	09 15				09 37	09 49		10 15				10 37	10 49		11 15				11 37	11 49
Stafford	a		09 00	09 29					10 00		10 29					11 00		11 29					12 00
Stoke-on-Trent	a		09 19	09 54					10 19		10 54					11 19		11 54					12 19
Congleton	a																						
Macclesfield	a			10 11							11 11							12 11					
Crewe ■	a	09 07						10 07							11 07							12 07	
Wilmslow	a																						
Stockport	a		09 49	10 27					10 49		11 27					11 49		12 27					12 49
M'chester Piccadilly ■	a		09 59	10 39					10 59		11 39					11 59		12 39					12 59
Warrington Bank Quay	a	09 26						10 26							11 26							12 26	
Wigan North Western	a	09 37						10 37							11 37							12 37	
Preston ■	a	09 51						10 51							11 51							12 51	
Lancaster ■	a	10 08						11 08							12 08							13 08	
Oxenholme Lake District	a	10 22													12 22							13 22	
Penrith North Lakes	a							11 44															
Carlisle ■	a	11 01						12 00							13 01							14 01	
Lockerbie	a																						
Haymarket	a	12 16													14 15								
Edinburgh ■	a	12 22			14 07							15 07			14 22				16 04				
Haymarket	a											15 15											
Motherwell	a											15 52											
Glasgow Central ■	a							13 17				16 23										15 17	
Inverkeithing	a																						
Kirkcaldy	a																						
Markinch	a																						
Ladybank	a																						
Cupar	a																						
Leuchars ■	a																						
Dundee	a																						
Arbroath	a																						
Montrose	a																						
Stonehaven	a																						
Aberdeen	a																						

A ▭ from Birmingham New Street ⌶ to Birmingham New Street
B ⌶ from Newport (South Wales)
C ⌶ to Edinburgh

Table 51

Saturdays from 15 September

South Coast and the South West - North West England, The North East and Scotland

Route Diagram - see first Page of Table 51

Station		XC ◇■ ⌶	XC ◇■ A ⌶	XC ■ ⌶	XC ◇■ ⌶	VT ◇■ ▭	XC ◇■ B ▭⌶	XC ◇■ C ⌶	XC ◇■ ⌶	XC ◇■ D ⌶	XC ■	XC ◇■ ⌶	VT ◇■ ▭	XC ◇■ B ▭⌶	XC ◇■ ⌶	XC ◇■ A ⌶	XC ■	XC ◇■ ⌶	VT ◇■ ▭	XC ◇■ B ▭⌶	XC ◇■ ⌶	XC ◇■ D ⌶
Bournemouth	d	08 45							09 45						10 45						11 45	
Brockenhurst ■	d	09 00							10 00						11 00						12 00	
Southampton Central	d	09 15			09 47				10 15						11 15			11 47			12 15	
Southampton Airport Pkway	d	09 22			09 54				10 22						11 22			11 54			12 22	
Winchester	d	09 31			10 03				10 31						11 31			12 03			12 31	
Basingstoke	d	09 47			10 19				10 47						11 47			12 19			12 47	
Guildford	d																					
Reading ■	d	10 11			10 40				11 11			11 40			12 11			12 40			13 11	
Oxford	d	10 36			11 07				11 36			12 07			12 36			13 07			13 36	
Banbury	d	10 54			11 24				11 54			12 24			12 54			13 24			13 54	
Leamington Spa ■	d	11 12			11 42				12 12			12 42			13 12			13 42			14 12	
Coventry	d	11 27							12 27						13 27						14 27	
Birmingham International	d	11 38							12 38						13 38						14 38	
Penzance	d		06 30													08 28						
St Erth	d		06 38													08 36						
Hayle	d		06 41																			
Camborne	d		06 51													08 46						
Redruth	d		06 57													08 52						
Truro	d		07 09													09 04						
St Austell	d		07 25													09 20						
Newquay (Summer Only)	d																					
Par	d		07 32													09 28						
Lostwithiel	d		07 39																			
Bodmin Parkway	d		07 46													09 39						
Liskeard ■	d		07 58													09 51						
Plymouth	d		08 25							09 25						10 25						11 25
Totnes	d		08 50							09 50						10 50						11 50
Paignton	d													10 07								
Torquay	d													10 13								
Newton Abbot	d		09 03							10 03				10 24		11 03						12 03
Teignmouth	d													10 31								
Dawlish	d													10 36								
Exeter St Davids ■	d		09 23							10 23				10 50		11 23						12 23
Tiverton Parkway	d		09 37							10 37				11 03		11 37						12 37
Taunton	d		09 51							10 51				11 18		11 51						12 51
Weston-super-Mare	d																					
Cardiff Central ■	d							10 45														
Newport (South Wales)	d							11 00														
Bristol Temple Meads ■	d		10 30				11 00			11 30				12 00		12 30				13 00		13 30
Bristol Parkway ■	d		10 40				11 10			11 40				12 10		12 40				13 10		13 40
Gloucester ■	d							11 46														
Cheltenham Spa	d		11 12				11 42	11 57		12 12				12 42		13 12				13 42		14 12
London Paddington	d																					
Birmingham New Street ■	a	11 48	11 56		12 18		12 26	12 45	12 48	12 56		13 18		13 26	13 48	13 56		14 18		14 26	14 48	14 56
Birmingham New Street ■	d	11 57	12 03	12 19	12 30	12 20	12 31	12 49	12 57	13 03	13 19	13 30	13 20	13 31	13 57	14 03	14 19	14 30	14 20	14 31	14 57	15 03
Tamworth	d		12 19	12 36				13 09			13 36					14 19	14 36					
Burton-on-Trent	d			12 48				13 21		13 27	13 50						14 47					15 27
Derby ■	a		12 41	13 05	13 08			13 34		13 41	14 05	14 08				14 41	14 59	15 05				15 41
Nottingham ■	a			13 33				14 05			14 33						15 33					
Chesterfield	a		13 02							14 02						15 02						16 02
Sheffield ■	a		13 17		13 41					14 17		14 41				15 17		15 41				16 18
Doncaster ■	a				14 18							15 17						16 18				
Wakefield Westgate ■	a		13 46							14 46						15 46						16 46
Leeds ■	a		14 02							15 02						16 02						17 02
York ■	a		14 26		14 40					15 28		15 40				16 26		16 41				17 26
Darlington ■	a		14 58		15 13					15 58		16 13				16 58		17 13				17 56
Durham	a		15 15		15 30					16 15		16 30				17 15		17 30				18 13
Chester-le-Street	a																					
Newcastle ■	a		15 29		15 45					16 29		16 45				17 29		17 45				18 29
Morpeth	a																					
Alnmouth for Alnwick	a		15 58							16 58						18 00						
Berwick-upon-Tweed	a		16 18													18 20						19 17
Dunbar	a									17 38												19 40
Wolverhampton ■	d	12 15				12 37	12 49		13 15				13 37	13 49	14 15				14 37	14 49	15 15	
Stafford	a	12 29					13 00		13 29					14 00	14 29					15 00	15 29	
Stoke-on-Trent	a	12 54					13 18		13 54					14 19	14 54					15 19	15 54	
Congleton	a																					
Macclesfield	a	13 11							14 11						15 11						16 11	
Crewe ■	a					13 07							14 07						15 07			
Wilmslow	a																					
Stockport	a	13 27					13 49		14 27					14 49	15 27					15 49	16 27	
M'chester Piccadilly ■	a	13 39					13 59		14 39					14 59	15 39					15 59	16 39	
Warrington Bank Quay	a					13 27							14 26						15 26			
Wigan North Western	a					13 38							14 37						15 37			
Preston ■	a					13 51							14 51						15 51			
Lancaster ■	a					14 08							15 08						16 08			
Oxenholme Lake District	a												15 22									
Penrith North Lakes	a					14 44													16 45			
Carlisle ■	a					15 00							16 01						17 00			
Lockerbie	a																					
Haymarket	a					16 16													18 14			
Edinburgh ■	a		17 07			16 22				18 05						19 08			18 22			20 06
Haymarket	a		17 15							18 14						19 15						20 17
Motherwell	a		17 52													19 52						
Glasgow Central ■	a		18 11										17 17			20 11						
Inverkeithing	a									18 28												20 33
Kirkcaldy	a									18 46												20 50
Markinch	a									18 56												21 00
Ladybank	a									19 03												21 08
Cupar	a									19 10												21 17
Leuchars ■	a									19 17												21 25
Dundee	a									19 32												21 43
Arbroath	a									19 49												
Montrose	a									20 03												
Stonehaven	a									20 23												
Aberdeen	a									20 43												

A ⌶ from Plymouth to Edinburgh
B ▭ from Birmingham New Street ⌶ to Birmingham New Street
C ⌶ from Newport (South Wales)
D ⌶ to Edinburgh

South Coast and the South West - North West England, The North East and Scotland

Route Diagram - see first Page of Table 51

		XC	XC	VT	XC	XC	XC	XC	XC	XC	VT	XC	XC	XC	XC	XC	XC	VT	XC	XC	XC	XC	XC
		■	◇■	◇■	◇■	◇■	◇■	◇■	■	◇■	◇■	◇■	◇■	◇■	◇■	■	◇■	◇■	◇■	◇■	◇■	◇■	■
					A	B		C				A		D	E						D	E	
			⊥	⊡	⊡⊥	⊥	⊥	⊥		⊥	⊡	⊡⊥	⊥	⊥	⊥		⊥	⊡	⊥	⊥	⊥	⊥	
Bournemouth	d						12 45						13 45							14 45			
Brockenhurst ■	d						13 00						14 00							15 00			
Southampton Central	d						13 15			13 47			14 15							15 15			
Southampton Airport Pkway	d						13 22			13 54			14 22							15 22			
Winchester	d						13 31			14 03			14 31							15 31			
Basingstoke	d						13 47			14 19			14 47							15 47			
Guildford	d																						
Reading ■	d		13 40				14 11			14 40			15 11				15 40			16 11			
Oxford	d		14 07				14 36			15 07			15 36				16 07			16 36			
Banbury	d		14 24				14 54			15 24			15 54				16 24			16 54			
Leamington Spa ■	d		14 42				15 12			15 42			16 12				16 42			17 12			
Coventry	d						15 27						16 27							17 27			
Birmingham International	d						15 38						16 38							17 38			
Penzance	d				09 43																		
St Erth	d				09 51																		
Hayle	d																						
Camborne	d				10 01																		
Redruth	d				10 07																		
Truro	d				10 19																		
St Austell	d				10 35																		
Newquay (Summer Only)	d																						
Par	d				10 42																		
Lostwithiel	d				10 49																		
Bodmin Parkway	d				10 56																		
Liskeard ■	d				11 09																		
Plymouth	d				11 48			12 23						13 25	13 25						14 25	14 25	
Totnes	d				12 13			12 49						13 50	13 50						14 50	14 50	
Paignton	d																		13 53				
Torquay	d																		13 59				
Newton Abbot	d				12 25			13 03						14 03	14 03				14 10		15 03	15 03	
Teignmouth	d																		14 17				
Dawlish	d																		14 22				
Exeter St Davids ■	d				12 48			13 25						14 24	14 23				14 36		15 23	15 23	
Tiverton Parkway	d				13 02			13 39						14 37	14 37				14 49		15 37	15 37	
Taunton	d				13 16			13 54						14 52	14 52				15 04		15 51	15 51	
Weston-super-Mare	d																		15 30				
Cardiff Central ■	d					13 45																	
Newport (South Wales)	d					14 00																	
Bristol Temple Meads ■	d				14 00			14 30				15 00		15 30	15 30				16 00		16 30	16 30	
Bristol Parkway ■	d				14 10			14 40				15 10		15 40	15 40				16 10		16 40	16 40	
Gloucester ■	d					14 46																	
Cheltenham Spa	d				14 42	14 57		15 12				15 42		16 12	16 12				16 42		17 12	17 12	
London Paddington	d																						
Birmingham New Street ■	a		15 18		15 26	15 45	15 48	15 55		16 18		16 26	16 48	16 56	16 56		17 18		17 26	17 48	17 56	17 56	
Birmingham New Street ■	d	15 19	15 30	15 20	15 31	15 49	15 57	16 03	16 19	16 30	16 20	16 31	16 57	17 03	17 03	17 19	17 30	17 20	17 31	17 57	18 03	18 03	18 19
Tamworth	d	15 36				16 09		16 19	16 38							17 36					18 19	18 19	18 36
Burton-on-Trent	d	15 48				16 21			16 50					17 26	17 26	17 48							18 47
Derby ■	a	15 59	16 05			16 34		16 40	17 05	17 08				17 41	17 41	17 59	18 05				18 41	18 41	18 59
Nottingham ■	a	16 33				17 05			17 33							18 32							19 33
Chesterfield	a							17 01						18 02	18 02						19 02	19 02	
Sheffield ■	a		16 41					17 19		17 44				18 18	18 18		18 42				19 18	19 18	
Doncaster ■	a		17 16														19 16						
Wakefield Westgate ■	a							17 47		18 12				18 46	18 46						19 49	19 49	
Leeds ■	a							18 02		18 31				19 01	19 01						20 05	20 05	
York ■	a		17 37					18 28		18 58				19 26	19 26		19 39				20 29	20 29	
Darlington ■	a		18 12					18 59		19 35				19 57	19 57		20 11				20 58	20 58	
Durham	a		18 29					19 17		19 52				20 14	20 14		20 28				21 15	21 15	
Chester-le-Street	a																						
Newcastle ■	a		18 44					19 31		20 08				20 28	20 28		20 42				21 29	21 29	
Morpeth	a														20 50								
Alnmouth for Alnwick	a							19 59															
Berwick-upon-Tweed	a							20 20							21 23							22 01	
Dunbar	a														21 47								
Wolverhampton ■	d			15 37	15 49		16 15				16 37	16 49	17 15					17 37	17 49	18 15			
Stafford	a				16 00		16 29					17 00	17 29						18 00	18 29			
Stoke-on-Trent	a				16 19		16 54					17 19	17 54						18 19	18 54			
Congleton	a																						
Macclesfield	a						17 11						18 11							19 11			
Crewe ■	a			16 08							17 07							18 07					
Wilmslow	a																						
Stockport	a				16 49		17 27					17 49	18 27						18 49	19 27			
M'chester Piccadilly ■	a				16 59		17 39					17 59	18 39						18 59	19 39			
Warrington Bank Quay	a			16 26							17 26							18 26					
Wigan North Western	a			16 37							17 37							18 37					
Preston ■	a			16 51							17 51							18 51					
Lancaster ■	a			17 09							18 08							19 08					
Oxenholme Lake District	a			17 24							18 22							19 22					
Penrith North Lakes	a										18 48												
Carlisle ■	a			18 03							19 04							20 01					
Lockerbie	a																						
Haymarket	a										20 16												
Edinburgh ■	a							21 09			20 22				22 14							23 10	
Haymarket	a							21 16															
Motherwell	a							22 00															
Glasgow Central ■	a			19 17				22 22										21 17					
Inverkeithing	a																						
Kirkcaldy	a																						
Markinch	a																						
Ladybank	a																						
Cupar	a																						
Leuchars ■	a																						
Dundee	a																						
Arbroath	a																						
Montrose	a																						
Stonehaven	a																						
Aberdeen	a																						

A ⊡ from Birmingham New Street ⊥ to Birmingham New Street
B ⊥ from Newport (South Wales)
C ⊥ to Edinburgh
D from 15 September until 20 October
E from 27 October

South Coast and the South West - North West England, The North East and Scotland

Route Diagram - see first Page of Table 51

		XC	VT	XC	XC	XC	XC	XC	XC	VT	XC	XC	XC	XC	VT	XC	XC	XC	XC	XC	XC	XC
		◇■	◇■	◇■	◇■	◇■	◇■	■	◇■	◇■	◇■	◇■	◇■	◇■	◇■	◇■	◇■	◇■	◇■	◇■	◇■	◇■
				A					B		A	C	C	C		A	C	C				D
		⊥	⊡	⊡⊥		⊥	⊥		⊥	⊡	⊡⊥	⊥	⊥	⊥	⊡	⊡⊥	⊥	⊥			⊥	⊥
Bournemouth	d					15 45						16 45					17 45					18 45
Brockenhurst ■	d					16 00						17 00					18 00					19 00
Southampton Central	d	15 47				16 15						17 15		17 47			18 15					19 15
Southampton Airport Pkway	d	15 54				16 22						17 22		17 54			18 22					19 22
Winchester	d	16 03				16 31						17 31		18 03			18 31					19 31
Basingstoke	d	16 19				16 47						17 47		18 19			18 47					19 47
Guildford	d																					
Reading ■	d	16 40				17 11			17 40			18 11		18 40			19 11		19 40			20 11
Oxford	d	17 07				17 36			18 07			18 36		19 07			19 36		20 07			20 36
Banbury	d	17 24				17 54			18 24			18 54		19 24			19 54		20 29			20 54
Leamington Spa ■	d	17 42				18 12			18 42			19 12		19 42			20 12		20 46			21 12
Coventry	d					18 27						19 27					20 27					21 27
Birmingham International	d					18 38						19 38					20 38					21 38
Penzance	d																					
St Erth	d																					
Hayle	d																					
Camborne	d																					
Redruth	d																					
Truro	d																					
St Austell	d																					
Newquay (Summer Only)	d																					
Par	d																					
Lostwithiel	d																					
Bodmin Parkway	d																					
Liskeard ■	d																					
Plymouth	d						15 25						16 25					17 23			18 25	
Totnes	d						15 50						16 50					17 49			18 50	
Paignton	d																					
Torquay	d																					
Newton Abbot	d						16 03						17 03					18 03			19 03	
Teignmouth	d																					
Dawlish	d																					
Exeter St Davids ■	d						16 23				16 53		17 23					18 25			19 23	
Tiverton Parkway	d						16 37				17 07		17 37					18 39			19 37	
Taunton	d						16 51				17 21		17 51					18 54			19 51	
Weston-super-Mare	d																					
Cardiff Central ■	d				16 45																	
Newport (South Wales)	d				17 00																	
Bristol Temple Meads ■	d			17 00			17 30				18 00		18 30			19 00		19 30		20 00	20 30	
Bristol Parkway ■	d			17 10			17 40				18 10		18 40			19 10		19 40		20 10	20 40	
Gloucester ■	d				17 46																	
Cheltenham Spa	d			17 42	17 58		18 12				18 42		19 12			19 42		20 12		20 42	21 12	
London Paddington	d																					
Birmingham New Street ■	a	18 18		18 26	18 45	18 48	18 56		19 18		19 26	19 48	19 58	20 18		20 26	20 48	20 53	21 18	21 38	21 53	21 48
Birmingham New Street ■	d	18 30	18 20	18 31	18 49	18 57	19 03	19 19	19 30	19 20	19 31	19 57	20 03	20 30	20 20	20 31	20 57	21 03				21 57
Tamworth	d				19 09			19 36					20 19					21 19				
Burton-on-Trent	d				19 21		19 27	19 48										21 31				
Derby ■	a	19 05			19 35		19 39	19 59	20 05				20 42	21 24				21 44				
Nottingham ■	a				20 05			20 35														
Chesterfield	a	19 29					20 04		20 29				21 04	21 45				22 07				
Sheffield ■	a	19 51					20 19		20 49				21 19	22 05				22 23				
Doncaster ■	a	20 17							21 21					22 30				22 51				
Wakefield Westgate ■	a						20 48						21 48					23 10				
Leeds ■	a						21 03						22 02					23 27				
York ■	a	20 40					21 57		21 45					22 57								
Darlington ■	a	21 13							22 13													
Durham	a	21 30							22 30													
Chester-le-Street	a																					
Newcastle ■	a	21 44							22 47													
Morpeth	a																					
Alnmouth for Alnwick	a																					
Berwick-upon-Tweed	a																					
Dunbar	a																					
Wolverhampton ■	d		18 37	18 49		19 15				19 37	19 49	20 15			20 37	20 49	21 15					22 16
Stafford	a			19 00		19 29					20 00	20 29			20 49	21 00	21 29					22 29
Stoke-on-Trent	a			19 19		19 54					20 19	20 54				21 20	21 52					22 50
Congleton	a																					
Macclesfield	a					20 11					20 36	21 11				21 38	22 11					23 07
Crewe ■	a		19 07							20 07					21 10							
Wilmslow	a																					
Stockport	a			19 49		20 27					20 49	21 27				21 53	22 27					23 21
M'chester Piccadilly ■	a			19 59		20 39					20 59	21 39				22 04	22 39					23 32
Warrington Bank Quay	a		19 26							20 26												
Wigan North Western	a		19 37							20 37												
Preston ■	a		19 54							20 59												
Lancaster ■	a																					
Oxenholme Lake District	a																					
Penrith North Lakes	a																					
Carlisle ■	a																					
Lockerbie	a																					
Haymarket	a																					
Edinburgh ■	a																					
Haymarket	a																					
Motherwell	a																					
Glasgow Central ■	a																					
Inverkeithing	a																					
Kirkcaldy	a																					
Markinch	a																					
Ladybank	a																					
Cupar	a																					
Leuchars ■	a																					
Dundee	a																					
Arbroath	a																					
Montrose	a																					
Stonehaven	a																					
Aberdeen	a																					

A ⊡ from Birmingham New Street ⊥ to Birmingham New Street
B ⊥ to Sheffield
C ⊥ to Birmingham New Street
D ⊥ to Reading

Table 51

Saturdays from 15 September

South Coast and the South West - North West England, The North East and Scotland

Route Diagram - see first Page of Table 51

		XC	XC	XC	XC	XC	XC	XC
			◇■	◇■	◇■	◇■		◇■
		A						
		🚌					🚌	H
Bournemouth	d					19 45		
Brockenhurst	d					20 00		
Southampton Central	d					20 15		
Southampton Airport Pkway	d					20 22		
Winchester	d					20 31		
Basingstoke	d					20 47		
Guildford	d							
Reading	d		20 40			21 11		21 40
Oxford	d		21 07			21 36		22 07
Banbury	d		21 25			21 54		22 29
Leamington Spa	d		21 45			22 12		22 46
Coventry	d		21 56			22 27		
Birmingham International	d		22 11			22 38		
Penzance	d							
St Erth	d							
Hayle	d							
Camborne	d							
Redruth	d							
Truro	d							
St Austell	d							
Newquay (Summer Only)	d							
Par	d							
Lostwithiel	d							
Bodmin Parkway	d							
Liskeard	d							
Plymouth	d							
Totnes	d							
Paignton	d							
Torquay	d							
Newton Abbot	d							
Teignmouth	d							
Dawlish	d							
Exeter St Davids	d							
Tiverton Parkway	d							
Taunton	d							
Weston-super-Mare	d							
Cardiff Central	d				20 50			
Newport (South Wales)	d				21 05			
Bristol Temple Meads	d							
Bristol Parkway	d							
Gloucester	d				21 49			
Cheltenham Spa	d				22 00			
London Paddington	d							
Birmingham New Street	a		22 21		22 42	22 48		23 16
Birmingham New Street	d	22 20		22 31			22 49	
Tamworth	d	22 55					23 24	
Burton-on-Trent	d	23 15					23s44	
Derby	a	23s45					00 04	
Nottingham	a	00 49						
Chesterfield	a							
Sheffield	a							
Doncaster	a							
Wakefield Westgate	a							
Leeds	a							
York	a							
Darlington	a							
Durham	a							
Chester-le-Street	a							
Newcastle	a							
Morpeth	a							
Alnmouth for Alnwick	a							
Berwick-upon-Tweed	a							
Dunbar	a							
Wolverhampton	d			22 49				
Stafford	a			23 01				
Stoke-on-Trent	a			23 20				
Congleton	a							
Macclesfield	a			23 38				
Crewe	a							
Wilmslow	a							
Stockport	a			23 53				
M'chester Piccadilly	a			00 10				
Warrington Bank Quay	a							
Wigan North Western	a							
Preston	a							
Lancaster	a							
Oxenholme Lake District	a							
Penrith North Lakes	a							
Carlisle	a							
Lockerbie	a							
Haymarket	a							
Edinburgh	a							
Haymarket	a							
Motherwell	a							
Glasgow Central	a							
Inverkeithing	a							
Kirkcaldy	a							
Markinch	a							
Ladybank	a							
Cupar	a							
Leuchars	a							
Dundee	a							
Arbroath	a							
Montrose	a							
Stonehaven	a							
Aberdeen	a							

A from 15 September until 20 October

Table 51

Sundays until 24 June

South Coast and the South West - North West England, The North East and Scotland

Route Diagram - see first Page of Table 51

		XC	VT	XC	XC	VT	XC	XC	VT	XC	XC	VT	XC	XC	XC	VT	XC	XC	XC	XC	VT	XC	XC
		◇■	◇■	◇■	◇■	◇■	◇■	◇■	◇■	◇■	◇■	◇■	◇■	◇■	◇■	◇■	◇■	◇■	◇■	◇■	◇■	◇■	◇■
								A							A			B	A				
			□	H	H	□	H	H	□	H	H	□	H	H	H	□	H	H	H	H	□	H	H
Bournemouth	d																			09 40			
Brockenhurst	d																			09 57			
Southampton Central	d													09 15						10 15			
Southampton Airport Pkway	d													09 22						10 22			
Winchester	d													09 31						10 31			
Basingstoke	d													09 47						10 47			
Guildford	d																						
Reading	d									09 11				10 11						11 11			
Oxford	d									09 37				10 37						11 37			
Banbury	d									09 54				10 54						11 54			
Leamington Spa	d									10 12				11 12						12 12			
Coventry	d									10 28				11 29						12 28			
Birmingham International	d									10 40				11 40						12 40			
Penzance	d																						
St Erth	d																						
Hayle	d																						
Camborne	d																						
Redruth	d																						
Truro	d																						
St Austell	d																						
Newquay (Summer Only)	d																						
Par	d																						
Lostwithiel	d																						
Bodmin Parkway	d																						
Liskeard	d																		09 25				
Plymouth	d																		09 50				
Totnes	d																						
Paignton	d																						
Torquay	d																						
Newton Abbot	d																		10 03				
Teignmouth	d																						
Dawlish	d																						
Exeter St Davids	d																		10 23				
Tiverton Parkway	d																		10 37				
Taunton	d																		10 51				
Weston-super-Mare	d																						
Cardiff Central	d																	10 45					
Newport (South Wales)	d																	10 59					
Bristol Temple Meads	d										09 15				10 30				11 30				
Bristol Parkway	d										09 25				10 40				11 40				
Gloucester	d										10 01							11 51					
Cheltenham Spa	d										10 12				11 12			12 03	12 12				
London Paddington	d																						
Birmingham New Street	a									10 50	10 50			11 50	11 50			12 45	12 50	12 50			
Birmingham New Street	d	22p31	08 35	08 50	09 03	09 09	10 01	10 03	10 09	11 01	11 03	11 09	11 49	12 01	12 03	12 09	12 30	12 49	13 03	12 58	13 10	13 30	13 31
Tamworth	d				09 19			10 18					12 07		12 19			13 07					
Burton-on-Trent	d				09 29			10 29			11 26		12 19					13 19	13 26				
Derby	a				09 42			10 39			11 40		12 34		12 43		13 01	13 33	13 42			14 00	
Nottingham	a												13 00					14 00					
Chesterfield	a				10 02			11 02			12 02				13 02		13 29		14 02			14 29	
Sheffield	a				10 16			11 17			12 18				13 18		13 43		14 17			14 45	
Doncaster	a																14 13					15 13	
Wakefield Westgate	a				10 44			11 44			12 44				13 45				14 44				
Leeds	a				11 02			12 01			13 02				14 02				15 02				
York	a				11 29			12 29			13 29				14 29		14 40		15 29			15 43	
Darlington	a				11 57			12 57			13 57				14 57		15 13		15 57			16 13	
Durham	a				12 14			13 14			14 14				15 14		15 30		16 14			16 30	
Chester-le-Street	a																						
Newcastle	a				12 29			13 32			14 28				15 28		15 44		16 28			16 44	
Morpeth	a										14 48												
Alnmouth for Alnwick	a							13 59							16 01				16 58				
Berwick-upon-Tweed	a							14 20							16 21								
Dunbar	a				13 39						15 40								17 39				
Wolverhampton	d	22p49	09 04	09 19		09 37	10 29		10 37	11 30		11 37		12 28		12 37				13 26	13 37		14 01
Stafford	a	23p01	09 16	09 32			10 43			11 42				12 42						13 39			
Stoke-on-Trent	a	23p20					11 02			12 03				13 02						13 58			14 31
Congleton	a																						
Macclesfield	a	23p38					11 19			12 21				13 20						14 16			14 49
Crewe	a		09 35	09 54		10 07			11 07			12 07				13 07					14 07		
Wilmslow	a			10 12																			
Stockport	a	23p53		10 21			11 37			12 35				13 38						14 29			15 02
M'chester Piccadilly	a	00 10		10 37			11 47			12 44				13 46						14 40			15 17
Warrington Bank Quay	a		09 54			10 26			11 26			12 26				13 26					14 26		
Wigan North Western	a		10 05			10 37			11 37			12 37				13 37					14 37		
Preston	a		10 22			10 51			11 51			12 51				13 51					14 50		
Lancaster	a					11 07			12 08			13 08				14 08					15 08		
Oxenholme Lake District	a					11 22			12 22			13 22									15 22		
Penrith North Lakes	a															14 44							
Carlisle	a					12 01			13 01			14 01				15 00					16 01		
Lockerbie	a																						
Haymarket	a								14 13							16 14							
Edinburgh	a				14 07			15 05	14 22		16 06				17 06	16 22			18 07				
Haymarket	a							15 14							17 14				18 16				
Motherwell	a							15 51							17 52								
Glasgow Central	a					13 17		16 13				15 16			18 12						17 17		
Inverkeithing	a																		18 28				
Kirkcaldy	a																		18 44				
Markinch	a																		18 53				
Ladybank	a																		19 01				
Cupar	a																		19 07				
Leuchars	a																		19 14				
Dundee	a																		19 29				
Arbroath	a																		19 46				
Montrose	a																		20 00				
Stonehaven	a																		20 23				
Aberdeen	a																		20 43				

A H to Edinburgh

B H from Newport (South Wales)

South Coast and the South West - North West England, The North East and Scotland

Route Diagram - see first Page of Table 51

		XC	XC	XC	VT	XC	XC	XC	XC	XC	XC	VT	XC	XC	XC	XC	VT	XC	XC	XC	XC	XC	VT
		◇1	◇1	◇1	◇1	◇1	◇1	◇1	◇1	◇1	◇1	◇1	◇1	◇1	◇1	◇1	◇1	◇1	◇1	◇1	◇1	◇1	◇1
		A		B				A		C				A		B				A		C	
		⌶	⌶	⌶	⊡	⌶	⌶	⌶	⌶	⌶	⌶	⊡	⌶	⌶	⌶	⌶	⊡	⌶	⌶	⌶	⌶	⌶	⊡
Bournemouth	d		10 40						11 40						12 40						13 40		
Brockenhurst 3	d		10 57						11 57						12 57						13 57		
Southampton Central	d		11 15						12 15						13 15						14 15		
Southampton Airport Pkway ✈	d		11 22						12 22						13 22						14 22		
Winchester	d		11 31						12 31						13 31						14 31		
Basingstoke	d		11 47						12 47						13 47						14 47		
Guildford	d					12 14																	
Reading 7	d		12 11			12 54			13 11		13 40				14 09			14 40			15 11		
Oxford	d		12 37			13 17			13 37		14 05				14 37			15 06			15 37		
Banbury	d		12 54			13 35			13 54		14 24				14 54			15 25			15 54		
Leamington Spa 8	d		13 12			13 52			14 12		14 42				15 12			15 43			16 12		
Coventry	d		13 26						14 26						15 26						16 26		
Birmingham International ✈	d		13 38						14 38						15 38						16 38		
Penzance	d									09 30													
St Erth	d									09 38													
Hayle	d																						
Camborne	d									09 48													
Redruth	d									09 54													
Truro	d									10 06													
St Austell	d									10 22													
Newquay (Summer Only)	d																					11 30	
Par	d									10 30												12 29	
Lostwithiel	d																						
Bodmin Parkway	d									10 41												12 41	
Liskeard 6	d									10 53												12 54	
Plymouth	d			10 25						11 25			12 00			12 25			12 52			13 23	
Totnes	d			10 50						11 50						12 50						13 49	
Paignton	d						10 50																
Torquay	d						10 56																
Newton Abbot	d			11 03			11 08			12 03			12 36			13 03			13 27			14 03	
Teignmouth	d						11 15																
Dawlish	d						11 20																
Exeter St Davids 6	d			11 23			11 32			12 23			12 57			13 23			13 48			14 25	
Tiverton Parkway	d			11 37			11 46			12 37			13 10			13 37						14 39	
Taunton	d			11 53			12 00			12 51			13 25			13 51						14 54	
Weston-super-Mare	d						12 21																
Cardiff Central 7	d	11 45						12 45						13 45						14 45			
Newport (South Wales)	d	11 59						12 59						13 59						14 59			
Bristol Temple Meads 10	d			12 30			13 00			13 30			14 00			14 30			15 00			15 30	
Bristol Parkway 7	d			12 40			13 10			13 40			14 10			14 40			15 10			15 40	
Gloucester 7	d	12 47						13 51						14 47						15 47			
Cheltenham Spa	d	12 58		13 12			13 42	14 02		14 12			14 42	14 58		15 12			15 42	15 58		16 12	
London Paddington	d																						
Birmingham New Street 12	a	13 41	13 48	13 50		14 19	14 26	14 45	14 48	14 50	15 09		15 27	15 41	15 48	15 50		16 12	16 26	16 41	16 48	16 50	
Birmingham New Street 12	d	13 49	13 58	14 03	14 10	14 30	14 31	14 49	14 58	15 03	15 30	15 10	15 31	15 49	15 58	16 03	16 10	16 30	16 31	16 49	16 58	17 03	17 10
Tamworth	d	14 07		14 19				15 09						16 07		16 19				17 07			
Burton-on-Trent	d	14 19						15 21		15 28				16 19						17 19		17 28	
Derby 6	a	14 34		14 42		15 04		15 34		15 42	16 02			16 34		16 42		17 04		17 34		17 39	
Nottingham 6	a	15 02						16 00						17 00						18 00			
Chesterfield	a			15 02						16 02						17 02						18 03	
Sheffield 7	a			15 17		15 47				16 18	16 48					17 17		17 48				18 19	
Doncaster 7	a					16 15					17 13							18 13					
Wakefield Westgate 7	a			15 44						16 44						17 47		18 33				18 47	
Leeds 10	a			16 02						17 02						18 02		18 51				19 04	
York 8	a			16 29		16 40				17 29	17 42					18 29		19 18				19 29	
Darlington 7	a			16 57		17 15				17 57	18 11					18 57		19 46				19 59	
Durham	a			17 14		17 33				18 14	18 29					19 14		20 03				20 17	
Chester-le-Street	a																						
Newcastle 8	a			17 30		17 47				18 28	18 43					19 30		20 19				20 31	
Morpeth	a																					20 52	
Alnmouth for Alnwick	a			18 01												20 04							
Berwick-upon-Tweed	a			18 22						19 17						20 24						21 25	
Dunbar	a									19 40												21 48	
Wolverhampton 7	d		14 25		14 37		15 01		15 26			15 37	16 01		16 26		16 37		17 01		17 26		17 37
Stafford	a		14 38						15 39						16 37						17 38		
Stoke-on-Trent	a		14 57				15 35		15 57				16 33		16 57				17 34		17 57		
Congleton	a																						
Macclesfield	a		15 14				15 57		16 14				16 54		17 14				17 54		18 14		
Crewe 10	a				15 07							16 07					17 07						18 07
Wilmslow	a																						
Stockport	a		15 26				16 09		16 26				17 07		17 29				18 07		18 28		
M'chester Piccadilly 10	a		15 38				16 22		16 38				17 19		17 40				18 19		18 40		
Warrington Bank Quay	a				15 26							16 26					17 26						18 26
Wigan North Western	a				15 37							16 37					17 37						18 37
Preston 8	a				15 51							16 51					17 51						18 51
Lancaster 6	a				16 08							17 08					18 08						19 08
Oxenholme Lake District	a											17 22					18 22						19 22
Penrith North Lakes	a				16 44												18 48						
Carlisle 8	a				17 00							18 01					19 04						20 01
Lockerbie	a																						
Haymarket	a				18 13																		
Edinburgh 10	a			19 06	18 22					20 05						21 08	20 22					22 16	
Haymarket	a			19 22												21 16							
Motherwell	a			20 00												21 53							
Glasgow Central 15	a			20 20								19 17				22 14							21 17
Inverkeithing	a																						
Kirkcaldy	a																						
Markinch	a																						
Ladybank	a																						
Cupar	a																						
Leuchars 3	a																						
Dundee	a																						
Arbroath	a																						
Montrose	a																						
Stonehaven	a																						
Aberdeen	a																						

A ⌶ from Newport (South Wales)
B ⌶ to Edinburgh
C ⌶ from Plymouth

South Coast and the South West - North West England, The North East and Scotland

Route Diagram - see first Page of Table 51

		XC	XC	XC	XC	XC	XC	VT	XC	XC	XC	XC	VT	XC	XC	XC	XC	XC	VT	XC	XC	XC
		◇1	◇1	◇1	◇1	◇1	◇1	◇1	◇1	◇1	◇1	◇1	■ 1	◇1	◇1	◇1	◇1	◇1	◇1	◇1	◇1	◇1
						A			B					C				D				
		⌶	⌶		⌶	⌶	⌶	⊡	⌶		⌶	⌶	⊡	⌶	⌶		⌶	⌶	⊡	⌶	⌶	
Bournemouth	d				14 40						15 40						16 40					
Brockenhurst 3	d				14 57						15 57						16 57					
Southampton Central	d				15 15						16 15						17 15					
Southampton Airport Pkway ✈	d				15 22						16 22						17 22					
Winchester	d				15 31						16 31						17 31					
Basingstoke	d				15 47						16 47						17 47					
Guildford	d																					
Reading 7	d	15 40			16 11		16 41				17 09			17 40			18 11			18 41		
Oxford	d	16 06			16 37		17 06				17 37			18 06			18 37			19 06		
Banbury	d	16 25			16 54		17 25				17 54			18 25			18 54			19 25		
Leamington Spa 8	d	16 43			17 12		17 43				18 12			18 43			19 12			19 43		
Coventry	d				17 26						18 26						19 26			19 54		
Birmingham International ✈	d				17 38						18 38						19 38			20 04		
Penzance	d								12 25													
St Erth	d								12 33													
Hayle	d								12 37													
Camborne	d								12 46													
Redruth	d								12 53													
Truro	d								13 04													
St Austell	d								13 21													
Newquay (Summer Only)	d																					
Par	d								13 28													
Lostwithiel	d								13 35													
Bodmin Parkway	d								13 42													
Liskeard 6	d								13 55													
Plymouth	d					14 23			14 35			15 23						16 25				
Totnes	d					14 49			15 00			15 49						16 49				
Paignton	d																					
Torquay	d																					
Newton Abbot	d					15 03			15 12			16 03						17 02				
Teignmouth	d																					
Dawlish	d																					
Exeter St Davids 6	d					15 25			15 33			16 24						17 24				
Tiverton Parkway	d					15 38			15 46			16 37						17 38				
Taunton	d					15 54			16 01			16 53						17 53				
Weston-super-Mare	d								16 30													
Cardiff Central 7	d			15 45						16 45						17 45						18 45
Newport (South Wales)	d			15 59						16 59						17 59						18 59
Bristol Temple Meads 10	d		16 00			16 30			17 00			17 30			18 00			18 30			19 00	
Bristol Parkway 7	d		16 10			16 40			17 10			17 40			18 10			18 40			19 10	
Gloucester 7	d			16 47						17 47						18 47						19 52
Cheltenham Spa	d		16 42	16 58		17 12			17 42	17 58		18 12			18 42	18 58		19 12			19 42	20 02
London Paddington	d																					
Birmingham New Street 12	a	17 12	17 26	17 41	17 48	17 49	18 09		18 27	18 41	18 48	18 51		19 11	19 26	19 41	19 48	19 56		20 15	20 26	20 44
Birmingham New Street 12	d	17 30	17 31	17 49	17 58	18 03	18 30	18 10	18 31	18 49	18 58	19 03	19 10	19 30	19 31	19 49	19 58	20 03	20 10		20 31	20 49
Tamworth	d			18 07		18 19				19 09						20 07		20 19				21 06
Burton-on-Trent	d			18 19						19 21		19 26				20 19						21 19
Derby 6	a	18 04		18 33		18 39	19 03			19 33		19 39		20 01		20 34		20 39				21 33
Nottingham 6	a			19 00						20 00						21 00						22 00
Chesterfield	a					19 04						20 01						21 02				
Sheffield 7	a	18 46				19 20	19 39					20 17		20 38				21 18				
Doncaster 7	a	19 15					20 16							21 19								
Wakefield Westgate 7	a					19 48						20 46						21 47				
Leeds 10	a					20 05						21 03						22 04				
York 8	a	19 43				20 29	20 45					21 31		21 44								
Darlington 7	a	20 11				20 59	21 12							22 22								
Durham	a	20 28				21 17	21 31							22 40								
Chester-le-Street	a																					
Newcastle 8	a	20 42				21 31	21 44							23 10								
Morpeth	a																					
Alnmouth for Alnwick	a					22 04																
Berwick-upon-Tweed	a																					
Dunbar	a																					
Wolverhampton 7	d		18 01		18 26			18 37	19 01		19 26		19 37		20 01		20 26		20 38		20 59	
Stafford	a				18 36						19 38						20 38		20 51			
Stoke-on-Trent	a		18 30		18 55				19 31		19 57				20 33		20 56				21 33	
Congleton	a																					
Macclesfield	a		18 48		19 14				19 49		20 14				20 56		21 15				21 51	
Crewe 10	a							19 07					20 07						21 10			
Wilmslow	a																					
Stockport	a		19 04		19 28				20 02		20 29				21 09		21 28				22 05	
M'chester Piccadilly 10	a		19 19		19 40				20 18		20 40				21 20		21 40				22 17	
Warrington Bank Quay	a							19 26					20 26									
Wigan North Western	a							19 37					20 37									
Preston 8	a							19 51					20 51									
Lancaster 6	a							20 08					21 08									
Oxenholme Lake District	a												21 22									
Penrith North Lakes	a							20 44														
Carlisle 8	a							21 00					22 01									
Lockerbie	a												22 22									
Haymarket	a							22 15														
Edinburgh 10	a	22 23				23 08		22 21														
Haymarket	a																					
Motherwell	a												23 09									
Glasgow Central 15	a												23 25									
Inverkeithing	a																					
Kirkcaldy	a																					
Markinch	a																					
Ladybank	a																					
Cupar	a																					
Leuchars 3	a																					
Dundee	a																					
Arbroath	a																					
Montrose	a																					
Stonehaven	a																					
Aberdeen	a																					

A ⌶ to Leeds
B ⌶ from Plymouth
C ⌶ to Sheffield
D ⌶ to Birmingham New Street

Table 51

Sundays until 24 June

South Coast and the South West - North West England, The North East and Scotland

Route Diagram - see first Page of Table 51

		XC	XC	VT	XC	XC	XC	XC	XC	XC	XC	XC	XC	XC
		◇■ ⌶	◇■ A ⌶	◇■ ⊡	◇■ ⌶	◇■ ⌶	◇■	◇■ B ⌶	◇■ C ⌶	◇■	◇■	◇■	◇■	◇■
Bournemouth	d	17 40						18 40			19 40			
Brockenhurst	d	17 57						18 57			19 57			
Southampton Central	d	18 15						19 15			20 15			
Southampton Airport Pkway	d	18 22						19 22			20 22			
Winchester	d	18 31						19 31			20 31			
Basingstoke	d	18 47						19 47			20 47			
Guildford	d													
Reading	d	19 11			19 40			20 11		20 41	21 11		21 40	
Oxford	d	19 37			20 06			20 37		21 06	21 37		22 06	
Banbury	d	19 54			20 25			20 54		21 24	21 54		22 24	
Leamington Spa	d	20 12			20 43			21 12		21 42	22 12		22 42	
Coventry	d	20 26			20 54			21 26		21 53	22 23		22 53	
Birmingham International	d	20 38			21 04			21 38		22 03	22 33		23 03	
Penzance	d		15 30											
St Erth	d		15 38											
Hayle	d													
Camborne	d		15 51											
Redruth	d		15 57											
Truro	d		16 09											
St Austell	d		16 25											
Newquay (Summer Only)	d													
Par	d		16 33											
Lostwithiel	d													
Bodmin Parkway	d		16 44											
Liskeard	d		16 56											
Plymouth	d		17 26						18 23					
Totnes	d		17 52						18 49					
Paignton	d					18 20								
Torquay	d					18 26								
Newton Abbot	d		18 04			18 37			19 03					
Teignmouth	d													
Dawlish	d													
Exeter St Davids	d		18 23			18 58			19 25					
Tiverton Parkway	d		18 38			19 11			19 38					
Taunton	d		18 52			19 25			19 54					
Weston-super-Mare	d													
Cardiff Central	d						19 45					20 45		
Newport (South Wales)	d						20 00					20 59		
Bristol Temple Meads	d		19 30			20 00			20 30					22 10
Bristol Parkway	d		19 40			20 10			20 40					22 20
Gloucester	d						20 50					21 48		
Cheltenham Spa	d		20 12			20 42	21 01		21 12			21 59		22 52
London Paddington	d													
Birmingham New Street	a	20 48	20 50		21 15	21 20	21 44	21 48	21 51	22 14	22 42	22 42	23 13	23 39
Birmingham New Street	d	20 58	21 03	21 12				21 59	22 03					
Tamworth	d		21 19						22 18					
Burton-on-Trent	d		21 30											
Derby	a		21 42						22 40					
Nottingham	a													
Chesterfield	a		22 02						23 04					
Sheffield	a		22 18						23 20					
Doncaster	a													
Wakefield Westgate	a		22 43											
Leeds	a		23 01						00 16					
York	a													
Darlington	a													
Durham	a													
Chester-le-Street	a													
Newcastle	a													
Morpeth	a													
Alnmouth for Alnwick	a													
Berwick-upon-Tweed	a													
Dunbar	a													
Wolverhampton	d	21 30		21 44				22 26						
Stafford	a	21 42		21 56				22 38						
Stoke-on-Trent	a	22 03						22 58						
Congleton	a													
Macclesfield	a	22 20						23 15						
Crewe	a			22 17										
Wilmslow	a													
Stockport	a	22 32						23 29						
M'chester Piccadilly	a	22 43						23 41						
Warrington Bank Quay	a			22 36										
Wigan North Western	a			22 47										
Preston	a			23 07										
Lancaster	a													
Oxenholme Lake District	a													
Penrith North Lakes	a													
Carlisle	a													
Lockerbie	a													
Haymarket	a													
Edinburgh	a													
Haymarket	a													
Motherwell	a													
Glasgow Central	a													
Inverkeithing	a													
Kirkcaldy	a													
Markinch	a													
Ladybank	a													
Cupar	a													
Leuchars	a													
Dundee	a													
Arbroath	a													
Montrose	a													
Stonehaven	a													
Aberdeen	a													

A ⌶ from Plymouth to Birmingham New Street B ⌶ to Reading C ⌶ to Birmingham New Street

Table 51

Sundays 1 July to 9 September

South Coast and the South West - North West England, The North East and Scotland

Route Diagram - see first Page of Table 51

		XC	XC	VT	XC	VT	XC	XC	VT	XC	XC	XC	VT	XC	XC	XC	XC	VT	XC	XC	XC	XC	XC	VT	XC
		◇■	🚌	◇■ ⊡	◇■ ⌶	◇■ ⊡	◇■ ⌶	◇■ A ⌶	◇■ ⊡	◇■ ⌶	🚌	◇■ ⌶	◇■ ⊡	◇■ ⌶	◇■ ⌶	🚌	◇■ A ⌶	◇■ ⊡	◇■ ⌶	◇■ B ⌶	◇■ A ⌶	◇■ ⌶	🚌	◇■ ⊡	◇■ ⌶
Bournemouth	d																					09 40			
Brockenhurst	d																					09 57			
Southampton Central	d														09 15							10 15			
Southampton Airport Pkway	d														09 22							10 22			
Winchester	d														09 31							10 31			
Basingstoke	d														09 47							10 47			
Guildford	d																								
Reading	d									09 11					10 11							11 11			
Oxford	d									09 37					10 37							11 37			
Banbury	d									09 54					10 54							11 54			
Leamington Spa	d									10 12	10 20				11 12	11 20						12 12	12 20		
Coventry	d										10a45					11a45							12a45		
Birmingham International	d																								
Penzance	d																								
St Erth	d																								
Hayle	d																								
Camborne	d																								
Redruth	d																								
Truro	d																								
St Austell	d																								
Newquay (Summer Only)	d																								
Par	d																								
Lostwithiel	d																								
Bodmin Parkway	d																								
Liskeard	d																								
Plymouth	d																				09 25				
Totnes	d																				09 50				
Paignton	d																								
Torquay	d																								
Newton Abbot	d																				10 03				
Teignmouth	d																								
Dawlish	d																								
Exeter St Davids	d																				10 23				
Tiverton Parkway	d																				10 37				
Taunton	d																				10 51				
Weston-super-Mare	d																								
Cardiff Central	d																			10 45					
Newport (South Wales)	d																			10 59					
Bristol Temple Meads	d											09 15					10 30				11 30				
Bristol Parkway	d											09 25					10 40				11 40				
Gloucester	d											10 01								11 51					
Cheltenham Spa	d											10 12					11 12			12 03	12 12				
London Paddington	d																								
Birmingham New Street	a									10 55		10 50			11 54		11 50			12 45	12 50	12 54			
Birmingham New Street	d	22p31	22p49	08 45	09 01	09 20	10 01	10 03	10 20	11 01		11 03	11 20	11 49	12 01		12 03	12 20	12 30	12 49	13 03	13 01		13 20	13 30
Tamworth	d		23p24					10 18						12 07			12 19			13 07					
Burton-on-Trent	d		23b44					10 29				11 26		12 19						13 19	13 26				
Derby	a		00 04					10 39				11 40		12 33			12 43		13 01	13 33	13 42				14 01
Nottingham	a													13 00						14 00					
Chesterfield	a							11 02				12 02					13 02		13 29		14 02				14 29
Sheffield	a							11 17				12 18					13 18		13 43		14 17				14 45
Doncaster	a																		14 13						15 13
Wakefield Westgate	a							11 44				12 44					13 45				14 44				
Leeds	a							12 01				13 02					14 02				15 02				
York	a							12 29				13 29					14 29		14 40		15 29				15 43
Darlington	a							12 57				13 57					14 57		15 13		15 57				16 13
Durham	a							13 14				14 14					15 14		15 30		16 14				16 30
Chester-le-Street	a																								
Newcastle	a							13 32				14 28					15 28		15 44		16 28				16 44
Morpeth	a											14 48													
Alnmouth for Alnwick	a							13 59									16 01				16 58				
Berwick-upon-Tweed	a							14 20									16 21								
Dunbar	a											15 40									17 39				
Wolverhampton	d	22p49		09 04	09 19	09 37	10 19		10 37	11 19			11 37		12 19			12 37				13 19		13 37	
Stafford	a	23p01		09 16	09 32		10 32			11 31					12 32							13 33			
Stoke-on-Trent	a	23p20					10 51			11 51					12 52							13 56			
Congleton	a																								
Macclesfield	a	23p38					11 08			12 09					13 10							14 14			
Crewe	a			09 35	09 54	10 06			11 07				12 07					13 07						14 07	
Wilmslow	a				10 12																				
Stockport	a	23p53			10 21		11 22			12 22					13 28							14 28			
M'chester Piccadilly	a	00 10			10 37		11 31			12 40					13 40							14 40			
Warrington Bank Quay	a			09 54		10 26			11 26				12 26					13 26						14 26	
Wigan North Western	a			10 05		10 37			11 37				12 37					13 37						14 37	
Preston	a			10 22		10 51			11 51				12 51					13 51						14 50	
Lancaster	a					11 07			12 08				13 08					14 08						15 08	
Oxenholme Lake District	a					11 22			12 22				13 22											15 22	
Penrith North Lakes	a																	14 44							
Carlisle	a					12 01			13 01				14 01					15 00						16 01	
Lockerbie	a																								
Haymarket	a								14 13									16 14							
Edinburgh	a							15 05	14 22			16 06					17 06	16 22			18 07				
Haymarket	a							15 14									17 14				18 16				
Motherwell	a							15 51									17 52								
Glasgow Central	a					13 17		16 13					15 16				18 12							17 17	
Inverkeithing	a																				18 28				
Kirkcaldy	a																				18 44				
Markinch	a																				18 53				
Ladybank	a																				19 01				
Cupar	a																				19 07				
Leuchars	a																				19 14				
Dundee	a																				19 29				
Arbroath	a																				19 46				
Montrose	a																				20 00				
Stonehaven	a																				20 23				
Aberdeen	a																				20 43				

A ⌶ to Edinburgh B ⌶ from Newport (South Wales) b Previous night, stops to set down only

South Coast and the South West - North West England, The North East and Scotland

Route Diagram - see first Page of Table 51

		XC	XC	XC	XC	XC	XC	VT	XC	XC	XC	XC	XC	XC	VT	XC	XC	XC	XC	XC	VT	XC	XC	XC	XC
		◇1	◇1	◇1	◇1	🚌	◇1	◇1	◇1	◇1	◇1	◇1	🚌	◇1	◇1	◇1	◇1	◇1	◇1	◇1	◇1	◇1	◇1	◇1	◇1
			A	B						A	C						A		B				A		C
		⊼	⊼	⊼	⊼		⊼	⊏	⊼	⊼	⊼	⊼		⊼	⊏	⊼	⊼	⊼	⊼	⊼	⊏	⊼	⊼	⊼	⊼
Bournemouth	d				10 40							11 40						12 40						13 40	
Brockenhurst	d				10 57							11 57						12 57						13 57	
Southampton Central	d				11 15							12 15						13 15						14 15	
Southampton Airport Pkway	d				11 22							12 22						13 22						14 22	
Winchester	d				11 31							12 31						13 31						14 31	
Basingstoke	d				11 47							12 47						13 47						14 47	
Guildford	d						12 14																		
Reading	d				12 11		12 54					13 11		13 40				14 11		14 40				15 11	
Oxford	d				12 37		13 17					13 37		14 05				14 37		15 06				15 37	
Banbury	d				12 54		13 35					13 54		14 24				14 54		15 25				15 54	
Leamington Spa	d				13 12	13 20	13 52					14 12	14 20	14 42				15 12		15 43				16 12	
Coventry	d					13a45							14a45					15 26						16 26	
Birmingham International	d																	15 38						16 38	
Penzance	d										09 30														
St Erth	d										09 38														
Hayle	d																								
Camborne	d										09 48														
Redruth	d										09 54														
Truro	d										10 06														
St Austell	d										10 22														
Newquay (Summer Only)	d																								11 30
Par	d										10 30														12 29
Lostwithiel	d																								
Bodmin Parkway	d										10 41														12 41
Liskeard	d										10 53														12 54
Plymouth	d			10 25							11 25					12 00			12 25			12 52			13 23
Totnes	d			10 50							11 50								12 50						13 49
Paignton	d								10 50																
Torquay	d								10 56																
Newton Abbot	d			11 03					11 08		12 03					12 36			13 03			13 27			14 03
Teignmouth	d								11 15																
Dawlish	d								11 20																
Exeter St Davids	d			11 23					11 32		12 23					12 57			13 23			13 48			14 25
Tiverton Parkway	d			11 37					11 46		12 37					13 10			13 37						14 39
Taunton	d			11 53					12 00		12 51					13 25			13 51						14 54
Weston-super-Mare	d								12 21																
Cardiff Central	d		11 45							12 45							13 45						14 45		
Newport (South Wales)	d		11 59							12 59							13 59						14 59		
Bristol Temple Meads	d			12 30					13 00		13 30					14 00			14 30			15 00			15 30
Bristol Parkway	d			12 40					13 10		13 40					14 10			14 40			15 10			15 40
Gloucester	d		12 47							13 51							14 47						15 47		
Cheltenham Spa	d		12 58	13 12					13 42	14 02	14 12					14 42	14 58		15 12			15 42	15 58		16 12
London Paddington	d																								
Birmingham New Street	a		13 41	13 50	13 54		14 19		14 26	14 45	14 50	14 54		15 09		15 27	15 41	15 48	15 50	16 12		16 26	16 41	16 48	16 50
Birmingham New Street	d	13 31	13 49	14 03	14 01		14 30	14 20	14 31	14 49	15 03	15 01		15 30	15 20	15 31	15 49	16 01	16 03	16 30	16 20	16 31	16 49	17 01	17 03
Tamworth	d		14 07	14 19						15 09							16 07		16 19				17 07		
Burton-on-Trent	d		14 19							15 21	15 28						16 19						17 19		17 28
Derby	a		14 34	14 42			15 04			15 34	15 42			16 02			16 34		16 42	17 04			17 34		17 39
Nottingham	a		15 02							16 00							17 00						18 00		
Chesterfield	a			15 02							16 02								17 02						18 03
Sheffield	a			15 17			15 47				16 18			16 48					17 17	17 48					18 19
Doncaster	a						16 15							17 13						18 13					
Wakefield Westgate	a			15 44							16 44								17 47	18 33					18 47
Leeds	a			16 02							17 02								18 02	18 51					19 04
York	a			16 29			16 40				17 29			17 42					18 29	19 18					19 29
Darlington	a			16 57			17 15				17 57			18 11					18 57	19 46					19 59
Durham	a			17 14			17 33				18 14			18 29					19 14	20 03					20 17
Chester-le-Street	a																								
Newcastle	a			17 30			17 47				18 28			18 43					19 30	20 19					20 31
Morpeth	a																								20 52
Alnmouth for Alnwick	a			18 01															20 04						
Berwick-upon-Tweed	a			18 22							19 17								20 24						21 25
Dunbar	a										19 40														21 48
Wolverhampton	d	13 49			14 19			14 37	14 49			15 19			15 37	15 49		16 19			16 37	16 49		17 19	
Stafford	a				14 33							15 33						16 34						17 35	
Stoke-on-Trent	a	14 19			14 56				15 19			15 56				16 19		16 56				17 19		17 56	
Congleton	a																								
Macclesfield	a				15 14							16 14						17 14						18 14	
Crewe	a							15 07							16 07						17 07				
Wilmslow	a																								
Stockport	a				15 28							16 28						17 28						18 28	
M'chester Piccadilly	a	14 57			15 40				15 59			16 40				16 59		17 40				17 56		18 40	
Warrington Bank Quay	a							15 26							16 26						17 26				
Wigan North Western	a							15 37							16 37						17 37				
Preston	a							15 51							16 51						17 51				
Lancaster	a							16 08							17 08						18 08				
Oxenholme Lake District	a														17 22						18 22				
Penrith North Lakes	a							16 44													18 48				
Carlisle	a							17 00							18 01						19 04				
Lockerbie	a																								
Haymarket	a							18 13																	
Edinburgh	a			19 06				18 22			20 05								21 08		20 22				22 16
Haymarket	a			19 22															21 16						
Motherwell	a			20 00															21 53						
Glasgow Central	a			20 20											19 17				22 14						
Inverkeithing	a																								
Kirkcaldy	a																								
Markinch	a																								
Ladybank	a																								
Cupar	a																								
Leuchars	a																								
Dundee	a																								
Arbroath	a																								
Montrose	a																								
Stonehaven	a																								
Aberdeen	a																								

A ⊼ from Newport (South Wales)
B ⊼ to Edinburgh
C ⊼ from Plymouth

South Coast and the South West - North West England, The North East and Scotland

Route Diagram - see first Page of Table 51

		XC	VT	XC	XC	XC	VT	XC	XC	XC	XC	XC	VT	XC	XC	XC	XC	XC	VT	XC	XC	XC	XC
		◇1	◇1	◇1	◇1	◇1	◇1	◇1	◇1	◇1	◇1	◇1	◇1	◇1	◇1	◇1	◇1	◇1	◇1	◇1	◇1	◇1	◇1
					A			B				C				D	D					D	B
		⊼	⊏	⊼	⊼	⊼	⊏	⊼		⊼	⊼	⊼	⊏	⊼		⊼	⊼	⊼	⊏	⊼		⊼	⊼
Bournemouth	d			14 40						15 40						16 40						17 40	
Brockenhurst	d			14 57						15 57						16 57						17 57	
Southampton Central	d			15 15						16 15						17 15						18 15	
Southampton Airport Pkway	d			15 22						16 22						17 22						18 22	
Winchester	d			15 31						16 31						17 31						18 31	
Basingstoke	d			15 47						16 47						17 47						18 47	
Guildford	d																						
Reading	d	15 40		16 11		16 40				17 11		17 40				18 11		18 41				19 11	
Oxford	d	16 06		16 37		17 06				17 37		18 06				18 37		19 06				19 37	
Banbury	d	16 25		16 54		17 25				17 54		18 25				18 54		19 25				19 54	
Leamington Spa	d	16 43		17 12		17 43				18 12		18 43				19 12		19 43				20 12	
Coventry	d			17 26						18 26						19 26		19 54				20 26	
Birmingham International	d			17 38						18 38						19 38		20 04				20 38	
Penzance	d							12 30															15 30
St Erth	d							12 40															15 38
Hayle	d							12 44															
Camborne	d							12 56															15 51
Redruth	d							13 02															15 57
Truro	d							13 14															16 09
St Austell	d							13 30															16 25
Newquay (Summer Only)	d																						
Par	d							13 38															16 33
Lostwithiel	d							13 45															
Bodmin Parkway	d							13 52															16 44
Liskeard	d							14 04															16 56
Plymouth	d				14 23			14 35			15 23						16 25						17 26
Totnes	d				14 49			15 00			15 49						16 49						17 52
Paignton	d																						
Torquay	d																						
Newton Abbot	d				15 03			15 12			16 03						17 02						18 04
Teignmouth	d																						
Dawlish	d																						
Exeter St Davids	d				15 25			15 33			16 24						17 24						18 23
Tiverton Parkway	d				15 38			15 46			16 37						17 38						18 38
Taunton	d				15 54			16 01			16 53						17 53						18 52
Weston-super-Mare	d							16 30															
Cardiff Central	d								16 45						17 45						18 45		
Newport (South Wales)	d								16 59						17 59						18 59		
Bristol Temple Meads	d				16 30			17 00			17 30			18 00			18 30			19 00			19 30
Bristol Parkway	d				16 40			17 10			17 40			18 10			18 40			19 10			19 40
Gloucester	d								17 47						18 47						19 52		
Cheltenham Spa	d				17 12			17 42	17 58		18 12			18 42	18 58		19 12			19 42	20 02		20 12
London Paddington	d																						
Birmingham New Street	a	17 12		17 48	17 49	18 09		18 27	18 41	18 48	18 51	19 11		19 26	19 41	19 48	19 56	20 15		20 26	20 44	20 48	20 50
Birmingham New Street	d	17 30	17 20	18 01	18 03	18 30	18 20	18 31	18 49	19 01	19 03	19 30	19 20	19 31	19 49	20 01	20 03		20 20	20 31	20 49	21 01	21 03
Tamworth	d				18 19				19 09						20 07		20 19				21 06		21 19
Burton-on-Trent	d								19 21		19 26				20 19						21 19		21 30
Derby	a	18 04			18 39	19 03			19 33		19 39	20 01			20 34		20 39				21 33		21 42
Nottingham	a								20 00						21 00						22 00		
Chesterfield	a				19 04						20 01						21 02						22 02
Sheffield	a	18 46			19 20	19 39					20 17	20 38					21 18						22 18
Doncaster	a	19 15				20 16						21 19											
Wakefield Westgate	a				19 48						20 46						21 47						22 43
Leeds	a				20 05						21 03						22 04						23 01
York	a	19 43			20 29	20 45					21 31	21 44											
Darlington	a	20 11			20 59	21 12						22 22											
Durham	a	20 28			21 17	21 31						22 40											
Chester-le-Street	a																						
Newcastle	a	20 42			21 31	21 44						23 10											
Morpeth	a																						
Alnmouth for Alnwick	a				22 04																		
Berwick-upon-Tweed	a																						
Dunbar	a																						
Wolverhampton	d		17 37	18 19			18 37	18 49		19 19			19 37	19 49		20 19			20 38	20 52		21 19	
Stafford	a			18 35						19 37						20 36			20 51			21 36	
Stoke-on-Trent	a			18 55				19 19		19 56				20 19		20 56				21 19		21 56	
Congleton	a																						
Macclesfield	a			19 14						20 14						21 15						22 14	
Crewe	a		18 07				19 07						20 07						21 10				
Wilmslow	a																						
Stockport	a			19 28						20 28						21 28						22 28	
M'chester Piccadilly	a			19 40				19 58		20 40				21 00		21 40				21 56		22 40	
Warrington Bank Quay	a		18 26				19 26						20 26										
Wigan North Western	a		18 37				19 37						20 37										
Preston	a		18 51				19 51						20 51										
Lancaster	a		19 08				20 08						21 08										
Oxenholme Lake District	a		19 22										21 22										
Penrith North Lakes	a						20 44																
Carlisle	a		20 01				21 00						22 01										
Lockerbie	a												22 22										
Haymarket	a						22 15																
Edinburgh	a	22 23			23 08		22 21																
Haymarket	a																						
Motherwell	a												23 07										
Glasgow Central	a		21 17										23 22										
Inverkeithing	a																						
Kirkcaldy	a																						
Markinch	a																						
Ladybank	a																						
Cupar	a																						
Leuchars	a																						
Dundee	a																						
Arbroath	a																						
Montrose	a																						
Stonehaven	a																						
Aberdeen	a																						

A ⊼ to Leeds
B ⊼ from Plymouth to Birmingham New Street
C ⊼ to Sheffield
D ⊼ to Birmingham New Street

Table 51

Sundays

1 July to 9 September

South Coast and the South West - North West England, The North East and Scotland

Route Diagram - see first Page of Table 51

		XC ◇1 ⌶	XC ◇1 ⌶	VT ◇1 🍴	XC ◇1	XC ◇1 A ⌶	XC ◇1 B ⌶	XC ◇1		XC ◇1	XC ◇1	XC ◇1
Bournemouth	d					18 40				19 40		
Brockenhurst 3	d					18 57				19 57		
Southampton Central	d					19 15				20 15		
Southampton Airport Pkway ✈	d					19 22				20 22		
Winchester	d					19 31				20 31		
Basingstoke	d					19 47				20 47		
Guildford	d											
Reading 7	d	19 40				20 11		20 41		21 11	21 40	
Oxford	d	20 06				20 37		21 06		21 37	22 06	
Banbury	d	20 25				20 54		21 24		21 54	22 24	
Leamington Spa 8	d	20 43				21 12		21 42		22 12	22 42	
Coventry	d	20 54				21 26		21 53		22 23	22 53	
Birmingham International ✈	d	21 04				21 38		22 03		22 33	23 03	
Penzance	d											
St Erth	d											
Hayle	d											
Camborne	d											
Redruth	d											
Truro	d											
St Austell	d											
Newquay (Summer Only)	d											
Par	d											
Lostwithiel	d											
Bodmin Parkway	d											
Liskeard 6	d											
Plymouth	d						18 23					
Totnes	d						18 49					
Paignton	d		18 20									
Torquay	d		18 26									
Newton Abbot	d		18 37				19 03					
Teignmouth	d											
Dawlish	d											
Exeter St Davids 6	d		18 58				19 25					
Tiverton Parkway	d		19 11				19 38					
Taunton	d		19 25				19 54					
Weston-super-Mare	d											
Cardiff Central 7	d				19 45							
Newport (South Wales)	d				20 00							
Bristol Temple Meads 10	d		20 00				20 30					22 10
Bristol Parkway 7	d		20 10				20 40					22 20
Gloucester 7	d				20 50							
Cheltenham Spa	d		20 42		21 01		21 12					22 52
London Paddington	d											
Birmingham New Street 12	a	21 15	21 20		21 44	21 48	21 51	22 14		22 42	23 13	23 39
Birmingham New Street 12	d			21 20		22 01	22 03					
Tamworth	d						22 18					
Burton-on-Trent	d											
Derby 6	a						22 40					
Nottingham 8	a											
Chesterfield	a						23 04					
Sheffield 7	a						23 20					
Doncaster 7	a											
Wakefield Westgate 7	a											
Leeds 10	a						00 16					
York 8	a											
Darlington 7	a											
Durham	a											
Chester-le-Street	a											
Newcastle 8	a											
Morpeth	a											
Alnmouth for Alnwick	a											
Berwick-upon-Tweed	a											
Dunbar	a											
Wolverhampton 7	d			21 38		22 19						
Stafford	a			21 56		22 36						
Stoke-on-Trent	a					22 55						
Congleton	a											
Macclesfield	a					23 12						
Crewe 10	a			22 17								
Wilmslow	a											
Stockport	a					23 27						
M'chester Piccadilly 10	a					23 41						
Warrington Bank Quay	a			22 36								
Wigan North Western	a			22 47								
Preston 8	a			23 07								
Lancaster 6	a											
Oxenholme Lake District	a											
Penrith North Lakes	a											
Carlisle 8	a											
Lockerbie	a											
Haymarket	a											
Edinburgh 10	a											
Haymarket	a											
Motherwell	a											
Glasgow Central 15	a											
Inverkeithing	a											
Kirkcaldy	a											
Markinch	a											
Ladybank	a											
Cupar	a											
Leuchars 3	a											
Dundee	a											
Arbroath	a											
Montrose	a											
Stonehaven	a											
Aberdeen	a											

A ⌶ to Reading

B ⌶ to Birmingham New Street

Table 51

Sundays

16 September to 21 October

South Coast and the South West - North West England, The North East and Scotland

Route Diagram - see first Page of Table 51

		XC 🚌	XC ◇1	XC 🚌	VT ◇1 🍴	XC ◇1 ⌶	VT ◇1 🍴	XC ◇1 ⌶	XC ◇1 ⌶	VT ◇1 🍴		XC ◇1 ⌶	XC ◇1 ⌶
Bournemouth	d												
Brockenhurst 3	d												
Southampton Central	d												
Southampton Airport Pkway ✈	d												
Winchester	d												
Basingstoke	d												
Guildford	d												
Reading 7	d												09 11
Oxford	d												09 37
Banbury	d												09 54
Leamington Spa 8	d												10 12
Coventry	d												10 28
Birmingham International ✈	d												10 40
Penzance	d												
St Erth	d												
Hayle	d												
Camborne	d												
Redruth	d												
Truro	d												
St Austell	d												
Newquay (Summer Only)	d												
Par	d												
Lostwithiel	d												
Bodmin Parkway	d												
Liskeard 6	d												
Plymouth	d												
Totnes	d												
Paignton	d												
Torquay	d												
Newton Abbot	d												
Teignmouth	d												
Dawlish	d												
Exeter St Davids 6	d												
Tiverton Parkway	d												
Taunton	d												
Weston-super-Mare	d												
Cardiff Central 7	d												
Newport (South Wales)	d												
Bristol Temple Meads 10	d												
Bristol Parkway 7	d												
Gloucester 7	d												
Cheltenham Spa	d												
London Paddington	d												
Birmingham New Street 12	a												10 50
Birmingham New Street 12	d	22p20	22p31	22p49	08 45	09 01	09 20	09 30	10 01	10 20		10 30	11 01
Tamworth	d	22p55		23p24									
Burton-on-Trent	d	23p15		23b44				10 16				11 16	
Derby 6	a	23b45		00 04				10 26				11 26	
Nottingham 8	a	00 49											
Chesterfield	a							11 02				12 02	
Sheffield 7	a							11 17				12 18	
Doncaster 7	a												
Wakefield Westgate 7	a							11 44				12 44	
Leeds 10	a							12 01				13 02	
York 8	a							12 29				13 31	
Darlington 7	a							12 57				14 00	
Durham	a							13 14				14 17	
Chester-le-Street	a												
Newcastle 8	a							13 31				14 32	
Morpeth	a												
Alnmouth for Alnwick	a												
Berwick-upon-Tweed	a												
Dunbar	a												
Wolverhampton 7	d		22p49		09 04	09 19	09 37		10 19	10 37			11 19
Stafford	a		23p01		09 16	09 32			10 32				11 31
Stoke-on-Trent	a		23p20						10 51				11 51
Congleton	a												
Macclesfield	a		23p38						11 08				12 09
Crewe 10	a				09 35	09 54	10 07			11 07			
Wilmslow	a					10 12							
Stockport	a		23p53			10 21			11 22				12 22
M'chester Piccadilly 10	a		00 10			10 31			11 31				12 40
Warrington Bank Quay	a				09 54		10 26			11 26			
Wigan North Western	a				10 05		10 37			11 37			
Preston 8	a				10 22		10 51			11 51			
Lancaster 6	a						11 07			12 08			
Oxenholme Lake District	a						11 22			12 22			
Penrith North Lakes	a												
Carlisle 8	a						12 01			13 01			
Lockerbie	a												
Haymarket	a									14 13			
Edinburgh 10	a									14 22			
Haymarket	a												
Motherwell	a												
Glasgow Central 15	a						13 17						
Inverkeithing	a												
Kirkcaldy	a												
Markinch	a												
Ladybank	a												
Cupar	a												
Leuchars 3	a												
Dundee	a												
Arbroath	a												
Montrose	a												
Stonehaven	a												
Aberdeen	a												

		XC ◇1 ⌶	VT ◇1 🍴	XC ◇1 ⌶	XC ◇1 ⌶	XC ◇1 ⌶	VT ◇1 🍴	XC ◇1 A ⌶		XC ◇1 ⌶	XC ◇1 ⌶	VT ◇1 🍴	XC ◇1 ⌶
Bournemouth	d									09 40			
Brockenhurst 3	d									09 57			
Southampton Central	d			09 15						10 15			
Southampton Airport Pkway ✈	d			09 22						10 22			
Winchester	d			09 31						10 31			
Basingstoke	d			09 47						10 47			
Guildford	d												
Reading 7	d			10 11						11 11			
Oxford	d			10 37						11 37			
Banbury	d			10 54						11 54			
Leamington Spa 8	d			11 12						12 12			
Coventry	d			11 29						12 28			
Birmingham International ✈	d			11 40						12 40			
Penzance	d												
St Erth	d												
Hayle	d												
Camborne	d												
Redruth	d												
Truro	d												
St Austell	d												
Newquay (Summer Only)	d												
Par	d												
Lostwithiel	d												
Bodmin Parkway	d												
Liskeard 6	d												
Plymouth	d												
Totnes	d												
Paignton	d												
Torquay	d												
Newton Abbot	d												
Teignmouth	d												
Dawlish	d												
Exeter St Davids 6	d												
Tiverton Parkway	d												
Taunton	d												
Weston-super-Mare	d												
Cardiff Central 7	d							10 45					
Newport (South Wales)	d							10 59					
Bristol Temple Meads 10	d	09 20				10 00							
Bristol Parkway 7	d	09 33				10 17							
Gloucester 7	d	10 29				11 27		11 51					
Cheltenham Spa	d	10 41				11 39		12 03					
London Paddington	d												
Birmingham New Street 12	a	11 20		11 51		12 17		12 45		12 50			
Birmingham New Street 12	d	11 30	11 20	12 01	12 03	12 30	12 20			13 01	13 03	13 20	13 31
Tamworth	d												
Burton-on-Trent	d	12 16				13 18							
Derby 6	a	12 26			12 54	13 29					13 55		
Nottingham 8	a												
Chesterfield	a	13 02			13 29	14 02					14 29		
Sheffield 7	a	13 18			13 43	14 17					14 45		
Doncaster 7	a				14 13						15 13		
Wakefield Westgate 7	a	13 45				14 44							
Leeds 10	a	14 02				15 02							
York 8	a	14 31			14 40	15 29					15 43		
Darlington 7	a	15 00			15 13	15 57					16 13		
Durham	a	15 19			15 30	16 14					16 30		
Chester-le-Street	a												
Newcastle 8	a	15 34			15 44	16 30					16 44		
Morpeth	a												
Alnmouth for Alnwick	a												
Berwick-upon-Tweed	a												
Dunbar	a												
Wolverhampton 7	d		11 37	12 19			12 37			13 19		13 37	13 49
Stafford	a			12 32						13 33			
Stoke-on-Trent	a			12 52						13 56			14 19
Congleton	a												
Macclesfield	a			13 10						14 14			
Crewe 10	a		12 07				13 07					14 07	
Wilmslow	a												
Stockport	a			13 28						14 28			
M'chester Piccadilly 10	a			13 40						14 40			14 57
Warrington Bank Quay	a		12 26				13 26					14 26	
Wigan North Western	a		12 37				13 37					14 37	
Preston 8	a		12 51				13 51					14 50	
Lancaster 6	a		13 08				14 08					15 08	
Oxenholme Lake District	a		13 22									15 22	
Penrith North Lakes	a						14 44						
Carlisle 8	a		14 01				15 00					16 01	
Lockerbie	a												
Haymarket	a						16 14						
Edinburgh 10	a						16 22						
Haymarket	a												
Motherwell	a												
Glasgow Central 15	a		15 16									17 17	
Inverkeithing	a												
Kirkcaldy	a												
Markinch	a												
Ladybank	a												
Cupar	a												
Leuchars 3	a												
Dundee	a												
Arbroath	a												
Montrose	a												
Stonehaven	a												
Aberdeen	a												

A ⌶ from Newport (South Wales)

b Previous night, stops to set down only

Sundays

16 September to 21 October

South Coast and the South West - North West England, The North East and Scotland

Route Diagram - see first Page of Table 51

		XC	XC	XC	XC	VT	XC	XC	XC	XC	XC	VT	XC	XC	XC	XC	XC	VT	XC	XC	XC	XC	XC
		◇1	◇1	◇1	◇1	◇1	◇1	◇1	◇1	◇1	◇1	◇1	◇1	◇1	◇1	◇1	◇1	◇1	◇1	◇1	◇1	◇1	◇1
		A		B				A						A		C				A			
		⊼	⊼	⊼	⊼	⊡	⊼	⊼	⊼	⊼	⊼	⊡	⊼	⊼	⊼	⊼	⊼	⊡	⊼	⊼	⊼	⊼	⊼
Bournemouth	d		10 40						11 40						12 40						13 40		
Brockenhurst	d		10 57						11 57						12 57						13 57		
Southampton Central	d		11 15						12 15						13 15						14 15		
Southampton Airport Pkway	d		11 22						12 22						13 22						14 22		
Winchester	d		11 31						12 31						13 31						14 31		
Basingstoke	d		11 47						12 47						13 47						14 47		
Guildford	d				12 14																		
Reading	d		12 11		12 54				13 11		13 41				14 09		14 40				15 09		15 40
Oxford	d		12 36		13 17				13 37		14 04				14 37		15 06				15 37		16 06
Banbury	d		12 53		13 35				13 54		14 24				14 54		15 25				15 54		16 25
Leamington Spa	d		13 12		13 52				14 12		14 42				15 12		15 43				16 12		16 43
Coventry	d		13 26						14 26						15 26						16 26		
Birmingham International	d		13 38						14 38						15 38						16 38		
Penzance	d															09 30							
St Erth	d															09 38							
Hayle	d																						
Camborne	d															09 48							
Redruth	d															09 54							
Truro	d															10 06							
St Austell	d															10 22							
Newquay (Summer Only)	d																						
Par	d															10 30							
Lostwithiel	d																						
Bodmin Parkway	d															10 41							
Liskeard	d															10 53							
Plymouth	d			09 25						10 25						11 25						12 23	
Totnes	d			09 50						10 50						11 50						12 49	
Paignton	d																						
Torquay	d																						
Newton Abbot	d			10 03						11 03						12 03						13 03	
Teignmouth	d																						
Dawlish	d																						
Exeter St Davids	d			10 23						11 23						12 23						13 25	
Tiverton Parkway	d			10 37						11 37						12 37						13 39	
Taunton	d			10 51						11 53						12 51						13 54	
WestonsuperMare	d																						
Cardiff Central	d	11 45						12 45						13 45						14 45			
Newport (South Wales)	d	11 59						12 59						13 59						14 59			
Bristol Temple Meads	d			11 30						12 30						13 30						14 30	
Bristol Parkway	d			11 43						12 49						13 43						14 45	
Gloucester	d	12 47		13 00				13 51		14 00				14 47		14 55				15 47		16 00	
Cheltenham Spa	d	12 58		13 12				14 02		14 12				14 58		15 12				15 58		16 12	
London Paddington	d																						
Birmingham New Street	a	13 41	13 48	13 50	14 19			14 45	14 48	14 50	15 09			15 41	15 48	15 50	16 12			16 41	16 48	16 50	17 12
Birmingham New Street	d		14 01	14 03	14 30	14 20	14 31	14 49	15 01	15 03	15 30	15 20	15 31	15 49	16 01	16 03	16 30	16 20	16 31	16 49	17 01	17 03	17 30
Tamworth	d			14 19				15 09						16 07		16 19				17 07			
Burton-on-Trent	d			14 29				15 21		15 28				16 19						17 19		17 28	
Derby	a			14 42	15 04			15 34		15 42	16 02			16 34		16 42	17 04			17 34		17 39	18 04
Nottingham	a							16 00						17 00						18 00			
Chesterfield	a			15 02						16 02						17 02						18 03	
Sheffield	a			15 17	15 47					16 18	16 48					17 17	17 48					18 19	18 46
Doncaster	a				16 15						17 13						18 13						19 15
Wakefield Westgate	a			15 44						16 44						17 47	18 33					18 47	
Leeds	a			16 02						17 02						18 02	18 51					19 04	
York	a			16 29	16 40					17 29	17 42					18 29	19 18					19 28	19 43
Darlington	a			16 57	17 15					17 57	18 11					18 57	19 46					19 59	20 11
Durham	a			17 14	17 33					18 14	18 29					19 14	20 03					20 17	20 28
Chester-le-Street	a																						
Newcastle	a			17 30	17 47					18 28	18 43					19 30	20 19					20 31	20 42
Morpeth	a																					20 52	
Alnmouth for Alnwick	a			18 01												20 04							
Berwick-upon-Tweed	a			18 22						19 17						20 24						21 25	
Dunbar	a									19 40												21 48	
Wolverhampton	d		14 19			14 37	14 49		15 19			15 37	15 49		16 19			16 37	16 49		17 19		
Stafford	a		14 33						15 33						16 34						17 35		
Stoke-on-Trent	a		14 55				15 19		15 56				16 19		16 56				17 19		17 56		
Congleton	a																						
Macclesfield	a		15 13						16 14						17 14						18 14		
Crewe	a					15 07						16 07						17 07					
Wilmslow	a																						
Stockport	a		15 27						16 28						17 28						18 28		
M'chester Piccadilly	a		15 39				15 59		16 40				16 59		17 40				17 56		18 40		
Warrington Bank Quay	a					15 26						16 26						17 26					
Wigan North Western	a					15 37						16 37						17 37					
Preston	a					15 51						16 51						17 51					
Lancaster	a					16 08						17 08						18 08					
Oxenholme Lake District	a											17 22						18 22					
Penrith North Lakes	a					16 44												18 48					
Carlisle	a					17 00						18 01						19 04					
Lockerbie	a																						
Haymarket	a					18 13																	
Edinburgh	a			19 06		18 22				20 05						21 08		20 22				22 16	22 23
Haymarket	a			19 22												21 16							
Motherwell	a			20 00												21 53							
Glasgow Central	a			20 20								19 17				22 14							
Inverkeithing	a																						
Kirkcaldy	a																						
Markinch	a																						
Ladybank	a																						
Cupar	a																						
Leuchars	a																						
Dundee	a																						
Arbroath	a																						
Montrose	a																						
Stonehaven	a																						
Aberdeen	a																						

A ⊼ from Newport (South Wales) B ⊼ to Edinburgh C ⊼ from Plymouth to Edinburgh

Sundays

16 September to 21 October

South Coast and the South West - North West England, The North East and Scotland

Route Diagram - see first Page of Table 51

		VT	XC	XC	XC	XC	XC	VT	XC	XC	XC	XC	XC	VT	XC	XC	XC	XC	XC	VT	XC	XC
		◇1	◇1	◇1	◇1	◇1	◇1	◇1	◇1	◇1	◇1	◇1	◇1	1	◇1	◇1	◇1	◇1	◇1	◇1	◇1	◇1
						A							B				C	C				
		⊡	⊼		⊼	⊼	⊼	⊡	⊼		⊼	⊼	⊼	⊡	⊼		⊼	⊼	⊼	⊡		
Bournemouth	d				14 40						15 40						16 40					
Brockenhurst	d				14 57						15 57						16 57					
Southampton Central	d				15 15						16 15						17 15					
Southampton Airport Pkway	d				15 22						16 22						17 22					
Winchester	d				15 31						16 31						17 31					
Basingstoke	d				15 47						16 47						17 47					
Guildford	d																					
Reading	d				16 09		16 41				17 09		17 40				18 11		18 41			
Oxford	d				16 37		17 06				17 37		18 06				18 37		19 06			
Banbury	d				16 54		17 25				17 54		18 25				18 54		19 25			
Leamington Spa	d				17 12		17 43				18 12		18 43				19 12		19 43			
Coventry	d				17 26						18 26						19 26		19 54			
Birmingham International	d				17 38						18 38						19 38		20 04			
Penzance	d																					
St Erth	d																					
Hayle	d																					
Camborne	d																					
Redruth	d																					
Truro	d																					
St Austell	d																					
Newquay (Summer Only)	d																					
Par	d																					
Lostwithiel	d																					
Bodmin Parkway	d																					
Liskeard	d																					
Plymouth	d					13 23						14 23						15 23				
Totnes	d					13 49						14 49						15 49				
Paignton	d																					
Torquay	d																					
Newton Abbot	d					14 03						15 03						16 03				
Teignmouth	d																					
Dawlish	d																					
Exeter St Davids	d					14 25						15 25						16 24				
Tiverton Parkway	d					14 38						15 38						16 37				
Taunton	d					14 54						15 54						16 53				
WestonsuperMare	d																					
Cardiff Central	d			15 45						16 45						17 45						18 45
Newport (South Wales)	d			15 59						16 59						17 59						18 59
Bristol Temple Meads	d					15 30						16 30						17 30				
Bristol Parkway	d					15 47						16 45						18 02				
Gloucester	d			16 47		17 00				17 47		18 00				18 47		19 00				19 52
Cheltenham Spa	d			16 58		17 12				17 58		18 12				18 58		19 12				20 02
London Paddington	d																					
Birmingham New Street	a			17 41	17 48	17 49	18 09			18 41	18 48	18 51	19 11			19 41	19 48	19 51	20 15			20 44
Birmingham New Street	d	17 20	17 31	17 49	18 01	18 03	18 30	18 20	18 31	18 49	19 01	19 03	19 30	19 20	19 31	19 49	20 01	20 03		20 20	20 31	20 49
Tamworth	d			18 07		18 19				19 09						20 07		20 19				21 06
Burton-on-Trent	d			18 19						19 21		19 26				20 19						21 19
Derby	a			18 33		18 38	19 03			19 33		19 39	20 01			20 34		20 39				21 33
Nottingham	a			19 00						20 00						21 00						22 00
Chesterfield	a					19 04						20 01						21 04				
Sheffield	a					19 20	19 39					20 17	20 38					21 19				
Doncaster	a						20 16						21 19									
Wakefield Westgate	a					19 48						20 46						21 47				
Leeds	a					20 05						21 03						22 04				
York	a					20 29	20 45					21 31	21 44									
Darlington	a					20 59	21 12						22 22									
Durham	a					21 17	21 31						22 40									
Chester-le-Street	a																					
Newcastle	a					21 31	21 44						23 10									
Morpeth	a																					
Alnmouth for Alnwick	a					22 04																
Berwick-upon-Tweed	a																					
Dunbar	a																					
Wolverhampton	d	17 37	17 49		18 19			18 37	18 49		19 19			19 37	19 49		20 19			20 38	20 52	
Stafford	a				18 35						19 37						20 36			20 51		
Stoke-on-Trent	a		18 19		18 56				19 19		19 56				20 19		20 56				21 19	
Congleton	a																					
Macclesfield	a				19 15						20 14						21 15					
Crewe	a	18 07						19 07						20 07						21 10		
Wilmslow	a																					
Stockport	a				19 28						20 28						21 28					
M'chester Piccadilly	a		18 56		19 40				19 58		20 40				21 00		21 40				21 56	
Warrington Bank Quay	a	18 26						19 26						20 26								
Wigan North Western	a	18 37						19 37						20 37								
Preston	a	18 51						19 51						20 51								
Lancaster	a	19 08						20 07						21 08								
Oxenholme Lake District	a	19 22												21 22								
Penrith North Lakes	a							20 44														
Carlisle	a	20 01						21 00						22 01								
Lockerbie	a													22 22								
Haymarket	a							22 15														
Edinburgh	a					23 08		22 21														
Haymarket	a																					
Motherwell	a													23 07								
Glasgow Central	a	21 17												23 22								
Inverkeithing	a																					
Kirkcaldy	a																					
Markinch	a																					
Ladybank	a																					
Cupar	a																					
Leuchars	a																					
Dundee	a																					
Arbroath	a																					
Montrose	a																					
Stonehaven	a																					
Aberdeen	a																					

A ⊼ to Leeds B ⊼ to Sheffield C ⊼ to Birmingham New Street

Table 51

Sundays

16 September to 21 October

South Coast and the South West - North West England, The North East and Scotland

Route Diagram - see first Page of Table 51

		XC	XC	XC	VT	XC	XC	XC	XC	XC	XC	XC	XC
		◇1	◇1	◇1	◇1	◇1	◇1	◇1	◇1	◇1	◇1	◇1	◇1
		A	A				B	C					
		⊼	⊼	⊼	☕		⊼	⊼			⊼		
Bournemouth	d	17 40					18 40			19 40			
Brockenhurst	d	17 57					18 57			19 57			
Southampton Central	d	18 15					19 15			20 15			
Southampton Airport Pkway ✈	d	18 22					19 22			20 22			
Winchester	d	18 31					19 31			20 31			
Basingstoke	d	18 47					19 47			20 47			
Guildford	d												
Reading	d	19 11		19 40			20 11		20 41	21 11		21 40	
Oxford	d	19 37		20 06			20 37		21 06	21 37		22 06	
Banbury	d	19 54		20 25			20 54		21 24	21 54		22 26	
Leamington Spa	d	20 12		20 43			21 12		21 42	22 12		22 43	
Coventry	d	20 26		20 54			21 26		21 53	22 23		22 54	
Birmingham International ✈	d	20 38		21 04			21 38		22 03	22 33		23 04	
Penzance	d							15 30					
St Erth	d							15 38					
Hayle	d												
Camborne	d							15 51					
Redruth	d							15 57					
Truro	d							16 09					
St Austell	d							16 25					
Newquay (Summer Only)	d												
Par	d							16 33					
Lostwithiel	d												
Bodmin Parkway	d							16 44					
Liskeard	d							16 56					
Plymouth	d		16 23					17 26			18 23		
Totnes	d		16 49					17 52			18 49		
Paignton	d												
Torquay	d												
Newton Abbot	d		17 02					18 04			19 03		
Teignmouth	d												
Dawlish	d												
Exeter St Davids	d		17 24					18 23			19 25		
Tiverton Parkway	d		17 39					18 38			19 39		
Taunton	d		17 53					18 52			19 54		
Weston-super-Mare	d												
Cardiff Central	d					19 45							
Newport (South Wales)	d					20 00							
Bristol Temple Meads	d		18 30					19 30			20 30		22 10
Bristol Parkway	d		19 00					19 45			20 43		22 24
Gloucester	d		20 00			20 50		21 00			22 00		23 21
Cheltenham Spa	d		20 12			21 01		21 12			22 12		23 33
London Paddington	d												
Birmingham New Street	a	20 48	20 51	21 15		21 44	21 48	21 51	22 14	22 42	22 50	23 14	00 11
Birmingham New Street	d	21 01	21 03		21 20		22 01	22 03					
Tamworth	d		21 19					22 18					
Burton-on-Trent	d		21 31										
Derby	a		21 42					22 40					
Nottingham	a												
Chesterfield	a		22 04					23 04					
Sheffield	a		22 19					23 20					
Doncaster	a												
Wakefield Westgate	a		22 45										
Leeds	a		23 03					00 11					
York	a												
Darlington	a												
Durham	a												
Chester-le-Street	a												
Newcastle	a												
Morpeth	a												
Alnmouth for Alnwick	a												
Berwick-upon-Tweed	a												
Dunbar	a												
Wolverhampton	d	21 19			21 38		22 19						
Stafford	a	21 36			21 56		22 36						
Stoke-on-Trent	a	21 56					22 55						
Congleton	a												
Macclesfield	a	22 14					23 12						
Crewe	a				22 17								
Wilmslow	a												
Stockport	a	22 28					23 27						
M'chester Piccadilly	a	22 40					23 41						
Warrington Bank Quay	a				22 36								
Wigan North Western	a				22 47								
Preston	a				23 07								
Lancaster	a												
Oxenholme Lake District	a												
Penrith North Lakes	a												
Carlisle	a												
Lockerbie	a												
Haymarket	a												
Edinburgh	a												
Haymarket	a												
Motherwell	a												
Glasgow Central	a												
Inverkeithing	a												
Kirkcaldy	a												
Markinch	a												
Ladybank	a												
Cupar	a												
Leuchars	a												
Dundee	a												
Arbroath	a												
Montrose	a												
Stonehaven	a												
Aberdeen	a												

A ⊼ to Birmingham New Street B ⊼ to Reading C ⊼ from Plymouth to Birmingham New Street

Table 51

Sundays

from 28 October

South Coast and the South West - North West England, The North East and Scotland

Route Diagram - see first Page of Table 51

		XC	XC	VT	XC	VT	XC	XC	VT	XC	XC	VT
		◇1		◇1	◇1	◇1	◇1	◇1	◇1	◇1	◇1	◇1
											A	
			🚌	☕	⊼	☕	⊼	⊼	☕	⊼	⊼	☕
Bournemouth	d											
Brockenhurst	d											
Southampton Central	d											
Southampton Airport Pkway ✈	d											
Winchester	d											
Basingstoke	d											
Guildford	d											
Reading	d									09 11		
Oxford	d									09 37		
Banbury	d									09 54		
Leamington Spa	d									10 12		
Coventry	d									10 28		
Birmingham International ✈	d									10 40		
Penzance	d											
St Erth	d											
Hayle	d											
Camborne	d											
Redruth	d											
Truro	d											
St Austell	d											
Newquay (Summer Only)	d											
Par	d											
Lostwithiel	d											
Bodmin Parkway	d											
Liskeard	d											
Plymouth	d											
Totnes	d											
Paignton	d											
Torquay	d											
Newton Abbot	d											
Teignmouth	d											
Dawlish	d											
Exeter St Davids	d											
Tiverton Parkway	d											
Taunton	d											
Weston-super-Mare	d											
Cardiff Central	d											
Newport (South Wales)	d											
Bristol Temple Meads	d											
Bristol Parkway	d											
Gloucester	d											
Cheltenham Spa	d											
London Paddington	d											
Birmingham New Street	a									10 50		
Birmingham New Street	d	22p31	22p49	08 45	09 01	09 20	10 01	10 03	10 20	11 01	11 03	11 20
Tamworth	d		23p24									
Burton-on-Trent	d		23b44									
Derby	a		00 04					11 18			12 18	
Nottingham	a											
Chesterfield	a							12 02			13 02	
Sheffield	a							12 18			13 18	
Doncaster	a											
Wakefield Westgate	a							12 44			13 45	
Leeds	a							13 02			14 02	
York	a							13 29			14 29	
Darlington	a							13 57			14 57	
Durham	a							14 14			15 14	
Chester-le-Street	a											
Newcastle	a							14 28			15 28	
Morpeth	a							14 46				
Alnmouth for Alnwick	a										16 01	
Berwick-upon-Tweed	a										16 21	
Dunbar	a							15 37				
Wolverhampton	d	22p49		09 04	09 19	09 37	10 19		10 37	11 19		11 37
Stafford	a	23p01		09 16	09 32		10 32			11 31		
Stoke-on-Trent	a	23p20					10 51			11 51		
Congleton	a											
Macclesfield	a	23p38					11 08			12 09		
Crewe	a			09 35	09 54	10 06			11 07			12 07
Wilmslow	a				10 12							
Stockport	a	23p53			10 21		11 22			12 22		
M'chester Piccadilly	a	00 10			10 31		11 31			12 34		
Warrington Bank Quay	a											
Wigan North Western	a											
Preston	a					11 29			12 44			13 26
Lancaster	a					12 08			13 08			14 08
Oxenholme Lake District	a					12 22			13 22			
Penrith North Lakes	a											14 44
Carlisle	a					13 01			14 01			15 00
Lockerbie	a											
Haymarket	a					14 13						16 14
Edinburgh	a					14 21		16 04			17 06	16 22
Haymarket	a										17 14	
Motherwell	a										17 52	
Glasgow Central	a								15 16		18 12	
Inverkeithing	a											
Kirkcaldy	a											
Markinch	a											
Ladybank	a											
Cupar	a											
Leuchars	a											
Dundee	a											
Arbroath	a											
Montrose	a											
Stonehaven	a											
Aberdeen	a											

		XC	XC	XC	XC	XC	VT	XC	XC	XC	XC	XC
				◇1	◇1	◇1	◇1	◇1	◇1	◇1	◇1	◇1
						A					A	
		🚌	🚌	⊼	⊼	⊼	☕	⊼	⊼	⊼	⊼	⊼
Bournemouth	d								09 40			10 40
Brockenhurst	d								09 57			10 57
Southampton Central	d				09 15				10 15			11 15
Southampton Airport Pkway ✈	d				09 22				10 22			11 22
Winchester	d				09 31				10 31			11 31
Basingstoke	d				09 47				10 47			11 47
Guildford	d											
Reading	d				10 11				11 11			12 11
Oxford	d				10 37				11 37			12 36
Banbury	d				10 54				11 54			12 53
Leamington Spa	d				11 12				12 12			13 12
Coventry	d				11 29				12 28			13 26
Birmingham International ✈	d				11 40				12 40			13 38
Penzance	d											
St Erth	d											
Hayle	d											
Camborne	d											
Redruth	d											
Truro	d											
St Austell	d											
Newquay (Summer Only)	d											
Par	d											
Lostwithiel	d											
Bodmin Parkway	d											
Liskeard	d											
Plymouth	d										09 25	
Totnes	d										09 50	
Paignton	d											
Torquay	d											
Newton Abbot	d										10 03	
Teignmouth	d											
Dawlish	d											
Exeter St Davids	d										10 23	
Tiverton Parkway	d										10 37	
Taunton	d										10 51	
Weston-super-Mare	d											
Cardiff Central	d											
Newport (South Wales)	d											
Bristol Temple Meads	d										11 30	
Bristol Parkway	d										11 40	
Gloucester	d	10 05									12 14	
Cheltenham Spa	d		10 10								12 26	
London Paddington	d											
Birmingham New Street	a	11 30	11 30		11 51				12 50		13 38	13 48
Birmingham New Street	d			11 45	12 01	12 03	12 20	12 45	13 01	13 31	14 03	14 01
Tamworth	d										14 19	
Burton-on-Trent	d											
Derby	a			12 56		13 17		14 01			14 42	
Nottingham	a											
Chesterfield	a			13 29		14 02		14 29			15 03	
Sheffield	a			13 43		14 17		14 45			15 17	
Doncaster	a			14 13				15 13				
Wakefield Westgate	a					14 44					15 44	
Leeds	a					15 02					16 02	
York	a			14 40		15 29		15 43			16 29	
Darlington	a			15 13		15 57		16 13			16 57	
Durham	a			15 30		16 14		16 30			17 14	
Chester-le-Street	a											
Newcastle	a			15 44		16 28		16 44			17 30	
Morpeth	a											
Alnmouth for Alnwick	a					16 58					18 01	
Berwick-upon-Tweed	a										18 22	
Dunbar	a					17 39						
Wolverhampton	d				12 19		12 37		13 19	13 49		14 19
Stafford	a				12 32				13 33			14 33
Stoke-on-Trent	a				12 52				13 56	14 19		14 55
Congleton	a											
Macclesfield	a				13 10				14 14			15 13
Crewe	a						13 07					
Wilmslow	a											
Stockport	a				13 28				14 28			15 27
M'chester Piccadilly	a				13 40				14 40	14 57		15 39
Warrington Bank Quay	a											
Wigan North Western	a											
Preston	a						14 33					
Lancaster	a						15 08					
Oxenholme Lake District	a						15 22					
Penrith North Lakes	a											
Carlisle	a						16 01					
Lockerbie	a											
Haymarket	a											
Edinburgh	a					18 07					19 06	
Haymarket	a					18 17					19 22	
Motherwell	a										20 00	
Glasgow Central	a						17 17				20 20	
Inverkeithing	a					18 31						
Kirkcaldy	a					18 46						
Markinch	a					18 55						
Ladybank	a					19 02						
Cupar	a					19 09						
Leuchars	a					19 16						
Dundee	a					19 31						
Arbroath	a					19 47						
Montrose	a					20 01						
Stonehaven	a					20 23						
Aberdeen	a					20 43						

A ⊼ to Edinburgh b Previous night, stops to set down only

South Coast and the South West - North West England, The North East and Scotland

Route Diagram - see first Page of Table 51

		XC	VT	XC	XC	XC	XC	XC	VT	XC	XC	XC	XC	XC	VT	XC	XC	XC	XC	XC	VT	XC	XC
		◇1	◇1	◇1	◇1	◇1	◇1	◇1	◇1	◇1	◇1	◇1	◇1	◇1	◇1	◇1	◇1	◇1	◇1	◇1	◇1	◇1	◇1
		⊼	⊏	⊼	⊼	⊼	⊼	⊼	⊏	A ⊼	⊼		B ⊼	⊼	⊏	⊼	C ⊼	⊼	D ⊼	⊼	⊏	⊼	
Bournemouth	d				11 40						12 40							13 40					
Brockenhurst 3	d				11 57						12 57							13 57					
Southampton Central	d				12 15						13 15							14 15					
Southampton Airport Pkway	d				12 22						13 22							14 22					
Winchester	d				12 31						13 31							14 31					
Basingstoke	d				12 47						13 47							14 47					
Guildford	d	12 14																					
Reading 7	d	12 54			13 11			13 41			14 09			14 40				15 09		15 40			
Oxford	d	13 17			13 37			14 06			14 37			15 06				15 37		16 06			
Banbury	d	13 35			13 54			14 24			14 54			15 25				15 54		16 25			
Leamington Spa 3	d	13 52			14 12			14 42			15 12			15 43				16 12		16 43			
Coventry	d				14 26						15 26							16 26					
Birmingham International	d				14 38						15 38							16 38					
Penzance	d									09 30													
St Erth	d									09 38													
Hayle	d																						
Camborne	d									09 48													
Redruth	d									09 54													
Truro	d									10 06													
St Austell	d									10 22													
Newquay (Summer Only)	d																						
Par	d									10 30													
Lostwithiel	d																						
Bodmin Parkway	d									10 41													
Liskeard 6	d									10 53													
Plymouth	d									11 25			12 25			12 52			13 23				
Totnes	d									11 50			12 50						13 49				
Paignton	d																						
Torquay	d																						
Newton Abbot	d									12 03			13 03			13 27			14 03				
Teignmouth	d																						
Dawlish	d																						
Exeter St Davids 6	d									12 23			13 23			13 48			14 25				
Tiverton Parkway	d									12 37			13 37						14 39				
Taunton	d									12 51			13 51						14 54				
WestonsuperMare	d																						
Cardiff Central 7	d																14 45						15 45
Newport (South Wales)	d																14 59						15 59
Bristol Temple Meads 10	d									13 30			14 30			15 00			15 30			16 00	
Bristol Parkway 7	d									13 40			14 40			15 10			15 40			16 10	
Gloucester 7	d									14 30							15 47						16 47
Cheltenham Spa	d									14 42			15 12			15 42	15 58		16 12			16 42	16 58
London Paddington	d																						
Birmingham New Street 12	a	14 19			14 48			15 09		15 23	15 48		15 50	16 12		16 26	16 41	16 48	16 50	17 12		17 26	17 41
Birmingham New Street 12	d	14 30	14 20	14 31	15 01	14 49	15 03	15 30	15 20	15 31	16 01	15 49	16 03	16 30	16 20	16 31	16 49	17 01	17 03	17 30	17 20	17 31	17 49
Tamworth	d					15 09						16 07	16 19				17 07						18 07
Burton-on-Trent	d					15 21	15 28					16 19					17 19		17 28				18 19
Derby 6	a	15 04				15 34	15 42	16 02				16 34	16 42	17 04			17 34		17 39	18 04			18 33
Nottingham 8	a					16 00						17 00					18 00						19 00
Chesterfield	a						16 02						17 02						18 03				
Sheffield 7	a	15 47					16 18	16 48					17 17	17 48					18 19	18 46			
Doncaster 7	a	16 15						17 13						18 13						19 15			
Wakefield Westgate 7	a						16 44						17 47	18 33					18 47				
Leeds 10	a						17 02						18 02	18 51					19 04				
York 8	a	16 40					17 29	17 42					18 29	19 18					19 29	19 43			
Darlington 7	a	17 15					17 57	18 11					18 57	19 46					19 59	20 11			
Durham	a	17 33					18 14	18 29					19 14	20 03					20 17	20 28			
ChesterleStreet	a																						
Newcastle 8	a	17 47					18 28	18 43					19 30	20 19					20 31	20 42			
Morpeth	a																		20 52				
Alnmouth for Alnwick	a												20 04										
BerwickuponTweed	a						19 17						20 24						21 25				
Dunbar	a						19 40												21 48				
Wolverhampton 7	d		14 37	14 49	15 19				15 37	15 49	16 19				16 37	16 49		17 19			17 37	17 49	
Stafford	a				15 33						16 34							17 35					
StokeonTrent	a			15 19	15 56					16 19	16 56					17 19		17 56				18 19	
Congleton	a																						
Macclesfield	a				16 14						17 14							18 14					
Crewe 10	a		15 07						16 07						17 07						18 07		
Wilmslow	a																						
Stockport	a				16 28						17 28							18 28					
M'chester Piccadilly 10	a			15 59	16 40					16 59	17 40					17 56		18 40				18 56	
Warrington Bank Quay	a		15 26						16 26						17 26						18 26		
Wigan North Western	a		15 37						16 37						17 37						18 37		
Preston 8	a		15 51						16 51						17 51						18 51		
Lancaster 6	a		16 08						17 08						18 08						19 08		
Oxenholme Lake District	a								17 22						18 22						19 22		
Penrith North Lakes	a		16 44												18 48								
Carlisle 8	a		17 00						18 01						19 04						20 01		
Lockerbie	a																						
Haymarket	a		18 13																				
Edinburgh 10	a		18 22				20 05						21 08		20 22				22 16	22 23			
Haymarket	a												21 16										
Motherwell	a												21 53										
Glasgow Central 15	a								19 17				22 14								21 17		
Inverkeithing	a																						
Kirkcaldy	a																						
Markinch	a																						
Ladybank	a																						
Cupar	a																						
Leuchars 3	a																						
Dundee	a																						
Arbroath	a																						
Montrose	a																						
Stonehaven	a																						
Aberdeen	a																						

A ⊼ from Plymouth
B ⊼ to Edinburgh
C ⊼ from Newport (South Wales)
D ⊼ from Birmingham New Street

South Coast and the South West - North West England, The North East and Scotland

Route Diagram - see first Page of Table 51

		XC	XC	XC	VT	XC	XC	XC	XC	XC	VT	XC	XC	XC	XC	XC	VT	XC	XC	XC	XC	XC
		◇1	◇1	◇1	◇1	◇1	◇1	◇1	◇1	◇1	2 1	◇1	◇1	◇1	◇1	◇1	◇1	◇1	◇1	◇1	◇1	◇1
		⊼	A ⊼	⊼	⊏	B ⊼		⊼	⊼	C ⊼	⊏	⊼		D ⊼	D ⊼	⊼	⊏	⊼		D ⊼	B ⊼	⊼
Bournemouth	d	14 40						15 40						16 40						17 40		
Brockenhurst 3	d	14 57						15 57						16 57						17 57		
Southampton Central	d	15 15						16 15						17 15						18 15		
Southampton Airport Pkway	d	15 22						16 22						17 22						18 22		
Winchester	d	15 31						16 31						17 31						18 31		
Basingstoke	d	15 47						16 47						17 47						18 47		
Guildford	d																					
Reading 7	d	16 09		16 41				17 09		17 40				18 11		18 41				19 09		19 40
Oxford	d	16 37		17 07				17 37		18 06				18 37		19 06				19 37		20 06
Banbury	d	16 54		17 25				17 54		18 25				18 54		19 25				19 54		20 25
Leamington Spa 3	d	17 12		17 43				18 12		18 43				19 12		19 43				20 12		20 43
Coventry	d	17 26						18 26						19 26		19 54				20 26		20 54
Birmingham International	d	17 38						18 38						19 38		20 04				20 38		21 04
Penzance	d					12 30															15 30	
St Erth	d					12 40															15 38	
Hayle	d					12 44																
Camborne	d					12 56															15 51	
Redruth	d					13 02															15 57	
Truro	d					13 14															16 09	
St Austell	d					13 30															16 25	
Newquay (Summer Only)	d																					
Par	d					13 38															16 33	
Lostwithiel	d					13 45																
Bodmin Parkway	d					13 52															16 44	
Liskeard 6	d					14 04															16 56	
Plymouth	d		14 23			14 35			15 23						16 25						17 26	
Totnes	d		14 49			15 00			15 49						16 49						17 52	
Paignton	d																					
Torquay	d																					
Newton Abbot	d		15 03			15 12			16 03						17 02						18 04	
Teignmouth	d																					
Dawlish	d																					
Exeter St Davids 6	d		15 25			15 33			16 24						17 24						18 23	
Tiverton Parkway	d		15 38			15 46			16 37						17 38						18 38	
Taunton	d		15 54			16 01			16 53						17 51						18 52	
WestonsuperMare	d					16 30																
Cardiff Central 7	d						16 45						17 45						18 45			
Newport (South Wales)	d						16 59						17 59						18 59			
Bristol Temple Meads 10	d		16 30			17 00			17 30			18 00			18 30			19 00			19 30	
Bristol Parkway 7	d		16 40			17 10			17 40			18 10			18 40			19 10			19 40	
Gloucester 7	d						17 47						18 47						19 52			
Cheltenham Spa	d		17 12			17 42	17 58		18 12			18 42	18 58		19 12			19 42	20 02		20 12	
London Paddington	d																					
Birmingham New Street 12	a	17 48	17 49	18 09		18 27	18 41	18 48	18 51	19 11		19 26	19 41	19 48	19 50	20 15		20 26	20 44	20 48	20 50	21 15
Birmingham New Street 12	d	18 01	18 03	18 30	18 20	18 31	18 49	19 01	19 03	19 30	19 20	19 31	19 49	20 01	20 03		20 20	20 31	20 49	21 01	21 03	
Tamworth	d		18 19				19 09						20 07		20 19				21 06		21 19	
Burton-on-Trent	d						19 21		19 26				20 19						21 19		21 30	
Derby 6	a		18 38	19 03			19 33		19 39	20 01			20 34		20 39				21 33		21 42	
Nottingham 8	a						20 00						21 00						22 00			
Chesterfield	a		19 04						20 01						21 02						22 02	
Sheffield 7	a		19 20	19 39					20 17	20 38					21 16						22 18	
Doncaster 7	a			20 16						21 19												
Wakefield Westgate 7	a		19 48						20 46						21 47						22 43	
Leeds 10	a		20 05						21 03						22 04						23 01	
York 8	a		20 29	20 45					21 31	21 44												
Darlington 7	a		20 59	21 12						22 22												
Durham	a		21 17	21 31						22 40												
ChesterleStreet	a																					
Newcastle 8	a		21 31	21 44						23 10												
Morpeth	a																					
Alnmouth for Alnwick	a		22 04																			
BerwickuponTweed	a																					
Dunbar	a																					
Wolverhampton 7	d	18 19			18 37	18 49		19 19			19 37	19 49		20 19			20 38	20 52		21 19		
Stafford	a	18 35						19 37						20 36			20 51			21 36		
StokeonTrent	a	18 56				19 19		19 56				20 19		20 56				21 19		21 56		
Congleton	a																					
Macclesfield	a	19 15						20 14						21 15						22 14		
Crewe 10	a				19 07						20 07						21 10					
Wilmslow	a																					
Stockport	a	19 28						20 28						21 28						22 28		
M'chester Piccadilly 10	a	19 40				19 58		20 40				21 00		21 40				21 56		22 40		
Warrington Bank Quay	a				19 26						20 26											
Wigan North Western	a				19 37						20 37											
Preston 8	a				19 51						20 51											
Lancaster 6	a				20 07						21 08											
Oxenholme Lake District	a										21 22											
Penrith North Lakes	a				20 44																	
Carlisle 8	a				21 00						22 01											
Lockerbie	a										22 22											
Haymarket	a				22 15																	
Edinburgh 10	a		23 08		22 21																	
Haymarket	a																					
Motherwell	a										23 07											
Glasgow Central 15	a										23 22											
Inverkeithing	a																					
Kirkcaldy	a																					
Markinch	a																					
Ladybank	a																					
Cupar	a																					
Leuchars 3	a																					
Dundee	a																					
Arbroath	a																					
Montrose	a																					
Stonehaven	a																					
Aberdeen	a																					

A ⊼ to Leeds
B ⊼ from Plymouth to Birmingham New Street
C ⊼ to Sheffield
D ⊼ to Birmingham New Street

Sundays
from 28 October

South Coast and the South West - North West England, The North East and Scotland

Route Diagram - see first Page of Table 51

		XC ◇■	VT ◇■	XC ◇■	XC ◇■ A	XC ◇■ B	XC ◇■	XC ◇■		XC ◇■	XC ◇■
Bournemouth	d				18 40			19 40			
Brockenhurst ■	d				18 57			19 57			
Southampton Central	d				19 15			20 15			
Southampton Airport Pkway	d				19 22			20 22			
Winchester	d				19 31			20 31			
Basingstoke	d				19 47			20 47			
Guildford	d										
Reading ■	d				20 11		20 41	21 09		21 40	
Oxford	d				20 37		21 06	21 37		22 06	
Banbury	d				20 54		21 24	21 54		22 26	
Leamington Spa ■	d				21 12		21 42	22 12		22 43	
Coventry	d				21 26		21 53	22 23		22 54	
Birmingham International	d				21 38		22 03	22 33		23 04	
Penzance	d										
St Erth	d										
Hayle	d										
Camborne	d										
Redruth	d										
Truro	d										
St Austell	d										
Newquay (Summer Only)	d										
Par	d										
Lostwithiel	d										
Bodmin Parkway	d										
Liskeard ■	d										
Plymouth	d					18 23					
Totnes	d					18 49					
Paignton	d	18 20									
Torquay	d	18 26									
Newton Abbot	d	18 37				19 03					
Teignmouth	d										
Dawlish	d										
Exeter St Davids ■	d	18 58				19 25					
Tiverton Parkway	d	19 11				19 38					
Taunton	d	19 25				19 54					
WestonsuperMare	d										
Cardiff Central ■	d			19 45							
Newport (South Wales)	d			20 00							
Bristol Temple Meads ■	d	20 00				20 30					22 10
Bristol Parkway ■	d	20 10				20 40					22 20
Gloucester ■	d			20 50							
Cheltenham Spa	d	20 42		21 01		21 12					22 52
London Paddington	d										
Birmingham New Street ■	a	21 20		21 44	21 48	21 51	22 14	22 42		23 14	23 39
Birmingham New Street ■	d		21 20		22 01	22 03					
Tamworth	d					22 19					
Burton-on-Trent	d										
Derby ■	a					22 43					
Nottingham ■	a										
Chesterfield	a										
Sheffield ■	a										
Doncaster ■	a										
Wakefield Westgate ■	a										
Leeds ■	a										
York ■	a										
Darlington ■	a										
Durham	a										
ChesterleStreet	a										
Newcastle ■	a										
Morpeth	a										
Alnmouth for Alnwick	a										
BerwickuponTweed	a										
Dunbar	a										
Wolverhampton ■	d		21 38		22 19						
Stafford	a		21 56		22 36						
StokeonTrent	a				22 55						
Congleton	a										
Macclesfield	a				23 12						
Crewe ■	a		22 17								
Wilmslow	a										
Stockport	a				23 27						
M'chester Piccadilly ■	a				23 41						
Warrington Bank Quay	a		22 36								
Wigan North Western	a		22 47								
Preston ■	a		23 07								
Lancaster ■	a										
Oxenholme Lake District	a										
Penrith North Lakes	a										
Carlisle ■	a										
Lockerbie	a										
Haymarket	a										
Edinburgh ■	a										
Haymarket	a										
Motherwell	a										
Glasgow Central ■	a										
Inverkeithing	a										
Kirkcaldy	a										
Markinch	a										
Ladybank	a										
Cupar	a										
Leuchars ■	a										
Dundee	a										
Arbroath	a										
Montrose	a										
Stonehaven	a										
Aberdeen	a										

A ⌶ to Reading

B ⌶ to Birmingham New Street

Network Diagram for Table 52

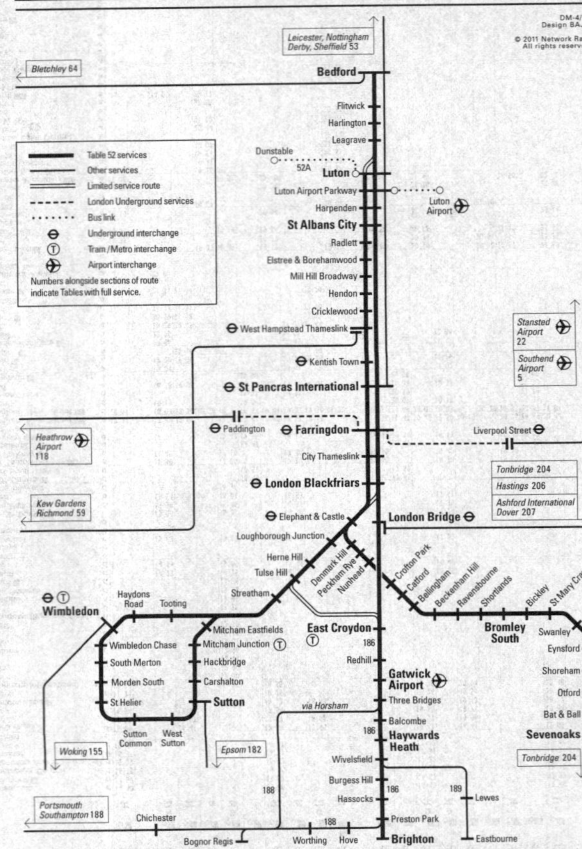

DM-4/11
Design BAJS

Bedford, Luton, St Albans and City of London - South London, Gatwick Airport and Brighton

Network Diagram - see first Page of Table 52

Miles	Miles	Miles	Miles			FC 1 A MO	FC 1 B MO	FC 1 C MO	FC 1 D MX	SE E MO	SE F MX	FC D MX	FC G MX	FC 1 A MO	FC 1 H MO	FC 1 D MX	SE E MO	SE F MX	FC D MX	FC MX G	SE G MX	FC G MX	FC 1 A MO
0	0	—	—	Bedford	d	21p40	21p42	21p42	21p52					22p10	22p12	22p16							22p40
9½	—	—	—	Flitwick	d	21p51	21p52	21p52	22p02					22p21	22p22	22p26							22p51
12½	—	—	—	Harlington	d	21p55	21p56	21p56	22p06					22p25	22p26	22p30							22p55
17	—	—	—	Leagrave	d	22p03	22p02	22p02	22p11					22p33	22p32	22p35							23p03
19½	19½	—	—	Luton	d	22p07	22p06	22p06	22p16			22p20		22p37	22p36	22p40			22p46				23p07
20½	—	—	—	Luton Airport Parkway	d	22p09	22p09	22p09	22p18			22p22		22p39	22p39	22p42			22p49				23p09
25	—	—	—	Harpenden	d	22p15	22p14	22p14	22p24			22p28		22p45	22p44	22p48			22p55				23p15
29¾	—	—	—	St Albans City	d	22p21	22p21	22p21	22p30			22p34		22p51	22p51	22p54			23p01				23p21
34¼	—	—	—	Radlett	d	22p26	22p26	22p26				22p39		22p56	22p56				23p06				23p26
37¼	—	—	—	Elstree & Borehamwood	d	22p31	22p31	22p31				22p43		23p01	23p01				23p11				23p31
40½	—	—	—	Mill Hill Broadway	d	22p35	22p35	22p35				22p47		23p05	23p05				23p15				23p35
42¾	—	—	—	Hendon	d	22p38	22p38	22p38				22p50		23p08	23p08				23p18				23p38
44¾	—	—	—	Cricklewood	d	22p42	22p42	22p42				22p54		23p12	23p12				23p22				23p42
45¾	—	—	—	West Hampstead Thameslink ⊖	d	22p44	22p44	22p44	22p44			22p56		23p14	23p14	23p10			23p24				23p44
48¼	—	—	—	Kentish Town ⊖	d	22p49	22p49	22p49				23p01		23p19	23p19				23p30				23p49
49¾	—	—	—	St Pancras International ⊖	a																		
50	0	—	—	St Pancras International ⊖	a	22p53	22p53	22p53	22p52			23p05		23p23	23p23	23p19			23p34				23p53
—	—	—	—		d	22p54	22p54	22p54	22p54			23p06		23p24	23p24	23p24			23p36	23p42			23p54
51	0	—	—	Farringdon ⊖	d	22p59	22p59	22p59	22p59			23p10		23p29	23p29	23p29			23p40	23p47			23p59
51¾	0	—	—	City Thameslink	d				23p03														
52¼	0	0	0	London Blackfriars ⊖	d	23p04	23p04	23p04	23p05	23p08	23p12	23p16		23p34	23p34	23p35	23p38	23p42	23p46	23p52			0005
1	1	—	—	Elephant & Castle ⊖	d					23p12	23p16	23p19					23p42	23p46	23p49				
3	3	—	—	Loughborough d	d							23b23											
4	4	—	—	Herne Hill	d							23p27							23p57				
53	—	—	—	London Bridge	a	23p10	23p10	23p10	23p11					23p40	23p40	23p41				0007			0011
—	—	—	—		d	23p11	23p11	23p11	23p12				23p29	23p41	23p41	23p42						23p59	0012
—	5	5	5	Tulse Hill	d							23p31	23p41						0001			0009	
—	62	62	0	Streatham	d							23p35	23p45						0005			0013	
—	—	—	1	Mitcham Eastfields	d																		
—	—	2	—	Mitcham unction	d																		
—	—	4	—	Hackbridge	d																		
—	—	4¾	—	Carshalton	d																		
—	8	—	—	Tooting	d							23p40	23p50						0010			0018	
—	9¼	—	—	Haydons Road	d							23p43	23p53						0013			0021	
—	10½	—	—	Wimbledon ⊖	d							23p49	23p57						0019			0025	
—	11½	—	—	Wimbledon Chase	d							23p52	0001						0022			0028	
—	12	—	—	South Merton	d							23p54	0003						0024			0030	
—	12½	—	—	Morden South	d							23p56	0005						0026			0032	
—	13	—	—	St Helier	d							23p58	0007						0028			0034	
—	14	—	—	Sutton Common	d							0001	0009						0030			0036	
—	15	—	—	West Sutton	d							0004	0012						0033			0039	
—	16	12½	6	Sutton (Surrey)	a							0009	0015						0039			0043	
63¼	—	—	10	East Croydon	d	23p25	23p25	23p27	23p25					23p57	23p57	23p57							0026
—	—	—	—	Denmark Hill	d					23p18	23p22						23p48	23p52			23p52		
—	—	—	—	Peckham Rye	d					23p21	23p25						23p51	23p55			23p55		
—	—	—	—	Nunhead	d					23p23	23p27						23p53	23p57			23p57		
—	—	—	—	Crofton Park	d					23p26	23p30						23p56	23p59			23p59		
—	—	—	—	Catford	d					23p29	23p33						23p59	0003			0003		
—	—	—	—	Bellingham	d					23p31	23p35						0001	0005			0005		
—	—	—	—	Beckenham Hill	d					23p33	23p37						0003	0007			0007		
—	—	—	—	Ravensbourne	d					23p35	23p39						0005	0009			0009		
—	—	—	—	Shortlands	d					23p37	23p41						0007	0011			0011		
—	—	—	—	Bromley South	d					23p40	23p44						0010	0014			0014		
—	—	—	—	Bickley	d					23p43	23p47						0013	0017			00a17		
—	—	—	—	St Mary Cray	d					23p47	23p51						0017	0021					
—	—	—	—	Swanley	d					23p52	23p56						0022	0026					
—	—	—	—	Eynsford	d					23p56	23p59						0026	0030					
—	—	—	—	Shoreham (Kent)	d					23p59	0004						0030	0034					
—	—	—	—	Otford	d					0003	0007						0033	0037					
—	—	—	—	Bat & Ball	d					0006	0010						0036	0040					
—	—	—	—	Sevenoaks	a					0009	0013						0039	0043					
73¾	—	—	—	Redhill	d																		
79½	—	—	—	Gatwick Airport ✈	d	23p42	23p42	23p50	23p41					0020	0020	0019							0049
82¼	—	—	—	Three Bridges	d	23p47	23p47	23p54	23p47					00a25	00a25	00a24							00a54
86¾	—	—	—	Balcombe	d				23p53														
90¾	—	—	—	Haywards Heath	d	23p56	23p56	0004	23p59														
93¾	—	—	—	Wivelsfield	d				0003														
94½	—	—	—	Burgess Hill	d	0002	0002	0009	0005														
96½	—	—	—	Hassocks	d	0006	0006	0012	0008														
102¼	—	—	—	Preston Park	d				0015														
103¾	—	—	—	Brighton	a	0016	0016	0022	0019														

A from 21 May until 25 une
B from 2 uly until 10 September
C from 17 September
D from 22 May
E from 21 May until 23 uly, MO from 20 August
F from 22 May until 20 uly, from 24 uly until 17 August, MXfrom 21 August
G until 18 May
H from 2 uly
b Previous night, stops to set down only

Bedford, Luton, St Albans and City of London - South London, Gatwick Airport and Brighton

Network Diagram - see first Page of Table 52

		FC 1 A MO	FC 1 B MX	FC 1 C MX	FC D	FC 1 E MO	FC 1 F MX	FC 1 C MX	FC D	FC 1 C MX	FC 1 E	FC 1 A MO	FC 1 B MX	FC D	FC D	SE G	SE H	SE I	SE J MX	SE K	FC D	FC 1 E MO	FC 1 F MX
Bedford	d	22p42	22p42	22p52		23p10	23p12	23p12		23p32	23p40	23p42	23p42		0002							0040	0042
Flitwick	d	22p52	22p52	23p02		23p21	23p22	23p22		23p42	23p51	23p52	23p52		0012							0051	0052
Harlington	d	22p56	22p56	23p06		23p25	23p26	23p26		23p46	23p55	23p56	23p56		0016							0055	0056
Leagrave	d	23p02	23p02	23p12		23p33	23p32	23p32		23p52	0003	0002	0002		0022							0102	0102
Luton	d	23p06	23p06	23p16		23p37	23p36	23p36		23p56	0007	0006	0006		0026							0106	0106
Luton Airport Parkway ✈	d	23p09	23p09	23p19		23p39	23p39	23p39		23p59	0009	0009	0009		0029							0109	0109
Harpenden	d	23p14	23p15	23p25		23p45	23p45	23p45		0005	0015	0014	0015		0035							0115	0115
St Albans City	d	23p21	23p21	23p31		23p51	23p51	23p51		0011	0021	0021	0021		0041							0121	0121
Radlett	d	23p26	23p26	23p36		23p56	23p56	23p56		0016	0026	0026	0026		0046							0126	0126
Elstree & Borehamwood	d	23p31	23p31	23p41		0001	0001	0001		0021	0031	0031	0031		0051							0131	0131
Mill Hill Broadway	d	23p35	23p35	23p45		0005	0005	0005		0025	0035	0035	0035		0055							0135	0135
Hendon	d	23p38	23p38	23p48		0008	0008	0008		0028	0038	0038	0038		0058							0138	0138
Cricklewood	d	23p42	23p42	23p52		0012	0012	0012		0032	0042	0042	0042		0102							0142	0142
West Hampstead Thameslink ⊖	d	23p44	23p44	23p54		0014	0014	0014		0034	0044	0044	0044		0104							0144	0144
Kentish Town ⊖	d	23p49	23p50	0002		0019	0020	0020		0040	0049	0049	0050		0110							0150	0150
St Pancras International ⊖	a																						
St Pancras International ⊖	a	23p53	23p53	0005		0023	0023	0025		0045	0053	0053	0053		0115							0153	0153
	d	23p54	23p54		0012	0024	0024		0030		0054	0054	0054	0100							0130	0154	0154
Farringdon ⊖	d	23p59	23p59		0017	0029	0029		0035				0059										
City Thameslink	d																						
London Blackfriars ⊖	d	0005	0005		0022	0035	0035		0040		0105	0105	0105	0110							0140	0205	0205
Elephant & Castle ⊖	d																						
Loughborough d	d																						
Herne Hill	d																						
London Bridge	a	0011	0011		0035	0041	0041		0055					0125							0155		
	d	0012	0012			0042	0042																
Tulse Hill	d																						
Streatham	d																						
Mitcham Eastfields	d																						
Mitcham unction	d																						
Hackbridge	d																						
Carshalton	d																						
Tooting	d																						
Haydons Road	d																						
Wimbledon ⊖	d																						
Wimbledon Chase	d																						
South Merton	d																						
Morden South	d																						
St Helier	d																						
Sutton Common	d																						
West Sutton	d																						
Sutton (Surrey)	a																						
East Croydon	d	0026	0027			0057	0057				0132	0132	0132									0232	0232
Denmark Hill	d																			0106			
Peckham Rye	d															01s08	01s08	01s08	01s08	0108			
Nunhead	d															01s10	01s10	01s10	01s10	0111			
Crofton Park	d															01s13	01s13	01s13	01s13	0114			
Catford	d															01s16	01s16	01s16	01s16	0116			
Bellingham	d															01s18	01s18	01s18	01s18	0119			
Beckenham Hill	d															01s20	01s20	01s20	01s20	0121			
Ravensbourne	d															01s22	01s22	01s22	01s22	0123			
Shortlands	d																			0125			
Bromley South	d															01s25	01s25	01s25	01s25	0128			
Bickley	d																			01a30			
St Mary Cray	d																						
Swanley	d																						
Eynsford	d																						
Shoreham (Kent)	d																						
Otford	d																						
Bat & Ball	d																						
Sevenoaks	a																						
Redhill	d																						
Gatwick Airport ✈	d	0049	0049			0122	0122				0152	0152	0152									0252	0252
Three Bridges	d	00a54	00a54			01a28	01a28				01a58	01a58	01a58									02a58	02a58
Balcombe	d																						
Haywards Heath	d																						
Wivelsfield	d																						
Burgess Hill	d																						
Hassocks	d																						
Preston Park	d																						
Brighton	a																						

A from 2 uly
B from 22 May
C until 18 May
D until 18 May
E from 21 May until 25 une
F from 22 May until 22 une, from 26 une
G 10 September
H 3 September
I 13 August
J from 29 August until 7 September
K from 30 uly until 10 August

Bedford, Luton, St Albans and City of London - South London, Gatwick Airport and Brighton

Network Diagram - see first Page of Table 52

Station		FC A	FC A 🚌	FC 1 B MO	FC 1 C MX	FC A 🚌	FC 1 A	FC 1 D	FC A 🚌	FC 1 B	FC 1 C MX	FC A 🚌	FC 1 A	FC 1 D	FC A 🚌	FC 1 B	FC 1 E MX	FC 1 B	FC 1 C MX	FC 1 A	SE	FC 1 B	FC 1 C MX
Bedford	d	01 02		01 40	01 42		02 02			02 40	02 42		03 02			03 40	03 42	04 06	04 08	04 08		04 18	04 20
Flitwick	d	01 12		01 51	01 52		02 12			02 51	02 52		03 12			03 51	03 52	04 17	04 18	04 18		04 29	04 30
Harlington	d	01 16		01 55	01 56		02 16			02 55	02 56		03 16			03 55	03 56	04 21	04 22	04 22		04 33	04 34
Leagrave	d	01 22		02 02	02 02		02 22			03 02	03 02		03 22			04 02	04 02	04 28	04 28	04 28		04 40	04 40
Luton	d	01 26		02 06	02 06		02 26			03 06	03 06		03 26			04 06	04 06	04 32	04 32	04 33		04 44	04 44
Luton Airport Parkway	d	01 29		02 09	02 09		02 29			03 09	03 09		03 29			04 09	04 09	04 35	04 35	04 35		04 47	04 47
Harpenden	d	01 35		02 15	02 15		02 35			03 15	03 15		03 35			04 15	04 15	04 41	04 41	04 41		04 53	04 53
St Albans City	d	01 41		02 21	02 21		02 41			03 21	03 21		03 41			04 21	04 21	04 47	04 47	04 47		04 59	04 59
Radlett	d	01 46		02 26	02 26		02 46			03 26	03 26		03 46			04 26	04 26					05 04	05 04
Elstree & Borehamwood	d	01 51		02 31	02 31		02 51			03 31	03 31		03 51			04 31	04 31					05 09	05 09
Mill Hill Broadway	d	01 55		02 35	02 35		02 55			03 35	03 35		03 55			04 35	04 35					05 13	05 13
Hendon	d	01 58		02 38	02 38		02 58			03 38	03 38		03 58			04 38	04 38					05 16	05 16
Cricklewood	d	02 02		02 42	02 42		03 02			03 42	03 42		04 02			04 42	04 42					05 20	05 20
West Hampstead Thameslink ⊖	d	02 04		02 44	02 44		03 04			03 44	03 44		04 04			04 44	04 44	05 04	05 04	05 04		05 22	05 22
Kentish Town ⊖	d	02 10		02 50	02 50		03 10			03 50	03 50		04 10			04 50	04 50					05 28	05 28
St Pancras International ⊖	a																						
St Pancras International ⊖	a	02 15		02 53	02 53		03 15			03 53	03 53		04 15			04 53	04 53	05 12	05 12	05 12		05 32	05 32
	d		02 30	02 54	02 54	03 00		03 28	03 30	03 54	03 54	04 00		04 24	04 30	04 54	04 54	05 12	05 12	05 12		05 32	05 32
Farringdon ⊖	d															04 59	04 59	05 18	05 18	05 18		05 38	05 38
City Thameslink	d																	05 21	05 21	05 21	05 26	05 41	05 41
London Blackfriars ⊖	d		02 40	03 05	03 05	03 10		03 39	03 40	04 05	04 05	04 10		04 35	04a40	05 04	05 04	05 24	05 24	05 24	05 28	05 44	05 44
Elephant & Castle ⊖	d																				05 32		
Loughborough Jn	d																						
Herne Hill	d																						
London Bridge	a		02 55			03 25			03 55			04 25						05 30	05 30	05 30		05 50	05 50
	d																	05 30	05 30	05 30		05 50	05 50
Tulse Hill	d																						
Streatham	d																						
Mitcham Eastfields	d																						
Mitcham Junction	d																						
Hackbridge	d																						
Carshalton	d																						
Tooting	d																						
Haydons Road	d																						
Wimbledon ⊖	d																						
Wimbledon Chase	d																						
South Merton	d																						
Morden South	d																						
St Helier	d																						
Sutton Common	d																						
West Sutton	d																						
Sutton (Surrey)	a																						
East Croydon	d			03 32	03 32			04 04		04 32	04 32			05 02		05 32	05 32	05 47	05 47	05 47		06 05	06 05
Denmark Hill	d																				05 39		
Peckham Rye	d																				05 41		
Nunhead	d																				05 44		
Crofton Park	d																				05 47		
Catford	d																				05 49		
Bellingham	d																				05 52		
Beckenham Hill	d																				05 54		
Ravensbourne	d																				05 56		
Shortlands	d																				05 58		
Bromley South	d																				06 01		
Bickley	d																				06 03		
St Mary Cray	d																				06 08		
Swanley	d																				06 12		
Eynsford	d																				06 17		
Shoreham (Kent)	d																				06 20		
Otford	d																				06 23		
Bat & Ball	d																				06 26		
Sevenoaks	a																				06 29		
Redhill	d																						
Gatwick Airport	d			03 52	03 52			04 24		04 52	04 52			05 22		05 54	05 54	06 04	06 04	06 04		06 22	06 22
Three Bridges	d			03a58	03a58			04a30		05 00	05 00			05 27		06 00	06 00	06 08	06 08	06 08		06 26	06 26
Balcombe	d																	06 14	06 14	06 14		06 33	06 33
Haywards Heath	d									05 11	05 11			05 36		06 11	06 11	06 19	06 19	06 19		06 39	06 39
Wivelsfield	d													05 40				06 23	06 23	06 23		06 43	06 43
Burgess Hill	d													05 43		06 16	06 16	06 25	06 25	06 25		06 45	06 45
Hassocks	d													05 46		06 20	06 20	06 29	06 29	06 29		06 49	06 49
Preston Park	d													05 53		06 27	06 27	06 35	06 35	06 35		06 55	06 55
Brighton	a									05 29	05 29			05 57		06 31	06 31	06 40	06 40	06 40		06 59	06 59

A until 18 May
B from 21 May until 25 June
C from 22 May until 22 June, from 26 June
D from 21 May
E until 22 June, also 14 May, from 26 June

Table 52 Mondays to Fridays

Bedford, Luton, St Albans and City of London - South London, Gatwick Airport and Brighton

Network Diagram - see first Page of Table 52

Station		FC 1 A	FC	FC	FC	FC 1	FC	FC 1	SE	FC	EM ◇1 🍴	FC 1	FC	FC 1 B	FC 1 C	FC	FC 1 B	FC 1 C	EM ◇1 🍴	FC A	FC D	FC 1 B
Bedford	d	04 20				05 00		05 20			05 36	05 40		05 52	05 54		05 56	05 58				06 12
Flitwick	d	04 30				05 10		05 30				05 50		06 02	06 04		06 06	06 08				06 22
Harlington	d	04 34				05 14		05 34				05 54					06 10	06 12				
Leagrave	d	04 40				05 20		05 39				05 59					06 15	06 17				
Luton	d	04 45		05 08		05 24		05 44		05 48		06 04	06 06	06 12	06 14		06 22	06 22	06 24			06 32
Luton Airport Parkway	d	04 47		05 10		05 27		05 46		05 50	05 53	06 06	06 08				06 24	06 24				
Harpenden	d	04 53		05 16		05 33		05 52		05 56		06 12	06 14	06 18	06 20		06 30	06 30				06 38
St Albans City	d	04 59		05 22		05 39		05 58		06 02		06 18	06 20	06 24	06 26		06 36	06 36		06 40	06 40	06 44
Radlett	d	05 04		05 28						06 07			06 25							06 45	06 45	
Elstree & Borehamwood	d	05 09		05 32						06 12			06 30							06 50	06 50	
Mill Hill Broadway	d	05 13		05 36						06 16			06 34							06 54	06 54	
Hendon	d	05 16		05 40						06 19			06 37							06 57	06 57	
Cricklewood	d	05 20		05 43						06 23			06 41							07 01	07 01	
West Hampstead Thameslink ⊖	d	05 22		05 46		05 54	06 04	06 12		06 26		06 30	06 44				06 50	06 50		07 04	07 04	
Kentish Town ⊖	d	05 28		05 50	05 54		06 08			06 30			06 48							07 08	07 08	
St Pancras International ⊖	a										06 16					←			06 48			
St Pancras International ⊖	a	05 32		05 54	05 58	06 02	06 12	06 20		06 34		06 38	06 52	06 44	06 44	06 52	06 57	06 57		07 12	07 12	07 04
	d	05 32	05 36	05 54	05 58	06 02	06 12	06 22		06 34		06 38	06 52	06 44	06 44	06 52	06 58	06 58		07 12	07 12	07 04
Farringdon ⊖	d	05 38	05 42	06 00	06 04	06 08	06 18	06 28		06 40		06 44	→	06 50	06 50	06 58	07 04	07 04		→	→	07 10
City Thameslink	d	05 41	05 44	06 03	06 07	06 11	06 21	06 31	06 39	06 43		06 47		06 53	06 53	07 01	07 07	07 07				07 13
London Blackfriars ⊖	d	05 44	05 47	06 06	06 10	06 14	06 24	06 34	06 42	06 46		06 50		06 58	06 58	07 04	07 09	07 09				07 16
Elephant & Castle ⊖	d		05 50	06 09	06 16		06 27		06 46	06 49				07 02	07 02	07 07						07 19
Loughborough Jn	d			06 13			06 31			06 53						07 11						07 23
Herne Hill	d		05 57	06 17			06 35			06 57						07 15						07 27
London Bridge	a	05 50				06 20		06 41				06 56					07 15	07 15				
	d	05 50				06 20		06 42				07 00					07 16	07 16				
Tulse Hill	d		06 02	06 22			06 42			07 02						07 20						07 31
Streatham	d		06 05	06 25			06 45			07 05						07 23						07 34
Mitcham Eastfields	d			06 29			06 49									07 27						
Mitcham Junction	d			06 32			06 52									07 30						
Hackbridge	d			06 35			06 55									07 33						
Carshalton	d			06 38			06 58									07 36						
Tooting	d		06 10							07 10												07 38
Haydons Road	d		06 13							07 13												07 41
Wimbledon ⊖	d		06 16							07 16												07 47
Wimbledon Chase	d		06 19							07 19												07 50
South Merton	d		06 21							07 21												07 52
Morden South	d		06 23							07 23												07 54
St Helier	d		06 25							07 25												07 56
Sutton Common	d		06 27							07 27												07 58
West Sutton	d		06 30							07 30												08 01
Sutton (Surrey)	a		06 33	06 43			07 03			07 35						07 39						08 07
East Croydon	d	06 05				06 35		06 55				07 15					07 31	07 31				
Denmark Hill	d				06 22				06 52					07 09	07 09							
Peckham Rye	d				06 25				06 55					07 12	07 12							
Nunhead	d				06 27				06 57					07 14	07 14							
Crofton Park	d				06 30				07 00					07 17	07 17							
Catford	d				06 33				07 03					07 20	07 20							
Bellingham	d				06 35				07 05					07 22	07 22							
Beckenham Hill	d				06 37				07 07					07 24	07 24							
Ravensbourne	d				06 39				07 09					07 26	07 26							
Shortlands	d				06 41				07 11					07 28	07 28							
Bromley South	d				06 44				07 14					07 31	07 31							
Bickley	d				06 47				07 17					07 34	07 34							
St Mary Cray	d				06 51				07 21					07 38	07 38							
Swanley	d				06 56				07 26					07 44	07 44							
Eynsford	d				07 00				07 30					07 48	07 48							
Shoreham (Kent)	d				07 04				07 34					07 52	07 52							
Otford	d				07 07				07 37					07 55	07 55							
Bat & Ball	d				07 10				07 40					07 58	07 58							
Sevenoaks	a				07 14				07 43					08 01	08 01							
Redhill	d																					
Gatwick Airport	d	06 22				06 52		07 11				07 31					07 47	07 47				
Three Bridges	d	06 26				06 56		07 15				07 35					07 51	07 51				
Balcombe	d	06 33						07 21									07 57	07 57				
Haywards Heath	d	06 39				07 06		07 26				07 46					08 02	08 02				
Wivelsfield	d	06 43				07 10						07 50					08 06	08 06				
Burgess Hill	d	06 45				07 12		07 31				07 52					08 08	08 08				
Hassocks	d	06 49				07 16		07 35				07 55					08 12	08 12				
Preston Park	d	06 55				07 22						08 02					08 18	08 18				
Brighton	a	06 59				07 27		07 44				08 06					08 23	08 23				

A until 18 May
B from 8 October
C until 5 October
D from 21 May

Bedford, Luton, St Albans and City of London - South London, Gatwick Airport and Brighton

Network Diagram - see first Page of Table 52

		FC ■ A	FC B	FC C	FC ■ D	FC	FC ■	EM ◇■	FC	FC ■	FC	FC	FC	EM ◇■	FC	FC	FC ■	FC	FC	FC	FC ■	EM ◇■	FC ■
Bedford	d	06 14			06 18		06 22	06 31		06 34					06 40		06 54				06 58	07 08	07 12
Flitwick	d	06 24					06 32		06 36	06 44					06 50		07 04				07 08		
Harlington	d						06 36		06 40						06 54						07 12		
Leagrave	d				06 34		06 41		06 45						06 59						07 18		07 28
Luton	d	06 34			06 39	06 43	06 46		06 50	06 54			07 00		07 04	07 10	07 14				07 22	07 24	07 32
Luton Airport Parkway	d				06 41	06 45	06 48		06 52				07 02	07 04	07 06	07 12					07 25		
Harpenden	d	06 40			06 47	06 51	06 54		06 58	07 00			07 08		07 12	07 18	07 20				07 31		07 38
St Albans City	d	06 46			06 53	06 57	07 00		07 04	07 06			07 16		07 18	07 24	07 26			07 34	07 38		07 44
Radlett	d					07 02			07 09				07 21			07 29				07 39			
Elstree & Borehamwood	d					07 06			07 13				07 25			07 33				07 43			
Mill Hill Broadway	d					07 10			07 17				07 30			07 37				07 48			
Hendon	d					07 13							07 33							07 51			
Cricklewood	d					07 17							07 37							07 55			
West Hampstead Thameslink	d				07 08	07 20			07 24				07 40			07 44				08 00			
Kentish Town	d					07 24							07 44							08 04			
St Pancras International	a		←	←				07 08			←	←		07 29				←	←			07 47	
St Pancras International	a	07 04	07 12	07 12	07 16	07 28	07 20		07 31	07 24	07 28	07 31	07 48		07 37	07 51	07 43	07 48	07 51	08 08	07 54		08 04
	d	07 04	07 12	07 12	07 16	07 28	07 20		07 32	07 24	07 28	07 32	07 48		07 38	07 52	07 44	07 48	07 52	08 08	07 56		08 04
Farringdon	d	07 10	07 18	07 18	07 22	→	07 26		→	07 30	07 34	07 38	→		07 44	→	07 50	07 54	07 58	→	08 02		08 10
City Thameslink	d	07 13	07 21	07 21	07 25		07 29			07 33	07 37	07 41			07 47		07 53	07 57	08 01		08 05		08 13
London Blackfriars	d	07 16	07 24	07 24	07 28		07 32			07 36	07 40	07 44			07 50		07 56	08 00	08 04		08 08		08a16
Elephant & Castle	d	07 19	07 28	07 28	07 33					07a39	07 44	07 47			07 54			08 04	08 07				
Loughborough Jn	d	07 23			07 37							07 51							08 11				
Herne Hill	d	07 27			07 41							07 57							08 17				
London Bridge	a						07 41														08 16		
	d						07 42														08 18		
Tulse Hill	d	07 31			07 45							08 05					08 10		08 21				
Streatham	d	07 34			07 48							08 08							08 24				
Mitcham Eastfields	d				07 52														08 28				
Mitcham Junction	d				07 55														08 31				
Hackbridge	d				07 58														08 34				
Carshalton	d				08 01														08 37				
Tooting	d	07 38										08 12											
Haydons Road	d	07 41										08 15											
Wimbledon	d	07 47										08 19											
Wimbledon Chase	d	07 50										08 22											
South Merton	d	07 52										08 24											
Morden South	d	07 54										08 26											
St Helier	d	07 56										08 28											
Sutton Common	d	07 58										08 30											
West Sutton	d	08 01										08 33											
Sutton (Surrey)	a	08 07			08 04							08 37							08 40				
East Croydon	d						07 55										08 26				08 37		
Denmark Hill	d		07 34	07 34							07 50				08 00			08 10					
Peckham Rye	d		07 36	07 36							07 53				08 03			08 13					
Nunhead	d		07 39	07 39							07 56				08 06			08 15					
Crofton Park	d		07 42	07 42											08 09			08 18					
Catford	d		07 44	07 44							08 00				08 12			08 21					
Bellingham	d		07 47	07 47							08 02				08 15			08 23					
Beckenham Hill	d		07 49	07 49											08 17			08 25					
Ravensbourne	d		07 51	07 51											08 19			08 27					
Shortlands	d		07 54	07 54											08 22			08 30					
Bromley South	d		07 57	07 57							08a10				08 25			08 33					
Bickley	d		08 00	08 00											08a28			08 35					
St Mary Cray	d		08 04	08 04														08 40					
Swanley	d		08 10	08 10														08 44					
Eynsford	d		08 15	08 15														08 49					
Shoreham (Kent)	d		08 18	08 18														08 52					
Otford	d		08 21	08 22														08 55					
Bat & Ball	d		08 24	08 25														08 58					
Sevenoaks	a		08 27	08 28														09 01					
Redhill	d																						
Gatwick Airport	d						08 12										08 42				08 53		
Three Bridges	d						08 16										08 46				08 58		
Balcombe	d						08 22										08 52						
Haywards Heath	d						08 27										08 58				09 08		
Wivelsfield	d						08 31										09 02						
Burgess Hill	d						08 33										09 04				09 13		
Hassocks	d						08 37										09 07						
Preston Park	d						08 43										09 14						
Brighton	a						08 48										09 18				09 25		

A until 5 October
B until 18 May
C from 21 May
D ■ from London Blackfriars

Bedford, Luton, St Albans and City of London - South London, Gatwick Airport and Brighton

Network Diagram - see first Page of Table 52

		FC	FC	EM ◇■ A	EM ◇■ B	FC	FC ■	FC	FC ■	FC ■ C	FC	EM ◇■	FC	FC ■	FC ■	FC	FC	FC	FC ■	EM ◇■	EM ◇■	FC ■
Bedford	d						07 16	07 22	07 30					07 33	07 44				07 48	07 55		07 58
Flitwick	d						07 26	07 32	07 40					07 43					07 58			08 08
Harlington	d						07 30	07 36						07 47					08 02			
Leagrave	d						07 35	07 41						07 52	08 00				08 08			
Luton	d		07 30				07 40	07 46	07 50			07 56		07 57	08 04		08 02		08 12		08 15	08 20
Luton Airport Parkway	d		07 32	07 41	07 41		07 42	07 48						07 59			08 04		08 15	08 12		
Harpenden	d		07 38				07 48	07 54	07 56					08 05	08 10		08 10		08 21			08 26
St Albans City	d		07 44			07 52	07 55	08 00	08 02				08 07	08 11	08 16		08 16	08 23	08 27			08 33
Radlett	d		07 49			07 57		08 05					08 12				08 21	08 28				
Elstree & Borehamwood	d		07 53			08 01		08 09					08 16				08 25	08 32				
Mill Hill Broadway	d		07 57			08 06		08 13					08 21				08 29	08 37				
Hendon	d					08 09							08 24					08 40				
Cricklewood	d					08 13							08 28					08 44				
West Hampstead Thameslink	d		08 04			08 16		08 20					08 32				08 36	08 48				
Kentish Town	d					08 20							08 36					08 52				
St Pancras International	a	←		08 07	08 07					←	←	08 24				←				08 39	08 43	
St Pancras International	a	08 08	08 11			08 24	08 15	08 27	08 19	08 24	08 27		08 40	08 32	08 35	08 40	08 43	08 56	08 47			08 51
	d	08 08	08 12			08 24	08 16	08 28	08 20	08 24	08 28		08 40	08 32	08 36	08 40	08 44	08 56	08 48			08 52
Farringdon	d	08 14	08 18			→	08 22	→	08 26	08 30	08 34		→	08 38	08 42	08 46	08 50	→	08 54			08 58
City Thameslink	d	08 17	08 21				08 25		08 29	08 33	08 37			08 41	08 45	08 49	08 53		08 57			09 01
London Blackfriars	d	08 20	08 24				08 28		08 32	08 36	08 40			08 44	08 48	08 52	08 56		09 00			09 04
Elephant & Castle	d		08 27				08 32				08 44			08 47	08a52	08 56	09 00					09a09
Loughborough Jn	d		08 31											08 51			09 04					
Herne Hill	d		08 36							08 46				08 57			09 11					
London Bridge	a																		09 11			
	d																		09 12			
Tulse Hill	d		08 40							08 50				09 01			09 16					
Streatham	d		08 44							08 54				09 05			09 20					
Mitcham Eastfields	d									08 58							09 24					
Mitcham Junction	d									09 01							09 27					
Hackbridge	d									09 04							09 30					
Carshalton	d									09 07							09 33					
Tooting	d		08 48											09 10								
Haydons Road	d		08 51											09 13								
Wimbledon	d		08 55											09 17								
Wimbledon Chase	d		08 58											09 20								
South Merton	d		09 00											09 22								
Morden South	d		09 02											09 24								
St Helier	d		09 04											09 26								
Sutton Common	d		09 06											09 28								
West Sutton	d		09 09											09 31								
Sutton (Surrey)	a		09 12							09 10				09 37			09 36					
East Croydon	d								08 58										09 25			
Denmark Hill	d						08 38				08 52					09 02						
Peckham Rye	d						08 41				08 55											
Nunhead	d						08 43				08 57											
Crofton Park	d						08 46				09 00											
Catford	d						08 49				09 03					09 09						
Bellingham	d						08 51				09 05											
Beckenham Hill	d						08 53				09 07											
Ravensbourne	d						08 55				09 09											
Shortlands	d						08 57				09 11											
Bromley South	d	08a37					09 00				09 14					09 18						
Bickley	d						09 03				09 17					09 20						
St Mary Cray	d						09 07				09 21					09 25						
Swanley	d						09 12				09 26					09 36						
Eynsford	d						09 16				09 30					09 40						
Shoreham (Kent)	d						09 20				09 34					09 44						
Otford	d						09 23				09 37					09 47						
Bat & Ball	d						09 26				09 40					09 50						
Sevenoaks	a						09 29				09 45					09 53						
Redhill	d																					
Gatwick Airport	d								09 13										09 41			
Three Bridges	d								09 17										09 45			
Balcombe	d																		09 51			
Haywards Heath	d								09 27										09 56			
Wivelsfield	d																		10 00			
Burgess Hill	d								09 32										10 02			
Hassocks	d								09 35										10 06			
Preston Park	d								09 42										10 12			
Brighton	a								09 46										10 17			

A from 17 September
B until 14 September
C ■ from London Blackfriars

Bedford, Luton, St Albans and City of London - South London, Gatwick Airport and Brighton

Network Diagram - see first Page of Table 52

Station		FC	FC	FC	FC ■	FC	FC	FC ■	FC	EM ◇■	FC	FC	FC ■	FC	FC	FC	FC ■	FC	FC	EM ◇■	FC	FC ■	EM ◇■
Bedford ■	d				08 04			08 24		08 29			08 40				08 54			09 02		09 10	09 18
Flitwick	d				08 14			08 34					08 50				09 04					09 20	
Harlington	d				08 18			08 38					08 54				09 08					09 24	
Leagrave	d				08 23			08 43					08 59				09 13					09 29	
Luton ■	d		08 20		08 28			08 48			08 54		09 04			09 14	09 18			09 18		09 34	
Luton Airport Parkway ■ ✈	d		08 22		08 30			08 50			08 56		09 06			09 16	09 20					09 36	09 34
Harpenden	d		08 28		08 36			08 56			09 02		09 12			09 22	09 26					09 42	
St Albans City	d		08 34	08 43	08 44		08 58	09 02			09 08	09 14	09 18			09 29	09 32				09 44	09 48	
Radlett	d		08 39	08 48			09 03				09 13	09 19				09 34					09 49		
Elstree & Borehamwood	d		08 43	08 52			09 07				09 17	09 23				09 38					09 53		
Mill Hill Broadway	d			08 57			09 12					09 28				09 43					09 58		
Hendon	d			09 00			09 15					09 31				09 46					10 01		
Cricklewood	d			09 04			09 19					09 35				09 50					10 05		
West Hampstead Thameslink ⊖	d		08 52	09 08			09 22				09 26	09 39				09 54					10 09		
Kentish Town ⊖	d			09 12			09 26					09 44			09 54	10 00					10 14		
St Pancras International ■ ⊖	a	←				←			←	09 06				←				←	←	09 44			10 00
St Pancras International ■ ⊖	a	08 56	08 59	09 16	09 03	09 16	09 30	09 21	09 30		09 33	09 47	09 39	09 47	09 58	10 03	09 51	09 58	10 03		10 18	10 09	
	d	08 56	09 00	09 16	09 04	09 16	09 30	09 22	09 30		09 34	09 48	09 40	09 48	10 00	10 04	09 54	10 00	10 04		10 18	10 09	
Farringdon ■ ⊖	d	09 02	09 06	→	09 10	09 22	→	09 28	09 36		09 40	→	09 45	09 53	→	→	09 59	10 05	10 09		→	10 14	
City Thameslink ■	d	09 05	09 09		09 13	09 25		09 31	09 39		09 43		09 48	09 57			10 03	10 09	10 13			10 18	
London Blackfriars ■ ⊖	d	09 08	09 12		09 16	09 28		09 34	09 42		09 46		09 50	10 00			10 05	10 12	10 16			10 20	
Elephant & Castle ⊖	d	09 12	09 16			09 31			09 46		09 49			10 03				10 16	10 19				
Loughborough Jn	d	09 16				09 35					09 53			10 07					10 23				
Herne Hill ■	d	09 25				09 41					09 57			10 11					10 27				
London Bridge ■	a				09 26			09 41					09 56				10 11					10 26	
	d				09 27			09 42					09 57				10 12					10 27	
Tulse Hill ■	d	09 31				09 46					10 01			10 16					10 31				
Streatham ■	d	09 35				09 50					10 05			10 20					10 35				
Mitcham Eastfields	d					09 54								10 24									
Mitcham Junction	d					09 57								10 27									
Hackbridge	d					10 00								10 30									
Carshalton	d					10 03								10 33									
Tooting	d	09 40									10 10								10 40				
Haydons Road	d	09 43									10 13								10 43				
Wimbledon ■ ⊖	d	09 47									10 17								10 47				
Wimbledon Chase	d	09 50									10 20								10 50				
South Merton	d	09 52									10 22								10 52				
Morden South	d	09 54									10 24								10 54				
St Helier	d	09 56									10 26								10 56				
Sutton Common	d	09 58									10 28								10 58				
West Sutton	d	10 01									10 31								11 01				
Sutton (Surrey) ■	a	10 05				10 06					10 35			10 36					11 05				
East Croydon	d				09 41			09 55					10 11				10 25					10 41	
Denmark Hill ■	d		09 22						09 52									10 22					
Peckham Rye ■	d		09 25						09 55									10 25					
Nunhead ■	d		09 27						09 57									10 27					
Crofton Park	d		09 30						10 00									10 30					
Catford	d		09 33						10 03									10 33					
Bellingham	d		09 35						10 05									10 35					
Beckenham Hill	d		09 37						10 07									10 37					
Ravensbourne	d		09 39						10 09									10 39					
Shortlands	d		09 41						10 11									10 41					
Bromley South ■	d		09 44						10 14									10 44					
Bickley ■	d		09 47						10 17									10 47					
St Mary Cray	d		09 51						10 21									10 51					
Swanley ■	d		09 56						10 26									10 56					
Eynsford	d		10 00						10 30									11 00					
Shoreham (Kent)	d		10 04						10 34									11 04					
Otford ■	d		10 07						10 37									11 07					
Bat & Ball	d		10 10						10 40									11 10					
Sevenoaks ■	a		10 13						10 43									11 13					
Redhill	d																						
Gatwick Airport ■ ✈	d				09 57			10 11					10 27				10 41					10 57	
Three Bridges ■	d				10 02			10 15					10 32				10 45					11 02	
Balcombe	d							10 21															
Haywards Heath ■	d				10 11			10 27					10 41				10 55					11 11	
Wivelsfield ■	d							10 31									10 59						
Burgess Hill ■	d							10 33									11 01						
Hassocks ■	d							10 36									11 04						
Preston Park	d							10 43									11 11						
Brighton ■	a				10 25			10 47					10 55				11 15					11 25	

Bedford, Luton, St Albans and City of London - South London, Gatwick Airport and Brighton

Network Diagram - see first Page of Table 52

Station		FC ■	FC	FC	FC	FC ■	FC	FC	FC	FC ■	FC	FC	EM ◇■	FC	FC	FC ■	FC	FC	FC	FC ■	EM ◇■	FC	FC
Bedford ■	d	09 18				09 24				09 40	09 48		09 49			09 54				10 10	10 18	10 18	
Flitwick	d	09 28				09 34				09 50	09 58					10 04				10 20		10 28	
Harlington	d					09 38				09 54						10 08				10 24			
Leagrave	d					09 43				09 59						10 13				10 29			
Luton ■	d	09 39			09 44	09 48				10 04	10 09		10 04		10 14	10 18				10 34		10 39	
Luton Airport Parkway ■ ✈	d	09 42			09 46	09 50				10 06	10 12				10 16	10 20				10 36	10 34	10 42	
Harpenden	d	09 48			09 52	09 56				10 12	10 18				10 22	10 26				10 42		10 48	
St Albans City	d	09 54			09 59	10 02			10 14	10 18	10 24				10 29	10 32			10 44	10 48		10 54	
Radlett	d				10 04				10 19						10 34				10 49				
Elstree & Borehamwood	d				10 08				10 23						10 38				10 53				
Mill Hill Broadway	d				10 13				10 28						10 43				10 58				
Hendon	d				10 16				10 31						10 46				11 01				
Cricklewood	d				10 20				10 35						10 50				11 05				
West Hampstead Thameslink ⊖	d				10 24				10 39						10 54				11 09				
Kentish Town ⊖	d			10 26	10 30				10 44					10 56	11 00				11 14				
St Pancras International ■ ⊖	a		←				←	←				←	10 29				←	←			11 01		←
St Pancras International ■ ⊖	a	10 13	10 18	10 29	10 33	10 23	10 29	10 33	10 48	10 38	10 43	10 48		10 59	11 03	10 51	10 59	11 03	11 18	11 09		11 13	11 18
	d	10 14	10 18	10 30	10 34	10 24	10 30	10 34	10 48	10 39	10 44	10 48		11 00	11 04	10 54	11 00	11 04	11 18	11 09		11 14	11 18
Farringdon ■ ⊖	d	10 20	10 24	→	→	10 29	10 35	10 39	→	10 44	10 50	10 54		→	→	10 59	11 05	11 09	→	11 14		11 20	11 24
City Thameslink ■	d	10 23	10 27			10 33	10 39	10 43		10 48	10 53	10 57				11 03	11 09	11 13		11 18		11 23	11 27
London Blackfriars ■ ⊖	d	10 26	10 30			10 35	10 42	10 46		10 50	10 56	11 00				11 05	11 12	11 16		11 20		11 26	11 30
Elephant & Castle ⊖	d	10a30	10 33				10 46	10 49			11a00	11 03					11 16	11 19				11a30	11 33
Loughborough Jn	d		10 37					10 53				11 07						11 23					11 37
Herne Hill ■	d		10 41					10 57				11 11						11 27					11 41
London Bridge ■	a					10 41				10 56						11 11				11 26			
	d					10 42				10 57						11 12				11 27			
Tulse Hill ■	d		10 46					11 01				11 16						11 31					11 46
Streatham ■	d		10 50					11 05				11 20						11 35					11 50
Mitcham Eastfields	d		10 54									11 24											11 54
Mitcham Junction	d		10 57									11 27											11 57
Hackbridge	d		11 00									11 30											12 00
Carshalton	d		11 03									11 33											12 03
Tooting	d							11 10										11 40					
Haydons Road	d							11 13										11 43					
Wimbledon ■ ⊖	d							11 17										11 47					
Wimbledon Chase	d							11 20										11 50					
South Merton	d							11 22										11 52					
Morden South	d							11 24										11 54					
St Helier	d							11 26										11 56					
Sutton Common	d							11 28										11 58					
West Sutton	d							11 31										12 01					
Sutton (Surrey) ■	a		11 06					11 35				11 36						12 05					12 06
East Croydon	d					10 55				11 11						11 25				11 41			
Denmark Hill ■	d						10 52										11 22						
Peckham Rye ■	d						10 55										11 25						
Nunhead ■	d						10 57										11 27						
Crofton Park	d						11 00										11 30						
Catford	d						11 03										11 33						
Bellingham	d						11 05										11 35						
Beckenham Hill	d						11 07										11 37						
Ravensbourne	d						11 09										11 39						
Shortlands	d						11 11										11 41						
Bromley South ■	d						11 14										11 44						
Bickley ■	d						11 17										11 47						
St Mary Cray	d						11 21										11 51						
Swanley ■	d						11 26										11 56						
Eynsford	d						11 30										12 00						
Shoreham (Kent)	d						11 34										12 04						
Otford ■	d						11 37										12 07						
Bat & Ball	d						11 40										12 10						
Sevenoaks ■	a						11 43										12 13						
Redhill	d																						
Gatwick Airport ■ ✈	d					11 11				11 27						11 41				11 57			
Three Bridges ■	d					11 15				11 32						11 45				12 02			
Balcombe	d					11 21																	
Haywards Heath ■	d					11 27				11 41						11 55				12 11			
Wivelsfield ■	d					11 31										11 59							
Burgess Hill ■	d					11 33										12 01							
Hassocks ■	d					11 36										12 04							
Preston Park	d					11 43										12 11							
Brighton ■	a					11 47				11 55						12 15				12 25			

Bedford, Luton, St Albans and City of London - South London, Gatwick Airport and Brighton

Network Diagram - see first Page of Table 52

		FC		FC	FC ■	FC	FC	FC	FC ■	FC	EM ◇■	FC		FC	FC ■	FC	FC	FC	FC ■	FC	EM ◇■	FC		FC	FC ■
Bedford	d				10 25				10 40		10 49				10 54				11 10		11 18				11 24
Flitwick	d				10 35				10 50						11 04				11 20						11 34
Harlington	d				10 39				10 54						11 08				11 24						11 38
Leagrave	d				10 44				10 59						11 13				11 29						11 43
Luton	d			10 44	10 49				11 04		11 05			11 14	11 18				11 34					11 44	11 48
Luton Airport Parkway	d			10 46	10 51				11 06					11 16	11 20				11 36		11 34			11 46	11 50
Harpenden	d			10 52	10 57				11 12					11 22	11 26				11 42					11 52	11 56
St Albans City	d			10 59	11 03			11 14	11 18					11 29	11 32			11 44	11 48					11 59	12 02
Radlett	d			11 04				11 19						11 34				11 49						12 04	
Elstree & Borehamwood	d			11 08				11 23						11 38				11 53						12 08	
Mill Hill Broadway	d			11 13				11 28						11 43				11 58						12 13	
Hendon	d			11 16				11 31						11 46				12 01						12 16	
Cricklewood	d			11 20				11 35						11 50				12 05						12 20	
West Hampstead Thameslink ⊖	d			11 24				11 39						11 54				12 09						12 24	
Kentish Town ⊖	d	11 26		11 30				11 44				11 56		12 00				12 14				12 26		12 30	
St Pancras International ⊖	a					←	←			←	11 29					←	←			←	12 00				
St Pancras International ⊖	a	11 29		11 33	11 21	11 29	11 33	11 47	11 38	11 47		11 59		12 03	11 51	11 59	12 03	12 17	12 09	12 17		12 29		12 33	12 21
	d	11 30		11 34	11 24	11 30	11 34	11 48	11 39	11 48		12 00		12 04	11 54	12 00	12 04	12 18	12 09	12 18		12 30		12 34	12 24
Farringdon ⊖	d	→		→	11 29	11 35	11 39	→	11 44	11 53		→		→	11 59	12 05	12 09	→	12 14	12 23		→		→	12 29
City Thameslink	d				11 33	11 39	11 43		11 48	11 57					12 03	12 09	12 13		12 18	12 27					12 33
London Blackfriars ⊖	d				11 35	11 42	11 46		11 50	12 00					12 05	12 12	12 16		12 20	12 30					12 35
Elephant & Castle ⊖	d					11 46	11 49			12 03						12 16	12 19			12 33					
Loughborough Jn	d						11 53			12 07							12 23			12 37					
Herne Hill	d						11 57			12 11							12 27			12 41					
London Bridge	a				11 41				11 56						12 11				12 26						12 41
	d				11 42				11 57						12 12				12 27						12 42
Tulse Hill	d						12 01			12 16							12 31			12 46					
Streatham	d						12 05			12 20							12 35			12 50					
Mitcham Eastfields	d									12 24										12 54					
Mitcham Junction	d									12 27										12 57					
Hackbridge	d									12 30										13 00					
Carshalton	d									12 33										13 03					
Tooting	d						12 10										12 40								
Haydons Road	d						12 13										12 43								
Wimbledon ⊖	d						12 17										12 47								
Wimbledon Chase	d						12 20										12 50								
South Merton	d						12 22										12 52								
Morden South	d						12 24										12 54								
St Helier	d						12 26										12 56								
Sutton Common	d						12 28										12 58								
West Sutton	d						12 31										13 01								
Sutton (Surrey)	a						12 35			12 36							13 05			13 06					
East Croydon	d				11 55				12 11						12 25				12 41						12 55
Denmark Hill	d					11 52										12 22									
Peckham Rye	d					11 55										12 25									
Nunhead	d					11 57										12 27									
Crofton Park	d					12 00										12 30									
Catford	d					12 03										12 33									
Bellingham	d					12 05										12 35									
Beckenham Hill	d					12 07										12 37									
Ravensbourne	d					12 09										12 39									
Shortlands	d					12 11										12 41									
Bromley South	d					12 14										12 44									
Bickley	d					12 17										12 47									
St Mary Cray	d					12 21										12 51									
Swanley	d					12 26										12 56									
Eynsford	d					12 30										13 00									
Shoreham (Kent)	d					12 34										13 04									
Otford	d					12 37										13 07									
Bat & Ball	d					12 40										13 10									
Sevenoaks	a					12 43										13 13									
Redhill	d																								
Gatwick Airport	d				12 11				12 27						12 41				12 57						13 11
Three Bridges	d				12 15				12 32						12 45				13 02						13 15
Balcombe	d				12 21																				13 21
Haywards Heath	d				12 27				12 41						12 55				13 11						13 27
Wivelsfield	d				12 31										12 59										13 31
Burgess Hill	d				12 33										13 01										13 33
Hassocks	d				12 36										13 04										13 36
Preston Park	d				12 43										13 11										13 43
Brighton	a				12 47				12 55						13 15				13 25						13 47

Bedford, Luton, St Albans and City of London - South London, Gatwick Airport and Brighton

Network Diagram - see first Page of Table 52

		FC	FC	FC	FC ■	FC	EM ◇■	FC		FC	FC ■	FC	FC	FC	FC ■	FC	EM ◇■	FC		FC	FC ■	FC	FC	FC	FC ■
Bedford	d				11 40		11 49				11 54				12 10		12 18				12 24				12 40
Flitwick	d				11 50						12 04				12 20						12 34				12 50
Harlington	d				11 54						12 08				12 24						12 38				12 54
Leagrave	d				11 59						12 13				12 29						12 43				12 59
Luton	d				12 04		12 05			12 14	12 18				12 34					12 44	12 48				13 04
Luton Airport Parkway	d				12 06					12 16	12 20				12 36		12 34			12 46	12 50				13 06
Harpenden	d				12 12					12 22	12 26				12 42					12 52	12 56				13 12
St Albans City	d			12 14	12 18					12 29	12 32			12 44	12 48					12 59	13 02			13 14	13 18
Radlett	d			12 19						12 34				12 49						13 04				13 19	
Elstree & Borehamwood	d			12 23						12 38				12 53						13 08				13 23	
Mill Hill Broadway	d			12 28						12 43				12 58						13 13				13 28	
Hendon	d			12 31						12 46				13 01						13 16				13 31	
Cricklewood	d			12 35						12 50				13 05						13 20				13 35	
West Hampstead Thameslink ⊖	d			12 39						12 54				13 09						13 24				13 39	
Kentish Town ⊖	d			12 44				12 56		13 00				13 14				13 26		13 30				13 44	
St Pancras International ⊖	a	←	←			←	12 29					←	←			←	13 00					←	←		
St Pancras International ⊖	a	12 29	12 33	12 47	12 39	12 47		12 59		13 03	12 51	12 59	13 03	13 17	13 08	13 17		13 29		13 33	13 21	13 29	13 33	13 47	13 38
	d	12 30	12 34	12 48	12 39	12 48		13 00		13 04	12 54	13 00	13 04	13 18	13 09	13 18		13 30		13 34	13 24	13 30	13 34	13 48	13 39
Farringdon ⊖	d	12 35	12 39	→	12 44	12 53		→		→	12 59	13 05	13 09	→	13 14	13 23		→		→	13 29	13 35	13 39	→	13 44
City Thameslink	d	12 39	12 43		12 48	12 57					13 03	13 09	13 13		13 18	13 27					13 33	13 39	13 43		13 48
London Blackfriars ⊖	d	12 42	12 46		12 50	13 00					13 05	13 12	13 16		13 20	13 30					13 35	13 42	13 46		13 50
Elephant & Castle ⊖	d	12 46	12 49			13 03						13 16	13 19			13 33						13 46	13 49		
Loughborough Jn	d		12 53			13 07							13 23			13 37							13 53		
Herne Hill	d		12 57			13 11							13 27			13 41							13 57		
London Bridge	a				12 56						13 11				13 26						13 41				13 56
	d				12 57						13 12				13 27						13 42				13 57
Tulse Hill	d		13 01			13 16							13 31			13 46							14 01		
Streatham	d		13 05			13 20							13 35			13 50							14 05		
Mitcham Eastfields	d					13 24										13 54									
Mitcham Junction	d					13 27										13 57									
Hackbridge	d					13 30										14 00									
Carshalton	d					13 33										14 03									
Tooting	d		13 10										13 40										14 10		
Haydons Road	d		13 13										13 43										14 13		
Wimbledon ⊖	d		13 17										13 47										14 17		
Wimbledon Chase	d		13 20										13 50										14 20		
South Merton	d		13 22										13 52										14 22		
Morden South	d		13 24										13 54										14 24		
St Helier	d		13 26										13 56										14 26		
Sutton Common	d		13 28										13 58										14 28		
West Sutton	d		13 31										14 01										14 31		
Sutton (Surrey)	a		13 35			13 36							14 05			14 06							14 35		
East Croydon	d				13 11						13 25				13 41						13 55				14 11
Denmark Hill	d	12 52										13 22										13 52			
Peckham Rye	d	12 55										13 25										13 55			
Nunhead	d	12 57										13 27										13 57			
Crofton Park	d	13 00										13 30										14 00			
Catford	d	13 03										13 33										14 03			
Bellingham	d	13 05										13 35										14 05			
Beckenham Hill	d	13 07										13 37										14 07			
Ravensbourne	d	13 09										13 39										14 09			
Shortlands	d	13 11										13 41										14 11			
Bromley South	d	13 14										13 44										14 14			
Bickley	d	13 17										13 47										14 17			
St Mary Cray	d	13 21										13 51										14 21			
Swanley	d	13 26										13 56										14 26			
Eynsford	d	13 30										14 00										14 30			
Shoreham (Kent)	d	13 34										14 04										14 34			
Otford	d	13 37										14 07										14 37			
Bat & Ball	d	13 40										14 10										14 40			
Sevenoaks	a	13 43										14 13										14 43			
Redhill	d																								
Gatwick Airport	d				13 27						13 41				13 57						14 11				14 27
Three Bridges	d				13 32						13 45				14 02						14 15				14 32
Balcombe	d																				14 21				
Haywards Heath	d				13 41						13 55				14 11						14 27				14 41
Wivelsfield	d										13 59										14 31				
Burgess Hill	d										14 01										14 33				
Hassocks	d										14 04										14 36				
Preston Park	d										14 11										14 43				
Brighton	a				13 55						14 15				14 25						14 47				14 55

Bedford, Luton, St Albans and City of London - South London, Gatwick Airport and Brighton

Network Diagram - see first Page of Table 52

Station		FC	EM ◇1	FC	FC	FC 1	FC	FC	FC	FC 1	FC	EM ◇1	FC	FC	FC 1	FC	FC	FC	FC 1	FC	EM ◇1	FC
Bedford	d		12 49			12 54				13 10		13 18			13 24				13 40		13 49	
Flitwick	d					13 04				13 20					13 34				13 50			
Harlington	d					13 08				13 24					13 38				13 54			
Leagrave	d					13 13				13 29					13 43				13 59			
Luton	d		13 05		13 14	13 18				13 34				13 44	13 48				14 04		14 05	
Luton Airport Parkway ✈	d				13 16	13 20				13 36		13 34		13 46	13 50				14 06			
Harpenden	d				13 22	13 26				13 42				13 52	13 56				14 12			
St Albans City	d				13 29	13 32			13 44	13 48				13 59	14 02			14 14	14 18			
Radlett	d				13 34				13 49					14 04				14 19				
Elstree & Borehamwood	d				13 38				13 53					14 08				14 23				
Mill Hill Broadway	d				13 43				13 58					14 13				14 28				
Hendon	d				13 46				14 01					14 16				14 31				
Cricklewood	d				13 50				14 05					14 20				14 35				
West Hampstead Thameslink ⊖	d				13 54				14 09					14 24				14 39				
Kentish Town ⊖	d			13 56	14 00				14 14				14 26	14 30				14 44				14 56
St Pancras International ⊖	a	←	13 29				←	←			←	14 01				←	←			←	14 29	
St Pancras International ⊖	a	13 47		13 59	14 03	13 51	13 59	14 03	14 17	14 09	14 17		14 29	14 33	14 21	14 29	14 33	14 47	14 38	14 47		14 59
	d	13 48		14 00	14 04	13 54	14 00	14 04	14 18	14 09	14 18		14 30	14 34	14 24	14 30	14 34	14 48	14 39	14 48		15 00
Farringdon ⊖	d	13 53		→	→	13 59	14 05	14 09	→	14 14	14 23		→	→	14 29	14 35	14 39	→	14 44	14 53		→
City Thameslink	d	13 57				14 03	14 09	14 13		14 18	14 27				14 33	14 39	14 43		14 48	14 57		
London Blackfriars ⊖	d	14 00				14 05	14 12	14 16		14 20	14 30				14 35	14 42	14 46		14 50	15 00		
Elephant & Castle ⊖	d	14 03					14 16	14 19			14 33					14 46	14 49			15 03		
Loughborough Junction	d	14 07						14 23			14 37						14 53			15 07		
Herne Hill	d	14 11						14 27			14 41						14 57			15 11		
London Bridge	a					14 11				14 26					14 41				14 56			
	d					14 12				14 27					14 42				14 57			
Tulse Hill	d	14 16						14 31			14 46						15 01			15 16		
Streatham	d	14 20						14 35			14 50						15 05			15 20		
Mitcham Eastfields	d	14 24									14 54									15 24		
Mitcham Junction	d	14 27									14 57									15 27		
Hackbridge	d	14 30									15 00									15 30		
Carshalton	d	14 33									15 03									15 33		
Tooting	d							14 40									15 10					
Haydons Road	d							14 43									15 13					
Wimbledon ⊖	d							14 47									15 17					
Wimbledon Chase	d							14 50									15 20					
South Merton	d							14 52									15 22					
Morden South	d							14 54									15 24					
St Helier	d							14 56									15 26					
Sutton Common	d							14 58									15 28					
West Sutton	d							15 01									15 31					
Sutton (Surrey)	a	14 36						15 05			15 06						15 35			15 36		
East Croydon	d					14 25				14 41					14 55				15 11			
Denmark Hill	d						14 22									14 52						
Peckham Rye	d						14 25									14 55						
Nunhead	d						14 27									14 57						
Crofton Park	d						14 30									15 00						
Catford	d						14 33									15 03						
Bellingham	d						14 35									15 05						
Beckenham Hill	d						14 37									15 07						
Ravensbourne	d						14 39									15 09						
Shortlands	d						14 41									15 11						
Bromley South	d						14 44									15 14						
Bickley	d						14 47									15 17						
St Mary Cray	d						14 51									15 21						
Swanley	d						14 56									15 26						
Eynsford	d						15 00									15 30						
Shoreham (Kent)	d						15 04									15 34						
Otford	d						15 07									15 37						
Bat & Ball	d						15 10									15 40						
Sevenoaks	a						15 13									15 43						
Redhill	d																					
Gatwick Airport ✈	d					14 41				14 57					15 11				15 27			
Three Bridges	d					14 45				15 02					15 15				15 32			
Balcombe	d														15 21							
Haywards Heath	d					14 55				15 11					15 27				15 41			
Wivelsfield	d					14 59									15 31							
Burgess Hill	d					15 01									15 33							
Hassocks	d					15 04									15 36							
Preston Park	d					15 11									15 43							
Brighton	a					15 15				15 25					15 47				15 55			

Bedford, Luton, St Albans and City of London - South London, Gatwick Airport and Brighton

Network Diagram - see first Page of Table 52

Station		FC	FC 1	FC	FC	FC	FC 1	FC	EM ◇1	FC	FC	FC 1	FC	FC	FC	FC 1	FC	EM ◇1	FC	FC	FC 1	FC	FC
Bedford	d		13 54				14 10		14 18			14 24				14 40		14 49			14 54		
Flitwick	d		14 04				14 20					14 34				14 50					15 04		
Harlington	d		14 08				14 24					14 38				14 54					15 08		
Leagrave	d		14 13				14 29					14 43				14 59					15 13		
Luton	d	14 14	14 18				14 34				14 44	14 48				15 04		15 05		15 14	15 18		
Luton Airport Parkway ✈	d	14 16	14 20				14 36		14 34		14 46	14 50				15 06				15 16	15 20		
Harpenden	d	14 22	14 26				14 42				14 52	14 56				15 12				15 22	15 26		
St Albans City	d	14 29	14 32			14 44	14 48				14 59	15 02			15 14	15 18				15 29	15 32		
Radlett	d	14 34				14 49					15 04				15 19					15 34			
Elstree & Borehamwood	d	14 38				14 53					15 08				15 23					15 38			
Mill Hill Broadway	d	14 43				14 58					15 13				15 28					15 43			
Hendon	d	14 46				15 01					15 16				15 31					15 46			
Cricklewood	d	14 50				15 05					15 20				15 35					15 50			
West Hampstead Thameslink ⊖	d	14 54				15 09					15 24				15 39					15 54			
Kentish Town ⊖	d	15 00				15 14				15 26	15 30				15 44				15 56	16 00			
St Pancras International ⊖	a			←	←			←	14 59				←	←			←	15 29				←	←
St Pancras International ⊖	a	15 03	14 51	14 59	15 03	15 17	15 08	15 17		15 29	15 33	15 21	15 29	15 33	15 47	15 38	15 47		15 59	16 03	15 51	15 59	16 03
	d	15 04	14 54	15 00	15 04	15 18	15 09	15 18		15 30	15 34	15 24	15 30	15 34	15 48	15 39	15 48		16 00	16 04	15 54	16 00	16 04
Farringdon ⊖	d	→	14 59	15 05	15 09	→	15 14	15 23		→	→	15 29	15 35	15 39	→	15 44	15 53		→	→	15 59	16 05	16 09
City Thameslink	d		15 03	15 09	15 13		15 18	15 27				15 33	15 39	15 43		15 48	15 57				16 03	16 09	16 13
London Blackfriars ⊖	d		15 05	15 12	15 16		15 20	15 30				15 35	15 42	15 46		15 50	16 00				16 05	16 12	16 16
Elephant & Castle ⊖	d			15 16	15 19			15 33					15 46	15 49			16 03					16 16	16 19
Loughborough Junction	d				15 23			15 37						15 53			16 07						16 23
Herne Hill	d				15 27			15 41						15 57			16 11						16 27
London Bridge	a		15 11				15 26					15 41				15 56					16 11		
	d		15 12				15 27					15 42				15 57					16 12		
Tulse Hill	d				15 31			15 46						16 01			16 16						16 32
Streatham	d				15 35			15 50						16 05			16 20						16 36
Mitcham Eastfields	d							15 54									16 24						
Mitcham Junction	d							15 57									16 27						
Hackbridge	d							16 00									16 30						
Carshalton	d							16 03									16 33						
Tooting	d				15 40									16 10									16 40
Haydons Road	d				15 43									16 13									16 43
Wimbledon ⊖	d				15 47									16 17									16 47
Wimbledon Chase	d				15 50									16 20									16 50
South Merton	d				15 52									16 22									16 52
Morden South	d				15 54									16 24									16 54
St Helier	d				15 56									16 26									16 56
Sutton Common	d				15 58									16 28									16 58
West Sutton	d				16 01									16 31									17 01
Sutton (Surrey)	a				16 05			16 06						16 35			16 36						17 05
East Croydon	d		15 25				15 41					15 55				16 11					16 25		
Denmark Hill	d			15 22									15 52									16 22	
Peckham Rye	d			15 25									15 55									16 25	
Nunhead	d			15 27									15 57									16 27	
Crofton Park	d			15 30									16 00									16 30	
Catford	d			15 33									16 03									16 33	
Bellingham	d			15 35									16 05									16 35	
Beckenham Hill	d			15 37									16 07									16 37	
Ravensbourne	d			15 39									16 09									16 39	
Shortlands	d			15 41									16 11									16 41	
Bromley South	d			15 44									16 14									16 44	
Bickley	d			15 47									16 17									16 47	
St Mary Cray	d			15 51									16 21									16 51	
Swanley	d			15 56									16 26									16 56	
Eynsford	d			16 00									16 30									17 00	
Shoreham (Kent)	d			16 04									16 34									17 04	
Otford	d			16 07									16 37									17 07	
Bat & Ball	d			16 10									16 40									17 10	
Sevenoaks	a			16 13									16 43									17 14	
Redhill	d																						
Gatwick Airport ✈	d		15 41				15 57					16 11				16 27					16 41		
Three Bridges	d		15 45				16 02					16 15				16 32					16 45		
Balcombe	d											16 21											
Haywards Heath	d		15 55				16 11					16 27				16 41					16 55		
Wivelsfield	d		15 59									16 31									16 59		
Burgess Hill	d		16 01									16 33									17 01		
Hassocks	d		16 04									16 36									17 04		
Preston Park	d		16 11									16 43									17 11		
Brighton	a		16 15				16 25					16 47				16 55					17 15		

Bedford, Luton, St Albans and City of London - South London, Gatwick Airport and Brighton

Network Diagram - see first Page of Table 52

		SE ■ A	FC	FC	FC ■	FC	FC	EM ◇■	FC	FC	FC ■	FC	FC	FC	FC ■	EM ◇■	FC ■	FC	FC	FC	FC	FC	FC ■
Bedford ■	d				15 10			15 18			15 24				15 40	15 49	15 52			15 56			16 10
Flitwick	d				15 20						15 34				15 50		16 02			16 06			16 20
Harlington	d				15 24						15 38				15 54					16 10			16 24
Leagrave	d				15 29						15 43				15 59					16 15			16 29
Luton ■	d				15 34					15 44	15 48				16 04	16 05	16 14		16 16	16 20			16 34
Luton Airport Parkway ■ ✈	d				15 36			15 34		15 46	15 50				16 06		16 17		16 18	16 22			16 36
Harpenden	d				15 42					15 52	15 56				16 12				16 24	16 28			16 42
St Albans City	d			15 44	15 48					15 59	16 02			16 14	16 18		16 25		16 30	16 34		16 44	16 48
Radlett	d			15 49						16 04				16 19					16 35			16 49	
Elstree & Borehamwood	d			15 53						16 08				16 23					16 39			16 53	
Mill Hill Broadway	d			15 58						16 13				16 28					16 44			16 58	
Hendon	d			16 01						16 16				16 31					16 47			17 01	
Cricklewood	d			16 05						16 20				16 35					16 51			17 05	
West Hampstead Thameslink ⊖	d			16 09						16 24				16 42					16 54	16 48		17 10	
Kentish Town ⊖	d		16 10	16 14					16 24	16 30				16 46					16 58			17 14	
St Pancras International ■ ⊖	a					←	←	15 59				←	←			16 29		←			←		
St Pancras International ■ ⊖	a		16 13	16 17	16 08	16 13	16 17		16 27	16 33	16 20	16 27	16 33	16 50	16 39		16 44	16 50	17 02	16 55	17 02	17 18	17 09
	d		16 14	16 18	16 09	16 14	16 18		16 28	16 34	16 22	16 28	16 34	16 52	16 40		16 46	16 52	17 02	16 58	17 02	17 18	17 10
Farringdon ■ ⊖	d		→	→	16 14	16 19	16 23		→	→	16 27	16 33	16 39	→	16 45		16 51	16 57	→	17 03	17 07	→	17 15
City Thameslink ■	d				16 18	16 23	16 27				16 31	16 37	16 43		16 49		16 55	17 01		17 07	17 11		17 19
London Blackfriars ■ ⊖	d	16 20			16 20	16 26	16 30				16 36	16 42	16 46		16 52		16 58	17 04		17 10	17 14		17 22
Elephant & Castle ⊖	d	16 24				16 30	16 33					16 46	16 49		16 56		17 02	17 08		17 14	17 18		
Loughborough d	d						16 37						16 53		17 00			17 12			17 22		
Herne Hill ■	d						16 41						16 57		17a04			17 16			17 26		
London Bridge ■	a				16 26						16 42												
	d				16 27						16 43												
Tulse Hill ■	d						16 46						17 02					17 20			17 31		
Streatham ■	d						16 50						17 06					17 24			17 36		
Mitcham Eastfields	d						16 55											17 28					
Mitcham unction	d						16 58											17 31					
Hackbridge	d						17 01											17 34					
Carshalton	d						17 04											17 37					
Tooting	d												17 10								17 40		
Haydons Road	d												17 13								17 43		
Wimbledon ■ ⊖	d												17 19								17 49		
Wimbledon Chase	d												17 22								17 52		
South Merton	d												17 24								17 54		
Morden South	d												17 26								17 56		
St Helier	d												17 28								17 58		
Sutton Common	d												17 30								18 00		
West Sutton	d												17 33								18 03		
Sutton (Surrey) ■	a						17 08						17 37					17 40			18 07		
East Croydon	d				16 41						17 00						17 26						17 47
Denmark Hill ■	d					16 39						16 52								17 20			
Peckham Rye ■	d					16 42						16 55								17 23			
Nunhead ■	d					16 44						16 57								17 26			
Crofton Park	d					16 47						17 00								17 29			
Catford	d					16 50						17 03								17 32			
Bellingham	d					16 52						17 05								17 35			
Beckenham Hill	d					16 54						17 07								17 37			
Ravensbourne	d					16 56						17 09								17 39			
Shortlands	d					16 58						17 11								17 43			
Bromley South ■	d	16 44				17 01						17 14								17 46			
Bickley ■	d					17a04						17 17											
St Mary Cray	d											17 21											
Swanley ■	d											17 30								17 55			
Eynsford	d											17 34								18 00			
Shoreham (Kent)	d											17 38								18 03			
Otford ■	d	17a00										17 41								18 06			
Bat & Ball	d											17 44								18 14			
Sevenoaks ■	a											17 49								18 23			
Redhill	d																						18 03
Gatwick Airport ■ ✈	d				16 57						17 16						17 42						18 14
Three Bridges ■	d				17 02						17 21						17 46						18 19
Balcombe	d										17 27						17 52						18 25
Haywards Heath ■	d				17 11						17 32						17 58						18 31
Wivelsfield ■	d										17 37												
Burgess Hill ■	d				17 17						17 39						18 03						18 36
Hassocks ■	d				17 21						17 43						18 07						18 40
Preston Park	d										17 50						18 14						18 47
Brighton ■	a				17 30						17 54						18 18						18 53

A from 21 May until 27 uly

Bedford, Luton, St Albans and City of London - South London, Gatwick Airport and Brighton

Network Diagram - see first Page of Table 52

		EM ◇■	FC ■	FC	FC	FC	FC ■	FC	FC ■	EM ◇■	FC ■	FC	FC	FC	FC	FC ■	FC	FC	FC ■	FC	EM ◇■	FC
Bedford ■	d	16 18	16 22				16 26		16 36	16 49						16 54			17 06		17 18	
Flitwick	d		16 32				16 36		16 46							17 04			17 16			
Harlington	d						16 40		16 50							17 08			17 20			
Leagrave	d						16 45		16 55							17 13			17 26			
Luton ■	d		16 42			16 46	16 50		17 00	17 05			17 10			17 18	17 22		17 30			17 38
Luton Airport Parkway ■ ✈	d	16 34	16 44			16 48	16 52		17 02				17 12			17 20	17 24		17 33		17 30	17 40
Harpenden	d					16 54	16 58		17 08				17 18			17 26	17 30		17 39			17 46
St Albans City	d		16 54			17 00	17 04		17 14			17 20	17 24			17 32	17 36	17 40	17 45			17 52
Radlett	d					17 05						17 25					17 41	17 45				17 57
Elstree & Borehamwood	d					17 09						17 29					17 45	17 49				18 01
Mill Hill Broadway	d					17 14						17 34					17 49	17 53				18 06
Hendon	d					17 17						17 37						17 57				18 09
Cricklewood	d					17 21						17 41						18 00				18 13
West Hampstead Thameslink ⊖	d					17 24	17 18		17 28			17 44		17 40		17 48	17 56	18 04				18 16
Kentish Town ⊖	d				17 18	17 28						17 48						18 08				18 20
St Pancras International ■ ⊖	a	17 00		←				←		17 29					←					←	18 01	
St Pancras International ■ ⊖	a		17 13	17 18	17 21	17 32	17 25	17 32	17 35			17 52	17 43	17 47	17 52	17 55	18 03	18 12	18 07	18 12		18 24
	d		17 14	17 18	17 22	17 32	17 28	17 32	17 36		17 40	17 52	17 44	17 48	17 52	17 56	18 04	18 12	18 08	18 12		18 24
Farringdon ■ ⊖	d		17 19	17 23	17 27	→	17 33	17 37	17 41		17 45	→	17 49	17 53	17 57	18 01	18 09	→	18 13	18 17		→
City Thameslink ■	d		17 23	17 27	17 31		17 37	17 41	17 45		17 49		17 53	17 57	18 01	18 05	18 13		18 17	18 21		
London Blackfriars ■ ⊖	d		17 25	17 30	17 36		17 40	17 44	17 48		17 51		17 56	18 00	18 04	18 10	18 16		18 20	18 24		
Elephant & Castle ⊖	d		17 29	17 34	17 40			17 48	17 52		17 55		18 00	18 05	18 08	18 14	18 20			18 28		
Loughborough d	d			17 38				17 52							18 12		18 24					
Herne Hill ■	d		17 36	17 43				17 57					18a06		18 17	18 21	18 28					
London Bridge ■	a																		18 27			
	d																		18 27			
Tulse Hill ■	d			17 48				18 02							18 22		18 32					
Streatham ■	d			17 52				18 06							18 26		18 36					
Mitcham Eastfields	d			17 55											18 29							
Mitcham unction	d			17 58											18 32							
Hackbridge	d			18 02											18 36							
Carshalton	d			18 04											18 38							
Tooting	d							18 10									18 40					
Haydons Road	d							18 13									18 43					
Wimbledon ■ ⊖	d							18 19									18 49					
Wimbledon Chase	d							18 22									18 52					
South Merton	d							18 24									18 54					
Morden South	d							18 26									18 56					
St Helier	d							18 28									18 58					
Sutton Common	d							18 30									19 00					
West Sutton	d							18 33									19 03					
Sutton (Surrey) ■	a			18 08				18 37							18 42		19 07					
East Croydon	d						18 09				18 25								18 41			
Denmark Hill ■	d				17 47									18 15						18 34		
Peckham Rye ■	d				17 50									18 18						18 38		
Nunhead ■	d				17 52									18 20						18 40		
Crofton Park	d				17 55									18 23						18 43		
Catford	d				17 58									18 26						18 46		
Bellingham	d				18 01									18 29						18 49		
Beckenham Hill	d				18 03									18 31						18 51		
Ravensbourne	d				18 05									18 33						18 53		
Shortlands	d				18 07									18 35						18 57		
Bromley South ■	d		17 48		18 10				18 11					18 38		18 31				19 00		
Bickley ■	d		17 50		18 12									18 40						19 03		
St Mary Cray	d		17 55		18 22				18 18					18 45		18 38				19 10		
Swanley ■	d		17a59		18 26				18 22					18 53		18a42				19 15		
Eynsford	d				18 31									18 57						19 19		
Shoreham (Kent)	d				18 34									19 01						19 23		
Otford ■	d				18 38				18a30					19 04						19 26		
Bat & Ball	d				18 41									19 07						19 29		
Sevenoaks ■	a				18 50									19 12						19 37		
Redhill	d										18 38											
Gatwick Airport ■ ✈	d						18 25				18 50								18 57			
Three Bridges ■	d						18 30				18a56								19 02			
Balcombe	d																		19 08			
Haywards Heath ■	d						18 39												19 14			
Wivelsfield ■	d						18 44															
Burgess Hill ■	d						18 46												19 19			
Hassocks ■	d						18 50												19 23			
Preston Park	d						18 57															
Brighton ■	a						19 02												19 33			

Bedford, Luton, St Albans and City of London - South London, Gatwick Airport and Brighton

Network Diagram - see first Page of Table 52

		FC	FC	EM	FC	FC	FC	FC		FC	EM	SE	FC	EM	FC	FC	FC	FC		FC	EM	FC	SE	FC	SE
		■		◇■		■	■	■			◇■	■ A		◇■		■				■	◇■			■	
Bedford ■	d	17 22				17 36	17 41				17 49					17 54		18 02		18 10	18 17			18 24	
Flitwick	d	17 32				17 46										18 04				18 20				18 34	
Harlington	d	17 36				17 50										18 08				18 24				18 38	
Leagrave	d	17 41				17 55										18 13				18 29				18 43	
Luton ■	d	17 46		17 51		18 00					18 05		18 06	18 15		18 18		18 22		18 34			18 44	18 48	
Luton Airport Parkway ■	d	17 48				18 02	17 59						18 08			18 20		18 24		18 36	18 33		18 46	18 50	
Harpenden	d	17 54				18 08							18 14			18 26		18 30		18 42			18 52	18 56	
St Albans City	d	18 00			18 06	18 14	18 09						18 20		18 26	18 32		18 36		18 48		18 52	18 58	19 02	
Radlett	d				18 11								18 25		18 31			18 41				18 57	19 03		
Elstree & Borehamwood	d				18 15								18 29		18 35			18 45				19 01	19 07		
Mill Hill Broadway	d				18 20								18 33		18 40			18 49					19 12		
Hendon	d				18 23										18 43								19 15		
Cricklewood	d				18 27										18 47								19 19		
West Hampstead Thameslink ⊖	d				18 30								18 40		18 50	18 46		18 56		19 02		19 10	19 22		
Kentish Town ⊖	d				18 34										18 54								19 26		
St Pancras International ■ ⊖	a		←	18 17				←		←	18 34			18 39			←				19 00				←
St Pancras International ■ ⊖	a	18 19	18 24		18 38	18 34	18 27	18 34		18 38			18 47		18 58	18 53	18 58	19 04		19 08		19 17	19 30	19 22	19 30
	d	18 20	18 24		18 38	18 34	18 30	18 34		18 38			18 48		19 00	18 54	19 00	19 04		19 09		19 18	19 30	19 24	19 30
Farringdon ■ ⊖	d	18 25	18 29		→	→	18 35	18 40		18 43			18 53		→	18 59	19 05	19 09		19 14		19 23	→	19 29	19 36
City Thameslink ■	d	18 29	18 33				18 39	18 43		18 47			18 57			19 03	19 09	19 13		19 18		19 27		19 33	19 39
London Blackfriars ■ ⊖	d	18 32	18 36				18 42	18 46		18 50		18 55	19 00			19 05	19 12	19 16		19 20		19 30		19 35	19 42
Elephant & Castle ⊖	d	18 36	18 40				18 46			18 54		18 59	19 04				19 16	19 19				19 33			19 46
Loughborough Jn	d		18 44							18 58			19 08					19 23				19 37			
Herne Hill ■	d		18 48							19 02			19 12					19 27				19 41			
London Bridge ■	a							18 54								19 11				19 26				19 41	
	d							18 57								19 12				19 27				19 42	
Tulse Hill ■	d		18 52							19 09			19 16					19 31				19 46			
Streatham ■	d		18 56							19 13			19 20					19 35				19 50			
Mitcham Eastfields	d		18 59										19 24									19 54			
Mitcham Junction	d		19 02										19 27									19 57			
Hackbridge	d		19 06										19 30									20 00			
Carshalton	d		19 08										19 33									20 03			
Tooting	d									19 18								19 40							
Haydons Road	d									19 21								19 43							
Wimbledon ■ ⊖	d									19 24								19 49							
Wimbledon Chase	d									19 27								19 52							
South Merton	d									19 29								19 54							
Morden South	d									19 31								19 56							
St Helier	d									19 33								19 58							
Sutton Common	d									19 35								20 00							
West Sutton	d									19 38								20 03							
Sutton (Surrey) ■	a		19 12							19 41			19 36					20 07				20 06			
East Croydon	d	19 01						19 11								19 25				19 41				19 55	
Denmark Hill ■	d						18 52										19 22								19 52
Peckham Rye ■	d						18 55										19 25								19 55
Nunhead ■	d						18 57										19 27								19 57
Crofton Park	d						19 00										19 30								20 00
Catford	d						19 03										19 33								20 03
Bellingham	d						19 05										19 35								20 05
Beckenham Hill	d						19 07										19 37								20 07
Ravensbourne	d						19 09										19 39								20 09
Shortlands	d						19 13										19 41								20 11
Bromley South ■	d						19 16					19 18					19 44								20 14
Bickley ■	d						19 19										19 47								20 17
St Mary Cray	d						19 23										19 51								20 21
Swanley ■	d						19 29										19 56								20 26
Eynsford	d						19 33										20 00								20 30
Shoreham (Kent)	d						19 37										20 04								20 34
Otford ■	d						19 40					19a34					20 07								20 37
Bat & Ball	d						19 43										20 10								20 40
Sevenoaks ■	a						19 50										20 13								20 43
Redhill	d																								
Gatwick Airport ■	d	19 18						19 26								19 41				19 57				20 11	
Three Bridges ■	d							19 31								19 45				20 02				20 15	
Balcombe	d							19 37								19 51									
Haywards Heath ■	d	19 30						19 42								19 57				20 11				20 25	
Wivelsfield ■	d															20 01								20 29	
Burgess Hill ■	d	19 35						19 48								20 03				20 16				20 31	
Hassocks ■	d	19 39						19 51								20 06				20 20				20 34	
Preston Park	d	19 46														20 13								20 41	
Brighton ■	a	19 52						20 01								20 17				20 29				20 45	

A from 21 May until 27 July

Bedford, Luton, St Albans and City of London - South London, Gatwick Airport and Brighton

Network Diagram - see first Page of Table 52

		FC	FC	EM		FC	FC	FC	FC	FC	EM	FC	FC	FC		FC	FC	FC	EM	FC	FC	FC	FC	EM
			■	◇■				■			◇■					■			◇■	A	■			◇■
Bedford ■	d	18 36	18 40	18 49				18 54			19 18					19 26			19 49		19 52			20 18
Flitwick	d		18 50					19 04								19 36					20 02			
Harlington	d		18 54					19 08								19 40					20 06			
Leagrave	d		18 59					19 13								19 45					20 11			
Luton ■	d	18 54	19 04	19 05			19 14	19 18		19 24				19 46		19 50			20 05		20 16		20 20	
Luton Airport Parkway ■	d	18 57	19 06				19 16	19 20		19 27	19 34			19 48		19 52					20 18		20 22	20 34
Harpenden	d	19 02	19 12				19 22	19 26		19 32				19 54		19 58					20 24		20 28	
St Albans City	d	19 08	19 18			19 22	19 28	19 32		19 38		19 52		20 00		20 04				20 22	20 30		20 34	
Radlett	d	19 13				19 27	19 33			19 43		19 57		20 05						20 27			20 39	
Elstree & Borehamwood	d	19 17				19 31	19 37			19 47		20 01		20 09						20 31			20 43	
Mill Hill Broadway	d						19 42							20 14									20 47	
Hendon	d						19 45							20 17									20 50	
Cricklewood	d						19 49							20 21									20 54	
West Hampstead Thameslink ⊖	d	19 26	19 32			19 40	19 52			19 56		20 10		20 24		20 17				20 40	20 44		20 56	
Kentish Town ⊖	d						19 56						20 26	20 30								20 56	21 01	
St Pancras International ■ ⊖	a			19 32					←		20 01						←	←	20 29					20 59
St Pancras International ■ ⊖	a	19 33	19 38			19 47	20 00	19 51	20 00	20 03		20 17	20 29	20 33		20 24	20 29	20 33		20 47	20 51	20 59	21 05	
	d	19 34	19 39			19 48	20 00	19 54	20 00	20 04		20 18	20 30	20 34		20 24	20 30	20 34		20 48	20 54	21 00	21 06	
Farringdon ■ ⊖	d	19 39	19 44			19 53	→	19 59	20 05	20 09		20 23	→	→		20 29	20 35	20 39		20 53	20 59	21 05	21 10	
City Thameslink ■	d	19 43	19 48			19 57		20 03	20 09	20 13		20 27				20 33	20 39	20 43		20 57	21 03	21 09	21 13	
London Blackfriars ■ ⊖	d	19 46	19 50			20 00		20 05	20 12	20 16		20 30				20 35	20 42	20 46		21 00	21 05	21 12	21 16	
Elephant & Castle ⊖	d	19 49				20 03			20 16	20 19		20 33					20 46	20 49		21 03		21 16	21 19	
Loughborough Jn	d	19 53				20 07				20 23		20 37						20 53		21 07			21 23	
Herne Hill ■	d	19 57				20 11				20 27		20 41						20 57		21 11			21 27	
London Bridge ■	a		19 56					20 11								20 41					21 11			
	d		19 57					20 12								20 42					21 12			
Tulse Hill ■	d	20 01				20 16				20 31		20 50						21 01		21 20			21 31	
Streatham ■	d	20 05				20 20				20 35		20 53						21 05		21 23			21 35	
Mitcham Eastfields	d					20 24						20 57								21 27				
Mitcham Junction	d					20 27						21 00								21 30				
Hackbridge	d					20 30						21 03								21 33				
Carshalton	d					20 33						21 06								21 36				
Tooting	d	20 10								20 40								21 10					21 40	
Haydons Road	d	20 13								20 43								21 13					21 43	
Wimbledon ■ ⊖	d	20 19								20 49								21 19					21 49	
Wimbledon Chase	d	20 22								20 52								21 22					21 52	
South Merton	d	20 24								20 54								21 24					21 54	
Morden South	d	20 26								20 56								21 26					21 56	
St Helier	d	20 28								20 58								21 28					21 58	
Sutton Common	d	20 30								21 00								21 30					22 00	
West Sutton	d	20 33								21 03								21 33					22 03	
Sutton (Surrey) ■	a	20 39				20 36				21 09		21 10						21 39		21 40			22 09	
East Croydon	d		20 11					20 25								20 55					21 25			
Denmark Hill ■	d								20 22								20 52					21 22		
Peckham Rye ■	d								20 25								20 55					21 25		
Nunhead ■	d								20 27								20 57					21 27		
Crofton Park	d								20 30								21 00					21 30		
Catford	d								20 33								21 03					21 33		
Bellingham	d								20 35								21 05					21 35		
Beckenham Hill	d								20 37								21 07					21 37		
Ravensbourne	d								20 39								21 09					21 39		
Shortlands	d								20 41								21 11					21 41		
Bromley South ■	d								20 44								21 14					21 44		
Bickley ■	d								20 47								21 17					21 47		
St Mary Cray	d								20 51								21 21					21 51		
Swanley ■	d								20 56								21 26					21 56		
Eynsford	d								21 00								21 30					22 00		
Shoreham (Kent)	d								21 04								21 34					22 04		
Otford ■	d								21 07								21 37					22 07		
Bat & Ball	d								21 10								21 40					22 10		
Sevenoaks ■	a								21 13								21 43					22 13		
Redhill	d																							
Gatwick Airport ■	d		20 27					20 41								21 11					21 41			
Three Bridges ■	d		20 32					20 45								21 15					21 45			
Balcombe	d							20 51													21 53			
Haywards Heath ■	d		20 41					20 57								21 25					21 59			
Wivelsfield ■	d							21 01								21 29					22 03			
Burgess Hill ■	d		20 46					21 03								21 31					22 05			
Hassocks ■	d							21 06								21 34					22 08			
Preston Park	d							21 13								21 41					22 15			
Brighton ■	a		20 57					21 17								21 45					22 19			

A from 21 May

Bedford, Luton, St Albans and City of London - South London, Gatwick Airport and Brighton

Network Diagram - see first Page of Table 52

		FC ■	SE A	FC	FC ■	EM ◇■	SE B	SE A	FC	EM ◇■	FC ■ B	FC ■ A	SE B	FC B	SE A	FC A	FC B	EM ◇■	FC B	FC ■ B	SE B	FC B	FC ■ A
Bedford ■	d	20 22			20 52	20 54				21 22	21 22	21 22						21 44		21 52			21 52
Flitwick	d	20 32			21 02						21 32	21 32								22 02			22 02
Harlington	d	20 36			21 06						21 36	21 36								22 06			22 06
Leagrave	d	20 41			21 11						21 41	21 41								22 11			22 11
Luton ■	d	20 46		20 50	21 16	21 08			21 20		21 46	21 46				21 50	21 50	22 01		22 16			22 16
Luton Airport Parkway ■	d	20 48		20 52	21 18				21 22	21 39	21 48	21 48				21 52	21 53			22 18			22 18
Harpenden	d	20 54		20 58	21 24				21 28		21 54	21 54				21 58	21 58			22 24			22 24
St Albans City	d	21 00		21 04	21 30				21 34		22 00	22 00				22 04	22 05			22 30			22 30
Radlett	d			21 09					21 39							22 09	22 10						
Elstree & Borehamwood	d			21 13					21 43							22 13	22 15						
Mill Hill Broadway	d			21 17					21 47							22 17	22 19						
Hendon	d			21 20					21 50							22 20	22 22						
Cricklewood	d			21 24					21 54							22 24	22 26						
West Hampstead Thameslink ⊖	d	21 14		21 26	21 44				21 56		22 14	22 14				22 26	22 28			22 44			22 44
Kentish Town ⊖	d			21 31					22 01							22 31	22 34						
St Pancras International ■ ⊖	a					21 33				22 04								22 29					
St Pancras International ■ ⊖	a	21 21		21 35	21 51				22 05		22 23	22 22				22 35	22 39			22 53			22 52
	d	21 24		21 36	21 54				22 06			22 24		22 30		22 36			22 45				22 54
Farringdon ■ ⊖	d	21 29		21 40	21 59				22 10			22 29		22 35		22 40			22 50				22 59
City Thameslink ■	d	21 33		21 43	22 03				22 13			22 33		22 37		22 43			22 52				23 03
London Blackfriars ■ ⊖	d	21 35	21 42	21 46	22 05			22 12	22 16			22 35		22 42	22 42	22 46			22 57				23 05
Elephant & Castle ⊖	d		21 46	21 49				22 16	22 19						22 46	22 49							
Loughborough Jn	d			21 53					22 23							22 53							
Herne Hill ■	d			21 57					22 27							22 57							
London Bridge ■	a	21 41			22 11							22 41		22 57					23 12				23 11
	d	21 42			22 12							22 42										23 01	23 12
Tulse Hill ■	d			22 01					22 31							23 01						23 11	
Streatham ■	d			22 05					22 35							23 05						23 15	
Mitcham Eastfields	d																						
Mitcham Junction	d																						
Hackbridge	d																						
Carshalton	d																						
Tooting	d			22 10					22 40							23 10						23 20	
Haydons Road	d			22 13					22 43							23 13						23 23	
Wimbledon ■ ⊖	d			22 19					22 49							23 17						23 27	
Wimbledon Chase	d			22 22					22 52							23 20						23 30	
South Merton	d			22 24					22 54							23 22						23 32	
Morden South	d			22 26					22 56							23 24						23 34	
St Helier	d			22 28					22 58							23 26						23 36	
Sutton Common	d			22 30					23 00							23 28						23 38	
West Sutton	d			22 33					23 03							23 31						23 41	
Sutton (Surrey) ■	a			22 39					23 09							23 35						23 45	
East Croydon	d	21 55			22 25							22 55											23 25
Denmark Hill ■	d		21 52				21 52	22 22					22 22		22 52						22 52		
Peckham Rye ■	d		21 55				21 55	22 25					22 25		22 55						22 55		
Nunhead ■	d		21 57				21 57	22 27					22 27		22 57						22 57		
Crofton Park	d		22 00				22 00	22 30					22 30		23 00						23 00		
Catford	d		22 03				22 03	22 33					22 33		23 03						23 03		
Bellingham	d		22 05				22 05	22 35					22 35		23 05						23 05		
Beckenham Hill	d		22 07				22 07	22 37					22 37		23 07						23 07		
Ravensbourne	d		22 09				22 09	22 39					22 39		23 09						23 09		
Shortlands	d		22 11				22 11	22 41					22 41		23 11						23 11		
Bromley South ■	d		22 14				22 14	22 44					22 44		23 14						23 14		
Bickley ■	d		22 17				22 17	22 47					22 47		23 17						23a17		
St Mary Cray	d		22 21				22 21	22 51					22 51		23 21								
Swanley ■	d		22 26				22 26	22 56					22 56		23 26								
Eynsford	d		22 30				22 30	23 00					23 00		23 30								
Shoreham (Kent)	d		22 34				22 34	23 04					23 04		23 34								
Otford ■	d		22 37				22 37	23 07					23 07		23 37								
Bat & Ball	d		22 40				22 40	23 10					23 10		23 40								
Sevenoaks ■	a		22 43				22 43	23 13					23 13		23 43								
Redhill	d																						
Gatwick Airport ■	d	22 11			22 41							23 11											23 41
Three Bridges ■	d	22 15			22 45							23 15											23 47
Balcombe	d				22 53																		23 53
Haywards Heath ■	d	22 25			22 59							23 25											23 59
Wivelsfield ■	d	22 29			23 03							23 29											00 03
Burgess Hill ■	d	22 31			23 05							23 31											00 05
Hassocks ■	d	22 34			23 08							23 34											00 08
Preston Park	d	22 41			23 15							23 41											00 15
Brighton ■	a	22 45			23 19							23 45											00 19

A from 21 May

B until 18 May

Bedford, Luton, St Albans and City of London - South London, Gatwick Airport and Brighton

Network Diagram - see first Page of Table 52

		FC A	SE B	FC B	FC A	FC A	FC ■ A	SE A	FC A	FC ■ B	EM ◇■	FC A	FC A	SE B	FC B	FC A	SE A	FC A	FC ■ B	EM ◇■ C	EM ◇■ D	FC ■ A	FC ■ B
Bedford ■	d						22 16			22 16	22 19								22 42	22 45	22 45	22 52	23 12
Flitwick	d						22 26			22 26									22 52			23 02	23 22
Harlington	d						22 30			22 30									22 56			23 06	23 26
Leagrave	d						22 35			22 35									23 02			23 12	23 32
Luton ■	d			22 20	22 20		22 40			22 40	22 34		22 46		22 46				23 06	23 00	23 02	23 16	23 36
Luton Airport Parkway ■	d			22 22	22 23		22 42			22 42	22 38		22 49		22 49				23 09			23 19	23 39
Harpenden	d			22 28	22 29		22 48			22 48			22 55		22 55				23 15			23 25	23 45
St Albans City	d			22 34	22 35		22 54			22 54			23 01		23 01				23 21			23 31	23 51
Radlett	d			22 39	22 40								23 06		23 06				23 26			23 36	23 56
Elstree & Borehamwood	d			22 43	22 45								23 11		23 11				23 31			23 41	00 01
Mill Hill Broadway	d			22 47	22 49								23 15		23 15				23 35			23 45	00 05
Hendon	d			22 50	22 52								23 18		23 18				23 38			23 48	00 08
Cricklewood	d			22 54	22 56								23 22		23 22				23 42			23 52	00 12
West Hampstead Thameslink ⊖	d			22 56	22 58		23 10			23 10			23 24		23 24				23 44			23 54	00 14
Kentish Town ⊖	d			23 01	23 04								23 30		23 30				23 50			00 02	00 20
St Pancras International ■ ⊖	a										23 01									23 26	23 34		
St Pancras International ■ ⊖	a			23 05	23 09		23 21			23 19			23 35		23 34				23 53			00 05	00 23
	d	23 00		23 06		23 15				23 24		23 30			23 36	23 42			23 54				00 24
Farringdon ■ ⊖	d	23 05		23 10		23 20				23 29		23 35			23 40	23 47			23 59				00 29
City Thameslink ■	d	23 07																					
London Blackfriars ■ ⊖	d	23 12	23 12	23 16		23 25				23 35		23 40		23 42	23 46	23 52			00 05				00 35
Elephant & Castle ⊖	d		23 16	23 19										23 46	23 49								
Loughborough Jn	d			23s23																			
Herne Hill ■	d			23 27											23 57								
London Bridge ■	a	23 27				23 40				23 41		23 54				00 07			00 11				00 41
	d								23 29	23 42								23 59	00 12				00 42
Tulse Hill ■	d			23 31					23 41						00 01			00 09					
Streatham ■	d			23 35					23 45						00 05			00 13					
Mitcham Eastfields	d																						
Mitcham Junction	d																						
Hackbridge	d																						
Carshalton	d																						
Tooting	d			23 40					23 50						00 10			00 18					
Haydons Road	d			23 43					23 53						00 13			00 21					
Wimbledon ■ ⊖	d			23 49					23 57						00 19			00 25					
Wimbledon Chase	d			23 52					00 01						00 22			00 28					
South Merton	d			23 54					00 03						00 24			00 30					
Morden South	d			23 56					00 05						00 26			00 32					
St Helier	d			23 58					00 07						00 28			00 34					
Sutton Common	d			00 01					00 09						00 30			00 36					
West Sutton	d			00 04					00 12						00 33			00 39					
Sutton (Surrey) ■	a			00 09					00 15						00 39			00 43					
East Croydon	d									23 57									00 27				00 57
Denmark Hill ■	d		23 22					23 22						23 52			23 52						
Peckham Rye ■	d		23 25					23 25						23 55			23 55						
Nunhead ■	d		23 27					23 27						23 57			23 57						
Crofton Park	d		23 30					23 30						23 59			23 59						
Catford	d		23 33					23 33						00 03			00 03						
Bellingham	d		23 35					23 35						00 05			00 05						
Beckenham Hill	d		23 37					23 37						00 07			00 07						
Ravensbourne	d		23 39					23 39						00 09			00 09						
Shortlands	d		23 41					23 41						00 11			00 11						
Bromley South ■	d		23 44					23 44						00 14			00 14						
Bickley ■	d		23 47					23a47						00 17			00a17						
St Mary Cray	d		23 51											00 21									
Swanley ■	d		23 56											00 26									
Eynsford	d		23 59											00 30									
Shoreham (Kent)	d		00 04											00 34									
Otford ■	d		00 07											00 37									
Bat & Ball	d		00 10											00 40									
Sevenoaks ■	a		00 13											00 43									
Redhill	d																						
Gatwick Airport ■	d									00 19									00 49				01 22
Three Bridges ■	d									00a24									00a54				01a28
Balcombe	d																						
Haywards Heath ■	d																						
Wivelsfield ■	d																						
Burgess Hill ■	d																						
Hassocks ■	d																						
Preston Park	d																						
Brighton ■	a																						

A until 18 May

B from 21 May

C from 27 July until 7 September, not from 13 August until 28 August

D not from 27 July until 10 August, from 29 August until 7 September

Table 52

Mondays to Fridays

Bedford, Luton, St Albans and City of London - South London, Gatwick Airport and Brighton

Network Diagram - see first Page of Table 52

Station		FC 1 A	FC 1 A	FC 1 B
Bedford	d	23 12	23 32	23 42
Flitwick	d	23 22	23 42	23 52
Harlington	d	23 26	23 46	23 56
Leagrave	d	23 32	23 52	00 02
Luton	d	23 36	23 56	00 06
Luton Airport Parkway ✈	d	23 39	23 59	00 09
Harpenden	d	23 45	00 05	00 15
St Albans City	d	23 51	00 11	00 21
Radlett	d	23 56	00 16	00 26
Elstree & Borehamwood	d	00 01	00 21	00 31
Mill Hill Broadway	d	00 05	00 25	00 35
Hendon	d	00 08	00 28	00 38
Cricklewood	d	00 12	00 32	00 42
West Hampstead Thameslink ⊖	d	00 14	00 34	00 44
Kentish Town ⊖	d	00 20	00 40	00 50
St Pancras International ⊖	a			
St Pancras International ⊖	a	00 25	00 45	00 53
	d			00 54
Farringdon ⊖	d			00 59
City Thameslink	d			
London Blackfriars ⊖	d			01 05
Elephant & Castle ⊖	d			
Loughborough d	d			
Herne Hill	d			
London Bridge	a			
	d			
Tulse Hill	d			
Streatham	d			
Mitcham Eastfields	d			
Mitcham Junction	d			
Hackbridge	d			
Carshalton	d			
Tooting	d			
Haydons Road	d			
Wimbledon ⊖	d			
Wimbledon Chase	d			
South Merton	d			
Morden South	d			
St Helier	d			
Sutton Common	d			
West Sutton	d			
Sutton (Surrey)	a			
East Croydon	d			01 32
Denmark Hill	d			
Peckham Rye	d			
Nunhead	d			
Crofton Park	d			
Catford	d			
Bellingham	d			
Beckenham Hill	d			
Ravensbourne	d			
Shortlands	d			
Bromley South	d			
Bickley	d			
St Mary Cray	d			
Swanley	d			
Eynsford	d			
Shoreham (Kent)	d			
Otford	d			
Bat & Ball	d			
Sevenoaks	a			
Redhill	d			
Gatwick Airport ✈	d			01 52
Three Bridges	d			01a58
Balcombe	d			
Haywards Heath	d			
Wivelsfield	d			
Burgess Hill	d			
Hassocks	d			
Preston Park	d			
Brighton	a			

A until 18 May

B from 21 May

Table 52

Saturdays
until 23 June

Bedford, Luton, St Albans - London

Network Diagram - see first Page of Table 52

Station		FC A 🚌	FC 1 B	FC 1 A	FC A 🚌	FC 1 B	FC 1 A	FC A 🚌	FC 1 A	FC 1 B		FC A 🚌	FC A	FC A 🚌	FC 1 B	FC A 🚌	FC 1 B	FC A 🚌	FC 1	FC A 🚌		FC 1 B	FC A 🚌	FC 1 B	FC A 🚌
Bedford	d		22p42	22p52		23p12	23p12		23p32	23p42			00 02		00 42		01 42					02 42		03 12	
Flitwick	d		22p52	23p02		23p22	23p22		23p42	23p52			00 12		00 52		01 52					02 52		03 22	
Harlington	d		22p56	23p06		23p26	23p26		23p46	23p56			00 16		00 56		01 56					02 56		03 26	
Leagrave	d		23p02	23p12		23p32	23p32		23p52	00 02			00 22		01 02		02 02					03 02		03 32	
Luton	d		23p06	23p16		23p36	23p36		23p56	00 06			00 26		01 06		02 06					03 06		03 36	
Luton Airport Parkway ✈	d		23p09	23p19		23p39	23p39		23p59	00 09			00 29		01 09		02 09					03 09		03 39	
Harpenden	d		23p15	23p25		23p45	23p45		00 05	00 15			00 35		01 15		02 15					03 15		03 45	
St Albans City	d		23p21	23p31		23p51	23p51		00 11	00 21			00 41		01 21		02 21					03 21		03 51	
Radlett	d		23p26	23p36		23p56	23p56		00 16	00 26			00 46		01 26		02 26					03 26		03 56	
Elstree & Borehamwood	d		23p31	23p41		00 01	00 01		00 21	00 31			00 51		01 31		02 31					03 31		04 01	
Mill Hill Broadway	d		23p35	23p45		00 05	00 05		00 25	00 35			00 55		01 35		02 35					03 35		04 05	
Hendon	d		23p38	23p48		00 08	00 08		00 28	00 38			00 58		01 38		02 38					03 38		04 08	
Cricklewood	d		23p42	23p52		00 12	00 12		00 32	00 42			01 02		01 42		02 42					03 42		04 12	
West Hampstead Thameslink ⊖	d		23p44	23p54		00 14	00 14		00 34	00 44			01 04		01 44		02 44					03 44		04 14	
Kentish Town ⊖	a		23p50	00 02		00 20	00 20		00 40	00 50			01 10		01 50		02 50					03 50		04 20	
St Pancras International ⊖	a																								
	d																								
St Pancras International ⊖	a		23p53	00 05		00 23	00 25		00 45	00 53			01 15		01 53		02 53					03 53		04 23	
	d	23p42	23p54		00 12	00 24		00 30		00 54		01 00		01 30	01 54	02 30	02 54	03 00	03 28	03 30		03 54	04 00	04 24	04 30
Farringdon ⊖	d	23p47	23p59		00 17	00 29		00 35		00 59															
City Thameslink	d																								
London Blackfriars ⊖	a	23p52	00 04		00 22	00 34		00 40		01 04		01 10		01 40	02 04	02 40	03 04	03 10	03 38	03 40		04 04	04 10	04 34	04 40
London Bridge	a	00 07			00 37			00 55				01 25		01 55		02 55		03 25		03 55			04 25		04 55

Station		FC 1	FC A 🚌	FC A 🚌	FC 1	FC		FC 1	FC	FC 1	EM ◇1 🍴	FC	FC	FC 1	FC	FC 1		FC	FC	FC 1	FC	FC 1	FC	FC	FC 1
Bedford	d	03 42			04 22			04 52		05 22	05 32			05 40		05 54				06 10		06 24			06 40
Flitwick	d	03 52			04 32			05 02		05 32				05 50		06 04				06 20		06 34			06 50
Harlington	d	03 56			04 36			05 06		05 36				05 54		06 08				06 24		06 38			06 54
Leagrave	d	04 02			04 42			05 12		05 42				05 59		06 13				06 29		06 43			06 59
Luton	d	04 06			04 46			05 16	05 30	05 46			06 00	06 04		06 18			06 30	06 34		06 48		07 00	07 04
Luton Airport Parkway ✈	d	04 09			04 49			05 19	05 32	05 49	05 54		06 02	06 06		06 20			06 32	06 36		06 50		07 02	07 06
Harpenden	d	04 15			04 55			05 25	05 38	05 55			06 08	06 12		06 26			06 38	06 42		06 56		07 08	07 12
St Albans City	d	04 21			05 01			05 31	05 44	06 01			06 14	06 18		06 32			06 44	06 48		07 02		07 14	07 18
Radlett	d	04 26			05 06				05 50				06 19						06 49					07 19	
Elstree & Borehamwood	d	04 31			05 11				05 54				06 23						06 53					07 23	
Mill Hill Broadway	d	04 35			05 15				05 58				06 28						06 58					07 28	
Hendon	d	04 38			05 18				06 02				06 31						07 01					07 31	
Cricklewood	d	04 42			05 22				06 05				06 35						07 05					07 35	
West Hampstead Thameslink ⊖	d	04 44			05 24	05 40		05 46	06 09	06 16		06 24	06 39			06 44		06 54	07 09				07 24	07 39	
Kentish Town ⊖	a	04 50			05 30	05 44			06 14			06 28	06 44					06 58	07 14				07 28	07 44	
St Pancras International ⊖	a										06 21				←						←				
	d																								
St Pancras International ⊖	a	04 53			05 33	05 48		05 53	06 17	06 23		06 32	06 47	06 38	06 47	06 52		07 02	07 17	07 08	07 17	07 21	07 32	07 47	07 38
	d	04 54	05 00	05 30	05 34	05 48		05 54	06 18	06 24		06 34	06 48	06 39	06 48	06 54		07 04	07 18	07 09	07 18	07 24	07 34	07 48	07 39
Farringdon ⊖	d	04 59	05 05	05 35	05 39	05 53		05 59	06 23	06 29		06 39	→	06 44	06 53	06 59		07 09	→	07 14	07 23	07 29	07 39	→	07 44
City Thameslink	d																								
London Blackfriars ⊖	a	05 04	05 10	05 40	05 44	05 59		06 04	06 29	06 34		06 45		06 49	06 59	07 04		07 15		07 19	07 29	07 34	07 45		07 49
London Bridge	a		05 25	05 55																					

Station		FC		EM ◇1 🍴	FC	FC 1	FC	FC	FC 1	FC	EM ◇1 🍴	FC		FC 1	FC	FC	FC 1	FC	EM ◇1 🍴	FC	FC 1	FC		FC	FC 1
Bedford	d			06 49		06 54			07 10		07 19			07 24			07 40		07 49		07 54				08 10
Flitwick	d					07 04			07 20					07 34			07 50				08 04				08 20
Harlington	d					07 08			07 24					07 38			07 54				08 08				08 24
Leagrave	d					07 13			07 29					07 43			07 59				08 13				08 29
Luton	d			07 04	07 14	07 18		07 30	07 34			07 44		07 48		08 00	08 04		08 05	08 14	08 18				08 34
Luton Airport Parkway ✈	d				07 16	07 20		07 32	07 36		07 35	07 46		07 50		08 02	08 06			08 16	08 20				08 36
Harpenden	d				07 22	07 26		07 38	07 42			07 52		07 56		08 08	08 12			08 22	08 26				08 42
St Albans City	d				07 29	07 32		07 44	07 48			07 59		08 02		08 14	08 18			08 29	08 32			08 44	08 48
Radlett	d				07 34			07 49				08 04				08 19				08 34				08 49	
Elstree & Borehamwood	d				07 38			07 53				08 08				08 23				08 38				08 53	
Mill Hill Broadway	d				07 43			07 58				08 13				08 28				08 43				08 58	
Hendon	d				07 46			08 01				08 16				08 31				08 46				09 01	
Cricklewood	d				07 50			08 05				08 20				08 35				08 50				09 05	
West Hampstead Thameslink ⊖	d				07 54			08 09				08 24				08 39				08 54				09 09	
Kentish Town ⊖	a				07 58			08 14				08 28				08 44				08 58				09 14	
St Pancras International ⊖	a	←		07 31			←			←	08 00				←			←	08 31			←			
	d																								
St Pancras International ⊖	a	07 47			08 02	07 51	08 02	08 17	08 08	08 17		08 32		08 21	08 32	08 47	08 38	08 47		09 02	08 51	09 02		09 17	09 08
	d	07 48			08 04	07 54	08 04	08 18	08 09	08 18		08 34		08 24	08 34	08 48	08 39	08 48		09 04	08 54	09 04		09 18	09 09
Farringdon ⊖	d	07 53			→	07 59	08 09	→	08 14	08 23		→		08 29	08 39	→	08 44	08 53		→	08 59	09 09		→	09 14
City Thameslink	d																				09 03	09 13			09 18
London Blackfriars ⊖	a	07 59				08 04	08 15		08 19	08 29				08 34	08 45		08 49	08 59			09 05	09 16			09 20
London Bridge	a																								

A 19 May

B not 19 May

Please refer to separate pages within this table for services operating between South London and Brighton

At weekends please use local bus and tube services to travel to/from St Pancras International and London Bridge when no trains are operating. See local publicity for details of alternative routes and services that are available across central London

Bedford, Luton, St Albans - London

Network Diagram - see first Page of Table 52

	FC	EM ◇■	FC	FC ■	FC	FC	FC ■		FC	EM ◇■	FC	FC ■	FC	FC	FC ■	FC	EM ◇■		FC	FC ■	FC	FC	FC ■	FC
Bedford d		08 19		08 24			08 40			08 49		08 54			09 10		09 19			09 24			09 40	
Flitwick d				08 34			08 50					09 04			09 20					09 34			09 50	
Harlington d				08 38			08 54					09 08			09 24					09 38			09 54	
Leagrave d				08 43			08 59					09 13			09 29					09 43			09 59	
Luton d			08 44	08 48			09 04			09 05	09 14	09 18			09 34				09 44	09 48			10 04	
Luton Airport Parkway d		08 35	08 46	08 50			09 06				09 16	09 20			09 36		09 35		09 46	09 50			10 06	
Harpenden d			08 52	08 56			09 12				09 22	09 26			09 42				09 52	09 56			10 12	
St Albans City d			08 59	09 02		09 14	09 18				09 29	09 32		09 44	09 48				09 59	10 02		10 14	10 18	
Radlett d			09 04			09 19					09 34			09 49					10 04			10 19		
Elstree & Borehamwood d			09 08			09 23					09 38			09 53					10 08			10 23		
Mill Hill Broadway d			09 13			09 28					09 43			09 58					10 13			10 28		
Hendon d			09 16			09 31					09 46			10 01					10 16			10 31		
Cricklewood d			09 20			09 35					09 50			10 05					10 20			10 35		
West Hampstead Thameslink ⊖ d			09 24			09 39					09 54			10 09					10 24			10 39		
Kentish Town ⊖ a			09 28			09 44					09 58			10 14					10 28			10 44		
St Pancras International ⊖ a	←	09 01			←				←	09 29			←			←	09 59				←			←
d																								
St Pancras International ⊖ a	09 17		09 32	09 21	09 32	09 47	09 38		09 47		10 02	09 51	10 02	10 17	10 08	10 17			10 32	10 21	10 32	10 47	10 38	10 47
d	09 18		09 34	09 24	09 34	09 48	09 39		09 48		10 04	09 54	10 04	10 18	10 09	10 18			10 34	10 24	10 34	10 48	10 39	10 48
Farringdon ⊖ d	09 23		→	09 29	09 39	→	09 44		09 53		→	09 59	10 09	→	10 14	10 23			→	10 29	10 39	→	10 44	10 53
City Thameslink d	09 27			09 33	09 43		09 48		09 57			10 03	10 13		10 18	10 27				10 33	10 43		10 48	10 57
London Blackfriars ⊖ a	09 30			09 35	09 46		09 50		10 00			10 05	10 16		10 20	10 30				10 35	10 46		10 50	11 00
London Bridge a																								

	EM ◇■	FC	FC ■		FC	FC	FC ■	FC	EM ◇■	FC	FC ■	FC	FC		FC ■	FC	EM ◇■	FC	FC ■	FC	FC	FC ■	FC
Bedford d	09 49		09 54				10 10		10 19		10 24				10 40		10 49		10 54			11 10	
Flitwick d			10 04				10 20				10 34				10 50				11 04			11 20	
Harlington d			10 08				10 24				10 38				10 54				11 08			11 24	
Leagrave d			10 13				10 29				10 43				10 59				11 13			11 29	
Luton d	10 05	10 14	10 18				10 34			10 44	10 48				11 04		11 05	11 14	11 18			11 34	
Luton Airport Parkway d		10 16	10 20				10 36		10 35	10 46	10 50				11 06			11 16	11 20			11 36	
Harpenden d		10 22	10 26				10 42			10 52	10 56				11 12			11 22	11 26			11 42	
St Albans City d		10 29	10 32			10 44	10 48			10 59	11 02		11 14		11 18			11 29	11 32		11 44	11 48	
Radlett d		10 34				10 49				11 04			11 19					11 34			11 49		
Elstree & Borehamwood d		10 38				10 53				11 08			11 23					11 38			11 53		
Mill Hill Broadway d		10 43				10 58				11 13			11 28					11 43			11 58		
Hendon d		10 46				11 01				11 16			11 31					11 46			12 01		
Cricklewood d		10 50				11 05				11 20			11 35					11 50			12 05		
West Hampstead Thameslink ⊖ d		10 54				11 09				11 24			11 39					11 54			12 09		
Kentish Town ⊖ a		10 58				11 14				11 28			11 44					11 58			12 14		
St Pancras International ⊖ a	10 29				←			←	11 01			←				←	11 29			←			←
d																							
St Pancras International ⊖ a		11 02	10 51		11 02	11 17	11 08	11 17		11 32	11 21	11 32	11 47		11 38	11 47		12 02	11 51	12 02	12 17	12 08	12 17
d		11 04	10 54		11 04	11 18	11 09	11 18		11 34	11 24	11 34	11 48		11 39	11 48		12 04	11 54	12 04	12 18	12 09	12 18
Farringdon ⊖ d		→	10 59		11 09	→	11 14	11 23		→	11 29	11 39	→		11 44	11 53		→	11 59	12 09	→	12 14	12 23
City Thameslink d			11 03		11 13		11 18	11 27			11 33	11 43			11 48	11 57			12 03	12 13		12 18	12 27
London Blackfriars ⊖ a			11 05		11 16		11 20	11 30			11 35	11 46			11 50	12 00			12 05	12 16		12 20	12 30
London Bridge a																							

	EM ◇■	FC	FC ■	FC	FC	FC ■	FC	EM ◇■	FC		FC ■	FC	FC	FC ■	FC	EM ◇■	FC	FC ■	FC		FC	FC ■	FC	EM ◇■
Bedford d	11 19		11 24			11 40		11 49			11 54			12 10		12 19		12 24				12 40		12 49
Flitwick d			11 34			11 50					12 04			12 20				12 34				12 50		
Harlington d			11 38			11 54					12 08			12 24				12 38				12 54		
Leagrave d			11 43			11 59					12 13			12 29				12 43				12 59		
Luton d		11 44	11 48			12 04		12 05	12 14		12 18			12 34			12 44	12 48				13 04		13 05
Luton Airport Parkway d	11 35	11 46	11 50			12 06			12 16		12 20			12 36		12 35	12 46	12 50				13 06		
Harpenden d		11 52	11 56			12 12			12 22		12 26			12 42			12 52	12 56				13 12		
St Albans City d		11 59	12 02		12 14	12 18			12 29		12 32		12 44	12 48			12 59	13 02			13 14	13 18		
Radlett d		12 04			12 19				12 34				12 49				13 04				13 19			
Elstree & Borehamwood d		12 08			12 23				12 38				12 53				13 08				13 23			
Mill Hill Broadway d		12 13			12 28				12 43				12 58				13 13				13 28			
Hendon d		12 16			12 31				12 46				13 01				13 16				13 31			
Cricklewood d		12 20			12 35				12 50				13 05				13 20				13 35			
West Hampstead Thameslink ⊖ d		12 24			12 39				12 54				13 09				13 24				13 39			
Kentish Town ⊖ a		12 28			12 44				12 58				13 14				13 28				13 44			
St Pancras International ⊖ a	12 01			←			←	12 29				←			←	13 01			←				←	13 29
d																								
St Pancras International ⊖ a		12 32	12 21	12 32	12 47	12 38	12 47		13 02		12 51	13 02	13 17	13 08	13 17		13 32	13 21	13 32		13 47	13 38	13 47	
d		12 34	12 24	12 34	12 48	12 39	12 48		13 04		12 54	13 04	13 18	13 09	13 18		13 34	13 24	13 34		13 48	13 39	13 48	
Farringdon ⊖ d		→	12 29	12 39	→	12 44	12 53		→		12 59	13 09	→	13 14	13 23		→	13 29	13 39		→	13 44	13 53	
City Thameslink d			12 33	12 43		12 48	12 57				13 03	13 13		13 18	13 27			13 33	13 43			13 48	13 57	
London Blackfriars ⊖ a			12 35	12 46		12 50	13 00				13 05	13 16		13 20	13 30			13 35	13 46			13 50	14 00	
London Bridge a																								

Please refer to separate pages within this table for services operating between South London and Brighton

At weekends please use local bus and tube services to travel to/from St Pancras International and London Bridge when no trains are operating. See local publicity for details of alternative routes and services that are available across central London

Bedford, Luton, St Albans - London

Network Diagram - see first Page of Table 52

	FC	FC ■	FC	FC	FC ■		FC	EM ◇■	FC	FC ■	FC	FC	FC ■	FC	EM ◇■		FC	FC ■	FC	FC	FC ■	FC	EM ◇■	FC
Bedford d		12 54			13 10			13 19		13 24			13 40		13 49			13 54			14 10		14 19	
Flitwick d		13 04			13 20					13 34			13 50					14 04			14 20			
Harlington d		13 08			13 24					13 38			13 54					14 08			14 24			
Leagrave d		13 13			13 29					13 43			13 59					14 13			14 29			
Luton d	13 14	13 18			13 34				13 44	13 48			14 04		14 05		14 14	14 18			14 34			14 44
Luton Airport Parkway d	13 16	13 20			13 36			13 35	13 46	13 50			14 06				14 16	14 20			14 36		14 35	14 46
Harpenden d	13 22	13 26			13 42				13 52	13 56			14 12				14 22	14 26			14 42			14 52
St Albans City d	13 29	13 32		13 44	13 48				13 59	14 02		14 14	14 18				14 29	14 32		14 44	14 48			14 59
Radlett d	13 34			13 49					14 04			14 19					14 34			14 49				15 04
Elstree & Borehamwood d	13 38			13 53					14 08			14 23					14 38			14 53				15 08
Mill Hill Broadway d	13 43			13 58					14 13			14 28					14 43			14 58				15 13
Hendon d	13 46			14 01					14 16			14 31					14 46			15 01				15 16
Cricklewood d	13 50			14 05					14 20			14 35					14 50			15 05				15 20
West Hampstead Thameslink ⊖ d	13 54			14 09					14 24			14 39					14 54			15 09				15 24
Kentish Town ⊖ a	13 58			14 14					14 28			14 44					14 58			15 14				15 28
St Pancras International ⊖ a			←				←	14 01			←			←	14 29				←			←	15 01	
d																								
St Pancras International ⊖ a	14 02	13 51	14 02	14 17	14 08		14 17		14 32	14 21	14 32	14 47	14 38	14 47			15 02	14 51	15 02	15 17	15 08	15 17		15 32
d	14 04	13 54	14 04	14 18	14 09		14 18		14 34	14 24	14 34	14 48	14 39	14 48			15 04	14 54	15 04	15 18	15 09	15 18		15 34
Farringdon ⊖ d	→	13 59	14 09	→	14 14		14 23		→	14 29	14 39	→	14 44	14 53			→	14 59	15 09	→	15 14	15 23		→
City Thameslink d		14 03	14 13		14 18		14 27			14 33	14 43		14 48	14 57				15 03	15 13		15 18	15 27		
London Blackfriars ⊖ a		14 05	14 16		14 20		14 30			14 35	14 46		14 50	15 00				15 05	15 16		15 20	15 30		
London Bridge a																								

	FC ■		FC	FC	FC ■	FC	EM ◇■	FC	FC ■	FC	FC		FC ■	FC	EM ◇■	FC	FC ■	FC	FC	FC ■	FC		EM ◇■	FC
Bedford d	14 24				14 40		14 49		14 54				15 10		15 19		15 24			15 40			15 49	
Flitwick d	14 34				14 50				15 04				15 20				15 34			15 50				
Harlington d	14 38				14 54				15 08				15 24				15 38			15 54				
Leagrave d	14 43				14 59				15 13				15 29				15 43			15 59				
Luton d	14 48				15 04		15 05	15 14	15 18				15 34			15 44	15 48			16 04			16 05	16 14
Luton Airport Parkway d	14 50				15 06			15 16	15 20				15 36		15 35	15 46	15 50			16 06				16 16
Harpenden d	14 56				15 12			15 22	15 26				15 42			15 52	15 56			16 12				16 22
St Albans City d	15 02			15 14	15 18			15 29	15 32		15 44		15 48			15 59	16 02		16 14	16 18				16 29
Radlett d				15 19				15 34			15 49					16 04			16 19					16 34
Elstree & Borehamwood d				15 23				15 38			15 53					16 08			16 23					16 38
Mill Hill Broadway d				15 28				15 43			15 58					16 13			16 28					16 43
Hendon d				15 31				15 46			16 01					16 16			16 31					16 46
Cricklewood d				15 35				15 50			16 05					16 20			16 35					16 50
West Hampstead Thameslink ⊖ d				15 39				15 54			16 09					16 24			16 39					16 54
Kentish Town ⊖ a				15 44				15 58			16 14					16 28			16 44					16 58
St Pancras International ⊖ a			←			←	15 29			←				←	16 01			←			←		16 29	
d																								
St Pancras International ⊖ a	15 21		15 32	15 47	15 38	15 47		16 02	15 51	16 02	16 17		16 08	16 17		16 32	16 21	16 32	16 47	16 38	16 47			17 02
d	15 24		15 34	15 48	15 39	15 48		16 04	15 54	16 04	16 18		16 09	16 18		16 34	16 24	16 34	16 48	16 39	16 48			17 04
Farringdon ⊖ d	15 29		15 39	→	15 44	15 53		→	15 59	16 09	→		16 14	16 23		→	16 29	16 39	→	16 44	16 53			→
City Thameslink d	15 33		15 43		15 48	15 57			16 03	16 13			16 18	16 27			16 33	16 43		16 48	16 57			
London Blackfriars ⊖ a	15 35		15 46		15 50	16 00			16 05	16 16			16 20	16 30			16 35	16 46		16 50	17 00			
London Bridge a																								

	FC ■	FC	FC	FC ■	FC	EM ◇■	FC		FC ■	FC	FC	FC ■	FC	EM ◇■	FC	FC ■	FC		FC	FC ■	FC	EM ◇■	FC	FC ■
Bedford d	15 54			16 10		16 19			16 24			16 40		16 49		16 54				17 10		17 19		17 24
Flitwick d	16 04			16 20					16 34			16 50				17 04				17 20				17 34
Harlington d	16 08			16 24					16 38			16 54				17 08				17 24				17 38
Leagrave d	16 13			16 29					16 43			16 59				17 13				17 29				17 43
Luton d	16 18			16 34			16 44		16 48			17 04		17 05	17 14	17 18				17 34			17 44	17 48
Luton Airport Parkway d	16 20			16 36		16 35	16 46		16 50			17 06			17 16	17 20				17 36		17 35	17 46	17 50
Harpenden d	16 26			16 42			16 52		16 56			17 12			17 22	17 26				17 42			17 52	17 56
St Albans City d	16 32		16 44	16 48			16 59		17 02		17 14	17 18			17 29	17 32			17 44	17 48			17 59	18 02
Radlett d			16 49				17 04				17 19				17 34				17 49				18 04	
Elstree & Borehamwood d			16 53				17 08				17 23				17 38				17 53				18 08	
Mill Hill Broadway d			16 58				17 13				17 28				17 43				17 58				18 13	
Hendon d			17 01				17 16				17 31				17 46				18 01				18 16	
Cricklewood d			17 05				17 20				17 35				17 50				18 05				18 20	
West Hampstead Thameslink ⊖ d			17 09				17 24				17 39				17 54				18 09				18 24	
Kentish Town ⊖ a			17 14				17 28				17 44				17 58				18 14				18 28	
St Pancras International ⊖ a		←			←	17 01				←			←	17 29			←				←	18 01		
d																								
St Pancras International ⊖ a	16 51	17 02	17 17	17 08	17 17		17 32		17 21	17 32	17 47	17 38	17 47		18 02	17 51	18 02		18 17	18 08	18 17		18 32	18 21
d	16 54	17 04	17 18	17 09	17 18		17 34		17 24	17 34	17 48	17 39	17 48		18 04	17 54	18 04		18 18	18 09	18 18		18 34	18 24
Farringdon ⊖ d	16 59	17 09	→	17 14	17 23		→		17 29	17 39	→	17 44	17 53		→	17 59	18 09		→	18 14	18 23		→	18 29
City Thameslink d	17 03	17 13		17 18	17 27				17 33	17 43		17 48	17 57			18 03	18 13			18 18	18 27			18 33
London Blackfriars ⊖ a	17 05	17 16		17 20	17 30				17 35	17 46		17 50	18 00			18 05	18 16			18 20	18 30			18 35
London Bridge a																								

Please refer to separate pages within this table for services operating between South London and Brighton

At weekends please use local bus and tube services to travel to/from St Pancras International and London Bridge when no trains are operating. See local publicity for details of alternative routes and services that are available across central London

Table 52

Bedford, Luton, St Albans - London

Saturdays until 23 June

Network Diagram - see first Page of Table 52

		FC	FC	FC [1]	FC	EM ◇[1]	FC	FC [1]	FC	FC	FC [1]	FC	EM ◇[1]	FC	FC [1]	FC	FC	FC [1]	FC	EM ◇[1]	FC	FC [1]
Bedford [7]	d			17 40		17 49		17 54			18 10		18 19		18 24			18 40		18 49		18 54
Flitwick	d			17 50				18 04			18 20				18 34			18 50				19 04
Harlington	d			17 54				18 08			18 24				18 38			18 54				19 08
Leagrave	d			17 59				18 13			18 29				18 43			18 59				19 13
Luton [10]	d			18 04		18 05	18 14	18 18			18 34			18 44	18 48			19 04		19 05	19 14	19 18
Luton Airport Parkway [7] ✈	d			18 06			18 16	18 20			18 36		18 35	18 46	18 50			19 06			19 16	19 20
Harpenden	d			18 12			18 22	18 26			18 42			18 52	18 56			19 12			19 22	19 26
St Albans City	d		18 14	18 18			18 29	18 32		18 44	18 48			18 59	19 02		19 14	19 18			19 29	19 32
Radlett	d		18 19				18 34			18 49				19 04			19 19				19 34	
Elstree & Borehamwood	d		18 23				18 38			18 53				19 08			19 23				19 38	
Mill Hill Broadway	d		18 28				18 43			18 58				19 13			19 28				19 43	
Hendon	d		18 31				18 46			19 01				19 16			19 31				19 46	
Cricklewood	d		18 35				18 50			19 05				19 20			19 35				19 50	
West Hampstead Thameslink ⊖	d		18 39				18 54			19 09				19 24			19 39				19 54	
Kentish Town ⊖	a		18 44				18 58			19 14				19 28			19 44				19 58	
St Pancras International [15] ⊖	a	←			←	18 29			←			←	18 59			←			←	19 29		
	d																					
St Pancras International [15] ⊖	a	18 32	18 47	18 38	18 47		19 02	18 51	19 02	19 17	19 08	19 17		19 32	19 21	19 32	19 47	19 38	19 47		20 02	19 51
	d	18 34	18 48	18 39	18 48		19 04	18 54	19 04	19 18	19 09	19 18		19 34	19 24	19 34	19 48	19 39	19 48		20 04	19 54
Farringdon [3] ⊖	d	18 39	→	18 44	18 53		→	18 59	19 09	→	19 14	19 23		→	19 29	19 39	→	19 44	19 53		→	19 59
City Thameslink [3]	d	18 43		18 48	18 57			19 03	19 13		19 18	19 27			19 33	19 43		19 48	19 57			20 03
London Blackfriars [3] ⊖	a	18 46		18 50	19 00			19 05	19 16		19 20	19 30			19 35	19 46		19 50	20 00			20 05
London Bridge [4]	a																					

		FC	EM ◇[1]	FC	FC [1]	FC	EM ◇[1]	FC	FC [1]	FC	EM ◇[1]	FC [1]	FC	EM ◇[1]	FC [1]	FC	EM ◇[1]	FC [1]	FC	EM ◇[1]	FC [1]	EM ◇[1]	FC
Bedford [7]	d		19 18		19 22		19 49		19 52		20 18	20 22		20 49	20 52		21 22	21 22		21 47	21 50	22 01	
Flitwick	d				19 32				20 02			20 32			21 02			21 32			22 00		
Harlington	d				19 36				20 06			20 36			21 06			21 36			22 04		
Leagrave	d				19 41				20 11			20 41			21 11			21 41			22 11		
Luton [10]	d				19 46	19 50	20 05		20 16	20 20		20 46	20 50	21 03	21 16	21 20		21 46	21 50	22 03	22 15	22 22	
Luton Airport Parkway [7] ✈	d		19 30		19 48	19 52			20 18	20 22	20 30	20 48	20 52		21 18	21 22	21 38	21 48	21 52		22 18	22 25	
Harpenden	d				19 54	19 58			20 24	20 28		20 54	20 58		21 24	21 28		21 54	21 58		22 24		
St Albans City	d			19 44	20 00	20 04		20 14	20 30	20 34		21 00	21 04		21 30	21 34		22 00	22 04		22 30		22 34
Radlett	d			19 49		20 09		20 19		20 39			21 09			21 39			22 09				22 39
Elstree & Borehamwood	d			19 53		20 13		20 23		20 43			21 13			21 43			22 13				22 43
Mill Hill Broadway	d			19 58		20 17		20 28		20 47			21 17			21 47			22 17				22 47
Hendon	d			20 01		20 20		20 31		20 50			21 20			21 50			22 20				22 50
Cricklewood	d			20 05		20 24		20 35		20 54			21 24			21 54			22 24				22 54
West Hampstead Thameslink ⊖	d			20 09	20 14	20 26		20 39	20 44	20 56		21 14	21 26		21 44	21 56		22 14	22 26		22 44		22 56
Kentish Town ⊖	a			20 14		20 31		20 44		21 01			21 31			22 01			22 31				23 01
St Pancras International [15] ⊖	a	←	20 01				20 29				21 01			21 29			22 05			22 29		22 47	
	d																						
St Pancras International [15] ⊖	a	20 02		20 17	20 21	20 35		20 47	20 51	21 05		21 21	21 35		21 51	22 05		22 21	22 35		22 52		23 05
	d	20 04		20 18	20 24	20 36		20 48	20 54	21 06		21 24	21 36		21 54	22 06		22 24	22 36		22 54		23 06
Farringdon [3] ⊖	d	20 09		20 23	20 29	20 40		20 53	20 59	21 10		21 29	21 40		21 59	22 10		22 29	22 40		22 59		23 10
City Thameslink [3]	d	20 13		20 27	20 33	20 43		20 57	21 03														
London Blackfriars [3] ⊖	a	20 16		20 30	20 35	20 46		21 00	21 05	21 16		21 34	21 46		22 04	22 16		22 34	22 46		23 04		23 16
London Bridge [4]	a																						

		FC [1]	EM ◇[1]	FC	FC [1]	FC [1]	FC [1]
Bedford [7]	d	22 16	22 39		22 40	23 10	23 40
Flitwick	d	22 27			22 51	23 21	23 51
Harlington	d	22 31			22 55	23 25	23 55
Leagrave	d	22 38			23 02	23 32	00 02
Luton [10]	d	22 42	22 59		23 06	23 36	00 06
Luton Airport Parkway [7] ✈	d	22 45			23 09	23 39	00 09
Harpenden	d	22 51			23 15	23 45	00 15
St Albans City	d	22 57		23 01	23 21	23 51	00 21
Radlett	d			23 06	23 27	23 56	00 26
Elstree & Borehamwood	d			23 11	23 31	00 01	00 31
Mill Hill Broadway	d			23 15	23 35	00 05	00 35
Hendon	d			23 18	23 39	00 08	00 38
Cricklewood	d			23 22	23 42	00 12	00 42
West Hampstead Thameslink ⊖	d	23 13		23 24	23 44	00 14	00 45
Kentish Town ⊖	a			23 30	23 50	00 20	00 50
St Pancras International [15] ⊖	a		23 37				
	d						
St Pancras International [15] ⊖	a	23 22		23 34	23 53	00 23	00 54
	d	23 24		23 36	23 54	00 24	00 54
Farringdon [3] ⊖	d	23 29		23 40	23 59	00 29	
City Thameslink [3]	d						
London Blackfriars [3] ⊖	a	23 34		23 46	00 04	00 34	01 04
London Bridge [4]	a						

Please refer to separate pages within this table for services operating between South London and Brighton

At weekends please use local bus and tube services to travel to/from St Pancras International and London Bridge when no trains are operating. See local publicity for details of alternative routes and services that are available across central London

Table 52

Bedford, Luton, St Albans - London

Saturdays from 30 June

Network Diagram - see first Page of Table 52

		FC [1]	FC [1]	FC [1]	FC [1]	FC [1]	FC [1]	FC [1]	FC [1]	FC [1]	FC [1]	FC	FC [1]	FC	FC [1]	EM ◇[1]	FC	FC	FC [1]	FC	FC [1]	FC	FC
Bedford [7]	d	22p42	23p12	23p42	00 42	01 42		02 42	03 12	03 42	04 22		04 52		05 22	05 32			05 40		05 54		
Flitwick	d	22p52	23p22	23p52	00 52	01 52		02 52	03 22	03 52	04 32		05 02		05 32				05 50		06 04		
Harlington	d	22p56	23p26	23p56	00 56	01 56		02 56	03 26	03 56	04 36		05 06		05 36				05 54		06 08		
Leagrave	d	23p02	23p32	00 02	01 02	02 02		03 02	03 32	04 02	04 42		05 12		05 42				05 59		06 13		
Luton [10]	d	23p06	23p36	00 06	01 06	02 06		03 06	03 36	04 06	04 46		05 16	05 30	05 46			06 00	06 04		06 18		06 30
Luton Airport Parkway [7] ✈	d	23p09	23p39	00 09	01 09	02 09		03 09	03 39	04 09	04 49		05 19	05 32	05 49	05 54		06 02	06 06		06 20		06 32
Harpenden	d	23p15	23p45	00 15	01 15	02 15		03 15	03 45	04 15	04 55		05 25	05 38	05 55			06 08	06 12		06 26		06 38
St Albans City	d	23p21	23p51	00 21	01 21	02 21		03 21	03 51	04 21	05 01		05 31	05 44	06 01			06 14	06 18		06 32		06 44
Radlett	d	23p26	23p56	00 26	01 26	02 26		03 26	03 56	04 26	05 06			05 50				06 19					06 49
Elstree & Borehamwood	d	23p31	00 01	00 31	01 31	02 31		03 31	04 01	04 31	05 11			05 54				06 23					06 53
Mill Hill Broadway	d	23p35	00 05	00 35	01 35	02 35		03 35	04 05	04 35	05 15			05 58				06 28					06 58
Hendon	d	23p38	00 08	00 38	01 38	02 38		03 38	04 08	04 38	05 18			06 02				06 31					07 01
Cricklewood	d	23p42	00 12	00 42	01 42	02 42		03 42	04 12	04 42	05 22			06 05				06 35					07 05
West Hampstead Thameslink ⊖	d	23p44	00 14	00 44	01 44	02 44		03 44	04 14	04 44	05 24	05 40	05 46	06 09	06 16		06 24	06 39			06 44	06 54	07 09
Kentish Town ⊖	a	23p50	00 20	00 50	01 50	02 50		03 50	04 20	04 50	05 30	05 44		06 14			06 28	06 44				06 58	07 14
St Pancras International [15] ⊖	a															06 21				←			
	d																						
St Pancras International [15] ⊖	a	23p53	00 23	00 53	01 53	02 53		03 53	04 23	04 53	05 33	05 48	05 53	06 17	06 23		06 32	06 47	06 38	06 47	06 52	07 02	07 17
	d	23p54	00 24	00 54	01 54	02 54	03 28	03 54	04 24	04 54	05 34	05 48	05 54	06 18	06 24		06 34	06 48	06 39	06 48	06 54	07 04	07 18
Farringdon [3] ⊖	d	23p59	00 29	00 59						04 59	05 39	05 53	05 59	06 23	06 29		06 39	→	06 44	06 53	06 59	07 09	→
City Thameslink [3]	d																						
London Blackfriars [3] ⊖	a	00 04	00 34	01 04	02 04	03 04	03 38	04 04	04 34	05 04	05 44	05 59	06 04	06 29	06 34		06 45		06 49	06 59	07 04	07 15	
London Bridge [4]	a																						

		FC [1]	FC	FC [1]	FC	FC	FC [1]	FC	EM ◇[1]	FC	FC [1]	FC	FC	FC [1]	FC	EM ◇[1]	FC	FC [1]	FC	FC	FC [1]	FC	EM ◇[1]
Bedford [7]	d	06 10		06 24			06 40		06 49		06 54			07 10		07 19		07 24			07 40		07 49
Flitwick	d	06 20		06 34			06 50				07 04			07 20				07 34			07 50		
Harlington	d	06 24		06 38			06 54				07 08			07 24				07 38			07 54		
Leagrave	d	06 29		06 43			06 59				07 13			07 29				07 43			07 59		
Luton [10]	d	06 34		06 48		07 00	07 04		07 04	07 14	07 18		07 30	07 34			07 44	07 48		08 00	08 04		08 05
Luton Airport Parkway [7] ✈	d	06 36		06 50		07 02	07 06			07 16	07 20		07 32	07 36		07 35	07 46	07 50		08 02	08 06		
Harpenden	d	06 42		06 56		07 08	07 12			07 22	07 26		07 38	07 42			07 52	07 56		08 08	08 12		
St Albans City	d	06 48		07 02		07 14	07 18			07 29	07 32		07 44	07 48			07 59	08 02		08 14	08 18		
Radlett	d					07 19				07 34			07 49				08 04			08 19			
Elstree & Borehamwood	d					07 23				07 38			07 53				08 08			08 23			
Mill Hill Broadway	d					07 28				07 43			07 58				08 13			08 28			
Hendon	d					07 31				07 46			08 01				08 16			08 31			
Cricklewood	d					07 35				07 50			08 05				08 20			08 35			
West Hampstead Thameslink ⊖	d				07 24	07 39				07 54			08 09				08 24			08 39			
Kentish Town ⊖	a				07 28	07 44				07 58			08 14				08 28			08 44			
St Pancras International [15] ⊖	a		←					←	07 31			←			←	08 00			←			←	08 31
	d																						
St Pancras International [15] ⊖	a	07 08	07 17	07 21	07 32	07 47	07 38	07 47		08 02	07 51	08 02	08 17	08 08	08 17		08 32	08 21	08 32	08 47	08 38	08 47	
	d	07 09	07 18	07 24	07 34	07 48	07 39	07 48		08 04	07 54	08 04	08 18	08 09	08 18		08 34	08 24	08 34	08 48	08 39	08 48	
Farringdon [3] ⊖	d	07 14	07 23	07 29	07 39	→	07 44	07 53		→	07 59	08 09	→	08 14	08 23		→	08 29	08 39	→	08 44	08 53	
City Thameslink [3]	d																						
London Blackfriars [3] ⊖	a	07 19	07 29	07 34	07 45		07 49	07 59			08 04	08 15		08 19	08 29			08 34	08 45		08 49	08 59	
London Bridge [4]	a																						

		FC	FC [1]	FC	FC	FC [1]	FC	EM ◇[1]	FC	FC [1]	FC	FC	FC [1]	FC	EM ◇[1]	FC	FC [1]	FC	FC	FC [1]	FC	EM ◇[1]
Bedford [7]	d		07 54			08 10		08 19		08 24			08 40		08 49		08 54			09 10		09 19
Flitwick	d		08 04			08 20				08 34			08 50				09 04			09 20		
Harlington	d		08 08			08 24				08 38			08 54				09 08			09 24		
Leagrave	d		08 13			08 29				08 43			08 59				09 13			09 29		
Luton [10]	d	08 14	08 18			08 34			08 44	08 48			09 04		09 05	09 14	09 18			09 34		
Luton Airport Parkway [7] ✈	d	08 16	08 20			08 36		08 35	08 46	08 50			09 06			09 16	09 20			09 36		09 35
Harpenden	d	08 22	08 26			08 42			08 52	08 56			09 12			09 22	09 26			09 42		
St Albans City	d	08 29	08 32		08 44	08 48			08 59	09 02		09 14	09 18			09 29	09 32		09 44	09 48		
Radlett	d	08 34			08 49				09 04			09 19				09 34			09 49			
Elstree & Borehamwood	d	08 38			08 53				09 08			09 23				09 38			09 53			
Mill Hill Broadway	d	08 43			08 58				09 13			09 28				09 43			09 58			
Hendon	d	08 46			09 01				09 16			09 31				09 46			10 01			
Cricklewood	d	08 50			09 05				09 20			09 35				09 50			10 05			
West Hampstead Thameslink ⊖	d	08 54			09 09				09 24			09 39				09 54			10 09			
Kentish Town ⊖	a	08 58			09 14				09 28			09 44				09 58			10 14			
St Pancras International [15] ⊖	a			←			←	09 01			←			←	09 29			←			←	09 59
	d																					
St Pancras International [15] ⊖	a	09 02	08 51	09 02	09 17	09 08	09 17		09 32	09 21	09 32	09 47	09 38	09 47		10 02	09 51	10 02	10 17	10 08	10 17	
	d	09 04	08 54	09 04	09 18	09 09	09 18		09 34	09 24	09 34	09 48	09 39	09 48		10 04	09 54	10 04	10 18	10 09	10 18	
Farringdon [3] ⊖	d	→	08 59	09 09	→	09 14	09 23		→	09 29	09 39	→	09 44	09 53		→	09 59	10 09	→	10 14	10 23	
City Thameslink [3]	d		09 03	09 13		09 18	09 27			09 33	09 43		09 48	09 57			10 03	10 13		10 18	10 27	
London Blackfriars [3] ⊖	a		09 05	09 16		09 20	09 30			09 35	09 46		09 50	10 00			10 05	10 16		10 20	10 30	
London Bridge [4]	a																					

Please refer to separate pages within this table for services operating between South London and Brighton

At weekends please use local bus and tube services to travel to/from St Pancras International and London Bridge when no trains are operating. See local publicity for details of alternative routes and services that are available across central London

Bedford, Luton, St Albans - London

Network Diagram - see first Page of Table 52

		FC	FC [1]	FC	FC	FC [1]	FC	EM ◇[1] ✠		FC	FC [1]	FC	FC	FC [1]	FC	EM ◇[1] ✠	FC	FC [1]		FC	FC	FC [1]	FC	EM ◇[1] ✠	FC
Bedford [7]	d		09 24			09 40		09 49			09 54			10 10		10 19		10 24				10 40		10 49	
Flitwick	d		09 34			09 50					10 04			10 20				10 34				10 50			
Harlington	d		09 38			09 54					10 08			10 24				10 38				10 54			
Leagrave	d		09 43			09 59					10 13			10 29				10 43				10 59			
Luton [10]	d	09 44	09 48			10 04		10 05		10 14	10 18			10 34			10 44	10 48				11 04		11 05	11 14
Luton Airport Parkway [7] ✈	d	09 46	09 50			10 06				10 16	10 20			10 36		10 35	10 46	10 50				11 06			11 16
Harpenden	d	09 52	09 56			10 12				10 22	10 26			10 42			10 52	10 56				11 12			11 22
St Albans City	d	09 59	10 02		10 14	10 18				10 29	10 32		10 44	10 48			10 59	11 02			11 14	11 18			11 29
Radlett	d	10 04			10 19					10 34			10 49				11 04				11 19				11 34
Elstree & Borehamwood	d	10 08			10 23					10 38			10 53				11 08				11 23				11 38
Mill Hill Broadway	d	10 13			10 28					10 43			10 58				11 13				11 28				11 43
Hendon	d	10 16			10 31					10 46			11 01				11 16				11 31				11 46
Cricklewood	d	10 20			10 35					10 50			11 05				11 20				11 35				11 50
West Hampstead Thameslink ⊖	d	10 24			10 39					10 54			11 09				11 24				11 39				11 54
Kentish Town ⊖	a	10 28			10 44					10 58			11 14				11 28				11 44				11 58
St Pancras International [15] ⊖	a			←			←	10 29				←			←	11 01				←			←	11 29	
	d																								
St Pancras International [15] ⊖	a	10 32	10 21	10 32	10 47	10 38	10 47			11 02	10 51	11 02	11 17	11 08	11 17		11 32	11 21		11 32	11 47	11 38	11 47		12 02
	d	10 34	10 24	10 34	10 48	10 39	10 48			11 04	10 54	11 04	11 18	11 09	11 18		11 34	11 24		11 34	11 48	11 39	11 48		12 04
Farringdon [3] ⊖	d	→	10 29	10 39	→	10 44	10 53			→	10 59	11 09	→	11 14	11 23		→	11 29		11 39	→	11 44	11 53		→
City Thameslink [3]	d		10 33	10 43		10 48	10 57				11 03	11 13		11 18	11 27			11 33		11 43		11 48	11 57		
London Blackfriars [3] ⊖	a		10 35	10 46		10 50	11 00				11 05	11 16		11 20	11 30			11 35		11 46		11 50	12 00		
London Bridge [4]	a																								

		FC [1]	FC	FC		FC [1]	FC	EM ◇[1] ✠	FC	FC [1]	FC	FC	FC [1]	FC		EM ◇[1] ✠	FC	FC [1]	FC	FC	FC [1]	FC	EM ◇[1] ✠	FC	
Bedford [7]	d	10 54				11 10		11 19		11 24			11 40			11 49		11 54			12 10		12 19		
Flitwick	d	11 04				11 20				11 34			11 50					12 04			12 20				
Harlington	d	11 08				11 24				11 38			11 54					12 08			12 24				
Leagrave	d	11 13				11 29				11 43			11 59					12 13			12 29				
Luton [10]	d	11 18				11 34			11 44	11 48			12 04			12 05	12 14	12 18			12 34			12 44	
Luton Airport Parkway [7] ✈	d	11 20				11 36		11 35	11 46	11 50			12 06				12 16	12 20			12 36		12 35	12 46	
Harpenden	d	11 26				11 42			11 52	11 56			12 12				12 22	12 26			12 42			12 52	
St Albans City	d	11 32		11 44		11 48			11 59	12 02		12 14	12 18				12 29	12 32		12 44	12 48			12 59	
Radlett	d			11 49					12 04			12 19					12 34			12 49				13 04	
Elstree & Borehamwood	d			11 53					12 08			12 23					12 38			12 53				13 08	
Mill Hill Broadway	d			11 58					12 13			12 28					12 43			12 58				13 13	
Hendon	d			12 01					12 16			12 31					12 46			13 01				13 16	
Cricklewood	d			12 05					12 20			12 35					12 50			13 05				13 20	
West Hampstead Thameslink ⊖	d			12 09					12 24			12 39					12 54			13 09				13 24	
Kentish Town ⊖	a			12 14					12 28			12 44					12 58			13 14				13 28	
St Pancras International [15] ⊖	a		←				←	12 01			←			←		12 29			←			←	13 01		
	d																								
St Pancras International [15] ⊖	a	11 51	12 02	12 17		12 08	12 17		12 32	12 21	12 32	12 47	12 38	12 47			13 02	12 51	13 02	13 17	13 08	13 17		13 32	
	d	11 54	12 04	12 18		12 09	12 18		12 34	12 24	12 34	12 48	12 39	12 48			13 04	12 54	13 04	13 18	13 09	13 18		13 34	
Farringdon [3] ⊖	d	11 59	12 09	→		12 14	12 23		→	12 29	12 39	→	12 44	12 53			→	12 59	13 09	→	13 14	13 23		→	
City Thameslink [3]	d	12 03	12 13			12 18	12 27			12 33	12 43		12 48	12 57				13 03	13 13		13 18	13 27			
London Blackfriars [3] ⊖	a	12 05	12 16			12 20	12 30			12 35	12 46		12 50	13 00				13 05	13 16		13 20	13 30			
London Bridge [4]	a																								

		FC [1]	FC	FC	FC [1]	FC	EM ◇[1] ✠	FC	FC [1]	FC		FC	FC [1]	FC	EM ◇[1] ✠	FC	FC [1]	FC	FC	FC [1]		FC	EM ◇[1] ✠	FC	FC [1]
Bedford [7]	d	12 24			12 40		12 49		12 54				13 10		13 19		13 24			13 40			13 49		13 54
Flitwick	d	12 34			12 50				13 04				13 20				13 34			13 50					14 04
Harlington	d	12 38			12 54				13 08				13 24				13 38			13 54					14 08
Leagrave	d	12 43			12 59				13 13				13 29				13 43			13 59					14 13
Luton [10]	d	12 48			13 04		13 05	13 14	13 18				13 34			13 44	13 48			14 04			14 05	14 14	14 18
Luton Airport Parkway [7] ✈	d	12 50			13 06			13 16	13 20				13 36		13 35	13 46	13 50			14 06				14 16	14 20
Harpenden	d	12 56			13 12			13 22	13 26				13 42			13 52	13 56			14 12				14 22	14 26
St Albans City	d	13 02		13 14	13 18			13 29	13 32			13 44	13 48			13 59	14 02		14 14	14 18				14 29	14 32
Radlett	d			13 19				13 34				13 49				14 04			14 19					14 34	
Elstree & Borehamwood	d			13 23				13 38				13 53				14 08			14 23					14 38	
Mill Hill Broadway	d			13 28				13 43				13 58				14 13			14 28					14 43	
Hendon	d			13 31				13 46				14 01				14 16			14 31					14 46	
Cricklewood	d			13 35				13 50				14 05				14 20			14 35					14 50	
West Hampstead Thameslink ⊖	d			13 39				13 54				14 09				14 24			14 39					14 54	
Kentish Town ⊖	a			13 44				13 58				14 14				14 28			14 44					14 58	
St Pancras International [15] ⊖	a		←			←	13 29			←				←	14 01			←				←	14 29		
	d																								
St Pancras International [15] ⊖	a	13 21	13 32	13 47	13 38	13 47		14 02	13 51	14 02		14 17	14 08	14 17		14 32	14 21	14 32	14 47	14 38		14 47		15 02	14 51
	d	13 24	13 34	13 48	13 39	13 48		14 04	13 54	14 04		14 18	14 09	14 18		14 34	14 24	14 34	14 48	14 39		14 48		15 04	14 54
Farringdon [3] ⊖	d	13 29	13 39	→	13 44	13 53		→	13 59	14 09		→	14 14	14 23		→	14 29	14 39	→	14 44		14 53		→	14 59
City Thameslink [3]	d	13 33	13 43		13 48	13 57			14 03	14 13			14 18	14 27			14 33	14 43		14 48		14 57			15 03
London Blackfriars [3] ⊖	a	13 35	13 46		13 50	14 00			14 05	14 16			14 20	14 30			14 35	14 46		14 50		15 00			15 05
London Bridge [4]	a																								

Please refer to separate pages within this table for services operating between South London and Brighton

At weekends please use local bus and tube services to travel to/from St Pancras International and London Bridge when no trains are operating. See local publicity for details of alternative routes and services that are available across central London

Bedford, Luton, St Albans - London

Network Diagram - see first Page of Table 52

		FC	FC	FC [1]	FC	EM ◇[1] ✠		FC	FC [1]	FC	FC	FC [1]	FC	EM ◇[1] ✠	FC	FC [1]		FC	FC	FC [1]	FC	EM ◇[1] ✠	FC	FC [1]	FC
Bedford [7]	d			14 10		14 19			14 24			14 40		14 49		14 54				15 10		15 19		15 24	
Flitwick	d			14 20					14 34			14 50				15 04				15 20				15 34	
Harlington	d			14 24					14 38			14 54				15 08				15 24				15 38	
Leagrave	d			14 29					14 43			14 59				15 13				15 29				15 43	
Luton [10]	d			14 34				14 44	14 48			15 04		15 05	15 14	15 18				15 34			15 44	15 48	
Luton Airport Parkway [7] ✈	d			14 36		14 35		14 46	14 50			15 06			15 16	15 20				15 36		15 35	15 46	15 50	
Harpenden	d			14 42				14 52	14 56			15 12			15 22	15 26				15 42			15 52	15 56	
St Albans City	d		14 44	14 48				14 59	15 02		15 14	15 18			15 29	15 32			15 44	15 48			15 59	16 02	
Radlett	d		14 49					15 04			15 19				15 34				15 49				16 04		
Elstree & Borehamwood	d		14 53					15 08			15 23				15 38				15 53				16 08		
Mill Hill Broadway	d		14 58					15 13			15 28				15 43				15 58				16 13		
Hendon	d		15 01					15 16			15 31				15 46				16 01				16 16		
Cricklewood	d		15 05					15 20			15 35				15 50				16 05				16 20		
West Hampstead Thameslink ⊖	d		15 09					15 24			15 39				15 54				16 09				16 24		
Kentish Town ⊖	a		15 14					15 28			15 44				15 58				16 14				16 28		
St Pancras International [15] ⊖	a	←			←	15 01				←			←	15 29				←			←	16 01			←
	d																								
St Pancras International [15] ⊖	a	15 02	15 17	15 08	15 17			15 32	15 21	15 32	15 47	15 38	15 47		16 02	15 51		16 02	16 17	16 08	16 17		16 32	16 21	16 32
	d	15 04	15 18	15 09	15 18			15 34	15 24	15 34	15 48	15 39	15 48		16 04	15 54		16 04	16 18	16 09	16 18		16 34	16 24	16 34
Farringdon [3] ⊖	d	15 09	→	15 14	15 23			→	15 29	15 39	→	15 44	15 53		→	15 59		16 09	→	16 14	16 23		→	16 29	16 39
City Thameslink [3]	d	15 13		15 18	15 27				15 33	15 43		15 48	15 57			16 03		16 13		16 18	16 27			16 33	16 43
London Blackfriars [3] ⊖	a	15 16		15 20	15 30				15 35	15 46		15 50	16 00			16 05		16 16		16 20	16 30			16 35	16 46
London Bridge [4]	a																								

		FC		FC [1]	FC	EM ◇[1] ✠	FC	FC [1]	FC	FC	FC [1]	FC		EM ◇[1] ✠	FC	FC [1]	FC	FC	FC [1]	FC	EM ◇[1] ✠	FC		FC [1]	FC
Bedford [7]	d			15 40		15 49		15 54			16 10			16 19		16 24			16 40		16 49			16 54	
Flitwick	d			15 50				16 04			16 20					16 34			16 50					17 04	
Harlington	d			15 54				16 08			16 24					16 38			16 54					17 08	
Leagrave	d			15 59				16 13			16 29					16 43			16 59					17 13	
Luton [10]	d			16 04		16 05	16 14	16 18			16 34				16 44	16 48			17 04		17 05	17 14		17 18	
Luton Airport Parkway [7] ✈	d			16 06			16 16	16 20			16 36			16 35	16 46	16 50			17 06			17 16		17 20	
Harpenden	d			16 12			16 22	16 26			16 42				16 52	16 56			17 12			17 22		17 26	
St Albans City	d	16 14		16 18			16 29	16 32		16 44	16 48				16 59	17 02		17 14	17 18			17 29		17 32	
Radlett	d	16 19					16 34			16 49					17 04			17 19				17 34			
Elstree & Borehamwood	d	16 23					16 38			16 53					17 08			17 23				17 38			
Mill Hill Broadway	d	16 28					16 43			16 58					17 13			17 28				17 43			
Hendon	d	16 31					16 46			17 01					17 16			17 31				17 46			
Cricklewood	d	16 35					16 50			17 05					17 20			17 35				17 50			
West Hampstead Thameslink ⊖	d	16 39					16 54			17 09					17 24			17 39				17 54			
Kentish Town ⊖	a	16 44					16 58			17 14					17 28			17 44				17 58			
St Pancras International [15] ⊖	a				←	16 29			←			←		17 01			←			←	17 29				←
	d																								
St Pancras International [15] ⊖	a	16 47		16 38	16 47		17 02	16 51	17 02	17 17	17 08	17 17			17 32	17 21	17 32	17 47	17 38	17 47		18 02		17 51	18 02
	d	16 48		16 39	16 48		17 04	16 54	17 04	17 18	17 09	17 18			17 34	17 24	17 34	17 48	17 39	17 48		18 04		17 54	18 04
Farringdon [3] ⊖	d	→		16 44	16 53		→	16 59	17 09	→	17 14	17 23			→	17 29	17 39	→	17 44	17 53		→		17 59	18 09
City Thameslink [3]	d			16 48	16 57			17 03	17 13		17 18	17 27				17 33	17 43		17 48	17 57				18 03	18 13
London Blackfriars [3] ⊖	a			16 50	17 00			17 05	17 16		17 20	17 30				17 35	17 46		17 50	18 00				18 05	18 16
London Bridge [4]	a																								

		FC	FC [1]	FC	EM ◇[1] ✠	FC	FC [1]	FC		FC	FC [1]	FC	EM ◇[1] ✠	FC	FC [1]	FC	FC	FC [1]		FC	EM ◇[1] ✠	FC	FC [1]	FC	FC
Bedford [7]	d		17 10		17 19		17 24				17 40		17 49		17 54			18 10			18 19		18 24		
Flitwick	d		17 20				17 34				17 50				18 04			18 20					18 34		
Harlington	d		17 24				17 38				17 54				18 08			18 24					18 38		
Leagrave	d		17 29				17 43				17 59				18 13			18 29					18 43		
Luton [10]	d		17 34			17 44	17 48				18 04		18 05	18 14	18 18			18 34				18 44	18 48		
Luton Airport Parkway [7] ✈	d		17 36		17 35	17 46	17 50				18 06			18 16	18 20			18 36			18 35	18 46	18 50		
Harpenden	d		17 42			17 52	17 56				18 12			18 22	18 26			18 42				18 52	18 56		
St Albans City	d	17 44	17 48			17 59	18 02			18 14	18 18			18 29	18 32		18 44	18 48				18 59	19 02		19 14
Radlett	d	17 49				18 04				18 19				18 34			18 49					19 04			19 19
Elstree & Borehamwood	d	17 53				18 08				18 23				18 38			18 53					19 08			19 23
Mill Hill Broadway	d	17 58				18 13				18 28				18 43			18 58					19 13			19 28
Hendon	d	18 01				18 16				18 31				18 46			19 01					19 16			19 31
Cricklewood	d	18 05				18 20				18 35				18 50			19 05					19 20			19 35
West Hampstead Thameslink ⊖	d	18 09				18 24				18 39				18 54			19 09					19 24			19 39
Kentish Town ⊖	a	18 14				18 28				18 44				18 58			19 14					19 28			19 44
St Pancras International [15] ⊖	a			←	18 01			←				←	18 29			←				←	18 59			←	
	d																								
St Pancras International [15] ⊖	a	18 17	18 08	18 17		18 32	18 21	18 32		18 47	18 38	18 47		19 02	18 51	19 02	19 17	19 08		19 17		19 32	19 21	19 32	19 47
	d	18 18	18 09	18 18		18 34	18 24	18 34		18 48	18 39	18 48		19 04	18 54	19 04	19 18	19 09		19 18		19 34	19 24	19 34	19 48
Farringdon [3] ⊖	d	→	18 14	18 23		→	18 29	18 39		→	18 44	18 53		→	18 59	19 09	→	19 14		19 23		→	19 29	19 39	→
City Thameslink [3]	d		18 18	18 27			18 33	18 43			18 48	18 57			19 03	19 13		19 18		19 27			19 33	19 43	
London Blackfriars [3] ⊖	a		18 20	18 30			18 35	18 46			18 50	19 00			19 05	19 16		19 20		19 30			19 35	19 46	
London Bridge [4]	a																								

Please refer to separate pages within this table for services operating between South London and Brighton

At weekends please use local bus and tube services to travel to/from St Pancras International and London Bridge when no trains are operating. See local publicity for details of alternative routes and services that are available across central London

Table 52

Bedford, Luton, St Albans - London

Saturdays from 30 June

Network Diagram - see first Page of Table 52

		FC 1	FC	EM ◇1 ✠	FC	FC 1	FC	EM ◇1 ✠	FC	FC 1	FC	EM ◇1 ✠	FC	FC 1	FC	EM ◇1 ✠	FC 1	FC	EM ◇1 ✠	FC 1	FC	EM ◇1 ✠
Bedford 7	d	18 40		18 49		18 54		19 18		19 22		19 49		19 52		20 18	20 22		20 49	20 52		21 22
Flitwick	d	18 50				19 04				19 32				20 02			20 32			21 02		
Harlington	d	18 54				19 08				19 36				20 06			20 36			21 06		
Leagrave	d	18 59				19 13				19 41				20 11			20 41			21 11		
Luton 10	d	19 04		19 05	19 14	19 18				19 46	19 50	20 05		20 16	20 20		20 46	20 50	21 03	21 16	21 20	
Luton Airport Parkway 7 ✈	d	19 06			19 16	19 20		19 30		19 48	19 52			20 18	20 22	20 30	20 48	20 52		21 18	21 22	21 38
Harpenden	d	19 12			19 22	19 26				19 54	19 58			20 24	20 28		20 54	20 58		21 24	21 28	
St Albans City	d	19 18			19 29	19 32			19 44	20 00	20 04		20 14	20 30	20 34		21 00	21 04		21 30	21 34	
Radlett	d				19 34				19 49		20 09		20 19		20 39			21 09			21 39	
Elstree & Borehamwood	d				19 38				19 53		20 13		20 23		20 43			21 13			21 43	
Mill Hill Broadway	d				19 43				19 58		20 17		20 28		20 47			21 17			21 47	
Hendon	d				19 46				20 01		20 20		20 31		20 50			21 20			21 50	
Cricklewood	d				19 50				20 05		20 24		20 35		20 54			21 24			21 54	
West Hampstead Thameslink ⊖	d				19 54				20 09	20 14	20 26		20 39	20 44	20 56		21 14	21 26		21 44	21 56	
Kentish Town ⊖	a				19 58				20 14		20 31		20 44		21 01			21 31			22 01	
St Pancras International 15 ⊖	a		←	19 29			←	20 01				20 29				21 01			21 29			22 05
	d																					
St Pancras International 15 ⊖	a	19 38	19 47		20 02	19 51	20 02		20 17	20 21	20 35		20 47	20 51	21 05		21 21	21 35		21 51	22 05	
	d	19 39	19 48		20 04	19 54	20 04		20 18	20 24	20 36		20 48	20 54	21 06		21 24	21 36		21 54	22 06	
Farringdon 3 ⊖	d	19 44	19 53		→	19 59	20 09		20 23	20 29	20 40		20 53	20 59	21 10		21 29	21 40		21 59	22 10	
City Thameslink 3	d	19 48	19 57			20 03	20 13		20 27	20 33	20 43		20 57	21 03								
London Blackfriars 3 ⊖	a	19 50	20 00			20 05	20 16		20 30	20 35	20 46		21 00	21 05	21 16		21 34	21 46		22 04	22 16	
London Bridge 4	a																					

		FC 1	FC	EM ◇1 ✠	FC 1	EM ◇1 ✠	FC	FC 1	FC	EM ◇1 ✠	FC 1	FC 1	FC 1
Bedford 7	d	21 22		21 47	21 52	22 01		22 16		22 39	22 42	23 12	23 42
Flitwick	d	21 32			22 02			22 26			22 52	23 22	23 52
Harlington	d	21 36			22 06			22 30			22 56	23 26	23 56
Leagrave	d	21 41			22 11			22 35			23 02	23 32	00 02
Luton 10	d	21 46	21 50	22 03	22 16	22 16	22 20	22 40	22 46	22 59	23 06	23 36	00 06
Luton Airport Parkway 7 ✈	d	21 48	21 52		22 18	22 19	22 22	22 42	22 49		23 09	23 39	00 09
Harpenden	d	21 54	21 58		22 24		22 28	22 48	22 55		23 15	23 45	00 15
St Albans City	d	22 00	22 04		22 30		22 34	22 54	23 01		23 21	23 51	00 21
Radlett	d		22 09				22 39		23 06		23 26	23 56	00 26
Elstree & Borehamwood	d		22 13				22 43		23 11		23 31	00 01	00 31
Mill Hill Broadway	d		22 17				22 47		23 15		23 35	00 05	00 35
Hendon	d		22 20				22 50		23 18		23 38	00 08	00 38
Cricklewood	d		22 24				22 54		23 22		23 42	00 12	00 42
West Hampstead Thameslink ⊖	d	22 14	22 26		22 44		22 56	23 10	23 24		23 44	00 14	00 44
Kentish Town ⊖	a		22 31				23 01		23 30		23 50	00 20	00 50
St Pancras International 15 ⊖	a			22 29		22 46				23 37			
	d												
St Pancras International 15 ⊖	a	22 21	22 35		22 52		23 05	23 19	23 34		23 53	00 23	00 53
	d	22 24	22 36		22 54		23 06	23 24	23 36		23 54	00 24	00 54
Farringdon 3 ⊖	d	22 29	22 40		22 59		23 10	23 29	23 40		23 59	00 29	
City Thameslink 3	d												
London Blackfriars 3 ⊖	a	22 34	22 46		23 04		23 16	23 34	23 46		00 04	00 34	01 04
London Bridge 4	a												

Sundays until 24 June

		FC 1	FC 1	FC 1	FC	FC 1	FC 1	FC 1	FC 1	FC	FC 1	EM ◇1 ✠	FC 1	FC	FC 1	EM ◇1 ✠	FC 1	FC	FC 1	EM ◇1 ✠	FC 1	FC	FC 1
Bedford 7	d	22p40	23p10	23p40	05 40	06 10	06 40	07 10	07 49		08 04	08 15	08 19		08 34	08 45	08 49		09 04	09 15	09 19		09 34
Flitwick	d	22p51	23p21	23p51	05 51	06 21	06 51	07 21	07 59		08 15		08 29		08 44		08 59		09 14		09 29		09 44
Harlington	d	22p55	23p25	23p55	05 55	06 25	06 55	07 25	08 03		08 19		08 33		08 48		09 03		09 18		09 33		09 48
Leagrave	d	23p02	23p32	00 02	06 03	06 33	07 03	07 33	08 10		08 26		08 40		08 56		09 10		09 26		09 40		09 56
Luton 10	d	23p06	23p36	00 06	06 07	06 37	07 07	07 37	08 14	08 18	08 30	08 34	08 44	08 48	09 00		09 14	09 18	09 30	09 35	09 44	09 48	10 00
Luton Airport Parkway 7 ✈	d	23p09	23p39	00 09	06 09	06 39	07 09	07 39	08 17	08 21	08 33		08 47	08 51	09 03	09 07	09 17	09 21	09 32		09 47	09 51	10 02
Harpenden	d	23p15	23p45	00 15	06 15	06 45	07 15	07 45	08 23	08 27	08 39		08 53	08 57	09 09		09 23	09 27	09 38		09 53	09 57	10 08
St Albans City	d	23p21	23p51	00 21	06 21	06 51	07 21	07 51	08 29	08 33	08 45		08 59	09 03	09 14		09 29	09 33	09 44		09 59	10 03	10 14
Radlett	d	23p27	23p56	00 26	06 27	06 57	07 27	07 57		08 38				09 08				09 38				10 08	
Elstree & Borehamwood	d	23p31	00 01	00 31	06 31	07 01	07 31	08 01		08 42				09 12				09 42				10 12	
Mill Hill Broadway	d	23p35	00 05	00 35	06 35	07 05	07 35	08 05		08 46				09 16				09 46				10 16	
Hendon	d	23p39	00 08	00 38	06 39	07 09	07 39	08 09		08 50				09 20				09 50				10 20	
Cricklewood	d	23p42	00 12	00 42	06 42	07 12	07 42	08 12		08 53				09 23				09 53				10 23	
West Hampstead Thameslink ⊖	d	23p44	00 14	00 45	06 45	07 15	07 45	08 15	08 45	08 56	08 59		09 15	09 26	09 29		09 45	09 56	09 59		10 15	10 26	10 29
Kentish Town ⊖	a	23p50	00 20	00 50	06 50	07 20	07 50	08 20		09 00				09 30				10 00				10 30	
St Pancras International 15 ⊖	a				06 59							09 11				09 47				10 18			
	d																						
St Pancras International 15 ⊖	a	23p53	00 23	00 54		07 24	07 53	08 23	08 53	09 05	09 08		09 23	09 35	09 38		09 54	10 05	10 08		10 22	10 35	10 38
	d	23p54	00 24	00 54		07 24	07 54	08 24	08 54	09 05	09 09		09 24	09 35	09 39		09 54	10 05	10 09		10 24	10 35	10 39
Farringdon 3 ⊖	d	23p59	00 29			07 29	07 59	08 29	08 58	09 10	09 14		09 29	09 40	09 44		09 59	10 10	10 14		10 29	10 40	10 44
City Thameslink 3	d																						
London Blackfriars 3 ⊖	a	00 04	00 34	01 04		07 34	08 04	08 34	09 04	09 14	09 19		09 34	09 44	09 49		10 04	10 14	10 19		10 34	10 44	10 49
London Bridge 4	a																						

Please refer to separate pages within this table for services operating between South London and Brighton

At weekends please use local bus and tube services to travel to/from St Pancras International and London Bridge when no trains are operating. See local publicity for details of alternative routes and services that are available across central London

Table 52

Bedford, Luton, St Albans - London

Sundays until 24 June

Network Diagram - see first Page of Table 52

		EM ◇1 ✠	FC 1	FC	FC 1	EM ◇1 ✠	FC 1	FC	FC 1	EM ◇1 ✠	FC 1	FC	FC 1	EM ◇1 ✠	FC 1	FC	FC 1	EM ◇1 ✠	FC 1	FC	FC 1	EM ◇1 ✠	FC 1
Bedford 7	d	09 45	09 49		10 04	10 15	10 19		10 34	10 45	10 49		11 04	11 15	11 19		11 34	11 45	11 49		12 04	12 15	12 19
Flitwick	d		09 59		10 14		10 29		10 44		10 59		11 14		11 29		11 44		11 59		12 14		12 29
Harlington	d		10 03		10 18		10 33		10 48		11 03		11 18		11 33		11 48		12 03		12 18		12 33
Leagrave	d		10 10		10 26		10 40		10 56		11 10		11 26		11 40		11 56		12 10		12 26		12 40
Luton 10	d		10 14		10 30	10 35	10 44		11 00		11 14		11 30	11 35	11 44		12 00		12 14		12 30	12 35	12 44
Luton Airport Parkway 7 ✈	d	10 06	10 17		10 32		10 47		11 02	11 06	11 17		11 32		11 47		12 02	12 06	12 17		12 32		12 47
Harpenden	d		10 23		10 38		10 53		11 08		11 23		11 38		11 53		12 08		12 23		12 38		12 53
St Albans City	d		10 29	10 33	10 44		10 59	11 03	11 14		11 29	11 33	11 44		11 59	12 03	12 14		12 29	12 33	12 44		12 59
Radlett	d			10 38				11 08				11 38				12 08				12 38			
Elstree & Borehamwood	d			10 42				11 12				11 42				12 12				12 42			
Mill Hill Broadway	d			10 46				11 16				11 46				12 16				12 46			
Hendon	d			10 50				11 20				11 50				12 20				12 50			
Cricklewood	d			10 53				11 23				11 53				12 23				12 53			
West Hampstead Thameslink ⊖	d		10 45	10 56	10 59		11 15	11 26	11 29		11 45	11 56	11 59		12 15	12 26	12 29		12 45	12 56	12 59		13 15
Kentish Town ⊖	a			11 00				11 30				12 00				12 30				13 00			
St Pancras International 15 ⊖	a	10 48				11 18				11 48				12 18				12 48				13 18	
	d																						
St Pancras International 15 ⊖	a		10 52	11 05	11 08		11 22	11 35	11 38		11 52	12 05	12 08		12 22	12 35	12 38		12 52	13 05	13 08		13 22
	d		10 54	11 05	11 09		11 24	11 35	11 39		11 54	12 05	12 09		12 24	12 35	12 39		12 54	13 05	13 09		13 24
Farringdon 3 ⊖	d		10 58	11 10	11 14		11 29	11 40	11 44		11 58	12 10	12 14		12 29	12 40	12 44		12 58	13 10	13 14		13 29
City Thameslink 3	d																						
London Blackfriars 3 ⊖	a		11 04	11 14	11 19		11 34	11 44	11 49		12 04	12 14	12 19		12 34	12 44	12 49		13 04	13 14	13 19		13 34
London Bridge 4	a																						

		FC	FC 1	EM ◇1 ☕	FC 1	FC	FC 1	EM ◇1 ☕	FC 1	FC	FC 1	EM ◇1 ✠	FC 1	FC	FC 1	FC 1	EM ◇1 ✠	FC	FC 1	FC 1	FC	FC 1
Bedford 7	d		12 34	12 45	12 49		13 04	13 15	13 19		13 34	13 45	13 49		14 04	14 19	14 30		14 34	14 49		15 04
Flitwick	d		12 45		12 59		13 14		13 29		13 44		13 59		14 14	14 29			14 44	14 59		15 14
Harlington	d		12 49		13 03		13 18		13 33		13 48		14 03		14 18	14 33			14 48	15 03		15 18
Leagrave	d		12 56		13 10		13 26		13 40		13 56		14 10		14 26	14 40			14 56	15 10		15 26
Luton 10	d		13 00		13 14		13 30	13 35	13 44		14 00		14 14		14 30	14 44	14 55		15 00	15 14		15 30
Luton Airport Parkway 7 ✈	d		13 03	13 06	13 17		13 32		13 47		14 02	14 08	14 17		14 32	14 47			15 02	15 17		15 32
Harpenden	d		13 09		13 23		13 38		13 53		14 08		14 23		14 38	14 53			15 08	15 23		15 38
St Albans City	d	13 03	13 15		13 29	13 33	13 44		13 59	14 03	14 14		14 29	14 33	14 44	14 59		15 03	15 14	15 29	15 33	15 44
Radlett	d	13 08				13 38				14 08				14 38				15 08			15 38	
Elstree & Borehamwood	d	13 12				13 42				14 12				14 42				15 12			15 42	
Mill Hill Broadway	d	13 16				13 46				14 16				14 46				15 16			15 46	
Hendon	d	13 20				13 50				14 20				14 50				15 20			15 50	
Cricklewood	d	13 23				13 53				14 23				14 53				15 23			15 53	
West Hampstead Thameslink ⊖	d	13 26	13 29		13 45	13 56	13 59		14 15	14 26	14 29		14 45	14 56	14 59	15 15		15 26	15 29	15 45	15 56	15 59
Kentish Town ⊖	a	13 30				14 00				14 30				15 00				15 30			16 00	
St Pancras International 15 ⊖	a			13 48				14 13				14 33					15 22					
	d																					
St Pancras International 15 ⊖	a	13 35	13 38		13 52	14 05	14 08		14 22	14 35	14 38		14 52	15 05	15 08	15 22		15 35	15 38	15 52	16 05	16 08
	d	13 35	13 39		13 54	14 05	14 09		14 24	14 35	14 39		14 54	15 05	15 09	15 24		15 35	15 39	15 54	16 05	16 09
Farringdon 3 ⊖	d	13 40	13 44		13 58	14 10	14 14		14 29	14 40	14 44		14 58	15 10	15 14	15 29		15 40	15 44	15 58	16 10	16 14
City Thameslink 3	d																					
London Blackfriars 3 ⊖	a	13 44	13 49		14 04	14 14	14 19		14 34	14 44	14 49		15 04	15 14	15 19	15 34		15 44	15 49	16 04	16 14	16 19
London Bridge 4	a																					

		EM ◇1 ✠	FC 1	EM ◇1 ✠	FC	FC 1	EM ◇1 ✠	FC 1	EM ◇1 ✠	FC	FC 1	FC 1	FC	FC 1	EM ◇1 ✠	FC 1	FC	FC 1	EM ◇1 ☕	FC 1	FC	FC 1	EM ◇1 ✠
Bedford 7	d	15 07	15 19	15 24		15 34	15 45	15 49			16 04	16 19		16 34	16 45	16 49		17 03	17 07	17 19		17 32	17 42
Flitwick	d		15 29			15 44		15 59			16 14	16 29		16 44		16 59				17 29			
Harlington	d		15 33			15 48		16 03			16 18	16 33		16 48		17 03				17 33			
Leagrave	d		15 40			15 56		16 10			16 26	16 40		16 56		17 10				17 40			
Luton 10	d		15 44	15 50		16 00		16 14	16 21		16 30	16 44		17 00		17 14		17 23	17 29	17 44		17 53	
Luton Airport Parkway 7 ✈	d	15 36	15 47			16 02	16 06	16 17			16 32	16 47		17 02	17 10	17 17		17 26		17 47		17 56	18 01
Harpenden	d		15 53			16 08		16 23			16 38	16 53		17 08		17 23		17 32		17 53		18 02	
St Albans City	d		15 59		16 03	16 14		16 29		16 33	16 44	16 59	17 03	17 14		17 29	17 33	17 44		17 59	18 03	18 14	
Radlett	d				16 08					16 38			17 08				17 38				18 08		
Elstree & Borehamwood	d				16 12					16 42			17 12				17 42				18 12		
Mill Hill Broadway	d				16 16					16 46			17 16				17 46				18 16		
Hendon	d				16 20					16 50			17 20				17 50				18 20		
Cricklewood	d				16 23					16 53			17 23				17 53				18 23		
West Hampstead Thameslink ⊖	d		16 15		16 26	16 29		16 45		16 56	16 59	17 15	17 26	17 29		17 45	17 56	17 59		18 15	18 26	18 29	
Kentish Town ⊖	a				16 30					17 00			17 30				18 00				18 30		
St Pancras International 15 ⊖	a	16 01		16 14			16 30		16 44						17 34				17 54				18 23
	d																						
St Pancras International 15 ⊖	a		16 22		16 35	16 38		16 52		17 05	17 08	17 22	17 35	17 38		17 52	18 05	18 08		18 22	18 35	18 38	
	d		16 24		16 35	16 39		16 54		17 05	17 09	17 24	17 35	17 39		17 54	18 05	18 09		18 24	18 35	18 39	
Farringdon 3 ⊖	d		16 29		16 40	16 44		16 58		17 10	17 14	17 29	17 40	17 44		17 58	18 10	18 14		18 29	18 40	18 44	
City Thameslink 3	d																						
London Blackfriars 3 ⊖	a		16 34		16 44	16 49		17 04		17 14	17 19	17 34	17 44	17 49		18 04	18 14	18 19		18 34	18 44	18 49	
London Bridge 4	a																						

Please refer to separate pages within this table for services operating between South London and Brighton

At weekends please use local bus and tube services to travel to/from St Pancras International and London Bridge when no trains are operating. See local publicity for details of alternative routes and services that are available across central London

Bedford, Luton, St Albans - London

Sundays

until 24 June

Network Diagram - see first Page of Table 52

		FC	EM	FC	FC	EM	FC	FC	EM	FC	FC	EM	FC	FC	EM	FC	FC	EM	FC	EM	FC	EM
		1	◇1		1	◇1		1	◇1		1	◇1		1	◇1		1	◇1	1	◇1	1	◇1
Bedford 7	d	17 49	18 13		18 19	18 42		18 49	19 09		19 19	19 42		19 49	20 03		20 10	20 29	20 40	21 04	21 10	21 36
Flitwick	d	17 59			18 29			18 59			19 29			19 59			20 21		20 51		21 21	
Harlington	d	18 03			18 33			19 03			19 33			20 03			20 25		20 55		21 25	
Leagrave	d	18 10			18 40			19 10			19 40			20 10			20 33		21 03		21 33	
Luton 10	d	18 14	18 31		18 44			19 14	19 29		19 44			20 14	20 21		20 37		21 07	21 23	21 37	21 55
Luton Airport Parkway 7 ✈	d	18 17			18 47	19 01		19 17			19 47	20 02		20 17			20 39	20 48	21 09		21 39	
Harpenden	d	18 23			18 53			19 23			19 53			20 23			20 45		21 15		21 45	
St Albans City	d	18 29		18 33	18 59		19 03	19 29		19 33	19 59		20 03	20 29		20 33	20 51		21 21		21 51	
Radlett	d			18 38			19 08			19 38			20 08			20 38	20 56		21 26		21 56	
Elstree & Borehamwood	d			18 42			19 12			19 42			20 12			20 42	21 01		21 31		22 01	
Mill Hill Broadway	d			18 46			19 16			19 46			20 16			20 46	21 05		21 35		22 05	
Hendon	d			18 50			19 20			19 50			20 20			20 50	21 08		21 38		22 08	
Cricklewood	d			18 53			19 23			19 53			20 23			20 53	21 12		21 42		22 12	
West Hampstead Thameslink ⊖	d	18 45		18 56	19 15		19 26	19 45		19 56	20 15		20 26	20 45		20 56	21 14		21 44		22 14	
Kentish Town ⊖	a			19 00			19 30			20 00			20 30			21 00	21 19		21 49		22 19	
St Pancras International 15 ⊖	a		18 53			19 23			19 51			20 24			20 45			21 12		21 45		22 20
	d																					
St Pancras International 15 ⊖	a	18 52		19 05	19 22		19 35	19 52		20 05	20 22		20 35	20 52		21 05	21 23		21 53		22 23	
	d	18 54		19 05	19 24		19 35	19 54		20 05	20 24		20 35	20 54		21 05	21 24		21 54		22 24	
Farringdon 3 ⊖	d	18 58		19 10	19 29		19 40	19 58		20 10	20 29		20 40	20 58		21 10	21 29		21 59		22 29	
City Thameslink 3	d																					
London Blackfriars 3 ⊖	a	19 04		19 14	19 34		19 44	20 04		20 14	20 34		20 44	21 04		21 14	21 34		22 04		22 34	
London Bridge 4	a																					

		FC	FC	EM	EM	FC	FC	FC
		1	1	◇1	◇1	1	1	1
Bedford 7	d	21 40	22 10	22 23	22 31	22 40	23 10	23 40
Flitwick	d	21 51	22 21			22 51	23 21	23 51
Harlington	d	21 55	22 25			22 55	23 25	23 55
Leagrave	d	22 03	22 33			23 03	23 33	00 03
Luton 10	d	22 07	22 37	22 42	22 50	23 07	23 37	00 07
Luton Airport Parkway 7 ✈	d	22 09	22 39			23 09	23 39	00 09
Harpenden	d	22 15	22 45			23 15	23 45	00 15
St Albans City	d	22 21	22 51			23 21	23 51	00 21
Radlett	d	22 26	22 56			23 26	23 56	00 26
Elstree & Borehamwood	d	22 31	23 01			23 31	00 01	00 31
Mill Hill Broadway	d	22 35	23 05			23 35	00 05	00 35
Hendon	d	22 38	23 08			23 38	00 08	00 38
Cricklewood	d	22 42	23 12			23 42	00 12	00 42
West Hampstead Thameslink ⊖	d	22 44	23 14			23 44	00 14	00 44
Kentish Town ⊖	a	22 49	23 19			23 49	00 19	00 49
St Pancras International 15 ⊖	a			23 08	23 27			
	d							
St Pancras International 15 ⊖	a	22 53	23 23			23 53	00 23	00 53
	d	22 54	23 24			23 54	00 24	00 54
Farringdon 3 ⊖	d	22 59	23 29			23 59	00 29	
City Thameslink 3	d							
London Blackfriars 3 ⊖	a	23 04	23 33			00 04	00 34	01 04
London Bridge 4	a							

Sundays

1 July to 16 September

		FC	FC	FC	FC	FC	FC	FC	FC	FC	FC	EM	FC	EM	FC	FC	EM	EM	FC	FC	FC	EM	EM
		1	1	1		1	1	1	1		1	◇1	1	◇1		1	◇1	◇1	1		1	◇1	◇1
												A		B			B	A				B	A
Bedford 7	d	22p42	23p12	23p42	05 42	06 12	06 42	07 12	07 50		08 06	08 15	08 20	08 32		08 36	08 45	08 45	08 50		09 06	09 09	09 15
Flitwick	d	22p52	23p22	23p52	05 52	06 22	06 52	07 22	08 00		08 16		08 30			08 46			09 00		09 16		
Harlington	d	22p56	23p26	23p56	05 56	06 26	06 56	07 26	08 04		08 20		08 34			08 50			09 04		09 20		
Leagrave	d	23p02	23p32	00 02	06 02	06 32	07 02	07 32	08 10		08 26		08 40			08 56			09 10		09 26		
Luton 10	d	23p06	23p36	00 06	06 06	06 36	07 06	07 36	08 14	08 18	08 30	08 34	08 44	08 48	08 48	09 00			09 14	09 18	09 30	09 25	09 35
Luton Airport Parkway 7 ✈	d	23p09	23p39	00 09	06 09	06 39	07 09	07 39	08 17	08 21	08 33		08 47		08 51	09 03	09 01	09 06	09 17	09 21	09 33		
Harpenden	d	23p15	23p45	00 15	06 14	06 44	07 14	07 44	08 22	08 26	08 38		08 52		08 56	09 08			09 22	09 26	09 38		
St Albans City	d	23p21	23p51	00 21	06 21	06 51	07 21	07 51	08 29	08 33	08 45		08 59		09 03	09 15			09 29	09 33	09 45		
Radlett	d	23p26	23p56	00 26	06 26	06 56	07 26	07 56		08 38					09 08					09 38			
Elstree & Borehamwood	d	23p31	00 01	00 31	06 31	07 01	07 31	08 01		08 42					09 12					09 42			
Mill Hill Broadway	d	23p35	00 05	00 35	06 35	07 05	07 35	08 05		08 46					09 16					09 46			
Hendon	d	23p38	00 08	00 38	06 38	07 08	07 38	08 08		08 50					09 20					09 50			
Cricklewood	d	23p42	00 12	00 42	06 42	07 12	07 42	08 12		08 53					09 23					09 53			
West Hampstead Thameslink ⊖	d	23p44	00 14	00 44	06 44	07 14	07 44	08 14	08 44	08 56	08 59		09 14		09 26	09 29			09 44	09 56	09 59		
Kentish Town ⊖	a	23p50	00 20	00 50	06 50	07 20	07 49	08 19		09 00					09 30					10 00			
St Pancras International 15 ⊖	a				06 58							09 11		09 13			09 27	09 48				09 49	10 18
	d																						
St Pancras International 15 ⊖	a	23p53	00 23	00 53		07 24	07 53	08 23	08 52	09 05	09 08		09 22		09 35	09 38			09 52	10 05	10 08		
	d	23p54	00 24	00 54		07 24	07 54	08 24	08 54	09 05	09 09		09 24		09 35	09 39			09 54	10 05	10 09		
Farringdon 3 ⊖	d	23p59	00 29			07 29	07 59	08 29	08 58	09 10	09 14		09 29		09 40	09 44			09 58	10 10	10 14		
City Thameslink 3	d																						
London Blackfriars 3 ⊖	a	00 04	00 34	01 04		07 34	08 04	08 34	09 04	09 14	09 19		09 34		09 44	09 49			10 04	10 14	10 19		
London Bridge 4	a																						

A 16 September **B** not 16 September

Please refer to separate pages within this table for services operating between South London and Brighton

At weekends please use local bus and tube services to travel to/from St Pancras International and London Bridge when no trains are operating. See local publicity for details of alternative routes and services that are available across central London

Bedford, Luton, St Albans - London

Sundays

1 July to 16 September

Network Diagram - see first Page of Table 52

		FC	FC	FC	EM	EM	FC	FC	FC	EM	EM	FC	FC	FC	EM	EM	FC	FC	FC	EM	EM	FC	FC
		1		1	◇1	◇1	1		1	◇1	◇1	1		1	◇1	◇1	1		1	◇1	◇1	1	
					A	B				A	B				A	B				A	B		
Bedford 7	d	09 20		09 36	09 39	09 45	09 50		10 06	10 09	10 15	10 20		10 36	10 41	10 45	10 50		11 06	11 12	11 15	11 20	
Flitwick	d	09 30		09 46			10 00		10 16			10 30		10 46			11 00		11 16			11 30	
Harlington	d	09 34		09 50			10 04		10 20			10 34		10 50			11 04		11 20			11 34	
Leagrave	d	09 40		09 56			10 10		10 26			10 40		10 56			11 10		11 26			11 40	
Luton 10	d	09 44	09 48	10 00			10 14	10 18	10 30	10 25	10 35	10 44	10 48	11 00			11 14	11 18	11 30	11 28	11 35	11 44	11 48
Luton Airport Parkway 7 ✈	d	09 47	09 51	10 03	09 56	10 06	10 17	10 21	10 33			10 47	10 51	11 03	10 57	11 06	11 17	11 21	11 33			11 47	11 51
Harpenden	d	09 52	09 56	10 08			10 22	10 26	10 38			10 52	10 56	11 08			11 22	11 26	11 38			11 52	11 56
St Albans City	d	09 59	10 03	10 15			10 29	10 33	10 45			10 59	11 03	11 15			11 29	11 33	11 45			11 59	12 03
Radlett	d		10 08					10 38					11 08					11 38					12 08
Elstree & Borehamwood	d		10 12					10 42					11 12					11 42					12 12
Mill Hill Broadway	d		10 16					10 46					11 16					11 46					12 16
Hendon	d		10 20					10 50					11 20					11 50					12 20
Cricklewood	d		10 23					10 53					11 23					11 53					12 23
West Hampstead Thameslink ⊖	d	10 14	10 26	10 29			10 44	10 56	10 59			11 14	11 26	11 29			11 44	11 56	11 59			12 14	12 26
Kentish Town ⊖	a		10 30					11 00					11 30					12 00					12 30
St Pancras International 15 ⊖	a				10 20	10 48				10 51	11 18				11 23	11 48				11 51	12 18		
	d																						
St Pancras International 15 ⊖	a	10 22	10 35	10 38			10 52	11 05	11 08			11 22	11 35	11 38			11 52	12 05	12 08			12 22	12 35
	d	10 24	10 35	10 39			10 54	11 05	11 09			11 24	11 35	11 39			11 54	12 05	12 09			12 24	12 35
Farringdon 3 ⊖	d	10 29	10 40	10 44			10 58	11 10	11 14			11 29	11 40	11 44			11 58	12 10	12 14			12 29	12 40
City Thameslink 3	d																						
London Blackfriars 3 ⊖	a	10 34	10 44	10 49			11 04	11 14	11 19			11 34	11 44	11 49			12 04	12 14	12 19			12 34	12 44
London Bridge 4	a																						

		FC	EM	EM	FC	FC	FC	EM	EM	FC	FC	FC	EM	EM	FC	FC	FC	EM	EM	FC	FC	FC
		1	◇1	◇1	1		1	◇1	◇1	1		1	◇1	◇1	1		1	◇1	◇1	1		1
			A	B				A	B				A	B				A	B			
Bedford 7	d	11 36	11 41	11 45	11 50		12 06	12 11	12 15	12 20		12 36	12 42	12 45	12 50		13 06	13 11	13 15	13 20		13 36
Flitwick	d	11 46			12 00		12 16			12 30		12 46			13 00		13 16			13 30		13 46
Harlington	d	11 50			12 04		12 20			12 34		12 50			13 04		13 20			13 34		13 50
Leagrave	d	11 56			12 10		12 26			12 40		12 56			13 10		13 26			13 40		13 56
Luton 10	d	12 00			12 14	12 18	12 30	12 27	12 35	12 44	12 48	13 00			13 14	13 18	13 30	13 29	13 35	13 44	13 48	14 00
Luton Airport Parkway 7 ✈	d	12 03	11 58	12 06	12 17	12 21	12 33			12 47	12 51	13 03	12 58	13 06	13 17	13 21	13 33			13 47	13 51	14 03
Harpenden	d	12 08			12 22	12 26	12 38			12 52	12 56	13 08			13 22	13 26	13 38			13 52	13 56	14 08
St Albans City	d	12 15			12 29	12 33	12 45			12 59	13 03	13 15			13 29	13 33	13 45			13 59	14 03	14 15
Radlett	d					12 38					13 08					13 38					14 08	
Elstree & Borehamwood	d					12 42					13 12					13 42					14 12	
Mill Hill Broadway	d					12 46					13 16					13 46					14 16	
Hendon	d					12 50					13 20					13 50					14 20	
Cricklewood	d					12 53					13 23					13 53					14 23	
West Hampstead Thameslink ⊖	d	12 29			12 44	12 56	12 59			13 14	13 26	13 29			13 44	13 56	13 59			14 14	14 26	14 29
Kentish Town ⊖	a					13 00					13 30					14 00					14 30	
St Pancras International 15 ⊖	a		12 24	12 48				12 50	13 18				13 24	13 48				13 54	14 12			
	d																					
St Pancras International 15 ⊖	a	12 38			12 52	13 05	13 08			13 22	13 35	13 38			13 52	14 05	14 08			14 22	14 35	14 38
	d	12 39			12 54	13 05	13 09			13 24	13 35	13 39			13 54	14 05	14 09			14 24	14 35	14 39
Farringdon 3 ⊖	d	12 44			12 58	13 10	13 14			13 29	13 40	13 44			13 58	14 10	14 14			14 29	14 40	14 44
City Thameslink 3	d																					
London Blackfriars 3 ⊖	a	12 49			13 04	13 14	13 19			13 34	13 44	13 49			14 04	14 14	14 19			14 34	14 44	14 49
London Bridge 4	a																					

		EM	EM	FC	FC	FC	FC	EM	EM	EM	FC	FC	FC	EM	FC	FC	FC	EM	EM	FC	FC	EM	EM
		◇1	◇1	1		1	1	◇1	◇1	◇1		1	1	◇1		1	1	◇1	◇1		1	◇1	◇1
		A	B					A	A	B				B				B	A			A	B
Bedford 7	d	13 42	13 45	13 50		14 06	14 20	14 23	14 28	14 32		14 36	14 50	15 02		15 06	15 20	15 23	15 24		15 36	15 40	15 43
Flitwick	d			14 00		14 16	14 30					14 46	15 00			15 16	15 30				15 46		
Harlington	d			14 04		14 20	14 34					14 50	15 04			15 20	15 34				15 50		
Leagrave	d			14 10		14 26	14 40					14 56	15 10			15 26	15 40				15 56		
Luton 10	d			14 14	14 18	14 30	14 44	14 39		14 49	14 48	15 00	15 14		15 18	15 30	15 44	15 39	15 42	15 48	16 00		
Luton Airport Parkway 7 ✈	d	13 58	14 04	14 17	14 21	14 33	14 47		14 44		14 51	15 03	15 17	15 18	15 21	15 33	15 47			15 51	16 03	15 56	15 59
Harpenden	d			14 22	14 26	14 38	14 52				14 56	15 08	15 22		15 26	15 38	15 52			15 56	16 08		
St Albans City	d			14 29	14 33	14 45	14 59				15 03	15 15	15 29		15 33	15 45	15 59			16 03	16 15		
Radlett	d				14 38						15 08				15 38					16 08			
Elstree & Borehamwood	d				14 42						15 12				15 42					16 12			
Mill Hill Broadway	d				14 46						15 16				15 46					16 16			
Hendon	d				14 50						15 20				15 50					16 20			
Cricklewood	d				14 53						15 23				15 53					16 23			
West Hampstead Thameslink ⊖	d			14 44	14 56	14 59	15 14				15 26	15 29	15 44		15 56	15 59	16 14			16 26	16 29		
Kentish Town ⊖	a				15 00						15 30				16 00					16 30			
St Pancras International 15 ⊖	a	14 24	14 30					15 03	15 08	15 12				15 44				16 02	16 07			16 20	16 23
	d																						
St Pancras International 15 ⊖	a			14 52	15 05	15 08	15 22				15 35	15 38	15 52		16 05	16 08	16 22			16 35	16 38		
	d			14 54	15 05	15 09	15 24				15 35	15 39	15 54		16 05	16 09	16 24			16 35	16 39		
Farringdon 3 ⊖	d			14 58	15 10	15 14	15 29				15 40	15 44	15 58		16 10	16 14	16 29			16 40	16 44		
City Thameslink 3	d																						
London Blackfriars 3 ⊖	a			15 04	15 14	15 19	15 34				15 44	15 49	16 04		16 14	16 19	16 34			16 44	16 49		
London Bridge 4	a																						

A not 16 September **B** 16 September

Please refer to separate pages within this table for services operating between South London and Brighton

At weekends please use local bus and tube services to travel to/from St Pancras International and London Bridge when no trains are operating. See local publicity for details of alternative routes and services that are available across central London

Table 52

Sundays

1 July to 16 September

Bedford, Luton, St Albans - London

Network Diagram - see first Page of Table 52

		EM	FC	EM	FC	FC	FC	EM	FC	FC	EM	FC	EM	FC	FC	EM	FC	FC	FC	EM	FC	EM
		◇1 A ⌶	1	◇1 B ⌶		1	1	◇1 A ⌶		1	◇1 B ⌶	1	◇1 A ▭		1	◇1 B ▭	1		1	◇1 A ⌶	1	◇1 B ⌶
Bedford 7	d		15 50			16 06	16 20	16 24		16 36	16 41	16 50	17 02		17 06	17 16	17 20		17 36	17 42	17 50	17 53
Flitwick	d		16 00			16 16	16 30			16 46		17 00			17 16		17 30		17 46		18 00	
Harlington	d		16 04			16 20	16 34			16 50		17 04			17 20		17 34		17 50		18 04	
Leagrave	d		16 10			16 26	16 40			16 56		17 10			17 26		17 40		17 56		18 10	
Luton 10	d	16 00	16 14	16 14	16 18	16 30	16 44		16 48	17 00		17 14	17 19	17 18	17 30	17 33	17 44	17 48	18 00		18 14	
Luton Airport Parkway 7 ✈	d		16 17		16 21	16 33	16 47	16 42	16 51	17 03	16 58	17 17		17 21	17 33		17 47	17 51	18 03	17 59	18 17	18 10
Harpenden	d		16 22		16 26	16 38	16 52		16 56	17 08		17 22		17 26	17 38		17 52	17 56	18 08		18 22	
St Albans City	d		16 29		16 33	16 45	16 59		17 03	17 15		17 29		17 33	17 45		17 59	18 03	18 15		18 29	
Radlett	d				16 38				17 08					17 38				18 08				
Elstree & Borehamwood	d				16 42				17 12					17 42				18 12				
Mill Hill Broadway	d				16 46				17 16					17 46				18 16				
Hendon	d				16 50				17 20					17 50				18 20				
Cricklewood	d				16 53				17 23					17 53				18 23				
West Hampstead Thameslink ⊖	d		16 44		16 56	16 59	17 14		17 26	17 29		17 44		17 56	17 59		18 14	18 26	18 29		18 44	
Kentish Town ⊖	a				17 00				17 30					18 00				18 30				
St Pancras International 15 ⊖	a	16 24		16 37				17 07			17 21		17 45			17 59				18 22		18 33
	d																					
St Pancras International 15 ⊖	a		16 52		17 05	17 08	17 22		17 35	17 38		17 52		18 05	18 08		18 22	18 35	18 38		18 52	
	d		16 54		17 05	17 09	17 24		17 35	17 39		17 54		18 05	18 09		18 24	18 35	18 39		18 54	
Farringdon 3 ⊖	d		16 58		17 10	17 14	17 29		17 40	17 44		17 58		18 10	18 14		18 29	18 40	18 44		18 58	
City Thameslink 3	d																					
London Blackfriars 3 ⊖	a		17 04		17 14	17 19	17 34		17 44	17 49		18 04		18 14	18 19		18 34	18 44	18 49		19 04	
London Bridge 4	a																					

		FC	EM	EM	FC	FC	EM	FC	EM	FC	EM	EM	FC	FC	EM	FC	EM	EM	FC	FC	EM	EM	FC
			◇1 B ⌶	◇1 A ⌶	1		◇1 A ⌶	1	◇1 B ⌶		◇1 B ⌶	◇1 A ⌶	1		◇1 A ⌶	1	◇1 B ⌶	◇1 A ⌶		1	◇1 B ⌶	◇1 A ⌶	1
Bedford 7	d		18 09	18 10	18 20		18 39	18 50	18 54		19 08	19 11	19 20		19 38	19 50	19 54	20 01		20 12	20 20	20 27	20 42
Flitwick	d				18 30			19 00					19 30			20 00				20 22			20 52
Harlington	d				18 34			19 04					19 34			20 04				20 26			20 56
Leagrave	d				18 40			19 10					19 40			20 10				20 32			21 02
Luton 10	d	18 18	18 27	18 28	18 44	18 48		19 14		19 18	19 25	19 28	19 44	19 48		20 14		20 17	20 18	20 36	20 35		21 06
Luton Airport Parkway 7 ✈	d	18 21			18 47	18 51	18 56	19 17	19 11	19 21			19 47	19 51	19 55	20 17	20 10		20 21	20 39		20 43	21 09
Harpenden	d	18 26			18 52	18 56		19 22		19 26			19 52	19 56		20 22			20 26	20 44			21 14
St Albans City	d	18 33			18 59	19 03		19 29		19 33			19 59	20 03		20 29			20 33	20 51			21 21
Radlett	d	18 38				19 08				19 38				20 08					20 38	20 56			21 26
Elstree & Borehamwood	d	18 42				19 12				19 42				20 12					20 42	21 01			21 31
Mill Hill Broadway	d	18 46				19 16				19 46				20 16					20 46	21 05			21 35
Hendon	d	18 50				19 20				19 50				20 20					20 50	21 08			21 38
Cricklewood	d	18 53				19 23				19 53				20 23					20 53	21 12			21 42
West Hampstead Thameslink ⊖	d	18 56			19 14	19 26		19 44		19 56			20 14	20 26		20 44			20 56	21 14			21 44
Kentish Town ⊖	a	19 00				19 30				20 00				20 30					21 00	21 19			21 49
St Pancras International 15 ⊖	a		18 50	18 51			19 19		19 34		19 48	19 51			20 18		20 33	20 40			20 58	21 06	
	d																						
St Pancras International 15 ⊖	a	19 05			19 22	19 35		19 52		20 05			20 22	20 35		20 52			21 05	21 23			21 53
	d	19 05			19 24	19 35		19 54		20 05			20 24	20 35		20 54			21 05	21 24			21 54
Farringdon 3 ⊖	d	19 10			19 29	19 40		19 58		20 10			20 29	20 40		20 58			21 10	21 29			21 59
City Thameslink 3	d																						
London Blackfriars 3 ⊖	a	19 14			19 34	19 44		20 04		20 14			20 34	20 44		21 04			21 14	21 34			22 04
London Bridge 4	a																						

		EM	EM	FC	EM	EM	EM	FC	FC	EM	EM	EM	EM	FC	FC	FC
		◇1 B ⌶	◇1 A ⌶	1	◇1 B ⌶	◇1 A ⌶	◇1 B ⌶	1	1	◇1 A ⌶	◇1 B ⌶	◇1 A ⌶	◇1 B ⌶	1	1	1
Bedford 7	d	20 45	21 01	21 12	21 18	21 31	21 35	21 42	22 12	22 16	22 22	22 27	22 41	22 42	23 12	23 42
Flitwick	d			21 22				21 52	22 22					22 52	23 22	23 52
Harlington	d			21 26				21 56	22 26					22 56	23 26	23 56
Leagrave	d			21 32				22 02	22 32					23 02	23 32	00 02
Luton 10	d		21 17	21 36	21 34	21 47	21 51	22 06	22 36	22 32	22 40	22 43	22 59	23 06	23 36	00 06
Luton Airport Parkway 7 ✈	d	21 01		21 39				22 09	22 39					23 09	23 39	00 09
Harpenden	d			21 44				22 14	22 44					23 14	23 45	00 14
St Albans City	d			21 51				22 21	22 51					23 21	23 51	00 21
Radlett	d			21 56				22 26	22 56					23 26	23 56	00 26
Elstree & Borehamwood	d			22 01				22 31	23 01					23 31	00 01	00 31
Mill Hill Broadway	d			22 05				22 35	23 05					23 35	00 05	00 35
Hendon	d			22 08				22 38	23 08					23 38	00 08	00 38
Cricklewood	d			22 12				22 42	23 12					23 42	00 12	00 42
West Hampstead Thameslink ⊖	d			22 14				22 44	23 14					23 44	00 14	00 44
Kentish Town ⊖	a			22 19				22 49	23 19					23 49	00 20	00 49
St Pancras International 15 ⊖	a	21 24	21 40		21 57	22 13	22 17			22 56	23 06	23 07	23 28			
	d															
St Pancras International 15 ⊖	a			22 23				22 53	23 23					23 53	00 23	00 53
	d			22 24				22 54	23 24					23 54	00 24	00 54
Farringdon 3 ⊖	d			22 29				22 59	23 29					23 59	00 29	
City Thameslink 3	d															
London Blackfriars 3 ⊖	a			22 34				23 04	23 33					00 04	00 34	01 04
London Bridge 4	a															

A not 16 September

B 16 September

Please refer to separate pages within this table for services operating between South London and Brighton

At weekends please use local bus and tube services to travel to/from St Pancras International and London Bridge when no trains are operating. See local publicity for details of alternative routes and services that are available across central London

Table 52

Sundays

from 23 September

Bedford, Luton, St Albans - London

Network Diagram - see first Page of Table 52

		FC	FC	FC	FC	FC	FC	FC	FC	FC	FC	EM	FC	FC	FC	EM	FC	FC	FC	EM	FC	FC	FC
		1	1	1		1	1	1	1		1	◇1 ⌶	1		1	◇1 ⌶	1		1	◇1 ⌶	1		1
Bedford 7	d	22p42	23p12	23p42	05 42	06 12	06 42	07 12	07 50		08 06	08 15	08 20		08 36	08 45	08 50		09 06	09 15	09 20		09 36
Flitwick	d	22p52	23p22	23p52	05 52	06 22	06 52	07 22	08 00		08 16		08 30		08 46		09 00		09 16		09 30		09 46
Harlington	d	22p56	23p26	23p56	05 56	06 26	06 56	07 26	08 04		08 20		08 34		08 50		09 04		09 20		09 34		09 50
Leagrave	d	23p02	23p32	00 02	06 02	06 32	07 02	07 32	08 10		08 26		08 40		08 56		09 10		09 26		09 40		09 56
Luton 10	d	23p06	23p36	00 06	06 06	06 36	07 06	07 36	08 14	08 18	08 30	08 34	08 44	08 48	09 00		09 14	09 18	09 30	09 35	09 44	09 48	10 00
Luton Airport Parkway 7 ✈	d	23p09	23p39	00 09	06 09	06 39	07 09	07 39	08 17	08 21	08 33		08 47	08 51	09 03	09 06	09 17	09 21	09 33		09 47	09 51	10 03
Harpenden	d	23p15	23p45	00 15	06 14	06 44	07 14	07 44	08 22	08 26	08 38		08 52	08 56	09 08		09 22	09 26	09 38		09 52	09 56	10 08
St Albans City	d	23p21	23p51	00 21	06 21	06 51	07 21	07 51	08 29	08 33	08 45		08 59	09 03	09 15		09 29	09 33	09 45		09 59	10 03	10 15
Radlett	d	23p26	23p56	00 26	06 26	06 56	07 26	07 56		08 38				09 08				09 38				10 08	
Elstree & Borehamwood	d	23p31	00 01	00 31	06 31	07 01	07 31	08 01		08 42				09 12				09 42				10 12	
Mill Hill Broadway	d	23p35	00 05	00 35	06 35	07 05	07 35	08 05		08 46				09 16				09 46				10 16	
Hendon	d	23p38	00 08	00 38	06 38	07 08	07 38	08 08		08 50				09 20				09 50				10 20	
Cricklewood	d	23p42	00 12	00 42	06 42	07 12	07 42	08 12		08 53				09 23				09 53				10 23	
West Hampstead Thameslink ⊖	d	23p44	00 14	00 44	06 44	07 14	07 44	08 14	08 44	08 56	08 59		09 14	09 26	09 29		09 44	09 56	09 59		10 14	10 26	10 29
Kentish Town ⊖	a	23p50	00 20	00 50	06 50	07 20	07 49	08 19		09 00				09 30				10 00				10 30	
St Pancras International 15 ⊖	a				06 58							09 11				09 48				10 18			
	d																						
St Pancras International 15 ⊖	a	23p53	00 23	00 53		07 24	07 53	08 23	08 52	09 05	09 08		09 22	09 35	09 38		09 52	10 05	10 08		10 22	10 35	10 38
	d	23p54	00 24	00 54		07 24	07 54	08 24	08 54	09 05	09 09		09 24	09 35	09 39		09 54	10 05	10 09		10 24	10 35	10 39
Farringdon 3 ⊖	d	23p59	00 29			07 29	07 59	08 29	08 58	09 10	09 14		09 29	09 40	09 44		09 58	10 10	10 14		10 29	10 40	10 44
City Thameslink 3	d																						
London Blackfriars 3 ⊖	a	00 04	00 34	01 04		07 34	08 04	08 34	09 04	09 14	09 19		09 34	09 44	09 49		10 04	10 14	10 19		10 34	10 44	10 49
London Bridge 4	a																						

		EM	FC	FC	FC	EM	FC	FC	FC	EM	FC	FC	FC	EM	FC	FC	FC	EM	FC	FC	FC	EM	FC
		◇1 ⌶	1		1	◇1 ⌶	1		1	◇1 ⌶	1		1	◇1 ⌶	1		1	◇1 ⌶	1		1	◇1 ⌶	1
Bedford 7	d	09 45	09 50		10 06	10 15	10 20		10 36	10 45	10 50		11 06	11 15	11 20		11 36	11 45	11 50		12 06	12 15	12 20
Flitwick	d		10 00		10 16		10 30		10 46		11 00		11 16		11 30		11 46		12 00		12 16		12 30
Harlington	d		10 04		10 20		10 34		10 50		11 04		11 20		11 34		11 50		12 04		12 20		12 34
Leagrave	d		10 10		10 26		10 40		10 56		11 10		11 26		11 40		11 56		12 10		12 26		12 40
Luton 10	d		10 14	10 18	10 30	10 35	10 44	10 48	11 00		11 14	11 18	11 30	11 35	11 44	11 48	12 00		12 14	12 18	12 30	12 35	12 44
Luton Airport Parkway 7 ✈	d	10 06	10 17	10 21	10 33		10 47	10 51	11 03	11 06	11 17	11 21	11 33		11 47	11 51	12 03	12 06	12 17	12 21	12 33		12 47
Harpenden	d		10 22	10 26	10 38		10 52	10 56	11 08		11 22	11 26	11 38		11 52	11 56	12 08		12 22	12 26	12 38		12 52
St Albans City	d		10 29	10 33	10 45		10 59	11 03	11 15		11 29	11 33	11 45		11 59	12 03	12 15		12 29	12 33	12 45		12 59
Radlett	d			10 38				11 08				11 38				12 08				12 38			
Elstree & Borehamwood	d			10 42				11 12				11 42				12 12				12 42			
Mill Hill Broadway	d			10 46				11 16				11 46				12 16				12 46			
Hendon	d			10 50				11 20				11 50				12 20				12 50			
Cricklewood	d			10 53				11 23				11 53				12 23				12 53			
West Hampstead Thameslink ⊖	d		10 44	10 56	10 59		11 14	11 26	11 29		11 44	11 56	11 59		12 14	12 26	12 29		12 44	12 56	12 59		13 14
Kentish Town ⊖	a			11 00				11 30				12 00				12 30				13 00			
St Pancras International 15 ⊖	a	10 48				11 18				11 48				12 18				12 48				13 18	
	d																						
St Pancras International 15 ⊖	a		10 52	11 05	11 08		11 22	11 35	11 38		11 52	12 05	12 08		12 22	12 35	12 38		12 52	13 05	13 08		13 22
	d		10 54	11 05	11 09		11 24	11 35	11 39		11 54	12 05	12 09		12 24	12 35	12 39		12 54	13 05	13 09		13 24
Farringdon 3 ⊖	d		10 58	11 10	11 14		11 29	11 40	11 44		11 58	12 10	12 14		12 29	12 40	12 44		12 58	13 10	13 14		13 29
City Thameslink 3	d																						
London Blackfriars 3 ⊖	a		11 04	11 14	11 19		11 34	11 44	11 49		12 04	12 14	12 19		12 34	12 44	12 49		13 04	13 14	13 19		13 34
London Bridge 4	a																						

		FC	FC	EM	FC	FC	FC	EM	FC	FC	FC	EM	FC	FC	FC	FC	EM	EM	FC	FC	FC	EM
			1	◇1 ▭	1		1	◇1 ▭	1		1	◇1 ⌶	1		1	1	◇1 A ⌶	◇1 B ⌶		1	1	◇1 A ⌶
Bedford 7	d		12 36	12 45	12 50		13 06	13 15	13 20		13 36	13 45	13 50		14 06	14 20	14 23	14 32		14 36	14 50	15 00
Flitwick	d		12 46		13 00		13 16		13 30		13 46		14 00		14 16	14 30				14 46	15 00	
Harlington	d		12 50		13 04		13 20		13 34		13 50		14 04		14 20	14 34				14 50	15 04	
Leagrave	d		12 56		13 10		13 26		13 40		13 56		14 10		14 26	14 40				14 56	15 10	
Luton 10	d	12 48	13 00		13 14	13 18	13 30	13 35	13 44	13 48	14 00		14 14	14 18	14 30	14 44	14 39	14 49	14 48	15 00	15 14	
Luton Airport Parkway 7 ✈	d	12 51	13 03	13 06	13 17	13 21	13 33		13 47	13 51	14 03	14 04	14 17	14 21	14 33	14 47			14 51	15 03	15 17	15 16
Harpenden	d	12 56	13 08		13 22	13 26	13 38		13 52	13 56	14 08		14 22	14 26	14 38	14 52			14 56	15 08	15 22	
St Albans City	d	13 03	13 15		13 29	13 33	13 45		13 59	14 03	14 15		14 29	14 33	14 45	14 59			15 03	15 15	15 29	
Radlett	d	13 08				13 38				14 08				14 38					15 08			
Elstree & Borehamwood	d	13 12				13 42				14 12				14 42					15 12			
Mill Hill Broadway	d	13 16				13 46				14 16				14 46					15 16			
Hendon	d	13 20				13 50				14 20				14 50					15 20			
Cricklewood	d	13 23				13 53				14 23				14 53					15 23			
West Hampstead Thameslink ⊖	d	13 26	13 29		13 44	13 56	13 59		14 14	14 26	14 29		14 44	14 56	14 59	15 14			15 26	15 29	15 44	
Kentish Town ⊖	a	13 30				14 00				14 30				15 00					15 30			
St Pancras International 15 ⊖	a			13 48				14 12				14 30					15 03	15 12				15 42
	d																					
St Pancras International 15 ⊖	a	13 35	13 38		13 52	14 05	14 08		14 22	14 35	14 38		14 52	15 05	15 08	15 22			15 35	15 38	15 52	
	d	13 35	13 39		13 54	14 05	14 09		14 24	14 35	14 39		14 54	15 05	15 09	15 24			15 35	15 39	15 54	
Farringdon 3 ⊖	d	13 40	13 44		13 58	14 10	14 14		14 29	14 40	14 44		14 58	15 10	15 14	15 29			15 40	15 44	15 58	
City Thameslink 3	d																					
London Blackfriars 3 ⊖	a	13 44	13 49		14 04	14 14	14 19		14 34	14 44	14 49		15 04	15 14	15 19	15 34			15 44	15 49	16 04	
London Bridge 4	a																					

A from 28 October

B from 23 September until 21 October

Please refer to separate pages within this table for services operating between South London and Brighton

At weekends please use local bus and tube services to travel to/from St Pancras International and London Bridge when no trains are operating. See local publicity for details of alternative routes and services that are available across central London

Bedford, Luton, St Albans - London

Sundays from 23 September

Network Diagram - see first Page of Table 52

		EM ◇1 A	FC	FC 1	FC 1	EM ◇1	FC	FC 1	EM ◇1 B	EM ◇1 A	FC 1	EM ◇1 A	EM ◇1 B	FC	FC 1	FC 1	FC	FC 1	EM ◇1 B	EM ◇1 A	FC 1	FC	FC 1
Bedford 7	d	15 02		15 06	15 20	15 23		15 36	15 41	15 43	15 50				16 06	16 20		16 36	16 39	16 41	16 50		17 06
Flitwick	d			15 16	15 30			15 46			16 00				16 16	16 30		16 46			17 00		17 16
Harlington	d			15 20	15 34			15 50			16 04				16 20	16 34		16 50			17 04		17 20
Leagrave	d			15 26	15 40			15 56			16 10				16 26	16 40		16 56			17 10		17 26
Luton 10	d		15 18	15 30	15 44	15 39	15 48	16 00			16 14	16 14	16 17	16 18	16 30	16 44	16 48	17 00			17 14	17 18	17 30
Luton Airport Parkway 7 ✈	d	15 18	15 21	15 33	15 47		15 51	16 03	15 57	15 59	16 17			16 21	16 33	16 47	16 51	17 03	16 56	16 58	17 17	17 21	17 33
Harpenden	d		15 26	15 38	15 52		15 56	16 08			16 22			16 26	16 38	16 52	16 56	17 08			17 22	17 26	17 38
St Albans City	d		15 33	15 45	15 59		16 03	16 15			16 29			16 33	16 45	16 59	17 03	17 15			17 29	17 33	17 45
Radlett	d		15 38				16 08							16 38			17 08					17 38	
Elstree & Borehamwood	d		15 42				16 12							16 42			17 12					17 42	
Mill Hill Broadway	d		15 46				16 16							16 46			17 16					17 46	
Hendon	d		15 50				16 20							16 50			17 20					17 50	
Cricklewood	d		15 53				16 23							16 53			17 23					17 53	
West Hampstead Thameslink ⊖	d		15 56	15 59	16 14		16 26	16 29			16 44			16 56	16 59	17 14	17 26	17 29			17 44	17 56	17 59
Kentish Town ⊖	a		16 00				16 30							17 00			17 30					18 00	
St Pancras International 15 ⊖	a	15 44				16 02			16 21	16 23		16 37	16 40						17 19	17 21			
	d																						
St Pancras International 15 ⊖	a		16 05	16 08	16 22		16 35	16 38			16 52			17 05	17 08	17 22	17 35	17 38			17 52	18 05	18 08
	d		16 05	16 09	16 24		16 35	16 39			16 54			17 05	17 09	17 24	17 35	17 39			17 54	18 05	18 09
Farringdon 3 ⊖	d		16 10	16 14	16 29		16 40	16 44			16 58			17 10	17 14	17 29	17 40	17 44			17 58	18 10	18 14
City Thameslink 3	d																						
London Blackfriars 3 ⊖	a		16 14	16 19	16 34		16 44	16 49			17 04			17 14	17 19	17 34	17 44	17 49			18 04	18 14	18 19
London Bridge 4	a																						

		EM ◇1	FC 1	FC	FC 1	FC 1	EM ◇1 B	EM ◇1 A	FC	EM ◇1 B	EM ◇1 A	FC 1	FC	FC 1	EM ◇1	FC	EM ◇1	FC 1	FC	FC 1	EM ◇1 B	EM ◇1 A
Bedford 7	d	17 16	17 20		17 36	17 50	17 52	17 53		18 07	18 09	18 20		18 50	18 54		19 08	19 20		19 50	19 53	19 54
Flitwick	d		17 30		17 46	18 00						18 30		19 00				19 30		20 00		
Harlington	d		17 34		17 50	18 04						18 34		19 04				19 34		20 04		
Leagrave	d		17 40		17 56	18 10						18 40		19 10				19 40		20 10		
Luton 10	d	17 33	17 44	17 48	18 00	18 14			18 18	18 25	18 27	18 44	18 48	19 14		19 18	19 25	19 44	19 48	20 14		
Luton Airport Parkway 7 ✈	d		17 47	17 51	18 03	18 17	18 09	18 10	18 21			18 47	18 51	19 17	19 11	19 21		19 47	19 51	20 17	20 09	20 10
Harpenden	d		17 52	17 56	18 08	18 22			18 26			18 52	18 56	19 22		19 26		19 52	19 56	20 22		
St Albans City	d		17 59	18 03	18 15	18 29			18 33			18 59	19 03	19 29		19 33		19 59	20 03	20 29		
Radlett	d			18 08					18 38				19 08			19 38			20 08			
Elstree & Borehamwood	d			18 12					18 42				19 12			19 42			20 12			
Mill Hill Broadway	d			18 16					18 46				19 16			19 46			20 16			
Hendon	d			18 20					18 50				19 20			19 50			20 20			
Cricklewood	d			18 23					18 53				19 23			19 53			20 23			
West Hampstead Thameslink ⊖	d		18 14	18 26	18 29	18 44			18 56			19 14	19 26	19 44		19 56		20 14	20 26	20 44		
Kentish Town ⊖	a			18 30					19 00				19 30			20 00			20 30			
St Pancras International 15 ⊖	a	17 59					18 32	18 33		18 48	18 50				19 34		19 48				20 32	20 33
	d																					
St Pancras International 15 ⊖	a		18 22	18 35	18 38	18 52			19 05			19 22	19 35	19 52		20 05		20 22	20 35	20 52		
	d		18 24	18 35	18 39	18 54			19 05			19 24	19 35	19 54		20 05		20 24	20 35	20 54		
Farringdon 3 ⊖	d		18 29	18 40	18 44	18 58			19 10			19 29	19 40	19 58		20 10		20 29	20 40	20 58		
City Thameslink 3	d																					
London Blackfriars 3 ⊖	a		18 34	18 44	18 49	19 04			19 14			19 34	19 44	20 04		20 14		20 34	20 44	21 04		
London Bridge 4	a																					

		FC	FC 1	EM ◇1	FC 1	EM ◇1	FC 1	EM ◇1 B	EM ◇1 A	EM ◇1 B	EM ◇1 A	FC 1	FC 1	EM ◇1 B	EM ◇1 A	EM ◇1 B	EM ◇1 A	FC 1	FC 1	FC 1
Bedford 7	d		20 12	20 20	20 42	20 45	21 12	21 16	21 18	21 33	21 35	21 42	22 12	22 22	22 22	22 39	22 41	22 42	23 12	23 42
Flitwick	d		20 22		20 52		21 22					21 52	22 22					22 52	23 22	23 52
Harlington	d		20 26		20 56		21 26					21 56	22 26					22 56	23 26	23 56
Leagrave	d		20 32		21 02		21 32					22 02	22 32					23 02	23 32	00 02
Luton 10	d	20 18	20 36	20 35	21 06		21 36	21 32	21 34	21 49	21 51	22 06	22 36	22 38	22 40	22 57	22 59	23 06	23 36	00 06
Luton Airport Parkway 7 ✈	d	20 21	20 39		21 09	21 01	21 39					22 09	22 39					23 09	23 39	00 09
Harpenden	d	20 26	20 44		21 14		21 44					22 14	22 44					23 14	23 45	00 14
St Albans City	d	20 33	20 51		21 21		21 51					22 21	22 51					23 21	23 51	00 21
Radlett	d	20 38	20 56		21 26		21 56					22 26	22 56					23 26	23 56	00 26
Elstree & Borehamwood	d	20 42	21 01		21 31		22 01					22 31	23 01					23 31	00 01	00 31
Mill Hill Broadway	d	20 46	21 05		21 35		22 05					22 35	23 05					23 35	00 05	00 35
Hendon	d	20 50	21 08		21 38		22 08					22 38	23 08					23 38	00 08	00 38
Cricklewood	d	20 53	21 12		21 42		22 12					22 42	23 12					23 42	00 12	00 42
West Hampstead Thameslink ⊖	d	20 56	21 14		21 44		22 14					22 44	23 14					23 44	00 14	00 44
Kentish Town ⊖	a	21 00	21 19		21 49		22 19					22 49	23 19					23 49	00 20	00 49
St Pancras International 15 ⊖	a			20 58		21 24		21 55	21 57	22 15	22 17			23 05	23 06	23 26	23 28			
	d																			
St Pancras International 15 ⊖	a	21 05	21 23		21 53		22 23					22 53	23 23					23 53	00 23	00 53
	d	21 05	21 24		21 54		22 24					22 54	23 24					23 54	00 24	00 54
Farringdon 3 ⊖	d	21 10	21 29		21 59		22 29					22 59	23 29					23 59	00 29	
City Thameslink 3	d																			
London Blackfriars 3 ⊖	a	21 14	21 34		22 04		22 34					23 04	23 33					00 04	00 34	01 04
London Bridge 4	a																			

A from 23 September until 21 October

B from 28 October

Please refer to separate pages within this table for services operating between South London and Brighton

At weekends please use local bus and tube services to travel to/from St Pancras International and London Bridge when no trains are operating. See local publicity for details of alternative routes and services that are available across central London

South London, Gatwick Airport - Brighton

Saturdays

Network Diagram - see first Page of Table 52

		FC 1 A	SE B	FC C	FC 1 D	FC 1 A	FC D	FC 1 D	SE B	FC C	SE E	FC D
St Pancras International 15 ⊖	d	22p54		23p06		23p24				23p36		
Farringdon 3 ⊖	d	22p59		23p10		23p29				23p40		
City Thameslink 3	d	23p03										
London Blackfriars 3 ⊖	a	23p05		23p16		23p34				23p46		
	d	23p05	23p12	23p16		23p35			23p42	23p46		
Elephant & Castle ⊖	d		23p16	23p19					23p46	23p49		
Loughborough Jn.	d			23b23								
Herne Hill 4	d			23p27						23p57		
Denmark Hill 4	d		23p22						23p52		23p52	
Peckham Rye 4	d		23p25						23p55		23p55	
Nunhead 4	d		23p27						23p57		23p57	
Crofton Park	d		23p30						23p59		23p59	
Catford	d		23p33						00 03		00 03	
Bellingham	d		23p35						00 05		00 05	
Beckenham Hill	d		23p37						00 07		00 07	
Ravensbourne	d		23p39						00 09		00 09	
Shortlands	d		23p41						00 11		00 11	
Bromley South 4	d		23p44						00 14		00 14	
Bickley 4	d		23p47						00 17		00a17	
St Mary Cray	d		23p51						00 21			
Swanley 4	d		23p56						00 26			
Eynsford	d		23p59						00 30			
Shoreham (Kent)	d		00 04						00 34			
Otford 4	d		00 07						00 37			
Bat & Ball	d		00 10						00 40			
Sevenoaks 4	a		00 13						00 43			
London Bridge 4	a											
	d				23p12		23p29	23p42				23p59
Tulse Hill 3	d			23p31			23p41			00 01		00 09
Streatham 4	d			23p35			23p45			00 05		00 13
Mitcham Eastfields	d											
Mitcham Junction	d											
Hackbridge	d											
Carshalton	d											
Tooting	d			23p40			23p50			00 10		00 18
Haydons Road	d			23p43			23p53			00 13		00 21
Wimbledon 6 ⊖	d			23p49			23p57			00 19		00 25
Wimbledon Chase	d			23p52			00 01			00 22		00 28
South Merton	d			23p54			00 03			00 24		00 30
Morden South	d			23p56			00 05			00 26		00 32
St Helier	d			23p58			00 07			00 28		00 34
Sutton Common	d			00 01			00 09			00 30		00 36
West Sutton	d			00 04			00 12			00 33		00 39
Sutton (Surrey) 4	a			00 09			00 15			00 39		00 43
East Croydon	d	23p25			23p25	23p57		23p57				
Redhill	d											
Gatwick Airport 10 ✈	d	23p41			23p41	00 19		00 19				
Three Bridges 4	d	23p47			23p47	00a24		00a24				
Balcombe	d	23p53			23p53							
Haywards Heath 3	d	23p59			23p59							
Wivelsfield 4	d	00 03			00 03							
Burgess Hill 4	d	00 05			00 05							
Hassocks 4	d	00 08			00 08							
Preston Park	d	00 15			00 15							
Brighton 10	a	00 19			00 19							

		SN F	FC D	FC 1 A	FC D	SN	FC D	FC 1 A	SN G	FC D	FC D	FC 1 A
St Pancras International 15 ⊖	d		23p42	23p54			00 12	00 24			00 30	00 54
Farringdon 3 ⊖	d		23p47	23p59			00 17	00 29			00 35	00 59
City Thameslink 3	d											
London Blackfriars 3 ⊖	a		23p52	00 04			00 22	00 34			00 40	01 04
	d		23p52	00 05			00 22	00 35			00 40	01 05
Elephant & Castle ⊖	d											
Loughborough Jn.	d											
Herne Hill 4	d											
Denmark Hill 4	d											
Peckham Rye 4	d											
Nunhead 4	d											
Crofton Park	d											
Catford	d											
Bellingham	d											
Beckenham Hill	d											
Ravensbourne	d											
Shortlands	d											
Bromley South 4	d											
Bickley 4	d											
St Mary Cray	d											
Swanley 4	d											
Eynsford	d											
Shoreham (Kent)	d											
Otford 4	d											
Bat & Ball	d											
Sevenoaks 4	a											
London Bridge 4	a		00 07				00 37				00 55	
	d	00 06			00 12	00 36				00 42		
Tulse Hill 3	d											
Streatham 4	d											
Mitcham Eastfields	d								00 38			
Mitcham Junction	d								00 41			
Hackbridge	d								00 45			
Carshalton	d								00 47			
Tooting	d											
Haydons Road	d											
Wimbledon 6 ⊖	d											
Wimbledon Chase	d											
South Merton	d											
Morden South	d											
St Helier	d											
Sutton Common	d											
West Sutton	d											
Sutton (Surrey) 4	a								00 51			
East Croydon	d	00a33		00 27	00 27	01a03		00 57		00 57		01 32
Redhill	d											
Gatwick Airport 10 ✈	d			00 49	00 50			01 22		01 22		01 52
Three Bridges 4	d			00a54	00a55			01a28		01a28		01a58
Balcombe	d											
Haywards Heath 3	d											
Wivelsfield 4	d											
Burgess Hill 4	d											
Hassocks 4	d											
Preston Park	d											
Brighton 10	a											

A not 19 May. From Bedford

B not 19 May

C not 19 May. From Luton

D 19 May

E 19 May. From London Victoria to Orpington

F To Caterham

G From London Victoria

b Previous night, stops to set down only

Please refer to separate pages within this table for services operating between Bedford and London

At weekends please use local bus and tube services to travel to/from St Pancras International and London Bridge when no trains are operating. See local publicity for details of alternative routes and services that are available across central London

South London, Gatwick Airport - Brighton

Network Diagram - see first Page of Table 52

		FC	FC	SE	SE	FC	FC	FC	FC	FC	FC	FC	FC	FC	FC	FC	FC	FC	FC	FC	FC	FC	FC
		1				1		1	1		1	1		1	1		1	1	1		1	1	
		A	A	B	C	A	A	D	A	A	D	A	A	A		A	A	D	A	A	D	A	A
			bus				bus			bus			bus			bus				bus			bus
St Pancras International ⊖	d		01 00				01 30	01 54		02 30	02 54		03 00		03 28	03 30		03 54		04 00	04 24		04 30
Farringdon ⊖	d																						
City Thameslink	d																						
London Blackfriars ⊖	a		01 10				01 40	02 04		02 40	03 04		03 10		03 38	03 40		04 04		04 10	04 34		04 40
	d		01 10				01 40	02 05		02 40	03 05		03 10		03 39	03 40		04 05		04 10	04 35		04 40
Elephant & Castle ⊖	d																						
Loughborough Jn.	d																						
Herne Hill	d																						
Denmark Hill	d				01 06																		
Peckham Rye	d			01s08	01 08																		
Nunhead	d			01s10	01 11																		
Crofton Park	d			01s13	01 14																		
Catford	d			01s16	01 16																		
Bellingham	d			01s18	01 19																		
Beckenham Hill	d			01s20	01 21																		
Ravensbourne	d			01s22	01 23																		
Shortlands	d				01 25																		
Bromley South	d			01s25	01 28																		
Bickley	d				01a30																		
St Mary Cray	d																						
Swanley	d																						
Eynsford	d																						
Shoreham (Kent)	d																						
Otford	d																						
Bat & Ball	d																						
Sevenoaks	a																						
London Bridge	a		01 25				01 55			02 55			03 25			03 55				04 25			04 55
	d	01 05				01 35			02 05			03 05		03 35			04 05		04 05			04 35	
Tulse Hill	d																						
Streatham	d																						
Mitcham Eastfields	d																						
Mitcham Junction	d																						
Hackbridge	d																						
Carshalton	d																						
Tooting	d																						
Haydons Road	d																						
Wimbledon ⊖	d																						
Wimbledon Chase	d																						
South Merton	d																						
Morden South	d																						
St Helier	d																						
Sutton Common	d																						
West Sutton	d																						
Sutton (Surrey)	a																						
East Croydon	d	01 31				02 02		02 32	02 32		03 32	03 32		04 02	04 04		04 31	04 32	04 32		05 02	05 02	
Redhill	d																						
Gatwick Airport ✈	d	01 52				02 22		02 52	02 52		03 52	03 52		04 24	04 24		04 51	04 52	04 52		05 22	05 22	
Three Bridges	d	01a58				02a28		02a58	02a58		03a58	03a58		04a30	04a30		04a58	04a58	04a58		05 27	05 27	
Balcombe	d																				05 33	05 33	
Haywards Heath	d																				05 39	05 39	
Wivelsfield	d																				05 43	05 43	
Burgess Hill	d																				05 45	05 45	
Hassocks	d																				05 48	05 48	
Preston Park	d																				05 55	05 55	
Brighton	a																				05 59	05 59	

A 19 May
B 1 September, 8 September. From London Victoria to Orpington
C 28 July, 4 August, 11 August. From London Victoria to Orpington
D not 19 May. From Bedford

Please refer to separate pages within this table for services operating between Bedford and London

At weekends please use local bus and tube services to travel to/from St Pancras International and London Bridge when no trains are operating. See local publicity for details of alternative routes and services that are available across central London

South London, Gatwick Airport - Brighton

Network Diagram - see first Page of Table 52

		FC	FC	FC	FC	FC	FC	FC	FC	SE	FC	FC	SE	FC	FC	SN	SE	FC	SN	SE	FC	SN
		1	1		1		1		1					1	1			1			1	
		A	B	B	B	B	A	C	A	D		E	F	B	A	G	D	B	H	F	B	I
				bus		bus																
St Pancras International ⊖	d	04 54		05 00		05 30	05 34	05 48	05 54			06 18			06 24							
Farringdon ⊖	d	04 59		05 05		05 35	05 39	05 53	05 59			06 23			06 29							
City Thameslink	d																					
London Blackfriars ⊖	a	05 04		05 10		05 40	05 44	05 59	06 04			06 29			06 34							
	d	05 04		05 10		05 40	05 45	06 00	06 05	06 12	06 16	06 30			06 35		06 42					
Elephant & Castle ⊖	d							06 03		06 16	06 19	06 33					06 46					
Loughborough Jn.	d																					
Herne Hill	d							06 11			06 27	06 41										
Denmark Hill	d									06 22			06 22				06 52			06 52		
Peckham Rye	d									06 25			06 25				06 55			06 55		
Nunhead	d									06 27			06 27				06 57			06 57		
Crofton Park	d									06 30			06 30				07 00			07 00		
Catford	d									06 33			06 33				07 03			07 03		
Bellingham	d									06 35			06 35				07 05			07 05		
Beckenham Hill	d									06 37			06 37				07 07			07 07		
Ravensbourne	d									06 39			06 39				07 09			07 09		
Shortlands	d									06 41			06 41				07 11			07 11		
Bromley South	d									06 44			06 44				07 14			07 14		
Bickley	d									06 47			06 47				07 17			07 17		
St Mary Cray	d									06 51			06 51				07 21			07 21		
Swanley	d									06 56			06 56				07 26			07 26		
Eynsford	d									07 00			07 00				07 30			07 30		
Shoreham (Kent)	d									07 04			07 04				07 34			07 34		
Otford	d									07 07			07 07				07 37			07 37		
Bat & Ball	d									07 10			07 10				07 40			07 40		
Sevenoaks	a									07 13			07 13				07 43			07 43		
London Bridge	a			05 25		05 55																
	d		05 05		05 52									06 27		06 36		06 42	06 50		06 57	
Tulse Hill	d							06 16			06 31	06 46										
Streatham	d							06 20			06 35	06 50										
Mitcham Eastfields	d							06 24				06 54										07 06
Mitcham Junction	d							06 27				06 57										07 09
Hackbridge	d							06 30				07 00										07 13
Carshalton	d							06 33				07 03										07 15
Tooting	d										06 40											
Haydons Road	d										06 43											
Wimbledon ⊖	d										06 47											
Wimbledon Chase	d										06 50											
South Merton	d										06 52											
Morden South	d										06 54											
St Helier	d										06 56											
Sutton Common	d										06 58											
West Sutton	d										07 01											
Sutton (Surrey)	a							06 36			07 05	07 06										07 19
East Croydon	d	05 32	05 32		06 05		06 05		06 25					06 41	06 55	07a03		06 55	07a06		07 11	
Redhill	d																					
Gatwick Airport ✈	d	05 54	05 54		06 20		06 20		06 41					06 57	07 11			07 11			07 27	
Three Bridges	d	06 00	06 00		06 25		06 25		06 45					07 02	07 15			07 15			07 32	
Balcombe	d	06 06	06 06		06 31		06 31								07 21			07 21				
Haywards Heath	d	06 11	06 11		06 37		06 37		06 55					07 11	07 27			07 27			07 41	
Wivelsfield	d	06 15	06 15		06 41		06 41		06 59						07 31			07 31				
Burgess Hill	d	06 17	06 17		06 43		06 43		07 01						07 33			07 33				
Hassocks	d	06 21	06 21		06 46		06 46		07 04						07 36			07 36				
Preston Park	d	06 27	06 27		06 53		06 53		07 11						07 43			07 43				
Brighton	a	06 31	06 31		06 57		06 57		07 15					07 25	07 47			07 47			07 55	

A From Bedford
B 19 May
C From West Hampstead Thameslink
D not 19 May
E From Luton
F 19 May. From London Victoria
G To Caterham
H To Tattenham Corner
I From London Victoria to Dorking

Please refer to separate pages within this table for services operating between Bedford and London

At weekends please use local bus and tube services to travel to/from St Pancras International and London Bridge when no trains are operating. See local publicity for details of alternative routes and services that are available across central London

South London, Gatwick Airport - Brighton

Network Diagram - see first Page of Table 52

		FC A	FC 1 B	FC C	FC 1 B	SN D	SE E	SN F	SE G	FC 1 H	SN I	FC A	FC 1 B	FC C	FC 1 B	SN D	SE E	SN F	SE G	FC 1 H	SN I	FC A	FC 1 B
St Pancras International 15 ⊖	d	06 34	06 39	06 48	06 54							07 04	07 09	07 18	07 24							07 34	07 39
Farringdon 3 ⊖	d	06 39	06 44	06 53	06 59							07 09	07 14	07 23	07 29							07 39	07 44
City Thameslink 3	d																						
London Blackfriars 3 ⊖	a	06 45	06 49	06 59	07 04							07 15	07 19	07 29	07 34							07 45	07 49
	d	06 46	06 50	07 00	07 05		07 12					07 16	07 20	07 30	07 35		07 42					07 46	07 50
Elephant & Castle ⊖	d	06 49		07 03			07 16					07 19		07 33			07 46					07 49	
Loughborough Jn.	d	06 53		07 07								07 23		07 37								07 53	
Herne Hill 4	d	06 57		07 11								07 27		07 41								07 57	
Denmark Hill 4	d						07 22		07 22								07 52		07 52				
Peckham Rye 4	d						07 25		07 25								07 55		07 55				
Nunhead 4	d						07 27		07 27								07 57		07 57				
Crofton Park	d						07 30		07 30								08 00		08 00				
Catford	d						07 33		07 33								08 03		08 03				
Bellingham	d						07 35		07 35								08 05		08 05				
Beckenham Hill	d						07 37		07 37								08 07		08 07				
Ravensbourne	d						07 39		07 39								08 09		08 09				
Shortlands	d						07 41		07 41								08 11		08 11				
Bromley South 4	d						07 44		07 44								08 14		08 14				
Bickley 4	d						07 47		07 47								08 17		08 17				
St Mary Cray	d						07 51		07 51								08 21		08 21				
Swanley 4	d						07 56		07 56								08 26		08 26				
Eynsford	d						08 00		08 00								08 30		08 30				
Shoreham (Kent)	d						08 04		08 04								08 34		08 34				
Otford 4	d						08 07		08 07								08 37		08 37				
Bat & Ball	d						08 10		08 10								08 40		08 40				
Sevenoaks 4	a						08 13		08 13								08 43		08 43				
London Bridge 4	a																						
	d					07 06		07 20		07 27						07 36		07 50		07 57			
Tulse Hill 3	d	07 01		07 16								07 31		07 46								08 01	
Streatham 4	d	07 05		07 20								07 35		07 50								08 05	
Mitcham Eastfields	d			07 24							07 36			07 54							08 06		
Mitcham Junction	d			07 27							07 39			07 57							08 09		
Hackbridge	d			07 30							07 43			08 00							08 13		
Carshalton	d			07 33							07 45			08 03							08 15		
Tooting	d	07 10										07 40										08 10	
Haydons Road	d	07 13										07 43										08 13	
Wimbledon 6 ⊖ ⛴	d	07 17										07 47										08 17	
Wimbledon Chase	d	07 20										07 50										08 20	
South Merton	d	07 22										07 52										08 22	
Morden South	d	07 24										07 54										08 24	
St Helier	d	07 26										07 56										08 26	
Sutton Common	d	07 28										07 58										08 28	
West Sutton	d	07 31										08 01										08 31	
Sutton (Surrey) 4	a	07 35		07 36							07 49	08 05		08 06							08 19	08 35	
East Croydon ⛴	d		07 11		07 25	07a33		07a36		07 41			07 41		07 55	08a03		08a06		08 11			08 11
Redhill	d																						
Gatwick Airport 10 ✈	d		07 27		07 41					07 57			07 57		08 11					08 27			08 27
Three Bridges 4	d		07 32		07 45					08 02			08 02		08 15					08 32			08 32
Balcombe	d														08 21								
Haywards Heath 3	d		07 41		07 55					08 11			08 11		08 27					08 41			08 41
Wivelsfield 4	d				07 59										08 31								
Burgess Hill 4	d				08 01										08 33								
Hassocks 4	d				08 04										08 36								
Preston Park	d				08 11										08 43								
Brighton 10	a		07 55		08 15					08 25			08 25		08 47					08 55			08 55

A From West Hampstead Thameslink
B From Bedford
C From Luton
D To Caterham
E not 19 May
F To Tattenham Corner
G 19 May. From London Victoria
H 19 May
I From London Victoria to Epsom

Please refer to separate pages within this table for services operating between Bedford and London

At weekends please use local bus and tube services to travel to/from St Pancras International and London Bridge when no trains are operating. See local publicity for details of alternative routes and services that are available across central London

South London, Gatwick Airport - Brighton

Network Diagram - see first Page of Table 52

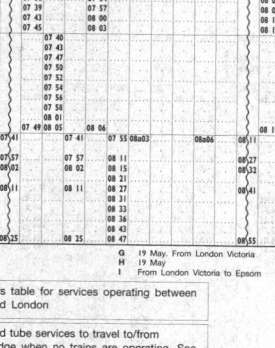

		FC A	FC 1 B	SN C	SE D	SN E	SE F	FC 1 G	SN H	FC A	FC 1 B	FC A	FC 1 B	SN C	SE D	SN E	SE F	FC 1 G	SN H	FC A	FC 1 B	FC A
St Pancras International 15 ⊖	d	07 48	07 54							08 04	08 09	08 18	08 24							08 34	08 39	08 48
Farringdon 3 ⊖	d	07 53	07 59							08 09	08 14	08 23	08 29							08 39	08 44	08 53
City Thameslink 3	d																					
London Blackfriars 3 ⊖	a	07 59	08 04							08 15	08 19	08 29	08 34							08 45	08 49	08 59
	d	08 00	08 05		08 12					08 16	08 20	08 30	08 35		08 42					08 46	08 50	09 00
Elephant & Castle ⊖	d	08 03			08 16					08 19		08 33			08 46					08 49		09 03
Loughborough Jn.	d	08 07								08 23		08 37								08 53		09 07
Herne Hill 4	d	08 11								08 27		08 41								08 57		09 11
Denmark Hill 4	d				08 22		08 22								08 52		08 52					
Peckham Rye 4	d				08 25		08 25								08 55		08 55					
Nunhead 4	d				08 27		08 27								08 57		08 57					
Crofton Park	d				08 30		08 30								09 00		09 00					
Catford	d				08 33		08 33								09 03		09 03					
Bellingham	d				08 35		08 35								09 05		09 05					
Beckenham Hill	d				08 37		08 37								09 07		09 07					
Ravensbourne	d				08 39		08 39								09 09		09 09					
Shortlands	d				08 41		08 41								09 11		09 11					
Bromley South 4	d				08 44		08 44								09 14		09 14					
Bickley 4	d				08 47		08 47								09 17		09 17					
St Mary Cray	d				08 51		08 51								09 21		09 21					
Swanley 4	d				08 56		08 56								09 26		09 26					
Eynsford	d				09 00		09 00								09 30		09 30					
Shoreham (Kent)	d				09 04		09 04								09 34		09 34					
Otford 4	d				09 07		09 07								09 37		09 37					
Bat & Ball	d				09 10		09 10								09 40		09 40					
Sevenoaks 4	a				09 13		09 13								09 43		09 43					
London Bridge 4	a																					
	d			08 06		08 20		08 27						08 36		08 50		08 57				
Tulse Hill 3	d	08 16								08 31		08 46								09 01		09 16
Streatham 4	d	08 20								08 35		08 50								09 05		09 20
Mitcham Eastfields	d	08 24							08 36			08 54							09 06			09 24
Mitcham Junction	d	08 27							08 39			08 57							09 09			09 27
Hackbridge	d	08 30							08 43			09 00							09 13			09 30
Carshalton	d	08 33							08 45			09 03							09 15			09 33
Tooting	d									08 40										09 10		
Haydons Road	d									08 43										09 13		
Wimbledon 6 ⊖ ⛴	d									08 47										09 17		
Wimbledon Chase	d									08 50										09 20		
South Merton	d									08 52										09 22		
Morden South	d									08 54										09 24		
St Helier	d									08 56										09 26		
Sutton Common	d									08 58										09 28		
West Sutton	d									09 01										09 31		
Sutton (Surrey) 4	a	08 36							08 49	09 05		09 06							09 19	09 35		09 36
East Croydon ⛴	d		08 25	08a33		08a36		08 40			08 41		08 55	09a03		09a06		09 11			09 11	
Redhill	d																					
Gatwick Airport 10 ✈	d		08 41					08 57			08 57		09 11					09 27			09 27	
Three Bridges 4	d		08 45					09 02			09 02		09 15					09 32			09 32	
Balcombe	d												09 21									
Haywards Heath 3	d		08 55					09 11			09 11		09 27					09 41			09 41	
Wivelsfield 4	d		08 59										09 31									
Burgess Hill 4	d		09 01										09 33									
Hassocks 4	d		09 04										09 36									
Preston Park	d		09 11										09 43									
Brighton 10	a		09 15					09 25			09 25		09 47					09 55			09 55	

A From Luton
B From Bedford
C To Caterham
D not 19 May
E To Tattenham Corner
F 19 May. From London Victoria
G 19 May
H From London Victoria to Epsom

Please refer to separate pages within this table for services operating between Bedford and London

At weekends please use local bus and tube services to travel to/from St Pancras International and London Bridge when no trains are operating. See local publicity for details of alternative routes and services that are available across central London

South London, Gatwick Airport - Brighton

Network Diagram - see first Page of Table 52

Station		FC A	SN B	SE C	SN D	SE E	FC F	SN G	FC H	FC A	FC I	FC A	SN B	SE C	SN D	SE E	FC F	SN G	FC H	FC A	FC I	FC A	SN B
St Pancras International	d	08 54							09 04	09 09	09 18	09 24							09 34	09 39	09 48	09 54	
Farringdon	d	08 59							09 09	09 14	09 23	09 29							09 39	09 44	09 53	09 59	
City Thameslink	d	09 03							09 13	09 18	09 27	09 33							09 43	09 48	09 57	10 03	
London Blackfriars	a	09 05							09 16	09 20	09 30	09 35							09 46	09 50	10 00	10 05	
	d	09 05		09 12					09 16	09 20	09 30	09 35		09 42					09 46	09 50	10 00	10 05	
Elephant & Castle	d			09 16					09 19		09 33			09 46					09 49		10 03		
Loughborough Jn.	d								09 23		09 37								09 53		10 07		
Herne Hill	d								09 27		09 41								09 57		10 11		
Denmark Hill	d			09 22		09 22								09 52		09 52							
Peckham Rye	d			09 25		09 25								09 55		09 55							
Nunhead	d			09 27		09 27								09 57		09 57							
Crofton Park	d			09 30		09 30								10 00		10 00							
Catford	d			09 33		09 33								10 03		10 03							
Bellingham	d			09 35		09 35								10 05		10 05							
Beckenham Hill	d			09 37		09 37								10 07		10 07							
Ravensbourne	d			09 39		09 39								10 09		10 09							
Shortlands	d			09 41		09 41								10 11		10 11							
Bromley South	d			09 44		09 44								10 14		10 14							
Bickley	d			09 47		09 47								10 17		10 17							
St Mary Cray	d			09 51		09 51								10 21		10 21							
Swanley	d			09 56		09 56								10 26		10 26							
Eynsford	d			10 00		10 00								10 30		10 30							
Shoreham (Kent)	d			10 04		10 04								10 34		10 34							
Otford	d			10 07		10 07								10 37		10 37							
Bat & Ball	d			10 10		10 10								10 40		10 40							
Sevenoaks	a			10 13		10 13								10 43		10 43							
London Bridge	a																						
	d		09 06		09 20		09 27						09 36		09 50		09 57						10 06
Tulse Hill	d								09 31		09 46								10 01		10 16		
Streatham	d								09 35		09 50								10 05		10 20		
Mitcham Eastfields	d							09 36			09 54							10 06			10 24		
Mitcham Junction	d							09 39			09 57							10 09			10 27		
Hackbridge	d							09 43			10 00							10 13			10 30		
Carshalton	d							09 45			10 03							10 15			10 33		
Tooting	d								09 40										10 10				
Haydons Road	d								09 43										10 13				
Wimbledon	d								09 47										10 17				
Wimbledon Chase	d								09 50										10 20				
South Merton	d								09 52										10 22				
Morden South	d								09 54										10 24				
St Helier	d								09 56										10 26				
Sutton Common	d								09 58										10 28				
West Sutton	d								10 01										10 31				
Sutton (Surrey)	a							09 49	10 05		10 06							10 19	10 35		10 36		
East Croydon	d	09 25	09a33		09a36		09 41			09 41		09 55	10a03		10a06		10 11			10 11		10 25	10a33
Redhill	d																						
Gatwick Airport	d	09 41					09 57			09 57		10 11					10 27			10 27		10 41	
Three Bridges	d	09 45					10 02			10 02		10 15					10 32			10 32		10 45	
Balcombe	d											10 21											
Haywards Heath	d	09 55					10 11			10 11		10 27					10 41			10 41		10 55	
Wivelsfield	d	09 59										10 31										10 59	
Burgess Hill	d	10 01										10 33										11 01	
Hassocks	d	10 04										10 36										11 04	
Preston Park	d	10 11										10 43										11 11	
Brighton	a	10 15					10 25			10 25		10 47					10 55			10 55		11 15	

A From Bedford
B To Caterham
C not 19 May
D To Tattenham Corner
E 19 May. From London Victoria
F 19 May
G From London Victoria to Epsom
H From Luton
I From St Albans City

Please refer to separate pages within this table for services operating between Bedford and London

At weekends please use local bus and tube services to travel to/from St Pancras International and London Bridge when no trains are operating. See local publicity for details of alternative routes and services that are available across central London

South London, Gatwick Airport - Brighton

Network Diagram - see first Page of Table 52

Station		SE A	SN B	SE C	FC D	SN E	FC F	FC G	FC H	FC G	SN I	SE A	SN B	SE C	FC D	SN E	FC F	FC G	FC H	FC G	SN I	SE A	SN B
St Pancras International	d						10 04	10 09	10 18	10 24							10 34	10 39	10 48	10 54			
Farringdon	d						10 09	10 14	10 23	10 29							10 39	10 44	10 53	10 59			
City Thameslink	d						10 13	10 18	10 27	10 33							10 43	10 48	10 57	11 03			
London Blackfriars	a						10 16	10 20	10 30	10 35							10 46	10 50	11 00	11 05			
	d	10 12					10 16	10 20	10 30	10 35		10 42					10 46	10 50	11 00	11 05		11 12	
Elephant & Castle	d	10 16					10 19		10 33			10 46					10 49		11 03			11 16	
Loughborough Jn.	d						10 23		10 37								10 53		11 07				
Herne Hill	d						10 27		10 41								10 57		11 11				
Denmark Hill	d	10 22		10 22								10 52		10 52								11 22	
Peckham Rye	d	10 25		10 25								10 55		10 55								11 25	
Nunhead	d	10 27		10 27								10 57		10 57								11 27	
Crofton Park	d	10 30		10 30								11 00		11 00								11 30	
Catford	d	10 33		10 33								11 03		11 03								11 33	
Bellingham	d	10 35		10 35								11 05		11 05								11 35	
Beckenham Hill	d	10 37		10 37								11 07		11 07								11 37	
Ravensbourne	d	10 39		10 39								11 09		11 09								11 39	
Shortlands	d	10 41		10 41								11 11		11 11								11 41	
Bromley South	d	10 44		10 44								11 14		11 14								11 44	
Bickley	d	10 47		10 47								11 17		11 17								11 47	
St Mary Cray	d	10 51		10 51								11 21		11 21								11 51	
Swanley	d	10 56		10 56								11 26		11 26								11 56	
Eynsford	d	11 00		11 00								11 30		11 30								12 00	
Shoreham (Kent)	d	11 04		11 04								11 34		11 34								12 04	
Otford	d	11 07		11 07								11 37		11 37								12 07	
Bat & Ball	d	11 10		11 10								11 40		11 40								12 10	
Sevenoaks	a	11 13		11 13								11 43		11 43								12 13	
London Bridge	a																						
	d		10 20		10 27						10 36		10 50		10 57						11 06		11 20
Tulse Hill	d						10 31		10 46								11 01		11 16				
Streatham	d						10 35		10 50								11 05		11 20				
Mitcham Eastfields	d					10 36			10 54							11 06			11 24				
Mitcham Junction	d					10 39			10 57							11 09			11 27				
Hackbridge	d					10 43			11 00							11 13			11 30				
Carshalton	d					10 45			11 03							11 15			11 33				
Tooting	d						10 40										11 10						
Haydons Road	d						10 43										11 13						
Wimbledon	d						10 47										11 17						
Wimbledon Chase	d						10 50										11 20						
South Merton	d						10 52										11 22						
Morden South	d						10 54										11 24						
St Helier	d						10 56										11 26						
Sutton Common	d						10 58										11 28						
West Sutton	d						11 01										11 31						
Sutton (Surrey)	a					10 49	11 05		11 06							11 19	11 35		11 36				
East Croydon	d		10a36		10 41			10 41		10 55	11a03		11a06		11 11			11 11		11 25	11a33		11a36
Redhill	d																						
Gatwick Airport	d				10 57			10 57		11 11					11 27			11 27		11 41			
Three Bridges	d				11 02			11 02		11 15					11 32			11 32		11 45			
Balcombe	d									11 21													
Haywards Heath	d				11 11			11 11		11 27					11 41			11 41		11 55			
Wivelsfield	d									11 31										11 59			
Burgess Hill	d									11 33										12 01			
Hassocks	d									11 36										12 04			
Preston Park	d									11 43										12 11			
Brighton	a				11 25			11 25		11 47					11 55			11 55		12 15			

A not 19 May
B To Tattenham Corner
C 19 May. From London Victoria
D 19 May
E From London Victoria to Epsom
F From Luton
G From Bedford
H From St Albans City
I To Caterham

Please refer to separate pages within this table for services operating between Bedford and London

At weekends please use local bus and tube services to travel to/from St Pancras International and London Bridge when no trains are operating. See local publicity for details of alternative routes and services that are available across central London

South London, Gatwick Airport - Brighton

Network Diagram - see first Page of Table 52

		SE	FC	SN	FC	FC	FC	FC	SN	SE	SN	SE	FC	SN	FC	FC	FC	FC	SN	SE	SN	SE
		A	B	C	D	E	F	E	G	H	I	A	B	C	D	E	F	E	G	H	I	A
St Pancras International ⊖	d				11 04	11 09	11 18	11 24							11 34	11 39	11 48	11 54				
Farringdon ⊖	d				11 09	11 14	11 23	11 29							11 39	11 44	11 53	11 59				
City Thameslink	d				11 13	11 18	11 27	11 33							11 43	11 48	11 57	12 03				
London Blackfriars ⊖	a				11 16	11 20	11 30	11 35							11 46	11 50	12 00	12 05				
	d				11 16	11 20	11 30	11 35		11 42					11 46	11 50	12 00	12 05		12 12		
Elephant & Castle ⊖	d				11 19		11 33			11 46					11 49		12 03			12 16		
Loughborough Jn.	d				11 23		11 37								11 53		12 07					
Herne Hill	d				11 27		11 41								11 57		12 11					
Denmark Hill	d	11 22								11 52		11 52								12 22		12 22
Peckham Rye	d	11 25								11 55		11 55								12 25		12 25
Nunhead	d	11 27								11 57		11 57								12 27		12 27
Crofton Park	d	11 30								12 00		12 00								12 30		12 30
Catford	d	11 33								12 03		12 03								12 33		12 33
Bellingham	d	11 35								12 05		12 05								12 35		12 35
Beckenham Hill	d	11 37								12 07		12 07								12 37		12 37
Ravensbourne	d	11 39								12 09		12 09								12 39		12 39
Shortlands	d	11 41								12 11		12 11								12 41		12 41
Bromley South	d	11 44								12 14		12 14								12 44		12 44
Bickley	d	11 47								12 17		12 17								12 47		12 47
St Mary Cray	d	11 51								12 21		12 21								12 51		12 51
Swanley	d	11 56								12 26		12 26								12 56		12 56
Eynsford	d	12 00								12 30		12 30								13 00		13 00
Shoreham (Kent)	d	12 04								12 34		12 34								13 04		13 04
Otford	d	12 07								12 37		12 37								13 07		13 07
Bat & Ball	d	12 10								12 40		12 40								13 10		13 10
Sevenoaks	a	12 13								12 43		12 43								13 13		13 13
London Bridge	a																					
	d		11 27						11 36		11 50		11 57						12 06		12 20	
Tulse Hill	d				11 31		11 46								12 01		12 16					
Streatham	d				11 35		11 50								12 05		12 20					
Mitcham Eastfields	d			11 36			11 54							12 06			12 24					
Mitcham Junction	d			11 39			11 57							12 09			12 27					
Hackbridge	d			11 43			12 00							12 13			12 30					
Carshalton	d			11 45			12 03							12 15			12 33					
Tooting	d				11 40										12 10							
Haydons Road	d				11 43										12 13							
Wimbledon ⊖	d				11 47										12 17							
Wimbledon Chase	d				11 50										12 20							
South Merton	d				11 52										12 22							
Morden South	d				11 54										12 24							
St Helier	d				11 56										12 26							
Sutton Common	d				11 58										12 28							
West Sutton	d				12 01										12 31							
Sutton (Surrey)	a			11 49	12 05		12 06							12 19	12 35		12 36					
East Croydon	d		11 41			11 41		11 55	12a03		12a06		12 11			12 11		12 25	12a33		12a36	
Redhill	d																					
Gatwick Airport	d		11 57			11 57		12 11					12 27			12 27		12 41				
Three Bridges	d		12 02			12 02		12 15					12 32			12 32		12 45				
Balcombe	d							12 21														
Haywards Heath	d		12 11			12 11		12 27					12 41			12 41		12 55				
Wivelsfield	d							12 31										12 59				
Burgess Hill	d							12 33										13 01				
Hassocks	d							12 36										13 04				
Preston Park	d							12 43										13 11				
Brighton	a		12 25			12 25		12 47					12 55			12 55		13 15				

A 19 May. From London Victoria
B 19 May
C From London Victoria to Epsom
D From Luton
E From Bedford
F From St Albans City
G To Caterham
H not 19 May
I To Tattenham Corner

Please refer to separate pages within this table for services operating between Bedford and London

At weekends please use local bus and tube services to travel to/from St Pancras International and London Bridge when no trains are operating. See local publicity for details of alternative routes and services that are available across central London

South London, Gatwick Airport - Brighton

Network Diagram - see first Page of Table 52

		FC	SN	FC	FC	FC	FC	SN	SE	SN	SE	FC	SN	FC	FC	FC	FC	SN	SE	SN	SE	FC	SN
		A	B	C	D	E	D	F	G	H	I	A	B	C	D	E	D	F	G	H	I	A	B
St Pancras International ⊖	d			12 04	12 09	12 18	12 24							12 34	12 39	12 48	12 54						
Farringdon ⊖	d			12 09	12 14	12 23	12 29							12 39	12 44	12 53	12 59						
City Thameslink	d			12 13	12 18	12 27	12 33							12 43	12 48	12 57	13 03						
London Blackfriars ⊖	a			12 16	12 20	12 30	12 35							12 46	12 50	13 00	13 05						
	d			12 16	12 20	12 30	12 35		12 42					12 46	12 50	13 00	13 05		13 12				
Elephant & Castle ⊖	d			12 19		12 33			12 46					12 49		13 03			13 16				
Loughborough Jn.	d			12 23		12 37								12 53		13 07							
Herne Hill	d			12 27		12 41								12 57		13 11							
Denmark Hill	d								12 52		12 52								13 22		13 22		
Peckham Rye	d								12 55		12 55								13 25		13 25		
Nunhead	d								12 57		12 57								13 27		13 27		
Crofton Park	d								13 00		13 00								13 30		13 30		
Catford	d								13 03		13 03								13 33		13 33		
Bellingham	d								13 05		13 05								13 35		13 35		
Beckenham Hill	d								13 07		13 07								13 37		13 37		
Ravensbourne	d								13 09		13 09								13 39		13 39		
Shortlands	d								13 11		13 11								13 41		13 41		
Bromley South	d								13 14		13 14								13 44		13 44		
Bickley	d								13 17		13 17								13 47		13 47		
St Mary Cray	d								13 21		13 21								13 51		13 51		
Swanley	d								13 26		13 26								13 56		13 56		
Eynsford	d								13 30		13 30								14 00		14 00		
Shoreham (Kent)	d								13 34		13 34								14 04		14 04		
Otford	d								13 37		13 37								14 07		14 07		
Bat & Ball	d								13 40		13 40								14 10		14 10		
Sevenoaks	a								13 43		13 43								14 13		14 13		
London Bridge	a																						
	d	12 27						12 36		12 50		12 57						13 06		13 20		13 27	
Tulse Hill	d			12 31		12 46								13 01		13 16							
Streatham	d			12 35		12 50								13 05		13 20							
Mitcham Eastfields	d		12 36			12 54							13 06			13 24							13 36
Mitcham Junction	d		12 39			12 57							13 09			13 27							13 39
Hackbridge	d		12 43			13 00							13 13			13 30							13 43
Carshalton	d		12 45			13 03							13 15			13 33							13 45
Tooting	d			12 40										13 10									
Haydons Road	d			12 43										13 13									
Wimbledon ⊖	d			12 47										13 17									
Wimbledon Chase	d			12 50										13 20									
South Merton	d			12 52										13 22									
Morden South	d			12 54										13 24									
St Helier	d			12 56										13 26									
Sutton Common	d			12 58										13 28									
West Sutton	d			13 01										13 31									
Sutton (Surrey)	a		12 49	13 05		13 06							13 19	13 35		13 36							13 49
East Croydon	d	12 41			12 41		12 55	13a03		13a06		13 11			13 11		13 25	13a33		13a36		13 41	
Redhill	d																						
Gatwick Airport	d	12 57			12 57		13 11					13 27			13 27		13 41					13 57	
Three Bridges	d	13 02			13 02		13 15					13 32			13 32		13 45					14 02	
Balcombe	d						13 21																
Haywards Heath	d	13 11			13 11		13 27					13 41			13 41		13 55					14 11	
Wivelsfield	d						13 31										13 59						
Burgess Hill	d						13 33										14 01						
Hassocks	d						13 36										14 04						
Preston Park	d						13 43										14 11						
Brighton	a	13 25			13 25		13 47					13 55			13 55		14 15					14 25	

A 19 May
B From London Victoria to Epsom
C From Luton
D From Bedford
E From St Albans City
F To Caterham
G not 19 May
H To Tattenham Corner
I 19 May. From London Victoria

Please refer to separate pages within this table for services operating between Bedford and London

At weekends please use local bus and tube services to travel to/from St Pancras International and London Bridge when no trains are operating. See local publicity for details of alternative routes and services that are available across central London

Table 52

Saturdays

South London, Gatwick Airport - Brighton

Network Diagram - see first Page of Table 52

Station		FC A	FC 1 B	FC C	FC 1 B	SN D	SE E	SN F	SE G	FC 1 H	SN I	FC A	FC 1 B	FC C	FC 1 B	SN D	SE E	SN F	SE G	FC 1 H	SN I	FC A
St Pancras International	d	13 04	13 09	13 18	13 24							13 34	13 39	13 48	13 54							14 04
Farringdon	d	13 09	13 14	13 23	13 29							13 39	13 44	13 53	13 59							14 09
City Thameslink	d	13 13	13 18	13 27	13 33							13 43	13 48	13 57	14 03							14 13
London Blackfriars	a	13 16	13 20	13 30	13 35							13 46	13 50	14 00	14 05							14 16
	d	13 16	13 20	13 30	13 35		13 42					13 46	13 50	14 00	14 05		14 12					14 16
Elephant & Castle	d	13 19		13 33			13 46					13 49		14 03			14 16					14 19
Loughborough Jn.	d	13 23		13 37								13 53		14 07								14 23
Herne Hill	d	13 27		13 41								13 57		14 11								14 27
Denmark Hill	d						13 52		13 52								14 22		14 22			
Peckham Rye	d						13 55		13 55								14 25		14 25			
Nunhead	d						13 57		13 57								14 27		14 27			
Crofton Park	d						14 00		14 00								14 30		14 30			
Catford	d						14 03		14 03								14 33		14 33			
Bellingham	d						14 05		14 05								14 35		14 35			
Beckenham Hill	d						14 07		14 07								14 37		14 37			
Ravensbourne	d						14 09		14 09								14 39		14 39			
Shortlands	d						14 11		14 11								14 41		14 41			
Bromley South	d						14 14		14 14								14 44		14 44			
Bickley	d						14 17		14 17								14 47		14 47			
St Mary Cray	d						14 21		14 21								14 51		14 51			
Swanley	d						14 26		14 26								14 56		14 56			
Eynsford	d						14 30		14 30								15 00		15 00			
Shoreham (Kent)	d						14 34		14 34								15 04		15 04			
Otford	d						14 37		14 37								15 07		15 07			
Bat & Ball	d						14 40		14 40								15 10		15 10			
Sevenoaks	a						14 43		14 43								15 13		15 13			
London Bridge	a																					
	d					13 36		13 50		13 57						14 06		14 20		14 27		
Tulse Hill	d	13 31		13 46								14 01		14 16								14 31
Streatham	d	13 35		13 50								14 05		14 20								14 35
Mitcham Eastfields	d			13 54							14 06			14 24							14 36	
Mitcham Junction	d			13 57							14 09			14 27							14 39	
Hackbridge	d			14 00							14 13			14 30							14 43	
Carshalton	d			14 03							14 15			14 33							14 45	
Tooting	d	13 40										14 10										14 40
Haydons Road	d	13 43										14 13										14 43
Wimbledon	d	13 47										14 17										14 47
Wimbledon Chase	d	13 50										14 20										14 50
South Merton	d	13 52										14 22										14 52
Morden South	d	13 54										14 24										14 54
St Helier	d	13 56										14 26										14 56
Sutton Common	d	13 58										14 28										14 58
West Sutton	d	14 01										14 31										15 01
Sutton (Surrey)	a	14 05		14 06							14 19	14 35		14 36							14 49	15 05
East Croydon	d		13 41		13 55	14a03		14a06		14 11			14 11		14 25	14a33		14a36		14 41		
Redhill	d																					
Gatwick Airport	d		13 57		14 11					14 27			14 27		14 41					14 57		
Three Bridges	d		14 02		14 15					14 32			14 32		14 45					15 02		
Balcombe	d				14 21																	
Haywards Heath	d		14 11		14 27					14 41			14 41		14 55					15 11		
Wivelsfield	d				14 31										14 59							
Burgess Hill	d				14 33										15 01							
Hassocks	d				14 36										15 04							
Preston Park	d				14 43										15 11							
Brighton	a		14 25		14 47					14 55			14 55		15 15					15 25		

A From Luton
B From Bedford
C From St Albans City
D To Caterham
E not 19 May
F To Tattenham Corner
G 19 May. From London Victoria
H 19 May
I From London Victoria to Epsom

Please refer to separate pages within this table for services operating between Bedford and London

At weekends please use local bus and tube services to travel to/from St Pancras International and London Bridge when no trains are operating. See local publicity for details of alternative routes and services that are available across central London

Table 52

Saturdays

South London, Gatwick Airport - Brighton

Network Diagram - see first Page of Table 52

Station		FC 1 A	FC B	FC 1 A	SN C	SE D	SN E	SE F	FC 1 G	SN H	FC I	FC 1 A	FC B	FC 1 A	SN C	SE D	SN E	SE F	FC 1 G	SN H	FC I	FC 1 A	FC B
St Pancras International	d	14 09	14 18	14 24							14 34	14 39	14 48	14 54							15 04	15 09	15 18
Farringdon	d	14 14	14 23	14 29							14 39	14 44	14 53	14 59							15 09	15 14	15 23
City Thameslink	d	14 18	14 27	14 33							14 43	14 48	14 57	15 03							15 13	15 18	15 27
London Blackfriars	a	14 20	14 30	14 35							14 46	14 50	15 00	15 05							15 16	15 20	15 30
	d	14 20	14 30	14 35		14 42					14 46	14 50	15 00	15 05		15 12					15 16	15 20	15 30
Elephant & Castle	d		14 33			14 46					14 49		15 03			15 16					15 19		15 33
Loughborough Jn.	d		14 37								14 53		15 07								15 23		15 37
Herne Hill	d		14 41								14 57		15 11								15 27		15 41
Denmark Hill	d					14 52		14 52								15 22		15 22					
Peckham Rye	d					14 55		14 55								15 25		15 25					
Nunhead	d					14 57		14 57								15 27		15 27					
Crofton Park	d					15 00		15 00								15 30		15 30					
Catford	d					15 03		15 03								15 33		15 33					
Bellingham	d					15 05		15 05								15 35		15 35					
Beckenham Hill	d					15 07		15 07								15 37		15 37					
Ravensbourne	d					15 09		15 09								15 39		15 39					
Shortlands	d					15 11		15 11								15 41		15 41					
Bromley South	d					15 14		15 14								15 44		15 44					
Bickley	d					15 17		15 17								15 47		15 47					
St Mary Cray	d					15 21		15 21								15 51		15 51					
Swanley	d					15 26		15 26								15 56		15 56					
Eynsford	d					15 30		15 30								16 00		16 00					
Shoreham (Kent)	d					15 34		15 34								16 04		16 04					
Otford	d					15 37		15 37								16 07		16 07					
Bat & Ball	d					15 40		15 40								16 10		16 10					
Sevenoaks	a					15 43		15 43								16 13		16 13					
London Bridge	a																						
	d				14 36		14 50		14 57						15 06		15 20		15 27				
Tulse Hill	d		14 46								15 01		15 16								15 31		15 46
Streatham	d		14 50								15 05		15 20								15 35		15 50
Mitcham Eastfields	d		14 54							15 06			15 24							15 36			15 54
Mitcham Junction	d		14 57							15 09			15 27							15 39			15 57
Hackbridge	d		15 00							15 13			15 30							15 43			16 00
Carshalton	d		15 03							15 15			15 33							15 45			16 03
Tooting	d										15 10										15 40		
Haydons Road	d										15 13										15 43		
Wimbledon	d										15 17										15 47		
Wimbledon Chase	d										15 20										15 50		
South Merton	d										15 22										15 52		
Morden South	d										15 24										15 54		
St Helier	d										15 26										15 56		
Sutton Common	d										15 28										15 58		
West Sutton	d										15 31										16 01		
Sutton (Surrey)	a		15 06							15 19	15 35		15 36							15 49	16 05		16 06
East Croydon	d	14 41		14 55	15a03		15a06		15 11			15 11		15 25	15a33		15a36		15 41			15 41	
Redhill	d																						
Gatwick Airport	d	14 57		15 11					15 27			15 27		15 41					15 57			15 57	
Three Bridges	d	15 02		15 15					15 32			15 32		15 45					16 02			16 02	
Balcombe	d			15 21																			
Haywards Heath	d	15 11		15 27					15 41			15 41		15 55					16 11			16 11	
Wivelsfield	d			15 31										15 59									
Burgess Hill	d			15 33										16 01									
Hassocks	d			15 36										16 04									
Preston Park	d			15 43										16 11									
Brighton	a	15 25		15 47					15 55			15 55		16 15					16 25			16 25	

A From Bedford
B From St Albans City
C To Caterham
D not 19 May
E To Tattenham Corner
F 19 May. From London Victoria
G 19 May
H From London Victoria to Epsom
I From Luton

Please refer to separate pages within this table for services operating between Bedford and London

At weekends please use local bus and tube services to travel to/from St Pancras International and London Bridge when no trains are operating. See local publicity for details of alternative routes and services that are available across central London

South London, Gatwick Airport - Brighton

Network Diagram - see first Page of Table 52

		FC ■ A	SN B	SE C	SN D	SE E	FC ■ F	SN G	FC H	FC ■ A	FC I	FC ■ A	SN B	SE C	SN D	SE E	FC ■ F	SN G	FC H	FC ■ A	FC I	FC ■ A	SN B
St Pancras International ⊖	d	15 24							15 34	15 39	15 48	15 54							16 04	16 09	16 18	16 24	
Farringdon ⊖	d	15 29							15 39	15 44	15 53	15 59							16 09	16 14	16 23	16 29	
City Thameslink	d	15 33							15 43	15 48	15 57	16 03							16 13	16 18	16 27	16 33	
London Blackfriars ⊖	a	15 35							15 46	15 50	16 00	16 05							16 16	16 20	16 30	16 35	
	d	15 35		15 42					15 46	15 50	16 00	16 05		16 12					16 16	16 20	16 30	16 35	
Elephant & Castle ⊖	d			15 46					15 49		16 03			16 16					16 19		16 33		
Loughborough Jn.	d								15 53		16 07								16 23		16 37		
Herne Hill	d								15 57		16 11								16 27		16 41		
Denmark Hill	d			15 52		15 52								16 22		16 22							
Peckham Rye	d			15 55		15 55								16 25		16 25							
Nunhead	d			15 57		15 57								16 27		16 27							
Crofton Park	d			16 00		16 00								16 30		16 30							
Catford	d			16 03		16 03								16 33		16 33							
Bellingham	d			16 05		16 05								16 35		16 35							
Beckenham Hill	d			16 07		16 07								16 37		16 37							
Ravensbourne	d			16 09		16 09								16 39		16 39							
Shortlands	d			16 11		16 11								16 41		16 41							
Bromley South	d			16 14		16 14								16 44		16 44							
Bickley	d			16 17		16 17								16 47		16 47							
St Mary Cray	d			16 21		16 21								16 51		16 51							
Swanley	d			16 26		16 26								16 56		16 56							
Eynsford	d			16 30		16 30								17 00		17 00							
Shoreham (Kent)	d			16 34		16 34								17 04		17 04							
Otford	d			16 37		16 37								17 07		17 07							
Bat & Ball	d			16 40		16 40								17 10		17 10							
Sevenoaks	a			16 43		16 43								17 13		17 13							
London Bridge	a																						
	d		15 36		15 50		15 57						16 06		16 20		16 27						16 36
Tulse Hill	d								16 01		16 16								16 31		16 46		
Streatham	d								16 05		16 20								16 35		16 50		
Mitcham Eastfields	d							16 06			16 24							16 36			16 54		
Mitcham Junction	d							16 09			16 27							16 39			16 57		
Hackbridge	d							16 13			16 30							16 43			17 00		
Carshalton	d							16 15			16 33							16 45			17 03		
Tooting	d								16 10										16 40				
Haydons Road	d								16 13										16 43				
Wimbledon ⊖	d								16 17										16 47				
Wimbledon Chase	d								16 20										16 50				
South Merton	d								16 22										16 52				
Morden South	d								16 24										16 54				
St Helier	d								16 26										16 56				
Sutton Common	d								16 28										16 58				
West Sutton	d								16 31										17 01				
Sutton (Surrey)	a							16 19	16 35		16 36							16 49	17 05		17 06		
East Croydon	d	15 55	16a03		16a06		16 11			16 11		16 25	16a33		16a36		16 41			16 41		16 55	17a03
Redhill	d																						
Gatwick Airport ✈	d	16 11					16 27			16 27		16 41					16 57			16 57		17 11	
Three Bridges	d	16 15					16 32			16 32		16 45					17 02			17 02		17 15	
Balcombe	d	16 21																				17 21	
Haywards Heath	d	16 27					16 41			16 41		16 55					17 11			17 11		17 27	
Wivelsfield	d	16 31										16 59										17 31	
Burgess Hill	d	16 33										17 01										17 33	
Hassocks	d	16 36										17 04										17 36	
Preston Park	d	16 43										17 11										17 43	
Brighton	a	16 47					16 55			16 55		17 15					17 25			17 25		17 47	

A From Bedford
B To Caterham
C not 19 May
D To Tattenham Corner
E 19 May. From London Victoria
F 19 May
G From London Victoria to Epsom
H From Luton
I From St Albans City

Please refer to separate pages within this table for services operating between Bedford and London

At weekends please use local bus and tube services to travel to/from St Pancras International and London Bridge when no trains are operating. See local publicity for details of alternative routes and services that are available across central London

South London, Gatwick Airport - Brighton

Network Diagram - see first Page of Table 52

		SE A	SN B	SE C	FC ■ D	SN E	FC F	FC ■ G	FC H	FC ■ G	SN I	SE A	SN B	SE C	FC ■ D	SN E	FC F	FC ■ G	FC H	FC ■ G	SN I	SE A
St Pancras International ⊖	d						16 34	16 39	16 48	16 54							17 04	17 09	17 18	17 24		
Farringdon ⊖	d						16 39	16 44	16 53	16 59							17 09	17 14	17 23	17 29		
City Thameslink	d						16 43	16 48	16 57	17 03							17 13	17 18	17 27	17 33		
London Blackfriars ⊖	a						16 46	16 50	17 00	17 05							17 16	17 20	17 30	17 35		
	d	16 42					16 46	16 50	17 00	17 05		17 12					17 16	17 20	17 30	17 35		17 42
Elephant & Castle ⊖	d	16 46					16 49		17 03			17 16					17 19		17 33			17 46
Loughborough Jn.	d						16 53		17 07								17 23		17 37			
Herne Hill	d						16 57		17 11								17 27		17 41			
Denmark Hill	d	16 52		16 52								17 22		17 22								17 52
Peckham Rye	d	16 55		16 55								17 25		17 25								17 55
Nunhead	d	16 57		16 57								17 27		17 27								17 57
Crofton Park	d	17 00		17 00								17 30		17 30								18 00
Catford	d	17 03		17 03								17 33		17 33								18 03
Bellingham	d	17 05		17 05								17 35		17 35								18 05
Beckenham Hill	d	17 07		17 07								17 37		17 37								18 07
Ravensbourne	d	17 09		17 09								17 39		17 39								18 09
Shortlands	d	17 11		17 11								17 41		17 41								18 11
Bromley South	d	17 14		17 14								17 44		17 44								18 14
Bickley	d	17 17		17 17								17 47		17 47								18 17
St Mary Cray	d	17 21		17 21								17 51		17 51								18 21
Swanley	d	17 26		17 26								17 56		17 56								18 26
Eynsford	d	17 30		17 30								18 00		18 00								18 30
Shoreham (Kent)	d	17 34		17 34								18 04		18 04								18 34
Otford	d	17 37		17 37								18 07		18 07								18 37
Bat & Ball	d	17 40		17 40								18 10		18 10								18 40
Sevenoaks	a	17 43		17 43								18 13		18 13								18 43
London Bridge	a																					
	d		16 50		16 57						17 06		17 20		17 27						17 36	
Tulse Hill	d						17 01		17 16								17 31		17 46			
Streatham	d						17 05		17 20								17 35		17 50			
Mitcham Eastfields	d					17 06			17 24							17 36			17 54			
Mitcham Junction	d					17 09			17 27							17 39			17 57			
Hackbridge	d					17 13			17 30							17 43			18 00			
Carshalton	d					17 15			17 33							17 45			18 03			
Tooting	d						17 10										17 40					
Haydons Road	d						17 13										17 43					
Wimbledon ⊖	d						17 17										17 47					
Wimbledon Chase	d						17 20										17 50					
South Merton	d						17 22										17 52					
Morden South	d						17 24										17 54					
St Helier	d						17 26										17 56					
Sutton Common	d						17 28										17 58					
West Sutton	d						17 31										18 01					
Sutton (Surrey)	a					17 19	17 35		17 36							17 49	18 05		18 06			
East Croydon	d		17a06		17 11			17 11		17 25	17a33		17a36		17 41			17 41		17 55	18a03	
Redhill	d																					
Gatwick Airport ✈	d				17 27			17 27		17 41					17 57			17 57		18 11		
Three Bridges	d				17 32			17 32		17 45					18 02			18 02		18 15		
Balcombe	d																			18 21		
Haywards Heath	d				17 41			17 41		17 55					18 11			18 11		18 27		
Wivelsfield	d									17 59										18 31		
Burgess Hill	d									18 01										18 33		
Hassocks	d									18 04										18 36		
Preston Park	d									18 11										18 43		
Brighton	a				17 55			17 55		18 15					18 25			18 25		18 47		

A not 19 May
B To Tattenham Corner
C 19 May. From London Victoria
D 19 May
E From London Victoria to Epsom
F From Luton
G From Bedford
H From St Albans City
I To Caterham

Please refer to separate pages within this table for services operating between Bedford and London

At weekends please use local bus and tube services to travel to/from St Pancras International and London Bridge when no trains are operating. See local publicity for details of alternative routes and services that are available across central London

Table 52

Saturdays

South London, Gatwick Airport - Brighton

Network Diagram - see first Page of Table 52

		SN	SE	FC	SN	FC	FC	FC	FC	SN	SE	SN	SE	FC	SN	FC	FC	FC	FC	SN	SE	SN	SE
		A	B	C	D	E	F	G	F	H	I	A	B	C	D	E	F	G	F	H	I	A	B
St Pancras International	d					17 34	17 39	17 48	17 54							18 04	18 09	18 18	18 24				
Farringdon	d					17 39	17 44	17 53	17 59							18 09	18 14	18 23	18 29				
City Thameslink	d					17 43	17 48	17 57	18 03							18 13	18 18	18 27	18 33				
London Blackfriars	a					17 46	17 50	18 00	18 05							18 16	18 20	18 30	18 35				
	d					17 46	17 50	18 00	18 05		18 12					18 16	18 20	18 30	18 35		18 42		
Elephant & Castle	d					17 49		18 03			18 16					18 19		18 33			18 46		
Loughborough Jn	d					17 53		18 07								18 23		18 37					
Herne Hill	d					17 57		18 11								18 27		18 41					
Denmark Hill	d		17 52								18 22		18 22								18 52		18 52
Peckham Rye	d		17 55								18 25		18 25								18 55		18 55
Nunhead	d		17 57								18 27		18 27								18 57		18 57
Crofton Park	d		18 00								18 30		18 30								19 00		19 00
Catford	d		18 03								18 33		18 33								19 03		19 03
Bellingham	d		18 05								18 35		18 35								19 05		19 05
Beckenham Hill	d		18 07								18 37		18 37								19 07		19 07
Ravensbourne	d		18 09								18 39		18 39								19 09		19 09
Shortlands	d		18 11								18 41		18 41								19 11		19 11
Bromley South	d		18 14								18 44		18 44								19 14		19 14
Bickley	d		18 17								18 47		18 47								19 17		19 17
St Mary Cray	d		18 21								18 51		18 51								19 21		19 21
Swanley	d		18 26								18 56		18 56								19 26		19 26
Eynsford	d		18 30								19 00		19 00								19 30		19 30
Shoreham (Kent)	d		18 34								19 04		19 04								19 34		19 34
Otford	d		18 37								19 07		19 07								19 37		19 37
Bat & Ball	d		18 40								19 10		19 10								19 40		19 40
Sevenoaks	a		18 43								19 13		19 13								19 43		19 43
London Bridge	a																						
	d	17 50		17 57						18 06		18 20		18 27						18 36		18 50	
Tulse Hill	d					18 01		18 16								18 31		18 46					
Streatham	d					18 05		18 20								18 35		18 50					
Mitcham Eastfields	d				18 06			18 24							18 36			18 54					
Mitcham Junction	d				18 09			18 27							18 39			18 57					
Hackbridge	d				18 13			18 30							18 43			19 00					
Carshalton	d				18 15			18 33							18 45			19 03					
Tooting	d					18 10										18 40							
Haydons Road	d					18 13										18 43							
Wimbledon	d					18 17										18 47							
Wimbledon Chase	d					18 20										18 50							
South Merton	d					18 22										18 52							
Morden South	d					18 24										18 54							
St Helier	d					18 26										18 56							
Sutton Common	d					18 28										18 58							
West Sutton	d					18 31										19 01							
Sutton (Surrey)	a				18 19	18 35		18 36							18 49	19 05		19 06					
East Croydon	d	18a06		18 11			18 11		18 25	18a33		18a36		18 41			18 41		18 55	19a03		19a06	
Redhill	d																						
Gatwick Airport	d			18 27			18 27		18 41					18 57			18 57		19 11				
Three Bridges	d			18 32			18 32		18 45					19 02			19 02		19 15				
Balcombe	d																		19 21				
Haywards Heath	d			18 41			18 41		18 55					19 11			19 11		19 27				
Wivelsfield	d								18 59										19 31				
Burgess Hill	d								19 01										19 33				
Hassocks	d								19 04										19 36				
Preston Park	d								19 11										19 43				
Brighton	a			18 55			18 55		19 15					19 25			19 25		19 47				

A To Tattenham Corner
B 19 May. From London Victoria
C 19 May
D From London Victoria to Epsom
E From Luton
F From Bedford
G From St Albans City
H To Caterham
I not 19 May

Please refer to separate pages within this table for services operating between Bedford and London

At weekends please use local bus and tube services to travel to/from St Pancras International and London Bridge when no trains are operating. See local publicity for details of alternative routes and services that are available across central London

Table 52

Saturdays

South London, Gatwick Airport - Brighton

Network Diagram - see first Page of Table 52

		FC	SN	FC	FC	FC	FC	SN	SE	SN	SE	FC	SN	FC	FC	FC	FC	SN	SE	SN	SE	FC
		A	B	C	D	E	D	F	G	H	I	A	B	C	D	E	D	F	G	H	I	A
St Pancras International	d			18 34	18 39	18 48	18 54							19 04	19 09	19 18	19 24					
Farringdon	d			18 39	18 44	18 53	18 59							19 09	19 14	19 23	19 29					
City Thameslink	d			18 43	18 48	18 57	19 03							19 13	19 18	19 27	19 33					
London Blackfriars	a			18 46	18 50	19 00	19 05							19 16	19 20	19 30	19 35					
	d			18 46	18 50	19 00	19 05		19 12					19 16	19 20	19 30	19 35		19 42			
Elephant & Castle	d			18 49		19 03			19 16					19 19		19 33			19 46			
Loughborough Jn	d			18 53		19 07								19 23		19 37						
Herne Hill	d			18 57		19 11								19 27		19 41						
Denmark Hill	d								19 22		19 22								19 52		19 52	
Peckham Rye	d								19 25		19 25								19 55		19 55	
Nunhead	d								19 27		19 27								19 57		19 57	
Crofton Park	d								19 30		19 30								20 00		20 00	
Catford	d								19 33		19 33								20 03		20 03	
Bellingham	d								19 35		19 35								20 05		20 05	
Beckenham Hill	d								19 37		19 37								20 07		20 07	
Ravensbourne	d								19 39		19 39								20 09		20 09	
Shortlands	d								19 41		19 41								20 11		20 11	
Bromley South	d								19 44		19 44								20 14		20 14	
Bickley	d								19 47		19 47								20 17		20 17	
St Mary Cray	d								19 51		19 51								20 21		20 21	
Swanley	d								19 56		19 56								20 26		20 26	
Eynsford	d								20 00		20 00								20 30		20 30	
Shoreham (Kent)	d								20 04		20 04								20 34		20 34	
Otford	d								20 07		20 07								20 37		20 37	
Bat & Ball	d								20 10		20 10								20 40		20 40	
Sevenoaks	a								20 13		20 13								20 43		20 43	
London Bridge	a																					
	d	18 57						19 06		19 20		19 27						19 36		19 50		19 57
Tulse Hill	d			19 01		19 16								19 31		19 46						
Streatham	d			19 05		19 20								19 35		19 50						
Mitcham Eastfields	d		19 06			19 24							19 36			19 54						
Mitcham Junction	d		19 09			19 27							19 39			19 57						
Hackbridge	d		19 13			19 30							19 43			20 00						
Carshalton	d		19 15			19 33							19 45			20 03						
Tooting	d			19 10										19 40								
Haydons Road	d			19 13										19 43								
Wimbledon	d			19 17										19 47								
Wimbledon Chase	d			19 20										19 50								
South Merton	d			19 22										19 52								
Morden South	d			19 24										19 54								
St Helier	d			19 26										19 56								
Sutton Common	d			19 28										19 58								
West Sutton	d			19 31										20 01								
Sutton (Surrey)	a		19 19	19 35		19 36							19 49	20 05		20 06						
East Croydon	d	19 11			19 11		19 25	19a33		19a36		19 41			19 41		19 55	20a03		20a06		20 11
Redhill	d																					
Gatwick Airport	d	19 27			19 27		19 41					19 57			19 57		20 11					20 27
Three Bridges	d	19 32			19 32		19 45					20 02			20 02		20 15					20 32
Balcombe	d																20 21					
Haywards Heath	d	19 41			19 41		19 55					20 11			20 11		20 27					20 41
Wivelsfield	d						19 59										20 31					
Burgess Hill	d						20 01										20 33					
Hassocks	d						20 04										20 36					
Preston Park	d						20 11										20 43					
Brighton	a	19 55			19 55		20 15					20 25			20 25		20 47					20 55

A 19 May
B From London Victoria to Epsom
C From Luton
D From Bedford
E From St Albans City
F To Caterham
G not 19 May
H To Tattenham Corner
I 19 May. From London Victoria

Please refer to separate pages within this table for services operating between Bedford and London

At weekends please use local bus and tube services to travel to/from St Pancras International and London Bridge when no trains are operating. See local publicity for details of alternative routes and services that are available across central London

South London, Gatwick Airport - Brighton

Network Diagram - see first Page of Table 52

		SN	FC	FC 1	FC	FC 1	SN	SE	SN	SE	SN	FC	FC	FC 1	SN	SE	SN	SE	SN	FC	FC	FC 1	SN
		A	B	C	D	C	E	F	G	H	A	B	D	C	E	F	G	H	A	B	D	C	E
St Pancras International 15 ⊖	d		19 34	19 39	19 48	19 54						20 04	20 18	20 24						20 36	20 48	20 54	
Farringdon 3 ⊖	d		19 39	19 44	19 53	19 59						20 09	20 23	20 29						20 40	20 53	20 59	
City Thameslink 3	d		19 43	19 48	19 57	20 03						20 13	20 27	20 33						20 43	20 57	21 03	
London Blackfriars 3 ⊖	a		19 46	19 50	20 00	20 05						20 16	20 30	20 35						20 46	21 00	21 05	
	d		19 46	19 50	20 00	20 05		20 12				20 16	20 30	20 35		20 42				20 46	21 00	21 05	
Elephant & Castle ⊖	d		19 49		20 03			20 16				20 19	20 33			20 46				20 49	21 03		
Loughborough Jn.	d		19 53		20 07							20 23	20 37							20 53	21 07		
Herne Hill 4	d		19 57		20 11							20 27	20 41							20 57	21 11		
Denmark Hill 4	d							20 22		20 22						20 52		20 52					
Peckham Rye 4	d							20 25		20 25						20 55		20 55					
Nunhead 4	d							20 27		20 27						20 57		20 57					
Crofton Park	d							20 30		20 30						21 00		21 00					
Catford	d							20 33		20 33						21 03		21 03					
Bellingham	d							20 35		20 35						21 05		21 05					
Beckenham Hill	d							20 37		20 37						21 07		21 07					
Ravensbourne	d							20 39		20 39						21 09		21 09					
Shortlands	d							20 41		20 41						21 11		21 11					
Bromley South 4	d							20 44		20 44						21 14		21 14					
Bickley 4	d							20 47		20 47						21 17		21 17					
St Mary Cray	d							20 51		20 51						21 21		21 21					
Swanley 4	d							20 56		20 56						21 26		21 26					
Eynsford	d							21 00		21 00						21 30		21 30					
Shoreham (Kent)	d							21 04		21 04						21 34		21 34					
Otford 4	d							21 07		21 07						21 37		21 37					
Bat & Ball	d							21 10		21 10						21 40		21 40					
Sevenoaks 4	a							21 13		21 13						21 43		21 43					
London Bridge 4	a																						
	d						20 06		20 20						20 36		20 50						21 06
Tulse Hill 3	d		20 01		20 16							20 31	20 46							21 01	21 16		
Streatham 4	d		20 05		20 20							20 35	20 50							21 05	21 20		
Mitcham Eastfields	d	20 06			20 24						20 36		20 54						21 06		21 24		
Mitcham Junction	d	20 09			20 27						20 39		20 57						21 09		21 27		
Hackbridge	d	20 13			20 30						20 43		21 00						21 13		21 30		
Carshalton	d	20 15			20 33						20 45		21 03						21 15		21 33		
Tooting	d		20 10									20 40								21 10			
Haydons Road	d		20 13									20 43								21 13			
Wimbledon 6 ⊖	d		20 17									20 47								21 17			
Wimbledon Chase	d		20 20									20 50								21 20			
South Merton	d		20 22									20 52								21 22			
Morden South	d		20 24									20 54								21 24			
St Helier	d		20 26									20 56								21 26			
Sutton Common	d		20 28									20 58								21 28			
West Sutton	d		20 31									21 01								21 31			
Sutton (Surrey) 4	a	20 19	20 35		20 36						20 49	21 05	21 06						21 19	21 35	21 42		
East Croydon	d			20 11		20 25	20a33		20a36					20 55	21a03		21a06					21 25	21a33
Redhill	d																						
Gatwick Airport 10 ✈	d			20 27		20 41								21 11								21 41	
Three Bridges 4	d			20 32		20 45								21 15								21 45	
Balcombe	d					20 51																21 53	
Haywards Heath 3	d			20 41		20 57								21 25								21 59	
Wivelsfield 4	d					21 01								21 29								22 03	
Burgess Hill 4	d					21 03								21 31								22 05	
Hassocks 4	d					21 06								21 34								22 08	
Preston Park	d					21 13								21 41								22 15	
Brighton 10	a			20 55		21 17								21 45								22 19	

A From London Victoria to Epsom
B From Luton
C From Bedford
D From St Albans City
E To Caterham
F not 19 May
G To Tattenham Corner
H 19 May. From London Victoria

Please refer to separate pages within this table for services operating between Bedford and London

At weekends please use local bus and tube services to travel to/from St Pancras International and London Bridge when no trains are operating. See local publicity for details of alternative routes and services that are available across central London

South London, Gatwick Airport - Brighton

Network Diagram - see first Page of Table 52

		SE	SN	SE	SN	FC	FC 1	SN	SE	SN	SE	SN	FC	FC 1	SN	SE	SN	SE	SN	FC	FC 1	SN	SE
		A	B	C	D	E	F	G	A	B	C	D	E	F	G	A	B	C	D	E	F	G	A
St Pancras International 15 ⊖	d					21 06	21 24						21 36	21 54						22 06	22 24		
Farringdon 3 ⊖	d					21 10	21 29						21 40	21 59						22 10	22 29		
City Thameslink 3	d																						
London Blackfriars 3 ⊖	a					21 16	21 34						21 46	22 04						22 16	22 34		
	d	21 12				21 16	21 35		21 42				21 46	22 05		22 12				22 16	22 35		22 42
Elephant & Castle ⊖	d	21 16				21 19			21 46				21 49			22 16				22 19			22 46
Loughborough Jn.	d					21 23							21 53							22 23			
Herne Hill 4	d					21 27							21 57							22 27			
Denmark Hill 4	d	21 22		21 22					21 52		21 52					22 22		22 22					22 52
Peckham Rye 4	d	21 25		21 25					21 55		21 55					22 25		22 25					22 55
Nunhead 4	d	21 27		21 27					21 57		21 57					22 27		22 27					22 57
Crofton Park	d	21 30		21 30					22 00		22 00					22 30		22 30					23 00
Catford	d	21 33		21 33					22 03		22 03					22 33		22 33					23 03
Bellingham	d	21 35		21 35					22 05		22 05					22 35		22 35					23 05
Beckenham Hill	d	21 37		21 37					22 07		22 07					22 37		22 37					23 07
Ravensbourne	d	21 39		21 39					22 09		22 09					22 39		22 39					23 09
Shortlands	d	21 41		21 41					22 11		22 11					22 41		22 41					23 11
Bromley South 4	d	21 44		21 44					22 14		22 14					22 44		22 44					23 14
Bickley 4	d	21 47		21 47					22 17		22 17					22 47		22 47					23 17
St Mary Cray	d	21 51		21 51					22 21		22 21					22 51		22 51					23 21
Swanley 4	d	21 56		21 56					22 26		22 26					22 56		22 56					23 26
Eynsford	d	22 00		22 00					22 30		22 30					23 00		23 00					23 30
Shoreham (Kent)	d	22 04		22 04					22 34		22 34					23 04		23 04					23 34
Otford 4	d	22 07		22 07					22 37		22 37					23 07		23 07					23 37
Bat & Ball	d	22 10		22 10					22 40		22 40					23 10		23 10					23 40
Sevenoaks 4	a	22 13		22 13					22 43		22 43					23 13		23 13					23 43
London Bridge 4	a																						
	d		21 20					21 36		21 50					22 06		22 20					22 36	
Tulse Hill 3	d					21 31							22 01							22 31			
Streatham 4	d					21 35							22 05							22 35			
Mitcham Eastfields	d				21 36							22 06							22 36				
Mitcham Junction	d				21 39							22 09							22 39				
Hackbridge	d				21 43							22 13							22 43				
Carshalton	d				21 45							22 15							22 45				
Tooting	d					21 40							22 10							22 40			
Haydons Road	d					21 43							22 13							22 43			
Wimbledon 6 ⊖	d					21 47							22 17							22 47			
Wimbledon Chase	d					21 50							22 20							22 50			
South Merton	d					21 52							22 22							22 52			
Morden South	d					21 54							22 24							22 54			
St Helier	d					21 56							22 26							22 56			
Sutton Common	d					21 58							22 28							22 58			
West Sutton	d					22 01							22 31							23 01			
Sutton (Surrey) 4	a				21 49	22 05						22 19	22 35						22 49	23 05			
East Croydon	d		21a36				21 55	22a04		22a07				22 25	22a35		22a37				22 55	23a03	
Redhill	d																						
Gatwick Airport 10 ✈	d						22 11							22 41							23 11		
Three Bridges 4	d						22 15							22 45							23 15		
Balcombe	d													22 53									
Haywards Heath 3	d						22 25							22 59							23 25		
Wivelsfield 4	d						22 29							23 03							23 29		
Burgess Hill 4	d						22 31							23 05							23 31		
Hassocks 4	d						22 34							23 08							23 34		
Preston Park	d						22 41							23 15							23 41		
Brighton 10	a						22 45							23 19							23 45		

A not 19 May
B To Tattenham Corner
C 19 May. From London Victoria
D From London Victoria to Epsom
E From Luton
F From Bedford
G To Caterham

Please refer to separate pages within this table for services operating between Bedford and London

At weekends please use local bus and tube services to travel to/from St Pancras International and London Bridge when no trains are operating. See local publicity for details of alternative routes and services that are available across central London

Table 52

Saturdays

South London, Gatwick Airport - Brighton

Network Diagram - see first Page of Table 52

Station		SN A	SE B	SN C	FC D	FC E	SN F	SE G	SE B	SN H	FC D	FC E	SN F	SE B	SE G	FC D	FC I	FC J
St Pancras International	d				22 36	22 54					23 06	23 24				23 36	23 54	23 54
Farringdon	d				22 40	22 59					23 10	23 29				23 40	23 59	23 59
City Thameslink	d																	
London Blackfriars	a				22 46	23 04					23 16	23 34				23 46	00 04	00 04
	d				22 46	23 05		23 12			23 16	23 35			23 42	23 46	00 05	00 05
Elephant & Castle	d				22 49			23 16			23 19				23 46	23 49		
Loughborough Jn.	d				22 53						23 23							
Herne Hill	d				22 57						23 27					23 57		
Denmark Hill	d		22 52					23 22	23 22					23 52	23 52			
Peckham Rye	d		22 55					23 25	23 25					23 55	23 55			
Nunhead	d		22 57					23 27	23 27					23 57	23 57			
Crofton Park	d		23 00					23 30	23 30					23 58	23 59			
Catford	d		23 03					23 33	23 33					00 03	00 03			
Bellingham	d		23 05					23 35	23 35					00 05	00 05			
Beckenham Hill	d		23 07					23 37	23 37					00 07	00 07			
Ravensbourne	d		23 09					23 39	23 39					00 09	00 09			
Shortlands	d		23 11					23 41	23 41					00 11	00 11			
Bromley South	d		23 14					23 44	23 44					00 14	00 14			
Bickley	d		23a17					23 47	23a47					00a17	00 17			
St Mary Cray	d							23 51							00 21			
Swanley	d							23 56							00 26			
Eynsford	d							23 59							00 30			
Shoreham (Kent)	d							00 04							00 34			
Otford	d							00 07							00 37			
Bat & Ball	d							00 10							00 40			
Sevenoaks	a							00 13							00 43			
London Bridge	a																	
	d	22 50					23 06						23 36					
Tulse Hill	d				23 01						23 31					00 01		
Streatham	d				23 05						23 35					00 05		
Mitcham Eastfields	d			23 06						23 43								
Mitcham Junction	d			23 09						23 46								
Hackbridge	d			23 13						23 50								
Carshalton	d			23 15						23 52								
Tooting	d				23 10						23 40					00 10		
Haydons Road	d				23 13						23 43					00 13		
Wimbledon	d				23 17						23 47					00 17		
Wimbledon Chase	d				23 20						23 50					00 20		
South Merton	d				23 22						23 52					00 22		
Morden South	d				23 24						23 54					00 24		
St Helier	d				23 26						23 56					00 26		
Sutton Common	d				23 28						23 58					00 28		
West Sutton	d				23 31						00 01					00 31		
Sutton (Surrey)	a			23 19	23 35					23 59	00 05					00 35		
East Croydon	d	23a06				23 25	23a33					23 57	00a03				00 27	00 27
Redhill	d																	
Gatwick Airport	d					23 41						00 19					00 49	00 50
Three Bridges	d					23 47						00a24					00a54	00a55
Balcombe	d					23 53												
Haywards Heath	d					23 59												
Wivelsfield	d					00 03												
Burgess Hill	d					00 05												
Hassocks	d					00 08												
Preston Park	d					00 15												
Brighton	a					00 19												

A To Tattenham Corner
B 19 May. From London Victoria to Orpington
C From London Victoria to Epsom
D From Luton
E From Bedford
F To Caterham
G not 19 May
H From London Victoria to Dorking
I from 30 June. From Bedford
J until 23 June. From Bedford

Please refer to separate pages within this table for services operating between Bedford and London

At weekends please use local bus and tube services to travel to/from St Pancras International and London Bridge when no trains are operating. See local publicity for details of alternative routes and services that are available across central London

Table 52

Sundays
until 9 September

South London, Gatwick Airport - Brighton

Network Diagram - see first Page of Table 52

Station		FC A	SE B	FC C	FC A	SE D	SE B	FC C	FC E	FC F	SN G	FC A	SN	FC A	SE H	SE I	SE J	SE J	FC K	FC L	SE J	FC A	SN
St Pancras International	d	22p54		23p06	23p24			23p36	23p54	23p54		00 24		00 54								07 24	
Farringdon	d	22p59		23p10	23p29			23p40	23p59	23p59		00 29										07 29	
City Thameslink	d																						
London Blackfriars	a	23p04		23p16	23p34			23p46	00 04	00 04		00 34		01 04								07 34	
	d	23p05	23p12	23p16	23p35		23p42	23p46	00 05	00 05		00 35		01 05			06 12	06 42	06 55	06 55	07 12	07 34	
Elephant & Castle	d		23p16	23p19			23p46	23p49									06 16	06 46			07 16		
Loughborough Jn.	d			23p23																			
Herne Hill	d			23p27				23p57															
Denmark Hill	d		23p22			23p52	23p52									01 06	06 22	06 52			07 22		
Peckham Rye	d		23p25			23p55	23p55								01s08	01 08	06 25	06 55			07 25		
Nunhead	d		23p27			23p57	23p57								01s10	01 11	06 27	06 57			07 27		
Crofton Park	d		23p30			23p58	23p59								01s13	01 14	06 30	07 00			07 30		
Catford	d		23p33			00 03	00 03								01s16	01 16	06 33	07 03			07 33		
Bellingham	d		23p35			00 05	00 05								01s18	01 19	06 35	07 05			07 35		
Beckenham Hill	d		23p37			00 07	00 07								01s20	01 21	06 37	07 07			07 37		
Ravensbourne	d		23p39			00 09	00 09								01s22	01 23	06 39	07 09			07 39		
Shortlands	d		23p41			00 11	00 11									01 25	06 41	07 11			07 41		
Bromley South	d		23p44			00 14	00 14								01s25	01 28	06 44	07 14			07 44		
Bickley	d		23p47			00a17	00 17									01a30	06 47	07 17			07 47		
St Mary Cray	d		23p51				00 21										06 51	07 21			07 51		
Swanley	d		23p56				00 26										06 56	07 26			07 56		
Eynsford	d		23p59				00 30										07 00	07 30			08 00		
Shoreham (Kent)	d		00 04				00 34										07 04	07 34			08 04		
Otford	d		00 07				00 37										07 07	07 37			08 07		
Bat & Ball	d		00 10				00 40										07 10	07 40			08 10		
Sevenoaks	a		00 13				00 43										07 13	07 43			08 13		
London Bridge	a																						
	d										00 06		00 36										07 21
Tulse Hill	d			23p31				00 01															07 39
Streatham	d			23p35				00 05															07 42
Mitcham Eastfields	d																						
Mitcham Junction	d																						
Hackbridge	d																						
Carshalton	d																						
Tooting	d			23p40				00 10															
Haydons Road	d			23p43				00 13															
Wimbledon	d			23p47				00 17															
Wimbledon Chase	d			23p50				00 20															
South Merton	d			23p52				00 22															
Morden South	d			23p54				00 24															
St Helier	d			23p56				00 26															
Sutton Common	d			23p58				00 28															
West Sutton	d			00 01				00 31															
Sutton (Surrey)	a			00 05				00 35															
East Croydon	d	23p25			23p57				00 27	00 27	00a33	00 57	01a03	01 32					07 25	07 25		07 55	08a01
Redhill	d																						
Gatwick Airport	d	23p41			00 19				00 49	00 50		01 22		01 52					07 42	07 42		08 12	
Three Bridges	d	23p47			00a24				00a54	00a55		01a28		01a58					07 47	07 47		08 17	
Balcombe	d	23p53																					
Haywards Heath	d	23p59																	07 56	07 56		08 26	
Wivelsfield	d	00 03																					
Burgess Hill	d	00 05																	08 01	08 01		08 31	
Hassocks	d	00 08																	08 05	08 05		08 35	
Preston Park	d	00 15																					
Brighton	a	00 19																	08 14	08 15		08 45	

A From Bedford
B not 20 May
C From Luton
D 20 May. From London Victoria to Orpington
E from 1 July until 9 September. From Bedford
F until 24 June. From Bedford
G To Caterham
H 2 September, 9 September. From London Victoria to Orpington
I 29 July, 5 August, 12 August. From London Victoria to Orpington
J 29 July, 5 August, 12 August
K until 24 June
L from 1 July until 22 July, from 19 August until 9 September

Please refer to separate pages within this table for services operating between Bedford and London

At weekends please use local bus and tube services to travel to/from St Pancras International and London Bridge when no trains are operating. See local publicity for details of alternative routes and services that are available across central London

South London, Gatwick Airport - Brighton

Sundays until 9 September

Network Diagram - see first Page of Table 52

		SE	SN	SN	SE	FC	SN	SE	SN	SN	SE	FC	SN	SE	SN	SN	SE	SN	SN	FC	FC	SE	SN
		A	B	C	D	E		A	B	C	D	E		A	B	C	D		C		E	A	B
St Pancras International ⊖	d					07 54						08 24									08 54		
Farringdon ⊖	d					07 59						08 29									08 58		
City Thameslink	d																						
London Blackfriars ⊖	a					08 04						08 34									09 04		
	d	07 38			07 42	08 04		08 08			08 12	08 34		08 38			08 42			08 56	09 04	09 08	
Elephant & Castle ⊖	d	07 42			07 46			08 12			08 16			08 42			08 46			09 00		09 12	
Loughborough Jn	d																			09 04			
Herne Hill	d																			09 08			
Denmark Hill	d	07 48			07 52			08 18			08 22			08 48			08 52					09 18	
Peckham Rye	d	07 51			07 55			08 21			08 25			08 51			08 55					09 21	
Nunhead	d	07 53			07 57			08 23			08 27			08 53			08 57					09 23	
Crofton Park	d	07 56			08 00			08 26			08 30			08 56			09 00					09 26	
Catford	d	07 59			08 03			08 29			08 33			08 59			09 03					09 29	
Bellingham	d	08 01			08 05			08 31			08 35			09 01			09 05					09 31	
Beckenham Hill	d	08 03			08 07			08 33			08 37			09 03			09 07					09 33	
Ravensbourne	d	08 05			08 09			08 35			08 39			09 05			09 09					09 35	
Shortlands	d	08 07			08 11			08 37			08 41			09 07			09 11					09 37	
Bromley South	d	08 10			08 14			08 40			08 44			09 10			09 14					09 40	
Bickley	d	08 13			08 17			08 43			08 47			09 13			09 17					09 43	
St Mary Cray	d	08 17			08 21			08 47			08 51			09 17			09 21					09 47	
Swanley	d	08 22			08 26			08 52			08 56			09 22			09 26					09 52	
Eynsford	d	08 26			08 30			08 56			09 00			09 26			09 30					09 56	
Shoreham (Kent)	d	08 30			08 34			09 00			09 04			09 30			09 34					10 00	
Otford	d	08 33			08 37			09 03			09 07			09 33			09 37					10 03	
Bat & Ball	d	08 36			08 40			09 06			09 10			09 36			09 40					10 06	
Sevenoaks	a	08 39			08 43			09 09			09 13			09 39			09 43					10 09	
London Bridge	a																						
	d		07 39				07 51		08 09				08 21		08 39			08 51					09 09
Tulse Hill	d						08 09						08 39					09 09		09 12			
Streatham	d						08 12						08 42					09 12		09 16			
Mitcham Eastfields	d			07 40						08 10						08 40			09 10	09 20			
Mitcham Junction	d			07 43						08 13						08 43			09 13	09 23			
Hackbridge	d			07 46						08 16						08 46			09 16	09 26			
Carshalton	d			07 49						08 19						08 49			09 19	09 29			
Tooting	d																						
Haydons Road	d																						
Wimbledon ⊖	d																						
Wimbledon Chase	d																						
South Merton	d																						
Morden South	d																						
St Helier	d																						
Sutton Common	d																						
West Sutton	d																						
Sutton (Surrey)	a			07 52						08 22						08 52			09 22	09 33			
East Croydon	d		08a07			08 25	08a30		08a37			08 55	09a01		09a07			09a30			09 25		09a37
Redhill	d																						
Gatwick Airport ✈	d					08 42						09 12									09 42		
Three Bridges	d					08 47						09 17									09 47		
Balcombe	d																						
Haywards Heath	d					08 56						09 26									09 56		
Wivelsfield	d																						
Burgess Hill	d					09 01						09 31									10 01		
Hassocks	d					09 05						09 35									10 05		
Preston Park	d																						
Brighton	a					09 15						09 45									10 15		

A until 22 July, from 19 August until 9 September
B To Tattenham Corner
C From London Victoria to Epsom
D 29 July, 5 August, 12 August
E From Bedford

Please refer to separate pages within this table for services operating between Bedford and London

At weekends please use local bus and tube services to travel to/from St Pancras International and London Bridge when no trains are operating. See local publicity for details of alternative routes and services that are available across central London

South London, Gatwick Airport - Brighton

Sundays until 9 September

Network Diagram - see first Page of Table 52

		SE	SN	FC	FC	SN	FC	FC	SE	SN	SE	SN	FC	FC	SN	FC	FC	FC	SE	SN	SE	SN
		A	B	C	D			D	E	F	A	B	C	D			G	H	E	F	A	B
St Pancras International ⊖	d			09 05	09 09			09 24					09 35	09 39			09 54	09 54				
Farringdon ⊖	d			09 10	09 14			09 29					09 40	09 44			09 59	09 58				
City Thameslink	d																					
London Blackfriars ⊖	a			09 14	09 19			09 34					09 44	09 49			10 04	10 04				
	d	09 12		09 15	09 19		09 26	09 34	09 38		09 42		09 45	09 49		09 56	10 04	10 04	10 08		10 12	
Elephant & Castle ⊖	d	09 16		09 18			09 30		09 42		09 46		09 48			10 00			10 12		10 16	
Loughborough Jn	d			09 22			09 34						09 52			10 04						
Herne Hill	d			09 26			09 38						09 56			10 08						
Denmark Hill	d	09 22							09 48		09 52								10 18		10 22	
Peckham Rye	d	09 25							09 51		09 55								10 21		10 25	
Nunhead	d	09 27							09 53		09 57								10 23		10 27	
Crofton Park	d	09 30							09 56		10 00								10 26		10 30	
Catford	d	09 33							09 59		10 03								10 29		10 33	
Bellingham	d	09 35							10 01		10 05								10 31		10 35	
Beckenham Hill	d	09 37							10 03		10 07								10 33		10 37	
Ravensbourne	d	09 39							10 05		10 09								10 35		10 39	
Shortlands	d	09 41							10 07		10 11								10 37		10 41	
Bromley South	d	09 44							10 10		10 14								10 40		10 44	
Bickley	d	09 47							10 13		10 17								10 43		10 47	
St Mary Cray	d	09 51							10 17		10 21								10 47		10 51	
Swanley	d	09 56							10 22		10 26								10 52		10 56	
Eynsford	d	10 00							10 26		10 30								10 56		11 00	
Shoreham (Kent)	d	10 04							10 30		10 34								11 00		11 04	
Otford	d	10 07							10 33		10 37								11 03		11 07	
Bat & Ball	d	10 10							10 36		10 40								11 06		11 10	
Sevenoaks	a	10 13							10 39		10 43								11 09		11 13	
London Bridge	a																					
	d					09 21				09 39					09 51					10 09		
Tulse Hill	d			09 30		09 39	09 42						10 00		10 09	10 12						
Streatham	d			09 34		09 42	09 46						10 04		10 12	10 16						
Mitcham Eastfields	d		09 40				09 50					10 10				10 20						10 40
Mitcham Junction	d		09 43				09 53					10 13				10 23						10 43
Hackbridge	d		09 46				09 56					10 16				10 26						10 46
Carshalton	d		09 49				09 59					10 19				10 29						10 49
Tooting	d			09 38									10 08									
Haydons Road	d			09 41									10 11									
Wimbledon ⊖	d			09 44									10 14									
Wimbledon Chase	d			09 47									10 17									
South Merton	d			09 49									10 19									
Morden South	d			09 51									10 21									
St Helier	d			09 53									10 23									
Sutton Common	d			09 55									10 25									
West Sutton	d			09 58									10 28									
Sutton (Surrey)	a		09 52	10 01			10 03					10 22	10 31			10 33						10 52
East Croydon	d				09a39	10a01		09 55		10a07				10a09	10a30		10 26	10 26		10a37		
Redhill	d																					
Gatwick Airport ✈	d							10 12									10 42	10 42				
Three Bridges	d							10 17									10 47	10 47				
Balcombe	d																					
Haywards Heath	d							10 26									10 56	10 56				
Wivelsfield	d																					
Burgess Hill	d							10 31									11 01	11 01				
Hassocks	d							10 35									11 05	11 05				
Preston Park	d																					
Brighton	a							10 45									11 15	11 15				

A 29 July, 5 August, 12 August
B From London Victoria to Epsom
C From Luton
D From Bedford
E until 22 July, from 19 August until 9 September
F To Tattenham Corner
G until 24 June. From Bedford
H from 1 July until 9 September. From Bedford

Please refer to separate pages within this table for services operating between Bedford and London

At weekends please use local bus and tube services to travel to/from St Pancras International and London Bridge when no trains are operating. See local publicity for details of alternative routes and services that are available across central London

Table 52

Sundays
until 9 September

South London, Gatwick Airport - Brighton

Network Diagram - see first Page of Table 52

		FC A	FC ■ B	SN	FC	FC ■ B	SE C	SN D		SE E	SN F	FC A	FC ■ B	SN	FC	FC ■ B	SE C	SN D		SE E	SN F	FC A	FC ■ B	SN	FC
St Pancras International ⊖	d	10 05	10 09			10 24						10 35	10 39			10 54						11 05	11 09		
Farringdon ⊖	d	10 10	10 14			10 29						10 40	10 44			10 58						11 10	11 14		
City Thameslink	d																								
London Blackfriars ⊖	a	10 14	10 19			10 34						10 44	10 49			11 04						11 14	11 19		
	d	10 15	10 19		10 26	10 34	10 38			10 42		10 45	10 49		10 56	11 04	11 08			11 12		11 15	11 19		11 26
Elephant & Castle ⊖	d	10 18			10 30		10 42			10 46		10 48			11 00		11 12			11 16		11 18			11 30
Loughborough Jn.	d	10 22			10 34							10 52			11 04							11 22			11 34
Herne Hill	d	10 26			10 38							10 56			11 08							11 26			11 38
Denmark Hill	d						10 48			10 52							11 18			11 22					
Peckham Rye	d						10 51			10 55							11 21			11 25					
Nunhead	d						10 53			10 57							11 23			11 27					
Crofton Park	d						10 56			11 00							11 26			11 30					
Catford	d						10 59			11 03							11 29			11 33					
Bellingham	d						11 01			11 05							11 31			11 35					
Beckenham Hill	d						11 03			11 07							11 33			11 37					
Ravensbourne	d						11 05			11 09							11 35			11 39					
Shortlands	d						11 07			11 11							11 37			11 41					
Bromley South	d						11 10			11 14							11 40			11 44					
Bickley	d						11 13			11 17							11 43			11 47					
St Mary Cray	d						11 17			11 21							11 47			11 51					
Swanley	d						11 22			11 26							11 52			11 56					
Eynsford	d						11 26			11 30							11 56			12 00					
Shoreham (Kent)	d						11 30			11 34							12 00			12 04					
Otford	d						11 33			11 37							12 03			12 07					
Bat & Ball	d						11 36			11 40							12 06			12 10					
Sevenoaks	a						11 39			11 43							12 09			12 13					
London Bridge	a																								
	d			10 21				10 39						10 51				11 09						11 21	
Tulse Hill	d	10 30		10 39	10 42							11 00		11 09	11 12							11 30		11 39	11 42
Streatham	d	10 34		10 42	10 46							11 04		11 12	11 16							11 34		11 42	11 46
Mitcham Eastfields	d				10 50						11 10				11 20						11 40				11 50
Mitcham Junction	d				10 53						11 13				11 23						11 43				11 53
Hackbridge	d				10 56						11 16				11 26						11 46				11 56
Carshalton	d				10 59						11 19				11 29						11 49				11 59
Tooting	d	10 38										11 08										11 38			
Haydons Road	d	10 41										11 11										11 41			
Wimbledon ⊖	d	10 44										11 14										11 44			
Wimbledon Chase	d	10 47										11 17										11 47			
South Merton	d	10 49										11 19										11 49			
Morden South	d	10 51										11 21										11 51			
St Helier	d	10 53										11 23										11 53			
Sutton Common	d	10 55										11 25										11 55			
West Sutton	d	10 58										11 28										11 58			
Sutton (Surrey)	a	11 01			11 03						11 22	11 31			11 33						11 52	12 01			12 03
East Croydon	d		10a39	11a01		10 55		11a07					11a09	11a30		11 25		11a37					11a39	12a01	
Redhill	d																								
Gatwick Airport	d					11 12										11 42									
Three Bridges	d					11 17										11 47									
Balcombe	d																								
Haywards Heath	d					11 26										11 56									
Wivelsfield	d																								
Burgess Hill	d					11 31										12 01									
Hassocks	d					11 35										12 05									
Preston Park	d																								
Brighton	a					11 45										12 15									

A From Luton
B From Bedford
C until 22 July, from 19 August until 9 September
D To Tattenham Corner
E 29 July, 5 August, 12 August
F From London Victoria to Epsom

Please refer to separate pages within this table for services operating between Bedford and London

At weekends please use local bus and tube services to travel to/from St Pancras International and London Bridge when no trains are operating. See local publicity for details of alternative routes and services that are available across central London

Table 52

Sundays
until 9 September

South London, Gatwick Airport - Brighton

Network Diagram - see first Page of Table 52

		FC ■ A	SE B	SN C		SE D	SN E	FC F	FC ■ A	SN	FC	FC ■ A	SE B	SN C		SE D	SN E	FC F	FC ■ A	SN	FC	FC ■ A	SE B	SN C	
St Pancras International ⊖	d	11 24						11 35	11 39			11 54						12 05	12 09			12 24			
Farringdon ⊖	d	11 29						11 40	11 44			11 58						12 10	12 14			12 29			
City Thameslink	d																								
London Blackfriars ⊖	a	11 34						11 44	11 49			12 04						12 14	12 19			12 34			
	d	11 34	11 38			11 42		11 45	11 49		11 56	12 04	12 08			12 12		12 15	12 19		12 26	12 34	12 38		
Elephant & Castle ⊖	d		11 42			11 46		11 48			12 00		12 12			12 16		12 18			12 30		12 42		
Loughborough Jn.	d							11 52			12 04							12 22			12 34				
Herne Hill	d							11 56			12 08							12 26			12 38				
Denmark Hill	d		11 48			11 52							12 18			12 22							12 48		
Peckham Rye	d		11 51			11 55							12 21			12 25							12 51		
Nunhead	d		11 53			11 57							12 23			12 27							12 53		
Crofton Park	d		11 56			12 00							12 26			12 30							12 56		
Catford	d		11 59			12 03							12 29			12 33							12 59		
Bellingham	d		12 01			12 05							12 31			12 35							13 01		
Beckenham Hill	d		12 03			12 07							12 33			12 37							13 03		
Ravensbourne	d		12 05			12 09							12 35			12 39							13 05		
Shortlands	d		12 07			12 11							12 37			12 41							13 07		
Bromley South	d		12 10			12 14							12 40			12 44							13 10		
Bickley	d		12 13			12 17							12 43			12 47							13 13		
St Mary Cray	d		12 17			12 21							12 47			12 51							13 17		
Swanley	d		12 22			12 26							12 52			12 56							13 22		
Eynsford	d		12 26			12 30							12 56			13 00							13 26		
Shoreham (Kent)	d		12 30			12 34							13 00			13 04							13 30		
Otford	d		12 33			12 37							13 03			13 07							13 33		
Bat & Ball	d		12 36			12 40							13 06			13 10							13 36		
Sevenoaks	a		12 39			12 43							13 09			13 13							13 39		
London Bridge	a																								
	d			11 39						11 51				12 09						12 21				12 39	
Tulse Hill	d							12 00		12 09	12 12							12 30		12 39	12 42				
Streatham	d							12 04		12 12	12 16							12 34		12 42	12 46				
Mitcham Eastfields	d						12 10				12 20						12 40				12 50				
Mitcham Junction	d						12 13				12 23						12 43				12 53				
Hackbridge	d						12 16				12 26						12 46				12 56				
Carshalton	d						12 19				12 29						12 49				12 59				
Tooting	d							12 08										12 38							
Haydons Road	d							12 11										12 41							
Wimbledon ⊖	d							12 14										12 44							
Wimbledon Chase	d							12 17										12 47							
South Merton	d							12 19										12 49							
Morden South	d							12 21										12 51							
St Helier	d							12 23										12 53							
Sutton Common	d							12 25										12 55							
West Sutton	d							12 28										12 58							
Sutton (Surrey)	a						12 22	12 31			12 33						12 52	13 01			13 03				
East Croydon	d	11 55		12a07					12a09	12a30		12 25		12a37					12a39	13a01		12 55		13a07	
Redhill	d																								
Gatwick Airport	d	12 12										12 42										13 12			
Three Bridges	d	12 17										12 47										13 17			
Balcombe	d																								
Haywards Heath	d	12 26										12 56										13 26			
Wivelsfield	d																								
Burgess Hill	d	12 31										13 01										13 31			
Hassocks	d	12 35										13 05										13 35			
Preston Park	d																								
Brighton	a	12 45										13 15										13 45			

A From Bedford
B until 22 July, from 19 August until 9 September
C To Tattenham Corner
D 29 July, 5 August, 12 August
E From London Victoria to Epsom
F From Luton

Please refer to separate pages within this table for services operating between Bedford and London

At weekends please use local bus and tube services to travel to/from St Pancras International and London Bridge when no trains are operating. See local publicity for details of alternative routes and services that are available across central London

Sundays
until 9 September

South London, Gatwick Airport - Brighton

Network Diagram - see first Page of Table 52

		SE A	SN B	FC C	FC ■ D	SN	FC	FC ■ D	SE E	SN F	SE A	SN B	FC C	FC ■ D	SN	FC	FC ■ D	SE E	SN F	SE A	SN B	FC C	FC ■ D
St Pancras International	d			12 35	12 39			12 54					13 05	13 09			13 24					13 35	13 39
Farringdon	d			12 40	12 44			12 58					13 10	13 14			13 29					13 40	13 44
City Thameslink	d																						
London Blackfriars	a			12 44	12 49			13 04					13 14	13 19			13 34					13 44	13 49
	d	12 42		12 45	12 49		12 56	13 04	13 08		13 12		13 15	13 19		13 26	13 34	13 38		13 42		13 45	13 49
Elephant & Castle	d	12 46		12 48			13 00		13 12		13 16		13 18			13 30		13 42		13 46		13 48	
Loughborough Jn.	d			12 52			13 04						13 22			13 34						13 52	
Herne Hill	d			12 56			13 08						13 26			13 38						13 56	
Denmark Hill	d	12 52							13 18		13 22							13 48		13 52			
Peckham Rye	d	12 55							13 21		13 25							13 51		13 55			
Nunhead	d	12 57							13 23		13 27							13 53		13 57			
Crofton Park	d	13 00							13 26		13 30							13 56		14 00			
Catford	d	13 03							13 29		13 33							13 59		14 03			
Bellingham	d	13 05							13 31		13 35							14 01		14 05			
Beckenham Hill	d	13 07							13 33		13 37							14 03		14 07			
Ravensbourne	d	13 09							13 35		13 39							14 05		14 09			
Shortlands	d	13 11							13 37		13 41							14 07		14 11			
Bromley South	d	13 14							13 40		13 44							14 10		14 14			
Bickley	d	13 17							13 43		13 47							14 13		14 17			
St Mary Cray	d	13 21							13 47		13 51							14 17		14 21			
Swanley	d	13 26							13 52		13 56							14 22		14 26			
Eynsford	d	13 30							13 56		14 00							14 26		14 30			
Shoreham (Kent)	d	13 34							14 00		14 04							14 30		14 34			
Otford	d	13 37							14 03		14 07							14 33		14 37			
Bat & Ball	d	13 40							14 06		14 10							14 36		14 40			
Sevenoaks	a	13 43							14 09		14 13							14 39		14 43			
London Bridge	a																						
	d					12 51				13 09					13 21				13 39				
Tulse Hill	d			13 00		13 09	13 12						13 30		13 39	13 42						14 00	
Streatham	d			13 04		13 12	13 16						13 34		13 42	13 46						14 04	
Mitcham Eastfields	d		13 10				13 20					13 40				13 50					14 10		
Mitcham Junction	d		13 13				13 23					13 43				13 53					14 13		
Hackbridge	d		13 16				13 26					13 46				13 56					14 16		
Carshalton	d		13 19				13 29					13 49				13 59					14 19		
Tooting	d			13 08									13 38									14 08	
Haydons Road	d			13 11									13 41									14 11	
Wimbledon	d			13 14									13 44									14 14	
Wimbledon Chase	d			13 17									13 47									14 17	
South Merton	d			13 19									13 49									14 19	
Morden South	d			13 21									13 51									14 21	
St Helier	d			13 23									13 53									14 23	
Sutton Common	d			13 25									13 55									14 25	
West Sutton	d			13 28									13 58									14 28	
Sutton (Surrey)	a		13 22	13 31			13 33					13 52	14 01			14 03					14 22	14 31	
East Croydon	d				13a09	13a30		13 25		13a37				13a39	14a01		13 55		14a07				14a09
Redhill	d																						
Gatwick Airport	d							13 42									14 12						
Three Bridges	d							13 47									14 17						
Balcombe	d																						
Haywards Heath	d							13 56									14 26						
Wivelsfield	d																						
Burgess Hill	d							14 01									14 31						
Hassocks	d							14 05									14 35						
Preston Park	d																						
Brighton	a							14 15									14 45						

A 29 July, 5 August, 12 August
B From London Victoria to Epsom
C From Luton
D From Bedford
E until 22 July, from 19 August until 9 September
F To Tattenham Corner

Please refer to separate pages within this table for services operating between Bedford and London

At weekends please use local bus and tube services to travel to/from St Pancras International and London Bridge when no trains are operating. See local publicity for details of alternative routes and services that are available across central London

Sundays
until 9 September

South London, Gatwick Airport - Brighton

Network Diagram - see first Page of Table 52

		SN	FC	FC ■ A	SE B	SN C	SE D	SN E	FC F	FC ■ A	SN	FC	FC ■ A	SE B	SN C	SE D	SN E	FC F	FC ■ A	SN	FC	FC ■ A	SE B
St Pancras International	d			13 54					14 05	14 09			14 24					14 35	14 39			14 54	
Farringdon	d			13 58					14 10	14 14			14 29					14 40	14 44			14 58	
City Thameslink	d																						
London Blackfriars	a			14 04					14 14	14 19			14 34					14 44	14 49			15 04	
	d		13 56	14 04	14 08		14 12		14 15	14 19		14 26	14 34	14 38		14 42		14 45	14 49		14 56	15 04	15 08
Elephant & Castle	d		14 00		14 12		14 16		14 18			14 30		14 42		14 46		14 48			15 00		15 12
Loughborough Jn.	d		14 04						14 22			14 34						14 52			15 04		
Herne Hill	d		14 08						14 26			14 38						14 56			15 08		
Denmark Hill	d				14 18		14 22							14 48		14 52							15 18
Peckham Rye	d				14 21		14 25							14 51		14 55							15 21
Nunhead	d				14 23		14 27							14 53		14 57							15 23
Crofton Park	d				14 26		14 30							14 56		15 00							15 26
Catford	d				14 29		14 33							14 59		15 03							15 29
Bellingham	d				14 31		14 35							15 01		15 05							15 31
Beckenham Hill	d				14 33		14 37							15 03		15 07							15 33
Ravensbourne	d				14 35		14 39							15 05		15 09							15 35
Shortlands	d				14 37		14 41							15 07		15 11							15 37
Bromley South	d				14 40		14 44							15 10		15 14							15 40
Bickley	d				14 43		14 47							15 13		15 17							15 43
St Mary Cray	d				14 47		14 51							15 17		15 21							15 47
Swanley	d				14 52		14 56							15 22		15 26							15 52
Eynsford	d				14 56		15 00							15 26		15 30							15 56
Shoreham (Kent)	d				15 00		15 04							15 30		15 34							16 00
Otford	d				15 03		15 07							15 33		15 37							16 03
Bat & Ball	d				15 06		15 10							15 36		15 40							16 06
Sevenoaks	a				15 09		15 13							15 39		15 43							16 09
London Bridge	a																						
	d	13 51				14 09					14 21				14 39					14 51			
Tulse Hill	d	14 09	14 12						14 30		14 39	14 42						15 00		15 09	15 12		
Streatham	d	14 12	14 16						14 34		14 42	14 46						15 04		15 12	15 16		
Mitcham Eastfields	d		14 20					14 40				14 50					15 10				15 20		
Mitcham Junction	d		14 23					14 43				14 53					15 13				15 23		
Hackbridge	d		14 26					14 46				14 56					15 16				15 26		
Carshalton	d		14 29					14 49				14 59					15 19				15 29		
Tooting	d								14 38									15 08					
Haydons Road	d								14 41									15 11					
Wimbledon	d								14 44									15 14					
Wimbledon Chase	d								14 47									15 17					
South Merton	d								14 49									15 19					
Morden South	d								14 51									15 21					
St Helier	d								14 53									15 23					
Sutton Common	d								14 55									15 25					
West Sutton	d								14 58									15 28					
Sutton (Surrey)	a		14 33					14 52	15 01			15 03					15 22	15 31			15 33		
East Croydon	d	14a30		14 25		14a37				14a39	15a01		14 55		15a07				15a09	15a30		15 25	
Redhill	d																						
Gatwick Airport	d			14 42									15 12									15 42	
Three Bridges	d			14 47									15 17									15 47	
Balcombe	d																						
Haywards Heath	d			14 56									15 26									15 56	
Wivelsfield	d																						
Burgess Hill	d			15 01									15 31									16 01	
Hassocks	d			15 05									15 35									16 05	
Preston Park	d																						
Brighton	a			15 15									15 45									16 15	

A From Bedford
B until 22 July, from 19 August until 9 September
C To Tattenham Corner
D 29 July, 5 August, 12 August
E From London Victoria to Epsom
F From Luton

Please refer to separate pages within this table for services operating between Bedford and London

At weekends please use local bus and tube services to travel to/from St Pancras International and London Bridge when no trains are operating. See local publicity for details of alternative routes and services that are available across central London

Table 52

Sundays until 9 September

South London, Gatwick Airport - Brighton

Network Diagram - see first Page of Table 52

		SN		SE	SN	FC	FC	SN	FC	FC	SE	SN		SE	SN	FC	FC	SN	FC	FC	SE	SN		SE	SN
							1			1							1			1					
		A		B	C	D	E			E	F	A		B	C	D	E			E	F	A		B	C
St Pancras International	d					15 05	15 09			15 24						15 35	15 39			15 54					
Farringdon	d					15 10	15 14			15 29						15 40	15 44			15 58					
City Thameslink	d																								
London Blackfriars	a					15 14	15 19			15 34						15 44	15 49			16 04					
	d			15 12		15 15	15 19		15 26	15 34	15 38			15 42		15 45	15 49		15 56	16 04	16 08			16 12	
Elephant & Castle	d			15 16		15 18			15 30		15 42			15 46		15 48			16 00		16 12			16 16	
Loughborough Jn.	d					15 22			15 34							15 52			16 04						
Herne Hill	d					15 26			15 38							15 56			16 08						
Denmark Hill	d			15 22							15 48			15 52							16 18			16 22	
Peckham Rye	d			15 25							15 51			15 55							16 21			16 25	
Nunhead	d			15 27							15 53			15 57							16 23			16 27	
Crofton Park	d			15 30							15 56			16 00							16 26			16 30	
Catford	d			15 33							15 59			16 03							16 29			16 33	
Bellingham	d			15 35							16 01			16 05							16 31			16 35	
Beckenham Hill	d			15 37							16 03			16 07							16 33			16 37	
Ravensbourne	d			15 39							16 05			16 09							16 35			16 39	
Shortlands	d			15 41							16 07			16 11							16 37			16 41	
Bromley South	d			15 44							16 10			16 14							16 40			16 44	
Bickley	d			15 47							16 13			16 17							16 43			16 47	
St Mary Cray	d			15 51							16 17			16 21							16 47			16 51	
Swanley	d			15 56							16 22			16 26							16 52			16 56	
Eynsford	d			16 00							16 26			16 30							16 56			17 00	
Shoreham (Kent)	d			16 04							16 30			16 34							17 00			17 04	
Otford	d			16 07							16 33			16 37							17 03			17 07	
Bat & Ball	d			16 10							16 36			16 40							17 06			17 10	
Sevenoaks	a			16 13							16 39			16 43							17 09			17 13	
London Bridge	a																								
	d	15 09						15 21				15 39						15 51				16 09			
Tulse Hill	d					15 30		15 39	15 42							16 00		16 09	16 12						
Streatham	d					15 34		15 42	15 46							16 04		16 12	16 16						
Mitcham Eastfields	d				15 40				15 50						16 10				16 20						16 40
Mitcham Junction	d				15 43				15 53						16 13				16 23						16 43
Hackbridge	d				15 46				15 56						16 16				16 26						16 46
Carshalton	d				15 49				15 59						16 19				16 29						16 49
Tooting	d					15 38										16 08									
Haydons Road	d					15 41										16 11									
Wimbledon	d					15 44										16 14									
Wimbledon Chase	d					15 47										16 17									
South Merton	d					15 49										16 19									
Morden South	d					15 51										16 21									
St Helier	d					15 53										16 23									
Sutton Common	d					15 55										16 25									
West Sutton	d					15 58										16 28									
Sutton (Surrey)	a				15 52	16 01			16 03						16 22	16 31			16 33						16 52
East Croydon	d	15a37					15a39	16a01		15 55		16a07					16a09	16a30		16 25		16a37			
Redhill	d																								
Gatwick Airport	d									16 12										16 42					
Three Bridges	d									16 17										16 47					
Balcombe	d																								
Haywards Heath	d									16 26										16 56					
Wivelsfield	d																								
Burgess Hill	d									16 31										17 01					
Hassocks	d									16 35										17 05					
Preston Park	d																								
Brighton	a									16 45										17 15					

A To Tattenham Corner
B 29 July, 5 August, 12 August
C From London Victoria to Epsom
D From Luton
E From Bedford
F until 22 July, from 19 August until 9 September

Please refer to separate pages within this table for services operating between Bedford and London

At weekends please use local bus and tube services to travel to/from St Pancras International and London Bridge when no trains are operating. See local publicity for details of alternative routes and services that are available across central London

Table 52

Sundays until 9 September

South London, Gatwick Airport - Brighton

Network Diagram - see first Page of Table 52

		FC	FC	SN	FC	FC	SE	SN		SE	SN	FC	FC	SN	FC	FC	SE	SN		SE	SN	FC	FC	SN	FC
			1			1							1			1							1		
		A	B			B	C	D		E	F	A	B			B	C	D		E	F	A	B		
St Pancras International	d	16 05	16 09			16 24						16 35	16 39			16 54						17 05	17 09		
Farringdon	d	16 10	16 14			16 29						16 40	16 44			16 58						17 10	17 14		
City Thameslink	d																								
London Blackfriars	a	16 14	16 19			16 34						16 44	16 49			17 04						17 14	17 19		
	d	16 15	16 19		16 26	16 34	16 38			16 42		16 45	16 49		16 56	17 04	17 08			17 12		17 15	17 19		17 26
Elephant & Castle	d	16 18			16 30		16 42			16 46		16 48			17 00		17 12			17 16		17 18			17 30
Loughborough Jn.	d	16 22			16 34							16 52			17 04							17 22			17 34
Herne Hill	d	16 26			16 38							16 56			17 08							17 26			17 38
Denmark Hill	d						16 48			16 52							17 18			17 22					
Peckham Rye	d						16 51			16 55							17 21			17 25					
Nunhead	d						16 53			16 57							17 23			17 27					
Crofton Park	d						16 56			17 00							17 26			17 30					
Catford	d						16 59			17 03							17 29			17 33					
Bellingham	d						17 01			17 05							17 31			17 35					
Beckenham Hill	d						17 03			17 07							17 33			17 37					
Ravensbourne	d						17 05			17 09							17 35			17 39					
Shortlands	d						17 07			17 11							17 37			17 41					
Bromley South	d						17 10			17 14							17 40			17 44					
Bickley	d						17 13			17 17							17 43			17 47					
St Mary Cray	d						17 17			17 21							17 47			17 51					
Swanley	d						17 22			17 26							17 52			17 56					
Eynsford	d						17 26			17 30							17 56			18 00					
Shoreham (Kent)	d						17 30			17 34							18 00			18 04					
Otford	d						17 33			17 37							18 03			18 07					
Bat & Ball	d						17 36			17 40							18 06			18 10					
Sevenoaks	a						17 39			17 43							18 09			18 13					
London Bridge	a																								
	d			16 21				16 39						16 51				17 09						17 21	
Tulse Hill	d	16 30		16 39	16 42							17 00		17 09	17 12							17 30		17 39	17 42
Streatham	d	16 34		16 42	16 46							17 04		17 12	17 16							17 34		17 42	17 46
Mitcham Eastfields	d				16 50						17 10				17 20						17 40				17 50
Mitcham Junction	d				16 53						17 13				17 23						17 43				17 53
Hackbridge	d				16 56						17 16				17 26						17 46				17 56
Carshalton	d				16 59						17 19				17 29						17 49				17 59
Tooting	d	16 38										17 08										17 38			
Haydons Road	d	16 41										17 11										17 41			
Wimbledon	d	16 44										17 14										17 44			
Wimbledon Chase	d	16 47										17 17										17 47			
South Merton	d	16 49										17 19										17 49			
Morden South	d	16 51										17 21										17 51			
St Helier	d	16 53										17 23										17 53			
Sutton Common	d	16 55										17 25										17 55			
West Sutton	d	16 58										17 28										17 58			
Sutton (Surrey)	a	17 01			17 03						17 22	17 31			17 33						17 52	18 01			18 03
East Croydon	d		16a39	17a01		16 55		17a07					17a09	17a30		17 25		17a37					17a39	18a01	
Redhill	d																								
Gatwick Airport	d					17 12										17 42									
Three Bridges	d					17 17										17 47									
Balcombe	d																								
Haywards Heath	d					17 26										17 56									
Wivelsfield	d																								
Burgess Hill	d					17 31										18 01									
Hassocks	d					17 35										18 05									
Preston Park	d																								
Brighton	a					17 45										18 15									

A From Luton
B From Bedford
C until 22 July, from 19 August until 9 September
D To Tattenham Corner
E 29 July, 5 August, 12 August
F From London Victoria to Epsom

Please refer to separate pages within this table for services operating between Bedford and London

At weekends please use local bus and tube services to travel to/from St Pancras International and London Bridge when no trains are operating. See local publicity for details of alternative routes and services that are available across central London

Sundays until 9 September

South London, Gatwick Airport - Brighton

Network Diagram - see first Page of Table 52

		FC	SE	SN		SE	SN	FC	FC	SN	FC	FC	SE	SN		SE	FC	FC	SN	FC	FC	SE	SN	SE
		A	B	C		D	E	F	A			A	B	C		D	F	A			A	B	C	D
St Pancras International	d	17 24						17 35	17 39			17 54					18 05	18 09			18 24			
Farringdon	d	17 29						17 40	17 44			17 58					18 10	18 14			18 29			
City Thameslink	d																							
London Blackfriars	a	17 34						17 44	17 49			18 04					18 14	18 19			18 34			
	d	17 34	17 38			17 42		17 45	17 49		17 56	18 04	18 08			18 12	18 15	18 19		18 26	18 34	18 38		18 42
Elephant & Castle	d		17 42			17 46		17 48			18 00		18 12			18 16	18 18			18 30		18 42		18 46
Loughborough Jn.	d							17 52			18 04						18 22			18 34				
Herne Hill	d							17 56			18 08						18 26			18 38				
Denmark Hill	d		17 48			17 52							18 18			18 22						18 48		18 52
Peckham Rye	d		17 51			17 55							18 21			18 25						18 51		18 55
Nunhead	d		17 53			17 57							18 23			18 27						18 53		18 57
Crofton Park	d		17 56			18 00							18 26			18 30						18 56		19 00
Catford	d		17 59			18 03							18 29			18 33						18 59		19 03
Bellingham	d		18 01			18 05							18 31			18 35						19 01		19 05
Beckenham Hill	d		18 03			18 07							18 33			18 37						19 03		19 07
Ravensbourne	d		18 05			18 09							18 35			18 39						19 05		19 09
Shortlands	d		18 07			18 11							18 37			18 41						19 07		19 11
Bromley South	d		18 10			18 14							18 40			18 44						19 10		19 14
Bickley	d		18 13			18 17							18 43			18 47						19 13		19 17
St Mary Cray	d		18 17			18 21							18 47			18 51						19 17		19 21
Swanley	d		18 22			18 26							18 52			18 56						19 22		19 26
Eynsford	d		18 26			18 30							18 56			19 00						19 26		19 30
Shoreham (Kent)	d		18 30			18 34							19 00			19 04						19 30		19 34
Otford	d		18 33			18 37							19 03			19 07						19 33		19 37
Bat & Ball	d		18 36			18 40							19 06			19 10						19 36		19 40
Sevenoaks	a		18 39			18 43							19 09			19 13						19 39		19 43
London Bridge	a																							
	d			17 39						17 51				18 09					18 21				18 39	
Tulse Hill	d							18 00		18 09	18 12						18 30		18 39	18 42				
Streatham	d							18 04		18 12	18 16						18 34		18 42	18 46				
Mitcham Eastfields	d						18 10				18 20									18 50				
Mitcham Junction	d						18 13				18 23									18 53				
Hackbridge	d						18 16				18 26									18 56				
Carshalton	d						18 19				18 29									18 59				
Tooting	d							18 08									18 38							
Haydons Road	d							18 11									18 41							
Wimbledon	d							18 14									18 44							
Wimbledon Chase	d							18 17									18 47							
South Merton	d							18 19									18 49							
Morden South	d							18 21									18 51							
St Helier	d							18 23									18 53							
Sutton Common	d							18 25									18 55							
West Sutton	d							18 28									18 58							
Sutton (Surrey)	a						18 22	18 31			18 33						19 01			19 03				
East Croydon	d	17 55		18a07					18a09	18a30		18 25		18a37				18a39	19a01		18 55		19a07	
Redhill	d																							
Gatwick Airport	d	18 12										18 42									19 12			
Three Bridges	d	18 17										18 47									19 17			
Balcombe	d																							
Haywards Heath	d	18 26										18 56									19 26			
Wivelsfield	d																							
Burgess Hill	d	18 31										19 01									19 31			
Hassocks	d	18 35										19 05									19 35			
Preston Park	d																							
Brighton	a	18 45										19 15									19 45			

A From Bedford
B until 22 July, from 19 August until 9 September
C To Tattenham Corner
D 29 July, 5 August, 12 August
E From London Victoria to Epsom
F From Luton

Please refer to separate pages within this table for services operating between Bedford and London

At weekends please use local bus and tube services to travel to/from St Pancras International and London Bridge when no trains are operating. See local publicity for details of alternative routes and services that are available across central London

Sundays until 9 September

South London, Gatwick Airport - Brighton

Network Diagram - see first Page of Table 52

		FC	FC	SN	FC	FC	SE	SN	SE	FC		SN	FC	FC	SE	SN	SE	FC	SN	FC		FC	SE	SN	SE
		A	B			B	C	D	E	A				B	C	D	E	A				B	C	D	E
St Pancras International	d	18 35	18 39			18 54				19 05				19 24				19 35				19 54			
Farringdon	d	18 40	18 44			18 58				19 10				19 29				19 40				19 58			
City Thameslink	d																								
London Blackfriars	a	18 44	18 49			19 04				19 14				19 34				19 44				20 04			
	d	18 45	18 49		18 56	19 04	19 08		19 12	19 15			19 26	19 34	19 38		19 42	19 45		19 56		20 04	20 08		20 12
Elephant & Castle	d	18 48			19 00		19 12		19 16	19 18			19 30		19 42		19 46	19 48		20 00			20 12		20 16
Loughborough Jn.	d	18 52			19 04					19 22			19 34					19 52		20 04					
Herne Hill	d	18 56			19 08					19 26			19 38					19 56		20 08					
Denmark Hill	d						19 18		19 22						19 48		19 52						20 18		20 22
Peckham Rye	d						19 21		19 25						19 51		19 55						20 21		20 25
Nunhead	d						19 23		19 27						19 53		19 57						20 23		20 27
Crofton Park	d						19 26		19 30						19 56		20 00						20 26		20 30
Catford	d						19 29		19 33						19 59		20 03						20 29		20 33
Bellingham	d						19 31		19 35						20 01		20 05						20 31		20 35
Beckenham Hill	d						19 33		19 37						20 03		20 07						20 33		20 37
Ravensbourne	d						19 35		19 39						20 05		20 09						20 35		20 39
Shortlands	d						19 37		19 41						20 07		20 11						20 37		20 41
Bromley South	d						19 40		19 44						20 10		20 14						20 40		20 44
Bickley	d						19 43		19 47						20 13		20 17						20 43		20 47
St Mary Cray	d						19 47		19 51						20 17		20 21						20 47		20 51
Swanley	d						19 52		19 56						20 22		20 26						20 52		20 56
Eynsford	d						19 56		20 00						20 26		20 30						20 56		21 00
Shoreham (Kent)	d						20 00		20 04						20 30		20 34						21 00		21 04
Otford	d						20 03		20 07						20 33		20 37						21 03		21 07
Bat & Ball	d						20 06		20 10						20 36		20 40						21 06		21 10
Sevenoaks	a						20 09		20 13						20 39		20 43						21 09		21 13
London Bridge	a																								
	d			18 51				19 09				19 21				19 39			19 51					20 09	
Tulse Hill	d	19 00		19 09	19 12					19 30		19 39	19 42					20 00	20 09	20 12					
Streatham	d	19 04		19 12	19 16					19 34		19 42	19 46					20 04	20 12	20 16					
Mitcham Eastfields	d				19 20								19 50							20 20					
Mitcham Junction	d				19 23								19 53							20 23					
Hackbridge	d				19 26								19 56							20 26					
Carshalton	d				19 29								19 59							20 29					
Tooting	d	19 08								19 38								20 08							
Haydons Road	d	19 11								19 41								20 11							
Wimbledon	d	19 14								19 44								20 14							
Wimbledon Chase	d	19 17								19 47								20 17							
South Merton	d	19 19								19 49								20 19							
Morden South	d	19 21								19 51								20 21							
St Helier	d	19 23								19 53								20 23							
Sutton Common	d	19 25								19 55								20 25							
West Sutton	d	19 28								19 58								20 28							
Sutton (Surrey)	a	19 31			19 33					20 01			20 03					20 31		20 33					
East Croydon	d		19a09	19a30		19 25		19a37				20a01		19 55		20a07			20a30			20 25		20a37	
Redhill	d																								
Gatwick Airport	d					19 42								20 12								20 42			
Three Bridges	d					19 47								20 17								20 47			
Balcombe	d																								
Haywards Heath	d					19 56								20 26								20 56			
Wivelsfield	d																								
Burgess Hill	d					20 01								20 31								21 01			
Hassocks	d					20 05								20 35								21 05			
Preston Park	d																								
Brighton	a					20 15								20 45								21 15			

A From Luton
B From Bedford
C until 22 July, from 19 August until 9 September
D To Tattenham Corner
E 29 July, 5 August, 12 August

Please refer to separate pages within this table for services operating between Bedford and London

At weekends please use local bus and tube services to travel to/from St Pancras International and London Bridge when no trains are operating. See local publicity for details of alternative routes and services that are available across central London

Table 52

Sundays
until 9 September

South London, Gatwick Airport - Brighton

Network Diagram - see first Page of Table 52

		FC	SN	FC	FC	SE	SN	SE	FC	FC	SN	SE	SN	SE	FC	FC	SN	SE	SN	SE	FC	SN	SE
		A			B	C	D	E	A	B		C	D	E	A	B		C	D	E	B		C
St Pancras International	d	20 05			20 24				20 35	20 54					21 05	21 24					21 54		
Farringdon	d	20 10			20 29				20 40	20 58					21 10	21 29					21 59		
City Thameslink	d																						
London Blackfriars	a	20 14			20 34				20 44	21 04					21 14	21 34					22 04		
	d	20 15		20 26	20 34	20 38		20 42	20 45	21 04		21 08		21 12	21 15	21 34		21 38		21 42	22 04		22 08
Elephant & Castle	d	20 18		20 30		20 42		20 46	20 48			21 12		21 16	21 18			21 42		21 46			22 12
Loughborough Jn.	d	20 22		20 34					20 52						21 22								
Herne Hill	d	20 26		20 38					20 56						21 26								
Denmark Hill	d					20 48		20 52				21 18		21 22				21 48		21 52			22 18
Peckham Rye	d					20 51		20 55				21 21		21 25				21 51		21 55			22 21
Nunhead	d					20 53		20 57				21 23		21 27				21 53		21 57			22 23
Crofton Park	d					20 56		21 00				21 26		21 30				21 56		22 00			22 26
Catford	d					20 59		21 03				21 29		21 33				21 59		22 03			22 29
Bellingham	d					21 01		21 05				21 31		21 35				22 01		22 05			22 31
Beckenham Hill	d					21 03		21 07				21 33		21 37				22 03		22 07			22 33
Ravensbourne	d					21 05		21 09				21 35		21 39				22 05		22 09			22 35
Shortlands	d					21 07		21 11				21 37		21 41				22 07		22 11			22 37
Bromley South	d					21 10		21 14				21 40		21 44				22 10		22 14			22 40
Bickley	d					21 13		21 17				21 43		21 47				22 13		22 17			22 43
St Mary Cray	d					21 17		21 21				21 47		21 51				22 17		22 21			22 47
Swanley	d					21 22		21 26				21 52		21 56				22 22		22 26			22 52
Eynsford	d					21 26		21 30				21 56		22 00				22 26		22 30			22 56
Shoreham (Kent)	d					21 30		21 34				22 00		22 04				22 30		22 34			23 00
Otford	d					21 33		21 37				22 03		22 07				22 33		22 37			23 03
Bat & Ball	d					21 36		21 40				22 06		22 10				22 36		22 40			23 06
Sevenoaks	a					21 39		21 43				22 09		22 13				22 39		22 43			23 09
London Bridge	a																						
	d		20 21				20 39				20 51		21 09				21 21		21 39			21 51	
Tulse Hill	d	20 30	20 39	20 42					21 00		21 09				21 30		21 39					22 09	
Streatham	d	20 34	20 42	20 46					21 04		21 12				21 34		21 42					22 12	
Mitcham Eastfields	d			20 50																			
Mitcham Junction	d			20 53																			
Hackbridge	d			20 56																			
Carshalton	d			20 59																			
Tooting	d	20 38							21 08						21 38								
Haydons Road	d	20 41							21 11						21 41								
Wimbledon	d	20 44							21 14						21 44								
Wimbledon Chase	d	20 47							21 17						21 47								
South Merton	d	20 49							21 19						21 49								
Morden South	d	20 51							21 21						21 51								
St Helier	d	20 53							21 23						21 53								
Sutton Common	d	20 55							21 25						21 55								
West Sutton	d	20 58							21 28						21 58								
Sutton (Surrey)	a	21 01		21 03					21 31						22 01								
East Croydon	d		21a01		20 55		21a07			21 25	21a30		21a37			21 55	22a01		22a07		22 25	22a30	
Redhill	d																						
Gatwick Airport	d				21 12					21 42						22 12					22 42		
Three Bridges	d				21 17					21 47						22 17					22 47		
Balcombe	d																						
Haywards Heath	d				21 26					21 56						22 26					22 56		
Wivelsfield	d																						
Burgess Hill	d				21 31					22 01						22 31					23 01		
Hassocks	d				21 35					22 05						22 35					23 05		
Preston Park	d																						
Brighton	a				21 45					22 15						22 45					23 15		

A From Luton
B From Bedford
C until 22 July, from 19 August until 9 September
D To Tattenham Corner
E 29 July, 5 August, 12 August

Please refer to separate pages within this table for services operating between Bedford and London

At weekends please use local bus and tube services to travel to/from St Pancras International and London Bridge when no trains are operating. See local publicity for details of alternative routes and services that are available across central London

Table 52

Sundays
until 9 September

South London, Gatwick Airport - Brighton

Network Diagram - see first Page of Table 52

		SN	SE	FC	SN	SE	SN	SE	FC	SN	SE	SN	SE	FC	SN	SE	SN	SE	FC
		A	B	C		D	A	B	C		D		B	C		D	E	B	C
St Pancras International	d			22 24					22 54					23 24					23 54
Farringdon	d			22 29					22 59					23 29					23 59
City Thameslink	d																		
London Blackfriars	a			22 34					23 04					23 33					00 04
	d		22 12	22 34		22 38		22 42	23 04		23 08		23 12	23 34		23 38		23 42	00 05
Elephant & Castle	d		22 16			22 42		22 46			23 12		23 16			23 42		23 46	
Loughborough Jn.	d																		
Herne Hill	d																		
Denmark Hill	d		22 22			22 48		22 52			23 18		23 22			23 48		23 52	
Peckham Rye	d		22 25			22 51		22 55			23 21		23 25			23 51		23 55	
Nunhead	d		22 27			22 53		22 57			23 23		23 27			23 53		23 57	
Crofton Park	d		22 30			22 56		23 00			23 26		23 30			23 56		23 59	
Catford	d		22 33			22 59		23 03			23 29		23 33			23 59		00 03	
Bellingham	d		22 35			23 01		23 05			23 31		23 35			00 01		00 05	
Beckenham Hill	d		22 37			23 03		23 07			23 33		23 37			00 03		00 07	
Ravensbourne	d		22 39			23 05		23 09			23 35		23 39			00 05		00 09	
Shortlands	d		22 41			23 07		23 11			23 37		23 41			00 07		00 11	
Bromley South	d		22 44			23 10		23 14			23 40		23 44			00 10		00 14	
Bickley	d		22 47			23 13		23 17			23 43		23 47			00 13		00 17	
St Mary Cray	d		22 51			23 17		23 21			23 47		23 51			00 17		00 21	
Swanley	d		22 56			23 22		23 26			23 52		23 56			00 22		00 26	
Eynsford	d		23 00			23 26		23 30			23 56		23 59			00 26		00 30	
Shoreham (Kent)	d		23 04			23 30		23 34			23 59		00 04			00 30		00 34	
Otford	d		23 07			23 33		23 37			00 03		00 07			00 33		00 37	
Bat & Ball	d		23 10			23 36		23 40			00 06		00 10			00 36		00 40	
Sevenoaks	a		23 13			23 39		23 43			00 09		00 13			00 39		00 43	
London Bridge	a																		
	d	22 09			22 21		22 39			22 51		23 09			23 21		23 39		
Tulse Hill	d				22 39					23 09					23 39				
Streatham	d				22 42					23 12					23 42				
Mitcham Eastfields	d																		
Mitcham Junction	d																		
Hackbridge	d																		
Carshalton	d																		
Tooting	d																		
Haydons Road	d																		
Wimbledon	d																		
Wimbledon Chase	d																		
South Merton	d																		
Morden South	d																		
St Helier	d																		
Sutton Common	d																		
West Sutton	d																		
Sutton (Surrey)	a																		
East Croydon	d	22a37		22 55	23a00		23a07		23 25	23a30		23a38		23 57	00a01		00a06		00 26
Redhill	d																		
Gatwick Airport	d			23 12					23 42					00 20					00 49
Three Bridges	d			23 17					23 47					00a25					00a54
Balcombe	d																		
Haywards Heath	d			23 26					23 56										
Wivelsfield	d																		
Burgess Hill	d			23 31					00 02										
Hassocks	d			23 35					00 06										
Preston Park	d																		
Brighton	a			23 45					00 16										

A To Tattenham Corner
B 29 July, 5 August, 12 August
C From Bedford
D until 22 July, from 19 August until 9 September
E To Caterham

Please refer to separate pages within this table for services operating between Bedford and London

At weekends please use local bus and tube services to travel to/from St Pancras International and London Bridge when no trains are operating. See local publicity for details of alternative routes and services that are available across central London

South London, Gatwick Airport - Brighton

Network Diagram - see first Page of Table 52

		FC 1 A	SE	FC B	FC 1 A	SE	FC B	FC 1 A	SN C	FC 1 A		SN	FC 1 A	FC 1	FC 1 A	SN	SE	SN D	SN E	FC 1 A		SN	SE	SN D	SN E
St Pancras International	d	22p54		23p06	23p24		23p36	23p54		00 24			00 54		07 24					07 54					
Farringdon	d	22p59		23p10	23p29		23p40	23p59		00 29					07 29					07 59					
City Thameslink	d																								
London Blackfriars	a	23p04		23p16	23p34		23p46	00 04		00 34			01 04		07 34					08 04					
	d	23p05	23p12	23p16	23p35	23p42	23p46	00 05		00 35			01 05	06 55	07 34		07 38			08 04			08 08		
Elephant & Castle	d		23p16	23p19		23p46	23p49										07 42						08 12		
Loughborough Jn.	d			23p23																					
Herne Hill	d			23p27			23p57																		
Denmark Hill	d		23p22			23p52											07 48						08 18		
Peckham Rye	d		23p25			23p55											07 51						08 21		
Nunhead	d		23p27			23p57											07 53						08 23		
Crofton Park	d		23p30			23p59											07 56						08 26		
Catford	d		23p33			00 03											07 59						08 29		
Bellingham	d		23p35			00 05											08 01						08 31		
Beckenham Hill	d		23p37			00 07											08 03						08 33		
Ravensbourne	d		23p39			00 09											08 05						08 35		
Shortlands	d		23p41			00 11											08 07						08 37		
Bromley South	d		23p44			00 14											08 10						08 40		
Bickley	d		23p47			00 17											08 13						08 43		
St Mary Cray	d		23p51			00 21											08 17						08 47		
Swanley	d		23p56			00 26											08 22						08 52		
Eynsford	d		23p59			00 30											08 26						08 56		
Shoreham (Kent)	d		00 04			00 34											08 30						09 00		
Otford	d		00 07			00 37											08 33						09 03		
Bat & Ball	d		00 10			00 40											08 36						09 06		
Sevenoaks	a		00 13			00 43											08 39						09 09		
London Bridge	a																								
	d								00 06			00 36				07 21		07 39				07 51		08 09	
Tulse Hill	d			23p31			00 01									07 39						08 09			
Streatham	d			23p35			00 05									07 42						08 12			
Mitcham Eastfields	d																		07 40						08 10
Mitcham Junction	d																		07 43						08 13
Hackbridge	d																		07 46						08 16
Carshalton	d																		07 49						08 19
Tooting	d			23p40			00 10																		
Haydons Road	d			23p43			00 13																		
Wimbledon	d			23p47			00 17																		
Wimbledon Chase	d			23p50			00 20																		
South Merton	d			23p52			00 22																		
Morden South	d			23p54			00 24																		
St Helier	d			23p56			00 26																		
Sutton Common	d			23p58			00 28																		
West Sutton	d			00 01			00 31																		
Sutton (Surrey)	a			00 05			00 35												07 52						08 22
East Croydon	d	23p25			23p57			00 27	00a33	00 57		01a03	01 32	07 25	07 57	08a01		08a07		08 28		08a30		08a37	
Redhill	d																								
Gatwick Airport	d	23p41			00 19			00 49		01 22			01 52	07 42	08 20					08 50					
Three Bridges	d	23p47			00a24			00a54		01a28			01a58	07 47	08 24					08 54					
Balcombe	d	23p53																							
Haywards Heath	d	23p59												07 56	08 34					09 04					
Wivelsfield	d	00 03																							
Burgess Hill	d	00 05												08 01	08 39					09 09					
Hassocks	d	00 08												08 05	08 42					09 12					
Preston Park	d	00 15																							
Brighton	a	00 19												08 15	08 52					09 22					

A From Bedford
B From Luton
C To Caterham
D To Tattenham Corner
E From London Victoria to Epsom

Please refer to separate pages within this table for services operating between Bedford and London

At weekends please use local bus and tube services to travel to/from St Pancras International and London Bridge when no trains are operating. See local publicity for details of alternative routes and services that are available across central London

South London, Gatwick Airport - Brighton

Network Diagram - see first Page of Table 52

		FC 1 A	SN	SE	SN B	SN C		SN	SN C	FC	FC 1 A	SE	SN B	SN C	FC D	FC 1 A		SN	FC	FC 1 A	SE	SN B	SN C	FC D	FC 1 A
St Pancras International	d	08 24									08 54				09 05	09 09				09 24				09 35	09 39
Farringdon	d	08 29									08 58				09 10	09 14				09 29				09 40	09 44
City Thameslink	d																								
London Blackfriars	a	08 34									09 04				09 14	09 19				09 34				09 44	09 49
	d	08 34		08 38						08 56	09 04	09 08			09 15	09 19			09 26	09 34	09 38			09 45	09 49
Elephant & Castle	d			08 42						09 00		09 12			09 18				09 30		09 42			09 48	
Loughborough Jn.	d									09 04					09 22				09 34					09 52	
Herne Hill	d									09 08					09 26				09 38					09 56	
Denmark Hill	d			08 48								09 18									09 48				
Peckham Rye	d			08 51								09 21									09 51				
Nunhead	d			08 53								09 23									09 53				
Crofton Park	d			08 56								09 26									09 56				
Catford	d			08 59								09 29									09 59				
Bellingham	d			09 01								09 31									10 01				
Beckenham Hill	d			09 03								09 33									10 03				
Ravensbourne	d			09 05								09 35									10 05				
Shortlands	d			09 07								09 37									10 07				
Bromley South	d			09 10								09 40									10 10				
Bickley	d			09 13								09 43									10 13				
St Mary Cray	d			09 17								09 47									10 17				
Swanley	d			09 22								09 52									10 22				
Eynsford	d			09 26								09 56									10 26				
Shoreham (Kent)	d			09 30								10 00									10 30				
Otford	d			09 33								10 03									10 33				
Bat & Ball	d			09 36								10 06									10 36				
Sevenoaks	a			09 39								10 09									10 39				
London Bridge	a																								
	d		08 21		08 39			08 51					09 09					09 21				09 39			
Tulse Hill	d		08 39					09 09		09 12					09 30			09 39	09 42					10 00	
Streatham	d		08 42					09 12		09 16					09 34			09 42	09 46					10 04	
Mitcham Eastfields	d					08 40			09 10	09 20				09 40					09 50				10 10		
Mitcham Junction	d					08 43			09 13	09 23				09 43					09 53				10 13		
Hackbridge	d					08 46			09 16	09 26				09 46					09 56				10 16		
Carshalton	d					08 49			09 19	09 29				09 49					09 59				10 19		
Tooting	d														09 38									10 08	
Haydons Road	d														09 41									10 11	
Wimbledon	d														09 44									10 14	
Wimbledon Chase	d														09 47									10 17	
South Merton	d														09 49									10 19	
Morden South	d														09 51									10 21	
St Helier	d														09 53									10 23	
Sutton Common	d														09 55									10 25	
West Sutton	d														09 58									10 28	
Sutton (Surrey)	a					08 52			09 22	09 33				09 52	10 01				10 03				10 22	10 31	
East Croydon	d	08 57	09a01		09a07			09a30			09 28		09a37			09a39		10a01		09 57		10a07			10a09
Redhill	d																								
Gatwick Airport	d	09 20									09 50									10 20					
Three Bridges	d	09 24									09 54									10 24					
Balcombe	d																								
Haywards Heath	d	09 34									10 04									10 36					
Wivelsfield	d																								
Burgess Hill	d	09 39									10 09									10 41					
Hassocks	d	09 42									10 12									10 44					
Preston Park	d																								
Brighton	a	09 52									10 22									10 54					

A From Bedford
B To Tattenham Corner
C From London Victoria to Epsom
D From Luton

Please refer to separate pages within this table for services operating between Bedford and London

At weekends please use local bus and tube services to travel to/from St Pancras International and London Bridge when no trains are operating. See local publicity for details of alternative routes and services that are available across central London

Table 52

Sundays
from 16 September

South London, Gatwick Airport - Brighton

Network Diagram - see first Page of Table 52

		SN		FC	FC 1 A	SE	SN B	SN C	FC D	FC 1 A	SN	FC		FC 1 A	SE	SN B	SN C	FC D	FC 1 A	SN	FC	FC 1 A		SE	SN B
St Pancras International ⊖	d				09 54				10 05	10 09				10 24				10 35	10 39			10 54			
Farringdon ⊖	d				09 58				10 10	10 14				10 29				10 40	10 44			10 58			
City Thameslink	d																								
London Blackfriars ⊖	a				10 04				10 14	10 19				10 34				10 44	10 49			11 04			
	d			09 56	10 04	10 08			10 15	10 19		10 26		10 34	10 38			10 45	10 49		10 56	11 04		11 08	
Elephant & Castle ⊖	d			10 00		10 12			10 18			10 30			10 42			10 48			11 00			11 12	
Loughborough Jn.	d			10 04					10 22			10 34						10 52			11 04				
Herne Hill	d			10 08					10 26			10 38						10 56			11 08				
Denmark Hill	d					10 18									10 48									11 18	
Peckham Rye	d					10 21									10 51									11 21	
Nunhead	d					10 23									10 53									11 23	
Crofton Park	d					10 26									10 56									11 26	
Catford	d					10 29									10 59									11 29	
Bellingham	d					10 31									11 01									11 31	
Beckenham Hill	d					10 33									11 03									11 33	
Ravensbourne	d					10 35									11 05									11 35	
Shortlands	d					10 37									11 07									11 37	
Bromley South	d					10 40									11 10									11 40	
Bickley	d					10 43									11 13									11 43	
St Mary Cray	d					10 47									11 17									11 47	
Swanley	d					10 52									11 22									11 52	
Eynsford	d					10 56									11 26									11 56	
Shoreham (Kent)	d					11 00									11 30									12 00	
Otford	d					11 03									11 33									12 03	
Bat & Ball	d					11 06									11 36									12 06	
Sevenoaks	a					11 09									11 39									12 09	
London Bridge	a																								
	d	09 51					10 09				10 21					10 39				10 51					11 09
Tulse Hill	d	10 09		10 12					10 30		10 39	10 42						11 00		11 09	11 12				
Streatham	d	10 12		10 16					10 34		10 42	10 46						11 04		11 12	11 16				
Mitcham Eastfields	d			10 20				10 40				10 50					11 10				11 20				
Mitcham Junction	d			10 23				10 43				10 53					11 13				11 23				
Hackbridge	d			10 26				10 46				10 56					11 16				11 26				
Carshalton	d			10 29				10 49				10 59					11 19				11 29				
Tooting	d								10 38									11 08							
Haydons Road	d								10 41									11 11							
Wimbledon ⊖	d								10 44									11 14							
Wimbledon Chase	d								10 47									11 17							
South Merton	d								10 49									11 19							
Morden South	d								10 51									11 21							
St Helier	d								10 53									11 23							
Sutton Common	d								10 55									11 25							
West Sutton	d								10 58									11 28							
Sutton (Surrey)	a			10 33				10 52	11 01			11 03					11 22	11 31			11 33				
East Croydon	d	10a30			10 28		10a37			10a39	11a01			10 57		11a07			11a09	11a30		11 28			11a37
Redhill	d																								
Gatwick Airport ✈	d				10 50									11 20								11 50			
Three Bridges	d				10 54									11 24								11 54			
Balcombe	d																								
Haywards Heath	d				11 04									11 36								12 04			
Wivelsfield	d																								
Burgess Hill	d				11 09									11 41								12 09			
Hassocks	d				11 12									11 44								12 12			
Preston Park	d																								
Brighton	a				11 22									11 54								12 22			

A From Bedford
B To Tattenham Corner
C From London Victoria to Epsom
D From Luton

Please refer to separate pages within this table for services operating between Bedford and London

At weekends please use local bus and tube services to travel to/from St Pancras International and London Bridge when no trains are operating. See local publicity for details of alternative routes and services that are available across central London

Table 52

Sundays
from 16 September

South London, Gatwick Airport - Brighton

Network Diagram - see first Page of Table 52

		SN A	FC B	FC 1 C	SN	FC	FC 1 C	SE		SN D	SN A	FC B	FC 1 C	SN	FC	FC 1 C	SE	SN D		SN A	FC B	FC 1 C	SN	FC	FC 1 C
St Pancras International ⊖	d		11 05	11 09			11 24					11 35	11 39			11 54					12 05	12 09			12 24
Farringdon ⊖	d		11 10	11 14			11 29					11 40	11 44			11 58					12 10	12 14			12 29
City Thameslink	d																								
London Blackfriars ⊖	a		11 14	11 19			11 34					11 44	11 49			12 04					12 14	12 19			12 34
	d		11 15	11 19		11 26	11 34	11 38				11 45	11 49		11 56	12 04	12 08				12 15	12 19		12 26	12 34
Elephant & Castle ⊖	d		11 18			11 30		11 42				11 48			12 00		12 12				12 18			12 30	
Loughborough Jn.	d		11 22			11 34						11 52			12 04						12 22			12 34	
Herne Hill	d		11 26			11 38						11 56			12 08						12 26			12 38	
Denmark Hill	d							11 48									12 18								
Peckham Rye	d							11 51									12 21								
Nunhead	d							11 53									12 23								
Crofton Park	d							11 56									12 26								
Catford	d							11 59									12 29								
Bellingham	d							12 01									12 31								
Beckenham Hill	d							12 03									12 33								
Ravensbourne	d							12 05									12 35								
Shortlands	d							12 07									12 37								
Bromley South	d							12 10									12 40								
Bickley	d							12 13									12 43								
St Mary Cray	d							12 17									12 47								
Swanley	d							12 22									12 52								
Eynsford	d							12 26									12 56								
Shoreham (Kent)	d							12 30									13 00								
Otford	d							12 33									13 03								
Bat & Ball	d							12 36									13 06								
Sevenoaks	a							12 39									13 09								
London Bridge	a																								
	d				11 21					11 39				11 51				12 09					12 21		
Tulse Hill	d		11 30		11 39	11 42						12 00		12 09	12 12						12 30		12 39	12 42	
Streatham	d		11 34		11 42	11 46						12 04		12 12	12 16						12 34		12 42	12 46	
Mitcham Eastfields	d	11 40				11 50					12 10				12 20					12 40				12 50	
Mitcham Junction	d	11 43				11 53					12 13				12 23					12 43				12 53	
Hackbridge	d	11 46				11 56					12 16				12 26					12 46				12 56	
Carshalton	d	11 49				11 59					12 19				12 29					12 49				12 59	
Tooting	d		11 38									12 08									12 38				
Haydons Road	d		11 41									12 11									12 41				
Wimbledon ⊖	d		11 44									12 14									12 44				
Wimbledon Chase	d		11 47									12 17									12 47				
South Merton	d		11 49									12 19									12 49				
Morden South	d		11 51									12 21									12 51				
St Helier	d		11 53									12 23									12 53				
Sutton Common	d		11 55									12 25									12 55				
West Sutton	d		11 58									12 28									12 58				
Sutton (Surrey)	a	11 52	12 01			12 03					12 22	12 31			12 33					12 52	13 01			13 03	
East Croydon	d			11a39	12a01		11 57			12a07			12a09	12a30		12 28		12a37				12 43	13a01		12 57
Redhill	d																								
Gatwick Airport ✈	d						12 20									12 50						13 01			13 20
Three Bridges	d						12 24									12 54						13a05			13 24
Balcombe	d																								
Haywards Heath	d						12 36									13 04									13 36
Wivelsfield	d																								
Burgess Hill	d						12 41									13 09									13 41
Hassocks	d						12 44									13 12									13 44
Preston Park	d																								
Brighton	a						12 54									13 22									13 54

A From London Victoria to Epsom
B From Luton
C From Bedford
D To Tattenham Corner

Please refer to separate pages within this table for services operating between Bedford and London

At weekends please use local bus and tube services to travel to/from St Pancras International and London Bridge when no trains are operating. See local publicity for details of alternative routes and services that are available across central London

South London, Gatwick Airport - Brighton

		SE	SN	SN	FC	FC	SN	FC	FC	SE	SN	SN	FC	FC	SN	FC	FC	SE	SN	SN	FC	FC
			A	B	C	1 D			1 D		A	B	C	1 D			1 D		A	B	C	1 D
St Pancras International 15 ⊖	d				12 35	12 39			12 54				13 05	13 09			13 24				13 35	13 39
Farringdon 3 ⊖	d				12 40	12 44			12 58				13 10	13 14			13 29				13 40	13 44
City Thameslink 3	d																					
London Blackfriars 3 ⊖	a				12 44	12 49			13 04				13 14	13 19			13 34				13 44	13 49
	d	12 38			12 45	12 49		12 56	13 04	13 08			13 15	13 19		13 26	13 34	13 38			13 45	13 49
Elephant & Castle ⊖	d	12 42			12 48			13 00		13 12			13 18			13 30		13 42			13 48	
Loughborough Jn.	d				12 52			13 04					13 22			13 34					13 52	
Herne Hill 4	d				12 56			13 08					13 26			13 38					13 56	
Denmark Hill 4	d	12 48								13 18								13 48				
Peckham Rye 4	d	12 51								13 21								13 51				
Nunhead 4	d	12 53								13 23								13 53				
Crofton Park	d	12 56								13 26								13 56				
Catford	d	12 59								13 29								13 59				
Bellingham	d	13 01								13 31								14 01				
Beckenham Hill	d	13 03								13 33								14 03				
Ravensbourne	d	13 05								13 35								14 05				
Shortlands	d	13 07								13 37								14 07				
Bromley South 4	d	13 10								13 40								14 10				
Bickley 4	d	13 13								13 43								14 13				
St Mary Cray	d	13 17								13 47								14 17				
Swanley 4	d	13 22								13 52								14 22				
Eynsford	d	13 26								13 56								14 26				
Shoreham (Kent)	d	13 30								14 00								14 30				
Otford 4	d	13 33								14 03								14 33				
Bat & Ball	d	13 36								14 06								14 36				
Sevenoaks 4	a	13 39								14 09								14 39				
London Bridge 4	a																					
	d		12 39				12 51				13 09				13 21				13 39			
Tulse Hill 3	d				13 00		13 09	13 12					13 30		13 39	13 42					14 00	
Streatham 4	d				13 04		13 12	13 16					13 34		13 42	13 46					14 04	
Mitcham Eastfields	d			13 10				13 20				13 40				13 50				14 10		
Mitcham Junction	d			13 13				13 23				13 43				13 53				14 13		
Hackbridge	d			13 16				13 26				13 46				13 56				14 16		
Carshalton	d			13 19				13 29				13 49				13 59				14 19		
Tooting	d				13 08								13 38								14 08	
Haydons Road	d				13 11								13 41								14 11	
Wimbledon 8 ⊖	d				13 14								13 44								14 14	
Wimbledon Chase	d				13 17								13 47								14 17	
South Merton	d				13 19								13 49								14 19	
Morden South	d				13 21								13 51								14 21	
St Helier	d				13 23								13 53								14 23	
Sutton Common	d				13 25								13 55								14 25	
West Sutton	d				13 28								13 58								14 28	
Sutton (Surrey) 4	a			13 22	13 31			13 33				13 52	14 01			14 03				14 22	14 31	
East Croydon	d		13a07			13 13	13a30		13 28		13a37			13a39	14a01		13 57		14a07			14 13
Redhill	d																					
Gatwick Airport 10 ✈	d					13 33			13 50								14 20					14 33
Three Bridges 4	d					13a38			13 54								14 24					14a38
Balcombe	d																					
Haywards Heath 3	d								14 04								14 36					
Wivelsfield 4	d																					
Burgess Hill 4	d								14 09								14 41					
Hassocks 4	d								14 12								14 44					
Preston Park	d																					
Brighton 10	a								14 22								14 54					

A To Tattenham Corner
B From London Victoria to Epsom
C From Luton
D From Bedford

Please refer to separate pages within this table for services operating between Bedford and London

At weekends please use local bus and tube services to travel to/from St Pancras International and London Bridge when no trains are operating. See local publicity for details of alternative routes and services that are available across central London

South London, Gatwick Airport - Brighton

		SN	FC	FC	SE	SN	SN	FC	FC	SN	FC	FC	SE	SN	SN	FC	FC	SN	FC	FC	SE	SN	SN
				1 A		B	C	D	1 A			1 A		B	C	D	1 A			1 A		B	C
St Pancras International 15 ⊖	d			13 54				14 05	14 09			14 24				14 35	14 39			14 54			
Farringdon 3 ⊖	d			13 58				14 10	14 14			14 29				14 40	14 44			14 58			
City Thameslink 3	d																						
London Blackfriars 3 ⊖	a			14 04				14 14	14 19			14 34				14 44	14 49			15 04			
	d		13 56	14 04	14 08			14 15	14 19		14 26	14 34	14 38			14 45	14 49		14 56	15 04	15 08		
Elephant & Castle ⊖	d		14 00		14 12			14 18			14 30		14 42			14 48			15 00		15 12		
Loughborough Jn.	d		14 04					14 22			14 34					14 52			15 04				
Herne Hill 4	d		14 08					14 26			14 38					14 56			15 08				
Denmark Hill 4	d				14 18								14 48								15 18		
Peckham Rye 4	d				14 21								14 51								15 21		
Nunhead 4	d				14 23								14 53								15 23		
Crofton Park	d				14 26								14 56								15 26		
Catford	d				14 29								14 59								15 29		
Bellingham	d				14 31								15 01								15 31		
Beckenham Hill	d				14 33								15 03								15 33		
Ravensbourne	d				14 35								15 05								15 35		
Shortlands	d				14 37								15 07								15 37		
Bromley South 4	d				14 40								15 10								15 40		
Bickley 4	d				14 43								15 13								15 43		
St Mary Cray	d				14 47								15 17								15 47		
Swanley 4	d				14 52								15 22								15 52		
Eynsford	d				14 56								15 26								15 56		
Shoreham (Kent)	d				15 00								15 30								16 00		
Otford 4	d				15 03								15 33								16 03		
Bat & Ball	d				15 06								15 36								16 06		
Sevenoaks 4	a				15 09								15 39								16 09		
London Bridge 4	a																						
	d	13 51				14 09				14 21				14 39				14 51				15 09	
Tulse Hill 3	d	14 09	14 12					14 30		14 39	14 42					15 00		15 09	15 12				
Streatham 4	d	14 12	14 16					14 34		14 42	14 46					15 04		15 12	15 16				
Mitcham Eastfields	d		14 20				14 40				14 50				15 10				15 20				15 40
Mitcham Junction	d		14 23				14 43				14 53				15 13				15 23				15 43
Hackbridge	d		14 26				14 46				14 56				15 16				15 26				15 46
Carshalton	d		14 29				14 49				14 59				15 19				15 29				15 49
Tooting	d							14 38								15 08							
Haydons Road	d							14 41								15 11							
Wimbledon 8 ⊖	d							14 44								15 14							
Wimbledon Chase	d							14 47								15 17							
South Merton	d							14 49								15 19							
Morden South	d							14 51								15 21							
St Helier	d							14 53								15 23							
Sutton Common	d							14 55								15 25							
West Sutton	d							14 58								15 28							
Sutton (Surrey) 4	a		14 33				14 52	15 01			15 03				15 22	15 31			15 33				15 52
East Croydon	d	14a30		14 28		14a37			14a39	15a01		14 57		15a07			15a09	15a30		15 28		15a37	
Redhill	d																						
Gatwick Airport 10 ✈	d			14 50								15 20								15 50			
Three Bridges 4	d			14 54								15 24								15 54			
Balcombe	d																						
Haywards Heath 3	d			15 04								15 36								16 04			
Wivelsfield 4	d																						
Burgess Hill 4	d			15 09								15 41								16 09			
Hassocks 4	d			15 12								15 44								16 12			
Preston Park	d																						
Brighton 10	a			15 22								15 54								16 22			

A From Bedford
B To Tattenham Corner
C From London Victoria to Epsom
D From Luton

Please refer to separate pages within this table for services operating between Bedford and London

At weekends please use local bus and tube services to travel to/from St Pancras International and London Bridge when no trains are operating. See local publicity for details of alternative routes and services that are available across central London

Table 52

Sundays from 16 September

South London, Gatwick Airport - Brighton

Network Diagram - see first Page of Table 52

		FC A	FC ■ B	SN	FC	FC ■ B	SE	SN C	SN D	FC A	FC ■ B	SN	FC	FC ■ B	SE	SN C	SN D	FC A	FC ■ B	SN	FC	FC ■ B	SE
St Pancras International ■ ⊖	d	15 05	15 09			15 24				15 35	15 39			15 54				16 05	16 09			16 24	
Farringdon ■ ⊖	d	15 10	15 14			15 29				15 40	15 44			15 58				16 10	16 14			16 29	
City Thameslink ■	d																						
London Blackfriars ■ ⊖	a	15 14	15 19			15 34				15 44	15 49			16 04				16 14	16 19			16 34	
	d	15 15	15 19		15 26	15 34	15 38			15 45	15 49		15 56	16 04	16 08			16 15	16 19		16 26	16 34	16 38
Elephant & Castle ⊖	d	15 18			15 30		15 42			15 48			16 00		16 12			16 18			16 30		16 42
Loughborough Jn.	d	15 22			15 34					15 52			16 04					16 22			16 34		
Herne Hill ■	d	15 26			15 38					15 56			16 08					16 26			16 38		
Denmark Hill ■	d						15 48								16 18								16 48
Peckham Rye ■	d						15 51								16 21								16 51
Nunhead ■	d						15 53								16 23								16 53
Crofton Park	d						15 56								16 26								16 56
Catford	d						15 59								16 29								16 59
Bellingham	d						16 01								16 31								17 01
Beckenham Hill	d						16 03								16 33								17 03
Ravensbourne	d						16 05								16 35								17 05
Shortlands	d						16 07								16 37								17 07
Bromley South ■	d						16 10								16 40								17 10
Bickley ■	d						16 13								16 43								17 13
St Mary Cray	d						16 17								16 47								17 17
Swanley ■	d						16 22								16 52								17 22
Eynsford	d						16 26								16 56								17 26
Shoreham (Kent)	d						16 30								17 00								17 30
Otford ■	d						16 33								17 03								17 33
Bat & Ball	d						16 36								17 06								17 36
Sevenoaks ■	a						16 39								17 09								17 39
London Bridge ■	a																						
	d			15 21				15 39				15 51				16 09				16 21			
Tulse Hill ■	d	15 30		15 39	15 42					16 00		16 09	16 12					16 30		16 39	16 42		
Streatham ■	d	15 34		15 42	15 46					16 04		16 12	16 16					16 34		16 42	16 46		
Mitcham Eastfields	d				15 50				16 10				16 20				16 40				16 50		
Mitcham Junction	d				15 53				16 13				16 23				16 43				16 53		
Hackbridge	d				15 56				16 16				16 26				16 46				16 56		
Carshalton	d				15 59				16 19				16 29				16 49				16 59		
Tooting	d	15 38								16 08								16 38					
Haydons Road	d	15 41								16 11								16 41					
Wimbledon ■ ⊖	d	15 44								16 14								16 44					
Wimbledon Chase	d	15 47								16 17								16 47					
South Merton	d	15 49								16 19								16 49					
Morden South	d	15 51								16 21								16 51					
St Helier	d	15 53								16 23								16 53					
Sutton Common	d	15 55								16 25								16 55					
West Sutton	d	15 58								16 28								16 58					
Sutton (Surrey) ■	a	16 01			16 03				16 22	16 31			16 33				16 52	17 01			17 03		
East Croydon	d		15a39	16a01		15 57		16a07			16a09	16a30		16 28		16a37			16a39	17a01		16 57	
Redhill	d																						
Gatwick Airport ■ ✈	d					16 20								16 50								17 20	
Three Bridges ■	d					16 24								16 54								17 24	
Balcombe	d																						
Haywards Heath ■	d					16 36								17 04								17 36	
Wivelsfield ■	d																						
Burgess Hill ■	d					16 41								17 09								17 41	
Hassocks ■	d					16 44								17 12								17 44	
Preston Park	d																						
Brighton ■	a					16 54								17 22								17 54	

A From Luton
B From Bedford
C To Tattenham Corner
D From London Victoria to Epsom

Please refer to separate pages within this table for services operating between Bedford and London

At weekends please use local bus and tube services to travel to/from St Pancras International and London Bridge when no trains are operating. See local publicity for details of alternative routes and services that are available across central London

Table 52

Sundays from 16 September

South London, Gatwick Airport - Brighton

Network Diagram - see first Page of Table 52

		SN A	SN B	FC C	FC ■ D	SN	FC	FC ■ D	SE	SN A	SN B	FC C	FC ■ D	SN	FC	FC ■ D	SE	SN A	SN B	FC C	FC ■ D	SN
St Pancras International ■ ⊖	d			16 35	16 39			16 54				17 05	17 09			17 24				17 35	17 39	
Farringdon ■ ⊖	d			16 40	16 44			16 58				17 10	17 14			17 29				17 40	17 44	
City Thameslink ■	d																					
London Blackfriars ■ ⊖	a			16 44	16 49			17 04				17 14	17 19			17 34				17 44	17 49	
	d			16 45	16 49		16 56	17 04	17 08			17 15	17 19		17 26	17 34	17 38			17 45	17 49	
Elephant & Castle ⊖	d			16 48			17 00		17 12			17 18			17 30		17 42			17 48		
Loughborough Jn.	d			16 52			17 04					17 22			17 34					17 52		
Herne Hill ■	d			16 56			17 08					17 26			17 38					17 56		
Denmark Hill ■	d								17 18								17 48					
Peckham Rye ■	d								17 21								17 51					
Nunhead ■	d								17 23								17 53					
Crofton Park	d								17 26								17 56					
Catford	d								17 29								17 59					
Bellingham	d								17 31								18 01					
Beckenham Hill	d								17 33								18 03					
Ravensbourne	d								17 35								18 05					
Shortlands	d								17 37								18 07					
Bromley South ■	d								17 40								18 10					
Bickley ■	d								17 43								18 13					
St Mary Cray	d								17 47								18 17					
Swanley ■	d								17 52								18 22					
Eynsford	d								17 56								18 26					
Shoreham (Kent)	d								18 00								18 30					
Otford ■	d								18 03								18 33					
Bat & Ball	d								18 06								18 36					
Sevenoaks ■	a								18 09								18 39					
London Bridge ■	a																					
	d	16 39				16 51				17 09				17 21				17 39				17 51
Tulse Hill ■	d			17 00		17 09	17 12					17 30		17 39	17 42					18 00		18 09
Streatham ■	d			17 04		17 12	17 16					17 34		17 42	17 46					18 04		18 12
Mitcham Eastfields	d		17 10				17 20				17 40				17 50				18 10			
Mitcham Junction	d		17 13				17 23				17 43				17 53				18 13			
Hackbridge	d		17 16				17 26				17 46				17 56				18 16			
Carshalton	d		17 19				17 29				17 49				17 59				18 19			
Tooting	d			17 08								17 38								18 08		
Haydons Road	d			17 11								17 41								18 11		
Wimbledon ■ ⊖	d			17 14								17 44								18 14		
Wimbledon Chase	d			17 17								17 47								18 17		
South Merton	d			17 19								17 49								18 19		
Morden South	d			17 21								17 51								18 21		
St Helier	d			17 23								17 53								18 23		
Sutton Common	d			17 25								17 55								18 25		
West Sutton	d			17 28								17 58								18 28		
Sutton (Surrey) ■	a		17 22	17 31			17 33				17 52	18 01			18 03				18 22	18 31		
East Croydon	d	17a07			17a09	17a30		17 28		17a37			17a39	18a01		17 57		18a07			18a09	18a30
Redhill	d																					
Gatwick Airport ■ ✈	d							17 50								18 20						
Three Bridges ■	d							17 54								18 24						
Balcombe	d																					
Haywards Heath ■	d							18 04								18 36						
Wivelsfield ■	d																					
Burgess Hill ■	d							18 09								18 41						
Hassocks ■	d							18 12								18 44						
Preston Park	d																					
Brighton ■	a							18 22								18 54						

A To Tattenham Corner
B From London Victoria to Epsom
C From Luton
D From Bedford

Please refer to separate pages within this table for services operating between Bedford and London

At weekends please use local bus and tube services to travel to/from St Pancras International and London Bridge when no trains are operating. See local publicity for details of alternative routes and services that are available across central London

Sundays

from 16 September

South London, Gatwick Airport - Brighton

Network Diagram - see first Page of Table 52

		FC	FC 1 A	SE	FC B	SN C	FC 1 A	SN	FC	FC 1 A	SE	FC B	SN C	FC 1 A	SN	FC	FC 1 A	SE	FC B	SN C	SN	FC	FC 1 A
St Pancras International 15 ⊖	d		17 54		18 05		18 09			18 24		18 35		18 39			18 54		19 05				19 24
Farringdon 3 ⊖	d		17 58		18 10		18 14			18 29		18 40		18 44			18 58		19 10				19 29
City Thameslink 3	d																						
London Blackfriars 3 ⊖	a		18 04		18 14		18 19			18 34		18 44		18 49			19 04		19 14				19 34
	d	17 56	18 04	18 08	18 15		18 19		18 26	18 34	18 38	18 45		18 49		18 56	19 04	19 08	19 15			19 26	19 34
Elephant & Castle ⊖	d	18 00		18 12	18 18				18 30		18 42	18 48				19 00		19 12	19 18			19 30	
Loughborough Jn.	d	18 04			18 22				18 34			18 52				19 04			19 22			19 34	
Herne Hill 4	d	18 08			18 26				18 38			18 56				19 08			19 26			19 38	
Denmark Hill 4	d			18 18							18 48							19 18					
Peckham Rye 4	d			18 21							18 51							19 21					
Nunhead 4	d			18 23							18 53							19 23					
Crofton Park	d			18 26							18 56							19 26					
Catford	d			18 29							18 59							19 29					
Bellingham	d			18 31							19 01							19 31					
Beckenham Hill	d			18 33							19 03							19 33					
Ravensbourne	d			18 35							19 05							19 35					
Shortlands	d			18 37							19 07							19 37					
Bromley South 4	d			18 40							19 10							19 40					
Bickley 4	d			18 43							19 13							19 43					
St Mary Cray	d			18 47							19 17							19 47					
Swanley 4	d			18 52							19 22							19 52					
Eynsford	d			18 56							19 26							19 56					
Shoreham (Kent)	d			19 00							19 30							20 00					
Otford 4	d			19 03							19 33							20 03					
Bat & Ball	d			19 06							19 36							20 06					
Sevenoaks 4	a			19 09							19 39							20 09					
London Bridge 4	a																						
	d					18 09		18 21					18 39		18 51					19 09	19 21		
Tulse Hill 3	d	18 12			18 30			18 39	18 42			19 00			19 09	19 12			19 30		19 39	19 42	
Streatham 4	d	18 16			18 34			18 42	18 46			19 04			19 12	19 16			19 34		19 42	19 46	
Mitcham Eastfields	d	18 20							18 50							19 20						19 50	
Mitcham Junction	d	18 23							18 53							19 23						19 53	
Hackbridge	d	18 26							18 56							19 26						19 56	
Carshalton	d	18 29							18 59							19 29						19 59	
Tooting	d				18 38							19 08							19 38				
Haydons Road	d				18 41							19 11							19 41				
Wimbledon 6 ⊖	d				18 44							19 14							19 44				
Wimbledon Chase	d				18 47							19 17							19 47				
South Merton	d				18 49							19 19							19 49				
Morden South	d				18 51							19 21							19 51				
St Helier	d				18 53							19 23							19 53				
Sutton Common	d				18 55							19 25							19 55				
West Sutton	d				18 58							19 28							19 58				
Sutton (Surrey) 4	a	18 33			19 01				19 03			19 31				19 33			20 01			20 03	
East Croydon	d		18 28			18a37	18 39	19a01		18 57			19a07	19 09	19a30		19 28			19a37	20a01		19 57
Redhill	d																						
Gatwick Airport 10 ✈	d		18 50				18 55			19 20				19 25			19 50						20 20
Three Bridges 4	d		18 54				18 59			19 24				19 29			19 54						20 24
Balcombe	d																						
Haywards Heath 3	d		19 04				19 09			19 36				19 39			20 04						20 34
Wivelsfield 4	d						19 13							19 43									
Burgess Hill 4	d		19 09				19 15			19 41				19 45			20 09						20 39
Hassocks 4	d		19 12				19 18			19 44				19 48			20 12						20 42
Preston Park	d						19 25							19 55									
Brighton 10	a		19 22				19 29			19 54				19 59			20 22						20 52

A From Bedford B From Luton C To Tattenham Corner

Please refer to separate pages within this table for services operating between Bedford and London

At weekends please use local bus and tube services to travel to/from St Pancras International and London Bridge when no trains are operating. See local publicity for details of alternative routes and services that are available across central London

Sundays

from 16 September

South London, Gatwick Airport - Brighton

Network Diagram - see first Page of Table 52

		SE	FC A	SN B	SN	FC	FC 1 C	SE	FC A	SN B	SN	FC	FC 1 C	SE	FC A	SN B	FC 1 C	SN	SE	FC A	SN B	FC 1 C
St Pancras International 15 ⊖	d		19 35				19 54		20 05				20 24		20 35		20 54			21 05		21 24
Farringdon 3 ⊖	d		19 40				19 58		20 10				20 29		20 40		20 58			21 10		21 29
City Thameslink 3	d																					
London Blackfriars 3 ⊖	a		19 44				20 04		20 14				20 34		20 44		21 04			21 14		21 34
	d	19 38	19 45			19 56	20 04	20 08	20 15			20 26	20 34	20 38	20 45		21 04		21 08	21 15		21 34
Elephant & Castle ⊖	d	19 42	19 48			20 00		20 12	20 18			20 30		20 42	20 48				21 12	21 18		
Loughborough Jn.	d		19 52			20 04			20 22			20 34			20 52					21 22		
Herne Hill 4	d		19 56			20 08			20 26			20 38			20 56					21 26		
Denmark Hill 4	d	19 48						20 18						20 48					21 18			
Peckham Rye 4	d	19 51						20 21						20 51					21 21			
Nunhead 4	d	19 53						20 23						20 53					21 23			
Crofton Park	d	19 56						20 26						20 56					21 26			
Catford	d	19 59						20 29						20 59					21 29			
Bellingham	d	20 01						20 31						21 01					21 31			
Beckenham Hill	d	20 03						20 33						21 03					21 33			
Ravensbourne	d	20 05						20 35						21 05					21 35			
Shortlands	d	20 07						20 37						21 07					21 37			
Bromley South 4	d	20 10						20 40						21 10					21 40			
Bickley 4	d	20 13						20 43						21 13					21 43			
St Mary Cray	d	20 17						20 47						21 17					21 47			
Swanley 4	d	20 22						20 52						21 22					21 52			
Eynsford	d	20 26						20 56						21 26					21 56			
Shoreham (Kent)	d	20 30						21 00						21 30					22 00			
Otford 4	d	20 33						21 03						21 33					22 03			
Bat & Ball	d	20 36						21 06						21 36					22 06			
Sevenoaks 4	a	20 39						21 09						21 39					22 09			
London Bridge 4	a																					
	d			19 39	19 51					20 09	20 21					20 39		20 51			21 09	
Tulse Hill 3	d		20 00		20 09	20 12			20 30		20 39	20 42			21 00			21 09		21 30		
Streatham 4	d		20 04		20 12	20 16			20 34		20 42	20 46			21 04			21 12		21 34		
Mitcham Eastfields	d					20 20						20 50										
Mitcham Junction	d					20 23						20 53										
Hackbridge	d					20 26						20 56										
Carshalton	d					20 29						20 59										
Tooting	d		20 08						20 38						21 08					21 38		
Haydons Road	d		20 11						20 41						21 11					21 41		
Wimbledon 6 ⊖	d		20 14						20 44						21 14					21 44		
Wimbledon Chase	d		20 17						20 47						21 17					21 47		
South Merton	d		20 19						20 49						21 19					21 49		
Morden South	d		20 21						20 51						21 21					21 51		
St Helier	d		20 23						20 53						21 23					21 53		
Sutton Common	d		20 25						20 55						21 25					21 55		
West Sutton	d		20 28						20 58						21 28					21 58		
Sutton (Surrey) 4	a		20 31			20 33			21 01			21 03			21 31					22 01		
East Croydon	d			20a07	20a30		20 28			20a37	21a01		20 57			21a07	21 28	21a30			21a37	21 57
Redhill	d																					
Gatwick Airport 10 ✈	d						20 50						21 20				21 50					22 20
Three Bridges 4	d						20 54						21 24				21 54					22 24
Balcombe	d																					
Haywards Heath 3	d						21 04						21 34				22 04					22 34
Wivelsfield 4	d																					
Burgess Hill 4	d						21 09						21 39				22 09					22 39
Hassocks 4	d						21 12						21 42				22 12					22 42
Preston Park	d																					
Brighton 10	a						21 22						21 52				22 22					22 52

A From Luton B To Tattenham Corner C From Bedford

Please refer to separate pages within this table for services operating between Bedford and London

At weekends please use local bus and tube services to travel to/from St Pancras International and London Bridge when no trains are operating. See local publicity for details of alternative routes and services that are available across central London

Table 52

South London, Gatwick Airport - Brighton

Sundays from 16 September

Network Diagram - see first Page of Table 52

		SN	SE	SN	FC	SN	SE	SN	FC	SN	SE	SN	FC	SN	SE	SN	FC	SN	SE	SN	FC
				A	B			A	B			A	B				B			C	B
St Pancras International	d				21 54				22 24				22 54				23 24				23 54
Farringdon	d				21 59				22 29				22 59				23 29				23 59
City Thameslink	d																				
London Blackfriars	a				22 04				22 34				23 04				23 33				00 04
	d		21 38		22 04		22 08		22 34		22 38		23 04		23 08		23 34		23 38		00 05
Elephant & Castle	d		21 42				22 12				22 42				23 12				23 42		
Loughborough Jn.	d																				
Herne Hill	d																				
Denmark Hill	d		21 48				22 18				22 48				23 18				23 48		
Peckham Rye	d		21 51				22 21				22 51				23 21				23 51		
Nunhead	d		21 53				22 23				22 53				23 23				23 53		
Crofton Park	d		21 56				22 26				22 56				23 26				23 56		
Catford	d		21 59				22 29				22 59				23 29				23 59		
Bellingham	d		22 01				22 31				23 01				23 31				00 01		
Beckenham Hill	d		22 03				22 33				23 03				23 33				00 03		
Ravensbourne	d		22 05				22 35				23 05				23 35				00 05		
Shortlands	d		22 07				22 37				23 07				23 37				00 07		
Bromley South	d		22 10				22 40				23 10				23 40				00 10		
Bickley	d		22 13				22 43				23 13				23 43				00 13		
St Mary Cray	d		22 17				22 47				23 17				23 47				00 17		
Swanley	d		22 22				22 52				23 22				23 52				00 22		
Eynsford	d		22 26				22 56				23 26				23 56				00 26		
Shoreham (Kent)	d		22 30				23 00				23 30				23 59				00 30		
Otford	d		22 33				23 03				23 33				00 03				00 33		
Bat & Ball	d		22 36				23 06				23 36				00 06				00 36		
Sevenoaks	a		22 39				23 09				23 39				00 09				00 39		
London Bridge	a																				
	d	21 21		21 39		21 51		22 09		22 21		22 39		22 51		23 09		23 21		23 39	
Tulse Hill	d	21 39				22 09				22 39				23 09				23 39			
Streatham	d	21 42				22 12				22 42				23 12				23 42			
Mitcham Eastfields	d																				
Mitcham Junction	d																				
Hackbridge	d																				
Carshalton	d																				
Tooting	d																				
Haydons Road	d																				
Wimbledon	d																				
Wimbledon Chase	d																				
South Merton	d																				
Morden South	d																				
St Helier	d																				
Sutton Common	d																				
West Sutton	d																				
Sutton (Surrey)	a																				
East Croydon	d	22a01		22a07	22 28	22a30		22a37	22 57	23a00		23a07	23 27	23a30		23a38	23 57	00a01		00a06	00 26
Redhill	d																				
Gatwick Airport	d				22 50				23 20				23 50				00 20				00 49
Three Bridges	d				22 54				23 24				23 54				00a25				00a54
Balcombe	d																				
Haywards Heath	d				23 04				23 34				00 04								
Wivelsfield	d																				
Burgess Hill	d				23 09				23 39				00 09								
Hassocks	d				23 12				23 42				00 12								
Preston Park	d																				
Brighton	a				23 22				23 52				00 22								

A To Tattenham Corner
B From Bedford
C To Caterham

Please refer to separate pages within this table for services operating between Bedford and London

At weekends please use local bus and tube services to travel to/from St Pancras International and London Bridge when no trains are operating. See local publicity for details of alternative routes and services that are available across central London

Table 52

Mondays to Fridays

Brighton, Gatwick Airport and South London - City of London, St Albans, Luton and Bedford

Network Diagram - see first Page of Table 52

Miles	Miles	Miles	Miles	Miles			FC	FC	FC	FC	EM MX	FC	FC	FC	FC	FC	FC	FC	FC	FC	FC	FC	FC	EM MX
							A MX	B MX	A MX	B MX		C MO	D MO	E MO	A MX	B MX	A MX	B MX	C MO	D MO	E MO	A MX	B MX	F
0	—	—	—	—	Brighton	d			21p37			21p44	21p45	21p45			22p07		22p14	22p15	22p15			
1½	—	—	—	—	Preston Park	d			21p41								22p11							
7¼	—	—	—	—	Hassocks	d			21p47			21p53	21p54	21p54			22p17		22p23	22p24	22p24			
9¼	—	—	—	—	Burgess Hill	d			21p51			21p56	21p57	21p57			22p21		22p26	22p27	22p27			
10	—	—	—	—	Wivelsfield	d			21p53								22p23							
13	—	—	—	—	Haywards Heath	d			22p02			22p02	22p03	22p03			22p32		22p32	22p33	22p33			
17	—	—	—	—	Balcombe	d											22p37							
21½	—	—	—	—	Three Bridges	d			22p12			22p11	22p12	22p12			22p43		22p41	22p42	22p42			
24¼	—	—	—	—	Gatwick Airport	d			22p17			22p16	22p17	22p17			22p47		22p46	22p47	22p47			
30	—	—	—	—	Redhill	d																		
40½	—	—	0	—	East Croydon	d			22p32			22p32	22p32	22p32			23p02		23p01	23p02	23p02			
—	—	—	—	—	Sevenoaks	d																		
—	—	—	—	—	Bat & Ball	d																		
—	—	—	—	—	Otford	d																		
—	—	—	—	—	Shoreham (Kent)	d																		
—	—	—	—	—	Eynsford	d																		
—	—	—	—	—	Swanley	d																		
—	—	—	—	—	St Mary Cray	d																		
—	—	—	—	—	Bickley	d																		
—	—	—	—	—	Bromley South	d																		
—	—	—	—	—	Shortlands	d																		
—	—	—	—	—	Ravensbourne	d																		
—	—	—	—	—	Beckenham Hill	d																		
—	—	—	—	—	Bellingham	d																		
—	—	—	—	—	Catford	d																		
—	—	—	—	—	Crofton Park	d																		
—	—	—	—	—	Nunhead	d																		
—	—	—	—	—	Peckham Rye	d																		
—	—	—	—	—	Denmark Hill	d																		
—	0	0	—	0	Sutton (Surrey)	d	21p47								22p17							22p47		
—	1	—	—	—	West Sutton	d	21p50								22p20							22p50		
—	2	—	—	—	Sutton Common	d	21p52								22p22							22p52		
—	3	—	—	—	St Helier	d	21p55								22p25							22p55		
—	3½	—	—	—	Morden South	d	21p57								22p27							22p57		
—	4	—	—	—	South Merton	d	21p59								22p29							22p59		
—	4½	—	—	—	Wimbledon Chase	d	22p01								22p31							23p01		
—	5½	—	—	—	Wimbledon	d	22p08								22p38							23p08		
—	6¾	—	—	—	Haydons Road	d	22p10								22p40							23p10		
—	8	—	—	—	Tooting	d	22p13								22p43							23p13		
—	—	—	—	1¼	Carshalton	d																		
—	—	—	—	2	Hackbridge	d																		
—	—	—	—	4	Mitcham unction	d																		
—	—	—	—	5	Mitcham Eastfields	d																		
—	9½	6	—	6	Streatham	d	22p19								22p49							23p19		
—	11	7½	5	—	Tulse Hill	d	22p23								22p53							23p23		
50¾	—	—	—	—	London Bridge	a			22p45			22p45	22p45	22p45			23p15		23p15	23p15	23p15			
—	—	—	—	—		d			22p45			22p45	22p45	22p45			23p15		23p15	23p15	23p15			
—	—	—	—	—	West Croydon	d																		
—	12	8½	—	—	Herne Hill	d	22p27								22p57							23p27		
—	13	9½	—	—	Loughborough d	d	22p30								23p00									
—	15	11½	—	—	Elephant & Castle	d	22p34								23p04							23p34		
51½	16	12½	10	—	London Blackfriars	d	22p38		22p52			22p52	22p52	22p52	23p08		23p22		23p22	23p22	23p22	23p38		
52	—	—	—	—	City Thameslink	d	22p40		22p54															
52¾	3	—	—	—	Farringdon	d	22p43		22p58			22p57	22p57	22p57	23p13		23p28		23p27	23p27	23p27	23p43		
53¾	0	—	—	—	St Pancras International	d					23p15													00 15
—	—	—	—	—	St Pancras International	a	22p47		23p02			23p01	23p01	23p01	23p17		23p32		23p31	23p31	23p31	23p47		
—	—	—	—	—		d	22p48	22p48	23p02	23p02		23p02	23p02	23p02	23p18	23p18	23p32	23p32	23p32	23p32	23p32	23p48	23p48	
55½	—	—	—	—	Kentish Town	d	22p51	22p51				23p06	23p06	23p06	23p21	23p21			23p36	23p36	23p36	23p51	23p51	
58	—	—	—	—	West Hampstead Thameslink	d	22p55	22p55	23p10	23p10		23p10	23p10	23p10	23p25	23p25	23p40	23p40	23p40	23p40	23p40	23p55	23p55	
59	—	—	—	—	Cricklewood	d	22p58	22p58				23p13	23p13	23p13	23p28	23p28			23p43	23p43	23p43	23p58	23p58	
61	—	—	—	—	Hendon	d	23p01	23p01				23p16	23p16	23p16	23p31	23p31			23p46	23p46	23p46	00 01	00 01	
63¼	—	—	—	—	Mill Hill Broadway	d	23p05	23p05				23p20	23p20	23p20	23p35	23p35			23p50	23p50	23p50	00 05	00 05	
66½	—	—	—	—	Elstree & Borehamwood	d	23p09	23p09				23p24	23p24	23p24	23p39	23p39			23p54	23p54	23p54	00 09	00 09	
69½	—	—	—	—	Radlett	d	23p14	23p14				23p29	23p29	23p29	23p44	23p44			23p59	23p59	23p59	00 14	00 14	
74	—	—	—	—	St Albans City	d	23p20	23p20	23p27	23p27		23p36	23p36	23p36	23p50	23p50	23p57	23p57	00 06	00 06	00 06	00 20	00 20	
78¾	—	—	—	—	Harpenden	d	23p26	23p26	23p33	23p33		23p42	23p42	23p42	23p56	23p56	00 03	00 03	00 12	00 12	00 12	00 26	00 26	
83¼	—	—	—	—	Luton Airport Parkway	d	23p32	23p32	23p39	23p39		23p48	23p48	23p48	00 02	00 02	00 09	00 09	00 18	00 18	00 18	00 32	00 32	
84¼	30¼	—	—	—	Luton	d	23p35	23p35	23p42	23p42	23p46	23p51	23p51	23p51	00 05	00 05	00 12	00 12	00 21	00 21	00 21	00 35	00 35	00 37
86¾	—	—	—	—	Leagrave	d	23p39	23p39	23p46	23p46		23p54	23p54	23p55	00 09	00 09	00 16	00 16	00 24	00 24	00 25	00 39	00 39	
91¾	—	—	—	—	Harlington	d	23p44	23p44	23p51	23p51		23p59	23p59	00 01	00 14	00 14	00 21	00 21	00 30	00 30	00 31	00 44	00 44	
94¼	—	—	—	—	Flitwick	d	23p48	23p48	23p55	23p55		00 04	00 04	00 06	00 18	00 18	00 25	00 25	00 34	00 34	00 36	00 48	00 48	
103¾	49¾	—	—	—	Bedford	a	00 02	00 02	00 08	00 08	00 11	00 17	00 17	00 17	00 32	00 32	00 38	00 38	00 47	00 47	00 47	01 02	01 02	00 52

A from 22 May
B until 18 May
C from 17 September
D from 2 uly until 10 September
E from 21 May until 25 une
F from 30 August until 7 September

Brighton, Gatwick Airport and South London - City of London, St Albans, Luton and Bedford

Network Diagram - see first Page of Table 52

Station		EM	FC	FC	EM	FC	FC	FC	FC	FC		FC	FC	FC	FC	FC	FC	FC	FC	FC		FC	FC	FC
		◇1 A MX	1 B MX	1 C MX	MX ◇1 D	1 E	1 F MO	1 G MO	1 H MO	B MX		C MX	MX C	1 I	1 B MX	1 F MO	1 G MO	1 H MO	1 C MX	I		I	1 B MX	1 G MO
Brighton	d		22p33				22p44	22p45	22p45						23p11	23p14	23p15	23p15	23p37				23p37	23p45
Preston Park	d		22p37																23p41				23p41	
Hassocks	d		22p43				22p53	22p54	22p54						23p20	23p23	23p24	23p24	23p47				23p47	23p54
Burgess Hill	d		22p47				22p56	22p57	22p57						23p23	23p26	23p27	23p27	23p51				23p51	23p57
Wivelsfield	d		22p49																23p53				23p53	
Haywards Heath	d		22p54				23p02	23p03	23p03						23p29	23p32	23p33	23p33	23p59				23p59	00 03
Balcombe	d		22p59																00 04				00 04	
Three Bridges	d		23p12				23p11	23p12	23p12						23p38	23p41	23p42	23p42	00 10				00 10	00 12
Gatwick Airport	d		23p17				23p16	23p17	23p17						23p43	23p46	23p47	23p47	00 15				00 15	00 17
Redhill	d																		00 23				00 23	00 24
East Croydon	d		23p32				23p32	23p32	23p32						00 04	00 03	00 04	00 04	00a35				00 36	00 36
Sevenoaks	d																							
Bat & Ball	d																							
Otford	d																							
Shoreham (Kent)	d																							
Eynsford	d																							
Swanley	d																							
St Mary Cray	d																							
Bickley	d																							
Bromley South	d																							
Shortlands	d																							
Ravensbourne	d																							
Beckenham Hill	d																							
Bellingham	d																							
Catford	d																							
Crofton Park	d																							
Nunhead	d																							
Peckham Rye	d																							
Denmark Hill	d																							
Sutton (Surrey)	d																							
West Sutton	d																							
Sutton Common	d																							
St Helier	d																							
Morden South	d																							
South Merton	d																							
Wimbledon Chase	d																							
Wimbledon	d																							
Haydons Road	d																							
Tooting	d																							
Carshalton	d																							
Hackbridge	d																							
Mitcham Junction	d																							
Mitcham Eastfields	d																							
Streatham	d																							
Tulse Hill	d																							
London Bridge	a		23p45				23p45	23p45	23p45						00 21	00 21	00 21	00 21					00 51	00 50
	d		23p45				23p45	23p45	23p45						00 22	00 22	00 22	00 22					00 52	00 51
West Croydon	d																							
Herne Hill	d																							
Loughborough Jn	d																							
Elephant & Castle	d																							
London Blackfriars	d		23p52				23p52	23p52	23p52	00 08			00 10		00 29	00 28	00 28	00 28		00 40			00 58	00 58
City Thameslink	d																							
Farringdon	d		23p58				23p57	23p57	23p57	00 13			00 20		00 33	00 33	00 33	00 33		00 50				
St Pancras International	d	00 15			00 15																			
St Pancras International	a		00 02				00 01	00 01	00 01	00 17			00 25		00 37	00 37	00 37	00 37		00 55			01 07	01 07
	d		00 02	00 02		00 02	00 02	00 02	00 02	00 18		00 18		00 32	00 38	00 38	00 38	00 38				01 02	01 08	01 08
Kentish Town	d					00 05	00 06	00 06	00 06	00 21		00 21		00 35	00 41	00 41	00 41	00 41				01 05	01 11	01 11
West Hampstead Thameslink	d		00 10	00 10		00 10	00 10	00 10	00 10	00 25		00 25		00 40	00 45	00 45	00 45	00 45				01 10	01 15	01 15
Cricklewood	d					00 13	00 13	00 13	00 13	00 28		00 28		00 43	00 48	00 48	00 48	00 48				01 13	01 18	01 18
Hendon	d					00 16	00 16	00 16	00 16	00 31		00 31		00 46	00 51	00 51	00 51	00 51				01 16	01 21	01 21
Mill Hill Broadway	d					00 20	00 20	00 20	00 20	00 35		00 35		00 50	00 55	00 55	00 55	00 55				01 20	01 25	01 25
Elstree & Borehamwood	d					00 24	00 24	00 24	00 24	00 39		00 39		00 54	00 59	00 59	00 59	00 59				01 24	01 29	01 29
Radlett	d					00 29	00 29	00 29	00 29	00 44		00 44		00 59	01 04	01 04	01 04	01 04				01 29	01 34	01 34
St Albans City	d		00 27	00 27		00 36	00 36	00 36	00 36	00 50		00 51		01 06	01 10	01 10	01 10	01 13				01 36	01 40	01 40
Harpenden	d		00 33	00 33		00 42	00 42	00 42	00 42	00 56		00 57		01 12	01 16	01 16	01 16	01 20				01 42	01 46	01 46
Luton Airport Parkway	d	00 35	00 39	00 39	00 44	00 48	00 48	00 48	00 48	01 02		01 03		01 18	01 22	01 22	01 22	01 26				01 48	01 52	01 52
Luton	d	00 39	00 42	00 42	00 47	00 51	00 51	00 51	00 51	01 05		01 06		01 21	01 25	01 25	01 25	01 29				01 51	01 55	01 55
Leagrave	d		00 46	00 46		00 54	00 54	00 54	00 55	01 09		01 09		01 24	01 29	01 29	01 29	01 32				01 54	01 59	01 59
Harlington	d		00 51	00 51		01 01	01 00	01 00	01 01	01 14		01 16		01 31	01 34	01 34	01 34	01 39				02 01	02 04	02 04
Flitwick	d		00 55	00 55		01 05	01 04	01 04	01 06	01 18		01 20		01 35	01 38	01 38	01 38	01 43				02 05	02 08	02 08
Bedford	a	00 54	01 08	01 08	01 12	01 18	01 17	01 17	01 17	01 32		01 32		01 48	01 52	01 52	01 52	01 55				02 18	02 22	02 22

A from 31 uly until 10 August
B from 22 May
C until 18 May
D not from 31 uly until 10 August, from 30 August until 7 September
E 14 May
F from 17 September
G from 2 uly until 10 September
H from 21 May until 25 une
I until 18 May

Brighton, Gatwick Airport and South London - City of London, St Albans, Luton and Bedford

Network Diagram - see first Page of Table 52

Station		FC	FC	FC	FC	FC	FC		FC	FC	FC	FC	FC	FC	FC	FC	FC		FC	EM	FC	SE	SE	FC	EM
		1 A MO	1 B MO	C	C	C	D MX		B MO	1 C	C	D MX	B MO	C	1 C	E	C		C	◇1				1	◇1
Brighton	d	23p45	23p45																						
Preston Park	d																								
Hassocks	d	23p54	23p54																						
Burgess Hill	d	23p57	23p57																						
Wivelsfield	d																								
Haywards Heath	d	00 03	00 03																						
Balcombe	d																								
Three Bridges	d	00 12	00 12				01 25		01 25			02 25	02 25			03 25					04 25			04 55	
Gatwick Airport	d	00 17	00 17				01 30		01 30			02 30	02 30			03 30					04 30			05 00	
Redhill	d	00 24	00 24																						
East Croydon	d	00 37	00 36				01 47		01 47			02 47	02 47			03 47					04 47			05 17	
Sevenoaks	d																								
Bat & Ball	d																								
Otford	d																								
Shoreham (Kent)	d																								
Eynsford	d																								
Swanley	d																								
St Mary Cray	d																								
Bickley	d																					04 41	05 02		
Bromley South	d																					04 44	05 05		
Shortlands	d																					04 47	05 08		
Ravensbourne	d																					04 49			
Beckenham Hill	d																					04 51			
Bellingham	d																					04 53			
Catford	d																					04 56			
Crofton Park	d																					04 58			
Nunhead	d																					05 01			
Peckham Rye	d																					05 04			
Denmark Hill	d																					05 07			
Sutton (Surrey)	d																								
West Sutton	d																								
Sutton Common	d																								
St Helier	d																								
Morden South	d																								
South Merton	d																								
Wimbledon Chase	d																								
Wimbledon	d																								
Haydons Road	d																								
Tooting	d																								
Carshalton	d																								
Hackbridge	d																								
Mitcham Junction	d																								
Mitcham Eastfields	d																								
Streatham	d																								
Tulse Hill	d																								
London Bridge	a	00 50	00 50																					05 34	
	d	00 51	00 51																					05 34	
West Croydon	d																								
Herne Hill	d																						05 23		
Loughborough Jn	d																								
Elephant & Castle	d																					05 13	05 29		
London Blackfriars	d	00 58	00 58	01 12		02 12	02 13		02 13		02 37	03 13	03 13	03 32		04 14	04 32				05 14	05 17	05 33	05 42	
City Thameslink	d																				05 16	05a19	05 35	05 44	
Farringdon	d																				05 20		05 38	05 48	
St Pancras International	d																			05 45					06 37
St Pancras International	a	01 07	01 07	01 27		02 27	02 23		02 23		02 52	03 23	03 23	03 47		04 22	04 47				05 24		05 42	05 52	
	d	01 08	01 08		01 34		02 24		02 24	02 32		03 24	03 24		03 52	04 24			04 52		05 24		05 43	05 52	
Kentish Town	d	01 11	01 11		01 37		02 28		02 28	02 35		03 28	03 28		03 55	04 28			04 55		05 28		05a47	05 56	
West Hampstead Thameslink	d	01 15	01 15		01 42		02 32		02 32	02 40		03 32	03 32		04 00	04 32			05 00		05 32			06 00	
Cricklewood	d	01 18	01 18		01 45		02 35		02 35	02 43		03 35	03 35		04 03	04 35			05 03		05 35			06 03	
Hendon	d	01 21	01 21		01 48		02 38		02 38	02 46		03 38	03 38		04 06	04 38			05 06		05 38			06 06	
Mill Hill Broadway	d	01 25	01 25		01 52		02 42		02 42	02 50		03 42	03 42		04 10	04 42			05 10		05 42			06 10	
Elstree & Borehamwood	d	01 29	01 29		01 56		02 46		02 46	02 54		03 46	03 46		04 14	04 46			05 14		05 46			06 14	
Radlett	d	01 34	01 34		02 01		02 51		02 51	02 59		03 51	03 51		04 19	04 51			05 19		05 51			06 18	
St Albans City	d	01 40	01 40		02 08		02 58		02 58	03 06		03 58	03 58		04 26	04 58			05 26		05 58			06 24	
Harpenden	d	01 46	01 47		02 14		03 04		03 04	03 12		04 04	04 04		04 32	05 04			05 32		06 03			06 30	
Luton Airport Parkway	d	01 52	01 53		02 20		03 10		03 10	03 18		04 10	04 10		04 38	05 10			05 38		06 09			06 36	
Luton	d	01 55	01 56		02 23		03 13		03 13	03 21		04 13	04 13		04 41	05 13			05 41	06 11	06 12			06 39	06a58
Leagrave	d	01 59	01 59		02 26		03 17		03 17	03 24		04 17	04 17		04 44	05 17			05 44		06 16			06 43	
Harlington	d	02 04	02 06		02 33		03 22		03 24	03 31		04 22	04 24		04 51	05 22			05 51		06 21			06 48	
Flitwick	d	02 08	02 10		02 37		03 26		03 28	03 35		04 26	04 29		04 55	05 26			05 55		06 25			06 52	
Bedford	a	02 22	02 22		02 50		03 39		03 39	03 48		04 39	04 40		05 08	05 39			06 08	06 26	06 39			07 04	

A from 17 September
B from 21 May until 25 une
C until 18 May
D from 22 May until 22 une, from 26 une
E from 21 May

Brighton, Gatwick Airport and South London - City of London, St Albans, Luton and Bedford

Network Diagram - see first Page of Table 52

	FC	FC	SE	FC	FC	EM	EM	FC	SE	FC	FC	FC	FC	EM	FC	FC	FC	SE	SE	FC
		1		1	1	◇1	◇1			1	1			◇1	1	1			1	1
				A	B					A	B	A	B		A	B				
Brighton 10 d				05 07	05 10					05 37	05 40				05 48	05 50				06 08
Preston Park d				05 11	05 14					05 41	05 44				05 52	05 54				06 12
Hassocks 4 d				05 19	05 20					05 47	05 50				05 58	06 00				06 19
Burgess Hill 4 d				05 23	05 24					05 51	05 54				06 02	06 04				06 23
Wivelsfield 4 d				05 25	05 26					05 54	05 56				06 04	06 06				06 25
Haywards Heath 3 d				05 30	05 31					05 59	06 01				06 09	06 11				06 30
Balcombe d				05 35	05 36					06 04	06 06									06 36
Three Bridges 4 d				05 41	05 42					06 11	06 12				06 19	06 20				06 42
Gatwick Airport 10 ✈ d		05 27		05 46	05 47					06 17	06 17				06 25	06 25				06 47
Redhill d		05 35													06 33	06 33				06 56
East Croydon d		05 47		06 02	06 02					06 32	06 32				06 44	06 44				07 09
Sevenoaks 4 d									05 40									06 13		
Bat & Ball d									05 43									06 16		
Otford 4 d									05 46									06 19	06 38	
Shoreham (Kent) d									05 49									06 22		
Eynsford d									05 53									06 26		
Swanley 4 d									05 58									06 31	06 48	
St Mary Cray 4 d									06 02									06 35		
Bickley d			05 41						06 06									06 39		
Bromley South d			05 44						06 10									06 42	06 57	
Shortlands 4 d			05 47						06 13									06 45		
Ravensbourne d			05 49						06 15									06 47		
Beckenham Hill d			05 51						06 17									06 49		
Bellingham d			05 53						06 19									06 51		
Catford d			05 56						06 22									06 54		
Crofton Park d			05 58						06 25									06 57		
Nunhead 4 d			06 01						06 27									06 59		
Peckham Rye 4 d			06 04						06 30									07 02		
Denmark Hill 4 d			06 07						06 33									07 05		
Sutton (Surrey) 4 d												06 03	06 05				06 34			
West Sutton d												06 06	06 08							
Sutton Common d												06 08	06 10							
St Helier d												06 11	06 13							
Morden South d												06 13	06 15							
South Merton d												06 15	06 17							
Wimbledon Chase d												06 17	06 19							
Wimbledon 6 ⊖ d												06 26	06 28							
Haydons Road d												06 28	06 30							
Tooting d												06 33	06 33							
Carshalton d																	06 37			
Hackbridge d																	06 39			
Mitcham Junction d																	06 42			
Mitcham Eastfields d																	06 45			
Streatham 4 d	05 46							06 06				06 38	06 38				06 49			
Tulse Hill 3 d	05 50							06 10				06 42	06 42				06 53			
London Bridge 4 ⊖ a		06 02		06 15	06 15					06 46	06 46				06 58	06 58				07 23
d		06 02		06 16	06 16					06 46	06 46				06 58	06 58				07 24
West Croydon d																				
Herne Hill 4 d	05 54							06 16				06 46	06 46				06 57			
Loughborough Jn d								06 19				06 49	06 49				07 00			
Elephant & Castle d	06 00		06 13					06 24	06 40			06 54	06 54				07 06	07 12	07 16	
London Blackfriars 3 ⊖ d	06 04	06 12	06 17	06 24	06 24			06 30	06 48	06 52	06 52	06 58	06 58		07 06	07 06	07 12	07 18	07 24	07 30
City Thameslink 3 d	06 06	06 14	06a19	06 26	06 26			06 32	06 50	06 54	06 54	07 00	07 00		07 08	07 08	07 14	07 20	07 26	07 33
Farringdon 3 ⊖ d	06 10	06 18		06 30	06 30			06 36	06 54	06 58	06 58	07 04	07 04		07 12	07 12	07 18	07 24	07 30	07 36
St Pancras International 15 ⊖ d						06 55	07 00							07 30						
St Pancras International 15 ⊖ a	06 14	06 22		06 34	06 34			06 40	06 58	07 02	07 02	07 08	07 08		07 16	07 16	07 22	07 28	07 34	07 40
d	06 14	06 22		06 34	06 34			06 40	06 58	07 02	07 02	07 08	07 08		07 18	07 18	07 22	07 28	07 34	07 40
Kentish Town ⊖ d	06 18							06 44	07 02									07 32		
West Hampstead Thameslink ⊖ d	06 22			06 42	06 42			06 48	07 06	07 10	07 10	07 16	07 16		07 26	07 26	07 30	07 36		
Cricklewood d	06 25							06 51	07 09									07 39		
Hendon d	06 28							06 54	07 12									07 42		
Mill Hill Broadway d	06 32							06 58	07 16			07 23	07 23					07 46		
Elstree & Borehamwood d	06 36							07 02	07 20			07 28	07 28				07 40	07 50		
Radlett d	06 42							07 06	07 24			07 32	07 32				07 44	07 54		
St Albans City d	06 48	06 44		06 58	06 58			07 12	07a31	07 23	07 23	07 38	07 38		07 42	07 42	07a51	08a01	07 53	
Harpenden d	06 54	06 50		07 04	07 04			07 18		07 29	07 29	07 43	07 43		07 47	07 47			07 59	
Luton Airport Parkway 7 ✈ d	07 00	06 56		07 10	07 10	07a15		07 24		07 34	07 34	07 49	07 49	07 51	07 53	07 53			08 05	08 06
Luton 10 d	07a03	06 59		07 13	07 13		07 23	07 27		07 37	07 37	07a53	07a53		07 57	07 57			08 08	08a10
Leagrave d		07 03		07 17	07 17			07 31		07 41	07 41				08 01	08 01			08 12	
Harlington d		07 08		07 22	07 22			07 36		07 46	07 46				08 06	08 06			08 18	
Flitwick d		07 12		07 26	07 26			07 40		07 50	07 50				08 10	08 10			08 22	
Bedford 7 a		07 24		07 40	07 40		07 38	07 52		08 03	08 03			08 06	08 23	08 23			08 35	

A from 8 October B until 5 October

Table 52 Mondays to Fridays

Brighton, Gatwick Airport and South London - City of London, St Albans, Luton and Bedford

Network Diagram - see first Page of Table 52

	EM	FC	SE	SE	FC	FC	SE	SE	SE	SE	FC	EM	FC	SE	EM	SE	FC	SE	SE	FC	SE
	◇1				1				1	1		◇1	1	1	◇1				1		1
									A	B											
Brighton 10 d					06 24								07 02								
Preston Park d					06 28								07 06								
Hassocks 4 d					06 35								07 13								
Burgess Hill 4 d					06 39								07 17								
Wivelsfield 4 d													07 20								
Haywards Heath 3 d					06 45								07 25								
Balcombe d					06 51																
Three Bridges 4 d					06 57								07 34								
Gatwick Airport 10 ✈ d					07 02								07 39								
Redhill d					07 11																
East Croydon d					07 23								07 54								
Sevenoaks 4 d				06 42				07 11										07 36			
Bat & Ball d				06 48				07 14										07 39			
Otford 4 d				06 51				07 18	07 23	07 23								07 43			
Shoreham (Kent) d				06 54				07 21										07 46			
Eynsford d				06 58				07 24										07 49			
Swanley 4 d				07 03				07 30	07 32	07 32								07 54	07 55		
St Mary Cray 4 d				07 07				07 34										07 59	08 00		
Bickley d			07 05	07 11			07 35	07 39								07 55		08 03			
Bromley South d			07 08	07 14			07 38	07 42	07 40	07 40						07 58		08 08	08 06		08 18
Shortlands 4 d			07 11	07 17			07 41	07 44								08 00		08 10			08 20
Ravensbourne d				07 19				07 47										08 13			08 23
Beckenham Hill d				07 21				07 49										08 15			08 25
Bellingham d				07 23				07 51								08 05		08 17			08 27
Catford d				07 26				07 53								08 08		08 20			08 30
Crofton Park d				07 29				07 56								08 10					
Nunhead 4 d				07 31				07 58								08 14					
Peckham Rye 4 d				07 34				08 01								08 16					08 36
Denmark Hill 4 d				07 37				08 04								08 19		08 26			08 39
Sutton (Surrey) 4 d		06 45				07 05					07 37						07 40			08 08	
West Sutton d		06 48				07 08											07 43				
Sutton Common d		06 50				07 10											07 45				
St Helier d		06 53				07 13											07 48				
Morden South d		06 55				07 15											07 50				
South Merton d		06 57				07 17											07 52				
Wimbledon Chase d		06 59				07 19											07 54				
Wimbledon 6 ⊖ d		07 06				07 26											07 58				
Haydons Road d		07 08				07 28											08 00				
Tooting d		07 11				07 31											08 03				
Carshalton d											07 40									08 11	
Hackbridge d											07 42									08 13	
Mitcham Junction d											07 45									08 16	
Mitcham Eastfields d											07 48									08 19	
Streatham 4 d		07 16				07 38					07 52						08 09			08 23	
Tulse Hill 3 d		07 20				07 43					07 57						08 13			08 28	
London Bridge 4 ⊖ a																					
d																					
West Croydon d																					
Herne Hill 4 d		07 24	07 31		07 41	07 47	07 57				08 01			08 13			08 20			08 32	
Loughborough Jn d		07 27	07 34			07 50	08 00				08 04			08 16			08 23			08 36	
Elephant & Castle d		07 32	07 38	07 44	07 48	07 54	08 05	08 13	07 59	08 00	08 09			08 21		08 25	08 28	08 35	08 31	08 40	08 45
London Blackfriars 3 ⊖ d		07 36	07 42	07 48	07 54	07 58	08 09	08 17	08 04	08 04	08 13		08 21	08 25		08 29	08 33	08 42	08 37	08 46	08 50
City Thameslink 3 d		07 38	07 44	07 50	07 56	08 01	08 11	08 19	08 06	08 06	08 15		08 23	08 27		08 31	08 35	08 44	08 39	08 48	08 52
Farringdon 3 ⊖ d		07 42	07 48	07 54	08 00	08 04	08 15	08 23	08 10	08 10	08 19		08 27	08 31		08 35	08 39	08 48	08 43	08 52	08 56
St Pancras International 15 ⊖ d	08 00											08 30			09 00						
St Pancras International 15 ⊖ a		07 46	07 52	07 58	08 04	08 08	08 19	08 27	08 14	08 14	08 23		08 31	08 35		08 39	08 43	08 52	08 47	08 56	09 00
d		07 46	07 52	07 58	08 04	08 10	08 20	08 28	08 16	08 16	08 24		08 32	08 36		08 40	08 44	08 52	08 48	08 56	09 00
Kentish Town ⊖ d				08 02		08 14		08 32			08 29						08 48	08a57		09 00	
West Hampstead Thameslink ⊖ d		07 54	08 00	08 06		08 18	08 28	08a38	08 24	08 24	08 34					08 50	08 54			09 04	
Cricklewood d				08 09		08 21					08 37						08 57			09 07	
Hendon d				08 12		08 24					08 40						09 00			09 10	
Mill Hill Broadway d			08 07	08 16		08 28	08 35				08 44					08 57	09 04			09 14	
Elstree & Borehamwood d			08 11	08 20		08 32	08 39				08 48					09 01	09 08			09 18	
Radlett d			08 15	08 24		08 36	08 43				08 52					09 06	09 12			09 22	
St Albans City d		08 09	08a22	08 30	08 25	08a43	08 50		08 37	08 37	08a59		08 52	08 57		09 13	09 18		09 09	09a29	09 20
Harpenden d		08 15		08 35	08 31		08 55		08 43	08 43				09 04		09 19	09 24		09 15		
Luton Airport Parkway 7 ✈ d		08 21		08 41	08 37		09 01		08 48	08 48		08 51	09 00	09 10		09 25	09 30		09 21		09 29
Luton 10 d	08 23	08 24		08a45	08 40		09a04		08 52	08 52			09 04	09 13	09 23	09a29	09a34		09 24		09 32
Leagrave d		08 27			08 44				08 56	08 56				09 17					09 27		
Harlington d		08 32			08 49				09 01	09 01				09 22					09 32		
Flitwick d		08 36			08 53				09 05	09 05			09 14	09 26					09 36		09 43
Bedford 7 a	08 37	08 49			09 05				09 17	09 17		09 07	09 26	09 38	09 37				09 49		09 56

A from 21 May, not from 30 July until 10 August B until 18 May, from 30 July until 10 August

Brighton, Gatwick Airport and South London - City of London, St Albans, Luton and Bedford

Network Diagram - see first Page of Table 52

		FC ■	SE	FC	SE ■	SE ■	EM ◇■ ⚒	FC ■	FC	SE	FC ■	SE ■	SE	EM ◇■ ⚒	FC	FC ■	SE	FC	FC ■	EM ◇■ ⚒	FC	FC ■
					A	B																
Brighton ■	d	07 24						07 50			08 02					08 16			08 34			09 00
Preston Park	d	07 28						07 54			08 06					08 20			08 38			
Hassocks ■	d	07 35						08 01			08 13					08 27			08 44			09 09
Burgess Hill ■	d	07 39									08 17					08 31			08 48			09 12
Wivelsfield ■	d										08 20					08 34			08 50			
Haywards Heath ■	d	07 47						08 09			08 25					08 39			09 00			09 18
Balcombe	d							08 15											09 06			
Three Bridges ■	d	07 56									08 34					08 48			09 12			09 27
Gatwick Airport ■ ✈	d	08 01						08 24			08 39					08 53			09 17			09 32
Redhill	d	08 09																				
East Croydon	d	08 23						08 39			08 54					09 09			09 32			09 47
Sevenoaks ■	d		07 53									08 24					08 43					
Bat & Ball	d		07 56									08 27					08 46					
Otford ■	d		08 00									08 31					08 49					
Shoreham (Kent)	d		08 03									08 34					08 52					
Eynsford	d		08 06									08 37					08 56					
Swanley ■	d		08 11									08 42					09 01					
St Mary Cray ■	d		08 16									08 46					09 05					
Bickley	d		08 20									08 51	08 55				09 09					
Bromley South	d		08 26							08 44		08 54	08 58				09 12					
Shortlands ■	d		08 29							08 46		08 56	09 00				09 15					
Ravensbourne	d									08 49			09 03				09 17					
Beckenham Hill	d									08 51			09 05				09 19					
Bellingham	d		08 33							08 53		09 01	09 07				09 21					
Catford	d		08 36							08 56		09 04	09 09				09 24					
Crofton Park	d		08 39							08 58			09 12				09 26					
Nunhead ■	d		08 41							09 01			09 14				09 29					
Peckham Rye ■	d		08 44							09 04		09 09	09 17				09 31					
Denmark Hill ■	d		08 47							09 07		09 12	09 19				09 34					
Sutton (Surrey) ■	d			08 08					08 39						08 41			09 13			09 11	
West Sutton	d			08 11											08 44						09 14	
Sutton Common	d			08 13											08 46						09 16	
St Helier	d			08 16											08 49						09 19	
Morden South	d			08 18											08 51						09 21	
South Merton	d			08 20											08 53						09 23	
Wimbledon Chase	d			08 22											08 55						09 25	
Wimbledon ■ ⊖	d			08 28											08 58						09 28	
Haydons Road	d			08 30											09 00						09 30	
Tooting	d			08 33											09 03						09 33	
Carshalton	d								08 42									09 16				
Hackbridge	d								08 44									09 18				
Mitcham Junction	d								08 47									09 21				
Mitcham Eastfields	d								08 50									09 24				
Streatham ■	d			08 39					08 54						09 08			09 28			09 38	
Tulse Hill ■	d	08 37		08 43					08 58						09 16			09 32			09 42	
London Bridge ■ ⊖	a										09 08								09 46			10 00
	d										09 09								09 46			10 00
West Croydon	d																					
Herne Hill ■	d	08 41		08 47	08 52	08 52		08 57	09 02						09 20			09 36			09 46	
Loughborough Jn	d			08 50	08 57	08 55			09 05						09 23			09 40			09 50	
Elephant & Castle	d	08 50	08 54	08 58	09 02	09 02		09 06	09 10	09 14		09 20	09 26		09 30	09 34	09 42	09 45			09 55	
London Blackfriars ■ ⊖	d	08 54	08 58	09 02	09 06	09 06		09 10	09 14	09 18	09 22	09 26	09 30		09 34	09 38	09 46	09 50	09 54		10 00	10 08
City Thameslink ■	d	08 56	09 00	09 04	09 08	09 08		09 12	09 16	09 20	09 24	09 28	09 32		09 36	09 40	09 48	09 52	09 56		10 02	10 10
Farringdon ■ ⊖	d	09 00	09 04	09 08	09 12	09 12		09 16	09 20	09 24	09 28	09 32	09 36		09 40	09 44	09 52	09 56	10 00		10 06	10 14
St Pancras International ■ ⊖	d						09 30							10 00						10 30		
St Pancras International ■ ⊖	a	09 04	09 08	09 12	09 16	09 16		09 20	09 24	09 28	09 32	09 36	09 40		09 44	09 48	09 56	10 00	10 04		10 10	10 18
	d	09 04	09 08	09 12	09 16	09 16		09 20	09 24	09 28	09 32	09 36	09 40		09 44	09 48	09 56	10 00	10 04		10 10	10 18
Kentish Town ⊖	d		09a13	09 16						09 34			09a45		09 48		10 00	10a05			10 14	
West Hampstead Thameslink ⊖	d			09 20					09 32	09 40					09 52		10 04				10 19	
Cricklewood	d			09 23						09 43					09 55		10 07				10 22	
Hendon	d			09 26						09 46					09 58		10 10				10 25	
Mill Hill Broadway	d			09 30						09 50					10 02		10 14				10 29	
Elstree & Borehamwood	d			09 34					09 42	09 54					10 06		10 18				10 33	
Radlett	d			09 38					09 46	09 58					10 10		10 22				10 37	
St Albans City	d	09 25		09 46				09 40	09a53	10 04	09 52	09 56			10 18	10 10	10a29		10 25		10 46	10 39
Harpenden	d	09 32		09 53				09 46		10 09		10 03			10 23	10 16			10 31		10 53	10 45
Luton Airport Parkway ■ ✈	d	09 38		09 59	09 44	09 44	09 51	09 52		10 15	10 01	10 09			10 29	10 22			10 37	10 51	10 59	10 51
Luton ■	d	09 41		10a03	09 47	09 47		09 55		10a19	10 04	10 12		10 23	10a33	10 25			10 40		11a03	10 54
Leagrave	d	09 45			09 50	09 50		09 59				10 16				10 29			10 44			10 57
Harlington	d	09 50						10 04				10 21				10 34			10 49			11 02
Flitwick	d	09 55			10 00	10 00		10 08			10 12	10 25				10 38			10 53			11 06
Bedford ■	a	10 08			10 12	10 12	10 07	10 20			10 24	10 38		10 37		10 50			11 05	11 06		11 19

A from 21 May

B until 18 May

Brighton, Gatwick Airport and South London - City of London, St Albans, Luton and Bedford

Network Diagram - see first Page of Table 52

		FC	SE	FC ■	EM ◇■ ⚒	FC	FC ■	FC	SE	FC ■	EM ◇■ ⚒	FC	SE	FC ■	FC	FC ■	EM ◇■ ⚒	FC	SE	FC ■	FC	FC ■
Brighton ■	d			09 07			09 34			09 37				10 04		10 07				10 34		10 37
Preston Park	d			09 11						09 41						10 11						10 41
Hassocks ■	d			09 17						09 47						10 17						10 47
Burgess Hill ■	d			09 21						09 51						10 21						10 51
Wivelsfield ■	d			09 23						09 53						10 23						10 53
Haywards Heath ■	d			09 32			09 48			10 02				10 18		10 32				10 48		11 02
Balcombe	d			09 37												10 37						
Three Bridges ■	d			09 43			09 57			10 12				10 27		10 43				10 57		11 12
Gatwick Airport ■ ✈	d			09 47			10 02			10 17				10 32		10 47				11 02		11 17
Redhill	d																					
East Croydon	d			10 02			10 17			10 32				10 47		11 02				11 17		11 32
Sevenoaks ■	d		09 13						09 42				10 02						10 32			
Bat & Ball	d		09 16						09 46				10 05						10 35			
Otford ■	d		09 21						09 50				10 08						10 38			
Shoreham (Kent)	d		09 24						09 53				10 11						10 41			
Eynsford	d		09 28						09 56				10 15						10 45			
Swanley ■	d		09 33						10 01				10 20						10 50			
St Mary Cray ■	d		09 37						10 05				10 24						10 54			
Bickley	d		09 42						10 10				10 28						10 58			
Bromley South	d		09 45						10 15				10 31						11 01			
Shortlands ■	d		09 48						10 18				10 34						11 04			
Ravensbourne	d		09 50						10 20				10 36						11 06			
Beckenham Hill	d		09 52						10 22				10 38						11 08			
Bellingham	d		09 54						10 24				10 40						11 10			
Catford	d		09 57						10 27				10 43						11 13			
Crofton Park	d		09 59						10 29				10 45						11 15			
Nunhead ■	d		10 02						10 32				10 48						11 18			
Peckham Rye ■	d		10 04						10 34				10 50						11 20			
Denmark Hill ■	d		10 07						10 37				10 54						11 24			
Sutton (Surrey) ■	d	09 38				09 37		10 08				10 07			10 38			10 37			11 08	
West Sutton	d					09 40						10 10						10 40				
Sutton Common	d					09 42						10 12						10 42				
St Helier	d					09 45						10 15						10 45				
Morden South	d					09 47						10 17						10 47				
South Merton	d					09 49						10 19						10 49				
Wimbledon Chase	d					09 51						10 21						10 51				
Wimbledon ■ ⊖	d					09 58						10 28						10 58				
Haydons Road	d					10 00						10 30						11 00				
Tooting	d					10 03						10 33						11 03				
Carshalton	d	09 41						10 11							10 41						11 11	
Hackbridge	d	09 43						10 13							10 43						11 13	
Mitcham Junction	d	09 46						10 16							10 46						11 16	
Mitcham Eastfields	d	09 49						10 19							10 49						11 19	
Streatham ■	d	09 53				10 08		10 23				10 38			10 53			11 08			11 23	
Tulse Hill ■	d	09 57				10 12		10 27				10 42			10 57			11 12			11 27	
London Bridge ■ ⊖	a			10 15			10 30			10 45				11 00		11 15				11 30		11 45
	d			10 16			10 30			10 45				11 00		11 15				11 30		11 45
West Croydon	d																					
Herne Hill ■	d	10 01				10 16		10 31				10 46			11 01			11 16			11 31	
Loughborough Jn	d	10 04				10 19		10 34				10 49			11 04			11 19			11 34	
Elephant & Castle	d	10 09	10 14			10 24		10 39	10 44			10 54	11 00		11 09			11 24	11 30		11 39	
London Blackfriars ■ ⊖	d	10 14	10 18	10 24		10 30	10 38	10 44	10 48	10 54		11 00	11 04	11 08	11 14	11 24		11 30	11 34	11 38	11 44	11 54
City Thameslink ■	d	10 16	10 20	10 26		10 32	10 40	10 46	10 50	10 56		11 02	11 06	11 10	11 16	11 26		11 32	11 36	11 40	11 46	11 56
Farringdon ■ ⊖	d	10 19	10 24	10 30		10 36	10 44	10 49	10 54	11 00		11 06	11 10	11 14	11 19	11 30		11 36	11 40	11 44	11 49	12 00
St Pancras International ■ ⊖	d				11 00						11 30						12 00					
St Pancras International ■ ⊖	a	10 23	10 28	10 34		10 40	10 48	10 53	10 58	11 04		11 10	11 14	11 18	11 23	11 34		11 40	11 44	11 48	11 53	12 04
	d	10 24	10 28	10 34		10 40	10 48	10 54	10 58	11 04		11 10	11 14	11 18	11 24	11 34		11 40	11 44	11 48	11 54	12 04
Kentish Town ⊖	d	10 27	10a33			10 44		10 57	11a03			11 14	11a19		11 27			11 44	11a49		11 57	
West Hampstead Thameslink ⊖	d	10 31				10 49		11 01				11 19			11 31			11 49			12 01	
Cricklewood	d	10 34				10 52		11 04				11 22			11 34			11 52			12 04	
Hendon	d	10 37				10 55		11 07				11 25			11 37			11 55			12 07	
Mill Hill Broadway	d	10 41				10 59		11 11				11 29			11 41			11 59			12 11	
Elstree & Borehamwood	d	10 45				11 03		11 15				11 33			11 45			12 03			12 15	
Radlett	d	10 49				11 09		11 19				11 37			11 49			12 07			12 19	
St Albans City	d	10a57		10 55		11 16	11 10	11a27		11 25		11 44		11 39	11a57	11 55		12 14		12 09	12a27	12 25
Harpenden	d			11 01		11 21	11 16			11 31		11 49		11 45		12 01		12 19		12 15		12 31
Luton Airport Parkway ■ ✈	d			11 07		11 27	11 22			11 37	11 51	11 55		11 51		12 07		12 25		12 21		12 37
Luton ■	d			11 10	11 23	11a31	11 25			11 40		11a59		11 54		12 10	12 23	12a29		12 24		12 40
Leagrave	d			11 14			11 28			11 44				11 57		12 14				12 27		12 44
Harlington	d			11 19			11 33			11 49				12 02		12 19				12 32		12 49
Flitwick	d			11 23			11 37			11 53				12 06		12 23				12 36		12 53
Bedford ■	a			11 35	11 37		11 50			12 05	12 06			12 19		12 35	12 37			12 49		13 05

Brighton, Gatwick Airport and South London - City of London, St Albans, Luton and Bedford

Network Diagram - see first Page of Table 52

		EM ◇1 ✕	FC	SE	FC 1	FC	FC 1	EM ◇1 ✕	FC	SE	FC 1	FC	FC 1	EM ◇1 ✕	FC	SE	FC 1	FC	FC 1	EM ◇1 ✕	FC	SE	FC 1
Brighton 10	d				11 04		11 07				11 34		11 37				12 04		12 07				12 34
Preston Park	d						11 11						11 41						12 11				
Hassocks 4	d						11 17						11 47						12 17				
Burgess Hill 4	d						11 21						11 51						12 21				
Wivelsfield 4	d						11 23						11 53						12 23				
Haywards Heath 3	d				11 18		11 32				11 48		12 02				12 18		12 32				12 48
Balcombe	d						11 37												12 37				
Three Bridges 4	d				11 27		11 43				11 57		12 12				12 27		12 43				12 57
Gatwick Airport 10 ✈	d				11 32		11 47				12 02		12 17				12 32		12 47				13 02
Redhill	d																						
East Croydon	d				11 47		12 02				12 17		12 32				12 47		13 02				13 17
Sevenoaks 4	d			11 02						11 32						12 02						12 32	
Bat & Ball	d			11 05						11 35						12 05						12 35	
Otford 4	d			11 08						11 38						12 08						12 38	
Shoreham (Kent)	d			11 11						11 41						12 11						12 41	
Eynsford	d			11 15						11 45						12 15						12 45	
Swanley 4	d			11 20						11 50						12 20						12 50	
St Mary Cray 4	d			11 24						11 54						12 24						12 54	
Bickley	d			11 28						11 58						12 28						12 58	
Bromley South	d			11 31						12 01						12 31						13 01	
Shortlands 4	d			11 34						12 04						12 34						13 04	
Ravensbourne	d			11 36						12 06						12 36						13 06	
Beckenham Hill	d			11 38						12 08						12 38						13 08	
Bellingham	d			11 40						12 10						12 40						13 10	
Catford	d			11 43						12 13						12 43						13 13	
Crofton Park	d			11 45						12 15						12 45						13 15	
Nunhead 4	d			11 48						12 18						12 48						13 18	
Peckham Rye 4	d			11 50						12 20						12 50						13 20	
Denmark Hill 4	d			11 54						12 24						12 54						13 24	
Sutton (Surrey) 4	d		11 07			11 38			11 37			12 08			12 07			12 38			12 37		
West Sutton	d		11 10						11 40						12 10						12 40		
Sutton Common	d		11 12						11 42						12 12						12 42		
St Helier	d		11 15						11 45						12 15						12 45		
Morden South	d		11 17						11 47						12 17						12 47		
South Merton	d		11 19						11 49						12 19						12 49		
Wimbledon Chase	d		11 21						11 51						12 21						12 51		
Wimbledon 6 ⊖	d		11 28						11 58						12 28						12 58		
Haydons Road	d		11 30						12 00						12 30						13 00		
Tooting	d		11 33						12 03						12 33						13 03		
Carshalton	d					11 41						12 11						12 41					
Hackbridge	d					11 43						12 13						12 43					
Mitcham Junction	d					11 46						12 16						12 46					
Mitcham Eastfields	d					11 49						12 19						12 49					
Streatham 4	d		11 38			11 53			12 08			12 23			12 38			12 53			13 08		
Tulse Hill 3	d		11 42			11 57			12 12			12 27			12 42			12 57			13 12		
London Bridge 4 ⊖	a				12 00		12 15				12 30		12 45				13 00		13 15				13 30
	d				12 00		12 15				12 30		12 45				13 00		13 15				13 30
West Croydon	d																						
Herne Hill 4	d		11 46			12 01			12 16			12 31			12 46			13 01			13 16		
Loughborough Jn	d		11 49			12 04			12 19			12 34			12 49			13 04			13 19		
Elephant & Castle	d		11 54	12 00		12 09			12 24	12 30		12 39			12 54	13 00		13 09			13 24	13 30	
London Blackfriars 3 ⊖	d		12 00	12 04	12 08	12 14	12 24		12 30	12 34	12 38	12 44	12 54		13 00	13 04	13 08	13 14	13 24		13 30	13 34	13 38
City Thameslink 3	d		12 02	12 06	12 10	12 16	12 26		12 32	12 36	12 40	12 46	12 56		13 02	13 06	13 10	13 16	13 26		13 32	13 36	13 40
Farringdon 3 ⊖	d		12 06	12 10	12 14	12 19	12 30		12 36	12 40	12 44	12 49	13 00		13 06	13 10	13 14	13 19	13 30		13 36	13 40	13 44
St Pancras International 15 ⊖	d	12 30						13 00						13 30						14 00			
St Pancras International 15 ⊖	a		12 10	12 14	12 18	12 23	12 34		12 40	12 44	12 48	12 53	13 04		13 10	13 14	13 18	13 23	13 34		13 40	13 44	13 48
	d		12 10	12 14	12 18	12 24	12 34		12 40	12 44	12 48	12 54	13 04		13 10	13 14	13 18	13 24	13 34		13 40	13 44	13 48
Kentish Town ⊖	d		12 14	12a19		12 27			12 44	12a49		12 57			13 14	13a19		13 27			13 44	13a49	
West Hampstead Thameslink ⊖	d		12 19			12 31			12 49			13 01			13 19			13 31			13 49		
Cricklewood	d		12 22			12 34			12 52			13 04			13 22			13 34			13 52		
Hendon	d		12 25			12 37			12 55			13 07			13 25			13 37			13 55		
Mill Hill Broadway	d		12 29			12 41			12 59			13 11			13 29			13 41			13 59		
Elstree & Borehamwood	d		12 33			12 45			13 03			13 15			13 33			13 45			14 03		
Radlett	d		12 37			12 49			13 07			13 19			13 37			13 49			14 07		
St Albans City	d		12 44		12 39	12a57	12 55		13 14		13 09	13a27	13 25		13 44		13 39	13a57	13 55		14 14		14 09
Harpenden	d		12 49		12 45		13 01		13 19		13 15		13 31		13 49		13 45		14 01		14 19		14 15
Luton Airport Parkway 7 ✈	d	12 51	12 55		12 51		13 07		13 25		13 21		13 37	13 51	13 55		13 51		14 07		14 25		14 21
Luton 10	d		12 58		12 54		13 10	13 22	13a29		13 24		13 40		13a59		13 54		14 10	14 23	14a29		14 24
Leagrave	d				12 57		13 14				13 27		13 44				13 57		14 14				14 27
Harlington	d				13 02		13 19				13 32		13 49				14 02		14 19				14 32
Flitwick	d				13 06		13 23				13 36		13 53				14 06		14 23				14 36
Bedford 7	a	13 06	13 24		13 19		13 35	13 37			13 49		14 05	14 06			14 19		14 35	14 37			14 49

Brighton, Gatwick Airport and South London - City of London, St Albans, Luton and Bedford

Network Diagram - see first Page of Table 52

		FC	FC 1	EM ◇1 ✕	FC	SE	FC 1	FC	FC 1	EM ◇1 ✕	FC	SE	FC 1	FC	FC 1	EM ◇1 ✕	FC	SE	FC 1	FC	FC 1	EM ◇1 ✕
Brighton 10	d		12 37				13 04		13 07				13 34		13 37				14 04		14 07	
Preston Park	d		12 41						13 11						13 41						14 11	
Hassocks 4	d		12 47						13 17						13 47						14 17	
Burgess Hill 4	d		12 51						13 21						13 51						14 21	
Wivelsfield 4	d		12 53						13 23						13 53						14 23	
Haywards Heath 3	d		13 02				13 18		13 32				13 48		14 02				14 18		14 32	
Balcombe	d								13 37												14 37	
Three Bridges 4	d		13 12				13 27		13 43				13 57		14 12				14 27		14 43	
Gatwick Airport 10 ✈	d		13 17				13 32		13 47				14 02		14 17				14 32		14 47	
Redhill	d																					
East Croydon	d		13 32				13 47		14 02				14 17		14 32				14 47		15 02	
Sevenoaks 4	d					13 02						13 32						14 02				
Bat & Ball	d					13 05						13 35						14 05				
Otford 4	d					13 08						13 38						14 08				
Shoreham (Kent)	d					13 11						13 41						14 11				
Eynsford	d					13 15						13 45						14 15				
Swanley 4	d					13 20						13 50						14 20				
St Mary Cray 4	d					13 24						13 54						14 24				
Bickley	d					13 28						13 58						14 28				
Bromley South	d					13 31						14 01						14 31				
Shortlands 4	d					13 34						14 04						14 34				
Ravensbourne	d					13 36						14 06						14 36				
Beckenham Hill	d					13 38						14 08						14 38				
Bellingham	d					13 40						14 10						14 40				
Catford	d					13 43						14 13						14 43				
Crofton Park	d					13 45						14 15						14 45				
Nunhead 4	d					13 48						14 18						14 48				
Peckham Rye 4	d					13 50						14 20						14 50				
Denmark Hill 4	d					13 54						14 24						14 54				
Sutton (Surrey) 4	d	13 08			13 07			13 38			13 37			14 08			14 07			14 38		
West Sutton	d				13 10						13 40						14 10					
Sutton Common	d				13 12						13 42						14 12					
St Helier	d				13 15						13 45						14 15					
Morden South	d				13 17						13 47						14 17					
South Merton	d				13 19						13 49						14 19					
Wimbledon Chase	d				13 21						13 51						14 21					
Wimbledon 6 ⊖	d				13 28						13 58						14 28					
Haydons Road	d				13 30						14 00						14 30					
Tooting	d				13 33						14 03						14 33					
Carshalton	d	13 11						13 41						14 11						14 41		
Hackbridge	d	13 13						13 43						14 13						14 43		
Mitcham Junction	d	13 16						13 46						14 16						14 46		
Mitcham Eastfields	d	13 19						13 49						14 19						14 49		
Streatham 4	d	13 23			13 38			13 53			14 08			14 23			14 38			14 53		
Tulse Hill 3	d	13 27			13 42			13 57			14 12			14 27			14 42			14 57		
London Bridge 4 ⊖	a		13 45				14 00		14 15				14 30		14 45				15 00		15 15	
	d		13 45				14 00		14 15				14 30		14 45				15 00		15 15	
West Croydon	d																					
Herne Hill 4	d	13 31			13 46			14 01			14 16			14 31			14 46			15 01		
Loughborough Jn	d	13 34			13 49			14 04			14 19			14 34			14 49			15 04		
Elephant & Castle	d	13 39			13 54	14 00		14 09			14 24	14 30		14 39			14 54	15 00		15 09		
London Blackfriars 3 ⊖	d	13 44	13 54		14 00	14 04	14 08	14 14	14 24		14 30	14 34	14 38	14 44	14 54		15 00	15 04	15 08	15 14	15 24	
City Thameslink 3	d	13 46	13 56		14 02	14 06	14 10	14 16	14 26		14 32	14 36	14 40	14 46	14 56		15 02	15 06	15 10	15 16	15 26	
Farringdon 3 ⊖	d	13 49	14 00		14 06	14 10	14 14	14 19	14 30		14 36	14 40	14 44	14 49	15 00		15 06	15 10	15 14	15 19	15 30	
St Pancras International 15 ⊖	d			14 30						15 00						15 30						16 00
St Pancras International 15 ⊖	a	13 53	14 04		14 10	14 14	14 18	14 23	14 34		14 40	14 44	14 48	14 53	15 04		15 10	15 14	15 18	15 23	15 34	
	d	13 54	14 04		14 10	14 14	14 18	14 24	14 34		14 40	14 44	14 48	14 54	15 04		15 10	15 14	15 18	15 24	15 34	
Kentish Town ⊖	d	13 57			14 14	14a19		14 27			14 44	14a49		14 57			15 14	15a19		15 27		
West Hampstead Thameslink ⊖	d	14 01			14 19			14 31			14 49			15 01			15 19			15 31		
Cricklewood	d	14 04			14 22			14 34			14 52			15 04			15 22			15 34		
Hendon	d	14 07			14 25			14 37			14 55			15 07			15 25			15 37		
Mill Hill Broadway	d	14 11			14 29			14 41			14 59			15 11			15 29			15 41		
Elstree & Borehamwood	d	14 15			14 33			14 45			15 03			15 15			15 33			15 45		
Radlett	d	14 19			14 37			14 49			15 07			15 19			15 37			15 49		
St Albans City	d	14a27	14 25		14 44		14 39	14a57	14 55		15 14		15 09	15a27	15 25		15 44		15 39	15a57	15 53	
Harpenden	d		14 31		14 49		14 45		15 01		15 19		15 15		15 31		15 49		15 45		15 59	
Luton Airport Parkway 7 ✈	d		14 37	14 51	14 55		14 51		15 07		15 25		15 21		15 37	15 51	15 55		15 51		16 04	
Luton 10	d		14 40		14a59		14 54		15 10	15 23	15a29		15 24		15 40		15a59		15 54		16 07	16 22
Leagrave	d		14 44				14 57		15 14				15 27		15 44				15 57		16 12	
Harlington	d		14 49				15 02		15 19				15 32		15 49				16 02		16 17	
Flitwick	d		14 53				15 06		15 23				15 36		15 53				16 06		16 21	
Bedford 7	a		15 05	15 06			15 19		15 35	15 37			15 49		16 05	16 06			16 19		16 33	16 37

Brighton, Gatwick Airport and South London - City of London, St Albans, Luton and Bedford

Network Diagram - see first Page of Table 52

		FC	SE	FC ■	FC	FC ■	EM ◇■	FC	SE		FC ■	FC	FC ■	EM ◇■	FC ■	FC	SE ■	FC	FC ■		EM ◇■	EM ◇■	FC ■	FC	FC
Brighton [10]	d			14 34		14 37					15 04				15 07				15 34				15 37		
Preston Park	d					14 41									15 11								15 41		
Hassocks [4]	d					14 47									15 17								15 47		
Burgess Hill [4]	d					14 51									15 21								15 51		
Wivelsfield [4]	d					14 53									15 23								15 53		
Haywards Heath [3]	d			14 48		15 02					15 18				15 32				15 48				15 58		
Balcombe	d														15 37										
Three Bridges [4]	d			14 57		15 12					15 27				15 43				15 57				16 07		
Gatwick Airport [10]	d			15 02		15 17					15 32				15 47				16 02				16 12		
Redhill	d																								
East Croydon	d			15 17		15 32					15 47				16 02				16 17				16 28		
Sevenoaks [4]	d		14 32						15 02								15 32								
Bat & Ball	d		14 35						15 05								15 35								
Otford [4]	d		14 38						15 08								15 38								
Shoreham (Kent)	d		14 41						15 11								15 41								
Eynsford	d		14 45						15 15								15 45								
Swanley [4]	d		14 50						15 20								15 50								
St Mary Cray [4]	d		14 54						15 24								15 54								
Bickley	d		14 58						15 28								15 58								
Bromley South	d		15 01						15 31								16 01								
Shortlands [4]	d		15 04						15 34								16 04								
Ravensbourne	d		15 06						15 36								16 06								
Beckenham Hill	d		15 08						15 38								16 08								
Bellingham	d		15 10						15 40								16 10								
Catford	d		15 13						15 43								16 13								
Crofton Park	d		15 15						15 45								16 15								
Nunhead [4]	d		15 18						15 48								16 18								
Peckham Rye [4]	d		15 20						15 50								16 20								
Denmark Hill [4]	d		15 24						15 54								16 24								
Sutton (Surrey) [4]	d	14 37			15 08			15 07				15 38				15 37		16 08							16 07
West Sutton	d	14 40						15 10								15 40									16 10
Sutton Common	d	14 42						15 12								15 42									16 12
St Helier	d	14 45						15 15								15 45									16 15
Morden South	d	14 47						15 17								15 47									16 17
South Merton	d	14 49						15 19								15 49									16 19
Wimbledon Chase	d	14 51						15 21								15 51									16 21
Wimbledon [6]	d	14 58						15 28								15 58									16 30
Haydons Road	d	15 00						15 30								16 00									16 32
Tooting	d	15 03						15 33								16 03									16 35
Carshalton	d				15 11							15 41						16 11							
Hackbridge	d				15 13							15 43						16 13							
Mitcham Junction	d				15 16							15 46						16 16							
Mitcham Eastfields	d				15 19							15 49						16 19							
Streatham [4]	d	15 08			15 23			15 38				15 53				16 08		16 23							16 40
Tulse Hill [3]	d	15 12			15 27			15 42				15 57				16 12		16 27	16 32						16 46
London Bridge [4]	a			15 30		15 45					16 00				16 15										
	d			15 30		15 45					16 00				16 16										
West Croydon	d																								
Herne Hill [4]	d	15 16			15 31			15 46				16 01				16 16		16 31							16 50
Loughborough Junction	d	15 19			15 34			15 49				16 04				16 19		16 34							16 53
Elephant & Castle	d	15 24	15 30		15 39			15 54	16 00			16 09	16 18			16 24	16 30	16 39	16 44					16 56	17 00
London Blackfriars [3]	d	15 30	15 34	15 38	15 44	15 54		16 00	16 04		16 08	16 14	16 22		16 26	16 30	16 38	16 44	16 52				16 56	17 00	17 04
City Thameslink [3]	d	15 32	15 36	15 40	15 46	15 56		16 02	16 06		16 10	16 16	16 24		16 28	16 32	16 40	16 46	16 54				16 58	17 02	17 06
Farringdon [3]	d	15 36	15 40	15 44	15 49	16 00		16 06	16 10		16 13	16 19	16 27		16 31	16 35	16 43	16 49	16 57				17 01	17 05	17 09
St Pancras International [15]	d						16 30							17 00							17 15	17 30			
St Pancras International [15]	a	15 40	15 44	15 48	15 53	16 04		16 10	16 14		16 17	16 23	16 31		16 35	16 39	16 47	16 53	17 01				17 05	17 09	17 13
	d	15 40	15 44	15 48	15 54	16 04		16 10	16 14		16 18	16 24	16 32		16 36	16 40	16 48	16 54	17 02				17 06	17 10	17 14
Kentish Town	d	15 44	15a49		15 57			16 14	16a19			16 28				16 44		16 58							17 18
West Hampstead Thameslink	d	15 49			16 01			16 19				16 32				16 48		17 02						17 18	17 22
Cricklewood	d	15 52			16 04			16 22				16 35				16 51		17 05							17 25
Hendon	d	15 55			16 07			16 25				16 38				16 54		17 08							17 28
Mill Hill Broadway	d	15 59			16 11			16 29				16 43				16 59		17 13						17 26	17 33
Elstree & Borehamwood	d	16 03			16 15			16 33				16 47				17 03		17 17						17 30	17 37
Radlett	d	16 07			16 19			16 38				16 51				17 07		17 21						17 34	17 43
St Albans City	d	16 14		16 09	16a27	16 25		16 46			16 39	16a59	16 52		16 56	17 14	17 08	17a29	17 20				17 26	17 40	17a51
Harpenden	d	16 19		16 15		16 31		16 51			16 45		16 58		17 02	17 19	17 14		17 26				17 32	17 47	
Luton Airport Parkway [7]	d	16 25		16 21		16 37	16 51	16 57			16 51				17 08	17 25	17 20						17 38	17 52	
Luton [10]	d	16a29		16 24		16 40	16 55	17a01			16 54		17 04		17 11	17a29	17 23		17 32		17a38		17 41	17a56	
Leagrave	d			16 27		16 44					16 57				17 15		17 27						17 45		
Harlington	d			16 32		16 49					17 02				17 20		17 32						17 50		
Flitwick	d			16 36		16 53					17 06		17 13		17 24		17 36		17 41				17 54		
Bedford [7]	a			16 49		17 05	17 09				17 19		17 25	17 33	17 36		17 49		17 53			18 03	18 06		

Brighton, Gatwick Airport and South London - City of London, St Albans, Luton and Bedford

Network Diagram - see first Page of Table 52

		SE ■	FC ■	SE	SE		FC ■	FC ■	EM ◇■	EM ◇■	FC	FC ■	SE	FC	FC ■		SE ■	EM ◇■	FC	SE ■	EM ◇■	SE ■	FC	FC	FC ■
			A	B	C																				
Brighton [10]	d						16 04	16 07				16 24			16 30										17 02
Preston Park	d							16 11							16 34										
Hassocks [4]	d							16 17							16 40										
Burgess Hill [4]	d							16 21							16 44										17 13
Wivelsfield [4]	d														16 46										
Haywards Heath [3]	d						16 18	16 26				16 38			16 51										17 18
Balcombe	d							16 32							16 56										
Three Bridges [4]	d						16 27	16 37				16 47			17 02										17 27
Gatwick Airport [10]	d						16 32	16 42				16 53			17 08										17 32
Redhill	d																								
East Croydon	d						16 47	16 58				17 09			17 23										17 47
Sevenoaks [4]	d	16 02		16 22	16 22								16 32							17 02					
Bat & Ball	d	16 05		16 25	16 25								16 35							17 05					
Otford [4]	d	16 08		16 28	16 28								16 38							17 08					
Shoreham (Kent)	d	16 11											16 41							17 11					
Eynsford	d	16 15											16 45							17 15					
Swanley [4]	d	16 20		16 37	16 37								16 50							17 20					
St Mary Cray [4]	d	16 24		16 41	16 41								16 54							17 24					
Bickley	d	16 28											16 58							17 28		17 42			
Bromley South	d	16 31		16 47	16 47								17 01							17 31		17 45			
Shortlands [4]	d	16 34											17 04							17 34					
Ravensbourne	d	16 36											17 06							17 36					
Beckenham Hill	d	16 38											17 08							17 38					
Bellingham	d	16 40		16 52	16 52								17 10							17 40					
Catford	d	16 43		16 55	16 55								17 13							17 43					
Crofton Park	d	16 45											17 15							17 45					
Nunhead [4]	d	16 48		16 59	16 59								17 18							17 48					
Peckham Rye [4]	d	16 50		17 02	17 02								17 20							17 50					
Denmark Hill [4]	d	16 54		17 05	17 05								17 24							17 54					
Sutton (Surrey) [4]	d		16 38								16 37			17 08					17 11					17 42	
West Sutton	d										16 40								17 14						
Sutton Common	d										16 42								17 16						
St Helier	d										16 45								17 19						
Morden South	d										16 47								17 21						
South Merton	d										16 49								17 23						
Wimbledon Chase	d										16 51								17 25						
Wimbledon [6]	d										17 00								17 30						
Haydons Road	d										17 02								17 32						
Tooting	d										17 05								17 35						
Carshalton	d		16 41											17 11										17 45	
Hackbridge	d		16 43											17 13										17 47	
Mitcham Junction	d		16 46											17 16										17 50	
Mitcham Eastfields	d		16 49											17 19										17 53	
Streatham [4]	d		16 53								17 10			17 23					17 40					17 57	
Tulse Hill [3]	d		16 57					17 12			17 16			17 27					17 44					18 01	
London Bridge [4]	a											17 27													18 13
	d											17 27													18 13
West Croydon	d																								
Herne Hill [4]	d		17 01								17 21			17 31			17 44		17 48					18 06	
Loughborough Junction	d										17 24			17 34			17 47		17 51					18 09	
Elephant & Castle	d	17 04	17 08	17 12	17 12			17 22			17 28		17 34	17 39			17 52		17 56	18 00		18 05	18 09	18 14	
London Blackfriars [3]	d	17 08	17 12	17 16	17 16		17 22	17 26			17 32	17 36	17 40	17 46	17 52		17 56		18 00	18 06		18 10	18 14	18 18	18 22
City Thameslink [3]	d	17 10	17 14	17 18	17 18		17 24	17 28			17 34	17 38	17 42	17 48	17 54		17 58		18 02	18 08		18 12	18 16	18 20	18 24
Farringdon [3]	d	17 13	17 17	17 23	17 23		17 27	17 31			17 37	17 41	17 45	17 51	17 57		18 01		18 05	18 11		18 15	18 19	18 23	18 27
St Pancras International [15]	d								17 45	18 00								18 25			18 30				
St Pancras International [15]	a	17 17	17 21	17 27	17 27		17 31	17 35			17 41	17 45	17 49	17 55	18 01		18 05		18 09	18 15		18 19	18 23	18 27	18 31
	d	17 18	17 22	17 28	17 28		17 32	17 36			17 42	17 46	17 50	17 56	18 02		18 06		18 10	18 16		18 20	18 24	18 28	18 32
Kentish Town	d			17 32	17 32						17 46			18 00					18 14					18 32	
West Hampstead Thameslink	d			17 36	17 36						17 50		17 58	18 04					18 18				18 32	18 36	
Cricklewood	d			17 39	17 39						17 53			18 07					18 21					18 39	
Hendon	d			17 42	17 42						17 56			18 10					18 24					18 42	
Mill Hill Broadway	d			17 47	17 47						18 01		18 06	18 15					18 29				18 40	18 47	
Elstree & Borehamwood	d			17 51	17 51						18 05		18 10	18 19					18 33				18 44	18 51	
Radlett	d			17 54	17 55						18 09		18 14	18 23					18 39				18 48	18 55	
St Albans City	d	17 38	17 44	18a03	18a03		17 50	17 56			18 16	18 06	18 20	18a31	18 20		18 26		18 46	18 36		18 42	18 54	19a03	18 50
Harpenden	d		17 51				17 56	18 02			18 21	18 14	18 26		18 26		18 32		18 52			18 48	19 00		18 56
Luton Airport Parkway [7]	d	17 48	17 57					18 08	18a08		18 27	18 20	18 32				18 38		18 58	18 47	18 53	18 54	19 06		
Luton [10]	d	17 51	18 00				18 02	18 11		18 23	18a31	18 23	18 36		18 32		18 41	18a49	19a01	18 50		18 57	19 09		19 02
Leagrave	d		18 04					18 15				18 27	18 40				18 45					19 01	19 13		
Harlington	d		18 09					18 20				18 32	18 45				18 50					19 06	19 18		
Flitwick	d	18 00	18 13				18 11	18 24				18 36	18 49		18 43		18 54			19 00		19 10	19 22		19 11
Bedford [7]	a	18 12	18 26				18 23	18 36		18 38		18 48	19 02		18 55		19 06			19 12	19 08	19 26	19 34		19 23

A ■ to Farringdon

B not from 30 July until 10 August

C from 30 July until 10 August

Brighton, Gatwick Airport and South London - City of London, St Albans, Luton and Bedford

Network Diagram - see first Page of Table 52

		FC ■	EM ◇■	FC	SE ■	FC	FC	FC ■	FC ■	EM ◇■	FC	SE ■ A	FC ■	FC	FC ■	EM ◇■	FC	SE	FC ■	FC	FC ■	EM ◇■
Brighton ■	d	17 07						17 24	17 37				18 02		18 07				18 34		18 37	
Preston Park	d	17 11						17 28	17 41						18 11						18 41	
Hassocks ■	d	17 17						17 34	17 47						18 17						18 47	
Burgess Hill ■	d	17 21						17 38	17 51				18 13		18 21						18 51	
Wivelsfield ■	d							17 40	17 53						18 23						18 53	
Haywards Heath ■	d	17 26						17 46	18 02				18 18		18 32				18 48		19 02	
Balcombe	d								18 07						18 37							
Three Bridges ■	d							17 55	18 13				18 27		18 43				18 57		19 12	
Gatwick Airport ■ ✈	d	17 39						18 00	18 17				18 32		18 47				19 02		19 17	
Redhill	d																					
East Croydon	d	17 58						18 16	18 32				18 47		19 02				19 17		19 32	
Sevenoaks ■	d				17 32							18 02						18 32				
Bat & Ball	d				17 35							18 05						18 35				
Otford ■	d				17 38							18 08						18 38				
Shoreham (Kent)	d				17 41							18 11						18 41				
Eynsford	d				17 45							18 15						18 45				
Swanley ■	d				17 50							18 20						18 50				
St Mary Cray ■	d				17 54							18 24						18 54				
Bickley	d				17 58							18 28						18 58				
Bromley South	d				18 01							18 31						19 01				
Shortlands ■	d				18 04							18 34						19 04				
Ravensbourne	d				18 06							18 36						19 06				
Beckenham Hill	d				18 08							18 38						19 08				
Bellingham	d				18 10							18 40						19 10				
Catford	d				18 13							18 43						19 13				
Crofton Park	d				18 15							18 45						19 15				
Nunhead ■	d				18 18							18 48						19 18				
Peckham Rye ■	d				18 20							18 50						19 20				
Denmark Hill ■	d				18 23							18 54						19 24				
Sutton (Surrey) ■	d			17 41		18 08					18 09			18 38			18 43			19 08		
West Sutton	d			17 44							18 12						18 46					
Sutton Common	d			17 46							18 14						18 48					
St Helier	d			17 49							18 17						18 51					
Morden South	d			17 51							18 19						18 53					
South Merton	d			17 53							18 21						18 55					
Wimbledon Chase	d			17 55							18 23						18 57					
Wimbledon ■ ⊖	d			18 00							18 28						19 00					
Haydons Road	d			18 02							18 30						19 02					
Tooting	d			18 05							18 33						19 05					
Carshalton	d					18 11								18 41						19 11		
Hackbridge	d					18 13								18 43						19 13		
Mitcham Junction	d					18 16								18 46						19 16		
Mitcham Eastfields	d					18 19								18 49						19 19		
Streatham ■	d			18 10		18 23					18 40			18 53			19 10			19 23		
Tulse Hill ■	d	18 12		18 16		18 28		18 32			18 44			18 57			19 14			19 27		
London Bridge ■ ⊖	a								18 46				19 00		19 15				19 30		19 45	
	d								18 46				19 01		19 17				19 30		19 45	
West Croydon	d																					
Herne Hill ■	d			18 20		18 32		18 41			18 48			19 02			19 17			19 31		
Loughborough Jn	d			18 23		18 35					18 51			19 05			19 20			19 34		
Elephant & Castle	d	18 22		18 28	18 32	18 40	18 44	18 48			18 56	19 00		19 10			19 25	19 30		19 39		
London Blackfriars ■ ⊖	d	18 26		18 32	18 36	18 44	18 48	18 52	18 56		19 00	19 06	19 10	19 18	19 24		19 30	19 34	19 38	19 46	19 54	
City Thameslink ■	d	18 28		18 34	18 38	18 46	18 50	18 54	18 58		19 02	19 08	19 12	19 20	19 26		19 32	19 36	19 40	19 48	19 56	
Farringdon ■ ⊖	d	18 31		18 37	18 41	18 49	18 53	18 57	19 01		19 05	19 11	19 15	19 23	19 30		19 36	19 40	19 44	19 51	20 00	
St Pancras International ■ ⊖	d		19 00							19 30						20 00						20 30
St Pancras International ■ ⊖	a	18 35		18 41	18 45	18 53	18 57	19 01	19 05		19 09	19 15	19 19	19 27	19 34		19 40	19 44	19 48	19 55	20 04	
	d	18 36		18 42	18 46	18 54	18 58	19 02	19 06		19 10	19 16	19 20	19 28	19 34		19 40	19 44	19 48	19 56	20 04	
Kentish Town ⊖	d			18 46			19 02				19 14			19 32			19 44	19a49		19 59		
West Hampstead Thameslink ⊖	d	18 44		18 52		19 02	19 06				19 18		19 28	19 36	19 41		19 49			20 03	20 11	
Cricklewood	d			18 55			19 09				19 21			19 39			19 52			20 06		
Hendon	d			18 58			19 12				19 24			19 42			19 55			20 09		
Mill Hill Broadway	d			19 03			19 17				19 28			19 46			19 59			20 13		
Elstree & Borehamwood	d			19 07		19 12	19 21				19 32		19 38	19 50			20 03			20 17		
Radlett	d			19 11		19 16	19 26				19 36			19 54			20 07			20 21		
St Albans City	d	18 58		19 18	19 06	19 22	19a33	19 20	19 26		19 42	19 36	19 46	20a01	19 55		20 14		20 09	20a29	20 25	
Harpenden	d	19 04		19 24	19 12	19 28		19 26	19 32		19 48	19 44	19 52		20 01		20 19		20 15		20 31	
Luton Airport Parkway ■ ✈	d	19 10		19 30	19 18	19 34			19 38	19 51	19 54		19 58		20 07		20 25		20 21		20 37	20 51
Luton ■	d	19 13	19 23	19a33	19 23	19 37		19 32	19 41		19a57	19 50	20 01		20 10	20 23	20a29		20 24		20 40	
Leagrave	d	19 17			19 27	19 41			19 45			19 54	20 04		20 14				20 27		20 44	
Harlington	d	19 22			19 32	19 46			19 50				20 09		20 19				20 32		20 49	
Flitwick	d	19 26			19 36	19 50		19 43	19 54				20 13		20 23				20 36		20 53	
Bedford ■	a	19 38	19 39		19 48	20 02		19 55	20 06	20 07		20 12	20 26		20 35	20 37			20 49		21 05	21 06

A ■ from London Blackfriars

Brighton, Gatwick Airport and South London - City of London, St Albans, Luton and Bedford

Network Diagram - see first Page of Table 52

		FC	SE	FC ■	FC	FC ■	EM ◇■	FC	SE	FC ■	FC	FC ■	FC	SE	FC ■	SE A	FC	EM ◇■	FC ■	EM ◇■	FC	SE B
Brighton ■	d					19 07				19 34		19 37			20 02				20 07			
Preston Park	d					19 11						19 41							20 11			
Hassocks ■	d					19 17						19 47							20 17			
Burgess Hill ■	d					19 21						19 51			20 13				20 21			
Wivelsfield ■	d					19 23						19 53							20 23			
Haywards Heath ■	d					19 32				19 48		20 02			20 19				20 32			
Balcombe	d					19 37													20 37			
Three Bridges ■	d			19 27		19 43				19 57		20 12			20 27				20 43			
Gatwick Airport ■ ✈	d			19 32		19 47				20 02		20 17			20 32				20 47			
Redhill	d																					
East Croydon	d			19 47		20 02				20 17		20 32			20 47				21 02			
Sevenoaks ■	d		19 02						19 32					20 02		20 32						20 32
Bat & Ball	d		19 05						19 35					20 05		20 35						20 35
Otford ■	d		19 08						19 38					20 08		20 38						20 38
Shoreham (Kent)	d		19 11						19 41					20 11		20 41						20 41
Eynsford	d		19 15						19 45					20 15		20 45						20 45
Swanley ■	d		19 20						19 50					20 20		20 50						20 50
St Mary Cray ■	d		19 24						19 54					20 24		20 54						20 54
Bickley	d		19 28						19 58					20 28		20 58						20 58
Bromley South	d		19 31						20 01					20 31		21 01						21 01
Shortlands ■	d		19 34						20 04					20 34		21 04						21 04
Ravensbourne	d		19 36						20 06					20 36		21 06						21 06
Beckenham Hill	d		19 38						20 08					20 38		21 08						21 08
Bellingham	d		19 40						20 10					20 40		21 10						21 10
Catford	d		19 43						20 13					20 43		21 13						21 13
Crofton Park	d		19 45						20 15					20 45		21 15						21 15
Nunhead ■	d		19 48						20 18					20 48		21 18						21 18
Peckham Rye ■	d		19 50						20 20					20 50		21 20						21 20
Denmark Hill ■	d		19 54						20 24					20 54		21a23						21 24
Sutton (Surrey) ■	d	19 13			19 42			19 37			20 12		20 07				20 42				20 37	
West Sutton	d	19 16						19 40					20 10								20 40	
Sutton Common	d	19 18						19 42					20 12								20 42	
St Helier	d	19 21						19 45					20 15								20 45	
Morden South	d	19 23						19 47					20 17								20 47	
South Merton	d	19 25						19 49					20 19								20 49	
Wimbledon Chase	d	19 27						19 51					20 21								20 51	
Wimbledon ■ ⊖	d	19 30						19 56					20 26								20 56	
Haydons Road	d	19 32						19 58					20 28								20 58	
Tooting	d	19 35						20 01					20 31								21 01	
Carshalton	d				19 45						20 15						20 45					
Hackbridge	d				19 47						20 17						20 47					
Mitcham Junction	d				19 50						20 20						20 50					
Mitcham Eastfields	d				19 53						20 23						20 53					
Streatham ■	d	19 40			19 57			20 06			20 27		20 36				20 57				21 06	
Tulse Hill ■	d	19 44			20 01			20 12			20 31		20 42				21 01				21 12	
London Bridge ■ ⊖	a			20 00		20 15				20 30		20 45			21 00				21 15			
	d			20 00		20 15				20 30		20 45			21 00				21 15			
West Croydon	d																					
Herne Hill ■	d	19 47			20 05			20 16			20 35		20 46				21 05				21 16	
Loughborough Jn	d	19 50			20 08			20 19			20 38		20 49				21 08				21 19	
Elephant & Castle	d	19 55	20 00		20 13			20 24	20 30		20 43		20 54	21 00			21 13				21 24	21 30
London Blackfriars ■ ⊖	d	20 00	20 04	20 08	20 18	20 24		20 30	20 34	20 38	20 48	20 54	21 00	21 04	21 08		21 18		21 24		21 30	21a34
City Thameslink ■	d	20 02	20 06	20 10	20 20	20 26		20 32	20 36	20 40	20 50	20 56	21 02	21 06	21 10		21 20		21 26		21 32	
Farringdon ■ ⊖	d	20 06	20 10	20 14	20 23	20 30		20 36	20 40	20 44	20 53	21 00	21 06	21 10	21 14		21 23		21 30		21 36	
St Pancras International ■ ⊖	d						21 00											21 30		22 00		
St Pancras International ■ ⊖	a	20 10	20 14	20 18	20 27	20 34		20 40	20 44	20 48	20 57	21 04	21 10	21 14	21 18		21 27		21 34		21 40	
	d	20 10	20 14	20 18	20 28	20 34		20 40	20 44	20 48	20 58	21 04	21 10	21 14	21 18		21 28		21 34		21 40	
Kentish Town ⊖	d	20 14	20a19		20 31			20 44	20a49		21 01		21 14	21a19			21 31				21 44	
West Hampstead Thameslink ⊖	d	20 19			20 35	20 41		20 49			21 05	21 11	21 19				21 35		21 41		21 49	
Cricklewood	d	20 22			20 38			20 52			21 08		21 22				21 38				21 52	
Hendon	d	20 25			20 41			20 55			21 11		21 25				21 41				21 55	
Mill Hill Broadway	d	20 29			20 45			20 59			21 15		21 29				21 45				21 59	
Elstree & Borehamwood	d	20 33			20 49			21 03			21 19		21 33				21 49				22 03	
Radlett	d	20 37			20 53			21 07			21 23		21 37				21 53				22 07	
St Albans City	d	20 44		20 39	21a01	20 55		21 14		21 09	21a31	21 25	21 44		21 39		22a01		21 55		22 14	
Harpenden	d	20 49		20 45		21 01		21 19		21 15		21 31	21 49		21 45				22 01		22 19	
Luton Airport Parkway ■ ✈	d	20 55		20 51		21 07		21 25		21 21		21 37	21 55		21 51			21 53	22 07		22 25	
Luton ■	d	20a59		20 54		21 10	21 23	21a29		21 24		21 40	21a59		21 54				22 10	22 24	22a29	
Leagrave	d			20 57		21 14				21 27		21 44			21 57				22 14			
Harlington	d			21 02		21 19				21 32		21 49			22 02				22 19			
Flitwick	d			21 06		21 23				21 36		21 53			22 06				22 23			
Bedford ■	a			21 19		21 35	21 37			21 49		22 05			22 19			22 08	22 35	22 39		

A until 18 May

B from 21 May

Brighton, Gatwick Airport and South London - City of London, St Albans, Luton and Bedford

Network Diagram - see first Page of Table 52

		FC ■	SE A	FC A	FC B	FC ■	SE B	FC ■ A	SE A	EM ◇■	FC	FC ■ B	SE B	FC ■ A	SE A	FC ■ A	FC B	FC A	FC A	FC A	FC ■ B
Brighton	d	20 34				20 37		21 11				21 11		21 37							21 37
Preston Park	d					20 41								21 41							21 41
Hassocks	d					20 47		21 20				21 20		21 47							21 47
Burgess Hill	d					20 51		21 23				21 23		21 51							21 51
Wivelsfield	d					20 53								21 53							21 53
Haywards Heath	d	20 48				21 02		21 32				21 32		22 02							22 02
Balcombe	d							21 37				21 37									
Three Bridges	d	20 57				21 12		21 43				21 43		22 12							22 12
Gatwick Airport	d	21 02				21 17		21 47				21 47		22 17							22 17
Redhill	d																				
East Croydon	d	21 17				21 32		22a02				22 02		22a32							22 32
Sevenoaks	d		21 02				21 02		21 32				21 32		22 02						
Bat & Ball	d		21 05				21 05		21 35				21 35		22 05						
Otford	d		21 08				21 08		21 38				21 38		22 08						
Shoreham (Kent)	d		21 11				21 11		21 41				21 41		22 11						
Eynsford	d		21 15				21 15		21 45				21 45		22 15						
Swanley	d		21 20				21 20		21 50				21 50		22 20						
St Mary Cray	d		21 24				21 24		21 54				21 54		22 24						
Bickley	d		21 28				21 28		21 58				21 58		22 28						
Bromley South	d		21 31				21 31		22 01				22 01		22 31						
Shortlands	d		21 34				21 34		22 04				22 04		22 34						
Ravensbourne	d		21 36				21 36		22 06				22 06		22 36						
Beckenham Hill	d		21 38				21 38		22 08				22 08		22 38						
Bellingham	d		21 40				21 40		22 10				22 10		22 40						
Catford	d		21 43				21 43		22 13				22 13		22 43						
Crofton Park	d		21 45				21 45		22 15				22 15		22 45						
Nunhead	d		21 48				21 48		22 18				22 18		22 48						
Peckham Rye	d		21 50				21 50		22 20				22 20		22 50						
Denmark Hill	d		21a53				21 54		22a23				22 24		22a53						
Sutton (Surrey)	d			21 12	21 12						21 17						21 47	22 12			
West Sutton	d										21 20						21 50	22 15			
Sutton Common	d										21 22						21 52	22 17			
St Helier	d										21 25						21 55	22 20			
Morden South	d										21 27						21 57	22 22			
South Merton	d										21 29						21 59	22 24			
Wimbledon Chase	d										21 31						22 01	22 26			
Wimbledon	d										21 38						22 08	22 30			
Haydons Road	d										21 40						22 10	22 32			
Tooting	d										21 43						22 13	22 35			
Carshalton	d			21 15	21 15																
Hackbridge	d			21 17	21 17																
Mitcham Junction	d			21 20	21 20																
Mitcham Eastfields	d			21 23	21 23																
Streatham	d			21 27	21 27						21 49						22 19	22 40			
Tulse Hill	d			21 31	21 31						21 53						22 23	22a44			
London Bridge	a	21 30				21 45						22 15									22 45
	d	21 30				21 45						22 15									22 45
West Croydon	d																				
Herne Hill	d			21 35	21 35						21 57						22 27				
Loughborough Jn	d			21 38	21 38						22 00						22 30				
Elephant & Castle	d			21 43	21 43		22 00				22 04		22 30				22 34				
London Blackfriars	d	21 38		21 48	21 48	21 54	22a04				22 08	22 22	22a34				22 38			22 40	22 52
City Thameslink	d	21 40		21 50	21 50	21 56					22 10	22 24					22 40			22 45	22 54
Farringdon	d	21 44		21 53	21 53	22 00					22 13	22 28					22 43			22 50	22 58
St Pancras International	d									22 25											
St Pancras International	a	21 48		21 57	21 57	22 04					22 17	22 32					22 47			22 55	23 02
	d	21 48		21 58	21 58	22 04					22 18	22 32				22 32	22 48		22 48		23 02
Kentish Town	d			22 01	22 01						22 21						22 51		22 51		
West Hampstead Thameslink	d			22 05	22 05	22 11					22 25	22 40				22 40	22 55		22 55		23 10
Cricklewood	d			22 08	22 08						22 28						22 58		22 58		
Hendon	d			22 11	22 11						22 31						23 01		23 01		
Mill Hill Broadway	d			22 15	22 15						22 35						23 05		23 05		
Elstree & Borehamwood	d			22 19	22 19						22 39						23 09		23 09		
Radlett	d			22 23	22 23						22 43						23 14		23 14		
St Albans City	d	22 09		22 30	22a31	22 25					22 50	22 57				22 57	23 20		23 20		23 27
Harpenden	d	22 15		22 36		22 31					22 56	23 03				23 03	23 26		23 26		23 33
Luton Airport Parkway	d	22 21		22 42		22 37				22 48	23 02	23 09				23 09	23 32		23 32		23 39
Luton	d	22 24		22 45		22 40					23 05	23 12				23 12	23 35		23 35		23 42
Leagrave	d	22 27		22 49		22 44					23 09	23 16				23 16	23 39		23 39		23 46
Harlington	d	22 32		22 54		22 49					23 14	23 21				23 21	23 44		23 44		23 51
Flitwick	d	22 36		22 58		22 53					23 18	23 25				23 25	23 48		23 48		23 55
Bedford	a	22 49		23 10		23 05				23 03	23 30	23 38				23 38	00 02		00 02		00 08

A until 18 May

B from 21 May

Brighton, Gatwick Airport and South London - City of London, St Albans, Luton and Bedford

Network Diagram - see first Page of Table 52

		FC ■ A	FC ■ A	FC A	SE B	SE A	EM ◇■	FC B	FC A	FC A	FC ■ A	FC A	FC ■ B	SE B	FC ■ A	FC B	FC A	FC A	FC ■ B	FC ■ A	FC ■ B	FC ■ A	FC ■ B
Brighton	d	22 07											22 07		22 33				22 33	23 11	23 11	23 37	23 37
Preston Park	d	22 11											22 11		22 37				22 37			23 41	23 41
Hassocks	d	22 17											22 17		22 43				22 43	23 20	23 20	23 47	23 47
Burgess Hill	d	22 21											22 21		22 47				22 47	23 23	23 23	23 51	23 51
Wivelsfield	d	22 23											22 23		22 49				22 49			23 53	23 53
Haywards Heath	d	22 32											22 32		22 54				22 54	23 29	23 29	23 59	23 59
Balcombe	d	22 37											22 37		22 59				22 59			00 04	00 04
Three Bridges	d	22 43											22 43		23 12				23 12	23 38	23 38	00 10	00 10
Gatwick Airport	d	22 47											22 47		23 17				23 17	23 43	23 43	00 15	00 15
Redhill	d																					00 23	00 23
East Croydon	d	23a02											23 02		23a32				23 32	00a01	00 04	00a35	00 36
Sevenoaks	d				22 02	22 32								22 32									
Bat & Ball	d				22 05	22 35								22 35									
Otford	d				22 08	22 38								22 38									
Shoreham (Kent)	d				22 11	22 41								22 41									
Eynsford	d				22 15	22 45								22 45									
Swanley	d				22 20	22 50								22 50									
St Mary Cray	d				22 24	22 54								22 54									
Bickley	d				22 28	22 58								22 58									
Bromley South	d				22 31	23 01								23 01									
Shortlands	d				22 34	23 04								23 04									
Ravensbourne	d				22 36	23 06								23 06									
Beckenham Hill	d				22 38	23 08								23 08									
Bellingham	d				22 40	23 10								23 10									
Catford	d				22 43	23 13								23 13									
Crofton Park	d				22 45	23 15								23 15									
Nunhead	d				22 48	23 18								23 18									
Peckham Rye	d				22 50	23 20								23 20									
Denmark Hill	d				22 54	23a23								23 24									
Sutton (Surrey)	d							22 17								22 47							
West Sutton	d							22 20								22 50							
Sutton Common	d							22 22								22 52							
St Helier	d							22 25								22 55							
Morden South	d							22 27								22 57							
South Merton	d							22 29								22 59							
Wimbledon Chase	d							22 31								23 01							
Wimbledon	d							22 38								23 08							
Haydons Road	d							22 40								23 10							
Tooting	d							22 43								23 13							
Carshalton	d																						
Hackbridge	d																						
Mitcham Junction	d																						
Mitcham Eastfields	d																						
Streatham	d							22 49								23 19							
Tulse Hill	d							22 53								23 23							
London Bridge	a												23 15						23 45		00 21		00 51
	d												23 15						23 45		00 22		00 52
West Croydon	d																						
Herne Hill	d							22 57								23 27							
Loughborough Jn	d							23 00															
Elephant & Castle	d				23 00			23 04						23 30		23 34							
London Blackfriars	d			22 55	23a04			23 08		23 10		23 20	23 22	23a34		23 38		23 40	23 52		00 29		00 58
City Thameslink	d			23 00						23 15		23 25											
Farringdon	d			23 05				23 13		23 20		23 30	23 28			23 43		23 50	23 58		00 33		
St Pancras International	d						23 15																
St Pancras International	a			23 10				23 17		23 25		23 35	23 32			23 47		23 55	00 02		00 37		01 07
	d		23 02					23 18	23 18		23 32		23 32			23 48	23 48		00 02		00 38		01 08
Kentish Town	d							23 21	23 21							23 51	23 51				00 41		01 11
West Hampstead Thameslink	d		23 10					23 25	23 25		23 40		23 40			23 55	23 55		00 10		00 45		01 15
Cricklewood	d							23 28	23 28							23 58	23 58				00 48		01 18
Hendon	d							23 31	23 31							00 01	00 01				00 51		01 21
Mill Hill Broadway	d							23 35	23 35							00 05	00 05				00 55		01 25
Elstree & Borehamwood	d							23 39	23 39							00 09	00 09				00 59		01 29
Radlett	d							23 44	23 44							00 14	00 14				01 04		01 34
St Albans City	d		23 27					23 50	23 50		23 57		23 57			00 20	00 20		00 27		01 10		01 40
Harpenden	d		23 33					23 56	23 56		00 03		00 03			00 26	00 26		00 33		01 16		01 46
Luton Airport Parkway	d		23 39					00 02	00 02		00 09		00 09			00 32	00 32		00 39		01 22		01 52
Luton	d		23 42				23 46	00 05	00 05		00 12		00 12			00 35	00 35		00 42		01 25		01 55
Leagrave	d		23 46					00 09	00 09		00 16		00 16			00 39	00 39		00 46		01 29		01 59
Harlington	d		23 51					00 14	00 14		00 21		00 21			00 44	00 44		00 51		01 34		02 04
Flitwick	d		23 55					00 18	00 18		00 25		00 25			00 48	00 48		00 55		01 38		02 08
Bedford	a		00 08				00 11	00 32	00 32		00 38		00 38			01 02	01 02		01 08		01 52		02 22

A until 18 May

B from 21 May

Brighton, Gatwick Airport - South London

Network Diagram - see first Page of Table 52

		FC	SN	FC	FC	FC	FC	FC	FC	FC	FC	FC	FC	FC	FC	FC	FC	FC	FC	FC	SN	FC	SN
		A	B	A	C	C	A	C	C	A	C	C	D	D	C	D	C	D	C	D	B	D	B
Brighton	d	22p33	23p02			23p11	23p11		23p37	23p37											03 50		05 21
Preston Park	d	22p37	23p06						23p41	23p41													
Hassocks	d	22p43	23p12			23p20	23p20		23p47	23p47													05 31
Burgess Hill	d	22p47	23p16			23p23	23p23		23p51	23p51													
Wivelsfield	d	22p49	23p19						23p53	23p53													
Haywards Heath	d	22p54	23p24			23p29	23p29		23p59	23p59											04 25		05 37
Balcombe	d	22p59							00 04	00 04													
Three Bridges	d	23p12	23p47			23p38	23p38		00 10	00 10			01 25	02 25		03 25		04 25		04 55	05 00	05 21	05 46
Gatwick Airport	d	23p17	23p53			23p43	23p43		00 15	00 15			01 30	02 30		03 30		04 30		05 00	05 05	05 27	05 53
Redhill	d		00 03						00 23	00 23												05 35	
East Croydon	d	23p32	00a16			00 04	00 04		00 36	00 36			01 50	02 47		03 47		04 47		05 17	05a29	05 47	06a10
Sutton (Surrey)	d																						
West Sutton	d																						
Sutton Common	d																						
St Helier	d																						
Morden South	d																						
South Merton	d																						
Wimbledon Chase	d																						
Wimbledon	d																						
Haydons Road	d																						
Tooting	d																						
Carshalton	d																						
Hackbridge	d																						
Mitcham Junction	d																						
Mitcham Eastfields	d																						
Streatham	d																						
Tulse Hill	d																						
London Bridge	a	23p45				00 19	00 21		00 52	00 51												06 02	
	d	23p45			23p55		00 22	00 25		00 52	00 57	01 57			03 17		04 17		05 20			06 02	
Sevenoaks	d																						
Bat & Ball	d																						
Otford	d																						
Shoreham (Kent)	d																						
Eynsford	d																						
Swanley	d																						
St Mary Cray	d																						
Bickley	d																						
Bromley South	d																						
Shortlands	d																						
Ravensbourne	d																						
Beckenham Hill	d																						
Bellingham	d																						
Catford	d																						
Crofton Park	d																						
Nunhead	d																						
Peckham Rye	d																						
Denmark Hill	d																						
Herne Hill	d																						
Loughborough Jn.	d																						
Elephant & Castle	d																						
London Blackfriars	a	23p52			00 10		00 28	00 40		00 58	01 12	02 12	02 13	03 13	03 32	04 13	04 32	05 13	05 35	05 43		06 08	
	d	23p52		00 08	00 10		00 29	00 40		00 58	01 12	02 12	02 14	03 13	03 32	04 14	04 32	05 14	05 35	05 44		06 08	
City Thameslink	d																						
Farringdon	d	23p58		00 13	00 20		00 33	00 50										05 20	05 45	05 50		06 12	
St Pancras International	a	00 02		00 17	00 25		00 37	00 55		01 07	01 27	02 27	02 24	03 23	03 47	04 22	04 47	05 24	05 50	05 54		06 16	

A not 19 May. To Bedford
B To London Victoria
C 19 May
D To Bedford

Please refer to separate pages within this table for services operating between London and Bedford

At weekends please use local bus and tube services to travel to/from St Pancras International and London Bridge when no trains are operating. See local publicity for details of alternative routes and services that are available across central London

Brighton, Gatwick Airport - South London

Network Diagram - see first Page of Table 52

		SE	SE	FC	FC	SN	SE	SN	SE	FC	FC	SN	SE	FC	SE	FC	FC	SE	SN	FC	FC	FC	FC
		A	B	C	D	E	F	E	B	C	D	E	F	G	B	C	D	F	H	I	C	D	G
Brighton	d			05 25	05 25	05 50		05 56		06 02	06 02	06 11				06 25	06 25				06 37	06 37	
Preston Park	d			05 29	05 29			06 00				06 15				06 29	06 29				06 41	06 41	
Hassocks	d			05 35	05 35			06 06				06 21				06 35	06 35				06 47	06 47	
Burgess Hill	d			05 39	05 39					06 12	06 12	06 25				06 39	06 39				06 51	06 51	
Wivelsfield	d			05 41	05 41			06 11				06 27				06 41	06 41				06 53	06 53	
Haywards Heath	d			05 46	05 46	06 12		06 16		06 18	06 17	06 40				06 46	06 46				07 02	07 02	
Balcombe	d			05 51	05 51											06 51	06 51						
Three Bridges	d			05 57	05 57	06 21		06 31		06 27	06 27	06 49				06 57	06 57				07 12	07 12	
Gatwick Airport	d			06 02	06 02	06 26		06 38		06 32	06 32	06 55				07 02	07 02				07 17	07 16	
Redhill	d																						
East Croydon	d			06 17	06 17	06a40		06a53		06 47	06 47	07a09				07 17	07 17				07 32	07 32	
Sutton (Surrey)	d													06 37					06 59	07 08			07 07
West Sutton	d													06 40									07 10
Sutton Common	d													06 42									07 12
St Helier	d													06 45									07 15
Morden South	d													06 47									07 17
South Merton	d													06 49									07 19
Wimbledon Chase	d													06 51									07 21
Wimbledon	d													06 58									07 28
Haydons Road	d													07 00									07 30
Tooting	d													07 03									07 33
Carshalton	d																		07 02	07 11			
Hackbridge	d																		07 05	07 13			
Mitcham Junction	d																		07 08	07 16			
Mitcham Eastfields	d																		07a11	07 19			
Streatham	d													07 08						07 23			07 38
Tulse Hill	d													07 12						07 27			07 42
London Bridge	a			06 30	06 32					07 00	07 02					07 30	07 32				07 45	07 47	
	d			06 30						07 00						07 30					07 45		
Sevenoaks	d		05 32				05 55		06 02				06 25		06 32			06 55					
Bat & Ball	d		05 35				05 58		06 05				06 28		06 35			06 58					
Otford	d		05 38				06 01		06 08				06 31		06 38			07 01					
Shoreham (Kent)	d		05 41				06 04		06 11				06 34		06 41			07 04					
Eynsford	d		05 45				06 08		06 15				06 38		06 45			07 08					
Swanley	d		05 50				06 13		06 20				06 43		06 50			07 13					
St Mary Cray	d		05 54				06 17		06 24				06 47		06 54			07 17					
Bickley	d	05 51	05 58				06 21		06 28				06 51		06 58			07 21					
Bromley South	d	05 54	06 01				06 24		06 31				06 54		07 01			07 24					
Shortlands	d	05 57	06 04				06 27		06 34				06 57		07 04			07 27					
Ravensbourne	d	05 59	06 06				06 29		06 36				06 59		07 06			07 29					
Beckenham Hill	d	06 01	06 08				06 31		06 38				07 01		07 08			07 31					
Bellingham	d	06 03	06 10				06 33		06 40				07 03		07 10			07 33					
Catford	d	06 06	06 13				06 36		06 43				07 06		07 13			07 36					
Crofton Park	d	06 08	06 15				06 38		06 45				07 08		07 15			07 38					
Nunhead	d	06 11	06 18				06 41		06 48				07 11		07 18			07 41					
Peckham Rye	d	06 13	06 20				06 43		06 50				07 13		07 20			07 43					
Denmark Hill	d	06a16	06 24				06a46		06 54				07a16		07 24			07a46					
Herne Hill	d													07 16						07 31			07 46
Loughborough Jn.	d													07 19						07 34			07 49
Elephant & Castle	d		06 30						07 00					07 24	07 30					07 39			07 54
London Blackfriars	a		06 34	06 37					07 04	07 07				07 27	07 34	07 37				07 42	07 52		07 57
	d			06 38						07 08				07 30		07 38				07 44	07 54		08 00
City Thameslink	d																						
Farringdon	d			06 42						07 12				07 36		07 44				07 49	08 00		08 06
St Pancras International	a			06 46						07 16				07 40		07 48				07 53	08 04		08 10

A 19 May. From Orpington to London Victoria
B not 19 May
C To Bedford
D 19 May
E To London Victoria
F 19 May. To London Victoria
G To Luton
H From Epsom to London Victoria
I To St Albans City

Please refer to separate pages within this table for services operating between London and Bedford

At weekends please use local bus and tube services to travel to/from St Pancras International and London Bridge when no trains are operating. See local publicity for details of alternative routes and services that are available across central London

Brighton, Gatwick Airport - South London

Network Diagram - see first Page of Table 52

Station		SE A	FC ■ B	FC C	FC ■ C	FC C	SE D	SN E	FC F	FC ■ B	FC ■ C	FC G	SE A	FC ■ B	FC C	FC ■ C	FC C	SE D	SN E	FC F	FC ■ B	FC ■ C
Brighton	d		07 04		07 04					07 07	07 07			07 34		07 34					07 37	07 37
Preston Park	d									07 11	07 11										07 41	07 41
Hassocks	d									07 17	07 17										07 47	07 47
Burgess Hill	d									07 21	07 21										07 51	07 51
Wivelsfield	d									07 23	07 23										07 53	07 53
Haywards Heath	d		07 18		07 18					07 32	07 32			07 48		07 48					08 02	08 02
Balcombe	d									07 37	07 37											
Three Bridges	d		07 27		07 27					07 42	07 42			07 57		07 57					08 12	08 12
Gatwick Airport	d		07 32		07 32					07 47	07 46			08 02		08 02					08 17	08 16
Redhill	d																					
East Croydon	d		07 47		07 47					08 02	08 01			08 17		08 17					08 32	08 32
Sutton (Surrey)	d			07 07		07 08		07 29	07 38			07 37			07 37		07 38		07 59	08 08		
West Sutton	d			07 10								07 40			07 40							
Sutton Common	d			07 12								07 42			07 42							
St Helier	d			07 15								07 45			07 45							
Morden South	d			07 17								07 47			07 47							
South Merton	d			07 19								07 49			07 49							
Wimbledon Chase	d			07 21								07 51			07 51							
Wimbledon	d			07 30								07 58			08 00							
Haydons Road	d			07 32								08 00			08 02							
Tooting	d			07 35								08 03			08 05							
Carshalton	d					07 11		07 32	07 41								07 41		08 02	08 11		
Hackbridge	d					07 13		07 35	07 43								07 43		08 05	08 13		
Mitcham Junction	d					07 16		07 38	07 46								07 46		08 08	08 16		
Mitcham Eastfields	d					07 19		07a41	07 49								07 49		08a11	08 19		
Streatham	d			07 40		07 23			07 53			08 08			08 10		07 53			08 23		
Tulse Hill	d			07 47		07 27			07 57			08 12			08 17		07 57			08 27		
London Bridge	a		08 00	08 00	08 02					08 15	08 17			08 30	08 30	08 32					08 45	08 47
	d		08 00							08 15				08 30							08 45	
Sevenoaks	d	07 02					07 25						07 32					07 55				
Bat & Ball	d	07 05					07 28						07 35					07 58				
Otford	d	07 08					07 31						07 38					08 01				
Shoreham (Kent)	d	07 11					07 34						07 41					08 04				
Eynsford	d	07 15					07 38						07 45					08 08				
Swanley	d	07 20					07 43						07 50					08 13				
St Mary Cray	d	07 24					07 47						07 54					08 17				
Bickley	d	07 28					07 51						07 58					08 21				
Bromley South	d	07 31					07 54						08 01					08 24				
Shortlands	d	07 34					07 57						08 04					08 27				
Ravensbourne	d	07 36					07 59						08 06					08 29				
Beckenham Hill	d	07 38					08 01						08 08					08 31				
Bellingham	d	07 40					08 03						08 10					08 33				
Catford	d	07 43					08 06						08 13					08 36				
Crofton Park	d	07 45					08 08						08 15					08 38				
Nunhead	d	07 48					08 11						08 18					08 41				
Peckham Rye	d	07 50					08 13						08 20					08 43				
Denmark Hill	d	07 54					08a16						08 24					08a46				
Herne Hill	d					07a31			08 01			08 16					08a01			08 31		
Loughborough Jn.	d								08 04			08 19								08 34		
Elephant & Castle	d	08 00							08 09			08 24	08 30							08 39		
London Blackfriars	a	08 04	08 07						08 12	08 22		08 27	08 34	08 37						08 42	08 52	
	d		08 08						08 14	08 24		08 30		08 38						08 44	08 54	
City Thameslink	d																					
Farringdon	d		08 14						08 19	08 30		08 36		08 44						08 49	09 00	
St Pancras International	a		08 18						08 23	08 34		08 40		08 48						08 53	09 04	

A not 19 May
B To Bedford
C 19 May
D 19 May. To London Victoria
E From Epsom to London Victoria
F To St Albans City
G To Luton

Please refer to separate pages within this table for services operating between London and Bedford

At weekends please use local bus and tube services to travel to/from St Pancras International and London Bridge when no trains are operating. See local publicity for details of alternative routes and services that are available across central London

Brighton, Gatwick Airport - South London

Network Diagram - see first Page of Table 52

Station		FC A	SE B	FC ■ C	FC D	FC ■ D	FC D	SE E	SN F	FC G	FC ■ C	FC ■ D	FC A	SE B	FC ■ C	FC D	FC ■ D	FC D	SE E	SN F	FC G	FC ■ C	FC ■ D
Brighton	d			08 04		08 04					08 07	08 07			08 34		08 34					08 37	08 37
Preston Park	d										08 11	08 11										08 41	08 41
Hassocks	d										08 17	08 17										08 47	08 47
Burgess Hill	d										08 21	08 21										08 51	08 51
Wivelsfield	d										08 23	08 23										08 53	08 53
Haywards Heath	d			08 18		08 18					08 32	08 32			08 48		08 48					09 02	09 02
Balcombe	d										08 37	08 37											
Three Bridges	d			08 27		08 27					08 42	08 42			08 57		08 57					09 12	09 12
Gatwick Airport	d			08 32		08 32					08 47	08 46			09 02		09 02					09 17	09 16
Redhill	d																						
East Croydon	d			08 47		08 47					09 02	09 01			09 17		09 17					09 32	09 32
Sutton (Surrey)	d	08 07			08 07		08 08		08 29	08 38			08 37			08 37		08 38		08 59	09 08		
West Sutton	d	08 10			08 10								08 40			08 40							
Sutton Common	d	08 12			08 12								08 42			08 42							
St Helier	d	08 15			08 15								08 45			08 45							
Morden South	d	08 17			08 17								08 47			08 47							
South Merton	d	08 19			08 19								08 49			08 49							
Wimbledon Chase	d	08 21			08 21								08 51			08 51							
Wimbledon	d	08 28			08 30								08 58			09 00							
Haydons Road	d	08 30			08 32								09 00			09 02							
Tooting	d	08 33			08 35								09 03			09 05							
Carshalton	d						08 11		08 32	08 41								08 41		09 02	09 11		
Hackbridge	d						08 13		08 35	08 43								08 43		09 05	09 13		
Mitcham Junction	d						08 16		08 38	08 46								08 46		09 08	09 16		
Mitcham Eastfields	d						08 19		08a41	08 49								08 49		09a11	09 19		
Streatham	d	08 38			08 40		08 23			08 53			09 08			09 10		08 53			09 23		
Tulse Hill	d	08 42			08 47		08 27			08 57			09 12			09 17		08 57			09 27		
London Bridge	a			09 00	09 00	09 02					09 15	09 17			09 30	09 30	09 32					09 45	09 47
	d			09 00							09 15				09 30							09 45	
Sevenoaks	d		08 02					08 25						08 32					08 55				
Bat & Ball	d		08 05					08 28						08 35					08 58				
Otford	d		08 08					08 31						08 38					09 01				
Shoreham (Kent)	d		08 11					08 34						08 41					09 04				
Eynsford	d		08 15					08 38						08 45					09 08				
Swanley	d		08 20					08 43						08 50					09 13				
St Mary Cray	d		08 24					08 47						08 54					09 17				
Bickley	d		08 28					08 51						08 58					09 21				
Bromley South	d		08 31					08 54						09 01					09 24				
Shortlands	d		08 34					08 57						09 04					09 27				
Ravensbourne	d		08 36					08 59						09 06					09 29				
Beckenham Hill	d		08 38					09 01						09 08					09 31				
Bellingham	d		08 40					09 03						09 10					09 33				
Catford	d		08 43					09 06						09 13					09 36				
Crofton Park	d		08 45					09 08						09 15					09 38				
Nunhead	d		08 48					09 11						09 18					09 41				
Peckham Rye	d		08 50					09 13						09 20					09 43				
Denmark Hill	d		08 54					09a16						09 24					09a46				
Herne Hill	d	08 46					08a31			09 01			09 16					09a01			09 31		
Loughborough Jn.	d	08 49								09 04			09 19								09 34		
Elephant & Castle	d	08 54	09 00							09 09			09 24	09 30							09 39		
London Blackfriars	a	08 57	09 04	09 07						09 12	09 22		09 27	09 34	09 37						09 42	09 52	
	d	09 00		09 08						09 14	09 24		09 30		09 38						09 44	09 54	
City Thameslink	d	09 02		09 10						09 16	09 26		09 32		09 40						09 46	09 56	
Farringdon	d	09 06		09 14						09 19	09 30		09 36		09 44						09 49	10 00	
St Pancras International	a	09 10		09 18						09 23	09 34		09 40		09 48						09 53	10 04	

A To Luton
B not 19 May
C To Bedford
D 19 May
E 19 May. To London Victoria
F From Epsom to London Victoria
G To St Albans City

Please refer to separate pages within this table for services operating between London and Bedford

At weekends please use local bus and tube services to travel to/from St Pancras International and London Bridge when no trains are operating. See local publicity for details of alternative routes and services that are available across central London

Saturdays
until 8 September

Brighton, Gatwick Airport - South London

Network Diagram - see first Page of Table 52

		FC A	SE B	FC C	FC D	FC D	FC D	SE E	SN F	FC G	FC C	FC D	FC A	SE B	FC C	FC D	FC D	FC D	SE E	SN F	FC G	FC C
Brighton	d			09 04		09 04					09 07	09 07			09 34		09 34					09 37
Preston Park	d										09 11	09 11										09 41
Hassocks	d										09 17	09 17										09 47
Burgess Hill	d										09 21	09 21										09 51
Wivelsfield	d										09 23	09 23										09 53
Haywards Heath	d			09 18		09 18					09 32	09 32			09 48		09 48					10 02
Balcombe	d										09 37	09 37										
Three Bridges	d			09 27		09 27					09 42	09 42			09 57		09 57					10 12
Gatwick Airport	d			09 32		09 32					09 47	09 46			10 02		10 02					10 17
Redhill	d																					
East Croydon	d			09 47		09 47					10 02	10 01			10 17		10 17					10 32
Sutton (Surrey)	d	09 07			09 07		09 08		09 29	09 38			09 37			09 37		09 38		09 59	10 08	
West Sutton	d	09 10			09 10								09 40			09 40						
Sutton Common	d	09 12			09 12								09 42			09 42						
St Helier	d	09 15			09 15								09 45			09 45						
Morden South	d	09 17			09 17								09 47			09 47						
South Merton	d	09 19			09 19								09 49			09 49						
Wimbledon Chase	d	09 21			09 21								09 51			09 51						
Wimbledon	d	09 28			09 30								09 58			10 00						
Haydons Road	d	09 30			09 32								10 00			10 02						
Tooting	d	09 33			09 35								10 03			10 05						
Carshalton	d						09 11		09 32	09 41								09 41		10 02	10 11	
Hackbridge	d						09 13		09 35	09 43								09 43		10 05	10 13	
Mitcham Junction	d						09 16		09 38	09 46								09 46		10 08	10 16	
Mitcham Eastfields	d						09 19		09a41	09 49								09 49		10a11	10 19	
Streatham	d	09 38			09 40		09 23			09 53			10 08			10 10		09 53			10 23	
Tulse Hill	d	09 42			09 47		09 27			09 57			10 12			10 17		09 57			10 27	
London Bridge	a			10 00	10 00	10 02					10 15	10 17			10 30	10 30	10 32					10 45
	d			10 00							10 15				10 30							10 45
Sevenoaks	d		09 02					09 25						09 32					09 55			
Bat & Ball	d		09 05					09 28						09 35					09 58			
Otford	d		09 08					09 31						09 38					10 01			
Shoreham (Kent)	d		09 11					09 34						09 41					10 04			
Eynsford	d		09 15					09 38						09 45					10 08			
Swanley	d		09 20					09 43						09 50					10 13			
St Mary Cray	d		09 24					09 47						09 54					10 17			
Bickley	d		09 28					09 51						09 58					10 21			
Bromley South	d		09 31					09 54						10 01					10 24			
Shortlands	d		09 34					09 57						10 04					10 27			
Ravensbourne	d		09 36					09 59						10 06					10 29			
Beckenham Hill	d		09 38					10 01						10 08					10 31			
Bellingham	d		09 40					10 03						10 10					10 33			
Catford	d		09 43					10 06						10 13					10 36			
Crofton Park	d		09 45					10 08						10 15					10 38			
Nunhead	d		09 48					10 11						10 18					10 41			
Peckham Rye	d		09 50					10 13						10 20					10 43			
Denmark Hill	d		09 54					10a16						10 24					10a46			
Herne Hill	d	09 46					09a31			10 01			10 16					10a01			10 31	
Loughborough Jn.	d	09 49								10 04			10 19								10 34	
Elephant & Castle	d	09 54	10 00							10 09			10 24	10 30							10 39	
London Blackfriars	a	09 57	10 04	10 07						10 12	10 22		10 27	10 34	10 37						10 42	10 52
	d	10 00		10 08						10 14	10 24		10 30		10 38						10 44	10 54
City Thameslink	d	10 02		10 10						10 16	10 26		10 32		10 40						10 46	10 56
Farringdon	d	10 06		10 14						10 19	10 30		10 36		10 44						10 49	11 00
St Pancras International	a	10 10		10 18						10 23	10 34		10 40		10 48						10 53	11 04

A To Luton
B not 19 May
C To Bedford
D 19 May
E 19 May. To London Victoria
F From Epsom to London Victoria
G To St Albans City

Please refer to separate pages within this table for services operating between London and Bedford

At weekends please use local bus and tube services to travel to/from St Pancras International and London Bridge when no trains are operating. See local publicity for details of alternative routes and services that are available across central London

Saturdays
until 8 September

Brighton, Gatwick Airport - South London

Network Diagram - see first Page of Table 52

		FC A	FC B	SE C	FC D	FC A	FC A	FC A	SE E	SN F	FC G	FC D	FC A	FC B	SE C	FC D	FC A	FC A	FC A	SE E	SN F	FC G	FC D
Brighton	d	09 37			10 04		10 04					10 07	10 07			10 34		10 34					10 37
Preston Park	d	09 41										10 11	10 11										10 41
Hassocks	d	09 47										10 17	10 17										10 47
Burgess Hill	d	09 51										10 21	10 21										10 51
Wivelsfield	d	09 53										10 23	10 23										10 53
Haywards Heath	d	10 02			10 18		10 18					10 32	10 32			10 48		10 48					11 02
Balcombe	d											10 37	10 37										
Three Bridges	d	10 12			10 27		10 27					10 42	10 42			10 57		10 57					11 12
Gatwick Airport	d	10 16			10 32		10 32					10 47	10 46			11 02		11 02					11 17
Redhill	d																						
East Croydon	d	10 32			10 47		10 47					11 02	11 01			11 17		11 17					11 32
Sutton (Surrey)	d		10 07			10 07		10 08		10 29	10 38			10 37			10 37		10 38		10 59	11 08	
West Sutton	d		10 10			10 10								10 40			10 40						
Sutton Common	d		10 12			10 12								10 42			10 42						
St Helier	d		10 15			10 15								10 45			10 45						
Morden South	d		10 17			10 17								10 47			10 47						
South Merton	d		10 19			10 19								10 49			10 49						
Wimbledon Chase	d		10 21			10 21								10 51			10 51						
Wimbledon	d		10 28			10 30								10 58			11 00						
Haydons Road	d		10 30			10 32								11 00			11 02						
Tooting	d		10 33			10 35								11 03			11 05						
Carshalton	d							10 11		10 32	10 41								10 41		11 02	11 11	
Hackbridge	d							10 13		10 35	10 43								10 43		11 05	11 13	
Mitcham Junction	d							10 16		10 38	10 46								10 46		11 08	11 16	
Mitcham Eastfields	d							10 19		10a41	10 49								10 49		11a11	11 19	
Streatham	d		10 38			10 40		10 23			10 53			11 08			11 10		10 53			11 23	
Tulse Hill	d		10 42			10 47		10 27			10 57			11 12			11 17		10 57			11 27	
London Bridge	a	10 47			11 00	11 00	11 02					11 15	11 17			11 30	11 30	11 32					11 45
	d				11 00							11 15				11 30							11 45
Sevenoaks	d			10 02					10 25						10 32					10 55			
Bat & Ball	d			10 05					10 28						10 35					10 58			
Otford	d			10 08					10 31						10 38					11 01			
Shoreham (Kent)	d			10 11					10 34						10 41					11 04			
Eynsford	d			10 15					10 38						10 45					11 08			
Swanley	d			10 20					10 43						10 50					11 13			
St Mary Cray	d			10 24					10 47						10 54					11 17			
Bickley	d			10 28					10 51						10 58					11 21			
Bromley South	d			10 31					10 54						11 01					11 24			
Shortlands	d			10 34					10 57						11 04					11 27			
Ravensbourne	d			10 36					10 59						11 06					11 29			
Beckenham Hill	d			10 38					11 01						11 08					11 31			
Bellingham	d			10 40					11 03						11 10					11 33			
Catford	d			10 43					11 06						11 13					11 36			
Crofton Park	d			10 45					11 08						11 15					11 38			
Nunhead	d			10 48					11 11						11 18					11 41			
Peckham Rye	d			10 50					11 13						11 20					11 43			
Denmark Hill	d			10 54					11a16						11 24					11a46			
Herne Hill	d		10 46					10a31			11 01			11 16					11a01			11 31	
Loughborough Jn.	d		10 49								11 04			11 19								11 34	
Elephant & Castle	d		10 54	11 00							11 09			11 24	11 30							11 39	
London Blackfriars	a		10 57	11 04	11 07						11 12	11 22		11 27	11 34	11 37						11 42	11 52
	d		11 00		11 08						11 14	11 24		11 30		11 38						11 44	11 54
City Thameslink	d		11 02		11 10						11 16	11 26		11 32		11 40						11 46	11 56
Farringdon	d		11 06		11 14						11 19	11 30		11 36		11 44						11 49	12 00
St Pancras International	a		11 10		11 18						11 23	11 34		11 40		11 48						11 53	12 04

A 19 May
B To Luton
C not 19 May
D To Bedford
E 19 May. To London Victoria
F From Epsom to London Victoria
G To St Albans City

Please refer to separate pages within this table for services operating between London and Bedford

At weekends please use local bus and tube services to travel to/from St Pancras International and London Bridge when no trains are operating. See local publicity for details of alternative routes and services that are available across central London

Brighton, Gatwick Airport - South London

Network Diagram - see first Page of Table 52

		FC 1	FC	SE	FC 1	FC	FC 1	FC	SE	SN	FC	FC 1	FC 1	FC	SE	FC 1	FC	FC 1	FC	SE	SN	FC	FC 1
		A	B	C	D	A	A	A	E	F	G	D	A	B	C	D	A	A	A	E	F	G	D
Brighton 10	d	10 37			11 04		11 04					11 07	11 07			11 34		11 34					11 37
Preston Park	d	10 41										11 11	11 11										11 41
Hassocks 4	d	10 47										11 17	11 17										11 47
Burgess Hill 4	d	10 51										11 21	11 21										11 51
Wivelsfield 4	d	10 53										11 23	11 23										11 53
Haywards Heath 3	d	11 02			11 18		11 18					11 32	11 32			11 48		11 48					12 02
Balcombe	d											11 37	11 37										
Three Bridges 4	d	11 12			11 27		11 27					11 42	11 42			11 57		11 57					12 12
Gatwick Airport 10 ✈	d	11 16			11 32		11 32					11 47	11 46			12 02		12 02					12 17
Redhill	d																						
East Croydon	d	11 32			11 47		11 47					12 02	12 01			12 17		12 17					12 32
Sutton (Surrey) 4	d		11 07			11 07		11 08		11 29	11 38			11 37			11 37		11 38		11 59	12 08	
West Sutton	d		11 10			11 10								11 40			11 40						
Sutton Common	d		11 12			11 12								11 42			11 42						
St Helier	d		11 15			11 15								11 45			11 45						
Morden South	d		11 17			11 17								11 47			11 47						
South Merton	d		11 19			11 19								11 49			11 49						
Wimbledon Chase	d		11 21			11 21								11 51			11 51						
Wimbledon 6	d		11 28			11 30								11 58			12 00						
Haydons Road	d		11 30			11 32								12 00			12 02						
Tooting	d		11 33			11 35								12 03			12 05						
Carshalton	d							11 11		11 32	11 41								11 41		12 02	12 11	
Hackbridge	d							11 13		11 35	11 43								11 43		12 05	12 13	
Mitcham Junction	d							11 16		11 38	11 46								11 46		12 08	12 16	
Mitcham Eastfields	d							11 19		11a41	11 49								11 49		12a11	12 19	
Streatham 4	d		11 38			11 40		11 23			11 53			12 08			12 10		11 53			12 23	
Tulse Hill 3	d		11 42			11 47		11 27			11 57			12 12			12 17		11 57			12 27	
London Bridge 4 ⊖	a	11 47			12 00	12 00	12 02					12 15	12 17			12 30	12 30	12 32					12 45
	d				12 00							12 15				12 30							12 45
Sevenoaks 4	d			11 02					11 25						11 32					11 55			
Bat & Ball	d			11 05					11 28						11 35					11 58			
Otford 4	d			11 08					11 31						11 38					12 01			
Shoreham (Kent)	d			11 11					11 34						11 41					12 04			
Eynsford	d			11 15					11 38						11 45					12 08			
Swanley 4	d			11 20					11 43						11 50					12 13			
St Mary Cray 4	d			11 24					11 47						11 54					12 17			
Bickley	d			11 28					11 51						11 58					12 21			
Bromley South	d			11 31					11 54						12 01					12 24			
Shortlands 4	d			11 34					11 57						12 04					12 27			
Ravensbourne	d			11 36					11 59						12 06					12 29			
Beckenham Hill	d			11 38					12 01						12 08					12 31			
Bellingham	d			11 40					12 03						12 10					12 33			
Catford	d			11 43					12 06						12 13					12 36			
Crofton Park	d			11 45					12 08						12 15					12 38			
Nunhead 4	d			11 48					12 11						12 18					12 41			
Peckham Rye 4	d			11 50					12 13						12 20					12 43			
Denmark Hill 4	d			11 54					12a16						12 24					12a46			
Herne Hill 4	d		11 46					11a31			12 01			12 16					12a01			12 31	
Loughborough Jn.	d		11 49								12 04			12 19								12 34	
Elephant & Castle	d		11 54	12 00							12 09			12 24	12 30							12 39	
London Blackfriars 3 ⊖	a		11 57	12 04	12 07						12 12	12 22		12 27	12 34	12 37						12 42	12 52
	d		12 00		12 08						12 14	12 24		12 30		12 38						12 44	12 54
City Thameslink 3	d		12 02		12 10						12 16	12 26		12 32		12 40						12 46	12 56
Farringdon 3 ⊖	d		12 06		12 14						12 19	12 30		12 36		12 44						12 49	13 00
St Pancras International 15 ⊖	a		12 10		12 18						12 23	12 34		12 40		12 48						12 53	13 04

A 19 May
B To Luton
C not 19 May
D To Bedford
E 19 May. To London Victoria
F From Epsom to London Victoria
G To St Albans City

Please refer to separate pages within this table for services operating between London and Bedford

At weekends please use local bus and tube services to travel to/from St Pancras International and London Bridge when no trains are operating. See local publicity for details of alternative routes and services that are available across central London

Brighton, Gatwick Airport - South London

Network Diagram - see first Page of Table 52

		FC 1	FC	SE	FC 1	FC	FC 1	FC	SE	SN	FC	FC 1	FC 1	FC	SE	FC 1	FC	FC 1	FC	SE	SN	FC
		A	B	C	D	A	A	A	E	F	G	D	A	B	C	D	A	A	A	E	F	G
Brighton 10	d	11 37			12 04		12 04					12 07	12 07			12 34		12 34				
Preston Park	d	11 41										12 11	12 11									
Hassocks 4	d	11 47										12 17	12 17									
Burgess Hill 4	d	11 51										12 21	12 21									
Wivelsfield 4	d	11 53										12 23	12 23									
Haywards Heath 3	d	12 02			12 18		12 18					12 32	12 32			12 48		12 48				
Balcombe	d											12 37	12 37									
Three Bridges 4	d	12 12			12 27		12 27					12 42	12 42			12 57		12 57				
Gatwick Airport 10 ✈	d	12 16			12 32		12 32					12 47	12 46			13 02		13 02				
Redhill	d																					
East Croydon	d	12 32			12 47		12 47					13 02	13 01			13 17		13 17				
Sutton (Surrey) 4	d		12 07			12 07		12 08		12 29	12 38			12 37			12 37		12 38		12 59	13 08
West Sutton	d		12 10			12 10								12 40			12 40					
Sutton Common	d		12 12			12 12								12 42			12 42					
St Helier	d		12 15			12 15								12 45			12 45					
Morden South	d		12 17			12 17								12 47			12 47					
South Merton	d		12 19			12 19								12 49			12 49					
Wimbledon Chase	d		12 21			12 21								12 51			12 51					
Wimbledon 6	d		12 28			12 30								12 58			13 00					
Haydons Road	d		12 30			12 32								13 00			13 02					
Tooting	d		12 33			12 35								13 03			13 05					
Carshalton	d							12 11		12 32	12 41								12 41		13 02	13 11
Hackbridge	d							12 13		12 35	12 43								12 43		13 05	13 13
Mitcham Junction	d							12 16		12 38	12 46								12 46		13 08	13 16
Mitcham Eastfields	d							12 19		12a41	12 49								12 49		13a11	13 19
Streatham 4	d		12 38			12 40		12 23			12 53			13 08			13 10		12 53			13 23
Tulse Hill 3	d		12 42			12 47		12 27			12 57			13 12			13 17		12 57			13 27
London Bridge 4 ⊖	a	12 47			13 00	13 00	13 02					13 15	13 17			13 30	13 30	13 32				
	d				13 00							13 15				13 30						
Sevenoaks 4	d			12 02					12 25						12 32					12 55		
Bat & Ball	d			12 05					12 28						12 35					12 58		
Otford 4	d			12 08					12 31						12 38					13 01		
Shoreham (Kent)	d			12 11					12 34						12 41					13 04		
Eynsford	d			12 15					12 38						12 45					13 08		
Swanley 4	d			12 20					12 43						12 50					13 13		
St Mary Cray 4	d			12 24					12 47						12 54					13 17		
Bickley	d			12 28					12 51						12 58					13 21		
Bromley South	d			12 31					12 54						13 01					13 24		
Shortlands 4	d			12 34					12 57						13 04					13 27		
Ravensbourne	d			12 36					12 59						13 06					13 29		
Beckenham Hill	d			12 38					13 01						13 08					13 31		
Bellingham	d			12 40					13 03						13 10					13 33		
Catford	d			12 43					13 06						13 13					13 36		
Crofton Park	d			12 45					13 08						13 15					13 38		
Nunhead 4	d			12 48					13 11						13 18					13 41		
Peckham Rye 4	d			12 50					13 13						13 20					13 43		
Denmark Hill 4	d			12 54					13a16						13 24					13a46		
Herne Hill 4	d		12 46					12a31			13 01			13 16					13a01			13 31
Loughborough Jn.	d		12 49								13 04			13 19								13 34
Elephant & Castle	d		12 54	13 00							13 09			13 24	13 30							13 39
London Blackfriars 3 ⊖	a		12 57	13 04	13 07						13 12	13 22		13 27	13 34	13 37						13 42
	d		13 00		13 08						13 14	13 24		13 30		13 38						13 44
City Thameslink 3	d		13 02		13 10						13 16	13 26		13 32		13 40						13 46
Farringdon 3 ⊖	d		13 06		13 14						13 19	13 30		13 36		13 44						13 49
St Pancras International 15 ⊖	a		13 10		13 18						13 23	13 34		13 40		13 48						13 53

A 19 May
B To Luton
C not 19 May
D To Bedford
E 19 May. To London Victoria
F From Epsom to London Victoria
G To St Albans City

Please refer to separate pages within this table for services operating between London and Bedford

At weekends please use local bus and tube services to travel to/from St Pancras International and London Bridge when no trains are operating. See local publicity for details of alternative routes and services that are available across central London

Table 52

Saturdays
until 8 September

Brighton, Gatwick Airport - South London

Network Diagram - see first Page of Table 52

		FC 1 A	FC 1 B	FC C	SE D	FC 1 A	FC B	FC 1 B	FC B	SE E	SN F	FC G	FC 1 A	FC 1 B	FC C	SE D	FC 1 A	FC B	FC 1 B	FC B	SE E	SN F	FC G
Brighton	d	12 37	12 37			13 04		13 04					13 07	13 07			13 34		13 34				
Preston Park	d	12 41	12 41										13 11	13 11									
Hassocks	d	12 47	12 47										13 17	13 17									
Burgess Hill	d	12 51	12 51										13 21	13 21									
Wivelsfield	d	12 53	12 53										13 23	13 23									
Haywards Heath	d	13 02	13 02			13 18		13 18					13 32	13 32			13 48		13 48				
Balcombe	d												13 37	13 37									
Three Bridges	d	13 12	13 12			13 27		13 27					13 42	13 42			13 57		13 57				
Gatwick Airport ✈	d	13 17	13 16			13 32		13 32					13 47	13 46			14 02		14 02				
Redhill	d																						
East Croydon	d	13 32	13 32			13 47		13 47					14 02	14 01			14 17		14 17				
Sutton (Surrey)	d			13 07			13 07		13 08		13 29	13 38			13 37			13 37		13 38		13 59	14 08
West Sutton	d			13 10			13 10								13 40			13 40					
Sutton Common	d			13 12			13 12								13 42			13 42					
St Helier	d			13 15			13 15								13 45			13 45					
Morden South	d			13 17			13 17								13 47			13 47					
South Merton	d			13 19			13 19								13 49			13 49					
Wimbledon Chase	d			13 21			13 21								13 51			13 51					
Wimbledon	d			13 28			13 30								13 58			14 00					
Haydons Road	d			13 30			13 32								14 00			14 02					
Tooting	d			13 33			13 35								14 03			14 05					
Carshalton	d								13 11		13 32	13 41								13 41		14 02	14 11
Hackbridge	d								13 13		13 35	13 43								13 43		14 05	14 13
Mitcham Junction	d								13 16		13 38	13 46								13 46		14 08	14 16
Mitcham Eastfields	d								13 19		13a41	13 49								13 49		14a11	14 19
Streatham	d			13 38			13 40		13 23			13 53			14 08			14 10		13 53			14 23
Tulse Hill	d			13 42			13 47		13 27			13 57			14 12			14 17		13 57			14 27
London Bridge ⊖	a	13 45	13 47			14 00	14 00	14 02					14 15	14 17			14 30	14 30	14 32				
	d	13 45				14 00							14 15				14 30						
Sevenoaks	d				13 02					13 25						13 32					13 55		
Bat & Ball	d				13 05					13 28						13 35					13 58		
Otford	d				13 08					13 31						13 38					14 01		
Shoreham (Kent)	d				13 11					13 34						13 41					14 04		
Eynsford	d				13 15					13 38						13 45					14 08		
Swanley	d				13 20					13 43						13 50					14 13		
St Mary Cray	d				13 24					13 47						13 54					14 17		
Bickley	d				13 28					13 51						13 58					14 21		
Bromley South	d				13 31					13 54						14 01					14 24		
Shortlands	d				13 34					13 57						14 04					14 27		
Ravensbourne	d				13 36					13 59						14 06					14 29		
Beckenham Hill	d				13 38					14 01						14 08					14 31		
Bellingham	d				13 40					14 03						14 10					14 33		
Catford	d				13 43					14 06						14 13					14 36		
Crofton Park	d				13 45					14 08						14 15					14 38		
Nunhead	d				13 48					14 11						14 18					14 41		
Peckham Rye	d				13 50					14 13						14 20					14 43		
Denmark Hill	d				13 54					14a16						14 24					14a46		
Herne Hill	d			13 46					13a31			14 01			14 16					14a01			14 31
Loughborough Jn.	d			13 49								14 04			14 19								14 34
Elephant & Castle	d			13 54	14 00							14 09			14 24	14 30							14 39
London Blackfriars ⊖	a	13 52		13 57	14 04	14 07						14 12	14 22		14 27	14 34	14 37						14 42
	d	13 54		14 00		14 08						14 14	14 24		14 30		14 38						14 44
City Thameslink	d	13 56		14 02		14 10						14 16	14 26		14 32		14 40						14 46
Farringdon ⊖	d	14 00		14 06		14 14						14 19	14 30		14 36		14 44						14 49
St Pancras International ⊖	a	14 04		14 10		14 18						14 23	14 34		14 40		14 48						14 53

A To Bedford
B 19 May
C To Luton
D not 19 May
E 19 May. To London Victoria
F From Epsom to London Victoria
G To St Albans City

Please refer to separate pages within this table for services operating between London and Bedford

At weekends please use local bus and tube services to travel to/from St Pancras International and London Bridge when no trains are operating. See local publicity for details of alternative routes and services that are available across central London

Table 52

Saturdays
until 8 September

Brighton, Gatwick Airport - South London

Network Diagram - see first Page of Table 52

		FC 1 A	FC 1 B	FC C	SE D	FC 1 A	FC B	FC 1 B	FC B	SE E	SN F	FC G	FC 1 A	FC 1 B	FC C	SE D	FC 1 A	FC B	FC 1 B	FC B	SE E	SN F
Brighton	d	13 37	13 37			14 04		14 04					14 07	14 07			14 34		14 34			
Preston Park	d	13 41	13 41										14 11	14 11								
Hassocks	d	13 47	13 47										14 17	14 17								
Burgess Hill	d	13 51	13 51										14 21	14 21								
Wivelsfield	d	13 53	13 53										14 23	14 23								
Haywards Heath	d	14 02	14 02			14 18		14 18					14 32	14 32			14 48		14 48			
Balcombe	d												14 37	14 37								
Three Bridges	d	14 12	14 12			14 27		14 27					14 42	14 42			14 57		14 57			
Gatwick Airport ✈	d	14 17	14 16			14 32		14 32					14 47	14 46			15 02		15 02			
Redhill	d																					
East Croydon	d	14 32	14 32			14 47		14 47					15 02	15 01			15 17		15 17			
Sutton (Surrey)	d			14 07			14 07		14 08		14 29	14 38			14 37			14 37		14 38		14 59
West Sutton	d			14 10			14 10								14 40			14 40				
Sutton Common	d			14 12			14 12								14 42			14 42				
St Helier	d			14 15			14 15								14 45			14 45				
Morden South	d			14 17			14 17								14 47			14 47				
South Merton	d			14 19			14 19								14 49			14 49				
Wimbledon Chase	d			14 21			14 21								14 51			14 51				
Wimbledon	d			14 28			14 30								14 58			15 00				
Haydons Road	d			14 30			14 32								15 00			15 02				
Tooting	d			14 33			14 35								15 03			15 05				
Carshalton	d								14 11		14 32	14 41								14 41		15 02
Hackbridge	d								14 13		14 35	14 43								14 43		15 05
Mitcham Junction	d								14 16		14 38	14 46								14 46		15 08
Mitcham Eastfields	d								14 19		14a41	14 49								14 49		15a11
Streatham	d			14 38			14 40		14 23			14 53			15 08			15 10		14 53		
Tulse Hill	d			14 42			14 47		14 27			14 57			15 12			15 17		14 57		
London Bridge ⊖	a	14 45	14 47			15 00	15 00	15 02					15 15	15 17			15 30	15 30	15 32			
	d	14 45				15 00							15 15				15 30					
Sevenoaks	d				14 02					14 25						14 32					14 55	
Bat & Ball	d				14 05					14 28						14 35					14 58	
Otford	d				14 08					14 31						14 38					15 01	
Shoreham (Kent)	d				14 11					14 34						14 41					15 04	
Eynsford	d				14 15					14 38						14 45					15 08	
Swanley	d				14 20					14 43						14 50					15 13	
St Mary Cray	d				14 24					14 47						14 54					15 17	
Bickley	d				14 28					14 51						14 58					15 21	
Bromley South	d				14 31					14 54						15 01					15 24	
Shortlands	d				14 34					14 57						15 04					15 27	
Ravensbourne	d				14 36					14 59						15 06					15 29	
Beckenham Hill	d				14 38					15 01						15 08					15 31	
Bellingham	d				14 40					15 03						15 10					15 33	
Catford	d				14 43					15 06						15 13					15 36	
Crofton Park	d				14 45					15 08						15 15					15 38	
Nunhead	d				14 48					15 11						15 18					15 41	
Peckham Rye	d				14 50					15 13						15 20					15 43	
Denmark Hill	d				14 54					15a16						15 24					15a46	
Herne Hill	d			14 46					14a31			15 01			15 16					15a01		
Loughborough Jn.	d			14 49								15 04			15 19							
Elephant & Castle	d			14 54	15 00							15 09			15 24	15 30						
London Blackfriars ⊖	a	14 52		14 57	15 04	15 07						15 12	15 22		15 27	15 34	15 37					
	d	14 54		15 00		15 08						15 14	15 24		15 30		15 38					
City Thameslink	d	14 56		15 02		15 10						15 16	15 26		15 32		15 40					
Farringdon ⊖	d	15 00		15 06		15 14						15 19	15 30		15 36		15 44					
St Pancras International ⊖	a	15 04		15 10		15 18						15 23	15 34		15 40		15 48					

A To Bedford
B 19 May
C To Luton
D not 19 May
E 19 May. To London Victoria
F From Epsom to London Victoria
G To St Albans City

Please refer to separate pages within this table for services operating between London and Bedford

At weekends please use local bus and tube services to travel to/from St Pancras International and London Bridge when no trains are operating. See local publicity for details of alternative routes and services that are available across central London

Brighton, Gatwick Airport - South London

Network Diagram - see first Page of Table 52

		FC A	FC ■ B	FC ■ C	FC D	SE E	FC ■ B	FC C	FC ■ C	FC C	SE F	SN G	FC A	FC ■ B	FC ■ C	FC D	SE E	FC ■ B	FC C	FC ■ C	FC C	SE F	SN G
Brighton ■	d		14 37	14 37			15 04		15 04					15 07	15 07			15 34		15 34			
Preston Park	d		14 41	14 41										15 11	15 11								
Hassocks ■	d		14 47	14 47										15 17	15 17								
Burgess Hill ■	d		14 51	14 51										15 21	15 21								
Wivelsfield ■	d		14 53	14 53										15 23	15 23								
Haywards Heath ■	d		15 02	15 02			15 18		15 18					15 32	15 32			15 48		15 48			
Balcombe	d													15 37	15 37								
Three Bridges ■	d		15 12	15 12			15 27		15 27					15 42	15 42			15 57		15 57			
Gatwick Airport ■ ✈	d		15 17	15 16			15 32		15 32					15 47	15 46			16 02		16 02			
Redhill	d																						
East Croydon	d		15 32	15 32			15 47		15 47					16 02	16 01			16 17		16 17			
Sutton (Surrey) ■	d	15 08			15 07			15 07		15 08		15 29	15 38			15 37			15 37		15 38		15 59
West Sutton	d				15 10			15 10								15 40			15 40				
Sutton Common	d				15 12			15 12								15 42			15 42				
St Helier	d				15 15			15 15								15 45			15 45				
Morden South	d				15 17			15 17								15 47			15 47				
South Merton	d				15 19			15 19								15 49			15 49				
Wimbledon Chase	d				15 21			15 21								15 51			15 51				
Wimbledon ■	d				15 28			15 30								15 58			16 00				
Haydons Road	d				15 30			15 32								16 00			16 02				
Tooting	d				15 33			15 35								16 03			16 05				
Carshalton	d	15 11								15 11		15 32	15 41								15 41		16 02
Hackbridge	d	15 13								15 13		15 35	15 43								15 43		16 05
Mitcham Junction	d	15 16								15 16		15 38	15 46								15 46		16 08
Mitcham Eastfields	d	15 19								15 19		15a41	15 49								15 49		16a11
Streatham ■	d	15 23			15 38			15 40		15 23			15 53			16 08			16 10		15 53		
Tulse Hill ■	d	15 27			15 42			15 47		15 27			15 57			16 12			16 17		15 57		
London Bridge ■ ⊖	a		15 45	15 47			16 00	16 00	16 02					16 15	16 17			16 30	16 30	16 32			
	d		15 45				16 00							16 15				16 30					
Sevenoaks ■	d					15 02					15 25						15 32					15 55	
Bat & Ball	d					15 05					15 28						15 35					15 58	
Otford ■	d					15 08					15 31						15 38					16 01	
Shoreham (Kent)	d					15 11					15 34						15 41					16 04	
Eynsford	d					15 15					15 38						15 45					16 08	
Swanley ■	d					15 20					15 43						15 50					16 13	
St Mary Cray ■	d					15 24					15 47						15 54					16 17	
Bickley	d					15 28					15 51						15 58					16 21	
Bromley South	d					15 31					15 54						16 01					16 24	
Shortlands ■	d					15 34					15 57						16 04					16 27	
Ravensbourne	d					15 36					15 59						16 06					16 29	
Beckenham Hill	d					15 38					16 01						16 08					16 31	
Bellingham	d					15 40					16 03						16 10					16 33	
Catford	d					15 43					16 06						16 13					16 36	
Crofton Park	d					15 45					16 08						16 15					16 38	
Nunhead ■	d					15 48					16 11						16 18					16 41	
Peckham Rye ■	d					15 50					16 13						16 20					16 43	
Denmark Hill ■	d					15 54					16a16						16 24					16a46	
Herne Hill ■	d	15 31			15 46					15a31			16 01			16 16				16a01			
Loughborough Jn.	d	15 34			15 49								16 04			16 19							
Elephant & Castle	d	15 39			15 54	16 00							16 09			16 24	16 30						
London Blackfriars ■ ⊖	a	15 42	15 52		15 57	16 04	16 07						16 12	16 22		16 27	16 34	16 37					
	d	15 44	15 54		16 00		16 08						16 14	16 24		16 30		16 38					
City Thameslink ■	d	15 46	15 56		16 02		16 10						16 16	16 26		16 32		16 40					
Farringdon ■ ⊖	d	15 49	16 00		16 06		16 14						16 19	16 30		16 36		16 44					
St Pancras International ■ ⊖	a	15 53	16 04		16 10		16 18						16 23	16 34		16 40		16 48					

A To St Albans City
B To Bedford
C 19 May
D To Luton
E not 19 May
F 19 May. To London Victoria
G From Epsom to London Victoria

Please refer to separate pages within this table for services operating between London and Bedford

At weekends please use local bus and tube services to travel to/from St Pancras International and London Bridge when no trains are operating. See local publicity for details of alternative routes and services that are available across central London

Brighton, Gatwick Airport - South London

Network Diagram - see first Page of Table 52

		FC A	FC ■ B	FC ■ C	FC D	SE E	FC ■ B	FC C	FC ■ C	FC C	SE F	SN G	FC A	FC ■ B	FC ■ C	FC D	SE E	FC ■ B	FC C	FC ■ C	FC C	SE F	SN G
Brighton ■	d		15 37	15 37			16 04		16 04					16 07	16 07			16 34		16 34			
Preston Park	d		15 41	15 41										16 11	16 11								
Hassocks ■	d		15 47	15 47										16 17	16 17								
Burgess Hill ■	d		15 51	15 51										16 21	16 21								
Wivelsfield ■	d		15 53	15 53										16 23	16 23								
Haywards Heath ■	d		16 02	16 02			16 18		16 18					16 32	16 32			16 48		16 48			
Balcombe	d													16 37	16 37								
Three Bridges ■	d		16 12	16 12			16 27		16 27					16 42	16 42			16 57		16 57			
Gatwick Airport ■ ✈	d		16 17	16 16			16 32		16 32					16 47	16 46			17 02		17 02			
Redhill	d																						
East Croydon	d		16 32	16 32			16 47		16 47					17 02	17 01			17 17		17 17			
Sutton (Surrey) ■	d	16 08			16 07			16 07		16 08		16 29	16 38			16 37			16 37		16 38		16 59
West Sutton	d				16 10			16 10								16 40			16 40				
Sutton Common	d				16 12			16 12								16 42			16 42				
St Helier	d				16 15			16 15								16 45			16 45				
Morden South	d				16 17			16 17								16 47			16 47				
South Merton	d				16 19			16 19								16 49			16 49				
Wimbledon Chase	d				16 21			16 21								16 51			16 51				
Wimbledon ■	d				16 28			16 30								16 58			17 00				
Haydons Road	d				16 30			16 32								17 00			17 02				
Tooting	d				16 33			16 35								17 03			17 05				
Carshalton	d	16 11								16 11		16 32	16 41								16 41		17 02
Hackbridge	d	16 13								16 13		16 35	16 43								16 43		17 05
Mitcham Junction	d	16 16								16 16		16 38	16 46								16 46		17 08
Mitcham Eastfields	d	16 19								16 19		16a41	16 49								16 49		17a11
Streatham ■	d	16 23			16 38			16 40		16 23			16 53			17 08			17 10		16 53		
Tulse Hill ■	d	16 27			16 42			16 47		16 27			16 57			17 12			17 17		16 57		
London Bridge ■ ⊖	a		16 45	16 47			17 00	17 00	17 02					17 15	17 17			17 30	17 30	17 32			
	d		16 45				17 00							17 15				17 30					
Sevenoaks ■	d					16 02					16 25						16 32					16 55	
Bat & Ball	d					16 05					16 28						16 35					16 58	
Otford ■	d					16 08					16 31						16 38					17 01	
Shoreham (Kent)	d					16 11					16 34						16 41					17 04	
Eynsford	d					16 15					16 38						16 45					17 08	
Swanley ■	d					16 20					16 43						16 50					17 13	
St Mary Cray ■	d					16 24					16 47						16 54					17 17	
Bickley	d					16 28					16 51						16 58					17 21	
Bromley South	d					16 31					16 54						17 01					17 24	
Shortlands ■	d					16 34					16 57						17 04					17 27	
Ravensbourne	d					16 36					16 59						17 06					17 29	
Beckenham Hill	d					16 38					17 01						17 08					17 31	
Bellingham	d					16 40					17 03						17 10					17 33	
Catford	d					16 43					17 06						17 13					17 36	
Crofton Park	d					16 45					17 08						17 15					17 38	
Nunhead ■	d					16 48					17 11						17 18					17 41	
Peckham Rye ■	d					16 50					17 13						17 20					17 43	
Denmark Hill ■	d					16 54					17a16						17 24					17a46	
Herne Hill ■	d	16 31			16 46					16a31			17 01			17 16				17a01			
Loughborough Jn.	d	16 34			16 49								17 04			17 19							
Elephant & Castle	d	16 39			16 54	17 00							17 09			17 24	17 30						
London Blackfriars ■ ⊖	a	16 42	16 52		16 57	17 04	17 07						17 12	17 22		17 27	17 34	17 37					
	d	16 44	16 54		17 00		17 08						17 14	17 24		17 30		17 38					
City Thameslink ■	d	16 46	16 56		17 02		17 10						17 16	17 26		17 32		17 40					
Farringdon ■ ⊖	d	16 49	17 00		17 06		17 14						17 19	17 30		17 36		17 44					
St Pancras International ■ ⊖	a	16 53	17 04		17 10		17 18						17 23	17 34		17 40		17 48					

A To St Albans City
B To Bedford
C 19 May
D To Luton
E not 19 May
F 19 May. To London Victoria
G From Epsom to London Victoria

Please refer to separate pages within this table for services operating between London and Bedford

At weekends please use local bus and tube services to travel to/from St Pancras International and London Bridge when no trains are operating. See local publicity for details of alternative routes and services that are available across central London

Table 52

Saturdays until 8 September

Brighton, Gatwick Airport - South London

Network Diagram - see first Page of Table 52

Station		FC A	FC ■ B	FC ■ C	FC ■ D	FC E	SE F	FC ■ G	FC D	FC ■ D	FC D	SE H	SN I	FC A	FC ■ G	FC ■ D	FC E	SE F	FC ■ G	FC D	FC ■ D	FC D
Brighton	d		16 37	16 37	16 37			17 04		17 04					17 07	17 07			17 34		17 34	
Preston Park	d		16 41	16 41	16 41										17 11	17 11						
Hassocks	d		16 47	16 47	16 47										17 17	17 17						
Burgess Hill	d		16 51	16 51	16 51										17 21	17 21						
Wivelsfield	d		16 53	16 53	16 53										17 23	17 23						
Haywards Heath	d		17 02	17 02	17 02			17 18		17 18					17 32	17 32			17 48		17 48	
Balcombe	d														17 37	17 37						
Three Bridges	d		17 11	17 12	17 12			17 27		17 27					17 42	17 42			17 57		17 57	
Gatwick Airport	d		17 16	17 17	17 16			17 32		17 32					17 47	17 46			18 02		18 02	
Redhill	d																					
East Croydon	d		17 31	17 32	17 32			17 47		17 47					18 02	18 01			18 17		18 17	
Sutton (Surrey)	d	17 08				17 07			17 07		17 08		17 29	17 38			17 37			17 37		17 38
West Sutton	d					17 10			17 10								17 40			17 40		
Sutton Common	d					17 12			17 12								17 42			17 42		
St Helier	d					17 15			17 15								17 45			17 45		
Morden South	d					17 17			17 17								17 47			17 47		
South Merton	d					17 19			17 19								17 49			17 49		
Wimbledon Chase	d					17 21			17 21								17 51			17 51		
Wimbledon	d					17 28			17 30								17 58			18 00		
Haydons Road	d					17 30			17 32								18 00			18 02		
Tooting	d					17 33			17 35								18 03			18 05		
Carshalton	d	17 11									17 11		17 32	17 41								17 41
Hackbridge	d	17 13									17 13		17 35	17 43								17 43
Mitcham Junction	d	17 16									17 16		17 38	17 46								17 46
Mitcham Eastfields	d	17 19									17 19		17a41	17 49								17 49
Streatham	d	17 23				17 38			17 40		17 23			17 53			18 08			18 10		17 53
Tulse Hill	d	17 27				17 42			17 47		17 27			17 57			18 12			18 17		17 57
London Bridge	a		17 45	17 45	17 47			18 00	18 00	18 02					18 15	18 17			18 30	18 30	18 32	
	d		17 45	17 45				18 00							18 15				18 30			
Sevenoaks	d						17 02					17 25						17 32				
Bat & Ball	d						17 05					17 28						17 35				
Otford	d						17 08					17 31						17 38				
Shoreham (Kent)	d						17 11					17 34						17 41				
Eynsford	d						17 15					17 38						17 45				
Swanley	d						17 20					17 43						17 50				
St Mary Cray	d						17 24					17 47						17 54				
Bickley	d						17 28					17 51						17 58				
Bromley South	d						17 31					17 54						18 01				
Shortlands	d						17 34					17 57						18 04				
Ravensbourne	d						17 36					17 59						18 06				
Beckenham Hill	d						17 38					18 01						18 08				
Bellingham	d						17 40					18 03						18 10				
Catford	d						17 43					18 06						18 13				
Crofton Park	d						17 45					18 08						18 15				
Nunhead	d						17 48					18 11						18 18				
Peckham Rye	d						17 50					18 13						18 20				
Denmark Hill	d						17 54					18a16						18 24				
Herne Hill	d	17 31				17 46					17a31			18 01			18 16					18a01
Loughborough Jn.	d	17 34				17 49								18 04			18 19					
Elephant & Castle	d	17 39				17 54	18 00							18 09			18 24	18 30				
London Blackfriars	a	17 42	17 52	17 52		17 57	18 04	18 07						18 12	18 22		18 27	18 34	18 37			
	d	17 44	17 54	17 54		18 00		18 08						18 14	18 24		18 30		18 38			
City Thameslink	d	17 46	17 56	17 56		18 02		18 10						18 16	18 26		18 32		18 40			
Farringdon	d	17 49	18 00	18 00		18 06		18 14						18 19	18 30		18 36		18 44			
St Pancras International	a	17 53	18 04	18 04		18 10		18 18						18 23	18 34		18 40		18 48			

A To St Albans City
B not 19 May. To Bedford
C 19 May. To Bedford
D 19 May
E To Luton
F not 19 May
G To Bedford
H 19 May. To London Victoria
I From Epsom to London Victoria

Please refer to separate pages within this table for services operating between London and Bedford

At weekends please use local bus and tube services to travel to/from St Pancras International and London Bridge when no trains are operating. See local publicity for details of alternative routes and services that are available across central London

Table 52

Saturdays until 8 September

Brighton, Gatwick Airport - South London

Network Diagram - see first Page of Table 52

Station		SE A	SN B	FC C	FC ■ D	FC ■ E	FC F	SE G	FC ■ D	FC E	FC ■ E	FC E	SE A	SN B	FC C	FC ■ D	FC ■ E	FC F	SE G	FC ■ D	FC E	FC ■ E	FC E
Brighton	d				17 37	17 37			18 04		18 04					18 07	18 07			18 34		18 34	
Preston Park	d				17 41	17 41										18 11	18 11						
Hassocks	d				17 47	17 47										18 17	18 17						
Burgess Hill	d				17 51	17 51										18 21	18 21						
Wivelsfield	d				17 53	17 53										18 23	18 23						
Haywards Heath	d				18 02	18 02			18 18		18 18					18 32	18 32			18 48		18 48	
Balcombe	d															18 37	18 37						
Three Bridges	d				18 12	18 12			18 27		18 27					18 42	18 42			18 57		18 57	
Gatwick Airport	d				18 17	18 16			18 32		18 32					18 47	18 46			19 02		19 02	
Redhill	d																						
East Croydon	d				18 32	18 32			18 47		18 47					19 02	19 01			19 17		19 17	
Sutton (Surrey)	d		17 59	18 08			18 07			18 07		18 08		18 29	18 38			18 37			18 37		18 38
West Sutton	d						18 10			18 10								18 40			18 40		
Sutton Common	d						18 12			18 12								18 42			18 42		
St Helier	d						18 15			18 15								18 45			18 45		
Morden South	d						18 17			18 17								18 47			18 47		
South Merton	d						18 19			18 19								18 49			18 49		
Wimbledon Chase	d						18 21			18 21								18 51			18 51		
Wimbledon	d						18 28			18 30								18 58			19 00		
Haydons Road	d						18 30			18 32								19 00			19 02		
Tooting	d						18 33			18 35								19 03			19 05		
Carshalton	d		18 02	18 11								18 11		18 32	18 41								18 41
Hackbridge	d		18 05	18 13								18 13		18 35	18 43								18 43
Mitcham Junction	d		18 08	18 16								18 16		18 38	18 46								18 46
Mitcham Eastfields	d		18a11	18 19								18 19		18a41	18 49								18 49
Streatham	d			18 23			18 38			18 40		18 23			18 53			19 08			19 10		18 53
Tulse Hill	d			18 27			18 42			18 47		18 27			18 57			19 12			19 17		18 57
London Bridge	a				18 45	18 47			19 00	19 00	19 02					19 15	19 17			19 30	19 30	19 32	
	d				18 45				19 00							19 15				19 30			
Sevenoaks	d	17 55						18 02					18 25						18 32				
Bat & Ball	d	17 58						18 05					18 28						18 35				
Otford	d	18 01						18 08					18 31						18 38				
Shoreham (Kent)	d	18 04						18 11					18 34						18 41				
Eynsford	d	18 08						18 15					18 38						18 45				
Swanley	d	18 13						18 20					18 43						18 50				
St Mary Cray	d	18 17						18 24					18 47						18 54				
Bickley	d	18 21						18 28					18 51						18 58				
Bromley South	d	18 24						18 31					18 54						19 01				
Shortlands	d	18 27						18 34					18 57						19 04				
Ravensbourne	d	18 29						18 36					18 59						19 06				
Beckenham Hill	d	18 31						18 38					19 01						19 08				
Bellingham	d	18 33						18 40					19 03						19 10				
Catford	d	18 36						18 43					19 06						19 13				
Crofton Park	d	18 38						18 45					19 08						19 15				
Nunhead	d	18 41						18 48					19 11						19 18				
Peckham Rye	d	18 43						18 50					19 13						19 20				
Denmark Hill	d	18a46						18 54					19a16						19 24				
Herne Hill	d			18 31			18 46					18a31			19 01			19 16					19a01
Loughborough Jn.	d			18 34			18 49								19 04			19 19					
Elephant & Castle	d			18 39			18 54	19 00							19 09			19 24	19 30				
London Blackfriars	a			18 42	18 52		18 57	19 04	19 07						19 12	19 22		19 27	19 34	19 37			
	d			18 44	18 54		19 00		19 08						19 14	19 24		19 30		19 38			
City Thameslink	d			18 46	18 56		19 02		19 10						19 16	19 26		19 32		19 40			
Farringdon	d			18 49	19 00		19 06		19 14						19 19	19 30		19 36		19 44			
St Pancras International	a			18 53	19 04		19 10		19 18						19 23	19 34		19 40		19 48			

A 19 May. To London Victoria
B From Epsom to London Victoria
C To St Albans City
D To Bedford
E 19 May
F To Luton
G not 19 May

Please refer to separate pages within this table for services operating between London and Bedford

At weekends please use local bus and tube services to travel to/from St Pancras International and London Bridge when no trains are operating. See local publicity for details of alternative routes and services that are available across central London

Brighton, Gatwick Airport - South London

Network Diagram - see first Page of Table 52

		SE	SN	FC	FC [1]	FC [1]	FC	SE	FC [1]	FC	FC [1]	FC	SE	SN	FC	FC [1]	FC [1]	FC	SE	FC [1]	FC	FC [1]
		A	B	C	C	D	E	F	C	D	D	D	A	B	C	C	D	E	F	C	D	D
Brighton	d				18 37	18 37			19 04		19 04					19 07	19 07			19 34		19 34
Preston Park	d				18 41	18 41										19 11	19 11					
Hassocks	d				18 47	18 47										19 17	19 17					
Burgess Hill	d				18 51	18 51										19 21	19 21					
Wivelsfield	d				18 53	18 53										19 23	19 23					
Haywards Heath	d				19 02	19 02			19 18		19 18					19 32	19 32			19 48		19 48
Balcombe	d															19 37	19 37					
Three Bridges	d				19 12	19 12			19 27		19 27					19 42	19 42			19 57		19 57
Gatwick Airport	d				19 17	19 16			19 32		19 32					19 47	19 46			20 02		20 02
Redhill	d																					
East Croydon	d				19 32	19 32			19 47		19 47					20 02	20 01			20 17		20 17
Sutton (Surrey)	d		18 59	19 08			19 07			19 07		19 08		19 29	19 38			19 37			19 37	
West Sutton	d						19 10			19 10								19 40			19 40	
Sutton Common	d						19 12			19 12								19 42			19 42	
St Helier	d						19 15			19 15								19 45			19 45	
Morden South	d						19 17			19 17								19 47			19 47	
South Merton	d						19 19			19 19								19 49			19 49	
Wimbledon Chase	d						19 21			19 21								19 51			19 51	
Wimbledon	d						19 28			19 30								19 58			20 00	
Haydons Road	d						19 30			19 32								20 00			20 02	
Tooting	d						19 33			19 35								20 03			20 05	
Carshalton	d		19 02	19 11								19 11		19 32	19 41							
Hackbridge	d		19 05	19 13								19 13		19 35	19 43							
Mitcham Junction	d		19 08	19 16								19 16		19 38	19 46							
Mitcham Eastfields	d		19a11	19 19								19 19		19a41	19 49							
Streatham	d			19 23			19 38			19 40		19 23			19 53			20 08			20 10	
Tulse Hill	d			19 27			19 42			19 47		19 27			19 57			20 12			20 17	
London Bridge	a				19 45	19 47			20 00	20 00	20 02					20 15	20 17			20 30	20 30	20 32
	d				19 45				20 00							20 15				20 30		
Sevenoaks	d	18 55						19 02					19 25						19 32			
Bat & Ball	d	18 58						19 05					19 28						19 35			
Otford	d	19 01						19 08					19 31						19 38			
Shoreham (Kent)	d	19 04						19 11					19 34						19 41			
Eynsford	d	19 08						19 15					19 38						19 45			
Swanley	d	19 13						19 20					19 43						19 50			
St Mary Cray	d	19 17						19 24					19 47						19 54			
Bickley	d	19 21						19 28					19 51						19 58			
Bromley South	d	19 24						19 31					19 54						20 01			
Shortlands	d	19 27						19 34					19 57						20 04			
Ravensbourne	d	19 29						19 36					19 59						20 06			
Beckenham Hill	d	19 31						19 38					20 01						20 08			
Bellingham	d	19 33						19 40					20 03						20 10			
Catford	d	19 36						19 43					20 06						20 13			
Crofton Park	d	19 38						19 45					20 08						20 15			
Nunhead	d	19 41						19 48					20 11						20 18			
Peckham Rye	d	19 43						19 50					20 13						20 20			
Denmark Hill	d	19a46						19 54					20a16						20 24			
Herne Hill	d			19 31			19 46					19a31			20 01			20 16				
Loughborough Jn.	d			19 34			19 49								20 04			20 19				
Elephant & Castle	d			19 39			19 54	20 00							20 09			20 24	20 30			
London Blackfriars	a			19 42	19 52		19 57	20 04	20 07						20 12	20 22		20 27	20 34	20 37		
	d			19 44	19 54		20 00		20 08						20 14	20 24		20 30		20 38		
City Thameslink	d			19 46	19 56		20 02		20 10						20 16	20 26		20 32		20 40		
Farringdon	d			19 49	20 00		20 06		20 14						20 19	20 30		20 36		20 44		
St Pancras International	a			19 53	20 04		20 10		20 18						20 23	20 34		20 40		20 48		

A 19 May. To London Victoria
B From Epsom to London Victoria
C To Bedford
D 19 May
E To Luton
F not 19 May

Please refer to separate pages within this table for services operating between London and Bedford

At weekends please use local bus and tube services to travel to/from St Pancras International and London Bridge when no trains are operating. See local publicity for details of alternative routes and services that are available across central London

Brighton, Gatwick Airport - South London

Network Diagram - see first Page of Table 52

		SE	SN	FC	FC [1]	FC [1]	SN ◇[1]	FC	SE	FC [1]	FC	FC [1]	SE	SN	FC	FC [1]	FC [1]	FC	SE	FC [1]	FC	FC [1]	SE
		A	B	C	D	E	F	C	G	D	E	E	A	B	C	D	E	C	G	D	E	E	A
Brighton	d				19 37	19 37	19 54			20 04		20 04				20 07	20 07			20 34		20 34	
Preston Park	d				19 41	19 41	19 58									20 11	20 11						
Hassocks	d				19 47	19 47	20 04									20 17	20 17						
Burgess Hill	d				19 51	19 51	20 08									20 21	20 21						
Wivelsfield	d				19 53	19 53	20 10									20 23	20 23						
Haywards Heath	d				20 02	20 02	20 22			20 18		20 18				20 32	20 32			20 48		20 48	
Balcombe	d															20 37	20 37						
Three Bridges	d				20 12	20 12	20 32			20 27		20 28				20 42	20 42			20 57		20 57	
Gatwick Airport	d				20 17	20 16	20 38			20 32		20 31				20 47	20 46			21 02		21 02	
Redhill	d						20 48																
East Croydon	d				20 32	20 32	20a59			20 47		20 47				21 02	21 01			21 17		21 17	
Sutton (Surrey)	d		19 59	20 08				20 07			20 08			20 29	20 38			20 37			20 37		
West Sutton	d							20 10			20 11							20 40			20 40		
Sutton Common	d							20 12			20 13							20 42			20 42		
St Helier	d							20 15			20 16							20 45			20 45		
Morden South	d							20 17			20 18							20 47			20 47		
South Merton	d							20 19			20 20							20 49			20 49		
Wimbledon Chase	d							20 21			20 22							20 51			20 51		
Wimbledon	d							20 28			20 30							20 58			21 00		
Haydons Road	d							20 30			20 32							21 00			21 02		
Tooting	d							20 33			20 35							21 03			21 05		
Carshalton	d		20 02	20 11										20 32	20 41								
Hackbridge	d		20 05	20 13										20 35	20 43								
Mitcham Junction	d		20 08	20 16										20 38	20 46								
Mitcham Eastfields	d		20a11	20 19										20a41	20 49								
Streatham	d			20 23				20 38			20 40				20 53			21 08			21 10		
Tulse Hill	d			20 27				20 42			20 47				20 57			21 12			21 17		
London Bridge	a				20 45	20 47				21 00	21 00	21 02				21 15	21 17			21 30	21 30	21 32	
	d				20 45					21 00						21 15				21 30			
Sevenoaks	d	19 55							20 02				20 25						20 32				20 55
Bat & Ball	d	19 58							20 05				20 28						20 35				20 58
Otford	d	20 01							20 08				20 31						20 38				21 01
Shoreham (Kent)	d	20 04							20 11				20 34						20 41				21 04
Eynsford	d	20 08							20 15				20 38						20 45				21 08
Swanley	d	20 13							20 20				20 43						20 50				21 13
St Mary Cray	d	20 17							20 24				20 47						20 54				21 17
Bickley	d	20 21							20 28				20 51						20 58				21 21
Bromley South	d	20 24							20 31				20 54						21 01				21 24
Shortlands	d	20 27							20 34				20 57						21 04				21 27
Ravensbourne	d	20 29							20 36				20 59						21 06				21 29
Beckenham Hill	d	20 31							20 38				21 01						21 08				21 31
Bellingham	d	20 33							20 40				21 03						21 10				21 33
Catford	d	20 36							20 43				21 06						21 13				21 36
Crofton Park	d	20 38							20 45				21 08						21 15				21 38
Nunhead	d	20 41							20 48				21 11						21 18				21 41
Peckham Rye	d	20 43							20 50				21 13						21 20				21 43
Denmark Hill	d	20a46							20 54				21a16						21 24				21a46
Herne Hill	d			20 31				20 46							21 01			21 16					
Loughborough Jn.	d			20 34				20 49							21 04			21 19					
Elephant & Castle	d			20 39				20 54	21 00						21 09			21 24	21 30				
London Blackfriars	a			20 42	20 52			20 57	21 04	21 07					21 12	21 22		21 27	21 34	21 37			
	d			20 44	20 54			21 00		21 08					21 14	21 24		21 30		21 38			
City Thameslink	d			20 46	20 56																		
Farringdon	d			20 49	21 00			21 06		21 14					21 19	21 30		21 36		21 44			
St Pancras International	a			20 53	21 04			21 10		21 18					21 23	21 34		21 40		21 48			

A 19 May. To London Victoria
B From Epsom to London Victoria
C To St Albans City
D To Bedford
E 19 May
F To London Victoria
G not 19 May

Please refer to separate pages within this table for services operating between London and Bedford

At weekends please use local bus and tube services to travel to/from St Pancras International and London Bridge when no trains are operating. See local publicity for details of alternative routes and services that are available across central London

Brighton, Gatwick Airport - South London

Network Diagram - see first Page of Table 52

		SN	FC	FC	FC	SN	SE	FC	FC	FC	FC	SE	SN	SE	FC	FC	FC	SE	SN	SN	SE	FC	FC
		A	B	C	D	E	F	D	C	C	D	G	A	F	D	C	C	G	A	E	F	D	C
Brighton	d			20 37	20 37	21 00				21 07	21 07						21 37			22 00			
Preston Park	d			20 41	20 41	21 04				21 11	21 11						21 41			22 04			
Hassocks	d			20 47	20 47	21 10				21 17	21 17						21 47			22 10			
Burgess Hill	d			20 51	20 51	21 14				21 21	21 21						21 51			22 14			
Wivelsfield	d			20 53	20 53	21 16				21 23	21 23						21 53			22 16			
Haywards Heath	d			21 02	21 02	21 22				21 32	21 32						22 02			22 22			
Balcombe	d									21 37	21 37												
Three Bridges	d			21 12	21 12	21 32				21 42	21 42						22 12			22 32			
Gatwick Airport	d			21 17	21 16	21 38				21 47	21 46						22 17			22 38			
Redhill	d					21 47														22 46			
East Croydon	d			21 32	21 32	21a59				22 02	22 01						22 32			22a59			
Sutton (Surrey)	d	20 59	21 08					21 07	21 15				21 29		21 37	21 45			21 59			22 07	22 15
West Sutton	d							21 10	21 18						21 40	21 48						22 10	22 18
Sutton Common	d							21 12	21 20						21 42	21 50						22 12	22 20
St Helier	d							21 15	21 23						21 45	21 53						22 15	22 23
Morden South	d							21 17	21 25						21 47	21 55						22 17	22 25
South Merton	d							21 19	21 27						21 49	21 57						22 19	22 27
Wimbledon Chase	d							21 21	21 29						21 51	21 59						22 21	22 29
Wimbledon	d							21 30	21 38						22 00	22 08						22 30	22 38
Haydons Road	d							21 32	21 40						22 02	22 10						22 32	22 40
Tooting	d							21 35	21 43						22 05	22 13						22 35	22 43
Carshalton	d	21 02	21 11										21 32						22 02				
Hackbridge	d	21 05	21 13										21 35						22 05				
Mitcham Junction	d	21 08	21 16										21 38						22 08				
Mitcham Eastfields	d	21a11	21 19										21a41						22a11				
Streatham	d		21 23					21 40	21 49						22 10	22 19						22 40	22 49
Tulse Hill	d		21 27					21 47	21 53						22 17	22 23						22 47	22 53
London Bridge	a			21 45	21 47			22 00		22 15	22 17				22 30		22 45					23 00	
	d			21 45						22 15							22 45						
Sevenoaks	d						21 02					21 25		21 32				21 55			22 02		
Bat & Ball	d						21 05					21 28		21 35				21 58			22 05		
Otford	d						21 08					21 31		21 38				22 01			22 08		
Shoreham (Kent)	d						21 11					21 34		21 41				22 04			22 11		
Eynsford	d						21 15					21 38		21 45				22 08			22 15		
Swanley	d						21 20					21 43		21 50				22 13			22 20		
St Mary Cray	d						21 24					21 47		21 54				22 17			22 24		
Bickley	d						21 28					21 51		21 58				22 21			22 28		
Bromley South	d						21 31					21 54		22 01				22 24			22 31		
Shortlands	d						21 34					21 57		22 04				22 27			22 34		
Ravensbourne	d						21 36					21 59		22 06				22 29			22 36		
Beckenham Hill	d						21 38					22 01		22 08				22 31			22 38		
Bellingham	d						21 40					22 03		22 10				22 33			22 40		
Catford	d						21 43					22 06		22 13				22 36			22 43		
Crofton Park	d						21 45					22 08		22 15				22 38			22 45		
Nunhead	d						21 48					22 11		22 18				22 41			22 48		
Peckham Rye	d						21 50					22 13		22 20				22 43			22 50		
Denmark Hill	d						21 54					22a16		22 24				22a46			22 54		
Herne Hill	d		21 31						21 57							22 27							22 57
Loughborough Jn.	d		21 34						22 00							22 30							23 00
Elephant & Castle	d		21 39				22 00		22 04					22 30		22 34					23 00		23 04
London Blackfriars	a		21 42	21 52			22 04		22 07	22 22				22 34		22 37	22 52				23 04		23 07
	d		21 44	21 54					22 08	22 22						22 38	22 52						23 08
City Thameslink	d																						
Farringdon	d		21 49	22 00					22 13	22 28						22 43	22 58						23 13
St Pancras International	a		21 53	22 04					22 17	22 32						22 47	23 02						23 17

A From Epsom to London Victoria
B To St Albans City
C To Bedford
D 19 May
E To London Victoria
F not 19 May
G 19 May. To London Victoria

Please refer to separate pages within this table for services operating between London and Bedford

At weekends please use local bus and tube services to travel to/from St Pancras International and London Bridge when no trains are operating. See local publicity for details of alternative routes and services that are available across central London

Brighton, Gatwick Airport - South London

Network Diagram - see first Page of Table 52

		FC	FC	SE	SN	SE	FC	FC	FC	FC	SN	SN	FC	FC	FC	FC
		A	B	C	D	E	A	F	G	B	D	H	B	A	B	A
Brighton	d	22 07	22 07					22 33	22 33	22 33		23 02	23 11	23 11	23 37	23 37
Preston Park	d	22 11	22 11					22 37	22 37	22 37		23 06			23 41	23 41
Hassocks	d	22 17	22 17					22 43	22 43	22 43		23 12	23 20	23 20	23 47	23 47
Burgess Hill	d	22 21	22 21					22 47	22 47	22 47		23 16	23 23	23 23	23 51	23 51
Wivelsfield	d	22 23	22 23					22 49	22 49	22 49		23 19			23 53	23 53
Haywards Heath	d	22 32	22 32					22 54	22 54	22 54		23 24	23 29	23 29	23 59	23 59
Balcombe	d	22 37	22 37					22 59	22 59	22 59					00 04	00 04
Three Bridges	d	22 43	22 42					23 12	23 12	23 12		23 47	23 38	23 38	00 10	00 10
Gatwick Airport	d	22 47	22 46					23 17	23 17	23 16		23 53	23 43	23 43	00 15	00 15
Redhill	d											00 03			00 23	00 23
East Croydon	d	23 02	23 01					23 32	23 32	23 32		00a16	00 04	00 04	00 36	00 36
Sutton (Surrey)	d				22 29		22 45				22 59					
West Sutton	d						22 48									
Sutton Common	d						22 50									
St Helier	d						22 53									
Morden South	d						22 55									
South Merton	d						22 57									
Wimbledon Chase	d						22 59									
Wimbledon	d						23 08									
Haydons Road	d						23 10									
Tooting	d						23 13									
Carshalton	d				22 32						23 02					
Hackbridge	d				22 35						23 05					
Mitcham Junction	d				22 38						23 08					
Mitcham Eastfields	d				22a41						23a11					
Streatham	d						23 19									
Tulse Hill	d						23 23									
London Bridge	a	23 15	23 17					23 44	23 46	23 47			00 19	00 21	00 52	00 51
	d	23 15						23 45	23 46					00 22		00 52
Sevenoaks	d			22 25		22 32										
Bat & Ball	d			22 28		22 35										
Otford	d			22 31		22 38										
Shoreham (Kent)	d			22 34		22 41										
Eynsford	d			22 38		22 45										
Swanley	d			22 43		22 50										
St Mary Cray	d			22 47		22 54										
Bickley	d			22 51		22 58										
Bromley South	d			22 54		23 01										
Shortlands	d			22 57		23 04										
Ravensbourne	d			22 59		23 06										
Beckenham Hill	d			23 01		23 08										
Bellingham	d			23 03		23 10										
Catford	d			23 06		23 13										
Crofton Park	d			23 08		23 15										
Nunhead	d			23 11		23 18										
Peckham Rye	d			23 13		23 20										
Denmark Hill	d			23a16		23 24										
Herne Hill	d						23 27									
Loughborough Jn.	d															
Elephant & Castle	d					23 30	23 34									
London Blackfriars	a	23 22				23 34	23 37	23 52	23 52					00 28		00 58
	d	23 22					23 38	23 52	23 52					00 28		00 58
City Thameslink	d															
Farringdon	d	23 28					23 43	23 58	23 58					00 33		
St Pancras International	a	23 32					23 47	00 02	00 02					00 37		01 07

A To Bedford
B 19 May
C 19 May. To London Victoria
D From Epsom to London Victoria
E not 19 May
F from 30 June until 8 September. To Bedford
G until 23 June. To Bedford
H To London Victoria

Please refer to separate pages within this table for services operating between London and Bedford

At weekends please use local bus and tube services to travel to/from St Pancras International and London Bridge when no trains are operating. See local publicity for details of alternative routes and services that are available across central London

Brighton, Gatwick Airport - South London

Network Diagram - see first Page of Table 52

Station		FC ■ A	SN ◇■ B	FC A	FC ■ A	FC ■ A	FC A	FC A	FC A	FC A	FC A	SN ■ B	FC A	SN ◇■ B	SE	FC ■ A	SN ◇■ B	SN ◇■ B	SE	FC ■ A	SN ◇■ B	FC C	SE
Brighton	d	22p33	23p02		23p11	23p37						03 50		05 21		05 25	05 50	05 56		06 02	06 11		
Preston Park	d	22p37	23p06			23p41										05 29		06 00			06 15		
Hassocks	d	22p43	23p12		23p20	23p47										05 35		06 06			06 21		
Burgess Hill	d	22p47	23p16		23p23	23p51								05 31		05 39				06 12	06 25		
Wivelsfield	d	22p49	23p19			23p53										05 41		06 11			06 27		
Haywards Heath	d	22p54	23p24		23p29	23p59						04 25		05 37		05 46	06 12	06 16		06 18	06 40		
Balcombe	d	22p59				00 04										05 51							
Three Bridges	d	23p12	23p47		23p38	00 10	01 25	02 25	03 25	04 25	04 55	05 00	05 21	05 46		05 57	06 21	06 31		06 27	06 49		
Gatwick Airport	d	23p17	23p53		23p43	00 15	01 30	02 30	03 30	04 30	05 00	05 05	05 27	05 53		06 02	06 26	06 38		06 32	06 55		
Redhill	d		00 03			00 23							05 35										
East Croydon	d	23p32	00a16		00 04	00 36	01 50	02 47	03 47	04 47	05 17	05a29	05 47	06a10		06 17	06a40	06a53		06 47	07a09		
Sutton (Surrey)	d																					06 37	
West Sutton	d																					06 40	
Sutton Common	d																					06 42	
St Helier	d																					06 45	
Morden South	d																					06 47	
South Merton	d																					06 49	
Wimbledon Chase	d																					06 51	
Wimbledon	d																					06 58	
Haydons Road	d																					07 00	
Tooting	d																					07 03	
Carshalton	d																						
Hackbridge	d																						
Mitcham Junction	d																						
Mitcham Eastfields	d																						
Streatham	d																					07 08	
Tulse Hill	d																					07 12	
London Bridge	a	23p45			00 21	00 51							06 02			06 30				07 00			
	d	23p45			00 22	00 52							06 02			06 30				07 00			
Sevenoaks	d														05 32				06 02				06 32
Bat & Ball	d														05 35				06 05				06 35
Otford	d														05 38				06 08				06 38
Shoreham (Kent)	d														05 41				06 11				06 41
Eynsford	d														05 45				06 15				06 45
Swanley	d														05 50				06 20				06 50
St Mary Cray	d														05 54				06 24				06 54
Bickley	d														05 58				06 28				06 58
Bromley South	d														06 01				06 31				07 01
Shortlands	d														06 04				06 34				07 04
Ravensbourne	d														06 06				06 36				07 06
Beckenham Hill	d														06 08				06 38				07 08
Bellingham	d														06 10				06 40				07 10
Catford	d														06 13				06 43				07 13
Crofton Park	d														06 15				06 45				07 15
Nunhead	d														06 18				06 48				07 18
Peckham Rye	d														06 20				06 50				07 20
Denmark Hill	d														06 24				06 54				07 24
Herne Hill	d																					07 16	
Loughborough Jn.	d																					07 19	
Elephant & Castle	d														06 30				07 00			07 24	07 30
London Blackfriars	a	23p52			00 28	00 58	02 13	03 13	04 13	05 13	05 43		06 08		06 34	06 37			07 04	07 07		07 27	07 34
	d	23p52		00 08	00 29	00 58	02 14	03 13	04 14	05 14	05 44		06 08			06 38				07 08		07 30	
City Thameslink	d																						
Farringdon	d	23p58		00 13	00 33					05 20	05 50		06 12			06 42				07 12		07 36	
St Pancras International	a	00 02		00 17	00 37	01 07	02 24	03 23	04 22	05 24	05 54		06 16			06 46				07 16		07 40	

A To Bedford
B To London Victoria
C To Luton

Please refer to separate pages within this table for services operating between London and Bedford

At weekends please use local bus and tube services to travel to/from St Pancras International and London Bridge when no trains are operating. See local publicity for details of alternative routes and services that are available across central London

Brighton, Gatwick Airport - South London

Network Diagram - see first Page of Table 52

Station		FC ■ A	SN B	FC C	FC ■ A	FC D	SE	FC ■ A	SN B	FC C	FC ■ A	FC D	SE	FC ■ A	SN B	FC C	FC ■ A	FC D	SE	FC ■ A	SN B	FC C	FC ■ A
Brighton	d	06 25			06 37			07 04			07 07			07 34			07 37			08 04			08 07
Preston Park	d	06 29			06 41						07 11						07 41						08 11
Hassocks	d	06 35			06 47						07 17						07 47						08 17
Burgess Hill	d	06 39			06 51						07 21						07 51						08 21
Wivelsfield	d	06 41			06 53						07 23						07 53						08 23
Haywards Heath	d	06 46			07 02			07 18			07 32			07 48			08 02			08 18			08 32
Balcombe	d	06 51									07 37												08 37
Three Bridges	d	06 57			07 12			07 27			07 42			07 57			08 12			08 27			08 42
Gatwick Airport	d	07 02			07 17			07 32			07 47			08 02			08 17			08 32			08 47
Redhill	d																						
East Croydon	d	07 17			07 32			07 47			08 02			08 17			08 32			08 47			09 02
Sutton (Surrey)	d		06 59	07 08		07 07			07 29	07 38		07 37			07 59	08 08		08 07			08 29	08 38	
West Sutton	d					07 10						07 40						08 10					
Sutton Common	d					07 12						07 42						08 12					
St Helier	d					07 15						07 45						08 15					
Morden South	d					07 17						07 47						08 17					
South Merton	d					07 19						07 49						08 19					
Wimbledon Chase	d					07 21						07 51						08 21					
Wimbledon	d					07 28						07 58						08 28					
Haydons Road	d					07 30						08 00						08 30					
Tooting	d					07 33						08 03						08 33					
Carshalton	d		07 02	07 11					07 32	07 41					08 02	08 11					08 32	08 41	
Hackbridge	d		07 05	07 13					07 35	07 43					08 05	08 13					08 35	08 43	
Mitcham Junction	d		07 08	07 16					07 38	07 46					08 08	08 16					08 38	08 46	
Mitcham Eastfields	d		07a11	07 19					07a41	07 49					08a11	08 19					08a41	08 49	
Streatham	d			07 23		07 38				07 53		08 08				08 23		08 38				08 53	
Tulse Hill	d			07 27		07 42				07 57		08 12				08 27		08 42				08 57	
London Bridge	a	07 30			07 45			08 00			08 15			08 30			08 45			09 00			09 15
	d	07 30			07 45			08 00			08 15			08 30			08 45			09 00			09 15
Sevenoaks	d						07 02						07 32						08 02				
Bat & Ball	d						07 05						07 35						08 05				
Otford	d						07 08						07 38						08 08				
Shoreham (Kent)	d						07 11						07 41						08 11				
Eynsford	d						07 15						07 45						08 15				
Swanley	d						07 20						07 50						08 20				
St Mary Cray	d						07 24						07 54						08 24				
Bickley	d						07 28						07 58						08 28				
Bromley South	d						07 31						08 01						08 31				
Shortlands	d						07 34						08 04						08 34				
Ravensbourne	d						07 36						08 06						08 36				
Beckenham Hill	d						07 38						08 08						08 38				
Bellingham	d						07 40						08 10						08 40				
Catford	d						07 43						08 13						08 43				
Crofton Park	d						07 45						08 15						08 45				
Nunhead	d						07 48						08 18						08 48				
Peckham Rye	d						07 50						08 20						08 50				
Denmark Hill	d						07 54						08 24						08 54				
Herne Hill	d			07 31		07 46				08 01		08 16				08 31		08 46				09 01	
Loughborough Jn.	d			07 34		07 49				08 04		08 19				08 34		08 49				09 04	
Elephant & Castle	d			07 39		07 54	08 00			08 09		08 24	08 30			08 39		08 54	09 00			09 09	
London Blackfriars	a	07 37		07 42	07 52	07 57	08 04	08 07		08 12	08 22	08 27	08 34	08 37		08 42	08 52	08 57	09 04	09 07		09 12	09 22
	d	07 38		07 44	07 54	08 00		08 08		08 14	08 24	08 30		08 38		08 44	08 54	09 00		09 08		09 14	09 24
City Thameslink	d																	09 02		09 10		09 16	09 26
Farringdon	d	07 44		07 49	08 00	08 06		08 14		08 19	08 30	08 36		08 44		08 49	09 00	09 06		09 14		09 19	09 30
St Pancras International	a	07 48		07 53	08 04	08 10		08 18		08 23	08 34	08 40		08 48		08 53	09 04	09 10		09 18		09 23	09 34

A To Bedford
B From Epsom to London Victoria
C To St Albans City
D To Luton

Please refer to separate pages within this table for services operating between London and Bedford

At weekends please use local bus and tube services to travel to/from St Pancras International and London Bridge when no trains are operating. See local publicity for details of alternative routes and services that are available across central London

Saturdays
from 22 September

Brighton, Gatwick Airport - South London

Network Diagram - see first Page of Table 52

Station		FC A		SE	FC ■ B	SN C	FC D	FC ■ B	FC A	SE	FC ■ B	SN C		FC D	FC ■ B	FC A	SE	FC ■ B	SN C	FC D	FC ■ B	FC A		SE	FC ■ B
Brighton	d				08 34			08 37			09 04				09 07			09 34			09 37				10 04
Preston Park	d							08 41							09 11						09 41				
Hassocks	d							08 47							09 17						09 47				
Burgess Hill	d							08 51							09 21						09 51				
Wivelsfield	d							08 53							09 23						09 53				
Haywards Heath	d				08 48			09 02			09 18				09 32			09 48			10 02				10 18
Balcombe	d														09 37										
Three Bridges	d				08 57			09 12			09 27				09 42			09 57			10 12				10 27
Gatwick Airport ✈	d				09 02			09 17			09 32				09 47			10 02			10 17				10 32
Redhill	d																								
East Croydon	d				09 17			09 32			09 47				10 02			10 17			10 32				10 47
Sutton (Surrey)	d	08 37				08 59	09 08		09 07			09 29		09 38		09 37			09 59	10 08		10 07			
West Sutton	d	08 40							09 10							09 40						10 10			
Sutton Common	d	08 42							09 12							09 42						10 12			
St Helier	d	08 45							09 15							09 45						10 15			
Morden South	d	08 47							09 17							09 47						10 17			
South Merton	d	08 49							09 19							09 49						10 19			
Wimbledon Chase	d	08 51							09 21							09 51						10 21			
Wimbledon	d	08 58							09 28							09 58						10 28			
Haydons Road	d	09 00							09 30							10 00						10 30			
Tooting	d	09 03							09 33							10 03						10 33			
Carshalton	d					09 02	09 11					09 32		09 41					10 02	10 11					
Hackbridge	d					09 05	09 13					09 35		09 43					10 05	10 13					
Mitcham Junction	d					09 08	09 16					09 38		09 46					10 08	10 16					
Mitcham Eastfields	d					09a11	09 19					09a41		09 49					10a11	10 19					
Streatham	d	09 08					09 23		09 38					09 53		10 08				10 23		10 38			
Tulse Hill	d	09 12					09 27		09 42					09 57		10 12				10 27		10 42			
London Bridge ⊖	a				09 30			09 45			10 00				10 15			10 30			10 45				11 00
	d				09 30			09 45			10 00				10 15			10 30			10 45				11 00
Sevenoaks	d			08 32						09 02							09 32							10 02	
Bat & Ball	d			08 35						09 05							09 35							10 05	
Otford	d			08 38						09 08							09 38							10 08	
Shoreham (Kent)	d			08 41						09 11							09 41							10 11	
Eynsford	d			08 45						09 15							09 45							10 15	
Swanley	d			08 50						09 20							09 50							10 20	
St Mary Cray	d			08 54						09 24							09 54							10 24	
Bickley	d			08 58						09 28							09 58							10 28	
Bromley South	d			09 01						09 31							10 01							10 31	
Shortlands	d			09 04						09 34							10 04							10 34	
Ravensbourne	d			09 06						09 36							10 06							10 36	
Beckenham Hill	d			09 08						09 38							10 08							10 38	
Bellingham	d			09 10						09 40							10 10							10 40	
Catford	d			09 13						09 43							10 13							10 43	
Crofton Park	d			09 15						09 45							10 15							10 45	
Nunhead	d			09 18						09 48							10 18							10 48	
Peckham Rye	d			09 20						09 50							10 20							10 50	
Denmark Hill	d			09 24						09 54							10 24							10 54	
Herne Hill	d	09 16					09 31		09 46					10 01		10 16				10 31		10 46			
Loughborough Jn	d	09 19					09 34		09 49					10 04		10 19				10 34		10 49			
Elephant & Castle	d	09 24		09 30			09 39		09 54	10 00				10 09		10 24	10 30			10 39		10 54		11 00	
London Blackfriars ⊖	a	09 27		09 34	09 37		09 42	09 52	09 57	10 04	10 07			10 12	10 22	10 27	10 34	10 37		10 42	10 52	10 57		11 04	11 07
	d	09 30			09 38		09 44	09 54	10 00		10 08			10 14	10 24	10 30		10 38		10 44	10 54	11 00			11 08
City Thameslink	d	09 32			09 40		09 46	09 56	10 02		10 10			10 16	10 26	10 32		10 40		10 46	10 56	11 02			11 10
Farringdon ⊖	d	09 36			09 44		09 49	10 00	10 06		10 14			10 19	10 30	10 36		10 44		10 49	11 00	11 06			11 14
St Pancras International ⊖	a	09 40			09 48		09 53	10 04	10 10		10 18			10 23	10 34	10 40		10 48		10 53	11 04	11 10			11 18

A To Luton
E To Bedford
C From Epsom to London Victoria
D To St Albans City

Please refer to separate pages within this table for services operating between London and Bedford

At weekends please use local bus and tube services to travel to/from St Pancras International and London Bridge when no trains are operating. See local publicity for details of alternative routes and services that are available across central London

Saturdays
from 22 September

Brighton, Gatwick Airport - South London

Network Diagram - see first Page of Table 52

Station		SN A	FC B	FC ■ C	FC D	SE	FC ■ C	SN A		FC B	FC ■ C	FC D	SE	FC ■ C	SN A	FC B	FC ■ C	FC D		SE	FC ■ C	SN A	FC B	FC ■ C	FC D
Brighton	d			10 07			10 34				10 37			11 04			11 07				11 34			11 37	
Preston Park	d			10 11							10 41						11 11							11 41	
Hassocks	d			10 17							10 47						11 17							11 47	
Burgess Hill	d			10 21							10 51						11 21							11 51	
Wivelsfield	d			10 23							10 53						11 23							11 53	
Haywards Heath	d			10 32			10 48				11 02			11 18			11 32				11 48			12 02	
Balcombe	d			10 37													11 37								
Three Bridges	d			10 42			10 57				11 12			11 27			11 42				11 57			12 12	
Gatwick Airport ✈	d			10 47			11 02				11 17			11 32			11 47				12 02			12 17	
Redhill	d																								
East Croydon	d			11 02			11 17				11 32			11 47			12 02				12 17			12 32	
Sutton (Surrey)	d	10 29	10 38		10 37			10 59		11 08		11 07			11 29	11 38		11 37				11 59	12 08		12 07
West Sutton	d				10 40							11 10						11 40							12 10
Sutton Common	d				10 42							11 12						11 42							12 12
St Helier	d				10 45							11 15						11 45							12 15
Morden South	d				10 47							11 17						11 47							12 17
South Merton	d				10 49							11 19						11 49							12 19
Wimbledon Chase	d				10 51							11 21						11 51							12 21
Wimbledon	d				10 58							11 28						11 58							12 28
Haydons Road	d				11 00							11 30						12 00							12 30
Tooting	d				11 03							11 33						12 03							12 33
Carshalton	d	10 32	10 41					11 02		11 11					11 32	11 41						12 02	12 11		
Hackbridge	d	10 35	10 43					11 05		11 13					11 35	11 43						12 05	12 13		
Mitcham Junction	d	10 38	10 46					11 08		11 16					11 38	11 46						12 08	12 16		
Mitcham Eastfields	d	10a41	10 49					11a11		11 19					11a41	11 49						12a11	12 19		
Streatham	d		10 53		11 08					11 23		11 38				11 53		12 08					12 23		12 38
Tulse Hill	d		10 57		11 12					11 27		11 42				11 57		12 12					12 27		12 42
London Bridge ⊖	a			11 15			11 30				11 45			12 00			12 15				12 30			12 45	
	d			11 15			11 30				11 45			12 00			12 15				12 30			12 45	
Sevenoaks	d					10 32							11 02							11 32					
Bat & Ball	d					10 35							11 05							11 35					
Otford	d					10 38							11 08							11 38					
Shoreham (Kent)	d					10 41							11 11							11 41					
Eynsford	d					10 45							11 15							11 45					
Swanley	d					10 50							11 20							11 50					
St Mary Cray	d					10 54							11 24							11 54					
Bickley	d					10 58							11 28							11 58					
Bromley South	d					11 01							11 31							12 01					
Shortlands	d					11 04							11 34							12 04					
Ravensbourne	d					11 06							11 36							12 06					
Beckenham Hill	d					11 08							11 38							12 08					
Bellingham	d					11 10							11 40							12 10					
Catford	d					11 13							11 43							12 13					
Crofton Park	d					11 15							11 45							12 15					
Nunhead	d					11 18							11 48							12 18					
Peckham Rye	d					11 20							11 50							12 20					
Denmark Hill	d					11 24							11 54							12 24					
Herne Hill	d		11 01		11 16					11 31		11 46				12 01		12 16					12 31		12 46
Loughborough Jn	d		11 04		11 19					11 34		11 49				12 04		12 19					12 34		12 49
Elephant & Castle	d		11 09		11 24	11 30				11 39		11 54	12 00			12 09		12 24		12 30			12 39		12 54
London Blackfriars ⊖	a		11 12	11 22	11 27	11 34	11 37			11 42	11 52	11 57	12 04	12 07		12 12	12 22	12 27		12 34	12 37		12 42	12 52	12 57
	d		11 14	11 24	11 30		11 38			11 44	11 54	12 00		12 08		12 14	12 24	12 30			12 38		12 44	12 54	13 00
City Thameslink	d		11 16	11 26	11 32		11 40			11 46	11 56	12 02		12 10		12 16	12 26	12 32			12 40		12 46	12 56	13 02
Farringdon ⊖	d		11 19	11 30	11 36		11 44			11 49	12 00	12 06		12 14		12 19	12 30	12 36			12 44		12 49	13 00	13 06
St Pancras International ⊖	a		11 23	11 34	11 40		11 48			11 53	12 04	12 10		12 18		12 23	12 34	12 40			12 48		12 53	13 04	13 10

A From Epsom to London Victoria
B To St Albans City
C To Bedford
D To Luton

Please refer to separate pages within this table for services operating between London and Bedford

At weekends please use local bus and tube services to travel to/from St Pancras International and London Bridge when no trains are operating. See local publicity for details of alternative routes and services that are available across central London

Brighton, Gatwick Airport - South London

Network Diagram - see first Page of Table 52

		SE	FC A	SN B	FC C	FC A	FC D	SE	FC A	SN B	FC C	FC A	FC D	SE	FC A	SN B	FC C	FC A	FC D	SE	FC A	SN B
Brighton	d		12 04			12 07			12 34			12 37			13 04			13 07			13 34	
Preston Park	d					12 11						12 41						13 11				
Hassocks	d					12 17						12 47						13 17				
Burgess Hill	d					12 21						12 51						13 21				
Wivelsfield	d					12 23						12 53						13 23				
Haywards Heath	d		12 18			12 32			12 48			13 02			13 18			13 32			13 48	
Balcombe	d					12 37												13 37				
Three Bridges	d		12 27			12 42			12 57			13 12			13 27			13 42			13 57	
Gatwick Airport ✈	d		12 32			12 47			13 02			13 17			13 32			13 47			14 02	
Redhill	d																					
East Croydon	d		12 47			13 02			13 17			13 32			13 47			14 02			14 17	
Sutton (Surrey)	d			12 29	12 38		12 37			12 59	13 08		13 07			13 29	13 38		13 37			13 59
West Sutton	d						12 40						13 10						13 40			
Sutton Common	d						12 42						13 12						13 42			
St Helier	d						12 45						13 15						13 45			
Morden South	d						12 47						13 17						13 47			
South Merton	d						12 49						13 19						13 49			
Wimbledon Chase	d						12 51						13 21						13 51			
Wimbledon	d						12 58						13 28						13 58			
Haydons Road	d						13 00						13 30						14 00			
Tooting	d						13 03						13 33						14 03			
Carshalton	d			12 32	12 41					13 02	13 11					13 32	13 41					14 02
Hackbridge	d			12 35	12 43					13 05	13 13					13 35	13 43					14 05
Mitcham Junction	d			12 38	12 46					13 08	13 16					13 38	13 46					14 08
Mitcham Eastfields	d			12a41	12 49					13a11	13 19					13a41	13 49					14a11
Streatham	d				12 53		13 08				13 23		13 38				13 53		14 08			
Tulse Hill	d				12 57		13 12				13 27		13 42				13 57		14 12			
London Bridge ⊖	a		13 00			13 15			13 30			13 45			14 00			14 15			14 30	
	d		13 00			13 15			13 30			13 45			14 00			14 15			14 30	
Sevenoaks	d	12 02						12 32						13 02						13 32		
Bat & Ball	d	12 05						12 35						13 05						13 35		
Otford	d	12 08						12 38						13 08						13 38		
Shoreham (Kent)	d	12 11						12 41						13 11						13 41		
Eynsford	d	12 15						12 45						13 15						13 45		
Swanley	d	12 20						12 50						13 20						13 50		
St Mary Cray	d	12 24						12 54						13 24						13 54		
Bickley	d	12 28						12 58						13 28						13 58		
Bromley South	d	12 31						13 01						13 31						14 01		
Shortlands	d	12 34						13 04						13 34						14 04		
Ravensbourne	d	12 36						13 06						13 36						14 06		
Beckenham Hill	d	12 38						13 08						13 38						14 08		
Bellingham	d	12 40						13 10						13 40						14 10		
Catford	d	12 43						13 13						13 43						14 13		
Crofton Park	d	12 45						13 15						13 45						14 15		
Nunhead	d	12 48						13 18						13 48						14 18		
Peckham Rye	d	12 50						13 20						13 50						14 20		
Denmark Hill	d	12 54						13 24						13 54						14 24		
Herne Hill	d				13 01		13 16				13 31		13 46				14 01		14 16			
Loughborough Jn.	d				13 04		13 19				13 34		13 49				14 04		14 19			
Elephant & Castle	d	13 00			13 09		13 24	13 30			13 39		13 54	14 00			14 09		14 24	14 30		
London Blackfriars ⊖	a	13 04	13 07		13 12	13 22	13 27	13 34	13 37		13 42	13 52	13 57	14 04	14 07		14 12	14 22	14 27	14 34	14 37	
	d		13 08		13 14	13 24	13 30		13 38		13 44	13 54	14 00		14 08		14 14	14 24	14 30		14 38	
City Thameslink	d		13 10		13 16	13 26	13 32		13 40		13 46	13 56	14 02		14 10		14 16	14 26	14 32		14 40	
Farringdon ⊖	d		13 14		13 19	13 30	13 36		13 44		13 49	14 00	14 06		14 14		14 19	14 30	14 36		14 44	
St Pancras International ⊖	a		13 18		13 23	13 34	13 40		13 48		13 53	14 04	14 10		14 18		14 23	14 34	14 40		14 48	

A To Bedford
B From Epsom to London Victoria
C To St Albans City
D To Luton

Please refer to separate pages within this table for services operating between London and Bedford

At weekends please use local bus and tube services to travel to/from St Pancras International and London Bridge when no trains are operating. See local publicity for details of alternative routes and services that are available across central London

Brighton, Gatwick Airport - South London

Network Diagram - see first Page of Table 52

		FC A	FC B	FC C	SE	FC B	SN D	FC A	FC B	FC C	SE	FC B	SN D	FC A	FC B	FC C	SE	FC B	SN D	FC A	FC B	FC C	SE
Brighton	d		13 37			14 04			14 07			14 34			14 37			15 04			15 07		
Preston Park	d		13 41						14 11						14 41						15 11		
Hassocks	d		13 47						14 17						14 47						15 17		
Burgess Hill	d		13 51						14 21						14 51						15 21		
Wivelsfield	d		13 53						14 23						14 53						15 23		
Haywards Heath	d		14 02			14 18			14 32			14 48			15 02			15 18			15 32		
Balcombe	d								14 37												15 37		
Three Bridges	d		14 12			14 27			14 42			14 57			15 12			15 27			15 42		
Gatwick Airport ✈	d		14 17			14 32			14 47			15 02			15 17			15 32			15 47		
Redhill	d																						
East Croydon	d		14 32			14 47			15 02			15 17			15 32			15 47			16 02		
Sutton (Surrey)	d	14 08		14 07			14 29	14 38		14 37			14 59	15 08		15 07			15 29	15 38		15 37	
West Sutton	d			14 10						14 40						15 10						15 40	
Sutton Common	d			14 12						14 42						15 12						15 42	
St Helier	d			14 15						14 45						15 15						15 45	
Morden South	d			14 17						14 47						15 17						15 47	
South Merton	d			14 19						14 49						15 19						15 49	
Wimbledon Chase	d			14 21						14 51						15 21						15 51	
Wimbledon	d			14 28						14 58						15 28						15 58	
Haydons Road	d			14 30						15 00						15 30						16 00	
Tooting	d			14 33						15 03						15 33						16 03	
Carshalton	d	14 11					14 32	14 41					15 02	15 11					15 32	15 41			
Hackbridge	d	14 13					14 35	14 43					15 05	15 13					15 35	15 43			
Mitcham Junction	d	14 16					14 38	14 46					15 08	15 16					15 38	15 46			
Mitcham Eastfields	d	14 19					14a41	14 49					15a11	15 19					15a41	15 49			
Streatham	d	14 23		14 38				14 53		15 08				15 23		15 38				15 53		16 08	
Tulse Hill	d	14 27		14 42				14 57		15 12				15 27		15 42				15 57		16 12	
London Bridge ⊖	a		14 45			15 00			15 15			15 30			15 45			16 00			16 15		
	d		14 45			15 00			15 15			15 30			15 45			16 00			16 15		
Sevenoaks	d				14 02						14 32						15 02						15 32
Bat & Ball	d				14 05						14 35						15 05						15 35
Otford	d				14 08						14 38						15 08						15 38
Shoreham (Kent)	d				14 11						14 41						15 11						15 41
Eynsford	d				14 15						14 45						15 15						15 45
Swanley	d				14 20						14 50						15 20						15 50
St Mary Cray	d				14 24						14 54						15 24						15 54
Bickley	d				14 28						14 58						15 28						15 58
Bromley South	d				14 31						15 01						15 31						16 01
Shortlands	d				14 34						15 04						15 34						16 04
Ravensbourne	d				14 36						15 06						15 36						16 06
Beckenham Hill	d				14 38						15 08						15 38						16 08
Bellingham	d				14 40						15 10						15 40						16 10
Catford	d				14 43						15 13						15 43						16 13
Crofton Park	d				14 45						15 15						15 45						16 15
Nunhead	d				14 48						15 18						15 48						16 18
Peckham Rye	d				14 50						15 20						15 50						16 20
Denmark Hill	d				14 54						15 24						15 54						16 24
Herne Hill	d	14 31		14 46				15 01		15 16				15 31		15 46				16 01		16 16	
Loughborough Jn.	d	14 34		14 49				15 04		15 19				15 34		15 49				16 04		16 19	
Elephant & Castle	d	14 39		14 54	15 00			15 09		15 24	15 30			15 39		15 54	16 00			16 09		16 24	16 30
London Blackfriars ⊖	a	14 42	14 52	14 57	15 04	15 07		15 12	15 22	15 27	15 34	15 37		15 42	15 52	15 57	16 04	16 07		16 12	16 22	16 27	16 34
	d	14 44	14 54	15 00		15 08		15 14	15 24	15 30		15 38		15 44	15 54	16 00		16 08		16 14	16 24	16 30	
City Thameslink	d	14 46	14 56	15 02		15 10		15 16	15 26	15 32		15 40		15 46	15 56	16 02		16 10		16 16	16 26	16 32	
Farringdon ⊖	d	14 49	15 00	15 06		15 14		15 19	15 30	15 36		15 44		15 49	16 00	16 06		16 14		16 19	16 30	16 36	
St Pancras International ⊖	a	14 53	15 04	15 10		15 18		15 23	15 34	15 40		15 48		15 53	16 04	16 10		16 18		16 23	16 34	16 40	

A To St Albans City
B To Bedford
C To Luton
D From Epsom to London Victoria

Please refer to separate pages within this table for services operating between London and Bedford

At weekends please use local bus and tube services to travel to/from St Pancras International and London Bridge when no trains are operating. See local publicity for details of alternative routes and services that are available across central London

Table 52

Saturdays
from 22 September

Brighton, Gatwick Airport - South London

Network Diagram - see first Page of Table 52

		FC 1 A	SN B	FC C	FC 1 A	FC D		SE	FC 1 A	SN B	FC C	FC 1 A	FC D	SE	FC 1 A	SN B		FC C	FC 1 A	FC D	SE	FC 1 A	SN B	FC C	FC 1 A
Brighton 10	d	15 34			15 37				16 04			16 07			16 34				16 37			17 04			17 07
Preston Park	d				15 41							16 11							16 41						17 11
Hassocks 4	d				15 47							16 17							16 47						17 17
Burgess Hill 4	d				15 51							16 21							16 51						17 21
Wivelsfield 4	d				15 53							16 23							16 53						17 23
Haywards Heath 3	d	15 48			16 02				16 18			16 32			16 48				17 02			17 18			17 32
Balcombe	d											16 37													17 37
Three Bridges 4	d	15 57			16 12				16 27			16 42			16 57				17 11			17 27			17 42
Gatwick Airport 10	d	16 02			16 17				16 32			16 47			17 02				17 16			17 32			17 47
Redhill	d																								
East Croydon	d	16 17			16 32				16 47			17 02			17 17				17 31			17 47			18 02
Sutton (Surrey) 4	d		15 59	16 08		16 07				16 29	16 38		16 37			16 59		17 08		17 07			17 29	17 38	
West Sutton	d					16 10							16 40							17 10					
Sutton Common	d					16 12							16 42							17 12					
St Helier	d					16 15							16 45							17 15					
Morden South	d					16 17							16 47							17 17					
South Merton	d					16 19							16 49							17 19					
Wimbledon Chase	d					16 21							16 51							17 21					
Wimbledon 6	d					16 28							16 58							17 28					
Haydons Road	d					16 30							17 00							17 30					
Tooting	d					16 33							17 03							17 33					
Carshalton	d		16 02	16 11						16 32	16 41					17 02		17 11					17 32	17 41	
Hackbridge	d		16 05	16 13						16 35	16 43					17 05		17 13					17 35	17 43	
Mitcham Junction	d		16 08	16 16						16 38	16 46					17 08		17 16					17 38	17 46	
Mitcham Eastfields	d		16a11	16 19						16a41	16 49					17a11		17 19					17a41	17 49	
Streatham 4	d			16 23		16 38					16 53		17 08					17 23		17 38				17 53	
Tulse Hill 3	d			16 27		16 42					16 57		17 12					17 27		17 42				17 57	
London Bridge 4 ⊖	a	16 30			16 45				17 00			17 15			17 30				17 45			18 00			18 15
	d	16 30			16 45				17 00			17 15			17 30				17 45			18 00			18 15
Sevenoaks 4	d							16 02						16 32							17 02				
Bat & Ball	d							16 05						16 35							17 05				
Otford 4	d							16 08						16 38							17 08				
Shoreham (Kent)	d							16 11						16 41							17 11				
Eynsford	d							16 15						16 45							17 15				
Swanley 4	d							16 20						16 50							17 20				
St Mary Cray 4	d							16 24						16 54							17 24				
Bickley	d							16 28						16 58							17 28				
Bromley South	d							16 31						17 01							17 31				
Shortlands 4	d							16 34						17 04							17 34				
Ravensbourne	d							16 36						17 06							17 36				
Beckenham Hill	d							16 38						17 08							17 38				
Bellingham	d							16 40						17 10							17 40				
Catford	d							16 43						17 13							17 43				
Crofton Park	d							16 45						17 15							17 45				
Nunhead 4	d							16 48						17 18							17 48				
Peckham Rye 4	d							16 50						17 20							17 50				
Denmark Hill 4	d							16 54						17 24							17 54				
Herne Hill 4	d			16 31		16 46					17 01		17 16					17 31		17 46				18 01	
Loughborough Jn	d			16 34		16 49					17 04		17 19					17 34		17 49				18 04	
Elephant & Castle	d			16 39		16 54		17 00			17 09		17 24	17 30				17 39		17 54	18 00			18 09	
London Blackfriars 3 ⊖	a	16 37		16 42	16 52	16 57		17 04	17 07		17 12	17 22	17 27	17 34	17 37			17 42	17 52	17 57	18 04	18 07		18 12	18 22
	d	16 38		16 44	16 54	17 00			17 08		17 14	17 24	17 30		17 38			17 44	17 54	18 00		18 08		18 14	18 24
City Thameslink 3	d	16 40		16 46	16 56	17 02			17 10		17 16	17 26	17 32		17 40			17 46	17 56	18 02		18 10		18 16	18 26
Farringdon 3 ⊖	d	16 44		16 49	17 00	17 06			17 14		17 19	17 30	17 36		17 44			17 49	18 00	18 06		18 14		18 19	18 30
St Pancras International 15 ⊖	a	16 48		16 53	17 04	17 10			17 18		17 23	17 34	17 40		17 48			17 53	18 04	18 10		18 18		18 23	18 34

A To Bedford
B From Epsom to London Victoria
C To St Albans City
D To Luton

Please refer to separate pages within this table for services operating between London and Bedford

At weekends please use local bus and tube services to travel to/from St Pancras International and London Bridge when no trains are operating. See local publicity for details of alternative routes and services that are available across central London

Table 52

Saturdays
from 22 September

Brighton, Gatwick Airport - South London

Network Diagram - see first Page of Table 52

		FC A		SE	FC 1 B	SN C	FC D	FC 1 B	FC A	SE	FC 1 B	SN C		FC D	FC 1 B	FC A	SE	FC 1 B	SN C	FC B	FC 1 B	FC A		SE	FC 1 B
Brighton 10	d				17 34			17 37			18 04				18 07			18 34			18 37				19 04
Preston Park	d							17 41							18 11						18 41				
Hassocks 4	d							17 47							18 17						18 47				
Burgess Hill 4	d							17 51							18 21						18 51				
Wivelsfield 4	d							17 53							18 23						18 53				
Haywards Heath 3	d				17 48			18 02			18 18				18 32			18 48			19 02				19 18
Balcombe	d														18 37										
Three Bridges 4	d				17 57			18 12			18 27				18 42			18 57			19 12				19 27
Gatwick Airport 10	d				18 02			18 17			18 32				18 47			19 02			19 17				19 32
Redhill	d																								
East Croydon	d				18 17			18 32			18 47				19 02			19 17			19 32				19 47
Sutton (Surrey) 4	d	17 37				17 59	18 08		18 07			18 29		18 38		18 37			18 59	19 08		19 07			
West Sutton	d	17 40							18 10							18 40						19 10			
Sutton Common	d	17 42							18 12							18 42						19 12			
St Helier	d	17 45							18 15							18 45						19 15			
Morden South	d	17 47							18 17							18 47						19 17			
South Merton	d	17 49							18 19							18 49						19 19			
Wimbledon Chase	d	17 51							18 21							18 51						19 21			
Wimbledon 6	d	17 58							18 28							18 58						19 28			
Haydons Road	d	18 00							18 30							19 00						19 30			
Tooting	d	18 03							18 33							19 03						19 33			
Carshalton	d					18 02	18 11					18 32		18 41					19 02	19 11					
Hackbridge	d					18 05	18 13					18 35		18 43					19 05	19 13					
Mitcham Junction	d					18 08	18 16					18 38		18 46					19 08	19 16					
Mitcham Eastfields	d					18a11	18 19					18a41		18 49					19a11	19 19					
Streatham 4	d	18 08					18 23		18 38					18 53		19 08				19 23		19 38			
Tulse Hill 3	d	18 12					18 27		18 42					18 57		19 12				19 27		19 42			
London Bridge 4 ⊖	a				18 30			18 45			19 00				19 15			19 30			19 45				20 00
	d				18 30			18 45			19 00				19 15			19 30			19 45				20 00
Sevenoaks 4	d			17 32						18 02							18 32							19 02	
Bat & Ball	d			17 35						18 05							18 35							19 05	
Otford 4	d			17 38						18 08							18 38							19 08	
Shoreham (Kent)	d			17 41						18 11							18 41							19 11	
Eynsford	d			17 45						18 15							18 45							19 15	
Swanley 4	d			17 50						18 20							18 50							19 20	
St Mary Cray 4	d			17 54						18 24							18 54							19 24	
Bickley	d			17 58						18 28							18 58							19 28	
Bromley South	d			18 01						18 31							19 01							19 31	
Shortlands 4	d			18 04						18 34							19 04							19 34	
Ravensbourne	d			18 06						18 36							19 06							19 36	
Beckenham Hill	d			18 08						18 38							19 08							19 38	
Bellingham	d			18 10						18 40							19 10							19 40	
Catford	d			18 13						18 43							19 13							19 43	
Crofton Park	d			18 15						18 45							19 15							19 45	
Nunhead 4	d			18 18						18 48							19 18							19 48	
Peckham Rye 4	d			18 20						18 50							19 20							19 50	
Denmark Hill 4	d			18 24						18 54							19 24							19 54	
Herne Hill 4	d	18 16					18 31		18 46					19 01		19 16				19 31		19 46			
Loughborough Jn	d	18 19					18 34		18 49					19 04		19 19				19 34		19 49			
Elephant & Castle	d	18 24		18 30			18 39		18 54	19 00				19 09		19 24	19 30			19 39		19 54		20 00	
London Blackfriars 3 ⊖	a	18 27		18 34	18 37		18 42	18 52	18 57	19 04	19 07			19 12	19 22	19 27	19 34	19 37		19 42	19 52	19 57		20 04	20 07
	d	18 30			18 38		18 44	18 54	19 00		19 08			19 14	19 24	19 30		19 38		19 44	19 54	20 00			20 08
City Thameslink 3	d	18 32			18 40		18 46	18 56	19 02		19 10			19 16	19 26	19 32		19 40		19 46	19 56	20 02			20 10
Farringdon 3 ⊖	d	18 36			18 44		18 49	19 00	19 06		19 14			19 19	19 30	19 36		19 44		19 49	20 00	20 06			20 14
St Pancras International 15 ⊖	a	18 40			18 48		18 53	19 04	19 10		19 18			19 23	19 34	19 40		19 48		19 53	20 04	20 10			20 18

A To Luton
B To Bedford
C From Epsom to London Victoria
D To St Albans City

Please refer to separate pages within this table for services operating between London and Bedford

At weekends please use local bus and tube services to travel to/from St Pancras International and London Bridge when no trains are operating. See local publicity for details of alternative routes and services that are available across central London

Brighton, Gatwick Airport - South London

Network Diagram - see first Page of Table 52

		SN	FC	FC	FC	SE	FC	SN	FC	FC	SN	FC	SE	FC	SN	FC	FC	FC	SE	FC	SN	FC	FC
				1			1			1	◇1			1			1			1			1
		A	B	B	C		B	A	D	B	E	C		B	A	D	B	C		B	A	D	B
Brighton	d			19 07			19 34			19 37	19 54			20 04			20 07			20 34			20 37
Preston Park	d			19 11						19 41	19 58						20 11						20 41
Hassocks	d			19 17						19 47	20 04						20 17						20 47
Burgess Hill	d			19 21						19 51	20 08						20 21						20 51
Wivelsfield	d			19 23						19 53	20 10						20 23						20 53
Haywards Heath	d			19 32			19 48			20 02	20 22			20 18			20 32			20 48			21 02
Balcombe	d			19 37													20 37						
Three Bridges	d			19 42			19 57			20 12	20 32			20 27			20 42			20 57			21 12
Gatwick Airport	d			19 47			20 02			20 17	20 38			20 32			20 47			21 02			21 17
Redhill	d										20 48												
East Croydon	d			20 02			20 17			20 32	20a59			20 47			21 02			21 17			21 32
Sutton (Surrey)	d	19 29	19 38		19 37			19 59	20 08			20 07			20 29	20 38		20 37			20 59	21 08	
West Sutton	d				19 40							20 10						20 40					
Sutton Common	d				19 42							20 12						20 42					
St Helier	d				19 45							20 15						20 45					
Morden South	d				19 47							20 17						20 47					
South Merton	d				19 49							20 19						20 49					
Wimbledon Chase	d				19 51							20 21						20 51					
Wimbledon	d				19 58							20 28						20 58					
Haydons Road	d				20 00							20 30						21 00					
Tooting	d				20 03							20 33						21 03					
Carshalton	d	19 32	19 41					20 02	20 11						20 32	20 41					21 02	21 11	
Hackbridge	d	19 35	19 43					20 05	20 13						20 35	20 43					21 05	21 13	
Mitcham Junction	d	19 38	19 46					20 08	20 16						20 38	20 46					21 08	21 16	
Mitcham Eastfields	d	19a41	19 49					20a11	20 19						20a41	20 49					21a11	21 19	
Streatham	d		19 53		20 08				20 23			20 38				20 53		21 08				21 23	
Tulse Hill	d		19 57		20 12				20 27			20 42				20 57		21 12				21 27	
London Bridge	a			20 15			20 30			20 45				21 00			21 15			21 30			21 45
	d			20 15			20 30			20 45				21 00			21 15			21 30			21 45
Sevenoaks	d					19 32							20 02						20 32				
Bat & Ball	d					19 35							20 05						20 35				
Otford	d					19 38							20 08						20 38				
Shoreham (Kent)	d					19 41							20 11						20 41				
Eynsford	d					19 45							20 15						20 45				
Swanley	d					19 50							20 20						20 50				
St Mary Cray	d					19 54							20 24						20 54				
Bickley	d					19 58							20 28						20 58				
Bromley South	d					20 01							20 31						21 01				
Shortlands	d					20 04							20 34						21 04				
Ravensbourne	d					20 06							20 36						21 06				
Beckenham Hill	d					20 08							20 38						21 08				
Bellingham	d					20 10							20 40						21 10				
Catford	d					20 13							20 43						21 13				
Crofton Park	d					20 15							20 45						21 15				
Nunhead	d					20 18							20 48						21 18				
Peckham Rye	d					20 20							20 50						21 20				
Denmark Hill	d					20 24							20 54						21 24				
Herne Hill	d		20 01		20 16				20 31			20 46				21 01		21 16				21 31	
Loughborough Jn.	d		20 04		20 19				20 34			20 49				21 04		21 19				21 34	
Elephant & Castle	d		20 09		20 24	20 30			20 39			20 54	21 00			21 09		21 24	21 30			21 39	
London Blackfriars	a		20 12	20 22	20 27	20 34	20 37		20 42	20 52		20 57	21 04	21 07		21 12	21 22	21 27	21 34	21 37		21 42	21 52
	d		20 14	20 24	20 30		20 38		20 44	20 54		21 00		21 08		21 14	21 24	21 30		21 38		21 44	21 54
City Thameslink	d		20 16	20 26	20 32		20 40		20 46	20 56													
Farringdon	d		20 19	20 30	20 36		20 44		20 49	21 00		21 06		21 14		21 19	21 30	21 36		21 44		21 49	22 00
St Pancras International	a		20 23	20 34	20 40		20 48		20 53	21 04		21 10		21 18		21 23	21 34	21 40		21 48		21 53	22 04

A From Epsom to London Victoria
B To Bedford
C To Luton
D To St Albans City
E To London Victoria

Please refer to separate pages within this table for services operating between London and Bedford

At weekends please use local bus and tube services to travel to/from St Pancras International and London Bridge when no trains are operating. See local publicity for details of alternative routes and services that are available across central London

Brighton, Gatwick Airport - South London

Network Diagram - see first Page of Table 52

		SN	SE	FC	FC	SN	SE	FC	FC	SN	SN	SE	FC	FC	SN	SE	FC	FC	SN	SN	FC	FC
		◇1			1				1		◇1			1				1		◇1	1	1
		A		B	B	C		B	B	C	A		B	B	C		B	B	C	A	B	B
Brighton	d	21 00			21 07				21 37		22 00			22 07				22 33		23 02	23 11	23 37
Preston Park	d	21 04			21 11				21 41		22 04			22 11				22 37		23 06		23 41
Hassocks	d	21 10			21 17				21 47		22 10			22 17				22 43		23 12	23 20	23 47
Burgess Hill	d	21 14			21 21				21 51		22 14			22 21				22 47		23 16	23 23	23 51
Wivelsfield	d	21 16			21 23				21 53		22 16			22 23				22 49		23 19		23 53
Haywards Heath	d	21 22			21 32				22 02		22 22			22 32				22 54		23 24	23 29	23 59
Balcombe	d				21 37									22 37				22 59				00 04
Three Bridges	d	21 32			21 42				22 12		22 32			22 43				23 12		23 47	23 38	00 10
Gatwick Airport	d	21 38			21 47				22 17		22 38			22 47				23 17		23 53	23 43	00 15
Redhill	d	21 47									22 46									00 03		00 23
East Croydon	d	21a59			22 02				22 32		22a59			23 02				23 32		00a16	00 04	00 36
Sutton (Surrey)	d			21 15		21 29		21 45		21 59			22 15		22 29		22 45		22 59			
West Sutton	d			21 18				21 48					22 18				22 48					
Sutton Common	d			21 20				21 50					22 20				22 50					
St Helier	d			21 23				21 53					22 23				22 53					
Morden South	d			21 25				21 55					22 25				22 55					
South Merton	d			21 27				21 57					22 27				22 57					
Wimbledon Chase	d			21 29				21 59					22 29				22 59					
Wimbledon	d			21 38				22 08					22 38				23 08					
Haydons Road	d			21 40				22 10					22 40				23 10					
Tooting	d			21 43				22 13					22 43				23 13					
Carshalton	d					21 32				22 02					22 32				23 02			
Hackbridge	d					21 35				22 05					22 35				23 05			
Mitcham Junction	d					21 38				22 08					22 38				23 08			
Mitcham Eastfields	d					21a41				22a11					22a41				23a11			
Streatham	d			21 49				22 19					22 49				23 19					
Tulse Hill	d			21 53				22 23					22 53				23 23					
London Bridge	a				22 15				22 45					23 15				23 44			00 21	00 51
	d				22 15				22 45					23 15				23 45			00 22	00 52
Sevenoaks	d		21 02				21 32					22 02				22 32						
Bat & Ball	d		21 05				21 35					22 05				22 35						
Otford	d		21 08				21 38					22 08				22 38						
Shoreham (Kent)	d		21 11				21 41					22 11				22 41						
Eynsford	d		21 15				21 45					22 15				22 45						
Swanley	d		21 20				21 50					22 20				22 50						
St Mary Cray	d		21 24				21 54					22 24				22 54						
Bickley	d		21 28				21 58					22 28				22 58						
Bromley South	d		21 31				22 01					22 31				23 01						
Shortlands	d		21 34				22 04					22 34				23 04						
Ravensbourne	d		21 36				22 06					22 36				23 06						
Beckenham Hill	d		21 38				22 08					22 38				23 08						
Bellingham	d		21 40				22 10					22 40				23 10						
Catford	d		21 43				22 13					22 43				23 13						
Crofton Park	d		21 45				22 15					22 45				23 15						
Nunhead	d		21 48				22 18					22 48				23 18						
Peckham Rye	d		21 50				22 20					22 50				23 20						
Denmark Hill	d		21 54				22 24					22 54				23 24						
Herne Hill	d			21 57				22 27					22 57				23 27					
Loughborough Jn.	d			22 00				22 30					23 00									
Elephant & Castle	d		22 00	22 04			22 30	22 34				23 00	23 04			23 30	23 34					
London Blackfriars	a		22 04	22 07	22 22		22 34	22 37	22 52			23 04	23 07	23 22		23 34	23 37	23 52			00 28	00 58
	d			22 08	22 22			22 38	22 52				23 08	23 22			23 38	23 52			00 28	00 58
City Thameslink	d																					
Farringdon	d			22 13	22 28			22 43	22 58				23 13	23 28			23 43	23 58			00 33	
St Pancras International	a			22 17	22 32			22 47	23 02				23 17	23 32			23 47	00 02			00 37	01 07

A To London Victoria
B To Bedford
C From Epsom to London Victoria

Please refer to separate pages within this table for services operating between London and Bedford

At weekends please use local bus and tube services to travel to/from St Pancras International and London Bridge when no trains are operating. See local publicity for details of alternative routes and services that are available across central London

Table 52

Sundays
until 24 June

Brighton, Gatwick Airport - South London

Network Diagram - see first Page of Table 52

Station		FC 1 A	SN ◇1 B	FC 1 C	FC A	FC 1 A	FC 1 C	FC 1 A	FC A	SN ◇1 B		FC	FC	FC 1 A	SN ◇1 B	SE D	FC 1 A	SN ◇1 B	SE D	FC 1 A		SE	SN E	SN F	FC 1 A
Brighton	d	22p33	23p02	23p11		23p11	23p37	23p37		03 50			05 45	06 15	06 19		06 45	07 04		07 15					07 45
Preston Park	d	22p37	23p06				23p41	23p41							06 22			07 07							
Hassocks	d	22p43	23p12	23p20		23p20	23p47	23p47					05 54	06 24	06 29		06 54	07 14		07 24					07 54
Burgess Hill	d	22p47	23p16	23p23		23p23	23p51	23p51					05 57	06 27	06 32		06 57	07 17		07 27					07 57
Wivelsfield	d	22p49	23p19				23p53	23p53							06 34			07 19							
Haywards Heath	d	22p54	23p24	23p29		23p29	23p59	23p59		04 26			06 03	06 33	06 39		07 03	07 25		07 33					08 03
Balcombe	d	22p59					00 04	00 04										07 30							
Three Bridges	d	23p12	23p47	23p38		23p38	00 10	00 10		04 58		05 12	06 12	06 42	06 48		07 12	07 36		07 42					08 12
Gatwick Airport	d	23p17	23p53	23p43		23p43	00 15	00 15		05 03		05 17	06 17	06 47	06 53		07 17	07 41		07 47					08 17
Redhill	d		00 03				00 23	00 23										07 49							
East Croydon	d	23p32	00a16	00 04		00 04	00 36	00 36		05a27		05 32	06 32	07 02	07a10		07 32	08a00		08 02					08 32
Sutton (Surrey)	d																						07 28	07 43	
West Sutton	d																								
Sutton Common	d																								
St Helier	d																								
Morden South	d																								
South Merton	d																								
Wimbledon Chase	d																								
Wimbledon	d																								
Haydons Road	d																								
Tooting	d																								
Carshalton	d																						07 31	07 46	
Hackbridge	d																						07 33	07 48	
Mitcham Junction	d																						07 37	07 52	
Mitcham Eastfields	d																						07a40	07a55	
Streatham	d																								
Tulse Hill	d																								
London Bridge ⊖	a	23p46		00 19		00 21	00 52	00 51						07 15			07 45			08 15					08 45
	d	23p46				00 22		00 52						07 15			07 45			08 15					08 45
Sevenoaks	d																					07 21			
Bat & Ball	d																					07 24			
Otford	d																					07 27			
Shoreham (Kent)	d																					07 30			
Eynsford	d																					07 34			
Swanley	d																					07 39			
St Mary Cray	d																					07 43			
Bickley	d															06 47			07 17			07 47			
Bromley South	d															06 50			07 20			07 50			
Shortlands	d															06 53			07 23			07 53			
Ravensbourne	d															06 55			07 25			07 55			
Beckenham Hill	d															06 57			07 27			07 57			
Bellingham	d															06 59			07 29			07 59			
Catford	d															07 02			07 32			08 02			
Crofton Park	d															07 04			07 34			08 04			
Nunhead	d															07 07			07 37			08 07			
Peckham Rye	d															07 09			07 39			08 09			
Denmark Hill	d															07 13			07 43			08 13			
Herne Hill	d																								
Loughborough Jn.	d																								
Elephant & Castle	d															07 19			07 49			08 19			
London Blackfriars ⊖	a	23p52				00 28		00 58				05 59	06 59	07 22		07 23	07 52		07 53	08 22		08 23			08 52
	d	23p52			00 08	00 28		00 58	01 29					07 22			07 52			08 22					08 52
City Thameslink	d																								
Farringdon ⊖	d	23p58			00 13	00 33								07 27			07 57			08 27					08 57
St Pancras International ⊖	a	00 02			00 17	00 37		01 07	01 37					07 32			08 02			08 32					09 02

A To Bedford
B To London Victoria
C 20 May
D From Orpington
E From Epsom to London Victoria
F From Dorking to London Victoria

Please refer to separate pages within this table for services operating between London and Bedford

At weekends please use local bus and tube services to travel to/from St Pancras International and London Bridge when no trains are operating. See local publicity for details of alternative routes and services that are available across central London

Table 52

Sundays
until 24 June

Brighton, Gatwick Airport - South London

Network Diagram - see first Page of Table 52

Station		SE	SN A	SN ◇1 B	SN C	FC 1 D		SE	SN A	SN C	FC 1 E	SE	SN A	SN C	SN A	FC 1 F		SN ◇1 B	FC 1 D	SE	FC F	SN C	SN A	FC	FC 1 D
Brighton	d			08 00		08 15					08 45							09 00	09 15						
Preston Park	d			08 03														09 03							
Hassocks	d			08 10		08 24					08 54							09 10	09 24						
Burgess Hill	d			08 13		08 27					08 57							09 13	09 27						
Wivelsfield	d			08 15														09 15							
Haywards Heath	d			08 25		08 33					09 03							09 25	09 33						
Balcombe	d			08 30														09 30							
Three Bridges	d			08 36		08 42					09 12							09 36	09 42						
Gatwick Airport	d			08 41		08 47					09 17							09 41	09 47						
Redhill	d			08 49														09 49							
East Croydon	d			09a00		09 02					09 32					09 47		10a00	10 02						10 17
Sutton (Surrey)	d		07 58		08 13				08 28	08 43			08 58	09 13	09 28						09 37	09 43	09 58	10 04	
West Sutton	d																				09 40				
Sutton Common	d																				09 42				
St Helier	d																				09 45				
Morden South	d																				09 47				
South Merton	d																				09 49				
Wimbledon Chase	d																				09 51				
Wimbledon	d																				09 56				
Haydons Road	d																				09 58				
Tooting	d																				10 01				
Carshalton	d		08 01		08 16				08 31	08 46			09 01	09 16	09 31							09 46	10 01	10 07	
Hackbridge	d		08 03		08 18				08 33	08 48			09 03	09 18	09 33							09 48	10 03	10 09	
Mitcham Junction	d		08 07		08 22				08 37	08 52			09 07	09 22	09 37							09 52	10 07	10 12	
Mitcham Eastfields	d		08a10		08a25				08a40	08a55			09a10	09a25	09a40							09a55	10a10	10 15	
Streatham	d																				10 06			10 19	
Tulse Hill	d																				10 10			10 23	
London Bridge ⊖	a					09 15					09 45					10 00			10 15						10 30
	d					09 15					09 45					10 00			10 15						10 30
Sevenoaks	d	07 51						08 21				08 51								09 21					
Bat & Ball	d	07 54						08 24				08 54								09 24					
Otford	d	07 57						08 27				08 57								09 27					
Shoreham (Kent)	d	08 00						08 30				09 00								09 30					
Eynsford	d	08 04						08 34				09 04								09 34					
Swanley	d	08 09						08 39				09 09								09 39					
St Mary Cray	d	08 13						08 43				09 13								09 43					
Bickley	d	08 17						08 47				09 17								09 47					
Bromley South	d	08 20						08 50				09 20								09 50					
Shortlands	d	08 23						08 53				09 23								09 53					
Ravensbourne	d	08 25						08 55				09 25								09 55					
Beckenham Hill	d	08 27						08 57				09 27								09 57					
Bellingham	d	08 29						08 59				09 29								09 59					
Catford	d	08 32						09 02				09 32								10 02					
Crofton Park	d	08 34						09 04				09 34								10 04					
Nunhead	d	08 37						09 07				09 37								10 07					
Peckham Rye	d	08 39						09 09				09 39								10 09					
Denmark Hill	d	08 43						09 13				09 43								10 13					
Herne Hill	d																				10 14			10 27	
Loughborough Jn.	d																				10 17			10 30	
Elephant & Castle	d	08 49						09 19				09 49								10 19	10 22			10 34	
London Blackfriars ⊖	a	08 53				09 22		09 23			09 52	09 53				10 07			10 22	10 23	10 25			10 37	10 37
	d					09 22					09 52					10 10			10 22		10 26				10 40
City Thameslink	d																								
Farringdon ⊖	d					09 27					09 57					10 14			10 27		10 31				10 44
St Pancras International ⊖	a					09 32					10 01					10 18			10 31		10 35				10 48

A From Epsom to London Victoria
B To London Victoria
C From Dorking to London Victoria
D To Bedford
E not 20 May. To Bedford
F To St Albans City

Please refer to separate pages within this table for services operating between London and Bedford

At weekends please use local bus and tube services to travel to/from St Pancras International and London Bridge when no trains are operating. See local publicity for details of alternative routes and services that are available across central London

Sundays until 24 June

Brighton, Gatwick Airport - South London

Network Diagram - see first Page of Table 52

		FC	SE	FC	SN	SN	FC	FC	SN	FC	SE	FC	SN	SN	FC	FC	FC	SE	FC	SN	SN	FC
		1						1	◇1	1						1	1					
		A		B	C	D		A	E	A		B	C	D		A	A		B	C	D	
Brighton	d	09 45							10 00	10 15							10 45					
Preston Park	d								10 03													
Hassocks	d	09 54							10 10	10 24							10 54					
Burgess Hill	d	09 57							10 13	10 27							10 57					
Wivelsfield	d								10 15													
Haywards Heath	d	10 03							10 25	10 33							11 03					
Balcombe	d								10 30													
Three Bridges	d	10 12							10 36	10 42							11 12					
Gatwick Airport ✈	d	10 17							10 41	10 47							11 17					
Redhill	d								10 49													
East Croydon	d	10 32						10 47	11a00	11 02						11 17	11 32					
Sutton (Surrey)	d			10 07	10 13	10 28	10 34					10 37	10 43	10 58	11 04				11 07	11 13	11 28	11 34
West Sutton	d			10 10								10 40							11 10			
Sutton Common	d			10 12								10 42							11 12			
St Helier	d			10 15								10 45							11 15			
Morden South	d			10 17								10 47							11 17			
South Merton	d			10 19								10 49							11 19			
Wimbledon Chase	d			10 21								10 51							11 21			
Wimbledon	d			10 26								10 56							11 26			
Haydons Road	d			10 28								10 58							11 28			
Tooting	d			10 31								11 01							11 31			
Carshalton	d				10 16	10 31	10 37						10 46	11 01	11 07					11 16	11 31	11 37
Hackbridge	d				10 18	10 33	10 39						10 48	11 03	11 09					11 18	11 33	11 39
Mitcham Junction	d				10 22	10 37	10 42						10 52	11 07	11 12					11 22	11 37	11 42
Mitcham Eastfields	d				10a25	10a40	10 45						10a55	11a10	11 15					11a25	11a40	11 45
Streatham	d			10 36			10 49					11 06			11 19				11 36			11 49
Tulse Hill	d			10 40			10 53					11 10			11 23				11 40			11 53
London Bridge ⊖	a	10 45						11 00		11 15						11 30	11 45					
	d	10 45						11 00		11 15						11 30	11 45					
Sevenoaks	d		09 51								10 21							10 51				
Bat & Ball	d		09 54								10 24							10 54				
Otford	d		09 57								10 27							10 57				
Shoreham (Kent)	d		10 00								10 30							11 00				
Eynsford	d		10 04								10 34							11 04				
Swanley	d		10 09								10 39							11 09				
St Mary Cray	d		10 13								10 43							11 13				
Bickley	d		10 17								10 47							11 17				
Bromley South	d		10 20								10 50							11 20				
Shortlands	d		10 23								10 53							11 23				
Ravensbourne	d		10 25								10 55							11 25				
Beckenham Hill	d		10 27								10 57							11 27				
Bellingham	d		10 29								10 59							11 29				
Catford	d		10 32								11 02							11 32				
Crofton Park	d		10 34								11 04							11 34				
Nunhead	d		10 37								11 07							11 37				
Peckham Rye	d		10 39								11 09							11 39				
Denmark Hill	d		10 43								11 13							11 43				
Herne Hill	d			10 44			10 57					11 14			11 27				11 44			11 57
Loughborough Jn.	d			10 47			11 00					11 17			11 30				11 47			12 00
Elephant & Castle	d		10 49	10 52			11 04				11 19	11 22			11 34			11 49	11 52			12 04
London Blackfriars ⊖	a	10 52	10 53	10 55			11 07	11 07		11 22	11 23	11 25			11 37	11 37	11 52	11 53	11 55			12 07
	d	10 52		10 56				11 10		11 22		11 26				11 40	11 52		11 56			
City Thameslink	d																					
Farringdon ⊖	d	10 57		11 01				11 14		11 27		11 31				11 44	11 57		12 01			
St Pancras International ⊖	a	11 01		11 05				11 18		11 31		11 35				11 48	12 01		12 05			

A To Bedford
B To St Albans City
C From Dorking to London Victoria
D From Epsom to London Victoria
E To London Victoria

Please refer to separate pages within this table for services operating between London and Bedford

At weekends please use local bus and tube services to travel to/from St Pancras International and London Bridge when no trains are operating. See local publicity for details of alternative routes and services that are available across central London

Sundays until 24 June

Brighton, Gatwick Airport - South London

Network Diagram - see first Page of Table 52

		FC	SN	FC	SE	FC	SN	SN	FC	FC	FC	SE	FC	SN	SN	FC	FC	SN	FC	SE	FC	SN	SN
		1	◇1	1						1	1						1	◇1	1				
		A	B	A		C	D	E		A	A		C	D	E		A	B	A		C	D	E
Brighton	d		11 00	11 15							11 45							12 00	12 15				
Preston Park	d		11 03															12 03					
Hassocks	d		11 10	11 24							11 54							12 10	12 24				
Burgess Hill	d		11 13	11 27							11 57							12 13	12 27				
Wivelsfield	d		11 15															12 15					
Haywards Heath	d		11 25	11 33							12 03							12 25	12 33				
Balcombe	d		11 30															12 30					
Three Bridges	d		11 36	11 42							12 12							12 36	12 42				
Gatwick Airport ✈	d		11 41	11 47							12 17							12 41	12 47				
Redhill	d		11 49															12 49					
East Croydon	d	11 47	12a00	12 02						12 17	12 32						12 47	13a00	13 02				
Sutton (Surrey)	d					11 37	11 43	11 58	12 04				12 07	12 13	12 28	12 34					12 37	12 43	12 58
West Sutton	d					11 40							12 10								12 40		
Sutton Common	d					11 42							12 12								12 42		
St Helier	d					11 45							12 15								12 45		
Morden South	d					11 47							12 17								12 47		
South Merton	d					11 49							12 19								12 49		
Wimbledon Chase	d					11 51							12 21								12 51		
Wimbledon	d					11 56							12 26								12 56		
Haydons Road	d					11 58							12 28								12 58		
Tooting	d					12 01							12 31								13 01		
Carshalton	d						11 46	12 01	12 07					12 16	12 31	12 37						12 46	13 01
Hackbridge	d						11 48	12 03	12 09					12 18	12 33	12 39						12 48	13 03
Mitcham Junction	d						11 52	12 07	12 12					12 22	12 37	12 42						12 52	13 07
Mitcham Eastfields	d						11a55	12a10	12 15					12a25	12a40	12 45						12a55	13a10
Streatham	d					12 06			12 19				12 36			12 49					13 06		
Tulse Hill	d					12 10			12 23				12 40			12 53					13 10		
London Bridge ⊖	a	12 00		12 15						12 30	12 45						13 00		13 15				
	d	12 00		12 15						12 30	12 45						13 00		13 15				
Sevenoaks	d				11 21							11 51								12 21			
Bat & Ball	d				11 24							11 54								12 24			
Otford	d				11 27							11 57								12 27			
Shoreham (Kent)	d				11 30							12 00								12 30			
Eynsford	d				11 34							12 04								12 34			
Swanley	d				11 39							12 09								12 39			
St Mary Cray	d				11 43							12 13								12 43			
Bickley	d				11 47							12 17								12 47			
Bromley South	d				11 50							12 20								12 50			
Shortlands	d				11 53							12 23								12 53			
Ravensbourne	d				11 55							12 25								12 55			
Beckenham Hill	d				11 57							12 27								12 57			
Bellingham	d				11 59							12 29								12 59			
Catford	d				12 02							12 32								13 02			
Crofton Park	d				12 04							12 34								13 04			
Nunhead	d				12 07							12 37								13 07			
Peckham Rye	d				12 09							12 39								13 09			
Denmark Hill	d				12 13							12 43								13 13			
Herne Hill	d					12 14			12 27				12 44			12 57					13 14		
Loughborough Jn.	d					12 17			12 30				12 47			13 00					13 17		
Elephant & Castle	d				12 19	12 22			12 34			12 49	12 52			13 04				13 19	13 22		
London Blackfriars ⊖	a	12 07		12 22	12 23	12 25			12 37	12 37	12 52	12 53	12 55			13 07	13 07		13 22	13 23	13 25		
	d	12 10		12 22		12 26				12 40	12 52		12 56				13 10		13 22		13 26		
City Thameslink	d																						
Farringdon ⊖	d	12 14		12 27		12 31				12 44	12 57		13 01				13 14		13 27		13 31		
St Pancras International ⊖	a	12 18		12 31		12 35				12 48	13 01		13 05				13 18		13 31		13 35		

A To Bedford
B To London Victoria
C To St Albans City
D From Dorking to London Victoria
E From Epsom to London Victoria

Please refer to separate pages within this table for services operating between London and Bedford

At weekends please use local bus and tube services to travel to/from St Pancras International and London Bridge when no trains are operating. See local publicity for details of alternative routes and services that are available across central London

Table 52

Sundays
until 24 June

Brighton, Gatwick Airport - South London

Network Diagram - see first Page of Table 52

		FC	FC	FC	SE	FC	SN	SN	FC	FC	SN	FC	SE	FC	SN	SN	FC	FC	FC	SE	FC	SN
			A	A		B	C	D		A	E	A		B	C	D		A	A		B	C
Brighton	d			12 45							13 00	13 15							13 45			
Preston Park	d										13 03											
Hassocks	d			12 54							13 10	13 24							13 54			
Burgess Hill	d			12 57							13 13	13 27							13 57			
Wivelsfield	d										13 15											
Haywards Heath	d			13 03							13 25	13 33							14 03			
Balcombe	d										13 30											
Three Bridges	d			13 12							13 36	13 42							14 12			
Gatwick Airport	d			13 17							13 41	13 47							14 17			
Redhill	d										13 49											
East Croydon	d		13 17	13 32						13 47	14a00	14 02						14 17	14 32			
Sutton (Surrey)	d	13 04				13 07	13 13	13 28	13 34					13 37	13 43	13 58	14 04				14 07	14 13
West Sutton	d					13 10								13 40							14 10	
Sutton Common	d					13 12								13 42							14 12	
St Helier	d					13 15								13 45							14 15	
Morden South	d					13 17								13 47							14 17	
South Merton	d					13 19								13 49							14 19	
Wimbledon Chase	d					13 21								13 51							14 21	
Wimbledon	d					13 26								13 56							14 26	
Haydons Road	d					13 28								13 58							14 28	
Tooting	d					13 31								14 01							14 31	
Carshalton	d	13 07					13 16	13 31	13 37						13 46	14 01	14 07					14 16
Hackbridge	d	13 09					13 18	13 33	13 39						13 48	14 03	14 09					14 18
Mitcham Junction	d	13 12					13 22	13 37	13 42						13 52	14 07	14 12					14 22
Mitcham Eastfields	d	13 15					13a25	13a40	13 45						13a55	14a10	14 15					14a25
Streatham	d	13 19				13 36			13 49					14 06			14 19				14 36	
Tulse Hill	d	13 23				13 40			13 53					14 10			14 23				14 40	
London Bridge	a		13 30	13 45						14 00		14 15						14 30	14 45			
	d		13 30	13 45						14 00		14 15						14 30	14 45			
Sevenoaks	d				12 51								13 21							13 51		
Bat & Ball	d				12 54								13 24							13 54		
Otford	d				12 57								13 27							13 57		
Shoreham (Kent)	d				13 00								13 30							14 00		
Eynsford	d				13 04								13 34							14 04		
Swanley	d				13 09								13 39							14 09		
St Mary Cray	d				13 13								13 43							14 13		
Bickley	d				13 17								13 47							14 17		
Bromley South	d				13 20								13 50							14 20		
Shortlands	d				13 23								13 53							14 23		
Ravensbourne	d				13 25								13 55							14 25		
Beckenham Hill	d				13 27								13 57							14 27		
Bellingham	d				13 29								13 59							14 29		
Catford	d				13 32								14 02							14 32		
Crofton Park	d				13 34								14 04							14 34		
Nunhead	d				13 37								14 07							14 37		
Peckham Rye	d				13 39								14 09							14 39		
Denmark Hill	d				13 43								14 13							14 43		
Herne Hill	d	13 27				13 44			13 57					14 14			14 27				14 44	
Loughborough Jn	d	13 30				13 47			14 00					14 17			14 30				14 47	
Elephant & Castle	d	13 34			13 49	13 52			14 04				14 19	14 22			14 34			14 49	14 52	
London Blackfriars	a	13 37	13 37	13 52	13 53	13 55			14 07	14 07		14 22	14 23	14 25			14 37	14 37	14 52	14 53	14 55	
	d		13 40	13 52		13 56				14 10		14 22		14 26				14 40	14 52		14 56	
City Thameslink	d																					
Farringdon	d		13 44	13 57		14 01				14 14		14 27		14 31				14 44	14 57		15 01	
St Pancras International	a		13 48	14 01		14 05				14 18		14 31		14 35				14 48	15 01		15 05	

A To Bedford
B To St Albans City
C From Dorking to London Victoria
D From Epsom to London Victoria
E To London Victoria

Please refer to separate pages within this table for services operating between London and Bedford

At weekends please use local bus and tube services to travel to/from St Pancras International and London Bridge when no trains are operating. See local publicity for details of alternative routes and services that are available across central London

Table 52

Sundays
until 24 June

Brighton, Gatwick Airport - South London

Network Diagram - see first Page of Table 52

		SN	FC	FC	SN	FC	SE	FC	SN	SN	FC	FC	FC	SE	FC	SN	SN	FC	FC	SN	FC	SE	FC
		A		B	C	B		D	E	A		B	B		D	E	A		B	C	B		D
Brighton	d				14 00	14 15							14 45							15 00	15 15		
Preston Park	d				14 03															15 03			
Hassocks	d				14 10	14 24							14 54							15 10	15 24		
Burgess Hill	d				14 13	14 27							14 57							15 13	15 27		
Wivelsfield	d				14 15															15 15			
Haywards Heath	d				14 25	14 33							15 03							15 25	15 33		
Balcombe	d				14 30															15 30			
Three Bridges	d				14 36	14 42							15 12							15 36	15 42		
Gatwick Airport	d				14 41	14 47							15 17							15 41	15 47		
Redhill	d				14 49															15 49			
East Croydon	d			14 47	15a00	15 02						15 17	15 32						15 47	16a00	16 02		
Sutton (Surrey)	d	14 28	14 34					14 37	14 43	14 58	15 04				15 07	15 13	15 28	15 34					15 37
West Sutton	d							14 40							15 10								15 40
Sutton Common	d							14 42							15 12								15 42
St Helier	d							14 45							15 15								15 45
Morden South	d							14 47							15 17								15 47
South Merton	d							14 49							15 19								15 49
Wimbledon Chase	d							14 51							15 21								15 51
Wimbledon	d							14 56							15 26								15 56
Haydons Road	d							14 58							15 28								15 58
Tooting	d							15 01							15 31								16 01
Carshalton	d	14 31	14 37						14 46	15 01	15 07					15 16	15 31	15 37					
Hackbridge	d	14 33	14 39						14 48	15 03	15 09					15 18	15 33	15 39					
Mitcham Junction	d	14 37	14 42						14 52	15 07	15 12					15 22	15 37	15 42					
Mitcham Eastfields	d	14a40	14 45						14a55	15a10	15 15					15a25	15a40	15 45					
Streatham	d		14 49					15 06			15 19				15 36			15 49					16 06
Tulse Hill	d		14 53					15 10			15 23				15 40			15 53					16 10
London Bridge	a			15 00		15 15						15 30	15 45						16 00		16 15		
	d			15 00		15 15						15 30	15 45						16 00		16 15		
Sevenoaks	d						14 21							14 51								15 21	
Bat & Ball	d						14 24							14 54								15 24	
Otford	d						14 27							14 57								15 27	
Shoreham (Kent)	d						14 30							15 00								15 30	
Eynsford	d						14 34							15 04								15 34	
Swanley	d						14 39							15 09								15 39	
St Mary Cray	d						14 43							15 13								15 43	
Bickley	d						14 47							15 17								15 47	
Bromley South	d						14 50							15 20								15 50	
Shortlands	d						14 53							15 23								15 53	
Ravensbourne	d						14 55							15 25								15 55	
Beckenham Hill	d						14 57							15 27								15 57	
Bellingham	d						14 59							15 29								15 59	
Catford	d						15 02							15 32								16 02	
Crofton Park	d						15 04							15 34								16 04	
Nunhead	d						15 07							15 37								16 07	
Peckham Rye	d						15 09							15 39								16 09	
Denmark Hill	d						15 13							15 43								16 13	
Herne Hill	d		14 57					15 14			15 27				15 44			15 57					16 14
Loughborough Jn	d		15 00					15 17			15 30				15 47			16 00					16 17
Elephant & Castle	d		15 04				15 19	15 22			15 34			15 49	15 52			16 04				16 19	16 22
London Blackfriars	a		15 07	15 07		15 22	15 23	15 25			15 37	15 37	15 52	15 53	15 55			16 07	16 07		16 22	16 23	16 25
	d			15 10		15 22		15 26				15 40	15 52		15 56				16 10		16 22		16 26
City Thameslink	d																						
Farringdon	d			15 14		15 27		15 31				15 44	15 57		16 01				16 14		16 27		16 31
St Pancras International	a			15 18		15 31		15 35				15 48	16 01		16 05				16 18		16 31		16 35

A From Epsom to London Victoria
B To Bedford
C To London Victoria
D To St Albans City
E From Dorking to London Victoria

Please refer to separate pages within this table for services operating between London and Bedford

At weekends please use local bus and tube services to travel to/from St Pancras International and London Bridge when no trains are operating. See local publicity for details of alternative routes and services that are available across central London

Brighton, Gatwick Airport - South London

Network Diagram - see first Page of Table 52

		SN	SN	FC	FC	FC		SE	FC	SN	SN	FC	FC	SN	FC	SE		FC	SN	SN	FC	FC	FC	SE	FC
					■	■							■	◇■	■							■	■		
		A	B		C	C			D	A	B		C	E	C			D	A	B		C	C		D
Brighton	d					15 45								16 00	16 15								16 45		
Preston Park	d													16 03											
Hassocks	d					15 54								16 10	16 24								16 54		
Burgess Hill	d					15 57								16 13	16 27								16 57		
Wivelsfield	d													16 15											
Haywards Heath	d					16 03								16 25	16 33								17 03		
Balcombe	d													16 30											
Three Bridges	d					16 12								16 36	16 42								17 12		
Gatwick Airport ✈	d					16 17								16 41	16 47								17 17		
Redhill	d													16 49											
East Croydon	d				16 17	16 32							16 47	17a00	17 02							17 17	17 32		
Sutton (Surrey)	d	15 43	15 58	16 04					16 07	16 13	16 28	16 34						16 37	16 43	16 58	17 04				17 07
West Sutton	d								16 10									16 40							17 10
Sutton Common	d								16 12									16 42							17 12
St Helier	d								16 15									16 45							17 15
Morden South	d								16 17									16 47							17 17
South Merton	d								16 19									16 49							17 19
Wimbledon Chase	d								16 21									16 51							17 21
Wimbledon	d								16 26									16 56							17 26
Haydons Road	d								16 28									16 58							17 28
Tooting	d								16 31									17 01							17 31
Carshalton	d	15 46	16 01	16 07						16 16	16 31	16 37							16 46	17 01	17 07				
Hackbridge	d	15 48	16 03	16 09						16 18	16 33	16 39							16 48	17 03	17 09				
Mitcham Junction	d	15 52	16 07	16 12						16 22	16 37	16 42							16 52	17 07	17 12				
Mitcham Eastfields	d	15a55	16a10	16 15						16a25	16a40	16 45							16a55	17a10	17 15				
Streatham	d			16 19					16 36			16 49						17 06			17 19				17 36
Tulse Hill	d			16 23					16 40			16 53						17 10			17 23				17 40
London Bridge ⊖	a				16 30	16 45							17 00		17 15							17 30	17 45		
	d				16 30	16 45							17 00		17 15							17 30	17 45		
Sevenoaks	d							15 51								16 21								16 51	
Bat & Ball	d							15 54								16 24								16 54	
Otford	d							15 57								16 27								16 57	
Shoreham (Kent)	d							16 00								16 30								17 00	
Eynsford	d							16 04								16 34								17 04	
Swanley	d							16 09								16 39								17 09	
St Mary Cray	d							16 13								16 43								17 13	
Bickley	d							16 17								16 47								17 17	
Bromley South	d							16 20								16 50								17 20	
Shortlands	d							16 23								16 53								17 23	
Ravensbourne	d							16 25								16 55								17 25	
Beckenham Hill	d							16 27								16 57								17 27	
Bellingham	d							16 29								16 59								17 29	
Catford	d							16 32								17 02								17 32	
Crofton Park	d							16 34								17 04								17 34	
Nunhead	d							16 37								17 07								17 37	
Peckham Rye	d							16 39								17 09								17 39	
Denmark Hill	d							16 43								17 13								17 43	
Herne Hill	d			16 27					16 44			16 57						17 14			17 27				17 44
Loughborough Jn.	d			16 30					16 47			17 00						17 17			17 30				17 47
Elephant & Castle	d			16 34				16 49	16 52			17 04				17 19		17 22			17 34			17 49	17 52
London Blackfriars ⊖	a			16 37	16 37	16 52		16 53	16 55			17 07	17 07		17 22	17 23		17 25			17 37	17 37	17 52	17 53	17 55
	d				16 40	16 52			16 56				17 10		17 22			17 26				17 40	17 52		17 56
City Thameslink	d																								
Farringdon ⊖	d				16 44	16 57			17 01				17 14		17 27			17 31				17 44	17 57		18 01
St Pancras International ⊖	a				16 48	17 01			17 05				17 18		17 31			17 35				17 48	18 01		18 05

A From Dorking to London Victoria
B From Epsom to London Victoria
C To Bedford
D To St Albans City
E To London Victoria

Please refer to separate pages within this table for services operating between London and Bedford

At weekends please use local bus and tube services to travel to/from St Pancras International and London Bridge when no trains are operating. See local publicity for details of alternative routes and services that are available across central London

Brighton, Gatwick Airport - South London

Network Diagram - see first Page of Table 52

		SN		SN	FC	FC	SN	FC	SE	FC	SN	SN		FC	FC	FC	SE	FC	SN	SN	FC	FC		SN	FC
						■	◇■	■							■	■						■		◇■	■
		A		B		C	D	C		E	A	B			C	C		E	A	B		C		D	C
Brighton	d						17 00	17 15								17 45								18 00	18 15
Preston Park	d						17 03																	18 03	
Hassocks	d						17 10	17 24								17 54								18 10	18 24
Burgess Hill	d						17 13	17 27								17 57								18 13	18 27
Wivelsfield	d						17 15																	18 15	
Haywards Heath	d						17 25	17 33								18 03								18 25	18 33
Balcombe	d						17 30																	18 30	
Three Bridges	d						17 36	17 42								18 12								18 36	18 42
Gatwick Airport ✈	d						17 41	17 47								18 17								18 41	18 47
Redhill	d						17 49																	18 49	
East Croydon	d					17 47	18a00	18 02							18 17	18 32						18 47		19a00	19 02
Sutton (Surrey)	d	17 13		17 28	17 34					17 37	17 43	17 58		18 04				18 07	18 13	18 28	18 34				
West Sutton	d									17 40								18 10							
Sutton Common	d									17 42								18 12							
St Helier	d									17 45								18 15							
Morden South	d									17 47								18 17							
South Merton	d									17 49								18 19							
Wimbledon Chase	d									17 51								18 21							
Wimbledon	d									17 56								18 26							
Haydons Road	d									17 58								18 28							
Tooting	d									18 01								18 31							
Carshalton	d	17 16		17 31	17 37						17 46	18 01		18 07					18 16	18 31	18 37				
Hackbridge	d	17 18		17 33	17 39						17 48	18 03		18 09					18 18	18 33	18 39				
Mitcham Junction	d	17 22		17 37	17 42						17 52	18 07		18 12					18 22	18 37	18 42				
Mitcham Eastfields	d	17a25		17a40	17 45						17a55	18a10		18 15					18a25	18a40	18 45				
Streatham	d				17 49					18 06				18 19				18 36			18 49				
Tulse Hill	d				17 53					18 10				18 23				18 40			18 53				
London Bridge ⊖	a					18 00		18 15							18 30	18 45						19 00			19 15
	d					18 00		18 15							18 30	18 45						19 00			19 15
Sevenoaks	d								17 21								17 51								
Bat & Ball	d								17 24								17 54								
Otford	d								17 27								17 57								
Shoreham (Kent)	d								17 30								18 00								
Eynsford	d								17 34								18 04								
Swanley	d								17 39								18 09								
St Mary Cray	d								17 43								18 13								
Bickley	d								17 47								18 17								
Bromley South	d								17 50								18 20								
Shortlands	d								17 53								18 23								
Ravensbourne	d								17 55								18 25								
Beckenham Hill	d								17 57								18 27								
Bellingham	d								17 59								18 29								
Catford	d								18 02								18 32								
Crofton Park	d								18 04								18 34								
Nunhead	d								18 07								18 37								
Peckham Rye	d								18 09								18 39								
Denmark Hill	d								18 13								18 43								
Herne Hill	d				17 57					18 14				18 27				18 44			18 57				
Loughborough Jn.	d				18 00					18 17				18 30				18 47			19 00				
Elephant & Castle	d				18 04				18 19	18 22				18 34			18 49	18 52			19 04				
London Blackfriars ⊖	a				18 07	18 07		18 22	18 23	18 25				18 37	18 37	18 52	18 53	18 55			19 07	19 07			19 22
	d					18 10		18 22		18 26					18 40	18 52		18 56				19 10			19 22
City Thameslink	d																								
Farringdon ⊖	d					18 14		18 27		18 31					18 44	18 57		19 01				19 14			19 27
St Pancras International ⊖	a					18 18		18 31		18 35					18 48	19 01		19 05				19 18			19 31

A From Dorking to London Victoria
B From Epsom to London Victoria
C To Bedford
D To London Victoria
E To St Albans City

Please refer to separate pages within this table for services operating between London and Bedford

At weekends please use local bus and tube services to travel to/from St Pancras International and London Bridge when no trains are operating. See local publicity for details of alternative routes and services that are available across central London

Table 52

Sundays until 24 June

Brighton, Gatwick Airport - South London

Network Diagram - see first Page of Table 52

		SE	FC	SN	SN	FC	FC ■	FC ■	SE	SN ◇■	FC	SN	FC	FC ■	SE	FC	SN	FC	FC ■	SE	SN ◇■	FC	SN
			A	B	C		D	D		E	D	B		D		D	B		D		E	D	B
Brighton	d							18 45		19 00				19 15					19 45		20 00		
Preston Park	d									19 03											20 03		
Hassocks	d							18 54		19 10				19 24					19 54		20 10		
Burgess Hill	d							18 57		19 13				19 27					19 57		20 13		
Wivelsfield	d									19 15											20 15		
Haywards Heath	d							19 03		19 25				19 33					20 03		20 25		
Balcombe	d									19 30											20 30		
Three Bridges	d							19 12		19 36				19 42					20 12		20 36		
Gatwick Airport ✈	d							19 17		19 41				19 47					20 17		20 41		
Redhill	d									19 49											20 49		
East Croydon	d						19 17	19 32		20a00				20 02					20 32		21a00		
Sutton (Surrey)	d		18 37	18 43	18 58	19 04					19 07	19 13	19 34			19 37	19 43	20 04				20 07	20 13
West Sutton	d		18 40								19 10					19 40						20 10	
Sutton Common	d		18 42								19 12					19 42						20 12	
St Helier	d		18 45								19 15					19 45						20 15	
Morden South	d		18 47								19 17					19 47						20 17	
South Merton	d		18 49								19 19					19 49						20 19	
Wimbledon Chase	d		18 51								19 21					19 51						20 21	
Wimbledon	d		18 56								19 26					19 56						20 26	
Haydons Road	d		18 58								19 28					19 58						20 28	
Tooting	d		19 01								19 31					20 01						20 31	
Carshalton	d			18 46	19 01	19 07						19 16	19 37				19 46	20 07					20 16
Hackbridge	d			18 48	19 03	19 09						19 18	19 39				19 48	20 09					20 18
Mitcham Junction	d			18 52	19 07	19 12						19 22	19 42				19 52	20 12					20 22
Mitcham Eastfields	d			18a55	19a10	19 15						19a25	19 45				19a55	20 15					20a25
Streatham	d		19 06			19 19					19 36		19 49			20 06		20 19				20 36	
Tulse Hill	d		19 10			19 23					19 40		19 53			20 10		20 23				20 40	
London Bridge ⊖	a						19 30	19 45						20 15					20 45				
	d						19 30	19 45						20 15					20 45				
Sevenoaks	d	18 21							18 51						19 21					19 51			
Bat & Ball	d	18 24							18 54						19 24					19 54			
Otford	d	18 27							18 57						19 27					19 57			
Shoreham (Kent)	d	18 30							19 00						19 30					20 00			
Eynsford	d	18 34							19 04						19 34					20 04			
Swanley	d	18 39							19 09						19 39					20 09			
St Mary Cray	d	18 43							19 13						19 43					20 13			
Bickley	d	18 47							19 17						19 47					20 17			
Bromley South	d	18 50							19 20						19 50					20 20			
Shortlands	d	18 53							19 23						19 53					20 23			
Ravensbourne	d	18 55							19 25						19 55					20 25			
Beckenham Hill	d	18 57							19 27						19 57					20 27			
Bellingham	d	18 59							19 29						19 59					20 29			
Catford	d	19 02							19 32						20 02					20 32			
Crofton Park	d	19 04							19 34						20 04					20 34			
Nunhead	d	19 07							19 37						20 07					20 37			
Peckham Rye	d	19 09							19 39						20 09					20 39			
Denmark Hill	d	19 13							19 43						20 13					20 43			
Herne Hill	d		19 14			19 27					19 44		19 57			20 14		20 27				20 44	
Loughborough Jn.	d		19 17			19 30					19 47		20 00			20 17		20 30				20 47	
Elephant & Castle	d	19 19	19 22			19 34			19 49		19 52		20 04		20 19	20 22		20 34		20 49		20 52	
London Blackfriars ⊖	a	19 23	19 25			19 37	19 37	19 52	19 53		19 55		20 07	20 22	20 23	20 25		20 37	20 52	20 53		20 55	
	d		19 26				19 40	19 52			20 03			20 22		20 33			20 52			21 03	
City Thameslink	d																						
Farringdon ⊖	d		19 31				19 44	19 57			20 08			20 27		20 38			20 57			21 08	
St Pancras International ⊖	a		19 35				19 48	20 01			20 13			20 31		20 43			21 01			21 13	

A To St Albans City
B From Dorking to London Victoria
C From Epsom to London Victoria
D To Bedford
E To London Victoria

Please refer to separate pages within this table for services operating between London and Bedford

At weekends please use local bus and tube services to travel to/from St Pancras International and London Bridge when no trains are operating. See local publicity for details of alternative routes and services that are available across central London

Table 52

Sundays until 24 June

Brighton, Gatwick Airport - South London

Network Diagram - see first Page of Table 52

		FC	FC ■	SE	FC	SN	FC	FC ■	SE	SN ◇■	FC	SN	FC	FC ■	SE	SN	FC	FC ■	SE	SN ◇■	SN	FC ■
			A		A	B		A		C	A	B		A		B		A		C	B	A
Brighton	d		20 15					20 45		21 04				21 15				21 45		22 04		22 15
Preston Park	d									21 07										22 07		
Hassocks	d		20 24					20 54		21 14				21 24				21 54		22 14		22 24
Burgess Hill	d		20 27					20 57		21 17				21 27				21 57		22 17		22 27
Wivelsfield	d									21 19										22 19		
Haywards Heath	d		20 33					21 03		21 25				21 33				22 03		22 25		22 33
Balcombe	d									21 30										22 30		
Three Bridges	d		20 42					21 12		21 36				21 42				22 12		22 36		22 42
Gatwick Airport ✈	d		20 47					21 17		21 41				21 47				22 17		22 41		22 47
Redhill	d									21 49										22 49		
East Croydon	d		21 02					21 32		22a00				22 02				22 32		23a00		23 02
Sutton (Surrey)	d	20 34			20 37	20 43	21 04				21 07	21 13	21 34			21 43	22 04				22 13	
West Sutton	d				20 40						21 10											
Sutton Common	d				20 42						21 12											
St Helier	d				20 45						21 15											
Morden South	d				20 47						21 17											
South Merton	d				20 49						21 19											
Wimbledon Chase	d				20 51						21 21											
Wimbledon	d				20 56						21 26											
Haydons Road	d				20 58						21 28											
Tooting	d				21 01						21 31											
Carshalton	d	20 37				20 46	21 07					21 16	21 37			21 46	22 07				22 16	
Hackbridge	d	20 39				20 48	21 09					21 18	21 39			21 48	22 09				22 18	
Mitcham Junction	d	20 42				20 52	21 12					21 22	21 42			21 52	22 12				22 22	
Mitcham Eastfields	d	20 45				20a55	21 15					21a25	21 45			21a55	22 15				22a25	
Streatham	d	20 49			21 06		21 19				21 36		21 49				22 19					
Tulse Hill	d	20 53			21 10		21 23				21 40		21 53				22 23					
London Bridge ⊖	a		21 15					21 45						22 15				22 45				23 15
	d		21 15					21 45						22 15				22 45				23 15
Sevenoaks	d			20 21					20 51						21 21				21 51			
Bat & Ball	d			20 24					20 54						21 24				21 54			
Otford	d			20 27					20 57						21 27				21 57			
Shoreham (Kent)	d			20 30					21 00						21 30				22 00			
Eynsford	d			20 34					21 04						21 34				22 04			
Swanley	d			20 39					21 09						21 39				22 09			
St Mary Cray	d			20 43					21 13						21 43				22 13			
Bickley	d			20 47					21 17						21 47				22 17			
Bromley South	d			20 50					21 20						21 50				22 20			
Shortlands	d			20 53					21 23						21 53				22 23			
Ravensbourne	d			20 55					21 25						21 55				22 25			
Beckenham Hill	d			20 57					21 27						21 57				22 27			
Bellingham	d			20 59					21 29						21 59				22 29			
Catford	d			21 02					21 32						22 02				22 32			
Crofton Park	d			21 04					21 34						22 04				22 34			
Nunhead	d			21 07					21 37						22 07				22 37			
Peckham Rye	d			21 09					21 39						22 09				22 39			
Denmark Hill	d			21 13					21 43						22 13				22 43			
Herne Hill	d	20 57			21 14		21 27				21 44		21 57				22 27					
Loughborough Jn.	d	21 00			21 17		21 30				21 47		22 00				22 30					
Elephant & Castle	d	21 04		21 19	21 22		21 34		21 49		21 52		22 04		22 19		22 34		22 49			
London Blackfriars ⊖	a	21 07	21 22	21 23	21 25		21 37	21 52	21 53		21 55		22 07	22 22	22 23		22 37	22 52	22 53			23 22
	d		21 22		21 33			21 52			22 03			22 22				22 52				23 22
City Thameslink	d																					
Farringdon ⊖	d		21 27		21 38			21 57			22 08			22 27				22 57				23 27
St Pancras International ⊖	a		21 31		21 43			22 01			22 13			22 31				23 01				23 31

A To Bedford
B From Dorking to London Victoria
C To London Victoria

Please refer to separate pages within this table for services operating between London and Bedford

At weekends please use local bus and tube services to travel to/from St Pancras International and London Bridge when no trains are operating. See local publicity for details of alternative routes and services that are available across central London

Brighton, Gatwick Airport - South London

Network Diagram - see first Page of Table 52

		SE	SN	FC	SN	SN	FC	SN	FC
				1	◇1		1		1
			A	B	C	A	B	A	B
Brighton 10	d			22 45	23 02		23 15		23 45
Preston Park	d				23 06				
Hassocks 4	d			22 54	23 12		23 24		23 54
Burgess Hill 4	d			22 57	23 16		23 27		23 57
Wivelsfield 4	d				23 18				
Haywards Heath 3	d			23 03	23 23		23 33		00 03
Balcombe	d				23 29				
Three Bridges 4	d			23 12	23 41		23 42		00 12
Gatwick Airport 10	d			23 17	23 46		23 47		00 17
Redhill	d				00 01				00 24
East Croydon	d			23 32	00a16		00 04		00 36
Sutton (Surrey) 4	d		22 43			23 13		23 43	
West Sutton	d								
Sutton Common	d								
St Helier	d								
Morden South	d								
South Merton	d								
Wimbledon Chase	d								
Wimbledon 6	d								
Haydons Road	d								
Tooting	d								
Carshalton	d		22 46			23 16		23 46	
Hackbridge	d		22 48			23 18		23 48	
Mitcham Junction	d		22 52			23 22		23 52	
Mitcham Eastfields	d		22a55			23a25		23a55	
Streatham 4	d								
Tulse Hill 3	d								
London Bridge 4	a			23 45			00 21		00 50
	d			23 45			00 22		00 51
Sevenoaks 4	d	22 21							
Bat & Ball	d	22 24							
Otford 4	d	22 27							
Shoreham (Kent)	d	22 30							
Eynsford	d	22 34							
Swanley 4	d	22 39							
St Mary Cray 4	d	22 43							
Bickley	d	22 47							
Bromley South	d	22 50							
Shortlands 4	d	22 53							
Ravensbourne	d	22 55							
Beckenham Hill	d	22 57							
Bellingham	d	22 59							
Catford	d	23 02							
Crofton Park	d	23 04							
Nunhead 4	d	23 07							
Peckham Rye 4	d	23 09							
Denmark Hill 4	d	23 13							
Herne Hill 4	d								
Loughborough Jn.	d								
Elephant & Castle	d	23 19							
London Blackfriars 3	a	23 23		23 52			00 27		00 57
	d			23 52			00 28		00 58
City Thameslink 3	d								
Farringdon 3	d			23 57			00 33		
St Pancras International 15	a			00 01			00 37		01 07

A From Dorking to London Victoria B To Bedford C To London Victoria

Please refer to separate pages within this table for services operating between London and Bedford

At weekends please use local bus and tube services to travel to/from St Pancras International and London Bridge when no trains are operating. See local publicity for details of alternative routes and services that are available across central London

Brighton, Gatwick Airport - South London

Network Diagram - see first Page of Table 52

		FC	SN	FC	FC	FC	FC	SN	FC	FC	FC	SE	FC	FC	SE	FC	FC	SN	SE	SE	FC	FC	SN
		1	◇1		1	1		◇1								1	1	◇1			1	1	◇1
		A	B	A	A	A	A	B	C	D	E	F	C	D	F	E	G	B	H	F	E	G	I
Brighton 10	d	22p33	23p02		23p11	23p37		03 50					05 45	05 45		06 11	06 15	06 19			06 44	06 45	07 00
Preston Park	d	22p37	23p06			23p41												06 22					07 03
Hassocks 4	d	22p43	23p12		23p20	23p47							05 54	05 54		06 20	06 24	06 29			06 53	06 54	07 10
Burgess Hill 4	d	22p47	23p16		23p23	23p51							05 57	05 57		06 26	06 27	06 32			06 56	06 57	07 13
Wivelsfield 4	d	22p49	23p19			23p53												06 34					07 15
Haywards Heath 3	d	22p54	23p24		23p29	23p59		04 26					06 03	06 03		06 32	06 33	06 39			07 02	07 03	07 20
Balcombe	d	22p59				00 04																	07 26
Three Bridges 4	d	23p12	23p47		23p38	00 10		04 58	05 12	05 12	05 12		06 12	06 12		06 41	06 42	06 48			07 11	07 12	07 32
Gatwick Airport 10	d	23p17	23p53		23p43	00 15		05 03	05 17	05 17	05 17		06 17	06 17		06 46	06 47	06 53			07 16	07 17	07 38
Redhill	d		00 03			00 23																	07 46
East Croydon	d	23p32	00a16		00 04	00 36		05a27	05 32	05 32	05 32		06 32	06 32		07 02	07 02	07a10			07 32	07 32	07a58
Sutton (Surrey) 4	d																						
West Sutton	d																						
Sutton Common	d																						
St Helier	d																						
Morden South	d																						
South Merton	d																						
Wimbledon Chase	d																						
Wimbledon 6	d																						
Haydons Road	d																						
Tooting	d																						
Carshalton	d																						
Hackbridge	d																						
Mitcham Junction	d																						
Mitcham Eastfields	d																						
Streatham 4	d																						
Tulse Hill 3	d																						
London Bridge 4	a	23p44			00 21	00 51										07 15	07 15				07 45	07 45	
	d	23p45			00 22	00 52										07 15	07 15				07 45	07 45	
Sevenoaks 4	d											05 32			06 02					06 32			
Bat & Ball	d											05 35			06 05					06 35			
Otford 4	d											05 38			06 08					06 38			
Shoreham (Kent)	d											05 41			06 11					06 41			
Eynsford	d											05 45			06 15					06 45			
Swanley 4	d											05 50			06 20					06 50			
St Mary Cray 4	d											05 54			06 24					06 54			
Bickley	d											05 58			06 28				06 47	06 58			
Bromley South	d											06 01			06 31				06 50	07 01			
Shortlands 4	d											06 04			06 34				06 53	07 04			
Ravensbourne	d											06 06			06 36				06 55	07 06			
Beckenham Hill	d											06 08			06 38				06 57	07 08			
Bellingham	d											06 10			06 40				06 59	07 10			
Catford	d											06 13			06 43				07 02	07 13			
Crofton Park	d											06 15			06 45				07 04	07 15			
Nunhead 4	d											06 18			06 48				07 07	07 18			
Peckham Rye 4	d											06 20			06 50				07 09	07 20			
Denmark Hill 4	d											06 24			06 54				07 13	07 24			
Herne Hill 4	d																						
Loughborough Jn.	d																						
Elephant & Castle	d											06 30			07 00				07 19	07 30			
London Blackfriars 3	a	23p52			00 28	00 58			05 59	05 59	05 59	06 34	06 59	06 59	07 04	07 22	07 22		07 23	07 34	07 52	07 52	
	d	23p52		00 08	00 28	00 58	01 29			05 59	05 59			06 59		07 22	07 22				07 52	07 52	
City Thameslink 3	d													07 02									
Farringdon 3	d	23p58		00 13	00 33					06 03						07 27	07 27				07 57	07 57	
St Pancras International 15	a	00 02		00 17	00 37	01 07	01 37			06 07	06 07			07 09		07 31	07 31				08 01	08 01	

A To Bedford
B To London Victoria
C from 1 July until 22 July, from 19 August until 9 September
D 29 July, 5 August, 12 August. To Bedford
E 16 September. To Bedford
F 29 July, 5 August, 12 August
G not 16 September. To Bedford
H from 1 July until 22 July, from 19 August until 16 September. From Orpington
I 16 September. To London Victoria

Please refer to separate pages within this table for services operating between London and Bedford

At weekends please use local bus and tube services to travel to/from St Pancras International and London Bridge when no trains are operating. See local publicity for details of alternative routes and services that are available across central London

Sundays
1 July to 16 September

Brighton, Gatwick Airport - South London

Network Diagram - see first Page of Table 52

		SN	SE	SE	FC	FC	SE	SN	SE	SN	FC	FC	SE	SN	SN	SN	SE	SN	FC	FC	SE	SN	SE
		◇■			■	■					■	■			◇■	◇■			■	■			
		A	B	C	D	E	F	G	C	H	D	E	F	G	I	A	C	H	D	E	F	G	C
Brighton	d	07 04			07 14	07 15					07 44	07 45			08 00	08 00			08 14	08 15			
Preston Park	d	07 07													08 03	08 03							
Hassocks	d	07 14			07 23	07 24					07 53	07 54			08 10	08 10			08 23	08 24			
Burgess Hill	d	07 17			07 26	07 27					07 56	07 57			08 13	08 13			08 26	08 27			
Wivelsfield	d	07 19													08 15	08 15							
Haywards Heath	d	07 25			07 32	07 33					08 02	08 03			08 20	08 25			08 32	08 33			
Balcombe	d	07 30													08 26	08 30							
Three Bridges	d	07 36			07 41	07 42					08 11	08 12			08 32	08 36			08 41	08 42			
Gatwick Airport	d	07 41			07 46	07 47					08 16	08 17			08 38	08 41			08 46	08 47			
Redhill	d	07 49													08 46	08 49							
East Croydon	d	08a00			08 01	08 02					08 32	08 32			08a58	09a00			09 01	09 02			
Sutton (Surrey)	d							07 28		07 43				07 58				08 13				08 28	
West Sutton	d																						
Sutton Common	d																						
St Helier	d																						
Morden South	d																						
South Merton	d																						
Wimbledon Chase	d																						
Wimbledon	d																						
Haydons Road	d																						
Tooting	d																						
Carshalton	d							07 31		07 46				08 01				08 16				08 31	
Hackbridge	d							07 33		07 48				08 03				08 18				08 33	
Mitcham Junction	d							07 37		07 52				08 07				08 22				08 37	
Mitcham Eastfields	d							07a40		07a55				08a10				08a25				08a40	
Streatham	d																						
Tulse Hill	d																						
London Bridge ⊖	a				08 15	08 15					08 45	08 45							09 15	09 15			
	d				08 15	08 15					08 45	08 45							09 15	09 15			
Sevenoaks	d			07 02			07 21		07 32				07 51				08 02				08 21		08 32
Bat & Ball	d			07 05			07 24		07 35				07 54				08 05				08 24		08 35
Otford	d			07 08			07 27		07 38				07 57				08 08				08 27		08 38
Shoreham (Kent)	d			07 11			07 30		07 41				08 00				08 11				08 30		08 41
Eynsford	d			07 15			07 34		07 45				08 04				08 15				08 34		08 45
Swanley	d			07 20			07 39		07 50				08 09				08 20				08 39		08 50
St Mary Cray	d			07 24			07 43		07 54				08 13				08 24				08 43		08 54
Bickley	d		07 17	07 28			07 47		07 58				08 17				08 28				08 47		08 58
Bromley South	d		07 20	07 31			07 50		08 01				08 20				08 31				08 50		09 01
Shortlands	d		07 23	07 34			07 53		08 04				08 23				08 34				08 53		09 04
Ravensbourne	d		07 25	07 36			07 55		08 06				08 25				08 36				08 55		09 06
Beckenham Hill	d		07 27	07 38			07 57		08 08				08 27				08 38				08 57		09 08
Bellingham	d		07 29	07 40			07 59		08 10				08 29				08 40				08 59		09 10
Catford	d		07 32	07 43			08 02		08 13				08 32				08 43				09 02		09 13
Crofton Park	d		07 34	07 45			08 04		08 15				08 34				08 45				09 04		09 15
Nunhead	d		07 37	07 48			08 07		08 18				08 37				08 48				09 07		09 18
Peckham Rye	d		07 39	07 50			08 09		08 20				08 39				08 50				09 09		09 20
Denmark Hill	d		07 43	07 54			08 13		08 24				08 43				08 54				09 13		09 24
Herne Hill	d																						
Loughborough Jn.	d																						
Elephant & Castle	d		07 49	08 00			08 19		08 30				08 49				09 00				09 19		09 30
London Blackfriars ⊖	a		07 53	08 04	08 22	08 22	08 23		08 34		08 52	08 52	08 53				09 04		09 22	09 22	09 23		09 34
	d				08 22	08 22					08 52	08 52							09 22	09 22			
City Thameslink	d																						
Farringdon ⊖	d				08 27	08 27					08 57	08 57							09 27	09 27			
St Pancras International ⊖	a				08 31	08 31					09 01	09 01							09 31	09 31			

A not 16 September. To London Victoria
B from 1 July until 22 July, from 19 August until 16 September. From Orpington
C 29 July, 5 August, 12 August
D 16 September. To Bedford
E not 16 September. To Bedford
F from 1 July until 22 July, from 19 August until 16 September
G From Epsom to London Victoria
H From Dorking to London Victoria
I 16 September. To London Victoria

Please refer to separate pages within this table for services operating between London and Bedford

At weekends please use local bus and tube services to travel to/from St Pancras International and London Bridge when no trains are operating. See local publicity for details of alternative routes and services that are available across central London

Sundays
1 July to 16 September

Brighton, Gatwick Airport - South London

Network Diagram - see first Page of Table 52

		SN	FC	FC	SE	SN	SE	SN	SN	FC	SN	SN	FC	FC	SE	FC	SE	SN	SN	FC	FC	FC
			■	■						■	◇■	◇■	■	■							■	■
		A	B	C	D	E	F	A	E	G	H	I	B	C	D	J	F	A	E		C	B
Brighton	d		08 44	08 45							09 00	09 00	09 14	09 15								09 44
Preston Park	d										09 03	09 03										
Hassocks	d		08 53	08 54							09 10	09 10	09 23	09 24								09 53
Burgess Hill	d		08 56	08 57							09 13	09 13	09 26	09 27								09 56
Wivelsfield	d										09 15	09 15										
Haywards Heath	d		09 02	09 03							09 20	09 25	09 32	09 33								10 02
Balcombe	d										09 26	09 30										
Three Bridges	d		09 11	09 12							09 32	09 36	09 41	09 42								10 11
Gatwick Airport	d		09 16	09 17							09 38	09 41	09 46	09 47								10 16
Redhill	d										09 46	09 49										
East Croydon	d		09 32	09 32						09 47	09a58	10a00	10 01	10 02							10 17	10 32
Sutton (Surrey)	d	08 43				08 58		09 13	09 28							09 37		09 43	09 58	10 04		
West Sutton	d															09 40						
Sutton Common	d															09 42						
St Helier	d															09 45						
Morden South	d															09 47						
South Merton	d															09 49						
Wimbledon Chase	d															09 51						
Wimbledon	d															09 56						
Haydons Road	d															09 58						
Tooting	d															10 01						
Carshalton	d	08 46				09 01		09 16	09 31									09 46	10 01	10 07		
Hackbridge	d	08 48				09 03		09 18	09 33									09 48	10 03	10 09		
Mitcham Junction	d	08 52				09 07		09 22	09 37									09 52	10 07	10 12		
Mitcham Eastfields	d	08a55				09a10		09a25	09a40									09a55	10a10	10 15		
Streatham	d															10 06				10 19		
Tulse Hill	d															10 10				10 23		
London Bridge ⊖	a		09 45	09 45						10 00			10 15	10 15							10 30	10 45
	d		09 45	09 45						10 00			10 15	10 15							10 30	10 45
Sevenoaks	d				08 51		09 02								09 21		09 32					
Bat & Ball	d				08 54		09 05								09 24		09 35					
Otford	d				08 57		09 08								09 27		09 38					
Shoreham (Kent)	d				09 00		09 11								09 30		09 41					
Eynsford	d				09 04		09 15								09 34		09 45					
Swanley	d				09 09		09 20								09 39		09 50					
St Mary Cray	d				09 13		09 24								09 43		09 54					
Bickley	d				09 17		09 28								09 47		09 58					
Bromley South	d				09 20		09 31								09 50		10 01					
Shortlands	d				09 23		09 34								09 53		10 04					
Ravensbourne	d				09 25		09 36								09 55		10 06					
Beckenham Hill	d				09 27		09 38								09 57		10 08					
Bellingham	d				09 29		09 40								09 59		10 10					
Catford	d				09 32		09 43								10 02		10 13					
Crofton Park	d				09 34		09 45								10 04		10 15					
Nunhead	d				09 37		09 48								10 07		10 18					
Peckham Rye	d				09 39		09 50								10 09		10 20					
Denmark Hill	d				09 43		09 54								10 13		10 24					
Herne Hill	d															10 14				10 27		
Loughborough Jn.	d															10 17				10 30		
Elephant & Castle	d				09 49		10 00								10 19	10 22	10 30			10 34		
London Blackfriars ⊖	a		09 52	09 52	09 53		10 04			10 07			10 22	10 22	10 23	10 25	10 34			10 37	10 37	10 52
	d		09 52	09 52						10 10			10 22	10 22		10 26					10 40	10 52
City Thameslink	d																					
Farringdon ⊖	d		09 57	09 57						10 14			10 27	10 27		10 31					10 44	10 57
St Pancras International ⊖	a		10 01	10 01						10 18			10 31	10 31		10 35					10 48	11 01

A From Dorking to London Victoria
B 16 September. To Bedford
C not 16 September. To Bedford
D from 1 July until 22 July, from 19 August until 16 September
E From Epsom to London Victoria
F 29 July, 5 August, 12 August
G not 16 September. To St Albans City
H 16 September. To London Victoria
I not 16 September. To London Victoria
J To Luton

Please refer to separate pages within this table for services operating between London and Bedford

At weekends please use local bus and tube services to travel to/from St Pancras International and London Bridge when no trains are operating. See local publicity for details of alternative routes and services that are available across central London

1 July to 16 September

Brighton, Gatwick Airport - South London

Network Diagram - see first Page of Table 52

		FC A	SE B	FC C	SE D	SN E	SN F	FC	FC G	SN H	SN I	FC J	FC A	SE B	FC C	SE D	SN E	SN F	FC	FC G	FC J	FC A	SE B
Brighton	d	09 45								10 00	10 00	10 14	10 15								10 44	10 45	
Preston Park	d									10 03	10 03												
Hassocks	d	09 54								10 10	10 10	10 23	10 24								10 53	10 54	
Burgess Hill	d	09 57								10 13	10 13	10 26	10 27								10 56	10 57	
Wivelsfield	d									10 15	10 15												
Haywards Heath	d	10 03								10 20	10 25	10 32	10 33								11 02	11 03	
Balcombe	d									10 26	10 30												
Three Bridges	d	10 12								10 32	10 36	10 41	10 42								11 11	11 12	
Gatwick Airport	d	10 17								10 38	10 41	10 46	10 47								11 16	11 17	
Redhill	d									10 46	10 49												
East Croydon	d	10 32							10 47	10a58	11a00	11 01	11 02							11 17	11 32	11 32	
Sutton (Surrey)	d			10 07		10 13	10 28	10 34							10 37		10 43	10 58	11 04				
West Sutton	d			10 10											10 40								
Sutton Common	d			10 12											10 42								
St Helier	d			10 15											10 45								
Morden South	d			10 17											10 47								
South Merton	d			10 19											10 49								
Wimbledon Chase	d			10 21											10 51								
Wimbledon	d			10 26											10 56								
Haydons Road	d			10 28											10 58								
Tooting	d			10 31											11 01								
Carshalton	d					10 16	10 31	10 37									10 46	11 01	11 07				
Hackbridge	d					10 18	10 33	10 39									10 48	11 03	11 09				
Mitcham Junction	d					10 22	10 37	10 42									10 52	11 07	11 12				
Mitcham Eastfields	d					10a25	10a40	10 45									10a55	11a10	11 15				
Streatham	d			10 36				10 49							11 06				11 19				
Tulse Hill	d			10 40				10 53							11 10				11 23				
London Bridge	a	10 45							11 00			11 15	11 15							11 30	11 45	11 45	
	d	10 45							11 00			11 15	11 15							11 30	11 45	11 45	
Sevenoaks	d		09 51		10 02									10 21		10 32							10 51
Bat & Ball	d		09 54		10 05									10 24		10 35							10 54
Otford	d		09 57		10 08									10 27		10 38							10 57
Shoreham (Kent)	d		10 00		10 11									10 30		10 41							11 00
Eynsford	d		10 04		10 15									10 34		10 45							11 04
Swanley	d		10 09		10 20									10 39		10 50							11 09
St Mary Cray	d		10 13		10 24									10 43		10 54							11 13
Bickley	d		10 17		10 28									10 47		10 58							11 17
Bromley South	d		10 20		10 31									10 50		11 01							11 20
Shortlands	d		10 23		10 34									10 53		11 04							11 23
Ravensbourne	d		10 25		10 36									10 55		11 06							11 25
Beckenham Hill	d		10 27		10 38									10 57		11 08							11 27
Bellingham	d		10 29		10 40									10 59		11 10							11 29
Catford	d		10 32		10 43									11 02		11 13							11 32
Crofton Park	d		10 34		10 45									11 04		11 15							11 34
Nunhead	d		10 37		10 48									11 07		11 18							11 37
Peckham Rye	d		10 39		10 50									11 09		11 20							11 39
Denmark Hill	d		10 43		10 54									11 13		11 24							11 43
Herne Hill	d			10 44				10 57							11 14				11 27				
Loughborough Jn.	d			10 47				11 00							11 17				11 30				
Elephant & Castle	d		10 49	10 52	11 00			11 04						11 19	11 22	11 30			11 34				11 49
London Blackfriars	a	10 52	10 53	10 55	11 04			11 07	11 07			11 22	11 22	11 23	11 25	11 34			11 37	11 37	11 52	11 52	11 53
	d	10 52		10 56					11 10			11 22	11 22		11 26					11 40	11 52	11 52	
City Thameslink	d																						
Farringdon	d	10 57		11 01					11 14			11 27	11 27		11 31					11 44	11 57	11 57	
St Pancras International	a	11 01		11 05					11 18			11 31	11 31		11 35					11 48	12 01	12 01	

A not 16 September. To Bedford
B from 1 July until 22 July, from 19 August until 16 September
C To Luton
D 29 July, 5 August, 12 August
E From Dorking to London Victoria
F From Epsom to London Victoria
G To Bedford
H 16 September. To London Victoria
I not 16 September. To London Victoria
J 16 September. To Bedford

Please refer to separate pages within this table for services operating between London and Bedford

At weekends please use local bus and tube services to travel to/from St Pancras International and London Bridge when no trains are operating. See local publicity for details of alternative routes and services that are available across central London

1 July to 16 September

Brighton, Gatwick Airport - South London

Network Diagram - see first Page of Table 52

		FC A	SE B	SN C	SN D	FC	FC E	SN F	SN G	FC H	FC I	SE J	FC A	SE B	SN C	SN D	FC	FC E	FC H	FC I	SE J	FC A
Brighton	d							11 00	11 00	11 14	11 15								11 44	11 45		
Preston Park	d							11 03	11 03													
Hassocks	d							11 10	11 10	11 23	11 24								11 53	11 54		
Burgess Hill	d							11 13	11 13	11 26	11 27								11 56	11 57		
Wivelsfield	d							11 15	11 15													
Haywards Heath	d							11 20	11 25	11 32	11 33								12 02	12 03		
Balcombe	d							11 26	11 30													
Three Bridges	d							11 32	11 36	11 41	11 42								12 11	12 12		
Gatwick Airport	d							11 38	11 41	11 46	11 47								12 16	12 17		
Redhill	d							11 46	11 49													
East Croydon	d						11 47	11a58	12a00	12 01	12 02							12 17	12 32	12 32		
Sutton (Surrey)	d	11 07		11 13	11 28	11 34							11 37		11 43	11 58	12 04					12 07
West Sutton	d	11 10											11 40									12 10
Sutton Common	d	11 12											11 42									12 12
St Helier	d	11 15											11 45									12 15
Morden South	d	11 17											11 47									12 17
South Merton	d	11 19											11 49									12 19
Wimbledon Chase	d	11 21											11 51									12 21
Wimbledon	d	11 26											11 56									12 26
Haydons Road	d	11 28											11 58									12 28
Tooting	d	11 31											12 01									12 31
Carshalton	d			11 16	11 31	11 37									11 46	12 01	12 07					
Hackbridge	d			11 18	11 33	11 39									11 48	12 03	12 09					
Mitcham Junction	d			11 22	11 37	11 42									11 52	12 07	12 12					
Mitcham Eastfields	d			11a25	11a40	11 45									11a55	12a10	12 15					
Streatham	d	11 36				11 49							12 06				12 19					12 36
Tulse Hill	d	11 40				11 53							12 10				12 23					12 40
London Bridge	a						12 00			12 15	12 15							12 30	12 45	12 45		
	d						12 00			12 15	12 15							12 30	12 45	12 45		
Sevenoaks	d		11 02									11 21		11 32							11 51	
Bat & Ball	d		11 05									11 24		11 35							11 54	
Otford	d		11 08									11 27		11 38							11 57	
Shoreham (Kent)	d		11 11									11 30		11 41							12 00	
Eynsford	d		11 15									11 34		11 45							12 04	
Swanley	d		11 20									11 39		11 50							12 09	
St Mary Cray	d		11 24									11 43		11 54							12 13	
Bickley	d		11 28									11 47		11 58							12 17	
Bromley South	d		11 31									11 50		12 01							12 20	
Shortlands	d		11 34									11 53		12 04							12 23	
Ravensbourne	d		11 36									11 55		12 06							12 25	
Beckenham Hill	d		11 38									11 57		12 08							12 27	
Bellingham	d		11 40									11 59		12 10							12 29	
Catford	d		11 43									12 02		12 13							12 32	
Crofton Park	d		11 45									12 04		12 15							12 34	
Nunhead	d		11 48									12 07		12 18							12 37	
Peckham Rye	d		11 50									12 09		12 20							12 39	
Denmark Hill	d		11 54									12 13		12 24							12 43	
Herne Hill	d	11 44				11 57							12 14				12 27					12 44
Loughborough Jn.	d	11 47				12 00							12 17				12 30					12 47
Elephant & Castle	d	11 52	12 00			12 04						12 19	12 22	12 30			12 34				12 49	12 52
London Blackfriars	a	11 55	12 04			12 07	12 07			12 22	12 22	12 23	12 25	12 34			12 37	12 37	12 52	12 52	12 53	12 55
	d	11 56					12 10			12 22	12 22		12 26					12 40	12 52	12 52		12 56
City Thameslink	d																					
Farringdon	d	12 01					12 14			12 27	12 27		12 31					12 44	12 57	12 57		13 01
St Pancras International	a	12 05					12 18			12 31	12 31		12 35					12 48	13 01	13 01		13 05

A To Luton
B 29 July, 5 August, 12 August
C From Dorking to London Victoria
D From Epsom to London Victoria
E To Bedford
F 16 September. To London Victoria
G not 16 September. To London Victoria
H 16 September. To Bedford
I not 16 September. To Bedford
J from 1 July until 22 July, from 19 August until 16 September

Please refer to separate pages within this table for services operating between London and Bedford

At weekends please use local bus and tube services to travel to/from St Pancras International and London Bridge when no trains are operating. See local publicity for details of alternative routes and services that are available across central London

Table 52

Sundays

1 July to 16 September

Brighton, Gatwick Airport - South London

Network Diagram - see first Page of Table 52

		SE A	SN B	SN C	FC	FC ■ D	SN ◇■ E	SN ◇■ F	FC ■ G	FC ■ H	SE I	FC J	SE A	SN B	SN C	FC	FC ■ D	FC ■ G	FC ■ H	SE I	FC J	SE A	SN B
Brighton	d						12 00	12 00	12 14	12 15								12 44	12 45				
Preston Park	d						12 03	12 03															
Hassocks	d						12 10	12 10	12 23	12 24								12 53	12 54				
Burgess Hill	d						12 13	12 13	12 26	12 27								12 56	12 57				
Wivelsfield	d						12 15	12 15															
Haywards Heath	d						12 20	12 25	12 32	12 33								13 02	13 03				
Balcombe	d						12 26	12 30															
Three Bridges	d						12 32	12 36	12 41	12 42								13 11	13 12				
Gatwick Airport ✈	d						12 38	12 41	12 46	12 47								13 16	13 17				
Redhill	d						12 46	12 49															
East Croydon	d					12 47	12a58	13a00	13 01	13 02							13 17	13 32	13 32				
Sutton (Surrey)	d		12 13	12 28	12 34							12 37		12 43	12 58	13 04					13 07		13 13
West Sutton	d											12 40									13 10		
Sutton Common	d											12 42									13 12		
St Helier	d											12 45									13 15		
Morden South	d											12 47									13 17		
South Merton	d											12 49									13 19		
Wimbledon Chase	d											12 51									13 21		
Wimbledon	d											12 56									13 26		
Haydons Road	d											12 58									13 28		
Tooting	d											13 01									13 31		
Carshalton	d		12 16	12 31	12 37									12 46	13 01	13 07							13 16
Hackbridge	d		12 18	12 33	12 39									12 48	13 03	13 09							13 18
Mitcham Junction	d		12 22	12 37	12 42									12 52	13 07	13 12							13 22
Mitcham Eastfields	d		12a25	12a40	12 45									12a55	13a10	13 15							13a25
Streatham	d				12 49							13 06				13 19					13 36		
Tulse Hill	d				12 53							13 10				13 23					13 40		
London Bridge ⊖	a					13 00			13 15	13 15							13 30	13 45	13 45				
	d					13 00			13 15	13 15							13 30	13 45	13 45				
Sevenoaks	d	12 02									12 21		12 32							12 51		13 02	
Bat & Ball	d	12 05									12 24		12 35							12 54		13 05	
Otford	d	12 08									12 27		12 38							12 57		13 08	
Shoreham (Kent)	d	12 11									12 30		12 41							13 00		13 11	
Eynsford	d	12 15									12 34		12 45							13 04		13 15	
Swanley	d	12 20									12 39		12 50							13 09		13 20	
St Mary Cray	d	12 24									12 43		12 54							13 13		13 24	
Bickley	d	12 28									12 47		12 58							13 17		13 28	
Bromley South	d	12 31									12 50		13 01							13 20		13 31	
Shortlands	d	12 34									12 53		13 04							13 23		13 34	
Ravensbourne	d	12 36									12 55		13 06							13 25		13 36	
Beckenham Hill	d	12 38									12 57		13 08							13 27		13 38	
Bellingham	d	12 40									12 59		13 10							13 29		13 40	
Catford	d	12 43									13 02		13 13							13 32		13 43	
Crofton Park	d	12 45									13 04		13 15							13 34		13 45	
Nunhead	d	12 48									13 07		13 18							13 37		13 48	
Peckham Rye	d	12 50									13 09		13 20							13 39		13 50	
Denmark Hill	d	12 54									13 13		13 24							13 43		13 54	
Herne Hill	d				12 57							13 14				13 27					13 44		
Loughborough Jn.	d				13 00							13 17				13 30					13 47		
Elephant & Castle	d	13 00			13 04						13 19	13 22	13 30			13 34				13 49	13 52	14 00	
London Blackfriars ⊖	a	13 04			13 07	13 07			13 22	13 22	13 23	13 25	13 34			13 37	13 37	13 52	13 52	13 53	13 55	14 04	
	d					13 10			13 22	13 22		13 26					13 40	13 52	13 52		13 56		
City Thameslink	d																						
Farringdon ⊖	d					13 14			13 27	13 27		13 31					13 44	13 57	13 57		14 01		
St Pancras International ⊖	a					13 18			13 31	13 31		13 35					13 48	14 01	14 01		14 05		

A 29 July, 5 August, 12 August
B From Dorking to London Victoria
C From Epsom to London Victoria
D To Bedford
E 16 September. To London Victoria
F not 16 September. To London Victoria
G 16 September. To Bedford
H not 16 September. To Bedford
I from 1 July until 22 July, from 19 August until 16 September
J To Luton

Please refer to separate pages within this table for services operating between London and Bedford

At weekends please use local bus and tube services to travel to/from St Pancras International and London Bridge when no trains are operating. See local publicity for details of alternative routes and services that are available across central London

Table 52

Sundays

1 July to 16 September

Brighton, Gatwick Airport - South London

Network Diagram - see first Page of Table 52

		SN A	FC	FC ■ B	SN ◇■ C	SN ◇■ D	FC ■ E	FC ■ F	SE G	FC H	SE I	SN J	SN A	FC	FC ■ B	FC ■ E	FC ■ F	SE G	FC H	SE I	SN J	SN A	FC
Brighton	d				13 00	13 00	13 14	13 15								13 44	13 45						
Preston Park	d				13 03	13 03																	
Hassocks	d				13 10	13 10	13 23	13 24								13 53	13 54						
Burgess Hill	d				13 13	13 13	13 26	13 27								13 56	13 57						
Wivelsfield	d				13 15	13 15																	
Haywards Heath	d				13 20	13 25	13 32	13 33								14 02	14 03						
Balcombe	d				13 26	13 30																	
Three Bridges	d				13 32	13 36	13 41	13 42								14 11	14 12						
Gatwick Airport ✈	d				13 38	13 41	13 46	13 47								14 16	14 17						
Redhill	d				13 46	13 49																	
East Croydon	d			13 47	13a58	14a00	14 01	14 02							14 17	14 32	14 32						
Sutton (Surrey)	d	13 28	13 34							13 37		13 43	13 58	14 04					14 07		14 13	14 28	14 34
West Sutton	d									13 40									14 10				
Sutton Common	d									13 42									14 12				
St Helier	d									13 45									14 15				
Morden South	d									13 47									14 17				
South Merton	d									13 49									14 19				
Wimbledon Chase	d									13 51									14 21				
Wimbledon	d									13 56									14 26				
Haydons Road	d									13 58									14 28				
Tooting	d									14 01									14 31				
Carshalton	d	13 31	13 37									13 46	14 01	14 07							14 16	14 31	14 37
Hackbridge	d	13 33	13 39									13 48	14 03	14 09							14 18	14 33	14 39
Mitcham Junction	d	13 37	13 42									13 52	14 07	14 12							14 22	14 37	14 42
Mitcham Eastfields	d	13a40	13 45									13a55	14a10	14 15							14a25	14a40	14 45
Streatham	d		13 49							14 06				14 19					14 36				14 49
Tulse Hill	d		13 53							14 10				14 23					14 40				14 53
London Bridge ⊖	a			14 00			14 15	14 15							14 30	14 45	14 45						
	d			14 00			14 15	14 15							14 30	14 45	14 45						
Sevenoaks	d								13 21		13 32							13 51		14 02			
Bat & Ball	d								13 24		13 35							13 54		14 05			
Otford	d								13 27		13 38							13 57		14 08			
Shoreham (Kent)	d								13 30		13 41							14 00		14 11			
Eynsford	d								13 34		13 45							14 04		14 15			
Swanley	d								13 39		13 50							14 09		14 20			
St Mary Cray	d								13 43		13 54							14 13		14 24			
Bickley	d								13 47		13 58							14 17		14 28			
Bromley South	d								13 50		14 01							14 20		14 31			
Shortlands	d								13 53		14 04							14 23		14 34			
Ravensbourne	d								13 55		14 06							14 25		14 36			
Beckenham Hill	d								13 57		14 08							14 27		14 38			
Bellingham	d								13 59		14 10							14 29		14 40			
Catford	d								14 02		14 13							14 32		14 43			
Crofton Park	d								14 04		14 15							14 34		14 45			
Nunhead	d								14 07		14 18							14 37		14 48			
Peckham Rye	d								14 09		14 20							14 39		14 50			
Denmark Hill	d								14 13		14 24							14 43		14 54			
Herne Hill	d		13 57							14 14				14 27					14 44				14 57
Loughborough Jn.	d		14 00							14 17				14 30					14 47				15 00
Elephant & Castle	d		14 04						14 19	14 22	14 30			14 34				14 49	14 52	15 00			15 04
London Blackfriars ⊖	a		14 07	14 07			14 22	14 22	14 23	14 25	14 34			14 37	14 37	14 52	14 52	14 53	14 55	15 04			15 07
	d			14 10			14 22	14 22		14 26					14 40	14 52	14 52		14 56				
City Thameslink	d																						
Farringdon ⊖	d			14 14			14 27	14 27		14 31					14 44	14 57	14 57		15 01				
St Pancras International ⊖	a			14 18			14 31	14 31		14 35					14 48	15 01	15 01		15 05				

A From Epsom to London Victoria
B To Bedford
C 16 September. To London Victoria
D not 16 September. To London Victoria
E 16 September. To Bedford
F not 16 September. To Bedford
G from 1 July until 22 July, from 19 August until 16 September
H To Luton
I 29 July, 5 August, 12 August
J From Dorking to London Victoria

Please refer to separate pages within this table for services operating between London and Bedford

At weekends please use local bus and tube services to travel to/from St Pancras International and London Bridge when no trains are operating. See local publicity for details of alternative routes and services that are available across central London

Brighton, Gatwick Airport - South London

Network Diagram - see first Page of Table 52

Station		FC A	SN B	SN C	FC D	FC E	SE F	FC G	SE H	SN I	SN J	FC	FC A	FC D	FC E	SE F	FC G	SE H	SN I	SN J	FC	FC A
Brighton	d		14 00	14 00	14 14	14 15								14 44	14 45							
Preston Park	d		14 03	14 03																		
Hassocks	d		14 10	14 10	14 23	14 24								14 53	14 54							
Burgess Hill	d		14 13	14 13	14 26	14 27								14 56	14 57							
Wivelsfield	d		14 15	14 15																		
Haywards Heath	d		14 20	14 25	14 32	14 33								15 02	15 03							
Balcombe	d		14 26	14 30																		
Three Bridges	d		14 32	14 36	14 41	14 42								15 11	15 12							
Gatwick Airport ✈	d		14 38	14 41	14 46	14 47								15 16	15 17							
Redhill	d		14 46	14 49																		
East Croydon	d	14 47	14a58	15a00	15 01	15 02							15 17	15 32	15 32							15 47
Sutton (Surrey)	d							14 37		14 43	14 58	15 04					15 07		15 13	15 28	15 34	
West Sutton	d							14 40									15 10					
Sutton Common	d							14 42									15 12					
St Helier	d							14 45									15 15					
Morden South	d							14 47									15 17					
South Merton	d							14 49									15 19					
Wimbledon Chase	d							14 51									15 21					
Wimbledon	d							14 56									15 26					
Haydons Road	d							14 58									15 28					
Tooting	d							15 01									15 31					
Carshalton	d									14 46	15 01	15 07							15 16	15 31	15 37	
Hackbridge	d									14 48	15 03	15 09							15 18	15 33	15 39	
Mitcham Junction	d									14 52	15 07	15 12							15 22	15 37	15 42	
Mitcham Eastfields	d									14a55	15a10	15 15							15a25	15a40	15 45	
Streatham	d							15 06				15 19					15 36				15 49	
Tulse Hill	d							15 10				15 23					15 40				15 53	
London Bridge ⊖	a	15 00			15 15	15 15							15 30	15 45	15 45							16 00
	d	15 00			15 15	15 15							15 30	15 45	15 45							16 00
Sevenoaks	d						14 21		14 32							14 51		15 02				
Bat & Ball	d						14 24		14 35							14 54		15 05				
Otford	d						14 27		14 38							14 57		15 08				
Shoreham (Kent)	d						14 30		14 41							15 00		15 11				
Eynsford	d						14 34		14 45							15 04		15 15				
Swanley	d						14 39		14 50							15 09		15 20				
St Mary Cray	d						14 43		14 54							15 13		15 24				
Bickley	d						14 47		14 58							15 17		15 28				
Bromley South	d						14 50		15 01							15 20		15 31				
Shortlands	d						14 53		15 04							15 23		15 34				
Ravensbourne	d						14 55		15 06							15 25		15 36				
Beckenham Hill	d						14 57		15 08							15 27		15 38				
Bellingham	d						14 59		15 10							15 29		15 40				
Catford	d						15 02		15 13							15 32		15 43				
Crofton Park	d						15 04		15 15							15 34		15 45				
Nunhead	d						15 07		15 18							15 37		15 48				
Peckham Rye	d						15 09		15 20							15 39		15 50				
Denmark Hill	d						15 13		15 24							15 43		15 54				
Herne Hill	d							15 14				15 27					15 44				15 57	
Loughborough Jn.	d							15 17				15 30					15 47				16 00	
Elephant & Castle	d						15 19	15 22	15 30			15 34				15 49	15 52	16 00			16 04	
London Blackfriars ⊖	a	15 07			15 22	15 22	15 23	15 25	15 34			15 37	15 37	15 52	15 52	15 53	15 55	16 04			16 07	16 07
	d	15 10			15 22	15 22		15 26					15 40	15 52	15 52		15 56					16 10
City Thameslink	d																					
Farringdon ⊖	d	15 14			15 27	15 27		15 31					15 44	15 57	15 57		16 01					16 14
St Pancras International ⊖	a	15 18			15 31	15 31		15 35					15 48	16 01	16 01		16 05					16 18

A To Bedford
B 16 September. To London Victoria
C not 16 September. To London Victoria
D 16 September. To Bedford
E not 16 September. To Bedford
F from 1 July until 22 July, from 19 August until 16 September
G To Luton
H 29 July, 5 August, 12 August
I From Dorking to London Victoria
J From Epsom to London Victoria

Please refer to separate pages within this table for services operating between London and Bedford

At weekends please use local bus and tube services to travel to/from St Pancras International and London Bridge when no trains are operating. See local publicity for details of alternative routes and services that are available across central London

Brighton, Gatwick Airport - South London

Network Diagram - see first Page of Table 52

Station		SN A	SN B	FC C	FC D	SE E	FC F	SE G	SN H	SN I	FC	FC J	FC C	FC D	SE E	FC F	SE G	SN H	SN I	FC	FC J	SN A	SN B
Brighton	d	15 00	15 00	15 14	15 15								15 44	15 45								16 00	16 00
Preston Park	d	15 03	15 03																			16 03	16 03
Hassocks	d	15 10	15 10	15 23	15 24								15 53	15 54								16 10	16 10
Burgess Hill	d	15 13	15 13	15 26	15 27								15 56	15 57								16 13	16 13
Wivelsfield	d	15 15	15 15																			16 15	16 15
Haywards Heath	d	15 20	15 25	15 32	15 33								16 02	16 03								16 20	16 25
Balcombe	d	15 26	15 30																			16 26	16 30
Three Bridges	d	15 32	15 36	15 41	15 42								16 11	16 12								16 32	16 36
Gatwick Airport ✈	d	15 38	15 41	15 46	15 47								16 16	16 17								16 38	16 41
Redhill	d	15 46	15 49																			16 46	16 49
East Croydon	d	15a58	16a00	16 01	16 02							16 17	16 32	16 32							16 47	16a58	17a00
Sutton (Surrey)	d						15 37		15 43	15 58	16 04					16 07		16 13	16 28	16 34			
West Sutton	d						15 40									16 10							
Sutton Common	d						15 42									16 12							
St Helier	d						15 45									16 15							
Morden South	d						15 47									16 17							
South Merton	d						15 49									16 19							
Wimbledon Chase	d						15 51									16 21							
Wimbledon	d						15 56									16 26							
Haydons Road	d						15 58									16 28							
Tooting	d						16 01									16 31							
Carshalton	d								15 46	16 01	16 07							16 16	16 31	16 37			
Hackbridge	d								15 48	16 03	16 09							16 18	16 33	16 39			
Mitcham Junction	d								15 52	16 07	16 12							16 22	16 37	16 42			
Mitcham Eastfields	d								15a55	16a10	16 15							16a25	16a40	16 45			
Streatham	d						16 06				16 19					16 36				16 49			
Tulse Hill	d						16 10				16 23					16 40				16 53			
London Bridge ⊖	a			16 15	16 15							16 30	16 45	16 45							17 00		
	d			16 15	16 15							16 30	16 45	16 45							17 00		
Sevenoaks	d					15 21		15 32							15 51		16 02						
Bat & Ball	d					15 24		15 35							15 54		16 05						
Otford	d					15 27		15 38							15 57		16 08						
Shoreham (Kent)	d					15 30		15 41							16 00		16 11						
Eynsford	d					15 34		15 45							16 04		16 15						
Swanley	d					15 39		15 50							16 09		16 20						
St Mary Cray	d					15 43		15 54							16 13		16 24						
Bickley	d					15 47		15 58							16 17		16 28						
Bromley South	d					15 50		16 01							16 20		16 31						
Shortlands	d					15 53		16 04							16 23		16 34						
Ravensbourne	d					15 55		16 06							16 25		16 36						
Beckenham Hill	d					15 57		16 08							16 27		16 38						
Bellingham	d					15 59		16 10							16 29		16 40						
Catford	d					16 02		16 13							16 32		16 43						
Crofton Park	d					16 04		16 15							16 34		16 45						
Nunhead	d					16 07		16 18							16 37		16 48						
Peckham Rye	d					16 09		16 20							16 39		16 50						
Denmark Hill	d					16 13		16 24							16 43		16 54						
Herne Hill	d						16 14				16 27					16 44				16 57			
Loughborough Jn.	d						16 17				16 30					16 47				17 00			
Elephant & Castle	d					16 19	16 22	16 30			16 34				16 49	16 52	17 00			17 04			
London Blackfriars ⊖	a			16 22	16 22	16 23	16 25	16 34			16 37	16 37	16 52	16 52	16 53	16 55	17 04			17 07	17 07		
	d			16 22	16 22		16 26					16 40	16 52	16 52		16 56					17 10		
City Thameslink	d																						
Farringdon ⊖	d			16 27	16 27		16 31					16 44	16 57	16 57		17 01					17 14		
St Pancras International ⊖	a			16 31	16 31		16 35					16 48	17 01	17 01		17 05					17 18		

A 16 September. To London Victoria
B not 16 September. To London Victoria
C 16 September. To Bedford
D not 16 September. To Bedford
E from 1 July until 22 July, from 19 August until 16 September
F To Luton
G 29 July, 5 August, 12 August
H From Dorking to London Victoria
I From Epsom to London Victoria
J To Bedford

Please refer to separate pages within this table for services operating between London and Bedford

At weekends please use local bus and tube services to travel to/from St Pancras International and London Bridge when no trains are operating. See local publicity for details of alternative routes and services that are available across central London

Table 52

Sundays

1 July to 16 September

Brighton, Gatwick Airport - South London

Network Diagram - see first Page of Table 52

		FC	FC	SE	FC	SE	SN	SN	FC	FC	FC	FC	SE	FC	SE	SN	SN	FC	FC	SN	SN	FC
		■	■							■	■	■							■	◇■	◇■	■
		A	B	C	D	E	F	G		H	A	B	C	D	E	F	G		H	I	J	A
Brighton ■	d	16 14	16 15								16 44	16 45								17 00	17 00	17 14
Preston Park	d																			17 03	17 03	
Hassocks ■	d	16 23	16 24								16 53	16 54								17 10	17 10	17 23
Burgess Hill ■	d	16 26	16 27								16 56	16 57								17 13	17 13	17 26
Wivelsfield ■	d																			17 15	17 15	
Haywards Heath ■	d	16 32	16 33								17 02	17 03								17 20	17 25	17 32
Balcombe	d																			17 26	17 30	
Three Bridges ■	d	16 41	16 42								17 11	17 12								17 32	17 36	17 41
Gatwick Airport ■ ✈	d	16 46	16 47								17 16	17 17								17 38	17 41	17 46
Redhill	d																			17 46	17 49	
East Croydon	d	17 01	17 02							17 17	17 32	17 32							17 47	17a58	18a00	18 01
Sutton (Surrey) ■	d				16 37		16 43	16 58	17 04					17 07		17 13	17 28	17 34				
West Sutton	d				16 40									17 10								
Sutton Common	d				16 42									17 12								
St Helier	d				16 45									17 15								
Morden South	d				16 47									17 17								
South Merton	d				16 49									17 19								
Wimbledon Chase	d				16 51									17 21								
Wimbledon ■	d				16 56									17 26								
Haydons Road	d				16 58									17 28								
Tooting	d				17 01									17 31								
Carshalton	d						16 46	17 01	17 07							17 16	17 31	17 37				
Hackbridge	d						16 48	17 03	17 09							17 18	17 33	17 39				
Mitcham Junction	d						16 52	17 07	17 12							17 22	17 37	17 42				
Mitcham Eastfields	d						16a55	17a10	17 15							17a25	17a40	17 45				
Streatham ■	d				17 06				17 19					17 36				17 49				
Tulse Hill ■	d				17 10				17 23					17 40				17 53				
London Bridge ■ ⊖	a	17 15	17 15							17 30	17 45	17 45							18 00			18 15
	d	17 15	17 15							17 30	17 45	17 45							18 00			18 15
Sevenoaks ■	d			16 21		16 32							16 51		17 02							
Bat & Ball	d			16 24		16 35							16 54		17 05							
Otford ■	d			16 27		16 38							16 57		17 08							
Shoreham (Kent)	d			16 30		16 41							17 00		17 11							
Eynsford	d			16 34		16 45							17 04		17 15							
Swanley ■	d			16 39		16 50							17 09		17 20							
St Mary Cray ■	d			16 43		16 54							17 13		17 24							
Bickley	d			16 47		16 58							17 17		17 28							
Bromley South	d			16 50		17 01							17 20		17 31							
Shortlands ■	d			16 53		17 04							17 23		17 34							
Ravensbourne	d			16 55		17 06							17 25		17 36							
Beckenham Hill	d			16 57		17 08							17 27		17 38							
Bellingham	d			16 59		17 10							17 29		17 40							
Catford	d			17 02		17 13							17 32		17 43							
Crofton Park	d			17 04		17 15							17 34		17 45							
Nunhead ■	d			17 07		17 18							17 37		17 48							
Peckham Rye ■	d			17 09		17 20							17 39		17 50							
Denmark Hill ■	d			17 13		17 24							17 43		17 54							
Herne Hill ■	d				17 14				17 27					17 44				17 57				
Loughborough Jn	d				17 17				17 30					17 47				18 00				
Elephant & Castle	d			17 19	17 22	17 30			17 34				17 49	17 52	18 00			18 04				
London Blackfriars ■ ⊖	a	17 22	17 22	17 23	17 25	17 34			17 37	17 37	17 52	17 52	17 53	17 55	18 04			18 07	18 07			18 22
	d	17 22	17 22		17 26					17 40	17 52	17 52		17 56					18 10			18 22
City Thameslink ■	d																					
Farringdon ■ ⊖	d	17 27	17 27		17 31					17 44	17 57	17 57		18 01					18 14			18 27
St Pancras International ■ ⊖	a	17 31	17 31		17 35					17 48	18 01	18 01		18 05					18 18			18 31

A 16 September. To Bedford
B not 16 September. To Bedford
C from 1 July until 22 July, from 19 August until 16 September
D To Luton
E 29 July, 5 August, 12 August
F From Dorking to London Victoria
G From Epsom to London Victoria
H To Bedford
I 16 September. To London Victoria
J not 16 September. To London Victoria

Please refer to separate pages within this table for services operating between London and Bedford

At weekends please use local bus and tube services to travel to/from St Pancras International and London Bridge when no trains are operating. See local publicity for details of alternative routes and services that are available across central London

Table 52

Sundays

1 July to 16 September

Brighton, Gatwick Airport - South London

Network Diagram - see first Page of Table 52

		FC	SE	FC	SE	SN	SN	FC	FC	FC	FC	SE	FC	SE	SN	SN	FC	FC	SN	SN	FC	FC	SE
		■							■	■	■							■	◇■	◇■	■	■	
		A	B	C	D	E	F		G	H	A	B	C	D	E	F		G	I	J	H	A	B
Brighton ■	d	17 15								17 44	17 45								18 00	18 00	18 14	18 15	
Preston Park	d																		18 03	18 03			
Hassocks ■	d	17 24								17 53	17 54								18 10	18 10	18 23	18 24	
Burgess Hill ■	d	17 27								17 56	17 57								18 13	18 13	18 26	18 27	
Wivelsfield ■	d																		18 15	18 15			
Haywards Heath ■	d	17 33								18 02	18 03								18 20	18 25	18 32	18 33	
Balcombe	d																		18 26	18 30			
Three Bridges ■	d	17 42								18 11	18 12								18 32	18 36	18 41	18 42	
Gatwick Airport ■ ✈	d	17 47								18 16	18 17								18 38	18 41	18 46	18 47	
Redhill	d																		18 46	18 49			
East Croydon	d	18 02							18 17	18 32	18 32							18 47	18a58	19a00	19 01	19 02	
Sutton (Surrey) ■	d			17 37		17 43	17 58	18 04					18 07		18 13	18 28	18 34						
West Sutton	d			17 40									18 10										
Sutton Common	d			17 42									18 12										
St Helier	d			17 45									18 15										
Morden South	d			17 47									18 17										
South Merton	d			17 49									18 19										
Wimbledon Chase	d			17 51									18 21										
Wimbledon ■	d			17 56									18 26										
Haydons Road	d			17 58									18 28										
Tooting	d			18 01									18 31										
Carshalton	d					17 46	18 01	18 07							18 16	18 31	18 37						
Hackbridge	d					17 48	18 03	18 09							18 18	18 33	18 39						
Mitcham Junction	d					17 52	18 07	18 12							18 22	18 37	18 42						
Mitcham Eastfields	d					17a55	18a10	18 15							18a25	18a40	18 45						
Streatham ■	d			18 06				18 19					18 36				18 49						
Tulse Hill ■	d			18 10				18 23					18 40				18 53						
London Bridge ■ ⊖	a	18 15							18 30	18 45	18 45							19 00			19 15	19 15	
	d	18 15							18 30	18 45	18 45							19 00			19 15	19 15	
Sevenoaks ■	d		17 21		17 32							17 51		18 02									18 21
Bat & Ball	d		17 24		17 35							17 54		18 05									18 24
Otford ■	d		17 27		17 38							17 57		18 08									18 27
Shoreham (Kent)	d		17 30		17 41							18 00		18 11									18 30
Eynsford	d		17 34		17 45							18 04		18 15									18 34
Swanley ■	d		17 39		17 50							18 09		18 20									18 39
St Mary Cray ■	d		17 43		17 54							18 13		18 24									18 43
Bickley	d		17 47		17 58							18 17		18 28									18 47
Bromley South	d		17 50		18 01							18 20		18 31									18 50
Shortlands ■	d		17 53		18 04							18 23		18 34									18 53
Ravensbourne	d		17 55		18 06							18 25		18 36									18 55
Beckenham Hill	d		17 57		18 08							18 27		18 38									18 57
Bellingham	d		17 59		18 10							18 29		18 40									18 59
Catford	d		18 02		18 13							18 32		18 43									19 02
Crofton Park	d		18 04		18 15							18 34		18 45									19 04
Nunhead ■	d		18 07		18 18							18 37		18 48									19 07
Peckham Rye ■	d		18 09		18 20							18 39		18 50									19 09
Denmark Hill ■	d		18 13		18 24							18 43		18 54									19 13
Herne Hill ■	d			18 14				18 27					18 44				18 57						
Loughborough Jn	d			18 17				18 30					18 47				19 00						
Elephant & Castle	d		18 19	18 22	18 30			18 34				18 49	18 52	19 00			19 04						19 19
London Blackfriars ■ ⊖	a	18 22	18 23	18 25	18 34			18 37	18 37	18 52	18 52	18 53	18 55	19 04			19 07	19 07			19 22	19 22	19 23
	d	18 22		18 26					18 40	18 52	18 52		18 56					19 10			19 22	19 22	
City Thameslink ■	d																						
Farringdon ■ ⊖	d	18 27		18 31					18 44	18 57	18 57		19 01					19 14			19 27	19 27	
St Pancras International ■ ⊖	a	18 31		18 35					18 48	19 01	19 01		19 05					19 18			19 31	19 31	

A not 16 September. To Bedford
B from 1 July until 22 July, from 19 August until 16 September
C To Luton
D 29 July, 5 August, 12 August
E From Dorking to London Victoria
F From Epsom to London Victoria
G To Bedford
H 16 September. To Bedford
I 16 September. To London Victoria
J not 16 September. To London Victoria

Please refer to separate pages within this table for services operating between London and Bedford

At weekends please use local bus and tube services to travel to/from St Pancras International and London Bridge when no trains are operating. See local publicity for details of alternative routes and services that are available across central London

Brighton, Gatwick Airport - South London

Sundays

1 July to 16 September

Network Diagram - see first Page of Table 52

		FC	SE	SN	SN	FC	FC	FC	FC	SE	SN	SN	FC	SE	SN	FC	FC	FC	SE	FC	SE	SN	FC
		A	B	C	D		A	E	F	G	H	I	A	B	C		E	F	G	A	B	C	
Brighton	d							18 44	18 45		19 00	19 00					19 14	19 15					
Preston Park	d										19 03	19 03											
Hassocks	d							18 53	18 54		19 10	19 10					19 23	19 24					
Burgess Hill	d							18 56	18 57		19 13	19 13					19 26	19 27					
Wivelsfield	d										19 15	19 15											
Haywards Heath	d							19 02	19 03		19 20	19 25					19 32	19 33					
Balcombe	d										19 26	19 30											
Three Bridges	d							19 11	19 12		19 32	19 36					19 41	19 42					
Gatwick Airport ✈	d							19 16	19 17		19 38	19 41					19 46	19 47					
Redhill	d										19 46	19 49											
East Croydon	d						19 17	19 32	19 32		19a58	20a00					20 01	20 02					
Sutton (Surrey)	d	18 37		18 43	18 58	19 04							19 07		19 13	19 34				19 37		19 43	20 04
West Sutton	d	18 40											19 10							19 40			
Sutton Common	d	18 42											19 12							19 42			
St Helier	d	18 45											19 15							19 45			
Morden South	d	18 47											19 17							19 47			
South Merton	d	18 49											19 19							19 49			
Wimbledon Chase	d	18 51											19 21							19 51			
Wimbledon	d	18 56											19 26							19 56			
Haydons Road	d	18 58											19 28							19 58			
Tooting	d	19 01											19 31							20 01			
Carshalton	d			18 46	19 01	19 07									19 16	19 37						19 46	20 07
Hackbridge	d			18 48	19 03	19 09									19 18	19 39						19 48	20 09
Mitcham Junction	d			18 52	19 07	19 12									19 22	19 42						19 52	20 12
Mitcham Eastfields	d			18a55	19a10	19 15									19a25	19 45						19a55	20 15
Streatham	d	19 06				19 19							19 36			19 49				20 06			20 19
Tulse Hill	d	19 10				19 23							19 40			19 53				20 10			20 23
London Bridge ⊖	a						19 30	19 45	19 45								20 15	20 15					
	d						19 30	19 45	19 45								20 15	20 15					
Sevenoaks	d		18 32							18 51				19 02					19 21		19 32		
Bat & Ball	d		18 35							18 54				19 05					19 24		19 35		
Otford	d		18 38							18 57				19 08					19 27		19 38		
Shoreham (Kent)	d		18 41							19 00				19 11					19 30		19 41		
Eynsford	d		18 45							19 04				19 15					19 34		19 45		
Swanley	d		18 50							19 09				19 20					19 39		19 50		
St Mary Cray	d		18 54							19 13				19 24					19 43		19 54		
Bickley	d		18 58							19 17				19 28					19 47		19 58		
Bromley South	d		19 01							19 20				19 31					19 50		20 01		
Shortlands	d		19 04							19 23				19 34					19 53		20 04		
Ravensbourne	d		19 06							19 25				19 36					19 55		20 06		
Beckenham Hill	d		19 08							19 27				19 38					19 57		20 08		
Bellingham	d		19 10							19 29				19 40					19 59		20 10		
Catford	d		19 13							19 32				19 43					20 02		20 13		
Crofton Park	d		19 15							19 34				19 45					20 04		20 15		
Nunhead	d		19 18							19 37				19 48					20 07		20 18		
Peckham Rye	d		19 20							19 39				19 50					20 09		20 20		
Denmark Hill	d		19 24							19 43				19 54					20 13		20 24		
Herne Hill	d	19 14				19 27							19 44			19 57				20 14			20 27
Loughborough Jn.	d	19 17				19 30							19 47			20 00				20 17			20 30
Elephant & Castle	d	19 22	19 30			19 34				19 49			19 52	20 00		20 04			20 19	20 22	20 30		20 34
London Blackfriars ⊖	a	19 25	19 34			19 37	19 37	19 52	19 52	19 53			19 55	20 04		20 07	20 22	20 22	20 23	20 25	20 34		20 37
	d	19 26					19 40	19 52	19 52				19 56				20 22	20 22		20 26			
City Thameslink	d																						
Farringdon ⊖	d	19 31					19 44	19 57	19 57				20 01				20 27	20 27		20 31			
St Pancras International ⊖	a	19 35					19 48	20 01	20 01				20 05				20 31	20 31		20 35			

A To Bedford
B 29 July, 5 August, 12 August
C From Dorking to London Victoria
D From Epsom to London Victoria
E 16 September. To Bedford
F not 16 September. To Bedford
G from 1 July until 22 July, from 19 August until 16 September
H 16 September. To London Victoria
I not 16 September. To London Victoria

Please refer to separate pages within this table for services operating between London and Bedford

At weekends please use local bus and tube services to travel to/from St Pancras International and London Bridge when no trains are operating. See local publicity for details of alternative routes and services that are available across central London

Brighton, Gatwick Airport - South London

Sundays

1 July to 16 September

Network Diagram - see first Page of Table 52

		FC	FC	SE	SN	SN	FC	SE	SN	FC	FC	FC	SE	FC	SE	SN	FC	FC	FC	SE	SN	SN
		A	B	C	D	E	F	G	H		A	B	C	F	G	H		A	B	C	D	E
Brighton	d	19 44	19 45		20 00	20 00					20 14	20 15						20 44	20 45		21 00	21 04
Preston Park	d				20 03	20 03															21 03	21 07
Hassocks	d	19 53	19 54		20 10	20 10					20 23	20 24						20 53	20 54		21 10	21 14
Burgess Hill	d	19 56	19 57		20 13	20 13					20 26	20 27						20 56	20 57		21 13	21 17
Wivelsfield	d				20 15	20 15															21 15	21 19
Haywards Heath	d	20 02	20 03		20 20	20 25					20 32	20 33						21 02	21 03		21 20	21 25
Balcombe	d				20 26	20 30															21 26	21 30
Three Bridges	d	20 11	20 12		20 32	20 36					20 41	20 42						21 11	21 12		21 32	21 36
Gatwick Airport ✈	d	20 16	20 17		20 38	20 41					20 46	20 47						21 16	21 17		21 38	21 41
Redhill	d				20 46	20 49															21 46	21 49
East Croydon	d	20 32	20 32		20a59	21a00					21 01	21 02						21 32	21 32		21a58	22a00
Sutton (Surrey)	d						20 07		20 13	20 34				20 37		20 43	21 04					
West Sutton	d						20 10							20 40								
Sutton Common	d						20 12							20 42								
St Helier	d						20 15							20 45								
Morden South	d						20 17							20 47								
South Merton	d						20 19							20 49								
Wimbledon Chase	d						20 21							20 51								
Wimbledon	d						20 26							20 56								
Haydons Road	d						20 28							20 58								
Tooting	d						20 31							21 01								
Carshalton	d								20 16	20 37						20 46	21 07					
Hackbridge	d								20 18	20 39						20 48	21 09					
Mitcham Junction	d								20 22	20 42						20 52	21 12					
Mitcham Eastfields	d								20a25	20 45						20a55	21 15					
Streatham	d						20 36			20 49				21 06			21 19					
Tulse Hill	d						20 40			20 53				21 10			21 23					
London Bridge ⊖	a	20 45	20 45								21 15	21 15						21 45	21 45			
	d	20 45	20 45								21 15	21 15						21 45	21 45			
Sevenoaks	d			19 51				20 02					20 21		20 32					20 51		
Bat & Ball	d			19 54				20 05					20 24		20 35					20 54		
Otford	d			19 57				20 08					20 27		20 38					20 57		
Shoreham (Kent)	d			20 00				20 11					20 30		20 41					21 00		
Eynsford	d			20 04				20 15					20 34		20 45					21 04		
Swanley	d			20 09				20 20					20 39		20 50					21 09		
St Mary Cray	d			20 13				20 24					20 43		20 54					21 13		
Bickley	d			20 17				20 28					20 47		20 58					21 17		
Bromley South	d			20 20				20 31					20 50		21 01					21 20		
Shortlands	d			20 23				20 34					20 53		21 04					21 23		
Ravensbourne	d			20 25				20 36					20 55		21 06					21 25		
Beckenham Hill	d			20 27				20 38					20 57		21 08					21 27		
Bellingham	d			20 29				20 40					20 59		21 10					21 29		
Catford	d			20 32				20 43					21 02		21 13					21 32		
Crofton Park	d			20 34				20 45					21 04		21 15					21 34		
Nunhead	d			20 37				20 48					21 07		21 18					21 37		
Peckham Rye	d			20 39				20 50					21 09		21 20					21 39		
Denmark Hill	d			20 43				20 54					21 13		21 24					21 43		
Herne Hill	d						20 44			20 57				21 14			21 27					
Loughborough Jn.	d						20 47			21 00				21 17			21 30					
Elephant & Castle	d			20 49			20 52	21 00		21 04			21 19	21 22	21 30		21 34			21 49		
London Blackfriars ⊖	a	20 52	20 52	20 53			20 55	21 04		21 07	21 22	21 22	21 23	21 25	21 34		21 37	21 52	21 52	21 53		
	d	20 52	20 52				20 56				21 22	21 22		21 26				21 52	21 52			
City Thameslink	d																					
Farringdon ⊖	d	20 57	20 57				21 01				21 27	21 27		21 31				21 57	21 57			
St Pancras International ⊖	a	21 01	21 01				21 05				21 31	21 31		21 35				22 01	22 01			

A 16 September. To Bedford
B not 16 September. To Bedford
C from 1 July until 22 July, from 19 August until 16 September
D 16 September. To London Victoria
E not 16 September. To London Victoria
F To Bedford
G 29 July, 5 August, 12 August
H From Dorking to London Victoria

Please refer to separate pages within this table for services operating between London and Bedford

At weekends please use local bus and tube services to travel to/from St Pancras International and London Bridge when no trains are operating. See local publicity for details of alternative routes and services that are available across central London

Table 52

Sundays

1 July to 16 September

Brighton, Gatwick Airport - South London

Network Diagram - see first Page of Table 52

		FC	SE	SN	FC	FC	FC	SE	SE	SN	FC	FC	FC	SE	SN	SE	SN	SN	FC	FC	SE	SE	SN
						1	1					1	1		◇1		◇1		1	1			
		A	B	C		D	E	F	B	C		D	E	F	G	B	H	C	D	E	F	B	C
Brighton 10	d					21 14	21 15					21 44	21 45		22 00		22 04		22 14	22 15			
Preston Park	d														22 03		22 07						
Hassocks 4	d					21 23	21 24					21 53	21 54		22 10		22 14		22 23	22 24			
Burgess Hill 4	d					21 26	21 27					21 56	21 57		22 13		22 17		22 26	22 27			
Wivelsfield 4	d														22 15		22 19						
Haywards Heath 3	d					21 32	21 33					22 02	22 03		22 20		22 25		22 32	22 33			
Balcombe	d														22 26		22 30						
Three Bridges 4	d					21 41	21 42					22 11	22 12		22 32		22 36		22 41	22 42			
Gatwick Airport 10 ✈	d					21 46	21 47					22 16	22 17		22 38		22 41		22 46	22 47			
Redhill	d														22 46		22 49						
East Croydon	d					22 01	22 02					22 32	22 32		22a58		23a00		23 01	23 02			
Sutton (Surrey) 4	d	21 07		21 13	21 34					21 43	22 04							22 13					22 43
West Sutton	d	21 10																					
Sutton Common	d	21 12																					
St Helier	d	21 15																					
Morden South	d	21 17																					
South Merton	d	21 19																					
Wimbledon Chase	d	21 21																					
Wimbledon 5	d	21 26																					
Haydons Road	d	21 28																					
Tooting	d	21 31																					
Carshalton	d			21 16	21 37					21 46	22 07							22 16					22 46
Hackbridge	d			21 18	21 39					21 48	22 09							22 18					22 48
Mitcham Junction	d			21 22	21 42					21 52	22 12							22 22					22 52
Mitcham Eastfields	d			21a25	21 45					21a55	22 15							22a25					22a55
Streatham 4	d	21 36			21 49						22 19												
Tulse Hill 3	d	21 40			21 53						22 23												
London Bridge 4 ⊖	a					22 15	22 15					22 45	22 45						23 15	23 15			
	d					22 15	22 15					22 45	22 45						23 15	23 15			
Sevenoaks 4	d		21 02					21 21	21 32					21 51		22 02					22 21	22 32	
Bat & Ball	d		21 05					21 24	21 35					21 54		22 05					22 24	22 35	
Otford 4	d		21 08					21 27	21 38					21 57		22 08					22 27	22 38	
Shoreham (Kent)	d		21 11					21 30	21 41					22 00		22 11					22 30	22 41	
Eynsford	d		21 15					21 34	21 45					22 04		22 15					22 34	22 45	
Swanley 4	d		21 20					21 39	21 50					22 09		22 20					22 39	22 50	
St Mary Cray 4	d		21 24					21 43	21 54					22 13		22 24					22 43	22 54	
Bickley	d		21 28					21 47	21 58					22 17		22 28					22 47	22 58	
Bromley South	d		21 31					21 50	22 01					22 20		22 31					22 50	23 01	
Shortlands 4	d		21 34					21 53	22 04					22 23		22 34					22 53	23 04	
Ravensbourne	d		21 36					21 55	22 06					22 25		22 36					22 55	23 06	
Beckenham Hill	d		21 38					21 57	22 08					22 27		22 38					22 57	23 08	
Bellingham	d		21 40					21 59	22 10					22 29		22 40					22 59	23 10	
Catford	d		21 43					22 02	22 13					22 32		22 43					23 02	23 13	
Crofton Park	d		21 45					22 04	22 15					22 34		22 45					23 04	23 15	
Nunhead 4	d		21 48					22 07	22 18					22 37		22 48					23 07	23 18	
Peckham Rye 4	d		21 50					22 09	22 20					22 39		22 50					23 09	23 20	
Denmark Hill 4	d		21 54					22 13	22 24					22 43		22 54					23 13	23 24	
Herne Hill 4	d	21 44			21 57						22 27												
Loughborough Jn.	d	21 47			22 00						22 30												
Elephant & Castle	d	21 52	22 00		22 04			22 19	22 30		22 34			22 49		23 00					23 19	23 30	
London Blackfriars 3 ⊖	a	21 55	22 04		22 07	22 22	22 22	22 23	22 34		22 37	22 52	22 52	22 53		23 04			23 22	23 22	23 23	23 34	
	d	21 56				22 22	22 22					22 52	22 52						23 22	23 22			
City Thameslink 3	d																						
Farringdon 3 ⊖	d	22 01				22 27	22 27					22 57	22 57						23 27	23 27			
St Pancras International 15 ⊖	a	22 05				22 31	22 31					23 01	23 01						23 31	23 31			

A To Bedford
B 29 July, 5 August, 12 August
C From Dorking to London Victoria
D 16 September. To Bedford
E not 16 September. To Bedford
F from 1 July until 22 July, from 19 August until 16 September
G 16 September. To London Victoria
H not 16 September. To London Victoria

Please refer to separate pages within this table for services operating between London and Bedford

At weekends please use local bus and tube services to travel to/from St Pancras International and London Bridge when no trains are operating. See local publicity for details of alternative routes and services that are available across central London

Table 52

Sundays

1 July to 16 September

Brighton, Gatwick Airport - South London

Network Diagram - see first Page of Table 52

		FC	FC	SN	SN	FC	FC	SN	FC	FC
		1	1	◇1		1	1		1	1
		A	B	C	D	A	B	D	B	A
Brighton 10	d	22 44	22 45	23 02		23 14	23 15		23 45	23 45
Preston Park	d			23 06						
Hassocks 4	d	22 53	22 54	23 12		23 23	23 24		23 54	23 54
Burgess Hill 4	d	22 56	22 57	23 16		23 26	23 27		23 57	23 57
Wivelsfield 4	d			23 18						
Haywards Heath 3	d	23 02	23 03	23 23		23 32	23 33		00 03	00 03
Balcombe	d			23 29						
Three Bridges 4	d	23 11	23 12	23 41		23 41	23 42		00 12	00 12
Gatwick Airport 10 ✈	d	23 16	23 17	23 46		23 46	23 47		00 17	00 17
Redhill	d			00 01					00 24	00 24
East Croydon	d	23 32	23 32	00a16		00 03	00 04		00 36	00 37
Sutton (Surrey) 4	d				23 13			23 43		
West Sutton	d									
Sutton Common	d									
St Helier	d									
Morden South	d									
South Merton	d									
Wimbledon Chase	d									
Wimbledon 5	d									
Haydons Road	d									
Tooting	d									
Carshalton	d				23 16			23 46		
Hackbridge	d				23 18			23 48		
Mitcham Junction	d				23 22			23 52		
Mitcham Eastfields	d				23a25			23a55		
Streatham 4	d									
Tulse Hill 3	d									
London Bridge 4 ⊖	a	23 45	23 45			00 21	00 21		00 50	00 50
	d	23 45	23 45			00 22	00 22		00 51	00 51
Sevenoaks 4	d									
Bat & Ball	d									
Otford 4	d									
Shoreham (Kent)	d									
Eynsford	d									
Swanley 4	d									
St Mary Cray 4	d									
Bickley	d									
Bromley South	d									
Shortlands 4	d									
Ravensbourne	d									
Beckenham Hill	d									
Bellingham	d									
Catford	d									
Crofton Park	d									
Nunhead 4	d									
Peckham Rye 4	d									
Denmark Hill 4	d									
Herne Hill 4	d									
Loughborough Jn.	d									
Elephant & Castle	d									
London Blackfriars 3 ⊖	a	23 52	23 52			00 27	00 27		00 57	00 57
	d	23 52	23 52			00 28	00 28		00 58	00 58
City Thameslink 3	d									
Farringdon 3 ⊖	d	23 57	23 57			00 33	00 33			
St Pancras International 15 ⊖	a	00 01	00 01			00 37	00 37		01 07	01 07

A 16 September. To Bedford
B not 16 September. To Bedford
C To London Victoria
D From Dorking to London Victoria

Please refer to separate pages within this table for services operating between London and Bedford

At weekends please use local bus and tube services to travel to/from St Pancras International and London Bridge when no trains are operating. See local publicity for details of alternative routes and services that are available across central London

Brighton, Gatwick Airport - South London

Sundays
from 23 September

Network Diagram - see first Page of Table 52

	FC	SN	FC	FC	FC	FC	SN	FC	FC	SN	SE	FC	SN	SE	FC	SE	SN	SN	FC	SE	SN	SN
	1	◇1		1	1		◇1		1	◇1		1	◇1		1				1			◇1
	A	B	A	A	A	A	B	A	A	B	C	A	B	C	A		D	E	A		D	B
Brighton 10 d	22p33	23p02		23p11	23p37		03 50		06 11	06 19		06 44	07 00		07 14				07 44			08 00
Preston Park d	22p37	23p06			23p41					06 22			07 03									08 03
Hassocks 4 d	22p43	23p12		23p20	23p47				06 20	06 29		06 53	07 10		07 23				07 53			08 10
Burgess Hill 4 d	22p47	23p16		23p23	23p51				06 26	06 32		06 56	07 13		07 26				07 56			08 13
Wivelsfield 4 d	22p49	23p19			23p53					06 34			07 15									08 15
Haywards Heath 3 d	22p54	23p24		23p29	23p59		04 26		06 32	06 39		07 02	07 20		07 32				08 02			08 20
Balcombe d	22p59				00 04								07 26									08 26
Three Bridges 4 d	23p12	23p47		23p38	00 10		04 58	05 12	06 41	06 48		07 11	07 32		07 41				08 11			08 32
Gatwick Airport 10 ✈ d	23p17	23p53		23p43	00 15		05 03	05 17	06 46	06 53		07 16	07 38		07 46				08 16			08 38
Redhill d		00 03			00 23								07 46									08 46
East Croydon d	23p32	00a16		00 04	00 36		05a27	05 32	07 02	07a10		07 32	07a58		08 01				08 32			08a58
Sutton (Surrey) 4 d																	07 28	07 43			07 58	
West Sutton d																						
Sutton Common d																						
St Helier d																						
Morden South d																						
South Merton d																						
Wimbledon Chase d																						
Wimbledon 6 d																						
Haydons Road d																						
Tooting d																						
Carshalton d																	07 31	07 46			08 01	
Hackbridge d																	07 33	07 48			08 03	
Mitcham Junction d																	07 37	07 52			08 07	
Mitcham Eastfields d																	07a40	07a55			08a10	
Streatham 4 d																						
Tulse Hill 3 d																						
London Bridge 4 ⊖ a	23p44			00 21	00 51				07 15			07 45			08 15				08 45			
d	23p45			00 22	00 52				07 15			07 45			08 15				08 45			
Sevenoaks 4 d																07 21				07 51		
Bat & Ball d																07 24				07 54		
Otford 4 d																07 27				07 57		
Shoreham (Kent) d																07 30				08 00		
Eynsford d																07 34				08 04		
Swanley 4 d																07 39				08 09		
St Mary Cray 4 d																07 43				08 13		
Bickley d											06 47			07 17		07 47				08 17		
Bromley South d											06 50			07 20		07 50				08 20		
Shortlands 4 d											06 53			07 23		07 53				08 23		
Ravensbourne d											06 55			07 25		07 55				08 25		
Beckenham Hill d											06 57			07 27		07 57				08 27		
Bellingham d											06 59			07 29		07 59				08 29		
Catford d											07 02			07 32		08 02				08 32		
Crofton Park d											07 04			07 34		08 04				08 34		
Nunhead 4 d											07 07			07 37		08 07				08 37		
Peckham Rye 4 d											07 09			07 39		08 09				08 39		
Denmark Hill 4 d											07 13			07 43		08 13				08 43		
Herne Hill 4 d																						
Loughborough Jn. d																						
Elephant & Castle d											07 19			07 49		08 19				08 49		
London Blackfriars 3 ⊖ a	23p52			00 28	00 58			05 59	07 22		07 23	07 52		07 53	08 22	08 23			08 52	08 53		
d	23p52		00 08	00 28	00 58	01 29		05 59	07 22			07 52			08 22				08 52			
City Thameslink 3 d																						
Farringdon 3 ⊖ d	23p58		00 13	00 33					07 27			07 57			08 27				08 57			
St Pancras International 15 ⊖ a	00 02		00 17	00 37	01 07	01 37		06 07	07 31			08 01			08 31				09 01			

A To Bedford
B To London Victoria
C From Orpington
D From Epsom to London Victoria
E From Dorking to London Victoria

Please refer to separate pages within this table for services operating between London and Bedford

At weekends please use local bus and tube services to travel to/from St Pancras International and London Bridge when no trains are operating. See local publicity for details of alternative routes and services that are available across central London

Brighton, Gatwick Airport - South London

Sundays
from 23 September

Network Diagram - see first Page of Table 52

	SN	FC	SE	SN	SN	FC	SE	SN	SN	SN	FC	SE	SN	FC	SN	SN	FC	FC	SE	FC	SN	SN
		1				1			◇1		1							1				
	A	B		C	A	B		C	D	A	B		C	E	A	C		B		E	A	C
Brighton 10 d		08 14				08 44			09 00		09 14							09 44				
Preston Park d									09 03													
Hassocks 4 d		08 23				08 53			09 10		09 23							09 53				
Burgess Hill 4 d		08 26				08 56			09 13		09 26							09 56				
Wivelsfield 4 d									09 15													
Haywards Heath 3 d		08 32				09 02			09 20		09 32							10 02				
Balcombe d									09 26													
Three Bridges 4 d		08 41				09 11			09 32		09 41							10 11				
Gatwick Airport 10 ✈ d		08 46				09 16			09 38		09 46							10 16				
Redhill d									09 46													
East Croydon d		09 01				09 32			09a58		10 01							10 32				
Sutton (Surrey) 4 d	08 13			08 28	08 43			08 58		09 13			09 28	09 37	09 43	09 58	10 04			10 07	10 13	10 28
West Sutton d														09 40						10 10		
Sutton Common d														09 42						10 12		
St Helier d														09 45						10 15		
Morden South d														09 47						10 17		
South Merton d														09 49						10 19		
Wimbledon Chase d														09 51						10 21		
Wimbledon 6 d														09 56						10 26		
Haydons Road d														09 58						10 28		
Tooting d														10 01						10 31		
Carshalton d	08 16			08 31	08 46			09 01		09 16			09 31		09 46	10 01	10 07				10 16	10 31
Hackbridge d	08 18			08 33	08 48			09 03		09 18			09 33		09 48	10 03	10 09				10 18	10 33
Mitcham Junction d	08 22			08 37	08 52			09 07		09 22			09 37		09 52	10 07	10 12				10 22	10 37
Mitcham Eastfields d	08a25			08a40	08a55			09a10		09a25			09a40		09a55	10a10	10 15				10a25	10a40
Streatham 4 d														10 06			10 19			10 36		
Tulse Hill 3 d														10 10			10 23			10 40		
London Bridge 4 ⊖ a		09 15				09 45					10 15							10 45				
d		09 15				09 45					10 15							10 45				
Sevenoaks 4 d			08 21				08 51					09 21							09 51			
Bat & Ball d			08 24				08 54					09 24							09 54			
Otford 4 d			08 27				08 57					09 27							09 57			
Shoreham (Kent) d			08 30				09 00					09 30							10 00			
Eynsford d			08 34				09 04					09 34							10 04			
Swanley 4 d			08 39				09 09					09 39							10 09			
St Mary Cray 4 d			08 43				09 13					09 43							10 13			
Bickley d			08 47				09 17					09 47							10 17			
Bromley South d			08 50				09 20					09 50							10 20			
Shortlands 4 d			08 53				09 23					09 53							10 23			
Ravensbourne d			08 55				09 25					09 55							10 25			
Beckenham Hill d			08 57				09 27					09 57							10 27			
Bellingham d			08 59				09 29					09 59							10 29			
Catford d			09 02				09 32					10 02							10 32			
Crofton Park d			09 04				09 34					10 04							10 34			
Nunhead 4 d			09 07				09 37					10 07							10 37			
Peckham Rye 4 d			09 09				09 39					10 09							10 39			
Denmark Hill 4 d			09 13				09 43					10 13							10 43			
Herne Hill 4 d														10 14			10 27			10 44		
Loughborough Jn. d														10 17			10 30			10 47		
Elephant & Castle d			09 19				09 49					10 19		10 22			10 34		10 49	10 52		
London Blackfriars 3 ⊖ a		09 22	09 23			09 52	09 53				10 22	10 23		10 25			10 37	10 52	10 53	10 55		
d		09 22				09 52					10 22			10 26				10 52		10 56		
City Thameslink 3 d																						
Farringdon 3 ⊖ d		09 27				09 57					10 27			10 31				10 57		11 01		
St Pancras International 15 ⊖ a		09 31				10 01					10 31			10 35				11 01		11 05		

A From Dorking to London Victoria
B To Bedford
C From Epsom to London Victoria
D To London Victoria
E To Luton

Please refer to separate pages within this table for services operating between London and Bedford

At weekends please use local bus and tube services to travel to/from St Pancras International and London Bridge when no trains are operating. See local publicity for details of alternative routes and services that are available across central London

Table 52

Sundays
from 23 September

Brighton, Gatwick Airport - South London

Network Diagram - see first Page of Table 52

	FC	FC ■ A	SN ◇■ B	FC ■ A	SE	FC C	SN D	SN E	FC	FC ■ A	FC ■ A	SE	FC C	SN D	SN E	FC	FC ■ A	SN ◇■ B	FC ■ A	SE	FC C
Brighton d			10 00	10 14							10 44							11 00	11 14		
Preston Park d			10 03															11 03			
Hassocks d			10 10	10 23							10 53							11 10	11 23		
Burgess Hill d			10 13	10 26							10 56							11 13	11 26		
Wivelsfield d			10 15															11 15			
Haywards Heath d			10 20	10 32							11 02							11 20	11 32		
Balcombe d			10 26															11 26			
Three Bridges d			10 32	10 41							11 11							11 32	11 41		
Gatwick Airport d			10 38	10 46							11 16							11 38	11 46		
Redhill d			10 46															11 46			
East Croydon d		10 47	10a58	11 01						11 17	11 32						11 47	11a58	12 01		
Sutton (Surrey) d	10 34					10 37	10 43	10 58	11 04				11 07	11 13	11 28	11 34					11 37
West Sutton d						10 40							11 10								11 40
Sutton Common d						10 42							11 12								11 42
St Helier d						10 45							11 15								11 45
Morden South d						10 47							11 17								11 47
South Merton d						10 49							11 19								11 49
Wimbledon Chase d						10 51							11 21								11 51
Wimbledon d						10 56							11 26								11 56
Haydons Road d						10 58							11 28								11 58
Tooting d						11 01							11 31								12 01
Carshalton d	10 37						10 46	11 01	11 07					11 16	11 31	11 37					
Hackbridge d	10 39						10 48	11 03	11 09					11 18	11 33	11 39					
Mitcham Junction d	10 42						10 52	11 07	11 12					11 22	11 37	11 42					
Mitcham Eastfields d	10 45						10a55	11a10	11 15					11a25	11a40	11 45					
Streatham d	10 49					11 06			11 19				11 36			11 49					12 06
Tulse Hill d	10 53					11 10			11 23				11 40			11 53					12 10
London Bridge a		11 00		11 15						11 30	11 45						12 00		12 15		
London Bridge d		11 00		11 15						11 30	11 45						12 00		12 15		
Sevenoaks d					10 21							10 51								11 21	
Bat & Ball d					10 24							10 54								11 24	
Otford d					10 27							10 57								11 27	
Shoreham (Kent) d					10 30							11 00								11 30	
Eynsford d					10 34							11 04								11 34	
Swanley d					10 39							11 09								11 39	
St Mary Cray d					10 43							11 13								11 43	
Bickley d					10 47							11 17								11 47	
Bromley South d					10 50							11 20								11 50	
Shortlands d					10 53							11 23								11 53	
Ravensbourne d					10 55							11 25								11 55	
Beckenham Hill d					10 57							11 27								11 57	
Bellingham d					10 59							11 29								11 59	
Catford d					11 02							11 32								12 02	
Crofton Park d					11 04							11 34								12 04	
Nunhead d					11 07							11 37								12 07	
Peckham Rye d					11 09							11 39								12 09	
Denmark Hill d					11 13							11 43								12 13	
Herne Hill d	10 57					11 14			11 27				11 44			11 57					12 14
Loughborough Jn. d	11 00					11 17			11 30				11 47			12 00					12 17
Elephant & Castle d	11 04				11 19	11 22			11 34			11 49	11 52			12 04				12 19	12 22
London Blackfriars a	11 07	11 07		11 22	11 23	11 25			11 37	11 37	11 52	11 53	11 55			12 07	12 07		12 22	12 23	12 25
London Blackfriars d		11 10		11 22		11 26				11 40	11 52		11 56				12 10		12 22		12 26
City Thameslink d																					
Farringdon d		11 14		11 27		11 31				11 44	11 57		12 01				12 14		12 27		12 31
St Pancras International a		11 18		11 31		11 35				11 48	12 01		12 05				12 18		12 31		12 35

A To Bedford
B To London Victoria
C To Luton
D From Dorking to London Victoria
E From Epsom to London Victoria

Please refer to separate pages within this table for services operating between London and Bedford

At weekends please use local bus and tube services to travel to/from St Pancras International and London Bridge when no trains are operating. See local publicity for details of alternative routes and services that are available across central London

Table 52

Sundays
from 23 September

Brighton, Gatwick Airport - South London

Network Diagram - see first Page of Table 52

	SN A	SN B	FC	FC ■ C	FC ■ C	SE	FC D	SN A	SN B	FC	FC ■ C	SN ◇■ E	FC ■ C	SE	FC D	SN A	SN B	FC	FC ■ C	FC ■ C	SE	FC D
Brighton d					11 44							12 00	12 14							12 44		
Preston Park d												12 03										
Hassocks d					11 53							12 10	12 23							12 53		
Burgess Hill d					11 56							12 13	12 26							12 56		
Wivelsfield d												12 15										
Haywards Heath d					12 02							12 20	12 32							13 02		
Balcombe d												12 26										
Three Bridges d					12 11							12 32	12 41							13 11		
Gatwick Airport d					12 16							12 38	12 46							13 16		
Redhill d												12 46										
East Croydon d				12 17	12 32						12 47	12a58	13 01						13 17	13 32		
Sutton (Surrey) d	11 43	11 58	12 04				12 07	12 13	12 28	12 34					12 37	12 43	12 58	13 04				13 07
West Sutton d							12 10								12 40							13 10
Sutton Common d							12 12								12 42							13 12
St Helier d							12 15								12 45							13 15
Morden South d							12 17								12 47							13 17
South Merton d							12 19								12 49							13 19
Wimbledon Chase d							12 21								12 51							13 21
Wimbledon d							12 26								12 56							13 26
Haydons Road d							12 28								12 58							13 28
Tooting d							12 31								13 01							13 31
Carshalton d	11 46	12 01	12 07					12 16	12 31	12 37						12 46	13 01	13 07				
Hackbridge d	11 48	12 03	12 09					12 18	12 33	12 39						12 48	13 03	13 09				
Mitcham Junction d	11 52	12 07	12 12					12 22	12 37	12 42						12 52	13 07	13 12				
Mitcham Eastfields d	11a55	12a10	12 15					12a25	12a40	12 45						12a55	13a10	13 15				
Streatham d			12 19				12 36			12 49					13 06			13 19				13 36
Tulse Hill d			12 23				12 40			12 53					13 10			13 23				13 40
London Bridge a				12 30	12 45						13 00		13 15						13 30	13 45		
London Bridge d				12 30	12 45						13 00		13 15						13 30	13 45		
Sevenoaks d						11 51								12 21							12 51	
Bat & Ball d						11 54								12 24							12 54	
Otford d						11 57								12 27							12 57	
Shoreham (Kent) d						12 00								12 30							13 00	
Eynsford d						12 04								12 34							13 04	
Swanley d						12 09								12 39							13 09	
St Mary Cray d						12 13								12 43							13 13	
Bickley d						12 17								12 47							13 17	
Bromley South d						12 20								12 50							13 20	
Shortlands d						12 23								12 53							13 23	
Ravensbourne d						12 25								12 55							13 25	
Beckenham Hill d						12 27								12 57							13 27	
Bellingham d						12 29								12 59							13 29	
Catford d						12 32								13 02							13 32	
Crofton Park d						12 34								13 04							13 34	
Nunhead d						12 37								13 07							13 37	
Peckham Rye d						12 39								13 09							13 39	
Denmark Hill d						12 43								13 13							13 43	
Herne Hill d			12 27				12 44			12 57					13 14			13 27				13 44
Loughborough Jn. d			12 30				12 47			13 00					13 17			13 30				13 47
Elephant & Castle d			12 34			12 49	12 52			13 04				13 19	13 22			13 34			13 49	13 52
London Blackfriars a			12 37	12 37	12 52	12 53	12 55			13 07	13 07		13 22	13 23	13 25			13 37	13 37	13 52	13 53	13 55
London Blackfriars d				12 40	12 52		12 56				13 10		13 22		13 26				13 40	13 52		13 56
City Thameslink d																						
Farringdon d				12 44	12 57		13 01				13 14		13 27		13 31				13 44	13 57		14 01
St Pancras International a				12 48	13 01		13 05				13 18		13 31		13 35				13 48	14 01		14 05

A From Dorking to London Victoria
B From Epsom to London Victoria
C To Bedford
D To Luton
E To London Victoria

Please refer to separate pages within this table for services operating between London and Bedford

At weekends please use local bus and tube services to travel to/from St Pancras International and London Bridge when no trains are operating. See local publicity for details of alternative routes and services that are available across central London

Brighton, Gatwick Airport - South London

from 23 September

Network Diagram - see first Page of Table 52

		SN	SN	FC	FC	SN	FC	SE	FC	SN	SN	FC	FC	FC	SE	FC	SN	SN	FC	FC	SN	FC
		A	B		C	D	C		E	A	B		C	C		E	A	B		C	D	C
Brighton	d					13 00	13 14							13 44							14 00	14 14
Preston Park	d					13 03															14 03	
Hassocks	d					13 10	13 23							13 53							14 10	14 23
Burgess Hill	d					13 13	13 26							13 56							14 13	14 26
Wivelsfield	d					13 15															14 15	
Haywards Heath	d					13 20	13 32							14 02							14 20	14 32
Balcombe	d					13 26															14 26	
Three Bridges	d					13 32	13 41							14 11							14 32	14 41
Gatwick Airport	d					13 38	13 46							14 16							14 38	14 46
Redhill	d					13 46															14 46	
East Croydon	d				13 47	13a58	14 01						14 17	14 32						14 47	14a58	15 01
Sutton (Surrey)	d	13 13	13 28	13 34					13 37	13 43	13 58	14 04				14 07	14 13	14 28	14 34			
West Sutton	d								13 40							14 10						
Sutton Common	d								13 42							14 12						
St Helier	d								13 45							14 15						
Morden South	d								13 47							14 17						
South Merton	d								13 49							14 19						
Wimbledon Chase	d								13 51							14 21						
Wimbledon	d								13 56							14 26						
Haydons Road	d								13 58							14 28						
Tooting	d								14 01							14 31						
Carshalton	d	13 16	13 31	13 37						13 46	14 01	14 07					14 16	14 31	14 37			
Hackbridge	d	13 18	13 33	13 39						13 48	14 03	14 09					14 18	14 33	14 39			
Mitcham Junction	d	13 22	13 37	13 42						13 52	14 07	14 12					14 22	14 37	14 42			
Mitcham Eastfields	d	13a25	13a40	13 45						13a55	14a10	14 15					14a25	14a40	14 45			
Streatham	d			13 49					14 06			14 19				14 36			14 49			
Tulse Hill	d			13 53					14 10			14 23				14 40			14 53			
London Bridge	a				14 00		14 15						14 30	14 45						15 00		15 15
	d				14 00		14 15						14 30	14 45						15 00		15 15
Sevenoaks	d							13 21							13 51							
Bat & Ball	d							13 24							13 54							
Otford	d							13 27							13 57							
Shoreham (Kent)	d							13 30							14 00							
Eynsford	d							13 34							14 04							
Swanley	d							13 39							14 09							
St Mary Cray	d							13 43							14 13							
Bickley	d							13 47							14 17							
Bromley South	d							13 50							14 20							
Shortlands	d							13 53							14 23							
Ravensbourne	d							13 55							14 25							
Beckenham Hill	d							13 57							14 27							
Bellingham	d							13 59							14 29							
Catford	d							14 02							14 32							
Crofton Park	d							14 04							14 34							
Nunhead	d							14 07							14 37							
Peckham Rye	d							14 09							14 39							
Denmark Hill	d							14 13							14 43							
Herne Hill	d			13 57					14 14			14 27				14 44			14 57			
Loughborough Jn	d			14 00					14 17			14 30				14 47			15 00			
Elephant & Castle	d			14 04				14 19	14 22			14 34			14 49	14 52			15 04			
London Blackfriars	a			14 07	14 07		14 22	14 23	14 25			14 37	14 37	14 52	14 53	14 55			15 07	15 07		15 22
	d				14 10		14 22		14 26				14 40	14 52		14 56				15 10		15 22
City Thameslink	d																					
Farringdon	d				14 14		14 27		14 31				14 44	14 57		15 01				15 14		15 27
St Pancras International	a				14 18		14 31		14 35				14 48	15 01		15 05				15 18		15 31

A From Dorking to London Victoria
B From Epsom to London Victoria
C To Bedford
D To London Victoria
E To Luton

Please refer to separate pages within this table for services operating between London and Bedford

At weekends please use local bus and tube services to travel to/from St Pancras International and London Bridge when no trains are operating. See local publicity for details of alternative routes and services that are available across central London

Brighton, Gatwick Airport - South London

from 23 September

Network Diagram - see first Page of Table 52

		SE	FC	SN	SN	FC	FC	FC	SE	FC	SN	SN	FC	FC	SN	FC	SE	FC	SN	SN	FC	FC	FC
			A	B	C		D	D		A	B	C		D	E	D		A	B	C		D	D
Brighton	d							14 44							15 00	15 14							15 44
Preston Park	d														15 03								
Hassocks	d							14 53							15 10	15 23							15 53
Burgess Hill	d							14 56							15 13	15 26							15 56
Wivelsfield	d														15 15								
Haywards Heath	d							15 02							15 20	15 32							16 02
Balcombe	d														15 26								
Three Bridges	d							15 11							15 32	15 41							16 11
Gatwick Airport	d							15 16							15 38	15 46							16 16
Redhill	d														15 46								
East Croydon	d						15 17	15 32						15 47	15a58	16 01						16 17	16 32
Sutton (Surrey)	d		14 37	14 43	14 58	15 04				15 07	15 13	15 28	15 34					15 37	15 43	15 58	16 04		
West Sutton	d		14 40							15 10								15 40					
Sutton Common	d		14 42							15 12								15 42					
St Helier	d		14 45							15 15								15 45					
Morden South	d		14 47							15 17								15 47					
South Merton	d		14 49							15 19								15 49					
Wimbledon Chase	d		14 51							15 21								15 51					
Wimbledon	d		14 56							15 26								15 56					
Haydons Road	d		14 58							15 28								15 58					
Tooting	d		15 01							15 31								16 01					
Carshalton	d			14 46	15 01	15 07					15 16	15 31	15 37						15 46	16 01	16 07		
Hackbridge	d			14 48	15 03	15 09					15 18	15 33	15 39						15 48	16 03	16 09		
Mitcham Junction	d			14 52	15 07	15 12					15 22	15 37	15 42						15 52	16 07	16 12		
Mitcham Eastfields	d			14a55	15a10	15 15					15a25	15a40	15 45						15a55	16a10	16 15		
Streatham	d		15 06			15 19				15 36			15 49					16 06			16 19		
Tulse Hill	d		15 10			15 23				15 40			15 53					16 10			16 23		
London Bridge	a						15 30	15 45						16 00		16 15						16 30	16 45
	d						15 30	15 45						16 00		16 15						16 30	16 45
Sevenoaks	d	14 21							14 51								15 21						
Bat & Ball	d	14 24							14 54								15 24						
Otford	d	14 27							14 57								15 27						
Shoreham (Kent)	d	14 30							15 00								15 30						
Eynsford	d	14 34							15 04								15 34						
Swanley	d	14 39							15 09								15 39						
St Mary Cray	d	14 43							15 13								15 43						
Bickley	d	14 47							15 17								15 47						
Bromley South	d	14 50							15 20								15 50						
Shortlands	d	14 53							15 23								15 53						
Ravensbourne	d	14 55							15 25								15 55						
Beckenham Hill	d	14 57							15 27								15 57						
Bellingham	d	14 59							15 29								15 59						
Catford	d	15 02							15 32								16 02						
Crofton Park	d	15 04							15 34								16 04						
Nunhead	d	15 07							15 37								16 07						
Peckham Rye	d	15 09							15 39								16 09						
Denmark Hill	d	15 13							15 43								16 13						
Herne Hill	d		15 14			15 27				15 44			15 57					16 14			16 27		
Loughborough Jn	d		15 17			15 30				15 47			16 00					16 17			16 30		
Elephant & Castle	d	15 19	15 22			15 34			15 49	15 52			16 04				16 19	16 22			16 34		
London Blackfriars	a	15 23	15 25			15 37	15 37	15 52	15 53	15 55			16 07	16 07		16 22	16 23	16 25			16 37	16 37	16 52
	d		15 26				15 40	15 52		15 56				16 10		16 22		16 26				16 40	16 52
City Thameslink	d																						
Farringdon	d		15 31				15 44	15 57		16 01				16 14		16 27		16 31				16 44	16 57
St Pancras International	a		15 35				15 48	16 01		16 05				16 18		16 31		16 35				16 48	17 01

A To Luton
B From Dorking to London Victoria
C From Epsom to London Victoria
D To Bedford
E To London Victoria

Please refer to separate pages within this table for services operating between London and Bedford

At weekends please use local bus and tube services to travel to/from St Pancras International and London Bridge when no trains are operating. See local publicity for details of alternative routes and services that are available across central London

Brighton, Gatwick Airport - South London

Sundays
from 23 September

Network Diagram - see first Page of Table 52

		SE	FC	SN	SN	FC	FC ■	SN ◇■	FC ■	SE	FC	SN	SN	FC	FC ■	FC ■	SE	FC	SN	SN	FC	FC ■	SN ◇■
			A	B	C		D	E	D		A	B	C		D	D		A	B	C		D	E
Brighton	d							16 00	16 14							16 44							17 00
Preston Park	d							16 03															17 03
Hassocks	d							16 10	16 23							16 53							17 10
Burgess Hill	d							16 13	16 26							16 56							17 13
Wivelsfield	d							16 15															17 15
Haywards Heath	d							16 20	16 32							17 02							17 20
Balcombe	d							16 26															17 26
Three Bridges	d							16 32	16 41							17 11							17 32
Gatwick Airport ✈	d							16 38	16 46							17 16							17 38
Redhill	d							16 46															17 46
East Croydon	d						16 47	16a58	17 01						17 17	17 32						17 47	17a58
Sutton (Surrey)	d		16 07	16 13	16 28	16 34					16 37	16 43	16 58	17 04				17 07	17 13	17 28	17 34		
West Sutton	d		16 10								16 40							17 10					
Sutton Common	d		16 12								16 42							17 12					
St Helier	d		16 15								16 45							17 15					
Morden South	d		16 17								16 47							17 17					
South Merton	d		16 19								16 49							17 19					
Wimbledon Chase	d		16 21								16 51							17 21					
Wimbledon	d		16 26								16 56							17 26					
Haydons Road	d		16 28								16 58							17 28					
Tooting	d		16 31								17 01							17 31					
Carshalton	d			16 16	16 31	16 37						16 46	17 01	17 07					17 16	17 31	17 37		
Hackbridge	d			16 18	16 33	16 39						16 48	17 03	17 09					17 18	17 33	17 39		
Mitcham Junction	d			16 22	16 37	16 42						16 52	17 07	17 12					17 22	17 37	17 42		
Mitcham Eastfields	d			16a25	16a40	16 45						16a55	17a10	17 15					17a25	17a40	17 45		
Streatham	d		16 36			16 49					17 06			17 19				17 36			17 49		
Tulse Hill	d		16 40			16 53					17 10			17 23				17 40			17 53		
London Bridge ⊖	a						17 00		17 15						17 30	17 45						18 00	
	d						17 00		17 15						17 30	17 45						18 00	
Sevenoaks	d	15 51								16 21							16 51						
Bat & Ball	d	15 54								16 24							16 54						
Otford	d	15 57								16 27							16 57						
Shoreham (Kent)	d	16 00								16 30							17 00						
Eynsford	d	16 04								16 34							17 04						
Swanley	d	16 09								16 39							17 09						
St Mary Cray	d	16 13								16 43							17 13						
Bickley	d	16 17								16 47							17 17						
Bromley South	d	16 20								16 50							17 20						
Shortlands	d	16 23								16 53							17 23						
Ravensbourne	d	16 25								16 55							17 25						
Beckenham Hill	d	16 27								16 57							17 27						
Bellingham	d	16 29								16 59							17 29						
Catford	d	16 32								17 02							17 32						
Crofton Park	d	16 34								17 04							17 34						
Nunhead	d	16 37								17 07							17 37						
Peckham Rye	d	16 39								17 09							17 39						
Denmark Hill	d	16 43								17 13							17 43						
Herne Hill	d		16 44			16 57					17 14			17 27				17 44			17 57		
Loughborough Jn.	d		16 47			17 00					17 17			17 30				17 47			18 00		
Elephant & Castle	d	16 49	16 52			17 04				17 19	17 22			17 34			17 49	17 52			18 04		
London Blackfriars ⊖	a	16 53	16 55			17 07	17 07		17 22	17 23	17 25			17 37	17 37	17 52	17 53	17 55			18 07	18 07	
	d		16 56				17 10		17 22		17 26				17 40	17 52		17 56				18 10	
City Thameslink	d																						
Farringdon ⊖	d		17 01				17 14		17 27		17 31				17 44	17 57		18 01				18 14	
St Pancras International ⊖	a		17 05				17 18		17 31		17 35				17 48	18 01		18 05				18 18	

A To Luton
B From Dorking to London Victoria
C From Epsom to London Victoria
D To Bedford
E To London Victoria

Please refer to separate pages within this table for services operating between London and Bedford

At weekends please use local bus and tube services to travel to/from St Pancras International and London Bridge when no trains are operating. See local publicity for details of alternative routes and services that are available across central London

Brighton, Gatwick Airport - South London

Sundays
from 23 September

Network Diagram - see first Page of Table 52

		FC ■	SE	FC	SN	SN	FC	FC ■	FC ■	SE	FC	SN	SN	FC	FC ■	SN ◇■	FC ■	SE	FC	SN	SN	FC
		A		B	C	D		A	A		B	C	D		A	E	A		A	C	D	
Brighton	d	17 14							17 44							18 00	18 14					
Preston Park	d															18 03						
Hassocks	d	17 23							17 53							18 10	18 23					
Burgess Hill	d	17 26							17 56							18 13	18 26					
Wivelsfield	d															18 15						
Haywards Heath	d	17 32							18 02							18 20	18 32					
Balcombe	d															18 26						
Three Bridges	d	17 41							18 11							18 32	18 41					
Gatwick Airport ✈	d	17 46							18 16							18 38	18 46					
Redhill	d															18 46						
East Croydon	d	18 01						18 17	18 32						18 47	18a58	19 01					
Sutton (Surrey)	d			17 37	17 43	17 58	18 04				18 07	18 13	18 28	18 34					18 37	18 43	18 58	19 04
West Sutton	d			17 40							18 10								18 40			
Sutton Common	d			17 42							18 12								18 42			
St Helier	d			17 45							18 15								18 45			
Morden South	d			17 47							18 17								18 47			
South Merton	d			17 49							18 19								18 49			
Wimbledon Chase	d			17 51							18 21								18 51			
Wimbledon	d			17 56							18 26								18 56			
Haydons Road	d			17 58							18 28								18 58			
Tooting	d			18 01							18 31								19 01			
Carshalton	d				17 46	18 01	18 07					18 16	18 31	18 37						18 46	19 01	19 07
Hackbridge	d				17 48	18 03	18 09					18 18	18 33	18 39						18 48	19 03	19 09
Mitcham Junction	d				17 52	18 07	18 12					18 22	18 37	18 42						18 52	19 07	19 12
Mitcham Eastfields	d				17a55	18a10	18 15					18a25	18a40	18 45						18a55	19a10	19 15
Streatham	d			18 06			18 19				18 36			18 49					19 06			19 19
Tulse Hill	d			18 10			18 23				18 40			18 53					19 10			19 23
London Bridge ⊖	a	18 15						18 30	18 45						19 00		19 15					
	d	18 15						18 30	18 45						19 00		19 15					
Sevenoaks	d		17 21							17 51								18 21				
Bat & Ball	d		17 24							17 54								18 24				
Otford	d		17 27							17 57								18 27				
Shoreham (Kent)	d		17 30							18 00								18 30				
Eynsford	d		17 34							18 04								18 34				
Swanley	d		17 39							18 09								18 39				
St Mary Cray	d		17 43							18 13								18 43				
Bickley	d		17 47							18 17								18 47				
Bromley South	d		17 50							18 20								18 50				
Shortlands	d		17 53							18 23								18 53				
Ravensbourne	d		17 55							18 25								18 55				
Beckenham Hill	d		17 57							18 27								18 57				
Bellingham	d		17 59							18 29								18 59				
Catford	d		18 02							18 32								19 02				
Crofton Park	d		18 04							18 34								19 04				
Nunhead	d		18 07							18 37								19 07				
Peckham Rye	d		18 09							18 39								19 09				
Denmark Hill	d		18 13							18 43								19 13				
Herne Hill	d			18 14			18 27				18 44			18 57					19 14			19 27
Loughborough Jn.	d			18 17			18 30				18 47			19 00					19 17			19 30
Elephant & Castle	d		18 19	18 22			18 34			18 49	18 52			19 04				19 19	19 22			19 34
London Blackfriars ⊖	a	18 22	18 23	18 25			18 37	18 37	18 52	18 53	18 55			19 07	19 07		19 22	19 23	19 25			19 37
	d	18 22		18 26				18 40	18 52		18 56				19 10		19 22		19 26			
City Thameslink	d																					
Farringdon ⊖	d	18 27		18 31				18 44	18 57		19 01				19 14		19 27		19 31			
St Pancras International ⊖	a	18 31		18 35				18 48	19 01		19 05				19 18		19 31		19 35			

A To Bedford
B To Luton
C From Dorking to London Victoria
D From Epsom to London Victoria
E To London Victoria

Please refer to separate pages within this table for services operating between London and Bedford

At weekends please use local bus and tube services to travel to/from St Pancras International and London Bridge when no trains are operating. See local publicity for details of alternative routes and services that are available across central London

Brighton, Gatwick Airport - South London

Network Diagram - see first Page of Table 52

		FC	FC	SE	SN	FC	SN	FC	FC	SE	FC	SN	FC	FC	SE	SN	FC	SN	FC	FC	SE	FC	SN
		1	1		◇1				1					1		◇1				1			
		A	A		B	A	C		A		A	C		A		B	A	C		A		A	C
Brighton 10	d		18 44		19 00				19 14					19 44		20 00				20 14			
Preston Park	d				19 03											20 03							
Hassocks 4	d		18 53		19 10				19 23					19 53		20 10				20 23			
Burgess Hill 4	d		18 56		19 13				19 26					19 56		20 13				20 26			
Wivelsfield 4	d				19 15											20 15							
Haywards Heath 3	d		19 02		19 20				19 32					20 02		20 20				20 32			
Balcombe	d				19 26											20 26							
Three Bridges 4	d		19 11		19 32				19 41					20 11		20 32				20 41			
Gatwick Airport 10 ✈	d		19 16		19 38				19 46					20 16		20 38				20 46			
Redhill	d				19 46											20 46							
East Croydon	d	19 17	19 32		19a58				20 01					20 32		20a59				21 01			
Sutton (Surrey) 4	d					19 07	19 13	19 34			19 37	19 43	20 04				20 07	20 13	20 34			20 37	20 43
West Sutton	d					19 10					19 40						20 10					20 40	
Sutton Common	d					19 12					19 42						20 12					20 42	
St Helier	d					19 15					19 45						20 15					20 45	
Morden South	d					19 17					19 47						20 17					20 47	
South Merton	d					19 19					19 49						20 19					20 49	
Wimbledon Chase	d					19 21					19 51						20 21					20 51	
Wimbledon 5	d					19 26					19 56						20 26					20 56	
Haydons Road	d					19 28					19 58						20 28					20 58	
Tooting	d					19 31					20 01						20 31					21 01	
Carshalton	d						19 16	19 37				19 46	20 07					20 16	20 37				20 46
Hackbridge	d						19 18	19 39				19 48	20 09					20 18	20 39				20 48
Mitcham Junction	d						19 22	19 42				19 52	20 12					20 22	20 42				20 52
Mitcham Eastfields	d						19a25	19 45				19a55	20 15					20a25	20 45				20a55
Streatham 4	d					19 36		19 49			20 06		20 19				20 36		20 49			21 06	
Tulse Hill 3	d					19 40		19 53			20 10		20 23				20 40		20 53			21 10	
London Bridge 4 ⊖	a	19 30	19 45						20 15					20 45						21 15			
	d	19 30	19 45						20 15					20 45						21 15			
Sevenoaks 4	d			18 51						19 21					19 51						20 21		
Bat & Ball	d			18 54						19 24					19 54						20 24		
Otford 4	d			18 57						19 27					19 57						20 27		
Shoreham (Kent)	d			19 00						19 30					20 00						20 30		
Eynsford	d			19 04						19 34					20 04						20 34		
Swanley 4	d			19 09						19 39					20 09						20 39		
St Mary Cray 4	d			19 13						19 43					20 13						20 43		
Bickley	d			19 17						19 47					20 17						20 47		
Bromley South	d			19 20						19 50					20 20						20 50		
Shortlands 4	d			19 23						19 53					20 23						20 53		
Ravensbourne	d			19 25						19 55					20 25						20 55		
Beckenham Hill	d			19 27						19 57					20 27						20 57		
Bellingham	d			19 29						19 59					20 29						20 59		
Catford	d			19 32						20 02					20 32						21 02		
Crofton Park	d			19 34						20 04					20 34						21 04		
Nunhead 4	d			19 37						20 07					20 37						21 07		
Peckham Rye 4	d			19 39						20 09					20 39						21 09		
Denmark Hill 4	d			19 43						20 13					20 43						21 13		
Herne Hill 4	d					19 44		19 57			20 14		20 27				20 44		20 57			21 14	
Loughborough Jn.	d					19 47		20 00			20 17		20 30				20 47		21 00			21 17	
Elephant & Castle	d			19 49		19 52		20 04		20 19	20 22		20 34		20 49		20 52		21 04		21 19	21 22	
London Blackfriars 3 ⊖	a	19 37	19 52	19 53		19 55		20 07	20 22	20 23	20 25		20 37	20 52	20 53		20 55		21 07	21 22	21 23	21 25	
	d	19 40	19 52			19 56			20 22		20 26			20 52			20 56			21 22		21 26	
City Thameslink 3	d																						
Farringdon 3 ⊖	d	19 44	19 57			20 01			20 27		20 31			20 57			21 01			21 27		21 31	
St Pancras International 15 ⊖	a	19 48	20 01			20 05			20 31		20 35			21 01			21 05			21 31		21 35	

A To Bedford
B To London Victoria
C From Dorking to London Victoria

Please refer to separate pages within this table for services operating between London and Bedford

At weekends please use local bus and tube services to travel to/from St Pancras International and London Bridge when no trains are operating. See local publicity for details of alternative routes and services that are available across central London

Brighton, Gatwick Airport - South London

Network Diagram - see first Page of Table 52

		FC	FC	SE	SN	FC	SN	FC	FC	SE	SN	FC	FC	SE	SN	SN	FC	SE	SN	FC	SN	SN
			1		◇1				1				1		◇1		1			1	◇1	
			A		B	A	C		A		C		A		B	C	A		C	A	B	C
Brighton 10	d		20 44		21 00				21 14				21 44		22 00		22 14			22 44	23 02	
Preston Park	d				21 03										22 03						23 06	
Hassocks 4	d		20 53		21 10				21 23				21 53		22 10		22 23			22 53	23 12	
Burgess Hill 4	d		20 56		21 13				21 26				21 56		22 13		22 26			22 56	23 16	
Wivelsfield 4	d				21 15										22 15						23 18	
Haywards Heath 3	d		21 02		21 20				21 32				22 02		22 20		22 32			23 02	23 23	
Balcombe	d				21 26										22 26						23 29	
Three Bridges 4	d		21 11		21 32				21 41				22 11		22 32		22 41			23 11	23 41	
Gatwick Airport 10 ✈	d		21 16		21 38				21 46				22 16		22 38		22 46			23 16	23 46	
Redhill	d				21 46										22 46						00 01	
East Croydon	d		21 32		21a58				22 01				22 32		22a58		23 01			23 32	00a16	
Sutton (Surrey) 4	d	21 04				21 07	21 13	21 34			21 43	22 04				22 13			22 43			23 13
West Sutton	d					21 10																
Sutton Common	d					21 12																
St Helier	d					21 15																
Morden South	d					21 17																
South Merton	d					21 19																
Wimbledon Chase	d					21 21																
Wimbledon 5	d					21 26																
Haydons Road	d					21 28																
Tooting	d					21 31																
Carshalton	d	21 07					21 16	21 37			21 46	22 07				22 16			22 46			23 16
Hackbridge	d	21 09					21 18	21 39			21 48	22 09				22 18			22 48			23 18
Mitcham Junction	d	21 12					21 22	21 42			21 52	22 12				22 22			22 52			23 22
Mitcham Eastfields	d	21 15					21a25	21 45			21a55	22 15				22a25			22a55			23a25
Streatham 4	d	21 19				21 36		21 49				22 19										
Tulse Hill 3	d	21 23				21 40		21 53				22 23										
London Bridge 4 ⊖	a		21 45						22 15				22 45				23 15			23 45		
	d		21 45						22 15				22 45				23 15			23 45		
Sevenoaks 4	d			20 51						21 21				21 51				22 21				
Bat & Ball	d			20 54						21 24				21 54				22 24				
Otford 4	d			20 57						21 27				21 57				22 27				
Shoreham (Kent)	d			21 00						21 30				22 00				22 30				
Eynsford	d			21 04						21 34				22 04				22 34				
Swanley 4	d			21 09						21 39				22 09				22 39				
St Mary Cray 4	d			21 13						21 43				22 13				22 43				
Bickley	d			21 17						21 47				22 17				22 47				
Bromley South	d			21 20						21 50				22 20				22 50				
Shortlands 4	d			21 23						21 53				22 23				22 53				
Ravensbourne	d			21 25						21 55				22 25				22 55				
Beckenham Hill	d			21 27						21 57				22 27				22 57				
Bellingham	d			21 29						21 59				22 29				22 59				
Catford	d			21 32						22 02				22 32				23 02				
Crofton Park	d			21 34						22 04				22 34				23 04				
Nunhead 4	d			21 37						22 07				22 37				23 07				
Peckham Rye 4	d			21 39						22 09				22 39				23 09				
Denmark Hill 4	d			21 43						22 13				22 43				23 13				
Herne Hill 4	d	21 27				21 44		21 57				22 27										
Loughborough Jn.	d	21 30				21 47		22 00				22 30										
Elephant & Castle	d	21 34		21 49		21 52		22 04		22 19		22 34		22 49				23 19				
London Blackfriars 3 ⊖	a	21 37	21 52	21 53		21 55		22 07	22 22	22 23		22 37	22 52	22 53			23 22	23 23		23 52		
	d		21 52			21 56			22 22				22 52				23 22			23 52		
City Thameslink 3	d																					
Farringdon 3 ⊖	d		21 57			22 01			22 27				22 57				23 27			23 57		
St Pancras International 15 ⊖	a		22 01			22 05			22 31				23 01				23 31			00 01		

A To Bedford
B To London Victoria
C From Dorking to London Victoria

Please refer to separate pages within this table for services operating between London and Bedford

At weekends please use local bus and tube services to travel to/from St Pancras International and London Bridge when no trains are operating. See local publicity for details of alternative routes and services that are available across central London

Table 52

Sundays from 23 September

Brighton, Gatwick Airport - South London

Network Diagram - see first Page of Table 52

	FC 1	SN	FC 1
	A	B	A
Brighton d	23 14		23 45
Preston Park d			
Hassocks d	23 23		23 54
Burgess Hill d	23 26		23 57
Wivelsfield d			
Haywards Heath d	23 32		00 03
Balcombe d			
Three Bridges d	23 41		00 12
Gatwick Airport d	23 46		00 17
Redhill d			00 24
East Croydon d	00 03		00 37
Sutton (Surrey) d		23 43	
West Sutton d			
Sutton Common d			
St Helier d			
Morden South d			
South Merton d			
Wimbledon Chase d			
Wimbledon d			
Haydons Road d			
Tooting d			
Carshalton d		23 46	
Hackbridge d		23 48	
Mitcham Junction d		23 52	
Mitcham Eastfields d		23a55	
Streatham d			
Tulse Hill d			
London Bridge a	00 21		00 50
d	00 22		00 51
Sevenoaks d			
Bat & Ball d			
Otford d			
Shoreham (Kent) d			
Eynsford d			
Swanley d			
St Mary Cray d			
Bickley d			
Bromley South d			
Shortlands d			
Ravensbourne d			
Beckenham Hill d			
Bellingham d			
Catford d			
Crofton Park d			
Nunhead d			
Peckham Rye d			
Denmark Hill d			
Herne Hill d			
Loughborough Jn d			
Elephant & Castle d			
London Blackfriars a	00 27		00 57
d	00 28		00 58
City Thameslink d			
Farringdon d	00 33		
St Pancras International a	00 37		01 07

A To Bedford

B From Dorking to London Victoria

Please refer to separate pages within this table for services operating between London and Bedford

At weekends please use local bus and tube services to travel to/from St Pancras International and London Bridge when no trains are operating. See local publicity for details of alternative routes and services that are available across central London

Table 52

Saturdays until 23 June

London, St Albans, Luton - Bedford

Network Diagram - see first Page of Table 52

	FC	FC	FC 1	FC 1	EM ◇1	FC	FC	FC 1	FC 1		FC	FC	FC 1	FC 1	EM ◇1	FC	FC	FC	FC 1		FC 1	FC	FC	FC 1
	A	B	A	B		A	B	A	B		A	B	A	B		A	B	B	B		A	B	B	A
London Bridge d			22p45					23p15					23p45					23p55			00 22	00 25		00 52
Elephant & Castle d	22p34					23p04					23p34													
London Blackfriars a	22p37		22p52			23p07		23p22			23p37		23p52					00 10			00 28	00 40		00 58
d	22p38		22p52			23p08		23p22			23p38		23p52			00 08		00 10			00 29	00 40		00 58
City Thameslink d	22p40		22p54																					
Farringdon d	22p43		22p58			23p13		23p28			23p43		23p58			00 13		00 20			00 33	00 50		
St Pancras International a	22p47		23p02			23p17		23p32			23p47		00 02			00 17		00 25			00 37	00 55		01 07
d	22p48	22p48	23p02	23p02	23p15	23p18	23p18	23p32	23p32		23p48	23p48	00 02	00 02	00 15	00 18	00 18		00 32		00 38		01 02	01 08
Kentish Town d	22p51	22p51				23p21	23p21				23p51	23p51				00 21	00 21		00 35		00 41		01 05	01 11
West Hampstead Thameslink d	22p55	22p55	23p10	23p10		23p25	23p25	23p40	23p40		23p55	23p55	00 10	00 10		00 25	00 25		00 40		00 45		01 10	01 15
Cricklewood d	22p58	22p58				23p28	23p28				23p58	23p58				00 28	00 28		00 43		00 48		01 13	01 18
Hendon d	23p01	23p01				23p31	23p31				00 01	00 01				00 31	00 31		00 46		00 51		01 16	01 21
Mill Hill Broadway d	23p05	23p05				23p35	23p35				00 05	00 05				00 35	00 35		00 50		00 55		01 20	01 25
Elstree & Borehamwood d	23p09	23p09				23p39	23p39				00 09	00 09				00 39	00 39		00 54		00 59		01 24	01 29
Radlett d	23p14	23p14				23p44	23p44				00 14	00 14				00 44	00 44		00 59		01 04		01 29	01 34
St Albans City d	23p20	23p20	23p27	23p27		23p50	23p50	23p57	23p57		00 20	00 20	00 27	00 27		00 50	00 50		01 06		01 10		01 36	01 40
Harpenden d	23p26	23p26	23p33	23p33		23p56	23p56	00 03	00 03		00 26	00 26	00 33	00 33		00 56	00 56		01 12		01 16		01 42	01 46
Luton Airport Parkway d	23p32	23p32	23p39	23p39		00 02	00 02	00 09	00 09		00 32	00 32	00 39	00 39	00 44	01 02	01 02		01 18		01 22		01 48	01 52
Luton d	23p35	23p35	23p42	23p42	23p46	00 05	00 05	00 12	00 12		00 35	00 35	00 42	00 42	00 47	01 05	01 05		01 21		01 25		01 51	01 55
Leagrave d	23p39	23p39	23p46	23p46		00 09	00 09	00 16	00 16		00 39	00 39	00 46	00 46		01 09	01 09		01 25		01 29		01 55	01 59
Harlington d	23p44	23p44	23p51	23p51		00 14	00 14	00 21	00 21		00 44	00 44	00 51	00 51		01 14	01 14		01 30		01 34		02 00	02 04
Flitwick d	23p48	23p48	23p55	23p55		00 18	00 18	00 25	00 25		00 48	00 48	00 55	00 55		01 18	01 18		01 34		01 38		02 04	02 08
Bedford a	00 02	00 02	00 08	00 08	00 11	00 32	00 32	00 38	00 38		01 02	01 02	01 08	01 08	01 12	01 32	01 32		01 47		01 52		02 17	02 22

	FC	FC	FC	FC	FC		FC	FC	FC	FC	FC	FC	EM ◇1	FC	FC		FC	SE	EM ◇1	FC 1	FC	EM ◇1	SE	EM ◇1
	B	B	B				B		B		B							A					A	
London Bridge d	00 57		01 57				03 17		04 17		05 20				06 02					06 30				
Elephant & Castle d																	06 09	06 30			06 39		07 00	
London Blackfriars a	01 12		02 12				03 32		04 32		05 35				06 08		06 12	06 34		06 37	06 42		07 04	
d	01 12		02 12	02 14	03 13		03 32	04 14	04 32	05 14	05 35	05 44			06 08		06 14			06 38	06 44			
City Thameslink d																								
Farringdon d										05 20	05 45	05 50			06 12		06 19			06 42	06 49			
St Pancras International a	01 27		02 27	02 24	03 23		03 47	04 22	04 47	05 24	05 50	05 54			06 16		06 23			06 46	06 53			
d		01 34		02 24	03 24			04 24		05 24		05 54	06 10		06 17		06 24		06 37	06 47	06 54	06 55		07 00
Kentish Town d		01 37		02 28	03 28			04 28		05 28		05 58					06 27				06 57			
West Hampstead Thameslink d		01 42		02 32	03 32			04 32		05 32		06 02			06 24		06 31			06 54	07 01			
Cricklewood d		01 45		02 35	03 35			04 35		05 35		06 05					06 34				07 04			
Hendon d		01 48		02 38	03 38			04 38		05 38		06 08					06 37				07 07			
Mill Hill Broadway d		01 52		02 42	03 42			04 42		05 42		06 12					06 41				07 11			
Elstree & Borehamwood d		01 56		02 46	03 46			04 46		05 46		06 16					06 45				07 15			
Radlett d		02 01		02 51	03 51			04 51		05 51		06 20					06 49				07 19			
St Albans City d		02 08		02 58	03 58			04 58		05 58		06 26			06 39		06 56			07 09	07 26			
Harpenden d		02 14		03 04	04 04			05 04		06 04		06 31			06 45		07 01			07 15	07 31			
Luton Airport Parkway d		02 20		03 10	04 10			05 10		06 10		06 37		←	06 51		07 07			07 21	07 37	07a15		
Luton d		02 23		03 13	04 13			05 13		06 13		06 40	06 33	06 40	06 54		07a11		06a58	07 24	07a41			07 23
Leagrave d		02 27		03 17	04 17			05 17		06 17		→		06 44	06 57					07 27				
Harlington d		02 32		03 22	04 22			05 22		06 22				06 49	07 02					07 32				
Flitwick d		02 36		03 26	04 26			05 26		06 26				06 53	07 06					07 36				
Bedford a		02 49		03 39	04 39			05 39		06 39			06 47	07 05	07 19					07 49				07 38

	FC 1		FC	EM ◇1	FC	SE	FC 1	FC	FC	EM ◇1	FC 1		FC 1	FC	SE	FC 1	FC	FC	EM ◇1	FC 1	FC		SE	FC 1
						A									A								A	
London Bridge d	07 00						07 30						07 45			08 00				08 15				08 30
Elephant & Castle d			07 09		07 24	07 30			07 39					07 54	08 00			08 09			08 24		08 30	
London Blackfriars a	07 07		07 12		07 27	07 34	07 37		07 42				07 52	07 57	08 04	08 07		08 12		08 22	08 27		08 34	08 37
d	07 08		07 14		07 30		07 38		07 44				07 54	08 00		08 08		08 14		08 24	08 30			08 38
City Thameslink d																								
Farringdon d	07 12		07 19		07 36		07 44		07 49				08 00	08 06		08 14		08 19		08 30	08 36			08 44
St Pancras International a	07 16		07 23		07 40		07 48		07 53				08 04	08 10		08 18		08 23		08 34	08 40			08 48
d	07 17		07 24	07 30	07 40		07 48		07 54	08 00			08 04	08 10		08 18		08 24	08 30	08 34	08 40			08 48
Kentish Town d			07 27		07 44				07 57					08 14				08 27			08 44			
West Hampstead Thameslink d	07 24		07 31		07 49				08 01					08 19				08 31			08 49			
Cricklewood d			07 34		07 52				08 04					08 22				08 34			08 52			
Hendon d			07 37		07 55				08 07					08 25				08 37			08 55			
Mill Hill Broadway d			07 41		07 59				08 11					08 29				08 41			08 59			
Elstree & Borehamwood d			07 45		08 03				08 15					08 33				08 45			09 03			
Radlett d			07 49		08 07			←	08 19					08 37			←	08 49			09 07			
St Albans City d	07 39		07 56		08 14		08 09	08 14	08a27				08 25	08 44		08 39	08 44	08a57		08 55	09 14			09 09
Harpenden d	07 45		08 01		→		08 15	08 19					08 31	→		08 45	08 49			09 01	→			09 15
Luton Airport Parkway d	07 51		08 07	07 51			08 21	08 25			←		08 37			08 51	08 55		08 51	09 07				09 21
Luton d	07 54		08 10				08 24	08a29		08 23	08 24		08 40			08 54	08a59			09 10				09 24
Leagrave d	07 57		08 14				→				08 27		08 44			08 57				09 14				→
Harlington d	08 02		08 19								08 32		08 49			09 02				09 19				
Flitwick d	08 06		08 23								08 36		08 53			09 06				09 23				
Bedford a	08 19		08 35	08 06						08 37	08 49		09 05			09 19			09 06	09 35				

A not 19 May

B 19 May

Please refer to separate pages within this table for services operating between Brighton and South London

At weekends please use local bus and tube services to travel to/from St Pancras International and London Bridge when no trains are operating. See local publicity for details of alternative routes and services that are available across central London

Saturdays until 23 June

London, St Albans, Luton - Bedford

Network Diagram - see first Page of Table 52

		FC	FC	EM ◇■ ⊼	FC ■	FC ■	FC	SE A	FC ■	FC	FC	EM ◇■ ⊼	FC ■	FC	SE A	FC ■	FC	FC	EM ◇■ ⊼	FC ■	FC ■	FC	SE A
London Bridge ■ ⊖	d					08 45			09 00				09 15			09 30					09 45		
Elephant & Castle	d		08 39				08 54	09 00			09 09			09 24	09 30			09 39				09 54	10 00
London Blackfriars ■ ⊖	a		08 42			08 52	08 57	09 04	09 07		09 12		09 22	09 27	09 34	09 37		09 42			09 52	09 57	10 04
	d		08 44			08 54	09 00		09 08		09 14		09 24	09 30		09 38		09 44			09 54	10 00	
City Thameslink ■	d						09 02		09 10		09 16		09 26	09 32		09 40		09 46			09 56	10 02	
Farringdon ■ ⊖	d		08 49			09 00	09 06		09 14		09 19		09 30	09 36		09 44		09 49			10 00	10 06	
St Pancras International ■ ⊖	a		08 53			09 04	09 10		09 18		09 23		09 34	09 40		09 48		09 53			10 04	10 10	
	d		08 54	09 00		09 04	09 10		09 18		09 24	09 30	09 34	09 40		09 48		09 54	10 00		10 04	10 10	
Kentish Town	d		08 57				09 14				09 27			09 44				09 57				10 14	
West Hampstead Thameslink	d		09 01				09 19				09 31			09 49				10 01				10 19	
Cricklewood	d		09 04				09 22				09 34			09 52				10 04				10 22	
Hendon	d		09 07				09 25				09 37			09 55				10 07				10 25	
Mill Hill Broadway	d		09 11				09 29				09 41			09 59				10 11				10 29	
Elstree & Borehamwood	d		09 15				09 33				09 45			10 03				10 15				10 33	
Radlett	d	←	09 19				09 37			←	09 49			10 07			←	10 19				10 37	
St Albans City	d	09 14	09a27			09 25	09 44		09 39	09 44	09a57		09 55	10 14		10 09	10 14	10a27			10 25	10 44	
Harpenden	d	09 19				09 31	→		09 45	09 49			10 01	→		10 15	10 19				10 31	→	
Luton Airport Parkway ■ ✈	d	09 25			←	09 37			09 51	09 55		09 51	10 07			10 21	10 25			←	10 37		
Luton ■	d	09a29		09 23	09 24	09 40			09 54	09a59			10 10			10 24	10a29		10 23	10 24	10 40		
Leagrave	d				09 27	09 44			09 57				10 14			→				10 27	10 44		
Harlington	d				09 32	09 49			10 02				10 19							10 32	10 49		
Flitwick	d				09 36	09 53			10 06				10 23							10 36	10 53		
Bedford ■	a			09 37	09 49	10 05			10 19			10 06	10 35						10 37	10 49	11 05		

		FC ■	FC	FC	EM ◇■ ⊼	FC ■	FC	SE A	FC ■	FC	FC	EM ◇■ ⊼	FC ■	FC ■	FC	SE A	FC ■	FC	FC	EM ◇■ ⊼	FC ■	FC
London Bridge ■ ⊖	d	10 00				10 15			10 30					10 45			11 00				11 15	
Elephant & Castle	d			10 09			10 24	10 30			10 39				10 54	11 00			11 09			11 24
London Blackfriars ■ ⊖	a	10 07		10 12		10 22	10 27	10 34	10 37		10 42			10 52	10 57	11 04	11 07		11 12		11 22	11 27
	d	10 08		10 14		10 24	10 30		10 38		10 44			10 54	11 00		11 08		11 14		11 24	11 30
City Thameslink ■	d	10 10		10 16		10 26	10 32		10 40		10 46			10 56	11 02		11 10		11 16		11 26	11 32
Farringdon ■ ⊖	d	10 14		10 19		10 30	10 36		10 44		10 49			11 00	11 06		11 14		11 19		11 30	11 36
St Pancras International ■ ⊖	a	10 18		10 23		10 34	10 40		10 48		10 53			11 04	11 10		11 18		11 23		11 34	11 40
	d	10 18		10 24	10 30	10 34	10 40		10 48		10 54	11 00		11 04	11 10		11 18		11 24	11 30	11 34	11 40
Kentish Town	d			10 27			10 44				10 57				11 14				11 27			11 44
West Hampstead Thameslink	d			10 31			10 49				11 01				11 19				11 31			11 49
Cricklewood	d			10 34			10 52				11 04				11 22				11 34			11 52
Hendon	d			10 37			10 55				11 07				11 25				11 37			11 55
Mill Hill Broadway	d			10 41			10 59				11 11				11 29				11 41			11 59
Elstree & Borehamwood	d			10 45			11 03				11 15				11 33				11 45			12 03
Radlett	d		←	10 49			11 07			←	11 19				11 37			←	11 49			12 07
St Albans City	d	10 39	10 44	10a57		10 55	11 14		11 09	11 14	11a27			11 25	11 44		11 39	11 44	11a57		11 55	12 14
Harpenden	d	10 45	10 49			11 01	→		11 15	11 19				11 31	→		11 45	11 49			12 01	→
Luton Airport Parkway ■ ✈	d	10 51	10 55		10 51	11 07			11 21	11 25			←	11 37			11 51	11 55		11 51	12 07	
Luton ■	d	10 54	10a59			11 10			11 24	11a29		11 23	11 24	11 40			11 54	11a59			12 10	
Leagrave	d	10 57				11 14			→				11 27	11 44			11 57				12 14	
Harlington	d	11 02				11 19							11 32	11 49			12 02				12 19	
Flitwick	d	11 06				11 23							11 36	11 53			12 06				12 23	
Bedford ■	a	11 19			11 06	11 35						11 37	11 49	12 05			12 19			12 06	12 35	

		SE A	FC ■	FC	FC	EM ◇■ ⊼	FC ■	FC ■	FC	SE A	FC ■	FC	FC	EM ◇■ ⊼	FC ■	FC	SE A	FC ■	FC	FC	EM ◇■ ⊼	FC ■	FC ■
London Bridge ■ ⊖	d		11 30					11 45			12 00				12 15			12 30					12 45
Elephant & Castle	d	11 30			11 39				11 54	12 00			12 09			12 24	12 30			12 39			
London Blackfriars ■ ⊖	a	11 34	11 37		11 42			11 52	11 57	12 04	12 07		12 12		12 22	12 27	12 34	12 37		12 42			12 52
	d		11 38		11 44			11 54	12 00		12 08		12 14		12 24	12 30		12 38		12 44			12 54
City Thameslink ■	d		11 40		11 46			11 56	12 02		12 10		12 16		12 26	12 32		12 40		12 46			12 56
Farringdon ■ ⊖	d		11 44		11 49			12 00	12 06		12 14		12 19		12 30	12 36		12 44		12 49			13 00
St Pancras International ■ ⊖	a		11 48		11 53			12 04	12 10		12 18		12 23		12 34	12 40		12 48		12 53			13 04
	d		11 48		11 54	12 00		12 04	12 10		12 18		12 24	12 30	12 34	12 40		12 48		12 54	13 00		13 04
Kentish Town	d				11 57				12 14				12 27			12 44				12 57			
West Hampstead Thameslink	d				12 01				12 19				12 31			12 49				13 01			
Cricklewood	d				12 04				12 22				12 34			12 52				13 04			
Hendon	d				12 07				12 25				12 37			12 55				13 07			
Mill Hill Broadway	d				12 11				12 29				12 41			12 59				13 11			
Elstree & Borehamwood	d				12 15				12 33				12 45			13 03				13 15			
Radlett	d			←	12 19				12 37			←	12 49			13 07			←	13 19			
St Albans City	d		12 09	12 14	12a27			12 25	12 44		12 39	12 44	12a57		12 55	13 14		13 09	13 14	13a27			13 25
Harpenden	d		12 15	12 19				12 31	→		12 45	12 49			13 01	→		13 15	13 19				13 31
Luton Airport Parkway ■ ✈	d		12 21	12 25			←	12 37			12 51	12 55		12 51	13 07			13 21	13 25			←	13 37
Luton ■	d		12 24	12a29		12 23	12 24	12 40			12 54	12a59			13 10			13 24	13a29		13 23	13 24	13 40
Leagrave	d		→				12 27	12 44			12 57				13 14			→				13 27	13 44
Harlington	d						12 32	12 49			13 02				13 19							13 32	13 49
Flitwick	d						12 36	12 53			13 06				13 23							13 36	13 53
Bedford ■	a					12 37	12 49	13 05			13 19			13 06	13 35						13 37	13 49	14 05

A not 19 May

Please refer to separate pages within this table for services operating between Brighton and South London

At weekends please use local bus and tube services to travel to/from St Pancras International and London Bridge when no trains are operating. See local publicity for details of alternative routes and services that are available across central London

Saturdays until 23 June

London, St Albans, Luton - Bedford

Network Diagram - see first Page of Table 52

		FC	SE A	FC ■	FC	FC	EM ◇■ ⊼	FC ■	FC	SE A	FC ■	FC	FC	EM ◇■ ⊼	FC ■	FC ■	FC	SE A	FC ■	FC	FC	EM ◇■ ⊼	FC ■
London Bridge ■ ⊖	d			13 00				13 15			13 30					13 45			14 00				14 15
Elephant & Castle	d	12 54	13 00			13 09			13 24	13 30			13 39				13 54	14 00			14 09		
London Blackfriars ■ ⊖	a	12 57	13 04	13 07		13 12		13 22	13 27	13 34	13 37		13 42			13 52	13 57	14 04	14 07		14 12		14 22
	d	13 00		13 08		13 14		13 24	13 30		13 38		13 44			13 54	14 00		14 08		14 14		14 24
City Thameslink ■	d	13 02		13 10		13 16		13 26	13 32		13 40		13 46			13 56	14 02		14 10		14 16		14 26
Farringdon ■ ⊖	d	13 06		13 14		13 19		13 30	13 36		13 44		13 49			14 00	14 06		14 14		14 19		14 30
St Pancras International ■ ⊖	a	13 10		13 18		13 23		13 34	13 40		13 48		13 53			14 04	14 10		14 18		14 23		14 34
	d	13 10		13 18		13 24	13 30	13 34	13 40		13 48		13 54	14 00		14 04	14 10		14 18		14 24	14 30	14 34
Kentish Town	d	13 14				13 27			13 44				13 57				14 14				14 27		
West Hampstead Thameslink	d	13 19				13 31			13 49				14 01				14 19				14 31		
Cricklewood	d	13 22				13 34			13 52				14 04				14 22				14 34		
Hendon	d	13 25				13 37			13 55				14 07				14 25				14 37		
Mill Hill Broadway	d	13 29				13 41			13 59				14 11				14 29				14 41		
Elstree & Borehamwood	d	13 33				13 45			14 03				14 15				14 33				14 45		
Radlett	d	13 37			←	13 49			14 07			←	14 19				14 37			←	14 49		
St Albans City	d	13 44		13 39	13 44	13a57		13 55	14 14		14 09	14 14	14a27			14 25	14 44		14 39	14 44	14a57		14 55
Harpenden	d	→		13 45	13 49			14 01	→		14 15	14 19				14 31	→		14 45	14 49			15 01
Luton Airport Parkway ■ ✈	d			13 51	13 55		13 51	14 07			14 21	14 25			←	14 37			14 51	14 55		14 51	15 07
Luton ■	d			13 54	13a59			14 10			14 24	14a29		14 23	14 24	14 40			14 54	14a59			15 10
Leagrave	d			13 57				14 14			→				14 27	14 44			14 57				15 14
Harlington	d			14 02				14 19							14 32	14 49			15 02				15 19
Flitwick	d			14 06				14 23							14 36	14 53			15 06				15 23
Bedford ■	a			14 19			14 06	14 35						14 37	14 49	15 05			15 19			15 06	15 35

		FC	SE A	FC ■	FC	FC	EM ◇■ ⊼	FC ■	FC ■	FC	SE A	FC ■	FC	FC	EM ◇■ ⊼	FC ■	FC	SE A	FC ■	FC	FC	EM ◇■ ⊼
London Bridge ■ ⊖	d			14 30					14 45			15 00				15 15			15 30			
Elephant & Castle	d	14 24	14 30			14 39				14 54	15 00			15 09			15 24	15 30			15 39	
London Blackfriars ■ ⊖	a	14 27	14 34	14 37		14 42			14 52	14 57	15 04	15 07		15 12		15 22	15 27	15 34	15 37		15 42	
	d	14 30		14 38		14 44			14 54	15 00		15 08		15 14		15 24	15 30		15 38		15 44	
City Thameslink ■	d	14 32		14 40		14 46			14 56	15 02		15 10		15 16		15 26	15 32		15 40		15 46	
Farringdon ■ ⊖	d	14 36		14 44		14 49			15 00	15 06		15 14		15 19		15 30	15 36		15 44		15 49	
St Pancras International ■ ⊖	a	14 40		14 48		14 53			15 04	15 10		15 18		15 23		15 34	15 40		15 48		15 53	
	d	14 40		14 48		14 54	15 00		15 04	15 10		15 18		15 24	15 30	15 34	15 40		15 48		15 54	16 00
Kentish Town	d	14 44				14 57				15 14				15 27			15 44				15 57	
West Hampstead Thameslink	d	14 49				15 01				15 19				15 31			15 49				16 01	
Cricklewood	d	14 52				15 04				15 22				15 34			15 52				16 04	
Hendon	d	14 55				15 07				15 25				15 37			15 55				16 07	
Mill Hill Broadway	d	14 59				15 11				15 29				15 41			15 59				16 11	
Elstree & Borehamwood	d	15 03				15 15				15 33				15 45			16 03				16 15	
Radlett	d	15 07			←	15 19				15 37			←	15 49			16 07			←	16 19	
St Albans City	d	15 14		15 09	15 14	15a27			15 25	15 44		15 39	15 44	15a57		15 55	16 14		16 09	16 14	16a27	
Harpenden	d	→		15 15	15 19				15 31	→		15 45	15 49			16 01	→		16 15	16 19		
Luton Airport Parkway ■ ✈	d			15 21	15 25			←	15 37			15 51	15 55		15 51	16 07			16 21	16 25		
Luton ■	d			15 24	15a29		15 23	15 24	15 40			15 54	15a59			16 10			16 24	16a29		16 23
Leagrave	d			→				15 27	15 44			15 57				16 14			→			
Harlington	d							15 32	15 49			16 02				16 19						
Flitwick	d							15 36	15 53			16 06				16 23						
Bedford ■	a						15 37	15 49	16 05			16 19			16 06	16 35						16 37

		FC ■	FC ■	FC	SE A	FC ■	FC	FC	EM ◇■ ⊼	FC ■	FC	SE A	FC ■	FC	FC	EM ◇■ ⊼	FC ■	FC ■	FC	SE A	FC ■	FC	FC
London Bridge ■ ⊖	d		15 45			16 00				16 15			16 30					16 45			17 00		
Elephant & Castle	d			15 54	16 00			16 09			16 24	16 30			16 39				16 54	17 00			17 09
London Blackfriars ■ ⊖	a		15 52	15 57	16 04	16 07		16 12		16 22	16 27	16 34	16 37		16 42			16 52	16 57	17 04	17 07		17 12
	d		15 54	16 00		16 08		16 14		16 24	16 30		16 38		16 44			16 54	17 00		17 08		17 14
City Thameslink ■	d		15 56	16 02		16 10		16 16		16 26	16 32		16 40		16 46			16 56	17 02		17 10		17 16
Farringdon ■ ⊖	d		16 00	16 06		16 14		16 19		16 30	16 36		16 44		16 49			17 00	17 06		17 14		17 19
St Pancras International ■ ⊖	a		16 04	16 10		16 18		16 23		16 34	16 40		16 48		16 53			17 04	17 10		17 18		17 23
	d		16 04	16 10		16 18		16 24	16 30	16 34	16 40		16 48		16 54	17 00		17 04	17 10		17 18		17 24
Kentish Town	d			16 14				16 27			16 44				16 57				17 14				17 27
West Hampstead Thameslink	d			16 19				16 31			16 49				17 01				17 19				17 31
Cricklewood	d			16 22				16 34			16 52				17 04				17 22				17 34
Hendon	d			16 25				16 37			16 55				17 07				17 25				17 37
Mill Hill Broadway	d			16 29				16 41			16 59				17 11				17 29				17 41
Elstree & Borehamwood	d			16 33				16 45			17 03				17 15				17 33				17 45
Radlett	d			16 37			←	16 49			17 07			←	17 19				17 37			←	17 49
St Albans City	d		16 25	16 44		16 39	16 44	16a57		16 55	17 14		17 09	17 14	17a27			17 25	17 44		17 39	17 44	17a57
Harpenden	d		16 31	→		16 45	16 49			17 01	→		17 15	17 19				17 31	→		17 45	17 49	
Luton Airport Parkway ■ ✈	d	←	16 37			16 51	16 55		16 51	17 07			17 21	17 25			←	17 37			17 51	17 55	
Luton ■	d	16 24	16 40			16 54	16a59			17 10			17 24	17a29		17 23	17 24	17 40			17 54	17a59	
Leagrave	d	16 27	16 44			16 57				17 14			→				17 27	17 44			17 57		
Harlington	d	16 32	16 49			17 02				17 19							17 32	17 49			18 02		
Flitwick	d	16 36	16 53			17 06				17 23							17 36	17 53			18 06		
Bedford ■	a	16 49	17 05			17 19			17 06	17 35						17 37	17 49	18 05			18 19		

A not 19 May

Please refer to separate pages within this table for services operating between Brighton and South London

At weekends please use local bus and tube services to travel to/from St Pancras International and London Bridge when no trains are operating. See local publicity for details of alternative routes and services that are available across central London

Table 52

London, St Albans, Luton - Bedford

Saturdays until 23 June

Network Diagram - see first Page of Table 52

		EM ◇1	FC 1	FC	SE A	FC 1	FC	FC	EM ◇1	FC 1	FC 1	FC	SE A	FC 1	FC	FC	EM ◇1	FC 1	FC	SE A	FC 1	FC
London Bridge ⊖	d		17 15			17 30					17 45			18 00				18 15			18 30	
Elephant & Castle	d			17 24	17 30			17 39				17 54	18 00			18 09			18 24	18 30		
London Blackfriars ⊖	a		17 22	17 27	17 34	17 37		17 42			17 52	17 57	18 04	18 07		18 12		18 22	18 27	18 34	18 37	
	d		17 24	17 30		17 38		17 44			17 54	18 00		18 08		18 14		18 24	18 30		18 38	
City Thameslink	d		17 26	17 32		17 40		17 46			17 56	18 02		18 10		18 16		18 26	18 32		18 40	
Farringdon ⊖	d		17 30	17 36		17 44		17 49			18 00	18 06		18 14		18 19		18 30	18 36		18 44	
St Pancras International ⊖	a		17 34	17 40		17 48		17 53			18 04	18 10		18 18		18 23		18 34	18 40		18 48	
	d	17 30	17 34	17 40		17 48		17 54	18 00		18 04	18 10		18 18		18 24	18 30	18 34	18 40		18 48	
Kentish Town	d			17 44				17 57				18 14				18 27			18 44			
West Hampstead Thameslink	d			17 49				18 01				18 19				18 31			18 49			
Cricklewood	d			17 52				18 04				18 22				18 34			18 52			
Hendon	d			17 55				18 07				18 25				18 37			18 55			
Mill Hill Broadway	d			17 59				18 11				18 29				18 41			18 59			
Elstree & Borehamwood	d			18 03				18 15				18 33				18 45			19 03			
Radlett	d			18 07			←	18 19				18 37			←	18 49			19 07			←
St Albans City	d		17 55	18 14		18 09	18 14	18a27			18 25	18 44		18 39	18 44	18a57		18 55	19 14		19 09	19 14
Harpenden	d		18 01	→		18 15	18 19				18 31	→		18 45	18 49			19 01	→		19 15	19 19
Luton Airport Parkway ✈	d	17 51	18 07			18 21	18 25			←	18 37			18 51	18 55		18 51	19 07			19 21	19 25
Luton	d		18 10			18 24	18a29		18 23	18 24	18 40			18 54	18a59			19 10			19 24	19a29
Leagrave	d		18 14			→				18 27	18 44			18 57				19 14			→	
Harlington	d		18 19							18 32	18 49			19 02				19 19				
Flitwick	d		18 23							18 36	18 53			19 06				19 23				
Bedford	a	18 06	18 35						18 37	18 49	19 05			19 19			19 06	19 35				

		FC	EM ◇1	FC 1	FC 1	FC	SE A	FC 1	FC	FC	EM ◇1	FC 1	FC	SE A	FC 1	FC	EM ◇1	FC 1	FC	FC 1	FC	FC	SE A
London Bridge ⊖	d				18 45			19 00				19 15			19 30					19 45			
Elephant & Castle	d	18 39				18 54	19 00			19 09			19 24	19 30		19 39						19 54	20 00
London Blackfriars ⊖	a	18 42			18 52	18 57	19 04	19 07		19 12		19 22	19 27	19 34	19 37	19 42				19 52		19 57	20 04
	d	18 44			18 54	19 00		19 08		19 14		19 24	19 30		19 38	19 44				19 54		20 00	
City Thameslink	d	18 46			18 56	19 02		19 10		19 16		19 26	19 32		19 40	19 46				19 56		20 02	
Farringdon ⊖	d	18 49			19 00	19 06		19 14		19 19		19 30	19 36		19 44	19 49				20 00		20 06	
St Pancras International ⊖	a	18 53			19 04	19 10		19 18		19 23		19 34	19 40		19 48	19 53				20 04		20 10	
	d	18 54	19 00		19 04	19 10		19 18		19 24	19 30	19 34	19 40		19 48	19 54	20 00			20 04		20 10	
Kentish Town	d	18 57				19 14				19 27			19 44			19 57						20 14	
West Hampstead Thameslink	d	19 01				19 19				19 31			19 49			20 01						20 19	
Cricklewood	d	19 04				19 22				19 34			19 52			20 04						20 22	
Hendon	d	19 07				19 25				19 37			19 55			20 07						20 25	
Mill Hill Broadway	d	19 11				19 29				19 41			19 59			20 11						20 29	
Elstree & Borehamwood	d	19 15				19 33				19 45			20 03			20 15						20 33	
Radlett	d	19 19				19 37			←	19 49			20 07			20 19			←		←	20 37	
St Albans City	d	19a27			19 25	19 44		19 39	19 44	19a57		19 55	20 14		20 09	20 27			20 14	20 25	20 27	20 44	
Harpenden	d				19 31	→		19 45	19 49			20 01	→		20 15	→			20 19	20 31	20 35	→	
Luton Airport Parkway ✈	d			←	19 37			19 51	19 55		19 51	20 07			20 21			←	20 25	20 37	20 41		
Luton	d		19 23	19 24	19 40			19 54	19a59			20 10			20 24		20 23	20 24	20a29	20 40	20 44		
Leagrave	d			19 27	19 44			19 57				20 14			→			20 27		20 44	20 48		
Harlington	d			19 32	19 49			20 02				20 19						20 32		20 49	20 53		
Flitwick	d			19 36	19 53			20 06				20 23						20 36		20 53	20 57		
Bedford	a		19 37	19 49	20 05			20 19			20 06	20 35					20 37	20 49		21 05	21 09		

		FC 1	FC	EM ◇1	FC	FC 1	FC	FC	SE A	FC 1	FC	FC	EM ◇1	FC 1	FC	SE A	FC 1	FC	EM ◇1	FC 1	FC	SE A	FC 1
London Bridge ⊖	d	20 00				20 15				20 30				20 45			21 00			21 15			21 30
Elephant & Castle	d		20 09					20 24	20 30			20 39			20 54	21 00		21 09			21 24	21 30	
London Blackfriars ⊖	a	20 07	20 12			20 22		20 27	20 34	20 37		20 42		20 52	20 57	21 04	21 07	21 12		21 22	21 27	21 34	21 37
	d	20 08	20 14			20 24		20 30		20 38		20 44		20 54	21 00		21 08	21 14		21 24	21 30		21 38
City Thameslink	d	20 10	20 16			20 26		20 32		20 40		20 46		20 56									
Farringdon ⊖	d	20 14	20 19			20 30		20 36		20 44		20 49		21 00	21 06		21 14	21 19		21 30	21 36		21 44
St Pancras International ⊖	a	20 18	20 23			20 34		20 40		20 48		20 53		21 04	21 10		21 18	21 23		21 34	21 40		21 48
	d	20 18	20 24	20 30		20 34		20 40		20 48		20 54	21 00	21 04	21 10		21 18	21 24	21 30	21 34	21 40		21 48
Kentish Town	d		20 27					20 44				20 57			21 14			21 27			21 44		
West Hampstead Thameslink	d		20 31					20 49				21 01			21 19			21 31			21 49		
Cricklewood	d		20 34					20 52				21 04			21 22			21 34			21 52		
Hendon	d		20 37					20 55				21 07			21 25			21 37			21 55		
Mill Hill Broadway	d		20 41					20 59				21 11			21 29			21 41			21 59		
Elstree & Borehamwood	d		20 45					21 03				21 15			21 33			21 45			22 03		
Radlett	d		20 49		←		←	21 07			←	21 19			21 37			21 49			22 07		
St Albans City	d	20 39	20 57		20 44	20 55	20 57	21 14		21 09	21 14	21a27		21 25	21a44		21 39	21a57		21 55	22a14		22 11
Harpenden	d	20 45	→		20 49	21 01	21 05	→		21 15	21 19			21 31			21 45			22 01			22 22
Luton Airport Parkway ✈	d	20 51		20 51	20 55	21 07	21 11			21 21	21 25			21 37			21 51		21 51	22 07			22 28
Luton	d	20 54			20a59	21 10	21 14			21 24	21a29		21 23	21 40			21 54			22 10			22 31
Leagrave	d	20 57				21 14	21 18			21 27				21 44			21 58			22 14			→
Harlington	d	21 02				21 19	21 23			21 32				21 49			22 03			22 21			
Flitwick	d	21 06				21 23	21 27			21 36				21 53			22 07			22 25			
Bedford	a	21 19		21 06		21 35	21 39			21 49			21 38	22 05			22 20		22 06	22 37			

A not 19 May

Please refer to separate pages within this table for services operating between Brighton and South London

At weekends please use local bus and tube services to travel to/from St Pancras International and London Bridge when no trains are operating. See local publicity for details of alternative routes and services that are available across central London

Table 52

London, St Albans, Luton - Bedford

Saturdays until 23 June

Network Diagram - see first Page of Table 52

		FC	EM ◇1	FC 1	FC 1	SE A	FC	EM ◇1	FC 1	SE A	FC	FC 1	SE A	FC	FC 1	SE A	FC	FC 1
London Bridge ⊖	d				21 45				22 15			22 45			23 15			23 46
Elephant & Castle	d	21 39				22 00	22 04			22 30	22 34		23 00	23 04		23 30	23 34	
London Blackfriars ⊖	a	21 42			21 52	22 04	22 07		22 22	22 34	22 37	22 52	23 04	23 07	23 22	23 34	23 37	23 52
	d	21 44			21 54		22 08		22 22		22 38	22 52		23 08	23 22		23 38	23 52
City Thameslink	d																	
Farringdon ⊖	d	21 49			22 00		22 13		22 28		22 43	22 58		23 13	23 28		23 43	23 58
St Pancras International ⊖	a	21 53			22 04		22 17		22 32		22 47	23 02		23 17	23 32		23 47	00 02
	d	21 54	22 00		22 04		22 18	22 25	22 32		22 48	23 02		23 18	23 32		23 48	00 02
Kentish Town	d	21 57					22 21				22 51			23 21			23 51	
West Hampstead Thameslink	d	22 01					22 25		22 40		22 55	23 10		23 25	23 40		23 55	00 10
Cricklewood	d	22 04					22 28				22 58			23 28			23 58	
Hendon	d	22 07					22 31				23 01			23 31			00 01	
Mill Hill Broadway	d	22 11					22 35				23 05			23 35			00 05	
Elstree & Borehamwood	d	22 15					22 39				23 09			23 39			00 09	
Radlett	d	22 19					22 43				23 14			23 44			00 14	
St Albans City	d	22a27			22 25		22 50		22 57		23 20	23 27		23 50	23 57		00 20	00 27
Harpenden	d				22 31		22 56		23 03		23 26	23 33		23 57	00 03		00 27	00 33
Luton Airport Parkway ✈	d			←	22 37		23 02	22 46	23 09		23 32	23 39		00 03	00 09		00 33	00 39
Luton	d		22 24	22 31	22 40		23 05		23 12		23 35	23 42		00 06	00 12		00 36	00 42
Leagrave	d			22 35	22 44		23 09		23 16		23 39	23 46		00 09	00 16		00 39	00 46
Harlington	d			22 41	22 51		23 16		23 23		23 46	23 53		00 16	00 23		00 46	00 53
Flitwick	d			22 45	22 55		23 20		23 27		23 50	23 57		00 21	00 27		00 51	00 57
Bedford	a		22 41	22 56	23 07		23 32	23 04	23 39		00 02	00 09		00 33	00 39		01 03	01 09

Saturdays 30 June to 8 September

		FC	FC 1	EM ◇1	FC	FC 1	FC	FC 1	EM ◇1 B	EM ◇1 C	FC 1	EM ◇1 D	FC	FC 1	FC 1	FC	FC	FC	FC	FC	EM ◇1	FC	FC
London Bridge ⊖	d		22p45			23p15		23p45						00 22	00 52								06 02
Elephant & Castle	d	22p34			23p04		23p34																
London Blackfriars ⊖	a	22p37	22p52		23p07	23p22	23p37	23p52						00 28	00 58								06 08
	d	22p38	22p52		23p08	23p22	23p38	23p52					00 08	00 29	00 58	02 14	03 13	04 14	05 14	05 44			06 08
City Thameslink	d	22p40	22p54																				
Farringdon ⊖	d	22p43	22p58		23p13	23p28	23p43	23p58					00 13	00 33					05 20	05 50			06 12
St Pancras International ⊖	a	22p47	23p02		23p17	23p32	23p47	00 02					00 17	00 37	01 07	02 24	03 23	04 22	05 24	05 54			06 16
	d	22p48	23p02	23p15	23p18	23p32	23p48	00 02	00 15	00 15		00 15	00 18	00 38	01 08	02 24	03 24	04 24	05 24	05 54	06 10		06 17
Kentish Town	d	22p51			23p21		23p51						00 21	00 41	01 11	02 28	03 28	04 28	05 28	05 58			
West Hampstead Thameslink	d	22p55	23p10		23p25	23p40	23p55	00 10					00 25	00 45	01 15	02 32	03 32	04 32	05 32	06 02			06 24
Cricklewood	d	22p58			23p28		23p58						00 28	00 48	01 18	02 35	03 35	04 35	05 35	06 05			
Hendon	d	23p01			23p31		00 01						00 31	00 51	01 21	02 38	03 38	04 38	05 38	06 08			
Mill Hill Broadway	d	23p05			23p35		00 05						00 35	00 55	01 25	02 42	03 42	04 42	05 42	06 12			
Elstree & Borehamwood	d	23p09			23p39		00 09						00 39	00 59	01 29	02 46	03 46	04 46	05 46	06 16			
Radlett	d	23p14			23p44		00 14						00 44	01 04	01 34	02 51	03 51	04 51	05 51	06 20			
St Albans City	d	23p20	23p27		23p50	23p57	00 20	00 27					00 50	01 10	01 40	02 58	03 58	04 58	05 58	06 26			06 39
Harpenden	d	23p26	23p33		23p56	00 03	00 26	00 33					00 56	01 16	01 46	03 04	04 04	05 04	06 04	06 31			06 45
Luton Airport Parkway ✈	d	23p32	23p39		00 02	00 09	00 32	00 39		00 35	←	00 44	01 02	01 22	01 52	03 10	04 10	05 10	06 10	06 37		←	06 51
Luton	d	23p35	23p42	23p46	00 05	00 12	00 35	00 42	00 37	00 39	00 42	00 47	01 05	01 25	01 55	03 13	04 13	05 13	06 13	06 40	06 33	06 40	06 54
Leagrave	d	23p39	23p46		00 09	00 16	00 39	→			00 46		01 09	01 29	01 59	03 17	04 17	05 17	06 17	→		06 44	06 57
Harlington	d	23p44	23p51		00 14	00 21	00 44				00 51		01 14	01 34	02 04	03 22	04 22	05 22	06 22			06 49	07 02
Flitwick	d	23p48	23p55		00 18	00 25	00 48				00 55		01 18	01 38	02 08	03 26	04 26	05 26	06 26			06 53	07 06
Bedford	a	00 02	00 08	00 11	00 32	00 38	01 02		00 52	00 54	01 08	01 12	01 32	01 52	02 22	03 39	04 39	05 39	06 39		06 47	07 05	07 19

		FC	SE	EM ◇1	FC 1	FC	EM ◇1	SE	EM ◇1	FC 1	FC	EM ◇1	FC	SE	FC 1	FC	FC	EM ◇1	FC 1	FC 1	FC	SE	FC 1
London Bridge ⊖	d				06 30					07 00					07 30					07 45			08 00
Elephant & Castle	d	06 09	06 30			06 39		07 00			07 09		07 24	07 30			07 39				07 54	08 00	
London Blackfriars ⊖	a	06 12	06 34		06 37	06 42		07 04		07 07	07 12		07 27	07 34	07 37		07 42			07 52	07 57	08 04	08 07
	d	06 14			06 38	06 44				07 08	07 14		07 30		07 38		07 44			07 54	08 00		08 08
City Thameslink	d																						
Farringdon ⊖	d	06 19			06 42	06 49				07 12	07 19		07 36		07 44		07 49			08 00	08 06		08 14
St Pancras International ⊖	a	06 23			06 46	06 53				07 16	07 23		07 40		07 48		07 53			08 04	08 10		08 18
	d	06 24		06 37	06 47	06 54	06 55		07 00	07 17	07 24	07 30	07 40		07 48		07 54	08 00		08 04	08 10		08 18
Kentish Town	d	06 27				06 57					07 27		07 44				07 57				08 14		
West Hampstead Thameslink	d	06 31			06 54	07 01				07 24	07 31		07 49				08 01				08 19		
Cricklewood	d	06 34				07 04					07 34		07 52				08 04				08 22		
Hendon	d	06 37				07 07					07 37		07 55				08 07				08 25		
Mill Hill Broadway	d	06 41				07 11					07 41		07 59				08 11				08 29		
Elstree & Borehamwood	d	06 45				07 15					07 45		08 03				08 15				08 33		
Radlett	d	06 49				07 19					07 49		08 07			←	08 19				08 37		
St Albans City	d	06 56			07 09	07 26				07 39	07 56		08 14		08 09	08 14	08a27			08 25	08 44		08 39
Harpenden	d	07 01			07 15	07 31				07 45	08 01		→		08 15	08 19				08 31	→		08 45
Luton Airport Parkway ✈	d	07 07			07 21	07 37	07a15			07 51	08 07	07 51			08 21	08 25			←	08 37			08 51
Luton	d	07a11		06a58	07 24	07a41			07 23	07 54	08 10				08 24	08a29		08 23	08 24	08 40			08 54
Leagrave	d				07 27					07 57	08 14				→				08 27	08 44			08 57
Harlington	d				07 32					08 02	08 19								08 32	08 49			09 02
Flitwick	d				07 36					08 06	08 23								08 36	08 53			09 06
Bedford	a				07 49				07 38	08 19	08 35	08 06						08 37	08 49	09 05			09 19

A not 19 May
B 1 September, 8 September
C 28 July, 4 August, 11 August
D from 30 June until 21 July, 18 August, 25 August

Please refer to separate pages within this table for services operating between Brighton and South London

At weekends please use local bus and tube services to travel to/from St Pancras International and London Bridge when no trains are operating. See local publicity for details of alternative routes and services that are available across central London

London, St Albans, Luton - Bedford

Network Diagram - see first Page of Table 52

		FC		FC	EM ◇1	FC 1	FC	SE	FC 1	FC	FC	EM ◇1		FC 1	FC 1	FC	SE	FC 1	FC	FC	EM ◇1	FC 1		FC	SE
London Bridge 4 ⊖	d					08 15			08 30						08 45			09 00				09 15			
Elephant & Castle	d			08 09			08 24	08 30			08 39					08 54	09 00			09 09				09 24	09 30
London Blackfriars 3 ⊖	a			08 12		08 22	08 27	08 34	08 37		08 42				08 52	08 57	09 04	09 07		09 12		09 22		09 27	09 34
	d			08 14		08 24	08 30		08 38		08 44				08 54	09 00		09 08		09 14		09 24		09 30	
City Thameslink 3	d															09 02		09 10		09 16		09 26		09 32	
Farringdon 3 ⊖	d			08 19		08 30	08 36		08 44		08 49				09 00	09 06		09 14		09 19		09 30		09 36	
St Pancras International 15 ⊖	a			08 23		08 34	08 40		08 48		08 53				09 04	09 10		09 18		09 23		09 34		09 40	
	d			08 24	08 30	08 34	08 40		08 48		08 54	09 00			09 04	09 10		09 18		09 24	09 30	09 34		09 40	
Kentish Town	d			08 27			08 44				08 57					09 14				09 27				09 44	
West Hampstead Thameslink	d			08 31			08 49				09 01					09 19				09 31				09 49	
Cricklewood	d			08 34			08 52				09 04					09 22				09 34				09 52	
Hendon	d			08 37			08 55				09 07					09 25				09 37				09 55	
Mill Hill Broadway	d			08 41			08 59				09 11					09 29				09 41				09 59	
Elstree & Borehamwood	d			08 45			09 03				09 15					09 33				09 45				10 03	
Radlett	d	←		08 49			09 07			←	09 19					09 37			←	09 49				10 07	
St Albans City	d	08 44		08a57		08 55	09 14		09 09	09 14	09a27				09 25	09 44		09 39	09 44	09a57		09 55		10 14	
Harpenden	d	08 49				09 01	→		09 15	09 19					09 31	→		09 45	09 49			10 01		→	
Luton Airport Parkway 7 ✈	d	08 55			08 51	09 07			09 21	09 25				←	09 37			09 51	09 55		09 51	10 07			
Luton 10	d	08a59				09 10			09 24	09a29		09 23		09 24	09 40			09 54	09a59			10 10			
Leagrave	d					09 14			→					09 27	09 44			09 57				10 14			
Harlington	d					09 19								09 32	09 49			10 02				10 19			
Flitwick	d					09 23								09 36	09 53			10 06				10 23			
Bedford 7	a				09 06	09 35						09 37		09 49	10 05			10 19			10 06	10 35			

		FC 1	FC	FC	EM ◇1	FC 1	FC 1	FC		SE	FC 1	FC	FC	EM ◇1	FC 1	FC	SE	FC 1		FC	FC	EM ◇1	FC 1	FC 1	FC
London Bridge 4 ⊖	d	09 30					09 45				10 00				10 15			10 30						10 45	
Elephant & Castle	d			09 39				09 54		10 00			10 09			10 24	10 30				10 39				10 54
London Blackfriars 3 ⊖	a	09 37		09 42			09 52	09 57		10 04	10 07		10 12		10 22	10 27	10 34	10 37			10 42			10 52	10 57
	d	09 38		09 44			09 54	10 00			10 08		10 14		10 24	10 30		10 38			10 44			10 54	11 00
City Thameslink 3	d	09 40		09 46			09 56	10 02			10 10		10 16		10 26	10 32		10 40			10 46			10 56	11 02
Farringdon 3 ⊖	d	09 44		09 49			10 00	10 06			10 14		10 19		10 30	10 36		10 44			10 49			11 00	11 06
St Pancras International 15 ⊖	a	09 48		09 53			10 04	10 10			10 18		10 23		10 34	10 40		10 48			10 53			11 04	11 10
	d	09 48		09 54	10 00		10 04	10 10			10 18		10 24	10 30	10 34	10 40		10 48			10 54	11 00		11 04	11 10
Kentish Town	d			09 57				10 14					10 27			10 44					10 57				11 14
West Hampstead Thameslink	d			10 01				10 19					10 31			10 49					11 01				11 19
Cricklewood	d			10 04				10 22					10 34			10 52					11 04				11 22
Hendon	d			10 07				10 25					10 37			10 55					11 07				11 25
Mill Hill Broadway	d			10 11				10 29					10 41			10 59					11 11				11 29
Elstree & Borehamwood	d			10 15				10 33					10 45			11 03					11 15				11 33
Radlett	d		←	10 19				10 37				←	10 49			11 07				←	11 19				11 37
St Albans City	d	10 09	10 14	10a27			10 25	10 44			10 39	10 44	10a57		10 55	11 14		11 09		11 14	11a27			11 25	11 44
Harpenden	d	10 15	10 19				10 31	→			10 45	10 49			11 01	→		11 15		11 19				11 31	→
Luton Airport Parkway 7 ✈	d	10 21	10 25			←	10 37				10 51	10 55		10 51	11 07			11 21		11 25			←	11 37	
Luton 10	d	10 24	10a29		10 23	10 24	10 40				10 54	10a59			11 10			11 24		11a29		11 23	11 24	11 40	
Leagrave	d	→				10 27	10 44				10 57				11 14			→					11 27	11 44	
Harlington	d					10 32	10 49				11 02				11 19								11 32	11 49	
Flitwick	d					10 36	10 53				11 06				11 23								11 36	11 53	
Bedford 7	a				10 37	10 49	11 05				11 19			11 06	11 35							11 37	11 49	12 05	

		SE	FC 1	FC		FC	EM ◇1	FC 1	FC	SE	FC 1	FC	FC	EM ◇1		FC 1	FC 1	FC	SE	FC 1	FC	FC	EM ◇1	FC 1	
London Bridge 4 ⊖	d		11 00					11 15			11 30						11 45			12 00				12 15	
Elephant & Castle	d	11 00				11 09			11 24	11 30			11 39					11 54	12 00			12 09			
London Blackfriars 3 ⊖	a	11 04	11 07			11 12		11 22	11 27	11 34	11 37		11 42				11 52	11 57	12 04	12 07		12 12		12 22	
	d		11 08			11 14		11 24	11 30		11 38		11 44				11 54	12 00		12 08		12 14		12 24	
City Thameslink 3	d		11 10			11 16		11 26	11 32		11 40		11 46				11 56	12 02		12 10		12 16		12 26	
Farringdon 3 ⊖	d		11 14			11 19		11 30	11 36		11 44		11 49				12 00	12 06		12 14		12 19		12 30	
St Pancras International 15 ⊖	a		11 18			11 23		11 34	11 40		11 48		11 53				12 04	12 10		12 18		12 23		12 34	
	d		11 18			11 24	11 30	11 34	11 40		11 48		11 54	12 00			12 04	12 10		12 18		12 24	12 30	12 34	
Kentish Town	d					11 27			11 44				11 57					12 14				12 27			
West Hampstead Thameslink	d					11 31			11 49				12 01					12 19				12 31			
Cricklewood	d					11 34			11 52				12 04					12 22				12 34			
Hendon	d					11 37			11 55				12 07					12 25				12 37			
Mill Hill Broadway	d					11 41			11 59				12 11					12 29				12 41			
Elstree & Borehamwood	d					11 45			12 03				12 15					12 33				12 45			
Radlett	d			←		11 49			12 07			←	12 19					12 37			←	12 49			
St Albans City	d		11 39	11 44		11a57		11 55	12 14		12 09	12 14	12a27				12 25	12 44		12 39	12 44	12a57		12 55	
Harpenden	d		11 45	11 49				12 01	→		12 15	12 19					12 31	→		12 45	12 49			13 01	
Luton Airport Parkway 7 ✈	d		11 51	11 55			11 51	12 07			12 21	12 25				←	12 37			12 51	12 55		12 51	13 07	
Luton 10	d		11 54	11a59				12 10			12 24	12a29		12 23		12 24	12 40			12 54	12a59			13 10	
Leagrave	d		11 57					12 14			→					12 27	12 44			12 57				13 14	
Harlington	d		12 02					12 19								12 32	12 49			13 02				13 19	
Flitwick	d		12 06					12 23								12 36	12 53			13 06				13 23	
Bedford 7	a		12 19				12 06	12 35						12 37		12 49	13 05			13 19			13 06	13 35	

Please refer to separate pages within this table for services operating between Brighton and South London

At weekends please use local bus and tube services to travel to/from St Pancras International and London Bridge when no trains are operating. See local publicity for details of alternative routes and services that are available across central London

London, St Albans, Luton - Bedford

Network Diagram - see first Page of Table 52

		FC	SE	FC 1	FC	FC	EM ◇1	FC 1	FC 1	FC		SE	FC 1	FC	FC	EM ◇1	FC 1	FC	SE	FC 1		FC	FC	EM ◇1	FC 1
London Bridge 4 ⊖	d			12 30					12 45				13 00				13 15			13 30					
Elephant & Castle	d	12 24	12 30			12 39				12 54		13 00			13 09			13 24	13 30				13 39		
London Blackfriars 3 ⊖	a	12 27	12 34	12 37		12 42			12 52	12 57		13 04	13 07		13 12		13 22	13 27	13 34	13 37			13 42		
	d	12 30		12 38		12 44			12 54	13 00			13 08		13 14		13 24	13 30		13 38			13 44		
City Thameslink 3	d	12 32		12 40		12 46			12 56	13 02			13 10		13 16		13 26	13 32		13 40			13 46		
Farringdon 3 ⊖	d	12 36		12 44		12 49			13 00	13 06			13 14		13 19		13 30	13 36		13 44			13 49		
St Pancras International 15 ⊖	a	12 40		12 48		12 53			13 04	13 10			13 18		13 23		13 34	13 40		13 48			13 53		
	d	12 40		12 48		12 54	13 00		13 04	13 10			13 18		13 24	13 30	13 34	13 40		13 48			13 54	14 00	
Kentish Town	d	12 44				12 57				13 14					13 27			13 44					13 57		
West Hampstead Thameslink	d	12 49				13 01				13 19					13 31			13 49					14 01		
Cricklewood	d	12 52				13 04				13 22					13 34			13 52					14 04		
Hendon	d	12 55				13 07				13 25					13 37			13 55					14 07		
Mill Hill Broadway	d	12 59				13 11				13 29					13 41			13 59					14 11		
Elstree & Borehamwood	d	13 03				13 15				13 33					13 45			14 03					14 15		
Radlett	d	13 07			←	13 19				13 37				←	13 49			14 07				←	14 19		
St Albans City	d	13 14		13 09	13 14	13a27			13 25	13 44			13 39	13 44	13a57		13 55	14 14		14 09		14 14	14a27		
Harpenden	d	→		13 15	13 19				13 31	→			13 45	13 49			14 01	→		14 15		14 19			
Luton Airport Parkway 7 ✈	d			13 21	13 25			←	13 37				13 51	13 55		13 51	14 07			14 21		14 25			←
Luton 10	d			13 24	13a29		13 23	13 24	13 40				13 54	13a59			14 10			14 24		14a29		14 23	14 24
Leagrave	d			→				13 27	13 44				13 57				14 14			→					14 27
Harlington	d							13 32	13 49				14 02				14 19								14 32
Flitwick	d							13 36	13 53				14 06				14 23								14 36
Bedford 7	a						13 37	13 49	14 05				14 19			14 06	14 35							14 37	14 49

		FC 1	FC	SE	FC 1	FC		FC	EM ◇1	FC 1	FC	SE	FC 1	FC	FC	EM ◇1		FC 1	FC 1	FC	SE	FC 1	FC	FC	EM ◇1
London Bridge 4 ⊖	d	13 45			14 00					14 15			14 30						14 45			15 00			
Elephant & Castle	d		13 54	14 00				14 09			14 24	14 30			14 39					14 54	15 00			15 09	
London Blackfriars 3 ⊖	a	13 52	13 57	14 04	14 07			14 12		14 22	14 27	14 34	14 37		14 42				14 52	14 57	15 04	15 07		15 12	
	d	13 54	14 00		14 08			14 14		14 24	14 30		14 38		14 44				14 54	15 00		15 08		15 14	
City Thameslink 3	d	13 56	14 02		14 10			14 16		14 26	14 32		14 40		14 46				14 56	15 02		15 10		15 16	
Farringdon 3 ⊖	d	14 00	14 06		14 14			14 19		14 30	14 36		14 44		14 49				15 00	15 06		15 14		15 19	
St Pancras International 15 ⊖	a	14 04	14 10		14 18			14 23		14 34	14 40		14 48		14 53				15 04	15 10		15 18		15 23	
	d	14 04	14 10		14 18			14 24	14 30	14 34	14 40		14 48		14 54	15 00			15 04	15 10		15 18		15 24	15 30
Kentish Town	d		14 14					14 27			14 44				14 57					15 14				15 27	
West Hampstead Thameslink	d		14 19					14 31			14 49				15 01					15 19				15 31	
Cricklewood	d		14 22					14 34			14 52				15 04					15 22				15 34	
Hendon	d		14 25					14 37			14 55				15 07					15 25				15 37	
Mill Hill Broadway	d		14 29					14 41			14 59				15 11					15 29				15 41	
Elstree & Borehamwood	d		14 33					14 45			15 03				15 15					15 33				15 45	
Radlett	d		14 37			←		14 49			15 07			←	15 19					15 37			←	15 49	
St Albans City	d	14 25	14 44		14 39	14 44		14a57		14 55	15 14		15 09	15 14	15a27				15 25	15 44		15 39	15 44	15a57	
Harpenden	d	14 31	→		14 45	14 49				15 01	→		15 15	15 19					15 31	→		15 45	15 49		
Luton Airport Parkway 7 ✈	d	14 37			14 51	14 55			14 51	15 07			15 21	15 25				←	15 37			15 51	15 55		15 51
Luton 10	d	14 40			14 54	14a59				15 10			15 24	15a29		15 23		15 24	15 40			15 54	15a59		
Leagrave	d	14 44			14 57					15 14			→					15 27	15 44			15 57			
Harlington	d	14 49			15 02					15 19								15 32	15 49			16 02			
Flitwick	d	14 53			15 06					15 23								15 36	15 53			16 06			
Bedford 7	a	15 05			15 19				15 06	15 35						15 37		15 49	16 05			16 19			16 06

		FC 1		FC	SE	FC 1	FC	FC	EM ◇1	FC 1	FC 1	FC		SE	FC 1	FC	FC	EM ◇1	FC 1	FC	SE	FC 1		FC	FC
London Bridge 4 ⊖	d	15 15				15 30					15 45				16 00				16 15			16 30			
Elephant & Castle	d			15 24	15 30			15 39				15 54		16 00			16 09			16 24	16 30				16 39
London Blackfriars 3 ⊖	a	15 22		15 27	15 34	15 37		15 42			15 52	15 57		16 04	16 07		16 12		16 22	16 27	16 34	16 37			16 42
	d	15 24		15 30		15 38		15 44			15 54	16 00			16 08		16 14		16 24	16 30		16 38			16 44
City Thameslink 3	d	15 26		15 32		15 40		15 46			15 56	16 02			16 10		16 16		16 26	16 32		16 40			16 46
Farringdon 3 ⊖	d	15 30		15 36		15 44		15 49			16 00	16 06			16 14		16 19		16 30	16 36		16 44			16 49
St Pancras International 15 ⊖	a	15 34		15 40		15 48		15 53			16 04	16 10			16 18		16 23		16 34	16 40		16 48			16 53
	d	15 34		15 40		15 48		15 54	16 00		16 04	16 10			16 18		16 24	16 30	16 34	16 40		16 48			16 54
Kentish Town	d			15 44				15 57				16 14					16 27			16 44					16 57
West Hampstead Thameslink	d			15 49				16 01				16 19					16 31			16 49					17 01
Cricklewood	d			15 52				16 04				16 22					16 34			16 52					17 04
Hendon	d			15 55				16 07				16 25					16 37			16 55					17 07
Mill Hill Broadway	d			15 59				16 11				16 29					16 41			16 59					17 11
Elstree & Borehamwood	d			16 03				16 15				16 33					16 45			17 03					17 15
Radlett	d			16 07			←	16 19				16 37				←	16 49			17 07				←	17 19
St Albans City	d	15 55		16 14		16 09	16 14	16a27			16 25	16 44			16 39	16 44	16a57		16 55	17 14		17 09		17 14	17a27
Harpenden	d	16 01		→		16 15	16 19				16 31	→			16 45	16 49			17 01	→		17 15		17 19	
Luton Airport Parkway 7 ✈	d	16 07				16 21	16 25			←	16 37				16 51	16 55		16 51	17 07			17 21		17 25	
Luton 10	d	16 10				16 24	16a29		16 23	16 24	16 40				16 54	16a59			17 10			17 24		17a29	
Leagrave	d	16 14				→				16 27	16 44				16 57				17 14			→			
Harlington	d	16 19								16 32	16 49				17 02				17 19						
Flitwick	d	16 23								16 36	16 53				17 06				17 23						
Bedford 7	a	16 35							16 37	16 49	17 05				17 19			17 06	17 35						

Please refer to separate pages within this table for services operating between Brighton and South London

At weekends please use local bus and tube services to travel to/from St Pancras International and London Bridge when no trains are operating. See local publicity for details of alternative routes and services that are available across central London

Table 52

London, St Albans, Luton - Bedford

Saturdays
30 June to 8 September

Network Diagram - see first Page of Table 52

		EM ◇1	FC 1	FC 1	FC	SE	FC 1	FC		FC	EM ◇1	FC 1	FC	SE	FC 1	FC	FC	EM ◇1		FC 1	FC 1	FC	SE	FC 1	FC
London Bridge 4 ⊖	d			16 45			17 00					17 15			17 30						17 45			18 00	
Elephant & Castle	d				16 54	17 00				17 09			17 24	17 30			17 39					17 54	18 00		
London Blackfriars 3 ⊖	a			16 52	16 57	17 04	17 07			17 12		17 22	17 27	17 34	17 37		17 42				17 52	17 57	18 04	18 07	
	d			16 54	17 00		17 08			17 14		17 24	17 30		17 38		17 44				17 54	18 00		18 08	
City Thameslink 3	d			16 56	17 02		17 10			17 16		17 26	17 32		17 40		17 46				17 56	18 02		18 10	
Farringdon 3 ⊖	d			17 00	17 06		17 14			17 19		17 30	17 36		17 44		17 49				18 00	18 06		18 14	
St Pancras International 15 ⊖	a			17 04	17 10		17 18			17 23		17 34	17 40		17 48		17 53				18 04	18 10		18 18	
	d	17 00		17 04	17 10		17 18			17 24	17 30	17 34	17 40		17 48		17 54	18 00			18 04	18 10		18 18	
Kentish Town	d				17 14					17 27			17 44				17 57					18 14			
West Hampstead Thameslink	d				17 19					17 31			17 49				18 01					18 19			
Cricklewood	d				17 22					17 34			17 52				18 04					18 22			
Hendon	d				17 25					17 37			17 55				18 07					18 25			
Mill Hill Broadway	d				17 29					17 41			17 59				18 11					18 29			
Elstree & Borehamwood	d				17 33					17 45			18 03				18 15					18 33			
Radlett	d				17 37			←		17 49			18 07			←	18 19					18 37			←
St Albans City	d			17 25	17 44		17 39	17 44		17a57		17 55	18 14		18 09	18 14	18a27				18 25	18 44		18 39	18 44
Harpenden	d			17 31	→		17 45	17 49				18 01	→		18 15	18 19					18 31	→		18 45	18 49
Luton Airport Parkway 7 ✈	d		←	17 37			17 51	17 55			17 51	18 07			18 21	18 25				←	18 37			18 51	18 55
Luton 10	d	17 23	17 24	17 40			17 54	17a59				18 10			18 24	18a29		18 23		18 24	18 40			18 54	18a59
Leagrave	d		17 27	17 44			17 57					18 14			→					18 27	18 44			18 57	
Harlington	d		17 32	17 49			18 02					18 19								18 32	18 49			19 02	
Flitwick	d		17 36	17 53			18 06					18 23								18 36	18 53			19 06	
Bedford 7	a	17 37	17 49	18 05			18 19				18 06	18 35						18 37		18 49	19 05			19 19	

		FC	EM ◇1	FC 1		FC	SE	FC 1	FC	FC	EM ◇1	FC 1	FC 1	FC		SE	FC 1	FC	FC	EM ◇1	FC 1	FC	SE	FC 1	
London Bridge 4 ⊖	d			18 15				18 30					18 45				19 00				19 15			19 30	
Elephant & Castle	d	18 09				18 24	18 30			18 39				18 54		19 00			19 09			19 24	19 30		
London Blackfriars 3 ⊖	a	18 12		18 22		18 27	18 34	18 37		18 42			18 52	18 57		19 04	19 07		19 12		19 22	19 27	19 34	19 37	
	d	18 14		18 24		18 30		18 38		18 44			18 54	19 00			19 08		19 14		19 24	19 30		19 38	
City Thameslink 3	d	18 16		18 26		18 32		18 40		18 46			18 56	19 02			19 10		19 16		19 26	19 32		19 40	
Farringdon 3 ⊖	d	18 19		18 30		18 36		18 44		18 49			19 00	19 06			19 14		19 19		19 30	19 36		19 44	
St Pancras International 15 ⊖	a	18 23		18 34		18 40		18 48		18 53			19 04	19 10			19 18		19 23		19 34	19 40		19 48	
	d	18 24	18 30	18 34		18 40		18 48		18 54	19 00		19 04	19 10			19 18		19 24	19 30	19 34	19 40		19 48	
Kentish Town	d	18 27				18 44				18 57				19 14					19 27			19 44			
West Hampstead Thameslink	d	18 31				18 49				19 01				19 19					19 31			19 49			
Cricklewood	d	18 34				18 52				19 04				19 22					19 34			19 52			
Hendon	d	18 37				18 55				19 07				19 25					19 37			19 55			
Mill Hill Broadway	d	18 41				18 59				19 11				19 29					19 41			19 59			
Elstree & Borehamwood	d	18 45				19 03				19 15				19 33					19 45			20 03			
Radlett	d	18 49				19 07			←	19 19				19 37				←	19 49			20 07			
St Albans City	d	18a57		18 55		19 14		19 09	19 14	19a27			19 25	19 44			19 39	19 44	19a57		19 55	20 14		20 09	
Harpenden	d			19 01		→		19 15	19 19				19 31	→			19 45	19 49			20 01	→		20 15	
Luton Airport Parkway 7 ✈	d		18 51	19 07				19 21	19 25			←	19 37				19 51	19 55		19 51	20 07			20 21	
Luton 10	d			19 10				19 24	19a29		19 23	19 24	19 40				19 54	19a59			20 10			20 24	
Leagrave	d			19 14				→				19 27	19 44				19 57				20 14			→	
Harlington	d			19 19								19 32	19 49				20 02				20 19				
Flitwick	d			19 23								19 36	19 53				20 06				20 23				
Bedford 7	a		19 06	19 35							19 37	19 49	20 05				20 19			20 06	20 35				

		FC	EM ◇1	FC 1	FC	FC 1	FC	FC	SE	FC 1		FC	EM ◇1	FC	FC 1	FC	FC	SE	FC 1	FC		FC	EM ◇1	FC 1	FC
London Bridge 4 ⊖	d					19 45				20 00					20 15				20 30					20 45	
Elephant & Castle	d	19 39						19 54	20 00			20 09					20 24	20 30				20 39			20 54
London Blackfriars 3 ⊖	a	19 42				19 52		19 57	20 04	20 07		20 12			20 22		20 27	20 34	20 37			20 42		20 52	20 57
	d	19 44				19 54		20 00		20 08		20 14			20 24		20 30		20 38			20 44		20 54	21 00
City Thameslink 3	d	19 46				19 56		20 02		20 10		20 16			20 26		20 32		20 40			20 46		20 56	
Farringdon 3 ⊖	d	19 49				20 00		20 06		20 14		20 19			20 30		20 36		20 44			20 49		21 00	21 06
St Pancras International 15 ⊖	a	19 53				20 04		20 10		20 18		20 23			20 34		20 40		20 48			20 53		21 04	21 10
	d	19 54	20 00			20 04		20 10		20 18		20 24	20 30		20 34		20 40		20 48			20 54	21 00	21 04	21 10
Kentish Town	d	19 57						20 14				20 27					20 44					20 57			21 14
West Hampstead Thameslink	d	20 01						20 19				20 31					20 49					21 01			21 19
Cricklewood	d	20 04						20 22				20 34					20 52					21 04			21 22
Hendon	d	20 07						20 25				20 37					20 55					21 07			21 25
Mill Hill Broadway	d	20 11						20 29				20 41					20 59					21 11			21 29
Elstree & Borehamwood	d	20 15						20 33				20 45					21 03					21 15			21 33
Radlett	d	20 19			←		←	20 37				20 49		←		←	21 07			←		21 19			21 37
St Albans City	d	20 27			20 14	20 25	20 27	20 44		20 39		20 57		20 44	20 55	20 57	21 14		21 09	21 14		21a27		21 25	21 44
Harpenden	d	→			20 19	20 31	20 35	→		20 45		→		20 49	21 01	21 05	→		21 15	21 19				21 31	→
Luton Airport Parkway 7 ✈	d			←	20 25	20 37	20 41			20 51			20 51	20 55	21 07	21 11			21 21	21 25				21 37	
Luton 10	d		20 23	20 24	20a29	20 40	20 44			20 54				20a59	21 10	21 14			21 24	21a29			21 23	21 40	
Leagrave	d			20 27		20 44	20 48			20 57					21 14	21 18			21 27					21 44	
Harlington	d			20 32		20 49	20 53			21 02					21 19	21 23			21 32					21 49	
Flitwick	d			20 36		20 53	20 57			21 06					21 23	21 27			21 36					21 53	
Bedford 7	a		20 37	20 49		21 05	21 09			21 19			21 06		21 35	21 39			21 49				21 38	22 05	

Please refer to separate pages within this table for services operating between Brighton and South London

At weekends please use local bus and tube services to travel to/from St Pancras International and London Bridge when no trains are operating. See local publicity for details of alternative routes and services that are available across central London

Table 52

London, St Albans, Luton - Bedford

Saturdays
30 June to 8 September

Network Diagram - see first Page of Table 52

		SE	FC 1	FC	FC	EM ◇1		FC 1	FC	SE	FC 1	FC	FC	EM ◇1	FC 1	SE		FC	EM ◇1	FC 1	SE	FC	FC 1	SE	FC
London Bridge 4 ⊖	d		21 00					21 15			21 30				21 45					22 15			22 45		
Elephant & Castle	d	21 00			21 09				21 24	21 30			21 39			22 00		22 04			22 30	22 34		23 00	23 04
London Blackfriars 3 ⊖	a	21 04	21 07		21 12			21 22	21 27	21 34	21 37		21 42		21 52	22 04		22 07		22 22	22 34	22 37	22 52	23 04	23 07
	d		21 08		21 14			21 24	21 30		21 38		21 44		21 54			22 08		22 22		22 38	22 52		23 08
City Thameslink 3	d																								
Farringdon 3 ⊖	d		21 14		21 19			21 30	21 36		21 44		21 49		22 00			22 13		22 28		22 43	22 58		23 13
St Pancras International 15 ⊖	a		21 18		21 23			21 34	21 40		21 48		21 53		22 04			22 17		22 32		22 47	23 02		23 17
	d		21 18		21 24	21 30		21 34	21 40		21 48		21 54	22 00	22 04			22 18	22 25	22 32		22 48	23 02		23 18
Kentish Town	d				21 27				21 44				21 57					22 21				22 51			23 21
West Hampstead Thameslink	d				21 31				21 49				22 01					22 25		22 40		22 55	23 10		23 25
Cricklewood	d				21 34				21 52				22 04					22 28				22 58			23 28
Hendon	d				21 37				21 55				22 07					22 31				23 01			23 31
Mill Hill Broadway	d				21 41				21 59				22 11					22 35				23 05			23 35
Elstree & Borehamwood	d				21 45				22 03				22 15					22 39				23 09			23 39
Radlett	d			←	21 49				22 07			←	22 19					22 43				23 14			23 44
St Albans City	d		21 39	21 44	21a57			21 55	22 14		22 09	22 14	22a27		22 25			22 50		22 57		23 20	23 27		23 50
Harpenden	d		21 45	21 49				22 01	→		22 15	22 19			22 31			22 56		23 03		23 26	23 33		23 56
Luton Airport Parkway 7 ✈	d		21 51	21 55		21 51		22 07			22 21	22 25			22 37			23 02	22 46	23 09		23 32	23 39		00 02
Luton 10	d		21 54	21a59				22 10			22 24	22a29		22 24	22 40			23 05		23 12		23 35	23 42		00 05
Leagrave	d		21 57					22 14			22 27				22 44			23 09		23 16		23 39	23 46		00 09
Harlington	d		22 02					22 19			22 32				22 49			23 14		23 21		23 44	23 51		00 14
Flitwick	d		22 06					22 23			22 36				22 53			23 18		23 25		23 48	23 55		00 18
Bedford 7	a		22 19			22 06		22 35			22 49			22 41	23 05			23 30	23 01	23 38		00 02	00 08		00 32

		FC 1		SE	FC	FC 1
London Bridge 4 ⊖	d	23 15				23 45
Elephant & Castle	d			23 30	23 34	
London Blackfriars 3 ⊖	a	23 22		23 34	23 37	23 52
	d	23 22			23 38	23 52
City Thameslink 3	d					
Farringdon 3 ⊖	d	23 28			23 43	23 58
St Pancras International 15 ⊖	a	23 32			23 47	00 02
	d	23 32			23 48	00 02
Kentish Town	d				23 51	
West Hampstead Thameslink	d	23 40			23 55	00 10
Cricklewood	d				23 58	
Hendon	d				00 01	
Mill Hill Broadway	d				00 05	
Elstree & Borehamwood	d				00 09	
Radlett	d				00 14	
St Albans City	d	23 57			00 20	00 27
Harpenden	d	00 03			00 26	00 33
Luton Airport Parkway 7 ✈	d	00 09			00 32	00 39
Luton 10	d	00 12			00 35	00 42
Leagrave	d	00 16			00 39	00 46
Harlington	d	00 21			00 44	00 51
Flitwick	d	00 25			00 48	00 55
Bedford 7	a	00 38			01 02	01 08

Saturdays
from 15 September

		FC	FC 1	EM ◇1	FC	FC 1	FC	FC 1	EM ◇1	FC		FC 1	FC 1	FC	FC	FC	FC	FC	EM ◇1	FC		FC	FC	SE	EM ◇1
London Bridge 4 ⊖	d		22p45			23p15		23p45				00 22	00 52									06 02			
Elephant & Castle	d	22p34			23p04		23p34																06 09	06 30	
London Blackfriars 3 ⊖	a	22p37	22p52		23p07	23p22	23p37	23p52				00 28	00 58									06 08	06 12	06 34	
	d	22p38	22p52		23p08	23p22	23p38	23p52		00 08		00 29	00 58	02 14	03 13	04 14	05 14	05 44				06 08	06 14		
City Thameslink 3	d	22p40	22p54																						
Farringdon 3 ⊖	d	22p43	22p58		23p13	23p28	23p43	23p58		00 13		00 33					05 20	05 50				06 12	06 19		
St Pancras International 15 ⊖	a	22p47	23p02		23p17	23p32	23p47	00 02		00 17		00 37	01 07	02 24	03 23	04 22	05 24	05 54				06 16	06 23		
	d	22p48	23p02	23p15	23p18	23p32	23p48	00 02	00 15	00 18		00 38	01 08	02 24	03 24	04 24	05 24	05 54	06 10			06 17	06 24		06 37
Kentish Town	d	22p51			23p21		23p51			00 21		00 41	01 11	02 28	03 28	04 28	05 28	05 58					06 27		
West Hampstead Thameslink	d	22p55	23p10		23p25	23p40	23p55	00 10		00 25		00 45	01 15	02 32	03 32	04 32	05 32	06 02				06 24	06 31		
Cricklewood	d	22p58			23p28		23p58			00 28		00 48	01 18	02 35	03 35	04 35	05 35	06 05					06 34		
Hendon	d	23p01			23p31		00 01			00 31		00 51	01 21	02 38	03 38	04 38	05 38	06 08					06 37		
Mill Hill Broadway	d	23p05			23p35		00 05			00 35		00 55	01 25	02 42	03 42	04 42	05 42	06 12					06 41		
Elstree & Borehamwood	d	23p09			23p39		00 09			00 39		00 59	01 29	02 46	03 46	04 46	05 46	06 16					06 45		
Radlett	d	23p14			23p44		00 14			00 44		01 04	01 34	02 51	03 51	04 51	05 51	06 20					06 49		
St Albans City	d	23p20	23p27		23p50	23p57	00 20	00 27		00 50		01 10	01 40	02 58	03 58	04 58	05 58	06 26				06 39	06 56		
Harpenden	d	23p26	23p33		23p56	00 03	00 26	00 33		00 56		01 16	01 46	03 04	04 04	05 04	06 04	06 31				06 45	07 01		
Luton Airport Parkway 7 ✈	d	23p32	23p39		00 02	00 09	00 32	00 39	00 44	01 02		01 22	01 52	03 10	04 10	05 10	06 10	06 37		←		06 51	07 07		
Luton 10	d	23p35	23p42	23p46	00 05	00 12	00 35	00 42	00 47	01 05		01 25	01 55	03 13	04 13	05 13	06 13	06 40	06 33	06 40		06 54	07a11		06a58
Leagrave	d	23p39	23p46		00 09	00 16	00 39	00 46		01 09		01 29	01 59	03 17	04 17	05 17	06 17	→		06 44		06 57			
Harlington	d	23p44	23p51		00 14	00 21	00 44	00 51		01 14		01 34	02 04	03 22	04 22	05 22	06 22			06 49		07 02			
Flitwick	d	23p48	23p55		00 18	00 25	00 48	00 55		01 18		01 38	02 08	03 26	04 26	05 26	06 26			06 53		07 06			
Bedford 7	a	00 02	00 08	00 11	00 32	00 38	01 02	01 08	01 12	01 32		01 52	02 22	03 39	04 39	05 39	06 39		06 47	07 05		07 19			

Please refer to separate pages within this table for services operating between Brighton and South London

At weekends please use local bus and tube services to travel to/from St Pancras International and London Bridge when no trains are operating. See local publicity for details of alternative routes and services that are available across central London

London, St Albans, Luton - Bedford

Network Diagram - see first Page of Table 52

Station		FC ■	FC	EM ◇■	SE	EM ◇■		FC ■	FC	EM ◇■	FC	SE	FC ■	FC	FC	EM ◇■		FC ■	FC ■	FC	SE	FC ■	FC	FC	EM ◇■
London Bridge 4 ⊖	d	06 30						07 00					07 30						07 45			08 00			
Elephant & Castle	d		06 39		07 00				07 09		07 24	07 30			07 39					07 54	08 00			08 09	
London Blackfriars 3 ⊖	a	06 37	06 42		07 04			07 07	07 12		07 27	07 34	07 37		07 42				07 52	07 57	08 04	08 07		08 12	
	d	06 38	06 44					07 08	07 14		07 30		07 38		07 44				07 54	08 00		08 08		08 14	
City Thameslink 3	d																								
Farringdon 3 ⊖	d	06 42	06 49					07 12	07 19		07 36		07 44		07 49				08 00	08 06		08 14		08 19	
St Pancras International 15 ⊖	a	06 46	06 53					07 16	07 23		07 40		07 48		07 53				08 04	08 10		08 18		08 23	
	d	06 47	06 54	06 55		07 00		07 17	07 24	07 30	07 40		07 48		07 54	08 00			08 04	08 10		08 18		08 24	08 30
Kentish Town	d		06 57						07 27		07 44				07 57					08 14				08 27	
West Hampstead Thameslink	d	06 54	07 01					07 24	07 31		07 49				08 01					08 19				08 31	
Cricklewood	d		07 04						07 34		07 52				08 04					08 22				08 34	
Hendon	d		07 07						07 37		07 55				08 07					08 25				08 37	
Mill Hill Broadway	d		07 11						07 41		07 59				08 11					08 29				08 41	
Elstree & Borehamwood	d		07 15						07 45		08 03				08 15					08 33				08 45	
Radlett	d		07 19						07 49		08 07			←	08 19					08 37			←	08 49	
St Albans City	d	07 09	07 26					07 39	07 56		08 14		08 09	08 14	08a27				08 25	08 44		08 39	08 44	08a57	
Harpenden	d	07 15	07 31					07 45	08 01		→		08 15	08 19					08 31	→		08 45	08 49		
Luton Airport Parkway 7 ✈	d	07 21	07 37	07a15				07 51	08 07	07 51			08 21	08 25				←	08 37			08 51	08 55		08 51
Luton 10	d	07 24	07a41			07 23		07 54	08 10				08 24	08a29		08 23		08 24	08 40			08 54	08a59		
Leagrave	d	07 27						07 57	08 14				→					08 27	08 44			08 57			
Harlington	d	07 32						08 02	08 19									08 32	08 49			09 02			
Flitwick	d	07 36						08 06	08 23									08 36	08 53			09 06			
Bedford 7	a	07 49				07 38		08 19	08 35	08 06						08 37		08 49	09 05			09 19			09 06

Station		FC ■		FC	SE	FC ■	FC	FC	EM ◇■	FC ■	FC ■	FC		SE	FC ■	FC	FC	EM ◇■	FC ■	FC	SE	FC ■		FC	FC
London Bridge 4 ⊖	d	08 15				08 30					08 45				09 00				09 15			09 30			
Elephant & Castle	d			08 24	08 30			08 39				08 54		09 00			09 09			09 24	09 30				09 39
London Blackfriars 3 ⊖	a	08 22		08 27	08 34	08 37		08 42			08 52	08 57		09 04	09 07		09 12		09 22	09 27	09 34	09 37			09 42
	d	08 24		08 30		08 38		08 44			08 54	09 00			09 08		09 14		09 24	09 30		09 38			09 44
City Thameslink 3	d											09 02			09 10		09 16		09 26	09 32		09 40			09 46
Farringdon 3 ⊖	d	08 30		08 36		08 44		08 49			09 00	09 06			09 14		09 19		09 30	09 36		09 44			09 49
St Pancras International 15 ⊖	a	08 34		08 40		08 48		08 53			09 04	09 10			09 18		09 23		09 34	09 40		09 48			09 53
	d	08 34		08 40		08 48		08 54	09 00		09 04	09 10			09 18		09 24	09 30	09 34	09 40		09 48			09 54
Kentish Town	d			08 44				08 57				09 14					09 27			09 44					09 57
West Hampstead Thameslink	d			08 49				09 01				09 19					09 31			09 49					10 01
Cricklewood	d			08 52				09 04				09 22					09 34			09 52					10 04
Hendon	d			08 55				09 07				09 25					09 37			09 55					10 07
Mill Hill Broadway	d			08 59				09 11				09 29					09 41			09 59					10 11
Elstree & Borehamwood	d			09 03				09 15				09 33					09 45			10 03					10 15
Radlett	d			09 07			←	09 19				09 37				←	09 49			10 07				←	10 19
St Albans City	d	08 55		09 14		09 09	09 14	09a27			09 25	09 44			09 39	09 44	09a57		09 55	10 14		10 09		10 14	10a27
Harpenden	d	09 01		→		09 15	09 19				09 31	→			09 45	09 49			10 01	→		10 15		10 19	
Luton Airport Parkway 7 ✈	d	09 07				09 21	09 25			←	09 37				09 51	09 55		09 51	10 07			10 21		10 25	
Luton 10	d	09 10				09 24	09a29		09 23	09 24	09 40				09 54	09a59			10 10			10 24		10a29	
Leagrave	d	09 14				→				09 27	09 44				09 57				10 14			→			
Harlington	d	09 19								09 32	09 49				10 02				10 19						
Flitwick	d	09 23								09 36	09 53				10 06				10 23						
Bedford 7	a	09 35							09 37	09 49	10 05				10 19			10 06	10 35						

Station		EM ◇■	FC ■	FC ■	FC	SE	FC ■	FC		FC	EM ◇■	FC ■	FC	SE	FC ■	FC	FC	EM ◇■		FC ■	FC ■	FC	SE	FC ■	FC
London Bridge 4 ⊖	d			09 45			10 00					10 15			10 30						10 45			11 00	
Elephant & Castle	d				09 54	10 00				10 09			10 24	10 30			10 39					10 54	11 00		
London Blackfriars 3 ⊖	a			09 52	09 57	10 04	10 07			10 12		10 22	10 27	10 34	10 37		10 42				10 52	10 57	11 04	11 07	
	d			09 54	10 00		10 08			10 14		10 24	10 30		10 38		10 44				10 54	11 00		11 08	
City Thameslink 3	d			09 56	10 02		10 10			10 16		10 26	10 32		10 40		10 46				10 56	11 02		11 10	
Farringdon 3 ⊖	d			10 00	10 06		10 14			10 19		10 30	10 36		10 44		10 49				11 00	11 06		11 14	
St Pancras International 15 ⊖	a			10 04	10 10		10 18			10 23		10 34	10 40		10 48		10 53				11 04	11 10		11 18	
	d	10 00		10 04	10 10		10 18			10 24	10 30	10 34	10 40		10 48		10 54	11 00			11 04	11 10		11 18	
Kentish Town	d				10 14					10 27			10 44				10 57					11 14			
West Hampstead Thameslink	d				10 19					10 31			10 49				11 01					11 19			
Cricklewood	d				10 22					10 34			10 52				11 04					11 22			
Hendon	d				10 25					10 37			10 55				11 07					11 25			
Mill Hill Broadway	d				10 29					10 41			10 59				11 11					11 29			
Elstree & Borehamwood	d				10 33					10 45			11 03				11 15					11 33			
Radlett	d				10 37			←		10 49			11 07			←	11 19					11 37			←
St Albans City	d			10 25	10 44		10 39	10 44		10a57		10 55	11 14		11 09	11 14	11a27				11 25	11 44		11 39	11 44
Harpenden	d			10 31	→		10 45	10 49				11 01	→		11 15	11 19					11 31	→		11 45	11 49
Luton Airport Parkway 7 ✈	d		←	10 37			10 51	10 55			10 51	11 07			11 21	11 25				←	11 37			11 51	11 55
Luton 10	d	10 23	10 24	10 40			10 54	10a59				11 10			11 24	11a29		11 23		11 24	11 40			11 54	11a59
Leagrave	d		10 27	10 44			10 57					11 14			→					11 27	11 44			11 57	
Harlington	d		10 32	10 49			11 02					11 19								11 32	11 49			12 02	
Flitwick	d		10 36	10 53			11 06					11 23								11 36	11 53			12 06	
Bedford 7	a	10 37	10 49	11 05			11 19				11 06	11 35						11 37		11 49	12 05			12 19	

Please refer to separate pages within this table for services operating between Brighton and South London

At weekends please use local bus and tube services to travel to/from St Pancras International and London Bridge when no trains are operating. See local publicity for details of alternative routes and services that are available across central London

Saturdays
from 15 September

London, St Albans, Luton - Bedford

Network Diagram - see first Page of Table 52

Station		FC	EM ◇■	FC ■		FC	SE	FC ■	FC	FC	EM ◇■	FC ■	FC ■	FC		SE	FC ■	FC	FC	EM ◇■	FC ■	FC	SE	FC ■	
London Bridge 4 ⊖	d			11 15				11 30					11 45				12 00				12 15			12 30	
Elephant & Castle	d	11 09				11 24	11 30			11 39				11 54		12 00			12 09			12 24	12 30		
London Blackfriars 3 ⊖	a	11 12		11 22		11 27	11 34	11 37		11 42			11 52	11 57		12 04	12 07		12 12		12 22	12 27	12 34	12 37	
	d	11 14		11 24		11 30		11 38		11 44			11 54	12 00			12 08		12 14		12 24	12 30		12 38	
City Thameslink 3	d	11 16		11 26		11 32		11 40		11 46			11 56	12 02			12 10		12 16		12 26	12 32		12 40	
Farringdon 3 ⊖	d	11 19		11 30		11 36		11 44		11 49			12 00	12 06			12 14		12 19		12 30	12 36		12 44	
St Pancras International 15 ⊖	a	11 23		11 34		11 40		11 48		11 53			12 04	12 10			12 18		12 23		12 34	12 40		12 48	
	d	11 24	11 30	11 34		11 40		11 48		11 54	12 00		12 04	12 10			12 18		12 24	12 30	12 34	12 40		12 48	
Kentish Town	d	11 27				11 44				11 57				12 14					12 27			12 44			
West Hampstead Thameslink	d	11 31				11 49				12 01				12 19					12 31			12 49			
Cricklewood	d	11 34				11 52				12 04				12 22					12 34			12 52			
Hendon	d	11 37				11 55				12 07				12 25					12 37			12 55			
Mill Hill Broadway	d	11 41				11 59				12 11				12 29					12 41			12 59			
Elstree & Borehamwood	d	11 45				12 03				12 15				12 33					12 45			13 03			
Radlett	d	11 49				12 07			←	12 19				12 37				←	12 49			13 07			
St Albans City	d	11a57		11 55		12 14		12 09	12 14	12a27			12 25	12 44			12 39	12 44	12a57		12 55	13 14		13 09	
Harpenden	d			12 01		→		12 15	12 19				12 31	→			12 45	12 49			13 01	→		13 15	
Luton Airport Parkway 7 ✈	d		11 51	12 07				12 21	12 25			←	12 37				12 51	12 55		12 51	13 07			13 21	
Luton 10	d			12 10				12 24	12a29		12 23	12 24	12 40				12 54	12a59			13 10			13 24	
Leagrave	d			12 14				→				12 27	12 44				12 57				13 14			→	
Harlington	d			12 19								12 32	12 49				13 02				13 19				
Flitwick	d			12 23								12 36	12 53				13 06				13 23				
Bedford 7	a		12 06	12 35							12 37	12 49	13 05				13 19			13 06	13 35				

Station		FC	FC	EM ◇■	FC ■	FC ■	FC	SE	FC ■	FC		FC	EM ◇■	FC ■	FC	SE	FC ■	FC	FC	EM ◇■		FC ■	FC ■	FC	SE
London Bridge 4 ⊖	d					12 45			13 00					13 15			13 30						13 45		
Elephant & Castle	d		12 39				12 54	13 00				13 09			13 24	13 30			13 39					13 54	14 00
London Blackfriars 3 ⊖	a		12 42			12 52	12 57	13 04	13 07			13 12		13 22	13 27	13 34	13 37		13 42				13 52	13 57	14 04
	d		12 44			12 54	13 00		13 08			13 14		13 24	13 30		13 38		13 44				13 54	14 00	
City Thameslink 3	d		12 46			12 56	13 02		13 10			13 16		13 26	13 32		13 40		13 46				13 56	14 02	
Farringdon 3 ⊖	d		12 49			13 00	13 06		13 14			13 19		13 30	13 36		13 44		13 49				14 00	14 06	
St Pancras International 15 ⊖	a		12 53			13 04	13 10		13 18			13 23		13 34	13 40		13 48		13 53				14 04	14 10	
	d		12 54	13 00		13 04	13 10		13 18			13 24	13 30	13 34	13 40		13 48		13 54	14 00			14 04	14 10	
Kentish Town	d		12 57				13 14					13 27			13 44				13 57					14 14	
West Hampstead Thameslink	d		13 01				13 19					13 31			13 49				14 01					14 19	
Cricklewood	d		13 04				13 22					13 34			13 52				14 04					14 22	
Hendon	d		13 07				13 25					13 37			13 55				14 07					14 25	
Mill Hill Broadway	d		13 11				13 29					13 41			13 59				14 11					14 29	
Elstree & Borehamwood	d		13 15				13 33					13 45			14 03				14 15					14 33	
Radlett	d	←	13 19				13 37			←		13 49			14 07			←	14 19					14 37	
St Albans City	d	13 14	13a27			13 25	13 44		13 39	13 44		13a57		13 55	14 14		14 09	14 14	14a27				14 25	14 44	
Harpenden	d	13 19				13 31	→		13 45	13 49				14 01	→		14 15	14 19					14 31	→	
Luton Airport Parkway 7 ✈	d	13 25			←	13 37			13 51	13 55			13 51	14 07			14 21	14 25				←	14 37		
Luton 10	d	13a29		13 23	13 24	13 40			13 54	13a59				14 10			14 24	14a29		14 23		14 24	14 40		
Leagrave	d				13 27	13 44			13 57					14 14			→					14 27	14 44		
Harlington	d				13 32	13 49			14 02					14 19								14 32	14 49		
Flitwick	d				13 36	13 53			14 06					14 23								14 36	14 53		
Bedford 7	a			13 37	13 49	14 05			14 19				14 06	14 35						14 37		14 49	15 05		

Station		FC ■	FC	FC	EM ◇■	FC ■		FC	SE	FC ■	FC	FC	EM ◇■	FC ■	FC ■	FC		SE	FC ■	FC	FC	EM ◇■	FC ■	FC	SE
London Bridge 4 ⊖	d	14 00				14 15				14 30					14 45				15 00				15 15		
Elephant & Castle	d			14 09				14 24	14 30			14 39				14 54		15 00			15 09			15 24	15 30
London Blackfriars 3 ⊖	a	14 07		14 12		14 22		14 27	14 34	14 37		14 42			14 52	14 57		15 04	15 07		15 12		15 22	15 27	15 34
	d	14 08		14 14		14 24		14 30		14 38		14 44			14 54	15 00			15 08		15 14		15 24	15 30	
City Thameslink 3	d	14 10		14 16		14 26		14 32		14 40		14 46			14 56	15 02			15 10		15 16		15 26	15 32	
Farringdon 3 ⊖	d	14 14		14 19		14 30		14 36		14 44		14 49			15 00	15 06			15 14		15 19		15 30	15 36	
St Pancras International 15 ⊖	a	14 18		14 23		14 34		14 40		14 48		14 53			15 04	15 10			15 18		15 23		15 34	15 40	
	d	14 18		14 24	14 30	14 34		14 40		14 48		14 54	15 00		15 04	15 10			15 18		15 24	15 30	15 34	15 40	
Kentish Town	d			14 27				14 44				14 57				15 14					15 27			15 44	
West Hampstead Thameslink	d			14 31				14 49				15 01				15 19					15 31			15 49	
Cricklewood	d			14 34				14 52				15 04				15 22					15 34			15 52	
Hendon	d			14 37				14 55				15 07				15 25					15 37			15 55	
Mill Hill Broadway	d			14 41				14 59				15 11				15 29					15 41			15 59	
Elstree & Borehamwood	d			14 45				15 03				15 15				15 33					15 45			16 03	
Radlett	d		←	14 49				15 07			←	15 19				15 37				←	15 49			16 07	
St Albans City	d	14 39	14 44	14a57		14 55		15 14		15 09	15 14	15a27			15 25	15 44			15 39	15 44	15a57		15 55	16 14	
Harpenden	d	14 45	14 49			15 01		→		15 15	15 19				15 31	→			15 45	15 49			16 01	→	
Luton Airport Parkway 7 ✈	d	14 51	14 55		14 51	15 07				15 21	15 25			←	15 37				15 51	15 55		15 51	16 07		
Luton 10	d	14 54	14a59			15 10				15 24	15a29		15 23	15 24	15 40				15 54	15a59			16 10		
Leagrave	d	14 57				15 14				→				15 27	15 44				15 57				16 14		
Harlington	d	15 02				15 19								15 32	15 49				16 02				16 19		
Flitwick	d	15 06				15 23								15 36	15 53				16 06				16 23		
Bedford 7	a	15 19			15 06	15 35							15 37	15 49	16 05				16 19			16 06	16 35		

Please refer to separate pages within this table for services operating between Brighton and South London

At weekends please use local bus and tube services to travel to/from St Pancras International and London Bridge when no trains are operating. See local publicity for details of alternative routes and services that are available across central London

Table 52

London, St Albans, Luton - Bedford

Saturdays

from 15 September

Network Diagram - see first Page of Table 52

		FC ■		FC	FC	EM ◇■	FC ■	FC ■	FC	SE	FC ■	FC		FC	EM ◇■	FC ■	FC	SE	FC ■	FC	FC	EM ◇■		FC ■	FC ■
London Bridge ⊖	d	15 30						15 45			16 00					16 15			16 30						16 45
Elephant & Castle	d				15 39				15 54	16 00				16 09			16 24	16 30			16 39				
London Blackfriars ⊖	a	15 37			15 42			15 52	15 57	16 04	16 07			16 12		16 22	16 27	16 34	16 37		16 42				16 52
	d	15 38			15 44			15 54	16 00		16 08			16 14		16 24	16 30		16 38		16 44				16 54
City Thameslink	d	15 40			15 46			15 56	16 02		16 10			16 16		16 26	16 32		16 40		16 46				16 56
Farringdon ⊖	d	15 44			15 49			16 00	16 06		16 14			16 19		16 30	16 36		16 44		16 49				17 00
St Pancras International ⊖	a	15 48			15 53			16 04	16 10		16 18			16 23		16 34	16 40		16 48		16 53				17 04
	d	15 48			15 54	16 00		16 04	16 10		16 18			16 24	16 30	16 34	16 40		16 48		16 54	17 00			17 04
Kentish Town	d				15 57				16 14					16 27			16 44				16 57				
West Hampstead Thameslink	d				16 01				16 19					16 31			16 49				17 01				
Cricklewood	d				16 04				16 22					16 34			16 52				17 04				
Hendon	d				16 07				16 25					16 37			16 55				17 07				
Mill Hill Broadway	d				16 11				16 29					16 41			16 59				17 11				
Elstree & Borehamwood	d				16 15				16 33					16 45			17 03				17 15				
Radlett	d			←	16 19				16 37			←		16 49			17 07			←	17 19				
St Albans City	d	16 09		16 14	16a27			16 25	16 44		16 39	16 44		16a57		16 55	17 14		17 09	17 14	17a27				17 25
Harpenden	d	16 15		16 19				16 31	→		16 45	16 49				17 01	→		17 15	17 19					17 31
Luton Airport Parkway ✈	d	16 21		16 25			←	16 37			16 51	16 55			16 51	17 07			17 21	17 25				←	17 37
Luton	d	16 24		16a29		16 23	16 24	16 40			16 54	16a59				17 10			17 24	17a29		17 23		17 24	17 40
Leagrave	d	→					16 27	16 44			16 57					17 14			→					17 27	17 44
Harlington	d						16 32	16 49			17 02					17 19								17 32	17 49
Flitwick	d						16 36	16 53			17 06					17 23								17 36	17 53
Bedford	a					16 37	16 49	17 05			17 19				17 06	17 35						17 37		17 49	18 05

		FC	SE	FC ■	FC	FC	EM ◇■	FC ■		FC	SE	FC ■	FC	FC	EM ◇■	FC ■	FC ■	FC		SE	FC ■	FC	FC	EM ◇■	FC ■
London Bridge ⊖	d			17 00				17 15				17 30					17 45				18 00				18 15
Elephant & Castle	d	16 54	17 00			17 09				17 24	17 30			17 39				17 54		18 00			18 09		
London Blackfriars ⊖	a	16 57	17 04	17 07		17 12		17 22		17 27	17 34	17 37		17 42			17 52	17 57		18 04	18 07		18 12		18 22
	d	17 00		17 08		17 14		17 24		17 30		17 38		17 44			17 54	18 00			18 08		18 14		18 24
City Thameslink	d	17 02		17 10		17 16		17 26		17 32		17 40		17 46			17 56	18 02			18 10		18 16		18 26
Farringdon ⊖	d	17 06		17 14		17 19		17 30		17 36		17 44		17 49			18 00	18 06			18 14		18 19		18 30
St Pancras International ⊖	a	17 10		17 18		17 23		17 34		17 40		17 48		17 53			18 04	18 10			18 18		18 23		18 34
	d	17 10		17 18		17 24	17 30	17 34		17 40		17 48		17 54	18 00		18 04	18 10			18 18		18 24	18 30	18 34
Kentish Town	d	17 14				17 27				17 44				17 57				18 14					18 27		
West Hampstead Thameslink	d	17 19				17 31				17 49				18 01				18 19					18 31		
Cricklewood	d	17 22				17 34				17 52				18 04				18 22					18 34		
Hendon	d	17 25				17 37				17 55				18 07				18 25					18 37		
Mill Hill Broadway	d	17 29				17 41				17 59				18 11				18 29					18 41		
Elstree & Borehamwood	d	17 33				17 45				18 03				18 15				18 33					18 45		
Radlett	d	17 37			←	17 49				18 07			←	18 19				18 37				←	18 49		
St Albans City	d	17 44		17 39	17 44	17a57		17 55		18 14		18 09	18 14	18a27			18 25	18 44			18 39	18 44	18a57		18 55
Harpenden	d	→		17 45	17 49			18 01		→		18 15	18 19				18 31	→			18 45	18 49			19 01
Luton Airport Parkway ✈	d			17 51	17 55		17 51	18 07				18 21	18 25			←	18 37				18 51	18 55		18 51	19 07
Luton	d			17 54	17a59			18 10				18 24	18a29		18 23	18 24	18 40				18 54	18a59			19 10
Leagrave	d			17 57				18 14				→				18 27	18 44				18 57				19 14
Harlington	d			18 02				18 19								18 32	18 49				19 02				19 19
Flitwick	d			18 06				18 23								18 36	18 53				19 06				19 23
Bedford	a			18 19			18 06	18 35							18 37	18 49	19 05				19 19			19 06	19 35

		FC	SE	FC ■		FC	FC	EM ◇■	FC ■	FC ■	FC	SE	FC ■	FC		FC	EM ◇■	FC ■	FC	SE	FC ■	FC	EM ◇■	FC ■	
London Bridge ⊖	d			18 30						18 45			19 00					19 15			19 30				
Elephant & Castle	d	18 24	18 30				18 39				18 54	19 00				19 09			19 24	19 30		19 39			
London Blackfriars ⊖	a	18 27	18 34	18 37			18 42			18 52	18 57	19 04	19 07			19 12		19 22	19 27	19 34	19 37	19 42			
	d	18 30		18 38			18 44			18 54	19 00		19 08			19 14		19 24	19 30		19 38	19 44			
City Thameslink	d	18 32		18 40			18 46			18 56	19 02		19 10			19 16		19 26	19 32		19 40	19 46			
Farringdon ⊖	d	18 36		18 44			18 49			19 00	19 06		19 14			19 19		19 30	19 36		19 44	19 49			
St Pancras International ⊖	a	18 40		18 48			18 53			19 04	19 10		19 18			19 23		19 34	19 40		19 48	19 53			
	d	18 40		18 48			18 54	19 00		19 04	19 10		19 18			19 24	19 30	19 34	19 40		19 48	19 54	20 00		
Kentish Town	d	18 44					18 57				19 14					19 27			19 44			19 57			
West Hampstead Thameslink	d	18 49					19 01				19 19					19 31			19 49			20 01			
Cricklewood	d	18 52					19 04				19 22					19 34			19 52			20 04			
Hendon	d	18 55					19 07				19 25					19 37			19 55			20 07			
Mill Hill Broadway	d	18 59					19 11				19 29					19 41			19 59			20 11			
Elstree & Borehamwood	d	19 03					19 15				19 33					19 45			20 03			20 15			
Radlett	d	19 07				←	19 19				19 37			←		19 49			20 07			20 19			
St Albans City	d	19 14		19 09		19 14	19a27			19 25	19 44		19 39	19 44		19a57		19 55	20 14		20 09	20 27			
Harpenden	d	→		19 15		19 19				19 31	→		19 45	19 49				20 01	→		20 15	→			
Luton Airport Parkway ✈	d			19 21		19 25			←	19 37			19 51	19 55			19 51	20 07			20 21			←	
Luton	d			19 24		19a29		19 23	19 24	19 40			19 54	19a59				20 10			20 24		20 23	20 24	
Leagrave	d			→					19 27	19 44			19 57					20 14			→			20 27	
Harlington	d								19 32	19 49			20 02					20 19						20 32	
Flitwick	d								19 36	19 53			20 06					20 23						20 36	
Bedford	a							19 37	19 49	20 05			20 19				20 06	20 35					20 37	20 49	

Please refer to separate pages within this table for services operating between Brighton and South London

At weekends please use local bus and tube services to travel to/from St Pancras International and London Bridge when no trains are operating. See local publicity for details of alternative routes and services that are available across central London

Table 52

London, St Albans, Luton - Bedford

Saturdays

from 15 September

Network Diagram - see first Page of Table 52

		FC	FC ■	FC	FC	SE	FC ■	FC	EM ◇■	FC		FC ■	FC	FC	SE	FC ■	FC	FC	EM ◇■	FC ■		FC	SE	FC ■	FC
London Bridge ⊖	d		19 45				20 00					20 15				20 30				20 45				21 00	
Elephant & Castle	d				19 54	20 00		20 09						20 24	20 30			20 39				20 54	21 00		
London Blackfriars ⊖	a		19 52		19 57	20 04	20 07	20 12				20 22		20 27	20 34	20 37		20 42		20 52		20 57	21 04	21 07	
	d		19 54		20 00		20 08	20 14				20 24		20 30		20 38		20 44		20 54		21 00		21 08	
City Thameslink	d		19 56		20 02		20 10	20 16				20 26		20 32		20 40		20 46		20 56					
Farringdon ⊖	d		20 00		20 06		20 14	20 19				20 30		20 36		20 44		20 49		21 00		21 06		21 14	
St Pancras International ⊖	a		20 04		20 10		20 18	20 23				20 34		20 40		20 48		20 53		21 04		21 10		21 18	
	d		20 04		20 10		20 18	20 24	20 30			20 34		20 40		20 48		20 54	21 00	21 04		21 10		21 18	
Kentish Town	d				20 14			20 27						20 44				20 57				21 14			
West Hampstead Thameslink	d				20 19			20 31						20 49				21 01				21 19			
Cricklewood	d				20 22			20 34						20 52				21 04				21 22			
Hendon	d				20 25			20 37						20 55				21 07				21 25			
Mill Hill Broadway	d				20 29			20 41						20 59				21 11				21 29			
Elstree & Borehamwood	d				20 33			20 45						21 03				21 15				21 33			
Radlett	d	←		←	20 37			20 49		←			←	21 07			←	21 19				21 37			←
St Albans City	d	20 14	20 25	20 27	20 44		20 39	20 57		20 44		20 55	20 57	21 14		21 09	21 14	21a27		21 25		21 44		21 39	21 44
Harpenden	d	20 19	20 31	20 35	→		20 45	→		20 49		21 01	21 05	→		21 15	21 19			21 31		→		21 45	21 49
Luton Airport Parkway ✈	d	20 25	20 37	20 41			20 51		20 51	20 55		21 07	21 11			21 21	21 25			21 37				21 51	21 55
Luton	d	20a29	20 40	20 44			20 54			20a59		21 10	21 14			21 24	21a29		21 23	21 40				21 54	21a59
Leagrave	d		20 44	20 48			20 57					21 14	21 18			21 27				21 44				21 57	
Harlington	d		20 49	20 53			21 02					21 19	21 23			21 32				21 49				22 02	
Flitwick	d		20 53	20 57			21 06					21 23	21 27			21 36				21 53				22 06	
Bedford	a		21 05	21 09			21 19		21 06			21 35	21 39			21 49			21 38	22 05				22 19	

		FC	EM ◇■	FC ■	FC	SE		FC ■	FC	FC	EM ◇■ A	EM ◇■ B	FC ■	SE	FC	EM ◇■		FC ■	SE	FC	FC ■	SE	FC	FC ■	SE
London Bridge ⊖	d			21 15				21 30					21 45					22 15			22 45			23 15	
Elephant & Castle	d	21 09			21 24	21 30				21 39				22 00	22 04				22 30	22 34		23 00	23 04		23 30
London Blackfriars ⊖	a	21 12		21 22	21 27	21 34		21 37		21 42			21 52	22 04	22 07			22 22	22 34	22 37	22 52	23 04	23 07	23 22	23 34
	d	21 14		21 24	21 30			21 38		21 44			21 54		22 08			22 22		22 38	22 52		23 08	23 22	
City Thameslink	d																								
Farringdon ⊖	d	21 19		21 30	21 36			21 44		21 49			22 00		22 13			22 28		22 43	22 58		23 13	23 28	
St Pancras International ⊖	a	21 23		21 34	21 40			21 48		21 53			22 04		22 17			22 32		22 47	23 02		23 17	23 32	
	d	21 24	21 30	21 34	21 40			21 48		21 54	22 00	22 00	22 04		22 18	22 25		22 32		22 48	23 02		23 18	23 32	
Kentish Town	d	21 27			21 44					21 57					22 21					22 51			23 21		
West Hampstead Thameslink	d	21 31			21 49					22 01					22 25			22 40		22 55	23 10		23 25	23 40	
Cricklewood	d	21 34			21 52					22 04					22 28					22 58			23 28		
Hendon	d	21 37			21 55					22 07					22 31					23 01			23 31		
Mill Hill Broadway	d	21 41			21 59					22 11					22 35					23 05			23 35		
Elstree & Borehamwood	d	21 45			22 03					22 15					22 39					23 09			23 39		
Radlett	d	21 49			22 07				←	22 19					22 43					23 14			23 44		
St Albans City	d	21a57		21 55	22 14			22 09	22 14	22a27			22 25		22 50			22 57		23 20	23 27		23 50	23 57	
Harpenden	d			22 01	→			22 15	22 19				22 31		22 56			23 03		23 26	23 33		23 56	00 03	
Luton Airport Parkway ✈	d		21 51	22 07				22 21	22 25				22 37		23 02	22 46		23 09		23 32	23 39		00 02	00 09	
Luton	d			22 10				22 24	22a29		22 24	22 24	22 40		23 05			23 12		23 35	23 42		00 05	00 12	
Leagrave	d			22 14				22 27					22 44		23 09			23 16		23 39	23 46		00 09	00 16	
Harlington	d			22 19				22 32					22 49		23 14			23 21		23 44	23 51		00 14	00 21	
Flitwick	d			22 23				22 36					22 53		23 18			23 25		23 48	23 55		00 18	00 25	
Bedford	a		22 06	22 35				22 49			22 39	22 41	23 05		23 30	23 01		23 38		00 02	00 08		00 32	00 38	

		FC		FC ■
London Bridge ⊖	d			23 45
Elephant & Castle	d	23 34		
London Blackfriars ⊖	a	23 37		23 52
	d	23 38		23 52
City Thameslink	d			
Farringdon ⊖	d	23 43		23 58
St Pancras International ⊖	a	23 47		00 02
	d	23 48		00 02
Kentish Town	d	23 51		
West Hampstead Thameslink	d	23 55		00 10
Cricklewood	d	23 58		
Hendon	d	00 01		
Mill Hill Broadway	d	00 05		
Elstree & Borehamwood	d	00 09		
Radlett	d	00 14		
St Albans City	d	00 20		00 27
Harpenden	d	00 26		00 33
Luton Airport Parkway ✈	d	00 32		00 39
Luton	d	00 35		00 42
Leagrave	d	00 39		00 46
Harlington	d	00 44		00 51
Flitwick	d	00 48		00 55
Bedford	a	01 02		01 08

A from 15 September until 20 October

B from 27 October

Please refer to separate pages within this table for services operating between Brighton and South London

At weekends please use local bus and tube services to travel to/from St Pancras International and London Bridge when no trains are operating. See local publicity for details of alternative routes and services that are available across central London

London, St Albans, Luton - Bedford

Network Diagram - see first Page of Table 52

Station		FC	FC ■	FC	FC ■	FC	FC ■	FC	FC ■	FC ■	FC	FC ■	SE	FC ■	SE	FC ■	SE	EM ◇■ ✠	FC ■	SE	EM ◇■ ✠	FC ■	SE
London Bridge ■ ⊖	d		22p45		23p15		23p46		00 22	00 52		07 15		07 45		08 15			08 45			09 15	
Elephant & Castle	d	22p34		23p04		23p34							07 19		07 49		08 19			08 49			09 19
London Blackfriars ■ ⊖	a	22p37	22p52	23p07	23p22	23p37	23p52		00 28	00 58		07 22	07 23	07 52	07 53	08 22	08 23		08 52	08 53		09 22	09 23
	d	22p38	22p52	23p08	23p22	23p38	23p52	00 08	00 28	00 58	01 29	07 22		07 52		08 22			08 52			09 22	
City Thameslink ■	d																						
Farringdon ■ ⊖	d	22p43	22p58	23p13	23p28	23p43	23p58	00 13	00 33			07 27		07 57		08 27			08 57			09 27	
St Pancras International ■ ⊖	a	22p47	23p02	23p17	23p32	23p47	00 02	00 17	00 37	01 07	01 37	07 32		08 02		08 32			09 02			09 32	
	d	22p48	23p02	23p18	23p32	23p48	00 02	00 18	00 38	01 08	01 38	07 33		08 03		08 33		09 00	09 03		09 30	09 33	
Kentish Town	d	22p51		23p21		23p51		00 21	00 41	01 11	01 41	07 37		08 07		08 37			09 09			09 37	
West Hampstead Thameslink	d	22p55	23p10	23p25	23p40	23p55	00 10	00 25	00 45	01 15	01 45	07 41		08 11		08 41			09 13			09 41	
Cricklewood	d	22p58		23p28		23p58		00 28	00 48	01 18	01 48	07 44		08 14		08 44			09 16			09 44	
Hendon	d	23p01		23p31		00 01		00 31	00 51	01 21	01 51	07 47		08 17		08 47			09 19			09 47	
Mill Hill Broadway	d	23p05		23p35		00 05		00 35	00 55	01 25	01 55	07 51		08 21		08 51			09 23			09 51	
Elstree & Borehamwood	d	23p09		23p39		00 09		00 39	00 59	01 29	01 59	07 55		08 25		08 55			09 27			09 55	
Radlett	d	23p14		23p44		00 14		00 44	01 04	01 34	02 04	08 01		08 31		09 01			09 32			10 01	
St Albans City	d	23p20	23p27	23p50	23p57	00 20	00 27	00 50	01 10	01 40	02 10	08 08		08 38		09 08			09 38			10 08	
Harpenden	d	23p26	23p33	23p57	00 03	00 27	00 33	00 57	01 17	01 47	02 17	08 15		08 45		09 15			09 45			10 15	
Luton Airport Parkway ■ ✈	d	23p32	23p39	00 03	00 09	00 33	00 39	01 03	01 23	01 53	02 23	08 21		08 51		09 21		09 25	09 51			10 21	
Luton ■	d	23p35	23p42	00 06	00 12	00 36	00 42	01 06	01 26	01 56	02 26	08 24		08 54		09 24			09 54		09 58	10 24	
Leagrave	d	23p39	23p46	00 09	00 16	00 39	00 46	01 09	01 29	01 59	02 29	08 27		08 57		09 27			09 57			10 27	
Harlington	d	23p46	23p53	00 16	00 23	00 46	00 53	01 16	01 36	02 06	02 36	08 34		09 04		09 34			10 04			10 34	
Flitwick	d	23p50	23p57	00 21	00 27	00 51	00 57	01 21	01 41	02 11	02 41	08 38		09 08		09 38			10 08			10 38	
Bedford ■	a	00 02	00 09	00 33	00 39	01 03	01 09	01 32	01 52	02 22	02 52	08 50		09 20		09 50		09 50	10 20		10 20	10 50	

Station		EM ◇■ ✠	FC ■ A	SE	FC ■	EM ◇■ ✠	FC ■	SE	FC	FC ■	FC	EM ◇■ ✠	FC ■	SE	FC	FC ■	FC	EM ◇■ ✠	FC ■	SE	FC	FC ■	FC
London Bridge ■ ⊖	d		09 45		10 00		10 15			10 30			10 45			11 00			11 15			11 30	
Elephant & Castle	d			09 49				10 19	10 22		10 34			10 49	10 52		11 04			11 19	11 22		11 34
London Blackfriars ■ ⊖	a		09 52	09 53	10 07		10 22	10 23	10 25	10 37	10 37		10 52	10 53	10 55	11 07	11 07		11 22	11 23	11 25	11 37	11 37
	d		09 52		10 10		10 22		10 26	10 40			10 52		10 56	11 10			11 22		11 26	11 40	
City Thameslink ■	d																						
Farringdon ■ ⊖	d		09 57		10 14		10 27		10 31	10 44			10 57		11 01	11 14			11 27		11 31	11 44	
St Pancras International ■ ⊖	a		10 01		10 18		10 31		10 35	10 48			11 01		11 05	11 18			11 31		11 35	11 48	
	d	10 00	10 02		10 20	10 30	10 32		10 36	10 50		11 00	11 02		11 06	11 20		11 30	11 32		11 36	11 50	
Kentish Town	d		10 06						10 40						11 10						11 40		
West Hampstead Thameslink	d		10 10		10 27		10 40		10 44				11 10		11 14	11 27			11 40		11 44	11 57	
Cricklewood	d		10 13						10 47						11 17						11 47		
Hendon	d		10 16						10 50						11 20						11 50		
Mill Hill Broadway	d		10 20						10 54						11 24						11 54		
Elstree & Borehamwood	d		10 24						10 58						11 28						11 58		
Radlett	d		10 29						11 02						11 32						12 02		
St Albans City	d		10 33		10a43		10 57		11a09	11 12			11 25		11a39	11 43			11 57		12a09	12 13	
Harpenden	d		10 40				11 02						11 32			11 49			12 02			12 19	
Luton Airport Parkway ■ ✈	d	10 26	10 46				11 08			11 21		11 25	11 38			11 55		11 59	12 08			12 25	
Luton ■	d		10 49			10 56	11 11			11 24		11 29	11 41			11 58		12 03	12 11			12 28	
Leagrave	d		10 52				11 14						11 44			12 01			12 14			12 31	
Harlington	d		10 59				11 21						11 51			12 08			12 21			12 38	
Flitwick	d		11 03				11 25						11 55			12 12			12 25			12 42	
Bedford ■	a	10 50	11 15			11 16	11 37			11 45		11 48	12 07			12 24		12 25	12 37			12 54	

Station		EM ◇■ ✠	FC ■	SE	FC	FC ■	FC	EM ◇■ ✠	FC ■	SE	FC	FC ■	FC	EM ◇■ ✠	FC ■	SE	FC	FC ■	FC	EM ◇■ ✠	FC ■	SE
London Bridge ■ ⊖	d		11 45			12 00			12 15			12 30			12 45			13 00			13 15	
Elephant & Castle	d			11 49	11 52		12 04			12 19	12 22		12 34			12 49	12 52		13 04			13 19
London Blackfriars ■ ⊖	a		11 52	11 53	11 55	12 07	12 07		12 22	12 23	12 25	12 37	12 37		12 52	12 53	12 55	13 07	13 07		13 22	13 23
	d		11 52		11 56	12 10			12 22		12 26	12 40			12 52		12 56	13 10			13 22	
City Thameslink ■	d																					
Farringdon ■ ⊖	d		11 57		12 01	12 14			12 27		12 31	12 44			12 57		13 01	13 14			13 27	
St Pancras International ■ ⊖	a		12 01		12 05	12 18			12 31		12 35	12 48			13 01		13 05	13 18			13 31	
	d	12 00	12 02		12 06	12 20		12 30	12 32		12 36	12 50		13 00	13 02		13 06	13 20		13 30	13 32	
Kentish Town	d				12 10						12 40						13 10					
West Hampstead Thameslink	d		12 10		12 14	12 27			12 40		12 44	12 57			13 10		13 14	13 27			13 40	
Cricklewood	d				12 17						12 47						13 17					
Hendon	d				12 20						12 50						13 20					
Mill Hill Broadway	d				12 24						12 54						13 24					
Elstree & Borehamwood	d				12 28						12 58						13 28					
Radlett	d				12 32						13 02						13 32					
St Albans City	d		12 25		12a39	12 43			12 57		13a09	13 13			13 25		13a39	13 43			13 57	
Harpenden	d		12 32			12 49			13 02			13 19			13 32			13 49			14 02	
Luton Airport Parkway ■ ✈	d	12 29	12 38			12 55		12 59	13 08			13 25		13 29	13 38			13 55		13 58	14 08	
Luton ■	d	12 33	12 41			12 58		13 03	13 11			13 28		13 33	13 41			13 58		14 03	14 11	
Leagrave	d		12 44			13 01			13 14			13 31			13 44			14 01			14 14	
Harlington	d		12 51			13 08			13 21			13 38			13 51			14 08			14 21	
Flitwick	d		12 55			13 12			13 25			13 42			13 55			14 12			14 25	
Bedford ■	a	12 55	13 07			13 24		13 25	13 37			13 54		13 56	14 07			14 24		14 24	14 37	

A not 20 May

Please refer to separate pages within this table for services operating between Brighton and South London

At weekends please use local bus and tube services to travel to/from St Pancras International and London Bridge when no trains are operating. See local publicity for details of alternative routes and services that are available across central London

London, St Albans, Luton - Bedford

Network Diagram - see first Page of Table 52

Station		FC	FC ■	FC	FC ■	SE	FC	FC	EM ◇■ ✠	FC ■	FC ■	SE	FC	FC	EM ◇■ ✠	FC ■	FC ■	FC ■	SE	FC	FC	EM ◇■ ✠	FC ■
London Bridge ■ ⊖	d		13 30		13 45					14 00	14 15						14 30	14 45					15 00
Elephant & Castle	d	13 22		13 34		13 49	13 52	14 04				14 19	14 22	14 34					14 49	14 52	15 04		
London Blackfriars ■ ⊖	a	13 25	13 37	13 37	13 52	13 53	13 55	14 07		14 07	14 22	14 23	14 25	14 37			14 37	14 52	14 53	14 55	15 07		15 07
	d	13 26	13 40		13 52		13 56			14 10	14 22		14 26				14 40	14 52		14 56			15 10
City Thameslink ■	d																						
Farringdon ■ ⊖	d	13 31	13 44		13 57		14 01			14 14	14 27		14 31				14 44	14 57		15 01			15 14
St Pancras International ■ ⊖	a	13 35	13 48		14 01		14 05			14 18	14 31		14 35				14 48	15 01		15 05			15 18
	d	13 36	13 50		14 02		14 06		14 05	14 20	14 32		14 36		14 35		14 50	15 02		15 06		15 05	15 20
Kentish Town	d	13 40					14 10						14 40							15 10			
West Hampstead Thameslink	d	13 44	13 57		14 10		14 14			14 27	14 40		14 44				14 57	15 10		15 14			15 27
Cricklewood	d	13 47					14 17						14 47							15 17			
Hendon	d	13 50					14 20						14 50							15 20			
Mill Hill Broadway	d	13 54					14 24						14 54							15 24			
Elstree & Borehamwood	d	13 58					14 28						14 58							15 28			
Radlett	d	14 02					14 32						15 02							15 32			
St Albans City	d	14a09	14 13		14 25		14a39			14 43	14 57		15a09				15 13	15 25		15a39			15 43
Harpenden	d		14 19		14 32					14 49	15 02						15 19	15 32					15 49
Luton Airport Parkway ■ ✈	d		14 25		14 38				14 29	14 55	15 08					←	15 25	15 38				15 29	15 55
Luton ■	d		14 28		14 41					14 58	15 11				15 02	15 11	15 28	15 41					15 58
Leagrave	d		14 31		14 44					15 01	→					15 14	15 31	15 44					16 01
Harlington	d		14 38		14 51					15 08						15 21	15 38	15 51					16 08
Flitwick	d		14 42		14 55					15 12						15 25	15 42	15 55					16 12
Bedford ■	a		14 54		15 07				14 54	15 24					15 24	15 37	15 54	16 07				15 54	16 24

Station		FC ■	SE	FC	FC	EM ◇■ ✠	FC ■	FC ■	FC ■	SE	FC	FC	EM ◇■ ✠	FC ■	FC ■	SE	FC	FC	EM ◇■ ✠	FC ■	FC ■	FC ■
London Bridge ■ ⊖	d	15 15						15 30	15 45					16 00	16 15						16 30	16 45
Elephant & Castle	d		15 19	15 22	15 34					15 49	15 52	16 04				16 19	16 22	16 34				
London Blackfriars ■ ⊖	a	15 22	15 23	15 25	15 37			15 37	15 52	15 53	15 55	16 07		16 07	16 22	16 23	16 25	16 37			16 37	16 52
	d	15 22		15 26				15 40	15 52		15 56			16 10	16 22		16 26				16 40	16 52
City Thameslink ■	d																					
Farringdon ■ ⊖	d	15 27		15 31				15 44	15 57		16 01			16 14	16 27		16 31				16 44	16 57
St Pancras International ■ ⊖	a	15 31		15 35				15 48	16 01		16 05			16 18	16 31		16 35				16 48	17 01
	d	15 32		15 36		15 35		15 50	16 02		16 06		16 05	16 20	16 32		16 36		16 35		16 50	17 02
Kentish Town	d			15 40							16 10						16 40					
West Hampstead Thameslink	d	15 40		15 44				15 57	16 10		16 14			16 27	16 40		16 44				16 57	17 10
Cricklewood	d			15 47							16 17						16 47					
Hendon	d			15 50							16 20						16 50					
Mill Hill Broadway	d			15 54							16 24						16 54					
Elstree & Borehamwood	d			15 58							16 28						16 58					
Radlett	d			16 02							16 32						17 02					
St Albans City	d	15 57		16a09				16 13	16 25		16a39			16 44	16 57		17a09				17 14	17 25
Harpenden	d	16 02						16 19	16 32					16 50	17 02						17 20	17 32
Luton Airport Parkway ■ ✈	d	16 08					←	16 25	16 38				16 29	16 56	17 08					←	17 26	17 38
Luton ■	d	16 11				16 02	16 11	16 28	16 41					16 59	17 11				17 04	17 11	17 29	17 41
Leagrave	d	→					16 14	16 31	16 44					17 02	→					17 14	17 32	17 44
Harlington	d						16 21	16 38	16 51					17 09						17 21	17 39	17 51
Flitwick	d						16 25	16 42	16 55					17 13						17 25	17 43	17 55
Bedford ■	a					16 24	16 37	16 54	17 07				16 54	17 25					17 24	17 37	17 55	18 07

Station		SE	FC	FC	EM ◇■ ✠	FC ■	FC ■	SE	FC	FC	EM ◇■ ✠	FC ■	FC ■	FC ■	SE	FC	FC	EM ◇■ ✠	FC ■	FC ■	SE	FC	FC
London Bridge ■ ⊖	d					17 00	17 15						17 30	17 45					18 00	18 15			
Elephant & Castle	d	16 49	16 52	17 04				17 19	17 22	17 34					17 49	17 52	18 04				18 19	18 22	18 34
London Blackfriars ■ ⊖	a	16 53	16 55	17 07		17 07	17 22	17 23	17 25	17 37			17 37	17 52	17 53	17 55	18 07		18 07	18 22	18 23	18 25	18 37
	d		16 56			17 10	17 22		17 26				17 40	17 52		17 56			18 10	18 22		18 26	
City Thameslink ■	d																						
Farringdon ■ ⊖	d		17 01			17 14	17 27		17 31				17 44	17 57		18 01			18 14	18 27		18 31	
St Pancras International ■ ⊖	a		17 05			17 18	17 31		17 35				17 48	18 01		18 05			18 18	18 31		18 35	
	d		17 06		17 05	17 20	17 32		17 36		17 35		17 50	18 02		18 06		18 05	18 20	18 32		18 36	
Kentish Town	d		17 10						17 40							18 10						18 40	
West Hampstead Thameslink	d		17 14			17 27	17 40		17 44				17 57	18 10		18 14			18 27	18 40		18 44	
Cricklewood	d		17 17						17 47							18 17						18 47	
Hendon	d		17 20						17 50							18 20						18 50	
Mill Hill Broadway	d		17 24						17 54							18 24						18 54	
Elstree & Borehamwood	d		17 28						17 58							18 28						18 58	
Radlett	d		17 32						18 02							18 32						19 02	
St Albans City	d		17a39			17 44	17 57		18a09				18 14	18 25		18a39			18 44	18 57		19a09	
Harpenden	d					17 50	18 02						18 20	18 32					18 50	19 02			
Luton Airport Parkway ■ ✈	d				17 31	17 56	18 08					←	18 26	18 38				18 31	18 56	19 08			
Luton ■	d					17 59	18 11				18 04	18 11	18 29	18 41					18 59	19 11			
Leagrave	d					18 02	→					18 14	18 32	18 44					19 02	→			
Harlington	d					18 09						18 21	18 39	18 51					19 09				
Flitwick	d					18 13						18 25	18 43	18 55					19 13				
Bedford ■	a				17 54	18 25					18 24	18 37	18 55	19 07				18 54	19 25				

Please refer to separate pages within this table for services operating between Brighton and South London

At weekends please use local bus and tube services to travel to/from St Pancras International and London Bridge when no trains are operating. See local publicity for details of alternative routes and services that are available across central London

Table 52

London, St Albans, Luton - Bedford

Sundays until 24 June

Network Diagram - see first Page of Table 52

Station		EM ◇1	FC 1	FC 1	FC 1	SE		FC	FC	EM ◇1	FC 1	FC 1	SE	FC	FC	EM ◇1		FC 1	FC 1	EM ◇1	FC 1	SE	FC	FC	EM ◇1
London Bridge 4 ⊖	d			18 30	18 45						19 00	19 15							19 30		19 45				
Elephant & Castle	d					18 49		18 52	19 04				19 19	19 22	19 34							19 49	19 52	20 04	
London Blackfriars 3 ⊖	a			18 37	18 52	18 53		18 55	19 07		19 07	19 22	19 23	19 25	19 37				19 37		19 52	19 53	19 55	20 07	
	d			18 40	18 52			18 56			19 10	19 22		19 26					19 40		19 52		20 03		
City Thameslink 3	d																								
Farringdon 3 ⊖	d			18 44	18 57			19 01			19 14	19 27		19 31					19 44		19 57		20 08		
St Pancras International 15 ⊖	a			18 48	19 01			19 05			19 18	19 31		19 35					19 48		20 01		20 13		
	d	18 35		18 50	19 02			19 06		19 05	19 20	19 32		19 36		19 35			19 50	20 00	20 02		20 14		20 30
Kentish Town	d							19 10						19 40									20 17		
West Hampstead Thameslink	d			18 57	19 10			19 14			19 27	19 40		19 44					19 57		20 10		20 21		
Cricklewood	d							19 17						19 47									20 24		
Hendon	d							19 20						19 50									20 27		
Mill Hill Broadway	d							19 24						19 54									20 31		
Elstree & Borehamwood	d							19 28						19 58									20 35		
Radlett	d							19 32						20 02									20 40		
St Albans City	d			19 14	19 25			19a39			19 44	19 57		20a09					20 14		20 25		20 46		
Harpenden	d			19 20	19 32						19 50	20 02							20 20		20 32		20 53		
Luton Airport Parkway 7 ✈	d		←	19 26	19 38					19 31	19 56	20 08						←	20 26	20 21	20 38		20 58		
Luton 10	d	19 03	19 11	19 29	19 41						19 59	20 11				20 04		20 11	20 29		20 41		21 01		20 54
Leagrave	d		19 14	19 32	19 44						20 02	→						20 14	20 33		20 44		→		
Harlington	d		19 21	19 39	19 51						20 09							20 21	20 39		20 51				
Flitwick	d		19 25	19 43	19 55						20 13							20 25	20 44		20 55				
Bedford 7	a	19 23	19 37	19 55	20 07					19 55	20 25					20 24		20 37	20 55	20 40	21 07				21 12

Station		FC		FC 1	SE	FC	FC	EM ◇1	FC 1	SE	FC	FC		EM ◇1	FC	FC 1	SE	FC	FC	FC 1	SE	FC		FC	EM ◇1
London Bridge 4 ⊖	d			20 15					20 45							21 15				21 45					
Elephant & Castle	d				20 19	20 22	20 34			20 49	20 52	21 04					21 19	21 22	21 34		21 49	21 52		22 04	
London Blackfriars 3 ⊖	a			20 22	20 23	20 25	20 37		20 52	20 53	20 55	21 07				21 22	21 23	21 25	21 37	21 52	21 53	21 55		22 07	
	d			20 22		20 33			20 52		21 03					21 22		21 33		21 52		22 03			
City Thameslink 3	d																								
Farringdon 3 ⊖	d			20 27		20 38			20 57		21 08					21 27		21 38		21 57		22 08			
St Pancras International 15 ⊖	a			20 31		20 43			21 01		21 13					21 31		21 43		22 01		22 13			
	d			20 32		20 44		21 00	21 02		21 14			21 30		21 32		21 44		22 02		22 14			22 30
Kentish Town	d					20 47					21 17							21 47				22 17			
West Hampstead Thameslink	d			20 40		20 51			21 10		21 21					21 40		21 51		22 10		22 21			
Cricklewood	d					20 54					21 24							21 54				22 24			
Hendon	d					20 57					21 27							21 57				22 27			
Mill Hill Broadway	d					21 01					21 31							22 01				22 31			
Elstree & Borehamwood	d					21 05					21 35							22 05				22 35			
Radlett	d					21 10					21 40							22 10				22 40			
St Albans City	d			20 57		21 16			21 25		21 46					21 57		22 16		22 27		22 46			
Harpenden	d			21 02		21 23			21 32		21 53					22 02		22 23		22 32		22 53			
Luton Airport Parkway 7 ✈	d	←		21 08		21 28		21 21	21 38		21 58				←	22 08		22 28		22 38		22 58			22 51
Luton 10	d	21 01		21 11		21 31			21 41		22 01			21 52	22 01	22 11		22 31		22 41		23 01			
Leagrave	d	21 05		21 14		21 35			21 44		→				22 05	22 14		22 35		22 45		23 05			
Harlington	d	21 11		21 21		21 41			21 51						22 11	22 21		22 41		22 51		23 11			
Flitwick	d	21 16		21 25		21 46			21 55						22 16	22 25		22 46		22 55		23 16			
Bedford 7	a	21 27		21 37		21 57		21 39	22 07					22 10	22 27	22 37		22 57		23 07		23 27			23 19

Station		FC 1	SE	FC	EM ◇1	FC 1	SE	FC 1		SE	FC 1
London Bridge 4 ⊖	d	22 15				22 45		23 15			23 45
Elephant & Castle	d		22 19	22 34			22 49			23 19	
London Blackfriars 3 ⊖	a	22 22	22 23	22 37		22 52	22 53	23 22		23 23	23 52
	d	22 22				22 52		23 22			23 52
City Thameslink 3	d										
Farringdon 3 ⊖	d	22 27				22 57		23 27			23 57
St Pancras International 15 ⊖	a	22 31				23 01		23 31			00 01
	d	22 32			23 00	23 02		23 32			00 02
Kentish Town	d	22 36				23 06		23 36			00 06
West Hampstead Thameslink	d	22 40				23 10		23 40			00 10
Cricklewood	d	22 43				23 13		23 43			00 13
Hendon	d	22 46				23 16		23 46			00 16
Mill Hill Broadway	d	22 50				23 20		23 50			00 20
Elstree & Borehamwood	d	22 54				23 24		23 54			00 24
Radlett	d	22 59				23 29		23 59			00 29
St Albans City	d	23 06				23 36		00 06			00 36
Harpenden	d	23 12				23 42		00 12			00 42
Luton Airport Parkway 7 ✈	d	23 18			23 27	23 48		00 18			00 48
Luton 10	d	23 21				23 51		00 21			00 51
Leagrave	d	23 25				23 55		00 25			00 55
Harlington	d	23 31				00 01		00 31			01 01
Flitwick	d	23 36				00 06		00 36			01 06
Bedford 7	a	23 47			23 55	00 17		00 47			01 17

Please refer to separate pages within this table for services operating between Brighton and South London

At weekends please use local bus and tube services to travel to/from St Pancras International and London Bridge when no trains are operating. See local publicity for details of alternative routes and services that are available across central London

Table 52

London, St Albans, Luton - Bedford

Sundays 1 July to 9 September

Network Diagram - see first Page of Table 52

Station		FC	FC 1	FC	FC 1	FC	FC 1	FC	FC 1	FC 1		FC	FC A	SE A	FC A	SE A	FC 1	SE B	SE A	FC 1		SE B	SE A	FC 1	SE B
London Bridge 4 ⊖	d		22p45		23p15		23p45		00 22	00 52							07 15			07 45				08 15	
Elephant & Castle	d	22p34		23p04		23p34								06 30		07 00		07 19	07 30			07 49	08 00		08 19
London Blackfriars 3 ⊖	a	22p37	22p52	23p07	23p22	23p37	23p52		00 28	00 58				06 34		07 04	07 22	07 23	07 34	07 52		07 53	08 04	08 22	08 23
	d	22p38	22p52	23p08	23p22	23p38	23p52	00 08	00 28	00 58		01 29	05 59		06 59		07 22			07 52				08 22	
City Thameslink 3	d														07 02										
Farringdon 3 ⊖	d	22p43	22p58	23p13	23p28	23p43	23p58	00 13	00 33				06 03				07 27			07 57				08 27	
St Pancras International 15 ⊖	a	22p47	23p02	23p17	23p32	23p47	00 02	00 17	00 37	01 07		01 37	06 07		07 09		07 31			08 01				08 31	
	d	22p48	23p02	23p18	23p32	23p48	00 02	00 18	00 38	01 08		01 38	06 08		07 09		07 32			08 02				08 32	
Kentish Town	d	22p51		23p21		23p51		00 21	00 41	01 11		01 41	06 11		07 13		07 36			08 06				08 36	
West Hampstead Thameslink	d	22p55	23p10	23p25	23p40	23p55	00 10	00 25	00 45	01 15		01 45	06 15		07 17		07 40			08 10				08 40	
Cricklewood	d	22p58		23p28		23p58		00 28	00 48	01 18		01 48	06 18		07 20		07 43			08 13				08 43	
Hendon	d	23p01		23p31		00 01		00 31	00 51	01 21		01 51	06 21		07 23		07 46			08 16				08 46	
Mill Hill Broadway	d	23p05		23p35		00 05		00 35	00 55	01 25		01 55	06 25		07 27		07 50			08 20				08 50	
Elstree & Borehamwood	d	23p09		23p39		00 09		00 39	00 59	01 29		01 59	06 29		07 31		07 54			08 24				08 54	
Radlett	d	23p14		23p44		00 14		00 44	01 04	01 34		02 04	06 34		07 36		07 59			08 29				08 59	
St Albans City	d	23p20	23p27	23p50	23p57	00 20	00 27	00 50	01 10	01 40		02 10	06 41		07 42		08 06			08 36				09 06	
Harpenden	d	23p26	23p33	23p56	00 03	00 26	00 33	00 56	01 16	01 46		02 16	06 47		07 48		08 12			08 42				09 12	
Luton Airport Parkway 7 ✈	d	23p32	23p39	00 02	00 09	00 32	00 39	01 02	01 22	01 52		02 22	06 53		07 54		08 18			08 48				09 18	
Luton 10	d	23p35	23p42	00 05	00 12	00 35	00 42	01 05	01 25	01 55		02 25	06 56		07 57		08 21			08 51				09 21	
Leagrave	d	23p39	23p46	00 09	00 16	00 39	00 46	01 09	01 29	01 59		02 29	07 00		08 01		08 24			08 54				09 24	
Harlington	d	23p44	23p51	00 14	00 21	00 44	00 51	01 14	01 34	02 04		02 34	07 05		08 06		08 30			09 00				09 30	
Flitwick	d	23p48	23p55	00 18	00 25	00 48	00 55	01 18	01 38	02 08		02 38	07 09		08 10		08 34			09 04				09 34	
Bedford 7	a	00 02	00 08	00 32	00 38	01 02	01 08	01 32	01 52	02 22		02 52	07 23		08 23		08 47			09 17				09 47	

Station		SE A	EM ◇1	FC 1	SE B	SE A		EM ◇1	FC 1	SE B	SE A	EM ◇1	FC 1	SE B	SE A	FC 1		EM ◇1	FC 1	SE B	FC	SE A	FC	FC 1	EM ◇1
London Bridge 4 ⊖	d			08 45					09 15				09 45			10 00			10 15					10 30	
Elephant & Castle	d	08 30			08 49	09 00				09 19	09 30			09 49	10 00					10 19	10 22	10 30	10 34		
London Blackfriars 3 ⊖	a	08 34		08 52	08 53	09 04			09 22	09 23	09 34		09 52	09 53	10 04	10 07			10 22	10 23	10 25	10 34	10 37	10 37	
	d			08 52					09 22				09 52			10 10			10 22		10 26			10 40	
City Thameslink 3	d																								
Farringdon 3 ⊖	d			08 57					09 27				09 57			10 14			10 27		10 31			10 44	
St Pancras International 15 ⊖	a			09 01					09 31				10 01			10 18			10 31		10 35			10 48	
	d		09 00	09 02				09 30	09 32			10 00	10 02			10 20		10 30	10 32		10 36			10 50	11 00
Kentish Town	d			09 06					09 36												10 40				
West Hampstead Thameslink	d			09 10					09 40				10 10			10 27			10 40		10 44			10 57	
Cricklewood	d			09 13					09 43												10 47				
Hendon	d			09 16					09 46												10 50				
Mill Hill Broadway	d			09 20					09 50												10 54				
Elstree & Borehamwood	d			09 24					09 54												10 58				
Radlett	d			09 29					09 59												11 02				
St Albans City	d			09 36					10 06				10 27			10a43			10 57		11 09			11 13	
Harpenden	d			09 42					10 12				10 33						11 03		11 15			11 19	
Luton Airport Parkway 7 ✈	d		09 21	09 48					10 18			10 23	10 39						11 09		11 20			11 25	11 21
Luton 10	d			09 51				09 52	10 21				10 42					10 52	11 12		11a24			11 28	11 25
Leagrave	d			09 54					10 24				10 45						11 15					→	
Harlington	d			10 00					10 30				10 51						11 21						
Flitwick	d			10 04					10 34				10 55						11 25						
Bedford 7	a		09 36	10 17				10 07	10 47			10 38	11 08					11 07	11 38						11 39

Station		FC 1		FC 1	SE B	FC	SE A	FC	FC 1	EM ◇1	FC 1	FC 1		SE B	FC	SE A	FC	FC 1	EM ◇1	FC 1	FC 1	SE B		FC	SE A
London Bridge 4 ⊖	d			10 45					11 00			11 15						11 30			11 45				
Elephant & Castle	d				10 49	10 52	11 00	11 04						11 19	11 22	11 30	11 34					11 49		11 52	12 00
London Blackfriars 3 ⊖	a			10 52	10 53	10 55	11 04	11 07	11 07			11 22		11 23	11 25	11 34	11 37	11 37			11 52	11 53		11 55	12 04
	d			10 52		10 56			11 10			11 22			11 26			11 40			11 52			11 56	
City Thameslink 3	d																								
Farringdon 3 ⊖	d			10 57		11 01			11 14			11 27			11 31			11 44			11 57			12 01	
St Pancras International 15 ⊖	a			11 01		11 05			11 18			11 31			11 35			11 48			12 01			12 05	
	d			11 02		11 06			11 20	11 30		11 32			11 36			11 50	12 00		12 02			12 06	
Kentish Town	d					11 10									11 40									12 10	
West Hampstead Thameslink	d			11 10		11 14			11 27			11 40			11 44			11 57			12 10			12 14	
Cricklewood	d					11 17									11 47									12 17	
Hendon	d					11 20									11 50									12 20	
Mill Hill Broadway	d					11 24									11 54									12 24	
Elstree & Borehamwood	d					11 28									11 58									12 28	
Radlett	d					11 33									12 02									12 33	
St Albans City	d			11 27		11 39			11 43			11 57			12 09			12 13			12 27			12 39	
Harpenden	d			11 33		11 45			11 49			12 03			12 15			12 19			12 33			12 45	
Luton Airport Parkway 7 ✈	d	←		11 39		11 50			11 55	11 51	←	12 09			12 20			12 25	12 23	←	12 39			12 50	
Luton 10	d	11 28		11 42		11a54			11 58	11 55	11 58	12 12			12a24			12 28	12 27	12 28	12 42			12a54	
Leagrave	d	11 31		11 45					→		12 01	12 15						→		12 31	12 45				
Harlington	d	11 38		11 51							12 07	12 21								12 37	12 51				
Flitwick	d	11 42		11 55							12 11	12 25								12 41	12 55				
Bedford 7	a	11 54		12 08						12 09	12 24	12 38							12 42	12 54	13 08				

A 29 July, 5 August, 12 August

B from 1 July until 22 July, from 19 August until 9 September

Please refer to separate pages within this table for services operating between Brighton and South London

At weekends please use local bus and tube services to travel to/from St Pancras International and London Bridge when no trains are operating. See local publicity for details of alternative routes and services that are available across central London

London, St Albans, Luton - Bedford

Network Diagram - see first Page of Table 52

		FC	FC	EM	FC	FC	SE	FC	SE	FC	FC	EM	FC	FC	SE	FC	SE	FC	FC	EM	FC	FC	SE
			1	◇1	1	1	A		B		1	◇1	1	1	A		B		1	◇1	1	1	A
London Bridge 4 ⊖	d		12 00			12 15					12 30			12 45					13 00			13 15	
Elephant & Castle	d	12 04					12§19	12 22	12§30	12 34					12§49	12 52	13§00	13 04					13§19
London Blackfriars 3 ⊖	a	12 07	12 07			12 22	12§23	12 25	12§34	12 37	12 37			12 52	12§53	12 55	13§04	13 07	13 07			13 22	13§23
	d		12 10			12 22		12 26			12 40			12 52		12 56			13 10			13 22	
City Thameslink 3	d																						
Farringdon 3 ⊖	d		12 14			12 27		12 31			12 44			12 57		13 01			13 14			13 27	
St Pancras International 15 ⊖	a		12 18			12 31		12 35			12 48			13 01		13 05			13 18			13 31	
	d		12 20	12 30		12 32		12 36			12 50	13 00		13 02		13 06			13 20	13 30		13 32	
Kentish Town	d							12 40								13 10							
West Hampstead Thameslink	d		12 27			12 40		12 44			12 57			13 10		13 14			13 27			13 40	
Cricklewood	d							12 47								13 17							
Hendon	d							12 50								13 20							
Mill Hill Broadway	d							12 54								13 24							
Elstree & Borehamwood	d							12 58								13 28							
Radlett	d							13 02								13 33							
St Albans City	d		12 43			12 57		13 09			13 13			13 27		13 39			13 43			13 57	
Harpenden	d		12 49			13 03		13 15			13 19			13 33		13 45			13 49			14 03	
Luton Airport Parkway 7 ✈	d		12 55	12 51	←	13 09		13 20			13 25	13 23	←	13 39		13 50			13 55	13 50	←	14 09	
Luton 10	d		12 58	12 55	12 58	13 12		13a24			13 28	13 27	13 28	13 42		13a54			13 58	13 55	13 58	14 12	
Leagrave	d		→		13 01	13 15					→		13 31	13 45					→		14 01	14 15	
Harlington	d				13 07	13 21							13 37	13 51							14 07	14 21	
Flitwick	d				13 11	13 25							13 41	13 55							14 11	14 25	
Bedford 7	a			13 09	13 24	13 38						13 42	13 54	14 08						14 09	14 24	14 38	

		FC	SE	FC	FC	EM	FC	SE	FC	SE	FC	FC	EM	FC	FC	SE	FC	SE	FC	FC	EM	FC
			B	1		◇1	1	A		B		1	◇1	1	1	A		B	1		◇1	1
London Bridge 4 ⊖	d			13 30			13 45					14 00			14 15				14 30			14 45
Elephant & Castle	d	13 22	13§30		13 34			13§49	13 52	14§00	14 04					14§19	14 22	14§30		14 34		
London Blackfriars 3 ⊖	a	13 25	13§34	13 37	13 37		13 52	13§53	13 55	14§04	14 07	14 07			14 22	14§23	14 25	14§34	14 37	14 37		14 52
	d	13 26		13 40			13 52		13 56			14 10			14 22		14 26		14 40			14 52
City Thameslink 3	d																					
Farringdon 3 ⊖	d	13 31		13 44			13 57		14 01			14 14			14 27		14 31		14 44			14 57
St Pancras International 15 ⊖	a	13 35		13 48			14 01		14 05			14 18			14 31		14 35		14 48			15 01
	d	13 36		13 50		14 00	14 02		14 06			14 20	14 30		14 32		14 36		14 50		15 00	15 02
Kentish Town	d	13 40							14 10								14 40					
West Hampstead Thameslink	d	13 44		13 57			14 10		14 14			14 27			14 40		14 44		14 57			15 10
Cricklewood	d	13 47							14 17								14 47					
Hendon	d	13 50							14 20								14 50					
Mill Hill Broadway	d	13 54							14 24								14 54					
Elstree & Borehamwood	d	13 58							14 28								14 58					
Radlett	d	14 02							14 33								15 02					
St Albans City	d	14 09		14 13			14 27		14 39			14 43			14 57		15 09		15 13			15 27
Harpenden	d	14 15		14 19			14 33		14 45			14 49			15 03		15 15		15 19			15 33
Luton Airport Parkway 7 ✈	d	14 20		14 25		14 23	14 39		14 50			14 55		←	15 09		15 20		15 25		15 23	15 39
Luton 10	d	14a24		14 28			14 42		14a54			14 58	14 54	14 58	15 12		15a24		15 28			15 42
Leagrave	d			14 31			14 45					→		15 01	15 15				15 31			15 45
Harlington	d			14 37			14 51							15 07	15 21				15 37			15 51
Flitwick	d			14 41			14 55							15 11	15 25				15 41			15 55
Bedford 7	a			14 54		14 38	15 08						15 09	15 24	15 38				15 54		15 38	16 08

		SE	FC	SE	FC	FC	EM	FC	FC	SE	FC	SE	FC	FC	EM	FC	SE	FC	SE	FC	FC	EM	FC
		A		B		1	◇1	1	1	A		B	1		◇1	1	A		B		1	◇1	1
London Bridge 4 ⊖	d					15 00			15 15				15 30			15 45					16 00		
Elephant & Castle	d	14§49	14 52	15§00	15 04					15§19	15 22	15§30		15 34			15§49	15 52	16§00	16 04			
London Blackfriars 3 ⊖	a	14§53	14 55	15§04	15 07	15 07			15 22	15§23	15 25	15§34	15 37	15 37		15 52	15§53	15 55	16§04	16 07	16 07		
	d		14 56			15 10			15 22		15 26		15 40			15 52		15 56			16 10		
City Thameslink 3	d																						
Farringdon 3 ⊖	d		15 01			15 14			15 27		15 31		15 44			15 57		16 01			16 14		
St Pancras International 15 ⊖	a		15 05			15 18			15 31		15 35		15 48			16 01		16 05			16 18		
	d		15 06			15 20	15 30		15 32		15 36		15 50		16 00	16 02		16 06			16 20	16 30	
Kentish Town	d		15 10								15 40							16 10					
West Hampstead Thameslink	d		15 14			15 27			15 40		15 44		15 57			16 10		16 14			16 27		
Cricklewood	d		15 17								15 47							16 17					
Hendon	d		15 20								15 50							16 20					
Mill Hill Broadway	d		15 24								15 54							16 24					
Elstree & Borehamwood	d		15 28								15 58							16 28					
Radlett	d		15 33								16 02							16 33					
St Albans City	d		15 39			15 43			15 57		16 09		16 13			16 27		16 39			16 43		
Harpenden	d		15 45			15 49			16 03		16 15		16 19			16 33		16 45			16 49		
Luton Airport Parkway 7 ✈	d		15 50			15 55		←	16 09		16 20		16 25		16 21	16 39		16 50			16 55		←
Luton 10	d		15a54			15 58	15 52	15 58	16 12		16a24		16 28			16 42		16a54			16 58	16 52	16 58
Leagrave	d					→		16 01	16 15				16 31			16 45					→		17 01
Harlington	d							16 07	16 21				16 37			16 51							17 07
Flitwick	d							16 11	16 25				16 41			16 55							17 11
Bedford 7	a						16 07	16 24	16 38				16 54		16 36	17 08						17 07	17 24

A from 1 July until 22 July, from 19 August until 9 September
B 29 July, 5 August, 12 August

Please refer to separate pages within this table for services operating between Brighton and South London

At weekends please use local bus and tube services to travel to/from St Pancras International and London Bridge when no trains are operating. See local publicity for details of alternative routes and services that are available across central London

Sundays
1 July to 9 September

London, St Albans, Luton - Bedford

Network Diagram - see first Page of Table 52

		FC	SE	FC	SE	FC	FC	EM	FC	SE	FC	SE	FC	FC	EM	FC	FC	SE	FC	SE	FC	FC	EM
		1	A		B	1		◇1	1	A		B		1	◇1	1	1	A		B	1		◇1
London Bridge 4 ⊖	d	16 15				16 30			16 45					17 00			17 15				17 30		
Elephant & Castle	d		16§19	16 22	16§30		16 34			16§49	16 52	17§00	17 04					17§19	17 22	17§30		17 34	
London Blackfriars 3 ⊖	a	16 22	16§23	16 25	16§34	16 37	16 37		16 52	16§53	16 55	17§04	17 07	17 07			17 22	17§23	17 25	17§34	17 37	17 37	
	d	16 22		16 26		16 40			16 52		16 56			17 10			17 22		17 26		17 40		
City Thameslink 3	d																						
Farringdon 3 ⊖	d	16 27		16 31		16 44			16 57		17 01			17 14			17 27		17 31		17 44		
St Pancras International 15 ⊖	a	16 31		16 35		16 48			17 01		17 05			17 18			17 31		17 35		17 48		
	d	16 32		16 36		16 50		17 00	17 02		17 06			17 20	17 30		17 32		17 36		17 50		18 00
Kentish Town	d			16 40							17 10								17 40				
West Hampstead Thameslink	d	16 40		16 44		16 57			17 10		17 14			17 27			17 40		17 44		17 57		
Cricklewood	d			16 47							17 17								17 47				
Hendon	d			16 50							17 20								17 50				
Mill Hill Broadway	d			16 54							17 24								17 54				
Elstree & Borehamwood	d			16 58							17 28								17 58				
Radlett	d			17 02							17 33								18 02				
St Albans City	d	16 57		17 09		17 13			17 27		17 39			17 43			17 57		18 09		18 13		
Harpenden	d	17 03		17 15		17 19			17 33		17 45			17 49			18 03		18 15		18 19		
Luton Airport Parkway 7 ✈	d	17 09		17 20		17 25		17 21	17 39		17 50			17 55		←	18 09		18 20		18 25		18 21
Luton 10	d	17 12		17a24		17 28			17 42		17a54			17 58	17 54	17 58	18 12		18a24		18 28		
Leagrave	d	17 15				17 31			17 45					→		18 01	18 15				18 31		
Harlington	d	17 21				17 37			17 51							18 07	18 21				18 37		
Flitwick	d	17 25				17 41			17 55							18 11	18 25				18 41		
Bedford 7	a	17 38				17 54		17 37	18 08						18 09	18 24	18 38				18 54		18 36

		FC	SE	FC	SE	FC	FC	EM	FC	FC	SE	FC	SE	FC	FC	EM	FC	SE	FC	SE	FC	FC
		1	A		B		1	◇1	1	1	A		B	1		◇1	1	A		B		1
London Bridge 4 ⊖	d	17 45					18 00			18 15				18 30			18 45					19 00
Elephant & Castle	d		17§49	17 52	18§00	18 04					18§19	18 22	18§30		18 34			18§49	18 52	19§00	19 04	
London Blackfriars 3 ⊖	a	17 52	17§53	17 55	18§04	18 07	18 07			18 22	18§23	18 25	18§34	18 37	18 37		18 52	18§53	18 55	19§04	19 07	19 07
	d	17 52		17 56			18 10			18 22		18 26		18 40			18 52		18 56			19 10
City Thameslink 3	d																					
Farringdon 3 ⊖	d	17 57		18 01			18 14			18 27		18 31		18 44			18 57		19 01			19 14
St Pancras International 15 ⊖	a	18 01		18 05			18 18			18 31		18 35		18 48			19 01		19 05			19 18
	d	18 02		18 06			18 20	18 30		18 32		18 36		18 50		19 00	19 02		19 06			19 20
Kentish Town	d			18 10								18 40							19 10			
West Hampstead Thameslink	d	18 10		18 14			18 27			18 40		18 44		18 57			19 10		19 14			19 27
Cricklewood	d			18 17								18 47							19 17			
Hendon	d			18 20								18 50							19 20			
Mill Hill Broadway	d			18 24								18 54							19 24			
Elstree & Borehamwood	d			18 28								18 58							19 28			
Radlett	d			18 33								19 02							19 33			
St Albans City	d	18 27		18 39			18 43			18 57		19 09		19 13			19 27		19 39			19 43
Harpenden	d	18 33		18 45			18 49			19 03		19 15		19 19			19 33		19 45			19 49
Luton Airport Parkway 7 ✈	d	18 39		18 50			18 55		←	19 09		19 20		19 25		19 21	19 39		19 50			19 55
Luton 10	d	18 42		18a54			18 58	18 53	18 58	19 12		19a24		19 28			19 42		19a54			19 58
Leagrave	d	18 45					→		19 01	19 15				19 31			19 45					→
Harlington	d	18 51							19 07	19 21				19 37			19 51					
Flitwick	d	18 55							19 11	19 25				19 41			19 55					
Bedford 7	a	19 08						19 07	19 24	19 38				19 54		19 36	20 08					

		EM	FC	FC	SE	FC	SE	FC	FC	EM	FC	SE	FC	SE	FC	EM	FC	SE	FC	SE	FC	EM	FC
		◇1	1	1	A		B	1		◇1	1	A		B		◇1	1	A		B		◇1	1
London Bridge 4 ⊖	d			19 15				19 30			19 45						20 15						20 45
Elephant & Castle	d				19§19	19 22	19§30		19 34			19§49	19 52	20§00	20 04			20§19	20 22	20§30	20 34		
London Blackfriars 3 ⊖	a			19 22	19§23	19 25	19§34	19 37	19 37		19 52	19§53	19 55	20§04	20 07		20 22	20§23	20 25	20§34	20 37		20 52
	d			19 22		19 26		19 40			19 52		19 56				20 22		20 26				20 52
City Thameslink 3	d																						
Farringdon 3 ⊖	d			19 27		19 31		19 44			19 57		20 01				20 27		20 31				20 57
St Pancras International 15 ⊖	a			19 31		19 35		19 48			20 01		20 05				20 31		20 35				21 01
	d	19 30		19 32		19 36		19 50		20 00	20 02		20 06			20 30	20 32		20 36			21 00	21 02
Kentish Town	d					19 40							20 10						20 40				
West Hampstead Thameslink	d			19 40		19 44		19 57			20 10		20 14				20 40		20 44				21 10
Cricklewood	d					19 47							20 17						20 47				
Hendon	d					19 50							20 20						20 50				
Mill Hill Broadway	d					19 54							20 24						20 54				
Elstree & Borehamwood	d					19 58							20 28						20 58				
Radlett	d					20 02							20 33						21 02				
St Albans City	d			19 57		20 09		20 13			20 27		20 39				20 57		21 09				21 27
Harpenden	d			20 03		20 15		20 19			20 33		20 45				21 03		21 15				21 33
Luton Airport Parkway 7 ✈	d		←	20 09		20 20		20 25		20 21	20 39		20 50				21 09		21 20			21 21	21 39
Luton 10	d	19 52	19 58	20 12		20 23		20 28			20 42		20 53			20 54	21 12		21 23				21 42
Leagrave	d		20 01	20 15		20 27		20 31			20 45		20 57				21 15		21 27				21 45
Harlington	d		20 07	20 21		20 32		20 37			20 51		21 02				21 21		21 32				21 51
Flitwick	d		20 11	20 25		20 36		20 41			20 55		21 06				21 25		21 36				21 55
Bedford 7	a	20 07	20 24	20 38		20 50		20 54		20 36	21 08		21 20			21 09	21 38		21 50			21 36	22 08

A from 1 July until 22 July, from 19 August until 9 September
B 29 July, 5 August, 12 August

Please refer to separate pages within this table for services operating between Brighton and South London

At weekends please use local bus and tube services to travel to/from St Pancras International and London Bridge when no trains are operating. See local publicity for details of alternative routes and services that are available across central London

Table 52

Sundays

1 July to 9 September

London, St Albans, Luton - Bedford

Network Diagram - see first Page of Table 52

		SE	FC	SE	FC	EM	FC	FC	SE	FC	SE	FC	FC	SE	FC	SE	FC	EM	FC	SE	SE	FC
						◇■		■					■					◇■	■			
		A		B					A		B			A		B				A	B	
London Bridge ■ ⊖	d							21 15					21 45						22 15			
Elephant & Castle	d	20 49	20 52	21 00	21 04				21 19	21 22	21 30	21 34		21 49	21 52	22 00	22 04			22 19	22 30	22 34
London Blackfriars ■ ⊖	a	20 53	20 55	21 04	21 07			21 22	21 23	21 25	21 34	21 37	21 52	21 53	21 55	22 04	22 07		22 22	22 23	22 34	22 37
	d		20 56					21 22		21 26			21 52		21 56				22 22			
City Thameslink ■	d																					
Farringdon ■ ⊖	d		21 01					21 27		21 31			21 57		22 01				22 27			
St Pancras International ■ ⊖	a		21 05					21 31		21 35			22 01		22 05				22 31			
	d		21 06			21 30		21 32		21 36			22 02		22 06			22 30	22 32			
Kentish Town	d		21 10							21 40					22 10				22 36			
West Hampstead Thameslink	d		21 14					21 40		21 44			22 10		22 14				22 40			
Cricklewood	d		21 17							21 47					22 17				22 43			
Hendon	d		21 20							21 50					22 20				22 46			
Mill Hill Broadway	d		21 24							21 54					22 24				22 50			
Elstree & Borehamwood	d		21 28							21 58					22 28				22 54			
Radlett	d		21 33							22 02					22 33				22 59			
St Albans City	d		21 39					21 57		22 09			22 27		22 39				23 06			
Harpenden	d		21 45					22 03		22 15			22 33		22 45				23 12			
Luton Airport Parkway ■ ✈	d		21 50				←	22 09		22 20			22 39		22 50			22 51	23 18			
Luton ■	d		21 53			21 52	21 53	22 12		22 23			22 42		22 53				23 21			
Leagrave	d		→				21 57	22 15		22 27			22 45		22 57				23 24			
Harlington	d						22 02	22 21		22 32			22 51		23 02				23 30			
Flitwick	d						22 06	22 25		22 36			22 55		23 06				23 34			
Bedford ■	a					22 07	22 20	22 38		22 50			23 08		23 20			23 06	23 47			

		EM	FC	SE	SE	FC	SE	SE	FC
		◇■	■			■			■
				A	B		A	B	
London Bridge ■ ⊖	d		22 45			23 15			23 45
Elephant & Castle	d			22 49	23 00		23 19	23 30	
London Blackfriars ■ ⊖	a		22 52	22 53	23 04	23 22	23 23	23 34	23 52
	d		22 52			23 22			23 52
City Thameslink ■	d								
Farringdon ■ ⊖	d		22 57			23 27			23 57
St Pancras International ■ ⊖	a		23 01			23 31			00 01
	d	23 00	23 02			23 32			00 02
Kentish Town	d		23 06			23 36			00 06
West Hampstead Thameslink	d		23 10			23 40			00 10
Cricklewood	d		23 13			23 43			00 13
Hendon	d		23 16			23 46			00 16
Mill Hill Broadway	d		23 20			23 50			00 20
Elstree & Borehamwood	d		23 24			23 54			00 24
Radlett	d		23 29			23 59			00 29
St Albans City	d		23 36			00 06			00 36
Harpenden	d		23 42			00 12			00 42
Luton Airport Parkway ■ ✈	d	23 21	23 48			00 18			00 48
Luton ■	d		23 51			00 21			00 51
Leagrave	d		23 54			00 24			00 54
Harlington	d		23 59			00 30			01 00
Flitwick	d		00 04			00 34			01 04
Bedford ■	a	23 36	00 17			00 47			01 17

Sundays

from 16 September

		FC	FC	FC	FC	FC	FC	FC	FC	FC	FC	FC	FC	SE	FC	SE	FC	SE	EM	FC	SE	EM	FC
			■		■		■		■	■			■		■		■		◇■	■		◇■	■
London Bridge ■ ⊖	d		22p45		23p15		23p45		00 22	00 52			07 15		07 45		08 15			08 45			09 15
Elephant & Castle	d	22p34		23p04		23p34								07 19		07 49		08 19			08 49		
London Blackfriars ■ ⊖	a	22p37	22p52	23p07	23p22	23p37	23p52		00 28	00 58			07 22	07 23	07 52	07 53	08 22	08 23		08 52	08 53		09 22
	d	22p38	22p52	23p08	23p22	23p38	23p52	00 08	00 28	00 58	01 29	05 59	07 22		07 52		08 22			08 52			09 22
City Thameslink ■	d																						
Farringdon ■ ⊖	d	22p43	22p58	23p13	23p28	23p43	23p58	00 13	00 33				07 27		07 57		08 27			08 57			09 27
St Pancras International ■ ⊖	a	22p47	23p02	23p17	23p32	23p47	00 02	00 17	00 37	01 07	01 37	06 07	07 31		08 01		08 31			09 01			09 31
	d	22p48	23p02	23p18	23p32	23p48	00 02	00 18	00 38	01 08	01 38	06 08	07 32		08 05		08 32		09 00	09 05		09 30	09 32
Kentish Town	d	22p51		23p21		23p51		00 21	00 41	01 11	01 41	06 11	07 36		08 09		08 36			09 09			09 36
West Hampstead Thameslink	d	22p55	23p10	23p25	23p40	23p55	00 10	00 25	00 45	01 15	01 45	06 15	07 40		08 13		08 40			09 13			09 40
Cricklewood	d	22p58		23p28		23p58		00 28	00 48	01 18	01 48	06 18	07 43		08 16		08 43			09 16			09 43
Hendon	d	23p01		23p31		00 01		00 31	00 51	01 21	01 51	06 21	07 46		08 19		08 46			09 19			09 46
Mill Hill Broadway	d	23p05		23p35		00 05		00 35	00 55	01 25	01 55	06 25	07 50		08 23		08 50			09 23			09 50
Elstree & Borehamwood	d	23p09		23p39		00 09		00 39	00 59	01 29	01 59	06 29	07 54		08 27		08 54			09 27			09 54
Radlett	d	23p14		23p44		00 14		00 44	01 04	01 34	02 04	06 34	07 59		08 31		08 59			09 31			09 59
St Albans City	d	23p20	23p27	23p50	23p57	00 20	00 27	00 50	01 10	01 40	02 10	06 41	08 06		08 38		09 06			09 38			10 06
Harpenden	d	23p26	23p33	23p56	00 03	00 26	00 33	00 56	01 16	01 46	02 16	06 47	08 12		08 44		09 12			09 44			10 12
Luton Airport Parkway ■ ✈	d	23p32	23p39	00 02	00 09	00 32	00 39	01 02	01 22	01 52	02 22	06 53	08 18		08 50		09 18		09 28	09 50			10 18
Luton ■	d	23p35	23p42	00 05	00 12	00 35	00 42	01 05	01 25	01 55	02 25	06 56	08 21		08 53		09 21			09 53		09 59	10 21
Leagrave	d	23p39	23p46	00 09	00 16	00 39	00 46	01 09	01 29	01 59	02 29	07 00	08 24		08 56		09 24			09 56			10 24
Harlington	d	23p44	23p51	00 14	00 21	00 44	00 51	01 14	01 34	02 04	02 34	07 05	08 30		09 02		09 30			10 02			10 30
Flitwick	d	23p48	23p55	00 18	00 25	00 48	00 55	01 18	01 38	02 08	02 38	07 09	08 34		09 06		09 34			10 06			10 34
Bedford ■	a	00 02	00 08	00 32	00 38	01 02	01 08	01 32	01 52	02 22	02 52	07 24	08 47		09 19		09 47		09 50	10 19		10 19	10 47

A from 1 July until 22 July, from 19 August until 9 September

B 29 July, 5 August, 12 August

Please refer to separate pages within this table for services operating between Brighton and South London

At weekends please use local bus and tube services to travel to/from St Pancras International and London Bridge when no trains are operating. See local publicity for details of alternative routes and services that are available across central London

Table 52

Sundays

from 16 September

London, St Albans, Luton - Bedford

Network Diagram - see first Page of Table 52

		SE	EM	FC	SE	EM	FC	SE	FC	FC	EM	FC	SE	FC	FC	FC	EM	FC	SE	FC	FC	FC	EM
			◇■	■		◇■	■				◇■	■			■		◇■	■			■		◇■
London Bridge ■ ⊖	d			09 45			10 15					10 45			11 00			11 15			11 30		
Elephant & Castle	d	09 19			09 49			10 19	10 22	10 34			10 49	10 52		11 04			11 19	11 22		11 34	
London Blackfriars ■ ⊖	a	09 23		09 52	09 53		10 22	10 23	10 25	10 37		10 52	10 53	10 55	11 07	11 07		11 22	11 23	11 25	11 37	11 37	
	d			09 52			10 22		10 26			10 52		10 56	11 10			11 22		11 26	11 40		
City Thameslink ■	d																						
Farringdon ■ ⊖	d			09 57			10 27		10 31			10 57		11 01	11 14			11 27		11 31	11 44		
St Pancras International ■ ⊖	a			10 01			10 31		10 35			11 01		11 05	11 18			11 31		11 35	11 48		
	d		10 00	10 02		10 30	10 32		10 36		11 00	11 02		11 06	11 20		11 30	11 32		11 36	11 50		12 00
Kentish Town	d								10 40					11 10						11 40			
West Hampstead Thameslink	d			10 10			10 40		10 44			11 10		11 14	11 27			11 40		11 44	11 57		
Cricklewood	d								10 47					11 17						11 47			
Hendon	d								10 50					11 20						11 50			
Mill Hill Broadway	d								10 54					11 24						11 54			
Elstree & Borehamwood	d								10 58					11 28						11 58			
Radlett	d								11 02					11 33						12 02			
St Albans City	d			10 27			10 57		11 09			11 27		11 39	11 43			11 57		12 09	12 13		
Harpenden	d			10 33			11 03		11 15			11 33		11 45	11 49			12 03		12 15	12 19		
Luton Airport Parkway ■ ✈	d		10 29	10 39			11 09		11 20		11 28	11 39		11 50	11 55		11 59	12 09		12 20	12 25		12 29
Luton ■	d			10 42		10 58	11 12		11a24		11 32	11 42		11a54	11 58		12 03	12 12		12a24	12 28		12 33
Leagrave	d			10 45			11 15					11 45			12 01			12 15			12 31		
Harlington	d			10 51			11 21					11 51			12 07			12 21			12 37		
Flitwick	d			10 55			11 25					11 55			12 11			12 25			12 41		
Bedford ■	a		10 51	11 08		11 19	11 38				11 52	12 08			12 24		12 24	12 38			12 54		12 54

		FC	SE	FC	FC	FC	EM	FC	SE	FC	FC	FC	EM	FC	SE	FC	FC	FC	EM	FC	SE	FC
		■			■		◇■	■			■		◇■	■			■		◇■	■		
London Bridge ■ ⊖	d	11 45			12 00			12 15			12 30			12 45			13 00			13 15		
Elephant & Castle	d		11 49	11 52		12 04			12 19	12 22		12 34			12 49	12 52		13 04			13 19	13 22
London Blackfriars ■ ⊖	a	11 52	11 53	11 55	12 07	12 07		12 22	12 23	12 25	12 37	12 37		12 52	12 53	12 55	13 07	13 07		13 22	13 23	13 25
	d	11 52		11 56	12 10			12 22		12 26	12 40			12 52		12 56	13 10			13 22		13 26
City Thameslink ■	d																					
Farringdon ■ ⊖	d	11 57		12 01	12 14			12 27		12 31	12 44			12 57		13 01	13 14			13 27		13 31
St Pancras International ■ ⊖	a	12 01		12 05	12 18			12 31		12 35	12 48			13 01		13 05	13 18			13 31		13 35
	d	12 02		12 06	12 20		12 30	12 32		12 36	12 50		13 00	13 02		13 06	13 20		13 30	13 32		13 36
Kentish Town	d			12 10						12 40						13 10						13 40
West Hampstead Thameslink	d	12 10		12 14	12 27			12 40		12 44	12 57			13 10		13 14	13 27			13 40		13 44
Cricklewood	d			12 17						12 47						13 17						13 47
Hendon	d			12 20						12 50						13 20						13 50
Mill Hill Broadway	d			12 24						12 54						13 24						13 54
Elstree & Borehamwood	d			12 28						12 58						13 28						13 58
Radlett	d			12 33						13 02						13 33						14 02
St Albans City	d	12 27		12 39	12 43			12 57		13 09	13 13			13 27		13 39	13 43			13 57		14 09
Harpenden	d	12 33		12 45	12 49			13 03		13 15	13 19			13 33		13 45	13 49			14 03		14 15
Luton Airport Parkway ■ ✈	d	12 39		12 50	12 55		12 59	13 09		13 20	13 25		13 29	13 39		13 50	13 55		13 58	14 09		14 20
Luton ■	d	12 42		12a54	12 58		13 03	13 12		13a24	13 28		13 33	13 42		13a54	13 58		14 03	14 12		14a24
Leagrave	d	12 45			13 01			13 15			13 31			13 45			14 01			14 15		
Harlington	d	12 51			13 07			13 21			13 37			13 51			14 07			14 21		
Flitwick	d	12 55			13 11			13 25			13 41			13 55			14 11			14 25		
Bedford ■	a	13 08			13 24		13 24	13 38			13 54		13 54	14 08			14 24		14 23	14 38		

		FC	FC	EM	FC	SE	FC	FC	FC	EM	FC	FC	SE	FC	FC	FC	EM	FC	SE	FC	FC	FC	EM
		■		◇■	■				■	◇■	■	■			■		◇■	■				■	◇■
																							A
London Bridge ■ ⊖	d	13 30			13 45				14 00			14 15			14 30			14 45				15 00	
Elephant & Castle	d		13 34			13 49	13 52	14 04					14 19	14 22		14 34			14 49	14 52	15 04		
London Blackfriars ■ ⊖	a	13 37	13 37		13 52	13 53	13 55	14 07	14 07			14 22	14 23	14 25	14 37	14 37		14 52	14 53	14 55	15 07	15 07	
	d	13 40			13 52		13 56		14 10			14 22		14 26	14 40			14 52		14 56		15 10	
City Thameslink ■	d																						
Farringdon ■ ⊖	d	13 44			13 57		14 01		14 14			14 27		14 31	14 44			14 57		15 01		15 14	
St Pancras International ■ ⊖	a	13 48			14 01		14 05		14 18			14 31		14 35	14 48			15 01		15 05		15 18	
	d	13 50		14 00	14 02		14 06		14 20	14 30		14 32		14 36	14 50		15 00	15 02		15 06		15 20	15 30
Kentish Town	d						14 10							14 40						15 10			
West Hampstead Thameslink	d	13 57			14 10		14 14		14 27			14 40		14 44	14 57			15 10		15 14		15 27	
Cricklewood	d						14 17							14 47						15 17			
Hendon	d						14 20							14 50						15 20			
Mill Hill Broadway	d						14 24							14 54						15 24			
Elstree & Borehamwood	d						14 28							14 58						15 28			
Radlett	d						14 33							15 02						15 33			
St Albans City	d	14 13			14 27		14 39		14 43			14 57		15 09	15 13			15 27		15 39		15 43	
Harpenden	d	14 19			14 33		14 45		14 49			15 03		15 15	15 19			15 33		15 45		15 49	
Luton Airport Parkway ■ ✈	d	14 25		14 21	14 39		14 50		14 55		←	15 09		15 20	15 25		15 23	15 39		15 50		15 55	
Luton ■	d	14 28			14 42		14a54		14 58	14 54	14 58	15 12		15a24	15 28			15 42		15a54		15 58	
Leagrave	d	14 31			14 45				→		15 01	15 15			15 31			15 45				→	
Harlington	d	14 37			14 51						15 07	15 21			15 37			15 51					
Flitwick	d	14 41			14 55						15 11	15 25			15 41			15 55					
Bedford ■	a	14 54		14 37	15 08					15 10	15 24	15 38			15 54		15 39	16 08					16 06

A from 28 October

Please refer to separate pages within this table for services operating between Brighton and South London

At weekends please use local bus and tube services to travel to/from St Pancras International and London Bridge when no trains are operating. See local publicity for details of alternative routes and services that are available across central London

London, St Albans, Luton - Bedford

Network Diagram - see first Page of Table 52

		EM ◇1 A	FC 1	FC 1		SE	FC	FC 1	FC	EM ◇1	FC 1	SE	FC	FC		FC 1	EM ◇1	FC 1	FC 1	SE	FC	FC 1	FC	EM ◇1
London Bridge 4 ⊖	d			15 15				15 30			15 45					16 00			16 15			16 30		
Elephant & Castle	d					15 19	15 22		15 34			15 49	15 52	16 04						16 19	16 22		16 34	
London Blackfriars 3 ⊖	a			15 22		15 23	15 25	15 37	15 37		15 52	15 53	15 55	16 07		16 07			16 22	16 23	16 25	16 37	16 37	
	d			15 22			15 26	15 40			15 52		15 56			16 10			16 22		16 26	16 40		
City Thameslink 3	d																							
Farringdon 3 ⊖	d			15 27			15 31	15 44			15 57		16 01			16 14			16 27		16 31	16 44		
St Pancras International 15 ⊖	a			15 31			15 35	15 48			16 01		16 05			16 18			16 31		16 35	16 48		
	d	15 30		15 32			15 36	15 50		16 00	16 02		16 06			16 20	16 30		16 32		16 36	16 50		17 00
Kentish Town	d						15 40						16 10								16 40			
West Hampstead Thameslink	d			15 40			15 44	15 57			16 10		16 14			16 27			16 40		16 44	16 57		
Cricklewood	d						15 47						16 17								16 47			
Hendon	d						15 50						16 20								16 50			
Mill Hill Broadway	d						15 54						16 24								16 54			
Elstree & Borehamwood	d						15 58						16 28								16 58			
Radlett	d						16 02						16 33								17 02			
St Albans City	d			15 57			16 09	16 13			16 27		16 39			16 43			16 57		17 09	17 13		
Harpenden	d			16 03			16 15	16 19			16 33		16 45			16 49			17 03		17 15	17 19		
Luton Airport Parkway 7 ✈	d		←	16 09			16 20	16 25		16 21	16 39		16 50			16 55		←	17 09		17 20	17 25		17 21
Luton 10	d	15 54	15 58	16 12			16a24	16 28			16 42		16a54			16 58	16 52	16 58	17 12		17a24	17 28		
Leagrave	d		16 01	16 15				16 31			16 45					→		17 01	17 15			17 31		
Harlington	d		16 07	16 21				16 37			16 51							17 07	17 21			17 37		
Flitwick	d		16 11	16 25				16 41			16 55							17 11	17 25			17 41		
Bedford 7	a	16 10	16 24	16 38				16 54		16 37	17 08						17 08	17 24	17 38			17 54		17 38

		FC 1	SE	FC	FC	FC 1	EM ◇1	FC 1	FC 1	SE		FC	FC 1	FC	EM ◇1	FC 1	SE	FC	FC	FC 1		EM ◇1	FC 1	FC 1	SE
London Bridge 4 ⊖	d	16 45				17 00			17 15				17 30			17 45				18 00				18 15	
Elephant & Castle	d		16 49	16 52	17 04					17 19		17 22		17 34			17 49	17 52	18 04						18 19
London Blackfriars 3 ⊖	a	16 52	16 53	16 55	17 07	17 07			17 22	17 23		17 25	17 37	17 37		17 52	17 53	17 55	18 07	18 07				18 22	18 23
	d	16 52		16 56		17 10			17 22			17 26	17 40			17 52		17 56		18 10				18 22	
City Thameslink 3	d																								
Farringdon 3 ⊖	d	16 57		17 01		17 14			17 27			17 31	17 44			17 57		18 01		18 14				18 27	
St Pancras International 15 ⊖	a	17 01		17 05		17 18			17 31			17 35	17 48			18 01		18 05		18 18				18 31	
	d	17 02		17 06		17 20	17 30		17 32			17 36	17 50		18 00	18 02		18 06		18 20		18 30		18 32	
Kentish Town	d			17 10								17 40						18 10							
West Hampstead Thameslink	d	17 10		17 14		17 27			17 40			17 44	17 57			18 10		18 14		18 27				18 40	
Cricklewood	d			17 17								17 47						18 17							
Hendon	d			17 20								17 50						18 20							
Mill Hill Broadway	d			17 24								17 54						18 24							
Elstree & Borehamwood	d			17 28								17 58						18 28							
Radlett	d			17 33								18 02						18 33							
St Albans City	d	17 27		17 39		17 43			17 57			18 09	18 13			18 27		18 39		18 43				18 57	
Harpenden	d	17 33		17 45		17 49			18 03			18 15	18 19			18 33		18 45		18 49				19 03	
Luton Airport Parkway 7 ✈	d	17 39		17 50		17 55		←	18 09			18 20	18 25		18 21	18 39		18 50		18 55			←	19 09	
Luton 10	d	17 42		17a54		17 58	17 52	17 58	18 12			18a24	18 28			18 42		18a54		18 58		18 53	18 58	19 12	
Leagrave	d	17 45				→		18 01	18 15				18 31			18 45				→			19 01	19 15	
Harlington	d	17 51						18 07	18 21				18 37			18 51							19 07	19 21	
Flitwick	d	17 55						18 11	18 25				18 41			18 55							19 11	19 25	
Bedford 7	a	18 08					18 08	18 24	18 38				18 54		18 38	19 08						19 08	19 24	19 38	

		FC	FC 1	FC	EM ◇1	FC 1		SE	FC	FC	FC 1	EM ◇1	FC 1	FC 1	SE	FC		FC 1	FC	EM ◇1	FC 1	SE	FC	FC	EM ◇1
London Bridge 4 ⊖	d		18 30			18 45					19 00			19 15				19 30			19 45				
Elephant & Castle	d	18 22		18 34				18 49	18 52	19 04					19 19	19 22			19 34			19 49	19 52	20 04	
London Blackfriars 3 ⊖	a	18 25	18 37	18 37		18 52		18 53	18 55	19 07	19 07			19 22	19 23	19 25		19 37	19 37		19 52	19 53	19 55	20 07	
	d	18 26	18 40			18 52			18 56		19 10			19 22		19 26		19 40			19 52		19 56		
City Thameslink 3	d																								
Farringdon 3 ⊖	d	18 31	18 44			18 57			19 01		19 14			19 27		19 31		19 44			19 57		20 01		
St Pancras International 15 ⊖	a	18 35	18 48			19 01			19 05		19 18			19 31		19 35		19 48			20 01		20 05		
	d	18 36	18 50		19 00	19 02			19 06		19 20	19 30		19 32		19 36		19 50		20 00	20 02		20 06		20 30
Kentish Town	d	18 40							19 10							19 40							20 10		
West Hampstead Thameslink	d	18 44	18 57			19 10			19 14		19 27			19 40		19 44		19 57			20 10		20 14		
Cricklewood	d	18 47							19 17							19 47							20 17		
Hendon	d	18 50							19 20							19 50							20 20		
Mill Hill Broadway	d	18 54							19 24							19 54							20 24		
Elstree & Borehamwood	d	18 58							19 28							19 58							20 28		
Radlett	d	19 02							19 33							20 02							20 33		
St Albans City	d	19 09	19 13			19 27			19 39		19 43			19 57		20 09		20 13			20 27		20 39		
Harpenden	d	19 15	19 19			19 33			19 45		19 49			20 03		20 15		20 19			20 33		20 45		
Luton Airport Parkway 7 ✈	d	19 20	19 25		19 21	19 39			19 50		19 55		←	20 09		20 20		20 25		20 21	20 39		20 50		
Luton 10	d	19a24	19 28			19 42			19a54		19 58	19 53	19 58	20 12		20 23		20 28			20 42		20 53		20 54
Leagrave	d		19 31			19 45					→		20 01	20 15		20 27		20 31			20 45		20 57		
Harlington	d		19 37			19 51							20 07	20 21		20 32		20 37			20 51		21 02		
Flitwick	d		19 41			19 55							20 11	20 25		20 36		20 41			20 55		21 06		
Bedford 7	a		19 54		19 38	20 08						20 08	20 24	20 38		20 50		20 54		20 37	21 08		21 20		21 10

A from 16 September until 21 October

Please refer to separate pages within this table for services operating between Brighton and South London

At weekends please use local bus and tube services to travel to/from St Pancras International and London Bridge when no trains are operating. See local publicity for details of alternative routes and services that are available across central London

London, St Albans, Luton - Bedford

Network Diagram - see first Page of Table 52

		FC 1		SE	FC	FC	EM ◇1	FC 1	SE	FC	FC	EM ◇1		FC	FC 1	SE	FC	FC	FC 1	SE	FC	FC		EM ◇1	FC 1
London Bridge 4 ⊖	d	20 15						20 45							21 15				21 45						22 15
Elephant & Castle	d			20 19	20 22	20 34			20 49	20 52	21 04					21 19	21 22	21 34		21 49	21 52	22 04			
London Blackfriars 3 ⊖	a	20 22		20 23	20 25	20 37		20 52	20 53	20 55	21 07				21 22	21 23	21 25	21 37	21 52	21 53	21 55	22 07			22 22
	d	20 22			20 26			20 52		20 56					21 22		21 26		21 52		21 56				22 22
City Thameslink 3	d																								
Farringdon 3 ⊖	d	20 27			20 31			20 57		21 01					21 27		21 31		21 57		22 01				22 27
St Pancras International 15 ⊖	a	20 31			20 35			21 01		21 05					21 31		21 35		22 01		22 05				22 31
	d	20 32			20 36		21 00	21 02		21 06		21 30			21 32		21 36		22 02		22 06			22 30	22 32
Kentish Town	d				20 40					21 10							21 40				22 10				22 36
West Hampstead Thameslink	d	20 40			20 44			21 10		21 14					21 40		21 44		22 10		22 14				22 40
Cricklewood	d				20 47					21 17							21 47				22 17				22 43
Hendon	d				20 50					21 20							21 50				22 20				22 46
Mill Hill Broadway	d				20 54					21 24							21 54				22 24				22 50
Elstree & Borehamwood	d				20 58					21 28							21 58				22 28				22 54
Radlett	d				21 02					21 33							22 02				22 33				22 59
St Albans City	d	20 57			21 09			21 27		21 39					21 57		22 09		22 27		22 39				23 06
Harpenden	d	21 03			21 15			21 33		21 45					22 03		22 15		22 33		22 45				23 12
Luton Airport Parkway 7 ✈	d	21 09			21 20		21 21	21 39		21 50				←	22 09		22 20		22 39		22 50			22 51	23 18
Luton 10	d	21 12			21 23			21 42		21 53		21 52		21 53	22 12		22 23		22 42		22 53				23 21
Leagrave	d	21 15			21 27			21 45		→				21 57	22 15		22 27		22 45		22 57				23 24
Harlington	d	21 21			21 32			21 51						22 02	22 21		22 32		22 51		23 02				23 30
Flitwick	d	21 25			21 36			21 55						22 06	22 25		22 36		22 55		23 06				23 34
Bedford 7	a	21 38			21 50		21 40	22 08				22 08		22 20	22 38		22 50		23 08		23 20			23 14	23 47

		SE	FC	EM ◇1	FC 1	SE	FC 1	SE		FC 1
London Bridge 4 ⊖	d				22 45		23 15			23 45
Elephant & Castle	d	22 19	22 34			22 49		23 19		
London Blackfriars 3 ⊖	a	22 23	22 37		22 52	22 53	23 22	23 23		23 52
	d				22 52		23 22			23 52
City Thameslink 3	d									
Farringdon 3 ⊖	d				22 57		23 27			23 57
St Pancras International 15 ⊖	a				23 01		23 31			00 01
	d			23 00	23 02		23 32			00 02
Kentish Town	d				23 06		23 36			00 06
West Hampstead Thameslink	d				23 10		23 40			00 10
Cricklewood	d				23 13		23 43			00 13
Hendon	d				23 16		23 46			00 16
Mill Hill Broadway	d				23 20		23 50			00 20
Elstree & Borehamwood	d				23 24		23 54			00 24
Radlett	d				23 29		23 59			00 29
St Albans City	d				23 36		00 06			00 36
Harpenden	d				23 42		00 12			00 42
Luton Airport Parkway 7 ✈	d			23 27	23 48		00 18			00 48
Luton 10	d				23 51		00 21			00 51
Leagrave	d				23 54		00 24			00 54
Harlington	d				23 59		00 30			01 00
Flitwick	d				00 04		00 34			01 04
Bedford 7	a			23 50	00 17		00 47			01 17

Please refer to separate pages within this table for services operating between Brighton and South London

At weekends please use local bus and tube services to travel to/from St Pancras International and London Bridge when no trains are operating. See local publicity for details of alternative routes and services that are available across central London

Route Diagram for Table 53

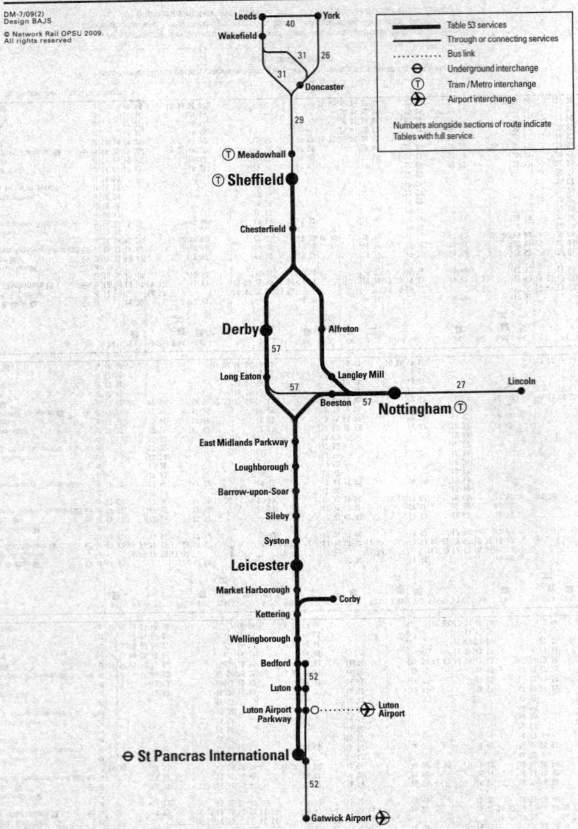

London - East Midlands - Sheffield

Route Diagram - see first Page of Table 53

Miles	Miles	Miles			NT MO	EM	EM MO	XC MO	XC MO	EM	EM MO	EM MX	EM MX	MX	EM MO	EM MX	EM MX	EM MO	EM	EM	EM	EM	EM		EM
					A	B	C	D	E	F	B	C			G	H F	I	J	K	C	L	F		B	
0	0	—	St Pancras International	d		20p30	20p30			21p30	21p30	21p30	22p00		22p25	22p25	22p30			22p30	22p30		23p00		23p00
29¼	29¼	—	Luton Airport Parkway	d											22p48	22p48	22p51			22p51	22p51		23p21		23p27
30¼	30¼	—	Luton	d		20p54	20p54			21p52	21p52	21p52	22p24												
49¾	49¾	—	Bedford	d		21p11	21p13			22p07	22p08	22p10	22p40		23p04	23p04	23p06			23p14	23p19		23p36		23p50
65¼	65¼	—	Wellingborough	d		21p24	21p26			22p20	22p21	22p23	22p53		23p17	23p17	23p20			23p28	23p32		23p50		00 04
72	72	0	Kettering	a		21p31	21p33			22p27	22p28	22p30	23p00		23p25	23p25	23p26			23p34	23p39		23p56		00 10
—	—	—		d		21p32	21p34			22p28	22p29	22p31	23p01		23p26	23p26	23p27			23p35	23p40		23p57		00 11
—	—	7½	Corby	d																					
—	—	21¾	Oakham	d																					
—	—	33¼	Melton Mowbray	d																					
83	83	—	Market Harborough	d		21p43	21p45			22p38	22p39	22p41	23p12		23p37	23p37	23p37	←	←	23p45	23p50		00 07		00 21
99¼	99¼	48½	Leicester	a		22p02	22p06			22p56	22p56	23p00	23p29		23p53	23p53	23p52	23p53	23p53	00 04	00 09		00 22		00 42
—	—	—		d		22p04	22p07			22p58	22p57	23p01	23p30		23p55	23p55	23p54	23p55	23p55	00 06	00 10		00 24		00 44
103	103	—	Syston	d											→	→									
105¾	105¾	—	Sileby	d																					
107¾	107¾	—	Barrow Upon Soar	d																					
111¾	111¾	—	Loughborough	d						23p08	23p08	23p12	23p41				00 04	00 06	00 06	00 16	00 21	←	00 34		00 54
117½	117½	—	East Midlands Parkway	d		22p20	22p23			23p16	23p20	23p24	23p50				00 12	00 14	00 14	00 29	00 28	00 29	00 42		01 07
123¼	—	—	Beeston	a									00 04				00 17			→	00 42	00 37			
126½	—	—	Nottingham	a									00 12				00 28				00 49	00 44			
—	—	—		d	21p30																				
—	—	—	Lincoln	a																					
138½	—	—	Langley Mill	d	21p52																				
144¾	—	—	Alfreton	d	22p00																				
—	120½	—	Long Eaton	a						23p19	23p27	23p31													
—	128½	—	Derby	a		22p32	22p36			23p30	23p38	23p42						00 34	00 34				00 53		01 21
—	—	—		d		22p34	22p37	22p44	22p44	23p32	23p39	23p43						00 35	00 40						
155	152¾	—	Chesterfield	d	22p13	22p56	22p58	23p05	23p05	23p51	23p59	00 03						00 58	01 18						
167¼	165	—	Sheffield	a	22p36	23p10	23p13	23p20	23p20	00 05	00 17	00 17						01 13	01 32						
—	—	—	Doncaster	a																					
—	—	—	Wakefield Kirkgate	a	23p26																				
—	—	—	Wakefield Westgate	a		23p40	00 01																		
—	—	—	Leeds	a	00 05	00 01	00 18	00 11	00 16																
—	—	—	York	a																					

		EM MO	EM MX	EM MX	EM MX	EM	EM MX	EM MX	EM	MX	EM MX	EM MX	EM	EM	EM	EM	EM MX	XC	XC		NT	EM	XC	NT	EM
		C	M	N	O	P	O Q	R		O	P	P	S	T	T	U V	W				X	U			
St Pancras International	d	23p00	23p15	23p15	00 01	00 01	00 15	00 15	00 15		00 30	00 30	00 45	00 15	01 00	01 15									
Luton Airport Parkway	d	23p27							00 35					00 44											
Luton	d		23p46	23p46				00 37	00 39					00 47											
Bedford	d	23p55	00 12	00 12				00 53	00 54					01 12											
Wellingborough	d	00 09	00 25	00 25	00 46	00 48		01 05	01 07		01 13	01 13	01 29	01 33	01 43	01 58									
Kettering	a	00 15	00 41	00 41	00 53	00 54	01 02	01 12	01 14		01 19	01 19	01 35	01 43	01 50	02 04									
	d	00 16	00 42	00 42	00 54	00 55	01 03	01 13	01 14		01 20	01 20	01 36	01 43		02 06									
Corby	d																								
Oakham	d																								
Melton Mowbray	d																								
Market Harborough	d	00 26	00 52	00 52	01 05	01 05		01 23	01 24		01 30	01 30	01 46	01 55		02 16									
Leicester	a	00 47	01 05	01 05	01 22	01 20	01 25	01 38	01 40		01 45	01 48	02 01	02 10		02 31									
	d	00 49	01 07	01 07		01 22	01 26				01 47	01 50	02 03												
Syston	d																								
Sileby	d																								
Barrow Upon Soar	d																								
Loughborough	d	00 59	01 17	01 17		01 32							02 13												
East Midlands Parkway	d	01 07	01 25	01 25		01 40																			
Beeston	a		01 33	01 38							02 03		02 24												
Nottingham	a		01 40	01 45							02 10		02 31												
	d		01 47	01 52							02 17		02 37				05 20							06 23	06 40
Lincoln	a																								
Langley Mill	d																							06 38	
Alfreton	d																							06 46	07 02
Long Eaton	a																								
Derby	a	01 26	02 05	02 10		01 51	01 49				02 36	02 12	02 55												
	d						01 50					02 14						05 56	06 00			06 20	06 34		
Chesterfield	d						02 10					02 34					05 49	06 15	06 15		06 26	06 42	06 54	06 58	07 13
Sheffield	a						02 23					02 47					06 15	06 28	06 28		06 46	07 13	07 07	07 18	07 31
Doncaster	a																	06 57	06 57						
Wakefield Kirkgate	a																				07 27			07 57	
Wakefield Westgate	a																						07 36		
Leeds	a																				07 51		07 52	08 21	
York	a																	07 26	07 26				08 22		

A from 21 May until 24 September
B 17 September, 24 September
C from 21 May until 25 June
D 17 September, 24 September. From Penzance
E from 21 May until 10 September. From Plymouth
F from 2 July until 10 September
G until 14 September. To Sheffield
H from 18 September until 28 September. To Sheffield
I until 14 September. From St Pancras International
J from 18 September until 28 September. From St Pancras International
K 17 September, 24 September. To Nottingham
L 17 September, 24 September. From St Pancras International
M from 31 July until 7 September, not from 14 August until 29 August. from Nottingham to Nottingham
N not from 31 July until 10 August, from 30 August until 7 September. from Nottingham to Nottingham
O 30 July, 6 August, 13 August, 3 September, 10 September
P from 31 July until 7 September, not from 14 August until 29 August
Q from 30 August until 7 September
R from 31 July until 10 August
S not from 31 July until 10 August, from 30 August until 7 September
T from 30 July until 10 September, not from 14 August until 29 August
U To Liverpool Lime Street
V until 24 September, not from 18 September until 21 September. To Newcastle. from Sheffield
W from 18 September until 28 September. To Newcastle. from Sheffield
X From Birmingham New Street to Glasgow Central

For connections from Gatwick Airport see Table 52

London - East Midlands - Sheffield

Route Diagram - see first Page of Table 53

Station		XC ◇1 A	EM ◇1	NT	EM		XC ◇1 B	EM ◇1	EM ◇ C	EM	XC ◇1 A	EM ◇1	EM ◇1	NT	EM ◇1		XC ◇1 D	EM ◇ E	XC ◇1 F	EM G	EM ◇1 H	EM	EM ◇1	EM ◇1	EM ◇1
St Pancras International	d							05 45				06 37			06 55						07 00		07 25	07 30	07 55
Luton Airport Parkway	d														07 16									07 51	
Luton	d							06 11				06 59									07 23				
Bedford	d							06 27													07 38			08 07	
Wellingborough	d							06 39				07 23									07 51			08 20	
Kettering	a							06 46				07 30									08 00			08 26	
	d							06 47				07 31	07 38								08 01			08 27	
Corby	d												07a48												
Oakham	d																								
Melton Mowbray	d																								
Market Harborough	d							06 57				07 41									08 12		08 21	08 37	
Leicester	a							07 11				07 56			08 04						08 29		08 36	08 52	09 02
	d				06 33			07 12		07 25		07 57			08 06					08 25	08 30		08 38	08 54	09 04
Syston	d				06 41					07 32										08 32					
Sileby	d				06 46					07 36										08 36					
Barrow Upon Soar	d				06 51					07 40										08 40					
Loughborough	d				06 56			07 24		07 45		08 08			08 16					08 45	08 41	←	08 48	09 04	
East Midlands Parkway	d				07 06			07 32		07 54					08 24					08 54	08 50	08 54	08 56		
Beeston	a				07 16					08 06					08 31					→		09 02		09 16	
Nottingham	a				07 23					08 15					08 39						09 02	09 13		09 26	
	d			07 13					07 45					08 11				08 45				09 21			
Lincoln	a																					10 17			
Langley Mill	d			07 29										08 31											
Alfreton	d			07 37					08 07					08 39				09 07							
Long Eaton	a							07 35															08 59		
Derby	a							07 47				08 24											09 15		09 26
	d	07 13	07 20				07 44	07 49			08 13	08 28					08 44		09 13				09 18		09 28
Chesterfield	d	07 32	07 42	07 50			08 03	08 09	08 18		08 32	08 47		08 51			09 03	09 18					09 37		09 47
Sheffield	a	07 48	08 00	08 08			08 17	08 25	08 38		08 45	09 04		09 16			09 17	09 38	09 43				09 52		10 00
Doncaster	a	08 24									09 18								10 18						
Wakefield Kirkgate	a			08 57										09 57											
Wakefield Westgate	a						08 46										09 46								
Leeds	a			09 20			09 03							10 18			10 02								
York	a	08 45					09 26				09 44						10 26		10 45						

Station			EM ◇1	EM ◇1	NT	XC ◇1 I	EM ◇ E	XC ◇1 J	EM G	EM ◇1	EM ◇1	H	EM	EM ◇1	EM ◇1	EM ◇1	EM ◇	NT ◇ K	XC ◇1 E	EM ◇ L	XC ◇1 G		EM	EM ◇1	EM ◇1
St Pancras International	d			08 00						08 15	08 25			08 30	08 55	09 00								09 15	09 25
Luton Airport Parkway	d													08 51											
Luton	d			08 23												09 23									
Bedford	d			08 38										09 07		09 38									
Wellingborough	d			08 51										09 20		09 51									
Kettering	a			09 00										09 27		10 00									
	d		08 32	09 01										09 27											
Corby	d		08a42	09a10													09 30								
Oakham	d																09 49								
Melton Mowbray	d																10 01								
Market Harborough	d									09 12				09 37										10 12	
Leicester	a									09 29	09 35			09 54	10 02									10 29	10 34
	d								09 25	09 30	09 35			09 54	10 04								10 25	10 30	10 35
Syston	d								09 32														10 32		
Sileby	d								09 36														10 36		
Barrow Upon Soar	d								09 40														10 40		
Loughborough	d								09 45		09 45		←	10 04									10 45		10 46
East Midlands Parkway	d								09 54	09 46	09 52		09 54				10 26						10 54	10 46	10 53
Beeston	a								→				10 02	10 17									→		
Nottingham	a									09 59			10 13	10 25										10 59	
	d				09 15		09 45						10 29					10 15		10 45					
Lincoln	a												11 31												
Langley Mill	d				09 32													10 32							
Alfreton	d				09 40		10 07											10 40		11 07					
Long Eaton	a										09 56														10 56
Derby	a										10 09				10 26		10 40								11 09
	d					09 44		10 11			10 18				10 28				10 44		11 11				11 18
Chesterfield	d				09 52	10 03	10 18				10 37				10 47			10 52	11 03	11 18					11 37
Sheffield	a				10 16	10 17	10 38	10 41			10 52				11 02			11 17	11 17	11 38	11 43				11 52
Doncaster	a							11 18													12 18				
Wakefield Kirkgate	a				10 57													11 57							
Wakefield Westgate	a					10 46													11 46						
Leeds	a				11 18	11 02												12 18	12 01						
York	a					11 26		11 46											12 26		12 46				

A From Birmingham New Street to Newcastle
B From Birmingham New Street to Edinburgh
C To Liverpool Lime Street
D From Bath Spa to Glasgow Central
E From Norwich to Liverpool Lime Street
F From Guildford to Newcastle
G To Lincoln
H From Leicester
I From Plymouth to Edinburgh
J From Reading to Newcastle
K From Plymouth to Glasgow Central
L From Winchester to Newcastle

For connections from Gatwick Airport see Table 52

...days to Fridays
until 28 September

London - East Midlands - Sheffield

Route Diagram - see first Page of Table 53

Station		EM A	EM ◇1	EM ◇1	EM ◇1	NT ◇	XC ◇1 B		EM ◇ C	XC ◇1 D	EM E	EM ◇1	EM ◇1	EM A	EM ◇1	EM ◇1	EM ◇1		NT ◇	XC ◇1 F	EM ◇ C	XC ◇1 G	EM E	EM ◇1	EM ◇1
St Pancras International	d		09 30	09 55	10 00							10 15	10 25		10 30	10 55	11 00							11 15	11 25
Luton Airport Parkway	d		09 51												10 51										
Luton	d				10 23												11 23								
Bedford	d		10 07		10 38										11 07		11 38								
Wellingborough	d		10 20		10 51										11 20		11 51								
Kettering	a		10 26		11 00										11 26		12 00								
	d		10 27		11 01										11 27		12 01								
Corby	d				11a10												12a10								
Oakham	d																								
Melton Mowbray	d																								
Market Harborough	d		10 37									11 12			11 37									12 12	
Leicester	a		10 54	11 02								11 29	11 33		11 52	12 02								12 29	12 33
	d		10 54	11 04							11 25	11 30	11 35		11 54	12 04							12 25	12 30	12 35
Syston	d										11 32												12 32		
Sileby	d										11 36												12 36		
Barrow Upon Soar	d										11 40												12 40		
Loughborough	d	←	11 04								11 45		11 45	←	12 04								12 46		12 45
East Midlands Parkway	d	10 54									11 54	11 46	11 53	11 54									12 58	12 46	12 53
Beeston	a	11 02	11 16								→			12 02	12 16								→		
Nottingham	a	11 14	11 25									11 59		12 13	12 26									12 59	
	d	11 17				11 15			11 45					12 27					12 15		12 45				
Lincoln	a	12 21												13 20											
Langley Mill	d					11 31													12 32						
Alfreton	d					11 39			12 07										12 40		13 07				
Long Eaton	a												11 56												12 56
Derby	a			11 26									12 09			12 26									13 09
	d			11 28			11 44			12 11			12 18			12 28				12 44		13 11			13 18
Chesterfield	d			11 47		11 52	12 04		12 18				12 37			12 47			12 52	13 03	13 18				13 37
Sheffield	a			12 04		12 16	12 17		12 38	12 41			12 52			13 04			13 16	13 17	13 38	13 41			13 52
Doncaster	a									13 18												14 18			
Wakefield Kirkgate	a					12 57													13 57						
Wakefield Westgate	a						12 46													13 46					
Leeds	a					13 18	13 03												14 18	14 02					
York	a						13 26			13 40										14 26		14 44			

Station		EM A	EM ◇1		EM ◇1	EM ◇1	NT ◇	XC ◇1 H	EM ◇ C	XC ◇1 D	EM E	EM ◇1	EM ◇1	A	EM	EM ◇1	EM ◇1	EM ◇1	NT ◇	XC ◇1 F	EM ◇ C	XC ◇1 G	EM E		EM ◇1
St Pancras International	d		11 30		11 55	12 00						12 15	12 25			12 30	12 55	13 00							13 15
Luton Airport Parkway	d		11 51													12 51									
Luton	d					12 23												13 22							
Bedford	d		12 07			12 38										13 07		13 38							
Wellingborough	d		12 20			12 51										13 20		13 50							
Kettering	a		12 26			13 00										13 26		13 59							
	d		12 27			13 01										13 27		14 01							
Corby	d					13a10												14a10							
Oakham	d																								
Melton Mowbray	d																								
Market Harborough	d		12 37									13 12				13 37									14 12
Leicester	a		12 53		13 02							13 30	13 33			13 54	14 02								14 29
	d		12 54		13 04						13 25	13 30	13 35			13 54	14 04						14 25		14 30
Syston	d										13 32												14 32		
Sileby	d										13 36												14 36		
Barrow Upon Soar	d										13 40												14 40		
Loughborough	d	←	13 04								13 45		13 45		←	14 04							14 45		
East Midlands Parkway	d	12 58									13 54	13 45	13 53		13 54								14 54		14 46
Beeston	a	13 07	13 16								→				14 02	14 16							→		
Nottingham	a	13 14	13 25									13 59			14 13	14 26									14 59
	d	13 17					13 15		13 45						14 29				14 15		14 45				
Lincoln	a	14 23													15 22										
Langley Mill	d						13 32												14 30						
Alfreton	d						13 40		14 07										14 38		15 07				
Long Eaton	a												13 56												
Derby	a				13 26								14 09				14 26								
	d				13 28			13 44		14 11			14 18				14 28			14 44		15 11			
Chesterfield	d				13 47		13 52	14 03	14 19				14 37				14 47		14 52	15 03	15 22				
Sheffield	a				14 00		14 16	14 17	14 38	14 41			14 52				15 03		15 16	15 17	15 38	15 41			
Doncaster	a									15 18												16 18			
Wakefield Kirkgate	a						14 57												15 57						
Wakefield Westgate	a							14 46												15 46					
Leeds	a						15 18	15 01											16 18	16 02					
York	a							15 26		15 45										16 28		16 45			

A From Leicester
B From Plymouth to Edinburgh
C From Norwich to Liverpool Lime Street
D From Reading to Newcastle
E To Lincoln
F From Penzance to Glasgow Central
G From Southampton Central to Newcastle
H From Plymouth to Aberdeen

For connections from Gatwick Airport see Table 52

Table 53

Mondays to Fridays

until 28 September

London - East Midlands - Sheffield

Route Diagram - see first Page of Table 53

		EM ◇1 🍴	EM A	EM ◇1 🍴	EM ◇1 🍴	EM ◇1 🍴	NT ◇	XC ◇1 B 🍴	EM ◇ C	XC ◇1 D 🍴	EM E	EM ◇1 🍴	EM ◇1 🍴	EM F	EM ◇1 🍴	EM ◇1 🍴	EM ◇1 🍴	NT ◇	XC ◇1 G 🍴	EM ◇ C	XC ◇1 H 🍴	EM I	EM ◇1 🍴
St Pancras International ⊖	d	13 25		13 30	13 55	14 00						14 15	14 25		14 30	14 55	15 00						15 15
Luton Airport Parkway 7 ✈	d			13 51											14 51								
Luton 10	d					14 23											15 23						
Bedford 7	d			14 07		14 38									15 07		15 38						
Wellingborough	d			14 20		14 51									15 20		15 51						
Kettering 4	a			14 26		15 00									15 26		16 00						
	d			14 27		15 01									15 27		16 01						
Corby	d					15a10											16a10						
Oakham	d																						
Melton Mowbray	d																						
Market Harborough	d			14 37								15 12			15 37								16 12
Leicester	a	14 33		14 54	15 02							15 29	15 33		15 54	16 02							16 29
	d	14 35		14 54	15 04						15 25	15 30	15 35		15 54	16 04						16 25	16 30
Syston	d										15 32											16 32	
Sileby	d										15 36											16 36	
Barrow Upon Soar	d										15 40											16 40	
Loughborough	d	14 45	←	15 04							15 45		15 45	←	16 04							16 45	
East Midlands Parkway ✈	d	14 53	14 54								15 54	15 46	15 53	15 54								16 54	16 46
Beeston	a		15 02	15 16							→			16 02	16 16							→	
Nottingham 8 ⇌	a		15 13	15 26								15 59		16 13	16 25								16 59
	d		15 27				15 15		15 45					16 14				16 15		16 45			
Lincoln	a		16 25											17 18									
Langley Mill	d						15 32											16 32					
Alfreton	d						15 40		16 07									16 40		17 07			
Long Eaton	a	14 56											15 56										
Derby 6	a	15 13			15 26								16 09			16 26							
	d	15 15			15 28			15 44		16 11			16 17			16 28			16 42		17 11		
Chesterfield	d	15 34			15 47		15 53	16 03	16 18				16 36			16 47		16 55	17 04	17 18			
Sheffield 7 ⇌	a	15 52			16 00		16 16	16 17	16 38	16 41			16 52			17 04		17 17	17 19	17 36	17 44		
Doncaster 7	a									17 18													
Wakefield Kirkgate 4	a						16 57											17 57					
Wakefield Westgate 7	a							16 49											17 47		18 13		
Leeds 10	a						17 18	17 04										18 18	18 03		18 31		
York 8	a							17 28		17 40									18 29		19 01		

		EM ◇1 🍴	EM A	EM ◇1 🍴	EM ◇1 🍴	EM ◇1 🍴	NT ◇	XC ◇1 J 🍴	EM ◇ C	XC ◇1 D 🍴	EM I	EM ◇1 🍴	EM ◇1 🍴	EM A	EM ◇1 🍴	EM ◇1 🍴	NT ◇	XC ◇1 K 🍴	EM ◇ C	XC ◇1 L 🍴	EM I	EM ◇1 🍴
St Pancras International ⊖	d	15 25		15 30	15 55	16 00						16 15	16 25		16 30	16 55						17 00
Luton Airport Parkway 7 ✈	d			15 51											16 51							
Luton 10	d					16 22									16 55							
Bedford 7	d			16 07		16 38									17 10							17 35
Wellingborough	d			16 20		16 50									17 23							17 48
Kettering 4	a			16 26		16 59									17 29							17 56
	d			16 27		17 00									17 30							18 04 18 08
Corby	d					17a09																18a18
Oakham	d																					
Melton Mowbray	d																					
Market Harborough	d			16 37								17 12			17 40							
Leicester	a	16 33		16 54	17 02							17 29	17 35		17 55	18 02						18 30
	d	16 35		16 54	17 04						17 25	17 30	17 35		17 55	18 04					18 25	18 32
Syston	d										17 32										18 32	
Sileby	d										17 36										18 36	
Barrow Upon Soar	d										17 40										18 40	
Loughborough	d	16 45	←	17 04							17 45		17 45	←	18 05						18 45	18 43
East Midlands Parkway ✈	d	16 53	16 54								17 54	17 46	17 52	17 54							18 54	18 50
Beeston	a		17 02	17 16							→			18 02	18 17						→	
Nottingham 8 ⇌	a		17 13	17 26								17 59		18 13	18 27							
	d		17 17				17 15		17 45					18 15			18 15		18 45			
Lincoln	a		18 26											19 23								
Langley Mill	d						17 32		18 02								18 32					
Alfreton	d						17 40		18 09								18 40		19 07			
Long Eaton	a	16 56											18 00									18 55
Derby 6	a	17 09			17 26								18 14			18 26						19 09
	d	17 18			17 28			17 41		18 11			18 18			18 28		18 42		19 11		19 18
Chesterfield	d	17 37			17 47		17 52	18 02	18 21				18 42			18 47	18 52	19 01	19 18	19 30		19 37
Sheffield 7 ⇌	a	17 52			18 02		18 14	18 18	18 39	18 44			18 58			19 01	19 17	19 19	19 39	19 47		19 51
Doncaster 7	a									19 14										20 15		
Wakefield Kirkgate 4	a						18 59										19 58					
Wakefield Westgate 7	a							18 47										19 50				
Leeds 10	a						19 23	19 03									20 19	20 05				
York 8	a							19 29		19 38								20 29		20 46		

A From Leicester
B From Plymouth to Dundee
C From Norwich to Liverpool Lime Street
D From Reading to Newcastle
E To Sleaford
F From Leicester to Sleaford
G From Plymouth to Glasgow Central
H From Southampton Central to Edinburgh
I To Lincoln
J From Plymouth to Edinburgh
K From Plymouth to Edinburgh. 🍴 to Leeds
L From Southampton Central to Newcastle. 🍴 to Doncaster

For connections from Gatwick Airport see Table 52

Table 53

Mondays to Fridays

until 28 September

London - East Midlands - Sheffield

Route Diagram - see first Page of Table 53

		EM ◇1 🍴	EM A	EM ◇1 🍴	EM ◇1 🍴	NT ◇	XC ◇1 B 🍴	EM ◇ C	EM ◇1 D 🍽🍴	XC ◇1 E 🍴	EM F	EM ◇1 🍴	EM A	EM ◇1 🍴	EM ◇1 🍴	EM ◇1 D 🍽🍴	XC ◇1 B	EM ◇1 🍴	EM ◇1 🍴	NT	XC ◇1 G	EM F
St Pancras International ⊖	d	17 15		17 30	17 55				17 45			18 15		18 00	18 25	18 30		18 55	19 00			
Luton Airport Parkway 7 ✈	d								18 09							18 53						
Luton 10	d	17 40												18 23	18 50				19 23			
Bedford 7	d			18 05										18 38		19 10			19 40			
Wellingborough	d			18 18					18 33			19 00		18 51		19 23			19 53			
Kettering 4	a			18 24					18 44			19 07		19 05		19 29			20 04			
	d			18 25					18 46			19 08		19 10		19 31			20 05			
Corby	d													19 20					20a14			
Oakham	d													19 40								
Melton Mowbray	d													19a52								
Market Harborough	d	18 18		18 35					18 59						19 27			19 52				
Leicester	a	18 36		18 54	19 04				19 21			19 32			19 44	19 56		20 11				
	d	18 37		18 56	19 04				19 25		19 25	19 34			19 45	19 57		20 13				20 25
Syston	d										19 32											20 32
Sileby	d										19 36											20 36
Barrow Upon Soar	d										19 40											20 40
Loughborough	d		←	19 06					19 36		19 45	19 45	←		19 56			20 23				20 45
East Midlands Parkway ✈	d	18 53	18 54	19 13					19 44		19 54	19 53	19 54			20 12		20 31				20 54
Beeston	a	19 02	19 07	19 18							→		20 07			20 17						→
Nottingham 8 ⇌	a	19 10	19 14	19 27					19 58			20 08	20 15			20 28						
	d		19 20			19 15		19 40	20 07			20 15				20 29				20 45		
Lincoln	a		20 17													21 22						
Langley Mill	d					19 32						20 33										
Alfreton	d					19 40		20 01				20 41										
Long Eaton	a								20 22						20 06							
Derby 6	a				19 28				20 35						20 19			20 46		21 05		
	d				19 28		19 41			20 11					20 21		20 44	20 48		21 06	21 13	
Chesterfield	d				19 47	19 52	20 02	20 12				20 53			20 41		21 03	21 09		21 28	21 34	
Sheffield 7 ⇌	a				20 03	20 15	20 18	20 28		20 48		21 14			20 56		21 18	21 25		21 54	21 51	
Doncaster 7	a									21 19											22 29	
Wakefield Kirkgate 4	a					20 57																
Wakefield Westgate 7	a						20 46					21 59					21 46					
Leeds 10	a					21 20	21 05					22 19					22 02					
York 8	a									21 45											22 53	

		EM ◇1 🍴	EM A	EM ◇1 🍴	EM ◇1 D 🍽🍴	EM ◇1 🍴	EM ◇1 🍴	NT	EM ◇1 🍴	XC ◇1 B	EM F	EM ◇1 🍴	EM A	EM ◇1 🍴	EM ◇1 H 🍴	EM ◇1 I 🍴	EM ◇1 🍴	EM ◇1 🍴	EM ◇1 🍴	EM ◇1 🍴	EM ◇1 🍴	EM ◇1 🍴	EM ◇1 H 🍴
St Pancras International ⊖	d	19 15		19 25	19 30	19 55	20 00		20 15			20 25		20 30	20 55	20 55	21 00	21 25		21 30	22 00		22 25
Luton Airport Parkway 7 ✈	d				19 51									20 51						21 53			22 48
Luton 10	d						20 23										21 23				22 24		
Bedford 7	d				20 07		20 38							21 07			21 38			22 09	22 40		23 04
Wellingborough	d				20 20		20 51							21 20			21 51			22 22	22 53		23 17
Kettering 4	a			20 15			21 00							21 26			21 57			22 30	23 00		23 25
	d			20 17			21 01							21 27			21 58		22 05	22 31	23 01	23 05	23 26
Corby	d						21a10												22a15			23a15	
Oakham	d																						
Melton Mowbray	d																						
Market Harborough	d	20 11		20 27	20 37				21 11					21 37			22 08	22 23		22 42	23 12		23 37
Leicester	a	20 28		20 42	20 54	21 04			21 25			21 33		21 53	22 02	22 02	22 26	22 40		23 01	23 29		23 53
	d	20 28		20 43	20 54	21 04			21 26		21 25	21 35		21 54	22 04	22 04	22 28	22 41		23 02	23 30		23 55
Syston	d										21 32												
Sileby	d										21 36												
Barrow Upon Soar	d										21 40												
Loughborough	d		←	20 54	21 04						21 45	21 45	←	22 04			22 38	22 52		23 13	23 41		00 06
East Midlands Parkway ✈	d	20 43	20 54	21 01					21 43		21 54	21 53	21 54				22 46	23 01		23 24	23 50		00 14
Beeston	a		21 03		21 18						→		22 07	22 16							00 04		
Nottingham 8 ⇌	a	21 04	21 15		21 29				21 58				22 15	22 26				23 11			00 12		
	d				21 43			21 11															
Lincoln	a																						
Langley Mill	d				22 01			21 38															
Alfreton	d				22 09			21 46															
Long Eaton	a			21 05								21 58								23 37			
Derby 6	a			21 16		21 32						22 10			22 26	22 26	22 59			23 50			00 34
	d					21 34				21 44					22 28	22 33							00 35
Chesterfield	d				22 21	21 55		22 00		22 07					22 47	23 08							00 58
Sheffield 7 ⇌	a				22 37	22 16		22 19		22 24					23 03	23 21							01 13
Doncaster 7	a																						
Wakefield Kirkgate 4	a																						
Wakefield Westgate 7	a				23 21	22 46				22 59													
Leeds 10	a				23 41	23 05				23 15													
York 8	a																						

A From Leicester
B From Plymouth
C From Norwich to Manchester Piccadilly
D 🍽 from Nottingham 🍴 to Nottingham
E From Reading to Newcastle. 🍴 to Sheffield
F To Nottingham
G From Southampton Central to Leeds
H until 14 September
I from 17 September until 28 September

For connections from Gatwick Airport see Table 52

London - East Midlands - Sheffield

Route Diagram - see first Page of Table 53

		EM ◇1 A ⌶	EM ◇1 B ⊡⌶		EM ◇1 C ⊡⌶
St Pancras International ⊖	d	22 25	23 15		23 15
Luton Airport Parkway 7 ✈	d	22 48			
Luton 10	d		23 46		23 46
Bedford 7	d	23 04	00 12		00 12
Wellingborough	d	23 17	00 25		00 25
Kettering 4	a	23 25	00 41		00 41
	d	23 26	00 42		00 42
Corby	d				
Oakham	d				
Melton Mowbray	d				
Market Harborough	d	23 37	00 52		00 52
Leicester	a	23 53	01 05		01 05
	d	23 55	01 07		01 07
Syston	d				
Sileby	d				
Barrow Upon Soar	d				
Loughborough	d	00 06	01 17		01 17
East Midlands Parkway ✈	d	00 14	01 25		01 25
Beeston	a		01 33		01 38
Nottingham 8	a		01 40		01 45
	d		01 47		01 52
Lincoln	a				
Langley Mill	d				
Alfreton	d				
Long Eaton	a				
Derby 6	a	00 34	02 05		02 10
	d	00 40			
Chesterfield	d	01 18			
Sheffield 7	a	01 32			
Doncaster 7	a				
Wakefield Kirkgate 4	a				
Wakefield Westgate 7	a				
Leeds 10	a				
York 8	a				

Mondays to Fridays

from 1 October

		NT MO	EM MO ◇1 D ⌶	EM MO ◇1 E ⌶	XC MO ◇1 F	EM MX ◇1 D ⌶	EM MX ◇1 E ⌶	EM MO ◇1 ⌶	EM MO ◇1 E ⌶	EM MO ◇1 ⌶	MX D	EM MX ◇1 ⌶	EM ◇1 G ⌶	EM MX ◇1 ⊡⌶	EM ◇1 H ⌶	EM ◇ I	XC ◇1 J ⌶	XC ◇1 ⌶	NT	EM ◇1 K ⌶		XC ◇1 H ⌶	NT L	EM ◇	XC ◇1 ⌶
St Pancras International ⊖	d		20p30	20p30		21p30	21p30	22p00	22p25	22p30		22p30	23p00	23p15	00 15										
Luton Airport Parkway 7 ✈	d								22p48	22p51		22p51	23p27		00 44										
Luton 10	d		20p54	20p54		21p52	21p52	22p24						23p46	00 47										
Bedford 7	d		21p11	21p11		22p08	22p08	22p40	23p04	23p14		23p14	23p50	00 12	01 12										
Wellingborough	d		21p24	21p24		22p21	22p21	22p53	23p17	23p28		23p28	00 04	00 25	01 33										
Kettering 4	a		21p31	21p31		22p28	22p28	23p00	23p25	23p34		23p34	00 10	00 41	01 43										
	d		21p32	21p32		22p29	22p29	23p01	23p26	23p35		23p35	00 11	00 42	01 43										
Corby	d																								
Oakham	d																								
Melton Mowbray	d																								
Market Harborough	d		21p43	21p43		22p39	22p39	23p12	23p37	23p45		23p45	00 21	00 52	01 55										
Leicester	a		22p02	22p02		22p54	22p56	23p29	23p53	00 04		00 04	00 42	01 05	02 10										
	d		22p04	22p04		22p55	22p57	23p30	23p55	00 06		00 06	00 44	01 07											
Syston	d																								
Sileby	d																								
Barrow Upon Soar	d																								
Loughborough	d					23p06	23p08	23p41	00 06	00 16		00 16	00 54	01 17											
East Midlands Parkway ✈	d		22p20	22p20		23p18	23p20	23p50	00 14	00 29		00 29	01 07	01 25											
Beeston	a							00 04		00 37		00 37		01 38											
Nottingham 8	a							00 12		00 44		00 48		01 45											
	d	21p30												01 52		05 20							06 23	06 40	
Lincoln	a																								
Langley Mill	d	21p52																					06 38		
Alfreton	d	22p00																					06 46	07 02	
Long Eaton	a					23p25	23p27																		
Derby 6	a		22p32	22p32		23p36	23p38		00 34				01 21	02 10											
	d		22p34	22p34	22p44	23p37	23p39		00 40								05 56	06 00		06 20		06 34			07 13
Chesterfield	d	22p13	22p55	22p56	23p05	23p57	23p59		01 18							05 49	06 15	06 15	06 26	06 42		06 54	06 58	07 13	07 32
Sheffield 7	a	22p36	23p09	23p10	23p20	00 17	00 17		01 32							06 15	06 28	06 28	06 46	07 13		07 07	07 18	07 31	07 48
Doncaster 7	a																06 57	06 57							08 24
Wakefield Kirkgate 4	a	23p26																	07 27				07 57		
Wakefield Westgate 7	a		23p40	23p40																		07 36			
Leeds 10	a	00 05	00 01	00 01	00 11														07 51			07 52	08 21		
York 8	a																07 26	07 26				08 22			08 45

A from 17 September until 28 September
B from 27 July until 7 September, not from 13 August until 28 August. ⊡ from Nottingham ⌶ to Nottingham
C not from 27 July until 10 August, from 29 August until 7 September. ⊡ from Nottingham ⌶ to Nottingham
D from 29 October
E from 1 October until 22 October
F from 1 October until 22 October. From Penzance
G ⊡ from Nottingham ⌶ to Nottingham
H To Liverpool Lime Street
I MO from 1 October until 22 October. To Newcastle. ⌶ from Sheffield
J To Newcastle. ⌶ from Sheffield
K From Birmingham New Street to Glasgow Central
L From Birmingham New Street to Newcastle

For connections from Gatwick Airport see Table 52

London - East Midlands - Sheffield

Route Diagram - see first Page of Table 53

		EM ◇1 ⌶	NT	EM	XC ◇1 A ⌶	EM ◇1 ⌶		EM ◇ B	EM	XC ◇1 C ⌶	EM ◇1 ⌶	EM ◇1 ⌶	NT	EM ◇1 ⌶	XC ◇1 D ⌶	EM ◇ E		XC ◇1 F ⌶	EM G	EM ◇1 ⌶	EM H	EM ◇1 ⌶	EM ◇1 ⌶	EM ◇1 ⌶	EM ◇1 ⌶
St Pancras International ⊖	d					05 45					06 37			06 55						07 00		07 25	07 30	07 55	
Luton Airport Parkway 7 ✈	d													07 16									07 51		
Luton 10	d					06 11					06 59									07 23					
Bedford 7	d					06 27														07 38			08 07		
Wellingborough	d					06 39					07 23									07 51			08 20		
Kettering 4	a					06 46					07 30									08 00			08 26		
	d					06 47					07 31	07 38								08 01			08 27		08 32
Corby	d											07a48													08a42
Oakham	d																								
Melton Mowbray	d																								
Market Harborough	d					06 57					07 41									08 12		08 21	08 37		
Leicester	a					07 11					07 56			08 04						08 29		08 36	08 52	09 02	
	d			06 33		07 12			07 25		07 57			08 06					08 25	08 30		08 38	08 54	09 04	
Syston	d			06 41					07 32										08 32						
Sileby	d			06 46					07 36										08 36						
Barrow Upon Soar	d			06 51					07 40										08 40						
Loughborough	d			06 56		07 24			07 45		08 08			08 16					08 45	08 41	←	08 48	09 04		
East Midlands Parkway ✈	d			07 06		07 32			07 54					08 24					08 54	08 50	08 54	08 56			
Beeston	a			07 16					08 06					08 31					→		09 02		09 16		
Nottingham 8	a			07 23					08 15					08 39						09 02	09 13		09 26		
	d		07 13					07 45					08 11			08 45					09 21				
Lincoln	a																				10 18				
Langley Mill	d		07 29										08 31												
Alfreton	d		07 37					08 07					08 39			09 07									
Long Eaton	a					07 35																08 59			
Derby 6	a					07 47					08 24											09 15		09 26	
	d	07 20			07 44	07 49				08 13	08 28				08 44			09 13				09 18		09 28	
Chesterfield	d	07 42	07 50		08 03	08 09		08 18		08 32	08 47		08 51		09 03	09 18						09 37		09 47	
Sheffield 7	a	08 00	08 08		08 17	08 25		08 38		08 45	09 04		09 16		09 17	09 38		09 43				09 52		10 00	
Doncaster 7	a									09 18								10 18							
Wakefield Kirkgate 4	a		08 57										09 57												
Wakefield Westgate 7	a				08 46										09 46										
Leeds 10	a		09 20		09 03								10 18		10 02										
York 8	a				09 26					09 44					10 26			10 45							

		EM ◇1 ⌶		NT	XC ◇1 I ⌶	EM ◇ E	XC ◇1 J ⌶	EM G	EM ◇1 ⌶	EM ◇1 ⌶	EM H	EM ◇1 ⌶		EM ◇1 ⌶	EM ◇1 ⌶	EM ◇ ⌶	NT ◇	XC ◇1 K ⌶	EM ◇ E	XC ◇1 L ⌶	EM G	EM ◇1 ⌶		EM ◇1 ⌶	EM H
St Pancras International ⊖	d	08 00							08 15	08 25		08 30		08 55	09 00							09 15		09 25	
Luton Airport Parkway 7 ✈	d											08 51													
Luton 10	d	08 23													09 23										
Bedford 7	d	08 38										09 07			09 38										
Wellingborough	d	08 51										09 20			09 51										
Kettering 4	a	09 00										09 27			10 00										
	d	09 01										09 27													
Corby	d	09a10														09 30									
Oakham	d															09 49									
Melton Mowbray	d															10 01									
Market Harborough	d								09 12			09 37										10 12			
Leicester	a								09 29	09 35		09 54		10 02								10 29		10 34	
	d							09 25	09 30	09 35		09 54		10 04							10 25	10 30		10 35	
Syston	d							09 32													10 32				
Sileby	d							09 36													10 36				
Barrow Upon Soar	d							09 40													10 40				
Loughborough	d							09 45		09 45	←	10 04									10 45			10 46	←
East Midlands Parkway ✈	d							09 54	09 46	09 52	09 54					10 26					10 54	10 46		10 53	10 54
Beeston	a							→			10 02	10 17									→				11 02
Nottingham 8	a								09 59		10 13	10 25										10 59			11 14
	d			09 15		09 45					10 29						10 15		10 45						11 17
Lincoln	a										11 33														12 23
Langley Mill	d			09 32													10 32								
Alfreton	d			09 40		10 07											10 40		11 07						
Long Eaton	a									09 56														10 56	
Derby 6	a									10 09				10 26		10 40								11 09	
	d				09 44		10 11			10 18				10 28				10 44		11 11				11 18	
Chesterfield	d			09 52	10 03	10 18				10 37				10 47			10 52	11 03	11 18					11 37	
Sheffield 7	a			10 16	10 17	10 38	10 41			10 52				11 02			11 17	11 17	11 38	11 43				11 52	
Doncaster 7	a						11 18													12 18					
Wakefield Kirkgate 4	a			10 57													11 57								
Wakefield Westgate 7	a				10 46													11 46							
Leeds 10	a			11 18	11 02												12 18	12 01							
York 8	a				11 26		11 46											12 26		12 46					

A From Birmingham New Street to Edinburgh
B To Liverpool Lime Street
C From Birmingham New Street to Newcastle
D From Bath Spa to Glasgow Central
E From Norwich to Liverpool Lime Street
F From Guildford to Newcastle
G To Lincoln
H From Leicester
I From Plymouth to Edinburgh
J From Reading to Newcastle
K From Plymouth to Glasgow Central
L From Winchester to Newcastle

For connections from Gatwick Airport see Table 52

London - East Midlands - Sheffield

Route Diagram - see first Page of Table 53

		EM ◇1 ✠	EM ◇1 ✠	EM ◇1 ✠	NT ◇	XC ◇1 A ✠	EM ◇ B	XC ◇1 C ✠		EM D	EM ◇1 ✠	EM ◇1 ✠	EM E	EM ◇1 ✠	EM ◇1 ✠	EM ◇1 ✠	NT ◇	XC ◇1 F ✠		EM ◇ B	XC ◇1 G ✠	EM D	EM ◇1 ✠	EM ◇1 ✠	EM E
St Pancras International ⊖	d	09 30	09 55	10 00							10 15	10 25		10 30	10 55	11 00							11 15	11 25	
Luton Airport Parkway 7 ✈	d	09 51												10 51											
Luton 10	d			10 23												11 23									
Bedford 7	d	10 07		10 38										11 07		11 38									
Wellingborough	d	10 20		10 51										11 20		11 51									
Kettering 4	a	10 26		11 00										11 26		12 00									
	d	10 27		11 01										11 27		12 01									
Corby	d			11a10												12a10									
Oakham	d																								
Melton Mowbray	d																								
Market Harborough	d	10 37									11 12			11 37									12 12		
Leicester	a	10 54	11 02								11 29	11 33		11 52	12 02								12 29	12 33	
	d	10 54	11 04							11 25	11 30	11 35		11 54	12 04							12 25	12 30	12 35	
Syston	d									11 32												12 32			
Sileby	d									11 36												12 36			
Barrow Upon Soar	d									11 40												12 40			
Loughborough	d	11 04								11 45		11 45	←	12 04								12 46		12 45	←
East Midlands Parkway ✈	d									11 54	11 46	11 53	11 54									12 58	12 46	12 53	12 58
Beeston	a	11 16								→			12 02	12 16								→			13 07
Nottingham 8 🚊	a	11 25									11 59		12 13	12 26									12 59		13 14
	d				11 15		11 45						12 27				12 15			12 45					13 17
Lincoln	a												13 22												14 26
Langley Mill	d				11 31												12 32								
Alfreton	d				11 39		12 07										12 40			13 07					
Long Eaton	a											11 56												12 56	
Derby 6	a		11 26									12 09			12 26									13 09	
	d		11 28			11 44		12 11				12 18			12 28			12 44			13 11			13 18	
Chesterfield	d		11 47		11 52	12 04	12 18					12 37			12 47		12 52	13 03		13 18				13 37	
Sheffield 7 🚊	a		12 04		12 16	12 17	12 38	12 41				12 52			13 04		13 16	13 17		13 38	13 41			13 52	
Doncaster 7	a							13 18													14 18				
Wakefield Kirkgate 4	a				12 57												13 57								
Wakefield Westgate 7	a					12 46												13 46							
Leeds 10	a				13 18	13 03											14 18	14 02							
York 8	a					13 26		13 40										14 26			14 44				

		EM ◇1 ✠	EM ◇1 ✠	EM ◇1 ✠		NT ◇	XC ◇1 H ✠	EM ◇ B	XC ◇1 C ✠	EM D	EM ◇1 ✠	EM ◇1 ✠	EM E	EM ◇1 ✠		EM ◇1 ✠	EM ◇1 ✠	NT ◇	XC ◇1 F ✠	EM ◇ B	XC ◇1 G ✠	EM D	EM ◇1 ✠	EM ◇1 ✠
St Pancras International ⊖	d	11 30	11 55	12 00							12 15	12 25		12 30		12 55	13 00						13 15	13 25
Luton Airport Parkway 7 ✈	d	11 51												12 51										
Luton 10	d			12 23													13 22							
Bedford 7	d	12 07		12 38										13 07			13 38							
Wellingborough	d	12 20		12 51										13 20			13 50							
Kettering 4	a	12 26		13 00										13 26			13 59							
	d	12 27		13 01										13 27			14 01							
Corby	d			13a10													14a10							
Oakham	d																							
Melton Mowbray	d																							
Market Harborough	d	12 37									13 12			13 37									14 12	
Leicester	a	12 53	13 02								13 30	13 33		13 54		14 02							14 29	14 33
	d	12 54	13 04							13 25	13 30	13 35		13 54		14 04						14 25	14 30	14 35
Syston	d									13 32												14 32		
Sileby	d									13 36												14 36		
Barrow Upon Soar	d									13 40												14 40		
Loughborough	d	13 04								13 45		13 45	←	14 04								14 45		14 45
East Midlands Parkway ✈	d									13 54	13 45	13 53	13 54									14 54	14 46	14 53
Beeston	a	13 16								→			14 02	14 16								→		
Nottingham 8 🚊	a	13 25									13 59		14 13	14 26									14 59	
	d					13 15		13 45					14 29					14 15		14 45				
Lincoln	a												15 24											
Langley Mill	d					13 32												14 30						
Alfreton	d					13 40		14 07										14 38		15 07				
Long Eaton	a											13 56												14 56
Derby 6	a		13 26									14 09				14 26								15 13
	d		13 28				13 44		14 11			14 18				14 28			14 44		15 11			15 15
Chesterfield	d		13 47			13 52	14 03	14 19				14 37				14 47		14 52	15 03	15 22				15 34
Sheffield 7 🚊	a		14 00			14 16	14 17	14 38	14 41			14 52				15 03		15 16	15 17	15 38	15 41			15 52
Doncaster 7	a								15 18												16 18			
Wakefield Kirkgate 4	a					14 57												15 57						
Wakefield Westgate 7	a						14 46												15 46					
Leeds 10	a					15 18	15 01											16 18	16 02					
York 8	a						15 26		15 45										16 28		16 45			

A From Plymouth to Edinburgh
B From Norwich to Liverpool Lime Street
C From Reading to Newcastle
D To Lincoln
E From Leicester
F From Penzance to Glasgow Central
G From Southampton Central to Newcastle
H From Plymouth to Aberdeen

For connections from Gatwick Airport see Table 52

London - East Midlands - Sheffield

Route Diagram - see first Page of Table 53

		EM A	EM ◇1 ✠	EM ◇1 ✠	EM ◇1 ✠	NT ◇	XC ◇1 B ✠	EM ◇ C	XC ◇1 D ✠	EM E		EM ◇1 ✠	EM ◇1 ✠	EM F	EM ◇1 ✠	EM ◇1 ✠	EM ◇1 ✠	NT ◇	XC ◇1 G ✠	EM ◇ C		XC ◇1 H ✠	EM I	EM ◇1 ✠	EM ◇1 ✠
St Pancras International ⊖	d		13 30	13 55	14 00							14 15	14 25		14 30	14 55	15 00							15 15	15 25
Luton Airport Parkway 7 ✈	d		13 51												14 51										
Luton 10	d				14 23												15 23								
Bedford 7	d		14 07		14 38										15 07		15 38								
Wellingborough	d		14 20		14 51										15 20		15 51								
Kettering 4	a		14 26		15 00										15 26		16 00								
	d		14 27		15 01										15 27		16 01								
Corby	d				15a10												16a10								
Oakham	d																								
Melton Mowbray	d																								
Market Harborough	d		14 37									15 12			15 37									16 12	
Leicester	a		14 54	15 02								15 29	15 33		15 54	16 02								16 29	16 33
	d		14 54	15 04						15 25		15 30	15 35		15 54	16 04							16 25	16 30	16 35
Syston	d									15 32													16 32		
Sileby	d									15 36													16 36		
Barrow Upon Soar	d									15 40													16 40		
Loughborough	d	←	15 04							15 45			15 45	←	16 04								16 45		16 45
East Midlands Parkway ✈	d	14 54								15 54		15 46	15 53	15 54									16 54	16 46	16 53
Beeston	a	15 02	15 16							→				16 02	16 16								→		
Nottingham 8 🚊	a	15 13	15 26									15 59		16 13	16 25									16 59	
	d	15 27				15 15		15 45						16 14				16 15		16 45					
Lincoln	a	16 27												17 19											
Langley Mill	d					15 32												16 32							
Alfreton	d					15 40		16 07										16 40		17 07					
Long Eaton	a												15 56												16 56
Derby 6	a			15 26									16 09			16 26									17 09
	d			15 28			15 44		16 11				16 17			16 28			16 42			17 11			17 18
Chesterfield	d			15 47		15 53	16 03	16 18					16 36			16 47		16 55	17 04	17 18					17 37
Sheffield 7 🚊	a			16 00		16 16	16 17	16 38	16 41				16 52			17 04		17 17	17 19	17 36		17 44			17 52
Doncaster 7	a								17 18																
Wakefield Kirkgate 4	a					16 57												17 57							
Wakefield Westgate 7	a						16 49												17 47			18 13			
Leeds 10	a					17 18	17 04											18 18	18 03			18 31			
York 8	a						17 28		17 40										18 29			19 01			

		EM A	EM ◇1 ✠	EM ◇1 ✠	EM ◇1 ✠	NT ◇		XC ◇1 J ✠	EM ◇ C	XC ◇1 D ✠	EM I	EM ◇1 ✠	EM ◇1 ✠	EM A	EM ◇1 ✠	EM ◇1 ✠		NT ◇	XC ◇1 K ✠	EM ◇ C	XC ◇1 L ✠	EM I	EM ◇1 ✠		EM ◇1 ✠
St Pancras International ⊖	d		15 30	15 55	16 00							16 15	16 25		16 30	16 55							17 00		17 15
Luton Airport Parkway 7 ✈	d		15 51												16 51										
Luton 10	d				16 22										16 55										17 40
Bedford 7	d		16 07		16 38										17 10								17 35		
Wellingborough	d		16 20		16 50										17 23								17 48		
Kettering 4	a		16 26		16 59										17 29								17 56		
	d		16 27		17 00										17 30								18 04	18 08	
Corby	d				17a09																			18a18	
Oakham	d																								
Melton Mowbray	d																								
Market Harborough	d		16 37									17 12			17 40										18 18
Leicester	a		16 54	17 02								17 29	17 35		17 55	18 02							18 30		18 36
	d		16 54	17 04							17 25	17 30	17 35		17 55	18 04						18 25	18 32		18 37
Syston	d										17 32											18 32			
Sileby	d										17 36											18 36			
Barrow Upon Soar	d										17 40											18 40			
Loughborough	d	←	17 04								17 45		17 45	←	18 05							18 45	18 43		
East Midlands Parkway ✈	d	16 54									17 54	17 46	17 52	17 54								18 54	18 50		18 53
Beeston	a	17 02	17 16								→			18 02	18 17							→			19 02
Nottingham 8 🚊	a	17 13	17 26									17 59		18 13	18 27										19 10
	d	17 17				17 15			17 45					18 15				18 15		18 45					
Lincoln	a	18 28												19 23											
Langley Mill	d					17 32			18 02									18 32							
Alfreton	d					17 40			18 09									18 40		19 07					
Long Eaton	a												18 00										18 55		
Derby 6	a			17 26									18 14			18 26							19 09		
	d			17 28				17 41		18 11			18 18			18 28			18 42		19 11		19 18		
Chesterfield	d			17 47		17 52		18 02	18 21				18 42			18 47		18 52	19 01	19 18	19 30		19 37		
Sheffield 7 🚊	a			18 02		18 14		18 18	18 39	18 44			18 58			19 01		19 17	19 19	19 39	19 47		19 51		
Doncaster 7	a									19 14											20 15				
Wakefield Kirkgate 4	a					18 59												19 58							
Wakefield Westgate 7	a							18 47											19 50						
Leeds 10	a					19 23		19 03										20 19	20 05						
York 8	a							19 29		19 38									20 29		20 46				

A From Leicester
B From Plymouth to Dundee
C From Norwich to Liverpool Lime Street
D From Reading to Newcastle
E To Sleaford
F From Leicester to Sleaford
G From Plymouth to Glasgow Central
H From Southampton Central to Edinburgh
I To Lincoln
J From Plymouth to Edinburgh
K From Plymouth to Edinburgh. ✠ to Leeds
L From Southampton Central to Newcastle. ✠ to Doncaster

For connections from Gatwick Airport see Table 52

London - East Midlands - Sheffield

Route Diagram - see first Page of Table 53

	EM A		EM ◇1 ⊼	EM ◇1 ⊼	NT ◇	XC ◇1 B ⊼	EM ◇ C	EM ◇1 D ⊡⊼	XC ◇1 E ⊼	EM F	EM ◇1 ⊼		EM A	EM ◇1 ⊼	EM ◇1 ⊼	EM ◇1 D ⊡⊼	XC ◇1 B	EM ◇1 ⊼	EM ◇1 ⊼	NT	XC ◇1 G		EM F	EM ◇1 ⊼
St Pancras International ⊖ d			17 30	17 55				17 45			18 15			18 00	18 25	18 30		18 55	19 00					19 15
Luton Airport Parkway 7 ✈ d								18 09								18 53								
Luton 10 d														18 23	18 50				19 23					
Bedford 7 d			18 05											18 38		19 10			19 40					
Wellingborough d			18 18					18 33			19 00			18 51		19 23			19 53					
Kettering 4 a			18 24					18 44			19 07			19 05		19 29			20 04					
d			18 25					18 46			19 08			19 10		19 31			20 05					
Corby d														19 20					20a14					
Oakham d														19 40										
Melton Mowbray d														19a52										
Market Harborough d			18 35					18 59							19 27			19 52						20 11
Leicester a			18 54	19 04				19 21			19 32				19 44	19 56		20 11						20 28
d			18 56	19 04				19 25		19 25	19 34				19 45	19 57		20 13					20 25	20 28
Syston d										19 32													20 32	
Sileby d										19 36													20 36	
Barrow Upon Soar d										19 40													20 40	
Loughborough d	←		19 06					19 36		19 45	19 45		←		19 56			20 23					20 45	
East Midlands Parkway ✈ d	18 54		19 13					19 44		19 54	19 53		19 54			20 12		20 31					20 54	20 43
Beeston a	19 07		19 18							→			20 07			20 17							→	
Nottingham 8 a	19 14		19 27					19 58			20 08		20 15			20 28								21 04
d	19 20				19 15		19 40	20 07			20 15					20 29				20 45				
Lincoln a	20 17															21 22								
Langley Mill d					19 32						20 33													
Alfreton d					19 40		20 01				20 41													
Long Eaton a								20 22							20 06									
Derby 6 a				19 28				20 35							20 19			20 46		21 05				
d				19 28		19 41			20 11						20 21		20 44	20 48		21 06	21 13			
Chesterfield d				19 47	19 52	20 02	20 12				20 53				20 41		21 03	21 09		21 28	21 34			
Sheffield 7 a				20 03	20 15	20 18	20 28		20 48		21 14				20 56		21 18	21 25		21 54	21 51			
Doncaster 7 a									21 19												22 29			
Wakefield Kirkgate 4 a					20 57																			
Wakefield Westgate 7 a						20 46					21 59						21 46							
Leeds 10 a					21 20	21 05					22 19						22 02							
York 8 a									21 45												22 53			

	EM A	EM ◇1 ⊼	EM ◇1 D ⊡⊼	EM ◇1 ⊼	EM ◇1 ⊼	NT	EM ◇1 ⊼		XC ◇1 B	EM F	EM ◇1 ⊼	EM A	EM ◇1 ⊼	EM ◇1 ⊼	EM ◇1 ⊼	EM ◇1 ⊼	EM ◇1 ⊼		EM ◇1 ⊼	EM ◇1 ⊼	EM ◇1 ⊼	EM ◇1 ⊼	EM ◇1 D ⊡⊼
St Pancras International ⊖ d		19 25	19 30	19 55	20 00		20 15				20 25		20 30	20 55	21 00	21 25			21 30	22 00		22 25	23 15
Luton Airport Parkway 7 ✈ d			19 51										20 51						21 53			22 48	
Luton 10 d					20 23										21 23					22 24			23 46
Bedford 7 d			20 07		20 38								21 07		21 38				22 09	22 40		23 04	00 12
Wellingborough d			20 20		20 51								21 20		21 51				22 22	22 53		23 17	00 25
Kettering 4 a		20 15			21 00								21 26		21 57				22 30	23 00		23 25	00 41
d		20 17			21 01								21 27		21 58		22 05		22 31	23 01	23 05	23 26	00 42
Corby d					21a10												22a15				23a15		
Oakham d																							
Melton Mowbray d																							
Market Harborough d		20 27	20 37				21 11						21 37		22 08	22 23			22 42	23 12		23 37	00 52
Leicester a		20 42	20 54	21 04			21 25				21 33		21 53	22 02	22 26	22 40			23 01	23 29		23 53	01 05
d		20 43	20 54	21 04			21 26			21 25	21 35		21 54	22 04	22 28	22 41			23 02	23 30		23 55	01 07
Syston d										21 32													
Sileby d										21 36													
Barrow Upon Soar d										21 40													
Loughborough d	←	20 54	21 04							21 45	21 45	←	22 04		22 38	22 52			23 13	23 41		00 06	01 17
East Midlands Parkway ✈ d	20 54	21 01					21 43			21 54	21 53	21 54			22 46	23 01			23 24	23 50		00 14	01 25
Beeston a	21 03		21 18							→		22 07	22 16							00 04			01 38
Nottingham 8 a	21 15		21 29				21 58					22 15	22 26			23 11				00 12			01 45
d			21 43			21 11																	01 52
Lincoln a																							
Langley Mill d			22 01			21 38																	
Alfreton d			22 09			21 46																	
Long Eaton a		21 05									21 58								23 37				
Derby 6 a		21 16		21 32							22 10			22 26	22 59				23 50			00 34	02 10
d				21 34					21 44					22 33								00 40	
Chesterfield d			22 21	21 55		22 00			22 07					23 08								01 18	
Sheffield 7 a			22 37	22 16		22 19			22 24					23 21								01 32	
Doncaster 7 a																							
Wakefield Kirkgate 4 a																							
Wakefield Westgate 7 a			23 21	22 46					22 59														
Leeds 10 a			23 41	23 05					23 15														
York 8 a																							

A From Leicester
B From Plymouth
C From Norwich to Manchester Piccadilly
D ⊡ from Nottingham ⊼ to Nottingham
E From Reading to Newcastle. ⊼ to Sheffield
F To Nottingham
G From Southampton Central to Leeds

For connections from Gatwick Airport see Table 52

London - East Midlands - Sheffield

Route Diagram - see first Page of Table 53

	EM ◇1 ⊼	EM ◇1 ⊼	EM ◇1 A ⊡⊼	EM ◇1 ⊼	EM ◇ B	XC ◇1 C ⊼	EM ◇1 ⊼	XC ◇1 D ⊼	EM ◇ B		XC ◇1 E ⊼	EM ◇1 ⊼	NT	EM	XC ◇1 F ⊼	EM ◇ B	EM	XC ◇1 E ⊼	EM ◇1 ⊼		EM ◇1 G ⊼	EM ◇1 ⊼	NT	EM ◇1 ⊼
St Pancras International ⊖ d	22p00	22p25	23p15	00 15															06 10		06 37			06 55
Luton Airport Parkway 7 ✈ d		22p48		00 44																				07 16
Luton 10 d	22p24		23p46	00 47															06 33		06 59			
Bedford 7 d	22p40	23p04	00 12	01 12															06 48					
Wellingborough d	22p53	23p17	00 25	01 33															07 01					
Kettering 4 a	23p00	23p25	00 41	01 43															07 07		07 27			
d	23p01	23p26	00 42	01 43															07 08		07 28	07 38		
Corby d																						07a48		
Oakham d																								
Melton Mowbray d																								
Market Harborough d	23p12	23p37	00 52	01 55															07 18		07 38			
Leicester a	23p29	23p53	01 05	02 10															07 35		07 53			08 04
d	23p30	23p55	01 07											06 36			07 25		07 36		07 55			08 06
Syston d														06 43			07 32							
Sileby d														06 47			07 36							
Barrow Upon Soar d														06 51			07 40							
Loughborough d	23p41	00 06	01 17											06 56			07 46		07 47		08 05			08 18
East Midlands Parkway ✈ d	23p50	00 14	01 25											07 06			07 57				08 13			
Beeston a	00 04		01 38											07 15			08 04							08 31
Nottingham 8 a	00 12		01 45											07 24			08 13							08 42
d			01 52		05 20				06 40				07 11			07 45							08 11	
Lincoln a																								
Langley Mill d													07 27										08 31	
Alfreton d									07 02				07 35			08 07							08 39	
Long Eaton a																			07 55					
Derby 6 a		00 34	02 10																08 09		08 26			
d		00 35				05 55	06 26	06 37			07 11	07 20			07 44			08 11	08 18		08 28			
Chesterfield d		00 58			05 49	06 31	06 45	06 56	07 13		07 30	07 42	07 50		08 03	08 18		08 30	08 37		08 47		08 51	
Sheffield 7 a		01 13			06 15	06 44	07 09	07 09	07 31		07 48	07 59	08 08		08 17	08 38		08 45	08 52		09 07		09 16	
Doncaster 7 a						07 16					08 23							09 18			09 53			
Wakefield Kirkgate 4 a													08 57										09 57	
Wakefield Westgate 7 a								07 36							08 45									
Leeds 10 a								07 52					09 20		09 03								10 18	
York 8 a						07 43		08 23			08 48				09 27			09 44			10 16			

	XC ◇1 H ⊼	EM ◇ I	XC ◇1 J ⊼	EM K	EM ◇1 ⊼		EM ◇1 L ⊼	EM	EM ◇1 ⊼	EM ◇1 ⊼	EM ◇1 ⊼	NT M	XC ◇1 I ⊼	EM ◇ N	XC ◇1 ⊼		EM K	EM ◇1 ⊼	EM ◇1 L ⊼	EM	EM ◇1 ⊼	EM ◇1 ⊼	EM ◇1 ⊼	NT
St Pancras International ⊖ d					07 00				07 30	07 55	08 00							08 15	08 25		08 30	08 55	09 00	
Luton Airport Parkway 7 ✈ d									07 51												08 51			
Luton 10 d					07 23						08 23												09 23	
Bedford 7 d					07 38				08 07		08 38										09 07		09 38	
Wellingborough d					07 51				08 20		08 51										09 20		09 51	
Kettering 4 a					08 00				08 27		09 00										09 26		10 00	
d					08 01				08 27		09 01										09 27		10 01	
Corby d											09a10												10a10	
Oakham d																								
Melton Mowbray d																								
Market Harborough d					08 12				08 37									09 12			09 37			
Leicester a					08 29				08 53	09 02								09 29	09 33		09 52	10 02		
d				08 25	08 30		08 38		08 54	09 04							09 25	09 30	09 35		09 54	10 04		
Syston d				08 32													09 32							
Sileby d				08 36													09 36							
Barrow Upon Soar d				08 40													09 40							
Loughborough d				08 45	08 41		08 49	←	09 04								09 45		09 45	←	10 04			
East Midlands Parkway ✈ d				08 57	08 50		08 56	08 57									09 54	09 46	09 53	09 54				
Beeston a				→				09 05	09 16								→			10 02	10 16			
Nottingham 8 a					09 03			09 14	09 26									09 59		10 13	10 26			
d		08 45						09 23				09 15		09 45						10 29				10 15
Lincoln a								10 17												11 30				
Langley Mill d												09 32												10 32
Alfreton d		09 07										09 40		10 07										10 40
Long Eaton a							09 00												09 56					
Derby 6 a							09 14			09 26									10 09			10 26		
d	08 44		09 11				09 18			09 28			09 44		10 11				10 18			10 28		
Chesterfield d	09 03	09 18					09 37			09 47		09 52	10 03	10 18					10 37			10 47		10 52
Sheffield 7 a	09 17	09 38	09 44				09 52			10 00		10 15	10 17	10 38	10 42				10 52			11 00		11 15
Doncaster 7 a			10 17												11 15									
Wakefield Kirkgate 4 a												10 57												11 57
Wakefield Westgate 7 a	09 46												10 46											
Leeds 10 a	10 02											11 18	11 02											12 18
York 8 a	10 26		10 40										11 26		11 40									

A ⊡ from Nottingham ⊼ to Nottingham
B To Liverpool Lime Street
C To Newcastle. ⊼ from Sheffield
D From Birmingham New Street to Glasgow Central
E From Birmingham New Street to Newcastle
F From Birmingham New Street to Edinburgh
G To Scarborough
H From Bristol Temple Meads to Glasgow Central
I From Norwich to Liverpool Lime Street
J From Guildford to Newcastle
K To Lincoln
L From Leicester
M From Plymouth to Edinburgh
N From Bournemouth to Newcastle

For connections from Gatwick Airport see Table 52

Table 53

Saturdays until 21 July

London - East Midlands - Sheffield

Route Diagram - see first Page of Table 53

		XC ◇■ A ✠	EM ◇ B	XC ◇■ C ✠	EM D	EM ◇■ ✠	EM ◇■ ✠	EM E	EM ◇■ ✠	EM ◇■ ✠	EM ◇■ ✠	NT	XC ◇■ F ✠	EM ◇ B	XC ◇■ G D ✠	EM	EM ◇■ ✠	EM ◇■ ✠	EM E	EM ◇■ ✠	EM ◇■ ✠	EM ◇■ ✠
St Pancras International ⊖	d					09 15	09 25		09 30	09 55	10 00						10 15	10 25		10 30	10 55	11 00
Luton Airport Parkway ✈	d								09 51											10 51		
Luton	d										10 23											11 23
Bedford	d								10 07		10 38									11 07		11 38
Wellingborough	d								10 20		10 51									11 20		11 51
Kettering	a								10 26		11 00									11 26		12 00
	d								10 27		11 01									11 27		12 01
Corby	d										11a10											12a10
Oakham	d																					
Melton Mowbray	d																					
Market Harborough	d					10 12			10 37								11 12			11 37		
Leicester	a					10 29	10 33		10 54	11 02							11 29	11 33		11 54	12 02	
	d				10 25	10 30	10 35		10 54	11 04						11 25	11 30	11 35		11 54	12 04	
Syston	d				10 32											11 32						
Sileby	d				10 36											11 36						
Barrow Upon Soar	d				10 40											11 40						
Loughborough	d				10 45		10 45	←	11 04							11 45		11 45	←	12 04		
East Midlands Parkway ✈	d				10 54	10 46	10 53	10 54								11 54	11 46	11 53	11 54			
Beeston	a				→			11 02	11 16							→			12 02	12 16		
Nottingham	a					10 59		11 13	11 26								11 59		12 13	12 26		
	d		10 45					11 17				11 15		11 45					12 27			
Lincoln	a							12 27											13 18			
Langley Mill	d											11 31										
Alfreton	d		11 07									11 39		12 07								
Long Eaton	a						10 56											11 56				
Derby	a						11 09			11 26								12 09			12 26	
	d	10 44		11 11			11 18			11 28			11 44		12 11			12 18			12 28	
Chesterfield	d	11 03	11 18				11 37			11 47		11 52	12 03	12 18				12 37			12 47	
Sheffield	a	11 17	11 38	11 41			11 52			12 00		12 16	12 16	12 38	12 41			12 52			13 04	
Doncaster	a			12 15											13 17							
Wakefield Kirkgate	a											12 57										
Wakefield Westgate	a	11 46											12 46									
Leeds	a	12 02										13 18	13 02									
York	a	12 26		12 39									13 26		13 40							

		NT	XC ◇■ H ✠	EM ◇ B	XC ◇■ C ✠	EM D	EM ◇■ ✠	EM ◇■ ✠	EM E	EM ◇■ ✠	EM ◇■ ✠	EM ◇■ ✠	NT	XC ◇■ I ✠	EM ◇ B	XC ◇■ G D ✠	EM	EM ◇■ ✠	EM ◇■ ✠	EM E	EM ◇■ ✠	EM ◇■ ✠	EM ◇■ ✠
St Pancras International ⊖	d						11 15	11 25		11 30	11 55	12 00						12 15	12 25		12 30	12 55	13 00
Luton Airport Parkway ✈	d									11 51											12 51		
Luton	d											12 23											13 23
Bedford	d									12 07		12 38									13 07		13 38
Wellingborough	d									12 20		12 51									13 20		13 51
Kettering	a									12 26		13 00									13 26		14 00
	d									12 27		13 01									13 27		14 01
Corby	d											13a10											14a10
Oakham	d																						
Melton Mowbray	d																						
Market Harborough	d						12 12			12 37								13 12			13 37		
Leicester	a						12 29	12 33		12 54	13 02							13 29	13 33		13 52	14 02	
	d					12 25	12 30	12 35		12 54	13 04						13 25	13 30	13 35		13 54	14 04	
Syston	d					12 32											13 32						
Sileby	d					12 36											13 36						
Barrow Upon Soar	d					12 40											13 40						
Loughborough	d					12 45		12 45	←	13 04							13 45		13 45	←	14 04		
East Midlands Parkway ✈	d					12 54	12 46	12 53	12 54								13 54	13 46	13 53	13 54			
Beeston	a					→			13 02	13 16							→			14 02	14 16		
Nottingham	a						12 59		13 13	13 27								13 59		14 13	14 26		
	d	12 15		12 45					13 17				13 15		13 45					14 29			
Lincoln	a								14 23											15 22			
Langley Mill	d	12 32											13 32										
Alfreton	d	12 40		13 07									13 40		14 07								
Long Eaton	a							12 56											13 56				
Derby	a							13 09			13 26								14 09			14 26	
	d		12 44		13 11			13 18			13 28			13 44		14 11			14 18			14 28	
Chesterfield	d	12 52	13 03	13 18				13 37			13 47		13 52	14 03	14 18				14 37			14 47	
Sheffield	a	13 15	13 17	13 38	13 41			13 52			14 00		14 15	14 17	14 38	14 41			14 52			15 00	
Doncaster	a				14 18											15 17							
Wakefield Kirkgate	a	13 57											14 57										
Wakefield Westgate	a		13 46											14 46									
Leeds	a	14 18	14 02										15 18	15 02									
York	a		14 26		14 40									15 28		15 40							

A From Plymouth to Glasgow Central
B From Norwich to Liverpool Lime Street
C From Southampton Central to Newcastle
D To Lincoln
E From Leicester
F From Plymouth to Edinburgh
G From Reading to Newcastle
H From Penzance to Glasgow Central
I From Plymouth to Aberdeen

For connections from Gatwick Airport see Table 52

Table 53

Saturdays until 21 July

London - East Midlands - Sheffield

Route Diagram - see first Page of Table 53

		NT	XC ◇■ A ✠	EM ◇ B	XC ◇■ C ✠	EM D	EM ◇■ ✠	EM ◇■ ✠	EM E	EM ◇■ ✠	EM ◇■ ✠	EM ◇■ ✠	NT	XC ◇■ F ✠	EM ◇ B	XC ◇■ G D ✠	EM	EM ◇■ ✠	EM ◇■ ✠	EM E	EM ◇■ ✠	EM ◇■ ✠
St Pancras International ⊖	d						13 15	13 25		13 30	13 55	14 00						14 15	14 25		14 30	14 55
Luton Airport Parkway ✈	d									13 51											14 51	
Luton	d											14 23										
Bedford	d									14 07		14 38									15 07	
Wellingborough	d									14 20		14 51									15 20	
Kettering	a									14 26		15 00									15 26	
	d									14 27		15 01									15 27	
Corby	d											15a10										
Oakham	d																					
Melton Mowbray	d																					
Market Harborough	d						14 12			14 37								15 12			15 37	
Leicester	a						14 29	14 33		14 54	15 02							15 29	15 33		15 53	16 02
	d					14 25	14 30	14 35		14 54	15 04						15 25	15 30	15 35		15 54	16 04
Syston	d					14 32											15 32					
Sileby	d					14 36											15 36					
Barrow Upon Soar	d					14 40											15 40					
Loughborough	d					14 45		14 45	←	15 04							15 45		15 45	←	16 04	
East Midlands Parkway ✈	d					14 54	14 46	14 53	14 54								15 54	15 46	15 53	15 54		
Beeston	a					→			15 02	15 16							→			16 02	16 16	
Nottingham	a						14 59		15 13	15 26								16 01		16 13	16 26	
	d	14 15		14 45					15 23				15 15		15 45					16 14		
Lincoln	a								16 21											17 16		
Langley Mill	d	14 30											15 32									
Alfreton	d	14 38		15 07									15 40		16 07							
Long Eaton	a							14 56											15 56			
Derby	a							15 09			15 26								16 09			16 26
	d		14 44		15 11			15 18			15 28			15 44		16 11			16 18			16 28
Chesterfield	d	14 52	15 03	15 18				15 37			15 47		15 53	16 03	16 18				16 37			16 47
Sheffield	a	15 15	15 17	15 38	15 41			15 52			16 00		16 14	16 18	16 38	16 41			16 52			17 00
Doncaster	a				16 18											17 16						
Wakefield Kirkgate	a	15 57											16 57									
Wakefield Westgate	a		15 46											16 46								
Leeds	a	16 18	16 02										17 18	17 02								
York	a		16 26		16 41									17 26		17 37						

		EM ◇■ ✠	NT	XC ◇■ H ✠	EM ◇ B	XC ◇■ C ✠	EM D	EM ◇■ ✠	EM ◇■ ✠	EM E	EM ◇■ ✠	EM ◇■ ✠	EM ◇■ ✠	NT	XC ◇■ I ✠	EM ◇ B	XC ◇■ G D ✠	EM	EM ◇■ ✠	EM ◇■ ✠	EM E	EM ◇■ ✠	EM ◇■ ✠
St Pancras International ⊖	d	15 00						15 15	15 25		15 30	15 55	16 00						16 15	16 25		16 30	16 55
Luton Airport Parkway ✈	d										15 51											16 51	
Luton	d	15 23											16 23										
Bedford	d	15 38									16 07		16 38									17 07	
Wellingborough	d	15 51									16 20		16 51									17 20	
Kettering	a	16 00									16 26		17 00									17 26	
	d	16 01									16 27		17 01									17 27	
Corby	d	16a10											17a10										
Oakham	d																						
Melton Mowbray	d																						
Market Harborough	d							16 12			16 37								17 12			17 37	
Leicester	a							16 29	16 33		16 54	17 02							17 29	17 33		17 52	18 02
	d						16 25	16 30	16 35		16 54	17 04						17 25	17 30	17 35		17 54	18 04
Syston	d						16 32											17 32					
Sileby	d						16 36											17 36					
Barrow Upon Soar	d						16 40											17 40					
Loughborough	d						16 45		16 45	←	17 04							17 45		17 45	←	18 04	
East Midlands Parkway ✈	d						16 54	16 45	16 52	16 54								17 54	17 46	17 53	17 54		
Beeston	a						→			17 02	17 16							→			18 02	18 16	
Nottingham	a							16 59		17 13	17 26								17 59		18 12	18 26	
	d		16 15		16 45					17 13				17 15		17 45					18 15		
Lincoln	a									18 22											19 25		
Langley Mill	d		16 32											17 32		18 03							
Alfreton	d		16 40		17 07									17 40		18 10							
Long Eaton	a								16 56											17 56			
Derby	a								17 09			17 26								18 09			18 26
	d			16 41		17 11			17 18			17 28			17 44		18 11			18 18			18 28
Chesterfield	d		16 55	17 02	17 18				17 37			17 47		17 52	18 03	18 22				18 39			18 47
Sheffield	a		17 17	17 19	17 34	17 44			17 52			18 04		18 14	18 18	18 39	18 42			18 59			19 04
Doncaster	a																19 16						
Wakefield Kirkgate	a		17 57											18 59									
Wakefield Westgate	a			17 47		18 12									18 46								
Leeds	a		18 18	18 02		18 31								19 23	19 01								
York	a			18 28		18 58									19 26		19 39						

A From Penzance to Glasgow Central
B From Norwich to Liverpool Lime Street
C From Southampton Central to Newcastle
D To Lincoln
E From Leicester
F From Newquay to Dundee
G From Reading to Newcastle
H From Paignton to Glasgow Central
I From Plymouth to Edinburgh

For connections from Gatwick Airport see Table 52

London - East Midlands - Sheffield

Saturdays until 21 July

Route Diagram - see first Page of Table 53

Station		EM ◇■ 🍴	NT	XC ◇■ A 🍴	EM ◇ B	XC ◇■ C 🍴		EM D	EM ◇■ 🍴	EM ◇■ 🍴	EM E	EM ◇■ F 🚗🍴	EM ◇■ 🍴	EM ◇■ 🍴	NT	XC ◇■ G 🍴	H	EM ◇ I	XC ◇■ J 🍴	EM	EM ◇■ 🍴	EM ◇■ E 🍴	EM	EM ◇■ 🍴	EM ◇■ 🍴
St Pancras International ⊖	d	17 00							17 15	17 25		17 30	17 55	18 00							18 15	18 25		18 30	18 55
Luton Airport Parkway 7 ✈	d											17 51												18 51	
Luton 10	d	17 23												18 23											
Bedford 7	d	17 38										18 07		18 38										19 07	
Wellingborough	d	17 51										18 20		18 51										19 20	
Kettering 4	a	18 00										18 26		19 00										19 26	
	d	18 01										18 27		19 01										19 27	
Corby	d	18a10												19a10											
Oakham	d																								
Melton Mowbray	d																								
Market Harborough	d								18 12			18 37									19 12			19 37	
Leicester	a								18 29	18 33		18 52	19 02								19 29	19 33		19 52	20 02
	d							18 25	18 30	18 35		18 54	19 04							19 25	19 30	19 35		19 54	20 04
Syston	d							18 32												19 32					
Sileby	d							18 36												19 36					
Barrow Upon Soar	d							18 40												19 40					
Loughborough	d							18 45		18 45	←	19 04								19 45		19 45	←	20 04	
East Midlands Parkway ✈	d							18 54	18 46	18 53	18 54									19 54	19 46	19 53	19 54		
Beeston	a							→			19 02	19 16								→			20 05	20 16	
Nottingham 8	a								18 59		19 14	19 26									19 59		20 15	20 26	
	d		18 15		18 45							19 29			19 15			19 40			20 15		20 29		
Lincoln	a											20 26											21 23		
Langley Mill	d		18 32												19 32						20 33				
Alfreton	d		18 40		19 07										19 40			20 01			20 41				
Long Eaton	a									18 56												19 56			
Derby 6	a									19 09			19 26									20 09			20 26
	d			18 44		19 11				19 18			19 28			19 44			20 11			20 18			20 28
Chesterfield	d		18 55	19 03	19 18	19 30				19 37			19 47		19 52	20 05		20 11	20 30		20 53	20 37			20 47
Sheffield 7	a		19 15	19 18	19 39	19 51				19 52			20 00		20 15	20 19		20 27	20 49		21 14	20 54			21 00
Doncaster 7	a					20 17													21 21						
Wakefield Kirkgate 4	a		19 58												20 57										
Wakefield Westgate 7	a			19 49												20 48					21 59				
Leeds 10	a		20 20	20 05											21 20	21 03					22 19				
York 8	a			20 29		20 40										21 57			21 44						

Station		EM ◇■ 🍴		XC ◇■ K	NT	XC ◇■ L	EM J	EM ◇■ 🍴	EM ◇■ 🍴	EM E	NT	EM ◇■ 🍴		EM ◇■ 🍴	EM ◇■ M 🍴	XC ◇■ D 🍴	EM	EM ◇■ 🍴	EM ◇■ E 🍴	EM	EM ◇■ 🍴	EM ◇■ 🍴	N	EM ◇■ N 🍴	EM ◇■ 🍴
St Pancras International ⊖	d	19 00						19 15	19 25			19 30		19 55	20 00			20 15	20 25		20 30	20 55		21 00	
Luton Airport Parkway 7 ✈	d											19 51									20 51				
Luton 10	d	19 23													20 23									21 23	
Bedford 7	d	19 38										20 07			20 38						21 07			21 38	
Wellingborough	d	19 51										20 20			20 51						21 20			21 51	
Kettering 4	a	20 00										20 26			21 00						21 26			22 00	
	d	20 01										20 27			21 01						21 27			22 01	22 05
Corby	d	20a10													21a10										22a15
Oakham	d																								
Melton Mowbray	d																								
Market Harborough	d							20 12				20 37						21 12			21 37			22 12	
Leicester	a							20 29	20 33			20 52		21 04				21 29	21 33		21 52	22 02		22 29	
	d						20 25	20 30	20 35			20 54		21 06			21 25	21 30	21 35		21 54	22 04		22 30	
Syston	d						20 32										21 32								
Sileby	d						20 36										21 36								
Barrow Upon Soar	d						20 40										21 40								
Loughborough	d						20 45		20 45	←		21 04					21 45		21 45	←	22 04			22 41	
East Midlands Parkway ✈	d						20 54	20 46	20 53	20 54							21 54	21 46	21 53	21 54	22 12				
Beeston	a						→			21 05		21 16					→			22 06	22 17				
Nottingham 8	a							20 59		21 15		21 26						22 01		22 14	22 27				
	d				20 40					21 25	21 15														
Lincoln	a									22 40															
Langley Mill	d				21 02						21 31														
Alfreton	d				21 10						21 39														
Long Eaton	a								20 56										21 57						
Derby 6	a								21 10					21 32					22 10			22 26		23 02	
	d			20 44		21 26								21 34		21 46						22 28			
Chesterfield	d			21 05	21 22	21 46					21 50			21 56		22 08						22 47			
Sheffield 7	a			21 19	21 40	22 05					22 13			22 15		22 23						23 00			
Doncaster 7	a					22 30										22 51									
Wakefield Kirkgate 4	a																								
Wakefield Westgate 7	a			21 49										22 44		23 10									
Leeds 10	a			22 02										23 04		23 27									
York 8	a					22 57																			

A From Plymouth to Edinburgh
B From Norwich to Liverpool Lime Street
C From Southampton Central to Newcastle
D To Nottingham
E From Leicester
F 🚗 from Nottingham 🍴 to Nottingham
G From Plymouth
H From Norwich to Manchester Piccadilly
I From Reading to Newcastle. 🍴 to Sheffield
J To Lincoln
K From Paignton
L From Southampton Central
M From Bournemouth
N from 30 June until 21 July

For connections from Gatwick Airport see Table 52

London - East Midlands - Sheffield

Saturdays until 21 July

Route Diagram - see first Page of Table 53

Station		XC ◇■ A	EM ◇■ B 🍴	EM ◇■ C 🍴	EM ◇■ C 🍴	EM ◇■ D 🍴	EM E 🚌	EM ◇■ F 🍴		EM ◇■ B 🍴	EM ◇■ C 🍴	EM ◇■ C 🍴	EM ◇■ D 🍴	EM E 🚌	EM ◇■ F 🍴	EM ◇■ C 🍴	EM ◇■ D 🍴	EM ◇■ D 🍴		EM ◇■ E 🍴	EM E 🚌
St Pancras International ⊖	d		21 00	21 25	21 30			21 25		21 30		22 00			22 00	22 25				22 25	
Luton Airport Parkway 7 ✈	d				21 51					21 51						22 46				22 46	
Luton 10	d		21 23									22 24			22 24						
Bedford 7	d		21 38		22 07					22 07		22 42			22 42	23 02				23 05	
Wellingborough	d		21 51		22 20					22 20		22 55			22 55	23 14				23 17	
Kettering 4	a		22 07		22 26					22 29		23 02			23 09	23 21				23 27	
	d		22 09		22 27		22 33			22 42	23 00	23 03			23 11	23 22				23 29	23 37
Corby	d		22 20								23a10				23 22						
Oakham	d																				
Melton Mowbray	d																				
Market Harborough	d			22 20	22 37	←	22a58					23 14		23 03		23 32	←	←			00a02
Leicester	a		23 09	22 36	22 51	23 09		23 24		23 42		23 31		23 38	00 12	23 46	23 42	00 12		00 26	
	d		23 16	22 37	22 52	23 16		23 31		23 48		23 32			00 19	23 46	23 48	00 19		00 33	
Syston	d		→							→					→						
Sileby	d																				
Barrow Upon Soar	d																				
Loughborough	d			22 48	23 04	23 27		23 41				23 44	←			23 59	23 59	00 30		00 43	
East Midlands Parkway ✈	d			22 55	23 12			23 53				23 52	23 53			00 07	00 11	00 42		00 55	
Beeston	a							→				23 59						00 50			
Nottingham 8	a			23 05								00 08	00 05					00 57			
	d																				
Lincoln	a																				
Langley Mill	d																				
Alfreton	d																				
Long Eaton	a				23 15											00 10	00 15			01 00	
Derby 6	a				23 26	23 51										00 21	00 26			01 11	
	d	22 33																			
Chesterfield	d	22 54																			
Sheffield 7	a	23 09																			
Doncaster 7	a																				
Wakefield Kirkgate 4	a																				
Wakefield Westgate 7	a																				
Leeds 10	a	23 51																			
York 8	a																				

Saturdays

28 July to 29 September

Station		EM ◇■ 🍴	EM ◇■ G 🍴	EM ◇■ H 🍴	EM ◇■ I J 🚗🍴	EM ◇■ K 🚗🍴	EM ◇■ L 🍴	EM ◇■ M 🍴	EM ◇■ K 🍴	EM ◇■ 🍴	K N	EM ◇■ K 🍴	EM ◇■ K 🍴	EM ◇■ O 🍴	EM ◇■ P 🍴	EM ◇	XC ◇■ Q O 🍴	EM ◇■ 🍴	XC ◇■ R 🍴	EM ◇		XC ◇■ 🍴	EM ◇■ 🍴	NT	EM
St Pancras International ⊖	d	22p00	22p25	22p25	23p15	23p15	00 01	00 15	00 15	00 30		00 45	00 15	01 00	01 15										
Luton Airport Parkway 7 ✈	d		22p48	22p48					00 35				00 44												
Luton 10	d	22p24			23p46	23p46		00 37	00 39				00 47												
Bedford 7	d	22p40	23p04	23p04	00 12	00 12		00 53	00 54				01 12												
Wellingborough	d	22p53	23p17	23p17	00 25	00 25	00 48	01 05	01 07	01 13		01 29	01 33	01 43	01 58										
Kettering 4	a	23p00	23p25	23p25	00 41	00 41	00 54	01 12	01 14	01 19		01 35	01 43	01 50	02 04										
	d	23p01	23p26	23p26	00 42	00 42	00 55	01 13	01 14	01 20		01 36	01 43		02 06										
Corby	d																								
Oakham	d																								
Melton Mowbray	d																								
Market Harborough	d	23p12	23p37	23p37	00 52	00 52	01 05	01 23	01 24	01 30		01 46	01 55		02 16										
Leicester	a	23p29	23p53	23p53	01 05	01 05	01 20	01 38	01 40	01 48		02 01	02 10		02 31										
	d	23p30	23p55	23p55	01 07	01 07	01 22			01 50		02 03													06 36
Syston	d																								06 43
Sileby	d																								06 47
Barrow Upon Soar	d																								06 51
Loughborough	d	23p41	00 06	00 06	01 17	01 17	01 32					02 13													06 56
East Midlands Parkway ✈	d	23p50	00 14	00 14	01 25	01 25	01 40																		07 06
Beeston	a	00 04			01 33	01 38						02 24													07 15
Nottingham 8	a	00 12			01 40	01 45						02 31													07 24
	d				01 47	01 52						02 37				05 20				06 40				07 11	
Lincoln	a																								
Langley Mill	d																							07 27	
Alfreton	d																			07 02				07 35	
Long Eaton	a																								
Derby 6	a		00 34	00 34	02 05	02 10	01 51			02 12		02 55													
	d		00 35	00 40						02 14							05 55	06 26	06 37			07 11	07 20		
Chesterfield	d		00 58	01 18						02 34						05 49	06 31	06 45	06 56	07 13		07 30	07 42	07 50	
Sheffield 7	a		01 13	01 32						02 47						06 15	06 44	07 09	07 09	07 31		07 48	07 59	08 08	
Doncaster 7	a																07 16					08 23			
Wakefield Kirkgate 4	a																							08 57	
Wakefield Westgate 7	a																		07 36						
Leeds 10	a																		07 52					09 20	
York 8	a																07 43		08 23			08 48			

A From Penzance
B until 23 June. To Derby
C from 30 June until 21 July
D until 23 June. From St Pancras International
E until 23 June
F until 23 June. To Nottingham
G not from 22 September until 29 September
H 22 September, 29 September
I 28 July, 4 August, 11 August, 1 September, 8 September. 🚗 from Nottingham 🍴 to Nottingham
J 18 August, 25 August, 15 September, 22 September, 29 September. 🚗 from Nottingham 🍴 to Nottingham
K 28 July, 4 August, 11 August, 1 September, 8 September
L 1 September, 8 September
M 28 July, 4 August, 11 August
N 18 August, 25 August, 15 September, 22 September, 29 September
O To Liverpool Lime Street
P To Newcastle. 🍴 from Sheffield
Q From Birmingham New Street to Glasgow Central
R From Birmingham New Street to Newcastle

For connections from Gatwick Airport see Table 52

London - East Midlands - Sheffield

Saturdays

28 July to 29 September

Route Diagram - see first Page of Table 53

		XC ◇1 A	EM ◇ B	EM	XC ◇1 C	EM ◇1		EM ◇1	EM ◇1	NT	EM ◇1	XC ◇1 D	EM ◇ E	XC ◇1 F	EM G	EM ◇1		EM ◇1 H	EM	EM ◇1	EM ◇1	EM ◇1	NT I	XC ◇1 E	EM ◇
St Pancras International	d					06 10		06 37			06 55					07 00				07 30	07 55	08 00			
Luton Airport Parkway	d										07 16									07 51					
Luton	d					06 33		06 59								07 23						08 23			
Bedford	d					06 48										07 38				08 07		08 38			
Wellingborough	d					07 01										07 51				08 20		08 51			
Kettering	a					07 07		07 27								08 00				08 27		09 00			
	d					07 08		07 28	07 38							08 01				08 27		09 01			
Corby	d								07a48													09a10			
Oakham	d																								
Melton Mowbray	d																								
Market Harborough	d					07 18		07 38								08 12				08 37					
Leicester	a					07 35		07 53			08 04					08 29				08 53	09 02				
	d			07 25		07 36		07 55			08 06				08 25	08 30		08 38		08 54	09 04				
Syston	d			07 32											08 32										
Sileby	d			07 36											08 36										
Barrow Upon Soar	d			07 40											08 40										
Loughborough	d			07 46		07 47		08 05			08 18				08 45	08 41		08 49	←	09 04					
East Midlands Parkway	d			07 57				08 13							08 57	08 50		08 56	08 57						
Beeston	a			08 04							08 31				→				09 05	09 16					
Nottingham	a			08 13							08 42					09 03			09 14	09 26					
	d		07 45							08 11			08 45						09 23				09 15		09 45
Lincoln	a																		10 17						
Langley Mill	d									08 31													09 32		
Alfreton	d		08 07							08 39			09 07										09 40		10 07
Long Eaton	a					07 55												09 00							
Derby	a					08 09		08 26										09 14			09 26				
	d	07 44			08 11	08 18		08 28				08 44		09 11				09 18			09 28			09 44	
Chesterfield	d	08 03	08 18		08 30	08 37		08 47		08 51		09 03	09 18					09 37			09 47		09 52	10 03	10 18
Sheffield	a	08 17	08 38		08 45	08 52		09 07		09 16		09 17	09 38	09 44				09 52			10 00		10 15	10 17	10 38
Doncaster	a				09 18			09 53						10 17											
Wakefield Kirkgate	a									09 57													10 57		
Wakefield Westgate	a	08 45										09 46												10 46	
Leeds	a	09 03								10 18		10 02											11 18	11 02	
York	a	09 27			09 44			10 16				10 26		10 40										11 26	

		XC ◇1 J		EM G	EM ◇1	EM ◇1 H	EM	EM ◇1	EM ◇1	EM ◇1	NT K	XC ◇1	E	EM ◇ L	XC ◇1 G	EM	EM ◇1 H	EM ◇1	EM	EM ◇1	EM ◇1	EM ◇1	I	NT	XC ◇1
St Pancras International	d				08 15	08 25		08 30	08 55	09 00							09 15	09 25		09 30	09 55	10 00			
Luton Airport Parkway	d							08 51												09 51					
Luton	d									09 23												10 23			
Bedford	d							09 07		09 38										10 07		10 38			
Wellingborough	d							09 20		09 51										10 20		10 51			
Kettering	a							09 26		10 00										10 26		11 00			
	d							09 27		10 01										10 27		11 01			
Corby	d									10a10												11a10			
Oakham	d																								
Melton Mowbray	d																								
Market Harborough	d				09 12			09 37									10 12			10 37					
Leicester	a				09 29	09 33		09 52	10 02								10 29	10 33		10 54	11 02				
	d			09 25	09 30	09 35		09 54	10 04							10 25	10 30	10 35		10 54	11 04				
Syston	d			09 32												10 32									
Sileby	d			09 36												10 36									
Barrow Upon Soar	d			09 40												10 40									
Loughborough	d			09 45		09 45	←	10 04								10 45		10 45	←	11 04					
East Midlands Parkway	d			09 54	09 46	09 53	09 54									10 54	10 46	10 53	10 54						
Beeston	a			→			10 02	10 16								→			11 02	11 16					
Nottingham	a				09 59		10 13	10 26									10 59		11 13	11 26					
	d						10 29				10 15			10 45					11 17					11 15	
Lincoln	a						11 30												12 27						
Langley Mill	d										10 32													11 31	
Alfreton	d										10 40			11 07										11 39	
Long Eaton	a					09 56												10 56							
Derby	a					10 09			10 26									11 09			11 26				
	d	10 11				10 18			10 28			10 44			11 11			11 18			11 28				11 44
Chesterfield	d					10 37			10 47		10 52	11 03		11 18				11 37			11 47			11 52	12 03
Sheffield	a	10 42				10 52			11 00		11 15	11 17		11 38	11 41			11 52			12 00			12 16	12 16
Doncaster	a	11 15													12 15										
Wakefield Kirkgate	a										11 57													12 57	
Wakefield Westgate	a											11 46													12 46
Leeds	a										12 18	12 02												13 18	13 02
York	a	11 40										12 26			12 39										13 26

A From Birmingham New Street to Edinburgh
B To Liverpool Lime Street
C From Birmingham New Street to Newcastle
D From Bristol Temple Meads to Glasgow Central
E From Norwich to Liverpool Lime Street
F From Guildford to Newcastle
G To Lincoln
H From Leicester
I From Plymouth to Edinburgh
J From Bournemouth to Newcastle
K From Plymouth to Glasgow Central
L From Southampton Central to Newcastle

For connections from Gatwick Airport see Table 52

Table 53

London - East Midlands - Sheffield

Saturdays

28 July to 29 September

Route Diagram - see first Page of Table 53

		EM ◇ A	XC ◇1 B	EM C	EM ◇1	EM ◇1	EM D	EM ◇1		EM ◇1	EM ◇1	NT	XC ◇1 E	EM ◇ A	XC ◇1 F	EM C	EM ◇1	EM ◇1		EM D	EM ◇1	EM ◇1	EM ◇1	NT	XC ◇1 G
St Pancras International	d				10 15	10 25		10 30		10 55	11 00						11 15	11 25			11 30	11 55	12 00		
Luton Airport Parkway	d							10 51													11 51				
Luton	d										11 23												12 23		
Bedford	d							11 07			11 38										12 07		12 38		
Wellingborough	d							11 20			11 51										12 20		12 51		
Kettering	a							11 26			12 00										12 26		13 00		
	d							11 27			12 01										12 27		13 01		
Corby	d										12a10												13a10		
Oakham	d																								
Melton Mowbray	d																								
Market Harborough	d				11 12			11 37									12 12				12 37				
Leicester	a				11 29	11 33		11 54		12 02							12 29	12 33			12 54	13 02			
	d			11 25	11 30	11 35		11 54		12 04						12 25	12 30	12 35			12 54	13 04			
Syston	d			11 32												12 32									
Sileby	d			11 36												12 36									
Barrow Upon Soar	d			11 40												12 40									
Loughborough	d			11 45		11 45	←	12 04								12 45		12 45		←	13 04				
East Midlands Parkway	d			11 54	11 46	11 53	11 54									12 54	12 46	12 53		12 54					
Beeston	a			→			12 02	12 16								→				13 02	13 16				
Nottingham	a				11 59		12 13	12 26									12 59			13 13	13 27				
	d	11 45					12 27					12 15		12 45						13 17				13 15	
Lincoln	a						13 18													14 23					
Langley Mill	d											12 32												13 32	
Alfreton	d	12 07										12 40		13 07										13 40	
Long Eaton	a					11 56												12 56							
Derby	a					12 09				12 26								13 09				13 26			
	d		12 11			12 18				12 28			12 44		13 11			13 18				13 28			13 44
Chesterfield	d	12 18				12 37				12 47		12 52	13 03	13 18				13 37				13 47		13 52	14 03
Sheffield	a	12 38	12 41			12 52				13 04		13 15	13 17	13 38	13 41			13 52				14 00		14 15	14 17
Doncaster	a		13 17												14 18										
Wakefield Kirkgate	a											13 57												14 57	
Wakefield Westgate	a												13 46												14 46
Leeds	a											14 18	14 02											15 18	15 02
York	a		13 40										14 26		14 40										15 28

		EM ◇ A	XC ◇1 B	EM C		EM ◇1	EM ◇1	EM D	EM ◇1	EM ◇1	EM ◇1	NT	XC ◇1 E	EM ◇ A		XC ◇1 F	EM C	EM ◇1	EM ◇1	EM D	EM ◇1	EM ◇1	EM ◇1	NT	
St Pancras International	d					12 15	12 25		12 30	12 55	13 00							13 15	13 25		13 30	13 55	14 00		
Luton Airport Parkway	d								12 51												13 51				
Luton	d										13 23												14 23		
Bedford	d								13 07		13 38										14 07		14 38		
Wellingborough	d								13 20		13 51										14 20		14 51		
Kettering	a								13 26		14 00										14 26		15 00		
	d								13 27		14 01										14 27		15 01		
Corby	d										14a10												15a10		
Oakham	d																								
Melton Mowbray	d																								
Market Harborough	d					13 12			13 37									14 12			14 37				
Leicester	a					13 29	13 33		13 52	14 02								14 29	14 33		14 54	15 02			
	d			13 25		13 30	13 35		13 54	14 04							14 25	14 30	14 35		14 54	15 04			
Syston	d			13 32													14 32								
Sileby	d			13 36													14 36								
Barrow Upon Soar	d			13 40													14 40								
Loughborough	d			13 45			13 45	←	14 04								14 45		14 45	←	15 04				
East Midlands Parkway	d			13 54		13 46	13 53	13 54									14 54	14 46	14 53	14 54					
Beeston	a			→				14 02	14 16								→			15 02	15 16				
Nottingham	a					13 59		14 13	14 26									14 59		15 13	15 26				
	d	13 45						14 29				14 15		14 45						15 23				15 15	
Lincoln	a							15 22												16 21					
Langley Mill	d											14 30												15 32	
Alfreton	d	14 07										14 38		15 07										15 40	
Long Eaton	a						13 56												14 56						
Derby	a						14 09			14 26									15 09			15 26			
	d		14 11				14 18			14 28			14 44			15 11			15 18			15 28			
Chesterfield	d	14 18					14 37			14 47		14 52	15 03	15 18					15 37			15 47		15 53	
Sheffield	a	14 38	14 41				14 52			15 00		15 15	15 17	15 38		15 41			15 52			16 00		16 14	
Doncaster	a		15 17													16 18									
Wakefield Kirkgate	a											15 57												16 57	
Wakefield Westgate	a												15 46												
Leeds	a											16 18	16 02											17 18	
York	a		15 40										16 26			16 41									

A From Norwich to Liverpool Lime Street
B From Reading to Newcastle
C To Lincoln
D From Leicester
E From Penzance to Glasgow Central
F From Southampton Central to Newcastle
G From Plymouth to Aberdeen

For connections from Gatwick Airport see Table 52

London - East Midlands - Sheffield

28 July to 29 September

Route Diagram - see first Page of Table 53

Station		XC A	EM B	XC C	EM D	EM	EM	EM E	EM	EM	EM	NT	XC F	EM B	XC G	EM D	EM	EM	EM E	EM	EM	EM	NT
St Pancras International ⊖	d					14 15	14 25		14 30	14 55	15 00						15 15	15 25		15 30	15 55	16 00	
Luton Airport Parkway ✈	d								14 51											15 51			
Luton	d										15 23											16 23	
Bedford	d								15 07		15 38									16 07		16 38	
Wellingborough	d								15 20		15 51									16 20		16 51	
Kettering	a								15 26		16 00									16 26		17 00	
	d								15 27		16 01									16 27		17 01	
Corby	d										16a10											17a10	
Oakham	d																						
Melton Mowbray	d																						
Market Harborough	d					15 12			15 37								16 12			16 37			
Leicester	a					15 29	15 33		15 53	16 02							16 29	16 33		16 54	17 02		
	d				15 25	15 30	15 35		15 54	16 04						16 25	16 30	16 35		16 54	17 04		
Syston	d				15 32											16 32							
Sileby	d				15 36											16 36							
Barrow Upon Soar	d				15 40											16 40							
Loughborough	d				15 45		15 45	←	16 04							16 45		16 45	←	17 04			
East Midlands Parkway ✈	d				15 54	15 46	15 53	15 54								16 54	16 45	16 52	16 54				
Beeston	a				→			16 02	16 16							→			17 02	17 16			
Nottingham	a					16 01		16 13	16 26								16 59		17 13	17 26			
	d		15 45					16 14				16 15		16 45					17 13				17 15
Lincoln	a							17 16											18 22				
Langley Mill	d											16 32											17 32
Alfreton	d		16 07									16 40		17 07									17 40
Long Eaton	a						15 56											16 56					
Derby	a						16 09			16 26								17 09			17 26		
	d	15 44		16 11			16 18			16 28			16 41		17 11			17 18			17 28		
Chesterfield	d	16 03	16 18				16 37			16 47		16 55	17 02	17 18				17 37			17 47		17 52
Sheffield	a	16 18	16 38	16 41			16 52			17 00		17 17	17 19	17 34	17 44			17 52			18 04		18 14
Doncaster	a			17 16																			
Wakefield Kirkgate	a											17 57											18 59
Wakefield Westgate	a	16 46											17 47		18 12								
Leeds	a	17 02										18 18	18 02		18 31								19 23
York	a	17 26		17 37									18 28		18 58								

Station		XC H	EM B	XC C	EM D	EM	EM	EM E	EM	EM	EM	NT	XC H	EM B	XC G	EM I	EM	EM	EM E	EM J	EM	EM	NT
St Pancras International ⊖	d					16 15	16 25		16 30	16 55	17 00						17 15	17 25		17 30	17 55	18 00	
Luton Airport Parkway ✈	d								16 51											17 51			
Luton	d										17 23											18 23	
Bedford	d								17 07		17 38									18 07		18 38	
Wellingborough	d								17 20		17 51									18 20		18 51	
Kettering	a								17 26		18 00									18 26		19 00	
	d								17 27		18 01									18 27		19 01	
Corby	d										18a10											19a10	
Oakham	d																						
Melton Mowbray	d																						
Market Harborough	d					17 12			17 37								18 12			18 37			
Leicester	a					17 29	17 33		17 52	18 02							18 29	18 33		18 52	19 02		
	d				17 25	17 30	17 35		17 54	18 04						18 25	18 30	18 35		18 54	19 04		
Syston	d				17 32											18 32							
Sileby	d				17 36											18 36							
Barrow Upon Soar	d				17 40											18 40							
Loughborough	d				17 45		17 45	←	18 04							18 45		18 45	←	19 04			
East Midlands Parkway ✈	d				17 54	17 46	17 53	17 54								18 54	18 46	18 53	18 54				
Beeston	a				→			18 02	18 16							→			19 02	19 16			
Nottingham	a					17 59		18 12	18 26								18 59		19 14	19 26			
	d		17 45					18 15				18 15		18 45						19 29			19 15
Lincoln	a							19 25												20 26			
Langley Mill	d		18 03									18 32											19 32
Alfreton	d		18 10									18 40		19 07									19 40
Long Eaton	a						17 56											18 56					
Derby	a						18 09			18 26								19 09			19 26		
	d	17 44		18 11			18 18			18 28			18 44		19 11			19 18			19 28		
Chesterfield	d	18 03	18 22				18 39			18 47		18 55	19 03	19 18	19 30			19 37			19 47		19 52
Sheffield	a	18 18	18 39	18 42			18 59			19 04		19 15	19 18	19 39	19 51			19 52			20 00		20 15
Doncaster	a			19 16											20 17								
Wakefield Kirkgate	a											19 58											20 57
Wakefield Westgate	a	18 46											19 49										
Leeds	a	19 01										20 20	20 05										21 20
York	a	19 26		19 39									20 29		20 40								

A From Newquay to Dundee
B From Norwich to Liverpool Lime Street
C From Reading to Newcastle
D To Lincoln
E From Leicester
F From Plymouth to Glasgow Central
G From Southampton Central to Newcastle
H From Plymouth to Newcastle
I To Nottingham
J from Nottingham to Nottingham

For connections from Gatwick Airport see Table 52

London - East Midlands - Sheffield

28 July to 29 September

Route Diagram - see first Page of Table 53

Station		XC A	EM B	XC C	XC D	EM E	EM	EM	EM F	EM	EM	EM	XC G	XC H	NT	XC I	EM E	EM	EM	EM F	NT	EM
St Pancras International ⊖	d						18 15	18 25		18 30	18 55	19 00						19 15	19 25			19 30
Luton Airport Parkway ✈	d									18 51												19 51
Luton	d											19 23										
Bedford	d									19 07		19 38										20 07
Wellingborough	d									19 20		19 51										20 20
Kettering	a									19 26		20 00										20 26
	d									19 27		20 01										20 27
Corby	d											20a10										
Oakham	d																					
Melton Mowbray	d																					
Market Harborough	d						19 12			19 37								20 12				20 37
Leicester	a						19 29	19 33		19 52	20 02							20 29	20 33			20 52
	d					19 25	19 30	19 35		19 54	20 04						20 25	20 30	20 35			20 54
Syston	d					19 32											20 32					
Sileby	d					19 36											20 36					
Barrow Upon Soar	d					19 40											20 40					
Loughborough	d					19 45		19 45	←	20 04							20 45		20 45	←		21 04
East Midlands Parkway ✈	d					19 54	19 46	19 53	19 54								20 54	20 46	20 53	20 54		
Beeston	a					→			20 05	20 16							→			21 05		21 16
Nottingham	a						19 59		20 15	20 26								20 59		21 15		21 26
	d		19 40				20 15		20 29						20 40					21 25	21 15	
Lincoln	a								21 23											22 40		
Langley Mill	d						20 33								21 02						21 31	
Alfreton	d		20 01				20 41								21 10						21 39	
Long Eaton	a							19 56											20 56			
Derby	a							20 09			20 26								21 10			
	d	19 44		20 11	20 11			20 18			20 28		20 44	20 44		21 26						
Chesterfield	d	20 05	20 11	20 30	20 30		20 53	20 37			20 47		21 05	21 05	21 22	21 46					21 50	
Sheffield	a	20 19	20 27	20 49	20 49		21 14	20 54			21 00		21 19	21 19	21 40	22 05					22 13	
Doncaster	a			21 21	21 21											22 30						
Wakefield Kirkgate	a																					
Wakefield Westgate	a	20 48					21 59						21 48	21 49								
Leeds	a	21 03					22 19						22 02	22 02								
York	a	21 57		21 44	21 45											22 57						

Station		EM	EM	XC J	XC G	EM K	EM	EM	EM F	EM	EM	EM L	XC M	EM N	EM L	EM L	EM O	EM L	EM P	EM P	EM Q	EM N	EM L
St Pancras International ⊖	d	19 55	20 00				20 15	20 25		20 30	20 55	21 00		21 00	21 25		21 25	21 30				21 30	
Luton Airport Parkway ✈	d									20 51								21 51				21 51	
Luton	d		20 23									21 23		21 23									
Bedford	d		20 38							21 07		21 38		21 38				22 07				22 07	
Wellingborough	d		20 51							21 20		21 51		21 51				22 20				22 20	
Kettering	a		21 00							21 26		22 00		22 02			22 15	22 26				22 29	
	d		21 01							21 27		22 01		22 03		22 05	22 16	22 27			22 34	22 36	23 00
Corby	d		21a10											22 14		22a15	22 27						23a10
Oakham	d																						
Melton Mowbray	d																						
Market Harborough	d						21 12			21 37		22 12			22 20			22 37	←	←	22a59		
Leicester	a	21 04					21 29	21 33		21 52	22 02	22 29		23 01	22 36		23 17	22 51	23 01	23 17		23 34	
	d	21 06				21 25	21 30	21 35		21 54	22 04	22 30		23 07	22 37		23 24	22 52	23 07	23 24		23 42	
Syston	d					21 32								→			→					→	
Sileby	d					21 36																	
Barrow Upon Soar	d					21 40																	
Loughborough	d					21 45		21 45	←	22 04		22 41			22 48			23 04	23 18	23 34			
East Midlands Parkway ✈	d					21 54	21 46	21 53	21 54	22 12					22 55			23 12		23 42			
Beeston	a					→			22 06	22 17													
Nottingham	a						22 01		22 14	22 27					23 05					23 52			
	d																						
Lincoln	a																						
Langley Mill	d																						
Alfreton	d																						
Long Eaton	a							21 57										23 15					
Derby	a	21 32						22 10			22 26	23 02						23 26	23 38				
	d	21 34		21 46	21 48						22 28		22 33										
Chesterfield	d	21 56		22 08	22 08						22 47		22 54										
Sheffield	a	22 15		22 23	22 23						23 00		23 09										
Doncaster	a			22 51	22 51																		
Wakefield Kirkgate	a																						
Wakefield Westgate	a	22 44		23 10	23 10																		
Leeds	a	23 04		23 27	23 27								23 51										
York	a																						

A From Plymouth
B From Norwich to Manchester Piccadilly
C from 28 July until 8 September. From Reading to Newcastle. to Sheffield
D 15 September, 22 September, 29 September. From Reading to Newcastle. to Sheffield
E To Lincoln
F From Leicester
G 15 September, 22 September, 29 September. From Plymouth
H from 28 July until 8 September. From Paignton
I From Southampton Central
J from 28 July until 8 September. From Bournemouth
K To Nottingham
L from 28 July until 8 September
M from 28 July until 8 September. From Penzance
N 15 September, 22 September, 29 September. To Derby
O 15 September, 22 September, 29 September. To Nottingham
P 15 September, 22 September, 29 September. From St Pancras International
Q 15 September, 22 September, 29 September

For connections from Gatwick Airport see Table 52

Table 53

Saturdays
28 July to 29 September

London - East Midlands - Sheffield

Route Diagram - see first Page of Table 53

		EM	EM	EM	EM	EM	EM	EM	EM
		◇1	◇1	◇1		◇1	◇1	◇1	
		A	B	C	D	B	C	D	D
					🚌				🚌
		🍴	🍴	🍴		🍴	🍴	🍴	
St Pancras International ⊖	d	22 00	22 00			22 25		22 25	
Luton Airport Parkway 7 ✈	d					22 46		22 46	
Luton 10	d	22 24	22 24						
Bedford 7	d	22 40	22 42			23 02		23 02	
Wellingborough	d	22 53	22 55			23 14		23 14	
Kettering 4	a	23 02	23 02			23 21		23 23	
	d	23 03	23 03			23 22		23 24	23 37
Corby	d	23 14							
Oakham	d								
Melton Mowbray	d								
Market Harborough	d		23 14	←	23 03	23 32	←		00a02
Leicester	a	23 59	23 31	23 34	23 38	23 46	23 59	00 16	
	d	00 06	23 32	23 42		23 46	00 06	00 23	
Syston	d	→							
Sileby	d								
Barrow Upon Soar	d								
Loughborough	d		23 44	23 52		23 59	00 17	00 33	
East Midlands Parkway ✈	d		23 52	23 59		00 07	00 26	00 41	
Beeston	a		23 59				00 32		
Nottingham 8 ⇌	a		00 08				00 42		
	d								
Lincoln	a								
Langley Mill	d								
Alfreton	d								
Long Eaton	a			00 04		00 10		00 44	
Derby 6	a			00 15		00 21		00 55	
	d								
Chesterfield	d								
Sheffield 7 ⇌	a								
Doncaster 7	a								
Wakefield Kirkgate 4	a								
Wakefield Westgate 7	a								
Leeds 10	a								
York 8	a								

Saturdays
from 6 October

		EM	EM	EM	EM	EM	XC	EM	XC	EM	XC	EM	NT	EM	XC	EM	EM	XC	EM	EM	EM	NT	EM
		◇1	◇1	◇1	◇1	◇	◇1	◇1	◇1	◇	◇1	◇1			◇1	◇		◇1	◇1	◇1	◇1		◇1
				E		F	G		H	F	I				J	F		I					
		🍴	🍴	🛒🍴	🍴		🍴	🍴	🍴		🍴	🍴			🍴			🍴	🍴	🍴	🍴		🍴
St Pancras International ⊖	d	22p00	22p25	23p15	00 15														06 10	06 37			06 55
Luton Airport Parkway 7 ✈	d		22p48		00 44																		07 16
Luton 10	d	22p24		23p46	00 47														06 33	06 59			
Bedford 7	d	22p40	23p04	00 12	01 12														06 48				
Wellingborough	d	22p53	23p17	00 25	01 33														07 01				
Kettering 4	a	23p00	23p25	00 41	01 43														07 07	07 27			
	d	23p01	23p26	00 42	01 43														07 08	07 28	07 38		
Corby	d																				07a48		
Oakham	d																						
Melton Mowbray	d																						
Market Harborough	d	23p12	23p37	00 52	01 55														07 18	07 38			
Leicester	a	23p29	23p53	01 05	02 10														07 35	07 53			08 04
	d	23p30	23p55	01 07										06 36			07 25		07 36	07 55			08 06
Syston	d													06 43			07 32						
Sileby	d													06 47			07 36						
Barrow Upon Soar	d													06 51			07 40						
Loughborough	d	23p41	00 06	01 17										06 56			07 46		07 47	08 05			08 18
East Midlands Parkway ✈	d	23p50	00 14	01 25										07 06			07 57			08 13			
Beeston	a	00 04		01 38										07 15			08 04						08 31
Nottingham 8 ⇌	a	00 12		01 45										07 24			08 13						08 42
	d			01 52		05 20				06 40			07 11			07 45						08 11	
Lincoln	a																						
Langley Mill	d												07 27									08 31	
Alfreton	d									07 02			07 35			08 07						08 39	
Long Eaton	a																		07 55				
Derby 6	a		00 34	02 10															08 09	08 26			
	d		00 40				05 55	06 26	06 37		07 11	07 20			07 44			08 11	08 18	08 28			
Chesterfield	d		01 18			05 49	06 31	06 45	06 56	07 13	07 30	07 42	07 50		08 03	08 18		08 30	08 37	08 47		08 51	
Sheffield 7 ⇌	a		01 32			06 15	06 44	07 09	07 09	07 31	07 48	07 59	08 08		08 17	08 38		08 45	08 52	09 07		09 16	
Doncaster 7	a						07 16				08 23							09 18		09 53			
Wakefield Kirkgate 4	a												08 57									09 57	
Wakefield Westgate 7	a								07 36						08 45								
Leeds 10	a								07 52				09 20		09 03							10 18	
York 8	a						07 43		08 23		08 48				09 27			09 44		10 16			

A 15 September, 22 September, 29 September. To Nottingham
B from 28 July until 8 September
C 15 September, 22 September, 29 September. From St Pancras International
D 15 September, 22 September, 29 September
E 🛒 from Nottingham 🍴 to Nottingham
F To Liverpool Lime Street
G To Newcastle. 🍴 from Sheffield
H From Birmingham New Street to Glasgow Central
I From Birmingham New Street to Newcastle
J From Birmingham New Street to Edinburgh

For connections from Gatwick Airport see Table 52

Table 53

Saturdays
from 6 October

London - East Midlands - Sheffield

Route Diagram - see first Page of Table 53

		XC	EM	XC	EM	EM	EM	EM	EM	EM	EM	NT	XC	EM	XC	EM	EM	EM	EM	EM	EM	EM	NT
		◇1	◇	◇1		◇1	◇1		◇1	◇1	◇1		◇1	◇	◇1		◇1	◇1		◇1	◇1	◇1	
		A	B	C	D			E					F	B	G	D			E				
		🍴		🍴		🍴	🍴		🍴	🍴	🍴		🍴		🍴		🍴	🍴		🍴	🍴	🍴	
St Pancras International ⊖	d					07 00			07 30	07 55	08 00						08 15	08 25		08 30	08 55	09 00	
Luton Airport Parkway 7 ✈	d								07 51											08 51			
Luton 10	d					07 23					08 23											09 23	
Bedford 7	d					07 38			08 07		08 38									09 07		09 38	
Wellingborough	d					07 51			08 20		08 51									09 20		09 51	
Kettering 4	a					08 00			08 27		09 00									09 26		10 00	
	d					08 01			08 27		09 01									09 27		10 01	
Corby	d										09a10											10a10	
Oakham	d																						
Melton Mowbray	d																						
Market Harborough	d					08 12			08 37								09 12			09 37			
Leicester	a					08 29			08 53	09 02							09 29	09 33		09 52	10 02		
	d				08 25	08 30	08 38		08 54	09 04						09 25	09 30	09 35		09 54	10 04		
Syston	d				08 32											09 32							
Sileby	d				08 36											09 36							
Barrow Upon Soar	d				08 40											09 40							
Loughborough	d				08 45	08 41	08 49	←	09 04							09 45		09 45	←	10 04			
East Midlands Parkway ✈	d				08 57	08 50	08 56	08 57								09 54	09 46	09 53	09 54				
Beeston	a				→			09 05	09 16							→			10 02	10 16			
Nottingham 8 ⇌	a					09 03		09 14	09 26								09 59		10 13	10 26			
	d		08 45					09 23				09 15		09 45					10 29				10 15
Lincoln	a							10 18											11 32				
Langley Mill	d											09 32											10 32
Alfreton	d		09 07									09 40		10 07									10 40
Long Eaton	a						09 00											09 56					
Derby 6	a						09 14			09 26								10 09			10 26		
	d	08 44		09 11			09 18			09 28			09 44		10 11			10 18			10 28		
Chesterfield	d	09 03	09 18				09 37			09 47		09 52	10 03	10 18				10 37			10 47		10 52
Sheffield 7 ⇌	a	09 17	09 38	09 44			09 52			10 00		10 15	10 17	10 38	10 42			10 52			11 00		11 15
Doncaster 7	a			10 17											11 15								
Wakefield Kirkgate 4	a											10 57											11 57
Wakefield Westgate 7	a	09 46											10 46										
Leeds 10	a	10 02										11 18	11 02										12 18
York 8	a	10 26		10 40									11 26		11 40								

		XC	EM	XC	EM	EM	EM	EM	EM	EM	EM	NT	XC	EM	XC	EM	EM	EM	EM	EM	EM	EM
		◇1	◇	◇1		◇1	◇1		◇1	◇1	◇1		◇1	◇	◇1		◇1	◇1		◇1	◇1	◇1
		H	B	I	D			E					F	B	J	D			E			
		🍴		🍴		🍴	🍴		🍴	🍴	🍴		🍴		🍴		🍴	🍴		🍴	🍴	🍴
St Pancras International ⊖	d					09 15	09 25		09 30	09 55	10 00						10 15	10 25		10 30	10 55	11 00
Luton Airport Parkway 7 ✈	d								09 51											10 51		
Luton 10	d										10 23											11 23
Bedford 7	d								10 07		10 38									11 07		11 38
Wellingborough	d								10 20		10 51									11 20		11 51
Kettering 4	a								10 26		11 00									11 26		12 00
	d								10 27		11 01									11 27		12 01
Corby	d										11a10											12a10
Oakham	d																					
Melton Mowbray	d																					
Market Harborough	d					10 12			10 37								11 12			11 37		
Leicester	a					10 29	10 33		10 54	11 02							11 29	11 33		11 54	12 02	
	d				10 25	10 30	10 35		10 54	11 04						11 25	11 30	11 35		11 54	12 04	
Syston	d				10 32											11 32						
Sileby	d				10 36											11 36						
Barrow Upon Soar	d				10 40											11 40						
Loughborough	d				10 45		10 45	←	11 04							11 45		11 45	←	12 04		
East Midlands Parkway ✈	d				10 54	10 46	10 53	10 54								11 54	11 46	11 53	11 54			
Beeston	a				→			11 02	11 16							→			12 02	12 16		
Nottingham 8 ⇌	a					10 59		11 13	11 26								11 59		12 13	12 26		
	d		10 45					11 17				11 15		11 45					12 27			
Lincoln	a							12 29											13 20			
Langley Mill	d											11 31										
Alfreton	d		11 07									11 39		12 07								
Long Eaton	a						10 56											11 56				
Derby 6	a						11 09			11 26								12 09			12 26	
	d	10 44		11 11			11 18			11 28			11 44		12 11			12 18			12 28	
Chesterfield	d	11 03	11 18				11 37			11 47		11 52	12 03	12 18				12 37			12 47	
Sheffield 7 ⇌	a	11 17	11 38	11 41			11 52			12 00		12 16	12 16	12 38	12 41			12 52			13 04	
Doncaster 7	a			12 15											13 17							
Wakefield Kirkgate 4	a											12 57										
Wakefield Westgate 7	a	11 46											12 46									
Leeds 10	a	12 02										13 18	13 02									
York 8	a	12 26		12 39									13 26		13 40							

A From Bristol Temple Meads to Glasgow Central
B From Norwich to Liverpool Lime Street
C From Guildford to Newcastle
D To Lincoln
E From Leicester
F From Plymouth to Edinburgh
G From Bournemouth to Newcastle
H From Plymouth to Glasgow Central
I From Southampton Central to Newcastle
J From Reading to Newcastle

For connections from Gatwick Airport see Table 52

London - East Midlands - Sheffield

Route Diagram - see first Page of Table 53

	NT	XC ◇1 A ✠	EM ◇ B	XC ◇1 C ✠	EM D	EM ◇1 ✠	EM ◇1 ✠	EM E	EM ◇1 ✠	EM ◇1 ✠	EM ◇1 ✠	NT	XC ◇1 F ✠	EM ◇ B	XC ◇1 G ✠	EM D	EM ◇1 ✠	EM ◇1 ✠	EM E	EM ◇1 ✠	EM ◇1 ✠	EM ◇1 ✠
St Pancras International ⊖ d						11 15	11 25		11 30	11 55	12 00						12 15	12 25		12 30	12 55	13 00
Luton Airport Parkway ✈ d									11 51											12 51		
Luton d											12 23											13 23
Bedford d									12 07		12 38									13 07		13 38
Wellingborough d									12 20		12 51									13 20		13 51
Kettering a									12 26		13 00									13 26		14 00
d									12 27		13 01									13 27		14 01
Corby d											13a10											14a10
Oakham d																						
Melton Mowbray d																						
Market Harborough d						12 12			12 37								13 12			13 37		
Leicester a						12 29	12 33		12 54	13 02							13 29	13 33		13 52	14 02	
d					12 25	12 30	12 35		12 54	13 04						13 25	13 30	13 35		13 54	14 04	
Syston d					12 32											13 32						
Sileby d					12 36											13 36						
Barrow Upon Soar d					12 40											13 40						
Loughborough d					12 45		12 45	←	13 04							13 45		13 45	←	14 04		
East Midlands Parkway ✈ d					12 54	12 46	12 53	12 54								13 54	13 46	13 53	13 54			
Beeston a					→			13 02	13 16							→			14 02	14 16		
Nottingham a						12 59		13 13	13 27								13 59		14 13	14 26		
d	12 15		12 45					13 17				13 15		13 45					14 29			
Lincoln a								14 26											15 24			
Langley Mill d	12 32											13 32										
Alfreton d	12 40		13 07									13 40		14 07								
Long Eaton a							12 56											13 56				
Derby a							13 09			13 26								14 09			14 26	
d		12 44		13 11			13 18			13 28			13 44		14 11			14 18			14 28	
Chesterfield d	12 52	13 03	13 18				13 37			13 47		13 52	14 03	14 18				14 37			14 47	
Sheffield a	13 15	13 17	13 38	13 41			13 52			14 00		14 15	14 17	14 38	14 41			14 52			15 00	
Doncaster a				14 18											15 17							
Wakefield Kirkgate a	13 57											14 57										
Wakefield Westgate a		13 46											14 46									
Leeds a	14 18	14 02										15 18	15 02									
York a		14 26		14 40									15 28		15 40							

	NT	XC ◇1 A ✠	EM ◇ B	XC ◇1 C ✠	EM D	EM ◇1 ✠	EM ◇1 ✠	EM E	EM ◇1 ✠	EM ◇1 ✠	EM ◇1 ✠	NT	XC ◇1 H ✠	EM ◇ B	XC ◇1 G ✠	EM D	EM ◇1 ✠	EM ◇1 ✠	EM E	EM ◇1 ✠	EM ◇1 ✠
St Pancras International ⊖ d						13 15	13 25		13 30	13 55	14 00						14 15	14 25		14 30	14 55
Luton Airport Parkway ✈ d									13 51											14 51	
Luton d											14 23										
Bedford d									14 07		14 38									15 07	
Wellingborough d									14 20		14 51									15 20	
Kettering a									14 26		15 00									15 26	
d									14 27		15 01									15 27	
Corby d											15a10										
Oakham d																					
Melton Mowbray d																					
Market Harborough d						14 12			14 37								15 12			15 37	
Leicester a						14 29	14 33		14 54	15 02							15 29	15 33		15 53	16 02
d					14 25	14 30	14 35		14 54	15 04						15 25	15 30	15 35		15 54	16 04
Syston d					14 32											15 32					
Sileby d					14 36											15 36					
Barrow Upon Soar d					14 40											15 40					
Loughborough d					14 45		14 45	←	15 04							15 45		15 45	←	16 04	
East Midlands Parkway ✈ d					14 54	14 46	14 53	14 54								15 54	15 46	15 53	15 54		
Beeston a					→			15 02	15 16							→			16 02	16 16	
Nottingham a						14 59		15 13	15 26								16 01		16 13	16 26	
d	14 15		14 45					15 23				15 15		15 45					16 14		
Lincoln a								16 23											17 17		
Langley Mill d	14 30											15 32									
Alfreton d	14 38		15 07									15 40		16 07							
Long Eaton a							14 56											15 56			
Derby a							15 09			15 26								16 09			16 26
d		14 44		15 11			15 18			15 28			15 44		16 11			16 18			16 28
Chesterfield d	14 52	15 03	15 18				15 37			15 47		15 53	16 03	16 18				16 37			16 47
Sheffield a	15 15	15 17	15 38	15 41			15 52			16 00		16 14	16 18	16 38	16 41			16 52			17 00
Doncaster a				16 18											17 16						
Wakefield Kirkgate a	15 57											16 57									
Wakefield Westgate a		15 46											16 46								
Leeds a	16 18	16 02										17 18	17 02								
York a		16 26		16 41									17 26		17 37						

A From Penzance to Glasgow Central
B From Norwich to Liverpool Lime Street
C From Southampton Central to Newcastle
D To Lincoln
E From Leicester
F From Plymouth to Aberdeen
G From Reading to Newcastle
H From Plymouth to Dundee

For connections from Gatwick Airport see Table 52

Table 53

Saturdays
from 6 October

London - East Midlands - Sheffield

Route Diagram - see first Page of Table 53

	EM ◇1 ✠	NT	XC ◇1 A ✠	EM ◇ B	XC ◇1 C ✠	EM D	EM ◇1 ✠	EM ◇1 ✠	EM E	EM ◇1 ✠	EM ◇1 ✠	EM ◇1 ✠	NT	XC ◇1 F ✠	EM ◇ B	XC ◇1 G ✠	EM D	EM ◇1 ✠	EM ◇1 ✠	EM E	EM ◇1 ✠	EM ◇1 ✠
St Pancras International ⊖ d	15 00						15 15	15 25		15 30	15 55	16 00						16 15	16 25		16 30	16 55
Luton Airport Parkway ✈ d										15 51											16 51	
Luton d	15 23											16 23										
Bedford d	15 38									16 07		16 38									17 07	
Wellingborough d	15 51									16 20		16 51									17 20	
Kettering a	16 00									16 26		17 00									17 26	
d	16 01									16 27		17 01									17 27	
Corby d	16a10											17a10										
Oakham d																						
Melton Mowbray d																						
Market Harborough d							16 12			16 37								17 12			17 37	
Leicester a							16 29	16 33		16 54	17 02							17 29	17 33		17 52	18 02
d						16 25	16 30	16 35		16 54	17 04						17 25	17 30	17 35		17 54	18 04
Syston d						16 32											17 32					
Sileby d						16 36											17 36					
Barrow Upon Soar d						16 40											17 40					
Loughborough d						16 45		16 45	←	17 04							17 45		17 45	←	18 04	
East Midlands Parkway ✈ d						16 54	16 45	16 52	16 54								17 54	17 46	17 53	17 54		
Beeston a						→			17 02	17 16							→			18 02	18 16	
Nottingham a							16 59		17 13	17 26								17 59		18 12	18 26	
d		16 15		16 45					17 13				17 15		17 45					18 15		
Lincoln a									18 24											19 27		
Langley Mill d		16 32											17 32		18 03							
Alfreton d		16 40		17 07									17 40		18 10							
Long Eaton a								16 56											17 56			
Derby a								17 09			17 26								18 09			18 26
d			16 41		17 11			17 18			17 28			17 44		18 11			18 18			18 28
Chesterfield d		16 55	17 02	17 18				17 37			17 47		17 52	18 03	18 22				18 39			18 47
Sheffield a		17 17	17 19	17 34	17 44			17 52			18 04		18 14	18 18	18 39	18 42			18 59			19 04
Doncaster a																19 16						
Wakefield Kirkgate a		17 57											18 59									
Wakefield Westgate a			17 47		18 12									18 46								
Leeds a		18 18	18 02		18 31								19 23	19 01								
York a			18 28		18 58									19 26		19 39						

	EM ◇1 ✠	NT	XC ◇1 F ✠	EM ◇ B	XC ◇1 C ✠	EM H	EM ◇1 ✠	EM ◇1 ✠	EM E	EM ◇1 I ✠	EM ◇1 ✠	EM ◇1 ✠	NT	XC ◇1 J ✠	EM ◇ K	XC ◇1 L ✠	EM D	EM ◇1 ✠	EM ◇1 ✠	EM E	EM ◇1 ✠	EM ◇1 ✠
St Pancras International ⊖ d	17 00						17 15	17 25		17 30	17 55	18 00						18 15	18 25		18 30	18 55
Luton Airport Parkway ✈ d										17 51											18 51	
Luton d	17 23											18 23										
Bedford d	17 38									18 07		18 38									19 07	
Wellingborough d	17 51									18 20		18 51									19 20	
Kettering a	18 00									18 26		19 00									19 26	
d	18 01									18 27		19 01									19 27	
Corby d	18a10											19a10										
Oakham d																						
Melton Mowbray d																						
Market Harborough d							18 12			18 37								19 12			19 37	
Leicester a							18 29	18 33		18 52	19 02							19 29	19 33		19 52	20 02
d						18 25	18 30	18 35		18 54	19 04						19 25	19 30	19 35		19 54	20 04
Syston d						18 32											19 32					
Sileby d						18 36											19 36					
Barrow Upon Soar d						18 40											19 40					
Loughborough d						18 45		18 45	←	19 04							19 45		19 45	←	20 04	
East Midlands Parkway ✈ d						18 54	18 46	18 53	18 54								19 54	19 46	19 53	19 54		
Beeston a						→			19 02	19 16							→			20 05	20 16	
Nottingham a							18 59		19 14	19 26								19 59		20 15	20 26	
d		18 15		18 45						19 29			19 15		19 40			20 15		20 29		
Lincoln a										20 26										21 23		
Langley Mill d		18 32											19 32					20 33				
Alfreton d		18 40		19 07									19 40		20 01			20 41				
Long Eaton a								18 56											19 56			
Derby a								19 09			19 26								20 09			20 26
d			18 44		19 11			19 18			19 28			19 44		20 11			20 18			20 28
Chesterfield d		18 55	19 03	19 18	19 30			19 37			19 47		19 52	20 05	20 11	20 30		20 53	20 37			20 47
Sheffield a		19 15	19 18	19 39	19 51			19 52			20 00		20 15	20 19	20 27	20 49		21 14	20 54			21 00
Doncaster a					20 17											21 21						
Wakefield Kirkgate a		19 58											20 57									
Wakefield Westgate a			19 49											20 48				21 59				
Leeds a		20 20	20 05										21 20	21 03				22 19				
York a			20 29		20 40									21 57		21 45						

A From Plymouth to Glasgow Central
B From Norwich to Liverpool Lime Street
C From Southampton Central to Newcastle
D To Lincoln
E From Leicester
F From Plymouth to Newcastle
G From Reading to Newcastle
H To Nottingham
I Restaurant from Nottingham ✠ to Nottingham
J From Plymouth
K From Norwich to Manchester Piccadilly
L From Reading to Newcastle. ✠ to Sheffield

For connections from Gatwick Airport see Table 52

Table 53

London - East Midlands - Sheffield

Saturdays from 6 October

Route Diagram - see first Page of Table 53

		EM	XC	NT	XC	EM	EM	EM	EM	NT	EM	EM	EM	XC	EM	EM	EM	EM	EM	EM	EM	EM
		◇1	◇1		◇1		◇1	◇1			◇1	◇1	◇1	◇1		◇1	◇1		◇1	◇1	◇1	◇1
			A		B	C			D					A	E			D			F	G
		🍴					🍴	🍴			🍴	🍴	🍴			🍴	🍴		🍴	🍴	🍴	🍴
St Pancras International ⊖	d	19 00					19 15	19 25			19 30	19 55	20 00			20 15	20 25		20 30	20 55	21 00	21 00
Luton Airport Parkway 7 ✈	d										19 51								20 51			
Luton 10	d	19 23											20 23								21 23	21 23
Bedford 7	d	19 38									20 07		20 38						21 07		21 38	21 38
Wellingborough	d	19 51									20 20		20 51						21 20		21 51	21 51
Kettering 4	a	20 00									20 26		21 00						21 26		22 00	22 02
	d	20 01									20 27		21 01						21 27		22 01	22 03
Corby	d	20a10											21a10									22 14
Oakham	d																					
Melton Mowbray	d																					
Market Harborough	d						20 12				20 37					21 12			21 37		22 12	
Leicester	a						20 29	20 33			20 52	21 04				21 29	21 33		21 52	22 02	22 29	23 01
	d					20 25	20 30	20 35			20 54	21 06			21 25	21 30	21 35		21 54	22 04	22 30	23 07 →
Syston	d					20 32									21 32							
Sileby	d					20 36									21 36							
Barrow Upon Soar	d					20 40									21 40							
Loughborough	d					20 45		20 45	←		21 04				21 45		21 45	←	22 04		22 41	
East Midlands Parkway ✈	d					20 54	20 46	20 53	20 54						21 54	21 46	21 53	21 54	22 12			
Beeston	a					→			21 05		21 16				→			22 06	22 17			
Nottingham 8 🚢	a						20 59		21 15		21 26					22 01		22 14	22 27			
	d			20 40					21 25	21 15												
Lincoln	a								22 40													
Langley Mill	d			21 02						21 31												
Alfreton	d			21 10						21 39												
Long Eaton	a							20 56									21 57					
Derby 6	a							21 10				21 32					22 10			22 26	23 02	
	d		20 44		21 26							21 34		21 48						22 28		
Chesterfield	d		21 05	21 22	21 46					21 50		21 56		22 08						22 47		
Sheffield 7 🚢	a		21 19	21 40	22 05					22 13		22 15		22 23						23 00		
Doncaster 7	a				22 30									22 51								
Wakefield Kirkgate 4	a																					
Wakefield Westgate 7	a		21 48									22 44		23 10								
Leeds 10	a		22 02									23 04		23 27								
York 8	a				22 57																	

		EM	EM	EM	EM	EM	EM	EM	EM	EM	EM	EM	EM	EM	EM	EM	EM	EM
		◇1	◇1	◇1	◇1	◇1	◇1		◇1	◇1	◇1	◇1	◇1		◇1	◇1	◇1	
		F	F	H	F	I	I	J	G F	H	F	I	J	F	I	J	J	
		🍴	🍴	🍴	🍴	🍴	🍴	🚌	🍴	🍴	🍴	🍴	🍴	🚌	🍴	🍴	🍴	🚌
St Pancras International ⊖	d	21 25		21 25	21 30				21 30		22 00	22 00			22 25		22 25	
Luton Airport Parkway 7 ✈	d				21 51				21 51						22 46		22 46	
Luton 10	d										22 24	22 24						
Bedford 7	d				22 07				22 07		22 40	22 42			23 02		23 02	
Wellingborough	d				22 20				22 20		22 53	22 55			23 14		23 14	
Kettering 4	a			22 15	22 26				22 29		23 02	23 02			23 21		23 23	
	d		22 05	22 16	22 27			22 34	22 36	23 00	23 03	23 03			23 22		23 24	23 37
Corby	d		22a15	22 27						23a10	23 14							
Oakham	d																	
Melton Mowbray	d																	
Market Harborough	d	22 20			22 37	←	←	22a59				23 14	←	23 03	23 32	←		00a02
Leicester	a	22 36		23 17	22 51	23 01	23 17		23 34		23 59	23 31	23 34	23 38	23 46	23 59	00 16	
	d	22 37		23 24	22 52	23 07	23 24		23 42		00 06	23 32	23 42		23 46	00 06	00 23	
Syston	d			→					→		→							
Sileby	d																	
Barrow Upon Soar	d																	
Loughborough	d	22 48			23 04	23 18	23 34					23 44	23 52		23 59	00 17	00 33	
East Midlands Parkway ✈	d	22 55			23 12		23 42					23 52	23 59		00 07	00 26	00 41	
Beeston	a											23 59				00 32		
Nottingham 8 🚢	a	23 05					23 52					00 08				00 42		
	d																	
Lincoln	a																	
Langley Mill	d																	
Alfreton	d																	
Long Eaton	a				23 15								00 04		00 10		00 44	
Derby 6	a				23 26	23 38							00 15		00 21		00 55	
	d																	
Chesterfield	d																	
Sheffield 7 🚢	a																	
Doncaster 7	a																	
Wakefield Kirkgate 4	a																	
Wakefield Westgate 7	a																	
Leeds 10	a																	
York 8	a																	

A From Plymouth
B From Southampton Central
C To Lincoln
D From Leicester
E To Nottingham
F from 27 October
G 6 October, 13 October, 20 October. To Derby
H 6 October, 13 October, 20 October. To Nottingham
I 6 October, 13 October, 20 October. From St Pancras International
J 6 October, 13 October, 20 October

For connections from Gatwick Airport see Table 52

Table 53

London - East Midlands - Sheffield

Sundays until 24 June

Route Diagram - see first Page of Table 53

		EM	EM	EM	EM	XC	EM	NT	XC	EM	EM	EM	NT	XC	EM	EM	EM	EM	EM	EM	EM	NT	XC
		◇1	◇1	◇1	◇1	◇1	◇		◇1	◇1		◇		◇1	◇	◇1			◇1				◇1
						A	B		C			B		D	B								E
		🍴	🍴	🍴	🍴	🍴			🍴	🍴	🚌			🍴		🍴	🚌	🚌	🍴	🚌	🚌		🍴
St Pancras International ⊖	d	21p25	21p30	22p00	22p25											09 00			09 30				
Luton Airport Parkway 7 ✈	d		21p51		22p46											09 25							
Luton 10	d			22p24															09 58				
Bedford 7	d		22p07	22p42	23p05											09 50			10 20				
Wellingborough	d		22p20	22p55	23p17											10 04			10 34				
Kettering 4	a		22p29	23p09	23p27											10 13			10 43				
	d		22p42	23p11	23p29											10 14	10 35		10 45	11 05			
Corby	d			23p22												10 29							
Oakham	d																						
Melton Mowbray	d																						
Market Harborough	d										10 41						11a00	11 00		11a30	11 45		
Leicester	a	23p24	23p42	00 12	00 26						11 11					11 15		11 30	11 39		12 15		
	d	23p31	23p48	00 19	00 33					10 05						11 21			11 45				
Syston	d																						
Sileby	d																						
Barrow Upon Soar	d																						
Loughborough	d	23p41	23p59	00 30	00 43					10 15						11 33			11 56				
East Midlands Parkway ✈	d	23p53	00 11	00 42	00 55					10 27						11 45			12 08				
Beeston	a			00 50												11 51							
Nottingham 8 🚢	a	00 05		00 57												11 58							
	d						09 31	10 06				10 41	11 15		11 46							12 19	
Lincoln	a																						
Langley Mill	d							10 27					11 31									12 35	
Alfreton	d						09 53	10 35				11 03	11 39		12 08							12 43	
Long Eaton	a		00 15		01 00					10 32									12 12				
Derby 6	a		00 26		01 11					10 43									12 23				
	d					09 44			10 44	10 48				11 44					12 25				12 44
Chesterfield	d					10 03	10 08	10 55	11 03	11 09		11 16	11 51	12 03	12 18				12 44			12 54	13 03
Sheffield 7 🚢	a					10 16	10 33	11 15	11 17	11 28		11 35	12 15	12 18	12 36				13 01			13 16	13 18
Doncaster 7	a									11 52													
Wakefield Kirkgate 4	a							11 53					12 52									13 52	
Wakefield Westgate 7	a					10 44			11 44					12 44									13 45
Leeds 10	a					11 02		12 19	12 01				13 18	13 02								14 18	14 02
York 8	a					11 29			12 29	12 15				13 29									14 29

		EM	EM	EM	EM	XC	NT	EM	EM	EM	XC	EM	EM	EM	EM	XC	NT	XC	EM	EM	EM	EM	EM
		◇	◇1			◇1		◇1			◇1	◇	◇1			◇1		◇1	◇1			◇	◇1
		F				G					H	F				G	I				B		
			🍴	🚌	🚌	🍴		🍴	🚌	🚌	🍴		🍴	🚌	🚌	🍴		🍴	🍴	🚌	🚌		🍴
St Pancras International ⊖	d		10 00					10 30					11 00						11 30				12 00
Luton Airport Parkway 7 ✈	d		10 26										11 25						11 59				12 29
Luton 10	d							10 56					11 29						12 03				12 33
Bedford 7	d		10 50					11 17					11 48						12 26				12 55
Wellingborough	d		11 04					11 28					12 02						12 39				13 08
Kettering 4	a		11 14					11 38					12 11						12 46				13 17
	d		11 15	11 35				11 40	12 05				12 12	12 35					12 48	13 05			13 19
Corby	d		11 31										12 27										13 29
Oakham	d																						
Melton Mowbray	d																						
Market Harborough	d			12a00	12 10				12a30	12 49				13a00	13 20					13a30	13 45		
Leicester	a		12 19		12 40			12 40		13 19			13 14		13 50				13 55		14 15		14 19
	d		12 29					12 53					13 29						14 02				14 26
Syston	d																						
Sileby	d																						
Barrow Upon Soar	d																						
Loughborough	d		12 40					13 05					13 40						14 13				14 36
East Midlands Parkway ✈	d		12 52					13 17					13 52						14 21				14 44
Beeston	a												13 59										14 49
Nottingham 8 🚢	a		13 04										14 06										14 56
	d	12 39					13 09					13 38					14 19					14 37	
Lincoln	a																						
Langley Mill	d	12 56					13 27					13 55					14 35					14 54	
Alfreton	d	13 04					13 35					14 03					14 43					15 02	
Long Eaton	a							13 21											14 25				
Derby 6	a							13 32											14 38				
	d					13 11		13 36			13 44					14 11		14 44	14 49				
Chesterfield	d	13 17				13 30	13 46	13 56			14 03	14 17				14 30	14 54	15 03	15 09			15 13	
Sheffield 7 🚢	a	13 33				13 43	14 07	14 13			14 17	14 35				14 45	15 15	15 17	15 29			15 34	
Doncaster 7	a					14 13										15 13							
Wakefield Kirkgate 4	a						14 52										15 52						
Wakefield Westgate 7	a										14 44							15 44					
Leeds 10	a						15 18				15 02						16 18	16 02					
York 8	a					14 40					15 29					15 43		16 29					

A From Birmingham New Street to Edinburgh
B To Liverpool Lime Street
C From Birmingham New Street to Glasgow Central
D From Bristol Temple Meads to Edinburgh
E From Bristol Temple Meads to Glasgow Central
F From Norwich to Liverpool Lime Street
G From Birmingham New Street to Newcastle
H From Plymouth to Aberdeen
I From Plymouth to Glasgow Central

For connections from Gatwick Airport see Table 52

London - East Midlands - Sheffield

Sundays until 24 June

Route Diagram - see first Page of Table 53

		EM		XC	EM	NT	EM	XC	EM	XC	EM	EM		NT	EM	EM	XC	EM	EM	XC	NT	EM		EM	XC
		🚌		◇1 A 🍴	◇1 🍴		◇1 🍴	◇1 B 🍴	◇ C	◇1 D 🍴	◇1 🍴	◇1 🍴			◇1 🍴	◇1 🍴	◇1 E 🍴	◇1 F 🍴	◇ G	◇1 D 🍴		◇1 🍴		◇1 🍴	◇1 H 🍴
St Pancras International ⊖	d				12 30		13 00				13 30				14 05			14 35				15 05			
Luton Airport Parkway 7 ✈	d				12 59		13 29				13 58				14 29							15 29			
Luton 10	d				13 03		13 33				14 03							15 02							
Bedford 7	d				13 25		13 56				14 24				14 54			15 24				15 54			
Wellingborough	d				13 39		14 09				14 38				15 08			15 38				16 08			
Kettering 4	a				13 47		14 16				14 45				15 14			15 45				16 16			
	d	13 35			14 12		14 17				14 46	14 55			15 15	15 45		15 46				16 17		16 45	
Corby	d											15a05				15a55								16a55	
Oakham	d																								
Melton Mowbray	d																								
Market Harborough	d	14a00					14 27				14 58				15 25			15 57				16 28			
Leicester	a				14 41		14 46				15 18				15 44			16 18				16 52			
	d				14 42		14 48				15 20				15 46			16 19				16 54			
Syston	d																								
Sileby	d																								
Barrow Upon Soar	d																								
Loughborough	d				14 53		14 58				15 31				15 56			16 30				17 05			
East Midlands Parkway ✈	d				15 02		15 06				15 39				16 04			16 39				17 13			
Beeston	a						15 12								16 09										
Nottingham 8 🚋	a						15 19								16 17							17 24			
	d					15 12			15 44					16 14					16 40		17 14				
Lincoln	a																								
Langley Mill	d					15 34								16 30					17 00		17 30				
Alfreton	d					15 44			16 06					16 38					17 08		17 38				
Long Eaton	a				15 05						15 43							16 42							
Derby 6	a				15 18						15 55							16 55							
	d			15 11	15 30			15 44		16 11	16 15						16 44	16 56		17 11					17 43
Chesterfield	d				15 51	15 53		16 03	16 23		16 36			16 50			17 03	17 17	17 22		17 51				18 04
Sheffield 7 🚋	a			15 47	16 06	16 15		16 18	16 39	16 48	16 52			17 15			17 17	17 32	17 40	17 48	18 14				18 19
Doncaster 7	a			16 15						17 13										18 13					
Wakefield Kirkgate 4	a					16 52								17 52							18 52				
Wakefield Westgate 7	a							16 44									17 47	18 06		18 33					18 47
Leeds 10	a					17 18		17 02						18 18			18 02	18 24		18 51	19 18				19 04
York 8	a			16 40				17 29		17 42							18 29			19 18					19 29

		EM	EM	EM	XC	EM	EM	EM		NT	XC	EM	EM	EM	XC	EM	EM	EM		NT	XC	EM	EM	XC	EM
		◇ G	◇1 🍴	◇1 🍴	◇1 I 🍴	◇1 🍴	◇1 🍴	◇1 🍴			◇1 J 🍴	◇ K	◇1 🍴	◇1 D 🍴	◇1 🍴	◇1 🍴	◇1 🍴	◇1 🍴		L	◇1 K 🍴	◇	◇1 M 🍴	◇1 🍴	◇1 🍴
St Pancras International ⊖	d		15 35	16 05		16 25	16 35						16 55	17 05		17 25	17 35						17 55		18 25
Luton Airport Parkway 7 ✈	d			16 29										17 31											
Luton 10	d		16 02				17 04										18 04								
Bedford 7	d		16 24	16 54			17 24							17 54			18 24								
Wellingborough	d		16 38	17 08			17 38							18 07			18 37								
Kettering 4	a		16 46	17 14			17 44							18 14			18 44								
	d		16 47	17 15			17 45	17 50						18 15			18 45	18 50							
Corby	d							18a00										19a00							
Oakham	d																								
Melton Mowbray	d																								
Market Harborough	d		16 58	17 25			17 55							18 25			18 55								
Leicester	a		17 18	17 44		17 53	18 16						18 20	18 44		18 53	19 16						19 20		19 46
	d		17 20	17 46		17 54	18 19						18 23	18 45		18 55	19 19						19 25		19 47
Syston	d																								
Sileby	d																								
Barrow Upon Soar	d																								
Loughborough	d		17 31	17 56			18 31							18 56			19 31								
East Midlands Parkway ✈	d		17 39	18 04		18 10	18 38						18 43	19 03		19 09	19 38						19 44		20 03
Beeston	a			18 09										19 10											
Nottingham 8 🚋	a			18 16									18 53	19 16									19 55		
	d	17 35								18 14		18 37								19 19		19 38			
Lincoln	a																								
Langley Mill	d	17 54								18 30		18 54								19 35					
Alfreton	d	18 02								18 38		19 02								19 43		20 00			
Long Eaton	a		17 43				18 43										19 42								
Derby 6	a		17 56			18 23	18 55									19 20	19 54								20 16
	d		18 04		18 11	18 24					18 43				19 05	19 22					19 41			20 03	20 17
Chesterfield	d	18 17				18 45				18 52	19 05	19 13				19 41				19 54	20 02	20 12			20 38
Sheffield 7 🚋	a	18 34	18 42		18 46	19 00				19 16	19 20	19 31			19 39	19 58				20 15	20 17	20 31		20 38	20 53
Doncaster 7	a				19 15										20 16									21 19	
Wakefield Kirkgate 4	a									19 52										20 52					
Wakefield Westgate 7	a										19 48										20 46				21 27
Leeds 10	a									20 18	20 05									21 16	21 03				21 44
York 8	a				19 43						20 29				20 45						21 31			21 44	

A From Guildford to Newcastle
B From Penzance to Edinburgh
C To Liverpool Lime Street
D From Reading to Newcastle
E From Plymouth to Glasgow Central
F 🍴 from Derby 🍴 to Derby
G From Norwich to Liverpool Lime Street
H From Newquay to Edinburgh
I From Reading to Edinburgh
J From Plymouth to Edinburgh. 🍴 to Leeds
K From Norwich to Manchester Piccadilly
L From Plymouth to Leeds
M From Reading to Newcastle. 🍴 to Sheffield

For connections from Gatwick Airport see Table 52

London - East Midlands - Sheffield

Sundays until 24 June

Route Diagram - see first Page of Table 53

		NT	EM	EM		EM	EM	XC	EM	EM	EM	EM	XC	NT		EM	EM	EM	EM	EM	EM	XC	EM	EM
			◇1 🍴	◇1 🍴		◇1 🍴	◇1 🍴	◇1 A	◇1 🍴	◇1 🍴	◇1 🍴	◇1 🍴	◇1 B			◇1 🍴	◇1 🍴	◇1 🍴	◇1 🍴	◇1 🍴	◇1 🍴	◇1 A	◇1 🍴	◇1 🍴
St Pancras International ⊖	d		18 05	18 35		18 55			19 25	19 05	19 35					19 55	20 00	20 25	20 30		21 00		21 30	22 30
Luton Airport Parkway 7 ✈	d		18 31							19 31							20 21				21 21			22 51
Luton 10	d			19 03							20 04								20 54				21 52	
Bedford 7	d		18 54	19 23						19 55	20 24						20 41		21 13		21 39		22 10	23 19
Wellingborough	d		19 08	19 37						20 08	20 38						20 54		21 26		21 53		22 23	23 32
Kettering 4	a		19 16	19 43						20 16	20 44						21 00		21 33		21 59		22 30	23 39
	d		19 23	19 44			19 45			20 23	20 45	20 46					21 01		21 34	21 55	22 00		22 31	23 40
Corby	d						19a55					20a56								22a05				
Oakham	d																							
Melton Mowbray	d																							
Market Harborough	d		19 34	19 54						20 34	20 55						21 11		21 45		22 10		22 41	23 50
Leicester	a		19 53	20 18		20 23			20 46	20 53	21 18					21 24	21 32	21 44	22 06		22 29		23 00	00 09
	d		19 54	20 20		20 25			20 47	20 55	21 20					21 26	21 33	21 45	22 07		22 31		23 01	00 10
Syston	d																							
Sileby	d																							
Barrow Upon Soar	d																							
Loughborough	d		20 05	20 31						21 05	21 31					21 37	21 44	21 56			22 41		23 12	00 21
East Midlands Parkway ✈	d		20 12	20 38		20 43			21 03	21 13	21 38					21 45	21 51	22 03	22 23		22 49		23 24	00 28
Beeston	a		20 18							21 22							21 59				22 54			00 42
Nottingham 8 🚋	a		20 25			20 53				21 29						21 56	22 06				23 01			00 49
	d	20 13												21 30										
Lincoln	a																							
Langley Mill	d	20 29												21 52										
Alfreton	d	20 37												22 00										
Long Eaton	a			20 42							21 44												23 31	
Derby 6	a			20 54					21 16		21 55							22 15	22 36				23 42	
	d							20 42	21 17				21 44						22 37			22 44	23 43	
Chesterfield	d	20 48						21 03	21 38				22 03	22 13					22 58			23 05	00 03	
Sheffield 7 🚋	a	21 14						21 18	21 53				22 18	22 36					23 13			23 20	00 17	
Doncaster 7	a																							
Wakefield Kirkgate 4	a													23 26										
Wakefield Westgate 7	a							21 47					22 43						00 01					
Leeds 10	a							22 04					23 01	00 05					00 18			00 16		
York 8	a																							

		EM
		◇1 🍴
St Pancras International ⊖	d	23 00
Luton Airport Parkway 7 ✈	d	23 27
Luton 10	d	
Bedford 7	d	23 55
Wellingborough	d	00 09
Kettering 4	a	00 15
	d	00 16
Corby	d	
Oakham	d	
Melton Mowbray	d	
Market Harborough	d	00 26
Leicester	a	00 47
	d	00 49
Syston	d	
Sileby	d	
Barrow Upon Soar	d	
Loughborough	d	00 59
East Midlands Parkway ✈	d	01 07
Beeston	a	
Nottingham 8 🚋	a	
	d	
Lincoln	a	
Langley Mill	d	
Alfreton	d	
Long Eaton	a	
Derby 6	a	01 26
	d	
Chesterfield	d	
Sheffield 7 🚋	a	
Doncaster 7	a	
Wakefield Kirkgate 4	a	
Wakefield Westgate 7	a	
Leeds 10	a	
York 8	a	

A From Plymouth
B From Penzance

For connections from Gatwick Airport see Table 52

Table 53

Sundays

1 July to 16 September

London - East Midlands - Sheffield

Route Diagram - see first Page of Table 53

		EM	EM	EM	EM	EM	EM	EM	EM	EM		EM	EM	EM	XC	EM	EM	NT	XC	EM		EM	EM	EM	EM
		◇■	◇■	◇■	◇■	◇■	◇■	◇■	◇■	◇■		◇■	◇■	◇■	◇■	◇	◇■		◇■	◇■		◇■	◇	◇■	◇■
		A	B	C	D	C	D	E	F	F		F	F	F	G H	C		I	E		C	H	C	B	
St Pancras International ⊖	d	21p30	22p00	22p00		22p25		22p25	00 01	00 15		00 30	01 00	01 15										09 00	09 00
Luton Airport Parkway ■ ✈	d	21p51				22p46		22p46																09 21	09 28
Luton ■	d		22p24	22p24																					
Bedford ■	d	22p07	22p40	22p42		23p02		23p02																09 36	09 50
Wellingborough	d	22p20	22p53	22p55		23p14		23p14	00 46			01 13	01 43	01 58										09 50	10 03
Kettering ■	a	22p29	23p02	23p02		23p21		23p23	00 53	01 02		01 19	01 51	02 04										09 56	10 14
	d	22p36	23p03	23p03		23p22		23p24	00 54	01 03		01 20		02 06			09 55							09 57	10 16
Corby	d		23p14														10a05								10 31
Oakham	d																								
Melton Mowbray	d																								
Market Harborough	d			23p14	←	23p32	←		01 05			01 30		02 16										10 07	
Leicester	a	23p34	23p59	23p31	23p34	23p46	23p59	00 16	01 22	01 26		01 45		02 31										10 21	11 17
	d	23p42	00 06	23p32	23p42	23p46	00 06	00 23		01 28		01 47								10 10		10 10		10 24	11 24
Syston	d	→	→																						→
Sileby	d																								
Barrow Upon Soar	d																								
Loughborough	d			23p44	23p52	23p59	00 17	00 33				01 57								10 20		10 21		10 34	
East Midlands Parkway ✈	d			23p52	23p59	00 07	00 26	00 41												10 28		10 29		10 42	
Beeston	a			23p59			00 32					02 07												10 47	
Nottingham ■ ⇌	a			00 08			00 42					02 14												10 54	
	d											02 20				09 31		10 06					10 41		
Lincoln	a																								
Langley Mill	d																	10 27							
Alfreton	d															09 53		10 35					11 03		
Long Eaton	a				00 04	00 10		00 44												10 31		10 32			
Derby ■	a				00 15	00 21		00 55		01 50		02 39								10 42		10 46			
	d									01 52					09 44				10 44	10 48		10 48			
Chesterfield	d									02 12					10 03	10 08		10 55	11 03	11 09		11 09	11 16		
Sheffield ■ ⇌	a									02 25					10 16	10 33		11 15	11 17	11 28		11 28	11 35		
Doncaster ■	a																			11 52		11 52			
Wakefield Kirkgate ■	a																	11 53							
Wakefield Westgate ■	a														10 44				11 44						
Leeds ■	a														11 02			12 19	12 01						
York ■	a														11 26				12 29	12 15		12 15			

		EM	NT	NT	XC	XC		EM	EM	EM	EM	EM	EM	EM	EM	NT		XC	XC	EM	EM	XC	EM	EM	EM
		◇■			◇■	◇■		◇	◇■	◇■	◇■	◇■	◇■	◇■	◇■			◇■	◇■	◇	◇■	◇■	◇■	◇■	◇■
		C	E	C	J	K	H	D	L	C	C	D	B	C			M	N	O	D	I	L	C	C	
St Pancras International ⊖	d	09 30								09 30		10 00		10 00	10 30								10 30		11 00
Luton Airport Parkway ■ ✈	d											10 23		10 29											11 21
Luton ■	d	09 52								09 59					10 52								10 58		11 25
Bedford ■	d	10 07								10 19		10 38		10 51	11 08								11 20		11 39
Wellingborough	d	10 20								10 32		10 52		11 05	11 19								11 31		11 53
Kettering ■	a	10 26								10 43		11 00		11 13	11 27								11 40		11 59
	d	10 28								10 44	10 55	11 01		11 13	11 27								11 40	11 55	12 00
Corby	d										11a05			11 29										12a05	
Oakham	d																								
Melton Mowbray	d																								
Market Harborough	d	10 38							←			11 12	←		11 37						←				12 10
Leicester	a	10 54							11 17	11 43		11 32	11 43	12 14	11 53						12 14		12 41		12 25
	d	10 56							11 24	11 49		11 34	11 49	12 21	11 54						12 21		12 47		12 27
Syston	d									→				→									→		
Sileby	d																								
Barrow Upon Soar	d																								
Loughborough	d	11 06							11 34			11 45	12 00		12 05						12 32				12 37
East Midlands Parkway ✈	d	11 14							11 42			11 53	12 07		12 12						12 40				12 45
Beeston	a								11 47																12 50
Nottingham ■ ⇌	a								11 54			12 04									12 51				12 57
	d		11 15	11 15				11 46								12 19				12 39					
Lincoln	a																								
Langley Mill	d		11 30	11 31												12 35				12 56					
Alfreton	d		11 39	11 39				12 08								12 43				13 04					
Long Eaton	a	11 17											12 11		12 16										
Derby ■	a	11 28											12 22		12 27										
	d	11 30			11 44	11 44							12 23		12 28			12 44	12 44			13 11			
Chesterfield	d	11 50	11 51	11 51	12 03	12 03		12 18					12 43		12 48	12 54		13 03	13 03	13 17		13 30			
Sheffield ■ ⇌	a	12 09	12 15	12 15	12 18	12 18		12 36					13 01		13 02	13 16		13 18	13 18	13 33		13 43			
Doncaster ■	a																					14 13			
Wakefield Kirkgate ■	a		12 52	12 52												13 52									
Wakefield Westgate ■	a				12 44	12 44												13 45	13 45						
Leeds ■	a		13 18	13 18	13 02	13 02										14 18		14 02	14 02						
York ■	a				13 29	13 31												14 29	14 31			14 40			

A 16 September. To Derby
B 16 September. To Nottingham
C not 16 September
D 16 September. From St Pancras International
E 16 September
F 29 July, 5 August, 12 August, 2 September, 9 September
G 16 September. To Newcastle
H To Liverpool Lime Street
I From Birmingham New Street to Newcastle
J not 16 September. From Bristol Temple Meads to Edinburgh
K 16 September. From Birmingham New Street to Newcastle
L 16 September. To Sheffield
M not 16 September. From Bristol Temple Meads to Glasgow Central
N 16 September. From Bristol Temple Meads to Newcastle
O From Norwich to Liverpool Lime Street

For connections from Gatwick Airport see Table 52

Table 53

Sundays

1 July to 16 September

London - East Midlands - Sheffield

Route Diagram - see first Page of Table 53

		EM		NT	EM	EM	XC	EM	EM	XC	EM	EM		EM	EM	EM	EM	NT	XC	EM	EM	EM		EM	EM
		◇■			◇■	◇■	◇■	◇	◇■	◇■	◇■	◇■		◇■	◇■	◇■	◇■		◇■	◇■	◇	◇		◇■	◇■
		A			B	C	D	E	A	F	G	C	C	B	C	C			H A	I	J		A	C	
St Pancras International ⊖	d				11 00	11 30					11 30			12 00	12 00	12 30									13 00
Luton Airport Parkway ■ ✈	d				11 28	11 51					11 59			12 23	12 29	12 51									13 23
Luton ■	d				11 32	11 55					12 03			12 27	12 33	12 55									13 27
Bedford ■	d				11 52	12 10					12 25			12 42	12 54	13 09									13 42
Wellingborough	d				12 06	12 23					12 38			12 56	13 07	13 23									13 56
Kettering ■	a				12 15	12 29					12 47			13 03	13 17	13 29									14 03
	d				12 15	12 30					12 48	12 55		13 04	13 19	13 30	13 55								14 04
Corby	d				12 30							13a05			13 29		14a05								
Oakham	d																								
Melton Mowbray	d																								
Market Harborough	d	←				12 40			←					13 15		13 40				←				←	14 15
Leicester	a	12 41			13 14	12 55			13 14		13 53			13 32	14 14	13 55				13 53				14 14	14 32
	d	12 47			13 23	12 57			13 23		13 59			13 34	14 26	13 57				13 59				14 26	14 34
Syston	d				→						→				→										
Sileby	d																								
Barrow Upon Soar	d																								
Loughborough	d	12 58				13 07			13 33					13 45		14 07				14 10				14 36	14 45
East Midlands Parkway ✈	d	13 05				13 15			13 41					13 53		14 15				14 21				14 44	14 53
Beeston	a								13 46					13 59										14 49	15 01
Nottingham ■ ⇌	a								13 53					14 07										14 56	15 09
	d			13 09				13 38										14 19			14 37	14 37			
Lincoln	a																								
Langley Mill	d			13 27				13 55										14 35			14 54	14 54			
Alfreton	d			13 35				14 03										14 43			15 02	15 02			
Long Eaton	a	13 09				13 21										14 18				14 25					
Derby ■	a	13 20				13 32										14 29				14 37					
	d	13 21				13 34	13 44			14 11						14 31			14 44	14 48					
Chesterfield	d	13 41		13 46		13 53	14 03	14 17		14 30						14 50		14 54	15 03	15 08	15 13	15 13			
Sheffield ■ ⇌	a	14 02		14 07		14 16	14 17	14 35		14 45						15 14		15 15	15 17	15 29	15 31	15 34			
Doncaster ■	a									15 13															
Wakefield Kirkgate ■	a			14 52														15 52							
Wakefield Westgate ■	a						14 44												15 44						
Leeds ■	a			15 18			15 02											16 18	16 02						
York ■	a						15 29			15 43									16 29						

		XC	EM	EM	EM	NT	XC	EM		EM	EM	EM	EM	XC	NT	XC	EM	EM		EM	EM	EM	EM	XC	EM
		◇■	◇■	◇■	◇■		◇■	◇■		◇■	◇	◇■	◇■	◇■		◇■	◇■	◇■		◇■	◇	◇■	◇■	◇■	◇■
		K	L	L	C		M	L			N	L	C	O		P	Q	R		E	C	L	O	C	
St Pancras International ⊖	d		12 30	13 00	13 30			13 30				14 00	14 00				14 30	14 30				15 00	15 00		15 30
Luton Airport Parkway ■ ✈	d		12 59	13 29	13 50			13 58				14 21	14 23									15 23	15 23		
Luton ■	d		13 03	13 33	13 55			14 03									14 54	14 54							15 52
Bedford ■	d		13 24	13 54	14 09			14 23				14 37	14 38				15 09	15 10				15 38	15 39		16 07
Wellingborough	d		13 38	14 07	14 23			14 37				14 51	14 52				15 23	15 24				15 52	15 53		16 20
Kettering ■	a		13 46	14 16	14 28			14 43				14 57	15 00				15 30	15 31				16 00	16 01		16 27
	d		14 08	14 18	14 29			14 46		14 55		14 58	15 01				15 31	15 32		15 45		16 01	16 02		16 28
Corby	d									15a05										15a55					
Oakham	d																								
Melton Mowbray	d																								
Market Harborough	d		14 24	14 29	14 40			14 58				15 08	15 12				15 42	15 43				16 12	16 13		16 38
Leicester	a		14 42	14 46	14 55			15 16				15 32	15 32				16 02	16 02				16 32	16 32		16 53
	d		14 44	14 48	14 57			15 18				15 34	15 34				16 04	16 04				16 34	16 34		16 54
Syston	d																								
Sileby	d																								
Barrow Upon Soar	d																								
Loughborough	d		14 55	14 59	15 07			15 29				15 44	15 45				16 15	16 15				16 45	16 45		17 04
East Midlands Parkway ✈	d		15 03	15 08	15 15			15 37				15 52	15 53				16 23	16 23				16 53	16 53		17 12
Beeston	a			15 13								15 59	15 59												
Nottingham ■ ⇌	a			15 21								16 06	16 07									17 04	17 05		
	d					15 12					15 44				16 14						16 40				
Lincoln	a																								
Langley Mill	d					15 34									16 30						17 00				
Alfreton	d					15 44					16 06				16 38						17 08				
Long Eaton	a		15 07		15 18			15 41									16 27	16 27							17 15
Derby ■	a		15 19		15 29			15 53									16 39	16 39							17 26
	d	15 11	15 21		15 31		15 44	15 55						16 11		16 44	16 48	16 48						17 11	17 29
Chesterfield	d		15 42		15 51	15 53	16 03	16 16			16 23				16 50	17 03	17 09	17 09			17 22				
Sheffield ■ ⇌	a	15 47	15 58		16 14	16 15	16 18	16 30			16 39			16 48	17 15	17 17	17 28	17 29			17 40			17 48	17 59
Doncaster ■	a	16 15												17 13										18 13	
Wakefield Kirkgate ■	a					16 52									17 52										
Wakefield Westgate ■	a						16 44									17 47	18 05	18 06						18 33	
Leeds ■	a					17 18	17 02								18 18	18 02	18 24	18 24						18 51	
York ■	a	16 40					17 29							17 42		18 29								19 18	

A 16 September. From St Pancras International
B 16 September. To Nottingham
C not 16 September
D From Plymouth to Aberdeen
E From Norwich to Liverpool Lime Street
F From Birmingham New Street to Newcastle
G 16 September. To Sheffield
H From Plymouth to Glasgow Central
I not 16 September. To Liverpool Lime Street
J 16 September. To Liverpool Lime Street
K From Guildford to Newcastle
L 16 September
M From Penzance to Edinburgh
N To Liverpool Lime Street
O From Reading to Newcastle
P From Penzance to Glasgow Central
Q not 16 September. ⌶ from Derby ⌶ to Derby
R 16 September. ⌶ from Derby ⌶ to Derby

For connections from Gatwick Airport see Table 52

London - East Midlands - Sheffield

1 July to 16 September

Route Diagram - see first Page of Table 53

Station		NT	XC ◇1 A	XC ◇1 B	EM ◇1 C	EM ◇1	EM ◇ D	EM ◇1 E	EM ◇1 C	XC ◇1 F	EM ◇1 E	EM ◇1 C	EM ◇1 E	NT G	XC ◇1 H	EM ◇1 E	EM ◇1 I	EM ◇1 C	EM ◇1 J	EM ◇1 E	EM ◇	EM ◇1
St Pancras International	d				15 30			16 00	16 00		16 25	16 25	16 30			16 30	16 55		16 55			17 00
Luton Airport Parkway	d							16 21	16 21													17 21
Luton	d				15 54								16 52			16 52						
Bedford	d				16 10			16 36	16 37				17 07			17 08						17 37
Wellingborough	d				16 24			16 50	16 51				17 20			17 21						17 51
Kettering	a				16 31			16 56	16 57				17 27			17 28						17 57
	d				16 32	16 45		16 57	16 58				17 28			17 29				17 50		17 58
Corby	d					16a55														18a00		
Oakham	d																					
Melton Mowbray	d																					
Market Harborough	d				16 43			17 07	17 08				17 38			17 39						18 08
Leicester	a				17 02			17 22	17 31		17 34	17 37	17 53			18 01	18 02		18 05			18 23
	d				17 04			17 24	17 32		17 36	17 39	17 54			18 03	18 04		18 11			18 25
Syston	d																					
Sileby	d																					
Barrow Upon Soar	d																					
Loughborough	d				17 15			17 34	17 43				18 04			18 13		←				18 35
East Midlands Parkway	d				17 23			17 42	17 50		17 52	17 55	18 12			18 21	18 19	18 21	18 25			18 43
Beeston	a							17 47	17 59							→						18 49
Nottingham	a							17 54	18 06								18 29		18 37			18 55
	d	17 14					17 35							18 14							18 37	
Lincoln	a																					
Langley Mill	d	17 30					17 54							18 30							18 54	
Alfreton	d	17 38					18 02							18 38							19 02	
Long Eaton	a				17 27								18 15					18 24				
Derby	a				17 39						18 04	18 07	18 26					18 35				
	d		17 43	17 43	17 49					18 11	18 12	18 15			18 43							
Chesterfield	d	17 51	18 04	18 04	18 10		18 17				18 31	18 36		18 52	19 05						19 13	
Sheffield	a	18 14	18 19	18 19	18 26		18 34			18 46	18 51	18 51		19 16	19 20						19 31	
Doncaster	a									19 15												
Wakefield Kirkgate	a	18 52												19 52								
Wakefield Westgate	a		18 47	18 47											19 48							
Leeds	a	19 18	19 04	19 04										20 18	20 05							
York	a		19 28	19 29						19 43					20 29							

Station		EM ◇1 C	EM ◇1 E	XC ◇1 K	EM ◇1 C	NT L	XC ◇1 H	EM ◇1 E	EM ◇1 I	EM ◇1	EM ◇1 M	EM ◇1 C	EM ◇1 N	EM ◇1 J	EM ◇ E C	EM ◇1 O	EM ◇1 E	XC ◇1	EM ◇1 C	EM ◇1 C	EM ◇1	EM ◇1	EM ◇1
St Pancras International	d	17 00	17 25		17 25			17 30	17 30			17 55	17 55			18 00	18 00		18 25	18 25	18 30	18 30	
Luton Airport Parkway	d	17 21														18 21	18 21						
Luton	d							17 52	17 54												18 53	18 53	
Bedford	d	17 38						18 08	18 09							18 36	18 38				19 07	19 08	
Wellingborough	d	17 51						18 21	18 23							18 50	18 51				19 21	19 22	
Kettering	a	17 58						18 28	18 30							18 56	18 58				19 27	19 28	
	d	17 59						18 29	18 31		18 50					18 57	18 59				19 28	19 29	19 45
Corby	d										19a00												19a55
Oakham	d																						
Melton Mowbray	d																						
Market Harborough	d	18 09						18 39	18 42	←						19 07	19 09				19 38	19 39	
Leicester	a	18 29	18 32		18 34			19 01	19 00	19 01		19 06	19 05			19 23	19 32		19 35	19 37	19 53	20 01	
	d	18 30	18 34		18 36			19 03	19 02	19 03		19 08	19 11			19 25	19 33		19 37	19 40	19 55	20 03	
Syston	d							→															
Sileby	d																						
Barrow Upon Soar	d																						
Loughborough	d	18 41							19 13	19 13				←		19 35	19 44				20 05	20 13	
East Midlands Parkway	d	18 48	18 48		18 53				19 21	19 21		19 26	19 25	19 26		19 43	19 51		19 53	19 56	20 13	20 21	
Beeston	a	18 58										→				19 49	19 59						
Nottingham	a	19 05											19 35	19 37		19 55	20 06						
	d					19 19									19 38								
Lincoln	a																						
Langley Mill	d					19 35																	
Alfreton	d					19 43									20 00								
Long Eaton	a								19 25	19 24											20 16	20 24	
Derby	a		18 59		19 04				19 37	19 35									20 05	20 08	20 27	20 35	
	d		19 01	19 05	19 10		19 41											20 03	20 07	20 10			
Chesterfield	d		19 20		19 29	19 54	20 02								20 12				20 28	20 31			
Sheffield	a		19 39	19 39	19 50	20 15	20 17								20 31			20 38	20 42	20 49			
Doncaster	a			20 16														21 19					
Wakefield Kirkgate	a					20 52																	
Wakefield Westgate	a						20 46												21 10	21 30			
Leeds	a					21 16	21 03												21 30	21 44			
York	a			20 45			21 31											21 44					

A 16 September. From Plymouth to Edinburgh
B not 16 September. From Newquay to Edinburgh
C 16 September
D From Norwich to Liverpool Lime Street
E not 16 September
F From Reading to Edinburgh
G From Plymouth to Edinburgh. 🍴 to Leeds
H 16 September. To Derby
I 16 September. From St Pancras International
J From Norwich to Manchester Piccadilly
K From Reading to Newcastle
L From Plymouth to Leeds
M not 16 September. To Nottingham
N not 16 September. From St Pancras International
O From Reading to Newcastle. 🍴 to Sheffield

For connections from Gatwick Airport see Table 52

London - East Midlands - Sheffield

1 July to 16 September

Route Diagram - see first Page of Table 53

Station		NT	EM ◇1 A	EM ◇1 B	EM ◇1 A	XC ◇1 C	XC ◇1 D	EM ◇1 A	EM ◇1 B	EM ◇1 B	EM ◇1 A	EM ◇1 B	EM ◇1	XC ◇1 E	XC ◇1 D	NT	EM ◇1 A	EM ◇1 B	EM ◇1 A	EM ◇1 B	EM ◇1 A	EM ◇1 B	EM ◇1 A
St Pancras International	d		18 55	18 55	19 00			19 25	19 00	19 25	19 30	19 30					19 55	19 55	20 00	20 00	20 25	20 25	20 30
Luton Airport Parkway	d				19 21				19 21										20 21	20 21			
Luton	d										19 52	19 53											20 54
Bedford	d				19 36				19 38		20 07	20 08							20 37	20 38			21 10
Wellingborough	d				19 50				19 51		20 20	20 22							20 50	20 51			21 23
Kettering	a				19 56				19 58		20 27	20 28							20 56	20 57			21 30
	d				19 57				19 59		20 28	20 29	20 46						20 57	20 58			21 31
Corby	d												20a56										
Oakham	d																						
Melton Mowbray	d																						
Market Harborough	d				20 09				20 09		20 38	20 39							21 07	21 08			21 42
Leicester	a		20 05	20 07	20 24			20 32	20 32	20 37	20 53	21 01					21 05	21 07	21 22	21 32	21 32	21 36	22 00
	d		20 07	20 08	20 26			20 34	20 33	20 40	20 55	21 03					21 07	21 09	21 24	21 33	21 34	21 37	22 02
Syston	d																						
Sileby	d																						
Barrow Upon Soar	d																						
Loughborough	d				20 36				20 44		21 05	21 13					21 18	21 20	21 34	21 44	21 44	21 48	
East Midlands Parkway	d		20 23	20 25	20 44			20 50	20 51	20 56	21 13	21 21					21 26	21 28	21 42	21 51	21 52	21 56	22 18
Beeston	a				20 50				20 59										21 47	21 59			
Nottingham	a		20 36	20 35	20 56				21 06								21 37	21 39	21 55	22 06			
	d	20 13														21 30							
Lincoln	a																						
Langley Mill	d	20 29														21 52							
Alfreton	d	20 37														22 00							
Long Eaton	a										21 16	21 24											
Derby	a							21 02		21 08	21 27	21 35									22 04	22 08	22 30
	d					20 42	20 43	21 03		21 10				21 44	21 44								22 32
Chesterfield	d	20 48				21 03	21 05	21 23		21 31				22 03	22 05	22 13							22 53
Sheffield	a	21 14				21 18	21 19	21 40		21 45				22 18	22 19	22 36							23 07
Doncaster	a																						
Wakefield Kirkgate	a															23 26							
Wakefield Westgate	a					21 47	21 47							22 43	22 45								23 36
Leeds	a					22 04	22 04							23 01	23 03	00 05							23 53
York	a																						

Station		EM ◇1 B	EM ◇1	EM ◇1 A	EM ◇1 B	XC ◇1 F	XC ◇1 C	EM ◇1 A	EM ◇1 B	EM ◇1 A	EM ◇1 B	EM ◇1 A	EM ◇1 B
St Pancras International	d	20 30		21 00	21 00			21 30	21 30	22 30	22 30	23 00	23 00
Luton Airport Parkway	d			21 21	21 21					22 51	22 51	23 21	23 27
Luton	d	20 54						21 52	21 52				
Bedford	d	21 11		21 36	21 40			22 07	22 08	23 06	23 14	23 36	23 50
Wellingborough	d	21 24		21 50	21 53			22 20	22 21	23 20	23 28	23 50	00 04
Kettering	a	21 31		21 56	22 00			22 27	22 28	23 26	23 34	23 56	00 10
	d	21 32	21 55	21 57	22 01			22 28	22 29	23 27	23 35	23 57	00 11
Corby	d		22a05										
Oakham	d												
Melton Mowbray	d												
Market Harborough	d	21 43		22 07	22 11			22 38	22 39	23 37	23 45	00 07	00 21
Leicester	a	22 02		22 22	22 28			22 56	22 56	23 52	00 04	00 22	00 42
	d	22 04		22 24	22 29			22 58	22 57	23 54	00 06	00 24	00 44
Syston	d												
Sileby	d												
Barrow Upon Soar	d												
Loughborough	d			22 34	22 39			23 08	23 08	00 04	00 16	00 34	00 54
East Midlands Parkway	d	22 20		22 42	22 52			23 16	23 20	00 12	00 29	00 42	01 07
Beeston	a			22 54	23 00					00 17	00 37		
Nottingham	a			23 01	23 07					00 28	00 44		
	d												
Lincoln	a												
Langley Mill	d												
Alfreton	d												
Long Eaton	a							23 19	23 27				
Derby	a	22 32						23 30	23 38			00 53	01 21
	d	22 34				22 44	22 44	23 32	23 39				
Chesterfield	d	22 56				23 05	23 05	23 51	23 59				
Sheffield	a	23 10				23 20	23 20	00 05	00 17				
Doncaster	a												
Wakefield Kirkgate	a												
Wakefield Westgate	a	23 40											
Leeds	a	00 01				00 11	00 16						
York	a												

A not 16 September
B 16 September
C not 16 September. From Plymouth
D 16 September. From Plymouth
E not 16 September. From Penzance
F 16 September. From Penzance

For connections from Gatwick Airport see Table 52

London - East Midlands - Sheffield

Sundays
from 23 September

Route Diagram - see first Page of Table 53

Station		XC	EM	EM	EM	EM	EM	EM	EM	EM		EM	NT	XC	EM	EM	EM	NT	NT	XC		XC	EM	EM	EM
		◇■	◇■	◇■	◇■	◇■	◇■	◇■	◇■	◇		◇■		◇■	◇■	◇	◇■			◇■		◇■	◇■	◇■	◇
		A	B	C	D	E	D	E	F	G	D			H	G	D	F	D	I		H C	D	G		
		⊼	⊼	⊼	⊼	⊼	⊼	⊼	⊼			⊼		⊼	⊼		⊼			⊼		⊼	⊼	⊼	
St Pancras International ⊖	d		21p30	22p00	22p00		22p25		22p25								09 00						09 00	09 30	
Luton Airport Parkway ■ ✈	d		21p51				22p46		22p46								09 28						09 28		
Luton ■	d			22p24	22p24																			09 59	
Bedford ■	d		22p07	22p40	22p42		23p02		23p02								09 50						09 50	10 19	
Wellingborough	d		22p20	22p53	22p55		23p14		23p14								10 03						10 03	10 32	
Kettering ■	a		22p29	23p02	23p02		23p21		23p23								10 10						10 14	10 38	
	d		22p36	23p03	23p03		23p22		23p24			09 55					10 11						10 16	10 40	
Corby	d			23p14								10a05											10 31		
Oakham	d																								
Melton Mowbray	d																								
Market Harborough	d				23p14	←	23p32	←									10 21							10 50	
Leicester	a		23p34	23p59	23p31	23p34	23p46	23p59	00 16								10 40						11 17	11 05	
	d		23p42	00 06	23p32	23p42	23p46	00 06	00 23						10 10		10 41						11 24	11 06	
Syston	d		→	→																			→		
Sileby	d																								
Barrow Upon Soar	d																								
Loughborough	d				23p44	23p52	23p59	00 17	00 33						10 20		10 52							11 17	
East Midlands Parkway ✈	d				23p52	23p59	00 07	00 26	00 41						10 28		10 59							11 24	
Beeston	a				23p59			00 32									11 05								
Nottingham ■ 🚋	a				00 08			00 42									11 14								
	d									09 31			10 06			10 41		11 15	11 15						11 46
Lincoln	a																								
Langley Mill	d												10 27					11 30	11 31						
Alfreton	d									09 53			10 35			11 03		11 39	11 39						12 08
Long Eaton	a					00 04	00 10		00 44						10 31									11 28	
Derby ■	a					00 15	00 21		00 55						10 42									11 39	
	d	09 44												10 44	10 48					11 44		11 44		11 48	
Chesterfield	d	10 03								10 08			10 55	11 03	11 09	11 16		11 51	11 51	12 03		12 03		12 10	12 18
Sheffield ■ 🚋	a	10 16								10 33			11 15	11 17	11 28	11 35		12 15	12 15	12 18		12 18		12 25	12 36
Doncaster ■	a														11 52										
Wakefield Kirkgate ■	a												11 53					12 52	12 52						
Wakefield Westgate ■	a	10 44												11 44						12 44		12 44			
Leeds ■	a	11 02											12 19	12 01				13 18	13 18	13 02		13 02			
York ■	a	11 26												12 29	12 15					13 29		13 31			

Station		EM	EM	EM	EM	EM		NT	XC	XC	EM	EM	EM	EM	XC	EM		EM	EM	EM	NT	XC	EM	EM	EM
		◇■	◇■	◇■	◇■	◇■			◇■	◇■	◇■	◇■	◇	◇■	◇■	◇■		◇■	◇■	◇■		◇■	◇■	◇■	◇
		E	J	D	D	E		K	L	C	D	G	E	M	J	D	D	E		N	C	D	O		
		⊼	⊼	⊼	⊼	⊼			⊼	⊼	⊼	⊼		⊼	⊼	⊼		⊼	⊼	⊼		⊼	⊼	⊼	
St Pancras International ⊖	d		09 30		10 00						10 00	10 30				10 30			11 00				11 00	11 30	
Luton Airport Parkway ■ ✈	d				10 29						10 29								11 28				11 28	11 59	
Luton ■	d		09 59									10 58				10 58			11 32				11 32	12 03	
Bedford ■	d		10 19		10 51						10 51	11 20				11 20			11 52				11 52	12 25	
Wellingborough	d		10 32		11 05						11 05	11 31				11 31			12 06				12 06	12 38	
Kettering ■	a		10 43		11 12						11 13	11 39				11 40			12 12				12 15	12 44	
	d		10 44	10 55	11 13						11 13	11 39				11 40		11 55	12 13				12 15	12 45	
Corby	d			11a05							11 29							12a05					12 30		
Oakham	d																								
Melton Mowbray	d																								
Market Harborough	d	←			11 24	←						11 49		←					12 23	←				12 55	
Leicester	a	11 17	11 43		11 41	11 43					12 14	12 05		12 14		12 41			12 38	12 41			13 14	13 16	
	d	11 24	11 49		11 42	11 49					12 21	12 06		12 21		12 47			12 40	12 47			13 23	13 18	
Syston	d		→								→					→							→		
Sileby	d																								
Barrow Upon Soar	d																								
Loughborough	d	11 34			11 53	12 00						12 17		12 32					12 50	12 58				13 28	
East Midlands Parkway ✈	d	11 42			12 02	12 07						12 24		12 40					12 58	13 05				13 36	
Beeston	a	11 47																	13 03						
Nottingham ■ 🚋	a	11 54			12 13									12 51					13 10						
	d							12 19					12 39								13 09				13 38
Lincoln	a																								
Langley Mill	d							12 35					12 56								13 27				13 55
Alfreton	d							12 43					13 04								13 35				14 03
Long Eaton	a					12 11						12 28								13 09				13 39	
Derby ■	a					12 22						12 39								13 20				13 50	
	d					12 23			12 44	12 44		12 48			13 11					13 21		13 44		13 52	
Chesterfield	d					12 43		12 54	13 03	13 03		13 09	13 17		13 30					13 41	13 46	14 03		14 11	14 17
Sheffield ■ 🚋	a					13 01		13 16	13 18	13 18		13 28	13 33		13 43					14 02	14 07	14 17		14 25	14 35
Doncaster ■	a														14 13										
Wakefield Kirkgate ■	a							13 52													14 52				
Wakefield Westgate ■	a								13 45	13 45												14 44			
Leeds ■	a							14 18	14 02	14 02											15 18	15 02			
York ■	a								14 29	14 31					14 40							15 29			

A from 23 September until 21 October. To Newcastle
B from 23 September until 21 October. To Derby
C from 23 September until 21 October. To Nottingham
D from 28 October
E from 23 September until 21 October. From St Pancras International
F from 23 September until 21 October
G To Liverpool Lime Street
H from 23 September until 21 October. From Birmingham New Street to Newcastle
I from 28 October. From Birmingham New Street to Edinburgh
J from 23 September until 21 October. To Sheffield
K from 28 October. From Birmingham New Street to Glasgow Central
L from 23 September until 21 October. From Bristol Temple Meads to Newcastle
M From Birmingham New Street to Newcastle
N From Bristol Temple Meads to Newcastle
O From Norwich to Liverpool Lime Street

For connections from Gatwick Airport see Table 52

London - East Midlands - Sheffield

Sundays
from 23 September

Route Diagram - see first Page of Table 53

Station		EM		XC	EM	EM	EM	NT	XC	EM	EM	EM		EM	EM	EM	EM	XC	EM	EM	EM	NT		EM	XC
		◇■		◇■	◇■	◇■	◇■		◇■	◇■	◇	◇		◇■	◇■	◇■	◇■	◇■	◇■	◇■	◇■			◇■	◇■
		A		B	C	D	D		E	A	F	G	H	D	A	D	I	C	D	A			J	K	
		⊼		⊼	⊼	⊼	⊼		⊼	⊼				⊼	⊼	⊼	⊼	⊼	⊼	⊼	⊼			⊼	⊼
St Pancras International ⊖	d				11 30		12 00							12 00	12 30				12 30	13 00				13 00	
Luton Airport Parkway ■ ✈	d				11 59		12 29							12 29	12 59				12 59	13 29				13 29	
Luton ■	d				12 03		12 33							12 33	13 03				13 03	13 33				13 33	
Bedford ■	d				12 25		12 54							12 54	13 24				13 24	13 54				13 54	
Wellingborough	d				12 38		13 07							13 07	13 38				13 38	14 07				14 07	
Kettering ■	a				12 47		13 14							13 17	13 46				13 46	14 14				14 16	
	d				12 48	12 55	13 15							13 19	13 47		13 55		14 08	14 15				14 18	
Corby	d					13a05								13 29			14a05								
Oakham	d																								
Melton Mowbray	d																								
Market Harborough	d	←					13 25			←					13 58	←			14 24	14 25	←			14 29	
Leicester	a	13 14			13 53		13 40			13 53				14 14	14 16	14 14			14 42	14 40	14 42			14 46	
	d	13 23			13 59		13 41			13 59				14 26	14 17	14 26			14 44	14 41	14 44			14 48	
Syston	d				→									→					→						
Sileby	d																								
Barrow Upon Soar	d																								
Loughborough	d	13 33					13 52			14 10					14 29	14 36				14 52	14 55			14 59	
East Midlands Parkway ✈	d	13 41					13 59			14 21					14 37	14 44				14 59	15 03			15 08	
Beeston	a	13 46					14 05									14 49				15 05				15 13	
Nottingham ■ 🚋	a	13 53					14 14									14 56				15 13				15 21	
	d							14 19			14 37	14 37										15 12			
Lincoln	a																								
Langley Mill	d							14 35			14 54	14 54										15 34			
Alfreton	d							14 43			15 02	15 02										15 44			
Long Eaton	a									14 25					14 41						15 07				
Derby ■	a									14 37					14 53						15 19				
	d			14 11					14 44	14 48					14 57			15 11			15 21				15 44
Chesterfield	d			14 30				14 54	15 03	15 08	15 13	15 13			15 18						15 42	15 53			16 03
Sheffield ■ 🚋	a			14 45				15 15	15 17	15 29	15 31	15 34			15 42			15 47			15 58	16 15			16 18
Doncaster ■	a			15 13														16 15							
Wakefield Kirkgate ■	a							15 52														16 52			
Wakefield Westgate ■	a								15 44																16 44
Leeds ■	a							16 18	16 02													17 18			17 02
York ■	a			15 43					16 29									16 40							17 29

Station		EM	EM	EM	EM	EM	EM	XC		NT	XC	EM	EM	EM	EM	EM	EM	XC		NT	XC	XC	EM	EM	EM
		◇■	◇■	◇	◇	◇■	◇■	◇■			◇■	◇■	◇■	◇■	◇	◇	◇■	◇■			◇■	◇■	◇■	◇■	◇■
				G	F	D	J	L			M	N	O	P	Q		L			R	S	D	J		
		⊼	⊼			⊼	⊼	⊼			⊼	⊼	⊼	⊼			⊼	⊼			⊼	⊼	⊼	⊼	⊼
St Pancras International ⊖	d	13 30				14 00	14 00					14 30	14 30				15 00						15 30	15 30	
Luton Airport Parkway ■ ✈	d	13 58				14 21	14 21										15 23								
Luton ■	d	14 03										14 54	14 54											15 54	
Bedford ■	d	14 23				14 37	14 37					15 10	15 10				15 39						16 06	16 10	
Wellingborough	d	14 37				14 51	14 51					15 24	15 24				15 53						16 20	16 24	
Kettering ■	a	14 43				14 57	14 57					15 31	15 31				16 01						16 27	16 31	
	d	14 46	14 55			14 58	14 58					15 32	15 32	15 45			16 02						16 28	16 32	16 45
Corby	d		15a05											15a55											16a55
Oakham	d																								
Melton Mowbray	d																								
Market Harborough	d	14 58				15 08	15 08					15 43	15 43				16 13						16 39	16 43	
Leicester	a	15 16				15 23	15 32					16 02	16 02				16 32						17 02	17 02	
	d	15 18				15 25	15 34					16 04	16 04				16 34						17 04	17 04	
Syston	d																								
Sileby	d																								
Barrow Upon Soar	d																								
Loughborough	d	15 29				15 35	15 44					16 15	16 15				16 45						17 15	17 15	
East Midlands Parkway ✈	d	15 37				15 43	15 52					16 23	16 23				16 53						17 23	17 23	
Beeston	a					15 48	15 59																		
Nottingham ■ 🚋	a					15 55	16 06										17 05								
	d			15 44	15 46					16 14					16 40	16 49				17 14					
Lincoln	a																								
Langley Mill	d									16 30					17 00	17 05				17 30					
Alfreton	d			16 06	16 08					16 38					17 08	17 13				17 38					
Long Eaton	a	15 41										16 27	16 27										17 27	17 27	
Derby ■	a	15 53										16 39	16 39										17 39	17 39	
	d	15 55						16 11			16 44	16 48	16 48					17 11			17 43	17 43	17 48	17 49	
Chesterfield	d	16 16		16 23	16 23					16 50	17 03	17 09	17 09		17 22	17 23				17 51	18 04	18 04	18 10	18 10	
Sheffield ■ 🚋	a	16 30		16 39	16 39			16 48		17 15	17 17	17 28	17 29		17 40	17 40		17 48		18 14	18 19	18 19	18 26	18 26	
Doncaster ■	a							17 13										18 13							
Wakefield Kirkgate ■	a									17 52										18 52					
Wakefield Westgate ■	a										17 47	18 06	18 06					18 33			18 47	18 47			
Leeds ■	a									18 18	18 02	18 24	18 24					18 51		19 18	19 04	19 04			
York ■	a							17 42			18 29							19 18			19 28	19 29			

A from 23 September until 21 October. From St Pancras International
B From Birmingham New Street to Newcastle
C from 23 September until 21 October. To Sheffield
D from 28 October
E From Plymouth to Glasgow Central
F from 28 October. To Liverpool Lime Street
G from 23 September until 21 October. To Liverpool Lime Street
H from 23 September until 21 October. To Nottingham
I From Guildford to Newcastle
J from 23 September until 21 October
K From Plymouth to Edinburgh
L From Reading to Newcastle
M From Penzance to Glasgow Central
N from 28 October. ⊡ from Derby ⊼ to Derby
O from 23 September until 21 October. ⊡ from Derby ⊼ to Derby
P from 23 September until 21 October. From Norwich to Liverpool Lime Street
Q from 28 October. From Norwich to Liverpool Lime Street
R from 23 September until 21 October. From Plymouth to Edinburgh
S from 28 October. From Plymouth to Edinburgh

For connections from Gatwick Airport see Table 52

London - East Midlands - Sheffield

Sundays from 23 September

Route Diagram - see first Page of Table 53

Station		EM ◇ A	EM ◇ B	EM ◇1 C	EM ◇1 D	XC ◇1 E	EM ◇1 C	EM ◇1 D	EM ◇1 C	NT	XC ◇1 F	EM ◇1 G C	EM ◇1	EM ◇1 H D	EM ◇1	EM ◇1 I	EM ◇	EM ◇1 J	XC ◇1 C	EM ◇1 D	EM ◇1 C	EM ◇1
St Pancras International	d			16 00	16 00		16 25	16 25	16 30			16 30	16 55		16 55			17 00		17 25	17 25	17 30
Luton Airport Parkway	d			16 21	16 21													17 21				
Luton	d								16 52			16 52										17 52
Bedford	d			16 37	16 37				17 08			17 08						17 38				18 08
Wellingborough	d			16 51	16 51				17 21			17 21						17 51				18 21
Kettering	a			16 57	16 57				17 28			17 28						17 58				18 28
	d			16 58	16 58				17 29			17 29				17 50		17 59				18 29
Corby	d															18a00						
Oakham	d																					
Melton Mowbray	d																					
Market Harborough	d			17 08	17 08				17 39			17 39						18 09				18 39
Leicester	a			17 23	17 31		17 35	17 37	17 54			18 01	18 02		18 05			18 29		18 33	18 34	18 54
	d			17 25	17 32		17 37	17 39	17 55			18 03	18 05		18 11			18 30		18 34	18 36	18 55
Syston	d																					
Sileby	d																					
Barrow Upon Soar	d																					
Loughborough	d			17 35	17 43				18 07			18 13		←				18 41				19 06
East Midlands Parkway	d			17 43	17 50		17 53	17 55	18 14			18 21	18 19	18 21	18 25			18 48		18 53	18 53	19 13
Beeston	a			17 48	17 59							→						18 58				
Nottingham	a			17 55	18 06								18 29		18 37			19 05				
	d	17 35	17 38							18 14							18 37					
Lincoln	a																					
Langley Mill	d	17 54	17 54							18 30							18 54					
Alfreton	d	18 02	18 02							18 38							19 02					
Long Eaton	a								18 18					18 24								19 17
Derby	a						18 05	18 07	18 29					18 35						19 04	19 04	19 28
	d					18 11	18 13	18 15			18 43								19 05	19 09	19 10	
Chesterfield	d	18 17	18 17				18 36	18 36		18 52	19 05						19 13			19 28	19 29	
Sheffield	a	18 34	18 34			18 46	18 51	18 51		19 16	19 20						19 31		19 39	19 50	19 50	
Doncaster	a					19 15													20 16			
Wakefield Kirkgate	a									19 52												
Wakefield Westgate	a										19 48											
Leeds	a									20 18	20 05											
York	a					19 43					20 29								20 45			

Station		NT	XC ◇1 K	EM ◇1 G C	EM ◇1	EM ◇1 H D	EM ◇1	EM ◇1 I	EM ◇ C	EM ◇1	D	EM ◇1 L	XC ◇1 C	EM ◇1 D	EM ◇1 C	EM ◇1	NT M	XC ◇1 N	XC ◇1 G	EM ◇1	C	EM ◇1 H	EM ◇1 D	EM ◇1	EM ◇1
St Pancras International	d			17 30	17 55		17 55			18 00		18 00		18 25	18 25	18 30				18 30		18 55		18 55	
Luton Airport Parkway	d									18 21		18 21													
Luton	d			17 52												18 53				18 53					
Bedford	d			18 08						18 38		18 38				19 08				19 08					
Wellingborough	d			18 21						18 51		18 51				19 22				19 22					
Kettering	a			18 28						18 58		18 58				19 28				19 28					
	d			18 29				18 50		18 59		18 59				19 29				19 29					19 45
Corby	d							19a00																	19a55
Oakham	d																								
Melton Mowbray	d																								
Market Harborough	d			18 39						19 09		19 09				19 39				19 39					
Leicester	a			19 01	19 02		19 05			19 24		19 32		19 35	19 37	19 54				20 01		20 02		20 07	
	d			19 03	19 04		19 11			19 25		19 33		19 37	19 40	19 56				20 03		20 06		20 08	
Syston	d																								
Sileby	d																								
Barrow Upon Soar	d																								
Loughborough	d			19 13		←				19 36		19 44				20 06				20 13			←		
East Midlands Parkway	d			19 21	19 18	19 21	19 25			19 43		19 51		19 53	19 56	20 14				20 21		20 20	20 21	20 25	
Beeston	a			→						19 49		19 59								→					
Nottingham	a				19 29		19 35			19 56		20 06										20 30		20 35	
	d	19 19							19 38								20 13								
Lincoln	a																								
Langley Mill	d	19 35															20 29								
Alfreton	d	19 43							20 00								20 37								
Long Eaton	a					19 24										20 24							20 24		
Derby	a					19 35								20 05	20 08	20 35							20 35		
	d		19 41										20 03	20 07	20 10			20 43	20 43						
Chesterfield	d	19 54	20 02						20 12					20 28	20 31		20 48	21 03	21 05						
Sheffield	a	20 15	20 17						20 31				20 38	20 49	20 49		21 14	21 16	21 19						
Doncaster	a												21 19												
Wakefield Kirkgate	a	20 52																							
Wakefield Westgate	a		20 46											21 27	21 30			21 47	21 47						
Leeds	a	21 16	21 03											21 44	21 44			22 04	22 04						
York	a		21 31										21 44												

A from 23 September until 21 October. From Norwich to Liverpool Lime Street
B from 28 October. From Norwich to Liverpool Lime Street
C from 28 October
D from 23 September until 21 October
E From Reading to Edinburgh
F From Plymouth to Edinburgh. ⊼ to Leeds
G from 23 September until 21 October. To Derby
H from 23 September until 21 October. From St Pancras International
I From Norwich to Manchester Piccadilly
J From Reading to Newcastle
K From Plymouth to Leeds
L From Reading to Newcastle. ⊼ to Sheffield
M from 28 October. From Plymouth
N from 23 September until 21 October. From Plymouth

For connections from Gatwick Airport see Table 52

Table 53

London - East Midlands - Sheffield

Sundays from 23 September

Route Diagram - see first Page of Table 53

Station		EM ◇1 A	EM ◇1 B	EM ◇1 A	EM ◇1 B	EM ◇1 A	EM ◇1 B	EM ◇1	XC ◇1 C	XC ◇1 D	NT	EM ◇1 A	EM ◇1 B	EM ◇1 A	EM ◇1 B	EM ◇1 A	EM ◇1 B	EM ◇1 A	EM ◇1 B	EM ◇1	EM ◇1 A	EM ◇1 B	XC ◇1 E
St Pancras International	d	19 00	19 00	19 25	19 25	19 30	19 30					19 55	19 55	20 00	20 00	20 25	20 25	20 30	20 30		21 00	21 00	
Luton Airport Parkway	d	19 21	19 21											20 21	20 21						21 21	21 21	
Luton	d					19 53	19 53											20 54	20 54				
Bedford	d	19 38	19 38			20 08	20 08							20 38	20 38			21 11	21 11		21 40	21 40	
Wellingborough	d	19 51	19 51			20 22	20 22							20 51	20 51			21 24	21 24		21 53	21 53	
Kettering	a	19 58	19 58			20 28	20 28							20 57	20 57			21 31	21 31		22 00	22 00	
	d	19 59	19 59			20 29	20 29	20 46						20 58	20 58			21 32	21 32	21 55	22 01	22 01	
Corby	d							20a56												22a05			
Oakham	d																						
Melton Mowbray	d																						
Market Harborough	d	20 09	20 09			20 39	20 39							21 08	21 08			21 43	21 43		22 11	22 11	
Leicester	a	20 24	20 32	20 35	20 37	20 54	21 01					21 05	21 07	21 23	21 32	21 32	21 36	22 02	22 02		22 26	22 28	
	d	20 25	20 33	20 37	20 40	20 56	21 03					21 07	21 09	21 25	21 33	21 34	21 37	22 04	22 04		22 27	22 29	
Syston	d																						
Sileby	d																						
Barrow Upon Soar	d																						
Loughborough	d	20 36	20 44			21 06	21 13					21 18	21 20	21 35	21 44	21 44	21 48				22 37	22 39	
East Midlands Parkway	d	20 43	20 51	20 53	20 56	21 14	21 21					21 26	21 28	21 43	21 51	21 52	21 56	22 20	22 20		22 50	22 52	
Beeston	a	20 49	20 59											21 49	21 59						22 58	23 00	
Nottingham	a	20 56	21 06									21 37	21 39	21 55	22 06						23 05	23 07	
	d										21 30												
Lincoln	a																						
Langley Mill	d										21 52												
Alfreton	d										22 00												
Long Eaton	a					21 23	21 24																
Derby	a			21 05	21 08	21 35	21 35									22 04	22 08	22 32	22 32				
	d			21 09	21 10				21 44	21 44								22 34	22 34				22 44
Chesterfield	d			21 30	21 31				22 03	22 05	22 13							22 55	22 56				23 05
Sheffield	a			21 44	21 45				22 18	22 19	22 36							23 09	23 10				23 20
Doncaster	a																						
Wakefield Kirkgate	a										23 26												
Wakefield Westgate	a								22 43	22 45								23 40	23 40				
Leeds	a								23 01	23 03	00 05							00 01	00 01				00 11
York	a																						

Station		EM ◇1 A	EM ◇1 B	EM ◇1 B	EM ◇1 A	EM ◇1
St Pancras International	d	21 30	21 30	22 30	22 30	23 00
Luton Airport Parkway	d			22 51	22 51	23 27
Luton	d	21 52	21 52			
Bedford	d	22 08	22 08	23 14	23 14	23 50
Wellingborough	d	22 21	22 21	23 28	23 28	00 04
Kettering	a	22 28	22 28	23 34	23 34	00 10
	d	22 29	22 29	23 35	23 35	00 11
Corby	d					
Oakham	d					
Melton Mowbray	d					
Market Harborough	d	22 39	22 39	23 45	23 45	00 21
Leicester	a	22 54	22 56	00 04	00 04	00 42
	d	22 55	22 57	00 06	00 06	00 44
Syston	d					
Sileby	d					
Barrow Upon Soar	d					
Loughborough	d	23 06	23 08	00 16	00 16	00 54
East Midlands Parkway	d	23 18	23 20	00 29	00 29	01 07
Beeston	a			00 37	00 37	
Nottingham	a			00 44	00 48	
	d					
Lincoln	a					
Langley Mill	d					
Alfreton	d					
Long Eaton	a	23 25	23 27			
Derby	a	23 36	23 38			01 21
	d	23 37	23 39			
Chesterfield	d	23 57	23 59			
Sheffield	a	00 17	00 17			
Doncaster	a					
Wakefield Kirkgate	a					
Wakefield Westgate	a					
Leeds	a					
York	a					

A from 28 October
B from 23 September until 21 October
C from 28 October. From Penzance
D from 23 September until 21 October. From Plymouth
E from 23 September until 21 October. From Penzance

For connections from Gatwick Airport see Table 52

Sheffield - East Midlands - London

Route Diagram - see first Page of Table 53

Miles	Miles	Miles			EM MX ◇■ A ⊼	EM MO ◇ B	EM MO ◇ C	EM MX ◇ D	EM ◇■ E ⊼	EM ◇■ ⊼	EM ◇■ ⊼	EM ◇■ ⊼	EM ◇■ ⊼	EM	NT	EM ◇■ ⊼	EM ◇■ F ⊼	EM ◇■ G ⊠⊼	EM ◇■ ⊼	EM ◇■ ⊼	EM ◇■ ⊠⊼	EM ◇■ ⊼	NT
—	—	—	York	d																			
—	—	—	Leeds	d																			
—	—	—	Wakefield Westgate	d																			
—	—	—	Wakefield Kirkgate	d																			
—	—	—	Doncaster	d																			
0	0	—	**Sheffield**	d	23p21	23p29	23p29	23p37	23p51						05 05		05 26	05 29			05 57		06 00
12¼	12¼	—	Chesterfield	d	23p45	23p43	23p43	00 02	00 04						05 20		05 38	05 41			06 10		06 16
—	36½	—	**Derby**	a	00 11				00 30								06 02	06 02			06 31		
—	—	—		d							04 55	05 17					06 04	06 04			06 32		
—	44	—	Long Eaton	d								05 27									06 43		
22½	—	—	Alfreton	d		23p54	23p54																06 30
34½	—	—	Langley Mill	d		00 02	00 02																06 37
—	—	—	Lincoln	d																			
40¼	—	—	**Nottingham**	a		00 25	00 32	00 40							06 12								07 02
—	—	—		d									05 31	05 43						06 28		06 49	
44	—	—	Beeston	d																06 34		06 55	
—	—	—	East Midlands Parkway	d							05 06		05 42				06 17	06 17		06 40		07 02	
55½	53¼	—	Loughborough	d							05 14		05 50	06 05			06 25	06 25			06 52		
59½	57¼	—	Barrow Upon Soar	d										06 09									
61½	59¼	—	Sileby	d										06 14									
64¼	62	—	Syston	d										06 20									
68	65¾	0	**Leicester**	a							05 24	05 42	06 02	06 28			06 37	06 37		06 54	07 04	07 16	
—	—	—		d						04 44	05 26	05 43	06 04				06 39	06 39		06 57	07 06	07 17	
84¼	82	—	Market Harborough	d							05 41	05 58	06 19				06 54	06 54		07 12		07 32	
—	—	15¼	Melton Mowbray	d												06 01							
—	—	26¾	Oakham	d												06 13							
—	—	41	Corby	d												06 34			07 08				
95¼	93	48½	Kettering	a						05 04	05 50	06 07	06 29			06 43	07 04	07 04	07 17	07 21	07 28	07 41	
—	—	—		d						05 05	05 51	06 08	06 30			06 44	07 06	07 06		07 22	07 29	07 42	
102¼	100	—	Wellingborough	d						05 23	05 59	06 16	06 38			06 53	07 14	07 14		07 30	07 38	07 50	
117½	115¼	—	Bedford	d						05 36		06 31				07 08					07 55		
137	134¾	—	Luton	d							06 24					07 24				07 56		08 15	
138	135¾	—	Luton Airport Parkway	d						05 53			07 04				07 41	07 41			08 12		
167¼	165	—	**St Pancras International**	a						06 16	06 48	07 08	07 29			07 47	08 07	08 07		08 24	08 39	08 43	

		XC ◇■ H	EM	EM ◇■ ⊠⊼	EM ◇■ ⊠⊼	EM ◇■ ⊼	EM ◇■ ⊠⊼	XC ◇■ I ⊼	EM ◇■ ⊼	EM	EM ◇■ ⊼	NT	XC ◇■ J ⊼	EM ◇■ K ⊠⊼	EM ◇■ L ⊼	EM ◇■ ⊼	EM ◇■ M ⊼	EM ◇■ ⊼	I	XC ◇■ N ⊼	EM	NT O	XC ◇■ ⊼	EM ◇■ ⊼
York	d																			06 32			07 23	
Leeds	d			05 25				06 00				06 05	06 15			06 34				07 05		07 05		
Wakefield Westgate	d			05 37				06 12					06 27			06 46				07 18				
Wakefield Kirkgate	d											06 21										07 25		
Doncaster	d			05 57									06 45										07 55	
Sheffield	d	06 01		06 27			06 47	06 50				07 03	07 18	07 27		07 32	07 41			07 53		08 05	08 20	
Chesterfield	d	06 27		06 39			06 59	07 04				07 20	07 30	07 39		07 45	07 55			08 06		08 24	08 32	
Derby	a	06 46		07 03			07 19	07 25					07 49	07 59			08 14			08 26			08 51	
	d			07 05			07 20		07 26					08 01			08 16							
Long Eaton	d								07 36								08 26							
Alfreton	d											07 33				07 58						08 35		
Langley Mill	d											07 40				08 06						08 42		
Lincoln	d														07 04						07 26			
Nottingham	a											08 02			07 57	08 21					08 30	09 02		
	d				07 10					07 31	07 50				08 02	08 28					08 32			
Beeston	d				07 17					07 37					08 08			←			08 38			
East Midlands Parkway	d				07 25		07 33			07 46	08 01					08 39	08 32	08 39			08 46			
Loughborough	d		06 53	07 22			07 41		07 47	07 55					08 22	→	08 40				08 55			
Barrow Upon Soar	d		06 57							07 59											08 59			
Sileby	d		07 03							08 04											09 03			
Syston	d		07 08							08 09											09 08			
Leicester	a		07 19	07 34	07 41		07 52		07 59	08 21	08 17			08 23	08 32		08 52	08 57			09 22			
	d			07 35	07 42		07 54		08 00		08 18			08 25	08 33		08 52	08 57						
Market Harborough	d				07 58				08 16						08 47			09 12						
Melton Mowbray	d																							
Oakham	d																							
Corby	d					08 02																		09 17
Kettering	a			07 57	08 08	08 11	08 14		08 26						08 56									09 26
	d			07 59	08 09		08 16		08 27						08 56									09 27
Wellingborough	d			08 07			08 24		08 38						09 04									09 35
Bedford	d				08 29				09 02						09 18									09 49
Luton	d								09 18															10 04
Luton Airport Parkway	d														09 34									
St Pancras International	a			08 55	09 06		09 09		09 44		09 29			09 34	10 00		10 05	10 16						10 29

A until 14 September
B from 21 May until 25 June, 17 September, 24 September. From Liverpool Lime Street
C from 2 July until 10 September. From Liverpool Lime Street
D From Liverpool Lime Street
E from 18 September until 28 September
F from 17 September until 28 September
G until 14 September
H To Reading
I To Plymouth
J To Southampton Central
K ⊡ from Nottingham ⊼ to Nottingham
L To St Pancras International
M From Leeds
N From Sleaford
O From Newcastle to Reading

For connections to Gatwick Airport see Table 52

Sheffield - East Midlands - London

Route Diagram - see first Page of Table 53

		EM ◇■ ⊼	EM ◇■ ⊼	EM ◇ A	EM ◇■ ⊼	XC ◇■ B ⊼	EM ◇■ ⊼	EM	NT	XC ◇■ C ⊼	EM ◇■ ⊼	EM ◇■ ⊼	EM ◇■ ⊼	EM ◇■ ⊼	EM ◇■ ⊼	EM	EM ◇ A	XC ◇■ D ⊼	NT	XC ◇■ E ⊼	EM ◇■ ⊼	EM ◇■ ⊼	EM ◇■ ⊼
York	d					07 44				08 24								08 44		09 35			
Leeds	d					08 11			08 02									09 11	09 05				
Wakefield Westgate	d					08 23												09 24					
Wakefield Kirkgate	d								08 23										09 23				
Doncaster	d									08 50										09 58			
Sheffield	d	08 27		08 38	08 47	08 54			09 05	09 23		09 27		09 35			09 38	09 54	10 05	10 23		10 27	
Chesterfield	d	08 39		08 53	08 59	09 06			09 22			09 39		09 47			09 53	10 06	10 22			10 39	
Derby	a	08 59			09 19	09 25				09 51		09 59		10 16				10 26		10 51		10 59	
	d	09 01			09 20							10 01		10 20								11 01	
Long Eaton	d				09 30									10 30									
Alfreton	d			09 03					09 32								10 04		10 33				
Langley Mill	d								09 40										10 40				
Lincoln	d							08 35								09 32							
Nottingham	a			09 30				09 30	10 00							10 30	10 30		11 00				
	d		09 02				09 28	09 32					10 02		10 28	10 32							11 02
Beeston	d		09 08					09 38					10 08			10 38							11 08
East Midlands Parkway	d				09 35		09 39	09 46						10 35	10 39	10 46							
Loughborough	d		09 20		09 42			09 55					10 20	10 42		10 55							11 20
Barrow Upon Soar	d							09 59								10 59							
Sileby	d							10 03								11 03							
Syston	d							10 08								11 08							
Leicester	a	09 23	09 31		09 54		09 57	10 21				10 23	10 33	10 54	10 57	11 21						11 23	11 31
	d	09 25	09 33		09 55		09 57					10 25	10 33	10 55	10 57							11 25	11 33
Market Harborough	d		09 47				10 12						10 47		11 12								11 47
Melton Mowbray	d																						
Oakham	d																						
Corby	d																				11 17		
Kettering	a		09 56										10 55								11 26		11 56
	d		09 56								10 27		10 56								11 27		11 56
Wellingborough	d		10 04								10 35		11 04								11 35		12 04
Bedford	d		10 18								10 49		11 18								11 49		12 18
Luton	d										11 05										12 05		
Luton Airport Parkway	d		10 34										11 34										12 34
St Pancras International	a	10 34	11 01		11 04		11 16				11 29	11 34	12 00	12 04	12 13						12 29	12 33	13 00

		EM ◇ A	EM ◇■ ⊼	XC ◇■ F ⊼	EM ◇■ ⊼	EM	NT ◇	XC ◇■ G ⊼	EM ◇■ ⊼	EM ◇■ ⊼	EM ◇■ ⊼	EM ◇ A	EM ◇■ ⊼	XC ◇■ H ⊼	EM ◇■ ⊼	EM	NT ◇ I	XC ◇■ ⊼	EM ◇■ ⊼	EM ◇■ ⊼	EM ◇■ ⊼	EM ◇■ ⊼
York	d			09 45				10 34						10 44				11 34				
Leeds	d			10 11			10 05							11 11			11 05					
Wakefield Westgate	d			10 23										11 24								
Wakefield Kirkgate	d						10 23										11 23					
Doncaster	d							10 58										11 58				
Sheffield	d	10 38	10 47	10 54			11 05	11 23		11 27		11 38	11 47	11 54			12 05	12 23		12 27		12 35
Chesterfield	d	10 52	10 59	11 06			11 22			11 39		11 53	11 59	12 06			12 22			12 39		12 48
Derby	a		11 19	11 25				11 51		11 59			12 19	12 26				12 51		12 59		13 15
	d		11 20							12 01			12 20							13 01		13 20
Long Eaton	d		11 30										12 30									13 30
Alfreton	d	11 03					11 33					12 03					12 33					
Langley Mill	d						11 40										12 40					
Lincoln	d					10 36										11 42						
Nottingham	a	11 30				11 30	12 00					12 30				12 30	13 01					
	d				11 28	11 32					12 02				12 28	12 32					13 02	
Beeston	d					11 38					12 08					12 38					13 08	
East Midlands Parkway	d		11 35		11 39	11 46							12 35		12 39	12 46						13 35
Loughborough	d		11 42			11 55					12 20		12 42			12 55					13 20	13 42
Barrow Upon Soar	d					11 59										12 59						
Sileby	d					12 03										13 03						
Syston	d					12 08										13 08						
Leicester	a		11 54		11 57	12 21				12 23	12 31		12 53		12 57	13 21				13 23	13 32	13 54
	d		11 55		11 57					12 25	12 33		12 55		12 57					13 25	13 33	13 55
Market Harborough	d				12 12						12 47				13 12						13 47	
Melton Mowbray	d																					
Oakham	d																					
Corby	d								12 17										13 17			
Kettering	a								12 26		12 56								13 26		13 56	
	d								12 27		12 56								13 27		13 56	
Wellingborough	d								12 35		13 04								13 35		14 04	
Bedford	d								12 49		13 18								13 49		14 18	
Luton	d								13 05										14 05			
Luton Airport Parkway	d										13 34										14 34	
St Pancras International	a		13 04		13 13				13 29	13 34	14 01		14 04		14 13				14 29	14 34	14 59	15 03

A From Liverpool Lime Street to Norwich
B From Newcastle to Plymouth
C From Newcastle to Southampton Central
D From Edinburgh to Plymouth
E From Edinburgh to Reading
F From Glasgow Central to Plymouth
G From Newcastle to Southampton Central
H From Dundee to Plymouth
I From Newcastle to Reading

For connections to Gatwick Airport see Table 52

until 28 September

Sheffield - East Midlands - London

Route Diagram - see first Page of Table 53

Station		EM ◇1 ⌶	EM	EM ◇ A	XC ◇1 B ⌶	NT ◇	XC ◇1 C ⌶	EM ◇1 ⌶	EM ◇1 ⌶	EM ◇1 ⌶	EM ◇ A	EM ◇1 ⌶	XC ◇1 D ⌶	EM ◇1 ⌶	EM	NT ◇	XC ◇1 E ⌶	EM ◇1 ⌶	EM ◇1 ⌶	EM ◇1 ⌶	EM ◇1 ⌶	EM ◇ A	XC ◇1 F ⌶
York [8]	d				11 45		12 34						12 44				13 34						13 44
Leeds [10]	d				12 12	12 05							13 11			13 05							14 11
Wakefield Westgate [7]	d				12 24								13 23										14 23
Wakefield Kirkgate [4]	d					12 23										13 23							
Doncaster [7]	d						12 59										13 58						
Sheffield [7]	d			12 38	12 54	13 05	13 23		13 27		13 38	13 47	13 54			14 05	14 23		14 27		14 35	14 38	14 54
Chesterfield	d			12 53	13 06	13 22			13 39		13 52	13 59	14 07			14 22			14 39		14 47	14 53	15 06
Derby [6]	a				13 25		13 51		13 59			14 19	14 26				14 51		14 59		15 16		15 25
	d								14 01			14 20							15 01		15 20		
Long Eaton	d											14 30									15 30		
Alfreton	d			13 03		13 33					14 03					14 33						15 04	
Langley Mill	d					13 40										14 40							
Lincoln	d		12 30												13 40								
Nottingham [8]	a		13 30	13 30		14 00					14 30				14 30	15 00						15 28	
	d	13 28	13 32							14 02				14 28	14 32					15 02			
Beeston	d		13 38							14 08					14 38					15 08			
East Midlands Parkway ✈	d	13 39	13 46									14 35		14 39	14 46						15 35		
Loughborough	d		13 55							14 20		14 42			14 55					15 20	15 42		
Barrow Upon Soar	d		13 59												14 59								
Sileby	d		14 03												15 03								
Syston	d		14 08												15 08								
Leicester	a	13 57	14 21						14 23	14 31		14 53		14 57	15 21				15 23	15 31	15 53		
	d	13 57							14 25	14 33		14 55		14 57					15 25	15 33	15 54		
Market Harborough	d	14 12								14 47				15 12						15 47			
Melton Mowbray	d																						
Oakham	d																						
Corby	d							14 17										15 17					
Kettering [4]	a							14 26		14 56								15 26		15 56			
	d							14 27		14 56								15 27		15 56			
Wellingborough	d							14 35		15 04								15 35		16 04			
Bedford [7]	d							14 49		15 18								15 49		16 18			
Luton [10]	d							15 05										16 05					
Luton Airport Parkway [7] ✈	d									15 34										16 34			
St Pancras International ⊖	a	15 13						15 29	15 34	15 59		16 04		16 13				16 29	16 33	17 00	17 05		

Station		EM ◇1 ⌶	EM	NT ◇	XC ◇1 G ⌶	EM ◇1 ⌶	EM ◇1 ⌶	EM ◇1 ⌶	EM ◇ A	EM ◇1 ⌶	XC ◇1 D ⌶	EM ◇1 ⌶	EM ◇1 ⌶	EM ◇1 H ⌶	EM	NT ◇	XC ◇1 E ⌶	EM ◇1 ⌶	EM ◇1 ⌶	EM ◇1 ⌶	EM ◇1 ⌶	EM ◇1 I ⌶
York [8]	d				14 34						14 44						15 34					
Leeds [10]	d			14 05							15 11					15 05						
Wakefield Westgate [7]	d										15 23											
Wakefield Kirkgate [4]	d			14 23												15 23						
Doncaster [7]	d				14 58												15 58					
Sheffield [7]	d			15 05	15 23		15 27		15 38	15 47	15 54					16 04	16 23	16 27		16 35		
Chesterfield	d			15 22			15 39		15 53		16 06					16 21		16 39		16 50		
Derby [6]	a				15 51		15 59			16 16	16 25						16 51	16 59		17 16		
	d						16 01			16 18				16 34				17 01		17 18		
Long Eaton	d									16 28										17 28		
Alfreton	d			15 33					16 04							16 32						
Langley Mill	d			15 40												16 40						
Lincoln	d		14 33												15 30							
Nottingham [8]	a		15 29	16 00					16 33						16 30	17 00						
	d	15 28	15 32					16 02				16 28			16 32				17 02		17 28	
Beeston	d		15 38					16 08							16 38				17 08			
East Midlands Parkway ✈	d	15 39	15 46							16 32		16 39		16 47	16 48					17 32	17 39	
Loughborough	d		15 55					16 20		16 40					16 57				17 20	17 40		
Barrow Upon Soar	d		15 59												17 01							
Sileby	d		16 03												17 05							
Syston	d		16 08												17 09							
Leicester	a	15 57	16 21				16 23	16 31		16 51		16 55			17 22			17 23	17 31	17 52	17 57	
	d	15 57					16 25	16 33		16 53		16 57						17 25	17 33	17 54	17 57	
Market Harborough	d	16 12						16 47				17 12							17 47		18 12	
Melton Mowbray	d													17 12								
Oakham	d													17 24								
Corby	d					16 17							17 17	17 52								
Kettering [4]	a					16 26		16 56		17 14			17 26	18 01					17 56	18 14		
	d					16 27		16 56		17 15			17 27	18 27					17 56	18 15		
Wellingborough	d					16 35		17 04					17 35	18 35					18 04			
Bedford [7]	d					16 49		17 18					17 49	18 49					18 17			←
Luton [10]	d					17 05						17 51	18 05	19 05				18 15				19 05
Luton Airport Parkway [7] ✈	d							17 30						→					18 33			
St Pancras International ⊖	a	17 18				17 29	17 33	18 01		18 08		18 17	18 34					18 39	19 00	19 06	19 19	19 32

A From Liverpool Lime Street to Norwich
B From Glasgow Central to Plymouth
C From Newcastle to Southampton Central
D From Glasgow Central to Penzance
E From Newcastle to Reading
F From Aberdeen to Penzance
G From Newcastle to Eastleigh
H To St Pancras International
I From Derby

For connections to Gatwick Airport see Table 52

until 28 September

Sheffield - East Midlands - London

Route Diagram - see first Page of Table 53

Station		EM	EM ◇ A	XC ◇1 B ⌶	NT ◇	XC ◇1 C ⌶	EM ◇1 ⌶	EM ◇1 ⌶	EM ◇1 ⌶	EM ◇1 ⌶	EM	EM ◇ A	XC ◇1 D ⌶	NT ◇	XC ◇1 C ⌶	EM ◇1 ⌶	EM ◇1 ⌶	EM ◇1 ⌶	EM ◇1 ⌶	EM ◇1 ⌶	EM	EM ◇ E	XC ◇1 B ⌶
York [8]	d			15 44		16 04							16 44		17 34								17 44
Leeds [10]	d			16 11	16 05	16 40							17 11	17 05									18 11
Wakefield Westgate [7]	d			16 23		16 52							17 23										18 23
Wakefield Kirkgate [4]	d				16 23									17 23									
Doncaster [7]	d														17 59								
Sheffield [7]	d		16 38	16 54	17 05	17 23	17 27		17 35			17 44	17 54	18 05	18 23		18 27		18 35			18 45	18 54
Chesterfield	d		16 56	17 06	17 22		17 39		17 50			18 02	18 07	18 22			18 39		18 47			19 01	19 06
Derby [6]	a			17 26		17 51	17 59		18 16				18 26		18 51		18 59		19 14				19 26
	d						18 01		18 18								19 01		19 18				
Long Eaton	d								18 28										19 28				
Alfreton	d		17 07		17 33							18 12		18 33								19 11	
Langley Mill	d				17 40									18 40									
Lincoln	d	16 34									17 28										18 35		
Nottingham [8]	a	17 30	17 31		18 00						18 32	18 34		19 00							19 29	19 38	
	d	17 32						18 02		18 28	18 33							19 02		19 28	19 32		
Beeston	d	17 38						18 08			18 39							19 08			19 38		
East Midlands Parkway ✈	d	17 48							18 32	18 39	18 48								19 32	19 39	19 46		
Loughborough	d	17 57						18 20	18 40		18 56							19 20	19 40		19 55		
Barrow Upon Soar	d	18 01									19 01										19 59		
Sileby	d	18 05									19 05										20 03		
Syston	d	18 09									19 10										20 08		
Leicester	a	18 22					18 23	18 31	18 51	18 55	19 22						19 23	19 31	19 51	19 55	20 20		
	d						18 25	18 33	18 53	18 57							19 25	19 33	19 53	19 57			
Market Harborough	d							18 47		19 12								19 47		20 12			
Melton Mowbray	d																						
Oakham	d																						
Corby	d															18 57							
Kettering [4]	a							18 56								19 06		19 56					
	d							18 56								19 27		19 56					
Wellingborough	d							19 04								19 35		20 04					
Bedford [7]	d							19 18								19 49		20 18					
Luton [10]	d															20 05							
Luton Airport Parkway [7] ✈	d							19 34										20 34					
St Pancras International ⊖	a						19 35	20 01	20 04	20 11						20 29	20 34	20 59	21 02	21 11			

Station		NT ◇	XC ◇1 F ⌶	EM ◇1 ⌶	EM ◇1 ⌶	EM ◇1 ⌶	EM ◇ A	XC ◇1 G ⌶	EM	NT ◇	XC ◇1 H ⌶	EM ◇1 ⌶	EM ◇1 ⌶	EM ◇1 ⌶	EM ◇1 ⌶	EM ◇1 I ⌶	EM ◇1 J ⌶	EM	EM ◇ E	XC ◇1 K ⌶	XC ◇1 H	EM ◇ E	EM ◇1 L ⌶
York [8]	d		18 34					18 45			19 34									19 44	20 35		
Leeds [10]	d	18 05						19 11		19 05										20 11			
Wakefield Westgate [7]	d							19 23												20 23			
Wakefield Kirkgate [4]	d	18 23								19 24													
Doncaster [7]	d		18 58								19 58										21 02		
Sheffield [7]	d	19 05	19 23		19 27		19 38	19 54		20 05	20 23				20 39				20 41	20 54	21 28	21 39	21 42
Chesterfield	d	19 22			19 39		19 53	20 06		20 22					20 53				20 58	21 06	21 41	21 55	22 00
Derby [6]	a		19 52		19 59			20 26			20 52				21 18					21 26	22 00		22 21
	d				20 01										21 20								
Long Eaton	d																						
Alfreton	d	19 33					20 04			20 33									21 09			22 05	
Langley Mill	d	19 40								20 40												22 12	
Lincoln	d																						
Nottingham [8]	a	20 00					20 31			21 00									21 38			22 38	
	d					20 02			20 32					21 02		21 28	21 28	21 32					
Beeston	d					20 08			20 38					21 08				21 38					
East Midlands Parkway ✈	d					20 16			20 46					21 15	21 33			21 46					
Loughborough	d					20 24			20 55					21 22	21 41	21 46	21 46	21 55					
Barrow Upon Soar	d								20 59									21 59					
Sileby	d								21 03									22 03					
Syston	d								21 08									22 08					
Leicester	a				20 23	20 34			21 22					21 32	21 52	21 58	21 58	22 21					
	d				20 25	20 36								21 33	21 55	21 59	21 59						
Market Harborough	d					20 50								21 47		22 13	22 13						
Melton Mowbray	d																						
Oakham	d																						
Corby	d			19 43								20 43	21 43										
Kettering [4]	a			19 52		20 59						20 53	21 52	21 56		22 22	22 22						
	d			20 27		20 59						21 17		21 57		22 23	22 23						
Wellingborough	d			20 35		21 07						21 26		22 05		22 31	22 31						
Bedford [7]	d			20 54		21 22						21 44		22 19		22 45	22 45						
Luton [10]	d			21 08								22 01		22 34		23 00	23 02						
Luton Airport Parkway [7] ✈	d					21 39								22 38									
St Pancras International ⊖	a			21 33	21 36	22 04						22 29		23 01	23 04	23 26	23 34						

A From Liverpool Lime Street to Norwich
B From Edinburgh to Plymouth
C From Newcastle to Reading
D From Glasgow Central to Plymouth
E From Liverpool Lime Street
F From Newcastle to Guildford
G From Glasgow Central to Bristol Temple Meads
H From Newcastle to Birmingham New Street
I from 27 July until 7 September, not from 13 August until 28 August
J not from 27 July until 10 August, from 29 August until 7 September
K From Edinburgh to Bristol Temple Meads. ⌶ to Leeds
L until 14 September

For connections to Gatwick Airport see Table 52

Sheffield - East Midlands - London

Mondays to Fridays
until 28 September

Route Diagram - see first Page of Table 53

	EM	XC	EM	EM	EM	EM	EM
	◇■	◇■	◇■		◇■	◇	◇■
	A	B			C	D	A
	✕	✕	✕		✕		✕
York ■ d		20 45					
Leeds ■ d		21 11					
Wakefield Westgate ■ d		21 23					
Wakefield Kirkgate ■ d							
Doncaster ■ d							
Sheffield ■ d	21 42	22 00			23 21	23 37	23 51
Chesterfield d	22 00	22 24			23 45	00 02	00 04
Derby ■ a	22 23	22 44			00 11		00 30
d							
Long Eaton d							
Alfreton d							
Langley Mill d							
Lincoln d							
Nottingham ■ a						00 40	
d				23 10			
Beeston d				23 16			
East Midlands Parkway d				23 25			
Loughborough d				23 33			
Barrow Upon Soar d							
Sileby d							
Syston d							
Leicester a				23 58			
d							
Market Harborough d							
Melton Mowbray d							
Oakham d							
Corby d			22 43				
Kettering ■ a			22 52				
d							
Wellingborough d							
Bedford ■ d							
Luton ■ d							
Luton Airport Parkway ■ d							
St Pancras International a							

Mondays to Fridays
from 1 October

	EM MO	EM MX	EM MX	EM	EM	EM	EM	EM	NT	EM
	◇	◇	◇■	◇■	◇■	◇■	◇■			◇■
	D	D								
			✕	✕	✕	✕	✕			✕
York ■ d										
Leeds ■ d										
Wakefield Westgate ■ d										
Wakefield Kirkgate ■ d										
Doncaster ■ d										
Sheffield ■ d	23p29	23p37	23p51						05 05	
Chesterfield d	23p43	00 02	00 04						05 20	
Derby ■ a			00 30							
d					04 55	05 17				
Long Eaton d						05 27				
Alfreton d	23p54									
Langley Mill d	00 02									
Lincoln d										
Nottingham ■ a	00 25	00 40							06 12	
d							05 31	05 43		
Beeston d										
East Midlands Parkway d					05 06		05 42			
Loughborough d					05 14		05 50	06 05		
Barrow Upon Soar d								06 09		
Sileby d								06 14		
Syston d								06 20		
Leicester a					05 24	05 42	06 02	06 28		
d				04 44	05 26	05 43	06 04			
Market Harborough d					05 41	05 58	06 19			
Melton Mowbray d										06 01
Oakham d										06 13
Corby d										06 34
Kettering ■ a				05 04	05 50	06 07	06 29			06 43
d				05 05	05 51	06 08	06 30			06 44
Wellingborough d				05 23	05 59	06 16	06 38			06 53
Bedford ■ d				05 36		06 31				07 08
Luton ■ d					06 24					07 24
Luton Airport Parkway ■ d				05 53			07 04			
St Pancras International a				06 16	06 48	07 08	07 29			07 47

	EM	EM	EM	EM	EM	NT	XC	EM	EM	EM	EM	EM
	◇■	◇■	◇■	◇■	◇■		◇■		◇■	◇■	◇■	◇■
							E					
	✕	✕	✕	⊠✕	✕				⊠✕	⊠✕	✕	⊠✕
York ■ d												
Leeds ■ d									05 25			
Wakefield Westgate ■ d									05 37			
Wakefield Kirkgate ■ d												
Doncaster ■ d									05 57			
Sheffield ■ d	05 26			05 57		06 00	06 01		06 27			06 47
Chesterfield d	05 38			06 10		06 16	06 27		06 39			06 59
Derby ■ a	06 02			06 31			06 46		07 03			07 19
d	06 04			06 32					07 05			07 20
Long Eaton d				06 43								
Alfreton d						06 30						
Langley Mill d						06 37						
Lincoln d												
Nottingham ■ a						07 02						
d			06 28		06 49					07 10		
Beeston d			06 34		06 55					07 17		
East Midlands Parkway d	06 17		06 40		07 02					07 25		07 33
Loughborough d	06 25			06 52				06 53	07 22			07 41
Barrow Upon Soar d								06 57				
Sileby d								07 03				
Syston d								07 08				
Leicester a	06 37		06 54	07 04	07 16			07 19	07 34	07 41		07 52
d	06 39		06 57	07 06	07 17				07 35	07 42		07 54
Market Harborough d	06 54		07 12		07 32					07 58		
Melton Mowbray d												
Oakham d												
Corby d		07 08									08 02	
Kettering ■ a	07 04	07 17	07 21	07 28	07 41				07 57	08 08	08 11	08 14
d	07 06		07 22	07 29	07 42				07 59	08 09		08 16
Wellingborough d	07 14		07 30	07 38	07 50				08 07			08 24
Bedford ■ d				07 55						08 29		
Luton ■ d			07 56		08 15							
Luton Airport Parkway ■ d	07 41			08 12								
St Pancras International a	08 07		08 24	08 39	08 43				08 55	09 06		09 09

A from 17 September until 28 September
B From Glasgow Central to Birmingham New Street. ✕ to Leeds
C until 14 September
D From Liverpool Lime Street
E To Reading

For connections to Gatwick Airport see Table 52

Sheffield - East Midlands - London

Mondays to Fridays
from 1 October

Route Diagram - see first Page of Table 53

	XC	EM	EM	EM	NT	XC	EM	EM	EM	EM	EM
	◇■	◇■		◇■		◇■	◇■	◇■	◇■	◇■	◇■
	A					B		C	D		E
	✕	✕		✕		✕	⊠✕	✕	✕	✕	✕
York ■ d											
Leeds ■ d	06 00				06 05	06 15			06 34		
Wakefield Westgate ■ d	06 12					06 27			06 46		
Wakefield Kirkgate ■ d					06 21						
Doncaster ■ d						06 45					
Sheffield ■ d	06 50				07 03	07 18	07 27		07 32	07 41	
Chesterfield d	07 04				07 20	07 30	07 39		07 45	07 55	
Derby ■ a	07 25					07 49	07 59			08 14	
d		07 26					08 01			08 16	
Long Eaton d		07 36								08 26	
Alfreton d					07 33				07 58		
Langley Mill d					07 40				08 06		
Lincoln d								07 04			
Nottingham ■ a					08 02			07 57	08 21		
d			07 31	07 50				08 02	08 28		
Beeston d			07 37					08 08			←
East Midlands Parkway d			07 46	08 01					08 39	08 32	08 39
Loughborough d		07 47	07 55					08 22	→	08 40	
Barrow Upon Soar d			07 59								
Sileby d			08 04								
Syston d			08 09								
Leicester a		07 59	08 21	08 17			08 23	08 32		08 52	08 57
d		08 00		08 18			08 25	08 33		08 52	08 57
Market Harborough d		08 16						08 47			09 12
Melton Mowbray d											
Oakham d											
Corby d											
Kettering ■ a		08 26						08 56			
d		08 27						08 56			
Wellingborough d		08 38						09 04			
Bedford ■ d		09 02						09 18			
Luton ■ d		09 18									
Luton Airport Parkway ■ d								09 34			
St Pancras International a		09 44		09 29			09 34	10 00		10 05	10 16

	XC	EM	NT	XC	EM	EM	EM	EM	EM	XC	EM
	◇■			◇■	◇■	◇■	◇■	◇	◇■	◇■	◇■
	A	F		G				H	I		
	✕			✕	✕	✕	✕		✕	✕	✕
York ■ d	06 32			07 23						07 44	
Leeds ■ d	07 05		07 05							08 11	
Wakefield Westgate ■ d	07 18									08 23	
Wakefield Kirkgate ■ d			07 25								
Doncaster ■ d				07 55							
Sheffield ■ d	07 53		08 05	08 20		08 27		08 38	08 47	08 54	
Chesterfield d	08 06		08 24	08 32		08 39		08 53	08 59	09 06	
Derby ■ a	08 26			08 51		08 59			09 19	09 25	
d						09 01			09 20		
Long Eaton d									09 30		
Alfreton d			08 35					09 03			
Langley Mill d			08 42								
Lincoln d		07 26									
Nottingham ■ a		08 32	09 02					09 30			
d		08 32					09 02				09 28
Beeston d		08 38					09 08				
East Midlands Parkway d		08 46							09 35		09 39
Loughborough d		08 55					09 20		09 42		
Barrow Upon Soar d		08 59									
Sileby d		09 03									
Syston d		09 08									
Leicester a		09 22				09 23	09 31		09 54		09 57
d						09 25	09 33		09 55		09 57
Market Harborough d							09 47				10 12
Melton Mowbray d											
Oakham d											
Corby d					09 17						
Kettering ■ a					09 26		09 56				
d					09 27		09 56				
Wellingborough d					09 35		10 04				
Bedford ■ d					09 49		10 18				
Luton ■ d					10 04						
Luton Airport Parkway ■ d							10 34				
St Pancras International a					10 29	10 34	11 01		11 04		11 16

	EM	NT	XC	EM	EM	EM	EM	EM	EM	XC
			◇■	◇■	◇■	◇■	◇■	◇■	◇	◇■
			J						H	K
			✕	✕	✕	✕	✕	✕		✕
York ■ d			08 24							08 44
Leeds ■ d		08 02								09 11
Wakefield Westgate ■ d										09 24
Wakefield Kirkgate ■ d		08 23								
Doncaster ■ d			08 50							
Sheffield ■ d		09 05	09 23		09 27		09 35		09 38	09 54
Chesterfield d		09 22			09 39		09 47		09 53	10 06
Derby ■ a			09 51		09 59		10 16			10 26
d					10 01		10 20			
Long Eaton d							10 30			
Alfreton d		09 32							10 04	
Langley Mill d		09 40								
Lincoln d	08 35									
Nottingham ■ a	09 32	10 00							10 30	
d	09 32					10 02		10 28		
Beeston d	09 38					10 08				
East Midlands Parkway d	09 46						10 35	10 39		
Loughborough d	09 55					10 20	10 42			
Barrow Upon Soar d	09 59									
Sileby d	10 03									
Syston d	10 08									
Leicester a	10 21				10 23	10 33	10 54	10 57		
d					10 25	10 33	10 55	10 57		
Market Harborough d						10 47		11 12		
Melton Mowbray d										
Oakham d										
Corby d										
Kettering ■ a						10 55				
d				10 27		10 56				
Wellingborough d				10 35		11 04				
Bedford ■ d				10 49		11 18				
Luton ■ d				11 05						
Luton Airport Parkway ■ d						11 34				
St Pancras International a				11 29	11 34	12 00	12 04	12 13		

	EM	NT	XC	EM	EM	EM	EM	EM	XC	EM	EM
			◇■	◇■	◇■	◇■	◇	◇■	◇■	◇■	
		L					H	M			
			✕	✕	✕	✕		✕	✕	✕	
York ■ d			09 35						09 45		
Leeds ■ d		09 05							10 11		
Wakefield Westgate ■ d									10 23		
Wakefield Kirkgate ■ d		09 23									
Doncaster ■ d			09 58								
Sheffield ■ d		10 05	10 23		10 27		10 38	10 47	10 54		
Chesterfield d		10 22			10 39		10 52	10 59	11 06		
Derby ■ a			10 51		10 59			11 19	11 25		
d					11 01			11 20			
Long Eaton d								11 30			
Alfreton d		10 33					11 03				
Langley Mill d		10 40									
Lincoln d	09 32										10 36
Nottingham ■ a	10 32	11 00					11 30				11 32
d	10 32					11 02				11 28	11 32
Beeston d	10 38					11 08					11 38
East Midlands Parkway d	10 46							11 35		11 39	11 46
Loughborough d	10 55					11 20		11 42			11 55
Barrow Upon Soar d	10 59										11 59
Sileby d	11 03										12 03
Syston d	11 08										12 08
Leicester a	11 21				11 23	11 31		11 54		11 57	12 21
d					11 25	11 33		11 55		11 57	
Market Harborough d						11 47				12 12	
Melton Mowbray d											
Oakham d											
Corby d				11 17							
Kettering ■ a				11 26		11 56					
d				11 27		11 56					
Wellingborough d				11 35		12 04					
Bedford ■ d				11 49		12 18					
Luton ■ d				12 05							
Luton Airport Parkway ■ d						12 34					
St Pancras International a				12 29	12 33	13 00		13 04		13 13	

A To Plymouth
B To Southampton Central
C ⊡ from Nottingham ✕ to Nottingham
D To St Pancras International
E From Leeds
F From Sleaford
G From Newcastle to Reading
H From Liverpool Lime Street to Norwich
I From Newcastle to Plymouth
J From Newcastle to Southampton Central
K From Edinburgh to Plymouth
L From Edinburgh to Reading
M From Glasgow Central to Plymouth

For connections to Gatwick Airport see Table 52

Sheffield - East Midlands - London

Mondays to Fridays
from 1 October

Route Diagram - see first Page of Table 53

		NT ◇	XC ◇■ A	EM ◇■	EM ◇■	EM ◇■	EM ◇ B	EM ◇■		XC ◇■ C	EM ◇■	EM	NT ◇	XC ◇■ D	EM ◇■	EM ◇■	EM ◇■	EM ◇■		EM ◇■	EM ◇ B	XC ◇■ E	EM	NT ◇	XC ◇■ A
York 8	d		10 34							10 44				11 34								11 45			12 34
Leeds 10	d	10 05								11 11			11 05									12 12		12 05	
Wakefield Westgate 7	d									11 24												12 24			
Wakefield Kirkgate 4	d	10 23											11 23											12 23	
Doncaster 7	d		10 58											11 58											12 59
Sheffield 7	d	11 05	11 23		11 27		11 38	11 47		11 54			12 05	12 23		12 27		12 35			12 38	12 54		13 05	13 23
Chesterfield	d	11 22			11 39		11 53	11 59		12 06			12 22			12 39		12 48			12 53	13 06		13 22	
Derby 6	a		11 51		11 59			12 19		12 26				12 51		12 59		13 15				13 25			13 51
	d				12 01			12 20								13 01		13 20							
Long Eaton	d							12 30										13 30							
Alfreton	d	11 33					12 03						12 33								13 03			13 33	
Langley Mill	d	11 40											12 40											13 40	
Lincoln	d											11 42											12 30		
Nottingham 8	a	12 00					12 30					12 32	13 01								13 30		13 32	14 00	
	d					12 02					12 28	12 32					13 02			13 28			13 32		
Beeston	d					12 08						12 38					13 08						13 38		
East Midlands Parkway	d							12 35			12 39	12 46						13 35		13 39			13 46		
Loughborough	d					12 20		12 42				12 55					13 20	13 42					13 55		
Barrow Upon Soar	d											12 59											13 59		
Sileby	d											13 03											14 03		
Syston	d											13 08											14 08		
Leicester	a				12 23	12 31		12 53			12 57	13 21				13 23	13 32	13 54		13 57			14 21		
	d				12 25	12 33		12 55			12 57					13 25	13 33	13 55		13 57					
Market Harborough	d					12 47					13 12						13 47			14 12					
Melton Mowbray	d																								
Oakham	d																								
Corby	d			12 17											13 17										
Kettering 4	a			12 26		12 56									13 26		13 56								
	d			12 27		12 56									13 27		13 56								
Wellingborough	d			12 35		13 04									13 35		14 04								
Bedford 7	d			12 49		13 18									13 49		14 18								
Luton 10	d			13 05											14 05										
Luton Airport Parkway 7	d					13 34											14 34								
St Pancras International	a			13 29	13 34	14 01		14 04			14 13				14 29	14 34	14 59	15 03		15 13					

		EM ◇■	EM ◇■	EM ◇■		EM ◇ B	EM ◇■	XC ◇■ F	EM ◇■	EM	NT ◇	XC ◇■ D	EM ◇■	EM ◇■		EM ◇■	EM ◇■	EM ◇ B	XC ◇■ G	EM ◇■	EM	NT ◇	XC ◇■ H	EM ◇■
York 8	d							12 44				13 34							13 44				14 34	
Leeds 10	d							13 11			13 05								14 11			14 05		
Wakefield Westgate 7	d							13 23											14 23					
Wakefield Kirkgate 4	d										13 23											14 23		
Doncaster 7	d											13 58											14 58	
Sheffield 7	d		13 27			13 38	13 47	13 54			14 05	14 23		14 27			14 35	14 38	14 54			15 05	15 23	
Chesterfield	d		13 39			13 52	13 59	14 07			14 22			14 39			14 47	14 53	15 06			15 22		
Derby 6	a		13 59				14 19	14 26				14 51		14 59			15 16		15 25				15 51	
	d		14 01				14 20							15 01			15 20							
Long Eaton	d						14 30										15 30							
Alfreton	d					14 03					14 33							15 04				15 33		
Langley Mill	d										14 40											15 40		
Lincoln	d									13 40											14 33			
Nottingham 8	a					14 30				14 32	15 00							15 28			15 31	16 00		
	d			14 02					14 28	14 32						15 02				15 28	15 32			
Beeston	d			14 08						14 38						15 08					15 38			
East Midlands Parkway	d						14 35		14 39	14 46							15 35			15 39	15 46			
Loughborough	d			14 20			14 42			14 55						15 20	15 42				15 55			
Barrow Upon Soar	d									14 59											15 59			
Sileby	d									15 03											16 03			
Syston	d									15 08											16 08			
Leicester	a		14 23	14 31			14 53		14 57	15 21				15 23		15 31	15 53			15 57	16 21			
	d		14 25	14 33			14 55		14 57					15 25		15 33	15 54			15 57				
Market Harborough	d			14 47					15 12							15 47				16 12				
Melton Mowbray	d																							
Oakham	d																							
Corby	d	14 17											15 17											16 17
Kettering 4	a	14 26		14 56									15 26			15 56								16 26
	d	14 27		14 56									15 27			15 56								16 27
Wellingborough	d	14 35		15 04									15 35			16 04								16 35
Bedford 7	d	14 49		15 18									15 49			16 18								16 49
Luton 10	d	15 05											16 05											17 05
Luton Airport Parkway 7	d			15 34												16 34								
St Pancras International	a	15 29	15 34	15 59			16 04		16 13				16 29	16 33		17 00	17 05			17 18				17 29

A From Newcastle to Southampton Central
B From Liverpool Lime Street to Norwich
C From Dundee to Plymouth
D From Newcastle to Reading
E From Glasgow Central to Plymouth
F From Glasgow Central to Penzance
G From Aberdeen to Penzance
H From Newcastle to Eastleigh

For connections to Gatwick Airport see Table 52

Sheffield - East Midlands - London

Mondays to Fridays
from 1 October

Route Diagram - see first Page of Table 53

		EM ◇■	EM ◇■	EM ◇ A	EM ◇■	XC ◇■ B	EM ◇■	EM ◇■	EM ◇■ C	EM		NT ◇	XC ◇■ D	EM ◇■	EM ◇■	EM ◇■	EM ◇■	EM ◇■ E	EM ◇ A	XC ◇■ F		EM	NT ◇	XC ◇■ D	EM ◇■
York 8	d					14 44							15 34							15 44				16 04	
Leeds 10	d					15 11						15 05								16 11			16 05	16 40	
Wakefield Westgate 7	d					15 23														16 23				16 52	
Wakefield Kirkgate 4	d											15 23											16 23		
Doncaster 7	d												15 58												
Sheffield 7	d	15 27		15 38	15 47	15 54						16 04	16 23	16 27		16 35			16 38	16 54			17 05	17 23	17 27
Chesterfield	d	15 39		15 53		16 06						16 21		16 39		16 50			16 56	17 06			17 22		17 39
Derby 6	a	15 59			16 16	16 25							16 51	16 59		17 16				17 26				17 51	17 59
	d	16 01			16 18				16 34					17 01		17 18									18 01
Long Eaton	d				16 28											17 28									
Alfreton	d			16 04								16 32							17 07				17 33		
Langley Mill	d											16 40											17 40		
Lincoln	d									15 30												16 34			
Nottingham 8	a			16 33						16 32		17 00							17 31			17 32	18 00		
	d		16 02				16 28			16 32					17 02		17 28					17 32			
Beeston	d		16 08							16 38					17 08							17 38			
East Midlands Parkway	d				16 32		16 39		16 47	16 48						17 32	17 39					17 48			
Loughborough	d		16 20		16 40					16 57					17 20	17 40						17 57			
Barrow Upon Soar	d									17 01												18 01			
Sileby	d									17 05												18 05			
Syston	d									17 09												18 09			
Leicester	a	16 23	16 31		16 51		16 55			17 22				17 23	17 31	17 52	17 57					18 22			18 23
	d	16 25	16 33		16 53		16 57							17 25	17 33	17 54	17 57								18 25
Market Harborough	d		16 47				17 12								17 47		18 12								
Melton Mowbray	d								17 12																
Oakham	d								17 24																
Corby	d							17 17	17 52																
Kettering 4	a		16 56		17 14			17 26	18 01						17 56	18 14									
	d		16 56		17 15			17 27	18 27						17 56	18 15									
Wellingborough	d		17 04					17 35	18 35						18 04										
Bedford 7	d		17 18					17 49	18 49						18 17			←							
Luton 10	d						17 51	18 05	19 05					18 15				19 05							
Luton Airport Parkway 7	d		17 30						→						18 33										
St Pancras International	a	17 33	18 01		18 08		18 17	18 34						18 39	19 00	19 06	19 19	19 32							19 35

		EM ◇■	EM ◇■	EM ◇■	EM	EM ◇ A		XC ◇■ G	NT ◇	XC ◇■ D	EM ◇■	EM ◇■	EM ◇■	EM ◇■	EM ◇■	EM		EM ◇ H	XC ◇■ F	NT ◇	XC ◇■ I	EM ◇■	EM ◇■	EM ◇■	EM ◇ A
York 8	d							16 44		17 34									17 44		18 34				
Leeds 10	d							17 11	17 05										18 11	18 05					
Wakefield Westgate 7	d							17 23											18 23						
Wakefield Kirkgate 4	d								17 23											18 23					
Doncaster 7	d									17 59											18 58				
Sheffield 7	d		17 35			17 44		17 54	18 05	18 23		18 27		18 35				18 45	18 54	19 05	19 23		19 27		19 38
Chesterfield	d		17 50			18 02		18 07	18 22			18 39		18 47				19 01	19 06	19 22			19 39		19 53
Derby 6	a		18 16					18 26		18 51		18 59		19 14					19 26		19 52		19 59		
	d		18 18									19 01		19 18									20 01		
Long Eaton	d		18 28											19 28											
Alfreton	d					18 12			18 33									19 11		19 33					20 04
Langley Mill	d								18 40											19 40					
Lincoln	d				17 26											18 35									
Nottingham 8	a				18 33	18 34			19 00							19 31		19 38		20 00					20 31
	d	18 02		18 28	18 33								19 02		19 28	19 32								20 02	
Beeston	d	18 08			18 39								19 08			19 38								20 08	
East Midlands Parkway	d		18 32	18 39	18 48									19 32	19 39	19 46								20 16	
Loughborough	d	18 20	18 40		18 56								19 20	19 40		19 55								20 24	
Barrow Upon Soar	d				19 01											19 59									
Sileby	d				19 05											20 03									
Syston	d				19 10											20 08									
Leicester	a	18 31	18 51	18 55	19 22							19 23	19 31	19 51	19 55	20 20							20 23	20 34	
	d	18 33	18 53	18 57								19 25	19 33	19 53	19 57								20 25	20 36	
Market Harborough	d	18 47		19 12									19 47		20 12									20 50	
Melton Mowbray	d																								
Oakham	d																								
Corby	d										18 57											19 43			
Kettering 4	a	18 56									19 06		19 56									19 52		20 59	
	d	18 56									19 27		19 56									20 27		20 59	
Wellingborough	d	19 04									19 35		20 04									20 35		21 07	
Bedford 7	d	19 18									19 49		20 18									20 54		21 22	
Luton 10	d										20 05											21 08			
Luton Airport Parkway 7	d	19 34											20 34											21 39	
St Pancras International	a	20 01	20 04	20 11							20 29	20 34	20 59	21 02	21 11							21 33	21 36	22 04	

A From Liverpool Lime Street to Norwich
B From Glasgow Central to Penzance
C To St Pancras International
D From Newcastle to Reading
E From Derby
F From Edinburgh to Plymouth
G From Glasgow Central to Plymouth
H From Liverpool Lime Street
I From Newcastle to Guildford

For connections to Gatwick Airport see Table 52

Table 53

Mondays to Fridays from 1 October

Sheffield - East Midlands - London

Route Diagram - see first Page of Table 53

		XC	EM	NT	XC	EM	EM	EM	EM	EM	EM	EM	XC	XC	EM	EM	XC	EM	EM	EM	EM
		◇1 A ⊼		◇	◇1 B ⊼	◇1 ⊼	◇1 ⊼	◇1 ⊼	◇1 ⊼	◇1 ⊼		◇ C	◇1 D ⊼	◇1 B	◇ C	◇1 ⊼	◇1 E ⊼	◇1 ⊼		◇ C	◇1 ⊼
York	d	18 45			19 34								19 44	20 35			20 45				
Leeds	d	19 11		19 05									20 11				21 11				
Wakefield Westgate	d	19 23											20 23				21 23				
Wakefield Kirkgate	d			19 24																	
Doncaster	d				19 58									21 02							
Sheffield	d	19 54		20 05	20 23				20 39			20 41	20 54	21 28	21 39	21 42	22 00			23 37	23 51
Chesterfield	d	20 06		20 22					20 53			20 58	21 06	21 41	21 55	22 00	22 24			00 02	00 04
Derby	a	20 26			20 52				21 18				21 26	22 00		22 23	22 44				00 30
	d								21 20												
Long Eaton	d																				
Alfreton	d			20 33								21 09			22 05						
Langley Mill	d			20 40											22 12						
Lincoln	d																				
Nottingham	a			21 00								21 38			22 38					00 40	
	d		20 32					21 02		21 28	21 32								23 10		
Beeston	d		20 38					21 08			21 38								23 16		
East Midlands Parkway	d		20 46					21 15	21 33		21 46								23 25		
Loughborough	d		20 55					21 22	21 41	21 46	21 55								23 33		
Barrow Upon Soar	d		20 59								21 59										
Sileby	d		21 03								22 03										
Syston	d		21 08								22 08										
Leicester	a		21 22					21 32	21 52	21 58	22 21								23 58		
	d							21 33	21 55	21 59											
Market Harborough	d							21 47		22 13											
Melton Mowbray	d																				
Oakham	d																				
Corby	d					20 43	21 43											22 43			
Kettering	a					20 53	21 52	21 56		22 22								22 52			
	d					21 17		21 57		22 23											
Wellingborough	d					21 26		22 05		22 31											
Bedford	d					21 44		22 19		22 45											
Luton	d					22 01		22 34		23 02											
Luton Airport Parkway	d							22 38													
St Pancras International	a					22 29		23 01	23 04	23 34											

Saturdays until 21 July

		EM	EM	EM	EM	EM	EM	EM	XC	EM	NT	EM	EM	EM	EM	EM	XC	EM	EM	NT	XC	EM	EM
		◇1 ⊼	◇ C	◇1 ⊼	◇1 ⊼	◇1 ⊼	◇1 ⊼	◇1 ⊼	◇1 F	◇1 ⊼			◇1 ⊼	◇1 ⊼	◇1 ⊼	◇1 ⊼	◇1 G ⊼	◇1 ⊼		H	◇1 I ⊼	◇1 ⊼	◇1 ⊼
York	d																						
Leeds	d																06 00				06 15		
Wakefield Westgate	d																06 12				06 29		
Wakefield Kirkgate	d																						
Doncaster	d																				06 47		
Sheffield	d	23p21	23p37			05 27			05 45		05 54		06 25				06 50			07 03	07 18		07 27
Chesterfield	d	23p45	00 02			05 39			05 57		06 20		06 37				07 03			07 20	07 30		07 39
Derby	a	00 11				05 59			06 36				06 59				07 24				07 49		07 59
	d				05 25	06 01		06 18					07 01			07 18							08 01
Long Eaton	d				05 35			06 28								07 28							
Alfreton	d										06 30									07 33			
Langley Mill	d										06 38									07 40			
Lincoln	d																						
Nottingham	a		00 40								07 04									08 02			
	d						06 02			06 28					07 02			07 28	07 31				
Beeston	d						06 08								07 08				07 37				
East Midlands Parkway	d				05 39			06 32		06 39						07 32		07 39	07 46				
Loughborough	d				05 47		06 20	06 40				06 50			07 20	07 40			07 55				
Barrow Upon Soar	d											06 57							07 59				
Sileby	d											07 05							08 03				
Syston	d											07 10							08 08				
Leicester	a				05 57	06 23	06 31	06 51		06 55		07 21	07 23		07 31	07 51		07 55	08 21				08 23
	d			04 40	05 59	06 25	06 33	06 53		06 57			07 25		07 33	07 53		07 57					08 25
Market Harborough	d				06 14		06 47			07 12					07 47			08 12					
Melton Mowbray	d																						
Oakham	d																						
Corby	d													07 08								08 15	
Kettering	a			05 00	06 23		06 56	07 15						07 20	07 56							08 24	
	d			05 01	06 26		06 56	07 26							07 56							08 26	
Wellingborough	d			05 09	06 34		07 04	07 34							08 04							08 34	
Bedford	d			05 32	06 49		07 19	07 49							08 19							08 49	
Luton	d				07 04			08 05														09 05	
Luton Airport Parkway	d			05 54			07 35								08 35								
St Pancras International	a			06 21	07 31	07 34	08 00	08 31		08 12			08 34		09 01	09 06		09 12				09 29	09 34

A From Glasgow Central to Bristol Temple Meads
B From Newcastle to Birmingham New Street
C From Liverpool Lime Street
D From Edinburgh to Bristol Temple Meads. ⊼ to Leeds
E From Glasgow Central to Birmingham New Street. ⊼ to Leeds
F To Reading
G To Paignton
H From Barnsley
I To Southampton Central

For connections to Gatwick Airport see Table 52

Table 53

Saturdays until 21 July

Sheffield - East Midlands - London

Route Diagram - see first Page of Table 53

		EM	EM	EM	XC	EM	NT	XC	EM	EM	EM	EM	EM	EM	EM	XC	EM	NT	XC	EM	EM	EM	EM
		◇1 A	◇1 ⊼	◇1 ⊼	◇1 B ⊼	C		◇1 D ⊼	◇1 ⊼	◇1 ⊼	◇1 ⊼	◇1 E ⊼	◇ F	◇1 ⊼	◇1 G ⊼	◇1 H ⊼			◇1 I ⊼	◇1 ⊼	◇1 ⊼	◇1 F ⊼	◇
York	d				06 40			07 24								07 44			08 34				
Leeds	d			06 34	07 10		07 05					07 34				08 12		08 05					
Wakefield Westgate	d			06 46	07 23							07 46				08 24							
Wakefield Kirkgate	d						07 25											08 23					
Doncaster	d							07 52											08 58				
Sheffield	d			07 32	07 56		08 05	08 20		08 27		08 32	08 38	08 47		08 54		09 05	09 23		09 27		09 38
Chesterfield	d			07 45	08 08		08 24	08 32		08 39		08 45	08 53	08 59		09 06		09 23			09 39		09 53
Derby	a				08 27			08 51		08 59				09 19		09 25			09 51		09 59		
	d		08 18							09 01				09 20							10 01		
Long Eaton	d		08 28											09 30									
Alfreton	d			07 56			08 35					08 56	09 03					09 32					10 03
Langley Mill	d			08 04			08 42											09 41					
Lincoln	d	07 04				07 26											08 35						
Nottingham	a	07 58		08 23		08 30	09 02					09 21	09 30				09 30	10 00					10 30
	d	08 02		08 28		08 32					09 02	09 28					09 32					10 02	
Beeston	d	08 08				08 38					09 08				←		09 38					10 08	
East Midlands Parkway	d		08 32	08 39		08 46						09 39		09 35	09 39		09 46						
Loughborough	d	08 20	08 40			08 55					09 20	→		09 42			09 55					10 20	
Barrow Upon Soar	d					08 59											09 59						
Sileby	d					09 03											10 03						
Syston	d					09 08											10 08						
Leicester	a	08 31	08 51	08 55		09 18				09 23	09 31			09 54	09 57		10 21				10 23	10 31	
	d	08 33	08 53	08 57						09 25	09 33			09 55	09 57						10 25	10 33	
Market Harborough	d	08 47		09 12							09 47				10 12							10 47	
Melton Mowbray	d																						
Oakham	d																						
Corby	d								09 17											10 17			
Kettering	a	08 56							09 26		09 56									10 26		10 56	
	d	08 56							09 27		09 56									10 27		10 56	
Wellingborough	d	09 04							09 35		10 04									10 35		11 04	
Bedford	d	09 19							09 49		10 19									10 49		11 19	
Luton	d								10 05											11 05			
Luton Airport Parkway	d	09 35									10 35											11 35	
St Pancras International	a	09 59	10 06	10 12					10 29	10 34	11 01			11 05	11 13					11 29	11 37	12 01	

		EM	XC	EM	EM	NT	XC	EM	EM	EM	EM	EM	XC	EM	EM	NT	XC	EM	EM	EM	EM	EM
		◇1 ⊼	◇1 J ⊼	◇1 ⊼			◇1 K ⊼	◇1 ⊼	◇1 ⊼	◇1 ⊼	◇ F	◇1 ⊼	◇1 L ⊼	◇1 ⊼			◇1 M ⊼	◇1 ⊼	◇1 ⊼	◇1 ⊼	◇ F	◇1 ⊼
York	d		08 44				09 35						09 46				10 34					
Leeds	d		09 11			09 05							10 12			10 05						
Wakefield Westgate	d		09 24										10 24									
Wakefield Kirkgate	d					09 23										10 23						
Doncaster	d						09 58										10 58					
Sheffield	d	09 47	09 54			10 04	10 23		10 27		10 38	10 47	10 54			11 05	11 23		11 27		11 38	11 47
Chesterfield	d	09 59	10 06			10 21			10 39		10 53	10 59	11 06			11 22			11 39		11 53	11 59
Derby	a	10 19	10 25				10 51		10 59			11 19	11 25				11 51		11 59			12 19
	d	10 20							11 01			11 20							12 01			12 20
Long Eaton	d	10 30										11 30										12 30
Alfreton	d					10 32					11 03					11 35					12 03	
Langley Mill	d					10 40										11 40						
Lincoln	d				09 19										10 36							
Nottingham	a				10 25	11 00					11 29				11 29	12 00					12 29	
	d			10 28	10 32					11 02				11 28	11 32					12 02		
Beeston	d				10 38					11 08					11 38					12 08		
East Midlands Parkway	d	10 35		10 39	10 46							11 35		11 39	11 46							12 35
Loughborough	d	10 42			10 55					11 20		11 42			11 55					12 20		12 42
Barrow Upon Soar	d				10 59										11 59							
Sileby	d				11 03										12 03							
Syston	d				11 08										12 08							
Leicester	a	10 54		10 57	11 20				11 23	11 31		11 54		11 57	12 19				12 23	12 31		12 54
	d	10 55		10 57					11 25	11 33		11 55		11 57					12 25	12 33		12 55
Market Harborough	d			11 12						11 47				12 12						12 47		
Melton Mowbray	d																					
Oakham	d																					
Corby	d							11 17										12 17				
Kettering	a							11 26		11 56								12 26		12 56		
	d							11 27		11 56								12 27		12 56		
Wellingborough	d							11 35		12 04								12 35		13 04		
Bedford	d							11 49		12 19								12 49		13 19		
Luton	d							12 05										13 05				
Luton Airport Parkway	d									12 35										13 35		
St Pancras International	a	12 05		12 13				12 29	12 34	13 01		13 05		13 13				13 29	13 34	14 01		14 05

A from Nottingham ⊼ to Nottingham
B To Plymouth
C From Sleaford
D From Newcastle to Reading
E To St Pancras International
F From Liverpool Lime Street to Norwich
G From Leeds
H To Penzance
I From Newcastle to Southampton Central
J From Edinburgh to Plymouth
K From Edinburgh to Reading
L From Glasgow Central to Paignton
M From Newcastle to Southampton Central

For connections to Gatwick Airport see Table 52

Sheffield - East Midlands - London

Route Diagram - see first Page of Table 53

	XC ◇■ A	EM ◇■	EM	NT	XC ◇■ B	EM ◇■	EM ◇■		EM ◇■	EM ◇ C	EM ◇■	XC ◇■ D	EM ◇■	EM	NT	XC ◇■ E	EM ◇■		EM ◇■	EM ◇■	EM ◇ C	EM ◇■	XC ◇■ D	EM ◇■
York d	10 45				11 34							11 45				12 34							12 45	
Leeds d	11 11			11 05								12 11			12 05								13 11	
Wakefield Westgate d	11 23											12 24											13 23	
Wakefield Kirkgate d				11 23											12 23									
Doncaster d					11 58											12 58								
Sheffield d	11 54			12 05	12 23		12 27			12 38	12 47	12 54			13 05	13 23			13 27		13 38	13 47	13 54	
Chesterfield d	12 07			12 22			12 39			12 53	12 59	13 06			13 22				13 39		13 53	13 59	14 07	
Derby a	12 26				12 51		12 59				13 19	13 25				13 51			13 59			14 19	14 27	
Derby d							13 01				13 20								14 01			14 20		
Long Eaton d											13 30											14 30		
Alfreton d				12 33						13 03					13 33						14 03			
Langley Mill d				12 40											13 40									
Lincoln d			11 42											12 30										
Nottingham a			12 30	13 01						13 30				13 30	14 00						14 29			
Nottingham d		12 28	12 32						13 02				13 28	13 32						14 02				14 28
Beeston d			12 38						13 08					13 38						14 08				
East Midlands Parkway d		12 39	12 46								13 35		13 39	13 46								14 35		14 39
Loughborough d			12 55						13 20		13 42			13 55						14 20		14 42		
Barrow Upon Soar d			12 59											13 59										
Sileby d			13 03											14 03										
Syston d			13 08											14 08										
Leicester a		12 57	13 19				13 23		13 31		13 54		13 57	14 19					14 23	14 31		14 54		14 57
Leicester d		12 57					13 25		13 33		13 55		13 57						14 25	14 33		14 55		14 57
Market Harborough d		13 12							13 47				14 12							14 47				15 12
Melton Mowbray d																								
Oakham d																								
Corby d						13 17											14 17							
Kettering a						13 26			13 56								14 26			14 56				
Kettering d						13 27			13 56								14 27			14 56				
Wellingborough d						13 35			14 04								14 35			15 04				
Bedford d						13 49			14 19								14 49			15 19				
Luton d						14 05											15 05							
Luton Airport Parkway d									14 35											15 35				
St Pancras International a		14 13				14 29	14 34		15 01		15 05		15 13				15 29		15 34	16 01		16 05		16 13

	EM	NT	XC ◇■ B		EM ◇■	EM ◇■	EM ◇■	EM ◇ C	EM ◇■	XC ◇■ F	EM ◇■	EM	NT		XC ◇■ E	EM ◇■	EM ◇■	EM ◇■	EM ◇ C	EM ◇■	XC ◇■ G	EM ◇■	EM
York d			13 34							13 44					14 34						14 44		
Leeds d		13 05								14 11			14 05								15 12		
Wakefield Westgate d										14 24											15 24		
Wakefield Kirkgate d		13 23											14 23										
Doncaster d			13 58												14 58								
Sheffield d		14 05	14 23			14 27		14 38	14 47	14 54			15 05		15 23		15 27		15 38	15 47	15 54		
Chesterfield d		14 22				14 39		14 53	14 59	15 06			15 22				15 39		15 53	15 59	16 07		
Derby a			14 51			14 59			15 19	15 26					15 51		15 59			16 19	16 26		
Derby d						15 01			15 20								16 01			16 20			
Long Eaton d									15 30											16 30			
Alfreton d		14 33						15 04					15 33						16 04				
Langley Mill d		14 40											15 40										
Lincoln d	13 40											14 35											15 27
Nottingham a	14 30	15 00						15 29				15 30	16 00						16 30				16 30
Nottingham d	14 32						15 02				15 28	15 32						16 02				16 28	16 32
Beeston d	14 38						15 08					15 38						16 08					16 38
East Midlands Parkway d	14 46								15 35		15 39	15 46								16 35		16 39	16 48
Loughborough d	14 55						15 20		15 42			15 55						16 19		16 42			16 57
Barrow Upon Soar d	14 59											15 59											17 01
Sileby d	15 03											16 03											17 05
Syston d	15 08											16 08											17 10
Leicester a	15 21					15 23	15 31		15 54		15 57	16 21					16 23	16 31		16 54		16 57	17 22
Leicester d						15 25	15 33		15 55		15 57						16 25	16 33		16 55		16 57	
Market Harborough d							15 47				16 12							16 47				17 12	
Melton Mowbray d																							
Oakham d																							
Corby d					15 17											16 17							
Kettering a					15 26		15 56									16 26		16 56					
Kettering d					15 27		15 56									16 27		16 56					
Wellingborough d					15 35		16 04									16 35		17 04					
Bedford d					15 49		16 19									16 49		17 19					
Luton d					16 05											17 05							
Luton Airport Parkway d							16 35											17 35					
St Pancras International a					16 29	16 34	17 01		17 05		17 13					17 29	17 34	18 01		18 05		18 13	

A From Dundee to Newquay
B From Newcastle to Reading
C From Liverpool Lime Street to Norwich
D From Glasgow Central to Penzance
E From Newcastle to Southampton Central
F From Aberdeen to Penzance
G From Glasgow Central to Plymouth

For connections to Gatwick Airport see Table 52

Sheffield - East Midlands - London

Saturdays until 21 July

Route Diagram - see first Page of Table 53

	NT	XC ◇■ A	EM ◇■	EM ◇■	EM ◇■	EM ◇■	EM ◇■	EM ◇ B	XC ◇■ C		EM	NT	XC ◇■ A	EM ◇■	EM ◇■	EM ◇■	EM ◇■	EM ◇■	EM		EM ◇ B	XC ◇■ D	NT	XC ◇■ A
York d		15 34							15 45				16 06									16 44		17 34
Leeds d	15 05								16 12			16 05	16 40									17 11	17 05	
Wakefield Westgate d									16 24				16 52									17 23		
Wakefield Kirkgate d	15 23											16 23											17 23	
Doncaster d		15 58																						17 58
Sheffield d	16 04	16 23		16 27		16 35		16 38	16 54			17 05	17 23		17 27		17 35				17 44	17 54	18 06	18 23
Chesterfield d	16 21			16 39		16 47		16 53	17 06			17 22			17 39		17 51				18 01	18 07	18 22	
Derby a		16 51		16 59		17 16			17 26				17 51		17 59		18 16					18 26		18 51
Derby d				17 01		17 18									18 01		18 18							
Long Eaton d						17 28											18 28							
Alfreton d	16 32							17 04				17 33								18 11		18 33	
Langley Mill d	16 40											17 40											18 40	
Lincoln d											16 34								17 26					
Nottingham a	17 00							17 29			17 30	18 00							18 31		18 33		19 00	
Nottingham d					17 02		17 28				17 32					18 02		18 28	18 32					
Beeston d					17 08						17 38					18 08			18 38					
East Midlands Parkway d						17 32	17 39				17 48						18 32	18 39	18 47					
Loughborough d					17 20	17 40					17 57					18 20	18 40		18 55					
Barrow Upon Soar d											18 01								19 00					
Sileby d											18 05								19 04					
Syston d											18 10								19 09					
Leicester a				17 23	17 31	17 51	17 55				18 22				18 23	18 31	18 51	18 55	19 21					
Leicester d				17 25	17 33	17 53	17 57								18 25	18 33	18 53	18 57						
Market Harborough d					17 47		18 12									18 47		19 12						
Melton Mowbray d																								
Oakham d																								
Corby d			17 17											18 17										
Kettering a			17 26		17 56									18 26		18 56								
Kettering d			17 27		17 56									18 27		18 56								
Wellingborough d			17 35		18 04									18 35		19 04								
Bedford d			17 49		18 19									18 49		19 18								
Luton d			18 05											19 05										
Luton Airport Parkway d					18 35											19 30								
St Pancras International a			18 29	18 34	18 59	19 06	19 12							19 29	19 34	20 01	20 05	20 12						

	EM ◇■	EM ◇■	EM ◇■	EM ◇ E	EM ◇■ F		XC ◇■ C	EM ◇■	EM	NT	XC ◇■ G	EM ◇■	EM ◇■	EM ◇■	EM ◇ B		XC ◇■ H	EM	EM ◇■ I	EM ◇■ J	EM ◇■	NT K	XC ◇■	EM ◇■
York d					17 50		17 44				18 34						18 44						19 34	
Leeds d							18 11			18 05							19 11					19 05		
Wakefield Westgate d							18 23										19 24							
Wakefield Kirkgate d										18 23												19 24		
Doncaster d					18 18						18 58												19 58	
Sheffield d		18 27		18 38	18 47		18 54			19 05	19 24		19 27		19 38		19 54					20 05	20 23	20 27
Chesterfield d		18 39		18 53			19 06			19 22			19 39		19 53		20 06					20 22		20 39
Derby a		18 59			19 19		19 25				19 52		19 59				20 26						20 51	21 00
Derby d		19 01			19 21								20 01											21 01
Long Eaton d					19 31																			
Alfreton d				19 03						19 33					20 04							20 33		
Langley Mill d										19 40												20 40		
Lincoln d									18 34															
Nottingham a				19 33					19 29	20 00					20 31							21 00		
Nottingham d			19 02					19 28	19 32					20 02				20 32		20 43	20 43			
Beeston d			19 08						19 38					20 08				20 38		20 49	20 49			
East Midlands Parkway d					19 35			19 41	19 46					20 16				20 46		20 55	20 55			21 14
Loughborough d			19 20		19 41				19 55					20 24				20 55		21 03	21 03			21 23
Barrow Upon Soar d									19 59									20 59						
Sileby d									20 03									21 03						
Syston d									20 08									21 08						
Leicester a		19 23	19 31		19 54			19 58	20 20				20 23	20 34				21 19		21 13	21 13			21 36
Leicester d		19 25	19 33		19 54			20 00					20 25	20 36						21 15	21 15			
Market Harborough d			19 47					20 15						20 50						21 29	21 29			
Melton Mowbray d																								
Oakham d																								
Corby d	19 17											19 43							20 43					
Kettering a	19 26		19 56		20 16							19 52		20 59					20 52	21 38	21 38			
Kettering d	19 27		19 56		20 17							20 26		20 59					21 24	21 38	21 38			
Wellingborough d	19 35		20 04									20 35		21 07					21 32	21 47	21 47			
Bedford d	19 49		20 18									20 49		21 22					21 47	22 01	22 01			
Luton d	20 05											21 03							22 03	22 16	22 22			
Luton Airport Parkway d			20 30											21 38						22 19	22 25			
St Pancras International a	20 29	20 34	21 01		21 06			21 15				21 29	21 34	22 05					22 29	22 46	22 47			

A From Newcastle to Reading
B From Liverpool Lime Street to Norwich
C From Edinburgh to Plymouth
D From Glasgow Central to Plymouth
E From Liverpool Lime Street
F From Scarborough
G From Newcastle to Guildford
H From Glasgow Central to Bristol Temple Meads
I from 30 June until 21 July
J until 23 June
K From Newcastle to Birmingham New Street

For connections to Gatwick Airport see Table 52

Table 53

Saturdays until 21 July

Sheffield - East Midlands - London

Route Diagram - see first Page of Table 53

		EM ◇1 A ⚒		EM B 🚌	EM ◇1 ⚒	EM	EM ◇ C	XC ◇1 D ⚒	XC ◇1 E	EM ◇ C	XC ◇1 F ⚒	EM ◇1 A ⚒		EM B 🚌	EM	EM ◇ C	EM ◇1 ⚒	EM ◇ C
York	d							19 44	20 34		20 45							
Leeds	d							20 11			21 11							
Wakefield Westgate	d							20 23			21 23							
Wakefield Kirkgate	d																	
Doncaster	d								21 00									
Sheffield	d						20 41	20 54	21 23	21 38	21 54					22 35	23 20	23 42
Chesterfield	d						20 59	21 06	21 35	21 54	22 06					22 51	23 33	23 57
Derby	a							21 26	21 52		22 25						00 13	
	d																	
Long Eaton	d																	
Alfreton	d						21 09			22 05						23 02		
Langley Mill	d									22 12								
Lincoln	d																	
Nottingham	a						21 33			22 33						23 32		00 34
	d				21 28	21 32									23 10			
Beeston	d					21 38									23 16			
East Midlands Parkway	d					21 46									23 25			
Loughborough	d				21 42	21 55									23 33			
Barrow Upon Soar	d					21 59												
Sileby	d					22 03												
Syston	d					22 13												
Leicester	a				21 52	22 21									23 52			
	d				21 54													
Market Harborough	d				22 08													
Melton Mowbray	d																	
Oakham	d																	
Corby	d	21 43		21 43								22 43		22 43				
Kettering	a	21 52		22 08	22 17							22 52		23 08				
	d				22 18													
Wellingborough	d				22 25													
Bedford	d				22 39													
Luton	d				22 59													
Luton Airport Parkway	d																	
St Pancras International	a				23 37													

Saturdays 28 July to 29 September

		EM ◇1 G ⚒	EM ◇ C	EM ◇1 H ⚒	EM ◇1 ⚒	EM ◇1 ⚒	EM ◇1 ⚒	EM ◇1 ⚒	EM ◇1 ⚒	XC ◇1 I		EM ◇1 ⚒	NT	EM	EM ◇1 ⚒	EM ◇1 ⚒	EM ◇1 ⚒	EM ◇1 ⚒	XC ◇1 J ⚒	EM ◇1 ⚒		EM	NT K	XC ◇1 L ⚒	EM ◇1 ⚒
York	d																								
Leeds	d																		06 00					06 15	
Wakefield Westgate	d																		06 12					06 29	
Wakefield Kirkgate	d																								
Doncaster	d																							06 47	
Sheffield	d	23p21	23p37	23p51			05 27			05 45			05 54		06 25				06 50				07 03	07 18	
Chesterfield	d	23p45	00 02	00 04			05 39			05 57			06 20		06 37				07 03				07 20	07 30	
Derby	a	00 11		00 30			05 59			06 36					06 59				07 24					07 49	
	d					05 25	06 01		06 18						07 01			07 18							
Long Eaton	d					05 35			06 28									07 28							
Alfreton	d												06 30										07 33		
Langley Mill	d												06 38										07 40		
Lincoln	d																								
Nottingham	a		00 40										07 04										08 02		
	d							06 02				06 28					07 02			07 28		07 31			
Beeston	d							06 08									07 08					07 37			
East Midlands Parkway	d					05 39			06 32			06 39						07 32		07 39		07 46			
Loughborough	d					05 47		06 20	06 40					06 50			07 20	07 40				07 55			
Barrow Upon Soar	d													06 57								07 59			
Sileby	d													07 05								08 03			
Syston	d													07 10								08 08			
Leicester	a					05 57	06 23	06 31	06 51			06 55		07 21	07 23		07 31	07 51		07 55		08 21			
	d				04 40	05 59	06 25	06 33	06 53			06 57			07 25		07 33	07 53		07 57					
Market Harborough	d					06 14		06 47				07 12					07 47			08 12					
Melton Mowbray	d																								
Oakham	d																								
Corby	d															07 08									08 15
Kettering	a				05 00	06 23		06 56	07 15							07 20	07 56								08 24
	d				05 01	06 26		06 56	07 26								07 56								08 26
Wellingborough	d				05 09	06 34		07 04	07 34								08 04								08 34
Bedford	d				05 32	06 49		07 19	07 49								08 19								08 49
Luton	d					07 04			08 05																09 05
Luton Airport Parkway	d				05 54			07 35									08 35								
St Pancras International	a				06 21	07 31	07 34	08 00	08 31			08 12			08 34		09 01	09 06		09 12					09 29

A from 30 June until 21 July
B until 23 June
C From Liverpool Lime Street
D From Edinburgh to Birmingham New Street. ⚒ to Leeds
E From Newcastle to Birmingham New Street
F From Glasgow Central to Birmingham New Street. ⚒ to Leeds
G not from 22 September until 29 September
H 22 September, 29 September
I from 28 July until 8 September. To Reading
J To Paignton
K From Barnsley
L To Southampton Central

For connections to Gatwick Airport see Table 52

Table 53

Saturdays 28 July to 29 September

Sheffield - East Midlands - London

Route Diagram - see first Page of Table 53

		EM ◇1 ⊠⚒	EM ◇1 A ⊡⚒	EM ◇1 ⚒	EM ◇1 ⊠⚒	XC ◇1 B ⚒		XC ◇1 C ⚒	EM D	NT	XC ◇1 E ⚒	EM ◇1 ⚒	EM ◇1 ⚒	EM ◇1 ⚒	EM ◇1 F ⚒	EM ◇ G		EM ◇1 ⚒	EM ◇1 H ⚒	XC ◇1 I ⚒	EM	NT	XC ◇1 J ⚒	EM ◇1 ⚒	EM ◇1 ⚒
York	d					06 17		06 40			07 24									07 44			08 34		
Leeds	d				06 34	07 10		07 10		07 05					07 34					08 12		08 05			
Wakefield Westgate	d				06 46	07 23		07 23							07 46					08 24					
Wakefield Kirkgate	d									07 25												08 23			
Doncaster	d										07 52												08 58		
Sheffield	d	07 27			07 32	07 56		07 56		08 05	08 20		08 27		08 32	08 38		08 47		08 54		09 05	09 23		09 27
Chesterfield	d	07 39			07 45	08 08		08 08		08 24	08 32		08 39		08 45	08 53		08 59		09 06		09 23			09 39
Derby	a	07 59				08 27		08 27			08 51		08 59					09 19		09 25			09 51		09 59
	d	08 01		08 18									09 01					09 20							10 01
Long Eaton	d			08 28														09 30							
Alfreton	d				07 56					08 35					08 56	09 03						09 32			
Langley Mill	d				08 04					08 42												09 41			
Lincoln	d		07 04						07 26												08 35				
Nottingham	a		07 58		08 23				08 30	09 02					09 21	09 30					09 30	10 00			
	d		08 02		08 28				08 32					09 02	09 28						09 32				
Beeston	d		08 08						08 38					09 08					←		09 38				
East Midlands Parkway	d			08 32	08 39				08 46						09 39			09 35	09 39		09 46				
Loughborough	d		08 20	08 40					08 55					09 20	→			09 42			09 55				
Barrow Upon Soar	d								08 59												09 59				
Sileby	d								09 03												10 03				
Syston	d								09 08												10 08				
Leicester	a	08 23	08 31	08 51	08 55				09 18				09 23	09 31				09 54	09 57		10 21				10 23
	d	08 25	08 33	08 53	08 57								09 25	09 33				09 55	09 57						10 25
Market Harborough	d		08 47		09 12									09 47					10 12						
Melton Mowbray	d																								
Oakham	d																								
Corby	d											09 17												10 17	
Kettering	a		08 56									09 26		09 56										10 26	
	d		08 56									09 27		09 56										10 27	
Wellingborough	d		09 04									09 35		10 04										10 35	
Bedford	d		09 19									09 49		10 19										10 49	
Luton	d											10 05												11 05	
Luton Airport Parkway	d		09 35											10 35											
St Pancras International	a	09 34	09 59	10 06	10 12							10 29	10 34	11 01				11 05	11 13					11 29	11 37

		EM ◇1 ⚒		EM ◇ G	EM ◇1 ⚒	XC ◇1 K ⚒	EM ◇1 ⚒	EM	NT	XC ◇1 L ⚒	EM ◇1 ⚒	EM ◇1 ⚒		EM ◇1 ⚒	EM ◇ G	EM ◇1 ⚒	XC ◇1 M ⚒	EM ◇1 ⚒	EM	NT	XC ◇1 N ⚒	EM ◇1 ⚒		EM ◇1 ⚒	EM ◇1 ⚒
York	d					08 44				09 35							09 46				10 34				
Leeds	d					09 11			09 05								10 12			10 05					
Wakefield Westgate	d					09 24											10 24								
Wakefield Kirkgate	d								09 23											10 23					
Doncaster	d									09 58											10 58				
Sheffield	d			09 38	09 47	09 54			10 04	10 23		10 27			10 38	10 47	10 54			11 05	11 23			11 27	
Chesterfield	d			09 53	09 59	10 06			10 21			10 39			10 53	10 59	11 06			11 22				11 39	
Derby	a				10 19	10 25				10 51		10 59				11 19	11 25				11 51			11 59	
	d				10 20							11 01				11 20								12 01	
Long Eaton	d				10 30											11 30									
Alfreton	d			10 03					10 32						11 03					11 35					
Langley Mill	d								10 40											11 40					
Lincoln	d							09 19											10 36						
Nottingham	a			10 30				10 25	11 00						11 29				11 29	12 00					
	d	10 02					10 28	10 32						11 02				11 28	11 32						12 02
Beeston	d	10 08						10 38						11 08					11 38						12 08
East Midlands Parkway	d				10 35		10 39	10 46								11 35		11 39	11 46						
Loughborough	d	10 20			10 42			10 55						11 20		11 42			11 55						12 20
Barrow Upon Soar	d							10 59											11 59						
Sileby	d							11 03											12 03						
Syston	d							11 08											12 08						
Leicester	a	10 31			10 54		10 57	11 20				11 23		11 31		11 54		11 57	12 19					12 23	12 31
	d	10 33			10 55		10 57					11 25		11 33		11 55		11 57						12 25	12 33
Market Harborough	d	10 47					11 12							11 47				12 12							12 47
Melton Mowbray	d																								
Oakham	d																								
Corby	d										11 17											12 17			
Kettering	a	10 56									11 26			11 56								12 26			12 56
	d	10 56									11 27			11 56								12 27			12 56
Wellingborough	d	11 04									11 35			12 04								12 35			13 04
Bedford	d	11 19									11 49			12 19								12 49			13 19
Luton	d										12 05											13 05			
Luton Airport Parkway	d	11 35												12 35											13 35
St Pancras International	a	12 01			12 05		12 13				12 29	12 34		13 01		13 05		13 13				13 29		13 34	14 01

A ⊡ from Nottingham ⚒ to Nottingham
B 15 September, 22 September, 29 September. To Plymouth
C from 28 July until 8 September. To Plymouth
D From Sleaford
E From Newcastle to Reading
F To St Pancras International
G From Liverpool Lime Street to Norwich
H From Leeds
I From Newcastle to Plymouth
J From Newcastle to Southampton Central
K From Edinburgh to Plymouth
L From Edinburgh to Reading
M From Glasgow Central to Paignton
N From Newcastle to Southampton Central

For connections to Gatwick Airport see Table 52

Sheffield - East Midlands - London

28 July to 29 September

Route Diagram - see first Page of Table 53

		EM ◇ A	EM ◇■	XC ◇■ B	EM ◇■	EM	NT	XC ◇■ C		EM ◇■	EM ◇■	EM ◇■	EM ◇ A	EM ◇■	XC ◇■ D	EM ◇■	EM	NT		XC ◇■ E	EM ◇■	EM ◇■	EM ◇■	EM ◇ A	EM ◇■
York	d			10 45				11 34							11 45					12 34					
Leeds	d			11 11			11 05								12 11			12 05							
Wakefield Westgate	d			11 23											12 24										
Wakefield Kirkgate	d						11 23											12 23							
Doncaster	d							11 58												12 58					
Sheffield	d	11 38	11 47	11 54			12 05	12 23			12 27		12 38	12 47	12 54			13 05		13 23		13 27		13 38	13 47
Chesterfield	d	11 53	11 59	12 07			12 22				12 39		12 53	12 59	13 06			13 22				13 39		13 53	13 59
Derby	a		12 19	12 26				12 51			12 59			13 19	13 25					13 51		13 59			14 19
	d		12 20								13 01			13 20								14 01			14 20
Long Eaton	d		12 30											13 30											14 30
Alfreton	d	12 03					12 33						13 03					13 33						14 03	
Langley Mill	d						12 40											13 40							
Lincoln	d					11 42											12 30								
Nottingham	a	12 29				12 30	13 01						13 30				13 30	14 00						14 29	
	d				12 28	12 32						13 02				13 28	13 32						14 02		
Beeston	d					12 38						13 08					13 38						14 08		
East Midlands Parkway	d		12 35		12 39	12 46								13 35		13 39	13 46								14 35
Loughborough	d		12 42			12 55						13 20		13 42			13 55						14 20		14 42
Barrow Upon Soar	d					12 59											13 59								
Sileby	d					13 03											14 03								
Syston	d					13 08											14 08								
Leicester	a		12 54		12 57	13 19					13 23	13 31		13 54		13 57	14 19					14 23	14 31		14 54
	d		12 55		12 57						13 25	13 33		13 55		13 57						14 25	14 33		14 55
Market Harborough	d				13 12							13 47				14 12							14 47		
Melton Mowbray	d																								
Oakham	d																								
Corby	d									13 17											14 17				
Kettering	a									13 26		13 56									14 26		14 56		
	d									13 27		13 56									14 27		14 56		
Wellingborough	d									13 35		14 04									14 35		15 04		
Bedford	d									13 49		14 19									14 49		15 19		
Luton	d									14 05											15 05				
Luton Airport Parkway	d											14 35											15 35		
St Pancras International	a		14 05		14 13					14 29	14 34	15 01		15 05		15 13					15 29	15 34	16 01		16 05

		XC ◇■ F	EM ◇■	EM		NT	XC ◇■ C	EM ◇■	EM ◇■	EM ◇■	EM ◇ A	EM ◇■	XC ◇■ G	EM ◇■		EM	NT	XC ◇■ E	EM ◇■	EM ◇■	EM ◇■	EM ◇ A	EM ◇■	XC ◇■ D
York	d	12 45					13 34						13 44					14 34						14 44
Leeds	d	13 11				13 05							14 11				14 05							15 12
Wakefield Westgate	d	13 23											14 24											15 24
Wakefield Kirkgate	d					13 23											14 23							
Doncaster	d						13 58											14 58						
Sheffield	d	13 54				14 05	14 23		14 27		14 38	14 47	14 54				15 05	15 23		15 27		15 38	15 47	15 54
Chesterfield	d	14 07				14 22			14 39		14 53	14 59	15 06				15 22			15 39		15 53	15 59	16 07
Derby	a	14 27					14 51		14 59			15 19	15 26					15 51		15 59			16 19	16 26
	d								15 01			15 20								16 01			16 20	
Long Eaton	d											15 30											16 30	
Alfreton	d					14 33					15 04						15 33					16 04		
Langley Mill	d					14 40											15 40							
Lincoln	d			13 40												14 35								
Nottingham	a			14 30		15 00					15 29					15 30	16 00					16 30		
	d		14 28	14 32						15 02				15 28		15 32					16 02			
Beeston	d			14 38						15 08						15 38					16 08			
East Midlands Parkway	d		14 39	14 46								15 35		15 39		15 46							16 35	
Loughborough	d			14 55						15 20		15 42				15 55					16 19		16 42	
Barrow Upon Soar	d			14 59												15 59								
Sileby	d			15 03												16 03								
Syston	d			15 08												16 08								
Leicester	a		14 57	15 21					15 23	15 31		15 54		15 57		16 21				16 23	16 31		16 54	
	d		14 57						15 25	15 33		15 55		15 57						16 25	16 33		16 55	
Market Harborough	d		15 12							15 47				16 12							16 47			
Melton Mowbray	d																							
Oakham	d																							
Corby	d							15 17											16 17					
Kettering	a							15 26		15 56									16 26		16 56			
	d							15 27		15 56									16 27		16 56			
Wellingborough	d							15 35		16 04									16 35		17 04			
Bedford	d							15 49		16 19									16 49		17 19			
Luton	d							16 05											17 05					
Luton Airport Parkway	d									16 35											17 35			
St Pancras International	a		16 13					16 29	16 34	17 01		17 05		17 13					17 29	17 34	18 01		18 05	

A From Liverpool Lime Street to Norwich
B From Dundee to Plymouth
C From Newcastle to Reading
D From Glasgow Central to Plymouth
E From Newcastle to Southampton Central
F From Glasgow Central to Penzance
G From Aberdeen to Penzance

For connections to Gatwick Airport see Table 52

Table 53

Sheffield - East Midlands - London

Saturdays

28 July to 29 September

Route Diagram - see first Page of Table 53

		EM ◇■	EM	NT	XC ◇■ A	EM ◇■	EM ◇■	EM ◇■	EM ◇■	EM ◇■		EM ◇ B	XC ◇■ C	EM	NT	XC ◇■ A	EM ◇■	EM ◇■	EM ◇■	EM ◇■		EM ◇■	EM	EM ◇ B	XC ◇■ D
York	d				15 34								15 45			16 06									16 44
Leeds	d			15 05									16 12		16 05	16 40									17 11
Wakefield Westgate	d												16 24			16 52									17 23
Wakefield Kirkgate	d			15 23											16 23										
Doncaster	d				15 58																				
Sheffield	d			16 04	16 23		16 27		16 35			16 38	16 54		17 05	17 23		17 27		17 35				17 44	17 54
Chesterfield	d			16 21			16 39		16 47			16 53	17 06		17 22			17 39		17 51				18 01	18 07
Derby	a				16 51		16 59		17 16				17 26			17 51		17 59		18 16					18 26
	d						17 01		17 18									18 01		18 18					
Long Eaton	d								17 28											18 28					
Alfreton	d			16 32								17 04			17 33									18 11	
Langley Mill	d			16 40											17 40										
Lincoln	d		15 27											16 34									17 26		
Nottingham	a		16 30	17 00								17 29		17 30	18 00								18 31	18 33	
	d	16 28	16 32					17 02		17 28				17 32					18 02			18 28	18 32		
Beeston	d		16 38					17 08						17 38					18 08				18 38		
East Midlands Parkway	d	16 39	16 48						17 32	17 39				17 48						18 32		18 39	18 47		
Loughborough	d		16 57					17 20	17 40					17 57					18 20	18 40			18 55		
Barrow Upon Soar	d		17 01											18 01									19 00		
Sileby	d		17 05											18 05									19 04		
Syston	d		17 10											18 10									19 09		
Leicester	a	16 57	17 22				17 23	17 31	17 51	17 55				18 22				18 23	18 31	18 51		18 55	19 21		
	d	16 57					17 25	17 33	17 53	17 57								18 25	18 33	18 53		18 57			
Market Harborough	d	17 12						17 47		18 12									18 47			19 12			
Melton Mowbray	d																								
Oakham	d																								
Corby	d					17 17											18 17								
Kettering	a					17 26		17 56									18 26		18 56						
	d					17 27		17 56									18 27		18 56						
Wellingborough	d					17 35		18 04									18 35		19 04						
Bedford	d					17 49		18 19									18 49		19 18						
Luton	d					18 05											19 05								
Luton Airport Parkway	d							18 35											19 30						
St Pancras International	a	18 13				18 29	18 34	18 59	19 06	19 12							19 29	19 34	20 01	20 05		20 12			

		NT	XC ◇■ A	EM ◇■	EM ◇■	EM ◇■		EM ◇ E	EM ◇■ F	XC ◇■ C	EM ◇■	EM	NT	XC ◇■ G	EM ◇■	EM ◇■		EM ◇■	EM ◇ B	XC ◇■ H	EM	EM ◇■	EM ◇■	NT	XC ◇■ I
York	d		17 34						17 50	17 44				18 34						18 44					19 34
Leeds	d	17 05								18 11			18 05							19 11				19 05	
Wakefield Westgate	d									18 23										19 24					
Wakefield Kirkgate	d	17 23											18 23											19 24	
Doncaster	d		17 58						18 18					18 58											19 58
Sheffield	d	18 06	18 23		18 27			18 38	18 47	18 54			19 05	19 24		19 27			19 38	19 54				20 05	20 23
Chesterfield	d	18 22			18 39			18 53		19 06			19 22			19 39			19 53	20 06				20 22	
Derby	a		18 51		18 59				19 19	19 25				19 52		19 59				20 26					20 51
	d				19 01				19 21							20 01									
Long Eaton	d								19 31																
Alfreton	d	18 33						19 03					19 33						20 04					20 33	
Langley Mill	d	18 40											19 40											20 40	
Lincoln	d											18 34													
Nottingham	a	19 00						19 33				19 29	20 00						20 31					21 00	
	d					19 02					19 28	19 32						20 02			20 32		20 43		
Beeston	d					19 08						19 38						20 08			20 38		20 49		
East Midlands Parkway	d								19 35		19 41	19 46						20 16			20 46		20 55		
Loughborough	d					19 20			19 41			19 55						20 24			20 55		21 03		
Barrow Upon Soar	d											19 59									20 59				
Sileby	d											20 03									21 03				
Syston	d											20 08									21 08				
Leicester	a				19 23	19 31			19 54		19 58	20 20				20 23		20 34			21 19		21 13		
	d				19 25	19 33			19 54		20 00					20 25		20 36					21 15		
Market Harborough	d					19 47					20 15							20 50					21 29		
Melton Mowbray	d																								
Oakham	d																								
Corby	d			19 17											19 43							20 43			
Kettering	a			19 26		19 56			20 16						19 52			20 59				20 52	21 38		
	d			19 27		19 56			20 17						20 26			20 59				21 24	21 38		
Wellingborough	d			19 35		20 04									20 35			21 07				21 32	21 47		
Bedford	d			19 49		20 18									20 49			21 22				21 47	22 01		
Luton	d			20 05											21 03							22 03	22 16		
Luton Airport Parkway	d					20 30												21 38					22 19		
St Pancras International	a			20 29	20 34	21 01			21 06		21 15				21 29	21 34		22 05				22 29	22 46		

A From Newcastle to Reading
B From Liverpool Lime Street to Norwich
C From Edinburgh to Plymouth
D From Glasgow Central to Plymouth
E From Liverpool Lime Street
F From Scarborough
G From Newcastle to Guildford
H From Glasgow Central to Bristol Temple Meads
I From Newcastle to Birmingham New Street

For connections to Gatwick Airport see Table 52

Table 53

Saturdays
28 July to 29 September

Sheffield - East Midlands - London

Route Diagram - see first Page of Table 53

		EM		EM	EM	EM	EM	EM	XC	XC	EM	XC		EM	EM	EM	EM	EM
		◇1 ⌶		◇1 A ⌶	B	◇1 ⌶		◇ C	◇1 D ⌶	◇1 E	◇ C	◇1 F ⌶		◇1 A ⌶		◇ C	◇1 ⌶	◇ C
York	d								19 44	20 34		20 45						
Leeds	d								20 11			21 11						
Wakefield Westgate	d								20 23			21 23						
Wakefield Kirkgate	d																	
Doncaster	d									21 00								
Sheffield	d	20 27						20 41	20 54	21 23	21 38	21 54				22 35	23 20	23 42
Chesterfield	d	20 39						20 59	21 06	21 35	21 54	22 06				22 51	23 33	23 57
Derby	a	21 00							21 26	21 52		22 25					00 13	
	d	21 01																
Long Eaton	d																	
Alfreton	d							21 09			22 05					23 02		
Langley Mill	d										22 12							
Lincoln	d																	
Nottingham	a							21 33			22 33					23 32		00 34
	d					21 28	21 32								23 10			
Beeston	d						21 38								23 16			
East Midlands Parkway	d	21 14					21 46								23 25			
Loughborough	d	21 23				21 42	21 55								23 33			
Barrow Upon Soar	d						21 59											
Sileby	d						22 03											
Syston	d						22 13											
Leicester	a	21 36				21 52	22 21								23 52			
	d					21 54												
Market Harborough	d					22 08												
Melton Mowbray	d																	
Oakham	d																	
Corby	d			21 43	21 43									22 43				
Kettering	a			21 52	22 08	22 17								22 52				
	d					22 18												
Wellingborough	d					22 25												
Bedford	d					22 39												
Luton	d					22 59												
Luton Airport Parkway	d																	
St Pancras International	a					23 37												

Saturdays
from 6 October

		EM	EM	EM	EM	EM	EM	EM	EM	NT		EM	EM	EM	EM	EM	XC	EM	EM	NT		XC	EM	EM	EM
		◇ C	◇1 ⌶	◇1 ⌶	◇1 ⌶	◇1 ⌶	◇1 ⌶	◇1 ⌶	◇1 ⌶				◇1 ⌶	◇1 ⌶	◇1 ⌶	◇1 ⌶	◇1 G ⌶	◇1 ⌶		H		◇1 I ⌶	◇1 ⌶	◇1 ⊠⌶	◇1 J ⊡⌶
York	d																								
Leeds	d																06 00					06 15			
Wakefield Westgate	d																06 12					06 29			
Wakefield Kirkgate	d																								
Doncaster	d																					06 47			
Sheffield	d	23p37	23p51			05 27				05 54			06 25				06 50			07 03		07 18		07 27	
Chesterfield	d	00 02	00 04			05 39				06 20			06 37				07 03			07 20		07 30		07 39	
Derby	a		00 30			05 59							06 59				07 24					07 49		07 59	
	d				05 25	06 01		06 18					07 01			07 18								08 01	
Long Eaton	d				05 35			06 28								07 28									
Alfreton	d									06 30										07 33					
Langley Mill	d									06 38										07 40					
Lincoln	d																								07 04
Nottingham	a	00 40								07 04										08 02					07 58
	d						06 02		06 28						07 02			07 28	07 31						08 02
Beeston	d						06 08								07 08				07 37						08 08
East Midlands Parkway	d				05 39			06 32	06 39							07 32		07 39	07 46						
Loughborough	d				05 47		06 20	06 40				06 50			07 20	07 40			07 55						08 20
Barrow Upon Soar	d											06 57							07 59						
Sileby	d											07 05							08 03						
Syston	d											07 10							08 08						
Leicester	a				05 57	06 23	06 31	06 51	06 55			07 21	07 23		07 31	07 51		07 55	08 21					08 23	08 31
	d			04 40	05 59	06 25	06 33	06 53	06 57				07 25		07 33	07 53		07 57						08 25	08 33
Market Harborough	d				06 14		06 47		07 12						07 47			08 12							08 47
Melton Mowbray	d																								
Oakham	d																								
Corby	d													07 08									08 15		
Kettering	a			05 00	06 23		06 56	07 15						07 20	07 56								08 24		08 56
	d			05 01	06 26		06 56	07 26							07 56								08 26		08 56
Wellingborough	d			05 09	06 34		07 04	07 34							08 04								08 34		09 04
Bedford	d			05 32	06 49		07 19	07 49							08 19								08 49		09 19
Luton	d				07 04			08 05															09 05		
Luton Airport Parkway	d			05 54			07 35								08 35										09 35
St Pancras International	a			06 21	07 31	07 34	08 00	08 31	08 12				08 34		09 01	09 06		09 12					09 29	09 34	09 59

A from 28 July until 8 September
B 15 September, 22 September, 29 September
C From Liverpool Lime Street
D From Edinburgh to Birmingham New Street. ⌶ to Leeds
E From Newcastle to Birmingham New Street
F From Glasgow Central to Birmingham New Street. ⌶ to Leeds
G To Plymouth
H From Barnsley
I To Southampton Central
J ⊡ from Nottingham ⌶ to Nottingham

For connections to Gatwick Airport see Table 52

Table 53

Saturdays
from 6 October

Sheffield - East Midlands - London

Route Diagram - see first Page of Table 53

		EM	EM	XC	EM	NT		XC	EM	EM	EM	EM	EM	EM	EM	XC		EM	NT	XC	EM	EM	EM	EM	EM
		◇1 ⌶	◇1 ⊠⌶	◇1 A ⌶	B			◇1 C ⌶	◇1 ⌶	◇1 ⌶	◇1 ⌶	◇1 D ⌶	◇ E	◇1 ⌶	◇1 F ⌶	◇1 G ⌶				◇1 H ⌶	◇1 ⌶	◇1 ⌶	◇1 E ⌶	◇	◇1 ⌶
York	d			06 17				07 24								07 44				08 34					
Leeds	d		06 34	07 10		07 05						07 34				08 12			08 05						
Wakefield Westgate	d		06 46	07 23								07 46				08 24									
Wakefield Kirkgate	d					07 25													08 23						
Doncaster	d							07 52												08 58					
Sheffield	d		07 32	07 56		08 05		08 20		08 27		08 32	08 38	08 47		08 54			09 05	09 23		09 27		09 38	09 47
Chesterfield	d		07 45	08 08		08 24		08 32		08 39		08 45	08 53	08 59		09 06			09 23			09 39		09 53	09 59
Derby	a			08 27				08 51		08 59				09 19		09 25				09 51		09 59			10 19
	d	08 18								09 01				09 20								10 01			10 20
Long Eaton	d	08 28												09 30											10 30
Alfreton	d		07 56			08 35						08 56	09 03						09 32					10 03	
Langley Mill	d		08 04			08 42													09 41						
Lincoln	d				07 26													08 35							
Nottingham	a		08 23		08 32	09 02						09 21	09 30					09 32	10 00					10 30	
	d		08 28		08 32						09 02	09 28						09 32					10 02		
Beeston	d				08 38						09 08				←			09 38					10 08		
East Midlands Parkway	d	08 32	08 39		08 46							09 39		09 35	09 39			09 46							10 35
Loughborough	d	08 40			08 55						09 20	→		09 42				09 55					10 20		10 42
Barrow Upon Soar	d				08 59													09 59							
Sileby	d				09 03													10 03							
Syston	d				09 08													10 08							
Leicester	a	08 51	08 55		09 18					09 23	09 31			09 54	09 57			10 21				10 23	10 31		10 54
	d	08 53	08 57							09 25	09 33			09 55	09 57							10 25	10 33		10 55
Market Harborough	d		09 12								09 47				10 12								10 47		
Melton Mowbray	d																								
Oakham	d																								
Corby	d								09 17												10 17				
Kettering	a								09 26		09 56										10 26		10 56		
	d								09 27		09 56										10 27		10 56		
Wellingborough	d								09 35		10 04										10 35		11 04		
Bedford	d								09 49		10 19										10 49		11 19		
Luton	d								10 05												11 05				
Luton Airport Parkway	d										10 35												11 35		
St Pancras International	a	10 06	10 12						10 29	10 34	11 01			11 05	11 13						11 29	11 37	12 01		12 05

		XC		EM	EM	NT	XC	EM	EM	EM	EM	EM		XC	EM	EM	NT	XC	EM	EM	EM	EM		EM	XC
		◇1 I ⌶		◇1 ⌶			◇1 J ⌶	◇1 ⌶	◇1 ⌶	◇1 ⌶	◇ E	◇1 ⌶		◇1 K ⌶	◇1 ⌶		L	◇1 ⌶	◇1 ⌶	◇1 ⌶	◇1 E ⌶	◇		◇1 M ⌶	◇1 ⌶
York	d	08 44					09 35							09 46				10 34							10 45
Leeds	d	09 11				09 05								10 12			10 05								11 11
Wakefield Westgate	d	09 24												10 24											11 23
Wakefield Kirkgate	d					09 23											10 23								
Doncaster	d						09 58											10 58							
Sheffield	d	09 54				10 04	10 23		10 27		10 38	10 47		10 54			11 05	11 23		11 27		11 38		11 47	11 54
Chesterfield	d	10 06				10 21			10 39		10 53	10 59		11 06			11 22			11 39		11 53		11 59	12 07
Derby	a	10 25					10 51		10 59			11 19		11 25				11 51		11 59				12 19	12 26
	d								11 01			11 20								12 01				12 20	
Long Eaton	d											11 30												12 30	
Alfreton	d					10 32					11 03						11 35					12 03			
Langley Mill	d					10 40											11 40								
Lincoln	d				09 19											10 36									
Nottingham	a				10 27	11 00					11 29					11 31	12 00					12 29			
	d			10 28	10 32					11 02					11 28	11 32					12 02				
Beeston	d				10 38					11 08						11 38					12 08				
East Midlands Parkway	d			10 39	10 46							11 35			11 39	11 46								12 35	
Loughborough	d				10 55					11 20		11 42				11 55					12 20			12 42	
Barrow Upon Soar	d				10 59											11 59									
Sileby	d				11 03											12 03									
Syston	d				11 08											12 08									
Leicester	a			10 57	11 20				11 23	11 31		11 54			11 57	12 19				12 23	12 31			12 54	
	d			10 57					11 25	11 33		11 55			11 57					12 25	12 33			12 55	
Market Harborough	d			11 12						11 47					12 12						12 47				
Melton Mowbray	d																								
Oakham	d																								
Corby	d							11 17											12 17						
Kettering	a							11 26		11 56									12 26		12 56				
	d							11 27		11 56									12 27		12 56				
Wellingborough	d							11 35		12 04									12 35		13 04				
Bedford	d							11 49		12 19									12 49		13 19				
Luton	d							12 05											13 05						
Luton Airport Parkway	d									12 35											13 35				
St Pancras International	a			12 13				12 29	12 34	13 01		13 05			13 13				13 29	13 34	14 01			14 05	

A To Plymouth
B From Sleaford
C From Newcastle to Reading
D To St Pancras International
E From Liverpool Lime Street to Norwich
F From Leeds
G From Newcastle to Plymouth
H From Newcastle to Southampton Central
I From Edinburgh to Plymouth
J From Edinburgh to Reading
K From Glasgow Central to Plymouth
L From Newcastle to Southampton Central
M From Dundee to Plymouth

For connections to Gatwick Airport see Table 52

Sheffield - East Midlands - London

Route Diagram - see first Page of Table 53

		EM ◇■ ⊼	EM	NT	XC ◇■ A ⊼	EM ◇■ ⊼	EM ◇■ ⊼	EM ◇■ ⊼	EM ◇ B	EM ◇■ ⊼	XC ◇■ C ⊼	EM ◇■ ⊼	EM	NT	XC ◇■ D ⊼	EM ◇■ ⊼	EM ◇■ ⊼	EM ◇■ ⊼	EM ◇ B	EM ◇■ ⊼	XC ◇■ E ⊼	EM ◇■ ⊼	EM
York [8]	d				11 34						11 45				12 34						12 45		
Leeds [10]	d			11 05							12 11			12 05							13 11		
Wakefield Westgate [7]	d										12 24										13 23		
Wakefield Kirkgate [4]	d			11 23										12 23									
Doncaster [7]	d				11 58										12 58								
Sheffield [7]	d			12 05	12 23		12 27		12 38	12 47	12 54			13 05	13 23		13 27		13 38	13 47	13 54		
Chesterfield	d			12 22			12 39		12 53	12 59	13 06			13 22			13 39		13 53	13 59	14 07		
Derby [6]	a				12 51		12 59			13 19	13 25				13 51		13 59			14 19	14 27		
	d						13 01			13 20							14 01			14 20			
Long Eaton	d									13 30										14 30			
Alfreton	d			12 33					13 03					13 33					14 03				
Langley Mill	d			12 40										13 40									
Lincoln	d		11 42										12 30										13 40
Nottingham [8]	a		12 30	13 01					13 30				13 32	14 00					14 29				14 32
	d	12 28	12 32					13 02				13 28	13 32					14 02				14 28	14 32
Beeston	d		12 38					13 08					13 38					14 08					14 38
East Midlands Parkway	d	12 39	12 46							13 35		13 39	13 46							14 35		14 39	14 46
Loughborough	d		12 55					13 20		13 42			13 55					14 20		14 42			14 55
Barrow Upon Soar	d		12 59										13 59										14 59
Sileby	d		13 03										14 03										15 03
Syston	d		13 08										14 08										15 08
Leicester	a	12 57	13 19				13 23	13 31		13 54		13 57	14 19				14 23	14 31		14 54		14 57	15 21
	d	12 57					13 25	13 33		13 55		13 57					14 25	14 33		14 55		14 57	
Market Harborough	d	13 12						13 47				14 12						14 47				15 12	
Melton Mowbray	d																						
Oakham	d																						
Corby	d					13 17										14 17							
Kettering [4]	a					13 26		13 56								14 26		14 56					
	d					13 27		13 56								14 27		14 56					
Wellingborough	d					13 35		14 04								14 35		15 04					
Bedford [7]	d					13 49		14 19								14 49		15 19					
Luton [10]	d					14 05										15 05							
Luton Airport Parkway [7]	d							14 35										15 35					
St Pancras International	a	14 13				14 29	14 34	15 01		15 05		15 13				15 29	15 34	16 01		16 05		16 13	

		NT	XC ◇■ A ⊼	EM ◇■ ⊼	EM ◇■ ⊼	EM ◇■ ⊼	EM ◇ B	EM ◇■ ⊼	XC ◇■ F ⊼	EM ◇■ ⊼	EM	NT	XC ◇■ D ⊼	EM ◇■ ⊼	EM ◇■ ⊼	EM ◇■ ⊼	EM ◇ B	EM ◇■ ⊼	XC ◇■ E ⊼	EM ◇■ ⊼	EM	NT
York [8]	d		13 34						13 44				14 34						14 44			
Leeds [10]	d	13 05							14 11			14 05							15 12			15 05
Wakefield Westgate [7]	d								14 24										15 24			
Wakefield Kirkgate [4]	d	13 23										14 23										15 23
Doncaster [7]	d		13 58										14 58									
Sheffield [7]	d	14 05	14 23		14 27		14 38	14 47	14 54			15 05	15 23		15 27		15 38	15 47	15 54			16 04
Chesterfield	d	14 22			14 39		14 53	14 59	15 06			15 22			15 39		15 53	15 59	16 07			16 21
Derby [6]	a		14 51		14 59			15 19	15 26				15 51		15 59			16 19	16 26			
	d				15 01			15 20							16 01			16 20				
Long Eaton	d							15 30										16 30				
Alfreton	d	14 33					15 04					15 33					16 04					16 32
Langley Mill	d	14 40										15 40										16 40
Lincoln	d										14 35										15 27	
Nottingham [8]	a	15 00					15 29				15 32	16 00					16 30				16 32	17 00
	d					15 02				15 28	15 32					16 02				16 28	16 32	
Beeston	d					15 08					15 38					16 08					16 38	
East Midlands Parkway	d							15 35		15 39	15 46							16 35		16 39	16 48	
Loughborough	d					15 20		15 42			15 55					16 19		16 42			16 57	
Barrow Upon Soar	d										15 59										17 01	
Sileby	d										16 03										17 05	
Syston	d										16 08										17 10	
Leicester	a				15 23	15 31		15 54		15 57	16 21				16 23	16 31		16 54		16 57	17 22	
	d				15 25	15 33		15 55		15 57					16 25	16 33		16 55		16 57		
Market Harborough	d					15 47				16 12						16 47				17 12		
Melton Mowbray	d																					
Oakham	d																					
Corby	d			15 17										16 17								
Kettering [4]	a			15 26		15 56								16 26		16 56						
	d			15 27		15 56								16 27		16 56						
Wellingborough	d			15 35		16 04								16 35		17 04						
Bedford [7]	d			15 49		16 19								16 49		17 19						
Luton [10]	d			16 05										17 05								
Luton Airport Parkway [7]	d					16 35										17 35						
St Pancras International	a			16 29	16 34	17 01		17 05		17 13				17 29	17 34	18 01		18 05		18 13		

A From Newcastle to Reading
B From Liverpool Lime Street to Norwich
C From Glasgow Central to Plymouth
D From Newcastle to Southampton Central
E From Glasgow Central to Penzance
F From Aberdeen to Penzance

For connections to Gatwick Airport see Table 52

Sheffield - East Midlands - London

Route Diagram - see first Page of Table 53

		XC ◇■ A ⊼	EM ◇■ ⊼	EM ◇■ ⊼	EM ◇■ ⊼	EM ◇■ ⊼	EM ◇■ ⊼	EM ◇ B	XC ◇■ C ⊼	EM	NT	XC ◇■ A ⊼	EM ◇■ ⊼	EM ◇■ ⊼	EM ◇■ ⊼	EM ◇■ ⊼	EM ◇■ ⊼	EM	EM ◇ B	XC ◇■ D ⊼	NT	XC ◇■ A ⊼	EM ◇■ ⊼
York [8]	d	15 34							15 45			16 06								16 44		17 34	
Leeds [10]	d								16 12		16 05	16 40								17 11	17 05		
Wakefield Westgate [7]	d								16 24			16 52								17 23			
Wakefield Kirkgate [4]	d										16 23										17 23		
Doncaster [7]	d	15 58																				17 58	
Sheffield [7]	d	16 23		16 27		16 35		16 38	16 54		17 05	17 23		17 27		17 35			17 44	17 54	18 06	18 23	
Chesterfield	d			16 39		16 47		16 53	17 06		17 22			17 39		17 51			18 01	18 07	18 22		
Derby [6]	a	16 51		16 59		17 16			17 26			17 51		17 59		18 16				18 26		18 51	
	d			17 01		17 18								18 01		18 18							
Long Eaton	d					17 28										18 28							
Alfreton	d							17 04			17 33								18 11		18 33		
Langley Mill	d										17 40										18 40		
Lincoln	d									16 34								17 26					
Nottingham [8]	a							17 29		17 30	18 00							18 33	18 33		19 00		
	d				17 02		17 28			17 32					18 02		18 28	18 33					
Beeston	d				17 08					17 38					18 08			18 39					
East Midlands Parkway	d					17 32	17 39			17 48						18 32	18 39	18 48					
Loughborough	d				17 20	17 40				17 57					18 20	18 40		18 56					
Barrow Upon Soar	d									18 01								19 01					
Sileby	d									18 05								19 05					
Syston	d									18 10								19 10					
Leicester	a			17 23	17 31	17 51	17 55			18 22				18 23	18 31	18 51	18 55	19 22					
	d			17 25	17 33	17 53	17 57							18 25	18 33	18 53	18 57						
Market Harborough	d				17 47		18 12								18 47		19 12						
Melton Mowbray	d																						
Oakham	d																						
Corby	d		17 17										18 17										19 17
Kettering [4]	a		17 26		17 56								18 26		18 56								19 26
	d		17 27		17 56								18 27		18 56								19 27
Wellingborough	d		17 35		18 04								18 35		19 04								19 35
Bedford [7]	d		17 49		18 19								18 49		19 18								19 49
Luton [10]	d		18 05										19 05										20 05
Luton Airport Parkway [7]	d				18 35										19 30								
St Pancras International	a		18 29	18 34	18 59	19 06	19 12						19 29	19 34	20 01	20 05	20 12						20 29

		EM ◇■ ⊼	EM ◇■ ⊼	EM ◇ E	EM ◇■ ⊼	XC ◇■ C ⊼	EM ◇■ ⊼	EM	NT	XC ◇■ F ⊼	EM ◇■ ⊼	EM ◇■ ⊼	EM ◇■ ⊼	EM ◇ B	XC ◇■ G ⊼	EM	EM ◇■ ⊼	EM ◇■ ⊼	NT	XC ◇■ H ⊼	EM ◇■ I ⊼	EM ◇■ J ⊼	EM 🚌
York [8]	d				17 50	17 44				18 34					18 44					19 34			
Leeds [10]	d					18 11			18 05						19 11				19 05				
Wakefield Westgate [7]	d					18 23									19 24								
Wakefield Kirkgate [4]	d								18 23										19 24				
Doncaster [7]	d				18 18					18 58										19 58			
Sheffield [7]	d	18 27		18 38	18 47	18 54			19 05	19 24		19 27		19 38	19 54				20 05	20 23	20 27		
Chesterfield	d	18 39		18 53		19 06			19 22			19 39		19 53	20 06				20 22		20 39		
Derby [6]	a	18 59			19 19	19 25				19 52		19 59			20 26					20 51	21 00		
	d	19 01			19 21							20 01									21 01		
Long Eaton	d				19 31																		
Alfreton	d			19 03					19 33					20 04					20 33				
Langley Mill	d								19 40										20 40				
Lincoln	d							18 34															
Nottingham [8]	a			19 33				19 31	20 00					20 31					21 00				
	d		19 02				19 28	19 32					20 02			20 32		20 43					
Beeston	d		19 08					19 38					20 08			20 38		20 49					
East Midlands Parkway	d				19 35		19 41	19 46					20 16			20 46		20 55			21 14		
Loughborough	d		19 20		19 41			19 55					20 24			20 55		21 03			21 23		
Barrow Upon Soar	d							19 59								20 59							
Sileby	d							20 03								21 03							
Syston	d							20 08								21 08							
Leicester	a	19 23	19 31		19 54		19 58	20 20				20 23	20 34			21 19		21 13			21 36		
	d	19 25	19 33		19 54		20 00					20 25	20 36					21 15					
Market Harborough	d		19 47				20 15						20 50					21 29					
Melton Mowbray	d																						
Oakham	d																						
Corby	d										19 43						20 43					21 43	21 43
Kettering [4]	a		19 56		20 16						19 52		20 59				20 52	21 38				21 52	22 08
	d		19 56		20 17						20 26		20 59				21 24	21 38					
Wellingborough	d		20 04								20 35		21 07				21 32	21 47					
Bedford [7]	d		20 18								20 49		21 22				21 47	22 01					
Luton [10]	d										21 03						22 03	22 16					
Luton Airport Parkway [7]	d		20 30										21 38					22 19					
St Pancras International	a	20 34	21 01		21 06		21 15				21 29	21 34	22 05				22 29	22 46					

A From Newcastle to Reading
B From Liverpool Lime Street to Norwich
C From Edinburgh to Plymouth
D From Glasgow Central to Plymouth
E From Liverpool Lime Street
F From Newcastle to Guildford
G From Glasgow Central to Bristol Temple Meads
H From Newcastle to Birmingham New Street
I from 27 October
J 6 October, 13 October, 20 October

For connections to Gatwick Airport see Table 52

Table 53

Saturdays from 6 October

Sheffield - East Midlands - London

Route Diagram - see first Page of Table 53

		EM		EM	EM	XC	XC	EM	XC	EM	EM	EM		EM	EM
		◇■			◇	◇■	◇■	◇	◇■	◇■		◇		◇■	◇
					A	B	C	A	D	E		A			A
		🛒				🛒			🛒	🛒				🛒	
York ■	d					19 44	20 34		20 45						
Leeds ■	d					20 11			21 11						
Wakefield Westgate ■	d					20 23			21 23						
Wakefield Kirkgate ■	d														
Doncaster ■	d						21 00								
Sheffield ■ 🚋	d				20 41	20 54	21 23	21 38	21 54			22 35		23 20	23 42
Chesterfield	d				20 59	21 06	21 35	21 54	22 06			22 51		23 33	23 57
Derby ■	a					21 26	21 52		22 25					00 13	
	d														
Long Eaton	d														
Alfreton	d				21 09			22 05				23 02			
Langley Mill	d							22 12							
Lincoln	d														
Nottingham ■ 🚋	a				21 33			22 33				23 32			00 34
	d	21 28		21 32							23 10				
Beeston	d			21 38							23 16				
East Midlands Parkway ✈	d			21 46							23 25				
Loughborough	d	21 42		21 55							23 33				
Barrow Upon Soar	d			21 59											
Sileby	d			22 03											
Syston	d			22 13											
Leicester	a	21 52		22 21							23 52				
	d	21 54													
Market Harborough	d	22 08													
Melton Mowbray	d														
Oakham	d														
Corby	d									22 43					
Kettering ■	a	22 17								22 52					
	d	22 18													
Wellingborough	d	22 25													
Bedford ■	d	22 39													
Luton ■	d	22 59													
Luton Airport Parkway ■ ✈	d														
St Pancras International ⊖	a	23 37													

Sundays until 24 June

		EM	EM	EM	EM	EM	EM	EM	EM	EM		EM	EM	EM	EM	EM	EM	EM	EM	EM		EM	EM	EM	XC
		◇■	◇		◇■			◇■				◇■			◇■			◇■		◇■				◇■	◇■
			A																						F
		🛒		🚌	🛒	🚌	🚌	🛒	🚌	🚌		🛒	🚌	🚌	🛒	🚌	🚌	🛒	🚌	🛒		🚌	🚌	🛒	🛒
York ■	d																								08 10
Leeds ■	d																								08 23
Wakefield Westgate ■	d																								
Wakefield Kirkgate ■	d																								
Doncaster ■	d																								
Sheffield ■ 🚋	d	23p20	23p42																					08 32	08 54
Chesterfield	d	23p33	23p57																					08 44	09 07
Derby ■	a	00 13																						09 03	09 28
	d				06 06							07 09						08 06						09 06	
Long Eaton	d																	08 16						09 16	
Alfreton	d																								
Langley Mill	d																								
Lincoln	d																								
Nottingham ■ 🚋	a		00 34																	08 30					
	d							06 44							07 37										
Beeston	d														07 43										
East Midlands Parkway ✈	d				06 20			06 55				07 22			07 50			08 21		08 42				09 21	
Loughborough	d											07 33			08 01			08 32		08 53				09 32	
Barrow Upon Soar	d																								
Sileby	d																								
Syston	d																								
Leicester	a				06 40			07 15				07 44			08 13			08 44		09 06				09 44	
	d				06 47	06 50		07 21	07 25			07 51	07 54		08 19	08 35		08 50		09 13		09 16		09 50	
Market Harborough	d			07 10		07a15	07 44		07a50	08 10			08a19	08 40		09a00	09 10		09 40			09a41	10 10		
Melton Mowbray	d																								
Oakham	d																								
Corby	d																			10 04					
Kettering ■	a			07 35	07 46		08 09	08 17		08 35		08 47		09 05	09 15		09 35	09 46	10 05	10 15			10 35	10 46	
	d				07 47			08 19				08 48			09 17			09 48		10 16				10 48	
Wellingborough	d				08 01			08 32				09 02			09 30			10 02		10 26				10 57	
Bedford ■	d				08 15			08 45				09 15			09 45			10 15		10 45				11 15	
Luton ■	d				08 34							09 35						10 35						11 35	
Luton Airport Parkway ■ ✈	d							09 07							10 06					11 06					
St Pancras International ⊖	a				09 11			09 47				10 18			10 48			11 18		11 48				12 18	

A From Liverpool Lime Street
B From Edinburgh to Birmingham New Street. 🛒 to Leeds
C From Newcastle to Birmingham New Street
D From Glasgow Central to Birmingham New Street. 🛒 to Leeds
E from 27 October
F To Plymouth

For connections to Gatwick Airport see Table 52

Table 53

Sundays until 24 June

Sheffield - East Midlands - London

Route Diagram - see first Page of Table 53

		EM	EM	EM	NT	EM		EM	EM	EM	EM	XC	NT	EM	EM	EM		EM	EM	EM	XC	NT	EM	EM	EM
				◇■					◇■		◇■	◇■				◇■			◇■	◇	◇■				◇■
											A	B				C				D	E				
		🚌	🚌	🛒		🚌		🚌	🛒	🚌	🚌🛒	🛒		🚌	🚌	🚌🛒		🚌	🛒		🛒		🚌	🚌	🛒
York ■	d																				09 28				
Leeds ■	d										08 42	09 00	09 05			09 46					10 00	10 02			
Wakefield Westgate ■	d										08 59	09 11				09 59					10 12				
Wakefield Kirkgate ■	d												09 21									10 18			
Doncaster ■	d											09 32									10 30				
Sheffield ■ 🚋	d				09 00				09 35		09 38	09 57	10 07			10 32				10 49	10 57	11 03			11 48
Chesterfield	d				09 17				09 47		09 53	10 09	10 23			10 45				11 04	11 09	11 20			12 00
Derby ■	a								10 07			10 32				11 07					11 28				12 20
	d								10 08							11 08									12 21
Long Eaton	d								10 18																12 31
Alfreton	d				09 28								10 33							11 14		11 30			
Langley Mill	d				09 35								10 41									11 38			
Lincoln	d																								
Nottingham ■ 🚋	a				09 53						10 23		10 57							11 39		11 54			
	d			09 25							10 34								11 29						
Beeston	d			09 32															11 36						
East Midlands Parkway ✈	d			09 40					10 23		10 45					11 21			11 43						12 36
Loughborough	d			09 52					10 30		10 54					11 29			11 52						12 43
Barrow Upon Soar	d																								
Sileby	d																								
Syston	d																								
Leicester	a			10 04					10 42		11 07					11 43			12 05						12 53
	d	09 55		10 11		10 20			10 48		11 13			11 17		11 50			12 12				12 15		12 59
Market Harborough	d	10a20	10 40			10a45		11 10		11 40				11a42	12 10			12 40					12a40	13 10	
Melton Mowbray	d																								
Oakham	d																								
Corby	d			11 04							12 04								13 06						
Kettering ■	a		11 05	11 15				11 35	11 44	12 05	12 15				12 35	12 45		13 05	13 15					13 35	14 02
	d			11 16					11 48		12 16					12 46			13 16						14 03
Wellingborough	d			11 26					11 58		12 26					12 56			13 26						14 13
Bedford ■	d			11 45					12 15		12 45					13 15			13 45						14 30
Luton ■	d								12 35							13 35									14 55
Luton Airport Parkway ■ ✈	d			12 06							13 06								14 08						
St Pancras International ⊖	a			12 48					13 18		13 48					14 13			14 33						15 22

		XC		NT	NT	EM	EM	EM	EM	XC	EM	NT		EM	EM	XC	EM	XC	EM	EM	EM	EM		XC	EM
		◇■					◇■	◇■	◇	◇■	◇■			◇■	◇	◇■	◇■	◇■	◇■	◇■	◇■	◇		◇■	◇■
		F							D	G					H	I		J			K		G		
		🛒				🚌	🛒	🛒		🛒	🛒			🛒		🛒	🛒	🛒	🛒	🛒	🛒			🛒	🛒
York ■	d	10 28								11 28						12 28								13 40	
Leeds ■	d	11 00		10 57	11 29					12 00		12 29				13 00								14 10	
Wakefield Westgate ■	d	11 12								12 12						13 12								14 23	
Wakefield Kirkgate ■	d			11 13	11 46							12 46													
Doncaster ■	d	11 30								12 30						13 30									
Sheffield ■ 🚋	d	11 57		12 00	12 31				12 49	12 57	13 27	13 31			13 49	13 57	14 16	14 22				14 46		14 54	
Chesterfield	d	12 09		12 18	12 49				13 03	13 09	13 39	13 48			14 03	14 09	14 29	14 32				15 00		15 06	
Derby ■	a	12 28								13 31	13 59					14 28	14 48	14 51						15 26	
	d										14 00						14 51								
Long Eaton	d										14 10						15 01								
Alfreton	d			12 28	12 59				13 14			13 59			14 14							15 11			
Langley Mill	d			12 36	13 07							14 06										15 18			
Lincoln	d																								
Nottingham ■ 🚋	a			12 52	13 24				13 39			14 22			14 39							15 40			
	d							13 30						14 24						15 18	15 36				
Beeston	d							13 37						14 30						15 24					
East Midlands Parkway ✈	d							13 46			14 15			14 36			15 05			15 30	15 46				
Loughborough	d							13 54			14 22			14 44			15 13			15 38					
Barrow Upon Soar	d																								
Sileby	d																								
Syston	d																								
Leicester	a							14 06			14 33			14 54			15 23			15 50	16 00				
	d					13 14		14 13			14 34			14 56			15 27			15 53	16 02				
Market Harborough	d					13a39		14 28			14 48			15 10						16 07					
Melton Mowbray	d																								
Oakham	d																								
Corby	d						14 25												15 25						16 25
Kettering ■	a						14 34	14 38			14 57			15 19					15 34	16 16					16 34
	d							14 39			14 58			15 20						16 17					
Wellingborough	d							14 47			15 06			15 27						16 25					
Bedford ■	d							15 07			15 24			15 45						16 45					
Luton ■	d										15 50						16 21								
Luton Airport Parkway ■ ✈	d							15 36						16 06						17 10					
St Pancras International ⊖	a							16 01			16 14			16 30			16 44			17 34	17 30				

A 🚌 from Nottingham 🛒 to Nottingham
B To Plymouth
C 🚌 from Derby 🛒 to Derby
D To Norwich
E From Leeds to Plymouth
F From Newcastle to Plymouth
G From Edinburgh to Plymouth
H From Manchester Piccadilly to Norwich
I From Edinburgh to Penzance
J To Reading
K From Liverpool Lime Street to Norwich

For connections to Gatwick Airport see Table 52

Sheffield - East Midlands - London

Sundays until 24 June

Route Diagram - see first Page of Table 53

Station		EM	NT	XC	EM	EM	EM	XC		EM	NT	EM	EM
		◇■ A ⊏⊼		◇■ B ⊼	◇■ ⊼	◇■ ⊼	◇ C	◇■ D ⊼		◇■ ⊼		◇■ ⊼	◇■ ⊼
York	d			14 34				14 40					
Leeds	d	13 59	14 06					15 10			15 06		
Wakefield Westgate	d	14 12						15 23					
Wakefield Kirkgate	d		14 22								15 22		
Doncaster	d			14 59									
Sheffield	d	15 01	15 07	15 23	15 35		15 43	15 54			16 07		
Chesterfield	d	15 15	15 24		15 47		15 57	16 07			16 23		
Derby	a	15 34		15 52	16 06			16 27					
	d	15 34			16 08								16 48
Long Eaton	d												16 58
Alfreton	d		15 34				16 08				16 33		
Langley Mill	d		15 42				16 15				16 41		
Lincoln	d												
Nottingham	a		15 59				16 32				16 56		
	d					16 18				16 45			
Beeston	d					16 24							
East Midlands Parkway	d	15 51			16 19	16 31				16 55			17 02
Loughborough	d	15 59				16 39							17 10
Barrow Upon Soar	d												
Sileby	d												
Syston	d												
Leicester	a	16 11			16 33	16 50				17 09			17 20
	d	16 13			16 41	16 53				17 10			17 23
Market Harborough	d	16 28				17 07							17 37
Melton Mowbray	d												
Oakham	d												
Corby	d											17 20	
Kettering	a	16 38				17 16						17 29	17 46
	d	16 39				17 17							17 47
Wellingborough	d	16 47				17 25							17 55
Bedford	d	17 07				17 42							18 13
Luton	d	17 29											18 31
Luton Airport Parkway	d					18 01							
St Pancras International	a	17 54			17 57	18 23				18 26			18 53

Station		XC	EM	EM	EM	XC		EM	NT	EM	EM	XC	EM
		◇■ B ⊼	◇■ ⊼	◇■ ⊼	◇ C	◇■ E ⊼		◇■ ⊼		◇■ ⊼	◇■ ⊼	◇■ F ⊼	◇■ ⊼
York	d	15 34				15 40						16 23	
Leeds	d					16 10			16 06				
Wakefield Westgate	d					16 22							
Wakefield Kirkgate	d								16 22				
Doncaster	d	15 59										16 51	
Sheffield	d	16 24	16 29		16 40	16 54			17 07			17 24	17 29
Chesterfield	d		16 43		16 56	17 06			17 23				17 43
Derby	a	16 53	17 03			17 26						17 53	18 03
	d		17 08								17 47		18 04
Long Eaton	d										17 57		
Alfreton	d				17 07				17 33				
Langley Mill	d				17 14				17 41				
Lincoln	d												
Nottingham	a				17 30				17 58				
	d			17 19				17 40					
Beeston	d			17 25									
East Midlands Parkway	d		17 21	17 31				17 51			18 01		18 17
Loughborough	d			17 39							18 09		
Barrow Upon Soar	d												
Sileby	d												
Syston	d												
Leicester	a		17 38	17 50				18 07			18 19		18 33
	d		17 39	17 53				18 09			18 21		18 34
Market Harborough	d			18 07							18 35		
Melton Mowbray	d												
Oakham	d												
Corby	d									18 20			
Kettering	a			18 16						18 29	18 44		
	d			18 17							18 45		
Wellingborough	d			18 25							18 52		
Bedford	d			18 42							19 09		
Luton	d										19 29		
Luton Airport Parkway	d			19 01									
St Pancras International	a		18 59	19 23				19 27			19 51		19 55

Station		EM	EM	XC		EM	EM	NT	XC	EM	EM	XC	EM
		◇■ ⊼	◇ C	◇■ G ⊼		◇■ ⊼	◇■ ⊼		◇■ B ⊼	◇■ ⊼	◇ H	◇■ E ⊼	◇■ ⊼
York	d			16 40					17 34	17 42		17 40	
Leeds	d			17 10				17 06				18 10	
Wakefield Westgate	d			17 22								18 22	
Wakefield Kirkgate	d							17 22					
Doncaster	d								17 59	18 06			
Sheffield	d		17 39	17 54				18 07	18 24	18 31	18 41	18 54	
Chesterfield	d		17 55	18 06				18 25		18 44	18 56	19 06	
Derby	a			18 25					18 53	19 04		19 25	
	d									19 05			
Long Eaton	d									19 15			
Alfreton	d		18 05					18 36			19 06		
Langley Mill	d		18 13					18 43			19 14		
Lincoln	d												
Nottingham	a		18 29					19 00			19 34		
	d	18 19					18 43						
Beeston	d	18 25											
East Midlands Parkway	d	18 31					18 53			19 20			
Loughborough	d	18 39					19 01			19 27			
Barrow Upon Soar	d												
Sileby	d												
Syston	d												
Leicester	a	18 52					19 12			19 38			
	d	18 54					19 14			19 39			
Market Harborough	d	19 08					19 28			19 53			
Melton Mowbray	d												
Oakham	d												
Corby	d					19 20							20 20
Kettering	a	19 17				19 29	19 37			20 02			20 29
	d	19 18					19 38			20 03			
Wellingborough	d	19 25					19 45			20 11			
Bedford	d	19 42					20 03			20 29			
Luton	d						20 21						
Luton Airport Parkway	d	20 02								20 48			
St Pancras International	a	20 24					20 45			21 12			

Station		EM		NT	XC	EM	EM	XC	NT	XC	EM	EM
		◇■ ⊼		I	◇■ ⊼	◇■ C ⊼	◇ J	◇■ ⊼	K	◇■ ⊼	◇■ ⊼	◇■ ⊼
York	d				18 34			18 40		19 24		
Leeds	d			18 06				19 10	19 06			
Wakefield Westgate	d							19 22				
Wakefield Kirkgate	d			18 22					19 22			
Doncaster	d				18 59					19 50		
Sheffield	d			19 07	19 24	19 31	19 40	19 54	20 06	20 20		20 24
Chesterfield	d			19 25		19 44	19 55	20 06	20 23			20 38
Derby	a				19 53	20 04		20 25		20 49		20 57
	d					20 05						20 59
Long Eaton	d					20 16						
Alfreton	d			19 36			20 06		20 34			
Langley Mill	d			19 43			20 13		20 41			
Lincoln	d											
Nottingham	a			20 00			20 30		20 57			
	d	19 43										
Beeston	d	19 49										
East Midlands Parkway	d	19 55				20 21						21 11
Loughborough	d	20 03				20 29						
Barrow Upon Soar	d											
Sileby	d											
Syston	d											
Leicester	a	20 13				20 41						21 28
	d	20 15				20 43						21 29
Market Harborough	d	20 29				20 58						21 44
Melton Mowbray	d											
Oakham	d											
Corby	d										21 25	
Kettering	a	20 38				21 08					21 34	21 54
	d	20 39				21 09						21 55
Wellingborough	d	20 46				21 17						22 03
Bedford	d	21 04				21 36						22 23
Luton	d	21 23				21 55						22 42
Luton Airport Parkway	d											
St Pancras International	a	21 45				22 20						23 08

A ⊏ from Leicester ⊼ to Leicester
B From Newcastle to Reading
C From Liverpool Lime Street to Norwich
D From Glasgow Central to Penzance
E From Glasgow Central to Plymouth
F From Edinburgh to Reading
G From Aberdeen to Plymouth
H From Liverpool Lime Street
I From Newcastle to Guildford
J From Glasgow Central to Bristol Temple Meads
K From Newcastle to Birmingham New Street

For connections to Gatwick Airport see Table 52

Table 53

Sheffield - East Midlands - London

Sundays until 24 June

Route Diagram - see first Page of Table 53

Station		EM	EM	XC	XC	EM	XC	EM	EM
		◇■ ⊼	◇ A	◇■ B ⊼	◇■ C ⊼	◇ A	◇■ D ⊼	◇■ ⊼	◇ A
York	d			19 40	20 24		20 40		
Leeds	d			20 10			21 10		
Wakefield Westgate	d			20 22			21 22		
Wakefield Kirkgate	d								
Doncaster	d				20 50				
Sheffield	d		20 40	20 54	21 20	21 40	21 54	22 35	23 29
Chesterfield	d		20 55	21 06	21 32	21 56	22 06	22 49	23 43
Derby	a			21 25	21 51		22 25	23 26	
	d								
Long Eaton	d								
Alfreton	d		21 06			22 07			23 54
Langley Mill	d		21 13			22 14			00 02
Lincoln	d								
Nottingham	a		21 34			22 35			00 25
	d	21 13							
Beeston	d								
East Midlands Parkway	d	21 23							
Loughborough	d	21 31							
Barrow Upon Soar	d								
Sileby	d								
Syston	d								
Leicester	a	21 41							
	d	21 43							
Market Harborough	d	21 57							
Melton Mowbray	d								
Oakham	d								
Corby	d								
Kettering	a	22 06							
	d	22 07							
Wellingborough	d	22 14							
Bedford	d	22 31							
Luton	d	22 50							
Luton Airport Parkway	d								
St Pancras International	a	23 27							

Sundays

1 July to 16 September

Station		EM	EM	EM	EM	EM	EM	EM	EM	EM		EM	EM
		◇■ ⊼	◇ A	◇■ E ⊼	◇■ E ⊼	◇■ F ⊼	◇■ G H ⊼	◇■ I ⊼	◇■ J ⊼	◇■ ⊼	E	◇■ J K ⊼	◇■ F ⊼
York	d												
Leeds	d												
Wakefield Westgate	d												
Wakefield Kirkgate	d												
Doncaster	d												
Sheffield	d	23p20	23p42				06 48						
Chesterfield	d	23p33	23p57				07 01						
Derby	a	00 13					07 21						
	d			06 13		07 16	07 22	07 22					07 54
Long Eaton	d												
Alfreton	d												
Langley Mill	d												
Lincoln	d												
Nottingham	a		00 34										
	d									07 25			
Beeston	d												
East Midlands Parkway	d			06 25	07 02	07 27	07 34	07 34		07 39		07 56	08 05
Loughborough	d					07 35						08 03	08 13
Barrow Upon Soar	d												
Sileby	d												
Syston	d								←				
Leicester	a			06 41	07 16	07 45	07 47	07 47	07 45	07 56		08 14	08 24
	d			06 48	07 22	07 52	07 48	07 48	07 52	07 57		08 20	08 25
Market Harborough	d					→	08 02	08 02		08 12			08 39
Melton Mowbray	d												
Oakham	d												
Corby	d												
Kettering	a			07 46	08 17		08 11	08 11	08 47	08 22		09 15	08 48
	d			07 47	08 19		08 12	08 12	08 48	08 23		09 17	08 49
Wellingborough	d			08 01	08 32		08 20	08 20	09 02	08 31		09 30	08 57
Bedford	d			08 15	08 45		08 32	08 32	09 15	08 45		09 45	09 09
Luton	d			08 34			08 48	08 48	09 35				09 25
Luton Airport Parkway	d				09 06				→	09 01		10 06	
St Pancras International	a			09 11	09 48		09 13	09 13		09 27		10 48	09 49

Station		EM	EM	EM	EM	EM	EM	EM		EM	EM	EM	XC
		◇■ J ⊼	◇■ J ⊼	◇■ E J ⊼	◇■ K ⊼	◇■ ⊼	◇■ J ⊼	◇■ J F ⊼	L	◇■ ⊼	◇■ ⊼	◇■ ⊼	◇■ ⊼
York	d												
Leeds	d												08 10
Wakefield Westgate	d												08 23
Wakefield Kirkgate	d												
Doncaster	d												
Sheffield	d						08 13					08 39	08 54
Chesterfield	d						08 26					08 52	09 07
Derby	a						08 45					09 11	09 28
	d		08 12				08 50					09 13	
Long Eaton	d		08 22				09 00					09 23	
Alfreton	d												
Langley Mill	d												
Lincoln	d												
Nottingham	a												
	d			08 22						09 15			
Beeston	d			08 28									
East Midlands Parkway	d		08 26	08 34		08 45	09 04			09 26		09 27	
Loughborough	d		08 34	08 42		08 54	09 12			09 34		09 35	
Barrow Upon Soar	d												
Sileby	d												
Syston	d												
Leicester	a		08 44	08 53		09 06	09 23			09 47		09 45	
	d		08 51	08 54		09 14	09 24			09 49		09 52	
Market Harborough	d			09 08			09 38			10 07			
Melton Mowbray	d												
Oakham	d												
Corby	d				09 30	10 04					10 25		
Kettering	a		09 46	09 17	09 39	10 15	09 47			10 17	10 34	10 47	
	d		09 48	09 18		10 16	09 48			10 18		10 48	
Wellingborough	d		10 02	09 26		10 26	09 57			10 26		10 58	
Bedford	d	←	10 15	09 39		10 45	10 09	←		10 41		11 15	
Luton	d	09 35	10 35				10 25	10 35				11 35	
Luton Airport Parkway	d		→	09 56		11 06				10 57		→	
St Pancras International	a	10 18		10 20		11 48	10 51	11 18		11 23			

A From Liverpool Lime Street
B From Edinburgh to Bristol Temple Meads. ⊼ to Leeds
C From Newcastle to Birmingham New Street
D From Glasgow Central to Birmingham New Street. ⊼ to Leeds
E 16 September
F 16 September. To St Pancras International
G 29 July, 5 August, 12 August, 2 September, 9 September
H from 1 July until 22 July, 19 August, 26 August
I 16 September. From Derby to St Pancras International
J not 16 September
K 16 September. From Derby
L To Plymouth

For connections to Gatwick Airport see Table 52

Sheffield - East Midlands - London

Route Diagram - see first Page of Table 53

		EM	NT	EM	EM	EM	EM	EM	EM	XC	XC	NT	EM	EM	EM		EM	EM	EM	EM	EM	XC	XC	NT
		◇■		◇■	◇■	◇■	◇■	◇■	◇■	◇■	◇■		◇■	◇■	◇■		◇■	◇■	◇■	◇■	◇	◇■	◇■	
		A		B	C	D	B	B	E	F	G		B	C	H	I	J	B	A	K	F	L		
		🍴		🍴	🍴	🍴	🍴	🍴	☐🍴	🍴	🍴		🍴	🍴	☐🍴		☐🍴	☐	🍴	🍴		🍴	🍴	
York	d																					09 28	09 30	
Leeds	d								08 42	09 00	09 00	09 05			09 44		09 46					10 00	10 00	10 02
Wakefield Westgate	d								08 55	09 11	09 11				09 58		09 58					10 12	10 12	
Wakefield Kirkgate	d											09 21												10 18
Doncaster	d									09 32	09 32											10 30	10 30	
Sheffield ⇌	d		09 00	09 17		09 37			09 41	09 57	09 57	10 07	10 17		10 26		10 28				10 49	10 57	10 57	11 03
Chesterfield	d		09 17	09 29		09 49			09 56	10 09	10 09	10 23	10 29		10 41		10 41				11 04	11 09	11 09	11 20
Derby	a			09 49		10 09				10 31	10 32		10 50				11 02					11 28	11 28	
	d			09 51		10 10							10 52				11 03							
Long Eaton	d			10 01		10 20							11 02											
Alfreton	d		09 28									10 33									11 14			11 30
Langley Mill	d		09 35									10 41												11 38
Lincoln	d																							
Nottingham ⇌	a		09 53						10 26			10 57			11 11						11 39			11 54
	d	09 34					10 15		10 34						11 18					11 29				
Beeston	d	09 41					10 22											←		11 36				
East Midlands Parkway ✈	d	09 48		10 05		10 25	10 30		10 45				11 06		11 30		11 16	11 30		11 43				
Loughborough	d	09 57		10 13		10 32	10 38		10 53				11 14		→		11 24	11 38		11 52				
Barrow Upon Soar	d																							
Sileby	d																							
Syston	d																							
Leicester	a	10 09		10 23		10 43	10 51		11 05				11 24				11 37	11 51		12 05				
	d	10 15		10 25		10 49	10 53		11 12				11 26				11 44	11 53		12 11				
Market Harborough	d			10 39			11 08						11 40					12 08						
Melton Mowbray	d																							
Oakham	d																							
Corby	d	11 04						11 25	12 02										12 30	13 05				
Kettering	a	11 15		10 48		11 44	11 18	11 34	12 12				11 49				12 45	12 18	12 39	13 14				
	d	11 16		10 51		11 48	11 19		12 16				11 50				12 46	12 19		13 16				
Wellingborough	d	11 26		10 59		11 58	11 27		12 26				11 58				12 56	12 27		13 26				
Bedford	d	11 45		11 12	←	12 15	11 41		12 45				12 11	←			13 15	12 42		13 45				
Luton	d			11 28	11 35	12 35							12 27	12 35			13 35							
Luton Airport Parkway ✈	d	12 06				→	11 58		13 06								→	12 58		14 04				
St Pancras International ⊖	a	12 48		11 51	12 18		12 24		13 48				12 50	13 18				13 24		14 30				

		EM	EM	EM	EM	EM	XC	XC	NT	EM	EM	EM	NT	EM	EM	EM	XC	XC	EM	EM		EM	NT
		◇■	◇■	◇■	◇■	◇■	◇■	◇■		◇■	◇■	◇■		◇■	◇■	◇	◇■	◇■	◇■	◇■		◇■	
		M	N	B	B	D	O	P		B	B	C			A	Q R	P	S	A		T		
		☐🍴	☐	🍴	🍴	🍴	🍴	🍴		🍴	🍴	🍴		🍴	🍴		🍴	🍴	🍴	🍴		🍴	
York	d						10 28	10 34									11 28	11 28					
Leeds	d	10 15					11 00	11 00	10 57				11 29				12 00	12 00					12 29
Wakefield Westgate	d	10 27					11 12	11 12									12 12	12 12					
Wakefield Kirkgate	d								11 13				11 46										12 46
Doncaster	d						11 30	11 30									12 30	12 30					
Sheffield ⇌	d	11 06				11 51	11 57	11 57	12 00	12 24			12 31			12 49	12 57	12 57	13 21	13 27			13 31
Chesterfield	d	11 25				12 04	12 09	12 09	12 18	12 37			12 49			13 03	13 09	13 09	13 34	13 39			13 48
Derby	a	11 47				12 23	12 28	12 28		12 57							13 30	13 31	13 53	13 58			
	d	11 48				12 27				13 02									13 55	14 01			
Long Eaton	d					12 37				13 12									14 05	14 11			
Alfreton	d								12 28				12 59			13 14							13 59
Langley Mill	d								12 36				13 07										14 06
Lincoln	d																						
Nottingham ⇌	a								12 52				13 24			13 39							14 22
	d			12 15							13 12				13 34								
Beeston	d			12 22							13 18				13 41								
East Midlands Parkway ✈	d	12 01		12 30		12 42				13 16	13 24				13 48				14 10	14 16			
Loughborough	d	12 09		12 38		12 49				13 24	13 32				13 57				14 19	14 23			
Barrow Upon Soar	d																						
Sileby	d																						
Syston	d																						
Leicester	a	12 21		12 52		13 00				13 34	13 42				14 09				14 31	14 34			
	d	12 23		12 53		13 09				13 36	13 44				14 10				14 32	14 35			
Market Harborough	d	12 38		13 08						13 50	13 58				14 25				14 47	14 49			
Melton Mowbray	d																						
Oakham	d																						
Corby	d				13 30									14 25									
Kettering	a	12 48		13 18	13 39	14 04				13 59	14 07			14 34	14 35				14 57	14 58			
	d	12 49		13 19		14 05				14 00	14 08				14 36				14 58	14 59			
Wellingborough	d	12 57		13 27		14 15				14 07	14 15				14 44				15 06	15 07			
Bedford	d	13 11	←	13 42		14 32				14 23	14 28	←			15 02				15 24	15 23		←	
Luton	d	13 29	13 35			14 49				14 39		14 49							15 42	15 39		15 42	
Luton Airport Parkway ✈	d			13 58		→					14 44				15 18				→				
St Pancras International ⊖	a	13 54	14 12	14 24						15 03	15 08	15 12			15 44					16 02		16 07	

A 16 September
B not 16 September
C 16 September. From Sheffield
D 16 September. To St Pancras International
E 16 September. ☐ from Nottingham 🍴 to Nottingham
F not 16 September. To Plymouth
G 16 September. To Plymouth
H not 16 September. To St Pancras International. ☐ from Nottingham 🍴 to Nottingham
I 16 September. To St Pancras International. ☐ from Derby 🍴 to Derby
J not 16 September. From Leeds
K not 16 September. To Norwich
L 16 September. From Leeds to Reading
M not 16 September. ☐ from Derby 🍴 to Derby
N 16 September. From Leeds
O not 16 September. From Newcastle to Plymouth
P 16 September. From Newcastle to Reading
Q To Norwich
R not 16 September. From Edinburgh to Reading
S not 16 September. To St Pancras International
T not 16 September. From Sheffield

For connections to Gatwick Airport see Table 52

Table 53 — Sundays — 1 July to 16 September

Sheffield - East Midlands - London

Route Diagram - see first Page of Table 53

		EM	EM	EM	XC	EM	EM	XC	EM	EM	EM	EM	EM	XC	XC	EM	EM		EM	EM	NT	XC	EM	EM
		◇■	◇■	◇	◇■	◇■	◇■	◇■	◇■	◇■	◇■	◇■	◇	◇■	◇■	◇■	◇■		◇■	◇■		◇■	◇■	◇■
		A	B	C	D	A	B	E		A	B	A	F	G	H	I		B	J		K	A	A	
		🍴	🍴		🍴	🍴	🍴	🍴	🍴	🍴	🍴	🍴		🍴	🍴	🍴	☐🍴		🍴	☐🍴		🍴	🍴	🍴
York	d				12 28									13 40	13 40							14 34		
Leeds	d				13 00									14 10	14 10		13 59			13 59	14 06			
Wakefield Westgate	d				13 12									14 23	14 23		14 12			14 12				
Wakefield Kirkgate	d																				14 22			
Doncaster	d				13 30																	14 59		
Sheffield ⇌	d			13 49	13 57	14 04	14 15	14 22					14 46	14 54	14 54		15 00			15 03	15 07	15 23	15 34	
Chesterfield	d			14 03	14 09	14 16	14 28	14 32					15 00	15 06	15 06		15 13			15 20	15 24		15 47	
Derby	a				14 28	14 36	14 48	14 51						15 25	15 26		15 33			15 43		15 52	16 06	
	d					14 37	14 49										15 35			15 48			16 08	
Long Eaton	d					14 47	14 59																	
Alfreton	d			14 14									15 11								15 34			
Langley Mill	d												15 18								15 42			
Lincoln	d																							
Nottingham ⇌	a			14 39									15 38								15 59			
	d	14 22	14 24							14 59	15 22	15 34							15 48					16 18
Beeston	d	14 28	14 30							15 06	15 28													16 24
East Midlands Parkway ✈	d	14 35	14 36			14 52	15 04			15 14	15 34	15 45					15 50		15 58	16 02			16 19	16 31
Loughborough	d	14 43	14 44			14 59	15 11			15 22	15 42						15 58			16 11				16 39
Barrow Upon Soar	d																							
Sileby	d																							
Syston	d																							
Leicester	a	14 54	14 54			15 10	15 22			15 34	15 52	16 02					16 11		16 12	16 23			16 33	16 50
	d	14 56	14 56			15 13	15 23			15 36	15 54	16 04					16 13		16 13	16 24			16 35	16 53
Market Harborough	d	15 10	15 10							15 51	16 08						16 28			16 39				17 07
Melton Mowbray	d																							
Oakham	d																							
Corby	d								15 25							16 25								
Kettering	a	15 19	15 19						15 34	16 01	16 17					16 34	16 38			16 49				17 16
	d	15 20	15 20							16 02	16 18						16 39			16 50				17 17
Wellingborough	d	15 27	15 27							16 10	16 25						16 47			16 58				17 25
Bedford	d	15 40	15 43							16 24	16 41						17 02			17 16				17 42
Luton	d					16 00	16 14										17 19			17 33				
Luton Airport Parkway ✈	d	15 56	15 59							16 42	16 58													17 59
St Pancras International ⊖	a	16 20	16 23			16 24	16 37			17 07	17 21	17 18					17 45		17 24	17 59			17 48	18 22

		EM	EM	XC	XC	EM	EM	EM	NT	EM	EM	EM	XC	EM	EM	EM	EM	XC	EM	EM	EM	NT
		◇	◇■	◇■	◇■	◇■	◇■	◇■		◇■	◇■	◇■	◇■	◇■	◇■	◇■	◇	◇■	◇■	◇■	◇■	
		F	B	L	M	B	B	A			B	A	K	A	B	A	F	N	B	A	B	
			🍴	🍴	🍴	🍴	🍴	🍴		🍴	🍴	🍴	🍴	🍴	🍴	🍴		🍴	🍴	🍴	🍴	
York	d			14 40	14 41								15 34					15 40				
Leeds	d			15 10	15 10				15 06									16 10				16 06
Wakefield Westgate	d			15 23	15 23													16 22				
Wakefield Kirkgate	d								15 22													16 22
Doncaster	d												15 59									
Sheffield ⇌	d	15 43	15 50	15 54	15 54				16 07				16 24	16 34	16 36		16 40	16 54				17 07
Chesterfield	d	15 57	16 02	16 07	16 07				16 23					16 47	16 50		16 56	17 06				17 23
Derby	a		16 22	16 27	16 27								16 53	17 06	17 10			17 26				
	d		16 25								16 48	16 47		17 08	17 17							
Long Eaton	d										16 58	16 57										
Alfreton	d	16 08							16 33								17 07					17 33
Langley Mill	d	16 15							16 41								17 14					17 41
Lincoln	d																					
Nottingham ⇌	a	16 32							16 56								17 30					17 58
	d					16 29	16 45	16 45								17 19			17 31	17 42	17 42	
Beeston	d					16 36										17 25			17 37			
East Midlands Parkway ✈	d		16 36			16 42	16 55	16 56			17 02	17 03		17 19	17 30	17 31			17 43	17 53	17 53	
Loughborough	d					16 50					17 10	17 10				17 39			17 51			
Barrow Upon Soar	d																					
Sileby	d																					
Syston	d																					
Leicester	a		16 51			17 00	17 09	17 12			17 20	17 22		17 33	17 51	17 51			18 01	18 10	18 10	
	d		16 54			17 02	17 14	17 14			17 23	17 23		17 35	17 53	17 53			18 03	18 12	18 11	
Market Harborough	d					17 16					17 37	17 37				18 07			18 17			
Melton Mowbray	d																					
Oakham	d																					
Corby	d									17 20												
Kettering	a					17 25				17 29	17 46	17 46				18 16			18 26			
	d					17 26					17 47	17 47				18 17			18 27			
Wellingborough	d					17 33					17 54	17 55				18 25			18 34			
Bedford	d					17 53					18 09	18 10				18 39			18 54			
Luton	d										18 27	18 28										
Luton Airport Parkway ✈	d					18 10										18 56			19 11			
St Pancras International ⊖	a		18 04			18 33	18 26	18 25			18 50	18 51		18 45	19 07	19 19			19 34	19 24	19 29	

A not 16 September
B 16 September
C From Manchester Piccadilly to Norwich
D From Edinburgh to Penzance
E To Reading
F From Liverpool Lime Street to Norwich
G not 16 September. From Edinburgh to Plymouth
H 16 September. From Newcastle to Penzance
I not 16 September. ☐ from Leicester 🍴 to Leicester
J 16 September. ☐ from Leicester 🍴 to Leicester
K From Newcastle to Reading
L not 16 September. From Glasgow Central to Penzance
M 16 September. From Newcastle to Plymouth
N From Glasgow Central to Plymouth

For connections to Gatwick Airport see Table 52

Sheffield - East Midlands - London

Sundays
1 July to 16 September

Route Diagram - see first Page of Table 53

		EM	EM	EM	XC	EM	EM	EM	EM	XC		XC	EM	EM	EM	NT	XC	EM	EM	EM		EM	XC	EM	EM
		◇1	◇1	◇1	◇1	◇1	◇1	◇1	◇	◇1		◇1	◇1	◇1	◇1		◇1	◇1	◇1	◇		◇1	◇1	◇1	◇1
			A	B	C	B	A	B	D	E		F	A		B		G	A	H	I	J	K		B	
		✠	✠	✠	✠	✠	✠	✠		✠		✠	✠	✠	✠		✠	✠	✠			✠	✠	✠	✠
York 8	d				16 23					16 40		16 41					17 34		17 42			17 42	17 40		
Leeds 10	d									17 10		17 10				17 06							18 10		
Wakefield Westgate 7	d									17 22		17 22											18 22		
Wakefield Kirkgate 4	d															17 22									
Doncaster 7	d				16 51												17 59		18 06			18 08			
Sheffield 7	d				17 24	17 29	17 30		17 39	17 54		17 54				18 07	18 24		18 32	18 41		18 46	18 54		
Chesterfield	d					17 43	17 44		17 55	18 06		18 06				18 25			18 44	18 56		19 01	19 06		
Derby 6	a				17 53	18 03	18 03			18 25		18 25					18 53		19 04			19 21	19 25		
	d		17 47	17 47		18 04	18 08												19 05			19 22			
Long Eaton	d		17 57	17 57															19 15			19 32			
Alfreton	d								18 05							18 36				19 06					
Langley Mill	d								18 13							18 43				19 14					
Lincoln	d																								
Nottingham 8	a								18 29							19 00				19 34					
	d							18 19					18 34		18 43			19 01							19 43
Beeston	d							18 25					18 40												19 49
East Midlands Parkway	d		18 01	18 01		18 17	18 20	18 32					18 46		18 53			19 11	19 20			19 37			19 55
Loughborough	d		18 09	18 09				18 39					18 54		19 01			19 18	19 27			19 44			20 03
Barrow Upon Soar	d																								
Sileby	d																								
Syston	d																								
Leicester	a		18 19	18 19		18 33	18 37	18 51					19 04		19 12			19 30	19 38			19 55			20 13
	d		18 21	18 23		18 34	18 37	18 53					19 06		19 14			19 31	19 41			19 56			20 15
Market Harborough	d		18 35	18 37				19 07					19 20		19 28			19 45	19 55			20 10			20 29
Melton Mowbray	d																								
Oakham	d																								
Corby	d	18 20												19 20										20 20	
Kettering 4	a	18 29	18 44	18 46				19 16					19 29	19 29	19 37			19 54	20 04			20 19		20 29	20 38
	d		18 45	18 47				19 17					19 30		19 38			19 55	20 05			20 20			20 39
Wellingborough	d		18 52	18 55				19 25					19 37		19 45			20 03	20 13			20 28			20 47
Bedford 7	d		19 08	19 11				19 38					19 54		20 01			20 20	20 27			20 45			21 01
Luton 10	d		19 25	19 28											20 17			20 35							21 17
Luton Airport Parkway 7	d							19 55					20 10						20 43			21 01			
St Pancras International	a		19 48	19 51		19 46	19 52	20 18					20 33		20 40			20 58	21 06			21 24			21 40

		EM	NT	XC	EM	EM		EM	XC	XC	NT	XC	EM	EM	EM	EM		EM	EM	EM	XC	XC	XC	EM	XC
		◇1		◇1	◇1	◇1		◇	◇1	◇1		◇1	◇1	◇1	◇1	◇1		◇1	◇1	◇	◇1	◇1	◇1	◇	◇1
		A		L	B	A		D	M	N		O		P	B	Q		B	A	I	R S	O	I	T	
		✠		✠	✠	✠			✠	✠		✠	✠	✠	✠	✠		✠	✠		✠	✠	✠		✠
York 8	d			18 34					18 40	18 41		19 24									19 40	19 40	20 24		20 40
Leeds 10	d		18 06						19 10	19 10	19 06										20 10	20 10			21 10
Wakefield Westgate 7	d								19 22	19 22											20 22	20 22			21 22
Wakefield Kirkgate 4	d		18 22								19 22														
Doncaster 7	d			18 59								19 50											20 50		
Sheffield 7	d		19 07	19 24	19 27	19 31		19 40	19 54	19 54	20 06	20 20		20 26	20 28					20 40	20 54	20 54	21 20	21 40	21 54
Chesterfield	d		19 25		19 42	19 44		19 55	20 06	20 06	20 23			20 40	20 41					20 55	21 06	21 06	21 32	21 56	22 06
Derby 6	a			19 53	20 02	20 03			20 25	20 25		20 49		20 59	21 00						21 25	21 25	21 51		22 25
	d				20 04	20 05								21 01	21 02										
Long Eaton	d				20 14	20 15																			
Alfreton	d		19 36					20 06			20 34									21 06				22 07	
Langley Mill	d		19 43					20 13			20 41									21 13				22 14	
Lincoln	d																								
Nottingham 8	a		20 00					20 30			20 57									21 34				22 35	
	d	19 57																21 13	21 21						
Beeston	d	20 03																							
East Midlands Parkway	d	20 09			20 19	20 20								21 13	21 13			21 23	21 32						
Loughborough	d	20 17			20 28	20 29												21 31	21 40						
Barrow Upon Soar	d																								
Sileby	d																								
Syston	d																								
Leicester	a	20 28			20 40	20 41								21 30	21 28	↑ 21 30		21 41	21 51						
	d	20 30			20 42	20 43								21 31	21 30	21 31		21 43	21 53						
Market Harborough	d	20 44			20 57	20 58								→	21 44	21 46		21 57	22 07						
Melton Mowbray	d																								
Oakham	d																								
Corby	d												21 25												
Kettering 4	a	20 53			21 07	21 08							21 34		21 53	21 56		22 06	22 16						
	d	20 54			21 08	21 09									21 54	21 57		22 07	22 17						
Wellingborough	d	21 01			21 16	21 17									22 01	22 05		22 14	22 25						
Bedford 7	d	21 18			21 31	21 35									22 16	22 22		22 27	22 41						
Luton 10	d	21 34			21 47	21 51									22 32	22 40		22 43	22 59						
Luton Airport Parkway 7	d																								
St Pancras International	a	21 57			22 13	22 17									22 56	23 06		23 07	23 28						

A 16 September
B not 16 September
C From Edinburgh to Reading
D From Liverpool Lime Street to Norwich
E not 16 September. From Aberdeen to Plymouth
F 16 September. From Newcastle to Plymouth
G From Newcastle to Reading
H not 16 September. From York Holgate Sidings
I From Liverpool Lime Street
J 16 September. From York Holgate Sidings
K From Glasgow Central to Plymouth
L From Newcastle to Guildford
M not 16 September. From Glasgow Central to Bristol Temple Meads
N 16 September. From Newcastle to Bristol Temple Meads
O From Newcastle to Birmingham New Street
P 16 September. To St Pancras International
Q 16 September. From Sheffield
R 16 September. From Edinburgh to Bristol Temple Meads
S not 16 September. From Edinburgh to Bristol Temple Meads. ✠ to Leeds
T From Glasgow Central to Birmingham New Street. ✠ to Leeds

For connections to Gatwick Airport see Table 52

Sheffield - East Midlands - London

Sundays
1 July to 16 September

Route Diagram - see first Page of Table 53

		EM		EM	EM	EM
		◇1		◇1	◇	◇
		A		B	C	D
		✠		✠		
York 8	d					
Leeds 10	d					
Wakefield Westgate 7	d					
Wakefield Kirkgate 4	d					
Doncaster 7	d					
Sheffield 7	d	22 35		22 35	23 29	23 29
Chesterfield	d	22 48		22 49	23 43	23 43
Derby 6	a	23 24		23 26		
	d					
Long Eaton	d					
Alfreton	d				23 54	23 54
Langley Mill	d				00 02	00 02
Lincoln	d					
Nottingham 8	a				00 25	00 32
	d					
Beeston	d					
East Midlands Parkway	d					
Loughborough	d					
Barrow Upon Soar	d					
Sileby	d					
Syston	d					
Leicester	a					
	d					
Market Harborough	d					
Melton Mowbray	d					
Oakham	d					
Corby	d					
Kettering 4	a					
	d					
Wellingborough	d					
Bedford 7	d					
Luton 10	d					
Luton Airport Parkway 7	d					
St Pancras International	a					

Sundays
from 23 September

		EM	EM	EM	EM	EM	EM	EM	EM	EM		EM	EM	EM	EM	EM	EM	XC	EM	EM		EM	NT	EM	EM
		◇1	◇	◇1	◇1	◇1	◇1	◇1	◇1	◇1		◇1	◇1	◇1	◇1	◇1	◇1	◇1	◇1	◇1		◇1		◇1	◇1
			E	F	G F	F	G	F	G		F	G	G F	G	F	H	G	G	F		G	F			
		✠		✠	✠	✠	✠	✠	✠	✠		✠	✠	✠	✠	✠	✠	✠	✠	✠		✠		✠	✠
York 8	d																								
Leeds 10	d																	08 10							
Wakefield Westgate 7	d																	08 23							
Wakefield Kirkgate 4	d																								
Doncaster 7	d																								
Sheffield 7	d	23p20	23p42													08 18	08 39	08 54					09 00	09 17	09 37
Chesterfield	d	23p33	23p57													08 31	08 52	09 07					09 17	09 29	09 49
Derby 6	a	00 13														08 50	09 11	09 28						09 49	10 09
	d			06 13	06 51		07 16			07 52		08 12				08 52	09 13							09 55	10 10
Long Eaton	d											08 22				09 02	09 23							10 05	10 20
Alfreton	d																						09 28		
Langley Mill	d																						09 35		
Lincoln	d																								
Nottingham 8	a		00 34																				09 53		
	d																					09 34			
Beeston	d																					09 41			
East Midlands Parkway	d			06 25	07 03	07 02	07 27	07 39	07 56	08 03		08 26	08 35		08 45	09 06	09 27		09 30			09 48		10 10	10 25
Loughborough	d						07 35		08 03	08 11		08 34	08 42		08 54	09 14	09 35		09 38			09 57		10 17	10 32
Barrow Upon Soar	d																								
Sileby	d																								
Syston	d																								
Leicester	a			06 41	07 19	07 16	07 45	07 53	08 14	08 22		08 44	08 53		09 06	09 24	09 45		09 50			10 09		10 28	10 43
	d			06 48	07 20	07 22	07 52	07 54	08 20	08 23		08 51	08 54		09 14	09 26	09 52		09 52			10 15		10 29	10 49
Market Harborough	d				07 38			08 11		08 40			09 11			09 40			10 10					10 43	
Melton Mowbray	d																								
Oakham	d																								
Corby	d													09 30	10 04					10 25		11 04			
Kettering 4	a			07 46	07 48	08 17	08 47	08 20	09 15	08 49		09 46	09 20	09 39	10 15	09 49	10 47		10 20	10 34		11 15		10 52	11 44
	d			07 47	07 49	08 19	08 48	08 21	09 17	08 50		09 48	09 21		10 16	09 50	10 48		10 21			11 16		10 53	11 48
Wellingborough	d			08 01	08 01	08 32	09 02	08 33	09 30	09 02		10 02	09 33		10 26	10 02	10 58		10 29			11 26		11 01	11 58
Bedford 7	d			08 15	08 15	08 45	09 15	08 45	09 45	09 15		10 15	09 45		10 45	10 15	11 15		10 45			11 45		11 15	12 15
Luton 10	d			08 34	08 34		09 35			09 35		10 35				10 35	11 35							11 35	12 35
Luton Airport Parkway 7	d					09 06		09 06	10 06				10 06		11 06				11 06			12 06			
St Pancras International	a			09 11	09 11	09 48	10 18	09 48	10 48	10 18		11 18	10 48		11 48	11 18	12 18		11 48			12 48		12 18	13 18

A not 16 September
B 16 September
C 16 September. From Liverpool Lime Street
D not 16 September. From Liverpool Lime Street
E From Liverpool Lime Street
F from 23 September until 21 October
G from 28 October
H To Plymouth

For connections to Gatwick Airport see Table 52

Table 53

Sundays from 23 September

Sheffield - East Midlands - London

Route Diagram - see first Page of Table 53

Station		EM ◇■ A ⌶	EM ◇■ A ⌶	EM ◇■ B ⊡⌶	XC ◇■ C ⌶	NT		EM ◇■ A ⌶	EM ◇■ D ⊡⌶	EM ◇■ E ⊡⌶	EM ◇■ F ⊡	XC ◇■ G ⌶	EM ◇■ A ⌶	EM ◇■ H ⌶	NT I	EM ◇■ ⊡⌶	A	EM ◇■ A ⌶	EM ◇■ J ⌶	EM ◇■ K ⌶	XC ◇■ ⌶	NT A	EM ◇■ L ⌶	EM ◇■ ⌶	NT
York ■	d											09 30									10 34				
Leeds ■	d			08 42	09 00	09 05			09 44	09 46		10 00			10 02	10 15					11 00	10 57			11 29
Wakefield Westgate ■	d			08 55	09 11				09 58	09 58		10 12				10 27					11 12				
Wakefield Kirkgate ■	d					09 21									10 18							11 13			11 46
Doncaster ■	d				09 32							10 30									11 30				
Sheffield ■	d			09 41	09 57	10 07		10 22	10 26	10 28		10 57			11 03	11 06				11 51	11 57	12 00	12 28		12 31
Chesterfield	d			09 56	10 09	10 23		10 34	10 41	10 41		11 09			11 20	11 25				12 04	12 09	12 18	12 41		12 49
Derby ■	a				10 32			10 54		11 02		11 28				11 47				12 23	12 28		13 00		
	d							10 55		11 03						11 51				12 27			13 02		
Long Eaton	d							11 05												12 37			13 12		
Alfreton	d					10 33									11 30							12 28			12 59
Langley Mill	d					10 41									11 38							12 36			13 07
Lincoln	d																								
Nottingham ■	a			10 26		10 57			11 11						11 54							12 52			13 24
	d	10 19		10 34					11 18					11 29				12 15							
Beeston	d	10 26									←			11 36				12 22							
East Midlands Parkway	d	10 33		10 45				11 10	11 29	11 16	11 29			11 43		12 03		12 29		12 42			13 16		
Loughborough	d	10 42		10 53				11 17	→	11 24	11 38			11 52		12 12		12 38		12 49			13 24		
Barrow Upon Soar	d																								
Sileby	d																								
Syston	d																								
Leicester	a	10 54		11 05				11 28		11 37	11 50			12 05		12 24		12 51		13 00			13 34		
	d	10 55		11 12				11 29		11 44	11 51			12 11		12 25		12 55		13 09			13 36		
Market Harborough	d	11 10						11 43			12 06					12 40		13 10					13 50		
Melton Mowbray	d																								
Oakham	d																								
Corby	d		11 25	12 02									12 30	13 05					13 30						
Kettering ■	a	11 20	11 34	12 12				11 52		12 45	12 16		12 39	13 14		12 50		13 20	13 39	14 04			13 59		
	d	11 21		12 16				11 53		12 46	12 18			13 16		12 51		13 21		14 05			14 00		
Wellingborough	d	11 29		12 26				12 01		12 56	12 26			13 26		12 59		13 29		14 15			14 07		
Bedford ■	d	11 45		12 45				12 15		13 15	12 45			13 45		13 15		13 45		14 32			14 23	←	
Luton ■	d							12 35		13 35						13 35				14 49			14 39	14 49	
Luton Airport Parkway ■	d	12 06		13 06							13 06			14 04				14 04		→					
St Pancras International	a	12 48		13 48				13 18		14 12	13 48			14 30		14 12		14 30					15 03	15 12	

Station		EM ◇■ ⌶		EM ◇■ A ⌶	EM ◇■ H ⌶	EM ◇ M	XC ◇■ N ⌶	EM ◇■ O ⌶	EM ◇■ H P ⌶	EM ◇■ ⌶	NT A	EM ◇■ ⌶	H	EM ◇■ Q ⌶	EM ◇ R H	XC ◇■ A ⌶	EM ◇■ S ⌶	EM ◇■ ⌶	XC ◇■ A ⌶	EM ◇■ H ⌶	EM ◇■ ⌶	EM ◇■ T ⌶	U	EM ◇	XC ◇■ ⌶
York ■	d						11 28									12 28									13 40
Leeds ■	d						12 00				12 29					13 00									14 10
Wakefield Westgate ■	d						12 12									13 12									14 23
Wakefield Kirkgate ■	d										12 46														
Doncaster ■	d						12 30									13 30									
Sheffield ■	d					12 49	12 57	13 24	13 27		13 31				13 49	13 57	14 15	14 21	14 22					14 46	14 54
Chesterfield	d					13 03	13 09	13 39	13 39		13 48				14 03	14 09	14 28	14 33	14 32					15 00	15 06
Derby ■	a						13 31	13 59	13 58							14 28	14 48	14 53	14 51						15 26
	d							14 03	14 01								14 49	14 54							
Long Eaton	d							14 13	14 11								14 59	15 04							
Alfreton	d					13 14					13 59				14 14									15 11	
Langley Mill	d										14 06													15 18	
Lincoln	d																								
Nottingham ■	a					13 39					14 22				14 39									15 38	
	d			13 34	13 34							14 24		14 24							15 22	15 22			
Beeston	d			13 41	13 41					←		14 30		14 30							15 28	15 28			
East Midlands Parkway	d			13 48	13 48			14 18	14 16	14 18		14 36		14 36			15 04	15 09			15 34	15 34			
Loughborough	d			13 57	13 57			→	14 23	14 25		14 44		14 44			15 11	15 16			15 42	15 42			
Barrow Upon Soar	d																								
Sileby	d																								
Syston	d																								
Leicester	a			14 09	14 09				14 34	14 36		14 54		14 54			15 22	15 27			15 52	15 52			
	d			14 10	14 10				14 35	14 37		14 56		14 56			15 23	15 28			15 54	15 54			
Market Harborough	d			14 25	14 25				14 49	14 51		15 10		15 10							16 08	16 08			
Melton Mowbray	d																								
Oakham	d																								
Corby	d	14 25																		15 25					
Kettering ■	a	14 34		14 35	14 35				14 58	15 00		15 19		15 19						15 34	16 17	16 17			
	d			14 36	14 36				14 59	15 01		15 20		15 20							16 18	16 18			
Wellingborough	d			14 44	14 44				15 07	15 09		15 27		15 27							16 25	16 25			
Bedford ■	d			15 00	15 02				15 23	15 23		15 41		15 43							16 39	16 41			
Luton ■	d								15 39	15 39							16 14	16 17							
Luton Airport Parkway ■	d			15 16	15 18							15 57		15 59							16 56	16 58			
St Pancras International	a			15 42	15 44				16 02	16 02		16 21		16 23			16 37	16 40			17 19	17 21			

A from 28 October
B from 23 September until 21 October. ⊡ from Nottingham ⌶ to Nottingham
C To Birmingham New Street
D from 28 October. To St Pancras International. ⊡ from Nottingham ⌶ to Nottingham
E from 23 September until 21 October. ⊡ from Derby ⌶ to Derby
F from 28 October. From Leeds
G From Leeds to Reading
H from 23 September until 21 October
I from 28 October. ⊡ from Derby ⌶ to Derby
J from 23 September until 21 October. To St Pancras International
K From Newcastle to Reading
L from 23 September until 21 October. From Sheffield
M To Norwich
N From Edinburgh to Birmingham New Street
O from 28 October. To St Pancras International
P from 28 October. From Sheffield
Q From Manchester Piccadilly to Norwich
R From Edinburgh to Penzance
S from 23 September until 21 October. To Reading
T From Liverpool Lime Street to Norwich
U from 23 September until 21 October. From Newcastle to Penzance

For connections to Gatwick Airport see Table 52

Table 53

Sundays from 23 September

Sheffield - East Midlands - London

Route Diagram - see first Page of Table 53

Station		EM ◇■ A ⌶	EM ◇■ B ⌶	EM ◇■ ⌶	EM ◇■ C ⌶	EM ◇■ D ⊡⌶	EM ◇■ E ⊡⌶	NT		XC ◇■ F ⌶	EM ◇ G	EM ◇■ B ⌶	EM ◇■ A ⌶	XC ◇■ H ⌶	XC ◇■ I ⌶	EM ◇■ B ⌶	EM ◇■ A ⌶	EM ◇■ B ⌶		EM ◇■ A ⌶	NT	EM ◇■ ⌶	EM ◇■ B ⌶	EM ◇■ A ⌶	XC ◇■ F ⌶
York ■	d									14 34				14 40	14 41										15 34
Leeds ■	d				13 59	13 59		14 06						15 10	15 10						15 06				
Wakefield Westgate ■	d				14 12	14 12								15 23	15 23										
Wakefield Kirkgate ■	d							14 22													15 22				
Doncaster ■	d									14 59															15 59
Sheffield ■	d				15 00	15 03		15 07		15 23	15 43	15 50	15 50	15 54	15 54						16 07				16 24
Chesterfield	d				15 16	15 20		15 24			15 57	16 02	16 02	16 07	16 07						16 23				
Derby ■	a				15 38	15 43				15 52		16 22	16 22	16 27	16 27										16 53
	d				15 50	15 48						16 25	16 25										16 48	16 48	
Long Eaton	d																						16 58	16 58	
Alfreton	d							15 34			16 08										16 33				
Langley Mill	d							15 42			16 15										16 41				
Lincoln	d																								
Nottingham ■	a							15 59			16 32										16 56				
	d	15 48	15 50													16 29	16 29	16 45		16 45					
Beeston	d						←									16 36	16 36								
East Midlands Parkway	d	15 58	16 00		16 04	16 02	16 04					16 36	16 36			16 42	16 42	16 55		16 55			17 02	17 02	
Loughborough	d				→	16 11	16 13									16 50	16 50						17 10	17 10	
Barrow Upon Soar	d																								
Sileby	d																								
Syston	d																								
Leicester	a	16 12	16 14			16 23	16 25					16 51	16 51			17 00	17 00	17 09		17 09			17 20	17 20	
	d	16 13	16 15			16 24	16 26					16 56	16 54			17 02	17 02	17 14		17 14			17 23	17 23	
Market Harborough	d					16 39	16 41									17 16	17 16						17 37	17 37	
Melton Mowbray	d																								
Oakham	d																								
Corby	d			16 25																		17 20			
Kettering ■	a			16 34		16 49	16 51									17 25	17 25					17 29	17 46	17 46	
	d					16 50	16 52									17 26	17 26						17 47	17 47	
Wellingborough	d					16 58	17 00									17 33	17 33						17 54	17 54	
Bedford ■	d					17 16	17 16									17 52	17 53						18 07	18 09	
Luton ■	d					17 33	17 33																18 25	18 27	
Luton Airport Parkway ■	d															18 09	18 10								
St Pancras International	a	17 24	17 24			17 59	17 59					18 04	18 04			18 32	18 33	18 24		18 26			18 48	18 50	

Station		EM ◇■ B ⌶	EM ◇■ A ⌶	EM ◇ G		XC ◇■ J ⌶	EM ◇■ ⌶	EM ◇■ B ⌶	EM ◇■ A ⌶	NT	EM ◇■ ⌶	EM ◇■ A ⌶	EM ◇■ B ⌶	XC ◇■ K ⌶		EM ◇■ ⌶	EM ◇ L	EM ◇ M	XC ◇■ N ⌶	XC ◇■ I ⌶	EM ◇■ B ⌶	EM ◇■ A ⌶	NT	XC ◇■ F ⌶
York ■	d					15 40								16 23					16 40	16 41				17 34
Leeds ■	d					16 10				16 06									17 10	17 10			17 06	
Wakefield Westgate ■	d					16 22													17 22	17 22				
Wakefield Kirkgate ■	d									16 22													17 22	
Doncaster ■	d													16 51										17 59
Sheffield ■	d	16 36	16 36	16 40		16 54				17 07				17 24		17 30	17 39	17 39	17 54	17 54			18 07	18 24
Chesterfield	d	16 50	16 50	16 56		17 06				17 23						17 44	17 55	17 55	18 06	18 06			18 25	
Derby ■	a	17 10	17 10			17 26								17 53		18 03			18 25	18 25				18 53
	d	17 17	17 17									17 47	17 48			18 08								
Long Eaton	d											17 57	17 58											
Alfreton	d			17 07						17 33							18 05	18 05					18 36	
Langley Mill	d			17 14						17 41							18 13	18 13					18 43	
Lincoln	d																							
Nottingham ■	a			17 30						17 58							18 29	18 33					19 00	
	d						17 31	17 42	17 42												18 34	18 34		
Beeston	d						17 37														18 40	18 40		
East Midlands Parkway	d	17 30	17 30				17 43	17 53	17 53			18 01	18 02			18 20					18 46	18 46		
Loughborough	d						17 51					18 09	18 10								18 54	18 54		
Barrow Upon Soar	d																							
Sileby	d																							
Syston	d																							
Leicester	a	17 51	17 51				18 01	18 10	18 10			18 19	18 20			18 37					19 04	19 04		
	d	17 53	17 53				18 03	18 12	18 11			18 21	18 22			18 37					19 06	19 06		
Market Harborough	d						18 17					18 35	18 36								19 20	19 20		
Melton Mowbray	d																							
Oakham	d																							
Corby	d										18 20													
Kettering ■	a						18 26				18 29	18 44	18 45								19 29	19 29		
	d						18 27					18 45	18 46								19 30	19 30		
Wellingborough	d						18 34					18 52	18 53								19 37	19 37		
Bedford ■	d						18 54					19 08	19 08								19 53	19 54		
Luton ■	d											19 25	19 25											
Luton Airport Parkway ■	d						19 11														20 09	20 10		
St Pancras International	a	19 05	19 07				19 34	19 27	19 29			19 48	19 48			19 52					20 32	20 33		

A from 23 September until 21 October
B from 28 October
C from 28 October. To St Pancras International
D from 23 September until 21 October. ⊡ from Leicester ⌶ to Leicester
E from 28 October. From Leeds. ⊡ from Leicester ⌶ to Leicester
F From Newcastle to Reading
G From Liverpool Lime Street to Norwich
H from 28 October. From Glasgow Central to Penzance
I from 23 September until 21 October. From Newcastle to Plymouth
J From Glasgow Central to Plymouth
K From Edinburgh to Reading
L from 23 September until 21 October. From Liverpool Lime Street to Norwich
M from 28 October. From Liverpool Lime Street to Norwich
N from 28 October. From Aberdeen to Plymouth

For connections to Gatwick Airport see Table 52

Sheffield - East Midlands - London

Route Diagram - see first Page of Table 53

		EM ◇■	EM ◇■ A	EM ◇■ B	EM ◇ C	EM ◇■ D	XC ◇■ E	EM ◇■	EM ◇■ A	EM ◇■ B	NT	XC ◇■ F	EM ◇■ A	EM ◇■ B	EM ◇ G H	XC ◇■ I	XC ◇■	NT J	XC ◇■	EM ◇■ A	EM ◇■ B	EM ◇■ A	EM ◇■
York ■	d					17 42	17 40					18 34				18 40	18 41		19 24				
Leeds ■	d						18 10				18 06					19 10	19 10	19 06					
Wakefield Westgate ■	d						18 22									19 22	19 22						
Wakefield Kirkgate ■	d										18 22							19 22					
Doncaster ■	d					18 08						18 59							19 50				
Sheffield ■	d				18 41	18 46	18 54				19 07	19 24	19 31	19 31	19 40	19 54	19 54	20 06	20 20		20 26	20 26	
Chesterfield	d				18 56	19 01	19 06				19 25		19 44	19 44	19 55	20 06	20 06	20 23			20 40	20 40	
Derby ■	a					19 21	19 25					19 53	20 03	20 03		20 25	20 25		20 49		20 59	20 59	
	d					19 22							20 05	20 05							21 01	21 01	
Long Eaton	d					19 32							20 15	20 15									
Alfreton	d				19 06						19 36				20 06			20 34					
Langley Mill	d				19 14						19 43				20 13			20 41					
Lincoln	d																						
Nottingham ■	a				19 34						20 00				20 30			20 57					
	d		19 01	19 01					19 57	19 57													21 21
Beeston	d								20 03	20 03													
East Midlands Parkway	d		19 11	19 11		19 37			20 09	20 09			20 20	20 20							21 13	21 13	21 32
Loughborough	d		19 18	19 18		19 44			20 17	20 17			20 29	20 29									21 40
Barrow Upon Soar	d																						
Sileby	d																						
Syston	d																						
Leicester	a		19 29	19 30		19 55			20 28	20 28			20 41	20 41							21 30	21 30	21 51
	d		19 31	19 31		19 56			20 30	20 30			20 43	20 43							21 31	21 31	21 52
Market Harborough	d		19 45	19 45		20 10			20 44	20 44			20 58	20 58							21 46	21 46	22 07
Melton Mowbray	d																						
Oakham	d																						
Corby	d	19 20						20 20												21 25			
Kettering ■	a	19 29	19 54	19 54		20 19		20 29	20 53	20 53			21 08	21 08						21 34	21 56	21 56	22 16
	d		19 55	19 55		20 20			20 54	20 54			21 09	21 09							21 57	21 57	22 17
Wellingborough	d		20 02	20 03		20 28			21 01	21 01			21 17	21 17							22 05	22 05	22 25
Bedford ■	d		20 20	20 20		20 45			21 16	21 18			21 33	21 35							22 22	22 22	22 39
Luton ■	d		20 35	20 35					21 32	21 34			21 49	21 51							22 38	22 40	22 57
Luton Airport Parkway ■	d					21 01																	
St Pancras International	a		20 58	20 58		21 24			21 55	21 57			22 15	22 17							23 05	23 06	23 26

		EM ◇■ B	EM ◇ C	XC ◇■ K	XC ◇■ L	XC ◇■ J	EM ◇ C	XC ◇■ M	EM ◇■	EM ◇ C
York ■	d			19 40	19 40	20 24		20 40		
Leeds ■	d			20 10	20 10			21 10		
Wakefield Westgate ■	d			20 22	20 22			21 22		
Wakefield Kirkgate ■	d									
Doncaster ■	d					20 50				
Sheffield ■	d		20 40	20 54	20 54	21 20	21 40	21 54	22 35	23 29
Chesterfield	d		20 55	21 06	21 06	21 32	21 56	22 06	22 49	23 43
Derby ■	a			21 25	21 25	21 51		22 25	23 26	
	d									
Long Eaton	d									
Alfreton	d		21 06				22 07			23 54
Langley Mill	d		21 13				22 14			00 02
Lincoln	d									
Nottingham ■	a		21 34				22 35			00 25
	d	21 21								
Beeston	d									
East Midlands Parkway	d	21 32								
Loughborough	d	21 40								
Barrow Upon Soar	d									
Sileby	d									
Syston	d									
Leicester	a	21 51								
	d	21 53								
Market Harborough	d	22 07								
Melton Mowbray	d									
Oakham	d									
Corby	d									
Kettering ■	a	22 16								
	d	22 17								
Wellingborough	d	22 25								
Bedford ■	d	22 41								
Luton ■	d	22 59								
Luton Airport Parkway ■	d									
St Pancras International	a	23 28								

A from 28 October
B from 23 September until 21 October
C From Liverpool Lime Street
D From York Holgate Sidings
E From Glasgow Central to Plymouth
F From Newcastle to Guildford
G From Liverpool Lime Street to Norwich
H from 28 October. From Glasgow Central to Bristol Temple Meads
I from 23 September until 21 October. From Newcastle to Bristol Temple Meads
J From Newcastle to Birmingham New Street
K from 23 September until 21 October. From Edinburgh to Bristol Temple Meads
L from 28 October. From Edinburgh to Bristol Temple Meads. ⌶ to Leeds
M From Glasgow Central to Birmingham New Street. ⌶ to Leeds

For connections to Gatwick Airport see Table 52

Nottingham - Mansfield - Worksop

Network Diagram - see first Page of Table 50

Miles			EM	EM	EM	EM	EM	EM	EM	EM	EM	EM	EM	EM	EM	EM	EM	EM	EM	EM	EM	EM	EM
0	**Nottingham ■**	d	05 40	06 05	07 00	08 25	08 53	09 25	09 55	10 25	10 55	11 25	11 55	12 25	12 55	13 25	13 55	14 25	14 55	15 25	15 55	16 25	16 55
5½	Bulwell	d	05 49	06 14	07 10	08 36	09 02		10 06		11 06		12 06		13 06		14 06		15 06		16 06		17 06
8¼	Hucknall	d	05 54	06 19	07 15	08 41	09 07	09 39	10 11	10 39	11 11	11 39	12 11	12 39	13 11	13 39	14 11	14 39	15 11	15 39	16 11	16 39	17 12
10¾	Newstead	d	05 59	06 24	07 21	08 46	09 12	09 44		10 44		11 44		12 44		13 44		14 44		15 44		16 44	17 17
13¾	Kirkby In Ashfield	d	06 05	06 30	07 31	08 52	09 18	09 49	10 19	10 49	11 19	11 49	12 19	12 49	13 19	13 49	14 19	14 49	15 19	15 49	16 19	16 49	17 23
14½	Sutton Parkway	d	06 08	06 33	07 34	08 55	09 21	09 52	10 22	10 52	11 22	11 52	12 22	12 52	13 22	13 52	14 22	14 52	15 22	15 52	16 22	16 52	17 27
17¼	**Mansfield**	d	06 13	06 38	07 40	09 00	09 26	09 57	10 27	10 57	11 27	11 57	12 27	12 57	13 27	13 57	14 27	14 57	15 27	15 57	16 27	16 57	17 32
18¾	Mansfield Woodhouse	d	06 18	06 47	07 45	09 04	09a33	10 02	10a34	11 02	11a34	12 02	12a34	13 02	13a34	14 02	14a34	15 02	15a34	16 02	16a34	17 02	17a39
21½	Shirebrook	d	06 24	06 54	07 51	09 11		10 08		11 08		12 08		13 08		14 08		15 08		16 08		17 08	
22¼	Langwith - Whaley Thorns	d	06 28	06 58	07 55	09 15		10 12		11 12		12 12		13 12		14 12		15 12		16 12		17 12	
25½	Creswell (Derbys)	d	06 32	07 02	07 59	09 19		10 16		11 16		12 16		13 16		14 16		15 16		16 16		17 16	
26¾	Whitwell	d	06 36	07 05	08 03	09 22		10 20		11 20		12 20		13 20		14 20		15 20		16 20		17 20	
31½	**Worksop**	a	06 48	07 20	08 18	09 33		10 33		11 33		12 33		13 33		14 33		15 33		16 33		17 33	

		EM	EM	EM	EM	EM	EM
Nottingham ■	d	17 25	17 55	18 55	19 55	20 55	22 05
Bulwell	d	17 39	18 11	19 05	20 05	21 05	22 19
Hucknall	d	17 44	18 16	19 10	20 16	21 16	22 24
Newstead	d	17 49	18 21	19 15	20 21	21 21	22 29
Kirkby In Ashfield	d	17 55	18 27	19 21	20 27	21 27	22 34
Sutton Parkway	d	17 58	18 30	19 24	20 30	21 30	22 37
Mansfield	d	18 03	18 35	19 29	20 35	21 35	22 42
Mansfield Woodhouse	d	18 08	18 39	19 33	20 39	21 40	22 47
Shirebrook	d	18 14	18 46	19 40	20 46	21 46	22 53
Langwith - Whaley Thorns	d	18 18	18 50	19 44	20 50	21 50	22 57
Creswell (Derbys)	d	18 22	18 54	19 48	20 54	21 54	23 01
Whitwell	d	18 26	18 57	19 51	20 57	21 58	23 05
Worksop	a	18 37	19 07	20 03	21 09	22 06	23 13

Saturdays

		EM	EM	EM	EM	EM	EM	EM	EM	EM	EM	EM	EM	EM	EM	EM	EM	EM	EM	EM	EM	EM	EM
Nottingham ■	d	05 40	06 05	06 59	08 25	08 53	09 25	09 55	10 25	10 55	11 25	11 55	12 25	12 55	13 25	13 55	14 25	14 55	15 25	15 55	16 25	16 55	17 25
Bulwell	d	05 49	06 14	07 09	08 36	09 02		10 06		11 06		12 06		13 06		14 06		15 06		16 06		17 06	17 39
Hucknall	d	05 54	06 19	07 14	08 41	09 07	09 39	10 11	10 39	11 11	11 39	12 11	12 39	13 11	13 39	14 11	14 39	15 11	15 39	16 11	16 39	17 12	17 44
Newstead	d	05 59	06 24	07 20	08 46	09 12	09 44		10 44		11 44		12 44		13 44		14 44		15 44		16 44	17 17	17 49
Kirkby In Ashfield	d	06 05	06 30	07 31	08 52	09 18	09 49	10 19	10 49	11 19	11 49	12 19	12 49	13 19	13 49	14 19	14 49	15 19	15 49	16 19	16 49	17 23	17 55
Sutton Parkway	d	06 08	06 33	07 34	08 55	09 21	09 52	10 22	10 52	11 22	11 52	12 22	12 52	13 22	13 52	14 22	14 52	15 22	15 52	16 22	16 52	17 27	17 58
Mansfield	d	06 13	06 38	07 40	09 00	09 26	09 57	10 27	10 57	11 27	11 57	12 27	12 57	13 27	13 57	14 27	14 57	15 27	15 57	16 27	16 57	17 32	18 03
Mansfield Woodhouse	d	06 18	06 47	07 45	09 04	09a33	10 02	10a34	11 02	11a34	12 02	12a34	13 02	13a34	14 02	14a34	15 02	15a34	16 02	16a34	17 02	17a39	18 08
Shirebrook	d	06 24	06 54	07 51	09 11		10 08		11 08		12 08		13 08		14 08		15 08		16 08		17 08		18 14
Langwith - Whaley Thorns	d	06 28	06 58	07 55	09 15		10 12		11 12		12 12		13 12		14 12		15 12		16 12		17 12		18 18
Creswell (Derbys)	d	06 32	07 02	07 59	09 19		10 16		11 16		12 16		13 16		14 16		15 16		16 16		17 16		18 22
Whitwell	d	06 36	07 05	08 03	09 22		10 20		11 20		12 20		13 20		14 20		15 20		16 20		17 20		18 26
Worksop	a	06 48	07 20	08 12	09 33		10 33		11 33		12 33		13 33		14 33		15 33		16 33		17 33		18 37

		EM	EM	EM	EM	EM	EM
Nottingham ■	d	17 55	18 55	19 55	20 55	22 05	23 05
Bulwell	d	18 11	19 05	20 05	21 05	22 19	23 18
Hucknall	d	18 16	19 10	20 16	21 16	22 24	23 23
Newstead	d	18 21	19 15	20 21	21 21	22 29	23 28
Kirkby In Ashfield	d	18 27	19 21	20 27	21 27	22 34	23 33
Sutton Parkway	d	18 30	19 24	20 30	21 30	22 37	23 36
Mansfield	d	18 35	19 29	20 35	21 35	22 42	23 41
Mansfield Woodhouse	d	18 39	19 33	20 39	21 40	22 47	23a46
Shirebrook	d	18 46	19 40	20 46	21 46	22 53	
Langwith - Whaley Thorns	d	18 50	19 44	20 50	21 50	22 57	
Creswell (Derbys)	d	18 54	19 48	20 54	21 54	23 01	
Whitwell	d	18 57	19 51	20 57	21 58	23 05	
Worksop	a	19 07	20 03	21 09	22 06	23 13	

Sundays

		EM A	EM B	EM	EM	EM C	EM D	EM	EM	EM	EM
Nottingham ■	d	07 20	08 07	09 36	11 26	13 26	13 27	15 25	16 53	18 29	20 27
Bulwell	d	07 40	08 16	09 46	11 36	13 36	13 37	15 35	17 03	18 40	20 37
Hucknall	d	07 45	08 21	09 51	11 41	13 41	13 42	15 40	17 08	18 45	20 42
Newstead	d	07 55	08 26	09 56	11 46	13 46	13 47	15 45	17 13	18 50	20 47
Kirkby In Ashfield	d	08 08	08 32	10 01	11 51	13 51	13 52	15 50	17 18	18 55	20 52
Sutton Parkway	d	08 15	08 35	10 04	11 54	13 54	13 55	15 53	17 21	18 58	20 55
Mansfield	d	08 30	08 40	10 09	11 59	13 59	14 00	15 58	17 26	19 03	21 00
Mansfield Woodhouse	d	08a40	08a47	10a16	12a06	14a06	14a07	16a05	17a33	19a10	21a07
Shirebrook	d										
Langwith - Whaley Thorns	d										
Creswell (Derbys)	d										
Whitwell	d										
Worksop	a										

A from 16 September
B until 9 September
C until 21 October
D from 28 October

Table 55

Worksop - Mansfield - Nottingham

Network Diagram - see first Page of Table 50

Miles			EM	EM	EM	EM	EM	EM	EM	EM	EM	EM	EM	EM	EM	EM	EM	EM	EM	EM	EM	EM	EM
0	**Worksop**	d	05 50		06 56		07 38	08 38		09 38		10 38		11 38		12 38		13 38		14 38		15 38	
4¾	Whitwell	d	05 59		07 05		07 47	08 47		09 47		10 47		11 47		12 47		13 47		14 47		15 47	
6	Creswell (Derbys)	d	06 02		07 08		07 50	08 50		09 50		10 50		11 50		12 50		13 50		14 50		15 50	
9¼	Langwith - Whaley Thorns	d	06 06		07 13		07 54	08 54		09 55		10 55		11 55		12 55		13 55		14 55		15 55	
10	Shirebrook	d	06 10		07 16		07 58	08 58		09 58		10 58		11 58		12 58		13 58		14 58		15 58	
12¾	Mansfield Woodhouse	d	06 17	07 07	07 25	07 39	08 06	09 06	09 37	10 07	10 37	11 07	11 37	12 07	12 37	13 07	13 37	14 07	14 37	15 07	15 37	16 07	16 37
14¼	**Mansfield**	d	06 22	07 11	07 29	07 43	08 10	09 10	09 40	10 10	10 40	11 10	11 40	12 10	12 40	13 10	13 40	14 10	14 40	15 10	15 40	16 10	16 40
17	Sutton Parkway	d	06 27	07 16	07 35	07 48	08 15	09 15	09 46	10 16	10 46	11 16	11 46	12 16	12 46	13 16	13 46	14 16	14 46	15 16	15 46	16 16	16 46
17¾	Kirkby In Ashfield	d	06 30	07 19	07 38	07 52	08 18	09 18	09 49	10 19	10 49	11 19	11 49	12 19	12 49	13 19	13 49	14 19	14 49	15 19	15 49	16 19	16 49
20¾	Newstead	d	06 35	07 26	07 43	07 57	08 23	09 23	09 54		10 54		11 54		12 54		13 54		14 54		15 54		16 54
23¼	Hucknall	d	06 39	07 31	07 48	08 02	08 28	09 27	09 58	10 26	10 58	11 26	11 58	12 26	12 58	13 26	13 58	14 26	14 58	15 26	15 58	16 26	16 58
26	Bulwell	d	06 43	07 35	07 53	08 06	08 32	09 31		10 30		11 30		12 30		13 30		14 30		15 30		16 30	
31½	**Nottingham** ■	a	06 58	07 48	08 04	08 18	08 44	09 44	10 14	10 44	11 14	11 44	12 14	12 44	13 19	13 44	14 14	14 44	15 14	15 44	16 14	16 44	17 14

		EM	EM	EM	EM	EM	EM	EM	EM
Worksop	d	16 42		17 46	18 41	19 22	20 15	21 20	22 21
Whitwell	d	16 51		17 55	18 50	19 31	20 24	21 29	22 30
Creswell (Derbys)	d	16 54		17 58	18 53	19 34	20 27	21 32	22 33
Langwith - Whaley Thorns	d	16 59		18 02	18 58	19 38	20 31	21 37	22 38
Shirebrook	d	17 02		18 07	19 01	19 42	20 35	21 40	22 41
Mansfield Woodhouse	d	17 10	17 43	18 14	19 09	19 49	20 43	21 48	22 49
Mansfield	d	17 14	17 46	18 18	19 13	19 53	20 50	21 53	22 53
Sutton Parkway	d	17 19	17 52	18 24	19 18	19 58	20 55	21 58	22 58
Kirkby In Ashfield	d	17 22	17 55	18 27	19 21	20 01	20 58	22 01	23 01
Newstead	d		17 59	18 31	19 26	20 06	21 03	22 06	23 06
Hucknall	d	17 30	18 04	18 36	19 30	20 10	21 07	22 10	23 10
Bulwell	d	17 34		18 40	19 34	20 14	21 14	22 14	23 14
Nottingham ■	a	17 48	18 20	18 51	19 47	20 36	21 26	22 28	23 26

Saturdays

		EM	EM	EM	EM	EM	EM	EM	EM	EM	EM	EM	EM	EM	EM	EM	EM	EM	EM	EM	EM	EM	EM
Worksop	d	05 50	06 56	07 38	08 38		09 38		10 38		11 38		12 38		13 38		14 38		15 38		16 42		17 46
Whitwell	d	05 59	07 05	07 47	08 47		09 47		10 47		11 47		12 47		13 47		14 47		15 47		16 51		17 55
Creswell (Derbys)	d	06 02	07 08	07 50	08 50		09 50		10 50		11 50		12 50		13 50		14 50		15 50		16 54		17 58
Langwith - Whaley Thorns	d	06 06	07 13	07 54	08 54		09 55		10 55		11 55		12 55		13 55		14 55		15 55		16 59		18 02
Shirebrook	d	06 10	07 16	07 58	08 58		09 58		10 58		11 58		12 58		13 58		14 58		15 58		17 02		18 07
Mansfield Woodhouse	d	06 17	07 25	08 06	09 06	09 37	10 07	10 37	11 07	11 37	12 07	12 37	13 07	13 37	14 07	14 37	15 07	15 37	16 07	16 37	17 10	17 43	18 14
Mansfield	d	06 22	07 29	08 10	09 10	09 40	10 10	10 40	11 10	11 40	12 10	12 40	13 10	13 40	14 10	14 40	15 10	15 40	16 10	16 40	17 14	17 46	18 18
Sutton Parkway	d	06 27	07 35	08 15	09 15	09 46	10 16	10 46	11 16	11 46	12 16	12 46	13 16	13 46	14 16	14 46	15 16	15 46	16 16	16 46	17 19	17 52	18 24
Kirkby In Ashfield	d	06 30	07 38	08 18	09 18	09 49	10 19	10 49	11 19	11 49	12 19	12 49	13 19	13 49	14 19	14 49	15 19	15 49	16 19	16 49	17 22	17 55	18 27
Newstead	d	06 35	07 43	08 23	09 23	09 54		10 54		11 54		12 54		13 54		14 54		15 54		16 54		17 59	18 31
Hucknall	d	06 39	07 48	08 28	09 27	09 58	10 26	10 58	11 26	11 58	12 26	12 58	13 26	13 58	14 26	14 58	15 26	15 58	16 26	16 58	17 30	18 04	18 36
Bulwell	d	06 43	07 53	08 32	09 31		10 30		11 30		12 30		13 30		14 30		15 30		16 30		17 34		18 40
Nottingham ■	a	06 58	08 05	08 44	09 44	10 15	10 44	11 14	11 44	12 14	12 44	13 15	13 44	14 14	14 44	15 14	15 44	16 15	16 44	17 14	17 48	18 19	18 51

		EM	EM	EM	EM	EM
Worksop	d	18 41	19 22	20 15	21 19	22 21
Whitwell	d	18 50	19 31	20 24	21 28	22 30
Creswell (Derbys)	d	18 53	19 34	20 27	21 31	22 33
Langwith - Whaley Thorns	d	18 58	19 38	20 31	21 36	22 38
Shirebrook	d	19 01	19 42	20 35	21 39	22 41
Mansfield Woodhouse	d	19 09	19 49	20 43	21 47	22 49
Mansfield	d	19 13	19 53	20 50	21 52	22 53
Sutton Parkway	d	19 18	19 58	20 55	21 57	22 58
Kirkby In Ashfield	d	19 21	20 01	20 58	22 00	23 01
Newstead	d	19 26	20 06	21 03	22 05	23 06
Hucknall	d	19 30	20 10	21 07	22 09	23 10
Bulwell	d	19 34	20 14	21 14	22 13	23 14
Nottingham ■	a	19 47	20 32	21 27	22 25	23 26

Sundays

		EM A	EM B 🚌	EM	EM	EM	EM	EM	EM	EM
Worksop	d									
Whitwell	d									
Creswell (Derbys)	d									
Langwith - Whaley Thorns	d									
Shirebrook	d									
Mansfield Woodhouse	d	08 52	08 45	10 30	12 12	14 10	16 09	17 36	19 17	21 10
Mansfield	d	08 55	08 57	10 33	12 15	14 13	16 12	17 39	19 20	21 13
Sutton Parkway	d	09 01	09 12	10 39	12 21	14 19	16 18	17 45	19 26	21 19
Kirkby In Ashfield	d	09 04	09 19	10 42	12 24	14 22	16 21	17 48	19 29	21 22
Newstead	d	09 08	09 32	10 46	12 28	14 26	16 25	17 52	19 33	21 26
Hucknall	d	09 13	09 42	10 51	12 33	14 31	16 30	17 57	19 38	21 31
Bulwell	d	09 17	09 47	10 55	12 37	14 35	16 34	18 01	19 42	21 35
Nottingham ■	a	09 27	10 07	11 07	12 49	14 47	16 46	18 13	19 54	21 47

A until 9 September

B from 16 September

Table 56

Nottingham - Derby - Matlock

Network Diagram - see first Page of Table 50

Miles			EM MX ◇■ A ⊐	EM MX ◇■ B ⊐	EM ◇■ C 🛒	EM ◇■ A 🛒	EM MX D	EM MX E	XC ◇■	EM	EM ◇■ 🛒	XC ◇■	EM ◇■ 🛒	EM ◇■ 🛒	XC ◇■	EM ◇■ ⊠🛒	EM ◇■ 🛒	EM	EM	XC ■	EM ◇■ ⊐	XC ◇■ 🛒	EM
0	**Nottingham** ■	d	01 47	01 52	02 17	02 37			06 00	06 18	06 28	06 37	06 49		06 56	07 10		07 19	07 31	07 37	08 02	08 08	08 15
3¼	Beeston	d							06 06	06 24	06a33	06 43	06a54		07 07	07a16		07 25	07a37	07 43	08a07		08 24
4¾	Attenborough	d							06 10	06 27					07 11			07 29					08 27
7¾	Long Eaton	d							06 17	06 35					07 18		07 36	07 40		07 51			08 35
13½	Spondon	d							06 24	06 42								07 47					08 42
16	**Derby** ■	a	02 05	02 10	02 36	02 55			06 30	06 49		07 00			07 31		07 47	07 53		08 02		08 32	08 48
—		d					05 40	06 04		06 50				07 20				07 54					08 50
21¼	Duffield	d					05 47	06 11		06 57								08 02					08 57
23¾	Belper	d					05 52	06 16		07 02				07a27				08 07					09 02
26½	Ambergate	d					05 58	06a22		07 08								08 13					09 08
28½	Whatstandwell	d					06 02			07 12								08 17					09 12
31½	Cromford	d					06 07			07 17								08 22					09 17
32¼	Matlock Bath	d					06 11			07 20								08 24					09 19
33¼	**Matlock**	a					06 14			07 24								08 27					09 24

		EM	XC ■	EM ◇■ 🛒	EM ◇■ 🛒	XC ◇■ 🛒	EM	EM	XC ■	EM ◇■ 🛒	EM ◇■ 🛒	XC ◇■ 🛒	EM	EM	XC ■	EM ◇■ 🛒	EM ◇■ 🛒	XC ◇■ 🛒	EM	EM	XC ■ 🛒	EM ◇■ 🛒	EM ◇■ 🛒
Nottingham ■	d	08 32	08 37		09 02	09 11	09 18	09 32	09 37		10 02	10 11	10 18	10 32	10 37		11 02	11 08	11 18	11 32	11 37		12 02
Beeston	d	08a38	08 43		09a07		09 24	09a38	09 43		10a07		10 24	10a38	10 43		11a07		11 24	11a38	11 43		12a07
Attenborough	d						09 27						10 27						11 27				
Long Eaton	d		08 51	09 00			09 35		09 51	09 56			10 35		10 51	10 56			11 35		11 51	11 57	
Spondon	d		08 57																				
Derby ■	a		09 02	09 15		09 31	09 48		10 02	10 09		10 33	10 49		11 02	11 09		11 31	11 48		12 02	12 09	
	d						09 50						10 50						11 54				
Duffield	d						09 57						10 57						12 01				
Belper	d						10 02						11 02						12 06				
Ambergate	d						10 08						11 08						12 12				
Whatstandwell	d						10 12						11 12						12 16				
Cromford	d						10 17						11 17						12 21				
Matlock Bath	d						10 20						11 20						12 24				
Matlock	a						10 24						11 24						12 28				

		XC ◇■	EM	EM	XC ■ 🛒	EM ◇■ 🛒	EM ◇■ 🛒	XC ◇■	EM	EM	XC ■ 🛒	EM ◇■ 🛒	EM ◇■ 🛒	XC ◇■ 🛒	EM	EM	XC ■ 🛒	EM ◇■ 🛒	EM ◇■ 🛒	XC ◇■	EM	EM
Nottingham ■	d	12 08	12 18	12 32	12 37		13 02	13 11	13 18	13 32	13 37		14 02	14 11	14 18	14 32	14 37		15 02	15 11	15 18	15 32
Beeston	d		12 24	12a38	12 43		13a07		13 24	13a38	13 43		14a07		14 24	14a38	14 43		15a07		15 24	15a38
Attenborough	d		12 27						13 27						14 27						15 27	
Long Eaton	d		12 35		12 51	12 57			13 35		13 51	13 57			14 35		14 51	14 57			15 35	
Spondon	d								13 43													
Derby ■	a	12 33	12 48		13 02	13 09		13 31	13 48		14 02	14 09		14 31	14 47		15 03	15 13		15 31	15 48	
	d		12 50						13 50						14 54						15 50	
Duffield	d		12 57						13 57						15 01						15 57	
Belper	d		13 02						14 02						15 06						16 02	
Ambergate	d		13 08						14 08						15 12						16 08	
Whatstandwell	d		13 12						14 12						15 16						16 12	
Cromford	d		13 17						14 17						15 21						16 17	
Matlock Bath	d		13 20						14 20						15 24						16 20	
Matlock	a		13 24						14 24						15 28						16 24	

		XC ■ 🛒	EM ◇■ 🛒	EM ◇■ 🛒	XC ◇■	EM	EM	XC ■ 🛒	EM ◇■ 🛒	EM	EM ◇■ 🛒	XC ◇■	EM	EM	XC ■ 🛒	EM ◇■ 🛒	EM ◇■ 🛒	XC ◇■	EM	EM	XC ■ 🛒	EM ◇■ 🛒	EM ◇■ 🛒
Nottingham ■	d	15 37		16 02	16 08	16 18	16 32	16 37		16 50	17 02	17 08	17 18	17 32	17 37		18 02	18 08	18 18	18 33	18 37		19 02
Beeston	d	15 43		16a07		16 24	16 38	16 43		16 55	17a07		17 24	17 38	17 43		18a07		18 24	18a39	18 43		19a07
Attenborough	d					16 27	16a41			16 58			17 27	17a41					18 27				
Long Eaton	d	15 51	15 57			16 35		16 51	16 57	17 07			17 35		17 51	18 01			18 37		18 51	18 56	
Spondon	d												17 42		17 57								
Derby ■	a	16 03	16 09		16 31	16 48		17 02	17 09	17 23		17 31	17 49		18 02	18 14		18 33	18 48		19 02	19 09	
	d					16 50							17 50						18 50				
Duffield	d					16 57							17 57						18 57				
Belper	d					17 02							18 02						19 02				
Ambergate	d					17 08							18 08						19 08				
Whatstandwell	d					17 12							18 12						19 12				
Cromford	d					17 17							18 17						19 17				
Matlock Bath	d					17 20							18 20						19 20				
Matlock	a					17 24							18 24						19 24				

A from 31 July until 7 September, not from 14 August until 29 August

B not from 31 July until 10 August, from 30 August until 7 September

C 30 July, 6 August, 13 August, 3 September, 10 September

D until 24 September, not from 18 September until 21 September

E from 18 September until 28 September

For connections from St Pancras International please refer to Table 53

Nottingham - Derby - Matlock

until 28 September

Network Diagram - see first Page of Table 50

		XC	EM	EM	XC	EM	EM	EM	EM	EM	XC	NT	EM	EM	EM	EM	XC	EM	EM	EM	EM	EM	EM
																			A	B	FX C		
Nottingham	d	19 08	19 18	19 32	19 37	20 02		20 07	20 11	20 32	20 37	20 45	21 02		21 16	21 32	21 37					22 16	23 10
Beeston	d		19 24	19a38	19 43	20a07			20 17	20a38	20 43		21a07		21 22	21a38	21 43					22 22	23a16
Attenborough	d		19 27		19 46				20 20						21 25		21 46					22 25	
Long Eaton	d		19 35		19 53		20 07	20 23	20 28		20 51			21 06	21 33		21 53	21 59				22 33	
Spondon	d																21 59						
Derby	a	19 32	19 48		20 02		20 19	20 35	20 44		21 02	21 05		21 16	21 49		22 04	22 10				22 49	
	d		19 50						20 56										22 16	22 16	22 16		
Duffield	d		19 57						21 03										22 23	22 23	22 35		
Belper	d		20 02						21 08										22 28	22 28	22 44		
Ambergate	d		20 08						21 14										22 34	22 34	22 51		
Whatstandwell	d		20 12						21 18										22 38	22 38	22 59		
Cromford	d		20 17						21 23										22 43	22 43	23 08		
Matlock Bath	d		20 20						21 26										22 46	22 46	23 11		
Matlock	a		20 24						21 29										22 49	22 51	23 16		

		EM	EM
Nottingham	d	23 15	
Beeston	d	23 21	
Attenborough	d	23 24	
Long Eaton	d	23 33	23 38
Spondon	d		
Derby	a	23 48	23 50
	d		
Duffield	d		
Belper	d		
Ambergate	d		
Whatstandwell	d		
Cromford	d		
Matlock Bath	d		
Matlock	a		

Mondays to Fridays

from 1 October

		EM	EM	EM	XC	EM	EM	XC	EM	EM	XC	EM	EM	EM	EM	XC	EM	XC	EM	EM	XC	EM	EM
		MX	D	MX E																			
Nottingham	d	01 52			06 00	06 18	06 28	06 37	06 49		06 56	07 10		07 19	07 31	07 37	08 02	08 08	08 15	08 32	08 37		09 02
Beeston	d				06 06	06 24	06a33	06 43	06a54		07 07	07a16		07 25	07a37	07 43	08a07		08 24	08a38	08 43		09a07
Attenborough	d				06 10	06 27					07 11			07 29					08 27				
Long Eaton	d				06 17	06 35					07 18		07 36	07 40		07 51			08 35		08 51	09 00	
Spondon	d				06 24	06 42								07 47					08 42		08 57		
Derby	a	02 10			06 30	06 49		07 00			07 31		07 47	07 53		08 02		08 32	08 48		09 02	09 15	
	d		05 40	06 04		06 50				07 20				07 54					08 50				
Duffield	d		05 47	06 11		06 57								08 02					08 57				
Belper	d		05 52	06 16		07 02				07a27				08 07					09 02				
Ambergate	d		05 58	06a22		07 08								08 13					09 08				
Whatstandwell	d		06 02			07 12								08 17					09 12				
Cromford	d		06 07			07 17								08 22					09 17				
Matlock Bath	d		06 11			07 20								08 24					09 19				
Matlock	a		06 14			07 25								08 28					09 26				

		XC	EM	EM	XC	EM	EM	XC	EM	EM	XC	EM	EM	XC	EM	EM	XC	EM	EM	XC	EM	EM	XC
Nottingham	d	09 11	09 18	09 32	09 37		10 02	10 11	10 18	10 32	10 37		11 02	11 08	11 18	11 32	11 37		12 02	12 08	12 18	12 32	12 37
Beeston	d		09 24	09a38	09 43		10a07		10 24	10a38	10 43		11a07		11 24	11a38	11 43		12a07		12 24	12a38	12 43
Attenborough	d		09 27						10 27						11 27						12 27		
Long Eaton	d		09 35		09 51	09 56			10 35		10 51	10 56			11 35		11 51	11 57			12 35		
Spondon	d																						12 51
Derby	a	09 31	09 48		10 02	10 09		10 33	10 49		11 02	11 09		11 31	11 48		12 02	12 09		12 33	12 48		13 02
	d		09 50						10 50						11 54						12 50		
Duffield	d		09 57						10 57						12 01						12 57		
Belper	d		10 02						11 02						12 06						13 02		
Ambergate	d		10 08						11 08						12 12						13 08		
Whatstandwell	d		10 12						11 12						12 16						13 12		
Cromford	d		10 17						11 17						12 21						13 17		
Matlock Bath	d		10 20						11 20						12 24						13 20		
Matlock	a		10 26						11 26						12 30						13 26		

A until 14 September
B 21 September, 28 September
C from 17 September until 27 September
D 1 October, 8 October, 15 October, from 22 October
E from 2 October until 19 October

For connections from St Pancras International please refer to Table 53

Nottingham - Derby - Matlock

from 1 October

Network Diagram - see first Page of Table 50

		EM	EM	XC	EM	EM	XC	EM	EM	XC	EM	EM	XC	EM	EM	XC	EM	EM	XC	EM	EM	XC
Nottingham	d		13 02	13 11	13 18	13 32	13 37		14 02	14 11	14 18	14 32	14 37		15 02	15 11	15 18	15 32	15 37		16 02	16 08
Beeston	d		13a07		13 24	13a38	13 43		14a07		14 24	14a38	14 43		15a07		15 24	15a38	15 43		16a07	
Attenborough	d				13 27						14 27						15 27					
Long Eaton	d	12 57			13 35		13 51	13 57			14 35		14 51	14 57			15 35		15 51	15 57		
Spondon	d				13 43																	
Derby	a	13 09		13 31	13 48		14 02	14 09		14 31	14 47		15 03	15 13		15 31	15 48		16 03	16 09		16 31
	d				13 50						14 54						15 50					
Duffield	d				13 57						15 01						15 57					
Belper	d				14 02						15 06						16 02					
Ambergate	d				14 08						15 12						16 08					
Whatstandwell	d				14 12						15 16						16 12					
Cromford	d				14 17						15 21						16 17					
Matlock Bath	d				14 20						15 24						16 20					
Matlock	a				14 26						15 29						16 26					

		EM	EM	XC	EM	EM	EM	XC	EM	EM	XC	EM	EM	XC	EM	EM	XC	EM	EM	XC	EM	EM	XC
Nottingham	d	16 18	16 32	16 37		16 50	17 02	17 08	17 18	17 32	17 37		18 02	18 08	18 18	18 33	18 37		19 02	19 08	19 18	19 32	19 37
Beeston	d	16 24	16 38	16 43		16 55	17a07		17 24	17 38	17 43		18a07		18 24	18a39	18 43		19a07		19 24	19a38	19 43
Attenborough	d	16 27	16a41			16 58			17 27	17a41					18 27						19 27		19 46
Long Eaton	d	16 35		16 51	16 57	17 07			17 35		17 51	18 01			18 37		18 51	18 56			19 35		19 53
Spondon	d								17 42		17 57												
Derby	a	16 48		17 02	17 09	17 23		17 31	17 49		18 02	18 14		18 33	18 48		19 02	19 09		19 32	19 48		20 02
	d	16 50							17 50						18 50						19 50		
Duffield	d	16 57							17 57						18 57						19 57		
Belper	d	17 02							18 02						19 02						20 02		
Ambergate	d	17 08							18 08						19 08						20 08		
Whatstandwell	d	17 12							18 12						19 12						20 12		
Cromford	d	17 17							18 17						19 17						20 17		
Matlock Bath	d	17 20							18 20						19 20						20 20		
Matlock	a	17 26							18 26						19 26						20 26		

		EM	EM	EM	EM	EM	XC	NT	EM	EM	EM	EM	XC	EM	EM	EM	EM	EM	EM	EM
															A	FX B				
Nottingham	d	20 02		20 07	20 11	20 32	20 37	20 45	21 02		21 16	21 32	21 37				22 16	23 10	23 15	
Beeston	d	20a07			20 17	20a38	20 43		21a07		21 22	21a38	21 43				22 22	23a16	23 21	
Attenborough	d				20 20						21 25		21 46				22 25		23 24	
Long Eaton	d		20 07	20 23	20 28		20 51			21 06	21 33		21 53	21 59			22 33		23 33	23 38
Spondon	d												21 59							
Derby	a		20 19	20 35	20 44		21 02	21 05		21 16	21 49		22 04	22 10			22 49		23 48	23 50
	d				20 56										22 16	22 16				
Duffield	d				21 03										22 23	22 35				
Belper	d				21 08										22 28	22 44				
Ambergate	d				21 14										22 34	22 51				
Whatstandwell	d				21 18										22 38	22 59				
Cromford	d				21 23										22 43	23 08				
Matlock Bath	d				21 27										22 46	23 11				
Matlock	a				21 32										22 51	23 16				

Saturdays

until 29 September

		EM	EM	EM	EM	XC	EM	EM	XC	EM	XC	EM	EM	EM	XC	EM	EM	XC	EM	EM	XC	EM	EM
		C	D	C																			
Nottingham	d	01 47	01 52	02 37		05 57	06 02	06 18	06 37		06 56	07 02	07 18	07 31	07 37		08 02	08 08	08 18	08 32	08 37		09 02
Beeston	d					06 03	06a07	06 24	06 43		07 02	07a07	07 24	07a37	07 43		08a07		08 24	08a38	08 43		09a07
Attenborough	d					06 06		06 27			07 06		07 27						08 27				
Long Eaton	d					06 17		06 34			07 14		07 35		07 51	07 56			08 35		08 51	09 01	
Spondon	d					06 24		06 43											08 42		08 58		
Derby	a	02 05	02 10	02 55		06 32		06 48	07 02		07 30		07 49		08 02	08 09		08 31	08 48		09 03	09 14	
	d				05 40			06 50		07 20			07 50						08 50				
Duffield	d				05 47			06 57					07 57						08 57				
Belper	d				05 52			07 02		07a27			08 02						09 02				
Ambergate	d				05 58			07 08					08 08						09 08				
Whatstandwell	d				06 02			07 12					08 12						09 12				
Cromford	d				06 07			07 17					08 17						09 17				
Matlock Bath	d				06 11			07 20					08 20						09 21				
Matlock	a				06 14			07 24					08 24						09 24				

A 5 October, 12 October, from 19 October
B from 1 October until 18 October
C 28 July, 4 August, 11 August, 1 September, 8 September
D until 21 July, 18 August, 25 August, 15 September, 22 September, 29 September

For connections from St Pancras International please refer to Table 53

Table 56

Saturdays
until 29 September

Nottingham - Derby - Matlock

Network Diagram - see first Page of Table 50

		XC	EM	EM	XC	EM	EM	XC	EM	EM	XC	EM	EM	XC	EM	EM	XC	EM	EM	XC	EM	EM	XC
		◇■ ✠			■	◇■ ✠	◇■ ✠	◇■ ✠			■	◇■ ✠	◇■ ✠	◇■ ✠			■ ✠	◇■ ✠	◇■ ✠	◇■			■ ✠
Nottingham ■ ⇌	d	09 08	09 18	09 32	09 37		10 02	10 08	10 18	10 32	10 37		11 02	11 11	11 18	11 32	11 37		12 02	12 08	12 18	12 32	12 37
Beeston	d		09 24	09a38	09 43		10a07		10 24	10a38	10 43		11a07		11 24	11a38	11 43		12a07		12 24	12a38	12 43
Attenborough	d		09 27						10 27						11 27						12 27		
Long Eaton	d		09 35		09 51	09 57			10 35		10 51	10 57			11 36		11 51	11 57			12 36		12 51
Spondon	d																						
Derby ■	a	09 31	09 48		10 02	10 09		10 31	10 49		11 02	11 09		11 31	11 48		12 02	12 09		12 31	12 48		13 02
	d		09 50						10 50						11 50						12 50		
Duffield	d		09 57						10 57						11 57						12 57		
Belper	d		10 02						11 02						12 02						13 02		
Ambergate	d		10 08						11 08						12 08						13 08		
Whatstandwell	d		10 12						11 12						12 12						13 12		
Cromford	d		10 17						11 17						12 17						13 17		
Matlock Bath	d		10 20						11 20						12 20						13 20		
Matlock	a		10 24						11 24						12 24						13 24		

		EM	EM	XC	EM	EM	XC	EM	EM	EM	XC	EM	EM	XC	EM	EM	XC	EM	EM	XC	EM	EM
		◇■ ✠	◇■ ✠	◇■			■ ✠	◇■ ✠	A	◇■ ✠	◇■ ✠			■ ✠	◇■ ✠	◇■ ✠	◇■ ✠			■ ✠	◇■ ✠	◇■ ✠
Nottingham ■ ⇌	d		13 02	13 08	13 18	13 32	13 37		13 52	14 02	14 08	14 18	14 32	14 37		15 02	15 08	15 18	15 32	15 37		16 02
Beeston	d		13a07		13 24	13a38	13 43		13 59	14a07		14 24	14a38	14 43		15a07		15 24	15a38	15 43		16a07
Attenborough	d				13 27							14 27						15 27				
Long Eaton	d	12 57			13 35		13 51	13 57	14 08			14 36		14 51	14 57			15 36		15 51	15 57	
Spondon	d				13 43																	
Derby ■	a	13 09		13 31	13 48		14 02	14 09	14 20		14 32	14 48		15 02	15 09		15 31	15 48		16 02	16 09	
	d				13 50							14 50						15 50				
Duffield	d				13 57							14 57						15 57				
Belper	d				14 02							15 02						16 02				
Ambergate	d				14 08							15 08						16 08				
Whatstandwell	d				14 12							15 12						16 12				
Cromford	d				14 17							15 17						16 17				
Matlock Bath	d				14 20							15 20						16 20				
Matlock	a				14 24							15 24						16 24				

		XC	EM	EM	XC	EM	EM	XC	EM	EM	XC	EM	EM	XC	EM	EM	XC	EM	EM	XC	EM	EM	XC
		◇■			■ ✠	◇■ ✠	◇■ ✠	◇■			■ ✠	◇■ ✠	◇■ ✠	◇■			■ ✠	◇■ ✠	◇■ ✠	◇■			■
Nottingham ■ ⇌	d	16 08	16 18	16 32	16 37		17 02	17 11	17 18	17 32	17 37		18 02	18 08	18 19	18 32	18 37		19 02	19 08	19 18	19 32	19 37
Beeston	d		16 24	16 38	16 43		17a07		17 24	17 38	17 43		18a07		18 24	18a38	18 43		19a07		19 24	19a38	19 43
Attenborough	d		16 27	16a41					17 27	17a41					18 26						19 27		19 46
Long Eaton	d		16 36		16 51	16 56			17 35		17 51	17 57			18 37		18 51	18 57			19 35		19 53
Spondon	d								17 42											19 27			
Derby ■	a	16 31	16 48		17 02	17 09		17 31	17 48		18 02	18 09		18 31	18 48		19 02	19 09		19 32	19 48		20 02
	d		16 50						17 50						18 50						19 50		
Duffield	d		16 57						17 57						18 57						19 57		
Belper	d		17 02						18 02						19 02						20 02		
Ambergate	d		17 08						18 08						19 08						20 08		
Whatstandwell	d		17 12						18 12						19 12						20 12		
Cromford	d		17 17						18 17						19 17						20 17		
Matlock Bath	d		17 20						18 20						19 20						20 20		
Matlock	a		17 24						18 24						19 24						20 24		

		EM	EM	EM	EM	XC	EM	EM	EM	EM	XC	EM	EM	EM	EM	EM	EM
		◇■ ✠	◇■ ✠			■	◇■ ✠	◇■ ✠			■	◇■ ✠				◇■ B ✠	
Nottingham ■ ⇌	d		20 02	20 09	20 32	20 37	20 43		21 08	21 32	21 37			22 15	23 10		23 15
Beeston	d		20a07	20 15	20a37	20 43	20a48		21 14	21a38	21 43			22 21	23a16		23 21
Attenborough	d			20 18					21 17		21 46			22 24			23 24
Long Eaton	d	19 57		20 27		20 51		20 57	21 26		21 53	21 57		22 33		23 16	23 32
Spondon	d										21 59						
Derby ■	a	20 09		20 42		21 02		21 10	21 41		22 04	22 10		22 48		23 26	23 47
	d			20 50									22 16				
Duffield	d			20 57									22 23				
Belper	d			21 02									22 28				
Ambergate	d			21 08									22 35				
Whatstandwell	d			21 12									22 39				
Cromford	d			21 17									22 44				
Matlock Bath	d			21 20									22 47				
Matlock	a			21 24									22 50				

A from 21 July until 8 September

B from 30 June until 8 September

For connections from St Pancras International please refer to Table 53

Table 56

Saturdays
from 6 October

Nottingham - Derby - Matlock

Network Diagram - see first Page of Table 50

		EM	EM	XC	EM	EM	XC	EM	XC	EM	EM	EM	XC	EM	EM	XC	EM	EM	XC	EM	EM	XC	EM
		◇■ 🛏		◇■	◇■ ✠		◇■	◇■ ✠	◇■	◇■ ✠			■	◇■ ✠	◇■ 🛏	◇■ ✠			■	◇■ ✠	◇■ ✠	◇■ ✠	
Nottingham ■ ⇌	d	01 52		05 57	06 02	06 18	06 37		06 56	07 02	07 18	07 31	07 37		08 02	08 08	08 18	08 32	08 37		09 02	09 08	09 18
Beeston	d			06 03	06a07	06 24	06 43		07 02	07a07	07 24	07a37	07 43		08a07		08 24	08a38	08 43		09a07		09 24
Attenborough	d			06 06		06 27			07 06		07 27						08 27						09 27
Long Eaton	d			06 17		06 34			07 14		07 35		07 51	07 56			08 35		08 51	09 01			09 35
Spondon	d			06 24		06 43											08 42		08 58				
Derby ■	a	02 10		06 32		06 48	07 02		07 30		07 49		08 02	08 09		08 31	08 48		09 03	09 14		09 31	09 48
	d		05 40			06 50		07 20			07 50						08 50						09 50
Duffield	d		05 47			06 57					07 57						08 57						09 57
Belper	d		05 52			07 02		07a27			08 02						09 02						10 02
Ambergate	d		05 58			07 08					08 08						09 08						10 08
Whatstandwell	d		06 02			07 12					08 12						09 12						10 12
Cromford	d		06 07			07 17					08 17						09 17						10 17
Matlock Bath	d		06 11			07 20					08 20						09 21						10 20
Matlock	a		06 16			07 25					08 25						09 26						10 26

		EM	XC	EM	EM	XC	EM	EM	XC	EM	EM	XC	EM	EM	XC	EM	EM	XC	EM	EM	XC	EM	EM
			■	◇■ ✠	◇■ ✠	◇■ ✠			■	◇■ ✠	◇■ ✠	◇■ ✠			■ ✠	◇■ ✠	◇■ ✠	◇■			■ ✠	◇■ ✠	◇■ ✠
Nottingham ■ ⇌	d	09 32	09 37		10 02	10 08	10 18	10 32	10 37		11 02	11 11	11 18	11 32	11 37		12 02	12 08	12 18	12 32	12 37		13 02
Beeston	d	09a38	09 43		10a07		10 24	10a38	10 43		11a07		11 24	11a38	11 43		12a07		12 24	12a38	12 43		13a07
Attenborough	d						10 27						11 27						12 27				
Long Eaton	d		09 51	09 57			10 35		10 51	10 57			11 36		11 51	11 57			12 36		12 51	12 57	
Spondon	d																						
Derby ■	a		10 02	10 09		10 31	10 49		11 02	11 09		11 31	11 48		12 02	12 09		12 31	12 48		13 02	13 09	
	d						10 50						11 50						12 50				
Duffield	d						10 57						11 57						12 57				
Belper	d						11 02						12 02						13 02				
Ambergate	d						11 08						12 08						13 08				
Whatstandwell	d						11 12						12 12						13 12				
Cromford	d						11 17						12 17						13 17				
Matlock Bath	d						11 20						12 20						13 20				
Matlock	a						11 26						12 26						13 26				

		XC	EM	EM	XC	EM	EM	XC	EM	EM	XC	EM	EM	XC	EM	EM	XC	EM	EM	XC	EM	EM
		◇■			■ ✠	◇■ ✠	◇■ ✠	◇■ ✠			■ ✠	◇■ ✠	◇■ ✠	◇■ ✠			■ ✠	◇■ ✠	◇■ ✠	◇■		
Nottingham ■ ⇌	d	13 08	13 18	13 32	13 37		14 02	14 08	14 18	14 32	14 37		15 02	15 08	15 18	15 32	15 37		16 02	16 08	16 18	16 32
Beeston	d		13 24	13a38	13 43		14a07		14 24	14a38	14 43		15a07		15 24	15a38	15 43		16a07		16 24	16 38
Attenborough	d		13 27						14 27						15 27						16 27	16a41
Long Eaton	d		13 35		13 51	13 57			14 36		14 51	14 57			15 36		15 51	15 57			16 36	
Spondon	d		13 43																			
Derby ■	a	13 31	13 48		14 02	14 09		14 32	14 48		15 02	15 09		15 31	15 48		16 02	16 09		16 31	16 48	
	d		13 50						14 50						15 50						16 50	
Duffield	d		13 57						14 57						15 57						16 57	
Belper	d		14 02						15 02						16 02						17 02	
Ambergate	d		14 08						15 08						16 08						17 08	
Whatstandwell	d		14 12						15 12						16 12						17 12	
Cromford	d		14 17						15 17						16 17						17 17	
Matlock Bath	d		14 20						15 20						16 20						17 20	
Matlock	a		14 26						15 26						16 26						17 26	

		XC	EM	EM	XC	EM	EM	XC	EM	EM	XC	EM	EM	XC	EM	EM	XC	EM	EM	XC	EM	EM	EM
		■ ✠	◇■ ✠	◇■ ✠	◇■			■ ✠	◇■ ✠	◇■ ✠	◇■			■ ✠	◇■ ✠	◇■ ✠	◇■			■	◇■ ✠	◇■ ✠	
Nottingham ■ ⇌	d	16 37		17 02	17 11	17 18	17 32	17 37		18 02	18 08	18 19	18 33	18 37		19 02	19 08	19 18	19 32	19 37		20 02	20 09
Beeston	d	16 43		17a07		17 24	17 38	17 43		18a07		18 24	18a39	18 43		19a07		19 24	19a38	19 43		20a07	20 15
Attenborough	d					17 27	17a41					18 27						19 27		19 46			20 18
Long Eaton	d	16 51	16 56			17 35		17 51	17 57			18 37		18 51	18 57			19 35		19 53	19 57		20 27
Spondon	d					17 42											19 27						
Derby ■	a	17 02	17 09		17 31	17 48		18 02	18 09		18 31	18 48		19 02	19 09		19 32	19 48		20 02	20 09		20 42
	d					17 50						18 50						19 50					20 50
Duffield	d					17 57						18 57						19 57					20 57
Belper	d					18 02						19 02						20 02					21 02
Ambergate	d					18 08						19 08						20 08					21 08
Whatstandwell	d					18 12						19 12						20 12					21 12
Cromford	d					18 17						19 17						20 17					21 17
Matlock Bath	d					18 20						19 20						20 20					21 20
Matlock	a					18 26						19 26						20 26					21 26

		EM	XC	EM	EM	EM	EM	XC	EM	EM	EM	EM	EM	EM
			■	◇■ ✠	◇■ ✠			■	◇■ ✠				◇■ A ✠	
Nottingham ■ ⇌	d	20 32	20 37	20 43		21 08	21 32	21 37			22 15	23 10		23 15
Beeston	d	20a37	20 43	20a48		21 14	21a38	21 43			22 21	23a16		23 21
Attenborough	d					21 17		21 46			22 24			23 24
Long Eaton	d		20 51		20 57	21 26		21 53	21 57		22 33		23 16	23 32
Spondon	d							21 59						
Derby ■	a		21 02		21 10	21 41		22 04	22 10		22 48		23 26	23 47
	d									22 16				
Duffield	d									22 23				
Belper	d									22 28				
Ambergate	d									22 35				
Whatstandwell	d									22 39				
Cromford	d									22 44				
Matlock Bath	d									22 47				
Matlock	a									22 52				

A from 27 October

For connections from St Pancras International please refer to Table 53

Nottingham - Derby - Matlock

Sundays
until 24 June

Network Diagram - see first Page of Table 50

		EM	EM	EM	EM	EM	EM	XC	EM	EM		EM	XC	XC	EM	EM	EM	XC	EM	EM		EM	EM	XC	EM
Nottingham	d			07 37	09 19	09 25		11 11	11 22	11 29			12 10	13 06		13 22	13 30	14 10	14 24			14 27		15 10	15 18
Beeston	d			07a42	09 24	09a31			11 27	11a35						13 27	13a36		14a29			14 33			15a23
Attenborough	d				09 28				11 31							13 31						14 37			
Long Eaton	d	00 16	01 01		09 36		10 32		11 39			12 13			13 22	13 39				14 26		14 44	15 06		
Spondon	d																								
Derby	a	00 26	01 11		09 47		10 43	11 31	11 47			12 23	12 30	13 26	13 32	13 50		14 29		14 38		14 56	15 18	15 30	
	d				09 52				11 52							13 52									
Duffield	d				09 59				11 59							13 59									
Belper	d				10 04				12 04							14 04									
Ambergate	d				10 10				12 10							14 10									
Whatstandwell	d				10 14				12 14							14 14									
Cromford	d				10 20				12 20							14 20									
Matlock Bath	d				10 22				12 22							14 22									
Matlock	a				10 25				12 25							14 25									

		EM	EM	XC	EM	EM		EM	XC	EM	EM	EM	XC	EM	EM	EM		XC	EM	EM	EM	XC	EM	EM	XC
Nottingham	d	15 21		16 10	16 18	16 22			17 10	17 19	17 23		18 10	18 19	18 23			19 10	19 22		19 43	20 10	20 21		21 08
Beeston	d	15 27			16a23	16 27				17a24	17 28			18a24	18 29				19 27		19a48		20 27		
Attenborough	d	15 31				16 31					17 32				18 32				19 31				20 31		
Long Eaton	d	15 39	15 44			16 38		16 43			17 40	17 44			18 40	18 44			19 38	19 43			20 38	20 43	
Spondon	d																								
Derby	a	15 50	15 55	16 30		16 50		16 55	17 29		17 51	17 56	18 30		18 51	18 55		19 30	19 50	19 54		20 29	20 51	20 54	21 31
	d	15 52									17 53								19 52						
Duffield	d	15 58									18 00								19 59						
Belper	d	16 03									18 05								20 04						
Ambergate	d	16 09									18 11								20 10						
Whatstandwell	d	16 13									18 15								20 14						
Cromford	d	16 19									18 21								20 20						
Matlock Bath	d	16 21									18 23								20 22						
Matlock	a	16 25									18 26								20 25						

		EM		EM	EM
Nottingham	d	21 24			
Beeston	d	21 29			
Attenborough	d	21 33			
Long Eaton	d	21 40		21 45	23 32
Spondon	d				
Derby	a	21 52		21 55	23 42
	d	21 54			
Duffield	d	22 01			
Belper	d	22 06			
Ambergate	d	22 12			
Whatstandwell	d	22 16			
Cromford	d	22 22			
Matlock Bath	d	22 24			
Matlock	a	22 27			

Sundays
1 July to 16 September

		EM A	EM B	EM A	EM C	EM B	EM	EM A	EM B	EM A		EM B	EM B	XC B	XC A	EM	EM A	EM A	EM B	XC A		EM B	EM A	XC B	XC A
Nottingham	d				02 20	08 22	09 22	09 34	10 15					11 10	11 11	11 22	11 29			12 10		12 15		13 06	13 06
Beeston	d					08a27	09 27	09a40	10a21							11 27	11a35					12a21			
Attenborough	d						09 31									11 31									
Long Eaton	d	00 05	00 11	00 45			09 39			10 31		10 32	11 18			11 39		12 12	12 17						
Spondon	d																						13 10		
Derby	a	00 15	00 21	00 55	02 39		09 50			10 42		10 46	11 28	11 32	11 31	11 47		12 22	12 27	12 30			13 20	13 25	13 26
	d						09 52									11 52									
Duffield	d						09 59									11 59									
Belper	d						10 04									12 04									
Ambergate	d						10 10									12 10									
Whatstandwell	d						10 14									12 14									
Cromford	d						10 20									12 20									
Matlock Bath	d						10 22									12 22									
Matlock	a						10 25									12 25									

A 16 September
B not 16 September
C 29 July, 5 August, 12 August, 2 September, 9 September

For connections from St Pancras International please refer to Table 53

Nottingham - Derby - Matlock

Sundays
1 July to 16 September

Network Diagram - see first Page of Table 50

		EM A	EM A	EM A	EM B	EM B		XC	EM A	EM A	EM B	EM B	EM A	EM B	EM A	EM B		EM A	XC	EM A	EM B	EM B	EM B	XC	EM A
Nottingham	d	13 12		13 22	13 22	13 34		14 10		14 22	14 24		14 25	14 27	14 59				15 10	15 22	15 22		15 29	16 10	16 18
Beeston	d	13a17		13 27	13 28	13a40				14a27	14a29		14 31	14 33	15a05					15 27	15a27		15 34		16a23
Attenborough	d			13 31	13 34								14 35	14 37						15 31			15 38		
Long Eaton	d		13 22	13 39	13 42				14 19			14 26	14 42	14 44		15 08		15 19		15 39		15 42	15 46		
Spondon	d																								
Derby	a		13 32	13 50	13 53			14 29	14 29			14 37	14 54	14 56		15 19		15 29	15 30	15 50		15 53	15 57	16 30	
	d			13 52	13 55															15 52			15 59		
Duffield	d			13 59	14 02															15 58			16 05		
Belper	d			14 04	14 07															16 03			16 10		
Ambergate	d			14 10	14 13															16 09			16 16		
Whatstandwell	d			14 14	14 17															16 13			16 20		
Cromford	d			14 20	14 23															16 19			16 26		
Matlock Bath	d			14 22	14 25															16 21			16 28		
Matlock	a			14 25	14 28															16 25			16 32		

		EM		EM	EM B	EM A	XC A	EM A	EM B	EM	EM B	EM A		XC B	EM A	EM B	EM A	EM B	EM B	XC	EM B	EM A		EM	EM A
Nottingham	d			16 22	16 29		17 10	17 19		17 23	17 31			18 10	18 19		18 23	18 23	18 34	19 10				19 22	19 43
Beeston	d			16 27	16a34			17a24		17 28	17a36				18a24		18 29	18 29	18a39					19 27	19a48
Attenborough	d			16 31						17 32							18 32	18 32						19 31	
Long Eaton	d	16 28		16 38		17 16			17 28	17 40		18 16				18 25	18 40	18 41			19 25	19 26		19 38	
Spondon	d																								
Derby	a	16 39		16 50		17 26	17 29		17 39	17 51		18 26		18 30		18 35	18 51	18 52		19 30	19 35	19 37		19 50	
	d									17 53														19 52	
Duffield	d									18 00														19 59	
Belper	d									18 05														20 04	
Ambergate	d									18 11														20 10	
Whatstandwell	d									18 15														20 14	
Cromford	d									18 21														20 20	
Matlock Bath	d									18 23														20 22	
Matlock	a									18 26														20 25	

		EM B	EM A	XC	EM B	EM	EM A	XC		EM B	EM A	EM B	EM A	EM B
Nottingham	d	19 57		20 10		20 21		21 08			21 23	21 24		
Beeston	d	20a02				20 27					21 29	21 29		
Attenborough	d					20 31					21 33	21 33		
Long Eaton	d		20 17		20 25	20 38	21 17			21 25	21 40	21 40	23 20	23 28
Spondon	d													
Derby	a		20 27	20 29	20 35	20 51	21 27	21 31		21 35	21 52	21 52	23 30	23 38
	d										21 54	21 54		
Duffield	d										22 01	22 01		
Belper	d										22 06	22 06		
Ambergate	d										22 12	22 12		
Whatstandwell	d										22 16	22 16		
Cromford	d										22 22	22 22		
Matlock Bath	d										22 24	22 24		
Matlock	a										22 27	22 27		

Sundays
from 23 September

		EM C	EM D	EM C	EM	EM C	EM D	EM	XC	EM D		EM	EM C	EM C	XC	EM D	EM D	EM C	XC	EM D		EM C	EM D	EM	XC
Nottingham	d				09 22	09 34	10 19		11 11			11 22	11 29		12 10	12 15			13 06			13 22	13 22	13 34	14 10
Beeston	d				09 27	09a40	10a25					11 27	11a35			12a21						13 28	13 28	13a40	
Attenborough	d				09 31							11 31										13 34	13 34		
Long Eaton	d	00 05	00 11	00 45	09 39			10 31		11 29		11 39		12 12			12 29	13 10		13 40		13 42	13 46		
Spondon	d																								
Derby	a	00 15	00 21	00 55	09 50			10 42	11 31	11 39		11 47		12 22	12 30		12 39	13 20	13 26	13 50		13 53	13 57		14 29
	d				09 52							11 52										13 55	13 59		
Duffield	d				09 59							11 59										14 02	14 06		
Belper	d				10 04							12 04										14 07	14 11		
Ambergate	d				10 10							12 10										14 13	14 17		
Whatstandwell	d				10 14							12 14										14 17	14 21		
Cromford	d				10 20							12 20										14 23	14 27		
Matlock Bath	d				10 22							12 22										14 25	14 29		
Matlock	a				10 25							12 25										14 28	14 32		

A not 16 September
B 16 September
C from 23 September until 21 October
D from 28 October

For connections from St Pancras International please refer to Table 53

Table 56

Sundays

from 23 September

Nottingham - Derby - Matlock

Network Diagram - see first Page of Table 50

		EM	EM	EM	EM	EM		XC	EM	EM	EM	XC	EM	EM	EM	EM		EM	EM	EM	XC	EM	EM	EM	EM
		◇1 ✠	◇1 A ✠	◇1 B ✠		◇1 A ✠		◇1 ✠	◇1 ✠	◇1 ✠		◇1 ✠	◇1 ✠		◇1 ✠	◇1 ✠			◇1 ✠	◇1 B ✠	◇1 ✠	◇1 A ✠		◇1 ✠	◇1 B ✠
Nottingham 8 ⇌	d	14 24			14 27			15 10	15 22		15 29	16 10		16 22	16 29			17 23	17 31		18 10		18 23	18 34	
Beeston	d	14a29			14 33				15a27		15 34			16 27	16a34			17 28	17a36				18 29	18a39	
Attenborough	d				14 37						15 38			16 31				17 32					18 32		
Long Eaton	d		14 26	14 42	14 44	15 08				15 42	15 46		16 28	16 38		17 28		17 40		18 19		18 25	18 41		19 18
Spondon	d																								
Derby 6	a		14 37	14 53	14 56	15 19		15 30		15 53	15 57	16 30	16 39	16 50		17 39		17 51		18 29	18 30	18 35	18 52		19 28
	d										15 59							17 53							
Duffield	d										16 05							18 00							
Belper	d										16 10							18 05							
Ambergate	d										16 16							18 11							
Whatstandwell	d										16 20							18 15							
Cromford	d										16 26							18 21							
Matlock Bath	d										16 28							18 23							
Matlock	a										16 32							18 26							

		XC		EM	EM	EM	XC	EM	EM	XC	EM	EM		EM	EM	EM
		◇1 ✠		◇1 A ✠		◇1 ✠	◇1	◇1 ✠		◇1	◇1 B ✠	◇1 A ✠			◇1 B ✠	◇1 A ✠
Nottingham 8 ⇌	d	19 10			19 22	19 57	20 10		20 21	21 08				21 24		
Beeston	d				19 27	20a02			20 27					21 29		
Attenborough	d				19 31				20 31					21 33		
Long Eaton	d			19 25	19 38			20 25	20 38		21 24	21 25		21 40	23 26	23 28
Spondon	d															
Derby 6	a	19 30		19 35	19 50		20 29	20 35	20 51	21 31	21 35	21 35		21 52	23 36	23 38
	d				19 52									21 54		
Duffield	d				19 59									22 01		
Belper	d				20 04									22 06		
Ambergate	d				20 10									22 12		
Whatstandwell	d				20 14									22 16		
Cromford	d				20 20									22 22		
Matlock Bath	d				20 22									22 24		
Matlock	a				20 25									22 27		

A from 23 September until 21 October

B from 28 October

For connections from St Pancras International please refer to Table 53

Table 56

Mondays to Fridays

until 28 September

Matlock - Derby - Nottingham

Network Diagram - see first Page of Table 50

Miles			EM	EM	EM	XC	EM	EM	EM	EM	EM		EM	EM	EM	XC	EM	EM	EM	EM	EM		EM	XC	EM
			MX A	MX B	MX ◇1 ✠	MO 1	◇1 C ✠	MO ◇1 D ✠	MX ◇1 E ✠	MX ◇1 F ✠	◇1 G ✠	MX H	◇1 F ✠	◇1 ✠	◇1 ✠			MX ◇1 I ✠	B				◇1 ✠	1 ✠	
0	**Matlock**	d	22p55																06 22						
1	Matlock Bath	d	22p57																06 24						
1¾	Cromford	d	23p00																06 27						
4¾	Whatstandwell	d	23p05																06 32						
6¾	Ambergate	d	23p10																06 37	06 37					06 56
9½	Belper	d	23p17																06 44	06 44					07 01
12	Duffield	d	23p21																06 48	06 48					07 05
17¼	**Derby** 6	a	23p29																06 56	06 56					07 13
—		d	23p31	23p31		23p59									05 17	06 00	06 24	06 32					07 01	07 10	
19¾	Spondon	d															06 29							07 18	
25½	Long Eaton	d	23p41	23p41											05a26		06 36	06a42						07 25	
28½	Attenborough	d	23p48	23p48													06 44				07 13			07 31	
30	Beeston	d	23p51	23p51	00 05		00 18	00 38	00 43	01 34	01 39		02 04	02 25		06 15	06 47				07 16			07 35	
33¼	**Nottingham** 8 ⇌	a	00 02	00 02	00 12	00 18	00 28	00 44	00 49	01 40	01 45		02 10	02 31		06 21	06 57				07 23		07 29	07 41	

		EM	EM	XC	EM	EM	XC		EM	EM	EM	XC	EM	EM	XC	EM	EM		XC	EM	EM	XC	EM	EM	XC
		◇1 ✠		1			1 ✠		◇1 ✠	◇1 ✠		1		◇1 ✠	1 ✠	◇1 ✠			◇1		◇1 ✠	1 ✠	◇1 ✠		◇1 ✠
Matlock	d										07 36						08 36							09 36	
Matlock Bath	d										07 38						08 38							09 38	
Cromford	d										07 41						08 41							09 41	
Whatstandwell	d										07 46						08 46							09 46	
Ambergate	d										07 51						08 51							09 51	
Belper	d										07 58						08 58							09 58	
Duffield	d										08 02						09 02							10 02	
Derby 6	a										08 10						09 10							10 10	
	d	07 26	07 33	07 40		07 53	08 10		08 16		08 20	08 40			09 05	09 20	09 24		09 39			10 05	10 20	10 24	10 41
Spondon	d			07 45							08 25														
Long Eaton	d	07a35	07 44	07 49		08 03	08 19		08a25		08 32				09 14	09a29	09 33					10 14	10a29	10 33	
Attenborough	d		07 52			08 13					08 39				09 21		09 40							10 40	
Beeston	d		07 55	07 58	08 06	08 16	08 27			08 32	08 42		09 02	09 17	09 24		09 43			10 02	10 17	10 22		10 43	
Nottingham 8 ⇌	a		08 05	08 08	08 15	08 26	08 33			08 39	08 50	09 05	09 13	09 26	09 33		09 53		10 05	10 13	10 25	10 32		10 53	11 05

		EM	EM		XC	EM	EM	XC	EM	EM	XC	EM	EM		XC	EM	EM	XC	EM	EM	XC	EM	EM		XC
			◇1 ✠		◇1	◇1 ✠		◇1 ✠		◇1 ✠	◇1	◇1 ✠			◇1 ✠		◇1 ✠	◇1 ✠	◇1 ✠		◇1 ✠		◇1 ✠		1
Matlock	d						10 36						11 36							12 36					
Matlock Bath	d						10 38						11 38							12 38					
Cromford	d						10 41						11 41							12 41					
Whatstandwell	d						10 46						11 46							12 46					
Ambergate	d						10 51						11 51							12 51					
Belper	d						10 58						11 58							12 58					
Duffield	d						11 02						12 02							13 02					
Derby 6	a						11 10						12 10							13 10					
	d				11 05	11 20	11 24	11 39			12 05	12 20	12 24		12 39			13 10	13 20	13 24	13 39				14 05
Spondon	d																			13 29					
Long Eaton	d				11 14	11a29	11 33				12 14	12a29	12 33					13 19	13a29	13 34					14 14
Attenborough	d						11 40						12 40							13 41					
Beeston	d	11 02	11 17		11 22		11 43		12 02	12 17	12 22		12 43			13 07	13 17	13 27		13 44		14 02	14 16		14 24
Nottingham 8 ⇌	a	11 14	11 25		11 32		11 53	12 05	12 13	12 26	12 32		12 53		13 05	13 14	13 25	13 33		13 53	14 05	14 13	14 26		14 32

		EM	EM	XC	EM	EM	XC	EM	EM		XC	EM	EM	XC	EM	EM	XC	EM	EM		XC	EM	EM	XC	EM
		◇1 ✠		◇1 ✠		◇1 ✠	1	◇1 ✠			◇1 ✠		◇1 ✠	1	◇1 ✠		◇1 ✠		◇1 ✠		1	◇1 ✠		◇1 ✠	
Matlock	d		13 36						14 36							15 36							16 36		
Matlock Bath	d		13 38						14 38							15 38							16 38		
Cromford	d		13 41						14 41							15 41							16 41		
Whatstandwell	d		13 46						14 46							15 46							16 46		
Ambergate	d		13 51						14 51							15 51							16 51		
Belper	d		13 58						14 58							15 58							16 58		
Duffield	d		14 02						15 02							16 02							17 02		
Derby 6	a		14 10						15 10							16 10							17 10		
	d	14 20	14 24	14 39			15 05	15 20	15 24		15 39			16 05	16 18	16 24	16 39				17 10	17 18	17 24	17 39	
Spondon	d																						17 29		
Long Eaton	d	14a29	14 33				15 14	15a29	15 33					16 14	16a27	16 33					17 19	17a28	17 36		
Attenborough	d		14 40						15 40							16 40							17 43		
Beeston	d		14 43		15 02	15 17	15 22		15 43			16 02	16 17	16 22		16 43		17 02	17 17		17 27		17 46		18 02
Nottingham 8 ⇌	a		14 53	15 05	15 13	15 26	15 32		15 53		16 05	16 13	16 25	16 32		16 54	17 05	17 13	17 26		17 33		17 54	18 05	18 13

A until 14 September

B from 18 September until 28 September

C from 2 July until 10 September

D 17 September, 24 September

E from 21 May until 25 June

F from 31 July until 7 September, not from 14 August until 29 August

G not from 31 July until 10 August, from 30 August until 7 September

H 30 July, 6 August, 13 August, 3 September, 10 September

I until 24 September, not from 18 September until 21 September

For connections to St Pancras International please refer to Table 53

Matlock - Derby - Nottingham

Mondays to Fridays
until 28 September

Network Diagram - see first Page of Table 50

		EM	EM ◇1 🍴	XC 1	EM ◇1 🍴	EM	XC ◇1	EM ◇1 🍴	EM	EM ◇1 🍴	XC 1	EM ◇1 🍴	EM	XC ◇1	EM	EM ◇1 🍴	XC 1	EM	XC ◇1	EM	EM ◇1 🍴	EM	XC ◇1
Matlock	d					17 36							18 36					19 36				20 36	
Matlock Bath	d					17 38							18 38					19 38				20 38	
Cromford	d					17 41							18 41					19 41				20 41	
Whatstandwell	d					17 46							18 46					19 46				20 46	
Ambergate	d					17 51							18 51					19 51				20 51	
Belper	d					17 58							18 58					19 58				20 58	
Duffield	d					18 02							19 02					20 02				21 02	
Derby	a					18 10							19 10					20 10				21 10	
	d	17 47		18 05	18 18	18 24	18 39				19 05	19 18	19 24	19 39			20 05	20 24	20 40			21 24	21 40
Spondon	d	17 53																					21 45
Long Eaton	d	18 01		18 14	18a27	18 33					19 14	19a27	19 33				20 14	20 33	20 49			21 33	21 52
Attenborough	d	18 09				18 40							19 40					20 40				21 40	21 58
Beeston	d	18 12	18 18	18 26		18 43		19 03	19 07	19 19	19 23		19 43		20 07	20 18	20 23	20 43	20 58	21 03	21 19	21 43	22 02
Nottingham	a	18 22	18 27	18 32		18 54	19 05	19 10	19 14	19 27	19 32		19 53	20 03	20 15	20 28	20 32	20 53	21 06	21 15	21 29	21 54	22 08

		EM	EM	EM ◇1 🍴	XC 1	EM FX A 🚌	EM B	EM FX A	XC 1
Matlock	d	21 39				22 25	22 55		
Matlock Bath	d	21 41				22 28	22 57		
Cromford	d	21 44				22 30	23 00		
Whatstandwell	d	21 49				22 38	23 05		
Ambergate	d	21 54				22 46	23 10		
Belper	d	22 01				22 53	23 17		
Duffield	d	22 05				23 01	23 21		
Derby	a	22 13				23 20	23 29		
	d				22 59		23 31	23 31	23 59
Spondon	d				23 04				
Long Eaton	d				23 11		23 41	23 41	
Attenborough	d				23 17		23 48	23 48	
Beeston	d		22 07	22 17	23 20		23 51	23 51	
Nottingham	a		22 15	22 26	23 27		00 02	00 02	00 18

Mondays to Fridays
from 1 October

		EM MX C	EM MX D	EM MX ◇1 🍴	XC MX 1	EM MO ◇1 E 🍴	EM MO ◇1 F 🍴	EM MX ◇1 🍴	EM ◇1 🍴	XC	EM	EM MX ◇1 ⊠🍴	EM G	EM D	EM	EM ◇1 🍴	XC 1 🍴	EM	EM ◇1 🍴	EM	XC 1	EM	EM
Matlock	d	22p55											06 22										
Matlock Bath	d	22p57											06 24										
Cromford	d	23p00											06 27										
Whatstandwell	d	23p05											06 32										
Ambergate	d	23p10											06 37	06 37				06 56					
Belper	d	23p17											06 44	06 44				07 01					
Duffield	d	23p21											06 48	06 48				07 05					
Derby	a	23p29											06 56	06 56				07 13					
	d	23p31	23p31		23p59				05 17	06 00	06 24	06 32				07 01	07 10		07 26	07 33	07 40		07 53
Spondon	d										06 29						07 18				07 45		
Long Eaton	d	23p41	23p41						05a26		06 36	06a42					07 25		07a35	07 44	07 49		08 03
Attenborough	d	23p48	23p48								06 44				07 13		07 31			07 52			08 13
Beeston	d	23p51	23p51	00 05		00 38	00 38	01 39		06 15	06 47				07 16		07 35			07 55	07 58	08 06	08 16
Nottingham	a	00 02	00 02	00 12	00 18	00 44	00 48	01 45		06 21	06 57				07 23	07 29	07 41			08 05	08 08	08 15	08 26

		XC 1 🍴	EM ◇1 🍴	EM ◇1 🍴	EM	XC 1	EM	EM ◇1 🍴	XC 1 🍴	EM ◇1 🍴	EM	XC ◇1	EM	EM ◇1 🍴	XC 1 🍴	EM ◇1 🍴	EM	XC ◇1 🍴	EM	EM ◇1 🍴	XC ◇1	EM ◇1 🍴	EM
Matlock	d				07 35						08 35						09 35						10 35
Matlock Bath	d				07 37						08 37						09 37						10 37
Cromford	d				07 40						08 40						09 40						10 40
Whatstandwell	d				07 45						08 45						09 45						10 45
Ambergate	d				07 50						08 50						09 50						10 50
Belper	d				07 58						08 58						09 58						10 58
Duffield	d				08 02						09 02						10 02						11 02
Derby	a				08 10						09 10						10 10						11 10
	d	08 10	08 16		08 20	08 40			09 05	09 20	09 24	09 39			10 05	10 20	10 24	10 41			11 05	11 20	11 24
Spondon	d				08 25																		
Long Eaton	d	08 19	08a25		08 32				09 14	09a29	09 33				10 14	10a29	10 33				11 14	11a29	11 33
Attenborough	d				08 39				09 21		09 40						10 40						11 40
Beeston	d	08 27		08 32	08 42		09 02	09 17	09 24		09 43		10 02	10 17	10 22		10 43		11 02	11 17	11 22		11 43
Nottingham	a	08 33		08 39	08 50	09 05	09 13	09 26	09 33		09 53	10 05	10 13	10 25	10 32		10 53	11 05	11 14	11 25	11 32		11 53

A from 17 September until 27 September
B not from 17 September until 20 September, from 24 September until 27 September
C from 23 October
D from 2 October until 19 October
E from 1 October until 22 October
F from 29 October
G 1 October, 8 October, 15 October, from 22 October

For connections to St Pancras International please refer to Table 53

Matlock - Derby - Nottingham

Mondays to Fridays
from 1 October

Network Diagram - see first Page of Table 50

		XC ◇1 🍴	EM	EM ◇1 🍴	XC ◇1	EM ◇1 🍴	EM	XC ◇1 🍴	EM	EM ◇1 🍴	XC ◇1 🍴	EM ◇1 🍴	EM	XC ◇1 🍴	EM	EM ◇1 🍴	XC 1	EM ◇1 🍴	EM	XC ◇1 🍴	EM	EM ◇1 🍴
Matlock	d						11 35						12 35						13 35			
Matlock Bath	d						11 37						12 37						13 37			
Cromford	d						11 40						12 40						13 40			
Whatstandwell	d						11 45						12 45						13 45			
Ambergate	d						11 50						12 50						13 50			
Belper	d						11 58						12 58						13 58			
Duffield	d						12 02						13 02						14 02			
Derby	a						12 10						13 10						14 10			
	d	11 39			12 05	12 20	12 24	12 39			13 10	13 20	13 24	13 39			14 05	14 20	14 24	14 39		
Spondon	d												13 29									
Long Eaton	d				12 14	12a29	12 33				13 19	13a29	13 34				14 14	14a29	14 33			
Attenborough	d						12 40						13 41						14 40			
Beeston	d		12 02	12 17	12 22		12 43		13 07	13 17	13 27		13 44		14 02	14 16	14 24		14 43		15 02	15 17
Nottingham	a	12 05	12 13	12 26	12 32		12 53	13 05	13 14	13 25	13 33		13 53	14 05	14 13	14 26	14 32		14 53	15 05	15 13	15 26

		XC 1	EM ◇1 🍴	EM	XC ◇1 🍴	EM	EM ◇1 🍴	XC 1	EM ◇1 🍴	EM	XC ◇1 🍴	EM	EM ◇1 🍴	XC 1	EM ◇1 🍴	EM	XC ◇1 🍴	EM	EM	EM ◇1 🍴	XC 1	EM ◇1 🍴	EM
Matlock	d			14 35						15 35						16 35							17 35
Matlock Bath	d			14 37						15 37						16 37							17 37
Cromford	d			14 40						15 40						16 40							17 40
Whatstandwell	d			14 45						15 45						16 45							17 45
Ambergate	d			14 50						15 50						16 50							17 50
Belper	d			14 58						15 58						16 58							17 58
Duffield	d			15 02						16 02						17 02							18 02
Derby	a			15 10						16 10						17 10							18 10
	d	15 05	15 20	15 24	15 39			16 05	16 18	16 24	16 39			17 10	17 18	17 24	17 39		17 47		18 05	18 18	18 24
Spondon	d															17 29			17 53				
Long Eaton	d	15 14	15a29	15 33				16 14	16a27	16 33				17 19	17a28	17 36			18 01		18 14	18a27	18 33
Attenborough	d			15 40						16 40						17 43			18 09				18 40
Beeston	d	15 22		15 43		16 02	16 17	16 22		16 43		17 02	17 17	17 27		17 46		18 02	18 12	18 18	18 26		18 43
Nottingham	a	15 32		15 53	16 05	16 13	16 25	16 32		16 54	17 05	17 13	17 26	17 33		17 54	18 05	18 13	18 22	18 27	18 32		18 54

		XC ◇1	EM ◇1 🍴	EM	EM ◇1 🍴	XC 1	EM ◇1 🍴	EM	XC ◇1	EM	EM ◇1 🍴	XC 1	EM	XC ◇1	EM	EM ◇1 🍴	EM	XC ◇1	EM	EM	EM ◇1 🍴	XC 1
Matlock	d							18 35					19 35				20 35		21 38			
Matlock Bath	d							18 37					19 37				20 37		21 40			
Cromford	d							18 40					19 40				20 40		21 43			
Whatstandwell	d							18 45					19 45				20 45		21 48			
Ambergate	d							18 50					19 50				20 50		21 53			
Belper	d							18 58					19 58				20 58		22 01			
Duffield	d							19 02					20 02				21 02		22 05			
Derby	a							19 10					20 10				21 10		22 13			
	d	18 39				19 05	19 18	19 24	19 39			20 05	20 24	20 40			21 24	21 40				22 59
Spondon	d																	21 45				23 04
Long Eaton	d					19 14	19a27	19 33				20 14	20 33	20 49			21 33	21 52				23 11
Attenborough	d							19 40					20 40				21 40	21 58				23 17
Beeston	d		19 03	19 07	19 19	19 23		19 43		20 07	20 18	20 23	20 43	20 58	21 03	21 19	21 43	22 02		22 07	22 17	23 20
Nottingham	a	19 05	19 10	19 14	19 27	19 32		19 53	20 03	20 15	20 28	20 32	20 53	21 06	21 15	21 29	21 54	22 08		22 15	22 26	23 27

		EM FX A 🚌	EM B	EM FX A	XC 1
Matlock	d	22 25	22 55		
Matlock Bath	d	22 28	22 57		
Cromford	d	22 30	23 00		
Whatstandwell	d	22 38	23 05		
Ambergate	d	22 46	23 10		
Belper	d	22 53	23 17		
Duffield	d	23 01	23 21		
Derby	a	23 20	23 29		
	d		23 31	23 31	23 59
Spondon	d				
Long Eaton	d		23 41	23 41	
Attenborough	d		23 48	23 48	
Beeston	d		23 51	23 51	
Nottingham	a		00 02	00 02	00 18

A from 1 October until 18 October
B 5 October, 12 October, from 19 October

For connections to St Pancras International please refer to Table 53

Saturdays
until 29 September

Matlock - Derby - Nottingham

Network Diagram - see first Page of Table 50

		EM	EM ◇1	XC 1	EM ◇1 A	EM ◇1 B	EM ◇1 A	EM ◇1	EM ◇1	EM	EM	EM	XC 1	EM ◇1	EM	XC 1	EM	EM C	XC 1	EM ◇1	EM ◇1	EM	XC 1
Matlock	d	22p55									06 22											07 36	
Matlock Bath	d	22p57									06 24											07 38	
Cromford	d	23p00									06 27											07 41	
Whatstandwell	d	23p05									06 32											07 46	
Ambergate	d	23p10									06 38											07 51	
Belper	d	23p17									06 44											07 58	
Duffield	d	23p21									06 48											08 02	
Derby 6	a	23p29									06 56											08 10	
	d	23p31		23p59				05 25	06 18	06 24			07 10	07 18	07 33	07 39		07 53	08 10	08 18		08 24	08 39
Spondon	d									06 29			07 15			07 44						08 29	
Long Eaton	d	23p41						05a34	06a27	06 35			07 22	07a27	07 42	07 52		08 03	08 19	08a27		08 36	
Attenborough	d	23p48								06 44		07 12	07 28		07 51							08 43	
Beeston	d	23p51	00 05		01 34	01 39	02 25			06 47		07 15	07 32		07 54	07 59	08 04	08 12	08 27		08 31	08 46	
Nottingham 8	a	00 02	00 12	00 18	01 40	01 45	02 31			06 57		07 24	07 38		08 05	08 08	08 13	08 19	08 34		08 42	08 53	09 05

		EM	EM ◇1	XC 1	EM ◇1	EM	XC ◇1	EM	EM ◇1	XC 1	EM ◇1	EM	XC ◇1	EM	EM ◇1	XC 1	EM ◇1	EM	XC ◇1	EM	EM ◇1	XC 1	EM ◇1
Matlock	d					08 36						09 36						10 36					
Matlock Bath	d					08 38						09 38						10 38					
Cromford	d					08 41						09 41						10 41					
Whatstandwell	d					08 46						09 46						10 46					
Ambergate	d					08 51						09 51						10 51					
Belper	d					08 58						09 58						10 58					
Duffield	d					09 02						10 02						11 02					
Derby 6	a					09 10						10 10						11 10					
	d			09 05	09 20	09 24	09 39			10 05	10 20	10 24	10 39			11 05	11 20	11 24	11 39			12 05	12 20
Spondon	d																						
Long Eaton	d			09 14	09a29	09 33				10 14	10a29	10 33				11 14	11a29	11 33				12 15	12a29
Attenborough	d			09 21		09 40						10 40						11 40					
Beeston	d	09 05	09 17	09 24		09 43		10 02	10 17	10 22		10 43		11 02	11 17	11 22		11 43		12 02	12 16	12 23	
Nottingham 8	a	09 14	09 26	09 33		09 53	10 05	10 13	10 26	10 33		10 53	11 05	11 13	11 26	11 33		11 53	12 05	12 13	12 26	12 33	

		EM	XC ◇1	EM	EM ◇1	XC 1	EM ◇1	EM	XC ◇1	EM	EM ◇1	XC 1	EM ◇1	EM	XC ◇1	EM	EM ◇1	XC 1	EM ◇1	EM	XC ◇1	EM
Matlock	d	11 36						12 36						13 36						14 36		
Matlock Bath	d	11 38						12 38						13 38						14 38		
Cromford	d	11 41						12 41						13 41						14 41		
Whatstandwell	d	11 46						12 46						13 46						14 46		
Ambergate	d	11 51						12 51						13 51						14 51		
Belper	d	11 58						12 58						13 58						14 58		
Duffield	d	12 02						13 02						14 02						15 02		
Derby 6	a	12 10						13 10						14 10						15 10		
	d	12 24	12 39			13 10	13 20	13 24	13 39			14 10	14 20	14 24	14 39			15 05	15 20	15 24	15 39	
Spondon	d							13 29														
Long Eaton	d	12 33				13 19	13a29	13 35				14 19	14a30	14 33				15 14	15a29	15 33		
Attenborough	d	12 40						13 42						14 40						15 40		
Beeston	d	12 43		13 02	13 16	13 27		13 45		14 02	14 17	14 27		14 43		15 02	15 17	15 24		15 43		16 02
Nottingham 8	a	12 53	13 05	13 13	13 27	13 33		13 53	14 05	14 13	14 26	14 33		14 53	15 05	15 13	15 26	15 33		15 53	16 05	16 13

		EM ◇1	XC 1	EM ◇1	EM	XC ◇1	EM	EM ◇1	XC 1	EM ◇1	EM	XC ◇1	EM	EM ◇1	XC 1	EM ◇1	EM	XC ◇1	EM	EM ◇1	XC 1	EM ◇1	EM
Matlock	d				15 36						16 36						17 36						18 36
Matlock Bath	d				15 38						16 38						17 38						18 38
Cromford	d				15 41						16 41						17 41						18 41
Whatstandwell	d				15 46						16 46						17 46						18 46
Ambergate	d				15 51						16 51						17 51						18 51
Belper	d				15 58						16 58						17 58						18 58
Duffield	d				16 02						17 02						18 02						19 02
Derby 6	a				16 10						17 10						18 10						19 10
	d		16 05	16 20	16 24	16 39			17 10	17 18	17 24	17 39			18 05	18 18	18 24	18 39			19 05	19 21	19 25
Spondon	d										17 29												
Long Eaton	d		16 14	16a29	16 33				17 19	17a27	17 36				18 14	18a27	18 33				19 14	19a30	19 34
Attenborough	d				16 40						17 43						18 40						19 41
Beeston	d	16 17	16 24		16 43		17 02	17 17	17 27		17 46		18 02	18 16	18 22		18 43		19 02	19 17	19 24		19 44
Nottingham 8	a	16 26	16 33		16 53	17 05	17 13	17 26	17 33		17 53	18 05	18 12	18 26	18 32		18 54	19 05	19 14	19 26	19 33		19 51

A 28 July, 4 August, 11 August, 1 September, 8 September
B until 21 July, 18 August, 25 August, 15 September, 22 September, 29 September
C from 21 July until 8 September

For connections to St Pancras International please refer to Table 53

Saturdays
until 29 September

Matlock - Derby - Nottingham

Network Diagram - see first Page of Table 50

		XC ◇1	EM	EM ◇1	XC 1 A	XC 1 B	EM	XC ◇1	EM	EM ◇1	EM	XC ◇1	EM	EM	EM ◇1	XC ◇1 C	XC ◇ D	EM
Matlock	d						19 36				20 36		21 36					22 55
Matlock Bath	d						19 38				20 38		21 38					22 57
Cromford	d						19 41				20 41		21 41					23 00
Whatstandwell	d						19 46				20 46		21 46					23 05
Ambergate	d						19 51				20 52		21 51					23 11
Belper	d						19 58				20 59		21 58					23 17
Duffield	d						20 02				21 03		22 02					23 21
Derby 6	a						20 10				21 11		22 10					23 29
	d	19 39			20 05	20 05	20 24	20 39			21 24	21 40				23 00	23 00	23 31
Spondon	d											21 45				23 05	23 05	
Long Eaton	d				20 14	20 14	20 33	20 49			21 33	21 52				23 12	23 12	23 41
Attenborough	d						20 40				21 40	21 58				23 18	23 18	23 48
Beeston	d		20 05	20 16	20 24	20 24	20 43	20 57	21 05	21 17	21 43	22 02		22 06	22 18	23 22	23 22	23 52
Nottingham 8	a	20 05	20 15	20 26	20 32	20 35	20 53	21 04	21 15	21 26	21 53	22 08		22 14	22 27	23 28	23 28	23 59

Saturdays
from 6 October

		EM	EM ◇1	XC 1	EM ◇1	EM ◇1	EM ◇1	EM	EM	EM	XC 1	EM ◇1	EM	XC 1	EM	XC 1	EM ◇1	EM ◇1	EM	XC 1	EM	EM ◇1	XC 1
Matlock	d	22p55							06 20										07 35				
Matlock Bath	d	22p57							06 22										07 37				
Cromford	d	23p00							06 25										07 40				
Whatstandwell	d	23p05							06 30										07 45				
Ambergate	d	23p10							06 36										07 50				
Belper	d	23p17							06 44										07 58				
Duffield	d	23p21							06 48										08 02				
Derby 6	a	23p29							06 56										08 10				
	d	23p31		23p59		05 25	06 18	06 24			07 10	07 18	07 33	07 39		08 10	08 18		08 24	08 39			09 05
Spondon	d							06 29			07 15			07 44					08 29				
Long Eaton	d	23p41				05a34	06a27	06 35			07 22	07a27	07 42	07 52		08 19	08a27		08 36				09 14
Attenborough	d	23p48						06 44		07 12	07 28		07 51						08 43				09 21
Beeston	d	23p51	00 05		01 39			06 47		07 15	07 32		07 54	07 59	08 04	08 27		08 31	08 46		09 05	09 17	09 24
Nottingham 8	a	00 02	00 12	00 18	01 45			06 57		07 24	07 38		08 05	08 08	08 13	08 34		08 42	08 53	09 05	09 14	09 26	09 33

		EM ◇1	EM	XC ◇1	EM	EM ◇1	XC 1	EM ◇1	EM	XC ◇1	EM	EM ◇1	XC 1	EM ◇1	EM	XC ◇1	EM	EM ◇1	XC 1	EM ◇1	EM	XC ◇1	EM
Matlock	d		08 35						09 35						10 35						11 35		
Matlock Bath	d		08 37						09 37						10 37						11 37		
Cromford	d		08 40						09 40						10 40						11 40		
Whatstandwell	d		08 45						09 45						10 45						11 45		
Ambergate	d		08 50						09 50						10 50						11 50		
Belper	d		08 58						09 58						10 58						11 58		
Duffield	d		09 02						10 02						11 02						12 02		
Derby 6	a		09 10						10 10						11 10						12 10		
	d	09 20	09 24	09 39			10 05	10 20	10 24	10 39			11 05	11 20	11 24	11 39			12 05	12 20	12 24	12 39	
Spondon	d																						
Long Eaton	d	09a29	09 33				10 14	10a29	10 33				11 14	11a29	11 33				12 15	12a29	12 33		
Attenborough	d		09 40						10 40						11 40						12 40		
Beeston	d		09 43		10 02	10 17	10 22		10 43		11 02	11 17	11 22		11 43		12 02	12 16	12 23		12 43		13 02
Nottingham 8	a		09 53	10 05	10 13	10 26	10 33		10 53	11 05	11 13	11 26	11 33		11 53	12 05	12 13	12 26	12 33		12 53	13 05	13 13

		EM ◇1	XC 1	EM ◇1	EM	XC ◇1	EM	EM ◇1	XC 1	EM ◇1	EM	XC ◇1	EM	EM ◇1	XC 1	EM ◇1	EM	XC ◇1	EM	EM ◇1	XC 1	EM ◇1
Matlock	d				12 35						13 35						14 35					
Matlock Bath	d				12 37						13 37						14 37					
Cromford	d				12 40						13 40						14 40					
Whatstandwell	d				12 45						13 45						14 45					
Ambergate	d				12 50						13 50						14 50					
Belper	d				12 58						13 58						14 58					
Duffield	d				13 02						14 02						15 02					
Derby 6	a				13 10						14 10						15 10					
	d		13 10	13 20	13 24	13 39			14 10	14 20	14 24	14 39			15 05	15 20	15 24	15 39			16 05	16 20
Spondon	d				13 29																	
Long Eaton	d		13 19	13a29	13 35				14 19	14a30	14 33				15 14	15a29	15 33				16 14	16a29
Attenborough	d				13 42						14 40						15 40					
Beeston	d	13 16	13 27		13 45		14 02	14 17	14 27		14 43		15 02	15 17	15 24		15 43		16 02	16 17	16 24	
Nottingham 8	a	13 27	13 33		13 53	14 05	14 13	14 26	14 33		14 53	15 05	15 13	15 26	15 33		15 53	16 05	16 13	16 26	16 33	

A until 8 September
B 15 September, 22 September, 29 September
C until 23 June
D from 30 June until 29 September

For connections to St Pancras International please refer to Table 53

		EM	XC ◇■ ⊼	EM	EM ◇■ ⊼	XC ■	EM ◇■ ⊼	EM		XC ◇■ ⊼	EM	EM ◇■ ⊼	XC ■	EM ◇■ ⊼	EM	XC ◇■	EM	EM ◇■ ⊼		XC ■	EM ◇■ ⊼	EM	XC ◇■	EM	EM ◇■ ⊼
Matlock	d	15 35						16 35							17 35							18 35			
Matlock Bath	d	15 37						16 37							17 37							18 37			
Cromford	d	15 40						16 40							17 40							18 40			
Whatstandwell	d	15 45						16 45							17 45							18 45			
Ambergate	d	15 50						16 50							17 50							18 50			
Belper	d	15 58						16 58							17 58							18 58			
Duffield	d	16 02						17 02							18 02							19 02			
Derby ■	a	16 10						17 10							18 10							19 10			
	d	16 24	16 39			17 10	17 18	17 24		17 39			18 05	18 18	18 24	18 39				19 05	19 21	19 25	19 39		
Spondon	d							17 29																	
Long Eaton	d	16 33				17 19	17a27	17 36					18 14	18a27	18 33					19 14	19a30	19 34			
Attenborough	d	16 40						17 43							18 40							19 41			
Beeston	d	16 43		17 02	17 17	17 27		17 46			18 02	18 16	18 22		18 43		19 02	19 17		19 24		19 44		20 05	20 16
Nottingham ■	a	16 53	17 05	17 13	17 26	17 33		17 53		18 05	18 12	18 26	18 32		18 54	19 05	19 14	19 26		19 33		19 51	20 05	20 15	20 26

		XC ■	EM	XC ◇■		EM	EM ◇■ ⊼	EM	XC ◇■	EM	EM	EM ◇■ ⊼	XC ◇	EM
Matlock	d		19 35					20 35		21 35				22 55
Matlock Bath	d		19 37					20 37		21 37				22 57
Cromford	d		19 40					20 40		21 40				23 00
Whatstandwell	d		19 45					20 45		21 45				23 05
Ambergate	d		19 50					20 50		21 50				23 11
Belper	d		19 58					20 58		21 58				23 17
Duffield	d		20 02					21 02		22 02				23 21
Derby ■	a		20 10					21 10		22 10				23 29
	d	20 05	20 24	20 39				21 24	21 40				23 00	23 31
Spondon	d								21 45				23 05	
Long Eaton	d	20 14	20 33	20 49				21 33	21 52				23 12	23 41
Attenborough	d		20 40					21 40	21 58				23 18	23 48
Beeston	d	20 24	20 43	20 57		21 05	21 17	21 43	22 02		22 06	22 18	23 22	23 52
Nottingham ■	a	20 35	20 53	21 04		21 15	21 26	21 53	22 08		22 14	22 27	23 28	23 59

Sundays
until 24 June

		EM ◇■ ⊼	EM ◇■ ⊼	EM	EM ◇■ ⊼	EM	EM ◇■ ⊼	EM	EM ◇■ ⊼	EM ◇■ ⊼		XC ◇■ ⊼	EM	XC ◇■ ⊼	EM ◇■ ⊼	EM ◇■ ⊼	EM ◇■ ⊼	XC ◇■ ⊼	EM ◇■ ⊼	EM ◇■ ⊼		EM	XC ◇■ ⊼	EM ◇■ ⊼	EM
Matlock	d							10 43					12 39									14 39			
Matlock Bath	d							10 45					12 41									14 41			
Cromford	d							10 48					12 44									14 44			
Whatstandwell	d							10 53					12 49									14 49			
Ambergate	d							10 59					12 54									14 54			
Belper	d							11 05					13 01									15 01			
Duffield	d							11 09					13 05									15 05			
Derby ■	a							11 15					13 13									15 13			
	d		08 06	08 18	09 06	09 18	10 08	11 18		12 21		12 40	13 18	13 40		14 00		14 40	14 51			15 18	15 40		16 18
Spondon	d																								
Long Eaton	d		08a15	08 28	09a15	09 28	10a17	11 28		12a30			13 28			14a09			15a00			15 28			16 27
Attenborough	d			08 35		09 34		11 35					13 35									15 35			16 35
Beeston	d	00 51		08 39		09 37		11 38	11 52				13 38		14 00		14 50			15 13		15 38		16 10	16 41
Nottingham ■	a	00 57		08 45		09 44		11 45	11 58			13 00	13 46	14 00	14 06		14 56	15 02		15 19		15 45	16 00	16 17	16 48

		XC ◇■ ⊼	EM ◇■ ⊼	EM	XC ◇■ ⊼	EM ◇■ ⊼		EM ◇■ ⊼	EM	XC ◇■	EM ◇■ ⊼	EM ◇■ ⊼	EM	XC ◇■	EM ◇■ ⊼	EM ◇■ ⊼		EM	XC ◇■	EM ◇■ ⊼	EM	XC ◇■	EM ◇■ ⊼	EM	EM
Matlock	d			16 39									18 39								20 39				22 45
Matlock Bath	d			16 41									18 41								20 41				22 47
Cromford	d			16 44									18 44								20 44				22 50
Whatstandwell	d			16 49									18 49								20 49				22 55
Ambergate	d			16 54									18 54								20 55				23 00
Belper	d			17 01									19 01								21 01				23 07
Duffield	d			17 05									19 05								21 06				23 11
Derby ■	a			17 13									19 13								21 13				23 18
	d	16 40	16 48	17 18	17 40	17 47			18 18	18 40	19 05		19 18	19 40	20 05			20 18	20 40		21 19	21 40		22 18	
Spondon	d																								
Long Eaton	d		16a57	17 28		17a56			18 28		19a14		19 28		20a15			20 27			21 29			22 28	
Attenborough	d			17 35					18 35				19 38					20 35			21 36			22 35	
Beeston	d			17 38				18 09	18 38			19 11	19 41			20 19		20 38		21 23	21 39		22 00	22 38	
Nottingham ■	a	17 00		17 45	18 00			18 16	18 46	19 00		19 16	19 48	20 00		20 25		20 45	21 00	21 29	21 46	22 00	22 06	22 45	

For connections to St Pancras International please refer to Table 53

		EM ◇■ ⊼
Matlock	d	
Matlock Bath	d	
Cromford	d	
Whatstandwell	d	
Ambergate	d	
Belper	d	
Duffield	d	
Derby ■	a	
	d	
Spondon	d	
Long Eaton	d	
Attenborough	d	
Beeston	d	22 55
Nottingham ■	a	23 01

Sundays
1 July to 16 September

		EM ◇■ A ⊼	EM ◇■ B ⊼	XC B 🚌	EM ◇■ C ⊼	EM ◇■ B ⊼	EM A	EM ◇■ A ⊼	EM ◇■ B ⊼	EM		EM ◇■ A ⊼	EM ◇■ B ⊼	EM ◇■ A ⊼	EM ◇■ A ⊼	EM	EM ◇■ B ⊼	XC ◇■ B ⊼	XC ◇■ A	EM ◇■ B ⊼		EM ◇■ A ⊼	XC ◇■ ⊼	EM ◇■ A ⊼	EM
Matlock	d															10 43									12 39
Matlock Bath	d															10 45									12 41
Cromford	d															10 48									12 44
Whatstandwell	d															10 53									12 49
Ambergate	d															10 59									12 54
Belper	d															11 05									13 01
Duffield	d															11 09									13 05
Derby ■	a															11 15									13 13
	d					08 12	08 18	08 50	09 13	09 18		09 51	10 10		10 52	11 18		11 40	11 40	12 27			12 40	13 02	13 18
Spondon	d			00s01																					
Long Eaton	d			00s12		08a21	08 28	08a59	09a22	09 28		10a00	10a19		11a01	11 28				12a36				13a11	13 28
Attenborough	d			00s23			08 35			09 34						11 35									13 35
Beeston	d	00 01	00 33	00s29	02 08		08 39			09 37				10 48		11 38	11 48					12 51			13 38
Nottingham ■	a	00 08	00 42	00 49	02 14		08 45			09 44				10 54		11 45	11 54	12 00	12 00			12 57	13 00		13 46

		EM ◇■ B ⊼	XC ◇■ ⊼	EM ◇■ A ⊼	EM ◇■ A ⊼	EM ◇■ B ⊼		EM ◇■ A ⊼	EM ◇■ B ⊼	XC ◇■ B ⊼	XC ◇■ A ⊼	EM ◇■ B ⊼	EM ◇■ A ⊼	EM ◇■ B ⊼	EM A	EM B		XC ◇■ ⊼	EM ◇■ B ⊼	EM ◇■ A ⊼	EM	XC ◇■ ⊼	EM ◇■ A ⊼	EM ◇■ B ⊼	EM A
Matlock	d														14 39	14 39									16 42
Matlock Bath	d														14 41	14 41									16 44
Cromford	d														14 44	14 44									16 47
Whatstandwell	d														14 49	14 49									16 52
Ambergate	d														14 54	14 57									16 58
Belper	d														15 01	15 03									17 05
Duffield	d														15 05	15 08									17 09
Derby ■	a														15 13	15 15									17 16
	d		13 40	13 55		14 01		14 37		14 40	14 42	14 49			15 18	15 18		15 40			16 18	16 40	16 47	16 48	17 18
Spondon	d																								
Long Eaton	d			14a04		14a10		14a46				14a58			15 28	15 28					16 27		16a56	16a57	17 28
Attenborough	d														15 35	15 35					16 35				17 35
Beeston	d	13 47			14 00				14 50				15 02	15 14	15 38	15 38			16 00	16 00	16 41				17 38
Nottingham ■	a	13 53	14 00		14 07				14 56	15 02	15 02		15 09	15 21	15 45	15 45		16 00	16 06	16 07	16 48	17 00			17 45

		EM B		EM ◇■ A ⊼	XC ◇■ ⊼	EM ◇■ ⊼	EM ◇■ B ⊼	EM	EM ◇■ A ⊼	XC ◇■ B	EM ◇■ B ⊼	EM ◇■ A ⊼		EM	EM ◇■ B ⊼	EM ◇■ A ⊼	XC ◇■	EM ◇■ B ⊼	EM ◇■ A ⊼	EM ◇■ B ⊼	EM B	EM A		EM ◇■ A ⊼	XC ◇■
Matlock	d	16 47												18 39											
Matlock Bath	d	16 49												18 41											
Cromford	d	16 52												18 44											
Whatstandwell	d	16 57												18 49											
Ambergate	d	17 01												18 54											
Belper	d	17 08												19 01											
Duffield	d	17 12												19 05											
Derby ■	a	17 20												19 13											
	d	17 21			17 40	17 47		18 18		18 40		19 05		19 18	19 22		19 40		20 04	20 05	20 18	20 18			20 40
Spondon	d																								
Long Eaton	d	17 31				17a56		18 28				19a14		19 28	19a31				20a13	20a14	20 27	20 27			
Attenborough	d	17 39						18 35						19 38							20 35	20 35			
Beeston	d	17 42		17 47			17 59	18 38	18 50		18 59			19 41		19 50		20 00			20 38	20 38		20 51	
Nottingham ■	a	17 48		17 54	18 00		18 06	18 46	18 55	19 00	19 05			19 48		19 55	20 00	20 06			20 45	20 47		20 56	21 00

A not 16 September
B 16 September
C 29 July, 5 August, 12 August, 2 September, 9 September

For connections to St Pancras International please refer to Table 53

Table 56

Sundays
1 uly to 16 September

Matlock - Derby - Nottingham

Network Diagram - see first Page of Table 50

		EM	EM	EM	EM	XC	EM	EM	EM	EM	EM
		◇■			◇■	◇■	◇■			◇■	◇■
		A	B	A	B		A			B	A
		⌶			⌶		⌶			⌶	⌶
Matlock	d		20 39	20 39					22 45		
Matlock Bath	d		20 41	20 41					22 47		
Cromford	d		20 44	20 44					22 50		
Whatstandwell	d		20 49	20 49					22 55		
Ambergate	d		20 55	20 55					23 00		
Belper	d		21 01	21 01					23 07		
Duffield	d		21 06	21 06					23 11		
Derby ■	a		21 13	21 13					23 18		
	d		21 19	21 23		21 40		22 18			
Spondon	d										
Long Eaton	d		21 29	21 35				22 28			
Attenborough	d		21 36	21 43				22 35			
Beeston	d	21 00	21 39	21 46	21 48		22 00	22 38		22 55	23 01
Nottingham ■	a	21 06	21 46	21 52	21 55	22 00	22 06	22 45		23 01	23 07

Sundays
from 23 September

		EM	EM	XC	EM	EM	EM	EM	EM	EM	EM	EM	EM	EM	XC	EM	XC	EM	EM	EM	EM	EM	XC
		◇■	◇■		◇■	◇■	◇■		◇■	◇■	◇■	◇■		◇■	◇■	◇■	◇■	◇■	◇■			◇■	◇■
		C	D	D	D	C	D		C	D	C	C		D		D		C	C	D	C	D	
		⌶	⌶		⌶	⌶	⌶		⌶	⌶	⌶	⌶		⌶	⌶	⌶	⌶	⌶	⌶			⌶	⌶
Matlock	d												10 43							12 39	12 39		
Matlock Bath	d												10 45							12 41	12 41		
Cromford	d												10 48							12 44	12 44		
Whatstandwell	d												10 53							12 49	12 49		
Ambergate	d												10 59							12 54	12 56		
Belper	d												11 05							13 01	13 03		
Duffield	d												11 09							13 05	13 07		
Derby ■	a												11 15							13 13	13 15		
	d				08 12	08 52	09 13	09 18	09 55	10 10	10 55		11 18		11 40	12 27	12 40	13 02		13 18	13 18		13 40
Spondon	d			00s01																			
Long Eaton	d			00s12	08a21	09a01	09a22	09 28	10a04	10a19	11a04		11 28			12a36		13a11		13 28	13 28		
Attenborough	d			00s23				09 34					11 35							13 35	13 35		
Beeston	d	00 01	00 33	00s29				09 37				11 06	11 38	11 48					13 04	13 38	13 38	13 47	
Nottingham ■	a	00 08	00 42	00 49				09 44				11 14	11 45	11 54	12 00		13 00		13 10	13 46	13 46	13 53	14 00

		EM	EM	EM	EM	XC	EM	EM	EM	EM	EM	EM	XC	EM	EM	XC	XC	EM	EM	EM	XC	EM	EM
		◇■	◇■	◇■	◇■	◇■	◇■	◇■	◇■	◇■		◇■	◇■	◇■		◇■	◇■	◇■		◇■	◇■	◇■	◇■
		D	C	C	D		D	C	C	D		C		D		D	C			C		D	C
		⌶	⌶	⌶	⌶	⌶	⌶	⌶	⌶	⌶		⌶	⌶	⌶		⌶		⌶		⌶	⌶	⌶	⌶
Matlock	d										14 39								16 47				
Matlock Bath	d										14 41								16 49				
Cromford	d										14 44								16 52				
Whatstandwell	d										14 49								16 57				
Ambergate	d										14 57								17 01				
Belper	d										15 03								17 08				
Duffield	d										15 08								17 12				
Derby ■	a										15 15								17 20				
	d	14 01	14 03			14 40	14 49	14 54			15 18		15 40		16 18	16 40	16 40	16 48	17 21		17 40	17 47	17 48
Spondon	d																						
Long Eaton	d	14a10	14a12				14a58	15a03			15 28				16 27			16a57	17 31			17a56	17a57
Attenborough	d										15 35				16 35				17 39				
Beeston	d			14 06	14 50				15 06	15 14	15 38	15 49		16 00	16 41				17 42	17 48			
Nottingham ■	a			14 14	14 56	15 02			15 13	15 21	15 45	15 55	16 00	16 06	16 48	17 00	17 00		17 48	17 55	18 00		

		EM	EM	XC	EM	EM	EM	EM	XC	EM	EM	EM	EM	EM	XC	EM	EM	EM	XC	EM	EM	EM
		◇■		◇■	◇■		◇■	◇■	◇■	◇■	◇■			◇■	◇■	◇■		◇■	◇■	◇■		
		D						C		D		D	C	C		D		C		D		
		⌶			⌶		⌶	⌶		⌶	⌶			⌶		⌶		⌶		⌶		
Matlock	d					18 39											20 39					22 45
Matlock Bath	d					18 41											20 41					22 47
Cromford	d					18 44											20 44					22 50
Whatstandwell	d					18 49											20 49					22 55
Ambergate	d					18 54											20 55					23 00
Belper	d					19 01											21 01					23 07
Duffield	d					19 05											21 06					23 11
Derby ■	a					19 13											21 13					23 18
	d		18 18	18 40		19 18	19 22		19 40		20 05	20 18	20 18		20 40		21 23		21 40		22 18	
Spondon	d																					
Long Eaton	d		18 28			19 28	19a31				20a14	20 27	20 27				21 35				22 28	
Attenborough	d		18 35			19 38						20 35	20 35				21 43				22 35	
Beeston	d	17 59	18 38		18 59	19 41		19 50		20 00		20 38	20 38	20 50		21 00	21 46	21 50		22 00	22 38	
Nottingham ■	a	18 06	18 46	19 00	19 05	19 48		19 56	20 00	20 06		20 45	20 47	20 56	21 00	21 06	21 52	21 55	22 00	22 06	22 45	

A 16 September
B not 16 September
C from 28 October
D from 23 September until 21 October

For connections to St Pancras International please refer to Table 53

Table 56

Sundays
from 23 September

Matlock - Derby - Nottingham

Network Diagram - see first Page of Table 50

		EM	EM
		◇■	◇■
		A	B
		⌶	⌶
Matlock	d		
Matlock Bath	d		
Cromford	d		
Whatstandwell	d		
Ambergate	d		
Belper	d		
Duffield	d		
Derby ■	a		
	d		
Spondon	d		
Long Eaton	d		
Attenborough	d		
Beeston	d	22 59	23 01
Nottingham ■	a	23 05	23 07

A from 28 October
B from 23 September until 21 October

For connections to St Pancras International please refer to Table 53

Nottingham, Derby and Leicester
Birmingham - Cardiff and Bristol

Network Diagram - see first Page of Table 50

Miles	Miles	Miles			XC MO ◇■ A ✠	AW MX	XC MX MO ◇■ B	XC ■ C	EM ◇■ D ✠	EM ◇■ D ✠	AW E	GW ◇■ F ▭	XC ◇■		EM ◇■ G ✠	EM ◇■ H I ⊠✠	GW F	GW ◇■ ▭	XC ◇■ J	GW ◇ K	XC ◇■ F ✠	GW ◇■ E ▭	AW L		XC ◇■ ✠
0	—	—	**Nottingham ■**	d																					
3¼	—	—	Beeston	d																					
4¾	—	—	Attenborough	d																					
7¾	—	—	Long Eaton	d																					
16	—	—	**Derby ■**	a																					
—	—	—		d	21p27		21p29		04 55	05 17					06 04	06 04									06 10
22¼	—	—	Willington	d																					
27	—	—	Burton-on-Trent	d	21p37		21p40																		06 20
40	—	—	Tamworth	d	21p48		21p50																		06 31
41¾	—	—	Wilnecote	d																					
—	0	—	**Leicester**	d				23p19	05a24	05a42					06a37	06a37									
—	1¾	—	South Wigston	d				23p24																	
—	4¾	—	Narborough	d				23p29																	
—	13½	—	Hinckley	d				23p38																	
—	18¾	—	Nuneaton	d				23p45																	
—	29¼	—	Coleshill Parkway	d				00 02																	
—	31	—	Water Orton	d																					
56¾	38¾	0	**Birmingham New Street ■**	a	22p05		22p07	00 15																	06 52
—	—	—		d	22p12		22p12						05 00						05 42		06 42				07 12
83¾	—	—	Worcester Shrub Hill ■	d								05 21								06 49		07 09			
98½	—	39¼	Ashchurch for Tewkesbury	d															06 34	07 05					
105¾	—	46½	Cheltenham Spa	d	22p52	23p00	23p31				05 37	05 54	06 03				06 24	06 31	06 43	07 16	07 22	07 30	07 45		07 52
112¼	—	—	Gloucester ■	a	23p03	23p12					05 48	06 03	06 16				06 34	06 40	06 53	07 26		07 39	07 57		
—	—	87	Bristol Parkway ■	a	00 01		00 01										07 23			08 19	07 57				08 25
—	—	92¾	**Bristol Temple Meads ■**	a	00 14		00 13										07 39			08 36	08 08				08 40
157	—	—	Newport (South Wales)	a		00 06					06 41		07 09						07 52				08 50		
168¾	—	—	**Cardiff Central ■**	a		00 35					07 00		07 26						08 08				09 07		

		XC ■	XC ◇■ M ✠	EM ◇■ N ⊠✠	XC ◇■ O	EM P	XC ◇■ Q ✠	XC ■ R	XC ◇■	S	XC ◇■ T	EM ◇■ N ⊠✠	EM ◇■ D ⊠✠	EM ◇■ F ✠	GW ◇■ E ▭	AW U	XC ◇■ ✠	XC ■ M	XC ◇■ ✠	V W	EM ◇■ P ✠	XC ◇■ Q ✠	EM X	XC ◇■ ✠	XC ◇■ ✠
Nottingham ■	d		06 00			06 18			06 37										06 56				07 19		
Beeston	d		06 06			06 24			06 43										07 07				07 25		
Attenborough	d		06 10			06 27													07 11				07 29		
Long Eaton	d		06 17			06 35													07 18		07 36		07 40		
Derby ■	a		06 30			06 49			07 00										07 31		07 47		07 53		
	d		06 36	06 32	06 48				07 06			07 05	07 20	07 26			07 27		07 36			07 50			
Willington	d																		07 44						
Burton-on-Trent	d		06 48		06 58				07 18								07 38		07 50			08 00			
Tamworth	d		07 01		07 09				07 30								07 50		08 03			08 11			
Wilnecote	d		07 05																08 07						
Leicester	d	06 16		07a04				06 43			07 10	07a34	07a52	07a59				07 24							07 49
South Wigston	d	06 22						06 49																	07 55
Narborough	d	06 27						06 54										07 33							08 00
Hinckley	d	06 35						07 02										07 42							08 08
Nuneaton	d	06 42						07 10			07 30							07 50							08 17
Coleshill Parkway	d	06 59						07 26			07 46							08 05							08 32
Water Orton	d							07 30										08 09							
Birmingham New Street ■	a	07 14	07 25		07 27			07 44	07 52		07 58						08 08	08 19	08 24			08 27			08 45
	d		07 30				07 42										08 12		08 30					08 42	
Worcester Shrub Hill ■	d																								
Ashchurch for Tewkesbury	d																								
Cheltenham Spa	d		08 16				08 25								08 31	08 45	08 52		09 12					09 25	
Gloucester ■	a		08 27												08 40	08 58			09 22						
Bristol Parkway ■	a						08 54										09 24							09 54	
Bristol Temple Meads ■	a						09 14										09 38							10 08	
Newport (South Wales)	a		09 12													09 51			10 09						
Cardiff Central ■	a		09 30													10 07			10 25						

A from 17 September until 22 October. From Edinburgh. ✠ to Birmingham New Street
B until 22 June. From Edinburgh
C from 21 May
D To St Pancras International
E To Maesteg
F To London Paddington
G from 17 September. From Sheffield to St Pancras International
H until 14 September. From Sheffield to St Pancras International
I To Westbury
J To Weymouth
K To Paignton
L To Plymouth. ✠ from Birmingham New Street
M ✠ from Birmingham New Street to Newport (South Wales)
N From Sheffield to St Pancras International
O From Sheffield to Reading
P To Matlock
Q From Manchester Piccadilly
R To Bournemouth
S From Cambridge
T From Leeds to St Pancras International
U From Leeds to Plymouth
V From St Pancras International to Sheffield
W From Leeds to Southampton Central
X From Stansted Airport

Nottingham, Derby and Leicester
Birmingham - Cardiff and Bristol

Network Diagram - see first Page of Table 50

		EM ◇■ A ⊠✠	XC ■	EM ◇■ A ✠	GW B		GW C	XC ◇■ D ✠	XC ■	XC ◇■ E ✠	EM F	XC ◇■ G ✠	XC ◇■ H A ✠	EM ◇■ I ✠	XC ◇■ ✠		XC ■ J	EM ◇■ A ✠	EM ◇■ K ✠	GW ◇■ L ▭	AW M	XC ◇■ ✠	XC ■ E	XC ◇■ F ✠	EM
Nottingham ■	d		07 37							08 08	08 15						08 37							09 11	09 18
Beeston	d		07 43								08 24						08 43								09 24
Attenborough	d										08 27														09 27
Long Eaton	d		07 51								08 35						08 51	09 00							09 35
Derby ■	a		08 02							08 32	08 48						09 02	09 15						09 31	09 48
	d	08 01	08 06	08 16				08 28		08 36		08 53		09 01			09 10		09 20			09 28		09 36	
Willington	d																								
Burton-on-Trent	d		08 18					08 38		08 49							09 21					09 38		09 49	
Tamworth	d		08 30					08 50		09 02							09 33							10 02	
Wilnecote	d		08 34														09 37								
Leicester	d	08a23		08a52					08 16				08 49	09a23					09a54				09 16		
South Wigston	d																								
Narborough	d								08 25														09 25		
Hinckley	d								08 34														09 34		
Nuneaton	d								08 42				09 10										09 42		
Coleshill Parkway	d								08 57				09 25										09 57		
Water Orton	d																						10 01		
Birmingham New Street ■	a		08 54					09 09	09 14	09 24		09 27	09 38				09 54					10 07	10 14	10 24	
	d							09 12		09 30					09 42							10 12		10 30	
Worcester Shrub Hill ■	d				09 06																				
Ashchurch for Tewkesbury	d				09 24																				
Cheltenham Spa	d				09 34		09 40	09 52		10 11					10 25					10 31	10 45	10 52		11 11	
Gloucester ■	a				09 42		09 51			10 22										10 40	10 57			11 22	
Bristol Parkway ■	a				10 22			10 25							10 54							11 26			
Bristol Temple Meads ■	a				10 37			10 41							11 12							11 37			
Newport (South Wales)	a									11 11											11 50			12 10	
Cardiff Central ■	a									11 27											12 12			12 28	

		XC ◇■ N ✠	XC ◇■ H ✠	EM ◇■ A ✠	XC ◇■ O ✠	XC ■ J	EM ◇■ A ✠	EM ◇■ P ✠	GW ■ C	GW	L	AW Q	XC ◇■ ✠	XC ■ E	XC ◇■ F ✠	EM R	XC ◇■ H A ✠	XC ◇■ O ✠	EM ◇■ ✠	XC ◇■ ✠	J	XC ■ A	EM ◇■ ✠	EM ◇■ ✠
Nottingham ■	d					09 37									10 11	10 18						10 37		
Beeston	d					09 43										10 24						10 43		
Attenborough	d															10 27								
Long Eaton	d					09 51	09 56									10 35						10 51	10 56	
Derby ■	a					10 02	10 09								10 33	10 49						11 02	11 09	
	d	09 53		10 01		10 10		10 20					10 28		10 37		10 53		11 01			11 10		11 20
Willington	d																							
Burton-on-Trent	d					10 21									10 49							11 21		
Tamworth	d					10 33							10 48		11 02							11 33		
Wilnecote	d					10 37																11 37		
Leicester	d		09 49	10a23				10a54						10 16				10 49	11a23					11a54
South Wigston	d													10 22										
Narborough	d													10 27										
Hinckley	d													10 35										
Nuneaton	d		10 10											10 42				11 09						
Coleshill Parkway	d		10 25											10 58				11 24						
Water Orton	d																							
Birmingham New Street ■	a	10 27	10 38			10 54							11 08	11 14	11 24		11 27	11 38				11 54		
	d				10 42								11 12		11 30					11 42				
Worcester Shrub Hill ■	d								11 06															
Ashchurch for Tewkesbury	d								11 24															
Cheltenham Spa	d				11 25				11 32	11 40		11 45	11 52		12 11					12 25				
Gloucester ■	a								11 42	11 51		11 57			12 22									
Bristol Parkway ■	a				11 54				12 22				12 28							12 55				
Bristol Temple Meads ■	a				12 08				12 34				12 40							13 10				
Newport (South Wales)	a											12 50			13 11									
Cardiff Central ■	a											13 07			13 29									

A From Sheffield to St Pancras International
B From Great Malvern to Westbury
C To Swindon
D From York to Plymouth
E ✠ to Newport (South Wales)
F To Matlock
G From Newcastle to Reading
H From Stansted Airport
I From Manchester Piccadilly to Paignton
J From St Pancras International to Sheffield
K To London Paddington
L To Maesteg
M From Newcastle to Plymouth
N From Newcastle to Southampton Central
O From Manchester Piccadilly
P From Great Malvern to Brighton
Q From Edinburgh to Plymouth
R From Edinburgh to Reading

Nottingham, Derby and Leicester Birmingham - Cardiff and Bristol

Network Diagram - see first Page of Table 50

Station		GW ◇1 A	XC ◇1 B	XC 1	XC ◇1 C	EM D	XC ◇1 E	XC ◇1 F	EM ◇1 G H	XC ◇1	XC 1 I	EM ◇1 G	EM ◇1 J	GW ◇ K L	GW	AW M	XC ◇1 N	XC 1 D	XC ◇1 O	EM F	XC ◇1 G	XC ◇1	EM ◇1
Nottingham 8	d				11 08	11 18					11 37								12 08	12 18			
Beeston	d					11 24					11 43									12 24			
Attenborough	d					11 27														12 27			
Long Eaton	d					11 35					11 51	11 57								12 35			
Derby 6	a				11 31	11 48					12 02	12 09							12 33	12 48			
	d		11 28		11 36		11 53		12 01		12 10		12 20				12 28		12 36		12 53		13 01
Willington	d																						
Burton-on-Trent	d				11 49						12 21								12 49				
Tamworth	d				12 02						12 33						12 48		13 02				
Wilnecote	d										12 37												
Leicester	d			11 16				11 49	12a23				12a53					12 16				12 49	13a23
South Wigston	d																	12 22					
Narborough	d			11 25														12 27					
Hinckley	d			11 34														12 35					
Nuneaton	d			11 42				12 10										12 41				13 09	
Coleshill Parkway	d			11 57				12 25										12 58				13 24	
Water Orton	d			12 01																			
Birmingham New Street 12	a		12 07	12 14	12 24		12 27	12 39			12 54						13 07	13 14	13 24		13 27	13 38	
	d		12 12		12 30					12 42							13 12		13 30				
Worcester Shrub Hill 7	d													13 06									
Ashchurch for Tewkesbury	d													13 24									
Cheltenham Spa	d	12 31	12 52		13 11					13 25				13 34	13 40	13 45	13 54		14 11				
Gloucester 7	a	12 40			13 22									13 42	13 51	13 57			14 22				
Bristol Parkway 7	a		13 25							13 57				14 22			14 27						
Bristol Temple Meads 10	a		13 38							14 09				14 38			14 41						
Newport (South Wales)	a				14 09											14 50			15 11				
Cardiff Central 7	a				14 29											15 07			15 29				

Station		XC ◇1 P	XC 1	EM ◇1 I	EM ◇1 G	GW ◇1 Q L	AW B	XC ◇1	XC 1 N	XC ◇1 D	EM E	XC ◇1 F	XC ◇1 G	EM ◇1 H	XC ◇1	XC 1 I	EM ◇1 G J	EM ◇1 K	GW ◇ R	GW	XC ◇1	XC 1
Nottingham 8	d		12 37							13 11	13 18					13 37						
Beeston	d		12 43								13 24					13 43						
Attenborough	d										13 27											
Long Eaton	d		12 51	12 57							13 35					13 51	13 57					
Derby 6	a		13 02	13 09						13 31	13 48					14 02	14 09					
	d		13 06		13 20			13 28		13 36		13 53		14 01		14 10		14 20			14 28	
Willington	d		13 14																			
Burton-on-Trent	d		13 21					13 38		13 49						14 21						
Tamworth	d		13 33							14 02						14 33					14 47	
Wilnecote	d															14 37						
Leicester	d				13a54				13 16				13 49	14a23				14a53				14 16
South Wigston	d																					14 22
Narborough	d								13 25													14 27
Hinckley	d								13 34													14 35
Nuneaton	d								13 42				14 10									14 41
Coleshill Parkway	d								13 57				14 25									14 58
Water Orton	d								14 01													
Birmingham New Street 12	a		13 54					14 06	14 14	14 24		14 27	14 38			14 54					15 07	15 13
	d	13 42						14 12		14 30					14 42						15 12	
Worcester Shrub Hill 7	d																		15 06			
Ashchurch for Tewkesbury	d																		15 24			
Cheltenham Spa	d	14 25				14 31	14 45	14 52		15 11					15 25				15 34	15 40	15 52	
Gloucester 7	a					14 40	14 56			15 22									15 42	15 51		
Bristol Parkway 7	a	14 57						15 25							15 56				16 22		16 27	
Bristol Temple Meads 10	a	15 10						15 39							16 08				16 37		16 40	
Newport (South Wales)	a						15 50			16 10												
Cardiff Central 7	a						16 10			16 29												

- A To London Paddington
- B From Glasgow Central to Plymouth
- C 🍴 to Newport (South Wales)
- D To Matlock
- E From Newcastle to Southampton Central
- F From Stansted Airport
- G From Sheffield to St Pancras International
- H From Manchester Piccadilly
- I From St Pancras International to Sheffield
- J From Great Malvern to Weymouth
- K To Swindon
- L To Maesteg
- M From Dundee to Plymouth
- N 🍴 from Birmingham New Street to Newport (South Wales)
- O From Newcastle to Reading
- P From Manchester Piccadilly to Exeter St Davids
- Q To London Paddington. The Cheltenham Spa Express
- R From Glasgow Central to Penzance

Nottingham, Derby and Leicester Birmingham - Cardiff and Bristol

Network Diagram - see first Page of Table 50

Station		XC ◇1 A	EM B	XC ◇1 C	XC ◇1 D	EM ◇1 E	XC ◇1 F	XC 1	EM ◇1 G	EM ◇1 E H	GW ◇1 I	AW J	XC ◇1	XC 1	XC ◇1 B	EM K D	XC ◇1	XC ◇1 E	EM ◇1 L	XC ◇1 G	XC 1 E	EM ◇1	EM ◇1
Nottingham 8	d	14 11	14 18					14 37							15 11	15 18					15 37		
Beeston	d		14 24					14 43								15 24					15 43		
Attenborough	d		14 27													15 27							
Long Eaton	d		14 35					14 51	14 57							15 35					15 51	15 57	
Derby 6	a	14 31	14 47					15 03	15 13						15 31	15 48					16 03	16 09	
	d	14 36		14 53		15 01		15 10		15 20			15 28		15 36		15 53		16 01		16 10		16 18
Willington	d							15 18															
Burton-on-Trent	d	14 49						15 24					15 38		15 49						16 21		
Tamworth	d	15 02						15 35							16 02						16 33		
Wilnecote	d																				16 37		
Leicester	d				14 49	15a23				15a53				15 16				15 49	16a23				16a51
South Wigston	d																						
Narborough	d													15 25									
Hinckley	d													15 34									
Nuneaton	d				15 10									15 42				16 09					
Coleshill Parkway	d				15 25									15 57				16 25					
Water Orton	d													16 01									
Birmingham New Street 12	a	15 24		15 27	15 38			15 54					16 04	16 14	16 24		16 27	16 38			16 54		
	d	15 30					15 42						16 12		16 30					16 42			
Worcester Shrub Hill 7	d																						
Ashchurch for Tewkesbury	d														17 05								
Cheltenham Spa	d	16 11					16 25				16 31	16 45	16 52		17 15					17 25			
Gloucester 7	a	16 22									16 40	16 56			17 26								
Bristol Parkway 7	a						16 56						17 25							17 58			
Bristol Temple Meads 10	a						17 10						17 39							18 10			
Newport (South Wales)	a	17 11										17 50			18 10								
Cardiff Central 7	a	17 28										18 10			18 27								

Station		GW M	GW ◇ N	AW I	XC ◇1 O	XC 1	XC ◇1	EM B	XC ◇1 C	XC ◇1 D	EM ◇1 E L	XC ◇1	XC 1 G	EM ◇1	EM ◇1 E H	GW ◇1 I	AW P	XC ◇1	XC 1	XC ◇1 B	EM C	XC ◇1 Q	XC ◇1
Nottingham 8	d						16 08	16 18					16 37							17 08	17 18		
Beeston	d							16 24					16 43								17 24		
Attenborough	d							16 27													17 27		
Long Eaton	d							16 35					16 51	16 57							17 35		
Derby 6	a						16 31	16 48					17 02	17 09						17 31	17 49		
	d				16 28		16 36		16 53		17 01		17 06		17 18			17 28		17 36		17 53	
Willington	d												17 14										
Burton-on-Trent	d						16 49						17 21					17 38		17 49			
Tamworth	d				16 47		17 02						17 33							18 02			
Wilnecote	d																						
Leicester	d					16 16				16 49	17a23				17a52				17 16				
South Wigston	d					16 22													17 22				
Narborough	d					16 27													17 27				
Hinckley	d					16 35													17 35				
Nuneaton	d					16 41				17 10									17 41				
Coleshill Parkway	d					16 58				17 25									17 58				
Water Orton	d																						
Birmingham New Street 12	a				17 09	17 14	17 24		17 27	17 38			17 52					18 07	18 14	18 24		18 27	
	d				17 12		17 30					17 42						18 12		18 30			18 42
Worcester Shrub Hill 7	d	17 06																					
Ashchurch for Tewkesbury	d	17 24					18 09																
Cheltenham Spa	d	17 33	17 40	17 45	17 52		18 18					18 25				18 34	18 45	18 52		19 15			19 25
Gloucester 7	a	17 42	17 49	17 57			18 29									18 44	18 56			19 27			
Bristol Parkway 7	a	18 22			18 28							18 55						19 27					19 56
Bristol Temple Meads 10	a	18 38			18 41							19 06						19 38					20 09
Newport (South Wales)	a			18 51			19 16										19 50			20 11			20 47
Cardiff Central 7	a			19 09			19 33										20 09			20 27			21 02

- A 🍴 to Newport (South Wales)
- B To Matlock
- C From Newcastle to Reading
- D From Stansted Airport
- E From Sheffield to St Pancras International
- F From Manchester Piccadilly to Paignton
- G From St Pancras International to Sheffield
- H To London Paddington
- I To Maesteg
- J From Aberdeen to Penzance
- K From Newcastle to Eastleigh
- L From Manchester Piccadilly
- M From Great Malvern to Westbury
- N To Southampton Central
- O From Glasgow Central to Penzance
- P From Edinburgh to Plymouth
- Q From Manchester Piccadilly. 🍴 to Bristol Temple Meads

Nottingham, Derby and Leicester Birmingham - Cardiff and Bristol

Network Diagram - see first Page of Table 50

Mondays to Fridays

		XC	EM	XC	EM	EM	GW	AW	XC	XC	GW	XC	EM	XC	XC	EM	XC	XC	EM	EM	GW	XC
		◇■	◇■	■	◇■	◇■			◇■	■		◇■		◇■	◇■	◇■	◇■	■	◇■	◇■	■	◇■
		A	B		C	B	D	E	F		G		H	I	A	B	J		C	B		K
			✠	✠	✠	✠			✠					✠		✠	✠	✠	✠	✠		✠
Nottingham ■ ⇌	d			17 37								18 08	18 18					18 37				
Beeston	d			17 43									18 24					18 43				
Attenborough	d												18 27									
Long Eaton	d			17 51	18 01								18 37					18 51	18 56			
Derby ■	a			18 02	18 14							18 33	18 48					19 02	19 09			
	d		18 01	18 10		18 18			18 28			18 37		18 53		19 01		19 10		19 18		19 28
Willington	d			18 16																		
Burton-on-Trent	d			18 22								18 49						19 21				19 38
Tamworth	d			18 34					18 47			19 02						19 33				
Wilnecote	d			18 37														19 37				
Leicester	d	17 49	18a23			18a51				18 16					18 49	19a23				19a51		
South Wigston	d	17 55								18 22												
Narborough	d	18 01								18 27												
Hinckley	d	18 09								18 35												
Nuneaton	d	18 16								18 41					19 10							
Coleshill Parkway	d	18 32								18 58					19 25							
Water Orton	d																					
Birmingham New Street ■	a	18 45		18 54					19 08	19 14		19 24		19 27	19 38			19 54				20 09
	d								19 12			19 30					19 42					20 12
Worcester Shrub Hill ■	d						19 07															
Ashchurch for Tewkesbury	d						19 24															
Cheltenham Spa	d						19 34	19 45	19 52		20 01	20 11					20 25				20 48	20 52
Gloucester ■	a						19 42	19 56			20 10	20 22									20 58	
Bristol Parkway ■	a						20 22		20 27								20 55				21 50	21 25
Bristol Temple Meads ■	a						20 38		20 40								21 07				22 11	21 36
Newport (South Wales)	a							20 51				21 11										
Cardiff Central ■	a							21 10				21 27										

		XC	GW	XC	XC	EM	XC	XC	EM	XC	XC	EM	XC	EM	XC	XC	XC	XC	NT	EM	GW	GW	XC
				FO	FX																		
		■		◇■	◇■		◇■	◇■	◇■	◇■	■	◇■	◇■		■	◇■	◇■	■		◇■			◇■
			G			H	L	A	B	M		C	N	H		O	A		P	B	G	D	Q
							✠	✠	✠			✠	✠			✠				✠			
Nottingham ■ ⇌	d			19 08	19 08	19 18					19 37			20 11				20 37	20 45				
Beeston	d					19 24					19 43			20 17				20 43					
Attenborough	d					19 27					19 46			20 20									
Long Eaton	d					19 35					19 53	20 07		20 28				20 51					
Derby ■	a			19 32	19 32	19 48					20 02	20 19		20 44				21 02	21 05				
	d			19 36	19 36		19 54		20 01		20 10		20 28			20 54		21 06		21 20			21 29
Willington	d																	21 14					
Burton-on-Trent	d			19 49	19 49						20 21							21 21					21 40
Tamworth	d			20 02	20 02						20 33		20 47					21 33					21 50
Wilnecote	d										20 37							21 37					
Leicester	d	19 16						19 49	20a23						20 18		20 49			21a52			
South Wigston	d	19 22													20 22								
Narborough	d	19 27													20 26								
Hinckley	d	19 35													20 35								
Nuneaton	d	19 41						20 09							20 41		21 09						
Coleshill Parkway	d	19 58						20 24							20 58		21 24						
Water Orton	d																						
Birmingham New Street ■	a	20 14		20 24	20 24		20 27	20 38			20 54		21 07		21 15	21 29	21 37	21 54					22 09
	d			20 30	20 30					20 42			21 12										22 12
Worcester Shrub Hill ■	d																					21 32	
Ashchurch for Tewkesbury	d																					21 52	
Cheltenham Spa	d		21 00	21 11	21 11					21 27			21 52								22 01	22 07	22 52
Gloucester ■	a		21 10	21 22	21 22								22 01								22 11	22 21	
Bristol Parkway ■	a									22 01			22 32									23 04	23 21
Bristol Temple Meads ■	a									22 13			22 44									23 19	23 40
Newport (South Wales)	a			22 15	22 15																		
Cardiff Central ■	a			22 31	22 35																		

A From Stansted Airport
B From Sheffield to St Pancras International
C From St Pancras International to Sheffield
D From Great Malvern
E To Maesteg
F From Glasgow Central to Plymouth
G To Swindon
H To Matlock
I From Newcastle to Reading
J From Manchester Piccadilly to Plymouth
K From Edinburgh to Plymouth
L From Newcastle to Guildford
M From Manchester Piccadilly
N From Glasgow Central. ✠ to Birmingham New Street
O From Newcastle
P To Sheffield
Q from 25 June. From Edinburgh

Mondays to Fridays

Nottingham, Derby and Leicester Birmingham - Cardiff and Bristol

Network Diagram - see first Page of Table 50

		AW	AW	GW	XC	XC	XC	XC	XC	LM	XC	XC	XC
		FO	FX							FO			
					◇■	■	◇■	◇■	■		■	◇■	◇■
					A		B	C				D	B
Nottingham ■ ⇌	d								21 37				
Beeston	d								21 43				
Attenborough	d								21 46				
Long Eaton	d								21 53				
Derby ■	a								22 04				
	d				21 29			22 02	22 10			22 45	
Willington	d												
Burton-on-Trent	d				21 40				22 21			22 56	
Tamworth	d				21 50				22 33			23 06	
Wilnecote	d								22 36				
Leicester	d					21 16	21 49				22 27		22 49
South Wigston	d					21 22					22 33		
Narborough	d					21 27					22 38		
Hinckley	d					21 35					22 46		
Nuneaton	d					21 42	22 10				22 54		23 10
Coleshill Parkway	d					21 59	22 25				23 10		23 25
Water Orton	d												
Birmingham New Street ■	a				22 07	22 14	22 38	22 51	23 00		23 25	23 25	23 41
	d				22 12					23 00			
Worcester Shrub Hill ■	d			22 28						23 46			
Ashchurch for Tewkesbury	d			22 51						00 01			
Cheltenham Spa	d	23 00	23 00	23 05	23 31					00 09			
Gloucester ■	a	23 12	23 12	23 17						00 20			
Bristol Parkway ■	a				00 01								
Bristol Temple Meads ■	a				00 13								
Newport (South Wales)	a	00 06	00 06										
Cardiff Central ■	a	00 33	00 35										

Saturdays

		AW	XC	LM	GW	XC	XC	GW	GW	XC	XC	EM	EM	GW	AW	XC	EM	XC	EM	XC	XC	XC	EM
			◇■			◇■	◇■		◇	◇■	■	◇■	◇■	◇■		◇■	◇■	◇■		◇■	◇■	■	◇■
			E		F			G	H	I		J	K	L	M	N	J	O	P	Q	R		K
										✠		✠	✠	⊡		✠	✠	✠			✠		✠
Nottingham ■ ⇌	d																	05 57	06 18				
Beeston	d																	06 03	06 24				
Attenborough	d																	06 06	06 27				
Long Eaton	d																	06 17	06 34				
Derby ■	a																	06 32	06 48				
	d		21p29									05 25	06 01			06 10	06 18	06 36		06 48			07 01
Willington	d																						
Burton-on-Trent	d		21p40													06 20		06 48		06 59			
Tamworth	d		21p50													06 31		07 01		07 09			
Wilnecote	d																	07 05					
Leicester	d										05 49	05a57	06a23				06a51					06 49	07a23
South Wigston	d										05 55											06 55	
Narborough	d										06 00											07 00	
Hinckley	d										06 08											07 08	
Nuneaton	d										06 14											07 14	
Coleshill Parkway	d										06 30											07 30	
Water Orton	d																					07 35	
Birmingham New Street ■	a		22p07								06 43					06 50		07 24		07 27		07 47	
	d		22p12	23p00		05 00	05 42			06 42						07 12		07 30			07 42		
Worcester Shrub Hill ■	d			23p46					06 47														
Ashchurch for Tewkesbury	d			00 01			06 33		07 03														
Cheltenham Spa	d	23p00	23p31	00 09	05 30	06 04	06 43	06 48	07 13	07 25				07 30	07 45	07 52		08 11			08 25		
Gloucester ■	a	23p12		00 20	05 40	06 13	06 54	06 58	07 24					07 40	07 57			08 22					
Bristol Parkway ■	a		00 01					07 39	08 19	07 54						08 24					08 54		
Bristol Temple Meads ■	a		00 13					07 54	08 34	08 05						08 38					09 08		
Newport (South Wales)	a	00 06				07 06	07 52								08 50			09 07					
Cardiff Central ■	a	00 33				07 22	08 08								09 10			09 23					

A until 22 June. From Edinburgh
B From Stansted Airport
C From Newcastle
D From Glasgow Central
E until 23 June. From Edinburgh
F To Swindon
G To Weston-super-Mare
H To Weymouth
I To Paignton
J To St Pancras International
K From Sheffield to St Pancras International
L To London Paddington
M To Maesteg
N To Plymouth. ✠ from Birmingham New Street
O ✠ from Birmingham New Street to Newport (South Wales)
P To Matlock
Q From Sheffield to Reading
R From Manchester Piccadilly

Nottingham, Derby and Leicester Birmingham - Cardiff and Bristol

Network Diagram - see first Page of Table 50

		XC	XC	EM	AW	XC		GW	XC	EM	XC	XC	EM	XC	XC	EM		EM	GW	XC	XC	XC	GW	XC	EM
		◇1	◇1	◇1		◇1		◇1	◇1		◇1	◇1	◇1	◇1	1	◇1		◇1		◇1	◇1	1		◇1	
		A 🛒	B	C 🛒	D	E 🛒		F	G H 🛒	I	J 🛒	K 🛒	L ⊠🛒	🛒	M	🛒	C	N 🛒	O P	🛒	Q 🛒	R	H	🛒	
Nottingham	d	06 37							06 56	07 18					07 37									08 08	08 18
Beeston	d	06 43							07 02	07 24					07 43										08 24
Attenborough	d								07 06	07 27															08 27
Long Eaton	d								07 14	07 35					07 51	07 56									08 35
Derby	a	07 02							07 30	07 49					08 02	08 09								08 31	08 48
	d	07 06		07 18		07 26			07 36		07 50		08 01		08 06			08 18		08 28	08 28			08 36	
Willington	d								07 43																
Burton-on-Trent	d	07 18				07 37			07 50		08 00				08 18					08 39	08 39			08 49	
Tamworth	d	07 30				07 48			08 02		08 11				08 30					08 49	08 49			09 02	
Wilnecote	d								08 05						08 34										
Leicester	d		07 16	07a51								07 49	08a23					08a51				08 16			
South Wigston	d																					08 22			
Narborough	d																					08 27			
Hinckley	d																					08 35			
Nuneaton	d		07 35									08 09										08 43			
Coleshill Parkway	d		07 51									08 24										09 01			
Water Orton	d																								
Birmingham New Street	a	07 52	08 04			08 08			08 24		08 27	08 38			08 54					09 08	09 09	09 14		09 24	
	d					08 12			08 30					08 42						09 12	09 12			09 30	
Worcester Shrub Hill	d																		09 08						
Ashchurch for Tewkesbury	d																		09 25						
Cheltenham Spa	d				08 45	08 52		09 00	09 11					09 25					09 35	09 52	09 52		10 01	10 11	
Gloucester	a				08 57			09 10	09 22										09 44				10 11	10 22	
Bristol Parkway	a					09 24								09 55					10 24	10 29	10 29				
Bristol Temple Meads	a					09 38								10 06					10 39	10 42	10 42				
Newport (South Wales)	a				09 50				10 07															11 08	
Cardiff Central	a				10 07				10 23															11 24	

		XC		XC	EM	XC	XC	EM	EM	AW	XC	XC		XC	GW	XC	EM	XC	XC	EM	XC	XC		EM	EM
		◇1		◇1	◇1	◇1	1	◇1	◇1		◇1	◇1		1	◇1	◇1		◇1	◇1	◇1	◇1	1		◇1	◇1
		S 🛒		J 🛒	K 🛒	T 🛒	U	K 🛒	D 🛒	V	W 🛒	🛒	F	R	H	X 🛒	J K	L 🛒	🛒	🛒	M 🛒	K		🛒	🛒
Nottingham	d						08 37									09 08	09 18					09 37			
Beeston	d						08 43										09 24					09 43			
Attenborough	d																09 27								
Long Eaton	d						08 51	09 01									09 35					09 51		09 57	
Derby	a						09 03	09 14								09 31	09 48					10 02		10 09	
	d	08 53			09 01		09 10		09 20		09 27	09 27				09 36		09 53		10 01		10 10			10 20
Willington	d																								
Burton-on-Trent	d						09 21				09 38	09 41				09 49						10 21			
Tamworth	d						09 33									10 02						10 33			
Wilnecote	d						09 37															10 37			
Leicester	d			08 49	09a23				09a54					09 16					09 49	10a23					10a54
South Wigston	d																								
Narborough	d													09 25											
Hinckley	d													09 34											
Nuneaton	d			09 09										09 41					10 09						
Coleshill Parkway	d			09 24										09 56					10 24						
Water Orton	d													10 01											
Birmingham New Street	a	09 27		09 38			09 54				10 04	10 04		10 14		10 24		10 27	10 38			10 54			
	d					09 42					10 12	10 12				10 30					10 42				
Worcester Shrub Hill	d																								
Ashchurch for Tewkesbury	d																								
Cheltenham Spa	d					10 25				10 45	10 52	10 52			11 00	11 11					11 25				
Gloucester	a									10 56					11 09	11 22									
Bristol Parkway	a					10 57					11 24	11 24									11 54				
Bristol Temple Meads	a					11 09					11 37	11 38									12 08				
Newport (South Wales)	a									11 50						12 07									
Cardiff Central	a									12 07						12 23									

A To Bournemouth. 🛒 from Derby
B From Cambridge
C To St Pancras International
D To Maesteg
E From Leeds to Paignton
F To London Paddington
G 🛒 from Birmingham New Street to Newport (South Wales)
H To Matlock
I From Leeds to Southampton Central
J From Stansted Airport
K From Sheffield to St Pancras International
L From Manchester Piccadilly
M From St Pancras International to Sheffield
N To Westbury
O from 15 September. From York to Plymouth
P until 8 September. From York to Plymouth
Q To Swindon
R 🛒 to Newport (South Wales)
S From Newcastle to Reading
T From Manchester Piccadilly to Paignton
U From Leicester to Sheffield
V from 15 September. From Newcastle to Plymouth
W until 8 September. From York to Penzance
X From Newcastle to Southampton Central

Nottingham, Derby and Leicester Birmingham - Cardiff and Bristol

Network Diagram - see first Page of Table 50

		GW	AW	XC	XC	GW	XC	EM		XC	XC	EM	XC	XC	EM	EM	XC	XC		GW	XC	EM	XC	XC	EM
		1		◇1	1		◇1			◇1	◇1	◇1	◇1	1	◇1	◇1	◇1	1		◇1	◇1		◇1	◇1	◇1
		A	B	C 🛒		D	E 🛒	F		G H 🛒	I 🛒	J 🛒	🛒	K	I 🛒	L 🛒	🛒		M	E F	N 🛒	H	I 🛒	🛒	🛒
Nottingham	d						10 08	10 18						10 37							11 11	11 18			
Beeston	d							10 24						10 43								11 24			
Attenborough	d							10 27														11 27			
Long Eaton	d							10 35						10 51	10 57							11 36			
Derby	a						10 31	10 49						11 02	11 09						11 31	11 48			
	d			10 28			10 37			10 53		11 01		11 10		11 20	11 27				11 36		11 54		12 01
Willington	d																								
Burton-on-Trent	d						10 49							11 21			11 39				11 49				
Tamworth	d			10 48			11 02							11 33							12 02				
Wilnecote	d													11 37											
Leicester	d				10 16						10 49	11a23				11a54		11 16						11 49	12a23
South Wigston	d				10 22																				
Narborough	d				10 27													11 25							
Hinckley	d				10 35													11 34							
Nuneaton	d				10 42						11 09							11 41						12 09	
Coleshill Parkway	d				10 58						11 24							11 56						12 24	
Water Orton	d																	12 02							
Birmingham New Street	a			11 04	11 14		11 24			11 27	11 38			11 54			12 07	12 14			12 24		12 27	12 38	
	d			11 12			11 30						11 42				12 12				12 30				
Worcester Shrub Hill	d	11 06																							
Ashchurch for Tewkesbury	d	11 24																							
Cheltenham Spa	d	11 34	11 45	11 52		12 01	12 11						12 25				12 52			13 00	13 11				
Gloucester	a	11 44	11 57			12 11	12 22													13 10	13 22				
Bristol Parkway	a	12 24		12 29									12 55				13 24								
Bristol Temple Meads	a	12 39		12 42									13 07				13 38								
Newport (South Wales)	a		12 50				13 11														14 08				
Cardiff Central	a		13 07				13 27														14 24				

		GW	XC	XC		EM	EM	AW	XC	XC	GW	XC	EM	XC		XC	EM	XC	XC	EM	EM	AW	XC	XC	
		◇	◇1	1		◇1	◇1		◇1	1		◇1		◇1		◇1	◇1	◇1	1	◇1	◇1		◇1	1	
		O	J 🛒	🛒	K	I 🛒	B 🛒	P	🛒	D	Q	F 🛒	R	🛒	H I	S 🛒	🛒	K 🛒	I 🛒	B 🛒	L 🛒	🛒	🛒		
Nottingham	d			11 37								12 08	12 18						12 37						
Beeston	d			11 43									12 24						12 43						
Attenborough	d												12 27												
Long Eaton	d			11 51		11 57							12 36						12 51	12 57					
Derby	a			12 02		12 09						12 31	12 48						13 02	13 09					
	d			12 10			12 20		12 29			12 36		12 53			13 01		13 06		13 20		13 28		
Willington	d																		13 14						
Burton-on-Trent	d			12 21								12 49							13 21				13 38		
Tamworth	d			12 33					12 49			13 02							13 33						
Wilnecote	d			12 37																					
Leicester	d						12a54			12 16						12 49	13a23				13a54			13 16	
South Wigston	d									12 22															
Narborough	d									12 27														13 25	
Hinckley	d									12 35														13 34	
Nuneaton	d									12 42						13 09								13 41	
Coleshill Parkway	d									12 58						13 24								13 56	
Water Orton	d																							14 00	
Birmingham New Street	a			12 54					13 09	13 14		13 24		13 27		13 38			13 54				14 07	14 14	
	d		12 42						13 12			13 30						13 42					14 12		
Worcester Shrub Hill	d	12 54																							
Ashchurch for Tewkesbury	d	13 10																							
Cheltenham Spa	d	13 20	13 26					13 45	13 52		14 01	14 11						14 25				14 45	14 52		
Gloucester	a	13 32						13 57			14 11	14 22										14 56			
Bristol Parkway	a	14 20	13 57						14 26									14 57					15 23		
Bristol Temple Meads	a	14 36	14 08						14 41									15 09					15 37		
Newport (South Wales)	a							14 50				15 11										15 50			
Cardiff Central	a							15 09				15 27										16 07			

A From Great Malvern to Brighton
B To Maesteg
C From Edinburgh to Plymouth
D To Swindon
E 🛒 to Newport (South Wales)
F To Matlock
G From Edinburgh to Reading
H From Stansted Airport
I From Sheffield to St Pancras International
J From Manchester Piccadilly
K From St Pancras International to Sheffield
L From Glasgow Central to Plymouth
M To London Paddington
N From Newcastle to Southampton Central
O From Worcester Foregate Street to Weymouth
P From Dundee to Plymouth
Q 🛒 from Birmingham New Street to Newport (South Wales)
R From Newcastle to Reading
S From Manchester Piccadilly to Exeter St Davids

Nottingham, Derby and Leicester
Birmingham - Cardiff and Bristol

Network Diagram - see first Page of Table 50

		GW ◇■ A	XC ◇■ B ⊼	EM C	XC ◇■ D ⊼	XC ◇■ E ⊼	EM ◇■ F ⊼	XC ◇■ G ⊼	XC ■ H ⊼	EM ◇■ ⊼	F	EM ◇■ I ⊼	GW ◇ J	XC ◇■ ⊼	XC ■ K	GW L	XC ◇■ C ⊼	EM M	XC ◇■ E ⊼	XC ◇■ F ⊼	G	EM ◇■ ⊼	XC ◇■ H ⊼	XC ■ ⊼	EM ◇■ ⊼
Nottingham ■	d		13 08	13 18					13 37								14 08	14 18						14 37	
Beeston	d			13 24					13 43									14 24						14 43	
Attenborough	d			13 27														14 27							
Long Eaton	d			13 35					13 51	13 57								14 36						14 51	14 57
Derby ■	a		13 31	13 48					14 02	14 09							14 32	14 48						15 02	15 09
	d		13 36		13 53		14 01		14 06			14 20		14 30			14 36		14 53			15 01		15 10	
Willington	d																							15 18	
Burton-on-Trent	d		13 49						14 18								14 49							15 24	
Tamworth	d		14 02						14 30					14 49			15 02							15 33	
Wilnecote	d								14 34																
Leicester	d					13 49	14a23					14a54			14 16					14 49		15a23			
South Wigston	d														14 22										
Narborough	d														14 27										
Hinckley	d														14 35										
Nuneaton	d					14 09									14 42					15 09					
Coleshill Parkway	d					14 24									14 58					15 24					
Water Orton	d																								
Birmingham New Street ■	a		14 24		14 27	14 38			14 54					15 08	15 14		15 24		15 27	15 38				15 54	
	d		14 30					14 42						15 12			15 30						15 42		
Worcester Shrub Hill ■	d												15 06												
Ashchurch for Tewkesbury	d												15 24												
Cheltenham Spa	d	15 00	15 11					15 25					15 34	15 52		16 01	16 11						16 25		
Gloucester ■	a	15 10	15 22										15 42			16 11	16 22								
Bristol Parkway ■	a							15 55					16 24	16 29									16 54		
Bristol Temple Meads ■	a							16 08					16 39	16 42									17 07		
Newport (South Wales)	a		16 08														17 10								
Cardiff Central ■	a		16 25														17 26								

		EM ◇■ F ⊼	AW N	XC ◇■ O ⊼	XC ■	GW ◇■ A		XC ◇■ ⊼	EM C	XC ◇■ D ⊼	XC ◇■ E ⊼	EM ◇■ F ⊼	XC ◇■ G ⊼	XC ■ H ⊼	EM ◇■ F ⊼	EM ◇■ ⊼	P	GW N	AW Q	XC ◇■ ⊼	XC ■ K	GW C	XC ◇■ M	EM	XC ◇■ ⊼
Nottingham ■	d							15 08	15 18					15 37									16 08	16 18	
Beeston	d								15 24					15 43										16 24	
Attenborough	d								15 27															16 27	
Long Eaton	d								15 36					15 51	15 57									16 36	
Derby ■	a							15 31	15 48					16 02	16 09								16 31	16 48	
	d	15 20		15 28				15 36		15 53		16 01		16 10		16 20				16 28			16 36		16 53
Willington	d																								
Burton-on-Trent	d			15 38				15 49						16 21									16 49		
Tamworth	d							16 02						16 33						16 48			17 02		
Wilnecote	d													16 37											
Leicester	d	15a54			15 16						15 49	16a23				16a54					16 16				
South Wigston	d																				16 22				
Narborough	d				15 25																16 27				
Hinckley	d				15 34																16 35				
Nuneaton	d				15 41						16 09										16 42				
Coleshill Parkway	d				15 57						16 24										16 58				
Water Orton	d				16 00																				
Birmingham New Street ■	a			16 04	16 14			16 24		16 27	16 38			16 54						17 07	17 14		17 24		17 27
	d			16 12				16 30					16 42							17 12			17 30		
Worcester Shrub Hill ■	d																	17 08							
Ashchurch for Tewkesbury	d																	17 24					18 08		
Cheltenham Spa	d		16 45	16 52		17 00		17 11					17 25					17 34	17 45	17 52		18 01	18 18		
Gloucester ■	a		16 56			17 10		17 22										17 44	17 56			18 11	18 29		
Bristol Parkway ■	a			17 24									17 54					18 24		18 29					
Bristol Temple Meads ■	a			17 38									18 07					18 39		18 42					
Newport (South Wales)	a		17 50					18 05											18 50				19 12		
Cardiff Central ■	a		18 10					18 21											19 10				19 29		

A To London Paddington
B ⊼ from Birmingham New Street to Newport (South Wales)
C To Matlock
D From Newcastle to Southampton Central
E From Stansted Airport
F From Sheffield to St Pancras International
G From Manchester Piccadilly
H From St Pancras International to Sheffield
I From Great Malvern to Weymouth
J From Glasgow Central to Penzance
K To Swindon
L ⊼ to Newport (South Wales)
M From Newcastle to Reading
N To Maesteg
O From Aberdeen to Penzance
P From Great Malvern to Westbury
Q From Glasgow Central to Plymouth

Nottingham, Derby and Leicester
Birmingham - Cardiff and Bristol

Network Diagram - see first Page of Table 50

		XC ◇■ A ⊼		EM ◇■ B ⊼	XC ◇■ C ⊼	XC ■ ⊼	EM ◇■ D ⊼	EM ◇■ B ⊼	AW E	XC ◇■ F ⊼	XC ■	GW ◇■ G		XC ◇■ H	EM I	XC ◇■ A ⊼	XC ◇■ B	EM ◇■ C ⊼	XC ◇■ ⊼	XC ■ D ⊼	EM ◇■ B ⊼	EM ◇■ ⊼	J	GW E	AW
Nottingham ■	d					16 37								17 11	17 18					17 37					
Beeston	d					16 43									17 24					17 43					
Attenborough	d														17 27										
Long Eaton	d					16 51	16 56								17 35					17 51	17 57				
Derby ■	a					17 02	17 09							17 31	17 48					18 02	18 09				
	d			17 01		17 06		17 18		17 28				17 36		17 53		18 01		18 10		18 18			
Willington	d					17 14														18 16					
Burton-on-Trent	d					17 21				17 38				17 49						18 22					
Tamworth	d					17 33								18 02						18 34					
Wilnecote	d																			18 37					
Leicester	d	16 49		17a23				17a51			17 16						17 49	18a23				18a51			
South Wigston	d										17 22														
Narborough	d										17 27														
Hinckley	d										17 35														
Nuneaton	d	17 09									17 41						18 09								
Coleshill Parkway	d	17 24									17 58						18 24								
Water Orton	d																								
Birmingham New Street ■	a	17 38				17 54				18 07	18 14			18 24		18 27	18 38			18 54					
	d				17 42					18 12				18 30					18 42						
Worcester Shrub Hill ■	d																							19 07	
Ashchurch for Tewkesbury	d																							19 24	
Cheltenham Spa	d				18 25				18 45	18 52		19 00		19 11					19 25					19 34	19 45
Gloucester ■	a								18 56			19 10		19 22										19 42	19 56
Bristol Parkway ■	a				18 54					19 25									19 55					20 24	
Bristol Temple Meads ■	a				19 05					19 39									20 06					20 39	
Newport (South Wales)	a								19 50					20 05					20 55						20 50
Cardiff Central ■	a								20 11					20 21					21 11						21 09

		XC ◇■ K ⊼	XC ■	GW L	XC ◇■	EM M	EM N	XC ◇■ I ⊼		XC ◇■ A	EM ◇■ B ⊼	XC ◇■ C ⊼	XC ■ ⊼	EM ◇■ D ⊼	EM ◇■ O ⊼	XC ◇■ F ⊼	XC ■	GW		XC ◇■ H	EM P	XC ◇■ A ⊼	XC ◇■ B ⊼	EM ◇■ Q ⊼	GW
Nottingham ■	d				18 08	18 19	18 19						18 37							19 08	19 18				
Beeston	d					18 24	18 24						18 43								19 24				
Attenborough	d					18 26	18 27														19 27				
Long Eaton	d					18 37	18 37						18 51	18 57							19 35				
Derby ■	a				18 31	18 48	18 48						19 02	19 09						19 32	19 48				
	d	18 28			18 36			18 53			19 01		19 10		19 21	19 27				19 36		19 54		20 01	
Willington	d																								
Burton-on-Trent	d				18 49								19 21			19 37				19 49					
Tamworth	d	18 46			19 02								19 33							20 02					
Wilnecote	d												19 37												
Leicester	d		18 16							18 49	19a23				19a54		19 16						19 49	20a23	
South Wigston	d		18 22														19 22								
Narborough	d		18 27														19 27								
Hinckley	d		18 35														19 35								
Nuneaton	d		18 42							19 09							19 42						20 09		
Coleshill Parkway	d		18 58							19 24							19 58						20 24		
Water Orton	d																								
Birmingham New Street ■	a	19 06	19 14		19 24			19 27		19 38			19 54			20 06	20 15			20 24		20 27	20 38		
	d	19 12			19 30							19 42				20 12				20 30					
Worcester Shrub Hill ■	d																								
Ashchurch for Tewkesbury	d																								
Cheltenham Spa	d	19 52		20 01	20 11							20 25				20 50		21 02		21 11					21 19
Gloucester ■	a			20 11	20 22													21 12		21 22					21 29
Bristol Parkway ■	a	20 29										20 54				21 22		21 53							
Bristol Temple Meads ■	a	20 42										21 05				21 35		22 05							
Newport (South Wales)	a				21 11															22 21					
Cardiff Central ■	a				21 29															22 43					

A From Stansted Airport
B From Sheffield to St Pancras International
C From Manchester Piccadilly
D From St Pancras International to Sheffield
E To Maesteg
F From Edinburgh to Plymouth
G To London Paddington
H To Matlock
I From Newcastle to Reading
J From Great Malvern
K From Glasgow Central to Plymouth
L To Westbury
M until 29 September. To Matlock
N from 6 October. To Matlock
O From Scarborough to St Pancras International
P From Newcastle to Guildford
Q To Swindon

Table 57

Nottingham, Derby and Leicester Birmingham - Cardiff and Bristol

Network Diagram - see first Page of Table 50

		XC	XC	EM		XC	EM	XC	XC	XC	EM	XC	XC	XC		GW	XC	XC	XC	XC	XC	XC	XC	XC
		◇■	■	◇■		◇■		■	◇■	◇■	◇■	■	◇■	■			◇■	◇■	■		◇■	■	◇■	◇■
		A		B		C	D		E	F	G		H		I	F	E	J	K	L	M	K		
		✠		✠		✠			✠		✠									🚌				
Nottingham	d		19 37				20 09					20 37							21 37					
Beeston	d		19 43				20 15					20 43							21 43					
Attenborough	d		19 46				20 18												21 46					
Long Eaton	d		19 53	19 57			20 27					20 51							21 53					
Derby	a		20 02	20 09			20 42					21 02							22 04					
	d		20 10			20 28			20 53		21 01	21 06	21 28					21 53	22 10	22 10	22 26		22 26	
Willington	d											21 14												
Burton-on-Trent	d		20 21									21 21	21 38						22 21	22 30	22 38		22 38	
Tamworth	d		20 33			20 46						21 33	21 49						22 33	22a55	22 48			23 00
Wilnecote	d		20 37									21 36							22 36					23 03
Leicester	d							20 16		20 49	21a36			21 18			21 49					22 16		
South Wigston	d							20 22						21 22								22 22		
Narborough	d							20 27						21 27								22 27		
Hinckley	d							20 35						21 35								22 35		
Nuneaton	d							20 42		21 09				21 42			22 09					22 42		
Coleshill Parkway	d							20 58		21 24				21 58			22 24					22 58		
Water Orton	d																							
Birmingham New Street	a		20 54			21 03		21 14	21 25	21 38		21 54	22 05	22 14			22 38	22 43	23 02		23 05	23 13	23 15	23 21
	d	20 42				21 12																		
Worcester Shrub Hill	d															21 31								
Ashchurch for Tewkesbury	d															21 51								
Cheltenham Spa	d	21 25				21 50										22 01								
Gloucester	a					21 59										22 10								
Bristol Parkway	a	21 58				22 30																		
Bristol Temple Meads	a	22 12				22 41																		
Newport (South Wales)	a																							
Cardiff Central	a																							

		XC	XC	XC	XC
		◇■	◇■		
		N	O	P	K
				🚌	🚌
Nottingham	d				
Beeston	d				
Attenborough	d				
Long Eaton	d				
Derby	a				
	d	22 26	22 26		22 35
Willington	d				
Burton-on-Trent	d			22 45	22 55
Tamworth	d			23 05	23a15
Wilnecote	d			23 10	
Leicester	d				
South Wigston	d				
Narborough	d				
Hinckley	d				
Nuneaton	d				
Coleshill Parkway	d				
Water Orton	d				
Birmingham New Street	a	23 34	23 38	23 40	
	d				
Worcester Shrub Hill	d				
Ashchurch for Tewkesbury	d				
Cheltenham Spa	d				
Gloucester	a				
Bristol Parkway	a				
Bristol Temple Meads	a				
Newport (South Wales)	a				
Cardiff Central	a				

A From Manchester Piccadilly
B From St Pancras International to Sheffield
C From Glasgow Central. ✠ to Birmingham New Street
D To Matlock
E From Newcastle
F From Stansted Airport
G From Sheffield
H From Edinburgh
I From Great Malvern
J until 23 June
K from 30 June until 8 September, from 27 October
L until 23 June. From Glasgow Central
M from 15 September until 20 October. From Glasgow Central
N from 27 October. From Glasgow Central
O from 30 June until 8 September. From Glasgow Central
P from 15 September until 20 October

Table 57

Nottingham, Derby and Leicester Birmingham - Cardiff and Bristol

Network Diagram - see first Page of Table 50

		EM	EM	EM	EM	GW	XC	GW	XC	XC		EM	EM	GW	XC	GW	XC	EM	EM	AW		XC	XC	GW	XC
		◇■	◇■	◇■	◇■		◇■		◇■	◇■			◇■	◇■	◇■		◇■	◇■	◇■			◇■	■		◇■
		A	A	A	B	C	D	E		F		G	B	H			F	I	J			K		C	L
		✠	✠	✠	✠		✠		✠	✠			✠	☕	✠		✠	✠	☕			✠			✠
Nottingham	d											09 19													11 11
Beeston	d											09 24													
Attenborough	d											09 28													
Long Eaton	d											09 36						10 32							
Derby	a											09 47						10 43							11 31
	d	06 06	07 09	08 06	09 06					09 28			10 08				10 34		11 08			11 30			11 36
Willington	d																								
Burton-on-Trent	d																					11 41			11 48
Tamworth	d																10 53								12 00
Wilnecote	d																								
Leicester	d	06a40	07a44	08a44	09a44								10a42						11a43				11 19		
South Wigston	d																								
Narborough	d																						11 28		
Hinckley	d																						11 36		
Nuneaton	d																						11 42		
Coleshill Parkway	d																						11 57		
Water Orton	d																								
Birmingham New Street	a									10 19							11 20					12 04	12 14		12 24
	d						09 12		10 12	10 30					11 12		11 30					12 12			12 30
Worcester Shrub Hill	d																								
Ashchurch for Tewkesbury	d																								
Cheltenham Spa	d					09 24	09 52	10 05	10 53	11 10				11 46	11 53	12 00	12 10			12 18		12 52		13 01	13 11
Gloucester	a					09 34		10 15	11 03					11 56	12 03	12 11				12 28				13 11	13 21
Bristol Parkway	a						10 21	10 52		11 39						12 54	12 39					13 21			
Bristol Temple Meads	a						10 32	11 07		11 52						13 10	12 51					13 32			
Newport (South Wales)	a								11 48						12 52					13 33					14 06
Cardiff Central	a								12 08						13 12					13 52					14 26

		EM	EM	GW	XC	XC		XC	XC	EM	AW	XC	XC	XC	GW	XC		EM	XC	XC	EM	XC	GW	XC	XC
		◇■	◇■	◇■	◇■	■		◇■	◇■	◇■		◇■	◇■	■		◇■			◇■	◇■	◇■	◇■	◇■	◇■	■
		B	M	H	N			L	O	M		P			Q	L		G	R	O	B	S	H	T	
		✠	✠	☕	✠			✠	✠	✠		✠	✠			✠			✠	✠	✠	✠	☕	✠	
Nottingham	d							12 10								13 06		13 22							
Beeston	d																	13 27							
Attenborough	d																	13 31							
Long Eaton	d		12 13							13 22								13 39							
Derby	a		12 23					12 30		13 32						13 26		13 50							
	d	12 21			12 30			12 36					13 32			13 36			13 54		14 00			14 31	
Willington	d																								
Burton-on-Trent	d							12 48					13 43			13 48									
Tamworth	d				12 48			13 00								14 00								14 50	
Wilnecote	d																								
Leicester	d	12a53				12 19			12 49					13 19						13 49	14a33				14 19
South Wigston	d					12 24																			14 24
Narborough	d					12 29								13 28											14 29
Hinckley	d					12 38								13 36											14 38
Nuneaton	d					12 45			13 08					13 43						14 08					14 45
Coleshill Parkway	d					13 00			13 23					13 59						14 23					15 00
Water Orton	d																								
Birmingham New Street	a				13 05	13 15		13 24	13 36				14 08	14 15		14 24			14 27	14 36				15 06	15 15
	d				13 12			13 30				13 42	14 12			14 30						14 42		15 12	
Worcester Shrub Hill	d														14 36										
Ashchurch for Tewkesbury	d														14 51										
Cheltenham Spa	d			13 46	13 52			14 12			14 18	14 24	14 52		15 01	15 11						15 25	15 46	15 52	
Gloucester	a			13 57				14 22			14 29				15 10	15 21							15 57		
Bristol Parkway	a				14 21							14 54	15 24		15 49							15 59		16 21	
Bristol Temple Meads	a				14 32							15 07	15 36		16 09							16 11		16 35	
Newport (South Wales)	a							15 08			15 34					16 06									
Cardiff Central	a							15 31			15 53					16 26									

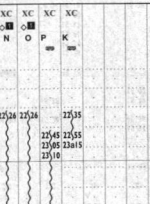

A To St Pancras International
B From Sheffield to St Pancras International
C To Swindon
D To Penzance
E To Taunton
F From Leeds to Plymouth
G To Matlock
H To London Paddington
I From Leicester to York
J From Leeds to St Pancras International
K From Leeds to Plymouth
L ✠ to Newport (South Wales)
M From St Pancras International to Sheffield
N From Newcastle to Plymouth
O From Stansted Airport
P From Edinburgh to Plymouth
Q To Weston-super-Mare
R To Reading
S From Manchester Piccadilly to Paignton
T From Edinburgh to Penzance

Nottingham, Derby and Leicester Birmingham - Cardiff and Bristol

Network Diagram - see first Page of Table 50

		XC		EM	EM	XC	XC	EM	AW	XC	GW	XC		XC	EM	GW	XC	EM	XC	EM	XC	EM		XC	GW
		◇■		◇■	◇■	◇■	◇■	◇■		◇■		◇■		■	◇■		◇■		◇■	◇■	◇■	◇■		◇■	◇■
		A		B	C	D	E	B		F	G	H		I			J	K	B	E C		F	L		
		⊼		⊼	⊼	⊼	⊼	⊼		⊼		⊼			⊼		⊼		⊼	⊼	⊼	⊼		⊼	⎍
Nottingham	d	14 10															15 10	15 21							
Beeston	d																15 27							
Attenborough	d																15 31							
Long Eaton	d			14 26				15 06										15 39		15 44					
Derby	a	14 29		14 38				15 18									15 30	15 50		15 55					
	d	14 35			14 51	14 53						15 26			15 34		15 35		15 54			16 08			
Willington	d																							
Burton-on-Trent	d	14 48										15 39					15 48								
Tamworth	d	15 00															16 00								
Wilnecote	d															16 03								
Leicester	d				15a23		14 49							15 19	16a11						15 49	16a33			
South Wigston	d																							
Narborough	d												15 28											
Hinckley	d												15 36											
Nuneaton	d						15 08							15 43							16 07				
Coleshill Parkway	d						15 23							15 58							16 22				
Water Orton	d																							
Birmingham New Street	a	15 21				15 27	15 36					16 02		16 15			16 24		16 27		16 36				
	d	15 30								15 42		16 12					16 30							16 42	
Worcester Shrub Hill	d														16 40									
Ashchurch for Tewkesbury	d														16 58									
Cheltenham Spa	d	16 11							16 18	16 25	16 33	16 51				17 08	17 11							17 25	17 46
Gloucester	a	16 21							16 29		16 43					17 16	17 21								17 56
Bristol Parkway	a								16 55		17 20				17 57								18 02	
Bristol Temple Meads	a								17 08		17 35				18 10								18 13	
Newport (South Wales)	a	17 06							17 37								18 07								
Cardiff Central	a	17 27							17 57								18 29								

		XC	XC	XC	EM	EM	XC	XC		EM	XC	AW	XC	XC	GW	XC	EM	EM		XC	EM	XC	EM	XC	XC
		◇■	■	◇■	◇■	◇■	◇■	◇■		◇■	◇■		◇■	■		◇■	◇■			◇■	◇■	◇■	◇■	◇■	◇■
		M		A	N	O	K	E	C	F		P			A	N	J		Q	B	E C	R	S		
		⊼		⊼	⊼	⊼	⊼	⊼		⊼	⊼		⊼			⊼	⊼			⊼	⊼		⊼	⊼	⊼
Nottingham	d			16 10												17 10		17 23							
Beeston	d																17 28							
Attenborough	d																17 32							
Long Eaton	d					16 43												17 40			17 44				
Derby	a			16 30		16 55										17 29		17 51			17 56				
	d	16 29		16 35	16 48		16 55			17 08			17 27			17 36	17 47			17 54			18 04		18 26
Willington	d																							
Burton-on-Trent	d			16 48									17 38			17 48									
Tamworth	d	16 48		17 00												18 00									18 45
Wilnecote	d																							
Leicester	d		16 19		17a20			16 49		17a38				17 18			18a19					17 49	18a33		
South Wigston	d		16 24											17 24											
Narborough	d		16 29											17 29											
Hinckley	d		16 38											17 38											
Nuneaton	d		16 45					17 08						17 45								18 08			
Coleshill Parkway	d		17 00					17 23						18 00								18 23			
Water Orton	d																							
Birmingham New Street	a	17 04	17 15	17 19			17 27	17 36					18 01	18 15		18 19				18 24		18 36			19 04
	d	17 12		17 30							17 42		18 12			18 30								18 42	19 12
Worcester Shrub Hill	d															18 40										
Ashchurch for Tewkesbury	d															18 55										
Cheltenham Spa	d	17 52		18 11							18 25	18 35	18 52		19 06	19 13								19 25	19 52
Gloucester	a			18 22								18 46			19 17	19 26									
Bristol Parkway	a	18 22									18 56		19 21		19 57									20 03	20 21
Bristol Temple Meads	a	18 40									19 08		19 35		20 11									20 14	20 35
Newport (South Wales)	a			19 07								19 54				20 11									
Cardiff Central	a			19 27								20 12				20 31									

A ⊼ to Newport (South Wales)
B From St Pancras International to Sheffield
C From Sheffield to St Pancras International
D From Sheffield to Reading
E From Stansted Airport
F From Manchester Piccadilly
G To Swindon
H From Edinburgh to Plymouth
I From Leeds to St Pancras International
J To Matlock
K From Newcastle to Reading
L To London Paddington
M From Glasgow Central to Penzance
N To St Pancras International
O From St Pancras International to Leeds
P From Glasgow Central to Plymouth
Q From Edinburgh to Reading
R From Manchester Piccadilly to Paignton
S From Aberdeen to Plymouth

Nottingham, Derby and Leicester Birmingham - Cardiff and Bristol

Network Diagram - see first Page of Table 50

		XC	GW	XC		XC	XC	EM	AW	XC	XC	XC	XC	EM		XC	XC	EM	GW	XC	GW	XC	XC	XC
		■	◇■	◇■		◇■	◇■	◇■		◇■	◇■	■	◇■			◇■	◇■	◇■		◇■		◇■	■	◇■
			A	B		C	D	E		F	G		H		I	D	J		F	K	L	M		
			⎍	⊼		⊼		⊼		⊼	⊼		⊼			⊼		⊼				⊼		
Nottingham	d			18 10									19 10	19 22										20 10
Beeston	d													19 27										
Attenborough	d													19 31										
Long Eaton	d													19 38										
Derby	a			18 30									19 30	19 50										20 29
	d			18 35		18 55		19 05			19 27		19 36			19 55		20 05				20 27		20 36
Willington	d																						
Burton-on-Trent	d			18 48							19 38		19 48										20 48
Tamworth	d			19 00									20 00									20 45		21 00
Wilnecote	d												20 04										
Leicester	d	18 16					18 49	19a38				19 19					19 49	20a41					20 19	
South Wigston	d											19 24										20 24	
Narborough	d	18 25										19 29										20 29	
Hinckley	d	18 34										19 37										20 38	
Nuneaton	d	18 41					19 08					19 43					20 08						20 44	
Coleshill Parkway	d	18 56					19 23					19 59					20 23						21 00	
Water Orton	d																						
Birmingham New Street	a	19 15		19 20		19 27	19 36				20 05	20 15	20 24			20 27	20 36					21 03	21 15	21 19
	d			19 30						19 42	20 12									20 42		21 12		
Worcester Shrub Hill	d																		20 37				
Ashchurch for Tewkesbury	d																		20 53				
Cheltenham Spa	d		20 05	20 11					20 18	20 25	20 52								21 03	21 25	21 46	21 52		
Gloucester	a		20 15	20 21					20 29										21 13		21 56	22 02		
Bristol Parkway	a									20 57	21 21								21 53	21 59		22 34		
Bristol Temple Meads	a									21 08	21 32								22 07	22 10		22 45		
Newport (South Wales)	a			21 06					21 31															
Cardiff Central	a			21 26					21 49															

		XC	XC	EM	GW	XC	XC	XC	XC	EM		XC	XC	XC	XC	EM
		◇■	◇■	◇■		◇■	◇■	■	◇■			◇■	◇■	◇■	■	◇■
		N	D	J		F	O			H	N	D	P		Q	
		⊼		⊼								⊼				⊼
Nottingham	d								21 08	21 24						
Beeston	d									21 29						
Attenborough	d									21 33						
Long Eaton	d									21 40						23 32
Derby	a								21 31	21 52						23 42
	d	20 54		20 59			21 27		21 36			21 53		22 26		
Willington	d														
Burton-on-Trent	d						21 37		21 48			22 03		22 37		
Tamworth	d						21 47		22 00			22 14		22 47		
Wilnecote	d								22 04							
Leicester	d		20 49	21a28				21 19					21 49		23 19	
South Wigston	d							21 24						23 24	
Narborough	d							21 29						23 29	
Hinckley	d							21 38						23 38	
Nuneaton	d		21 08					21 45					22 08		23 45	
Coleshill Parkway	d		21 23					22 00					22 23		00 02	
Water Orton	d														
Birmingham New Street	a	21 28	21 36				22 04	22 15	22 23			22 30	22 36	23 04	00 15	
	d					21 43	22 12									
Worcester Shrub Hill	d														
Ashchurch for Tewkesbury	d														
Cheltenham Spa	d				22 01	22 24	22 52									
Gloucester	a				22 12											
Bristol Parkway	a					22 53	23 22									
Bristol Temple Meads	a					23 07	23 33									
Newport (South Wales)	a														
Cardiff Central	a														

A To London Paddington
B ⊼ to Birmingham New Street
C From Newcastle to Reading
D From Stansted Airport
E From York to St Pancras International
F From Manchester Piccadilly
G From Glasgow Central to Plymouth
H To Matlock
I From Newcastle to Guildford
J From Sheffield to St Pancras International
K To Swindon
L From Glasgow Central. ⊼ to Birmingham New Street
M 20 May, 27 May
N From Newcastle
O From Edinburgh
P From Glasgow Central
Q From St Pancras International to Sheffield

Table 57

Nottingham, Derby and Leicester Birmingham - Cardiff and Bristol

Sundays

1 July to 9 September

Network Diagram - see first Page of Table 50

		EM	EM	EM	GW	XC	GW	XC	XC	GW		XC	EM	EM	GW	XC	AW	XC	XC	EM		XC	EM	EM	GW
		◇■	◇■	◇■		◇■		◇■	◇■	◇■		◇■		◇■		◇■		◇■		◇■		■	◇■	◇■	
		A	B	A	C	D	E		F	G	H	I	A				H		J			A	K C		
		⌶	⌶	⌶		⌶		⌶	⌶	☕		⌶		⌶		⌶		⌶	🚌	⌶			⌶	⌶	
Nottingham ■ ⇌	d												09 22												
Beeston	d												09 27												
Attenborough	d												09 31												
Long Eaton	d												09 39							10 32				11 18	
Derby ■	a												09 50							10 46				11 28	
	d	07 22	07 54	08 50								09 37		09 51				10 32	10 35				10 52		
Willington	d																								
Burton-on-Trent	d																		10 55						
Tamworth	d																		11 20						
Wilnecote	d																								
Leicester	d	07a47	08a24	09a23										10a23								11 19	11a24		
South Wigston	d																								
Narborough	d																					11 28			
Hinckley	d																					11 36			
Nuneaton	d																					11 42			
Coleshill Parkway	d																		11a50			11 57			
Water Orton	d																								
Birmingham New Street ■	a											10 48						11 48				12 14			
	d					09 12		10 12	10 30			11 12				11 30		12 12							
Worcester Shrub Hill ■	d																								
Ashchurch for Tewkesbury	d																								
Cheltenham Spa	d				09 24	09 52	10 05	10 53	11 10	11 46		11 52			12 00	12 11	12 18	12 54							13 01
Gloucester ■	a				09 34		10 15	11 03		11 56					12 11	12 21	12 28								13 11
Bristol Parkway ■	a					10 21	10 52		11 39			12 21			12 54			13 23							
Bristol Temple Meads ■	a					10 32	11 07		11 52			12 33			13 10			13 35							
Newport (South Wales)	a							11 48								13 06	13 33								
Cardiff Central ■	a							12 08								13 26	13 52								

		XC	GW	XC	XC	XC		EM	EM	XC	AW	XC	XC	XC	XC	EM		EM	GW	XC	XC	XC	XC	XC	EM
		◇■	◇■	◇■		■		◇■	◇■	◇■		◇■	◇■		■	◇■		◇■		◇■	◇■	◇■	◇■		
		L	G	M				N	K	L		O			A		K	P	L	Q	R S		I		
		⌶	☕	⌶	🚌			☕	⌶	⌶		⌶	⌶	🚌		⌶		⌶		⌶	⌶	⌶	⌶	🚌	
Nottingham ■ ⇌	d																								13 22
Beeston	d																								13 27
Attenborough	d																								13 31
Long Eaton	d								12 17									13 22							13 39
Derby ■	a								12 27									13 32							13 50
	d			11 34	11 35			11 48					12 32	12 35		13 02							13 32	13 35	
Willington	d																								
Burton-on-Trent	d				11 55									12 55										13 55	
Tamworth	d				12 20									13 20										14 20	
Wilnecote	d																								
Leicester	d					12 19		12a21							13 19	13a34					13 49				
South Wigston	d					12 24																			
Narborough	d					12 29									13 28										
Hinckley	d					12 38									13 36										
Nuneaton	d					12 45									13 43						14 08				
Coleshill Parkway	d				12a50	13 00								13a50	13 59						14 23			14a50	
Water Orton	d																								
Birmingham New Street ■	a			12 48		13 15							13 47		14 15						14 36		14 48		
	d	12 30		13 12						13 30		13 42	14 12							14 30		14 42			
Worcester Shrub Hill ■	d																		14 36						
Ashchurch for Tewkesbury	d																		14 51						
Cheltenham Spa	d	13 11	13 46	13 52						14 12	14 18	14 24	14 52						15 01	15 11		15 25			
Gloucester ■	a	13 21	13 57							14 22	14 29								15 10	15 21					
Bristol Parkway ■	a			14 21								14 54	15 24						15 49			15 59			
Bristol Temple Meads ■	a			14 32								15 07	15 36						16 09			16 11			
Newport (South Wales)	a	14 06								15 08	15 34									16 06					
Cardiff Central ■	a	14 26								15 31	15 53									16 26					

- A From Sheffield to St Pancras International
- B To St Pancras International
- C To Swindon
- D To Penzance
- E To Taunton
- F To Plymouth
- G To London Paddington
- H From Leeds to Plymouth
- I To Matlock
- J From Leicester to York
- K From St Pancras International to Sheffield
- L ⌶ to Newport (South Wales)
- M From York to Plymouth
- N From Leeds to St Pancras International
- O From Newcastle to Plymouth
- P To Weston-super-Mare
- Q From Stansted Airport
- R From Manchester Piccadilly to Paignton
- S From Edinburgh to Reading

Table 57

Nottingham, Derby and Leicester Birmingham - Cardiff and Bristol

Sundays

1 July to 9 September

Network Diagram - see first Page of Table 50

		EM		EM	GW	XC	XC	XC	EM	XC	XC	AW		XC	GW	XC	EM	XC	EM	GW	XC	EM		XC	XC
		◇■		◇■	◇■	◇■	■	◇■	◇■	◇■	◇■			◇■		◇■	◇■	■	◇■		◇■			◇■	◇■
		A		B	C	D		E	A	F	G		H	I	J	B		K			L		M	G	
		⌶		⌶	☕	⌶		⌶	⌶	⌶	⌶			⌶		⌶	⌶		⌶		⌶			⌶	⌶
Nottingham ■ ⇌	d							14 10													15 10	15 22			
Beeston	d																					15 27			
Attenborough	d																					15 31			
Long Eaton	d			14 19													15 19					15 39			
Derby ■	a			14 29				14 29									15 29				15 30	15 50			
	d	13 55				14 31		14 35	14 37	14 53						15 26			15 35		15 35			15 54	
Willington	d																								
Burton-on-Trent	d							14 48								15 38					15 48				
Tamworth	d					14 50		15 00													16 00				
Wilnecote	d																				16 03				
Leicester	d	14a31					14 19		15a10		14 49							15 19	16a11						15 49
South Wigston	d						14 24																		
Narborough	d						14 29											15 28							
Hinckley	d						14 38											15 36							
Nuneaton	d						14 45				15 08							15 43							16 07
Coleshill Parkway	d						15 00				15 23							15 58							16 22
Water Orton	d																								
Birmingham New Street ■	a					15 06	15 15	15 21		15 27	15 36					16 01		16 15			16 24			16 27	16 36
	d					15 12		15 30						15 42		16 12					16 30				
Worcester Shrub Hill ■	d																			16 40					
Ashchurch for Tewkesbury	d																			16 58					
Cheltenham Spa	d				15 46	15 52		16 11				16 18		16 25	16 33	16 51				17 08	17 11				
Gloucester ■	a				15 57			16 21				16 29			16 43					17 16	17 21				
Bristol Parkway ■	a					16 21								16 55		17 20				17 57					
Bristol Temple Meads ■	a					16 35								17 08		17 35				18 10					
Newport (South Wales)	a							17 06				17 37									18 07				
Cardiff Central ■	a							17 27				17 57									18 29				

		EM	XC	GW	XC	XC	XC	EM		EM	XC	XC	EM	EM	XC	AW	XC	XC		GW	XC	EM	EM	XC	XC
		◇■	◇■	◇■	◇■	■	◇■	◇■		◇■	◇■	◇■	◇■	◇■	◇■		◇■	■			◇■	◇■		◇■	◇■
		A	H	C	N		E O		P	M	G	A	B	H		Q			E	P	L	R	G		
		⌶	⌶	☕	⌶		⌶	⌶		⌶	⌶	⌶	⌶	⌶	⌶		⌶				⌶	⌶		⌶	
Nottingham ■ ⇌	d						16 10														17 10		17 23		
Beeston	d																						17 28		
Attenborough	d																						17 32		
Long Eaton	d							16 28						17 16									17 40		
Derby ■	a						16 30	16 39						17 26							17 29		17 51		
	d	16 08			16 29		16 35			16 47	16 55		17 08				17 27				17 36	17 47		17 54	
Willington	d																								
Burton-on-Trent	d						16 48										17 38				17 48				
Tamworth	d				16 48		17 00														18 00				
Wilnecote	d																								
Leicester	d	16a33				16 19				17a22		16 49	17a33					17 18				18a19			17 49
South Wigston	d					16 24												17 24							
Narborough	d					16 29												17 29							
Hinckley	d					16 38												17 38							
Nuneaton	d					16 45						17 08						17 45							18 08
Coleshill Parkway	d					17 00						17 23						18 00							18 23
Water Orton	d																								
Birmingham New Street ■	a				17 04	17 15	17 19				17 27	17 36					18 01	18 15			18 19			18 24	18 36
	d		16 42		17 12		17 30								17 42		18 12				18 30				
Worcester Shrub Hill ■	d																			18 40					
Ashchurch for Tewkesbury	d																			18 55					
Cheltenham Spa	d		17 25	17 46	17 52		18 11								18 25	18 35	18 52			19 06	19 13				
Gloucester ■	a			17 56			18 22									18 46				19 17	19 26				
Bristol Parkway ■	a		18 02		18 22										18 56		19 21			19 57					
Bristol Temple Meads ■	a		18 13		18 40										19 08		19 35			20 11					
Newport (South Wales)	a						19 07									19 54					20 11				
Cardiff Central ■	a						19 27									20 12					20 31				

- A From Sheffield to St Pancras International
- B From St Pancras International to Sheffield
- C To London Paddington
- D From Edinburgh to Penzance
- E ⌶ to Newport (South Wales)
- F From Sheffield to Reading
- G From Stansted Airport
- H From Manchester Piccadilly
- I To Swindon
- J From Edinburgh to Plymouth
- K From Leeds to St Pancras International
- L To Matlock
- M From Newcastle to Reading
- N From Glasgow Central to Penzance
- O From St Pancras International to Leeds
- P To St Pancras International
- Q From Glasgow Central to Plymouth
- R From Edinburgh to Reading

Nottingham, Derby and Leicester Birmingham - Cardiff and Bristol

Network Diagram - see first Page of Table 50

	EM ◇■ A ⊥	XC ◇■ B ⊥	XC ◇■ C ⊥		XC ■	XC ◇■ D ⊥	XC ◇■ E	EM ◇■ F ⊥	GW ◇■ G	AW H	XC ◇■ I ⊥	XC ◇■ ⊥	XC ■		XC ◇■ J ⊥	EM K	XC ◇■ E ⊥	XC ◇■ A	EM ◇■ H ⊥	GW L	XC ◇■ M	GW	XC ◇■ ⊥
Nottingham d															19 10	19 22							
Beeston d																19 27							
Attenborough d																19 31							
Long Eaton d																19 38							
Derby a															19 30	19 50							
d	18 04		18 26			18 55		19 05				19 27			19 36		19 56		20 04				20 27
Willington d																							
Burton-on-Trent d												19 38			19 48								
Tamworth d			18 45												20 00								20 45
Wilnecote d															20 04								
Leicester d	18a33				18 16		18 49	19a38					19 19					19 49	20a40				
South Wigston d													19 24										
Narborough d					18 25								19 29										
Hinckley d					18 34								19 37										
Nuneaton d					18 41		19 08						19 43					20 08					
Coleshill Parkway d					18 56		19 23						19 59					20 23					
Water Orton d																							
Birmingham New Street a			19 04		19 15	19 27	19 36					20 05	20 15		20 24		20 27	20 36					21 03
d		18 42	19 12								19 42	20 12									20 42		21 12
Worcester Shrub Hill d																				20 37			
Ashchurch for Tewkesbury d																				20 53			
Cheltenham Spa d		19 25	19 52						20 05	20 18	20 25	20 52								21 03	21 25	21 46	21 52
Gloucester a									20 15	20 29										21 13		21 56	22 02
Bristol Parkway a		20 03	20 21								20 57	21 21								21 53	21 59		22 34
Bristol Temple Meads a		20 14	20 35								21 08	21 32								22 07	22 10		22 45
Newport (South Wales) a										21 31													
Cardiff Central a										21 49													

	XC ■	XC ◇■	XC ◇■ N ⊥	EM ◇■ A ⊥	GW	XC ◇■ H	XC ◇■ O	XC ■	XC ◇■		EM J N	XC ◇■ P ⊥	XC ◇■	XC ■ Q	EM ◇■ ⊥
Nottingham d		20 10							21 08		21 23				
Beeston d											21 29				
Attenborough d											21 33				
Long Eaton d											21 40				23 20
Derby a		20 29							21 31		21 52				23 30
d		20 36	20 54	21 02			21 27		21 36			21 53	22 26		
Willington d															
Burton-on-Trent d		20 48					21 37		21 48			22 03	22 37		
Tamworth d		21 00					21 47		22 00			22 14	22 47		
Wilnecote d									22 04						
Leicester d	20 19			21a28				21 19						23 19	
South Wigston d	20 24							21 24						23 24	
Narborough d	20 29							21 29						23 29	
Hinckley d	20 38							21 38						23 38	
Nuneaton d	20 44							21 45						23 45	
Coleshill Parkway d	21 00							22 00						00 02	
Water Orton d															
Birmingham New Street a	21 15	21 19	21 28				22 04	22 15	22 23			22 30	23 04	00 15	
d						21 43	22 12								
Worcester Shrub Hill d															
Ashchurch for Tewkesbury d															
Cheltenham Spa d					22 01	22 24	22 52								
Gloucester a					22 12										
Bristol Parkway a						22 53	23 22								
Bristol Temple Meads a						23 07	23 33								
Newport (South Wales) a															
Cardiff Central a															

A From Sheffield to St Pancras International
B From Manchester Piccadilly to Paignton
C From Aberdeen to Plymouth
D From Newcastle to Reading
E From Stansted Airport
F From York Holgate Sidings to St Pancras International
G To London Paddington
H From Manchester Piccadilly
I From Glasgow Central to Plymouth
J To Matlock
K From Newcastle to Guildford
L To Swindon
M From Glasgow Central. ⊥ to Birmingham New Street
N From Newcastle
O From Edinburgh
P From Glasgow Central
Q From St Pancras International to Sheffield

Nottingham, Derby and Leicester Birmingham - Cardiff and Bristol

Network Diagram - see first Page of Table 50

	EM ◇■ A ⊥	EM ◇■ A ⊥	EM ◇■ A ⊥	GW (bus)	EM ◇■ B ⊥	GW C	XC ◇■ D ⊥	GW C	XC ◇■ ⊥		XC ◇■ E ⊥	EM F	EM ◇■ B ⊥	GW C	XC ◇■ ⊥	XC ◇■ E ⊥	EM ◇■ G ⊥	AW D	XC ◇■ ⊥		XC ■ H	EM ◇■ I	XC ◇■ J ⊥	EM ◇■ ⊥
Nottingham d												09 22												
Beeston d												09 27												
Attenborough d												09 31												
Long Eaton d												09 39					10 31							12 12
Derby a												09 50					10 42							12 22
d	06 13	07 16	08 12		09 13						09 28		10 10			10 34						11 03	11 30	
Willington d																								
Burton-on-Trent d																							11 41	
Tamworth d																								
Wilnecote d																								
Leicester d	06a41	07a45	08a44		09a45								10a43								11 19	11a37		
South Wigston d																								
Narborough d																					11 28			
Hinckley d																					11 36			
Nuneaton d																					11 42			
Coleshill Parkway d																					11 57			
Water Orton d																								
Birmingham New Street a											10 16					11 25					12 14		12 21	
d							09 12		10 12		10 30				11 12	11 30			12 12					
Worcester Shrub Hill d																								
Ashchurch for Tewkesbury d																								
Cheltenham Spa d				08 45		09 24	09 52	10 24	10 53		11 11			11 24	11 53	12 10		12 18	12 51					
Gloucester a				09 05		09 34	10 01	10 34	11 03		11 20			11 34	12 03	12 19		12 28	13 02					
Bristol Parkway a				10 45			11 11				12 17					13 17			14 03					
Bristol Temple Meads a							11 35				12 35					13 35			14 32					
Newport (South Wales) a									11 48						12 52			13 33						
Cardiff Central a									12 08						13 12			13 52						

	GW C	XC ◇■ K ⊥	XC ◇■ D ⊥	XC ■	EM ◇■ B ⊥		XC ◇■ L ⊥	EM ◇■ J ⊥	XC ◇■ K ⊥	AW C	GW M	XC ◇■ ⊥	XC ■ L	XC ◇■ F ⊥	EM		XC ◇■ N ⊥	GW K	XC ◇■ O ⊥	XC ◇■ B ⊥	EM ◇■ P ⊥	GW ◇■ Q	XC ◇■ ⊥	XC ■
Nottingham d															13 22									
Beeston d															13 28									
Attenborough d															13 34									
Long Eaton d								13 10							13 42									
Derby a								13 20							13 53									
d					12 27		12 31							13 32			13 54				14 01		14 31	
Willington d																								
Burton-on-Trent d							12 42							13 43										
Tamworth d																							14 50	
Wilnecote d																								
Leicester d				12 19	13a00								13 19							13 49	14a34			14 19
South Wigston d				12 24																				14 24
Narborough d				12 29									13 28											14 29
Hinckley d				12 38									13 36											14 38
Nuneaton d				12 45									13 43							14 08				14 45
Coleshill Parkway d				13 00									13 59							14 23				15 00
Water Orton d																								
Birmingham New Street a				13 15			13 20						14 15	14 26			14 27			14 36			15 06	15 15
d		12 30	13 12						13 30			14 12							14 30				15 12	
Worcester Shrub Hill d																		14 36						
Ashchurch for Tewkesbury d																		14 51						
Cheltenham Spa d	13 01	13 11	13 51						14 12	14 18	14 46	14 52						15 01	15 11			15 46	15 52	
Gloucester a	13 11	13 21	14 02						14 22	14 29	14 56	15 09						15 12	15 21			15 57	16 02	
Bristol Parkway a			15 08									16 11											17 09	
Bristol Temple Meads a			15 32									16 32											17 35	
Newport (South Wales) a		14 06							15 08	15 34									16 06					
Cardiff Central a		14 26							15 31	15 53									16 26					

A To St Pancras International
B From Sheffield to St Pancras International
C To Swindon
D To Plymouth
E From Leeds to Plymouth
F To Matlock
G From Leicester to York
H From Leeds to St Pancras International
I From Leeds to Reading
J From St Pancras International to Sheffield
K ⊥ to Newport (South Wales)
L From Newcastle to Reading
M To Penzance
N To Reading
O From Stansted Airport
P To London Paddington
Q From Newcastle to Plymouth

Table 57

Sundays
16 September to 21 October

Nottingham, Derby and Leicester
Birmingham - Cardiff and Bristol

Network Diagram - see first Page of Table 50

	XC		EM	EM	XC	XC	EM	AW	GW	XC	XC		GW	XC	EM	EM	XC	EM	XC	EM	GW		XC	XC
	◇■ A ⊼		◇■ B ⊼	◇■ C ⊼	◇■ D ⊼	◇■ E ⊼	◇■ B ⊼		F	◇■ G ⊼	■			◇■ H ⊼	◇■ B ⊼	◇■ I ⊼	◇■ J ⊼	E	◇■ C ⊼	◇■ K ⊼	◇■ L		◇■ ⊼	■
Nottingham ■ d	14 10													15 10				15 29						
Beeston d																		15 34						
Attenborough d																		15 38						
Long Eaton d			14 26				15 08									15 42		15 46						
Derby ■ a	14 29		14 37				15 19							15 30		15 53		15 57						
d	14 35			14 49	14 53					15 27				15 35	15 48		15 54			16 25			16 28	
Willington d																								
Burton-on-Trent d	14 48									15 38				15 48										
Tamworth d	15 00													16 00									16 48	
Wilnecote d														16 03										
Leicester d				15a22		14 49					15 19				16a23				15 49	16a51				16 19
South Wigston d																								16 24
Narborough d											15 28													16 29
Hinckley d											15 36													16 38
Nuneaton d						15 08					15 43								16 07					16 45
Coleshill Parkway d						15 23					15 58								16 22					17 00
Water Orton d																								
Birmingham New Street ■ a	15 21				15 27	15 36				16 01	16 15			16 24			16 27		16 36				17 04	17 15
d	15 30									16 12				16 30									17 12	
Worcester Shrub Hill ■ d													16 40											
Ashchurch for Tewkesbury d													16 58											
Cheltenham Spa d	16 11							16 18	16 32	16 52			17 08	17 11							17 46		17 52	
Gloucester ■ a	16 21							16 29	16 42	17 01			17 17	17 21							17 56		18 01	
Bristol Parkway ■ a										18 07													19 13	
Bristol Temple Meads ■ a										18 40													19 35	
Newport (South Wales) a	17 06							17 37						18 07										
Cardiff Central ■ a	17 27							17 57						18 29										

	XC	EM	EM	XC	XC	EM	AW		XC	XC	EM	EM	EM	XC	XC	EM	GW		XC	XC	GW	XC	XC	XC
	◇■ A ⊼	◇■ M ⊼	◇■ N ⊼	◇■ I ⊼	◇■ E ⊼	◇■ C ⊼			◇■ L ⊼	■	◇■ B ⊼	◇■ N ⊼	J	◇■ I ⊼	◇■ E	◇■ C ⊼		L	◇■ ⊼	■ K	◇■ O	◇■ I ⊼	◇■ E ⊼	◇■
Nottingham ■ d	16 10												17 23									18 10		
Beeston d													17 28											
Attenborough d													17 32											
Long Eaton d		16 28									17 28		17 40											
Derby ■ a	16 30	16 39									17 39		17 51									18 30		
d	16 35		16 48	16 55		17 17			17 27			17 47		17 54		18 08			18 26			18 35	18 55	
Willington d																								
Burton-on-Trent d	16 48								17 38													18 48		
Tamworth d	17 00																		18 45			19 00		
Wilnecote d																								
Leicester d			17a20		16 49	17a51				17 18		18a19			17 49	18a37				18 16				18 49
South Wigston d										17 24														
Narborough d										17 29										18 25				
Hinckley d										17 38										18 34				
Nuneaton d					17 08					17 45					18 08					18 41				19 08
Coleshill Parkway d					17 23					18 00					18 23					18 56				19 23
Water Orton d																								
Birmingham New Street ■ a	17 19			17 27	17 36				18 01	18 15				18 25	18 36				19 04	19 15		19 20	19 27	19 36
d	17 30								18 12										19 12			19 30		
Worcester Shrub Hill ■ d																	18 40							
Ashchurch for Tewkesbury d																	18 56							
Cheltenham Spa d	18 11						18 35		18 52								19 07		19 52		20 05	20 11		
Gloucester ■ a	18 22						18 46		19 01								19 18		20 01		20 15	20 21		
Bristol Parkway ■ a									20 03										21 13					
Bristol Temple Meads ■ a									20 35										21 32					
Newport (South Wales) a	19 07						19 54															21 06		
Cardiff Central ■ a	19 27						20 12															21 26		

A ⊼ to Newport (South Wales)
B From St Pancras International to Sheffield
C From Sheffield to St Pancras International
D From Sheffield to Reading
E From Stansted Airport
F To Swindon
G From Newcastle to Penzance
H From Leeds to St Pancras International
I From Newcastle to Reading
J To Matlock
K To London Paddington
L From Newcastle to Plymouth
M From St Pancras International to Leeds
N To St Pancras International
O ⊼ to Birmingham New Street

Table 57

Sundays
16 September to 21 October

Nottingham, Derby and Leicester
Birmingham - Cardiff and Bristol

Network Diagram - see first Page of Table 50

	EM	AW	XC		XC	XC	EM	XC	XC	EM	GW	XC	XC		XC	XC	EM	GW	XC	XC	XC	EM	XC
	◇■ A ⊼		◇■ B ⊼		■	◇■ ⊼	C	◇■ D ⊼	◇■ E	◇■ F ⊼	G	H ◇■ ⊼	■		◇■ B	◇■ F ⊼	◇■ ⊼	I	◇■ ⊼	■	◇■ C	B	◇■ ⊼
Nottingham ■ d						19 10	19 22								20 10						21 08	21 24	
Beeston d							19 27															21 29	
Attenborough d							19 31															21 33	
Long Eaton d							19 38															21 40	
Derby ■ a						19 30	19 50								20 29						21 31	21 52	
d	19 22		19 27			19 36		19 56		20 05		20 27			20 36	20 54	21 01		21 27		21 36		21 53
Willington d																							
Burton-on-Trent d			19 38			19 48									20 48				21 37		21 48		22 03
Tamworth d						19 59						20 45			21 00				21 48		22 00		22 14
Wilnecote d						20 03															22 04		
Leicester d	19a55				19 19				19 49	20a41			20 19				21a30			21 19			
South Wigston d					19 24								20 24							21 24			
Narborough d					19 29								20 29							21 29			
Hinckley d					19 37								20 38							21 38			
Nuneaton d					19 43				20 08				20 44							21 45			
Coleshill Parkway d					19 59				20 23				21 00							22 00			
Water Orton d																							
Birmingham New Street ■ a			20 05		20 15	20 24		20 27	20 36			21 03	21 15		21 19	21 28			22 05	22 15	22 23		22 30
d			20 12									21 12							22 12				
Worcester Shrub Hill ■ d																		21 36					
Ashchurch for Tewkesbury d																		21 52					
Cheltenham Spa d		20 18	20 52								21 46	21 52						22 02	22 52				
Gloucester ■ a		20 29	21 01								21 56	22 05						22 13	23 03				
Bristol Parkway ■ a			22 06									23 12							00 01				
Bristol Temple Meads ■ a			22 22									23 30							00 14				
Newport (South Wales) a		21 31																					
Cardiff Central ■ a		21 49																					

	XC	XC	EM
	◇■ J	■	◇■ K ⊼
Nottingham ■ d			
Beeston d			
Attenborough d			
Long Eaton d			23 28
Derby ■ a			23 38
d	22 26		
Willington d			
Burton-on-Trent d	22 37		
Tamworth d	22 47		
Wilnecote d			
Leicester d		23 19	
South Wigston d		23 24	
Narborough d		23 29	
Hinckley d		23 38	
Nuneaton d		23 45	
Coleshill Parkway d		00 02	
Water Orton d			
Birmingham New Street ■ a	23 04	00 15	
d			
Worcester Shrub Hill ■ d			
Ashchurch for Tewkesbury d			
Cheltenham Spa d			
Gloucester ■ a			
Bristol Parkway ■ a			
Bristol Temple Meads ■ a			
Newport (South Wales) a			
Cardiff Central ■ a			

A From York Holgate Sidings to St Pancras International
B From Newcastle
C To Matlock
D From Newcastle to Guildford
E From Stansted Airport
F From Sheffield to St Pancras International
G To Swindon
H From Newcastle. ⊼ to Birmingham New Street
I From Edinburgh. ⊼ to Birmingham New Street
J From Glasgow Central
K From St Pancras International to Sheffield

Nottingham, Derby and Leicester Birmingham - Cardiff and Bristol

Network Diagram - see first Page of Table 50

		EM	EM	EM	GW	GW	GW	XC	XC	GW		XC	EM	EM	XC	EM	XC	EM	XC	EM		GW	AW	XC	EM
		◇■	◇■	◇■								◇■		◇■	◇■	◇■	■	◇■	◇■	◇■				■	◇■
		A	A	B	C	D	C			C		E	F	B	G H		B	I	J					K	
		🍴	🍴	🍴				🚌	🚌			🍴		🍴	🍴	🍴		🍴	🍴	🍴					🍽
Nottingham ■ 🚆	d												09 22												
Beeston	d												09 27												
Attenborough	d												09 31												
Long Eaton	d												09 39			10 31				11 29					
Derby ■	a												09 50			10 42				11 39					
	d	06 51	07 52	08 52								09 45		09 55	10 34			10 55	11 30						11 51
Willington	d																								
Burton-on-Trent	d																		11 41						
Tamworth	d														10 56				11 54						
Wilnecote	d																								
Leicester	d	07a19	08a22	09a24										10a28			11 19	11a28						12 19	12a24
South Wigston	d																							12 24	
Narborough	d																11 28							12 29	
Hinckley	d																11 36							12 38	
Nuneaton	d																11 42							12 45	
Coleshill Parkway	d																11 57							13 00	
Water Orton	d																								
Birmingham New Street ■	a											10 56			11 16		12 14		12 17					13 15	
	d								09 35			11 03													
Worcester Shrub Hill ■	d																								
Ashchurch for Tewkesbury	d																								
Cheltenham Spa	d				09 24	10 05	10 24	10 40	10a55	11 24		12 03										12 08	12 18		
Gloucester ■	a				09 34	10 15	10 34	11 00		11 34												12 19	12 28		
Bristol Parkway ■	a					10 52						12 34										13 00			
Bristol Temple Meads ■	a					11 07						12 46										13 12			
Newport (South Wales)	a																						13 33		
Cardiff Central ■	a																						13 52		

		GW	AW	XC	EM	XC		EM	XC	EM	EM	GW	XC	XC	EM	XC		GW	XC	XC	GW	XC	EM	XC	AW
				◇■	◇■	■		◇■	◇■	◇■			◇■	◇■	◇■	◇■		◇■	◇■	■		◇■	◇■	◇■	
		C		L	J			B	M	J	F	C	N	O B	P		Q	R			N	J O			
				🍴	🍴			🍴	🍴	🍴			🍴	🍴	🍴	🍴		🍽	🍴			🍴	🍴	🍴	
Nottingham ■ 🚆	d										13 22											14 10			
Beeston	d										13 28														
Attenborough	d										13 34														
Long Eaton	d				12 29					13 40	13 46												14 42		
Derby ■	a				12 39					13 50	13 57											14 29	14 53		
	d			12 31				13 02	13 32						14 03				14 31			14 35			
Willington	d																								
Burton-on-Trent	d			12 42					13 44													14 48			
Tamworth	d			12 51					13 59										14 50			15 00			
Wilnecote	d																								
Leicester	d					13 19		13a34						13 49	14a36					14 19				14 49	
South Wigston	d																			14 24					
Narborough	d					13 28														14 29					
Hinckley	d					13 36														14 38					
Nuneaton	d					13 43								14 08						14 45				15 08	
Coleshill Parkway	d					13 59								14 23						15 00				15 23	
Water Orton	d																								
Birmingham New Street ■	a			13 09		14 15			14 19					14 36					15 06	15 15		15 21		15 36	
	d			13 29									14 30			14 42			15 12			15 30			
Worcester Shrub Hill ■	d																				15 36				
Ashchurch for Tewkesbury	d																				15 51				
Cheltenham Spa	d	13 01	14 18	14 27								14 46	15 11			15 25		15 46	15 52		16 01	16 11			16 18
Gloucester ■	a	13 11	14 29	14 43								14 56	15 21					15 57			16 10	16 21			16 29
Bristol Parkway ■	a			15 18												15 59			16 21		16 49				
Bristol Temple Meads ■	a			15 29												16 11			16 35		17 09				
Newport (South Wales)	a		15 34										16 06									17 06			17 37
Cardiff Central ■	a		15 53										16 26									17 27			17 57

- A To St Pancras International
- B From Sheffield to St Pancras International
- C To Swindon
- D To Taunton
- E From Leeds to Plymouth
- F To Matlock
- G From Leeds
- H From Leicester to York
- I From York
- J From St Pancras International to Sheffield
- K From Leeds to St Pancras International
- L From Newcastle to Plymouth
- M From Edinburgh
- N 🍴 to Newport (South Wales)
- O From Stansted Airport
- P From Manchester Piccadilly to Paignton
- Q To London Paddington
- R From Edinburgh to Penzance

from 28 October

Nottingham, Derby and Leicester Birmingham - Cardiff and Bristol

Network Diagram - see first Page of Table 50

		XC		XC	EM	GW	GW	XC	EM	EM	XC	EM		XC	EM	XC	GW	XC	XC	XC	EM	EM		XC	XC
		◇■		■	◇■			◇■	◇■	◇■	◇■			◇■	◇■	◇■	◇■	◇■	■	◇■	◇■	◇■		◇■	◇■
		A			B	C			D	E	F	G	H	B	A	I	J		K	L	M		F	H	
		🍴			🍴			🍴	🍴	🍴	🍴			🍴	🍴	🍴	🍽	🍴		🍴	🍴	🍴		🍴	🍴
Nottingham ■ 🚆	d							15 10				15 29								16 10					
Beeston	d											15 34													
Attenborough	d											15 38													
Long Eaton	d									15 42		15 46									16 28				
Derby ■	a							15 30		15 53		15 57								16 30	16 39				
	d				14 54			15 35	15 50		15 54				16 25			16 29		16 35		16 48		16 55	
Willington	d																								
Burton-on-Trent	d							15 48												16 48					
Tamworth	d							16 00										16 47		17 00					
Wilnecote	d							16 03																	
Leicester	d			15 19	15a27				16a25					15 49	16a51				16 19			17a20			16 49
South Wigston	d																		16 24						
Narborough	d			15 28															16 29						
Hinckley	d			15 36															16 38						
Nuneaton	d			15 43										16 07					16 45						17 08
Coleshill Parkway	d			15 58										16 22					17 00						17 23
Water Orton	d																								
Birmingham New Street ■	a			16 15				16 24			16 27			16 36				17 03	17 15	17 19				17 27	17 36
	d	15 42						16 30								16 42		17 12		17 30					
Worcester Shrub Hill ■	d						16 40																		
Ashchurch for Tewkesbury	d						16 58																		
Cheltenham Spa	d	16 25				16 32	17 08	17 11								17 25	17 46	17 52		18 11					
Gloucester ■	a					16 42	17 16	17 21									17 56			18 22					
Bristol Parkway ■	a	17 00					17 57									18 02		18 22							
Bristol Temple Meads ■	a	17 11					18 10									18 13		18 40							
Newport (South Wales)	a							18 07												19 07					
Cardiff Central ■	a							18 29												19 27					

		EM	XC	AW	XC	XC	EM	EM		EM	XC	XC	EM	GW	XC	XC	XC	GW		XC	XC	XC	EM	AW	XC
		◇■	◇■		◇■	■	◇■	◇■			◇■	◇■	◇■		◇■	◇■	■	◇■		◇■	◇■	◇■	◇■		◇■
		B	A		N		E	M		G O	H	B		P	Q		I		R F	H	S		A		
		🍴	🍴		🍴		🍴	🍴			🍴		🍴		🍴	🍴		🍽		🍴	🍴		🍴		🍴
Nottingham ■ 🚆	d									17 23										18 10					
Beeston	d									17 28															
Attenborough	d									17 32															
Long Eaton	d						17 28			17 40															
Derby ■	a						17 39			17 51										18 30					
	d	17 17			17 27			17 48			17 54		18 08			18 26				18 35	18 55		19 22		
Willington	d																								
Burton-on-Trent	d				17 38															18 48					
Tamworth	d															18 45				19 00					
Wilnecote	d																								
Leicester	d	17a51				17 18		18a20				17 49	18a37				18 16					18 49	19a55		
South Wigston	d					17 24																			
Narborough	d					17 29											18 25								
Hinckley	d					17 38											18 34								
Nuneaton	d					17 45						18 08					18 41					19 08			
Coleshill Parkway	d					18 00						18 23					18 56					19 23			
Water Orton	d																								
Birmingham New Street ■	a				18 01	18 15					18 24	18 36				19 04	19 15			19 20	19 27	19 36			
	d		17 42		18 12										18 42	19 12				19 30					19 42
Worcester Shrub Hill ■	d													18 40											
Ashchurch for Tewkesbury	d													18 55											
Cheltenham Spa	d		18 25	18 35	18 52									19 06	19 25	19 52		20 05		20 11				20 18	20 25
Gloucester ■	a			18 46										19 17				20 15		20 21				20 29	
Bristol Parkway ■	a		18 56		19 21									19 57	20 03	20 21									20 57
Bristol Temple Meads ■	a		19 08		19 35									20 11	20 14	20 35									21 08
Newport (South Wales)	a			19 54																21 06				21 31	
Cardiff Central ■	a			20 12																21 26				21 49	

- A From Manchester Piccadilly
- B From Sheffield to St Pancras International
- C To Swindon
- D From Leeds to St Pancras International
- E From St Pancras International to Sheffield
- F From Newcastle to Reading
- G To Matlock
- H From Stansted Airport
- I To London Paddington
- J From Glasgow Central to Penzance
- K 🍴 to Newport (South Wales)
- L From St Pancras International to Leeds
- M To St Pancras International
- N From Glasgow Central to Plymouth
- O From Edinburgh to Reading
- P From Manchester Piccadilly to Plymouth
- Q From Aberdeen to Plymouth
- R 🍴 to Birmingham New Street
- S From York to St Pancras International

Nottingham, Derby and Leicester Birmingham - Cardiff and Bristol

Network Diagram - see first Page of Table 50

		XC	XC	XC		EM	XC	XC	EM	GW	XC	GW	XC	XC		XC	XC	EM	GW	XC	XC	XC	XC	EM
		◇1 A ✠	1	◇1 ✠		B	◇1 C ✠	◇1 D	◇1 E ✠		◇1 F	G	◇1 H ✠	1		◇1 I	◇1 E ✠	◇1 ✠	F	◇1 J	◇1	1	◇1 B	
Nottingham	d			19 10		19 22										20 10							21 08	21 24
Beeston	d					19 27																		21 29
Attenborough	d					19 31																		21 33
Long Eaton	d					19 38																		21 40
Derby	a			19 30		19 50										20 29							21 31	21 52
	d	19 27		19 36			19 56		20 05				20 27			20 36	20 54	21 01			21 27		21 36	
Willington	d																							
Burton-on-Trent	d	19 38		19 48												20 48					21 37		21 48	
Tamworth	d			19 59									20 45			21 00					21 47		22 00	
Wilnecote	d			20 03																			22 04	
Leicester	d		19 19					19 49	20a41					20 19				21a30				21 19		
South Wigston	d		19 24											20 24								21 24		
Narborough	d		19 29											20 29								21 29		
Hinckley	d		19 37											20 38								21 38		
Nuneaton	d		19 43					20 08						20 44								21 45		
Coleshill Parkway	d		19 59					20 23						21 00								22 00		
Water Orton	d																							
Birmingham New Street	a	20 05	20 15	20 24			20 27	20 36					21 03	21 15		21 19	21 28				22 04	22 15	22 23	
	d	20 12									20 42		21 12							21 43	22 12			
Worcester Shrub Hill	d									20 37														
Ashchurch for Tewkesbury	d									20 53														
Cheltenham Spa	d	20 52								21 03	21 25	21 46	21 52						22 01	22 24	22 52			
Gloucester	a									21 13		21 56	22 02						22 12					
Bristol Parkway	a	21 21								21 53	21 59		22 34							22 53	23 22			
Bristol Temple Meads	a	21 32								22 07	22 10		22 45							23 07	23 33			
Newport (South Wales)	a																							
Cardiff Central	a																							

		XC	XC	XC	EM
		◇1 I ✠	◇1 K	1	◇1 L ✠
Nottingham	d				
Beeston	d				
Attenborough	d				
Long Eaton	d				23 26
Derby	a				23 36
	d	21 53	22 26		
Willington	d				
Burton-on-Trent	d	22 03	22 37		
Tamworth	d	22 14	22 47		
Wilnecote	d				
Leicester	d			23 19	
South Wigston	d			23 24	
Narborough	d			23 29	
Hinckley	d			23 38	
Nuneaton	d			23 45	
Coleshill Parkway	d			00 02	
Water Orton	d				
Birmingham New Street	a	22 30	23 04	00 15	
	d				
Worcester Shrub Hill	d				
Ashchurch for Tewkesbury	d				
Cheltenham Spa	d				
Gloucester	a				
Bristol Parkway	a				
Bristol Temple Meads	a				
Newport (South Wales)	a				
Cardiff Central	a				

A From Glasgow Central to Plymouth
B To Matlock
C From Newcastle to Guildford
D From Stansted Airport
E From Sheffield to St Pancras International
F From Manchester Piccadilly
G To Swindon
H From Glasgow Central. ✠ to Birmingham New Street
I From Newcastle
J From Edinburgh
K From Glasgow Central
L From St Pancras International to Sheffield

Bristol and Cardiff - Birmingham Leicester, Derby and Nottingham

Network Diagram - see first Page of Table 50

Miles	Miles	Miles			XC	XC	XC	XC	XC	XC	GW	XC	XC		XC	XC	XC	XC	XC	XC	XC	XC	XC		XC
					MX 1	MX ◇1	MO ◇1 A	◇1 B	1	◇1 C ✠		1 ✠	◇1 B ✠		◇1 D ✠	1	1	◇1 E ✠	1 ✠	◇1 B ✠	◇1 D ✠	1	1		◇1 F ✠
0	—	—	Cardiff Central	d		21p50																			
11¾	—	—	Newport (South Wales)	d		22p05																			
—	—	0	Bristol Temple Meads	d			22p10																		06 27
—	—	5¾	Bristol Parkway	d			22p24																		06 40
56½	—	—	Gloucester	d		22p47	23p21				06 00														
63	—	46¼	Cheltenham Spa	d		22p58	23p33				06 11														07 12
70¼	—	53½	Ashchurch for Tewkesbury	d							06 20														
85	—	—	Worcester Shrub Hill	a							06 40														07 56
112	0	92¾	Birmingham New Street	a		00 01	00 11																		
—	—	—		d	23p09			05 22	05 52	06 00		06 19	06 22		06 30	06 49	06 52	07 03	07 19	07 22	07 30	07 49	07 52		08 03
119¾	7¾	—	Water Orton	d																					
—	9½	—	Coleshill Parkway	d				05 35	06 05				06 35				07 05			07 35			08 05		
—	20	—	Nuneaton	d				05 52	06 21				06 52				07 22			07 51			08 22		
—	25¼	—	Hinckley	d					06 29								07 29			07 58			08 29		
—	34	—	Narborough	d					06 37								07 37			08 06			08 37		
—	37	—	South Wigston	d					06 42								07 42			08 10			08 42		
—	38¾	—	Leicester	a				06 13	06 50				07 17				07 48			08 15			08 48		
127	—	—	Wilnecote	d	23p24							06 35							07 34						
128¾	—	—	Tamworth	d	23p28							06 39				07 07		07 19	07 38			08 07			08 19
141¾	—	—	Burton-on-Trent	d	23p40							06 51				07 19		07 29	07 50			08 19			08 29
146½	—	—	Willington	d	23p45											07 25						08 25			
152¾	—	—	Derby	a	23p55					06 32		07 05			07 11	07 34		07 42	08 05		08 11	08 34			08 42
—	—	—		d	23p59							07 10				07 40			08 10			08 40			
161	—	—	Long Eaton	d								07 25				07 49			08 19						
164	—	—	Attenborough	d								07 31													
165½	—	—	Beeston	d								07 35				07 58			08 27						
168¾	—	—	Nottingham	a	00 18							07 41				08 08			08 33			09 05			

		XC	GW	XC	XC	XC	XC	XC	XC		XC	XC	XC	XC	XC	XC	XC	XC	XC		XC	GW	XC	XC	XC
		◇1 G ✠	H	1 I ✠	◇1 J ✠	◇1 ✠	◇1	1 K	◇1 ✠		1 B ✠	◇1 L ✠	◇1 M ✠	◇1 N ✠	◇1 ✠	1 O	◇1 ✠	◇1 B	◇1 ✠	P	◇1 Q R ✠	N	◇1 ✠	◇1 ✠	1
Cardiff Central	d						06 40						07 00		07 45									08 45	
Newport (South Wales)	d						06 55						07 15		08 02									09 02	
Bristol Temple Meads	d				07 00				07 30				08 00				08 30				09 00	08 41			
Bristol Parkway	d				07 10				07 40				08 10				08 40				09 10	08 52			
Gloucester	d	07 10	07 14				07 46								08 46							09 37		09 46	
Cheltenham Spa	d	07 21	07 25		07 42		07 57		08 12				08 42		08 57		09 12				09 42	09 48		09 57	
Ashchurch for Tewkesbury	d	07 29	07 34				08 05															09 56			
Worcester Shrub Hill	a		07 54																			10 14			
Birmingham New Street	a	08 16			08 26		08 45		08 56				09 26		09 45		09 56				10 26			10 45	
	d	08 22		08 19		08 30	08 49	08 52	09 03		09 19	09 22		09 30	09 49	09 52	10 03	10 19	10 22				10 30	10 49	10 52
Water Orton	d							09 03																	11 03
Coleshill Parkway	d	08 35						09 07				09 35				10 07			10 35						11 07
Nuneaton	d	08 52						09 22				09 52				10 23			10 52						11 23
Hinckley	d							09 30								10 30									11 30
Narborough	d							09 39								10 39									11 39
South Wigston	d															10 44									
Leicester	a	09 14						09 49				10 15				10 50			11 15						11 48
Wilnecote	d						09 05																	11 05	
Tamworth	d			08 36			09 09				09 36				10 07		10 19	10 36						11 09	
Burton-on-Trent	d			08 48			09 21		09 26		09 48				10 19			10 48						11 21	
Willington	d														10 25										
Derby	a			08 59		09 05	09 34		09 39		09 59			10 05	10 34		10 40	10 59					11 05	11 33	
	d			09 05			09 39				10 05				10 41			11 05						11 39	
Long Eaton	d			09 14							10 14							11 14							
Attenborough	d			09 21																					
Beeston	d			09 24							10 22							11 22							
Nottingham	a			09 33			10 05				10 32				11 05			11 32						12 05	

A from 17 September until 22 October
B To Stansted Airport
C To Glasgow Central
D To Newcastle
E To Edinburgh
F From Bath Spa to Glasgow Central
G To Stansted Airport. ✠ from Birmingham New Street
H To Great Malvern
I To Manchester Piccadilly
J From Guildford to Newcastle
K From Plymouth to Edinburgh
L To Manchester Piccadilly. ✠ from Bristol Temple Meads
M From Reading to Newcastle
N ✠ from Newport (South Wales)
O From Plymouth to Glasgow Central
P From Paignton to Manchester Piccadilly
Q From Warminster to Great Malvern
R From Winchester to Newcastle

Bristol and Cardiff - Birmingham Leicester, Derby and Nottingham

Network Diagram - see first Page of Table 50

		XC ◇1 A 🍴	XC ◇1	XC ◇1 B 🍴	XC ◇1 C 🍴		XC ◇1 D 🍴	XC ◇1 E 🍴	XC 1	XC ◇1 F 🍴	XC ◇1 🍴	XC ◇1 B 🍴	XC ◇1 C 🍴	GW ◇ G	XC ◇1 H 🍴	E	XC ◇1 🍴	XC 1 I	XC ◇1 🍴	XC 1 B	XC ◇1 J 🍴	XC ◇1 D 🍴	XC ◇1 E 🍴	XC ◇1 🍴	XC 1
Cardiff Central 7	d							09 45									10 45							11 45	
Newport (South Wales)	d							10 00									11 00							12 02	
Bristol Temple Meads 10	d	09 30			10 00					10 30			11 00	10 41					11 30			12 00			
Bristol Parkway 7	d	09 40			10 10					10 40			11 10	10 52					11 40			12 10			
Gloucester 7	d							10 46						11 35			11 46							12 46	
Cheltenham Spa	d	10 12			10 42			10 57		11 12			11 42	11 48			11 57		12 12			12 42		12 57	
Ashchurch for Tewkesbury	d													11 56										13 05	
Worcester Shrub Hill 7	a													12 14											
Birmingham New Street 12	a	10 56			11 26			11 45		11 58			12 26				12 45		12 56			13 26		13 45	
	d	11 03	11 19	11 22			11 30	11 49	11 52	12 03	12 19	12 22			12 30		12 49	12 52	13 03	13 19	13 22		13 30	13 49	13 52
Water Orton	d																	13 03							
Coleshill Parkway	d			11 35					12 07			12 35						13 07			13 35				14 07
Nuneaton	d			11 52					12 23			12 52						13 22			13 52				14 23
Hinckley	d								12 30									13 29							14 30
Narborough	d								12 38									13 38							14 39
South Wigston	d								12 43																14 43
Leicester	a			12 13					12 49			13 13						13 50			14 14				14 50
Wilnecote	d																13 05							14 05	
Tamworth	d		11 36					12 07		12 19	12 37						13 09			13 36				14 09	
Burton-on-Trent	d	11 26	11 48					12 19			12 50						13 20		13 28	13 48				14 21	
Willington	d							12 25																	
Derby 6	a	11 39	11 59				12 05	12 33		12 41	13 05				13 08		13 34		13 40	13 59			14 05	14 34	
	d		12 05					12 39			13 10						13 39			14 05				14 39	
Long Eaton	d		12 14								13 19									14 14					
Attenborough	d																								
Beeston	d		12 22								13 27									14 24					
Nottingham 8	a		12 32					13 05			13 33						14 05			14 32				15 05	

			XC ◇1 F 🍴	XC 1	XC ◇1 B 🍴	XC ◇1 C 🍴	GW ◇ K	XC ◇1 H 🍴	XC ◇1 E 🍴	XC 1 L	XC ◇1 🍴		XC 1 B	XC ◇1 M 🍴	XC ◇1 D 🍴	XC ◇1 E 🍴	XC ◇1 🍴	XC 1 N	XC ◇1 🍴	XC 1	XC 1	B	XC ◇1 C 🍴	XC ◇1 G 🍴	GW ◇
Cardiff Central 7	d								12 45								13 45								
Newport (South Wales)	d								13 01								14 00								
Bristol Temple Meads 10	d		12 30			13 00	12 41				13 30				14 00				14 30					15 00	14 41
Bristol Parkway 7	d		12 40			13 10	12 52				13 40				14 10				14 40					15 10	14 52
Gloucester 7	d						13 37		13 46								14 46								15 36
Cheltenham Spa	d		13 12			13 42	13 48		13 57		14 12				14 42		14 57		15 12					15 42	15 48
Ashchurch for Tewkesbury	d						13 56																		15 56
Worcester Shrub Hill 7	a						14 14																		16 15
Birmingham New Street 12	a		13 56			14 26			14 45		14 56				15 26		15 45		15 56					16 26	
	d		14 03	14 19	14 22			14 30	14 49	14 52	15 03		15 19	15 22		15 30	15 49	15 52	16 03	16 09	16 19		16 22		
Water Orton	d									15 03										16 19					
Coleshill Parkway	d				14 35					15 07				15 35				16 07		16 23			16 35		
Nuneaton	d				14 52					15 22				15 52				16 23		16 39			16 52		
Hinckley	d									15 30								16 30		16 46					
Narborough	d									15 38								16 39		16 55					
South Wigston	d																	16 43							
Leicester	a				15 14					15 50				16 14				16 50		17 06			17 14		
Wilnecote	d								15 05								16 05								
Tamworth	d		14 19	14 36					15 09				15 36				16 09		16 19		16 39				
Burton-on-Trent	d			14 48					15 21		15 26		15 48				16 21				16 51				
Willington	d																								
Derby 6	a		14 40	15 00				15 06	15 34		15 39		16 00			16 06	16 34		16 40		17 05				
	d			15 05					15 39				16 05				16 39				17 10				
Long Eaton	d			15 14									16 14								17 19				
Attenborough	d																								
Beeston	d			15 22									16 22								17 27				
Nottingham 8	a			15 32					16 05				16 32				17 05				17 33				

A From Plymouth to Edinburgh
B To Stansted Airport
C To Manchester Piccadilly
D From Reading to Newcastle
E 🍴 from Newport (South Wales)
F From Penzance to Glasgow Central
G From Southampton Central to Great Malvern
H From Southampton Central to Newcastle
I From Plymouth to Aberdeen
J From Paignton to Manchester Piccadilly
K From Brighton to Great Malvern
L From Plymouth to Dundee
M From Penzance to Manchester Piccadilly
N From Plymouth to Glasgow Central

Bristol and Cardiff - Birmingham Leicester, Derby and Nottingham

Network Diagram - see first Page of Table 50

		XC ◇1 A 🍴	XC ◇1 B 🍴	XC ◇1 C	XC MX ◇1 D 🍴	XC MO ◇1 D 🍴	XC 1		XC 1	XC ◇1 E	XC ◇1 F 🍴	XC ◇1 G 🍴	XC 1	XC ◇1	XC 1 D	XC ◇1 🍴	XC 1	E	XC ◇1 H	XC ◇1 I 🍴	GW J	XC ◇1 🍴	XC ◇1	XC 1 K	XC ◇1 🍴
Cardiff Central 7	d		14 45											15 45									16 45		
Newport (South Wales)	d		15 01											16 00									17 00		
Bristol Temple Meads 10	d				15 30	15 30					16 00					16 30				17 00	16 41				17 30
Bristol Parkway 7	d				15 40	15 40					16 10					16 40				17 10	16 52				17 40
Gloucester 7	d		15 46											16 46							17 37		17 46		
Cheltenham Spa	d		15 57		16 11	16 12					16 42			16 57		17 12				17 42	17 48		17 58		18 12
Ashchurch for Tewkesbury	d																				17 56				
Worcester Shrub Hill 7	a																				18 18				
Birmingham New Street 12	a		16 45		16 56	16 56					17 26			17 45		17 56				18 26			18 45		18 55
	d	16 30	16 49	16 52	17 03	17 03	17 09		17 19	17 22		17 30	17 39	17 49	17 52	18 03	18 19		18 22			18 30	18 49	18 52	19 03
Water Orton	d						17 23						17 50		18 03										
Coleshill Parkway	d			17 05			17 27			17 35					18 07				18 35					19 07	
Nuneaton	d			17 22			17 44			17 52					18 23				18 52					19 23	
Hinckley	d			17 29			17 51								18 30									19 30	
Narborough	d			17 39											18 39									19 39	
South Wigston	d						18 03								18 44									19 44	
Leicester	a			17 50			18 09			18 15					18 50				19 13					19 50	
Wilnecote	d		17 05										17 58										19 05		
Tamworth	d		17 09						17 36				18 02	18 09		18 19	18 36						19 09		
Burton-on-Trent	d		17 21		17 26	17 26			17 48				18 13	18 21			18 48						19 22		19 26
Willington	d												18 19												
Derby 6	a	17 08	17 34		17 38	17 38			17 59			18 05	18 31	18 34		18 40	18 59					19 05	19 34		19 39
	d		17 39						18 05					18 39			19 05						19 39		
Long Eaton	d								18 14								19 14								
Attenborough	d																								
Beeston	d								18 26								19 23								
Nottingham 8	a		18 05						18 32					19 05			19 32						20 03		

		XC 1	XC ◇1 E		XC ◇1 L 🍴	XC ◇1 G 🍴	XC ◇1 M 🍴	XC 1	XC ◇1 N 🍴	XC ◇1 C	XC ◇1 H I 🍴	GW O	XC ◇1		XC ◇1 N	XC ◇1 🍴	XC 1	XC ◇1	XC ◇1	XC 1 P	XC ◇1	GW Q	GW ◇1 🛏		XC 1
Cardiff Central 7	d						17 45								18 45				19 50						
Newport (South Wales)	d						18 00								19 01				20 05						
Bristol Temple Meads 10	d				18 00				18 30		19 00	18 41				19 30		20 00			20 30	20 41			
Bristol Parkway 7	d				18 10				18 40		19 10	18 52				19 40		20 10			20 40	20 52			
Gloucester 7	d						18 46					19 38			19 46			20 46	20 58			21 34	21 52		
Cheltenham Spa	d				18 42		18 57		19 12		19 42	19 48			19 58	20 12		20 56	21 09		21 17	21 45	22 04		
Ashchurch for Tewkesbury	d											19 56			20 05							21 54			
Worcester Shrub Hill 7	a											20 15										22 14	22 24		
Birmingham New Street 12	a				19 26		19 45		19 56		20 28				20 45	20 52		21 46	21 51		22 06				
	d	19 19	19 22			19 30	19 49	19 52	20 03	20 22			20 30		20 49	21 03	20 52			22 03					22 22
Water Orton	d							20 03																	
Coleshill Parkway	d		19 35					20 07		20 35							21 05								22 35
Nuneaton	d		19 52					20 23		20 52							21 22								22 52
Hinckley	d							20 30									21 29								22 59
Narborough	d							20 39									21 38								23 08
South Wigston	d							20 44									21 42								23 12
Leicester	a		20 16					20 50		21 14							21 50								23 18
Wilnecote	d						20 05								21 05										
Tamworth	d	19 36					20 09		20 19						21 09	21 19				22 28					
Burton-on-Trent	d	19 48					20 21								21 21	21 30				22 40					
Willington	d																								
Derby 6	a	19 59				20 05	20 34		20 42				21 11		21 34	21 43				22 54					
	d	20 05					20 40								21 40					22 59					
Long Eaton	d	20 14					20 49								21 52					23 11					
Attenborough	d														21 58					23 17					
Beeston	d	20 23					20 58								22 02					23 20					
Nottingham 8	a	20 32					21 06								22 08					23 27					

A From Southampton Central to Edinburgh
B 🍴 from Newport (South Wales)
C To Cambridge
D From Plymouth to Edinburgh
E To Stansted Airport
F From Paignton to Manchester Piccadilly
G From Reading to Newcastle
H To Manchester Piccadilly
I From Warminster to Great Malvern
J From Southampton Central to Newcastle
K From Plymouth to Leeds
L From Exeter St Davids to Manchester Piccadilly
M 🍴 from Newport (South Wales) to Birmingham New Street
N From Plymouth to Leeds. 🍴 to Birmingham New Street
O From Southampton Central to Leeds
P From Plymouth
Q From London Paddington

Bristol and Cardiff - Birmingham Leicester, Derby and Nottingham

Network Diagram - see first Page of Table 50

		XC ■	XC ◇■	XC ◇■ A	XC ◇■
Cardiff Central	d		21 05		21 50
Newport (South Wales)	d		21 21		22 05
Bristol Temple Meads	d			22 00	
Bristol Parkway	d			22 10	
Gloucester	d		22 04		22 47
Cheltenham Spa	d		22 15	22 42	22 58
Ashchurch for Tewkesbury	d		22 23		
Worcester Shrub Hill	a				
Birmingham New Street	a		23 36	23 44	00 01
	d	23 09			
Water Orton	d				
Coleshill Parkway	d				
Nuneaton	d				
Hinckley	d				
Narborough	d				
South Wigston	d				
Leicester	a				
Wilnecote	d	23 24			
Tamworth	d	23 28			
Burton-on-Trent	d	23 40			
Willington	d	23 45			
Derby	a	23 55			
	d	23 59			
Long Eaton	d				
Attenborough	d				
Beeston	d				
Nottingham	a	00 18			

Saturdays

		XC ■	XC ◇■	XC ◇■ B	GW	XC ■	XC ◇■ C ⊥	XC ■ ⊥	XC ◇■ B ⊥	XC ◇■ D ⊥	XC ■	XC ■	XC ◇■ E ⊥	XC ■ ⊥	XC ◇■ B ⊥	XC ◇■ D ⊥	XC ■	XC ■	XC ◇■ C ⊥	XC ◇■ F ⊥	GW	XC ■ ⊥	XC ◇■ G ⊥
Cardiff Central	d		21p50																				
Newport (South Wales)	d		22p05																				
Bristol Temple Meads	d																		06 15				07 00
Bristol Parkway	d																		06 25				07 10
Gloucester	d		22p47		05 50														07 01	07 07	07 15		
Cheltenham Spa	d		22p58		06 00														07 12	07 18	07 25		07 42
Ashchurch for Tewkesbury	d				06 09															07 25	07 34		
Worcester Shrub Hill	a				06 33																07 52		
Birmingham New Street	a		00 01																07 56	08 08			08 26
	d	23p09		05 22		05 52	05 57	06 19	06 22	06 30	06 49	06 52	07 03	07 19	07 22	07 30	07 49	07 52	08 03	08 22		08 19	
Water Orton	d											07 02											
Coleshill Parkway	d			05 35		06 05			06 35			07 06			07 35			08 05		08 35			
Nuneaton	d			05 52		06 21			06 52			07 22			07 52			08 22		08 52			
Hinckley	d					06 28						07 29						08 29					
Narborough	d					06 36						07 37						08 38					
South Wigston	d					06 41						07 42						08 42					
Leicester	a			06 13		06 47			07 13			07 48			08 13			08 48		09 13			
Wilnecote	d	23p24						06 35						07 34									
Tamworth	d	23p28					06 13	06 39		06 46	07 07		07 19	07 38		07 46	08 07		08 19			08 36	
Burton-on-Trent	d	23p40					06 24	06 51		06 56	07 19		07 29	07 50		07 56	08 17		08 29			08 48	
Willington	d	23p45									07 25						08 25						
Derby	a	23p55					06 35	07 05		07 09	07 34		07 42	08 05		08 09	08 34		08 42			08 59	
	d	23p59						07 10			07 39			08 10			08 39					09 05	
Long Eaton	d							07 22			07 52			08 19								09 14	
Attenborough	d							07 28														09 21	
Beeston	d							07 32			07 59			08 27								09 24	
Nottingham	a	00 18						07 38			08 08			08 34			09 05					09 33	

A From Paignton
B To Stansted Airport
C To Glasgow Central
D To Newcastle
E To Edinburgh
F To Stansted Airport. ⊥ from Birmingham New Street
G To Manchester Piccadilly

Bristol and Cardiff - Birmingham Leicester, Derby and Nottingham

Network Diagram - see first Page of Table 50

		XC ◇■ A ⊥	XC ◇■	XC ■	XC ◇■ B ⊥	XC ■ ⊥	XC ◇■ C ⊥	XC ◇■ D ⊥	XC ◇■ E ⊥	XC ◇■ F ⊥	XC ■	XC ◇■ G ⊥	XC ■	XC ◇■ C ⊥	XC ◇■ H ⊥	GW I	XC ◇■ J ⊥	XC ◇■ F ⊥	XC ■	XC ◇■ B ⊥	XC ■	XC ◇■ C ⊥	XC ◇■ D ⊥
Cardiff Central	d		06 40					07 00		07 45								08 45					
Newport (South Wales)	d		06 55					07 15		08 00								09 00					
Bristol Temple Meads	d				07 30			08 00				08 30			09 00	08 41				09 30			10 00
Bristol Parkway	d				07 40			08 10				08 40			09 10	08 52				09 40			10 10
Gloucester	d		07 46							08 47						09 38		09 46					
Cheltenham Spa	d		07 57		08 12			08 42		08 58		09 12			09 42	09 48		09 57		10 12			10 42
Ashchurch for Tewkesbury	d		08 04													09 57							
Worcester Shrub Hill	a															10 14							
Birmingham New Street	a		08 45		08 56			09 26		09 45		09 56			10 26			10 45		10 56			11 26
	d	08 30	08 49	08 52	09 03	09 19	09 22		09 30	09 49	09 52	10 03	10 19	10 22			10 30	10 49	10 52	11 03	11 19	11 22	
Water Orton	d			09 03															11 03				
Coleshill Parkway	d			09 07			09 35				10 07			10 35					11 07			11 35	
Nuneaton	d			09 23			09 52				10 24			10 52					11 23			11 52	
Hinckley	d			09 30							10 31								11 30				
Narborough	d			09 39							10 39								11 39				
South Wigston	d										10 44												
Leicester	a			09 48			10 14				10 50			11 14					11 48			12 14	
Wilnecote	d		09 05															11 05					
Tamworth	d		09 09			09 36				10 07		10 19	10 36					11 09			11 36		
Burton-on-Trent	d		09 21		09 28	09 48				10 19			10 48					11 21		11 28	11 48		
Willington	d									10 25													
Derby	a	09 06	09 34		09 41	09 59			10 05	10 34		10 41	10 59				11 05	11 34		11 41	11 59		
	d		09 39			10 05				10 39			11 05					11 39			12 05		
Long Eaton	d					10 14							11 14								12 15		
Attenborough	d																						
Beeston	d					10 22							11 22								12 23		
Nottingham	a		10 05			10 33				11 05			11 33					12 05			12 33		

		XC ◇■ K ⊥	XC ◇■ F ⊥	XC ■	XC ◇■ L ⊥	XC ■ ⊥	XC ◇■ C ⊥	XC ◇■ M ⊥	GW ◇ N	XC ◇■ J ⊥	XC ◇■ F ⊥	XC ■	XC ◇■ O ⊥	XC ■	XC ◇■ C ⊥	XC ◇■ H ⊥	XC ◇■ K ⊥	XC ◇■ F ⊥	XC ■	XC ◇■ L ⊥	XC ■	XC ◇■ C ⊥
Cardiff Central	d		09 45								10 45							11 45				
Newport (South Wales)	d		10 00								11 00							12 00				
Bristol Temple Meads	d				10 30			11 00	10 41				11 30			12 00				12 30		
Bristol Parkway	d				10 40			11 10	10 52				11 40			12 10				12 40		
Gloucester	d		10 46						11 38		11 46							12 46				
Cheltenham Spa	d		10 57		11 12			11 42	11 48		11 57		12 12			12 42		12 57		13 12		
Ashchurch for Tewkesbury	d								11 58									13 05				
Worcester Shrub Hill	a								12 15													
Birmingham New Street	a		11 45		11 56			12 26			12 45		12 56			13 26		13 45		13 56		
	d	11 30	11 49	11 52	12 03	12 19	12 22			12 30	12 49	12 52	13 03	13 19	13 22		13 30	13 49	13 52	14 03	14 19	14 22
Water Orton	d											13 03										
Coleshill Parkway	d			12 08			12 35					13 07			13 35				14 08			14 35
Nuneaton	d			12 24			12 52					13 23			13 52				14 24			14 52
Hinckley	d			12 31								13 30							14 31			
Narborough	d			12 39								13 39							14 39			
South Wigston	d			12 43															14 44			
Leicester	a			12 49			13 14					13 48			14 14				14 50			15 14
Wilnecote	d										13 05							14 05				
Tamworth	d		12 07		12 19	12 36					13 09			13 36				14 09		14 19	14 36	
Burton-on-Trent	d		12 19			12 48					13 21		13 27	13 50				14 21			14 47	
Willington	d		12 25																			
Derby	a	12 05	12 34		12 41	13 05				13 08	13 34		13 41	14 05			14 08	14 35		14 41	14 59	
	d		12 39			13 10					13 39			14 10				14 39			15 05	
Long Eaton	d					13 19								14 19							15 14	
Attenborough	d																					
Beeston	d					13 27								14 27							15 24	
Nottingham	a		13 05			13 33					14 05			14 33				15 05			15 33	

A From Guildford to Newcastle
B From Plymouth to Edinburgh
C To Stansted Airport
D To Manchester Piccadilly
E From Bournemouth to Newcastle
F ⊥ from Newport (South Wales)
G From Plymouth to Glasgow Central
H From Paignton to Manchester Piccadilly
I From Warminster to Great Malvern
J From Southampton Central to Newcastle
K From Reading to Newcastle
L From Penzance to Glasgow Central
M From Plymouth to Manchester Piccadilly
N From Southampton Central to Worcester Foregate Street
O From Plymouth to Aberdeen

Bristol and Cardiff - Birmingham
Leicester, Derby and Nottingham

Network Diagram - see first Page of Table 50

		XC ◇1 A [trolley]	GW ◇ B	XC ◇1 C [trolley]	XC ◇1 D [trolley]	XC 1	XC ◇1 E [trolley]	XC ◇1 F [trolley]		XC 1	XC ◇1 G H [trolley]	XC ◇1 I [trolley]	XC ◇1 D [trolley]	XC ◇1 [trolley]	XC 1 J	XC ◇1 [trolley]	XC 1 G	XC ◇1 [trolley]	A	XC ◇1 K C [trolley]	GW ◇ D	XC ◇1 [trolley]	XC ◇1 L [trolley]	XC 1	XC ◇1 [trolley]
Cardiff Central 7	d				12 45									13 45									14 45		
Newport (South Wales)	d				13 00									14 00									15 00		
Bristol Temple Meads 10	d	13 00	12 41				13 30	13 30				14 00				14 30				15 00	14 41				15 30
Bristol Parkway 7	d	13 10	12 52				13 40	13 40				14 10				14 40				15 10	14 52				15 40
Gloucester 7	d		13 38		13 46									14 46							15 38		15 46		
Cheltenham Spa	d	13 42	13 48		13 57		14 12	14 12				14 42		14 57		15 12				15 42	15 48		15 57		16 12
Ashchurch for Tewkesbury	d		13 57																		15 57				
Worcester Shrub Hill 7	a		14 15																		16 14				
Birmingham New Street 12	a	14 26			14 45		14 56	14 56				15 26		15 45		15 55				16 26			16 45		16 56
	d			14 30	14 49	14 52	15 03	15 03		15 19	15 22		15 30	15 49	15 52	16 03	16 19	16 22				16 30	16 49	16 52	17 03
Water Orton	d					15 03																		17 03	
Coleshill Parkway	d					15 07					15 35				16 08			16 35						17 07	
Nuneaton	d					15 23					15 52				16 24			16 52						17 23	
Hinckley	d					15 30									16 31									17 30	
Narborough	d					15 39									16 39									17 39	
South Wigston	d														16 44										
Leicester	a					15 48					16 14				16 50			17 14						17 48	
Wilnecote	d				15 05									16 05									17 05		
Tamworth	d				15 09					15 36				16 09		16 19	16 38						17 09		
Burton-on-Trent	d				15 21		15 27	15 27		15 48				16 21			16 50						17 21		17 26
Willington	d																								
Derby 6	a			15 05	15 34		15 38	15 41		15 59			16 05	16 34		16 40	17 05					17 08	17 34		17 41
	d				15 39					16 05				16 39			17 10						17 39		
Long Eaton	d									16 14							17 19								
Attenborough	d																								
Beeston	d									16 24							17 27								
Nottingham 8	a				16 05					16 33				17 05			17 33						18 05		

		XC 1	XC ◇1 G	XC ◇1 M [trolley]		XC ◇1 I [trolley]	XC ◇1	XC 1	XC ◇1 L [trolley]	XC 1	XC ◇1 G A	XC ◇1 N [trolley]	GW C	XC ◇1 [trolley]		XC ◇1 O	XC 1	XC ◇1 P [trolley]	XC 1 Q	XC 1 G	XC ◇1 R I	XC ◇1 S [trolley]	XC ◇1 [trolley]	XC ◇1 [trolley]
Cardiff Central 7	d						15 45									16 45								17 45
Newport (South Wales)	d						16 00									17 00								18 00
Bristol Temple Meads 10	d			16 00					16 30			17 00	16 41					17 30				18 00		
Bristol Parkway 7	d			16 10					16 40			17 10	16 52					17 40				18 10		
Gloucester 7	d						16 46						17 38			17 46								18 46
Cheltenham Spa	d			16 42			16 57		17 12			17 42	17 48			17 58		18 12				18 42		18 57
Ashchurch for Tewkesbury	d												17 57											
Worcester Shrub Hill 7	a												18 15											
Birmingham New Street 12	a			17 26			17 45		17 56			18 26				18 45		18 56				19 26		19 45
	d	17 19	17 22			17 30	17 49	17 52	18 03	18 19	18 22			18 30		18 49	18 52	19 03	19 19	19 19	19 22		19 30	19 49
Water Orton	d																							
Coleshill Parkway	d		17 35					18 05			18 35						19 05				19 35			
Nuneaton	d		17 52					18 22			18 52						19 22				19 52			
Hinckley	d							18 29									19 29							
Narborough	d							18 38									19 38							
South Wigston	d							18 42									19 42							
Leicester	a		18 14					18 48			19 13						19 48				20 14			
Wilnecote	d						18 05									19 05								20 05
Tamworth	d	17 36					18 09		18 19	18 36						19 09			19 36	19 36				20 09
Burton-on-Trent	d	17 48					18 21			18 47						19 21		19 27	19 48	19 48				20 21
Willington	d						18 28																	
Derby 6	a	17 59				18 05	18 34		18 41	18 59				19 05		19 35		19 39	19 59	19 59			20 05	20 34
	d	18 05					18 39			19 05						19 39			20 05	20 05				20 39
Long Eaton	d	18 14								19 14									20 14	20 14				20 49
Attenborough	d																							
Beeston	d	18 22								19 24									20 24	20 24				20 57
Nottingham 8	a	18 32					19 05			19 33						20 05			20 32	20 35				21 04

A To Manchester Piccadilly
B From Brighton to Great Malvern
C From Southampton Central to Newcastle
D [trolley] from Newport (South Wales)
E until 8 September. From Newquay to Dundee
F from 15 September. From Plymouth to Dundee
G To Stansted Airport
H From Penzance to Manchester Piccadilly
I From Reading to Newcastle
J From Plymouth to Glasgow Central
K From Southampton Central to Great Malvern
L From Plymouth to Newcastle
M From Paignton to Manchester Piccadilly
N From Warminster to Great Malvern
O From Plymouth to York
P until 8 September
Q from 15 September
R From Exeter St Davids to Manchester Piccadilly
S [trolley] from Newport (South Wales) to Birmingham New Street

Bristol and Cardiff - Birmingham
Leicester, Derby and Nottingham

Network Diagram - see first Page of Table 50

		XC 1	XC ◇1 A [trolley]	XC ◇1 B	XC ◇1 C [trolley]	GW ◇ D	GW E	XC ◇1 F	XC ◇1	XC 1		XC ◇1 G H [trolley]	XC ◇1 I [trolley]	XC ◇1 J [trolley]	XC ◇1 K	XC ◇1 L [trolley]	XC ◇1 M [trolley]	XC ◇1 N [trolley]	XC ◇1 O	XC ◇1 P		XC ◇1 N	GW	XC [bus]	XC 1
Cardiff Central 7	d								18 45										20 00	20 00		20 00			
Newport (South Wales)	d								19 00										20 15	20 15		20 15			
Bristol Temple Meads 10	d		18 30		19 00	18 41	18 41					19 30	19 30		20 00	20 30	20 30	20 30					20 43		
Bristol Parkway 7	d		18 40		19 10	18 52	18 52					19 40	19 40		20 10	20 40	20 40	20 40					20 52		
Gloucester 7	d					19 38	19 38		19 46										21 07	21 07		21 07	21 38		
Cheltenham Spa	d		19 12		19 42	19 48	19 48		19 57			20 12	20 12		20 42	21 12	21 12	21 12	21 18	21 18		21 18	21 48		
Ashchurch for Tewkesbury	d					19 57	19 57												21 25	21 25		21 25	21 58		
Worcester Shrub Hill 7	a					20 15	20 15																22 18		
Birmingham New Street 12	a		19 58		20 26				20 40			20 54	20 53		21 38	21 52	21 52	21 53	22 07	22 07		22 07			
	d	19 52	20 03	20 22				20 30	20 49	20 52			21 03	21 03		21 56	21 57			22 10		22 10		22 20	22 22
Water Orton	d	20 03																							
Coleshill Parkway	d	20 07		20 35						21 05															22 35
Nuneaton	d	20 23		20 52						21 21															22 52
Hinckley	d	20 30								21 29															22 59
Narborough	d	20 39								21 37															23 08
South Wigston	d	20 43								21 42															23 12
Leicester	a	20 49		21 13						21 48															23 18
Wilnecote	d								21 04																
Tamworth	d		20 19						21 09				21 19	21 20						22a27		22 27		22 55	
Burton-on-Trent	d								21 21				21 31	21 30								22 39		23 15	
Willington	d																					22 45		23 30	
Derby 6	a		20 42					21 24	21 34				21 44	21 41		22 31	22 32					22 55		23s45	
	d								21 40													23 00			
Long Eaton	d								21 52													23 12		00s12	
Attenborough	d								21 58													23 18		00s23	
Beeston	d								22 02													23 22		00s29	
Nottingham 8	a								22 08													23 28		00 49	

		XC ◇1	XC 1 P	XC Q [bus]
Cardiff Central 7	d	20 50		
Newport (South Wales)	d	21 05		
Bristol Temple Meads 10	d			
Bristol Parkway 7	d			
Gloucester 7	d	21 49		
Cheltenham Spa	d	22 00		
Ashchurch for Tewkesbury	d			
Worcester Shrub Hill 7	a			
Birmingham New Street 12	a	22 42		
	d		22 49	22 49
Water Orton	d			
Coleshill Parkway	d			
Nuneaton	d			
Hinckley	d			
Narborough	d			
South Wigston	d			
Leicester	a			
Wilnecote	d		23 04	23 19
Tamworth	d		23 08	23 24
Burton-on-Trent	d		23 20	23s44
Willington	d			
Derby 6	a		23 33	00 04
	d			
Long Eaton	d			
Attenborough	d			
Beeston	d			
Nottingham 8	a			

A From Plymouth to Leeds. [trolley] to Birmingham New Street
B To Cambridge
C To Manchester Piccadilly
D until 8 September. From Weymouth to Great Malvern
E from 15 September. From Warminster to Great Malvern
F From Southampton Central to York
G until 8 September. From Newquay to Manchester Piccadilly
H from 15 September. From Plymouth to Leeds. [trolley] to Birmingham New Street
I until 8 September. From Bournemouth to Leeds
J From Paignton
K until 23 June. From Penzance to Leeds. [trolley] to Birmingham New Street
L from 30 June until 8 September. From Penzance to Leeds. [trolley] to Birmingham New Street
M from 15 September. From Plymouth
N from 15 September until 20 October
O from 30 June until 8 September, from 27 October
P until 23 June
Q from 30 June

Sundays until 24 June

Bristol and Cardiff - Birmingham Leicester, Derby and Nottingham

Network Diagram - see first Page of Table 50

		XC ◇■ A ⌶	XC ■	XC ◇■ B ⌶	XC ◇■ A ⌶	XC ■	XC ◇■ C ⌶	XC ◇■ ⌶	XC ◇■ B ⌶	XC ■	XC ◇■ C ⌶	XC ◇■ D ⌶	XC ◇■ E ⌶	XC ◇■ F ⌶	XC ■	XC ◇■ C ⌶	XC ◇■ D ⌶	XC ◇■ E ⌶	XC ◇■ G ⌶	XC ■ C	XC ◇■ H ⌶	XC ◇■ ⌶	GW
Cardiff Central 7	d												10 45					11 45					
Newport (South Wales)	d												10 59					11 59					
Bristol Temple Meads 10	d				09 15				10 30					11 30					12 30			13 00	12 41
Bristol Parkway 7	d				09 25				10 40					11 40					12 40			13 10	12 52
Gloucester 7	d				10 01								11 51					12 47					13 37
Cheltenham Spa	d				10 12				11 12				12 03	12 12				12 58	13 12			13 42	13 49
Ashchurch for Tewkesbury	d																						13 57
Worcester Shrub Hill 7	a																						14 17
Birmingham New Street 12	a				10 50				11 50				12 45	12 50				13 41	13 50			14 26	
	d	09 03	09 52	10 03	11 03	10 52	11 22	11 49	12 03	11 52	12 22	12 30	12 49	13 03	12 52	13 22	13 30	13 49	14 03	13 52	14 22		
Water Orton	d																						
Coleshill Parkway	d		10 05			11 05	11 35			12 05	12 35				13 05	13 35				14 04	14 35		
Nuneaton	d		10 22			11 22	11 52			12 22	12 52				13 22	13 51				14 20	14 52		
Hinckley	d		10 29			11 29				12 29					13 29					14 27			
Narborough	d		10 37			11 37				12 38					13 37					14 37			
South Wigston	d		10 42							12 42										14 41			
Leicester	a		10 50			11 50	12 13			12 48	13 12				13 50	14 12				14 50	15 12		
Wilnecote	d																						
Tamworth	d	09 19		10 18				12 07	12 19				13 07					14 07	14 19				
Burton-on-Trent	d	09 29		10 29	11 26			12 19					13 19	13 26				14 19					
Willington	d																						
Derby 6	a	09 42		10 39	11 40			12 34	12 43			13 01	13 33	13 42			14 00	14 34	14 42				
	d							12 40					13 40					14 40					
Long Eaton	d																						
Attenborough	d																						
Beeston	d																						
Nottingham 8	a							13 00					14 00					15 02					

		XC ◇■ I ⌶	XC ◇■ E ⌶	XC ◇■ J ⌶	XC ■ C	XC ◇■ ⌶	XC ◇■ K L ⌶	XC ◇■ E ⌶	XC ◇■ G ⌶	XC ◇■ ⌶	XC ■ C	XC ◇■ K L	XC ◇■ E ⌶	XC ◇■ ⌶	XC ◇■ ⌶	M	GW	XC ◇■ C ⌶	XC ■ N	XC ◇■ O	XC ◇■ ⌶	XC ◇■ P ⌶	XC ◇■	XC ◇■ ⌶
Cardiff Central 7	d		12 45						13 45						14 45								15 45	
Newport (South Wales)	d		12 59						13 59						14 59								15 59	
Bristol Temple Meads 10	d			13 30			14 00			14 30			15 00				14 41	15 30			16 00			16 30
Bristol Parkway 7	d			13 40			14 10			14 40			15 10				14 53	15 40			16 10			16 40
Gloucester 7	d		13 51						14 47						15 47		15 52						16 47	
Cheltenham Spa	d		14 02	14 12			14 42		14 58	15 12			15 42		15 58		16 03	16 12			16 42		16 58	17 12
Ashchurch for Tewkesbury	d																16 11							
Worcester Shrub Hill 7	a																16 34							
Birmingham New Street 12	a		14 45	14 50			15 27		15 41	15 50			16 26		16 41			16 50			17 26		17 41	17 49
	d	14 30	14 49	15 03	14 52	15 22		15 30	15 49	16 03	15 52	16 22		16 30	16 49			17 03	16 52	17 22		17 30	17 49	18 03
Water Orton	d																							
Coleshill Parkway	d				15 05	15 35					16 05	16 35							17 05	17 35				
Nuneaton	d				15 22	15 52					16 22	16 52							17 22	17 52				
Hinckley	d				15 29						16 29								17 29					
Narborough	d				15 37						16 37								17 37					
South Wigston	d										16 42								17 42					
Leicester	a				15 48	16 13					16 48	17 12							17 47	18 12				
Wilnecote	d		15 04																					
Tamworth	d		15 09						16 07	16 19					17 07								18 07	18 19
Burton-on-Trent	d		15 21	15 28					16 19						17 19			17 28					18 19	
Willington	d																							
Derby 6	a	15 04	15 34	15 42				16 02	16 34	16 42				17 04	17 34			17 39				18 04	18 33	18 39
	d		15 40						16 40						17 40								18 40	
Long Eaton	d																							
Attenborough	d																							
Beeston	d																							
Nottingham 8	a		16 00						17 00						18 00								19 00	

A To Edinburgh
B To Glasgow Central
C To Stansted Airport
D To Newcastle
E ⌶ from Newport (South Wales)
F From Plymouth to Aberdeen
G From Plymouth to Glasgow Central
H From Paignton to Manchester Piccadilly
I From Guildford to Newcastle
J From Penzance to Edinburgh
K From Plymouth to Manchester Piccadilly
L From Reading to Newcastle
M From Newquay to Edinburgh
N To Manchester Piccadilly
O From Reading to Edinburgh
P From Plymouth to Edinburgh

Sundays until 24 June

Bristol and Cardiff - Birmingham Leicester, Derby and Nottingham

Network Diagram - see first Page of Table 50

		XC ■	XC ◇■ A	XC ◇■ B ⌶	GW	XC ◇■ C ⌶	XC ◇■	XC ◇■ D ⌶	XC ■	XC ◇■ A	XC ◇■ E ⌶	XC ◇■ C ⌶	XC ◇■	XC ■	XC ◇■ F ⌶	XC ◇■ G	XC ◇■ E ⌶	GW	XC ◇■ H	XC ◇■ ⌶	XC ■ I	XC ◇■ ⌶
Cardiff Central 7	d						16 45						17 45						18 45			
Newport (South Wales)	d						16 59						17 59						18 59			
Bristol Temple Meads 10	d			17 00	16 41			17 30			18 00				18 30		19 00	18 41		19 30		20 00
Bristol Parkway 7	d			17 10	16 52			17 40			18 10				18 40		19 10	18 52		19 40		20 10
Gloucester 7	d				17 35		17 47						18 47					19 38	19 52			
Cheltenham Spa	d			17 42	17 46		17 58	18 12			18 42		18 58		19 12		19 42	19 48	20 02	20 12		20 42
Ashchurch for Tewkesbury	d				17 54													19 57				
Worcester Shrub Hill 7	a				18 14													20 18				
Birmingham New Street 12	a			18 27			18 41	18 51			19 26		19 41		19 56		20 26		20 44	20 50		21 20
	d	17 52	18 22			18 30	18 49	19 03	18 52	19 22		19 30	19 49	19 52	20 03	20 22			20 49	21 03	20 52	
Water Orton	d																					
Coleshill Parkway	d	18 05	18 35						19 05	19 35				20 05		20 35					21 05	
Nuneaton	d	18 22	18 52						19 22	19 52				20 22		20 52					21 22	
Hinckley	d	18 29							19 29					20 29							21 29	
Narborough	d	18 37							19 37					20 38							21 38	
South Wigston	d	18 42							19 41					20 42							21 42	
Leicester	a	18 49	19 12						19 48	20 12				20 48		21 12					21 48	
Wilnecote	d						19 04															
Tamworth	d						19 09						20 07		20 19				21 06	21 19		
Burton-on-Trent	d						19 21	19 26					20 19						21 19	21 30		
Willington	d																					
Derby 6	a					19 03	19 33	19 39				20 01	20 34		20 39				21 33	21 42		
	d						19 40						20 40						21 40			
Long Eaton	d																					
Attenborough	d																					
Beeston	d																					
Nottingham 8	a						20 00						21 00						22 00			

		XC ◇■	XC ◇■ F ⌶	XC ■	XC ◇■	XC ◇■
Cardiff Central 7	d	19 45			20 45	
Newport (South Wales)	d	20 00			20 59	
Bristol Temple Meads 10	d		20 30			22 10
Bristol Parkway 7	d		20 40			22 20
Gloucester 7	d	20 50			21 48	
Cheltenham Spa	d	21 01	21 12		21 59	22 52
Ashchurch for Tewkesbury	d					
Worcester Shrub Hill 7	a					
Birmingham New Street 12	a	21 44	21 51		22 42	23 39
	d		22 03	21 52		
Water Orton	d					
Coleshill Parkway	d			22 05		
Nuneaton	d			22 22		
Hinckley	d			22 29		
Narborough	d			22 37		
South Wigston	d			22 42		
Leicester	a			22 48		
Wilnecote	d					
Tamworth	d		22 18			
Burton-on-Trent	d					
Willington	d					
Derby 6	a		22 40			
	d					
Long Eaton	d					
Attenborough	d					
Beeston	d					
Nottingham 8	a					

A To Stansted Airport
B From Penzance to Manchester Piccadilly
C From Reading to Newcastle
D From Plymouth to Leeds
E To Manchester Piccadilly
F From Plymouth to Leeds. ⌶ to Birmingham New Street
G To Cambridge
H From Penzance to Leeds. ⌶ to Birmingham New Street
I From Paignton

Bristol and Cardiff - Birmingham
Leicester, Derby and Nottingham

Network Diagram - see first Page of Table 50

		XC	XC	XC	XC	XC	XC	XC	XC	XC		XC	XC	XC	XC	XC	XC	XC	XC	XC		XC	XC	XC	GW
		🚌	■	◇■ A ✠	◇■ B ✠	■	◇■ C ✠	◇■ ✠	◇■ A ✠	■		◇■ C ✠	◇■ D ✠	◇■ E ✠	◇■ F ✠	■	◇■ C ✠	◇■ D ✠	◇■ E ✠	◇■ G ✠		■ C	◇■ H ✠	◇■ ✠	
Cardiff Central 7	d													10 45					11 45						
Newport (South Wales)	d													10 59					11 59						
Bristol Temple Meads 10	d				09 15				10 30						11 30					12 30				13 00	12 41
Bristol Parkway 7	d				09 25				10 40						11 40					12 40				13 10	12 52
Gloucester 7	d				10 01									11 51					12 47						13 37
Cheltenham Spa	d				10 12				11 12					12 03	12 12				12 58	13 12				13 42	13 49
Ashchurch for Tewkesbury	d																								13 57
Worcester Shrub Hill 7	a																								14 17
Birmingham New Street 12	a				10 50				11 50					12 45	12 50				13 41	13 50				14 26	
	d	22p49	09 52	10 03	11 03	10 52	11 22	11 49	12 03	11 52		12 22	12 30	12 49	13 03	12 52	13 22	13 30	13 49	14 03		13 52	14 22		
Water Orton	d																								
Coleshill Parkway	d		10 05			11 05	11 35			12 05		12 35				13 05	13 35					14 04	14 35		
Nuneaton	d		10 22			11 22	11 52			12 22		12 52				13 22	13 51					14 20	14 52		
Hinckley	d		10 29			11 29				12 29						13 29						14 27			
Narborough	d		10 37			11 37				12 38						13 37						14 37			
South Wigston	d		10 42							12 42												14 41			
Leicester	a		10 50			11 48	12 13			12 48		13 12				13 50	14 12					14 50	15 12		
Wilnecote	d	23p19																							
Tamworth	d	23p24		10 18				12 07	12 19					13 07					14 07	14 19					
Burton-on-Trent	d	23b44		10 29	11 26			12 19						13 19	13 26				14 19						
Willington	d																								
Derby 6	a	00 04		10 39	11 40			12 33	12 43				13 01	13 33	13 42			14 01	14 34	14 42					
	d							12 40						13 40					14 42						
Long Eaton	d																								
Attenborough	d																								
Beeston	d																								
Nottingham 8	a							13 00						14 00					15 02						

		XC	XC	XC	XC	XC		XC	XC	XC	XC	XC	XC	XC	XC	XC		GW	XC	XC	XC	XC	XC	XC	XC
		◇■ I ✠	◇■ E ✠	◇■ J ✠	■	◇■ C ✠		◇■ K L ✠	◇■ E ✠	◇■ G ✠	◇■ ✠	■ C	◇■ K L	◇■ E ✠	◇■ ✠	◇■ ✠	M		◇■ C ✠	■ N	◇■ O	◇■ ✠	◇■ C ✠	■	◇■
Cardiff Central 7	d		12 45							13 45						14 45									
Newport (South Wales)	d		12 59							13 59						14 59									
Bristol Temple Meads 10	d			13 30				14 00			14 30			15 00				14 41	15 30				16 30		
Bristol Parkway 7	d			13 40				14 10			14 40			15 10				14 53	15 40				16 40		
Gloucester 7	d		13 51							14 47						15 47		15 52							
Cheltenham Spa	d		14 02	14 12				14 42		14 58	15 12			15 42		15 58		16 03	16 12				17 12		
Ashchurch for Tewkesbury	d																	16 11							
Worcester Shrub Hill 7	a																	16 34							
Birmingham New Street 12	a		14 45	14 50				15 27		15 41	15 50			16 26		16 41			16 50				17 49		
	d	14 30	14 49	15 03	14 52	15 22			15 30	15 49	16 03	15 52	16 22		16 30	16 49			17 03	16 52	17 22	17 30	18 03	17 52	18 22
Water Orton	d																								
Coleshill Parkway	d				15 05	15 35						16 05	16 35							17 05	17 35			18 05	18 35
Nuneaton	d				15 22	15 52						16 22	16 52							17 22	17 52			18 22	18 52
Hinckley	d				15 29							16 29								17 29				18 29	
Narborough	d				15 37							16 37								17 37				18 37	
South Wigston	d											16 42								17 42				18 42	
Leicester	a				15 48	16 13						16 48	17 12							17 47	18 12			18 49	19 12
Wilnecote	d		15 04																						
Tamworth	d		15 09							16 07	16 19					17 07							18 19		
Burton-on-Trent	d		15 21	15 28						16 19						17 19			17 28						
Willington	d																								
Derby 6	a	15 04	15 34	15 42					16 02	16 34	16 42				17 04	17 34			17 39			18 04	18 39		
	d		15 40							16 40						17 40									
Long Eaton	d																								
Attenborough	d																								
Beeston	d																								
Nottingham 8	a		16 00							17 00						18 00									

A To Glasgow Central
B To Edinburgh
C To Stansted Airport
D To Newcastle
E ✠ from Newport (South Wales)
F From Plymouth to Aberdeen
G From Plymouth to Glasgow Central
H From Paignton to Manchester Piccadilly
I From Guildford to Newcastle
J From Penzance to Edinburgh
K From Plymouth to Manchester Piccadilly
L From Reading to Newcastle
M From Newquay to Edinburgh
N From Reading to Edinburgh
O From Plymouth to Edinburgh
b Previous night, stops to set down only

Bristol and Cardiff - Birmingham
Leicester, Derby and Nottingham

Network Diagram - see first Page of Table 50

		XC		GW	XC	XC	XC	XC	XC	XC	XC	XC		XC	XC	XC	GW	XC	XC	XC	XC	XC		XC	XC
		◇■ A ✠			◇■ B ✠	◇■	◇■ C ✠	■	◇■ D	◇■ E ✠	◇■ B ✠	◇■		■	◇■ F ✠	◇■ E ✠		◇■	◇■ G ✠	■ H	◇■ ✠	◇■	F	◇■ ✠	■
Cardiff Central 7	d					16 45						17 45						18 45				19 45			
Newport (South Wales)	d					16 59						17 59						18 59				20 00			
Bristol Temple Meads 10	d	17 00		16 41			17 30			18 00					18 30	19 00	18 41		19 30		20 00			20 30	
Bristol Parkway 7	d	17 10		16 52			17 40			18 10					18 40	19 10	18 52		19 40		20 10			20 40	
Gloucester 7	d			17 35		17 47						18 47					19 38	19 52				20 50			
Cheltenham Spa	d	17 42		17 46		17 58	18 12			18 42		18 58			19 12	19 42	19 48	20 02	20 12		20 42	21 01		21 12	
Ashchurch for Tewkesbury	d			17 54													19 57								
Worcester Shrub Hill 7	a			18 14													20 18								
Birmingham New Street 12	a	18 27				18 41	18 51			19 26		19 41			19 56	20 26		20 44	20 50		21 20	21 44		21 51	
	d				18 30	18 49	19 03	18 52	19 22		19 30	19 49		19 52	20 03			20 49	21 03	20 52				22 03	21 52
Water Orton	d																								
Coleshill Parkway	d							19 05	19 35					20 05						21 05					22 05
Nuneaton	d							19 22	19 52					20 22						21 22					22 22
Hinckley	d							19 29						20 29						21 29					22 29
Narborough	d							19 37						20 38						21 38					22 37
South Wigston	d							19 41						20 42						21 42					22 42
Leicester	a							19 48	20 12					20 48						21 48					22 48
Wilnecote	d					19 04																			
Tamworth	d					19 09						20 07			20 19			21 06	21 19					22 18	
Burton-on-Trent	d					19 21	19 26					20 19						21 19	21 30						
Willington	d																								
Derby 6	a				19 03	19 33	19 39				20 01	20 34			20 39			21 33	21 42					22 40	
	d					19 40						20 40						21 40							
Long Eaton	d																								
Attenborough	d																								
Beeston	d																								
Nottingham 8	a					20 00						21 00						22 00							

		XC
		◇■
Cardiff Central 7	d	
Newport (South Wales)	d	
Bristol Temple Meads 10	d	22 10
Bristol Parkway 7	d	22 20
Gloucester 7	d	
Cheltenham Spa	d	22 52
Ashchurch for Tewkesbury	d	
Worcester Shrub Hill 7	a	
Birmingham New Street 12	a	23 39
	d	
Water Orton	d	
Coleshill Parkway	d	
Nuneaton	d	
Hinckley	d	
Narborough	d	
South Wigston	d	
Leicester	a	
Wilnecote	d	
Tamworth	d	
Burton-on-Trent	d	
Willington	d	
Derby 6	a	
	d	
Long Eaton	d	
Attenborough	d	
Beeston	d	
Nottingham 8	a	

A From Penzance to Manchester Piccadilly
B From Reading to Newcastle
C From Plymouth to Leeds
D To Stansted Airport
E To Manchester Piccadilly
F From Plymouth to Leeds. ✠ to Birmingham New Street
G From Penzance to Leeds. ✠ to Birmingham New Street
H From Paignton

Table 57

16 September to 21 October

Bristol and Cardiff - Birmingham
Leicester, Derby and Nottingham

Network Diagram - see first Page of Table 50

		XC 🚌	XC 🚌	XC ◇1 A 🍴	XC 1	XC ◇1 A 🍴	XC 1	XC ◇1 A 🍴	XC ◇1 B 🍴	XC 1		XC ◇1 A 🍴	XC ◇1 A 🍴	XC ◇1 B 🍴	XC ◇1 C 🍴	XC 1	XC ◇1 A 🍴	XC ◇1 B 🍴	XC ◇1 C 🍴	XC ◇1 D 🍴		GW	XC 1	XC ◇1 B 🍴	XC ◇1 E 🍴
Cardiff Central 7	d														10 45				11 45						
Newport (South Wales)	d														10 59				11 59						
Bristol Temple Meads 10	d							09 20					10 00							11 30					
Bristol Parkway 7	d							09 33					10 17							11 43					
Gloucester 7	d							10 29					11 27		11 51				12 47	13 00		13 37			
Cheltenham Spa	d							10 41					11 39		12 03				12 58	13 12		13 48			
Ashchurch for Tewkesbury	d																					13 57			
Worcester Shrub Hill 7	a																					14 15			
Birmingham New Street 12	a							11 20					12 17		12 45				13 41	13 50					
	d	22p20	22p49	09 30	09 52	10 30	10 52	11 30	11 22	11 52		12 03	12 30	12 22		12 52	13 03	13 22		14 03			13 52	14 22	14 30
Water Orton	d																								
Coleshill Parkway	d				10 05		11 05		11 35	12 05				12 35		13 05		13 35					14 04	14 35	
Nuneaton	d				10 22		11 22		11 52	12 22				12 52		13 22		13 51					14 20	14 52	
Hinckley	d				10 29		11 29			12 29						13 29							14 27		
Narborough	d				10 37		11 37			12 38						13 37							14 37		
South Wigston	d				10 42					12 42													14 41		
Leicester	a				10 50		11 50		12 13	12 48				13 12		13 50		14 12					14 50	15 12	
Wilnecote	d		23p19																						
Tamworth	d	22p55	23p24																	14 19					
Burton-on-Trent	d	23p15	23b44	10 16		11 16		12 16					13 18							14 29					
Willington	d	23p30																							
Derby 6	a	23b45	00 04	10 26		11 26		12 26				12 54	13 29				13 55			14 42					15 04
	d																								
Long Eaton	d	00s12																							
Attenborough	d	00s23																							
Beeston	d	00s29																							
Nottingham 8	a	00 49																							

		XC ◇1 C 🍴	XC ◇1 F 🍴	XC 1	XC ◇1 B 🍴	XC ◇1 G 🍴		XC ◇1 C 🍴	XC ◇1 H 🍴	XC 1 B	XC ◇1 G	XC ◇1 C 🍴	XC ◇1 🍴	GW F	XC ◇1 🍴	XC 1	B	XC ◇1 I	XC ◇1 🍴	XC ◇1 F	XC ◇1 🍴	GW	XC 1 B	XC ◇1 G	XC ◇1 🍴
Cardiff Central 7	d	12 45						13 45					14 45							15 45					
Newport (South Wales)	d	12 59						13 59					14 59							15 59					
Bristol Temple Meads 10	d		12 30						13 30						14 30						15 30				
Bristol Parkway 7	d		12 49						13 43						14 45						15 47				
Gloucester 7	d	13 51	14 00					14 47	14 55				15 47	15 52	16 00					16 47	17 00	17 35			
Cheltenham Spa	d	14 02	14 12					14 58	15 12				15 58	16 03	16 12					16 58	17 12	17 46			
Ashchurch for Tewkesbury	d													16 11								17 54			
Worcester Shrub Hill 7	a													16 33								18 14			
Birmingham New Street 12	a	14 45	14 50					15 41	15 50				16 41		16 50					17 41	17 49				
	d	14 49	15 03	14 52	15 22	15 30		15 49	16 03	15 52	16 22	16 30	16 49		17 03	16 52		17 22	17 30	17 49	18 03		17 52	18 22	18 30
Water Orton	d																								
Coleshill Parkway	d			15 05	15 35					16 05	16 35					17 05		17 35					18 05	18 35	
Nuneaton	d			15 22	15 52					16 22	16 52					17 22		17 52					18 22	18 52	
Hinckley	d			15 29						16 29						17 29							18 29		
Narborough	d			15 37						16 37						17 37							18 37		
South Wigston	d									16 42						17 42							18 42		
Leicester	a			15 48	16 13					16 48	17 12					17 47		18 12					18 49	19 12	
Wilnecote	d	15 04																							
Tamworth	d	15 09						16 07	16 19				17 07							18 07	18 19				
Burton-on-Trent	d	15 21	15 28					16 19					17 19		17 28					18 19					
Willington	d																								
Derby 6	a	15 34	15 42			16 02		16 34	16 42			17 04	17 34		17 39				18 04	18 33	18 38				19 03
	d	15 40						16 40					17 40							18 40					
Long Eaton	d																								
Attenborough	d																								
Beeston	d																								
Nottingham 8	a	16 00						17 00					18 00							19 00					

A To Newcastle
B To Stansted Airport
C 🍴 from Newport (South Wales)
D From Plymouth to Glasgow Central
E From Guildford to Newcastle
F From Plymouth to Edinburgh
G From Reading to Newcastle
H From Penzance to Glasgow Central
I From Reading to Edinburgh
b Previous night, stops to set down only

Table 57

16 September to 21 October

Bristol and Cardiff - Birmingham
Leicester, Derby and Nottingham

Network Diagram - see first Page of Table 50

		XC ◇1		XC ◇1 A 🍴	XC 1	XC ◇1 B	XC ◇1 C 🍴	XC ◇1	XC ◇1 D 🍴	XC 1	XC ◇1 E	XC ◇1		XC ◇1 D 🍴	GW	XC 1	XC ◇1	XC ◇1 F 🍴	XC 1	XC ◇1 G 🍴	XC ◇1				
Cardiff Central 7	d	16 45						17 45				18 45					19 45								
Newport (South Wales)	d	16 59						17 59				18 59					20 00								
Bristol Temple Meads 10	d			16 30					17 30					18 30				19 30		20 30	22 10				
Bristol Parkway 7	d			16 45					18 02					19 00				19 45		20 43	22 24				
Gloucester 7	d	17 47		18 00				18 47	19 00			19 52		20 00	20 25		20 50	21 00		22 00	23 21				
Cheltenham Spa	d	17 58		18 12				18 58	19 12			20 02		20 12	20 35		21 01	21 12		22 12	23 33				
Ashchurch for Tewkesbury	d														20 44										
Worcester Shrub Hill 7	a														21 02										
Birmingham New Street 12	a	18 41		18 51				19 41	19 51			20 44		20 51			21 44	21 51		22 50	00 11				
	d	18 49		19 03	18 52	19 22	19 30	19 49	20 03	19 52	20 22	20 49		21 03		20 52		22 03	21 52						
Water Orton	d																								
Coleshill Parkway	d				19 05	19 35				20 05	20 35					21 05			22 05						
Nuneaton	d				19 22	19 52				20 22	20 52					21 22			22 22						
Hinckley	d				19 29					20 29						21 29			22 29						
Narborough	d				19 37					20 38						21 38			22 37						
South Wigston	d				19 41					20 42						21 42			22 42						
Leicester	a				19 48	20 12				20 48	21 12					21 48			22 48						
Wilnecote	d	19 04																							
Tamworth	d	19 09						20 07	20 19			21 06		21 19				22 18							
Burton-on-Trent	d	19 21		19 26				20 19				21 19		21 31											
Willington	d																								
Derby 6	a	19 33		19 39			20 01	20 34	20 39			21 33		21 42				22 40							
	d	19 40						20 40				21 40													
Long Eaton	d																								
Attenborough	d																								
Beeston	d																								
Nottingham 8	a	20 00						21 00				22 00													

from 28 October

		XC 🚌	XC 1	XC ◇1 H 🍴	XC 🚌	XC 1	XC ◇1 I 🍴	XC 🚌	XC ◇1 B 🍴	XC 🚌		XC ◇1 J 🍴	XC 1 K	XC ◇1 🍴	XC 🚌 B	XC ◇1 J 🍴	XC ◇1 🍴	XC 1	XC 🚌 B	XC ◇1 🍴	L	XC ◇1 🍴	XC 1 B	XC ◇1 M 🍴	XC ◇1 🍴
Cardiff Central 7	d																								
Newport (South Wales)	d																								
Bristol Temple Meads 10	d																					11 30			
Bristol Parkway 7	d																					11 40			
Gloucester 7	d																					12 14			
Cheltenham Spa	d									10 10												12 26			
Ashchurch for Tewkesbury	d																								
Worcester Shrub Hill 7	a																								
Birmingham New Street 12	a									11 30												13 38			
	d	22p49	09 52	10 03		10 52	11 03		11 22			11 45	11 52	12 03		12 22	12 45	12 52		13 22		14 03	13 52	14 22	14 30
Water Orton	d																								
Coleshill Parkway	d		10 05		10 15	11 05		11 15	11 35				12 05		12 15	12 35		13 05	13 15	13 35			14 04	14 35	
Nuneaton	d		10 22			11 22			11 52				12 22			12 52		13 22		13 51			14 20	14 52	
Hinckley	d		10 29			11 29							12 29					13 29					14 27		
Narborough	d		10 37			11 37							12 38					13 37					14 37		
South Wigston	d		10 42										12 42										14 41		
Leicester	a		10 50			11 50			12 13				12 48			13 12		13 50		14 12			14 50	15 12	
Wilnecote	d	23p19																							
Tamworth	d	23p24			10 40			11 40							12 40				13 40			14 19			
Burton-on-Trent	d	23b44			11 05			12 05							13 05				14 05						
Willington	d																								
Derby 6	a	00 04		11 18	11 30		12 18	12 30				12 56		13 17	13 30		14 01		14 30			14 42			15 04
	d																								
Long Eaton	d																								
Attenborough	d																								
Beeston	d																								
Nottingham 8	a																								

A From Plymouth to Leeds
B To Stansted Airport
C From Reading to Newcastle
D From Plymouth to Leeds. 🍴 to Birmingham New Street
E To Cambridge
F From Penzance to Leeds. 🍴 to Birmingham New Street
G From Plymouth
H To Edinburgh
I To Glasgow Central
J To Newcastle
K To Aberdeen
L From Plymouth to Glasgow Central
M From Guildford to Newcastle
b Previous night, stops to set down only

Bristol and Cardiff - Birmingham Leicester, Derby and Nottingham

Network Diagram - see first Page of Table 50

		XC ◇1 ☕	XC 1	XC ◇1 A ☕	XC ◇1 B ☕	XC ◇1 C ☕	GW	XC ◇1 D ☕	XC ◇1	XC ◇1 E ☕	XC 1	XC ◇1 B	XC ◇1 F ☕	XC ◇1 D ☕	XC ◇1 G ☕	GW	XC ◇1 H ☕	XC 1 B	XC ◇1 I	XC ◇1 J ☕	XC ◇1 ☕	XC ◇1 K	XC ◇1 ☕
Cardiff Central [7]	d														14 45							15 45	
Newport (South Wales)	d														14 59							15 59	
Bristol Temple Meads [10]	d					13 30	13 41			14 30			15 00			14 41	15 30			16 00			16 30
Bristol Parkway [7]	d					13 40	13 52			14 40			15 10			14 53	15 40			16 10			16 40
Gloucester [7]	d					14 30	14 37								15 47	15 52						16 47	
Cheltenham Spa	d					14 42	14 49			15 12			15 42		15 58	16 03	16 12			16 42		16 58	17 12
Ashchurch for Tewkesbury	d						14 57									16 11							
Worcester Shrub Hill [7]	a						15 18									16 34							
Birmingham New Street [12]	a					15 23				15 50			16 26		16 41		16 50			17 26		17 41	17 49
	d	14 49	14 52	15 03	15 22			15 30	15 49	16 03	15 52	16 22		16 30	16 49		17 03	16 52	17 22		17 30	17 49	18 03
Water Orton	d																						
Coleshill Parkway	d		15 05		15 35						16 05	16 35						17 05	17 35				
Nuneaton	d		15 22		15 52						16 22	16 52						17 22	17 52				
Hinckley	d		15 29								16 29							17 29					
Narborough	d		15 37								16 37							17 37					
South Wigston	d										16 42							17 42					
Leicester	a		15 48		16 13						16 48	17 12						17 47	18 12				
Wilnecote	d	15 04																					
Tamworth	d	15 09							16 07	16 19					17 07							18 07	18 19
Burton-on-Trent	d	15 21		15 28					16 19						17 19		17 28					18 19	
Willington	d																						
Derby [6]	a	15 34		15 42				16 02	16 34	16 42				17 04	17 34		17 39				18 04	18 33	18 38
	d	15 40							16 40						17 40							18 40	
Long Eaton	d																						
Attenborough	d																						
Beeston	d																						
Nottingham [8] ⇌	a	16 00							17 00						18 00							19 00	

		XC 1	XC ◇1 B	XC ◇1 C ☕	GW	XC ◇1 D ☕	XC ◇1	XC ◇1 L ☕	XC 1	XC ◇1 B	XC ◇1 I ☕	XC ◇1 D ☕	XC ◇1	XC ◇1 M ☕	XC 1	XC ◇1 N	XC ◇1 I ☕	GW	XC ◇1	XC ◇1 O ☕	XC 1	XC ◇1 P ☕
Cardiff Central [7]	d						16 45						17 45						18 45			
Newport (South Wales)	d						16 59						17 59						18 59			
Bristol Temple Meads [10]	d			17 00	16 41			17 30			18 00			18 30			19 00	18 41		19 30		20 00
Bristol Parkway [7]	d			17 10	16 52			17 40			18 10			18 40			19 10	18 52		19 40		20 10
Gloucester [7]	d				17 35		17 47						18 47					19 38	19 52			
Cheltenham Spa	d			17 42	17 46		17 58	18 12			18 42		18 58	19 12			19 42	19 48	20 02	20 12		20 42
Ashchurch for Tewkesbury	d				17 54													19 57				
Worcester Shrub Hill [7]	a				18 14													20 18				
Birmingham New Street [12]	a			18 27			18 41	18 51			19 26		19 41	19 50			20 26		20 44	20 50		21 20
	d	17 52	18 22			18 30	18 49	19 03	18 52	19 22		19 30	19 49	20 03	19 52	20 22			20 49	21 03	20 52	
Water Orton	d																					
Coleshill Parkway	d	18 05	18 35						19 05	19 35					20 05	20 35					21 05	
Nuneaton	d	18 22	18 52						19 22	19 52					20 22	20 52					21 22	
Hinckley	d	18 29							19 29						20 29						21 29	
Narborough	d	18 37							19 37						20 38						21 38	
South Wigston	d	18 42							19 41						20 42						21 42	
Leicester	a	18 49	19 12						19 48	20 12					20 48	21 12					21 48	
Wilnecote	d						19 04															
Tamworth	d						19 09						20 07	20 19					21 06	21 19		
Burton-on-Trent	d						19 21	19 26					20 19						21 19	21 30		
Willington	d																					
Derby [6]	a					19 03	19 33	19 39				20 01	20 34	20 39					21 33	21 42		
	d						19 40						20 40						21 40			
Long Eaton	d																					
Attenborough	d																					
Beeston	d																					
Nottingham [8] ⇌	a						20 00						21 00						22 00			

A To Edinburgh
B To Stansted Airport
C From Penzance to Manchester Piccadilly
D From Reading to Newcastle
E From Plymouth to Glasgow Central
F From Plymouth to Manchester Piccadilly
G ☕ from Newport (South Wales)
H From Plymouth to Edinburgh. ☕ from Birmingham New Street
I To Manchester Piccadilly
J From Reading to Edinburgh
K From Plymouth to Edinburgh
L From Plymouth to Leeds
M From Plymouth to Leeds. ☕ to Birmingham New Street
N To Cambridge
O From Penzance to Leeds. ☕ to Birmingham New Street
P From Paignton

Bristol and Cardiff - Birmingham Leicester, Derby and Nottingham

Network Diagram - see first Page of Table 50

		XC ◇1	XC ◇1 A ☕	XC 1	XC ◇1
Cardiff Central [7]	d	19 45			
Newport (South Wales)	d	20 00			
Bristol Temple Meads [10]	d		20 30		22 10
Bristol Parkway [7]	d		20 40		22 20
Gloucester [7]	d	20 50			
Cheltenham Spa	d	21 01	21 12		22 52
Ashchurch for Tewkesbury	d				
Worcester Shrub Hill [7]	a				
Birmingham New Street [12]	a	21 44	21 51		23 39
	d		22 03	21 52	
Water Orton	d				
Coleshill Parkway	d			22 05	
Nuneaton	d			22 22	
Hinckley	d			22 29	
Narborough	d			22 37	
South Wigston	d			22 42	
Leicester	a			22 48	
Wilnecote	d				
Tamworth	d		22 19		
Burton-on-Trent	d				
Willington	d				
Derby [6]	a		22 43		
	d				
Long Eaton	d				
Attenborough	d				
Beeston	d				
Nottingham [8] ⇌	a				

A From Plymouth. ☕ to Birmingham New Street

Network Diagram for Tables 59, 60, 61, 62, 64, 66

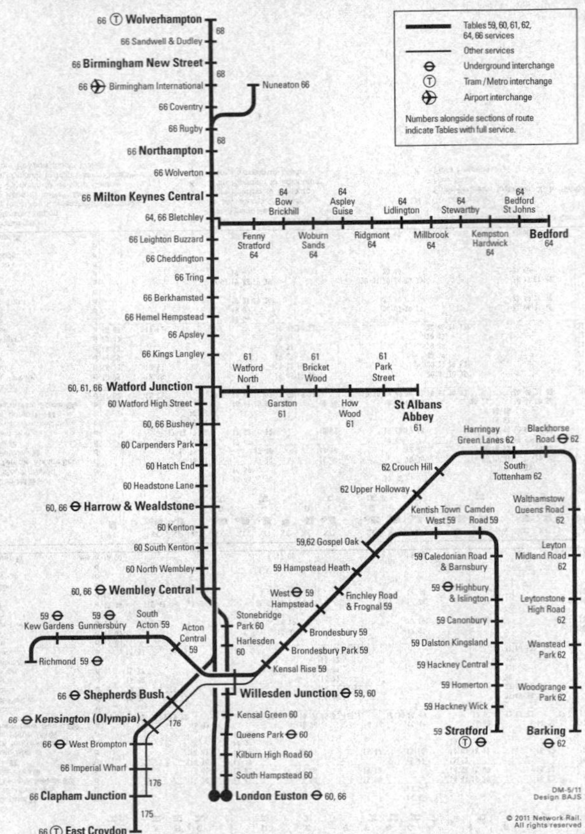

Mondays to Fridays

until 26 July

Stratford - Highbury and Islington, West Hampstead, Willesden Junction, Clapham Junction and Richmond

Network Diagram - see first Page of Table 59

Miles	Miles			LO MX	LO MX	LO	LO	LO	LO	LO	LO	LO	LO	LO		LO	LO	LO	LO	LO	LO	LO	LO	LO	LO
0	—	**Stratford** [7] ⊖	d		23p45			05 47			06 05	06 12	06 20	06 27		06 35	06 42	06 50	06 55	07 00	07 12	07 20	07 27	07 35	07 42
1	—	Hackney Wick	d		23p48			05 50			06 08	06 15	06 23	06 30		06 38	06 45	06 54	06 58	07 03	07 15	07 23	07 30	07 38	07 45
1¾	—	Homerton	d		23p51			05 53			06 11	06 18	06 26	06 33		06 41	06 48	06 56	07 01	07 06	07 18	07 26	07 33	07 42	07 48
2½	—	Hackney Central	d		23p53			05 55			06 13	06 20	06 28	06 35		06 43	06 50	06 58	07 03	07 08	07 20	07 28	07 35	07 43	07 50
3¼	—	Dalston Kingsland	d		23p55			05 57			06 15	06 22	06 30	06 37		06 45	06 52	07 00	07 05	07 10	07 22	07 30	07 37	07 45	07 52
4¼	—	Canonbury	d		23p57			05 59			06 17	06 24	06 32	06 39		06 47	06 54	07 02	07 07	07 12	07 24	07 32	07 39	07 47	07 54
4¾	—	**Highbury & Islington** ⊖	d		23p59			06 02			06 19	06 27	06 35	06 41		06 50	06 57	07 05	07 10	07 15	07 27	07 35	07 42	07 50	07 57
5¼	—	Caledonian Rd & Barnsbury	d		00 02			06 04			06 21	06 29	06 37	06 43		06 52	06 59	07 07	07 12	07 17	07 29	07 37	07 44	07 52	07 59
6¼	—	Camden Road	d		00 05			06 07			06 24	06 32	06 40	06 46		06 55	07 02	07 10	07 15	07 20	07 32	07 40	07 47	07 55	08 02
6½	—	Kentish Town West	d		00 07			06 09			06 27	06 34	06 42	06 49		06 57	07 04	07 13	07 17	07 22	07 34	07 42	07 49	07 57	08 04
7½	—	**Gospel Oak**	d		00 10			06 12			06 30	06 37	06 45	06 51		07 00	07 07	07 15	07 20	07 25	07 37	07 45	07 52	08 00	08 07
8	—	Hampstead Heath	d		00 12			06 14			06 32	06 39	06 47	06 53		07 02	07 09	07 17	07 22	07 27	07 39	07 47	07 54	08 02	08 09
9	—	Finchley Road & Frognal	d		00 14			06 16			06 34	06 41	06 49	06 55		07 04	07 11	07 19	07 24	07 29	07 41	07 49	07 56	08 04	08 11
9½	—	West Hampstead ⊖	d		00 16			06 18			06 36	06 43	06 51	06 57		07 06	07 13	07 21	07 26	07 31	07 43	07 51	07 58	08 06	08 13
10	—	Brondesbury	d		00 18			06 20			06 38	06 45	06 53	06 58		07 08	07 15	07 22	07 28	07 33	07 45	07 53	08 00	08 08	08 15
10¼	—	Brondesbury Park	d		00 19			06 21			06 39	06 46	06 54	07 00		07 09	07 16	07 24	07 29	07 34	07 46	07 54	08 01	08 09	08 16
11	—	Kensal Rise	d		00 21			06 23			06 41	06 48	06 56	07 02		07 11	07 18	07 26	07 31	07 36	07 48	07 56	08 03	08 11	08 18
12	0	**Willesden Jn. High Level** ⊖	a					06 27			06 45	06 52	07 00	07 06		07 15	07 22	07 30	07 35	07 40	07 52	08 00	08 07	08 15	08 22
—	—		d	23p40		06 01	06 09	06 28	06 33	06 41	06 46	06 53	07 01	07 07		07 16	07 23	07 31	07 36	07 41	07 53	08 01	08 08	08 16	08 23
12	—	**Willesden Jn Low Level** ⊖	a		00 29																				
—	2	**Shepherd's Bush** ⊖	d	23p48		06 08			06 40		06 54		07 09			07 24		07 39		07 49		08 09		08 24	
—	2¾	**Kensington (Olympia)** ⊖	d	23p50		06 10			06 42		06 56		07 11			07 26		07 41		07 51		08 11		08 26	
—	3½	West Brompton ⊖	d	23p52		06 13			06 45		06 58		07 13			07 28		07 43		07 53		08 13		08 28	
—	4½	Imperial Wharf	d	23p55		06 16			06 48		07 01		07 16			07 31		07 46		07 56		08 16		08 31	
—	6	**Clapham Junction** [10]	a	00 02		06 23			06 54		07 09		07 24			07 39		07 54		08 04		08 24		08 39	
13½	—	Acton Central	d				06 14	06 33		06 46		06 58		07 13			07 28		07 41		07 58		08 13		08 28
14½	—	South Acton	d				06 16	06 36		06 49		07 01		07 16			07 31		07 44		08 01		08 16		08 31
15¼	—	Gunnersbury ⊖	d				06 20	06 39		06 53		07 04		07 19			07 34		07 48		08 04		08 19		08 34
16¼	—	Kew Gardens ⊖	d				06 23	06 42		06 56		07 07		07 22			07 37		07 51		08 07		08 22		08 37
17½	—	**Richmond** ⊖	a				06 30	06 49		07 04		07 14		07 30			07 44		07 57		08 14		08 28		08 43

		LO		LO	LO	LO	LO	LO	LO	LO	LO	LO	LO	LO		LO	LO	LO	LO	LO	LO	LO	LO	LO	LO
Stratford [7] ⊖	d	07 50		07 57	08 03	08 12	08 20	08 27	08 35	08 42	08 50	08 57	09 03	09 15			09 25	09 35	09 45		09 55	10 05	10 15		10 25
Hackney Wick	d	07 53		08 00	08 06	08 15	08 23	08 30	08 38	08 45	08 53	09 00	09 06	09 18			09 28	09 38	09 48		09 58	10 08	10 18		10 28
Homerton	d	07 56		08 03	08 09	08 18	08 26	08 33	08 41	08 48	08 56	09 03	09 09	09 21			09 31	09 41	09 51		10 01	10 11	10 21		10 31
Hackney Central	d	07 58		08 05	08 11	08 20	08 28	08 35	08 43	08 50	08 58	09 05	09 11	09 23			09 33	09 43	09 53		10 03	10 13	10 23		10 33
Dalston Kingsland	d	08 00		08 07	08 13	08 22	08 30	08 37	08 45	08 52	09 00	09 07	09 13	09 25			09 35	09 45	09 55		10 05	10 15	10 25		10 35
Canonbury	d	08 02		08 09	08 15	08 24	08 32	08 39	08 47	08 54	09 02	09 09	09 15	09 27			09 37	09 47	09 57		10 07	10 17	10 27		10 37
Highbury & Islington ⊖	d	08 05		08 12	08 18	08 27	08 35	08 42	08 50	08 57	09 05	09 12	09 18	09 30			09 40	09 50	10 00		10 10	10 20	10 30		10 40
Caledonian Rd & Barnsbury	d	08 07		08 14	08 20	08 29	08 37	08 44	08 52	08 59	09 07	09 14	09 20	09 32			09 42	09 52	10 02		10 12	10 22	10 32		10 42
Camden Road	d	08 10		08 17	08 23	08 32	08 40	08 47	08 55	09 02	09 10	09 17	09 23	09 35			09 45	09 55	10 05		10 15	10 25	10 35		10 45
Kentish Town West	d	08 12		08 19	08 25	08 34	08 42	08 49	08 59	09 04	09 12	09 19	09 25	09 37			09 47	09 57	10 07		10 17	10 27	10 37		10 47
Gospel Oak	d	08 15		08 22	08 28	08 37	08 45	08 52	09 02	09 08	09 15	09 22	09 27	09 40			09 50	10 00	10 10		10 20	10 30	10 40		10 50
Hampstead Heath	d	08 17		08 24	08 30	08 39	08 47	08 54	09 04	09 10	09 17	09 24	09 29	09 42			09 52	10 02	10 12		10 22	10 32	10 42		10 52
Finchley Road & Frognal	d	08 19		08 26	08 32	08 41	08 49	08 56	09 06	09 12	09 19	09 26	09 31	09 44			09 54	10 04	10 14		10 24	10 34	10 44		10 54
West Hampstead ⊖	d	08 21		08 28	08 34	08 43	08 51	08 58	09 08	09 14	09 21	09 28	09 33	09 46			09 56	10 06	10 16		10 26	10 36	10 46		10 56
Brondesbury	d	08 23		08 30	08 36	08 45	08 53	09 00	09 10	09 15	09 23	09 30	09 35	09 48			09 58	10 08	10 18		10 28	10 38	10 48		10 58
Brondesbury Park	d	08 24		08 31	08 37	08 46	08 54	09 01	09 11	09 17	09 24	09 31	09 36	09 49			09 59	10 09	10 19		10 29	10 39	10 49		10 59
Kensal Rise	d	08 26		08 33	08 39	08 48	08 56	09 03	09 13	09 19	09 26	09 33	09 38	09 51			10 01	10 11	10 21		10 31	10 41	10 51		11 01
Willesden Jn. High Level ⊖	a	08 30		08 37	08 43	08 52	09 00	09 07	09 16	09 23	09 30	09 37	09 42	09 55			10 05	10 15	10 25		10 35	10 45	10 55		11 05
	d	08 31		08 38	08 46	08 53	09 01	09 08	09 17	09 24	09 31	09 38	09 44	09 56		10 01	10 06	10 16	10 26	10 31	10 36	10 46	10 56	11 01	11 06
Willesden Jn Low Level ⊖	a																								
Shepherd's Bush ⊖	d	08 39			08 54		09 09		09 25		09 39		09 54			10 09		10 26		10 39		10 54		11 09	
Kensington (Olympia) ⊖	d	08 41			08 56		09 11		09 27		09 41		09 56			10 11		10 28		10 41		10 56		11 11	
West Brompton ⊖	d	08 43			08 58		09 13		09 29		09 43		09 58			10 13		10 30		10 43		10 58		11 13	
Imperial Wharf	d	08 46			09 01		09 16		09 32		09 46		10 01			10 16		10 33		10 46		11 01		11 16	
Clapham Junction [10]	a	08 54			09 09		09 25		09 39		09 54		10 08			10 23		10 40		10 53		11 09		11 23	
Acton Central	d			08 43		08 58		09 13		09 29		09 43		10 01			10 11		10 31		10 41		11 01		11 11
South Acton	d			08 46		09 01		09 16		09 31		09 46		10 04			10 14		10 34		10 44		11 04		11 14
Gunnersbury ⊖	d			08 51		09 04		09 19		09 37		09 49		10 08			10 19		10 38		10 48		11 08		11 18
Kew Gardens ⊖	d			08 54		09 07		09 22		09 40		09 52		10 11			10 22		10 41		10 51		11 11		11 21
Richmond ⊖	a			08 58		09 13		09 28		09 45		09 58		10 16			10 27		10 46		10 56		11 16		11 26

Stratford - Highbury and Islington, West Hampstead, Willesden Junction, Clapham Junction and Richmond

Network Diagram - see first Page of Table 59

		LO	LO	LO	LO	LO	LO	LO	LO	LO	LO	LO	LO	LO	LO	LO	LO	LO	LO	LO	LO	LO	LO
Stratford 7 ⊖	d	10 35	10 45		10 55	11 05	11 15		11 25	11 37	11 45		11 55	12 05	12 15		12 25	12 35	12 45		12 55	13 05	13 15
Hackney Wick	d	10 38	10 48		10 58	11 08	11 18		11 28	11 40	11 48		11 58	12 08	12 18		12 28	12 38	12 48		12 58	13 08	13 18
Homerton	d	10 41	10 51		11 01	11 11	11 21		11 31	11 43	11 51		12 01	12 11	12 21		12 31	12 41	12 51		13 01	13 11	13 21
Hackney Central	d	10 43	10 53		11 03	11 13	11 23		11 33	11 45	11 53		12 03	12 13	12 23		12 33	12 43	12 53		13 03	13 13	13 23
Dalston Kingsland	d	10 45	10 55		11 05	11 15	11 25		11 35	11 47	11 55		12 05	12 15	12 25		12 35	12 45	12 55		13 05	13 15	13 25
Canonbury	d	10 47	10 57		11 07	11 17	11 27		11 37	11 49	11 57		12 07	12 17	12 27		12 37	12 47	12 57		13 07	13 17	13 27
Highbury & Islington ⊖	d	10 50	11 00		11 10	11 20	11 30		11 40	11 52	12 00		12 10	12 20	12 30		12 40	12 50	13 00		13 10	13 20	13 30
Caledonian Rd & Barnsbury	d	10 52	11 02		11 12	11 22	11 32		11 42	11 54	12 02		12 12	12 22	12 32		12 42	12 52	13 02		13 12	13 22	13 32
Camden Road	d	10 55	11 05		11 15	11 25	11 35		11 45	11 57	12 05		12 15	12 25	12 35		12 45	12 55	13 05		13 15	13 25	13 35
Kentish Town West	d	10 57	11 07		11 17	11 27	11 37		11 47	11 59	12 07		12 17	12 27	12 37		12 47	12 57	13 07		13 17	13 27	13 37
Gospel Oak	d	11 00	11 10		11 20	11 30	11 40		11 51	12 02	12 10		12 20	12 30	12 40		12 50	13 00	13 10		13 20	13 30	13 41
Hampstead Heath	d	11 02	11 12		11 22	11 32	11 42		11 53	12 04	12 12		12 22	12 32	12 42		12 52	13 02	13 12		13 22	13 32	13 43
Finchley Road & Frognal	d	11 04	11 14		11 24	11 34	11 44		11 55	12 06	12 14		12 24	12 34	12 44		12 54	13 04	13 14		13 24	13 34	13 45
West Hampstead ⊖	d	11 06	11 16		11 26	11 36	11 46		11 57	12 08	12 16		12 26	12 36	12 46		12 56	13 06	13 16		13 26	13 36	13 47
Brondesbury	d	11 08	11 18		11 28	11 38	11 48		11 59	12 10	12 18		12 28	12 38	12 48		12 58	13 08	13 18		13 28	13 38	13 49
Brondesbury Park	d	11 09	11 19		11 29	11 39	11 49		12 00	12 11	12 19		12 29	12 39	12 49		12 59	13 09	13 19		13 29	13 39	13 50
Kensal Rise	d	11 11	11 21		11 31	11 41	11 51		12 02	12 13	12 21		12 31	12 41	12 51		13 01	13 11	13 21		13 31	13 41	13 52
Willesden Jn. High Level ⊖	a	11 15	11 25		11 35	11 44	11 55		12 06	12 16	12 25		12 35	12 45	12 55		13 05	13 15	13 25		13 35	13 45	13 56
	d	11 16	11 26	11 31	11 36	11 45	11 56	12 01	12 07	12 17	12 26	12 31	12 36	12 46	12 56	13 01	13 06	13 16	13 26	13 31	13 36	13 46	13 57
Willesden Jn Low Level ⊖	a																						
Shepherd's Bush ⊖	d	11 24		11 39		11 54		12 09		12 25		12 39		12 54		13 09		13 24		13 39		13 54	
Kensington (Olympia) ⊖	d	11 26		11 41		11 56		12 11		12 27		12 41		12 56		13 11		13 26		13 41		13 56	
West Brompton ⊖	d	11 28		11 43		11 58		12 13		12 29		12 43		12 58		13 13		13 28		13 43		13 58	
Imperial Wharf	d	11 31		11 46		12 01		12 16		12 32		12 46		13 01		13 16		13 31		13 46		14 01	
Clapham Junction 10	a	11 39		11 53		12 09		12 23		12 40		12 55		13 08		13 25		13 38		13 55		14 09	
Acton Central	d		11 31		11 41		12 01		12 12		12 31		12 41		13 01		13 11		13 31		13 41		14 02
South Acton	d		11 34		11 44		12 04		12 15		12 34		12 44		13 04		13 14		13 34		13 44		14 05
Gunnersbury ⊖	d		11 38		11 48		12 08		12 19		12 38		12 48		13 08		13 18		13 38		13 48		14 09
Kew Gardens ⊖	d		11 41		11 51		12 11		12 22		12 41		12 51		13 11		13 21		13 41		13 51		14 12
Richmond ⊖	a		11 46		11 56		12 16		12 27		12 46		12 56		13 16		13 26		13 46		13 56		14 17

		LO	LO	LO	LO	LO	LO	LO	LO	LO	LO	LO	LO	LO	LO	LO	LO	LO	LO	LO	LO	LO	LO
Stratford 7 ⊖	d		13 25	13 35	13 45		13 55	14 05	14 15		14 25	14 35	14 45		14 55	15 05	15 15		15 25	15 35	15 42	15 50	15 59
Hackney Wick	d		13 28	13 38	13 48		13 58	14 08	14 18		14 28	14 38	14 48		14 58	15 08	15 18		15 28	15 38	15 45	15 53	16 02
Homerton	d		13 31	13 41	13 51		14 01	14 11	14 21		14 31	14 41	14 51		15 01	15 11	15 21		15 31	15 41	15 48	15 56	16 05
Hackney Central	d		13 33	13 43	13 53		14 03	14 13	14 23		14 33	14 43	14 53		15 03	15 13	15 23		15 33	15 43	15 50	15 58	16 07
Dalston Kingsland	d		13 35	13 45	13 55		14 05	14 15	14 25		14 35	14 45	14 55		15 05	15 15	15 25		15 35	15 45	15 52	16 00	16 09
Canonbury	d		13 37	13 47	13 57		14 07	14 17	14 27		14 37	14 47	14 57		15 07	15 17	15 27		15 37	15 47	15 54	16 02	16 11
Highbury & Islington ⊖	d		13 40	13 50	14 00		14 10	14 20	14 30		14 40	14 50	15 00		15 10	15 20	15 30		15 40	15 50	15 57	16 05	16 14
Caledonian Rd & Barnsbury	d		13 42	13 52	14 02		14 12	14 22	14 32		14 42	14 52	15 02		15 12	15 22	15 32		15 42	15 52	15 59	16 07	16 16
Camden Road	d		13 45	13 55	14 05		14 15	14 25	14 35		14 45	14 55	15 05		15 15	15 25	15 35		15 45	15 55	16 03	16 10	16 19
Kentish Town West	d		13 47	13 57	14 07		14 17	14 27	14 37		14 47	14 57	15 07		15 17	15 27	15 37		15 48	15 57	16 06	16 12	16 21
Gospel Oak	d		13 50	14 00	14 10		14 20	14 30	14 40		14 50	15 00	15 10		15 20	15 30	15 40		15 50	16 02	16 08	16 15	16 24
Hampstead Heath	d		13 52	14 02	14 12		14 22	14 32	14 42		14 52	15 02	15 12		15 22	15 32	15 42		15 52	16 04	16 10	16 17	16 26
Finchley Road & Frognal	d		13 54	14 04	14 14		14 24	14 34	14 44		14 54	15 04	15 14		15 24	15 34	15 44		15 54	16 06	16 12	16 19	16 28
West Hampstead ⊖	d		13 56	14 06	14 16		14 26	14 36	14 46		14 56	15 06	15 16		15 26	15 36	15 46		15 56	16 08	16 14	16 21	16 30
Brondesbury	d		13 58	14 08	14 18		14 28	14 38	14 48		14 58	15 08	15 18		15 28	15 38	15 48		15 58	16 10	16 15	16 23	16 32
Brondesbury Park	d		13 59	14 09	14 19		14 29	14 39	14 49		14 59	15 09	15 19		15 29	15 39	15 49		15 59	16 11	16 17	16 24	16 33
Kensal Rise	d		14 01	14 11	14 21		14 31	14 41	14 51		15 01	15 11	15 21		15 31	15 41	15 51		16 01	16 13	16 19	16 26	16 35
Willesden Jn. High Level ⊖	a		14 05	14 15	14 25		14 35	14 45	14 55		15 05	15 15	15 25		15 35	15 45	15 55		16 05	16 16	16 23	16 30	16 39
	d	14 01	14 06	14 16	14 26	14 31	14 36	14 46	14 56	15 01	15 06	15 16	15 26	15 31	15 36	15 46	15 56	16 01	16 06	16 17	16 24	16 31	16 40
Willesden Jn Low Level ⊖	a																						
Shepherd's Bush ⊖	d	14 09		14 24		14 39		14 54		15 09		15 26		15 39		15 54		16 09		16 25		16 39	
Kensington (Olympia) ⊖	d	14 11		14 26		14 41		14 56		15 11		15 28		15 41		15 56		16 11		16 27		16 41	
West Brompton ⊖	d	14 13		14 28		14 43		14 58		15 13		15 30		15 43		15 58		16 13		16 29		16 43	
Imperial Wharf	d	14 16		14 31		14 46		15 01		15 16		15 33		15 46		16 01		16 16		16 32		16 46	
Clapham Junction 10	a	14 23		14 39		14 53		15 09		15 23		15 40		15 53		16 09		16 23		16 39		16 54	
Acton Central	d		14 11		14 31		14 41		15 01		15 11		15 31		15 41		16 01		16 11		16 29		16 45
South Acton	d		14 14		14 34		14 44		15 04		15 14		15 34		15 44		16 04		16 14		16 31		16 48
Gunnersbury ⊖	d		14 18		14 38		14 48		15 08		15 18		15 38		15 48		16 08		16 18		16 34		16 51
Kew Gardens ⊖	d		14 21		14 41		14 51		15 11		15 21		15 41		15 51		16 11		16 21		16 37		16 54
Richmond ⊖	a		14 26		14 46		14 56		15 16		15 26		15 46		15 56		16 16		16 27		16 43		17 00

Stratford - Highbury and Islington, West Hampstead, Willesden Junction, Clapham Junction and Richmond

Network Diagram - see first Page of Table 59

		LO	LO	LO	LO	LO	LO	LO	LO	LO	LO	LO	LO	LO	LO	LO	LO	LO	LO	LO	LO	LO	LO
Stratford 7 ⊖	d		16 12	16 20	16 27	16 35	16 42	16 50	16 57	17 05	17 12	17 21	17 27	17 36	17 42	17 51	17 57	18 05	18 12	18 20	18 27	18 35	18 42
Hackney Wick	d		16 15	16 23	16 30	16 38	16 45	16 53	17 00	17 08	17 15	17 23	17 30	17 38	17 45	17 54	18 00	18 08	18 15	18 23	18 30	18 38	18 45
Homerton	d		16 18	16 26	16 33	16 40	16 48	16 56	17 03	17 11	17 18	17 26	17 33	17 41	17 48	17 57	18 03	18 11	18 18	18 26	18 33	18 41	18 48
Hackney Central	d		16 20	16 28	16 35	16 42	16 50	16 58	17 05	17 13	17 20	17 28	17 35	17 43	17 50	17 59	18 05	18 13	18 20	18 28	18 35	18 43	18 50
Dalston Kingsland	d		16 22	16 30	16 37	16 44	16 52	17 00	17 07	17 15	17 22	17 30	17 37	17 45	17 52	18 01	18 07	18 15	18 22	18 31	18 37	18 45	18 52
Canonbury	d		16 24	16 32	16 39	16 46	16 54	17 02	17 09	17 17	17 24	17 32	17 39	17 47	17 54	18 03	18 09	18 17	18 24	18 32	18 39	18 47	18 54
Highbury & Islington ⊖	d		16 27	16 35	16 42	16 49	16 57	17 05	17 12	17 20	17 27	17 35	17 42	17 50	17 57	18 06	18 12	18 20	18 27	18 35	18 42	18 50	18 57
Caledonian Rd & Barnsbury	d		16 29	16 37	16 44	16 51	16 59	17 07	17 14	17 22	17 29	17 37	17 44	17 52	17 59	18 08	18 14	18 22	18 29	18 37	18 44	18 52	18 59
Camden Road	d		16 32	16 40	16 47	16 54	17 02	17 10	17 17	17 25	17 32	17 40	17 47	17 55	18 02	18 12	18 17	18 25	18 32	18 40	18 47	18 55	19 02
Kentish Town West	d		16 34	16 42	16 49	16 58	17 04	17 13	17 19	17 27	17 34	17 42	17 49	17 58	18 05	18 15	18 19	18 27	18 34	18 42	18 49	18 57	19 05
Gospel Oak	d		16 37	16 45	16 52	17 03	17 08	17 17	17 23	17 30	17 37	17 45	17 52	18 02	18 08	18 18	18 22	18 30	18 37	18 45	18 52	19 00	19 09
Hampstead Heath	d		16 39	16 47	16 54	17 05	17 10	17 19	17 25	17 32	17 39	17 47	17 54	18 04	18 10	18 20	18 24	18 32	18 39	18 47	18 54	19 02	19 11
Finchley Road & Frognal	d		16 41	16 49	16 56	17 07	17 12	17 21	17 27	17 34	17 41	17 49	17 56	18 06	18 12	18 22	18 26	18 34	18 41	18 49	18 56	19 04	19 13
West Hampstead ⊖	d		16 43	16 51	16 58	17 09	17 14	17 23	17 29	17 36	17 43	17 51	17 58	18 08	18 14	18 24	18 28	18 36	18 43	18 51	18 58	19 06	19 15
Brondesbury	d		16 45	16 53	17 00	17 10	17 16	17 25	17 30	17 38	17 45	17 53	18 00	18 09	18 16	18 26	18 30	18 38	18 45	18 53	19 00	19 08	19 16
Brondesbury Park	d		16 46	16 54	17 01	17 12	17 17	17 26	17 32	17 39	17 46	17 54	18 01	18 11	18 17	18 27	18 31	18 39	18 46	18 54	19 01	19 09	19 18
Kensal Rise	d		16 48	16 56	17 03	17 14	17 19	17 28	17 34	17 41	17 48	17 56	18 03	18 13	18 19	18 29	18 33	18 41	18 48	18 56	19 03	19 11	19 20
Willesden Jn. High Level ⊖	a		16 52	17 00	17 07	17 18	17 23	17 31	17 38	17 45	17 52	18 00	18 07	18 17	18 23	18 32	18 37	18 45	18 52	19 00	19 07	19 15	19 24
	d	16 46	16 53	17 01	17 08	17 19	17 24	17 32	17 39	17 46	17 53	18 01	18 08	18 18	18 24	18 33	18 38	18 46	18 53	19 01	19 08	19 16	19 25
Willesden Jn Low Level ⊖	a																						
Shepherd's Bush ⊖	d	16 53		17 09		17 26		17 40		17 54		18 09		18 25		18 41		18 54		19 09		19 23	
Kensington (Olympia) ⊖	d	16 55		17 11		17 28		17 42		17 56		18 11		18 27		18 43		18 56		19 11		19 25	
West Brompton ⊖	d	16 58		17 13		17 31		17 44		17 58		18 13		18 30		18 45		18 58		19 13		19 28	
Imperial Wharf	d	17 01		17 16		17 34		17 47		18 01		18 16		18 33		18 48		19 01		19 16		19 31	
Clapham Junction 10	a	17 07		17 24		17 39		17 54		18 09		18 25		18 40		18 54		19 09		19 24		19 39	
Acton Central	d		16 58		17 13		17 29		17 44		17 58		18 13		18 29		18 43		18 58		19 13		19 30
South Acton	d		17 01		17 16		17 34		17 46		18 00		18 16		18 32		18 46		19 01		19 16		19 32
Gunnersbury ⊖	d		17 04		17 19		17 39		17 49		18 03		18 19		18 38		18 47		19 06		19 19		19 38
Kew Gardens ⊖	d		17 07		17 22		17 42		17 52		18 06		18 22		18 41		18 50		19 09		19 22		19 41
Richmond ⊖	a		17 13		17 28		17 46		17 58		18 13		18 28		18 45		18 56		19 14		19 29		19 46

		LO	LO	LO	LO	LO	LO	LO	LO	LO	LO	LO	LO	LO	LO	LO	LO	LO	LO	LO	LO	LO	LO
Stratford 7 ⊖	d	18 48	18 57	19 05	19 15		19 25	19 37	19 45		19 55	20 05	20 15		20 25	20 35	20 45		20 55	21 05	21 15		21 25
Hackney Wick	d	18 51	19 00	19 08	19 18		19 28	19 40	19 48		19 58	20 08	20 18		20 28	20 38	20 48		20 58	21 08	21 18		21 28
Homerton	d	18 54	19 03	19 11	19 21		19 31	19 43	19 51		20 01	20 11	20 21		20 31	20 41	20 51		21 01	21 11	21 21		21 31
Hackney Central	d	18 56	19 05	19 13	19 23		19 33	19 45	19 53		20 03	20 13	20 23		20 33	20 43	20 53		21 03	21 13	21 23		21 33
Dalston Kingsland	d	18 58	19 07	19 15	19 25		19 35	19 47	19 55		20 05	20 15	20 25		20 35	20 45	20 55		21 05	21 15	21 25		21 35
Canonbury	d	19 00	19 09	19 17	19 27		19 37	19 49	19 57		20 07	20 17	20 27		20 37	20 47	20 57		21 07	21 17	21 27		21 37
Highbury & Islington ⊖	d	19 03	19 12	19 20	19 30		19 40	19 52	20 00		20 10	20 20	20 30		20 40	20 50	21 00		21 10	21 20	21 30		21 40
Caledonian Rd & Barnsbury	d	19 05	19 14	19 22	19 32		19 42	19 54	20 02		20 12	20 22	20 32		20 42	20 52	21 02		21 12	21 22	21 32		21 42
Camden Road	d	19 08	19 17	19 25	19 35		19 45	19 57	20 05		20 15	20 25	20 35		20 45	20 55	21 05		21 15	21 25	21 35		21 45
Kentish Town West	d	19 10	19 19	19 27	19 37		19 47	19 59	20 07		20 18	20 27	20 37		20 47	20 57	21 07		21 17	21 27	21 37		21 47
Gospel Oak	d	19 13	19 24	19 30	19 40		19 50	20 01	20 10		20 22	20 30	20 40		20 50	21 00	21 10		21 20	21 30	21 40		21 50
Hampstead Heath	d	19 15	19 26	19 32	19 42		19 52	20 03	20 12		20 24	20 32	20 42		20 52	21 02	21 12		21 22	21 32	21 42		21 52
Finchley Road & Frognal	d	19 17	19 28	19 34	19 44		19 54	20 05	20 14		20 26	20 34	20 44		20 54	21 04	21 14		21 24	21 34	21 44		21 54
West Hampstead ⊖	d	19 19	19 30	19 36	19 46		19 56	20 07	20 16		20 28	20 36	20 46		20 56	21 06	21 16		21 26	21 36	21 46		21 56
Brondesbury	d	19 21	19 32	19 38	19 48		19 58	20 09	20 18		20 29	20 38	20 48		20 57	21 08	21 18		21 28	21 38	21 48		21 58
Brondesbury Park	d	19 22	19 33	19 39	19 49		19 59	20 10	20 19		20 31	20 39	20 49		20 59	21 09	21 19		21 29	21 39	21 49		21 59
Kensal Rise	d	19 24	19 35	19 41	19 51		20 01	20 12	20 21		20 33	20 41	20 51		21 01	21 11	21 21		21 31	21 41	21 51		22 01
Willesden Jn. High Level ⊖	a	19 30	19 39	19 45	19 55		20 05	20 16	20 25		20 36	20 45	20 55		21 05	21 15	21 25		21 35	21 45	21 55		22 05
	d	19 31	19 40	19 46	19 56	20 01	20 06	20 17	20 26	20 31	20 37	20 46	20 57	21 01	21 06	21 16	21 26	21 31	21 36	21 46	21 56	22 01	22 06
Willesden Jn Low Level ⊖	a																						
Shepherd's Bush ⊖	d	19 39		19 54		20 09		20 26		20 39		20 54		21 09		21 26		21 39		21 54		22 09	
Kensington (Olympia) ⊖	d	19 41		19 56		20 11		20 28		20 41		20 56		21 11		21 28		21 41		21 56		22 11	
West Brompton ⊖	d	19 43		19 58		20 13		20 30		20 43		20 58		21 13		21 31		21 43		21 58		22 13	
Imperial Wharf	d	19 46		20 01		20 16		20 33		20 46		21 01		21 16		21 34		21 46		22 01		22 16	
Clapham Junction 10	a	19 54		20 09		20 23		20 41		20 53		21 09		21 23		21 41		21 53		22 09		22 23	
Acton Central	d		19 45		20 01		20 11		20 31		20 42		21 02		21 11		21 31		21 41		22 01		22 11
South Acton	d		19 48		20 04		20 14		20 34		20 44		21 05		21 13		21 34		21 44		22 04		22 14
Gunnersbury ⊖	d		19 51		20 09		20 18		20 38		20 49		21 08		21 18		21 38		21 48		22 08		22 18
Kew Gardens ⊖	d		19 54		20 12		20 21		20 41		20 52		21 11		21 21		21 41		21 51		22 11		22 21
Richmond ⊖	a		19 59		20 17		20 26		20 46		20 56		21 16		21 26		21 46		21 56		22 16		22 26

Stratford - Highbury and Islington, West Hampstead, Willesden Junction, Clapham Junction and Richmond

Network Diagram - see first Page of Table 59

		LO	LO	LO	LO	LO	LO	LO	LO	LO	LO	LO	LO
Stratford ⊖	d	21 35	21 45		21 55	22 15	22 25		22 45	22 55	23 15		23 45
Hackney Wick	d	21 38	21 48		21 58	22 18	22 28		22 48	22 58	23 18		23 48
Homerton	d	21 41	21 51		22 01	22 21	22 31		22 51	23 01	23 21		23 51
Hackney Central	d	21 43	21 53		22 03	22 23	22 33		22 53	23 03	23 23		23 53
Dalston Kingsland	d	21 45	21 55		22 05	22 25	22 35		22 55	23 05	23 25		23 55
Canonbury	d	21 47	21 57		22 07	22 27	22 37		22 57	23 07	23 27		23 57
Highbury & Islington ⊖	d	21 50	22 00		22 10	22 30	22 40		23 00	23 10	23 30		23 59
Caledonian Rd & Barnsbury	d	21 52	22 02		22 12	22 32	22 42		23 02	23 12	23 32		00 02
Camden Road	d	21 55	22 05		22 15	22 35	22a46		23 05	23a16	23 35		00 05
Kentish Town West	d	21 57	22 07		22 17	22 37			23 07		23 37		00 07
Gospel Oak	d	22 00	22 10		22 20	22 40			23 10		23 40		00 10
Hampstead Heath	d	22 02	22 12		22 22	22 42			23 12		23 42		00 12
Finchley Road & Frognal	d	22 04	22 14		22 24	22 44			23 14		23 44		00 14
West Hampstead ⊖	d	22 06	22 16		22 26	22 46			23 16		23 46		00 16
Brondesbury	d	22 08	22 18		22 28	22 48			23 18		23 48		00 18
Brondesbury Park	d	22 09	22 19		22 29	22 49			23 19		23 49		00 19
Kensal Rise	d	22 11	22 21		22 31	22 51			23 21		23 51		00 21
Willesden Jn. High Level ⊖	a	22 15	22 25		22 35	22 55			23 25				
	d	22 16	22 26	22 31	22 36	22 56		23 01	23 26			23 40	
Willesden Jn Low Level ⊖	a										23 56		00 29
Shepherd's Bush ⊖	d	22 26		22 39				23 09				23 48	
Kensington (Olympia) ⊖	d	22 28		22 41				23 11				23 50	
West Brompton ⊖	d	22 30		22 43				23 13				23 52	
Imperial Wharf	d	22 33		22 46				23 16				23 55	
Clapham Junction 10	a	22 40		22 53				23 23				00 02	
Acton Central	d		22 31		22 41	23 01			23 31				
South Acton	d		22 34		22 44	23 04			23 34				
Gunnersbury ⊖	d		22 38		22 48	23 08			23 38				
Kew Gardens ⊖	d		22 41		22 51	23 11			23 41				
Richmond ⊖	a		22 46		22 56	23 16			23 46				

		LO MO	LO A	LO B	LO MO	LO A	LO A	LO MO	LO MO	LO A	LO A	LO MO	LO A	LO MO	LO MO	LO A	LO B	LO A	LO MO	LO A	LO MO	LO C	LO C
Stratford ⊖	d	22p52	22p52		23p00	23p02	23p07	23p07	23p15	23p15	23p22	23p22	23p30	23p30	23p37	23p38	23p45	23p45	23p45	23p52	23p52	00 01	00 07
Hackney Wick	d	22p55	22p55		23p05	23p05	23p10	23p10	23p18	23p18	23p25	23p25	23p33	23p35	23p40	23p41	23p48	23p48	23p49	23p55	23p55	00 03	00 10
Homerton	d	22p58	22p58		23p06	23p06	23p13	23p13	23p19	23p21	23p28	23p28	23p36	23p36	23p43	23p44	23p51	23p51	23p51	23p58	23p58	00 06	00 13
Hackney Central	d	23p00	23p00		23p08	23p08	23p15	23p15	23p21	23p23	23p30	23p30	23p38	23p38	23p45	23p46	23p53	23p53	23p53	23p59	00 01	00 08	00 15
Dalston Kingsland	d	23p02	23p02		23p10	23p10	23p17	23p17	23p23	23p25	23p32	23p32	23p40	23p40	23p47	23p48	23p55	23p55	23p55	00 02	00 03	00 10	00 17
Canonbury	d	23p04	23p04		23p12	23p12	23p19	23p19	23p25	23p27	23p34	23p34	23p42	23p42	23p49	23p50	23p57	23p57	23p57	00 04	00 05	00 12	00 19
Highbury & Islington ⊖	d	23p08	23p08		23p16	23p16	23p23	23p23	23p28	23p31	23p38	23p38	23p46	23p46	23p53	23p53	23p59	00 01	00 01	00 08	00 08	00 16	00 23
Caledonian Rd & Barnsbury	d	23p10	23p10		23p18	23p18	23p25	23p25	23p30	23p33	23p40	23p40	23p48	23p48	23p55	23p55	00 02	00 03	00 03	00 10	00 10	00 18	00 25
Camden Road	d	23p14	23p14		23p22	23p22	23p29	23p29	23p34	23p37	23p44	23p45	23p53	23p52	23p59	23p59	00 05	00 07	00 07	00 14	00 14	00 22	00a31
Kentish Town West	d	23p16	23p16		23p24	23p24	23p31	23p31	23p37	23p39	23p46	23p47	23p55	23p54	00 01	00 02	00 07	00 09	00 09	00 16	00 16	00 24	
Gospel Oak	d	23p19	23p19		23p27	23p27	23p34	23p34	23p40	23p42	23p49	23p50	23p59	23p57	00 04	00 05	00 10	00 12	00 12	00 19	00 19	00 27	
Hampstead Heath	d	23p21	23p21		23p29	23p29	23p36	23p36	23p42	23p44	23p51	23p52	00 01	23p59	00 06	00 07	00 12	00 14	00 14	00 21	00 21	00 29	
Finchley Road & Frognal	d	23p23	23p23		23p31	23p31	23p38	23p38	23p44	23p46	23p53	23p54	00 03	00 01	00 08	00 09	00 14	00 16	00 16	00 23	00 23	00 31	
West Hampstead ⊖	d	23p25	23p25		23p33	23p33	23p40	23p40	23p47	23p48	23p55	23p56	00 05	00 03	00 10	00 11	00 16	00 18	00 18	00 25	00 25	00 33	
Brondesbury	d	23p27	23p27		23p35	23p35	23p42	23p42	23p48	23p50	23p57	23p58	00 06	00 05	00 12	00 13	00 18	00 20	00 20	00 27	00 27	00 35	
Brondesbury Park	d	23p28	23p28		23p36	23p36	23p43	23p43	23p50	23p51	23p58	23p59	00 08	00 06	00 13	00 14	00 19	00 21	00 21	00 28	00 28	00 36	
Kensal Rise	d	23p30	23p30		23p38	23p38	23p45	23p45	23p52	23p53	00 01	00 01	00 10	00 08	00 15	00 16	00 21	00 23	00 23	00 30	00 30	00 38	
Willesden Jn. High Level ⊖	a	23p34	23p35		23p42	23p42	23p49	23p49	23p57	23p57	00 04	00 04	00 13	00 12	00 19	00 20		00 27	00 27	00 34	00 34	00 42	
	d	23p35	23p36	23p40	23p43	23p43	23p50	23p50	23p59	23p59	00 05	00 05	00 14	00 13	00 20	00 21		00 28	00 28	00 35	00 35	00 43	
Willesden Jn Low Level ⊖	a																00 29						
Shepherd's Bush ⊖	d			23p48	23p53	23p57			00 09	00 09			00 24	00 23				00 38	00 38			00 53	
Kensington (Olympia) ⊖	d			23p50	23p56	23p59			00 11	00 11			00 26	00 26				00 41	00 41			00 56	
West Brompton ⊖	d			23p52	23p58	00 02			00 14	00 14			00 29	00 28				00 43	00 43			00 58	
Imperial Wharf	d			23p55	00 01	00 05			00 17	00 17			00 32	00 31				00 46	00 46			01 01	
Clapham Junction 10	a			00 02	00 09	00 13			00 22	00 22			00 39	00 39				00 54	00 54			01 09	
Acton Central	d	23p40	23p41				23p55	23p55			00 10	00 10			00 25	00 26				00 40	00 40		
South Acton	d	23p43	23p43				23p58	23p58			00 13	00 13			00 28	00 29				00 43	00 43		
Gunnersbury ⊖	d	23p48	23p48				00 02	00 03			00 18	00 18			00 32	00 33				00 47	00 48		
Kew Gardens ⊖	d	23p51	23p51				00 05	00 06			00 21	00 21			00 35	00 36				00 50	00 51		
Richmond ⊖	a	00 01	00 01				00 14	00 16			00 30	00 31			00 45	00 45				00 59	01 00		

A MX from 31 July until 10 August

B 27 July

C not 27 July

Stratford - Highbury and Islington, West Hampstead, Willesden Junction, Clapham Junction and Richmond

Network Diagram - see first Page of Table 59

		LO MO	LO A	LO A	LO MO	LO MO	LO A	LO B	LO A	LO MO	LO B	LO MO	LO A	LO	LO	LO	LO	LO	LO	LO	LO	LO	LO
Stratford ⊖	d	00 15	00 15	00 22	00 22	00 30	00 32	00 37	00 45	00 45	00 52	01 00	01 00			05 47			06 00	06 07	06 15	06 23	06 34
Hackney Wick	d	00 18	00 18	00 25	00 25	00 33	00 35	00 40	00 48	00 48	00 55	01 03	01 04			05 50			06 04	06 10	06 18	06 26	06 38
Homerton	d	00 21	00 21	00 28	00 28	00 36	00 36	00 43	00 51	00 51	00 58	01 06	01 06			05 53			06 06	06 13	06 21	06 29	06 39
Hackney Central	d	00 23	00 23	00 30	00 30	00 38	00 38	00 45	00 53	00 53	01 00	01 08	01 08			05 55			06 08	06 15	06 23	06 31	06 41
Dalston Kingsland	d	00 25	00 25	00 32	00 32	00 40	00 40	00 47	00 55	00 55	01 02	01 10	01 10			05 57			06 10	06 17	06 25	06 33	06 43
Canonbury	d	00 27	00 27	00 34	00 34	00 42	00 42	00 49	00 57	00 57	01 04	01 12	01 12			05 59			06 12	06 19	06 27	06 35	06 45
Highbury & Islington ⊖	d	00 31	00 31	00 37	00 38	00 46	00 46	00 53	01 01	01 01	01 08	01 16	01 17			06 02			06 16	06 23	06 31	06 38	06 49
Caledonian Rd & Barnsbury	d	00 33	00 33	00 39	00 40	00 48	00 48	00 55	01 03	01 03	01 10	01 18	01 19			06 04			06 18	06 25	06 33	06 40	06 51
Camden Road	d	00 37	00 37	00a46	00a46	00 52	00 52	01a00	01 07	01 07	01a16	01 22	01 23			06 07			06 22	06 29	06 37	06 44	06 55
Kentish Town West	d	00 39	00 39			00 54	00 54		01 09	01 09		01 24	01 26			06 09			06 24	06 31	06 39	06 46	06 57
Gospel Oak	d	00 42	00 42			00 57	00 57		01 12	01 12		01 27	01 28			06 12			06 27	06 34	06 42	06 49	07 00
Hampstead Heath	d	00 44	00 44			00 59	00 59		01 14	01 14		01 29	01 30			06 14			06 29	06 36	06 44	06 51	07 02
Finchley Road & Frognal	d	00 46	00 46			01 01	01 01		01 16	01 16		01 31	01 32			06 16			06 31	06 38	06 46	06 53	07 04
West Hampstead ⊖	d	00 48	00 48			01 03	01 03		01 18	01 18		01 33	01 35			06 18			06 33	06 40	06 48	06 55	07 06
Brondesbury	d	00 50	00 50			01 05	01 05		01 20	01 20		01 35	01 36			06 20			06 35	06 42	06 50	06 57	07 07
Brondesbury Park	d	00 51	00 51			01 06	01 06		01 21	01 21		01 36	01 38			06 21			06 36	06 43	06 51	06 58	07 09
Kensal Rise	d	00 53	00 53			01 08	01 08		01 23	01 23		01 38	01 40			06 23			06 38	06 45	06 53	07 00	07 11
Willesden Jn. High Level ⊖	a															06 27			06 42	06 49	06 57	07 04	07 15
	d													06 02	06 06	06 28	06 33	06 41	06 43	06 50	06 58	07 05	07 16
Willesden Jn Low Level ⊖	a	01 01	01 02			01 21	01 21		01 41	01 42		01 57	01 50										
Shepherd's Bush ⊖	d													06 09			06 41		06 53		07 08		07 26
Kensington (Olympia) ⊖	d													06 11			06 43		06 56		07 11		07 28
West Brompton ⊖	d													06 14			06 46		06 58		07 13		07 31
Imperial Wharf	d													06 17			06 49		07 01		07 16		07 34
Clapham Junction 10	a													06 23			06 56		07 09		07 24		07 41
Acton Central	d														06 11	06 33		06 46		06 55		07 10	
South Acton	d														06 14	06 36		06 49		06 58		07 13	
Gunnersbury ⊖	d														06 18	06 40		06 53		07 02		07 17	
Kew Gardens ⊖	d														06 21	06 43		06 56		07 05		07 20	
Richmond ⊖	a														06 30	06 52		07 06		07 14		07 29	

		LO	LO	LO	LO	LO	LO	LO	LO	LO	LO	LO	LO	LO	LO	LO	LO	LO	LO	LO	LO	LO	LO
Stratford ⊖	d	06 40	06 45	06 52	07 00	07 07	07 15	07 22	07 26	07 30	07 37	07 45	07 52	07 56	08 00	08 07	08 15	08 22	08 26	08 30	08 37	08 45	08 52
Hackney Wick	d	06 43	06 49	06 55	07 03	07 10	07 18	07 25	07 29	07 33	07 41	07 48	07 55	07 59	08 03	08 10	08 18	08 25	08 29	08 33	08 40	08 48	08 55
Homerton	d	06 46	06 51	06 58	07 06	07 13	07 21	07 28	07 32	07 36	07 43	07 51	07 58	08 02	08 06	08 13	08 21	08 28	08 32	08 36	08 43	08 51	08 58
Hackney Central	d	06 48	06 53	07 00	07 08	07 15	07 23	07 30	07 34	07 38	07 45	07 53	08 00	08 04	08 08	08 15	08 23	08 30	08 34	08 38	08 45	08 53	09 00
Dalston Kingsland	d	06 50	06 55	07 02	07 10	07 17	07 25	07 32	07 36	07 40	07 48	07 55	08 02	08 06	08 10	08 17	08 25	08 32	08 36	08 40	08 47	08 55	09 02
Canonbury	d	06 52	06 57	07 04	07 12	07 19	07 27	07 34	07 39	07 42	07 50	07 57	08 04	08 09	08 12	08 19	08 27	08 34	08 39	08 42	08 49	08 57	09 04
Highbury & Islington ⊖	d	06 56	07 01	07 08	07 16	07 23	07 31	07 38	07 42	07 46	07 53	08 01	08 08	08 12	08 16	08 23	08 31	08 38	08 42	08 46	08 53	09 01	09 08
Caledonian Rd & Barnsbury	d	06 58	07 03	07 10	07 18	07 25	07 33	07 40	07 44	07 48	07 55	08 03	08 10	08 14	08 18	08 25	08 33	08 40	08 44	08 48	08 55	09 03	09 10
Camden Road	d	07 02	07 07	07 14	07 22	07 29	07 37	07 44	07a50	07 52	07 59	08 07	08 14	08a20	08 22	08 29	08 37	08 44	08a50	08 54	09 01	09 07	09 14
Kentish Town West	d	07 04	07 09	07 16	07 24	07 31	07 39	07 46		07 54	08 02	08 09	08 16		08 24	08 31	08 39	08 46		08 56	09 03	09 09	09 16
Gospel Oak	d	07 06	07 12	07 19	07 27	07 34	07 42	07 49		07 57	08 04	08 12	08 19		08 27	08 34	08 42	08 49		08 59	09 06	09 12	09 19
Hampstead Heath	d	07 08	07 14	07 21	07 29	07 36	07 44	07 51		07 59	08 06	08 14	08 21		08 29	08 36	08 44	08 51		09 01	09 08	09 14	09 21
Finchley Road & Frognal	d	07 10	07 16	07 23	07 31	07 38	07 46	07 53		08 01	08 08	08 16	08 23		08 31	08 38	08 46	08 53		09 03	09 10	09 16	09 23
West Hampstead ⊖	d	07 12	07 18	07 25	07 33	07 40	07 48	07 55		08 03	08 11	08 18	08 25		08 33	08 40	08 48	08 55		09 05	09 12	09 18	09 25
Brondesbury	d	07 14	07 20	07 27	07 35	07 42	07 50	07 57		08 05	08 12	08 20	08 27		08 35	08 42	08 50	08 57		09 07	09 13	09 20	09 27
Brondesbury Park	d	07 15	07 21	07 28	07 36	07 43	07 51	07 58		08 06	08 14	08 21	08 28		08 36	08 43	08 51	08 58		09 08	09 15	09 21	09 28
Kensal Rise	d	07 17	07 23	07 30	07 38	07 45	07 53	08 00		08 08	08 16	08 23	08 30		08 38	08 45	08 53	09 00		09 10	09 17	09 23	09 30
Willesden Jn. High Level ⊖	a	07 20	07 27	07 34	07 42	07 49	07 57	08 04		08 12	08 20	08 27	08 34		08 42	08 49	08 57	09 04		09 14	09 21	09 27	09 34
	d	07 21	07 28	07 35	07 43	07 50	07 58	08 05		08 13	08 21	08 28	08 35		08 43	08 50	08 58	09 05		09 15	09 22	09 28	09 35
Willesden Jn Low Level ⊖	a																						
Shepherd's Bush ⊖	d		07 38		07 53		08 08			08 23		08 38			08 53		09 08			09 25		09 38	
Kensington (Olympia) ⊖	d		07 41		07 56		08 11			08 26		08 41			08 56		09 11			09 28		09 41	
West Brompton ⊖	d		07 43		07 58		08 13			08 28		08 43			08 58		09 13			09 30		09 43	
Imperial Wharf	d		07 46		08 01		08 16			08 31		08 46			09 01		09 16			09 33		09 46	
Clapham Junction 10	a		07 54		08 09		08 24			08 39		08 54			09 09		09 24			09 41		09 54	
Acton Central	d	07 26		07 40		07 55		08 10			08 26		08 40			08 55		09 10			09 26		09 40
South Acton	d	07 29		07 43		07 58		08 13			08 28		08 43			08 58		09 13			09 29		09 43
Gunnersbury ⊖	d	07 32		07 49		08 02		08 18			08 32		08 50			09 03		09 17			09 32		09 50
Kew Gardens ⊖	d	07 35		07 51		08 05		08 21			08 35		08 53			09 06		09 20			09 35		09 52
Richmond ⊖	a	07 44		08 00		08 14		08 30			08 45		09 01			09 15		09 29			09 44		10 01

A MX from 31 July until 10 August

B not 27 July

Stratford - Highbury and Islington, West Hampstead, Willesden Junction, Clapham Junction and Richmond

Network Diagram - see first Page of Table 59

		LO	LO	LO	LO	LO	LO	LO	LO	LO	LO	LO	LO	LO	LO	LO	LO	LO	LO	LO	LO	LO	LO
Stratford 7	⊖ d	08 56	09 00	09 07	09 15	09 22	09 26	09 30	09 37	09 45	09 52	10 00	10 07	10 15	10 22	10 30	10 37	10 46	10 52	11 00	11 07	11 12	11 20
Hackney Wick	d	08 59	09 03	09 10	09 18	09 25	09 29	09 33	09 40	09 48	09 55	10 04	10 11	10 18	10 25	10 33	10 40	10 49	10 55	11 03	11 10	11 13	11 23
Homerton	d	09 02	09 06	09 13	09 21	09 28	09 32	09 36	09 43	09 51	09 58	10 06	10 13	10 21	10 28	10 35	10 43	10 51	10 58	11 06	11 13	11 16	11 26
Hackney Central	d	09 04	09 08	09 15	09 23	09 30	09 34	09 38	09 45	09 53	10 00	10 08	10 15	10 23	10 30	10 37	10 45	10 53	11 00	11 08	11 15	11 18	11 28
Dalston Kingsland	d	09 06	09 10	09 17	09 25	09 32	09 36	09 40	09 47	09 55	10 02	10 10	10 17	10 25	10 32	10 38	10 47	10 56	11 02	11 10	11 17	11 20	11 30
Canonbury	d	09 09	09 12	09 19	09 27	09 34	09 39	09 42	09 49	09 57	10 04	10 12	10 19	10 27	10 34	10 40	10 49	10 58	11 04	11 12	11 19	11 22	11 32
Highbury & Islington	⊖ d	09 12	09 16	09 23	09 31	09 38	09 42	09 46	09 53	10 01	10 08	10 16	10 23	10 31	10 38	10 43	10 53	11 02	11 08	11 16	11 23	11 26	11 37
Caledonian Rd & Barnsbury	d	09 14	09 18	09 25	09 33	09 40	09 44	09 48	09 55	10 03	10 10	10 18	10 25	10 33	10 40	10 45	10 55	11 04	11 10	11 18	11 25	11 28	11 39
Camden Road	d	09a20	09 22	09 29	09 37	09 44	09a53	09 52	09 59	10 07	10 14	10 22	10 29	10 37	10 44	10 49	10 59	11 08	11 15	11 22	11 29	11 33	11 43
Kentish Town West	d		09 24	09 31	09 39	09 46		09 54	10 01	10 09	10 16	10 24	10 31	10 39	10 46	10 52	11 01	11 10	11 17	11 24	11 31	11 35	11 45
Gospel Oak	d		09 27	09 34	09 42	09 49		09 57	10 04	10 12	10 19	10 28	10 35	10 42	10 49	10 54	11 04	11 13	11 24	11 27	11 34	11 38	11 47
Hampstead Heath	d		09 29	09 36	09 44	09 51		09 59	10 06	10 14	10 21	10 30	10 37	10 44	10 51	10 56	11 06	11 15	11 26	11 29	11 36	11 40	11 49
Finchley Road & Frognal	d		09 31	09 38	09 46	09 53		10 01	10 08	10 16	10 23	10 32	10 39	10 46	10 53	10 58	11 08	11 17	11 28	11 31	11 38	11 42	11 51
West Hampstead	⊖ d		09 33	09 40	09 48	09 55		10 03	10 10	10 18	10 25	10 35	10 41	10 48	10 55	11 01	11 10	11 19	11 30	11 33	11 40	11 44	11 53
Brondesbury	d		09 35	09 42	09 50	09 57		10 05	10 12	10 20	10 27	10 36	10 43	10 50	10 57	11 02	11 12	11 21	11 32	11 35	11 42	11 46	11 55
Brondesbury Park	d		09 36	09 43	09 51	09 58		10 06	10 13	10 21	10 28	10 38	10 44	10 51	10 58	11 04	11 13	11 22	11 33	11 36	11 43	11 47	11 56
Kensal Rise	d		09 38	09 45	09 53	10 00		10 08	10 15	10 23	10 30	10 40	10 46	10 53	11 00	11 06	11 15	11 24	11 35	11 38	11 45	11 49	11 58
Willesden Jn. High Level	⊖ a		09 42	09 49	09 57	10 04		10 12	10 19	10 27	10 34	10 44	10 50	10 57	11 04	11 12	11 19	11 28	11 40	11 42	11 49	11 55	12 02
	d		09 43	09 50	09 58	10 05		10 13	10 20	10 28	10 35	10 45	10 51	10 58	11 05	11 13	11 20	11 29	11 41	11 43	11 50	11 57	12 06
Willesden Jn Low Level	⊖ a																						
Shepherd's Bush	⊖ d		09 53		10 08			10 24		10 38		10 55		11 08		11 23		11 39		11 53		12 09	
Kensington (Olympia)	⊖ d		09 56		10 11			10 26		10 41		10 57		11 11		11 26		11 42		11 56		12 12	
West Brompton	⊖ d		09 58		10 13			10 29		10 43		11 00		11 13		11 28		11 44		11 58		12 14	
Imperial Wharf	d		10 01		10 16			10 32		10 46		11 03		11 16		11 31		11 47		12 01		12 17	
Clapham Junction 10	a		10 09		10 24			10 40		10 54		11 10		11 24		11 39		11 55		12 09		12 25	
Acton Central	d			09 55		10 10			10 25		10 40		10 56		11 10		11 25		11 46		11 55		12 11
South Acton	d			09 58		10 13			10 28		10 43		10 59		11 13		11 28		11 48		11 58		12 13
Gunnersbury	⊖ d			10 02		10 20			10 32		10 49		11 02		11 20		11 32		11 53		12 02		12 19
Kew Gardens	⊖ d			10 05		10 23			10 35		10 52		11 05		11 23		11 35		11 56		12 05		12 22
Richmond	⊖ a			10 14		10 31			10 45		11 01		11 15		11 31		11 44		12 05		12 15		12 31

		LO	LO	LO	LO	LO	LO	LO	LO	LO	LO	LO	LO	LO	LO	LO	LO	LO	LO	LO	LO	LO	LO
Stratford 7	⊖ d	11 30	11 37	11 45	11 52	12 02	12 07	12 15	12 22	12 32	12 39	12 45	12 52	13 02	13 07	13 15	13 22	13 30	13 37	13 45	13 52	14 02	14 07
Hackney Wick	d	11 33	11 40	11 48	11 56	12 04	12 10	12 18	12 25	12 35	12 42	12 48	12 57	13 05	13 10	13 18	13 25	13 33	13 41	13 48	13 55	14 05	14 10
Homerton	d	11 36	11 43	11 49	11 58	12 06	12 13	12 21	12 28	12 36	12 45	12 51	13 00	13 06	13 13	13 21	13 28	13 36	13 43	13 51	13 58	14 06	14 13
Hackney Central	d	11 38	11 45	11 51	12 00	12 08	12 15	12 23	12 30	12 38	12 47	12 53	13 02	13 08	13 15	13 23	13 30	13 38	13 45	13 53	14 00	14 08	14 15
Dalston Kingsland	d	11 40	11 47	11 53	12 03	12 10	12 17	12 25	12 32	12 40	12 49	12 55	13 04	13 10	13 17	13 25	13 32	13 40	13 47	13 55	14 02	14 10	14 17
Canonbury	d	11 42	11 49	11 55	12 05	12 12	12 19	12 27	12 34	12 42	12 51	12 57	13 06	13 12	13 19	13 27	13 34	13 42	13 49	13 57	14 04	14 12	14 19
Highbury & Islington	⊖ d	11 46	11 53	11 59	12 08	12 16	12 23	12 31	12 37	12 46	12 54	13 01	13 08	13 16	13 22	13 31	13 38	13 46	13 53	14 01	14 08	14 16	14 23
Caledonian Rd & Barnsbury	d	11 48	11 55	12 01	12 10	12 18	12 28	12 33	12 39	12 48	12 56	13 03	13 10	13 18	13 24	13 33	13 40	13 48	13 55	14 03	14 10	14 18	14 25
Camden Road	d	11 52	11 59	12 05	12 15	12 22	12 32	12 37	12 43	12 52	13 00	13 07	13 14	13 22	13 28	13 38	13 44	13 52	13 59	14 07	14 14	14 22	14 29
Kentish Town West	d	11 54	12 01	12 08	12 17	12 24	12 35	12 39	12 46	12 54	13 03	13 09	13 17	13 24	13 31	13 40	13 48	13 54	14 01	14 09	14 16	14 24	14 31
Gospel Oak	d	11 57	12 04	12 12	12 19	12 27	12 39	12 42	12 48	12 59	13 06	13 12	13 19	13 27	13 33	13 44	13 51	13 58	14 05	14 12	14 19	14 27	14 34
Hampstead Heath	d	11 59	12 06	12 13	12 21	12 29	12 41	12 44	12 50	13 01	13 08	13 14	13 21	13 29	13 35	13 46	13 53	14 00	14 07	14 14	14 21	14 29	14 36
Finchley Road & Frognal	d	12 01	12 08	12 15	12 23	12 31	12 43	12 46	12 52	13 03	13 10	13 16	13 24	13 31	13 37	13 48	13 55	14 02	14 09	14 16	14 23	14 31	14 38
West Hampstead	⊖ d	12 03	12 10	12 17	12 25	12 33	12 45	12 48	12 55	13 05	13 12	13 18	13 26	13 33	13 39	13 50	13 57	14 04	14 11	14 18	14 25	14 33	14 40
Brondesbury	d	12 05	12 12	12 19	12 27	12 35	12 47	12 50	12 56	13 07	13 14	13 20	13 28	13 35	13 41	13 51	13 58	14 05	14 12	14 20	14 27	14 35	14 42
Brondesbury Park	d	12 06	12 13	12 20	12 28	12 36	12 48	12 51	12 58	13 08	13 15	13 21	13 29	13 36	13 42	13 53	14 00	14 07	14 14	14 21	14 28	14 36	14 43
Kensal Rise	d	12 08	12 15	12 22	12 30	12 38	12 50	12 53	13 00	13 10	13 17	13 23	13 31	13 38	13 44	13 55	14 02	14 09	14 16	14 23	14 30	14 38	14 45
Willesden Jn. High Level	⊖ a	12 12	12 19	12 27	12 34	12 42	12 53	12 57	13 04	13 13	13 20	13 27	13 34	13 42	13 48	13 58	14 05	14 13	14 20	14 27	14 34	14 42	14 49
	d	12 13	12 20	12 28	12 35	12 43	12 53	12 58	13 05	13 14	13 21	13 28	13 35	13 43	13 50	13 59	14 06	14 14	14 21	14 28	14 35	14 43	14 50
Willesden Jn Low Level	⊖ a																						
Shepherd's Bush	⊖ d	12 23		12 38		12 53		13 08		13 24		13 38		13 53		14 09		14 25		14 38		14 53	
Kensington (Olympia)	⊖ d	12 26		12 41		12 56		13 11		13 27		13 41		13 56		14 11		14 27		14 41		14 56	
West Brompton	⊖ d	12 28		12 43		12 58		13 13		13 29		13 43		13 58		14 14		14 30		14 43		14 58	
Imperial Wharf	d	12 31		12 46		13 01		13 16		13 32		13 46		14 01		14 17		14 33		14 46		15 01	
Clapham Junction 10	a	12 39		12 54		13 09		13 24		13 40		13 54		14 09		14 24		14 41		14 54		15 09	
Acton Central	d		12 25		12 40		12 58		13 10		13 26		13 40		13 55		14 11		14 26		14 40		14 55
South Acton	d		12 28		12 43		13 01		13 13		13 29		13 43		13 58		14 14		14 28		14 43		14 58
Gunnersbury	⊖ d		12 32		12 49		13 03		13 19		13 32		13 49		14 02		14 19		14 32		14 49		15 02
Kew Gardens	⊖ d		12 35		12 52		13 06		13 22		13 35		13 52		14 05		14 22		14 35		14 52		15 05
Richmond	⊖ a		12 45		13 01		13 15		13 31		13 45		14 01		14 15		14 31		14 45		15 01		15 15

Stratford - Highbury and Islington, West Hampstead, Willesden Junction, Clapham Junction and Richmond

Network Diagram - see first Page of Table 59

		LO	LO	LO	LO	LO	LO	LO	LO	LO	LO	LO	LO	LO	LO	LO	LO	LO	LO	LO	LO	LO	LO
Stratford 7	⊖ d	14 15	14 22	14 32	14 37	14 45	14 52	15 00	15 07	15 16	15 22	15 28	15 37	15 45	15 52	16 00	16 07	16 11	16 15	16 22	16 32	16 37	16 41
Hackney Wick	d	14 18	14 25	14 35	14 40	14 48	14 56	15 03	15 11	15 19	15 25	15 29	15 40	15 48	15 55	16 03	16 10	16 14	16 18	16 25	16 35	16 40	16 44
Homerton	d	14 21	14 28	14 36	14 43	14 51	14 58	15 05	15 13	15 21	15 28	15 32	15 43	15 51	15 58	16 06	16 13	16 17	16 21	16 28	16 36	16 43	16 47
Hackney Central	d	14 23	14 30	14 38	14 45	14 53	15 00	15 07	15 15	15 23	15 30	15 34	15 45	15 53	16 00	16 08	16 15	16 19	16 23	16 30	16 38	16 45	16 49
Dalston Kingsland	d	14 25	14 32	14 40	14 47	14 55	15 02	15 10	15 18	15 25	15 32	15 36	15 47	15 55	16 02	16 10	16 17	16 21	16 25	16 32	16 40	16 47	16 51
Canonbury	d	14 27	14 34	14 42	14 49	14 57	15 04	15 12	15 20	15 27	15 34	15 38	15 49	15 57	16 04	16 12	16 19	16 24	16 27	16 34	16 42	16 49	16 54
Highbury & Islington	⊖ d	14 31	14 38	14 46	14 53	15 01	15 08	15 16	15 24	15 31	15 38	15 41	15 53	16 01	16 08	16 16	16 23	16 27	16 31	16 38	16 46	16 53	16 57
Caledonian Rd & Barnsbury	d	14 33	14 40	14 48	14 55	15 03	15 10	15 18	15 26	15 33	15 40	15 43	15 55	16 03	16 10	16 18	16 25	16 29	16 33	16 40	16 48	16 55	16 59
Camden Road	d	14 37	14 44	14 52	14 59	15 07	15 14	15 22	15 30	15 37	15 44	15 47	15 59	16 07	16 14	16 22	16 29	16a38	16 37	16 44	16 52	16 59	17a08
Kentish Town West	d	14 39	14 46	14 54	15 01	15 09	15 16	15 24	15 32	15 39	15 46	15 50	16 01	16 10	16 16	16 24	16 31		16 39	16 46	16 54	17 01	
Gospel Oak	d	14 42	14 49	14 57	15 04	15 12	15 19	15 27	15 35	15 42	15 49	15 53	16 04	16 12	16 19	16 27	16 34		16 42	16 49	16 57	17 04	
Hampstead Heath	d	14 44	14 51	14 59	15 06	15 14	15 21	15 29	15 37	15 44	15 51	15 55	16 06	16 14	16 21	16 29	16 36		16 44	16 51	16 59	17 06	
Finchley Road & Frognal	d	14 46	14 53	15 01	15 08	15 16	15 23	15 31	15 39	15 46	15 53	15 57	16 08	16 16	16 23	16 31	16 38		16 46	16 53	17 01	17 08	
West Hampstead	⊖ d	14 48	14 55	15 03	15 10	15 18	15 25	15 33	15 41	15 48	15 55	15 59	16 10	16 18	16 25	16 33	16 40		16 48	16 55	17 03	17 10	
Brondesbury	d	14 50	14 57	15 05	15 12	15 20	15 27	15 35	15 43	15 50	15 57	16 00	16 12	16 20	16 27	16 35	16 42		16 50	16 57	17 05	17 12	
Brondesbury Park	d	14 51	14 58	15 06	15 13	15 21	15 28	15 36	15 44	15 51	15 58	16 02	16 13	16 21	16 28	16 36	16 43		16 51	16 58	17 06	17 13	
Kensal Rise	d	14 53	15 00	15 08	15 15	15 23	15 30	15 38	15 46	15 53	16 00	16 04	16 15	16 23	16 30	16 38	16 45		16 53	17 00	17 08	17 15	
Willesden Jn. High Level	⊖ a	14 57	15 04	15 12	15 19	15 27	15 34	15 42	15 50	15 57	16 04	16 08	16 19	16 27	16 34	16 42	16 49		16 57	17 05	17 12	17 19	
	d	14 58	15 05	15 13	15 20	15 28	15 35	15 43	15 51	15 58	16 05	16 09	16 20	16 28	16 35	16 43	16 50		16 58	17 06	17 13	17 20	
Willesden Jn Low Level	⊖ a																						
Shepherd's Bush	⊖ d	15 08		15 23		15 38		15 53		16 08		16 24		16 38		16 53			17 08		17 23		
Kensington (Olympia)	⊖ d	15 11		15 26		15 41		15 56		16 11		16 26		16 41		16 56			17 11		17 26		
West Brompton	⊖ d	15 13		15 28		15 43		15 58		16 13		16 29		16 43		16 58			17 13		17 28		
Imperial Wharf	d	15 16		15 31		15 46		16 01		16 16		16 32		16 46		17 01			17 16		17 31		
Clapham Junction 10	a	15 24		15 39		15 54		16 09		16 24		16 40		16 53		17 09			17 24		17 39		
Acton Central	d		15 10		15 25		15 40		15 56		16 10		16 25		16 40		16 55			17 11		17 25	
South Acton	d		15 13		15 28		15 43		15 59		16 13		16 28		16 43		16 58			17 14		17 28	
Gunnersbury	⊖ d		15 19		15 32		15 49		16 04		16 19		16 32		16 49		17 02			17 18		17 32	
Kew Gardens	⊖ d		15 21		15 35		15 51		16 07		16 22		16 35		16 52		17 05			17 21		17 35	
Richmond	⊖ a		15 30		15 45		16 00		16 18		16 31		16 44		17 01		17 14			17 30		17 44	

		LO	LO	LO	LO	LO	LO	LO	LO	LO	LO	LO	LO	LO	LO	LO	LO	LO	LO	LO	LO	LO	LO
Stratford 7	⊖ d	16 45	16 52	17 00	17 07	17 11	17 15	17 22	17 30	17 37	17 41	17 45	17 52	18 00	18 07	18 11	18 15	18 22	18 30	18 37	18 41	18 45	18 52
Hackney Wick	d	16 48	16 55	17 03	17 10	17 14	17 18	17 25	17 33	17 40	17 44	17 48	17 56	18 03	18 10	18 14	18 18	18 27	18 33	18 40	18 44	18 48	18 55
Homerton	d	16 51	16 58	17 06	17 13	17 17	17 21	17 28	17 36	17 43	17 47	17 51	17 58	18 06	18 13	18 17	18 21	18 29	18 36	18 43	18 47	18 51	18 58
Hackney Central	d	16 53	17 00	17 08	17 15	17 19	17 23	17 30	17 38	17 45	17 49	17 53	18 00	18 08	18 15	18 19	18 23	18 31	18 38	18 45	18 49	18 53	19 00
Dalston Kingsland	d	16 55	17 02	17 10	17 17	17 21	17 25	17 32	17 40	17 47	17 51	17 55	18 02	18 10	18 17	18 21	18 25	18 35	18 40	18 47	18 51	18 55	19 02
Canonbury	d	16 57	17 04	17 12	17 19	17 24	17 27	17 34	17 42	17 49	17 54	17 57	18 04	18 12	18 19	18 24	18 27	18 37	18 42	18 49	18 54	18 57	19 04
Highbury & Islington	⊖ d	17 01	17 08	17 16	17 23	17 27	17 31	17 38	17 46	17 53	17 57	18 01	18 08	18 16	18 23	18 27	18 33	18 40	18 46	18 53	18 57	19 01	19 08
Caledonian Rd & Barnsbury	d	17 03	17 10	17 18	17 25	17 29	17 33	17 40	17 48	17 55	17 59	18 03	18 10	18 18	18 25	18 29	18 35	18 42	18 48	18 55	18 59	19 03	19 10
Camden Road	d	17 07	17 14	17 22	17 29	17a38	17 37	17 44	17 52	17 59	18a08	18 07	18 14	18 22	18 29	18a38	18 39	18 46	18 52	18 59	19a08	19 07	19 14
Kentish Town West	d	17 09	17 16	17 24	17 31		17 39	17 46	17 54	18 01		18 09	18 16	18 24	18 31		18 42	18 48	18 54	19 01		19 09	19 16
Gospel Oak	d	17 12	17 19	17 27	17 34		17 42	17 49	17 57	18 04		18 12	18 19	18 27	18 34		18 44	18 51	18 57	19 04		19 12	19 19
Hampstead Heath	d	17 14	17 21	17 29	17 36		17 44	17 51	17 59	18 06		18 14	18 21	18 29	18 36		18 46	18 53	18 59	19 06		19 14	19 21
Finchley Road & Frognal	d	17 16	17 23	17 31	17 38		17 46	17 53	18 01	18 08		18 16	18 23	18 31	18 38		18 48	18 55	19 01	19 08		19 16	19 23
West Hampstead	⊖ d	17 18	17 25	17 33	17 40		17 48	17 55	18 03	18 10		18 18	18 25	18 33	18 40		18 50	18 57	19 03	19 10		19 18	19 25
Brondesbury	d	17 20	17 27	17 35	17 42		17 50	17 57	18 05	18 12		18 20	18 27	18 35	18 42		18 52	18 58	19 05	19 12		19 20	19 27
Brondesbury Park	d	17 21	17 28	17 36	17 43		17 51	17 58	18 06	18 13		18 21	18 28	18 36	18 43		18 53	19 00	19 06	19 13		19 21	19 28
Kensal Rise	d	17 23	17 30	17 38	17 45		17 53	18 00	18 08	18 15		18 23	18 30	18 38	18 45		18 55	19 02	19 08	19 15		19 23	19 30
Willesden Jn. High Level	⊖ a	17 27	17 35	17 42	17 49		17 57	18 04	18 12	18 19		18 27	18 34	18 42	18 49		18 58	19 06	19 13	19 19		19 27	19 34
	d	17 28	17 36	17 43	17 50		17 58	18 05	18 13	18 20		18 28	18 35	18 43	18 50		18 59	19 07	19 14	19 20		19 28	19 35
Willesden Jn Low Level	⊖ a																						
Shepherd's Bush	⊖ d	17 38		17 53			18 08		18 23			18 38		18 53			19 09		19 24			19 38	
Kensington (Olympia)	⊖ d	17 41		17 56			18 11		18 26			18 41		18 56			19 12		19 27			19 41	
West Brompton	⊖ d	17 43		17 58			18 13		18 28			18 43		18 58			19 14		19 29			19 43	
Imperial Wharf	d	17 46		18 01			18 16		18 31			18 46		19 01			19 17		19 32			19 46	
Clapham Junction 10	a	17 54		18 09			18 24		18 39			18 54		19 09			19 25		19 40			19 54	
Acton Central	d		17 41		17 55			18 10		18 24			18 40		18 55			19 12		19 25			19 40
South Acton	d		17 44		17 58			18 13		18 27			18 43		18 58			19 14		19 28			19 43
Gunnersbury	⊖ d		17 48		18 02			18 17		18 31			18 47		19 01			19 17		19 31			19 48
Kew Gardens	⊖ d		17 51		18 05			18 20		18 34			18 50		19 04			19 20		19 34			19 51
Richmond	⊖ a		18 00		18 14			18 30		18 43			19 00		19 13			19 30		19 44			20 00

Stratford - Highbury and Islington, West Hampstead, Willesden Junction, Clapham Junction and Richmond

Network Diagram - see first Page of Table 59

		LO	LO	LO	LO	LO	LO	LO	LO	LO	LO	LO	LO	LO	LO	LO	LO	LO	LO	LO	LO	LO	LO
Stratford 7 ⊖	d	19 00	19 07	19 11	19 15	19 22	19 30	19 38	19 45	19 54	20 00	20 07	20 14	20 22	20 32	20 37	20 45	20 52	21 02	21 07	21 15	21 25	21 30
Hackney Wick	d	19 03	19 10	19 14	19 18	19 25	19 33	19 43	19 47	19 58	20 03	20 10	20 17	20 25	20 35	20 40	20 48	20 55	21 05	21 10	21 18	21 28	21 35
Homerton	d	19 06	19 13	19 17	19 21	19 28	19 35	19 45	19 50	20 00	20 06	20 13	20 19	20 28	20 36	20 43	20 51	20 58	21 07	21 13	21 21	21 31	21 36
Hackney Central	d	19 08	19 15	19 19	19 23	19 30	19 37	19 47	19 52	20 02	20 08	20 15	20 21	20 30	20 38	20 45	20 53	21 00	21 09	21 15	21 23	21 33	21 38
Dalston Kingsland	d	19 10	19 17	19 21	19 25	19 32	19 40	19 50	19 54	20 05	20 10	20 17	20 22	20 32	20 40	20 47	20 55	21 02	21 11	21 17	21 25	21 35	21 40
Canonbury	d	19 12	19 19	19 24	19 27	19 34	19 42	19 52	19 56	20 07	20 12	20 19	20 24	20 34	20 42	20 49	20 57	21 04	21 13	21 19	21 27	21 37	21 42
Highbury & Islington ⊖	d	19 16	19 23	19 27	19 31	19 38	19 45	19 56	20 00	20 10	20 16	20 23	20 29	20 38	20 46	20 52	21 01	21 08	21 16	21 23	21 31	21 41	21 47
Caledonian Rd & Barnsbury	d	19 18	19 25	19 29	19 33	19 40	19 47	19 58	20 02	20 12	20 18	20 25	20 31	20 40	20 48	20 54	21 03	21 10	21 18	21 25	21 33	21 43	21 49
Camden Road	d	19 22	19 29	19a38	19 37	19 44	19 51	20 02	20 06	20 16	20 22	20 29	20 37	20 43	20 52	20 58	21 07	21 14	21 22	21 29	21 37	21 47	21 54
Kentish Town West	d	19 24	19 31		19 39	19 46	19 54	20 04	20 08	20 19	20 24	20 31	20 39	20 46	20 55	21 01	21 09	21 16	21 25	21 31	21 39	21 50	21 56
Gospel Oak	d	19 27	19 34		19 42	19 49	19 57	20 07	20 11	20 22	20 27	20 34	20 42	20 50	20 57	21 04	21 13	21 20	21 27	21 34	21 42	21 52	21 59
Hampstead Heath	d	19 29	19 36		19 44	19 51	19 59	20 09	20 13	20 24	20 29	20 36	20 44	20 52	20 59	21 06	21 15	21 22	21 29	21 36	21 44	21 54	22 01
Finchley Road & Frognal	d	19 31	19 38		19 46	19 53	20 01	20 11	20 15	20 26	20 31	20 38	20 46	20 54	21 01	21 08	21 17	21 24	21 31	21 38	21 46	21 56	22 03
West Hampstead ⊖	d	19 33	19 40		19 48	19 55	20 03	20 13	20 17	20 28	20 33	20 40	20 48	20 56	21 04	21 10	21 19	21 26	21 33	21 40	21 48	21 59	22 05
Brondesbury	d	19 35	19 42		19 50	19 57	20 05	20 15	20 19	20 30	20 35	20 42	20 50	20 58	21 05	21 12	21 21	21 28	21 35	21 42	21 50	22 00	22 07
Brondesbury Park	d	19 36	19 43		19 51	19 58	20 06	20 16	20 20	20 31	20 36	20 43	20 51	20 59	21 07	21 13	21 22	21 29	21 36	21 43	21 51	22 02	22 08
Kensal Rise	d	19 38	19 45		19 53	20 00	20 08	20 18	20 22	20 33	20 38	20 45	20 53	21 01	21 09	21 15	21 24	21 31	21 38	21 45	21 53	22 04	22 10
Willesden Jn. High Level ⊖	a	19 42	19 50		19 57	20 04	20 12	20 22	20 26	20 37	20 42	20 49	20 57	21 05	21 13	21 19	21 27	21 35	21 42	21 49	21 57	22 08	22 15
	d	19 43	19 51		19 58	20 05	20 13	20 23	20 28	20 38	20 43	20 50	20 58	21 06	21 14	21 20	21 28	21 36	21 43	21 50	21 58	22 09	22 16
Willesden Jn Low Level ⊖	a																						
Shepherd's Bush ⊖	d	19 53			20 08		20 23		20 38		20 53		21 08		21 23		21 38		21 53		22 08		22 26
Kensington (Olympia) ⊖	d	19 56			20 11		20 26		20 41		20 56		21 11		21 26		21 41		21 56		22 11		22 29
West Brompton ⊖	d	19 58			20 13		20 28		20 43		20 58		21 13		21 28		21 43		21 58		22 13		22 31
Imperial Wharf	d	20 01			20 16		20 31		20 46		21 01		21 16		21 31		21 46		22 01		22 16		22 34
Clapham Junction 10	a	20 09			20 24		20 39		20 54		21 09		21 24		21 39		21 54		22 09		22 24		22 42
Acton Central	d		19 56			20 10		20 28		20 44		20 55		21 11		21 25		21 41		21 55		22 14	
South Acton	d		19 58			20 14		20 31		20 47		20 58		21 14		21 28		21 44		21 58		22 16	
Gunnersbury ⊖	d		20 02			20 18		20 34		20 52		21 02		21 18		21 32		21 48		22 02		22 23	
Kew Gardens ⊖	d		20 05			20 21		20 37		20 55		21 05		21 21		21 35		21 51		22 05		22 26	
Richmond ⊖	a		20 14			20 30		20 48		21 05		21 15		21 30		21 45		22 00		22 15		22 36	

		LO	LO	LO	LO	LO	LO	LO	LO	LO	LO	LO	LO	LO	LO	LO	LO	LO	LO	LO
Stratford 7 ⊖	d	21 37	21 45	21 52	22 00	22 07	22 15	22 22	22 30	22 37	22 45	22 52	23 02	23 07	23 15	23 22	23 30	23 38	23 45	23 52
Hackney Wick	d	21 41	21 49	21 55	22 03	22 10	22 18	22 25	22 34	22 40	22 48	22 55	23 05	23 10	23 18	23 25	23 33	23 41	23 48	23 55
Homerton	d	21 43	21 51	21 58	22 06	22 13	22 21	22 28	22 35	22 43	22 51	22 58	23 06	23 13	23 21	23 28	23 36	23 44	23 51	23 58
Hackney Central	d	21 45	21 53	22 00	22 08	22 15	22 23	22 30	22 37	22 45	22 53	23 00	23 08	23 15	23 23	23 30	23 38	23 46	23 53	23 59
Dalston Kingsland	d	21 48	21 55	22 02	22 10	22 17	22 25	22 32	22 40	22 47	22 55	23 02	23 10	23 17	23 25	23 32	23 40	23 48	23 55	00 02
Canonbury	d	21 51	21 57	22 04	22 12	22 19	22 27	22 34	22 42	22 49	22 57	23 04	23 12	23 19	23 27	23 34	23 42	23 50	23 57	00 04
Highbury & Islington ⊖	d	21 55	22 01	22 08	22 16	22 23	22 31	22 38	22 46	22 53	23 01	23 08	23 16	23 23	23 31	23 38	23 46	23 53	00 01	00 08
Caledonian Rd & Barnsbury	d	21 57	22 03	22 10	22 18	22 25	22 33	22 40	22 48	22 55	23 03	23 10	23 18	23 25	23 33	23 40	23 48	23 55	00 03	00 10
Camden Road	d	22 01	22 07	22 14	22 22	22 29	22 37	22 44	22 52	22 59	23 07	23 14	23 22	23 29	23 37	23 44	23 53	23 59	00 07	00 14
Kentish Town West	d	22 03	22 09	22 16	22 25	22 32	22 39	22 46	22 54	23 01	23 09	23 16	23 24	23 31	23 39	23 46	23 55	00 02	00 09	00 16
Gospel Oak	d	22 06	22 12	22 19	22 29	22 35	22 43	22 50	22 57	23 04	23 12	23 19	23 27	23 34	23 42	23 49	23 59	00 05	00 12	00 19
Hampstead Heath	d	22 08	22 14	22 21	22 31	22 37	22 45	22 52	22 59	23 06	23 14	23 21	23 29	23 36	23 44	23 51	00 01	00 07	00 14	00 21
Finchley Road & Frognal	d	22 10	22 16	22 23	22 33	22 39	22 47	22 54	23 01	23 08	23 16	23 23	23 31	23 38	23 46	23 53	00 03	00 09	00 16	00 23
West Hampstead ⊖	d	22 12	22 18	22 25	22 35	22 42	22 50	22 57	23 03	23 10	23 18	23 25	23 33	23 40	23 48	23 55	00 05	00 11	00 18	00 25
Brondesbury	d	22 14	22 20	22 27	22 36	22 43	22 51	22 58	23 05	23 12	23 20	23 27	23 35	23 42	23 50	23 57	00 06	00 13	00 20	00 27
Brondesbury Park	d	22 15	22 21	22 28	22 38	22 45	22 53	23 00	23 06	23 13	23 21	23 28	23 36	23 43	23 51	23 58	00 08	00 14	00 21	00 28
Kensal Rise	d	22 17	22 23	22 30	22 40	22 47	22 55	23 02	23 08	23 15	23 23	23 30	23 38	23 45	23 53	00 01	00 10	00 16	00 23	00 30
Willesden Jn. High Level ⊖	a	22 22	22 27	22 34	22 43	22 51	22 58	23 05	23 12	23 19	23 27	23 35	23 42	23 49	23 57	00 04	00 13	00 20	00 27	00 34
	d	22 23	22 28	22 35	22 44	22 52	22 59	23 06	23 13	23 20	23 28	23 36	23 43	23 50	23 59	00 05	00 14	00 21	00 28	00 35
Willesden Jn Low Level ⊖	a																			
Shepherd's Bush ⊖	d		22 38		22 54		23 09		23 23		23 38		23 57		00 09		00 24		00 38	
Kensington (Olympia) ⊖	d		22 41		22 56		23 11		23 26		23 41		23 59		00 11		00 26		00 41	
West Brompton ⊖	d		22 43		22 59		23 14		23 28		23 43		00 02		00 14		00 29		00 43	
Imperial Wharf	d		22 46		23 02		23 17		23 31		23 46		00 05		00 17		00 32		00 46	
Clapham Junction 10	a		22 54		23 10		23 25		23 39		23 54		00 13		00 22		00 39		00 54	
Acton Central	d	22 28		22 40		22 57		23 11		23 25		23 41		23 55		00 10		00 26		00 40
South Acton	d	22 30		22 43		22 59		23 13		23 28		23 43		23 58		00 13		00 29		00 43
Gunnersbury ⊖	d	22 34		22 48		23 02		23 19		23 32		23 48		00 02		00 18		00 33		00 47
Kew Gardens ⊖	d	22 37		22 51		23 05		23 22		23 35		23 51		00 05		00 21		00 36		00 50
Richmond ⊖	a	22 48		23 00		23 15		23 31		23 45		00 01		00 14		00 30		00 45		00 59

Stratford - Highbury and Islington, West Hampstead, Willesden Junction, Clapham Junction and Richmond

Network Diagram - see first Page of Table 59

		LO A	LO MX	LO A	LO A	LO A	LO A	LO A	LO A	LO MX	LO A	LO A	LO A	LO A	LO A	LO A	LO A	LO A	LO A	LO A	LO A	LO	LO
Stratford 7 ⊖	d	22p52		23p00	23p07	23p15	23p22	23p30	23p37	23p45	23p45	23p52	00 01	00 07	00 15	00 22	00 30	00 37	00 45	00 52	01 00		
Hackney Wick	d	22p55		23p05	23p10	23p18	23p25	23p35	23p40	23p48	23p49	23p55	00 03	00 10	00 18	00 25	00 33	00 40	00 48	00 55	01 03		
Homerton	d	22p58		23p06	23p13	23p19	23p28	23p36	23p43	23p51	23p51	23p58	00 06	00 13	00 21	00 28	00 36	00 43	00 51	00 58	01 06		
Hackney Central	d	23p00		23p08	23p15	23p21	23p30	23p38	23p45	23p53	23p53	00 01	00 08	00 15	00 23	00 30	00 38	00 45	00 53	01 00	01 08		
Dalston Kingsland	d	23p02		23p10	23p17	23p23	23p32	23p40	23p47	23p55	23p55	00 03	00 10	00 17	00 25	00 32	00 40	00 47	00 55	01 02	01 10		
Canonbury	d	23p04		23p12	23p19	23p25	23p34	23p42	23p49	23p57	23p57	00 05	00 12	00 19	00 27	00 34	00 42	00 49	00 57	01 04	01 12		
Highbury & Islington ⊖	d	23p08		23p16	23p23	23p28	23p38	23p46	23p53	23p59	00 01	00 08	00 16	00 23	00 31	00 38	00 46	00 53	01 01	01 08	01 16		
Caledonian Rd & Barnsbury	d	23p10		23p18	23p25	23p30	23p40	23p48	23p55	00 02	00 03	00 10	00 18	00 25	00 33	00 40	00 48	00 55	01 03	01 10	01 18		
Camden Road	d	23p14		23p22	23p29	23p34	23p45	23p52	23p59	00 05	00 07	00 14	00 22	00a31	00 37	00a46	00 52	01a01	01 07	01a16	01 22		
Kentish Town West	d	23p16		23p24	23p31	23p37	23p47	23p54	00 01	00 07	00 09	00 16	00 24		00 39		00 54		01 09		01 24		
Gospel Oak	d	23p19		23p27	23p34	23p40	23p50	23p57	00 04	00 10	00 12	00 19	00 27		00 42		00 57		01 12		01 27		
Hampstead Heath	d	23p21		23p29	23p36	23p42	23p52	23p59	00 06	00 12	00 14	00 21	00 29		00 44		00 59		01 14		01 29		
Finchley Road & Frognal	d	23p23		23p31	23p38	23p44	23p54	00 01	00 08	00 14	00 16	00 23	00 31		00 46		01 01		01 16		01 31		
West Hampstead ⊖	d	23p25		23p33	23p40	23p47	23p56	00 03	00 10	00 16	00 18	00 25	00 33		00 48		01 03		01 18		01 33		
Brondesbury	d	23p27		23p35	23p42	23p48	23p58	00 05	00 12	00 18	00 20	00 27	00 35		00 50		01 05		01 20		01 35		
Brondesbury Park	d	23p28		23p36	23p43	23p50	23p59	00 06	00 13	00 19	00 21	00 28	00 36		00 51		01 06		01 21		01 36		
Kensal Rise	d	23p30		23p38	23p45	23p52	00 01	00 08	00 15	00 21	00 23	00 30	00 38		00 53		01 08		01 23		01 38		
Willesden Jn. High Level ⊖	a	23p34		23p42	23p49	23p57	00 04	00 12	00 19		00 27	00 34	00 42										
	d	23p35	23p40	23p43	23p50	23p59	00 05	00 13	00 20		00 28	00 35	00 43									06 01	06 09
Willesden Jn Low Level ⊖	a									00 29					01 01		01 21		01 42		01 57		
Shepherd's Bush ⊖	d		23p48	23p53		00 09		00 23			00 38		00 53									06 08	
Kensington (Olympia) ⊖	d		23p50	23p56		00 11		00 26			00 41		00 56									06 10	
West Brompton ⊖	d		23p52	23p58		00 14		00 28			00 43		00 58									06 13	
Imperial Wharf	d		23p55	00 01		00 17		00 31			00 46		01 01									06 16	
Clapham Junction 10	a		00 02	00 09		00 22		00 39			00 54		01 09									06 23	
Acton Central	d	23p40			23p55		00 10		00 25			00 40											06 14
South Acton	d	23p43			23p58		00 13		00 28			00 43											06 16
Gunnersbury ⊖	d	23p48			00 03		00 18		00 32			00 48											06 20
Kew Gardens ⊖	d	23p51			00 06		00 21		00 35			00 51											06 23
Richmond ⊖	a	00 01			00 16		00 31		00 45			01 00											06 30

		LO	LO	LO	LO	LO	LO	LO	LO	LO	LO	LO	LO	LO	LO	LO	LO	LO	LO	LO	LO	LO	LO
Stratford 7 ⊖	d	05 47			06 05	06 12	06 20	06 27	06 35	06 42	06 50	06 55	07 00	07 12	07 20	07 27	07 35	07 42	07 50	07 57	08 03	08 12	08 20
Hackney Wick	d	05 50			06 08	06 15	06 23	06 30	06 38	06 45	06 54	06 58	07 03	07 15	07 23	07 30	07 38	07 45	07 53	08 00	08 06	08 15	08 23
Homerton	d	05 53			06 11	06 18	06 26	06 33	06 41	06 48	06 56	07 01	07 06	07 18	07 26	07 33	07 42	07 48	07 56	08 03	08 09	08 18	08 26
Hackney Central	d	05 55			06 13	06 20	06 28	06 35	06 43	06 50	06 58	07 03	07 08	07 20	07 28	07 35	07 43	07 50	07 58	08 05	08 11	08 20	08 28
Dalston Kingsland	d	05 57			06 15	06 22	06 30	06 37	06 45	06 52	07 00	07 05	07 10	07 22	07 30	07 37	07 45	07 52	08 00	08 07	08 13	08 22	08 30
Canonbury	d	05 59			06 17	06 24	06 32	06 39	06 47	06 54	07 02	07 07	07 12	07 24	07 32	07 39	07 47	07 54	08 02	08 09	08 15	08 24	08 32
Highbury & Islington ⊖	d	06 02			06 19	06 27	06 35	06 41	06 50	06 57	07 05	07 10	07 15	07 27	07 35	07 42	07 50	07 57	08 05	08 12	08 18	08 27	08 35
Caledonian Rd & Barnsbury	d	06 04			06 21	06 29	06 37	06 43	06 52	06 59	07 07	07 12	07 17	07 29	07 37	07 44	07 52	07 59	08 07	08 14	08 20	08 29	08 37
Camden Road	d	06 07			06 24	06 32	06 40	06 46	06 55	07 02	07 10	07 15	07 20	07 32	07 40	07 47	07 55	08 02	08 10	08 17	08 23	08 32	08 40
Kentish Town West	d	06 09			06 27	06 34	06 42	06 49	06 57	07 04	07 13	07 17	07 22	07 34	07 42	07 49	07 57	08 04	08 12	08 19	08 25	08 34	08 42
Gospel Oak	d	06 12			06 30	06 37	06 45	06 51	07 00	07 07	07 15	07 20	07 25	07 37	07 45	07 52	08 00	08 07	08 15	08 22	08 28	08 37	08 45
Hampstead Heath	d	06 14			06 32	06 39	06 47	06 53	07 02	07 09	07 17	07 22	07 27	07 39	07 47	07 54	08 02	08 09	08 17	08 24	08 30	08 39	08 47
Finchley Road & Frognal	d	06 16			06 34	06 41	06 49	06 55	07 04	07 11	07 19	07 24	07 29	07 41	07 49	07 56	08 04	08 11	08 19	08 26	08 32	08 41	08 49
West Hampstead ⊖	d	06 18			06 36	06 43	06 51	06 57	07 06	07 13	07 21	07 26	07 31	07 43	07 51	07 58	08 06	08 13	08 21	08 28	08 34	08 43	08 51
Brondesbury	d	06 20			06 38	06 45	06 53	06 58	07 08	07 15	07 22	07 28	07 33	07 45	07 53	08 00	08 08	08 15	08 23	08 30	08 36	08 45	08 53
Brondesbury Park	d	06 21			06 39	06 46	06 54	07 00	07 09	07 16	07 24	07 29	07 34	07 46	07 54	08 01	08 09	08 16	08 24	08 31	08 37	08 46	08 54
Kensal Rise	d	06 23			06 41	06 48	06 56	07 02	07 11	07 18	07 26	07 31	07 36	07 48	07 56	08 03	08 11	08 18	08 26	08 33	08 39	08 48	08 56
Willesden Jn. High Level ⊖	a	06 27			06 45	06 52	07 00	07 06	07 15	07 22	07 30	07 35	07 40	07 52	08 00	08 07	08 15	08 22	08 30	08 37	08 43	08 52	09 00
	d	06 28	06 33	06 41	06 46	06 53	07 01	07 07	07 16	07 23	07 31	07 36	07 41	07 53	08 01	08 08	08 16	08 23	08 31	08 38	08 46	08 53	09 01
Willesden Jn Low Level ⊖	a																						
Shepherd's Bush ⊖	d		06 40		06 54		07 09		07 24		07 39		07 49		08 09		08 24		08 39		08 54		09 09
Kensington (Olympia) ⊖	d		06 42		06 56		07 11		07 26		07 41		07 51		08 11		08 26		08 41		08 56		09 11
West Brompton ⊖	d		06 45		06 58		07 13		07 28		07 43		07 53		08 13		08 28		08 43		08 58		09 13
Imperial Wharf	d		06 48		07 01		07 16		07 31		07 46		07 56		08 16		08 31		08 46		09 01		09 16
Clapham Junction 10	a		06 54		07 09		07 24		07 39		07 54		08 04		08 24		08 39		08 54		09 09		09 25
Acton Central	d	06 33		06 46		06 58		07 13		07 28		07 41		07 58		08 13		08 28		08 43		08 58	
South Acton	d	06 36		06 49		07 01		07 16		07 31		07 44		08 01		08 16		08 31		08 46		09 01	
Gunnersbury ⊖	d	06 39		06 53		07 04		07 19		07 34		07 48		08 04		08 19		08 34		08 51		09 04	
Kew Gardens ⊖	d	06 42		06 56		07 07		07 22		07 37		07 51		08 07		08 22		08 37		08 54		09 07	
Richmond ⊖	a	06 49		07 04		07 14		07 30		07 44		07 57		08 14		08 28		08 43		08 58		09 13	

A 13 August

Stratford - Highbury and Islington, West Hampstead, Willesden Junction, Clapham Junction and Richmond

Network Diagram - see first Page of Table 59

Station			LO	LO	LO	LO	LO	LO	LO	LO	LO	LO	LO
Stratford 7	⊖	d	08 27	08 35	08 42	08 50	08 57	09 03	09 15		09 25	09 35	09 45
Hackney Wick		d	08 30	08 38	08 45	08 53	09 00	09 06	09 18		09 28	09 38	09 48
Homerton		d	08 33	08 41	08 48	08 56	09 03	09 09	09 21		09 31	09 41	09 51
Hackney Central		d	08 35	08 43	08 50	08 58	09 05	09 11	09 23		09 33	09 43	09 53
Dalston Kingsland		d	08 37	08 45	08 52	09 00	09 07	09 13	09 25		09 35	09 45	09 55
Canonbury		d	08 39	08 47	08 54	09 02	09 09	09 15	09 27		09 37	09 47	09 57
Highbury & Islington	⊖	d	08 42	08 50	08 57	09 05	09 12	09 18	09 30		09 40	09 50	10 00
Caledonian Rd & Barnsbury		d	08 44	08 52	08 59	09 07	09 14	09 20	09 32		09 42	09 52	10 02
Camden Road		d	08 47	08 55	09 02	09 10	09 17	09 23	09 35		09 45	09 55	10 05
Kentish Town West		d	08 49	08 59	09 04	09 12	09 19	09 25	09 37		09 47	09 57	10 07
Gospel Oak		d	08 52	09 02	09 08	09 15	09 22	09 27	09 40		09 50	10 00	10 10
Hampstead Heath		d	08 54	09 04	09 10	09 17	09 24	09 29	09 42		09 52	10 02	10 12
Finchley Road & Frognal		d	08 56	09 06	09 12	09 19	09 26	09 31	09 44		09 54	10 04	10 14
West Hampstead	⊖	d	08 58	09 08	09 14	09 21	09 28	09 33	09 46		09 56	10 06	10 16
Brondesbury		d	09 00	09 10	09 15	09 23	09 30	09 35	09 48		09 58	10 08	10 18
Brondesbury Park		d	09 01	09 11	09 17	09 24	09 31	09 36	09 49		09 59	10 09	10 19
Kensal Rise		d	09 03	09 13	09 19	09 26	09 33	09 38	09 51		10 01	10 11	10 21
Willesden Jn. High Level	⊖	a	09 07	09 16	09 23	09 30	09 37	09 42	09 55		10 05	10 15	10 25
		d	09 08	09 17	09 24	09 31	09 38	09 44	09 56	10 01	10 06	10 16	10 26
Willesden Jn Low Level	⊖	a											
Shepherd's Bush	⊖	d		09 25		09 39		09 54		10 09		10 26	
Kensington (Olympia)	⊖	d		09 27		09 41		09 56		10 11		10 28	
West Brompton	⊖	d		09 29		09 43		09 58		10 13		10 30	
Imperial Wharf		d		09 32		09 46		10 01		10 16		10 33	
Clapham Junction 10		a		09 39		09 54		10 08		10 23		10 40	
Acton Central		d	09 13		09 29		09 43		10 01		10 11		10 31
South Acton		d	09 16		09 31		09 46		10 04		10 14		10 34
Gunnersbury	⊖	d	09 19		09 37		09 49		10 08		10 19		10 38
Kew Gardens	⊖	d	09 22		09 40		09 52		10 11		10 22		10 41
Richmond	⊖	a	09 28		09 45		09 58		10 16		10 27		10 46

Station			LO	LO	LO	LO	LO	LO	LO	LO	LO	LO	LO
Stratford 7	⊖	d		09 55	10 05	10 15		10 25	10 35	10 45		10 55	11 05
Hackney Wick		d		09 58	10 08	10 18		10 28	10 38	10 48		10 58	11 08
Homerton		d		10 01	10 11	10 21		10 31	10 41	10 51		11 01	11 11
Hackney Central		d		10 03	10 13	10 23		10 33	10 43	10 53		11 03	11 13
Dalston Kingsland		d		10 05	10 15	10 25		10 35	10 45	10 55		11 05	11 15
Canonbury		d		10 07	10 17	10 27		10 37	10 47	10 57		11 07	11 17
Highbury & Islington	⊖	d		10 10	10 20	10 30		10 40	10 50	11 00		11 10	11 20
Caledonian Rd & Barnsbury		d		10 12	10 22	10 32		10 42	10 52	11 02		11 12	11 22
Camden Road		d		10 15	10 25	10 35		10 45	10 55	11 05		11 15	11 25
Kentish Town West		d		10 17	10 27	10 37		10 47	10 57	11 07		11 17	11 27
Gospel Oak		d		10 20	10 30	10 40		10 50	11 00	11 10		11 20	11 30
Hampstead Heath		d		10 22	10 32	10 42		10 52	11 02	11 12		11 22	11 32
Finchley Road & Frognal		d		10 24	10 34	10 44		10 54	11 04	11 14		11 24	11 34
West Hampstead	⊖	d		10 26	10 36	10 46		10 56	11 06	11 16		11 26	11 36
Brondesbury		d		10 28	10 38	10 48		10 58	11 08	11 18		11 28	11 38
Brondesbury Park		d		10 29	10 39	10 49		10 59	11 09	11 19		11 29	11 39
Kensal Rise		d		10 31	10 41	10 51		11 01	11 11	11 21		11 31	11 41
Willesden Jn. High Level	⊖	a		10 35	10 45	10 55		11 05	11 15	11 25		11 35	11 44
		d	10 31	10 36	10 46	10 56	11 01	11 06	11 16	11 26	11 31	11 36	11 45
Willesden Jn Low Level	⊖	a											
Shepherd's Bush	⊖	d	10 39		10 54		11 09		11 24		11 39		11 54
Kensington (Olympia)	⊖	d	10 41		10 56		11 11		11 26		11 41		11 56
West Brompton	⊖	d	10 43		10 58		11 13		11 28		11 43		11 58
Imperial Wharf		d	10 46		11 01		11 16		11 31		11 46		12 01
Clapham Junction 10		a	10 53		11 09		11 23		11 39		11 53		12 09
Acton Central		d		10 41		11 01		11 11		11 31		11 41	
South Acton		d		10 44		11 04		11 14		11 34		11 44	
Gunnersbury	⊖	d		10 48		11 08		11 18		11 38		11 48	
Kew Gardens	⊖	d		10 51		11 11		11 21		11 41		11 51	
Richmond	⊖	a		10 56		11 16		11 26		11 46		11 56	

Station			LO	LO	LO	LO	LO	LO	LO	LO	LO	LO	LO
Stratford 7	⊖	d	11 15		11 25	11 37	11 45		11 55	12 05	12 15		12 25
Hackney Wick		d	11 18		11 28	11 40	11 48		11 58	12 08	12 18		12 28
Homerton		d	11 21		11 31	11 43	11 51		12 01	12 11	12 21		12 31
Hackney Central		d	11 23		11 33	11 45	11 53		12 03	12 13	12 23		12 33
Dalston Kingsland		d	11 25		11 35	11 47	11 55		12 05	12 15	12 25		12 35
Canonbury		d	11 27		11 37	11 49	11 57		12 07	12 17	12 27		12 37
Highbury & Islington	⊖	d	11 30		11 40	11 52	12 00		12 10	12 20	12 30		12 40
Caledonian Rd & Barnsbury		d	11 32		11 42	11 54	12 02		12 12	12 22	12 32		12 42
Camden Road		d	11 35		11 45	11 57	12 05		12 15	12 25	12 35		12 45
Kentish Town West		d	11 37		11 47	11 59	12 07		12 17	12 27	12 37		12 47
Gospel Oak		d	11 40		11 51	12 02	12 10		12 20	12 30	12 40		12 50
Hampstead Heath		d	11 42		11 53	12 04	12 12		12 22	12 32	12 42		12 52
Finchley Road & Frognal		d	11 44		11 55	12 06	12 14		12 24	12 34	12 44		12 54
West Hampstead	⊖	d	11 46		11 57	12 08	12 16		12 26	12 36	12 46		12 56
Brondesbury		d	11 48		11 59	12 10	12 18		12 28	12 38	12 48		12 58
Brondesbury Park		d	11 49		12 00	12 11	12 19		12 29	12 39	12 49		12 59
Kensal Rise		d	11 51		12 02	12 13	12 21		12 31	12 41	12 51		13 01
Willesden Jn. High Level	⊖	a	11 55		12 06	12 16	12 25		12 35	12 45	12 55		13 05
		d	11 56	12 01	12 07	12 17	12 26	12 31	12 36	12 46	12 56	13 01	13 06
Willesden Jn Low Level	⊖	a											
Shepherd's Bush	⊖	d		12 09		12 25		12 39		12 54		13 09	
Kensington (Olympia)	⊖	d		12 11		12 27		12 41		12 56		13 11	
West Brompton	⊖	d		12 13		12 29		12 43		12 58		13 13	
Imperial Wharf		d		12 16		12 32		12 46		13 01		13 16	
Clapham Junction 10		a		12 23		12 40		12 53		13 08		13 25	
Acton Central		d	12 01		12 12		12 31		12 41		13 01		13 11
South Acton		d	12 04		12 15		12 34		12 44		13 04		13 14
Gunnersbury	⊖	d	12 08		12 19		12 38		12 48		13 08		13 18
Kew Gardens	⊖	d	12 11		12 22		12 41		12 51		13 11		13 21
Richmond	⊖	a	12 16		12 27		12 46		12 56		13 16		13 26

Station			LO	LO	LO	LO	LO	LO	LO	LO	LO	LO	LO
Stratford 7	⊖	d	12 35	12 45		12 55	13 05	13 15		13 25	13 35	13 45	
Hackney Wick		d	12 38	12 48		12 58	13 08	13 18		13 28	13 38	13 48	
Homerton		d	12 41	12 51		13 01	13 11	13 21		13 31	13 41	13 51	
Hackney Central		d	12 43	12 53		13 03	13 13	13 23		13 33	13 43	13 53	
Dalston Kingsland		d	12 45	12 55		13 05	13 15	13 25		13 35	13 45	13 55	
Canonbury		d	12 47	12 57		13 07	13 17	13 27		13 37	13 47	13 57	
Highbury & Islington	⊖	d	12 50	13 00		13 10	13 20	13 30		13 40	13 50	14 00	
Caledonian Rd & Barnsbury		d	12 52	13 02		13 12	13 22	13 32		13 42	13 52	14 02	
Camden Road		d	12 55	13 05		13 15	13 25	13 35		13 45	13 55	14 05	
Kentish Town West		d	12 57	13 07		13 17	13 27	13 37		13 47	13 57	14 07	
Gospel Oak		d	13 00	13 10		13 20	13 30	13 41		13 50	14 00	14 10	
Hampstead Heath		d	13 02	13 12		13 22	13 32	13 43		13 52	14 02	14 12	
Finchley Road & Frognal		d	13 04	13 14		13 24	13 34	13 45		13 54	14 04	14 14	
West Hampstead	⊖	d	13 06	13 16		13 26	13 36	13 47		13 56	14 06	14 16	
Brondesbury		d	13 08	13 18		13 28	13 38	13 49		13 58	14 08	14 18	
Brondesbury Park		d	13 09	13 19		13 29	13 39	13 50		13 59	14 09	14 19	
Kensal Rise		d	13 11	13 21		13 31	13 41	13 52		14 01	14 11	14 21	
Willesden Jn. High Level	⊖	a	13 15	13 25		13 35	13 45	13 56		14 05	14 15	14 25	
		d	13 16	13 26	13 31	13 36	13 46	13 57	14 01	14 06	14 16	14 26	14 31
Willesden Jn Low Level	⊖	a											
Shepherd's Bush	⊖	d	13 24		13 39		13 54		14 09		14 24		14 39
Kensington (Olympia)	⊖	d	13 26		13 41		13 56		14 11		14 26		14 41
West Brompton	⊖	d	13 28		13 43		13 58		14 13		14 28		14 43
Imperial Wharf		d	13 31		13 46		14 01		14 16		14 31		14 46
Clapham Junction 10		a	13 38		13 55		14 09		14 23		14 39		14 53
Acton Central		d		13 31		13 41		14 02		14 11		14 31	
South Acton		d		13 34		13 44		14 05		14 14		14 34	
Gunnersbury	⊖	d		13 38		13 48		14 09		14 18		14 38	
Kew Gardens	⊖	d		13 41		13 51		14 12		14 21		14 41	
Richmond	⊖	a		13 46		13 56		14 17		14 26		14 46	

Stratford - Highbury and Islington, West Hampstead, Willesden Junction, Clapham Junction and Richmond

Network Diagram - see first Page of Table 59

Station			LO	LO	LO	LO	LO	LO	LO	LO	LO	LO	LO
Stratford 7	⊖	d	13 55	14 05	14 15		14 25	14 35	14 45		14 55	15 05	15 15
Hackney Wick		d	13 58	14 08	14 18		14 28	14 38	14 48		14 58	15 08	15 18
Homerton		d	14 01	14 11	14 21		14 31	14 41	14 51		15 01	15 11	15 21
Hackney Central		d	14 03	14 13	14 23		14 33	14 43	14 53		15 03	15 13	15 23
Dalston Kingsland		d	14 05	14 15	14 25		14 35	14 45	14 55		15 05	15 15	15 25
Canonbury		d	14 07	14 17	14 27		14 37	14 47	14 57		15 07	15 17	15 27
Highbury & Islington	⊖	d	14 10	14 20	14 30		14 40	14 50	15 00		15 10	15 20	15 30
Caledonian Rd & Barnsbury		d	14 12	14 22	14 32		14 42	14 52	15 02		15 12	15 22	15 32
Camden Road		d	14 15	14 25	14 35		14 45	14 55	15 05		15 15	15 25	15 35
Kentish Town West		d	14 17	14 27	14 37		14 47	14 57	15 07		15 17	15 27	15 37
Gospel Oak		d	14 20	14 30	14 40		14 50	15 00	15 10		15 20	15 30	15 40
Hampstead Heath		d	14 22	14 32	14 42		14 52	15 02	15 12		15 22	15 32	15 42
Finchley Road & Frognal		d	14 24	14 34	14 44		14 54	15 04	15 14		15 24	15 34	15 44
West Hampstead	⊖	d	14 26	14 36	14 46		14 56	15 06	15 16		15 26	15 36	15 46
Brondesbury		d	14 28	14 38	14 48		14 58	15 08	15 18		15 28	15 38	15 48
Brondesbury Park		d	14 29	14 39	14 49		14 59	15 09	15 19		15 29	15 39	15 49
Kensal Rise		d	14 31	14 41	14 51		15 01	15 11	15 21		15 31	15 41	15 51
Willesden Jn. High Level	⊖	a	14 35	14 45	14 55		15 05	15 15	15 25		15 35	15 45	15 55
		d	14 36	14 46	14 56	15 01	15 06	15 16	15 26	15 31	15 36	15 46	15 56
Willesden Jn Low Level	⊖	a											
Shepherd's Bush	⊖	d		14 54		15 09		15 26		15 39		15 54	
Kensington (Olympia)	⊖	d		14 56		15 11		15 28		15 41		15 56	
West Brompton	⊖	d		14 58		15 13		15 30		15 43		15 58	
Imperial Wharf		d		15 01		15 16		15 33		15 46		16 01	
Clapham Junction 10		a		15 09		15 23		15 40		15 53		16 09	
Acton Central		d	14 41		15 01		15 11		15 31		15 41		16 01
South Acton		d	14 44		15 04		15 14		15 34		15 44		16 04
Gunnersbury	⊖	d	14 48		15 08		15 18		15 38		15 48		16 08
Kew Gardens	⊖	d	14 51		15 11		15 21		15 41		15 51		16 11
Richmond	⊖	a	14 56		15 16		15 26		15 46		15 56		16 16

Station			LO	LO	LO	LO	LO	LO	LO	LO	LO	LO	LO
Stratford 7	⊖	d		15 25	15 35	15 42	15 50	15 59		16 12	16 20	16 27	16 35
Hackney Wick		d		15 28	15 38	15 45	15 53	16 02		16 15	16 23	16 30	16 38
Homerton		d		15 31	15 41	15 48	15 56	16 05		16 18	16 26	16 33	16 40
Hackney Central		d		15 33	15 43	15 50	15 58	16 07		16 20	16 28	16 35	16 42
Dalston Kingsland		d		15 35	15 45	15 52	16 00	16 09		16 22	16 30	16 37	16 44
Canonbury		d		15 37	15 47	15 54	16 02	16 11		16 24	16 32	16 39	16 46
Highbury & Islington	⊖	d		15 40	15 50	15 57	16 05	16 14		16 27	16 35	16 42	16 49
Caledonian Rd & Barnsbury		d		15 42	15 52	15 59	16 07	16 16		16 29	16 37	16 44	16 51
Camden Road		d		15 45	15 55	16 03	16 10	16 19		16 32	16 40	16 47	16 54
Kentish Town West		d		15 48	15 57	16 06	16 12	16 21		16 34	16 42	16 49	16 58
Gospel Oak		d		15 50	16 02	16 08	16 15	16 24		16 37	16 45	16 52	17 03
Hampstead Heath		d		15 52	16 04	16 10	16 17	16 26		16 39	16 47	16 54	17 05
Finchley Road & Frognal		d		15 54	16 06	16 12	16 19	16 28		16 41	16 49	16 56	17 07
West Hampstead	⊖	d		15 56	16 08	16 14	16 21	16 30		16 43	16 51	16 58	17 09
Brondesbury		d		15 58	16 10	16 15	16 23	16 32		16 45	16 53	17 00	17 10
Brondesbury Park		d		15 59	16 11	16 17	16 24	16 33		16 46	16 54	17 01	17 12
Kensal Rise		d		16 01	16 13	16 19	16 26	16 35		16 48	16 56	17 03	17 14
Willesden Jn. High Level	⊖	a		16 05	16 16	16 23	16 30	16 39		16 52	17 00	17 07	17 18
		d	16 01	16 06	16 17	16 24	16 31	16 40	16 46	16 53	17 01	17 08	17 19
Willesden Jn Low Level	⊖	a											
Shepherd's Bush	⊖	d	16 09		16 25		16 39		16 53		17 09		17 26
Kensington (Olympia)	⊖	d	16 11		16 27		16 41		16 55		17 11		17 28
West Brompton	⊖	d	16 13		16 29		16 43		16 58		17 13		17 31
Imperial Wharf		d	16 16		16 32		16 46		17 01		17 16		17 34
Clapham Junction 10		a	16 23		16 39		16 54		17 07		17 24		17 39
Acton Central		d		16 11		16 29		16 45		16 58		17 13	
South Acton		d		16 14		16 31		16 48		17 01		17 16	
Gunnersbury	⊖	d		16 18		16 34		16 51		17 04		17 19	
Kew Gardens	⊖	d		16 21		16 37		16 54		17 07		17 22	
Richmond	⊖	a		16 27		16 43		17 00		17 13		17 28	

Station			LO	LO	LO	LO	LO	LO	LO	LO	LO	LO	LO
Stratford 7	⊖	d	16 42	16 50	16 57	17 05	17 12	17 21	17 27	17 36	17 42	17 51	17 57
Hackney Wick		d	16 45	16 53	17 00	17 08	17 15	17 23	17 30	17 38	17 45	17 54	18 00
Homerton		d	16 48	16 56	17 03	17 11	17 18	17 26	17 33	17 41	17 48	17 57	18 03
Hackney Central		d	16 50	16 58	17 05	17 13	17 20	17 28	17 35	17 43	17 50	17 59	18 05
Dalston Kingsland		d	16 52	17 00	17 07	17 15	17 22	17 30	17 37	17 45	17 52	18 01	18 07
Canonbury		d	16 54	17 02	17 09	17 17	17 24	17 32	17 39	17 47	17 54	18 03	18 09
Highbury & Islington	⊖	d	16 57	17 05	17 12	17 20	17 27	17 35	17 42	17 50	17 57	18 06	18 12
Caledonian Rd & Barnsbury		d	16 59	17 07	17 14	17 22	17 29	17 37	17 44	17 52	17 59	18 08	18 14
Camden Road		d	17 02	17 10	17 17	17 25	17 32	17 40	17 47	17 55	18 02	18 12	18 17
Kentish Town West		d	17 04	17 13	17 19	17 27	17 34	17 42	17 49	17 58	18 05	18 15	18 19
Gospel Oak		d	17 08	17 17	17 23	17 30	17 37	17 45	17 52	18 02	18 08	18 18	18 22
Hampstead Heath		d	17 10	17 19	17 25	17 32	17 39	17 47	17 54	18 04	18 10	18 20	18 24
Finchley Road & Frognal		d	17 12	17 21	17 27	17 34	17 41	17 49	17 56	18 06	18 12	18 22	18 26
West Hampstead	⊖	d	17 14	17 23	17 29	17 36	17 43	17 51	17 58	18 08	18 14	18 24	18 28
Brondesbury		d	17 16	17 25	17 30	17 38	17 45	17 53	18 00	18 09	18 16	18 26	18 30
Brondesbury Park		d	17 17	17 26	17 32	17 39	17 46	17 54	18 01	18 11	18 17	18 27	18 31
Kensal Rise		d	17 19	17 28	17 34	17 41	17 48	17 56	18 03	18 13	18 19	18 29	18 33
Willesden Jn. High Level	⊖	a	17 23	17 31	17 38	17 45	17 52	18 00	18 07	18 17	18 23	18 32	18 37
		d	17 24	17 32	17 39	17 46	17 53	18 01	18 08	18 18	18 24	18 33	18 38
Willesden Jn Low Level	⊖	a											
Shepherd's Bush	⊖	d		17 40		17 54		18 09		18 25		18 41	
Kensington (Olympia)	⊖	d		17 42		17 56		18 11		18 27		18 43	
West Brompton	⊖	d		17 44		17 58		18 13		18 30		18 45	
Imperial Wharf		d		17 47		18 01		18 16		18 33		18 48	
Clapham Junction 10		a		17 54		18 09		18 25		18 40		18 54	
Acton Central		d	17 29		17 44		17 58		18 13		18 29		18 43
South Acton		d	17 34		17 46		18 00		18 16		18 32		18 46
Gunnersbury	⊖	d	17 39		17 49		18 03		18 19		18 38		18 49
Kew Gardens	⊖	d	17 42		17 52		18 06		18 22		18 41		18 52
Richmond	⊖	a	17 46		17 58		18 13		18 28		18 45		18 58

Station			LO	LO	LO	LO	LO	LO	LO	LO	LO	LO	LO
Stratford 7	⊖	d	18 05	18 12	18 20	18 27	18 35	18 42	18 48	18 57	19 05	19 15	
Hackney Wick		d	18 08	18 15	18 23	18 30	18 38	18 45	18 51	19 00	19 08	19 18	
Homerton		d	18 11	18 18	18 26	18 33	18 41	18 48	18 54	19 03	19 11	19 21	
Hackney Central		d	18 13	18 20	18 28	18 35	18 43	18 50	18 56	19 05	19 13	19 23	
Dalston Kingsland		d	18 15	18 22	18 31	18 37	18 45	18 52	18 58	19 07	19 15	19 25	
Canonbury		d	18 17	18 24	18 32	18 39	18 47	18 54	19 00	19 09	19 17	19 27	
Highbury & Islington	⊖	d	18 20	18 27	18 35	18 42	18 50	18 57	19 03	19 12	19 20	19 30	
Caledonian Rd & Barnsbury		d	18 22	18 29	18 37	18 44	18 52	18 59	19 05	19 14	19 22	19 32	
Camden Road		d	18 25	18 32	18 40	18 47	18 55	19 02	19 08	19 17	19 25	19 35	
Kentish Town West		d	18 27	18 34	18 42	18 49	18 57	19 05	19 10	19 19	19 27	19 37	
Gospel Oak		d	18 30	18 37	18 45	18 52	19 00	19 09	19 13	19 24	19 30	19 40	
Hampstead Heath		d	18 32	18 39	18 47	18 54	19 02	19 11	19 15	19 26	19 32	19 42	
Finchley Road & Frognal		d	18 34	18 41	18 49	18 56	19 04	19 13	19 17	19 28	19 34	19 44	
West Hampstead	⊖	d	18 36	18 43	18 51	18 58	19 06	19 15	19 19	19 30	19 36	19 46	
Brondesbury		d	18 38	18 45	18 53	19 00	19 08	19 16	19 21	19 32	19 38	19 48	
Brondesbury Park		d	18 39	18 46	18 54	19 01	19 09	19 18	19 22	19 33	19 39	19 49	
Kensal Rise		d	18 41	18 48	18 56	19 03	19 11	19 20	19 24	19 35	19 41	19 51	
Willesden Jn. High Level	⊖	a	18 45	18 52	19 00	19 07	19 15	19 24	19 30	19 39	19 45	19 55	
		d	18 46	18 53	19 01	19 08	19 16	19 25	19 31	19 40	19 46	19 56	20 01
Willesden Jn Low Level	⊖	a											
Shepherd's Bush	⊖	d	18 54		19 09		19 23		19 39		19 54		20 09
Kensington (Olympia)	⊖	d	18 56		19 11		19 25		19 41		19 56		20 11
West Brompton	⊖	d	18 58		19 13		19 28		19 43		19 58		20 13
Imperial Wharf		d	19 01		19 16		19 31		19 46		20 01		20 16
Clapham Junction 10		a	19 09		19 24		19 39		19 54		20 09		20 23
Acton Central		d		18 58		19 13		19 30		19 45		20 01	
South Acton		d		19 01		19 16		19 32		19 48		20 04	
Gunnersbury	⊖	d		19 06		19 19		19 38		19 51		20 09	
Kew Gardens	⊖	d		19 09		19 22		19 41		19 54		20 12	
Richmond	⊖	a		19 14		19 29		19 46		19 59		20 17	

Table 59

Mondays to Fridays

13 August to 28 August

Stratford - Highbury and Islington, West Hampstead, Willesden Junction, Clapham Junction and Richmond

Network Diagram - see first Page of Table 59

Station		LO	LO	LO	LO	LO	LO	LO	LO	LO	LO	LO	LO	LO	LO	LO	LO	LO	LO	LO	LO	LO	LO
Stratford 7	⊖ d	19 25	19 37	19 45		19 55	20 05	20 15		20 25	20 35	20 45		20 55	21 05	21 15		21 25	21 35	21 45		21 55	22 15
Hackney Wick	d	19 28	19 40	19 48		19 58	20 08	20 18		20 28	20 38	20 48		20 58	21 08	21 18		21 28	21 38	21 48		21 58	22 18
Homerton	d	19 31	19 43	19 51		20 01	20 11	20 21		20 31	20 41	20 51		21 01	21 11	21 21		21 31	21 41	21 51		22 01	22 21
Hackney Central	d	19 33	19 45	19 53		20 03	20 13	20 23		20 33	20 43	20 53		21 03	21 13	21 23		21 33	21 43	21 53		22 03	22 23
Dalston Kingsland	d	19 35	19 47	19 55		20 05	20 15	20 25		20 35	20 45	20 55		21 05	21 15	21 25		21 35	21 45	21 55		22 05	22 25
Canonbury	d	19 37	19 49	19 57		20 07	20 17	20 27		20 37	20 47	20 57		21 07	21 17	21 27		21 37	21 47	21 57		22 07	22 27
Highbury & Islington	⊖ d	19 40	19 52	20 00		20 10	20 20	20 30		20 40	20 50	21 00		21 10	21 20	21 30		21 40	21 50	22 00		22 10	22 30
Caledonian Rd & Barnsbury	d	19 42	19 54	20 02		20 12	20 22	20 32		20 42	20 52	21 02		21 12	21 22	21 32		21 42	21 52	22 02		22 12	22 32
Camden Road	d	19 45	19 57	20 05		20 15	20 25	20 35		20 45	20 55	21 05		21 15	21 25	21 35		21 45	21 55	22 05		22 15	22 35
Kentish Town West	d	19 47	19 59	20 07		20 18	20 27	20 37		20 47	20 57	21 07		21 17	21 27	21 37		21 47	21 57	22 07		22 17	22 37
Gospel Oak	d	19 50	20 01	20 10		20 22	20 30	20 40		20 50	21 00	21 10		21 20	21 30	21 40		21 50	22 00	22 10		22 20	22 40
Hampstead Heath	d	19 52	20 03	20 12		20 24	20 32	20 42		20 52	21 02	21 12		21 22	21 32	21 42		21 52	22 02	22 12		22 22	22 42
Finchley Road & Frognal	d	19 54	20 05	20 14		20 26	20 34	20 44		20 54	21 04	21 14		21 24	21 34	21 44		21 54	22 04	22 14		22 24	22 44
West Hampstead	⊖ d	19 56	20 07	20 16		20 28	20 36	20 46		20 56	21 06	21 16		21 26	21 36	21 46		21 56	22 06	22 16		22 26	22 46
Brondesbury	d	19 58	20 09	20 18		20 29	20 38	20 48		20 57	21 08	21 18		21 28	21 38	21 48		21 58	22 08	22 18		22 28	22 48
Brondesbury Park	d	19 59	20 10	20 19		20 31	20 39	20 49		20 59	21 09	21 19		21 29	21 39	21 49		21 59	22 09	22 19		22 29	22 49
Kensal Rise	d	20 01	20 12	20 21		20 33	20 41	20 51		21 01	21 11	21 21		21 31	21 41	21 51		22 01	22 11	22 21		22 31	22 51
Willesden Jn. High Level	⊖ a	20 05	20 16	20 25		20 36	20 45	20 55		21 05	21 15	21 25		21 35	21 45	21 55		22 05	22 15	22 25		22 35	22 55
	d	20 06	20 17	20 26	20 31	20 37	20 46	20 57	21 01	21 06	21 16	21 26	21 31	21 36	21 46	21 56	22 01	22 06	22 16	22 26	22 31	22 36	22 56
Willesden Jn Low Level	⊖ a																						
Shepherd's Bush	⊖ d		20 26		20 39		20 54		21 09		21 26		21 39		21 54		22 09		22 26		22 39		
Kensington (Olympia)	⊖ d		20 28		20 41		20 56		21 11		21 28		21 41		21 56		22 11		22 28		22 41		
West Brompton	⊖ d		20 30		20 43		20 58		21 13		21 31		21 43		21 58		22 13		22 30		22 43		
Imperial Wharf	d		20 33		20 46		21 01		21 16		21 34		21 46		22 01		22 16		22 33		22 46		
Clapham Junction 10	a		20 41		20 53		21 09		21 23		21 41		21 53		22 09		22 23		22 40		22 53		
Acton Central	d	20 11		20 31		20 42		21 02		21 11		21 31		21 41		22 01		22 11		22 31		22 41	23 01
South Acton	d	20 14		20 34		20 44		21 05		21 13		21 34		21 44		22 04		22 14		22 34		22 44	23 04
Gunnersbury	⊖ d	20 18		20 38		20 49		21 08		21 18		21 38		21 48		22 08		22 18		22 38		22 48	23 08
Kew Gardens	⊖ d	20 21		20 41		20 52		21 11		21 21		21 41		21 51		22 11		22 21		22 41		22 51	23 11
Richmond	⊖ a	20 26		20 46		20 56		21 16		21 26		21 46		21 56		22 16		22 26		22 46		22 56	23 16

Station		LO	LO	LO	LO	LO	LO	LO
Stratford 7	⊖ d	22 25		22 45	22 55	23 15		23 45
Hackney Wick	d	22 28		22 48	22 58	23 18		23 48
Homerton	d	22 31		22 51	23 01	23 21		23 51
Hackney Central	d	22 33		22 53	23 03	23 23		23 53
Dalston Kingsland	d	22 35		22 55	23 05	23 25		23 55
Canonbury	d	22 37		22 57	23 07	23 27		23 57
Highbury & Islington	⊖ d	22 40		23 00	23 10	23 30		23 59
Caledonian Rd & Barnsbury	d	22 42		23 02	23 12	23 32		00 02
Camden Road	d	22a46		23 05	23a16	23 35		00 05
Kentish Town West	d			23 07		23 37		00 07
Gospel Oak	d			23 10		23 40		00 10
Hampstead Heath	d			23 12		23 42		00 12
Finchley Road & Frognal	d			23 14		23 44		00 14
West Hampstead	⊖ d			23 16		23 46		00 16
Brondesbury	d			23 18		23 48		00 18
Brondesbury Park	d			23 19		23 49		00 19
Kensal Rise	d			23 21		23 51		00 21
Willesden Jn. High Level	⊖ a			23 25				
	d		23 01	23 26			23 40	
Willesden Jn Low Level	⊖ a					23 56		00 29
Shepherd's Bush	⊖ d		23 09				23 48	
Kensington (Olympia)	⊖ d		23 11				23 50	
West Brompton	⊖ d		23 13				23 52	
Imperial Wharf	d		23 16				23 55	
Clapham Junction 10	a		23 23				00 02	
Acton Central	d			23 31				
South Acton	d			23 34				
Gunnersbury	⊖ d			23 38				
Kew Gardens	⊖ d			23 41				
Richmond	⊖ a			23 46				

Table 59

Mondays to Fridays

29 August to 7 September

Stratford - Highbury and Islington, West Hampstead, Willesden Junction, Clapham Junction and Richmond

Network Diagram - see first Page of Table 59

Station		LO A	LO B	LO C	LO A	LO B	LO B	LO A	LO A	LO B	LO B	LO A	LO B	LO A	LO A	LO B	LO C	LO B	LO A	LO B	LO A	LO D	LO D
Stratford 7	⊖ d	22p52	22p52		23p00	23p02	23p07	23p07	23p15	23p15	23p22	23p22	23p30	23p30	23p37	23p38	23p45	23p45	23p45	23p52	23p52	00 01	00 07
Hackney Wick	d	22p55	22p55		23p05	23p05	23p10	23p10	23p18	23p18	23p25	23p25	23p33	23p35	23p40	23p41	23p48	23p48	23p49	23p55	23p55	00 03	00 10
Homerton	d	22p58	22p58		23p06	23p06	23p13	23p13	23p19	23p21	23p28	23p28	23p36	23p36	23p43	23p44	23p51	23p51	23p51	23p58	23p58	00 06	00 13
Hackney Central	d	23p00	23p00		23p08	23p08	23p15	23p15	23p21	23p23	23p30	23p30	23p38	23p38	23p45	23p46	23p53	23p53	23p53	23p59	00 01	00 08	00 15
Dalston Kingsland	d	23p02	23p02		23p10	23p10	23p17	23p17	23p23	23p25	23p32	23p32	23p40	23p40	23p47	23p48	23p55	23p55	23p55	00 02	00 03	00 10	00 17
Canonbury	d	23p04	23p04		23p12	23p12	23p19	23p19	23p25	23p27	23p34	23p34	23p42	23p42	23p49	23p50	23p57	23p57	23p57	00 04	00 05	00 12	00 19
Highbury & Islington	⊖ d	23p08	23p08		23p16	23p16	23p23	23p23	23p28	23p31	23p38	23p38	23p46	23p46	23p53	23p53	23p59	00 01	00 01	00 08	00 08	00 16	00 23
Caledonian Rd & Barnsbury	d	23p10	23p10		23p18	23p18	23p25	23p25	23p30	23p33	23p40	23p40	23p48	23p48	23p55	23p55	00 02	00 03	00 03	00 10	00 10	00 18	00 25
Camden Road	d	23p14	23p14		23p22	23p22	23p29	23p29	23p34	23p37	23p44	23p45	23p53	23p52	23p59	23p59	00 05	00 07	00 07	00 14	00 14	00 22	00a31
Kentish Town West	d	23p16	23p16		23p24	23p24	23p31	23p31	23p37	23p39	23p46	23p47	23p55	23p54	00 01	00 02	00 07	00 09	00 09	00 16	00 16	00 24	
Gospel Oak	d	23p19	23p19		23p27	23p27	23p34	23p34	23p40	23p42	23p49	23p50	23p59	23p57	00 04	00 05	00 10	00 12	00 12	00 19	00 19	00 27	
Hampstead Heath	d	23p21	23p21		23p29	23p29	23p36	23p36	23p42	23p44	23p51	23p52	00 01	23p59	00 06	00 07	00 12	00 14	00 14	00 21	00 21	00 29	
Finchley Road & Frognal	d	23p23	23p23		23p31	23p31	23p38	23p38	23p44	23p46	23p53	23p54	00 03	00 01	00 08	00 09	00 14	00 16	00 16	00 23	00 23	00 31	
West Hampstead	⊖ d	23p25	23p25		23p33	23p33	23p40	23p40	23p47	23p48	23p55	23p56	00 05	00 03	00 10	00 11	00 16	00 18	00 18	00 25	00 25	00 33	
Brondesbury	d	23p27	23p27		23p35	23p35	23p42	23p42	23p48	23p50	23p57	23p58	00 06	00 05	00 12	00 13	00 18	00 20	00 20	00 27	00 27	00 35	
Brondesbury Park	d	23p28	23p28		23p36	23p36	23p43	23p43	23p50	23p51	23p58	23p59	00 08	00 06	00 13	00 14	00 19	00 21	00 21	00 28	00 28	00 36	
Kensal Rise	d	23p30	23p30		23p38	23p38	23p45	23p45	23p52	23p53	00 01	00 01	00 10	00 08	00 15	00 16	00 21	00 23	00 23	00 30	00 30	00 38	
Willesden Jn. High Level	⊖ a	23p34	23p35		23p42	23p42	23p49	23p49	23p57	23p57	00 04	00 04	00 13	00 12	00 19	00 20		00 27	00 27	00 34	00 34	00 42	
	d	23p35	23p36	23p40	23p43	23p43	23p50	23p50	23p59	23p59	00 05	00 05	00 14	00 13	00 20	00 21		00 28	00 28	00 35	00 35	00 43	
Willesden Jn Low Level	⊖ a																00 29						
Shepherd's Bush	⊖ d			23p48	23p53	23p57			00 09	00 09			00 24	00 23				00 38	00 38			00 53	
Kensington (Olympia)	⊖ d			23p50	23p56	23p59			00 11	00 11			00 26	00 26				00 41	00 41			00 56	
West Brompton	⊖ d			23p52	23p58	00 02			00 14	00 14			00 29	00 28				00 43	00 43			00 58	
Imperial Wharf	d			23p55	00 01	00 05			00 17	00 17			00 32	00 31				00 46	00 46			01 01	
Clapham Junction 10	a			00 02	00 09	00 13			00 22	00 23			00 39	00 39				00 54	00 54			01 09	
Acton Central	d	23p40	23p41				23p55	23p55			00 10	00 10			00 25	00 26				00 40	00 40		
South Acton	d	23p43	23p43				23p58	23p58			00 13	00 13			00 28	00 29				00 43	00 43		
Gunnersbury	⊖ d	23p48	23p48				00 02	00 03			00 18	00 18			00 32	00 33				00 47	00 48		
Kew Gardens	⊖ d	23p51	23p51				00 05	00 06			00 21	00 21			00 35	00 36				00 50	00 51		
Richmond	⊖ a	00 01	00 01				00 14	00 16			00 30	00 30			00 44	00 45				00 59	01 00		

Station		LO A	LO B	LO B	LO A	LO A	LO B	LO D	LO B	LO A	LO D	LO A	LO B	LO	LO	LO	LO	LO	LO	LO	LO	LO	LO
Stratford 7	⊖ d	00 15	00 15	00 22	00 22	00 30	00 32	00 37	00 45	00 45	00 52	01 00	01 00			05 47			06 00	06 07	06 15	06 23	06 34
Hackney Wick	d	00 18	00 18	00 25	00 25	00 33	00 35	00 40	00 48	00 48	00 55	01 03	01 04			05 50			06 04	06 10	06 18	06 26	06 38
Homerton	d	00 21	00 21	00 28	00 28	00 36	00 36	00 43	00 51	00 51	00 58	01 06	01 06			05 53			06 06	06 13	06 21	06 29	06 39
Hackney Central	d	00 23	00 23	00 30	00 30	00 38	00 38	00 45	00 53	00 53	01 00	01 08	01 08			05 55			06 08	06 15	06 23	06 31	06 41
Dalston Kingsland	d	00 25	00 25	00 32	00 32	00 40	00 40	00 47	00 55	00 55	01 02	01 10	01 10			05 57			06 10	06 17	06 25	06 33	06 43
Canonbury	d	00 27	00 27	00 34	00 34	00 42	00 42	00 49	00 57	00 57	01 04	01 12	01 12			05 59			06 12	06 19	06 27	06 35	06 45
Highbury & Islington	⊖ d	00 31	00 31	00 37	00 38	00 46	00 46	00 53	01 01	01 01	01 08	01 16	01 17			06 02			06 16	06 23	06 31	06 38	06 49
Caledonian Rd & Barnsbury	d	00 33	00 33	00 39	00 40	00 48	00 48	00 55	01 03	01 03	01 10	01 18	01 19			06 04			06 18	06 25	06 33	06 40	06 51
Camden Road	d	00 37	00 37	00a49	00a46	00 52	00 52	01a03	01 07	01 07	01a16	01 22	01 23			06 07			06 22	06 29	06 37	06 44	06 55
Kentish Town West	d	00 39	00 39			00 54	00 54		01 09	01 09		01 24	01 26			06 09			06 24	06 31	06 39	06 46	06 57
Gospel Oak	d	00 42	00 42			00 57	00 57		01 12	01 12		01 27	01 28			06 12			06 27	06 34	06 42	06 49	07 00
Hampstead Heath	d	00 44	00 44			00 59	00 59		01 14	01 14		01 29	01 30			06 14			06 29	06 36	06 44	06 51	07 02
Finchley Road & Frognal	d	00 46	00 46			01 01	01 01		01 16	01 16		01 31	01 32			06 16			06 31	06 38	06 46	06 53	07 04
West Hampstead	⊖ d	00 48	00 48			01 03	01 03		01 18	01 18		01 33	01 35			06 18			06 33	06 40	06 48	06 55	07 06
Brondesbury	d	00 50	00 50			01 05	01 05		01 20	01 20		01 35	01 36			06 20			06 35	06 42	06 50	06 57	07 07
Brondesbury Park	d	00 51	00 51			01 06	01 06		01 21	01 21		01 36	01 38			06 21			06 36	06 43	06 51	06 58	07 09
Kensal Rise	d	00 53	00 53			01 08	01 08		01 23	01 23		01 38	01 40			06 23			06 38	06 45	06 53	07 00	07 11
Willesden Jn. High Level	⊖ a															06 27			06 42	06 49	06 57	07 04	07 15
	d													06 02	06 06	06 28	06 33	06 41	06 43	06 50	06 58	07 05	07 16
Willesden Jn Low Level	⊖ a	01 01	01 02			01 21	01 21		01 41	01 42		01 57	01 50										
Shepherd's Bush	⊖ d													06 09			06 41		06 53		07 08		07 26
Kensington (Olympia)	⊖ d													06 11			06 43		06 56		07 11		07 28
West Brompton	⊖ d													06 14			06 46		06 58		07 13		07 31
Imperial Wharf	d													06 17			06 49		07 01		07 16		07 34
Clapham Junction 10	a													06 23			06 56		07 09		07 24		07 41
Acton Central	d														06 11	06 33		06 46		06 55		07 10	
South Acton	d														06 14	06 36		06 49		06 58		07 13	
Gunnersbury	⊖ d														06 18	06 40		06 53		07 02		07 17	
Kew Gardens	⊖ d														06 21	06 43		06 56		07 05		07 20	
Richmond	⊖ a														06 30	06 52		07 05		07 14		07 29	

A 3 September
B not 29 August, 3 September
C 29 August
D not 29 August

Stratford - Highbury and Islington, West Hampstead, Willesden Junction, Clapham Junction and Richmond

Network Diagram - see first Page of Table 59

		LO	LO	LO	LO	LO	LO	LO	LO	LO	LO	LO	LO	LO	LO	LO	LO	LO	LO	LO	LO	LO	LO
Stratford 7 ⊖	d	06 40	06 45	06 52	07 00	07 07	07 15	07 22	07 26	07 30	07 37	07 45	07 52	07 56	08 00	08 07	08 15	08 22	08 26	08 30	08 37	08 45	08 52
Hackney Wick	d	06 43	06 49	06 55	07 03	07 10	07 18	07 25	07 29	07 33	07 41	07 48	07 55	07 59	08 03	08 10	08 18	08 25	08 29	08 33	08 40	08 48	08 55
Homerton	d	06 46	06 51	06 58	07 06	07 13	07 21	07 28	07 32	07 36	07 43	07 51	07 58	08 02	08 06	08 13	08 21	08 28	08 32	08 36	08 43	08 51	08 58
Hackney Central	d	06 48	06 53	07 00	07 08	07 15	07 23	07 30	07 34	07 38	07 45	07 53	08 00	08 04	08 08	08 15	08 23	08 30	08 34	08 38	08 45	08 53	09 00
Dalston Kingsland	d	06 50	06 55	07 02	07 10	07 17	07 25	07 32	07 36	07 40	07 48	07 55	08 02	08 06	08 10	08 17	08 25	08 32	08 36	08 40	08 47	08 55	09 02
Canonbury	d	06 52	06 57	07 04	07 12	07 19	07 27	07 34	07 39	07 42	07 50	07 57	08 04	08 09	08 12	08 19	08 27	08 34	08 39	08 42	08 49	08 57	09 04
Highbury & Islington ⊖	d	06 56	07 01	07 08	07 16	07 23	07 31	07 38	07 42	07 46	07 53	08 01	08 08	08 12	08 16	08 23	08 31	08 38	08 42	08 46	08 53	09 01	09 08
Caledonian Rd & Barnsbury	d	06 58	07 03	07 10	07 18	07 25	07 33	07 40	07 44	07 48	07 55	08 03	08 10	08 14	08 18	08 25	08 33	08 40	08 44	08 48	08 55	09 03	09 10
Camden Road	d	07 02	07 07	07 14	07 22	07 29	07 37	07 44	07a53	07 52	07 59	08 07	08 14	08a23	08 22	08 29	08 37	08 44	08a53	08 54	09 01	09 07	09 14
Kentish Town West	d	07 04	07 09	07 16	07 24	07 31	07 39	07 46		07 54	08 02	08 09	08 16		08 24	08 31	08 39	08 46		08 56	09 03	09 09	09 16
Gospel Oak	d	07 06	07 12	07 19	07 27	07 34	07 42	07 49		07 57	08 04	08 12	08 19		08 27	08 34	08 42	08 49		08 59	09 06	09 12	09 19
Hampstead Heath	d	07 08	07 14	07 21	07 29	07 36	07 44	07 51		07 59	08 06	08 14	08 21		08 29	08 36	08 44	08 51		09 01	09 08	09 14	09 21
Finchley Road & Frognal	d	07 10	07 16	07 23	07 31	07 38	07 46	07 53		08 01	08 08	08 16	08 23		08 31	08 38	08 46	08 53		09 03	09 10	09 16	09 23
West Hampstead ⊖	d	07 12	07 18	07 25	07 33	07 40	07 48	07 55		08 03	08 11	08 18	08 25		08 33	08 40	08 48	08 55		09 05	09 12	09 18	09 25
Brondesbury	d	07 14	07 20	07 27	07 35	07 42	07 50	07 57		08 05	08 12	08 20	08 27		08 35	08 42	08 50	08 57		09 07	09 13	09 20	09 27
Brondesbury Park	d	07 15	07 21	07 28	07 36	07 43	07 51	07 58		08 06	08 14	08 21	08 28		08 36	08 43	08 51	08 58		09 08	09 15	09 21	09 28
Kensal Rise	d	07 17	07 23	07 30	07 38	07 45	07 53	08 00		08 08	08 16	08 23	08 30		08 38	08 45	08 53	09 00		09 10	09 17	09 23	09 30
Willesden Jn. High Level ⊖	a	07 20	07 27	07 34	07 42	07 49	07 57	08 04		08 12	08 20	08 27	08 34		08 42	08 49	08 57	09 04		09 14	09 21	09 27	09 34
	d	07 21	07 28	07 35	07 43	07 50	07 58	08 05		08 13	08 21	08 28	08 35		08 43	08 50	08 58	09 05		09 15	09 22	09 28	09 35
Willesden Jn Low Level ⊖	a																						
Shepherd's Bush ⊖	d		07 38		07 53		08 08			08 23		08 38			08 53		09 08			09 25		09 38	
Kensington (Olympia) ⊖	d		07 41		07 56		08 11			08 26		08 41			08 56		09 11			09 28		09 41	
West Brompton ⊖	d		07 43		07 58		08 13			08 28		08 43			08 58		09 13			09 30		09 43	
Imperial Wharf	d		07 46		08 01		08 16			08 31		08 46			09 01		09 16			09 33		09 46	
Clapham Junction 10	a		07 54		08 09		08 24			08 39		08 54			09 09		09 24			09 41		09 54	
Acton Central	d	07 26		07 40		07 55		08 10			08 26		08 40			08 55		09 10			09 26		09 40
South Acton	d	07 29		07 43		07 58		08 13			08 28		08 43			08 58		09 13			09 29		09 43
Gunnersbury ⊖	d	07 32		07 49		08 02		08 18			08 32		08 48			09 02		09 17			09 32		09 49
Kew Gardens ⊖	d	07 35		07 51		08 05		08 21			08 35		08 51			09 05		09 20			09 35		09 52
Richmond ⊖	a	07 44		08 00		08 14		08 30			08 45		09 00			09 14		09 29			09 44		10 01

		LO	LO	LO	LO	LO	LO	LO	LO	LO	LO	LO	LO	LO	LO	LO	LO	LO	LO	LO	LO	LO	LO
Stratford 7 ⊖	d	08 56	09 00	09 07	09 15	09 22	09 26	09 30	09 37	09 45	09 52	10 00	10 07	10 15	10 22	10 30	10 37	10 46	10 52	11 00	11 07	11 12	11 20
Hackney Wick	d	08 59	09 03	09 10	09 18	09 25	09 29	09 33	09 40	09 48	09 56	10 04	10 11	10 18	10 25	10 33	10 40	10 49	10 55	11 03	11 10	11 13	11 24
Homerton	d	09 02	09 06	09 13	09 21	09 28	09 32	09 36	09 43	09 51	09 58	10 06	10 13	10 21	10 28	10 35	10 43	10 51	10 58	11 06	11 13	11 16	11 26
Hackney Central	d	09 04	09 08	09 15	09 23	09 30	09 34	09 38	09 45	09 53	10 00	10 08	10 15	10 23	10 30	10 37	10 45	10 53	11 00	11 08	11 15	11 18	11 28
Dalston Kingsland	d	09 06	09 10	09 17	09 25	09 32	09 36	09 40	09 47	09 55	10 02	10 10	10 17	10 25	10 32	10 38	10 47	10 56	11 02	11 10	11 17	11 20	11 31
Canonbury	d	09 09	09 12	09 19	09 27	09 34	09 39	09 42	09 49	09 57	10 04	10 12	10 19	10 27	10 34	10 40	10 49	10 58	11 04	11 12	11 19	11 22	11 33
Highbury & Islington ⊖	d	09 12	09 16	09 23	09 31	09 38	09 42	09 46	09 53	10 01	10 08	10 16	10 23	10 31	10 38	10 43	10 53	11 02	11 08	11 16	11 23	11 26	11 37
Caledonian Rd & Barnsbury	d	09 14	09 18	09 25	09 33	09 40	09 44	09 48	09 55	10 03	10 10	10 18	10 25	10 33	10 40	10 45	10 55	11 04	11 10	11 18	11 25	11 28	11 39
Camden Road	d	09a23	09 22	09 29	09 37	09 44	09a53	09 52	09 59	10 07	10 14	10 22	10 29	10 37	10 44	10 49	10 59	11 08	11 15	11 22	11 29	11 33	11 43
Kentish Town West	d		09 24	09 31	09 39	09 46		09 54	10 01	10 09	10 16	10 24	10 31	10 39	10 46	10 52	11 01	11 10	11 17	11 24	11 31	11 35	11 45
Gospel Oak	d		09 27	09 34	09 42	09 49		09 57	10 04	10 12	10 19	10 28	10 35	10 42	10 49	10 54	11 04	11 13	11 24	11 27	11 34	11 38	11 47
Hampstead Heath	d		09 29	09 36	09 44	09 51		09 59	10 06	10 14	10 21	10 30	10 37	10 44	10 51	10 56	11 06	11 15	11 26	11 29	11 36	11 40	11 49
Finchley Road & Frognal	d		09 31	09 38	09 46	09 53		10 01	10 08	10 16	10 23	10 32	10 39	10 46	10 53	10 58	11 08	11 17	11 28	11 31	11 38	11 42	11 51
West Hampstead ⊖	d		09 33	09 40	09 48	09 55		10 03	10 10	10 18	10 25	10 35	10 41	10 48	10 55	11 01	11 10	11 19	11 30	11 33	11 40	11 44	11 53
Brondesbury	d		09 35	09 42	09 50	09 57		10 05	10 12	10 20	10 27	10 36	10 43	10 50	10 57	11 02	11 12	11 21	11 32	11 35	11 42	11 46	11 55
Brondesbury Park	d		09 36	09 43	09 51	09 58		10 06	10 13	10 21	10 28	10 38	10 44	10 51	10 58	11 04	11 13	11 22	11 33	11 36	11 43	11 47	11 56
Kensal Rise	d		09 38	09 45	09 53	10 00		10 08	10 15	10 23	10 30	10 40	10 46	10 53	11 00	11 06	11 15	11 24	11 35	11 38	11 45	11 49	11 58
Willesden Jn. High Level ⊖	a		09 42	09 49	09 57	10 04		10 12	10 19	10 27	10 34	10 44	10 50	10 57	11 04	11 12	11 19	11 28	11 40	11 42	11 49	11 55	12 02
	d		09 43	09 50	09 58	10 05		10 13	10 20	10 28	10 35	10 45	10 51	10 58	11 05	11 13	11 20	11 29	11 41	11 43	11 50	11 57	12 06
Willesden Jn Low Level ⊖	a																						
Shepherd's Bush ⊖	d		09 53		10 08			10 24		10 38		10 55		11 08		11 23		11 39		11 53		12 09	
Kensington (Olympia) ⊖	d		09 56		10 11			10 26		10 41		10 57		11 11		11 26		11 42		11 56		12 12	
West Brompton ⊖	d		09 58		10 13			10 29		10 43		11 00		11 13		11 28		11 44		11 58		12 14	
Imperial Wharf	d		10 01		10 16			10 32		10 46		11 03		11 16		11 31		11 47		12 01		12 17	
Clapham Junction 10	a		10 09		10 24			10 40		10 54		11 10		11 24		11 39		11 55		12 09		12 25	
Acton Central	d			09 55		10 10			10 25		10 40		10 56		11 10		11 25		11 46		11 55		12 11
South Acton	d			09 58		10 13			10 28		10 43		10 59		11 13		11 28		11 48		11 58		12 13
Gunnersbury ⊖	d			10 02		10 19			10 32		10 48		11 02		11 19		11 32		11 53		12 02		12 19
Kew Gardens ⊖	d			10 05		10 22			10 35		10 51		11 05		11 22		11 35		11 56		12 05		12 22
Richmond ⊖	a			10 14		10 30			10 44		11 00		11 15		11 30		11 44		12 05		12 15		12 31

Stratford - Highbury and Islington, West Hampstead, Willesden Junction, Clapham Junction and Richmond

Network Diagram - see first Page of Table 59

		LO	LO	LO	LO	LO	LO	LO	LO	LO	LO	LO	LO	LO	LO	LO	LO	LO	LO	LO	LO	LO	LO
Stratford 7 ⊖	d	11 30	11 37	11 45	11 52	12 02	12 07	12 15	12 22	12 32	12 39	12 45	12 52	13 02	13 07	13 15	13 22	13 30	13 37	13 45	13 52	14 02	14 07
Hackney Wick	d	11 33	11 40	11 48	11 56	12 06	12 10	12 18	12 25	12 35	12 42	12 48	12 57	13 05	13 10	13 18	13 25	13 33	13 41	13 48	13 55	14 05	14 10
Homerton	d	11 36	11 43	11 49	11 58	12 06	12 13	12 21	12 28	12 36	12 45	12 51	13 00	13 06	13 13	13 21	13 28	13 36	13 43	13 51	13 58	14 06	14 13
Hackney Central	d	11 38	11 45	11 51	12 00	12 08	12 15	12 23	12 30	12 38	12 47	12 53	13 02	13 08	13 15	13 23	13 30	13 38	13 45	13 53	14 00	14 08	14 15
Dalston Kingsland	d	11 40	11 47	11 53	12 03	12 10	12 17	12 25	12 32	12 40	12 49	12 55	13 04	13 10	13 17	13 25	13 32	13 40	13 47	13 55	14 02	14 10	14 17
Canonbury	d	11 42	11 49	11 55	12 05	12 12	12 19	12 27	12 34	12 42	12 51	12 57	13 06	13 12	13 19	13 27	13 34	13 42	13 49	13 57	14 04	14 12	14 19
Highbury & Islington ⊖	d	11 46	11 53	11 59	12 08	12 16	12 23	12 31	12 37	12 46	12 54	13 01	13 08	13 16	13 22	13 31	13 38	13 46	13 53	14 01	14 08	14 16	14 23
Caledonian Rd & Barnsbury	d	11 48	11 55	12 01	12 10	12 18	12 28	12 33	12 39	12 48	12 56	13 03	13 10	13 18	13 24	13 33	13 40	13 48	13 55	14 03	14 10	14 18	14 25
Camden Road	d	11 52	11 59	12 05	12 15	12 22	12 32	12 37	12 43	12 52	13 00	13 07	13 14	13 22	13 28	13 38	13 44	13 52	13 59	14 07	14 14	14 22	14 29
Kentish Town West	d	11 54	12 01	12 08	12 17	12 24	12 35	12 39	12 46	12 54	13 03	13 09	13 17	13 24	13 31	13 40	13 48	13 54	14 01	14 09	14 16	14 24	14 31
Gospel Oak	d	11 57	12 04	12 12	12 19	12 27	12 39	12 42	12 48	12 59	13 06	13 12	13 19	13 27	13 33	13 44	13 51	13 58	14 05	14 12	14 19	14 27	14 34
Hampstead Heath	d	11 59	12 06	12 13	12 21	12 29	12 41	12 44	12 50	13 01	13 08	13 14	13 21	13 29	13 35	13 46	13 53	14 00	14 07	14 14	14 21	14 29	14 36
Finchley Road & Frognal	d	12 01	12 08	12 15	12 23	12 31	12 43	12 46	12 52	13 03	13 10	13 16	13 24	13 31	13 37	13 48	13 55	14 02	14 09	14 16	14 23	14 31	14 38
West Hampstead ⊖	d	12 03	12 10	12 17	12 25	12 33	12 45	12 48	12 55	13 05	13 12	13 18	13 26	13 33	13 39	13 50	13 57	14 04	14 11	14 18	14 25	14 33	14 40
Brondesbury	d	12 05	12 12	12 19	12 27	12 35	12 47	12 50	12 56	13 07	13 14	13 20	13 28	13 35	13 41	13 51	13 58	14 05	14 12	14 20	14 27	14 35	14 42
Brondesbury Park	d	12 06	12 13	12 20	12 28	12 36	12 48	12 51	12 58	13 08	13 15	13 21	13 29	13 36	13 42	13 53	14 00	14 07	14 14	14 21	14 28	14 36	14 43
Kensal Rise	d	12 08	12 15	12 22	12 30	12 38	12 50	12 53	13 00	13 10	13 17	13 23	13 31	13 38	13 44	13 55	14 02	14 09	14 16	14 23	14 30	14 38	14 45
Willesden Jn. High Level ⊖	a	12 12	12 19	12 27	12 34	12 42	12 53	12 57	13 04	13 13	13 20	13 27	13 34	13 42	13 48	13 58	14 05	14 13	14 20	14 27	14 34	14 42	14 49
	d	12 13	12 20	12 28	12 35	12 43	12 53	12 58	13 05	13 14	13 21	13 28	13 35	13 43	13 50	13 59	14 06	14 14	14 21	14 28	14 35	14 43	14 50
Willesden Jn Low Level ⊖	a																						
Shepherd's Bush ⊖	d	12 23		12 38		12 53		13 08		13 24		13 38		13 53		14 09		14 25		14 38		14 53	
Kensington (Olympia) ⊖	d	12 26		12 41		12 56		13 11		13 27		13 41		13 56		14 11		14 27		14 41		14 56	
West Brompton ⊖	d	12 28		12 43		12 58		13 13		13 29		13 43		13 58		14 14		14 30		14 43		14 58	
Imperial Wharf	d	12 31		12 46		13 01		13 16		13 32		13 46		14 01		14 17		14 33		14 46		15 01	
Clapham Junction 10	a	12 39		12 54		13 09		13 24		13 40		13 54		14 09		14 24		14 41		14 54		15 09	
Acton Central	d		12 25		12 40		12 58		13 10		13 26		13 40		13 55		14 11		14 26		14 40		14 55
South Acton	d		12 28		12 43		13 01		13 13		13 29		13 43		13 58		14 14		14 28		14 43		14 58
Gunnersbury ⊖	d		12 32		12 49		13 03		13 19		13 32		13 49		14 02		14 19		14 32		14 49		15 02
Kew Gardens ⊖	d		12 35		12 52		13 06		13 22		13 35		13 52		14 05		14 22		14 35		14 52		15 05
Richmond ⊖	a		12 44		13 01		13 15		13 31		13 45		14 01		14 15		14 31		14 45		15 01		15 15

		LO	LO	LO	LO	LO	LO	LO	LO	LO	LO	LO	LO	LO	LO	LO	LO	LO	LO	LO	LO	LO	LO
Stratford 7 ⊖	d	14 15	14 22	14 32	14 37	14 45	14 52	15 00	15 06	15 16	15 22	15 28	15 37	15 45	15 52	16 00	16 07	16 11	16 15	16 22	16 32	16 37	16 41
Hackney Wick	d	14 18	14 25	14 35	14 40	14 48	14 56	15 03	15 10	15 19	15 25	15 29	15 40	15 48	15 55	16 03	16 10	16 14	16 18	16 25	16 35	16 40	16 44
Homerton	d	14 21	14 28	14 36	14 43	14 51	14 58	15 05	15 12	15 21	15 28	15 32	15 43	15 51	15 58	16 06	16 13	16 17	16 21	16 28	16 36	16 43	16 47
Hackney Central	d	14 23	14 30	14 38	14 45	14 53	15 00	15 07	15 14	15 23	15 30	15 34	15 45	15 53	16 00	16 08	16 15	16 19	16 23	16 30	16 38	16 45	16 49
Dalston Kingsland	d	14 25	14 32	14 40	14 47	14 55	15 02	15 10	15 17	15 25	15 32	15 36	15 47	15 55	16 02	16 10	16 17	16 21	16 25	16 32	16 40	16 47	16 51
Canonbury	d	14 27	14 34	14 42	14 49	14 57	15 04	15 12	15 19	15 27	15 34	15 38	15 49	15 57	16 04	16 12	16 19	16 24	16 27	16 34	16 42	16 49	16 54
Highbury & Islington ⊖	d	14 31	14 38	14 46	14 53	15 01	15 08	15 16	15 23	15 31	15 38	15 41	15 53	16 01	16 08	16 16	16 23	16 27	16 31	16 38	16 46	16 53	16 57
Caledonian Rd & Barnsbury	d	14 33	14 40	14 48	14 55	15 03	15 10	15 18	15 25	15 33	15 40	15 43	15 55	16 03	16 10	16 18	16 25	16 29	16 33	16 40	16 48	16 55	16 59
Camden Road	d	14 37	14 44	14 52	14 59	15 07	15 14	15 22	15 29	15 37	15 44	15 47	15 59	16 07	16 14	16 22	16 29	16a38	16 37	16 44	16 52	16 59	17a08
Kentish Town West	d	14 39	14 46	14 54	15 01	15 09	15 16	15 24	15 31	15 39	15 46	15 50	16 01	16 10	16 16	16 24	16 31		16 39	16 46	16 54	17 01	
Gospel Oak	d	14 42	14 49	14 57	15 04	15 12	15 19	15 27	15 34	15 42	15 49	15 53	16 04	16 12	16 19	16 27	16 34		16 42	16 49	16 57	17 04	
Hampstead Heath	d	14 44	14 51	14 59	15 06	15 14	15 21	15 29	15 36	15 44	15 51	15 55	16 06	16 14	16 21	16 29	16 36		16 44	16 51	16 59	17 06	
Finchley Road & Frognal	d	14 46	14 53	15 01	15 08	15 16	15 23	15 31	15 38	15 46	15 53	15 57	16 08	16 16	16 23	16 31	16 38		16 46	16 53	17 01	17 08	
West Hampstead ⊖	d	14 48	14 55	15 03	15 10	15 18	15 25	15 33	15 40	15 48	15 55	15 59	16 10	16 18	16 25	16 33	16 40		16 48	16 55	17 03	17 10	
Brondesbury	d	14 50	14 57	15 05	15 12	15 20	15 27	15 35	15 42	15 50	15 57	16 00	16 12	16 20	16 27	16 35	16 42		16 50	16 57	17 05	17 12	
Brondesbury Park	d	14 51	14 58	15 06	15 13	15 21	15 28	15 36	15 43	15 51	15 58	16 02	16 13	16 21	16 28	16 36	16 43		16 51	16 58	17 06	17 13	
Kensal Rise	d	14 53	15 00	15 08	15 15	15 23	15 30	15 38	15 45	15 53	16 00	16 04	16 15	16 23	16 30	16 38	16 45		16 53	17 00	17 08	17 15	
Willesden Jn. High Level ⊖	a	14 57	15 04	15 12	15 19	15 27	15 34	15 42	15 49	15 57	16 04	16 08	16 19	16 27	16 34	16 42	16 49		16 57	17 05	17 12	17 19	
	d	14 58	15 05	15 13	15 20	15 28	15 35	15 43	15 50	15 58	16 05	16 09	16 20	16 28	16 35	16 43	16 50		16 58	17 06	17 13	17 20	
Willesden Jn Low Level ⊖	a																						
Shepherd's Bush ⊖	d	15 08		15 23		15 38		15 53		16 08		16 24		16 38		16 53			17 08		17 23		
Kensington (Olympia) ⊖	d	15 11		15 26		15 41		15 56		16 11		16 26		16 41		16 56			17 11		17 26		
West Brompton ⊖	d	15 13		15 28		15 43		15 58		16 13		16 29		16 43		16 58			17 13		17 28		
Imperial Wharf	d	15 16		15 31		15 46		16 01		16 16		16 32		16 46		17 01			17 16		17 31		
Clapham Junction 10	a	15 24		15 39		15 54		16 09		16 24		16 40		16 54		17 09			17 24		17 39		
Acton Central	d		15 10		15 25		15 40		15 55		16 10		16 25		16 40		16 55			17 11		17 25	
South Acton	d		15 13		15 28		15 43		15 58		16 13		16 28		16 43		16 58			17 14		17 28	
Gunnersbury ⊖	d		15 18		15 32		15 48		16 02		16 18		16 32		16 48		17 02			17 18		17 32	
Kew Gardens ⊖	d		15 21		15 35		15 51		16 05		16 21		16 35		16 51		17 05			17 21		17 35	
Richmond ⊖	a		15 30		15 45		16 00		16 14		16 30		16 44		17 00		17 14			17 30		17 44	

29 August to 7 September

Stratford - Highbury and Islington, West Hampstead, Willesden Junction, Clapham Junction and Richmond

Network Diagram - see first Page of Table 59

		LO	LO	LO	LO	LO	LO	LO	LO	LO	LO	LO	LO	LO	LO	LO	LO	LO	LO	LO	LO	LO	LO
Stratford 7	⊖ d	16 45	16 52	17 00	17 07	17 11	17 15	17 22	17 30	17 37	17 41	17 45	17 52	18 00	18 07	18 11	18 15	18 22	18 30	18 37	18 41	18 45	18 52
Hackney Wick	d	16 48	16 55	17 03	17 10	17 14	17 18	17 25	17 33	17 40	17 44	17 48	17 56	18 03	18 10	18 14	18 18	18 25	18 33	18 40	18 44	18 48	18 55
Homerton	d	16 51	16 58	17 06	17 13	17 17	17 21	17 28	17 36	17 43	17 47	17 51	17 58	18 06	18 13	18 17	18 21	18 28	18 36	18 43	18 47	18 51	18 58
Hackney Central	d	16 53	17 00	17 08	17 15	17 19	17 23	17 30	17 38	17 45	17 49	17 53	18 00	18 08	18 15	18 19	18 23	18 30	18 38	18 45	18 49	18 53	19 00
Dalston Kingsland	d	16 55	17 02	17 10	17 17	17 21	17 25	17 32	17 40	17 47	17 51	17 55	18 02	18 10	18 17	18 21	18 25	18 32	18 40	18 47	18 51	18 55	19 02
Canonbury	d	16 57	17 04	17 12	17 19	17 24	17 27	17 34	17 42	17 49	17 54	17 57	18 04	18 12	18 19	18 24	18 27	18 34	18 42	18 49	18 54	18 57	19 04
Highbury & Islington	⊖ d	17 01	17 08	17 16	17 23	17 27	17 31	17 38	17 46	17 53	17 57	18 01	18 08	18 16	18 23	18 27	18 31	18 38	18 46	18 53	18 57	19 01	19 08
Caledonian Rd & Barnsbury	d	17 03	17 10	17 18	17 25	17 29	17 33	17 40	17 48	17 55	17 59	18 03	18 10	18 18	18 25	18 29	18 33	18 40	18 48	18 55	18 59	19 03	19 10
Camden Road	d	17 07	17 14	17 22	17 29	17a38	17 37	17 44	17 52	17 59	18a08	18 07	18 14	18 22	18 29	18a38	18 37	18 44	18 52	18 59	19a08	19 07	19 14
Kentish Town West	d	17 09	17 16	17 24	17 31		17 39	17 46	17 54	18 01		18 09	18 16	18 24	18 31		18 39	18 46	18 54	19 01		19 09	19 16
Gospel Oak	d	17 12	17 19	17 27	17 34		17 42	17 49	17 57	18 04		18 12	18 19	18 27	18 34		18 42	18 49	18 57	19 04		19 12	19 19
Hampstead Heath	d	17 14	17 21	17 29	17 36		17 44	17 51	17 59	18 06		18 14	18 21	18 29	18 36		18 44	18 51	18 59	19 06		19 14	19 21
Finchley Road & Frognal	d	17 16	17 23	17 31	17 38		17 46	17 53	18 01	18 08		18 16	18 23	18 31	18 38		18 46	18 53	19 01	19 08		19 16	19 23
West Hampstead	⊖ d	17 18	17 25	17 33	17 40		17 48	17 55	18 03	18 10		18 18	18 25	18 33	18 40		18 48	18 55	19 03	19 10		19 18	19 25
Brondesbury	d	17 20	17 27	17 35	17 42		17 50	17 57	18 05	18 12		18 20	18 27	18 35	18 42		18 50	18 57	19 05	19 12		19 20	19 27
Brondesbury Park	d	17 21	17 28	17 36	17 43		17 51	17 58	18 06	18 13		18 21	18 28	18 36	18 43		18 51	18 58	19 06	19 13		19 21	19 28
Kensal Rise	d	17 23	17 30	17 38	17 45		17 53	18 00	18 08	18 15		18 23	18 30	18 38	18 45		18 53	19 00	19 08	19 15		19 23	19 30
Willesden Jn. High Level	⊖ a	17 27	17 35	17 42	17 49		17 57	18 04	18 12	18 19		18 27	18 34	18 42	18 49		18 57	19 04	19 13	19 19		19 27	19 34
	d	17 28	17 36	17 43	17 50		17 58	18 05	18 13	18 20		18 28	18 35	18 43	18 50		18 58	19 05	19 14	19 20		19 28	19 35
Willesden Jn Low Level	⊖ a																						
Shepherd's Bush	⊖ d	17 38		17 53			18 08		18 23			18 38		18 53			19 08		19 24			19 38	
Kensington (Olympia)	⊖ d	17 41		17 56			18 11		18 26			18 41		18 56			19 11		19 27			19 41	
West Brompton	⊖ d	17 43		17 58			18 13		18 28			18 43		18 58			19 13		19 29			19 43	
Imperial Wharf	d	17 46		18 01			18 16		18 31			18 46		19 01			19 16		19 32			19 46	
Clapham Junction 10	a	17 54		18 09			18 24		18 39			18 54		19 09			19 24		19 40			19 54	
Acton Central	d		17 41		17 55			18 10		18 24			18 40		18 55			19 10		19 25			19 40
South Acton	d		17 44		17 58			18 13		18 27			18 43		18 58			19 13		19 28			19 43
Gunnersbury	⊖ d		17 48		18 02			18 17		18 31			18 47		19 01			19 18		19 31			19 48
Kew Gardens	⊖ d		17 51		18 05			18 20		18 34			18 50		19 04			19 21		19 34			19 51
Richmond	⊖ a		18 00		18 14			18 29		18 43			19 00		19 13			19 30		19 43			20 00

		LO	LO	LO	LO	LO	LO	LO	LO	LO	LO	LO	LO	LO	LO	LO	LO	LO	LO	LO	LO	LO	LO
Stratford 7	⊖ d	19 00	19 07	19 11	19 15	19 22	19 30	19 38	19 45	19 54	20 00	20 07	20 14	20 22	20 32	20 37	20 45	20 52	21 02	21 07	21 15	21 22	21 30
Hackney Wick	d	19 03	19 10	19 14	19 18	19 25	19 33	19 43	19 47	19 58	20 03	20 10	20 17	20 25	20 35	20 40	20 48	20 55	21 05	21 10	21 18	21 25	21 35
Homerton	d	19 06	19 13	19 17	19 21	19 28	19 35	19 45	19 50	20 00	20 06	20 13	20 19	20 28	20 36	20 43	20 51	20 58	21 07	21 13	21 21	21 28	21 36
Hackney Central	d	19 08	19 15	19 19	19 23	19 30	19 37	19 47	19 52	20 02	20 08	20 15	20 21	20 30	20 38	20 45	20 53	21 00	21 09	21 15	21 23	21 30	21 38
Dalston Kingsland	d	19 10	19 17	19 21	19 25	19 32	19 40	19 50	19 54	20 05	20 10	20 17	20 22	20 32	20 40	20 47	20 55	21 02	21 11	21 17	21 25	21 32	21 40
Canonbury	d	19 12	19 19	19 24	19 27	19 34	19 42	19 52	19 56	20 07	20 12	20 19	20 24	20 34	20 42	20 49	20 57	21 04	21 13	21 19	21 27	21 34	21 42
Highbury & Islington	⊖ d	19 16	19 23	19 27	19 31	19 38	19 45	19 56	20 00	20 10	20 16	20 23	20 29	20 38	20 46	20 52	21 01	21 08	21 16	21 23	21 31	21 38	21 47
Caledonian Rd & Barnsbury	d	19 18	19 25	19 29	19 33	19 40	19 47	19 58	20 02	20 12	20 18	20 25	20 31	20 40	20 48	20 54	21 03	21 10	21 18	21 25	21 33	21 40	21 49
Camden Road	d	19 22	19 29	19a38	19 37	19 44	19 51	20 02	20 06	20 16	20 22	20 29	20 37	20 43	20 52	20 58	21 07	21 14	21 22	21 29	21 37	21 44	21 54
Kentish Town West	d	19 24	19 31		19 39	19 46	19 54	20 04	20 08	20 19	20 24	20 31	20 39	20 46	20 55	21 01	21 09	21 16	21 25	21 31	21 39	21 46	21 56
Gospel Oak	d	19 27	19 34		19 42	19 49	19 57	20 07	20 11	20 22	20 27	20 34	20 42	20 50	20 57	21 04	21 13	21 20	21 27	21 34	21 42	21 49	21 59
Hampstead Heath	d	19 29	19 36		19 44	19 51	19 59	20 09	20 13	20 24	20 29	20 36	20 44	20 52	20 59	21 06	21 15	21 22	21 29	21 36	21 44	21 51	22 01
Finchley Road & Frognal	d	19 31	19 38		19 46	19 53	20 01	20 11	20 15	20 26	20 31	20 38	20 46	20 54	21 01	21 08	21 17	21 24	21 31	21 38	21 46	21 53	22 03
West Hampstead	⊖ d	19 33	19 40		19 48	19 55	20 03	20 13	20 17	20 28	20 33	20 40	20 48	20 56	21 04	21 10	21 19	21 26	21 33	21 40	21 48	21 55	22 05
Brondesbury	d	19 35	19 42		19 50	19 57	20 05	20 15	20 19	20 30	20 35	20 42	20 50	20 58	21 05	21 12	21 21	21 28	21 35	21 42	21 50	21 57	22 07
Brondesbury Park	d	19 36	19 43		19 51	19 58	20 06	20 16	20 20	20 31	20 36	20 43	20 51	20 59	21 07	21 13	21 22	21 29	21 36	21 43	21 51	21 58	22 08
Kensal Rise	d	19 38	19 45		19 53	20 00	20 08	20 18	20 22	20 33	20 38	20 45	20 53	21 01	21 09	21 15	21 24	21 31	21 38	21 45	21 53	22 00	22 10
Willesden Jn. High Level	⊖ a	19 42	19 50		19 57	20 04	20 12	20 22	20 26	20 37	20 42	20 49	20 57	21 05	21 13	21 19	21 27	21 35	21 42	21 49	21 57	22 04	22 15
	d	19 43	19 51		19 58	20 05	20 13	20 23	20 28	20 38	20 43	20 50	20 58	21 06	21 14	21 20	21 28	21 36	21 43	21 50	21 58	22 06	22 16
Willesden Jn Low Level	⊖ a																						
Shepherd's Bush	⊖ d	19 53			20 08		20 23		20 38		20 53		21 08		21 23		21 38		21 53		22 08		22 26
Kensington (Olympia)	⊖ d	19 56			20 11		20 26		20 41		20 56		21 11		21 26		21 41		21 56		22 11		22 29
West Brompton	⊖ d	19 58			20 13		20 28		20 43		20 58		21 13		21 28		21 43		21 58		22 13		22 31
Imperial Wharf	d	20 01			20 16		20 31		20 46		21 01		21 16		21 31		21 46		22 01		22 16		22 34
Clapham Junction 10	a	20 09			20 24		20 39		20 54		21 09		21 24		21 39		21 54		22 09		22 24		22 42
Acton Central	d		19 56			20 10		20 28		20 44		20 55		21 11		21 25		21 41		21 55		22 11	
South Acton	d		19 58			20 14		20 31		20 47		20 58		21 14		21 28		21 44		21 58		22 13	
Gunnersbury	⊖ d		20 02			20 18		20 34		20 52		21 02		21 18		21 32		21 48		22 02		22 18	
Kew Gardens	⊖ d		20 05			20 21		20 37		20 55		21 05		21 21		21 35		21 51		22 05		22 21	
Richmond	⊖ a		20 14			20 30		20 47		21 05		21 14		21 30		21 44		22 00		22 14		22 30	

29 August to 7 September

Stratford - Highbury and Islington, West Hampstead, Willesden Junction, Clapham Junction and Richmond

Network Diagram - see first Page of Table 59

		LO	LO	LO	LO	LO	LO	LO	LO	LO	LO	LO	LO	LO	LO	LO	LO	LO	LO	LO
Stratford 7	⊖ d	21 37	21 45	21 52	22 00	22 07	22 15	22 22	22 32	22 37	22 45	22 52	23 02	23 07	23 15	23 22	23 30	23 38	23 45	23 52
Hackney Wick	d	21 40	21 49	21 55	22 03	22 10	22 18	22 25	22 35	22 40	22 48	22 55	23 05	23 10	23 18	23 25	23 33	23 41	23 48	23 55
Homerton	d	21 43	21 51	21 58	22 06	22 13	22 21	22 28	22 37	22 43	22 51	22 58	23 06	23 13	23 21	23 28	23 36	23 44	23 51	23 58
Hackney Central	d	21 45	21 53	22 00	22 08	22 15	22 23	22 30	22 39	22 45	22 53	23 00	23 08	23 15	23 23	23 30	23 38	23 46	23 53	23 59
Dalston Kingsland	d	21 47	21 55	22 02	22 10	22 17	22 25	22 32	22 41	22 47	22 55	23 02	23 10	23 17	23 25	23 32	23 40	23 48	23 55	00 02
Canonbury	d	21 49	21 57	22 04	22 12	22 19	22 27	22 34	22 43	22 49	22 57	23 04	23 12	23 19	23 27	23 34	23 42	23 50	23 57	00 04
Highbury & Islington	⊖ d	21 53	22 01	22 08	22 16	22 23	22 31	22 38	22 46	22 53	23 01	23 08	23 16	23 23	23 31	23 38	23 46	23 53	00 01	00 08
Caledonian Rd & Barnsbury	d	21 55	22 03	22 10	22 18	22 25	22 33	22 40	22 48	22 55	23 03	23 10	23 18	23 25	23 33	23 40	23 48	23 55	00 03	00 10
Camden Road	d	21 59	22 07	22 14	22 22	22 29	22 37	22 44	22 52	22 59	23 07	23 14	23 22	23 29	23 37	23 44	23 53	23 59	00 07	00 14
Kentish Town West	d	22 01	22 09	22 16	22 25	22 32	22 39	22 46	22 55	23 01	23 09	23 16	23 24	23 31	23 39	23 46	23 55	00 02	00 09	00 16
Gospel Oak	d	22 04	22 12	22 19	22 29	22 35	22 43	22 50	22 57	23 04	23 12	23 19	23 27	23 34	23 42	23 49	23 59	00 05	00 12	00 19
Hampstead Heath	d	22 06	22 14	22 21	22 31	22 37	22 45	22 52	22 59	23 06	23 14	23 21	23 29	23 36	23 44	23 51	00 01	00 07	00 14	00 21
Finchley Road & Frognal	d	22 08	22 16	22 23	22 33	22 39	22 47	22 54	23 01	23 08	23 16	23 23	23 31	23 38	23 46	23 53	00 03	00 09	00 16	00 23
West Hampstead	⊖ d	22 10	22 18	22 25	22 35	22 42	22 50	22 57	23 03	23 10	23 18	23 25	23 33	23 40	23 48	23 55	00 05	00 11	00 18	00 25
Brondesbury	d	22 12	22 20	22 27	22 36	22 43	22 51	22 58	23 05	23 12	23 20	23 27	23 35	23 42	23 50	23 57	00 06	00 13	00 20	00 27
Brondesbury Park	d	22 13	22 21	22 28	22 38	22 45	22 53	23 00	23 06	23 13	23 21	23 28	23 36	23 43	23 51	23 58	00 08	00 14	00 21	00 28
Kensal Rise	d	22 15	22 23	22 30	22 40	22 47	22 55	23 02	23 08	23 15	23 23	23 30	23 38	23 45	23 53	00 01	00 10	00 16	00 23	00 30
Willesden Jn. High Level	⊖ a	22 19	22 27	22 34	22 43	22 51	22 58	23 05	23 12	23 19	23 27	23 35	23 42	23 49	23 57	00 04	00 13	00 20	00 27	00 34
	d	22 20	22 28	22 35	22 44	22 52	22 59	23 06	23 13	23 20	23 28	23 36	23 43	23 50	23 59	00 05	00 14	00 21	00 28	00 35
Willesden Jn Low Level	⊖ a																			
Shepherd's Bush	⊖ d		22 38		22 54		23 09		23 23		23 38		23 57		00 09		00 24		00 38	
Kensington (Olympia)	⊖ d		22 41		22 56		23 11		23 26		23 41		23 59		00 11		00 26		00 41	
West Brompton	⊖ d		22 43		22 59		23 14		23 28		23 43		00 02		00 14		00 29		00 43	
Imperial Wharf	d		22 46		23 02		23 17		23 31		23 46		00 05		00 17		00 32		00 46	
Clapham Junction 10	a		22 54		23 10		23 25		23 39		23 54		00 13		00 23		00 39		00 54	
Acton Central	d	22 25		22 40		22 57		23 11		23 25		23 41		23 55		00 10		00 26		00 40
South Acton	d	22 28		22 43		22 59		23 13		23 28		23 43		23 58		00 13		00 29		00 43
Gunnersbury	⊖ d	22 32		22 48		23 02		23 18		23 32		23 48		00 02		00 18		00 33		00 47
Kew Gardens	⊖ d	22 35		22 51		23 05		23 21		23 35		23 51		00 05		00 21		00 36		00 50
Richmond	⊖ a	22 44		23 00		23 15		23 30		23 44		00 01		00 14		00 30		00 45		00 59

Mondays to Fridays

from 10 September

		LO	LO MX	LO	LO	LO	LO	LO	LO	LO MX	LO	LO	LO	LO	LO	LO	LO	LO	LO	LO	LO	LO	LO
		A		A	A	A	A	A	A		A	A	A	A	A	A	A	A	A	A	A		
Stratford 7	⊖ d	22p52		23p00	23p07	23p15	23p22	23p30	23p37	23p45	23p45	23p52	00 01	00 07	00 15	00 22	00 30	00 37	00 45	00 52	01 00		
Hackney Wick	d	22p55		23p05	23p10	23p18	23p25	23p35	23p40	23p48	23p49	23p55	00 03	00 10	00 18	00 25	00 33	00 40	00 48	00 55	01 03		
Homerton	d	22p58		23p06	23p13	23p19	23p28	23p36	23p43	23p51	23p51	23p58	00 06	00 13	00 21	00 28	00 36	00 43	00 51	00 58	01 06		
Hackney Central	d	23p00		23p08	23p15	23p21	23p30	23p38	23p45	23p53	23p53	00 01	00 08	00 15	00 23	00 30	00 38	00 45	00 53	01 00	01 08		
Dalston Kingsland	d	23p02		23p10	23p17	23p23	23p32	23p40	23p47	23p55	23p55	00 03	00 10	00 17	00 25	00 32	00 40	00 47	00 55	01 02	01 10		
Canonbury	d	23p04		23p12	23p19	23p25	23p34	23p42	23p49	23p57	23p57	00 05	00 12	00 19	00 27	00 34	00 42	00 49	00 57	01 04	01 12		
Highbury & Islington	⊖ d	23p08		23p16	23p23	23p28	23p38	23p46	23p53	23p59	00 01	00 08	00 16	00 23	00 31	00 38	00 46	00 53	01 01	01 08	01 16		
Caledonian Rd & Barnsbury	d	23p10		23p18	23p25	23p30	23p40	23p48	23p55	00 02	00 03	00 10	00 18	00 25	00 33	00 40	00 48	00 55	01 03	01 10	01 18		
Camden Road	d	23p14		23p22	23p29	23p34	23p45	23p52	23p59	00 05	00 07	00 14	00 22	00a31	00 37	00a46	00 52	01a01	01 07	01a16	01 22		
Kentish Town West	d	23p16		23p24	23p31	23p37	23p47	23p54	00 01	00 07	00 09	00 16	00 24		00 39		00 54		01 09		01 24		
Gospel Oak	d	23p19		23p27	23p34	23p40	23p50	23p57	00 04	00 10	00 12	00 19	00 27		00 42		00 57		01 12		01 27		
Hampstead Heath	d	23p21		23p29	23p36	23p42	23p52	23p59	00 06	00 12	00 14	00 21	00 29		00 44		00 59		01 14		01 29		
Finchley Road & Frognal	d	23p23		23p31	23p38	23p44	23p54	00 01	00 08	00 14	00 16	00 23	00 31		00 46		01 01		01 16		01 31		
West Hampstead	⊖ d	23p25		23p33	23p40	23p47	23p56	00 03	00 10	00 16	00 18	00 25	00 33		00 48		01 03		01 18		01 33		
Brondesbury	d	23p27		23p35	23p42	23p48	23p58	00 05	00 12	00 18	00 20	00 27	00 35		00 50		01 05		01 20		01 35		
Brondesbury Park	d	23p28		23p36	23p43	23p50	23p59	00 06	00 13	00 19	00 21	00 28	00 36		00 51		01 06		01 21		01 36		
Kensal Rise	d	23p30		23p38	23p45	23p52	00 01	00 08	00 15	00 21	00 23	00 30	00 38		00 53		01 08		01 23		01 38		
Willesden Jn. High Level	⊖ a	23p34		23p42	23p49	23p57	00 04	00 12	00 19		00 27	00 34	00 42										
	d	23p35	23p40	23p43	23p50	23p59	00 05	00 13	00 20		00 28	00 35	00 43									06 01	06 09
Willesden Jn Low Level	⊖ a									00 29					01 01		01 21		01 42		01 57		
Shepherd's Bush	⊖ d		23p48	23p53		00 09		00 23			00 38		00 53									06 08	
Kensington (Olympia)	⊖ d		23p50	23p56		00 11		00 26			00 41		00 56									06 10	
West Brompton	⊖ d		23p52	23p58		00 14		00 28			00 43		00 58									06 13	
Imperial Wharf	d		23p55	00 01		00 17		00 31			00 46		01 01									06 16	
Clapham Junction 10	a		00 02	00 09		00 22		00 39			00 54		01 09									06 23	
Acton Central	d	23p40			23p55		00 10		00 25			00 40											06 14
South Acton	d	23p43			23p58		00 13		00 28			00 43											06 16
Gunnersbury	⊖ d	23p48			00 03		00 18		00 32			00 48											06 20
Kew Gardens	⊖ d	23p51			00 06		00 21		00 35			00 51											06 23
Richmond	⊖ a	00 01			00 16		00 30		00 44			01 00											06 30

A 10 September

Stratford - Highbury and Islington, West Hampstead, Willesden Junction, Clapham Junction and Richmond

Network Diagram - see first Page of Table 59

		LO	LO	LO	LO	LO	LO	LO	LO	LO	LO	LO	LO	LO	LO	LO	LO	LO	LO	LO	LO	LO	LO
Stratford 7 ⊖	d	05 47			06 05	06 12	06 20	06 27	06 35	06 42	06 50	06 55	07 00	07 12	07 20	07 27	07 35	07 42	07 50	07 57	08 03	08 12	08 20
Hackney Wick	d	05 50			06 08	06 15	06 23	06 30	06 38	06 45	06 54	06 58	07 03	07 15	07 23	07 30	07 38	07 45	07 53	08 00	08 06	08 15	08 23
Homerton	d	05 53			06 11	06 18	06 26	06 33	06 41	06 48	06 56	07 01	07 06	07 18	07 26	07 33	07 42	07 48	07 56	08 03	08 09	08 18	08 26
Hackney Central	d	05 55			06 13	06 20	06 28	06 35	06 43	06 50	06 58	07 03	07 08	07 20	07 28	07 35	07 43	07 50	07 58	08 05	08 11	08 20	08 28
Dalston Kingsland	d	05 57			06 15	06 22	06 30	06 37	06 45	06 52	07 00	07 05	07 10	07 22	07 30	07 37	07 45	07 52	08 00	08 07	08 13	08 22	08 30
Canonbury	d	05 59			06 17	06 24	06 32	06 39	06 47	06 54	07 02	07 07	07 12	07 24	07 32	07 39	07 47	07 54	08 02	08 09	08 15	08 24	08 32
Highbury & Islington ⊖	d	06 02			06 19	06 27	06 35	06 41	06 50	06 57	07 05	07 10	07 15	07 27	07 35	07 42	07 50	07 57	08 05	08 12	08 18	08 27	08 35
Caledonian Rd & Barnsbury	d	06 04			06 21	06 29	06 37	06 43	06 52	06 59	07 07	07 12	07 17	07 29	07 37	07 44	07 52	07 59	08 07	08 14	08 20	08 29	08 37
Camden Road	d	06 07			06 24	06 32	06 40	06 46	06 55	07 02	07 10	07 15	07 20	07 32	07 40	07 47	07 55	08 02	08 10	08 17	08 23	08 32	08 40
Kentish Town West	d	06 09			06 27	06 34	06 42	06 49	06 57	07 04	07 13	07 17	07 22	07 34	07 42	07 49	07 57	08 04	08 12	08 19	08 25	08 34	08 42
Gospel Oak	d	06 12			06 30	06 37	06 45	06 51	07 00	07 07	07 15	07 20	07 25	07 37	07 45	07 52	08 00	08 07	08 15	08 22	08 28	08 37	08 45
Hampstead Heath	d	06 14			06 32	06 39	06 47	06 53	07 02	07 09	07 17	07 22	07 27	07 39	07 47	07 54	08 02	08 09	08 17	08 24	08 30	08 39	08 47
Finchley Road & Frognal	d	06 16			06 34	06 41	06 49	06 55	07 04	07 11	07 19	07 24	07 29	07 41	07 49	07 56	08 04	08 11	08 19	08 26	08 32	08 41	08 49
West Hampstead ⊖	d	06 18			06 36	06 43	06 51	06 57	07 06	07 13	07 21	07 26	07 31	07 43	07 51	07 58	08 06	08 13	08 21	08 28	08 34	08 43	08 51
Brondesbury	d	06 20			06 38	06 45	06 53	06 58	07 08	07 15	07 22	07 28	07 33	07 45	07 53	08 00	08 08	08 15	08 23	08 30	08 36	08 45	08 53
Brondesbury Park	d	06 21			06 39	06 46	06 54	07 00	07 09	07 16	07 24	07 29	07 34	07 46	07 54	08 01	08 09	08 16	08 24	08 31	08 37	08 46	08 54
Kensal Rise	d	06 23			06 41	06 48	06 56	07 02	07 11	07 18	07 26	07 31	07 36	07 48	07 56	08 03	08 11	08 18	08 26	08 33	08 39	08 48	08 56
Willesden Jn. High Level ⊖	a	06 27			06 45	06 52	07 00	07 06	07 15	07 22	07 30	07 35	07 40	07 52	08 00	08 07	08 15	08 22	08 30	08 37	08 43	08 52	09 00
	d	06 28	06 33	06 41	06 46	06 53	07 01	07 07	07 16	07 23	07 31	07 36	07 41	07 53	08 01	08 08	08 16	08 23	08 31	08 38	08 46	08 53	09 01
Willesden Jn Low Level ⊖	a																						
Shepherd's Bush ⊖	d		06 40		06 54		07 09		07 24		07 39		07 49		08 09		08 24		08 39		08 54		09 09
Kensington (Olympia) ⊖	d		06 42		06 56		07 11		07 26		07 41		07 51		08 11		08 26		08 41		08 56		09 11
West Brompton ⊖	d		06 45		06 58		07 13		07 28		07 43		07 53		08 13		08 28		08 43		08 58		09 13
Imperial Wharf	d		06 48		07 01		07 16		07 31		07 46		07 56		08 16		08 31		08 46		09 01		09 16
Clapham Junction 10	a		06 54		07 09		07 24		07 42		07 54		08 04		08 24		08 39		08 54		09 09		09 25
Acton Central	d	06 33		06 46		06 58		07 13		07 28		07 41		07 58		08 13		08 28		08 43		08 58	
South Acton	d	06 36		06 49		07 01		07 16		07 31		07 44		08 01		08 16		08 31		08 46		09 01	
Gunnersbury ⊖	d	06 39		06 53		07 04		07 19		07 34		07 48		08 04		08 19		08 34		08 51		09 04	
Kew Gardens ⊖	d	06 42		06 56		07 07		07 22		07 37		07 51		08 07		08 22		08 37		08 54		09 07	
Richmond ⊖	a	06 49		07 04		07 14		07 30		07 44		07 57		08 14		08 28		08 43		08 58		09 13	

		LO	LO	LO	LO	LO	LO	LO	LO	LO	LO	LO	LO	LO	LO	LO	LO	LO	LO	LO	LO	LO	LO
Stratford 7 ⊖	d	08 27	08 35	08 42	08 50	08 57	09 03	09 15		09 25	09 35	09 45		09 55	10 05	10 15		10 25	10 35	10 45		10 55	11 05
Hackney Wick	d	08 30	08 38	08 45	08 53	09 00	09 06	09 18		09 28	09 38	09 48		09 58	10 08	10 18		10 28	10 38	10 48		10 58	11 08
Homerton	d	08 33	08 41	08 48	08 56	09 03	09 09	09 21		09 31	09 41	09 51		10 01	10 11	10 21		10 31	10 41	10 51		11 01	11 11
Hackney Central	d	08 35	08 43	08 50	08 58	09 05	09 11	09 23		09 33	09 43	09 53		10 03	10 13	10 23		10 33	10 43	10 53		11 03	11 13
Dalston Kingsland	d	08 37	08 45	08 52	09 00	09 07	09 13	09 25		09 35	09 45	09 55		10 05	10 15	10 25		10 35	10 45	10 55		11 05	11 15
Canonbury	d	08 39	08 47	08 54	09 02	09 09	09 15	09 27		09 37	09 47	09 57		10 07	10 17	10 27		10 37	10 47	10 57		11 07	11 17
Highbury & Islington ⊖	d	08 42	08 50	08 57	09 05	09 12	09 18	09 30		09 40	09 50	10 00		10 10	10 20	10 30		10 40	10 50	11 00		11 10	11 20
Caledonian Rd & Barnsbury	d	08 44	08 52	08 59	09 07	09 14	09 20	09 32		09 42	09 52	10 02		10 12	10 22	10 32		10 42	10 52	11 02		11 12	11 22
Camden Road	d	08 47	08 55	09 02	09 10	09 17	09 23	09 35		09 45	09 55	10 05		10 15	10 25	10 35		10 45	10 55	11 05		11 15	11 25
Kentish Town West	d	08 49	08 59	09 04	09 12	09 19	09 25	09 37		09 47	09 57	10 07		10 17	10 27	10 37		10 47	10 57	11 07		11 17	11 27
Gospel Oak	d	08 52	09 02	09 08	09 15	09 22	09 27	09 40		09 50	10 00	10 10		10 20	10 30	10 40		10 50	11 00	11 10		11 20	11 30
Hampstead Heath	d	08 54	09 04	09 10	09 17	09 24	09 29	09 42		09 52	10 02	10 12		10 22	10 32	10 42		10 52	11 02	11 12		11 22	11 32
Finchley Road & Frognal	d	08 56	09 06	09 12	09 19	09 26	09 31	09 44		09 54	10 04	10 14		10 24	10 34	10 44		10 54	11 04	11 14		11 24	11 34
West Hampstead ⊖	d	08 58	09 08	09 14	09 21	09 28	09 33	09 46		09 56	10 06	10 16		10 26	10 36	10 46		10 56	11 06	11 16		11 26	11 36
Brondesbury	d	09 00	09 10	09 15	09 23	09 30	09 35	09 48		09 58	10 08	10 18		10 28	10 38	10 48		10 58	11 08	11 18		11 28	11 38
Brondesbury Park	d	09 01	09 11	09 17	09 24	09 31	09 36	09 49		09 59	10 09	10 19		10 29	10 39	10 49		10 59	11 09	11 19		11 29	11 39
Kensal Rise	d	09 03	09 13	09 19	09 26	09 33	09 38	09 51		10 01	10 11	10 21		10 31	10 41	10 51		11 01	11 11	11 21		11 31	11 41
Willesden Jn. High Level ⊖	a	09 07	09 16	09 23	09 30	09 37	09 42	09 55		10 05	10 15	10 25		10 35	10 45	10 55		11 05	11 15	11 25		11 35	11 44
	d	09 08	09 17	09 24	09 31	09 38	09 44	09 56	10 01	10 06	10 16	10 26	10 31	10 36	10 46	10 56	11 01	11 06	11 16	11 26	11 31	11 36	11 45
Willesden Jn Low Level ⊖	a																						
Shepherd's Bush ⊖	d		09 25		09 39		09 54		10 09		10 26		10 39		10 54		11 09		11 24		11 39		11 54
Kensington (Olympia) ⊖	d		09 27		09 41		09 56		10 11		10 28		10 41		10 56		11 11		11 26		11 41		11 56
West Brompton ⊖	d		09 29		09 43		09 58		10 13		10 30		10 43		10 58		11 13		11 28		11 43		11 58
Imperial Wharf	d		09 32		09 46		10 01		10 16		10 33		10 46		11 01		11 16		11 31		11 46		12 01
Clapham Junction 10	a		09 39		09 54		10 08		10 23		10 40		10 53		11 09		11 23		11 39		11 53		12 09
Acton Central	d	09 13		09 29		09 43		10 01		10 11		10 31		10 41		11 01		11 11		11 31		11 41	
South Acton	d	09 16		09 31		09 46		10 04		10 14		10 34		10 44		11 04		11 14		11 34		11 44	
Gunnersbury ⊖	d	09 19		09 37		09 49		10 08		10 19		10 38		10 48		11 08		11 18		11 38		11 48	
Kew Gardens ⊖	d	09 22		09 40		09 52		10 11		10 22		10 41		10 51		11 11		11 21		11 41		11 51	
Richmond ⊖	a	09 28		09 45		09 58		10 16		10 27		10 46		10 56		11 16		11 26		11 46		11 56	

Stratford - Highbury and Islington, West Hampstead, Willesden Junction, Clapham Junction and Richmond

Network Diagram - see first Page of Table 59

		LO	LO	LO	LO	LO	LO	LO	LO	LO	LO	LO	LO	LO	LO	LO	LO	LO	LO	LO	LO	LO	LO
Stratford 7 ⊖	d	11 15		11 25	11 37	11 45		11 55	12 05	12 15		12 25	12 35	12 45		12 55	13 05	13 15		13 25	13 35	13 45	
Hackney Wick	d	11 18		11 28	11 40	11 48		11 58	12 08	12 18		12 28	12 38	12 48		12 58	13 08	13 18		13 28	13 38	13 48	
Homerton	d	11 21		11 31	11 43	11 51		12 01	12 11	12 21		12 31	12 41	12 51		13 01	13 11	13 21		13 31	13 41	13 51	
Hackney Central	d	11 23		11 33	11 45	11 53		12 03	12 13	12 23		12 33	12 43	12 53		13 03	13 13	13 23		13 33	13 43	13 53	
Dalston Kingsland	d	11 25		11 35	11 47	11 55		12 05	12 15	12 25		12 35	12 45	12 55		13 05	13 15	13 25		13 35	13 45	13 55	
Canonbury	d	11 27		11 37	11 49	11 57		12 07	12 17	12 27		12 37	12 47	12 57		13 07	13 17	13 27		13 37	13 47	13 57	
Highbury & Islington ⊖	d	11 30		11 40	11 52	12 00		12 10	12 20	12 30		12 40	12 50	13 00		13 10	13 20	13 30		13 40	13 50	14 00	
Caledonian Rd & Barnsbury	d	11 32		11 42	11 54	12 02		12 12	12 22	12 32		12 42	12 52	13 02		13 12	13 22	13 32		13 42	13 52	14 02	
Camden Road	d	11 35		11 45	11 57	12 05		12 15	12 25	12 35		12 45	12 55	13 05		13 15	13 25	13 35		13 45	13 55	14 05	
Kentish Town West	d	11 37		11 47	11 59	12 07		12 17	12 27	12 37		12 47	12 57	13 07		13 17	13 27	13 37		13 47	13 57	14 07	
Gospel Oak	d	11 40		11 51	12 02	12 10		12 20	12 30	12 40		12 50	13 00	13 10		13 20	13 30	13 41		13 50	14 00	14 10	
Hampstead Heath	d	11 42		11 53	12 04	12 12		12 22	12 32	12 42		12 52	13 02	13 12		13 22	13 32	13 43		13 52	14 02	14 12	
Finchley Road & Frognal	d	11 44		11 55	12 06	12 14		12 24	12 34	12 44		12 54	13 04	13 14		13 24	13 34	13 45		13 54	14 04	14 14	
West Hampstead ⊖	d	11 46		11 57	12 08	12 16		12 26	12 36	12 46		12 56	13 06	13 16		13 26	13 36	13 47		13 56	14 06	14 16	
Brondesbury	d	11 48		11 59	12 10	12 18		12 28	12 38	12 48		12 58	13 08	13 18		13 28	13 38	13 49		13 58	14 08	14 18	
Brondesbury Park	d	11 49		12 00	12 11	12 19		12 29	12 39	12 49		12 59	13 09	13 19		13 29	13 39	13 50		13 59	14 09	14 19	
Kensal Rise	d	11 51		12 02	12 13	12 21		12 31	12 41	12 51		13 01	13 11	13 21		13 31	13 41	13 52		14 01	14 11	14 21	
Willesden Jn. High Level ⊖	a	11 55		12 06	12 16	12 25		12 35	12 45	12 55		13 05	13 15	13 25		13 35	13 45	13 56		14 05	14 15	14 25	
	d	11 56	12 01	12 07	12 17	12 26	12 31	12 36	12 46	12 56	13 01	13 06	13 16	13 26	13 31	13 36	13 46	13 57	14 01	14 06	14 16	14 26	14 31
Willesden Jn Low Level ⊖	a																						
Shepherd's Bush ⊖	d		12 09		12 25		12 39		12 54		13 09		13 24		13 39		13 54		14 09		14 24		14 39
Kensington (Olympia) ⊖	d		12 11		12 27		12 41		12 56		13 11		13 26		13 41		13 56		14 11		14 26		14 41
West Brompton ⊖	d		12 13		12 29		12 43		12 58		13 13		13 28		13 43		13 58		14 13		14 28		14 43
Imperial Wharf	d		12 16		12 32		12 46		13 01		13 16		13 31		13 46		14 01		14 16		14 31		14 46
Clapham Junction 10	a		12 23		12 40		12 55		13 08		13 25		13 38		13 55		14 09		14 23		14 39		14 53
Acton Central	d	12 01		12 12		12 31		12 41		13 01		13 11		13 31		13 41		14 02		14 11		14 31	
South Acton	d	12 04		12 15		12 34		12 44		13 04		13 14		13 34		13 44		14 05		14 14		14 34	
Gunnersbury ⊖	d	12 08		12 19		12 38		12 48		13 08		13 18		13 38		13 48		14 09		14 18		14 38	
Kew Gardens ⊖	d	12 11		12 22		12 41		12 51		13 11		13 21		13 41		13 51		14 12		14 21		14 41	
Richmond ⊖	a	12 16		12 27		12 46		12 56		13 16		13 26		13 46		13 56		14 17		14 26		14 46	

		LO	LO	LO	LO	LO	LO	LO	LO	LO	LO	LO	LO	LO	LO	LO	LO	LO	LO	LO	LO	LO	LO
Stratford 7 ⊖	d	13 55	14 05	14 15		14 25	14 35	14 45		14 55	15 05	15 15		15 25	15 35	15 42	15 50	15 59		16 12	16 20	16 27	16 35
Hackney Wick	d	13 58	14 08	14 18		14 28	14 38	14 48		14 58	15 08	15 18		15 28	15 38	15 45	15 53	16 02		16 15	16 23	16 30	16 38
Homerton	d	14 01	14 11	14 21		14 31	14 41	14 51		15 01	15 11	15 21		15 31	15 41	15 48	15 56	16 05		16 18	16 26	16 33	16 40
Hackney Central	d	14 03	14 13	14 23		14 33	14 43	14 53		15 03	15 13	15 23		15 33	15 43	15 50	15 58	16 07		16 20	16 28	16 35	16 42
Dalston Kingsland	d	14 05	14 15	14 25		14 35	14 45	14 55		15 05	15 15	15 25		15 35	15 45	15 52	16 00	16 09		16 22	16 30	16 37	16 44
Canonbury	d	14 07	14 17	14 27		14 37	14 47	14 57		15 07	15 17	15 27		15 37	15 47	15 54	16 02	16 11		16 24	16 32	16 39	16 46
Highbury & Islington ⊖	d	14 10	14 20	14 30		14 40	14 50	15 00		15 10	15 20	15 30		15 40	15 50	15 57	16 05	16 14		16 27	16 35	16 42	16 49
Caledonian Rd & Barnsbury	d	14 12	14 22	14 32		14 42	14 52	15 02		15 12	15 22	15 32		15 42	15 52	15 59	16 07	16 16		16 29	16 37	16 44	16 51
Camden Road	d	14 15	14 25	14 35		14 45	14 55	15 05		15 15	15 25	15 35		15 45	15 55	16 03	16 10	16 19		16 32	16 40	16 47	16 54
Kentish Town West	d	14 17	14 27	14 37		14 47	14 57	15 07		15 17	15 27	15 37		15 48	15 57	16 06	16 12	16 21		16 34	16 42	16 49	16 58
Gospel Oak	d	14 20	14 30	14 40		14 50	15 00	15 10		15 20	15 30	15 40		15 50	16 02	16 08	16 15	16 24		16 37	16 45	16 52	17 03
Hampstead Heath	d	14 22	14 32	14 42		14 52	15 02	15 12		15 22	15 32	15 42		15 52	16 04	16 10	16 17	16 26		16 39	16 47	16 54	17 05
Finchley Road & Frognal	d	14 24	14 34	14 44		14 54	15 04	15 14		15 24	15 34	15 44		15 54	16 06	16 12	16 19	16 28		16 41	16 49	16 56	17 07
West Hampstead ⊖	d	14 26	14 36	14 46		14 56	15 06	15 16		15 26	15 36	15 46		15 56	16 08	16 14	16 21	16 30		16 43	16 51	16 58	17 09
Brondesbury	d	14 28	14 38	14 48		14 58	15 08	15 18		15 28	15 38	15 48		15 58	16 10	16 15	16 23	16 32		16 45	16 53	17 00	17 10
Brondesbury Park	d	14 29	14 39	14 49		14 59	15 09	15 19		15 29	15 39	15 49		15 59	16 11	16 17	16 24	16 33		16 46	16 54	17 01	17 12
Kensal Rise	d	14 31	14 41	14 51		15 01	15 11	15 21		15 31	15 41	15 51		16 01	16 13	16 19	16 26	16 35		16 48	16 56	17 03	17 14
Willesden Jn. High Level ⊖	a	14 35	14 45	14 55		15 05	15 15	15 25		15 35	15 45	15 55		16 05	16 16	16 23	16 30	16 39		16 52	17 00	17 07	17 18
	d	14 36	14 46	14 56	15 01	15 06	15 16	15 26	15 31	15 36	15 46	15 56	16 01	16 06	16 17	16 24	16 31	16 40	16 46	16 53	17 01	17 08	17 19
Willesden Jn Low Level ⊖	a																						
Shepherd's Bush ⊖	d		14 54		15 09		15 26		15 39		15 54		16 09		16 25		16 39		16 53		17 09		17 26
Kensington (Olympia) ⊖	d		14 56		15 11		15 28		15 41		15 56		16 11		16 27		16 41		16 55		17 11		17 28
West Brompton ⊖	d		14 58		15 13		15 30		15 43		15 58		16 13		16 29		16 43		16 58		17 13		17 31
Imperial Wharf	d		15 01		15 16		15 33		15 46		16 01		16 16		16 32		16 46		17 01		17 16		17 34
Clapham Junction 10	a		15 09		15 23		15 40		15 53		16 09		16 23		16 39		16 54		17 07		17 24		17 39
Acton Central	d	14 41		15 01		15 11		15 31		15 41		16 01		16 11		16 29		16 45		16 58		17 13	
South Acton	d	14 44		15 04		15 14		15 34		15 44		16 04		16 14		16 31		16 48		17 01		17 16	
Gunnersbury ⊖	d	14 48		15 08		15 18		15 38		15 48		16 08		16 18		16 34		16 51		17 04		17 19	
Kew Gardens ⊖	d	14 51		15 11		15 21		15 41		15 51		16 11		16 21		16 37		16 54		17 07		17 22	
Richmond ⊖	a	14 56		15 16		15 26		15 46		15 56		16 16		16 27		16 43		17 00		17 13		17 28	

Table 59

Mondays to Fridays
from 10 September

Stratford - Highbury and Islington, West Hampstead, Willesden Junction, Clapham Junction and Richmond

Network Diagram - see first Page of Table 59

		LO	LO	LO	LO	LO	LO	LO	LO	LO	LO	LO	LO	LO	LO	LO	LO	LO	LO	LO	LO	LO	LO
Stratford [7] ⊖	d	16 42	16 50	16 57	17 05	17 12	17 21	17 27	17 36	17 42	17 51	17 57	18 05	18 12	18 20	18 27	18 35	18 42	18 48	18 57	19 05	19 15	
Hackney Wick	d	16 45	16 53	17 00	17 08	17 15	17 23	17 30	17 38	17 45	17 54	18 00	18 08	18 15	18 23	18 30	18 38	18 45	18 51	19 00	19 08	19 18	
Homerton	d	16 48	16 56	17 03	17 11	17 18	17 26	17 33	17 41	17 48	17 57	18 03	18 11	18 18	18 26	18 33	18 41	18 48	18 54	19 03	19 11	19 21	
Hackney Central	d	16 50	16 58	17 05	17 13	17 20	17 28	17 35	17 43	17 50	17 59	18 05	18 13	18 20	18 28	18 35	18 43	18 50	18 56	19 05	19 13	19 23	
Dalston Kingsland	d	16 52	17 00	17 07	17 15	17 22	17 30	17 37	17 45	17 52	18 01	18 07	18 15	18 22	18 31	18 37	18 45	18 52	18 58	19 07	19 15	19 25	
Canonbury	d	16 54	17 02	17 09	17 17	17 24	17 32	17 39	17 47	17 54	18 03	18 09	18 17	18 24	18 32	18 39	18 47	18 54	19 00	19 09	19 17	19 27	
Highbury & Islington ⊖	d	16 57	17 05	17 12	17 20	17 27	17 35	17 42	17 50	17 57	18 06	18 12	18 20	18 27	18 35	18 42	18 50	18 57	19 03	19 12	19 20	19 30	
Caledonian Rd & Barnsbury	d	16 59	17 07	17 14	17 22	17 29	17 37	17 44	17 52	17 59	18 08	18 14	18 22	18 29	18 37	18 44	18 52	18 59	19 05	19 14	19 22	19 32	
Camden Road	d	17 02	17 10	17 17	17 25	17 32	17 40	17 47	17 55	18 02	18 12	18 17	18 25	18 32	18 40	18 47	18 55	19 02	19 08	19 17	19 25	19 35	
Kentish Town West	d	17 04	17 13	17 19	17 27	17 34	17 42	17 49	17 58	18 05	18 15	18 19	18 27	18 34	18 42	18 49	18 57	19 05	19 10	19 19	19 27	19 37	
Gospel Oak	d	17 08	17 17	17 23	17 30	17 37	17 45	17 52	18 02	18 08	18 18	18 22	18 30	18 37	18 45	18 52	19 00	19 09	19 13	19 24	19 30	19 40	
Hampstead Heath	d	17 10	17 19	17 25	17 32	17 39	17 47	17 54	18 04	18 10	18 20	18 24	18 32	18 39	18 47	18 54	19 02	19 11	19 15	19 26	19 32	19 42	
Finchley Road & Frognal	d	17 12	17 21	17 27	17 34	17 41	17 49	17 56	18 06	18 12	18 22	18 26	18 34	18 41	18 49	18 56	19 04	19 13	19 17	19 28	19 34	19 44	
West Hampstead ⊖	d	17 14	17 23	17 29	17 36	17 43	17 51	17 58	18 08	18 14	18 24	18 28	18 36	18 43	18 51	18 58	19 06	19 15	19 19	19 30	19 36	19 46	
Brondesbury	d	17 16	17 25	17 30	17 38	17 45	17 53	18 00	18 09	18 16	18 26	18 30	18 38	18 45	18 53	19 00	19 08	19 16	19 21	19 32	19 38	19 48	
Brondesbury Park	d	17 17	17 26	17 32	17 39	17 46	17 54	18 01	18 11	18 17	18 27	18 31	18 39	18 46	18 54	19 01	19 09	19 18	19 22	19 33	19 39	19 49	
Kensal Rise	d	17 19	17 28	17 34	17 41	17 48	17 56	18 03	18 13	18 19	18 29	18 33	18 41	18 48	18 56	19 03	19 11	19 20	19 24	19 35	19 41	19 51	
Willesden Jn. High Level ⊖	a	17 23	17 31	17 38	17 45	17 52	18 00	18 07	18 17	18 23	18 32	18 37	18 45	18 52	19 00	19 07	19 15	19 24	19 30	19 39	19 45	19 55	
	d	17 24	17 32	17 39	17 46	17 53	18 01	18 08	18 18	18 24	18 33	18 38	18 46	18 53	19 01	19 08	19 16	19 25	19 31	19 40	19 46	19 56	20 01
Willesden Jn Low Level ⊖	a																						
Shepherd's Bush ⊖	d		17 40		17 54		18 09		18 25		18 41		18 54		19 09		19 23		19 39		19 54		20 09
Kensington (Olympia) ⊖	d		17 42		17 56		18 11		18 27		18 43		18 56		19 11		19 25		19 41		19 56		20 11
West Brompton ⊖	d		17 44		17 58		18 13		18 30		18 45		18 58		19 13		19 28		19 43		19 58		20 13
Imperial Wharf	d		17 47		18 01		18 16		18 33		18 48		19 01		19 16		19 31		19 46		20 01		20 16
Clapham Junction [10]	a		17 54		18 09		18 25		18 40		18 54		19 09		19 24		19 39		19 54		20 09		20 23
Acton Central	d	17 29		17 44		17 58		18 13		18 29		18 43		18 58		19 13		19 30		19 45		20 01	
South Acton	d	17 34		17 46		18 00		18 16		18 32		18 46		19 01		19 16		19 32		19 48		20 04	
Gunnersbury ⊖	d	17 39		17 49		18 03		18 19		18 38		18 49		19 06		19 19		19 38		19 51		20 09	
Kew Gardens ⊖	d	17 42		17 52		18 06		18 22		18 41		18 52		19 09		19 22		19 41		19 54		20 12	
Richmond ⊖	a	17 46		17 58		18 13		18 28		18 45		18 58		19 14		19 29		19 46		19 59		20 17	

		LO	LO	LO	LO	LO	LO	LO	LO	LO	LO	LO	LO	LO	LO	LO	LO	LO	LO	LO	LO	LO	LO
Stratford [7] ⊖	d	19 25	19 37	19 45		19 55	20 05	20 15		20 25	20 35	20 45		20 55	21 05	21 15		21 25	21 35	21 45		21 55	22 15
Hackney Wick	d	19 28	19 40	19 48		19 58	20 08	20 18		20 28	20 38	20 48		20 58	21 08	21 18		21 28	21 38	21 48		21 58	22 18
Homerton	d	19 31	19 43	19 51		20 01	20 11	20 21		20 31	20 41	20 51		21 01	21 11	21 21		21 31	21 41	21 51		22 01	22 21
Hackney Central	d	19 33	19 45	19 53		20 03	20 13	20 23		20 33	20 43	20 53		21 03	21 13	21 23		21 33	21 43	21 53		22 03	22 23
Dalston Kingsland	d	19 35	19 47	19 55		20 05	20 15	20 25		20 35	20 45	20 55		21 05	21 15	21 25		21 35	21 45	21 55		22 05	22 25
Canonbury	d	19 37	19 49	19 57		20 07	20 17	20 27		20 37	20 47	20 57		21 07	21 17	21 27		21 37	21 47	21 57		22 07	22 27
Highbury & Islington ⊖	d	19 40	19 52	20 00		20 10	20 20	20 30		20 40	20 50	21 00		21 10	21 20	21 30		21 40	21 50	22 00		22 10	22 30
Caledonian Rd & Barnsbury	d	19 42	19 54	20 02		20 12	20 22	20 32		20 42	20 52	21 02		21 12	21 22	21 32		21 42	21 52	22 02		22 12	22 32
Camden Road	d	19 45	19 57	20 05		20 15	20 25	20 35		20 45	20 55	21 05		21 15	21 25	21 35		21 45	21 55	22 05		22 15	22 35
Kentish Town West	d	19 47	19 59	20 07		20 18	20 27	20 37		20 47	20 57	21 07		21 17	21 27	21 37		21 47	21 57	22 07		22 17	22 37
Gospel Oak	d	19 50	20 01	20 10		20 22	20 30	20 40		20 50	21 00	21 10		21 20	21 30	21 40		21 50	22 00	22 10		22 20	22 40
Hampstead Heath	d	19 52	20 03	20 12		20 24	20 32	20 42		20 52	21 02	21 12		21 22	21 32	21 42		21 52	22 02	22 12		22 22	22 42
Finchley Road & Frognal	d	19 54	20 05	20 14		20 26	20 34	20 44		20 54	21 04	21 14		21 24	21 34	21 44		21 54	22 04	22 14		22 24	22 44
West Hampstead ⊖	d	19 56	20 07	20 16		20 28	20 36	20 46		20 56	21 06	21 16		21 26	21 36	21 46		21 56	22 06	22 16		22 26	22 46
Brondesbury	d	19 58	20 09	20 18		20 29	20 38	20 48		20 57	21 08	21 18		21 28	21 38	21 48		21 58	22 08	22 18		22 28	22 48
Brondesbury Park	d	19 59	20 10	20 19		20 31	20 39	20 49		20 59	21 09	21 19		21 29	21 39	21 49		21 59	22 09	22 19		22 29	22 49
Kensal Rise	d	20 01	20 12	20 21		20 33	20 41	20 51		21 01	21 11	21 21		21 31	21 41	21 51		22 01	22 11	22 21		22 31	22 51
Willesden Jn. High Level ⊖	a	20 05	20 16	20 25		20 36	20 45	20 55		21 05	21 15	21 25		21 35	21 45	21 55		22 05	22 15	22 25		22 35	22 55
	d	20 06	20 17	20 26	20 31	20 37	20 46	20 57	21 01	21 06	21 16	21 26	21 31	21 36	21 46	21 56	22 01	22 06	22 16	22 26	22 31	22 36	22 56
Willesden Jn Low Level ⊖	a																						
Shepherd's Bush ⊖	d		20 26		20 39		20 54		21 09		21 26		21 39		21 54		22 09		22 26		22 39		
Kensington (Olympia) ⊖	d		20 28		20 41		20 56		21 11		21 28		21 41		21 56		22 11		22 28		22 41		
West Brompton ⊖	d		20 30		20 43		20 58		21 13		21 31		21 43		21 58		22 13		22 30		22 43		
Imperial Wharf	d		20 33		20 46		21 01		21 16		21 34		21 46		22 01		22 16		22 33		22 46		
Clapham Junction [10]	a		20 41		20 53		21 09		21 23		21 41		21 53		22 09		22 23		22 40		22 53		
Acton Central	d	20 11		20 31		20 42		21 02		21 11		21 31		21 41		22 01		22 11		22 31		22 41	23 01
South Acton	d	20 14		20 34		20 44		21 05		21 13		21 34		21 44		22 04		22 14		22 34		22 44	23 04
Gunnersbury ⊖	d	20 18		20 38		20 49		21 08		21 18		21 38		21 48		22 08		22 18		22 38		22 48	23 08
Kew Gardens ⊖	d	20 21		20 41		20 52		21 11		21 21		21 41		21 51		22 11		22 21		22 41		22 51	23 11
Richmond ⊖	a	20 26		20 46		20 56		21 16		21 26		21 46		21 56		22 16		22 26		22 46		22 56	23 16

Table 59

Mondays to Fridays
from 10 September

Stratford - Highbury and Islington, West Hampstead, Willesden Junction, Clapham Junction and Richmond

Network Diagram - see first Page of Table 59

		LO	LO	LO	LO	LO	LO	LO
Stratford [7] ⊖	d	22 25		22 45	22 55	23 15		23 45
Hackney Wick	d	22 28		22 48	22 58	23 18		23 48
Homerton	d	22 31		22 51	23 01	23 21		23 51
Hackney Central	d	22 33		22 53	23 03	23 23		23 53
Dalston Kingsland	d	22 35		22 55	23 05	23 25		23 55
Canonbury	d	22 37		22 57	23 07	23 27		23 57
Highbury & Islington ⊖	d	22 40		23 00	23 10	23 30		23 59
Caledonian Rd & Barnsbury	d	22 42		23 02	23 12	23 32		00 02
Camden Road	d	22a46		23 05	23a16	23 35		00 05
Kentish Town West	d			23 07		23 37		00 07
Gospel Oak	d			23 10		23 40		00 10
Hampstead Heath	d			23 12		23 42		00 12
Finchley Road & Frognal	d			23 14		23 44		00 14
West Hampstead ⊖	d			23 16		23 46		00 16
Brondesbury	d			23 18		23 48		00 18
Brondesbury Park	d			23 19		23 49		00 19
Kensal Rise	d			23 21		23 51		00 21
Willesden Jn. High Level ⊖	a			23 25				
	d		23 01	23 26			23 40	
Willesden Jn Low Level ⊖	a					23 56		00 29
Shepherd's Bush ⊖	d		23 09				23 48	
Kensington (Olympia) ⊖	d		23 11				23 50	
West Brompton ⊖	d		23 13				23 52	
Imperial Wharf	d		23 16				23 55	
Clapham Junction [10]	a		23 23				00 02	
Acton Central	d			23 31				
South Acton	d			23 34				
Gunnersbury ⊖	d			23 38				
Kew Gardens ⊖	d			23 41				
Richmond ⊖	a			23 46				

Saturdays
until 21 July

		LO	LO	LO	LO	LO	LO	LO	LO	LO	LO	LO	LO	LO	LO	LO	LO	LO	LO	LO	LO	LO	LO
Stratford [7] ⊖	d		23p45			05 42		05 55	06 05	06 15		06 25	06 35	06 45		06 55	07 05	07 15		07 25	07 35	07 45	
Hackney Wick	d		23p48			05 45		05 58	06 08	06 18		06 28	06 38	06 48		06 58	07 08	07 18		07 28	07 38	07 48	
Homerton	d		23p51			05 48		06 01	06 11	06 21		06 31	06 41	06 51		07 01	07 11	07 21		07 31	07 41	07 51	
Hackney Central	d		23p53			05 50		06 03	06 13	06 23		06 33	06 43	06 53		07 03	07 13	07 23		07 33	07 43	07 53	
Dalston Kingsland	d		23p55			05 52		06 05	06 15	06 25		06 35	06 45	06 55		07 05	07 15	07 25		07 35	07 45	07 55	
Canonbury	d		23p57			05 54		06 07	06 17	06 27		06 37	06 47	06 57		07 07	07 17	07 27		07 37	07 47	07 57	
Highbury & Islington ⊖	d		23p59			05 57		06 10	06 20	06 30		06 40	06 50	07 00		07 10	07 20	07 30		07 40	07 50	08 00	
Caledonian Rd & Barnsbury	d		00 02			05 59		06 12	06 22	06 32		06 42	06 52	07 02		07 12	07 22	07 32		07 42	07 52	08 02	
Camden Road	d		00 05			06 02		06 15	06 25	06 35		06 45	06 55	07 05		07 15	07 25	07 35		07 45	07 55	08 05	
Kentish Town West	d		00 07			06 07		06 17	06 27	06 37		06 47	06 57	07 07		07 17	07 27	07 37		07 47	07 57	08 07	
Gospel Oak	d		00 10			06 11		06 20	06 30	06 40		06 50	07 00	07 10		07 20	07 30	07 40		07 50	08 00	08 10	
Hampstead Heath	d		00 12			06 13		06 22	06 32	06 42		06 52	07 02	07 12		07 22	07 32	07 42		07 52	08 02	08 12	
Finchley Road & Frognal	d		00 14			06 15		06 24	06 34	06 44		06 54	07 04	07 14		07 24	07 34	07 44		07 54	08 04	08 14	
West Hampstead ⊖	d		00 16			06 17		06 26	06 36	06 46		06 56	07 06	07 16		07 26	07 36	07 46		07 56	08 06	08 16	
Brondesbury	d		00 18			06 19		06 28	06 38	06 48		06 58	07 08	07 18		07 28	07 38	07 48		07 58	08 08	08 18	
Brondesbury Park	d		00 19			06 20		06 29	06 39	06 49		06 59	07 09	07 19		07 29	07 39	07 49		07 59	08 09	08 19	
Kensal Rise	d		00 21			06 22		06 31	06 41	06 51		07 01	07 11	07 21		07 31	07 41	07 51		08 01	08 11	08 21	
Willesden Jn. High Level ⊖	a					06 25		06 35	06 45	06 55		07 05	07 15	07 25		07 35	07 45	07 55		08 05	08 15	08 25	
	d	23p40		06 02	06 06	06 26	06 31	06 36	06 46	06 56	07 01	07 06	07 16	07 26	07 31	07 36	07 46	07 56	08 01	08 06	08 16	08 26	08 31
Willesden Jn Low Level ⊖	a		00 29																				
Shepherd's Bush ⊖	d	23p48		06 10			06 39		06 54		07 09		07 24		07 39		07 54		08 09		08 24		08 39
Kensington (Olympia) ⊖	d	23p50		06 12			06 41		06 56		07 11		07 26		07 41		07 56		08 11		08 26		08 41
West Brompton ⊖	d	23p52		06 14			06 43		06 58		07 13		07 28		07 43		07 58		08 13		08 28		08 43
Imperial Wharf	d	23p55		06 17			06 46		07 01		07 16		07 31		07 46		08 01		08 16		08 31		08 46
Clapham Junction [10]	a	00 02		06 25			06 53		07 09		07 23		07 39		07 53		08 09		08 23		08 39		08 53
Acton Central	d				06 11	06 31		06 41		07 01		07 11		07 31		07 41		08 01		08 11		08 31	
South Acton	d				06 14	06 34		06 44		07 04		07 14		07 34		07 44		08 04		08 14		08 34	
Gunnersbury ⊖	d				06 19	06 37		06 47		07 07		07 17		07 37		07 48		08 08		08 18		08 38	
Kew Gardens ⊖	d				06 22	06 40		06 50		07 10		07 20		07 40		07 51		08 11		08 21		08 41	
Richmond ⊖	a				06 29	06 44		06 56		07 16		07 26		07 46		07 56		08 16		08 26		08 46	

Stratford - Highbury and Islington, West Hampstead, Willesden Junction, Clapham Junction and Richmond

Network Diagram - see first Page of Table 59

		LO	LO	LO	LO	LO	LO	LO	LO	LO	LO	LO	LO	LO	LO	LO	LO	LO	LO	LO	LO	LO	LO
Stratford [7]	⊖ d	07 55	08 05	08 15		08 25	08 35	08 45		08 55	09 05	09 15		09 25	09 35	09 45		09 55	10 05	10 15		10 25	10 35
Hackney Wick	d	07 58	08 08	08 18		08 28	08 38	08 48		08 58	09 08	09 18		09 28	09 38	09 48		09 58	10 08	10 18		10 28	10 38
Homerton	d	08 01	08 11	08 21		08 31	08 41	08 51		09 01	09 11	09 21		09 31	09 41	09 51		10 01	10 11	10 21		10 31	10 41
Hackney Central	d	08 03	08 13	08 23		08 33	08 43	08 53		09 03	09 13	09 23		09 33	09 43	09 53		10 03	10 13	10 23		10 33	10 43
Dalston Kingsland	d	08 05	08 15	08 25		08 35	08 45	08 55		09 05	09 15	09 25		09 35	09 45	09 55		10 05	10 15	10 25		10 35	10 45
Canonbury	d	08 07	08 17	08 27		08 37	08 47	08 57		09 07	09 17	09 27		09 37	09 47	09 57		10 07	10 17	10 27		10 37	10 47
Highbury & Islington	⊖ d	08 10	08 20	08 30		08 40	08 50	09 00		09 10	09 20	09 30		09 40	09 50	10 00		10 10	10 20	10 30		10 40	10 50
Caledonian Rd & Barnsbury	d	08 12	08 22	08 32		08 42	08 52	09 02		09 12	09 22	09 32		09 42	09 52	10 02		10 12	10 22	10 32		10 42	10 52
Camden Road	d	08 15	08 25	08 35		08 45	08 55	09 05		09 15	09 25	09 35		09 45	09 55	10 05		10 15	10 25	10 35		10 45	10 55
Kentish Town West	d	08 17	08 27	08 37		08 47	08 57	09 07		09 17	09 27	09 37		09 47	09 57	10 07		10 17	10 27	10 37		10 47	10 57
Gospel Oak	d	08 20	08 30	08 40		08 50	09 00	09 10		09 20	09 30	09 40		09 50	10 00	10 10		10 20	10 30	10 40		10 50	11 00
Hampstead Heath	d	08 22	08 32	08 42		08 52	09 02	09 12		09 22	09 32	09 42		09 52	10 02	10 12		10 22	10 32	10 42		10 52	11 02
Finchley Road & Frognal	d	08 24	08 34	08 44		08 54	09 04	09 14		09 24	09 34	09 44		09 54	10 04	10 14		10 24	10 34	10 44		10 54	11 04
West Hampstead	⊖ d	08 26	08 36	08 46		08 56	09 06	09 16		09 26	09 36	09 46		09 56	10 06	10 16		10 26	10 36	10 46		10 56	11 06
Brondesbury	d	08 28	08 38	08 48		08 58	09 08	09 18		09 28	09 38	09 48		09 58	10 08	10 18		10 28	10 38	10 48		10 58	11 08
Brondesbury Park	d	08 29	08 39	08 49		08 59	09 09	09 19		09 29	09 39	09 49		09 59	10 09	10 19		10 29	10 39	10 49		10 59	11 09
Kensal Rise	d	08 31	08 41	08 51		09 01	09 11	09 21		09 31	09 41	09 51		10 01	10 11	10 21		10 31	10 41	10 51		11 01	11 11
Willesden Jn. High Level	⊖ a	08 35	08 45	08 55		09 05	09 15	09 25		09 35	09 45	09 55		10 05	10 15	10 25		10 35	10 45	10 55		11 05	11 15
	d	08 36	08 46	08 56	09 01	09 06	09 16	09 26	09 31	09 36	09 46	09 56	10 01	10 06	10 16	10 26	10 31	10 36	10 46	10 56	11 01	11 06	11 16
Willesden Jn Low Level	⊖ a																						
Shepherd's Bush	⊖ d		08 54		09 09		09 24		09 39		09 54		10 09		10 24		10 39		10 54		11 09		11 24
Kensington (Olympia)	⊖ d		08 56		09 11		09 26		09 41		09 56		10 11		10 26		10 41		10 56		11 11		11 26
West Brompton	⊖ d		08 58		09 13		09 28		09 43		09 58		10 13		10 28		10 43		10 58		11 13		11 28
Imperial Wharf	d		09 01		09 16		09 31		09 46		10 01		10 16		10 31		10 46		11 01		11 16		11 31
Clapham Junction [10]	a		09 09		09 23		09 39		09 53		10 09		10 23		10 39		10 53		11 09		11 23		11 39
Acton Central	d	08 41		09 01		09 11		09 31		09 41		10 01		10 11		10 31		10 41		11 01		11 11	
South Acton	d	08 44		09 04		09 14		09 34		09 44		10 04		10 14		10 34		10 45		11 04		11 14	
Gunnersbury	⊖ d	08 48		09 08		09 18		09 38		09 48		10 08		10 18		10 38		10 48		11 08		11 18	
Kew Gardens	⊖ d	08 51		09 11		09 21		09 41		09 51		10 11		10 21		10 41		10 51		11 11		11 21	
Richmond	⊖ a	08 56		09 16		09 26		09 46		09 56		10 16		10 26		10 46		10 56		11 16		11 26	

		LO	LO	LO	LO	LO	LO	LO	LO	LO	LO	LO	LO	LO	LO	LO	LO	LO	LO	LO	LO	LO	LO
Stratford [7]	⊖ d	10 45		10 55	11 05	11 15		11 25	11 35	11 45		11 55	12 05	12 15		12 25	12 35	12 45		12 55	13 05	13 15	
Hackney Wick	d	10 48		10 58	11 08	11 18		11 28	11 38	11 48		11 58	12 08	12 18		12 28	12 38	12 48		12 58	13 08	13 18	
Homerton	d	10 51		11 01	11 11	11 21		11 31	11 41	11 51		12 01	12 11	12 21		12 31	12 41	12 51		13 01	13 11	13 21	
Hackney Central	d	10 53		11 03	11 13	11 23		11 33	11 43	11 53		12 03	12 13	12 23		12 33	12 43	12 53		13 03	13 13	13 23	
Dalston Kingsland	d	10 55		11 05	11 15	11 25		11 35	11 45	11 55		12 05	12 15	12 25		12 35	12 45	12 55		13 05	13 15	13 25	
Canonbury	d	10 57		11 07	11 17	11 27		11 37	11 47	11 57		12 07	12 17	12 27		12 37	12 47	12 57		13 07	13 17	13 27	
Highbury & Islington	⊖ d	11 00		11 10	11 20	11 30		11 40	11 50	12 00		12 10	12 20	12 30		12 40	12 50	13 00		13 10	13 20	13 30	
Caledonian Rd & Barnsbury	d	11 02		11 12	11 22	11 32		11 42	11 52	12 02		12 12	12 22	12 32		12 42	12 52	13 02		13 12	13 22	13 32	
Camden Road	d	11 05		11 15	11 25	11 35		11 45	11 55	12 05		12 15	12 25	12 35		12 45	12 55	13 05		13 15	13 25	13 35	
Kentish Town West	d	11 07		11 17	11 27	11 37		11 47	11 57	12 07		12 17	12 27	12 37		12 47	12 57	13 07		13 17	13 27	13 37	
Gospel Oak	d	11 10		11 20	11 30	11 40		11 50	12 00	12 10		12 20	12 30	12 40		12 50	13 00	13 10		13 20	13 30	13 40	
Hampstead Heath	d	11 12		11 22	11 32	11 42		11 52	12 02	12 12		12 22	12 32	12 42		12 52	13 02	13 12		13 22	13 32	13 42	
Finchley Road & Frognal	d	11 14		11 24	11 34	11 44		11 54	12 04	12 14		12 24	12 34	12 44		12 54	13 04	13 14		13 24	13 34	13 44	
West Hampstead	⊖ d	11 16		11 26	11 36	11 46		11 56	12 06	12 16		12 26	12 36	12 46		12 56	13 06	13 16		13 26	13 36	13 46	
Brondesbury	d	11 18		11 28	11 38	11 48		11 58	12 08	12 18		12 28	12 38	12 48		12 58	13 08	13 18		13 28	13 38	13 48	
Brondesbury Park	d	11 19		11 29	11 39	11 49		11 59	12 09	12 19		12 29	12 39	12 49		12 59	13 09	13 19		13 29	13 39	13 49	
Kensal Rise	d	11 21		11 31	11 41	11 51		12 01	12 11	12 21		12 31	12 41	12 51		13 01	13 11	13 21		13 31	13 41	13 51	
Willesden Jn. High Level	⊖ a	11 25		11 35	11 45	11 55		12 05	12 15	12 25		12 35	12 45	12 55		13 05	13 15	13 25		13 35	13 45	13 55	
	d	11 26	11 31	11 36	11 46	11 56	12 01	12 06	12 16	12 26	12 31	12 36	12 46	12 56	13 01	13 06	13 16	13 26	13 31	13 36	13 46	13 56	14 01
Willesden Jn Low Level	⊖ a																						
Shepherd's Bush	⊖ d		11 39		11 54		12 09		12 24		12 39		12 54		13 09		13 24		13 39		13 54		14 09
Kensington (Olympia)	⊖ d		11 41		11 56		12 11		12 26		12 41		12 56		13 11		13 26		13 41		13 56		14 11
West Brompton	⊖ d		11 43		11 58		12 13		12 28		12 43		12 58		13 13		13 28		13 43		13 58		14 13
Imperial Wharf	d		11 46		12 01		12 16		12 31		12 46		13 01		13 16		13 31		13 46		14 01		14 16
Clapham Junction [10]	a		11 53		12 09		12 23		12 39		12 53		13 09		13 23		13 39		13 55		14 09		14 23
Acton Central	d	11 31		11 41		12 01		12 11		12 31		12 41		13 01		13 11		13 31		13 41		14 01	
South Acton	d	11 34		11 44		12 04		12 14		12 34		12 44		13 04		13 14		13 34		13 44		14 04	
Gunnersbury	⊖ d	11 38		11 48		12 08		12 18		12 38		12 48		13 08		13 18		13 38		13 48		14 08	
Kew Gardens	⊖ d	11 41		11 51		12 11		12 21		12 41		12 51		13 11		13 21		13 41		13 51		14 11	
Richmond	⊖ a	11 46		11 56		12 16		12 26		12 46		12 56		13 16		13 26		13 46		13 56		14 16	

Stratford - Highbury and Islington, West Hampstead, Willesden Junction, Clapham Junction and Richmond

Network Diagram - see first Page of Table 59

		LO	LO	LO	LO		LO	LO	LO	LO	LO	LO	LO	LO	LO	LO	LO	LO	LO	LO	LO	LO
Stratford [7]	⊖ d	13 25	13 35	13 45				17 55	18 05	18 15		18 25	18 35	18 45		18 55	19 05	19 15		19 25	19 35	19 45
Hackney Wick	d	13 28	13 38	13 48				17 58	18 08	18 18		18 28	18 38	18 48		18 58	19 08	19 18		19 28	19 38	19 48
Homerton	d	13 31	13 41	13 51				18 01	18 11	18 21		18 31	18 41	18 51		19 01	19 11	19 21		19 31	19 41	19 51
Hackney Central	d	13 33	13 43	13 53				18 03	18 13	18 23		18 33	18 43	18 53		19 03	19 13	19 23		19 33	19 43	19 53
Dalston Kingsland	d	13 35	13 45	13 55				18 05	18 15	18 25		18 35	18 45	18 55		19 05	19 15	19 25		19 35	19 45	19 55
Canonbury	d	13 37	13 47	13 57				18 07	18 17	18 27		18 37	18 47	18 57		19 07	19 17	19 27		19 37	19 47	19 57
Highbury & Islington	⊖ d	13 40	13 50	14 00				18 10	18 20	18 30		18 40	18 50	19 00		19 10	19 20	19 30		19 40	19 50	20 00
Caledonian Rd & Barnsbury	d	13 42	13 52	14 02				18 12	18 22	18 32		18 42	18 52	19 02		19 12	19 22	19 32		19 42	19 52	20 02
Camden Road	d	13 45	13 55	14 05				18 15	18 25	18 35		18 45	18 55	19 05		19 15	19 25	19 35		19 45	19 55	20 05
Kentish Town West	d	13 47	13 57	14 07				18 17	18 27	18 37		18 47	18 57	19 07		19 17	19 27	19 37		19 47	19 57	20 07
Gospel Oak	d	13 50	14 00	14 10				18 20	18 30	18 40		18 50	19 00	19 10		19 20	19 30	19 40		19 50	20 00	20 10
Hampstead Heath	d	13 52	14 02	14 12		and at the same minutes past each hour until		18 22	18 32	18 42		18 52	19 02	19 12		19 22	19 32	19 42		19 52	20 02	20 12
Finchley Road & Frognal	d	13 54	14 04	14 14				18 24	18 34	18 44		18 54	19 04	19 14		19 24	19 34	19 44		19 54	20 04	20 14
West Hampstead	⊖ d	13 56	14 06	14 16				18 26	18 36	18 46		18 56	19 06	19 16		19 26	19 36	19 46		19 56	20 06	20 16
Brondesbury	d	13 58	14 08	14 18				18 28	18 38	18 48		18 58	19 08	19 18		19 28	19 38	19 48		19 58	20 08	20 18
Brondesbury Park	d	13 59	14 09	14 19				18 29	18 39	18 49		18 59	19 09	19 19		19 29	19 39	19 49		19 59	20 09	20 19
Kensal Rise	d	14 01	14 11	14 21				18 31	18 41	18 51		19 01	19 11	19 21		19 31	19 41	19 51		20 01	20 11	20 21
Willesden Jn. High Level	⊖ a	14 05	14 15	14 25				18 35	18 45	18 55		19 05	19 15	19 25		19 35	19 45	19 55		20 05	20 15	20 25
	d	14 06	14 16	14 26	14 31		18 31	18 36	18 46	18 56	19 01	19 05	19 16	19 26	19 31	19 36	19 46	19 56	20 01	20 06	20 16	20 26
Willesden Jn Low Level	⊖ a																					
Shepherd's Bush	⊖ d		14 24		14 39		18 39		18 54		19 09		19 24		19 39		19 54		20 09		20 24	
Kensington (Olympia)	⊖ d		14 26		14 41		18 41		18 56		19 11		19 26		19 41		19 56		20 11		20 26	
West Brompton	⊖ d		14 28		14 43		18 43		18 58		19 13		19 28		19 43		19 58		20 13		20 28	
Imperial Wharf	d		14 31		14 46		18 46		19 01		19 16		19 31		19 46		20 01		20 16		20 31	
Clapham Junction [10]	a		14 39		14 53		18 53		19 09		19 23		19 39		19 53		20 09		20 23		20 39	
Acton Central	d	14 11		14 31				18 41		19 01		19 10		19 31		19 41		20 01		20 11		20 31
South Acton	d	14 14		14 34				18 44		19 04		19 13		19 34		19 44		20 04		20 14		20 34
Gunnersbury	⊖ d	14 18		14 38				18 48		19 08		19 17		19 38		19 48		20 08		20 18		20 38
Kew Gardens	⊖ d	14 21		14 41				18 51		19 11		19 20		19 41		19 51		20 11		20 21		20 41
Richmond	⊖ a	14 26		14 46				18 56		19 17		19 27		19 47		19 57		20 17		20 27		20 47

		LO	LO	LO	LO	LO	LO	LO	LO	LO	LO	LO	LO	LO	LO	LO	LO	LO	LO	LO	LO	LO	LO
Stratford [7]	⊖ d		19 55	20 05	20 15		20 25	20 35	20 45		20 55	21 05	21 15		21 25	21 35	21 45		21 55	22 15	22 25		22 45
Hackney Wick	d		19 58	20 08	20 18		20 28	20 38	20 48		20 58	21 08	21 18		21 28	21 38	21 48		21 58	22 18	22 28		22 48
Homerton	d		20 01	20 11	20 21		20 31	20 41	20 51		21 01	21 11	21 21		21 31	21 41	21 51		22 01	22 21	22 31		22 51
Hackney Central	d		20 03	20 13	20 23		20 33	20 43	20 53		21 03	21 13	21 23		21 33	21 43	21 53		22 03	22 23	22 33		22 53
Dalston Kingsland	d		20 05	20 15	20 25		20 35	20 45	20 55		21 05	21 15	21 25		21 35	21 45	21 55		22 05	22 25	22 35		22 55
Canonbury	d		20 07	20 17	20 27		20 37	20 47	20 57		21 07	21 17	21 27		21 37	21 47	21 57		22 07	22 27	22 37		22 57
Highbury & Islington	⊖ d		20 10	20 20	20 30		20 40	20 50	21 00		21 10	21 20	21 30		21 40	21 50	22 00		22 10	22 30	22 40		23 00
Caledonian Rd & Barnsbury	d		20 12	20 22	20 32		20 42	20 52	21 02		21 12	21 22	21 32		21 42	21 52	22 02		22 12	22 32	22 42		23 02
Camden Road	d		20 15	20 25	20 35		20 45	20 55	21 05		21 15	21 25	21 35		21 45	21 55	22 05		22 15	22 35	22a45		23 05
Kentish Town West	d		20 17	20 27	20 37		20 47	20 57	21 07		21 17	21 27	21 37		21 47	21 57	22 07		22 17	22 37			23 07
Gospel Oak	d		20 20	20 30	20 40		20 50	21 00	21 10		21 20	21 30	21 40		21 50	22 00	22 10		22 20	22 40			23 10
Hampstead Heath	d		20 22	20 32	20 42		20 52	21 02	21 12		21 22	21 32	21 42		21 52	22 02	22 12		22 22	22 42			23 12
Finchley Road & Frognal	d		20 24	20 34	20 44		20 54	21 04	21 14		21 24	21 34	21 44		21 54	22 04	22 14		22 24	22 44			23 14
West Hampstead	⊖ d		20 26	20 36	20 46		20 56	21 06	21 16		21 26	21 36	21 46		21 56	22 06	22 16		22 26	22 46			23 16
Brondesbury	d		20 28	20 38	20 48		20 58	21 08	21 18		21 28	21 38	21 48		21 58	22 08	22 18		22 28	22 48			23 18
Brondesbury Park	d		20 29	20 39	20 49		20 59	21 09	21 19		21 29	21 39	21 49		21 59	22 09	22 19		22 29	22 49			23 19
Kensal Rise	d		20 31	20 41	20 51		21 01	21 11	21 21		21 31	21 41	21 51		22 01	22 11	22 21		22 31	22 51			23 21
Willesden Jn. High Level	⊖ a		20 35	20 45	20 55		21 05	21 15	21 25		21 35	21 45	21 55		22 05	22 15	22 25		22 35	22 55			23 25
	d	20 31	20 36	20 46	20 56	21 01	21 06	21 16	21 26	21 31	21 36	21 46	21 56	22 01	22 06	22 16	22 26	22 31	22 36	22 56		23 01	23 26
Willesden Jn Low Level	⊖ a																						
Shepherd's Bush	⊖ d	20 39		20 54		21 11		21 24		21 39		21 54		22 11		22 24		22 39				23 09	
Kensington (Olympia)	⊖ d	20 41		20 56		21 13		21 26		21 41		21 56		22 13		22 26		22 41				23 11	
West Brompton	⊖ d	20 43		20 58		21 15		21 28		21 43		21 58		22 15		22 28		22 43				23 13	
Imperial Wharf	d	20 46		21 01		21 18		21 31		21 46		22 01		22 18		22 31		22 46				23 16	
Clapham Junction [10]	a	20 53		21 09		21 25		21 39		21 53		22 09		22 25		22 39		22 53				23 23	
Acton Central	d		20 41		21 01		21 11		21 31		21 41		22 01		22 11		22 31		22 41	23 01			23 31
South Acton	d		20 44		21 04		21 14		21 34		21 44		22 04		22 14		22 34		22 44	23 04			23 34
Gunnersbury	⊖ d		20 48		21 08		21 18		21 38		21 48		22 08		22 18		22 38		22 48	23 08			23 38
Kew Gardens	⊖ d		20 51		21 11		21 21		21 41		21 51		22 11		22 21		22 41		22 51	23 11			23 41
Richmond	⊖ a		20 57		21 17		21 27		21 47		21 57		22 17		22 27		22 47		22 57	23 17			23 47

Table 59

Stratford - Highbury and Islington, West Hampstead, Willesden Junction, Clapham Junction and Richmond

Saturdays
until 21 July

Network Diagram - see first Page of Table 59

			LO	LO	LO
Stratford 7	⊖	d	22 55	23 15	23 45
Hackney Wick		d	22 58	23 18	23 48
Homerton		d	23 01	23 21	23 51
Hackney Central		d	23 03	23 23	23 53
Dalston Kingsland		d	23 05	23 25	23 55
Canonbury		d	23 07	23 27	23 57
Highbury & Islington	⊖	d	23 10	23 30	23 59
Caledonian Rd & Barnsbury		d	23 12	23 32	00 02
Camden Road		d	23a15	23 35	00 05
Kentish Town West		d		23 37	00 07
Gospel Oak		d		23 40	00 10
Hampstead Heath		d		23 42	00 12
Finchley Road & Frognal		d		23 44	00 14
West Hampstead	⊖	d		23 46	00 16
Brondesbury		d		23 48	00 18
Brondesbury Park		d		23 49	00 19
Kensal Rise		d		23 51	00 21
Willesden Jn. High Level	⊖	a		23 54	
		d			
Willesden Jn Low Level	⊖	a			00 29
Shepherd's Bush	⊖	d			
Kensington (Olympia)	⊖	d			
West Brompton	⊖	d			
Imperial Wharf		d			
Clapham Junction 10		a			
Acton Central		d			
South Acton		d			
Gunnersbury	⊖	d			
Kew Gardens	⊖	d			
Richmond	⊖	a			

Saturdays
28 July to 11 August

			LO	LO	LO	LO	LO	LO	LO	LO	LO	LO	LO	LO	LO	LO	LO	LO	LO	LO	LO	LO	LO	LO
Stratford 7	⊖	d	22p52	23p02	23p07	23p15	23p22	23p30	23p38	23p45	23p52	00 01	00 07	00 15	00 22	00 30	00 37	00 45	00 52	01 00			05 47	
Hackney Wick		d	22p55	23p05	23p10	23p18	23p25	23p33	23p41	23p48	23p55	00 03	00 10	00 20	00 25	00 33	00 40	00 48	00 55	01 03			05 50	
Homerton		d	22p58	23p06	23p13	23p21	23p28	23p36	23p44	23p51	23p58	00 06	00 13	00 21	00 28	00 36	00 43	00 50	00 58	01 06			05 53	
Hackney Central		d	23p00	23p08	23p15	23p23	23p30	23p38	23p46	23p53	23p59	00 08	00 15	00 23	00 30	00 38	00 45	00 52	01 00	01 08			05 55	
Dalston Kingsland		d	23p02	23p10	23p17	23p25	23p32	23p40	23p48	23p55	00 02	00 10	00 17	00 25	00 32	00 40	00 47	00 54	01 02	01 10			05 57	
Canonbury		d	23p04	23p12	23p19	23p27	23p34	23p42	23p50	23p57	00 04	00 12	00 19	00 27	00 34	00 42	00 49	00 56	01 04	01 12			05 59	
Highbury & Islington	⊖	d	23p08	23p16	23p23	23p31	23p38	23p46	23p53	00 01	00 08	00 16	00 23	00 31	00 38	00 46	00 53	00 59	01 08	01 17			06 02	
Caledonian Rd & Barnsbury		d	23p10	23p18	23p25	23p33	23p40	23p48	23p55	00 03	00 10	00 18	00 25	00 33	00 40	00 48	00 55	01 01	01 10	01 19			06 04	
Camden Road		d	23p14	23p22	23p29	23p37	23p44	23p53	23p59	00 07	00 14	00 22	00a34	00 37	00a49	00 52	01a04	01 05	01a21	01 23			06 07	
Kentish Town West		d	23p16	23p24	23p31	23p39	23p46	23p55	00 02	00 09	00 16	00 24		00 39		00 55		01 08		01 26			06 11	
Gospel Oak		d	23p19	23p27	23p34	23p42	23p49	23p59	00 05	00 12	00 19	00 28		00 43		00 57		01 10		01 28			06 13	
Hampstead Heath		d	23p21	23p29	23p36	23p44	23p51	00 01	00 07	00 14	00 21	00 30		00 45		00 59		01 12		01 30			06 15	
Finchley Road & Frognal		d	23p23	23p31	23p38	23p46	23p53	00 03	00 09	00 16	00 23	00 32		00 47		01 01		01 14		01 32			06 17	
West Hampstead	⊖	d	23p25	23p33	23p40	23p48	23p55	00 05	00 11	00 18	00 25	00 34		00 49		01 03		01 17		01 35			06 19	
Brondesbury		d	23p27	23p35	23p42	23p50	23p57	00 06	00 13	00 20	00 27	00 36		00 51		01 05		01 18		01 36			06 20	
Brondesbury Park		d	23p28	23p36	23p43	23p51	23p58	00 08	00 14	00 21	00 28	00 37		00 52		01 06		01 20		01 38			06 22	
Kensal Rise		d	23p30	23p38	23p45	23p53	00 01	00 10	00 16	00 23	00 30	00 39		00 54		01 08		01 22		01 40			06 24	
Willesden Jn. High Level	⊖	a	23p35	23p42	23p49	23p57	00 04	00 13	00 20	00 27	00 34	00 42											06 27	
		d	23p36	23p43	23p50	23p59	00 05	00 14	00 21	00 28	00 35	00 43									06 02	06 06	06 28	06 33
Willesden Jn Low Level	⊖	a												01 01		01 21		01 41		01 50				
Shepherd's Bush	⊖	d		23p57		00 09		00 24		00 38		00 53									06 09			06 41
Kensington (Olympia)	⊖	d		23p59		00 11		00 26		00 41		00 56									06 11			06 43
West Brompton	⊖	d		00 02		00 14		00 29		00 43		00 58									06 14			06 46
Imperial Wharf		d		00 05		00 17		00 32		00 46		01 01									06 17			06 49
Clapham Junction 10		a		00 13		00 22		00 39		00 54		01 09									06 23			06 56
Acton Central		d	23p41		23p55		00 10		00 26		00 40											06 11	06 33	
South Acton		d	23p43		23p58		00 13		00 29		00 43											06 14	06 35	
Gunnersbury	⊖	d	23p48		00 02		00 18		00 33		00 47											06 18	06 42	
Kew Gardens	⊖	d	23p51		00 05		00 21		00 36		00 50											06 21	06 45	
Richmond	⊖	a	00 01		00 14		00 30		00 45		00 59											06 31	06 55	

Table 59

Saturdays
28 July to 11 August

Stratford - Highbury and Islington, West Hampstead, Willesden Junction, Clapham Junction and Richmond

Network Diagram - see first Page of Table 59

			LO	LO	LO	LO	LO	LO	LO	LO	LO	LO	LO	LO	LO	LO	LO	LO	LO	LO	LO	LO	LO	LO
Stratford 7	⊖	d		06 00	06 07	06 15	06 24	06 30	06 37	06 45	06 52	07 02	07 07	07 15	07 22	07 30	07 37	07 45	07 52	08 00	08 07	08 15	08 22	08 30
Hackney Wick		d		06 04	06 10	06 18	06 29	06 33	06 40	06 48	06 58	07 05	07 10	07 18	07 25	07 33	07 40	07 48	07 55	08 03	08 10	08 18	08 25	08 33
Homerton		d		06 06	06 13	06 19	06 31	06 36	06 43	06 49	07 00	07 06	07 13	07 21	07 28	07 36	07 43	07 51	07 58	08 06	08 13	08 21	08 28	08 36
Hackney Central		d		06 08	06 15	06 21	06 33	06 38	06 45	06 51	07 02	07 08	07 15	07 23	07 30	07 38	07 45	07 53	08 00	08 08	08 15	08 23	08 30	08 38
Dalston Kingsland		d		06 10	06 17	06 23	06 35	06 40	06 47	06 54	07 05	07 10	07 17	07 25	07 32	07 40	07 47	07 55	08 02	08 10	08 17	08 25	08 32	08 40
Canonbury		d		06 12	06 19	06 25	06 37	06 42	06 49	06 56	07 07	07 12	07 19	07 27	07 34	07 42	07 49	07 57	08 04	08 12	08 19	08 27	08 34	08 42
Highbury & Islington	⊖	d		06 16	06 23	06 28	06 41	06 46	06 53	06 58	07 10	07 16	07 23	07 31	07 38	07 46	07 53	08 01	08 08	08 16	08 23	08 31	08 38	08 46
Caledonian Rd & Barnsbury		d		06 18	06 25	06 30	06 43	06 48	06 55	07 01	07 12	07 18	07 25	07 33	07 40	07 48	07 55	08 03	08 10	08 18	08 25	08 33	08 40	08 48
Camden Road		d		06 22	06 29	06 34	06 46	06 52	06 59	07 04	07 16	07 22	07 29	07 37	07 44	07 52	07 59	08 07	08 14	08 22	08 29	08 37	08 44	08 52
Kentish Town West		d		06 24	06 31	06 36	06 48	06 54	07 01	07 07	07 19	07 24	07 31	07 39	07 46	07 54	08 01	08 09	08 16	08 24	08 31	08 39	08 47	08 54
Gospel Oak		d		06 27	06 34	06 39	06 50	06 57	07 04	07 11	07 21	07 27	07 34	07 42	07 49	07 57	08 04	08 12	08 19	08 27	08 34	08 44	08 51	08 58
Hampstead Heath		d		06 29	06 36	06 41	06 52	06 59	07 06	07 13	07 23	07 29	07 36	07 44	07 51	07 59	08 06	08 14	08 21	08 29	08 36	08 46	08 53	09 00
Finchley Road & Frognal		d		06 31	06 38	06 43	06 54	07 01	07 08	07 15	07 25	07 31	07 38	07 46	07 53	08 01	08 08	08 16	08 23	08 31	08 38	08 48	08 55	09 02
West Hampstead	⊖	d		06 33	06 40	06 45	06 56	07 03	07 10	07 17	07 28	07 33	07 40	07 48	07 55	08 03	08 10	08 18	08 25	08 33	08 40	08 50	08 57	09 04
Brondesbury		d		06 35	06 42	06 47	06 58	07 05	07 12	07 19	07 29	07 35	07 42	07 50	07 57	08 05	08 12	08 20	08 27	08 35	08 42	08 52	08 59	09 05
Brondesbury Park		d		06 36	06 43	06 48	06 59	07 06	07 13	07 20	07 31	07 36	07 43	07 51	07 58	08 06	08 13	08 21	08 28	08 36	08 43	08 53	09 00	09 07
Kensal Rise		d		06 38	06 45	06 50	07 01	07 08	07 15	07 22	07 33	07 38	07 45	07 53	08 00	08 08	08 15	08 23	08 30	08 38	08 45	08 55	09 02	09 09
Willesden Jn. High Level	⊖	a		06 42	06 49	06 55	07 05	07 12	07 19	07 26	07 36	07 42	07 49	07 57	08 04	08 12	08 19	08 27	08 34	08 42	08 49	08 58	09 06	09 12
		d	06 41	06 43	06 50	06 56	07 06	07 13	07 20	07 27	07 37	07 43	07 50	07 58	08 05	08 13	08 20	08 28	08 35	08 43	08 50	08 59	09 07	09 13
Willesden Jn Low Level	⊖	a																						
Shepherd's Bush	⊖	d		06 53		07 08		07 23		07 38		07 53		08 08		08 23		08 38		08 53		09 09		09 23
Kensington (Olympia)	⊖	d		06 56		07 11		07 26		07 41		07 56		08 11		08 26		08 41		08 56		09 12		09 26
West Brompton	⊖	d		06 58		07 13		07 28		07 43		07 58		08 13		08 28		08 43		08 58		09 14		09 28
Imperial Wharf		d		07 01		07 16		07 31		07 46		08 01		08 16		08 31		08 46		09 01		09 17		09 31
Clapham Junction 10		a		07 09		07 24		07 39		07 54		08 09		08 24		08 39		08 54		09 09		09 25		09 39
Acton Central		d	06 46		06 55		07 11		07 25		07 42		07 55		08 10		08 25		08 40		08 55		09 12	
South Acton		d	06 49		06 58		07 14		07 28		07 45		07 58		08 13		08 28		08 43		08 58		09 14	
Gunnersbury	⊖	d	06 52		07 02		07 18		07 32		07 48		08 02		08 18		08 32		08 48		09 02		09 18	
Kew Gardens	⊖	d	06 55		07 05		07 21		07 35		07 51		08 05		08 21		08 35		08 51		09 05		09 21	
Richmond	⊖	a	07 05		07 15		07 30		07 45		08 01		08 15		08 31		08 45		09 01		09 15		09 31	

			LO	LO	LO	LO	LO	LO	LO	LO	LO	LO	LO	LO	LO	LO	LO	LO	LO	LO	LO	LO	LO	LO
Stratford 7	⊖	d	08 37	08 45	08 52	09 00	09 07	09 15	09 22	09 30	09 37	09 45	09 52	10 00	10 07	10 15	10 22	10 30	10 37	10 45	10 52	11 00	11 07	11 15
Hackney Wick		d	08 40	08 48	08 55	09 04	09 10	09 18	09 25	09 33	09 40	09 48	09 55	10 03	10 10	10 18	10 25	10 33	10 40	10 48	10 55	11 03	11 10	11 18
Homerton		d	08 43	08 51	08 58	09 06	09 13	09 21	09 28	09 36	09 43	09 51	09 58	10 06	10 13	10 21	10 28	10 36	10 43	10 51	10 58	11 06	11 13	11 21
Hackney Central		d	08 45	08 53	09 00	09 08	09 15	09 23	09 30	09 38	09 45	09 53	10 00	10 08	10 15	10 23	10 30	10 38	10 45	10 53	11 00	11 08	11 15	11 23
Dalston Kingsland		d	08 47	08 55	09 02	09 10	09 17	09 25	09 32	09 40	09 47	09 55	10 02	10 10	10 17	10 25	10 32	10 40	10 47	10 55	11 02	11 10	11 17	11 25
Canonbury		d	08 49	08 57	09 04	09 12	09 19	09 27	09 34	09 42	09 49	09 57	10 04	10 12	10 19	10 27	10 34	10 42	10 49	10 57	11 04	11 12	11 19	11 27
Highbury & Islington	⊖	d	08 53	09 01	09 08	09 16	09 23	09 31	09 38	09 46	09 53	10 01	10 08	10 16	10 23	10 31	10 38	10 46	10 53	11 01	11 08	11 16	11 23	11 31
Caledonian Rd & Barnsbury		d	08 55	09 03	09 10	09 18	09 25	09 33	09 40	09 48	09 55	10 03	10 10	10 18	10 25	10 33	10 40	10 48	10 55	11 03	11 10	11 18	11 25	11 33
Camden Road		d	08 59	09 07	09 14	09 22	09 29	09 37	09 44	09 52	09 59	10 07	10 14	10 22	10 29	10 37	10 44	10 52	10 59	11 07	11 14	11 22	11 29	11 37
Kentish Town West		d	09 02	09 09	09 16	09 24	09 31	09 39	09 46	09 54	10 01	10 09	10 16	10 24	10 31	10 39	10 46	10 54	11 01	11 09	11 16	11 24	11 31	11 39
Gospel Oak		d	09 04	09 12	09 19	09 28	09 35	09 42	09 49	09 57	10 04	10 12	10 19	10 27	10 34	10 42	10 49	10 57	11 04	11 12	11 19	11 27	11 34	11 42
Hampstead Heath		d	09 06	09 14	09 21	09 30	09 37	09 44	09 51	09 59	10 06	10 14	10 21	10 29	10 36	10 44	10 51	10 59	11 06	11 14	11 21	11 29	11 36	11 44
Finchley Road & Frognal		d	09 08	09 16	09 23	09 32	09 39	09 46	09 53	10 01	10 08	10 16	10 23	10 31	10 38	10 46	10 53	11 01	11 08	11 16	11 23	11 31	11 38	11 46
West Hampstead	⊖	d	09 10	09 18	09 25	09 34	09 41	09 48	09 55	10 03	10 10	10 18	10 25	10 33	10 40	10 48	10 55	11 03	11 10	11 18	11 25	11 33	11 40	11 48
Brondesbury		d	09 12	09 20	09 27	09 36	09 42	09 50	09 57	10 05	10 12	10 20	10 27	10 35	10 42	10 50	10 57	11 05	11 12	11 20	11 27	11 35	11 42	11 50
Brondesbury Park		d	09 13	09 21	09 28	09 37	09 44	09 51	09 58	10 06	10 13	10 21	10 28	10 36	10 43	10 51	10 58	11 06	11 13	11 21	11 28	11 36	11 43	11 51
Kensal Rise		d	09 15	09 23	09 30	09 39	09 46	09 53	10 00	10 08	10 15	10 23	10 30	10 38	10 45	10 53	11 00	11 08	11 15	11 23	11 30	11 38	11 45	11 53
Willesden Jn. High Level	⊖	a	09 19	09 27	09 34	09 43	09 49	09 57	10 04	10 12	10 19	10 27	10 34	10 42	10 49	10 58	11 04	11 12	11 19	11 27	11 34	11 42	11 49	11 57
		d	09 20	09 28	09 35	09 44	09 50	09 58	10 05	10 13	10 20	10 28	10 35	10 43	10 50	10 59	11 05	11 13	11 20	11 28	11 35	11 43	11 50	11 58
Willesden Jn Low Level	⊖	a																						
Shepherd's Bush	⊖	d		09 38		09 54		10 08		10 23		10 38		10 53		11 09		11 23		11 38		11 53		12 08
Kensington (Olympia)	⊖	d		09 41		09 56		10 11		10 26		10 41		10 56		11 11		11 26		11 41		11 56		12 11
West Brompton	⊖	d		09 43		09 59		10 13		10 28		10 43		10 58		11 14		11 28		11 43		11 58		12 13
Imperial Wharf		d		09 46		10 02		10 16		10 31		10 46		11 01		11 17		11 31		11 46		12 01		12 16
Clapham Junction 10		a		09 54		10 10		10 24		10 39		10 54		11 09		11 25		11 39		11 54		12 09		12 24
Acton Central		d	09 25		09 40		09 55		10 10		10 25		10 40		10 55		11 10		11 25		11 40		11 55	
South Acton		d	09 28		09 43		09 57		10 13		10 28		10 43		10 58		11 13		11 28		11 43		11 58	
Gunnersbury	⊖	d	09 32		09 48		10 02		10 18		10 32		10 48		11 02		11 19		11 32		11 49		12 02	
Kew Gardens	⊖	d	09 35		09 51		10 05		10 21		10 35		10 51		11 05		11 22		11 35		11 52		12 05	
Richmond	⊖	a	09 44		10 01		10 15		10 31		10 45		11 01		11 15		11 31		11 45		12 01		12 15	

Stratford - Highbury and Islington, West Hampstead, Willesden Junction, Clapham Junction and Richmond

Network Diagram - see first Page of Table 59

		LO	LO	LO	LO	LO	LO	LO	LO	LO	LO	LO	LO	LO	LO	LO	LO	LO	LO	LO	LO	LO	LO
Stratford [7] ⊖	d	11 22	11 30	11 37	11 45	11 52	12 00	12 07	12 15	12 22	12 27	12 37	12 45	12 52	13 00	13 07	13 15	13 22	13 30	13 37	13 45	13 52	14 00
Hackney Wick	d	11 25	11 33	11 40	11 48	11 55	12 03	12 10	12 18	12 25	12 30	12 40	12 48	12 55	13 03	13 10	13 18	13 25	13 33	13 40	13 48	13 55	14 03
Homerton	d	11 28	11 36	11 43	11 51	11 58	12 06	12 13	12 21	12 28	12 31	12 43	12 50	12 58	13 06	13 13	13 21	13 28	13 36	13 43	13 51	13 58	14 06
Hackney Central	d	11 30	11 38	11 45	11 53	12 00	12 08	12 15	12 23	12 30	12 33	12 45	12 52	13 00	13 08	13 15	13 23	13 30	13 38	13 45	13 53	14 00	14 08
Dalston Kingsland	d	11 32	11 40	11 47	11 55	12 02	12 10	12 17	12 25	12 32	12 35	12 47	12 54	13 02	13 10	13 17	13 25	13 32	13 40	13 47	13 55	14 02	14 10
Canonbury	d	11 34	11 42	11 49	11 57	12 04	12 12	12 19	12 27	12 34	12 37	12 49	12 56	13 04	13 12	13 19	13 27	13 34	13 42	13 49	13 57	14 04	14 12
Highbury & Islington ⊖	d	11 38	11 46	11 53	12 01	12 08	12 16	12 23	12 31	12 38	12 40	12 53	12 59	13 06	13 16	13 23	13 31	13 38	13 46	13 53	14 01	14 08	14 16
Caledonian Rd & Barnsbury	d	11 40	11 48	11 55	12 03	12 10	12 18	12 25	12 33	12 40	12 42	12 55	13 01	13 08	13 18	13 25	13 33	13 40	13 48	13 55	14 03	14 10	14 18
Camden Road	d	11 44	11 52	11 59	12 07	12 14	12 22	12 29	12 37	12 44	12 46	12 59	13 04	13 11	13 22	13 29	13 37	13 44	13 52	13 59	14 07	14 14	14 22
Kentish Town West	d	11 46	11 54	12 01	12 09	12 16	12 24	12 31	12 39	12 46	12 49	13 01	13 07	13 14	13 24	13 31	13 39	13 46	13 54	14 01	14 09	14 16	14 24
Gospel Oak	d	11 49	11 57	12 04	12 12	12 19	12 27	12 34	12 42	12 49	12 51	13 04	13 09	13 17	13 27	13 34	13 42	13 49	13 57	14 04	14 12	14 19	14 27
Hampstead Heath	d	11 51	11 59	12 06	12 14	12 21	12 29	12 36	12 44	12 51	12 53	13 06	13 11	13 19	13 29	13 36	13 44	13 51	13 59	14 06	14 14	14 21	14 29
Finchley Road & Frognal	d	11 53	12 01	12 08	12 16	12 23	12 31	12 38	12 46	12 53	12 55	13 08	13 13	13 21	13 31	13 38	13 46	13 53	14 01	14 08	14 16	14 23	14 31
West Hampstead ⊖	d	11 55	12 03	12 10	12 18	12 25	12 33	12 40	12 48	12 55	12 58	13 10	13 16	13 24	13 33	13 40	13 48	13 55	14 03	14 10	14 18	14 25	14 33
Brondesbury	d	11 57	12 05	12 12	12 20	12 27	12 35	12 42	12 50	12 57	12 59	13 12	13 17	13 25	13 35	13 42	13 50	13 57	14 05	14 12	14 20	14 27	14 35
Brondesbury Park	d	11 58	12 06	12 13	12 21	12 28	12 36	12 43	12 51	12 58	13 01	13 13	13 19	13 27	13 36	13 43	13 51	13 58	14 06	14 13	14 21	14 28	14 36
Kensal Rise	d	12 00	12 08	12 15	12 23	12 30	12 38	12 45	12 53	13 00	13 03	13 15	13 21	13 29	13 38	13 45	13 53	14 00	14 08	14 15	14 23	14 30	14 38
Willesden Jn. High Level ⊖	a	12 04	12 12	12 19	12 27	12 34	12 42	12 49	12 57	13 04	13 07	13 19	13 26	13 33	13 42	13 49	13 57	14 04	14 12	14 19	14 27	14 34	14 42
	d	12 05	12 13	12 20	12 28	12 35	12 43	12 50	12 58	13 05	13 10	13 20	13 27	13 34	13 43	13 50	13 58	14 05	14 13	14 20	14 28	14 35	14 43
Willesden Jn Low Level ⊖	a																						
Shepherd's Bush ⊖	d		12 23		12 38		12 53		13 08		13 23		13 38		13 53		14 08		14 23		14 38		14 53
Kensington (Olympia) ⊖	d		12 26		12 41		12 56		13 11		13 26		13 41		13 56		14 11		14 26		14 41		14 56
West Brompton ⊖	d		12 28		12 43		12 58		13 13		13 28		13 43		13 58		14 13		14 28		14 43		14 58
Imperial Wharf	d		12 31		12 46		13 01		13 16		13 31		13 46		14 01		14 16		14 31		14 46		15 01
Clapham Junction [10]	a		12 39		12 54		13 09		13 24		13 39		13 54		14 09		14 24		14 39		14 54		15 09
Acton Central	d	12 10		12 25		12 40		12 55		13 10		13 25		13 40		13 55		14 10		14 25		14 40	
South Acton	d	12 13		12 28		12 43		12 58		13 13		13 28		13 43		13 58		14 13		14 28		14 43	
Gunnersbury ⊖	d	12 18		12 32		12 48		13 02		13 18		13 32		13 48		14 02		14 18		14 32		14 48	
Kew Gardens ⊖	d	12 21		12 35		12 51		13 05		13 21		13 35		13 51		14 05		14 21		14 35		14 51	
Richmond ⊖	a	12 31		12 45		13 01		13 15		13 31		13 45		14 01		14 15		14 31		14 45		15 01	

		LO	LO	LO	LO	LO	LO	LO	LO	LO	LO	LO	LO	LO	LO	LO	LO	LO	LO	LO	LO	LO	LO
Stratford [7] ⊖	d	14 07	14 15	14 22	14 30	14 37	14 45	14 52	15 00	15 07	15 15	15 22	15 30	15 37	15 45	15 52	16 00	16 07	16 15	16 22	16 32	16 37	16 45
Hackney Wick	d	14 10	14 18	14 25	14 33	14 40	14 48	14 55	15 03	15 10	15 18	15 25	15 33	15 40	15 48	15 55	16 03	16 10	16 18	16 25	16 35	16 40	16 48
Homerton	d	14 13	14 21	14 28	14 36	14 43	14 51	14 58	15 06	15 13	15 21	15 28	15 36	15 43	15 51	15 58	16 06	16 13	16 21	16 28	16 37	16 43	16 51
Hackney Central	d	14 15	14 23	14 30	14 38	14 45	14 53	15 00	15 08	15 15	15 23	15 30	15 38	15 45	15 53	16 00	16 08	16 15	16 23	16 30	16 39	16 45	16 53
Dalston Kingsland	d	14 17	14 25	14 32	14 40	14 47	14 55	15 02	15 10	15 17	15 25	15 32	15 40	15 47	15 55	16 02	16 10	16 17	16 25	16 32	16 41	16 47	16 55
Canonbury	d	14 19	14 27	14 34	14 42	14 49	14 57	15 04	15 12	15 19	15 27	15 34	15 42	15 49	15 57	16 04	16 12	16 19	16 27	16 34	16 43	16 49	16 57
Highbury & Islington ⊖	d	14 23	14 31	14 38	14 46	14 53	15 01	15 08	15 16	15 23	15 31	15 38	15 46	15 53	16 01	16 08	16 16	16 23	16 31	16 38	16 46	16 53	17 01
Caledonian Rd & Barnsbury	d	14 25	14 33	14 40	14 48	14 55	15 03	15 10	15 18	15 25	15 33	15 40	15 48	15 55	16 03	16 10	16 18	16 25	16 33	16 40	16 48	16 55	17 03
Camden Road	d	14 29	14 37	14 44	14 52	14 59	15 07	15 14	15 22	15 29	15 37	15 44	15 52	15 59	16 07	16 14	16 22	16 29	16 37	16 44	16 52	16 59	17 07
Kentish Town West	d	14 31	14 39	14 46	14 54	15 01	15 09	15 16	15 24	15 31	15 39	15 46	15 54	16 01	16 09	16 16	16 24	16 31	16 39	16 46	16 55	17 01	17 09
Gospel Oak	d	14 34	14 42	14 49	14 57	15 04	15 12	15 19	15 27	15 34	15 42	15 49	15 57	16 04	16 12	16 19	16 27	16 34	16 42	16 49	16 57	17 04	17 12
Hampstead Heath	d	14 36	14 44	14 51	14 59	15 06	15 14	15 21	15 29	15 36	15 44	15 51	15 59	16 06	16 14	16 21	16 29	16 36	16 44	16 51	16 59	17 06	17 14
Finchley Road & Frognal	d	14 38	14 46	14 53	15 01	15 08	15 16	15 23	15 31	15 38	15 46	15 53	16 01	16 08	16 16	16 23	16 31	16 38	16 46	16 53	17 01	17 08	17 16
West Hampstead ⊖	d	14 40	14 48	14 55	15 03	15 10	15 18	15 25	15 33	15 40	15 48	15 55	16 03	16 10	16 18	16 25	16 33	16 40	16 48	16 55	17 03	17 10	17 18
Brondesbury	d	14 42	14 50	14 57	15 05	15 12	15 20	15 27	15 35	15 42	15 50	15 57	16 05	16 12	16 20	16 27	16 35	16 42	16 50	16 57	17 04	17 12	17 20
Brondesbury Park	d	14 43	14 51	14 58	15 06	15 13	15 21	15 28	15 36	15 43	15 51	15 58	16 06	16 13	16 21	16 28	16 36	16 43	16 51	16 58	17 06	17 13	17 21
Kensal Rise	d	14 45	14 53	15 00	15 08	15 15	15 23	15 30	15 38	15 45	15 53	16 00	16 08	16 15	16 23	16 30	16 38	16 45	16 53	17 00	17 08	17 15	17 23
Willesden Jn. High Level ⊖	a	14 49	14 57	15 04	15 12	15 19	15 27	15 34	15 42	15 49	15 57	16 04	16 12	16 19	16 27	16 34	16 42	16 49	16 57	17 04	17 12	17 19	17 27
	d	14 50	14 58	15 05	15 13	15 20	15 28	15 35	15 43	15 50	15 58	16 05	16 13	16 20	16 28	16 35	16 43	16 50	16 58	17 05	17 13	17 20	17 28
Willesden Jn Low Level ⊖	a																						
Shepherd's Bush ⊖	d		15 08		15 23		15 38		15 53		16 08		16 23		16 38		16 53		17 08		17 23		17 38
Kensington (Olympia) ⊖	d		15 11		15 26		15 41		15 56		16 11		16 26		16 41		16 56		17 11		17 26		17 41
West Brompton ⊖	d		15 13		15 28		15 43		15 58		16 13		16 28		16 43		16 58		17 13		17 28		17 43
Imperial Wharf	d		15 16		15 31		15 46		16 01		16 16		16 31		16 46		17 01		17 16		17 31		17 46
Clapham Junction [10]	a		15 24		15 39		15 54		16 09		16 24		16 39		16 54		17 09		17 24		17 39		17 54
Acton Central	d	14 55		15 10		15 25		15 40		15 55		16 10		16 25		16 40		16 55		17 10		17 25	
South Acton	d	14 58		15 13		15 28		15 43		15 58		16 13		16 28		16 43		16 58		17 13		17 28	
Gunnersbury ⊖	d	15 02		15 18		15 32		15 48		16 02		16 18		16 32		16 48		17 02		17 18		17 32	
Kew Gardens ⊖	d	15 05		15 21		15 35		15 51		16 05		16 21		16 35		16 51		17 05		17 21		17 35	
Richmond ⊖	a	15 15		15 31		15 45		16 01		16 15		16 31		16 45		17 01		17 15		17 31		17 45	

Stratford - Highbury and Islington, West Hampstead, Willesden Junction, Clapham Junction and Richmond

Network Diagram - see first Page of Table 59

		LO	LO	LO	LO	LO	LO	LO	LO	LO	LO	LO	LO	LO	LO	LO	LO	LO	LO	LO	LO	LO	LO
Stratford [7] ⊖	d	16 52	17 00	17 07	17 15	17 22	17 30	17 37	17 45	17 52	18 00	18 07	18 15	18 22	18 30	18 37	18 45	18 52	19 00	19 07	19 15	19 22	19 30
Hackney Wick	d	16 55	17 03	17 10	17 18	17 25	17 33	17 40	17 48	17 55	18 03	18 10	18 18	18 25	18 33	18 40	18 48	18 55	19 03	19 10	19 18	19 25	19 33
Homerton	d	16 58	17 06	17 13	17 21	17 28	17 36	17 43	17 51	17 58	18 06	18 13	18 21	18 28	18 36	18 43	18 51	18 58	19 06	19 13	19 21	19 28	19 36
Hackney Central	d	17 00	17 08	17 15	17 23	17 30	17 38	17 45	17 53	18 00	18 08	18 15	18 23	18 30	18 38	18 45	18 53	19 00	19 08	19 15	19 23	19 30	19 38
Dalston Kingsland	d	17 02	17 10	17 17	17 25	17 32	17 40	17 47	17 55	18 02	18 10	18 17	18 25	18 32	18 40	18 47	18 55	19 02	19 10	19 17	19 25	19 32	19 40
Canonbury	d	17 04	17 12	17 19	17 27	17 34	17 42	17 49	17 57	18 04	18 12	18 19	18 27	18 34	18 42	18 49	18 57	19 04	19 12	19 19	19 27	19 34	19 42
Highbury & Islington ⊖	d	17 08	17 16	17 23	17 31	17 38	17 46	17 53	18 01	18 08	18 16	18 23	18 31	18 38	18 46	18 53	19 01	19 08	19 16	19 23	19 31	19 38	19 46
Caledonian Rd & Barnsbury	d	17 10	17 18	17 25	17 33	17 40	17 48	17 55	18 03	18 10	18 18	18 25	18 33	18 40	18 48	18 55	19 03	19 10	19 18	19 25	19 33	19 40	19 48
Camden Road	d	17 14	17 22	17 29	17 37	17 44	17 52	17 59	18 07	18 14	18 22	18 29	18 37	18 44	18 52	18 59	19 07	19 14	19 22	19 28	19 37	19 44	19 52
Kentish Town West	d	17 16	17 24	17 31	17 39	17 46	17 54	18 01	18 09	18 16	18 24	18 31	18 39	18 46	18 54	19 01	19 09	19 16	19 24	19 31	19 39	19 46	19 54
Gospel Oak	d	17 19	17 27	17 34	17 42	17 49	17 57	18 04	18 12	18 19	18 27	18 33	18 42	18 49	18 57	19 04	19 12	19 19	19 27	19 33	19 42	19 49	19 57
Hampstead Heath	d	17 21	17 29	17 36	17 44	17 51	17 59	18 06	18 14	18 21	18 29	18 35	18 44	18 51	18 59	19 06	19 14	19 21	19 29	19 35	19 44	19 51	19 59
Finchley Road & Frognal	d	17 23	17 31	17 38	17 46	17 53	18 01	18 08	18 16	18 23	18 31	18 37	18 46	18 53	19 01	19 08	19 16	19 23	19 31	19 37	19 46	19 53	20 01
West Hampstead ⊖	d	17 25	17 33	17 40	17 48	17 55	18 03	18 10	18 18	18 25	18 33	18 39	18 48	18 55	19 03	19 10	19 18	19 25	19 33	19 40	19 48	19 55	20 03
Brondesbury	d	17 27	17 35	17 42	17 50	17 57	18 05	18 12	18 20	18 27	18 35	18 41	18 50	18 57	19 05	19 12	19 20	19 27	19 35	19 41	19 50	19 57	20 05
Brondesbury Park	d	17 28	17 36	17 43	17 51	17 58	18 06	18 13	18 21	18 28	18 36	18 42	18 51	18 58	19 06	19 13	19 21	19 28	19 36	19 43	19 51	19 58	20 06
Kensal Rise	d	17 30	17 38	17 45	17 53	18 00	18 08	18 15	18 23	18 30	18 38	18 44	18 53	19 00	19 08	19 15	19 23	19 30	19 38	19 45	19 53	20 00	20 08
Willesden Jn. High Level ⊖	a	17 34	17 42	17 49	17 57	18 04	18 12	18 19	18 27	18 34	18 42	18 48	18 57	19 04	19 12	19 19	19 27	19 34	19 42	19 49	19 57	20 04	20 12
	d	17 35	17 43	17 50	17 58	18 05	18 13	18 20	18 28	18 35	18 43	18 49	18 58	19 05	19 13	19 20	19 28	19 35	19 43	19 50	19 58	20 05	20 13
Willesden Jn Low Level ⊖	a																						
Shepherd's Bush ⊖	d		17 53		18 08		18 23		18 38		18 53		19 08		19 23		19 38		19 53		20 08		20 23
Kensington (Olympia) ⊖	d		17 56		18 11		18 26		18 41		18 56		19 11		19 26		19 41		19 56		20 11		20 26
West Brompton ⊖	d		17 58		18 13		18 28		18 43		18 58		19 13		19 28		19 43		19 58		20 13		20 28
Imperial Wharf	d		18 01		18 16		18 31		18 46		19 01		19 16		19 31		19 46		20 01		20 16		20 31
Clapham Junction [10]	a		18 09		18 24		18 39		18 54		19 09		19 24		19 39		19 54		20 09		20 24		20 39
Acton Central	d	17 40		17 55		18 10		18 25		18 40		18 54		19 10		19 25		19 40		19 55		20 11	
South Acton	d	17 43		17 58		18 13		18 28		18 43		18 57		19 13		19 28		19 43		19 58		20 14	
Gunnersbury ⊖	d	17 48		18 02		18 18		18 32		18 48		19 02		19 18		19 32		19 48		20 02		20 18	
Kew Gardens ⊖	d	17 51		18 05		18 21		18 35		18 51		19 05		19 21		19 35		19 51		20 05		20 21	
Richmond ⊖	a	18 01		18 15		18 31		18 45		19 01		19 15		19 31		19 45		20 01		20 15		20 31	

		LO	LO	LO	LO	LO	LO	LO	LO	LO	LO	LO	LO	LO	LO	LO	LO	LO	LO	LO	LO	LO	LO
Stratford [7] ⊖	d	19 37	19 45	19 52	20 00	20 07	20 15	20 22	20 30	20 37	20 45	20 52	21 00	21 07	21 15	21 22	21 30	21 37	21 45	21 52	22 00	22 07	22 15
Hackney Wick	d	19 40	19 48	19 55	20 03	20 10	20 18	20 25	20 33	20 40	20 48	20 55	21 03	21 10	21 18	21 25	21 33	21 40	21 48	21 55	22 03	22 10	22 18
Homerton	d	19 43	19 51	19 58	20 06	20 13	20 21	20 28	20 36	20 43	20 51	20 58	21 06	21 13	21 21	21 28	21 36	21 43	21 51	21 58	22 06	22 13	22 21
Hackney Central	d	19 45	19 53	20 00	20 08	20 15	20 23	20 30	20 38	20 45	20 53	21 00	21 08	21 15	21 23	21 30	21 38	21 45	21 53	22 00	22 08	22 15	22 23
Dalston Kingsland	d	19 47	19 55	20 02	20 10	20 17	20 25	20 32	20 40	20 47	20 55	21 02	21 10	21 17	21 25	21 32	21 40	21 47	21 55	22 02	22 10	22 17	22 25
Canonbury	d	19 49	19 57	20 04	20 12	20 19	20 27	20 34	20 42	20 49	20 57	21 04	21 12	21 19	21 27	21 34	21 42	21 49	21 57	22 04	22 12	22 19	22 27
Highbury & Islington ⊖	d	19 53	20 01	20 08	20 16	20 23	20 31	20 38	20 46	20 53	21 01	21 08	21 16	21 23	21 31	21 38	21 46	21 53	22 01	22 08	22 16	22 23	22 31
Caledonian Rd & Barnsbury	d	19 55	20 03	20 10	20 18	20 25	20 33	20 40	20 48	20 55	21 03	21 10	21 18	21 25	21 33	21 40	21 48	21 55	22 03	22 10	22 18	22 25	22 33
Camden Road	d	19 59	20 07	20 14	20 22	20 29	20 37	20 44	20 52	20 59	21 07	21 14	21 22	21 29	21 37	21 44	21 52	21 59	22 07	22 14	22 21	22 28	22 37
Kentish Town West	d	20 01	20 09	20 16	20 24	20 31	20 39	20 46	20 54	21 01	21 09	21 16	21 24	21 31	21 39	21 46	21 54	22 01	22 09	22 16	22 23	22 30	22 39
Gospel Oak	d	20 04	20 12	20 19	20 27	20 34	20 42	20 49	20 57	21 04	21 12	21 19	21 27	21 34	21 42	21 49	21 57	22 04	22 12	22 19	22 26	22 33	22 42
Hampstead Heath	d	20 06	20 14	20 21	20 29	20 36	20 44	20 51	20 59	21 06	21 14	21 21	21 29	21 36	21 44	21 51	21 59	22 06	22 14	22 21	22 28	22 35	22 44
Finchley Road & Frognal	d	20 08	20 16	20 23	20 31	20 38	20 46	20 53	21 01	21 08	21 16	21 23	21 31	21 38	21 46	21 53	22 01	22 08	22 16	22 23	22 30	22 37	22 46
West Hampstead ⊖	d	20 10	20 18	20 25	20 33	20 40	20 48	20 55	21 03	21 10	21 18	21 25	21 33	21 40	21 48	21 55	22 03	22 10	22 18	22 25	22 32	22 39	22 48
Brondesbury	d	20 12	20 20	20 27	20 35	20 42	20 50	20 57	21 05	21 12	21 20	21 27	21 35	21 42	21 50	21 57	22 05	22 12	22 20	22 27	22 34	22 40	22 50
Brondesbury Park	d	20 13	20 21	20 28	20 36	20 43	20 51	20 58	21 06	21 13	21 21	21 28	21 36	21 43	21 51	21 58	22 06	22 13	22 21	22 28	22 35	22 42	22 51
Kensal Rise	d	20 15	20 23	20 30	20 38	20 45	20 53	21 00	21 08	21 15	21 23	21 30	21 38	21 45	21 53	22 00	22 08	22 15	22 23	22 30	22 37	22 44	22 53
Willesden Jn. High Level ⊖	a	20 19	20 27	20 34	20 42	20 49	20 57	21 04	21 12	21 19	21 27	21 34	21 42	21 49	21 57	22 04	22 12	22 19	22 27	22 34	22 40	22 47	22 57
	d	20 20	20 28	20 35	20 43	20 50	20 58	21 05	21 13	21 20	21 28	21 35	21 43	21 50	21 58	22 05	22 13	22 20	22 28	22 35	22 41	22 48	22 58
Willesden Jn Low Level ⊖	a																						
Shepherd's Bush ⊖	d		20 38		20 53		21 09		21 23		21 38		21 53		22 09		22 23		22 38		22 53		23 08
Kensington (Olympia) ⊖	d		20 41		20 56		21 12		21 26		21 41		21 56		22 12		22 26		22 41		22 56		23 11
West Brompton ⊖	d		20 43		20 58		21 14		21 28		21 43		21 58		22 14		22 28		22 43		22 58		23 13
Imperial Wharf	d		20 46		21 01		21 17		21 31		21 46		22 01		22 19		22 31		22 46		23 01		23 16
Clapham Junction [10]	a		20 54		21 09		21 25		21 39		21 54		22 09		22 25		22 39		22 54		23 09		23 24
Acton Central	d	20 26		20 40		20 55		21 10		21 25		21 40		21 55		22 10		22 25		22 40		22 55	
South Acton	d	20 28		20 43		20 58		21 13		21 28		21 43		21 58		22 13		22 28		22 43		22 57	
Gunnersbury ⊖	d	20 32		20 48		21 02		21 18		21 32		21 48		22 02		22 18		22 32		22 48		23 02	
Kew Gardens ⊖	d	20 35		20 51		21 05		21 21		21 35		21 51		22 05		22 21		22 35		22 51		23 05	
Richmond ⊖	a	20 45		21 01		21 15		21 31		21 45		22 01		22 15		22 31		22 45		23 01		23 15	

Table 59

Saturdays
28 July to 11 August

Stratford - Highbury and Islington, West Hampstead, Willesden Junction, Clapham Junction and Richmond

Network Diagram - see first Page of Table 59

		LO	LO	LO	LO	LO	LO	LO	LO	LO	LO	LO	LO	LO
Stratford 7 ⊖	d	22 22	22 30	22 37	22 45	22 52	23 00	23 07	23 15	23 22	23 30	23 37	23 45	23 52
Hackney Wick	d	22 25	22 33	22 40	22 48	22 55	23 03	23 10	23 18	23 25	23 33	23 40	23 48	23 55
Homerton	d	22 28	22 36	22 43	22 51	22 58	23 06	23 13	23 21	23 28	23 36	23 43	23 51	23 58
Hackney Central	d	22 30	22 38	22 45	22 53	23 00	23 08	23 15	23 23	23 30	23 38	23 45	23 53	00 01
Dalston Kingsland	d	22 32	22 40	22 47	22 55	23 02	23 10	23 17	23 25	23 32	23 40	23 47	23 55	00 03
Canonbury	d	22 34	22 42	22 49	22 57	23 04	23 12	23 19	23 27	23 34	23 42	23 49	23 57	00 04
Highbury & Islington ⊖	d	22 38	22 46	22 53	23 01	23 08	23 16	23 23	23 31	23 38	23 46	23 53	00 01	00 08
Caledonian Rd & Barnsbury	d	22 40	22 48	22 55	23 03	23 10	23 18	23 25	23 33	23 40	23 48	23 55	00 03	00 10
Camden Road	d	22 44	22 52	22 59	23 07	23 14	23 22	23 29	23 37	23 44	23 52	23 59	00 07	00 14
Kentish Town West	d	22 46	22 54	23 02	23 09	23 16	23 24	23 31	23 39	23 46	23 54	00 01	00 09	00 16
Gospel Oak	d	22 49	22 57	23 04	23 12	23 19	23 27	23 34	23 42	23 49	23 57	00 04	00 12	00 19
Hampstead Heath	d	22 51	22 59	23 06	23 14	23 21	23 29	23 36	23 44	23 51	23 59	00 06	00 14	00 21
Finchley Road & Frognal	d	22 53	23 01	23 08	23 16	23 23	23 31	23 38	23 46	23 53	00 01	00 08	00 16	00 23
West Hampstead ⊖	d	22 55	23 04	23 11	23 18	23 25	23 33	23 40	23 48	23 55	00 03	00 10	00 18	00 25
Brondesbury	d	22 57	23 05	23 12	23 20	23 27	23 35	23 42	23 50	23 57	00 05	00 12	00 20	00 27
Brondesbury Park	d	22 58	23 07	23 14	23 21	23 28	23 36	23 43	23 51	23 58	00 06	00 13	00 21	00 28
Kensal Rise	d	23 00	23 09	23 16	23 23	23 30	23 38	23 45	23 53	00 01	00 08	00 15	00 23	00 30
Willesden Jn. High Level ⊖	a	23 04	23 12	23 20	23 27	23 34	23 42	23 49	23 57	00 04	00 12	00 19	00 27	00 34
	d	23 05	23 14	23 21	23 28	23 35	23 43	23 50	23 59	00 05	00 13	00 20	00 28	00 35
Willesden Jn Low Level ⊖	a													
Shepherd's Bush ⊖	d		23 24		23 38		23 53		00 09		00 23		00 38	
Kensington (Olympia) ⊖	d		23 27		23 41		23 56		00 11		00 26		00 41	
West Brompton ⊖	d		23 29		23 43		23 58		00 14		00 28		00 43	
Imperial Wharf	d		23 32		23 46		00 01		00 17		00 31		00 46	
Clapham Junction 10	a		23 40		23 54		00 09		00 22		00 39		00 54	
Acton Central	d	23 10		23 26		23 40		23 55		00 10		00 25		00 40
South Acton	d	23 13		23 28		23 43		23 58		00 13		00 28		00 43
Gunnersbury ⊖	d	23 18		23 32		23 48		00 02		00 18		00 32		00 48
Kew Gardens ⊖	d	23 21		23 35		23 51		00 05		00 21		00 35		00 51
Richmond ⊖	a	23 31		23 45		00 02		00 14		00 31		00 45		01 00

Saturdays
18 August to 25 August

		LO	LO	LO	LO	LO	LO	LO	LO	LO	LO	LO
Stratford 7 ⊖	d		23p45			05 42		05 55	06 05	06 15		06 25
Hackney Wick	d		23p48			05 45		05 58	06 08	06 18		06 28
Homerton	d		23p51			05 48		06 01	06 11	06 21		06 31
Hackney Central	d		23p53			05 50		06 03	06 13	06 23		06 33
Dalston Kingsland	d		23p55			05 52		06 05	06 15	06 25		06 35
Canonbury	d		23p57			05 54		06 07	06 17	06 27		06 37
Highbury & Islington ⊖	d		23p59			05 57		06 10	06 20	06 30		06 40
Caledonian Rd & Barnsbury	d		00 02			05 59		06 12	06 22	06 32		06 42
Camden Road	d		00 05			06 02		06 15	06 25	06 35		06 45
Kentish Town West	d		00 07			06 07		06 17	06 27	06 37		06 47
Gospel Oak	d		00 10			06 11		06 20	06 30	06 40		06 50
Hampstead Heath	d		00 12			06 13		06 22	06 32	06 42		06 52
Finchley Road & Frognal	d		00 14			06 15		06 24	06 34	06 44		06 54
West Hampstead ⊖	d		00 16			06 17		06 26	06 36	06 46		06 56
Brondesbury	d		00 18			06 19		06 28	06 38	06 48		06 58
Brondesbury Park	d		00 19			06 20		06 29	06 39	06 49		06 59
Kensal Rise	d		00 21			06 22		06 31	06 41	06 51		07 01
Willesden Jn. High Level ⊖	a					06 25		06 35	06 45	06 55		07 05
	d	23p40		06 02	06 06	06 26	06 31	06 36	06 46	06 56	07 01	07 06
Willesden Jn Low Level ⊖	a		00 29									
Shepherd's Bush ⊖	d	23p48		06 10			06 39		06 54		07 09	
Kensington (Olympia) ⊖	d	23p50		06 12			06 41		06 56		07 11	
West Brompton ⊖	d	23p52		06 14			06 43		06 58		07 13	
Imperial Wharf	d	23p55		06 17			06 46		07 01		07 16	
Clapham Junction 10	a	00 02		06 25			06 53		07 09		07 23	
Acton Central	d				06 11	06 31		06 41		07 01		07 11
South Acton	d				06 14	06 34		06 44		07 04		07 14
Gunnersbury ⊖	d				06 19	06 37		06 47		07 07		07 17
Kew Gardens ⊖	d				06 22	06 40		06 50		07 10		07 20
Richmond ⊖	a				06 29	06 44		06 56		07 16		07 26

		LO	LO	LO	LO	LO	LO	LO	LO	LO	LO	LO
Stratford 7 ⊖	d	06 35	06 45		06 55	07 05	07 15		07 25	07 35	07 45	
Hackney Wick	d	06 38	06 48		06 58	07 08	07 18		07 28	07 38	07 48	
Homerton	d	06 41	06 51		07 01	07 11	07 21		07 31	07 41	07 51	
Hackney Central	d	06 43	06 53		07 03	07 13	07 23		07 33	07 43	07 53	
Dalston Kingsland	d	06 45	06 55		07 05	07 15	07 25		07 35	07 45	07 55	
Canonbury	d	06 47	06 57		07 07	07 17	07 27		07 37	07 47	07 57	
Highbury & Islington ⊖	d	06 50	07 00		07 10	07 20	07 30		07 40	07 50	08 00	
Caledonian Rd & Barnsbury	d	06 52	07 02		07 12	07 22	07 32		07 42	07 52	08 02	
Camden Road	d	06 55	07 05		07 15	07 25	07 35		07 45	07 55	08 05	
Kentish Town West	d	06 57	07 07		07 17	07 27	07 37		07 47	07 57	08 07	
Gospel Oak	d	07 00	07 10		07 20	07 30	07 40		07 50	08 00	08 10	
Hampstead Heath	d	07 02	07 12		07 22	07 32	07 42		07 52	08 02	08 12	
Finchley Road & Frognal	d	07 04	07 14		07 24	07 34	07 44		07 54	08 04	08 14	
West Hampstead ⊖	d	07 06	07 16		07 26	07 36	07 46		07 56	08 06	08 16	
Brondesbury	d	07 08	07 18		07 28	07 38	07 48		07 58	08 08	08 18	
Brondesbury Park	d	07 09	07 19		07 29	07 39	07 49		07 59	08 09	08 19	
Kensal Rise	d	07 11	07 21		07 31	07 41	07 51		08 01	08 11	08 21	
Willesden Jn. High Level ⊖	a	07 15	07 25		07 35	07 45	07 55		08 05	08 15	08 25	
	d	07 16	07 26	07 31	07 36	07 46	07 56	08 01	08 06	08 16	08 26	08 31
Willesden Jn Low Level ⊖	a											
Shepherd's Bush ⊖	d	07 24		07 39		07 54		08 09		08 24		08 39
Kensington (Olympia) ⊖	d	07 26		07 41		07 56		08 11		08 26		08 41
West Brompton ⊖	d	07 28		07 43		07 58		08 13		08 28		08 43
Imperial Wharf	d	07 31		07 46		08 01		08 16		08 31		08 46
Clapham Junction 10	a	07 39		07 53		08 09		08 23		08 39		08 53
Acton Central	d		07 31		07 41		08 01		08 11		08 31	
South Acton	d		07 34		07 44		08 04		08 14		08 34	
Gunnersbury ⊖	d		07 37		07 48		08 08		08 18		08 38	
Kew Gardens ⊖	d		07 40		07 51		08 11		08 21		08 41	
Richmond ⊖	a		07 46		07 56		08 16		08 26		08 46	

Table 59

Saturdays
18 August to 25 August

Stratford - Highbury and Islington, West Hampstead, Willesden Junction, Clapham Junction and Richmond

Network Diagram - see first Page of Table 59

		LO	LO	LO	LO	LO	LO	LO	LO	LO	LO	LO
Stratford 7 ⊖	d	07 55	08 05	08 15		08 25	08 35	08 45		08 55	09 05	09 15
Hackney Wick	d	07 58	08 08	08 18		08 28	08 38	08 48		08 58	09 08	09 18
Homerton	d	08 01	08 11	08 21		08 31	08 41	08 51		09 01	09 11	09 21
Hackney Central	d	08 03	08 13	08 23		08 33	08 43	08 53		09 03	09 13	09 23
Dalston Kingsland	d	08 05	08 15	08 25		08 35	08 45	08 55		09 05	09 15	09 25
Canonbury	d	08 07	08 17	08 27		08 37	08 47	08 57		09 07	09 17	09 27
Highbury & Islington ⊖	d	08 10	08 20	08 30		08 40	08 50	09 00		09 10	09 20	09 30
Caledonian Rd & Barnsbury	d	08 12	08 22	08 32		08 42	08 52	09 02		09 12	09 22	09 32
Camden Road	d	08 15	08 25	08 35		08 45	08 55	09 05		09 15	09 25	09 35
Kentish Town West	d	08 17	08 27	08 37		08 47	08 57	09 07		09 17	09 27	09 37
Gospel Oak	d	08 20	08 30	08 40		08 50	09 00	09 10		09 20	09 30	09 40
Hampstead Heath	d	08 22	08 32	08 42		08 52	09 02	09 12		09 22	09 32	09 42
Finchley Road & Frognal	d	08 24	08 34	08 44		08 54	09 04	09 14		09 24	09 34	09 44
West Hampstead ⊖	d	08 26	08 36	08 46		08 56	09 06	09 16		09 26	09 36	09 46
Brondesbury	d	08 28	08 38	08 48		08 58	09 08	09 18		09 28	09 38	09 48
Brondesbury Park	d	08 29	08 39	08 49		08 59	09 09	09 19		09 29	09 39	09 49
Kensal Rise	d	08 31	08 41	08 51		09 01	09 11	09 21		09 31	09 41	09 51
Willesden Jn. High Level ⊖	a	08 35	08 45	08 55		09 05	09 15	09 25		09 35	09 45	09 55
	d	08 36	08 46	08 56	09 01	09 06	09 16	09 26	09 31	09 36	09 46	09 56
Willesden Jn Low Level ⊖	a											
Shepherd's Bush ⊖	d		08 54		09 09		09 24		09 39		09 54	
Kensington (Olympia) ⊖	d		08 56		09 11		09 26		09 41		09 56	
West Brompton ⊖	d		08 58		09 13		09 28		09 43		09 58	
Imperial Wharf	d		09 01		09 16		09 31		09 46		10 01	
Clapham Junction 10	a		09 09		09 23		09 39		09 53		10 09	
Acton Central	d	08 41		09 01		09 11		09 31		09 41		10 01
South Acton	d	08 44		09 04		09 14		09 34		09 44		10 04
Gunnersbury ⊖	d	08 48		09 08		09 18		09 38		09 48		10 08
Kew Gardens ⊖	d	08 51		09 11		09 21		09 41		09 51		10 11
Richmond ⊖	a	08 56		09 16		09 26		09 46		09 56		10 16

		LO	LO	LO	LO	LO	LO	LO	LO	LO	LO	LO
Stratford 7 ⊖	d		09 25	09 35	09 45		09 55	10 05	10 15		10 25	10 35
Hackney Wick	d		09 28	09 38	09 48		09 58	10 08	10 18		10 28	10 38
Homerton	d		09 31	09 41	09 51		10 01	10 11	10 21		10 31	10 41
Hackney Central	d		09 33	09 43	09 53		10 03	10 13	10 23		10 33	10 43
Dalston Kingsland	d		09 35	09 45	09 55		10 05	10 15	10 25		10 35	10 45
Canonbury	d		09 37	09 47	09 57		10 07	10 17	10 27		10 37	10 47
Highbury & Islington ⊖	d		09 40	09 50	10 00		10 10	10 20	10 30		10 40	10 50
Caledonian Rd & Barnsbury	d		09 42	09 52	10 02		10 12	10 22	10 32		10 42	10 52
Camden Road	d		09 45	09 55	10 05		10 15	10 25	10 35		10 45	10 55
Kentish Town West	d		09 47	09 57	10 07		10 17	10 27	10 37		10 47	10 57
Gospel Oak	d		09 50	10 00	10 10		10 20	10 30	10 40		10 50	11 00
Hampstead Heath	d		09 52	10 02	10 12		10 22	10 32	10 42		10 52	11 02
Finchley Road & Frognal	d		09 54	10 04	10 14		10 24	10 34	10 44		10 54	11 04
West Hampstead ⊖	d		09 56	10 06	10 16		10 26	10 36	10 46		10 56	11 06
Brondesbury	d		09 58	10 08	10 18		10 28	10 38	10 48		10 58	11 08
Brondesbury Park	d		09 59	10 09	10 19		10 29	10 39	10 49		10 59	11 09
Kensal Rise	d		10 01	10 11	10 21		10 31	10 41	10 51		11 01	11 11
Willesden Jn. High Level ⊖	a		10 05	10 15	10 25		10 35	10 45	10 55		11 05	11 15
	d	10 01	10 06	10 16	10 26	10 31	10 36	10 46	10 56	11 01	11 06	11 16
Willesden Jn Low Level ⊖	a											
Shepherd's Bush ⊖	d	10 09		10 24		10 39		10 54		11 09		11 24
Kensington (Olympia) ⊖	d	10 11		10 26		10 41		10 56		11 11		11 26
West Brompton ⊖	d	10 13		10 28		10 43		10 58		11 13		11 28
Imperial Wharf	d	10 16		10 31		10 46		11 01		11 16		11 31
Clapham Junction 10	a	10 23		10 39		10 53		11 09		11 23		11 39
Acton Central	d		10 11		10 31		10 41		11 01		11 11	
South Acton	d		10 14		10 34		10 45		11 04		11 14	
Gunnersbury ⊖	d		10 18		10 38		10 48		11 08		11 18	
Kew Gardens ⊖	d		10 21		10 41		10 51		11 11		11 21	
Richmond ⊖	a		10 26		10 46		10 56		11 16		11 26	

		LO	LO	LO	LO	LO	LO	LO	LO	LO	LO	LO
Stratford 7 ⊖	d	10 45		10 55	11 05	11 15		11 25	11 35	11 45		11 55
Hackney Wick	d	10 48		10 58	11 08	11 18		11 28	11 38	11 48		11 58
Homerton	d	10 51		11 01	11 11	11 21		11 31	11 41	11 51		12 01
Hackney Central	d	10 53		11 03	11 13	11 23		11 33	11 43	11 53		12 03
Dalston Kingsland	d	10 55		11 05	11 15	11 25		11 35	11 45	11 55		12 05
Canonbury	d	10 57		11 07	11 17	11 27		11 37	11 47	11 57		12 07
Highbury & Islington ⊖	d	11 00		11 10	11 20	11 30		11 40	11 50	12 00		12 10
Caledonian Rd & Barnsbury	d	11 02		11 12	11 22	11 32		11 42	11 52	12 02		12 12
Camden Road	d	11 05		11 15	11 25	11 35		11 45	11 55	12 05		12 15
Kentish Town West	d	11 07		11 17	11 27	11 37		11 47	11 57	12 07		12 17
Gospel Oak	d	11 10		11 20	11 30	11 40		11 50	12 00	12 10		12 20
Hampstead Heath	d	11 12		11 22	11 32	11 42		11 52	12 02	12 12		12 22
Finchley Road & Frognal	d	11 14		11 24	11 34	11 44		11 54	12 04	12 14		12 24
West Hampstead ⊖	d	11 16		11 26	11 36	11 46		11 56	12 06	12 16		12 26
Brondesbury	d	11 18		11 28	11 38	11 48		11 58	12 08	12 18		12 28
Brondesbury Park	d	11 19		11 29	11 39	11 49		11 59	12 09	12 19		12 29
Kensal Rise	d	11 21		11 31	11 41	11 51		12 01	12 11	12 21		12 31
Willesden Jn. High Level ⊖	a	11 25		11 35	11 45	11 55		12 05	12 15	12 25		12 35
	d	11 26	11 31	11 36	11 46	11 56	12 01	12 06	12 16	12 26	12 31	12 36
Willesden Jn Low Level ⊖	a											
Shepherd's Bush ⊖	d		11 39		11 54		12 09		12 24		12 39	
Kensington (Olympia) ⊖	d		11 41		11 56		12 11		12 26		12 41	
West Brompton ⊖	d		11 43		11 58		12 13		12 28		12 43	
Imperial Wharf	d		11 46		12 01		12 16		12 31		12 46	
Clapham Junction 10	a		11 53		12 09		12 23		12 39		12 53	
Acton Central	d	11 31		11 41		12 01		12 11		12 31		12 41
South Acton	d	11 34		11 44		12 04		12 14		12 34		12 44
Gunnersbury ⊖	d	11 38		11 48		12 08		12 18		12 38		12 48
Kew Gardens ⊖	d	11 41		11 51		12 11		12 21		12 41		12 51
Richmond ⊖	a	11 46		11 56		12 16		12 26		12 46		12 56

		LO	LO	LO	LO	LO	LO	LO	LO	LO	LO	LO
Stratford 7 ⊖	d	12 05	12 15		12 25	12 35	12 45		12 55	13 05	13 15	
Hackney Wick	d	12 08	12 18		12 28	12 38	12 48		12 58	13 08	13 18	
Homerton	d	12 11	12 21		12 31	12 41	12 51		13 01	13 11	13 21	
Hackney Central	d	12 13	12 23		12 33	12 43	12 53		13 03	13 13	13 23	
Dalston Kingsland	d	12 15	12 25		12 35	12 45	12 55		13 05	13 15	13 25	
Canonbury	d	12 17	12 27		12 37	12 47	12 57		13 07	13 17	13 27	
Highbury & Islington ⊖	d	12 20	12 30		12 40	12 50	13 00		13 10	13 20	13 30	
Caledonian Rd & Barnsbury	d	12 22	12 32		12 42	12 52	13 02		13 12	13 22	13 32	
Camden Road	d	12 25	12 35		12 45	12 55	13 05		13 15	13 25	13 35	
Kentish Town West	d	12 27	12 37		12 47	12 57	13 07		13 17	13 27	13 37	
Gospel Oak	d	12 30	12 40		12 50	13 00	13 10		13 20	13 30	13 40	
Hampstead Heath	d	12 32	12 42		12 52	13 02	13 12		13 22	13 32	13 42	
Finchley Road & Frognal	d	12 34	12 44		12 54	13 04	13 14		13 24	13 34	13 44	
West Hampstead ⊖	d	12 36	12 46		12 56	13 06	13 16		13 26	13 36	13 46	
Brondesbury	d	12 38	12 48		12 58	13 08	13 18		13 28	13 38	13 48	
Brondesbury Park	d	12 39	12 49		12 59	13 09	13 19		13 29	13 39	13 49	
Kensal Rise	d	12 41	12 51		13 01	13 11	13 21		13 31	13 41	13 51	
Willesden Jn. High Level ⊖	a	12 45	12 55		13 05	13 15	13 25		13 35	13 45	13 55	
	d	12 46	12 56	13 01	13 06	13 16	13 26	13 31	13 36	13 46	13 56	14 01
Willesden Jn Low Level ⊖	a											
Shepherd's Bush ⊖	d	12 54		13 09		13 24		13 39		13 54		14 09
Kensington (Olympia) ⊖	d	12 56		13 11		13 26		13 41		13 56		14 11
West Brompton ⊖	d	12 58		13 13		13 28		13 43		13 58		14 13
Imperial Wharf	d	13 01		13 16		13 31		13 46		14 01		14 16
Clapham Junction 10	a	13 09		13 23		13 39		13 55		14 09		14 23
Acton Central	d		13 01		13 11		13 31		13 41		14 01	
South Acton	d		13 04		13 14		13 34		13 44		14 04	
Gunnersbury ⊖	d		13 08		13 18		13 38		13 48		14 08	
Kew Gardens ⊖	d		13 11		13 21		13 41		13 51		14 11	
Richmond ⊖	a		13 16		13 26		13 46		13 56		14 16	

Stratford - Highbury and Islington, West Hampstead, Willesden Junction, Clapham Junction and Richmond

Network Diagram - see first Page of Table 59

Station			LO	LO	LO	LO		LO	LO	LO	LO	LO	LO	LO	LO	LO	LO	LO	LO	LO	LO	LO	LO
Stratford 7	⊖	d	13 25	13 35	13 45				17 55	18 05	18 15		18 25	18 35	18 45		18 55	19 05	19 15		19 25	19 35	19 45
Hackney Wick		d	13 28	13 38	13 48				17 58	18 08	18 18		18 28	18 38	18 48		18 58	19 08	19 18		19 28	19 38	19 48
Homerton		d	13 31	13 41	13 51				18 01	18 11	18 21		18 31	18 41	18 51		19 01	19 11	19 21		19 31	19 41	19 51
Hackney Central		d	13 33	13 43	13 53				18 03	18 13	18 23		18 33	18 43	18 53		19 03	19 13	19 23		19 33	19 43	19 53
Dalston Kingsland		d	13 35	13 45	13 55				18 05	18 15	18 25		18 35	18 45	18 55		19 05	19 15	19 25		19 35	19 45	19 55
Canonbury		d	13 37	13 47	13 57				18 07	18 17	18 27		18 37	18 47	18 57		19 07	19 17	19 27		19 37	19 47	19 57
Highbury & Islington	⊖	d	13 40	13 50	14 00				18 10	18 20	18 30		18 40	18 50	19 00		19 10	19 20	19 30		19 40	19 50	20 00
Caledonian Rd & Barnsbury		d	13 42	13 52	14 02				18 12	18 22	18 32		18 42	18 52	19 02		19 12	19 22	19 32		19 42	19 52	20 02
Camden Road		d	13 45	13 55	14 05				18 15	18 25	18 35		18 45	18 55	19 05		19 15	19 25	19 35		19 45	19 55	20 05
Kentish Town West		d	13 47	13 57	14 07				18 17	18 27	18 37		18 47	18 57	19 07		19 17	19 27	19 37		19 47	19 57	20 07
Gospel Oak		d	13 50	14 00	14 10		and at the same minutes past each hour until		18 20	18 30	18 40		18 50	19 00	19 10		19 20	19 30	19 40		19 50	20 00	20 10
Hampstead Heath		d	13 52	14 02	14 12				18 22	18 32	18 42		18 52	19 02	19 12		19 22	19 32	19 42		19 52	20 02	20 12
Finchley Road & Frognal		d	13 54	14 04	14 14				18 24	18 34	18 44		18 54	19 04	19 14		19 24	19 34	19 44		19 54	20 04	20 14
West Hampstead	⊖	d	13 56	14 06	14 16				18 26	18 36	18 46		18 56	19 06	19 16		19 26	19 36	19 46		19 56	20 06	20 16
Brondesbury		d	13 58	14 08	14 18				18 28	18 38	18 48		18 58	19 08	19 18		19 28	19 38	19 48		19 58	20 08	20 18
Brondesbury Park		d	13 59	14 09	14 19				18 29	18 39	18 49		18 59	19 09	19 19		19 29	19 39	19 49		19 59	20 09	20 19
Kensal Rise		d	14 01	14 11	14 21				18 31	18 41	18 51		19 01	19 11	19 21		19 31	19 41	19 51		20 01	20 11	20 21
Willesden Jn. High Level	⊖	a	14 05	14 15	14 25				18 35	18 45	18 55		19 05	19 15	19 25		19 35	19 45	19 55		20 05	20 15	20 25
		d	14 06	14 16	14 26	14 31		18 31	18 36	18 46	18 56	19 01	19 05	19 16	19 26	19 31	19 36	19 46	19 56	20 01	20 06	20 16	20 26
Willesden Jn Low Level	⊖	a																					
Shepherd's Bush	⊖	d		14 24		14 39		18 39		18 54		19 09		19 24		19 39		19 54		20 09		20 24	
Kensington (Olympia)	⊖	d		14 26		14 41		18 41		18 56		19 11		19 26		19 41		19 56		20 11		20 26	
West Brompton	⊖	d		14 28		14 43		18 43		18 58		19 13		19 28		19 43		19 58		20 13		20 28	
Imperial Wharf		d		14 31		14 46		18 46		19 01		19 16		19 31		19 46		20 01		20 16		20 31	
Clapham Junction 10		a		14 39		14 53		18 53		19 09		19 23		19 39		19 53		20 09		20 23		20 39	
Acton Central		d	14 11		14 31				18 41		19 01		19 10		19 31		19 41		20 01		20 11		20 31
South Acton		d	14 14		14 34				18 44		19 04		19 13		19 34		19 44		20 04		20 14		20 34
Gunnersbury	⊖	d	14 18		14 38				18 48		19 08		19 17		19 38		19 48		20 08		20 18		20 38
Kew Gardens	⊖	d	14 21		14 41				18 51		19 11		19 20		19 41		19 51		20 11		20 21		20 41
Richmond	⊖	a	14 26		14 46				18 56		19 17		19 27		19 47		19 57		20 17		20 27		20 47

Station			LO	LO	LO	LO	LO	LO	LO	LO	LO	LO	LO	LO	LO	LO	LO	LO	LO	LO	LO	LO	LO	LO
Stratford 7	⊖	d		19 55	20 05	20 15		20 25	20 35	20 45		20 55	21 05	21 15		21 25	21 35	21 45		21 55	22 15	22 25		22 45
Hackney Wick		d		19 58	20 08	20 18		20 28	20 38	20 48		20 58	21 08	21 18		21 28	21 38	21 48		21 58	22 18	22 28		22 48
Homerton		d		20 01	20 11	20 21		20 31	20 41	20 51		21 01	21 11	21 21		21 31	21 41	21 51		22 01	22 21	22 31		22 51
Hackney Central		d		20 03	20 13	20 23		20 33	20 43	20 53		21 03	21 13	21 23		21 33	21 43	21 53		22 03	22 23	22 33		22 53
Dalston Kingsland		d		20 05	20 15	20 25		20 35	20 45	20 55		21 05	21 15	21 25		21 35	21 45	21 55		22 05	22 25	22 35		22 55
Canonbury		d		20 07	20 17	20 27		20 37	20 47	20 57		21 07	21 17	21 27		21 37	21 47	21 57		22 07	22 27	22 37		22 57
Highbury & Islington	⊖	d		20 10	20 20	20 30		20 40	20 50	21 00		21 10	21 20	21 30		21 40	21 50	22 00		22 10	22 30	22 40		23 00
Caledonian Rd & Barnsbury		d		20 12	20 22	20 32		20 42	20 52	21 02		21 12	21 22	21 32		21 42	21 52	22 02		22 12	22 32	22 42		23 02
Camden Road		d		20 15	20 25	20 35		20 45	20 55	21 05		21 15	21 25	21 35		21 45	21 55	22 05		22 15	22 35	22a45		23 05
Kentish Town West		d		20 17	20 27	20 37		20 47	20 57	21 07		21 17	21 27	21 37		21 47	21 57	22 07		22 17	22 37			23 07
Gospel Oak		d		20 20	20 30	20 40		20 50	21 00	21 10		21 20	21 30	21 40		21 50	22 00	22 10		22 20	22 40			23 10
Hampstead Heath		d		20 22	20 32	20 42		20 52	21 02	21 12		21 22	21 32	21 42		21 52	22 02	22 12		22 22	22 42			23 12
Finchley Road & Frognal		d		20 24	20 34	20 44		20 54	21 04	21 14		21 24	21 34	21 44		21 54	22 04	22 14		22 24	22 44			23 14
West Hampstead	⊖	d		20 26	20 36	20 46		20 56	21 06	21 16		21 26	21 36	21 46		21 56	22 06	22 16		22 26	22 46			23 16
Brondesbury		d		20 28	20 38	20 48		20 58	21 08	21 18		21 28	21 38	21 48		21 58	22 08	22 18		22 28	22 48			23 18
Brondesbury Park		d		20 29	20 39	20 49		20 59	21 09	21 19		21 29	21 39	21 49		21 59	22 09	22 19		22 29	22 49			23 19
Kensal Rise		d		20 31	20 41	20 51		21 01	21 11	21 21		21 31	21 41	21 51		22 01	22 11	22 21		22 31	22 51			23 21
Willesden Jn. High Level	⊖	a		20 35	20 45	20 55		21 05	21 15	21 25		21 35	21 45	21 55		22 05	22 15	22 25		22 35	22 55			23 25
		d	20 31	20 36	20 46	20 56	21 01	21 06	21 16	21 26	21 31	21 36	21 46	21 56	22 01	22 06	22 16	22 26	22 31	22 36	22 56		23 01	23 26
Willesden Jn Low Level	⊖	a																						
Shepherd's Bush	⊖	d	20 39		20 54		21 11		21 24		21 39		21 54		22 11		22 24		22 39				23 09	
Kensington (Olympia)	⊖	d	20 41		20 56		21 13		21 26		21 41		21 56		22 13		22 26		22 41				23 11	
West Brompton	⊖	d	20 43		20 58		21 15		21 28		21 43		21 58		22 15		22 28		22 43				23 13	
Imperial Wharf		d	20 46		21 01		21 18		21 31		21 46		22 01		22 18		22 31		22 46				23 16	
Clapham Junction 10		a	20 53		21 09		21 25		21 39		21 53		22 09		22 25		22 39		22 53				23 23	
Acton Central		d		20 41		21 01		21 11		21 31		21 41		22 01		22 11		22 31		22 41	23 01			23 31
South Acton		d		20 44		21 04		21 14		21 34		21 44		22 04		22 14		22 34		22 44	23 04			23 34
Gunnersbury	⊖	d		20 48		21 08		21 18		21 38		21 48		22 08		22 18		22 38		22 48	23 08			23 38
Kew Gardens	⊖	d		20 51		21 11		21 21		21 41		21 51		22 11		22 21		22 41		22 51	23 11			23 41
Richmond	⊖	a		20 57		21 17		21 27		21 47		21 57		22 17		22 27		22 47		22 57	23 17			23 47

Stratford - Highbury and Islington, West Hampstead, Willesden Junction, Clapham Junction and Richmond

Network Diagram - see first Page of Table 59

Station			LO	LO	LO
Stratford 7	⊖	d	22 55	23 15	23 45
Hackney Wick		d	22 58	23 18	23 48
Homerton		d	23 01	23 21	23 51
Hackney Central		d	23 03	23 23	23 53
Dalston Kingsland		d	23 05	23 25	23 55
Canonbury		d	23 07	23 27	23 57
Highbury & Islington	⊖	d	23 10	23 30	23 59
Caledonian Rd & Barnsbury		d	23 12	23 32	00 02
Camden Road		d	23a15	23 35	00 05
Kentish Town West		d		23 37	00 07
Gospel Oak		d		23 40	00 10
Hampstead Heath		d		23 42	00 12
Finchley Road & Frognal		d		23 44	00 14
West Hampstead	⊖	d		23 46	00 16
Brondesbury		d		23 48	00 18
Brondesbury Park		d		23 49	00 19
Kensal Rise		d		23 51	00 21
Willesden Jn. High Level	⊖	a		23 54	
		d			
Willesden Jn Low Level	⊖	a			00 29
Shepherd's Bush	⊖	d			
Kensington (Olympia)	⊖	d			
West Brompton	⊖	d			
Imperial Wharf		d			
Clapham Junction 10		a			
Acton Central		d			
South Acton		d			
Gunnersbury	⊖	d			
Kew Gardens	⊖	d			
Richmond	⊖	a			

Saturdays

1 September to 8 September

Station			LO	LO	LO	LO	LO	LO	LO	LO	LO	LO	LO	LO	LO	LO	LO	LO	LO	LO	LO	LO	LO	LO
Stratford 7	⊖	d	22p52	23p02	23p07	23p15	23p22	23p30	23p38	23p45	23p52	00 01	00 07	00 15	00 22	00 30	00 37	00 45	00 52	01 00			05 47	
Hackney Wick		d	22p55	23p05	23p10	23p18	23p25	23p33	23p41	23p48	23p55	00 03	00 10	00 20	00 25	00 33	00 40	00 48	00 55	01 03			05 50	
Homerton		d	22p58	23p06	23p13	23p21	23p28	23p36	23p44	23p51	23p58	00 06	00 13	00 21	00 28	00 36	00 43	00 50	00 58	01 06			05 53	
Hackney Central		d	23p00	23p08	23p15	23p23	23p30	23p38	23p46	23p53	23p59	00 08	00 15	00 23	00 30	00 38	00 45	00 52	01 00	01 08			05 55	
Dalston Kingsland		d	23p02	23p10	23p17	23p25	23p32	23p40	23p48	23p55	00 02	00 10	00 17	00 25	00 32	00 40	00 47	00 54	01 02	01 10			05 57	
Canonbury		d	23p04	23p12	23p19	23p27	23p34	23p42	23p50	23p57	00 04	00 12	00 19	00 27	00 34	00 42	00 49	00 56	01 04	01 12			05 59	
Highbury & Islington	⊖	d	23p08	23p16	23p23	23p31	23p38	23p46	23p53	00 01	00 08	00 16	00 23	00 31	00 38	00 46	00 53	00 59	01 08	01 17			06 02	
Caledonian Rd & Barnsbury		d	23p10	23p18	23p25	23p33	23p40	23p48	23p55	00 03	00 10	00 18	00 25	00 33	00 40	00 48	00 55	01 01	01 10	01 19			06 04	
Camden Road		d	23p14	23p22	23p29	23p37	23p44	23p53	23p59	00 07	00 14	00 22	00a34	00 37	00a49	00 52	01a04	01 05	01a21	01 23			06 07	
Kentish Town West		d	23p16	23p24	23p31	23p39	23p46	23p55	00 02	00 09	00 16	00 24		00 39		00 55		01 08		01 26			06 11	
Gospel Oak		d	23p19	23p27	23p34	23p42	23p49	23p59	00 05	00 12	00 19	00 28		00 43		00 57		01 10		01 28			06 13	
Hampstead Heath		d	23p21	23p29	23p36	23p44	23p51	00 01	00 07	00 14	00 21	00 30		00 45		00 59		01 12		01 30			06 15	
Finchley Road & Frognal		d	23p23	23p31	23p38	23p46	23p53	00 03	00 09	00 16	00 23	00 32		00 47		01 01		01 14		01 32			06 17	
West Hampstead	⊖	d	23p25	23p33	23p40	23p48	23p55	00 05	00 11	00 18	00 25	00 34		00 49		01 03		01 17		01 35			06 19	
Brondesbury		d	23p27	23p35	23p42	23p50	23p57	00 06	00 13	00 20	00 27	00 36		00 51		01 05		01 18		01 36			06 20	
Brondesbury Park		d	23p28	23p36	23p43	23p51	23p58	00 08	00 14	00 21	00 28	00 37		00 52		01 06		01 20		01 38			06 22	
Kensal Rise		d	23p30	23p38	23p45	23p53	00 01	00 10	00 16	00 23	00 30	00 39		00 54		01 08		01 22		01 40			06 24	
Willesden Jn. High Level	⊖	a	23p35	23p42	23p49	23p57	00 04	00 13	00 20	00 27	00 34	00 42											06 27	
		d	23p36	23p43	23p50	23p59	00 05	00 14	00 21	00 28	00 35	00 43									06 02	06 06	06 28	06 33
Willesden Jn Low Level	⊖	a												01 03		01 21		01 41		01 50				
Shepherd's Bush	⊖	d		23p57		00 09		00 24		00 38		00 53									06 09			06 41
Kensington (Olympia)	⊖	d		23p59		00 11		00 26		00 41		00 56									06 11			06 43
West Brompton	⊖	d		00 02		00 14		00 29		00 43		00 58									06 14			06 46
Imperial Wharf		d		00 05		00 17		00 32		00 46		01 01									06 17			06 49
Clapham Junction 10		a		00 13		00 23		00 39		00 54		01 09									06 23			06 56
Acton Central		d	23p41		23p55		00 10		00 26		00 40											06 11	06 33	
South Acton		d	23p43		23p58		00 13		00 29		00 43											06 14	06 35	
Gunnersbury	⊖	d	23p48		00 02		00 18		00 33		00 47											06 18	06 42	
Kew Gardens	⊖	d	23p51		00 05		00 21		00 36		00 50											06 21	06 45	
Richmond	⊖	a	00 01		00 14		00 30		00 45		00 59											06 31	06 55	

Stratford - Highbury and Islington, West Hampstead, Willesden Junction, Clapham Junction and Richmond

Network Diagram - see first Page of Table 59

Station		LO	LO	LO	LO	LO	LO	LO	LO	LO	LO	LO
Stratford 7 ⊖	d		06 00	06 07	06 15	06 24	06 30	06 37	06 45	06 52	07 02	07 07
Hackney Wick	d		06 04	06 10	06 18	06 29	06 33	06 40	06 48	06 58	07 05	07 10
Homerton	d		06 06	06 13	06 19	06 31	06 36	06 43	06 49	07 00	07 06	07 13
Hackney Central	d		06 08	06 15	06 21	06 33	06 38	06 45	06 51	07 02	07 08	07 15
Dalston Kingsland	d		06 10	06 17	06 23	06 35	06 40	06 47	06 54	07 05	07 10	07 17
Canonbury	d		06 12	06 19	06 25	06 37	06 42	06 49	06 56	07 07	07 12	07 19
Highbury & Islington ⊖	d		06 16	06 23	06 28	06 41	06 46	06 53	06 58	07 10	07 16	07 23
Caledonian Rd & Barnsbury	d		06 18	06 25	06 30	06 43	06 48	06 55	07 01	07 12	07 18	07 25
Camden Road	d		06 22	06 29	06 34	06 46	06 52	06 59	07 04	07 16	07 22	07 29
Kentish Town West	d		06 24	06 31	06 36	06 48	06 54	07 01	07 07	07 19	07 24	07 31
Gospel Oak	d		06 27	06 34	06 39	06 50	06 57	07 04	07 11	07 21	07 27	07 34
Hampstead Heath	d		06 29	06 36	06 41	06 52	06 59	07 06	07 13	07 23	07 29	07 36
Finchley Road & Frognal	d		06 31	06 38	06 43	06 54	07 01	07 08	07 15	07 25	07 31	07 38
West Hampstead ⊖	d		06 33	06 40	06 45	06 56	07 03	07 10	07 17	07 28	07 33	07 40
Brondesbury	d		06 35	06 42	06 47	06 58	07 05	07 12	07 19	07 29	07 35	07 42
Brondesbury Park	d		06 36	06 43	06 48	06 59	07 06	07 13	07 20	07 31	07 36	07 43
Kensal Rise	d		06 38	06 45	06 50	07 01	07 08	07 15	07 22	07 33	07 38	07 45
Willesden Jn. High Level ⊖	a		06 42	06 49	06 55	07 05	07 12	07 19	07 26	07 36	07 42	07 49
	d	06 41	06 43	06 50	06 56	07 06	07 13	07 20	07 27	07 37	07 43	07 50
Willesden Jn Low Level ⊖	a											
Shepherd's Bush ⊖	d		06 53		07 08		07 23		07 38		07 53	
Kensington (Olympia) ⊖	d		06 56		07 11		07 26		07 41		07 56	
West Brompton ⊖	d		06 58		07 13		07 28		07 43		07 58	
Imperial Wharf	d		07 01		07 16		07 31		07 46		08 01	
Clapham Junction 10	a		07 09		07 24		07 39		07 54		08 09	
Acton Central	d	06 46		06 55		07 11		07 25		07 42		07 55
South Acton	d	06 49		06 58		07 14		07 28		07 45		07 58
Gunnersbury ⊖	d	06 52		07 02		07 18		07 32		07 48		08 02
Kew Gardens ⊖	d	06 55		07 05		07 21		07 35		07 51		08 05
Richmond ⊖	a	07 05		07 15		07 30		07 45		08 01		08 15

Station		LO	LO	LO	LO	LO	LO	LO	LO	LO	LO	LO
Stratford 7 ⊖	d	07 15	07 22	07 30	07 37	07 45	07 52	08 00	08 07	08 15	08 22	08 30
Hackney Wick	d	07 18	07 25	07 33	07 40	07 48	07 55	08 03	08 10	08 18	08 25	08 33
Homerton	d	07 21	07 28	07 36	07 43	07 51	07 58	08 06	08 13	08 21	08 28	08 36
Hackney Central	d	07 23	07 30	07 38	07 45	07 53	08 00	08 08	08 15	08 23	08 30	08 38
Dalston Kingsland	d	07 25	07 32	07 40	07 47	07 55	08 02	08 10	08 17	08 25	08 32	08 40
Canonbury	d	07 27	07 34	07 42	07 49	07 57	08 04	08 12	08 19	08 27	08 34	08 42
Highbury & Islington ⊖	d	07 31	07 38	07 46	07 53	08 01	08 08	08 16	08 23	08 31	08 38	08 46
Caledonian Rd & Barnsbury	d	07 33	07 40	07 48	07 55	08 03	08 10	08 18	08 25	08 33	08 40	08 48
Camden Road	d	07 37	07 44	07 52	07 59	08 07	08 14	08 22	08 29	08 37	08 44	08 52
Kentish Town West	d	07 39	07 46	07 54	08 01	08 09	08 16	08 24	08 31	08 39	08 47	08 54
Gospel Oak	d	07 42	07 49	07 57	08 04	08 12	08 19	08 27	08 34	08 44	08 51	08 58
Hampstead Heath	d	07 44	07 51	07 59	08 06	08 14	08 21	08 29	08 36	08 46	08 53	09 00
Finchley Road & Frognal	d	07 46	07 53	08 01	08 08	08 16	08 23	08 31	08 38	08 48	08 55	09 02
West Hampstead ⊖	d	07 48	07 55	08 03	08 10	08 18	08 25	08 33	08 40	08 50	08 57	09 04
Brondesbury	d	07 50	07 57	08 05	08 12	08 20	08 27	08 35	08 42	08 52	08 59	09 05
Brondesbury Park	d	07 51	07 58	08 06	08 13	08 21	08 28	08 36	08 43	08 53	09 00	09 07
Kensal Rise	d	07 53	08 00	08 08	08 15	08 23	08 30	08 38	08 45	08 55	09 02	09 09
Willesden Jn. High Level ⊖	a	07 57	08 04	08 12	08 19	08 27	08 34	08 42	08 49	08 58	09 06	09 12
	d	07 58	08 05	08 13	08 20	08 28	08 35	08 43	08 50	08 59	09 07	09 13
Willesden Jn Low Level ⊖	a											
Shepherd's Bush ⊖	d	08 08		08 23		08 38		08 53		09 09		09 23
Kensington (Olympia) ⊖	d	08 11		08 26		08 41		08 56		09 12		09 26
West Brompton ⊖	d	08 13		08 28		08 43		08 58		09 14		09 28
Imperial Wharf	d	08 16		08 31		08 46		09 01		09 17		09 31
Clapham Junction 10	a	08 24		08 39		08 54		09 09		09 25		09 39
Acton Central	d		08 10		08 25		08 40		08 55		09 12	
South Acton	d		08 13		08 28		08 43		08 58		09 14	
Gunnersbury ⊖	d		08 18		08 32		08 48		09 02		09 18	
Kew Gardens ⊖	d		08 21		08 35		08 51		09 05		09 21	
Richmond ⊖	a		08 30		08 45		09 00		09 15		09 30	

Station		LO	LO	LO	LO	LO	LO	LO	LO	LO	LO	LO
Stratford 7 ⊖	d	08 37	08 45	08 52	09 00	09 07	09 15	09 22	09 30	09 37	09 45	09 52
Hackney Wick	d	08 40	08 48	08 55	09 04	09 10	09 18	09 25	09 33	09 40	09 48	09 55
Homerton	d	08 43	08 51	08 58	09 06	09 13	09 21	09 28	09 36	09 43	09 51	09 58
Hackney Central	d	08 45	08 53	09 00	09 08	09 15	09 23	09 30	09 38	09 45	09 53	10 00
Dalston Kingsland	d	08 47	08 55	09 02	09 10	09 17	09 25	09 32	09 40	09 47	09 55	10 02
Canonbury	d	08 49	08 57	09 04	09 12	09 19	09 27	09 34	09 42	09 49	09 57	10 04
Highbury & Islington ⊖	d	08 53	09 01	09 08	09 16	09 23	09 31	09 38	09 46	09 53	10 01	10 08
Caledonian Rd & Barnsbury	d	08 55	09 03	09 10	09 18	09 25	09 33	09 40	09 48	09 55	10 03	10 10
Camden Road	d	08 59	09 07	09 14	09 22	09 29	09 37	09 44	09 52	09 59	10 07	10 14
Kentish Town West	d	09 02	09 09	09 16	09 24	09 31	09 39	09 46	09 54	10 01	10 09	10 16
Gospel Oak	d	09 04	09 12	09 19	09 28	09 35	09 42	09 49	09 57	10 04	10 12	10 19
Hampstead Heath	d	09 06	09 14	09 21	09 30	09 37	09 44	09 51	09 59	10 06	10 14	10 21
Finchley Road & Frognal	d	09 08	09 16	09 23	09 32	09 39	09 46	09 53	10 01	10 08	10 16	10 23
West Hampstead ⊖	d	09 10	09 18	09 25	09 34	09 41	09 48	09 55	10 03	10 10	10 18	10 25
Brondesbury	d	09 12	09 20	09 27	09 36	09 42	09 50	09 57	10 05	10 12	10 20	10 27
Brondesbury Park	d	09 13	09 21	09 28	09 37	09 44	09 51	09 58	10 06	10 13	10 21	10 28
Kensal Rise	d	09 15	09 23	09 30	09 39	09 46	09 53	10 00	10 08	10 15	10 23	10 30
Willesden Jn. High Level ⊖	a	09 19	09 27	09 34	09 43	09 49	09 57	10 04	10 12	10 19	10 27	10 34
	d	09 20	09 28	09 35	09 44	09 50	09 58	10 05	10 13	10 20	10 28	10 35
Willesden Jn Low Level ⊖	a											
Shepherd's Bush ⊖	d		09 38		09 54		10 08		10 23		10 38	
Kensington (Olympia) ⊖	d		09 41		09 56		10 11		10 26		10 41	
West Brompton ⊖	d		09 43		09 59		10 13		10 28		10 43	
Imperial Wharf	d		09 46		10 02		10 16		10 31		10 46	
Clapham Junction 10	a		09 54		10 10		10 24		10 39		10 54	
Acton Central	d	09 25		09 40		09 55		10 10		10 25		10 40
South Acton	d	09 28		09 43		09 57		10 13		10 28		10 43
Gunnersbury ⊖	d	09 32		09 48		10 02		10 18		10 32		10 48
Kew Gardens ⊖	d	09 35		09 51		10 05		10 21		10 35		10 51
Richmond ⊖	a	09 44		10 00		10 15		10 31		10 45		11 00

Station		LO	LO	LO	LO	LO	LO	LO	LO	LO	LO	LO
Stratford 7 ⊖	d	10 00	10 07	10 15	10 22	10 30	10 37	10 45	10 52	11 00	11 07	11 15
Hackney Wick	d	10 03	10 10	10 18	10 25	10 33	10 40	10 48	10 55	11 03	11 10	11 18
Homerton	d	10 06	10 13	10 21	10 28	10 36	10 43	10 51	10 58	11 06	11 13	11 21
Hackney Central	d	10 08	10 15	10 23	10 30	10 38	10 45	10 53	11 00	11 08	11 15	11 23
Dalston Kingsland	d	10 10	10 17	10 25	10 32	10 40	10 47	10 55	11 02	11 10	11 17	11 25
Canonbury	d	10 12	10 19	10 27	10 34	10 42	10 49	10 57	11 04	11 12	11 19	11 27
Highbury & Islington ⊖	d	10 16	10 23	10 31	10 38	10 46	10 53	11 01	11 08	11 16	11 23	11 31
Caledonian Rd & Barnsbury	d	10 18	10 25	10 33	10 40	10 48	10 55	11 03	11 10	11 18	11 25	11 33
Camden Road	d	10 22	10 29	10 37	10 44	10 52	10 59	11 07	11 14	11 22	11 29	11 37
Kentish Town West	d	10 24	10 31	10 39	10 46	10 54	11 01	11 09	11 16	11 24	11 31	11 39
Gospel Oak	d	10 27	10 34	10 42	10 49	10 57	11 04	11 12	11 19	11 27	11 34	11 42
Hampstead Heath	d	10 29	10 36	10 44	10 51	10 59	11 06	11 14	11 21	11 29	11 36	11 44
Finchley Road & Frognal	d	10 31	10 38	10 46	10 53	11 01	11 08	11 16	11 23	11 31	11 38	11 46
West Hampstead ⊖	d	10 33	10 40	10 48	10 55	11 03	11 10	11 18	11 25	11 33	11 40	11 48
Brondesbury	d	10 35	10 42	10 50	10 57	11 05	11 12	11 20	11 27	11 35	11 42	11 50
Brondesbury Park	d	10 36	10 43	10 51	10 58	11 06	11 13	11 21	11 28	11 36	11 43	11 51
Kensal Rise	d	10 38	10 45	10 53	11 00	11 08	11 15	11 23	11 30	11 38	11 45	11 53
Willesden Jn. High Level ⊖	a	10 42	10 49	10 58	11 04	11 12	11 19	11 27	11 34	11 42	11 49	11 57
	d	10 43	10 50	10 59	11 05	11 13	11 20	11 28	11 35	11 43	11 50	11 58
Willesden Jn Low Level ⊖	a											
Shepherd's Bush ⊖	d	10 53		11 09		11 23		11 38		11 53		12 08
Kensington (Olympia) ⊖	d	10 56		11 11		11 26		11 41		11 56		12 11
West Brompton ⊖	d	10 58		11 14		11 28		11 43		11 58		12 13
Imperial Wharf	d	11 01		11 17		11 31		11 46		12 01		12 16
Clapham Junction 10	a	11 09		11 25		11 39		11 54		12 09		12 24
Acton Central	d		10 55		11 10		11 25		11 40		11 55	
South Acton	d		10 58		11 13		11 28		11 43		11 58	
Gunnersbury ⊖	d		11 02		11 18		11 32		11 48		12 02	
Kew Gardens ⊖	d		11 05		11 21		11 35		11 51		12 05	
Richmond ⊖	a		11 15		11 30		11 45		12 01		12 15	

Stratford - Highbury and Islington, West Hampstead, Willesden Junction, Clapham Junction and Richmond

Network Diagram - see first Page of Table 59

Station		LO	LO	LO	LO	LO	LO	LO	LO	LO	LO	LO
Stratford 7 ⊖	d	11 22	11 30	11 37	11 45	11 52	12 00	12 07	12 15	12 22	12 27	12 37
Hackney Wick	d	11 25	11 33	11 40	11 48	11 55	12 03	12 10	12 18	12 25	12 30	12 40
Homerton	d	11 28	11 36	11 43	11 51	11 58	12 06	12 13	12 21	12 28	12 31	12 43
Hackney Central	d	11 30	11 38	11 45	11 53	12 00	12 08	12 15	12 23	12 30	12 33	12 45
Dalston Kingsland	d	11 32	11 40	11 47	11 55	12 02	12 10	12 17	12 25	12 32	12 35	12 47
Canonbury	d	11 34	11 42	11 49	11 57	12 04	12 12	12 19	12 27	12 34	12 37	12 49
Highbury & Islington ⊖	d	11 38	11 46	11 53	12 01	12 08	12 16	12 23	12 31	12 38	12 40	12 53
Caledonian Rd & Barnsbury	d	11 40	11 48	11 55	12 03	12 10	12 18	12 25	12 33	12 40	12 42	12 55
Camden Road	d	11 44	11 52	11 59	12 07	12 14	12 22	12 29	12 37	12 44	12 46	12 59
Kentish Town West	d	11 46	11 54	12 01	12 09	12 16	12 24	12 31	12 39	12 46	12 49	13 01
Gospel Oak	d	11 49	11 57	12 04	12 12	12 19	12 27	12 34	12 42	12 49	12 51	13 04
Hampstead Heath	d	11 51	11 59	12 06	12 14	12 21	12 29	12 36	12 44	12 51	12 53	13 06
Finchley Road & Frognal	d	11 53	12 01	12 08	12 16	12 23	12 31	12 38	12 46	12 53	12 55	13 08
West Hampstead ⊖	d	11 55	12 03	12 10	12 18	12 25	12 33	12 40	12 48	12 55	12 58	13 10
Brondesbury	d	11 57	12 05	12 12	12 20	12 27	12 35	12 42	12 50	12 57	12 59	13 12
Brondesbury Park	d	11 58	12 06	12 13	12 21	12 28	12 36	12 43	12 51	12 58	13 01	13 13
Kensal Rise	d	12 00	12 08	12 15	12 23	12 30	12 38	12 45	12 53	13 00	13 03	13 15
Willesden Jn. High Level ⊖	a	12 04	12 12	12 19	12 27	12 34	12 42	12 49	12 57	13 04	13 07	13 19
	d	12 05	12 13	12 20	12 28	12 35	12 43	12 50	12 58	13 05	13 10	13 20
Willesden Jn Low Level ⊖	a											
Shepherd's Bush ⊖	d		12 23		12 38		12 53		13 08		13 23	
Kensington (Olympia) ⊖	d		12 26		12 41		12 56		13 11		13 26	
West Brompton ⊖	d		12 28		12 43		12 58		13 13		13 28	
Imperial Wharf	d		12 31		12 46		13 01		13 16		13 31	
Clapham Junction 10	a		12 39		12 54		13 09		13 24		13 39	
Acton Central	d	12 10		12 25		12 40		12 55		13 10		13 25
South Acton	d	12 13		12 28		12 43		12 58		13 13		13 28
Gunnersbury ⊖	d	12 18		12 32		12 48		13 02		13 18		13 32
Kew Gardens ⊖	d	12 21		12 35		12 51		13 05		13 21		13 35
Richmond ⊖	a	12 30		12 45		13 00		13 15		13 30		13 45

Station		LO	LO	LO	LO	LO	LO	LO	LO	LO	LO	LO
Stratford 7 ⊖	d	12 45	12 52	13 00	13 07	13 15	13 22	13 30	13 37	13 45	13 52	14 00
Hackney Wick	d	12 48	12 55	13 03	13 10	13 18	13 25	13 33	13 40	13 48	13 55	14 03
Homerton	d	12 50	12 58	13 06	13 13	13 21	13 28	13 36	13 43	13 51	13 58	14 06
Hackney Central	d	12 52	13 00	13 08	13 15	13 23	13 30	13 38	13 45	13 53	14 00	14 08
Dalston Kingsland	d	12 54	13 02	13 10	13 17	13 25	13 32	13 40	13 47	13 55	14 02	14 10
Canonbury	d	12 56	13 04	13 12	13 19	13 27	13 34	13 42	13 49	13 57	14 04	14 12
Highbury & Islington ⊖	d	12 59	13 06	13 16	13 23	13 31	13 38	13 46	13 53	14 01	14 08	14 16
Caledonian Rd & Barnsbury	d	13 01	13 08	13 18	13 25	13 33	13 40	13 48	13 55	14 03	14 10	14 18
Camden Road	d	13 04	13 11	13 22	13 29	13 37	13 44	13 52	13 59	14 07	14 14	14 22
Kentish Town West	d	13 07	13 14	13 24	13 31	13 39	13 46	13 54	14 01	14 09	14 16	14 24
Gospel Oak	d	13 09	13 17	13 27	13 34	13 42	13 49	13 57	14 04	14 12	14 19	14 27
Hampstead Heath	d	13 11	13 19	13 29	13 36	13 44	13 51	13 59	14 06	14 14	14 21	14 29
Finchley Road & Frognal	d	13 13	13 21	13 31	13 38	13 46	13 53	14 01	14 08	14 16	14 23	14 31
West Hampstead ⊖	d	13 16	13 24	13 33	13 40	13 48	13 55	14 03	14 10	14 18	14 25	14 33
Brondesbury	d	13 17	13 25	13 35	13 42	13 50	13 57	14 05	14 12	14 20	14 27	14 35
Brondesbury Park	d	13 19	13 27	13 36	13 43	13 51	13 58	14 06	14 13	14 21	14 28	14 36
Kensal Rise	d	13 21	13 29	13 38	13 45	13 53	14 00	14 08	14 15	14 23	14 30	14 38
Willesden Jn. High Level ⊖	a	13 26	13 33	13 42	13 49	13 57	14 04	14 12	14 19	14 27	14 34	14 42
	d	13 27	13 34	13 43	13 50	13 58	14 05	14 13	14 20	14 28	14 35	14 43
Willesden Jn Low Level ⊖	a											
Shepherd's Bush ⊖	d	13 38		13 53		14 08		14 23		14 38		14 53
Kensington (Olympia) ⊖	d	13 41		13 56		14 11		14 26		14 41		14 56
West Brompton ⊖	d	13 43		13 58		14 13		14 28		14 43		14 58
Imperial Wharf	d	13 46		14 01		14 16		14 31		14 46		15 01
Clapham Junction 10	a	13 54		14 09		14 24		14 39		14 54		15 09
Acton Central	d		13 40		13 55		14 10		14 25		14 40	
South Acton	d		13 43		13 58		14 13		14 28		14 43	
Gunnersbury ⊖	d		13 48		14 02		14 18		14 32		14 48	
Kew Gardens ⊖	d		13 51		14 05		14 21		14 35		14 51	
Richmond ⊖	a		14 00		14 15		14 30		14 45		15 00	

Station		LO	LO	LO	LO	LO	LO	LO	LO	LO	LO	LO
Stratford 7 ⊖	d	14 07	14 15	14 22	14 30	14 37	14 45	14 52	15 00	15 07	15 15	15 22
Hackney Wick	d	14 10	14 18	14 25	14 33	14 40	14 48	14 55	15 03	15 10	15 18	15 25
Homerton	d	14 13	14 21	14 28	14 36	14 43	14 51	14 58	15 06	15 13	15 21	15 28
Hackney Central	d	14 15	14 23	14 30	14 38	14 45	14 53	15 00	15 08	15 15	15 23	15 30
Dalston Kingsland	d	14 17	14 25	14 32	14 40	14 47	14 55	15 02	15 10	15 17	15 25	15 32
Canonbury	d	14 19	14 27	14 34	14 42	14 49	14 57	15 04	15 12	15 19	15 27	15 34
Highbury & Islington ⊖	d	14 23	14 31	14 38	14 46	14 53	15 01	15 08	15 16	15 23	15 31	15 38
Caledonian Rd & Barnsbury	d	14 25	14 33	14 40	14 48	14 55	15 03	15 10	15 18	15 25	15 33	15 40
Camden Road	d	14 29	14 37	14 44	14 52	14 59	15 07	15 14	15 22	15 29	15 37	15 44
Kentish Town West	d	14 31	14 39	14 46	14 54	15 01	15 09	15 16	15 24	15 31	15 39	15 46
Gospel Oak	d	14 34	14 42	14 49	14 57	15 04	15 12	15 19	15 27	15 34	15 42	15 49
Hampstead Heath	d	14 36	14 44	14 51	14 59	15 06	15 14	15 21	15 29	15 36	15 44	15 51
Finchley Road & Frognal	d	14 38	14 46	14 53	15 01	15 08	15 16	15 23	15 31	15 38	15 46	15 53
West Hampstead ⊖	d	14 40	14 48	14 55	15 03	15 10	15 18	15 25	15 33	15 40	15 48	15 55
Brondesbury	d	14 42	14 50	14 57	15 05	15 12	15 20	15 27	15 35	15 42	15 50	15 57
Brondesbury Park	d	14 43	14 51	14 58	15 06	15 13	15 21	15 28	15 36	15 43	15 51	15 58
Kensal Rise	d	14 45	14 53	15 00	15 08	15 15	15 23	15 30	15 38	15 45	15 53	16 00
Willesden Jn. High Level ⊖	a	14 49	14 57	15 04	15 12	15 19	15 27	15 34	15 42	15 49	15 57	16 04
	d	14 50	14 58	15 05	15 13	15 20	15 28	15 35	15 43	15 50	15 58	16 05
Willesden Jn Low Level ⊖	a											
Shepherd's Bush ⊖	d		15 08		15 23		15 38		15 53		16 08	
Kensington (Olympia) ⊖	d		15 11		15 26		15 41		15 56		16 11	
West Brompton ⊖	d		15 13		15 28		15 43		15 58		16 13	
Imperial Wharf	d		15 16		15 31		15 46		16 01		16 16	
Clapham Junction 10	a		15 24		15 39		15 54		16 09		16 24	
Acton Central	d	14 55		15 10		15 25		15 40		15 55		16 10
South Acton	d	14 58		15 13		15 28		15 43		15 58		16 13
Gunnersbury ⊖	d	15 02		15 18		15 32		15 48		16 02		16 18
Kew Gardens ⊖	d	15 05		15 21		15 35		15 51		16 05		16 21
Richmond ⊖	a	15 15		15 30		15 45		16 00		16 15		16 30

Station		LO	LO	LO	LO	LO	LO	LO	LO	LO	LO	LO
Stratford 7 ⊖	d	15 30	15 37	15 45	15 52	16 00	16 07	16 15	16 22	16 32	16 37	16 45
Hackney Wick	d	15 33	15 40	15 48	15 55	16 03	16 10	16 18	16 25	16 35	16 40	16 48
Homerton	d	15 36	15 43	15 51	15 58	16 06	16 13	16 21	16 28	16 37	16 43	16 51
Hackney Central	d	15 38	15 45	15 53	16 00	16 08	16 15	16 23	16 30	16 39	16 45	16 53
Dalston Kingsland	d	15 40	15 47	15 55	16 02	16 10	16 17	16 25	16 32	16 41	16 47	16 55
Canonbury	d	15 42	15 49	15 57	16 04	16 12	16 19	16 27	16 34	16 43	16 49	16 57
Highbury & Islington ⊖	d	15 46	15 53	16 01	16 08	16 16	16 23	16 31	16 38	16 46	16 53	17 01
Caledonian Rd & Barnsbury	d	15 48	15 55	16 03	16 10	16 18	16 25	16 33	16 40	16 48	16 55	17 03
Camden Road	d	15 52	15 59	16 07	16 14	16 22	16 29	16 37	16 44	16 52	16 59	17 07
Kentish Town West	d	15 54	16 01	16 09	16 16	16 24	16 31	16 39	16 46	16 55	17 01	17 09
Gospel Oak	d	15 57	16 04	16 12	16 19	16 27	16 34	16 42	16 49	16 57	17 04	17 12
Hampstead Heath	d	15 59	16 06	16 14	16 21	16 29	16 36	16 44	16 51	16 59	17 06	17 14
Finchley Road & Frognal	d	16 01	16 08	16 16	16 23	16 31	16 38	16 46	16 53	17 01	17 08	17 16
West Hampstead ⊖	d	16 03	16 10	16 18	16 25	16 33	16 40	16 48	16 55	17 03	17 10	17 18
Brondesbury	d	16 05	16 12	16 20	16 27	16 35	16 42	16 50	16 57	17 04	17 12	17 20
Brondesbury Park	d	16 06	16 13	16 21	16 28	16 36	16 43	16 51	16 58	17 06	17 13	17 21
Kensal Rise	d	16 08	16 15	16 23	16 30	16 38	16 45	16 53	17 00	17 08	17 15	17 23
Willesden Jn. High Level ⊖	a	16 12	16 19	16 27	16 34	16 42	16 49	16 57	17 04	17 12	17 19	17 27
	d	16 13	16 20	16 28	16 35	16 43	16 50	16 58	17 05	17 13	17 20	17 28
Willesden Jn Low Level ⊖	a											
Shepherd's Bush ⊖	d	16 23		16 38		16 53		17 08		17 23		17 38
Kensington (Olympia) ⊖	d	16 26		16 41		16 56		17 11		17 26		17 41
West Brompton ⊖	d	16 28		16 43		16 58		17 13		17 28		17 43
Imperial Wharf	d	16 31		16 46		17 01		17 16		17 31		17 46
Clapham Junction 10	a	16 39		16 54		17 09		17 24		17 39		17 54
Acton Central	d		16 25		16 40		16 55		17 10		17 25	
South Acton	d		16 28		16 43		16 58		17 13		17 28	
Gunnersbury ⊖	d		16 32		16 48		17 02		17 18		17 32	
Kew Gardens ⊖	d		16 35		16 51		17 05		17 21		17 35	
Richmond ⊖	a		16 45		17 00		17 15		17 30		17 45	

Stratford - Highbury and Islington, West Hampstead, Willesden Junction, Clapham Junction and Richmond

Network Diagram - see first Page of Table 59

		LO	LO	LO	LO	LO	LO	LO	LO	LO	LO	LO	LO	LO	LO	LO	LO	LO	LO	LO	LO	LO	LO
Stratford 7 ⊖	d	16 52	17 00	17 07	17 15	17 22	17 30	17 37	17 45	17 52	18 00	18 07	18 15	18 22	18 30	18 37	18 45	18 52	19 00	19 07	19 15	19 22	19 30
Hackney Wick	d	16 55	17 03	17 10	17 18	17 25	17 33	17 40	17 48	17 55	18 03	18 10	18 18	18 25	18 33	18 40	18 48	18 55	19 03	19 10	19 18	19 25	19 33
Homerton	d	16 58	17 06	17 13	17 21	17 28	17 36	17 43	17 51	17 58	18 06	18 13	18 21	18 28	18 36	18 43	18 51	18 58	19 06	19 13	19 21	19 28	19 36
Hackney Central	d	17 00	17 08	17 15	17 23	17 30	17 38	17 45	17 53	18 00	18 08	18 15	18 23	18 30	18 38	18 45	18 53	19 00	19 08	19 15	19 23	19 30	19 38
Dalston Kingsland	d	17 02	17 10	17 17	17 25	17 32	17 40	17 47	17 55	18 02	18 10	18 17	18 25	18 32	18 40	18 47	18 55	19 02	19 10	19 17	19 25	19 32	19 40
Canonbury	d	17 04	17 12	17 19	17 27	17 34	17 42	17 49	17 57	18 04	18 12	18 19	18 27	18 34	18 42	18 49	18 57	19 04	19 12	19 19	19 27	19 34	19 42
Highbury & Islington ⊖	d	17 08	17 16	17 23	17 31	17 38	17 46	17 53	18 01	18 08	18 16	18 23	18 31	18 38	18 46	18 53	19 01	19 08	19 16	19 23	19 31	19 38	19 46
Caledonian Rd & Barnsbury	d	17 10	17 18	17 25	17 33	17 40	17 48	17 55	18 03	18 10	18 18	18 25	18 33	18 40	18 48	18 55	19 03	19 10	19 18	19 25	19 33	19 40	19 48
Camden Road	d	17 14	17 22	17 29	17 37	17 44	17 52	17 59	18 07	18 14	18 22	18 29	18 37	18 44	18 52	18 59	19 07	19 14	19 22	19 28	19 37	19 44	19 52
Kentish Town West	d	17 16	17 24	17 31	17 39	17 46	17 54	18 01	18 09	18 16	18 24	18 31	18 39	18 46	18 54	19 01	19 09	19 16	19 24	19 31	19 39	19 46	19 54
Gospel Oak	d	17 19	17 27	17 34	17 42	17 49	17 57	18 04	18 12	18 19	18 27	18 33	18 42	18 49	18 57	19 04	19 12	19 19	19 27	19 33	19 42	19 49	19 57
Hampstead Heath	d	17 21	17 29	17 36	17 44	17 51	17 59	18 06	18 14	18 21	18 29	18 35	18 44	18 51	18 59	19 06	19 14	19 21	19 29	19 35	19 44	19 51	19 59
Finchley Road & Frognal	d	17 23	17 31	17 38	17 46	17 53	18 01	18 08	18 16	18 23	18 31	18 37	18 46	18 53	19 01	19 08	19 16	19 23	19 31	19 37	19 46	19 53	20 01
West Hampstead ⊖	d	17 25	17 33	17 40	17 48	17 55	18 03	18 10	18 18	18 25	18 33	18 39	18 48	18 55	19 03	19 10	19 18	19 25	19 33	19 40	19 48	19 55	20 03
Brondesbury	d	17 27	17 35	17 42	17 50	17 57	18 05	18 12	18 20	18 27	18 35	18 41	18 50	18 57	19 05	19 12	19 20	19 27	19 35	19 41	19 50	19 57	20 05
Brondesbury Park	d	17 28	17 36	17 43	17 51	17 58	18 06	18 13	18 21	18 28	18 36	18 42	18 51	18 58	19 06	19 13	19 21	19 28	19 36	19 43	19 51	19 58	20 06
Kensal Rise	d	17 30	17 38	17 45	17 53	18 00	18 08	18 15	18 23	18 30	18 38	18 44	18 53	19 00	19 08	19 15	19 23	19 30	19 38	19 45	19 53	20 00	20 08
Willesden Jn. High Level ⊖	a	17 34	17 42	17 49	17 57	18 04	18 12	18 19	18 27	18 34	18 42	18 48	18 57	19 04	19 12	19 19	19 27	19 34	19 42	19 49	19 57	20 04	20 12
	d	17 35	17 43	17 50	17 58	18 05	18 13	18 20	18 28	18 35	18 43	18 49	18 58	19 05	19 13	19 20	19 28	19 35	19 43	19 50	19 58	20 05	20 13
Willesden Jn Low Level ⊖	a																						
Shepherd's Bush ⊖	d		17 53		18 08		18 23		18 38		18 53		19 08		19 23		19 38		19 53		20 08		20 23
Kensington (Olympia) ⊖	d		17 56		18 11		18 26		18 41		18 56		19 11		19 26		19 41		19 56		20 11		20 26
West Brompton ⊖	d		17 58		18 13		18 28		18 43		18 58		19 13		19 28		19 43		19 58		20 13		20 28
Imperial Wharf	d		18 01		18 16		18 31		18 46		19 01		19 16		19 31		19 46		20 01		20 16		20 31
Clapham Junction 10	a		18 09		18 24		18 39		18 54		19 09		19 24		19 39		19 54		20 09		20 24		20 39
Acton Central	d	17 40		17 55		18 10		18 25		18 40		18 54		19 10		19 25		19 40		19 55		20 11	
South Acton	d	17 43		17 58		18 13		18 28		18 43		18 57		19 13		19 28		19 43		19 58		20 14	
Gunnersbury ⊖	d	17 48		18 02		18 18		18 32		18 48		19 02		19 18		19 32		19 48		20 02		20 18	
Kew Gardens ⊖	d	17 51		18 05		18 21		18 35		18 51		19 05		19 21		19 35		19 51		20 05		20 21	
Richmond ⊖	a	18 00		18 15		18 30		18 45		19 00		19 15		19 30		19 45		20 00		20 15		20 30	

		LO	LO	LO	LO	LO	LO	LO	LO	LO	LO	LO	LO	LO	LO	LO	LO	LO	LO	LO	LO	LO	LO
Stratford 7 ⊖	d	19 37	19 45	19 52	20 00	20 07	20 15	20 22	20 30	20 37	20 45	20 52	21 00	21 07	21 15	21 22	21 30	21 37	21 45	21 52	22 00	22 07	22 15
Hackney Wick	d	19 40	19 48	19 55	20 03	20 10	20 18	20 25	20 33	20 40	20 48	20 55	21 03	21 10	21 18	21 25	21 33	21 40	21 48	21 55	22 03	22 10	22 18
Homerton	d	19 43	19 51	19 58	20 06	20 13	20 21	20 28	20 36	20 43	20 51	20 58	21 06	21 13	21 21	21 28	21 36	21 43	21 51	21 58	22 06	22 13	22 21
Hackney Central	d	19 45	19 53	20 00	20 08	20 15	20 23	20 30	20 38	20 45	20 53	21 00	21 08	21 15	21 23	21 30	21 38	21 45	21 53	22 00	22 08	22 15	22 23
Dalston Kingsland	d	19 47	19 55	20 02	20 10	20 17	20 25	20 32	20 40	20 47	20 55	21 02	21 10	21 17	21 25	21 32	21 40	21 47	21 55	22 02	22 10	22 17	22 25
Canonbury	d	19 49	19 57	20 04	20 12	20 19	20 27	20 34	20 42	20 49	20 57	21 04	21 12	21 19	21 27	21 34	21 42	21 49	21 57	22 04	22 12	22 19	22 27
Highbury & Islington ⊖	d	19 53	20 01	20 08	20 16	20 23	20 31	20 38	20 46	20 53	21 01	21 08	21 16	21 23	21 31	21 38	21 46	21 53	22 01	22 08	22 16	22 23	22 31
Caledonian Rd & Barnsbury	d	19 55	20 03	20 10	20 18	20 25	20 33	20 40	20 48	20 55	21 03	21 10	21 18	21 25	21 33	21 40	21 48	21 55	22 03	22 10	22 18	22 25	22 33
Camden Road	d	19 59	20 07	20 14	20 22	20 29	20 37	20 44	20 52	20 59	21 07	21 14	21 22	21 29	21 37	21 44	21 52	21 59	22 07	22 14	22 21	22 28	22 37
Kentish Town West	d	20 01	20 09	20 16	20 24	20 31	20 39	20 46	20 54	21 01	21 09	21 16	21 24	21 31	21 39	21 46	21 54	22 01	22 09	22 16	22 23	22 30	22 39
Gospel Oak	d	20 04	20 12	20 19	20 27	20 34	20 42	20 49	20 57	21 04	21 12	21 19	21 27	21 34	21 42	21 49	21 57	22 04	22 12	22 19	22 26	22 33	22 42
Hampstead Heath	d	20 06	20 14	20 21	20 29	20 36	20 44	20 51	20 59	21 06	21 14	21 21	21 29	21 36	21 44	21 51	21 59	22 06	22 14	22 21	22 28	22 35	22 44
Finchley Road & Frognal	d	20 08	20 16	20 23	20 31	20 38	20 46	20 53	21 01	21 08	21 16	21 23	21 31	21 38	21 46	21 53	22 01	22 08	22 16	22 23	22 30	22 37	22 46
West Hampstead ⊖	d	20 10	20 18	20 25	20 33	20 40	20 48	20 55	21 03	21 10	21 18	21 25	21 33	21 40	21 48	21 55	22 03	22 10	22 18	22 25	22 32	22 39	22 48
Brondesbury	d	20 12	20 20	20 27	20 35	20 42	20 50	20 57	21 05	21 12	21 20	21 27	21 35	21 42	21 50	21 57	22 05	22 12	22 20	22 27	22 34	22 40	22 50
Brondesbury Park	d	20 13	20 21	20 28	20 36	20 43	20 51	20 58	21 06	21 13	21 21	21 28	21 36	21 43	21 51	21 58	22 06	22 13	22 21	22 28	22 35	22 42	22 51
Kensal Rise	d	20 15	20 23	20 30	20 38	20 45	20 53	21 00	21 08	21 15	21 23	21 30	21 38	21 45	21 53	22 00	22 08	22 15	22 23	22 30	22 37	22 44	22 53
Willesden Jn. High Level ⊖	a	20 19	20 27	20 34	20 42	20 49	20 57	21 04	21 12	21 19	21 27	21 34	21 42	21 49	21 57	22 04	22 12	22 19	22 27	22 34	22 40	22 47	22 57
	d	20 20	20 28	20 35	20 43	20 50	20 58	21 05	21 13	21 20	21 28	21 35	21 43	21 50	21 58	22 05	22 13	22 20	22 28	22 35	22 41	22 48	22 58
Willesden Jn Low Level ⊖	a																						
Shepherd's Bush ⊖	d		20 38		20 53		21 09		21 23		21 38		21 53		22 09		22 23		22 38		22 53		23 08
Kensington (Olympia) ⊖	d		20 41		20 56		21 12		21 26		21 41		21 56		22 12		22 26		22 41		22 56		23 11
West Brompton ⊖	d		20 43		20 58		21 14		21 28		21 43		21 58		22 14		22 28		22 43		22 58		23 13
Imperial Wharf	d		20 46		21 01		21 17		21 31		21 46		22 01		22 19		22 31		22 46		23 01		23 16
Clapham Junction 10	a		20 54		21 09		21 25		21 39		21 54		22 09		22 25		22 39		22 54		23 09		23 24
Acton Central	d	20 26		20 40		20 55		21 10		21 25		21 40		21 55		22 10		22 25		22 40		22 55	
South Acton	d	20 28		20 43		20 58		21 13		21 28		21 43		21 58		22 13		22 28		22 43		22 57	
Gunnersbury ⊖	d	20 32		20 48		21 02		21 18		21 32		21 48		22 02		22 18		22 32		22 48		23 02	
Kew Gardens ⊖	d	20 35		20 51		21 05		21 21		21 35		21 51		22 05		22 21		22 35		22 51		23 05	
Richmond ⊖	a	20 45		21 00		21 15		21 30		21 45		22 00		22 15		22 30		22 45		23 00		23 15	

Table 59 — Saturdays
1 September to 8 September

Stratford - Highbury and Islington, West Hampstead, Willesden Junction, Clapham Junction and Richmond

Network Diagram - see first Page of Table 59

		LO	LO	LO	LO	LO	LO	LO	LO	LO	LO	LO	LO	LO
Stratford 7 ⊖	d	22 22	22 30	22 37	22 45	22 52	23 00	23 07	23 15	23 22	23 30	23 37	23 45	23 52
Hackney Wick	d	22 25	22 33	22 40	22 48	22 55	23 03	23 10	23 18	23 25	23 33	23 40	23 48	23 55
Homerton	d	22 28	22 36	22 43	22 51	22 58	23 06	23 13	23 21	23 28	23 36	23 43	23 51	23 58
Hackney Central	d	22 30	22 38	22 45	22 53	23 00	23 08	23 15	23 23	23 30	23 38	23 45	23 53	00 01
Dalston Kingsland	d	22 32	22 40	22 47	22 55	23 02	23 10	23 17	23 25	23 32	23 40	23 47	23 55	00 03
Canonbury	d	22 34	22 42	22 49	22 57	23 04	23 12	23 19	23 27	23 34	23 42	23 49	23 57	00 04
Highbury & Islington ⊖	d	22 38	22 46	22 53	23 01	23 08	23 16	23 23	23 31	23 38	23 46	23 53	00 01	00 08
Caledonian Rd & Barnsbury	d	22 40	22 48	22 55	23 03	23 10	23 18	23 25	23 33	23 40	23 48	23 55	00 03	00 10
Camden Road	d	22 44	22 52	22 59	23 07	23 14	23 22	23 29	23 37	23 44	23 52	23 59	00 07	00 14
Kentish Town West	d	22 46	22 54	23 02	23 09	23 16	23 24	23 31	23 39	23 46	23 54	00 01	00 09	00 16
Gospel Oak	d	22 49	22 57	23 04	23 12	23 19	23 27	23 34	23 42	23 49	23 57	00 04	00 12	00 19
Hampstead Heath	d	22 51	22 59	23 06	23 14	23 21	23 29	23 36	23 44	23 51	23 59	00 06	00 14	00 21
Finchley Road & Frognal	d	22 53	23 01	23 08	23 16	23 23	23 31	23 38	23 46	23 53	00 01	00 08	00 16	00 23
West Hampstead ⊖	d	22 55	23 04	23 11	23 18	23 25	23 33	23 40	23 48	23 55	00 03	00 10	00 18	00 25
Brondesbury	d	22 57	23 05	23 12	23 20	23 27	23 35	23 42	23 50	23 57	00 05	00 12	00 20	00 27
Brondesbury Park	d	22 58	23 07	23 14	23 21	23 28	23 36	23 43	23 51	23 58	00 06	00 13	00 21	00 28
Kensal Rise	d	23 00	23 09	23 16	23 23	23 30	23 38	23 45	23 53	00 01	00 08	00 15	00 23	00 30
Willesden Jn. High Level ⊖	a	23 04	23 12	23 20	23 27	23 34	23 42	23 49	23 57	00 04	00 12	00 19	00 27	00 34
	d	23 05	23 14	23 21	23 28	23 35	23 43	23 50	23 59	00 05	00 13	00 20	00 28	00 35
Willesden Jn Low Level ⊖	a													
Shepherd's Bush ⊖	d		23 24		23 38		23 53		00 09		00 23		00 38	
Kensington (Olympia) ⊖	d		23 27		23 41		23 56		00 11		00 26		00 41	
West Brompton ⊖	d		23 29		23 43		23 58		00 14		00 28		00 43	
Imperial Wharf	d		23 32		23 46		00 01		00 17		00 31		00 46	
Clapham Junction 10	a		23 40		23 54		00 09		00 22		00 39		00 54	
Acton Central	d	23 10		23 26		23 40		23 55		00 10		00 25		00 40
South Acton	d	23 13		23 28		23 43		23 58		00 13		00 28		00 43
Gunnersbury ⊖	d	23 18		23 32		23 48		00 02		00 18		00 32		00 48
Kew Gardens ⊖	d	23 21		23 35		23 51		00 05		00 21		00 35		00 51
Richmond ⊖	a	23 30		23 45		00 01		00 14		00 31		00 44		01 00

Saturdays
from 15 September

		LO	LO	LO	LO	LO	LO	LO	LO	LO	LO	LO	LO	LO	LO	LO	LO	LO	LO	LO	LO	LO	LO
Stratford 7 ⊖	d		23p45			05 42		05 55	06 05	06 15		06 25	06 35	06 45		06 55	07 05	07 15		07 25	07 35	07 45	
Hackney Wick	d		23p48			05 45		05 58	06 08	06 18		06 28	06 38	06 48		06 58	07 08	07 18		07 28	07 38	07 48	
Homerton	d		23p51			05 48		06 01	06 11	06 21		06 31	06 41	06 51		07 01	07 11	07 21		07 31	07 41	07 51	
Hackney Central	d		23p53			05 50		06 03	06 13	06 23		06 33	06 43	06 53		07 03	07 13	07 23		07 33	07 43	07 53	
Dalston Kingsland	d		23p55			05 52		06 05	06 15	06 25		06 35	06 45	06 55		07 05	07 15	07 25		07 35	07 45	07 55	
Canonbury	d		23p57			05 54		06 07	06 17	06 27		06 37	06 47	06 57		07 07	07 17	07 27		07 37	07 47	07 57	
Highbury & Islington ⊖	d		23p59			05 57		06 10	06 20	06 30		06 40	06 50	07 00		07 10	07 20	07 30		07 40	07 50	08 00	
Caledonian Rd & Barnsbury	d		00 02			05 59		06 12	06 22	06 32		06 42	06 52	07 02		07 12	07 22	07 32		07 42	07 52	08 02	
Camden Road	d		00 05			06 02		06 15	06 25	06 35		06 45	06 55	07 05		07 15	07 25	07 35		07 45	07 55	08 05	
Kentish Town West	d		00 07			06 07		06 17	06 27	06 37		06 47	06 57	07 07		07 17	07 27	07 37		07 47	07 57	08 07	
Gospel Oak	d		00 10			06 11		06 20	06 30	06 40		06 50	07 00	07 10		07 20	07 30	07 40		07 50	08 00	08 10	
Hampstead Heath	d		00 12			06 13		06 22	06 32	06 42		06 52	07 02	07 12		07 22	07 32	07 42		07 52	08 02	08 12	
Finchley Road & Frognal	d		00 14			06 15		06 24	06 34	06 44		06 54	07 04	07 14		07 24	07 34	07 44		07 54	08 04	08 14	
West Hampstead ⊖	d		00 16			06 17		06 26	06 36	06 46		06 56	07 06	07 16		07 26	07 36	07 46		07 56	08 06	08 16	
Brondesbury	d		00 18			06 19		06 28	06 38	06 48		06 58	07 08	07 18		07 28	07 38	07 48		07 58	08 08	08 18	
Brondesbury Park	d		00 19			06 20		06 29	06 39	06 49		06 59	07 09	07 19		07 29	07 39	07 49		07 59	08 09	08 19	
Kensal Rise	d		00 21			06 22		06 31	06 41	06 51		07 01	07 11	07 21		07 31	07 41	07 51		08 01	08 11	08 21	
Willesden Jn. High Level ⊖	a					06 25		06 35	06 45	06 55		07 05	07 15	07 25		07 35	07 45	07 55		08 05	08 15	08 25	
	d	23p40		06 02	06 06	06 26	06 31	06 36	06 46	06 56	07 01	07 06	07 16	07 26	07 31	07 36	07 46	07 56	08 01	08 06	08 16	08 26	08 31
Willesden Jn Low Level ⊖	a		00 29																				
Shepherd's Bush ⊖	d	23p48		06 10			06 39		06 54		07 09		07 24		07 39		07 54		08 09		08 24		08 39
Kensington (Olympia) ⊖	d	23p50		06 12			06 41		06 56		07 11		07 26		07 41		07 56		08 11		08 26		08 41
West Brompton ⊖	d	23p52		06 14			06 43		06 58		07 13		07 28		07 43		07 58		08 13		08 28		08 43
Imperial Wharf	d	23p55		06 17			06 46		07 01		07 16		07 31		07 46		08 01		08 16		08 31		08 46
Clapham Junction 10	a	00 02		06 25			06 53		07 09		07 23		07 39		07 53		08 09		08 23		08 39		08 53
Acton Central	d				06 11	06 31		06 41		07 01		07 11		07 31		07 41		08 01		08 11		08 31	
South Acton	d				06 14	06 34		06 44		07 04		07 14		07 34		07 44		08 04		08 14		08 34	
Gunnersbury ⊖	d				06 19	06 37		06 47		07 07		07 17		07 37		07 48		08 08		08 18		08 38	
Kew Gardens ⊖	d				06 22	06 40		06 50		07 10		07 20		07 40		07 51		08 11		08 21		08 41	
Richmond ⊖	a				06 29	06 44		06 56		07 16		07 26		07 46		07 56		08 16		08 26		08 46	

Table 59

Saturdays
from 15 September

Stratford - Highbury and Islington, West Hampstead, Willesden Junction, Clapham Junction and Richmond

Network Diagram - see first Page of Table 59

		LO	LO	LO	LO	LO	LO	LO	LO	LO	LO	LO	LO	LO	LO	LO	LO	LO	LO	LO	LO	LO	LO
Stratford ⊖	d	07 55	08 05	08 15		08 25	08 35	08 45		08 55	09 05	09 15		09 25	09 35	09 45		09 55	10 05	10 15		10 25	10 35
Hackney Wick	d	07 58	08 08	08 18		08 28	08 38	08 48		08 58	09 08	09 18		09 28	09 38	09 48		09 58	10 08	10 18		10 28	10 38
Homerton	d	08 01	08 11	08 21		08 31	08 41	08 51		09 01	09 11	09 21		09 31	09 41	09 51		10 01	10 11	10 21		10 31	10 41
Hackney Central	d	08 03	08 13	08 23		08 33	08 43	08 53		09 03	09 13	09 23		09 33	09 43	09 53		10 03	10 13	10 23		10 33	10 43
Dalston Kingsland	d	08 05	08 15	08 25		08 35	08 45	08 55		09 05	09 15	09 25		09 35	09 45	09 55		10 05	10 15	10 25		10 35	10 45
Canonbury	d	08 07	08 17	08 27		08 37	08 47	08 57		09 07	09 17	09 27		09 37	09 47	09 57		10 07	10 17	10 27		10 37	10 47
Highbury & Islington ⊖	d	08 10	08 20	08 30		08 40	08 50	09 00		09 10	09 20	09 30		09 40	09 50	10 00		10 10	10 20	10 30		10 40	10 50
Caledonian Rd & Barnsbury	d	08 12	08 22	08 32		08 42	08 52	09 02		09 12	09 22	09 32		09 42	09 52	10 02		10 12	10 22	10 32		10 42	10 52
Camden Road	d	08 15	08 25	08 35		08 45	08 55	09 05		09 15	09 25	09 35		09 45	09 55	10 05		10 15	10 25	10 35		10 45	10 55
Kentish Town West	d	08 17	08 27	08 37		08 47	08 57	09 07		09 17	09 27	09 37		09 47	09 57	10 07		10 17	10 27	10 37		10 47	10 57
Gospel Oak	d	08 20	08 30	08 40		08 50	09 00	09 10		09 20	09 30	09 40		09 50	10 00	10 10		10 20	10 30	10 40		10 50	11 00
Hampstead Heath	d	08 22	08 32	08 42		08 52	09 02	09 12		09 22	09 32	09 42		09 52	10 02	10 12		10 22	10 32	10 42		10 52	11 02
Finchley Road & Frognal	d	08 24	08 34	08 44		08 54	09 04	09 14		09 24	09 34	09 44		09 54	10 04	10 14		10 24	10 34	10 44		10 54	11 04
West Hampstead ⊖	d	08 26	08 36	08 46		08 56	09 06	09 16		09 26	09 36	09 46		09 56	10 06	10 16		10 26	10 36	10 46		10 56	11 06
Brondesbury	d	08 28	08 38	08 48		08 58	09 08	09 18		09 28	09 38	09 48		09 58	10 08	10 18		10 28	10 38	10 48		10 58	11 08
Brondesbury Park	d	08 29	08 39	08 49		08 59	09 09	09 19		09 29	09 39	09 49		09 59	10 09	10 19		10 29	10 39	10 49		10 59	11 09
Kensal Rise	d	08 31	08 41	08 51		09 01	09 11	09 21		09 31	09 41	09 51		10 01	10 11	10 21		10 31	10 41	10 51		11 01	11 11
Willesden Jn. High Level ⊖	a	08 35	08 45	08 55		09 05	09 15	09 25		09 35	09 45	09 55		10 05	10 15	10 25		10 35	10 45	10 55		11 05	11 15
	d	08 36	08 46	08 56	09 01	09 06	09 16	09 26	09 31	09 36	09 46	09 56	10 01	10 06	10 16	10 26	10 31	10 36	10 46	10 56	11 01	11 06	11 16
Willesden Jn Low Level ⊖	a																						
Shepherd's Bush ⊖	d		08 54		09 09		09 24		09 39		09 54		10 09		10 24		10 39		10 54		11 09		11 24
Kensington (Olympia) ⊖	d		08 56		09 11		09 26		09 41		09 56		10 11		10 26		10 41		10 56		11 11		11 26
West Brompton ⊖	d		08 58		09 13		09 28		09 43		09 58		10 13		10 28		10 43		10 58		11 13		11 28
Imperial Wharf	d		09 01		09 16		09 31		09 46		10 01		10 16		10 31		10 46		11 01		11 16		11 31
Clapham Junction 10	a		09 09		09 23		09 39		09 53		10 09		10 23		10 39		10 53		11 09		11 23		11 39
Acton Central	d	08 41		09 01		09 11		09 31		09 41		10 01		10 11		10 31		10 41		11 01		11 11	
South Acton	d	08 44		09 04		09 14		09 34		09 44		10 04		10 14		10 34		10 45		11 04		11 14	
Gunnersbury ⊖	d	08 48		09 08		09 18		09 38		09 48		10 08		10 18		10 38		10 48		11 08		11 18	
Kew Gardens ⊖	d	08 51		09 11		09 21		09 41		09 51		10 11		10 21		10 41		10 51		11 11		11 21	
Richmond ⊖	a	08 56		09 16		09 26		09 46		09 56		10 16		10 26		10 46		10 56		11 16		11 26	

		LO	LO	LO	LO	LO	LO	LO	LO	LO	LO	LO	LO	LO	LO	LO	LO	LO	LO	LO	LO	LO	LO
Stratford ⊖	d	10 45		10 55	11 05	11 15		11 25	11 35	11 45		11 55	12 05	12 15		12 25	12 35	12 45		12 55	13 05	13 15	
Hackney Wick	d	10 48		10 58	11 08	11 18		11 28	11 38	11 48		11 58	12 08	12 18		12 28	12 38	12 48		12 58	13 08	13 18	
Homerton	d	10 51		11 01	11 11	11 21		11 31	11 41	11 51		12 01	12 11	12 21		12 31	12 41	12 51		13 01	13 11	13 21	
Hackney Central	d	10 53		11 03	11 13	11 23		11 33	11 43	11 53		12 03	12 13	12 23		12 33	12 43	12 53		13 03	13 13	13 23	
Dalston Kingsland	d	10 55		11 05	11 15	11 25		11 35	11 45	11 55		12 05	12 15	12 25		12 35	12 45	12 55		13 05	13 15	13 25	
Canonbury	d	10 57		11 07	11 17	11 27		11 37	11 47	11 57		12 07	12 17	12 27		12 37	12 47	12 57		13 07	13 17	13 27	
Highbury & Islington ⊖	d	11 00		11 10	11 20	11 30		11 40	11 50	12 00		12 10	12 20	12 30		12 40	12 50	13 00		13 10	13 20	13 30	
Caledonian Rd & Barnsbury	d	11 02		11 12	11 22	11 32		11 42	11 52	12 02		12 12	12 22	12 32		12 42	12 52	13 02		13 12	13 22	13 32	
Camden Road	d	11 05		11 15	11 25	11 35		11 45	11 55	12 05		12 15	12 25	12 35		12 45	12 55	13 05		13 15	13 25	13 35	
Kentish Town West	d	11 07		11 17	11 27	11 37		11 47	11 57	12 07		12 17	12 27	12 37		12 47	12 57	13 07		13 17	13 27	13 37	
Gospel Oak	d	11 10		11 20	11 30	11 40		11 50	12 00	12 10		12 20	12 30	12 40		12 50	13 00	13 10		13 20	13 30	13 40	
Hampstead Heath	d	11 12		11 22	11 32	11 42		11 52	12 02	12 12		12 22	12 32	12 42		12 52	13 02	13 12		13 22	13 32	13 42	
Finchley Road & Frognal	d	11 14		11 24	11 34	11 44		11 54	12 04	12 14		12 24	12 34	12 44		12 54	13 04	13 14		13 24	13 34	13 44	
West Hampstead ⊖	d	11 16		11 26	11 36	11 46		11 56	12 06	12 16		12 26	12 36	12 46		12 56	13 06	13 16		13 26	13 36	13 46	
Brondesbury	d	11 18		11 28	11 38	11 48		11 58	12 08	12 18		12 28	12 38	12 48		12 58	13 08	13 18		13 28	13 38	13 48	
Brondesbury Park	d	11 19		11 29	11 39	11 49		11 59	12 09	12 19		12 29	12 39	12 49		12 59	13 09	13 19		13 29	13 39	13 49	
Kensal Rise	d	11 21		11 31	11 41	11 51		12 01	12 11	12 21		12 31	12 41	12 51		13 01	13 11	13 21		13 31	13 41	13 51	
Willesden Jn. High Level ⊖	a	11 25		11 35	11 45	11 55		12 05	12 15	12 25		12 35	12 45	12 55		13 05	13 15	13 25		13 35	13 45	13 55	
	d	11 26	11 31	11 36	11 46	11 56	12 01	12 06	12 16	12 26	12 31	12 36	12 46	12 56	13 01	13 06	13 16	13 26	13 31	13 36	13 46	13 56	14 01
Willesden Jn Low Level ⊖	a																						
Shepherd's Bush ⊖	d		11 39		11 54		12 09		12 24		12 39		12 54		13 09		13 24		13 39		13 54		14 09
Kensington (Olympia) ⊖	d		11 41		11 56		12 11		12 26		12 41		12 56		13 11		13 26		13 41		13 56		14 11
West Brompton ⊖	d		11 43		11 58		12 13		12 28		12 43		12 58		13 13		13 28		13 43		13 58		14 13
Imperial Wharf	d		11 46		12 01		12 16		12 31		12 46		13 01		13 16		13 31		13 46		14 01		14 16
Clapham Junction 10	a		11 53		12 09		12 23		12 39		12 53		13 09		13 23		13 39		13 55		14 09		14 23
Acton Central	d	11 31		11 41		12 01		12 11		12 31		12 41		13 01		13 11		13 31		13 41		14 01	
South Acton	d	11 34		11 44		12 04		12 14		12 34		12 44		13 04		13 14		13 34		13 44		14 04	
Gunnersbury ⊖	d	11 38		11 48		12 08		12 18		12 38		12 48		13 08		13 18		13 38		13 48		14 08	
Kew Gardens ⊖	d	11 41		11 51		12 11		12 21		12 41		12 51		13 11		13 21		13 41		13 51		14 11	
Richmond ⊖	a	11 46		11 56		12 16		12 26		12 46		12 56		13 16		13 26		13 46		13 56		14 16	

Table 59

Saturdays
from 15 September

Stratford - Highbury and Islington, West Hampstead, Willesden Junction, Clapham Junction and Richmond

Network Diagram - see first Page of Table 59

		LO	LO	LO	LO		LO	LO	LO	LO	LO	LO	LO	LO	LO	LO	LO	LO	LO	LO	LO	LO
Stratford ⊖	d	13 25	13 35	13 45				17 55	18 05	18 15		18 25	18 35	18 45		18 55	19 05	19 15		19 25	19 35	19 45
Hackney Wick	d	13 28	13 38	13 48				17 58	18 08	18 18		18 28	18 38	18 48		18 58	19 08	19 18		19 28	19 38	19 48
Homerton	d	13 31	13 41	13 51				18 01	18 11	18 21		18 31	18 41	18 51		19 01	19 11	19 21		19 31	19 41	19 51
Hackney Central	d	13 33	13 43	13 53				18 03	18 13	18 23		18 33	18 43	18 53		19 03	19 13	19 23		19 33	19 43	19 53
Dalston Kingsland	d	13 35	13 45	13 55				18 05	18 15	18 25		18 35	18 45	18 55		19 05	19 15	19 25		19 35	19 45	19 55
Canonbury	d	13 37	13 47	13 57				18 07	18 17	18 27		18 37	18 47	18 57		19 07	19 17	19 27		19 37	19 47	19 57
Highbury & Islington ⊖	d	13 40	13 50	14 00				18 10	18 20	18 30		18 40	18 50	19 00		19 10	19 20	19 30		19 40	19 50	20 00
Caledonian Rd & Barnsbury	d	13 42	13 52	14 02				18 12	18 22	18 32		18 42	18 52	19 02		19 12	19 22	19 32		19 42	19 52	20 02
Camden Road	d	13 45	13 55	14 05				18 15	18 25	18 35		18 45	18 55	19 05		19 15	19 25	19 35		19 45	19 55	20 05
Kentish Town West	d	13 47	13 57	14 07				18 17	18 27	18 37		18 47	18 57	19 07		19 17	19 27	19 37		19 47	19 57	20 07
Gospel Oak	d	13 50	14 00	14 10				18 20	18 30	18 40		18 50	19 00	19 10		19 20	19 30	19 40		19 50	20 00	20 10
Hampstead Heath	d	13 52	14 02	14 12		and at the same minutes past each hour until		18 22	18 32	18 42		18 52	19 02	19 12		19 22	19 32	19 42		19 52	20 02	20 12
Finchley Road & Frognal	d	13 54	14 04	14 14				18 24	18 34	18 44		18 54	19 04	19 14		19 24	19 34	19 44		19 54	20 04	20 14
West Hampstead ⊖	d	13 56	14 06	14 16				18 26	18 36	18 46		18 56	19 06	19 16		19 26	19 36	19 46		19 56	20 06	20 16
Brondesbury	d	13 58	14 08	14 18				18 28	18 38	18 48		18 58	19 08	19 18		19 28	19 38	19 48		19 58	20 08	20 18
Brondesbury Park	d	13 59	14 09	14 19				18 29	18 39	18 49		18 59	19 09	19 19		19 29	19 39	19 49		19 59	20 09	20 19
Kensal Rise	d	14 01	14 11	14 21				18 31	18 41	18 51		19 01	19 11	19 21		19 31	19 41	19 51		20 01	20 11	20 21
Willesden Jn. High Level ⊖	a	14 05	14 15	14 25				18 35	18 45	18 55		19 05	19 15	19 25		19 35	19 45	19 55		20 05	20 15	20 25
	d	14 06	14 16	14 26	14 31		18 31	18 36	18 46	18 56	19 01	19 05	19 16	19 26	19 31	19 36	19 46	19 56	20 01	20 06	20 16	20 26
Willesden Jn Low Level ⊖	a																					
Shepherd's Bush ⊖	d		14 24		14 39		18 39		18 54		19 09		19 24		19 39		19 54		20 09		20 24	
Kensington (Olympia) ⊖	d		14 26		14 41		18 41		18 56		19 11		19 26		19 41		19 56		20 11		20 26	
West Brompton ⊖	d		14 28		14 43		18 43		18 58		19 13		19 28		19 43		19 58		20 13		20 28	
Imperial Wharf	d		14 31		14 46		18 46		19 01		19 16		19 31		19 46		20 01		20 16		20 31	
Clapham Junction 10	a		14 39		14 53		18 53		19 09		19 23		19 39		19 53		20 09		20 23		20 39	
Acton Central	d	14 11		14 31				18 41		19 01		19 10		19 31		19 41		20 01		20 11		20 31
South Acton	d	14 14		14 34				18 44		19 04		19 13		19 34		19 44		20 04		20 14		20 34
Gunnersbury ⊖	d	14 18		14 38				18 48		19 08		19 17		19 38		19 48		20 08		20 18		20 38
Kew Gardens ⊖	d	14 21		14 41				18 51		19 11		19 20		19 41		19 51		20 11		20 21		20 41
Richmond ⊖	a	14 26		14 46				18 56		19 17		19 27		19 47		19 57		20 17		20 27		20 47

		LO	LO	LO	LO	LO	LO	LO	LO	LO	LO	LO	LO	LO	LO	LO	LO	LO	LO	LO	LO	LO	LO
Stratford ⊖	d		19 55	20 05	20 15		20 25	20 35	20 45		20 55	21 05	21 15		21 25	21 35	21 45		21 55	22 15	22 25		22 45
Hackney Wick	d		19 58	20 08	20 18		20 28	20 38	20 48		20 58	21 08	21 18		21 28	21 38	21 48		21 58	22 18	22 28		22 48
Homerton	d		20 01	20 11	20 21		20 31	20 41	20 51		21 01	21 11	21 21		21 31	21 41	21 51		22 01	22 21	22 31		22 51
Hackney Central	d		20 03	20 13	20 23		20 33	20 43	20 53		21 03	21 13	21 23		21 33	21 43	21 53		22 03	22 23	22 33		22 53
Dalston Kingsland	d		20 05	20 15	20 25		20 35	20 45	20 55		21 05	21 15	21 25		21 35	21 45	21 55		22 05	22 25	22 35		22 55
Canonbury	d		20 07	20 17	20 27		20 37	20 47	20 57		21 07	21 17	21 27		21 37	21 47	21 57		22 07	22 27	22 37		22 57
Highbury & Islington ⊖	d		20 10	20 20	20 30		20 40	20 50	21 00		21 10	21 20	21 30		21 40	21 50	22 00		22 10	22 30	22 40		23 00
Caledonian Rd & Barnsbury	d		20 12	20 22	20 32		20 42	20 52	21 02		21 12	21 22	21 32		21 42	21 52	22 02		22 12	22 32	22 42		23 02
Camden Road	d		20 15	20 25	20 35		20 45	20 55	21 05		21 15	21 25	21 35		21 45	21 55	22 05		22 15	22 35	22a45		23 05
Kentish Town West	d		20 17	20 27	20 37		20 47	20 57	21 07		21 17	21 27	21 37		21 47	21 57	22 07		22 17	22 37			23 07
Gospel Oak	d		20 20	20 30	20 40		20 50	21 00	21 10		21 20	21 30	21 40		21 50	22 00	22 10		22 20	22 40			23 10
Hampstead Heath	d		20 22	20 32	20 42		20 52	21 02	21 12		21 22	21 32	21 42		21 52	22 02	22 12		22 22	22 42			23 12
Finchley Road & Frognal	d		20 24	20 34	20 44		20 54	21 04	21 14		21 24	21 34	21 44		21 54	22 04	22 14		22 24	22 44			23 14
West Hampstead ⊖	d		20 26	20 36	20 46		20 56	21 06	21 16		21 26	21 36	21 46		21 56	22 06	22 16		22 26	22 46			23 16
Brondesbury	d		20 28	20 38	20 48		20 58	21 08	21 18		21 28	21 38	21 48		21 58	22 08	22 18		22 28	22 48			23 18
Brondesbury Park	d		20 29	20 39	20 49		20 59	21 09	21 19		21 29	21 39	21 49		21 59	22 09	22 19		22 29	22 49			23 19
Kensal Rise	d		20 31	20 41	20 51		21 01	21 11	21 21		21 31	21 41	21 51		22 01	22 11	22 21		22 31	22 51			23 21
Willesden Jn. High Level ⊖	a		20 35	20 45	20 55		21 05	21 15	21 25		21 35	21 45	21 55		22 05	22 15	22 25		22 35	22 55			23 25
	d	20 31	20 36	20 46	20 56	21 01	21 06	21 16	21 26	21 31	21 36	21 46	21 56	22 01	22 06	22 16	22 26	22 31	22 36	22 56		23 01	23 26
Willesden Jn Low Level ⊖	a																						
Shepherd's Bush ⊖	d	20 39		20 54		21 11		21 24		21 39		21 54		22 11		22 24		22 39				23 09	
Kensington (Olympia) ⊖	d	20 41		20 56		21 13		21 26		21 41		21 56		22 13		22 26		22 41				23 11	
West Brompton ⊖	d	20 43		20 58		21 15		21 28		21 43		21 58		22 15		22 28		22 43				23 13	
Imperial Wharf	d	20 46		21 01		21 18		21 31		21 46		22 01		22 18		22 31		22 46				23 16	
Clapham Junction 10	a	20 53		21 09		21 25		21 39		21 53		22 09		22 25		22 39		22 53				23 23	
Acton Central	d		20 41		21 01		21 11		21 31		21 41		22 01		22 11		22 31		22 41	23 01			23 31
South Acton	d		20 44		21 04		21 14		21 34		21 44		22 04		22 14		22 34		22 44	23 04			23 34
Gunnersbury ⊖	d		20 48		21 08		21 18		21 38		21 48		22 08		22 18		22 38		22 48	23 08			23 38
Kew Gardens ⊖	d		20 51		21 11		21 21		21 41		21 51		22 11		22 21		22 41		22 51	23 11			23 41
Richmond ⊖	a		20 57		21 17		21 27		21 47		21 57		22 17		22 27		22 47		22 57	23 17			23 47

Stratford - Highbury and Islington, West Hampstead, Willesden Junction, Clapham Junction and Richmond

Network Diagram - see first Page of Table 59

Station		LO	LO	LO
Stratford 7 ⊖	d	22 55	23 15	23 45
Hackney Wick	d	22 58	23 18	23 48
Homerton	d	23 01	23 21	23 51
Hackney Central	d	23 03	23 23	23 53
Dalston Kingsland	d	23 05	23 25	23 55
Canonbury	d	23 07	23 27	23 57
Highbury & Islington ⊖	d	23 10	23 30	23 59
Caledonian Rd & Barnsbury	d	23 12	23 32	00 02
Camden Road	d	23a15	23 35	00 05
Kentish Town West	d		23 37	00 07
Gospel Oak	d		23 40	00 10
Hampstead Heath	d		23 42	00 12
Finchley Road & Frognal	d		23 44	00 14
West Hampstead ⊖	d		23 46	00 16
Brondesbury	d		23 48	00 18
Brondesbury Park	d		23 49	00 19
Kensal Rise	d		23 51	00 21
Willesden Jn. High Level ⊖	a		23 54	
	d			
Willesden Jn Low Level ⊖	a			00 29
Shepherd's Bush ⊖	d			
Kensington (Olympia) ⊖	d			
West Brompton ⊖	d			
Imperial Wharf	d			
Clapham Junction 10	a			
Acton Central	d			
South Acton	d			
Gunnersbury ⊖	d			
Kew Gardens ⊖	d			
Richmond ⊖	a			

Sundays
until 22 July

Station		LO	LO	LO	LO	LO	LO	LO A	LO B	LO	LO	LO	LO	LO	LO	LO	LO	LO	LO	LO	LO	LO	LO
Stratford 7 ⊖	d	23p45									09 15		09 30		09 45		10 00		10 20		10 35		10 45
Hackney Wick	d	23p48									09 18		09 33		09 48		10 03		10 23		10 38		10 48
Homerton	d	23p51									09 21		09 36		09 51		10 06		10 26		10 41		10 51
Hackney Central	d	23p53									09 23		09 38		09 53		10 08		10 28		10 43		10 53
Dalston Kingsland	d	23p55									09 25		09 40		09 55		10 10		10 30		10 45		10 55
Canonbury	d	23p57									09 27		09 42		09 57		10 12		10 32		10 47		10 57
Highbury & Islington ⊖	d	23p59									09 30		09 45		10 00		10 15		10 35		10 50		11 00
Caledonian Rd & Barnsbury	d	00 02									09 32		09 47		10 02		10 17		10 37		10 52		11 02
Camden Road	d	00 05									09 35		09 50		10 05		10 20		10 40		10 55		11 05
Kentish Town West	d	00 07									09 37		09 52		10 07		10 22		10 42		10 57		11 07
Gospel Oak	d	00 10						09 24	09 27		09 40		09 55		10 10		10 25		10 45		11 00		11 10
Hampstead Heath	d	00 12						09 26	09 28		09 42		09 57		10 12		10 27		10 47		11 02		11 12
Finchley Road & Frognal	d	00 14						09 28	09 29		09 44		09 59		10 14		10 29		10 49		11 04		11 14
West Hampstead ⊖	d	00 16						09 30	09 30		09 46		10 01		10 16		10 31		10 51		11 06		11 16
Brondesbury	d	00 18						09 32	09 32		09 48		10 03		10 18		10 33		10 53		11 08		11 18
Brondesbury Park	d	00 19						09 33	09 33		09 49		10 04		10 19		10 34		10 54		11 09		11 19
Kensal Rise	d	00 21						09 35	09 35		09 51		10 06		10 21		10 36		10 56		11 11		11 21
Willesden Jn. High Level ⊖	a							09 39	09 47		09 55		10 10		10 25		10 40		11 00		11 15		11 25
	d		08 32	08 56	09 02	09 26	09 32	09 40		09 48	09 56	10 02	10 11	10 16	10 26	10 32	10 41	10 46	11 01	11 02	11 16	11 16	11 26
Willesden Jn Low Level ⊖	a	00 29																					
Shepherd's Bush ⊖	d		08 40		09 10		09 40			09 54		10 10		10 24		10 40		10 55		11 10	11 24		
Kensington (Olympia) ⊖	d		08 42		09 12		09 42			09 56		10 12		10 26		10 42		10 56		11 12	11 26		
West Brompton ⊖	d		08 44		09 14		09 44			09 58		10 14		10 28		10 44		10 58		11 14	11 28		
Imperial Wharf	d		08 47		09 17		09 47			10 01		10 17		10 31		10 47		11 01		11 17	11 31		
Clapham Junction 10	a		08 54		09 23		09 53			10 09		10 23		10 38		10 53		11 08		11 28	11 40		
Acton Central	d			09 01		09 31		09 45			10 01		10 16		10 31		10 46		11 06			11 21	11 31
South Acton	d			09 03		09 34		09 47			10 04		10 19		10 34		10 49		11 09			11 24	11 34
Gunnersbury ⊖	d			09 08		09 38		09 50			10 08		10 22		10 38		10 52		11 12			11 28	11 38
Kew Gardens ⊖	d			09 11		09 41		09 53			10 11		10 25		10 41		10 55		11 15			11 31	11 41
Richmond ⊖	a			09 19		09 49		10 03			10 18		10 31		10 46		11 01		11 21			11 38	11 46

A not 20 May, 3 June

B 20 May, 3 June

Stratford - Highbury and Islington, West Hampstead, Willesden Junction, Clapham Junction and Richmond

Network Diagram - see first Page of Table 59

Station		LO	LO	LO	LO	LO	LO	LO	LO	LO	LO	LO	LO	LO	LO	LO	LO	LO	LO	LO	LO	LO	LO
Stratford 7 ⊖	d		10 55	11 05	11 15		11 25	11 35	11 45		11 55	12 05	12 15		12 25	12 35	12 45		12 55	13 05	13 15		13 25
Hackney Wick	d		10 58	11 08	11 18		11 28	11 38	11 48		11 58	12 08	12 18		12 28	12 38	12 48		12 58	13 08	13 18		13 28
Homerton	d		11 01	11 11	11 21		11 31	11 41	11 51		12 01	12 11	12 21		12 31	12 41	12 51		13 01	13 11	13 21		13 31
Hackney Central	d		11 03	11 13	11 23		11 33	11 43	11 53		12 03	12 13	12 23		12 33	12 43	12 53		13 03	13 13	13 23		13 33
Dalston Kingsland	d		11 05	11 15	11 25		11 35	11 45	11 55		12 05	12 15	12 25		12 35	12 45	12 55		13 05	13 15	13 25		13 35
Canonbury	d		11 07	11 17	11 27		11 37	11 47	11 57		12 07	12 17	12 27		12 37	12 47	12 57		13 07	13 17	13 27		13 37
Highbury & Islington ⊖	d		11 10	11 20	11 30		11 40	11 50	12 00		12 10	12 20	12 30		12 40	12 50	13 00		13 10	13 20	13 30		13 40
Caledonian Rd & Barnsbury	d		11 12	11 22	11 32		11 42	11 52	12 02		12 12	12 22	12 32		12 42	12 52	13 02		13 12	13 22	13 32		13 42
Camden Road	d		11 15	11 25	11 35		11 45	11 55	12 05		12 15	12 25	12 35		12 45	12 55	13 05		13 15	13 25	13 35		13 45
Kentish Town West	d		11 17	11 27	11 37		11 47	11 57	12 07		12 17	12 27	12 37		12 47	12 57	13 07		13 17	13 27	13 37		13 47
Gospel Oak	d		11 20	11 30	11 40		11 50	12 00	12 10		12 20	12 30	12 40		12 50	13 00	13 10		13 20	13 30	13 40		13 50
Hampstead Heath	d		11 22	11 32	11 42		11 52	12 02	12 12		12 22	12 32	12 42		12 52	13 02	13 12		13 22	13 32	13 42		13 52
Finchley Road & Frognal	d		11 24	11 34	11 44		11 54	12 04	12 14		12 24	12 34	12 44		12 54	13 04	13 14		13 24	13 34	13 44		13 54
West Hampstead ⊖	d		11 26	11 36	11 46		11 56	12 06	12 16		12 26	12 36	12 46		12 56	13 06	13 16		13 26	13 36	13 46		13 56
Brondesbury	d		11 28	11 38	11 48		11 58	12 08	12 18		12 28	12 38	12 48		12 58	13 08	13 18		13 28	13 38	13 48		13 58
Brondesbury Park	d		11 29	11 39	11 49		11 59	12 09	12 19		12 29	12 39	12 49		12 59	13 09	13 19		13 29	13 39	13 49		13 59
Kensal Rise	d		11 31	11 41	11 51		12 01	12 11	12 21		12 31	12 41	12 51		13 01	13 11	13 21		13 31	13 41	13 51		14 01
Willesden Jn. High Level ⊖	a		11 35	11 45	11 55		12 05	12 15	12 25		12 35	12 45	12 55		13 05	13 15	13 25		13 35	13 45	13 55		14 05
	d	11 32	11 36	11 46	11 56	12 02	12 06	12 16	12 26	12 32	12 36	12 46	12 56	13 02	13 06	13 16	13 26	13 32	13 36	13 46	13 56	14 02	14 06
Willesden Jn Low Level ⊖	a																						
Shepherd's Bush ⊖	d	11 40		11 54		12 10		12 24		12 40		12 54		13 10		13 24		13 40		13 54		14 10	
Kensington (Olympia) ⊖	d	11 42		11 56		12 12		12 26		12 42		12 56		13 12		13 26		13 42		13 56		14 12	
West Brompton ⊖	d	11 44		11 58		12 14		12 28		12 44		12 58		13 14		13 28		13 44		13 58		14 14	
Imperial Wharf	d	11 47		12 01		12 17		12 31		12 47		13 01		13 17		13 31		13 47		14 01		14 17	
Clapham Junction 10	a	11 53		12 09		12 23		12 39		12 53		13 09		13 23		13 39		13 53		14 09		14 23	
Acton Central	d		11 41		12 01		12 11		12 31		12 41		13 01		13 11		13 31		13 41		14 01		14 11
South Acton	d		11 44		12 04		12 14		12 34		12 44		13 04		13 14		13 34		13 44		14 04		14 14
Gunnersbury ⊖	d		11 48		12 08		12 18		12 38		12 48		13 08		13 18		13 38		13 48		14 08		14 18
Kew Gardens ⊖	d		11 51		12 11		12 21		12 41		12 51		13 11		13 21		13 41		13 51		14 11		14 21
Richmond ⊖	a		11 56		12 16		12 26		12 46		12 56		13 16		13 26		13 46		13 56		14 16		14 26

Station		LO	LO	LO	LO	LO	LO	LO	LO	LO	LO	LO	LO	LO	LO	LO	LO	LO	LO	LO	LO	LO	LO
Stratford 7 ⊖	d	13 35	13 45		13 55	14 05	14 15		14 25	14 35	14 45		14 55	15 05	15 15		15 25	15 35	15 45		15 55	16 05	16 15
Hackney Wick	d	13 38	13 48		13 58	14 08	14 18		14 28	14 38	14 48		14 58	15 08	15 18		15 28	15 38	15 48		15 58	16 08	16 18
Homerton	d	13 41	13 51		14 01	14 11	14 21		14 31	14 41	14 51		15 01	15 11	15 21		15 31	15 41	15 51		16 01	16 11	16 21
Hackney Central	d	13 43	13 53		14 03	14 13	14 23		14 33	14 43	14 53		15 03	15 13	15 23		15 33	15 43	15 53		16 03	16 13	16 23
Dalston Kingsland	d	13 45	13 55		14 05	14 15	14 25		14 35	14 45	14 55		15 05	15 15	15 25		15 35	15 45	15 55		16 05	16 15	16 25
Canonbury	d	13 47	13 57		14 07	14 17	14 27		14 37	14 47	14 57		15 07	15 17	15 27		15 37	15 47	15 57		16 07	16 17	16 27
Highbury & Islington ⊖	d	13 50	14 00		14 10	14 20	14 30		14 40	14 50	15 00		15 10	15 20	15 30		15 40	15 50	16 00		16 10	16 20	16 30
Caledonian Rd & Barnsbury	d	13 52	14 02		14 12	14 22	14 32		14 42	14 52	15 02		15 12	15 22	15 32		15 42	15 52	16 02		16 12	16 22	16 32
Camden Road	d	13 55	14 05		14 15	14 25	14 35		14 45	14 55	15 05		15 15	15 25	15 35		15 45	15 55	16 05		16 15	16 25	16 35
Kentish Town West	d	13 57	14 07		14 17	14 27	14 37		14 47	14 57	15 07		15 17	15 27	15 37		15 47	15 57	16 07		16 17	16 27	16 37
Gospel Oak	d	14 00	14 10		14 20	14 30	14 40		14 50	15 00	15 10		15 20	15 30	15 40		15 50	16 00	16 10		16 20	16 30	16 40
Hampstead Heath	d	14 02	14 12		14 22	14 32	14 42		14 52	15 02	15 12		15 22	15 32	15 42		15 52	16 02	16 12		16 22	16 32	16 42
Finchley Road & Frognal	d	14 04	14 14		14 24	14 34	14 44		14 54	15 04	15 14		15 24	15 34	15 44		15 54	16 04	16 14		16 24	16 34	16 44
West Hampstead ⊖	d	14 06	14 16		14 26	14 36	14 46		14 56	15 06	15 16		15 26	15 36	15 46		15 56	16 06	16 16		16 26	16 36	16 46
Brondesbury	d	14 08	14 18		14 28	14 38	14 48		14 58	15 08	15 18		15 28	15 38	15 48		15 58	16 08	16 18		16 28	16 38	16 48
Brondesbury Park	d	14 09	14 19		14 29	14 39	14 49		14 59	15 09	15 19		15 29	15 39	15 49		15 59	16 09	16 19		16 29	16 39	16 49
Kensal Rise	d	14 11	14 21		14 31	14 41	14 51		15 01	15 11	15 21		15 31	15 41	15 51		16 01	16 11	16 21		16 31	16 41	16 51
Willesden Jn. High Level ⊖	a	14 15	14 25		14 35	14 45	14 55		15 05	15 15	15 25		15 35	15 45	15 55		16 05	16 15	16 25		16 35	16 45	16 55
	d	14 16	14 26	14 32	14 36	14 46	14 56	15 02	15 06	15 16	15 26	15 32	15 36	15 46	15 56	16 02	16 06	16 16	16 26	16 32	16 36	16 46	16 56
Willesden Jn Low Level ⊖	a																						
Shepherd's Bush ⊖	d	14 24		14 40		14 54		15 10		15 24		15 40		15 54		16 10		16 24		16 40		16 54	
Kensington (Olympia) ⊖	d	14 26		14 42		14 56		15 12		15 26		15 42		15 56		16 12		16 26		16 42		16 56	
West Brompton ⊖	d	14 28		14 44		14 58		15 14		15 28		15 44		15 58		16 14		16 28		16 44		16 58	
Imperial Wharf	d	14 31		14 47		15 01		15 17		15 31		15 47		16 01		16 17		16 31		16 47		17 01	
Clapham Junction 10	a	14 39		14 54		15 09		15 23		15 39		15 53		16 09		16 23		16 39		16 54		17 10	
Acton Central	d		14 31		14 41		15 01		15 11		15 31		15 41		16 01		16 11		16 31		16 41		17 01
South Acton	d		14 34		14 44		15 04		15 14		15 34		15 44		16 04		16 14		16 34		16 44		17 04
Gunnersbury ⊖	d		14 38		14 48		15 08		15 18		15 38		15 48		16 08		16 18		16 38		16 48		17 08
Kew Gardens ⊖	d		14 41		14 51		15 11		15 21		15 41		15 51		16 11		16 21		16 41		16 51		17 11
Richmond ⊖	a		14 46		14 56		15 16		15 26		15 46		15 56		16 16		16 26		16 46		16 56		17 16

Table 59

Stratford - Highbury and Islington, West Hampstead, Willesden Junction, Clapham Junction and Richmond

Sundays until 22 July

Network Diagram - see first Page of Table 59

		LO	LO	LO	LO	LO	LO	LO	LO	LO	LO	LO	LO	LO	LO	LO	LO	LO	LO	LO	LO	LO	LO
Stratford [7] ⊖	d		16 25	16 35	16 45		16 55	17 05	17 15		17 25	17 35	17 45		17 55	18 05	18 15		18 25	18 35	18 45		18 55
Hackney Wick	d		16 28	16 38	16 48		16 58	17 08	17 18		17 28	17 38	17 48		17 58	18 08	18 18		18 28	18 38	18 48		18 58
Homerton	d		16 31	16 41	16 51		17 01	17 11	17 21		17 31	17 41	17 51		18 01	18 11	18 21		18 31	18 41	18 51		19 01
Hackney Central	d		16 33	16 43	16 53		17 03	17 13	17 23		17 33	17 43	17 53		18 03	18 13	18 23		18 33	18 43	18 53		19 03
Dalston Kingsland	d		16 35	16 45	16 55		17 05	17 15	17 25		17 35	17 45	17 55		18 05	18 15	18 25		18 35	18 45	18 55		19 05
Canonbury	d		16 37	16 47	16 57		17 07	17 17	17 27		17 37	17 47	17 57		18 07	18 17	18 27		18 37	18 47	18 57		19 07
Highbury & Islington ⊖	d		16 40	16 50	17 00		17 10	17 20	17 30		17 40	17 50	18 00		18 10	18 20	18 30		18 40	18 50	19 00		19 10
Caledonian Rd & Barnsbury	d		16 42	16 52	17 02		17 12	17 22	17 32		17 42	17 52	18 02		18 12	18 22	18 32		18 42	18 52	19 02		19 12
Camden Road	d		16 45	16 55	17 05		17 15	17 25	17 35		17 45	17 55	18 05		18 15	18 25	18 35		18 45	18 55	19 05		19 15
Kentish Town West	d		16 47	16 57	17 07		17 17	17 27	17 37		17 47	17 57	18 07		18 17	18 27	18 37		18 47	18 57	19 07		19 17
Gospel Oak	d		16 50	17 00	17 10		17 20	17 30	17 40		17 50	18 00	18 10		18 20	18 30	18 40		18 50	19 00	19 10		19 20
Hampstead Heath	d		16 52	17 02	17 12		17 22	17 32	17 42		17 52	18 02	18 12		18 22	18 32	18 42		18 52	19 02	19 12		19 22
Finchley Road & Frognal	d		16 54	17 04	17 14		17 24	17 34	17 44		17 54	18 04	18 14		18 24	18 34	18 44		18 54	19 04	19 14		19 24
West Hampstead ⊖	d		16 56	17 06	17 16		17 26	17 36	17 46		17 56	18 06	18 16		18 26	18 36	18 46		18 56	19 06	19 16		19 26
Brondesbury	d		16 58	17 08	17 18		17 28	17 38	17 48		17 58	18 08	18 18		18 28	18 38	18 48		18 58	19 08	19 18		19 28
Brondesbury Park	d		16 59	17 09	17 19		17 29	17 39	17 49		17 59	18 09	18 19		18 29	18 39	18 49		18 59	19 09	19 19		19 29
Kensal Rise	d		17 01	17 11	17 21		17 31	17 41	17 51		18 01	18 11	18 21		18 31	18 41	18 51		19 01	19 11	19 21		19 31
Willesden Jn. High Level ⊖	a		17 05	17 15	17 25		17 35	17 45	17 55		18 05	18 15	18 25		18 35	18 45	18 55		19 05	19 15	19 25		19 35
	d	17 02	17 06	17 16	17 26	17 32	17 36	17 46	17 56	18 02	18 06	18 16	18 26	18 32	18 36	18 46	18 56	19 02	19 06	19 16	19 26	19 32	19 36
Willesden Jn Low Level ⊖	a																						
Shepherd's Bush ⊖	d	17 10		17 24		17 40		17 54		18 10		18 24		18 40		18 54		19 10		19 24		19 40	
Kensington (Olympia) ⊖	d	17 12		17 26		17 42		17 56		18 12		18 26		18 42		18 56		19 12		19 26		19 42	
West Brompton ⊖	d	17 14		17 28		17 44		17 58		18 14		18 28		18 44		18 58		19 14		19 28		19 44	
Imperial Wharf	d	17 17		17 31		17 47		18 01		18 17		18 31		18 47		19 01		19 17		19 31		19 47	
Clapham Junction [10]	a	17 24		17 40		17 54		18 10		18 24		18 38		18 54		19 10		19 26		19 40		19 54	
Acton Central	d		17 11		17 31		17 41		18 01		18 11		18 31		18 41		19 01		19 11		19 31		19 41
South Acton	d		17 14		17 34		17 44		18 04		18 14		18 34		18 44		19 04		19 14		19 34		19 44
Gunnersbury ⊖	d		17 18		17 38		17 48		18 08		18 18		18 38		18 48		19 08		19 18		19 38		19 48
Kew Gardens ⊖	d		17 21		17 41		17 51		18 11		18 21		18 41		18 51		19 11		19 21		19 41		19 51
Richmond ⊖	a		17 26		17 46		17 56		18 16		18 26		18 46		18 56		19 16		19 26		19 46		19 56

		LO	LO	LO	LO	LO	LO	LO	LO	LO	LO	LO	LO	LO	LO	LO	LO	LO	LO	LO	LO	LO	LO
Stratford [7] ⊖	d	19 05	19 15		19 25	19 35	19 45		19 55	20 05	20 15		20 25	20 35	20 45		20 55	21 05	21 15		21 30	21 45	
Hackney Wick	d	19 08	19 18		19 28	19 38	19 48		19 58	20 08	20 18		20 28	20 38	20 48		20 58	21 08	21 18		21 33	21 48	
Homerton	d	19 11	19 21		19 31	19 41	19 51		20 01	20 11	20 21		20 31	20 41	20 51		21 01	21 11	21 21		21 36	21 51	
Hackney Central	d	19 13	19 23		19 33	19 43	19 53		20 03	20 13	20 23		20 33	20 43	20 53		21 03	21 13	21 23		21 38	21 53	
Dalston Kingsland	d	19 15	19 25		19 35	19 45	19 55		20 05	20 15	20 25		20 35	20 45	20 55		21 05	21 15	21 25		21 40	21 55	
Canonbury	d	19 17	19 27		19 37	19 47	19 57		20 07	20 17	20 27		20 37	20 47	20 57		21 07	21 17	21 27		21 42	21 57	
Highbury & Islington ⊖	d	19 20	19 30		19 40	19 50	20 00		20 10	20 20	20 30		20 40	20 50	21 00		21 10	21 20	21 30		21 45	22 00	
Caledonian Rd & Barnsbury	d	19 22	19 32		19 42	19 52	20 02		20 12	20 22	20 32		20 42	20 52	21 02		21 12	21 22	21 32		21 47	22 02	
Camden Road	d	19 25	19 35		19 45	19 55	20 05		20 15	20 25	20 35		20 45	20 55	21 05		21 15	21 25	21 35		21 50	22 05	
Kentish Town West	d	19 27	19 37		19 47	19 57	20 07		20 17	20 27	20 37		20 47	20 57	21 07		21 17	21 27	21 37		21 52	22 07	
Gospel Oak	d	19 30	19 40		19 50	20 00	20 10		20 20	20 30	20 40		20 50	21 00	21 10		21 20	21 30	21 40		21 55	22 10	
Hampstead Heath	d	19 32	19 42		19 52	20 02	20 12		20 22	20 32	20 42		20 52	21 02	21 12		21 22	21 32	21 42		21 57	22 12	
Finchley Road & Frognal	d	19 34	19 44		19 54	20 04	20 14		20 24	20 34	20 44		20 54	21 04	21 14		21 24	21 34	21 44		21 59	22 14	
West Hampstead ⊖	d	19 36	19 46		19 56	20 06	20 16		20 26	20 36	20 46		20 56	21 06	21 16		21 26	21 36	21 46		22 01	22 16	
Brondesbury	d	19 38	19 48		19 58	20 08	20 18		20 28	20 38	20 48		20 58	21 08	21 18		21 28	21 38	21 48		22 03	22 18	
Brondesbury Park	d	19 39	19 49		19 59	20 09	20 19		20 29	20 39	20 49		20 59	21 09	21 19		21 29	21 39	21 49		22 04	22 19	
Kensal Rise	d	19 41	19 51		20 01	20 11	20 21		20 31	20 41	20 51		21 01	21 11	21 21		21 31	21 41	21 51		22 06	22 21	
Willesden Jn. High Level ⊖	a	19 45	19 55		20 05	20 15	20 25		20 35	20 45	20 55		21 05	21 15	21 25		21 35	21 45	21 55		22 10	22 25	
	d	19 46	19 56	20 02	20 06	20 16	20 26	20 32	20 36	20 46	20 56	21 02	21 06	21 16	21 26	21 32	21 39	21 46	21 56	22 02	22 11	22 26	22 32
Willesden Jn Low Level ⊖	a																						
Shepherd's Bush ⊖	d	19 54		20 10		20 24		20 40		20 54		21 10		21 24		21 40		21 54		22 10			22 40
Kensington (Olympia) ⊖	d	19 56		20 12		20 26		20 42		20 56		21 12		21 26		21 42		21 56		22 12			22 42
West Brompton ⊖	d	19 58		20 14		20 28		20 44		20 58		21 14		21 28		21 44		21 58		22 14			22 44
Imperial Wharf	d	20 01		20 17		20 31		20 47		21 01		21 17		21 31		21 47		22 01		22 17			22 47
Clapham Junction [10]	a	20 10		20 24		20 40		20 54		21 10		21 24		21 39		21 54		22 09		22 24			22 54
Acton Central	d		20 01		20 11		20 31		20 41		21 01		21 11		21 31		21 44		22 01		22 16	22 31	
South Acton	d		20 04		20 14		20 34		20 44		21 04		21 14		21 34		21 47		22 04		22 19	22 34	
Gunnersbury ⊖	d		20 08		20 18		20 38		20 48		21 08		21 18		21 38		21 50		22 08		22 22	22 38	
Kew Gardens ⊖	d		20 11		20 21		20 41		20 51		21 11		21 21		21 41		21 53		22 11		22 25	22 41	
Richmond ⊖	a		20 16		20 26		20 46		20 56		21 16		21 26		21 46		21 57		22 16		22 31	22 46	

Table 59

Stratford - Highbury and Islington, West Hampstead, Willesden Junction, Clapham Junction and Richmond

Sundays until 22 July

Network Diagram - see first Page of Table 59

		LO	LO	LO	LO
Stratford [7] ⊖	d	22 00			
Hackney Wick	d	22 03			
Homerton	d	22 06			
Hackney Central	d	22 08			
Dalston Kingsland	d	22 10			
Canonbury	d	22 12			
Highbury & Islington ⊖	d	22 15			
Caledonian Rd & Barnsbury	d	22 17			
Camden Road	d	22 20			
Kentish Town West	d	22 22			
Gospel Oak	d	22 25		22 55	23 30
Hampstead Heath	d	22 27		22 57	23 32
Finchley Road & Frognal	d	22 29		22 59	23 34
West Hampstead ⊖	d	22 31		23 01	23 36
Brondesbury	d	22 33		23 03	23 38
Brondesbury Park	d	22 34		23 04	23 39
Kensal Rise	d	22 36		23 06	23 41
Willesden Jn. High Level ⊖	a	22 40		23 10	
	d	22 41	22 46	23 11	
Willesden Jn Low Level ⊖	a				23 54
Shepherd's Bush ⊖	d		22 54		
Kensington (Olympia) ⊖	d		22 56		
West Brompton ⊖	d		22 58		
Imperial Wharf	d		23 01		
Clapham Junction [10]	a		23 11		
Acton Central	d	22 46		23 16	
South Acton	d	22 49		23 19	
Gunnersbury ⊖	d	22 52		23 22	
Kew Gardens ⊖	d	22 55		23 25	
Richmond ⊖	a	23 01		23 32	

Sundays 29 July to 12 August

		LO	LO	LO	LO	LO	LO	LO	LO	LO	LO	LO	LO	LO	LO	LO	LO	LO	LO	LO	LO	LO	LO
Stratford [7] ⊖	d	22p52	23p00	23p07	23p15	23p22	23p30	23p37	23p45	23p52	00 01	00 07	00 15	00 22	00 30	00 37	00 45	00 52	01 00			05 47	
Hackney Wick	d	22p55	23p03	23p10	23p18	23p25	23p33	23p40	23p48	23p55	00 05	00 10	00 20	00 25	00 35	00 40	00 50	00 55	01 05			05 50	
Homerton	d	22p58	23p06	23p13	23p21	23p28	23p36	23p43	23p51	23p58	00 06	00 13	00 21	00 28	00 36	00 43	00 51	00 58	01 06			05 53	
Hackney Central	d	23p00	23p08	23p15	23p23	23p30	23p38	23p45	23p53	00 01	00 08	00 15	00 23	00 30	00 38	00 45	00 53	01 00	01 08			05 55	
Dalston Kingsland	d	23p02	23p10	23p17	23p25	23p32	23p40	23p47	23p55	00 03	00 10	00 17	00 25	00 32	00 40	00 47	00 55	01 02	01 10			05 57	
Canonbury	d	23p04	23p12	23p19	23p27	23p34	23p42	23p49	23p57	00 04	00 12	00 19	00 27	00 34	00 42	00 49	00 57	01 04	01 12			05 59	
Highbury & Islington ⊖	d	23p08	23p16	23p23	23p31	23p38	23p46	23p53	00 01	00 08	00 16	00 23	00 31	00 38	00 46	00 53	01 01	01 08	01 16			06 02	
Caledonian Rd & Barnsbury	d	23p10	23p18	23p25	23p33	23p40	23p48	23p55	00 03	00 10	00 18	00 25	00 33	00 40	00 48	00 55	01 03	01 10	01 18			06 04	
Camden Road	d	23p14	23p22	23p29	23p37	23p44	23p52	23p59	00 07	00 14	00 22	00a34	00 37	00a49	00 52	01a04	01 07	01a19	01 22			06 07	
Kentish Town West	d	23p16	23p24	23p31	23p39	23p46	23p54	00 01	00 09	00 16	00 24		00 39		00 54		01 09		01 24			06 09	
Gospel Oak	d	23p19	23p27	23p34	23p42	23p49	23p57	00 04	00 12	00 19	00 27		00 42		00 57		01 12		01 27			06 12	
Hampstead Heath	d	23p21	23p29	23p36	23p44	23p51	23p59	00 06	00 14	00 21	00 29		00 44		00 59		01 14		01 29			06 14	
Finchley Road & Frognal	d	23p23	23p31	23p38	23p46	23p53	00 01	00 08	00 16	00 23	00 31		00 46		01 01		01 16		01 31			06 16	
West Hampstead ⊖	d	23p25	23p33	23p40	23p48	23p55	00 03	00 10	00 18	00 25	00 33		00 48		01 03		01 18		01 33			06 18	
Brondesbury	d	23p27	23p35	23p42	23p50	23p57	00 05	00 12	00 20	00 27	00 35		00 50		01 05		01 20		01 35			06 20	
Brondesbury Park	d	23p28	23p36	23p43	23p51	23p58	00 06	00 13	00 21	00 28	00 36		00 51		01 06		01 21		01 36			06 21	
Kensal Rise	d	23p30	23p38	23p45	23p53	00 01	00 08	00 15	00 23	00 30	00 38		00 53		01 08		01 23		01 38			06 23	
Willesden Jn. High Level ⊖	a	23p34	23p42	23p49	23p57	00 04	00 12	00 19	00 27	00 34	00 42											06 27	
	d	23p35	23p43	23p50	23p59	00 05	00 13	00 20	00 28	00 35	00 43									06 02	06 06	06 28	06 33
Willesden Jn Low Level ⊖	a												01 01		01 21		01 41		01 50				
Shepherd's Bush ⊖	d		23p53		00 09		00 23		00 38		00 53									06 09			06 41
Kensington (Olympia) ⊖	d		23p56		00 11		00 26		00 41		00 56									06 11			06 43
West Brompton ⊖	d		23p58		00 14		00 28		00 43		00 58									06 14			06 46
Imperial Wharf	d		00 01		00 17		00 31		00 46		01 01									06 17			06 49
Clapham Junction [10]	a		00 09		00 22		00 39		00 54		01 09									06 23			06 55
Acton Central	d	23p40		23p55		00 10		00 25		00 40											06 11	06 33	
South Acton	d	23p43		23p58		00 13		00 28		00 43											06 14	06 36	
Gunnersbury ⊖	d	23p48		00 02		00 18		00 32		00 48											06 18	06 40	
Kew Gardens ⊖	d	23p51		00 05		00 21		00 35		00 51											06 21	06 43	
Richmond ⊖	a	00 02		00 14		00 31		00 45		01 00											06 30	06 52	

Stratford - Highbury and Islington, West Hampstead, Willesden Junction, Clapham Junction and Richmond

Network Diagram - see first Page of Table 59

		LO	LO	LO	LO	LO	LO	LO	LO	LO	LO	LO	LO	LO	LO	LO	LO	LO	LO	LO	LO	LO	LO
Stratford 7 ⊖	d		06 00	06 07	06 15	06 23	06 30	06 37	06 45	06 52	07 00	07 07	07 15	07 22	07 30	07 37	07 45	07 52	08 00	08 07	08 15	08 22	08 30
Hackney Wick	d		06 05	06 10	06 20	06 26	06 35	06 40	06 50	06 55	07 05	07 10	07 20	07 25	07 35	07 40	07 50	07 55	08 05	08 10	08 20	08 25	08 35
Homerton	d		06 06	06 13	06 21	06 29	06 36	06 43	06 51	06 58	07 06	07 13	07 21	07 28	07 36	07 43	07 51	07 58	08 06	08 13	08 21	08 28	08 36
Hackney Central	d		06 08	06 15	06 23	06 31	06 38	06 45	06 53	07 00	07 08	07 15	07 23	07 30	07 38	07 45	07 53	08 00	08 08	08 15	08 23	08 30	08 38
Dalston Kingsland	d		06 10	06 17	06 25	06 33	06 40	06 47	06 55	07 02	07 10	07 17	07 25	07 32	07 40	07 47	07 55	08 02	08 10	08 17	08 25	08 32	08 40
Canonbury	d		06 12	06 19	06 27	06 35	06 42	06 49	06 57	07 04	07 12	07 19	07 27	07 34	07 42	07 49	07 57	08 04	08 12	08 19	08 27	08 34	08 42
Highbury & Islington ⊖	d		06 16	06 23	06 31	06 38	06 46	06 53	07 01	07 08	07 16	07 23	07 31	07 38	07 46	07 53	08 01	08 08	08 16	08 23	08 31	08 38	08 46
Caledonian Rd & Barnsbury	d		06 18	06 25	06 33	06 40	06 48	06 55	07 03	07 10	07 18	07 25	07 33	07 40	07 48	07 55	08 03	08 10	08 18	08 25	08 33	08 40	08 48
Camden Road	d		06 22	06 29	06 37	06 44	06 52	06 59	07 07	07 14	07 22	07 29	07 37	07 44	07 52	07 59	08 07	08 14	08 22	08 29	08 37	08 44	08 52
Kentish Town West	d		06 24	06 31	06 39	06 46	06 54	07 01	07 09	07 16	07 24	07 31	07 39	07 46	07 54	08 01	08 09	08 16	08 24	08 31	08 39	08 46	08 54
Gospel Oak	d		06 27	06 34	06 42	06 49	06 57	07 04	07 12	07 19	07 27	07 34	07 42	07 49	07 57	08 04	08 12	08 19	08 27	08 34	08 42	08 49	08 57
Hampstead Heath	d		06 29	06 36	06 44	06 51	06 59	07 06	07 14	07 21	07 29	07 36	07 44	07 51	07 59	08 06	08 14	08 21	08 29	08 36	08 44	08 51	08 59
Finchley Road & Frognal	d		06 31	06 38	06 46	06 53	07 01	07 08	07 16	07 23	07 31	07 38	07 46	07 53	08 01	08 08	08 16	08 23	08 31	08 38	08 46	08 53	09 01
West Hampstead ⊖	d		06 33	06 40	06 48	06 55	07 03	07 10	07 18	07 25	07 33	07 40	07 48	07 55	08 03	08 10	08 18	08 25	08 33	08 40	08 48	08 55	09 03
Brondesbury	d		06 35	06 42	06 50	06 57	07 05	07 12	07 20	07 27	07 35	07 42	07 50	07 57	08 05	08 12	08 20	08 27	08 35	08 42	08 50	08 57	09 05
Brondesbury Park	d		06 36	06 43	06 51	06 58	07 06	07 13	07 21	07 28	07 36	07 43	07 51	07 58	08 06	08 13	08 21	08 28	08 36	08 43	08 51	08 58	09 06
Kensal Rise	d		06 38	06 45	06 53	07 00	07 08	07 15	07 23	07 30	07 38	07 45	07 53	08 00	08 08	08 15	08 23	08 30	08 38	08 45	08 53	09 00	09 08
Willesden Jn. High Level ⊖	a		06 42	06 49	06 57	07 04	07 12	07 19	07 27	07 34	07 42	07 49	07 57	08 04	08 12	08 19	08 27	08 34	08 42	08 49	08 57	09 04	09 12
	d	06 41	06 43	06 50	06 58	07 05	07 13	07 20	07 28	07 35	07 43	07 50	07 58	08 05	08 13	08 20	08 28	08 35	08 43	08 50	08 58	09 05	09 13
Willesden Jn Low Level ⊖	a																						
Shepherd's Bush ⊖	d		06 53		07 08		07 23		07 38		07 53		08 08		08 23		08 38		08 53		09 08		09 23
Kensington (Olympia) ⊖	d		06 56		07 11		07 26		07 41		07 56		08 11		08 26		08 41		08 56		09 11		09 26
West Brompton ⊖	d		06 58		07 13		07 28		07 43		07 58		08 13		08 28		08 43		08 58		09 13		09 28
Imperial Wharf	d		07 01		07 16		07 31		07 46		08 01		08 16		08 31		08 46		09 01		09 16		09 31
Clapham Junction 10	a		07 08		07 23		07 38		07 53		08 07		08 23		08 38		08 53		09 07		09 23		09 38
Acton Central	d	06 46		06 55		07 10		07 27		07 40		07 55		08 10		08 25		08 40		08 55		09 10	
South Acton	d	06 49		06 58		07 13		07 29		07 43		07 57		08 13		08 28		08 43		08 58		09 13	
Gunnersbury ⊖	d	06 52		07 02		07 18		07 34		07 48		08 02		08 18		08 32		08 48		09 02		09 18	
Kew Gardens ⊖	d	06 55		07 05		07 21		07 37		07 51		08 05		08 21		08 35		08 51		09 05		09 21	
Richmond ⊖	a	07 05		07 14		07 30		07 48		08 00		08 15		08 32		08 44		09 01		09 14		09 31	

		LO	LO	LO	LO	LO	LO	LO	LO	LO	LO	LO	LO	LO	LO	LO	LO	LO	LO	LO	LO		LO
Stratford 7 ⊖	d	08 37	08 45	08 52	09 00	09 07	09 15	09 22	09 30	09 37	09 45	09 52	10 00	10 07	10 15	10 22	10 30	10 37	10 45	10 52	11 00		15 00
Hackney Wick	d	08 40	08 50	08 55	09 05	09 10	09 20	09 25	09 35	09 40	09 50	09 55	10 05	10 10	10 20	10 25	10 35	10 40	10 50	10 55	11 05		15 05
Homerton	d	08 43	08 51	08 58	09 06	09 13	09 21	09 28	09 36	09 43	09 51	09 58	10 06	10 13	10 21	10 28	10 36	10 43	10 51	10 58	11 06		15 06
Hackney Central	d	08 45	08 53	09 00	09 08	09 15	09 23	09 30	09 38	09 45	09 53	10 00	10 08	10 15	10 23	10 30	10 38	10 45	10 53	11 00	11 08		15 08
Dalston Kingsland	d	08 47	08 55	09 02	09 10	09 17	09 25	09 32	09 40	09 47	09 55	10 02	10 10	10 17	10 25	10 32	10 40	10 47	10 55	11 02	11 10		15 10
Canonbury	d	08 49	08 57	09 04	09 12	09 19	09 27	09 34	09 42	09 49	09 57	10 04	10 12	10 19	10 27	10 34	10 42	10 49	10 57	11 04	11 12		15 12
Highbury & Islington ⊖	d	08 53	09 01	09 08	09 16	09 23	09 31	09 38	09 46	09 53	10 01	10 08	10 16	10 23	10 31	10 38	10 46	10 53	11 01	11 08	11 16		15 16
Caledonian Rd & Barnsbury	d	08 55	09 03	09 10	09 18	09 25	09 33	09 40	09 48	09 55	10 03	10 10	10 18	10 25	10 33	10 40	10 48	10 55	11 03	11 10	11 18		15 18
Camden Road	d	08 59	09 07	09 14	09 22	09 29	09 37	09 44	09 52	09 59	10 07	10 14	10 22	10 29	10 37	10 44	10 52	10 59	11 07	11 14	11 22		15 22
Kentish Town West	d	09 01	09 09	09 16	09 24	09 31	09 39	09 46	09 54	10 01	10 09	10 16	10 24	10 31	10 39	10 46	10 54	11 01	11 09	11 16	11 24		15 24
Gospel Oak	d	09 04	09 12	09 19	09 27	09 34	09 42	09 49	09 57	10 04	10 12	10 19	10 27	10 34	10 42	10 49	10 57	11 04	11 12	11 19	11 27		15 27
Hampstead Heath	d	09 06	09 14	09 21	09 29	09 36	09 44	09 51	09 59	10 06	10 14	10 21	10 29	10 36	10 44	10 51	10 59	11 06	11 14	11 21	11 29	and at the same minutes past each hour until	15 29
Finchley Road & Frognal	d	09 08	09 16	09 23	09 31	09 38	09 46	09 53	10 01	10 08	10 16	10 23	10 31	10 38	10 46	10 53	11 01	11 08	11 16	11 23	11 31		15 31
West Hampstead ⊖	d	09 10	09 18	09 25	09 33	09 40	09 48	09 55	10 03	10 10	10 18	10 25	10 33	10 40	10 48	10 55	11 03	11 10	11 18	11 25	11 33		15 33
Brondesbury	d	09 12	09 20	09 27	09 35	09 42	09 50	09 57	10 05	10 12	10 20	10 27	10 35	10 42	10 50	10 57	11 05	11 12	11 20	11 27	11 35		15 35
Brondesbury Park	d	09 13	09 21	09 28	09 36	09 43	09 51	09 58	10 06	10 13	10 21	10 28	10 36	10 43	10 51	10 58	11 06	11 13	11 21	11 28	11 36		15 36
Kensal Rise	d	09 15	09 23	09 30	09 38	09 45	09 53	10 00	10 08	10 15	10 23	10 30	10 38	10 45	10 53	11 00	11 08	11 15	11 23	11 30	11 38		15 38
Willesden Jn. High Level ⊖	a	09 19	09 27	09 34	09 42	09 49	09 57	10 04	10 12	10 19	10 27	10 34	10 42	10 49	10 57	11 04	11 12	11 19	11 27	11 34	11 42		15 42
	d	09 20	09 28	09 35	09 43	09 50	09 58	10 05	10 13	10 20	10 28	10 35	10 43	10 50	10 58	11 05	11 13	11 20	11 28	11 35	11 43		15 43
Willesden Jn Low Level ⊖	a																						
Shepherd's Bush ⊖	d		09 38		09 53		10 08		10 23		10 38		10 53		11 08		11 23		11 38		11 53		15 53
Kensington (Olympia) ⊖	d		09 41		09 56		10 11		10 26		10 41		10 56		11 11		11 26		11 41		11 56		15 56
West Brompton ⊖	d		09 43		09 58		10 13		10 28		10 43		10 58		11 13		11 28		11 43		11 58		15 58
Imperial Wharf	d		09 46		10 01		10 16		10 31		10 46		11 01		11 16		11 31		11 46		12 01		16 01
Clapham Junction 10	a		09 53		10 07		10 23		10 38		10 53		11 07		11 23		11 38		11 53		12 08		16 08
Acton Central	d	09 25		09 40		09 55		10 10		10 25		10 40		10 55		11 10		11 25		11 40			
South Acton	d	09 28		09 43		09 58		10 13		10 28		10 43		10 58		11 13		11 28		11 43			
Gunnersbury ⊖	d	09 32		09 49		10 02		10 18		10 32		10 48		11 02		11 18		11 32		11 48			
Kew Gardens ⊖	d	09 35		09 52		10 05		10 21		10 35		10 51		11 05		11 21		11 35		11 51			
Richmond ⊖	a	09 45		10 01		10 14		10 31		10 45		11 01		11 15		11 31		11 45		12 01			

Stratford - Highbury and Islington, West Hampstead, Willesden Junction, Clapham Junction and Richmond

Network Diagram - see first Page of Table 59

		LO	LO	LO	LO	LO	LO	LO	LO		LO	LO	LO	LO	LO	LO	LO	LO	LO	LO	LO	LO
Stratford 7 ⊖	d	15 07	15 15	15 22	15 30	15 37	15 45	15 52	16 00		22 00	22 07	22 15	22 22	22 30	22 37	22 45	22 52	23 00	23 07	23 15	23 22
Hackney Wick	d	15 10	15 20	15 25	15 35	15 40	15 50	15 55	16 05		22 05	22 10	22 20	22 25	22 35	22 40	22 50	22 55	23 05	23 10	23 18	23 25
Homerton	d	15 13	15 21	15 28	15 36	15 43	15 51	15 58	16 06		22 06	22 13	22 21	22 28	22 36	22 43	22 51	22 58	23 06	23 13	23 19	23 28
Hackney Central	d	15 15	15 23	15 30	15 38	15 45	15 53	16 00	16 08		22 08	22 15	22 23	22 30	22 38	22 45	22 53	23 00	23 08	23 15	23 21	23 30
Dalston Kingsland	d	15 17	15 25	15 32	15 40	15 47	15 55	16 02	16 10		22 10	22 17	22 25	22 32	22 40	22 47	22 55	23 02	23 10	23 17	23 23	23 32
Canonbury	d	15 19	15 27	15 34	15 42	15 49	15 57	16 04	16 12		22 12	22 19	22 27	22 34	22 42	22 49	22 57	23 04	23 12	23 19	23 25	23 34
Highbury & Islington ⊖	d	15 23	15 31	15 38	15 46	15 53	16 01	16 08	16 16		22 16	22 23	22 31	22 38	22 46	22 53	23 01	23 08	23 16	23 23	23 28	23 38
Caledonian Rd & Barnsbury	d	15 25	15 33	15 40	15 48	15 55	16 03	16 10	16 18		22 18	22 25	22 33	22 40	22 48	22 55	23 03	23 10	23 18	23 25	23 30	23 40
Camden Road	d	15 29	15 37	15 44	15 52	15 59	16 07	16 14	16 22		22 22	22 29	22 37	22 44	22 52	22 59	23 07	23 14	23 22	23 29	23 34	23 45
Kentish Town West	d	15 31	15 39	15 46	15 54	16 01	16 09	16 16	16 24		22 24	22 31	22 39	22 46	22 54	23 01	23 09	23 16	23 24	23 31	23 37	23 47
Gospel Oak	d	15 34	15 42	15 49	15 57	16 04	16 12	16 19	16 27		22 27	22 34	22 42	22 49	22 57	23 04	23 12	23 19	23 27	23 34	23 40	23 50
Hampstead Heath	d	15 36	15 44	15 51	15 59	16 06	16 14	16 21	16 29	and at the same minutes past each hour until	22 29	22 36	22 44	22 51	22 59	23 06	23 14	23 21	23 29	23 36	23 42	23 52
Finchley Road & Frognal	d	15 38	15 46	15 53	16 01	16 08	16 16	16 23	16 31		22 31	22 38	22 46	22 53	23 01	23 08	23 16	23 23	23 31	23 38	23 44	23 54
West Hampstead ⊖	d	15 40	15 48	15 55	16 03	16 10	16 18	16 25	16 33		22 33	22 40	22 48	22 55	23 03	23 10	23 18	23 25	23 33	23 40	23 47	23 56
Brondesbury	d	15 42	15 50	15 57	16 05	16 12	16 20	16 27	16 35		22 35	22 42	22 50	22 57	23 05	23 12	23 20	23 27	23 35	23 42	23 48	23 58
Brondesbury Park	d	15 43	15 51	15 58	16 06	16 13	16 21	16 28	16 36		22 36	22 43	22 51	22 58	23 06	23 13	23 21	23 28	23 36	23 43	23 50	23 59
Kensal Rise	d	15 45	15 53	16 00	16 08	16 15	16 23	16 30	16 38		22 38	22 45	22 53	23 00	23 08	23 15	23 23	23 30	23 38	23 45	23 52	00 01
Willesden Jn. High Level ⊖	a	15 49	15 57	16 04	16 12	16 19	16 27	16 34	16 42		22 42	22 49	22 57	23 04	23 12	23 19	23 27	23 34	23 42	23 49	23 57	00 04
	d	15 50	15 58	16 05	16 13	16 20	16 28	16 35	16 43		22 43	22 50	22 58	23 05	23 13	23 20	23 28	23 35	23 43	23 50	23 59	00 05
Willesden Jn Low Level ⊖	a																					
Shepherd's Bush ⊖	d		16 08		16 23		16 38		16 53		22 53		23 08		23 23		23 38		23 53		00 09	
Kensington (Olympia) ⊖	d		16 11		16 26		16 41		16 56		22 56		23 11		23 26		23 41		23 56		00 11	
West Brompton ⊖	d		16 13		16 28		16 43		16 58		22 58		23 13		23 28		23 43		23 58		00 14	
Imperial Wharf	d		16 16		16 31		16 46		17 01		23 01		23 16		23 31		23 46		00 01		00 17	
Clapham Junction 10	a		16 24		16 39		16 54		17 09		23 09		23 24		23 39		23 54		00 09		00 22	
Acton Central	d	15 55		16 10		16 25		16 40				22 55		23 10		23 25		23 40		23 55		00 10
South Acton	d	15 58		16 13		16 28		16 43				22 58		23 13		23 28		23 43		23 58		00 13
Gunnersbury ⊖	d	16 02		16 18		16 32		16 48				23 02		23 18		23 32		23 48		00 03		00 18
Kew Gardens ⊖	d	16 05		16 21		16 35		16 51				23 05		23 21		23 35		23 51		00 06		00 21
Richmond ⊖	a	16 15		16 31		16 45		17 01				23 15		23 31		23 45		00 01		00 16		00 31

		LO	LO	LO	LO
Stratford 7 ⊖	d	23 30	23 37	23 45	23 52
Hackney Wick	d	23 35	23 40	23 49	23 55
Homerton	d	23 36	23 43	23 51	23 58
Hackney Central	d	23 38	23 45	23 53	00 01
Dalston Kingsland	d	23 40	23 47	23 55	00 03
Canonbury	d	23 42	23 49	23 57	00 05
Highbury & Islington ⊖	d	23 46	23 53	00 01	00 08
Caledonian Rd & Barnsbury	d	23 48	23 55	00 03	00 10
Camden Road	d	23 52	23 59	00 07	00 14
Kentish Town West	d	23 54	00 01	00 09	00 16
Gospel Oak	d	23 57	00 04	00 12	00 19
Hampstead Heath	d	23 59	00 06	00 14	00 21
Finchley Road & Frognal	d	00 01	00 08	00 16	00 23
West Hampstead ⊖	d	00 03	00 10	00 18	00 25
Brondesbury	d	00 05	00 12	00 20	00 27
Brondesbury Park	d	00 06	00 13	00 21	00 28
Kensal Rise	d	00 08	00 15	00 23	00 30
Willesden Jn. High Level ⊖	a	00 12	00 19	00 27	00 34
	d	00 13	00 20	00 28	00 35
Willesden Jn Low Level ⊖	a				
Shepherd's Bush ⊖	d	00 23		00 38	
Kensington (Olympia) ⊖	d	00 26		00 41	
West Brompton ⊖	d	00 28		00 43	
Imperial Wharf	d	00 31		00 46	
Clapham Junction 10	a	00 39		00 54	
Acton Central	d		00 25		00 40
South Acton	d		00 28		00 43
Gunnersbury ⊖	d		00 32		00 48
Kew Gardens ⊖	d		00 35		00 51
Richmond ⊖	a		00 45		01 00

Table 59

Sundays
19 August to 26 August

Stratford - Highbury and Islington, West Hampstead, Willesden Junction, Clapham Junction and Richmond

Network Diagram - see first Page of Table 59

		LO	LO	LO	LO	LO	LO	LO	LO	LO	LO	LO	LO	LO	LO	LO	LO	LO	LO	LO	LO	LO	LO
Stratford 7	⊖ d	23p45								09 15		09 30		09 45		10 00		10 20		10 35		10 45	
Hackney Wick	d	23p48								09 18		09 33		09 48		10 03		10 23		10 38		10 48	
Homerton	d	23p51								09 21		09 36		09 51		10 06		10 26		10 41		10 51	
Hackney Central	d	23p53								09 23		09 38		09 53		10 08		10 28		10 43		10 53	
Dalston Kingsland	d	23p55								09 25		09 40		09 55		10 10		10 30		10 45		10 55	
Canonbury	d	23p57								09 27		09 42		09 57		10 12		10 32		10 47		10 57	
Highbury & Islington	⊖ d	23p59								09 30		09 45		10 00		10 15		10 35		10 50		11 00	
Caledonian Rd & Barnsbury	d	00 02								09 32		09 47		10 02		10 17		10 37		10 52		11 02	
Camden Road	d	00 05								09 35		09 50		10 05		10 20		10 40		10 55		11 05	
Kentish Town West	d	00 07								09 37		09 52		10 07		10 22		10 42		10 57		11 07	
Gospel Oak	d	00 10						09 24		09 40		09 55		10 10		10 25		10 45		11 00		11 10	
Hampstead Heath	d	00 12						09 26		09 42		09 57		10 12		10 27		10 47		11 02		11 12	
Finchley Road & Frognal	d	00 14						09 28		09 44		09 59		10 14		10 29		10 49		11 04		11 14	
West Hampstead	⊖ d	00 16						09 30		09 46		10 01		10 16		10 31		10 51		11 06		11 16	
Brondesbury	d	00 18						09 32		09 48		10 03		10 18		10 33		10 53		11 08		11 18	
Brondesbury Park	d	00 19						09 33		09 49		10 04		10 19		10 34		10 54		11 09		11 19	
Kensal Rise	d	00 21						09 35		09 51		10 06		10 21		10 36		10 56		11 11		11 21	
Willesden Jn. High Level	⊖ a							09 39		09 55		10 10		10 25		10 40		11 00		11 15		11 25	
	d		08 32	08 56	09 02	09 26	09 32	09 40	09 48	09 56	10 02	10 11	10 16	10 26	10 32	10 41	10 46	11 01	11 02	11 16	11 16	11 26	11 32
Willesden Jn Low Level	⊖ a	00 29																					
Shepherd's Bush	⊖ d		08 40		09 10		09 40		09 54		10 10		10 24		10 40		10 55		11 10	11 24			11 40
Kensington (Olympia)	⊖ d		08 42		09 12		09 42		09 56		10 12		10 26		10 42		10 56		11 12	11 26			11 42
West Brompton	⊖ d		08 44		09 14		09 44		09 58		10 14		10 28		10 44		10 58		11 14	11 28			11 44
Imperial Wharf	d		08 47		09 17		09 47		10 01		10 17		10 31		10 47		11 01		11 17	11 31			11 47
Clapham Junction 10	a		08 54		09 23		09 53		10 09		10 23		10 38		10 53		11 08		11 28	11 40			11 53
Acton Central	d			09 01		09 31		09 45		10 01		10 16		10 31		10 46		11 06			11 21	11 31	
South Acton	d			09 03		09 34		09 47		10 04		10 19		10 34		10 49		11 09			11 24	11 34	
Gunnersbury	⊖ d			09 08		09 38		09 50		10 08		10 22		10 38		10 52		11 12			11 28	11 38	
Kew Gardens	⊖ d			09 11		09 41		09 53		10 11		10 25		10 41		10 55		11 15			11 31	11 41	
Richmond	⊖ a			09 19		09 49		10 03		10 18		10 31		10 46		11 01		11 21			11 38	11 46	

		LO	LO	LO	LO	LO	LO	LO	LO	LO	LO	LO	LO	LO	LO	LO	LO	LO	LO	LO	LO	LO	LO
Stratford 7	⊖ d	10 55	11 05	11 15		11 25	11 35	11 45		11 55	12 05	12 15		12 25	12 35	12 45		12 55	13 05	13 15		13 25	13 35
Hackney Wick	d	10 58	11 08	11 18		11 28	11 38	11 48		11 58	12 08	12 18		12 28	12 38	12 48		12 58	13 08	13 18		13 28	13 38
Homerton	d	11 01	11 11	11 21		11 31	11 41	11 51		12 01	12 11	12 21		12 31	12 41	12 51		13 01	13 11	13 21		13 31	13 41
Hackney Central	d	11 03	11 13	11 23		11 33	11 43	11 53		12 03	12 13	12 23		12 33	12 43	12 53		13 03	13 13	13 23		13 33	13 43
Dalston Kingsland	d	11 05	11 15	11 25		11 35	11 45	11 55		12 05	12 15	12 25		12 35	12 45	12 55		13 05	13 15	13 25		13 35	13 45
Canonbury	d	11 07	11 17	11 27		11 37	11 47	11 57		12 07	12 17	12 27		12 37	12 47	12 57		13 07	13 17	13 27		13 37	13 47
Highbury & Islington	⊖ d	11 10	11 20	11 30		11 40	11 50	12 00		12 10	12 20	12 30		12 40	12 50	13 00		13 10	13 20	13 30		13 40	13 50
Caledonian Rd & Barnsbury	d	11 12	11 22	11 32		11 42	11 52	12 02		12 12	12 22	12 32		12 42	12 52	13 02		13 12	13 22	13 32		13 42	13 52
Camden Road	d	11 15	11 25	11 35		11 45	11 55	12 05		12 15	12 25	12 35		12 45	12 55	13 05		13 15	13 25	13 35		13 45	13 55
Kentish Town West	d	11 17	11 27	11 37		11 47	11 57	12 07		12 17	12 27	12 37		12 47	12 57	13 07		13 17	13 27	13 37		13 47	13 57
Gospel Oak	d	11 20	11 30	11 40		11 50	12 00	12 10		12 20	12 30	12 40		12 50	13 00	13 10		13 20	13 30	13 40		13 50	14 00
Hampstead Heath	d	11 22	11 32	11 42		11 52	12 02	12 12		12 22	12 32	12 42		12 52	13 02	13 12		13 22	13 32	13 42		13 52	14 02
Finchley Road & Frognal	d	11 24	11 34	11 44		11 54	12 04	12 14		12 24	12 34	12 44		12 54	13 04	13 14		13 24	13 34	13 44		13 54	14 04
West Hampstead	⊖ d	11 26	11 36	11 46		11 56	12 06	12 16		12 26	12 36	12 46		12 56	13 06	13 16		13 26	13 36	13 46		13 56	14 06
Brondesbury	d	11 28	11 38	11 48		11 58	12 08	12 18		12 28	12 38	12 48		12 58	13 08	13 18		13 28	13 38	13 48		13 58	14 08
Brondesbury Park	d	11 29	11 39	11 49		11 59	12 09	12 19		12 29	12 39	12 49		12 59	13 09	13 19		13 29	13 39	13 49		13 59	14 09
Kensal Rise	d	11 31	11 41	11 51		12 01	12 11	12 21		12 31	12 41	12 51		13 01	13 11	13 21		13 31	13 41	13 51		14 01	14 11
Willesden Jn. High Level	⊖ a	11 35	11 45	11 55		12 05	12 15	12 25		12 35	12 45	12 55		13 05	13 15	13 25		13 35	13 45	13 55		14 05	14 15
	d	11 36	11 46	11 56	12 02	12 06	12 16	12 26	12 32	12 36	12 46	12 56	13 02	13 06	13 16	13 26	13 32	13 36	13 46	13 56	14 02	14 06	14 16
Willesden Jn Low Level	⊖ a																						
Shepherd's Bush	⊖ d		11 54		12 10		12 24		12 40		12 54		13 10		13 24		13 40		13 54		14 10		14 24
Kensington (Olympia)	⊖ d		11 56		12 12		12 26		12 42		12 56		13 12		13 26		13 42		13 56		14 12		14 26
West Brompton	⊖ d		11 58		12 14		12 28		12 44		12 58		13 14		13 28		13 44		13 58		14 14		14 28
Imperial Wharf	d		12 01		12 17		12 31		12 47		13 01		13 17		13 31		13 47		14 01		14 17		14 31
Clapham Junction 10	a		12 09		12 23		12 39		12 53		13 09		13 23		13 39		13 53		14 09		14 23		14 39
Acton Central	d	11 41		12 01		12 11		12 31		12 41		13 01		13 11		13 31		13 41		14 01		14 11	
South Acton	d	11 44		12 04		12 14		12 34		12 44		13 04		13 14		13 34		13 44		14 04		14 14	
Gunnersbury	⊖ d	11 48		12 08		12 18		12 38		12 48		13 08		13 18		13 38		13 48		14 08		14 18	
Kew Gardens	⊖ d	11 51		12 11		12 21		12 41		12 51		13 11		13 21		13 41		13 51		14 11		14 21	
Richmond	⊖ a	11 56		12 16		12 26		12 46		12 56		13 16		13 26		13 46		13 56		14 16		14 26	

Table 59

Sundays
19 August to 26 August

Stratford - Highbury and Islington, West Hampstead, Willesden Junction, Clapham Junction and Richmond

Network Diagram - see first Page of Table 59

		LO	LO	LO	LO	LO	LO	LO	LO	LO	LO	LO	LO	LO	LO	LO	LO	LO	LO	LO	LO	LO	LO
Stratford 7	⊖ d	13 45		13 55	14 05	14 15		14 25	14 35	14 45		14 55	15 05	15 15		15 25	15 35	15 45		15 55	16 05	16 15	
Hackney Wick	d	13 48		13 58	14 08	14 18		14 28	14 38	14 48		14 58	15 08	15 18		15 28	15 38	15 48		15 58	16 08	16 18	
Homerton	d	13 51		14 01	14 11	14 21		14 31	14 41	14 51		15 01	15 11	15 21		15 31	15 41	15 51		16 01	16 11	16 21	
Hackney Central	d	13 53		14 03	14 13	14 23		14 33	14 43	14 53		15 03	15 13	15 23		15 33	15 43	15 53		16 03	16 13	16 23	
Dalston Kingsland	d	13 55		14 05	14 15	14 25		14 35	14 45	14 55		15 05	15 15	15 25		15 35	15 45	15 55		16 05	16 15	16 25	
Canonbury	d	13 57		14 07	14 17	14 27		14 37	14 47	14 57		15 07	15 17	15 27		15 37	15 47	15 57		16 07	16 17	16 27	
Highbury & Islington	⊖ d	14 00		14 10	14 20	14 30		14 40	14 50	15 00		15 10	15 20	15 30		15 40	15 50	16 00		16 10	16 20	16 30	
Caledonian Rd & Barnsbury	d	14 02		14 12	14 22	14 32		14 42	14 52	15 02		15 12	15 22	15 32		15 42	15 52	16 02		16 12	16 22	16 32	
Camden Road	d	14 05		14 15	14 25	14 35		14 45	14 55	15 05		15 15	15 25	15 35		15 45	15 55	16 05		16 15	16 25	16 35	
Kentish Town West	d	14 07		14 17	14 27	14 37		14 47	14 57	15 07		15 17	15 27	15 37		15 47	15 57	16 07		16 17	16 27	16 37	
Gospel Oak	d	14 10		14 20	14 30	14 40		14 50	15 00	15 10		15 20	15 30	15 40		15 50	16 00	16 10		16 20	16 30	16 40	
Hampstead Heath	d	14 12		14 22	14 32	14 42		14 52	15 02	15 12		15 22	15 32	15 42		15 52	16 02	16 12		16 22	16 32	16 42	
Finchley Road & Frognal	d	14 14		14 24	14 34	14 44		14 54	15 04	15 14		15 24	15 34	15 44		15 54	16 04	16 14		16 24	16 34	16 44	
West Hampstead	⊖ d	14 16		14 26	14 36	14 46		14 56	15 06	15 16		15 26	15 36	15 46		15 56	16 06	16 16		16 26	16 36	16 46	
Brondesbury	d	14 18		14 28	14 38	14 48		14 58	15 08	15 18		15 28	15 38	15 48		15 58	16 08	16 18		16 28	16 38	16 48	
Brondesbury Park	d	14 19		14 29	14 39	14 49		14 59	15 09	15 19		15 29	15 39	15 49		15 59	16 09	16 19		16 29	16 39	16 49	
Kensal Rise	d	14 21		14 31	14 41	14 51		15 01	15 11	15 21		15 31	15 41	15 51		16 01	16 11	16 21		16 31	16 41	16 51	
Willesden Jn. High Level	⊖ a	14 25		14 35	14 45	14 55		15 05	15 15	15 25		15 35	15 45	15 55		16 05	16 15	16 25		16 35	16 45	16 55	
	d	14 26	14 32	14 36	14 46	14 56	15 02	15 06	15 16	15 26	15 32	15 36	15 46	15 56	16 02	16 06	16 16	16 26	16 32	16 36	16 46	16 56	17 02
Willesden Jn Low Level	⊖ a																						
Shepherd's Bush	⊖ d		14 40		14 54		15 10		15 24		15 40		15 54		16 10		16 24		16 40		16 54		17 10
Kensington (Olympia)	⊖ d		14 42		14 56		15 12		15 26		15 42		15 56		16 12		16 26		16 42		16 56		17 12
West Brompton	⊖ d		14 44		14 58		15 14		15 28		15 44		15 58		16 14		16 28		16 44		16 58		17 14
Imperial Wharf	d		14 47		15 01		15 17		15 31		15 47		16 01		16 17		16 31		16 47		17 01		17 17
Clapham Junction 10	a		14 54		15 09		15 23		15 39		15 53		16 09		16 23		16 39		16 54		17 10		17 24
Acton Central	d	14 31		14 41		15 01		15 11		15 31		15 41		16 01		16 11		16 31		16 41		17 01	
South Acton	d	14 34		14 44		15 04		15 14		15 34		15 44		16 04		16 14		16 34		16 44		17 04	
Gunnersbury	⊖ d	14 38		14 48		15 08		15 18		15 38		15 48		16 08		16 18		16 38		16 48		17 08	
Kew Gardens	⊖ d	14 41		14 51		15 11		15 21		15 41		15 51		16 11		16 21		16 41		16 51		17 11	
Richmond	⊖ a	14 46		14 56		15 16		15 26		15 46		15 56		16 16		16 26		16 46		16 56		17 16	

		LO	LO	LO	LO	LO	LO	LO	LO	LO	LO	LO	LO	LO	LO	LO	LO	LO	LO	LO	LO	LO	LO
Stratford 7	⊖ d	16 25	16 35	16 45		16 55	17 05	17 15		17 25	17 35	17 45		17 55	18 05	18 15		18 25	18 35	18 45		18 55	19 05
Hackney Wick	d	16 28	16 38	16 48		16 58	17 08	17 18		17 28	17 38	17 48		17 58	18 08	18 18		18 28	18 38	18 48		18 58	19 08
Homerton	d	16 31	16 41	16 51		17 01	17 11	17 21		17 31	17 41	17 51		18 01	18 11	18 21		18 31	18 41	18 51		19 01	19 11
Hackney Central	d	16 33	16 43	16 53		17 03	17 13	17 23		17 33	17 43	17 53		18 03	18 13	18 23		18 33	18 43	18 53		19 03	19 13
Dalston Kingsland	d	16 35	16 45	16 55		17 05	17 15	17 25		17 35	17 45	17 55		18 05	18 15	18 25		18 35	18 45	18 55		19 05	19 15
Canonbury	d	16 37	16 47	16 57		17 07	17 17	17 27		17 37	17 47	17 57		18 07	18 17	18 27		18 37	18 47	18 57		19 07	19 17
Highbury & Islington	⊖ d	16 40	16 50	17 00		17 10	17 20	17 30		17 40	17 50	18 00		18 10	18 20	18 30		18 40	18 50	19 00		19 10	19 20
Caledonian Rd & Barnsbury	d	16 42	16 52	17 02		17 12	17 22	17 32		17 42	17 52	18 02		18 12	18 22	18 32		18 42	18 52	19 02		19 12	19 22
Camden Road	d	16 45	16 55	17 05		17 15	17 25	17 35		17 45	17 55	18 05		18 15	18 25	18 35		18 45	18 55	19 05		19 15	19 25
Kentish Town West	d	16 47	16 57	17 07		17 17	17 27	17 37		17 47	17 57	18 07		18 17	18 27	18 37		18 47	18 57	19 07		19 17	19 27
Gospel Oak	d	16 50	17 00	17 10		17 20	17 30	17 40		17 50	18 00	18 10		18 20	18 30	18 40		18 50	19 00	19 10		19 20	19 30
Hampstead Heath	d	16 52	17 02	17 12		17 22	17 32	17 42		17 52	18 02	18 12		18 22	18 32	18 42		18 52	19 02	19 12		19 22	19 32
Finchley Road & Frognal	d	16 54	17 04	17 14		17 24	17 34	17 44		17 54	18 04	18 14		18 24	18 34	18 44		18 54	19 04	19 14		19 24	19 34
West Hampstead	⊖ d	16 56	17 06	17 16		17 26	17 36	17 46		17 56	18 06	18 16		18 26	18 36	18 46		18 56	19 06	19 16		19 26	19 36
Brondesbury	d	16 58	17 08	17 18		17 28	17 38	17 48		17 58	18 08	18 18		18 28	18 38	18 48		18 58	19 08	19 18		19 28	19 38
Brondesbury Park	d	16 59	17 09	17 19		17 29	17 39	17 49		17 59	18 09	18 19		18 29	18 39	18 49		18 59	19 09	19 19		19 29	19 39
Kensal Rise	d	17 01	17 11	17 21		17 31	17 41	17 51		18 01	18 11	18 21		18 31	18 41	18 51		19 01	19 11	19 21		19 31	19 41
Willesden Jn. High Level	⊖ a	17 05	17 15	17 25		17 35	17 45	17 55		18 05	18 15	18 25		18 35	18 45	18 55		19 05	19 15	19 25		19 35	19 45
	d	17 06	17 16	17 26	17 32	17 36	17 46	17 56	18 02	18 06	18 16	18 26	18 32	18 36	18 46	18 56	19 02	19 06	19 16	19 26	19 32	19 36	19 46
Willesden Jn Low Level	⊖ a																						
Shepherd's Bush	⊖ d		17 24		17 40		17 54		18 10		18 24		18 40		18 54		19 10		19 24		19 40		19 54
Kensington (Olympia)	⊖ d		17 26		17 42		17 56		18 12		18 26		18 42		18 56		19 12		19 26		19 42		19 56
West Brompton	⊖ d		17 28		17 44		17 58		18 14		18 28		18 44		18 58		19 14		19 28		19 44		19 58
Imperial Wharf	d		17 31		17 47		18 01		18 17		18 31		18 47		19 01		19 17		19 31		19 47		20 01
Clapham Junction 10	a		17 40		17 54		18 10		18 24		18 38		18 54		19 10		19 26		19 40		19 54		20 10
Acton Central	d	17 11		17 31		17 41		18 01		18 11		18 31		18 41		19 01		19 11		19 31		19 41	
South Acton	d	17 14		17 34		17 44		18 04		18 14		18 34		18 44		19 04		19 14		19 34		19 44	
Gunnersbury	⊖ d	17 18		17 38		17 48		18 08		18 18		18 38		18 48		19 08		19 18		19 38		19 48	
Kew Gardens	⊖ d	17 21		17 41		17 51		18 11		18 21		18 41		18 51		19 11		19 21		19 41		19 51	
Richmond	⊖ a	17 26		17 46		17 56		18 16		18 26		18 46		18 56		19 16		19 26		19 46		19 56	

Stratford - Highbury and Islington, West Hampstead, Willesden Junction, Clapham Junction and Richmond

Network Diagram - see first Page of Table 59

Station		LO	LO	LO	LO	LO	LO	LO	LO	LO	LO	LO
Stratford 7 ⊖	d	19 15		19 25	19 35	19 45		19 55	20 05	20 15		20 25
Hackney Wick	d	19 18		19 28	19 38	19 48		19 58	20 08	20 18		20 28
Homerton	d	19 21		19 31	19 41	19 51		20 01	20 11	20 21		20 31
Hackney Central	d	19 23		19 33	19 43	19 53		20 03	20 13	20 23		20 33
Dalston Kingsland	d	19 25		19 35	19 45	19 55		20 05	20 15	20 25		20 35
Canonbury	d	19 27		19 37	19 47	19 57		20 07	20 17	20 27		20 37
Highbury & Islington ⊖	d	19 30		19 40	19 50	20 00		20 10	20 20	20 30		20 40
Caledonian Rd & Barnsbury	d	19 32		19 42	19 52	20 02		20 12	20 22	20 32		20 42
Camden Road	d	19 35		19 45	19 55	20 05		20 15	20 25	20 35		20 45
Kentish Town West	d	19 37		19 47	19 57	20 07		20 17	20 27	20 37		20 47
Gospel Oak	d	19 40		19 50	20 00	20 10		20 20	20 30	20 40		20 50
Hampstead Heath	d	19 42		19 52	20 02	20 12		20 22	20 32	20 42		20 52
Finchley Road & Frognal	d	19 44		19 54	20 04	20 14		20 24	20 34	20 44		20 54
West Hampstead ⊖	d	19 46		19 56	20 06	20 16		20 26	20 36	20 46		20 56
Brondesbury	d	19 48		19 58	20 08	20 18		20 28	20 38	20 48		20 58
Brondesbury Park	d	19 49		19 59	20 09	20 19		20 29	20 39	20 49		20 59
Kensal Rise	d	19 51		20 01	20 11	20 21		20 31	20 41	20 51		21 01
Willesden Jn. High Level ⊖	a	19 55		20 05	20 15	20 25		20 35	20 45	20 55		21 05
	d	19 56	20 02	20 06	20 16	20 26	20 32	20 36	20 46	20 56	21 02	21 06
Willesden Jn Low Level ⊖	a											
Shepherd's Bush ⊖	d		20 10		20 24		20 40		20 54		21 10	
Kensington (Olympia) ⊖	d		20 12		20 26		20 42		20 56		21 12	
West Brompton ⊖	d		20 14		20 28		20 44		20 58		21 14	
Imperial Wharf	d		20 17		20 31		20 47		21 01		21 17	
Clapham Junction 10	a		20 24		20 40		20 54		21 10		21 24	
Acton Central	d	20 01		20 11		20 31		20 41		21 01		21 11
South Acton	d	20 04		20 14		20 34		20 44		21 04		21 14
Gunnersbury ⊖	d	20 08		20 18		20 38		20 48		21 08		21 18
Kew Gardens ⊖	d	20 11		20 21		20 41		20 51		21 11		21 21
Richmond ⊖	a	20 16		20 26		20 46		20 56		21 16		21 26

Station		LO	LO	LO	LO	LO	LO	LO	LO	LO	LO	LO
Stratford 7 ⊖	d	20 35	20 45		20 55	21 05	21 15		21 30	21 45		22 00
Hackney Wick	d	20 38	20 48		20 58	21 08	21 18		21 33	21 48		22 03
Homerton	d	20 41	20 51		21 01	21 11	21 21		21 36	21 51		22 06
Hackney Central	d	20 43	20 53		21 03	21 13	21 23		21 38	21 53		22 08
Dalston Kingsland	d	20 45	20 55		21 05	21 15	21 25		21 40	21 55		22 10
Canonbury	d	20 47	20 57		21 07	21 17	21 27		21 42	21 57		22 12
Highbury & Islington ⊖	d	20 50	21 00		21 10	21 20	21 30		21 45	22 00		22 15
Caledonian Rd & Barnsbury	d	20 52	21 02		21 12	21 22	21 32		21 47	22 02		22 17
Camden Road	d	20 55	21 05		21 15	21 25	21 35		21 50	22 05		22 20
Kentish Town West	d	20 57	21 07		21 17	21 27	21 37		21 52	22 07		22 22
Gospel Oak	d	21 00	21 10		21 20	21 30	21 40		21 55	22 10		22 25
Hampstead Heath	d	21 02	21 12		21 22	21 32	21 42		21 57	22 12		22 27
Finchley Road & Frognal	d	21 04	21 14		21 24	21 34	21 44		21 59	22 14		22 29
West Hampstead ⊖	d	21 06	21 16		21 26	21 36	21 46		22 01	22 16		22 31
Brondesbury	d	21 08	21 18		21 28	21 38	21 48		22 03	22 18		22 33
Brondesbury Park	d	21 09	21 19		21 29	21 39	21 49		22 04	22 19		22 34
Kensal Rise	d	21 11	21 21		21 31	21 41	21 51		22 06	22 21		22 36
Willesden Jn. High Level ⊖	a	21 15	21 25		21 35	21 45	21 55		22 10	22 25		22 40
	d	21 16	21 26	21 32	21 39	21 46	21 56	22 02	22 11	22 26	22 32	22 41
Willesden Jn Low Level ⊖	a											
Shepherd's Bush ⊖	d	21 24		21 40		21 54		22 10			22 40	
Kensington (Olympia) ⊖	d	21 26		21 42		21 56		22 12			22 42	
West Brompton ⊖	d	21 28		21 44		21 58		22 14			22 44	
Imperial Wharf	d	21 31		21 47		22 01		22 17			22 47	
Clapham Junction 10	a	21 39		21 54		22 09		22 24			22 54	
Acton Central	d		21 31		21 44		22 01		22 16	22 31		22 46
South Acton	d		21 34		21 47		22 04		22 19	22 34		22 49
Gunnersbury ⊖	d		21 38		21 50		22 08		22 22	22 38		22 52
Kew Gardens ⊖	d		21 41		21 53		22 11		22 25	22 41		22 55
Richmond ⊖	a		21 46		21 57		22 16		22 31	22 46		23 01

Station		LO	LO	LO
Stratford 7 ⊖	d			
Hackney Wick	d			
Homerton	d			
Hackney Central	d			
Dalston Kingsland	d			
Canonbury	d			
Highbury & Islington ⊖	d			
Caledonian Rd & Barnsbury	d			
Camden Road	d			
Kentish Town West	d			
Gospel Oak	d		22 55	23 30
Hampstead Heath	d		22 57	23 32
Finchley Road & Frognal	d		22 59	23 34
West Hampstead ⊖	d		23 01	23 36
Brondesbury	d		23 03	23 38
Brondesbury Park	d		23 04	23 39
Kensal Rise	d		23 06	23 41
Willesden Jn. High Level ⊖	a		23 10	
	d	22 46	23 11	
Willesden Jn Low Level ⊖	a			23 54
Shepherd's Bush ⊖	d	22 54		
Kensington (Olympia) ⊖	d	22 56		
West Brompton ⊖	d	22 58		
Imperial Wharf	d	23 01		
Clapham Junction 10	a	23 11		
Acton Central	d		23 16	
South Acton	d		23 19	
Gunnersbury ⊖	d		23 22	
Kew Gardens ⊖	d		23 25	
Richmond ⊖	a		23 32	

Stratford - Highbury and Islington, West Hampstead, Willesden Junction, Clapham Junction and Richmond

Network Diagram - see first Page of Table 59

Station		LO	LO	LO	LO	LO	LO	LO	LO	LO	LO	LO
Stratford 7 ⊖	d	22p52	23p00	23p07	23p15	23p22	23p30	23p37	23p45	23p52	00 01	00 07
Hackney Wick	d	22p55	23p03	23p10	23p18	23p25	23p33	23p40	23p48	23p55	00 05	00 10
Homerton	d	22p58	23p06	23p13	23p21	23p28	23p36	23p43	23p51	23p58	00 06	00 13
Hackney Central	d	23p00	23p08	23p15	23p23	23p30	23p38	23p45	23p53	00 01	00 08	00 15
Dalston Kingsland	d	23p02	23p10	23p17	23p25	23p32	23p40	23p47	23p55	00 03	00 10	00 17
Canonbury	d	23p04	23p12	23p19	23p27	23p34	23p42	23p49	23p57	00 04	00 12	00 19
Highbury & Islington ⊖	d	23p08	23p16	23p23	23p31	23p38	23p46	23p53	00 01	00 08	00 16	00 23
Caledonian Rd & Barnsbury	d	23p10	23p18	23p25	23p33	23p40	23p48	23p55	00 03	00 10	00 18	00 25
Camden Road	d	23p14	23p22	23p29	23p37	23p44	23p52	23p59	00 07	00 14	00 22	00a34
Kentish Town West	d	23p16	23p24	23p31	23p39	23p46	23p54	00 01	00 09	00 16	00 24	
Gospel Oak	d	23p19	23p27	23p34	23p42	23p49	23p57	00 04	00 12	00 19	00 27	
Hampstead Heath	d	23p21	23p29	23p36	23p44	23p51	23p59	00 06	00 14	00 21	00 29	
Finchley Road & Frognal	d	23p23	23p31	23p38	23p46	23p53	00 01	00 08	00 16	00 23	00 31	
West Hampstead ⊖	d	23p25	23p33	23p40	23p48	23p55	00 03	00 10	00 18	00 25	00 33	
Brondesbury	d	23p27	23p35	23p42	23p50	23p57	00 05	00 12	00 20	00 27	00 35	
Brondesbury Park	d	23p28	23p36	23p43	23p51	23p58	00 06	00 13	00 21	00 28	00 36	
Kensal Rise	d	23p30	23p38	23p45	23p53	00 01	00 08	00 15	00 23	00 30	00 38	
Willesden Jn. High Level ⊖	a	23p34	23p42	23p49	23p57	00 04	00 12	00 19	00 27	00 34	00 42	
	d	23p35	23p43	23p50	23p59	00 05	00 13	00 20	00 28	00 35	00 43	
Willesden Jn Low Level ⊖	a											
Shepherd's Bush ⊖	d		23p53		00 09		00 23		00 38		00 53	
Kensington (Olympia) ⊖	d		23p56		00 11		00 26		00 41		00 56	
West Brompton ⊖	d		23p58		00 14		00 28		00 43		00 58	
Imperial Wharf	d		00 01		00 17		00 31		00 46		01 01	
Clapham Junction 10	a		00 09		00 22		00 39		00 54		01 09	
Acton Central	d	23p40		23p55		00 10		00 25		00 40		
South Acton	d	23p43		23p58		00 13		00 28		00 43		
Gunnersbury ⊖	d	23p48		00 02		00 18		00 32		00 48		
Kew Gardens ⊖	d	23p51		00 05		00 21		00 35		00 51		
Richmond ⊖	a	00 01		00 14		00 31		00 44		01 00		

Station		LO	LO	LO	LO	LO	LO	LO	LO	LO	LO	LO
Stratford 7 ⊖	d	00 15	00 22	00 30	00 37	00 45	00 52	01 00			05 47	
Hackney Wick	d	00 20	00 25	00 35	00 40	00 50	00 55	01 05			05 50	
Homerton	d	00 21	00 28	00 36	00 43	00 51	00 58	01 06			05 53	
Hackney Central	d	00 23	00 30	00 38	00 45	00 53	01 00	01 08			05 55	
Dalston Kingsland	d	00 25	00 32	00 40	00 47	00 55	01 02	01 10			05 57	
Canonbury	d	00 27	00 34	00 42	00 49	00 57	01 04	01 12			05 59	
Highbury & Islington ⊖	d	00 31	00 38	00 46	00 53	01 01	01 08	01 16			06 02	
Caledonian Rd & Barnsbury	d	00 33	00 40	00 48	00 55	01 03	01 10	01 18			06 04	
Camden Road	d	00 37	00a49	00 52	01a04	01 07	01a19	01 22			06 07	
Kentish Town West	d	00 39		00 54		01 09		01 24			06 09	
Gospel Oak	d	00 42		00 57		01 12		01 27			06 12	
Hampstead Heath	d	00 44		00 59		01 14		01 29			06 14	
Finchley Road & Frognal	d	00 46		01 01		01 16		01 31			06 16	
West Hampstead ⊖	d	00 48		01 03		01 18		01 33			06 18	
Brondesbury	d	00 50		01 05		01 20		01 35			06 20	
Brondesbury Park	d	00 51		01 06		01 21		01 36			06 21	
Kensal Rise	d	00 53		01 08		01 23		01 38			06 23	
Willesden Jn. High Level ⊖	a										06 27	
	d								06 02	06 06	06 28	06 33
Willesden Jn Low Level ⊖	a	01 03		01 21		01 41		01 50				
Shepherd's Bush ⊖	d								06 09			06 41
Kensington (Olympia) ⊖	d								06 11			06 43
West Brompton ⊖	d								06 14			06 46
Imperial Wharf	d								06 17			06 49
Clapham Junction 10	a								06 23			06 55
Acton Central	d									06 11	06 33	
South Acton	d									06 14	06 36	
Gunnersbury ⊖	d									06 18	06 40	
Kew Gardens ⊖	d									06 21	06 43	
Richmond ⊖	a									06 30	06 52	

Station		LO	LO	LO	LO	LO	LO	LO	LO	LO	LO	LO
Stratford 7 ⊖	d		06 00	06 07	06 15	06 23	06 30	06 37	06 45	06 52	07 00	07 07
Hackney Wick	d		06 05	06 10	06 20	06 26	06 35	06 40	06 50	06 55	07 05	07 10
Homerton	d		06 06	06 13	06 21	06 29	06 36	06 43	06 51	06 58	07 06	07 13
Hackney Central	d		06 08	06 15	06 23	06 31	06 38	06 45	06 53	07 00	07 08	07 15
Dalston Kingsland	d		06 10	06 17	06 25	06 33	06 40	06 47	06 55	07 02	07 10	07 17
Canonbury	d		06 12	06 19	06 27	06 35	06 42	06 49	06 57	07 04	07 12	07 19
Highbury & Islington ⊖	d		06 16	06 23	06 31	06 38	06 46	06 53	07 01	07 08	07 16	07 23
Caledonian Rd & Barnsbury	d		06 18	06 25	06 33	06 40	06 48	06 55	07 03	07 10	07 18	07 25
Camden Road	d		06 22	06 29	06 37	06 44	06 52	06 59	07 07	07 14	07 22	07 29
Kentish Town West	d		06 24	06 31	06 39	06 46	06 54	07 01	07 09	07 16	07 24	07 31
Gospel Oak	d		06 27	06 34	06 42	06 49	06 57	07 04	07 12	07 19	07 27	07 34
Hampstead Heath	d		06 29	06 36	06 44	06 51	06 59	07 06	07 14	07 21	07 29	07 36
Finchley Road & Frognal	d		06 31	06 38	06 46	06 53	07 01	07 08	07 16	07 23	07 31	07 38
West Hampstead ⊖	d		06 33	06 40	06 48	06 55	07 03	07 10	07 18	07 25	07 33	07 40
Brondesbury	d		06 35	06 42	06 50	06 57	07 05	07 12	07 20	07 27	07 35	07 42
Brondesbury Park	d		06 36	06 43	06 51	06 58	07 06	07 13	07 21	07 28	07 36	07 43
Kensal Rise	d		06 38	06 45	06 53	07 00	07 08	07 15	07 23	07 30	07 38	07 45
Willesden Jn. High Level ⊖	a		06 42	06 49	06 57	07 04	07 12	07 19	07 27	07 34	07 42	07 49
	d	06 41	06 43	06 50	06 58	07 05	07 13	07 20	07 28	07 35	07 43	07 50
Willesden Jn Low Level ⊖	a											
Shepherd's Bush ⊖	d		06 53		07 08		07 23		07 38		07 53	
Kensington (Olympia) ⊖	d		06 56		07 11		07 26		07 41		07 56	
West Brompton ⊖	d		06 58		07 13		07 28		07 43		07 58	
Imperial Wharf	d		07 01		07 16		07 31		07 46		08 01	
Clapham Junction 10	a		07 08		07 23		07 38		07 53		08 07	
Acton Central	d	06 46		06 55		07 10		07 27		07 40		07 55
South Acton	d	06 49		06 58		07 13		07 29		07 43		07 57
Gunnersbury ⊖	d	06 52		07 02		07 18		07 34		07 48		08 01
Kew Gardens ⊖	d	06 55		07 05		07 21		07 37		07 51		08 04
Richmond ⊖	a	07 05		07 14		07 30		07 47		08 00		08 14

Station		LO	LO	LO	LO	LO	LO	LO	LO	LO	LO	LO
Stratford 7 ⊖	d	07 15	07 22	07 30	07 37	07 45	07 52	08 00	08 07	08 15	08 22	08 30
Hackney Wick	d	07 20	07 25	07 35	07 40	07 50	07 55	08 05	08 10	08 20	08 25	08 35
Homerton	d	07 21	07 28	07 36	07 43	07 51	07 58	08 06	08 13	08 21	08 28	08 36
Hackney Central	d	07 23	07 30	07 38	07 45	07 53	08 00	08 08	08 15	08 23	08 30	08 38
Dalston Kingsland	d	07 25	07 32	07 40	07 47	07 55	08 02	08 10	08 17	08 25	08 32	08 40
Canonbury	d	07 27	07 34	07 42	07 49	07 57	08 04	08 12	08 19	08 27	08 34	08 42
Highbury & Islington ⊖	d	07 31	07 38	07 46	07 53	08 01	08 08	08 16	08 23	08 31	08 38	08 46
Caledonian Rd & Barnsbury	d	07 33	07 40	07 48	07 55	08 03	08 10	08 18	08 25	08 33	08 40	08 48
Camden Road	d	07 37	07 44	07 52	07 59	08 07	08 14	08 22	08 29	08 37	08 44	08 52
Kentish Town West	d	07 39	07 46	07 54	08 01	08 09	08 16	08 24	08 31	08 39	08 46	08 54
Gospel Oak	d	07 42	07 49	07 57	08 04	08 12	08 19	08 27	08 34	08 42	08 49	08 57
Hampstead Heath	d	07 44	07 51	07 59	08 06	08 14	08 21	08 29	08 36	08 44	08 51	08 59
Finchley Road & Frognal	d	07 46	07 53	08 01	08 08	08 16	08 23	08 31	08 38	08 46	08 53	09 01
West Hampstead ⊖	d	07 48	07 55	08 03	08 10	08 18	08 25	08 33	08 40	08 48	08 55	09 03
Brondesbury	d	07 50	07 57	08 05	08 12	08 20	08 27	08 35	08 42	08 50	08 57	09 05
Brondesbury Park	d	07 51	07 58	08 06	08 13	08 21	08 28	08 36	08 43	08 51	08 58	09 06
Kensal Rise	d	07 53	08 00	08 08	08 15	08 23	08 30	08 38	08 45	08 53	09 00	09 08
Willesden Jn. High Level ⊖	a	07 57	08 04	08 12	08 19	08 27	08 34	08 42	08 49	08 57	09 04	09 12
	d	07 58	08 05	08 13	08 20	08 28	08 35	08 43	08 50	08 58	09 05	09 13
Willesden Jn Low Level ⊖	a											
Shepherd's Bush ⊖	d	08 08		08 23		08 38		08 53		09 08		09 23
Kensington (Olympia) ⊖	d	08 11		08 26		08 41		08 56		09 11		09 26
West Brompton ⊖	d	08 13		08 28		08 43		08 58		09 13		09 28
Imperial Wharf	d	08 16		08 31		08 46		09 01		09 16		09 31
Clapham Junction 10	a	08 23		08 38		08 53		09 07		09 23		09 38
Acton Central	d		08 10		08 25		08 40		08 55		09 10	
South Acton	d		08 13		08 28		08 43		08 58		09 13	
Gunnersbury ⊖	d		08 18		08 32		08 48		09 02		09 18	
Kew Gardens ⊖	d		08 21		08 35		08 51		09 05		09 21	
Richmond ⊖	a		08 30		08 44		09 00		09 14		09 30	

Table 59

Sundays
2 September to 9 September

Stratford - Highbury and Islington, West Hampstead, Willesden Junction, Clapham Junction and Richmond

Network Diagram - see first Page of Table 59

Station		LO	LO	LO	LO	LO	LO	LO	LO	LO	LO	LO	LO	LO	LO	LO	LO	LO	LO	LO	LO		LO
Stratford 7 ⊖	d	08 37	08 45	08 52	09 00	09 07	09 15	09 22	09 30	09 37	09 45	09 52	10 00	10 07	10 15	10 22	10 30	10 37	10 45	10 52	11 00	and at the same minutes past each hour until	15 00
Hackney Wick	d	08 40	08 50	08 55	09 05	09 10	09 20	09 25	09 35	09 40	09 50	09 55	10 05	10 10	10 20	10 25	10 35	10 40	10 50	10 55	11 05		15 05
Homerton	d	08 43	08 51	08 58	09 06	09 13	09 21	09 28	09 36	09 43	09 51	09 58	10 06	10 13	10 21	10 28	10 36	10 43	10 51	10 58	11 06		15 06
Hackney Central	d	08 45	08 53	09 00	09 08	09 15	09 23	09 30	09 38	09 45	09 53	10 00	10 08	10 15	10 23	10 30	10 38	10 45	10 53	11 00	11 08		15 08
Dalston Kingsland	d	08 47	08 55	09 02	09 10	09 17	09 25	09 32	09 40	09 47	09 55	10 02	10 10	10 17	10 25	10 32	10 40	10 47	10 55	11 02	11 10		15 10
Canonbury	d	08 49	08 57	09 04	09 12	09 19	09 27	09 34	09 42	09 49	09 57	10 04	10 12	10 19	10 27	10 34	10 42	10 49	10 57	11 04	11 12		15 12
Highbury & Islington ⊖	d	08 53	09 01	09 08	09 16	09 23	09 31	09 38	09 46	09 53	10 01	10 08	10 16	10 23	10 31	10 38	10 46	10 53	11 01	11 08	11 16		15 16
Caledonian Rd & Barnsbury	d	08 55	09 03	09 10	09 18	09 25	09 33	09 40	09 48	09 55	10 03	10 10	10 18	10 25	10 33	10 40	10 48	10 55	11 03	11 10	11 18		15 18
Camden Road	d	08 59	09 07	09 14	09 22	09 29	09 37	09 44	09 52	09 59	10 07	10 14	10 22	10 29	10 37	10 44	10 52	10 59	11 07	11 14	11 22		15 22
Kentish Town West	d	09 01	09 09	09 16	09 24	09 31	09 39	09 46	09 54	10 01	10 09	10 16	10 24	10 31	10 39	10 46	10 54	11 01	11 09	11 16	11 24		15 24
Gospel Oak	d	09 04	09 12	09 19	09 27	09 34	09 42	09 49	09 57	10 04	10 12	10 19	10 27	10 34	10 42	10 49	10 57	11 04	11 12	11 19	11 27		15 27
Hampstead Heath	d	09 06	09 14	09 21	09 29	09 36	09 44	09 51	09 59	10 06	10 14	10 21	10 29	10 36	10 44	10 51	10 59	11 06	11 14	11 21	11 29		15 29
Finchley Road & Frognal	d	09 08	09 16	09 23	09 31	09 38	09 46	09 53	10 01	10 08	10 16	10 23	10 31	10 38	10 46	10 53	11 01	11 08	11 16	11 23	11 31		15 31
West Hampstead ⊖	d	09 10	09 18	09 25	09 33	09 40	09 48	09 55	10 03	10 10	10 18	10 25	10 33	10 40	10 48	10 55	11 03	11 10	11 18	11 25	11 33		15 33
Brondesbury	d	09 12	09 20	09 27	09 35	09 42	09 50	09 57	10 05	10 12	10 20	10 27	10 35	10 42	10 50	10 57	11 05	11 12	11 20	11 27	11 35		15 35
Brondesbury Park	d	09 13	09 21	09 28	09 36	09 43	09 51	09 58	10 06	10 13	10 21	10 28	10 36	10 43	10 51	10 58	11 06	11 13	11 21	11 28	11 36		15 36
Kensal Rise	d	09 15	09 23	09 30	09 38	09 45	09 53	10 00	10 08	10 15	10 23	10 30	10 38	10 45	10 53	11 00	11 08	11 15	11 23	11 30	11 38		15 38
Willesden Jn. High Level ⊖	a	09 19	09 27	09 34	09 42	09 49	09 57	10 04	10 12	10 19	10 27	10 34	10 42	10 49	10 57	11 04	11 12	11 19	11 27	11 34	11 42		15 42
	d	09 20	09 28	09 35	09 43	09 50	09 58	10 05	10 13	10 20	10 28	10 35	10 43	10 50	10 58	11 05	11 13	11 20	11 28	11 35	11 43		15 43
Willesden Jn Low Level ⊖	a																						
Shepherd's Bush ⊖	d		09 38		09 53		10 08		10 23		10 38		10 53		11 08		11 23		11 38		11 53		15 53
Kensington (Olympia) ⊖	d		09 41		09 56		10 11		10 26		10 41		10 56		11 11		11 26		11 41		11 56		15 56
West Brompton ⊖	d		09 43		09 58		10 13		10 28		10 43		10 58		11 13		11 28		11 43		11 58		15 58
Imperial Wharf	d		09 46		10 01		10 16		10 31		10 46		11 01		11 16		11 31		11 46		12 01		16 01
Clapham Junction 10	a		09 53		10 07		10 23		10 38		10 53		11 07		11 23		11 38		11 53		12 08		16 08
Acton Central	d	09 25		09 40		09 55		10 10		10 25		10 40		10 55		11 10		11 25		11 40			
South Acton	d	09 28		09 43		09 58		10 13		10 28		10 43		10 58		11 13		11 28		11 43			
Gunnersbury ⊖	d	09 32		09 49		10 02		10 18		10 32		10 48		11 02		11 18		11 32		11 48			
Kew Gardens ⊖	d	09 35		09 52		10 05		10 21		10 35		10 51		11 05		11 21		11 35		11 51			
Richmond ⊖	a	09 44		10 01		10 14		10 30		10 44		11 00		11 14		11 30		11 44		12 00			

Station		LO	LO	LO	LO	LO	LO	LO	LO		LO	LO	LO	LO	LO	LO	LO	LO	LO	LO	LO	LO
Stratford 7 ⊖	d	15 07	15 15	15 22	15 30	15 37	15 45	15 52	16 00	and at the same minutes past each hour until	22 00	22 07	22 15	22 22	22 30	22 37	22 45	22 52	23 00	23 07	23 15	23 22
Hackney Wick	d	15 10	15 20	15 25	15 35	15 40	15 50	15 55	16 05		22 05	22 10	22 20	22 25	22 35	22 40	22 50	22 55	23 05	23 10	23 18	23 25
Homerton	d	15 13	15 21	15 28	15 36	15 43	15 51	15 58	16 06		22 06	22 13	22 21	22 28	22 36	22 43	22 51	22 58	23 06	23 13	23 19	23 28
Hackney Central	d	15 15	15 23	15 30	15 38	15 45	15 53	16 00	16 08		22 08	22 15	22 23	22 30	22 38	22 45	22 53	23 00	23 08	23 15	23 21	23 30
Dalston Kingsland	d	15 17	15 25	15 32	15 40	15 47	15 55	16 02	16 10		22 10	22 17	22 25	22 32	22 40	22 47	22 55	23 02	23 10	23 17	23 23	23 32
Canonbury	d	15 19	15 27	15 34	15 42	15 49	15 57	16 04	16 12		22 12	22 19	22 27	22 34	22 42	22 49	22 57	23 04	23 12	23 19	23 25	23 34
Highbury & Islington ⊖	d	15 23	15 31	15 38	15 46	15 53	16 01	16 08	16 16		22 16	22 23	22 31	22 38	22 46	22 53	23 01	23 08	23 16	23 23	23 28	23 38
Caledonian Rd & Barnsbury	d	15 25	15 33	15 40	15 48	15 55	16 03	16 10	16 18		22 18	22 25	22 33	22 40	22 48	22 55	23 03	23 10	23 18	23 25	23 30	23 40
Camden Road	d	15 29	15 37	15 44	15 52	15 59	16 07	16 14	16 22		22 22	22 29	22 37	22 44	22 52	22 59	23 07	23 14	23 22	23 29	23 34	23 45
Kentish Town West	d	15 31	15 39	15 46	15 54	16 01	16 09	16 16	16 24		22 24	22 31	22 39	22 46	22 54	23 01	23 09	23 16	23 24	23 31	23 37	23 47
Gospel Oak	d	15 34	15 42	15 49	15 57	16 04	16 12	16 19	16 27		22 27	22 34	22 42	22 49	22 57	23 04	23 12	23 19	23 27	23 34	23 40	23 50
Hampstead Heath	d	15 36	15 44	15 51	15 59	16 06	16 14	16 21	16 29		22 29	22 36	22 44	22 51	22 59	23 06	23 14	23 21	23 29	23 36	23 42	23 52
Finchley Road & Frognal	d	15 38	15 46	15 53	16 01	16 08	16 16	16 23	16 31		22 31	22 38	22 46	22 53	23 01	23 08	23 16	23 23	23 31	23 38	23 44	23 54
West Hampstead ⊖	d	15 40	15 48	15 55	16 03	16 10	16 18	16 25	16 33		22 33	22 40	22 48	22 55	23 03	23 10	23 18	23 25	23 33	23 40	23 47	23 56
Brondesbury	d	15 42	15 50	15 57	16 05	16 12	16 20	16 27	16 35		22 35	22 42	22 50	22 57	23 05	23 12	23 20	23 27	23 35	23 42	23 48	23 58
Brondesbury Park	d	15 43	15 51	15 58	16 06	16 13	16 21	16 28	16 36		22 36	22 43	22 51	22 58	23 06	23 13	23 21	23 28	23 36	23 43	23 50	23 59
Kensal Rise	d	15 45	15 53	16 00	16 08	16 15	16 23	16 30	16 38		22 38	22 45	22 53	23 00	23 08	23 15	23 23	23 30	23 38	23 45	23 52	00 01
Willesden Jn. High Level ⊖	a	15 49	15 57	16 04	16 12	16 19	16 27	16 34	16 42		22 42	22 49	22 57	23 04	23 12	23 19	23 27	23 34	23 42	23 49	23 57	00 04
	d	15 50	15 58	16 05	16 13	16 20	16 28	16 35	16 43		22 43	22 50	22 58	23 05	23 13	23 20	23 28	23 35	23 43	23 50	23 59	00 05
Willesden Jn Low Level ⊖	a																					
Shepherd's Bush ⊖	d		16 08		16 23		16 38		16 53		22 53		23 08		23 23		23 38		23 53		00 09	
Kensington (Olympia) ⊖	d		16 11		16 26		16 41		16 56		22 56		23 11		23 26		23 41		23 56		00 11	
West Brompton ⊖	d		16 13		16 28		16 43		16 58		22 58		23 13		23 28		23 43		23 58		00 14	
Imperial Wharf	d		16 16		16 31		16 46		17 01		23 01		23 16		23 31		23 46		00 01		00 17	
Clapham Junction 10	a		16 24		16 39		16 54		17 09		23 09		23 24		23 39		23 54		00 09		00 22	
Acton Central	d	15 55		16 10		16 25		16 40				22 55		23 10		23 25		23 40		23 55		00 10
South Acton	d	15 58		16 13		16 28		16 43				22 58		23 13		23 28		23 43		23 58		00 13
Gunnersbury ⊖	d	16 02		16 18		16 32		16 48				23 02		23 18		23 32		23 48		00 03		00 18
Kew Gardens ⊖	d	16 05		16 21		16 35		16 51				23 05		23 21		23 35		23 51		00 06		00 21
Richmond ⊖	a	16 14		16 30		16 44		17 00				23 14		23 30		23 44		00 01		00 16		00 30

Table 59

Sundays
2 September to 9 September

Stratford - Highbury and Islington, West Hampstead, Willesden Junction, Clapham Junction and Richmond

Network Diagram - see first Page of Table 59

Station		LO	LO	LO	LO
Stratford 7 ⊖	d	23 30	23 37	23 45	23 52
Hackney Wick	d	23 35	23 40	23 49	23 55
Homerton	d	23 36	23 43	23 51	23 58
Hackney Central	d	23 38	23 45	23 53	00 01
Dalston Kingsland	d	23 40	23 47	23 55	00 03
Canonbury	d	23 42	23 49	23 57	00 05
Highbury & Islington ⊖	d	23 46	23 53	00 01	00 08
Caledonian Rd & Barnsbury	d	23 48	23 55	00 03	00 10
Camden Road	d	23 52	23 59	00 07	00 14
Kentish Town West	d	23 54	00 01	00 09	00 16
Gospel Oak	d	23 57	00 04	00 12	00 19
Hampstead Heath	d	23 59	00 06	00 14	00 21
Finchley Road & Frognal	d	00 01	00 08	00 16	00 23
West Hampstead ⊖	d	00 03	00 10	00 18	00 25
Brondesbury	d	00 05	00 12	00 20	00 27
Brondesbury Park	d	00 06	00 13	00 21	00 28
Kensal Rise	d	00 08	00 15	00 23	00 30
Willesden Jn. High Level ⊖	a	00 12	00 19	00 27	00 34
	d	00 13	00 20	00 28	00 35
Willesden Jn Low Level ⊖	a				
Shepherd's Bush ⊖	d	00 23		00 38	
Kensington (Olympia) ⊖	d	00 26		00 41	
West Brompton ⊖	d	00 28		00 43	
Imperial Wharf	d	00 31		00 46	
Clapham Junction 10	a	00 39		00 54	
Acton Central	d		00 25		00 40
South Acton	d		00 28		00 43
Gunnersbury ⊖	d		00 32		00 48
Kew Gardens ⊖	d		00 35		00 51
Richmond ⊖	a		00 44		01 00

Sundays
from 16 September

Station		LO	LO	LO	LO	LO	LO	LO	LO	LO	LO	LO	LO	LO	LO	LO	LO	LO	LO	LO	LO	LO	LO
Stratford 7 ⊖	d	23p45								09 15		09 30		09 45		10 00		10 20		10 35		10 45	
Hackney Wick	d	23p48								09 18		09 33		09 48		10 03		10 23		10 38		10 48	
Homerton	d	23p51								09 21		09 36		09 51		10 06		10 26		10 41		10 51	
Hackney Central	d	23p53								09 23		09 38		09 53		10 08		10 28		10 43		10 53	
Dalston Kingsland	d	23p55								09 25		09 40		09 55		10 10		10 30		10 45		10 55	
Canonbury	d	23p57								09 27		09 42		09 57		10 12		10 32		10 47		10 57	
Highbury & Islington ⊖	d	23p59								09 30		09 45		10 00		10 15		10 35		10 50		11 00	
Caledonian Rd & Barnsbury	d	00 02								09 32		09 47		10 02		10 17		10 37		10 52		11 02	
Camden Road	d	00 05								09 35		09 50		10 05		10 20		10 40		10 55		11 05	
Kentish Town West	d	00 07								09 37		09 52		10 07		10 22		10 42		10 57		11 07	
Gospel Oak	d	00 10						09 24		09 40		09 55		10 10		10 25		10 45		11 00		11 10	
Hampstead Heath	d	00 12						09 26		09 42		09 57		10 12		10 27		10 47		11 02		11 12	
Finchley Road & Frognal	d	00 14						09 28		09 44		09 59		10 14		10 29		10 49		11 04		11 14	
West Hampstead ⊖	d	00 16						09 30		09 46		10 01		10 16		10 31		10 51		11 06		11 16	
Brondesbury	d	00 18						09 32		09 48		10 03		10 18		10 33		10 53		11 08		11 18	
Brondesbury Park	d	00 19						09 33		09 49		10 04		10 19		10 34		10 54		11 09		11 19	
Kensal Rise	d	00 21						09 35		09 51		10 06		10 21		10 36		10 56		11 11		11 21	
Willesden Jn. High Level ⊖	a							09 39		09 55		10 10		10 25		10 40		11 00		11 15		11 25	
	d		08 32	08 56	09 02	09 26	09 32	09 40	09 48	09 56	10 02	10 11	10 16	10 26	10 32	10 41	10 46	11 01	11 02	11 16	11 16	11 26	11 32
Willesden Jn Low Level ⊖	a	00 29																					
Shepherd's Bush ⊖	d		08 40		09 10		09 40		09 54		10 10		10 24		10 40		10 55		11 10	11 24			11 40
Kensington (Olympia) ⊖	d		08 42		09 12		09 42		09 56		10 12		10 26		10 42		10 56		11 12	11 26			11 42
West Brompton ⊖	d		08 44		09 14		09 44		09 58		10 14		10 28		10 44		10 58		11 14	11 28			11 44
Imperial Wharf	d		08 47		09 17		09 47		10 01		10 17		10 31		10 47		11 01		11 17	11 31			11 47
Clapham Junction 10	a		08 54		09 23		09 53		10 09		10 23		10 38		10 53		11 08		11 28	11 40			11 53
Acton Central	d			09 01		09 31		09 45		10 01		10 16		10 31		10 46		11 06			11 21	11 31	
South Acton	d			09 03		09 34		09 47		10 04		10 19		10 34		10 49		11 09			11 24	11 34	
Gunnersbury ⊖	d			09 08		09 38		09 50		10 08		10 22		10 38		10 52		11 12			11 28	11 38	
Kew Gardens ⊖	d			09 11		09 41		09 53		10 11		10 25		10 41		10 55		11 15			11 31	11 41	
Richmond ⊖	a			09 19		09 49		10 03		10 18		10 31		10 46		11 01		11 21			11 38	11 46	

Stratford - Highbury and Islington, West Hampstead, Willesden Junction, Clapham Junction and Richmond

Network Diagram - see first Page of Table 59

		LO	LO	LO	LO	LO	LO	LO	LO	LO	LO	LO	LO	LO	LO	LO	LO	LO	LO	LO	LO	LO	LO
Stratford 7 ⊖	d	10 55	11 05	11 15		11 25	11 35	11 45		11 55	12 05	12 15		12 25	12 35	12 45		12 55	13 05	13 15		13 25	13 35
Hackney Wick	d	10 58	11 08	11 18		11 28	11 38	11 48		11 58	12 08	12 18		12 28	12 38	12 48		12 58	13 08	13 18		13 28	13 38
Homerton	d	11 01	11 11	11 21		11 31	11 41	11 51		12 01	12 11	12 21		12 31	12 41	12 51		13 01	13 11	13 21		13 31	13 41
Hackney Central	d	11 03	11 13	11 23		11 33	11 43	11 53		12 03	12 13	12 23		12 33	12 43	12 53		13 03	13 13	13 23		13 33	13 43
Dalston Kingsland	d	11 05	11 15	11 25		11 35	11 45	11 55		12 05	12 15	12 25		12 35	12 45	12 55		13 05	13 15	13 25		13 35	13 45
Canonbury	d	11 07	11 17	11 27		11 37	11 47	11 57		12 07	12 17	12 27		12 37	12 47	12 57		13 07	13 17	13 27		13 37	13 47
Highbury & Islington ⊖	d	11 10	11 20	11 30		11 40	11 50	12 00		12 10	12 20	12 30		12 40	12 50	13 00		13 10	13 20	13 30		13 40	13 50
Caledonian Rd & Barnsbury	d	11 12	11 22	11 32		11 42	11 52	12 02		12 12	12 22	12 32		12 42	12 52	13 02		13 12	13 22	13 32		13 42	13 52
Camden Road	d	11 15	11 25	11 35		11 45	11 55	12 05		12 15	12 25	12 35		12 45	12 55	13 05		13 15	13 25	13 35		13 45	13 55
Kentish Town West	d	11 17	11 27	11 37		11 47	11 57	12 07		12 17	12 27	12 37		12 47	12 57	13 07		13 17	13 27	13 37		13 47	13 57
Gospel Oak	d	11 20	11 30	11 40		11 50	12 00	12 10		12 20	12 30	12 40		12 50	13 00	13 10		13 20	13 30	13 40		13 50	14 00
Hampstead Heath	d	11 22	11 32	11 42		11 52	12 02	12 12		12 22	12 32	12 42		12 52	13 02	13 12		13 22	13 32	13 42		13 52	14 02
Finchley Road & Frognal	d	11 24	11 34	11 44		11 54	12 04	12 14		12 24	12 34	12 44		12 54	13 04	13 14		13 24	13 34	13 44		13 54	14 04
West Hampstead ⊖	d	11 26	11 36	11 46		11 56	12 06	12 16		12 26	12 36	12 46		12 56	13 06	13 16		13 26	13 36	13 46		13 56	14 06
Brondesbury	d	11 28	11 38	11 48		11 58	12 08	12 18		12 28	12 38	12 48		12 58	13 08	13 18		13 28	13 38	13 48		13 58	14 08
Brondesbury Park	d	11 29	11 39	11 49		11 59	12 09	12 19		12 29	12 39	12 49		12 59	13 09	13 19		13 29	13 39	13 49		13 59	14 09
Kensal Rise	d	11 31	11 41	11 51		12 01	12 11	12 21		12 31	12 41	12 51		13 01	13 11	13 21		13 31	13 41	13 51		14 01	14 11
Willesden Jn. High Level ⊖	a	11 35	11 45	11 55		12 05	12 15	12 25		12 35	12 45	12 55		13 05	13 15	13 25		13 35	13 45	13 55		14 05	14 15
	d	11 36	11 46	11 56	12 02	12 06	12 16	12 26	12 32	12 36	12 46	12 56	13 02	13 06	13 16	13 26	13 32	13 36	13 46	13 56	14 02	14 06	14 16
Willesden Jn Low Level ⊖	a																						
Shepherd's Bush ⊖	d		11 54		12 10		12 24		12 40		12 54		13 10		13 24		13 40		13 54		14 10		14 24
Kensington (Olympia) ⊖	d		11 56		12 12		12 26		12 42		12 56		13 12		13 26		13 42		13 56		14 12		14 26
West Brompton ⊖	d		11 58		12 14		12 28		12 44		12 58		13 14		13 28		13 44		13 58		14 14		14 28
Imperial Wharf	d		12 01		12 17		12 31		12 47		13 01		13 17		13 31		13 47		14 01		14 17		14 31
Clapham Junction 10	a		12 09		12 23		12 39		12 53		13 09		13 23		13 39		13 53		14 09		14 23		14 39
Acton Central	d	11 41		12 01		12 11		12 31		12 41		13 01		13 11		13 31		13 41		14 01		14 11	
South Acton	d	11 44		12 04		12 14		12 34		12 44		13 04		13 14		13 34		13 44		14 04		14 14	
Gunnersbury ⊖	d	11 48		12 08		12 18		12 38		12 48		13 08		13 18		13 38		13 48		14 08		14 18	
Kew Gardens ⊖	d	11 51		12 11		12 21		12 41		12 51		13 11		13 21		13 41		13 51		14 11		14 21	
Richmond ⊖	a	11 56		12 16		12 26		12 46		12 56		13 16		13 26		13 46		13 56		14 16		14 26	

		LO	LO	LO	LO	LO	LO	LO	LO	LO	LO	LO	LO	LO	LO	LO	LO	LO	LO	LO	LO	LO	LO
Stratford 7 ⊖	d	13 45		13 55	14 05	14 15		14 25	14 35	14 45		14 55	15 05	15 15		15 25	15 35	15 45		15 55	16 05	16 15	
Hackney Wick	d	13 48		13 58	14 08	14 18		14 28	14 38	14 48		14 58	15 08	15 18		15 28	15 38	15 48		15 58	16 08	16 18	
Homerton	d	13 51		14 01	14 11	14 21		14 31	14 41	14 51		15 01	15 11	15 21		15 31	15 41	15 51		16 01	16 11	16 21	
Hackney Central	d	13 53		14 03	14 13	14 23		14 33	14 43	14 53		15 03	15 13	15 23		15 33	15 43	15 53		16 03	16 13	16 23	
Dalston Kingsland	d	13 55		14 05	14 15	14 25		14 35	14 45	14 55		15 05	15 15	15 25		15 35	15 45	15 55		16 05	16 15	16 25	
Canonbury	d	13 57		14 07	14 17	14 27		14 37	14 47	14 57		15 07	15 17	15 27		15 37	15 47	15 57		16 07	16 17	16 27	
Highbury & Islington ⊖	d	14 00		14 10	14 20	14 30		14 40	14 50	15 00		15 10	15 20	15 30		15 40	15 50	16 00		16 10	16 20	16 30	
Caledonian Rd & Barnsbury	d	14 02		14 12	14 22	14 32		14 42	14 52	15 02		15 12	15 22	15 32		15 42	15 52	16 02		16 12	16 22	16 32	
Camden Road	d	14 05		14 15	14 25	14 35		14 45	14 55	15 05		15 15	15 25	15 35		15 45	15 55	16 05		16 15	16 25	16 35	
Kentish Town West	d	14 07		14 17	14 27	14 37		14 47	14 57	15 07		15 17	15 27	15 37		15 47	15 57	16 07		16 17	16 27	16 37	
Gospel Oak	d	14 10		14 20	14 30	14 40		14 50	15 00	15 10		15 20	15 30	15 40		15 50	16 00	16 10		16 20	16 30	16 40	
Hampstead Heath	d	14 12		14 22	14 32	14 42		14 52	15 02	15 12		15 22	15 32	15 42		15 52	16 02	16 12		16 22	16 32	16 42	
Finchley Road & Frognal	d	14 14		14 24	14 34	14 44		14 54	15 04	15 14		15 24	15 34	15 44		15 54	16 04	16 14		16 24	16 34	16 44	
West Hampstead ⊖	d	14 16		14 26	14 36	14 46		14 56	15 06	15 16		15 26	15 36	15 46		15 56	16 06	16 16		16 26	16 36	16 46	
Brondesbury	d	14 18		14 28	14 38	14 48		14 58	15 08	15 18		15 28	15 38	15 48		15 58	16 08	16 18		16 28	16 38	16 48	
Brondesbury Park	d	14 19		14 29	14 39	14 49		14 59	15 09	15 19		15 29	15 39	15 49		15 59	16 09	16 19		16 29	16 39	16 49	
Kensal Rise	d	14 21		14 31	14 41	14 51		15 01	15 11	15 21		15 31	15 41	15 51		16 01	16 11	16 21		16 31	16 41	16 51	
Willesden Jn. High Level ⊖	a	14 25		14 35	14 45	14 55		15 05	15 15	15 25		15 35	15 45	15 55		16 05	16 15	16 25		16 35	16 45	16 55	
	d	14 26	14 32	14 36	14 46	14 56	15 02	15 06	15 16	15 26	15 32	15 36	15 46	15 56	16 02	16 06	16 16	16 26	16 32	16 36	16 46	16 56	17 02
Willesden Jn Low Level ⊖	a																						
Shepherd's Bush ⊖	d		14 40		14 54		15 10		15 24		15 40		15 54		16 10		16 24		16 40		16 54		17 10
Kensington (Olympia) ⊖	d		14 42		14 56		15 12		15 26		15 42		15 56		16 12		16 26		16 42		16 56		17 12
West Brompton ⊖	d		14 44		14 58		15 14		15 28		15 44		15 58		16 14		16 28		16 44		16 58		17 14
Imperial Wharf	d		14 47		15 01		15 17		15 31		15 47		16 01		16 17		16 31		16 47		17 01		17 17
Clapham Junction 10	a		14 54		15 09		15 23		15 39		15 53		16 09		16 23		16 39		16 54		17 10		17 24
Acton Central	d	14 31		14 41		15 01		15 11		15 31		15 41		16 01		16 11		16 31		16 41		17 01	
South Acton	d	14 34		14 44		15 04		15 14		15 34		15 44		16 04		16 14		16 34		16 44		17 04	
Gunnersbury ⊖	d	14 38		14 48		15 08		15 18		15 38		15 48		16 08		16 18		16 38		16 48		17 08	
Kew Gardens ⊖	d	14 41		14 51		15 11		15 21		15 41		15 51		16 11		16 21		16 41		16 51		17 11	
Richmond ⊖	a	14 46		14 56		15 16		15 26		15 46		15 56		16 16		16 26		16 46		16 56		17 16	

Table 59

Stratford - Highbury and Islington, West Hampstead, Willesden Junction, Clapham Junction and Richmond

Sundays
from 16 September

Network Diagram - see first Page of Table 59

		LO	LO	LO	LO	LO	LO	LO	LO	LO	LO	LO	LO	LO	LO	LO	LO	LO	LO	LO	LO	LO	LO
Stratford 7 ⊖	d	16 25	16 35	16 45		16 55	17 05	17 15		17 25	17 35	17 45		17 55	18 05	18 15		18 25	18 35	18 45		18 55	19 05
Hackney Wick	d	16 28	16 38	16 48		16 58	17 08	17 18		17 28	17 38	17 48		17 58	18 08	18 18		18 28	18 38	18 48		18 58	19 08
Homerton	d	16 31	16 41	16 51		17 01	17 11	17 21		17 31	17 41	17 51		18 01	18 11	18 21		18 31	18 41	18 51		19 01	19 11
Hackney Central	d	16 33	16 43	16 53		17 03	17 13	17 23		17 33	17 43	17 53		18 03	18 13	18 23		18 33	18 43	18 53		19 03	19 13
Dalston Kingsland	d	16 35	16 45	16 55		17 05	17 15	17 25		17 35	17 45	17 55		18 05	18 15	18 25		18 35	18 45	18 55		19 05	19 15
Canonbury	d	16 37	16 47	16 57		17 07	17 17	17 27		17 37	17 47	17 57		18 07	18 17	18 27		18 37	18 47	18 57		19 07	19 17
Highbury & Islington ⊖	d	16 40	16 50	17 00		17 10	17 20	17 30		17 40	17 50	18 00		18 10	18 20	18 30		18 40	18 50	19 00		19 10	19 20
Caledonian Rd & Barnsbury	d	16 42	16 52	17 02		17 12	17 22	17 32		17 42	17 52	18 02		18 12	18 22	18 32		18 42	18 52	19 02		19 12	19 22
Camden Road	d	16 45	16 55	17 05		17 15	17 25	17 35		17 45	17 55	18 05		18 15	18 25	18 35		18 45	18 55	19 05		19 15	19 25
Kentish Town West	d	16 47	16 57	17 07		17 17	17 27	17 37		17 47	17 57	18 07		18 17	18 27	18 37		18 47	18 57	19 07		19 17	19 27
Gospel Oak	d	16 50	17 00	17 10		17 20	17 30	17 40		17 50	18 00	18 10		18 20	18 30	18 40		18 50	19 00	19 10		19 20	19 30
Hampstead Heath	d	16 52	17 02	17 12		17 22	17 32	17 42		17 52	18 02	18 12		18 22	18 32	18 42		18 52	19 02	19 12		19 22	19 32
Finchley Road & Frognal	d	16 54	17 04	17 14		17 24	17 34	17 44		17 54	18 04	18 14		18 24	18 34	18 44		18 54	19 04	19 14		19 24	19 34
West Hampstead ⊖	d	16 56	17 06	17 16		17 26	17 36	17 46		17 56	18 06	18 16		18 26	18 36	18 46		18 56	19 06	19 16		19 26	19 36
Brondesbury	d	16 58	17 08	17 18		17 28	17 38	17 48		17 58	18 08	18 18		18 28	18 38	18 48		18 58	19 08	19 18		19 28	19 38
Brondesbury Park	d	16 59	17 09	17 19		17 29	17 39	17 49		17 59	18 09	18 19		18 29	18 39	18 49		18 59	19 09	19 19		19 29	19 39
Kensal Rise	d	17 01	17 11	17 21		17 31	17 41	17 51		18 01	18 11	18 21		18 31	18 41	18 51		19 01	19 11	19 21		19 31	19 41
Willesden Jn. High Level ⊖	a	17 05	17 15	17 25		17 35	17 45	17 55		18 05	18 15	18 25		18 35	18 45	18 55		19 05	19 15	19 25		19 35	19 45
	d	17 06	17 16	17 26	17 32	17 36	17 46	17 56	18 02	18 06	18 16	18 26	18 32	18 36	18 46	18 56	19 02	19 06	19 16	19 26	19 32	19 36	19 46
Willesden Jn Low Level ⊖	a																						
Shepherd's Bush ⊖	d		17 24		17 40		17 54		18 10		18 24		18 40		18 54		19 10		19 24		19 40		19 54
Kensington (Olympia) ⊖	d		17 26		17 42		17 56		18 12		18 26		18 42		18 56		19 12		19 26		19 42		19 56
West Brompton ⊖	d		17 28		17 44		17 58		18 14		18 28		18 44		18 58		19 14		19 28		19 44		19 58
Imperial Wharf	d		17 31		17 47		18 01		18 17		18 31		18 47		19 01		19 17		19 31		19 47		20 01
Clapham Junction 10	a		17 40		17 54		18 10		18 24		18 38		18 54		19 10		19 26		19 40		19 54		20 10
Acton Central	d	17 11		17 31		17 41		18 01		18 11		18 31		18 41		19 01		19 11		19 31		19 41	
South Acton	d	17 14		17 34		17 44		18 04		18 14		18 34		18 44		19 04		19 14		19 34		19 44	
Gunnersbury ⊖	d	17 18		17 38		17 48		18 08		18 18		18 38		18 48		19 08		19 18		19 38		19 48	
Kew Gardens ⊖	d	17 21		17 41		17 51		18 11		18 21		18 41		18 51		19 11		19 21		19 41		19 51	
Richmond ⊖	a	17 26		17 46		17 56		18 16		18 26		18 46		18 56		19 16		19 26		19 46		19 56	

		LO	LO	LO	LO	LO	LO	LO	LO	LO	LO	LO	LO	LO	LO	LO	LO	LO	LO	LO	LO	LO	LO
Stratford 7 ⊖	d	19 15		19 25	19 35	19 45		19 55	20 05	20 15		20 25	20 35	20 45		20 55	21 05	21 15		21 30	21 45		22 00
Hackney Wick	d	19 18		19 28	19 38	19 48		19 58	20 08	20 18		20 28	20 38	20 48		20 58	21 08	21 18		21 33	21 48		22 03
Homerton	d	19 21		19 31	19 41	19 51		20 01	20 11	20 21		20 31	20 41	20 51		21 01	21 11	21 21		21 36	21 51		22 06
Hackney Central	d	19 23		19 33	19 43	19 53		20 03	20 13	20 23		20 33	20 43	20 53		21 03	21 13	21 23		21 38	21 53		22 08
Dalston Kingsland	d	19 25		19 35	19 45	19 55		20 05	20 15	20 25		20 35	20 45	20 55		21 05	21 15	21 25		21 40	21 55		22 10
Canonbury	d	19 27		19 37	19 47	19 57		20 07	20 17	20 27		20 37	20 47	20 57		21 07	21 17	21 27		21 42	21 57		22 12
Highbury & Islington ⊖	d	19 30		19 40	19 50	20 00		20 10	20 20	20 30		20 40	20 50	21 00		21 10	21 20	21 30		21 45	22 00		22 15
Caledonian Rd & Barnsbury	d	19 32		19 42	19 52	20 02		20 12	20 22	20 32		20 42	20 52	21 02		21 12	21 22	21 32		21 47	22 02		22 17
Camden Road	d	19 35		19 45	19 55	20 05		20 15	20 25	20 35		20 45	20 55	21 05		21 15	21 25	21 35		21 50	22 05		22 20
Kentish Town West	d	19 37		19 47	19 57	20 07		20 17	20 27	20 37		20 47	20 57	21 07		21 17	21 27	21 37		21 52	22 07		22 22
Gospel Oak	d	19 40		19 50	20 00	20 10		20 20	20 30	20 40		20 50	21 00	21 10		21 20	21 30	21 40		21 55	22 10		22 25
Hampstead Heath	d	19 42		19 52	20 02	20 12		20 22	20 32	20 42		20 52	21 02	21 12		21 22	21 32	21 42		21 57	22 12		22 27
Finchley Road & Frognal	d	19 44		19 54	20 04	20 14		20 24	20 34	20 44		20 54	21 04	21 14		21 24	21 34	21 44		21 59	22 14		22 29
West Hampstead ⊖	d	19 46		19 56	20 06	20 16		20 26	20 36	20 46		20 56	21 06	21 16		21 26	21 36	21 46		22 01	22 16		22 31
Brondesbury	d	19 48		19 58	20 08	20 18		20 28	20 38	20 48		20 58	21 08	21 18		21 28	21 38	21 48		22 03	22 18		22 33
Brondesbury Park	d	19 49		19 59	20 09	20 19		20 29	20 39	20 49		20 59	21 09	21 19		21 29	21 39	21 49		22 04	22 19		22 34
Kensal Rise	d	19 51		20 01	20 11	20 21		20 31	20 41	20 51		21 01	21 11	21 21		21 31	21 41	21 51		22 06	22 21		22 36
Willesden Jn. High Level ⊖	a	19 55		20 05	20 15	20 25		20 35	20 45	20 55		21 05	21 15	21 25		21 35	21 45	21 55		22 10	22 25		22 40
	d	19 56	20 02	20 06	20 16	20 26	20 32	20 36	20 46	20 56	21 02	21 06	21 16	21 26	21 32	21 39	21 46	21 56	22 02	22 11	22 26	22 32	22 41
Willesden Jn Low Level ⊖	a																						
Shepherd's Bush ⊖	d		20 10		20 24		20 40		20 54		21 10		21 24		21 40		21 54		22 10			22 40	
Kensington (Olympia) ⊖	d		20 12		20 26		20 42		20 56		21 12		21 26		21 42		21 56		22 12			22 42	
West Brompton ⊖	d		20 14		20 28		20 44		20 58		21 14		21 28		21 44		21 58		22 14			22 44	
Imperial Wharf	d		20 17		20 31		20 47		21 01		21 17		21 31		21 47		22 01		22 17			22 47	
Clapham Junction 10	a		20 24		20 40		20 54		21 10		21 24		21 39		21 54		22 09		22 24			22 54	
Acton Central	d	20 01		20 11		20 31		20 41		21 01		21 11		21 31		21 44		22 01		22 16	22 31		22 46
South Acton	d	20 04		20 14		20 34		20 44		21 04		21 14		21 34		21 47		22 04		22 19	22 34		22 49
Gunnersbury ⊖	d	20 08		20 18		20 38		20 48		21 08		21 18		21 38		21 50		22 08		22 22	22 38		22 52
Kew Gardens ⊖	d	20 11		20 21		20 41		20 51		21 11		21 21		21 41		21 53		22 11		22 25	22 41		22 55
Richmond ⊖	a	20 16		20 26		20 46		20 56		21 16		21 26		21 46		21 57		22 16		22 31	22 46		23 01

Table 59

Sundays from 16 September

Stratford - Highbury and Islington, West Hampstead, Willesden Junction, Clapham Junction and Richmond

Network Diagram - see first Page of Table 59

Station			LO	LO	LO
Stratford 7	⊖	d			
Hackney Wick		d			
Homerton		d			
Hackney Central		d			
Dalston Kingsland		d			
Canonbury		d			
Highbury & Islington	⊖	d			
Caledonian Rd & Barnsbury		d			
Camden Road		d			
Kentish Town West		d			
Gospel Oak		d		22 55	23 30
Hampstead Heath		d		22 57	23 32
Finchley Road & Frognal		d		22 59	23 34
West Hampstead	⊖	d		23 01	23 36
Brondesbury		d		23 03	23 38
Brondesbury Park		d		23 04	23 39
Kensal Rise		d		23 06	23 41
Willesden Jn. High Level	⊖	a		23 10	
		d	22 46	23 11	
Willesden Jn Low Level	⊖	a			23 54
Shepherd's Bush	⊖	d	22 54		
Kensington (Olympia)	⊖	d	22 56		
West Brompton	⊖	d	22 58		
Imperial Wharf		d	23 01		
Clapham Junction 10		a	23 11		
Acton Central		d		23 16	
South Acton		d		23 19	
Gunnersbury	⊖	d		23 22	
Kew Gardens	⊖	d		23 25	
Richmond	⊖	a		23 32	

Table 59

Mondays to Fridays until 26 July

Richmond and Clapham Junction - Willesden Junction, West Hampstead, Highbury and Islington and Stratford

Network Diagram - see first Page of Table 59

Miles	Miles	Station			LO MX	LO	LO	LO	LO	LO	LO	LO	LO	LO	LO		LO	LO	LO	LO	LO	LO	LO	LO	LO	LO
0	—	**Richmond**	⊖	d	23p00				05 54	06 09		06 24		06 37			06 53		07 06		07 24		07 36		07 53	
1½	—	Kew Gardens	⊖	d	23p03				05 57	06 12		06 27		06 40			06 56		07 09		07 27		07 39		07 56	
2½	—	Gunnersbury	⊖	d	23p06				06 00	06 15		06 30		06 43			06 59		07 12		07 30		07 42		07 59	
3¼	—	South Acton		d	23p09				06 03	06 18		06 33		06 46			07 02		07 15		07 33		07 45		08 02	
4	—	Acton Central		d	23p12				06 06	06 21		06 36		06 51			07 06		07 21		07 36		07 51		08 06	
—	0	**Clapham Junction** 10		d		05 47					06 14		06 29		06 44			06 59		07 14		07 29		07 44		07 59
—	1½	Imperial Wharf		d		05 51					06 18		06 33		06 48			07 03		07 18		07 33		07 48		08 03
—	2½	West Brompton	⊖	d		05 54					06 21		06 36		06 51			07 06		07 21		07 36		07 51		08 06
—	3¼	**Kensington (Olympia)**	⊖	d		05 57					06 24		06 39		06 54			07 09		07 24		07 39		07 54		08 09
—	4	**Shepherd's Bush**	⊖	d		05 59					06 26		06 41		06 56			07 11		07 26		07 41		07 56		08 11
5¾	—	**Willesden Jn Low Level**	⊖	d				05 58																		
5¾	6	**Willesden Jn. High Level**	⊖	a	23p17	06 08			06 11	06 26	06 34	06 41	06 50	06 56	07 04		07 11	07 19	07 26	07 35	07 41	07 49	07 56	08 05	08 11	08 19
—	—			d	23p18				06 12	06 27	06 35	06 42	06 50	06 57	07 05		07 12	07 20	07 27	07 35	07 42	07 50	07 57	08 06	08 12	08 20
6¾	—	Kensal Rise		d	23p20			06 02	06 14	06 29	06 37	06 44	06 52	06 59	07 07		07 14	07 22	07 29	07 37	07 44	07 52	07 59	08 08	08 14	08 22
7½	—	Brondesbury Park		d	23p22			06 04	06 16	06 31	06 39	06 46	06 54	07 01	07 09		07 16	07 24	07 31	07 39	07 46	07 54	08 01	08 10	08 16	08 24
7¾	—	Brondesbury		d	23p24			06 06	06 18	06 33	06 41	06 48	06 56	07 03	07 11		07 18	07 26	07 33	07 41	07 48	07 56	08 03	08 12	08 18	08 26
8¼	—	West Hampstead	⊖	d	23p26			06 08	06 20	06 35	06 43	06 50	06 58	07 05	07 13		07 20	07 28	07 35	07 43	07 50	07 58	08 05	08 14	08 20	08 28
8¾	—	Finchley Road & Frognal		d	23p27			06 09	06 21	06 36	06 44	06 51	06 59	07 06	07 14		07 21	07 29	07 36	07 44	07 51	07 59	08 06	08 15	08 21	08 29
9¾	—	Hampstead Heath		d	23p30			06 12	06 24	06 39	06 47	06 54	07 02	07 09	07 17		07 24	07 32	07 39	07 47	07 54	08 02	08 09	08 18	08 24	08 32
10¼	—	**Gospel Oak**		d	23p32			06 14	06 26	06 41	06 49	06 56	07 04	07 11	07 19		07 26	07 34	07 41	07 49	07 56	08 04	08 11	08 20	08 26	08 34
11	—	Kentish Town West		d	23p34			06 16	06 28	06 43	06 51	06 58	07 06	07 13	07 21		07 28	07 36	07 43	07 51	07 58	08 06	08 13	08 22	08 28	08 36
11¼	—	Camden Road		d	23p38		06 11	06 20	06 32	06 47	06 55	07 02	07 10	07 17	07 25		07 32	07 40	07 47	07 55	08 02	08 10	08 17	08 26	08 32	08 40
12½	—	Caledonian Rd & Barnsbury		d	23p41		06 14	06 23	06 35	06 50	06 58	07 05	07 13	07 20	07 28		07 35	07 43	07 50	07 58	08 05	08 13	08 20	08 29	08 35	08 43
13	—	**Highbury & Islington**	⊖	d	23p44		06 16	06 26	06 38	06 53	07 01	07 08	07 16	07 23	07 31		07 38	07 46	07 53	08 01	08 08	08 16	08 23	08 32	08 38	08 46
13½	—	Canonbury	⊖	d	23p46		06 18	06 28	06 40	06 55	07 03	07 10	07 18	07 25	07 33		07 40	07 48	07 55	08 03	08 10	08 18	08 25	08 34	08 40	08 48
14½	—	Dalston Kingsland		d	23p48		06 20	06 30	06 42	06 57	07 05	07 12	07 20	07 27	07 35		07 42	07 50	07 57	08 05	08 12	08 20	08 27	08 36	08 42	08 50
15¼	—	Hackney Central		d	23p50		06 22	06 32	06 44	06 59	07 07	07 14	07 22	07 29	07 37		07 44	07 52	07 59	08 07	08 14	08 22	08 29	08 38	08 44	08 52
16	—	Homerton		d	23p52		06 24	06 34	06 46	07 01	07 09	07 16	07 24	07 31	07 39		07 46	07 54	08 01	08 09	08 16	08 24	08 31	08 40	08 46	08 54
16¾	—	Hackney Wick		d	23p54		06 26	06 36	06 48	07 03	07 11	07 18	07 26	07 33	07 41		07 48	07 56	08 03	08 11	08 18	08 26	08 33	08 42	08 48	08 56
17¾	—	**Stratford** 7	⊖	a	00 04		06 32	06 44	06 55	07 10	07 18	07 25	07 33	07 39	07 48		07 55	08 03	08 09	08 18	08 25	08 33	08 39	08 49	08 54	09 03

Station			LO		LO	LO	LO	LO	LO	LO	LO	LO	LO	LO	LO		LO	LO	LO	LO	LO	LO	LO	LO	LO	LO
Richmond	⊖	d	08 08			08 22		08 36		08 52		09 10		09 27			09 36		09 57		10 08		10 28		10 38	
Kew Gardens	⊖	d	08 11			08 25		08 39		08 55		09 13		09 30			09 39		10 00		10 11		10 31		10 41	
Gunnersbury	⊖	d	08 14			08 28		08 42		08 58		09 16		09 33			09 42		10 03		10 14		10 34		10 44	
South Acton		d	08 17			08 31		08 45		09 01		09 19		09 36			09 45		10 06		10 17		10 37		10 47	
Acton Central		d	08 21			08 36		08 51		09 06		09 22		09 40			09 50		10 10		10 20		10 40		10 50	
Clapham Junction 10		d			08 09		08 29		08 44		08 59		09 15		09 30			09 45		10 00		10 15		10 30		10 45
Imperial Wharf		d			08 13		08 33		08 48		09 03		09 19		09 34			09 49		10 04		10 19		10 36		10 49
West Brompton	⊖	d			08 16		08 36		08 51		09 06		09 22		09 37			09 52		10 07		10 22		10 39		10 52
Kensington (Olympia)	⊖	d			08 19		08 39		08 54		09 09		09 25		09 40			09 55		10 10		10 25		10 42		10 55
Shepherd's Bush	⊖	d			08 21		08 41		08 56		09 11		09 27		09 42			09 57		10 12		10 27		10 44		10 57
Willesden Jn Low Level	⊖	d																								
Willesden Jn. High Level	⊖	a	08 26		08 31	08 41	08 49	08 56	09 05	09 11	09 19	09 27	09 35	09 45	09 51		09 55	10 05	10 15	10 21	10 25	10 35	10 45	10 51	10 55	11 05
		d	08 27		08 35	08 42	08 50	08 57	09 06	09 13	09 20	09 28	09 36	09 46			09 56	10 06	10 16		10 26	10 36	10 46		10 56	11 06
Kensal Rise		d	08 29		08 38	08 44	08 52	08 59	09 08	09 15	09 24	09 30	09 38	09 48			09 58	10 08	10 18		10 28	10 38	10 48		10 58	11 08
Brondesbury Park		d	08 31		08 40	08 46	08 54	09 01	09 10	09 17	09 26	09 32	09 40	09 50			10 00	10 10	10 20		10 30	10 40	10 50		11 00	11 10
Brondesbury		d	08 33		08 41	08 48	08 56	09 03	09 12	09 19	09 27	09 34	09 42	09 52			10 02	10 12	10 22		10 32	10 42	10 52		11 02	11 12
West Hampstead	⊖	d	08 35		08 43	08 50	08 58	09 05	09 14	09 21	09 30	09 36	09 44	09 54			10 04	10 14	10 24		10 34	10 44	10 54		11 04	11 14
Finchley Road & Frognal		d	08 36		08 45	08 51	08 59	09 06	09 15	09 22	09 31	09 37	09 45	09 55			10 05	10 15	10 25		10 35	10 45	10 55		11 05	11 15
Hampstead Heath		d	08 39		08 47	08 54	09 02	09 09	09 18	09 25	09 34	09 40	09 48	09 58			10 08	10 18	10 28		10 38	10 48	10 58		11 08	11 18
Gospel Oak		d	08 41		08 51	08 56	09 04	09 11	09 20	09 27	09 36	09 42	09 50	10 00			10 10	10 20	10 30		10 40	10 50	11 00		11 10	11 20
Kentish Town West		d	08 43		08 53	08 58	09 06	09 13	09 22	09 29	09 38	09 44	09 52	10 02			10 12	10 22	10 32		10 42	10 52	11 02		11 12	11 22
Camden Road		d	08 47		08 56	09 02	09 10	09 17	09 26	09 33	09 42	09 48	09 56	10 06			10 16	10 26	10 36		10 46	10 56	11 06		11 16	11 26
Caledonian Rd & Barnsbury		d	08 50		08 59	09 05	09 13	09 20	09 29	09 36	09 45	09 51	09 59	10 09			10 19	10 29	10 39		10 49	10 59	11 09		11 19	11 29
Highbury & Islington	⊖	d	08 53		09 02	09 08	09 16	09 23	09 32	09 39	09 48	09 54	10 02	10 12			10 22	10 32	10 42		10 52	11 02	11 12		11 22	11 32
Canonbury	⊖	d	08 55		09 04	09 10	09 18	09 25	09 34	09 41	09 50	09 56	10 04	10 14			10 24	10 34	10 44		10 54	11 04	11 14		11 24	11 34
Dalston Kingsland		d	08 57		09 06	09 12	09 20	09 27	09 36	09 43	09 52	09 58	10 06	10 16			10 26	10 36	10 46		10 56	11 06	11 16		11 26	11 36
Hackney Central		d	08 59		09 08	09 14	09 22	09 29	09 38	09 45	09 54	10 00	10 08	10 18			10 28	10 38	10 48		10 58	11 08	11 18		11 28	11 38
Homerton		d	09 01		09 10	09 16	09 24	09 31	09 40	09 47	09 56	10 02	10 10	10 20			10 30	10 40	10 50		11 00	11 10	11 20		11 30	11 40
Hackney Wick		d	09 03		09 13	09 18	09 26	09 33	09 42	09 49	09 58	10 04	10 12	10 22			10 32	10 42	10 52		11 02	11 12	11 22		11 32	11 42
Stratford 7	⊖	a	09 09		09 21	09 26	09 33	09 38	09 50	09 55	10 05	10 10	10 19	10 28			10 38	10 49	10 58		11 09	11 19	11 29		11 40	11 49

Richmond and Clapham Junction - Willesden Junction, West Hampstead, Highbury and Islington and Stratford

Network Diagram - see first Page of Table 59

	LO		LO	LO	LO	LO	LO	LO	LO	LO	LO	LO	LO		LO	LO	LO	LO	LO	LO	LO	LO	LO	LO
Richmond ⊖ d	10 58			11 08		11 28		11 38		11 58		12 08			12 28		12 38		12 58		13 08		13 28	
Kew Gardens ⊖ d	11 01			11 11		11 31		11 41		12 01		12 11			12 31		12 41		13 01		13 11		13 31	
Gunnersbury ⊖ d	11 04			11 14		11 34		11 44		12 04		12 14			12 34		12 44		13 04		13 14		13 34	
South Acton d	11 07			11 17		11 37		11 47		12 07		12 17			12 37		12 47		13 07		13 17		13 37	
Acton Central d	11 10			11 20		11 40		11 50		12 10		12 20			12 40		12 50		13 10		13 20		13 40	
Clapham Junction 10 d			11 00		11 15		11 30		11 45		12 00		12 15			12 30		12 45		13 00		13 15		13 30
Imperial Wharf d			11 04		11 19		11 34		11 49		12 04		12 19			12 35		12 49		13 04		13 19		13 36
West Brompton ⊖ d			11 07		11 22		11 37		11 52		12 07		12 22			12 38		12 52		13 07		13 22		13 39
Kensington (Olympia) ⊖ d			11 10		11 25		11 40		11 55		12 10		12 25			12 41		12 55		13 10		13 25		13 42
Shepherd's Bush ⊖ d			11 12		11 27		11 42		11 57		12 12		12 27			12 43		12 57		13 12		13 27		13 44
Willesden Jn Low Level ⊖ d																								
Willesden Jn. High Level ⊖ a	11 15		11 21	11 25	11 35	11 45	11 51	11 55	12 05	12 15	12 21	12 25	12 35		12 45	12 51	12 55	13 05	13 15	13 21	13 25	13 35	13 45	13 51
d	11 16			11 26	11 36	11 46		11 56	12 06	12 16		12 26	12 36		12 46		12 56	13 06	13 16		13 26	13 36	13 46	
Kensal Rise d	11 18			11 28	11 38	11 48		11 58	12 08	12 18		12 28	12 38		12 48		12 58	13 08	13 18		13 28	13 38	13 48	
Brondesbury Park d	11 20			11 30	11 40	11 50		12 00	12 10	12 20		12 30	12 40		12 50		13 00	13 10	13 20		13 30	13 40	13 50	
Brondesbury d	11 22			11 32	11 42	11 52		12 02	12 12	12 22		12 32	12 42		12 52		13 02	13 12	13 22		13 32	13 42	13 52	
West Hampstead ⊖ d	11 24			11 34	11 44	11 54		12 04	12 14	12 24		12 34	12 44		12 54		13 04	13 14	13 24		13 34	13 44	13 54	
Finchley Road & Frognal d	11 25			11 35	11 45	11 55		12 05	12 15	12 25		12 35	12 45		12 55		13 05	13 15	13 25		13 35	13 45	13 55	
Hampstead Heath d	11 28			11 38	11 48	11 58		12 08	12 18	12 28		12 38	12 48		12 58		13 08	13 18	13 28		13 38	13 48	13 58	
Gospel Oak d	11 30			11 40	11 50	12 00		12 10	12 20	12 30		12 40	12 50		13 00		13 10	13 20	13 30		13 40	13 50	14 00	
Kentish Town West d	11 32			11 42	11 52	12 02		12 12	12 22	12 32		12 42	12 52		13 02		13 12	13 22	13 32		13 42	13 52	14 02	
Camden Road d	11 36			11 46	11 56	12 06		12 16	12 26	12 36		12 46	12 56		13 06		13 16	13 26	13 36		13 46	13 56	14 06	
Caledonian Rd & Barnsbury d	11 39			11 49	11 59	12 09		12 19	12 29	12 39		12 49	12 59		13 09		13 19	13 29	13 39		13 49	13 59	14 09	
Highbury & Islington ⊖ d	11 42			11 52	12 02	12 12		12 22	12 32	12 42		12 52	13 02		13 12		13 22	13 32	13 42		13 52	14 02	14 12	
Canonbury ⊖ d	11 45			11 54	12 04	12 14		12 24	12 34	12 44		12 54	13 04		13 14		13 24	13 34	13 45		13 54	14 04	14 14	
Dalston Kingsland d	11 47			11 56	12 06	12 16		12 26	12 36	12 46		12 56	13 06		13 16		13 26	13 36	13 47		13 56	14 06	14 16	
Hackney Central d	11 49			11 58	12 08	12 18		12 28	12 38	12 48		12 58	13 08		13 18		13 28	13 38	13 49		13 58	14 08	14 18	
Homerton d	11 51			12 00	12 10	12 20		12 30	12 40	12 50		13 00	13 10		13 20		13 30	13 40	13 51		14 00	14 10	14 20	
Hackney Wick d	11 53			12 02	12 12	12 22		12 32	12 42	12 52		13 02	13 12		13 22		13 33	13 42	13 53		14 02	14 12	14 22	
Stratford 7 ⊖ a	11 59			12 09	12 19	12 29		12 39	12 51	12 59		13 09	13 19		13 29		13 39	13 49	13 59		14 09	14 19	14 29	

	LO		LO	LO	LO	LO	LO	LO	LO	LO	LO	LO	LO		LO	LO	LO	LO	LO	LO	LO	LO	LO	LO
Richmond ⊖ d	13 38			13 58		14 10		14 28		14 38		14 58			15 08		15 26		15 38		15 53		16 09	
Kew Gardens ⊖ d	13 41			14 01		14 13		14 31		14 41		15 01			15 11		15 29		15 41		15 56		16 12	
Gunnersbury ⊖ d	13 44			14 04		14 16		14 34		14 44		15 04			15 14		15 32		15 44		15 59		16 15	
South Acton d	13 47			14 07		14 19		14 37		14 47		15 07			15 17		15 35		15 47		16 02		16 18	
Acton Central d	13 50			14 10		14 22		14 40		14 50		15 10			15 20		15 38		15 50		16 06		16 21	
Clapham Junction 10 d			13 45		14 00		14 15		14 30		14 45		15 00			15 15		15 30		15 44		15 59		16 14
Imperial Wharf d			13 49		14 04		14 19		14 34		14 55		15 04			15 19		15 34		15 49		16 03		16 18
West Brompton ⊖ d			13 52		14 07		14 22		14 37		14 58		15 07			15 22		15 37		15 52		16 06		16 21
Kensington (Olympia) ⊖ d			13 55		14 10		14 25		14 40		15 01		15 10			15 25		15 40		15 55		16 09		16 24
Shepherd's Bush ⊖ d			13 57		14 12		14 27		14 42		15 03		15 12			15 27		15 42		15 57		16 11		16 26
Willesden Jn Low Level ⊖ d																								
Willesden Jn. High Level ⊖ a	13 55		14 05	14 15	14 21	14 27	14 35	14 45	14 51	14 55	15 10	15 15	15 21		15 25	15 35	15 44	15 51	15 55	16 05	16 11	16 20	16 26	16 34
d	13 56		14 06	14 16		14 28	14 36	14 46		14 56	15 11	15 16			15 26	15 36	15 45		15 56	16 06	16 12	16 20	16 27	16 35
Kensal Rise d	13 58		14 08	14 18		14 30	14 38	14 48		14 58	15 14	15 18			15 28	15 38	15 47		15 58	16 08	16 14	16 22	16 29	16 37
Brondesbury Park d	14 00		14 10	14 20		14 32	14 40	14 50		15 00	15 16	15 20			15 30	15 40	15 49		16 00	16 10	16 16	16 24	16 31	16 40
Brondesbury d	14 02		14 12	14 22		14 34	14 42	14 52		15 02	15 17	15 22			15 32	15 42	15 51		16 02	16 12	16 18	16 26	16 33	16 41
West Hampstead ⊖ d	14 04		14 14	14 24		14 36	14 44	14 54		15 04	15 19	15 24			15 34	15 44	15 53		16 04	16 14	16 20	16 28	16 35	16 43
Finchley Road & Frognal d	14 05		14 15	14 25		14 37	14 45	14 55		15 05	15 21	15 25			15 35	15 45	15 54		16 05	16 15	16 21	16 29	16 36	16 44
Hampstead Heath d	14 08		14 18	14 28		14 40	14 48	14 58		15 08	15 23	15 28			15 38	15 48	15 57		16 08	16 18	16 24	16 32	16 39	16 47
Gospel Oak d	14 10		14 20	14 30		14 42	14 50	15 00		15 10	15 26	15 30			15 40	15 50	16 00		16 10	16 20	16 26	16 34	16 41	16 49
Kentish Town West d	14 12		14 22	14 32		14 44	14 52	15 02		15 12	15 28	15 32			15 42	15 52	16 02		16 12	16 22	16 28	16 36	16 43	16 51
Camden Road d	14 16		14 26	14 36		14 48	14 56	15 06		15 16	15 32	15 36			15 46	15 56	16 05		16 16	16 26	16 32	16 40	16 47	16 55
Caledonian Rd & Barnsbury d	14 19		14 29	14 39		14 51	14 59	15 09		15 19	15 35	15 39			15 49	15 59	16 08		16 19	16 29	16 35	16 43	16 50	16 58
Highbury & Islington ⊖ d	14 22		14 32	14 42		14 54	15 02	15 12		15 22	15 38	15 42			15 52	16 02	16 11		16 22	16 32	16 38	16 46	16 53	17 01
Canonbury ⊖ d	14 24		14 34	14 44		14 56	15 04	15 14		15 24	15 40	15 44			15 54	16 04	16 13		16 24	16 34	16 40	16 48	16 55	17 03
Dalston Kingsland d	14 26		14 36	14 46		14 58	15 06	15 16		15 26	15 42	15 46			15 56	16 06	16 15		16 26	16 36	16 42	16 50	16 57	17 05
Hackney Central d	14 28		14 38	14 48		15 00	15 08	15 18		15 28	15 44	15 48			15 58	16 08	16 17		16 28	16 38	16 44	16 52	16 59	17 07
Homerton d	14 30		14 40	14 50		15 02	15 10	15 20		15 30	15 46	15 50			16 00	16 10	16 19		16 30	16 40	16 46	16 54	17 01	17 09
Hackney Wick d	14 32		14 42	14 52		15 04	15 12	15 22		15 32	15 49	15 52			16 02	16 12	16 21		16 32	16 42	16 48	16 56	17 03	17 11
Stratford 7 ⊖ a	14 39		14 49	14 59		15 12	15 19	15 30		15 39	15 54	15 57			16 09	16 19	16 27		16 39	16 48	16 54	17 03	17 10	17 18

Richmond and Clapham Junction - Willesden Junction, West Hampstead, Highbury and Islington and Stratford

Network Diagram - see first Page of Table 59

	LO		LO	LO	LO	LO	LO	LO	LO	LO	LO	LO	LO		LO	LO	LO	LO	LO	LO	LO	LO	LO	LO
Richmond ⊖ d	16 23			16 36		16 53		17 06		17 23		17 36			17 53		18 06		18 22		18 36		18 54	
Kew Gardens ⊖ d	16 26			16 39		16 56		17 09		17 26		17 39			17 56		18 09		18 26		18 39		18 57	
Gunnersbury ⊖ d	16 29			16 42		16 59		17 12		17 29		17 42			17 59		18 12		18 29		18 42		19 00	
South Acton d	16 32			16 45		17 02		17 15		17 32		17 45			18 02		18 15		18 31		18 45		19 03	
Acton Central d	16 36			16 51		17 06		17 21		17 36		17 51			18 06		18 21		18 34		18 51		19 06	
Clapham Junction 10 d			16 29		16 44		16 59		17 14		17 29		17 44			17 59		18 14		18 29		18 44		18 59
Imperial Wharf d			16 33		16 48		17 03		17 18		17 33		17 48			18 03		18 18		18 33		18 48		19 03
West Brompton ⊖ d			16 36		16 51		17 06		17 21		17 36		17 51			18 06		18 21		18 36		18 51		19 06
Kensington (Olympia) ⊖ d			16 39		16 54		17 09		17 24		17 39		17 54			18 09		18 24		18 39		18 54		19 09
Shepherd's Bush ⊖ d			16 41		16 56		17 11		17 26		17 41		17 56			18 11		18 26		18 41		18 56		19 11
Willesden Jn Low Level ⊖ d																								
Willesden Jn. High Level ⊖ a	16 41		16 49	16 56	17 04	17 11	17 19	17 26	17 34	17 41	17 49	17 56	18 04		18 11	18 19	18 26	18 34	18 39	18 49	18 56	19 04	19 11	19 19
d	16 42		16 50	16 57	17 05	17 12	17 20	17 27	17 35	17 42	17 50	17 57	18 05		18 12	18 20	18 27	18 35	18 40	18 50	18 57	19 05	19 12	19 20
Kensal Rise d	16 44		16 52	16 59	17 07	17 14	17 22	17 29	17 37	17 44	17 52	17 59	18 07		18 14	18 22	18 29	18 37	18 43	18 52	18 59	19 07	19 14	19 22
Brondesbury Park d	16 46		16 54	17 01	17 09	17 16	17 24	17 31	17 39	17 46	17 54	18 01	18 09		18 16	18 24	18 31	18 39	18 45	18 54	19 01	19 09	19 16	19 24
Brondesbury d	16 48		16 56	17 03	17 11	17 18	17 26	17 33	17 41	17 48	17 56	18 03	18 11		18 18	18 26	18 33	18 41	18 46	18 56	19 03	19 11	19 18	19 26
West Hampstead ⊖ d	16 50		16 58	17 05	17 13	17 20	17 28	17 35	17 43	17 50	17 58	18 05	18 13		18 20	18 28	18 35	18 43	18 48	18 58	19 05	19 13	19 20	19 28
Finchley Road & Frognal d	16 51		16 59	17 06	17 14	17 21	17 29	17 36	17 44	17 51	17 59	18 06	18 14		18 21	18 29	18 36	18 44	18 50	18 59	19 06	19 14	19 21	19 29
Hampstead Heath d	16 54		17 02	17 09	17 17	17 24	17 32	17 39	17 47	17 54	18 02	18 09	18 17		18 24	18 32	18 39	18 47	18 52	19 02	19 09	19 17	19 24	19 32
Gospel Oak d	16 56		17 04	17 11	17 19	17 26	17 34	17 41	17 49	17 56	18 04	18 11	18 19		18 26	18 34	18 41	18 49	18 55	19 04	19 11	19 19	19 26	19 34
Kentish Town West d	16 58		17 06	17 13	17 21	17 28	17 36	17 43	17 51	17 58	18 06	18 13	18 21		18 28	18 36	18 43	18 51	18 57	19 06	19 13	19 21	19 28	19 36
Camden Road d	17 02		17 10	17 17	17 25	17 32	17 40	17 47	17 55	18 02	18 10	18 17	18 25		18 32	18 40	18 47	18 55	19 00	19 10	19 17	19 25	19 32	19 40
Caledonian Rd & Barnsbury d	17 05		17 13	17 20	17 28	17 35	17 43	17 50	17 58	18 05	18 13	18 20	18 28		18 35	18 44	18 50	18 58	19 03	19 13	19 20	19 28	19 35	19 43
Highbury & Islington ⊖ d	17 08		17 16	17 23	17 31	17 38	17 46	17 53	18 01	18 08	18 16	18 23	18 31		18 38	18 46	18 53	19 01	19 06	19 16	19 23	19 31	19 38	19 46
Canonbury ⊖ d	17 10		17 18	17 25	17 33	17 40	17 48	17 55	18 03	18 10	18 18	18 25	18 33		18 40	18 48	18 55	19 03	19 08	19 18	19 25	19 33	19 40	19 48
Dalston Kingsland d	17 12		17 20	17 27	17 35	17 42	17 50	17 57	18 05	18 12	18 20	18 27	18 35		18 42	18 50	18 57	19 05	19 10	19 20	19 27	19 35	19 42	19 50
Hackney Central d	17 14		17 22	17 29	17 37	17 44	17 52	17 59	18 07	18 14	18 22	18 29	18 37		18 44	18 52	18 59	19 07	19 12	19 22	19 29	19 37	19 44	19 52
Homerton d	17 16		17 24	17 31	17 39	17 46	17 54	18 01	18 09	18 16	18 24	18 31	18 39		18 46	18 54	19 01	19 09	19 14	19 24	19 31	19 39	19 46	19 54
Hackney Wick d	17 18		17 26	17 33	17 41	17 48	17 56	18 03	18 11	18 18	18 26	18 33	18 41		18 48	18 56	19 03	19 11	19 17	19 26	19 33	19 41	19 48	19 56
Stratford 7 ⊖ a	17 24		17 33	17 38	17 50	17 54	18 05	18 08	18 20	18 24	18 35	18 39	18 50		18 54	19 05	19 08	19 20	19 24	19 33	19 40	19 48	19 55	20 03

	LO		LO	LO	LO	LO	LO	LO	LO	LO	LO	LO	LO		LO	LO	LO	LO	LO	LO	LO	LO	LO	LO
Richmond ⊖ d	19 09			19 26		19 41		19 56		20 11		20 26			20 40		20 58		21 10		21 28		21 38	
Kew Gardens ⊖ d	19 12			19 29		19 44		19 59		20 14		20 29			20 43		21 01		21 13		21 31		21 41	
Gunnersbury ⊖ d	19 15			19 32		19 47		20 02		20 17		20 32			20 46		21 04		21 16		21 34		21 44	
South Acton d	19 18			19 35		19 50		20 05		20 20		20 35			20 49		21 07		21 19		21 37		21 47	
Acton Central d	19 23			19 40		19 54		20 08		20 23		20 40			20 52		21 10		21 23		21 40		21 50	
Clapham Junction 10 d			19 15		19 30		19 45		20 00		20 15		20 30			20 45		21 00		21 15		21 30		21 45
Imperial Wharf d			19 19		19 34		19 49		20 04		20 19		20 34			20 49		21 04		21 19		21 34		21 49
West Brompton ⊖ d			19 22		19 37		19 52		20 07		20 22		20 37			20 52		21 07		21 22		21 37		21 52
Kensington (Olympia) ⊖ d			19 25		19 40		19 55		20 10		20 25		20 40			20 55		21 10		21 25		21 40		21 55
Shepherd's Bush ⊖ d			19 27		19 42		19 57		20 12		20 27		20 42			20 57		21 12		21 27		21 42		21 57
Willesden Jn Low Level ⊖ d																								
Willesden Jn. High Level ⊖ a	19 28		19 35	19 45	19 51	19 59	20 05	20 15	20 21	20 28	20 35	20 45	20 51		20 57	21 05	21 16	21 21	21 28	21 35	21 45	21 51	21 55	22 05
d	19 29		19 36	19 46		20 00	20 06	20 16		20 29	20 36	20 46			20 59	21 06	21 17		21 29	21 36	21 46		21 56	22 06
Kensal Rise d	19 31		19 38	19 48		20 02	20 08	20 18		20 31	20 38	20 48			21 01	21 08	21 19		21 31	21 38	21 48		21 58	22 08
Brondesbury Park d	19 33		19 40	19 50		20 04	20 10	20 20		20 33	20 40	20 50			21 03	21 10	21 21		21 33	21 40	21 50		22 00	22 10
Brondesbury d	19 35		19 42	19 52		20 06	20 12	20 22		20 35	20 42	20 52			21 05	21 12	21 23		21 35	21 42	21 52		22 02	22 12
West Hampstead ⊖ d	19 37		19 44	19 54		20 08	20 14	20 24		20 37	20 44	20 54			21 07	21 14	21 25		21 37	21 44	21 54		22 04	22 14
Finchley Road & Frognal d	19 38		19 45	19 55		20 09	20 15	20 25		20 38	20 45	20 55			21 08	21 15	21 26		21 38	21 45	21 55		22 05	22 15
Hampstead Heath d	19 41		19 48	19 58		20 12	20 18	20 28		20 41	20 48	20 58			21 11	21 18	21 29		21 41	21 48	21 58		22 08	22 18
Gospel Oak d	19 43		19 50	20 00		20 14	20 20	20 30		20 43	20 50	21 00			21 13	21 20	21 30		21 43	21 50	22 00		22 10	22 20
Kentish Town West d	19 45		19 52	20 02		20 16	20 22	20 32		20 45	20 52	21 02			21 15	21 22	21 32		21 45	21 52	22 02		22 12	22 22
Camden Road d	19 49		19 56	20 06		20 20	20 26	20 36		20 49	20 56	21 06			21 19	21 26	21 36		21 49	21 56	22 06		22 16	22 26
Caledonian Rd & Barnsbury d	19 52		19 59	20 09		20 23	20 29	20 39		20 52	20 59	21 09			21 22	21 29	21 39		21 52	21 59	22 09		22 19	22 29
Highbury & Islington ⊖ d	19 55		20 02	20 12		20 26	20 33	20 42		20 55	21 02	21 12			21 25	21 32	21 42		21 55	22 02	22 12		22 22	22 32
Canonbury ⊖ d	19 57		20 04	20 14		20 28	20 35	20 44		20 57	21 04	21 14			21 27	21 34	21 44		21 57	22 04	22 14		22 24	22 34
Dalston Kingsland d	19 59		20 06	20 16		20 30	20 37	20 46		20 59	21 06	21 16			21 29	21 36	21 46		21 59	22 06	22 16		22 26	22 36
Hackney Central d	20 01		20 08	20 18		20 32	20 39	20 48		21 01	21 08	21 18			21 31	21 38	21 48		22 01	22 08	22 18		22 28	22 38
Homerton d	20 03		20 10	20 20		20 34	20 41	20 50		21 03	21 10	21 20			21 33	21 40	21 50		22 03	22 10	22 20		22 30	22 40
Hackney Wick d	20 05		20 12	20 22		20 36	20 43	20 52		21 05	21 12	21 22			21 35	21 42	21 52		22 05	22 12	22 22		22 32	22 42
Stratford 7 ⊖ a	20 11		20 19	20 28		20 42	20 51	20 58		21 11	21 19	21 28			21 41	21 49	21 59		22 13	22 19	22 29		22 39	22 49

until 26 July

Richmond and Clapham Junction - Willesden Junction, West Hampstead, Highbury and Islington and Stratford

Network Diagram - see first Page of Table 59

Station		LO	LO	LO	LO	LO	LO	LO	LO	LO	LO
Richmond ⊖	d	21 56			22 28			23 00		23 28	
Kew Gardens ⊖	d	21 59			22 31			23 03		23 31	
Gunnersbury ⊖	d	22 02			22 34			23 06		23 34	
South Acton	d	22 05			22 37			23 09		23 37	
Acton Central	d	22 10			22 40			23 12		23 40	
Clapham Junction 10	d		22 00	22 15		22 30	22 45		23 00		23 30
Imperial Wharf	d		22 04	22 19		22 34	22 49		23 04		23 34
West Brompton ⊖	d		22 07	22 22		22 37	22 52		23 07		23 37
Kensington (Olympia) ⊖	d		22 10	22 25		22 40	22 55		23 10		23 40
Shepherd's Bush ⊖	d		22 12	22 27		22 42	22 57		23 12		23 42
Willesden Jn Low Level ⊖	d										
Willesden Jn. High Level ⊖	a	22 15	22 21	22 36	22 45	22 51	23 06	23 17	23 23	23 45	23 51
	d	22 16			22 46			23 18			
Kensal Rise	d	22 18			22 48			23 20			
Brondesbury Park	d	22 20			22 50			23 22			
Brondesbury	d	22 22			22 52			23 24			
West Hampstead ⊖	d	22 24			22 54			23 26			
Finchley Road & Frognal	d	22 25			22 55			23 27			
Hampstead Heath	d	22 28			22 58			23 30			
Gospel Oak	d	22 30			23 00			23 32			
Kentish Town West	d	22 32			23 02			23 34			
Camden Road	d	22 36			23 06			23 38			
Caledonian Rd & Barnsbury	d	22 39			23 09			23 41			
Highbury & Islington ⊖	d	22 42			23 12			23 44			
Canonbury ⊖	d	22 44			23 14			23 46			
Dalston Kingsland	d	22 46			23 16			23 48			
Hackney Central	d	22 48			23 18			23 50			
Homerton	d	22 50			23 20			23 52			
Hackney Wick	d	22 52			23 22			23 54			
Stratford 7 ⊖	a	22 58			23 29			00 04			

Mondays to Fridays

27 July to 10 August

Station		LO A	LO B	LO A	LO A	LO A	LO C	LO MO	LO C	LO MO	LO A	LO A
Richmond ⊖	d	22p55	23p00		23p11		23p25	23p25			23p41	
Kew Gardens ⊖	d	22p58	23p03		23p14		23p28	23p28			23p44	
Gunnersbury ⊖	d	23p01	23p06		23p17		23p31	23p31			23p47	
South Acton	d	23p04	23p09		23p20		23p34	23p34			23p50	
Acton Central	d	23p07	23p12		23p22		23p37	23p37			23p52	
Clapham Junction 10	d			22p59		23p14			23p29	23p29		23p44
Imperial Wharf	d			23p03		23p18			23p33	23p33		23p48
West Brompton ⊖	d			23p06		23p21			23p36	23p36		23p51
Kensington (Olympia) ⊖	d			23p10		23p25			23p40	23p40		23p55
Shepherd's Bush ⊖	d			23p12		23p27			23p42	23p42		23p57
Willesden Jn Low Level ⊖	d											
Willesden Jn. High Level ⊖	a	23p12	23p17	23p20	23p27	23p35	23p42	23p42	23p50	23p50	23p57	00 05
	d	23p14	23p18	23p21	23p29	23p36	23p43	23p44	23p51	23p51	23p59	00 06
Kensal Rise	d	23p16	23p20	23p23	23p31	23p38	23p45	23p46	23p53	23p53	00 01	00 08
Brondesbury Park	d	23p18	23p22	23p25	23p33	23p40	23p47	23p48	23p55	23p55	00 03	00 10
Brondesbury	d	23p20	23p24	23p27	23p35	23p42	23p49	23p50	23p57	23p57	00 05	00 12
West Hampstead ⊖	d	23p22	23p26	23p29	23p37	23p44	23p51	23p52	23p59	23p59	00 07	00 14
Finchley Road & Frognal	d	23p24	23p27	23p31	23p39	23p46	23p53	23p54	00 01	00 01	00 09	00 16
Hampstead Heath	d	23p26	23p30	23p33	23p41	23p48	23p55	23p56	00 03	00 03	00 11	00 18
Gospel Oak	d	23p30	23p32	23p37	23p45	23p52	00 01	00 01	00 07	00 07	00 15	00 22
Kentish Town West	d	23p32	23p34	23p39	23p47	23p54	00 02	00 02	00 09	00 09	00 17	00 24
Camden Road	d	23p36	23p38	23p43	23p51	23p58	00 06	00 06	00 12	00 13	00 21	00 28
Caledonian Rd & Barnsbury	d	23p39	23p41	23p46	23p54	00 01	00 09	00 09	00 15	00 16	00 24	00 31
Highbury & Islington ⊖	d	23p41	23p44	23p48	23p56	00 03	00 11	00 11	00 18	00 18	00 26	00 33
Canonbury ⊖	d	23p43	23p46	23p50	23p59	00 05	00 13	00 13	00 20	00 20	00 28	00 35
Dalston Kingsland	d	23p46	23p48	23p53	00 02	00 08	00 16	00 16	00 22	00 23	00 31	00 38
Hackney Central	d	23p48	23p50	23p55	00 03	00 10	00 18	00 18	00 24	00 25	00 33	00 40
Homerton	d	23p50	23p52	23p57	00 05	00 12	00 20	00 20	00 26	00 27	00 35	00 42
Hackney Wick	d	23p52	23p54	23p59	00 07	00 14	00 22	00 22	00 29	00 29	00 37	00 44
Stratford 7 ⊖	a	00 04	00 04	00 09	00 19	00 24	00 34	00 34	00 40	00 39	00 49	00 54

Station		LO A	LO A	LO MO	LO C	LO	LO	LO	LO	LO	LO	LO
Richmond ⊖	d	23p55									05 54	
Kew Gardens ⊖	d	23p59									05 57	
Gunnersbury ⊖	d	00 01									06 00	
South Acton	d	00 04									06 03	
Acton Central	d	00 07									06 06	
Clapham Junction 10	d		23p59	00 12	00 17	05 47						
Imperial Wharf	d		00 03	00 16	00 23	05 51						
West Brompton ⊖	d		00 06	00 19	00 26	05 54						
Kensington (Olympia) ⊖	d		00 10	00 22	00 29	05 58						
Shepherd's Bush ⊖	d		00 12	00 24	00 31	06 00						
Willesden Jn Low Level ⊖	d								05 58			
Willesden Jn. High Level ⊖	a	00 12	00 20	00 37	00 44	06 12					06 11	
	d	00 14	00 21								06 12	
Kensal Rise	d	00 16	00 23						06 02		06 14	
Brondesbury Park	d	00 18	00 25						06 04		06 16	
Brondesbury	d	00 20	00 27						06 06		06 18	
West Hampstead ⊖	d	00 22	00 29						06 08		06 20	
Finchley Road & Frognal	d	00 24	00 31						06 09		06 21	
Hampstead Heath	d	00 26	00 33						06 12		06 24	
Gospel Oak	d	00 30	00 37						06 14		06 26	
Kentish Town West	d	00 32	00 39						06 16		06 28	
Camden Road	d	00 36	00 43				06 11	06 15	06 20	06 28	06 32	06 40
Caledonian Rd & Barnsbury	d	00 39	00 46				06 14	06 18	06 23	06 31	06 35	06 43
Highbury & Islington ⊖	d	00 41	00 48				06 16	06 21	06 26	06 34	06 38	06 47
Canonbury ⊖	d	00 43	00 50				06 18	06 23	06 28	06 36	06 40	06 48
Dalston Kingsland	d	00 46	00 53				06 20	06 25	06 30	06 38	06 42	06 50
Hackney Central	d	00 48	00 55				06 22	06 27	06 32	06 40	06 44	06 52
Homerton	d	00 50	00 57				06 24	06 29	06 34	06 42	06 46	06 54
Hackney Wick	d	00 52	00 59				06 26	06 31	06 36	06 44	06 51	06 56
Stratford 7 ⊖	a	01 04	01 09				06 37	06 41	06 48	06 54	07 00	07 08

A not 27 July

B 27 July

C MX from 31 July until 10 August

27 July to 10 August

Richmond and Clapham Junction - Willesden Junction, West Hampstead, Highbury and Islington and Stratford

Network Diagram - see first Page of Table 59

Station		LO	LO	LO	LO	LO	LO	LO	LO	LO	LO	LO
Richmond ⊖	d	06 10			06 25		06 42			06 54		07 11
Kew Gardens ⊖	d	06 13			06 28		06 45			06 57		07 15
Gunnersbury ⊖	d	06 16			06 31		06 48			07 00		07 18
South Acton	d	06 19			06 34		06 51			07 03		07 20
Acton Central	d	06 22			06 37		06 54			07 06		07 24
Clapham Junction 10	d		06 14			06 29		06 44			06 59	
Imperial Wharf	d		06 18			06 33		06 48			07 03	
West Brompton ⊖	d		06 21			06 36		06 51			07 06	
Kensington (Olympia) ⊖	d		06 25			06 40		06 55			07 10	
Shepherd's Bush ⊖	d		06 27			06 42		06 57			07 12	
Willesden Jn Low Level ⊖	d											
Willesden Jn. High Level ⊖	a	06 27	06 35		06 42	06 50	06 57	07 05		07 12	07 20	07 29
	d	06 29	06 36		06 44	06 51	06 59	07 06		07 14	07 21	07 30
Kensal Rise	d	06 31	06 38		06 46	06 53	07 01	07 08		07 16	07 23	07 32
Brondesbury Park	d	06 33	06 40		06 48	06 55	07 03	07 10		07 18	07 25	07 33
Brondesbury	d	06 35	06 42		06 50	06 57	07 05	07 12		07 20	07 27	07 35
West Hampstead ⊖	d	06 37	06 44		06 52	06 59	07 07	07 14		07 22	07 29	07 37
Finchley Road & Frognal	d	06 39	06 46		06 54	07 01	07 09	07 16		07 24	07 31	07 39
Hampstead Heath	d	06 41	06 48		06 56	07 03	07 11	07 18		07 26	07 33	07 41
Gospel Oak	d	06 45	06 52		07 00	07 07	07 15	07 22		07 30	07 37	07 45
Kentish Town West	d	06 47	06 54		07 02	07 09	07 17	07 24		07 32	07 39	07 47
Camden Road	d	06 51	06 58	07 03	07 06	07 13	07 21	07 28	07 33	07 36	07 43	07 51
Caledonian Rd & Barnsbury	d	06 54	07 01	07 06	07 09	07 16	07 24	07 31	07 36	07 39	07 46	07 54
Highbury & Islington ⊖	d	06 56	07 03	07 08	07 11	07 18	07 26	07 33	07 38	07 41	07 48	07 56
Canonbury ⊖	d	06 58	07 05	07 10	07 13	07 20	07 28	07 35	07 40	07 43	07 50	07 58
Dalston Kingsland	d	07 01	07 08	07 13	07 16	07 23	07 31	07 38	07 43	07 46	07 53	08 01
Hackney Central	d	07 03	07 10	07 15	07 18	07 25	07 33	07 40	07 45	07 48	07 55	08 03
Homerton	d	07 05	07 12	07 17	07 20	07 27	07 35	07 42	07 47	07 50	07 57	08 05
Hackney Wick	d	07 07	07 14	07 19	07 22	07 29	07 37	07 44	07 49	07 52	07 59	08 07
Stratford 7 ⊖	a	07 19	07 24	07 30	07 34	07 39	07 49	07 54	08 00	08 04	08 09	08 19

Station		LO	LO	LO	LO	LO	LO	LO	LO	LO	LO	LO
Richmond ⊖	d			07 25		07 41			07 55		08 10	
Kew Gardens ⊖	d			07 28		07 45			07 58		08 13	
Gunnersbury ⊖	d			07 31		07 48			08 01		08 16	
South Acton	d			07 34		07 50			08 03		08 19	
Acton Central	d			07 37		07 54			08 06		08 22	
Clapham Junction 10	d	07 14			07 29		07 44			07 59		08 14
Imperial Wharf	d	07 18			07 33		07 48			08 03		08 18
West Brompton ⊖	d	07 21			07 36		07 51			08 06		08 21
Kensington (Olympia) ⊖	d	07 25			07 40		07 55			08 10		08 25
Shepherd's Bush ⊖	d	07 27			07 42		07 57			08 12		08 27
Willesden Jn Low Level ⊖	d											
Willesden Jn. High Level ⊖	a	07 35		07 42	07 50	07 57	08 05		08 11	08 20	08 27	08 35
	d	07 36		07 44	07 51	07 59	08 06		08 14	08 21	08 29	08 36
Kensal Rise	d	07 38		07 46	07 53	08 01	08 08		08 16	08 23	08 31	08 38
Brondesbury Park	d	07 40		07 48	07 55	08 03	08 10		08 18	08 25	08 33	08 40
Brondesbury	d	07 42		07 50	07 57	08 05	08 12		08 20	08 27	08 35	08 42
West Hampstead ⊖	d	07 44		07 52	07 59	08 07	08 14		08 22	08 29	08 37	08 44
Finchley Road & Frognal	d	07 46		07 54	08 01	08 09	08 16		08 24	08 31	08 39	08 46
Hampstead Heath	d	07 48		07 56	08 03	08 11	08 18		08 26	08 33	08 41	08 48
Gospel Oak	d	07 52		08 00	08 07	08 15	08 22		08 30	08 37	08 45	08 52
Kentish Town West	d	07 54		08 02	08 09	08 17	08 24		08 32	08 39	08 47	08 54
Camden Road	d	07 58	08 03	08 06	08 13	08 21	08 28	08 33	08 36	08 43	08 51	08 58
Caledonian Rd & Barnsbury	d	08 01	08 06	08 09	08 16	08 24	08 31	08 36	08 39	08 46	08 54	09 01
Highbury & Islington ⊖	d	08 03	08 08	08 11	08 18	08 26	08 33	08 38	08 41	08 48	08 56	09 03
Canonbury ⊖	d	08 05	08 10	08 13	08 20	08 28	08 35	08 40	08 43	08 50	08 58	09 05
Dalston Kingsland	d	08 08	08 13	08 16	08 23	08 31	08 38	08 43	08 46	08 53	09 01	09 08
Hackney Central	d	08 10	08 15	08 18	08 25	08 33	08 40	08 45	08 48	08 55	09 03	09 10
Homerton	d	08 12	08 17	08 20	08 27	08 35	08 42	08 47	08 50	08 57	09 05	09 12
Hackney Wick	d	08 14	08 19	08 22	08 29	08 37	08 44	08 49	08 52	08 59	09 07	09 14
Stratford 7 ⊖	a	08 24	08 30	08 34	08 39	08 49	08 54	09 00	09 04	09 09	09 19	09 24

Station		LO	LO	LO	LO	LO	LO	LO	LO	LO	LO	LO
Richmond ⊖	d		08 25		08 41		08 55		09 11		09 25	
Kew Gardens ⊖	d		08 28		08 45		08 58		09 14		09 28	
Gunnersbury ⊖	d		08 31		08 48		09 01		09 17		09 31	
South Acton	d		08 34		08 50		09 03		09 20		09 33	
Acton Central	d		08 37		08 54		09 07		09 24		09 37	
Clapham Junction 10	d			08 29		08 44		08 59		09 14		09 29
Imperial Wharf	d			08 33		08 48		09 03		09 18		09 33
West Brompton ⊖	d			08 36		08 51		09 06		09 21		09 36
Kensington (Olympia) ⊖	d			08 40		08 55		09 10		09 25		09 40
Shepherd's Bush ⊖	d			08 42		08 57		09 12		09 27		09 42
Willesden Jn Low Level ⊖	d											
Willesden Jn. High Level ⊖	a		08 42	08 50	08 57	09 05	09 12	09 20	09 27	09 35	09 42	09 50
	d		08 44	08 51	08 59	09 06	09 14	09 21	09 29	09 36	09 44	09 51
Kensal Rise	d		08 46	08 53	09 01	09 08	09 16	09 23	09 31	09 38	09 46	09 53
Brondesbury Park	d		08 48	08 55	09 03	09 10	09 18	09 25	09 33	09 40	09 48	09 55
Brondesbury	d		08 50	08 57	09 05	09 12	09 20	09 27	09 35	09 42	09 50	09 57
West Hampstead ⊖	d		08 52	08 59	09 07	09 14	09 22	09 29	09 37	09 44	09 52	09 59
Finchley Road & Frognal	d		08 54	09 01	09 09	09 16	09 24	09 31	09 39	09 46	09 54	10 01
Hampstead Heath	d		08 56	09 03	09 11	09 18	09 26	09 33	09 41	09 48	09 56	10 03
Gospel Oak	d		09 00	09 07	09 15	09 22	09 30	09 37	09 45	09 52	10 00	10 07
Kentish Town West	d		09 02	09 09	09 17	09 24	09 32	09 39	09 47	09 54	10 02	10 09
Camden Road	d	09 03	09 06	09 13	09 21	09 28	09 36	09 43	09 51	09 58	10 06	10 13
Caledonian Rd & Barnsbury	d	09 06	09 09	09 16	09 24	09 31	09 39	09 46	09 54	10 01	10 09	10 16
Highbury & Islington ⊖	d	09 08	09 11	09 18	09 26	09 33	09 41	09 48	09 56	10 03	10 11	10 18
Canonbury ⊖	d	09 10	09 13	09 20	09 28	09 35	09 43	09 50	09 58	10 05	10 13	10 20
Dalston Kingsland	d	09 13	09 16	09 23	09 31	09 38	09 46	09 53	10 01	10 08	10 16	10 23
Hackney Central	d	09 15	09 18	09 25	09 33	09 40	09 48	09 55	10 03	10 10	10 18	10 25
Homerton	d	09 17	09 20	09 27	09 35	09 42	09 50	09 57	10 05	10 12	10 20	10 27
Hackney Wick	d	09 19	09 22	09 29	09 37	09 44	09 52	09 59	10 07	10 14	10 22	10 29
Stratford 7 ⊖	a	09 30	09 34	09 39	09 49	09 54	10 04	10 09	10 19	10 24	10 34	10 39

Station		LO	LO	LO	LO	LO	LO	LO	LO	LO	LO	LO
Richmond ⊖	d	09 42		09 55		10 10		10 25		10 41		10 55
Kew Gardens ⊖	d	09 45		09 58		10 13		10 28		10 44		10 58
Gunnersbury ⊖	d	09 50		10 01		10 16		10 31		10 47		11 01
South Acton	d	09 52		10 04		10 19		10 34		10 50		11 04
Acton Central	d	09 56		10 07		10 22		10 37		10 52		11 07
Clapham Junction 10	d		09 44		09 59		10 14		10 29		10 44	
Imperial Wharf	d		09 48		10 03		10 18		10 36		10 48	
West Brompton ⊖	d		09 51		10 06		10 21		10 39		10 51	
Kensington (Olympia) ⊖	d		09 55		10 10		10 25		10 42		10 55	
Shepherd's Bush ⊖	d		09 57		10 12		10 27		10 45		10 57	
Willesden Jn Low Level ⊖	d											
Willesden Jn. High Level ⊖	a	09 59	10 05	10 12	10 20	10 27	10 35	10 42	10 52	10 55	11 06	11 12
	d	10 00	10 07	10 14	10 21	10 29	10 36	10 44	10 53	10 57	11 07	11 14
Kensal Rise	d	10 02	10 09	10 16	10 23	10 31	10 38	10 46	10 56	11 01	11 09	11 16
Brondesbury Park	d	10 04	10 11	10 18	10 25	10 33	10 40	10 48	10 58	11 03	11 11	11 18
Brondesbury	d	10 06	10 13	10 20	10 27	10 35	10 42	10 50	10 59	11 05	11 13	11 20
West Hampstead ⊖	d	10 08	10 15	10 22	10 29	10 37	10 44	10 52	11 02	11 07	11 15	11 22
Finchley Road & Frognal	d	10 10	10 17	10 24	10 31	10 39	10 46	10 54	11 03	11 09	11 17	11 24
Hampstead Heath	d	10 12	10 19	10 26	10 33	10 41	10 48	10 56	11 06	11 11	11 19	11 26
Gospel Oak	d	10 16	10 23	10 30	10 37	10 45	10 52	11 00	11 09	11 16	11 23	11 30
Kentish Town West	d	10 18	10 25	10 32	10 39	10 47	10 54	11 02	11 11	11 18	11 25	11 32
Camden Road	d	10 22	10 29	10 36	10 43	10 51	10 58	11 06	11 15	11 21	11 29	11 36
Caledonian Rd & Barnsbury	d	10 25	10 32	10 39	10 46	10 54	11 01	11 09	11 18	11 24	11 32	11 39
Highbury & Islington ⊖	d	10 28	10 35	10 41	10 48	10 56	11 03	11 11	11 20	11 27	11 34	11 41
Canonbury ⊖	d	10 30	10 37	10 43	10 50	10 58	11 05	11 13	11 22	11 29	11 36	11 43
Dalston Kingsland	d	10 32	10 39	10 46	10 53	11 01	11 08	11 16	11 25	11 31	11 39	11 46
Hackney Central	d	10 34	10 41	10 48	10 55	11 03	11 10	11 18	11 27	11 33	11 41	11 48
Homerton	d	10 36	10 43	10 50	10 57	11 05	11 12	11 20	11 29	11 35	11 43	11 50
Hackney Wick	d	10 38	10 46	10 52	10 59	11 07	11 14	11 22	11 31	11 38	11 45	11 52
Stratford 7 ⊖	a	10 50	10 56	11 04	11 09	11 20	11 24	11 34	11 41	11 49	11 56	12 04

Richmond and Clapham Junction - Willesden Junction, West Hampstead, Highbury and Islington and Stratford

Network Diagram - see first Page of Table 59

		LO	LO	LO	LO	LO	LO	LO	LO	LO	LO	LO	LO	LO	LO	LO	LO	LO	LO	LO	LO	LO	LO
Richmond ⊖	d		11 11		11 25		11 40		11 55		12 11		12 25		12 41		12 55		13 10		13 25		13 41
Kew Gardens ⊖	d		11 14		11 28		11 43		11 58		12 14		12 28		12 44		12 58		13 13		13 28		13 44
Gunnersbury ⊖	d		11 17		11 31		11 46		12 01		12 17		12 31		12 47		13 01		13 16		13 31		13 47
South Acton	d		11 20		11 34		11 49		12 04		12 20		12 34		12 50		13 04		13 19		13 34		13 50
Acton Central	d		11 22		11 37		11 52		12 07		12 22		12 37		12 53		13 07		13 23		13 37		13 52
Clapham Junction 10	d	10 59		11 14		11 29		11 44		11 59		12 14		12 29		12 44		12 59		13 14		13 29	
Imperial Wharf	d	11 03		11 18		11 33		11 48		12 03		12 18		12 35		12 48		13 03		13 18		13 36	
West Brompton ⊖	d	11 06		11 21		11 36		11 51		12 06		12 21		12 38		12 51		13 06		13 21		13 39	
Kensington (Olympia) ⊖	d	11 10		11 25		11 40		11 55		12 10		12 25		12 41		12 55		13 10		13 25		13 42	
Shepherd's Bush ⊖	d	11 12		11 27		11 42		11 57		12 12		12 27		12 44		12 57		13 12		13 27		13 45	
Willesden Jn Low Level ⊖	d																						
Willesden Jn. High Level ⊖	a	11 20	11 27	11 35	11 42	11 50	11 57	12 05	12 12	12 20	12 28	12 35	12 42	12 51	12 56	13 05	13 12	13 20	13 27	13 35	13 42	13 52	13 57
	d	11 21	11 29	11 36	11 44	11 51	11 59	12 06	12 14	12 21	12 30	12 36	12 44	12 52	12 59	13 06	13 14	13 21	13 29	13 36	13 44	13 53	13 59
Kensal Rise	d	11 23	11 31	11 38	11 46	11 53	12 01	12 08	12 16	12 23	12 32	12 38	12 46	12 55	13 01	13 08	13 16	13 23	13 31	13 38	13 46	13 56	14 01
Brondesbury Park	d	11 25	11 33	11 40	11 48	11 55	12 03	12 10	12 18	12 25	12 34	12 40	12 48	12 57	13 03	13 10	13 18	13 25	13 33	13 40	13 48	13 58	14 03
Brondesbury	d	11 27	11 35	11 42	11 50	11 57	12 05	12 12	12 20	12 27	12 36	12 42	12 50	12 58	13 05	13 12	13 20	13 27	13 35	13 42	13 50	13 59	14 05
West Hampstead ⊖	d	11 29	11 37	11 44	11 52	11 59	12 07	12 14	12 22	12 29	12 38	12 44	12 52	13 01	13 07	13 14	13 22	13 29	13 37	13 44	13 52	14 02	14 07
Finchley Road & Frognal	d	11 31	11 39	11 46	11 54	12 01	12 09	12 16	12 24	12 31	12 40	12 46	12 54	13 02	13 09	13 16	13 24	13 31	13 39	13 46	13 54	14 03	14 09
Hampstead Heath	d	11 33	11 41	11 48	11 56	12 03	12 11	12 18	12 26	12 33	12 42	12 48	12 56	13 05	13 11	13 18	13 26	13 33	13 41	13 48	13 56	14 06	14 11
Gospel Oak	d	11 37	11 45	11 52	12 00	12 07	12 16	12 22	12 30	12 37	12 46	12 52	13 00	13 09	13 15	13 22	13 30	13 37	13 45	13 52	14 00	14 10	14 15
Kentish Town West	d	11 39	11 47	11 54	12 02	12 09	12 18	12 24	12 32	12 39	12 48	12 54	13 02	13 11	13 17	13 24	13 32	13 39	13 47	13 54	14 02	14 12	14 17
Camden Road	d	11 43	11 51	11 58	12 06	12 13	12 22	12 28	12 36	12 43	12 52	12 58	13 06	13 14	13 21	13 28	13 36	13 43	13 51	13 58	14 06	14 15	14 21
Caledonian Rd & Barnsbury	d	11 46	11 54	12 01	12 09	12 16	12 25	12 31	12 39	12 46	12 55	13 01	13 09	13 17	13 24	13 31	13 39	13 46	13 54	14 01	14 09	14 18	14 24
Highbury & Islington ⊖	d	11 48	11 56	12 03	12 11	12 18	12 27	12 33	12 41	12 48	12 57	13 03	13 11	13 20	13 26	13 33	13 41	13 48	13 57	14 03	14 11	14 21	14 26
Canonbury ⊖	d	11 50	11 58	12 05	12 13	12 20	12 29	12 35	12 43	12 50	12 59	13 05	13 13	13 22	13 28	13 35	13 43	13 50	13 59	14 05	14 13	14 23	14 28
Dalston Kingsland	d	11 53	12 01	12 08	12 16	12 23	12 32	12 38	12 46	12 53	13 02	13 08	13 16	13 24	13 31	13 38	13 46	13 53	14 01	14 08	14 16	14 25	14 31
Hackney Central	d	11 55	12 03	12 10	12 18	12 25	12 34	12 40	12 48	12 55	13 04	13 10	13 18	13 26	13 33	13 40	13 48	13 55	14 03	14 10	14 18	14 27	14 33
Homerton	d	11 57	12 05	12 12	12 20	12 27	12 36	12 42	12 50	12 57	13 06	13 12	13 20	13 28	13 35	13 42	13 50	13 57	14 05	14 12	14 20	14 29	14 35
Hackney Wick	d	11 59	12 07	12 14	12 22	12 29	12 38	12 44	12 52	12 59	13 08	13 14	13 22	13 31	13 37	13 44	13 52	13 59	14 08	14 14	14 22	14 32	14 37
Stratford 7 ⊖	a	12 10	12 19	12 24	12 34	12 40	12 49	12 54	13 04	13 10	13 19	13 24	13 34	13 41	13 49	13 54	14 04	14 10	14 19	14 24	14 34	14 41	14 49

		LO	LO	LO	LO	LO	LO	LO	LO	LO	LO	LO	LO	LO	LO	LO	LO	LO	LO	LO	LO	LO	LO
Richmond ⊖	d		13 55		14 11		14 25		14 40		14 55			15 11		15 25			15 41		15 56		
Kew Gardens ⊖	d		13 58		14 14		14 28		14 43		14 58			15 14		15 28			15 44		16 00		
Gunnersbury ⊖	d		14 01		14 17		14 31		14 46		15 01			15 17		15 31			15 47		16 03		
South Acton	d		14 04		14 20		14 34		14 49		15 04			15 20		15 34			15 50		16 05		
Acton Central	d		14 07		14 22		14 37		14 52		15 07			15 22		15 37			15 52		16 08		
Clapham Junction 10	d	13 44		13 59		14 14		14 29		14 44		14 59			15 14		15 29			15 44		15 59	
Imperial Wharf	d	13 48		14 03		14 18		14 33		14 55		15 03			15 18		15 33			15 48		16 03	
West Brompton ⊖	d	13 51		14 06		14 21		14 36		14 58		15 06			15 21		15 36			15 51		16 06	
Kensington (Olympia) ⊖	d	13 55		14 10		14 25		14 40		15 01		15 10			15 25		15 40			15 55		16 10	
Shepherd's Bush ⊖	d	13 57		14 12		14 27		14 42		15 04		15 12			15 27		15 42			15 57		16 12	
Willesden Jn Low Level ⊖	d																						
Willesden Jn. High Level ⊖	a	14 05	14 12	14 20	14 28	14 35	14 42	14 50	14 57	15 11	15 13	15 20		15 27	15 35	15 42	15 50		15 57	16 05	16 13	16 20	
	d	14 06	14 14	14 21	14 29	14 36	14 44	14 51	14 59	15 11	15 14	15 21		15 29	15 36	15 44	15 51		15 59	16 06	16 14	16 21	
Kensal Rise	d	14 08	14 16	14 23	14 32	14 38	14 46	14 53	15 01	15 14	15 16	15 23		15 31	15 38	15 46	15 53		16 01	16 08	16 17	16 23	
Brondesbury Park	d	14 10	14 18	14 25	14 34	14 40	14 48	14 55	15 03	15 16	15 18	15 25		15 33	15 40	15 48	15 55		16 03	16 10	16 19	16 25	
Brondesbury	d	14 12	14 20	14 27	14 35	14 42	14 50	14 57	15 05	15 17	15 20	15 27		15 35	15 42	15 50	15 57		16 05	16 12	16 20	16 27	
West Hampstead ⊖	d	14 14	14 22	14 29	14 38	14 44	14 52	14 59	15 07	15 20	15 22	15 29		15 37	15 44	15 53	15 59		16 07	16 14	16 23	16 29	
Finchley Road & Frognal	d	14 16	14 24	14 31	14 39	14 46	14 54	15 01	15 09	15 21	15 24	15 31		15 39	15 46	15 55	16 01		16 09	16 16	16 24	16 31	
Hampstead Heath	d	14 18	14 26	14 33	14 42	14 48	14 56	15 03	15 11	15 24	15 26	15 33		15 41	15 48	15 57	16 03		16 11	16 18	16 27	16 33	
Gospel Oak	d	14 22	14 30	14 37	14 45	14 52	15 00	15 07	15 15	15 28	15 30	15 37		15 45	15 52	16 01	16 07		16 15	16 22	16 31	16 37	
Kentish Town West	d	14 24	14 32	14 39	14 47	14 54	15 02	15 09	15 17	15 30	15 32	15 39		15 47	15 54	16 03	16 09		16 17	16 24	16 33	16 39	
Camden Road	d	14 28	14 36	14 43	14 51	14 58	15 06	15 13	15 21	15 33	15 36	15 43	15 49	15 51	15 58	16 07	16 13	16 19	16 21	16 28	16 36	16 43	16 49
Caledonian Rd & Barnsbury	d	14 31	14 39	14 46	14 54	15 01	15 09	15 16	15 24	15 36	15 39	15 46	15 52	15 54	16 01	16 10	16 16	16 22	16 24	16 31	16 39	16 46	16 52
Highbury & Islington ⊖	d	14 33	14 41	14 48	14 56	15 03	15 11	15 18	15 26	15 39	15 41	15 49	15 54	15 57	16 03	16 12	16 18	16 24	16 26	16 33	16 42	16 48	16 54
Canonbury ⊖	d	14 35	14 43	14 50	14 58	15 05	15 13	15 20	15 28	15 41	15 43	15 51	15 56	15 59	16 05	16 14	16 20	16 26	16 28	16 35	16 44	16 50	16 56
Dalston Kingsland	d	14 38	14 46	14 53	15 01	15 08	15 16	15 23	15 31	15 43	15 46	15 54	15 59	16 01	16 08	16 17	16 23	16 29	16 31	16 38	16 46	16 53	16 59
Hackney Central	d	14 40	14 48	14 55	15 03	15 10	15 18	15 25	15 33	15 45	15 48	15 56	16 01	16 03	16 10	16 19	16 25	16 31	16 33	16 40	16 48	16 55	17 01
Homerton	d	14 42	14 50	14 57	15 05	15 12	15 20	15 27	15 35	15 47	15 50	15 58	16 03	16 05	16 12	16 21	16 27	16 33	16 35	16 42	16 50	16 57	17 03
Hackney Wick	d	14 44	14 52	14 59	15 07	15 14	15 22	15 29	15 37	15 50	15 52	16 00	16 05	16 08	16 14	16 23	16 29	16 35	16 37	16 44	16 53	16 59	17 05
Stratford 7 ⊖	a	14 54	15 04	15 09	15 19	15 24	15 34	15 39	15 49	15 59	16 04	16 10	16 15	16 19	16 24	16 35	16 40	16 45	16 49	16 54	17 05	17 09	17 15

Richmond and Clapham Junction - Willesden Junction, West Hampstead, Highbury and Islington and Stratford

Network Diagram - see first Page of Table 59

		LO	LO	LO	LO	LO	LO	LO	LO	LO	LO	LO	LO	LO	LO	LO	LO	LO	LO	LO	LO	LO	LO
Richmond ⊖	d	16 10		16 25			16 41		16 55			17 11		17 25			17 41		17 55			18 11	
Kew Gardens ⊖	d	16 13		16 28			16 45		16 58			17 15		17 28			17 45		17 58			18 15	
Gunnersbury ⊖	d	16 16		16 31			16 49		17 01			17 18		17 31			17 48		18 01			18 18	
South Acton	d	16 19		16 33			16 51		17 04			17 20		17 34			17 50		18 04			18 20	
Acton Central	d	16 22		16 37			16 54		17 07			17 24		17 37			17 54		18 07			18 24	
Clapham Junction 10	d		16 14		16 29			16 44		16 59			17 14		17 29			17 44		17 59			18 14
Imperial Wharf	d		16 18		16 33			16 48		17 03			17 18		17 33			17 48		18 03			18 18
West Brompton ⊖	d		16 21		16 36			16 51		17 06			17 21		17 36			17 51		18 06			18 21
Kensington (Olympia) ⊖	d		16 25		16 40			16 55		17 10			17 25		17 40			17 55		18 10			18 25
Shepherd's Bush ⊖	d		16 27		16 42			16 57		17 12			17 27		17 42			17 57		18 12			18 27
Willesden Jn Low Level ⊖	d																						
Willesden Jn. High Level ⊖	a	16 27	16 35	16 42	16 50		16 57	17 05	17 12	17 20		17 27	17 35	17 42	17 50		17 57	18 05	18 12	18 20		18 27	18 35
	d	16 29	16 36	16 44	16 51		16 59	17 06	17 14	17 21		17 29	17 36	17 44	17 51		17 59	18 06	18 14	18 21		18 29	18 36
Kensal Rise	d	16 31	16 38	16 46	16 53		17 01	17 08	17 16	17 23		17 31	17 38	17 46	17 53		18 01	18 08	18 16	18 23		18 31	18 38
Brondesbury Park	d	16 33	16 40	16 48	16 55		17 03	17 10	17 18	17 25		17 33	17 40	17 48	17 55		18 03	18 10	18 18	18 25		18 33	18 40
Brondesbury	d	16 35	16 42	16 50	16 57		17 05	17 12	17 20	17 27		17 35	17 42	17 50	17 57		18 05	18 12	18 20	18 27		18 35	18 42
West Hampstead ⊖	d	16 37	16 44	16 52	16 59		17 07	17 14	17 22	17 29		17 37	17 44	17 52	17 59		18 07	18 14	18 22	18 29		18 37	18 44
Finchley Road & Frognal	d	16 39	16 46	16 54	17 01		17 09	17 16	17 24	17 31		17 39	17 46	17 54	18 01		18 09	18 16	18 24	18 31		18 39	18 46
Hampstead Heath	d	16 41	16 48	16 56	17 03		17 11	17 18	17 26	17 33		17 41	17 48	17 56	18 03		18 11	18 18	18 26	18 33		18 41	18 48
Gospel Oak	d	16 45	16 52	17 00	17 07		17 15	17 22	17 30	17 37		17 45	17 52	18 00	18 07		18 15	18 22	18 30	18 37		18 45	18 52
Kentish Town West	d	16 47	16 54	17 02	17 09		17 17	17 24	17 32	17 39		17 47	17 54	18 02	18 09		18 17	18 24	18 32	18 39		18 47	18 54
Camden Road	d	16 51	16 58	17 06	17 13	17 19	17 21	17 28	17 36	17 43	17 49	17 51	17 58	18 06	18 13	18 19	18 21	18 28	18 36	18 43	18 49	18 51	18 58
Caledonian Rd & Barnsbury	d	16 54	17 01	17 09	17 16	17 22	17 24	17 31	17 39	17 46	17 52	17 54	18 01	18 09	18 16	18 22	18 24	18 31	18 39	18 46	18 52	18 54	19 01
Highbury & Islington ⊖	d	16 56	17 03	17 11	17 18	17 24	17 26	17 33	17 41	17 48	17 54	17 56	18 03	18 11	18 18	18 24	18 26	18 33	18 41	18 48	18 54	18 56	19 03
Canonbury ⊖	d	16 58	17 05	17 13	17 20	17 26	17 28	17 35	17 43	17 50	17 56	17 58	18 05	18 13	18 20	18 26	18 28	18 35	18 43	18 50	18 56	18 58	19 05
Dalston Kingsland	d	17 01	17 08	17 16	17 23	17 29	17 31	17 38	17 46	17 53	17 59	18 01	18 08	18 16	18 23	18 29	18 31	18 38	18 46	18 53	18 59	19 01	19 08
Hackney Central	d	17 03	17 10	17 18	17 25	17 31	17 33	17 40	17 48	17 55	18 01	18 03	18 10	18 18	18 25	18 31	18 33	18 40	18 48	18 55	19 01	19 03	19 10
Homerton	d	17 05	17 12	17 20	17 27	17 33	17 35	17 42	17 50	17 57	18 03	18 05	18 12	18 20	18 27	18 33	18 35	18 42	18 50	18 57	19 03	19 05	19 12
Hackney Wick	d	17 07	17 14	17 22	17 29	17 35	17 37	17 44	17 52	17 59	18 05	18 07	18 14	18 22	18 29	18 35	18 37	18 44	18 52	18 59	19 05	19 07	19 14
Stratford 7 ⊖	a	17 19	17 24	17 34	17 39	17 45	17 49	17 54	18 04	18 09	18 15	18 19	18 24	18 34	18 39	18 45	18 49	18 54	19 04	19 09	19 15	19 19	19 24

		LO	LO	LO	LO	LO	LO	LO	LO	LO	LO	LO	LO	LO	LO	LO	LO	LO	LO	LO	LO	LO	LO
Richmond ⊖	d	18 25		18 42		18 55		19 11		19 25		19 40		19 55		20 10		20 25		20 40		20 55	
Kew Gardens ⊖	d	18 28		18 45		18 58		19 14		19 28		19 43		19 58		20 13		20 28		20 43		20 58	
Gunnersbury ⊖	d	18 31		18 48		19 01		19 17		19 31		19 46		20 01		20 16		20 31		20 46		21 01	
South Acton	d	18 34		18 51		19 04		19 20		19 34		19 49		20 04		20 19		20 34		20 49		21 04	
Acton Central	d	18 37		18 54		19 07		19 22		19 37		19 52		20 07		20 22		20 37		20 52		21 07	
Clapham Junction 10	d		18 29		18 44		18 59		19 14		19 29		19 44		19 59		20 14		20 29		20 44		20 59
Imperial Wharf	d		18 33		18 48		19 03		19 18		19 33		19 48		20 03		20 18		20 33		20 48		21 03
West Brompton ⊖	d		18 36		18 51		19 06		19 21		19 36		19 51		20 06		20 21		20 36		20 51		21 06
Kensington (Olympia) ⊖	d		18 40		18 55		19 10		19 25		19 40		19 55		20 10		20 25		20 40		20 55		21 09
Shepherd's Bush ⊖	d		18 42		18 57		19 12		19 27		19 42		19 57		20 12		20 27		20 42		20 57		21 12
Willesden Jn Low Level ⊖	d																						
Willesden Jn. High Level ⊖	a	18 42	18 50	18 57	19 05	19 12	19 20	19 27	19 35	19 42	19 50	19 57	20 05	20 12	20 20	20 27	20 37	20 42	20 50	20 55	21 05	21 13	21 19
	d	18 44	18 51	18 59	19 06	19 14	19 21	19 29	19 36	19 44	19 51	19 59	20 06	20 14	20 21	20 29	20 38	20 44	20 51	20 57	21 06	21 14	21 20
Kensal Rise	d	18 46	18 53	19 01	19 08	19 16	19 23	19 31	19 38	19 46	19 53	20 01	20 08	20 16	20 23	20 31	20 40	20 46	20 53	20 59	21 08	21 16	21 23
Brondesbury Park	d	18 48	18 55	19 03	19 10	19 18	19 25	19 33	19 40	19 48	19 55	20 03	20 10	20 18	20 25	20 33	20 42	20 48	20 55	21 01	21 10	21 18	21 25
Brondesbury	d	18 50	18 57	19 05	19 12	19 20	19 27	19 35	19 42	19 50	19 57	20 05	20 12	20 20	20 27	20 35	20 44	20 50	20 57	21 03	21 12	21 20	21 27
West Hampstead ⊖	d	18 52	18 59	19 07	19 14	19 22	19 29	19 37	19 44	19 52	19 59	20 07	20 14	20 22	20 29	20 37	20 46	20 52	20 59	21 05	21 14	21 22	21 29
Finchley Road & Frognal	d	18 54	19 01	19 09	19 16	19 24	19 31	19 39	19 46	19 54	20 01	20 09	20 16	20 24	20 31	20 39	20 48	20 54	21 01	21 07	21 16	21 24	21 31
Hampstead Heath	d	18 56	19 03	19 11	19 18	19 26	19 33	19 41	19 48	19 56	20 03	20 11	20 18	20 26	20 33	20 41	20 50	20 56	21 03	21 09	21 18	21 26	21 33
Gospel Oak	d	19 00	19 07	19 15	19 22	19 30	19 37	19 45	19 52	20 00	20 07	20 15	20 22	20 30	20 37	20 45	20 54	21 00	21 07	21 12	21 22	21 30	21 37
Kentish Town West	d	19 02	19 09	19 17	19 24	19 32	19 39	19 47	19 54	20 02	20 09	20 17	20 24	20 32	20 39	20 47	20 56	21 02	21 09	21 14	21 24	21 32	21 39
Camden Road	d	19 06	19 13	19 21	19 28	19 36	19 43	19 51	19 58	20 06	20 13	20 21	20 28	20 36	20 43	20 51	21 00	21 06	21 13	21 17	21 28	21 36	21 43
Caledonian Rd & Barnsbury	d	19 09	19 16	19 24	19 31	19 39	19 46	19 54	20 01	20 09	20 16	20 24	20 31	20 39	20 46	20 54	21 03	21 09	21 16	21 20	21 31	21 39	21 46
Highbury & Islington ⊖	d	19 11	19 18	19 26	19 33	19 41	19 48	19 56	20 03	20 11	20 18	20 26	20 33	20 41	20 48	20 56	21 05	21 11	21 18	21 23	21 33	21 41	21 48
Canonbury ⊖	d	19 13	19 20	19 28	19 35	19 43	19 50	19 58	20 05	20 13	20 20	20 28	20 35	20 43	20 50	20 58	21 07	21 13	21 20	21 25	21 35	21 43	21 50
Dalston Kingsland	d	19 16	19 23	19 31	19 38	19 46	19 53	20 01	20 08	20 16	20 23	20 31	20 38	20 46	20 53	21 01	21 10	21 16	21 23	21 28	21 38	21 46	21 53
Hackney Central	d	19 18	19 25	19 33	19 40	19 48	19 55	20 03	20 10	20 18	20 25	20 33	20 40	20 48	20 55	21 03	21 12	21 18	21 25	21 31	21 40	21 48	21 55
Homerton	d	19 20	19 27	19 35	19 42	19 50	19 57	20 05	20 12	20 20	20 27	20 35	20 42	20 50	20 57	21 05	21 14	21 20	21 27	21 34	21 42	21 50	21 57
Hackney Wick	d	19 22	19 29	19 37	19 44	19 52	19 59	20 07	20 14	20 22	20 29	20 37	20 44	20 52	20 59	21 07	21 16	21 22	21 29	21 36	21 44	21 52	21 59
Stratford 7 ⊖	a	19 34	19 39	19 49	19 54	20 04	20 09	20 18	20 24	20 34	20 40	20 49	20 54	21 04	21 10	21 19	21 26	21 34	21 39	21 49	21 54	22 04	22 09

Table 59

Mondays to Fridays

27 July to 10 August

Richmond and Clapham Junction - Willesden Junction, West Hampstead, Highbury and Islington and Stratford

Network Diagram - see first Page of Table 59

Station		LO	LO	LO	LO	LO	LO	LO	LO	LO	LO	LO
Richmond ⊖	d	21 11		21 25		21 41		21 55		22 11		22 25
Kew Gardens ⊖	d	21 14		21 28		21 44		21 58		22 14		22 28
Gunnersbury ⊖	d	21 18		21 31		21 48		22 01		22 18		22 31
South Acton	d	21 21		21 34		21 51		22 04		22 21		22 34
Acton Central	d	21 23		21 37		21 53		22 07		22 23		22 37
Clapham Junction 10	d		21 14		21 29		21 44		21 59		22 14	
Imperial Wharf	d		21 18		21 33		21 48		22 03		22 18	
West Brompton ⊖	d		21 21		21 36		21 51		22 06		22 21	
Kensington (Olympia) ⊖	d		21 25		21 40		21 55		22 10		22 25	
Shepherd's Bush ⊖	d		21 27		21 42		21 57		22 12		22 27	
Willesden Jn Low Level ⊖	d											
Willesden Jn. High Level ⊖	a	21 27	21 35	21 42	21 50	21 57	22 05	22 12	22 20	22 27	22 35	22 42
	d	21 29	21 37	21 44	21 51	21 59	22 06	22 14	22 21	22 29	22 36	22 44
Kensal Rise	d	21 31	21 39	21 46	21 53	22 01	22 08	22 16	22 23	22 31	22 38	22 46
Brondesbury Park	d	21 33	21 41	21 48	21 55	22 03	22 10	22 18	22 25	22 33	22 40	22 48
Brondesbury	d	21 35	21 43	21 50	21 57	22 05	22 12	22 20	22 27	22 35	22 42	22 50
West Hampstead ⊖	d	21 37	21 45	21 52	21 59	22 07	22 14	22 23	22 29	22 37	22 44	22 52
Finchley Road & Frognal	d	21 39	21 47	21 54	22 01	22 09	22 15	22 24	22 31	22 39	22 46	22 54
Hampstead Heath	d	21 41	21 49	21 56	22 03	22 11	22 18	22 27	22 33	22 41	22 48	22 56
Gospel Oak	d	21 45	21 54	22 00	22 07	22 15	22 22	22 30	22 37	22 45	22 52	23 00
Kentish Town West	d	21 47	21 56	22 02	22 09	22 17	22 24	22 32	22 39	22 47	22 54	23 02
Camden Road	d	21 51	22 01	22 06	22 13	22 21	22 28	22 36	22 43	22 51	22 58	23 06
Caledonian Rd & Barnsbury	d	21 54	22 04	22 09	22 16	22 24	22 31	22 39	22 46	22 54	23 01	23 09
Highbury & Islington ⊖	d	21 56	22 06	22 11	22 18	22 26	22 33	22 41	22 48	22 56	23 03	23 11
Canonbury ⊖	d	21 58	22 08	22 13	22 20	22 28	22 35	22 43	22 50	22 58	23 05	23 13
Dalston Kingsland	d	22 01	22 11	22 16	22 23	22 31	22 38	22 46	22 53	23 01	23 08	23 16
Hackney Central	d	22 03	22 13	22 18	22 25	22 33	22 40	22 48	22 55	23 03	23 10	23 18
Homerton	d	22 05	22 15	22 20	22 27	22 35	22 42	22 50	22 57	23 05	23 12	23 20
Hackney Wick	d	22 07	22 17	22 22	22 29	22 37	22 44	22 52	22 59	23 07	23 14	23 22
Stratford 7 ⊖	a	22 19	22 27	22 34	22 40	22 49	22 54	23 04	23 10	23 19	23 24	23 34

Station		LO	LO	LO	LO	LO	LO	LO	LO	LO	LO	LO
Richmond ⊖	d		22 40		22 55		23 11		23 25		23 41	
Kew Gardens ⊖	d		22 43		22 58		23 14		23 28		23 44	
Gunnersbury ⊖	d		22 46		23 01		23 17		23 31		23 47	
South Acton	d		22 49		23 04		23 20		23 34		23 50	
Acton Central	d		22 52		23 07		23 22		23 37		23 52	
Clapham Junction 10	d	22 29		22 44		22 59		23 14		23 29		23 44
Imperial Wharf	d	22 33		22 48		23 03		23 18		23 33		23 48
West Brompton ⊖	d	22 36		22 51		23 06		23 21		23 36		23 51
Kensington (Olympia) ⊖	d	22 40		22 55		23 10		23 25		23 40		23 55
Shepherd's Bush ⊖	d	22 42		22 57		23 12		23 27		23 42		23 57
Willesden Jn Low Level ⊖	d											
Willesden Jn. High Level ⊖	a	22 50	22 57	23 05	23 12	23 20	23 27	23 35	23 42	23 50	23 57	00 05
	d	22 51	22 59	23 06	23 14	23 21	23 29	23 36	23 43	23 51	23 59	00 06
Kensal Rise	d	22 53	23 01	23 08	23 16	23 23	23 31	23 38	23 45	23 53	00 01	00 08
Brondesbury Park	d	22 55	23 03	23 10	23 18	23 25	23 33	23 40	23 47	23 55	00 03	00 10
Brondesbury	d	22 57	23 05	23 12	23 20	23 27	23 35	23 42	23 49	23 57	00 05	00 12
West Hampstead ⊖	d	22 59	23 07	23 14	23 22	23 29	23 37	23 44	23 51	23 59	00 07	00 14
Finchley Road & Frognal	d	23 01	23 09	23 16	23 24	23 31	23 39	23 46	23 53	00 01	00 09	00 16
Hampstead Heath	d	23 03	23 11	23 18	23 26	23 33	23 41	23 48	23 55	00 03	00 11	00 18
Gospel Oak	d	23 07	23 15	23 22	23 30	23 37	23 45	23 52	00 01	00 07	00 15	00 22
Kentish Town West	d	23 09	23 17	23 24	23 32	23 39	23 47	23 54	00 02	00 09	00 17	00 24
Camden Road	d	23 13	23 21	23 28	23 36	23 43	23 51	23 58	00 06	00 12	00 21	00 28
Caledonian Rd & Barnsbury	d	23 16	23 24	23 31	23 39	23 46	23 54	00 01	00 09	00 15	00 24	00 31
Highbury & Islington ⊖	d	23 18	23 26	23 33	23 41	23 48	23 56	00 03	00 11	00 18	00 26	00 33
Canonbury ⊖	d	23 20	23 28	23 35	23 43	23 50	23 59	00 05	00 13	00 20	00 28	00 35
Dalston Kingsland	d	23 23	23 31	23 38	23 46	23 53	00 02	00 08	00 16	00 22	00 31	00 38
Hackney Central	d	23 25	23 33	23 40	23 48	23 55	00 03	00 10	00 18	00 24	00 33	00 40
Homerton	d	23 27	23 35	23 42	23 50	23 57	00 05	00 12	00 20	00 26	00 35	00 42
Hackney Wick	d	23 29	23 37	23 44	23 52	23 59	00 07	00 14	00 22	00 29	00 37	00 44
Stratford 7 ⊖	a	23 39	23 49	23 54	00 04	00 09	00 19	00 24	00 34	00 40	00 49	00 54

Station		LO	LO
Richmond ⊖	d	23 55	
Kew Gardens ⊖	d	23 59	
Gunnersbury ⊖	d	00 01	
South Acton	d	00 04	
Acton Central	d	00 07	
Clapham Junction 10	d		23 59
Imperial Wharf	d		00 03
West Brompton ⊖	d		00 06
Kensington (Olympia) ⊖	d		00 10
Shepherd's Bush ⊖	d		00 12
Willesden Jn Low Level ⊖	d		
Willesden Jn. High Level ⊖	a	00 12	00 20
	d	00 14	00 21
Kensal Rise	d	00 16	00 23
Brondesbury Park	d	00 18	00 25
Brondesbury	d	00 20	00 27
West Hampstead ⊖	d	00 22	00 29
Finchley Road & Frognal	d	00 24	00 31
Hampstead Heath	d	00 26	00 33
Gospel Oak	d	00 30	00 37
Kentish Town West	d	00 32	00 39
Camden Road	d	00 36	00 43
Caledonian Rd & Barnsbury	d	00 39	00 46
Highbury & Islington ⊖	d	00 41	00 48
Canonbury ⊖	d	00 43	00 50
Dalston Kingsland	d	00 46	00 53
Hackney Central	d	00 48	00 55
Homerton	d	00 50	00 57
Hackney Wick	d	00 52	00 59
Stratford 7 ⊖	a	01 04	01 09

Table 59

Mondays to Fridays

13 August to 28 August

Richmond and Clapham Junction - Willesden Junction, West Hampstead, Highbury and Islington and Stratford

Network Diagram - see first Page of Table 59

Station		LO A	LO MX	LO A	LO A	LO A	LO A	LO A	LO A	LO A	LO A	LO A
Richmond ⊖	d	22p55	23p00		23p11		23p25		23p41		23p55	
Kew Gardens ⊖	d	22p58	23p03		23p14		23p28		23p44		23p59	
Gunnersbury ⊖	d	23p01	23p06		23p17		23p31		23p47		00 01	
South Acton	d	23p04	23p09		23p20		23p34		23p50		00 04	
Acton Central	d	23p07	23p12		23p22		23p37		23p52		00 07	
Clapham Junction 10	d			22p59		23p14		23p29		23p44		23p59
Imperial Wharf	d			23p03		23p18		23p33		23p48		00 03
West Brompton ⊖	d			23p06		23p21		23p36		23p51		00 06
Kensington (Olympia) ⊖	d			23p10		23p25		23p40		23p55		00 10
Shepherd's Bush ⊖	d			23p12		23p27		23p42		23p57		00 12
Willesden Jn Low Level ⊖	d											
Willesden Jn. High Level ⊖	a	23p12	23p17	23p20	23p27	23p35	23p42	23p50	23p57	00 05	00 12	00 20
	d	23p14	23p18	23p21	23p29	23p36	23p44	23p51	23p59	00 06	00 14	00 21
Kensal Rise	d	23p16	23p20	23p23	23p31	23p38	23p46	23p53	00 01	00 08	00 16	00 23
Brondesbury Park	d	23p18	23p22	23p25	23p33	23p40	23p48	23p55	00 03	00 10	00 18	00 25
Brondesbury	d	23p20	23p24	23p27	23p35	23p42	23p50	23p57	00 05	00 12	00 20	00 27
West Hampstead ⊖	d	23p22	23p26	23p29	23p37	23p44	23p52	23p59	00 07	00 14	00 22	00 29
Finchley Road & Frognal	d	23p24	23p27	23p31	23p39	23p46	23p54	00 01	00 09	00 16	00 24	00 31
Hampstead Heath	d	23p26	23p30	23p33	23p41	23p48	23p56	00 03	00 11	00 18	00 26	00 33
Gospel Oak	d	23p30	23p32	23p37	23p45	23p52	00 01	00 07	00 15	00 22	00 30	00 37
Kentish Town West	d	23p32	23p34	23p39	23p47	23p54	00 02	00 09	00 17	00 24	00 32	00 39
Camden Road	d	23p36	23p38	23p43	23p51	23p58	00 06	00 13	00 21	00 28	00 36	00 43
Caledonian Rd & Barnsbury	d	23p39	23p41	23p46	23p54	00 01	00 09	00 16	00 24	00 31	00 39	00 46
Highbury & Islington ⊖	d	23p41	23p44	23p48	23p56	00 03	00 11	00 18	00 26	00 33	00 41	00 48
Canonbury ⊖	d	23p43	23p46	23p50	23p59	00 05	00 13	00 20	00 28	00 35	00 43	00 50
Dalston Kingsland	d	23p46	23p48	23p53	00 02	00 08	00 16	00 23	00 31	00 38	00 46	00 53
Hackney Central	d	23p48	23p50	23p55	00 03	00 10	00 18	00 25	00 33	00 40	00 48	00 55
Homerton	d	23p50	23p52	23p57	00 05	00 12	00 20	00 27	00 35	00 42	00 50	00 57
Hackney Wick	d	23p52	23p54	23p59	00 07	00 14	00 22	00 29	00 37	00 44	00 52	00 59
Stratford 7 ⊖	a	00 04	00 04	00 09	00 19	00 24	00 34	00 39	00 49	00 54	01 04	01 09

Station		LO A	LO	LO	LO	LO	LO	LO	LO	LO	LO	LO
Richmond ⊖	d					05 54	06 09		06 24		06 37	
Kew Gardens ⊖	d					05 57	06 12		06 27		06 40	
Gunnersbury ⊖	d					06 00	06 15		06 30		06 43	
South Acton	d					06 03	06 18		06 33		06 46	
Acton Central	d					06 06	06 21		06 36		06 51	
Clapham Junction 10	d	00 12	05 47					06 14		06 29		06 44
Imperial Wharf	d	00 16	05 51					06 18		06 33		06 48
West Brompton ⊖	d	00 19	05 54					06 21		06 36		06 51
Kensington (Olympia) ⊖	d	00 22	05 57					06 24		06 39		06 54
Shepherd's Bush ⊖	d	00 24	05 59					06 26		06 41		06 56
Willesden Jn Low Level ⊖	d				05 58							
Willesden Jn. High Level ⊖	a	00 37	06 08			06 11	06 26	06 34	06 41	06 50	06 56	07 04
	d					06 12	06 27	06 35	06 42	06 50	06 57	07 05
Kensal Rise	d				06 02	06 14	06 29	06 37	06 44	06 52	06 59	07 07
Brondesbury Park	d				06 04	06 16	06 31	06 39	06 46	06 54	07 01	07 09
Brondesbury	d				06 06	06 18	06 33	06 41	06 48	06 56	07 03	07 11
West Hampstead ⊖	d				06 08	06 20	06 35	06 43	06 50	06 58	07 05	07 13
Finchley Road & Frognal	d				06 09	06 21	06 36	06 44	06 51	06 59	07 06	07 14
Hampstead Heath	d				06 12	06 24	06 39	06 47	06 54	07 02	07 09	07 17
Gospel Oak	d				06 14	06 26	06 41	06 49	06 56	07 04	07 11	07 19
Kentish Town West	d				06 16	06 28	06 43	06 51	06 58	07 06	07 13	07 21
Camden Road	d			06 11	06 20	06 32	06 47	06 55	07 02	07 10	07 17	07 25
Caledonian Rd & Barnsbury	d			06 14	06 23	06 35	06 50	06 58	07 05	07 13	07 20	07 28
Highbury & Islington ⊖	d			06 16	06 26	06 38	06 53	07 01	07 08	07 16	07 23	07 31
Canonbury ⊖	d			06 18	06 28	06 40	06 55	07 03	07 10	07 18	07 25	07 33
Dalston Kingsland	d			06 20	06 30	06 42	06 57	07 05	07 12	07 20	07 27	07 35
Hackney Central	d			06 22	06 32	06 44	06 59	07 07	07 14	07 22	07 29	07 37
Homerton	d			06 24	06 34	06 46	07 01	07 09	07 16	07 24	07 31	07 39
Hackney Wick	d			06 26	06 36	06 48	07 03	07 11	07 18	07 26	07 33	07 41
Stratford 7 ⊖	a			06 32	06 44	06 55	07 10	07 18	07 25	07 33	07 39	07 48

Station		LO	LO	LO	LO	LO	LO	LO	LO	LO	LO	LO
Richmond ⊖	d	06 53		07 06		07 24		07 36		07 53		08 08
Kew Gardens ⊖	d	06 56		07 09		07 27		07 39		07 56		08 11
Gunnersbury ⊖	d	06 59		07 12		07 30		07 42		07 59		08 14
South Acton	d	07 02		07 15		07 33		07 45		08 02		08 17
Acton Central	d	07 06		07 21		07 36		07 51		08 06		08 21
Clapham Junction 10	d		06 59		07 14		07 29		07 44		07 59	
Imperial Wharf	d		07 03		07 18		07 33		07 48		08 03	
West Brompton ⊖	d		07 06		07 21		07 36		07 51		08 06	
Kensington (Olympia) ⊖	d		07 09		07 24		07 39		07 54		08 09	
Shepherd's Bush ⊖	d		07 11		07 26		07 41		07 56		08 11	
Willesden Jn Low Level ⊖	d											
Willesden Jn. High Level ⊖	a	07 11	07 19	07 26	07 35	07 41	07 49	07 56	08 05	08 11	08 19	08 26
	d	07 12	07 20	07 27	07 35	07 42	07 50	07 57	08 06	08 12	08 20	08 27
Kensal Rise	d	07 14	07 22	07 29	07 37	07 44	07 52	07 59	08 08	08 14	08 22	08 29
Brondesbury Park	d	07 16	07 24	07 31	07 39	07 46	07 54	08 01	08 10	08 16	08 24	08 31
Brondesbury	d	07 18	07 26	07 33	07 41	07 48	07 56	08 03	08 12	08 18	08 26	08 33
West Hampstead ⊖	d	07 20	07 28	07 35	07 43	07 50	07 58	08 05	08 14	08 20	08 28	08 35
Finchley Road & Frognal	d	07 21	07 29	07 36	07 44	07 51	07 59	08 06	08 15	08 21	08 29	08 36
Hampstead Heath	d	07 24	07 32	07 39	07 47	07 54	08 02	08 09	08 18	08 24	08 32	08 39
Gospel Oak	d	07 26	07 34	07 41	07 49	07 56	08 04	08 11	08 20	08 26	08 34	08 41
Kentish Town West	d	07 28	07 36	07 43	07 51	07 58	08 06	08 13	08 22	08 28	08 36	08 43
Camden Road	d	07 32	07 40	07 47	07 55	08 02	08 10	08 17	08 26	08 32	08 40	08 47
Caledonian Rd & Barnsbury	d	07 35	07 43	07 50	07 58	08 05	08 13	08 20	08 29	08 35	08 43	08 50
Highbury & Islington ⊖	d	07 38	07 46	07 53	08 01	08 08	08 16	08 23	08 32	08 38	08 46	08 53
Canonbury ⊖	d	07 40	07 48	07 55	08 03	08 10	08 18	08 25	08 34	08 40	08 48	08 55
Dalston Kingsland	d	07 42	07 50	07 57	08 05	08 12	08 20	08 27	08 36	08 42	08 50	08 57
Hackney Central	d	07 44	07 52	07 59	08 07	08 14	08 22	08 29	08 38	08 44	08 52	08 59
Homerton	d	07 46	07 54	08 01	08 09	08 16	08 24	08 31	08 40	08 46	08 54	09 01
Hackney Wick	d	07 48	07 56	08 03	08 11	08 18	08 26	08 33	08 42	08 48	08 56	09 03
Stratford 7 ⊖	a	07 55	08 03	08 09	08 18	08 25	08 33	08 39	08 49	08 54	09 03	09 09

Station		LO	LO	LO	LO	LO	LO	LO	LO	LO	LO	LO
Richmond ⊖	d		08 22		08 36		08 52		09 10		09 27	
Kew Gardens ⊖	d		08 25		08 39		08 55		09 13		09 30	
Gunnersbury ⊖	d		08 28		08 42		08 58		09 16		09 33	
South Acton	d		08 31		08 45		09 01		09 19		09 36	
Acton Central	d		08 36		08 51		09 06		09 22		09 40	
Clapham Junction 10	d	08 09		08 29		08 44		08 59		09 15		09 30
Imperial Wharf	d	08 13		08 33		08 48		09 03		09 19		09 34
West Brompton ⊖	d	08 16		08 36		08 51		09 06		09 22		09 37
Kensington (Olympia) ⊖	d	08 19		08 39		08 54		09 09		09 25		09 40
Shepherd's Bush ⊖	d	08 21		08 41		08 56		09 11		09 27		09 42
Willesden Jn Low Level ⊖	d											
Willesden Jn. High Level ⊖	a	08 34	08 41	08 49	08 56	09 05	09 11	09 19	09 27	09 35	09 45	09 51
	d	08 35	08 42	08 50	08 57	09 06	09 13	09 20	09 28	09 36	09 46	
Kensal Rise	d	08 38	08 44	08 52	08 59	09 08	09 15	09 24	09 30	09 38	09 48	
Brondesbury Park	d	08 40	08 46	08 54	09 01	09 10	09 17	09 26	09 32	09 40	09 50	
Brondesbury	d	08 41	08 48	08 56	09 03	09 12	09 19	09 27	09 34	09 42	09 52	
West Hampstead ⊖	d	08 43	08 50	08 58	09 05	09 14	09 21	09 30	09 36	09 44	09 54	
Finchley Road & Frognal	d	08 45	08 51	08 59	09 06	09 15	09 22	09 31	09 37	09 45	09 55	
Hampstead Heath	d	08 47	08 54	09 02	09 09	09 18	09 25	09 34	09 40	09 48	09 58	
Gospel Oak	d	08 51	08 56	09 04	09 11	09 20	09 27	09 36	09 42	09 50	10 00	
Kentish Town West	d	08 53	08 58	09 06	09 13	09 22	09 29	09 38	09 44	09 52	10 02	
Camden Road	d	08 56	09 02	09 10	09 17	09 26	09 33	09 42	09 48	09 56	10 06	
Caledonian Rd & Barnsbury	d	08 59	09 05	09 13	09 20	09 29	09 36	09 45	09 51	09 59	10 09	
Highbury & Islington ⊖	d	09 02	09 08	09 16	09 23	09 32	09 39	09 48	09 54	10 02	10 12	
Canonbury ⊖	d	09 04	09 10	09 18	09 25	09 34	09 41	09 50	09 56	10 04	10 14	
Dalston Kingsland	d	09 06	09 12	09 20	09 27	09 36	09 43	09 52	09 58	10 06	10 16	
Hackney Central	d	09 08	09 14	09 22	09 29	09 38	09 45	09 54	10 00	10 08	10 18	
Homerton	d	09 10	09 16	09 24	09 31	09 40	09 47	09 56	10 02	10 10	10 20	
Hackney Wick	d	09 13	09 18	09 26	09 33	09 42	09 49	09 58	10 04	10 12	10 22	
Stratford 7 ⊖	a	09 18	09 26	09 33	09 38	09 50	09 55	10 05	10 10	10 19	10 28	

A 13 August

Richmond and Clapham Junction - Willesden Junction, West Hampstead, Highbury and Islington and Stratford

Network Diagram - see first Page of Table 59

		LO	LO	LO	LO	LO	LO	LO	LO	LO	LO	LO	LO	LO	LO	LO	LO	LO	LO	LO	LO	LO	LO
Richmond	⊖ d	09 36		09 57		10 08		10 28		10 38		10 58		11 08		11 28		11 38		11 58		12 08	
Kew Gardens	⊖ d	09 39		10 00		10 11		10 31		10 41		11 01		11 11		11 31		11 41		12 01		12 11	
Gunnersbury	⊖ d	09 42		10 03		10 14		10 34		10 44		11 04		11 14		11 34		11 44		12 04		12 14	
South Acton	d	09 45		10 06		10 17		10 37		10 47		11 07		11 17		11 37		11 47		12 07		12 17	
Acton Central	d	09 50		10 10		10 20		10 40		10 50		11 10		11 20		11 40		11 50		12 10		12 20	
Clapham Junction 10	d		09 45		10 00		10 15		10 30		10 45		11 00		11 15		11 30		11 45		12 00		12 15
Imperial Wharf	d		09 49		10 04		10 19		10 36		10 49		11 04		11 19		11 34		11 49		12 04		12 19
West Brompton	⊖ d		09 52		10 07		10 22		10 39		10 52		11 07		11 22		11 37		11 52		12 07		12 22
Kensington (Olympia)	⊖ d		09 55		10 10		10 25		10 42		10 55		11 10		11 25		11 40		11 55		12 10		12 25
Shepherd's Bush	⊖ d		09 57		10 12		10 27		10 44		10 57		11 12		11 27		11 42		11 57		12 12		12 27
Willesden Jn Low Level	⊖ d																						
Willesden Jn. High Level	⊖ a	09 55	10 05	10 15	10 21	10 25	10 35	10 45	10 51	10 55	11 05	11 15	11 21	11 25	11 35	11 45	11 51	11 55	12 05	12 15	12 21	12 25	12 35
	d	09 56	10 06	10 16		10 26	10 36	10 46		10 56	11 06	11 16		11 26	11 36	11 46		11 56	12 06	12 16		12 26	12 36
Kensal Rise	d	09 58	10 08	10 18		10 28	10 38	10 48		10 58	11 08	11 18		11 28	11 38	11 48		11 58	12 08	12 18		12 28	12 38
Brondesbury Park	d	10 00	10 10	10 20		10 30	10 40	10 50		11 00	11 10	11 20		11 30	11 40	11 50		12 00	12 10	12 20		12 30	12 40
Brondesbury	d	10 02	10 12	10 22		10 32	10 42	10 52		11 02	11 12	11 22		11 32	11 42	11 52		12 02	12 12	12 22		12 32	12 42
West Hampstead	⊖ d	10 04	10 14	10 24		10 34	10 44	10 54		11 04	11 14	11 24		11 34	11 44	11 54		12 04	12 14	12 24		12 34	12 44
Finchley Road & Frognal	d	10 05	10 15	10 25		10 35	10 45	10 55		11 05	11 15	11 25		11 35	11 45	11 55		12 05	12 15	12 25		12 35	12 45
Hampstead Heath	d	10 08	10 18	10 28		10 38	10 48	10 58		11 08	11 18	11 28		11 38	11 48	11 58		12 08	12 18	12 28		12 38	12 48
Gospel Oak	d	10 10	10 20	10 30		10 40	10 50	11 00		11 10	11 20	11 30		11 40	11 50	12 00		12 10	12 20	12 30		12 40	12 50
Kentish Town West	d	10 12	10 22	10 32		10 42	10 52	11 02		11 12	11 22	11 32		11 42	11 52	12 02		12 12	12 22	12 32		12 42	12 52
Camden Road	d	10 16	10 26	10 36		10 46	10 56	11 06		11 16	11 26	11 36		11 46	11 56	12 06		12 16	12 26	12 36		12 46	12 56
Caledonian Rd & Barnsbury	d	10 19	10 29	10 39		10 49	10 59	11 09		11 19	11 29	11 39		11 49	11 59	12 09		12 19	12 29	12 39		12 49	12 59
Highbury & Islington	⊖ d	10 22	10 32	10 42		10 52	11 02	11 12		11 22	11 32	11 42		11 52	12 02	12 12		12 22	12 32	12 42		12 52	13 02
Canonbury	⊖ d	10 24	10 34	10 44		10 54	11 04	11 14		11 24	11 34	11 45		11 54	12 04	12 14		12 24	12 34	12 44		12 54	13 04
Dalston Kingsland	d	10 26	10 36	10 46		10 56	11 06	11 16		11 26	11 36	11 47		11 56	12 06	12 16		12 26	12 36	12 46		12 56	13 06
Hackney Central	d	10 28	10 38	10 48		10 58	11 08	11 18		11 28	11 38	11 49		11 58	12 08	12 18		12 28	12 38	12 48		12 58	13 08
Homerton	d	10 30	10 40	10 50		11 00	11 10	11 20		11 30	11 40	11 51		12 00	12 10	12 20		12 30	12 40	12 50		13 00	13 10
Hackney Wick	d	10 32	10 42	10 52		11 02	11 12	11 22		11 32	11 42	11 53		12 02	12 12	12 22		12 32	12 42	12 52		13 02	13 12
Stratford 7	⊖ a	10 38	10 49	10 58		11 09	11 19	11 29		11 40	11 49	11 59		12 09	12 19	12 29		12 39	12 51	12 59		13 09	13 19

		LO	LO	LO	LO	LO	LO	LO	LO	LO	LO	LO	LO	LO	LO	LO	LO	LO	LO	LO	LO	LO	LO
Richmond	⊖ d	12 28		12 38		12 58		13 08		13 28		13 38		13 58		14 10		14 28		14 38		14 58	
Kew Gardens	⊖ d	12 31		12 41		13 01		13 11		13 31		13 41		14 01		14 13		14 31		14 41		15 01	
Gunnersbury	⊖ d	12 34		12 44		13 04		13 14		13 34		13 44		14 04		14 16		14 34		14 44		15 04	
South Acton	d	12 37		12 47		13 07		13 17		13 37		13 47		14 07		14 19		14 37		14 47		15 07	
Acton Central	d	12 40		12 50		13 10		13 20		13 40		13 50		14 10		14 22		14 40		14 50		15 10	
Clapham Junction 10	d		12 30		12 45		13 00		13 15		13 30		13 45		14 00		14 15		14 30		14 45		15 00
Imperial Wharf	d		12 35		12 49		13 04		13 19		13 36		13 49		14 04		14 19		14 34		14 55		15 04
West Brompton	⊖ d		12 38		12 52		13 07		13 22		13 39		13 52		14 07		14 22		14 37		14 58		15 07
Kensington (Olympia)	⊖ d		12 41		12 55		13 10		13 25		13 42		13 55		14 10		14 25		14 40		15 01		15 10
Shepherd's Bush	⊖ d		12 43		12 57		13 12		13 27		13 44		13 57		14 12		14 27		14 42		15 03		15 12
Willesden Jn Low Level	⊖ d																						
Willesden Jn. High Level	⊖ a	12 45	12 51	12 55	13 05	13 15	13 21	13 25	13 35	13 45	13 51	13 55	14 05	14 15	14 21	14 27	14 35	14 45	14 51	14 55	15 10	15 15	15 21
	d	12 46		12 56	13 06	13 16		13 26	13 36	13 46		13 56	14 06	14 16		14 28	14 36	14 46		14 56	15 11	15 16	
Kensal Rise	d	12 48		12 58	13 08	13 18		13 28	13 38	13 48		13 58	14 08	14 18		14 30	14 38	14 48		14 58	15 14	15 18	
Brondesbury Park	d	12 50		13 00	13 10	13 20		13 30	13 40	13 50		14 00	14 10	14 20		14 32	14 40	14 50		15 00	15 16	15 20	
Brondesbury	d	12 52		13 02	13 12	13 22		13 32	13 42	13 52		14 02	14 12	14 22		14 34	14 42	14 52		15 02	15 17	15 22	
West Hampstead	⊖ d	12 54		13 04	13 14	13 24		13 34	13 44	13 54		14 04	14 14	14 24		14 36	14 44	14 54		15 04	15 19	15 24	
Finchley Road & Frognal	d	12 55		13 05	13 15	13 25		13 35	13 45	13 55		14 05	14 15	14 25		14 37	14 45	14 55		15 05	15 21	15 25	
Hampstead Heath	d	12 58		13 08	13 18	13 28		13 38	13 48	13 58		14 08	14 18	14 28		14 40	14 48	14 58		15 08	15 23	15 28	
Gospel Oak	d	13 00		13 10	13 20	13 30		13 40	13 50	14 00		14 10	14 20	14 30		14 42	14 50	15 00		15 10	15 26	15 30	
Kentish Town West	d	13 02		13 12	13 22	13 32		13 42	13 52	14 02		14 12	14 22	14 32		14 44	14 52	15 02		15 12	15 28	15 32	
Camden Road	d	13 06		13 16	13 26	13 36		13 46	13 56	14 06		14 16	14 26	14 36		14 48	14 56	15 06		15 16	15 32	15 36	
Caledonian Rd & Barnsbury	d	13 09		13 19	13 29	13 39		13 49	13 59	14 09		14 19	14 29	14 39		14 51	14 59	15 09		15 19	15 35	15 39	
Highbury & Islington	⊖ d	13 12		13 22	13 32	13 42		13 52	14 02	14 12		14 22	14 32	14 42		14 54	15 02	15 12		15 22	15 38	15 42	
Canonbury	⊖ d	13 14		13 24	13 34	13 45		13 54	14 04	14 14		14 24	14 34	14 44		14 56	15 04	15 14		15 24	15 40	15 44	
Dalston Kingsland	d	13 16		13 26	13 36	13 47		13 56	14 06	14 16		14 26	14 36	14 46		14 58	15 06	15 16		15 26	15 42	15 46	
Hackney Central	d	13 18		13 28	13 38	13 49		13 58	14 08	14 18		14 28	14 38	14 48		15 00	15 08	15 18		15 28	15 44	15 48	
Homerton	d	13 20		13 30	13 40	13 51		14 00	14 10	14 20		14 30	14 40	14 50		15 02	15 10	15 20		15 30	15 46	15 50	
Hackney Wick	d	13 22		13 33	13 42	13 53		14 02	14 12	14 22		14 32	14 42	14 52		15 04	15 12	15 22		15 32	15 49	15 52	
Stratford 7	⊖ a	13 29		13 39	13 49	13 59		14 09	14 19	14 29		14 39	14 49	14 59		15 12	15 19	15 30		15 39	15 54	15 57	

Richmond and Clapham Junction - Willesden Junction, West Hampstead, Highbury and Islington and Stratford

Network Diagram - see first Page of Table 59

		LO	LO	LO	LO	LO	LO	LO	LO	LO	LO	LO	LO	LO	LO	LO	LO	LO	LO	LO	LO	LO	LO
Richmond	⊖ d	15 08		15 26		15 38		15 53		16 09		16 23		16 36		16 53		17 06		17 23		17 36	
Kew Gardens	⊖ d	15 11		15 29		15 41		15 56		16 12		16 26		16 39		16 56		17 09		17 26		17 39	
Gunnersbury	⊖ d	15 14		15 32		15 44		15 59		16 15		16 29		16 42		16 59		17 12		17 29		17 42	
South Acton	d	15 17		15 35		15 47		16 02		16 18		16 32		16 45		17 02		17 15		17 32		17 45	
Acton Central	d	15 20		15 38		15 50		16 06		16 21		16 36		16 51		17 06		17 21		17 36		17 51	
Clapham Junction 10	d		15 15		15 30		15 44		15 59		16 14		16 29		16 44		16 59		17 14		17 29		17 44
Imperial Wharf	d		15 19		15 34		15 49		16 03		16 18		16 33		16 48		17 03		17 18		17 33		17 48
West Brompton	⊖ d		15 22		15 37		15 52		16 06		16 21		16 36		16 51		17 06		17 21		17 36		17 51
Kensington (Olympia)	⊖ d		15 25		15 40		15 55		16 09		16 24		16 39		16 54		17 09		17 24		17 39		17 54
Shepherd's Bush	⊖ d		15 27		15 42		15 57		16 11		16 26		16 41		16 56		17 11		17 26		17 41		17 56
Willesden Jn Low Level	⊖ d																						
Willesden Jn. High Level	⊖ a	15 25	15 35	15 44	15 51	15 55	16 05	16 11	16 20	16 26	16 34	16 41	16 49	16 56	17 04	17 11	17 19	17 26	17 34	17 41	17 49	17 56	18 04
	d	15 26	15 36	15 45		15 56	16 06	16 12	16 20	16 27	16 35	16 42	16 50	16 57	17 05	17 12	17 20	17 27	17 35	17 42	17 50	17 57	18 05
Kensal Rise	d	15 28	15 38	15 47		15 58	16 08	16 14	16 22	16 29	16 37	16 44	16 52	16 59	17 07	17 14	17 22	17 29	17 37	17 44	17 52	17 59	18 07
Brondesbury Park	d	15 30	15 40	15 49		16 00	16 10	16 16	16 24	16 31	16 40	16 46	16 54	17 01	17 09	17 16	17 24	17 31	17 39	17 46	17 54	18 01	18 09
Brondesbury	d	15 32	15 42	15 51		16 02	16 12	16 18	16 26	16 33	16 41	16 48	16 56	17 03	17 11	17 18	17 26	17 33	17 41	17 48	17 56	18 03	18 11
West Hampstead	⊖ d	15 34	15 44	15 53		16 04	16 14	16 20	16 28	16 35	16 43	16 50	16 58	17 05	17 13	17 20	17 28	17 35	17 43	17 50	17 58	18 05	18 13
Finchley Road & Frognal	d	15 35	15 45	15 54		16 05	16 15	16 21	16 29	16 36	16 44	16 51	16 59	17 06	17 14	17 21	17 29	17 36	17 44	17 51	17 59	18 06	18 14
Hampstead Heath	d	15 38	15 48	15 57		16 08	16 18	16 24	16 32	16 39	16 47	16 54	17 02	17 09	17 17	17 24	17 32	17 39	17 47	17 54	18 02	18 09	18 17
Gospel Oak	d	15 40	15 50	16 00		16 10	16 20	16 26	16 34	16 41	16 49	16 56	17 04	17 11	17 19	17 26	17 34	17 41	17 49	17 56	18 04	18 11	18 19
Kentish Town West	d	15 42	15 52	16 02		16 12	16 22	16 28	16 36	16 43	16 51	16 58	17 06	17 13	17 21	17 28	17 36	17 43	17 51	17 58	18 06	18 13	18 21
Camden Road	d	15 46	15 56	16 05		16 16	16 26	16 32	16 40	16 47	16 55	17 02	17 10	17 17	17 25	17 32	17 40	17 47	17 55	18 02	18 10	18 17	18 25
Caledonian Rd & Barnsbury	d	15 49	15 59	16 08		16 19	16 29	16 35	16 43	16 50	16 58	17 05	17 13	17 20	17 28	17 35	17 43	17 50	17 58	18 05	18 13	18 20	18 28
Highbury & Islington	⊖ d	15 52	16 02	16 11		16 22	16 32	16 38	16 46	16 53	17 01	17 08	17 16	17 23	17 31	17 38	17 46	17 53	18 01	18 08	18 16	18 23	18 31
Canonbury	⊖ d	15 54	16 04	16 13		16 24	16 34	16 40	16 48	16 55	17 03	17 10	17 18	17 25	17 33	17 40	17 48	17 55	18 03	18 10	18 18	18 25	18 33
Dalston Kingsland	d	15 56	16 06	16 15		16 26	16 36	16 42	16 50	16 57	17 05	17 12	17 20	17 27	17 35	17 42	17 50	17 57	18 05	18 12	18 20	18 27	18 35
Hackney Central	d	15 58	16 08	16 17		16 28	16 38	16 44	16 52	16 59	17 07	17 14	17 22	17 29	17 37	17 44	17 52	17 59	18 07	18 14	18 22	18 29	18 37
Homerton	d	16 00	16 10	16 19		16 30	16 40	16 46	16 54	17 01	17 09	17 16	17 24	17 31	17 39	17 46	17 54	18 01	18 09	18 16	18 24	18 31	18 39
Hackney Wick	d	16 02	16 12	16 21		16 32	16 42	16 48	16 56	17 03	17 11	17 18	17 26	17 33	17 41	17 48	17 56	18 03	18 11	18 18	18 26	18 33	18 41
Stratford 7	⊖ a	16 09	16 19	16 27		16 39	16 48	16 54	17 03	17 10	17 18	17 24	17 33	17 38	17 50	17 54	18 05	18 08	18 20	18 24	18 35	18 39	18 50

		LO	LO	LO	LO	LO	LO	LO	LO	LO	LO	LO	LO	LO	LO	LO	LO	LO	LO	LO	LO	LO	LO
Richmond	⊖ d	17 53		18 06		18 22		18 36		18 54		19 09		19 26		19 41		19 56		20 11		20 26	
Kew Gardens	⊖ d	17 56		18 09		18 26		18 39		18 57		19 12		19 29		19 44		19 59		20 14		20 29	
Gunnersbury	⊖ d	17 59		18 12		18 29		18 42		19 00		19 15		19 32		19 47		20 02		20 17		20 32	
South Acton	d	18 02		18 15		18 31		18 45		19 03		19 18		19 35		19 50		20 05		20 20		20 35	
Acton Central	d	18 06		18 21		18 34		18 51		19 06		19 23		19 40		19 54		20 08		20 23		20 40	
Clapham Junction 10	d		17 59		18 14		18 29		18 44		18 59		19 15		19 30		19 45		20 00		20 15		20 30
Imperial Wharf	d		18 03		18 18		18 33		18 48		19 03		19 19		19 34		19 49		20 04		20 19		20 34
West Brompton	⊖ d		18 06		18 21		18 36		18 51		19 06		19 22		19 37		19 52		20 07		20 22		20 37
Kensington (Olympia)	⊖ d		18 09		18 24		18 39		18 54		19 09		19 25		19 40		19 55		20 10		20 25		20 40
Shepherd's Bush	⊖ d		18 11		18 26		18 41		18 56		19 11		19 27		19 42		19 57		20 12		20 27		20 42
Willesden Jn Low Level	⊖ d																						
Willesden Jn. High Level	⊖ a	18 11	18 19	18 26	18 34	18 39	18 49	18 56	19 04	19 11	19 19	19 28	19 35	19 45	19 51	19 59	20 05	20 15	20 21	20 28	20 35	20 45	20 51
	d	18 12	18 20	18 27	18 35	18 40	18 50	18 57	19 05	19 12	19 20	19 29	19 36	19 46		20 00	20 06	20 16		20 29	20 36	20 46	
Kensal Rise	d	18 14	18 22	18 29	18 37	18 43	18 52	18 59	19 07	19 14	19 22	19 31	19 38	19 48		20 02	20 08	20 18		20 31	20 38	20 48	
Brondesbury Park	d	18 16	18 24	18 31	18 39	18 45	18 54	19 01	19 09	19 16	19 24	19 33	19 40	19 50		20 04	20 10	20 20		20 33	20 40	20 50	
Brondesbury	d	18 18	18 26	18 33	18 41	18 46	18 56	19 03	19 11	19 18	19 26	19 35	19 42	19 52		20 06	20 12	20 22		20 35	20 42	20 52	
West Hampstead	⊖ d	18 20	18 28	18 35	18 43	18 48	18 58	19 05	19 13	19 20	19 28	19 37	19 44	19 54		20 08	20 14	20 24		20 37	20 44	20 54	
Finchley Road & Frognal	d	18 21	18 29	18 36	18 44	18 50	18 59	19 06	19 14	19 21	19 29	19 38	19 45	19 55		20 09	20 15	20 25		20 38	20 45	20 55	
Hampstead Heath	d	18 24	18 32	18 39	18 47	18 52	19 02	19 09	19 17	19 24	19 32	19 41	19 48	19 58		20 12	20 18	20 28		20 41	20 48	20 58	
Gospel Oak	d	18 26	18 34	18 41	18 49	18 55	19 04	19 11	19 19	19 26	19 34	19 43	19 50	20 00		20 14	20 20	20 30		20 43	20 50	21 00	
Kentish Town West	d	18 28	18 36	18 43	18 51	18 57	19 06	19 13	19 21	19 28	19 36	19 45	19 52	20 02		20 16	20 22	20 32		20 45	20 52	21 02	
Camden Road	d	18 32	18 40	18 47	18 55	19 00	19 10	19 17	19 25	19 32	19 40	19 49	19 56	20 06		20 20	20 26	20 36		20 49	20 56	21 06	
Caledonian Rd & Barnsbury	d	18 35	18 44	18 50	18 58	19 03	19 13	19 20	19 28	19 35	19 43	19 52	19 59	20 09		20 23	20 29	20 39		20 52	20 59	21 09	
Highbury & Islington	⊖ d	18 38	18 46	18 53	19 01	19 06	19 16	19 23	19 31	19 38	19 46	19 55	20 02	20 12		20 26	20 33	20 42		20 55	21 02	21 12	
Canonbury	⊖ d	18 40	18 48	18 55	19 03	19 08	19 18	19 25	19 33	19 40	19 48	19 57	20 04	20 14		20 28	20 35	20 44		20 57	21 04	21 14	
Dalston Kingsland	d	18 42	18 50	18 57	19 05	19 10	19 20	19 27	19 35	19 42	19 50	19 59	20 06	20 16		20 30	20 37	20 46		20 59	21 06	21 16	
Hackney Central	d	18 44	18 52	18 59	19 07	19 12	19 22	19 29	19 37	19 44	19 52	20 01	20 08	20 18		20 32	20 39	20 48		21 01	21 08	21 18	
Homerton	d	18 46	18 54	19 01	19 09	19 14	19 24	19 31	19 39	19 46	19 54	20 03	20 10	20 20		20 34	20 41	20 50		21 03	21 10	21 20	
Hackney Wick	d	18 48	18 56	19 03	19 11	19 17	19 26	19 33	19 41	19 48	19 56	20 05	20 12	20 22		20 36	20 43	20 52		21 05	21 12	21 22	
Stratford 7	⊖ a	18 54	19 05	19 08	19 20	19 24	19 33	19 40	19 48	19 55	20 03	20 11	20 19	20 28		20 42	20 51	20 58		21 11	21 19	21 28	

Richmond and Clapham Junction - Willesden Junction, West Hampstead, Highbury and Islington and Stratford

Network Diagram - see first Page of Table 59

Station		LO	LO	LO	LO	LO	LO	LO	LO	LO	LO	LO
Richmond ⊖	d	20 40		20 58		21 10		21 28		21 38		21 56
Kew Gardens ⊖	d	20 43		21 01		21 13		21 31		21 41		21 59
Gunnersbury ⊖	d	20 46		21 04		21 16		21 34		21 44		22 02
South Acton	d	20 49		21 07		21 19		21 37		21 47		22 05
Acton Central	d	20 52		21 10		21 23		21 40		21 50		22 10
Clapham Junction 10	d		20 45		21 00		21 15		21 30		21 45	
Imperial Wharf	d		20 49		21 04		21 19		21 34		21 49	
West Brompton ⊖	d		20 52		21 07		21 22		21 37		21 52	
Kensington (Olympia) ⊖	d		20 55		21 10		21 25		21 40		21 55	
Shepherd's Bush ⊖	d		20 57		21 12		21 27		21 42		21 57	
Willesden Jn Low Level ⊖	d											
Willesden Jn. High Level ⊖	a	20 57	21 05	21 16	21 21	21 28	21 35	21 45	21 51	21 55	22 05	22 15
	d	20 59	21 06	21 17		21 29	21 36	21 46		21 56	22 06	22 16
Kensal Rise	d	21 01	21 08	21 19		21 31	21 38	21 48		21 58	22 08	22 18
Brondesbury Park	d	21 03	21 10	21 21		21 33	21 40	21 50		22 00	22 10	22 20
Brondesbury	d	21 05	21 12	21 23		21 35	21 42	21 52		22 02	22 12	22 22
West Hampstead ⊖	d	21 07	21 14	21 25		21 37	21 44	21 54		22 04	22 14	22 24
Finchley Road & Frognal	d	21 08	21 15	21 26		21 38	21 45	21 55		22 05	22 15	22 25
Hampstead Heath	d	21 11	21 18	21 29		21 41	21 48	21 58		22 08	22 18	22 28
Gospel Oak	d	21 13	21 20	21 30		21 43	21 50	22 00		22 10	22 20	22 30
Kentish Town West	d	21 15	21 22	21 32		21 45	21 52	22 02		22 12	22 22	22 32
Camden Road	d	21 19	21 26	21 36		21 49	21 56	22 06		22 16	22 26	22 36
Caledonian Rd & Barnsbury	d	21 22	21 29	21 39		21 52	21 59	22 09		22 19	22 29	22 39
Highbury & Islington ⊖	d	21 25	21 32	21 42		21 55	22 02	22 12		22 22	22 32	22 42
Canonbury ⊖	d	21 27	21 34	21 44		21 57	22 04	22 14		22 24	22 34	22 44
Dalston Kingsland	d	21 29	21 36	21 46		21 59	22 06	22 16		22 26	22 36	22 46
Hackney Central	d	21 31	21 38	21 48		22 01	22 08	22 18		22 28	22 38	22 48
Homerton	d	21 33	21 40	21 50		22 03	22 10	22 20		22 30	22 40	22 50
Hackney Wick	d	21 35	21 42	21 52		22 05	22 12	22 22		22 32	22 42	22 52
Stratford 7 ⊖	a	21 41	21 49	21 59		22 13	22 19	22 29		22 39	22 49	22 58

Station		LO	LO	LO	LO	LO	LO	LO	LO	LO
Richmond ⊖	d			22 28			23 00		23 28	
Kew Gardens ⊖	d			22 31			23 03		23 31	
Gunnersbury ⊖	d			22 34			23 06		23 34	
South Acton	d			22 37			23 09		23 37	
Acton Central	d			22 40			23 12		23 40	
Clapham Junction 10	d	22 00	22 15		22 30	22 45		23 00		23 30
Imperial Wharf	d	22 04	22 19		22 34	22 49		23 04		23 34
West Brompton ⊖	d	22 07	22 22		22 37	22 52		23 07		23 37
Kensington (Olympia) ⊖	d	22 10	22 25		22 40	22 55		23 10		23 40
Shepherd's Bush ⊖	d	22 12	22 27		22 42	22 57		23 12		23 42
Willesden Jn Low Level ⊖	d									
Willesden Jn. High Level ⊖	a	22 21	22 36	22 45	22 51	23 06	23 17	23 23	23 45	23 51
	d			22 46			23 18			
Kensal Rise	d			22 48			23 20			
Brondesbury Park	d			22 50			23 22			
Brondesbury	d			22 52			23 24			
West Hampstead ⊖	d			22 54			23 26			
Finchley Road & Frognal	d			22 55			23 27			
Hampstead Heath	d			22 58			23 30			
Gospel Oak	d			23 00			23 32			
Kentish Town West	d			23 02			23 34			
Camden Road	d			23 06			23 38			
Caledonian Rd & Barnsbury	d			23 09			23 41			
Highbury & Islington ⊖	d			23 12			23 44			
Canonbury ⊖	d			23 14			23 46			
Dalston Kingsland	d			23 16			23 48			
Hackney Central	d			23 18			23 50			
Homerton	d			23 20			23 52			
Hackney Wick	d			23 22			23 54			
Stratford 7 ⊖	a			23 29			00 04			

Mondays to Fridays
29 August to 7 September

Station		LO A	LO B	LO A	LO A	LO A	LO C	LO D	LO C	LO D	LO A	LO A
Richmond ⊖	d	22p55	23p00		23p10		23p25	23p25			23p40	
Kew Gardens ⊖	d	22p58	23p03		23p13		23p28	23p28			23p43	
Gunnersbury ⊖	d	23p01	23p06		23p16		23p31	23p31			23p46	
South Acton	d	23p04	23p09		23p19		23p34	23p34			23p49	
Acton Central	d	23p07	23p12		23p22		23p37	23p37			23p52	
Clapham Junction 10	d			22p59		23p14			23p29	23p29		23p44
Imperial Wharf	d			23p03		23p18			23p33	23p33		23p48
West Brompton ⊖	d			23p06		23p21			23p36	23p36		23p51
Kensington (Olympia) ⊖	d			23p10		23p25			23p40	23p40		23p55
Shepherd's Bush ⊖	d			23p12		23p27			23p42	23p42		23p57
Willesden Jn Low Level ⊖	d											
Willesden Jn. High Level ⊖	a	23p12	23p17	23p20	23p27	23p35	23p42	23p42	23p50	23p50	23p57	00 05
	d	23p14	23p18	23p21	23p29	23p36	23p43	23p44	23p51	23p51	23p59	00 06
Kensal Rise	d	23p16	23p20	23p23	23p31	23p38	23p45	23p46	23p53	23p53	00 01	00 08
Brondesbury Park	d	23p18	23p22	23p25	23p33	23p40	23p47	23p48	23p55	23p55	00 03	00 10
Brondesbury	d	23p20	23p24	23p27	23p35	23p42	23p49	23p50	23p57	23p57	00 05	00 12
West Hampstead ⊖	d	23p22	23p26	23p29	23p37	23p44	23p51	23p52	23p59	23p59	00 07	00 14
Finchley Road & Frognal	d	23p24	23p27	23p31	23p39	23p46	23p53	23p54	00 01	00 01	00 09	00 16
Hampstead Heath	d	23p26	23p30	23p33	23p41	23p48	23p55	23p56	00 03	00 03	00 11	00 18
Gospel Oak	d	23p30	23p32	23p37	23p45	23p52	00 01	00 01	00 07	00 07	00 15	00 22
Kentish Town West	d	23p32	23p34	23p39	23p47	23p54	00 02	00 02	00 09	00 09	00 17	00 24
Camden Road	d	23p36	23p38	23p43	23p51	23p58	00 06	00 06	00 12	00 13	00 21	00 28
Caledonian Rd & Barnsbury	d	23p39	23p41	23p46	23p54	00 01	00 09	00 09	00 15	00 16	00 24	00 31
Highbury & Islington ⊖	d	23p41	23p44	23p48	23p56	00 03	00 11	00 11	00 18	00 18	00 26	00 33
Canonbury ⊖	d	23p43	23p46	23p50	23p59	00 05	00 13	00 13	00 20	00 20	00 28	00 35
Dalston Kingsland	d	23p46	23p48	23p53	00 02	00 08	00 16	00 16	00 22	00 23	00 31	00 38
Hackney Central	d	23p48	23p50	23p55	00 03	00 10	00 18	00 18	00 24	00 25	00 33	00 40
Homerton	d	23p50	23p52	23p57	00 05	00 12	00 20	00 20	00 26	00 27	00 35	00 42
Hackney Wick	d	23p52	23p54	23p59	00 07	00 14	00 22	00 22	00 29	00 29	00 37	00 44
Stratford 7 ⊖	a	00 04	00 04	00 09	00 19	00 24	00 34	00 34	00 40	00 39	00 49	00 54

Station		LO A	LO A	LO D	LO C	LO	LO	LO	LO	LO	LO	LO
Richmond ⊖	d	23p55									05 54	
Kew Gardens ⊖	d	23p59									05 57	
Gunnersbury ⊖	d	00 01									06 00	
South Acton	d	00 04									06 03	
Acton Central	d	00 07									06 06	
Clapham Junction 10	d		23p59	00 12	00 17	05 47						
Imperial Wharf	d		00 03	00 16	00 23	05 51						
West Brompton ⊖	d		00 06	00 19	00 26	05 54						
Kensington (Olympia) ⊖	d		00 10	00 22	00 29	05 58						
Shepherd's Bush ⊖	d		00 12	00 24	00 31	06 00						
Willesden Jn Low Level ⊖	d								05 58			
Willesden Jn. High Level ⊖	a	00 12	00 20	00 37	00 44	06 12					06 11	
	d	00 14	00 21								06 12	
Kensal Rise	d	00 16	00 23						06 02		06 14	
Brondesbury Park	d	00 18	00 25						06 04		06 16	
Brondesbury	d	00 20	00 27						06 06		06 18	
West Hampstead ⊖	d	00 22	00 29						06 08		06 20	
Finchley Road & Frognal	d	00 24	00 31						06 09		06 21	
Hampstead Heath	d	00 26	00 33						06 12		06 24	
Gospel Oak	d	00 30	00 37						06 14		06 26	
Kentish Town West	d	00 32	00 39						06 16		06 28	
Camden Road	d	00 36	00 43				06 11	06 15	06 20	06 28	06 32	06 40
Caledonian Rd & Barnsbury	d	00 39	00 46				06 14	06 18	06 23	06 31	06 35	06 43
Highbury & Islington ⊖	d	00 41	00 48				06 16	06 21	06 26	06 34	06 38	06 47
Canonbury ⊖	d	00 43	00 50				06 18	06 23	06 28	06 36	06 40	06 48
Dalston Kingsland	d	00 46	00 53				06 20	06 25	06 30	06 38	06 42	06 50
Hackney Central	d	00 48	00 55				06 22	06 27	06 32	06 40	06 44	06 52
Homerton	d	00 50	00 57				06 24	06 29	06 34	06 42	06 46	06 54
Hackney Wick	d	00 52	00 59				06 26	06 31	06 36	06 44	06 48	06 56
Stratford 7 ⊖	a	01 04	01 09				06 37	06 41	06 48	06 54	07 00	07 08

A not 29 August
B 29 August
C not 29 August, 3 September
D 3 September

Richmond and Clapham Junction - Willesden Junction, West Hampstead, Highbury and Islington and Stratford

Network Diagram - see first Page of Table 59

Station		LO	LO	LO	LO	LO	LO	LO	LO	LO	LO	LO
Richmond ⊖	d	06 10			06 25		06 42			06 54		07 11
Kew Gardens ⊖	d	06 13			06 28		06 45			06 57		07 14
Gunnersbury ⊖	d	06 16			06 31		06 48			07 00		07 18
South Acton	d	06 19			06 34		06 51			07 03		07 20
Acton Central	d	06 22			06 37		06 54			07 06		07 24
Clapham Junction 10	d		06 14			06 29		06 44			06 59	
Imperial Wharf	d		06 18			06 33		06 48			07 03	
West Brompton ⊖	d		06 21			06 36		06 51			07 06	
Kensington (Olympia) ⊖	d		06 25			06 40		06 55			07 10	
Shepherd's Bush ⊖	d		06 27			06 42		06 57			07 12	
Willesden Jn Low Level ⊖	d											
Willesden Jn. High Level ⊖	a	06 27	06 35		06 42	06 50	06 57	07 05		07 12	07 20	07 29
	d	06 29	06 36		06 44	06 51	06 59	07 06		07 14	07 21	07 30
Kensal Rise	d	06 31	06 38		06 46	06 53	07 01	07 08		07 16	07 23	07 32
Brondesbury Park	d	06 33	06 40		06 48	06 55	07 03	07 10		07 18	07 25	07 33
Brondesbury	d	06 35	06 42		06 50	06 57	07 05	07 12		07 20	07 27	07 35
West Hampstead ⊖	d	06 37	06 44		06 52	06 59	07 07	07 14		07 22	07 29	07 37
Finchley Road & Frognal	d	06 39	06 46		06 54	07 01	07 09	07 16		07 24	07 31	07 39
Hampstead Heath	d	06 41	06 48		06 56	07 03	07 11	07 18		07 26	07 33	07 41
Gospel Oak	d	06 45	06 52		07 00	07 07	07 15	07 22		07 30	07 37	07 45
Kentish Town West	d	06 47	06 54		07 02	07 09	07 17	07 24		07 32	07 39	07 47
Camden Road	d	06 51	06 58	07 03	07 06	07 13	07 21	07 28	07 33	07 36	07 43	07 51
Caledonian Rd & Barnsbury	d	06 54	07 01	07 06	07 09	07 16	07 24	07 31	07 36	07 39	07 46	07 54
Highbury & Islington ⊖	d	06 56	07 03	07 08	07 11	07 18	07 26	07 33	07 38	07 41	07 48	07 56
Canonbury ⊖	d	06 58	07 05	07 10	07 13	07 20	07 28	07 35	07 40	07 43	07 50	07 58
Dalston Kingsland	d	07 01	07 08	07 13	07 16	07 23	07 31	07 38	07 43	07 46	07 53	08 01
Hackney Central	d	07 03	07 10	07 15	07 18	07 25	07 33	07 40	07 45	07 48	07 55	08 03
Homerton	d	07 05	07 12	07 17	07 20	07 27	07 35	07 42	07 47	07 50	07 57	08 05
Hackney Wick	d	07 07	07 14	07 19	07 22	07 29	07 37	07 44	07 49	07 52	07 59	08 07
Stratford 7 ⊖	a	07 19	07 24	07 30	07 34	07 39	07 49	07 54	08 00	08 04	08 09	08 19

Station		LO	LO	LO	LO	LO	LO	LO	LO	LO	LO	LO
Richmond ⊖	d			07 25		07 41			07 55		08 10	
Kew Gardens ⊖	d			07 28		07 44			07 58		08 13	
Gunnersbury ⊖	d			07 31		07 48			08 01		08 16	
South Acton	d			07 34		07 50			08 03		08 19	
Acton Central	d			07 37		07 54			08 06		08 22	
Clapham Junction 10	d	07 14			07 29		07 44			07 59		08 14
Imperial Wharf	d	07 18			07 33		07 48			08 03		08 18
West Brompton ⊖	d	07 21			07 36		07 51			08 06		08 21
Kensington (Olympia) ⊖	d	07 25			07 40		07 55			08 10		08 25
Shepherd's Bush ⊖	d	07 27			07 42		07 57			08 12		08 27
Willesden Jn Low Level ⊖	d											
Willesden Jn. High Level ⊖	a	07 35		07 42	07 50	07 57	08 05		08 11	08 20	08 27	08 35
	d	07 36		07 44	07 51	07 59	08 06		08 14	08 21	08 29	08 36
Kensal Rise	d	07 38		07 46	07 53	08 01	08 08		08 16	08 23	08 31	08 38
Brondesbury Park	d	07 40		07 48	07 55	08 03	08 10		08 18	08 25	08 33	08 40
Brondesbury	d	07 42		07 50	07 57	08 05	08 12		08 20	08 27	08 35	08 42
West Hampstead ⊖	d	07 44		07 52	07 59	08 07	08 14		08 22	08 29	08 37	08 44
Finchley Road & Frognal	d	07 46		07 54	08 01	08 09	08 16		08 24	08 31	08 39	08 46
Hampstead Heath	d	07 48		07 56	08 03	08 11	08 18		08 26	08 33	08 41	08 48
Gospel Oak	d	07 52		08 00	08 07	08 15	08 22		08 30	08 37	08 45	08 52
Kentish Town West	d	07 54		08 02	08 09	08 17	08 24		08 32	08 39	08 47	08 54
Camden Road	d	07 58	08 03	08 06	08 13	08 21	08 28	08 33	08 36	08 43	08 51	08 58
Caledonian Rd & Barnsbury	d	08 01	08 06	08 09	08 16	08 24	08 31	08 36	08 39	08 46	08 54	09 01
Highbury & Islington ⊖	d	08 03	08 08	08 11	08 18	08 26	08 33	08 38	08 41	08 48	08 56	09 03
Canonbury ⊖	d	08 05	08 10	08 13	08 20	08 28	08 35	08 40	08 43	08 50	08 58	09 05
Dalston Kingsland	d	08 08	08 13	08 16	08 23	08 31	08 38	08 43	08 46	08 53	09 01	09 08
Hackney Central	d	08 10	08 15	08 18	08 25	08 33	08 40	08 45	08 48	08 55	09 03	09 10
Homerton	d	08 12	08 17	08 20	08 27	08 35	08 42	08 47	08 50	08 57	09 05	09 12
Hackney Wick	d	08 14	08 19	08 22	08 29	08 37	08 44	08 49	08 52	08 59	09 07	09 14
Stratford 7 ⊖	a	08 24	08 30	08 34	08 39	08 49	08 54	09 00	09 04	09 09	09 19	09 24

Station		LO	LO	LO	LO	LO	LO	LO	LO	LO	LO	LO
Richmond ⊖	d		08 25		08 41		08 55		09 11		09 25	
Kew Gardens ⊖	d		08 28		08 44		08 58		09 14		09 28	
Gunnersbury ⊖	d		08 31		08 48		09 01		09 17		09 31	
South Acton	d		08 34		08 50		09 03		09 20		09 33	
Acton Central	d		08 37		08 54		09 07		09 24		09 37	
Clapham Junction 10	d			08 29		08 44		08 59		09 14		09 29
Imperial Wharf	d			08 33		08 48		09 03		09 18		09 33
West Brompton ⊖	d			08 36		08 51		09 06		09 21		09 36
Kensington (Olympia) ⊖	d			08 40		08 55		09 10		09 25		09 40
Shepherd's Bush ⊖	d			08 42		08 57		09 12		09 27		09 42
Willesden Jn Low Level ⊖	d											
Willesden Jn. High Level ⊖	a		08 42	08 50	08 57	09 05	09 12	09 20	09 27	09 35	09 42	09 50
	d		08 44	08 51	08 59	09 06	09 14	09 21	09 29	09 36	09 44	09 51
Kensal Rise	d		08 46	08 53	09 01	09 08	09 16	09 23	09 31	09 38	09 46	09 53
Brondesbury Park	d		08 48	08 55	09 03	09 10	09 18	09 25	09 33	09 40	09 48	09 55
Brondesbury	d		08 50	08 57	09 05	09 12	09 20	09 27	09 35	09 42	09 50	09 57
West Hampstead ⊖	d		08 52	08 59	09 07	09 14	09 22	09 29	09 37	09 44	09 52	09 59
Finchley Road & Frognal	d		08 54	09 01	09 09	09 16	09 24	09 31	09 39	09 46	09 54	10 01
Hampstead Heath	d		08 56	09 03	09 11	09 18	09 26	09 33	09 41	09 48	09 56	10 03
Gospel Oak	d		09 00	09 07	09 15	09 22	09 30	09 37	09 45	09 52	10 00	10 07
Kentish Town West	d		09 02	09 09	09 17	09 24	09 32	09 39	09 47	09 54	10 02	10 09
Camden Road	d	09 03	09 06	09 13	09 21	09 28	09 36	09 43	09 51	09 58	10 06	10 13
Caledonian Rd & Barnsbury	d	09 06	09 09	09 16	09 24	09 31	09 39	09 46	09 54	10 01	10 09	10 16
Highbury & Islington ⊖	d	09 08	09 11	09 18	09 26	09 33	09 41	09 48	09 56	10 03	10 11	10 18
Canonbury ⊖	d	09 10	09 13	09 20	09 28	09 35	09 43	09 50	09 58	10 05	10 13	10 20
Dalston Kingsland	d	09 13	09 16	09 23	09 31	09 38	09 46	09 53	10 01	10 08	10 16	10 23
Hackney Central	d	09 15	09 18	09 25	09 33	09 40	09 48	09 55	10 03	10 10	10 18	10 25
Homerton	d	09 17	09 20	09 27	09 35	09 42	09 50	09 57	10 05	10 12	10 20	10 27
Hackney Wick	d	09 19	09 22	09 29	09 37	09 44	09 52	09 59	10 07	10 14	10 22	10 29
Stratford 7 ⊖	a	09 30	09 34	09 39	09 49	09 54	10 04	10 09	10 19	10 24	10 34	10 39

Station		LO	LO	LO	LO	LO	LO	LO	LO	LO	LO	LO
Richmond ⊖	d	09 42		09 55		10 10		10 25		10 41		10 55
Kew Gardens ⊖	d	09 45		09 58		10 13		10 28		10 44		10 58
Gunnersbury ⊖	d	09 48		10 01		10 16		10 31		10 47		11 01
South Acton	d	09 51		10 04		10 19		10 34		10 50		11 04
Acton Central	d	09 56		10 07		10 22		10 37		10 53		11 07
Clapham Junction 10	d		09 44		09 59		10 14		10 29		10 44	
Imperial Wharf	d		09 48		10 03		10 18		10 36		10 48	
West Brompton ⊖	d		09 51		10 06		10 21		10 39		10 51	
Kensington (Olympia) ⊖	d		09 55		10 10		10 25		10 42		10 55	
Shepherd's Bush ⊖	d		09 57		10 12		10 27		10 45		10 57	
Willesden Jn Low Level ⊖	d											
Willesden Jn. High Level ⊖	a	09 59	10 05	10 12	10 20	10 27	10 35	10 42	10 52	10 55	11 06	11 12
	d	10 00	10 07	10 14	10 21	10 29	10 36	10 44	10 53	10 57	11 07	11 14
Kensal Rise	d	10 02	10 09	10 16	10 23	10 31	10 38	10 46	10 56	11 01	11 09	11 16
Brondesbury Park	d	10 04	10 11	10 18	10 25	10 33	10 40	10 48	10 58	11 03	11 11	11 18
Brondesbury	d	10 06	10 13	10 20	10 27	10 35	10 42	10 50	10 59	11 05	11 13	11 20
West Hampstead ⊖	d	10 08	10 15	10 22	10 29	10 37	10 44	10 52	11 02	11 07	11 15	11 22
Finchley Road & Frognal	d	10 10	10 17	10 24	10 31	10 39	10 46	10 54	11 03	11 09	11 17	11 24
Hampstead Heath	d	10 12	10 19	10 26	10 33	10 41	10 48	10 56	11 06	11 11	11 19	11 26
Gospel Oak	d	10 16	10 23	10 30	10 37	10 45	10 52	11 00	11 09	11 16	11 23	11 30
Kentish Town West	d	10 18	10 25	10 32	10 39	10 47	10 54	11 02	11 11	11 18	11 25	11 32
Camden Road	d	10 22	10 29	10 36	10 43	10 51	10 58	11 06	11 15	11 21	11 29	11 36
Caledonian Rd & Barnsbury	d	10 25	10 32	10 39	10 46	10 54	11 01	11 09	11 18	11 24	11 32	11 39
Highbury & Islington ⊖	d	10 28	10 35	10 41	10 48	10 56	11 03	11 11	11 20	11 27	11 34	11 41
Canonbury ⊖	d	10 30	10 37	10 43	10 50	10 58	11 05	11 13	11 22	11 29	11 36	11 43
Dalston Kingsland	d	10 32	10 39	10 46	10 53	11 01	11 08	11 16	11 25	11 31	11 39	11 46
Hackney Central	d	10 34	10 41	10 48	10 55	11 03	11 10	11 18	11 27	11 33	11 41	11 48
Homerton	d	10 36	10 43	10 50	10 57	11 05	11 12	11 20	11 29	11 35	11 43	11 50
Hackney Wick	d	10 38	10 46	10 52	10 59	11 07	11 14	11 22	11 31	11 38	11 45	11 52
Stratford 7 ⊖	a	10 50	10 56	11 04	11 09	11 20	11 24	11 34	11 41	11 49	11 56	12 04

Richmond and Clapham Junction - Willesden Junction, West Hampstead, Highbury and Islington and Stratford

Network Diagram - see first Page of Table 59

		LO	LO	LO	LO	LO	LO	LO	LO	LO	LO	LO
Richmond	⊖ d		11 10		11 25		11 40		11 55		12 10	
Kew Gardens	⊖ d		11 13		11 28		11 43		11 58		12 13	
Gunnersbury	⊖ d		11 16		11 31		11 46		12 01		12 16	
South Acton	d		11 19		11 34		11 49		12 04		12 19	
Acton Central	d		11 22		11 37		11 52		12 07		12 22	
Clapham Junction 10	d	10 59		11 14		11 29		11 44		11 59		12 14
Imperial Wharf	d	11 03		11 18		11 33		11 48		12 03		12 18
West Brompton	⊖ d	11 06		11 21		11 36		11 51		12 06		12 21
Kensington (Olympia)	⊖ d	11 10		11 25		11 40		11 55		12 10		12 25
Shepherd's Bush	⊖ d	11 12		11 27		11 42		11 57		12 12		12 27
Willesden Jn Low Level	⊖ d											
Willesden Jn. High Level	⊖ a	11 20	11 27	11 35	11 42	11 50	11 57	12 05	12 12	12 20	12 28	12 35
	d	11 21	11 29	11 36	11 44	11 51	11 59	12 06	12 14	12 21	12 30	12 36
Kensal Rise	d	11 23	11 31	11 38	11 46	11 53	12 01	12 08	12 16	12 23	12 32	12 38
Brondesbury Park	d	11 25	11 33	11 40	11 48	11 55	12 03	12 10	12 18	12 25	12 34	12 40
Brondesbury	d	11 27	11 35	11 42	11 50	11 57	12 05	12 12	12 20	12 27	12 36	12 42
West Hampstead	⊖ d	11 29	11 37	11 44	11 52	11 59	12 07	12 14	12 22	12 29	12 38	12 44
Finchley Road & Frognal	d	11 31	11 39	11 46	11 54	12 01	12 09	12 16	12 24	12 31	12 40	12 46
Hampstead Heath	d	11 33	11 41	11 48	11 56	12 03	12 11	12 18	12 26	12 33	12 42	12 48
Gospel Oak	d	11 37	11 45	11 52	12 00	12 07	12 16	12 22	12 30	12 37	12 46	12 52
Kentish Town West	d	11 39	11 47	11 54	12 02	12 09	12 18	12 24	12 32	12 39	12 48	12 54
Camden Road	d	11 43	11 51	11 58	12 06	12 13	12 22	12 28	12 36	12 43	12 52	12 58
Caledonian Rd & Barnsbury	d	11 46	11 54	12 01	12 09	12 16	12 25	12 31	12 39	12 46	12 55	13 01
Highbury & Islington	⊖ d	11 48	11 56	12 03	12 11	12 18	12 27	12 33	12 41	12 48	12 57	13 03
Canonbury	⊖ d	11 50	11 58	12 05	12 13	12 20	12 29	12 35	12 43	12 50	12 59	13 05
Dalston Kingsland	d	11 53	12 01	12 08	12 16	12 23	12 32	12 38	12 46	12 53	13 02	13 08
Hackney Central	d	11 55	12 03	12 10	12 18	12 25	12 34	12 40	12 48	12 55	13 04	13 10
Homerton	d	11 57	12 05	12 12	12 20	12 27	12 36	12 42	12 50	12 57	13 06	13 12
Hackney Wick	d	11 59	12 07	12 14	12 22	12 29	12 38	12 44	12 52	12 59	13 08	13 14
Stratford 7	⊖ a	12 10	12 19	12 24	12 34	12 40	12 49	12 54	13 04	13 09	13 19	13 24

		LO	LO	LO	LO	LO	LO	LO	LO	LO	LO	LO
Richmond	⊖ d	12 25		12 40		12 55		13 10		13 25		13 41
Kew Gardens	⊖ d	12 28		12 43		12 58		13 13		13 28		13 44
Gunnersbury	⊖ d	12 31		12 46		13 01		13 16		13 31		13 47
South Acton	d	12 34		12 49		13 04		13 19		13 34		13 50
Acton Central	d	12 37		12 52		13 07		13 22		13 37		13 52
Clapham Junction 10	d		12 29		12 44		12 59		13 14		13 29	
Imperial Wharf	d		12 35		12 48		13 03		13 18		13 36	
West Brompton	⊖ d		12 38		12 51		13 06		13 21		13 39	
Kensington (Olympia)	⊖ d		12 41		12 55		13 10		13 25		13 42	
Shepherd's Bush	⊖ d		12 44		12 57		13 12		13 27		13 45	
Willesden Jn Low Level	⊖ d											
Willesden Jn. High Level	⊖ a	12 42	12 51	12 55	13 05	13 12	13 20	13 27	13 35	13 42	13 52	13 57
	d	12 44	12 52	12 59	13 06	13 14	13 21	13 29	13 36	13 44	13 53	13 59
Kensal Rise	d	12 46	12 55	13 01	13 08	13 16	13 23	13 31	13 38	13 46	13 56	14 01
Brondesbury Park	d	12 48	12 57	13 03	13 10	13 18	13 25	13 33	13 40	13 48	13 58	14 03
Brondesbury	d	12 50	12 58	13 05	13 12	13 20	13 27	13 35	13 42	13 50	13 59	14 05
West Hampstead	⊖ d	12 52	13 01	13 07	13 14	13 22	13 29	13 37	13 44	13 52	14 02	14 07
Finchley Road & Frognal	d	12 54	13 02	13 09	13 16	13 24	13 31	13 39	13 46	13 54	14 03	14 09
Hampstead Heath	d	12 56	13 05	13 11	13 18	13 26	13 33	13 41	13 48	13 56	14 06	14 11
Gospel Oak	d	13 00	13 09	13 15	13 22	13 30	13 37	13 45	13 52	14 00	14 10	14 15
Kentish Town West	d	13 02	13 11	13 17	13 24	13 32	13 39	13 47	13 54	14 02	14 12	14 17
Camden Road	d	13 06	13 14	13 21	13 28	13 36	13 43	13 51	13 58	14 06	14 15	14 21
Caledonian Rd & Barnsbury	d	13 09	13 17	13 24	13 31	13 39	13 46	13 54	14 01	14 09	14 18	14 24
Highbury & Islington	⊖ d	13 11	13 20	13 26	13 33	13 41	13 48	13 57	14 03	14 11	14 21	14 26
Canonbury	⊖ d	13 13	13 22	13 28	13 35	13 43	13 50	13 59	14 05	14 13	14 23	14 28
Dalston Kingsland	d	13 16	13 24	13 31	13 38	13 46	13 53	14 01	14 08	14 16	14 25	14 31
Hackney Central	d	13 18	13 26	13 33	13 40	13 48	13 55	14 03	14 10	14 18	14 27	14 33
Homerton	d	13 20	13 28	13 35	13 42	13 50	13 57	14 05	14 12	14 20	14 29	14 35
Hackney Wick	d	13 22	13 31	13 37	13 44	13 52	13 59	14 08	14 14	14 22	14 32	14 37
Stratford 7	⊖ a	13 34	13 41	13 49	13 54	14 04	14 10	14 19	14 24	14 34	14 41	14 49

		LO	LO	LO	LO	LO	LO	LO	LO	LO	LO	LO
Richmond	⊖ d		13 55		14 11		14 25		14 40		14 55	
Kew Gardens	⊖ d		13 58		14 14		14 28		14 43		14 58	
Gunnersbury	⊖ d		14 01		14 17		14 31		14 46		15 01	
South Acton	d		14 04		14 20		14 34		14 49		15 04	
Acton Central	d		14 07		14 22		14 37		14 52		15 07	
Clapham Junction 10	d	13 44		13 59		14 14		14 29		14 44		14 59
Imperial Wharf	d	13 48		14 03		14 18		14 33		14 55		15 03
West Brompton	⊖ d	13 51		14 06		14 21		14 36		14 58		15 06
Kensington (Olympia)	⊖ d	13 55		14 10		14 25		14 40		15 01		15 10
Shepherd's Bush	⊖ d	13 57		14 12		14 27		14 42		15 04		15 12
Willesden Jn Low Level	⊖ d											
Willesden Jn. High Level	⊖ a	14 05	14 12	14 20	14 28	14 35	14 42	14 50	14 57	15 11	15 13	15 20
	d	14 06	14 14	14 21	14 29	14 36	14 44	14 51	14 59	15 11	15 14	15 21
Kensal Rise	d	14 08	14 16	14 23	14 32	14 38	14 46	14 53	15 01	15 14	15 16	15 23
Brondesbury Park	d	14 10	14 18	14 25	14 34	14 40	14 48	14 55	15 03	15 16	15 18	15 25
Brondesbury	d	14 12	14 20	14 27	14 35	14 42	14 50	14 57	15 05	15 17	15 20	15 27
West Hampstead	⊖ d	14 14	14 22	14 29	14 38	14 44	14 52	14 59	15 07	15 20	15 22	15 29
Finchley Road & Frognal	d	14 16	14 24	14 31	14 39	14 46	14 54	15 01	15 09	15 21	15 24	15 31
Hampstead Heath	d	14 18	14 26	14 33	14 42	14 48	14 56	15 03	15 11	15 24	15 26	15 33
Gospel Oak	d	14 22	14 30	14 37	14 45	14 52	15 00	15 07	15 15	15 28	15 30	15 37
Kentish Town West	d	14 24	14 32	14 39	14 47	14 54	15 02	15 09	15 17	15 30	15 32	15 39
Camden Road	d	14 28	14 36	14 43	14 51	14 58	15 06	15 13	15 21	15 33	15 36	15 43
Caledonian Rd & Barnsbury	d	14 31	14 39	14 46	14 54	15 01	15 09	15 16	15 24	15 36	15 39	15 46
Highbury & Islington	⊖ d	14 33	14 41	14 48	14 56	15 03	15 11	15 18	15 26	15 39	15 41	15 48
Canonbury	⊖ d	14 35	14 43	14 50	14 58	15 05	15 13	15 20	15 28	15 41	15 43	15 50
Dalston Kingsland	d	14 38	14 46	14 53	15 01	15 08	15 16	15 23	15 31	15 43	15 46	15 53
Hackney Central	d	14 40	14 48	14 55	15 03	15 10	15 18	15 25	15 33	15 45	15 48	15 55
Homerton	d	14 42	14 50	14 57	15 05	15 12	15 20	15 27	15 35	15 47	15 50	15 57
Hackney Wick	d	14 44	14 52	14 59	15 07	15 14	15 22	15 29	15 37	15 50	15 52	15 59
Stratford 7	⊖ a	14 54	15 04	15 09	15 19	15 24	15 36	15 39	15 49	15 59	16 04	16 09

		LO	LO	LO	LO	LO	LO	LO	LO	LO	LO	LO
Richmond	⊖ d		15 10		15 25			15 40		15 56		
Kew Gardens	⊖ d		15 13		15 28			15 43		15 59		
Gunnersbury	⊖ d		15 16		15 31			15 46		16 02		
South Acton	d		15 19		15 34			15 49		16 05		
Acton Central	d		15 22		15 37			15 52		16 08		
Clapham Junction 10	d			15 14		15 29			15 44		15 59	
Imperial Wharf	d			15 18		15 33			15 48		16 03	
West Brompton	⊖ d			15 21		15 36			15 51		16 06	
Kensington (Olympia)	⊖ d			15 25		15 40			15 55		16 10	
Shepherd's Bush	⊖ d			15 27		15 42			15 57		16 12	
Willesden Jn Low Level	⊖ d											
Willesden Jn. High Level	⊖ a		15 27	15 35	15 42	15 50		15 57	16 05	16 13	16 20	
	d		15 29	15 36	15 44	15 51		15 59	16 06	16 14	16 21	
Kensal Rise	d		15 31	15 38	15 46	15 53		16 01	16 08	16 16	16 23	
Brondesbury Park	d		15 33	15 40	15 48	15 55		16 03	16 10	16 18	16 25	
Brondesbury	d		15 35	15 42	15 50	15 57		16 05	16 12	16 20	16 27	
West Hampstead	⊖ d		15 37	15 44	15 53	15 59		16 07	16 14	16 22	16 29	
Finchley Road & Frognal	d		15 39	15 46	15 55	16 01		16 09	16 16	16 24	16 31	
Hampstead Heath	d		15 41	15 48	15 57	16 03		16 11	16 18	16 26	16 33	
Gospel Oak	d		15 45	15 52	16 01	16 07		16 15	16 22	16 30	16 37	
Kentish Town West	d		15 47	15 54	16 03	16 09		16 17	16 24	16 32	16 39	
Camden Road	d	15 49	15 51	15 58	16 07	16 13	16 19	16 21	16 28	16 36	16 43	16 49
Caledonian Rd & Barnsbury	d	15 52	15 54	16 01	16 10	16 16	16 22	16 24	16 31	16 39	16 46	16 52
Highbury & Islington	⊖ d	15 54	15 57	16 03	16 12	16 18	16 24	16 26	16 33	16 41	16 48	16 54
Canonbury	⊖ d	15 56	15 59	16 05	16 14	16 20	16 26	16 28	16 35	16 43	16 50	16 56
Dalston Kingsland	d	15 59	16 01	16 08	16 17	16 23	16 29	16 31	16 38	16 46	16 53	16 59
Hackney Central	d	16 01	16 03	16 10	16 19	16 25	16 31	16 33	16 40	16 48	16 55	17 01
Homerton	d	16 03	16 05	16 12	16 21	16 27	16 33	16 35	16 42	16 50	16 57	17 03
Hackney Wick	d	16 05	16 08	16 14	16 23	16 29	16 35	16 37	16 44	16 52	16 59	17 05
Stratford 7	⊖ a	16 15	16 19	16 24	16 35	16 40	16 45	16 49	16 54	17 04	17 09	17 15

Richmond and Clapham Junction - Willesden Junction, West Hampstead, Highbury and Islington and Stratford

Network Diagram - see first Page of Table 59

		LO	LO	LO	LO	LO	LO	LO	LO	LO	LO	LO
Richmond	⊖ d	16 10		16 25			16 41		16 55			17 11
Kew Gardens	⊖ d	16 13		16 28			16 44		16 58			17 14
Gunnersbury	⊖ d	16 16		16 31			16 48		17 01			17 18
South Acton	d	16 19		16 33			16 50		17 04			17 20
Acton Central	d	16 22		16 37			16 54		17 07			17 24
Clapham Junction 10	d		16 14		16 29			16 44		16 59		
Imperial Wharf	d		16 18		16 33			16 48		17 03		
West Brompton	⊖ d		16 21		16 36			16 51		17 06		
Kensington (Olympia)	⊖ d		16 25		16 40			16 55		17 10		
Shepherd's Bush	⊖ d		16 27		16 42			16 57		17 12		
Willesden Jn Low Level	⊖ d											
Willesden Jn. High Level	⊖ a	16 27	16 35	16 42	16 50		16 57	17 05	17 12	17 20		17 27
	d	16 29	16 36	16 44	16 51		16 59	17 06	17 14	17 21		17 29
Kensal Rise	d	16 31	16 38	16 46	16 53		17 01	17 08	17 16	17 23		17 31
Brondesbury Park	d	16 33	16 40	16 48	16 55		17 03	17 10	17 18	17 25		17 33
Brondesbury	d	16 35	16 42	16 50	16 57		17 05	17 12	17 20	17 27		17 35
West Hampstead	⊖ d	16 37	16 44	16 52	16 59		17 07	17 14	17 22	17 29		17 37
Finchley Road & Frognal	d	16 39	16 46	16 54	17 01		17 09	17 16	17 24	17 31		17 39
Hampstead Heath	d	16 41	16 48	16 56	17 03		17 11	17 18	17 26	17 33		17 41
Gospel Oak	d	16 45	16 52	17 00	17 07		17 15	17 22	17 30	17 37		17 45
Kentish Town West	d	16 47	16 54	17 02	17 09		17 17	17 24	17 32	17 39		17 47
Camden Road	d	16 51	16 58	17 06	17 13	17 19	17 21	17 28	17 36	17 43	17 49	17 51
Caledonian Rd & Barnsbury	d	16 54	17 01	17 09	17 16	17 22	17 24	17 31	17 39	17 46	17 52	17 54
Highbury & Islington	⊖ d	16 56	17 03	17 11	17 18	17 24	17 26	17 33	17 41	17 48	17 54	17 56
Canonbury	⊖ d	16 58	17 05	17 13	17 20	17 26	17 28	17 35	17 43	17 50	17 56	17 58
Dalston Kingsland	d	17 01	17 08	17 16	17 23	17 29	17 31	17 38	17 46	17 53	17 59	18 01
Hackney Central	d	17 03	17 10	17 18	17 25	17 31	17 33	17 40	17 48	17 55	18 01	18 03
Homerton	d	17 05	17 12	17 20	17 27	17 33	17 35	17 42	17 50	17 57	18 03	18 05
Hackney Wick	d	17 07	17 14	17 22	17 29	17 35	17 37	17 44	17 52	17 59	18 05	18 07
Stratford 7	⊖ a	17 19	17 24	17 34	17 39	17 45	17 49	17 54	18 04	18 09	18 15	18 19

		LO	LO	LO	LO	LO	LO	LO	LO	LO	LO	LO
Richmond	⊖ d		17 25			17 41		17 55			18 11	
Kew Gardens	⊖ d		17 28			17 44		17 58			18 14	
Gunnersbury	⊖ d		17 31			17 48		18 01			18 18	
South Acton	d		17 34			17 50		18 04			18 20	
Acton Central	d		17 37			17 54		18 07			18 24	
Clapham Junction 10	d	17 14		17 29			17 44		17 59			18 14
Imperial Wharf	d	17 18		17 33			17 48		18 03			18 18
West Brompton	⊖ d	17 21		17 36			17 51		18 06			18 21
Kensington (Olympia)	⊖ d	17 25		17 40			17 55		18 10			18 25
Shepherd's Bush	⊖ d	17 27		17 42			17 57		18 12			18 27
Willesden Jn Low Level	⊖ d											
Willesden Jn. High Level	⊖ a	17 35	17 42	17 50		17 57	18 05	18 12	18 20		18 27	18 35
	d	17 36	17 44	17 51		17 59	18 06	18 14	18 21		18 29	18 36
Kensal Rise	d	17 38	17 46	17 53		18 01	18 08	18 16	18 23		18 31	18 38
Brondesbury Park	d	17 40	17 48	17 55		18 03	18 10	18 18	18 25		18 33	18 40
Brondesbury	d	17 42	17 50	17 57		18 05	18 12	18 20	18 27		18 35	18 42
West Hampstead	⊖ d	17 44	17 52	17 59		18 07	18 14	18 22	18 29		18 37	18 44
Finchley Road & Frognal	d	17 46	17 54	18 01		18 09	18 16	18 24	18 31		18 39	18 46
Hampstead Heath	d	17 48	17 56	18 03		18 11	18 18	18 26	18 33		18 41	18 48
Gospel Oak	d	17 52	18 00	18 07		18 15	18 22	18 30	18 37		18 45	18 52
Kentish Town West	d	17 54	18 02	18 09		18 17	18 24	18 32	18 39		18 47	18 54
Camden Road	d	17 58	18 06	18 13	18 19	18 21	18 28	18 36	18 43	18 49	18 51	18 58
Caledonian Rd & Barnsbury	d	18 01	18 09	18 16	18 22	18 24	18 31	18 39	18 46	18 52	18 54	19 01
Highbury & Islington	⊖ d	18 03	18 11	18 18	18 24	18 26	18 33	18 41	18 48	18 54	18 56	19 03
Canonbury	⊖ d	18 05	18 13	18 20	18 26	18 28	18 35	18 43	18 50	18 56	18 58	19 05
Dalston Kingsland	d	18 08	18 16	18 23	18 29	18 31	18 38	18 46	18 53	18 59	19 01	19 08
Hackney Central	d	18 10	18 18	18 25	18 31	18 33	18 40	18 48	18 55	19 01	19 03	19 10
Homerton	d	18 12	18 20	18 27	18 33	18 35	18 42	18 50	18 57	19 03	19 05	19 12
Hackney Wick	d	18 14	18 22	18 29	18 35	18 37	18 44	18 52	18 59	19 05	19 07	19 14
Stratford 7	⊖ a	18 24	18 34	18 39	18 45	18 49	18 54	19 04	19 09	19 15	19 19	19 24

		LO	LO	LO	LO	LO	LO	LO	LO	LO	LO	LO
Richmond	⊖ d	18 25		18 42		18 55		19 10		19 25		19 40
Kew Gardens	⊖ d	18 28		18 45		18 58		19 13		19 28		19 43
Gunnersbury	⊖ d	18 31		18 48		19 01		19 16		19 31		19 46
South Acton	d	18 34		18 51		19 04		19 19		19 34		19 49
Acton Central	d	18 37		18 54		19 07		19 22		19 37		19 52
Clapham Junction 10	d		18 29		18 44		18 59		19 14		19 29	
Imperial Wharf	d		18 33		18 48		19 03		19 18		19 33	
West Brompton	⊖ d		18 36		18 51		19 06		19 21		19 36	
Kensington (Olympia)	⊖ d		18 40		18 55		19 10		19 25		19 40	
Shepherd's Bush	⊖ d		18 42		18 57		19 12		19 27		19 42	
Willesden Jn Low Level	⊖ d											
Willesden Jn. High Level	⊖ a	18 42	18 50	18 57	19 05	19 12	19 20	19 27	19 35	19 42	19 50	19 57
	d	18 44	18 51	18 59	19 06	19 14	19 21	19 29	19 36	19 44	19 51	19 59
Kensal Rise	d	18 46	18 53	19 01	19 08	19 16	19 23	19 31	19 38	19 46	19 53	20 01
Brondesbury Park	d	18 48	18 55	19 03	19 10	19 18	19 25	19 33	19 40	19 48	19 55	20 03
Brondesbury	d	18 50	18 57	19 05	19 12	19 20	19 27	19 35	19 42	19 50	19 57	20 05
West Hampstead	⊖ d	18 52	18 59	19 07	19 14	19 22	19 29	19 37	19 44	19 52	19 59	20 07
Finchley Road & Frognal	d	18 54	19 01	19 09	19 16	19 24	19 31	19 39	19 46	19 54	20 01	20 09
Hampstead Heath	d	18 56	19 03	19 11	19 18	19 26	19 33	19 41	19 48	19 56	20 03	20 11
Gospel Oak	d	19 00	19 07	19 15	19 22	19 30	19 37	19 45	19 52	20 00	20 07	20 15
Kentish Town West	d	19 02	19 09	19 17	19 24	19 32	19 39	19 47	19 54	20 02	20 09	20 17
Camden Road	d	19 06	19 13	19 21	19 28	19 36	19 43	19 51	19 58	20 06	20 13	20 21
Caledonian Rd & Barnsbury	d	19 09	19 16	19 24	19 31	19 39	19 46	19 54	20 01	20 09	20 16	20 24
Highbury & Islington	⊖ d	19 11	19 18	19 26	19 33	19 41	19 48	19 56	20 03	20 11	20 18	20 26
Canonbury	⊖ d	19 13	19 20	19 28	19 35	19 43	19 50	19 58	20 05	20 13	20 20	20 28
Dalston Kingsland	d	19 16	19 23	19 31	19 38	19 46	19 53	20 01	20 08	20 16	20 23	20 31
Hackney Central	d	19 18	19 25	19 33	19 40	19 48	19 55	20 03	20 10	20 18	20 25	20 33
Homerton	d	19 20	19 27	19 35	19 42	19 50	19 57	20 05	20 12	20 20	20 27	20 35
Hackney Wick	d	19 22	19 29	19 37	19 44	19 52	19 59	20 07	20 14	20 22	20 29	20 37
Stratford 7	⊖ a	19 34	19 39	19 49	19 54	20 04	20 09	20 18	20 24	20 34	20 40	20 49

		LO	LO	LO	LO	LO	LO	LO	LO	LO	LO	LO
Richmond	⊖ d		19 55		20 10		20 25		20 40		20 55	
Kew Gardens	⊖ d		19 58		20 13		20 28		20 43		20 58	
Gunnersbury	⊖ d		20 01		20 16		20 31		20 46		21 01	
South Acton	d		20 04		20 19		20 34		20 49		21 04	
Acton Central	d		20 07		20 22		20 37		20 52		21 07	
Clapham Junction 10	d	19 44		19 59		20 14		20 29		20 44		20 59
Imperial Wharf	d	19 48		20 03		20 18		20 33		20 48		21 03
West Brompton	⊖ d	19 51		20 06		20 21		20 36		20 51		21 06
Kensington (Olympia)	⊖ d	19 55		20 10		20 25		20 40		20 55		21 09
Shepherd's Bush	⊖ d	19 57		20 12		20 27		20 42		20 57		21 12
Willesden Jn Low Level	⊖ d											
Willesden Jn. High Level	⊖ a	20 05	20 12	20 20	20 27	20 37	20 42	20 50	20 55	21 05	21 13	21 19
	d	20 06	20 14	20 21	20 29	20 38	20 44	20 51	20 57	21 06	21 14	21 20
Kensal Rise	d	20 08	20 16	20 23	20 31	20 40	20 46	20 53	20 59	21 08	21 16	21 23
Brondesbury Park	d	20 10	20 18	20 25	20 33	20 42	20 48	20 55	21 01	21 10	21 18	21 25
Brondesbury	d	20 12	20 20	20 27	20 35	20 44	20 50	20 57	21 03	21 12	21 20	21 27
West Hampstead	⊖ d	20 14	20 22	20 29	20 37	20 46	20 52	20 59	21 05	21 14	21 22	21 29
Finchley Road & Frognal	d	20 16	20 24	20 31	20 39	20 48	20 54	21 01	21 07	21 16	21 24	21 31
Hampstead Heath	d	20 18	20 26	20 33	20 41	20 50	20 56	21 03	21 09	21 18	21 26	21 33
Gospel Oak	d	20 22	20 30	20 37	20 45	20 54	21 00	21 07	21 12	21 22	21 30	21 37
Kentish Town West	d	20 24	20 32	20 39	20 47	20 56	21 02	21 09	21 14	21 24	21 32	21 39
Camden Road	d	20 28	20 36	20 43	20 51	21 00	21 06	21 13	21 17	21 28	21 36	21 43
Caledonian Rd & Barnsbury	d	20 31	20 39	20 46	20 54	21 03	21 09	21 16	21 20	21 31	21 39	21 46
Highbury & Islington	⊖ d	20 33	20 41	20 48	20 56	21 05	21 11	21 18	21 23	21 33	21 41	21 48
Canonbury	⊖ d	20 35	20 43	20 50	20 58	21 07	21 13	21 20	21 25	21 35	21 43	21 50
Dalston Kingsland	d	20 38	20 46	20 53	21 01	21 10	21 16	21 23	21 28	21 38	21 46	21 53
Hackney Central	d	20 40	20 48	20 55	21 03	21 12	21 18	21 25	21 31	21 40	21 48	21 55
Homerton	d	20 42	20 50	20 57	21 05	21 14	21 20	21 27	21 34	21 42	21 50	21 57
Hackney Wick	d	20 44	20 52	20 59	21 07	21 16	21 22	21 29	21 36	21 44	21 52	21 59
Stratford 7	⊖ a	20 54	21 04	21 10	21 19	21 26	21 34	21 39	21 49	21 54	22 04	22 09

Table 59

Mondays to Fridays
29 August to 7 September

Richmond and Clapham Junction - Willesden Junction, West Hampstead, Highbury and Islington and Stratford

Network Diagram - see first Page of Table 59

		LO	LO	LO	LO	LO	LO	LO	LO	LO	LO	LO
Richmond	⊖ d	21 10		21 25		21 40		21 55		22 10		22 25
Kew Gardens	⊖ d	21 13		21 28		21 43		21 58		22 13		22 28
Gunnersbury	⊖ d	21 16		21 31		21 46		22 01		22 16		22 31
South Acton	d	21 19		21 34		21 49		22 04		22 19		22 34
Acton Central	d	21 22		21 37		21 52		22 07		22 22		22 37
Clapham Junction 10	d		21 14		21 29		21 44		21 59		22 14	
Imperial Wharf	d		21 18		21 33		21 48		22 03		22 18	
West Brompton	⊖ d		21 21		21 36		21 51		22 06		22 21	
Kensington (Olympia)	⊖ d		21 25		21 40		21 55		22 10		22 25	
Shepherd's Bush	⊖ d		21 27		21 42		21 57		22 12		22 27	
Willesden Jn Low Level	⊖ d											
Willesden Jn. High Level	⊖ a	21 27	21 35	21 42	21 50	21 57	22 05	22 12	22 20	22 27	22 35	22 42
	d	21 29	21 37	21 44	21 51	21 59	22 06	22 14	22 21	22 29	22 36	22 44
Kensal Rise	d	21 31	21 39	21 46	21 53	22 01	22 08	22 16	22 23	22 31	22 38	22 46
Brondesbury Park	d	21 33	21 41	21 48	21 55	22 03	22 10	22 18	22 25	22 33	22 40	22 48
Brondesbury	d	21 35	21 43	21 50	21 57	22 05	22 12	22 20	22 27	22 35	22 42	22 50
West Hampstead	⊖ d	21 37	21 45	21 52	21 59	22 07	22 14	22 23	22 29	22 37	22 44	22 52
Finchley Road & Frognal	d	21 39	21 47	21 54	22 01	22 09	22 15	22 24	22 31	22 39	22 46	22 54
Hampstead Heath	d	21 41	21 49	21 56	22 03	22 11	22 18	22 27	22 33	22 41	22 48	22 56
Gospel Oak	d	21 45	21 54	22 00	22 07	22 15	22 22	22 30	22 37	22 45	22 52	23 00
Kentish Town West	d	21 47	21 56	22 02	22 09	22 17	22 24	22 32	22 39	22 47	22 54	23 02
Camden Road	d	21 51	22 01	22 06	22 13	22 21	22 28	22 36	22 43	22 51	22 58	23 06
Caledonian Rd & Barnsbury	d	21 54	22 04	22 09	22 16	22 24	22 31	22 39	22 46	22 54	23 01	23 09
Highbury & Islington	⊖ d	21 56	22 06	22 11	22 18	22 26	22 33	22 41	22 48	22 56	23 03	23 11
Canonbury	⊖ d	21 58	22 08	22 13	22 20	22 28	22 35	22 43	22 50	22 58	23 05	23 13
Dalston Kingsland	d	22 01	22 11	22 16	22 23	22 31	22 38	22 46	22 53	23 01	23 08	23 16
Hackney Central	d	22 03	22 13	22 18	22 25	22 33	22 40	22 48	22 55	23 03	23 10	23 18
Homerton	d	22 05	22 15	22 20	22 27	22 35	22 42	22 50	22 57	23 05	23 12	23 20
Hackney Wick	d	22 07	22 17	22 22	22 29	22 37	22 44	22 52	22 59	23 07	23 14	23 22
Stratford 7	⊖ a	22 19	22 27	22 34	22 40	22 49	22 54	23 04	23 10	23 19	23 24	23 34

		LO	LO	LO	LO	LO	LO	LO	LO	LO	LO	LO
Richmond	⊖ d		22 40		22 55		23 10		23 25		23 40	
Kew Gardens	⊖ d		22 43		22 58		23 13		23 28		23 43	
Gunnersbury	⊖ d		22 46		23 01		23 16		23 31		23 46	
South Acton	d		22 49		23 04		23 19		23 34		23 49	
Acton Central	d		22 52		23 07		23 22		23 37		23 52	
Clapham Junction 10	d	22 29		22 44		22 59		23 14		23 29		23 44
Imperial Wharf	d	22 33		22 48		23 03		23 18		23 33		23 48
West Brompton	⊖ d	22 36		22 51		23 06		23 21		23 36		23 51
Kensington (Olympia)	⊖ d	22 40		22 55		23 10		23 25		23 40		23 55
Shepherd's Bush	⊖ d	22 42		22 57		23 12		23 27		23 42		23 57
Willesden Jn Low Level	⊖ d											
Willesden Jn. High Level	⊖ a	22 50	22 57	23 05	23 12	23 20	23 27	23 35	23 42	23 50	23 57	00 05
	d	22 51	22 59	23 06	23 14	23 21	23 29	23 36	23 43	23 51	23 59	00 06
Kensal Rise	d	22 53	23 01	23 08	23 16	23 23	23 31	23 38	23 45	23 53	00 01	00 08
Brondesbury Park	d	22 55	23 03	23 10	23 18	23 25	23 33	23 40	23 47	23 55	00 03	00 10
Brondesbury	d	22 57	23 05	23 12	23 20	23 27	23 35	23 42	23 49	23 57	00 05	00 12
West Hampstead	⊖ d	22 59	23 07	23 14	23 22	23 29	23 37	23 44	23 51	23 59	00 07	00 14
Finchley Road & Frognal	d	23 01	23 09	23 16	23 24	23 31	23 39	23 46	23 53	00 01	00 09	00 16
Hampstead Heath	d	23 03	23 11	23 18	23 26	23 33	23 41	23 48	23 55	00 03	00 11	00 18
Gospel Oak	d	23 07	23 15	23 22	23 30	23 37	23 45	23 52	00 01	00 07	00 15	00 22
Kentish Town West	d	23 09	23 17	23 24	23 32	23 39	23 47	23 54	00 02	00 09	00 17	00 24
Camden Road	d	23 13	23 21	23 28	23 36	23 43	23 51	23 58	00 06	00 12	00 21	00 28
Caledonian Rd & Barnsbury	d	23 16	23 24	23 31	23 39	23 46	23 54	00 01	00 09	00 15	00 24	00 31
Highbury & Islington	⊖ d	23 18	23 26	23 33	23 41	23 48	23 56	00 03	00 11	00 18	00 26	00 33
Canonbury	⊖ d	23 20	23 28	23 35	23 43	23 50	23 59	00 05	00 13	00 20	00 28	00 35
Dalston Kingsland	d	23 23	23 31	23 38	23 46	23 53	00 02	00 08	00 16	00 22	00 31	00 38
Hackney Central	d	23 25	23 33	23 40	23 48	23 55	00 03	00 10	00 18	00 24	00 33	00 40
Homerton	d	23 27	23 35	23 42	23 50	23 57	00 05	00 12	00 20	00 26	00 35	00 42
Hackney Wick	d	23 29	23 37	23 44	23 52	23 59	00 07	00 14	00 22	00 29	00 37	00 44
Stratford 7	⊖ a	23 39	23 49	23 54	00 04	00 09	00 19	00 24	00 34	00 40	00 49	00 54

		LO	LO
Richmond	⊖ d	23 55	
Kew Gardens	⊖ d	23 59	
Gunnersbury	⊖ d	00 01	
South Acton	d	00 04	
Acton Central	d	00 07	
Clapham Junction 10	d		23 59
Imperial Wharf	d		00 03
West Brompton	⊖ d		00 06
Kensington (Olympia)	⊖ d		00 10
Shepherd's Bush	⊖ d		00 12
Willesden Jn Low Level	⊖ d		
Willesden Jn. High Level	⊖ a	00 12	00 20
	d	00 14	00 21
Kensal Rise	d	00 16	00 23
Brondesbury Park	d	00 18	00 25
Brondesbury	d	00 20	00 27
West Hampstead	⊖ d	00 22	00 29
Finchley Road & Frognal	d	00 24	00 31
Hampstead Heath	d	00 26	00 33
Gospel Oak	d	00 30	00 37
Kentish Town West	d	00 32	00 39
Camden Road	d	00 36	00 43
Caledonian Rd & Barnsbury	d	00 39	00 46
Highbury & Islington	⊖ d	00 41	00 48
Canonbury	⊖ d	00 43	00 50
Dalston Kingsland	d	00 46	00 53
Hackney Central	d	00 48	00 55
Homerton	d	00 50	00 57
Hackney Wick	d	00 52	00 59
Stratford 7	⊖ a	01 04	01 09

Table 59

Mondays to Fridays
from 10 September

Richmond and Clapham Junction - Willesden Junction, West Hampstead, Highbury and Islington and Stratford

Network Diagram - see first Page of Table 59

		LO A	LO MX	LO A	LO A	LO A	LO A	LO A	LO A	LO A	LO A	LO A
Richmond	⊖ d	22p55	23p00		23p10		23p25		23p40		23p55	
Kew Gardens	⊖ d	22p58	23p03		23p13		23p28		23p43		23p59	
Gunnersbury	⊖ d	23p01	23p06		23p16		23p31		23p46		00 01	
South Acton	d	23p04	23p09		23p19		23p34		23p49		00 04	
Acton Central	d	23p07	23p12		23p22		23p37		23p52		00 07	
Clapham Junction 10	d			22p59		23p14		23p29		23p44		23p59
Imperial Wharf	d			23p03		23p18		23p33		23p48		00 03
West Brompton	⊖ d			23p06		23p21		23p36		23p51		00 06
Kensington (Olympia)	⊖ d			23p10		23p25		23p40		23p55		00 10
Shepherd's Bush	⊖ d			23p12		23p27		23p42		23p57		00 12
Willesden Jn Low Level	⊖ d											
Willesden Jn. High Level	⊖ a	23p12	23p17	23p20	23p27	23p35	23p42	23p50	23p57	00 05	00 12	00 20
	d	23p14	23p18	23p21	23p29	23p36	23p44	23p51	23p59	00 06	00 14	00 21
Kensal Rise	d	23p16	23p20	23p23	23p31	23p38	23p46	23p53	00 01	00 08	00 16	00 23
Brondesbury Park	d	23p18	23p22	23p25	23p33	23p40	23p48	23p55	00 03	00 10	00 18	00 25
Brondesbury	d	23p20	23p24	23p27	23p35	23p42	23p50	23p57	00 05	00 12	00 20	00 27
West Hampstead	⊖ d	23p22	23p26	23p29	23p37	23p44	23p52	23p59	00 07	00 14	00 22	00 29
Finchley Road & Frognal	d	23p24	23p27	23p31	23p39	23p46	23p54	00 01	00 09	00 16	00 24	00 31
Hampstead Heath	d	23p26	23p30	23p33	23p41	23p48	23p56	00 03	00 11	00 18	00 26	00 33
Gospel Oak	d	23p30	23p32	23p37	23p45	23p52	00 01	00 07	00 15	00 22	00 30	00 37
Kentish Town West	d	23p32	23p34	23p39	23p47	23p54	00 02	00 09	00 17	00 24	00 32	00 39
Camden Road	d	23p36	23p38	23p43	23p51	23p58	00 06	00 13	00 21	00 28	00 36	00 43
Caledonian Rd & Barnsbury	d	23p39	23p41	23p46	23p54	00 01	00 09	00 16	00 24	00 31	00 39	00 46
Highbury & Islington	⊖ d	23p41	23p44	23p48	23p56	00 03	00 11	00 18	00 26	00 33	00 41	00 48
Canonbury	⊖ d	23p43	23p46	23p50	23p59	00 05	00 13	00 20	00 28	00 35	00 43	00 50
Dalston Kingsland	d	23p46	23p48	23p53	00 02	00 08	00 16	00 23	00 31	00 38	00 46	00 53
Hackney Central	d	23p48	23p50	23p55	00 03	00 10	00 18	00 25	00 33	00 40	00 48	00 55
Homerton	d	23p50	23p52	23p57	00 05	00 12	00 20	00 27	00 35	00 42	00 50	00 57
Hackney Wick	d	23p52	23p54	23p59	00 07	00 14	00 22	00 29	00 37	00 44	00 52	00 59
Stratford 7	⊖ a	00 04	00 01	00 09	00 19	00 24	00 34	00 39	00 49	00 54	01 04	01 09

		LO A	LO	LO	LO	LO	LO	LO	LO	LO	LO	LO
Richmond	⊖ d					05 54	06 09		06 24		06 37	
Kew Gardens	⊖ d					05 57	06 12		06 27		06 40	
Gunnersbury	⊖ d					06 00	06 15		06 30		06 43	
South Acton	d					06 03	06 18		06 33		06 46	
Acton Central	d					06 06	06 21		06 36		06 51	
Clapham Junction 10	d	00 12	05 47					06 14		06 29		06 44
Imperial Wharf	d	00 16	05 51					06 18		06 33		06 48
West Brompton	⊖ d	00 19	05 54					06 21		06 36		06 51
Kensington (Olympia)	⊖ d	00 22	05 57					06 24		06 39		06 54
Shepherd's Bush	⊖ d	00 24	05 59					06 26		06 41		06 56
Willesden Jn Low Level	⊖ d				05 58							
Willesden Jn. High Level	⊖ a	00 37	06 08			06 11	06 26	06 34	06 41	06 50	06 56	07 04
	d					06 12	06 27	06 35	06 42	06 50	06 57	07 05
Kensal Rise	d				06 02	06 14	06 29	06 37	06 44	06 52	06 59	07 07
Brondesbury Park	d				06 04	06 16	06 31	06 39	06 46	06 54	07 01	07 09
Brondesbury	d				06 06	06 18	06 33	06 41	06 48	06 56	07 03	07 11
West Hampstead	⊖ d				06 08	06 20	06 35	06 43	06 50	06 58	07 05	07 13
Finchley Road & Frognal	d				06 09	06 21	06 36	06 44	06 51	06 59	07 06	07 14
Hampstead Heath	d				06 12	06 24	06 39	06 47	06 54	07 02	07 09	07 17
Gospel Oak	d				06 14	06 26	06 41	06 49	06 56	07 04	07 11	07 19
Kentish Town West	d				06 16	06 28	06 43	06 51	06 58	07 06	07 13	07 21
Camden Road	d			06 11	06 20	06 32	06 47	06 55	07 02	07 10	07 17	07 25
Caledonian Rd & Barnsbury	d			06 14	06 23	06 35	06 50	06 58	07 05	07 13	07 20	07 28
Highbury & Islington	⊖ d			06 16	06 26	06 38	06 53	07 01	07 08	07 16	07 23	07 31
Canonbury	⊖ d			06 18	06 28	06 40	06 55	07 03	07 10	07 18	07 25	07 33
Dalston Kingsland	d			06 20	06 30	06 42	06 57	07 05	07 12	07 20	07 27	07 35
Hackney Central	d			06 22	06 32	06 44	06 59	07 07	07 14	07 22	07 29	07 37
Homerton	d			06 24	06 34	06 46	07 01	07 09	07 16	07 24	07 31	07 39
Hackney Wick	d			06 26	06 36	06 48	07 03	07 11	07 18	07 26	07 33	07 41
Stratford 7	⊖ a			06 32	06 44	06 55	07 10	07 18	07 25	07 33	07 39	07 48

		LO	LO	LO	LO	LO	LO	LO	LO	LO	LO	LO
Richmond	⊖ d	06 53		07 06		07 24		07 36		07 53		08 08
Kew Gardens	⊖ d	06 56		07 09		07 27		07 39		07 56		08 11
Gunnersbury	⊖ d	06 59		07 12		07 30		07 42		07 59		08 14
South Acton	d	07 02		07 15		07 33		07 45		08 02		08 17
Acton Central	d	07 06		07 21		07 36		07 51		08 06		08 21
Clapham Junction 10	d		06 59		07 14		07 29		07 44		07 59	
Imperial Wharf	d		07 03		07 18		07 33		07 48		08 03	
West Brompton	⊖ d		07 06		07 21		07 36		07 51		08 06	
Kensington (Olympia)	⊖ d		07 09		07 24		07 39		07 54		08 09	
Shepherd's Bush	⊖ d		07 11		07 26		07 41		07 56		08 11	
Willesden Jn Low Level	⊖ d											
Willesden Jn. High Level	⊖ a	07 11	07 19	07 26	07 35	07 41	07 49	07 56	08 05	08 11	08 19	08 26
	d	07 12	07 20	07 27	07 35	07 42	07 50	07 57	08 06	08 12	08 20	08 27
Kensal Rise	d	07 14	07 22	07 29	07 37	07 44	07 52	07 59	08 08	08 14	08 22	08 29
Brondesbury Park	d	07 16	07 24	07 31	07 39	07 46	07 54	08 01	08 10	08 16	08 24	08 31
Brondesbury	d	07 18	07 26	07 33	07 41	07 48	07 56	08 03	08 12	08 18	08 26	08 33
West Hampstead	⊖ d	07 20	07 28	07 35	07 43	07 50	07 58	08 05	08 14	08 20	08 28	08 35
Finchley Road & Frognal	d	07 21	07 29	07 36	07 44	07 51	07 59	08 06	08 15	08 21	08 29	08 36
Hampstead Heath	d	07 24	07 32	07 39	07 47	07 54	08 02	08 09	08 18	08 24	08 32	08 39
Gospel Oak	d	07 26	07 34	07 41	07 49	07 56	08 04	08 11	08 20	08 26	08 34	08 41
Kentish Town West	d	07 28	07 36	07 43	07 51	07 58	08 06	08 13	08 22	08 28	08 36	08 43
Camden Road	d	07 32	07 40	07 47	07 55	08 02	08 10	08 17	08 26	08 32	08 40	08 47
Caledonian Rd & Barnsbury	d	07 35	07 43	07 50	07 58	08 05	08 13	08 20	08 29	08 35	08 43	08 50
Highbury & Islington	⊖ d	07 38	07 46	07 53	08 01	08 08	08 16	08 23	08 32	08 38	08 46	08 53
Canonbury	⊖ d	07 40	07 48	07 55	08 03	08 10	08 18	08 25	08 34	08 40	08 48	08 55
Dalston Kingsland	d	07 42	07 50	07 57	08 05	08 12	08 20	08 27	08 36	08 42	08 50	08 57
Hackney Central	d	07 44	07 52	07 59	08 07	08 14	08 22	08 29	08 38	08 44	08 52	08 59
Homerton	d	07 46	07 54	08 01	08 09	08 16	08 24	08 31	08 40	08 46	08 54	09 01
Hackney Wick	d	07 48	07 56	08 03	08 11	08 18	08 26	08 33	08 42	08 48	08 56	09 03
Stratford 7	⊖ a	07 55	08 03	08 09	08 18	08 25	08 33	08 39	08 49	08 54	09 03	09 09

		LO	LO	LO	LO	LO	LO	LO	LO	LO	LO	LO
Richmond	⊖ d		08 22		08 36		08 52		09 10		09 27	
Kew Gardens	⊖ d		08 25		08 39		08 55		09 13		09 30	
Gunnersbury	⊖ d		08 28		08 42		08 58		09 16		09 33	
South Acton	d		08 31		08 45		09 01		09 19		09 36	
Acton Central	d		08 36		08 51		09 06		09 22		09 40	
Clapham Junction 10	d	08 09		08 29		08 44		08 59		09 15		09 30
Imperial Wharf	d	08 13		08 33		08 48		09 03		09 19		09 34
West Brompton	⊖ d	08 16		08 36		08 51		09 06		09 22		09 37
Kensington (Olympia)	⊖ d	08 19		08 39		08 54		09 09		09 25		09 40
Shepherd's Bush	⊖ d	08 21		08 41		08 56		09 11		09 27		09 42
Willesden Jn Low Level	⊖ d											
Willesden Jn. High Level	⊖ a	08 31	08 41	08 49	08 56	09 05	09 11	09 19	09 27	09 35	09 45	09 51
	d	08 35	08 42	08 50	08 57	09 06	09 13	09 20	09 28	09 36	09 46	
Kensal Rise	d	08 38	08 44	08 52	08 59	09 08	09 15	09 24	09 30	09 38	09 48	
Brondesbury Park	d	08 40	08 46	08 54	09 01	09 10	09 17	09 26	09 32	09 40	09 50	
Brondesbury	d	08 41	08 48	08 56	09 03	09 12	09 19	09 27	09 34	09 42	09 52	
West Hampstead	⊖ d	08 43	08 50	08 58	09 05	09 14	09 21	09 30	09 36	09 44	09 54	
Finchley Road & Frognal	d	08 45	08 51	08 59	09 06	09 15	09 22	09 31	09 37	09 45	09 55	
Hampstead Heath	d	08 47	08 54	09 02	09 09	09 18	09 25	09 34	09 40	09 48	09 58	
Gospel Oak	d	08 51	08 56	09 04	09 11	09 20	09 27	09 36	09 42	09 50	10 00	
Kentish Town West	d	08 53	08 58	09 06	09 13	09 22	09 29	09 38	09 44	09 52	10 02	
Camden Road	d	08 56	09 02	09 10	09 17	09 26	09 33	09 42	09 48	09 56	10 06	
Caledonian Rd & Barnsbury	d	08 59	09 05	09 13	09 20	09 29	09 36	09 45	09 51	09 59	10 09	
Highbury & Islington	⊖ d	09 02	09 08	09 16	09 23	09 32	09 39	09 48	09 54	10 02	10 12	
Canonbury	⊖ d	09 04	09 10	09 18	09 25	09 34	09 41	09 50	09 56	10 04	10 14	
Dalston Kingsland	d	09 06	09 12	09 20	09 27	09 36	09 43	09 52	09 58	10 06	10 16	
Hackney Central	d	09 08	09 14	09 22	09 29	09 38	09 45	09 54	10 00	10 08	10 18	
Homerton	d	09 10	09 16	09 24	09 31	09 40	09 47	09 56	10 02	10 10	10 20	
Hackney Wick	d	09 13	09 18	09 26	09 33	09 42	09 49	09 58	10 04	10 12	10 22	
Stratford 7	⊖ a	09 18	09 26	09 33	09 38	09 50	09 55	10 05	10 10	10 19	10 28	

A 10 September

Richmond and Clapham Junction - Willesden Junction, West Hampstead, Highbury and Islington and Stratford

Network Diagram - see first Page of Table 59

		LO	LO	LO	LO	LO	LO	LO	LO	LO	LO	LO	LO	LO	LO	LO	LO	LO	LO	LO	LO	LO	LO
Richmond ⊖	d	09 36		09 57		10 08		10 28		10 38		10 58		11 08		11 28		11 38		11 58		12 08	
Kew Gardens ⊖	d	09 39		10 00		10 11		10 31		10 41		11 01		11 11		11 31		11 41		12 01		12 11	
Gunnersbury ⊖	d	09 42		10 03		10 14		10 34		10 44		11 04		11 14		11 34		11 44		12 04		12 14	
South Acton	d	09 45		10 06		10 17		10 37		10 47		11 07		11 17		11 37		11 47		12 07		12 17	
Acton Central	d	09 50		10 10		10 20		10 40		10 50		11 10		11 20		11 40		11 50		12 10		12 20	
Clapham Junction 10	d		09 45		10 00		10 15		10 30		10 45		11 00		11 15		11 30		11 45		12 00		12 15
Imperial Wharf	d		09 49		10 04		10 19		10 36		10 49		11 04		11 19		11 34		11 49		12 04		12 19
West Brompton ⊖	d		09 52		10 07		10 22		10 39		10 52		11 07		11 22		11 37		11 52		12 07		12 22
Kensington (Olympia) ⊖	d		09 55		10 10		10 25		10 42		10 55		11 10		11 25		11 40		11 55		12 10		12 25
Shepherd's Bush ⊖	d		09 57		10 12		10 27		10 44		10 57		11 12		11 27		11 42		11 57		12 12		12 27
Willesden Jn Low Level ⊖	d																						
Willesden Jn. High Level ⊖	a	09 55	10 05	10 15	10 21	10 25	10 35	10 45	10 51	10 55	11 05	11 15	11 21	11 25	11 35	11 45	11 51	11 55	12 05	12 15	12 21	12 25	12 35
	d	09 56	10 06	10 16		10 26	10 36	10 46		10 56	11 06	11 16		11 26	11 36	11 46		11 56	12 06	12 16		12 26	12 36
Kensal Rise	d	09 58	10 08	10 18		10 28	10 38	10 48		10 58	11 08	11 18		11 28	11 38	11 48		11 58	12 08	12 18		12 28	12 38
Brondesbury Park	d	10 00	10 10	10 20		10 30	10 40	10 50		11 00	11 10	11 20		11 30	11 40	11 50		12 00	12 10	12 20		12 30	12 40
Brondesbury	d	10 02	10 12	10 22		10 32	10 42	10 52		11 02	11 12	11 22		11 32	11 42	11 52		12 02	12 12	12 22		12 32	12 42
West Hampstead ⊖	d	10 04	10 14	10 24		10 34	10 44	10 54		11 04	11 14	11 24		11 34	11 44	11 54		12 04	12 14	12 24		12 34	12 44
Finchley Road & Frognal	d	10 05	10 15	10 25		10 35	10 45	10 55		11 05	11 15	11 25		11 35	11 45	11 55		12 05	12 15	12 25		12 35	12 45
Hampstead Heath	d	10 08	10 18	10 28		10 38	10 48	10 58		11 08	11 18	11 28		11 38	11 48	11 58		12 08	12 18	12 28		12 38	12 48
Gospel Oak	d	10 10	10 20	10 30		10 40	10 50	11 00		11 10	11 20	11 30		11 40	11 50	12 00		12 10	12 20	12 30		12 40	12 50
Kentish Town West	d	10 12	10 22	10 32		10 42	10 52	11 02		11 12	11 22	11 32		11 42	11 52	12 02		12 12	12 22	12 32		12 42	12 52
Camden Road	d	10 16	10 26	10 36		10 46	10 56	11 06		11 16	11 26	11 36		11 46	11 56	12 06		12 16	12 26	12 36		12 46	12 56
Caledonian Rd & Barnsbury	d	10 19	10 29	10 39		10 49	10 59	11 09		11 19	11 29	11 39		11 49	11 59	12 09		12 19	12 29	12 39		12 49	12 59
Highbury & Islington ⊖	d	10 22	10 32	10 42		10 52	11 02	11 12		11 22	11 32	11 42		11 52	12 02	12 12		12 22	12 32	12 42		12 52	13 02
Canonbury ⊖	d	10 24	10 34	10 44		10 54	11 04	11 14		11 24	11 34	11 45		11 54	12 04	12 14		12 24	12 34	12 44		12 54	13 04
Dalston Kingsland	d	10 26	10 36	10 46		10 56	11 06	11 16		11 26	11 36	11 47		11 56	12 06	12 16		12 26	12 36	12 46		12 56	13 06
Hackney Central	d	10 28	10 38	10 48		10 58	11 08	11 18		11 28	11 38	11 49		11 58	12 08	12 18		12 28	12 38	12 48		12 58	13 08
Homerton	d	10 30	10 40	10 50		11 00	11 10	11 20		11 30	11 40	11 51		12 00	12 10	12 20		12 30	12 40	12 50		13 00	13 10
Hackney Wick	d	10 32	10 42	10 52		11 02	11 12	11 22		11 32	11 42	11 53		12 02	12 12	12 22		12 32	12 42	12 52		13 02	13 12
Stratford 7 ⊖	a	10 38	10 49	10 58		11 09	11 19	11 29		11 40	11 49	11 59		12 09	12 19	12 29		12 39	12 51	12 59		13 09	13 19

		LO	LO	LO	LO	LO	LO	LO	LO	LO	LO	LO	LO	LO	LO	LO	LO	LO	LO	LO	LO	LO	LO
Richmond ⊖	d	12 28		12 38		12 58		13 08		13 28		13 38		13 58		14 10		14 28		14 38		14 58	
Kew Gardens ⊖	d	12 31		12 41		13 01		13 11		13 31		13 41		14 01		14 13		14 31		14 41		15 01	
Gunnersbury ⊖	d	12 34		12 44		13 04		13 14		13 34		13 44		14 04		14 16		14 34		14 44		15 04	
South Acton	d	12 37		12 47		13 07		13 17		13 37		13 47		14 07		14 19		14 37		14 47		15 07	
Acton Central	d	12 40		12 50		13 10		13 20		13 40		13 50		14 10		14 22		14 40		14 50		15 10	
Clapham Junction 10	d		12 30		12 45		13 00		13 15		13 30		13 45		14 00		14 15		14 30		14 45		15 00
Imperial Wharf	d		12 35		12 49		13 04		13 19		13 36		13 49		14 04		14 19		14 34		14 55		15 04
West Brompton ⊖	d		12 38		12 52		13 07		13 22		13 39		13 52		14 07		14 22		14 37		14 58		15 07
Kensington (Olympia) ⊖	d		12 41		12 55		13 10		13 25		13 42		13 55		14 10		14 25		14 40		15 01		15 10
Shepherd's Bush ⊖	d		12 43		12 57		13 12		13 27		13 44		13 57		14 12		14 27		14 42		15 03		15 12
Willesden Jn Low Level ⊖	d																						
Willesden Jn. High Level ⊖	a	12 45	12 51	12 55	13 05	13 15	13 21	13 25	13 35	13 45	13 51	13 55	14 05	14 15	14 21	14 27	14 35	14 45	14 51	14 55	15 10	15 15	15 21
	d	12 46		12 56	13 06	13 16		13 26	13 36	13 46		13 56	14 06	14 16		14 28	14 36	14 46		14 56	15 11	15 16	
Kensal Rise	d	12 48		12 58	13 08	13 18		13 28	13 38	13 48		13 58	14 08	14 18		14 30	14 38	14 48		14 58	15 14	15 18	
Brondesbury Park	d	12 50		13 00	13 10	13 20		13 30	13 40	13 50		14 00	14 10	14 20		14 32	14 40	14 50		15 00	15 16	15 20	
Brondesbury	d	12 52		13 02	13 12	13 22		13 32	13 42	13 52		14 02	14 12	14 22		14 34	14 42	14 52		15 02	15 17	15 22	
West Hampstead ⊖	d	12 54		13 04	13 14	13 24		13 34	13 44	13 54		14 04	14 14	14 24		14 36	14 44	14 54		15 04	15 19	15 24	
Finchley Road & Frognal	d	12 55		13 05	13 15	13 25		13 35	13 45	13 55		14 05	14 15	14 25		14 37	14 45	14 55		15 05	15 21	15 25	
Hampstead Heath	d	12 58		13 08	13 18	13 28		13 38	13 48	13 58		14 08	14 18	14 28		14 40	14 48	14 58		15 08	15 23	15 28	
Gospel Oak	d	13 00		13 10	13 20	13 30		13 40	13 50	14 00		14 10	14 20	14 30		14 42	14 50	15 00		15 10	15 26	15 30	
Kentish Town West	d	13 02		13 12	13 22	13 32		13 42	13 52	14 02		14 12	14 22	14 32		14 44	14 52	15 02		15 12	15 28	15 32	
Camden Road	d	13 06		13 16	13 26	13 36		13 46	13 56	14 06		14 16	14 26	14 36		14 48	14 56	15 06		15 16	15 32	15 36	
Caledonian Rd & Barnsbury	d	13 09		13 19	13 29	13 39		13 49	13 59	14 09		14 19	14 29	14 39		14 51	14 59	15 09		15 19	15 35	15 39	
Highbury & Islington ⊖	d	13 12		13 22	13 32	13 42		13 52	14 02	14 12		14 22	14 32	14 42		14 54	15 02	15 12		15 22	15 38	15 42	
Canonbury ⊖	d	13 14		13 24	13 34	13 45		13 54	14 04	14 14		14 24	14 34	14 44		14 56	15 04	15 14		15 24	15 40	15 44	
Dalston Kingsland	d	13 16		13 26	13 36	13 47		13 56	14 06	14 16		14 26	14 36	14 46		14 58	15 06	15 16		15 26	15 42	15 46	
Hackney Central	d	13 18		13 28	13 38	13 49		13 58	14 08	14 18		14 28	14 38	14 48		15 00	15 08	15 18		15 28	15 44	15 48	
Homerton	d	13 20		13 30	13 40	13 51		14 00	14 10	14 20		14 30	14 40	14 50		15 02	15 10	15 20		15 30	15 46	15 50	
Hackney Wick	d	13 22		13 33	13 42	13 53		14 02	14 12	14 22		14 32	14 42	14 52		15 04	15 12	15 22		15 32	15 49	15 52	
Stratford 7 ⊖	a	13 29		13 39	13 49	13 59		14 09	14 19	14 29		14 39	14 49	14 59		15 12	15 19	15 30		15 39	15 54	15 57	

Richmond and Clapham Junction - Willesden Junction, West Hampstead, Highbury and Islington and Stratford

Network Diagram - see first Page of Table 59

		LO	LO	LO	LO	LO	LO	LO	LO	LO	LO	LO	LO	LO	LO	LO	LO	LO	LO	LO	LO	LO	LO
Richmond ⊖	d	15 08		15 26		15 38		15 53		16 09		16 23		16 36		16 53		17 06		17 23		17 36	
Kew Gardens ⊖	d	15 11		15 29		15 41		15 56		16 12		16 26		16 39		16 56		17 09		17 26		17 39	
Gunnersbury ⊖	d	15 14		15 32		15 44		15 59		16 15		16 29		16 42		16 59		17 12		17 29		17 42	
South Acton	d	15 17		15 35		15 47		16 02		16 18		16 32		16 45		17 02		17 15		17 32		17 45	
Acton Central	d	15 20		15 38		15 50		16 06		16 21		16 36		16 51		17 06		17 21		17 36		17 51	
Clapham Junction 10	d		15 15		15 30		15 44		15 59		16 14		16 29		16 44		16 59		17 14		17 29		17 44
Imperial Wharf	d		15 19		15 34		15 49		16 03		16 18		16 33		16 48		17 03		17 18		17 33		17 48
West Brompton ⊖	d		15 22		15 37		15 52		16 06		16 21		16 36		16 51		17 06		17 21		17 36		17 51
Kensington (Olympia) ⊖	d		15 25		15 40		15 55		16 09		16 24		16 39		16 54		17 09		17 24		17 39		17 54
Shepherd's Bush ⊖	d		15 27		15 42		15 57		16 11		16 26		16 41		16 56		17 11		17 26		17 41		17 56
Willesden Jn Low Level ⊖	d																						
Willesden Jn. High Level ⊖	a	15 25	15 35	15 44	15 51	15 55	16 05	16 11	16 20	16 26	16 34	16 41	16 49	16 56	17 04	17 11	17 19	17 26	17 34	17 41	17 49	17 56	18 04
	d	15 26	15 36	15 45		15 56	16 06	16 12	16 20	16 27	16 35	16 42	16 50	16 57	17 05	17 12	17 20	17 27	17 35	17 42	17 50	17 57	18 05
Kensal Rise	d	15 28	15 38	15 47		15 58	16 08	16 14	16 22	16 29	16 37	16 44	16 52	16 59	17 07	17 14	17 22	17 29	17 37	17 44	17 52	17 59	18 07
Brondesbury Park	d	15 30	15 40	15 49		16 00	16 10	16 16	16 24	16 31	16 40	16 46	16 54	17 01	17 09	17 16	17 24	17 31	17 39	17 46	17 54	18 01	18 09
Brondesbury	d	15 32	15 42	15 51		16 02	16 12	16 18	16 26	16 33	16 41	16 48	16 56	17 03	17 11	17 18	17 26	17 33	17 41	17 48	17 56	18 03	18 11
West Hampstead ⊖	d	15 34	15 44	15 53		16 04	16 14	16 20	16 28	16 35	16 43	16 50	16 58	17 05	17 13	17 20	17 28	17 35	17 43	17 50	17 58	18 05	18 13
Finchley Road & Frognal	d	15 35	15 45	15 54		16 05	16 15	16 21	16 29	16 36	16 44	16 51	16 59	17 06	17 14	17 21	17 29	17 36	17 44	17 51	17 59	18 06	18 14
Hampstead Heath	d	15 38	15 48	15 57		16 08	16 18	16 24	16 32	16 39	16 47	16 54	17 02	17 09	17 17	17 24	17 32	17 39	17 47	17 54	18 02	18 09	18 17
Gospel Oak	d	15 40	15 50	16 00		16 10	16 20	16 26	16 34	16 41	16 49	16 56	17 04	17 11	17 19	17 26	17 34	17 41	17 49	17 56	18 04	18 11	18 19
Kentish Town West	d	15 42	15 52	16 02		16 12	16 22	16 28	16 36	16 43	16 51	16 58	17 06	17 13	17 21	17 28	17 36	17 43	17 51	17 58	18 06	18 13	18 21
Camden Road	d	15 46	15 56	16 05		16 16	16 26	16 32	16 40	16 47	16 55	17 02	17 10	17 17	17 25	17 32	17 40	17 47	17 55	18 02	18 10	18 17	18 25
Caledonian Rd & Barnsbury	d	15 49	15 59	16 08		16 19	16 29	16 35	16 43	16 50	16 58	17 05	17 13	17 20	17 28	17 35	17 43	17 50	17 58	18 05	18 13	18 20	18 28
Highbury & Islington ⊖	d	15 52	16 02	16 11		16 22	16 32	16 38	16 46	16 53	17 01	17 08	17 16	17 23	17 31	17 38	17 46	17 53	18 01	18 08	18 16	18 23	18 31
Canonbury ⊖	d	15 54	16 04	16 13		16 24	16 34	16 40	16 48	16 55	17 03	17 10	17 18	17 25	17 33	17 40	17 48	17 55	18 03	18 10	18 18	18 25	18 33
Dalston Kingsland	d	15 56	16 06	16 15		16 26	16 36	16 42	16 50	16 57	17 05	17 12	17 20	17 27	17 35	17 42	17 50	17 57	18 05	18 12	18 20	18 27	18 35
Hackney Central	d	15 58	16 08	16 17		16 28	16 38	16 44	16 52	16 59	17 07	17 14	17 22	17 29	17 37	17 44	17 52	17 59	18 07	18 14	18 22	18 29	18 37
Homerton	d	16 00	16 10	16 19		16 30	16 40	16 46	16 54	17 01	17 09	17 16	17 24	17 31	17 39	17 46	17 54	18 01	18 09	18 16	18 24	18 31	18 39
Hackney Wick	d	16 02	16 12	16 21		16 32	16 42	16 48	16 56	17 03	17 11	17 18	17 26	17 33	17 41	17 48	17 56	18 03	18 11	18 18	18 26	18 33	18 41
Stratford 7 ⊖	a	16 09	16 19	16 27		16 39	16 48	16 54	17 03	17 10	17 18	17 24	17 33	17 38	17 50	17 54	18 05	18 08	18 20	18 24	18 35	18 39	18 50

		LO	LO	LO	LO	LO	LO	LO	LO	LO	LO	LO	LO	LO	LO	LO	LO	LO	LO	LO	LO	LO	LO
Richmond ⊖	d	17 53		18 06		18 22		18 36		18 54		19 09		19 26		19 41		19 56		20 11		20 26	
Kew Gardens ⊖	d	17 56		18 09		18 26		18 39		18 57		19 12		19 29		19 44		19 59		20 14		20 29	
Gunnersbury ⊖	d	17 59		18 12		18 29		18 42		19 00		19 15		19 32		19 47		20 02		20 17		20 32	
South Acton	d	18 02		18 15		18 31		18 45		19 03		19 18		19 35		19 50		20 05		20 20		20 35	
Acton Central	d	18 06		18 21		18 34		18 51		19 06		19 23		19 40		19 54		20 08		20 23		20 40	
Clapham Junction 10	d		17 59		18 14		18 29		18 44		18 59		19 15		19 30		19 45		20 00		20 15		20 30
Imperial Wharf	d		18 03		18 18		18 33		18 48		19 03		19 19		19 34		19 49		20 04		20 19		20 34
West Brompton ⊖	d		18 06		18 21		18 36		18 51		19 06		19 22		19 37		19 52		20 07		20 22		20 37
Kensington (Olympia) ⊖	d		18 09		18 24		18 39		18 54		19 09		19 25		19 40		19 55		20 10		20 25		20 40
Shepherd's Bush ⊖	d		18 11		18 26		18 41		18 56		19 11		19 27		19 42		19 57		20 12		20 27		20 42
Willesden Jn Low Level ⊖	d																						
Willesden Jn. High Level ⊖	a	18 11	18 19	18 26	18 34	18 39	18 49	18 56	19 04	19 11	19 19	19 28	19 35	19 45	19 51	19 59	20 05	20 15	20 21	20 28	20 35	20 45	20 51
	d	18 12	18 20	18 27	18 35	18 40	18 50	18 57	19 05	19 12	19 20	19 29	19 36	19 46		20 00	20 06	20 16		20 29	20 36	20 46	
Kensal Rise	d	18 14	18 22	18 29	18 37	18 43	18 52	18 59	19 07	19 14	19 22	19 31	19 38	19 48		20 02	20 08	20 18		20 31	20 38	20 48	
Brondesbury Park	d	18 16	18 24	18 31	18 39	18 45	18 54	19 01	19 09	19 16	19 24	19 33	19 40	19 50		20 04	20 10	20 20		20 33	20 40	20 50	
Brondesbury	d	18 18	18 26	18 33	18 41	18 46	18 56	19 03	19 11	19 18	19 26	19 35	19 42	19 52		20 06	20 12	20 22		20 35	20 42	20 52	
West Hampstead ⊖	d	18 20	18 28	18 35	18 43	18 48	18 58	19 05	19 13	19 20	19 28	19 37	19 44	19 54		20 08	20 14	20 24		20 37	20 44	20 54	
Finchley Road & Frognal	d	18 21	18 29	18 36	18 44	18 50	18 59	19 06	19 14	19 21	19 29	19 38	19 45	19 55		20 09	20 15	20 25		20 38	20 45	20 55	
Hampstead Heath	d	18 24	18 32	18 39	18 47	18 52	19 02	19 09	19 17	19 24	19 32	19 41	19 48	19 58		20 12	20 18	20 28		20 41	20 48	20 58	
Gospel Oak	d	18 26	18 34	18 41	18 49	18 55	19 04	19 11	19 19	19 26	19 34	19 43	19 50	20 00		20 14	20 20	20 30		20 43	20 50	21 00	
Kentish Town West	d	18 28	18 36	18 43	18 51	18 57	19 06	19 13	19 21	19 28	19 36	19 45	19 52	20 02		20 16	20 22	20 32		20 45	20 52	21 02	
Camden Road	d	18 32	18 40	18 47	18 55	19 00	19 10	19 17	19 25	19 32	19 40	19 49	19 56	20 06		20 20	20 26	20 36		20 49	20 56	21 06	
Caledonian Rd & Barnsbury	d	18 35	18 44	18 50	18 58	19 03	19 13	19 20	19 28	19 35	19 43	19 52	19 59	20 09		20 23	20 29	20 39		20 52	20 59	21 09	
Highbury & Islington ⊖	d	18 38	18 46	18 53	19 01	19 06	19 16	19 23	19 31	19 38	19 46	19 55	20 02	20 12		20 26	20 33	20 42		20 55	21 02	21 12	
Canonbury ⊖	d	18 40	18 48	18 55	19 03	19 08	19 18	19 25	19 33	19 40	19 48	19 57	20 04	20 14		20 28	20 35	20 44		20 57	21 04	21 14	
Dalston Kingsland	d	18 42	18 50	18 57	19 05	19 10	19 20	19 27	19 35	19 42	19 50	19 59	20 06	20 16		20 30	20 37	20 46		20 59	21 06	21 16	
Hackney Central	d	18 44	18 52	18 59	19 07	19 12	19 22	19 29	19 37	19 44	19 52	20 01	20 08	20 18		20 32	20 39	20 48		21 01	21 08	21 18	
Homerton	d	18 46	18 54	19 01	19 09	19 14	19 24	19 31	19 39	19 46	19 54	20 03	20 10	20 20		20 34	20 41	20 50		21 03	21 10	21 20	
Hackney Wick	d	18 48	18 56	19 03	19 11	19 17	19 26	19 33	19 41	19 48	19 56	20 05	20 12	20 22		20 36	20 43	20 52		21 05	21 12	21 22	
Stratford 7 ⊖	a	18 54	19 05	19 08	19 20	19 24	19 33	19 40	19 48	19 55	20 03	20 11	20 19	20 28		20 42	20 51	20 58		21 11	21 19	21 28	

Table 59

Mondays to Fridays
from 10 September

Richmond and Clapham Junction - Willesden Junction, West Hampstead, Highbury and Islington and Stratford

Network Diagram - see first Page of Table 59

	LO	LO	LO	LO	LO	LO	LO	LO	LO	LO	LO	LO	LO	LO	LO	LO	LO	LO	LO	LO
Richmond ⊖ d	20 40		20 58		21 10		21 28		21 38		21 56			22 28			23 00		23 28	
Kew Gardens ⊖ d	20 43		21 01		21 13		21 31		21 41		21 59			22 31			23 03		23 31	
Gunnersbury ⊖ d	20 46		21 04		21 16		21 34		21 44		22 02			22 34			23 06		23 34	
South Acton d	20 49		21 07		21 19		21 37		21 47		22 05			22 37			23 09		23 37	
Acton Central d	20 52		21 10		21 23		21 40		21 50		22 10			22 40			23 12		23 40	
Clapham Junction [10] d		20 45		21 00		21 15		21 30		21 45		22 00	22 15		22 30	22 45		23 00		23 30
Imperial Wharf d		20 49		21 04		21 19		21 34		21 49		22 04	22 19		22 34	22 49		23 04		23 34
West Brompton ⊖ d		20 52		21 07		21 22		21 37		21 52		22 07	22 22		22 37	22 52		23 07		23 37
Kensington (Olympia) ⊖ d		20 55		21 10		21 25		21 40		21 55		22 10	22 25		22 40	22 55		23 10		23 40
Shepherd's Bush ⊖ d		20 57		21 12		21 27		21 42		21 57		22 12	22 27		22 42	22 57		23 12		23 42
Willesden Jn Low Level ⊖ d																				
Willesden Jn. High Level ⊖ a	20 57	21 05	21 16	21 21	21 28	21 35	21 45	21 51	21 55	22 05	22 15	22 21	22 36	22 45	22 51	23 06	23 17	23 23	23 45	23 51
d	20 59	21 06	21 17		21 29	21 36	21 46		21 56	22 06	22 16			22 46			23 18			
Kensal Rise d	21 01	21 08	21 19		21 31	21 38	21 48		21 58	22 08	22 18			22 48			23 20			
Brondesbury Park d	21 03	21 10	21 21		21 33	21 40	21 50		22 00	22 10	22 20			22 50			23 22			
Brondesbury d	21 05	21 12	21 23		21 35	21 42	21 52		22 02	22 12	22 22			22 52			23 24			
West Hampstead ⊖ d	21 07	21 14	21 25		21 37	21 44	21 54		22 04	22 14	22 24			22 54			23 26			
Finchley Road & Frognal d	21 08	21 15	21 26		21 38	21 45	21 55		22 05	22 15	22 25			22 55			23 27			
Hampstead Heath d	21 11	21 18	21 29		21 41	21 48	21 58		22 08	22 18	22 28			22 58			23 30			
Gospel Oak d	21 13	21 20	21 30		21 43	21 50	22 00		22 10	22 20	22 30			23 00			23 32			
Kentish Town West d	21 15	21 22	21 32		21 45	21 52	22 02		22 12	22 22	22 32			23 02			23 34			
Camden Road d	21 19	21 26	21 36		21 49	21 56	22 06		22 16	22 26	22 36			23 06			23 38			
Caledonian Rd & Barnsbury d	21 22	21 29	21 39		21 52	21 59	22 09		22 19	22 29	22 39			23 09			23 41			
Highbury & Islington ⊖ d	21 25	21 32	21 42		21 55	22 02	22 12		22 22	22 32	22 42			23 12			23 44			
Canonbury ⊖ d	21 27	21 34	21 44		21 57	22 04	22 14		22 24	22 34	22 44			23 14			23 46			
Dalston Kingsland d	21 29	21 36	21 46		21 59	22 06	22 16		22 26	22 36	22 46			23 16			23 48			
Hackney Central d	21 31	21 38	21 48		22 01	22 08	22 18		22 28	22 38	22 48			23 18			23 50			
Homerton d	21 33	21 40	21 50		22 03	22 10	22 20		22 30	22 40	22 50			23 20			23 52			
Hackney Wick d	21 35	21 42	21 52		22 05	22 12	22 22		22 32	22 42	22 52			23 22			23 54			
Stratford [7] ⊖ a	21 41	21 49	21 59		22 13	22 19	22 29		22 39	22 49	22 58			23 29			00 01			

Saturdays
until 21 July

	LO	LO	LO	LO	LO	LO	LO	LO	LO	LO	LO	LO	LO	LO	LO	LO	LO	LO	LO	LO	LO	LO
Richmond ⊖ d	23p00			05 58	06 10		06 28		06 40		06 58		07 10		07 28		07 40		07 58		08 08	
Kew Gardens ⊖ d	23p03			06 01	06 13		06 31		06 43		07 01		07 13		07 31		07 43		08 01		08 11	
Gunnersbury ⊖ d	23p06			06 04	06 16		06 34		06 46		07 04		07 16		07 34		07 46		08 04		08 14	
South Acton d	23p09			06 07	06 19		06 37		06 49		07 07		07 19		07 37		07 49		08 07		08 17	
Acton Central d	23p12			06 10	06 23		06 40		06 53		07 10		07 23		07 40		07 52		08 10		08 20	
Clapham Junction [10] d		05 47				06 15		06 30		06 45		07 00		07 15		07 30		07 45		08 00		08 15
Imperial Wharf d		05 51				06 19		06 34		06 49		07 04		07 19		07 34		07 49		08 04		08 19
West Brompton ⊖ d		05 54				06 22		06 37		06 52		07 07		07 22		07 37		07 52		08 07		08 22
Kensington (Olympia) ⊖ d		05 57				06 25		06 40		06 55		07 10		07 25		07 40		07 55		08 10		08 25
Shepherd's Bush ⊖ d		05 59				06 27		06 42		06 57		07 12		07 27		07 42		07 57		08 12		08 27
Willesden Jn Low Level ⊖ d			05 57																			
Willesden Jn. High Level ⊖ a	23p17	06 08		06 15	06 28	06 35	06 45	06 53	06 58	07 05	07 15	07 23	07 28	07 35	07 45	07 51	07 57	08 05	08 15	08 21	08 25	08 35
d	23p18			06 16	06 29	06 36	06 46		06 59	07 06	07 16		07 29	07 36	07 46		07 58	08 06	08 16		08 26	08 36
Kensal Rise d	23p20		06 01	06 18	06 31	06 38	06 48		07 01	07 08	07 18		07 31	07 38	07 48		08 00	08 08	08 18		08 28	08 38
Brondesbury Park d	23p22		06 03	06 20	06 33	06 40	06 50		07 03	07 10	07 20		07 33	07 40	07 50		08 02	08 10	08 20		08 30	08 40
Brondesbury d	23p24		06 05	06 22	06 35	06 42	06 52		07 05	07 12	07 22		07 35	07 42	07 52		08 04	08 12	08 22		08 32	08 42
West Hampstead ⊖ d	23p26		06 07	06 24	06 37	06 44	06 54		07 07	07 14	07 24		07 37	07 44	07 54		08 06	08 14	08 24		08 34	08 44
Finchley Road & Frognal d	23p27		06 08	06 25	06 38	06 45	06 55		07 08	07 15	07 25		07 38	07 45	07 55		08 07	08 15	08 25		08 35	08 45
Hampstead Heath d	23p30		06 11	06 28	06 41	06 48	06 58		07 11	07 18	07 28		07 41	07 48	07 58		08 10	08 18	08 28		08 38	08 48
Gospel Oak d	23p32		06 13	06 30	06 43	06 50	07 00		07 13	07 20	07 30		07 43	07 50	08 00		08 12	08 20	08 30		08 41	08 50
Kentish Town West d	23p34		06 15	06 32	06 45	06 52	07 02		07 15	07 22	07 32		07 45	07 52	08 02		08 14	08 22	08 32		08 43	08 52
Camden Road d	23p38		06 19	06 36	06 49	06 56	07 06		07 19	07 26	07 36		07 49	07 56	08 06		08 18	08 26	08 36		08 46	08 56
Caledonian Rd & Barnsbury d	23p41		06 22	06 39	06 52	06 59	07 09		07 22	07 29	07 39		07 52	07 59	08 09		08 21	08 29	08 39		08 49	08 59
Highbury & Islington ⊖ d	23p44		06 25	06 42	06 55	07 02	07 12		07 25	07 32	07 42		07 55	08 02	08 12		08 24	08 32	08 42		08 52	09 02
Canonbury ⊖ d	23p46		06 27	06 44	06 57	07 04	07 14		07 27	07 34	07 44		07 57	08 04	08 14		08 26	08 34	08 44		08 54	09 04
Dalston Kingsland d	23p48		06 29	06 46	06 59	07 06	07 16		07 29	07 36	07 46		07 59	08 06	08 16		08 28	08 36	08 46		08 56	09 06
Hackney Central d	23p50		06 31	06 48	07 01	07 08	07 18		07 31	07 38	07 48		08 01	08 08	08 18		08 30	08 38	08 48		08 58	09 08
Homerton d	23p52		06 33	06 50	07 03	07 10	07 20		07 33	07 40	07 50		08 03	08 10	08 20		08 32	08 40	08 50		09 00	09 10
Hackney Wick d	23p54		06 35	06 52	07 05	07 12	07 22		07 35	07 42	07 52		08 05	08 12	08 22		08 34	08 42	08 52		09 02	09 12
Stratford [7] ⊖ a	00 04		06 42	06 59	07 11	07 19	07 29		07 41	07 49	07 59		08 11	08 19	08 29		08 41	08 49	08 59		09 09	09 19

Table 59

Saturdays
until 21 July

Richmond and Clapham Junction - Willesden Junction, West Hampstead, Highbury and Islington and Stratford

Network Diagram - see first Page of Table 59

	LO	LO	LO	LO	LO	LO	LO		LO	LO	LO	LO	LO	LO	LO	LO	LO	LO	LO	LO	LO
Richmond ⊖ d	08 28		08 38		08 58		09 08		14 08		14 28		14 38		14 58		15 08		15 28		15 38
Kew Gardens ⊖ d	08 31		08 41		09 01		09 11		14 11		14 31		14 41		15 01		15 11		15 31		15 41
Gunnersbury ⊖ d	08 34		08 44		09 04		09 14		14 14		14 34		14 44		15 04		15 14		15 34		15 44
South Acton d	08 37		08 47		09 07		09 17		14 17		14 37		14 47		15 07		15 17		15 37		15 47
Acton Central d	08 40		08 50		09 10		09 20		14 20		14 40		14 50		15 10		15 20		15 40		15 50
Clapham Junction [10] d		08 30		08 45		09 00				14 15		14 30		14 45		15 00		15 15		15 30	
Imperial Wharf d		08 34		08 49		09 04				14 19		14 34		14 49		15 04		15 19		15 34	
West Brompton ⊖ d		08 37		08 52		09 07				14 22		14 37		14 52		15 07		15 22		15 37	
Kensington (Olympia) ⊖ d		08 40		08 55		09 10				14 25		14 40		14 55		15 10		15 25		15 40	
Shepherd's Bush ⊖ d		08 42		08 57		09 12				14 27		14 42		14 57		15 12		15 27		15 42	
Willesden Jn Low Level ⊖ d																					
Willesden Jn. High Level ⊖ a	08 45	08 51	08 55	09 05	09 15	09 21	09 25	and at the same minutes past each hour until	14 25	14 35	14 45	14 51	14 55	15 05	15 15	15 21	15 25	15 35	15 45	15 51	15 55
d	08 46		08 56	09 06	09 16		09 26		14 26	14 36	14 46		14 56	15 06	15 16		15 26	15 36	15 46		15 56
Kensal Rise d	08 48		08 58	09 08	09 18		09 28		14 28	14 38	14 48		14 58	15 08	15 18		15 28	15 38	15 48		15 58
Brondesbury Park d	08 50		09 00	09 10	09 20		09 30		14 30	14 40	14 50		15 00	15 10	15 20		15 30	15 40	15 50		16 00
Brondesbury d	08 52		09 02	09 12	09 22		09 32		14 32	14 42	14 52		15 02	15 12	15 22		15 32	15 42	15 52		16 02
West Hampstead ⊖ d	08 54		09 04	09 14	09 24		09 34		14 34	14 44	14 54		15 04	15 14	15 24		15 34	15 44	15 54		16 04
Finchley Road & Frognal d	08 55		09 05	09 15	09 25		09 35		14 35	14 45	14 55		15 05	15 15	15 25		15 35	15 45	15 55		16 05
Hampstead Heath d	08 58		09 08	09 18	09 28		09 38		14 38	14 48	14 58		15 08	15 18	15 28		15 38	15 48	15 58		16 08
Gospel Oak d	09 00		09 10	09 20	09 30		09 40		14 40	14 50	15 00		15 10	15 20	15 30		15 40	15 50	16 00		16 10
Kentish Town West d	09 02		09 12	09 22	09 32		09 42		14 42	14 52	15 02		15 12	15 22	15 32		15 42	15 52	16 02		16 12
Camden Road d	09 06		09 16	09 26	09 36		09 46		14 46	14 56	15 06		15 16	15 26	15 36		15 46	15 56	16 06		16 16
Caledonian Rd & Barnsbury d	09 09		09 19	09 29	09 39		09 49		14 49	14 59	15 09		15 19	15 29	15 39		15 49	15 59	16 09		16 19
Highbury & Islington ⊖ d	09 12		09 22	09 32	09 42		09 52		14 52	15 02	15 12		15 22	15 32	15 42		15 52	16 02	16 12		16 22
Canonbury ⊖ d	09 14		09 24	09 34	09 44		09 54		14 54	15 04	15 14		15 24	15 34	15 44		15 54	16 04	16 14		16 24
Dalston Kingsland d	09 16		09 26	09 36	09 46		09 56		14 56	15 06	15 16		15 26	15 36	15 46		15 56	16 06	16 16		16 26
Hackney Central d	09 18		09 28	09 38	09 48		09 58		14 58	15 08	15 18		15 28	15 38	15 48		15 58	16 08	16 18		16 28
Homerton d	09 20		09 30	09 40	09 50		10 00		15 00	15 10	15 20		15 30	15 40	15 50		16 00	16 10	16 20		16 30
Hackney Wick d	09 22		09 32	09 42	09 52		10 02		15 02	15 12	15 22		15 32	15 42	15 52		16 02	16 12	16 22		16 32
Stratford [7] ⊖ a	09 29		09 39	09 49	09 59		10 09		15 09	15 19	15 29		15 39	15 49	15 59		16 10	16 21	16 30		16 40

	LO	LO	LO	LO	LO	LO	LO	LO	LO	LO	LO	LO	LO	LO	LO	LO	LO	LO	LO	LO	LO	LO
Richmond ⊖ d		15 58		16 08		16 28		16 38		16 58		17 08		17 28		17 38		17 58		18 08		18 28
Kew Gardens ⊖ d		16 01		16 11		16 31		16 41		17 01		17 11		17 31		17 41		18 01		18 11		18 31
Gunnersbury ⊖ d		16 04		16 14		16 34		16 44		17 04		17 14		17 34		17 44		18 04		18 14		18 34
South Acton d		16 07		16 17		16 37		16 47		17 07		17 17		17 37		17 47		18 07		18 17		18 37
Acton Central d		16 10		16 20		16 40		16 50		17 10		17 20		17 40		17 50		18 10		18 20		18 40
Clapham Junction [10] d	15 45		16 00		16 15		16 30		16 45		17 00		17 15		17 30		17 45		18 00		18 15	
Imperial Wharf d	15 49		16 04		16 19		16 34		16 49		17 04		17 19		17 34		17 49		18 04		18 19	
West Brompton ⊖ d	15 52		16 07		16 22		16 37		16 52		17 07		17 22		17 37		17 52		18 07		18 22	
Kensington (Olympia) ⊖ d	15 55		16 10		16 25		16 40		16 55		17 10		17 25		17 40		17 55		18 10		18 25	
Shepherd's Bush ⊖ d	15 57		16 12		16 27		16 42		16 57		17 12		17 27		17 42		17 57		18 12		18 27	
Willesden Jn Low Level ⊖ d																						
Willesden Jn. High Level ⊖ a	16 05	16 15	16 21	16 25	16 35	16 45	16 53	16 55	17 05	17 15	17 21	17 25	17 35	17 45	17 51	17 55	18 05	18 15	18 21	18 25	18 35	18 45
d	16 06	16 16		16 26	16 36	16 46		16 56	17 06	17 16		17 26	17 36	17 46		17 56	18 06	18 16		18 26	18 36	18 46
Kensal Rise d	16 08	16 18		16 28	16 38	16 48		16 58	17 08	17 18		17 28	17 38	17 48		17 58	18 08	18 18		18 28	18 38	18 48
Brondesbury Park d	16 10	16 20		16 30	16 40	16 50		17 00	17 10	17 20		17 30	17 40	17 50		18 00	18 10	18 20		18 30	18 40	18 50
Brondesbury d	16 12	16 22		16 32	16 42	16 52		17 02	17 12	17 22		17 32	17 42	17 52		18 02	18 12	18 22		18 32	18 42	18 52
West Hampstead ⊖ d	16 14	16 24		16 34	16 44	16 54		17 04	17 14	17 24		17 34	17 44	17 54		18 04	18 14	18 24		18 34	18 44	18 54
Finchley Road & Frognal d	16 15	16 25		16 35	16 45	16 55		17 05	17 15	17 25		17 35	17 45	17 55		18 05	18 15	18 25		18 35	18 45	18 55
Hampstead Heath d	16 18	16 28		16 38	16 48	16 58		17 08	17 18	17 28		17 38	17 48	17 58		18 08	18 18	18 28		18 38	18 48	18 58
Gospel Oak d	16 20	16 30		16 40	16 50	17 00		17 11	17 20	17 30		17 40	17 50	18 00		18 10	18 20	18 30		18 40	18 50	19 00
Kentish Town West d	16 22	16 32		16 42	16 52	17 02		17 13	17 22	17 32		17 42	17 52	18 02		18 12	18 22	18 32		18 42	18 52	19 02
Camden Road d	16 26	16 36		16 46	16 56	17 06		17 16	17 26	17 36		17 46	17 56	18 06		18 16	18 26	18 36		18 46	18 56	19 06
Caledonian Rd & Barnsbury d	16 29	16 39		16 49	16 59	17 09		17 19	17 29	17 39		17 49	17 59	18 09		18 19	18 29	18 39		18 49	18 59	19 09
Highbury & Islington ⊖ d	16 32	16 42		16 52	17 02	17 12		17 22	17 32	17 42		17 52	18 02	18 12		18 22	18 32	18 42		18 52	19 02	19 12
Canonbury ⊖ d	16 34	16 44		16 54	17 04	17 14		17 24	17 34	17 44		17 54	18 04	18 14		18 24	18 34	18 44		18 54	19 04	19 14
Dalston Kingsland d	16 36	16 46		16 56	17 06	17 16		17 26	17 36	17 46		17 56	18 06	18 16		18 26	18 36	18 46		18 56	19 06	19 16
Hackney Central d	16 38	16 48		16 58	17 08	17 18		17 28	17 38	17 48		17 58	18 08	18 18		18 28	18 38	18 48		18 58	19 08	19 18
Homerton d	16 40	16 50		17 00	17 10	17 20		17 30	17 40	17 50		18 00	18 10	18 20		18 30	18 40	18 50		19 00	19 10	19 20
Hackney Wick d	16 42	16 52		17 02	17 12	17 22		17 32	17 42	17 52		18 02	18 12	18 22		18 32	18 42	18 52		19 02	19 12	19 22
Stratford [7] ⊖ a	16 51	17 00		17 10	17 21	17 30		17 40	17 51	18 00		18 10	18 21	18 30		18 40	18 51	19 00		19 10	19 21	19 30

Richmond and Clapham Junction - Willesden Junction, West Hampstead, Highbury and Islington and Stratford

Network Diagram - see first Page of Table 59

		LO	LO	LO	LO	LO	LO	LO	LO	LO	LO	LO	LO	LO	LO	LO	LO	LO	LO	LO	LO	LO	LO
Richmond ⊖	d		18 38		18 58		19 08		19 28		19 38		19 58		20 08		20 28		20 38		20 58		21 08
Kew Gardens ⊖	d		18 41		19 01		19 11		19 31		19 41		20 01		20 11		20 31		20 41		21 01		21 11
Gunnersbury ⊖	d		18 44		19 04		19 14		19 34		19 44		20 04		20 14		20 34		20 44		21 04		21 14
South Acton	d		18 47		19 07		19 17		19 37		19 47		20 07		20 17		20 37		20 47		21 07		21 17
Acton Central	d		18 50		19 10		19 20		19 40		19 50		20 10		20 20		20 40		20 50		21 10		21 20
Clapham Junction 10	d	18 30		18 45		19 00		19 15		19 30		19 45		20 00		20 15		20 30		20 45		21 00	
Imperial Wharf	d	18 34		18 49		19 04		19 19		19 34		19 49		20 04		20 19		20 34		20 49		21 04	
West Brompton ⊖	d	18 37		18 52		19 07		19 22		19 37		19 52		20 07		20 22		20 37		20 52		21 07	
Kensington (Olympia) ⊖	d	18 40		18 55		19 10		19 25		19 40		19 55		20 10		20 25		20 40		20 55		21 10	
Shepherd's Bush ⊖	d	18 42		18 57		19 12		19 27		19 42		19 57		20 12		20 27		20 42		20 57		21 12	
Willesden Jn Low Level ⊖	d																						
Willesden Jn. High Level ⊖	a	18 51	18 55	19 05	19 15	19 21	19 25	19 35	19 45	19 51	19 55	20 05	20 15	20 21	20 25	20 35	20 45	20 51	20 55	21 05	21 15	21 21	21 25
	d		18 56	19 06	19 16		19 26	19 36	19 46		19 56	20 06	20 16		20 26	20 36	20 46		20 56	21 06	21 16		21 26
Kensal Rise	d		18 58	19 08	19 18		19 28	19 38	19 48		19 58	20 08	20 18		20 28	20 38	20 48		20 58	21 08	21 18		21 28
Brondesbury Park	d		19 00	19 10	19 20		19 30	19 40	19 50		20 00	20 10	20 20		20 30	20 40	20 50		21 00	21 10	21 20		21 30
Brondesbury	d		19 02	19 12	19 22		19 32	19 42	19 52		20 02	20 12	20 22		20 32	20 42	20 52		21 02	21 12	21 22		21 32
West Hampstead ⊖	d		19 04	19 14	19 24		19 34	19 44	19 54		20 04	20 14	20 24		20 34	20 44	20 54		21 04	21 14	21 24		21 34
Finchley Road & Frognal	d		19 05	19 15	19 25		19 35	19 45	19 55		20 05	20 15	20 25		20 35	20 45	20 55		21 05	21 15	21 25		21 35
Hampstead Heath	d		19 08	19 18	19 28		19 38	19 48	19 58		20 08	20 18	20 28		20 38	20 48	20 58		21 08	21 18	21 28		21 38
Gospel Oak	d		19 10	19 20	19 30		19 40	19 50	20 00		20 10	20 20	20 30		20 40	20 50	21 00		21 10	21 20	21 30		21 40
Kentish Town West	d		19 12	19 22	19 32		19 42	19 52	20 02		20 12	20 22	20 32		20 42	20 52	21 02		21 12	21 22	21 32		21 42
Camden Road	d		19 16	19 26	19 36		19 46	19 56	20 06		20 16	20 26	20 36		20 46	20 56	21 06		21 16	21 26	21 36		21 46
Caledonian Rd & Barnsbury	d		19 19	19 29	19 39		19 49	19 59	20 09		20 19	20 29	20 39		20 49	20 59	21 09		21 19	21 29	21 39		21 49
Highbury & Islington ⊖	d		19 22	19 32	19 42		19 52	20 02	20 12		20 22	20 32	20 42		20 52	21 02	21 12		21 22	21 32	21 42		21 52
Canonbury ⊖	d		19 24	19 34	19 44		19 54	20 04	20 14		20 24	20 34	20 44		20 54	21 04	21 14		21 24	21 34	21 44		21 54
Dalston Kingsland	d		19 26	19 36	19 46		19 56	20 06	20 16		20 26	20 36	20 46		20 56	21 06	21 16		21 26	21 36	21 46		21 56
Hackney Central	d		19 28	19 38	19 48		19 58	20 08	20 18		20 28	20 38	20 48		20 58	21 08	21 18		21 28	21 38	21 48		21 58
Homerton	d		19 30	19 40	19 50		20 00	20 10	20 20		20 30	20 40	20 50		21 00	21 10	21 20		21 30	21 40	21 50		22 00
Hackney Wick	d		19 32	19 42	19 52		20 02	20 12	20 22		20 32	20 42	20 52		21 02	21 12	21 22		21 32	21 42	21 52		22 02
Stratford 7 ⊖	a		19 40	19 51	20 00		20 10	20 21	20 30		20 40	20 51	21 01		21 09	21 19	21 29		21 39	21 49	21 59		22 09

		LO	LO	LO	LO	LO	LO	LO	LO	LO	LO	LO	LO	LO	LO	LO
Richmond ⊖	d		21 28		21 38		21 58			22 28			23 00		23 28	
Kew Gardens ⊖	d		21 31		21 41		22 01			22 31			23 03		23 31	
Gunnersbury ⊖	d		21 34		21 44		22 04			22 34			23 06		23 34	
South Acton	d		21 37		21 47		22 07			22 37			23 09		23 37	
Acton Central	d		21 40		21 50		22 10			22 40			23 12		23 40	
Clapham Junction 10	d	21 15		21 30		21 45		22 00	22 15		22 30	22 45		23 00		23 30
Imperial Wharf	d	21 19		21 34		21 49		22 04	22 19		22 34	22 51		23 04		23 34
West Brompton ⊖	d	21 22		21 37		21 52		22 07	22 22		22 37	22 54		23 07		23 37
Kensington (Olympia) ⊖	d	21 25		21 40		21 55		22 10	22 25		22 40	22 59		23 10		23 40
Shepherd's Bush ⊖	d	21 27		21 42		21 57		22 12	22 27		22 42	23 01		23 12		23 42
Willesden Jn Low Level ⊖	d															
Willesden Jn. High Level ⊖	a	21 35	21 45	21 51	21 55	22 05	22 15	22 21	22 36	22 45	22 52	23 09	23 17	23 21	23 45	23 51
	d	21 36	21 46		21 56	22 06	22 16			22 46			23 18			
Kensal Rise	d	21 38	21 48		21 58	22 08	22 18			22 48			23 20			
Brondesbury Park	d	21 40	21 50		22 00	22 10	22 20			22 50			23 22			
Brondesbury	d	21 42	21 52		22 02	22 12	22 22			22 52			23 24			
West Hampstead ⊖	d	21 44	21 54		22 04	22 14	22 24			22 54			23 26			
Finchley Road & Frognal	d	21 45	21 55		22 05	22 15	22 25			22 55			23 27			
Hampstead Heath	d	21 48	21 58		22 08	22 18	22 28			22 58			23 30			
Gospel Oak	d	21 50	22 00		22 10	22 20	22 30			23 00			23 32			
Kentish Town West	d	21 52	22 02		22 12	22 22	22 32			23 02			23 34			
Camden Road	d	21 56	22 06		22 16	22 26	22 36			23 06			23 38			
Caledonian Rd & Barnsbury	d	21 59	22 09		22 19	22 29	22 39			23 09			23 41			
Highbury & Islington ⊖	d	22 02	22 12		22 22	22 32	22 42			23 12			23 44			
Canonbury ⊖	d	22 04	22 14		22 24	22 34	22 44			23 14			23 46			
Dalston Kingsland	d	22 06	22 16		22 26	22 36	22 46			23 16			23 48			
Hackney Central	d	22 08	22 18		22 28	22 38	22 48			23 18			23 50			
Homerton	d	22 10	22 20		22 30	22 40	22 50			23 20			23 52			
Hackney Wick	d	22 12	22 22		22 32	22 42	22 52			23 22			23 54			
Stratford 7 ⊖	a	22 19	22 29		22 39	22 49	22 59			23 29			23 59			

Richmond and Clapham Junction - Willesden Junction, West Hampstead, Highbury and Islington and Stratford

Network Diagram - see first Page of Table 59

		LO	LO	LO	LO	LO	LO	LO	LO	LO	LO	LO	LO	LO	LO	LO	LO	LO	LO	LO	LO	LO	LO
Richmond ⊖	d	22p55		23p11		23p25		23p41		23p55								05 54		06 10		06 25	
Kew Gardens ⊖	d	22p58		23p14		23p28		23p44		23p59								05 57		06 13		06 28	
Gunnersbury ⊖	d	23p01		23p17		23p31		23p47		00 01								06 01		06 16		06 31	
South Acton	d	23p04		23p20		23p34		23p50		00 04								06 04		06 19		06 34	
Acton Central	d	23p07		23p22		23p37		23p52		00 07								06 07		06 22		06 37	
Clapham Junction 10	d		22p59		23p14		23p29		23p44		23p59	00 15	05 47								06 14		06 29
Imperial Wharf	d		23p03		23p18		23p33		23p48		00 03	00 19	05 51								06 18		06 33
West Brompton ⊖	d		23p06		23p21		23p36		23p51		00 06	00 22	05 54								06 21		06 36
Kensington (Olympia) ⊖	d		23p10		23p25		23p40		23p55		00 10	00 25	05 58								06 25		06 40
Shepherd's Bush ⊖	d		23p12		23p27		23p42		23p57		00 12	00 27	06 00								06 27		06 42
Willesden Jn Low Level ⊖	d															05 58							
Willesden Jn. High Level ⊖	a	23p12	23p20	23p27	23p35	23p42	23p50	23p57	00 05	00 12	00 20	00 40	06 12					06 12		06 27	06 35	06 42	06 50
	d	23p14	23p21	23p29	23p36	23p43	23p51	23p59	00 06	00 14	00 21							06 13		06 29	06 36	06 44	06 51
Kensal Rise	d	23p16	23p23	23p31	23p38	23p45	23p53	00 01	00 08	00 16	00 23					06 02		06 15		06 31	06 38	06 46	06 53
Brondesbury Park	d	23p18	23p25	23p33	23p40	23p47	23p55	00 03	00 10	00 18	00 25					06 04		06 17		06 33	06 40	06 48	06 55
Brondesbury	d	23p20	23p27	23p35	23p42	23p49	23p57	00 05	00 12	00 20	00 27					06 06		06 19		06 35	06 42	06 50	06 57
West Hampstead ⊖	d	23p22	23p29	23p37	23p44	23p51	23p59	00 07	00 14	00 22	00 29					06 08		06 21		06 37	06 44	06 52	06 59
Finchley Road & Frognal	d	23p24	23p31	23p39	23p46	23p53	00 01	00 09	00 16	00 24	00 31					06 09		06 22		06 39	06 46	06 54	07 01
Hampstead Heath	d	23p26	23p33	23p41	23p48	23p55	00 03	00 11	00 18	00 26	00 33					06 12		06 25		06 41	06 48	06 56	07 03
Gospel Oak	d	23p30	23p37	23p45	23p52	00 01	00 07	00 15	00 22	00 30	00 37					06 14		06 27		06 45	06 52	07 00	07 07
Kentish Town West	d	23p32	23p39	23p47	23p54	00 02	00 09	00 17	00 24	00 32	00 39					06 16		06 29		06 47	06 54	07 02	07 09
Camden Road	d	23p36	23p43	23p51	23p58	00 06	00 12	00 21	00 28	00 36	00 43			06 11	06 16	06 20	06 29	06 36	06 40	06 51	06 58	07 06	07 13
Caledonian Rd & Barnsbury	d	23p39	23p46	23p54	00 01	00 09	00 15	00 24	00 31	00 39	00 46			06 14	06 19	06 23	06 32	06 39	06 43	06 54	07 01	07 09	07 16
Highbury & Islington ⊖	d	23p41	23p48	23p56	00 03	00 11	00 18	00 26	00 33	00 41	00 48			06 16	06 21	06 26	06 35	06 42	06 47	06 56	07 03	07 11	07 18
Canonbury ⊖	d	23p43	23p50	23p59	00 05	00 13	00 20	00 28	00 35	00 43	00 50			06 18	06 23	06 28	06 37	06 44	06 48	06 58	07 05	07 13	07 20
Dalston Kingsland	d	23p46	23p53	00 02	00 08	00 16	00 22	00 31	00 38	00 46	00 53			06 20	06 25	06 30	06 39	06 46	06 50	07 01	07 08	07 16	07 23
Hackney Central	d	23p48	23p55	00 03	00 10	00 18	00 24	00 33	00 40	00 48	00 55			06 22	06 27	06 32	06 41	06 48	06 52	07 03	07 10	07 18	07 25
Homerton	d	23p50	23p57	00 05	00 12	00 20	00 26	00 35	00 42	00 50	00 57			06 24	06 29	06 34	06 43	06 50	06 54	07 05	07 12	07 20	07 27
Hackney Wick	d	23p52	23p59	00 07	00 14	00 22	00 29	00 37	00 44	00 52	00 59			06 26	06 31	06 36	06 45	06 52	06 56	07 07	07 14	07 22	07 29
Stratford 7 ⊖	a	00 04	00 09	00 19	00 24	00 34	00 40	00 49	00 54	01 04	01 09			06 38	06 41	06 46	06 55	07 02	07 10	07 19	07 24	07 34	07 39

		LO	LO	LO	LO	LO	LO	LO	LO	LO	LO	LO	LO	LO	LO	LO	LO	LO	LO	LO	LO	LO	LO
Richmond ⊖	d	06 40		06 55		07 11		07 25		07 41		07 55		08 11		08 25		08 41		08 55		09 11	
Kew Gardens ⊖	d	06 43		06 58		07 14		07 28		07 44		07 58		08 14		08 28		08 44		08 58		09 14	
Gunnersbury ⊖	d	06 46		07 01		07 17		07 31		07 47		08 01		08 17		08 31		08 47		09 01		09 17	
South Acton	d	06 49		07 04		07 22		07 34		07 50		08 04		08 20		08 34		08 50		09 04		09 20	
Acton Central	d	06 52		07 07		07 24		07 37		07 52		08 07		08 22		08 37		08 52		09 07		09 22	
Clapham Junction 10	d		06 44		06 59		07 14		07 29		07 44		07 59		08 14		08 29		08 44		08 59		09 14
Imperial Wharf	d		06 48		07 03		07 18		07 33		07 48		08 03		08 18		08 33		08 48		09 03		09 18
West Brompton ⊖	d		06 51		07 06		07 21		07 36		07 51		08 06		08 21		08 36		08 51		09 06		09 21
Kensington (Olympia) ⊖	d		06 55		07 10		07 25		07 40		07 55		08 10		08 25		08 40		08 55		09 10		09 25
Shepherd's Bush ⊖	d		06 57		07 12		07 27		07 42		07 57		08 12		08 27		08 42		08 57		09 12		09 27
Willesden Jn Low Level ⊖	d																						
Willesden Jn. High Level ⊖	a	06 57	07 05	07 12	07 20	07 28	07 35	07 42	07 50	07 57	08 05	08 12	08 22	08 27	08 35	08 42	08 50	08 57	09 05	09 12	09 20	09 27	09 35
	d	06 59	07 06	07 14	07 21	07 29	07 36	07 44	07 51	07 59	08 06	08 14	08 24	08 29	08 36	08 44	08 51	08 59	09 06	09 14	09 21	09 29	09 36
Kensal Rise	d	07 01	07 08	07 16	07 23	07 31	07 38	07 46	07 53	08 01	08 08	08 16	08 27	08 31	08 38	08 46	08 53	09 01	09 08	09 16	09 23	09 31	09 38
Brondesbury Park	d	07 03	07 10	07 18	07 25	07 33	07 40	07 48	07 55	08 03	08 10	08 18	08 29	08 33	08 40	08 48	08 55	09 03	09 10	09 18	09 25	09 33	09 40
Brondesbury	d	07 05	07 12	07 20	07 27	07 35	07 42	07 50	07 57	08 05	08 12	08 20	08 30	08 35	08 42	08 50	08 57	09 05	09 12	09 20	09 27	09 35	09 42
West Hampstead ⊖	d	07 07	07 14	07 22	07 29	07 37	07 44	07 52	07 59	08 07	08 14	08 22	08 32	08 37	08 44	08 52	08 59	09 07	09 14	09 22	09 29	09 37	09 44
Finchley Road & Frognal	d	07 09	07 16	07 24	07 31	07 39	07 46	07 54	08 01	08 09	08 16	08 24	08 34	08 39	08 46	08 54	09 01	09 09	09 16	09 24	09 31	09 39	09 46
Hampstead Heath	d	07 11	07 18	07 26	07 33	07 41	07 48	07 56	08 03	08 11	08 18	08 26	08 36	08 41	08 48	08 56	09 03	09 11	09 18	09 26	09 33	09 41	09 48
Gospel Oak	d	07 15	07 22	07 30	07 37	07 45	07 52	08 00	08 07	08 15	08 22	08 30	08 39	08 45	08 52	09 00	09 07	09 15	09 22	09 30	09 37	09 45	09 52
Kentish Town West	d	07 17	07 24	07 32	07 39	07 47	07 54	08 02	08 09	08 17	08 24	08 32	08 41	08 47	08 54	09 02	09 09	09 17	09 24	09 32	09 39	09 47	09 54
Camden Road	d	07 20	07 31	07 36	07 43	07 51	07 58	08 06	08 13	08 21	08 28	08 36	08 43	08 51	08 58	09 06	09 13	09 21	09 28	09 36	09 43	09 51	09 58
Caledonian Rd & Barnsbury	d	07 23	07 34	07 39	07 46	07 54	08 01	08 09	08 16	08 24	08 31	08 39	08 46	08 54	09 01	09 09	09 16	09 24	09 31	09 39	09 46	09 54	10 01
Highbury & Islington ⊖	d	07 25	07 36	07 41	07 48	07 56	08 03	08 11	08 18	08 26	08 33	08 41	08 49	08 56	09 03	09 11	09 18	09 26	09 33	09 41	09 48	09 56	10 03
Canonbury ⊖	d	07 27	07 38	07 43	07 50	07 58	08 05	08 13	08 20	08 28	08 35	08 43	08 51	08 58	09 05	09 13	09 20	09 28	09 35	09 43	09 50	09 58	10 05
Dalston Kingsland	d	07 29	07 40	07 46	07 53	08 01	08 08	08 16	08 23	08 31	08 38	08 46	08 53	09 01	09 08	09 16	09 23	09 31	09 38	09 46	09 53	10 01	10 08
Hackney Central	d	07 31	07 42	07 48	07 55	08 03	08 10	08 18	08 25	08 33	08 40	08 48	08 55	09 03	09 10	09 18	09 25	09 33	09 40	09 48	09 55	10 03	10 10
Homerton	d	07 33	07 44	07 50	07 57	08 05	08 12	08 20	08 27	08 35	08 42	08 50	08 57	09 05	09 12	09 20	09 27	09 35	09 42	09 50	09 57	10 05	10 12
Hackney Wick	d	07 36	07 47	07 52	07 59	08 07	08 14	08 22	08 29	08 37	08 44	08 52	08 59	09 07	09 14	09 22	09 29	09 37	09 44	09 52	09 59	10 07	10 14
Stratford 7 ⊖	a	07 48	07 57	08 04	08 09	08 19	08 24	08 34	08 39	08 49	08 54	09 04	09 09	09 19	09 24	09 34	09 39	09 49	09 54	10 04	10 09	10 19	10 24

Richmond and Clapham Junction - Willesden Junction, West Hampstead, Highbury and Islington and Stratford

Network Diagram - see first Page of Table 59

	LO	LO	LO	LO	LO	LO	LO	LO	LO	LO	LO
Richmond ⊖ d	09 25		09 40		09 55		10 11		10 25		10 41
Kew Gardens ⊖ d	09 28		09 43		09 58		10 14		10 28		10 44
Gunnersbury ⊖ d	09 31		09 46		10 01		10 17		10 31		10 47
South Acton d	09 34		09 49		10 04		10 20		10 34		10 50
Acton Central d	09 37		09 52		10 07		10 22		10 37		10 52
Clapham Junction 10 d		09 29		09 44		09 59		10 14		10 29	
Imperial Wharf d		09 33		09 48		10 03		10 18		10 33	
West Brompton ⊖ d		09 36		09 51		10 06		10 21		10 36	
Kensington (Olympia) ⊖ d		09 40		09 55		10 10		10 25		10 40	
Shepherd's Bush ⊖ d		09 42		09 57		10 12		10 27		10 42	
Willesden Jn Low Level ⊖ d											
Willesden Jn. High Level ⊖ a	09 42	09 50	09 57	10 05	10 12	10 20	10 27	10 35	10 42	10 50	10 57
d	09 44	09 51	09 59	10 06	10 14	10 21	10 29	10 36	10 44	10 51	10 59
Kensal Rise d	09 46	09 53	10 01	10 08	10 16	10 23	10 31	10 38	10 46	10 53	11 01
Brondesbury Park d	09 48	09 55	10 03	10 10	10 18	10 25	10 33	10 40	10 48	10 55	11 03
Brondesbury d	09 50	09 57	10 05	10 12	10 20	10 27	10 35	10 42	10 50	10 57	11 05
West Hampstead ⊖ d	09 52	09 59	10 07	10 14	10 22	10 29	10 37	10 44	10 52	10 59	11 07
Finchley Road & Frognal d	09 54	10 01	10 09	10 16	10 24	10 31	10 39	10 46	10 54	11 01	11 09
Hampstead Heath d	09 56	10 03	10 11	10 18	10 26	10 33	10 41	10 48	10 56	11 03	11 11
Gospel Oak d	10 00	10 07	10 15	10 22	10 30	10 37	10 45	10 52	11 00	11 07	11 15
Kentish Town West d	10 02	10 09	10 17	10 24	10 32	10 39	10 47	10 54	11 02	11 09	11 17
Camden Road d	10 06	10 13	10 21	10 28	10 36	10 43	10 51	10 58	11 06	11 13	11 21
Caledonian Rd & Barnsbury d	10 09	10 16	10 24	10 31	10 39	10 46	10 54	11 01	11 09	11 16	11 24
Highbury & Islington ⊖ d	10 11	10 18	10 26	10 33	10 41	10 48	10 56	11 03	11 11	11 18	11 26
Canonbury ⊖ d	10 13	10 20	10 28	10 35	10 43	10 50	10 58	11 05	11 13	11 20	11 28
Dalston Kingsland d	10 16	10 23	10 31	10 38	10 46	10 53	11 01	11 08	11 16	11 23	11 31
Hackney Central d	10 18	10 25	10 33	10 40	10 48	10 55	11 03	11 10	11 18	11 25	11 33
Homerton d	10 20	10 27	10 35	10 42	10 50	10 57	11 05	11 12	11 20	11 27	11 35
Hackney Wick d	10 22	10 29	10 37	10 44	10 52	10 59	11 07	11 14	11 22	11 29	11 37
Stratford 7 ⊖ a	10 34	10 39	10 49	10 54	11 04	11 09	11 19	11 24	11 34	11 39	11 49

	LO	LO	LO	LO	LO	LO	LO	LO	LO	LO	LO
Richmond ⊖ d		10 55		11 11		11 25		11 41		11 55	
Kew Gardens ⊖ d		10 58		11 14		11 28		11 44		11 58	
Gunnersbury ⊖ d		11 01		11 17		11 31		11 47		12 01	
South Acton d		11 04		11 20		11 35		11 50		12 04	
Acton Central d		11 07		11 22		11 38		11 52		12 07	
Clapham Junction 10 d	10 44		10 59		11 14		11 29		11 44		11 59
Imperial Wharf d	10 48		11 03		11 18		11 33		11 48		12 03
West Brompton ⊖ d	10 51		11 06		11 21		11 36		11 51		12 06
Kensington (Olympia) ⊖ d	10 55		11 10		11 25		11 40		11 55		12 10
Shepherd's Bush ⊖ d	10 57		11 12		11 27		11 42		11 57		12 12
Willesden Jn Low Level ⊖ d											
Willesden Jn. High Level ⊖ a	11 05	11 12	11 20	11 27	11 35	11 43	11 50	11 57	12 05	12 12	12 20
d	11 06	11 14	11 21	11 29	11 36	11 44	11 51	11 59	12 06	12 14	12 21
Kensal Rise d	11 08	11 16	11 23	11 31	11 38	11 46	11 53	12 01	12 08	12 16	12 23
Brondesbury Park d	11 10	11 18	11 25	11 33	11 40	11 48	11 55	12 03	12 10	12 18	12 25
Brondesbury d	11 12	11 20	11 27	11 35	11 42	11 50	11 57	12 05	12 12	12 20	12 27
West Hampstead ⊖ d	11 14	11 22	11 29	11 37	11 44	11 52	11 59	12 07	12 14	12 22	12 29
Finchley Road & Frognal d	11 16	11 24	11 31	11 39	11 46	11 54	12 01	12 09	12 16	12 24	12 31
Hampstead Heath d	11 18	11 26	11 33	11 41	11 48	11 56	12 03	12 11	12 18	12 26	12 33
Gospel Oak d	11 22	11 30	11 37	11 45	11 52	12 00	12 07	12 15	12 22	12 30	12 37
Kentish Town West d	11 24	11 32	11 39	11 47	11 54	12 02	12 09	12 17	12 24	12 32	12 39
Camden Road d	11 28	11 36	11 43	11 51	11 58	12 06	12 13	12 21	12 28	12 36	12 43
Caledonian Rd & Barnsbury d	11 31	11 39	11 46	11 54	12 01	12 09	12 16	12 24	12 31	12 39	12 46
Highbury & Islington ⊖ d	11 33	11 41	11 48	11 56	12 03	12 11	12 18	12 26	12 33	12 41	12 48
Canonbury ⊖ d	11 35	11 43	11 50	11 58	12 05	12 13	12 20	12 28	12 35	12 43	12 50
Dalston Kingsland d	11 38	11 46	11 53	12 01	12 08	12 16	12 23	12 31	12 38	12 46	12 53
Hackney Central d	11 40	11 48	11 55	12 03	12 10	12 18	12 25	12 33	12 40	12 48	12 55
Homerton d	11 42	11 50	11 57	12 05	12 12	12 20	12 27	12 35	12 42	12 50	12 57
Hackney Wick d	11 44	11 52	11 59	12 07	12 14	12 22	12 29	12 37	12 45	12 52	12 59
Stratford 7 ⊖ a	11 54	12 04	12 09	12 19	12 24	12 35	12 39	12 49	12 55	13 04	13 09

	LO	LO	LO	LO	LO	LO	LO	LO	LO	LO	LO
Richmond ⊖ d	12 11		12 25		12 41		12 55		13 11		13 25
Kew Gardens ⊖ d	12 14		12 28		12 44		12 58		13 14		13 28
Gunnersbury ⊖ d	12 17		12 31		12 47		13 01		13 17		13 31
South Acton d	12 20		12 34		12 50		13 04		13 20		13 34
Acton Central d	12 22		12 37		12 52		13 07		13 22		13 37
Clapham Junction 10 d		12 14		12 29		12 44		12 59		13 14	
Imperial Wharf d		12 18		12 33		12 48		13 03		13 18	
West Brompton ⊖ d		12 21		12 36		12 51		13 06		13 21	
Kensington (Olympia) ⊖ d		12 25		12 40		12 55		13 10		13 25	
Shepherd's Bush ⊖ d		12 27		12 42		12 57		13 12		13 27	
Willesden Jn Low Level ⊖ d											
Willesden Jn. High Level ⊖ a	12 27	12 35	12 42	12 50	12 57	13 05	13 12	13 20	13 27	13 35	13 42
d	12 29	12 36	12 44	12 51	12 59	13 06	13 14	13 21	13 29	13 36	13 44
Kensal Rise d	12 31	12 38	12 46	12 53	13 01	13 08	13 16	13 23	13 31	13 38	13 46
Brondesbury Park d	12 33	12 40	12 48	12 55	13 03	13 10	13 18	13 25	13 33	13 40	13 48
Brondesbury d	12 35	12 42	12 50	12 57	13 05	13 12	13 20	13 27	13 35	13 42	13 50
West Hampstead ⊖ d	12 37	12 44	12 52	12 59	13 07	13 14	13 22	13 29	13 37	13 44	13 52
Finchley Road & Frognal d	12 39	12 46	12 54	13 01	13 09	13 16	13 24	13 31	13 39	13 46	13 54
Hampstead Heath d	12 41	12 48	12 56	13 03	13 11	13 18	13 26	13 33	13 41	13 48	13 56
Gospel Oak d	12 45	12 52	13 00	13 07	13 15	13 22	13 30	13 37	13 45	13 52	14 00
Kentish Town West d	12 47	12 54	13 02	13 09	13 17	13 24	13 32	13 39	13 47	13 54	14 02
Camden Road d	12 51	12 58	13 06	13 13	13 21	13 28	13 36	13 43	13 51	13 58	14 06
Caledonian Rd & Barnsbury d	12 54	13 01	13 09	13 16	13 24	13 31	13 39	13 46	13 54	14 01	14 09
Highbury & Islington ⊖ d	12 56	13 03	13 11	13 18	13 26	13 33	13 41	13 48	13 56	14 03	14 11
Canonbury ⊖ d	12 58	13 05	13 13	13 20	13 28	13 35	13 43	13 50	13 58	14 05	14 13
Dalston Kingsland d	13 01	13 08	13 16	13 23	13 31	13 38	13 46	13 53	14 01	14 08	14 16
Hackney Central d	13 03	13 10	13 18	13 25	13 33	13 40	13 48	13 55	14 03	14 10	14 18
Homerton d	13 05	13 12	13 20	13 27	13 35	13 42	13 50	13 57	14 05	14 12	14 20
Hackney Wick d	13 07	13 14	13 22	13 29	13 37	13 44	13 52	13 59	14 07	14 14	14 22
Stratford 7 ⊖ a	13 19	13 24	13 34	13 39	13 49	13 54	14 04	14 09	14 19	14 24	14 34

	LO	LO	LO	LO	LO	LO	LO	LO	LO	LO	LO
Richmond ⊖ d		13 41		13 55		14 11		14 25		14 41	
Kew Gardens ⊖ d		13 44		13 58		14 14		14 28		14 44	
Gunnersbury ⊖ d		13 47		14 01		14 17		14 31		14 47	
South Acton d		13 50		14 04		14 20		14 34		14 50	
Acton Central d		13 52		14 07		14 22		14 37		14 52	
Clapham Junction 10 d	13 29		13 44		13 59		14 14		14 29		14 44
Imperial Wharf d	13 33		13 48		14 03		14 18		14 33		14 48
West Brompton ⊖ d	13 36		13 51		14 06		14 21		14 36		14 51
Kensington (Olympia) ⊖ d	13 40		13 55		14 10		14 25		14 40		14 55
Shepherd's Bush ⊖ d	13 42		13 57		14 12		14 27		14 42		14 57
Willesden Jn Low Level ⊖ d											
Willesden Jn. High Level ⊖ a	13 50	13 57	14 05	14 12	14 20	14 27	14 35	14 42	14 50	14 57	15 05
d	13 51	13 59	14 06	14 14	14 21	14 29	14 36	14 44	14 51	14 59	15 06
Kensal Rise d	13 53	14 01	14 08	14 16	14 23	14 31	14 38	14 46	14 53	15 01	15 08
Brondesbury Park d	13 55	14 03	14 10	14 18	14 25	14 33	14 40	14 48	14 55	15 03	15 10
Brondesbury d	13 57	14 05	14 12	14 20	14 27	14 35	14 42	14 50	14 57	15 05	15 12
West Hampstead ⊖ d	13 59	14 07	14 14	14 22	14 29	14 37	14 44	14 52	14 59	15 07	15 14
Finchley Road & Frognal d	14 01	14 09	14 16	14 24	14 31	14 39	14 46	14 54	15 01	15 09	15 16
Hampstead Heath d	14 03	14 11	14 18	14 26	14 33	14 41	14 48	14 56	15 03	15 11	15 18
Gospel Oak d	14 07	14 15	14 22	14 30	14 37	14 45	14 52	15 00	15 07	15 15	15 22
Kentish Town West d	14 09	14 17	14 24	14 32	14 39	14 47	14 54	15 02	15 09	15 17	15 24
Camden Road d	14 13	14 21	14 28	14 36	14 43	14 51	14 58	15 06	15 13	15 21	15 28
Caledonian Rd & Barnsbury d	14 16	14 24	14 31	14 39	14 46	14 54	15 01	15 09	15 16	15 24	15 31
Highbury & Islington ⊖ d	14 18	14 26	14 33	14 41	14 48	14 56	15 03	15 11	15 18	15 26	15 33
Canonbury ⊖ d	14 20	14 28	14 35	14 43	14 50	14 58	15 05	15 13	15 20	15 28	15 35
Dalston Kingsland d	14 23	14 31	14 38	14 46	14 53	15 01	15 08	15 16	15 23	15 31	15 38
Hackney Central d	14 25	14 33	14 40	14 48	14 55	15 03	15 10	15 18	15 25	15 33	15 40
Homerton d	14 27	14 35	14 42	14 50	14 57	15 05	15 12	15 20	15 27	15 35	15 42
Hackney Wick d	14 29	14 37	14 44	14 52	14 59	15 07	15 14	15 22	15 29	15 37	15 44
Stratford 7 ⊖ a	14 39	14 49	14 54	15 04	15 09	15 19	15 24	15 34	15 39	15 49	15 54

Richmond and Clapham Junction - Willesden Junction, West Hampstead, Highbury and Islington and Stratford

Network Diagram - see first Page of Table 59

	LO	LO	LO	LO	LO	LO	LO	LO	LO	LO	LO
Richmond ⊖ d	14 55		15 11		15 25		15 41		15 55		16 11
Kew Gardens ⊖ d	14 58		15 14		15 28		15 44		15 58		16 14
Gunnersbury ⊖ d	15 01		15 17		15 31		15 47		16 01		16 17
South Acton d	15 04		15 20		15 34		15 50		16 04		16 20
Acton Central d	15 07		15 22		15 37		15 52		16 07		16 22
Clapham Junction 10 d		14 59		15 14		15 29		15 44		15 59	
Imperial Wharf d		15 03		15 18		15 33		15 48		16 03	
West Brompton ⊖ d		15 06		15 21		15 36		15 51		16 06	
Kensington (Olympia) ⊖ d		15 10		15 25		15 40		15 55		16 10	
Shepherd's Bush ⊖ d		15 12		15 27		15 42		15 57		16 12	
Willesden Jn Low Level ⊖ d											
Willesden Jn. High Level ⊖ a	15 12	15 20	15 27	15 35	15 42	15 50	15 57	16 05	16 12	16 20	16 27
d	15 14	15 21	15 29	15 36	15 44	15 51	15 59	16 06	16 14	16 21	16 29
Kensal Rise d	15 16	15 23	15 31	15 38	15 46	15 53	16 01	16 08	16 16	16 23	16 31
Brondesbury Park d	15 18	15 25	15 33	15 40	15 48	15 55	16 03	16 10	16 18	16 25	16 33
Brondesbury d	15 20	15 27	15 35	15 42	15 50	15 57	16 05	16 12	16 20	16 27	16 35
West Hampstead ⊖ d	15 22	15 29	15 37	15 44	15 52	15 59	16 07	16 14	16 22	16 29	16 37
Finchley Road & Frognal d	15 24	15 31	15 39	15 46	15 54	16 01	16 09	16 16	16 24	16 31	16 39
Hampstead Heath d	15 26	15 33	15 41	15 48	15 56	16 03	16 11	16 18	16 26	16 33	16 41
Gospel Oak d	15 30	15 37	15 45	15 52	16 00	16 07	16 15	16 22	16 30	16 37	16 45
Kentish Town West d	15 32	15 39	15 47	15 54	16 02	16 09	16 17	16 24	16 32	16 39	16 47
Camden Road d	15 36	15 43	15 51	15 58	16 06	16 13	16 21	16 28	16 36	16 43	16 51
Caledonian Rd & Barnsbury d	15 39	15 46	15 54	16 01	16 09	16 16	16 24	16 31	16 39	16 46	16 54
Highbury & Islington ⊖ d	15 41	15 48	15 56	16 03	16 11	16 18	16 26	16 33	16 41	16 48	16 56
Canonbury ⊖ d	15 43	15 50	15 58	16 05	16 13	16 20	16 28	16 35	16 43	16 50	16 58
Dalston Kingsland d	15 46	15 53	16 01	16 08	16 16	16 23	16 31	16 38	16 46	16 53	17 01
Hackney Central d	15 48	15 55	16 03	16 10	16 18	16 25	16 33	16 40	16 48	16 55	17 03
Homerton d	15 50	15 57	16 05	16 12	16 20	16 27	16 35	16 42	16 50	16 57	17 05
Hackney Wick d	15 52	15 59	16 07	16 14	16 22	16 29	16 37	16 44	16 52	16 59	17 07
Stratford 7 ⊖ a	16 04	16 09	16 19	16 24	16 34	16 40	16 49	16 54	17 04	17 09	17 19

	LO	LO	LO		LO	LO	LO	LO	LO	LO
Richmond ⊖ d		16 25				22 41		22 55		23 11
Kew Gardens ⊖ d		16 28				22 44		22 58		23 14
Gunnersbury ⊖ d		16 31				22 47		23 01		23 17
South Acton d		16 34				22 50		23 04		23 20
Acton Central d		16 37				22 52		23 07		23 22
Clapham Junction 10 d	16 14		16 29		22 29		22 44		22 59	
Imperial Wharf d	16 18		16 33		22 33		22 48		23 03	
West Brompton ⊖ d	16 21		16 36		22 36		22 51		23 06	
Kensington (Olympia) ⊖ d	16 25		16 40		22 40		22 55		23 10	
Shepherd's Bush ⊖ d	16 27		16 42		22 42		22 57		23 12	
Willesden Jn Low Level ⊖ d										
Willesden Jn. High Level ⊖ a	16 35	16 42	16 50	and at the same minutes past each hour until	22 50	22 57	23 05	23 12	23 20	23 27
d	16 36	16 44	16 51		22 51	22 59	23 06	23 14	23 21	23 29
Kensal Rise d	16 38	16 46	16 53		22 53	23 01	23 08	23 16	23 23	23 31
Brondesbury Park d	16 40	16 48	16 55		22 55	23 03	23 10	23 18	23 25	23 33
Brondesbury d	16 42	16 50	16 57		22 57	23 05	23 12	23 20	23 27	23 35
West Hampstead ⊖ d	16 44	16 52	16 59		22 59	23 07	23 14	23 22	23 29	23 37
Finchley Road & Frognal d	16 46	16 54	17 01		23 01	23 09	23 16	23 24	23 31	23 39
Hampstead Heath d	16 48	16 56	17 03		23 03	23 11	23 18	23 26	23 33	23 41
Gospel Oak d	16 52	17 00	17 07		23 07	23 15	23 22	23 30	23 37	23 45
Kentish Town West d	16 54	17 02	17 09		23 09	23 17	23 24	23 32	23 39	23 47
Camden Road d	16 58	17 06	17 13		23 13	23 21	23 28	23 36	23 43	23 51
Caledonian Rd & Barnsbury d	17 01	17 09	17 16		23 16	23 24	23 31	23 39	23 46	23 54
Highbury & Islington ⊖ d	17 03	17 11	17 18		23 18	23 26	23 33	23 41	23 48	23 56
Canonbury ⊖ d	17 05	17 13	17 20		23 20	23 28	23 35	23 43	23 50	23 59
Dalston Kingsland d	17 08	17 16	17 23		23 23	23 31	23 38	23 46	23 53	00 02
Hackney Central d	17 10	17 18	17 25		23 25	23 33	23 40	23 48	23 55	00 03
Homerton d	17 12	17 20	17 27		23 27	23 35	23 42	23 50	23 57	00 05
Hackney Wick d	17 14	17 22	17 29		23 29	23 37	23 44	23 52	23 59	00 07
Stratford 7 ⊖ a	17 24	17 34	17 39		23 39	23 49	23 54	00 04	00 09	00 19

	LO	LO	LO	LO	LO	LO	LO
Richmond ⊖ d		23 25		23 41		23 55	
Kew Gardens ⊖ d		23 28		23 44		23 59	
Gunnersbury ⊖ d		23 31		23 47		00 01	
South Acton d		23 34		23 50		00 04	
Acton Central d		23 37		23 52		00 07	
Clapham Junction 10 d	23 14		23 29		23 44		23 59
Imperial Wharf d	23 18		23 33		23 48		00 03
West Brompton ⊖ d	23 21		23 36		23 51		00 06
Kensington (Olympia) ⊖ d	23 25		23 40		23 55		00 10
Shepherd's Bush ⊖ d	23 27		23 42		23 57		00 12
Willesden Jn Low Level ⊖ d							
Willesden Jn. High Level ⊖ a	23 35	23 42	23 50	23 57	00 05	00 12	00 20
d	23 36	23 44	23 51	23 59	00 06	00 14	00 21
Kensal Rise d	23 38	23 46	23 53	00 01	00 08	00 16	00 23
Brondesbury Park d	23 40	23 48	23 55	00 03	00 10	00 18	00 25
Brondesbury d	23 42	23 50	23 57	00 05	00 12	00 20	00 27
West Hampstead ⊖ d	23 44	23 52	23 59	00 07	00 14	00 22	00 29
Finchley Road & Frognal d	23 46	23 54	00 01	00 09	00 16	00 24	00 31
Hampstead Heath d	23 48	23 56	00 03	00 11	00 18	00 26	00 33
Gospel Oak d	23 52	00 01	00 07	00 15	00 22	00 30	00 37
Kentish Town West d	23 54	00 02	00 09	00 17	00 24	00 32	00 39
Camden Road d	23 58	00 06	00 13	00 21	00 28	00 36	00 43
Caledonian Rd & Barnsbury d	00 01	00 09	00 16	00 24	00 31	00 39	00 46
Highbury & Islington ⊖ d	00 03	00 11	00 18	00 26	00 33	00 41	00 48
Canonbury ⊖ d	00 05	00 13	00 20	00 28	00 35	00 43	00 50
Dalston Kingsland d	00 08	00 16	00 23	00 31	00 38	00 46	00 53
Hackney Central d	00 10	00 18	00 25	00 33	00 40	00 48	00 55
Homerton d	00 12	00 20	00 27	00 35	00 42	00 50	00 57
Hackney Wick d	00 14	00 22	00 29	00 37	00 44	00 52	00 59
Stratford 7 ⊖ a	00 24	00 34	00 39	00 49	00 54	01 04	01 09

Richmond and Clapham Junction - Willesden Junction, West Hampstead, Highbury and Islington and Stratford

Network Diagram - see first Page of Table 59

	LO	LO	LO	LO	LO	LO	LO	LO	LO	LO	LO	LO	LO	LO	LO	LO	LO	LO	LO	LO	LO	LO
Richmond ⊖ d	23p00			05 58	06 10		06 28		06 40		06 58		07 10		07 28		07 40		07 58		08 08	
Kew Gardens ⊖ d	23p03			06 01	06 13		06 31		06 43		07 01		07 13		07 31		07 43		08 01		08 11	
Gunnersbury ⊖ d	23p06			06 04	06 16		06 34		06 46		07 04		07 16		07 34		07 46		08 04		08 14	
South Acton d	23p09			06 07	06 19		06 37		06 49		07 07		07 19		07 37		07 49		08 07		08 17	
Acton Central d	23p12			06 10	06 23		06 40		06 53		07 10		07 23		07 40		07 52		08 10		08 20	
Clapham Junction 10 d		05 47				06 15		06 30		06 45		07 00		07 15		07 30		07 45		08 00		08 15
Imperial Wharf d		05 51				06 19		06 34		06 49		07 04		07 19		07 34		07 49		08 04		08 19
West Brompton ⊖ d		05 54				06 22		06 37		06 52		07 07		07 22		07 37		07 52		08 07		08 22
Kensington (Olympia) ⊖ d		05 57				06 25		06 40		06 55		07 10		07 25		07 40		07 55		08 10		08 25
Shepherd's Bush ⊖ d		05 59				06 27		06 42		06 57		07 12		07 27		07 42		07 57		08 12		08 27
Willesden Jn Low Level ⊖ d			05 57																			
Willesden Jn. High Level ⊖ a	23p17	06 08		06 15	06 28	06 35	06 45	06 53	06 58	07 05	07 15	07 23	07 28	07 35	07 45	07 51	07 57	08 05	08 15	08 21	08 25	08 35
d	23p18			06 16	06 29	06 36	06 46		06 59	07 06	07 16		07 29	07 36	07 46		07 58	08 06	08 16		08 26	08 36
Kensal Rise d	23p20		06 01	06 18	06 31	06 38	06 48		07 01	07 08	07 18		07 31	07 38	07 48		08 00	08 08	08 18		08 28	08 38
Brondesbury Park d	23p22		06 03	06 20	06 33	06 40	06 50		07 03	07 10	07 20		07 33	07 40	07 50		08 02	08 10	08 20		08 30	08 40
Brondesbury d	23p24		06 05	06 22	06 35	06 42	06 52		07 05	07 12	07 22		07 35	07 42	07 52		08 04	08 12	08 22		08 32	08 42
West Hampstead ⊖ d	23p26		06 07	06 24	06 37	06 44	06 54		07 07	07 14	07 24		07 37	07 44	07 54		08 06	08 14	08 24		08 34	08 44
Finchley Road & Frognal d	23p27		06 08	06 25	06 38	06 45	06 55		07 08	07 15	07 25		07 38	07 45	07 55		08 07	08 15	08 25		08 35	08 45
Hampstead Heath d	23p30		06 11	06 28	06 41	06 48	06 58		07 11	07 18	07 28		07 41	07 48	07 58		08 10	08 18	08 28		08 38	08 48
Gospel Oak d	23p32		06 13	06 30	06 43	06 50	07 00		07 13	07 20	07 30		07 43	07 50	08 00		08 12	08 20	08 30		08 41	08 50
Kentish Town West d	23p34		06 15	06 32	06 45	06 52	07 02		07 15	07 22	07 32		07 45	07 52	08 02		08 14	08 22	08 32		08 43	08 52
Camden Road d	23p38		06 19	06 36	06 49	06 56	07 06		07 19	07 26	07 36		07 49	07 56	08 06		08 18	08 26	08 36		08 46	08 56
Caledonian Rd & Barnsbury d	23p41		06 22	06 39	06 52	06 59	07 09		07 22	07 29	07 39		07 52	07 59	08 09		08 21	08 29	08 39		08 49	08 59
Highbury & Islington ⊖ d	23p44		06 25	06 42	06 55	07 02	07 12		07 25	07 32	07 42		07 55	08 02	08 12		08 24	08 32	08 42		08 52	09 02
Canonbury ⊖ d	23p46		06 27	06 44	06 57	07 04	07 14		07 27	07 34	07 44		07 57	08 04	08 14		08 26	08 34	08 44		08 54	09 04
Dalston Kingsland d	23p48		06 29	06 46	06 59	07 06	07 16		07 29	07 36	07 46		07 59	08 06	08 16		08 28	08 36	08 46		08 56	09 06
Hackney Central d	23p50		06 31	06 48	07 01	07 08	07 18		07 31	07 38	07 48		08 01	08 08	08 18		08 30	08 38	08 48		08 58	09 08
Homerton d	23p52		06 33	06 50	07 03	07 10	07 20		07 33	07 40	07 50		08 03	08 10	08 20		08 32	08 40	08 50		09 00	09 10
Hackney Wick d	23p54		06 35	06 52	07 05	07 12	07 22		07 35	07 42	07 52		08 05	08 12	08 22		08 34	08 42	08 52		09 02	09 12
Stratford 7 ⊖ a	00 04		06 42	06 59	07 11	07 19	07 29		07 41	07 49	07 59		08 11	08 19	08 29		08 41	08 49	08 59		09 09	09 19

	LO	LO	LO	LO	LO	LO	LO		LO	LO	LO	LO	LO	LO	LO	LO	LO	LO	LO	LO	LO
Richmond ⊖ d	08 28		08 38		08 58		09 08		14 08		14 28		14 38		14 58		15 08		15 28		15 38
Kew Gardens ⊖ d	08 31		08 41		09 01		09 11		14 11		14 31		14 41		15 01		15 11		15 31		15 41
Gunnersbury ⊖ d	08 34		08 44		09 04		09 14		14 14		14 34		14 44		15 04		15 14		15 34		15 44
South Acton d	08 37		08 47		09 07		09 17		14 17		14 37		14 47		15 07		15 17		15 37		15 47
Acton Central d	08 40		08 50		09 10		09 20		14 20		14 40		14 50		15 10		15 20		15 40		15 50
Clapham Junction 10 d		08 30		08 45		09 00				14 15		14 30		14 45		15 00		15 15		15 30	
Imperial Wharf d		08 34		08 49		09 04				14 19		14 34		14 49		15 04		15 19		15 34	
West Brompton ⊖ d		08 37		08 52		09 07				14 22		14 37		14 52		15 07		15 22		15 37	
Kensington (Olympia) ⊖ d		08 40		08 55		09 10				14 25		14 40		14 55		15 10		15 25		15 40	
Shepherd's Bush ⊖ d		08 42		08 57		09 12				14 27		14 42		14 57		15 12		15 27		15 42	
Willesden Jn Low Level ⊖ d																					
Willesden Jn. High Level ⊖ a	08 45	08 51	08 55	09 05	09 15	09 21	09 25	and at the same minutes past each hour until	14 25	14 35	14 45	14 51	14 55	15 05	15 15	15 21	15 25	15 35	15 45	15 51	15 55
d	08 46		08 56	09 06	09 16		09 26		14 26	14 36	14 46		14 56	15 06	15 16		15 26	15 36	15 46		15 56
Kensal Rise d	08 48		08 58	09 08	09 18		09 28		14 28	14 38	14 48		14 58	15 08	15 18		15 28	15 38	15 48		15 58
Brondesbury Park d	08 50		09 00	09 10	09 20		09 30		14 30	14 40	14 50		15 00	15 10	15 20		15 30	15 40	15 50		16 00
Brondesbury d	08 52		09 02	09 12	09 22		09 32		14 32	14 42	14 52		15 02	15 12	15 22		15 32	15 42	15 52		16 02
West Hampstead ⊖ d	08 54		09 04	09 14	09 24		09 34		14 34	14 44	14 54		15 04	15 14	15 24		15 34	15 44	15 54		16 04
Finchley Road & Frognal d	08 55		09 05	09 15	09 25		09 35		14 35	14 45	14 55		15 05	15 15	15 25		15 35	15 45	15 55		16 05
Hampstead Heath d	08 58		09 08	09 18	09 28		09 38		14 38	14 48	14 58		15 08	15 18	15 28		15 38	15 48	15 58		16 08
Gospel Oak d	09 00		09 10	09 20	09 30		09 40		14 40	14 50	15 00		15 10	15 20	15 30		15 40	15 50	16 00		16 10
Kentish Town West d	09 02		09 12	09 22	09 32		09 42		14 42	14 52	15 02		15 12	15 22	15 32		15 42	15 52	16 02		16 12
Camden Road d	09 06		09 16	09 26	09 36		09 46		14 46	14 56	15 06		15 16	15 26	15 36		15 46	15 56	16 06		16 16
Caledonian Rd & Barnsbury d	09 09		09 19	09 29	09 39		09 49		14 49	14 59	15 09		15 19	15 29	15 39		15 49	15 59	16 09		16 19
Highbury & Islington ⊖ d	09 12		09 22	09 32	09 42		09 52		14 52	15 02	15 12		15 22	15 32	15 42		15 52	16 02	16 12		16 22
Canonbury ⊖ d	09 14		09 24	09 34	09 44		09 54		14 54	15 04	15 14		15 24	15 34	15 44		15 54	16 04	16 14		16 24
Dalston Kingsland d	09 16		09 26	09 36	09 46		09 56		14 56	15 06	15 16		15 26	15 36	15 46		15 56	16 06	16 16		16 26
Hackney Central d	09 18		09 28	09 38	09 48		09 58		14 58	15 08	15 18		15 28	15 38	15 48		15 58	16 08	16 18		16 28
Homerton d	09 20		09 30	09 40	09 50		10 00		15 00	15 10	15 20		15 30	15 40	15 50		16 00	16 10	16 20		16 30
Hackney Wick d	09 22		09 32	09 42	09 52		10 02		15 02	15 12	15 22		15 32	15 42	15 52		16 02	16 12	16 22		16 32
Stratford 7 ⊖ a	09 29		09 39	09 49	09 59		10 09		15 09	15 19	15 29		15 39	15 49	15 59		16 10	16 21	16 30		16 39

Richmond and Clapham Junction - Willesden Junction, West Hampstead, Highbury and Islington and Stratford

18 August to 25 August

Network Diagram - see first Page of Table 59

	LO	LO	LO	LO	LO	LO	LO	LO	LO	LO	LO	LO	LO	LO	LO	LO	LO	LO	LO	LO	LO	LO
Richmond ⊖ d		15 58		16 08		16 28		16 38		16 58		17 08		17 28		17 38		17 58		18 08		18 28
Kew Gardens ⊖ d		16 01		16 11		16 31		16 41		17 01		17 11		17 31		17 41		18 01		18 11		18 31
Gunnersbury ⊖ d		16 04		16 14		16 34		16 44		17 04		17 14		17 34		17 44		18 04		18 14		18 34
South Acton d		16 07		16 17		16 37		16 47		17 07		17 17		17 37		17 47		18 07		18 17		18 37
Acton Central d		16 10		16 20		16 40		16 50		17 10		17 20		17 40		17 50		18 10		18 20		18 40
Clapham Junction 10 d	15 45		16 00		16 15		16 30		16 45		17 00		17 15		17 30		17 45		18 00		18 15	
Imperial Wharf d	15 49		16 04		16 19		16 34		16 49		17 04		17 19		17 34		17 49		18 04		18 19	
West Brompton ⊖ d	15 52		16 07		16 22		16 37		16 52		17 07		17 22		17 37		17 52		18 07		18 22	
Kensington (Olympia) ⊖ d	15 55		16 10		16 25		16 40		16 55		17 10		17 25		17 40		17 55		18 10		18 25	
Shepherd's Bush ⊖ d	15 57		16 12		16 27		16 42		16 57		17 12		17 27		17 42		17 57		18 12		18 27	
Willesden Jn Low Level ⊖ d																						
Willesden Jn. High Level ⊖ a	16 05	16 15	16 21	16 25	16 35	16 45	16 53	16 55	17 05	17 15	17 21	17 25	17 35	17 45	17 51	17 55	18 05	18 15	18 21	18 25	18 35	18 45
d	16 06	16 16		16 26	16 36	16 46		16 56	17 06	17 16		17 26	17 36	17 46		17 56	18 06	18 16		18 26	18 36	18 46
Kensal Rise d	16 08	16 18		16 28	16 38	16 48		16 58	17 08	17 18		17 28	17 38	17 48		17 58	18 08	18 18		18 28	18 38	18 48
Brondesbury Park d	16 10	16 20		16 30	16 40	16 50		17 00	17 10	17 20		17 30	17 40	17 50		18 00	18 10	18 20		18 30	18 40	18 50
Brondesbury d	16 12	16 22		16 32	16 42	16 52		17 02	17 12	17 22		17 32	17 42	17 52		18 02	18 12	18 22		18 32	18 42	18 52
West Hampstead ⊖ d	16 14	16 24		16 34	16 44	16 54		17 04	17 14	17 24		17 34	17 44	17 54		18 04	18 14	18 24		18 34	18 44	18 54
Finchley Road & Frognal d	16 15	16 25		16 35	16 45	16 55		17 05	17 15	17 25		17 35	17 45	17 55		18 05	18 15	18 25		18 35	18 45	18 55
Hampstead Heath d	16 18	16 28		16 38	16 48	16 58		17 08	17 18	17 28		17 38	17 48	17 58		18 08	18 18	18 28		18 38	18 48	18 58
Gospel Oak d	16 20	16 30		16 40	16 50	17 00		17 11	17 20	17 30		17 40	17 50	18 00		18 10	18 20	18 30		18 40	18 50	19 00
Kentish Town West d	16 22	16 32		16 42	16 52	17 02		17 13	17 22	17 32		17 42	17 52	18 02		18 12	18 22	18 32		18 42	18 52	19 02
Camden Road d	16 26	16 36		16 46	16 56	17 06		17 16	17 26	17 36		17 46	17 56	18 06		18 16	18 26	18 36		18 46	18 56	19 06
Caledonian Rd & Barnsbury d	16 29	16 39		16 49	16 59	17 09		17 19	17 29	17 39		17 49	17 59	18 09		18 19	18 29	18 39		18 49	18 59	19 09
Highbury & Islington ⊖ d	16 32	16 42		16 52	17 02	17 12		17 22	17 32	17 42		17 52	18 02	18 12		18 22	18 32	18 42		18 52	19 02	19 12
Canonbury ⊖ d	16 34	16 44		16 54	17 04	17 14		17 24	17 34	17 44		17 54	18 04	18 14		18 24	18 34	18 44		18 54	19 04	19 14
Dalston Kingsland d	16 36	16 46		16 56	17 06	17 16		17 26	17 36	17 46		17 56	18 06	18 16		18 26	18 36	18 46		18 56	19 06	19 16
Hackney Central d	16 38	16 48		16 58	17 08	17 18		17 28	17 38	17 48		17 58	18 08	18 18		18 28	18 38	18 48		18 58	19 08	19 18
Homerton d	16 40	16 50		17 00	17 10	17 20		17 30	17 40	17 50		18 00	18 10	18 20		18 30	18 40	18 50		19 00	19 10	19 20
Hackney Wick d	16 42	16 52		17 02	17 12	17 22		17 32	17 42	17 52		18 02	18 12	18 22		18 32	18 42	18 52		19 02	19 12	19 22
Stratford 7 ⊖ a	16 51	17 00		17 10	17 21	17 30		17 40	17 51	18 00		18 10	18 21	18 30		18 40	18 51	19 00		19 10	19 21	19 30

	LO	LO	LO	LO	LO	LO	LO	LO	LO	LO	LO	LO	LO	LO	LO	LO	LO	LO	LO	LO	LO	LO
Richmond ⊖ d		18 38		18 58		19 08		19 28		19 38		19 58		20 08		20 28		20 38		20 58		21 08
Kew Gardens ⊖ d		18 41		19 01		19 11		19 31		19 41		20 01		20 11		20 31		20 41		21 01		21 11
Gunnersbury ⊖ d		18 44		19 04		19 14		19 34		19 44		20 04		20 14		20 34		20 44		21 04		21 14
South Acton d		18 47		19 07		19 17		19 37		19 47		20 07		20 17		20 37		20 47		21 07		21 17
Acton Central d		18 50		19 10		19 20		19 40		19 50		20 10		20 20		20 40		20 50		21 10		21 20
Clapham Junction 10 d	18 30		18 45		19 00		19 15		19 30		19 45		20 00		20 15		20 30		20 45		21 00	
Imperial Wharf d	18 34		18 49		19 04		19 19		19 34		19 49		20 04		20 19		20 34		20 49		21 04	
West Brompton ⊖ d	18 37		18 52		19 07		19 22		19 37		19 52		20 07		20 22		20 37		20 52		21 07	
Kensington (Olympia) ⊖ d	18 40		18 55		19 10		19 25		19 40		19 55		20 10		20 25		20 40		20 55		21 10	
Shepherd's Bush ⊖ d	18 42		18 57		19 12		19 27		19 42		19 57		20 12		20 27		20 42		20 57		21 12	
Willesden Jn Low Level ⊖ d																						
Willesden Jn. High Level ⊖ a	18 51	18 55	19 05	19 15	19 21	19 25	19 35	19 45	19 51	19 55	20 05	20 15	20 21	20 25	20 35	20 45	20 51	20 55	21 05	21 15	21 21	21 25
d		18 56	19 06	19 16		19 26	19 36	19 46		19 56	20 06	20 16		20 26	20 36	20 46		20 56	21 06	21 16		21 26
Kensal Rise d		18 58	19 08	19 18		19 28	19 38	19 48		19 58	20 08	20 18		20 28	20 38	20 48		20 58	21 08	21 18		21 28
Brondesbury Park d		19 00	19 10	19 20		19 30	19 40	19 50		20 00	20 10	20 20		20 30	20 40	20 50		21 00	21 10	21 20		21 30
Brondesbury d		19 02	19 12	19 22		19 32	19 42	19 52		20 02	20 12	20 22		20 32	20 42	20 52		21 02	21 12	21 22		21 32
West Hampstead ⊖ d		19 04	19 14	19 24		19 34	19 44	19 54		20 04	20 14	20 24		20 34	20 44	20 54		21 04	21 14	21 24		21 34
Finchley Road & Frognal d		19 05	19 15	19 25		19 35	19 45	19 55		20 05	20 15	20 25		20 35	20 45	20 55		21 05	21 15	21 25		21 35
Hampstead Heath d		19 08	19 18	19 28		19 38	19 48	19 58		20 08	20 18	20 28		20 38	20 48	20 58		21 08	21 18	21 28		21 38
Gospel Oak d		19 10	19 20	19 30		19 40	19 50	20 00		20 10	20 20	20 30		20 40	20 50	21 00		21 10	21 20	21 30		21 40
Kentish Town West d		19 12	19 22	19 32		19 42	19 52	20 02		20 12	20 22	20 32		20 42	20 52	21 02		21 12	21 22	21 32		21 42
Camden Road d		19 16	19 26	19 36		19 46	19 56	20 06		20 16	20 26	20 36		20 46	20 56	21 06		21 16	21 26	21 36		21 46
Caledonian Rd & Barnsbury d		19 19	19 29	19 39		19 49	19 59	20 09		20 19	20 29	20 39		20 49	20 59	21 09		21 19	21 29	21 39		21 49
Highbury & Islington ⊖ d		19 22	19 32	19 42		19 52	20 02	20 12		20 22	20 32	20 42		20 52	21 02	21 12		21 22	21 32	21 42		21 52
Canonbury ⊖ d		19 24	19 34	19 44		19 54	20 04	20 14		20 24	20 34	20 44		20 54	21 04	21 14		21 24	21 34	21 44		21 54
Dalston Kingsland d		19 26	19 36	19 46		19 56	20 06	20 16		20 26	20 36	20 46		20 56	21 06	21 16		21 26	21 36	21 46		21 56
Hackney Central d		19 28	19 38	19 48		19 58	20 08	20 18		20 28	20 38	20 48		20 58	21 08	21 18		21 28	21 38	21 48		21 58
Homerton d		19 30	19 40	19 50		20 00	20 10	20 20		20 30	20 40	20 50		21 00	21 10	21 20		21 30	21 40	21 50		22 00
Hackney Wick d		19 32	19 42	19 52		20 02	20 12	20 22		20 32	20 42	20 52		21 02	21 12	21 22		21 32	21 42	21 52		22 02
Stratford 7 ⊖ a		19 40	19 51	20 00		20 10	20 21	20 30		20 40	20 51	21 01		21 09	21 19	21 29		21 39	21 49	21 59		22 09

Table 59

Saturdays
18 August to 25 August

Richmond and Clapham Junction - Willesden Junction, West Hampstead, Highbury and Islington and Stratford

Network Diagram - see first Page of Table 59

Station		LO	LO	LO	LO	LO	LO	LO	LO	LO	LO	LO	LO	LO	LO	LO
Richmond	⊖ d		21 28		21 38		21 58			22 28			23 00		23 28	
Kew Gardens	⊖ d		21 31		21 41		22 01			22 31			23 03		23 31	
Gunnersbury	⊖ d		21 34		21 44		22 04			22 34			23 06		23 34	
South Acton	d		21 37		21 47		22 07			22 37			23 09		23 37	
Acton Central	d		21 40		21 50		22 10			22 40			23 12		23 40	
Clapham Junction 10	d	21 15		21 30		21 45		22 00	22 15		22 30	22 45		23 00		23 30
Imperial Wharf	d	21 19		21 34		21 49		22 04	22 19		22 34	22 51		23 04		23 34
West Brompton	⊖ d	21 22		21 37		21 52		22 07	22 22		22 37	22 54		23 07		23 37
Kensington (Olympia)	⊖ d	21 25		21 40		21 55		22 10	22 25		22 40	22 59		23 10		23 40
Shepherd's Bush	⊖ d	21 27		21 42		21 57		22 12	22 27		22 42	23 01		23 12		23 42
Willesden Jn Low Level	⊖ d															
Willesden Jn. High Level	⊖ a	21 35	21 45	21 51	21 55	22 05	22 15	22 21	22 36	22 45	22 52	23 09	23 17	23 21	23 45	23 51
	d	21 36	21 46		21 56	22 06	22 16			22 46			23 18			
Kensal Rise	d	21 38	21 48		21 58	22 08	22 18			22 48			23 20			
Brondesbury Park	d	21 40	21 50		22 00	22 10	22 20			22 50			23 22			
Brondesbury	d	21 42	21 52		22 02	22 12	22 22			22 52			23 24			
West Hampstead	⊖ d	21 44	21 54		22 04	22 14	22 24			22 54			23 26			
Finchley Road & Frognal	d	21 45	21 55		22 05	22 15	22 25			22 55			23 27			
Hampstead Heath	d	21 48	21 58		22 08	22 18	22 28			22 58			23 30			
Gospel Oak	d	21 50	22 00		22 10	22 20	22 30			23 00			23 32			
Kentish Town West	d	21 52	22 02		22 12	22 22	22 32			23 02			23 34			
Camden Road	d	21 56	22 06		22 16	22 26	22 36			23 06			23 38			
Caledonian Rd & Barnsbury	d	21 59	22 09		22 19	22 29	22 39			23 09			23 41			
Highbury & Islington	⊖ d	22 02	22 12		22 22	22 32	22 42			23 12			23 44			
Canonbury	⊖ d	22 04	22 14		22 24	22 34	22 44			23 14			23 46			
Dalston Kingsland	d	22 06	22 16		22 26	22 36	22 46			23 16			23 48			
Hackney Central	d	22 08	22 18		22 28	22 38	22 48			23 18			23 50			
Homerton	d	22 10	22 20		22 30	22 40	22 50			23 20			23 52			
Hackney Wick	d	22 12	22 22		22 32	22 42	22 52			23 22			23 54			
Stratford 7	⊖ a	22 19	22 29		22 39	22 49	22 59			23 29			23 59			

Saturdays
1 September to 8 September

Station		LO	LO	LO	LO	LO	LO	LO	LO	LO	LO	LO
Richmond	⊖ d	22p55		23p10		23p25		23p40		23p55		
Kew Gardens	⊖ d	22p58		23p13		23p28		23p43		23p59		
Gunnersbury	⊖ d	23p01		23p16		23p31		23p46		00 01		
South Acton	d	23p04		23p19		23p34		23p49		00 04		
Acton Central	d	23p07		23p22		23p37		23p52		00 07		
Clapham Junction 10	d		22p59		23p14		23p29		23p44		23p59	00 15
Imperial Wharf	d		23p03		23p18		23p33		23p48		00 03	00 19
West Brompton	⊖ d		23p06		23p21		23p36		23p51		00 06	00 22
Kensington (Olympia)	⊖ d		23p10		23p25		23p40		23p55		00 10	00 25
Shepherd's Bush	⊖ d		23p12		23p27		23p42		23p57		00 12	00 27
Willesden Jn Low Level	⊖ d											
Willesden Jn. High Level	⊖ a	23p12	23p20	23p27	23p35	23p42	23p50	23p57	00 05	00 12	00 20	00 40
	d	23p14	23p21	23p29	23p36	23p43	23p51	23p59	00 06	00 14	00 21	
Kensal Rise	d	23p16	23p23	23p31	23p38	23p45	23p53	00 01	00 08	00 16	00 23	
Brondesbury Park	d	23p18	23p25	23p33	23p40	23p47	23p55	00 03	00 10	00 18	00 25	
Brondesbury	d	23p20	23p27	23p35	23p42	23p49	23p57	00 05	00 12	00 20	00 27	
West Hampstead	⊖ d	23p22	23p29	23p37	23p44	23p51	23p59	00 07	00 14	00 22	00 29	
Finchley Road & Frognal	d	23p24	23p31	23p39	23p46	23p53	00 01	00 09	00 16	00 24	00 31	
Hampstead Heath	d	23p26	23p33	23p41	23p48	23p55	00 03	00 11	00 18	00 26	00 33	
Gospel Oak	d	23p30	23p37	23p45	23p52	00 01	00 07	00 15	00 22	00 30	00 37	
Kentish Town West	d	23p32	23p39	23p47	23p54	00 02	00 09	00 17	00 24	00 32	00 39	
Camden Road	d	23p36	23p43	23p51	23p58	00 06	00 12	00 21	00 28	00 36	00 43	
Caledonian Rd & Barnsbury	d	23p39	23p46	23p54	00 01	00 09	00 15	00 24	00 31	00 39	00 46	
Highbury & Islington	⊖ d	23p41	23p48	23p56	00 03	00 11	00 18	00 26	00 33	00 41	00 48	
Canonbury	⊖ d	23p43	23p50	23p59	00 05	00 13	00 20	00 28	00 35	00 43	00 50	
Dalston Kingsland	d	23p46	23p53	00 02	00 08	00 16	00 22	00 31	00 38	00 46	00 53	
Hackney Central	d	23p48	23p55	00 03	00 10	00 18	00 24	00 33	00 40	00 48	00 55	
Homerton	d	23p50	23p57	00 05	00 12	00 20	00 26	00 35	00 42	00 50	00 57	
Hackney Wick	d	23p52	23p59	00 07	00 14	00 22	00 29	00 37	00 44	00 52	00 59	
Stratford 7	⊖ a	00 04	00 09	00 19	00 24	00 34	00 40	00 49	00 54	01 04	01 09	

Station		LO	LO	LO	LO	LO	LO	LO	LO	LO	LO	LO
Richmond	⊖ d						05 54		06 10		06 25	
Kew Gardens	⊖ d						05 57		06 13		06 28	
Gunnersbury	⊖ d						06 00		06 16		06 31	
South Acton	d						06 03		06 19		06 34	
Acton Central	d						06 06		06 22		06 37	
Clapham Junction 10	d	05 47								06 14		06 29
Imperial Wharf	d	05 51								06 18		06 33
West Brompton	⊖ d	05 54								06 21		06 36
Kensington (Olympia)	⊖ d	05 58								06 25		06 40
Shepherd's Bush	⊖ d	06 00								06 27		06 42
Willesden Jn Low Level	⊖ d				05 58							
Willesden Jn. High Level	⊖ a	06 12					06 11		06 27	06 35	06 42	06 50
	d						06 12		06 29	06 36	06 44	06 51
Kensal Rise	d				06 02		06 14		06 31	06 38	06 46	06 53
Brondesbury Park	d				06 04		06 16		06 33	06 40	06 48	06 55
Brondesbury	d				06 06		06 18		06 35	06 42	06 50	06 57
West Hampstead	⊖ d				06 08		06 20		06 37	06 44	06 52	06 59
Finchley Road & Frognal	d				06 09		06 21		06 39	06 46	06 54	07 01
Hampstead Heath	d				06 12		06 24		06 41	06 48	06 56	07 03
Gospel Oak	d				06 14		06 26		06 45	06 52	07 00	07 07
Kentish Town West	d				06 16		06 28		06 47	06 54	07 02	07 09
Camden Road	d		06 11	06 16	06 20	06 29	06 35	06 40	06 51	06 58	07 06	07 13
Caledonian Rd & Barnsbury	d		06 14	06 19	06 23	06 32	06 38	06 43	06 54	07 01	07 09	07 16
Highbury & Islington	⊖ d		06 16	06 21	06 26	06 35	06 41	06 47	06 56	07 03	07 11	07 18
Canonbury	⊖ d		06 18	06 23	06 28	06 37	06 43	06 48	06 58	07 05	07 13	07 20
Dalston Kingsland	d		06 20	06 25	06 30	06 39	06 45	06 50	07 01	07 08	07 16	07 23
Hackney Central	d		06 22	06 27	06 32	06 41	06 47	06 52	07 03	07 10	07 18	07 25
Homerton	d		06 24	06 29	06 34	06 43	06 49	06 54	07 05	07 12	07 20	07 27
Hackney Wick	d		06 26	06 31	06 36	06 45	06 51	06 56	07 07	07 14	07 22	07 29
Stratford 7	⊖ a		06 38	06 41	06 46	06 55	07 01	07 10	07 19	07 24	07 34	07 39

Table 59

Saturdays
1 September to 8 September

Richmond and Clapham Junction - Willesden Junction, West Hampstead, Highbury and Islington and Stratford

Network Diagram - see first Page of Table 59

Station		LO	LO	LO	LO	LO	LO	LO	LO	LO	LO	LO
Richmond	⊖ d	06 40		06 55		07 11		07 25		07 41		07 55
Kew Gardens	⊖ d	06 43		06 58		07 14		07 28		07 44		07 58
Gunnersbury	⊖ d	06 46		07 01		07 17		07 31		07 47		08 01
South Acton	d	06 49		07 04		07 22		07 34		07 50		08 04
Acton Central	d	06 52		07 07		07 24		07 37		07 52		08 07
Clapham Junction 10	d		06 44		06 59		07 14		07 29		07 44	
Imperial Wharf	d		06 48		07 03		07 18		07 33		07 48	
West Brompton	⊖ d		06 51		07 06		07 21		07 36		07 51	
Kensington (Olympia)	⊖ d		06 55		07 10		07 25		07 40		07 55	
Shepherd's Bush	⊖ d		06 57		07 12		07 27		07 42		07 57	
Willesden Jn Low Level	⊖ d											
Willesden Jn. High Level	⊖ a	06 57	07 05	07 12	07 20	07 28	07 35	07 42	07 50	07 57	08 05	08 12
	d	06 59	07 06	07 14	07 21	07 29	07 36	07 44	07 51	07 59	08 06	08 14
Kensal Rise	d	07 01	07 08	07 16	07 23	07 31	07 38	07 46	07 53	08 01	08 08	08 16
Brondesbury Park	d	07 03	07 10	07 18	07 25	07 33	07 40	07 48	07 55	08 03	08 10	08 18
Brondesbury	d	07 05	07 12	07 20	07 27	07 35	07 42	07 50	07 57	08 05	08 12	08 20
West Hampstead	⊖ d	07 07	07 14	07 22	07 29	07 37	07 44	07 52	07 59	08 07	08 14	08 22
Finchley Road & Frognal	d	07 09	07 16	07 24	07 31	07 39	07 46	07 54	08 01	08 09	08 16	08 24
Hampstead Heath	d	07 11	07 18	07 26	07 33	07 41	07 48	07 56	08 03	08 11	08 18	08 26
Gospel Oak	d	07 15	07 22	07 30	07 37	07 45	07 52	08 00	08 07	08 15	08 22	08 30
Kentish Town West	d	07 17	07 24	07 32	07 39	07 47	07 54	08 02	08 09	08 17	08 24	08 32
Camden Road	d	07 20	07 31	07 36	07 43	07 51	07 58	08 06	08 13	08 21	08 28	08 36
Caledonian Rd & Barnsbury	d	07 23	07 34	07 39	07 46	07 54	08 01	08 09	08 16	08 24	08 31	08 39
Highbury & Islington	⊖ d	07 25	07 36	07 41	07 48	07 56	08 03	08 11	08 18	08 26	08 33	08 41
Canonbury	⊖ d	07 27	07 38	07 43	07 50	07 58	08 05	08 13	08 20	08 28	08 35	08 43
Dalston Kingsland	d	07 29	07 40	07 46	07 53	08 01	08 08	08 16	08 23	08 31	08 38	08 46
Hackney Central	d	07 31	07 42	07 48	07 55	08 03	08 10	08 18	08 25	08 33	08 40	08 48
Homerton	d	07 33	07 44	07 50	07 57	08 05	08 12	08 20	08 27	08 35	08 42	08 50
Hackney Wick	d	07 36	07 47	07 52	07 59	08 07	08 14	08 22	08 29	08 37	08 44	08 52
Stratford 7	⊖ a	07 48	07 57	08 04	08 09	08 19	08 24	08 34	08 39	08 49	08 54	09 04

Station		LO	LO	LO	LO	LO	LO	LO	LO	LO	LO	LO
Richmond	⊖ d		08 11		08 25		08 41		08 55		09 11	
Kew Gardens	⊖ d		08 14		08 28		08 44		08 58		09 14	
Gunnersbury	⊖ d		08 17		08 31		08 47		09 01		09 17	
South Acton	d		08 20		08 34		08 50		09 04		09 20	
Acton Central	d		08 22		08 37		08 52		09 07		09 22	
Clapham Junction 10	d	07 59		08 14		08 29		08 44		08 59		09 14
Imperial Wharf	d	08 03		08 18		08 33		08 48		09 03		09 18
West Brompton	⊖ d	08 06		08 21		08 36		08 51		09 06		09 21
Kensington (Olympia)	⊖ d	08 10		08 25		08 40		08 55		09 10		09 25
Shepherd's Bush	⊖ d	08 12		08 27		08 42		08 57		09 12		09 27
Willesden Jn Low Level	⊖ d											
Willesden Jn. High Level	⊖ a	08 22	08 27	08 35	08 42	08 50	08 57	09 05	09 12	09 20	09 27	09 35
	d	08 24	08 29	08 36	08 44	08 51	08 59	09 06	09 14	09 21	09 29	09 36
Kensal Rise	d	08 27	08 31	08 38	08 46	08 53	09 01	09 08	09 16	09 23	09 31	09 38
Brondesbury Park	d	08 29	08 33	08 40	08 48	08 55	09 03	09 10	09 18	09 25	09 33	09 40
Brondesbury	d	08 30	08 35	08 42	08 50	08 57	09 05	09 12	09 20	09 27	09 35	09 42
West Hampstead	⊖ d	08 32	08 37	08 44	08 52	08 59	09 07	09 14	09 22	09 29	09 37	09 44
Finchley Road & Frognal	d	08 34	08 39	08 46	08 54	09 01	09 09	09 16	09 24	09 31	09 39	09 46
Hampstead Heath	d	08 36	08 41	08 48	08 56	09 03	09 11	09 18	09 26	09 33	09 41	09 48
Gospel Oak	d	08 39	08 45	08 52	09 00	09 07	09 15	09 22	09 30	09 37	09 45	09 52
Kentish Town West	d	08 41	08 47	08 54	09 02	09 09	09 17	09 24	09 32	09 39	09 47	09 54
Camden Road	d	08 43	08 51	08 58	09 06	09 13	09 21	09 28	09 36	09 43	09 51	09 58
Caledonian Rd & Barnsbury	d	08 46	08 54	09 01	09 09	09 16	09 24	09 31	09 39	09 46	09 54	10 01
Highbury & Islington	⊖ d	08 49	08 56	09 03	09 11	09 18	09 26	09 33	09 41	09 48	09 56	10 03
Canonbury	⊖ d	08 51	08 58	09 05	09 13	09 20	09 28	09 35	09 43	09 50	09 58	10 05
Dalston Kingsland	d	08 53	09 01	09 08	09 16	09 23	09 31	09 38	09 46	09 53	10 01	10 08
Hackney Central	d	08 55	09 03	09 10	09 18	09 25	09 33	09 40	09 48	09 55	10 03	10 10
Homerton	d	08 57	09 05	09 12	09 20	09 27	09 35	09 42	09 50	09 57	10 05	10 12
Hackney Wick	d	08 59	09 07	09 14	09 22	09 29	09 37	09 44	09 52	09 59	10 07	10 14
Stratford 7	⊖ a	09 09	09 19	09 24	09 34	09 39	09 49	09 54	10 04	10 09	10 19	10 24

Station		LO	LO	LO	LO	LO	LO	LO	LO	LO	LO	LO
Richmond	⊖ d	09 25		09 40		09 55		10 11		10 25		10 41
Kew Gardens	⊖ d	09 28		09 43		09 58		10 14		10 28		10 44
Gunnersbury	⊖ d	09 31		09 46		10 01		10 17		10 31		10 47
South Acton	d	09 34		09 49		10 04		10 20		10 34		10 50
Acton Central	d	09 37		09 52		10 07		10 22		10 37		10 52
Clapham Junction 10	d		09 29		09 44		09 59		10 14		10 29	
Imperial Wharf	d		09 33		09 48		10 03		10 18		10 33	
West Brompton	⊖ d		09 36		09 51		10 06		10 21		10 36	
Kensington (Olympia)	⊖ d		09 40		09 55		10 10		10 25		10 40	
Shepherd's Bush	⊖ d		09 42		09 57		10 12		10 27		10 42	
Willesden Jn Low Level	⊖ d											
Willesden Jn. High Level	⊖ a	09 42	09 50	09 57	10 05	10 12	10 20	10 27	10 35	10 42	10 50	10 57
	d	09 44	09 51	09 59	10 06	10 14	10 21	10 29	10 36	10 44	10 51	10 59
Kensal Rise	d	09 46	09 53	10 01	10 08	10 16	10 23	10 31	10 38	10 46	10 53	11 01
Brondesbury Park	d	09 48	09 55	10 03	10 10	10 18	10 25	10 33	10 40	10 48	10 55	11 03
Brondesbury	d	09 50	09 57	10 05	10 12	10 20	10 27	10 35	10 42	10 50	10 57	11 05
West Hampstead	⊖ d	09 52	09 59	10 07	10 14	10 22	10 29	10 37	10 44	10 52	10 59	11 07
Finchley Road & Frognal	d	09 54	10 01	10 09	10 16	10 24	10 31	10 39	10 46	10 54	11 01	11 09
Hampstead Heath	d	09 56	10 03	10 11	10 18	10 26	10 33	10 41	10 48	10 56	11 03	11 11
Gospel Oak	d	10 00	10 07	10 15	10 22	10 30	10 37	10 45	10 52	11 00	11 07	11 15
Kentish Town West	d	10 02	10 09	10 17	10 24	10 32	10 39	10 47	10 54	11 02	11 09	11 17
Camden Road	d	10 06	10 13	10 21	10 28	10 36	10 43	10 51	10 58	11 06	11 13	11 21
Caledonian Rd & Barnsbury	d	10 09	10 16	10 24	10 31	10 39	10 46	10 54	11 01	11 09	11 16	11 24
Highbury & Islington	⊖ d	10 11	10 18	10 26	10 33	10 41	10 48	10 56	11 03	11 11	11 18	11 26
Canonbury	⊖ d	10 13	10 20	10 28	10 35	10 43	10 50	10 58	11 05	11 13	11 20	11 28
Dalston Kingsland	d	10 16	10 23	10 31	10 38	10 46	10 53	11 01	11 08	11 16	11 23	11 31
Hackney Central	d	10 18	10 25	10 33	10 40	10 48	10 55	11 03	11 10	11 18	11 25	11 33
Homerton	d	10 20	10 27	10 35	10 42	10 50	10 57	11 05	11 12	11 20	11 27	11 35
Hackney Wick	d	10 22	10 29	10 37	10 44	10 52	10 59	11 07	11 14	11 22	11 29	11 37
Stratford 7	⊖ a	10 34	10 39	10 49	10 54	11 04	11 09	11 19	11 24	11 34	11 39	11 49

Station		LO	LO	LO	LO	LO	LO	LO	LO	LO	LO	LO
Richmond	⊖ d		10 55		11 11		11 25		11 41		11 55	
Kew Gardens	⊖ d		10 58		11 14		11 28		11 44		11 58	
Gunnersbury	⊖ d		11 01		11 17		11 31		11 47		12 01	
South Acton	d		11 04		11 20		11 35		11 50		12 04	
Acton Central	d		11 07		11 22		11 38		11 52		12 07	
Clapham Junction 10	d	10 44		10 59		11 14		11 29		11 44		11 59
Imperial Wharf	d	10 48		11 03		11 18		11 33		11 48		12 03
West Brompton	⊖ d	10 51		11 06		11 21		11 36		11 51		12 06
Kensington (Olympia)	⊖ d	10 55		11 10		11 25		11 40		11 55		12 10
Shepherd's Bush	⊖ d	10 57		11 12		11 27		11 42		11 57		12 12
Willesden Jn Low Level	⊖ d											
Willesden Jn. High Level	⊖ a	11 05	11 12	11 20	11 27	11 35	11 43	11 50	11 57	12 05	12 12	12 20
	d	11 06	11 14	11 21	11 29	11 36	11 44	11 51	11 59	12 06	12 14	12 21
Kensal Rise	d	11 08	11 16	11 23	11 31	11 38	11 46	11 53	12 01	12 08	12 16	12 23
Brondesbury Park	d	11 10	11 18	11 25	11 33	11 40	11 48	11 55	12 03	12 10	12 18	12 25
Brondesbury	d	11 12	11 20	11 27	11 35	11 42	11 50	11 57	12 05	12 12	12 20	12 27
West Hampstead	⊖ d	11 14	11 22	11 29	11 37	11 44	11 52	11 59	12 07	12 14	12 22	12 29
Finchley Road & Frognal	d	11 16	11 24	11 31	11 39	11 46	11 54	12 01	12 09	12 16	12 24	12 31
Hampstead Heath	d	11 18	11 26	11 33	11 41	11 48	11 56	12 03	12 11	12 18	12 26	12 33
Gospel Oak	d	11 22	11 30	11 37	11 45	11 52	12 00	12 07	12 15	12 22	12 30	12 37
Kentish Town West	d	11 24	11 32	11 39	11 47	11 54	12 02	12 09	12 17	12 24	12 32	12 39
Camden Road	d	11 28	11 36	11 43	11 51	11 58	12 06	12 13	12 21	12 28	12 36	12 43
Caledonian Rd & Barnsbury	d	11 31	11 39	11 46	11 54	12 01	12 09	12 16	12 24	12 31	12 39	12 46
Highbury & Islington	⊖ d	11 33	11 41	11 48	11 56	12 03	12 11	12 18	12 26	12 33	12 41	12 48
Canonbury	⊖ d	11 35	11 43	11 50	11 58	12 05	12 13	12 20	12 28	12 35	12 43	12 50
Dalston Kingsland	d	11 38	11 46	11 53	12 01	12 08	12 16	12 23	12 31	12 38	12 46	12 53
Hackney Central	d	11 40	11 48	11 55	12 03	12 10	12 18	12 25	12 33	12 40	12 48	12 55
Homerton	d	11 42	11 50	11 57	12 05	12 12	12 20	12 27	12 35	12 42	12 50	12 57
Hackney Wick	d	11 44	11 52	11 59	12 07	12 14	12 22	12 29	12 37	12 45	12 52	12 59
Stratford 7	⊖ a	11 54	12 04	12 09	12 19	12 24	12 35	12 39	12 49	12 55	13 04	13 09

Richmond and Clapham Junction - Willesden Junction, West Hampstead, Highbury and Islington and Stratford

Network Diagram - see first Page of Table 59

			LO	LO	LO	LO	LO	LO	LO	LO	LO	LO	LO	LO	LO	LO	LO	LO	LO	LO	LO	LO	LO	LO
Richmond	⊖	d	12 11		12 25		12 41		12 55		13 11		13 25		13 41		13 55		14 11		14 25		14 41	
Kew Gardens	⊖	d	12 14		12 28		12 44		12 58		13 14		13 28		13 44		13 58		14 14		14 28		14 44	
Gunnersbury	⊖	d	12 17		12 31		12 47		13 01		13 17		13 31		13 47		14 01		14 17		14 31		14 47	
South Acton		d	12 20		12 34		12 50		13 04		13 20		13 34		13 50		14 04		14 20		14 34		14 50	
Acton Central		d	12 22		12 37		12 52		13 07		13 22		13 37		13 52		14 07		14 22		14 37		14 52	
Clapham Junction 10		d		12 14		12 29		12 44		12 59		13 14		13 29		13 44		13 59		14 14		14 29		14 44
Imperial Wharf		d		12 18		12 33		12 48		13 03		13 18		13 33		13 48		14 03		14 18		14 33		14 48
West Brompton	⊖	d		12 21		12 36		12 51		13 06		13 21		13 36		13 51		14 06		14 21		14 36		14 51
Kensington (Olympia)	⊖	d		12 25		12 40		12 55		13 10		13 25		13 40		13 55		14 10		14 25		14 40		14 55
Shepherd's Bush	⊖	d		12 27		12 42		12 57		13 12		13 27		13 42		13 57		14 12		14 27		14 42		14 57
Willesden Jn Low Level	⊖	d																						
Willesden Jn. High Level	⊖	a	12 27	12 35	12 42	12 50	12 57	13 05	13 12	13 20	13 27	13 35	13 42	13 50	13 57	14 05	14 12	14 20	14 27	14 35	14 42	14 50	14 57	15 05
		d	12 29	12 36	12 44	12 51	12 59	13 06	13 14	13 21	13 29	13 36	13 44	13 51	13 59	14 06	14 14	14 21	14 29	14 36	14 44	14 51	14 59	15 06
Kensal Rise		d	12 31	12 38	12 46	12 53	13 01	13 08	13 16	13 23	13 31	13 38	13 46	13 53	14 01	14 08	14 16	14 23	14 31	14 38	14 46	14 53	15 01	15 08
Brondesbury Park		d	12 33	12 40	12 48	12 55	13 03	13 10	13 18	13 25	13 33	13 40	13 48	13 55	14 03	14 10	14 18	14 25	14 33	14 40	14 48	14 55	15 03	15 10
Brondesbury		d	12 35	12 42	12 50	12 57	13 05	13 12	13 20	13 27	13 35	13 42	13 50	13 57	14 05	14 12	14 20	14 27	14 35	14 42	14 50	14 57	15 05	15 12
West Hampstead	⊖	d	12 37	12 44	12 52	12 59	13 07	13 14	13 22	13 29	13 37	13 44	13 52	13 59	14 07	14 14	14 22	14 29	14 37	14 44	14 52	14 59	15 07	15 14
Finchley Road & Frognal		d	12 39	12 46	12 54	13 01	13 09	13 16	13 24	13 31	13 39	13 46	13 54	14 01	14 09	14 16	14 24	14 31	14 39	14 46	14 54	15 01	15 09	15 16
Hampstead Heath		d	12 41	12 48	12 56	13 03	13 11	13 18	13 26	13 33	13 41	13 48	13 56	14 03	14 11	14 18	14 26	14 33	14 41	14 48	14 56	15 03	15 11	15 18
Gospel Oak		d	12 45	12 52	13 00	13 07	13 15	13 22	13 30	13 37	13 45	13 52	14 00	14 07	14 15	14 22	14 30	14 37	14 45	14 52	15 00	15 07	15 15	15 22
Kentish Town West		d	12 47	12 54	13 02	13 09	13 17	13 24	13 32	13 39	13 47	13 54	14 02	14 09	14 17	14 24	14 32	14 39	14 47	14 54	15 02	15 09	15 17	15 24
Camden Road		d	12 51	12 58	13 06	13 13	13 21	13 28	13 36	13 43	13 51	13 58	14 06	14 13	14 21	14 28	14 36	14 43	14 51	14 58	15 06	15 13	15 21	15 28
Caledonian Rd & Barnsbury		d	12 54	13 01	13 09	13 16	13 24	13 31	13 39	13 46	13 54	14 01	14 09	14 16	14 24	14 31	14 39	14 46	14 54	15 01	15 09	15 16	15 24	15 31
Highbury & Islington	⊖	d	12 56	13 03	13 11	13 18	13 26	13 33	13 41	13 48	13 56	14 03	14 11	14 18	14 26	14 33	14 41	14 48	14 56	15 03	15 11	15 18	15 26	15 33
Canonbury	⊖	d	12 58	13 05	13 13	13 20	13 28	13 35	13 43	13 50	13 58	14 05	14 13	14 20	14 28	14 35	14 43	14 50	14 58	15 05	15 13	15 20	15 28	15 35
Dalston Kingsland		d	13 01	13 08	13 16	13 23	13 31	13 38	13 46	13 53	14 01	14 08	14 16	14 23	14 31	14 38	14 46	14 53	15 01	15 08	15 16	15 23	15 31	15 38
Hackney Central		d	13 03	13 10	13 18	13 25	13 33	13 40	13 48	13 55	14 03	14 10	14 18	14 25	14 33	14 40	14 48	14 55	15 03	15 10	15 18	15 25	15 33	15 40
Homerton		d	13 05	13 12	13 20	13 27	13 35	13 42	13 50	13 57	14 05	14 12	14 20	14 27	14 35	14 42	14 50	14 57	15 05	15 12	15 20	15 27	15 35	15 42
Hackney Wick		d	13 07	13 14	13 22	13 29	13 37	13 44	13 52	13 59	14 07	14 14	14 22	14 29	14 37	14 44	14 52	14 59	15 07	15 14	15 22	15 29	15 37	15 44
Stratford 7	⊖	a	13 19	13 24	13 34	13 39	13 49	13 54	14 04	14 09	14 19	14 24	14 34	14 39	14 49	14 54	15 04	15 09	15 19	15 24	15 34	15 39	15 49	15 54

			LO	LO	LO	LO	LO	LO	LO	LO	LO	LO	LO	LO	LO	LO		LO	LO	LO	LO	LO	LO
Richmond	⊖	d	14 55		15 11		15 25		15 41		15 55		16 11		16 25				22 41		22 55		23 11
Kew Gardens	⊖	d	14 58		15 14		15 28		15 44		15 58		16 14		16 28				22 44		22 58		23 14
Gunnersbury	⊖	d	15 01		15 17		15 31		15 47		16 01		16 17		16 31				22 47		23 01		23 17
South Acton		d	15 04		15 20		15 34		15 50		16 04		16 20		16 34				22 50		23 04		23 20
Acton Central		d	15 07		15 22		15 37		15 52		16 07		16 22		16 37				22 52		23 07		23 22
Clapham Junction 10		d		14 59		15 14		15 29		15 44		15 59		16 14		16 29		22 29		22 44		22 59	
Imperial Wharf		d		15 03		15 18		15 33		15 48		16 03		16 18		16 33		22 33		22 48		23 03	
West Brompton	⊖	d		15 06		15 21		15 36		15 51		16 06		16 21		16 36		22 36		22 51		23 06	
Kensington (Olympia)	⊖	d		15 10		15 25		15 40		15 55		16 10		16 25		16 40		22 40		22 55		23 10	
Shepherd's Bush	⊖	d		15 12		15 27		15 42		15 57		16 12		16 27		16 42		22 42		22 57		23 12	
Willesden Jn Low Level	⊖	d																					
Willesden Jn. High Level	⊖	a	15 12	15 20	15 27	15 35	15 42	15 50	15 57	16 05	16 12	16 20	16 27	16 35	16 42	16 50	and at	22 50	22 57	23 05	23 12	23 20	23 27
		d	15 14	15 21	15 29	15 36	15 44	15 51	15 59	16 06	16 14	16 21	16 29	16 36	16 44	16 51	the same	22 51	22 59	23 06	23 14	23 21	23 29
Kensal Rise		d	15 16	15 23	15 31	15 38	15 46	15 53	16 01	16 08	16 16	16 23	16 31	16 38	16 46	16 53	minutes	22 53	23 01	23 08	23 16	23 23	23 31
Brondesbury Park		d	15 18	15 25	15 33	15 40	15 48	15 55	16 03	16 10	16 18	16 25	16 33	16 40	16 48	16 55	past	22 55	23 03	23 10	23 18	23 25	23 33
Brondesbury		d	15 20	15 27	15 35	15 42	15 50	15 57	16 05	16 12	16 20	16 27	16 35	16 42	16 50	16 57	each	22 57	23 05	23 12	23 20	23 27	23 35
West Hampstead	⊖	d	15 22	15 29	15 37	15 44	15 52	15 59	16 07	16 14	16 22	16 29	16 37	16 44	16 52	16 59	hour until	22 59	23 07	23 14	23 22	23 29	23 37
Finchley Road & Frognal		d	15 24	15 31	15 39	15 46	15 54	16 01	16 09	16 16	16 24	16 31	16 39	16 46	16 54	17 01		23 01	23 09	23 16	23 24	23 31	23 39
Hampstead Heath		d	15 26	15 33	15 41	15 48	15 56	16 03	16 11	16 18	16 26	16 33	16 41	16 48	16 56	17 03		23 03	23 11	23 18	23 26	23 33	23 41
Gospel Oak		d	15 30	15 37	15 45	15 52	16 00	16 07	16 15	16 22	16 30	16 37	16 45	16 52	17 00	17 07		23 07	23 15	23 22	23 30	23 37	23 45
Kentish Town West		d	15 32	15 39	15 47	15 54	16 02	16 09	16 17	16 24	16 32	16 39	16 47	16 54	17 02	17 09		23 09	23 17	23 24	23 32	23 39	23 47
Camden Road		d	15 36	15 43	15 51	15 58	16 06	16 13	16 21	16 28	16 36	16 43	16 51	16 58	17 06	17 13		23 13	23 21	23 28	23 36	23 43	23 51
Caledonian Rd & Barnsbury		d	15 39	15 46	15 54	16 01	16 09	16 16	16 24	16 31	16 39	16 46	16 54	17 01	17 09	17 16		23 16	23 24	23 31	23 39	23 46	23 54
Highbury & Islington	⊖	d	15 41	15 48	15 56	16 03	16 11	16 18	16 26	16 33	16 41	16 48	16 56	17 03	17 11	17 18		23 18	23 26	23 33	23 41	23 48	23 56
Canonbury	⊖	d	15 43	15 50	15 58	16 05	16 13	16 20	16 28	16 35	16 43	16 50	16 58	17 05	17 13	17 20		23 20	23 28	23 35	23 43	23 50	23 59
Dalston Kingsland		d	15 46	15 53	16 01	16 08	16 16	16 23	16 31	16 38	16 46	16 53	17 01	17 08	17 16	17 23		23 23	23 31	23 38	23 46	23 53	00 02
Hackney Central		d	15 48	15 55	16 03	16 10	16 18	16 25	16 33	16 40	16 48	16 55	17 03	17 10	17 18	17 25		23 25	23 33	23 40	23 48	23 55	00 03
Homerton		d	15 50	15 57	16 05	16 12	16 20	16 27	16 35	16 42	16 50	16 57	17 05	17 12	17 20	17 27		23 27	23 35	23 42	23 50	23 57	00 05
Hackney Wick		d	15 52	15 59	16 07	16 14	16 22	16 29	16 37	16 44	16 52	16 59	17 07	17 14	17 22	17 29		23 29	23 37	23 44	23 52	23 59	00 07
Stratford 7	⊖	a	16 04	16 09	16 19	16 24	16 34	16 40	16 49	16 54	17 04	17 09	17 19	17 24	17 34	17 39		23 39	23 49	23 54	00 04	00 09	00 19

Richmond and Clapham Junction - Willesden Junction, West Hampstead, Highbury and Islington and Stratford

Network Diagram - see first Page of Table 59

			LO	LO	LO	LO	LO	LO	LO
Richmond	⊖	d		23 25		23 41		23 55	
Kew Gardens	⊖	d		23 28		23 44		23 59	
Gunnersbury	⊖	d		23 31		23 47		00 01	
South Acton		d		23 34		23 50		00 04	
Acton Central		d		23 37		23 52		00 07	
Clapham Junction 10		d	23 14		23 29		23 44		23 59
Imperial Wharf		d	23 18		23 33		23 48		00 03
West Brompton	⊖	d	23 21		23 36		23 51		00 06
Kensington (Olympia)	⊖	d	23 25		23 40		23 55		00 10
Shepherd's Bush	⊖	d	23 27		23 42		23 57		00 12
Willesden Jn Low Level	⊖	d							
Willesden Jn. High Level	⊖	a	23 35	23 42	23 50	23 57	00 05	00 12	00 20
		d	23 36	23 44	23 51	23 59	00 06	00 14	00 21
Kensal Rise		d	23 38	23 46	23 53	00 01	00 08	00 16	00 23
Brondesbury Park		d	23 40	23 48	23 55	00 03	00 10	00 18	00 25
Brondesbury		d	23 42	23 50	23 57	00 05	00 12	00 20	00 27
West Hampstead	⊖	d	23 44	23 52	23 59	00 07	00 14	00 22	00 29
Finchley Road & Frognal		d	23 46	23 54	00 01	00 09	00 16	00 24	00 31
Hampstead Heath		d	23 48	23 56	00 03	00 11	00 18	00 26	00 33
Gospel Oak		d	23 52	00 01	00 07	00 15	00 22	00 30	00 37
Kentish Town West		d	23 54	00 02	00 09	00 17	00 24	00 32	00 39
Camden Road		d	23 58	00 06	00 13	00 21	00 28	00 36	00 43
Caledonian Rd & Barnsbury		d	00 01	00 09	00 16	00 24	00 31	00 39	00 46
Highbury & Islington	⊖	d	00 03	00 11	00 18	00 26	00 33	00 41	00 48
Canonbury	⊖	d	00 05	00 13	00 20	00 28	00 35	00 43	00 50
Dalston Kingsland		d	00 08	00 16	00 23	00 31	00 38	00 46	00 53
Hackney Central		d	00 10	00 18	00 25	00 33	00 40	00 48	00 55
Homerton		d	00 12	00 20	00 27	00 35	00 42	00 50	00 57
Hackney Wick		d	00 14	00 22	00 29	00 37	00 44	00 52	00 59
Stratford 7	⊖	a	00 24	00 34	00 39	00 49	00 54	01 04	01 09

Saturdays
from 15 September

			LO	LO	LO	LO	LO	LO	LO	LO	LO	LO	LO	LO	LO	LO	LO	LO	LO	LO	LO	LO	LO	LO
Richmond	⊖	d	23p00			05 58	06 10		06 28		06 40		06 58		07 10		07 28		07 40		07 58		08 08	
Kew Gardens	⊖	d	23p03			06 01	06 13		06 31		06 43		07 01		07 13		07 31		07 43		08 01		08 11	
Gunnersbury	⊖	d	23p06			06 04	06 16		06 34		06 46		07 04		07 16		07 34		07 46		08 04		08 14	
South Acton		d	23p09			06 07	06 19		06 37		06 49		07 07		07 19		07 37		07 49		08 07		08 17	
Acton Central		d	23p12			06 10	06 23		06 40		06 53		07 10		07 23		07 40		07 52		08 10		08 20	
Clapham Junction 10		d		05 47				06 15		06 30		06 45		07 00		07 15		07 30		07 45		08 00		08 15
Imperial Wharf		d		05 51				06 19		06 34		06 49		07 04		07 19		07 34		07 49		08 04		08 19
West Brompton	⊖	d		05 54				06 22		06 37		06 52		07 07		07 22		07 37		07 52		08 07		08 22
Kensington (Olympia)	⊖	d		05 57				06 25		06 40		06 55		07 10		07 25		07 40		07 55		08 10		08 25
Shepherd's Bush	⊖	d		05 59				06 27		06 42		06 57		07 12		07 27		07 42		07 57		08 12		08 27
Willesden Jn Low Level	⊖	d			05 57																			
Willesden Jn. High Level	⊖	a	23p17	06 08		06 15	06 28	06 35	06 45	06 53	06 58	07 05	07 15	07 23	07 28	07 35	07 45	07 51	07 57	08 05	08 15	08 21	08 25	08 35
		d	23p18			06 16	06 29	06 36	06 46		06 59	07 06	07 16		07 29	07 36	07 46		07 58	08 06	08 16		08 26	08 36
Kensal Rise		d	23p20		06 01	06 18	06 31	06 38	06 48		07 01	07 08	07 18		07 31	07 38	07 48		08 00	08 08	08 18		08 28	08 38
Brondesbury Park		d	23p22		06 03	06 20	06 33	06 40	06 50		07 03	07 10	07 20		07 33	07 40	07 50		08 02	08 10	08 20		08 30	08 40
Brondesbury		d	23p24		06 05	06 22	06 35	06 42	06 52		07 05	07 12	07 22		07 35	07 42	07 52		08 04	08 12	08 22		08 32	08 42
West Hampstead	⊖	d	23p26		06 07	06 24	06 37	06 44	06 54		07 07	07 14	07 24		07 37	07 44	07 54		08 06	08 14	08 24		08 34	08 44
Finchley Road & Frognal		d	23p27		06 08	06 25	06 38	06 45	06 55		07 08	07 15	07 25		07 38	07 45	07 55		08 07	08 15	08 25		08 35	08 45
Hampstead Heath		d	23p30		06 11	06 28	06 41	06 48	06 58		07 11	07 18	07 28		07 41	07 48	07 58		08 10	08 18	08 28		08 38	08 48
Gospel Oak		d	23p32		06 13	06 30	06 43	06 50	07 00		07 13	07 20	07 30		07 43	07 50	08 00		08 12	08 20	08 30		08 41	08 50
Kentish Town West		d	23p34		06 15	06 32	06 45	06 52	07 02		07 15	07 22	07 32		07 45	07 52	08 02		08 14	08 22	08 32		08 43	08 52
Camden Road		d	23p38		06 19	06 36	06 49	06 56	07 06		07 19	07 26	07 36		07 49	07 56	08 06		08 18	08 26	08 36		08 46	08 56
Caledonian Rd & Barnsbury		d	23p41		06 22	06 39	06 52	06 59	07 09		07 22	07 29	07 39		07 52	07 59	08 09		08 21	08 29	08 39		08 49	08 59
Highbury & Islington	⊖	d	23p44		06 25	06 42	06 55	07 02	07 12		07 25	07 32	07 42		07 55	08 02	08 12		08 24	08 32	08 42		08 52	09 02
Canonbury	⊖	d	23p46		06 27	06 44	06 57	07 04	07 14		07 27	07 34	07 44		07 57	08 04	08 14		08 26	08 34	08 44		08 54	09 04
Dalston Kingsland		d	23p48		06 29	06 46	06 59	07 06	07 16		07 29	07 36	07 46		07 59	08 06	08 16		08 28	08 36	08 46		08 56	09 06
Hackney Central		d	23p50		06 31	06 48	07 01	07 08	07 18		07 31	07 38	07 48		08 01	08 08	08 18		08 30	08 38	08 48		08 58	09 08
Homerton		d	23p52		06 33	06 50	07 03	07 10	07 20		07 33	07 40	07 50		08 03	08 10	08 20		08 32	08 40	08 50		09 00	09 10
Hackney Wick		d	23p54		06 35	06 52	07 05	07 12	07 22		07 35	07 42	07 52		08 05	08 12	08 22		08 34	08 42	08 52		09 02	09 12
Stratford 7	⊖	a	00 01		06 42	06 59	07 11	07 19	07 29		07 41	07 49	07 59		08 11	08 19	08 29		08 41	08 49	08 59		09 09	09 19

Table 59

Saturdays
from 15 September

Richmond and Clapham Junction - Willesden Junction, West Hampstead, Highbury and Islington and Stratford

Network Diagram - see first Page of Table 59

		LO	LO	LO	LO	LO	LO	LO		LO	LO	LO	LO	LO	LO	LO	LO	LO	LO	LO	LO	LO
Richmond	⊖ d	08 28		08 38		08 58		09 08		14 08		14 28		14 38		14 58		15 08		15 28		15 38
Kew Gardens	⊖ d	08 31		08 41		09 01		09 11		14 11		14 31		14 41		15 01		15 11		15 31		15 41
Gunnersbury	⊖ d	08 34		08 44		09 04		09 14		14 14		14 34		14 44		15 04		15 14		15 34		15 44
South Acton	d	08 37		08 47		09 07		09 17		14 17		14 37		14 47		15 07		15 17		15 37		15 47
Acton Central	d	08 40		08 50		09 10		09 20		14 20		14 40		14 50		15 10		15 20		15 40		15 50
Clapham Junction 10	d		08 30		08 45		09 00				14 15		14 30		14 45		15 00		15 15		15 30	
Imperial Wharf	d		08 34		08 49		09 04				14 19		14 34		14 49		15 04		15 19		15 34	
West Brompton	⊖ d		08 37		08 52		09 07				14 22		14 37		14 52		15 07		15 22		15 37	
Kensington (Olympia)	⊖ d		08 40		08 55		09 10				14 25		14 40		14 55		15 10		15 25		15 40	
Shepherd's Bush	⊖ d		08 42		08 57		09 12				14 27		14 42		14 57		15 12		15 27		15 42	
Willesden Jn Low Level	⊖ d																					
Willesden Jn. High Level	⊖ a	08 45	08 51	08 55	09 05	09 15	09 21	09 25	and at the same minutes past each hour until	14 25	14 35	14 45	14 51	14 55	15 05	15 15	15 21	15 25	15 35	15 45	15 51	15 55
	d	08 46		08 56	09 06	09 16		09 26		14 26	14 36	14 46		14 56	15 06	15 16		15 26	15 36	15 46		15 56
Kensal Rise	d	08 48		08 58	09 08	09 18		09 28		14 28	14 38	14 48		14 58	15 08	15 18		15 28	15 38	15 48		15 58
Brondesbury Park	d	08 50		09 00	09 10	09 20		09 30		14 30	14 40	14 50		15 00	15 10	15 20		15 30	15 40	15 50		16 00
Brondesbury	d	08 52		09 02	09 12	09 22		09 32		14 32	14 42	14 52		15 02	15 12	15 22		15 32	15 42	15 52		16 02
West Hampstead	⊖ d	08 54		09 04	09 14	09 24		09 34		14 34	14 44	14 54		15 04	15 14	15 24		15 34	15 44	15 54		16 04
Finchley Road & Frognal	d	08 55		09 05	09 15	09 25		09 35		14 35	14 45	14 55		15 05	15 15	15 25		15 35	15 45	15 55		16 05
Hampstead Heath	d	08 58		09 08	09 18	09 28		09 38		14 38	14 48	14 58		15 08	15 18	15 28		15 38	15 48	15 58		16 08
Gospel Oak	d	09 00		09 10	09 20	09 30		09 40		14 40	14 50	15 00		15 10	15 20	15 30		15 40	15 50	16 00		16 10
Kentish Town West	d	09 02		09 12	09 22	09 32		09 42		14 42	14 52	15 02		15 12	15 22	15 32		15 42	15 52	16 02		16 12
Camden Road	d	09 06		09 16	09 26	09 36		09 46		14 46	14 56	15 06		15 16	15 26	15 36		15 46	15 56	16 06		16 16
Caledonian Rd & Barnsbury	d	09 09		09 19	09 29	09 39		09 49		14 49	14 59	15 09		15 19	15 29	15 39		15 49	15 59	16 09		16 19
Highbury & Islington	⊖ d	09 12		09 22	09 32	09 42		09 52		14 52	15 02	15 12		15 22	15 32	15 42		15 52	16 02	16 12		16 22
Canonbury	⊖ d	09 14		09 24	09 34	09 44		09 54		14 54	15 04	15 14		15 24	15 34	15 44		15 54	16 04	16 14		16 24
Dalston Kingsland	d	09 16		09 26	09 36	09 46		09 56		14 56	15 06	15 16		15 26	15 36	15 46		15 56	16 06	16 16		16 26
Hackney Central	d	09 18		09 28	09 38	09 48		09 58		14 58	15 08	15 18		15 28	15 38	15 48		15 58	16 08	16 18		16 28
Homerton	d	09 20		09 30	09 40	09 50		10 00		15 00	15 10	15 20		15 30	15 40	15 50		16 00	16 10	16 20		16 30
Hackney Wick	d	09 22		09 32	09 42	09 52		10 02		15 02	15 12	15 22		15 32	15 42	15 52		16 02	16 12	16 22		16 32
Stratford 7	⊖ a	09 29		09 39	09 49	09 59		10 09		15 09	15 19	15 29		15 39	15 49	15 59		16 10	16 21	16 30		16 40

		LO	LO	LO	LO	LO	LO	LO	LO	LO	LO	LO	LO	LO	LO	LO	LO	LO	LO	LO	LO	LO	LO
Richmond	⊖ d		15 58		16 08		16 28		16 38		16 58		17 08		17 28		17 38		17 58		18 08		18 28
Kew Gardens	⊖ d		16 01		16 11		16 31		16 41		17 01		17 11		17 31		17 41		18 01		18 11		18 31
Gunnersbury	⊖ d		16 04		16 14		16 34		16 44		17 04		17 14		17 34		17 44		18 04		18 14		18 34
South Acton	d		16 07		16 17		16 37		16 47		17 07		17 17		17 37		17 47		18 07		18 17		18 37
Acton Central	d		16 10		16 20		16 40		16 50		17 10		17 20		17 40		17 50		18 10		18 20		18 40
Clapham Junction 10	d	15 45		16 00		16 15		16 30		16 45		17 00		17 15		17 30		17 45		18 00		18 15	
Imperial Wharf	d	15 49		16 04		16 19		16 34		16 49		17 04		17 19		17 34		17 49		18 04		18 19	
West Brompton	⊖ d	15 52		16 07		16 22		16 37		16 52		17 07		17 22		17 37		17 52		18 07		18 22	
Kensington (Olympia)	⊖ d	15 55		16 10		16 25		16 40		16 55		17 10		17 25		17 40		17 55		18 10		18 25	
Shepherd's Bush	⊖ d	15 57		16 12		16 27		16 42		16 57		17 12		17 27		17 42		17 57		18 12		18 27	
Willesden Jn Low Level	⊖ d																						
Willesden Jn. High Level	⊖ a	16 05	16 15	16 21	16 25	16 35	16 45	16 53	16 55	17 05	17 15	17 21	17 25	17 35	17 45	17 51	17 55	18 05	18 15	18 21	18 25	18 35	18 45
	d	16 06	16 16		16 26	16 36	16 46		16 56	17 06	17 16		17 26	17 36	17 46		17 56	18 06	18 16		18 26	18 36	18 46
Kensal Rise	d	16 08	16 18		16 28	16 38	16 48		16 58	17 08	17 18		17 28	17 38	17 48		17 58	18 08	18 18		18 28	18 38	18 48
Brondesbury Park	d	16 10	16 20		16 30	16 40	16 50		17 00	17 10	17 20		17 30	17 40	17 50		18 00	18 10	18 20		18 30	18 40	18 50
Brondesbury	d	16 12	16 22		16 32	16 42	16 52		17 02	17 12	17 22		17 32	17 42	17 52		18 02	18 12	18 22		18 32	18 42	18 52
West Hampstead	⊖ d	16 14	16 24		16 34	16 44	16 54		17 04	17 14	17 24		17 34	17 44	17 54		18 04	18 14	18 24		18 34	18 44	18 54
Finchley Road & Frognal	d	16 15	16 25		16 35	16 45	16 55		17 05	17 15	17 25		17 35	17 45	17 55		18 05	18 15	18 25		18 35	18 45	18 55
Hampstead Heath	d	16 18	16 28		16 38	16 48	16 58		17 08	17 18	17 28		17 38	17 48	17 58		18 08	18 18	18 28		18 38	18 48	18 58
Gospel Oak	d	16 20	16 30		16 40	16 50	17 00		17 11	17 20	17 30		17 40	17 50	18 00		18 10	18 20	18 30		18 40	18 50	19 00
Kentish Town West	d	16 22	16 32		16 42	16 52	17 02		17 13	17 22	17 32		17 42	17 52	18 02		18 12	18 22	18 32		18 42	18 52	19 02
Camden Road	d	16 26	16 36		16 46	16 56	17 06		17 16	17 26	17 36		17 46	17 56	18 06		18 16	18 26	18 36		18 46	18 56	19 06
Caledonian Rd & Barnsbury	d	16 29	16 39		16 49	16 59	17 09		17 19	17 29	17 39		17 49	17 59	18 09		18 19	18 29	18 39		18 49	18 59	19 09
Highbury & Islington	⊖ d	16 32	16 42		16 52	17 02	17 12		17 22	17 32	17 42		17 52	18 02	18 12		18 22	18 32	18 42		18 52	19 02	19 12
Canonbury	⊖ d	16 34	16 44		16 54	17 04	17 14		17 24	17 34	17 44		17 54	18 04	18 14		18 24	18 34	18 44		18 54	19 04	19 14
Dalston Kingsland	d	16 36	16 46		16 56	17 06	17 16		17 26	17 36	17 46		17 56	18 06	18 16		18 26	18 36	18 46		18 56	19 06	19 16
Hackney Central	d	16 38	16 48		16 58	17 08	17 18		17 28	17 38	17 48		17 58	18 08	18 18		18 28	18 38	18 48		18 58	19 08	19 18
Homerton	d	16 40	16 50		17 00	17 10	17 20		17 30	17 40	17 50		18 00	18 10	18 20		18 30	18 40	18 50		19 00	19 10	19 20
Hackney Wick	d	16 42	16 52		17 02	17 12	17 22		17 32	17 42	17 52		18 02	18 12	18 22		18 32	18 42	18 52		19 02	19 12	19 22
Stratford 7	⊖ a	16 51	17 00		17 10	17 21	17 30		17 40	17 51	18 00		18 10	18 21	18 30		18 40	18 51	19 00		19 10	19 21	19 30

Table 59

Saturdays
from 15 September

Richmond and Clapham Junction - Willesden Junction, West Hampstead, Highbury and Islington and Stratford

Network Diagram - see first Page of Table 59

		LO	LO	LO	LO	LO	LO	LO	LO	LO	LO	LO	LO	LO	LO	LO	LO	LO	LO	LO	LO	LO	LO
Richmond	⊖ d		18 38		18 58		19 08		19 28		19 38		19 58		20 08		20 28		20 38		20 58		21 08
Kew Gardens	⊖ d		18 41		19 01		19 11		19 31		19 41		20 01		20 11		20 31		20 41		21 01		21 11
Gunnersbury	⊖ d		18 44		19 04		19 14		19 34		19 44		20 04		20 14		20 34		20 44		21 04		21 14
South Acton	d		18 47		19 07		19 17		19 37		19 47		20 07		20 17		20 37		20 47		21 07		21 17
Acton Central	d		18 50		19 10		19 20		19 40		19 50		20 10		20 20		20 40		20 50		21 10		21 20
Clapham Junction 10	d	18 30		18 45		19 00		19 15		19 30		19 45		20 00		20 15		20 30		20 45		21 00	
Imperial Wharf	d	18 34		18 49		19 04		19 19		19 34		19 49		20 04		20 19		20 34		20 49		21 04	
West Brompton	⊖ d	18 37		18 52		19 07		19 22		19 37		19 52		20 07		20 22		20 37		20 52		21 07	
Kensington (Olympia)	⊖ d	18 40		18 55		19 10		19 25		19 40		19 55		20 10		20 25		20 40		20 55		21 10	
Shepherd's Bush	⊖ d	18 42		18 57		19 12		19 27		19 42		19 57		20 12		20 27		20 42		20 57		21 12	
Willesden Jn Low Level	⊖ d																						
Willesden Jn. High Level	⊖ a	18 51	18 55	19 05	19 15	19 21	19 25	19 35	19 45	19 51	19 55	20 05	20 15	20 21	20 25	20 35	20 45	20 51	20 55	21 05	21 15	21 21	21 25
	d		18 56	19 06	19 16		19 26	19 36	19 46		19 56	20 06	20 16		20 26	20 36	20 46		20 56	21 06	21 16		21 26
Kensal Rise	d		18 58	19 08	19 18		19 28	19 38	19 48		19 58	20 08	20 18		20 28	20 38	20 48		20 58	21 08	21 18		21 28
Brondesbury Park	d		19 00	19 10	19 20		19 30	19 40	19 50		20 00	20 10	20 20		20 30	20 40	20 50		21 00	21 10	21 20		21 30
Brondesbury	d		19 02	19 12	19 22		19 32	19 42	19 52		20 02	20 12	20 22		20 32	20 42	20 52		21 02	21 12	21 22		21 32
West Hampstead	⊖ d		19 04	19 14	19 24		19 34	19 44	19 54		20 04	20 14	20 24		20 34	20 44	20 54		21 04	21 14	21 24		21 34
Finchley Road & Frognal	d		19 05	19 15	19 25		19 35	19 45	19 55		20 05	20 15	20 25		20 35	20 45	20 55		21 05	21 15	21 25		21 35
Hampstead Heath	d		19 08	19 18	19 28		19 38	19 48	19 58		20 08	20 18	20 28		20 38	20 48	20 58		21 08	21 18	21 28		21 38
Gospel Oak	d		19 10	19 20	19 30		19 40	19 50	20 00		20 10	20 20	20 30		20 40	20 50	21 00		21 10	21 20	21 30		21 40
Kentish Town West	d		19 12	19 22	19 32		19 42	19 52	20 02		20 12	20 22	20 32		20 42	20 52	21 02		21 12	21 22	21 32		21 42
Camden Road	d		19 16	19 26	19 36		19 46	19 56	20 06		20 16	20 26	20 36		20 46	20 56	21 06		21 16	21 26	21 36		21 46
Caledonian Rd & Barnsbury	d		19 19	19 29	19 39		19 49	19 59	20 09		20 19	20 29	20 39		20 49	20 59	21 09		21 19	21 29	21 39		21 49
Highbury & Islington	⊖ d		19 22	19 32	19 42		19 52	20 02	20 12		20 22	20 32	20 42		20 52	21 02	21 12		21 22	21 32	21 42		21 52
Canonbury	⊖ d		19 24	19 34	19 44		19 54	20 04	20 14		20 24	20 34	20 44		20 54	21 04	21 14		21 24	21 34	21 44		21 54
Dalston Kingsland	d		19 26	19 36	19 46		19 56	20 06	20 16		20 26	20 36	20 46		20 56	21 06	21 16		21 26	21 36	21 46		21 56
Hackney Central	d		19 28	19 38	19 48		19 58	20 08	20 18		20 28	20 38	20 48		20 58	21 08	21 18		21 28	21 38	21 48		21 58
Homerton	d		19 30	19 40	19 50		20 00	20 10	20 20		20 30	20 40	20 50		21 00	21 10	21 20		21 30	21 40	21 50		22 00
Hackney Wick	d		19 32	19 42	19 52		20 02	20 12	20 22		20 32	20 42	20 52		21 02	21 12	21 22		21 32	21 42	21 52		22 02
Stratford 7	⊖ a		19 40	19 51	20 00		20 10	20 21	20 30		20 40	20 51	21 01		21 09	21 19	21 29		21 39	21 49	21 59		22 09

		LO	LO	LO	LO	LO	LO	LO	LO	LO	LO	LO	LO	LO	LO	LO
Richmond	⊖ d		21 28		21 38		21 58			22 28			23 00		23 28	
Kew Gardens	⊖ d		21 31		21 41		22 01			22 31			23 03		23 31	
Gunnersbury	⊖ d		21 34		21 44		22 04			22 34			23 06		23 34	
South Acton	d		21 37		21 47		22 07			22 37			23 09		23 37	
Acton Central	d		21 40		21 50		22 10			22 40			23 12		23 40	
Clapham Junction 10	d	21 15		21 30		21 45		22 00	22 15		22 30	22 45		23 00		23 30
Imperial Wharf	d	21 19		21 34		21 49		22 04	22 19		22 34	22 51		23 04		23 34
West Brompton	⊖ d	21 22		21 37		21 52		22 07	22 22		22 37	22 54		23 07		23 37
Kensington (Olympia)	⊖ d	21 25		21 40		21 55		22 10	22 25		22 40	22 59		23 10		23 40
Shepherd's Bush	⊖ d	21 27		21 42		21 57		22 12	22 27		22 42	23 01		23 12		23 42
Willesden Jn Low Level	⊖ d															
Willesden Jn. High Level	⊖ a	21 35	21 45	21 51	21 55	22 05	22 15	22 21	22 36	22 45	22 52	23 09	23 17	23 21	23 45	23 51
	d	21 36	21 46		21 56	22 06	22 16			22 46			23 18			
Kensal Rise	d	21 38	21 48		21 58	22 08	22 18			22 48			23 20			
Brondesbury Park	d	21 40	21 50		22 00	22 10	22 20			22 50			23 22			
Brondesbury	d	21 42	21 52		22 02	22 12	22 22			22 52			23 24			
West Hampstead	⊖ d	21 44	21 54		22 04	22 14	22 24			22 54			23 26			
Finchley Road & Frognal	d	21 45	21 55		22 05	22 15	22 25			22 55			23 27			
Hampstead Heath	d	21 48	21 58		22 08	22 18	22 28			22 58			23 30			
Gospel Oak	d	21 50	22 00		22 10	22 20	22 30			23 00			23 32			
Kentish Town West	d	21 52	22 02		22 12	22 22	22 32			23 02			23 34			
Camden Road	d	21 56	22 06		22 16	22 26	22 36			23 06			23 38			
Caledonian Rd & Barnsbury	d	21 59	22 09		22 19	22 29	22 39			23 09			23 41			
Highbury & Islington	⊖ d	22 02	22 12		22 22	22 32	22 42			23 12			23 44			
Canonbury	⊖ d	22 04	22 14		22 24	22 34	22 44			23 14			23 46			
Dalston Kingsland	d	22 06	22 16		22 26	22 36	22 46			23 16			23 48			
Hackney Central	d	22 08	22 18		22 28	22 38	22 48			23 18			23 50			
Homerton	d	22 10	22 20		22 30	22 40	22 50			23 20			23 52			
Hackney Wick	d	22 12	22 22		22 32	22 42	22 52			23 22			23 54			
Stratford 7	⊖ a	22 19	22 29		22 39	22 49	22 59			23 29			23 59			

Richmond and Clapham Junction - Willesden Junction, West Hampstead, Highbury and Islington and Stratford

Network Diagram - see first Page of Table 59

Station		LO	LO	LO	LO	LO	LO	LO	LO	LO	LO	LO
Richmond ⊖	d			08 59		09 17	09 29		09 47	09 59		10 10
Kew Gardens ⊖	d			09 02		09 20	09 32		09 50	10 02		10 13
Gunnersbury ⊖	d			09 05		09 23	09 35		09 53	10 05		10 16
South Acton	d			09 08		09 26	09 38		09 56	10 08		10 19
Acton Central	d			09 11		09 29	09 41		09 59	10 11		10 22
Clapham Junction 10	d	08 30			09 00			09 30			10 00	
Imperial Wharf	d	08 34			09 04			09 34			10 04	
West Brompton ⊖	d	08 37			09 07			09 37			10 07	
Kensington (Olympia) ⊖	d	08 40			09 10			09 40			10 10	
Shepherd's Bush ⊖	d	08 42			09 12			09 42			10 12	
Willesden Jn Low Level ⊖	d		09 00									
Willesden Jn. High Level ⊖	a	08 51		09 16	09 21	09 34	09 45	09 51	10 04	10 16	10 21	10 27
	d			09 17		09 35	09 47		10 05	10 17		10 28
Kensal Rise	d		09 04	09 19		09 37	09 49		10 07	10 19		10 30
Brondesbury Park	d		09 06	09 21		09 39	09 51		10 09	10 21		10 32
Brondesbury	d		09 08	09 23		09 41	09 53		10 11	10 23		10 34
West Hampstead ⊖	d		09 10	09 25		09 43	09 55		10 13	10 25		10 36
Finchley Road & Frognal	d		09 11	09 26		09 44	09 56		10 14	10 26		10 37
Hampstead Heath	d		09 14	09 30		09 47	09 59		10 17	10 29		10 40
Gospel Oak	d		09 16	09 32		09 49	10 01		10 19	10 31		10 42
Kentish Town West	d		09 18	09 34		09 51	10 03		10 21	10 33		10 44
Camden Road	d		09 22	09 37		09 55	10 07		10 25	10 37		10 48
Caledonian Rd & Barnsbury	d		09 25	09 40		09 58	10 10		10 28	10 40		10 51
Highbury & Islington ⊖	d		09 28	09 43		10 01	10 13		10 31	10 43		10 54
Canonbury ⊖	d		09 30	09 45		10 03	10 15		10 33	10 45		10 56
Dalston Kingsland	d		09 32	09 47		10 05	10 17		10 35	10 47		10 58
Hackney Central	d		09 34	09 49		10 07	10 19		10 37	10 49		11 00
Homerton	d		09 36	09 51		10 09	10 21		10 39	10 51		11 02
Hackney Wick	d		09 38	09 53		10 11	10 23		10 41	10 53		11 04
Stratford 7 ⊖	a		09 48	10 00		10 18	10 30		10 48	11 00		11 11

Station		LO	LO	LO	LO	LO	LO	LO	LO	LO	LO	LO
Richmond ⊖	d		10 29		10 40		10 59		11 10		11 29	
Kew Gardens ⊖	d		10 32		10 43		11 02		11 13		11 32	
Gunnersbury ⊖	d		10 35		10 46		11 05		11 16		11 35	
South Acton	d		10 38		10 49		11 08		11 19		11 38	
Acton Central	d		10 41		10 52		11 11		11 22		11 41	
Clapham Junction 10	d	10 20		10 30		10 45		11 00		11 20		11 30
Imperial Wharf	d	10 24		10 34		10 49		11 04		11 24		11 34
West Brompton ⊖	d	10 27		10 37		10 52		11 07		11 27		11 37
Kensington (Olympia) ⊖	d	10 30		10 40		10 55		11 10		11 30		11 40
Shepherd's Bush ⊖	d	10 32		10 42		10 57		11 12		11 32		11 42
Willesden Jn Low Level ⊖	d											
Willesden Jn. High Level ⊖	a	10 40	10 46	10 51	10 57	11 05	11 16	11 21	11 27	11 40	11 46	11 52
	d	10 41	10 47		10 58	11 06	11 17		11 28	11 41	11 47	
Kensal Rise	d	10 43	10 49		11 00	11 08	11 19		11 30	11 43	11 49	
Brondesbury Park	d	10 45	10 51		11 02	11 10	11 21		11 32	11 45	11 51	
Brondesbury	d	10 47	10 53		11 04	11 12	11 23		11 34	11 47	11 53	
West Hampstead ⊖	d	10 49	10 55		11 06	11 14	11 25		11 36	11 49	11 55	
Finchley Road & Frognal	d	10 50	10 56		11 07	11 15	11 26		11 37	11 50	11 56	
Hampstead Heath	d	10 53	10 59		11 10	11 18	11 29		11 40	11 53	11 59	
Gospel Oak	d	10 55	11 01		11 12	11 20	11 31		11 42	11 55	12 01	
Kentish Town West	d	10 57	11 03		11 14	11 22	11 33		11 44	11 57	12 03	
Camden Road	d	11 01	11 07		11 18	11 26	11 37		11 48	12 01	12 07	
Caledonian Rd & Barnsbury	d	11 04	11 10		11 21	11 29	11 40		11 51	12 04	12 10	
Highbury & Islington ⊖	d	11 07	11 13		11 24	11 32	11 43		11 54	12 07	12 13	
Canonbury ⊖	d	11 09	11 15		11 26	11 34	11 45		11 56	12 09	12 15	
Dalston Kingsland	d	11 11	11 17		11 28	11 36	11 47		11 58	12 11	12 17	
Hackney Central	d	11 13	11 19		11 30	11 38	11 49		12 00	12 13	12 19	
Homerton	d	11 15	11 21		11 32	11 40	11 51		12 02	12 15	12 21	
Hackney Wick	d	11 17	11 23		11 34	11 42	11 53		12 04	12 17	12 23	
Stratford 7 ⊖	a	11 24	11 30		11 41	11 49	12 00		12 11	12 24	12 30	

Station		LO	LO	LO	LO	LO	LO	LO	LO	LO	LO	LO
Richmond ⊖	d	11 40		11 59		12 10		12 29		12 40		12 59
Kew Gardens ⊖	d	11 43		12 02		12 13		12 32		12 43		13 02
Gunnersbury ⊖	d	11 46		12 05		12 16		12 35		12 46		13 05
South Acton	d	11 49		12 08		12 19		12 38		12 49		13 08
Acton Central	d	11 52		12 11		12 22		12 41		12 52		13 11
Clapham Junction 10	d		11 45		12 00		12 15		12 30		12 45	
Imperial Wharf	d		11 49		12 04		12 19		12 34		12 49	
West Brompton ⊖	d		11 52		12 07		12 22		12 37		12 52	
Kensington (Olympia) ⊖	d		11 55		12 10		12 25		12 40		12 55	
Shepherd's Bush ⊖	d		11 57		12 12		12 27		12 42		12 57	
Willesden Jn Low Level ⊖	d											
Willesden Jn. High Level ⊖	a	11 57	12 05	12 16	12 21	12 27	12 35	12 46	12 51	12 57	13 05	13 16
	d	11 58	12 06	12 17		12 28	12 36	12 47		12 58	13 06	13 17
Kensal Rise	d	12 00	12 08	12 19		12 30	12 38	12 49		13 00	13 08	13 19
Brondesbury Park	d	12 02	12 10	12 21		12 32	12 40	12 51		13 02	13 10	13 21
Brondesbury	d	12 04	12 12	12 23		12 34	12 42	12 53		13 04	13 12	13 23
West Hampstead ⊖	d	12 06	12 14	12 25		12 36	12 44	12 55		13 06	13 14	13 25
Finchley Road & Frognal	d	12 07	12 15	12 26		12 37	12 45	12 56		13 07	13 15	13 26
Hampstead Heath	d	12 10	12 18	12 29		12 40	12 48	12 59		13 10	13 18	13 29
Gospel Oak	d	12 12	12 20	12 31		12 42	12 50	13 01		13 12	13 20	13 31
Kentish Town West	d	12 14	12 22	12 33		12 44	12 52	13 03		13 14	13 22	13 33
Camden Road	d	12 18	12 26	12 37		12 48	12 56	13 07		13 18	13 26	13 37
Caledonian Rd & Barnsbury	d	12 21	12 29	12 40		12 51	12 59	13 10		13 21	13 29	13 40
Highbury & Islington ⊖	d	12 24	12 32	12 43		12 54	13 02	13 13		13 24	13 32	13 43
Canonbury ⊖	d	12 26	12 34	12 45		12 56	13 04	13 15		13 26	13 34	13 45
Dalston Kingsland	d	12 28	12 36	12 47		12 58	13 06	13 17		13 28	13 36	13 47
Hackney Central	d	12 30	12 38	12 49		13 00	13 08	13 19		13 30	13 38	13 49
Homerton	d	12 32	12 40	12 51		13 02	13 10	13 21		13 32	13 40	13 51
Hackney Wick	d	12 34	12 42	12 53		13 04	13 12	13 23		13 34	13 42	13 53
Stratford 7 ⊖	a	12 41	12 49	13 00		13 11	13 19	13 30		13 41	13 49	14 00

Station		LO	LO	LO	LO	LO	LO	LO	LO	LO	LO	LO
Richmond ⊖	d		13 10		13 29		13 40		13 59		14 10	
Kew Gardens ⊖	d		13 13		13 32		13 43		14 02		14 13	
Gunnersbury ⊖	d		13 16		13 35		13 46		14 05		14 16	
South Acton	d		13 19		13 38		13 49		14 08		14 19	
Acton Central	d		13 22		13 41		13 52		14 11		14 22	
Clapham Junction 10	d	13 00		13 15		13 30		13 45		14 00		14 15
Imperial Wharf	d	13 04		13 19		13 34		13 49		14 04		14 19
West Brompton ⊖	d	13 07		13 22		13 37		13 52		14 07		14 22
Kensington (Olympia) ⊖	d	13 10		13 25		13 40		13 55		14 10		14 25
Shepherd's Bush ⊖	d	13 12		13 27		13 42		13 57		14 12		14 27
Willesden Jn Low Level ⊖	d											
Willesden Jn. High Level ⊖	a	13 21	13 27	13 35	13 46	13 51	13 57	14 05	14 16	14 22	14 27	14 35
	d		13 28	13 36	13 47		13 58	14 06	14 17		14 28	14 36
Kensal Rise	d		13 30	13 38	13 49		14 00	14 08	14 19		14 30	14 38
Brondesbury Park	d		13 32	13 40	13 51		14 02	14 10	14 21		14 32	14 40
Brondesbury	d		13 34	13 42	13 53		14 04	14 12	14 23		14 34	14 42
West Hampstead ⊖	d		13 36	13 44	13 55		14 06	14 14	14 25		14 36	14 44
Finchley Road & Frognal	d		13 37	13 45	13 56		14 07	14 15	14 26		14 37	14 45
Hampstead Heath	d		13 40	13 48	13 59		14 10	14 18	14 29		14 40	14 48
Gospel Oak	d		13 42	13 50	14 01		14 12	14 20	14 31		14 42	14 50
Kentish Town West	d		13 44	13 52	14 03		14 14	14 22	14 33		14 44	14 52
Camden Road	d		13 48	13 56	14 07		14 18	14 26	14 37		14 48	14 56
Caledonian Rd & Barnsbury	d		13 51	13 59	14 10		14 21	14 29	14 40		14 51	14 59
Highbury & Islington ⊖	d		13 54	14 02	14 13		14 24	14 32	14 43		14 54	15 02
Canonbury ⊖	d		13 56	14 04	14 15		14 26	14 34	14 45		14 56	15 04
Dalston Kingsland	d		13 58	14 06	14 17		14 28	14 36	14 47		14 58	15 06
Hackney Central	d		14 00	14 08	14 19		14 30	14 38	14 49		15 00	15 08
Homerton	d		14 02	14 10	14 21		14 32	14 40	14 51		15 02	15 10
Hackney Wick	d		14 04	14 12	14 23		14 34	14 42	14 53		15 04	15 12
Stratford 7 ⊖	a		14 11	14 19	14 30		14 41	14 49	15 00		15 11	15 19

Richmond and Clapham Junction - Willesden Junction, West Hampstead, Highbury and Islington and Stratford

Network Diagram - see first Page of Table 59

Station		LO	LO	LO	LO	LO	LO	
Richmond ⊖	d	14 29		14 40		14 59		
Kew Gardens ⊖	d	14 32		14 43		15 02		
Gunnersbury ⊖	d	14 35		14 46		15 05		
South Acton	d	14 38		14 49		15 08		
Acton Central	d	14 41		14 52		15 11		
Clapham Junction 10	d		14 30		14 45		15 00	
Imperial Wharf	d		14 34		14 49		15 04	
West Brompton ⊖	d		14 37		14 52		15 07	
Kensington (Olympia) ⊖	d		14 40		14 55		15 10	
Shepherd's Bush ⊖	d		14 42		14 57		15 12	
Willesden Jn Low Level ⊖	d							
Willesden Jn. High Level ⊖	a	14 46	14 51	14 57	15 05	15 16	15 21	and at the same minutes past each hour until
	d	14 47		14 58	15 06	15 17		
Kensal Rise	d	14 49		15 00	15 08	15 19		
Brondesbury Park	d	14 51		15 02	15 10	15 21		
Brondesbury	d	14 53		15 04	15 12	15 23		
West Hampstead ⊖	d	14 55		15 06	15 14	15 25		
Finchley Road & Frognal	d	14 56		15 07	15 15	15 26		
Hampstead Heath	d	14 59		15 10	15 18	15 29		
Gospel Oak	d	15 01		15 12	15 20	15 31		
Kentish Town West	d	15 03		15 14	15 22	15 33		
Camden Road	d	15 07		15 18	15 26	15 37		
Caledonian Rd & Barnsbury	d	15 10		15 21	15 29	15 40		
Highbury & Islington ⊖	d	15 13		15 24	15 32	15 43		
Canonbury ⊖	d	15 15		15 26	15 34	15 45		
Dalston Kingsland	d	15 17		15 28	15 36	15 47		
Hackney Central	d	15 19		15 30	15 38	15 49		
Homerton	d	15 21		15 32	15 40	15 51		
Hackney Wick	d	15 23		15 34	15 42	15 53		
Stratford 7 ⊖	a	15 30		15 41	15 49	16 00		

Station		LO	LO	LO	LO	LO	LO	LO	LO	LO	LO	LO	LO	LO	LO
Richmond ⊖	d		20 10		20 29		20 40		20 59		21 17		21 29		21 47
Kew Gardens ⊖	d		20 13		20 32		20 43		21 02		21 20		21 32		21 50
Gunnersbury ⊖	d		20 16		20 35		20 46		21 05		21 23		21 35		21 53
South Acton	d		20 19		20 38		20 49		21 08		21 26		21 38		21 56
Acton Central	d		20 22		20 41		20 52		21 11		21 29		21 41		21 59
Clapham Junction 10	d	20 00		20 15		20 30		20 45		21 00		21 20		21 30	
Imperial Wharf	d	20 04		20 19		20 34		20 49		21 04		21 24		21 34	
West Brompton ⊖	d	20 07		20 22		20 37		20 52		21 07		21 27		21 37	
Kensington (Olympia) ⊖	d	20 10		20 25		20 40		20 55		21 10		21 30		21 40	
Shepherd's Bush ⊖	d	20 12		20 27		20 42		20 57		21 12		21 32		21 42	
Willesden Jn Low Level ⊖	d														
Willesden Jn. High Level ⊖	a	20 21	20 27	20 36	20 46	20 51	20 57	21 08	21 16	21 21	21 34	21 41	21 46	21 51	22 04
	d		20 28		20 47		20 58		21 17		21 35		21 47		22 05
Kensal Rise	d		20 30		20 49		21 00		21 19		21 37		21 49		22 07
Brondesbury Park	d		20 32		20 51		21 02		21 21		21 39		21 51		22 09
Brondesbury	d		20 34		20 53		21 04		21 23		21 41		21 53		22 11
West Hampstead ⊖	d		20 36		20 55		21 06		21 25		21 43		21 55		22 13
Finchley Road & Frognal	d		20 37		20 56		21 07		21 26		21 44		21 56		22 14
Hampstead Heath	d		20 40		20 59		21 10		21 29		21 47		21 59		22 17
Gospel Oak	d		20 42		21 01		21 12		21 31		21 49		22 01		22a22
Kentish Town West	d		20 44		21 03		21 14		21 33		21 51		22 03		
Camden Road	d		20 48		21 07		21 18		21 37		21 55		22 07		
Caledonian Rd & Barnsbury	d		20 51		21 10		21 21		21 40		21 58		22 10		
Highbury & Islington ⊖	d		20 54		21 13		21 24		21 43		22 01		22 13		
Canonbury ⊖	d		20 56		21 15		21 26		21 45		22 03		22 15		
Dalston Kingsland	d		20 58		21 17		21 28		21 47		22 05		22 17		
Hackney Central	d		21 00		21 19		21 30		21 49		22 07		22 19		
Homerton	d		21 02		21 21		21 32		21 51		22 09		22 21		
Hackney Wick	d		21 04		21 23		21 34		21 53		22 11		22 23		
Stratford 7 ⊖	a		21 11		21 30		21 41		22 00		22 18		22 31		

Station		LO	LO	LO	LO	LO	LO	LO	LO
Richmond ⊖	d		21 59			22 28		22 58	
Kew Gardens ⊖	d		22 02			22 31		23 02	
Gunnersbury ⊖	d		22 05			22 34		23 05	
South Acton	d		22 08			22 37		23 08	
Acton Central	d		22 11			22 40		23 11	
Clapham Junction 10	d	21 45		22 00	22 20		22 44		23 15
Imperial Wharf	d	21 49		22 04	22 24		22 48		23 19
West Brompton ⊖	d	21 52		22 07	22 27		22 51		23 22
Kensington (Olympia) ⊖	d	21 55		22 10	22 30		22 54		23 25
Shepherd's Bush ⊖	d	21 57		22 12	22 32		22 56		23 27
Willesden Jn Low Level ⊖	d								
Willesden Jn. High Level ⊖	a	22 08	22 16	22 23	22 41	22 45	23 08	23 16	23 36
	d		22 17			22 46		23 17	
Kensal Rise	d		22 19			22 48		23 19	
Brondesbury Park	d		22 21			22 50		23 21	
Brondesbury	d		22 23			22 52		23 23	
West Hampstead ⊖	d		22 25			22 54		23 25	
Finchley Road & Frognal	d		22 26			22 55		23 26	
Hampstead Heath	d		22 29			22 58		23 29	
Gospel Oak	d		22a36			23a03		23a35	
Kentish Town West	d								
Camden Road	d								
Caledonian Rd & Barnsbury	d								
Highbury & Islington ⊖	d								
Canonbury ⊖	d								
Dalston Kingsland	d								
Hackney Central	d								
Homerton	d								
Hackney Wick	d								
Stratford 7 ⊖	a								

Table 59

Sundays
29 July to 12 August

Richmond and Clapham Junction - Willesden Junction, West Hampstead, Highbury and Islington and Stratford

Network Diagram - see first Page of Table 59

		LO	LO	LO	LO	LO	LO	LO	LO	LO	LO	LO	LO	LO	LO	LO	LO	LO	LO	LO	LO	LO	LO
Richmond ⊖	d	22p55		23p11		23p25		23p41		23p55								05 54		06 10		06 25	
Kew Gardens ⊖	d	22p58		23p14		23p28		23p44		23p59								05 57		06 13		06 28	
Gunnersbury ⊖	d	23p01		23p17		23p31		23p47		00 01								06 00		06 16		06 31	
South Acton	d	23p04		23p20		23p34		23p50		00 04								06 03		06 19		06 34	
Acton Central	d	23p07		23p22		23p37		23p52		00 07								06 06		06 22		06 37	
Clapham Junction 10	d		22p59		23p14		23p29		23p44		23p59	00 12	05 47								06 14		06 29
Imperial Wharf	d		23p03		23p18		23p33		23p48		00 03	00 16	05 51								06 18		06 33
West Brompton ⊖	d		23p06		23p21		23p36		23p51		00 06	00 19	05 54								06 21		06 36
Kensington (Olympia) ⊖	d		23p10		23p25		23p40		23p55		00 10	00 22	05 58								06 25		06 40
Shepherd's Bush ⊖	d		23p12		23p27		23p42		23p57		00 12	00 24	06 00								06 27		06 42
Willesden Jn Low Level ⊖	d															05 58							
Willesden Jn. High Level ⊖	a	23p12	23p20	23p27	23p35	23p42	23p50	23p57	00 05	00 12	00 20	00 37	06 12					06 11		06 27	06 35	06 42	06 50
	d	23p14	23p21	23p29	23p36	23p44	23p51	23p59	00 06	00 14	00 21							06 12		06 29	06 36	06 44	06 51
Kensal Rise	d	23p16	23p23	23p31	23p38	23p46	23p53	00 01	00 08	00 16	00 23					06 02		06 14		06 31	06 38	06 46	06 53
Brondesbury Park	d	23p18	23p25	23p33	23p40	23p48	23p55	00 03	00 10	00 18	00 25					06 04		06 16		06 33	06 40	06 48	06 55
Brondesbury	d	23p20	23p27	23p35	23p42	23p50	23p57	00 05	00 12	00 20	00 27					06 06		06 18		06 35	06 42	06 50	06 57
West Hampstead ⊖	d	23p22	23p29	23p37	23p44	23p52	23p59	00 07	00 14	00 22	00 29					06 08		06 20		06 37	06 44	06 52	06 59
Finchley Road & Frognal	d	23p24	23p31	23p39	23p46	23p54	00 01	00 09	00 16	00 24	00 31					06 09		06 21		06 39	06 46	06 54	07 01
Hampstead Heath	d	23p26	23p33	23p41	23p48	23p56	00 03	00 11	00 18	00 26	00 33					06 12		06 24		06 41	06 48	06 56	07 03
Gospel Oak	d	23p30	23p37	23p45	23p52	00 01	00 07	00 15	00 22	00 30	00 37					06 14		06 26		06 45	06 52	07 00	07 07
Kentish Town West	d	23p32	23p39	23p47	23p54	00 02	00 09	00 17	00 24	00 32	00 39					06 16		06 28		06 47	06 54	07 02	07 09
Camden Road	d	23p36	23p43	23p51	23p58	00 06	00 13	00 21	00 28	00 36	00 43			06 11	06 15	06 20	06 28	06 32	06 40	06 51	06 58	07 06	07 13
Caledonian Rd & Barnsbury	d	23p39	23p46	23p54	00 01	00 09	00 16	00 24	00 31	00 39	00 46			06 14	06 18	06 23	06 31	06 35	06 43	06 54	07 01	07 09	07 16
Highbury & Islington ⊖	d	23p41	23p48	23p56	00 03	00 11	00 18	00 26	00 33	00 41	00 48			06 16	06 21	06 26	06 34	06 38	06 47	06 56	07 03	07 11	07 18
Canonbury ⊖	d	23p43	23p50	23p59	00 05	00 13	00 20	00 28	00 35	00 43	00 50			06 18	06 23	06 28	06 36	06 40	06 48	06 58	07 05	07 13	07 20
Dalston Kingsland	d	23p46	23p53	00 02	00 08	00 16	00 23	00 31	00 38	00 46	00 53			06 20	06 25	06 30	06 38	06 42	06 50	07 01	07 08	07 16	07 23
Hackney Central	d	23p48	23p55	00 03	00 10	00 18	00 25	00 33	00 40	00 48	00 55			06 22	06 27	06 32	06 40	06 44	06 52	07 03	07 10	07 18	07 25
Homerton	d	23p50	23p57	00 05	00 12	00 20	00 27	00 35	00 42	00 50	00 57			06 24	06 29	06 34	06 42	06 46	06 54	07 05	07 12	07 20	07 27
Hackney Wick	d	23p52	23p59	00 07	00 14	00 22	00 29	00 37	00 44	00 52	00 59			06 26	06 31	06 36	06 44	06 48	06 56	07 07	07 14	07 22	07 29
Stratford 7 ⊖	a	00 04	00 09	00 19	00 24	00 34	00 39	00 49	00 54	01 04	01 09			06 38	06 41	06 46	06 54	06 58	07 08	07 19	07 24	07 34	07 39

		LO	LO	LO	LO	LO	LO	LO	LO	LO	LO	LO	LO	LO	LO	LO	LO	LO	LO	LO	LO	LO	LO
Richmond ⊖	d	06 40		06 55		07 10		07 25		07 40		07 55		08 12		08 26		08 40		08 55		09 10	
Kew Gardens ⊖	d	06 43		06 58		07 13		07 28		07 43		07 58		08 15		08 29		08 43		08 58		09 13	
Gunnersbury ⊖	d	06 46		07 01		07 16		07 31		07 46		08 01		08 18		08 32		08 46		09 01		09 16	
South Acton	d	06 49		07 04		07 19		07 34		07 49		08 04		08 21		08 35		08 49		09 04		09 19	
Acton Central	d	06 52		07 07		07 22		07 37		07 52		08 07		08 23		08 38		08 52		09 07		09 23	
Clapham Junction 10	d		06 44		06 59		07 14		07 29		07 44		07 59		08 14		08 29		08 44		08 59		09 14
Imperial Wharf	d		06 48		07 03		07 18		07 33		07 48		08 03		08 18		08 33		08 48		09 03		09 18
West Brompton ⊖	d		06 51		07 06		07 21		07 36		07 51		08 06		08 21		08 36		08 51		09 06		09 21
Kensington (Olympia) ⊖	d		06 55		07 10		07 25		07 40		07 55		08 10		08 25		08 40		08 55		09 10		09 25
Shepherd's Bush ⊖	d		06 57		07 12		07 27		07 42		07 57		08 12		08 27		08 42		08 57		09 12		09 27
Willesden Jn Low Level ⊖	d																						
Willesden Jn. High Level ⊖	a	06 57	07 05	07 12	07 20	07 27	07 35	07 42	07 50	07 57	08 05	08 12	08 20	08 27	08 35	08 43	08 50	08 57	09 05	09 12	09 20	09 28	09 35
	d	06 59	07 06	07 14	07 21	07 29	07 36	07 44	07 51	07 59	08 06	08 14	08 21	08 29	08 36	08 45	08 51	08 59	09 06	09 14	09 21	09 30	09 36
Kensal Rise	d	07 01	07 08	07 16	07 23	07 31	07 38	07 46	07 53	08 01	08 08	08 16	08 23	08 31	08 38	08 47	08 53	09 01	09 08	09 16	09 23	09 32	09 38
Brondesbury Park	d	07 03	07 10	07 18	07 25	07 33	07 40	07 48	07 55	08 03	08 10	08 18	08 25	08 33	08 40	08 49	08 55	09 03	09 10	09 18	09 25	09 34	09 40
Brondesbury	d	07 05	07 12	07 20	07 27	07 35	07 42	07 50	07 57	08 05	08 12	08 20	08 27	08 35	08 42	08 51	08 57	09 05	09 12	09 20	09 27	09 36	09 42
West Hampstead ⊖	d	07 07	07 14	07 22	07 29	07 37	07 44	07 52	07 59	08 07	08 14	08 22	08 29	08 37	08 44	08 53	08 59	09 07	09 14	09 22	09 29	09 38	09 44
Finchley Road & Frognal	d	07 09	07 16	07 24	07 31	07 39	07 46	07 54	08 01	08 09	08 16	08 24	08 31	08 39	08 46	08 55	09 01	09 09	09 16	09 24	09 31	09 40	09 46
Hampstead Heath	d	07 11	07 18	07 26	07 33	07 41	07 48	07 56	08 03	08 11	08 18	08 26	08 33	08 41	08 48	08 57	09 03	09 11	09 18	09 26	09 33	09 42	09 48
Gospel Oak	d	07 15	07 22	07 30	07 37	07 45	07 52	08 00	08 07	08 15	08 22	08 30	08 37	08 45	08 52	09 01	09 07	09 15	09 22	09 30	09 37	09 46	09 52
Kentish Town West	d	07 17	07 24	07 32	07 39	07 47	07 54	08 02	08 09	08 17	08 24	08 32	08 39	08 47	08 54	09 03	09 09	09 17	09 24	09 32	09 39	09 48	09 54
Camden Road	d	07 21	07 28	07 36	07 43	07 51	07 58	08 06	08 13	08 21	08 28	08 36	08 43	08 51	08 58	09 07	09 13	09 21	09 28	09 36	09 43	09 52	09 58
Caledonian Rd & Barnsbury	d	07 24	07 31	07 39	07 46	07 54	08 01	08 09	08 16	08 24	08 31	08 39	08 46	08 54	09 01	09 10	09 16	09 24	09 31	09 39	09 46	09 55	10 01
Highbury & Islington ⊖	d	07 26	07 33	07 41	07 48	07 56	08 03	08 11	08 18	08 26	08 33	08 41	08 48	08 56	09 03	09 12	09 18	09 26	09 33	09 41	09 48	09 57	10 03
Canonbury ⊖	d	07 28	07 35	07 43	07 50	07 58	08 05	08 13	08 20	08 28	08 35	08 43	08 50	08 58	09 05	09 14	09 20	09 28	09 35	09 43	09 50	09 59	10 05
Dalston Kingsland	d	07 31	07 38	07 46	07 53	08 01	08 08	08 16	08 23	08 31	08 38	08 46	08 53	09 01	09 08	09 17	09 23	09 31	09 38	09 46	09 53	10 02	10 08
Hackney Central	d	07 33	07 40	07 48	07 55	08 03	08 10	08 18	08 25	08 33	08 40	08 48	08 55	09 03	09 10	09 19	09 25	09 33	09 40	09 48	09 55	10 04	10 10
Homerton	d	07 35	07 42	07 50	07 57	08 05	08 12	08 20	08 27	08 35	08 42	08 50	08 57	09 05	09 12	09 21	09 27	09 35	09 42	09 50	09 57	10 06	10 12
Hackney Wick	d	07 37	07 44	07 52	07 59	08 07	08 14	08 22	08 29	08 37	08 44	08 52	08 59	09 07	09 14	09 23	09 29	09 37	09 44	09 52	09 59	10 08	10 14
Stratford 7 ⊖	a	07 49	07 54	08 04	08 09	08 19	08 24	08 34	08 39	08 49	08 54	09 04	09 09	09 19	09 24	09 35	09 39	09 49	09 54	10 04	10 09	10 19	10 24

Table 59

Sundays
29 July to 12 August

Richmond and Clapham Junction - Willesden Junction, West Hampstead, Highbury and Islington and Stratford

Network Diagram - see first Page of Table 59

		LO	LO	LO	LO	LO	LO	LO	LO	LO	LO	LO	LO	LO	LO	LO	LO	LO	LO	LO	LO	LO	LO
Richmond ⊖	d	09 25		09 41		09 55		10 10		10 25		10 41		10 55		11 11		11 25		11 41		11 55	
Kew Gardens ⊖	d	09 28		09 44		09 58		10 13		10 28		10 44		10 58		11 14		11 28		11 44		11 58	
Gunnersbury ⊖	d	09 31		09 47		10 01		10 16		10 31		10 47		11 01		11 17		11 31		11 47		12 01	
South Acton	d	09 34		09 50		10 04		10 19		10 34		10 50		11 04		11 20		11 34		11 50		12 04	
Acton Central	d	09 37		09 52		10 07		10 22		10 37		10 52		11 07		11 23		11 37		11 52		12 07	
Clapham Junction 10	d		09 29		09 44		09 59		10 14		10 29		10 44		10 59		11 14		11 29		11 44		11 59
Imperial Wharf	d		09 33		09 48		10 03		10 18		10 33		10 48		11 03		11 18		11 33		11 48		12 03
West Brompton ⊖	d		09 36		09 51		10 06		10 21		10 36		10 51		11 06		11 21		11 36		11 51		12 06
Kensington (Olympia) ⊖	d		09 40		09 55		10 10		10 25		10 40		10 55		11 10		11 25		11 40		11 55		12 10
Shepherd's Bush ⊖	d		09 42		09 57		10 12		10 27		10 42		10 57		11 12		11 27		11 42		11 57		12 12
Willesden Jn Low Level ⊖	d																						
Willesden Jn. High Level ⊖	a	09 42	09 50	09 57	10 05	10 12	10 20	10 27	10 35	10 42	10 50	10 57	11 05	11 12	11 20	11 28	11 35	11 42	11 50	11 57	12 05	12 12	12 20
	d	09 44	09 51	09 59	10 06	10 14	10 21	10 29	10 36	10 44	10 51	10 59	11 06	11 14	11 21	11 30	11 36	11 44	11 51	11 59	12 06	12 14	12 21
Kensal Rise	d	09 46	09 53	10 01	10 08	10 16	10 23	10 31	10 38	10 46	10 53	11 01	11 08	11 16	11 23	11 32	11 38	11 46	11 53	12 01	12 08	12 16	12 23
Brondesbury Park	d	09 48	09 55	10 03	10 10	10 18	10 25	10 33	10 40	10 48	10 55	11 03	11 10	11 18	11 25	11 34	11 40	11 48	11 55	12 03	12 10	12 18	12 25
Brondesbury	d	09 50	09 57	10 05	10 12	10 20	10 27	10 35	10 42	10 50	10 57	11 05	11 12	11 20	11 27	11 36	11 42	11 50	11 57	12 05	12 12	12 20	12 27
West Hampstead ⊖	d	09 52	09 59	10 07	10 14	10 22	10 29	10 37	10 44	10 52	10 59	11 07	11 14	11 22	11 29	11 38	11 44	11 52	11 59	12 07	12 14	12 22	12 29
Finchley Road & Frognal	d	09 54	10 01	10 09	10 16	10 24	10 31	10 39	10 46	10 54	11 01	11 09	11 16	11 24	11 31	11 40	11 46	11 54	12 01	12 09	12 16	12 24	12 31
Hampstead Heath	d	09 56	10 03	10 11	10 18	10 26	10 33	10 41	10 48	10 56	11 03	11 11	11 18	11 26	11 33	11 42	11 48	11 56	12 03	12 11	12 18	12 26	12 33
Gospel Oak	d	10 00	10 07	10 15	10 22	10 30	10 37	10 45	10 52	11 00	11 07	11 15	11 22	11 30	11 37	11 46	11 52	12 00	12 07	12 15	12 22	12 30	12 37
Kentish Town West	d	10 02	10 09	10 17	10 24	10 32	10 39	10 47	10 54	11 02	11 09	11 17	11 24	11 32	11 39	11 48	11 54	12 02	12 09	12 17	12 24	12 32	12 39
Camden Road	d	10 06	10 13	10 21	10 28	10 36	10 43	10 51	10 58	11 06	11 13	11 21	11 28	11 36	11 43	11 52	11 58	12 06	12 13	12 21	12 28	12 36	12 43
Caledonian Rd & Barnsbury	d	10 09	10 16	10 24	10 31	10 39	10 46	10 54	11 01	11 09	11 16	11 24	11 31	11 39	11 46	11 55	12 01	12 09	12 16	12 24	12 31	12 39	12 46
Highbury & Islington ⊖	d	10 11	10 18	10 26	10 33	10 41	10 48	10 56	11 03	11 11	11 18	11 26	11 33	11 41	11 48	11 57	12 03	12 11	12 18	12 26	12 33	12 41	12 48
Canonbury ⊖	d	10 13	10 20	10 28	10 35	10 43	10 50	10 58	11 05	11 13	11 20	11 28	11 35	11 43	11 50	11 59	12 05	12 13	12 20	12 28	12 35	12 43	12 50
Dalston Kingsland	d	10 16	10 23	10 31	10 38	10 46	10 53	11 01	11 08	11 16	11 23	11 31	11 38	11 46	11 53	12 02	12 08	12 16	12 23	12 31	12 38	12 46	12 53
Hackney Central	d	10 18	10 25	10 33	10 40	10 48	10 55	11 03	11 10	11 18	11 25	11 33	11 40	11 48	11 55	12 04	12 10	12 18	12 25	12 33	12 40	12 48	12 55
Homerton	d	10 20	10 27	10 35	10 42	10 50	10 57	11 05	11 12	11 20	11 27	11 35	11 42	11 50	11 57	12 06	12 12	12 20	12 27	12 35	12 42	12 50	12 57
Hackney Wick	d	10 22	10 29	10 37	10 44	10 52	10 59	11 07	11 14	11 22	11 29	11 37	11 44	11 52	11 59	12 08	12 14	12 22	12 29	12 37	12 44	12 52	12 59
Stratford 7 ⊖	a	10 34	10 39	10 49	10 54	11 04	11 09	11 19	11 24	11 34	11 39	11 49	11 54	12 04	12 09	12 20	12 24	12 34	12 39	12 49	12 54	13 04	13 09

		LO	LO	LO	LO	LO	LO	LO	LO	LO		LO	LO	LO	LO	LO	LO	LO	LO	LO	LO	LO	LO
Richmond ⊖	d	12 11		12 25		12 41		12 55		13 11		22 11		22 25		22 41		22 55		23 11		23 25	
Kew Gardens ⊖	d	12 14		12 28		12 44		12 58		13 14		22 14		22 28		22 44		22 58		23 14		23 28	
Gunnersbury ⊖	d	12 17		12 31		12 47		13 01		13 17		22 17		22 31		22 47		23 01		23 17		23 31	
South Acton	d	12 20		12 34		12 50		13 04		13 20		22 20		22 34		22 50		23 04		23 20		23 34	
Acton Central	d	12 23		12 37		12 52		13 07		13 22		22 22		22 37		22 52		23 07		23 22		23 37	
Clapham Junction 10	d		12 14		12 29		12 44		12 59				22 14		22 29		22 44		22 59		23 14		23 29
Imperial Wharf	d		12 18		12 33		12 48		13 03				22 18		22 33		22 48		23 03		23 18		23 33
West Brompton ⊖	d		12 21		12 36		12 51		13 06				22 21		22 36		22 51		23 06		23 21		23 36
Kensington (Olympia) ⊖	d		12 25		12 40		12 55		13 10				22 25		22 40		22 55		23 10		23 25		23 40
Shepherd's Bush ⊖	d		12 27		12 42		12 57		13 12				22 27		22 42		22 57		23 12		23 27		23 42
Willesden Jn Low Level ⊖	d																						
Willesden Jn. High Level ⊖	a	12 28	12 35	12 42	12 50	12 57	13 05	13 12	13 20	13 27	and at the same minutes past each hour until	22 27	22 35	22 42	22 50	22 57	23 05	23 12	23 20	23 27	23 35	23 42	23 50
	d	12 30	12 36	12 44	12 51	12 59	13 06	13 14	13 21	13 29		22 29	22 36	22 44	22 51	22 59	23 06	23 14	23 21	23 29	23 36	23 44	23 51
Kensal Rise	d	12 32	12 38	12 46	12 53	13 01	13 08	13 16	13 23	13 31		22 31	22 38	22 46	22 53	23 01	23 08	23 16	23 23	23 31	23 38	23 46	23 53
Brondesbury Park	d	12 34	12 40	12 48	12 55	13 03	13 10	13 18	13 25	13 33		22 33	22 40	22 48	22 55	23 03	23 10	23 18	23 25	23 33	23 40	23 48	23 55
Brondesbury	d	12 36	12 42	12 50	12 57	13 05	13 12	13 20	13 27	13 35		22 35	22 42	22 50	22 57	23 05	23 12	23 20	23 27	23 35	23 42	23 50	23 57
West Hampstead ⊖	d	12 38	12 44	12 52	12 59	13 07	13 14	13 22	13 29	13 37		22 37	22 44	22 52	22 59	23 07	23 14	23 22	23 29	23 37	23 44	23 52	23 59
Finchley Road & Frognal	d	12 40	12 46	12 54	13 01	13 09	13 16	13 24	13 31	13 39		22 39	22 46	22 54	23 01	23 09	23 16	23 24	23 31	23 39	23 46	23 54	00 01
Hampstead Heath	d	12 42	12 48	12 56	13 03	13 11	13 18	13 26	13 33	13 41		22 41	22 48	22 56	23 03	23 11	23 18	23 26	23 33	23 41	23 48	23 56	00 03
Gospel Oak	d	12 46	12 52	13 00	13 07	13 15	13 22	13 30	13 37	13 45		22 45	22 52	23 00	23 07	23 15	23 22	23 30	23 37	23 45	23 52	00 01	00 07
Kentish Town West	d	12 48	12 54	13 02	13 09	13 17	13 24	13 32	13 39	13 47		22 47	22 54	23 02	23 09	23 17	23 24	23 32	23 39	23 47	23 54	00 02	00 09
Camden Road	d	12 52	12 58	13 06	13 13	13 21	13 28	13 36	13 43	13 51		22 51	22 58	23 06	23 13	23 21	23 28	23 36	23 43	23 51	23 58	00 06	00 13
Caledonian Rd & Barnsbury	d	12 55	13 01	13 09	13 16	13 24	13 31	13 39	13 46	13 54		22 54	23 01	23 09	23 16	23 24	23 31	23 39	23 46	23 54	00 01	00 09	00 16
Highbury & Islington ⊖	d	12 57	13 03	13 11	13 18	13 26	13 33	13 41	13 48	13 56		22 56	23 03	23 11	23 18	23 26	23 33	23 41	23 48	23 56	00 03	00 11	00 18
Canonbury ⊖	d	12 59	13 05	13 13	13 20	13 28	13 35	13 43	13 50	13 58		22 58	23 05	23 13	23 20	23 28	23 35	23 43	23 50	23 59	00 05	00 13	00 20
Dalston Kingsland	d	13 02	13 08	13 16	13 23	13 31	13 38	13 46	13 53	14 01		23 01	23 08	23 16	23 23	23 31	23 38	23 46	23 53	00 02	00 08	00 16	00 23
Hackney Central	d	13 04	13 10	13 18	13 25	13 33	13 40	13 48	13 55	14 03		23 03	23 10	23 18	23 25	23 33	23 40	23 48	23 55	00 03	00 10	00 18	00 25
Homerton	d	13 06	13 12	13 20	13 27	13 35	13 42	13 50	13 57	14 05		23 05	23 12	23 20	23 27	23 35	23 42	23 50	23 57	00 05	00 12	00 20	00 27
Hackney Wick	d	13 08	13 14	13 22	13 29	13 37	13 44	13 52	13 59	14 07		23 07	23 14	23 22	23 29	23 37	23 44	23 52	23 59	00 07	00 14	00 22	00 29
Stratford 7 ⊖	a	13 20	13 24	13 34	13 39	13 49	13 54	14 04	14 09	14 19		23 19	23 24	23 34	23 39	23 49	23 54	00 04	00 09	00 19	00 24	00 34	00 39

Sundays

29 July to 12 August

Richmond and Clapham Junction - Willesden Junction, West Hampstead, Highbury and Islington and Stratford

Network Diagram - see first Page of Table 59

		LO	LO	LO	LO
Richmond	⊖ d	23 41		23 55	
Kew Gardens	⊖ d	23 44		23 59	
Gunnersbury	⊖ d	23 47		00 01	
South Acton	d	23 50		00 04	
Acton Central	d	23 52		00 07	
Clapham Junction 10	d		23 44		23 59
Imperial Wharf	d		23 48		00 03
West Brompton	⊖ d		23 51		00 06
Kensington (Olympia)	⊖ d		23 55		00 10
Shepherd's Bush	⊖ d		23 57		00 12
Willesden Jn Low Level	⊖ d				
Willesden Jn. High Level	⊖ a	23 57	00 05	00 12	00 20
	d	23 59	00 06	00 14	00 21
Kensal Rise	d	00 01	00 08	00 16	00 23
Brondesbury Park	d	00 03	00 10	00 18	00 25
Brondesbury	d	00 05	00 12	00 20	00 27
West Hampstead	⊖ d	00 07	00 14	00 22	00 29
Finchley Road & Frognal	d	00 09	00 16	00 24	00 31
Hampstead Heath	d	00 11	00 18	00 26	00 33
Gospel Oak	d	00 15	00 22	00 30	00 37
Kentish Town West	d	00 17	00 24	00 32	00 39
Camden Road	d	00 21	00 28	00 36	00 43
Caledonian Rd & Barnsbury	d	00 24	00 31	00 39	00 46
Highbury & Islington	⊖ d	00 26	00 33	00 41	00 48
Canonbury	⊖ d	00 28	00 35	00 43	00 50
Dalston Kingsland	d	00 31	00 38	00 46	00 53
Hackney Central	d	00 33	00 40	00 48	00 55
Homerton	d	00 35	00 42	00 50	00 57
Hackney Wick	d	00 37	00 44	00 52	00 59
Stratford 7	⊖ a	00 49	00 54	01 04	01 09

Sundays

19 August to 26 August

		LO	LO	LO	LO	LO	LO	LO	LO	LO	LO	LO
Richmond	⊖ d			08 59		09 17	09 29		09 47	09 59		10 10
Kew Gardens	⊖ d			09 02		09 20	09 32		09 50	10 02		10 13
Gunnersbury	⊖ d			09 05		09 23	09 35		09 53	10 05		10 16
South Acton	d			09 08		09 26	09 38		09 56	10 08		10 19
Acton Central	d			09 11		09 29	09 41		09 59	10 11		10 22
Clapham Junction 10	d	08 30			09 00			09 30			10 00	
Imperial Wharf	d	08 34			09 04			09 34			10 04	
West Brompton	⊖ d	08 37			09 07			09 37			10 07	
Kensington (Olympia)	⊖ d	08 40			09 10			09 40			10 10	
Shepherd's Bush	⊖ d	08 42			09 12			09 42			10 12	
Willesden Jn Low Level	⊖ d		09 00									
Willesden Jn. High Level	⊖ a	08 51		09 16	09 21	09 34	09 46	09 51	10 04	10 16	10 21	10 27
	d			09 17		09 35	09 47		10 05	10 17		10 28
Kensal Rise	d		09 04	09 19		09 37	09 49		10 07	10 19		10 30
Brondesbury Park	d		09 06	09 21		09 39	09 51		10 09	10 21		10 32
Brondesbury	d		09 08	09 23		09 41	09 53		10 11	10 23		10 34
West Hampstead	⊖ d		09 10	09 25		09 43	09 55		10 13	10 25		10 36
Finchley Road & Frognal	d		09 11	09 26		09 44	09 56		10 14	10 26		10 37
Hampstead Heath	d		09 14	09 30		09 47	09 59		10 17	10 29		10 40
Gospel Oak	d		09 16	09 32		09 49	10 01		10 19	10 31		10 42
Kentish Town West	d		09 18	09 34		09 51	10 03		10 21	10 33		10 44
Camden Road	d		09 22	09 37		09 55	10 07		10 25	10 37		10 48
Caledonian Rd & Barnsbury	d		09 25	09 40		09 58	10 10		10 28	10 40		10 51
Highbury & Islington	⊖ d		09 28	09 43		10 01	10 13		10 31	10 43		10 54
Canonbury	⊖ d		09 30	09 45		10 03	10 15		10 33	10 45		10 56
Dalston Kingsland	d		09 32	09 47		10 05	10 16		10 35	10 47		10 58
Hackney Central	d		09 34	09 49		10 07	10 18		10 37	10 49		11 00
Homerton	d		09 36	09 51		10 09	10 20		10 39	10 51		11 02
Hackney Wick	d		09 38	09 53		10 11	10 22		10 41	10 53		11 04
Stratford 7	⊖ a		09 48	10 00		10 18	10 30		10 48	11 00		11 11

		LO	LO	LO	LO	LO	LO	LO	LO	LO	LO	LO
Richmond	⊖ d		10 29		10 40		10 59		11 10		11 29	
Kew Gardens	⊖ d		10 32		10 43		11 02		11 13		11 32	
Gunnersbury	⊖ d		10 35		10 46		11 05		11 16		11 35	
South Acton	d		10 38		10 49		11 08		11 19		11 38	
Acton Central	d		10 41		10 52		11 11		11 22		11 41	
Clapham Junction 10	d	10 20		10 30		10 45		11 00		11 20		11 30
Imperial Wharf	d	10 24		10 34		10 49		11 04		11 24		11 34
West Brompton	⊖ d	10 27		10 37		10 52		11 07		11 27		11 37
Kensington (Olympia)	⊖ d	10 30		10 40		10 55		11 10		11 30		11 40
Shepherd's Bush	⊖ d	10 32		10 42		10 57		11 12		11 32		11 42
Willesden Jn Low Level	⊖ d											
Willesden Jn. High Level	⊖ a	10 40	10 46	10 51	10 57	11 05	11 16	11 21	11 27	11 40	11 46	11 52
	d	10 41	10 47		10 58	11 06	11 17		11 28	11 41	11 47	
Kensal Rise	d	10 43	10 49		11 00	11 08	11 19		11 30	11 43	11 49	
Brondesbury Park	d	10 45	10 51		11 02	11 10	11 21		11 32	11 45	11 51	
Brondesbury	d	10 47	10 53		11 04	11 12	11 23		11 34	11 47	11 53	
West Hampstead	⊖ d	10 49	10 55		11 06	11 14	11 25		11 36	11 49	11 55	
Finchley Road & Frognal	d	10 50	10 56		11 07	11 15	11 26		11 37	11 50	11 56	
Hampstead Heath	d	10 53	10 59		11 10	11 18	11 29		11 40	11 53	11 59	
Gospel Oak	d	10 55	11 01		11 12	11 20	11 31		11 42	11 55	12 01	
Kentish Town West	d	10 57	11 03		11 14	11 22	11 33		11 44	11 57	12 03	
Camden Road	d	11 01	11 07		11 18	11 26	11 37		11 48	12 01	12 07	
Caledonian Rd & Barnsbury	d	11 04	11 10		11 21	11 29	11 40		11 51	12 04	12 10	
Highbury & Islington	⊖ d	11 07	11 13		11 24	11 32	11 43		11 54	12 07	12 13	
Canonbury	⊖ d	11 09	11 15		11 26	11 34	11 45		11 56	12 09	12 15	
Dalston Kingsland	d	11 11	11 17		11 28	11 36	11 47		11 58	12 11	12 17	
Hackney Central	d	11 13	11 19		11 30	11 38	11 49		12 00	12 13	12 19	
Homerton	d	11 15	11 21		11 32	11 40	11 51		12 02	12 15	12 21	
Hackney Wick	d	11 17	11 23		11 34	11 42	11 53		12 04	12 17	12 23	
Stratford 7	⊖ a	11 24	11 30		11 41	11 49	12 00		12 11	12 24	12 30	

Sundays

19 August to 26 August

Richmond and Clapham Junction - Willesden Junction, West Hampstead, Highbury and Islington and Stratford

Network Diagram - see first Page of Table 59

		LO	LO	LO	LO	LO	LO	LO	LO	LO	LO	LO	LO	LO	LO	LO	LO	LO	LO	LO	LO	LO	LO
Richmond	⊖ d	11 40		11 59		12 10		12 29		12 40		12 59		13 10		13 29		13 40		13 59		14 10	
Kew Gardens	⊖ d	11 43		12 02		12 13		12 32		12 43		13 02		13 13		13 32		13 43		14 02		14 13	
Gunnersbury	⊖ d	11 46		12 05		12 16		12 35		12 46		13 05		13 16		13 35		13 46		14 05		14 16	
South Acton	d	11 49		12 08		12 19		12 38		12 49		13 08		13 19		13 38		13 49		14 08		14 19	
Acton Central	d	11 52		12 11		12 22		12 41		12 52		13 11		13 22		13 41		13 52		14 11		14 22	
Clapham Junction 10	d		11 45		12 00		12 15		12 30		12 45		13 00		13 15		13 30		13 45		14 00		14 15
Imperial Wharf	d		11 49		12 04		12 19		12 34		12 49		13 04		13 19		13 34		13 49		14 04		14 19
West Brompton	⊖ d		11 52		12 07		12 22		12 37		12 52		13 07		13 22		13 37		13 52		14 07		14 22
Kensington (Olympia)	⊖ d		11 55		12 10		12 25		12 40		12 55		13 10		13 25		13 40		13 55		14 10		14 25
Shepherd's Bush	⊖ d		11 57		12 12		12 27		12 42		12 57		13 12		13 27		13 42		13 57		14 12		14 27
Willesden Jn Low Level	⊖ d																						
Willesden Jn. High Level	⊖ a	11 57	12 05	12 16	12 21	12 27	12 35	12 46	12 51	12 57	13 05	13 16	13 21	13 27	13 35	13 46	13 51	13 57	14 05	14 16	14 22	14 27	14 35
	d	11 58	12 06	12 17		12 28	12 36	12 47		12 58	13 06	13 17		13 28	13 36	13 47		13 58	14 06	14 17		14 28	14 36
Kensal Rise	d	12 00	12 08	12 19		12 30	12 38	12 49		13 00	13 08	13 19		13 30	13 38	13 49		14 00	14 08	14 19		14 30	14 38
Brondesbury Park	d	12 02	12 10	12 21		12 32	12 40	12 51		13 02	13 10	13 21		13 32	13 40	13 51		14 02	14 10	14 21		14 32	14 40
Brondesbury	d	12 04	12 12	12 23		12 34	12 42	12 53		13 04	13 12	13 23		13 34	13 42	13 53		14 04	14 12	14 23		14 34	14 42
West Hampstead	⊖ d	12 06	12 14	12 25		12 36	12 44	12 55		13 06	13 14	13 25		13 36	13 44	13 55		14 06	14 14	14 25		14 36	14 44
Finchley Road & Frognal	d	12 07	12 15	12 26		12 37	12 45	12 56		13 07	13 15	13 26		13 37	13 45	13 56		14 07	14 15	14 26		14 37	14 45
Hampstead Heath	d	12 10	12 18	12 29		12 40	12 48	12 59		13 10	13 18	13 29		13 40	13 48	13 59		14 10	14 18	14 29		14 40	14 48
Gospel Oak	d	12 12	12 20	12 31		12 42	12 50	13 01		13 12	13 20	13 31		13 42	13 50	14 01		14 12	14 20	14 31		14 42	14 50
Kentish Town West	d	12 14	12 22	12 33		12 44	12 52	13 03		13 14	13 22	13 33		13 44	13 52	14 03		14 14	14 22	14 33		14 44	14 52
Camden Road	d	12 18	12 26	12 37		12 48	12 56	13 07		13 18	13 26	13 37		13 48	13 56	14 07		14 18	14 26	14 37		14 48	14 56
Caledonian Rd & Barnsbury	d	12 21	12 29	12 40		12 51	12 59	13 10		13 21	13 29	13 40		13 51	13 59	14 10		14 21	14 29	14 40		14 51	14 59
Highbury & Islington	⊖ d	12 24	12 32	12 43		12 54	13 02	13 13		13 24	13 32	13 43		13 54	14 02	14 13		14 24	14 32	14 43		14 54	15 02
Canonbury	⊖ d	12 26	12 34	12 45		12 56	13 04	13 15		13 26	13 34	13 45		13 56	14 04	14 15		14 26	14 34	14 45		14 56	15 04
Dalston Kingsland	d	12 28	12 36	12 47		12 58	13 06	13 17		13 28	13 36	13 47		13 58	14 06	14 17		14 28	14 36	14 47		14 58	15 06
Hackney Central	d	12 30	12 38	12 49		13 00	13 08	13 19		13 30	13 38	13 49		14 00	14 08	14 19		14 30	14 38	14 49		15 00	15 08
Homerton	d	12 32	12 40	12 51		13 02	13 10	13 21		13 32	13 40	13 51		14 02	14 10	14 21		14 32	14 40	14 51		15 02	15 10
Hackney Wick	d	12 34	12 42	12 53		13 04	13 12	13 23		13 34	13 42	13 53		14 04	14 12	14 23		14 34	14 42	14 53		15 04	15 12
Stratford 7	⊖ a	12 41	12 49	13 00		13 11	13 19	13 30		13 41	13 49	14 00		14 11	14 19	14 30		14 41	14 49	15 00		15 11	15 19

		LO	LO	LO	LO	LO	LO		LO	LO	LO	LO	LO	LO	LO	LO	LO	LO	LO	LO	LO	LO
Richmond	⊖ d	14 29		14 40		14 59				20 10		20 29		20 40		20 59		21 17		21 29		21 47
Kew Gardens	⊖ d	14 32		14 43		15 02				20 13		20 32		20 43		21 02		21 20		21 32		21 50
Gunnersbury	⊖ d	14 35		14 46		15 05				20 16		20 35		20 46		21 05		21 23		21 35		21 53
South Acton	d	14 38		14 49		15 08				20 19		20 38		20 49		21 08		21 26		21 38		21 56
Acton Central	d	14 41		14 52		15 11				20 22		20 41		20 52		21 11		21 29		21 41		21 59
Clapham Junction 10	d		14 30		14 45		15 00		20 00		20 15		20 30		20 45		21 00		21 20		21 30	
Imperial Wharf	d		14 34		14 49		15 04		20 04		20 19		20 34		20 49		21 04		21 24		21 34	
West Brompton	⊖ d		14 37		14 52		15 07		20 07		20 22		20 37		20 52		21 07		21 27		21 37	
Kensington (Olympia)	⊖ d		14 40		14 55		15 10		20 10		20 25		20 40		20 55		21 10		21 30		21 40	
Shepherd's Bush	⊖ d		14 42		14 57		15 12		20 12		20 27		20 42		20 57		21 12		21 32		21 42	
Willesden Jn Low Level	⊖ d																					
Willesden Jn. High Level	⊖ a	14 46	14 51	14 57	15 05	15 16	15 21	and at the same minutes past each hour until	20 21	20 27	20 36	20 46	20 51	20 57	21 08	21 16	21 21	21 34	21 41	21 46	21 51	22 04
	d	14 47		14 58	15 06	15 17				20 28		20 47		20 58		21 17		21 35		21 47		22 05
Kensal Rise	d	14 49		15 00	15 08	15 19				20 30		20 49		21 00		21 19		21 37		21 49		22 07
Brondesbury Park	d	14 51		15 02	15 10	15 21				20 32		20 51		21 02		21 21		21 39		21 51		22 09
Brondesbury	d	14 53		15 04	15 12	15 23				20 34		20 53		21 04		21 23		21 41		21 53		22 11
West Hampstead	⊖ d	14 55		15 06	15 14	15 25				20 36		20 55		21 06		21 25		21 43		21 55		22 13
Finchley Road & Frognal	d	14 56		15 07	15 15	15 26				20 37		20 56		21 07		21 26		21 44		21 56		22 14
Hampstead Heath	d	14 59		15 10	15 18	15 29				20 40		20 59		21 10		21 29		21 47		21 59		22 17
Gospel Oak	d	15 01		15 12	15 20	15 31				20 42		21 01		21 12		21 31		21 49		22 01		22a22
Kentish Town West	d	15 03		15 14	15 22	15 33				20 44		21 03		21 14		21 33		21 51		22 03		
Camden Road	d	15 07		15 18	15 26	15 37				20 48		21 07		21 18		21 37		21 55		22 07		
Caledonian Rd & Barnsbury	d	15 10		15 21	15 29	15 40				20 51		21 10		21 21		21 40		21 58		22 10		
Highbury & Islington	⊖ d	15 13		15 24	15 32	15 43				20 54		21 13		21 24		21 43		22 01		22 13		
Canonbury	⊖ d	15 15		15 26	15 34	15 45				20 56		21 15		21 26		21 45		22 03		22 15		
Dalston Kingsland	d	15 17		15 28	15 36	15 47				20 58		21 17		21 28		21 47		22 05		22 17		
Hackney Central	d	15 19		15 30	15 38	15 49				21 00		21 19		21 30		21 49		22 07		22 19		
Homerton	d	15 21		15 32	15 40	15 51				21 02		21 21		21 32		21 51		22 09		22 21		
Hackney Wick	d	15 23		15 34	15 42	15 53				21 04		21 23		21 34		21 53		22 11		22 23		
Stratford 7	⊖ a	15 30		15 41	15 49	16 00				21 11		21 30		21 41		22 00		22 18		22 31		

Table 59

Sundays
19 August to 26 August

Richmond and Clapham Junction - Willesden Junction, West Hampstead, Highbury and Islington and Stratford

Network Diagram - see first Page of Table 59

		LO	LO	LO	LO	LO	LO	LO	LO
Richmond	⊖ d		21 59			22 28		22 58	
Kew Gardens	⊖ d		22 02			22 31		23 02	
Gunnersbury	⊖ d		22 05			22 34		23 05	
South Acton	d		22 08			22 37		23 08	
Acton Central	d		22 11			22 40		23 11	
Clapham Junction 10	d	21 45		22 00	22 20		22 44		23 15
Imperial Wharf	d	21 49		22 04	22 24		22 48		23 19
West Brompton	⊖ d	21 52		22 07	22 27		22 51		23 22
Kensington (Olympia)	⊖ d	21 55		22 10	22 30		22 54		23 25
Shepherd's Bush	⊖ d	21 57		22 12	22 32		22 56		23 27
Willesden Jn Low Level	⊖ d								
Willesden Jn. High Level	⊖ a	22 08	22 16	22 23	22 41	22 45	23 08	23 16	23 36
	d		22 17			22 46		23 17	
Kensal Rise	d		22 19			22 48		23 19	
Brondesbury Park	d		22 21			22 50		23 21	
Brondesbury	d		22 23			22 52		23 23	
West Hampstead	⊖ d		22 25			22 54		23 25	
Finchley Road & Frognal	d		22 26			22 55		23 26	
Hampstead Heath	d		22 29			22 58		23 29	
Gospel Oak	d		22a36			23a03		23a35	
Kentish Town West	d								
Camden Road	d								
Caledonian Rd & Barnsbury	d								
Highbury & Islington	⊖ d								
Canonbury	⊖ d								
Dalston Kingsland	d								
Hackney Central	d								
Homerton	d								
Hackney Wick	d								
Stratford 7	⊖ a								

Sundays
2 September to 9 September

		LO	LO	LO	LO	LO	LO	LO	LO	LO	LO	LO	LO	LO	LO	LO	LO	LO	LO	LO	LO	LO	LO
Richmond	⊖ d	22p55		23p11		23p25		23p41		23p55								05 54		06 10		06 25	
Kew Gardens	⊖ d	22p58		23p14		23p28		23p44		23p59								05 57		06 13		06 28	
Gunnersbury	⊖ d	23p01		23p17		23p31		23p47		00 01								06 00		06 16		06 31	
South Acton	d	23p04		23p20		23p34		23p50		00 04								06 03		06 19		06 34	
Acton Central	d	23p07		23p22		23p37		23p52		00 07								06 06		06 22		06 37	
Clapham Junction 10	d		22p59		23p14		23p29		23p44		23p59	00 12	05 47								06 14		06 29
Imperial Wharf	d		23p03		23p18		23p33		23p48		00 03	00 16	05 51								06 18		06 33
West Brompton	⊖ d		23p06		23p21		23p36		23p51		00 06	00 19	05 54								06 21		06 36
Kensington (Olympia)	⊖ d		23p10		23p25		23p40		23p55		00 10	00 22	05 58								06 25		06 40
Shepherd's Bush	⊖ d		23p12		23p27		23p42		23p57		00 12	00 24	06 00								06 27		06 42
Willesden Jn Low Level	⊖ d															05 58							
Willesden Jn. High Level	⊖ a	23p12	23p20	23p27	23p35	23p42	23p50	23p57	00 05	00 12	00 20	00 37	06 12					06 11		06 27	06 35	06 42	06 50
	d	23p14	23p21	23p29	23p36	23p44	23p51	23p59	00 06	00 14	00 21							06 12		06 29	06 36	06 44	06 51
Kensal Rise	d	23p16	23p23	23p31	23p38	23p46	23p53	00 01	00 08	00 16	00 23					06 02		06 14		06 31	06 38	06 46	06 53
Brondesbury Park	d	23p18	23p25	23p33	23p40	23p48	23p55	00 03	00 10	00 18	00 25					06 04		06 16		06 33	06 40	06 48	06 55
Brondesbury	d	23p20	23p27	23p35	23p42	23p50	23p57	00 05	00 12	00 20	00 27					06 06		06 18		06 35	06 42	06 50	06 57
West Hampstead	⊖ d	23p22	23p29	23p37	23p44	23p52	23p59	00 07	00 14	00 22	00 29					06 08		06 20		06 37	06 44	06 52	06 59
Finchley Road & Frognal	d	23p24	23p31	23p39	23p46	23p54	00 01	00 09	00 16	00 24	00 31					06 09		06 21		06 39	06 46	06 54	07 01
Hampstead Heath	d	23p26	23p33	23p41	23p48	23p56	00 03	00 11	00 18	00 26	00 33					06 12		06 24		06 41	06 48	06 56	07 03
Gospel Oak	d	23p30	23p37	23p45	23p52	00 01	00 07	00 15	00 22	00 30	00 37					06 14		06 26		06 45	06 52	07 00	07 07
Kentish Town West	d	23p32	23p39	23p47	23p54	00 02	00 09	00 17	00 24	00 32	00 39					06 16		06 28		06 47	06 54	07 02	07 09
Camden Road	d	23p36	23p43	23p51	23p58	00 06	00 13	00 21	00 28	00 36	00 43			06 11	06 15	06 20	06 28	06 32	06 40	06 51	06 58	07 06	07 13
Caledonian Rd & Barnsbury	d	23p39	23p46	23p54	00 01	00 09	00 16	00 24	00 31	00 39	00 46			06 14	06 18	06 23	06 31	06 35	06 43	06 54	07 01	07 09	07 16
Highbury & Islington	⊖ d	23p41	23p48	23p56	00 03	00 11	00 18	00 26	00 33	00 41	00 48			06 16	06 21	06 26	06 34	06 38	06 47	06 56	07 03	07 11	07 18
Canonbury	⊖ d	23p43	23p50	23p59	00 05	00 13	00 20	00 28	00 35	00 43	00 50			06 18	06 23	06 28	06 36	06 40	06 48	06 58	07 05	07 13	07 20
Dalston Kingsland	d	23p46	23p53	00 02	00 08	00 16	00 23	00 31	00 38	00 46	00 53			06 20	06 25	06 30	06 38	06 42	06 50	07 01	07 08	07 16	07 23
Hackney Central	d	23p48	23p55	00 03	00 10	00 18	00 25	00 33	00 40	00 48	00 55			06 22	06 27	06 32	06 40	06 44	06 52	07 03	07 10	07 18	07 25
Homerton	d	23p50	23p57	00 05	00 12	00 20	00 27	00 35	00 42	00 50	00 57			06 24	06 29	06 34	06 42	06 46	06 54	07 05	07 12	07 20	07 27
Hackney Wick	d	23p52	23p59	00 07	00 14	00 22	00 29	00 37	00 44	00 52	00 59			06 26	06 31	06 36	06 44	06 48	06 56	07 07	07 14	07 22	07 29
Stratford 7	⊖ a	00 04	00 09	00 19	00 24	00 34	00 39	00 49	00 54	01 04	01 09			06 38	06 41	06 46	06 54	06 58	07 08	07 19	07 24	07 34	07 39

Table 59

Sundays
2 September to 9 September

Richmond and Clapham Junction - Willesden Junction, West Hampstead, Highbury and Islington and Stratford

Network Diagram - see first Page of Table 59

		LO	LO	LO	LO	LO	LO	LO	LO	LO	LO	LO	LO	LO	LO	LO	LO	LO	LO	LO	LO	LO	LO
Richmond	⊖ d	06 40		06 55		07 10		07 25		07 40		07 55		08 12		08 25		08 40		08 55		09 10	
Kew Gardens	⊖ d	06 43		06 58		07 13		07 28		07 43		07 58		08 15		08 28		08 43		08 58		09 13	
Gunnersbury	⊖ d	06 46		07 01		07 16		07 31		07 46		08 01		08 18		08 31		08 46		09 01		09 16	
South Acton	d	06 49		07 04		07 19		07 34		07 49		08 04		08 21		08 34		08 49		09 04		09 19	
Acton Central	d	06 52		07 07		07 22		07 37		07 52		08 07		08 23		08 37		08 52		09 07		09 23	
Clapham Junction 10	d		06 44		06 59		07 14		07 29		07 44		07 59		08 14		08 29		08 44		08 59		09 14
Imperial Wharf	d		06 48		07 03		07 18		07 33		07 48		08 03		08 18		08 33		08 48		09 03		09 18
West Brompton	⊖ d		06 51		07 06		07 21		07 36		07 51		08 06		08 21		08 36		08 51		09 06		09 21
Kensington (Olympia)	⊖ d		06 55		07 10		07 25		07 40		07 55		08 10		08 25		08 40		08 55		09 10		09 25
Shepherd's Bush	⊖ d		06 57		07 12		07 27		07 42		07 57		08 12		08 27		08 42		08 57		09 12		09 27
Willesden Jn Low Level	⊖ d																						
Willesden Jn. High Level	⊖ a	06 57	07 05	07 12	07 20	07 27	07 35	07 42	07 50	07 57	08 05	08 12	08 20	08 27	08 35	08 42	08 50	08 57	09 05	09 12	09 20	09 28	09 35
	d	06 59	07 06	07 14	07 21	07 29	07 36	07 44	07 51	07 59	08 06	08 14	08 21	08 29	08 36	08 44	08 51	08 59	09 06	09 14	09 21	09 30	09 36
Kensal Rise	d	07 01	07 08	07 16	07 23	07 31	07 38	07 46	07 53	08 01	08 08	08 16	08 23	08 31	08 38	08 46	08 53	09 01	09 08	09 16	09 23	09 32	09 38
Brondesbury Park	d	07 03	07 10	07 18	07 25	07 33	07 40	07 48	07 55	08 03	08 10	08 18	08 25	08 33	08 40	08 48	08 55	09 03	09 10	09 18	09 25	09 34	09 40
Brondesbury	d	07 05	07 12	07 20	07 27	07 35	07 42	07 50	07 57	08 05	08 12	08 20	08 27	08 35	08 42	08 50	08 57	09 05	09 12	09 20	09 27	09 36	09 42
West Hampstead	⊖ d	07 07	07 14	07 22	07 29	07 37	07 44	07 52	07 59	08 07	08 14	08 22	08 29	08 37	08 44	08 52	08 59	09 07	09 14	09 22	09 29	09 38	09 44
Finchley Road & Frognal	d	07 09	07 16	07 24	07 31	07 39	07 46	07 54	08 01	08 09	08 16	08 24	08 31	08 39	08 46	08 54	09 01	09 09	09 16	09 24	09 31	09 40	09 46
Hampstead Heath	d	07 11	07 18	07 26	07 33	07 41	07 48	07 56	08 03	08 11	08 18	08 26	08 33	08 41	08 48	08 56	09 03	09 11	09 18	09 26	09 33	09 42	09 48
Gospel Oak	d	07 15	07 22	07 30	07 37	07 45	07 52	08 00	08 07	08 15	08 22	08 30	08 37	08 45	08 52	09 00	09 07	09 15	09 22	09 30	09 37	09 46	09 52
Kentish Town West	d	07 17	07 24	07 32	07 39	07 47	07 54	08 02	08 09	08 17	08 24	08 32	08 39	08 47	08 54	09 02	09 09	09 17	09 24	09 32	09 39	09 48	09 54
Camden Road	d	07 21	07 28	07 36	07 43	07 51	07 58	08 06	08 13	08 21	08 28	08 36	08 43	08 51	08 58	09 06	09 13	09 21	09 28	09 36	09 43	09 52	09 58
Caledonian Rd & Barnsbury	d	07 24	07 31	07 39	07 46	07 54	08 01	08 09	08 16	08 24	08 31	08 39	08 46	08 54	09 01	09 09	09 16	09 24	09 31	09 39	09 46	09 55	10 01
Highbury & Islington	⊖ d	07 26	07 33	07 41	07 48	07 56	08 03	08 11	08 18	08 26	08 33	08 41	08 48	08 56	09 03	09 11	09 18	09 26	09 33	09 41	09 48	09 57	10 03
Canonbury	⊖ d	07 28	07 35	07 43	07 50	07 58	08 05	08 13	08 20	08 28	08 35	08 43	08 50	08 58	09 05	09 13	09 20	09 28	09 35	09 43	09 50	09 59	10 05
Dalston Kingsland	d	07 31	07 38	07 46	07 53	08 01	08 08	08 16	08 23	08 31	08 38	08 46	08 53	09 01	09 08	09 16	09 23	09 31	09 38	09 46	09 53	10 02	10 08
Hackney Central	d	07 33	07 40	07 48	07 55	08 03	08 10	08 18	08 25	08 33	08 40	08 48	08 55	09 03	09 10	09 18	09 25	09 33	09 40	09 48	09 55	10 04	10 10
Homerton	d	07 35	07 42	07 50	07 57	08 05	08 12	08 20	08 27	08 35	08 42	08 50	08 57	09 05	09 12	09 20	09 27	09 35	09 42	09 50	09 57	10 06	10 12
Hackney Wick	d	07 37	07 44	07 52	07 59	08 07	08 14	08 22	08 29	08 37	08 44	08 52	08 59	09 07	09 14	09 22	09 29	09 37	09 44	09 52	09 59	10 08	10 14
Stratford 7	⊖ a	07 49	07 54	08 04	08 09	08 19	08 24	08 34	08 39	08 49	08 54	09 04	09 09	09 19	09 24	09 34	09 39	09 49	09 54	10 04	10 09	10 19	10 24

		LO	LO	LO	LO	LO	LO	LO		LO	LO	LO	LO	LO	LO	LO	LO	LO	LO	LO	LO	LO
Richmond	⊖ d	09 25		09 40		09 55		10 10		22 10		22 25		22 40		22 55		23 10		23 25		23 40
Kew Gardens	⊖ d	09 28		09 43		09 58		10 13		22 13		22 28		22 43		22 58		23 13		23 28		23 43
Gunnersbury	⊖ d	09 31		09 46		10 01		10 16		22 16		22 31		22 46		23 01		23 16		23 31		23 46
South Acton	d	09 34		09 49		10 04		10 19		22 19		22 34		22 49		23 04		23 19		23 34		23 49
Acton Central	d	09 37		09 52		10 07		10 22		22 22		22 37		22 52		23 07		23 22		23 37		23 52
Clapham Junction 10	d		09 29		09 44		09 59				22 14		22 29		22 44		22 59		23 14		23 29	
Imperial Wharf	d		09 33		09 48		10 03				22 18		22 33		22 48		23 03		23 18		23 33	
West Brompton	⊖ d		09 36		09 51		10 06				22 21		22 36		22 51		23 06		23 21		23 36	
Kensington (Olympia)	⊖ d		09 40		09 55		10 10				22 25		22 40		22 55		23 10		23 25		23 40	
Shepherd's Bush	⊖ d		09 42		09 57		10 12				22 27		22 42		22 57		23 12		23 27		23 42	
Willesden Jn Low Level	⊖ d																					
Willesden Jn. High Level	⊖ a	09 42	09 50	09 57	10 05	10 12	10 20	10 27	and at the same minutes past each hour until	22 27	22 35	22 42	22 50	22 57	23 05	23 12	23 20	23 27	23 35	23 42	23 50	23 57
	d	09 44	09 51	09 59	10 06	10 14	10 21	10 29		22 29	22 36	22 44	22 51	22 59	23 06	23 14	23 21	23 29	23 36	23 44	23 51	23 59
Kensal Rise	d	09 46	09 53	10 01	10 08	10 16	10 23	10 31		22 31	22 38	22 46	22 53	23 01	23 08	23 16	23 23	23 31	23 38	23 46	23 53	00 01
Brondesbury Park	d	09 48	09 55	10 03	10 10	10 18	10 25	10 33		22 33	22 40	22 48	22 55	23 03	23 10	23 18	23 25	23 33	23 40	23 48	23 55	00 03
Brondesbury	d	09 50	09 57	10 05	10 12	10 20	10 27	10 35		22 35	22 42	22 50	22 57	23 05	23 12	23 20	23 27	23 35	23 42	23 50	23 57	00 05
West Hampstead	⊖ d	09 52	09 59	10 07	10 14	10 22	10 29	10 37		22 37	22 44	22 52	22 59	23 07	23 14	23 22	23 29	23 37	23 44	23 52	23 59	00 07
Finchley Road & Frognal	d	09 54	10 01	10 09	10 16	10 24	10 31	10 39		22 39	22 46	22 54	23 01	23 09	23 16	23 24	23 31	23 39	23 46	23 54	00 01	00 09
Hampstead Heath	d	09 56	10 03	10 11	10 18	10 26	10 33	10 41		22 41	22 48	22 56	23 03	23 11	23 18	23 26	23 33	23 41	23 48	23 56	00 03	00 11
Gospel Oak	d	10 00	10 07	10 15	10 22	10 30	10 37	10 45		22 45	22 52	23 00	23 07	23 15	23 22	23 30	23 37	23 45	23 52	00 01	00 07	00 15
Kentish Town West	d	10 02	10 09	10 17	10 24	10 32	10 39	10 47		22 47	22 54	23 02	23 09	23 17	23 24	23 32	23 39	23 47	23 54	00 02	00 09	00 17
Camden Road	d	10 06	10 13	10 21	10 28	10 36	10 43	10 51		22 51	22 58	23 06	23 13	23 21	23 28	23 36	23 43	23 51	23 58	00 06	00 13	00 21
Caledonian Rd & Barnsbury	d	10 09	10 16	10 24	10 31	10 39	10 46	10 54		22 54	23 01	23 09	23 16	23 24	23 31	23 39	23 46	23 54	00 01	00 09	00 16	00 24
Highbury & Islington	⊖ d	10 11	10 18	10 26	10 33	10 41	10 48	10 56		22 56	23 03	23 11	23 18	23 26	23 33	23 41	23 48	23 56	00 03	00 11	00 18	00 26
Canonbury	⊖ d	10 13	10 20	10 28	10 35	10 43	10 50	10 58		22 58	23 05	23 13	23 20	23 28	23 35	23 43	23 50	23 59	00 05	00 13	00 20	00 28
Dalston Kingsland	d	10 16	10 23	10 31	10 38	10 46	10 53	11 01		23 01	23 08	23 16	23 23	23 31	23 38	23 46	23 53	00 02	00 08	00 16	00 23	00 31
Hackney Central	d	10 18	10 25	10 33	10 40	10 48	10 55	11 03		23 03	23 10	23 18	23 25	23 33	23 40	23 48	23 55	00 03	00 10	00 18	00 25	00 33
Homerton	d	10 20	10 27	10 35	10 42	10 50	10 57	11 05		23 05	23 12	23 20	23 27	23 35	23 42	23 50	23 57	00 05	00 12	00 20	00 27	00 35
Hackney Wick	d	10 22	10 29	10 37	10 44	10 52	10 59	11 07		23 07	23 14	23 22	23 29	23 37	23 44	23 52	23 59	00 07	00 14	00 22	00 29	00 37
Stratford 7	⊖ a	10 34	10 39	10 49	10 54	11 04	11 09	11 19		23 19	23 24	23 34	23 39	23 49	23 54	00 04	00 09	00 19	00 24	00 34	00 39	00 49

Sundays
2 September to 9 September

Richmond and Clapham Junction - Willesden Junction, West Hampstead, Highbury and Islington and Stratford

Network Diagram - see first Page of Table 59

		LO	LO	LO
Richmond ⊖	d		23 55	
Kew Gardens ⊖	d		23 59	
Gunnersbury ⊖	d		00 01	
South Acton	d		00 04	
Acton Central	d		00 07	
Clapham Junction 10	d	23 44		23 59
Imperial Wharf	d	23 48		00 03
West Brompton ⊖	d	23 51		00 06
Kensington (Olympia) ⊖	d	23 55		00 10
Shepherd's Bush ⊖	d	23 57		00 12
Willesden Jn Low Level ⊖	d			
Willesden Jn. High Level ⊖	a	00 05	00 12	00 20
	d	00 06	00 14	00 21
Kensal Rise	d	00 08	00 16	00 23
Brondesbury Park	d	00 10	00 18	00 25
Brondesbury	d	00 12	00 20	00 27
West Hampstead ⊖	d	00 14	00 22	00 29
Finchley Road & Frognal	d	00 16	00 24	00 31
Hampstead Heath	d	00 18	00 26	00 33
Gospel Oak	d	00 22	00 30	00 37
Kentish Town West	d	00 24	00 32	00 39
Camden Road	d	00 28	00 36	00 43
Caledonian Rd & Barnsbury	d	00 31	00 39	00 46
Highbury & Islington ⊖	d	00 33	00 41	00 48
Canonbury ⊖	d	00 35	00 43	00 50
Dalston Kingsland	d	00 38	00 46	00 53
Hackney Central	d	00 40	00 48	00 55
Homerton	d	00 42	00 50	00 57
Hackney Wick	d	00 44	00 52	00 59
Stratford 7 ⊖	a	00 54	01 04	01 09

Sundays
from 16 September

		LO	LO	LO	LO	LO	LO	LO	LO	LO	LO	LO	LO	LO	LO	LO	LO	LO	LO	LO	LO	LO	LO
Richmond ⊖	d			08 59		09 17	09 28		09 47	09 59		10 10		10 29		10 40		10 59		11 10		11 29	
Kew Gardens ⊖	d			09 02		09 20	09 31		09 50	10 02		10 13		10 32		10 43		11 02		11 13		11 32	
Gunnersbury ⊖	d			09 05		09 23	09 34		09 53	10 05		10 16		10 35		10 46		11 05		11 16		11 35	
South Acton	d			09 08		09 26	09 37		09 56	10 08		10 19		10 38		10 49		11 08		11 19		11 38	
Acton Central	d			09 11		09 29	09 40		09 59	10 11		10 22		10 41		10 52		11 11		11 22		11 41	
Clapham Junction 10	d	08 30			09 00			09 30			10 00		10 20		10 30		10 45		11 00		11 20		11 30
Imperial Wharf	d	08 34			09 04			09 34			10 04		10 24		10 34		10 49		11 04		11 24		11 34
West Brompton ⊖	d	08 37			09 07			09 37			10 07		10 27		10 37		10 52		11 07		11 27		11 37
Kensington (Olympia) ⊖	d	08 40			09 10			09 40			10 10		10 30		10 40		10 55		11 10		11 30		11 40
Shepherd's Bush ⊖	d	08 42			09 12			09 42			10 12		10 32		10 42		10 57		11 12		11 32		11 42
Willesden Jn Low Level ⊖	d		09 00																				
Willesden Jn. High Level ⊖	a	08 51		09 16	09 21	09 34	09 46	09 51	10 04	10 16	10 21	10 27	10 40	10 46	10 51	10 57	11 05	11 16	11 21	11 27	11 40	11 46	11 52
	d			09 17		09 35	09 46		10 05	10 17		10 28	10 41	10 47		10 58	11 06	11 17		11 28	11 41	11 47	
Kensal Rise	d		09 04	09 19		09 37	09 48		10 07	10 19		10 30	10 43	10 49		11 00	11 08	11 19		11 30	11 43	11 49	
Brondesbury Park	d		09 06	09 21		09 39	09 50		10 09	10 21		10 32	10 45	10 51		11 02	11 10	11 21		11 32	11 45	11 51	
Brondesbury	d		09 08	09 23		09 41	09 52		10 11	10 23		10 34	10 47	10 53		11 04	11 12	11 23		11 34	11 47	11 53	
West Hampstead ⊖	d		09 10	09 25		09 43	09 54		10 13	10 25		10 36	10 49	10 55		11 06	11 14	11 25		11 36	11 49	11 55	
Finchley Road & Frognal	d		09 11	09 26		09 44	09 55		10 14	10 26		10 37	10 50	10 56		11 07	11 15	11 26		11 37	11 50	11 56	
Hampstead Heath	d		09 14	09 30		09 47	09 58		10 17	10 29		10 40	10 53	10 59		11 10	11 18	11 29		11 40	11 53	11 59	
Gospel Oak	d		09 16	09 32		09 49	10 00		10 19	10 31		10 42	10 55	11 01		11 12	11 20	11 31		11 42	11 55	12 01	
Kentish Town West	d		09 18	09 34		09 51	10 02		10 21	10 33		10 44	10 57	11 03		11 14	11 22	11 33		11 44	11 57	12 03	
Camden Road	d		09 22	09 37		09 55	10 06		10 25	10 37		10 48	11 01	11 07		11 18	11 26	11 37		11 48	12 01	12 07	
Caledonian Rd & Barnsbury	d		09 25	09 40		09 58	10 09		10 28	10 40		10 51	11 04	11 10		11 21	11 29	11 40		11 51	12 04	12 10	
Highbury & Islington ⊖	d		09 28	09 43		10 01	10 12		10 31	10 43		10 54	11 07	11 13		11 24	11 32	11 43		11 54	12 07	12 13	
Canonbury ⊖	d		09 30	09 45		10 03	10 14		10 33	10 45		10 56	11 09	11 15		11 26	11 34	11 45		11 56	12 09	12 15	
Dalston Kingsland	d		09 32	09 47		10 05	10 16		10 35	10 47		10 58	11 11	11 17		11 28	11 36	11 47		11 58	12 11	12 17	
Hackney Central	d		09 34	09 49		10 07	10 18		10 37	10 49		11 00	11 13	11 19		11 30	11 38	11 49		12 00	12 13	12 19	
Homerton	d		09 36	09 51		10 09	10 20		10 39	10 51		11 02	11 15	11 21		11 32	11 40	11 51		12 02	12 15	12 21	
Hackney Wick	d		09 38	09 53		10 11	10 22		10 41	10 53		11 04	11 17	11 23		11 34	11 42	11 53		12 04	12 17	12 23	
Stratford 7 ⊖	a		09 48	10 00		10 18	10 30		10 48	11 00		11 11	11 24	11 30		11 41	11 49	12 00		12 11	12 24	12 30	

Sundays
from 16 September

Richmond and Clapham Junction - Willesden Junction, West Hampstead, Highbury and Islington and Stratford

Network Diagram - see first Page of Table 59

		LO	LO	LO	LO	LO	LO	LO	LO	LO	LO	LO	LO	LO	LO	LO	LO	LO	LO	LO	LO	LO	LO
Richmond ⊖	d	11 40		11 59		12 10		12 29		12 40		12 59		13 10		13 29		13 40		13 59		14 10	
Kew Gardens ⊖	d	11 43		12 02		12 13		12 32		12 43		13 02		13 13		13 32		13 43		14 02		14 13	
Gunnersbury ⊖	d	11 46		12 05		12 16		12 35		12 46		13 05		13 16		13 35		13 46		14 05		14 16	
South Acton	d	11 49		12 08		12 19		12 38		12 49		13 08		13 19		13 38		13 49		14 08		14 19	
Acton Central	d	11 52		12 11		12 22		12 41		12 52		13 11		13 22		13 41		13 52		14 11		14 22	
Clapham Junction 10	d		11 45		12 00		12 15		12 30		12 45		13 00		13 15		13 30		13 45		14 00		14 15
Imperial Wharf	d		11 49		12 04		12 19		12 34		12 49		13 04		13 19		13 34		13 49		14 04		14 19
West Brompton ⊖	d		11 52		12 07		12 22		12 37		12 52		13 07		13 22		13 37		13 52		14 07		14 22
Kensington (Olympia) ⊖	d		11 55		12 10		12 25		12 40		12 55		13 10		13 25		13 40		13 55		14 10		14 25
Shepherd's Bush ⊖	d		11 57		12 12		12 27		12 42		12 57		13 12		13 27		13 42		13 57		14 12		14 27
Willesden Jn Low Level ⊖	d																						
Willesden Jn. High Level ⊖	a	11 57	12 05	12 16	12 21	12 27	12 35	12 46	12 51	12 57	13 05	13 16	13 21	13 27	13 35	13 46	13 51	13 57	14 05	14 16	14 22	14 27	14 35
	d	11 58	12 06	12 17		12 28	12 36	12 47		12 58	13 06	13 17		13 28	13 36	13 47		13 58	14 06	14 17		14 28	14 36
Kensal Rise	d	12 00	12 08	12 19		12 30	12 38	12 49		13 00	13 08	13 19		13 30	13 38	13 49		14 00	14 08	14 19		14 30	14 38
Brondesbury Park	d	12 02	12 10	12 21		12 32	12 40	12 51		13 02	13 10	13 21		13 32	13 40	13 51		14 02	14 10	14 21		14 32	14 40
Brondesbury	d	12 04	12 12	12 23		12 34	12 42	12 53		13 04	13 12	13 23		13 34	13 42	13 53		14 04	14 12	14 23		14 34	14 42
West Hampstead ⊖	d	12 06	12 14	12 25		12 36	12 44	12 55		13 06	13 14	13 25		13 36	13 44	13 55		14 06	14 14	14 25		14 36	14 44
Finchley Road & Frognal	d	12 07	12 15	12 26		12 37	12 45	12 56		13 07	13 15	13 26		13 37	13 45	13 56		14 07	14 15	14 26		14 37	14 45
Hampstead Heath	d	12 10	12 18	12 29		12 40	12 48	12 59		13 10	13 18	13 29		13 40	13 48	13 59		14 10	14 18	14 29		14 40	14 48
Gospel Oak	d	12 12	12 20	12 31		12 42	12 50	13 01		13 12	13 20	13 31		13 42	13 50	14 01		14 12	14 20	14 31		14 42	14 50
Kentish Town West	d	12 14	12 22	12 33		12 44	12 52	13 03		13 14	13 22	13 33		13 44	13 52	14 03		14 14	14 22	14 33		14 44	14 52
Camden Road	d	12 18	12 26	12 37		12 48	12 56	13 07		13 18	13 26	13 37		13 48	13 56	14 07		14 18	14 26	14 37		14 48	14 56
Caledonian Rd & Barnsbury	d	12 21	12 29	12 40		12 51	12 59	13 10		13 21	13 29	13 40		13 51	13 59	14 10		14 21	14 29	14 40		14 51	14 59
Highbury & Islington ⊖	d	12 24	12 32	12 43		12 54	13 02	13 13		13 24	13 32	13 43		13 54	14 02	14 13		14 24	14 32	14 43		14 54	15 02
Canonbury ⊖	d	12 26	12 34	12 45		12 56	13 04	13 15		13 26	13 34	13 45		13 56	14 04	14 15		14 26	14 34	14 45		14 56	15 04
Dalston Kingsland	d	12 28	12 36	12 47		12 58	13 06	13 17		13 28	13 36	13 47		13 58	14 06	14 17		14 28	14 36	14 47		14 58	15 06
Hackney Central	d	12 30	12 38	12 49		13 00	13 08	13 19		13 30	13 38	13 49		14 00	14 08	14 19		14 30	14 38	14 49		15 00	15 08
Homerton	d	12 32	12 40	12 51		13 02	13 10	13 21		13 32	13 40	13 51		14 02	14 10	14 21		14 32	14 40	14 51		15 02	15 10
Hackney Wick	d	12 34	12 42	12 53		13 04	13 12	13 23		13 34	13 42	13 53		14 04	14 12	14 23		14 34	14 42	14 53		15 04	15 12
Stratford 7 ⊖	a	12 41	12 49	13 00		13 11	13 19	13 30		13 41	13 49	14 00		14 11	14 19	14 30		14 41	14 49	15 00		15 11	15 19

		LO	LO	LO	LO	LO	LO		LO	LO	LO	LO	LO	LO	LO	LO	LO	LO	LO	LO	LO	LO
Richmond ⊖	d	14 29		14 40		14 59				20 10		20 29		20 40		20 59		21 17		21 29		21 47
Kew Gardens ⊖	d	14 32		14 43		15 02				20 13		20 32		20 43		21 02		21 20		21 32		21 50
Gunnersbury ⊖	d	14 35		14 46		15 05				20 16		20 35		20 46		21 05		21 23		21 35		21 53
South Acton	d	14 38		14 49		15 08				20 19		20 38		20 49		21 08		21 26		21 38		21 56
Acton Central	d	14 41		14 52		15 11				20 22		20 41		20 52		21 11		21 29		21 41		21 59
Clapham Junction 10	d		14 30		14 45		15 00		20 00		20 15		20 30		20 45		21 00		21 20		21 30	
Imperial Wharf	d		14 34		14 49		15 04		20 04		20 19		20 34		20 49		21 04		21 24		21 34	
West Brompton ⊖	d		14 37		14 52		15 07		20 07		20 22		20 37		20 52		21 07		21 27		21 37	
Kensington (Olympia) ⊖	d		14 40		14 55		15 10		20 10		20 25		20 40		20 55		21 10		21 30		21 40	
Shepherd's Bush ⊖	d		14 42		14 57		15 12		20 12		20 27		20 42		20 57		21 12		21 32		21 42	
Willesden Jn Low Level ⊖	d																					
Willesden Jn. High Level ⊖	a	14 46	14 51	14 57	15 05	15 16	15 21	and at	20 21	20 27	20 36	20 46	20 51	20 57	21 08	21 16	21 21	21 34	21 41	21 46	21 51	22 04
	d	14 47		14 58	15 06	15 17		the same		20 28		20 47		20 58		21 17		21 35		21 47		22 05
Kensal Rise	d	14 49		15 00	15 08	15 19		minutes		20 30		20 49		21 00		21 19		21 37		21 49		22 07
Brondesbury Park	d	14 51		15 02	15 10	15 21		past		20 32		20 51		21 02		21 21		21 39		21 51		22 09
Brondesbury	d	14 53		15 04	15 12	15 23		each		20 34		20 53		21 04		21 23		21 41		21 53		22 11
West Hampstead ⊖	d	14 55		15 06	15 14	15 25		hour until		20 36		20 55		21 06		21 25		21 43		21 55		22 13
Finchley Road & Frognal	d	14 56		15 07	15 15	15 26				20 37		20 56		21 07		21 26		21 44		21 56		22 14
Hampstead Heath	d	14 59		15 10	15 18	15 29				20 40		20 59		21 10		21 29		21 47		21 59		22 17
Gospel Oak	d	15 01		15 12	15 20	15 31				20 42		21 01		21 12		21 31		21 49		22 01		22a22
Kentish Town West	d	15 03		15 14	15 22	15 33				20 44		21 03		21 14		21 33		21 51		22 03		
Camden Road	d	15 07		15 18	15 26	15 37				20 48		21 07		21 18		21 37		21 55		22 07		
Caledonian Rd & Barnsbury	d	15 10		15 21	15 29	15 40				20 51		21 10		21 21		21 40		21 58		22 10		
Highbury & Islington ⊖	d	15 13		15 24	15 32	15 43				20 54		21 13		21 24		21 43		22 01		22 13		
Canonbury ⊖	d	15 15		15 26	15 34	15 45				20 56		21 15		21 26		21 45		22 03		22 15		
Dalston Kingsland	d	15 17		15 28	15 36	15 47				20 58		21 17		21 28		21 47		22 05		22 17		
Hackney Central	d	15 19		15 30	15 38	15 49				21 00		21 19		21 30		21 49		22 07		22 19		
Homerton	d	15 21		15 32	15 40	15 51				21 02		21 21		21 32		21 51		22 09		22 21		
Hackney Wick	d	15 23		15 34	15 42	15 53				21 04		21 23		21 34		21 53		22 11		22 23		
Stratford 7 ⊖	a	15 30		15 41	15 49	16 00				21 11		21 30		21 41		22 00		22 19		22 31		

Table 59

Sundays
from 16 September

Richmond and Clapham Junction - Willesden Junction, West Hampstead, Highbury and Islington and Stratford

Network Diagram - see first Page of Table 59

		LO	LO	LO	LO	LO	LO	LO	LO
Richmond ⊖	d		21 59			22 28		22 58	
Kew Gardens ⊖	d		22 02			22 31		23 02	
Gunnersbury ⊖	d		22 05			22 34		23 05	
South Acton	d		22 08			22 37		23 08	
Acton Central	d		22 11			22 40		23 11	
Clapham Junction 10	d	21 45		22 00	22 20		22 44		23 15
Imperial Wharf	d	21 49		22 04	22 24		22 48		23 19
West Brompton ⊖	d	21 52		22 07	22 27		22 51		23 22
Kensington (Olympia) ⊖	d	21 55		22 10	22 30		22 54		23 25
Shepherd's Bush ⊖	d	21 57		22 12	22 32		22 56		23 27
Willesden Jn Low Level ⊖	d								
Willesden Jn. High Level ⊖	a	22 08	22 16	22 23	22 41	22 45	23 08	23 16	23 36
	d		22 17			22 46		23 17	
Kensal Rise	d		22 19			22 48		23 19	
Brondesbury Park	d		22 21			22 50		23 21	
Brondesbury	d		22 23			22 52		23 23	
West Hampstead ⊖	d		22 25			22 54		23 25	
Finchley Road & Frognal	d		22 26			22 55		23 26	
Hampstead Heath	d		22 29			22 58		23 29	
Gospel Oak	d		22a36			23a03		23a35	
Kentish Town West	d								
Camden Road	d								
Caledonian Rd & Barnsbury	d								
Highbury & Islington ⊖	d								
Canonbury ⊖	d								
Dalston Kingsland	d								
Hackney Central	d								
Homerton	d								
Hackney Wick	d								
Stratford 7 ⊖	a								

Table 60

Mondays to Fridays
until 26 July

London, Queen's Park and Harrow & Wealdstone - Watford Junction

Network Diagram - see first Page of Table 59

Miles			LO MO A	LO MX	LO MO A	LO MX	LO	LO	LO	LO	LO	LO	LO	LO	LO	and at the same minutes past each hour until	LO	LO	LO	LO	LO	LO
0	**London Euston** 15 ⊖	d	23p17	23p27	23p47	23p57	05 37	06 07	06 37	06 57	07 17	07 37	07 57	08 17	08 37		15 37	15 57	16 17	16 37	16 57	17 17
2½	South Hampstead	d	23p23	23p33	23p53	00 03	05 43	06 13	06 43	07 03	07 23	07 43	08 03	08 23	08 43		15 43	16 03	16 23	16 43	17 03	17 23
3	Kilburn High Road	d	23p24	23p34	23p54	00 04	05 44	06 14	06 44	07 04	07 24	07 44	08 04	08 24	08 44		15 44	16 04	16 24	16 44	17 04	17 24
3¾	**Queen's Park (London)** ⊖	d	23p26	23p36	23p56	00 06	05 46	06 16	06 46	07 06	07 26	07 46	08 06	08 26	08 46		15 46	16 06	16 27	16 47	17 07	17 27
4½	Kensal Green	d	23p28	23p38	23p58	00 08	05 48	06 18	06 48	07 08	07 28	07 48	08 08	08 28	08 48		15 48	16 08	16 29	16 49	17 09	17 29
5½	**Willesden Jn Low Level**	d	23p31	23p41	00 01	00 11	05 51	06 21	06 51	07 11	07 31	07 51	08 11	08 31	08 51		15 51	16 11	16 32	16 52	17 12	17 32
6	Harlesden	d	23p33	23p43	00 03	00 13	05 53	06 23	06 53	07 13	07 33	07 53	08 13	08 33	08 53		15 53	16 13	16 34	16 54	17 14	17 34
7	Stonebridge Park	d	23p35	23p45	00 05	00 15	05 55	06 25	06 55	07 15	07 35	07 55	08 15	08 35	08 55		15 55	16 15	16 36	16 56	17 16	17 36
8	Wembley Central	d	23p38	23p48	00 08	00 18	05 58	06 28	06 58	07 18	07 38	07 58	08 18	08 38	08 58		15 58	16 18	16 39	16 59	17 19	17 39
9	North Wembley	d	23p40	23p50	00 10	00 20	06 00	06 30	07 00	07 20	07 40	08 00	08 20	08 40	09 00		16 00	16 20	16 41	17 01	17 21	17 41
9½	South Kenton	d	23p42	23p52	00 12	00 22	06 02	06 32	07 02	07 22	07 42	08 02	08 22	08 42	09 02		16 02	16 22	16 43	17 03	17 23	17 43
10¼	Kenton	d	23p44	23p54	00 14	00 24	06 04	06 34	07 04	07 24	07 44	08 04	08 24	08 44	09 04		16 04	16 24	16 45	17 05	17 25	17 45
11¼	**Harrow & Wealdstone**	d	23p46	23p56	00 16	00 26	06 06	06 36	07 06	07 26	07 46	08 06	08 26	08 46	09 06		16 06	16 26	16 48	17 08	17 28	17 48
12½	Headstone Lane	d	23p49	23p59	00 19	00 29	06 09	06 39	07 09	07 29	07 49	08 09	08 29	08 49	09 09		16 09	16 29	16 51	17 11	17 31	17 51
13¼	Hatch End	d	23p51	00 01	00 21	00 31	06 11	06 41	07 11	07 31	07 51	08 11	08 31	08 51	09 11		16 11	16 31	16 53	17 13	17 33	17 53
14¾	Carpenders Park	d	23p54	00 04	00 24	00 34	06 14	06 44	07 14	07 34	07 54	08 14	08 34	08 54	09 14		16 14	16 34	16 56	17 16	17 36	17 56
16	Bushey	d	23p57	00 07	00 27	00 37	06 17	06 47	07 17	07 37	07 57	08 17	08 37	08 57	09 17		16 17	16 37	16 59	17 19	17 39	17 59
16¾	Watford High Street	d	23p59	00 10	00 30	00 40	06 20	06 50	07 20	07 40	08 00	08 20	08 40	09 00	09 20		16 20	16 40	17 01	17 21	17 41	18 01
17¾	**Watford Junction**	a	00 04	00 14	00 35	00 44	06 24	06 54	07 24	07 45	08 04	08 28	08 44	09 04	09 24		16 24	16 44	17 08	17 28	17 48	18 08

		LO	LO	LO	LO	LO	LO	LO	LO	LO	LO	LO	LO	LO	LO	LO	LO	LO	LO
London Euston 15 ⊖	d	17 37	17 57	18 17	18 37	18 57	19 17	19 37	19 57	20 17	20 37	20 57	21 17	21 37	21 57	22 27	22 57	23 27	23 57
South Hampstead	d	17 43	18 03	18 23	18 43	19 03	19 23	19 43	20 03	20 23	20 43	21 03	21 23	21 43	22 03	22 33	23 03	23 33	00 03
Kilburn High Road	d	17 44	18 04	18 24	18 44	19 04	19 24	19 44	20 04	20 24	20 44	21 04	21 24	21 44	22 04	22 34	23 04	23 34	00 04
Queen's Park (London) ⊖	d	17 47	18 07	18 27	18 47	19 07	19 26	19 46	20 06	20 26	20 46	21 06	21 26	21 46	22 06	22 36	23 06	23 36	00 06
Kensal Green	d	17 49	18 09	18 29	18 49	19 09	19 28	19 48	20 08	20 28	20 48	21 08	21 28	21 48	22 08	22 38	23 08	23 38	00 08
Willesden Jn Low Level	d	17 52	18 12	18 32	18 52	19 12	19 31	19 51	20 11	20 31	20 51	21 11	21 31	21 51	22 11	22 41	23 11	23 41	00 11
Harlesden	d	17 54	18 14	18 34	18 54	19 14	19 33	19 53	20 13	20 33	20 53	21 13	21 33	21 53	22 13	22 43	23 13	23 43	00 13
Stonebridge Park	d	17 56	18 16	18 36	18 56	19 16	19 35	19 55	20 15	20 35	20 55	21 15	21 35	21 55	22 15	22 45	23 15	23 45	00 15
Wembley Central	d	17 59	18 19	18 39	18 59	19 19	19 38	19 58	20 18	20 38	20 58	21 18	21 38	21 58	22 18	22 48	23 18	23 48	00 18
North Wembley	d	18 01	18 21	18 41	19 01	19 21	19 40	20 00	20 20	20 40	21 00	21 20	21 40	22 00	22 20	22 50	23 20	23 50	00 20
South Kenton	d	18 03	18 23	18 43	19 03	19 23	19 42	20 02	20 22	20 42	21 02	21 22	21 42	22 02	22 22	22 52	23 22	23 52	00 22
Kenton	d	18 05	18 25	18 45	19 05	19 25	19 44	20 04	20 24	20 44	21 04	21 24	21 44	22 04	22 24	22 54	23 24	23 54	00 24
Harrow & Wealdstone	d	18 08	18 28	18 48	19 08	19 28	19 46	20 06	20 26	20 46	21 06	21 26	21 46	22 06	22 26	22 56	23 26	23 56	00 26
Headstone Lane	d	18 11	18 31	18 51	19 11	19 31	19 49	20 09	20 29	20 49	21 09	21 29	21 49	22 09	22 29	22 59	23 29	23 59	00 29
Hatch End	d	18 13	18 33	18 53	19 13	19 33	19 51	20 11	20 31	20 51	21 11	21 31	21 51	22 11	22 31	23 01	23 31	00 01	00 31
Carpenders Park	d	18 16	18 36	18 56	19 16	19 36	19 54	20 14	20 34	20 54	21 14	21 34	21 54	22 14	22 34	23 04	23 34	00 04	00 34
Bushey	d	18 19	18 39	18 59	19 19	19 39	19 57	20 17	20 37	20 57	21 17	21 37	21 57	22 17	22 37	23 07	23 37	00 07	00 37
Watford High Street	d	18 21	18 41	19 01	19 21	19 41	20 00	20 20	20 40	21 00	21 20	21 40	22 00	22 20	22 40	23 10	23 40	00 10	00 40
Watford Junction	a	18 28	18 48	19 08	19 28	19 48	20 04	20 28	20 44	21 08	21 28	21 44	22 04	22 25	22 44	23 14	23 44	00 14	00 44

Mondays to Fridays
27 July to 7 September

		LO MO	LO MX	LO MO	LO MX	LO	LO	LO	LO	LO	LO	LO	LO	LO	LO	LO	LO	LO B	LO C	LO	LO
London Euston 15 ⊖	d	23p17	23p27	23p47	23p57	05 37	06 07	06 37	06 57	07 17	07 37	07 57	08 17	08 37	08 57	09 17	09 37	09 57	09 57	10 17	10 37
South Hampstead	d	23p23	23p33	23p53	00 03	05 43	06 13	06 43	07 03	07 23	07 43	08 03	08 23	08 43	09 03	09 23	09 43	10 03	10 03	10 23	10 43
Kilburn High Road	d	23p24	23p34	23p54	00 04	05 44	06 14	06 44	07 04	07 24	07 44	08 04	08 24	08 44	09 04	09 24	09 44	10 04	10 04	10 24	10 44
Queen's Park (London) ⊖	d	23p26	23p36	23p56	00 06	05 46	06 16	06 46	07 06	07 26	07 46	08 06	08 26	08 46	09 06	09 26	09 46	10 05	10 06	10 26	10 46
Kensal Green	d	23p28	23p38	23p58	00 08	05 48	06 18	06 48	07 08	07 28	07 48	08 08	08 28	08 48	09 08	09 28	09 48	10 07	10 08	10 28	10 48
Willesden Jn Low Level	d	23p31	23p41	00 01	00 11	05 51	06 21	06 51	07 11	07 31	07 51	08 11	08 31	08 51	09 11	09 31	09 51	10 10	10 11	10 31	10 51
Harlesden	d	23p33	23p43	00 03	00 13	05 53	06 23	06 53	07 13	07 33	07 53	08 13	08 33	08 53	09 13	09 33	09 53	10 12	10 13	10 33	10 53
Stonebridge Park	d	23p35	23p45	00 05	00 15	05 55	06 25	06 55	07 15	07 35	07 55	08 15	08 35	08 55	09 15	09 35	09 55	10 14	10 15	10 35	10 55
Wembley Central	d	23p38	23p48	00 08	00 18	05 58	06 28	06 58	07 18	07 38	07 58	08 18	08 38	08 58	09 18	09 38	09 58	10 17	10 18	10 38	10 58
North Wembley	d	23p40	23p50	00 10	00 20	06 00	06 30	07 00	07 20	07 40	08 00	08 20	08 40	09 00	09 20	09 40	10 00	10 19	10 20	10 40	11 00
South Kenton	d	23p42	23p52	00 12	00 22	06 02	06 32	07 02	07 22	07 42	08 02	08 22	08 42	09 02	09 22	09 42	10 02	10 21	10 22	10 42	11 02
Kenton	d	23p44	23p54	00 14	00 24	06 04	06 34	07 04	07 24	07 44	08 04	08 24	08 44	09 04	09 24	09 44	10 04	10 23	10 24	10 44	11 04
Harrow & Wealdstone	d	23p46	23p56	00 16	00 26	06 06	06 36	07 06	07 26	07 46	08 06	08 26	08 46	09 06	09 26	09 46	10 06	10 25	10 26	10 46	11 06
Headstone Lane	d	23p49	23p59	00 19	00 29	06 09	06 39	07 09	07 29	07 49	08 09	08 29	08 49	09 09	09 29	09 49	10 09	10 28	10 29	10 49	11 09
Hatch End	d	23p51	00 01	00 21	00 31	06 11	06 41	07 11	07 31	07 51	08 11	08 31	08 51	09 11	09 31	09 51	10 11	10 30	10 31	10 51	11 11
Carpenders Park	d	23p54	00 04	00 24	00 34	06 14	06 44	07 14	07 34	07 54	08 14	08 34	08 54	09 14	09 34	09 54	10 14	10 33	10 34	10 54	11 14
Bushey	d	23p57	00 07	00 27	00 37	06 17	06 47	07 17	07 37	07 57	08 17	08 37	08 57	09 17	09 37	09 57	10 17	10 36	10 37	10 57	11 17
Watford High Street	d	23p59	00 10	00 30	00 40	06 20	06 50	07 20	07 40	08 00	08 20	08 40	09 00	09 20	09 40	10 00	10 20	10 39	10 40	11 00	11 20
Watford Junction	a	00 04	00 14	00 35	00 44	06 24	06 54	07 24	07 44	08 04	08 28	08 44	09 04	09 24	09 44	10 04	10 24	10 44	10 44	11 04	11 24

A from 21 May until 23 July

B not from 13 August until 28 August

C from 13 August until 28 August

Stations Queen's Park to Harrow & Wealdstone inclusive are also served by London Underground Bakerloo Line Services

Mondays to Fridays

27 July to 7 September

London, Queen's Park and Harrow & Wealdstone - Watford Junction

Network Diagram - see first Page of Table 59

	LO	and at the same minutes past each hour until	LO	LO	LO	LO	LO A		LO B	LO	LO	LO	LO	LO	LO	LO	LO A		LO B	LO	LO	LO	LO
London Euston 15 ⊖ d	10 57		15 57	16 17	16 37	16 57	17 17		17 17	17 37	17 57	18 17	18 37	18 57	19 17	19 37	19 57		19 57	20 17	20 37	20 57	21 17
South Hampstead d	11 03		16 03	16 23	16 43	17 03	17 23		17 23	17 43	18 03	18 23	18 43	19 03	19 23	19 43	20 03		20 03	20 23	20 43	21 03	21 23
Kilburn High Road d	11 04		16 04	16 24	16 44	17 04	17 24		17 24	17 44	18 04	18 24	18 44	19 04	19 24	19 44	20 04		20 04	20 24	20 44	21 04	21 24
Queen's Park (London) ⊖ d	11 06		16 06	16 27	16 47	17 07	17 27		17 27	17 47	18 07	18 27	18 47	19 07	19 26	19 46	20 06		20 06	20 26	20 46	21 06	21 26
Kensal Green d	11 08		16 08	16 29	16 49	17 09	17 29		17 29	17 49	18 09	18 29	18 49	19 09	19 28	19 48	20 07		20 08	20 28	20 48	21 08	21 28
Willesden Jn Low Level d	11 11		16 11	16 32	16 52	17 12	17 31		17 32	17 52	18 12	18 32	18 52	19 12	19 31	19 51	20 09		20 11	20 31	20 51	21 11	21 31
Harlesden d	11 13		16 13	16 34	16 54	17 14	17 33		17 34	17 54	18 14	18 34	18 54	19 14	19 33	19 53	20 11		20 13	20 33	20 53	21 13	21 33
Stonebridge Park d	11 15		16 15	16 36	16 56	17 16	17 35		17 36	17 56	18 16	18 36	18 56	19 16	19 35	19 55	20 12		20 15	20 35	20 55	21 15	21 35
Wembley Central d	11 18		16 18	16 39	16 59	17 19	17 38		17 39	17 59	18 19	18 39	18 59	19 19	19 38	19 58	20 16		20 18	20 38	20 58	21 18	21 38
North Wembley d	11 20		16 20	16 41	17 01	17 21	17 40		17 41	18 01	18 21	18 41	19 01	19 21	19 40	20 00	20 18		20 20	20 40	21 00	21 20	21 40
South Kenton d	11 22		16 22	16 43	17 03	17 23	17 42		17 43	18 03	18 23	18 43	19 03	19 23	19 42	20 02	20 20		20 22	20 42	21 02	21 22	21 42
Kenton d	11 24		16 24	16 45	17 05	17 25	17 44		17 45	18 05	18 25	18 45	19 05	19 25	19 44	20 04	20 22		20 24	20 44	21 04	21 24	21 44
Harrow & Wealdstone d	11 26		16 26	16 48	17 08	17 28	17 47		17 48	18 08	18 28	18 48	19 08	19 28	19 46	20 06	20 23		20 26	20 46	21 06	21 26	21 46
Headstone Lane d	11 29		16 29	16 51	17 11	17 31	17 50		17 51	18 11	18 31	18 51	19 11	19 31	19 49	20 09	20 26		20 29	20 49	21 09	21 29	21 49
Hatch End d	11 31		16 31	16 53	17 13	17 33	17 52		17 53	18 13	18 33	18 53	19 13	19 33	19 51	20 11	20 28		20 31	20 51	21 11	21 31	21 51
Carpenders Park d	11 34		16 34	16 56	17 16	17 36	17 55		17 56	18 16	18 36	18 56	19 16	19 36	19 54	20 14	20 31		20 34	20 54	21 14	21 34	21 54
Bushey d	11 37		16 37	16 59	17 19	17 39	17 58		17 59	18 19	18 39	18 59	19 19	19 39	19 57	20 17	20 34		20 37	20 57	21 17	21 37	21 57
Watford High Street d	11 40		16 40	17 01	17 21	17 41	18 00		18 01	18 21	18 41	19 01	19 21	19 41	20 00	20 20	20 38		20 40	21 00	21 20	21 40	22 00
Watford Junction a	11 44		16 44	17 08	17 28	17 48	18 07		18 08	18 28	18 48	19 08	19 28	19 48	20 04	20 28	20 44		20 44	21 08	21 28	21 44	22 04

	LO	LO	LO	LO		LO	LO
London Euston 15 ⊖ d	21 37	21 57	22 27	22 57		23 27	23 57
South Hampstead d	21 43	22 03	22 33	23 03		23 33	00 03
Kilburn High Road d	21 44	22 04	22 34	23 04		23 34	00 04
Queen's Park (London) ⊖ d	21 46	22 06	22 36	23 06		23 36	00 06
Kensal Green d	21 48	22 08	22 38	23 08		23 38	00 08
Willesden Jn Low Level d	21 51	22 11	22 41	23 11		23 41	00 11
Harlesden d	21 53	22 13	22 43	23 13		23 43	00 13
Stonebridge Park d	21 55	22 15	22 45	23 15		23 45	00 15
Wembley Central d	21 58	22 18	22 48	23 18		23 48	00 18
North Wembley d	22 00	22 20	22 50	23 20		23 50	00 20
South Kenton d	22 02	22 22	22 52	23 22		23 52	00 22
Kenton d	22 04	22 24	22 54	23 24		23 54	00 24
Harrow & Wealdstone d	22 06	22 26	22 56	23 26		23 56	00 26
Headstone Lane d	22 09	22 29	22 59	23 29		23 59	00 29
Hatch End d	22 11	22 31	23 01	23 31		00 01	00 31
Carpenders Park d	22 14	22 34	23 04	23 34		00 04	00 34
Bushey d	22 17	22 37	23 07	23 37		00 07	00 37
Watford High Street d	22 20	22 40	23 10	23 40		00 10	00 40
Watford Junction a	22 25	22 44	23 14	23 44		00 14	00 44

Mondays to Fridays

from 10 September

	LO MO	LO MX	LO MO	LO MX	LO	LO	LO	LO	LO		LO	LO	LO	LO	and at the same minutes past each hour until	LO	LO	LO		LO	LO	LO	LO
London Euston 15 ⊖ d	23p17	23p27	23p47	23p57	05 37	06 07	06 37	06 57	07 17		07 37	07 57	08 17	08 37		15 37	15 57	16 17		16 37	16 57	17 17	17 37
South Hampstead d	23p23	23p33	23p53	00 03	05 43	06 13	06 43	07 03	07 23		07 43	08 03	08 23	08 43		15 43	16 03	16 23		16 43	17 03	17 23	17 43
Kilburn High Road d	23p24	23p34	23p54	00 04	05 44	06 14	06 44	07 04	07 24		07 44	08 04	08 24	08 44		15 44	16 04	16 24		16 44	17 04	17 24	17 44
Queen's Park (London) ⊖ d	23p26	23p36	23p56	00 06	05 46	06 16	06 46	07 06	07 26		07 46	08 06	08 26	08 46		15 46	16 06	16 27		16 47	17 07	17 27	17 47
Kensal Green d	23p28	23p38	23p58	00 08	05 48	06 18	06 48	07 08	07 28		07 48	08 08	08 28	08 48		15 48	16 08	16 29		16 49	17 09	17 29	17 49
Willesden Jn Low Level d	23p31	23p41	00 01	00 11	05 51	06 21	06 51	07 11	07 31		07 51	08 11	08 31	08 51		15 51	16 11	16 32		16 52	17 12	17 32	17 52
Harlesden d	23p33	23p43	00 03	00 13	05 53	06 23	06 53	07 13	07 33		07 53	08 13	08 33	08 53		15 53	16 13	16 34		16 54	17 14	17 34	17 54
Stonebridge Park d	23p35	23p45	00 05	00 15	05 55	06 25	06 55	07 15	07 35		07 55	08 15	08 35	08 55		15 55	16 15	16 36		16 56	17 16	17 36	17 56
Wembley Central d	23p38	23p48	00 08	00 18	05 58	06 28	06 58	07 18	07 38		07 58	08 18	08 38	08 58		15 58	16 18	16 39		16 59	17 19	17 39	17 59
North Wembley d	23p40	23p50	00 10	00 20	06 00	06 30	07 00	07 20	07 40		08 00	08 20	08 40	09 00		16 00	16 20	16 41		17 01	17 21	17 41	18 01
South Kenton d	23p42	23p52	00 12	00 22	06 02	06 32	07 02	07 22	07 42		08 02	08 22	08 42	09 02		16 02	16 22	16 43		17 03	17 23	17 43	18 03
Kenton d	23p44	23p54	00 14	00 24	06 04	06 34	07 04	07 24	07 44		08 04	08 24	08 44	09 04		16 04	16 24	16 45		17 05	17 25	17 45	18 05
Harrow & Wealdstone d	23p46	23p56	00 16	00 26	06 06	06 36	07 06	07 26	07 46		08 06	08 26	08 46	09 06		16 06	16 26	16 48		17 08	17 28	17 48	18 08
Headstone Lane d	23p49	23p59	00 19	00 29	06 09	06 39	07 09	07 29	07 49		08 09	08 29	08 49	09 09		16 09	16 29	16 51		17 11	17 31	17 51	18 11
Hatch End d	23p51	00 01	00 21	00 31	06 11	06 41	07 11	07 31	07 51		08 11	08 31	08 51	09 11		16 11	16 31	16 53		17 13	17 33	17 53	18 13
Carpenders Park d	23p54	00 04	00 24	00 34	06 14	06 44	07 14	07 34	07 54		08 14	08 34	08 54	09 14		16 14	16 34	16 56		17 16	17 36	17 56	18 16
Bushey d	23p57	00 07	00 27	00 37	06 17	06 47	07 17	07 37	07 57		08 17	08 37	08 57	09 17		16 17	16 37	16 59		17 19	17 39	17 59	18 19
Watford High Street d	23p59	00 10	00 30	00 40	06 20	06 50	07 20	07 40	08 00		08 20	08 40	09 00	09 20		16 20	16 40	17 01		17 21	17 41	18 01	18 21
Watford Junction a	00 04	00 14	00 35	00 44	06 24	06 54	07 24	07 44	08 04		08 28	08 44	09 04	09 24		16 24	16 44	17 08		17 28	17 48	18 08	18 28

	LO	LO	LO	LO	LO		LO	LO	LO	LO	LO	LO	LO	LO	LO		LO	LO	LO
London Euston 15 ⊖ d	17 57	18 17	18 37	18 57	19 17		19 37	19 57	20 17	20 37	20 57	21 17	21 37	21 57	22 27		22 57	23 27	23 57
South Hampstead d	18 03	18 23	18 43	19 03	19 23		19 43	20 03	20 23	20 43	21 03	21 23	21 43	22 03	22 33		23 03	23 33	00 03
Kilburn High Road d	18 04	18 24	18 44	19 04	19 24		19 44	20 04	20 24	20 44	21 04	21 24	21 44	22 04	22 34		23 04	23 34	00 04
Queen's Park (London) ⊖ d	18 07	18 27	18 47	19 07	19 26		19 46	20 06	20 26	20 46	21 06	21 26	21 46	22 06	22 36		23 06	23 36	00 06
Kensal Green d	18 09	18 29	18 49	19 09	19 28		19 48	20 08	20 28	20 48	21 08	21 28	21 48	22 08	22 38		23 08	23 38	00 08
Willesden Jn Low Level d	18 12	18 32	18 52	19 12	19 31		19 51	20 11	20 31	20 51	21 11	21 31	21 51	22 11	22 41		23 11	23 41	00 11
Harlesden d	18 14	18 34	18 54	19 14	19 33		19 53	20 13	20 33	20 53	21 13	21 33	21 53	22 13	22 43		23 13	23 43	00 13
Stonebridge Park d	18 16	18 36	18 56	19 16	19 35		19 55	20 15	20 35	20 55	21 15	21 35	21 55	22 15	22 45		23 15	23 45	00 15
Wembley Central d	18 19	18 39	18 59	19 19	19 38		19 58	20 18	20 38	20 58	21 18	21 38	21 58	22 18	22 48		23 18	23 48	00 18
North Wembley d	18 21	18 41	19 01	19 21	19 40		20 00	20 20	20 40	21 00	21 20	21 40	22 00	22 20	22 50		23 20	23 50	00 20
South Kenton d	18 23	18 43	19 03	19 23	19 42		20 02	20 22	20 42	21 02	21 22	21 42	22 02	22 22	22 52		23 22	23 52	00 22
Kenton d	18 25	18 45	19 05	19 25	19 44		20 04	20 24	20 44	21 04	21 24	21 44	22 04	22 24	22 54		23 24	23 54	00 24
Harrow & Wealdstone d	18 28	18 48	19 08	19 28	19 46		20 06	20 26	20 46	21 06	21 26	21 46	22 06	22 26	22 56		23 26	23 56	00 26
Headstone Lane d	18 31	18 51	19 11	19 31	19 49		20 09	20 29	20 49	21 09	21 29	21 49	22 09	22 29	22 59		23 29	23 59	00 29
Hatch End d	18 33	18 53	19 13	19 33	19 51		20 11	20 31	20 51	21 11	21 31	21 51	22 11	22 31	23 01		23 31	00 01	00 31
Carpenders Park d	18 36	18 56	19 16	19 36	19 54		20 14	20 34	20 54	21 14	21 34	21 54	22 14	22 34	23 04		23 34	00 04	00 34
Bushey d	18 39	18 59	19 19	19 39	19 57		20 17	20 37	20 57	21 17	21 37	21 57	22 17	22 37	23 07		23 37	00 07	00 37
Watford High Street d	18 41	19 01	19 21	19 41	20 00		20 20	20 40	21 00	21 20	21 40	22 00	22 20	22 40	23 10		23 40	00 10	00 40
Watford Junction a	18 48	19 08	19 28	19 48	20 04		20 28	20 44	21 08	21 28	21 44	22 04	22 25	22 44	23 14		23 44	00 14	00 44

A not from 13 August until 28 August

B from 13 August until 28 August

Stations Queen's Park to Harrow & Wealdstone inclusive are also served by London Underground Bakerloo Line Services

Saturdays

until 21 July

London, Queen's Park and Harrow & Wealdstone - Watford Junction

Network Diagram - see first Page of Table 59

	LO	LO	LO	LO	LO	LO	LO	LO	LO	and at the same minutes past each hour until	LO		LO	LO	LO	LO	and at the same minutes past each hour until	LO	LO	LO		LO
London Euston 15 ⊖ d	23p27	23p57	05 37	06 07	06 37	06 57	07 17	07 37	07 57		14 57		15 17	15 37	15 57	16 17		19 17	19 37	19 57		20 17
South Hampstead d	23p33	00 03	05 43	06 13	06 43	07 03	07 23	07 43	08 03		15 03		15 23	15 43	16 03	16 23		19 23	19 43	20 03		20 23
Kilburn High Road d	23p34	00 04	05 44	06 14	06 44	07 04	07 24	07 44	08 04		15 04		15 24	15 44	16 04	16 24		19 24	19 44	20 04		20 24
Queen's Park (London) ⊖ d	23p36	00 06	05 46	06 16	06 46	07 06	07 26	07 46	08 06		15 06		15 26	15 46	16 06	16 26		19 26	19 46	20 06		20 26
Kensal Green d	23p38	00 08	05 48	06 18	06 48	07 08	07 28	07 48	08 08		15 08		15 28	15 48	16 08	16 28		19 28	19 48	20 08		20 28
Willesden Jn Low Level d	23p41	00 11	05 51	06 21	06 51	07 11	07 31	07 51	08 11		15 11		15 31	15 51	16 11	16 31		19 31	19 51	20 11		20 31
Harlesden d	23p43	00 13	05 53	06 23	06 53	07 13	07 33	07 53	08 13		15 13		15 33	15 53	16 13	16 33		19 33	19 53	20 13		20 33
Stonebridge Park d	23p45	00 15	05 55	06 25	06 55	07 15	07 35	07 55	08 15		15 15		15 35	15 55	16 15	16 35		19 35	19 55	20 15		20 35
Wembley Central d	23p48	00 18	05 58	06 28	06 58	07 18	07 38	07 58	08 18		15 18		15 38	15 58	16 18	16 38		19 38	19 58	20 18		20 38
North Wembley d	23p50	00 20	06 00	06 30	07 00	07 20	07 40	08 00	08 20		15 20		15 40	16 00	16 20	16 40		19 40	20 00	20 20		20 40
South Kenton d	23p52	00 22	06 02	06 32	07 02	07 22	07 42	08 02	08 22		15 22		15 42	16 02	16 22	16 42		19 42	20 02	20 22		20 42
Kenton d	23p54	00 24	06 04	06 34	07 04	07 24	07 44	08 04	08 24		15 24		15 44	16 04	16 24	16 44		19 44	20 04	20 24		20 44
Harrow & Wealdstone d	23p56	00 26	06 06	06 36	07 06	07 26	07 46	08 06	08 26		15 26		15 46	16 06	16 26	16 46		19 46	20 06	20 26		20 46
Headstone Lane d	23p59	00 29	06 09	06 39	07 09	07 29	07 49	08 09	08 29		15 29		15 49	16 09	16 29	16 49		19 49	20 09	20 29		20 49
Hatch End d	00 01	00 31	06 11	06 41	07 11	07 31	07 51	08 11	08 31		15 31		15 51	16 11	16 31	16 51		19 51	20 11	20 31		20 51
Carpenders Park d	00 04	00 34	06 14	06 44	07 14	07 34	07 54	08 14	08 34		15 34		15 54	16 14	16 34	16 54		19 54	20 14	20 34		20 54
Bushey d	00 07	00 37	06 17	06 47	07 17	07 37	07 57	08 17	08 37		15 37		15 57	16 17	16 37	16 57		19 57	20 17	20 37		20 57
Watford High Street d	00 10	00 40	06 20	06 50	07 20	07 40	08 00	08 20	08 40		15 40		16 00	16 20	16 40	17 00		20 00	20 20	20 40		21 00
Watford Junction a	00 14	00 44	06 26	06 55	07 24	07 45	08 04	08 24	08 44		15 44		16 04	16 28	16 48	17 08		20 08	20 28	20 48		21 04

	LO	LO	LO	LO	LO	LO	LO	LO		LO
London Euston 15 ⊖ d	20 37	20 57	21 17	21 37	21 57	22 27	22 57	23 27		23 57
South Hampstead d	20 43	21 03	21 23	21 43	22 03	22 33	23 03	23 33		00 03
Kilburn High Road d	20 44	21 04	21 24	21 44	22 04	22 34	23 04	23 34		00 04
Queen's Park (London) ⊖ d	20 46	21 06	21 26	21 46	22 06	22 36	23 06	23 36		00 06
Kensal Green d	20 48	21 08	21 28	21 48	22 08	22 38	23 08	23 38		00 08
Willesden Jn Low Level d	20 51	21 11	21 31	21 51	22 11	22 41	23 11	23 41		00 11
Harlesden d	20 53	21 13	21 33	21 53	22 13	22 43	23 13	23 43		00 13
Stonebridge Park d	20 55	21 15	21 35	21 55	22 15	22 45	23 15	23 45		00 15
Wembley Central d	20 58	21 18	21 38	21 58	22 18	22 48	23 18	23 48		00 18
North Wembley d	21 00	21 20	21 40	22 00	22 20	22 50	23 20	23 50		00 20
South Kenton d	21 02	21 22	21 42	22 02	22 22	22 52	23 22	23 52		00 22
Kenton d	21 04	21 24	21 44	22 04	22 24	22 54	23 24	23 54		00 24
Harrow & Wealdstone d	21 06	21 26	21 46	22 06	22 26	22 56	23 26	23 56		00 26
Headstone Lane d	21 09	21 29	21 49	22 09	22 29	22 59	23 29	23 59		00 29
Hatch End d	21 11	21 31	21 51	22 11	22 31	23 01	23 31	00 01		00 31
Carpenders Park d	21 14	21 34	21 54	22 14	22 34	23 04	23 34	00 04		00 34
Bushey d	21 17	21 37	21 57	22 17	22 37	23 07	23 37	00 07		00 37
Watford High Street d	21 20	21 40	22 00	22 20	22 40	23 10	23 40	00 10		00 40
Watford Junction a	21 24	21 44	22 08	22 24	22 44	23 14	23 44	00 14		00 44

Saturdays

28 July to 8 September

	LO	LO	LO	LO	LO	LO	LO	and at the same minutes past each hour until	LO		LO	LO	LO	LO	LO	and at the same minutes past each hour until	LO	LO		LO	LO	LO A
London Euston 15 ⊖ d	23p27	23p57	05 37	06 07	06 37	06 57	07 17		14 17		14 37	14 57	15 17	15 37	15 57		19 57	20 17		20 37	20 57	21 17
South Hampstead d	23p33	00 03	05 43	06 13	06 43	07 03	07 23		14 23		14 43	15 03	15 23	15 43	16 03		20 03	20 23		20 43	21 03	21 23
Kilburn High Road d	23p34	00 04	05 44	06 14	06 44	07 04	07 24		14 24		14 44	15 04	15 24	15 44	16 04		20 04	20 24		20 44	21 04	21 24
Queen's Park (London) ⊖ d	23p36	00 06	05 46	06 16	06 46	07 06	07 26		14 26		14 46	15 06	15 26	15 46	16 06		20 06	20 26		20 46	21 06	21 26
Kensal Green d	23p38	00 08	05 48	06 18	06 48	07 08	07 28		14 28		14 48	15 08	15 28	15 48	16 08		20 08	20 28		20 48	21 08	21 28
Willesden Jn Low Level d	23p41	00 11	05 51	06 21	06 51	07 11	07 31		14 31		14 51	15 11	15 31	15 51	16 11		20 11	20 31		20 51	21 11	21 31
Harlesden d	23p43	00 13	05 53	06 23	06 53	07 13	07 33		14 33		14 53	15 13	15 33	15 53	16 13		20 13	20 33		20 53	21 13	21 33
Stonebridge Park d	23p45	00 15	05 55	06 25	06 55	07 15	07 35		14 35		14 55	15 15	15 35	15 55	16 15		20 15	20 35		20 55	21 15	21 35
Wembley Central d	23p48	00 18	05 58	06 28	06 58	07 18	07 38		14 38		14 58	15 18	15 38	15 58	16 18		20 18	20 38		20 58	21 18	21 38
North Wembley d	23p50	00 20	06 00	06 30	07 00	07 20	07 40		14 40		15 00	15 20	15 40	16 00	16 20		20 20	20 40		21 00	21 20	21 40
South Kenton d	23p52	00 22	06 02	06 32	07 02	07 22	07 42		14 42		15 02	15 22	15 42	16 02	16 22		20 22	20 42		21 02	21 22	21 42
Kenton d	23p54	00 24	06 04	06 34	07 04	07 24	07 44		14 44		15 04	15 24	15 44	16 04	16 24		20 24	20 44		21 04	21 24	21 44
Harrow & Wealdstone d	23p56	00 26	06 06	06 36	07 06	07 26	07 46		14 46		15 06	15 26	15 46	16 06	16 26		20 26	20 46		21 06	21 26	21 46
Headstone Lane d	23p59	00 29	06 09	06 39	07 09	07 29	07 49		14 49		15 09	15 29	15 49	16 09	16 29		20 29	20 49		21 09	21 29	21 49
Hatch End d	00 01	00 31	06 11	06 41	07 11	07 31	07 51		14 51		15 11	15 31	15 51	16 11	16 31		20 31	20 51		21 11	21 31	21 51
Carpenders Park d	00 04	00 34	06 14	06 44	07 14	07 34	07 54		14 54		15 14	15 34	15 54	16 14	16 34		20 34	20 54		21 14	21 34	21 54
Bushey d	00 07	00 37	06 17	06 47	07 17	07 37	07 57		14 57		15 17	15 37	15 57	16 17	16 37		20 37	20 57		21 17	21 37	21 57
Watford High Street d	00 10	00 40	06 20	06 50	07 20	07 40	08 00		15 00		15 20	15 40	16 00	16 20	16 40		20 40	21 00		21 20	21 40	22 00
Watford Junction a	00 14	00 44	06 24	06 55	07 24	07 44	08 04		15 04		15 24	15 44	16 08	16 28	16 48		20 48	21 04		21 24	21 44	22 07

	LO B	LO	LO	LO	LO	LO		LO
London Euston 15 ⊖ d	21 17	21 37	21 57	22 27	22 57	23 27		23 57
South Hampstead d	21 23	21 43	22 03	22 33	23 03	23 33		00 03
Kilburn High Road d	21 24	21 44	22 04	22 34	23 04	23 34		00 04
Queen's Park (London) ⊖ d	21 26	21 46	22 06	22 36	23 06	23 36		00 06
Kensal Green d	21 28	21 48	22 08	22 38	23 08	23 38		00 08
Willesden Jn Low Level d	21 31	21 51	22 11	22 41	23 11	23 41		00 11
Harlesden d	21 33	21 53	22 13	22 43	23 13	23 43		00 13
Stonebridge Park d	21 35	21 55	22 15	22 45	23 15	23 45		00 15
Wembley Central d	21 38	21 58	22 18	22 48	23 18	23 48		00 18
North Wembley d	21 40	22 00	22 20	22 50	23 20	23 50		00 20
South Kenton d	21 42	22 02	22 22	22 52	23 22	23 52		00 22
Kenton d	21 44	22 04	22 24	22 54	23 24	23 54		00 24
Harrow & Wealdstone d	21 46	22 06	22 26	22 56	23 26	23 56		00 26
Headstone Lane d	21 49	22 09	22 29	22 59	23 29	23 59		00 29
Hatch End d	21 51	22 11	22 31	23 01	23 31	00 01		00 31
Carpenders Park d	21 54	22 14	22 34	23 04	23 34	00 04		00 34
Bushey d	21 57	22 17	22 37	23 07	23 37	00 07		00 37
Watford High Street d	22 00	22 20	22 40	23 10	23 40	00 10		00 40
Watford Junction a	22 08	22 24	22 44	23 14	23 44	00 14		00 44

A not from 18 August until 25 August

B 18 August, 25 August

Stations Queen's Park to Harrow & Wealdstone inclusive are also served by London Underground Bakerloo Line Services

Saturdays
from 15 September

London, Queen's Park and Harrow & Wealdstone - Watford Junction

Network Diagram - see first Page of Table 59

	LO	LO	LO	LO	LO	LO	LO		LO	LO	LO	LO		LO	LO	LO	LO	LO	LO	LO
London Euston ⊖ d	23p27	23p57	05 37	06 07	06 37	06 57	07 17	and at the same minutes past each hour until	15 17	15 37	15 57	16 17	and at the same minutes past each hour until	19 17	19 37	19 57	20 17	20 37	20 57	21 17
South Hampstead d	23p33	00 03	05 43	06 13	06 43	07 03	07 23		15 23	15 43	16 03	16 23		19 23	19 43	20 03	20 23	20 43	21 03	21 23
Kilburn High Road d	23p34	00 04	05 44	06 14	06 44	07 04	07 24		15 24	15 44	16 04	16 24		19 24	19 44	20 04	20 24	20 44	21 04	21 24
Queen's Park (London) ⊖ d	23p36	00 06	05 46	06 16	06 46	07 06	07 26		15 26	15 46	16 06	16 26		19 26	19 46	20 06	20 26	20 46	21 06	21 26
Kensal Green d	23p38	00 08	05 48	06 18	06 48	07 08	07 28		15 28	15 48	16 08	16 28		19 28	19 48	20 08	20 28	20 48	21 08	21 28
Willesden Jn Low Level d	23p41	00 11	05 51	06 21	06 51	07 11	07 31		15 31	15 51	16 11	16 31		19 31	19 51	20 11	20 31	20 51	21 11	21 31
Harlesden d	23p43	00 13	05 53	06 23	06 53	07 13	07 33		15 33	15 53	16 13	16 33		19 33	19 53	20 13	20 33	20 53	21 13	21 33
Stonebridge Park d	23p45	00 15	05 55	06 25	06 55	07 15	07 35		15 35	15 55	16 15	16 35		19 35	19 55	20 15	20 35	20 55	21 15	21 35
Wembley Central d	23p48	00 18	05 58	06 28	06 58	07 18	07 38		15 38	15 58	16 18	16 38		19 38	19 58	20 18	20 38	20 58	21 18	21 38
North Wembley d	23p50	00 20	06 00	06 30	07 00	07 20	07 40		15 40	16 00	16 20	16 40		19 40	20 00	20 20	20 40	21 00	21 20	21 40
South Kenton d	23p52	00 22	06 02	06 32	07 02	07 22	07 42		15 42	16 02	16 22	16 42		19 42	20 02	20 22	20 42	21 02	21 22	21 42
Kenton d	23p54	00 24	06 04	06 34	07 04	07 24	07 44		15 44	16 04	16 24	16 44		19 44	20 04	20 24	20 44	21 04	21 24	21 44
Harrow & Wealdstone d	23p56	00 26	06 06	06 36	07 06	07 26	07 46		15 46	16 06	16 26	16 46		19 46	20 06	20 26	20 46	21 06	21 26	21 46
Headstone Lane d	23p59	00 29	06 09	06 39	07 09	07 29	07 49		15 49	16 09	16 29	16 49		19 49	20 09	20 29	20 49	21 09	21 29	21 49
Hatch End d	00 01	00 31	06 11	06 41	07 11	07 31	07 51		15 51	16 11	16 31	16 51		19 51	20 11	20 31	20 51	21 11	21 31	21 51
Carpenders Park d	00 04	00 34	06 14	06 44	07 14	07 34	07 54		15 54	16 14	16 34	16 54		19 54	20 14	20 34	20 54	21 14	21 34	21 54
Bushey d	00 07	00 37	06 17	06 47	07 17	07 37	07 57		15 57	16 17	16 37	16 57		19 57	20 17	20 37	20 57	21 17	21 37	21 57
Watford High Street d	00 10	00 40	06 20	06 50	07 20	07 40	08 00		16 00	16 20	16 40	17 00		20 00	20 20	20 40	21 00	21 20	21 40	22 00
Watford Junction a	00 14	00 44	06 24	06 55	07 24	07 44	08 04		16 04	16 28	16 48	17 08		20 08	20 28	20 48	21 04	21 24	21 44	22 08

	LO	LO	LO	LO	LO	LO
London Euston ⊖ d	21 37	21 57	22 27	22 57	23 27	23 57
South Hampstead d	21 43	22 03	22 33	23 03	23 33	00 03
Kilburn High Road d	21 44	22 04	22 34	23 04	23 34	00 04
Queen's Park (London) ⊖ d	21 46	22 06	22 36	23 06	23 36	00 06
Kensal Green d	21 48	22 08	22 38	23 08	23 38	00 08
Willesden Jn Low Level d	21 51	22 11	22 41	23 11	23 41	00 11
Harlesden d	21 53	22 13	22 43	23 13	23 43	00 13
Stonebridge Park d	21 55	22 15	22 45	23 15	23 45	00 15
Wembley Central d	21 58	22 18	22 48	23 18	23 48	00 18
North Wembley d	22 00	22 20	22 50	23 20	23 50	00 20
South Kenton d	22 02	22 22	22 52	23 22	23 52	00 22
Kenton d	22 04	22 24	22 54	23 24	23 54	00 24
Harrow & Wealdstone d	22 06	22 26	22 56	23 26	23 56	00 26
Headstone Lane d	22 09	22 29	22 59	23 29	23 59	00 29
Hatch End d	22 11	22 31	23 01	23 31	00 01	00 31
Carpenders Park d	22 14	22 34	23 04	23 34	00 04	00 34
Bushey d	22 17	22 37	23 07	23 37	00 07	00 37
Watford High Street d	22 20	22 40	23 10	23 40	00 10	00 40
Watford Junction a	22 24	22 44	23 14	23 44	00 14	00 44

Sundays
until 22 July

	LO	LO	LO	LO	LO	LO	LO	LO	LO	LO	LO	LO	LO		LO	LO	LO	LO	LO	LO	LO
London Euston ⊖ d	23p27	23p57	06 47	07 17	07 47	08 17	08 47	09 17	09 37	09 57	10 17	10 37	10 57	and at the same minutes past each hour until	14 57	15 17	15 37	15 57	16 17	16 37	16 57
South Hampstead d	23p33	00 03	06 53	07 23	07 53	08 23	08 53	09 23	09 43	10 03	10 23	10 43	11 03		15 03	15 23	15 43	16 03	16 23	16 43	17 03
Kilburn High Road d	23p34	00 04	06 54	07 24	07 54	08 24	08 54	09 24	09 44	10 04	10 24	10 44	11 04		15 04	15 24	15 44	16 04	16 24	16 44	17 04
Queen's Park (London) ⊖ d	23p36	00 06	06 56	07 26	07 56	08 26	08 56	09 26	09 46	10 06	10 26	10 46	11 06		15 06	15 26	15 46	16 06	16 26	16 46	17 06
Kensal Green d	23p38	00 08	06 58	07 28	07 58	08 28	08 58	09 28	09 48	10 08	10 28	10 48	11 08		15 08	15 28	15 48	16 08	16 28	16 48	17 08
Willesden Jn Low Level d	23p41	00 11	07 01	07 31	08 01	08 31	09 01	09 31	09 51	10 11	10 31	10 51	11 11		15 11	15 31	15 51	16 11	16 31	16 51	17 11
Harlesden d	23p43	00 13	07 03	07 33	08 03	08 33	09 03	09 33	09 53	10 13	10 33	10 53	11 13		15 13	15 33	15 53	16 13	16 33	16 53	17 13
Stonebridge Park d	23p45	00 15	07 05	07 36	08 05	08 35	09 05	09 35	09 55	10 15	10 35	10 55	11 15		15 15	15 35	15 55	16 15	16 35	16 55	17 15
Wembley Central d	23p48	00 18	07 08	07 38	08 08	08 38	09 08	09 38	09 58	10 18	10 38	10 58	11 18		15 18	15 38	15 58	16 18	16 38	16 58	17 18
North Wembley d	23p50	00 20	07 10	07 40	08 10	08 40	09 10	09 40	10 00	10 20	10 40	11 00	11 20		15 20	15 40	16 00	16 20	16 40	17 00	17 20
South Kenton d	23p52	00 22	07 12	07 42	08 12	08 42	09 12	09 42	10 02	10 22	10 42	11 02	11 22		15 22	15 42	16 02	16 22	16 42	17 02	17 22
Kenton d	23p54	00 24	07 14	07 44	08 14	08 44	09 14	09 44	10 04	10 24	10 44	11 04	11 24		15 24	15 44	16 04	16 24	16 44	17 04	17 24
Harrow & Wealdstone d	23p56	00 26	07 16	07 46	08 16	08 46	09 16	09 46	10 06	10 26	10 46	11 06	11 26		15 26	15 46	16 06	16 26	16 46	17 06	17 26
Headstone Lane d	23p59	00 29	07 19	07 49	08 19	08 49	09 19	09 49	10 09	10 29	10 49	11 09	11 29		15 29	15 49	16 09	16 29	16 49	17 09	17 29
Hatch End d	00 01	00 31	07 21	07 51	08 21	08 51	09 21	09 51	10 11	10 31	10 51	11 11	11 31		15 31	15 51	16 11	16 31	16 51	17 11	17 31
Carpenders Park d	00 04	00 34	07 24	07 54	08 24	08 54	09 24	09 54	10 14	10 34	10 54	11 14	11 34		15 34	15 54	16 14	16 34	16 54	17 14	17 34
Bushey d	00 07	00 37	07 27	07 57	08 27	08 57	09 27	09 57	10 17	10 37	10 57	11 17	11 37		15 37	15 57	16 17	16 37	16 57	17 17	17 37
Watford High Street d	00 10	00 40	07 30	08 00	08 30	09 00	09 30	10 00	10 20	10 40	11 00	11 20	11 40		15 40	16 00	16 20	16 40	17 00	17 20	17 40
Watford Junction a	00 14	00 44	07 35	08 06	08 34	09 04	09 35	10 04	10 24	10 45	11 04	11 24	11 44		15 44	16 04	16 28	16 48	17 08	17 24	17 44

	LO	LO	LO	LO	LO	LO	LO	LO	LO	LO	LO	LO	LO	LO	LO	LO	LO	LO	LO
London Euston ⊖ d	17 17	17 37	17 57	18 17	18 37	18 57	19 17	19 37	19 57	20 17	20 37	20 57	21 17	21 37	21 57	22 17	22 47	23 17	23 47
South Hampstead d	17 23	17 43	18 03	18 23	18 43	19 03	19 23	19 43	20 03	20 23	20 43	21 03	21 23	21 43	22 03	22 23	22 53	23 23	23 53
Kilburn High Road d	17 24	17 44	18 04	18 24	18 44	19 04	19 24	19 44	20 04	20 24	20 44	21 04	21 24	21 44	22 04	22 24	22 54	23 24	23 54
Queen's Park (London) ⊖ d	17 26	17 46	18 06	18 26	18 46	19 06	19 26	19 46	20 06	20 26	20 46	21 06	21 26	21 46	22 06	22 26	22 56	23 26	23 56
Kensal Green d	17 28	17 48	18 08	18 28	18 48	19 08	19 28	19 48	20 08	20 28	20 48	21 08	21 28	21 48	22 08	22 28	22 58	23 28	23 58
Willesden Jn Low Level d	17 31	17 51	18 11	18 31	18 51	19 11	19 31	19 51	20 11	20 31	20 51	21 11	21 31	21 51	22 11	22 31	23 01	23 31	00 01
Harlesden d	17 33	17 53	18 13	18 33	18 53	19 13	19 33	19 53	20 13	20 33	20 53	21 13	21 33	21 53	22 13	22 33	23 03	23 33	00 03
Stonebridge Park d	17 35	17 55	18 15	18 35	18 55	19 15	19 35	19 55	20 15	20 35	20 55	21 15	21 35	21 55	22 15	22 35	23 05	23 35	00 05
Wembley Central d	17 38	17 58	18 18	18 38	18 58	19 18	19 38	19 58	20 18	20 38	20 58	21 18	21 38	21 58	22 18	22 38	23 08	23 38	00 08
North Wembley d	17 40	18 00	18 20	18 40	19 00	19 20	19 40	20 00	20 20	20 40	21 00	21 20	21 40	22 00	22 20	22 40	23 10	23 40	00 10
South Kenton d	17 42	18 02	18 22	18 42	19 02	19 22	19 42	20 02	20 22	20 42	21 02	21 22	21 42	22 02	22 22	22 42	23 12	23 42	00 12
Kenton d	17 44	18 04	18 24	18 44	19 04	19 24	19 44	20 04	20 24	20 44	21 04	21 24	21 44	22 04	22 24	22 44	23 14	23 44	00 14
Harrow & Wealdstone d	17 46	18 06	18 26	18 46	19 06	19 26	19 46	20 06	20 26	20 46	21 06	21 26	21 46	22 06	22 26	22 46	23 16	23 46	00 16
Headstone Lane d	17 49	18 09	18 29	18 49	19 09	19 29	19 49	20 09	20 29	20 49	21 09	21 29	21 49	22 09	22 29	22 49	23 19	23 49	00 19
Hatch End d	17 51	18 11	18 31	18 51	19 11	19 31	19 51	20 11	20 31	20 51	21 11	21 31	21 51	22 11	22 31	22 51	23 21	23 51	00 21
Carpenders Park d	17 54	18 14	18 34	18 54	19 14	19 34	19 54	20 14	20 34	20 54	21 14	21 34	21 54	22 14	22 34	22 54	23 24	23 54	00 24
Bushey d	17 57	18 17	18 37	18 57	19 17	19 37	19 57	20 17	20 37	20 57	21 17	21 37	21 57	22 17	22 37	22 57	23 27	23 57	00 27
Watford High Street d	18 00	18 20	18 40	19 00	19 20	19 40	20 00	20 20	20 40	21 00	21 20	21 40	22 00	22 20	22 40	23 00	23 30	23 59	00 30
Watford Junction a	18 08	18 28	18 48	19 08	19 28	19 48	20 04	20 28	20 48	21 04	21 24	21 45	22 04	22 24	22 44	23 04	23 34	00 04	00 35

Stations Queen's Park to Harrow & Wealdstone inclusive are also served by London Underground Bakerloo Line Services

Sundays
29 July to 9 September

London, Queen's Park and Harrow & Wealdstone - Watford Junction

Network Diagram - see first Page of Table 59

	LO	LO	LO	LO	LO	LO A	LO B	LO	LO	LO	LO	LO	LO	LO		LO	LO	LO	LO	LO	LO
London Euston ⊖ d	23p27	23p57	06 47	07 17	07 47	08 17	08 17	08 47	09 17	09 37	09 57	10 17	10 37	10 57	and at the same minutes past each hour until	14 57	15 17	15 37	15 57	16 17	16 37
South Hampstead d	23p33	00 03	06 53	07 23	07 53	08 23	08 23	08 53	09 23	09 43	10 03	10 23	10 43	11 03		15 03	15 23	15 43	16 03	16 23	16 43
Kilburn High Road d	23p34	00 04	06 54	07 24	07 54	08 24	08 24	08 54	09 24	09 44	10 04	10 24	10 44	11 04		15 04	15 24	15 44	16 04	16 24	16 44
Queen's Park (London) ⊖ d	23p36	00 06	06 56	07 26	07 56	08 26	08 26	08 56	09 26	09 46	10 06	10 26	10 46	11 06		15 06	15 26	15 46	16 06	16 26	16 46
Kensal Green d	23p38	00 08	06 58	07 28	07 58	08 28	08 28	08 58	09 28	09 48	10 08	10 28	10 48	11 08		15 08	15 28	15 48	16 08	16 28	16 48
Willesden Jn Low Level d	23p41	00 11	07 01	07 31	08 01	08 31	08 31	09 01	09 31	09 51	10 11	10 31	10 51	11 11		15 11	15 31	15 51	16 11	16 31	16 51
Harlesden d	23p43	00 13	07 03	07 33	08 03	08 33	08 33	09 03	09 33	09 53	10 13	10 33	10 53	11 13		15 13	15 33	15 53	16 13	16 33	16 53
Stonebridge Park d	23p45	00 15	07 05	07 35	08 05	08 35	08 35	09 05	09 35	09 55	10 15	10 35	10 55	11 15		15 15	15 35	15 55	16 15	16 35	16 55
Wembley Central d	23p48	00 18	07 08	07 38	08 08	08 38	08 38	09 08	09 38	09 58	10 18	10 38	10 58	11 18		15 18	15 38	15 58	16 18	16 38	16 58
North Wembley d	23p50	00 20	07 10	07 40	08 10	08 40	08 40	09 10	09 40	10 00	10 20	10 40	11 00	11 20		15 20	15 40	16 00	16 20	16 40	17 00
South Kenton d	23p52	00 22	07 12	07 42	08 12	08 42	08 42	09 12	09 42	10 02	10 22	10 42	11 02	11 22		15 22	15 42	16 02	16 22	16 42	17 02
Kenton d	23p54	00 24	07 14	07 44	08 14	08 44	08 44	09 14	09 44	10 04	10 24	10 44	11 04	11 24		15 24	15 44	16 04	16 24	16 44	17 04
Harrow & Wealdstone d	23p56	00 26	07 16	07 46	08 16	08 46	08 46	09 16	09 46	10 06	10 26	10 46	11 06	11 26		15 26	15 46	16 06	16 26	16 46	17 06
Headstone Lane d	23p59	00 29	07 19	07 49	08 19	08 49	08 49	09 19	09 49	10 09	10 29	10 49	11 09	11 29		15 29	15 49	16 09	16 29	16 49	17 09
Hatch End d	00 01	00 31	07 21	07 51	08 21	08 51	08 51	09 21	09 51	10 11	10 31	10 51	11 11	11 31		15 31	15 51	16 11	16 31	16 51	17 11
Carpenders Park d	00 04	00 34	07 24	07 54	08 24	08 54	08 54	09 24	09 54	10 14	10 34	10 54	11 14	11 34		15 34	15 54	16 14	16 34	16 54	17 14
Bushey d	00 07	00 37	07 27	07 57	08 27	08 57	08 57	09 27	09 57	10 17	10 37	10 57	11 17	11 37		15 37	15 57	16 17	16 37	16 57	17 17
Watford High Street d	00 10	00 40	07 30	08 00	08 30	09 00	09 00	09 30	10 00	10 20	10 40	11 00	11 20	11 40		15 40	16 00	16 20	16 40	17 00	17 20
Watford Junction a	00 14	00 44	07 34	08 04	08 34	09 04	09 05	09 35	10 04	10 24	10 45	11 04	11 24	11 44		15 44	16 08	16 28	16 48	17 08	17 24

	LO	LO	LO	LO	LO	LO	LO	LO	LO	LO	LO	LO	LO	LO	LO	LO	LO	LO	LO	LO
London Euston ⊖ d	16 57	17 17	17 37	17 57	18 17	18 37	18 57	19 17	19 37	19 57	20 17	20 37	20 57	21 17	21 37	21 57	22 17	22 47	23 17	23 47
South Hampstead d	17 03	17 23	17 43	18 03	18 23	18 43	19 03	19 23	19 43	20 03	20 23	20 43	21 03	21 23	21 43	22 03	22 23	22 53	23 23	23 53
Kilburn High Road d	17 04	17 24	17 44	18 04	18 24	18 44	19 04	19 24	19 44	20 04	20 24	20 44	21 04	21 24	21 44	22 04	22 24	22 54	23 24	23 54
Queen's Park (London) ⊖ d	17 06	17 26	17 46	18 06	18 26	18 46	19 06	19 26	19 46	20 06	20 26	20 46	21 06	21 26	21 46	22 06	22 26	22 56	23 26	23 56
Kensal Green d	17 08	17 28	17 48	18 08	18 28	18 48	19 08	19 28	19 48	20 08	20 28	20 48	21 08	21 28	21 48	22 08	22 28	22 58	23 28	23 58
Willesden Jn Low Level d	17 11	17 31	17 51	18 11	18 31	18 51	19 11	19 31	19 51	20 11	20 31	20 51	21 11	21 31	21 51	22 11	22 31	23 01	23 31	00 01
Harlesden d	17 13	17 33	17 53	18 13	18 33	18 53	19 13	19 33	19 53	20 13	20 33	20 53	21 13	21 33	21 53	22 13	22 33	23 03	23 33	00 03
Stonebridge Park d	17 15	17 35	17 55	18 15	18 35	18 55	19 15	19 35	19 55	20 15	20 35	20 55	21 15	21 35	21 55	22 15	22 35	23 05	23 35	00 05
Wembley Central d	17 18	17 38	17 58	18 18	18 38	18 58	19 18	19 38	19 58	20 18	20 38	20 58	21 18	21 38	21 58	22 18	22 38	23 08	23 38	00 08
North Wembley d	17 20	17 40	18 00	18 20	18 40	19 00	19 20	19 40	20 00	20 20	20 40	21 00	21 20	21 40	22 00	22 20	22 40	23 10	23 40	00 10
South Kenton d	17 22	17 42	18 02	18 22	18 42	19 02	19 22	19 42	20 02	20 22	20 42	21 02	21 22	21 42	22 02	22 22	22 42	23 12	23 42	00 12
Kenton d	17 24	17 44	18 04	18 24	18 44	19 04	19 24	19 44	20 04	20 24	20 44	21 04	21 24	21 44	22 04	22 24	22 44	23 14	23 44	00 14
Harrow & Wealdstone d	17 26	17 46	18 06	18 26	18 46	19 06	19 26	19 46	20 06	20 26	20 46	21 06	21 26	21 46	22 06	22 26	22 46	23 16	23 46	00 16
Headstone Lane d	17 29	17 49	18 09	18 29	18 49	19 09	19 29	19 49	20 09	20 29	20 49	21 09	21 29	21 49	22 09	22 29	22 49	23 19	23 49	00 19
Hatch End d	17 31	17 51	18 11	18 31	18 51	19 11	19 31	19 51	20 11	20 31	20 51	21 11	21 31	21 51	22 11	22 31	22 51	23 21	23 51	00 21
Carpenders Park d	17 34	17 54	18 14	18 34	18 54	19 14	19 34	19 54	20 14	20 34	20 54	21 14	21 34	21 54	22 14	22 34	22 54	23 24	23 54	00 24
Bushey d	17 37	17 57	18 17	18 37	18 57	19 17	19 37	19 57	20 17	20 37	20 57	21 17	21 37	21 57	22 17	22 37	22 57	23 27	23 57	00 27
Watford High Street d	17 40	18 00	18 20	18 40	19 00	19 20	19 40	20 00	20 20	20 40	21 00	21 20	21 40	22 00	22 20	22 40	23 00	23 30	23 59	00 30
Watford Junction a	17 44	18 08	18 28	18 48	19 08	19 28	19 48	20 08	20 28	20 48	21 04	21 24	21 45	22 04	22 24	22 44	23 04	23 34	00 04	00 35

Sundays
from 16 September

	LO	LO	LO	LO	LO	LO	LO	LO	LO	LO	LO	LO	LO		LO	LO	LO	LO	LO	LO	LO
London Euston ⊖ d	23p27	23p57	06 47	07 17	07 47	08 17	08 47	09 17	09 37	09 57	10 17	10 37	10 57	and at the same minutes past each hour until	14 57	15 17	15 37	15 57	16 17	16 37	16 57
South Hampstead d	23p33	00 03	06 53	07 23	07 53	08 23	08 53	09 23	09 43	10 03	10 23	10 43	11 03		15 03	15 23	15 43	16 03	16 23	16 43	17 03
Kilburn High Road d	23p34	00 04	06 54	07 24	07 54	08 24	08 54	09 24	09 44	10 04	10 24	10 44	11 04		15 04	15 24	15 44	16 04	16 24	16 44	17 04
Queen's Park (London) ⊖ d	23p36	00 06	06 56	07 26	07 56	08 26	08 56	09 26	09 46	10 06	10 26	10 46	11 06		15 06	15 26	15 46	16 06	16 26	16 46	17 06
Kensal Green d	23p38	00 08	06 58	07 28	07 58	08 28	08 58	09 28	09 48	10 08	10 28	10 48	11 08		15 08	15 28	15 48	16 08	16 28	16 48	17 08
Willesden Jn Low Level d	23p41	00 11	07 01	07 31	08 01	08 31	09 01	09 31	09 51	10 11	10 31	10 51	11 11		15 11	15 31	15 51	16 11	16 31	16 51	17 11
Harlesden d	23p43	00 13	07 03	07 33	08 03	08 33	09 03	09 33	09 53	10 13	10 33	10 53	11 13		15 13	15 33	15 53	16 13	16 33	16 53	17 13
Stonebridge Park d	23p45	00 15	07 05	07 35	08 05	08 35	09 05	09 35	09 55	10 15	10 35	10 55	11 15		15 15	15 35	15 55	16 15	16 35	16 55	17 15
Wembley Central d	23p48	00 18	07 08	07 38	08 08	08 38	09 08	09 38	09 58	10 18	10 38	10 58	11 18		15 18	15 38	15 58	16 18	16 38	16 58	17 18
North Wembley d	23p50	00 20	07 10	07 40	08 10	08 40	09 10	09 40	10 00	10 20	10 40	11 00	11 20		15 20	15 40	16 00	16 20	16 40	17 00	17 20
South Kenton d	23p52	00 22	07 12	07 42	08 12	08 42	09 12	09 42	10 02	10 22	10 42	11 02	11 22		15 22	15 42	16 02	16 22	16 42	17 02	17 22
Kenton d	23p54	00 24	07 14	07 44	08 14	08 44	09 14	09 44	10 04	10 24	10 44	11 04	11 24		15 24	15 44	16 04	16 24	16 44	17 04	17 24
Harrow & Wealdstone d	23p56	00 26	07 16	07 46	08 16	08 46	09 16	09 46	10 06	10 26	10 46	11 06	11 26		15 26	15 46	16 06	16 26	16 46	17 06	17 26
Headstone Lane d	23p59	00 29	07 19	07 49	08 19	08 49	09 19	09 49	10 09	10 29	10 49	11 09	11 29		15 29	15 49	16 09	16 29	16 49	17 09	17 29
Hatch End d	00 01	00 31	07 21	07 51	08 21	08 51	09 21	09 51	10 11	10 31	10 51	11 11	11 31		15 31	15 51	16 11	16 31	16 51	17 11	17 31
Carpenders Park d	00 04	00 34	07 24	07 54	08 24	08 54	09 24	09 54	10 14	10 34	10 54	11 14	11 34		15 34	15 54	16 14	16 34	16 54	17 14	17 34
Bushey d	00 07	00 37	07 27	07 57	08 27	08 57	09 27	09 57	10 17	10 37	10 57	11 17	11 37		15 37	15 57	16 17	16 37	16 57	17 17	17 37
Watford High Street d	00 10	00 40	07 30	08 00	08 30	09 00	09 30	10 00	10 20	10 40	11 00	11 20	11 40		15 40	16 00	16 20	16 40	17 00	17 20	17 40
Watford Junction a	00 14	00 44	07 34	08 04	08 34	09 05	09 35	10 04	10 24	10 45	11 04	11 24	11 44		15 44	16 04	16 28	16 48	17 08	17 24	17 44

	LO	LO	LO	LO	LO	LO	LO	LO	LO	LO	LO	LO	LO	LO	LO	LO	LO	LO	LO
London Euston ⊖ d	17 17	17 37	17 57	18 17	18 37	18 57	19 17	19 37	19 57	20 17	20 37	20 57	21 17	21 37	21 57	22 17	22 47	23 17	23 47
South Hampstead d	17 23	17 43	18 03	18 23	18 43	19 03	19 23	19 43	20 03	20 23	20 43	21 03	21 23	21 43	22 03	22 23	22 53	23 23	23 53
Kilburn High Road d	17 24	17 44	18 04	18 24	18 44	19 04	19 24	19 44	20 04	20 24	20 44	21 04	21 24	21 44	22 04	22 24	22 54	23 24	23 54
Queen's Park (London) ⊖ d	17 26	17 46	18 06	18 26	18 46	19 06	19 26	19 46	20 06	20 26	20 46	21 06	21 26	21 46	22 06	22 26	22 56	23 26	23 56
Kensal Green d	17 28	17 48	18 08	18 28	18 48	19 08	19 28	19 48	20 08	20 28	20 48	21 08	21 28	21 48	22 08	22 28	22 58	23 28	23 58
Willesden Jn Low Level d	17 31	17 51	18 11	18 31	18 51	19 11	19 31	19 51	20 11	20 31	20 51	21 11	21 31	21 51	22 11	22 31	23 01	23 31	00 01
Harlesden d	17 33	17 53	18 13	18 33	18 53	19 13	19 33	19 53	20 13	20 33	20 53	21 13	21 33	21 53	22 13	22 33	23 03	23 33	00 03
Stonebridge Park d	17 35	17 55	18 15	18 35	18 55	19 15	19 35	19 55	20 15	20 35	20 55	21 15	21 35	21 55	22 15	22 35	23 05	23 35	00 05
Wembley Central d	17 38	17 58	18 18	18 38	18 58	19 18	19 38	19 58	20 18	20 38	20 58	21 18	21 38	21 58	22 18	22 38	23 08	23 38	00 08
North Wembley d	17 40	18 00	18 20	18 40	19 00	19 20	19 40	20 00	20 20	20 40	21 00	21 20	21 40	22 00	22 20	22 40	23 10	23 40	00 10
South Kenton d	17 42	18 02	18 22	18 42	19 02	19 22	19 42	20 02	20 22	20 42	21 02	21 22	21 42	22 02	22 22	22 42	23 12	23 42	00 12
Kenton d	17 44	18 04	18 24	18 44	19 04	19 24	19 44	20 04	20 24	20 44	21 04	21 24	21 44	22 04	22 24	22 44	23 14	23 44	00 14
Harrow & Wealdstone d	17 46	18 06	18 26	18 46	19 06	19 26	19 46	20 06	20 26	20 46	21 06	21 26	21 46	22 06	22 26	22 46	23 16	23 46	00 16
Headstone Lane d	17 49	18 09	18 29	18 49	19 09	19 29	19 49	20 09	20 29	20 49	21 09	21 29	21 49	22 09	22 29	22 49	23 19	23 49	00 19
Hatch End d	17 51	18 11	18 31	18 51	19 11	19 31	19 51	20 11	20 31	20 51	21 11	21 31	21 51	22 11	22 31	22 51	23 21	23 51	00 21
Carpenders Park d	17 54	18 14	18 34	18 54	19 14	19 34	19 54	20 14	20 34	20 54	21 14	21 34	21 54	22 14	22 34	22 54	23 24	23 54	00 24
Bushey d	17 57	18 17	18 37	18 57	19 17	19 37	19 57	20 17	20 37	20 57	21 17	21 37	21 57	22 17	22 37	22 57	23 27	23 57	00 27
Watford High Street d	18 00	18 20	18 40	19 00	19 20	19 40	20 00	20 20	20 40	21 00	21 20	21 40	22 00	22 20	22 40	23 00	23 30	23 59	00 30
Watford Junction a	18 08	18 28	18 48	19 08	19 28	19 48	20 04	20 28	20 48	21 04	21 24	21 45	22 04	22 24	22 44	23 04	23 34	00 04	00 35

A not from 2 September until 9 September

B 2 September, 9 September

Stations Queen's Park to Harrow & Wealdstone inclusive are also served by London Underground Bakerloo Line Services

until 26 July

Watford Junction - Harrow & Wealdstone, Queen's Park and London

Network Diagram - see first Page of Table 59

Miles	Station		LO MX	LO MO A	LO	LO	LO	LO	LO	LO	LO	LO	LO	LO	LO	LO	LO	LO	LO	LO	LO	
0	**Watford Junction**	d	23p21	23p21	05 11	05 41	06 11	06 40	07 00	07 20	07 40	08 00	08 20	08 40	09 00	09 21	09 41	10 01	10 21	10 41	11 01	and at the same minutes past each hour until
1	Watford High Street	d	23p24	23p24	05 14	05 44	06 14	06 43	07 03	07 23	07 43	08 03	08 23	08 43	09 03	09 24	09 44	10 04	10 24	10 44	11 04	
1¾	Bushey	d	23p26	23p26	05 16	05 46	06 16	06 45	07 05	07 25	07 45	08 05	08 25	08 45	09 05	09 26	09 46	10 06	10 26	10 46	11 06	
3	Carpenders Park	d	23p29	23p29	05 19	05 49	06 19	06 48	07 08	07 28	07 48	08 08	08 28	08 48	09 08	09 29	09 49	10 09	10 29	10 49	11 09	
4½	Hatch End	d	23p32	23p32	05 22	05 52	06 22	06 51	07 11	07 31	07 51	08 11	08 31	08 51	09 11	09 32	09 52	10 12	10 32	10 52	11 12	
5¼	Headstone Lane	d	23p34	23p34	05 24	05 54	06 24	06 53	07 13	07 33	07 53	08 13	08 33	08 53	09 13	09 34	09 54	10 14	10 34	10 54	11 14	
6½	**Harrow & Wealdstone**	d	23p37	23p37	05 27	05 57	06 27	06 56	07 16	07 36	07 56	08 16	08 36	08 56	09 16	09 37	09 57	10 17	10 37	10 57	11 17	
7½	Kenton	d	23p39	23p39	05 29	05 59	06 29	06 59	07 19	07 39	07 59	08 19	08 39	08 59	09 19	09 39	09 59	10 19	10 39	10 59	11 19	
8¼	South Kenton	d	23p41	23p41	05 31	06 01	06 31	07 01	07 21	07 41	08 01	08 21	08 41	09 01	09 21	09 41	10 01	10 21	10 41	11 01	11 21	
8¾	North Wembley	d	23p43	23p43	05 33	06 03	06 33	07 03	07 23	07 43	08 03	08 23	08 43	09 03	09 23	09 43	10 03	10 23	10 43	11 03	11 23	
9¾	Wembley Central	d	23p45	23p45	05 35	06 05	06 35	07 05	07 25	07 45	08 05	08 25	08 45	09 05	09 25	09 45	10 05	10 25	10 45	11 05	11 25	
10¾	Stonebridge Park	d	23p48	23p48	05 38	06 08	06 38	07 08	07 28	07 48	08 08	08 28	08 48	09 08	09 28	09 48	10 08	10 28	10 48	11 08	11 28	
11¾	Harlesden	d	23p50	23p50	05 40	06 10	06 40	07 10	07 30	07 50	08 10	08 30	08 50	09 10	09 30	09 50	10 10	10 30	10 50	11 10	11 30	
12¼	**Willesden Jn Low Level**	d	23p52	23p52	05 42	06 12	06 42	07 13	07 33	07 53	08 13	08 33	08 53	09 13	09 33	09 52	10 12	10 32	10 52	11 12	11 32	
13¼	Kensal Green	d	23p55	23p55	05 45	06 15	06 45	07 15	07 35	07 55	08 15	08 35	08 55	09 15	09 35	09 55	10 15	10 35	10 55	11 15	11 35	
14	**Queen's Park (London)** ⊖	d	23p57	23p57	05 47	06 17	06 47	07 18	07 38	07 58	08 18	08 38	08 58	09 18	09 38	09 57	10 17	10 37	10 57	11 17	11 37	
14¾	Kilburn High Road	d	23p59	23p59	05 49	06 19	06 49	07 20	07 40	08 00	08 20	08 40	09 00	09 20	09 40	09 59	10 19	10 39	10 59	11 19	11 39	
15¼	South Hampstead	d	00 01	00 01	05 51	06 21	06 51	07 22	07 42	08 02	08 22	08 42	09 02	09 22	09 42	10 01	10 21	10 41	11 01	11 21	11 41	
17¾	**London Euston** 15 ⊖	a	00 10	00 12	05 59	06 32	06 58	07 29	07 52	08 12	08 31	08 52	09 12	09 29	09 52	10 11	10 30	10 49	11 11	11 30	11 50	

Station		LO	LO	LO	LO	LO	LO	LO	LO	LO	LO	LO	LO	LO	LO	LO	LO	LO	LO	LO	LO	LO	LO
Watford Junction	d	15 01	15 21	15 41	16 01	16 21	16 41	17 01	17 21	17 41	18 01	18 21	18 41	19 01	19 21	19 41	20 01	20 21	20 41	21 01	21 21	21 41	22 01
Watford High Street	d	15 04	15 24	15 44	16 04	16 24	16 44	17 04	17 24	17 44	18 04	18 24	18 44	19 04	19 24	19 44	20 04	20 24	20 44	21 04	21 24	21 44	22 04
Bushey	d	15 06	15 26	15 46	16 06	16 26	16 46	17 06	17 26	17 46	18 06	18 26	18 46	19 06	19 26	19 46	20 06	20 26	20 46	21 06	21 26	21 46	22 06
Carpenders Park	d	15 09	15 29	15 49	16 09	16 29	16 49	17 09	17 29	17 49	18 09	18 29	18 49	19 09	19 29	19 49	20 09	20 29	20 49	21 09	21 29	21 49	22 09
Hatch End	d	15 12	15 32	15 52	16 12	16 32	16 52	17 12	17 32	17 52	18 12	18 32	18 52	19 12	19 32	19 52	20 12	20 32	20 52	21 12	21 32	21 52	22 12
Headstone Lane	d	15 14	15 34	15 54	16 14	16 34	16 54	17 14	17 34	17 54	18 14	18 34	18 54	19 14	19 34	19 54	20 14	20 34	20 54	21 14	21 34	21 54	22 14
Harrow & Wealdstone	d	15 17	15 37	15 57	16 17	16 37	16 57	17 17	17 37	17 57	18 17	18 37	18 57	19 17	19 37	19 57	20 17	20 37	20 57	21 17	21 37	21 57	22 17
Kenton	d	15 19	15 39	15 59	16 19	16 39	16 59	17 19	17 39	17 59	18 19	18 39	18 59	19 19	19 39	19 59	20 19	20 39	20 59	21 19	21 39	21 59	22 19
South Kenton	d	15 21	15 41	16 01	16 21	16 41	17 01	17 21	17 41	18 01	18 21	18 41	19 01	19 21	19 41	20 01	20 21	20 41	21 01	21 21	21 41	22 01	22 21
North Wembley	d	15 23	15 43	16 03	16 23	16 43	17 03	17 23	17 43	18 03	18 23	18 43	19 03	19 23	19 43	20 03	20 23	20 43	21 03	21 23	21 43	22 03	22 23
Wembley Central	d	15 25	15 45	16 05	16 25	16 45	17 05	17 25	17 45	18 05	18 25	18 45	19 05	19 25	19 45	20 05	20 25	20 45	21 05	21 25	21 45	22 05	22 25
Stonebridge Park	d	15 28	15 48	16 08	16 28	16 48	17 08	17 28	17 48	18 08	18 28	18 48	19 08	19 28	19 48	20 08	20 28	20 48	21 08	21 28	21 48	22 08	22 28
Harlesden	d	15 30	15 50	16 10	16 30	16 50	17 10	17 30	17 50	18 10	18 30	18 50	19 10	19 30	19 50	20 10	20 30	20 50	21 10	21 30	21 50	22 10	22 30
Willesden Jn Low Level	d	15 32	15 52	16 12	16 32	16 52	17 12	17 32	17 52	18 12	18 32	18 52	19 12	19 32	19 52	20 12	20 32	20 52	21 12	21 32	21 52	22 12	22 32
Kensal Green	d	15 35	15 55	16 15	16 35	16 55	17 15	17 35	17 55	18 15	18 35	18 55	19 15	19 35	19 55	20 15	20 35	20 55	21 15	21 35	21 55	22 15	22 35
Queen's Park (London) ⊖	d	15 37	15 57	16 17	16 37	16 57	17 17	17 37	17 57	18 17	18 37	18 57	19 17	19 37	19 57	20 17	20 37	20 57	21 17	21 37	21 57	22 17	22 37
Kilburn High Road	d	15 39	15 59	16 19	16 39	16 59	17 19	17 39	17 59	18 19	18 39	18 59	19 19	19 39	19 59	20 19	20 39	20 59	21 19	21 39	21 59	22 19	22 39
South Hampstead	d	15 41	16 01	16 21	16 41	17 01	17 21	17 41	18 01	18 21	18 41	19 01	19 21	19 41	20 01	20 21	20 41	21 01	21 21	21 41	22 01	22 21	22 41
London Euston 15 ⊖	a	15 50	16 11	16 30	16 49	17 11	17 30	17 53	18 13	18 30	18 50	19 11	19 30	19 52	20 10	20 30	20 48	21 11	21 30	21 51	22 11	22 30	22 50

Station		LO	LO	LO
Watford Junction	d	22 21	22 51	23 21
Watford High Street	d	22 24	22 54	23 24
Bushey	d	22 26	22 56	23 26
Carpenders Park	d	22 29	22 59	23 29
Hatch End	d	22 32	23 02	23 32
Headstone Lane	d	22 34	23 04	23 34
Harrow & Wealdstone	d	22 37	23 07	23 37
Kenton	d	22 39	23 09	23 39
South Kenton	d	22 41	23 11	23 41
North Wembley	d	22 43	23 13	23 43
Wembley Central	d	22 45	23 15	23 45
Stonebridge Park	d	22 48	23 18	23 48
Harlesden	d	22 50	23 20	23 50
Willesden Jn Low Level	d	22 52	23 22	23 52
Kensal Green	d	22 55	23 25	23 55
Queen's Park (London) ⊖	d	22 57	23 27	23 57
Kilburn High Road	d	22 59	23 29	23 59
South Hampstead	d	23 01	23 31	00 01
London Euston 15 ⊖	a	23 10	23 39	00 10

Mondays to Fridays

27 July to 7 September

Station		LO MX B	LO C	LO MO	LO	LO	LO	LO	LO	LO	LO	LO	LO	LO	LO	LO	LO	LO	LO	LO	LO	
Watford Junction	d	23p21	23p21	23p21	05 11	05 41	06 11	06 40	07 00	07 20	07 40	08 00	08 20	08 40	09 00	09 21	09 41	10 01	10 21	10 41	11 01	and at the same minutes past each hour until
Watford High Street	d	23p24	23p24	23p24	05 14	05 44	06 14	06 43	07 03	07 23	07 43	08 03	08 23	08 43	09 03	09 24	09 44	10 04	10 24	10 44	11 04	
Bushey	d	23p26	23p26	23p26	05 16	05 46	06 16	06 45	07 05	07 25	07 45	08 05	08 25	08 45	09 05	09 26	09 46	10 06	10 26	10 46	11 06	
Carpenders Park	d	23p29	23p29	23p29	05 19	05 49	06 19	06 48	07 08	07 28	07 48	08 08	08 28	08 48	09 08	09 29	09 49	10 09	10 29	10 49	11 09	
Hatch End	d	23p32	23p32	23p32	05 22	05 52	06 22	06 51	07 11	07 31	07 51	08 11	08 31	08 51	09 11	09 32	09 52	10 12	10 32	10 52	11 12	
Headstone Lane	d	23p34	23p34	23p34	05 24	05 54	06 24	06 53	07 13	07 33	07 53	08 13	08 33	08 53	09 13	09 34	09 54	10 14	10 34	10 54	11 14	
Harrow & Wealdstone	d	23p37	23p37	23p37	05 27	05 57	06 27	06 56	07 16	07 36	07 56	08 16	08 36	08 56	09 16	09 37	09 57	10 17	10 37	10 57	11 17	
Kenton	d	23p39	23p39	23p39	05 29	05 59	06 29	06 59	07 19	07 39	07 59	08 19	08 39	08 59	09 19	09 39	09 59	10 19	10 39	10 59	11 19	
South Kenton	d	23p41	23p41	23p41	05 31	06 01	06 31	07 01	07 21	07 41	08 01	08 21	08 41	09 01	09 21	09 41	10 01	10 21	10 41	11 01	11 21	
North Wembley	d	23p43	23p43	23p43	05 33	06 03	06 33	07 03	07 23	07 43	08 03	08 23	08 43	09 03	09 23	09 43	10 03	10 23	10 43	11 03	11 23	
Wembley Central	d	23p45	23p45	23p45	05 35	06 05	06 35	07 05	07 25	07 45	08 05	08 25	08 45	09 05	09 25	09 45	10 05	10 25	10 45	11 05	11 25	
Stonebridge Park	d	23p48	23p48	23p48	05 38	06 08	06 38	07 08	07 28	07 48	08 08	08 28	08 48	09 08	09 28	09 48	10 08	10 28	10 48	11 08	11 28	
Harlesden	d	23p50	23p50	23p50	05 40	06 10	06 40	07 10	07 30	07 50	08 10	08 30	08 50	09 10	09 30	09 50	10 10	10 30	10 50	11 10	11 30	
Willesden Jn Low Level	d	23p52	23p52	23p52	05 42	06 12	06 42	07 13	07 33	07 53	08 13	08 33	08 53	09 13	09 33	09 52	10 12	10 32	10 52	11 12	11 32	
Kensal Green	d	23p55	23p55	23p55	05 45	06 15	06 45	07 15	07 35	07 55	08 15	08 35	08 55	09 15	09 35	09 55	10 15	10 35	10 55	11 15	11 35	
Queen's Park (London) ⊖	d	23p57	23p57	23p57	05 47	06 17	06 47	07 18	07 38	07 58	08 18	08 38	08 58	09 18	09 38	09 57	10 17	10 37	10 57	11 17	11 37	
Kilburn High Road	d	23p59	23p59	23p59	05 49	06 19	06 49	07 20	07 40	08 00	08 20	08 40	09 00	09 20	09 40	09 59	10 19	10 39	10 59	11 19	11 39	
South Hampstead	d	00 01	00 01	00 01	05 51	06 21	06 51	07 22	07 42	08 02	08 22	08 42	09 02	09 22	09 42	10 01	10 21	10 41	11 01	11 21	11 41	
London Euston 15 ⊖	a	00 09	00 10	00 12	05 59	06 32	06 58	07 29	07 52	08 12	08 31	08 52	09 12	09 29	09 52	10 11	10 30	10 49	11 11	11 30	11 50	

A from 21 May until 23 July
B from 31 July until 7 September
C 27 July

Stations Harrow & Wealdstone to Queen's Park inclusive are also served by London Underground Bakerloo Line Services

27 July to 7 September

Watford Junction - Harrow & Wealdstone, Queen's Park and London

Network Diagram - see first Page of Table 59

Station		LO	LO	LO	LO	LO	LO	LO	LO	LO	LO	LO	LO	LO	LO	LO	LO	LO	LO	LO	LO	LO	LO
Watford Junction	d	15 01	15 21	15 41	16 01	16 21	16 41	17 01	17 21	17 41	18 01	18 21	18 41	19 01	19 21	19 41	20 01	20 21	20 41	21 01	21 21	21 41	22 01
Watford High Street	d	15 04	15 24	15 44	16 04	16 24	16 44	17 04	17 24	17 44	18 04	18 24	18 44	19 04	19 24	19 44	20 04	20 24	20 44	21 04	21 24	21 44	22 04
Bushey	d	15 06	15 26	15 46	16 06	16 26	16 46	17 06	17 26	17 46	18 06	18 26	18 46	19 06	19 26	19 46	20 06	20 26	20 46	21 06	21 26	21 46	22 06
Carpenders Park	d	15 09	15 29	15 49	16 09	16 29	16 49	17 09	17 29	17 49	18 09	18 29	18 49	19 09	19 29	19 49	20 09	20 29	20 49	21 09	21 29	21 49	22 09
Hatch End	d	15 12	15 32	15 52	16 12	16 32	16 52	17 12	17 32	17 52	18 12	18 32	18 52	19 12	19 32	19 52	20 12	20 32	20 52	21 12	21 32	21 52	22 12
Headstone Lane	d	15 14	15 34	15 54	16 14	16 34	16 54	17 14	17 34	17 54	18 14	18 34	18 54	19 14	19 34	19 54	20 14	20 34	20 54	21 14	21 34	21 54	22 14
Harrow & Wealdstone	d	15 17	15 37	15 57	16 17	16 37	16 57	17 17	17 37	17 57	18 17	18 37	18 57	19 17	19 37	19 57	20 17	20 37	20 57	21 17	21 37	21 57	22 17
Kenton	d	15 19	15 39	15 59	16 19	16 39	16 59	17 19	17 39	17 59	18 19	18 39	18 59	19 19	19 39	19 59	20 19	20 39	20 59	21 19	21 39	21 59	22 19
South Kenton	d	15 21	15 41	16 01	16 21	16 41	17 01	17 21	17 41	18 01	18 21	18 41	19 01	19 21	19 41	20 01	20 21	20 41	21 01	21 21	21 41	22 01	22 21
North Wembley	d	15 23	15 43	16 03	16 23	16 43	17 03	17 23	17 43	18 03	18 23	18 43	19 03	19 23	19 43	20 03	20 23	20 43	21 03	21 23	21 43	22 03	22 23
Wembley Central	d	15 25	15 45	16 05	16 25	16 45	17 05	17 25	17 45	18 05	18 25	18 45	19 05	19 25	19 45	20 05	20 25	20 45	21 05	21 25	21 45	22 05	22 25
Stonebridge Park	d	15 28	15 48	16 08	16 28	16 48	17 08	17 28	17 48	18 08	18 28	18 48	19 08	19 28	19 48	20 08	20 28	20 48	21 08	21 28	21 48	22 08	22 28
Harlesden	d	15 30	15 50	16 10	16 30	16 50	17 10	17 30	17 50	18 10	18 30	18 50	19 10	19 30	19 50	20 10	20 30	20 50	21 10	21 30	21 50	22 10	22 30
Willesden Jn Low Level	d	15 32	15 52	16 12	16 32	16 52	17 12	17 32	17 52	18 12	18 32	18 52	19 12	19 32	19 52	20 12	20 32	20 52	21 12	21 32	21 52	22 12	22 32
Kensal Green	d	15 35	15 55	16 15	16 35	16 55	17 15	17 35	17 55	18 15	18 35	18 55	19 15	19 35	19 55	20 15	20 35	20 55	21 15	21 35	21 55	22 15	22 35
Queen's Park (London) ⊖	d	15 37	15 57	16 17	16 37	16 57	17 17	17 37	17 57	18 17	18 37	18 57	19 17	19 37	19 57	20 17	20 37	20 57	21 17	21 37	21 57	22 17	22 37
Kilburn High Road	d	15 39	15 59	16 19	16 39	16 59	17 19	17 39	17 59	18 19	18 39	18 59	19 19	19 39	19 59	20 19	20 39	20 59	21 19	21 39	21 59	22 19	22 39
South Hampstead	d	15 41	16 01	16 21	16 41	17 01	17 21	17 41	18 01	18 21	18 41	19 01	19 21	19 41	20 01	20 21	20 41	21 01	21 21	21 41	22 01	22 21	22 41
London Euston 15 ⊖	a	15 50	16 11	16 30	16 49	17 11	17 30	17 53	18 13	18 30	18 50	19 11	19 30	19 52	20 10	20 30	20 48	21 11	21 30	21 51	22 11	22 30	22 50

Station		LO	LO	LO
Watford Junction	d	22 21	22 51	23 21
Watford High Street	d	22 24	22 54	23 24
Bushey	d	22 26	22 56	23 26
Carpenders Park	d	22 29	22 59	23 29
Hatch End	d	22 32	23 02	23 32
Headstone Lane	d	22 34	23 04	23 34
Harrow & Wealdstone	d	22 37	23 07	23 37
Kenton	d	22 39	23 09	23 39
South Kenton	d	22 41	23 11	23 41
North Wembley	d	22 43	23 13	23 43
Wembley Central	d	22 45	23 15	23 45
Stonebridge Park	d	22 48	23 18	23 48
Harlesden	d	22 50	23 20	23 50
Willesden Jn Low Level	d	22 52	23 22	23 52
Kensal Green	d	22 55	23 25	23 55
Queen's Park (London) ⊖	d	22 57	23 27	23 57
Kilburn High Road	d	22 59	23 29	23 59
South Hampstead	d	23 01	23 31	00 01
London Euston 15 ⊖	a	23 10	23 39	00 09

Mondays to Fridays

from 10 September

Station		LO MX	LO MO	LO	LO	LO	LO	LO	LO	LO	LO	LO	LO	LO	LO	LO	LO	LO	LO	LO		LO
Watford Junction	d	23p21	23p21	05 11	05 41	06 11	06 40	07 00	07 20	07 40	08 00	08 20	08 40	09 00	09 21	09 41	10 01	10 21	10 41	11 01	and at the same minutes past each hour until	15 01
Watford High Street	d	23p24	23p24	05 14	05 44	06 14	06 43	07 03	07 23	07 43	08 03	08 23	08 43	09 03	09 24	09 44	10 04	10 24	10 44	11 04		15 04
Bushey	d	23p26	23p26	05 16	05 46	06 16	06 45	07 05	07 25	07 45	08 05	08 25	08 45	09 05	09 26	09 46	10 06	10 26	10 46	11 06		15 06
Carpenders Park	d	23p29	23p29	05 19	05 49	06 19	06 48	07 08	07 28	07 48	08 08	08 28	08 48	09 08	09 29	09 49	10 09	10 29	10 49	11 09		15 09
Hatch End	d	23p32	23p32	05 22	05 52	06 22	06 51	07 11	07 31	07 51	08 11	08 31	08 51	09 11	09 32	09 52	10 12	10 32	10 52	11 12		15 12
Headstone Lane	d	23p34	23p34	05 24	05 54	06 24	06 53	07 13	07 33	07 53	08 13	08 33	08 53	09 13	09 34	09 54	10 14	10 34	10 54	11 14		15 14
Harrow & Wealdstone	d	23p37	23p37	05 27	05 57	06 27	06 56	07 16	07 36	07 56	08 16	08 36	08 56	09 16	09 37	09 57	10 17	10 37	10 57	11 17		15 17
Kenton	d	23p39	23p39	05 29	05 59	06 29	06 59	07 19	07 39	07 59	08 19	08 39	08 59	09 19	09 39	09 59	10 19	10 39	10 59	11 19		15 19
South Kenton	d	23p41	23p41	05 31	06 01	06 31	07 01	07 21	07 41	08 01	08 21	08 41	09 01	09 21	09 41	10 01	10 21	10 41	11 01	11 21		15 21
North Wembley	d	23p43	23p43	05 33	06 03	06 33	07 03	07 23	07 43	08 03	08 23	08 43	09 03	09 23	09 43	10 03	10 23	10 43	11 03	11 23		15 23
Wembley Central	d	23p45	23p45	05 35	06 05	06 35	07 05	07 25	07 45	08 05	08 25	08 45	09 05	09 25	09 45	10 05	10 25	10 45	11 05	11 25		15 25
Stonebridge Park	d	23p48	23p48	05 38	06 08	06 38	07 08	07 28	07 48	08 08	08 28	08 48	09 08	09 28	09 48	10 08	10 28	10 48	11 08	11 28		15 28
Harlesden	d	23p50	23p50	05 40	06 10	06 40	07 10	07 30	07 50	08 10	08 30	08 50	09 10	09 30	09 50	10 10	10 30	10 50	11 10	11 30		15 30
Willesden Jn Low Level	d	23p52	23p52	05 42	06 12	06 42	07 13	07 33	07 53	08 13	08 33	08 53	09 13	09 33	09 52	10 12	10 32	10 52	11 12	11 32		15 32
Kensal Green	d	23p55	23p55	05 45	06 15	06 45	07 15	07 35	07 55	08 15	08 35	08 55	09 15	09 35	09 55	10 15	10 35	10 55	11 15	11 35		15 35
Queen's Park (London) ⊖	d	23p57	23p57	05 47	06 17	06 47	07 18	07 38	07 58	08 18	08 38	08 58	09 18	09 38	09 57	10 17	10 37	10 57	11 17	11 37		15 37
Kilburn High Road	d	23p59	23p59	05 49	06 19	06 49	07 20	07 40	08 00	08 20	08 40	09 00	09 20	09 40	09 59	10 19	10 39	10 59	11 19	11 39		15 39
South Hampstead	d	00 01	00 01	05 51	06 21	06 51	07 22	07 42	08 02	08 22	08 42	09 02	09 22	09 42	10 01	10 21	10 41	11 01	11 21	11 41		15 41
London Euston 15 ⊖	a	00 09	00 12	05 59	06 32	06 58	07 29	07 52	08 12	08 31	08 52	09 12	09 29	09 52	10 11	10 30	10 49	11 11	11 30	11 50		15 50

Station		LO	LO	LO	LO	LO	LO	LO	LO	LO	LO	LO	LO	LO	LO	LO	LO	LO	LO	LO	LO	LO	LO
Watford Junction	d	15 21	15 41	16 01	16 21	16 41	17 01	17 21	17 41	18 01	18 21	18 41	19 01	19 21	19 41	20 01	20 21	20 41	21 01	21 21	21 41	22 01	22 21
Watford High Street	d	15 24	15 44	16 04	16 24	16 44	17 04	17 24	17 44	18 04	18 24	18 44	19 04	19 24	19 44	20 04	20 24	20 44	21 04	21 24	21 44	22 04	22 24
Bushey	d	15 26	15 46	16 06	16 26	16 46	17 06	17 26	17 46	18 06	18 26	18 46	19 06	19 26	19 46	20 06	20 26	20 46	21 06	21 26	21 46	22 06	22 26
Carpenders Park	d	15 29	15 49	16 09	16 29	16 49	17 09	17 29	17 49	18 09	18 29	18 49	19 09	19 29	19 49	20 09	20 29	20 49	21 09	21 29	21 49	22 09	22 29
Hatch End	d	15 32	15 52	16 12	16 32	16 52	17 12	17 32	17 52	18 12	18 32	18 52	19 12	19 32	19 52	20 12	20 32	20 52	21 12	21 32	21 52	22 12	22 32
Headstone Lane	d	15 34	15 54	16 14	16 34	16 54	17 14	17 34	17 54	18 14	18 34	18 54	19 14	19 34	19 54	20 14	20 34	20 54	21 14	21 34	21 54	22 14	22 34
Harrow & Wealdstone	d	15 37	15 57	16 17	16 37	16 57	17 17	17 37	17 57	18 17	18 37	18 57	19 17	19 37	19 57	20 17	20 37	20 57	21 17	21 37	21 57	22 17	22 37
Kenton	d	15 39	15 59	16 19	16 39	16 59	17 19	17 39	17 59	18 19	18 39	18 59	19 19	19 39	19 59	20 19	20 39	20 59	21 19	21 39	21 59	22 19	22 39
South Kenton	d	15 41	16 01	16 21	16 41	17 01	17 21	17 41	18 01	18 21	18 41	19 01	19 21	19 41	20 01	20 21	20 41	21 01	21 21	21 41	22 01	22 21	22 41
North Wembley	d	15 43	16 03	16 23	16 43	17 03	17 23	17 43	18 03	18 23	18 43	19 03	19 23	19 43	20 03	20 23	20 43	21 03	21 23	21 43	22 03	22 23	22 43
Wembley Central	d	15 45	16 05	16 25	16 45	17 05	17 25	17 45	18 05	18 25	18 45	19 05	19 25	19 45	20 05	20 25	20 45	21 05	21 25	21 45	22 05	22 25	22 45
Stonebridge Park	d	15 48	16 08	16 28	16 48	17 08	17 28	17 48	18 08	18 28	18 48	19 08	19 28	19 48	20 08	20 28	20 48	21 08	21 28	21 48	22 08	22 28	22 48
Harlesden	d	15 50	16 10	16 30	16 50	17 10	17 30	17 50	18 10	18 30	18 50	19 10	19 30	19 50	20 10	20 30	20 50	21 10	21 30	21 50	22 10	22 30	22 50
Willesden Jn Low Level	d	15 52	16 12	16 32	16 52	17 12	17 32	17 52	18 12	18 32	18 52	19 12	19 32	19 52	20 12	20 32	20 52	21 12	21 32	21 52	22 12	22 32	22 52
Kensal Green	d	15 55	16 15	16 35	16 55	17 15	17 35	17 55	18 15	18 35	18 55	19 15	19 35	19 55	20 15	20 35	20 55	21 15	21 35	21 55	22 15	22 35	22 55
Queen's Park (London) ⊖	d	15 57	16 17	16 37	16 57	17 17	17 37	17 57	18 17	18 37	18 57	19 17	19 37	19 57	20 17	20 37	20 57	21 17	21 37	21 57	22 17	22 37	22 57
Kilburn High Road	d	15 59	16 19	16 39	16 59	17 19	17 39	17 59	18 19	18 39	18 59	19 19	19 39	19 59	20 19	20 39	20 59	21 19	21 39	21 59	22 19	22 39	22 59
South Hampstead	d	16 01	16 21	16 41	17 01	17 21	17 41	18 01	18 21	18 41	19 01	19 21	19 41	20 01	20 21	20 41	21 01	21 21	21 41	22 01	22 21	22 41	23 01
London Euston 15 ⊖	a	16 11	16 30	16 49	17 11	17 30	17 53	18 13	18 30	18 50	19 11	19 30	19 52	20 10	20 30	20 48	21 11	21 30	21 51	22 11	22 30	22 50	23 10

Stations Harrow & Wealdstone to Queen's Park inclusive are also served by London Underground Bakerloo Line Services

Watford Junction - Harrow & Wealdstone, Queen's Park and London

Mondays to Fridays
from 10 September

Network Diagram - see first Page of Table 59

		LO	LO
Watford Junction	d	22 51	23 21
Watford High Street	d	22 54	23 24
Bushey	d	22 56	23 26
Carpenders Park	d	22 59	23 29
Hatch End	d	23 02	23 32
Headstone Lane	d	23 04	23 34
Harrow & Wealdstone	d	23 07	23 37
Kenton	d	23 09	23 39
South Kenton	d	23 11	23 41
North Wembley	d	23 13	23 43
Wembley Central	d	23 15	23 45
Stonebridge Park	d	23 18	23 48
Harlesden	d	23 20	23 50
Willesden Jn Low Level	d	23 22	23 52
Kensal Green	d	23 25	23 55
Queen's Park (London) ⊖	d	23 27	23 57
Kilburn High Road	d	23 29	23 59
South Hampstead	d	23 31	00 01
London Euston 15 ⊖	a	23 39	00 09

Saturdays
until 21 July

		LO	LO	LO	LO	LO	LO	LO	LO	LO	LO	LO	LO	LO	LO	LO	LO	LO	LO		LO	LO
Watford Junction	d	23p21	05 11	05 41	06 11	06 41	07 01	07 21	07 41	08 01	08 21	08 41	09 01	09 21	09 41	10 01	10 21	10 41	11 01		21 01	21 21
Watford High Street	d	23p24	05 14	05 44	06 14	06 44	07 04	07 24	07 44	08 04	08 24	08 44	09 04	09 24	09 44	10 04	10 24	10 44	11 04		21 04	21 24
Bushey	d	23p26	05 16	05 46	06 16	06 46	07 06	07 26	07 46	08 06	08 26	08 46	09 06	09 26	09 46	10 06	10 26	10 46	11 06		21 06	21 26
Carpenders Park	d	23p29	05 19	05 49	06 19	06 49	07 09	07 29	07 49	08 09	08 29	08 49	09 09	09 29	09 49	10 09	10 29	10 49	11 09		21 09	21 29
Hatch End	d	23p32	05 22	05 52	06 22	06 52	07 12	07 32	07 52	08 12	08 32	08 52	09 12	09 32	09 52	10 12	10 32	10 52	11 12		21 12	21 32
Headstone Lane	d	23p34	05 24	05 54	06 24	06 54	07 14	07 34	07 54	08 14	08 34	08 54	09 14	09 34	09 54	10 14	10 34	10 54	11 14	and at	21 14	21 34
Harrow & Wealdstone	d	23p37	05 27	05 57	06 27	06 57	07 17	07 37	07 57	08 17	08 37	08 57	09 17	09 37	09 57	10 17	10 37	10 57	11 17	the same	21 17	21 37
Kenton	d	23p39	05 29	05 59	06 29	06 59	07 19	07 39	07 59	08 19	08 39	08 59	09 19	09 39	09 59	10 19	10 39	10 59	11 19	minutes	21 19	21 39
South Kenton	d	23p41	05 31	06 01	06 31	07 01	07 21	07 41	08 01	08 21	08 41	09 01	09 21	09 41	10 01	10 21	10 41	11 01	11 21	past	21 21	21 41
North Wembley	d	23p43	05 33	06 03	06 33	07 03	07 23	07 43	08 03	08 23	08 43	09 03	09 23	09 43	10 03	10 23	10 43	11 03	11 23	each	21 23	21 43
Wembley Central	d	23p45	05 35	06 05	06 35	07 05	07 25	07 45	08 05	08 25	08 45	09 05	09 25	09 45	10 05	10 25	10 45	11 05	11 25	hour until	21 25	21 45
Stonebridge Park	d	23p48	05 38	06 08	06 38	07 08	07 28	07 48	08 08	08 28	08 48	09 08	09 28	09 48	10 08	10 28	10 48	11 08	11 28		21 28	21 48
Harlesden	d	23p50	05 40	06 10	06 40	07 10	07 30	07 50	08 10	08 30	08 50	09 10	09 30	09 50	10 10	10 30	10 50	11 10	11 30		21 30	21 50
Willesden Jn Low Level	d	23p52	05 42	06 12	06 42	07 12	07 32	07 52	08 12	08 32	08 52	09 12	09 32	09 52	10 12	10 32	10 52	11 12	11 32		21 32	21 52
Kensal Green	d	23p55	05 45	06 15	06 45	07 15	07 35	07 55	08 15	08 35	08 55	09 15	09 35	09 55	10 15	10 35	10 55	11 15	11 35		21 35	21 55
Queen's Park (London) ⊖	d	23p57	05 47	06 17	06 47	07 17	07 37	07 57	08 17	08 37	08 57	09 17	09 37	09 57	10 17	10 37	10 57	11 17	11 37		21 37	21 57
Kilburn High Road	d	23p59	05 49	06 19	06 49	07 19	07 39	07 59	08 19	08 39	08 59	09 19	09 39	09 59	10 19	10 39	10 59	11 19	11 39		21 39	21 59
South Hampstead	d	00 01	05 51	06 21	06 51	07 21	07 41	08 01	08 21	08 41	09 01	09 21	09 41	10 01	10 21	10 41	11 01	11 21	11 41		21 41	22 01
London Euston 15 ⊖	a	00 10	06 00	06 30	06 59	07 30	07 49	08 13	08 30	08 50	09 12	09 30	09 50	10 13	10 30	10 49	11 13	11 30	11 50		21 50	22 10

		LO	LO	LO	LO	LO
Watford Junction	d	21 41	22 01	22 21	22 51	23 21
Watford High Street	d	21 44	22 04	22 24	22 54	23 24
Bushey	d	21 46	22 06	22 26	22 56	23 26
Carpenders Park	d	21 49	22 09	22 29	22 59	23 29
Hatch End	d	21 52	22 12	22 32	23 02	23 32
Headstone Lane	d	21 54	22 14	22 34	23 04	23 34
Harrow & Wealdstone	d	21 57	22 17	22 37	23 07	23 37
Kenton	d	21 59	22 19	22 39	23 09	23 39
South Kenton	d	22 01	22 21	22 41	23 11	23 41
North Wembley	d	22 03	22 23	22 43	23 13	23 43
Wembley Central	d	22 05	22 25	22 45	23 15	23 45
Stonebridge Park	d	22 08	22 28	22 48	23 17	23 48
Harlesden	d	22 10	22 30	22 50	23 19	23 50
Willesden Jn Low Level	d	22 12	22 32	22 52	23 21	23 52
Kensal Green	d	22 15	22 35	22 55	23 23	23 55
Queen's Park (London) ⊖	d	22 17	22 37	22 57	23 25	23 57
Kilburn High Road	d	22 19	22 39	22 59	23 27	23 59
South Hampstead	d	22 21	22 41	23 01	23 29	00 01
London Euston 15 ⊖	a	22 30	22 53	23 11	23 38	00 10

Saturdays
28 July to 8 September

		LO	LO	LO	LO	LO	LO	LO	LO	LO	LO	LO	LO	LO	LO	LO	LO	LO	LO		LO	LO
Watford Junction	d	23p21	05 11	05 41	06 11	06 41	07 01	07 21	07 41	08 01	08 21	08 41	09 01	09 21	09 41	10 01	10 21	10 41	11 01		21 01	21 21
Watford High Street	d	23p24	05 14	05 44	06 14	06 44	07 04	07 24	07 44	08 04	08 24	08 44	09 04	09 24	09 44	10 04	10 24	10 44	11 04		21 04	21 24
Bushey	d	23p26	05 16	05 46	06 16	06 46	07 06	07 26	07 46	08 06	08 26	08 46	09 06	09 26	09 46	10 06	10 26	10 46	11 06		21 06	21 26
Carpenders Park	d	23p29	05 19	05 49	06 19	06 49	07 09	07 29	07 49	08 09	08 29	08 49	09 09	09 29	09 49	10 09	10 29	10 49	11 09		21 09	21 29
Hatch End	d	23p32	05 22	05 52	06 22	06 52	07 12	07 32	07 52	08 12	08 32	08 52	09 12	09 32	09 52	10 12	10 32	10 52	11 12		21 12	21 32
Headstone Lane	d	23p34	05 24	05 54	06 24	06 54	07 14	07 34	07 54	08 14	08 34	08 54	09 14	09 34	09 54	10 14	10 34	10 54	11 14	and at	21 14	21 34
Harrow & Wealdstone	d	23p37	05 27	05 57	06 27	06 57	07 17	07 37	07 57	08 17	08 37	08 57	09 17	09 37	09 57	10 17	10 37	10 57	11 17	the same	21 17	21 37
Kenton	d	23p39	05 29	05 59	06 29	06 59	07 19	07 39	07 59	08 19	08 39	08 59	09 19	09 39	09 59	10 19	10 39	10 59	11 19	minutes	21 19	21 39
South Kenton	d	23p41	05 31	06 01	06 31	07 01	07 21	07 41	08 01	08 21	08 41	09 01	09 21	09 41	10 01	10 21	10 41	11 01	11 21	past	21 21	21 41
North Wembley	d	23p43	05 33	06 03	06 33	07 03	07 23	07 43	08 03	08 23	08 43	09 03	09 23	09 43	10 03	10 23	10 43	11 03	11 23	each	21 23	21 43
Wembley Central	d	23p45	05 35	06 05	06 35	07 05	07 25	07 45	08 05	08 25	08 45	09 05	09 25	09 45	10 05	10 25	10 45	11 05	11 25	hour until	21 25	21 45
Stonebridge Park	d	23p48	05 38	06 08	06 38	07 08	07 28	07 48	08 08	08 28	08 48	09 08	09 28	09 48	10 08	10 28	10 48	11 08	11 28		21 28	21 48
Harlesden	d	23p50	05 40	06 10	06 40	07 10	07 30	07 50	08 10	08 30	08 50	09 10	09 30	09 50	10 10	10 30	10 50	11 10	11 30		21 30	21 50
Willesden Jn Low Level	d	23p52	05 42	06 12	06 42	07 12	07 32	07 52	08 12	08 32	08 52	09 12	09 32	09 52	10 12	10 32	10 52	11 12	11 32		21 32	21 52
Kensal Green	d	23p55	05 45	06 15	06 45	07 15	07 35	07 55	08 15	08 35	08 55	09 15	09 35	09 55	10 15	10 35	10 55	11 15	11 35		21 35	21 55
Queen's Park (London) ⊖	d	23p57	05 47	06 17	06 47	07 17	07 37	07 57	08 17	08 37	08 57	09 17	09 37	09 57	10 17	10 37	10 57	11 17	11 37		21 37	21 57
Kilburn High Road	d	23p59	05 49	06 19	06 49	07 19	07 39	07 59	08 19	08 39	08 59	09 19	09 39	09 59	10 19	10 39	10 59	11 19	11 39		21 39	21 59
South Hampstead	d	00 01	05 51	06 21	06 51	07 21	07 41	08 01	08 21	08 41	09 01	09 21	09 41	10 01	10 21	10 41	11 01	11 21	11 41		21 41	22 01
London Euston 15 ⊖	a	00 09	06 00	06 31	06 59	07 30	07 49	08 13	08 30	08 50	09 12	09 30	09 50	10 13	10 30	10 49	11 13	11 30	11 50		21 50	22 10

Stations Harrow & Wealdstone to Queen's Park inclusive are also served by London Underground Bakerloo Line Services

Saturdays
28 July to 8 September

Watford Junction - Harrow & Wealdstone, Queen's Park and London

Network Diagram - see first Page of Table 59

		LO	LO	LO	LO A	LO B	LO A	LO B
Watford Junction	d	21 41	22 01	22 21	22 51	22 51	23 21	23 21
Watford High Street	d	21 44	22 04	22 24	22 54	22 54	23 24	23 24
Bushey	d	21 46	22 06	22 26	22 56	22 56	23 26	23 26
Carpenders Park	d	21 49	22 09	22 29	22 59	22 59	23 29	23 29
Hatch End	d	21 52	22 12	22 32	23 02	23 02	23 32	23 32
Headstone Lane	d	21 54	22 14	22 34	23 04	23 04	23 34	23 34
Harrow & Wealdstone	d	21 57	22 17	22 37	23 07	23 07	23 37	23 37
Kenton	d	21 59	22 19	22 39	23 09	23 09	23 39	23 39
South Kenton	d	22 01	22 21	22 41	23 11	23 11	23 41	23 41
North Wembley	d	22 03	22 23	22 43	23 13	23 13	23 43	23 43
Wembley Central	d	22 05	22 25	22 45	23 15	23 15	23 45	23 45
Stonebridge Park	d	22 08	22 28	22 48	23 17	23 18	23 48	23 48
Harlesden	d	22 10	22 30	22 50	23 19	23 20	23 50	23 50
Willesden Jn Low Level	d	22 12	22 32	22 52	23 21	23 22	23 52	23 52
Kensal Green	d	22 15	22 35	22 55	23 23	23 25	23 55	23 55
Queen's Park (London) ⊖	d	22 17	22 37	22 57	23 25	23 27	23 57	23 57
Kilburn High Road	d	22 19	22 39	22 59	23 27	23 29	23 59	23 59
South Hampstead	d	22 21	22 41	23 01	23 29	23 31	00 01	00 01
London Euston 15 ⊖	a	22 30	22 53	23 11	23 38	23 38	00 10	00 12

Saturdays
from 15 September

		LO	LO	LO	LO	LO	LO	LO	LO	LO	LO	LO	LO	LO	LO	LO	LO	LO	LO		LO	LO
Watford Junction	d	23p21	05 11	05 41	06 11	06 41	07 01	07 21	07 41	08 01	08 21	08 41	09 01	09 21	09 41	10 01	10 21	10 41	11 01		21 01	21 21
Watford High Street	d	23p24	05 14	05 44	06 14	06 44	07 04	07 24	07 44	08 04	08 24	08 44	09 04	09 24	09 44	10 04	10 24	10 44	11 04		21 04	21 24
Bushey	d	23p26	05 16	05 46	06 16	06 46	07 06	07 26	07 46	08 06	08 26	08 46	09 06	09 26	09 46	10 06	10 26	10 46	11 06		21 06	21 26
Carpenders Park	d	23p29	05 19	05 49	06 19	06 49	07 09	07 29	07 49	08 09	08 29	08 49	09 09	09 29	09 49	10 09	10 29	10 49	11 09		21 09	21 29
Hatch End	d	23p32	05 22	05 52	06 22	06 52	07 12	07 32	07 52	08 12	08 32	08 52	09 12	09 32	09 52	10 12	10 32	10 52	11 12		21 12	21 32
Headstone Lane	d	23p34	05 24	05 54	06 24	06 54	07 14	07 34	07 54	08 14	08 34	08 54	09 14	09 34	09 54	10 14	10 34	10 54	11 14	and at	21 14	21 34
Harrow & Wealdstone	d	23p37	05 27	05 57	06 27	06 57	07 17	07 37	07 57	08 17	08 37	08 57	09 17	09 37	09 57	10 17	10 37	10 57	11 17	the same	21 17	21 37
Kenton	d	23p39	05 29	05 59	06 29	06 59	07 19	07 39	07 59	08 19	08 39	08 59	09 19	09 39	09 59	10 19	10 39	10 59	11 19	minutes	21 19	21 39
South Kenton	d	23p41	05 31	06 01	06 31	07 01	07 21	07 41	08 01	08 21	08 41	09 01	09 21	09 41	10 01	10 21	10 41	11 01	11 21	past	21 21	21 41
North Wembley	d	23p43	05 33	06 03	06 33	07 03	07 23	07 43	08 03	08 23	08 43	09 03	09 23	09 43	10 03	10 23	10 43	11 03	11 23	each	21 23	21 43
Wembley Central	d	23p45	05 35	06 05	06 35	07 05	07 25	07 45	08 05	08 25	08 45	09 05	09 25	09 45	10 05	10 25	10 45	11 05	11 25	hour until	21 25	21 45
Stonebridge Park	d	23p48	05 38	06 08	06 38	07 08	07 28	07 48	08 08	08 28	08 48	09 08	09 28	09 48	10 08	10 28	10 48	11 08	11 28		21 28	21 48
Harlesden	d	23p50	05 40	06 10	06 40	07 10	07 30	07 50	08 10	08 30	08 50	09 10	09 30	09 50	10 10	10 30	10 50	11 10	11 30		21 30	21 50
Willesden Jn Low Level	d	23p52	05 42	06 12	06 42	07 12	07 32	07 52	08 12	08 32	08 52	09 12	09 32	09 52	10 12	10 32	10 52	11 12	11 32		21 32	21 52
Kensal Green	d	23p55	05 45	06 15	06 45	07 15	07 35	07 55	08 15	08 35	08 55	09 15	09 35	09 55	10 15	10 35	10 55	11 15	11 35		21 35	21 55
Queen's Park (London) ⊖	d	23p57	05 47	06 17	06 47	07 17	07 37	07 57	08 17	08 37	08 57	09 17	09 37	09 57	10 17	10 37	10 57	11 17	11 37		21 37	21 57
Kilburn High Road	d	23p59	05 49	06 19	06 49	07 19	07 39	07 59	08 19	08 39	08 59	09 19	09 39	09 59	10 19	10 39	10 59	11 19	11 39		21 39	21 59
South Hampstead	d	00 01	05 51	06 21	06 51	07 21	07 41	08 01	08 21	08 41	09 01	09 21	09 41	10 01	10 21	10 41	11 01	11 21	11 41		21 41	22 01
London Euston 15 ⊖	a	00 09	06 00	06 30	06 59	07 30	07 49	08 13	08 30	08 50	09 12	09 30	09 50	10 13	10 30	10 49	11 13	11 30	11 50		21 50	22 10

		LO	LO	LO	LO	LO
Watford Junction	d	21 41	22 01	22 21	22 51	23 21
Watford High Street	d	21 44	22 04	22 24	22 54	23 24
Bushey	d	21 46	22 06	22 26	22 56	23 26
Carpenders Park	d	21 49	22 09	22 29	22 59	23 29
Hatch End	d	21 52	22 12	22 32	23 02	23 32
Headstone Lane	d	21 54	22 14	22 34	23 04	23 34
Harrow & Wealdstone	d	21 57	22 17	22 37	23 07	23 37
Kenton	d	21 59	22 19	22 39	23 09	23 39
South Kenton	d	22 01	22 21	22 41	23 11	23 41
North Wembley	d	22 03	22 23	22 43	23 13	23 43
Wembley Central	d	22 05	22 25	22 45	23 15	23 45
Stonebridge Park	d	22 08	22 28	22 48	23 17	23 48
Harlesden	d	22 10	22 30	22 50	23 19	23 50
Willesden Jn Low Level	d	22 12	22 32	22 52	23 21	23 52
Kensal Green	d	22 15	22 35	22 55	23 23	23 55
Queen's Park (London) ⊖	d	22 17	22 37	22 57	23 25	23 57
Kilburn High Road	d	22 19	22 39	22 59	23 27	23 59
South Hampstead	d	22 21	22 41	23 01	23 29	00 01
London Euston 15 ⊖	a	22 30	22 53	23 11	23 38	00 10

Sundays
until 22 July

		LO	LO		LO	LO	LO	LO	LO	LO	LO	LO	LO	LO		LO	LO	LO	LO	LO	LO
Watford Junction	d	23p21	06 51		09 21	09 41	10 01	10 21	10 41	11 01	11 21	11 41	12 01	12 21		18 21	18 41	19 01	19 21	19 41	20 01
Watford High Street	d	23p24	06 54		09 24	09 44	10 04	10 24	10 44	11 04	11 24	11 44	12 04	12 24		18 24	18 44	19 04	19 24	19 44	20 04
Bushey	d	23p26	06 56		09 26	09 46	10 06	10 26	10 46	11 06	11 26	11 46	12 06	12 26		18 26	18 46	19 06	19 26	19 46	20 06
Carpenders Park	d	23p29	06 59		09 29	09 49	10 09	10 29	10 49	11 09	11 29	11 49	12 09	12 29		18 29	18 49	19 09	19 29	19 49	20 09
Hatch End	d	23p32	07 02		09 32	09 52	10 12	10 32	10 52	11 12	11 32	11 52	12 12	12 32		18 32	18 52	19 12	19 32	19 52	20 12
Headstone Lane	d	23p34	07 04		09 34	09 54	10 14	10 34	10 54	11 14	11 34	11 54	12 14	12 34	and at	18 34	18 54	19 14	19 34	19 54	20 14
Harrow & Wealdstone	d	23p37	07 07	and	09 37	09 57	10 17	10 37	10 57	11 17	11 37	11 57	12 17	12 37	the same	18 37	18 57	19 17	19 37	19 57	20 17
Kenton	d	23p39	07 09	every 30	09 39	09 59	10 19	10 39	10 59	11 19	11 39	11 59	12 19	12 39	minutes	18 39	18 59	19 19	19 39	19 59	20 19
South Kenton	d	23p41	07 11	minutes	09 41	10 01	10 21	10 41	11 01	11 21	11 41	12 01	12 21	12 41	past	18 41	19 01	19 21	19 41	20 01	20 21
North Wembley	d	23p43	07 13	until	09 43	10 03	10 23	10 43	11 03	11 23	11 43	12 03	12 23	12 43	each	18 43	19 03	19 23	19 43	20 03	20 23
Wembley Central	d	23p45	07 15		09 45	10 05	10 25	10 45	11 05	11 25	11 45	12 05	12 25	12 45	hour until	18 45	19 05	19 25	19 45	20 05	20 25
Stonebridge Park	d	23p48	07 18		09 48	10 08	10 28	10 48	11 08	11 28	11 48	12 08	12 28	12 48		18 48	19 08	19 28	19 48	20 08	20 28
Harlesden	d	23p50	07 20		09 50	10 10	10 30	10 50	11 10	11 30	11 50	12 10	12 30	12 50		18 50	19 10	19 30	19 50	20 10	20 30
Willesden Jn Low Level	d	23p52	07 22		09 52	10 12	10 32	10 52	11 12	11 32	11 52	12 12	12 32	12 52		18 52	19 12	19 32	19 52	20 12	20 32
Kensal Green	d	23p55	07 25		09 55	10 15	10 35	10 55	11 15	11 35	11 55	12 15	12 35	12 55		18 55	19 15	19 35	19 55	20 15	20 35
Queen's Park (London) ⊖	d	23p57	07 27		09 57	10 17	10 37	10 57	11 17	11 37	11 57	12 17	12 37	12 57		18 57	19 17	19 37	19 57	20 17	20 37
Kilburn High Road	d	23p59	07 29		09 59	10 19	10 39	10 59	11 19	11 39	11 59	12 19	12 39	12 59		18 59	19 19	19 39	19 59	20 19	20 39
South Hampstead	d	00 01	07 31		10 01	10 21	10 41	11 01	11 21	11 41	12 01	12 21	12 41	13 01		19 01	19 21	19 41	20 01	20 21	20 41
London Euston 15 ⊖	a	00 10	07 40		10 10	10 30	10 50	11 13	11 30	11 50	12 11	12 31	12 50	13 10		19 10	19 31	19 49	20 10	20 31	20 49

A 18 August, 25 August

B not from 18 August until 25 August

Stations Harrow & Wealdstone to Queen's Park inclusive are also served by London Underground Bakerloo Line Services

Watford Junction - Harrow & Wealdstone, Queen's Park and London

Sundays until 22 July

Network Diagram - see first Page of Table 59

		LO	LO	LO	LO	LO	LO	LO	LO	LO
Watford Junction	d	20 21	20 41	21 01	21 21	21 41	22 01	22 21	22 51	23 21
Watford High Street	d	20 24	20 44	21 04	21 24	21 44	22 04	22 24	22 54	23 24
Bushey	d	20 26	20 46	21 06	21 26	21 46	22 06	22 26	22 56	23 26
Carpenders Park	d	20 29	20 49	21 09	21 29	21 49	22 09	22 29	22 59	23 29
Hatch End	d	20 32	20 52	21 12	21 32	21 52	22 12	22 32	23 02	23 32
Headstone Lane	d	20 34	20 54	21 14	21 34	21 54	22 14	22 34	23 04	23 34
Harrow & Wealdstone	d	20 37	20 57	21 17	21 37	21 57	22 17	22 37	23 07	23 37
Kenton	d	20 39	20 59	21 19	21 39	21 59	22 19	22 39	23 09	23 39
South Kenton	d	20 41	21 01	21 21	21 41	22 01	22 21	22 41	23 11	23 41
North Wembley	d	20 43	21 03	21 23	21 43	22 03	22 23	22 43	23 13	23 43
Wembley Central	d	20 45	21 05	21 25	21 45	22 05	22 25	22 45	23 15	23 45
Stonebridge Park	d	20 48	21 08	21 28	21 48	22 08	22 28	22 48	23 18	23 48
Harlesden	d	20 50	21 10	21 30	21 50	22 10	22 30	22 50	23 20	23 50
Willesden Jn Low Level	d	20 52	21 12	21 32	21 52	22 12	22 32	22 52	23 22	23 52
Kensal Green	d	20 55	21 15	21 35	21 55	22 15	22 35	22 55	23 25	23 55
Queen's Park (London) ⊖	d	20 57	21 17	21 37	21 57	22 17	22 37	22 57	23 27	23 57
Kilburn High Road	d	20 59	21 19	21 39	21 59	22 19	22 39	22 59	23 29	23 59
South Hampstead	d	21 01	21 21	21 41	22 01	22 21	22 41	23 01	23 31	00 01
London Euston 15 ⊖	a	21 13	21 30	21 51	22 10	22 30	22 51	23 10	23 40	00 12

Sundays 29 July to 9 September

		LO A	LO B	LO		LO	LO	LO	LO	LO	LO	LO	LO	LO	LO		LO	LO	LO	LO	LO
Watford Junction	d	23p21	23p21	06 51		09 21	09 41	10 01	10 21	10 41	11 01	11 21	11 41	12 01	12 21		18 21	18 41	19 01	19 21	19 41
Watford High Street	d	23p24	23p24	06 54		09 24	09 44	10 04	10 24	10 44	11 04	11 24	11 44	12 04	12 24		18 24	18 44	19 04	19 24	19 44
Bushey	d	23p26	23p26	06 56		09 26	09 46	10 06	10 26	10 46	11 06	11 26	11 46	12 06	12 26		18 26	18 46	19 06	19 26	19 46
Carpenders Park	d	23p29	23p29	06 59		09 29	09 49	10 09	10 29	10 49	11 09	11 29	11 49	12 09	12 29		18 29	18 49	19 09	19 29	19 49
Hatch End	d	23p32	23p32	07 02		09 32	09 52	10 12	10 32	10 52	11 12	11 32	11 52	12 12	12 32		18 32	18 52	19 12	19 32	19 52
Headstone Lane	d	23p34	23p34	07 04		09 34	09 54	10 14	10 34	10 54	11 14	11 34	11 54	12 14	12 34	and at	18 34	18 54	19 14	19 34	19 54
Harrow & Wealdstone	d	23p37	23p37	07 07	and	09 37	09 57	10 17	10 37	10 57	11 17	11 37	11 57	12 17	12 37	the same	18 37	18 57	19 17	19 37	19 57
Kenton	d	23p39	23p39	07 09	every 30	09 39	09 59	10 19	10 39	10 59	11 19	11 39	11 59	12 19	12 39	minutes	18 39	18 59	19 19	19 39	19 59
South Kenton	d	23p41	23p41	07 11	minutes	09 41	10 01	10 21	10 41	11 01	11 21	11 41	12 01	12 21	12 41	past	18 41	19 01	19 21	19 41	20 01
North Wembley	d	23p43	23p43	07 13	until	09 43	10 03	10 23	10 43	11 03	11 23	11 43	12 03	12 23	12 43	each	18 43	19 03	19 23	19 43	20 03
Wembley Central	d	23p45	23p45	07 15		09 45	10 05	10 25	10 45	11 05	11 25	11 45	12 05	12 25	12 45	hour until	18 45	19 05	19 25	19 45	20 05
Stonebridge Park	d	23p48	23p48	07 18		09 48	10 08	10 28	10 48	11 08	11 28	11 48	12 08	12 28	12 48		18 48	19 08	19 28	19 48	20 08
Harlesden	d	23p50	23p50	07 20		09 50	10 10	10 30	10 50	11 10	11 30	11 50	12 10	12 30	12 50		18 50	19 10	19 30	19 50	20 10
Willesden Jn Low Level	d	23p52	23p52	07 22		09 52	10 12	10 32	10 52	11 12	11 32	11 52	12 12	12 32	12 52		18 52	19 12	19 32	19 52	20 12
Kensal Green	d	23p55	23p55	07 25		09 55	10 15	10 35	10 55	11 15	11 35	11 55	12 15	12 35	12 55		18 55	19 15	19 35	19 55	20 15
Queen's Park (London) ⊖	d	23p57	23p57	07 27		09 57	10 17	10 37	10 57	11 17	11 37	11 57	12 17	12 37	12 57		18 57	19 17	19 37	19 57	20 17
Kilburn High Road	d	23p59	23p59	07 29		09 59	10 19	10 39	10 59	11 19	11 39	11 59	12 19	12 39	12 59		18 59	19 19	19 39	19 59	20 19
South Hampstead	d	00 01	00 01	07 31		10 01	10 21	10 41	11 01	11 21	11 41	12 01	12 21	12 41	13 01		19 01	19 21	19 41	20 01	20 21
London Euston 15 ⊖	a	00 10	00 12	07 40		10 10	10 30	10 50	11 13	11 30	11 50	12 11	12 31	12 50	13 10		19 10	19 31	19 49	20 10	20 31

		LO	LO	LO	LO	LO	LO	LO	LO	LO	LO
Watford Junction	d	20 01	20 21	20 41	21 01	21 21	21 41	22 01	22 21	22 51	23 21
Watford High Street	d	20 04	20 24	20 44	21 04	21 24	21 44	22 04	22 24	22 54	23 24
Bushey	d	20 06	20 26	20 46	21 06	21 26	21 46	22 06	22 26	22 56	23 26
Carpenders Park	d	20 09	20 29	20 49	21 09	21 29	21 49	22 09	22 29	22 59	23 29
Hatch End	d	20 12	20 32	20 52	21 12	21 32	21 52	22 12	22 32	23 02	23 32
Headstone Lane	d	20 14	20 34	20 54	21 14	21 34	21 54	22 14	22 34	23 04	23 34
Harrow & Wealdstone	d	20 17	20 37	20 57	21 17	21 37	21 57	22 17	22 37	23 07	23 37
Kenton	d	20 19	20 39	20 59	21 19	21 39	21 59	22 19	22 39	23 09	23 39
South Kenton	d	20 21	20 41	21 01	21 21	21 41	22 01	22 21	22 41	23 11	23 41
North Wembley	d	20 23	20 43	21 03	21 23	21 43	22 03	22 23	22 43	23 13	23 43
Wembley Central	d	20 25	20 45	21 05	21 25	21 45	22 05	22 25	22 45	23 15	23 45
Stonebridge Park	d	20 28	20 48	21 08	21 28	21 48	22 08	22 28	22 48	23 18	23 48
Harlesden	d	20 30	20 50	21 10	21 30	21 50	22 10	22 30	22 50	23 20	23 50
Willesden Jn Low Level	d	20 32	20 52	21 12	21 32	21 52	22 12	22 32	22 52	23 22	23 52
Kensal Green	d	20 35	20 55	21 15	21 35	21 55	22 15	22 35	22 55	23 25	23 55
Queen's Park (London) ⊖	d	20 37	20 57	21 17	21 37	21 57	22 17	22 37	22 57	23 27	23 57
Kilburn High Road	d	20 39	20 59	21 19	21 39	21 59	22 19	22 39	22 59	23 29	23 59
South Hampstead	d	20 41	21 01	21 21	21 41	22 01	22 21	22 41	23 01	23 31	00 01
London Euston 15 ⊖	a	20 49	21 13	21 30	21 51	22 10	22 30	22 49	23 10	23 40	00 12

Sundays from 16 September

		LO	LO		LO	LO	LO	LO	LO	LO	LO	LO	LO	LO		LO	LO	LO	LO	LO	LO
Watford Junction	d	23p21	06 51		09 21	09 41	10 01	10 21	10 41	11 01	11 21	11 41	12 01	12 21		18 21	18 41	19 01	19 21	19 41	20 01
Watford High Street	d	23p24	06 54		09 24	09 44	10 04	10 24	10 44	11 04	11 24	11 44	12 04	12 24		18 24	18 44	19 04	19 24	19 44	20 04
Bushey	d	23p26	06 56		09 26	09 46	10 06	10 26	10 46	11 06	11 26	11 46	12 06	12 26		18 26	18 46	19 06	19 26	19 46	20 06
Carpenders Park	d	23p29	06 59		09 29	09 49	10 09	10 29	10 49	11 09	11 29	11 49	12 09	12 29		18 29	18 49	19 09	19 29	19 49	20 09
Hatch End	d	23p32	07 02		09 32	09 52	10 12	10 32	10 52	11 12	11 32	11 52	12 12	12 32		18 32	18 52	19 12	19 32	19 52	20 12
Headstone Lane	d	23p34	07 04		09 34	09 54	10 14	10 34	10 54	11 14	11 34	11 54	12 14	12 34	and at	18 34	18 54	19 14	19 34	19 54	20 14
Harrow & Wealdstone	d	23p37	07 07	and	09 37	09 57	10 17	10 37	10 57	11 17	11 37	11 57	12 17	12 37	the same	18 37	18 57	19 17	19 37	19 57	20 17
Kenton	d	23p39	07 09	every 30	09 39	09 59	10 19	10 39	10 59	11 19	11 39	11 59	12 19	12 39	minutes	18 39	18 59	19 19	19 39	19 59	20 19
South Kenton	d	23p41	07 11	minutes	09 41	10 01	10 21	10 41	11 01	11 21	11 41	12 01	12 21	12 41	past	18 41	19 01	19 21	19 41	20 01	20 21
North Wembley	d	23p43	07 13	until	09 43	10 03	10 23	10 43	11 03	11 23	11 43	12 03	12 23	12 43	each	18 43	19 03	19 23	19 43	20 03	20 23
Wembley Central	d	23p45	07 15		09 45	10 05	10 25	10 45	11 05	11 25	11 45	12 05	12 25	12 45	hour until	18 45	19 05	19 25	19 45	20 05	20 25
Stonebridge Park	d	23p48	07 18		09 48	10 08	10 28	10 48	11 08	11 28	11 48	12 08	12 28	12 48		18 48	19 08	19 28	19 48	20 08	20 28
Harlesden	d	23p50	07 20		09 50	10 10	10 30	10 50	11 10	11 30	11 50	12 10	12 30	12 50		18 50	19 10	19 30	19 50	20 10	20 30
Willesden Jn Low Level	d	23p52	07 22		09 52	10 12	10 32	10 52	11 12	11 32	11 52	12 12	12 32	12 52		18 52	19 12	19 32	19 52	20 12	20 32
Kensal Green	d	23p55	07 25		09 55	10 15	10 35	10 55	11 15	11 35	11 55	12 15	12 35	12 55		18 55	19 15	19 35	19 55	20 15	20 35
Queen's Park (London) ⊖	d	23p57	07 27		09 57	10 17	10 37	10 57	11 17	11 37	11 57	12 17	12 37	12 57		18 57	19 17	19 37	19 57	20 17	20 37
Kilburn High Road	d	23p59	07 29		09 59	10 19	10 39	10 59	11 19	11 39	11 59	12 19	12 39	12 59		18 59	19 19	19 39	19 59	20 19	20 39
South Hampstead	d	00 01	07 31		10 01	10 21	10 41	11 01	11 21	11 41	12 01	12 21	12 41	13 01		19 01	19 21	19 41	20 01	20 21	20 41
London Euston 15 ⊖	a	00 10	07 40		10 10	10 30	10 50	11 13	11 30	11 50	12 11	12 31	12 50	13 10		19 10	19 31	19 49	20 10	20 31	20 49

A 19 August, 26 August

B not from 19 August until 26 August

Stations Harrow & Wealdstone to Queen's Park inclusive are also served by London Underground Bakerloo Line Services

Watford Junction - Harrow & Wealdstone, Queen's Park and London

Sundays from 16 September

Network Diagram - see first Page of Table 59

		LO	LO	LO	LO	LO	LO	LO	LO	LO
Watford Junction	d	20 21	20 41	21 01	21 21	21 41	22 01	22 21	22 51	23 21
Watford High Street	d	20 24	20 44	21 04	21 24	21 44	22 04	22 24	22 54	23 24
Bushey	d	20 26	20 46	21 06	21 26	21 46	22 06	22 26	22 56	23 26
Carpenders Park	d	20 29	20 49	21 09	21 29	21 49	22 09	22 29	22 59	23 29
Hatch End	d	20 32	20 52	21 12	21 32	21 52	22 12	22 32	23 02	23 32
Headstone Lane	d	20 34	20 54	21 14	21 34	21 54	22 14	22 34	23 04	23 34
Harrow & Wealdstone	d	20 37	20 57	21 17	21 37	21 57	22 17	22 37	23 07	23 37
Kenton	d	20 39	20 59	21 19	21 39	21 59	22 19	22 39	23 09	23 39
South Kenton	d	20 41	21 01	21 21	21 41	22 01	22 21	22 41	23 11	23 41
North Wembley	d	20 43	21 03	21 23	21 43	22 03	22 23	22 43	23 13	23 43
Wembley Central	d	20 45	21 05	21 25	21 45	22 05	22 25	22 45	23 15	23 45
Stonebridge Park	d	20 48	21 08	21 28	21 48	22 08	22 28	22 48	23 18	23 48
Harlesden	d	20 50	21 10	21 30	21 50	22 10	22 30	22 50	23 20	23 50
Willesden Jn Low Level	d	20 52	21 12	21 32	21 52	22 12	22 32	22 52	23 22	23 52
Kensal Green	d	20 55	21 15	21 35	21 55	22 15	22 35	22 55	23 25	23 55
Queen's Park (London) ⊖	d	20 57	21 17	21 37	21 57	22 17	22 37	22 57	23 27	23 57
Kilburn High Road	d	20 59	21 19	21 39	21 59	22 19	22 39	22 59	23 29	23 59
South Hampstead	d	21 01	21 21	21 41	22 01	22 21	22 41	23 01	23 31	00 01
London Euston 15 ⊖	a	21 13	21 30	21 51	22 10	22 30	22 49	23 10	23 40	00 12

Stations Harrow & Wealdstone to Queen's Park inclusive are also served by London Underground Bakerloo Line Services

Table 61

Watford Junction - St. Albans

Mondays to Fridays
until 19 October

Miles			LM	LM	LM	LM	LM	LM	LM	LM	LM	LM	LM	LM	LM	LM	LM	LM	LM	LM	LM	LM	LM
0	**Watford Junction**	d	05 57	06 39	07 21	08 04	09 01	09 46	10 31	11 16	12 01	12 46	13 31	14 16	15 01	15 46	16 31	17 21	18 10	18 55	19 38	20 31	21 31
0½	Watford North	d	05 59	06 41	07 23	08 06	09 03	09 48	10 33	11 18	12 03	12 48	13 33	14 18	15 03	15 48	16 33	17 23	18 12	18 57	19 40	20 33	21 33
1¾	Garston (Hertfordshire)	d	06 02	06 44	07 26	08 09	09 06	09 51	10 36	11 21	12 06	12 51	13 36	14 21	15 06	15 51	16 36	17 26	18 15	19 00	19 43	20 36	21 36
3¼	Bricket Wood	d	06 05	06 47	07 29	08 12	09 09	09 54	10 39	11 24	12 09	12 54	13 39	14 24	15 09	15 54	16 39	17 29	18 18	19 03	19 46	20 39	21 39
4½	How Wood	d	06 07	06 49	07 31	08 14	09 11	09 56	10 41	11 26	12 11	12 56	13 41	14 26	15 11	15 56	16 41	17 31	18 20	19 05	19 48	20 41	21 41
5	Park Street	d	06 09	06 51	07 33	08 16	09 13	09 58	10 43	11 28	12 13	12 58	13 43	14 28	15 13	15 58	16 43	17 33	18 22	19 07	19 50	20 43	21 43
6½	**St Albans Abbey**	a	06 13	06 55	07 37	08 20	09 17	10 02	10 47	11 32	12 17	13 02	13 47	14 32	15 17	16 02	16 47	17 37	18 26	19 11	19 54	20 47	21 47

Mondays to Fridays
from 22 October

		LM	LM	LM	LM	LM	LM	LM	LM	LM	LM	LM	LM	LM	LM	LM	LM	LM	LM	LM	LM
Watford Junction	d	05 46	06 32	07 18	08 04	08 53	09 39	10 25	11 25	12 25	13 25	14 15	15 01	15 48	16 35	17 21	18 08	18 54	19 40	20 30	21 31
Watford North	d	05 48	06 34	07 20	08 06	08 55	09 41	10 27	11 27	12 27	13 27	14 17	15 03	15 50	16 37	17 23	18 10	18 56	19 42	20 32	21 33
Garston (Hertfordshire)	d	05 51	06 37	07 23	08 09	08 58	09 44	10 30	11 30	12 30	13 30	14 20	15 06	15 53	16 40	17 26	18 13	18 59	19 45	20 35	21 36
Bricket Wood	d	05 54	06 40	07 26	08 12	09 01	09 47	10 33	11 33	12 33	13 33	14 23	15 09	15 56	16 43	17 29	18 16	19 02	19 48	20 38	21 39
How Wood	d	05 56	06 42	07 28	08 14	09 03	09 49	10 35	11 35	12 35	13 35	14 25	15 11	15 58	16 45	17 31	18 18	19 04	19 50	20 40	21 41
Park Street	d	05 58	06 44	07 30	08 16	09 05	09 51	10 37	11 37	12 37	13 37	14 27	15 13	16 00	16 47	17 33	18 20	19 06	19 52	20 42	21 43
St Albans Abbey	a	06 04	06 50	07 36	08 22	09 11	09 57	10 43	11 43	12 43	13 43	14 33	15 19	16 06	16 53	17 39	18 26	19 12	19 58	20 48	21 49

Saturdays
until 20 October

		LM	LM	LM	LM	LM	LM	LM	LM	LM	LM	LM	LM	LM	LM	LM	LM	LM	LM	LM	LM	LM
Watford Junction	d	06 01	06 45	07 31	08 15	09 01	09 46	10 31	11 16	12 01	12 46	13 31	14 16	15 01	15 46	16 31	17 16	18 01	18 46	19 31	20 31	21 31
Watford North	d	06 03	06 47	07 33	08 17	09 03	09 48	10 33	11 18	12 03	12 48	13 33	14 18	15 03	15 48	16 33	17 18	18 03	18 48	19 33	20 33	21 33
Garston (Hertfordshire)	d	06 06	06 50	07 36	08 20	09 06	09 51	10 36	11 21	12 06	12 51	13 36	14 21	15 06	15 51	16 36	17 21	18 06	18 51	19 36	20 36	21 36
Bricket Wood	d	06 09	06 53	07 39	08 23	09 09	09 54	10 39	11 24	12 09	12 54	13 39	14 24	15 09	15 54	16 39	17 24	18 09	18 54	19 39	20 39	21 39
How Wood	d	06 11	06 55	07 41	08 25	09 11	09 56	10 41	11 26	12 11	12 56	13 41	14 26	15 11	15 56	16 41	17 26	18 11	18 56	19 41	20 41	21 41
Park Street	d	06 13	06 57	07 43	08 27	09 13	09 58	10 43	11 28	12 13	12 58	13 43	14 28	15 13	15 58	16 43	17 28	18 13	18 58	19 43	20 43	21 43
St Albans Abbey	a	06 17	07 01	07 47	08 31	09 17	10 02	10 47	11 32	12 17	13 02	13 47	14 32	15 17	16 02	16 47	17 32	18 17	19 02	19 47	20 47	21 47

Saturdays
from 27 October

		LM	LM	LM	LM	LM	LM	LM	LM	LM	LM	LM	LM	LM	LM	LM	LM	LM	LM	LM	LM
Watford Junction	d	05 49	06 35	07 21	08 07	08 53	09 39	10 25	11 25	12 25	13 25	14 15	15 01	15 48	16 35	17 21	18 08	18 54	19 40	20 30	21 31
Watford North	d	05 51	06 37	07 23	08 09	08 55	09 41	10 27	11 27	12 27	13 27	14 17	15 03	15 50	16 37	17 23	18 10	18 56	19 42	20 32	21 33
Garston (Hertfordshire)	d	05 54	06 40	07 26	08 12	08 58	09 44	10 30	11 30	12 30	13 30	14 20	15 06	15 53	16 40	17 26	18 13	18 59	19 45	20 35	21 36
Bricket Wood	d	05 57	06 43	07 29	08 15	09 01	09 47	10 33	11 33	12 33	13 33	14 23	15 09	15 56	16 43	17 29	18 16	19 02	19 48	20 38	21 39
How Wood	d	05 59	06 45	07 31	08 17	09 03	09 49	10 35	11 35	12 35	13 35	14 25	15 11	15 58	16 45	17 31	18 18	19 04	19 50	20 40	21 41
Park Street	d	06 01	06 47	07 33	08 19	09 05	09 51	10 37	11 37	12 37	13 37	14 27	15 13	16 00	16 47	17 33	18 20	19 06	19 52	20 42	21 43
St Albans Abbey	a	06 07	06 53	07 39	08 25	09 11	09 57	10 43	11 43	12 43	13 43	14 33	15 19	16 06	16 53	17 39	18 26	19 12	19 58	20 48	21 49

Sundays
until 21 October

		LM	LM	LM	LM	LM	LM	LM	LM	LM	LM	LM	LM	LM	LM	LM
Watford Junction	d	08 07	09 07	10 20	11 20	12 07	13 07	14 07	15 07	16 07	17 07	18 07	19 07	20 07	21 02	22 04
Watford North	d	08 09	09 09	10 22	11 22	12 09	13 09	14 09	15 09	16 09	17 09	18 09	19 09	20 09	21 04	22 06
Garston (Hertfordshire)	d	08 12	09 12	10 25	11 25	12 12	13 12	14 12	15 12	16 12	17 12	18 12	19 12	20 12	21 07	22 09
Bricket Wood	d	08 15	09 15	10 28	11 28	12 15	13 15	14 15	15 15	16 15	17 15	18 15	19 15	20 15	21 10	22 12
How Wood	d	08 17	09 17	10 30	11 30	12 17	13 17	14 17	15 17	16 17	17 17	18 17	19 17	20 17	21 12	22 14
Park Street	d	08 19	09 19	10 32	11 32	12 19	13 19	14 19	15 19	16 19	17 19	18 19	19 19	20 19	21 14	22 16
St Albans Abbey	a	08 23	09 23	10 36	11 36	12 23	13 23	14 23	15 23	16 23	17 23	18 23	19 23	20 23	21 18	22 20

Sundays
from 28 October

		LM	LM	LM	LM	LM	LM	LM	LM	LM	LM	LM	LM	LM	LM	LM
Watford Junction	d	08 07	09 07	10 20	11 20	12 07	13 07	14 07	15 07	16 07	17 07	18 07	19 07	20 07	21 02	22 04
Watford North	d	08 09	09 09	10 22	11 22	12 09	13 09	14 09	15 09	16 09	17 09	18 09	19 09	20 09	21 04	22 06
Garston (Hertfordshire)	d	08 12	09 12	10 25	11 25	12 12	13 12	14 12	15 12	16 12	17 12	18 12	19 12	20 12	21 07	22 09
Bricket Wood	d	08 15	09 15	10 28	11 28	12 15	13 15	14 15	15 15	16 15	17 15	18 15	19 15	20 15	21 10	22 12
How Wood	d	08 17	09 17	10 30	11 30	12 17	13 17	14 17	15 17	16 17	17 17	18 17	19 17	20 17	21 12	22 14
Park Street	d	08 19	09 19	10 32	11 32	12 19	13 19	14 19	15 19	16 19	17 19	18 19	19 19	20 19	21 14	22 16
St Albans Abbey	a	08 25	09 25	10 38	11 38	12 25	13 25	14 25	15 25	16 25	17 25	18 25	19 25	20 25	21 20	22 22

For connections from London Euston please refer to Table 66

Table 61

St. Albans - Watford Junction

Mondays to Fridays
until 19 October

Miles			LM	LM	LM	LM	LM	LM	LM	LM	LM	LM	LM	LM	LM	LM	LM	LM	LM	LM	LM	LM	LM
0	**St Albans Abbey**	d	06 18	07 00	07 42	08 25	09 22	10 07	10 52	11 37	12 22	13 07	13 52	14 37	15 22	16 07	16 52	17 42	18 32	19 16	20 00	20 52	21 52
1½	Park Street	d	06 21	07 03	07 45	08 28	09 25	10 10	10 55	11 40	12 25	13 10	13 55	14 40	15 25	16 10	16 55	17 45	18 35	19 19	20 03	20 55	21 55
2¼	How Wood	d	06 23	07 05	07 47	08 30	09 27	10 12	10 57	11 42	12 27	13 12	13 57	14 42	15 27	16 12	16 57	17 47	18 37	19 21	20 05	20 57	21 57
3	Bricket Wood	d	06 26	07 08	07 50	08 33	09 30	10 15	11 00	11 45	12 30	13 15	14 00	14 45	15 30	16 15	17 00	17 50	18 40	19 24	20 08	21 00	22 00
4¾	Garston (Hertfordshire)	d	06 29	07 11	07 53	08 36	09 33	10 18	11 03	11 48	12 33	13 18	14 03	14 48	15 33	16 18	17 03	17 53	18 43	19 27	20 11	21 03	22 03
5½	Watford North	d	06 31	07 13	07 55	08 38	09 35	10 20	11 05	11 50	12 35	13 20	14 05	14 50	15 35	16 20	17 05	17 55	18 45	19 29	20 13	21 05	22 05
6½	**Watford Junction**	a	06 34	07 16	07 58	08 41	09 38	10 23	11 08	11 53	12 38	13 23	14 08	14 53	15 38	16 24	17 08	17 58	18 48	19 32	20 16	21 08	22 08

Mondays to Fridays
from 22 October

		LM	LM	LM	LM	LM	LM	LM	LM	LM	LM	LM	LM	LM	LM	LM	LM	LM	LM	LM	LM
St Albans Abbey	d	06 09	06 55	07 41	08 27	09 16	10 02	10 48	11 48	12 48	13 48	14 38	15 24	16 11	16 58	17 44	18 31	19 17	20 03	20 53	21 54
Park Street	d	06 12	06 58	07 44	08 30	09 19	10 05	10 51	11 51	12 51	13 51	14 41	15 27	16 14	17 01	17 47	18 34	19 20	20 06	20 56	21 57
How Wood	d	06 14	07 00	07 46	08 32	09 21	10 07	10 53	11 53	12 53	13 53	14 43	15 29	16 16	17 03	17 49	18 36	19 22	20 08	20 58	21 59
Bricket Wood	d	06 17	07 03	07 49	08 35	09 24	10 10	10 56	11 56	12 56	13 56	14 46	15 32	16 19	17 06	17 52	18 39	19 25	20 11	21 01	22 02
Garston (Hertfordshire)	d	06 20	07 06	07 52	08 38	09 27	10 13	10 59	11 59	12 59	13 59	14 49	15 35	16 22	17 09	17 55	18 42	19 28	20 14	21 04	22 05
Watford North	d	06 22	07 08	07 54	08 40	09 29	10 15	11 01	12 01	13 01	14 01	14 51	15 37	16 24	17 11	17 57	18 44	19 30	20 16	21 06	22 07
Watford Junction	a	06 27	07 13	07 59	08 45	09 34	10 20	11 06	12 06	13 06	14 06	14 56	15 42	16 29	17 16	18 02	18 49	19 35	20 21	21 10	22 12

Saturdays
until 20 October

		LM	LM	LM	LM	LM	LM	LM	LM	LM	LM	LM	LM	LM	LM	LM	LM	LM	LM	LM	LM	LM
St Albans Abbey	d	06 22	07 06	07 52	08 36	09 22	10 07	10 52	11 37	12 22	13 07	13 52	14 37	15 22	16 07	16 52	17 37	18 22	19 07	19 52	20 52	21 52
Park Street	d	06 25	07 09	07 55	08 39	09 25	10 10	10 55	11 40	12 25	13 10	13 55	14 40	15 25	16 10	16 55	17 40	18 25	19 10	19 55	20 55	21 55
How Wood	d	06 27	07 11	07 57	08 41	09 27	10 12	10 57	11 42	12 27	13 12	13 57	14 42	15 27	16 12	16 57	17 42	18 27	19 12	19 57	20 57	21 57
Bricket Wood	d	06 30	07 14	08 00	08 44	09 30	10 15	11 00	11 45	12 30	13 15	14 00	14 45	15 30	16 15	17 00	17 45	18 30	19 15	20 00	21 00	22 00
Garston (Hertfordshire)	d	06 33	07 17	08 03	08 47	09 33	10 18	11 03	11 48	12 33	13 18	14 03	14 48	15 33	16 18	17 03	17 48	18 33	19 18	20 03	21 03	22 03
Watford North	d	06 35	07 19	08 05	08 49	09 35	10 20	11 05	11 50	12 35	13 20	14 05	14 50	15 35	16 20	17 05	17 50	18 35	19 20	20 05	21 05	22 05
Watford Junction	a	06 38	07 22	08 08	08 52	09 38	10 23	11 08	11 53	12 38	13 23	14 08	14 53	15 38	16 23	17 08	17 53	18 38	19 23	20 08	21 08	22 08

Saturdays
from 27 October

		LM	LM	LM	LM	LM	LM	LM	LM	LM	LM	LM	LM	LM	LM	LM	LM	LM	LM	LM	LM
St Albans Abbey	d	06 12	06 58	07 44	08 30	09 16	10 02	10 48	11 48	12 48	13 48	14 38	15 24	16 11	16 58	17 44	18 31	19 17	20 03	20 53	21 54
Park Street	d	06 15	07 01	07 47	08 33	09 19	10 05	10 51	11 51	12 51	13 51	14 41	15 27	16 14	17 01	17 47	18 34	19 20	20 06	20 56	21 57
How Wood	d	06 17	07 03	07 49	08 35	09 21	10 07	10 53	11 53	12 53	13 53	14 43	15 29	16 16	17 03	17 49	18 36	19 22	20 08	20 58	21 59
Bricket Wood	d	06 20	07 06	07 52	08 38	09 24	10 10	10 56	11 56	12 56	13 56	14 46	15 32	16 19	17 06	17 52	18 39	19 25	20 11	21 01	22 02
Garston (Hertfordshire)	d	06 23	07 09	07 55	08 41	09 27	10 13	10 59	11 59	12 59	13 59	14 49	15 35	16 22	17 09	17 55	18 42	19 28	20 14	21 04	22 05
Watford North	d	06 25	07 11	07 57	08 43	09 29	10 15	11 01	12 01	13 01	14 01	14 51	15 37	16 24	17 11	17 57	18 44	19 30	20 16	21 06	22 07
Watford Junction	a	06 30	07 16	08 02	08 48	09 34	10 20	11 06	12 06	13 06	14 06	14 56	15 42	16 29	17 16	18 02	18 49	19 35	20 21	21 10	22 12

Sundays
until 21 October

		LM	LM	LM	LM	LM	LM	LM	LM	LM	LM	LM	LM	LM	LM	LM
St Albans Abbey	d	08 28	09 28	10 42	11 42	12 28	13 28	14 28	15 28	16 28	17 28	18 28	19 28	20 28	21 23	22 25
Park Street	d	08 31	09 31	10 45	11 45	12 31	13 31	14 31	15 31	16 31	17 31	18 31	19 31	20 31	21 26	22 28
How Wood	d	08 33	09 33	10 47	11 47	12 33	13 33	14 33	15 33	16 33	17 33	18 33	19 33	20 33	21 28	22 30
Bricket Wood	d	08 36	09 36	10 50	11 50	12 36	13 36	14 36	15 36	16 36	17 36	18 36	19 36	20 36	21 31	22 33
Garston (Hertfordshire)	d	08 39	09 39	10 53	11 53	12 39	13 39	14 39	15 39	16 39	17 39	18 39	19 39	20 39	21 34	22 36
Watford North	d	08 41	09 41	10 55	11 55	12 41	13 41	14 41	15 41	16 41	17 41	18 41	19 41	20 41	21 36	22 38
Watford Junction	a	08 44	09 44	10 58	11 58	12 44	13 44	14 44	15 44	16 44	17 44	18 44	19 44	20 44	21 39	22 41

Sundays
from 28 October

		LM	LM	LM	LM	LM	LM	LM	LM	LM	LM	LM	LM	LM	LM	LM
St Albans Abbey	d	08 30	09 30	10 43	11 43	12 30	13 30	14 30	15 30	16 30	17 30	18 30	19 30	20 30	21 25	22 27
Park Street	d	08 33	09 33	10 46	11 46	12 33	13 33	14 33	15 33	16 33	17 33	18 33	19 33	20 33	21 28	22 30
How Wood	d	08 35	09 35	10 48	11 48	12 35	13 35	14 35	15 35	16 35	17 35	18 35	19 35	20 35	21 30	22 32
Bricket Wood	d	08 38	09 38	10 51	11 51	12 38	13 38	14 38	15 38	16 38	17 38	18 38	19 38	20 38	21 33	22 35
Garston (Hertfordshire)	d	08 41	09 41	10 54	11 54	12 41	13 41	14 41	15 41	16 41	17 41	18 41	19 41	20 41	21 36	22 38
Watford North	d	08 43	09 43	10 56	11 56	12 43	13 43	14 43	15 43	16 43	17 43	18 43	19 43	20 43	21 38	22 40
Watford Junction	a	08 48	09 48	11 00	12 01	12 47	13 47	14 47	15 47	16 47	17 47	18 47	19 47	20 48	21 43	22 45

For connections to London Euston please refer to Table 66

Gospel Oak - Barking

Mondays to Fridays

until 26 July

Network Diagram - see first Page of Table 59

Miles			LO MX	LO	LO	LO	LO	LO	LO	LO	LO	LO	LO	LO	LO	LO	LO	LO	LO	LO	LO	LO	LO
0	**Gospel Oak**	d	23p35	06 20	06 35	06 50	07 05	07 20	07 35	07 50	08 05	08 20	08 35	08 50	09 05	09 20	09 35	09 50	10 05	10 20	10 35	10 50	11 05
1¼	Upper Holloway	d	23p39	06 24	06 39	06 54	07 09	07 24	07 39	07 54	08 09	08 24	08 39	08 54	09 09	09 24	09 39	09 54	10 09	10 24	10 39	10 54	11 09
2	Crouch Hill	d	23p42	06 27	06 42	06 57	07 12	07 27	07 42	07 57	08 12	08 27	08 42	08 57	09 12	09 27	09 42	09 57	10 12	10 27	10 42	10 57	11 12
3	Harringay Green Lanes	d	23p45	06 30	06 45	07 00	07 15	07 30	07 45	08 00	08 15	08 30	08 45	09 00	09 15	09 30	09 45	10 00	10 15	10 30	10 45	11 00	11 15
4¼	South Tottenham	d	23p48	06 33	06 48	07 03	07 18	07 33	07 48	08 03	08 18	08 33	08 48	09 03	09 18	09 33	09 48	10 03	10 18	10 33	10 48	11 03	11 18
5¾	Blackhorse Road ⊖	d	23p51	06 36	06 51	07 06	07 21	07 36	07 51	08 06	08 21	08 36	08 51	09 06	09 21	09 36	09 51	10 06	10 21	10 36	10 51	11 06	11 21
6½	Walthamstow Queens Road	d	23p54	06 39	06 54	07 09	07 24	07 39	07 54	08 09	08 24	08 39	08 54	09 09	09 24	09 39	09 54	10 09	10 24	10 39	10 54	11 09	11 24
7½	Leyton Midland Road	d	23p57	06 42	06 57	07 12	07 27	07 42	07 57	08 12	08 27	08 42	08 57	09 12	09 27	09 42	09 57	10 12	10 27	10 42	10 57	11 12	11 27
8¼	Leytonstone High Road	d	23p59	06 45	07 00	07 15	07 30	07 45	08 00	08 15	08 30	08 45	09 00	09 15	09 30	09 45	10 00	10 15	10 30	10 45	11 00	11 15	11 30
9½	Wanstead Park	d	00 03	06 48	07 03	07 18	07 33	07 48	08 03	08 18	08 33	08 48	09 03	09 18	09 33	09 48	10 03	10 18	10 33	10 48	11 03	11 18	11 33
10½	Woodgrange Park	d	00 05	06 50	07 05	07 20	07 35	07 50	08 05	08 20	08 35	08 50	09 05	09 20	09 35	09 50	10 05	10 20	10 35	10 50	11 05	11 20	11 35
12¼	**Barking** ⊖	a	00 14	06 57	07 11	07 27	07 41	07 56	08 11	08 26	08 42	08 56	09 11	09 26	09 41	09 56	10 12	10 26	10 41	10 56	11 11	11 26	11 41

		LO	LO	LO	LO	LO	LO		LO	LO	LO	LO	LO	LO	LO	LO	LO	LO	LO	LO	LO	LO
Gospel Oak	d	11 20	11 35	11 50	12 05	12 20	12 35	and at the same minutes past each hour until	18 35	18 50	19 05	19 20	19 35	19 50	20 05	20 20	20 35	20 50	21 05	21 20	21 35	21 50
Upper Holloway	d	11 24	11 39	11 54	12 09	12 24	12 39		18 39	18 54	19 09	19 24	19 39	19 54	20 09	20 24	20 39	20 54	21 09	21 24	21 39	21 54
Crouch Hill	d	11 27	11 42	11 57	12 12	12 27	12 42		18 42	18 57	19 12	19 27	19 42	19 57	20 12	20 27	20 42	20 57	21 12	21 27	21 42	21 57
Harringay Green Lanes	d	11 30	11 45	12 00	12 15	12 30	12 45		18 45	19 00	19 15	19 30	19 45	20 00	20 15	20 30	20 45	21 00	21 15	21 30	21 45	22 00
South Tottenham	d	11 33	11 48	12 03	12 18	12 33	12 48		18 48	19 03	19 18	19 33	19 48	20 03	20 18	20 33	20 48	21 03	21 18	21 33	21 48	22 03
Blackhorse Road ⊖	d	11 36	11 51	12 06	12 21	12 36	12 51		18 51	19 06	19 21	19 36	19 51	20 06	20 21	20 36	20 51	21 06	21 21	21 36	21 51	22 06
Walthamstow Queens Road	d	11 39	11 54	12 09	12 24	12 39	12 54		18 54	19 09	19 24	19 39	19 54	20 09	20 24	20 39	20 54	21 09	21 24	21 39	21 54	22 09
Leyton Midland Road	d	11 42	11 57	12 12	12 27	12 42	12 57		18 57	19 12	19 27	19 42	19 57	20 12	20 27	20 42	20 57	21 12	21 27	21 42	21 57	22 12
Leytonstone High Road	d	11 45	12 00	12 15	12 30	12 45	13 00		19 00	19 15	19 30	19 45	20 00	20 15	20 30	20 45	21 00	21 15	21 30	21 45	22 00	22 15
Wanstead Park	d	11 48	12 03	12 18	12 33	12 48	13 03		19 03	19 18	19 33	19 48	20 03	20 18	20 33	20 48	21 03	21 18	21 33	21 48	22 03	22 18
Woodgrange Park	d	11 50	12 05	12 20	12 35	12 50	13 05		19 05	19 20	19 35	19 50	20 05	20 20	20 35	20 50	21 05	21 20	21 35	21 50	22 05	22 20
Barking ⊖	a	11 56	12 12	12 26	12 41	12 56	13 11		19 11	19 26	19 41	19 57	20 11	20 26	20 42	20 56	21 11	21 26	21 41	21 56	22 11	22 26

		LO	LO	LO	LO
Gospel Oak	d	22 05	22 35	23 05	23 35
Upper Holloway	d	22 09	22 39	23 09	23 39
Crouch Hill	d	22 12	22 42	23 12	23 42
Harringay Green Lanes	d	22 15	22 45	23 15	23 45
South Tottenham	d	22 18	22 48	23 18	23 48
Blackhorse Road ⊖	d	22 21	22 51	23 21	23 51
Walthamstow Queens Road	d	22 24	22 54	23 24	23 54
Leyton Midland Road	d	22 27	22 57	23 27	23 57
Leytonstone High Road	d	22 30	23 00	23 30	23 59
Wanstead Park	d	22 33	23 03	23 33	00 03
Woodgrange Park	d	22 35	23 05	23 35	00 05
Barking ⊖	a	22 42	23 11	23 41	00 14

Mondays to Fridays

27 July to 10 August

		LO A	LO MX B	LO	LO	LO	LO	LO	LO	LO	LO	LO	LO	LO	LO	LO	LO	LO	LO	LO	LO	LO	LO
Gospel Oak	d	23p35	23p35	06 20	06 35	06 50	07 05	07 20	07 35	07 50	08 05	08 20	08 35	08 50	09 05	09 20	09 35	09 50	10 05	10 20	10 35	10 50	11 05
Upper Holloway	d	23p39	23p39	06 24	06 39	06 54	07 09	07 24	07 39	07 54	08 09	08 24	08 39	08 54	09 09	09 24	09 39	09 54	10 09	10 24	10 39	10 54	11 09
Crouch Hill	d	23p42	23p42	06 27	06 42	06 57	07 12	07 27	07 42	07 57	08 12	08 27	08 42	08 57	09 12	09 27	09 42	09 57	10 12	10 27	10 42	10 57	11 12
Harringay Green Lanes	d	23p45	23p45	06 30	06 45	07 00	07 15	07 30	07 45	08 00	08 15	08 30	08 45	09 00	09 15	09 30	09 45	10 00	10 15	10 30	10 45	11 00	11 15
South Tottenham	d	23p48	23p48	06 33	06 48	07 03	07 18	07 33	07 48	08 03	08 18	08 33	08 48	09 03	09 18	09 33	09 48	10 03	10 18	10 33	10 48	11 03	11 18
Blackhorse Road ⊖	d	23p51	23p51	06 36	06 51	07 06	07 21	07 36	07 51	08 06	08 21	08 36	08 51	09 06	09 21	09 36	09 51	10 06	10 21	10 36	10 51	11 06	11 21
Walthamstow Queens Road	d	23p54	23p54	06 39	06 54	07 09	07 24	07 39	07 54	08 09	08 24	08 39	08 54	09 09	09 24	09 39	09 54	10 09	10 24	10 39	10 54	11 09	11 24
Leyton Midland Road	d	23p57	23p57	06 42	06 57	07 12	07 27	07 42	07 57	08 12	08 27	08 42	08 57	09 12	09 27	09 42	09 57	10 12	10 27	10 42	10 57	11 12	11 27
Leytonstone High Road	d	23p59	00 01	06 45	07 00	07 15	07 30	07 45	08 00	08 15	08 30	08 45	09 00	09 15	09 30	09 45	10 00	10 15	10 30	10 45	11 00	11 15	11 30
Wanstead Park	d	00 03	00 03	06 48	07 03	07 18	07 33	07 48	08 03	08 18	08 33	08 48	09 03	09 18	09 33	09 48	10 03	10 18	10 33	10 48	11 03	11 18	11 33
Woodgrange Park	d	00 05	00 05	06 50	07 05	07 20	07 35	07 50	08 05	08 20	08 35	08 50	09 05	09 20	09 35	09 50	10 05	10 20	10 35	10 50	11 05	11 20	11 35
Barking ⊖	a	00 14	00 14	06 59	07 14	07 30	07 44	07 59	08 14	08 29	08 44	08 59	09 15	09 29	09 44	09 59	10 14	10 29	10 44	11 01	11 14	11 29	11 44

		LO	LO	LO	LO	LO	LO	LO	LO	LO	LO	LO	LO	LO	LO	LO		LO	LO	LO	LO	LO
Gospel Oak	d	11 20	11 35	11 50	12 05	12 20	12 35	12 50	13 05	13 20	13 35	13 50	14 05	14 20	14 35	14 50	and at the same minutes past each hour until	17 50	18 05	18 20	18 35	18 50
Upper Holloway	d	11 24	11 39	11 54	12 09	12 24	12 39	12 54	13 09	13 24	13 39	13 55	14 09	14 24	14 39	14 54		17 54	18 09	18 24	18 39	18 54
Crouch Hill	d	11 27	11 42	11 57	12 12	12 27	12 42	12 57	13 12	13 27	13 42	13 57	14 12	14 27	14 42	14 57		17 57	18 12	18 27	18 42	18 57
Harringay Green Lanes	d	11 30	11 45	12 00	12 15	12 30	12 45	13 00	13 15	13 30	13 45	14 00	14 15	14 30	14 45	15 00		18 00	18 15	18 30	18 45	19 00
South Tottenham	d	11 33	11 48	12 03	12 18	12 33	12 48	13 03	13 18	13 33	13 48	14 03	14 18	14 33	14 48	15 03		18 03	18 18	18 33	18 48	19 03
Blackhorse Road ⊖	d	11 36	11 51	12 06	12 21	12 36	12 51	13 06	13 21	13 36	13 51	14 07	14 21	14 36	14 51	15 06		18 06	18 21	18 36	18 51	19 06
Walthamstow Queens Road	d	11 39	11 54	12 09	12 24	12 39	12 54	13 09	13 24	13 39	13 54	14 09	14 24	14 39	14 54	15 09		18 09	18 24	18 39	18 54	19 09
Leyton Midland Road	d	11 42	11 57	12 12	12 27	12 42	12 57	13 12	13 27	13 42	13 57	14 13	14 27	14 42	14 57	15 12		18 12	18 27	18 42	18 57	19 12
Leytonstone High Road	d	11 45	12 00	12 15	12 30	12 45	13 00	13 15	13 30	13 45	14 00	14 15	14 30	14 45	15 00	15 15		18 15	18 30	18 45	19 00	19 15
Wanstead Park	d	11 48	12 03	12 18	12 33	12 48	13 03	13 18	13 33	13 48	14 03	14 18	14 33	14 48	15 03	15 18		18 18	18 33	18 48	19 03	19 18
Woodgrange Park	d	11 50	12 05	12 20	12 35	12 50	13 05	13 20	13 35	13 50	14 05	14 21	14 35	14 50	15 05	15 20		18 20	18 35	18 50	19 05	19 20
Barking ⊖	a	11 59	12 14	12 29	12 44	12 59	13 14	13 29	13 44	13 59	14 14	14 30	14 44	14 59	15 14	15 29		18 29	18 44	18 59	19 14	19 31

		LO	LO	LO	LO	LO	LO	LO	LO	LO	LO	LO	LO	LO	LO	LO	LO
Gospel Oak	d	19 05	19 20	19 35	19 50	20 05	20 20	20 35	20 50	21 05	21 20	21 35	21 50	22 05	22 35	23 05	23 35
Upper Holloway	d	19 09	19 24	19 39	19 54	20 09	20 24	20 39	20 54	21 09	21 24	21 39	21 54	22 09	22 39	23 09	23 39
Crouch Hill	d	19 12	19 27	19 42	19 57	20 12	20 27	20 42	20 57	21 12	21 27	21 42	21 57	22 12	22 42	23 12	23 42
Harringay Green Lanes	d	19 15	19 30	19 45	20 00	20 15	20 30	20 45	21 00	21 15	21 30	21 45	22 00	22 15	22 45	23 15	23 45
South Tottenham	d	19 18	19 33	19 48	20 03	20 18	20 33	20 48	21 03	21 18	21 33	21 48	22 03	22 18	22 48	23 18	23 48
Blackhorse Road ⊖	d	19 21	19 36	19 51	20 06	20 21	20 36	20 51	21 06	21 21	21 36	21 51	22 06	22 21	22 51	23 21	23 51
Walthamstow Queens Road	d	19 24	19 39	19 54	20 09	20 24	20 39	20 54	21 09	21 24	21 39	21 54	22 09	22 24	22 54	23 24	23 54
Leyton Midland Road	d	19 27	19 42	19 57	20 12	20 27	20 42	20 57	21 12	21 27	21 42	21 57	22 12	22 27	22 57	23 27	23 57
Leytonstone High Road	d	19 30	19 45	20 00	20 15	20 30	20 45	21 00	21 15	21 30	21 45	22 00	22 15	22 30	23 00	23 30	00 01
Wanstead Park	d	19 33	19 48	20 03	20 18	20 33	20 48	21 03	21 18	21 33	21 48	22 03	22 18	22 33	23 03	23 33	00 03
Woodgrange Park	d	19 35	19 50	20 05	20 20	20 35	20 50	21 05	21 20	21 35	21 50	22 05	22 20	22 35	23 05	23 35	00 05
Barking ⊖	a	19 44	19 59	20 14	20 29	20 45	20 59	21 14	21 29	21 44	21 59	22 14	22 29	22 44	23 14	23 44	00 14

A 27 July

B from 31 July until 10 August

Table 62

Gospel Oak - Barking

Mondays to Fridays

13 August to 28 August

Network Diagram - see first Page of Table 59

		LO MX	LO	LO	LO	LO	LO	LO	LO	LO	LO	LO	LO	LO	LO	LO	LO	LO	LO	LO	LO	LO	LO
Gospel Oak	d	23p35	06 20	06 35	06 50	07 05	07 20	07 35	07 50	08 05	08 20	08 35	08 50	09 05	09 20	09 35	09 50	10 05	10 20	10 35	10 50	11 05	11 20
Upper Holloway	d	23p39	06 24	06 39	06 54	07 09	07 24	07 39	07 54	08 09	08 24	08 39	08 54	09 09	09 24	09 39	09 54	10 09	10 24	10 39	10 54	11 09	11 24
Crouch Hill	d	23p42	06 27	06 42	06 57	07 12	07 27	07 42	07 57	08 12	08 27	08 42	08 57	09 12	09 27	09 42	09 57	10 12	10 27	10 42	10 57	11 12	11 27
Harringay Green Lanes	d	23p45	06 30	06 45	07 00	07 15	07 30	07 45	08 00	08 15	08 30	08 45	09 00	09 15	09 30	09 45	10 00	10 15	10 30	10 45	11 00	11 15	11 30
South Tottenham	d	23p48	06 33	06 48	07 03	07 18	07 33	07 48	08 03	08 18	08 33	08 48	09 03	09 18	09 33	09 48	10 03	10 18	10 33	10 48	11 03	11 18	11 33
Blackhorse Road ⊖	d	23p51	06 36	06 51	07 06	07 21	07 36	07 51	08 06	08 21	08 36	08 51	09 06	09 21	09 36	09 51	10 06	10 21	10 36	10 51	11 06	11 21	11 36
Walthamstow Queens Road	d	23p54	06 39	06 54	07 09	07 24	07 39	07 54	08 09	08 24	08 39	08 54	09 09	09 24	09 39	09 54	10 09	10 24	10 39	10 54	11 09	11 24	11 39
Leyton Midland Road	d	23p57	06 42	06 57	07 12	07 27	07 42	07 57	08 12	08 27	08 42	08 57	09 12	09 27	09 42	09 57	10 12	10 27	10 42	10 57	11 12	11 27	11 42
Leytonstone High Road	d	23p59	06 45	07 00	07 15	07 30	07 45	08 00	08 15	08 30	08 45	09 00	09 15	09 30	09 45	10 00	10 15	10 30	10 45	11 00	11 15	11 30	11 45
Wanstead Park	d	00 03	06 48	07 03	07 18	07 33	07 48	08 03	08 18	08 33	08 48	09 03	09 18	09 33	09 48	10 03	10 18	10 33	10 48	11 03	11 18	11 33	11 48
Woodgrange Park	d	00 05	06 50	07 05	07 20	07 35	07 50	08 05	08 20	08 35	08 50	09 05	09 20	09 35	09 50	10 05	10 20	10 35	10 50	11 05	11 20	11 35	11 50
Barking ⊖	a	00 14	06 57	07 11	07 27	07 41	07 56	08 11	08 26	08 42	08 56	09 11	09 26	09 41	09 56	10 12	10 26	10 41	10 56	11 11	11 26	11 41	11 56

		LO	LO	LO	LO	LO		LO	LO	LO	LO	LO	LO	LO	LO	LO	LO	LO	LO	LO	LO	LO
Gospel Oak	d	11 35	11 50	12 05	12 20	12 35	and at the same minutes past each hour until	18 35	18 50	19 05	19 20	19 35	19 50	20 05	20 20	20 35	20 50	21 05	21 20	21 35	21 50	22 05
Upper Holloway	d	11 39	11 54	12 09	12 24	12 39		18 39	18 54	19 09	19 24	19 39	19 54	20 09	20 24	20 39	20 54	21 09	21 24	21 39	21 54	22 09
Crouch Hill	d	11 42	11 57	12 12	12 27	12 42		18 42	18 57	19 12	19 27	19 42	19 57	20 12	20 27	20 42	20 57	21 12	21 27	21 42	21 57	22 12
Harringay Green Lanes	d	11 45	12 00	12 15	12 30	12 45		18 45	19 00	19 15	19 30	19 45	20 00	20 15	20 30	20 45	21 00	21 15	21 30	21 45	22 00	22 15
South Tottenham	d	11 48	12 03	12 18	12 33	12 48		18 48	19 03	19 18	19 33	19 48	20 03	20 18	20 33	20 48	21 03	21 18	21 33	21 48	22 03	22 18
Blackhorse Road ⊖	d	11 51	12 06	12 21	12 36	12 51		18 51	19 06	19 21	19 36	19 51	20 06	20 21	20 36	20 51	21 06	21 21	21 36	21 51	22 06	22 21
Walthamstow Queens Road	d	11 54	12 09	12 24	12 39	12 54		18 54	19 09	19 24	19 39	19 54	20 09	20 24	20 39	20 54	21 09	21 24	21 39	21 54	22 09	22 24
Leyton Midland Road	d	11 57	12 12	12 27	12 42	12 57		18 57	19 12	19 27	19 42	19 57	20 12	20 27	20 42	20 57	21 12	21 27	21 42	21 57	22 12	22 27
Leytonstone High Road	d	12 00	12 15	12 30	12 45	13 00		19 00	19 15	19 30	19 45	20 00	20 15	20 30	20 45	21 00	21 15	21 30	21 45	22 00	22 15	22 30
Wanstead Park	d	12 03	12 18	12 33	12 48	13 03		19 03	19 18	19 33	19 48	20 03	20 18	20 33	20 48	21 03	21 18	21 33	21 48	22 03	22 18	22 33
Woodgrange Park	d	12 05	12 20	12 35	12 50	13 05		19 05	19 20	19 35	19 50	20 05	20 20	20 35	20 50	21 05	21 20	21 35	21 50	22 05	22 20	22 35
Barking ⊖	a	12 12	12 26	12 41	12 56	13 11		19 11	19 26	19 41	19 57	20 11	20 26	20 42	20 56	21 11	21 26	21 41	21 56	22 11	22 26	22 42

		LO	LO	LO
Gospel Oak	d	22 35	23 05	23 35
Upper Holloway	d	22 39	23 09	23 39
Crouch Hill	d	22 42	23 12	23 42
Harringay Green Lanes	d	22 45	23 15	23 45
South Tottenham	d	22 48	23 18	23 48
Blackhorse Road ⊖	d	22 51	23 21	23 51
Walthamstow Queens Road	d	22 54	23 24	23 54
Leyton Midland Road	d	22 57	23 27	23 57
Leytonstone High Road	d	23 00	23 30	23 59
Wanstead Park	d	23 03	23 33	00 03
Woodgrange Park	d	23 05	23 35	00 05
Barking ⊖	a	23 11	23 41	00 14

Mondays to Fridays

29 August to 7 September

		LO A	LO B	LO	LO	LO	LO	LO	LO	LO	LO	LO	LO	LO	LO	LO	LO	LO	LO	LO	LO	LO	LO
Gospel Oak	d	23p35	23p35	06 20	06 35	06 50	07 05	07 20	07 35	07 50	08 05	08 20	08 35	08 50	09 05	09 20	09 35	09 50	10 05	10 20	10 35	10 50	11 05
Upper Holloway	d	23p39	23p39	06 24	06 39	06 54	07 09	07 24	07 39	07 54	08 09	08 24	08 39	08 54	09 09	09 27	09 39	09 54	10 09	10 24	10 39	10 54	11 09
Crouch Hill	d	23p42	23p42	06 27	06 42	06 57	07 12	07 27	07 42	07 57	08 12	08 27	08 42	08 57	09 12	09 30	09 42	09 57	10 12	10 27	10 42	10 57	11 12
Harringay Green Lanes	d	23p45	23p45	06 30	06 45	07 00	07 15	07 30	07 45	08 00	08 15	08 30	08 45	09 00	09 15	09 33	09 45	10 00	10 15	10 30	10 45	11 00	11 15
South Tottenham	d	23p48	23p48	06 33	06 48	07 03	07 18	07 33	07 48	08 03	08 18	08 33	08 48	09 03	09 18	09 36	09 48	10 03	10 18	10 33	10 48	11 03	11 18
Blackhorse Road ⊖	d	23p51	23p51	06 36	06 51	07 06	07 21	07 36	07 51	08 06	08 21	08 36	08 51	09 06	09 21	09 39	09 51	10 06	10 21	10 36	10 51	11 06	11 21
Walthamstow Queens Road	d	23p54	23p54	06 39	06 54	07 09	07 24	07 39	07 54	08 09	08 24	08 39	08 54	09 09	09 24	09 42	09 54	10 09	10 24	10 39	10 54	11 09	11 24
Leyton Midland Road	d	23p57	23p57	06 42	06 57	07 12	07 27	07 42	07 57	08 12	08 27	08 42	08 57	09 12	09 27	09 45	09 57	10 12	10 27	10 42	10 57	11 12	11 27
Leytonstone High Road	d	23p59	00 01	06 45	07 00	07 15	07 30	07 45	08 00	08 15	08 30	08 45	09 00	09 15	09 30	09 48	10 00	10 15	10 30	10 45	11 00	11 15	11 30
Wanstead Park	d	00 03	00 03	06 48	07 03	07 18	07 33	07 48	08 03	08 18	08 33	08 48	09 03	09 18	09 33	09 51	10 03	10 18	10 33	10 48	11 03	11 18	11 33
Woodgrange Park	d	00 05	00 05	06 50	07 05	07 20	07 35	07 50	08 05	08 20	08 35	08 50	09 05	09 20	09 35	09 53	10 05	10 20	10 35	10 50	11 05	11 20	11 35
Barking ⊖	a	00 14	00 14	06 59	07 14	07 30	07 44	07 59	08 14	08 29	08 44	08 59	09 15	09 29	09 44	10 02	10 14	10 29	10 44	11 01	11 14	11 29	11 44

		LO	LO	LO	LO	LO	LO	LO	LO	LO	LO	LO	LO	LO	LO	LO		LO	LO	LO	LO	LO
Gospel Oak	d	11 20	11 35	11 50	12 05	12 20	12 35	12 50	13 05	13 20	13 35	13 50	14 05	14 20	14 35	14 50	and at the same minutes past each hour until	17 50	18 05	18 20	18 35	18 50
Upper Holloway	d	11 24	11 39	11 54	12 09	12 24	12 39	12 54	13 09	13 24	13 39	13 55	14 09	14 24	14 39	14 54		17 54	18 09	18 24	18 39	18 54
Crouch Hill	d	11 27	11 42	11 57	12 12	12 27	12 42	12 57	13 12	13 27	13 42	13 57	14 12	14 27	14 42	14 57		17 57	18 12	18 27	18 42	18 57
Harringay Green Lanes	d	11 30	11 45	12 00	12 15	12 30	12 45	13 00	13 15	13 30	13 45	14 00	14 15	14 30	14 45	15 00		18 00	18 15	18 30	18 45	19 00
South Tottenham	d	11 33	11 48	12 03	12 18	12 33	12 48	13 03	13 18	13 33	13 48	14 03	14 18	14 33	14 48	15 03		18 03	18 18	18 33	18 48	19 03
Blackhorse Road ⊖	d	11 36	11 51	12 06	12 21	12 36	12 51	13 06	13 21	13 36	13 51	14 07	14 21	14 36	14 51	15 06		18 06	18 21	18 36	18 51	19 06
Walthamstow Queens Road	d	11 39	11 54	12 09	12 24	12 39	12 54	13 09	13 24	13 39	13 54	14 09	14 24	14 39	14 54	15 09		18 09	18 24	18 39	18 54	19 09
Leyton Midland Road	d	11 42	11 57	12 12	12 27	12 42	12 57	13 12	13 27	13 42	13 57	14 13	14 27	14 42	14 57	15 12		18 12	18 27	18 42	18 57	19 12
Leytonstone High Road	d	11 45	12 00	12 15	12 30	12 45	13 00	13 15	13 30	13 45	14 00	14 15	14 30	14 45	15 00	15 15		18 15	18 30	18 45	19 00	19 15
Wanstead Park	d	11 48	12 03	12 18	12 33	12 48	13 03	13 18	13 33	13 48	14 03	14 18	14 33	14 48	15 03	15 18		18 18	18 33	18 48	19 03	19 18
Woodgrange Park	d	11 50	12 05	12 20	12 35	12 50	13 05	13 20	13 35	13 50	14 05	14 21	14 35	14 50	15 05	15 20		18 20	18 35	18 50	19 05	19 20
Barking ⊖	a	11 59	12 14	12 29	12 44	12 59	13 14	13 29	13 44	13 59	14 14	14 30	14 44	14 59	15 14	15 29		18 29	18 44	18 59	19 14	19 31

		LO	LO	LO	LO	LO	LO	LO	LO	LO	LO	LO	LO	LO	LO	LO	LO
Gospel Oak	d	19 05	19 20	19 35	19 50	20 05	20 20	20 35	20 50	21 05	21 20	21 35	21 50	22 05	22 35	23 05	23 35
Upper Holloway	d	19 09	19 24	19 39	19 54	20 09	20 24	20 39	20 54	21 09	21 24	21 39	21 54	22 09	22 39	23 09	23 39
Crouch Hill	d	19 12	19 27	19 42	19 57	20 12	20 27	20 42	20 57	21 12	21 27	21 42	21 57	22 12	22 42	23 12	23 42
Harringay Green Lanes	d	19 15	19 30	19 45	20 00	20 15	20 30	20 45	21 00	21 15	21 30	21 45	22 00	22 15	22 45	23 15	23 45
South Tottenham	d	19 18	19 33	19 48	20 03	20 18	20 33	20 48	21 03	21 18	21 33	21 48	22 03	22 18	22 48	23 18	23 48
Blackhorse Road ⊖	d	19 21	19 36	19 51	20 06	20 21	20 36	20 51	21 06	21 21	21 36	21 51	22 06	22 21	22 51	23 21	23 51
Walthamstow Queens Road	d	19 24	19 39	19 54	20 09	20 24	20 39	20 54	21 09	21 24	21 39	21 54	22 09	22 24	22 54	23 24	23 54
Leyton Midland Road	d	19 27	19 42	19 57	20 12	20 27	20 42	20 57	21 12	21 27	21 42	21 57	22 12	22 27	22 57	23 27	23 57
Leytonstone High Road	d	19 30	19 45	20 00	20 15	20 30	20 45	21 00	21 15	21 30	21 45	22 00	22 15	22 30	23 00	23 30	00 01
Wanstead Park	d	19 33	19 48	20 03	20 18	20 33	20 48	21 03	21 18	21 33	21 48	22 03	22 18	22 33	23 03	23 33	00 03
Woodgrange Park	d	19 35	19 50	20 05	20 20	20 35	20 50	21 05	21 20	21 35	21 50	22 05	22 20	22 35	23 05	23 35	00 05
Barking ⊖	a	19 44	19 59	20 14	20 29	20 45	20 59	21 14	21 29	21 44	21 59	22 14	22 29	22 44	23 14	23 44	00 14

A 29 August

B not 29 August, 3 September

Table 62

Gospel Oak - Barking

Mondays to Fridays
from 10 September

Network Diagram - see first Page of Table 59

		LO MX	LO	LO	LO	LO	LO	LO	LO	LO	LO	LO	LO	LO	LO	LO	LO	LO	LO	LO	LO	LO	LO
Gospel Oak	d	23p35	06 20	06 35	06 50	07 05	07 20	07 35	07 50	08 05	08 20	08 35	08 50	09 05	09 20	09 35	09 50	10 05	10 20	10 35	10 50	11 05	11 20
Upper Holloway	d	23p39	06 24	06 39	06 54	07 09	07 24	07 39	07 54	08 09	08 24	08 39	08 54	09 09	09 24	09 39	09 54	10 09	10 24	10 39	10 54	11 09	11 24
Crouch Hill	d	23p42	06 27	06 42	06 57	07 12	07 27	07 42	07 57	08 12	08 27	08 42	08 57	09 12	09 27	09 42	09 57	10 12	10 27	10 42	10 57	11 12	11 27
Harringay Green Lanes	d	23p45	06 30	06 45	07 00	07 15	07 30	07 45	08 00	08 15	08 30	08 45	09 00	09 15	09 30	09 45	10 00	10 15	10 30	10 45	11 00	11 15	11 30
South Tottenham	d	23p48	06 33	06 48	07 03	07 18	07 33	07 48	08 03	08 18	08 33	08 48	09 03	09 18	09 33	09 48	10 03	10 18	10 33	10 48	11 03	11 18	11 33
Blackhorse Road ⊖	d	23p51	06 36	06 51	07 06	07 21	07 36	07 51	08 06	08 21	08 36	08 51	09 06	09 21	09 36	09 51	10 06	10 21	10 36	10 51	11 06	11 21	11 36
Walthamstow Queens Road	d	23p54	06 39	06 54	07 09	07 24	07 39	07 54	08 09	08 24	08 39	08 54	09 09	09 24	09 39	09 54	10 09	10 24	10 39	10 54	11 09	11 24	11 39
Leyton Midland Road	d	23p57	06 42	06 57	07 12	07 27	07 42	07 57	08 12	08 27	08 42	08 57	09 12	09 27	09 42	09 57	10 12	10 27	10 42	10 57	11 12	11 27	11 42
Leytonstone High Road	d	23p59	06 45	07 00	07 15	07 30	07 45	08 00	08 15	08 30	08 45	09 00	09 15	09 30	09 45	10 00	10 15	10 30	10 45	11 00	11 15	11 30	11 45
Wanstead Park	d	00 03	06 48	07 03	07 18	07 33	07 48	08 03	08 18	08 33	08 48	09 03	09 18	09 33	09 48	10 03	10 18	10 33	10 48	11 03	11 18	11 33	11 48
Woodgrange Park	d	00 05	06 50	07 05	07 20	07 35	07 50	08 05	08 20	08 35	08 50	09 05	09 20	09 35	09 50	10 05	10 20	10 35	10 50	11 05	11 20	11 35	11 50
Barking ⊖	a	00 12	06 57	07 11	07 27	07 41	07 56	08 11	08 26	08 42	08 56	09 11	09 26	09 41	09 56	10 12	10 26	10 41	10 56	11 11	11 26	11 41	11 56

		LO	LO	LO	LO	LO		LO	LO	LO	LO	LO	LO	LO	LO	LO	LO	LO	LO	LO	LO	LO
Gospel Oak	d	11 35	11 50	12 05	12 20	12 35	and at the same minutes past each hour until	18 35	18 50	19 05	19 20	19 35	19 50	20 05	20 20	20 35	20 50	21 05	21 20	21 35	21 50	22 05
Upper Holloway	d	11 39	11 54	12 09	12 24	12 39		18 39	18 54	19 09	19 24	19 39	19 54	20 09	20 24	20 39	20 54	21 09	21 24	21 39	21 54	22 09
Crouch Hill	d	11 42	11 57	12 12	12 27	12 42		18 42	18 57	19 12	19 27	19 42	19 57	20 12	20 27	20 42	20 57	21 12	21 27	21 42	21 57	22 12
Harringay Green Lanes	d	11 45	12 00	12 15	12 30	12 45		18 45	19 00	19 15	19 30	19 45	20 00	20 15	20 30	20 45	21 00	21 15	21 30	21 45	22 00	22 15
South Tottenham	d	11 48	12 03	12 18	12 33	12 48		18 48	19 03	19 18	19 33	19 48	20 03	20 18	20 33	20 48	21 03	21 18	21 33	21 48	22 03	22 18
Blackhorse Road ⊖	d	11 51	12 06	12 21	12 36	12 51		18 51	19 06	19 21	19 36	19 51	20 06	20 21	20 36	20 51	21 06	21 21	21 36	21 51	22 06	22 21
Walthamstow Queens Road	d	11 54	12 09	12 24	12 39	12 54		18 54	19 09	19 24	19 39	19 54	20 09	20 24	20 39	20 54	21 09	21 24	21 39	21 54	22 09	22 24
Leyton Midland Road	d	11 57	12 12	12 27	12 42	12 57		18 57	19 12	19 27	19 42	19 57	20 12	20 27	20 42	20 57	21 12	21 27	21 42	21 57	22 12	22 27
Leytonstone High Road	d	12 00	12 15	12 30	12 45	13 00		19 00	19 15	19 30	19 45	20 00	20 15	20 30	20 45	21 00	21 15	21 30	21 45	22 00	22 15	22 30
Wanstead Park	d	12 03	12 18	12 33	12 48	13 03		19 03	19 18	19 33	19 48	20 03	20 18	20 33	20 48	21 03	21 18	21 33	21 48	22 03	22 18	22 33
Woodgrange Park	d	12 05	12 20	12 35	12 50	13 05		19 05	19 20	19 35	19 50	20 05	20 20	20 35	20 50	21 05	21 20	21 35	21 50	22 05	22 20	22 35
Barking ⊖	a	12 12	12 26	12 41	12 56	13 11		19 11	19 26	19 41	19 57	20 11	20 26	20 42	20 56	21 11	21 26	21 41	21 56	22 11	22 26	22 42

		LO	LO	LO
Gospel Oak	d	22 35	23 05	23 35
Upper Holloway	d	22 39	23 09	23 39
Crouch Hill	d	22 42	23 12	23 42
Harringay Green Lanes	d	22 45	23 15	23 45
South Tottenham	d	22 48	23 18	23 48
Blackhorse Road ⊖	d	22 51	23 21	23 51
Walthamstow Queens Road	d	22 54	23 24	23 54
Leyton Midland Road	d	22 57	23 27	23 57
Leytonstone High Road	d	23 00	23 30	23 59
Wanstead Park	d	23 03	23 33	00 03
Woodgrange Park	d	23 05	23 35	00 05
Barking ⊖	a	23 11	23 41	00 12

Saturdays
until 21 July

		LO	LO	LO	LO	LO	LO		LO	LO	LO	LO	LO	LO	LO	LO		LO	LO	LO	LO
Gospel Oak	d	23p35	06 20	06 35	06 50	07 05	07 20	and at the same minutes past each hour until	10 20	10 35	10 50	11 05	11 20	11 35	11 50	12 05	and at the same minutes past each hour until	15 05	15 20	15 35	15 50
Upper Holloway	d	23p39	06 24	06 39	06 54	07 09	07 24		10 24	10 39	10 54	11 09	11 24	11 39	11 54	12 09		15 09	15 24	15 39	15 54
Crouch Hill	d	23p42	06 27	06 42	06 57	07 12	07 27		10 27	10 42	10 57	11 12	11 27	11 42	11 57	12 12		15 12	15 27	15 42	15 57
Harringay Green Lanes	d	23p45	06 30	06 45	07 00	07 15	07 30		10 30	10 45	11 00	11 15	11 30	11 45	12 00	12 15		15 15	15 30	15 45	16 00
South Tottenham	d	23p48	06 33	06 48	07 03	07 18	07 33		10 33	10 48	11 03	11 18	11 33	11 48	12 03	12 18		15 18	15 33	15 48	16 03
Blackhorse Road ⊖	d	23p51	06 36	06 51	07 06	07 21	07 36		10 36	10 51	11 06	11 21	11 36	11 51	12 06	12 21		15 21	15 36	15 51	16 06
Walthamstow Queens Road	d	23p54	06 39	06 54	07 09	07 24	07 39		10 39	10 54	11 09	11 24	11 39	11 54	12 09	12 24		15 24	15 39	15 54	16 09
Leyton Midland Road	d	23p57	06 42	06 57	07 12	07 27	07 42		10 42	10 57	11 12	11 27	11 42	11 57	12 12	12 27		15 27	15 42	15 57	16 12
Leytonstone High Road	d	23p59	06 45	07 00	07 15	07 30	07 45		10 45	11 00	11 15	11 30	11 45	12 00	12 15	12 30		15 30	15 45	16 00	16 15
Wanstead Park	d	00 03	06 48	07 03	07 18	07 33	07 48		10 48	11 03	11 18	11 33	11 48	12 03	12 18	12 33		15 33	15 48	16 03	16 18
Woodgrange Park	d	00 05	06 50	07 05	07 20	07 35	07 50		10 50	11 05	11 20	11 35	11 50	12 05	12 20	12 35		15 35	15 50	16 05	16 20
Barking ⊖	a	00 14	06 57	07 09	07 24	07 39	07 54		10 54	11 09	11 24	11 42	11 54	12 09	12 24	12 39		15 39	15 54	16 09	16 24

		LO	LO	LO	LO	LO	LO	LO	LO	LO	LO	LO	LO	LO	LO	LO	LO	LO	LO	LO	LO	LO	LO
Gospel Oak	d	16 05	16 20	16 35	16 50	17 05	17 20	17 35	17 50	18 05	18 20	18 35	18 50	19 05	19 20	19 35	19 50	20 05	20 20	20 35	20 50	21 05	21 20
Upper Holloway	d	16 09	16 24	16 39	16 54	17 09	17 24	17 39	17 54	18 09	18 24	18 39	18 54	19 09	19 24	19 39	19 54	20 09	20 24	20 39	20 54	21 09	21 24
Crouch Hill	d	16 12	16 27	16 42	16 57	17 12	17 27	17 42	17 57	18 12	18 27	18 42	18 57	19 12	19 27	19 42	19 57	20 12	20 27	20 42	20 57	21 12	21 27
Harringay Green Lanes	d	16 15	16 30	16 45	17 00	17 15	17 30	17 45	18 00	18 15	18 30	18 45	19 00	19 15	19 30	19 45	20 00	20 15	20 30	20 45	21 00	21 15	21 30
South Tottenham	d	16 18	16 33	16 48	17 03	17 18	17 33	17 48	18 03	18 18	18 33	18 48	19 03	19 18	19 33	19 48	20 03	20 18	20 33	20 48	21 03	21 18	21 33
Blackhorse Road ⊖	d	16 21	16 36	16 51	17 06	17 21	17 36	17 51	18 06	18 21	18 36	18 51	19 06	19 21	19 36	19 51	20 06	20 21	20 36	20 51	21 06	21 21	21 36
Walthamstow Queens Road	d	16 24	16 39	16 54	17 09	17 24	17 39	17 54	18 09	18 24	18 39	18 54	19 09	19 24	19 39	19 54	20 09	20 24	20 39	20 54	21 09	21 24	21 39
Leyton Midland Road	d	16 27	16 42	16 57	17 12	17 27	17 42	17 57	18 12	18 27	18 42	18 57	19 12	19 27	19 42	19 57	20 12	20 27	20 42	20 57	21 12	21 27	21 42
Leytonstone High Road	d	16 30	16 45	17 00	17 15	17 30	17 45	18 00	18 15	18 30	18 45	19 00	19 15	19 30	19 45	20 00	20 15	20 30	20 45	21 00	21 15	21 30	21 45
Wanstead Park	d	16 33	16 48	17 03	17 18	17 33	17 48	18 03	18 18	18 33	18 48	19 03	19 18	19 33	19 48	20 03	20 18	20 33	20 48	21 03	21 18	21 33	21 48
Woodgrange Park	d	16 35	16 50	17 05	17 20	17 35	17 50	18 05	18 20	18 35	18 50	19 05	19 20	19 35	19 50	20 05	20 20	20 35	20 50	21 05	21 20	21 35	21 50
Barking ⊖	a	16 42	16 57	17 12	17 27	17 42	17 54	18 09	18 24	18 39	18 54	19 09	19 24	19 39	19 54	20 12	20 24	20 39	20 54	21 09	21 24	21 39	21 54

		LO	LO	LO	LO	LO	LO
Gospel Oak	d	21 35	21 50	22 05	22 35	23 05	23 35
Upper Holloway	d	21 39	21 54	22 09	22 39	23 09	23 39
Crouch Hill	d	21 42	21 57	22 12	22 42	23 12	23 42
Harringay Green Lanes	d	21 45	22 00	22 15	22 45	23 15	23 45
South Tottenham	d	21 48	22 03	22 18	22 48	23 18	23 48
Blackhorse Road ⊖	d	21 51	22 06	22 21	22 51	23 21	23 51
Walthamstow Queens Road	d	21 54	22 09	22 24	22 54	23 24	23 54
Leyton Midland Road	d	21 57	22 12	22 27	22 57	23 27	23 57
Leytonstone High Road	d	22 00	22 15	22 30	23 00	23 30	00 01
Wanstead Park	d	22 03	22 18	22 33	23 03	23 33	00 03
Woodgrange Park	d	22 05	22 20	22 35	23 05	23 35	00 05
Barking ⊖	a	22 09	22 24	22 39	23 09	23 39	00 12

Table 62

Gospel Oak - Barking

Saturdays
28 July to 11 August

Network Diagram - see first Page of Table 59

		LO	LO	LO	LO	LO		LO	LO	LO	LO	LO	LO	LO	LO	LO		LO	LO	LO	LO
Gospel Oak	d	23p35	06 20	06 35	06 50	07 05	and at the same minutes past each hour until	16 05	16 20	16 35	16 50	17 05	17 20	17 35	17 50	18 05	and at the same minutes past each hour until	22 05	22 35	23 05	23 35
Upper Holloway	d	23p39	06 24	06 39	06 54	07 09		16 09	16 24	16 39	16 54	17 09	17 24	17 39	17 54	18 09		22 09	22 39	23 09	23 39
Crouch Hill	d	23p42	06 27	06 42	06 57	07 12		16 12	16 27	16 42	16 57	17 12	17 27	17 42	17 57	18 12		22 12	22 42	23 12	23 42
Harringay Green Lanes	d	23p45	06 30	06 45	07 00	07 15		16 15	16 30	16 45	17 00	17 15	17 30	17 45	18 00	18 15		22 15	22 45	23 15	23 45
South Tottenham	d	23p48	06 33	06 48	07 03	07 18		16 18	16 33	16 48	17 03	17 18	17 33	17 48	18 03	18 18		22 18	22 48	23 18	23 48
Blackhorse Road ⊖	d	23p51	06 36	06 51	07 06	07 21		16 21	16 36	16 51	17 06	17 21	17 36	17 51	18 06	18 21		22 21	22 51	23 21	23 51
Walthamstow Queens Road	d	23p54	06 39	06 54	07 09	07 24		16 24	16 39	16 54	17 09	17 24	17 39	17 54	18 09	18 24		22 24	22 54	23 24	23 54
Leyton Midland Road	d	23p57	06 42	06 57	07 12	07 27		16 27	16 42	16 57	17 12	17 27	17 42	17 57	18 12	18 27		22 27	22 57	23 27	23 57
Leytonstone High Road	d	00 01	06 45	07 00	07 15	07 30		16 30	16 45	17 00	17 15	17 30	17 45	18 00	18 15	18 30		22 30	23 00	23 30	00 01
Wanstead Park	d	00 03	06 48	07 03	07 18	07 33		16 33	16 48	17 03	17 18	17 33	17 48	18 03	18 18	18 33		22 33	23 03	23 33	00 03
Woodgrange Park	d	00 05	06 50	07 05	07 20	07 35		16 35	16 50	17 05	17 20	17 35	17 50	18 05	18 20	18 35		22 35	23 05	23 35	00 05
Barking ⊖	a	00 14	06 59	07 14	07 29	07 44		16 44	16 59	17 14	17 29	17 46	17 59	18 14	18 29	18 44		22 44	23 14	23 44	00 14

Saturdays
18 August to 25 August

		LO	LO	LO	LO	LO	LO		LO	LO	LO	LO	LO	LO	LO	LO		LO	LO	LO	LO
Gospel Oak	d	23p35	06 20	06 35	06 50	07 05	07 20	and at the same minutes past each hour until	10 20	10 35	10 50	11 05	11 20	11 35	11 50	12 05	and at the same minutes past each hour until	15 05	15 20	15 35	15 50
Upper Holloway	d	23p39	06 24	06 39	06 54	07 09	07 24		10 24	10 39	10 54	11 09	11 24	11 39	11 54	12 09		15 09	15 24	15 39	15 54
Crouch Hill	d	23p42	06 27	06 42	06 57	07 12	07 27		10 27	10 42	10 57	11 12	11 27	11 42	11 57	12 12		15 12	15 27	15 42	15 57
Harringay Green Lanes	d	23p45	06 30	06 45	07 00	07 15	07 30		10 30	10 45	11 00	11 15	11 30	11 45	12 00	12 15		15 15	15 30	15 45	16 00
South Tottenham	d	23p48	06 33	06 48	07 03	07 18	07 33		10 33	10 48	11 03	11 18	11 33	11 48	12 03	12 18		15 18	15 33	15 48	16 03
Blackhorse Road ⊖	d	23p51	06 36	06 51	07 06	07 21	07 36		10 36	10 51	11 06	11 21	11 36	11 51	12 06	12 21		15 21	15 36	15 51	16 06
Walthamstow Queens Road	d	23p54	06 39	06 54	07 09	07 24	07 39		10 39	10 54	11 09	11 24	11 39	11 54	12 09	12 24		15 24	15 39	15 54	16 09
Leyton Midland Road	d	23p57	06 42	06 57	07 12	07 27	07 42		10 42	10 57	11 12	11 27	11 42	11 57	12 12	12 27		15 27	15 42	15 57	16 12
Leytonstone High Road	d	23p59	06 45	07 00	07 15	07 30	07 45		10 45	11 00	11 15	11 30	11 45	12 00	12 15	12 30		15 30	15 45	16 00	16 15
Wanstead Park	d	00 03	06 48	07 03	07 18	07 33	07 48		10 48	11 03	11 18	11 33	11 48	12 03	12 18	12 33		15 33	15 48	16 03	16 18
Woodgrange Park	d	00 05	06 50	07 05	07 20	07 35	07 50		10 50	11 05	11 20	11 35	11 50	12 05	12 20	12 35		15 35	15 50	16 05	16 20
Barking ⊖	a	00 14	06 57	07 09	07 24	07 39	07 54		10 54	11 09	11 24	11 42	11 54	12 09	12 24	12 39		15 39	15 54	16 09	16 24

		LO	LO	LO	LO	LO	LO	LO	LO	LO	LO	LO	LO	LO	LO	LO	LO	LO	LO	LO	LO	LO	LO
Gospel Oak	d	16 05	16 20	16 35	16 50	17 05	17 20	17 35	17 50	18 05	18 20	18 35	18 50	19 05	19 20	19 35	19 50	20 05	20 20	20 35	20 50	21 05	21 20
Upper Holloway	d	16 09	16 24	16 39	16 54	17 09	17 24	17 39	17 54	18 09	18 24	18 39	18 54	19 09	19 24	19 39	19 54	20 09	20 24	20 39	20 54	21 09	21 24
Crouch Hill	d	16 12	16 27	16 42	16 57	17 12	17 27	17 42	17 57	18 12	18 27	18 42	18 57	19 12	19 27	19 42	19 57	20 12	20 27	20 42	20 57	21 12	21 27
Harringay Green Lanes	d	16 15	16 30	16 45	17 00	17 15	17 30	17 45	18 00	18 15	18 30	18 45	19 00	19 15	19 30	19 45	20 00	20 15	20 30	20 45	21 00	21 15	21 30
South Tottenham	d	16 18	16 33	16 48	17 03	17 18	17 33	17 48	18 03	18 18	18 33	18 48	19 03	19 18	19 33	19 48	20 03	20 18	20 33	20 48	21 03	21 18	21 33
Blackhorse Road ⊖	d	16 21	16 36	16 51	17 06	17 21	17 36	17 51	18 06	18 21	18 36	18 51	19 06	19 21	19 36	19 51	20 06	20 21	20 36	20 51	21 06	21 21	21 36
Walthamstow Queens Road	d	16 24	16 39	16 54	17 09	17 24	17 39	17 54	18 09	18 24	18 39	18 54	19 09	19 24	19 39	19 54	20 09	20 24	20 39	20 54	21 09	21 24	21 39
Leyton Midland Road	d	16 27	16 42	16 57	17 12	17 27	17 42	17 57	18 12	18 27	18 42	18 57	19 12	19 27	19 42	19 57	20 12	20 27	20 42	20 57	21 12	21 27	21 42
Leytonstone High Road	d	16 30	16 45	17 00	17 15	17 30	17 45	18 00	18 15	18 30	18 45	19 00	19 15	19 30	19 45	20 00	20 15	20 30	20 45	21 00	21 15	21 30	21 45
Wanstead Park	d	16 33	16 48	17 03	17 18	17 33	17 48	18 03	18 18	18 33	18 48	19 03	19 18	19 33	19 48	20 03	20 18	20 33	20 48	21 03	21 18	21 33	21 48
Woodgrange Park	d	16 35	16 50	17 05	17 20	17 35	17 50	18 05	18 20	18 35	18 50	19 05	19 20	19 35	19 50	20 05	20 20	20 35	20 50	21 05	21 20	21 35	21 50
Barking ⊖	a	16 42	16 57	17 12	17 27	17 42	17 54	18 09	18 24	18 39	18 54	19 09	19 24	19 39	19 54	20 12	20 24	20 39	20 54	21 09	21 24	21 39	21 54

		LO	LO	LO	LO	LO	LO
Gospel Oak	d	21 35	21 50	22 05	22 35	23 05	23 35
Upper Holloway	d	21 39	21 54	22 09	22 39	23 09	23 39
Crouch Hill	d	21 42	21 57	22 12	22 42	23 12	23 42
Harringay Green Lanes	d	21 45	22 00	22 15	22 45	23 15	23 45
South Tottenham	d	21 48	22 03	22 18	22 48	23 18	23 48
Blackhorse Road ⊖	d	21 51	22 06	22 21	22 51	23 21	23 51
Walthamstow Queens Road	d	21 54	22 09	22 24	22 54	23 24	23 54
Leyton Midland Road	d	21 57	22 12	22 27	22 57	23 27	23 57
Leytonstone High Road	d	22 00	22 15	22 30	23 00	23 30	00 01
Wanstead Park	d	22 03	22 18	22 33	23 03	23 33	00 03
Woodgrange Park	d	22 05	22 20	22 35	23 05	23 35	00 05
Barking ⊖	a	22 09	22 24	22 39	23 09	23 39	00 12

Saturdays
1 September to 8 September

		LO	LO	LO	LO	LO	LO	LO	LO	LO	LO	LO	LO	LO	LO	LO	LO		LO	LO	LO	LO
Gospel Oak	d	23p35	06 20	06 35	06 50	07 05	07 20	07 35	07 50	08 05	08 20	08 35	08 49	09 05	09 20	09 35	09 50	and at the same minutes past each hour until	16 50	17 05	17 20	17 35
Upper Holloway	d	23p39	06 24	06 39	06 54	07 09	07 24	07 39	07 54	08 09	08 24	08 39	08 54	09 09	09 24	09 39	09 54		16 54	17 09	17 24	17 39
Crouch Hill	d	23p42	06 27	06 42	06 57	07 12	07 27	07 42	07 57	08 12	08 27	08 42	08 57	09 12	09 27	09 42	09 57		16 57	17 12	17 27	17 42
Harringay Green Lanes	d	23p45	06 30	06 45	07 00	07 15	07 30	07 45	08 00	08 15	08 30	08 45	09 00	09 15	09 30	09 45	10 00		17 00	17 15	17 30	17 45
South Tottenham	d	23p48	06 33	06 48	07 03	07 18	07 33	07 48	08 03	08 18	08 33	08 48	09 03	09 18	09 33	09 48	10 03		17 03	17 18	17 33	17 48
Blackhorse Road ⊖	d	23p51	06 36	06 51	07 06	07 21	07 36	07 51	08 06	08 21	08 36	08 51	09 06	09 21	09 36	09 51	10 06		17 06	17 21	17 36	17 51
Walthamstow Queens Road	d	23p54	06 39	06 54	07 09	07 24	07 39	07 54	08 09	08 24	08 39	08 54	09 09	09 24	09 39	09 54	10 09		17 09	17 24	17 39	17 54
Leyton Midland Road	d	23p57	06 42	06 57	07 12	07 27	07 42	07 57	08 12	08 27	08 42	08 57	09 12	09 27	09 42	09 57	10 12		17 12	17 27	17 42	17 57
Leytonstone High Road	d	00 01	06 45	07 00	07 15	07 30	07 45	08 00	08 15	08 30	08 45	09 00	09 15	09 30	09 45	10 00	10 15		17 15	17 30	17 45	18 00
Wanstead Park	d	00 03	06 48	07 03	07 18	07 33	07 48	08 03	08 18	08 33	08 48	09 03	09 18	09 33	09 48	10 03	10 18		17 18	17 33	17 48	18 03
Woodgrange Park	d	00 05	06 50	07 05	07 20	07 35	07 50	08 05	08 20	08 35	08 50	09 05	09 20	09 35	09 50	10 05	10 20		17 20	17 35	17 50	18 05
Barking ⊖	a	00 14	06 59	07 14	07 29	07 44	07 59	08 14	08 29	08 44	08 59	09 14	09 29	09 44	09 59	10 14	10 29		17 29	17 46	17 59	18 14

		LO	LO		LO	LO	LO	LO
Gospel Oak	d	17 50	18 05	and at the same minutes past each hour until	22 05	22 35	23 05	23 35
Upper Holloway	d	17 54	18 09		22 09	22 39	23 09	23 39
Crouch Hill	d	17 57	18 12		22 12	22 42	23 12	23 42
Harringay Green Lanes	d	18 00	18 15		22 15	22 45	23 15	23 45
South Tottenham	d	18 03	18 18		22 18	22 48	23 18	23 48
Blackhorse Road ⊖	d	18 06	18 21		22 21	22 51	23 21	23 51
Walthamstow Queens Road	d	18 09	18 24		22 24	22 54	23 24	23 54
Leyton Midland Road	d	18 12	18 27		22 27	22 57	23 27	23 57
Leytonstone High Road	d	18 15	18 30		22 30	23 00	23 30	00 01
Wanstead Park	d	18 18	18 33		22 33	23 03	23 33	00 03
Woodgrange Park	d	18 20	18 35		22 35	23 05	23 35	00 05
Barking ⊖	a	18 29	18 44		22 44	23 14	23 44	00 14

Gospel Oak - Barking

Saturdays

from 15 September

Network Diagram - see first Page of Table 59

		LO	LO	LO	LO	LO	LO		LO	LO	LO	LO	LO	LO	LO	LO		LO	LO	LO	LO
Gospel Oak	d	23p35	06 20	06 35	06 50	07 05	07 20		10 20	10 35	10 50	11 05	11 20	11 35	11 50	12 05		15 05	15 20	15 35	15 50
Upper Holloway	d	23p39	06 24	06 39	06 54	07 09	07 24		10 24	10 39	10 54	11 09	11 24	11 39	11 54	12 09		15 09	15 24	15 39	15 54
Crouch Hill	d	23p42	06 27	06 42	06 57	07 12	07 27	and at	10 27	10 42	10 57	11 12	11 27	11 42	11 57	12 12	and at	15 12	15 27	15 42	15 57
Harringay Green Lanes	d	23p45	06 30	06 45	07 00	07 15	07 30	the same	10 30	10 45	11 00	11 15	11 30	11 45	12 00	12 15	the same	15 15	15 30	15 45	16 00
South Tottenham	d	23p48	06 33	06 48	07 03	07 18	07 33	minutes	10 33	10 48	11 03	11 18	11 33	11 48	12 03	12 18	minutes	15 18	15 33	15 48	16 03
Blackhorse Road ⊖	d	23p51	06 36	06 51	07 06	07 21	07 36	past	10 36	10 51	11 06	11 21	11 36	11 51	12 06	12 21	past	15 21	15 36	15 51	16 06
Walthamstow Queens Road	d	23p54	06 39	06 54	07 09	07 24	07 39	each	10 39	10 54	11 09	11 24	11 39	11 54	12 09	12 24	each	15 24	15 39	15 54	16 09
Leyton Midland Road	d	23p57	06 42	06 57	07 12	07 27	07 42	hour until	10 42	10 57	11 12	11 27	11 42	11 57	12 12	12 27	hour until	15 27	15 42	15 57	16 12
Leytonstone High Road	d	23p59	06 45	07 00	07 15	07 30	07 45		10 45	11 00	11 15	11 30	11 45	12 00	12 15	12 30		15 30	15 45	16 00	16 15
Wanstead Park	d	00 03	06 48	07 03	07 18	07 33	07 48		10 48	11 03	11 18	11 33	11 48	12 03	12 18	12 33		15 33	15 48	16 03	16 18
Woodgrange Park	d	00 05	06 50	07 05	07 20	07 35	07 50		10 50	11 05	11 20	11 35	11 50	12 05	12 20	12 35		15 35	15 50	16 05	16 20
Barking ⊖	a	00 12	06 57	07 09	07 24	07 39	07 54		10 54	11 09	11 24	11 42	11 54	12 09	12 24	12 39		15 39	15 54	16 09	16 24

		LO	LO	LO	LO	LO	LO	LO	LO	LO	LO	LO	LO	LO	LO	LO	LO	LO	LO	LO	LO	LO	LO
Gospel Oak	d	16 05	16 20	16 35	16 50	17 05	17 20	17 35	17 50	18 05	18 20	18 35	18 50	19 05	19 20	19 35	19 50	20 05	20 20	20 35	20 50	21 05	21 20
Upper Holloway	d	16 09	16 24	16 39	16 54	17 09	17 24	17 39	17 54	18 09	18 24	18 39	18 54	19 09	19 24	19 39	19 54	20 09	20 24	20 39	20 54	21 09	21 24
Crouch Hill	d	16 12	16 27	16 42	16 57	17 12	17 27	17 42	17 57	18 12	18 27	18 42	18 57	19 12	19 27	19 42	19 57	20 12	20 27	20 42	20 57	21 12	21 27
Harringay Green Lanes	d	16 15	16 30	16 45	17 00	17 15	17 30	17 45	18 00	18 15	18 30	18 45	19 00	19 15	19 30	19 45	20 00	20 15	20 30	20 45	21 00	21 15	21 30
South Tottenham	d	16 18	16 33	16 48	17 03	17 18	17 33	17 48	18 03	18 18	18 33	18 48	19 03	19 18	19 33	19 48	20 03	20 18	20 33	20 48	21 03	21 18	21 33
Blackhorse Road ⊖	d	16 21	16 36	16 51	17 06	17 21	17 36	17 51	18 06	18 21	18 36	18 51	19 06	19 21	19 36	19 51	20 06	20 21	20 36	20 51	21 06	21 21	21 36
Walthamstow Queens Road	d	16 24	16 39	16 54	17 09	17 24	17 39	17 54	18 09	18 24	18 39	18 54	19 09	19 24	19 39	19 54	20 09	20 24	20 39	20 54	21 09	21 24	21 39
Leyton Midland Road	d	16 27	16 42	16 57	17 12	17 27	17 42	17 57	18 12	18 27	18 42	18 57	19 12	19 27	19 42	19 57	20 12	20 27	20 42	20 57	21 12	21 27	21 42
Leytonstone High Road	d	16 30	16 45	17 00	17 15	17 30	17 45	18 00	18 15	18 30	18 45	19 00	19 15	19 30	19 45	20 00	20 15	20 30	20 45	21 00	21 15	21 30	21 45
Wanstead Park	d	16 33	16 48	17 03	17 18	17 33	17 48	18 03	18 18	18 33	18 48	19 03	19 18	19 33	19 48	20 03	20 18	20 33	20 48	21 03	21 18	21 33	21 48
Woodgrange Park	d	16 35	16 50	17 05	17 20	17 35	17 50	18 05	18 20	18 35	18 50	19 05	19 20	19 35	19 50	20 05	20 20	20 35	20 50	21 05	21 20	21 35	21 50
Barking ⊖	a	16 42	16 57	17 12	17 27	17 42	17 54	18 09	18 24	18 39	18 54	19 09	19 24	19 39	19 54	20 12	20 24	20 39	20 54	21 09	21 24	21 39	21 54

		LO	LO	LO	LO	LO	LO
Gospel Oak	d	21 35	21 50	22 05	22 35	23 05	23 35
Upper Holloway	d	21 39	21 54	22 09	22 39	23 09	23 39
Crouch Hill	d	21 42	21 57	22 12	22 42	23 12	23 42
Harringay Green Lanes	d	21 45	22 00	22 15	22 45	23 15	23 45
South Tottenham	d	21 48	22 03	22 18	22 48	23 18	23 48
Blackhorse Road ⊖	d	21 51	22 06	22 21	22 51	23 21	23 51
Walthamstow Queens Road	d	21 54	22 09	22 24	22 54	23 24	23 54
Leyton Midland Road	d	21 57	22 12	22 27	22 57	23 27	23 57
Leytonstone High Road	d	22 00	22 15	22 30	23 00	23 30	00 01
Wanstead Park	d	22 03	22 18	22 33	23 03	23 33	00 03
Woodgrange Park	d	22 05	22 20	22 35	23 05	23 35	00 05
Barking ⊖	a	22 09	22 24	22 39	23 09	23 39	00 12

Sundays

until 22 July

		LO	LO	LO	LO	LO		LO	LO	LO	LO	LO	LO	LO	LO	LO
Gospel Oak	d	23p35	08 55	09 10	09 25	09 40		20 40	20 55	21 10	21 25	21 40	21 55	22 10	22 40	23 10
Upper Holloway	d	23p39	08 59	09 14	09 29	09 44		20 44	20 59	21 14	21 29	21 44	21 59	22 14	22 44	23 14
Crouch Hill	d	23p42	09 02	09 17	09 32	09 47	and at	20 47	21 02	21 17	21 32	21 47	22 02	22 17	22 47	23 17
Harringay Green Lanes	d	23p45	09 05	09 20	09 35	09 50	the same	20 50	21 05	21 20	21 35	21 50	22 05	22 20	22 50	23 20
South Tottenham	d	23p48	09 08	09 23	09 38	09 53	minutes	20 53	21 08	21 23	21 38	21 53	22 08	22 23	22 53	23 23
Blackhorse Road ⊖	d	23p51	09 11	09 26	09 41	09 56	past	20 56	21 11	21 26	21 41	21 56	22 11	22 26	22 56	23 26
Walthamstow Queens Road	d	23p54	09 14	09 29	09 44	09 59	each	20 59	21 14	21 29	21 44	21 59	22 14	22 29	22 59	23 29
Leyton Midland Road	d	23p57	09 17	09 32	09 47	10 02	hour until	21 02	21 17	21 32	21 47	22 02	22 17	22 32	23 02	23 32
Leytonstone High Road	d	00 01	09 20	09 35	09 50	10 05		21 05	21 20	21 35	21 50	22 05	22 20	22 35	23 05	23 35
Wanstead Park	d	00 03	09 23	09 38	09 53	10 08		21 08	21 23	21 38	21 53	22 08	22 23	22 38	23 08	23 38
Woodgrange Park	d	00 05	09 25	09 40	09 55	10 10		21 10	21 25	21 40	21 55	22 10	22 25	22 40	23 10	23 40
Barking ⊖	a	00 12	09 29	09 44	09 59	10 14		21 14	21 29	21 47	21 59	22 14	22 29	22 44	23 14	23 44

Sundays

29 July to 12 August

		LO	LO	LO	LO	LO		LO	LO	LO	LO	LO
Gospel Oak	d	23p35	08 55	09 10	09 25	09 40		21 40	21 55	22 10	22 40	23 10
Upper Holloway	d	23p39	08 59	09 14	09 29	09 44		21 44	21 59	22 14	22 44	23 14
Crouch Hill	d	23p42	09 02	09 17	09 32	09 47	and at	21 47	22 02	22 17	22 47	23 17
Harringay Green Lanes	d	23p45	09 05	09 20	09 35	09 50	the same	21 50	22 05	22 20	22 50	23 20
South Tottenham	d	23p48	09 08	09 23	09 38	09 53	minutes	21 53	22 08	22 23	22 53	23 23
Blackhorse Road ⊖	d	23p51	09 11	09 26	09 41	09 56	past	21 56	22 11	22 26	22 56	23 26
Walthamstow Queens Road	d	23p54	09 14	09 29	09 44	09 59	each	21 59	22 14	22 29	22 59	23 29
Leyton Midland Road	d	23p57	09 17	09 32	09 47	10 02	hour until	22 02	22 17	22 32	23 02	23 32
Leytonstone High Road	d	00 01	09 20	09 35	09 50	10 05		22 05	22 20	22 35	23 05	23 35
Wanstead Park	d	00 03	09 23	09 38	09 53	10 08		22 08	22 23	22 38	23 08	23 38
Woodgrange Park	d	00 05	09 25	09 40	09 55	10 10		22 10	22 25	22 40	23 10	23 40
Barking ⊖	a	00 14	09 34	09 49	10 04	10 19		22 19	22 34	22 49	23 19	23 49

Gospel Oak - Barking

Sundays

19 August to 26 August

Network Diagram - see first Page of Table 59

		LO	LO	LO	LO	LO		LO	LO	LO	LO	LO	LO	LO	LO	LO
Gospel Oak	d	23p35	08 55	09 10	09 25	09 40		20 40	20 55	21 10	21 25	21 40	21 55	22 10	22 40	23 10
Upper Holloway	d	23p39	08 59	09 14	09 29	09 44		20 44	20 59	21 14	21 29	21 44	21 59	22 14	22 44	23 14
Crouch Hill	d	23p42	09 02	09 17	09 32	09 47	and at	20 47	21 02	21 17	21 32	21 47	22 02	22 17	22 47	23 17
Harringay Green Lanes	d	23p45	09 05	09 20	09 35	09 50	the same	20 50	21 05	21 20	21 35	21 50	22 05	22 20	22 50	23 20
South Tottenham	d	23p48	09 08	09 23	09 38	09 53	minutes	20 53	21 08	21 23	21 38	21 53	22 08	22 23	22 53	23 23
Blackhorse Road ⊖	d	23p51	09 11	09 26	09 41	09 56	past	20 56	21 11	21 26	21 41	21 56	22 11	22 26	22 56	23 26
Walthamstow Queens Road	d	23p54	09 14	09 29	09 44	09 59	each	20 59	21 14	21 29	21 44	21 59	22 14	22 29	22 59	23 29
Leyton Midland Road	d	23p57	09 17	09 32	09 47	10 02	hour until	21 02	21 17	21 32	21 47	22 02	22 17	22 32	23 02	23 32
Leytonstone High Road	d	00 01	09 20	09 35	09 50	10 05		21 05	21 20	21 35	21 50	22 05	22 20	22 35	23 05	23 35
Wanstead Park	d	00 03	09 23	09 38	09 53	10 08		21 08	21 23	21 38	21 53	22 08	22 23	22 38	23 08	23 38
Woodgrange Park	d	00 05	09 25	09 40	09 55	10 10		21 10	21 25	21 40	21 55	22 10	22 25	22 40	23 10	23 40
Barking ⊖	a	00 12	09 29	09 44	09 59	10 14		21 14	21 29	21 47	21 59	22 14	22 29	22 44	23 14	23 44

Sundays

2 September to 9 September

		LO	LO	LO	LO	LO		LO	LO	LO	LO	LO
Gospel Oak	d	23p35	08 55	09 10	09 25	09 40		21 40	21 55	22 10	22 40	23 10
Upper Holloway	d	23p39	08 59	09 14	09 29	09 44		21 44	21 59	22 14	22 44	23 14
Crouch Hill	d	23p42	09 02	09 17	09 32	09 47	and at	21 47	22 02	22 17	22 47	23 17
Harringay Green Lanes	d	23p45	09 05	09 20	09 35	09 50	the same	21 50	22 05	22 20	22 50	23 20
South Tottenham	d	23p48	09 08	09 23	09 38	09 53	minutes	21 53	22 08	22 23	22 53	23 23
Blackhorse Road ⊖	d	23p51	09 11	09 26	09 41	09 56	past	21 56	22 11	22 26	22 56	23 26
Walthamstow Queens Road	d	23p54	09 14	09 29	09 44	09 59	each	21 59	22 14	22 29	22 59	23 29
Leyton Midland Road	d	23p57	09 17	09 32	09 47	10 02	hour until	22 02	22 17	22 32	23 02	23 32
Leytonstone High Road	d	00 01	09 20	09 35	09 50	10 05		22 05	22 20	22 35	23 05	23 35
Wanstead Park	d	00 03	09 23	09 38	09 53	10 08		22 08	22 23	22 38	23 08	23 38
Woodgrange Park	d	00 05	09 25	09 40	09 55	10 10		22 10	22 25	22 40	23 10	23 40
Barking ⊖	a	00 14	09 34	09 49	10 04	10 19		22 19	22 34	22 49	23 19	23 49

Sundays

from 16 September

		LO	LO	LO	LO	LO		LO	LO	LO	LO	LO	LO	LO	LO	LO
Gospel Oak	d	23p35	08 55	09 10	09 25	09 40		20 40	20 55	21 10	21 25	21 40	21 55	22 10	22 40	23 10
Upper Holloway	d	23p39	08 59	09 14	09 29	09 44		20 44	20 59	21 14	21 29	21 44	21 59	22 14	22 44	23 14
Crouch Hill	d	23p42	09 02	09 17	09 32	09 47	and at	20 47	21 02	21 17	21 32	21 47	22 02	22 17	22 47	23 17
Harringay Green Lanes	d	23p45	09 05	09 20	09 35	09 50	the same	20 50	21 05	21 20	21 35	21 50	22 05	22 20	22 50	23 20
South Tottenham	d	23p48	09 08	09 23	09 38	09 53	minutes	20 53	21 08	21 23	21 38	21 53	22 08	22 23	22 53	23 23
Blackhorse Road ⊖	d	23p51	09 11	09 26	09 41	09 56	past	20 56	21 11	21 26	21 41	21 56	22 11	22 26	22 56	23 26
Walthamstow Queens Road	d	23p54	09 14	09 29	09 44	09 59	each	20 59	21 14	21 29	21 44	21 59	22 14	22 29	22 59	23 29
Leyton Midland Road	d	23p57	09 17	09 32	09 47	10 02	hour until	21 02	21 17	21 32	21 47	22 02	22 17	22 32	23 02	23 32
Leytonstone High Road	d	00 01	09 20	09 35	09 50	10 05		21 05	21 20	21 35	21 50	22 05	22 20	22 35	23 05	23 35
Wanstead Park	d	00 03	09 23	09 38	09 53	10 08		21 08	21 23	21 38	21 53	22 08	22 23	22 38	23 08	23 38
Woodgrange Park	d	00 05	09 25	09 40	09 55	10 10		21 10	21 25	21 40	21 55	22 10	22 25	22 40	23 10	23 40
Barking ⊖	a	00 12	09 29	09 44	09 59	10 14		21 14	21 29	21 47	21 59	22 14	22 29	22 44	23 14	23 44

Table 62

Barking - Gospel Oak

Mondays to Fridays

until 26 July

Network Diagram - see first Page of Table 59

Miles			LO MO A	LO MX	LO	LO	LO	LO	LO	LO	LO	LO B	LO	LO	LO	LO	LO	LO	LO	LO	LO	LO	LO
0	**Barking** ⊖	d	23p38	23p47	06 17	06 32	06 47	07 02	07 17	07 32	07 47		08 02	08 17	08 32	08 47	09 02	09 17	09 32	09 47	10 02	10 17	10 32
1¾	Woodgrange Park	d	23p41	23p50	06 20	06 35	06 50	07 05	07 20	07 35	07 50	07 59	08 05	08 20	08 35	08 50	09 05	09 20	09 35	09 50	10 05	10 20	10 35
2¾	Wanstead Park	d	23p44	23p53	06 23	06 38	06 53	07 08	07 23	07 38	07 53	08 02	08 08	08 23	08 38	08 53	09 08	09 23	09 38	09 53	10 08	10 23	10 38
4	Leytonstone High Road	d	23p48	23p57	06 27	06 42	06 57	07 12	07 27	07 42	07 57	08 05	08 12	08 27	08 42	08 57	09 12	09 27	09 42	09 57	10 12	10 27	10 42
4¾	Leyton Midland Road	d	23p50	23p59	06 29	06 44	06 59	07 14	07 29	07 44	07 59	08 08	08 14	08 29	08 44	08 59	09 14	09 29	09 44	09 59	10 14	10 29	10 44
5¾	Walthamstow Queens Road	d	23p53	00 02	06 32	06 47	07 02	07 17	07 32	07 47	08 02	08 11	08 17	08 32	08 47	09 02	09 17	09 32	09 47	10 02	10 17	10 32	10 47
6½	Blackhorse Road ⊖	d	23p56	00 05	06 35	06 50	07 05	07 20	07 35	07 50	08 05	08 14	08 20	08 35	08 50	09 05	09 20	09 35	09 50	10 05	10 20	10 35	10 50
8¼	South Tottenham	d	23p59	00 09	06 39	06 54	07 09	07 24	07 39	07 54	08 09	08 18	08 24	08 39	08 54	09 09	09 24	09 39	09 54	10 09	10 24	10 39	10 54
9¼	Harringay Green Lanes	d	00 03	00 12	06 42	06 57	07 12	07 27	07 42	07 57	08 12	08 21	08 27	08 42	08 57	09 12	09 27	09 42	09 57	10 12	10 27	10 42	10 57
10¼	Crouch Hill	d	00 06	00 15	06 45	07 00	07 15	07 30	07 45	08 00	08 15	08 24	08 30	08 45	09 00	09 15	09 30	09 45	10 00	10 19	10 30	10 45	11 00
11	Upper Holloway	d	00 08	00 17	06 47	07 02	07 17	07 32	07 47	08 02	08 17	08a27	08 32	08 47	09 02	09 17	09 32	09 47	10 02	10 22	10 32	10 47	11 02
12¼	**Gospel Oak**	a	00 13	00 27	06 55	07 09	07 23	07 39	07 53	08 08	08 23		08 38	08 53	09 08	09 23	09 38	09 53	10 08	10 29	10 38	10 54	11 11

		LO	LO	LO	LO	LO	LO	LO	LO	LO	LO	LO	LO	LO	LO	LO	LO	LO	LO	LO	LO	LO	LO
Barking ⊖	d	10 47	11 02	11 17	11 32	11 47	12 02	12 17	12 32	12 47	13 02	13 17	13 32	13 47	14 02	14 17	14 32	14 47	15 02	15 17	15 32	15 47	16 02
Woodgrange Park	d	10 50	11 05	11 20	11 35	11 50	12 05	12 20	12 35	12 50	13 05	13 20	13 35	13 50	14 05	14 20	14 35	14 50	15 05	15 20	15 35	15 50	16 05
Wanstead Park	d	10 53	11 08	11 23	11 38	11 53	12 08	12 23	12 38	12 53	13 08	13 23	13 38	13 53	14 08	14 23	14 38	14 53	15 08	15 23	15 38	15 53	16 08
Leytonstone High Road	d	10 57	11 12	11 27	11 42	11 57	12 12	12 27	12 42	12 57	13 12	13 27	13 42	13 57	14 12	14 27	14 42	14 57	15 12	15 27	15 42	15 57	16 12
Leyton Midland Road	d	10 59	11 14	11 29	11 44	11 59	12 14	12 29	12 44	12 59	13 14	13 29	13 44	13 59	14 14	14 29	14 44	14 59	15 14	15 29	15 44	15 59	16 14
Walthamstow Queens Road	d	11 02	11 17	11 32	11 47	12 02	12 17	12 32	12 47	13 02	13 17	13 32	13 47	14 02	14 17	14 32	14 47	15 02	15 17	15 32	15 47	16 02	16 17
Blackhorse Road ⊖	d	11 05	11 20	11 35	11 50	12 05	12 20	12 35	12 50	13 05	13 20	13 35	13 50	14 05	14 20	14 35	14 50	15 05	15 20	15 35	15 50	16 05	16 20
South Tottenham	d	11 09	11 24	11 39	11 54	12 09	12 24	12 39	12 54	13 09	13 24	13 39	13 54	14 09	14 24	14 39	14 54	15 09	15 24	15 39	15 54	16 09	16 24
Harringay Green Lanes	d	11 12	11 27	11 42	11 57	12 12	12 27	12 42	12 57	13 12	13 27	13 42	13 57	14 12	14 27	14 42	14 57	15 12	15 27	15 42	15 57	16 12	16 27
Crouch Hill	d	11 15	11 30	11 45	12 00	12 15	12 30	12 45	13 00	13 15	13 30	13 45	14 00	14 15	14 30	14 45	15 00	15 15	15 30	15 45	16 00	16 15	16 30
Upper Holloway	d	11 17	11 32	11 47	12 02	12 17	12 32	12 47	13 02	13 17	13 32	13 47	14 02	14 17	14 32	14 47	15 02	15 17	15 32	15 47	16 02	16 17	16 32
Gospel Oak	a	11 23	11 41	11 55	12 11	12 23	12 41	12 54	13 11	13 23	13 41	13 53	14 08	14 23	14 38	14 53	15 08	15 24	15 38	15 53	16 08	16 23	16 40

		LO	LO	LO	LO	LO	LO	LO	LO	LO	LO	LO	LO	LO	LO	LO	LO	LO	LO	LO	LO	LO
Barking ⊖	d	16 17	16 32	16 47	17 02	17 17	17 32	17 47	18 02	18 17	18 32	18 47	19 02	19 17	19 32	19 47	20 02	20 17	20 32	20 47	21 02	21 17
Woodgrange Park	d	16 20	16 35	16 50	17 05	17 20	17 35	17 50	18 05	18 20	18 35	18 50	19 05	19 20	19 35	19 50	20 05	20 20	20 35	20 50	21 05	21 20
Wanstead Park	d	16 23	16 38	16 53	17 08	17 23	17 38	17 53	18 08	18 23	18 38	18 53	19 08	19 23	19 38	19 53	20 08	20 23	20 38	20 53	21 08	21 23
Leytonstone High Road	d	16 27	16 42	16 57	17 12	17 27	17 42	17 57	18 12	18 27	18 42	18 57	19 12	19 27	19 42	19 57	20 12	20 27	20 42	20 57	21 12	21 27
Leyton Midland Road	d	16 29	16 44	16 59	17 14	17 29	17 44	17 59	18 14	18 29	18 44	18 59	19 14	19 29	19 44	19 59	20 14	20 29	20 44	20 59	21 14	21 29
Walthamstow Queens Road	d	16 32	16 47	17 02	17 17	17 32	17 47	18 02	18 17	18 32	18 47	19 02	19 17	19 32	19 47	20 02	20 17	20 32	20 47	21 02	21 17	21 32
Blackhorse Road ⊖	d	16 35	16 50	17 05	17 20	17 35	17 50	18 05	18 20	18 35	18 50	19 05	19 20	19 35	19 50	20 05	20 20	20 35	20 50	21 05	21 20	21 35
South Tottenham	d	16 39	16 54	17 09	17 24	17 39	17 54	18 09	18 24	18 39	18 54	19 09	19 24	19 39	19 54	20 09	20 24	20 39	20 54	21 09	21 24	21 39
Harringay Green Lanes	d	16 42	16 57	17 12	17 27	17 42	17 57	18 12	18 27	18 42	18 57	19 12	19 27	19 42	19 57	20 12	20 27	20 42	20 57	21 12	21 27	21 42
Crouch Hill	d	16 45	17 00	17 15	17 30	17 45	18 00	18 15	18 30	18 45	19 00	19 15	19 30	19 45	20 00	20 15	20 30	20 45	21 00	21 15	21 30	21 45
Upper Holloway	d	16 47	17 02	17 17	17 32	17 47	18 02	18 17	18 32	18 47	19 02	19 17	19 32	19 47	20 02	20 17	20 32	20 47	21 02	21 17	21 32	21 47
Gospel Oak	a	16 53	17 08	17 23	17 38	17 53	18 08	18 23	18 38	18 53	19 09	19 26	19 38	19 53	20 08	20 23	20 38	20 53	21 08	21 24	21 38	21 54

		LO	LO	LO	LO	LO	LO	LO
Barking ⊖	d	21 32	21 47	22 02	22 17	22 47	23 17	23 47
Woodgrange Park	d	21 35	21 50	22 05	22 20	22 50	23 20	23 50
Wanstead Park	d	21 38	21 53	22 08	22 23	22 53	23 23	23 53
Leytonstone High Road	d	21 42	21 57	22 12	22 27	22 57	23 27	23 57
Leyton Midland Road	d	21 44	21 59	22 14	22 29	22 59	23 29	23 59
Walthamstow Queens Road	d	21 47	22 02	22 17	22 32	23 02	23 32	00 02
Blackhorse Road ⊖	d	21 50	22 05	22 20	22 35	23 05	23 35	00 05
South Tottenham	d	21 54	22 09	22 24	22 39	23 09	23 39	00 09
Harringay Green Lanes	d	21 57	22 12	22 27	22 42	23 12	23 42	00 12
Crouch Hill	d	22 00	22 16	22 30	22 45	23 15	23 45	00 15
Upper Holloway	d	22 02	22 18	22 32	22 47	23 17	23 47	00 17
Gospel Oak	a	22 11	22 23	22 38	22 53	23 25	23 58	00 27

Mondays to Fridays

27 July to 10 August

		LO MO	LO C	LO	LO	LO	LO	LO	LO	LO	LO	LO	LO	LO	LO	LO	LO	LO	LO	LO	LO	LO	LO
Barking ⊖	d	23p38	23p47	06 17	06 32	06 47	07 02	07 17	07 32	07 47	08 02	08 17	08 32	08 47	09 02	09 17	09 32	09 47	10 02	10 17	10 32	10 47	11 02
Woodgrange Park	d	23p41	23p50	06 20	06 35	06 50	07 05	07 20	07 35	07 50	08 05	08 20	08 35	08 50	09 05	09 20	09 35	09 50	10 05	10 20	10 35	10 50	11 05
Wanstead Park	d	23p44	23p53	06 23	06 38	06 53	07 08	07 23	07 38	07 53	08 08	08 23	08 38	08 53	09 08	09 23	09 38	09 53	10 08	10 23	10 38	10 53	11 08
Leytonstone High Road	d	23p48	23p57	06 27	06 42	06 57	07 12	07 27	07 42	07 57	08 12	08 27	08 42	08 57	09 12	09 27	09 42	09 57	10 12	10 27	10 42	10 57	11 12
Leyton Midland Road	d	23p50	23p59	06 29	06 44	06 59	07 14	07 29	07 44	07 59	08 14	08 29	08 44	08 59	09 14	09 29	09 44	09 59	10 14	10 29	10 44	10 59	11 14
Walthamstow Queens Road	d	23p53	00 02	06 32	06 47	07 02	07 17	07 32	07 47	08 02	08 17	08 32	08 47	09 02	09 17	09 32	09 47	10 02	10 17	10 32	10 47	11 02	11 17
Blackhorse Road ⊖	d	23p56	00 05	06 35	06 50	07 05	07 20	07 35	07 50	08 05	08 20	08 35	08 50	09 05	09 20	09 35	09 50	10 05	10 20	10 35	10 50	11 05	11 20
South Tottenham	d	23p59	00 09	06 39	06 54	07 09	07 24	07 39	07 54	08 09	08 24	08 39	08 54	09 09	09 24	09 39	09 54	10 09	10 24	10 39	10 54	11 09	11 24
Harringay Green Lanes	d	00 03	00 12	06 42	06 57	07 12	07 27	07 42	07 57	08 12	08 27	08 42	08 57	09 12	09 27	09 42	09 57	10 12	10 27	10 42	10 57	11 12	11 27
Crouch Hill	d	00 06	00 15	06 45	07 00	07 15	07 30	07 45	08 00	08 15	08 30	08 45	09 00	09 15	09 30	09 45	10 00	10 19	10 30	10 45	11 00	11 15	11 30
Upper Holloway	d	00 08	00 17	06 47	07 02	07 17	07 32	07 47	08 02	08 17	08 32	08 47	09 02	09 17	09 32	09 47	10 02	10 22	10 32	10 47	11 02	11 17	11 32
Gospel Oak	a	00 18	00 27	06 59	07 13	07 28	07 43	07 58	08 13	08 28	08 43	08 58	09 13	09 28	09 43	09 58	10 13	10 34	10 43	10 58	11 14	11 28	11 43

		LO	LO	LO	LO	LO	LO	LO	LO	LO	LO	LO	LO	LO	LO	LO	LO	LO	LO	LO	LO	LO	LO
Barking ⊖	d	11 17	11 32	11 47	12 02	12 17	12 32	12 47	13 02	13 17	13 32	13 47	14 02	14 17	14 32	14 47	15 02	15 17	15 32	15 47	16 02	16 17	16 32
Woodgrange Park	d	11 20	11 35	11 50	12 05	12 20	12 35	12 50	13 05	13 20	13 35	13 50	14 05	14 20	14 35	14 50	15 05	15 20	15 35	15 50	16 05	16 20	16 35
Wanstead Park	d	11 23	11 38	11 53	12 08	12 23	12 38	12 53	13 08	13 23	13 38	13 53	14 08	14 23	14 38	14 53	15 08	15 23	15 38	15 53	16 08	16 23	16 38
Leytonstone High Road	d	11 27	11 42	11 57	12 12	12 27	12 42	12 57	13 12	13 27	13 42	13 57	14 12	14 27	14 42	14 57	15 12	15 27	15 42	15 57	16 12	16 27	16 42
Leyton Midland Road	d	11 29	11 44	11 59	12 14	12 29	12 44	12 59	13 14	13 29	13 44	13 59	14 14	14 29	14 44	14 59	15 14	15 29	15 44	15 59	16 14	16 29	16 44
Walthamstow Queens Road	d	11 32	11 47	12 02	12 17	12 32	12 47	13 02	13 17	13 32	13 47	14 02	14 17	14 32	14 47	15 02	15 17	15 32	15 47	16 02	16 17	16 32	16 47
Blackhorse Road ⊖	d	11 35	11 50	12 05	12 20	12 35	12 50	13 05	13 20	13 35	13 50	14 05	14 20	14 35	14 50	15 05	15 20	15 35	15 50	16 05	16 20	16 35	16 50
South Tottenham	d	11 39	11 54	12 09	12 24	12 39	12 54	13 09	13 24	13 39	13 54	14 09	14 24	14 39	14 54	15 09	15 24	15 39	15 54	16 09	16 24	16 39	16 54
Harringay Green Lanes	d	11 42	11 57	12 12	12 27	12 42	12 57	13 12	13 27	13 42	13 57	14 12	14 27	14 42	14 57	15 12	15 27	15 42	15 57	16 12	16 27	16 42	16 57
Crouch Hill	d	11 45	12 00	12 15	12 30	12 45	13 00	13 15	13 30	13 45	14 00	14 15	14 30	14 45	15 02	15 15	15 30	15 45	16 00	16 15	16 30	16 45	17 00
Upper Holloway	d	11 47	12 02	12 17	12 32	12 47	13 02	13 17	13 32	13 47	14 02	14 23	14 32	14 47	15 06	15 17	15 32	15 47	16 02	16 17	16 32	16 47	17 02
Gospel Oak	a	11 58	12 16	12 28	12 46	12 58	13 16	13 28	13 43	13 58	14 13	14 33	14 43	14 58	15 18	15 28	15 43	15 58	16 13	16 28	16 45	16 58	17 13

A from 21 May until 23 July   B not 4 June, 5 June   C not 30 July, 6 August

Table 62

Barking - Gospel Oak

Mondays to Fridays

27 July to 10 August

Network Diagram - see first Page of Table 59

		LO	LO	LO	LO	LO	LO	LO	LO	LO	LO	LO	LO	LO	LO	LO	LO	LO	LO	LO	LO	LO
Barking ⊖	d	16 47	17 02	17 17	17 32	17 47	18 02	18 17	18 32	18 47	19 02	19 17	19 32	19 47	20 02	20 17	20 32	20 47	21 02	21 17	21 32	21 47
Woodgrange Park	d	16 50	17 05	17 20	17 35	17 50	18 05	18 20	18 35	18 50	19 05	19 20	19 35	19 50	20 05	20 20	20 35	20 50	21 05	21 20	21 35	21 50
Wanstead Park	d	16 53	17 08	17 23	17 38	17 53	18 08	18 23	18 38	18 53	19 08	19 23	19 38	19 53	20 08	20 23	20 38	20 53	21 08	21 23	21 38	21 53
Leytonstone High Road	d	16 57	17 12	17 27	17 42	17 57	18 12	18 27	18 42	18 57	19 12	19 27	19 42	19 57	20 12	20 27	20 42	20 57	21 12	21 27	21 42	21 57
Leyton Midland Road	d	16 59	17 14	17 29	17 44	17 59	18 14	18 29	18 44	18 59	19 14	19 29	19 44	19 59	20 14	20 29	20 44	20 59	21 14	21 29	21 44	21 59
Walthamstow Queens Road	d	17 02	17 17	17 32	17 47	18 02	18 17	18 32	18 47	19 02	19 17	19 32	19 47	20 02	20 17	20 32	20 47	21 02	21 17	21 32	21 47	22 02
Blackhorse Road ⊖	d	17 05	17 20	17 35	17 50	18 05	18 20	18 35	18 50	19 05	19 20	19 35	19 50	20 05	20 20	20 35	20 50	21 05	21 20	21 35	21 50	22 05
South Tottenham	d	17 09	17 24	17 39	17 54	18 09	18 24	18 39	18 54	19 09	19 24	19 39	19 54	20 09	20 24	20 39	20 54	21 09	21 24	21 39	21 54	22 09
Harringay Green Lanes	d	17 12	17 27	17 42	17 57	18 12	18 27	18 42	18 57	19 12	19 27	19 42	19 57	20 12	20 27	20 42	20 57	21 12	21 27	21 42	21 57	22 12
Crouch Hill	d	17 15	17 30	17 45	18 00	18 15	18 30	18 45	19 00	19 15	19 30	19 45	20 00	20 15	20 30	20 45	21 00	21 15	21 30	21 45	22 00	22 15
Upper Holloway	d	17 17	17 32	17 47	18 09	18 17	18 32	18 47	19 02	19 18	19 32	19 47	20 02	20 23	20 32	20 47	21 02	21 17	21 32	21 47	22 03	22 17
Gospel Oak	a	17 28	17 43	17 58	18 19	18 28	18 43	18 58	19 13	19 33	19 43	20 02	20 13	20 34	20 43	20 58	21 15	21 28	21 43	21 58	22 18	22 32

		LO	LO	LO	LO	LO
Barking ⊖	d	22 02	22 17	22 47	23 17	23 47
Woodgrange Park	d	22 05	22 20	22 50	23 20	23 50
Wanstead Park	d	22 08	22 23	22 53	23 23	23 53
Leytonstone High Road	d	22 12	22 27	22 57	23 27	23 57
Leyton Midland Road	d	22 14	22 29	22 59	23 29	23 59
Walthamstow Queens Road	d	22 17	22 32	23 02	23 32	00 02
Blackhorse Road ⊖	d	22 20	22 35	23 05	23 35	00 05
South Tottenham	d	22 24	22 39	23 09	23 39	00 09
Harringay Green Lanes	d	22 27	22 42	23 12	23 42	00 12
Crouch Hill	d	22 30	22 45	23 15	23 45	00 15
Upper Holloway	d	22 32	22 47	23 17	23 47	00 17
Gospel Oak	a	22 43	22 58	23 31	23 58	00 27

Mondays to Fridays

13 August to 28 August

		LO A	LO B	LO MX	LO	LO	LO	LO	LO	LO	LO	LO	LO	LO	LO	LO	LO	LO	LO	LO	LO	LO	LO
Barking ⊖	d	23p38	23p38	23p47	06 17	06 32	06 47	07 02	07 17	07 32	07 47		08 02	08 17	08 32	08 47	09 02	09 17	09 32	09 47	10 02	10 17	10 32
Woodgrange Park	d	23p41	23p41	23p50	06 20	06 35	06 50	07 05	07 20	07 35	07 50	07 59	08 05	08 20	08 35	08 50	09 05	09 20	09 35	09 50	10 05	10 20	10 35
Wanstead Park	d	23p44	23p44	23p53	06 23	06 38	06 53	07 08	07 23	07 38	07 53	08 02	08 08	08 23	08 38	08 53	09 08	09 23	09 38	09 53	10 08	10 23	10 38
Leytonstone High Road	d	23p48	23p48	23p57	06 27	06 42	06 57	07 12	07 27	07 42	07 57	08 05	08 12	08 27	08 42	08 57	09 12	09 27	09 42	09 57	10 12	10 27	10 42
Leyton Midland Road	d	23p50	23p50	23p59	06 29	06 44	06 59	07 14	07 29	07 44	07 59	08 08	08 14	08 29	08 44	08 59	09 14	09 29	09 44	09 59	10 14	10 29	10 44
Walthamstow Queens Road	d	23p53	23p53	00 02	06 32	06 47	07 02	07 17	07 32	07 47	08 02	08 11	08 17	08 32	08 47	09 02	09 17	09 32	09 47	10 02	10 17	10 32	10 47
Blackhorse Road ⊖	d	23p56	23p56	00 05	06 35	06 50	07 05	07 20	07 35	07 50	08 05	08 14	08 20	08 35	08 50	09 05	09 20	09 35	09 50	10 05	10 20	10 35	10 50
South Tottenham	d	23p59	23p59	00 09	06 39	06 54	07 09	07 24	07 39	07 54	08 09	08 18	08 24	08 39	08 54	09 09	09 24	09 39	09 54	10 09	10 24	10 39	10 54
Harringay Green Lanes	d	00 03	00 03	00 12	06 42	06 57	07 12	07 27	07 42	07 57	08 12	08 21	08 27	08 42	08 57	09 12	09 27	09 42	09 57	10 12	10 27	10 42	10 57
Crouch Hill	d	00 06	00 06	00 15	06 45	07 00	07 15	07 30	07 45	08 00	08 15	08 24	08 30	08 45	09 00	09 15	09 30	09 45	10 00	10 19	10 30	10 45	11 00
Upper Holloway	d	00 08	00 08	00 17	06 47	07 02	07 17	07 32	07 47	08 02	08 17	08a27	08 32	08 47	09 02	09 17	09 32	09 47	10 02	10 22	10 32	10 47	11 02
Gospel Oak	a	00 13	00 18	00 27	06 55	07 09	07 23	07 39	07 53	08 08	08 23		08 38	08 53	09 08	09 23	09 38	09 53	10 08	10 29	10 38	10 54	11 11

		LO	LO	LO	LO	LO	LO	LO	LO	LO	LO	LO	LO	LO	LO	LO	LO	LO	LO	LO	LO	LO	LO
Barking ⊖	d	10 47	11 02	11 17	11 32	11 47	12 02	12 17	12 32	12 47	13 02	13 17	13 32	13 47	14 02	14 17	14 32	14 47	15 02	15 17	15 32	15 47	16 02
Woodgrange Park	d	10 50	11 05	11 20	11 35	11 50	12 05	12 20	12 35	12 50	13 05	13 20	13 35	13 50	14 05	14 20	14 35	14 50	15 05	15 20	15 35	15 50	16 05
Wanstead Park	d	10 53	11 08	11 23	11 38	11 53	12 08	12 23	12 38	12 53	13 08	13 23	13 38	13 53	14 08	14 23	14 38	14 53	15 08	15 23	15 38	15 53	16 08
Leytonstone High Road	d	10 57	11 12	11 27	11 42	11 57	12 12	12 27	12 42	12 57	13 12	13 27	13 42	13 57	14 12	14 27	14 42	14 57	15 12	15 27	15 42	15 57	16 12
Leyton Midland Road	d	10 59	11 14	11 29	11 44	11 59	12 14	12 29	12 44	12 59	13 14	13 29	13 44	13 59	14 14	14 29	14 44	14 59	15 14	15 29	15 44	15 59	16 14
Walthamstow Queens Road	d	11 02	11 17	11 32	11 47	12 02	12 17	12 32	12 47	13 02	13 17	13 32	13 47	14 02	14 17	14 32	14 47	15 02	15 17	15 32	15 47	16 02	16 17
Blackhorse Road ⊖	d	11 05	11 20	11 35	11 50	12 05	12 20	12 35	12 50	13 05	13 20	13 35	13 50	14 05	14 20	14 35	14 50	15 05	15 20	15 35	15 50	16 05	16 20
South Tottenham	d	11 09	11 24	11 39	11 54	12 09	12 24	12 39	12 54	13 09	13 24	13 39	13 54	14 09	14 24	14 39	14 54	15 09	15 24	15 39	15 54	16 09	16 24
Harringay Green Lanes	d	11 12	11 27	11 42	11 57	12 12	12 27	12 42	12 57	13 12	13 27	13 42	13 57	14 12	14 27	14 42	14 57	15 12	15 27	15 42	15 57	16 12	16 27
Crouch Hill	d	11 15	11 30	11 45	12 00	12 15	12 30	12 45	13 00	13 15	13 30	13 45	14 00	14 15	14 30	14 45	15 00	15 15	15 30	15 45	16 00	16 15	16 30
Upper Holloway	d	11 17	11 32	11 47	12 02	12 17	12 32	12 47	13 02	13 17	13 32	13 47	14 02	14 17	14 32	14 47	15 02	15 17	15 32	15 47	16 02	16 17	16 32
Gospel Oak	a	11 23	11 41	11 55	12 11	12 23	12 41	12 54	13 11	13 23	13 41	13 53	14 08	14 23	14 38	14 53	15 08	15 24	15 38	15 53	16 08	16 23	16 40

		LO	LO	LO	LO	LO	LO	LO	LO	LO	LO	LO	LO	LO	LO	LO	LO	LO	LO	LO	LO	LO
Barking ⊖	d	16 17	16 32	16 47	17 02	17 17	17 32	17 47	18 02	18 17	18 32	18 47	19 02	19 17	19 32	19 47	20 02	20 17	20 32	20 47	21 02	21 17
Woodgrange Park	d	16 20	16 35	16 50	17 05	17 20	17 35	17 50	18 05	18 20	18 35	18 50	19 05	19 20	19 35	19 50	20 05	20 20	20 35	20 50	21 05	21 20
Wanstead Park	d	16 23	16 38	16 53	17 08	17 23	17 38	17 53	18 08	18 23	18 38	18 53	19 08	19 23	19 38	19 53	20 08	20 23	20 38	20 53	21 08	21 23
Leytonstone High Road	d	16 27	16 42	16 57	17 12	17 27	17 42	17 57	18 12	18 27	18 42	18 57	19 12	19 27	19 42	19 57	20 12	20 27	20 42	20 57	21 12	21 27
Leyton Midland Road	d	16 29	16 44	16 59	17 14	17 29	17 44	17 59	18 14	18 29	18 44	18 59	19 14	19 29	19 44	19 59	20 14	20 29	20 44	20 59	21 14	21 29
Walthamstow Queens Road	d	16 32	16 47	17 02	17 17	17 32	17 47	18 02	18 17	18 32	18 47	19 02	19 17	19 32	19 47	20 02	20 17	20 32	20 47	21 02	21 17	21 32
Blackhorse Road ⊖	d	16 35	16 50	17 05	17 20	17 35	17 50	18 05	18 20	18 35	18 50	19 05	19 20	19 35	19 50	20 05	20 20	20 35	20 50	21 05	21 20	21 35
South Tottenham	d	16 39	16 54	17 09	17 24	17 39	17 54	18 09	18 24	18 39	18 54	19 09	19 24	19 39	19 54	20 09	20 24	20 39	20 54	21 09	21 24	21 39
Harringay Green Lanes	d	16 42	16 57	17 12	17 27	17 42	17 57	18 12	18 27	18 42	18 57	19 12	19 27	19 42	19 57	20 12	20 27	20 42	20 57	21 12	21 27	21 42
Crouch Hill	d	16 45	17 00	17 15	17 30	17 45	18 00	18 15	18 30	18 45	19 00	19 15	19 30	19 45	20 00	20 15	20 30	20 45	21 00	21 15	21 30	21 45
Upper Holloway	d	16 47	17 02	17 17	17 32	17 47	18 02	18 17	18 32	18 47	19 02	19 17	19 32	19 47	20 02	20 17	20 32	20 47	21 02	21 17	21 32	21 47
Gospel Oak	a	16 53	17 08	17 23	17 38	17 53	18 08	18 23	18 38	18 53	19 09	19 26	19 38	19 53	20 08	20 23	20 38	20 53	21 08	21 24	21 38	21 54

		LO	LO	LO	LO	LO	LO	LO
Barking ⊖	d	21 32	21 47	22 02	22 17	22 47	23 17	23 47
Woodgrange Park	d	21 35	21 50	22 05	22 20	22 50	23 20	23 50
Wanstead Park	d	21 38	21 53	22 08	22 23	22 53	23 23	23 53
Leytonstone High Road	d	21 42	21 57	22 12	22 27	22 57	23 27	23 57
Leyton Midland Road	d	21 44	21 59	22 14	22 29	22 59	23 29	23 59
Walthamstow Queens Road	d	21 47	22 02	22 17	22 32	23 02	23 32	00 02
Blackhorse Road ⊖	d	21 50	22 05	22 20	22 35	23 05	23 35	00 05
South Tottenham	d	21 54	22 09	22 24	22 39	23 09	23 39	00 09
Harringay Green Lanes	d	21 57	22 12	22 27	22 42	23 12	23 42	00 12
Crouch Hill	d	22 00	22 16	22 30	22 45	23 15	23 45	00 15
Upper Holloway	d	22 02	22 18	22 32	22 47	23 17	23 47	00 17
Gospel Oak	a	22 11	22 23	22 38	22 53	23 25	23 58	00 27

A 20 August, 27 August   B 13 August

Barking - Gospel Oak

Mondays to Fridays
29 August to 7 September

Network Diagram - see first Page of Table 59

		LO A	LO B	LO	LO	LO	LO	LO	LO	LO	LO	LO	LO	LO	LO	LO	LO	LO	LO	LO	LO	LO	LO
Barking ⊖	d	23p38	23p47	06 17	06 32	06 47	07 02	07 17	07 32	07 47	08 02	08 17	08 32	08 47	09 02	09 17	09 32	09 47	10 02	10 17	10 32	10 47	11 02
Woodgrange Park	d	23p41	23p50	06 20	06 35	06 50	07 05	07 20	07 35	07 50	08 05	08 20	08 35	08 50	09 05	09 20	09 35	09 50	10 05	10 20	10 35	10 50	11 05
Wanstead Park	d	23p44	23p53	06 23	06 38	06 53	07 08	07 23	07 38	07 53	08 08	08 23	08 38	08 53	09 08	09 23	09 38	09 53	10 08	10 23	10 38	10 53	11 08
Leytonstone High Road	d	23p48	23p57	06 27	06 42	06 57	07 12	07 27	07 42	07 57	08 12	08 27	08 42	08 57	09 12	09 27	09 42	09 57	10 12	10 27	10 42	10 57	11 12
Leyton Midland Road	d	23p50	23p59	06 29	06 44	06 59	07 14	07 29	07 44	07 59	08 14	08 29	08 44	08 59	09 14	09 29	09 44	09 59	10 14	10 29	10 44	10 59	11 14
Walthamstow Queens Road	d	23p53	00 02	06 32	06 47	07 02	07 17	07 32	07 47	08 02	08 17	08 32	08 47	09 02	09 17	09 32	09 47	10 02	10 17	10 32	10 47	11 02	11 17
Blackhorse Road ⊖	d	23p56	00 05	06 35	06 50	07 05	07 20	07 35	07 50	08 05	08 20	08 35	08 50	09 05	09 20	09 35	09 50	10 05	10 20	10 35	10 50	11 05	11 20
South Tottenham	d	23p59	00 09	06 39	06 54	07 09	07 24	07 39	07 54	08 09	08 24	08 39	08 54	09 09	09 24	09 39	09 54	10 09	10 24	10 39	10 54	11 09	11 24
Harringay Green Lanes	d	00 03	00 12	06 42	06 57	07 12	07 27	07 42	07 57	08 12	08 27	08 42	08 57	09 12	09 27	09 42	09 57	10 12	10 27	10 42	10 57	11 12	11 27
Crouch Hill	d	00 06	00 15	06 45	07 00	07 15	07 30	07 45	08 00	08 15	08 30	08 45	09 00	09 15	09 30	09 45	10 00	10 19	10 30	10 45	11 00	11 15	11 30
Upper Holloway	d	00 08	00 17	06 47	07 02	07 17	07 32	07 47	08 02	08 17	08 32	08 47	09 02	09 17	09 32	09 47	10 02	10 22	10 32	10 47	11 02	11 17	11 32
Gospel Oak	a	00 18	00 27	06 59	07 13	07 28	07 43	07 58	08 13	08 28	08 43	08 58	09 13	09 28	09 43	09 58	10 13	10 34	10 43	10 58	11 14	11 28	11 43

		LO	LO	LO	LO	LO	LO	LO	LO	LO	LO	LO	LO	LO	LO	LO	LO	LO	LO	LO	LO	LO	LO
Barking ⊖	d	11 17	11 32	11 47	12 02	12 17	12 32	12 47	13 02	13 17	13 32	13 47	14 02	14 17	14 32	14 47	15 02	15 17	15 32	15 47	16 02	16 17	16 32
Woodgrange Park	d	11 20	11 35	11 50	12 05	12 20	12 35	12 50	13 05	13 20	13 35	13 50	14 05	14 20	14 35	14 50	15 05	15 20	15 35	15 50	16 05	16 20	16 35
Wanstead Park	d	11 23	11 38	11 53	12 08	12 23	12 38	12 53	13 08	13 23	13 38	13 53	14 08	14 23	14 38	14 53	15 08	15 23	15 38	15 53	16 08	16 23	16 38
Leytonstone High Road	d	11 27	11 42	11 57	12 12	12 27	12 42	12 57	13 12	13 27	13 42	13 57	14 12	14 27	14 42	14 57	15 12	15 27	15 42	15 57	16 12	16 27	16 42
Leyton Midland Road	d	11 29	11 44	11 59	12 14	12 29	12 44	12 59	13 14	13 29	13 44	13 59	14 14	14 29	14 44	14 59	15 14	15 29	15 44	15 59	16 14	16 29	16 44
Walthamstow Queens Road	d	11 32	11 47	12 02	12 17	12 32	12 47	13 02	13 17	13 32	13 47	14 02	14 17	14 32	14 47	15 02	15 17	15 32	15 47	16 02	16 17	16 32	16 47
Blackhorse Road ⊖	d	11 35	11 50	12 05	12 20	12 35	12 50	13 05	13 20	13 35	13 50	14 05	14 20	14 35	14 50	15 05	15 20	15 35	15 50	16 05	16 20	16 35	16 50
South Tottenham	d	11 39	11 54	12 09	12 24	12 39	12 54	13 09	13 24	13 39	13 54	14 09	14 24	14 39	14 54	15 09	15 24	15 39	15 54	16 09	16 24	16 39	16 54
Harringay Green Lanes	d	11 42	11 57	12 12	12 27	12 42	12 57	13 12	13 27	13 42	13 57	14 12	14 27	14 42	14 57	15 12	15 27	15 42	15 57	16 12	16 27	16 42	16 57
Crouch Hill	d	11 45	12 00	12 15	12 30	12 45	13 00	13 15	13 30	13 45	14 00	14 15	14 30	14 45	15 02	15 15	15 30	15 45	16 00	16 15	16 30	16 45	17 00
Upper Holloway	d	11 47	12 02	12 17	12 32	12 47	13 02	13 17	13 32	13 47	14 02	14 23	14 32	14 47	15 06	15 17	15 32	15 47	16 02	16 17	16 32	16 47	17 02
Gospel Oak	a	11 58	12 16	12 28	12 46	12 58	13 16	13 28	13 43	13 58	14 13	14 33	14 43	14 58	15 18	15 28	15 43	15 58	16 13	16 28	16 45	16 58	17 13

		LO	LO	LO	LO	LO	LO	LO	LO	LO	LO	LO	LO	LO	LO	LO	LO	LO	LO	LO	LO	LO
Barking ⊖	d	16 47	17 02	17 17	17 32	17 47	18 02	18 17	18 32	18 47	19 02	19 17	19 32	19 47	20 02	20 17	20 32	20 47	21 02	21 17	21 32	21 47
Woodgrange Park	d	16 50	17 05	17 20	17 35	17 50	18 05	18 20	18 35	18 50	19 05	19 20	19 35	19 50	20 05	20 20	20 35	20 50	21 05	21 20	21 35	21 50
Wanstead Park	d	16 53	17 08	17 23	17 38	17 53	18 08	18 23	18 38	18 53	19 08	19 23	19 38	19 53	20 08	20 23	20 38	20 53	21 08	21 23	21 38	21 53
Leytonstone High Road	d	16 57	17 12	17 27	17 42	17 57	18 12	18 27	18 42	18 57	19 12	19 27	19 42	19 57	20 12	20 27	20 42	20 57	21 12	21 27	21 42	21 57
Leyton Midland Road	d	16 59	17 14	17 29	17 44	17 59	18 14	18 29	18 44	18 59	19 14	19 29	19 44	19 59	20 14	20 29	20 44	20 59	21 14	21 29	21 44	21 59
Walthamstow Queens Road	d	17 02	17 17	17 32	17 47	18 02	18 17	18 32	18 47	19 02	19 17	19 32	19 47	20 02	20 17	20 32	20 47	21 02	21 17	21 32	21 47	22 02
Blackhorse Road ⊖	d	17 05	17 20	17 35	17 50	18 05	18 20	18 35	18 50	19 05	19 20	19 35	19 50	20 05	20 20	20 35	20 50	21 05	21 20	21 35	21 50	22 05
South Tottenham	d	17 09	17 24	17 39	17 54	18 09	18 24	18 39	18 54	19 09	19 24	19 39	19 54	20 09	20 24	20 39	20 54	21 09	21 24	21 39	21 54	22 09
Harringay Green Lanes	d	17 12	17 27	17 42	17 57	18 12	18 27	18 42	18 57	19 12	19 27	19 42	19 57	20 12	20 27	20 42	20 57	21 12	21 27	21 42	21 57	22 12
Crouch Hill	d	17 15	17 30	17 45	18 00	18 15	18 30	18 45	19 00	19 15	19 30	19 45	20 00	20 15	20 30	20 45	21 00	21 15	21 30	21 45	22 00	22 15
Upper Holloway	d	17 17	17 32	17 47	18 09	18 17	18 32	18 47	19 02	19 18	19 32	19 47	20 02	20 23	20 32	20 47	21 02	21 17	21 32	21 47	22 03	22 17
Gospel Oak	a	17 28	17 43	17 58	18 19	18 28	18 43	18 58	19 13	19 33	19 43	20 02	20 13	20 34	20 43	20 58	21 15	21 28	21 43	21 58	22 18	22 32

		LO	LO	LO	LO	LO
Barking ⊖	d	22 02	22 17	22 47	23 17	23 47
Woodgrange Park	d	22 05	22 20	22 50	23 20	23 50
Wanstead Park	d	22 08	22 23	22 53	23 23	23 53
Leytonstone High Road	d	22 12	22 27	22 57	23 27	23 57
Leyton Midland Road	d	22 14	22 29	22 59	23 29	23 59
Walthamstow Queens Road	d	22 17	22 32	23 02	23 32	00 02
Blackhorse Road ⊖	d	22 20	22 35	23 05	23 35	00 05
South Tottenham	d	22 24	22 39	23 09	23 39	00 09
Harringay Green Lanes	d	22 27	22 42	23 12	23 42	00 12
Crouch Hill	d	22 30	22 45	23 15	23 45	00 15
Upper Holloway	d	22 32	22 47	23 17	23 47	00 17
Gospel Oak	a	22 43	22 58	23 31	23 58	00 27

Mondays to Fridays
from 10 September

		LO MO C	LO D	LO MX	LO	LO	LO	LO	LO	LO	LO	LO	LO	LO	LO	LO	LO	LO	LO	LO	LO	LO	LO
Barking ⊖	d	23p38	23p38	23p47	06 17	06 32	06 47	07 02	07 17	07 32	07 47		08 02	08 17	08 32	08 47	09 02	09 17	09 32	09 47	10 02	10 17	10 32
Woodgrange Park	d	23p41	23p41	23p50	06 20	06 35	06 50	07 05	07 20	07 35	07 50	07 59	08 05	08 20	08 35	08 50	09 05	09 20	09 35	09 50	10 05	10 20	10 35
Wanstead Park	d	23p44	23p44	23p53	06 23	06 38	06 53	07 08	07 23	07 38	07 53	08 02	08 08	08 23	08 38	08 53	09 08	09 23	09 38	09 53	10 08	10 23	10 38
Leytonstone High Road	d	23p48	23p48	23p57	06 27	06 42	06 57	07 12	07 27	07 42	07 57	08 05	08 12	08 27	08 42	08 57	09 12	09 27	09 42	09 57	10 12	10 27	10 42
Leyton Midland Road	d	23p50	23p50	23p59	06 29	06 44	06 59	07 14	07 29	07 44	07 59	08 08	08 14	08 29	08 44	08 59	09 14	09 29	09 44	09 59	10 14	10 29	10 44
Walthamstow Queens Road	d	23p53	23p53	00 02	06 32	06 47	07 02	07 17	07 32	07 47	08 02	08 11	08 17	08 32	08 47	09 02	09 17	09 32	09 47	10 02	10 17	10 32	10 47
Blackhorse Road ⊖	d	23p56	23p56	00 05	06 35	06 50	07 05	07 20	07 35	07 50	08 05	08 14	08 20	08 35	08 50	09 05	09 20	09 35	09 50	10 05	10 20	10 35	10 50
South Tottenham	d	23p59	23p59	00 09	06 39	06 54	07 09	07 24	07 39	07 54	08 09	08 18	08 24	08 39	08 54	09 09	09 24	09 39	09 54	10 09	10 24	10 39	10 54
Harringay Green Lanes	d	00 03	00 03	00 12	06 42	06 57	07 12	07 27	07 42	07 57	08 12	08 21	08 27	08 42	08 57	09 12	09 27	09 42	09 57	10 12	10 27	10 42	10 57
Crouch Hill	d	00 06	00 06	00 15	06 45	07 00	07 15	07 30	07 45	08 00	08 15	08 24	08 30	08 45	09 00	09 15	09 30	09 45	10 00	10 19	10 30	10 45	11 00
Upper Holloway	d	00 08	00 08	00 17	06 47	07 02	07 17	07 32	07 47	08 02	08 17	08a27	08 32	08 47	09 02	09 17	09 32	09 47	10 02	10 22	10 32	10 47	11 02
Gospel Oak	a	00 13	00 18	00 24	06 55	07 09	07 23	07 39	07 53	08 08	08 23		08 38	08 53	09 08	09 23	09 38	09 53	10 08	10 29	10 38	10 54	11 11

		LO	LO	LO	LO	LO	LO	LO	LO	LO	LO	LO	LO	LO	LO	LO	LO	LO	LO	LO	LO	LO	LO
Barking ⊖	d	10 47	11 02	11 17	11 32	11 47	12 02	12 17	12 32	12 47	13 02	13 17	13 32	13 47	14 02	14 17	14 32	14 47	15 02	15 17	15 32	15 47	16 02
Woodgrange Park	d	10 50	11 05	11 20	11 35	11 50	12 05	12 20	12 35	12 50	13 05	13 20	13 35	13 50	14 05	14 20	14 35	14 50	15 05	15 20	15 35	15 50	16 05
Wanstead Park	d	10 53	11 08	11 23	11 38	11 53	12 08	12 23	12 38	12 53	13 08	13 23	13 38	13 53	14 08	14 23	14 38	14 53	15 08	15 23	15 38	15 53	16 08
Leytonstone High Road	d	10 57	11 12	11 27	11 42	11 57	12 12	12 27	12 42	12 57	13 12	13 27	13 42	13 57	14 12	14 27	14 42	14 57	15 12	15 27	15 42	15 57	16 12
Leyton Midland Road	d	10 59	11 14	11 29	11 44	11 59	12 14	12 29	12 44	12 59	13 14	13 29	13 44	13 59	14 14	14 29	14 44	14 59	15 14	15 29	15 44	15 59	16 14
Walthamstow Queens Road	d	11 02	11 17	11 32	11 47	12 02	12 17	12 32	12 47	13 02	13 17	13 32	13 47	14 02	14 17	14 32	14 47	15 02	15 17	15 32	15 47	16 02	16 17
Blackhorse Road ⊖	d	11 05	11 20	11 35	11 50	12 05	12 20	12 35	12 50	13 05	13 20	13 35	13 50	14 05	14 20	14 35	14 50	15 05	15 20	15 35	15 50	16 05	16 20
South Tottenham	d	11 09	11 24	11 39	11 54	12 09	12 24	12 39	12 54	13 09	13 24	13 39	13 54	14 09	14 24	14 39	14 54	15 09	15 24	15 39	15 54	16 09	16 24
Harringay Green Lanes	d	11 12	11 27	11 42	11 57	12 12	12 27	12 42	12 57	13 12	13 27	13 42	13 57	14 12	14 27	14 42	14 57	15 12	15 27	15 42	15 57	16 12	16 27
Crouch Hill	d	11 15	11 30	11 45	12 00	12 15	12 30	12 45	13 00	13 15	13 30	13 45	14 00	14 15	14 30	14 45	15 00	15 15	15 30	15 45	16 00	16 15	16 30
Upper Holloway	d	11 17	11 32	11 47	12 02	12 17	12 32	12 47	13 02	13 17	13 32	13 47	14 02	14 17	14 32	14 47	15 02	15 17	15 32	15 47	16 02	16 17	16 32
Gospel Oak	a	11 23	11 41	11 55	12 11	12 23	12 41	12 54	13 11	13 23	13 41	13 53	14 08	14 23	14 38	14 53	15 08	15 24	15 38	15 53	16 08	16 23	16 40

A 3 September
B not 3 September
C from 17 September
D 10 September

Barking - Gospel Oak

Mondays to Fridays
from 10 September

Network Diagram - see first Page of Table 59

		LO	LO	LO	LO	LO	LO	LO	LO	LO	LO	LO	LO	LO	LO	LO	LO	LO	LO	LO	LO	LO
Barking ⊖	d	16 17	16 32	16 47	17 02	17 17	17 32	17 47	18 02	18 17	18 32	18 47	19 02	19 17	19 32	19 47	20 02	20 17	20 32	20 47	21 02	21 17
Woodgrange Park	d	16 20	16 35	16 50	17 05	17 20	17 35	17 50	18 05	18 20	18 35	18 50	19 05	19 20	19 35	19 50	20 05	20 20	20 35	20 50	21 05	21 20
Wanstead Park	d	16 23	16 38	16 53	17 08	17 23	17 38	17 53	18 08	18 23	18 38	18 53	19 08	19 23	19 38	19 53	20 08	20 23	20 38	20 53	21 08	21 23
Leytonstone High Road	d	16 27	16 42	16 57	17 12	17 27	17 42	17 57	18 12	18 27	18 42	18 57	19 12	19 27	19 42	19 57	20 12	20 27	20 42	20 57	21 12	21 27
Leyton Midland Road	d	16 29	16 44	16 59	17 14	17 29	17 44	17 59	18 14	18 29	18 44	18 59	19 14	19 29	19 44	19 59	20 14	20 29	20 44	20 59	21 14	21 29
Walthamstow Queens Road	d	16 32	16 47	17 02	17 17	17 32	17 47	18 02	18 17	18 32	18 47	19 02	19 17	19 32	19 47	20 02	20 17	20 32	20 47	21 02	21 17	21 32
Blackhorse Road ⊖	d	16 35	16 50	17 05	17 20	17 35	17 50	18 05	18 20	18 35	18 50	19 05	19 20	19 35	19 50	20 05	20 20	20 35	20 50	21 05	21 20	21 35
South Tottenham	d	16 39	16 54	17 09	17 24	17 39	17 54	18 09	18 24	18 39	18 54	19 09	19 24	19 39	19 54	20 09	20 24	20 39	20 54	21 09	21 24	21 39
Harringay Green Lanes	d	16 42	16 57	17 12	17 27	17 42	17 57	18 12	18 27	18 42	18 57	19 12	19 27	19 42	19 57	20 12	20 27	20 42	20 57	21 12	21 27	21 42
Crouch Hill	d	16 45	17 00	17 15	17 30	17 45	18 00	18 15	18 30	18 45	19 00	19 15	19 30	19 45	20 00	20 15	20 30	20 45	21 00	21 15	21 30	21 45
Upper Holloway	d	16 47	17 02	17 17	17 32	17 47	18 02	18 17	18 32	18 47	19 02	19 17	19 32	19 47	20 02	20 17	20 32	20 47	21 02	21 17	21 32	21 47
Gospel Oak	a	16 53	17 08	17 23	17 38	17 53	18 08	18 23	18 38	18 53	19 09	19 26	19 38	19 53	20 08	20 23	20 38	20 53	21 08	21 24	21 38	21 54

		LO	LO	LO	LO	LO	LO	LO
Barking ⊖	d	21 32	21 47	22 02	22 17	22 47	23 17	23 47
Woodgrange Park	d	21 35	21 50	22 05	22 20	22 50	23 20	23 50
Wanstead Park	d	21 38	21 53	22 08	22 23	22 53	23 23	23 53
Leytonstone High Road	d	21 42	21 57	22 12	22 27	22 57	23 27	23 57
Leyton Midland Road	d	21 44	21 59	22 14	22 29	22 59	23 29	23 59
Walthamstow Queens Road	d	21 47	22 02	22 17	22 32	23 02	23 32	00 02
Blackhorse Road ⊖	d	21 50	22 05	22 20	22 35	23 05	23 35	00 05
South Tottenham	d	21 54	22 09	22 24	22 39	23 09	23 39	00 09
Harringay Green Lanes	d	21 57	22 12	22 27	22 42	23 12	23 42	00 12
Crouch Hill	d	22 00	22 16	22 30	22 45	23 15	23 45	00 15
Upper Holloway	d	22 02	22 18	22 32	22 47	23 17	23 47	00 17
Gospel Oak	a	22 11	22 23	22 38	22 53	23 25	23 53	00 24

Saturdays
until 21 July

		LO	LO	LO	LO	LO	LO	LO	LO	LO	LO	LO	LO	LO	LO	LO	LO	LO	LO	LO	LO	LO	LO
Barking ⊖	d	23p47	06 17	06 32	06 47	07 02	07 17	07 32	07 47	08 02	08 17	08 32	08 47	09 02	09 17	09 32	09 47	10 02	10 17	10 32	10 47	11 02	11 17
Woodgrange Park	d	23p50	06 20	06 35	06 50	07 05	07 20	07 35	07 50	08 05	08 20	08 35	08 50	09 05	09 20	09 35	09 50	10 05	10 20	10 35	10 50	11 05	11 20
Wanstead Park	d	23p53	06 23	06 38	06 53	07 08	07 23	07 38	07 53	08 08	08 23	08 38	08 53	09 08	09 23	09 38	09 53	10 08	10 23	10 38	10 53	11 08	11 23
Leytonstone High Road	d	23p57	06 27	06 42	06 57	07 12	07 27	07 42	07 57	08 12	08 27	08 42	08 57	09 12	09 27	09 42	09 57	10 12	10 27	10 42	10 57	11 12	11 27
Leyton Midland Road	d	23p59	06 29	06 44	06 59	07 14	07 29	07 44	07 59	08 14	08 29	08 44	08 59	09 14	09 29	09 44	09 59	10 14	10 29	10 44	10 59	11 14	11 29
Walthamstow Queens Road	d	00 02	06 32	06 47	07 02	07 17	07 32	07 47	08 02	08 17	08 32	08 47	09 02	09 17	09 32	09 47	10 02	10 17	10 32	10 47	11 02	11 17	11 32
Blackhorse Road ⊖	d	00 05	06 35	06 50	07 05	07 20	07 35	07 50	08 05	08 20	08 35	08 50	09 05	09 20	09 35	09 50	10 05	10 20	10 35	10 50	11 05	11 20	11 35
South Tottenham	d	00 09	06 39	06 54	07 09	07 24	07 39	07 54	08 09	08 24	08 39	08 54	09 09	09 24	09 39	09 54	10 09	10 24	10 39	10 54	11 09	11 24	11 39
Harringay Green Lanes	d	00 12	06 42	06 57	07 12	07 27	07 42	07 57	08 12	08 27	08 42	08 57	09 12	09 27	09 42	09 57	10 12	10 27	10 42	10 57	11 12	11 27	11 42
Crouch Hill	d	00 15	06 45	07 00	07 15	07 30	07 45	08 00	08 15	08 30	08 45	09 00	09 15	09 30	09 45	10 00	10 15	10 30	10 45	11 00	11 15	11 30	11 45
Upper Holloway	d	00 17	06 47	07 02	07 17	07 32	07 47	08 02	08 17	08 32	08 47	09 02	09 17	09 32	09 47	10 02	10 17	10 32	10 48	11 02	11 17	11 32	11 47
Gospel Oak	a	00 27	06 54	07 08	07 23	07 38	07 53	08 08	08 23	08 38	08 53	09 08	09 24	09 38	09 53	10 08	10 23	10 39	10 53	11 11	11 23	11 39	11 53

		LO	LO	LO	LO	LO	LO	LO		LO	LO	LO	LO	LO	LO	LO	LO	LO	LO	LO	LO	LO
Barking ⊖	d	11 32	11 47	12 02	12 17	12 32	12 47	13 02	and at the same minutes past each hour until	18 02	18 17	18 32	18 47	19 02	19 17	19 32	19 47	20 02	20 17	20 32	20 47	21 02
Woodgrange Park	d	11 35	11 50	12 05	12 20	12 35	12 50	13 05		18 05	18 20	18 35	18 50	19 05	19 20	19 35	19 50	20 05	20 20	20 35	20 50	21 05
Wanstead Park	d	11 38	11 53	12 08	12 23	12 38	12 53	13 08		18 08	18 23	18 38	18 53	19 08	19 23	19 38	19 53	20 08	20 23	20 38	20 53	21 08
Leytonstone High Road	d	11 42	11 57	12 12	12 27	12 42	12 57	13 12		18 12	18 27	18 42	18 57	19 12	19 27	19 42	19 57	20 12	20 27	20 42	20 57	21 12
Leyton Midland Road	d	11 44	11 59	12 14	12 29	12 44	12 59	13 14		18 14	18 29	18 44	18 59	19 14	19 29	19 44	19 59	20 14	20 29	20 44	20 59	21 14
Walthamstow Queens Road	d	11 47	12 02	12 17	12 32	12 47	13 02	13 17		18 17	18 32	18 47	19 02	19 17	19 32	19 47	20 02	20 17	20 32	20 47	21 02	21 17
Blackhorse Road ⊖	d	11 50	12 05	12 20	12 35	12 50	13 05	13 20		18 20	18 35	18 50	19 05	19 20	19 35	19 50	20 05	20 20	20 35	20 50	21 05	21 20
South Tottenham	d	11 54	12 09	12 24	12 39	12 54	13 09	13 24		18 24	18 39	18 54	19 09	19 24	19 39	19 54	20 09	20 24	20 39	20 54	21 09	21 24
Harringay Green Lanes	d	11 57	12 12	12 27	12 42	12 57	13 12	13 27		18 27	18 42	18 57	19 12	19 27	19 42	19 57	20 12	20 27	20 42	20 57	21 12	21 27
Crouch Hill	d	12 00	12 15	12 30	12 45	13 00	13 15	13 30		18 30	18 45	19 00	19 15	19 30	19 45	20 00	20 15	20 30	20 45	21 00	21 15	21 30
Upper Holloway	d	12 02	12 17	12 32	12 47	13 02	13 17	13 32		18 32	18 47	19 02	19 17	19 32	19 47	20 02	20 17	20 32	20 47	21 02	21 17	21 32
Gospel Oak	a	12 09	12 23	12 40	12 53	13 08	13 23	13 38		18 38	18 53	19 08	19 23	19 41	19 53	20 08	20 23	20 38	20 53	21 08	21 23	21 38

		LO	LO	LO	LO	LO	LO	LO	LO
Barking ⊖	d	21 17	21 32	21 47	22 02	22 17	22 47	23 17	23 47
Woodgrange Park	d	21 20	21 35	21 50	22 05	22 20	22 50	23 20	23 50
Wanstead Park	d	21 23	21 38	21 53	22 08	22 23	22 53	23 23	23 53
Leytonstone High Road	d	21 27	21 42	21 57	22 12	22 27	22 57	23 27	23 57
Leyton Midland Road	d	21 29	21 44	21 59	22 14	22 29	22 59	23 29	23 59
Walthamstow Queens Road	d	21 32	21 47	22 02	22 17	22 32	23 02	23 32	00 02
Blackhorse Road ⊖	d	21 35	21 50	22 05	22 20	22 35	23 05	23 35	00 05
South Tottenham	d	21 39	21 54	22 09	22 24	22 39	23 09	23 39	00 09
Harringay Green Lanes	d	21 42	21 57	22 12	22 27	22 42	23 12	23 42	00 12
Crouch Hill	d	21 45	22 00	22 15	22 30	22 45	23 15	23 45	00 15
Upper Holloway	d	21 47	22 02	22 17	22 32	22 47	23 17	23 47	00 17
Gospel Oak	a	21 53	22 08	22 22	22 38	22 52	23 22	23 52	00 24

Saturdays
28 July to 11 August

		LO	LO	LO	LO	LO	LO	LO	LO	LO	LO	LO	LO	LO	LO	LO	LO	LO	LO	LO	LO	LO	LO
Barking ⊖	d	23p47	06 17	06 32	06 47	07 02	07 17	07 32	07 47	08 02	08 17	08 32	08 47	09 02	09 17	09 32	09 47	10 02	10 17	10 34	10 47	11 02	11 17
Woodgrange Park	d	23p50	06 20	06 35	06 50	07 05	07 20	07 35	07 50	08 05	08 20	08 35	08 50	09 05	09 20	09 35	09 50	10 05	10 20	10 37	10 50	11 05	11 20
Wanstead Park	d	23p53	06 23	06 38	06 53	07 08	07 23	07 38	07 53	08 08	08 23	08 38	08 53	09 08	09 23	09 38	09 53	10 08	10 23	10 40	10 53	11 08	11 23
Leytonstone High Road	d	23p57	06 27	06 42	06 57	07 12	07 27	07 42	07 57	08 12	08 27	08 42	08 57	09 12	09 27	09 42	09 57	10 12	10 27	10 44	10 57	11 12	11 27
Leyton Midland Road	d	23p59	06 29	06 44	06 59	07 14	07 29	07 44	07 59	08 14	08 29	08 44	08 59	09 14	09 29	09 44	09 59	10 14	10 29	10 46	10 59	11 14	11 29
Walthamstow Queens Road	d	00 02	06 32	06 47	07 02	07 17	07 32	07 47	08 02	08 17	08 32	08 47	09 02	09 17	09 32	09 47	10 02	10 17	10 32	10 49	11 02	11 17	11 32
Blackhorse Road ⊖	d	00 05	06 35	06 50	07 05	07 20	07 35	07 50	08 05	08 20	08 35	08 50	09 05	09 20	09 35	09 50	10 05	10 20	10 35	10 52	11 05	11 20	11 35
South Tottenham	d	00 09	06 39	06 54	07 09	07 24	07 39	07 54	08 09	08 24	08 39	08 54	09 09	09 24	09 39	09 54	10 09	10 24	10 39	10 56	11 09	11 24	11 39
Harringay Green Lanes	d	00 12	06 42	06 57	07 12	07 27	07 42	07 57	08 12	08 27	08 42	08 57	09 12	09 27	09 42	09 57	10 12	10 27	10 42	10 59	11 12	11 27	11 42
Crouch Hill	d	00 15	06 45	07 00	07 15	07 30	07 45	08 00	08 15	08 30	08 45	09 00	09 15	09 30	09 45	10 00	10 15	10 30	10 45	11 02	11 15	11 30	11 45
Upper Holloway	d	00 17	06 47	07 02	07 17	07 32	07 47	08 02	08 17	08 32	08 47	09 02	09 17	09 32	09 47	10 02	10 17	10 32	10 47	11 04	11 17	11 32	11 47
Gospel Oak	a	00 27	06 59	07 13	07 28	07 43	07 58	08 13	08 28	08 45	08 57	09 13	09 27	09 43	09 58	10 13	10 28	10 42	10 58	11 18	11 28	11 43	11 58

Table 62

Saturdays

28 July to 11 August

Barking - Gospel Oak

Network Diagram - see first Page of Table 59

		LO		LO	LO	LO	LO	LO	LO	LO	LO	LO	LO	LO	LO	LO	LO	LO	LO	LO	LO	LO	LO
Barking ⊖	d	11 32		18 32	18 47	19 02	19 17	19 32	19 47	20 02	20 17	20 32	20 47	21 02	21 17	21 32	21 47	22 02	22 17	22 47	23 17	23 47
Woodgrange Park	d	11 35		18 35	18 50	19 05	19 20	19 35	19 50	20 05	20 20	20 35	20 50	21 05	21 20	21 35	21 50	22 05	22 20	22 50	23 20	23 50
Wanstead Park	d	11 38	and at	18 38	18 53	19 08	19 23	19 38	19 53	20 08	20 23	20 38	20 53	21 08	21 23	21 38	21 53	22 08	22 23	22 53	23 23	23 53
Leytonstone High Road	d	11 42	the same	18 42	18 57	19 12	19 27	19 42	19 57	20 12	20 27	20 42	20 57	21 12	21 27	21 42	21 57	22 12	22 27	22 57	23 27	23 57
Leyton Midland Road	d	11 44	minutes	18 44	18 59	19 14	19 29	19 44	19 59	20 14	20 29	20 44	20 59	21 14	21 29	21 44	21 59	22 14	22 29	22 59	23 29	23 59
Walthamstow Queens Road	d	11 47	past	18 47	19 02	19 17	19 32	19 47	20 02	20 17	20 32	20 47	21 02	21 17	21 32	21 47	22 02	22 17	22 32	23 02	23 32	00 02
Blackhorse Road ⊖	d	11 50	each	18 50	19 05	19 20	19 35	19 50	20 05	20 20	20 35	20 50	21 05	21 20	21 35	21 50	22 05	22 20	22 35	23 05	23 35	00 05
South Tottenham	d	11 54	hour until	18 54	19 09	19 24	19 39	19 54	20 09	20 24	20 39	20 54	21 09	21 24	21 39	21 54	22 09	22 24	22 39	23 09	23 39	00 09
Harringay Green Lanes	d	11 57		18 57	19 12	19 27	19 42	19 57	20 12	20 27	20 42	20 57	21 12	21 27	21 42	21 57	22 12	22 27	22 42	23 12	23 42	00 12
Crouch Hill	d	12 00		19 00	19 15	19 30	19 45	20 00	20 15	20 30	20 45	21 00	21 15	21 30	21 45	22 00	22 15	22 30	22 45	23 15	23 45	00 15
Upper Holloway	d	12 02		19 02	19 17	19 33	19 47	20 02	20 17	20 32	20 47	21 02	21 17	21 32	21 47	22 02	22 17	22 32	22 47	23 17	23 47	00 17
Gospel Oak	a	12 13		19 13	19 28	19 47	19 58	20 13	20 28	20 43	20 58	21 13	21 28	21 43	21 58	22 13	22 27	22 42	22 57	23 27	23 57	00 27

Saturdays

18 August to 25 August

		LO	LO	LO	LO	LO	LO	LO	LO	LO	LO	LO	LO	LO	LO	LO	LO	LO	LO	LO	LO	LO	LO
Barking ⊖	d	23p47	06 17	06 32	06 47	07 02	07 17	07 32	07 47	08 02	08 17	08 32	08 47	09 02	09 17	09 32	09 47	10 02	10 17	10 32	10 47	11 02	11 17
Woodgrange Park	d	23p50	06 20	06 35	06 50	07 05	07 20	07 35	07 50	08 05	08 20	08 35	08 50	09 05	09 20	09 35	09 50	10 05	10 20	10 35	10 50	11 05	11 20
Wanstead Park	d	23p53	06 23	06 38	06 53	07 08	07 23	07 38	07 53	08 08	08 23	08 38	08 53	09 08	09 23	09 38	09 53	10 08	10 23	10 38	10 53	11 08	11 23
Leytonstone High Road	d	23p57	06 27	06 42	06 57	07 12	07 27	07 42	07 57	08 12	08 27	08 42	08 57	09 12	09 27	09 42	09 57	10 12	10 27	10 42	10 57	11 12	11 27
Leyton Midland Road	d	23p59	06 29	06 44	06 59	07 14	07 29	07 44	07 59	08 14	08 29	08 44	08 59	09 14	09 29	09 44	09 59	10 14	10 29	10 44	10 59	11 14	11 29
Walthamstow Queens Road	d	00 02	06 32	06 47	07 02	07 17	07 32	07 47	08 02	08 17	08 32	08 47	09 02	09 17	09 32	09 47	10 02	10 17	10 32	10 47	11 02	11 17	11 32
Blackhorse Road ⊖	d	00 05	06 35	06 50	07 05	07 20	07 35	07 50	08 05	08 20	08 35	08 50	09 05	09 20	09 35	09 50	10 05	10 20	10 35	10 50	11 05	11 20	11 35
South Tottenham	d	00 09	06 39	06 54	07 09	07 24	07 39	07 54	08 09	08 24	08 39	08 54	09 09	09 24	09 39	09 54	10 09	10 24	10 39	10 54	11 09	11 24	11 39
Harringay Green Lanes	d	00 12	06 42	06 57	07 12	07 27	07 42	07 57	08 12	08 27	08 42	08 57	09 12	09 27	09 42	09 57	10 12	10 27	10 42	10 57	11 12	11 27	11 42
Crouch Hill	d	00 15	06 45	07 00	07 15	07 30	07 45	08 00	08 15	08 30	08 45	09 00	09 15	09 30	09 45	10 00	10 15	10 30	10 45	11 00	11 15	11 30	11 45
Upper Holloway	d	00 17	06 47	07 02	07 17	07 32	07 47	08 02	08 17	08 32	08 47	09 02	09 17	09 32	09 47	10 02	10 17	10 32	10 48	11 02	11 17	11 32	11 47
Gospel Oak	a	00 27	06 54	07 08	07 23	07 38	07 53	08 08	08 23	08 38	08 53	09 08	09 24	09 38	09 53	10 08	10 23	10 39	10 53	11 11	11 23	11 39	11 53

		LO	LO	LO	LO	LO	LO	LO		LO	LO	LO	LO	LO	LO	LO	LO	LO	LO	LO	LO	LO
Barking ⊖	d	11 32	11 47	12 02	12 17	12 32	12 47	13 02		18 02	18 17	18 32	18 47	19 02	19 17	19 32	19 47	20 02	20 17	20 32	20 47	21 02
Woodgrange Park	d	11 35	11 50	12 05	12 20	12 35	12 50	13 05		18 05	18 20	18 35	18 50	19 05	19 20	19 35	19 50	20 05	20 20	20 35	20 50	21 05
Wanstead Park	d	11 38	11 53	12 08	12 23	12 38	12 53	13 08	and at	18 08	18 23	18 38	18 53	19 08	19 23	19 38	19 53	20 08	20 23	20 38	20 53	21 08
Leytonstone High Road	d	11 42	11 57	12 12	12 27	12 42	12 57	13 12	the same	18 12	18 27	18 42	18 57	19 12	19 27	19 42	19 57	20 12	20 27	20 42	20 57	21 12
Leyton Midland Road	d	11 44	11 59	12 14	12 29	12 44	12 59	13 14	minutes	18 14	18 29	18 44	18 59	19 14	19 29	19 44	19 59	20 14	20 29	20 44	20 59	21 14
Walthamstow Queens Road	d	11 47	12 02	12 17	12 32	12 47	13 02	13 17	past	18 17	18 32	18 47	19 02	19 17	19 32	19 47	20 02	20 17	20 32	20 47	21 02	21 17
Blackhorse Road ⊖	d	11 50	12 05	12 20	12 35	12 50	13 05	13 20	each	18 20	18 35	18 50	19 05	19 20	19 35	19 50	20 05	20 20	20 35	20 50	21 05	21 20
South Tottenham	d	11 54	12 09	12 24	12 39	12 54	13 09	13 24	hour until	18 24	18 39	18 54	19 09	19 24	19 39	19 54	20 09	20 24	20 39	20 54	21 09	21 24
Harringay Green Lanes	d	11 57	12 12	12 27	12 42	12 57	13 12	13 27		18 27	18 42	18 57	19 12	19 27	19 42	19 57	20 12	20 27	20 42	20 57	21 12	21 27
Crouch Hill	d	12 00	12 15	12 30	12 45	13 00	13 15	13 30		18 30	18 45	19 00	19 15	19 30	19 45	20 00	20 15	20 30	20 45	21 00	21 15	21 30
Upper Holloway	d	12 02	12 17	12 32	12 47	13 02	13 17	13 32		18 32	18 47	19 02	19 17	19 32	19 47	20 02	20 17	20 32	20 47	21 02	21 17	21 32
Gospel Oak	a	12 09	12 23	12 40	12 53	13 08	13 23	13 38		18 38	18 53	19 08	19 23	19 41	19 53	20 08	20 23	20 38	20 53	21 08	21 23	21 38

		LO	LO	LO	LO	LO	LO	LO	LO
Barking ⊖	d	21 17	21 32	21 47	22 02	22 17	22 47	23 17	23 47
Woodgrange Park	d	21 20	21 35	21 50	22 05	22 20	22 50	23 20	23 50
Wanstead Park	d	21 23	21 38	21 53	22 08	22 23	22 53	23 23	23 53
Leytonstone High Road	d	21 27	21 42	21 57	22 12	22 27	22 57	23 27	23 57
Leyton Midland Road	d	21 29	21 44	21 59	22 14	22 29	22 59	23 29	23 59
Walthamstow Queens Road	d	21 32	21 47	22 02	22 17	22 32	23 02	23 32	00 02
Blackhorse Road ⊖	d	21 35	21 50	22 05	22 20	22 35	23 05	23 35	00 05
South Tottenham	d	21 39	21 54	22 09	22 24	22 39	23 09	23 39	00 09
Harringay Green Lanes	d	21 42	21 57	22 12	22 27	22 42	23 12	23 42	00 12
Crouch Hill	d	21 45	22 00	22 15	22 30	22 45	23 15	23 45	00 15
Upper Holloway	d	21 47	22 02	22 17	22 32	22 47	23 17	23 47	00 17
Gospel Oak	a	21 53	22 08	22 22	22 38	22 52	23 22	23 52	00 24

Saturdays

1 September to 8 September

		LO	LO	LO	LO	LO	LO	LO	LO	LO	LO	LO	LO	LO	LO	LO	LO	LO	LO	LO	LO	LO	LO
Barking ⊖	d	23p47	06 17	06 32	06 47	07 02	07 17	07 32	07 47	08 02	08 17	08 32	08 47	09 02	09 17	09 32	09 47	10 02	10 17	10 34	10 47	11 02	11 17
Woodgrange Park	d	23p50	06 20	06 35	06 50	07 05	07 20	07 35	07 50	08 05	08 20	08 35	08 50	09 05	09 20	09 35	09 50	10 05	10 20	10 37	10 50	11 05	11 20
Wanstead Park	d	23p53	06 23	06 38	06 53	07 08	07 23	07 38	07 53	08 08	08 23	08 38	08 53	09 08	09 23	09 38	09 53	10 08	10 23	10 40	10 53	11 08	11 23
Leytonstone High Road	d	23p57	06 27	06 42	06 57	07 12	07 27	07 42	07 57	08 12	08 27	08 42	08 57	09 12	09 27	09 42	09 57	10 12	10 27	10 44	10 57	11 12	11 27
Leyton Midland Road	d	23p59	06 29	06 44	06 59	07 14	07 29	07 44	07 59	08 14	08 29	08 44	08 59	09 14	09 29	09 44	09 59	10 14	10 29	10 46	10 59	11 14	11 29
Walthamstow Queens Road	d	00 02	06 32	06 47	07 02	07 17	07 32	07 47	08 02	08 17	08 32	08 47	09 02	09 17	09 32	09 47	10 02	10 17	10 32	10 49	11 02	11 17	11 32
Blackhorse Road ⊖	d	00 05	06 35	06 50	07 05	07 20	07 35	07 50	08 05	08 20	08 35	08 50	09 05	09 20	09 35	09 50	10 05	10 20	10 35	10 52	11 05	11 20	11 35
South Tottenham	d	00 09	06 39	06 54	07 09	07 24	07 39	07 54	08 09	08 24	08 39	08 54	09 09	09 24	09 39	09 54	10 09	10 24	10 39	10 56	11 09	11 24	11 39
Harringay Green Lanes	d	00 12	06 42	06 57	07 12	07 27	07 42	07 57	08 12	08 27	08 42	08 57	09 12	09 27	09 42	09 57	10 12	10 27	10 42	10 59	11 12	11 27	11 42
Crouch Hill	d	00 15	06 45	07 00	07 15	07 30	07 45	08 00	08 15	08 30	08 45	09 00	09 15	09 30	09 45	10 00	10 15	10 30	10 45	11 02	11 15	11 30	11 45
Upper Holloway	d	00 17	06 47	07 02	07 17	07 32	07 47	08 02	08 17	08 32	08 47	09 02	09 17	09 32	09 47	10 02	10 17	10 32	10 48	11 04	11 17	11 32	11 47
Gospel Oak	a	00 27	06 59	07 13	07 28	07 43	07 58	08 13	08 28	08 45	08 57	09 13	09 27	09 43	09 58	10 13	10 28	10 42	10 58	11 18	11 28	11 43	11 58

		LO		LO	LO	LO	LO	LO	LO	LO	LO	LO	LO	LO	LO	LO	LO	LO	LO	LO	LO	LO
Barking ⊖	d	11 32		18 32	18 47	19 02	19 17	19 32	19 47	20 02	20 17	20 32	20 47	21 02	21 17	21 32	21 47	22 02	22 17	22 47	23 17	23 47
Woodgrange Park	d	11 35		18 35	18 50	19 05	19 20	19 35	19 50	20 05	20 20	20 35	20 50	21 05	21 20	21 35	21 50	22 05	22 20	22 50	23 20	23 50
Wanstead Park	d	11 38	and at	18 38	18 53	19 08	19 23	19 38	19 53	20 08	20 23	20 38	20 53	21 08	21 23	21 38	21 53	22 08	22 23	22 53	23 23	23 53
Leytonstone High Road	d	11 42	the same	18 42	18 57	19 12	19 27	19 42	19 57	20 12	20 27	20 42	20 57	21 12	21 27	21 42	21 57	22 12	22 27	22 57	23 27	23 57
Leyton Midland Road	d	11 44	minutes	18 44	18 59	19 14	19 29	19 44	19 59	20 14	20 29	20 44	20 59	21 14	21 29	21 44	21 59	22 14	22 29	22 59	23 29	23 59
Walthamstow Queens Road	d	11 47	past	18 47	19 02	19 17	19 32	19 47	20 02	20 17	20 32	20 47	21 02	21 17	21 32	21 47	22 02	22 17	22 32	23 02	23 32	00 02
Blackhorse Road ⊖	d	11 50	each	18 50	19 05	19 20	19 35	19 50	20 05	20 20	20 35	20 50	21 05	21 20	21 35	21 50	22 05	22 20	22 35	23 05	23 35	00 05
South Tottenham	d	11 54	hour until	18 54	19 09	19 24	19 39	19 54	20 09	20 24	20 39	20 54	21 09	21 24	21 39	21 54	22 09	22 24	22 39	23 09	23 39	00 09
Harringay Green Lanes	d	11 57		18 57	19 12	19 27	19 42	19 57	20 12	20 27	20 42	20 57	21 12	21 27	21 42	21 57	22 12	22 27	22 42	23 12	23 42	00 12
Crouch Hill	d	12 00		19 00	19 15	19 30	19 45	20 00	20 15	20 30	20 45	21 00	21 15	21 30	21 45	22 00	22 15	22 30	22 45	23 15	23 45	00 15
Upper Holloway	d	12 02		19 02	19 17	19 33	19 47	20 02	20 17	20 32	20 47	21 02	21 17	21 32	21 47	22 02	22 17	22 32	22 47	23 17	23 47	00 17
Gospel Oak	a	12 13		19 13	19 28	19 47	19 58	20 13	20 28	20 43	20 58	21 13	21 28	21 43	21 58	22 13	22 27	22 42	22 57	23 27	23 57	00 27

Table 62

Saturdays

from 15 September

Barking - Gospel Oak

Network Diagram - see first Page of Table 59

		LO	LO	LO	LO	LO	LO	LO	LO	LO	LO	LO	LO	LO	LO	LO	LO	LO	LO	LO	LO	LO	LO
Barking ⊖	d	23p47	06 17	06 32	06 47	07 02	07 17	07 32	07 47	08 02	08 17	08 32	08 47	09 02	09 17	09 32	09 47	10 02	10 17	10 32	10 47	11 02	11 17
Woodgrange Park	d	23p50	06 20	06 35	06 50	07 05	07 20	07 35	07 50	08 05	08 20	08 35	08 50	09 05	09 20	09 35	09 50	10 05	10 20	10 35	10 50	11 05	11 20
Wanstead Park	d	23p53	06 23	06 38	06 53	07 08	07 23	07 38	07 53	08 08	08 23	08 38	08 53	09 08	09 23	09 38	09 53	10 08	10 23	10 38	10 53	11 08	11 23
Leytonstone High Road	d	23p57	06 27	06 42	06 57	07 12	07 27	07 42	07 57	08 12	08 27	08 42	08 57	09 12	09 27	09 42	09 57	10 12	10 27	10 42	10 57	11 12	11 27
Leyton Midland Road	d	23p59	06 29	06 44	06 59	07 14	07 29	07 44	07 59	08 14	08 29	08 44	08 59	09 14	09 29	09 44	09 59	10 14	10 29	10 44	10 59	11 14	11 29
Walthamstow Queens Road	d	00 02	06 32	06 47	07 02	07 17	07 32	07 47	08 02	08 17	08 32	08 47	09 02	09 17	09 32	09 47	10 02	10 17	10 32	10 47	11 02	11 17	11 32
Blackhorse Road ⊖	d	00 05	06 35	06 50	07 05	07 20	07 35	07 50	08 05	08 20	08 35	08 50	09 05	09 20	09 35	09 50	10 05	10 20	10 35	10 50	11 05	11 20	11 35
South Tottenham	d	00 09	06 39	06 54	07 09	07 24	07 39	07 54	08 09	08 24	08 39	08 54	09 09	09 24	09 39	09 54	10 09	10 24	10 39	10 54	11 09	11 24	11 39
Harringay Green Lanes	d	00 12	06 42	06 57	07 12	07 27	07 42	07 57	08 12	08 27	08 42	08 57	09 12	09 27	09 42	09 57	10 12	10 27	10 42	10 57	11 12	11 27	11 42
Crouch Hill	d	00 15	06 45	07 00	07 15	07 30	07 45	08 00	08 15	08 30	08 45	09 00	09 15	09 30	09 45	10 00	10 15	10 30	10 45	11 00	11 15	11 30	11 45
Upper Holloway	d	00 17	06 47	07 02	07 17	07 32	07 47	08 02	08 17	08 32	08 47	09 02	09 17	09 32	09 47	10 02	10 17	10 32	10 48	11 02	11 17	11 32	11 47
Gospel Oak	a	00 24	06 54	07 08	07 23	07 38	07 53	08 08	08 23	08 38	08 53	09 08	09 24	09 38	09 53	10 08	10 23	10 39	10 53	11 11	11 23	11 39	11 53

		LO	LO	LO	LO	LO	LO	LO		LO	LO	LO	LO	LO	LO	LO	LO	LO	LO	LO	LO	LO
Barking ⊖	d	11 32	11 47	12 02	12 17	12 32	12 47	13 02		18 02	18 17	18 32	18 47	19 02	19 17	19 32	19 47	20 02	20 17	20 32	20 47	21 02
Woodgrange Park	d	11 35	11 50	12 05	12 20	12 35	12 50	13 05		18 05	18 20	18 35	18 50	19 05	19 20	19 35	19 50	20 05	20 20	20 35	20 50	21 05
Wanstead Park	d	11 38	11 53	12 08	12 23	12 38	12 53	13 08	and at	18 08	18 23	18 38	18 53	19 08	19 23	19 38	19 53	20 08	20 23	20 38	20 53	21 08
Leytonstone High Road	d	11 42	11 57	12 12	12 27	12 42	12 57	13 12	the same	18 12	18 27	18 42	18 57	19 12	19 27	19 42	19 57	20 12	20 27	20 42	20 57	21 12
Leyton Midland Road	d	11 44	11 59	12 14	12 29	12 44	12 59	13 14	minutes	18 14	18 29	18 44	18 59	19 14	19 29	19 44	19 59	20 14	20 29	20 44	20 59	21 14
Walthamstow Queens Road	d	11 47	12 02	12 17	12 32	12 47	13 02	13 17	past	18 17	18 32	18 47	19 02	19 17	19 32	19 47	20 02	20 17	20 32	20 47	21 02	21 17
Blackhorse Road ⊖	d	11 50	12 05	12 20	12 35	12 50	13 05	13 20	each	18 20	18 35	18 50	19 05	19 20	19 35	19 50	20 05	20 20	20 35	20 50	21 05	21 20
South Tottenham	d	11 54	12 09	12 24	12 39	12 54	13 09	13 24	hour until	18 24	18 39	18 54	19 09	19 24	19 39	19 54	20 09	20 24	20 39	20 54	21 09	21 24
Harringay Green Lanes	d	11 57	12 12	12 27	12 42	12 57	13 12	13 27		18 27	18 42	18 57	19 12	19 27	19 42	19 57	20 12	20 27	20 42	20 57	21 12	21 27
Crouch Hill	d	12 00	12 15	12 30	12 45	13 00	13 15	13 30		18 30	18 45	19 00	19 15	19 30	19 45	20 00	20 15	20 30	20 45	21 00	21 15	21 30
Upper Holloway	d	12 02	12 17	12 32	12 47	13 02	13 17	13 32		18 32	18 47	19 02	19 17	19 32	19 47	20 02	20 17	20 32	20 47	21 02	21 17	21 32
Gospel Oak	a	12 09	12 23	12 40	12 53	13 08	13 23	13 38		18 38	18 53	19 08	19 23	19 41	19 53	20 08	20 23	20 38	20 53	21 08	21 23	21 38

		LO	LO	LO	LO	LO	LO	LO	LO
Barking ⊖	d	21 17	21 32	21 47	22 02	22 17	22 47	23 17	23 47
Woodgrange Park	d	21 20	21 35	21 50	22 05	22 20	22 50	23 20	23 50
Wanstead Park	d	21 23	21 38	21 53	22 08	22 23	22 53	23 23	23 53
Leytonstone High Road	d	21 27	21 42	21 57	22 12	22 27	22 57	23 27	23 57
Leyton Midland Road	d	21 29	21 44	21 59	22 14	22 29	22 59	23 29	23 59
Walthamstow Queens Road	d	21 32	21 47	22 02	22 17	22 32	23 02	23 32	00 02
Blackhorse Road ⊖	d	21 35	21 50	22 05	22 20	22 35	23 05	23 35	00 05
South Tottenham	d	21 39	21 54	22 09	22 24	22 39	23 09	23 39	00 09
Harringay Green Lanes	d	21 42	21 57	22 12	22 27	22 42	23 12	23 42	00 12
Crouch Hill	d	21 45	22 00	22 15	22 30	22 45	23 15	23 45	00 15
Upper Holloway	d	21 47	22 02	22 17	22 32	22 47	23 17	23 47	00 17
Gospel Oak	a	21 53	22 08	22 22	22 38	22 52	23 22	23 52	00 24

Sundays

until 22 July

		LO	LO	LO	LO	LO		LO	LO	LO	LO	LO	LO
Barking ⊖	d	23p47	08 53	09 08	09 23	09 38		21 38	21 53	22 08	22 38	23 08	23 38
Woodgrange Park	d	23p50	08 56	09 11	09 26	09 41		21 41	21 56	22 11	22 41	23 11	23 41
Wanstead Park	d	23p53	08 59	09 14	09 29	09 44	and at	21 44	21 59	22 14	22 44	23 14	23 44
Leytonstone High Road	d	23p57	09 03	09 18	09 33	09 48	the same	21 48	22 03	22 18	22 48	23 18	23 48
Leyton Midland Road	d	23p59	09 05	09 20	09 35	09 50	minutes	21 50	22 05	22 20	22 50	23 20	23 50
Walthamstow Queens Road	d	00 02	09 08	09 23	09 38	09 53	past	21 53	22 08	22 23	22 53	23 23	23 53
Blackhorse Road ⊖	d	00 05	09 11	09 26	09 41	09 56	each	21 56	22 11	22 26	22 56	23 26	23 56
South Tottenham	d	00 09	09 15	09 30	09 45	10 00	hour until	22 00	22 15	22 30	23 00	23 30	23 59
Harringay Green Lanes	d	00 12	09 18	09 33	09 48	10 03		22 03	22 18	22 33	23 03	23 33	00 03
Crouch Hill	d	00 15	09 21	09 36	09 51	10 06		22 06	22 21	22 36	23 06	23 36	00 06
Upper Holloway	d	00 17	09 23	09 38	09 53	10 08		22 08	22 23	22 38	23 08	23 38	00 08
Gospel Oak	a	00 24	09 28	09 43	09 58	10 13		22 13	22 28	22 43	23 13	23 43	00 13

Sundays

29 July to 12 August

		LO	LO	LO	LO	LO		LO	LO	LO	LO	LO	LO
Barking ⊖	d	23p47	08 53	09 08	09 23	09 38		21 38	21 53	22 08	22 38	23 08	23 38
Woodgrange Park	d	23p50	08 56	09 11	09 26	09 41		21 41	21 56	22 11	22 41	23 11	23 41
Wanstead Park	d	23p53	08 59	09 14	09 29	09 44	and at	21 44	21 59	22 14	22 44	23 14	23 44
Leytonstone High Road	d	23p57	09 03	09 18	09 33	09 48	the same	21 48	22 03	22 18	22 48	23 18	23 48
Leyton Midland Road	d	23p59	09 05	09 20	09 35	09 50	minutes	21 50	22 05	22 20	22 50	23 20	23 50
Walthamstow Queens Road	d	00 02	09 08	09 23	09 38	09 53	past	21 53	22 08	22 23	22 53	23 23	23 53
Blackhorse Road ⊖	d	00 05	09 11	09 26	09 41	09 56	each	21 56	22 11	22 26	22 56	23 26	23 56
South Tottenham	d	00 09	09 15	09 30	09 45	10 00	hour until	22 00	22 15	22 30	23 00	23 30	23 59
Harringay Green Lanes	d	00 12	09 18	09 33	09 48	10 03		22 03	22 18	22 33	23 03	23 33	00 03
Crouch Hill	d	00 15	09 21	09 36	09 51	10 06		22 06	22 21	22 36	23 06	23 36	00 06
Upper Holloway	d	00 17	09 23	09 38	09 53	10 08		22 08	22 23	22 38	23 08	23 38	00 08
Gospel Oak	a	00 27	09 33	09 48	10 03	10 18		22 18	22 33	22 48	23 18	23 48	00 18

Sundays

19 August to 26 August

Barking - Gospel Oak

Network Diagram - see first Page of Table 59

		LO	LO	LO	LO	LO		LO	LO	LO	LO	LO	LO
Barking ⊖	d	23p47	08 53	09 08	09 23	09 38	and at the same minutes past each hour until	21 38	21 53	22 08	22 38	23 08	23 38
Woodgrange Park	d	23p50	08 56	09 11	09 26	09 41		21 41	21 56	22 11	22 41	23 11	23 41
Wanstead Park	d	23p53	08 59	09 14	09 29	09 44		21 44	21 59	22 14	22 44	23 14	23 44
Leytonstone High Road	d	23p57	09 03	09 18	09 33	09 48		21 48	22 03	22 18	22 48	23 18	23 48
Leyton Midland Road	d	23p59	09 05	09 20	09 35	09 50		21 50	22 05	22 20	22 50	23 20	23 50
Walthamstow Queens Road	d	00 02	09 08	09 23	09 38	09 53		21 53	22 08	22 23	22 53	23 23	23 53
Blackhorse Road ⊖	d	00 05	09 11	09 26	09 41	09 56		21 56	22 11	22 26	22 56	23 26	23 56
South Tottenham	d	00 09	09 15	09 30	09 45	10 00		22 00	22 15	22 30	23 00	23 30	23 59
Harringay Green Lanes	d	00 12	09 18	09 33	09 48	10 03		22 03	22 18	22 33	23 03	23 33	00 03
Crouch Hill	d	00 15	09 21	09 36	09 51	10 06		22 06	22 21	22 36	23 06	23 36	00 06
þper Holloway	d	00 17	09 23	09 38	09 53	10 08		22 08	22 23	22 38	23 08	23 38	00 08
Gospel Oak	a	00 24	09 28	09 43	09 58	10 13		22 13	22 28	22 43	23 13	23 43	00 13

Sundays

2 September to 9 September

		LO	LO	LO	LO	LO		LO	LO	LO	LO	LO	LO
Barking ⊖	d	23p47	08 53	09 08	09 23	09 38	and at the same minutes past each hour until	21 38	21 53	22 08	22 38	23 08	23 38
Woodgrange Park	d	23p50	08 56	09 11	09 26	09 41		21 41	21 56	22 11	22 41	23 11	23 41
Wanstead Park	d	23p53	08 59	09 14	09 29	09 44		21 44	21 59	22 14	22 44	23 14	23 44
Leytonstone High Road	d	23p57	09 03	09 18	09 33	09 48		21 48	22 03	22 18	22 48	23 18	23 48
Leyton Midland Road	d	23p59	09 05	09 20	09 35	09 50		21 50	22 05	22 20	22 50	23 20	23 50
Walthamstow Queens Road	d	00 02	09 08	09 23	09 38	09 53		21 53	22 08	22 23	22 53	23 23	23 53
Blackhorse Road ⊖	d	00 05	09 11	09 26	09 41	09 56		21 56	22 11	22 26	22 56	23 26	23 56
South Tottenham	d	00 09	09 15	09 30	09 45	10 00		22 00	22 15	22 30	23 00	23 30	23 59
Harringay Green Lanes	d	00 12	09 18	09 33	09 48	10 03		22 03	22 18	22 33	23 03	23 33	00 03
Crouch Hill	d	00 15	09 21	09 36	09 51	10 06		22 06	22 21	22 36	23 06	23 36	00 06
þper Holloway	d	00 17	09 23	09 38	09 53	10 08		22 08	22 23	22 38	23 08	23 38	00 08
Gospel Oak	a	00 27	09 33	09 48	10 03	10 18		22 18	22 33	22 48	23 18	23 48	00 18

Sundays

from 16 September

		LO	LO	LO	LO	LO		LO	LO	LO	LO	LO	LO
Barking ⊖	d	23p47	08 53	09 08	09 23	09 38	and at the same minutes past each hour until	21 38	21 53	22 08	22 38	23 08	23 38
Woodgrange Park	d	23p50	08 56	09 11	09 26	09 41		21 41	21 56	22 11	22 41	23 11	23 41
Wanstead Park	d	23p53	08 59	09 14	09 29	09 44		21 44	21 59	22 14	22 44	23 14	23 44
Leytonstone High Road	d	23p57	09 03	09 18	09 33	09 48		21 48	22 03	22 18	22 48	23 18	23 48
Leyton Midland Road	d	23p59	09 05	09 20	09 35	09 50		21 50	22 05	22 20	22 50	23 20	23 50
Walthamstow Queens Road	d	00 02	09 08	09 23	09 38	09 53		21 53	22 08	22 23	22 53	23 23	23 53
Blackhorse Road ⊖	d	00 05	09 11	09 26	09 41	09 56		21 56	22 11	22 26	22 56	23 26	23 56
South Tottenham	d	00 09	09 15	09 30	09 45	10 00		22 00	22 15	22 30	23 00	23 30	23 59
Harringay Green Lanes	d	00 12	09 18	09 33	09 48	10 03		22 03	22 18	22 33	23 03	23 33	00 03
Crouch Hill	d	00 15	09 21	09 36	09 51	10 06		22 06	22 21	22 36	23 06	23 36	00 06
þper Holloway	d	00 17	09 23	09 38	09 53	10 08		22 08	22 23	22 38	23 08	23 38	00 08
Gospel Oak	a	00 24	09 28	09 43	09 58	10 13		22 13	22 28	22 43	23 13	23 43	00 13

Mondays to Fridays

Bletchley - Bedford

Network Diagram - see first Page of Table 59

Miles			LM	LM	LM	LM	LM	LM	LM	LM	LM	LM	LM	LM	LM	LM	LM	LM
0	**Bletchley**	d	05 41	06 41	07 32	08 39	10 01	11 01	12 01	13 01	14 01	15 01	15 47	16 47	17 31	18 31	20 01	21 01
1	Fenny Stratford	d	05 44	06 44	07 35	08 42	10 04	11 04	12 04	13 04	14 04	15 04	15 50	16 50	17 34	18 34	20 04	21 04
2	Bow Brickhill	d	05 48	06 48	07 39	08 46	10 08	11 08	12 08	13 08	14 08	15 08	15 54	16 54	17 38	18 38	20 08	21 08
4	Woburn Sands	d	05 52	06 52	07 43	08 50	10 12	11 12	12 12	13 12	14 12	15 12	15 58	16 58	17 42	18 42	20 12	21 12
5	Aspley Guise	d	05 55	06 55	07 46	08 53	10 15	11 15	12 15	13 15	14 15	15 15	16 01	17 01	17 45	18 45	20 15	21 15
6¾	Ridgmont	d	05 58	06 58	07 49	08 56	10 18	11 18	12 18	13 18	14 18	15 18	16 04	17 04	17 48	18 48	20 18	21 18
8½	Lidlington	d	06 02	07 02	07 53	09 00	10 22	11 22	12 22	13 22	14 22	15 22	16 08	17 08	17 52	18 52	20 22	21 22
10	Millbrook (Bedfordshire)	d	06 05	07 05	07 56	09 03	10 25	11 25	12 25	13 25	14 25	15 25	16 11	17 11	17 55	18 55	20 25	21 25
11¼	Stewartby	d	06 09	07 09	08 00	09 07	10 29	11 29	12 29	13 29	14 29	15 29	16 15	17 15	17 59	18 59	20 29	21 29
13	Kempston Hardwick	d	06 12	07 12	08 03	09 10	10 32	11 32	12 32	13 32	14 32	15 32	16 18	17 18	18 02	19 02	20 32	21 32
16	Bedford St Johns	d	06 19	07 20	08 10	09 17	10 39	11 39	12 39	13 39	14 39	15 39	16 25	17 25	18 09	19 09	20 39	21 39
16¾	**Bedford** [7]	a	06 25	07 25	08 16	09 23	10 45	11 45	12 45	13 45	14 45	15 45	16 31	17 31	18 15	19 15	20 45	21 45

Saturdays

		LM	LM	LM	LM	LM	LM	LM	LM	LM	LM	LM	LM	LM	LM	LM	LM
Bletchley	d	05 41	06 37	07 32	08 39	10 01	11 01	12 01	13 01	14 01	15 01	15 47	16 47	17 31	18 31	20 01	21 01
Fenny Stratford	d	05 44	06 40	07 35	08 42	10 04	11 04	12 04	13 04	14 04	15 04	15 50	16 50	17 34	18 34	20 04	21 04
Bow Brickhill	d	05 48	06 44	07 39	08 46	10 08	11 08	12 08	13 08	14 08	15 08	15 54	16 54	17 38	18 38	20 08	21 08
Woburn Sands	d	05 52	06 48	07 43	08 50	10 12	11 12	12 12	13 12	14 12	15 12	15 58	16 58	17 42	18 42	20 12	21 12
Aspley Guise	d	05 55	06 51	07 46	08 53	10 15	11 15	12 15	13 15	14 15	15 15	16 01	17 01	17 45	18 45	20 15	21 15
Ridgmont	d	05 58	06 54	07 49	08 56	10 18	11 18	12 18	13 18	14 18	15 18	16 04	17 04	17 48	18 48	20 18	21 18
Lidlington	d	06 02	06 58	07 53	09 00	10 22	11 22	12 22	13 22	14 22	15 22	16 08	17 08	17 52	18 52	20 22	21 22
Millbrook (Bedfordshire)	d	06 05	07 01	07 56	09 03	10 25	11 25	12 25	13 25	14 25	15 25	16 11	17 11	17 55	18 55	20 25	21 25
Stewartby	d	06 09	07 05	08 00	09 07	10 29	11 29	12 29	13 29	14 29	15 29	16 15	17 15	17 59	18 59	20 29	21 29
Kempston Hardwick	d	06 12	07 08	08 03	09 10	10 32	11 32	12 32	13 32	14 32	15 32	16 18	17 18	18 02	19 02	20 32	21 32
Bedford St Johns	d	06 19	07 15	08 10	09 17	10 39	11 39	12 39	13 39	14 39	15 39	16 25	17 25	18 09	19 09	20 39	21 39
Bedford [7]	a	06 25	07 21	08 16	09 23	10 45	11 45	12 45	13 45	14 45	15 45	16 31	17 31	18 15	19 15	20 45	21 45

Table 64

Mondays to Fridays

Bedford - Bletchley

Network Diagram - see first Page of Table 59

Miles			LM	LM	LM	LM	LM	LM	LM	LM	LM	LM	LM	LM	LM	LM	LM	LM
0	**Bedford** [7]	d	06 31	07 31	08 31	09 33	10 55	11 55	12 55	13 55	14 55	15 55	16 37	17 37	18 25	19 35	20 55	21 56
0¾	Bedford St Johns	d	06 34	07 34	08 34	09 36	10 58	11 58	12 58	13 58	14 58	15 58	16 40	17 40	18 28	19 38	20 58	21 59
3¾	Kempston Hardwick	d	06 41	07 41	08 41	09 43	11 05	12 05	13 05	14 05	15 05	16 05	16 47	17 47	18 35	19 45	21 05	22 06
5½	Stewartby	d	06 44	07 44	08 44	09 46	11 08	12 08	13 08	14 08	15 08	16 08	16 50	17 50	18 38	19 48	21 08	22 09
6¾	Millbrook (Bedfordshire)	d	06 48	07 48	08 48	09 50	11 12	12 12	13 12	14 12	15 12	16 12	16 54	17 54	18 42	19 52	21 12	22 13
8¼	Lidlington	d	06 51	07 51	08 51	09 53	11 15	12 15	13 15	14 15	15 15	16 15	16 57	17 57	18 45	19 55	21 15	22 16
10	Ridgmont	d	06 56	07 56	08 56	09 58	11 20	12 20	13 20	14 20	15 20	16 20	17 02	18 02	18 50	20 00	21 20	22 21
11¾	Aspley Guise	d	06 59	07 59	08 59	10 01	11 23	12 23	13 23	14 23	15 23	16 23	17 05	18 05	18 53	20 03	21 23	22 24
12¾	Woburn Sands	d	07 02	08 02	09 02	10 04	11 26	12 26	13 26	14 26	15 26	16 26	17 08	18 08	18 56	20 06	21 26	22 27
14¾	Bow Brickhill	d	07 06	08 06	09 06	10 08	11 30	12 30	13 30	14 30	15 30	16 30	17 12	18 12	19 00	20 10	21 30	22 31
15¾	Fenny Stratford	d	07 09	08 09	09 09	10 11	11 33	12 33	13 33	14 33	15 33	16 33	17 15	18 15	19 03	20 13	21 33	22 34
16¾	**Bletchley**	a	07 14	08 14	09 14	10 16	11 38	12 38	13 38	14 38	15 38	16 38	17 20	18 20	19 08	20 18	21 38	22 39

Saturdays

		LM	LM	LM	LM	LM	LM	LM	LM	LM	LM	LM	LM	LM	LM	LM	LM
Bedford [7]	d	06 31	07 31	08 31	09 33	10 55	11 55	12 55	13 55	14 55	15 55	16 37	17 37	18 25	19 35	20 55	21 56
Bedford St Johns	d	06 34	07 34	08 34	09 36	10 58	11 58	12 58	13 58	14 58	15 58	16 40	17 40	18 28	19 38	20 58	21 59
Kempston Hardwick	d	06 41	07 41	08 41	09 43	11 05	12 05	13 05	14 05	15 05	16 05	16 47	17 47	18 35	19 45	21 05	22 06
Stewartby	d	06 44	07 44	08 44	09 46	11 08	12 08	13 08	14 08	15 08	16 08	16 50	17 50	18 38	19 48	21 08	22 09
Millbrook (Bedfordshire)	d	06 48	07 48	08 48	09 50	11 12	12 12	13 12	14 12	15 12	16 12	16 54	17 54	18 42	19 52	21 12	22 13
Lidlington	d	06 51	07 51	08 51	09 53	11 15	12 15	13 15	14 15	15 15	16 15	16 57	17 57	18 45	19 55	21 15	22 16
Ridgmont	d	06 56	07 56	08 56	09 58	11 20	12 20	13 20	14 20	15 20	16 20	17 02	18 02	18 50	20 00	21 20	22 21
Aspley Guise	d	06 59	07 59	08 59	10 01	11 23	12 23	13 23	14 23	15 23	16 23	17 05	18 05	18 53	20 03	21 23	22 24
Woburn Sands	d	07 02	08 02	09 02	10 04	11 26	12 26	13 26	14 26	15 26	16 26	17 08	18 08	18 56	20 06	21 26	22 27
Bow Brickhill	d	07 06	08 06	09 06	10 08	11 30	12 30	13 30	14 30	15 30	16 30	17 12	18 12	19 00	20 10	21 30	22 31
Fenny Stratford	d	07 09	08 09	09 09	10 11	11 33	12 33	13 33	14 33	15 33	16 33	17 15	18 15	19 03	20 13	21 33	22 34
Bletchley	a	07 14	08 14	09 14	10 16	11 38	12 38	13 38	14 38	15 38	16 38	17 20	18 20	19 08	20 18	21 38	22 39

No Sunday Service

For connections to Milton Keynes Central please refer to Table 66

Route Diagram for Table 65

London-Scotland
See Tables 400-404
for Sleeper trains.

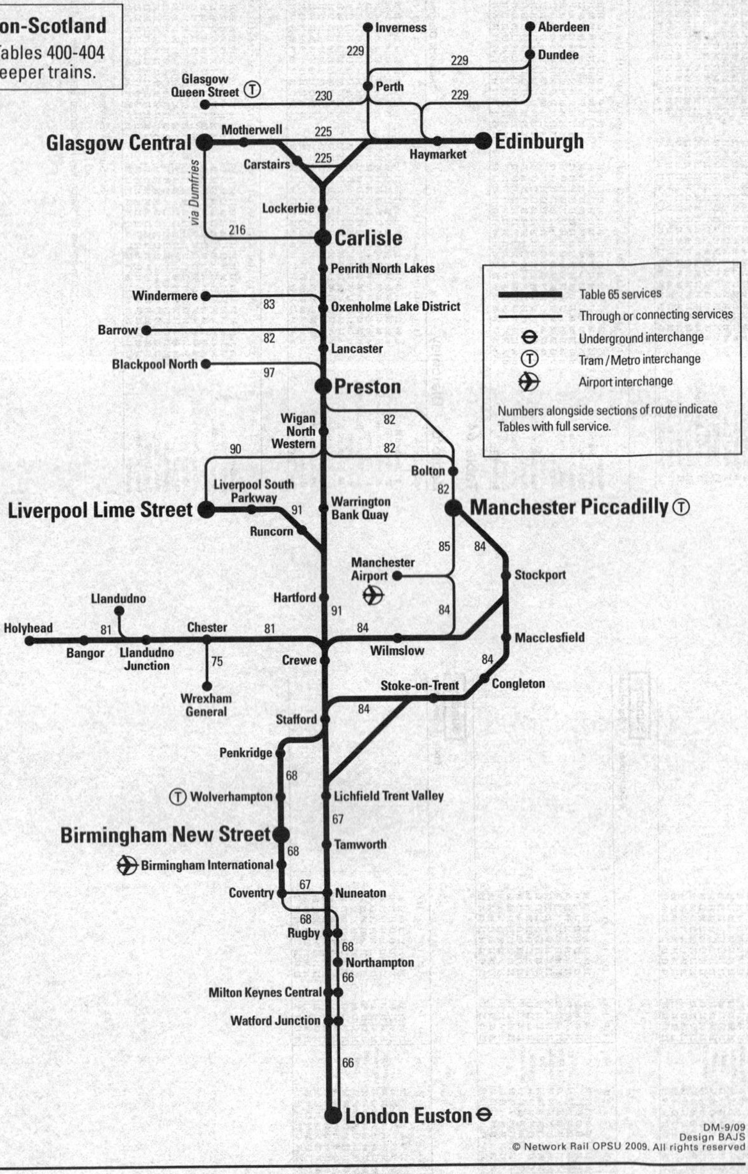

DM-9/09
Design BAJS

Table 65

London and West Midlands - North West England and Scotland

Mondays to Fridays

until 29 June

Route Diagram - see first Page of Table 65

Miles	Miles	Miles	Miles	Miles			XC	XC	VT	VT	VT	TP	TP	NT	TP	NT	SR		SR		VT	VT	VT
							MX	MX	MO	MX	MO	MX	MX	MO	MX	MX	MO		MX		MO	MO	MO
										R							R		R				
							◇1	◇1	◇1	1	◇1	◇1	◇1		◇1						◇1	◇1	◇1
							A	B	C		C			C			D		E		C	C	C
																	🛏		🛏				
									☕	☕	☕						☕		☕		☕	☕	☕
0	—	—	—	—	**London Euston** 15 ⊖	d			19p25	19p30							20p55		21p15		21p21	21p25	21p51
17½	—	—	—	—	Watford Junction	d											21b17		21b33				
49¾	—	—	—	—	Milton Keynes Central	d																22p14	22p38
82½	0	—	—	—	Rugby	d																	23p18
97	—	—	—	—	Nuneaton	d															22p52		23p29
110	—	—	—	—	Tamworth Low Level	d																	
116¼	—	0	—	—	Lichfield Trent Valley	d																	
—	11½	—	—	—	Coventry	d																	
—	22	—	—	—	Birmingham International ✈	d																	
—	30½	—	—	—	**Birmingham New Street** 12	d	22p30	22p30															
—	43¼	—	—	—	Wolverhampton 7	d	22p48	22p48															
—	53¼	—	—	—	Penkridge	d																	
133½	59½	—	—	—	**Stafford**	a	23p00	23p00													23p16		23c53
—	—	—	—	—		d	23p01	23p01													23p17		
—	75¾	30¼	—	—	**Stoke-on-Trent**	a	23p21	23p20														23p29	
—	87½	42	—	—	Congleton	a																	
—	95¼	50¼	—	—	Macclesfield	a																23p45	
158	—	—	0	—	**Crewe** 10	a															23p43		00s21
—	—	—	—	—		d											23b39		23b54		23p45		
—	—	—	—	—	Chester	a																	
—	—	—	—	—	Wrexham General	a																	
—	—	—	—	—	Llandudno	a																	
—	—	—	—	—	Bangor (Gwynedd)	a																	
—	—	—	—	—	Holyhead	a																	
—	—	—	—	—	Wilmslow	a																	
—	107¼	62¼	—	—	Stockport	a																23p59	00s50
—	113	68	—	—	**Manchester Piccadilly** 10	a	00 12	00 12														00 12	01 00
169¾	—	—	11¾	—	Hartford	a																	
182	—	—	—	—	Warrington Bank Quay	a			21p16	21p15													
—	—	—	—	—		d			21p16	21p15													
—	—	—	22½	—	Runcorn	a															00 07		
—	—	—	30	—	Liverpool South Parkway 7 ✈	a																	
—	—	—	35½	—	**Liverpool Lime Street** 10	a															00 30		
—	—	—	—	—		d																	
—	—	—	—	—	Manchester Airport ✈	d						22p00	22p29										
—	—	—	—	—	**Manchester Piccadilly** 10	d						22p16	22p46										
—	—	79¼	—	—	Bolton	d					←	22p33	23p07										
193¾	—	—	—	—	Wigan North Western	a			21p27	21p26	21p27	22p48											
—	—	—	—	—		d			21p27	21p26	21p27	22p51		23p14		23p48							
209	—	99¼	—	—	**Preston** 8	a			→	21p39	21p40	23p09	23p33	23p36		00 13							
—	—	—	—	—	**Preston** 8	d				21p41	21p42	23p13	23p35	23p39	23p51		00u30		00u52				
—	—	—	—	—	Blackpool North	a							00 02	00 05	00 16								
230	—	—	—	—	**Lancaster** 6	a				21p55	21p56	23p28											
—	—	—	—	—		d				21p56	21p57	23p29											
—	—	—	—	—	Barrow-in-Furness	a						00 31											
249	—	—	—	—	Oxenholme Lake District	a				22p09	22p10												
—	—	—	—	—		d				22p09	22p11												
—	—	—	—	—	Windermere	a																	
281¼	—	—	—	—	Penrith North Lakes	d				22p35	22p36												
299	—	—	—	—	**Carlisle** 8	a				22p50	22p51												
—	—	—	—	—		d				22p51	22p53												
324¼	—	—	0	—	Lockerbie	d																	
372½	—	—	—	0	Carstairs	a																	
388½	—	—	—	—	Motherwell	a																	
401¼	—	—	—	—	**Glasgow Central** 15	a				00 06	00 02												
—	—	—	75	26¼	Haymarket	a																	
—	—	—	76¼	27½	**Edinburgh** 10	a																	
—	—	—	—	97¼	Perth	a												05s39		05s39			
—	—	—	135½	—	Dundee	a											06s08		06s08				
—	—	—	206¾	—	Aberdeen	a											07 36		07 36				
—	—	—	—	215¼	Inverness	a												08 38		08 38			

A until 22 June
B from 26 June until 29 June
C from 21 May until 25 June
D from 21 May until 25 June. Conveys a portion for Fort William, arrives at 0954
E Conveys a portion for Fort William, arrives at 0954
b Previous night, stops to pick up only
c Previous night, stops to set down only

OVERNIGHT SLEEPERS. For sleeper trains, operated by First ScotRail, please refer to Tables 400 - 404

London and West Midlands - North West England and Scotland

Route Diagram - see first Page of Table 65

Station		VT	LM	SR	SR	TP	NT	TP	NT	NT	LM	TP	XC	VT	TP	LM	TP	NT	TP	NT
		MX	MX	MO	MX		MX		MX	MO										
				R	R															
		◇1	◇1			◇1		◇1			◇1	◇1	◇1	◇1	◇1	◇1	◇1		◇1	
				A																
London Euston 15 ⊖	d	22p00		23p27	23p50															
Watford Junction	d			23c47	00u10															
Milton Keynes Central	d	22p31																		
Rugby	d	22p54																		
Nuneaton	d	23p04																		
Tamworth Low Level	d	23b15																		
Lichfield Trent Valley	d	23b22																		
Coventry	d																			
Birmingham International ✈	d																			
Birmingham New Street 12	d		23p09										05 57							
Wolverhampton 7	d		23p36										06 16							
Penkridge	d		23p46																	
Stafford	a	23b38	23p52										06 29							
	d		23p53										06 30							
Stoke-on-Trent	a												06 50							
Congleton	a												07 02							
Macclesfield	a												07 11							
Crewe 10	a	00s03	00 16																	
	d						00 44				05 40			05 57		06 02				
Chester	a																			
Wrexham General	a																			
Llandudno	a																			
Bangor (Gwynedd)	a																			
Holyhead	a																			
Wilmslow	a																			
Stockport	a	00s26											07 27							
Manchester Piccadilly 10	a	00 35											07 37							
Hartford	a															06 14				
Warrington Bank Quay	a													06 13						
	d													06 14						
Runcorn	a										05 58					06 27				
Liverpool South Parkway 7 ✈	a										06 10					06 36				
Liverpool Lime Street 10	a										06 22					06 49				
	d																			06 57
Manchester Airport ✈	d					00 01	01 20	04 00							05 45		06 18			
Manchester Piccadilly 10	d					00 16	01a36	04 15				05 46			06 03		06 33			
Bolton	d					00s31		04s29							06 19		06 50	07 01		
Wigan North Western	a							04 44				06 15		06 24				07 19		07 30
	d							04 44				06 15		06 25						07 31
Preston 8	a					01s05		05s04				06 35		06 37	06 42		07 11			07 56
Preston 8	d								05 22	05 22		06 37		06 40	06 44		07 14		07 20	
Blackpool North	a					01 30		05 33				07 06								
Lancaster 6	a								05 42	05 42				06 54	06 59		07 30		07 36	
	d								05 42	05 42				06 54	07 00		07 30		07 36	
Barrow-in-Furness	a								06 47	06 47									08 39	
Oxenholme Lake District	a													07 08	07 15					
	d													07 10	07 15					
Windermere	a																			
Penrith North Lakes	d													07 35			08 07			
Carlisle 8	a			05s04	05s16				09 21	09 22				07 50	07 55		08 24			
	d													07 51	07 56		08 25			
Lockerbie	d													08 10	08 16					
Carstairs	a			06s20	06s20															
Motherwell	a			06s56	06s56															
Glasgow Central 15	a			07 20	07 20									09 14			09 45			
Haymarket	a														09s17					
Edinburgh 10	a			07 16	07 16										09 22					
Perth	a																			
Dundee	a																			
Aberdeen	a																			
Inverness	a																			

A from 21 May until 25 June.

b Previous night, stops to set down only

c Previous night, stops to pick up only

OVERNIGHT SLEEPERS. For sleeper trains, operated by First ScotRail, please refer to Tables 400 - 404

Table 65

Mondays to Fridays

until 29 June

London and West Midlands - North West England and Scotland

Route Diagram - see first Page of Table 65

		LM	LM	VT	XC	TP	VT	VT	VT	TP	NT	NT	LM	LM	VT	XC	VT	TP	LM	VT	VT
		◇1	1	◇1	◇1	◇1	◇1	◇1	◇1	◇1			◇1	◇1	◇1	◇1	◇1	◇1	◇1	◇1	◇1
				⊠	🛒	🛒	⊠	⊠	⊠	🛒					⊠	🛒	⊠	🛒		⊠	⊠
London Euston 15 ⊖	d						05 27	05 39	06 17								06 55			07 07	07 10
Watford Junction	d						05u45	06u02													
Milton Keynes Central	d						06 10	06 22	06 47								07 27				07 41
Rugby	d							06 45													
Nuneaton	d						06 39														
Tamworth Low Level	d																				
Lichfield Trent Valley	d																				
Coventry	d																				
Birmingham International ✈	d																		07 17		
Birmingham New Street 12	d		06 01	06 19	06 22								06 36	07 01	07 20	07 31			07 36		
Wolverhampton 7	d		06 19	06 36	06 40								06 53	07 19	07 37	07 49			07 53		
Penkridge	d		06 29											07 29					08 03		
Stafford	a		06 35		06 53		07 03						07 08	07 36		08 00			08 09	08 22	
	d		06 36		06 55		07 03						07 08	07 36		08 01			08 09	08 23	
Stoke-on-Trent	a				07 13				07 45							08 19	08 24				
Congleton	a																				
Macclesfield	a				07 30				08 01							08 36	08 41				
Crewe 10	a		06 56	07 07			07 22	07 30					07 33	07 56	08 07				08 30		08 47
	d	06 32	06 57	07 09			07 24	07 32					07 34	07 57	08 09				08 31		08 49
Chester	a																				09 12
Wrexham General	a																				
Llandudno	a																				
Bangor (Gwynedd)	a																				
Holyhead	a																				
Wilmslow	a																				
Stockport	a				07 45				08 16							08 50	08 55				
Manchester Piccadilly 10	a				07 59				08 28							08 59	09 07				
Hartford	a	06 46	07 10										07 47	08 09							
Warrington Bank Quay	a			07 26				07 49							08 26						
	d			07 27				07 49							08 27						
Runcorn	a	06 59	07 22				07 41						08 00	08 22					08 50	08 55	
Liverpool South Parkway 7 ✈	a	07 08	07 31										08 09	08 31					08 59		
Liverpool Lime Street 10	a	07 22	07 43				08 01						08 21	08 44					09 10	09 15	
	d											07 57									
Manchester Airport ✈	d					07 00				07 25								07 56			
Manchester Piccadilly 10	d					07 15				07 45								08 15			
Bolton	d					07 31				07 59								08 32			
Wigan North Western	a			07 37				08 00				08 30			08 37						
	d			07 38				08 00				08 31			08 38						
Preston 8	a			07 51		07 57		08 13		08 22		08 56			08 51			08 58			
Preston 8	d			07 53		07 59		08 15		08 24	08 38				08 53			08 59			
Blackpool North	a					08 29												09 25			
Lancaster 6	a			08 08				08 29		08 39	08 58				09 08						
	d			08 08				08 30		08 40	08 58				09 08						
Barrow-in-Furness	a										10 04										
Oxenholme Lake District	a			08 21				08 43		08 54											
	d			08 22				08 43		08 54											
Windermere	a																				
Penrith North Lakes	d									09 20					09 45						
Carlisle 8	a			09 01				09 21		09 34	12 39				09 59						
	d			09 01				09 22		09 36					10 01						
Lockerbie	d									09 55											
Carstairs	a																				
Motherwell	a																				
Glasgow Central 15	a							10 36							11 16						
Haymarket	a			10 16						10s56											
Edinburgh 10	a			10 21						11 04											
Perth	a																				
Dundee	a																				
Aberdeen	a																				
Inverness	a																				

OVERNIGHT SLEEPERS. For sleeper trains, operated by First ScotRail, please refer to Tables 400 - 404

Table 65

Mondays to Fridays

until 29 June

London and West Midlands - North West England and Scotland

Route Diagram - see first Page of Table 65

		VT	XC		TP	VT	NT	LM	VT	XC	VT	TP				LM	VT	VT	XC	VT	TP		NT		LM
		◇1	◇1		◇1	◇1		◇1	◇1	◇1	◇1	◇1				◇1	◇1	◇1	◇1	◇1	◇1				◇1
		☒	🛒		🛒	☒			☒	🛒	☒	🛒					☒	☒	🛒	☒	🛒				
London Euston 15 ⊖	d	07 20				07 30					08 00						08 07	08 20		08 30					
Watford Junction	d																								
Milton Keynes Central	d	07 50																08 50							
Rugby	d																								
Nuneaton	d																								
Tamworth Low Level	d																								
Lichfield Trent Valley	d																								
Coventry	d		07 27																08 27						
Birmingham International ✈	d		07 38																08 38						
Birmingham New Street 12	d		07 57					08 01	08 20	08 31						08 36			08 57						09 01
Wolverhampton 7 ⛴	d		08 15					08 19	08 37	08 49						08 53			09 15						09 19
Penkridge	d							08 29								09 03									
Stafford	a		08 29					08 35		09 00						09 09	09 22		09 29						09 34
	d		08 30					08 36		09 01						09 09	09 23		09 30						09 35
Stoke-on-Trent	a	08 48	08 54							09 19	09 24							09 48	09 54						
Congleton	a																								
Macclesfield	a		09 11								09 41								10 11						
Crewe 10	a							08 56	09 07							09 30									09 56
	d							08 57	09 09							09 31									09 57
Chester	a																								
Wrexham General	a																								
Llandudno	a																								
Bangor (Gwynedd)	a																								
Holyhead	a																								
Wilmslow	a																								
Stockport	a	09 16	09 27							09 49	09 55							10 16	10 27						
Manchester Piccadilly 10 ⛴	a	09 28	09 39							09 59	10 07							10 28	10 39						
Hartford	a							09 11																	10 10
Warrington Bank Quay	a					09 14			09 26											10 14					
	d					09 14			09 27											10 14					
Runcorn	a							09 22								09 50	09 55								10 22
Liverpool South Parkway 7 ✈	a							09 31								09 59									10 31
Liverpool Lime Street 10	a							09 43								10 10	10 15								10 43
	d						08 57																09 57		
Manchester Airport ✈	d				08 25							09 00									09 29				
Manchester Piccadilly 10 ⛴	d				08 46							09 16									09 46				
Bolton	d				09 07							09 33									10 07				
Wigan North Western	a					09 25	09 30		09 37											10 25			10 30		
	d					09 25	09 31		09 38											10 25			10 31		
Preston 8	a				09 33	09 38	09 54		09 51			09 55								10 38	10 33		10 54		
Preston 8	d				09 38	09 41	09 55		09 53			09 58	10 07							10 41	10 38	10 45	10 55		
Blackpool North	a				10 05		10 19														11 05		11 20		
Lancaster 6	a					09 54			10 08			10 13	10 22							10 54		11 00			
	d					09 55			10 08			10 14	10 23							10 55		11 01			
Barrow-in-Furness	a												11 17												
Oxenholme Lake District	a								10 22											11 08		11 17			
	d								10 23											11 08		11 18			
Windermere	a																					11 39			
Penrith North Lakes	d					10 31																			
Carlisle 8	a					10 46			11 02			11 07								11 46					
	d					10 47			11 04			11 10								11 47					
Lockerbie	d											11 29													
Carstairs	a																								
Motherwell	a																								
Glasgow Central 15	a					12 01						12 28								13 01					
Haymarket	a								12 14																
Edinburgh 10	a								12 21																
Perth	a																								
Dundee	a																								
Aberdeen	a																								
Inverness	a																								

OVERNIGHT SLEEPERS. For sleeper trains, operated by First ScotRail, please refer to Tables 400 - 404

Table 65

Mondays to Fridays

until 29 June

London and West Midlands - North West England and Scotland

Route Diagram - see first Page of Table 65

		VT	XC	VT	TP		LM	VT	VT		VT	XC	TP	VT	NT	LM	VT	XC	TP			LM	XC	LM	TP
		◇■	◇■	◇■	◇■		◇■	◇■	◇■		◇■	◇■	◇■	◇■		◇■	◇■	◇■	◇■			◇■	◇■	◇■	◇■
																			A						
		⊠	🛒	⊠	🛒			⊠	⊠		⊠	🛒	🛒	⊠			⊠	🛒	🛒				🛒		🛒
London Euston [15] ⊖	d			09 00				09 07	09 10		09 20			09 30											
Watford Junction	d																								
Milton Keynes Central	d								09 41		09 50														
Rugby	d																								
Nuneaton	d																								
Tamworth Low Level	d																								
Lichfield Trent Valley	d																								
Coventry	d											09 27											10 27		
Birmingham International ✈	d											09 38											10 38		
Birmingham New Street [12]	d	09 20	09 31				09 36					09 57				10 01	10 20	10 31				10 36	10 57	11 01	
Wolverhampton [7] ⛴	d	09 37	09 49				09 53					10 15				10 19	10 37	10 49				10 53	11 15	11 19	
Penkridge	d						10 03															11 03			
Stafford	a		10 00				10 09	10 22				10 29				10 34		11 00				11 09	11 28	11 34	
	d		10 01				10 09	10 23				10 30				10 35		11 01				11 09	11 30	11 35	
Stoke-on-Trent	a		10 19	10 24							10 48	10 54						11 19					11 54		
Congleton	a																								
Macclesfield	a			10 41								11 11											12 11		
Crewe [10]	a	10 07					10 30		10 47							10 56	11 07					11 30		11 56	
	d	10 09					10 31		10 49							10 57	11 09					11 31		11 57	
Chester	a								11 09																
Wrexham General	a																								
Llandudno	a																								
Bangor (Gwynedd)	a								12 16																
Holyhead	a								12 50																
Wilmslow	a																								
Stockport	a		10 49	10 55							11 16	11 27						11 49					12 27		
Manchester Piccadilly [10] ⛴	a		10 59	11 07							11 28	11 39						11 59					12 39		
Hartford	a															11 11								12 10	
Warrington Bank Quay	a	10 26												11 14			11 26								
	d	10 27												11 14			11 27								
Runcorn	a						10 50	10 55								11 21						11 50		12 22	
Liverpool South Parkway [7] ✈	a						10 59									11 30						11 59		12 31	
Liverpool Lime Street [10]	a						11 10	11 15								11 43						12 10		12 43	
	d														10 57										
Manchester Airport ✈	d				10 00								10 29						11 00						11 29
Manchester Piccadilly [10] ⛴	d				10 16								10 46						11 16						11 46
Bolton	d				10 33								11 07						11 33						12 07
Wigan North Western	a	10 37												11 25	11 30		11 37								
	d	10 38												11 25	11 31		11 38								
Preston [8]	a	10 51			10 55								11 33	11 38	11 54		11 51		11 57						12 33
Preston [8]	d	10 53			10 58								11 38	11 41	11 55		11 53		11 58						12 38
Blackpool North	a												12 05		12 19										13 05
Lancaster [6]	a	11 08			11 13									11 54			12 08		12 13						
	d	11 08			11 14									11 55			12 08		12 14						
Barrow-in-Furness	a																		13 11						
Oxenholme Lake District	a				11 28												12 22								
	d				11 28												12 24								
Windermere	a																								
Penrith North Lakes	d	11 45			11 53									12 30											
Carlisle [8]	a	12 00			12 10									12 45			13 01								
	d	12 01			12 11									12 47			13 03								
Lockerbie	d				12 30																				
Carstairs	a																								
Motherwell	a																								
Glasgow Central [15]	a	13 17												14 01											
Haymarket	a				13s33												14 15								
Edinburgh [10]	a				13 39												14 21								
Perth	a																								
Dundee	a																								
Aberdeen	a																								
Inverness	a																								

A 🛒 to Preston

OVERNIGHT SLEEPERS. For sleeper trains, operated by First ScotRail, please refer to Tables 400 - 404

Table 65

Mondays to Fridays

until 29 June

London and West Midlands - North West England and Scotland

Route Diagram - see first Page of Table 65

		VT	VT	VT	VT		VT	VT	XC	VT	NT	VT	TP		LM		VT	VT	VT	XC	TP	TP	VT	NT	LM
																							R		
		◇1	◇1	◇1	◇1		◇1	◇1	◇1	◇1		◇1	◇1		◇1		◇1	◇1	◇1	◇1	◇1	◇1	1		◇1
		☕	☒	☒	☒		☒	☒	⚯	☕		☕	⚯				☕	☕	☕	⚯		⚯	☒		
London Euston 15 ⊖	d	09 43	10 00	10 07	10 10		10 20	10 30		11 00							11 07	11 10	11 20				11 30		
Watford Junction	d																								
Milton Keynes Central	d	10 13			10 41		10 50											11 41	11 50						
Rugby	d																								
Nuneaton	d																								
Tamworth Low Level	d																								
Lichfield Trent Valley	d																								
Coventry	d	10 42																		11 27					
Birmingham International ✈	d	10 53																		11 38					
Birmingham New Street 12	d	11 20							11 31						11 36					11 57					12 01
Wolverhampton 7 ⛴	d	11 37							11 49						11 53					12 15					12 19
Penkridge	d														12 03										
Stafford	a			11 22					12 00						12 09		12 22			12 29					12 34
	d			11 23					12 01						12 09		12 23			12 30					12 35
Stoke-on-Trent	a		11 24				11 48		12 19	12 24									12 48	12 54					
Congleton	a																								
Macclesfield	a		11 41							12 41										13 11					
Crewe 10	a	12 07			11 47										12 30			12 47							12 56
	d	12 09			11 49										12 31			12 49							12 57
Chester	a				12 12													13 12							
Wrexham General	a																								
Llandudno	a																								
Bangor (Gwynedd)	a																								
Holyhead	a																								
Wilmslow	a																								
Stockport	a		11 55				12 16		12 49	12 55									13 16	13 27					
Manchester Piccadilly 10 ⛴	a		12 07				12 28		12 59	13 07									13 28	13 39					
Hartford	a																								13 11
Warrington Bank Quay	a	12 26						12 14															13 14		
	d	12 27						12 14															13 14		
Runcorn	a			11 55											12 50		12 55								13 21
Liverpool South Parkway 7 ✈	a														12 59										13 30
Liverpool Lime Street 10	a			12 15											13 10		13 15								13 43
	d										11 57													12 57	
Manchester Airport ✈	d												12 00									12 29			
Manchester Piccadilly 10 ⛴	d												12 16									12 46			
Bolton	d											←	12 33									13 07			
Wigan North Western	a	12 37						12 25			12 30	12 37											13 25	13 30	
	d	12 38						12 25			12 31	12 38											13 25	13 31	
Preston 8	a	→						12 38			12 54	12 51	12 55									13 33	13 38	13 54	
Preston 8	d							12 41			12 55	12 53	12 58								13 04	13 38	13 41	13 55	
Blackpool North	a										13 19											14 05		14 19	
Lancaster 6	a							13 00				13 08	13 13								13 19		13 54		
	d											13 08	13 14								13 20		13 55		
Barrow-in-Furness	a																								
Oxenholme Lake District	a											13 22	13 28								13 36		14 08		
	d											13 24	13 28								13 37		14 08		
Windermere	a																				13 56				
Penrith North Lakes	d												13 53												
Carlisle 8	a											14 01	14 10										14 46		
	d											14 03	14 11										14 47		
Lockerbie	d												14 30												
Carstairs	a																								
Motherwell	a																								
Glasgow Central 15	a											15 25											16 06		
Haymarket	a												15s34												
Edinburgh 10	a												15 39												
Perth	a																								
Dundee	a																								
Aberdeen	a																								
Inverness	a																								

OVERNIGHT SLEEPERS. For sleeper trains, operated by First ScotRail, please refer to Tables 400 - 404

Table 65

Mondays to Fridays

until 29 June

London and West Midlands - North West England and Scotland

Route Diagram - see first Page of Table 65

		VT	XC	VT	TP	TP FX	LM	VT	VT	VT	XC	TP	VT	NT	LM	VT	XC	VT	TP	LM
		◇1	◇1	◇1	◇1	◇1	◇1	◇1	◇1	◇1	◇1	◇1	◇1		◇1	◇1	◇1	◇1	◇1	◇1
						A														
		🍴	🛒	🍴	🛒	🛒		🍴	🍴	🍴	🛒	🛒	🍴			🍴	🛒	🍴	🛒	
London Euston 15 ⊖	d			12 00				12 07	12 10	12 20			12 30					13 00		
Watford Junction	d																			
Milton Keynes Central	d								12 41	12 50										
Rugby	d																			
Nuneaton	d																			
Tamworth Low Level	d																			
Lichfield Trent Valley	d																			
Coventry	d										12 27									
Birmingham International ✈	d										12 38									
Birmingham New Street 12	d	12 20	12 31				12 36				12 57				13 01	13 20	13 31			13 36
Wolverhampton 7 ⛴	d	12 37	12 49				12 53				13 15				13 19	13 37	13 49			13 53
Penkridge	d						13 03													14 03
Stafford	a		13 00				13 09	13 22			13 29				13 34		14 00			14 09
	d		13 01				13 09	13 23			13 30				13 35		14 01			14 09
Stoke-on-Trent	a		13 19	13 24						13 48	13 54						14 19	14 24		
Congleton	a																			
Macclesfield	a			13 41							14 11							14 41		
Crewe 10	a	13 07					13 30		13 47						13 56	14 07				14 30
	d	13 09					13 31		13 49						13 57	14 09				14 31
Chester	a								14 12											
Wrexham General	a																			
Llandudno	a																			
Bangor (Gwynedd)	a																			
Holyhead	a																			
Wilmslow	a																			
Stockport	a		13 49	13 55						14 16	14 27						14 49	14 55		
Manchester Piccadilly 10 ⛴	a		13 59	14 07						14 28	14 39						14 59	15 07		
Hartford	a														14 11					
Warrington Bank Quay	a	13 26											14 14			14 26				
	d	13 27											14 14			14 27				
Runcorn	a						13 50	13 55							14 21					14 50
Liverpool South Parkway 7 ✈	a						13 59								14 30					14 59
Liverpool Lime Street 10	a						14 10	14 15							14 43					15 10
	d													13 57						
Manchester Airport ✈	d				13 00	13 00						13 29							14 00	
Manchester Piccadilly 10 ⛴	d				13 16	13 16						13 46							14 16	
Bolton	d				13 33	13 33						14 07							14 33	
Wigan North Western	a	13 37											14 25	14 30		14 37				
	d	13 38											14 25	14 31		14 38				
Preston 8	a	13 51			13 55	13 55						14 33	14 38	14 54		14 51			14 55	
Preston 8	d	13 53			13 58	14 04						14 38	14 41	14 55		14 53			14 58	
Blackpool North	a											15 05		15 21						
Lancaster 6	a	14 08			14 13	14 19							15 00			15 08			15 13	
	d	14 08			14 14	14 20										15 09			15 14	
Barrow-in-Furness	a					15 15														
Oxenholme Lake District	a															15 22			15 28	
	d															15 24			15 28	
Windermere	a																			
Penrith North Lakes	d	14 45																	15 53	
Carlisle 8	a	15 00			15 06											16 01			16 10	
	d	15 02			15 07											16 03			16 11	
Lockerbie	d				15 27														16 30	
Carstairs	a																			
Motherwell	a																			
Glasgow Central 15	a				16 30											17 14				
Haymarket	a	16 17																	17s31	
Edinburgh 10	a	16 21																	17 39	
Perth	a																			
Dundee	a																			
Aberdeen	a																			
Inverness	a																			

A 🛒 to Preston

OVERNIGHT SLEEPERS. For sleeper trains, operated by First ScotRail, please refer to Tables 400 - 404

London and West Midlands - North West England and Scotland

Route Diagram - see first Page of Table 65

		VT	VT	VT	XC	TP	VT		NT	LM	VT	XC	TP	VT FO	VT		LM		VT	VT	VT	XC	TP	VT FX	VT FO
																									■
		◇1	◇1	◇1	◇1	◇1	◇1			◇1	◇1	◇1	◇1	◇	◇1		◇1		◇1	◇1	◇1	◇1	◇1	◇1	1
													A												
		⊡	⊡	⊡	⊼	⊼	⊠				⊡	⊼	⊼	⊡	⊡				⊡	⊡	⊡	⊼	⊼	⊡	⊡
London Euston 15 ⊖	d	13 07	13 10	13 20			13 30							13 33	14 00				14 07	14 10	14 20			14 30	14 30
Watford Junction	d																								
Milton Keynes Central	d		13 41	13 50																14 41	14 50				
Rugby	d																								
Nuneaton	d																								
Tamworth Low Level	d																								
Lichfield Trent Valley	d																								
Coventry	d				13 27																	14 27			
Birmingham International ✈	d				13 38																	14 38			
Birmingham New Street 12	d				13 57					14 01	14 20	14 31					14 36					14 57			
Wolverhampton 7	d				14 15					14 19	14 37	14 49					14 53					15 15			
Penkridge	d																15 03								
Stafford	a	14 22			14 29					14 34		15 00					15 09		15 22			15 29			
	d	14 23			14 30					14 35		15 01					15 09		15 23			15 30			
Stoke-on-Trent	a			14 48	14 54							15 19			15 24						15 48	15 54			
Congleton	a																								
Macclesfield	a				15 11										15 41							16 11			
Crewe 10	a		14 47							14 56	15 07			15 16			15 30			15 47					
	d		14 49							14 57	15 09			15 19			15 31			15 49					
Chester	a		15 12																	16 12					
Wrexham General	a																								
Llandudno	a																								
Bangor (Gwynedd)	a																								
Holyhead	a																								
Wilmslow	a																								
Stockport	a			15 16	15 27							15 49			15 55						16 16	16 27			
Manchester Piccadilly 10	a			15 28	15 39							15 59			16 07						16 28	16 39			
Hartford	a									15 11															
Warrington Bank Quay	a						15 14				15 26			15 38										16 17	16 16
	d						15 14				15 27			15 39										16 17	16 17
Runcorn	a	14 55								15 21							15 50		15 55						
Liverpool South Parkway 7 ✈	a									15 30							15 59								
Liverpool Lime Street 10	a	15 15								15 43							16 10		16 15						
	d								14 57																
Manchester Airport ✈	d					14 29							15 00										15 29		
Manchester Piccadilly 10	d					14 46							15 16										15 46		
Bolton	d					15 07							15 33										16 07		
Wigan North Western	a						15 25		15 30		15 37			15 49										16 29	16 28
	d						15 25		15 31		15 38			15 50										16 29	16 29
Preston 8	a					15 33	15 38		15 54		15 51		15 57	16 03									16 35	16 42	16 42
Preston 8	d					15 38	15 41		15 55		15 53		15 58	16 06									16 38	16 43	16 43
Blackpool North	a					16 05			16 20														17 07		
Lancaster 6	a										16 08		16 14	16 26										17 00	17 00
	d										16 08		16 15												17 00
Barrow-in-Furness	a												17 18												
Oxenholme Lake District	a						16 04																		17 15
	d						16 06																		17 16
Windermere	a																								
Penrith North Lakes	d						16 31				16 45														17 42
Carlisle 8	a						16 46				17 00														18 00
	d						16 47				17 02														18 00
Lockerbie	d																								
Carstairs	a																								
Motherwell	a																								
Glasgow Central 15	a						18 01																		19 14
Haymarket	a										18 12														
Edinburgh 10	a										18 22														
Perth	a																								
Dundee	a																								
Aberdeen	a																								
Inverness	a																								

A ⊼ to Preston

OVERNIGHT SLEEPERS. For sleeper trains, operated by First ScotRail, please refer to Tables 400 - 404

Table 65

Mondays to Fridays

until 29 June

London and West Midlands - North West England and Scotland

Route Diagram - see first Page of Table 65

		NT	LM	VT	XC	TP	TP FX	LM	XC	LM	TP	TP	VT	VT	VT	VT	VT	VT	XC	VT	NT
			◇1	◇1	◇1	◇1	◇1	◇1	◇1	◇1	◇1	◇1	R 1	◇1	◇1	◇1	◇1	◇1	◇1	◇1	
							A														
				🍽	🛒	🛒	🛒		🛒			🛒	🍽	🍽	🍽	🍽	🍽	⊠	🛒	🍽	
London Euston 15 ⊖	d												14 43	15 00	15 07	15 10	15 20	15 30		16 00	
Watford Junction	d																				
Milton Keynes Central	d												15 13			15 41	15 50				
Rugby	d																				
Nuneaton	d																				
Tamworth Low Level	d																				
Lichfield Trent Valley	d																				
Coventry	d								15 27				15 42								
Birmingham International ✈	d								15 38				15 53								
Birmingham New Street 12	d		15 01	15 20	15 31			15 36	15 57	16 01			16 20						16 31		
Wolverhampton 7	d		15 19	15 37	15 50			15 53	16 15	16 19			16 37						16 49		
Penkridge	d							16 03													
Stafford	a		15 34		16 01			16 09	16 30	16 34					16 22				17 00		
	d		15 35		16 02			16 09	16 31	16 35					16 23				17 01		
Stoke-on-Trent	a				16 20				16 54					16 24			16 48		17 19	17 24	
Congleton	a																				
Macclesfield	a								17 11					16 41						17 41	
Crewe 10	a		15 56	16 07				16 30		16 56			17 07			16 47					
	d		15 57	16 09				16 31		16 57			17 09			16 49					
Chester	a															17 12					
Wrexham General	a																				
Llandudno	a																				
Bangor (Gwynedd)	a																				
Holyhead	a																				
Wilmslow	a																				
Stockport	a				16 49				17 27					16 54			17 16		17 49	17 55	
Manchester Piccadilly 10	a				16 59				17 39					17 07			17 28		17 59	18 07	
Hartford	a		16 10							17 11											
Warrington Bank Quay	a			16 26									17 26					17 14			
	d			16 27									17 27					17 14			
Runcorn	a		16 22					16 50		17 21					16 55						
Liverpool South Parkway 7 ✈	a		16 31					16 59		17 30											
Liverpool Lime Street 10	a		16 44					17 10		17 43					17 15						
	d	15 57																			16 57
Manchester Airport ✈	d					16 00	16 00					16 29									
Manchester Piccadilly 10	d					16 16	16 16					16 46									
Bolton	d					16 33	16 33					17 06									
Wigan North Western	a	16 30		16 37									17 37					17 25			17 30
	d	16 30		16 38									17 38					17 25			17 31
Preston 8	a	16 54		16 51		16 55	16 55					17 30	→					17 38			17 54
Preston 8	d	16 56		16 53		17 00	17 04				17 04	17 32						17 41			17 55
Blackpool North	a	17 20										18 02									18 23
Lancaster 6	a			17 08		17 15	17 23				17 23							17 54			
	d			17 08		17 16	17 25				17 25							17 55			
Barrow-in-Furness	a																				
Oxenholme Lake District	a			17 22		17 30	17 43				17 43							18 08			
	d			17 23		17 30	17 49				17 49							18 08			
Windermere	a						18 08				18 08										
Penrith North Lakes	d			17 49																	
Carlisle 8	a			18 05		18 10												18 47			
	d			18 06		18 11												18 47			
Lockerbie	d					18 30															
Carstairs	a																				
Motherwell	a																				
Glasgow Central 15	a			19 19														19 57			
Haymarket	a					19s31															
Edinburgh 10	a					19 39															
Perth	a																				
Dundee	a																				
Aberdeen	a																				
Inverness	a																				

A 🛒 to Preston

OVERNIGHT SLEEPERS. For sleeper trains, operated by First ScotRail, please refer to Tables 400 - 404

London and West Midlands - North West England and Scotland

Route Diagram - see first Page of Table 65

		VT	TP		NT		LM	VT	VT		XC	VT	LM	TP	VT	VT	XC	TP				LM	NT	VT	VT
		R 1 ☕	◇1 🛒				◇1	◇1 ☕	◇1 ☕		◇1 🛒	◇1 ⊠	◇1	◇1 🛒	R 1 ☕	◇1 ☕	◇1 🛒	◇1 🛒				◇1		◇1 ⊠	◇1 ⊠
London Euston 15 ⊖	d							16 07	16 20			16 30				16 33								16 57	17 00
Watford Junction	d																								
Milton Keynes Central	d								16u50																
Rugby	d															17 22									
Nuneaton	d																								
Tamworth Low Level	d																							18 00	
Lichfield Trent Valley	d																							18 07	
Coventry	d										16 27														
Birmingham International ✈	d										16 38														
Birmingham New Street 12	d						16 36				16 57		17 01		17 20		17 31					17 36			
Wolverhampton 7	d						16 53				17 15		17 19		17 37		17 50					17 53			
Penkridge	d						17 03						17 29									18 02			
Stafford	a						17 09	17 22			17 29		17 35			17 52	18 01					18 09			
	d						17 09	17 23			17 30		17 36			17 56	18 02					18 09			
Stoke-on-Trent	a								17 48		17 54						18 20								18 24
Congleton	a																								
Macclesfield	a										18 11														18 41
Crewe 10	a						17 30						17 56		18 07	18 16						18 30			
	d						17 31						17 57		18 09	18 18						18 31			
Chester	a																								
Wrexham General	a																								
Llandudno	a																								
Bangor (Gwynedd)	a																								
Holyhead	a																								
Wilmslow	a																								
Stockport	a								18 16		18 27						18 49								18 55
Manchester Piccadilly 10	a								18 28		18 39						18 59								19 07
Hartford	a												18 11									18 44			
Warrington Bank Quay	a														18 26	18 35								18 49	
	d														18 27	18 36								18 50	
Runcorn	a						17 50	17 55					18 21									18 56			
Liverpool South Parkway 7 ✈	a						17 59						18 30									19 05			
Liverpool Lime Street 10	a						18 10	18 15					18 43									19 16			
	d				17 19																				
Manchester Airport ✈	d		17 00											17 29				18 00							
Manchester Piccadilly 10	d		17 15											17 46				18 16							
Bolton	d	←	17 32											18 07				18 33							
Wigan North Western	a	17 37			18 02										18 37	18 46								19 00	
	d	17 38													18 38	18 47								19 01	
Preston 8	a	17 51	17 55									18 30		18 38	18 51	19 01		18 55						19 14	
Preston 8	d	17 53	17 58	18 08								18 30		18 40	18 53			19 00	19 04				19 08	19 15	
Blackpool North	a													19 10									19 33		
Lancaster 6	a	18 08	18 13	18 23											19 08			19 15	19 20					19 30	
	d	18 08	18 14	18 24											19 08			19 16	19 20					19 30	
Barrow-in-Furness	a			19 29															20 24						
Oxenholme Lake District	a	18 22	18 28												19 22			19 30						19 43	
	d	18 23	18 28												19 24			19 32						19 45	
Windermere	a																								
Penrith North Lakes	d	18 49	18 53															19 57						20 10	
Carlisle 8	a	19 04	19 09												20 01			20 13						20 25	
	d	19 04	19 11												20 03			20 13						20 25	
Lockerbie	d																							20 44	
Carstairs	a																								
Motherwell	a		20s16																					21 26	
Glasgow Central 15	a		20 33									20 38			21 17									21 47	
Haymarket	a	20 16																21s31							
Edinburgh 10	a	20 22																21 39							
Perth	a																								
Dundee	a																								
Aberdeen	a																								
Inverness	a																								

OVERNIGHT SLEEPERS. For sleeper trains, operated by First ScotRail, please refer to Tables 400 - 404

until 29 June

London and West Midlands - North West England and Scotland

Route Diagram - see first Page of Table 65

		VT	VT	VT	XC		LM	TP	VT	VT	TP	NT	VT	VT	XC		VT		LM	VT	VT	VT	XC	LM
		◇1	◇1	◇1	◇1		◇1	◇1	◇1	◇1	◇1		◇1	◇1	◇1		◇1		◇1	◇1	◇1	◇1	◇1	◇1
																					A			
		⊠	⊠	⊠	🛒			🛒	⊠	☕			⊠	⊠	🛒		⊠			⊠	⊠	⊠	🛒	
London Euston 15 ⊖	d	17 07	17 10	17 20					17 30				17 33	17 57			18 00			18 07	18 10	18 20		
Watford Junction	d																							
Milton Keynes Central	d		17u40	17u50																	18u40	18u50		
Rugby	d												18 23											
Nuneaton	d		18 12																		19 13			
Tamworth Low Level	d													19 00										
Lichfield Trent Valley	d													19 08										
Coventry	d				17 27																		18 27	
Birmingham International ✈	d				17 38																		18 38	
Birmingham New Street 12	d				17 57		18 01			18 20					18 31				18 36				18 57	19 01
Wolverhampton 7	d				18 15		18 19			18 37					18 49				18 53				19 15	19 19
Penkridge	d						18 29												19 03					19 29
Stafford	a	18 23			18 29		18 35						18 52		19 00				19 09	19 23			19 27	19 36
	d	18 24			18 30		18 35						18 55		19 01				19 09	19 24			19 29	19 36
Stoke-on-Trent	a			18 49	18 54										19 19		19 24					19 48	19 54	
Congleton	a																							
Macclesfield	a				19 11												19 41						20 11	
Crewe 10	a	18 42	18 53				19 00			19 07			19 14						19 30	19 42	19 53			20 01
	d	18 44	18 56				19 02			19 09			19 16						19 31	19 44	19 56			
Chester	a		19 15																		20 15			
Wrexham General	a																				20 38			
Llandudno	a																							
Bangor (Gwynedd)	a																				21 25			
Holyhead	a																				21 59			
Wilmslow	a																							
Stockport	a			19 16	19 27										19 48		19 55					20 16	20 27	
Manchester Piccadilly 10	a			19 28	19 39										19 59		20 07					20 28	20 39	
Hartford	a																		19 47					
Warrington Bank Quay	a								19 14	19 26				19 49										
	d								19 14	19 27				19 50										
Runcorn	a	19 02					19 22						19 33						19 57	20 01				
Liverpool South Parkway 7 ✈	a						19 31												20 06					
Liverpool Lime Street 10	a	19 22					19 44						19 51						20 18	20 19				
	d											19 23												
Manchester Airport ✈	d							18 29			19 00													
Manchester Piccadilly 10	d							18 46			19 16													
Bolton	d							19 07			19 33													
Wigan North Western	a								19 25	19 37		19 54		20 00										
	d								19 25	19 38		19 55		20 01										
Preston 8	a							19 33	19 38	19 51	19 55	20 18		20 14										
Preston 8	d							19 38	19 41	19 53	19 58	20 19		20 15										
Blackpool North	a							20 06				20 42												
Lancaster 6	a								19 54	20 08	20 13			20 30										
	d								19 55	20 08	20 14			20 30										
Barrow-in-Furness	a										21 17													
Oxenholme Lake District	a								20 08															
	d								20 08															
Windermere	a																							
Penrith North Lakes	d									20 45														
Carlisle 8	a								20 46	21 00				21 17										
	d								20 47	21 02				21 18										
Lockerbie	d													21 37										
Carstairs	a																							
Motherwell	a													22 21										
Glasgow Central 15	a								22 01					22 39										
Haymarket	a									22 14														
Edinburgh 10	a									22 22														
Perth	a																							
Dundee	a																							
Aberdeen	a																							
Inverness	a																							

A ⊠ to Chester

OVERNIGHT SLEEPERS. For sleeper trains, operated by First ScotRail, please refer to Tables 400 - 404

until 29 June

London and West Midlands - North West England and Scotland

Route Diagram - see first Page of Table 65

			TP	VT	VT	TP	NT	VT	XC		LM		XC	VT	TP	VT FO	VT ThFO	VT MT WO	VT ThFO	VT	VT		VT	VT	VT FO
																		R	R	R	R		R	R	
			◇1	◇1	◇1	◇1		◇1	◇1		◇1		◇1	◇1	◇1	◇	◇	1	1	1	1		1	1	◇
													A												
				☒	☕			☒	🍴				🍴	☒		☕	☕	☕	☕	☕	☕		☕	☕	☕
London Euston 15 ⊖	d			18 30				18 33						18 43		18 46	18 57	19 00	19 00	19 07	19 10		19 20	19 30	
Watford Junction	d																								
Milton Keynes Central	d													19 13							19u40		19 50		
Rugby	d							19 23								19 39									
Nuneaton	d																			20 03					
Tamworth Low Level	d															19s59									
Lichfield Trent Valley	d															20s07									
Coventry	d												19 27	19 42											
Birmingham International ✈	d												19 38	19 53											
Birmingham New Street 12	d				19 20				19 31		19 36		19 57	20 20											
Wolverhampton 7	d				19 37				19 49		19 53		20 16	20 36											
Penkridge	d										20 03														
Stafford	a							19 53	20 00		20 09		20 29	20 49		20s35				20 26					
	d							19 56	20 01		20 09		20 30	20 52						20 27					
Stoke-on-Trent	a								20 19				20 54					20 24	20 24				20 48		
Congleton	a																								
Macclesfield	a												21 11					20 41	20 41						
Crewe 10	a				20 07			20 15			20 30			21 15		21s01	20s33				20 48				
	d				20 09			20 17			20 31										20 50				
Chester	a																				21 10				
Wrexham General	a																								
Llandudno	a																								
Bangor (Gwynedd)	a																								
Holyhead	a																								
Wilmslow	a																								
Stockport	a								20 48				21 27					20 55	20 55				21 16		
Manchester Piccadilly 10	a								20 58				21 39				21 09	21 07	21 10				21 28		
Hartford	a										20 45														
Warrington Bank Quay	a			20 14	20 26											21s20								21 15	
	d			20 14	20 27																			21 15	
Runcorn	a							20 34			20 56									21 01					
Liverpool South Parkway 7 ✈	a										21 05														
Liverpool Lime Street 10	a							20 53			21 16									21 21					
	d						20 25																		
Manchester Airport ✈	d		19 29			20 00									20 29										
Manchester Piccadilly 10	d		19 46			20 16									20 46										
Bolton	d		20 07			20 33									21 07										←
Wigan North Western	a			20 25	20 37		20 57									21s31								21 26	21s31
	d			20 25	20 38		20 57																	21 26	
Preston 8	a		20 33	20 38	20 51	20 57	21 22								21 33	→								21 39	21 46
Preston 8	d		20 38	20 41	20 53	20 59	21 24								21 38									21 41	
Blackpool North	a		21 06				21 52								22 06										
Lancaster 6	a			20 54	21 08	21 14																		21 55	
	d			20 55	21 08	21 15																		21 56	
Barrow-in-Furness	a					22 18																			
Oxenholme Lake District	a			21 08	21 22																			22 09	
	d			21 09	21 24																			22 09	
Windermere	a																								
Penrith North Lakes	d			21 34																				22 35	
Carlisle 8	a			21 49	22 01																			22 50	
	d			21 51	22 03																			22 51	
Lockerbie	d																								
Carstairs	a																								
Motherwell	a																								
Glasgow Central 15	a			23 04	23 18																			00 06	
Haymarket	a																								
Edinburgh 10	a																								
Perth	a																								
Dundee	a																								
Aberdeen	a																								
Inverness	a																								

A 🍴 to Birmingham New Street

OVERNIGHT SLEEPERS. For sleeper trains, operated by First ScotRail, please refer to Tables 400 - 404

London and West Midlands - North West England and Scotland

Route Diagram - see first Page of Table 65

		XC	VT	LM	VT	XC	AW	VT	NT	TP	VT	VT	AW	VT	TP	LM	VT	VT	XC	TP	VT
													FX				FO	FX			FO
		◇1	◇1	◇1	◇1	◇1		◇1		◇1	◇1	◇1		◇1	◇1	◇1	◇1	◇1	◇1	◇1	◇1
						A											B	C			B
			☕		☕	🛒		☕			☕	☕	🚌	☕			☕	☕			☕
London Euston 15 ⊖	d		20 00		20 07			20 10			20 30	21 00					21 07	21 07			21 10
Watford Junction	d																				21u25
Milton Keynes Central	d							20 40				21 31					21 38	21 38			
Rugby	d																				22 04
Nuneaton	d				21 03												22 08	22 08			
Tamworth Low Level	d										21 34										
Lichfield Trent Valley	d										21 42										
Coventry	d					20 27													21 27		
Birmingham International ✈	d					20 38													21 38		
Birmingham New Street 12	d	20 31		20 36		20 57								21 20		21 36			21 57		
Wolverhampton 7	d	20 49		20 53		21 16								21 41		21 53			22 16		
Penkridge	d			21 03												22 03					
Stafford	a			21 09	21 27	21 31								21 53		22 09			22 29		22 34
	d			21 09	21 27	21 32								21 55		22 09			22 30		22 34
Stoke-on-Trent	a	21 17	21 23			21 54						22 28							22 53		
Congleton	a																				
Macclesfield	a		21 40			22 11						22 44							23 11		
Crewe 10	a			21 30				21 48						22 17		22 30	22 46	22 49			22 53
	d			21 31			21 36	21 50						22 18		22 31	22 48	22 51			22 54
Chester	a						21 59	22 15													
Wrexham General	a																				
Llandudno	a																				
Bangor (Gwynedd)	a																				
Holyhead	a																				
Wilmslow	a																				
Stockport	a	21 46	21 55			22 25						22 58							23 25		
Manchester Piccadilly 10 🚊	a	21 59	22 07			22 35						23 11							23 37		
Hartford	a			21 43												22 43					
Warrington Bank Quay	a										22 22			22 36							23 12
	d										22 23		22 28	22 36							23 12
Runcorn	a			21 54	21 59											22 56	23 05	23 08			
Liverpool South Parkway 7 ✈	a			22 05												23 07					
Liverpool Lime Street 10	a			22 15	22 20											23 23	23 24	23 27			
	d																				
Manchester Airport ✈	d									21 29					22 00					22 29	
Manchester Piccadilly 10 🚊	d									21 46			23a38		22 16					22 46	
Bolton	d									22 07					22 33					23 07	
Wigan North Western	a										22 33			22 46	22 48						23 23
	d										22 34			22 46	22 51						23 23
Preston 8	a									22 36	22 53			23 01	23 09					23 33	23 39
Preston 8	d								21 51	22 38					23 13					23 35	
Blackpool North	a									23 04										00 02	
Lancaster 6	a								22 11						23 28						
	d								22 11						23 29						
Barrow-in-Furness	a								23 16						00 31						
Oxenholme Lake District	a																				
	d																				
Windermere	a																				
Penrith North Lakes	d																				
Carlisle 8	a																				
	d																				
Lockerbie	d																				
Carstairs	a																				
Motherwell	a																				
Glasgow Central 15	a																				
Haymarket	a																				
Edinburgh 10	a																				
Perth	a																				
Dundee	a																				
Aberdeen	a																				
Inverness	a																				

A 🛒 to Birmingham New Street

B also from 25 June until 28 June

C until 21 June

OVERNIGHT SLEEPERS. For sleeper trains, operated by First ScotRail, please refer to Tables 400 - 404

London and West Midlands - North West England and Scotland

Route Diagram - see first Page of Table 65

		VT			TP	NT	SR	VT	XC	XC	XC	LM		VT	LM	SR	SR	AW
		FX				FX			FX		FO					FO	FX	FX
		◇1			◇1			◇1	◇1	◇1	◇1	◇1		◇1	◇1			
		A					B		A	C	D							
London Euston 15 ⊖	d	21 10					21 15	21 40						22 00		23 50	23 50	
Watford Junction	d	21u25					21u33									00u10	00u10	
Milton Keynes Central	d													22 31				
Rugby	d	22 04												22 54				
Nuneaton	d													23 04				
Tamworth Low Level	d													23s15				
Lichfield Trent Valley	d													23s22				
Coventry	d																	
Birmingham International ✈	d																	
Birmingham New Street 12	d								22 30	22 30	22 30	22 36			23 09			
Wolverhampton 7	d								22 48	22 48	22 48	22 57			23 36			
Penkridge	d											23 07			23 46			
Stafford	a	22 35							23 00	23 00	23 00	23 13		23s38	23 52			
	d	22 35							23 01	23 01	23 01	23 13			23 53			
Stoke-on-Trent	a							23 06	23 21	23 20	23 21							
Congleton	a																	
Macclesfield	a							23 23										
Crewe 10	a	22 56										23 43		00s03	00 16			
	d	22 57					23u54											
Chester	a																	
Wrexham General	a																	
Llandudno	a																	
Bangor (Gwynedd)	a																	
Holyhead	a																	
Wilmslow	a																	
Stockport	a							23 37						00s26				
Manchester Piccadilly 10	a							23 46	00 12	00 12	00 13			00 35				
Hartford	a																	
Warrington Bank Quay	a	23 15																
	d	23 15																23 59
Runcorn	a																	
Liverpool South Parkway 7 ✈	a																	
Liverpool Lime Street 10	a																	
	d																	
Manchester Airport ✈	d																	
Manchester Piccadilly 10	d																	01a09
Bolton	d																	
Wigan North Western	a	23 26																
	d	23 26				23 48												
Preston 8	a	23 42				00 13												
Preston 8	d				23 51		00u52											
Blackpool North	a				00 16													
Lancaster 6	a																	
	d																	
Barrow-in-Furness	a																	
Oxenholme Lake District	a																	
	d																	
Windermere	a																	
Penrith North Lakes	d																	
Carlisle 8	a															05s15	05s16	
	d																	
Lockerbie	d																	
Carstairs	a															06s20	06s20	
Motherwell	a															06s56	06s56	
Glasgow Central 15	a															07 20	07 20	
Haymarket	a																	
Edinburgh 10	a															07 15	07 16	
Perth	a						05s39											
Dundee	a						06s08											
Aberdeen	a						07 36											
Inverness	a						08 38											

A until 21 June

B Conveys a portion for Fort William, arrives at 0954

C from 25 June until 29 June

D until 22 June

OVERNIGHT SLEEPERS. For sleeper trains, operated by First ScotRail, please refer to Tables 400 - 404

2 July to 14 September

London and West Midlands - North West England and Scotland

Route Diagram - see first Page of Table 65

		XC MX		VT MO	VT MX	VT MO	TP MX	TP MX	NT MO	TP MX		NT MX	SR MO	SR MX	VT MO	VT MO	VT MO	VT MX		LM MX	SR MO	VT
					R								R	R							R	
		◇1		◇1	1	◇1	◇1	◇1		◇1					◇1	◇1	◇1	◇1		◇1		◇1
													A	A								B
													🛏	🛏							🛏	
				☕	☕	☕							☕	☕	☕	☕	☕	☕			☕	☕
London Euston 15 ⊖	d			19p25	19p30								20p55	21p15	21p21	21p25	21p51	22p00			23p27	23p30
Watford Junction	d												21b17	21b33							23b47	
Milton Keynes Central	d															22p14	22p38	22p31				
Rugby	d																23p18	22p54				
Nuneaton	d														22p52		23p29	23p04				
Tamworth Low Level	d																	23c15				
Lichfield Trent Valley	d																	23c22				
Coventry	d																					
Birmingham International ✈	d																					
Birmingham New Street 12	d	22p30																		23p09		
Wolverhampton 7	d	22p48																		23p36		
Penkridge	d																			23p46		
Stafford	a	23p00													23p16		23c53	23c38		23p52		
	d	23p01													23p17					23p53		
Stoke-on-Trent	a	23p20														23p29						00s53
Congleton	a																					
Macclesfield	a															23p45						01s10
Crewe 10	a														23p43		00s21	00s03		00 16		
	d												23b39	23b54	23p45							
Chester	a																					
Wrexham General	a																					
Llandudno	a																					
Bangor (Gwynedd)	a																					
Holyhead	a																					
Wilmslow	a																					
Stockport	a															23p59	00s50	00s26				01s24
Manchester Piccadilly 10	a	00 12														00 12	01 00	00 35				01 37
Hartford	a																					
Warrington Bank Quay	a			21p16	21p15																	
	d			21p16	21p15																	
Runcorn	a														00 07							
Liverpool South Parkway 7 ✈	a																					
Liverpool Lime Street 10	a														00 30							
	d																					
Manchester Airport ✈	d						22p00	22p29														
Manchester Piccadilly 10	d						22p16	22p46														
Bolton	d					←	22p33	23p07														
Wigan North Western	a			21p27	21p26	21p27	22p48															
	d			21p27	21p26	21p27	22p51		23p14			23p48										
Preston 8	a			→	21p39	21p40	23p09	23p33	23p36			00 13										
Preston 8	d				21p41	21p42	23p13	23p35	23p39	23p51			00u30	00u52								
Blackpool North	a							00 02	00 05	00 16												
Lancaster 6	a				21p55	21p56	23p28															
	d				21p56	21p57	23p29															
Barrow-in-Furness	a						00 31															
Oxenholme Lake District	a				22p09	22p10																
	d				22p09	22p11																
Windermere	a																					
Penrith North Lakes	d				22p35	22p36																
Carlisle 8	a				22p50	22p51															05s04	
	d				22p51	22p53																
Lockerbie	d																					
Carstairs	a																				06s20	
Motherwell	a																				06s56	
Glasgow Central 15	a				00 06	00 02															07 20	
Haymarket	a																					
Edinburgh 10	a																				07 16	
Perth	a												05s39	05s39								
Dundee	a												06s08	06s08								
Aberdeen	a												07 36	07 36								
Inverness	a												08 38	08 38								

A Conveys a portion for Fort William, arrives at 0954

B 30 July, 6 August, 13 August, 3 September, 10 September

b Previous night, stops to pick up only

c Previous night, stops to set down only

OVERNIGHT SLEEPERS. For sleeper trains, operated by First ScotRail, please refer to Tables 400 - 404

London and West Midlands - North West England and Scotland

Route Diagram - see first Page of Table 65

		VT	VT	VT	SR	SR	TP	VT	VT	NT	VT	VT	VT	VT	TP	NT	NT	LM	TP	XC	VT
		MX		MX	MX	MX			MX	MX		MX		MX		MX	MO				
					R	R															
		◇1	◇1	◇1			◇1	◇1	◇1		◇1	◇1	◇1	◇1	◇1			◇1	◇1	◇1	◇1
		A	B	A	C	D		B	A		B	A	B	A							
					🛏	🛏															
		☕	☕	☕	☕	☕		☕	☕		☕	☕	☕	☕							⊠
London Euston 15 ⊖	d	23p30	23p45	23p45	23p50	23p50		00ʃ30	00ʃ30		01ʃ00	01ʃ00	01ʃ30	01ʃ30							
Watford Junction	d				00u10	00u14															
Milton Keynes Central	d																				
Rugby	d		00s33	00s47							01s48	01s48									
Nuneaton	d		00s44	00s58							01s59	02s05									
Tamworth Low Level	d																				
Lichfield Trent Valley	d																				
Coventry	d																				
Birmingham International ✈	d																				
Birmingham New Street 12	d																			05 57	
Wolverhampton 7	d																			06 16	
Penkridge	d																				
Stafford	a		01s08	01s22							02s23	02s29								06 29	
	d																			06 30	
Stoke-on-Trent	a	00s53						01s53	01s53				02s53	02s55						06 50	
Congleton	a																			07 02	
Macclesfield	a	01s10						02s10	02s10				03s12	03s12						07 11	
Crewe 10	a		01s27	01s41							02s42	02s50									
	d									00 44								05 40			05 57
Chester	a																				
Wrexham General	a																				
Llandudno	a																				
Bangor (Gwynedd)	a																				
Holyhead	a																				
Wilmslow	a																				
Stockport	a	01s24						02s24	02s26				03s30	03s30						07 27	
Manchester Piccadilly 10	a	01ʃ43						02ʃ37	02ʃ39				03ʃ43	03ʃ43						07 37	
Hartford	a																				
Warrington Bank Quay	a																				06 13
	d																				06 14
Runcorn	a		01s46	02s02							03s01	03s09						05 58			
Liverpool South Parkway 7 ✈	a																	06 10			
Liverpool Lime Street 10	a		02ʃ07	02ʃ21							03ʃ19	03ʃ27						06 22			
	d																				
Manchester Airport ✈	d						00 01			01 20					04 00						
Manchester Piccadilly 10	d						00 16			01a36					04 15				05 46		
Bolton	d						00s31								04s29						
Wigan North Western	a														04 44				06 15		06 24
	d														04 44				06 15		06 25
Preston 8	a						01s05								05s04				06 35		06 37
Preston 8	d															05 22	05 22		06 37		06 40
Blackpool North	a						01 30								05 33				07 06		
Lancaster 6	a															05 42	05 42				06 54
	d															05 42	05 42				06 54
Barrow-in-Furness	a															06 47	06 47				
Oxenholme Lake District	a																				07 08
	d																				07 10
Windermere	a																				
Penrith North Lakes	d																				07 35
Carlisle 8	a				05s16	05s15										09 21	09 22				07 50
	d																				07 51
Lockerbie	d																				08 10
Carstairs	a				06s20	06s19															
Motherwell	a				06s56	06s55															
Glasgow Central 15	a				07ʃ20	07ʃ20															09 14
Haymarket	a																				
Edinburgh 10	a				07ʃ16	07ʃ16															
Perth	a																				
Dundee	a																				
Aberdeen	a																				
Inverness	a																				

A from 31 July until 7 September, not from 14 August until 29 August

B 30 July, 6 August, 13 August, 3 September, 10 September

C not from 31 July until 10 August, from 30 August until 7 September.

D from 31 July until 7 September, not from 14 August until 29 August.

OVERNIGHT SLEEPERS. For sleeper trains, operated by First ScotRail, please refer to Tables 400 - 404

London and West Midlands - North West England and Scotland

Route Diagram - see first Page of Table 65

		TP		LM	TP	NT	TP	NT	LM	LM	VT	XC		TP		VT	VT	VT	TP	NT	NT	LM		LM	VT
		◇1		◇1	◇1		◇1		◇1	1	◇1	◇1		◇1		◇1	◇1	◇1	◇1			◇1		◇1	◇1
		🛒			🛒						⊠	🛒		🛒		⊠	⊠	⊠	🛒						⊠
London Euston 15 ⊖	d															05 27	05 39	06 17							
Watford Junction	d															05u45	06u02								
Milton Keynes Central	d															06 10	06 22	06 47							
Rugby	d																06 45								
Nuneaton	d															06 39									
Tamworth Low Level	d																								
Lichfield Trent Valley	d																								
Coventry	d																								
Birmingham International ✈	d																								
Birmingham New Street 12	d									06 01	06 19	06 22										06 36		07 01	07 20
Wolverhampton 7 ⛴	d									06 19	06 36	06 40										06 53		07 19	07 37
Penkridge	d									06 29														07 29	
Stafford	a									06 35		06 53				07 03						07 08		07 36	
	d									06 36		06 55				07 03						07 08		07 36	
Stoke-on-Trent	a											07 13						07 45							
Congleton	a																								
Macclesfield	a											07 30						08 01							
Crewe 10	a									06 56	07 07					07 22	07 30					07 33		07 56	08 07
	d			06 02					06 32	06 57	07 09					07 24	07 32					07 34		07 57	08 09
Chester	a																								
Wrexham General	a																								
Llandudno	a																								
Bangor (Gwynedd)	a																								
Holyhead	a																								
Wilmslow	a																								
Stockport	a											07 45						08 16							
Manchester Piccadilly 10 ⛴	a											07 59						08 28							
Hartford	a			06 14					06 46	07 10												07 47		08 09	
Warrington Bank Quay	a										07 26						07 49								08 26
	d										07 27						07 49								08 27
Runcorn	a			06 27					06 59	07 22						07 41						08 00		08 22	
Liverpool South Parkway 7 ✈	a			06 36					07 08	07 31												08 09		08 31	
Liverpool Lime Street 10	a			06 49					07 22	07 43						08 01						08 21		08 44	
	d							06 57													07 57				
Manchester Airport ✈	d	05 45			06 18									07 00					07 25						
Manchester Piccadilly 10 ⛴	d	06 03			06 33									07 15					07 45						
Bolton	d	06 19			06 50	07 01								07 31					07 59						
Wigan North Western	a					07 19		07 30			07 37						08 00				08 30				08 37
	d							07 31			07 38						08 00				08 31				08 38
Preston 8	a	06 42			07 11			07 56			07 51			07 57			08 13		08 22		08 56				08 51
Preston 8	d	06 44			07 14		07 20				07 53			07 59			08 15		08 24	08 38					08 53
Blackpool North	a													08 29											
Lancaster 6	a	06 59			07 30		07 36				08 08						08 29		08 39	08 58					09 08
	d	07 00			07 30		07 36				08 08						08 30		08 40	08 58					09 08
Barrow-in-Furness	a						08 39													10 04					
Oxenholme Lake District	a	07 15									08 21						08 43		08 54						
	d	07 15									08 22						08 43		08 54						
Windermere	a																								
Penrith North Lakes	d				08 07														09 20						09 45
Carlisle 8	a	07 55			08 24						09 01						09 21		09 34	12 39					09 59
	d	07 56			08 25						09 01						09 22		09 36						10 01
Lockerbie	d	08 16																	09 55						
Carstairs	a																								
Motherwell	a																								
Glasgow Central 15	a				09 45												10 36								11 16
Haymarket	a	09s17									10 16								10s56						
Edinburgh 10	a	09 22									10 21								11 04						
Perth	a																								
Dundee	a																								
Aberdeen	a																								
Inverness	a																								

OVERNIGHT SLEEPERS. For sleeper trains, operated by First ScotRail, please refer to Tables 400 - 404

London and West Midlands - North West England and Scotland

Route Diagram - see first Page of Table 65

		XC	VT	TP		LM	VT	VT		VT	XC	TP	VT	NT	LM	VT	XC	VT		TP			LM	VT	VT
		◇1	◇1	◇1		◇1	◇1	◇1		◇1	◇1	◇1	◇1		◇1	◇1	◇1	◇1		◇1			◇1	◇1	◇1
		🛒	⊠	🛒			⊠	⊠		⊠	🛒	🛒	⊠			⊠	🛒	⊠		🛒				⊠	⊠
London Euston 15 ⊖	d		06 55				07 07	07 10		07 20			07 30					08 00						08 07	08 20
Watford Junction	d																								
Milton Keynes Central	d		07 27					07 41		07 50															08 50
Rugby	d																								
Nuneaton	d																								
Tamworth Low Level	d																								
Lichfield Trent Valley	d																								
Coventry	d										07 27														
Birmingham International ✈	d					07 17					07 38														
Birmingham New Street 12	d	07 31				07 36					07 57				08 01	08 20	08 31						08 36		
Wolverhampton 7	d	07 49				07 53					08 15				08 19	08 37	08 49						08 53		
Penkridge	d					08 03									08 29								09 03		
Stafford	a	08 00				08 09	08 22				08 29				08 35		09 00						09 09	09 22	
	d	08 01				08 09	08 23				08 30				08 36		09 01						09 09	09 23	
Stoke-on-Trent	a	08 19	08 24							08 48	08 54						09 19	09 24							09 48
Congleton	a																								
Macclesfield	a	08 36	08 41								09 11							09 41							
Crewe 10	a					08 30		08 47							08 56	09 07							09 30		
	d					08 31		08 49							08 57	09 09							09 31		
Chester	a							09 12																	
Wrexham General	a																								
Llandudno	a																								
Bangor (Gwynedd)	a																								
Holyhead	a																								
Wilmslow	a																								
Stockport	a	08 50	08 55							09 16	09 27						09 49	09 55							10 16
Manchester Piccadilly 10	a	08 59	09 07							09 28	09 39						09 59	10 07							10 28
Hartford	a														09 11										
Warrington Bank Quay	a												09 14			09 26									
	d												09 14			09 27									
Runcorn	a					08 50	08 55								09 22								09 50	09 55	
Liverpool South Parkway 7 ✈	a					08 59									09 31								09 59		
Liverpool Lime Street 10	a					09 10	09 15								09 43								10 10	10 15	
	d													08 57											
Manchester Airport ✈	d			07 56								08 25								09 00					
Manchester Piccadilly 10	d			08 15								08 46								09 16					
Bolton	d			08 32								09 07								09 33					
Wigan North Western	a												09 25	09 30		09 37									
	d												09 25	09 31		09 38									
Preston 8	a			08 58								09 33	09 38	09 54		09 51				09 55					
Preston 8	d			08 59								09 38	09 41	09 55		09 53				09 58	10 07				
Blackpool North	a			09 25								10 05		10 19											
Lancaster 6	a												09 54			10 08				10 13	10 22				
	d												09 55			10 08				10 14	10 23				
Barrow-in-Furness	a																				11 17				
Oxenholme Lake District	a															10 22									
	d															10 23									
Windermere	a																								
Penrith North Lakes	d												10 31												
Carlisle 8	a												10 46			11 02				11 07					
	d												10 47			11 04				11 10					
Lockerbie	d																			11 29					
Carstairs	a																								
Motherwell	a																								
Glasgow Central 15	a												12 01							12 28					
Haymarket	a															12 14									
Edinburgh 10	a															12 21									
Perth	a																								
Dundee	a																								
Aberdeen	a																								
Inverness	a																								

OVERNIGHT SLEEPERS. For sleeper trains, operated by First ScotRail, please refer to Tables 400 - 404

Table 65

Mondays to Fridays

2 July to 14 September

London and West Midlands - North West England and Scotland

Route Diagram - see first Page of Table 65

Station		XC	VT	TP			NT	LM	VT	XC	TP		LM	XC	LM		TP	VT	VT	VT	VT	VT	VT	VT	XC
		◇1	◇1	◇1				◇1	◇1	◇1	◇1		◇1	◇1	◇1		◇1	◇1	◇1	◇1	◇1	◇1	◇1	◇1	◇1
		🛒	⊠	🛒					⊠	🛒	🛒			🛒			🛒	⊠	⊠	⊠	⊠	⊠	⊠	⊠	🛒
London Euston 15 ⊖	d		08 30															08 43	09 00	09 07	09 10	09 10	09 20	09 30	
Watford Junction	d																								
Milton Keynes Central	d																	09 13			09 40	09 41	09 50		
Rugby	d																								
Nuneaton	d																								
Tamworth Low Level	d																								
Lichfield Trent Valley	d																								
Coventry	d	08 27												09 27				09 42							
Birmingham International ✈	d	08 38												09 38				09 53							
Birmingham New Street 12	d	08 57						09 01	09 20	09 31			09 36	09 57	10 01			10 20							10 31
Wolverhampton 7	d	09 15						09 19	09 37	09 49			09 53	10 15	10 19			10 37							10 49
Penkridge	d												10 03												
Stafford	a	09 29						09 34		10 00			10 09	10 29	10 34					10 22					11 00
	d	09 30						09 35		10 01			10 09	10 30	10 35					10 23					11 01
Stoke-on-Trent	a	09 54								10 19				10 54					10 24				10 48		11 19
Congleton	a																								
Macclesfield	a	10 11												11 11					10 41						
Crewe 10	a							09 56	10 07				10 30		10 56			11 07			10 47	10 47			
	d							09 57	10 09				10 31		10 57			11 09			10 49	10 49			
Chester	a																				11 09	11 09			
Wrexham General	a																								
Llandudno	a																								
Bangor (Gwynedd)	a																					12 16			
Holyhead	a																					12 50			
Wilmslow	a																								
Stockport	a	10 27								10 49				11 27					10 55				11 16		11 49
Manchester Piccadilly 10	a	10 39								10 59				11 39					11 07				11 28		11 59
Hartford	a							10 10							11 11										
Warrington Bank Quay	a		10 14						10 26									11 26						11 14	
	d		10 14						10 27									11 27						11 14	
Runcorn	a							10 22					10 50		11 21					10 55					
Liverpool South Parkway 7 ✈	a							10 31					10 59		11 30										
Liverpool Lime Street 10	a							10 43					11 10		11 43					11 15					
	d						09 57																		
Manchester Airport ✈	d			09 29							10 00						10 29								
Manchester Piccadilly 10	d			09 46							10 16						10 46								
Bolton	d			10 07							10 33						11 07								
Wigan North Western	a		10 25				10 30		10 37									11 37						11 25	
	d		10 25				10 31		10 38									11 38						11 25	
Preston 8	a		10 38	10 33			10 54		10 51		10 55						11 33	→						11 38	
Preston 8	d		10 41	10 38	10 45		10 55		10 53		10 58						11 38							11 41	
Blackpool North	a			11 05			11 20										12 05								
Lancaster 6	a		10 54		11 00				11 08		11 13													11 54	
	d		10 55		11 01				11 08		11 14													11 55	
Barrow-in-Furness	a																								
Oxenholme Lake District	a		11 08		11 17						11 28														
	d		11 08		11 18						11 28														
Windermere	a				11 39																				
Penrith North Lakes	d								11 45		11 53													12 30	
Carlisle 8	a		11 46						12 00		12 10													12 45	
	d		11 47						12 01		12 11													12 47	
Lockerbie	d										12 30														
Carstairs	a																								
Motherwell	a																								
Glasgow Central 15	a		13 01						13 17															14 01	
Haymarket	a										13s33														
Edinburgh 10	a										13 39														
Perth	a																								
Dundee	a																								
Aberdeen	a																								
Inverness	a																								

OVERNIGHT SLEEPERS. For sleeper trains, operated by First ScotRail, please refer to Tables 400 - 404

London and West Midlands - North West England and Scotland

Route Diagram - see first Page of Table 65

			VT	NT	VT	TP		LM	VT	VT	VT		XC	TP	VT	NT	LM	VT	XC	VT	TP			LM	VT
			◇1		◇1	◇1		◇1	◇1	◇1	◇1		◇1	◇1	◇1		◇1	◇1	◇1	◇1	◇1			◇1	◇1
						A																			
			⊠		⊠	⊤			⊠	⊠	⊠		⊤	⊤	⊠			⊏	⊤	⊏	⊤				⊏
London Euston 15 ⊖	d		10 00						10 07	10 10	10 20				10 30					11 00					11 07
Watford Junction	d																								
Milton Keynes Central	d									10 41	10 50														
Rugby	d																								
Nuneaton	d																								
Tamworth Low Level	d																								
Lichfield Trent Valley	d																								
Coventry	d												10 27												
Birmingham International ✈	d												10 38												
Birmingham New Street 12	d							10 36					10 57				11 01	11 20	11 31					11 36	
Wolverhampton 7 ⇌	d							10 53					11 15				11 19	11 37	11 49					11 53	
Penkridge	d							11 03																12 03	
Stafford	a							11 09	11 22				11 28				11 34		12 00					12 09	12 22
	d							11 09	11 23				11 30				11 35		12 01					12 09	12 23
Stoke-on-Trent	a		11 24								11 48		11 54						12 19	12 24					
Congleton	a																								
Macclesfield	a		11 41										12 11							12 41					
Crewe 10	a							11 30		11 47							11 56	12 07						12 30	
	d							11 31		11 49							11 57	12 09						12 31	
Chester	a									12 12															
Wrexham General	a																								
Llandudno	a																								
Bangor (Gwynedd)	a																								
Holyhead	a																								
Wilmslow	a																								
Stockport	a		11 55								12 16		12 27						12 49	12 55					
Manchester Piccadilly 10 ⇌	a		12 07								12 28		12 39						12 59	13 07					
Hartford	a																12 10								
Warrington Bank Quay	a														12 14			12 26							
	d														12 14			12 27							
Runcorn	a							11 50	11 55								12 22							12 50	12 55
Liverpool South Parkway 7 ✈	a							11 59									12 31							12 59	
Liverpool Lime Street 10	a							12 10	12 15								12 43							13 10	13 15
	d			10 57												11 57									
Manchester Airport ✈	d					11 00								11 29							12 00				
Manchester Piccadilly 10 ⇌	d					11 16								11 46							12 16				
Bolton	d				←	11 33								12 07							12 33				
Wigan North Western	a			11 30	11 37										12 25	12 30		12 37							
	d			11 31	11 38										12 25	12 31		12 38							
Preston 8	a			11 54	11 51	11 57								12 33	12 38	12 54		12 51			12 55				
Preston 8	d			11 55	11 53	11 58								12 38	12 41	12 55		12 53			12 58				
Blackpool North	a			12 19										13 05		13 19									
Lancaster 6	a				12 08	12 13									12 56			13 08			13 13				
	d				12 08	12 14									12 56			13 08			13 14				
Barrow-in-Furness	a					13 11																			
Oxenholme Lake District	a				12 22										13 08			13 22			13 28				
	d				12 24										13 09			13 24			13 28				
Windermere	a																								
Penrith North Lakes	d														13 34						13 53				
Carlisle 8	a				13 01										13 49			14 01			14 10				
	d				13 03										13 50			14 03			14 11				
Lockerbie	d																				14 30				
Carstairs	a														14 46										
Motherwell	a																								
Glasgow Central 15	a														15 25			15 17							
Haymarket	a				14 15																15s34				
Edinburgh 10	a				14 21																15 39				
Perth	a																								
Dundee	a																								
Aberdeen	a																								
Inverness	a																								

A ⊤ to Preston

OVERNIGHT SLEEPERS. For sleeper trains, operated by First ScotRail, please refer to Tables 400 - 404

Table 65

Mondays to Fridays

2 July to 14 September

London and West Midlands - North West England and Scotland

Route Diagram - see first Page of Table 65

		VT	VT	XC	TP	TP	VT		NT	LM	VT	XC	VT	TP	TP FX		LM		VT	VT	VT	XC	TP	VT	VT
		◇1	◇1	◇1	◇1	◇1	R 1			◇1	◇1	◇1	◇1	◇1	◇1		◇1		◇1	◇1	◇1	◇1	◇1	◇1	◇1
															A									B	C
		☕	☕	🛒		🛒	⊠				☕	🛒	☕	🛒	🛒				☕	☕	☕	🛒	🛒	☕	☕
London Euston 15 ⊖	d	11 10	11 20				11 30						12 00						12 07	12 10	12 20			12 30	12 30
Watford Junction	d																								
Milton Keynes Central	d	11 41	11 50																	12 41	12 50				
Rugby	d																								
Nuneaton	d																								
Tamworth Low Level	d																								
Lichfield Trent Valley	d																								
Coventry	d			11 27																		12 27			
Birmingham International ✈	d			11 38																		12 38			
Birmingham New Street 12	d			11 57						12 01	12 20	12 31					12 36					12 57			
Wolverhampton 7 ⛴	d			12 15						12 19	12 37	12 49					12 53					13 15			
Penkridge	d																13 03								
Stafford	a			12 29						12 34		13 00					13 09		13 22			13 29			
	d			12 30						12 35		13 01					13 09		13 23			13 30			
Stoke-on-Trent	a		12 48	12 54								13 19	13 24								13 48	13 54			
Congleton	a																								
Macclesfield	a			13 11									13 41									14 11			
Crewe 10	a	12 47								12 56	13 07						13 30			13 47					
	d	12 49								12 57	13 09						13 31			13 49					
Chester	a	13 12																		14 12					
Wrexham General	a																								
Llandudno	a																								
Bangor (Gwynedd)	a																								
Holyhead	a																								
Wilmslow	a																								
Stockport	a		13 16	13 27								13 49	13 55								14 16	14 27			
Manchester Piccadilly 10 ⛴	a		13 28	13 39								13 59	14 07								14 28	14 39			
Hartford	a									13 11															
Warrington Bank Quay	a						13 14				13 26													14 14	14 14
	d						13 14				13 27													14 14	14 14
Runcorn	a									13 21							13 50		13 55						
Liverpool South Parkway 7 ✈	a									13 30							13 59								
Liverpool Lime Street 10	a									13 43							14 10		14 15						
	d								12 57																
Manchester Airport ✈	d					12 29								13 00	13 00								13 29		
Manchester Piccadilly 10 ⛴	d					12 46								13 16	13 16								13 46		
Bolton	d					13 07								13 33	13 33								14 07		
Wigan North Western	a						13 25		13 30		13 37													14 25	14 25
	d						13 25		13 31		13 38													14 25	14 25
Preston 8	a					13 33	13 38		13 54		13 51			13 55	13 55								14 33	14 38	14 38
Preston 8	d				13 04	13 38	13 41		13 55		13 53			13 58	14 04								14 38	14 41	14 41
Blackpool North	a					14 05			14 19														15 05		
Lancaster 6	a				13 19		13 54				14 08			14 13	14 19									14 54	15 00
	d				13 20		13 55				14 08			14 14	14 20									14 55	
Barrow-in-Furness	a														15 15										
Oxenholme Lake District	a				13 36		14 08																		
	d				13 37		14 08																		
Windermere	a				13 56																				
Penrith North Lakes	d										14 45														
Carlisle 8	a						14 46				15 00			15 06										15 30	
	d						14 47				15 02			15 07										15 45	
Lockerbie	d													15 27										15 47	
Carstairs	a																								
Motherwell	a																								
Glasgow Central 15	a						16 00							16 30										17 04	
Haymarket	a										16 17														
Edinburgh 10	a										16 21														
Perth	a																								
Dundee	a																								
Aberdeen	a																								
Inverness	a																								

A 🛒 to Preston

B from 27 July until 7 September, not from 13 August until 28 August

C not from 27 July until 10 August, from 29 August until 7 September

OVERNIGHT SLEEPERS. For sleeper trains, operated by First ScotRail, please refer to Tables 400 - 404

London and West Midlands - North West England and Scotland

Route Diagram - see first Page of Table 65

		NT	LM		VT	XC	VT	TP		LM	VT	VT	VT		XC	TP	VT	NT	LM	VT	XC	TP	VT		
			◇1		◇1	◇1	◇1	◇1		◇1	◇1	◇1	◇1		◇1	◇1	◇1		◇1	◇1	◇1	◇1	◇		
																						A	B		
					☕	🛒	☕	🛒			☕	☕	☕		🛒	🛒	⊠			☕	🛒	🛒	☕		
London Euston [15] ⊖	d						13 00				13 07	13 10	13 20				13 30						13 33		
Watford Junction	d																								
Milton Keynes Central	d											13 41	13 50												
Rugby	d																								
Nuneaton	d																								
Tamworth Low Level	d																								
Lichfield Trent Valley	d																								
Coventry	d														13 27										
Birmingham International ✈	d														13 38										
Birmingham New Street [12]	d		13 01		13 20	13 31				13 36					13 57				14 01	14 20	14 31				
Wolverhampton [7]	d		13 19		13 37	13 49				13 53					14 15				14 19	14 37	14 49				
Penkridge	d									14 03															
Stafford	a		13 34			14 00				14 09	14 22				14 29				14 34		15 00				
	d		13 35			14 01				14 09	14 23				14 30				14 35		15 01				
Stoke-on-Trent	a					14 19	14 24						14 48		14 54						15 19				
Congleton	a																								
Macclesfield	a						14 41								15 11										
Crewe [10]	a		13 56		14 07					14 30		14 47							14 56	15 07			15 16		
	d		13 57		14 09					14 31		14 49							14 57	15 09			15 19		
Chester	a											15 12													
Wrexham General	a																								
Llandudno	a																								
Bangor (Gwynedd)	a																								
Holyhead	a																								
Wilmslow	a																								
Stockport	a					14 49	14 55						15 16		15 27						15 49				
Manchester Piccadilly [10]	a					14 59	15 07						15 28		15 39						15 59				
Hartford	a		14 11																15 11						
Warrington Bank Quay	a				14 26												15 14			15 26			15 38		
	d				14 27												15 14			15 27			15 39		
Runcorn	a		14 21							14 50	14 55								15 21						
Liverpool South Parkway [7] ✈	a		14 30							14 59									15 30						
Liverpool Lime Street [10]	a		14 43							15 10	15 15								15 43						
	d	13 57																14 57							
Manchester Airport ✈	d							14 00								14 29						15 00			
Manchester Piccadilly [10]	d							14 16								14 46						15 16			
Bolton	d							14 33								15 07						15 33			
Wigan North Western	a	14 30			14 37												15 25	15 30		15 37			15 49		
	d	14 31			14 38												15 25	15 31		15 38			15 50		
Preston [8]	a	14 54			14 51			14 55								15 33	15 38	15 54		15 51		15 57	16 03		
Preston [8]	d	14 55			14 53			14 58								15 38	15 41	15 55		15 53		15 58	16 06		
Blackpool North	a	15 21														16 05		16 20							
Lancaster [6]	a				15 08			15 13												16 08		16 14	16 26		
	d				15 09			15 14												16 08		16 15			
Barrow-in-Furness	a																					17 18			
Oxenholme Lake District	a				15 22			15 28									16 04								
	d				15 24			15 28									16 06								
Windermere	a																								
Penrith North Lakes	d							15 53									16 31			16 45					
Carlisle [8]	a				16 01			16 10									16 46			17 00					
	d				16 03			16 11									16 47			17 02					
Lockerbie	d							16 30																	
Carstairs	a																								
Motherwell	a																								
Glasgow Central [15]	a				17 14												18 01								
Haymarket	a							17s31												18 12					
Edinburgh [10]	a							17 39												18 22					
Perth	a																								
Dundee	a																								
Aberdeen	a																								
Inverness	a																								

A 🛒 to Preston

B 6 July, 13 July, 20 July, 17 August, 24 August, 14 September

OVERNIGHT SLEEPERS. For sleeper trains, operated by First ScotRail, please refer to Tables 400 - 404

London and West Midlands - North West England and Scotland

Route Diagram - see first Page of Table 65

		LM	XC	LM	TP	VT	VT	VT	VT		VT	VT FX	VT FO	XC	VT	NT	VT	TP	TP FX			LM	VT	VT	VT
		◇1	◇1	◇1	◇1	◇1	◇1	◇1	◇1		◇1	◇1	R 1	◇1	◇1		◇1	◇1	◇1			◇1	◇1	◇1	◇1
												A	B						C						
			🍴		🍴	⊡	⊡	⊡	⊡		⊡	⊡	⊡	🍴	⊡		⊡	🍴	🍴				⊡	⊡	⊡
London Euston [15] ⊖	d					13 43	14 00	14 07	14 10		14 20	14 30	14 30		15 00								15 07	15 10	15 20
Watford Junction	d																								
Milton Keynes Central	d					14 13			14 41		14 50													15 41	15 50
Rugby	d																								
Nuneaton	d																								
Tamworth Low Level	d																								
Lichfield Trent Valley	d																								
Coventry	d		14 27			14 42																			
Birmingham International ✈	d		14 38			14 53																			
Birmingham New Street [12]	d	14 36	14 57	15 01		15 20								15 31								15 36			
Wolverhampton [7] 🚌	d	14 53	15 15	15 19		15 37								15 50								15 53			
Penkridge	d	15 03																				16 03			
Stafford	a	15 09	15 29	15 34				15 22						16 01								16 09	16 22		
	d	15 09	15 30	15 35				15 23						16 02								16 09	16 23		
Stoke-on-Trent	a		15 54				15 24				15 48			16 20	16 24										16 48
Congleton	a																								
Macclesfield	a		16 11				15 41								16 41										
Crewe [10]	a	15 30		15 56		16 07			15 47													16 30		16 47	
	d	15 31		15 57		16 09			15 49													16 31		16 49	
Chester	a								16 12															17 12	
Wrexham General	a																								
Llandudno	a																								
Bangor (Gwynedd)	a																								
Holyhead	a																								
Wilmslow	a																								
Stockport	a		16 27				15 55				16 16			16 49	16 54										17 16
Manchester Piccadilly [10] 🚌	a		16 39				16 07				16 28			16 59	17 07										17 28
Hartford	a			16 10																					
Warrington Bank Quay	a					16 26						16 16	16 16												
	d					16 27						16 17	16 17												
Runcorn	a	15 50		16 22				15 55														16 50	16 55		
Liverpool South Parkway [7] ✈	a	15 59		16 31																		16 59			
Liverpool Lime Street [10]	a	16 10		16 44				16 15														17 10	17 15		
	d															15 57									
Manchester Airport ✈	d				15 29													16 00	16 00						
Manchester Piccadilly [10] 🚌	d				15 46													16 16	16 16						
Bolton	d				16 07												←	16 33	16 33						
Wigan North Western	a					16 37						16 28	16 28			16 30	16 37								
	d					16 38						16 29	16 29			16 30	16 38								
Preston [8]	a				16 35	→						16 42	16 42			16 54	16 51	16 55	16 55						
Preston [8]	d				16 38							16 43	16 43			16 56	16 53	17 00	17 04						
Blackpool North	a				17 07											17 20									
Lancaster [6]	a											17 00	17 00				17 08	17 15	17 23						
	d												17 00				17 08	17 16	17 25						
Barrow-in-Furness	a																								
Oxenholme Lake District	a												17 15				17 22	17 30	17 43						
	d												17 16				17 23	17 30	17 49						
Windermere	a																		18 08						
Penrith North Lakes	d												17 42				17 49								
Carlisle [8]	a												18 00				18 05	18 10							
	d												18 00				18 06	18 11							
Lockerbie	d																	18 30							
Carstairs	a																								
Motherwell	a																								
Glasgow Central [15]	a												19 14				19 19								
Haymarket	a																	19s31							
Edinburgh [10]	a																	19 39							
Perth	a																								
Dundee	a																								
Aberdeen	a																								
Inverness	a																								

A not from 30 July until 9 August, from 29 August until 6 September

B also from 30 July until 9 August, from 29 August until 6 September

C 🍴 to Preston

OVERNIGHT SLEEPERS. For sleeper trains, operated by First ScotRail, please refer to Tables 400 - 404

London and West Midlands - North West England and Scotland

Route Diagram - see first Page of Table 65

Station		XC	TP	TP	VT		NT	LM	VT	XC	VT	TP	TP	NT			LM	VT	VT	XC	VT	LM	TP	VT	VT
		◇1	◇1	◇1	◇1			◇1	1	◇1	◇1	◇1					◇1	◇1	◇1	◇1	◇1	◇1	◇1	1	◇1
London Euston 15 ⊖	d				15 30						16 00							16 07	16 20		16 30				16 33
Watford Junction	d																								
Milton Keynes Central	d																		16u50						
Rugby	d																								17 22
Nuneaton	d																								
Tamworth Low Level	d																								
Lichfield Trent Valley	d																								
Coventry	d	15 27																		16 27					
Birmingham International ✈	d	15 38																		16 38					
Birmingham New Street 12	d	15 57						16 01	16 20	16 31							16 36			16 57		17 01		17 20	
Wolverhampton 7	d	16 15						16 19	16 37	16 49							16 53			17 15		17 19		17 37	
Penkridge	d																17 03					17 29			
Stafford	a	16 30						16 34		17 00							17 09	17 22		17 29		17 35			17 52
	d	16 31						16 35		17 01							17 09	17 23		17 30		17 36			17 56
Stoke-on-Trent	a	16 54								17 19	17 24								17 48	17 54					
Congleton	a																								
Macclesfield	a	17 11									17 41									18 11					
Crewe 10	a							16 56	17 07								17 30					17 56		18 07	18 16
	d							16 57	17 09								17 31					17 57		18 09	18 18
Chester	a																								
Wrexham General	a																								
Llandudno	a																								
Bangor (Gwynedd)	a																								
Holyhead	a																								
Wilmslow	a																								
Stockport	a	17 27								17 49	17 55								18 16	18 27					
Manchester Piccadilly 10	a	17 39								17 59	18 07								18 28	18 39					
Hartford	a							17 11														18 11			
Warrington Bank Quay	a				17 14				17 26															18 26	18 35
	d				17 14				17 27															18 27	18 36
Runcorn	a							17 21									17 50	17 55				18 21			
Liverpool South Parkway 7 ✈	a							17 30									17 59					18 30			
Liverpool Lime Street 10	a							17 43									18 10	18 15				18 43			
	d						16 57							17 19											
Manchester Airport ✈	d			16 29								17 00											17 29		
Manchester Piccadilly 10	d			16 46								17 15											17 46		
Bolton	d			17 06								17 32											18 07		
Wigan North Western	a				17 25		17 30		17 37					18 02										18 37	18 46
	d				17 25		17 31		17 38															18 38	18 47
Preston 8	a			17 30	17 38		17 54		17 51			17 55									18 30		18 30	18 51	19 01
Preston 8	d		17 04	17 32	17 41		17 55		17 53			17 58	18 08								18 30		18 40	18 53	
Blackpool North	a			18 02			18 23																19 10		
Lancaster 6	a		17 23		17 54				18 08			18 13	18 23											19 08	
	d		17 25		17 55				18 08			18 14	18 24											19 08	
Barrow-in-Furness	a												19 29												
Oxenholme Lake District	a		17 43		18 08				18 22			18 28												19 22	
	d		17 49		18 08				18 23			18 28												19 24	
Windermere	a		18 08																						
Penrith North Lakes	d								18 49			18 53													
Carlisle 8	a				18 47				19 04			19 09												20 01	
	d				18 47				19 04			19 11												20 03	
Lockerbie	d																								
Carstairs	a																								
Motherwell	a											20s16													
Glasgow Central 15	a				19 57							20 33									20 38			21 17	
Haymarket	a								20 16																
Edinburgh 10	a								20 22																
Perth	a																								
Dundee	a																								
Aberdeen	a																								
Inverness	a																								

OVERNIGHT SLEEPERS. For sleeper trains, operated by First ScotRail, please refer to Tables 400 - 404

Table 65

Mondays to Fridays

2 July to 14 September

London and West Midlands - North West England and Scotland

Route Diagram - see first Page of Table 65

			XC	TP			LM	NT	VT	VT	VT		VT	VT	XC	LM	TP	VT	VT	TP	NT		VT	VT	XC
			◇1	◇1			◇1		◇1	◇1	◇1		◇1	◇1	◇1	◇1	◇1	◇1	◇1	◇1			◇1	◇1	◇1
			🛒	🛒					⊠	⊠	⊠		⊠	⊠	🛒		🛒	⊠	☕				⊠	⊠	🛒
London Euston 15 ⊖	d								16 57	17 00	17 07		17 10	17 20				17 30					17 33	17 57	
Watford Junction	d																								
Milton Keynes Central	d												17u40	17u50											
Rugby	d																						18 23		
Nuneaton	d												18 12												
Tamworth Low Level	d								18 00															19 00	
Lichfield Trent Valley	d								18 07															19 08	
Coventry	d														17 27										
Birmingham International ✈	d														17 38										
Birmingham New Street 12	d		17 31				17 36								17 57	18 01			18 20						18 31
Wolverhampton 7	d		17 50				17 53								18 15	18 19			18 37						18 49
Penkridge	d						18 02									18 29									
Stafford	a		18 01				18 09				18 23				18 29	18 35							18 52		19 00
	d		18 02				18 09				18 24				18 30	18 35							18 55		19 01
Stoke-on-Trent	a		18 20							18 24				18 49	18 54										19 19
Congleton	a																								
Macclesfield	a									18 41					19 11										
Crewe 10	a						18 30				18 42		18 53			19 00			19 07				19 14		
	d						18 31				18 44		18 56			19 02			19 09				19 16		
Chester	a												19 15												
Wrexham General	a																								
Llandudno	a																								
Bangor (Gwynedd)	a																								
Holyhead	a																								
Wilmslow	a																								
Stockport	a		18 49							18 55				19 16	19 27										19 48
Manchester Piccadilly 10	a		18 59							19 07				19 28	19 39										19 59
Hartford	a						18 44																		
Warrington Bank Quay	a								18 49									19 14	19 26					19 49	
	d								18 50									19 14	19 27					19 50	
Runcorn	a						18 56				19 02					19 22							19 33		
Liverpool South Parkway 7 ✈	a						19 05									19 31									
Liverpool Lime Street 10	a						19 16				19 22					19 44							19 51		
	d																				19 23				
Manchester Airport ✈	d			18 00													18 29			19 00					
Manchester Piccadilly 10	d			18 16													18 46			19 16					
Bolton	d			18 33													19 07			19 33					
Wigan North Western	a								19 00									19 25	19 37		19 54			20 00	
	d								19 01									19 25	19 38		19 55			20 01	
Preston 8	a			18 55					19 14								19 33	19 38	19 51	19 55	20 18			20 14	
Preston 8	d			19 00	19 04			19 08	19 15								19 38	19 41	19 53	19 58	20 19			20 15	
Blackpool North	a							19 33									20 06				20 42				
Lancaster 6	a			19 15	19 20				19 30									19 54	20 08	20 13				20 30	
	d			19 16	19 20				19 30									19 55	20 08	20 14				20 30	
Barrow-in-Furness	a				20 24															21 17					
Oxenholme Lake District	a			19 30					19 43									20 08							
	d			19 32					19 45									20 08							
Windermere	a																								
Penrith North Lakes	d			19 57					20 10										20 45						
Carlisle 8	a			20 13					20 25									20 46	21 00					21 17	
	d			20 13					20 25									20 47	21 02					21 18	
Lockerbie	d								20 44															21 37	
Carstairs	a																								
Motherwell	a								21 26															22 21	
Glasgow Central 15	a								21 47									22 01						22 39	
Haymarket	a			21s31															22 14						
Edinburgh 10	a			21 39															22 22						
Perth	a																								
Dundee	a																								
Aberdeen	a																								
Inverness	a																								

OVERNIGHT SLEEPERS. For sleeper trains, operated by First ScotRail, please refer to Tables 400 - 404

London and West Midlands - North West England and Scotland

Route Diagram - see first Page of Table 65

		VT		LM	VT	VT		VT	XC	LM	TP	VT	VT	TP	NT	VT		XC		LM	XC	VT	TP	
		◇1		◇1	◇1	◇1		◇1	◇1	◇1	◇1	◇1	◇1	◇1		◇1		◇1		◇1	◇1	◇1	◇1	
						A															B			
		⊠			⊠	⊠		⊠	[trolley]			⊠	[buffet]			⊠		[trolley]			[trolley]	⊠		
London Euston 15 ⊖	d	18 00			18 07	18 10		18 20				18 30				18 33						18 43		
Watford Junction	d																							
Milton Keynes Central	d					18u40		18u50														19 13		
Rugby	d															19 23								
Nuneaton	d					19 13																		
Tamworth Low Level	d																							
Lichfield Trent Valley	d																							
Coventry	d								18 27												19 27	19 42		
Birmingham International ✈	d								18 38												19 38	19 53		
Birmingham New Street 12	d			18 36					18 57	19 01			19 20					19 31		19 36	19 57	20 20		
Wolverhampton 7	d			18 53					19 15	19 19			19 37					19 49		19 53	20 16	20 36		
Penkridge	d			19 03						19 29										20 03				
Stafford	a			19 09	19 23				19 27	19 36						19 53		20 00		20 09	20 29	20 49		
	d			19 09	19 24				19 29	19 36						19 56		20 01		20 09	20 30	20 52		
Stoke-on-Trent	a	19 24						19 48	19 54									20 19			20 54			
Congleton	a																							
Macclesfield	a	19 41							20 11												21 11			
Crewe 10	a			19 30	19 42	19 53				20 01			20 07			20 15				20 30		21 15		
	d			19 31	19 44	19 56							20 09			20 17				20 31				
Chester	a					20 15																		
Wrexham General	a					20 38																		
Llandudno	a																							
Bangor (Gwynedd)	a					21 25																		
Holyhead	a					21 59																		
Wilmslow	a																							
Stockport	a	19 55						20 16	20 27									20 48			21 27			
Manchester Piccadilly 10	a	20 07						20 28	20 39									20 58			21 39			
Hartford	a			19 47																20 45				
Warrington Bank Quay	a											20 14	20 26											
	d											20 14	20 27											
Runcorn	a			19 57	20 01											20 34				20 56				
Liverpool South Parkway 7 ✈	a			20 06																21 05				
Liverpool Lime Street 10	a			20 18	20 19											20 53				21 16				
	d														20 25									
Manchester Airport ✈	d										19 29			20 00									20 29	
Manchester Piccadilly 10	d										19 46			20 16									20 46	
Bolton	d										20 07			20 33									21 07	
Wigan North Western	a											20 25	20 37		20 57									
	d											20 25	20 38		20 57									
Preston 8	a										20 33	20 38	20 51	20 57	21 22								21 33	
Preston 8	d										20 38	20 41	20 53	20 59	21 24								21 38	
Blackpool North	a										21 06				21 52								22 06	
Lancaster 6	a											20 54	21 08	21 14										
	d											20 55	21 08	21 15										
Barrow-in-Furness	a													22 18										
Oxenholme Lake District	a											21 08	21 22											
	d											21 09	21 24											
Windermere	a																							
Penrith North Lakes	d											21 34												
Carlisle 8	a											21 49	22 01											
	d											21 51	22 03											
Lockerbie	d																							
Carstairs	a																							
Motherwell	a																							
Glasgow Central 15	a											23 04	23 18											
Haymarket	a																							
Edinburgh 10	a																							
Perth	a																							
Dundee	a																							
Aberdeen	a																							
Inverness	a																							

A ⊠ to Chester

B [trolley] to Birmingham New Street

OVERNIGHT SLEEPERS. For sleeper trains, operated by First ScotRail, please refer to Tables 400 - 404

Table 65

Mondays to Fridays

2 July to 14 September

London and West Midlands - North West England and Scotland

Route Diagram - see first Page of Table 65

		VT FO	VT ThFO		VT MT WO	VT ThFO	VT	VT	VT	VT FO	XC	VT	LM		VT	XC		VT	NT	TP	VT	VT	AW FX		VT
					R	R	R	R	R																
		◇	◇		1	1	1	1	1	◇	◇1	◇1	◇1		◇1	◇1 A		◇1		◇1	◇1	◇1			◇1
		☕	☕		☕	☕	☕	☕	☕	☕		☕			☕	🍴		☕			☕	☕	☕		☕
London Euston 15 ⊖	d	18 46	18 57		19 00	19 00	19 07	19 20	19 30			20 00			20 07			20 10			20 30	21 00			
Watford Junction	d																								
Milton Keynes Central	d							19 50										20 40				21 31			
Rugby	d	19 39																							
Nuneaton	d						20 03								21 03										
Tamworth Low Level	d	19s59																			21 34				
Lichfield Trent Valley	d	20s07																			21 42				
Coventry	d															20 27									
Birmingham International ✈	d															20 38									
Birmingham New Street 12	d										20 31		20 36			20 57									21 20
Wolverhampton 7 🚌	d										20 49		20 53			21 16									21 41
Penkridge	d												21 03												
Stafford	a	20s35					20 26						21 09		21 27	21 31									21 53
	d						20 27						21 09		21 27	21 32									21 55
Stoke-on-Trent	a				20 24	20 24		20 48			21 17	21 23				21 54						22 28			
Congleton	a																								
Macclesfield	a				20 41	20 41						21 40				22 11						22 44			
Crewe 10	a	21s01	20s33										21 30					21 48							22 17
	d												21 31					21 50							22 18
Chester	a																	22 15							
Wrexham General	a																								
Llandudno	a																								
Bangor (Gwynedd)	a																								
Holyhead	a																								
Wilmslow	a																								
Stockport	a				20 55	20 55		21 16			21 46	21 55				22 25						22 58			
Manchester Piccadilly 10 🚌	a		21 09		21 07	21 10		21 28			21 59	22 07				22 35						23 11			
Hartford	a												21 43												
Warrington Bank Quay	a	21s20							21 15												22 22				22 36
	d								21 15												22 23		22 28		22 36
Runcorn	a						21 01						21 54		21 59										
Liverpool South Parkway 7 ✈	a												22 05												
Liverpool Lime Street 10	a						21 21						22 15		22 20										
	d																								
Manchester Airport ✈	d																			21 29					
Manchester Piccadilly 10 🚌	d																			21 46			23a38		
Bolton	d									⟵										22 07					
Wigan North Western	a	21s31							21 26	21s31											22 33				22 46
	d								21 26												22 34				22 46
Preston 8	a	⟶							21 39	21 46										22 36	22 53				23 01
Preston 8	d								21 41										21 51	22 38					
Blackpool North	a																			23 04					
Lancaster 6	a								21 55										22 11						
	d								21 56										22 11						
Barrow-in-Furness	a																		23 16						
Oxenholme Lake District	a								22 09																
	d								22 09																
Windermere	a																								
Penrith North Lakes	d								22 35																
Carlisle 8	a								22 50																
	d								22 51																
Lockerbie	d																								
Carstairs	a																								
Motherwell	a																								
Glasgow Central 15	a								00 06																
Haymarket	a																								
Edinburgh 10	a																								
Perth	a																								
Dundee	a																								
Aberdeen	a																								
Inverness	a																								

A 🍴 to Birmingham New Street

OVERNIGHT SLEEPERS. For sleeper trains, operated by First ScotRail, please refer to Tables 400 - 404

2 July to 14 September

London and West Midlands - North West England and Scotland

Route Diagram - see first Page of Table 65

Station		TP		LM	VT	XC	TP	VT			TP	NT FX	SR	VT	XC	LM	VT	LM		VT	VT FX	VT	SR FO
													R										R
		◇1		◇1	◇1	◇1	◇1	◇1			◇1			◇1	◇1	◇1	◇1	◇1		◇1	◇1	◇1	
													A							B	C	D	E
London Euston	d				21 07			21 10					21 15	21 40			22 00			23§30	23§45	23§45	23 50
Watford Junction	d							21u25					21u33							§	§	§	00u10
Milton Keynes Central	d				21 38												22 31			§	§	§	
Rugby	d							22 04									22 54			§	00s47	00s47	
Nuneaton	d				22 08												23 04			§	00s58	01s02	
Tamworth Low Level	d																23s15			§	§	§	
Lichfield Trent Valley	d																23s22			§	§	§	
Coventry	d					21 27														§	§	§	
Birmingham International	d					21 38														§	§	§	
Birmingham New Street	d			21 36		21 57									22 30	22 36		23 09		§	§	§	
Wolverhampton	d			21 53		22 16									22 48	22 57		23 36		§	§	§	
Penkridge	d			22 03												23 07		23 46		§	§	§	
Stafford	a			22 09		22 29		22 34							23 00	23 13	23s38	23 52		§	01s22	01s31	
	d			22 09		22 30		22 34							23 01	23 13		23 53		§	§	§	
Stoke-on-Trent	a					22 53								23 06	23 20					00s53	§	§	
Congleton	a																			§	§	§	
Macclesfield	a					23 11								23 23						01s10	§	§	
Crewe	a			22 30	22 46			22 53								23 43	00s03	00 16		§	01s41	01s55	
	d			22 31	22 48			22 54					23u54							§	§	§	
Chester	a																			§	§	§	
Wrexham General	a																			§	§	§	
Llandudno	a																			§	§	§	
Bangor (Gwynedd)	a																			§	§	§	
Holyhead	a																			§	§	§	
Wilmslow	a																			§	§	§	
Stockport	a					23 25								23 37			00s26			01s24	§	§	
Manchester Piccadilly	a					23 37								23 46	00 12		00 35			01§43	§	§	
Hartford	a			22 43																	§	§	
Warrington Bank Quay	a							23 12													§	§	
	d							23 12													§	§	
Runcorn	a			22 56	23 05																02s02	02s16	
Liverpool South Parkway	a			23 07																	§	§	
Liverpool Lime Street	a			23 23	23 24																02§21	02§34	
	d																						
Manchester Airport	d	22 00					22 29																
Manchester Piccadilly	d	22 16					22 46																
Bolton	d	22 33					23 07																
Wigan North Western	a	22 48						23 23															
	d	22 51						23 23				23 48											
Preston	a	23 09					23 33	23 39				00 13											
Preston	d	23 13					23 35				23 51		00u52										
Blackpool North	a						00 02				00 16												
Lancaster	a	23 28																					
	d	23 29																					
Barrow-in-Furness	a	00 31																					
Oxenholme Lake District	a																						
	d																						
Windermere	a																						
Penrith North Lakes	d																						
Carlisle	a																						05s15
	d																						
Lockerbie	d																						
Carstairs	a																						06s20
Motherwell	a																						06s56
Glasgow Central	a																						07 20
Haymarket	a																						
Edinburgh	a																						07 15
Perth	a												05s39										
Dundee	a												06s08										
Aberdeen	a												07 36										
Inverness	a												08 38										

A Conveys a portion for Fort William, arrives 0954
B from 27 July until 7 September, not from 13 August until 28 August
C from 30 July until 6 September, not from 13 August until 28 August
D 27 July, 3 August, 10 August, 31 August, 7 September

OVERNIGHT SLEEPERS. For sleeper trains, operated by First ScotRail, please refer to Tables 400 - 404

Table 65

London and West Midlands - North West England and Scotland

Mondays to Fridays

2 July to 14 September

Route Diagram - see first Page of Table 65

		SR FX ◻R A 🛏	SR FX ◻R B 🛏	AW FX 🚌
London Euston 15 ⊖	d	23§50	23§50	
Watford Junction	d	00u10	00u14	
Milton Keynes Central	d			
Rugby	d			
Nuneaton	d			
Tamworth Low Level	d			
Lichfield Trent Valley	d			
Coventry	d			
Birmingham International ✈	d			
Birmingham New Street 12	d			
Wolverhampton 7	d			
Penkridge	d			
Stafford	a			
	d			
Stoke-on-Trent	a			
Congleton	a			
Macclesfield	a			
Crewe 10	a			
	d			
Chester	a			
Wrexham General	a			
Llandudno	a			
Bangor (Gwynedd)	a			
Holyhead	a			
Wilmslow	a			
Stockport	a			
Manchester Piccadilly 10	a			
Hartford	a			
Warrington Bank Quay	a			
	d			23 59
Runcorn	a			
Liverpool South Parkway 7 ✈	a			
Liverpool Lime Street 10	a			
	d			
Manchester Airport ✈	d			
Manchester Piccadilly 10	d			01a09
Bolton	d			
Wigan North Western	a			
	d			
Preston 8	a			
Preston 8	d			
Blackpool North	a			
Lancaster 6	a			
	d			
Barrow-in-Furness	a			
Oxenholme Lake District	a			
	d			
Windermere	a			
Penrith North Lakes	d			
Carlisle 8	a	05s16	05s15	
	d			
Lockerbie	d			
Carstairs	a	06s20	06s19	
Motherwell	a	06s56	06s55	
Glasgow Central 15	a	07§20	07§20	
Haymarket	a			
Edinburgh 10	a	07§16	07§16	
Perth	a			
Dundee	a			
Aberdeen	a			
Inverness	a			

A not from 30 July until 9 August, from 29 August until 6 September.

B from 30 July until 6 September, not from 13 August until 28 August.

OVERNIGHT SLEEPERS. For sleeper trains, operated by First ScotRail, please refer to Tables 400 - 404

London and West Midlands - North West England and Scotland

Route Diagram - see first Page of Table 65

		XC		VT	VT	VT	TP	TP	NT	TP		NT	SR		SR		VT	VT	VT	VT		LM	SR		
		MX		MO	MX	MO	MX	MX	MO	MX		MX	MO		MX		MO	MO	MO	MX		MX	MO		
		◇1		◇1	R 1	◇1	◇1	◇1		◇1			R A		R A		◇1	◇1	◇1	◇1		◇1	R B		
London Euston 15 ⊖	d			19p28	19p30								20p55		21p15		21p21	21p25	21p51	22p00			23p27		
Watford Junction	d												21b17		21b33								23b47		
Milton Keynes Central	d																	22p14	22p38	22p31					
Rugby	d																		23p18	22p54					
Nuneaton	d																22p52		23p29	23p04					
Tamworth Low Level	d																			23c15					
Lichfield Trent Valley	d																			23c22					
Coventry	d																								
Birmingham International ✈	d																								
Birmingham New Street 12	d	22p30																				23p09			
Wolverhampton 7	d	22p48																				23p36			
Penkridge	d																					23p46			
Stafford	a	23p00															23p16		23c53	23c38		23p52			
	d	23p01															23p17					23p53			
Stoke-on-Trent	a	23p20																23p29							
Congleton	a																								
Macclesfield	a																	23p45							
Crewe 10	a																23p43		00s21	00s03		00 16			
	d												23b39		23b54		23p45								
Chester	a																								
Wrexham General	a																								
Llandudno	a																								
Bangor (Gwynedd)	a																								
Holyhead	a																								
Wilmslow	a																								
Stockport	a																	23p59	00s50	00s26					
Manchester Piccadilly 10	a	00 12																00 12	01 00	00 35					
Hartford	a																								
Warrington Bank Quay	a			21p16	21p15																				
	d			21p16	21p15																				
Runcorn	a																00 07								
Liverpool South Parkway 7 ✈	a																								
Liverpool Lime Street 10	a																00 30								
	d																								
Manchester Airport ✈	d						22p00	22p29																	
Manchester Piccadilly 10	d						22p16	22p46																	
Bolton	d					←	22p33	23p07																	
Wigan North Western	a			21p27	21p26	21p27	22p48																		
	d			21p27	21p26	21p27	22p51		23p14			23p48													
Preston 8	a			→	21p39	21p40	23p09	23p33	23p36			00 13													
Preston 8	d				21p41	21p42	23p13	23p35	23p39	23p51			00u30		00u52										
Blackpool North	a							00 02	00 05	00 16															
Lancaster 6	a				21p55	21p56	23p28																		
	d				21p56	21p57	23p29																		
Barrow-in-Furness	a						00 31																		
Oxenholme Lake District	a				22p09	22p10																			
	d				22p09	22p11																			
Windermere	a																								
Penrith North Lakes	d				22p35	22p36																			
Carlisle 8	a				22p50	22p51																	05s04		
	d				22p51	22p53																			
Lockerbie	d																								
Carstairs	a																						06s20		
Motherwell	a																							06s56	
Glasgow Central 15	a				00 06	00 02																		07 20	
Haymarket	a																								
Edinburgh 10	a																						07 16		
Perth	a													05s39		05s39									
Dundee	a												06s08		06s08										
Aberdeen	a												07 36		07 36										
Inverness	a													08 38		08 38									

A Conveys a portion for Fort William, arrives at 0954

b Previous night, stops to pick up only

c Previous night, stops to set down only

OVERNIGHT SLEEPERS. For sleeper trains, operated by First ScotRail, please refer to Tables 400 - 404

London and West Midlands - North West England and Scotland

Route Diagram - see first Page of Table 65

		SR MX	TP	NT MX	TP	NT MX		NT MO	LM	TP	XC	VT	TP	LM	TP	NT		TP	NT	LM	LM	VT	XC	TP
		R	◇1		◇1				◇1	◇1	◇1	◇1	◇1	◇1	◇1			◇1		◇1	1	◇1	◇1	◇1
		🛏										⊠	T		T							⊠	T	T
London Euston 15 ⊖	d	23p50																						
Watford Junction	d	00u10																						
Milton Keynes Central	d																							
Rugby	d																							
Nuneaton	d																							
Tamworth Low Level	d																							
Lichfield Trent Valley	d																							
Coventry	d																							
Birmingham International ✈	d																							
Birmingham New Street 12	d										05 57										06 01	06 19	06 22	
Wolverhampton 7 🚌	d										06 16										06 19	06 36	06 40	
Penkridge	d																				06 29			
Stafford	a										06 29										06 35		06 53	
	d										06 30										06 36		06 55	
Stoke-on-Trent	a										06 50												07 13	
Congleton	a										07 02													
Macclesfield	a										07 11												07 30	
Crewe 10	a																				06 56	07 07		
	d			00 44					05 40			05 57		06 02						06 32	06 57	07 09		
Chester	a																							
Wrexham General	a																							
Llandudno	a																							
Bangor (Gwynedd)	a																							
Holyhead	a																							
Wilmslow	a																							
Stockport	a										07 27												07 45	
Manchester Piccadilly 10 🚌	a										07 37												07 59	
Hartford	a													06 14						06 46	07 10			
Warrington Bank Quay	a											06 13										07 26		
	d											06 14										07 27		
Runcorn	a								05 58					06 27						06 59	07 22			
Liverpool South Parkway 7 ✈	a								06 10					06 36						07 08	07 31			
Liverpool Lime Street 10	a								06 22					06 49						07 22	07 43			
	d																		06 57					
Manchester Airport ✈	d		00 01	01 20	04 00								05 45		06 18									07 00
Manchester Piccadilly 10 🚌	d		00 16	01a36	04 15					05 46			06 03		06 33									07 15
Bolton	d		00s31		04s29								06 19		06 50	07 01								07 31
Wigan North Western	a				04 44					06 15		06 24				07 19			07 30			07 37		
	d				04 44					06 15		06 25							07 31			07 38		
Preston 8	a		01s05		05s04					06 35		06 37	06 42		07 11				07 56			07 51		07 57
Preston 8	d					05 22		05 22		06 37		06 40	06 44		07 14			07 20				07 53		07 59
Blackpool North	a		01 30		05 33					07 06														08 29
Lancaster 6	a					05 42		05 42				06 54	06 59		07 30			07 36				08 08		
	d					05 42		05 42				06 54	07 00		07 30			07 36				08 08		
Barrow-in-Furness	a					06 47		06 47										08 39						
Oxenholme Lake District	a											07 08	07 15									08 21		
	d											07 10	07 15									08 22		
Windermere	a																							
Penrith North Lakes	d											07 35			08 07									
Carlisle 8	a	05s16				09 21		09 22				07 50	07 55		08 24							09 01		
	d											07 51	07 56		08 25							09 01		
Lockerbie	d											08 10	08 16											
Carstairs	a	06s20																						
Motherwell	a	06s56																						
Glasgow Central 15	a	07 20										09 14			09 45									
Haymarket	a												09s17									10 16		
Edinburgh 10	a	07 16											09 22									10 21		
Perth	a																							
Dundee	a																							
Aberdeen	a																							
Inverness	a																							

OVERNIGHT SLEEPERS. For sleeper trains, operated by First ScotRail, please refer to Tables 400 - 404

London and West Midlands - North West England and Scotland

Route Diagram - see first Page of Table 65

		VT		VT	VT	TP	NT	NT	LM	LM	VT	XC		VT	TP		LM	VT	VT	VT	XC	TP		VT
		◇1		◇1	◇1	◇1			◇1	◇1	◇1	◇1		◇1	◇1		◇1	◇1	◇1	◇1	◇1	◇1		◇1
		⊠		⊠	⊠	⊼					⊠	⊼		⊠	⊼			⊠	⊠	⊠	⊼	⊼		⊠
London Euston 15 ⊖	d	05 27		05 39	06 17									06 55				07 07	07 10	07 20				07 30
Watford Junction	d	05u45		06u02																				
Milton Keynes Central	d	06 10		06 22	06 47									07 27					07 41	07 50				
Rugby	d			06 45																				
Nuneaton	d	06 39																						
Tamworth Low Level	d																							
Lichfield Trent Valley	d																							
Coventry	d																				07 27			
Birmingham International ✈	d																07 17				07 38			
Birmingham New Street 12	d								06 36	07 01	07 20	07 31					07 36				07 57			
Wolverhampton 7	d								06 53	07 19	07 37	07 49					07 53				08 15			
Penkridge	d									07 29							08 03							
Stafford	a	07 03							07 08	07 36		08 00					08 09	08 22			08 29			
	d	07 03							07 08	07 36		08 01					08 09	08 23			08 30			
Stoke-on-Trent	a				07 45							08 19		08 24						08 48	08 54			
Congleton	a																							
Macclesfield	a				08 01							08 36		08 41							09 11			
Crewe 10	a	07 22		07 30					07 33	07 56	08 07						08 30		08 47					
	d	07 24		07 32					07 34	07 57	08 09						08 31		08 49					
Chester	a																		09 12					
Wrexham General	a																							
Llandudno	a																							
Bangor (Gwynedd)	a																							
Holyhead	a																							
Wilmslow	a																							
Stockport	a				08 16							08 50		08 55						09 16	09 27			
Manchester Piccadilly 10	a				08 28							08 59		09 07						09 28	09 39			
Hartford	a								07 47	08 09														
Warrington Bank Quay	a			07 49							08 26													09 14
	d			07 49							08 27													09 14
Runcorn	a	07 41							08 00	08 22							08 50	08 55						
Liverpool South Parkway 7 ✈	a								08 09	08 31							08 59							
Liverpool Lime Street 10	a	08 01							08 21	08 44							09 10	09 15						
	d							07 57																
Manchester Airport ✈	d					07 25									07 56							08 25		
Manchester Piccadilly 10	d					07 45									08 15							08 46		
Bolton	d					07 59									08 32							09 07		
Wigan North Western	a			08 00				08 30			08 37													09 25
	d			08 00				08 31			08 38													09 25
Preston 8	a			08 13		08 22		08 56			08 51				08 58							09 33		09 38
Preston 8	d			08 15		08 24	08 38				08 53				08 59							09 38		09 41
Blackpool North	a														09 25							10 05		
Lancaster 6	a			08 29		08 39	08 58				09 08													09 54
	d			08 30		08 40	08 58				09 08													09 55
Barrow-in-Furness	a						10 04																	
Oxenholme Lake District	a			08 43		08 54																		
	d			08 43		08 54																		
Windermere	a																							
Penrith North Lakes	d					09 20					09 45													10 31
Carlisle 8	a			09 21		09 34	12 39				09 59													10 46
	d			09 22		09 36					10 01													10 47
Lockerbie	d					09 55																		
Carstairs	a																							
Motherwell	a																							
Glasgow Central 15	a			10 36							11 16													12 01
Haymarket	a					10s56																		
Edinburgh 10	a					11 04																		
Perth	a																							
Dundee	a																							
Aberdeen	a																							
Inverness	a																							

OVERNIGHT SLEEPERS. For sleeper trains, operated by First ScotRail, please refer to Tables 400 - 404

Table 65

Mondays to Fridays

from 17 September

London and West Midlands - North West England and Scotland

Route Diagram - see first Page of Table 65

		NT	LM	VT	XC	VT	TP				LM	VT	VT	XC	VT	TP		NT	LM		VT	XC	VT	TP
			◇1	◇1	◇1	◇1	◇1				◇1	◇1	◇1	◇1	◇1	◇1			◇1		◇1	◇1	◇1	◇1
				⊠	⊥	⊠	⊥					⊠	⊠	⊥	⊠	⊥					⊠	⊥	⊠	⊥
London Euston 15 ⊖	d					08 00						08 07	08 20		08 30								09 00	
Watford Junction	d																							
Milton Keynes Central	d												08 50											
Rugby	d																							
Nuneaton	d																							
Tamworth Low Level	d																							
Lichfield Trent Valley	d																							
Coventry	d													08 27										
Birmingham International ✈	d													08 38										
Birmingham New Street 12	d		08 01	08 20	08 31						08 36			08 57					09 01		09 20	09 31		
Wolverhampton 7 ⛴	d		08 19	08 37	08 49						08 53			09 15					09 19		09 37	09 49		
Penkridge	d		08 29								09 03													
Stafford	a		08 35		09 00						09 09	09 22		09 29					09 34			10 00		
	d		08 36		09 01						09 09	09 23		09 30					09 35			10 01		
Stoke-on-Trent	a				09 19	09 24							09 48	09 54								10 19	10 24	
Congleton	a																							
Macclesfield	a					09 41								10 11									10 41	
Crewe 10	a		08 56	09 07							09 30								09 56		10 07			
	d		08 57	09 09							09 31								09 57		10 09			
Chester	a																							
Wrexham General	a																							
Llandudno	a																							
Bangor (Gwynedd)	a																							
Holyhead	a																							
Wilmslow	a																							
Stockport	a				09 49	09 55							10 16	10 27								10 49	10 55	
Manchester Piccadilly 10 ⛴	a				09 59	10 07							10 28	10 39								10 59	11 07	
Hartford	a		09 11																10 10					
Warrington Bank Quay	a			09 26											10 14						10 26			
	d			09 27											10 14						10 27			
Runcorn	a		09 22								09 50	09 55							10 22					
Liverpool South Parkway 7 ✈	a		09 31								09 59								10 31					
Liverpool Lime Street 10	a		09 43								10 10	10 15							10 43					
	d	08 57																09 57						
Manchester Airport ✈	d						09 00									09 29								10 00
Manchester Piccadilly 10 ⛴	d						09 16									09 46								10 16
Bolton	d						09 33									10 07								10 33
Wigan North Western	a	09 30		09 37											10 25			10 30			10 37			
	d	09 31		09 38											10 25			10 31			10 38			
Preston 8	a	09 54		09 51			09 55								10 38	10 33		10 54			10 51			10 55
Preston 8	d	09 55		09 53			09 58	10 07							10 41	10 38	10 45	10 55			10 53			10 58
Blackpool North	a	10 19														11 05		11 20						
Lancaster 6	a			10 08			10 13	10 22							10 54		11 00				11 08			11 13
	d			10 08			10 14	10 23							10 55		11 01				11 08			11 14
Barrow-in-Furness	a							11 17																
Oxenholme Lake District	a			10 22											11 08		11 17							11 28
	d			10 23											11 08		11 18							11 28
Windermere	a																11 39							
Penrith North Lakes	d																				11 45			11 53
Carlisle 8	a			11 02			11 07								11 46						12 00			12 10
	d			11 04			11 10								11 47						12 01			12 11
Lockerbie	d						11 29																	12 30
Carstairs	a																							
Motherwell	a																							
Glasgow Central 15	a						12 28								13 01						13 17			
Haymarket	a			12 14																				13s33
Edinburgh 10	a			12 21																				13 39
Perth	a																							
Dundee	a																							
Aberdeen	a																							
Inverness	a																							

OVERNIGHT SLEEPERS. For sleeper trains, operated by First ScotRail, please refer to Tables 400 - 404

London and West Midlands - North West England and Scotland

Route Diagram - see first Page of Table 65

		LM	VT	VT	VT		VT	XC	TP	VT	NT	LM	VT	XC	VT		TP		LM	VT	VT	VT	XC	TP	VT
		◇■	◇■	◇■	◇■		◇■	◇■	◇■	◇■		◇■	◇■	◇■	◇■		◇■		◇■	◇■	◇■	◇■	◇■	◇■	◇■
																	A								
			⊠	⊠	⊠		⊠	🛒	🛒	⊠			⊠	🛒	⊠		🛒			⊠	⊠	⊠	🛒	🛒	⊠
London Euston [15] ⊖	d		09 07	09 10	09 10		09 20			09 30					10 00					10 07	10 10	10 20			10 30
Watford Junction	d																								
Milton Keynes Central	d			09 40	09 41		09 50														10 41	10 50			
Rugby	d																								
Nuneaton	d																								
Tamworth Low Level	d																								
Lichfield Trent Valley	d																								
Coventry	d							09 27															10 27		
Birmingham International ✈	d							09 38															10 38		
Birmingham New Street [12]	d	09 36						09 57				10 01	10 20	10 31					10 36				10 57		
Wolverhampton [7] 🚢	d	09 53						10 15				10 19	10 37	10 49					10 53				11 15		
Penkridge	d	10 03																	11 03						
Stafford	a	10 09	10 22					10 29				10 34		11 00					11 09	11 22			11 28		
	d	10 09	10 23					10 30				10 35		11 01					11 09	11 23			11 30		
Stoke-on-Trent	a						10 48	10 54						11 19	11 24							11 48	11 54		
Congleton	a																								
Macclesfield	a							11 11							11 41								12 11		
Crewe [10]	a	10 30		10 47	10 47							10 56	11 07						11 30		11 47				
	d	10 31		10 49	10 49							10 57	11 09						11 31		11 49				
Chester	a			11 09	11 09																12 12				
Wrexham General	a																								
Llandudno	a																								
Bangor (Gwynedd)	a				12 16																				
Holyhead	a				12 50																				
Wilmslow	a																								
Stockport	a						11 16	11 27						11 49	11 55							12 16	12 27		
Manchester Piccadilly [10] 🚢	a						11 28	11 39						11 59	12 07							12 28	12 39		
Hartford	a											11 11													
Warrington Bank Quay	a									11 14			11 26												12 14
	d									11 14			11 27												12 14
Runcorn	a	10 50	10 55									11 21							11 50	11 55					
Liverpool South Parkway [7] ✈	a	10 59										11 30							11 59						
Liverpool Lime Street [10]	a	11 10	11 15									11 43							12 10	12 15					
	d										10 57														
Manchester Airport ✈	d								10 29								11 00							11 29	
Manchester Piccadilly [10] 🚢	d								10 46								11 16							11 46	
Bolton	d								11 07								11 33							12 07	
Wigan North Western	a									11 25	11 30		11 37												12 25
	d									11 25	11 31		11 38												12 25
Preston [8]	a								11 33	11 38	11 54		11 51				11 57							12 33	12 38
Preston [8]	d								11 38	11 41	11 55		11 53				11 58							12 38	12 41
Blackpool North	a								12 05		12 19													13 05	
Lancaster [6]	a									11 54			12 08				12 13								13 00
	d									11 55			12 08				12 14								
Barrow-in-Furness	a																13 11								
Oxenholme Lake District	a												12 22												
	d												12 24												
Windermere	a																								
Penrith North Lakes	d									12 30															
Carlisle [8]	a									12 45			13 01												
	d									12 47			13 03												
Lockerbie	d																								
Carstairs	a																								
Motherwell	a																								
Glasgow Central [15]	a									14 01															
Haymarket	a												14 15												
Edinburgh [10]	a												14 21												
Perth	a																								
Dundee	a																								
Aberdeen	a																								
Inverness	a																								

A 🛒 to Preston

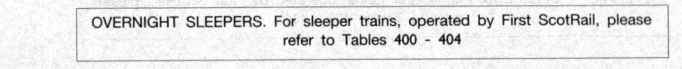

OVERNIGHT SLEEPERS. For sleeper trains, operated by First ScotRail, please refer to Tables 400 - 404

London and West Midlands - North West England and Scotland

Route Diagram - see first Page of Table 65

		NT	LM	VT	XC	VT	TP	LM	VT	VT	VT	XC	TP	TP	VT	NT	LM	VT	XC	VT	TP
															R						
			◇1	◇1	◇1	◇1	◇1	◇1	◇1	◇1	◇1	◇1	◇1	◇1	1		◇1	◇1	◇1	◇1	◇1
				☕	🛒	☕	🛒		☕	☕	☕	🛒		🛒	✕			☕	🛒	☕	🛒
London Euston 15 ⊖	d					11 00			11 07	11 10	11 20				11 30					12 00	
Watford Junction	d																				
Milton Keynes Central	d									11 41	11 50										
Rugby	d																				
Nuneaton	d																				
Tamworth Low Level	d																				
Lichfield Trent Valley	d																				
Coventry	d											11 27									
Birmingham International ✈	d											11 38									
Birmingham New Street 12	d		11 01	11 20	11 31			11 36				11 57					12 01	12 20	12 31		
Wolverhampton 7 ⛴	d		11 19	11 37	11 49			11 53				12 15					12 19	12 37	12 49		
Penkridge	d							12 03													
Stafford	a		11 34		12 00			12 09	12 22			12 29					12 34		13 00		
	d		11 35		12 01			12 09	12 23			12 30					12 35		13 01		
Stoke-on-Trent	a				12 19	12 24					12 48	12 54							13 19	13 24	
Congleton	a																				
Macclesfield	a					12 41						13 11								13 41	
Crewe 10	a		11 56	12 07				12 30		12 47							12 56	13 07			
	d		11 57	12 09				12 31		12 49							12 57	13 09			
Chester	a									13 12											
Wrexham General	a																				
Llandudno	a																				
Bangor (Gwynedd)	a																				
Holyhead	a																				
Wilmslow	a																				
Stockport	a				12 49	12 55					13 16	13 27							13 49	13 55	
Manchester Piccadilly 10 ⛴	a				12 59	13 07					13 28	13 39							13 59	14 07	
Hartford	a		12 10														13 11				
Warrington Bank Quay	a			12 26											13 14			13 26			
	d			12 27											13 14			13 27			
Runcorn	a		12 22					12 50	12 55								13 21				
Liverpool South Parkway 7 ✈	a		12 31					12 59									13 30				
Liverpool Lime Street 10	a		12 43					13 10	13 15								13 43				
	d	11 57														12 57					
Manchester Airport ✈	d						12 00							12 29							13 00
Manchester Piccadilly 10 ⛴	d						12 16							12 46							13 16
Bolton	d						12 33							13 07							13 33
Wigan North Western	a	12 30		12 37											13 25	13 30		13 37			
	d	12 31		12 38											13 25	13 31		13 38			
Preston 8	a	12 54		12 51			12 55							13 33	13 38	13 54		13 51			13 55
Preston 8	d	12 55		12 53			12 58						13 04	13 38	13 41	13 55		13 53			13 58
Blackpool North	a	13 19												14 05		14 19					
Lancaster 6	a			13 08			13 13						13 19		13 54			14 08			14 13
	d			13 08			13 14						13 20		13 55			14 08			14 14
Barrow-in-Furness	a																				
Oxenholme Lake District	a			13 22			13 28						13 36		14 08						
	d			13 24			13 28						13 37		14 08						
Windermere	a												13 56								
Penrith North Lakes	d						13 53											14 45			
Carlisle 8	a			14 01			14 10								14 46			15 00			15 06
	d			14 03			14 11								14 47			15 02			15 07
Lockerbie	d						14 30														15 27
Carstairs	a																				
Motherwell	a																				
Glasgow Central 15	a			15 17											16 00						16 30
Haymarket	a						15s34											16 17			
Edinburgh 10	a						15 39											16 21			
Perth	a																				
Dundee	a																				
Aberdeen	a																				
Inverness	a																				

OVERNIGHT SLEEPERS. For sleeper trains, operated by First ScotRail, please refer to Tables 400 - 404

London and West Midlands - North West England and Scotland

Route Diagram - see first Page of Table 65

		TP FX		LM	VT	VT	VT		XC	TP	VT	NT	LM	VT	XC	VT	TP			LM	VT	VT	VT	XC	TP
		◇1		◇1	◇1	◇1	◇1		◇1	◇1	◇1		◇1	◇1	◇1	◇1	◇1			◇1	◇1	◇1	◇1	◇1	◇1
		A																							
		╤o			☕	☕	☕		╤o	╤o	☕			☕	╤o	☕	╤o				☕	☕	☕	╤o	╤o
London Euston 15 ⊖	d				12 07	12 10	12 20				12 30					13 00					13 07	13 10	13 20		
Watford Junction	d																								
Milton Keynes Central	d					12 41	12 50															13 41	13 50		
Rugby	d																								
Nuneaton	d																								
Tamworth Low Level	d																								
Lichfield Trent Valley	d																								
Coventry	d								12 27															13 27	
Birmingham International ✈	d								12 38															13 38	
Birmingham New Street 12	d			12 36					12 57				13 01	13 20	13 31					13 36				13 57	
Wolverhampton 7 ⛴	d			12 53					13 15				13 19	13 37	13 49					13 53				14 15	
Penkridge	d			13 03																14 03					
Stafford	a			13 09	13 22				13 29				13 34		14 00					14 09	14 22			14 29	
	d			13 09	13 23				13 30				13 35		14 01					14 09	14 23			14 30	
Stoke-on-Trent	a						13 48		13 54						14 19	14 24							14 48	14 54	
Congleton	a																								
Macclesfield	a								14 11							14 41								15 11	
Crewe 10	a			13 30		13 47							13 56	14 07						14 30		14 47			
	d			13 31		13 49							13 57	14 09						14 31		14 49			
Chester	a					14 12																15 12			
Wrexham General	a																								
Llandudno	a																								
Bangor (Gwynedd)	a																								
Holyhead	a																								
Wilmslow	a																								
Stockport	a						14 16		14 27						14 49	14 55							15 16	15 27	
Manchester Piccadilly 10 ⛴	a						14 28		14 39						14 59	15 07							15 28	15 39	
Hartford	a												14 11												
Warrington Bank Quay	a										14 14			14 26											
	d										14 14			14 27											
Runcorn	a			13 50	13 55								14 21							14 50	14 55				
Liverpool South Parkway 7 ✈	a			13 59									14 30							14 59					
Liverpool Lime Street 10	a			14 10	14 15								14 43							15 10	15 15				
	d											13 57													
Manchester Airport ✈	d	13 00								13 29							14 00								14 29
Manchester Piccadilly 10 ⛴	d	13 16								13 46							14 16								14 46
Bolton	d	13 33								14 07							14 33								15 07
Wigan North Western	a										14 25	14 30		14 37											
	d										14 25	14 31		14 38											
Preston 8	a	13 55								14 33	14 38	14 54		14 51			14 55								15 33
Preston 8	d	14 04								14 38	14 41	14 55		14 53			14 58								15 38
Blackpool North	a									15 05		15 21													16 05
Lancaster 6	a	14 19									15 00			15 08			15 13								
	d	14 20												15 09			15 14								
Barrow-in-Furness	a	15 15																							
Oxenholme Lake District	a													15 22			15 28								
	d													15 24			15 28								
Windermere	a																								
Penrith North Lakes	d																15 53								
Carlisle 8	a													16 01			16 10								
	d													16 03			16 11								
Lockerbie	d																16 30								
Carstairs	a																								
Motherwell	a																								
Glasgow Central 15	a													17 14											
Haymarket	a																17s31								
Edinburgh 10	a																17 39								
Perth	a																								
Dundee	a																								
Aberdeen	a																								
Inverness	a																								

A ╤o to Preston

OVERNIGHT SLEEPERS. For sleeper trains, operated by First ScotRail, please refer to Tables 400 - 404

Table 65

Mondays to Fridays

from 17 September

London and West Midlands - North West England and Scotland

Route Diagram - see first Page of Table 65

		VT	NT	LM	VT	XC	TP	VT FO	VT	LM	VT	VT	VT	XC	TP	VT FX	VT FO	NT	LM	VT	XC
		◇1		◇1	◇1	◇1	◇1	◇	◇1	◇1	◇1	◇1	◇1	◇1	◇1	◇1	R 1		◇1	◇1	◇1
		⊠			🍴	🛒	A 🛒	🍴	🍴		🍴	🍴	🍴	🛒	🛒	🍴	🍴			🍴	🛒
London Euston [15] ⊖	d	13 30						13 33	14 00		14 07	14 10	14 20			14 30	14 30				
Watford Junction	d																				
Milton Keynes Central	d											14 41	14 50								
Rugby	d																				
Nuneaton	d																				
Tamworth Low Level	d																				
Lichfield Trent Valley	d																				
Coventry	d													14 27							
Birmingham International ✈	d													14 38							
Birmingham New Street [12]	d			14 01	14 20	14 31				14 36				14 57					15 01	15 20	15 31
Wolverhampton [7]	d			14 19	14 37	14 49				14 53				15 15					15 19	15 37	15 50
Penkridge	d									15 03											
Stafford	a			14 34		15 00				15 09	15 22			15 29					15 34		16 01
	d			14 35		15 01				15 09	15 23			15 30					15 35		16 02
Stoke-on-Trent	a					15 19			15 24				15 48	15 54							16 20
Congleton	a																				
Macclesfield	a								15 41					16 11							
Crewe [10]	a			14 56	15 07			15 16		15 30		15 47							15 56	16 07	
	d			14 57	15 09			15 19		15 31		15 49							15 57	16 09	
Chester	a											16 12									
Wrexham General	a																				
Llandudno	a																				
Bangor (Gwynedd)	a																				
Holyhead	a																				
Wilmslow	a																				
Stockport	a					15 49			15 55				16 16	16 27							16 49
Manchester Piccadilly [10]	a					15 59			16 07				16 28	16 39							16 59
Hartford	a			15 11															16 10		
Warrington Bank Quay	a	15 14			15 26			15 38								16 16	16 16			16 26	
	d	15 14			15 27			15 39								16 17	16 17			16 27	
Runcorn	a			15 21						15 50	15 55								16 22		
Liverpool South Parkway [7] ✈	a			15 30						15 59									16 31		
Liverpool Lime Street [10]	a			15 43						16 10	16 15								16 44		
	d		14 57															15 57			
Manchester Airport ✈	d						15 00								15 29						
Manchester Piccadilly [10]	d						15 16								15 46						
Bolton	d						15 33								16 07						
Wigan North Western	a	15 25	15 30		15 37			15 49								16 28	16 28	16 30		16 37	
	d	15 25	15 31		15 38			15 50								16 29	16 29	16 30		16 38	
Preston [8]	a	15 38	15 54		15 51		15 57	16 03							16 35	16 42	16 42	16 54		16 51	
Preston [8]	d	15 41	15 55		15 53		15 58	16 06							16 38	16 43	16 43	16 56		16 53	
Blackpool North	a		16 20												17 07			17 20			
Lancaster [6]	a				16 08		16 14	16 26								17 00	17 00			17 08	
	d				16 08		16 15										17 00			17 08	
Barrow-in-Furness	a						17 18														
Oxenholme Lake District	a	16 04															17 15			17 22	
	d	16 06															17 16			17 23	
Windermere	a																				
Penrith North Lakes	d	16 31			16 45												17 42			17 49	
Carlisle [8]	a	16 46			17 00												18 00			18 05	
	d	16 47			17 02												18 00			18 06	
Lockerbie	d																				
Carstairs	a																				
Motherwell	a																				
Glasgow Central [15]	a	18 01															19 14			19 19	
Haymarket	a				18 12																
Edinburgh [10]	a				18 22																
Perth	a																				
Dundee	a																				
Aberdeen	a																				
Inverness	a																				

A 🛒 to Preston

OVERNIGHT SLEEPERS. For sleeper trains, operated by First ScotRail, please refer to Tables 400 - 404

from 17 September

London and West Midlands - North West England and Scotland

Route Diagram - see first Page of Table 65

		VT	TP	TP FX	LM	VT	VT	VT	XC	TP	TP	VT	NT	LM	VT	XC	VT	TP	TP	NT	NT
															R						
		◇1	◇1	◇1	◇1	◇1	◇1	◇1	◇1	◇1	◇1	◇1		◇1	1	◇1	◇1	◇1			
				A																B	C
		₽	🛒	🛒		₽	₽	₽	🛒		🛒	⊠			₽	🛒	₽	🛒			
London Euston 15 ⊖	d	15 00				15 07	15 10	15 20				15 30					16 00				
Watford Junction	d																				
Milton Keynes Central	d						15 41	15 50													
Rugby	d																				
Nuneaton	d																				
Tamworth Low Level	d																				
Lichfield Trent Valley	d																				
Coventry	d								15 27												
Birmingham International ✈	d								15 38												
Birmingham New Street 12	d				15 36				15 57					16 01	16 20	16 31					
Wolverhampton 7	d				15 53				16 15					16 19	16 37	16 49					
Penkridge	d				16 03																
Stafford	a				16 09	16 22			16 30					16 34		17 00					
	d				16 09	16 23			16 31					16 35		17 01					
Stoke-on-Trent	a	16 24						16 48	16 54							17 19	17 24				
Congleton	a																				
Macclesfield	a	16 41							17 11								17 41				
Crewe 10	a				16 30		16 47							16 56	17 07						
	d				16 31		16 49							16 57	17 09						
Chester	a						17 12														
Wrexham General	a																				
Llandudno	a																				
Bangor (Gwynedd)	a																				
Holyhead	a																				
Wilmslow	a																				
Stockport	a	16 54						17 16	17 27							17 49	17 55				
Manchester Piccadilly 10	a	17 07						17 28	17 39							17 59	18 07				
Hartford	a													17 11							
Warrington Bank Quay	a											17 14			17 26						
	d											17 14			17 27						
Runcorn	a				16 50	16 55								17 21							
Liverpool South Parkway 7 ✈	a				16 59									17 30							
Liverpool Lime Street 10	a				17 10	17 15								17 43							
	d												16 57							17 19	17 19
Manchester Airport ✈	d		16 00	16 00							16 29							17 00			
Manchester Piccadilly 10	d		16 16	16 16							16 46							17 15			
Bolton	d		16 33	16 33							17 06							17 32			
Wigan North Western	a											17 25	17 30		17 37					18 02	18 06
	d											17 25	17 31		17 38						
Preston 8	a		16 55	16 55							17 30	17 38	17 54		17 51			17 55			
Preston 8	d		17 00	17 04						17 04	17 32	17 41	17 55		17 53			17 58	18 08		
Blackpool North	a										18 02		18 23								
Lancaster 6	a		17 15	17 23						17 23		17 54			18 08			18 13	18 23		
	d		17 16	17 25						17 25		17 55			18 08			18 14	18 24		
Barrow-in-Furness	a																		19 29		
Oxenholme Lake District	a		17 30	17 43						17 43		18 08			18 22			18 28			
	d		17 30	17 49						17 49		18 08			18 23			18 28			
Windermere	a			18 08						18 08											
Penrith North Lakes	d														18 49			18 53			
Carlisle 8	a		18 10									18 47			19 04			19 09			
	d		18 11									18 47			19 04			19 11			
Lockerbie	d		18 30																		
Carstairs	a																				
Motherwell	a																	20s16			
Glasgow Central 15	a											19 57						20 33			
Haymarket	a		19s31												20 16						
Edinburgh 10	a		19 39												20 22						
Perth	a																				
Dundee	a																				
Aberdeen	a																				
Inverness	a																				

A 🛒 to Preston

B from 17 September until 28 September

C from 1 October

OVERNIGHT SLEEPERS. For sleeper trains, operated by First ScotRail, please refer to Tables 400 - 404

London and West Midlands - North West England and Scotland

Route Diagram - see first Page of Table 65

		LM	VT	VT	XC		VT	LM	TP	VT	VT	XC	TP				LM	NT	VT	VT	VT	VT	VT	XC	LM
										R															
		◇1	◇1	◇1	◇1		◇1	◇1	◇1	1	◇1	◇1	◇1				◇1		◇1	◇1	◇1	◇1	◇1	◇1	◇1
			☕	☕	🛒		⊠		🛒	☕	☕	🛒	🛒						⊠	⊠	⊠	⊠	⊠	🛒	
London Euston 15 ⊖	d		16 07	16 20			16 30				16 33								16 57	17 00	17 07	17 10	17 20		
Watford Junction	d																								
Milton Keynes Central	d			16u50																		17u40	17u50		
Rugby	d										17 22														
Nuneaton	d																					18 12			
Tamworth Low Level	d																		18 00						
Lichfield Trent Valley	d																		18 07						
Coventry	d				16 27																			17 27	
Birmingham International ✈	d				16 38																			17 38	
Birmingham New Street 12	d	16 36			16 57			17 01		17 20		17 31					17 36							17 57	18 01
Wolverhampton 7	d	16 53			17 15			17 19		17 37		17 50					17 53							18 15	18 19
Penkridge	d	17 03						17 29									18 02								18 29
Stafford	a	17 09	17 22		17 29			17 35			17 52	18 01					18 09				18 23			18 29	18 35
	d	17 09	17 23		17 30			17 36			17 56	18 02					18 09				18 24			18 30	18 35
Stoke-on-Trent	a			17 48	17 54							18 20								18 24			18 49	18 54	
Congleton	a																								
Macclesfield	a				18 11															18 41				19 11	
Crewe 10	a	17 30						17 56		18 07	18 16						18 30				18 42	18 53			19 00
	d	17 31						17 57		18 09	18 18						18 31				18 44	18 56			19 02
Chester	a																					19 15			
Wrexham General	a																								
Llandudno	a																								
Bangor (Gwynedd)	a																								
Holyhead	a																								
Wilmslow	a																								
Stockport	a			18 16	18 27							18 49								18 55			19 16	19 27	
Manchester Piccadilly 10	a			18 28	18 39							18 59								19 07			19 28	19 39	
Hartford	a							18 11									18 44								
Warrington Bank Quay	a									18 26	18 35								18 49						
	d									18 27	18 36								18 50						
Runcorn	a	17 50	17 55					18 21									18 56				19 02				19 22
Liverpool South Parkway 7 ✈	a	17 59						18 30									19 05								19 31
Liverpool Lime Street 10	a	18 10	18 15					18 43									19 16				19 22				19 44
	d																								
Manchester Airport ✈	d								17 29				18 00												
Manchester Piccadilly 10	d								17 46				18 16												
Bolton	d								18 07				18 33												
Wigan North Western	a									18 37	18 46								19 00						
	d									18 38	18 47								19 01						
Preston 8	a						18 30		18 38	18 51	19 01		18 55						19 14						
Preston 8	d						18 30		18 40	18 53			19 00	19 04				19 08	19 15						
Blackpool North	a								19 10									19 33							
Lancaster 6	a									19 08			19 15	19 20					19 30						
	d									19 08			19 16	19 20					19 30						
Barrow-in-Furness	a													20 24											
Oxenholme Lake District	a									19 22			19 30						19 43						
	d									19 24			19 32						19 45						
Windermere	a																								
Penrith North Lakes	d												19 57						20 10						
Carlisle 8	a									20 01			20 13						20 25						
	d									20 03			20 13						20 25						
Lockerbie	d																		20 44						
Carstairs	a																								
Motherwell	a																		21 26						
Glasgow Central 15	a						20 38			21 17									21 47						
Haymarket	a												21s31												
Edinburgh 10	a												21 39												
Perth	a																								
Dundee	a																								
Aberdeen	a																								
Inverness	a																								

OVERNIGHT SLEEPERS. For sleeper trains, operated by First ScotRail, please refer to Tables 400 - 404

from 17 September

London and West Midlands - North West England and Scotland

Route Diagram - see first Page of Table 65

		TP	VT	VT	TP	NT	VT	VT	XC	VT	LM	VT	VT	VT	XC	LM	TP	VT	VT	TP
		◇1	◇1	◇1	◇1		◇1	◇1	◇1	◇1	◇1	◇1	◇1	◇1	◇1	◇1	◇1	◇1	◇1	◇1
													A							
		⊼	⊠	☕			⊠	⊠	⊼	⊠		⊠	⊠	⊠	⊼			⊠	☕	
London Euston 15 ⊖	d		17 30				17 33	17 57		18 00		18 07	18 10	18 20				18 30		
Watford Junction	d																			
Milton Keynes Central	d												18u40	18u50						
Rugby	d						18 23													
Nuneaton	d												19 13							
Tamworth Low Level	d							19 00												
Lichfield Trent Valley	d							19 08												
Coventry	d														18 27					
Birmingham International ✈	d														18 38					
Birmingham New Street 12	d			18 20					18 31		18 36				18 57	19 01			19 20	
Wolverhampton 7	d			18 37					18 49		18 53				19 15	19 19			19 37	
Penkridge	d										19 03					19 29				
Stafford	a						18 52		19 00		19 09	19 23			19 27	19 36				
	d						18 55		19 01		19 09	19 24			19 29	19 36				
Stoke-on-Trent	a								19 19	19 24				19 48	19 54					
Congleton	a																			
Macclesfield	a									19 41					20 11					
Crewe 10	a			19 07			19 14				19 30	19 42	19 53			20 01			20 07	
	d			19 09			19 16				19 31	19 44	19 56						20 09	
Chester	a												20 15							
Wrexham General	a												20 38							
Llandudno	a																			
Bangor (Gwynedd)	a												21 25							
Holyhead	a												21 59							
Wilmslow	a																			
Stockport	a								19 48	19 55				20 16	20 27					
Manchester Piccadilly 10	a								19 59	20 07				20 28	20 39					
Hartford	a										19 47									
Warrington Bank Quay	a		19 14	19 26				19 49										20 14	20 26	
	d		19 14	19 27				19 50										20 14	20 27	
Runcorn	a						19 33				19 57	20 01								
Liverpool South Parkway 7 ✈	a										20 06									
Liverpool Lime Street 10	a						19 51				20 18	20 19								
	d					19 23														
Manchester Airport ✈	d	18 29			19 00												19 29			20 00
Manchester Piccadilly 10	d	18 46			19 16												19 46			20 16
Bolton	d	19 07			19 33												20 07			20 33
Wigan North Western	a		19 25	19 37		19 54		20 00										20 25	20 37	
	d		19 25	19 38		19 55		20 01										20 25	20 38	
Preston 8	a	19 33	19 38	19 51	19 55	20 18		20 14									20 33	20 38	20 51	20 57
Preston 8	d	19 38	19 41	19 53	19 58	20 19		20 15									20 38	20 41	20 53	20 59
Blackpool North	a	20 06				20 42											21 06			
Lancaster 6	a		19 54	20 08	20 13			20 30										20 54	21 08	21 14
	d		19 55	20 08	20 14			20 30										20 55	21 08	21 15
Barrow-in-Furness	a				21 17															22 18
Oxenholme Lake District	a		20 08															21 08	21 22	
	d		20 08															21 09	21 24	
Windermere	a																			
Penrith North Lakes	d			20 45														21 34		
Carlisle 8	a		20 46	21 00				21 17										21 49	22 01	
	d		20 47	21 02				21 18										21 51	22 03	
Lockerbie	d							21 37												
Carstairs	a																			
Motherwell	a							22 21												
Glasgow Central 15	a		22 01					22 39										23 04	23 18	
Haymarket	a			22 14																
Edinburgh 10	a			22 22																
Perth	a																			
Dundee	a																			
Aberdeen	a																			
Inverness	a																			

A ⊠ to Chester

OVERNIGHT SLEEPERS. For sleeper trains, operated by First ScotRail, please refer to Tables 400 - 404

Mondays to Fridays

from 17 September

London and West Midlands - North West England and Scotland

Route Diagram - see first Page of Table 65

		NT	VT	XC		LM	XC		VT	TP		VT FO	VT ThFO	VT MT WO	VT ThFO	VT	VT		VT	VT FO	XC	VT	LM	VT	XC
														R	R	R	R		R						
			◇1	◇1		◇1	◇1		◇1	◇1		◇	◇	1	1	1	1		1	◇	◇1	◇1	◇1	◇1	◇1
							A																		A
			⊠	⊼			⊼		⊠			☕	☕	☕	☕	☕	☕		☕	☕		☕		☕	⊼
London Euston 15 ⊖	d		18 33						18 43			18 46	18 57	19 00	19 00	19 07	19 20		19 30			20 00		20 07	
Watford Junction	d																								
Milton Keynes Central	d								19 13								19u50								
Rugby	d		19 23									19 39													
Nuneaton	d															20 03								21 03	
Tamworth Low Level	d											19s59													
Lichfield Trent Valley	d											20s07													
Coventry	d						19 27		19 42																20 27
Birmingham International ✈	d						19 38		19 53																20 38
Birmingham New Street 12	d			19 31		19 36	19 57		20 20												20 31		20 36		20 57
Wolverhampton 7	d			19 49		19 53	20 16		20 36												20 49		20 53		21 16
Penkridge	d					20 03																	21 03		
Stafford	a		19 53	20 00		20 09	20 29		20 49			20s35				20 26							21 09	21 27	21 31
	d		19 56	20 01		20 09	20 30		20 52							20 27							21 09	21 27	21 32
Stoke-on-Trent	a			20 19			20 54							20 24	20 24		20 48				21 17	21 23			21 54
Congleton	a																								
Macclesfield	a						21 11							20 41	20 41							21 40			22 11
Crewe 10	a		20 15			20 30			21 15			21s01	20s33										21 30		
	d		20 17			20 31																	21 31		
Chester	a																								
Wrexham General	a																								
Llandudno	a																								
Bangor (Gwynedd)	a																								
Holyhead	a																								
Wilmslow	a																								
Stockport	a			20 48			21 27							20 55	20 55		21 16				21 46	21 55			22 25
Manchester Piccadilly 10	a			20 58			21 39						21 09	21 07	21 10		21 28				21 59	22 07			22 35
Hartford	a					20 45																	21 43		
Warrington Bank Quay	a											21s20							21 15						
	d																		21 15						
Runcorn	a		20 34			20 56										21 01							21 54	21 59	
Liverpool South Parkway 7 ✈	a					21 05																	22 05		
Liverpool Lime Street 10	a		20 53			21 16										21 21							22 15	22 20	
	d	20 25																							
Manchester Airport ✈	d									20 29															
Manchester Piccadilly 10	d									20 46															
Bolton	d									21 07										←					
Wigan North Western	a	20 57										21s31							21 26	21s31					
	d	20 57																	21 26						
Preston 8	a	21 22								21 33		↪							21 39	21 46					
Preston 8	d	21 24								21 38									21 41						
Blackpool North	a	21 52								22 06															
Lancaster 6	a																		21 55						
	d																		21 56						
Barrow-in-Furness	a																								
Oxenholme Lake District	a																		22 09						
	d																		22 09						
Windermere	a																								
Penrith North Lakes	d																		22 35						
Carlisle 8	a																		22 50						
	d																		22 51						
Lockerbie	d																								
Carstairs	a																								
Motherwell	a																								
Glasgow Central 15	a																		00 06						
Haymarket	a																								
Edinburgh 10	a																								
Perth	a																								
Dundee	a																								
Aberdeen	a																								
Inverness	a																								

A ⊼ to Birmingham New Street

OVERNIGHT SLEEPERS. For sleeper trains, operated by First ScotRail, please refer to Tables 400 - 404

Table 65

Mondays to Fridays

from 17 September

London and West Midlands - North West England and Scotland

Route Diagram - see first Page of Table 65

		VT	NT	TP	VT	VT	AW FX	VT	TP	LM	VT	XC	TP	VT	TP	NT FX	SR	VT
		◇1		◇1	◇1	◇1		◇1	◇1	◇1	◇1	◇1	◇1	◇1	◇1		A	◇1
London Euston 15 ⊖	d	20 10			20 30	21 00					21 07			21 10			21 15	21 40
Watford Junction	d													21u25			21u33	
Milton Keynes Central	d	20 40				21 31					21 38							
Rugby	d													22 04				
Nuneaton	d										22 08							
Tamworth Low Level	d				21 34													
Lichfield Trent Valley	d				21 42													
Coventry	d											21 27						
Birmingham International ✈	d											21 38						
Birmingham New Street 12	d							21 20		21 36		21 57						
Wolverhampton 7	d							21 41		21 53		22 16						
Penkridge	d									22 03								
Stafford	a							21 53		22 09		22 29		22 34				
	d							21 55		22 09		22 30		22 34				
Stoke-on-Trent	a					22 28						22 53						23 06
Congleton	a																	
Macclesfield	a					22 44						23 11						23 23
Crewe 10	a	21 48						22 17		22 30	22 46			22 53				
	d	21 50						22 18		22 31	22 48			22 54			23u54	
Chester	a	22 15																
Wrexham General	a																	
Llandudno	a																	
Bangor (Gwynedd)	a																	
Holyhead	a																	
Wilmslow	a																	
Stockport	a					22 58						23 25						23 37
Manchester Piccadilly 10	a					23 11						23 37						23 46
Hartford	a									22 43								
Warrington Bank Quay	a				22 22			22 36						23 12				
	d				22 23		22 28	22 36						23 12				
Runcorn	a									22 56	23 05							
Liverpool South Parkway 7 ✈	a									23 07								
Liverpool Lime Street 10	a									23 23	23 24							
	d																	
Manchester Airport ✈	d			21 29					22 00				22 29					
Manchester Piccadilly 10	d			21 46			23a38		22 16				22 46					
Bolton	d			22 07					22 33				23 07					
Wigan North Western	a				22 33			22 46	22 48					23 23				
	d				22 34			22 46	22 51					23 23		23 48		
Preston 8	a			22 36	22 53			23 01	23 09				23 33	23 39		00 13		
Preston 8	d		21 51	22 38					23 13				23 35		23 51		00u52	
Blackpool North	a			23 04									00 02		00 16			
Lancaster 6	a		22 11						23 28									
	d		22 11						23 29									
Barrow-in-Furness	a		23 16						00 31									
Oxenholme Lake District	a																	
	d																	
Windermere	a																	
Penrith North Lakes	d																	
Carlisle 8	a																	
	d																	
Lockerbie	d																	
Carstairs	a																	
Motherwell	a																	
Glasgow Central 15	a																	
Haymarket	a																	
Edinburgh 10	a																	
Perth	a																05s39	
Dundee	a																06s08	
Aberdeen	a																07 36	
Inverness	a																08 38	

A Conveys a portion for Fort William, arrives at 0954

OVERNIGHT SLEEPERS. For sleeper trains, operated by First ScotRail, please refer to Tables 400 - 404

Table 65

Mondays to Fridays

from 17 September

London and West Midlands - North West England and Scotland

Route Diagram - see first Page of Table 65

		XC	LM	VT	LM	SR FO		SR FX			AW FX
						R		R			
		◇1	◇1	◇1	◇1						
London Euston 15 ⊖	d			22 00			23 50		23 50		
Watford Junction	d						00u10		00u10		
Milton Keynes Central	d			22 31							
Rugby	d			22 54							
Nuneaton	d			23 04							
Tamworth Low Level	d			23s15							
Lichfield Trent Valley	d			23s22							
Coventry	d										
Birmingham International ✈	d										
Birmingham New Street 12	d	22 30	22 36		23 09						
Wolverhampton 7	d	22 48	22 57		23 36						
Penkridge	d		23 07		23 46						
Stafford	a	23 00	23 13	23s38	23 52						
	d	23 01	23 13		23 53						
Stoke-on-Trent	a	23 20									
Congleton	a										
Macclesfield	a										
Crewe 10	a		23 43	00s03	00 16						
	d										
Chester	a										
Wrexham General	a										
Llandudno	a										
Bangor (Gwynedd)	a										
Holyhead	a										
Wilmslow	a										
Stockport	a			00s26							
Manchester Piccadilly 10	a	00 12		00 35							
Hartford	a										
Warrington Bank Quay	a										
	d										23 59
Runcorn	a										
Liverpool South Parkway 7 ✈	a										
Liverpool Lime Street 10	a										
	d										
Manchester Airport ✈	d										
Manchester Piccadilly 10	d										01a09
Bolton	d										
Wigan North Western	a										
	d										
Preston 8	a										
Preston 8	d										
Blackpool North	a										
Lancaster 6	a										
	d										
Barrow-in-Furness	a										
Oxenholme Lake District	a										
	d										
Windermere	a										
Penrith North Lakes	d										
Carlisle 8	a						05s15		05s16		
	d										
Lockerbie	d										
Carstairs	a						06s20		06s20		
Motherwell	a						06s56		06s56		
Glasgow Central 15	a						07 20		07 20		
Haymarket	a										
Edinburgh 10	a					07 15		07 16			
Perth	a										
Dundee	a										
Aberdeen	a										
Inverness	a										

OVERNIGHT SLEEPERS. For sleeper trains, operated by First ScotRail, please refer to Tables 400 - 404

Table 65

Saturdays

until 30 June

London and West Midlands - North West England and Scotland

Route Diagram - see first Page of Table 65

		VT	TP	TP	XC	XC	TP	SR	VT	LM	SR	TP	NT	TP	TP	LM	XC	VT	TP	LM	TP
		R 1	◇1	◇1	◇1	◇1	◇1	R	◇1	◇1	R	◇1		◇1	◇1	1	◇1	◇1	◇1	1	◇1
					A	B		C													
London Euston 15 ⊖	d	19p30						21p15	22p00		23p50										
Watford Junction	d							21b33			00u10										
Milton Keynes Central	d								22p31												
Rugby	d								22p54												
Nuneaton	d								23p04												
Tamworth Low Level	d								23c15												
Lichfield Trent Valley	d								23c22												
Coventry	d																				
Birmingham International ✈	d																				
Birmingham New Street 12	d				22p30	22p30				23p09							05 57				
Wolverhampton 7	d				22p48	22p48				23p36							06 16				
Penkridge	d									23p46											
Stafford	a				23p00	23p00			23c38	23p52							06 29				
	d				23p01	23p01				23p53							06 30				
Stoke-on-Trent	a				23p20	23p21											06 50				
Congleton	a																07 02				
Macclesfield	a																07 11				
Crewe 10	a								00s03	00 16											
	d							23b54					00 44			05 48		05 57		06 12	
Chester	a																				
Wrexham General	a																				
Llandudno	a																				
Bangor (Gwynedd)	a																				
Holyhead	a																				
Wilmslow	a																				
Stockport	a								00s26								07 27				
Manchester Piccadilly 10	a				00 12	00 13			00 35								07 38				
Hartford	a																				
Warrington Bank Quay	a	21p15																06 13			
	d	21p15																06 14			
Runcorn	a															06 07				06 31	
Liverpool South Parkway 7 ✈	a															06 15				06 39	
Liverpool Lime Street 10	a															06 26				06 53	
	d																				
Manchester Airport ✈	d		22p00	22p29								00 01	01 20	04 00					05 45		06 18
Manchester Piccadilly 10	d		22p16	22p46								00 16	01a36	04 15	05 43				06 03		06 33
Bolton	d		22p33	23p07								00s31		04s29	05 59				06 19		06 50
Wigan North Western	a	21p26	22p48															06 24			
	d	21p26	22p51															06 25			
Preston 8	a	21p39	23p09	23p33								01s05		05s04	06 26			06 37	06 42		07 11
Preston 8	d	21p41	23p13	23p35			23p51	00u52							06 37			06 40	06 44		07 14
Blackpool North	a			00 02			00 16					01 30		05 33	07 06						
Lancaster 6	a	21p55	23p28															06 54	06 59		07 30
	d	21p56	23p29															06 54	07 00		07 30
Barrow-in-Furness	a		00 31																		
Oxenholme Lake District	a	22p09																07 08	07 15		
	d	22p09																07 10	07 15		
Windermere	a																				
Penrith North Lakes	d	22p35																07 37			08 07
Carlisle 8	a	22p50									05s15							07 50	07 55		08 24
	d	22p51																07 51	07 56		08 25
Lockerbie	d																	08 10	08 16		
Carstairs	a										06s20										
Motherwell	a										06s56										
Glasgow Central 15	a	00 06									07 20							09 13			09 45
Haymarket	a																		09s17		
Edinburgh 10	a										07 15								09 22		
Perth	a							05s39													
Dundee	a							06s08													
Aberdeen	a							07 36													
Inverness	a							08 38													

A 30 June

B not 30 June

C Conveys a portion for Fort William, arrrives at 0954

b Previous night, stops to pick up only

c Previous night, stops to set down only

OVERNIGHT SLEEPERS. For sleeper trains, operated by First ScotRail, please refer to Tables 400 - 404

Table 65

Saturdays
until 30 June

London and West Midlands - North West England and Scotland

Route Diagram - see first Page of Table 65

		NT	TP	NT	LM	LM		VT	XC	TP		LM	TP	VT	LM	NT		NT	VT	XC	VT	TP		LM	VT
			◇1		◇1	◇1		◇1	◇1	◇1		◇1	◇1	◇1	◇1				◇1	◇1	◇1	◇1		◇1	◇1
								🍴	🛒	🛒			🛒	🍴					🍴	🛒	🍴	🛒			🍴
London Euston 15 ⊖	d													06 05							06 55				07 07
Watford Junction	d													06u20											
Milton Keynes Central	d													06 41							07 27				
Rugby	d													07 03											
Nuneaton	d																								
Tamworth Low Level	d																								
Lichfield Trent Valley	d																								
Coventry	d																								
Birmingham International ✈	d																								
Birmingham New Street 12	d					06 01		06 20	06 31			06 36			07 01				07 20	07 31				07 36	
Wolverhampton 7 ⛴	d					06 18		06 37	06 49			06 54			07 18				07 37	07 49				07 53	
Penkridge	d					06 29									07 30									08 03	
Stafford	a					06 35			07 00			07 08		07 33	07 36					08 00				08 09	08 22
	d					06 36			07 01			07 08		07 34	07 38					08 01				08 09	08 23
Stoke-on-Trent	a								07 18											08 19	08 24				
Congleton	a																								
Macclesfield	a								07 36											08 36	08 41				
Crewe 10	a					06 56		07 07				07 33		07 53	07 58				08 07					08 30	08 41
	d				06 32	06 57		07 09				07 35		07 55	08 00				08 09					08 31	08 43
Chester	a																								
Wrexham General	a																								
Llandudno	a																								
Bangor (Gwynedd)	a																								
Holyhead	a																								
Wilmslow	a																								
Stockport	a								07 49											08 49	08 55				
Manchester Piccadilly 10 ⛴	a								07 59											08 59	09 07				
Hartford	a				06 46	07 10						07 48			08 11										
Warrington Bank Quay	a							07 26						08 11					08 27						
	d							07 27						08 12					08 27						
Runcorn	a				06 59	07 20						08 02			08 24									08 50	09 00
Liverpool South Parkway 7 ✈	a				07 08	07 30						08 11			08 33									08 59	
Liverpool Lime Street 10	a				07 22	07 42						08 24			08 46									09 12	09 21
	d			06 57																					
Manchester Airport ✈	d									07 00			07 25									07 56			
Manchester Piccadilly 10 ⛴	d									07 15			07 45									08 15			
Bolton	d	07 01								07 31			07 59									08 32			
Wigan North Western	a	07 19		07 30				07 37						08 22					08 38						
	d			07 31				07 38						08 23				08 30	08 38						
Preston 8	a			07 54				07 51		07 57			08 22	08 36				08 54	08 51			08 58			
Preston 8	d		07 20	07 55				07 53		07 59			08 24	08 37		08 42		08 55	08 53			08 59			
Blackpool North	a			08 21						08 29								09 21				09 25			
Lancaster 6	a		07 36					08 08					08 39	08 52		09 02			09 08						
	d		07 36					08 08					08 40	08 52		09 03			09 08						
Barrow-in-Furness	a		08 39													10 07									
Oxenholme Lake District	a							08 21						09 05											
	d							08 22						09 06											
Windermere	a																								
Penrith North Lakes	d													09 32					09 45						
Carlisle 8	a							09 00					09 30	09 47		12 39			10 02						
	d							09 02					09 30	09 48					10 04						
Lockerbie	d												09 50												
Carstairs	a																								
Motherwell	a																								
Glasgow Central 15	a													11 03					11 17						
Haymarket	a							10 16					10s48												
Edinburgh 10	a							10 22					10 56												
Perth	a																								
Dundee	a																								
Aberdeen	a																								
Inverness	a																								

OVERNIGHT SLEEPERS. For sleeper trains, operated by First ScotRail, please refer to Tables 400 - 404

Table 65

Saturdays
until 30 June

London and West Midlands - North West England and Scotland

Route Diagram - see first Page of Table 65

		VT		XC	TP	VT	TP	NT	LM	VT	XC	VT		TP			LM	VT	VT	VT	XC	TP		VT	TP
		◇1		◇1	◇1	◇1	◇1		◇1	◇1	◇1	◇1		◇1			◇1	◇1	◇1	◇1	◇1	◇1		◇1	◇1
					A									A											
		🍴		🛒	🛒	🍴				🍴	🍴	🍴		🛒				🍴	🍴	🍴	🛒	🛒		🍴	
London Euston 15 ⊖	d	07 20				07 30						08 00						08 07	08 10	08 20				08 30	
Watford Junction	d																								
Milton Keynes Central	d	07 50																	08 41	08 50					
Rugby	d																								
Nuneaton	d																								
Tamworth Low Level	d																								
Lichfield Trent Valley	d																								
Coventry	d			07 27																	08 27				
Birmingham International ✈	d			07 38																	08 38				
Birmingham New Street 12	d			07 57					08 01	08 20	08 31						08 36				08 57				
Wolverhampton 7 ⛴	d			08 15					08 19	08 37	08 49						08 53				09 15				
Penkridge	d								08 29								09 03								
Stafford	a			08 29					08 35		09 00						09 09	09 22			09 29				
	d			08 30					08 36		09 01						09 09	09 23			09 30				
Stoke-on-Trent	a	08 48		08 54							09 19	09 24								09 48	09 54				
Congleton	a																								
Macclesfield	a			09 11								09 41									10 11				
Crewe 10	a								08 56	09 07							09 30		09 47						
	d								08 57	09 09							09 31		09 49						
Chester	a																		10 12						
Wrexham General	a																								
Llandudno	a																								
Bangor (Gwynedd)	a																								
Holyhead	a																								
Wilmslow	a																								
Stockport	a	09 16		09 27							09 49	09 55								10 16	10 27				
Manchester Piccadilly 10 ⛴	a	09 28		09 39							09 59	10 07								10 28	10 39				
Hartford	a								09 11																
Warrington Bank Quay	a					09 14				09 26														10 14	
	d					09 14				09 27														10 14	
Runcorn	a								09 21								09 50	09 55							
Liverpool South Parkway 7 ✈	a								09 30								09 59								
Liverpool Lime Street 10	a								09 43								10 10	10 15							
	d							08 57																	
Manchester Airport ✈	d				08 25									09 00								09 29			
Manchester Piccadilly 10 ⛴	d				08 46									09 16								09 46			
Bolton	d				09 07									09 33								10 07			
Wigan North Western	a					09 25		09 30		09 37														10 25	
	d					09 25		09 31		09 38														10 25	
Preston 8	a				09 30	09 38		09 54		09 51				09 55								10 33		10 38	
Preston 8	d				09 32	09 41	09 45	09 55		09 53				10 08	09 58							10 38		10 41	10 45
Blackpool North	a							10 21						10 35								11 05			
Lancaster 6	a				09 47	09 54	10 00			10 08					10 13									10 54	11 00
	d				09 48	09 55	10 01			10 08					10 14									10 55	11 01
Barrow-in-Furness	a						11 04																		
Oxenholme Lake District	a				10 04					10 22														11 08	11 17
	d				10 05					10 24														11 08	11 18
Windermere	a				10 26																				11 39
Penrith North Lakes	d					10 30									10 53										
Carlisle 8	a					10 46				11 01					11 10									11 46	
	d					10 47				11 03					11 11									11 47	
Lockerbie	d														11 30										
Carstairs	a																								
Motherwell	a																								
Glasgow Central 15	a					12 01									12 32									13 01	
Haymarket	a									12 16															
Edinburgh 10	a									12 22															
Perth	a																								
Dundee	a																								
Aberdeen	a																								
Inverness	a																								

A 🛒 to Preston

OVERNIGHT SLEEPERS. For sleeper trains, operated by First ScotRail, please refer to Tables 400 - 404

Table 65

Saturdays
until 30 June

London and West Midlands - North West England and Scotland

Route Diagram - see first Page of Table 65

		NT	LM	VT	XC	TP		LM		VT	VT	VT	VT	XC	TP	VT	NT	LM		VT	XC	VT	TP		LM
			◇1	◇1	◇1	◇1		◇1		◇1	◇1	◇1	◇1	◇1	◇1	◇1		◇1		◇1	◇1	◇1	◇1		◇1
																							A		
London Euston 15 ⊖	d									08 50	09 00	09 07	09 20			09 30						10 00			
Watford Junction	d									09 05															
Milton Keynes Central	d									09 25			09 50												
Rugby	d																								
Nuneaton	d																								
Tamworth Low Level	d																								
Lichfield Trent Valley	d																								
Coventry	d													09 27											
Birmingham International ✈	d													09 38											
Birmingham New Street 12	d		09 01	09 20	09 31			09 36						09 57				10 01		10 20	10 31				10 36
Wolverhampton 7	d		09 19	09 37	09 49			09 53						10 15				10 19		10 37	10 49				10 53
Penkridge	d							10 03																	11 03
Stafford	a		09 34		10 00			10 09				10 22		10 29				10 35			11 00				11 09
	d		09 35		10 01			10 09				10 23		10 30				10 35			11 01				11 09
Stoke-on-Trent	a				10 19						10 24		10 48	10 54							11 19	11 24			
Congleton	a																								
Macclesfield	a										10 41			11 11								11 41			
Crewe 10	a		09 56	10 07				10 30		10 32								10 56		11 07					11 30
	d		09 57	10 09				10 31		10 43								10 57		11 09					11 31
Chester	a									11 10															
Wrexham General	a																								
Llandudno	a																								
Bangor (Gwynedd)	a									12 19															
Holyhead	a									12 55															
Wilmslow	a																								
Stockport	a				10 49						10 55		11 16	11 27							11 49	11 55			
Manchester Piccadilly 10	a				10 59						11 07		11 28	11 39							11 59	12 07			
Hartford	a		10 10															11 11							
Warrington Bank Quay	a			10 26												11 14				11 26					
	d			10 27												11 14				11 27					
Runcorn	a		10 22					10 50				10 55						11 21							11 50
Liverpool South Parkway 7 ✈	a		10 31					10 59										11 30							11 59
Liverpool Lime Street 10	a		10 44					11 10				11 15						11 43							12 10
	d	09 57															10 57								
Manchester Airport ✈	d					10 00									10 29								11 00		
Manchester Piccadilly 10	d					10 16									10 46								11 16		
Bolton	d					10 33									11 07								11 33		
Wigan North Western	a	10 30		10 37												11 25	11 30			11 37					
	d	10 31		10 38												11 25	11 31			11 38					
Preston 8	a	10 54		10 51		10 55									11 33	11 38	11 54			11 51			11 55		
Preston 8	d	10 55		10 53		10 58									11 38	11 41	11 55			11 53			11 58		
Blackpool North	a	11 21													12 05		12 21								
Lancaster 6	a			11 08		11 13										11 54				12 08			12 13		
	d			11 08		11 14										11 55				12 08			12 14		
Barrow-in-Furness	a																						13 11		
Oxenholme Lake District	a					11 28														12 22					
	d					11 28														12 24					
Windermere	a																								
Penrith North Lakes	d			11 45		11 53										12 30									
Carlisle 8	a			12 00		12 10										12 46				13 01					
	d			12 03		12 11										12 47				13 03					
Lockerbie	d					12 30																			
Carstairs	a																								
Motherwell	a																								
Glasgow Central 15	a			13 17												14 01									
Haymarket	a					13s33														14 15					
Edinburgh 10	a					13 39														14 22					
Perth	a																								
Dundee	a																								
Aberdeen	a																								
Inverness	a																								

A 🛒 to Preston

OVERNIGHT SLEEPERS. For sleeper trains, operated by First ScotRail, please refer to Tables 400 - 404

Table 65

Saturdays
until 30 June

London and West Midlands - North West England and Scotland

Route Diagram - see first Page of Table 65

		VT	VT	VT		XC	TP	VT	TP	NT	LM	VT	XC	VT		TP		LM	VT	VT	VT	XC	TP	TP
		◇1	◇1	◇1		◇1	◇1	◇1	◇1		◇1	◇1	◇1	◇1		◇1		◇1	◇1	◇1	◇1	◇1	◇1	◇1
									A															
		☕	☕	☕		🛒	🛒	☕				☕	☕	☕		🛒			☕	☕	☕	🛒		🛒
London Euston 15 ⊖	d	10 07	10 10	10 20				10 30						11 00					11 07	11 10	11 20			
Watford Junction	d																							
Milton Keynes Central	d		10 41	10 50																11 41	11 50			
Rugby	d																							
Nuneaton	d																							
Tamworth Low Level	d																							
Lichfield Trent Valley	d																							
Coventry	d					10 27																11 27		
Birmingham International ✈	d					10 38																11 38		
Birmingham New Street 12	d					10 57					11 01	11 20	11 31					11 36				11 57		
Wolverhampton 7 ⛴	d					11 15					11 19	11 37	11 49					11 53				12 15		
Penkridge	d																	12 03						
Stafford	a	11 22				11 29					11 35		12 00					12 09	12 22			12 29		
	d	11 23				11 30					11 35		12 01					12 09	12 23			12 30		
Stoke-on-Trent	a			11 48		11 54							12 19	12 24							12 48	12 54		
Congleton	a																							
Macclesfield	a					12 11								12 41								13 11		
Crewe 10	a		11 47								11 56	12 07						12 30		12 47				
	d		11 49								11 57	12 09						12 31		12 49				
Chester	a		12 12																	13 12				
Wrexham General	a																							
Llandudno	a																							
Bangor (Gwynedd)	a																							
Holyhead	a																							
Wilmslow	a																							
Stockport	a			12 16		12 27							12 49	12 55							13 16	13 27		
Manchester Piccadilly 10 ⛴	a			12 28		12 39							12 59	13 07							13 28	13 39		
Hartford	a										12 10													
Warrington Bank Quay	a							12 14				12 26												
	d							12 14				12 27												
Runcorn	a	11 55									12 22							12 50	12 55					
Liverpool South Parkway 7 ✈	a										12 31							12 59						
Liverpool Lime Street 10	a	12 15									12 44							13 10	13 15					
	d									11 57														
Manchester Airport ✈	d						11 29									12 00								12 29
Manchester Piccadilly 10 ⛴	d						11 46									12 16								12 46
Bolton	d						12 07									12 33								13 07
Wigan North Western	a							12 25		12 30		12 37												
	d							12 25		12 31		12 38												
Preston 8	a						12 33	12 38		12 54		12 51				12 55								13 33
Preston 8	d						12 38	12 41	12⟆48	12 55		12 53				12 58							13 04	13 38
Blackpool North	a						13 05		13⟆12	13 21														14 05
Lancaster 6	a							12 54				13 08				13 13							13 19	
	d							12 55				13 08				13 14							13 20	
Barrow-in-Furness	a																							
Oxenholme Lake District	a							13 08				13 22				13 28							13 36	
	d							13 08				13 24				13 28							13 37	
Windermere	a																						13 56	
Penrith North Lakes	d															13 53								
Carlisle 8	a							13 46				14 01				14 10								
	d							13 47				14 03				14 11								
Lockerbie	d															14 30								
Carstairs	a																							
Motherwell	a																							
Glasgow Central 15	a							15 01				15 17												
Haymarket	a															15s30								
Edinburgh 10	a															15 39								
Perth	a																							
Dundee	a																							
Aberdeen	a																							
Inverness	a																							

A 30 June

OVERNIGHT SLEEPERS. For sleeper trains, operated by First ScotRail, please refer to Tables 400 - 404

Table 65

Saturdays
until 30 June

London and West Midlands - North West England and Scotland

Route Diagram - see first Page of Table 65

		VT	NT	LM	VT	XC	VT	TP	TP			LM	VT	VT	VT	XC	TP	TP	VT	NT		LM	VT	XC	VT
		◇1		◇1	◇1	◇1	◇1	◇1	◇1			◇1	◇1	◇1	◇1	◇1	◇1	◇1	◇1			◇1	◇1	◇1	◇1
								A	B								A								
		☕			☕	☕	☕	🍴	🍴				☕	☕	☕	🍴	🍴	🍴	☕				☕	☕	☕
London Euston 15 ⊖	d	11 30					12 00						12 07	12 10	12 20				12 30						13 00
Watford Junction	d																								
Milton Keynes Central	d													12 41	12 50										
Rugby	d																								
Nuneaton	d																								
Tamworth Low Level	d																								
Lichfield Trent Valley	d																								
Coventry	d															12 27									
Birmingham International ✈	d															12 38									
Birmingham New Street 12	d			12 01	12 20	12 31						12 36				12 57						13 01	13 20	13 31	
Wolverhampton 7 🚌	d			12 19	12 37	12 49						12 53				13 15						13 19	13 37	13 49	
Penkridge	d											13 03													
Stafford	a			12 35		13 00						13 09	13 22			13 29						13 35		14 00	
	d			12 35		13 01						13 09	13 23			13 30						13 35		14 01	
Stoke-on-Trent	a					13 18	13 24								13 48	13 54								14 19	14 24
Congleton	a																								
Macclesfield	a						13 41									14 11									14 41
Crewe 10	a			12 56	13 07							13 30		13 47								13 56	14 07		
	d			12 57	13 09							13 31		13 49								13 57	14 09		
Chester	a													14 12											
Wrexham General	a																								
Llandudno	a																								
Bangor (Gwynedd)	a																								
Holyhead	a																								
Wilmslow	a																								
Stockport	a					13 49	13 55								14 16	14 27								14 49	14 55
Manchester Piccadilly 10 🚌	a					13 59	14 07								14 28	14 39								14 59	15 07
Hartford	a			13 11																		14 11			
Warrington Bank Quay	a	13 14			13 27														14 14				14 26		
	d	13 14			13 27														14 14				14 27		
Runcorn	a			13 21								13 50	13 55									14 21			
Liverpool South Parkway 7 ✈	a			13 30								13 59										14 30			
Liverpool Lime Street 10	a			13 43								14 10	14 15									14 43			
	d		12 57																	13 57					
Manchester Airport ✈	d							13 00	13 00									13 29							
Manchester Piccadilly 10 🚌	d							13 16	13 16									13 46							
Bolton	d							13 33	13 33									14 07							
Wigan North Western	a	13 25	13 30		13 38														14 25	14 30			14 37		
	d	13 25	13 31		13 38														14 25	14 31			14 38		
Preston 8	a	13 38	13 54		13 51			13 55	13 55									14 33	14 38	14 54			14 51		
Preston 8	d	13 41	13 55		13 53			13 58	13 58								13 58	14 38	14 41	14 55			14 53		
Blackpool North	a		14 21															15 05		15 21					
Lancaster 6	a	13 54			14 08			14 13	14 13								14 13		14 54				15 08		
	d	13 55			14 08			14 14	14 14								14 14		14 55				15 09		
Barrow-in-Furness	a																								
Oxenholme Lake District	a	14 08							14 28														15 22		
	d	14 08							14 28														15 24		
Windermere	a																								
Penrith North Lakes	d				14 45														15 30						
Carlisle 8	a	14 46			15 00			15 06	15 06								15 06		15 46				16 01		
	d	14 47			15 02			15 07	15 07								15 07		15 47				16 03		
Lockerbie	d							15 27	15 27								15 27								
Carstairs	a																								
Motherwell	a																								
Glasgow Central 15	a	16 01						16 30	16 30								16 30		17 01				17 17		
Haymarket	a				16 16																				
Edinburgh 10	a				16 22																				
Perth	a																								
Dundee	a																								
Aberdeen	a																								
Inverness	a																								

A 30 June **B** not 30 June

OVERNIGHT SLEEPERS. For sleeper trains, operated by First ScotRail, please refer to Tables 400 - 404

Table 65

Saturdays
until 30 June

London and West Midlands - North West England and Scotland

Route Diagram - see first Page of Table 65

		TP			LM	VT		VT	VT	XC	TP	VT	NT	LM	VT	XC		VT	TP		LM	VT	VT	XC	TP
		◇1			◇1	◇1		◇1	◇1	◇1	◇1	◇1		◇1	◇1	◇1		◇1	◇1		◇1	◇1	◇1	◇1	◇1
																			A						
		⊥				⊡		⊡	⊡	⊥	⊥	⊡			⊡	⊡		⊡	⊥			⊡	⊡	⊥	⊥
London Euston 15 ⊖	d					13 07		13 10	13 20			13 30						14 00				14 07	14 20		
Watford Junction	d																								
Milton Keynes Central	d							13 41	13 50														14 50		
Rugby	d																								
Nuneaton	d																								
Tamworth Low Level	d																								
Lichfield Trent Valley	d																								
Coventry	d									13 27														14 27	
Birmingham International ✈	d									13 38														14 38	
Birmingham New Street 12	d				13 36					13 57				14 01	14 20	14 31					14 36			14 57	
Wolverhampton 7 ⛴	d				13 53					14 15				14 19	14 37	14 49					14 53			15 15	
Penkridge	d				14 03																15 03				
Stafford	a				14 09	14 22				14 29				14 35		15 00					15 09	15 22		15 29	
	d				14 09	14 23				14 30				14 35		15 01					15 09	15 23		15 30	
Stoke-on-Trent	a								14 48	14 54						15 19		15 24					15 48	15 54	
Congleton	a																								
Macclesfield	a									15 11								15 41						16 11	
Crewe 10	a				14 30			14 47						14 56	15 07						15 30				
	d				14 31			14 49						14 57	15 09						15 31				
Chester	a							15 12																	
Wrexham General	a																								
Llandudno	a																								
Bangor (Gwynedd)	a																								
Holyhead	a																								
Wilmslow	a																								
Stockport	a								15 16	15 27						15 49		15 55					16 16	16 27	
Manchester Piccadilly 10 ⛴	a								15 28	15 39						15 59		16 07					16 28	16 39	
Hartford	a													15 11											
Warrington Bank Quay	a											15 14			15 26										
	d											15 14			15 27										
Runcorn	a				14 50	14 55								15 21							15 50	15 55			
Liverpool South Parkway 7 ✈	a				14 59									15 30							15 59				
Liverpool Lime Street 10	a				15 10	15 15								15 43							16 10	16 15			
	d												14 57												
Manchester Airport ✈	d	14 00									14 29								15 00						15 29
Manchester Piccadilly 10 ⛴	d	14 16									14 46								15 16						15 46
Bolton	d	14 33									15 07								15 33						16 07
Wigan North Western	a											15 25	15 30		15 37										
	d											15 25	15 31		15 38										
Preston 8	a	14 55									15 33	15 38	15 54		15 51				15 57						16 33
Preston 8	d	14 58	15 04								15 38	15 41	15 55		15 53				15 58						16 38
Blackpool North	a										16 05		16 21												17 07
Lancaster 6	a	15 13	15 20									15 54			16 08				16 14						
	d	15 14	15 20									15 55			16 08				16 15						
Barrow-in-Furness	a		16 15																17 18						
Oxenholme Lake District	a	15 28										16 08													
	d	15 28										16 08													
Windermere	a																								
Penrith North Lakes	d	15 53													16 45										
Carlisle 8	a	16 10										16 46			17 00										
	d	16 11										16 47			17 03										
Lockerbie	d	16 30																							
Carstairs	a																								
Motherwell	a																								
Glasgow Central 15	a											18 01													
Haymarket	a	17s31													18 14										
Edinburgh 10	a	17 39													18 22										
Perth	a																								
Dundee	a																								
Aberdeen	a																								
Inverness	a																								

A ⊥ to Preston

OVERNIGHT SLEEPERS. For sleeper trains, operated by First ScotRail, please refer to Tables 400 - 404

Table 65

Saturdays

until 30 June

London and West Midlands - North West England and Scotland

Route Diagram - see first Page of Table 65

		VT		NT	LM	VT	XC	VT	TP			LM		VT	VT	VT	XC	TP	VT	NT	LM	VT		XC	VT
		◇1			◇1	◇1	◇1	◇1	◇1			◇1		◇1	◇1	◇1	◇1	◇1	◇1		◇1	◇1		◇1	◇1
		🍽				🍽	🍽	🍽	🛒					🍽	🍽	🍽	🛒	🛒	🍽			🍽		🍽	🍽
London Euston 15 ⊖	d	14 30						15 00						15 07	15 10	15 20			15 30						16 00
Watford Junction	d																								
Milton Keynes Central	d														15 41	15 50									
Rugby	d																								
Nuneaton	d																								
Tamworth Low Level	d																								
Lichfield Trent Valley	d																								
Coventry	d																15 27								
Birmingham International ✈	d																15 38								
Birmingham New Street 12	d				15 01	15 20	15 31					15 36					15 57				16 01	16 20		16 31	
Wolverhampton 7 ⛴	d				15 19	15 37	15 49					15 53					16 15				16 19	16 37		16 49	
Penkridge	d											16 03													
Stafford	a				15 35		16 00					16 09		16 22			16 29				16 35			17 00	
	d				15 35		16 01					16 09		16 23			16 30				16 35			17 01	
Stoke-on-Trent	a						16 18	16 24								16 48	16 54							17 19	17 24
Congleton	a																								
Macclesfield	a							16 41									17 11								17 41
Crewe 10	a				15 56	16 08						16 30			16 47						16 56	17 07			
	d				15 57	16 09						16 31			16 49						16 57	17 09			
Chester	a														17 12										
Wrexham General	a																								
Llandudno	a																								
Bangor (Gwynedd)	a																								
Holyhead	a																								
Wilmslow	a																								
Stockport	a						16 48	16 54								17 16	17 27							17 49	17 55
Manchester Piccadilly 10 ⛴	a						16 59	17 07								17 28	17 39							17 59	18 07
Hartford	a				16 10																17 11				
Warrington Bank Quay	a	16 14				16 26													17 14			17 26			
	d	16 14				16 27													17 14			17 27			
Runcorn	a				16 22							16 50		16 55							17 21				
Liverpool South Parkway 7 ✈	a				16 31							16 59									17 30				
Liverpool Lime Street 10	a				16 44							17 10		17 15							17 43				
	d			15 57																16 57					
Manchester Airport ✈	d								16 00									16 29							
Manchester Piccadilly 10 ⛴	d								16 16									16 46							
Bolton	d								16 33									17 06							
Wigan North Western	a	16 25		16 30		16 37													17 25	17 30		17 37			
	d	16 25		16 31		16 38													17 25	17 31		17 38			
Preston 8	a	16 38		16 54		16 51			16 55									17 30	17 38	17 54		17 51			
Preston 8	d	16 41		16 55		16 53			17 00	17 04								17 32	17 41	17 55		17 53			
Blackpool North	a			17 21														18 02		18 24					
Lancaster 6	a	16 54				17 09			17 16	17 20									17 54			18 08			
	d	16 55				17 10			17 16	17 21									17 55			18 08			
Barrow-in-Furness	a																								
Oxenholme Lake District	a					17 24			17 30	17 37									18 08			18 22			
	d					17 25			17 30	17 38									18 08			18 23			
Windermere	a									18 00															
Penrith North Lakes	d	17 30																				18 49			
Carlisle 8	a	17 46				18 03			18 10										18 46			19 04			
	d	17 47				18 04			18 11										18 47			19 04			
Lockerbie	d								18 30																
Carstairs	a																								
Motherwell	a																								
Glasgow Central 15	a	19 01				19 17													20 01						
Haymarket	a								19s31													20 16			
Edinburgh 10	a								19 39													20 22			
Perth	a																								
Dundee	a																								
Aberdeen	a																								
Inverness	a																								

OVERNIGHT SLEEPERS. For sleeper trains, operated by First ScotRail, please refer to Tables 400 - 404

Table 65

Saturdays
until 30 June

London and West Midlands - North West England and Scotland

Route Diagram - see first Page of Table 65

		TP	NT		LM	VT	VT	XC		LM	TP	VT	VT	TP	VT	XC	VT	TP			LM	VT	VT	XC	LM
		◇1			◇1	◇1	◇1	◇1		◇1	◇1	◇1	◇1	◇1	◇1	◇1	◇1	◇1			◇1	◇1	◇1	◇1	◇1
																		A							
		☕				🍴	🍴	☕				🍴	🍴	☕	🍴	☕	🍴	☕				🍴	🍴	☕	
London Euston 15 ⊖	d					16 07	16 20					16 30	16 33				17 00					17 07	17 20		
Watford Junction	d																								
Milton Keynes Central	d						16 50																17 50		
Rugby	d																								
Nuneaton	d																					18 03			
Tamworth Low Level	d												17 38												
Lichfield Trent Valley	d												17 45												
Coventry	d							16 27																17 27	
Birmingham International ✈	d							16 38																17 38	
Birmingham New Street 12	d				16 36			16 57		17 01					17 20	17 31					17 36			17 57	18 01
Wolverhampton 7 ⛴	d				16 53			17 15		17 19					17 37	17 49					17 53			18 15	18 19
Penkridge	d				17 03					17 29											18 03				18 29
Stafford	a				17 09	17 22		17 29		17 35			17 58			18 00					18 09	18 26		18 29	18 35
	d				17 09	17 23		17 30		17 36			17 59			18 01					18 09	18 27		18 30	18 35
Stoke-on-Trent	a						17 48	17 54								18 19	18 24						18 48	18 54	
Congleton	a																								
Macclesfield	a							18 11									18 41							19 11	
Crewe 10	a				17 30					17 56					18 07						18 30				18 56
	d				17 31					17 57					18 09						18 33				18 59
Chester	a																								
Wrexham General	a																								
Llandudno	a																								
Bangor (Gwynedd)	a																								
Holyhead	a																								
Wilmslow	a																								
Stockport	a						18 16	18 27								18 49	18 55						19 16	19 27	
Manchester Piccadilly 10 ⛴	a						18 28	18 39								18 59	19 07						19 28	19 39	
Hartford	a									18 11											18 43				19 12
Warrington Bank Quay	a											18 14			18 26										
	d											18 14			18 27										
Runcorn	a				17 50	17 55				18 21			18 31								18 52	18 59			19 22
Liverpool South Parkway 7 ✈	a				17 59					18 30											19 02				19 31
Liverpool Lime Street 10	a				18 10	18 15				18 43			18 52								19 14	19 17			19 44
	d		17 19																						
Manchester Airport ✈	d	17 00												17 29				18 00							
Manchester Piccadilly 10 ⛴	d	17 15												17 46				18 16							
Bolton	d	17 32												18 07				18 33							
Wigan North Western	a		18 04									18 25			18 37										
	d											18 25			18 38										
Preston 8	a	17 55										18 38		18 38	18 51			18 55							
Preston 8	d	17 58									18 02	18 41		18 40	18 53			18 58							
Blackpool North	a													19 10											
Lancaster 6	a	18 13									18 18	18 54			19 08			19 13							
	d	18 14									18 18	18 55			19 08			19 15							
Barrow-in-Furness	a										19 26							20 19							
Oxenholme Lake District	a	18 28										19 08			19 22										
	d	18 28										19 08			19 24										
Windermere	a																								
Penrith North Lakes	d	18 53										19 34													
Carlisle 8	a	19 09										19 49			20 01										
	d	19 11										19 51			20 03										
Lockerbie	d	19 30																							
Carstairs	a																								
Motherwell	a	20s16																							
Glasgow Central 15	a	20 33										21 01			21 17										
Haymarket	a																								
Edinburgh 10	a																								
Perth	a																								
Dundee	a																								
Aberdeen	a																								
Inverness	a																								

A ☕ to Preston

OVERNIGHT SLEEPERS. For sleeper trains, operated by First ScotRail, please refer to Tables 400 - 404

Table 65

Saturdays
until 30 June

London and West Midlands - North West England and Scotland

Route Diagram - see first Page of Table 65

		TP	VT	VT	XC	VT	LM	TP	NT	VT	VT	VT	XC	LM	TP	VT	VT	VT	TP	NT
		◇1	◇1	◇1	◇1	◇1	◇1	◇1		◇1	◇1	◇1	◇1	◇1	◇1	◇1	◇1	◇1	◇1	
																A	B			
		🛒	☕	☕	☕	☕				☕	☕	☕	🛒			☕	☕	☕		
London Euston 15 ⊖	d		17 30			18 00				18 07	18 10	18 20				18 30	18 30			
Watford Junction	d																			
Milton Keynes Central	d										18 41	18 50								
Rugby	d																			
Nuneaton	d																			
Tamworth Low Level	d																			
Lichfield Trent Valley	d																			
Coventry	d												18 27							
Birmingham International ✈	d												18 38							
Birmingham New Street 12	d			18 20	18 31		18 36						18 57	19 01				19 20		
Wolverhampton 7	d			18 37	18 49		18 53						19 15	19 19				19 37		
Penkridge	d						19 03							19 29						
Stafford	a				19 00		19 09			19 22			19 29	19 35						
	d				19 01		19 09			19 23			19 30	19 36						
Stoke-on-Trent	a				19 19	19 24						19 48	19 54							
Congleton	a																			
Macclesfield	a					19 41							20 11							
Crewe 10	a			19 07			19 30				19 47			19 58				20 07		
	d			19 09							19 49			19 58				20 09		
Chester	a										20 12									
Wrexham General	a																			
Llandudno	a																			
Bangor (Gwynedd)	a																			
Holyhead	a																			
Wilmslow	a																			
Stockport	a				19 49	19 55						20 16	20 27							
Manchester Piccadilly 10	a				19 59	20 07						20 28	20 39							
Hartford	a													20 11						
Warrington Bank Quay	a		19 14	19 26												20 14	20 14	20 26		
	d		19 14	19 27												20 14	20 14	20 27		
Runcorn	a									19 55				20 24						
Liverpool South Parkway 7 ✈	a													20 33						
Liverpool Lime Street 10	a									20 15				20 46						
	d								19 23											20 25
Manchester Airport ✈	d	18 29						19 00							19 29				20 00	
Manchester Piccadilly 10	d	18 46						19 16							19 46				20 16	
Bolton	d	19 07						19 33							20 07				20 33	
Wigan North Western	a		19 25	19 37					19 54							20 25	20 25	20 37		20 57
	d		19 25	19 38					19 55							20 25	20 25	20 38		20 57
Preston 8	a	19 33	19 38	19 54				19 58	20 18						20 33	20 38	20 38	20 59	20 57	21 22
Preston 8	d	19 38	19 41					20 01	20 19						20 38	20 41	20 41		21 02	21 24
Blackpool North	a	20 06							20 44						21 06					21 53
Lancaster 6	a		19 54					20 17								20 54	20 54		21 17	
	d		19 55					20 17								20 55	20 55		21 18	
Barrow-in-Furness	a							21 20											22 21	
Oxenholme Lake District	a		20 08													21 08	21 08			
	d		20 08													21 09	21 08			
Windermere	a																			
Penrith North Lakes	d		20 34													21 34	21 34			
Carlisle 8	a		20 49													21 49	21 49			
	d		20 51													21 51	21 51			
Lockerbie	d																			
Carstairs	a																			
Motherwell	a															22 44	22 44			
Glasgow Central 15	a		22 01													23 04	23 04			
Haymarket	a																			
Edinburgh 10	a																			
Perth	a																			
Dundee	a																			
Aberdeen	a																			
Inverness	a																			

A not 30 June   **B** 30 June

OVERNIGHT SLEEPERS. For sleeper trains, operated by First ScotRail, please refer to Tables 400 - 404

Table 65

Saturdays
until 30 June

London and West Midlands - North West England and Scotland

Route Diagram - see first Page of Table 65

		VT	XC	VT	VT	VT	XC	TP	VT	LM		VT	XC	LM	XC		VT	VT	LM	XC		NT	TP	TP	
		◇1	◇1	◇1	◇1	◇1	◇1	◇1	◇1	◇1		◇1	◇1	◇1	◇1		◇1	◇1	◇1	◇1			◇1	◇1	
							A																		
		🍴	🍴	🍴	🍴	🍴	🛒		🍴			🍴	🍴		🛒		🍴	🍴							
London Euston 15 ⊖	d	18 33		19 00	19 07	19 20			19 30								20 11	20 20							
Watford Junction	d																								
Milton Keynes Central	d					19 50												21 05							
Rugby	d																21 15								
Nuneaton	d				20 03													21 33							
Tamworth Low Level	d	19 38																							
Lichfield Trent Valley	d	19 45																							
Coventry	d						19 27													21 27					
Birmingham International ✈	d						19 38													21 38					
Birmingham New Street 12	d		19 31				19 57			20 01		20 20	20 31	20 36	20 57				21 36	21 57					
Wolverhampton 7 ⛴	d		19 49				20 15			20 22		20 37	20 49	20 53	21 15				21 59	22 16					
Penkridge	d									20 31				21 03					22 09						
Stafford	a	19 58	20 00		20 26		20 29			20 37		20 49	21 00	21 09	21 29		21 46		22 15	22 29					
	d	19 59	20 01		20 27		20 30			20 38		20 50	21 01	21 09	21 30		21 46		22 16	22 30					
Stoke-on-Trent	a		20 19	20 24		20 48	20 54						21 20		21 52			22 05		22 50					
Congleton	a																								
Macclesfield	a		20 36	20 41			21 11						21 38		22 10			22 21		23 07					
Crewe 10	a				20 45				21 04	20 58		21 10		21 30			22 05		22 40						
	d				20 47				21 05	21 06							22 06								
Chester	a																								
Wrexham General	a																								
Llandudno	a																								
Bangor (Gwynedd)	a																								
Holyhead	a																								
Wilmslow	a																								
Stockport	a		20 49	20 55		21 16	21 27						21 53		22 26			22 35		23 21					
Manchester Piccadilly 10 ⛴	a		20 59	21 07		21 28	21 39						22 04		22 39			22 51		23 32					
Hartford	a									21 19															
Warrington Bank Quay	a								21 22																
	d								21 22																
Runcorn	a	20 31			21 05					21 29							22 24								
Liverpool South Parkway 7 ✈	a									21 38															
Liverpool Lime Street 10	a	20 52			21 25					21 50							22 46								
	d																								
Manchester Airport ✈	d							20 29															21 29	22 00	
Manchester Piccadilly 10 ⛴	d							20 46															21 46	22 16	
Bolton	d							21 07															22 07	22 33	
Wigan North Western	a								21 33																
	d								21 33																
Preston 8	a							21 33	21 49														22 36	22 54	
Preston 8	d							21 38														21 59	22 38	22 55	
Blackpool North	a							22 06															23 04		
Lancaster 6	a																					22 19		23 11	
	d																					22 19		23 11	
Barrow-in-Furness	a																					23 24		00 15	
Oxenholme Lake District	a																								
	d																								
Windermere	a																								
Penrith North Lakes	d																								
Carlisle 8	a																								
	d																								
Lockerbie	d																								
Carstairs	a																								
Motherwell	a																								
Glasgow Central 15	a																								
Haymarket	a																								
Edinburgh 10	a																								
Perth	a																								
Dundee	a																								
Aberdeen	a																								
Inverness	a																								

A 🛒 to Birmingham New Street

OVERNIGHT SLEEPERS. For sleeper trains, operated by First ScotRail, please refer to Tables 400 - 404

Table 65

Saturdays

until 30 June

London and West Midlands - North West England and Scotland

Route Diagram - see first Page of Table 65

		VT	TP	XC	LM
		◇1	◇1	◇1	◇1
		🍴			
London Euston 15 ⊖	d	20 31			
Watford Junction	d	20u46			
Milton Keynes Central	d				
Rugby	d	21 36			
Nuneaton	d				
Tamworth Low Level	d	21 53			
Lichfield Trent Valley	d	22 00			
Coventry	d				
Birmingham International ✈	d				
Birmingham New Street 12	d			22 31	22 36
Wolverhampton 7	d			22 49	22 56
Penkridge	d				23 06
Stafford	a			23 01	23 13
	d			23 02	23 13
Stoke-on-Trent	a			23 20	
Congleton	a				
Macclesfield	a			23 38	
Crewe 10	a	22 35			23 37
	d	22 37			
Chester	a				
Wrexham General	a				
Llandudno	a				
Bangor (Gwynedd)	a				
Holyhead	a				
Wilmslow	a				
Stockport	a			23 53	
Manchester Piccadilly 10	a			00 10	
Hartford	a				
Warrington Bank Quay	a	22 53			
	d	22 54			
Runcorn	a				
Liverpool South Parkway 7 ✈	a				
Liverpool Lime Street 10	a				
	d				
Manchester Airport ✈	d		22 29		
Manchester Piccadilly 10	d		22 46		
Bolton	d		23 07		
Wigan North Western	a	23 04			
	d	23 05			
Preston 8	a	23 19	23 33		
Preston 8	d		23 35		
Blackpool North	a		00 02		
Lancaster 6	a				
	d				
Barrow-in-Furness	a				
Oxenholme Lake District	a				
	d				
Windermere	a				
Penrith North Lakes	d				
Carlisle 8	a				
	d				
Lockerbie	d				
Carstairs	a				
Motherwell	a				
Glasgow Central 15	a				
Haymarket	a				
Edinburgh 10	a				
Perth	a				
Dundee	a				
Aberdeen	a				
Inverness	a				

OVERNIGHT SLEEPERS. For sleeper trains, operated by First ScotRail, please refer to Tables 400 - 404

London and West Midlands - North West England and Scotland

Route Diagram - see first Page of Table 65

		VT	TP	TP	XC	TP	SR	VT	LM		VT	VT	SR	TP	VT	NT	VT	VT		TP	TP	LM	XC
		R					R						R										
		1	◇1	◇1	◇1	◇1		◇1	◇1		◇1	◇1		◇1	◇1		◇1	◇1		◇1	◇1	1	◇1
							A				B	B			B		B	B					
							🛏						🛏										
		☕					☕	☕			☕	☕	☕		☕		☕	☕					
London Euston 15 ⊖	d	19p30					21p15	22p00			23p30	23p45	23p50		00ʃ30		01ʃ00	01ʃ30					
Watford Junction	d						21b33						00u10										
Milton Keynes Central	d							22p31															
Rugby	d							22p54				00s47					01s55						
Nuneaton	d							23p04				01s02					02s06						
Tamworth Low Level	d							23c15															
Lichfield Trent Valley	d							23c22															
Coventry	d																						
Birmingham International ✈	d																						
Birmingham New Street 12	d				22p30				23p09														05 57
Wolverhampton 7	d				22p48				23p36														06 16
Penkridge	d								23p46														
Stafford	a				23p00			23c38	23p52			01s31					02s31						06 29
	d				23p01				23p53														06 30
Stoke-on-Trent	a				23p20						00s53				01s53			03s04					06 50
Congleton	a																						07 02
Macclesfield	a										01s10				02s10			03s20					07 11
Crewe 10	a							00s03	00 16			01s55					03s00						
	d						23b54									00 44						05 48	
Chester	a																						
Wrexham General	a																						
Llandudno	a																						
Bangor (Gwynedd)	a																						
Holyhead	a																						
Wilmslow	a																						
Stockport	a							00s26			01s24				02s24			03s34					07 27
Manchester Piccadilly 10	a				00 12			00 35			01ʃ43				02ʃ37			03ʃ45					07 38
Hartford	a																						
Warrington Bank Quay	a	21p15																					
	d	21p15																					
Runcorn	a											02s16					03s19					06 07	
Liverpool South Parkway 7 ✈	a																					06 15	
Liverpool Lime Street 10	a											02ʃ34					03ʃ38					06 26	
	d																						
Manchester Airport ✈	d		22p00	22p29										00 01		01 20				04 00			
Manchester Piccadilly 10	d		22p16	22p46										00 16		01a36				04 15	05 43		
Bolton	d		22p33	23p07										00s31						04s29	05 59		
Wigan North Western	a	21p26	22p48																				
	d	21p26	22p51																				
Preston 8	a	21p39	23p09	23p33										01s05						05s04	06 26		
Preston 8	d	21p41	23p13	23p35		23p51	00u52														06 37		
Blackpool North	a			00 02		00 16								01 30						05 33	07 06		
Lancaster 6	a	21p55	23p28																				
	d	21p56	23p29																				
Barrow-in-Furness	a		00 31																				
Oxenholme Lake District	a	22p09																					
	d	22p09																					
Windermere	a																						
Penrith North Lakes	d	22p35																					
Carlisle 8	a	22p50											05s15										
	d	22p51																					
Lockerbie	d																						
Carstairs	a												06s20										
Motherwell	a												06s56										
Glasgow Central 15	a	00 06											07 20										
Haymarket	a																						
Edinburgh 10	a						03 58						07 15										
Perth	a						05s39																
Dundee	a						06s08																
Aberdeen	a						07 36																
Inverness	a						08 38																

A Conveys a portion from Fort William, arrives at 0954

B 28 July, 4 August, 11 August, 1 September, 8 September

b Previous night, stops to pick up only

c Previous night, stops to set down only

OVERNIGHT SLEEPERS. For sleeper trains, operated by First ScotRail, please refer to Tables 400 - 404

Table 65

Saturdays

7 July to 8 September

London and West Midlands - North West England and Scotland

Route Diagram - see first Page of Table 65

		VT	TP	LM	TP	NT		TP	NT	LM	LM	VT	XC	TP		LM		TP	VT	LM	NT	NT	VT	XC	VT
		◇1	◇1	1	◇1			◇1		◇1	◇1	◇1	◇1	◇1		◇1		◇1	◇1	◇1			◇1	◇1	◇1
		⊐	⚲		⚲							⊐	⚲	⚲				⚲	⊐				⊐	⚲	⊐
London Euston 15 ⊖	d																		06 05						06 55
Watford Junction	d																		06u20						
Milton Keynes Central	d																		06 41						07 27
Rugby	d																		07 03						
Nuneaton	d																								
Tamworth Low Level	d																								
Lichfield Trent Valley	d																								
Coventry	d																								
Birmingham International ✈	d																								
Birmingham New Street 12	d										06 01	06 20	06 31			06 36				07 01			07 20	07 31	
Wolverhampton 7	d										06 18	06 37	06 49			06 54				07 18			07 37	07 49	
Penkridge	d										06 29									07 30					
Stafford	a										06 35		07 00			07 08			07 33	07 36				08 00	
	d										06 36		07 01			07 08			07 34	07 38				08 01	
Stoke-on-Trent	a												07 18											08 19	08 24
Congleton	a																								
Macclesfield	a												07 36											08 36	08 41
Crewe 10	a										06 56	07 07				07 33			07 53	07 58			08 07		
	d	05 57		06 12						06 32	06 57	07 09				07 35			07 55	08 00			08 09		
Chester	a																								
Wrexham General	a																								
Llandudno	a																								
Bangor (Gwynedd)	a																								
Holyhead	a																								
Wilmslow	a																								
Stockport	a												07 49											08 49	08 55
Manchester Piccadilly 10	a												07 59											08 59	09 07
Hartford	a									06 46	07 10					07 48				08 11					
Warrington Bank Quay	a	06 13										07 26							08 11				08 27		
	d	06 14										07 27							08 12				08 27		
Runcorn	a			06 31						06 59	07 20					08 02				08 24					
Liverpool South Parkway 7 ✈	a			06 39						07 08	07 30					08 11				08 33					
Liverpool Lime Street 10	a			06 53						07 22	07 42					08 24				08 46					
	d								06 57																
Manchester Airport ✈	d		05 45		06 18									07 00				07 25							
Manchester Piccadilly 10	d		06 03		06 33									07 15				07 45							
Bolton	d		06 19		06 50	07 01								07 31				07 59							
Wigan North Western	a	06 24				07 19			07 30			07 37							08 22				08 38		
	d	06 25							07 31			07 38							08 23			08 30	08 38		
Preston 8	a	06 37	06 42		07 11				07 54			07 51		07 57				08 22	08 36			08 54	08 51		
Preston 8	d	06 40	06 44		07 14			07 20	07 55			07 53		07 59				08 24	08 37		08 42	08 55	08 53		
Blackpool North	a								08 21					08 29								09 21			
Lancaster 6	a	06 54	06 59		07 30			07 36				08 08						08 39	08 52		09 02		09 08		
	d	06 54	07 00		07 30			07 36				08 08						08 40	08 52		09 03		09 08		
Barrow-in-Furness	a							08 39													10 07				
Oxenholme Lake District	a	07 08	07 15									08 21							09 05						
	d	07 10	07 15									08 22							09 06						
Windermere	a																								
Penrith North Lakes	d	07 37			08 07														09 32				09 45		
Carlisle 8	a	07 50	07 55		08 24							09 00						09 30	09 47		12 39		10 02		
	d	07 51	07 56		08 25							09 02						09 30	09 48				10 04		
Lockerbie	d	08 10	08 16															09 50							
Carstairs	a																								
Motherwell	a																								
Glasgow Central 15	a	09 13			09 45														11 03				11 17		
Haymarket	a		09s17									10 16						10s48							
Edinburgh 10	a		09 22									10 22						10 56							
Perth	a																								
Dundee	a																								
Aberdeen	a																								
Inverness	a																								

OVERNIGHT SLEEPERS. For sleeper trains, operated by First ScotRail, please refer to Tables 400 - 404

Table 65

Saturdays

7 July to 8 September

London and West Midlands - North West England and Scotland

Route Diagram - see first Page of Table 65

		TP			LM	VT	VT	XC	TP	VT	TP	NT		LM	VT	XC	VT	TP			LM	VT		VT	VT
		◇1			◇1	◇1	◇1	◇1	◇1	◇1	◇1			◇1	◇1	◇1	◇1	◇1			◇1	◇1		◇1	◇1
									A									A							
		🛒				☕	☕	🛒	🛒	☕					☕	☕	☕	🛒				☕		☕	☕
London Euston 15 ⊖	d					07 07	07 20			07 30							08 00					08 07		08 10	08 20
Watford Junction	d																								
Milton Keynes Central	d						07 50																	08 41	08 50
Rugby	d																								
Nuneaton	d																								
Tamworth Low Level	d																								
Lichfield Trent Valley	d																								
Coventry	d							07 27																	
Birmingham International ✈	d							07 38																	
Birmingham New Street 12	d				07 36			07 57						08 01	08 20	08 31					08 36				
Wolverhampton 7	d				07 53			08 15						08 19	08 37	08 49					08 53				
Penkridge	d				08 03									08 29							09 03				
Stafford	a				08 09	08 22		08 29						08 35		09 00					09 09	09 22			
	d				08 09	08 23		08 30						08 36		09 01					09 09	09 23			
Stoke-on-Trent	a						08 48	08 54								09 19	09 24								09 48
Congleton	a																								
Macclesfield	a							09 11									09 41								
Crewe 10	a				08 30	08 41								08 56	09 07						09 30			09 47	
	d				08 31	08 43								08 57	09 09						09 31			09 49	
Chester	a																							10 12	
Wrexham General	a																								
Llandudno	a																								
Bangor (Gwynedd)	a																								
Holyhead	a																								
Wilmslow	a																								
Stockport	a						09 16	09 27								09 49	09 55								10 16
Manchester Piccadilly 10	a						09 28	09 39								09 59	10 07								10 28
Hartford	a													09 11											
Warrington Bank Quay	a									09 14					09 26										
	d									09 14					09 27										
Runcorn	a				08 50	09 00								09 21							09 50	09 55			
Liverpool South Parkway 7 ✈	a				08 59									09 30							09 59				
Liverpool Lime Street 10	a				09 12	09 21								09 43							10 10	10 15			
	d											08 57													
Manchester Airport ✈	d	07 56							08 25									09 00							
Manchester Piccadilly 10	d	08 15							08 46									09 16							
Bolton	d	08 32							09 07									09 33							
Wigan North Western	a									09 25		09 30			09 37										
	d									09 25		09 31			09 38										
Preston 8	a	08 58							09 30	09 38		09 54			09 51			09 55							
Preston 8	d	08 59							09 32	09 41	09 45	09 55			09 53			10 08	09 58						
Blackpool North	a	09 25										10 21						10 35							
Lancaster 6	a								09 47	09 54	10 00				10 08				10 13						
	d								09 48	09 55	10 01				10 08				10 14						
Barrow-in-Furness	a										11 04														
Oxenholme Lake District	a								10 04						10 22										
	d								10 05						10 24										
Windermere	a								10 26																
Penrith North Lakes	d									10 30									10 53						
Carlisle 8	a									10 46					11 01				11 10						
	d									10 47					11 03				11 11						
Lockerbie	d																		11 30						
Carstairs	a																								
Motherwell	a																								
Glasgow Central 15	a									12 01									12 32						
Haymarket	a														12 16										
Edinburgh 10	a														12 22										
Perth	a																								
Dundee	a																								
Aberdeen	a																								
Inverness	a																								

A 🛒 to Preston

OVERNIGHT SLEEPERS. For sleeper trains, operated by First ScotRail, please refer to Tables 400 - 404

Saturdays

7 July to 8 September

London and West Midlands - North West England and Scotland

Route Diagram - see first Page of Table 65

		XC	TP	VT	TP	NT	LM	VT	XC	TP	LM	XC	LM	TP	VT	VT	VT	VT	VT	VT	XC	VT
		◇1	◇1	◇1	◇1		◇1	◇1	◇1	◇1	◇1	◇1	◇1	◇1	◇1	◇1	◇1	◇1	◇1	◇1	◇1	◇1
London Euston 15 ⊖	d			08 30											08 43	08 50	09 00	09 07	09 20	09 30		10 00
Watford Junction	d															09 05						
Milton Keynes Central	d														09 13	09 25			09 50			
Rugby	d																					
Nuneaton	d																					
Tamworth Low Level	d																					
Lichfield Trent Valley	d																					
Coventry	d	08 27										09 27			09 42							
Birmingham International ✈	d	08 38										09 38			09 53							
Birmingham New Street 12	d	08 57					09 01	09 20	09 31		09 36	09 57	10 01		10 20						10 31	
Wolverhampton 7	d	09 15					09 19	09 37	09 49		09 53	10 15	10 19		10 37						10 49	
Penkridge	d										10 03											
Stafford	a	09 29					09 34		10 00		10 09	10 29	10 35					10 22			11 00	
	d	09 30					09 35		10 01		10 09	10 30	10 35					10 23			11 01	
Stoke-on-Trent	a	09 54							10 19			10 54					10 24		10 48		11 19	11 24
Congleton	a																					
Macclesfield	a	10 11										11 11					10 41					11 41
Crewe 10	a						09 56	10 07			10 30		10 56		11 07	10 32						
	d						09 57	10 09			10 31		10 57		11 09	10 43						
Chester	a															11 10						
Wrexham General	a																					
Llandudno	a																					
Bangor (Gwynedd)	a															12 19						
Holyhead	a															12 55						
Wilmslow	a																					
Stockport	a	10 27							10 49			11 27					10 55		11 16		11 49	11 55
Manchester Piccadilly 10	a	10 39							10 59			11 39					11 07		11 28		11 59	12 07
Hartford	a						10 10						11 11									
Warrington Bank Quay	a			10 14				10 26							11 26					11 14		
	d			10 14				10 27							11 27					11 14		
Runcorn	a						10 22				10 50		11 21									
Liverpool South Parkway 7 ✈	a						10 31				10 59		11 30					10 55				
Liverpool Lime Street 10	a						10 44				11 10		11 43					11 15				
	d					09 57																
Manchester Airport ✈	d		09 29							10 00				10 29								
Manchester Piccadilly 10	d		09 46							10 16				10 46								
Bolton	d		10 07							10 33				11 07								
Wigan North Western	a			10 25		10 30		10 37							11 37					11 25		
	d			10 25		10 31		10 38							11 38					11 25		
Preston 8	a		10 33	10 38		10 54		10 51		10 55				11 33	→					11 38		
Preston 8	d		10 38	10 41	10 45	10 55		10 53		10 58				11 38						11 41		
Blackpool North	a		11 05			11 21								12 05								
Lancaster 6	a			10 54	11 00			11 08		11 13										11 54		
	d			10 55	11 01			11 08		11 14										11 55		
Barrow-in-Furness	a																					
Oxenholme Lake District	a			11 08	11 17					11 28												
	d			11 08	11 18					11 28												
Windermere	a				11 39																	
Penrith North Lakes	d							11 45		11 53										12 30		
Carlisle 8	a			11 46				12 00		12 10										12 46		
	d			11 47				12 03		12 11										12 47		
Lockerbie	d									12 30												
Carstairs	a																					
Motherwell	a																					
Glasgow Central 15	a			13 01				13 17												14 01		
Haymarket	a									13s33												
Edinburgh 10	a									13 39												
Perth	a																					
Dundee	a																					
Aberdeen	a																					
Inverness	a																					

OVERNIGHT SLEEPERS. For sleeper trains, operated by First ScotRail, please refer to Tables 400 - 404

Table 65

Saturdays

7 July to 8 September

London and West Midlands - North West England and Scotland

Route Diagram - see first Page of Table 65

		NT	VT	TP	LM	VT	VT	VT	XC	TP	VT	TP	NT	LM	VT	XC	VT	TP	LM	VT
			◇1	◇1	◇1	◇1	◇1	◇1	◇1	◇1	◇1	◇1		◇1	◇1	◇1	◇1	◇1	◇1	◇1
				A																
			ℙ	⊼		ℙ	ℙ	ℙ	⊼	⊼	ℙ				ℙ	ℙ	ℙ	⊼		ℙ
London Euston 15 ⊖	d					10 07	10 10	10 20			10 30						11 00			11 07
Watford Junction	d																			
Milton Keynes Central	d						10 41	10 50												
Rugby	d																			
Nuneaton	d																			
Tamworth Low Level	d																			
Lichfield Trent Valley	d																			
Coventry	d								10 27											
Birmingham International ✈	d								10 38											
Birmingham New Street 12	d				10 36				10 57					11 01	11 20	11 31			11 36	
Wolverhampton 7	d				10 53				11 15					11 19	11 37	11 49			11 53	
Penkridge	d				11 03														12 03	
Stafford	a				11 09	11 22			11 29					11 35		12 00			12 09	12 22
	d				11 09	11 23			11 30					11 35		12 01			12 09	12 23
Stoke-on-Trent	a							11 48	11 54							12 19	12 24			
Congleton	a																			
Macclesfield	a								12 11								12 41			
Crewe 10	a				11 30		11 47							11 56	12 07				12 30	
	d				11 31		11 49							11 57	12 09				12 31	
Chester	a						12 12													
Wrexham General	a																			
Llandudno	a																			
Bangor (Gwynedd)	a																			
Holyhead	a																			
Wilmslow	a																			
Stockport	a							12 16	12 27							12 49	12 55			
Manchester Piccadilly 10	a							12 28	12 39							12 59	13 07			
Hartford	a													12 10						
Warrington Bank Quay	a										12 14				12 26					
	d										12 14				12 27					
Runcorn	a				11 50	11 55								12 22					12 50	12 55
Liverpool South Parkway 7 ✈	a				11 59									12 31					12 59	
Liverpool Lime Street 10	a				12 10	12 15								12 44					13 10	13 15
	d	10 57											11 57							
Manchester Airport ✈	d			11 00						11 29								12 00		
Manchester Piccadilly 10	d			11 16						11 46								12 16		
Bolton	d		←	11 33						12 07								12 33		
Wigan North Western	a	11 30	11 37								12 25		12 30		12 37					
	d	11 31	11 38								12 25		12 31		12 38					
Preston 8	a	11 54	11 51	11 55						12 33	12 38		12 54		12 51			12 55		
Preston 8	d	11 55	11 53	11 58						12 38	12 41	12 48	12 55		12 53			12 58		
Blackpool North	a	12 21								13 05		13 12	13 21							
Lancaster 6	a		12 08	12 13							12 54				13 08			13 13		
	d		12 08	12 14							12 55				13 08			13 14		
Barrow-in-Furness	a			13 11																
Oxenholme Lake District	a		12 22								13 08				13 22			13 28		
	d		12 24								13 08				13 24			13 28		
Windermere	a																			
Penrith North Lakes	d																	13 53		
Carlisle 8	a		13 01								13 46				14 01			14 10		
	d		13 03								13 47				14 03			14 11		
Lockerbie	d																	14 30		
Carstairs	a																			
Motherwell	a																			
Glasgow Central 15	a										15 01				15 17					
Haymarket	a		14 15															15s30		
Edinburgh 10	a		14 22															15 39		
Perth	a																			
Dundee	a																			
Aberdeen	a																			
Inverness	a																			

A ⊼ to Preston

OVERNIGHT SLEEPERS. For sleeper trains, operated by First ScotRail, please refer to Tables 400 - 404

Table 65

Saturdays

7 July to 8 September

London and West Midlands - North West England and Scotland

Route Diagram - see first Page of Table 65

		VT	VT	XC	TP	TP	VT	NT	LM	VT		XC	VT	TP		LM	VT	VT	VT	XC		TP	TP	VT	NT
		◇1	◇1	◇1	◇1	◇1	◇1		◇1	◇1		◇1	◇1	◇1		◇1	◇1	◇1	◇1	◇1		◇1	◇1	◇1	
																						A			
		☕	☕	🛒		🛒	☕			☕		☕	☕	🛒			☕	☕	☕	🛒		🛒	🛒	☕	
London Euston 15 ⊖	d	11 10	11 20				11 30						12 00				12 07	12 10	12 20					12 30	
Watford Junction	d																								
Milton Keynes Central	d	11 41	11 50															12 41	12 50						
Rugby	d																								
Nuneaton	d																								
Tamworth Low Level	d																								
Lichfield Trent Valley	d																								
Coventry	d			11 27																12 27					
Birmingham International ✈	d			11 38																12 38					
Birmingham New Street 12	d			11 57					12 01	12 20		12 31				12 36				12 57					
Wolverhampton 7 🚌	d			12 15					12 19	12 37		12 49				12 53				13 15					
Penkridge	d															13 03									
Stafford	a			12 29					12 35			13 00				13 09	13 22			13 29					
	d			12 30					12 35			13 01				13 09	13 23			13 30					
Stoke-on-Trent	a		12 48	12 54								13 18	13 24						13 48	13 54					
Congleton	a																								
Macclesfield	a			13 11									13 41							14 11					
Crewe 10	a	12 47							12 56	13 07						13 30		13 47							
	d	12 49							12 57	13 09						13 31		13 49							
Chester	a	13 12																14 12							
Wrexham General	a																								
Llandudno	a																								
Bangor (Gwynedd)	a																								
Holyhead	a																								
Wilmslow	a																								
Stockport	a		13 16	13 27								13 49	13 55						14 16	14 27					
Manchester Piccadilly 10 🚌	a		13 28	13 39								13 59	14 07						14 28	14 39					
Hartford	a								13 11																
Warrington Bank Quay	a						13 14			13 26														14 14	
	d						13 14			13 27														14 14	
Runcorn	a								13 21							13 50	13 55								
Liverpool South Parkway 7 ✈	a								13 30							13 59									
Liverpool Lime Street 10	a								13 43							14 10	14 15								
	d							12 57																	13 57
Manchester Airport ✈	d					12 29								13 00									13 29		
Manchester Piccadilly 10 🚌	d					12 46								13 16									13 46		
Bolton	d					13 07								13 33									14 07		
Wigan North Western	a						13 25	13 30		13 37														14 25	14 30
	d						13 25	13 31		13 38														14 25	14 31
Preston 8	a					13 33	13 38	13 54		13 51				13 55									14 33	14 38	14 54
Preston 8	d				13 04	13 38	13 41	13 55		13 53				13 58								13 58	14 38	14 41	14 55
Blackpool North	a					14 05		14 21															15 05		15 21
Lancaster 6	a				13 19		13 54			14 08				14 13								14 13		14 54	
	d				13 20		13 55			14 08				14 14								14 14		14 55	
Barrow-in-Furness	a																								
Oxenholme Lake District	a				13 36		14 08																		
	d				13 37		14 08																		
Windermere	a				13 56																				
Penrith North Lakes	d									14 45														15 30	
Carlisle 8	a						14 46			15 00				15 06								15 06		15 46	
	d						14 47			15 02				15 07								15 07		15 47	
Lockerbie	d													15 27								15 27			
Carstairs	a																								
Motherwell	a																								
Glasgow Central 15	a						16 01							16 30								16 30		17 01	
Haymarket	a									16 16															
Edinburgh 10	a									16 22															
Perth	a																								
Dundee	a																								
Aberdeen	a																								
Inverness	a																								

A from 7 July until 4 August, 8 September

OVERNIGHT SLEEPERS. For sleeper trains, operated by First ScotRail, please refer to Tables 400 - 404

Table 65

Saturdays

7 July to 8 September

London and West Midlands - North West England and Scotland

Route Diagram - see first Page of Table 65

		LM	VT	XC	VT	TP				LM	VT	VT	VT	XC	TP	VT	NT		LM	VT	XC	TP		LM	XC
		◇1	◇1	◇1	◇1	◇1				◇1	◇1	◇1	◇1	◇1	◇1	◇1			◇1	◇1	◇1	◇1		◇1	◇1
																						A			
			🍴	🍴	🍴	🛒					🍴	🍴	🍴	🛒	🛒	🍴				🍴	🍴	🛒			🛒
London Euston 15 ⊖	d				13 00						13 07	13 10	13 20			13 30									
Watford Junction	d																								
Milton Keynes Central	d											13 41	13 50												
Rugby	d																								
Nuneaton	d																								
Tamworth Low Level	d																								
Lichfield Trent Valley	d																								
Coventry	d													13 27											14 27
Birmingham International ✈	d													13 38											14 38
Birmingham New Street 12	d	13 01	13 20	13 31						13 36				13 57					14 01	14 20	14 31			14 36	14 57
Wolverhampton 7	d	13 19	13 37	13 49						13 53				14 15					14 19	14 37	14 49			14 53	15 15
Penkridge	d									14 03														15 03	
Stafford	a	13 35		14 00						14 09	14 22			14 29					14 35		15 00			15 09	15 29
	d	13 35		14 01						14 09	14 23			14 30					14 35		15 01			15 09	15 30
Stoke-on-Trent	a			14 19	14 24								14 48	14 54							15 19				15 54
Congleton	a																								
Macclesfield	a				14 41									15 11											16 11
Crewe 10	a	13 56	14 07							14 30		14 47							14 56	15 07				15 30	
	d	13 57	14 09							14 31		14 49							14 57	15 09				15 31	
Chester	a											15 12													
Wrexham General	a																								
Llandudno	a																								
Bangor (Gwynedd)	a																								
Holyhead	a																								
Wilmslow	a																								
Stockport	a			14 49	14 55								15 16	15 27							15 49				16 27
Manchester Piccadilly 10	a			14 59	15 07								15 28	15 39							15 59				16 39
Hartford	a	14 11																	15 11						
Warrington Bank Quay	a		14 26													15 14				15 26					
	d		14 27													15 14				15 27					
Runcorn	a	14 21								14 50	14 55								15 21					15 50	
Liverpool South Parkway 7 ✈	a	14 30								14 59									15 30					15 59	
Liverpool Lime Street 10	a	14 43								15 10	15 15								15 43					16 10	
	d																14 57								
Manchester Airport ✈	d					14 00									14 29							15 00			
Manchester Piccadilly 10	d					14 16									14 46							15 16			
Bolton	d					14 33									15 07							15 33			
Wigan North Western	a		14 37													15 25	15 30			15 37					
	d		14 38													15 25	15 31			15 38					
Preston 8	a		14 51			14 55									15 33	15 38	15 54			15 51		15 57			
Preston 8	d		14 53			14 58	15 04								15 38	15 41	15 55			15 53		15 58			
Blackpool North	a														16 05		16 21								
Lancaster 6	a		15 08			15 13	15 20									15 54				16 08		16 14			
	d		15 09			15 14	15 20									15 55				16 08		16 15			
Barrow-in-Furness	a						16 15															17 18			
Oxenholme Lake District	a		15 22			15 28										16 08									
	d		15 24			15 28										16 08									
Windermere	a																								
Penrith North Lakes	d					15 53														16 45					
Carlisle 8	a		16 01			16 10										16 46				17 00					
	d		16 03			16 11										16 47				17 03					
Lockerbie	d					16 30																			
Carstairs	a																								
Motherwell	a																								
Glasgow Central 15	a		17 17													18 01									
Haymarket	a					17s31														18 14					
Edinburgh 10	a					17 39														18 22					
Perth	a																								
Dundee	a																								
Aberdeen	a																								
Inverness	a																								

A 🛒 to Preston

OVERNIGHT SLEEPERS. For sleeper trains, operated by First ScotRail, please refer to Tables 400 - 404

Table 65

Saturdays

7 July to 8 September

London and West Midlands - North West England and Scotland

Route Diagram - see first Page of Table 65

		LM	TP		VT	VT	VT	VT	VT	XC	VT	NT	VT		TP			LM	VT	VT	VT	XC	TP		VT
		◇1	◇1		◇1	◇1	◇1	◇1	◇1	◇1	◇1		◇1		◇1			◇1	◇1	◇1	◇1	◇1	◇1		◇1
			🛒		☕	☕	☕	☕	☕	☕	☕		☕		🛒				☕	☕	☕	🛒	🛒		☕
London Euston 15 ⊖	d				13 43	14 00	14 07	14 20	14 30		15 00								15 07	15 10	15 20				15 30
Watford Junction	d																								
Milton Keynes Central	d				14 13			14 50												15 41	15 50				
Rugby	d																								
Nuneaton	d																								
Tamworth Low Level	d																								
Lichfield Trent Valley	d																								
Coventry	d				14 42																	15 27			
Birmingham International ✈	d				14 53																	15 38			
Birmingham New Street 12	d	15 01			15 20					15 31								15 36				15 57			
Wolverhampton 7 ⛴	d	15 19			15 37					15 49								15 53				16 15			
Penkridge	d																	16 03							
Stafford	a	15 35					15 22			16 00								16 09	16 22			16 29			
	d	15 35					15 23			16 01								16 09	16 23			16 30			
Stoke-on-Trent	a					15 24		15 48		16 18	16 24										16 48	16 54			
Congleton	a																								
Macclesfield	a					15 41					16 41											17 11			
Crewe 10	a	15 56			16 08													16 30		16 47					
	d	15 57			16 09													16 31		16 49					
Chester	a																			17 12					
Wrexham General	a																								
Llandudno	a																								
Bangor (Gwynedd)	a																								
Holyhead	a																								
Wilmslow	a																								
Stockport	a					15 55		16 16		16 48	16 54										17 16	17 27			
Manchester Piccadilly 10 ⛴	a					16 07		16 28		16 59	17 07										17 28	17 39			
Hartford	a	16 10																							
Warrington Bank Quay	a				16 26				16 14																17 14
	d				16 27				16 14																17 14
Runcorn	a	16 22					15 55											16 50	16 55						
Liverpool South Parkway 7 ✈	a	16 31																16 59							
Liverpool Lime Street 10	a	16 44					16 15											17 10	17 15						
	d											15 57													
Manchester Airport ✈	d		15 29												16 00								16 29		
Manchester Piccadilly 10 ⛴	d		15 46												16 16								16 46		
Bolton	d		16 07										←		16 33								17 06		
Wigan North Western	a				16 37				16 25			16 30	16 37												17 25
	d				16 38				16 25			16 31	16 38												17 25
Preston 8	a		16 33		→				16 38			16 54	16 51		16 55								17 30		17 38
Preston 8	d		16 38						16 41			16 55	16 53		17 00	17 04							17 32		17 41
Blackpool North	a		17 07									17 21											18 02		
Lancaster 6	a								16 54				17 09		17 16	17 20									17 54
	d								16 55				17 10		17 16	17 21									17 55
Barrow-in-Furness	a																								
Oxenholme Lake District	a												17 24		17 30	17 37									18 08
	d												17 25		17 30	17 38									18 08
Windermere	a															18 00									
Penrith North Lakes	d								17 30																
Carlisle 8	a								17 46				18 03		18 10										18 46
	d								17 47				18 04		18 11										18 47
Lockerbie	d														18 30										
Carstairs	a																								
Motherwell	a																								
Glasgow Central 15	a								19 01				19 17												20 01
Haymarket	a														19s31										
Edinburgh 10	a														19 39										
Perth	a																								
Dundee	a																								
Aberdeen	a																								
Inverness	a																								

OVERNIGHT SLEEPERS. For sleeper trains, operated by First ScotRail, please refer to Tables 400 - 404

London and West Midlands - North West England and Scotland

Route Diagram - see first Page of Table 65

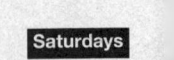

		NT	LM	VT	XC	VT	TP	NT			LM	VT	VT	XC	LM	TP	VT	VT	TP		VT	XC	VT	TP
			◇1	◇1	◇1	◇1	◇1				◇1	◇1	◇1	◇1	◇1	◇1	◇1	◇1	◇1		◇1	◇1	◇1	◇1
																								A
				🍴	🍴	🍴	🛒					🍴	🍴	🛒			🍴	🍴	🛒		🍴	🛒	🍴	🛒
London Euston 15 ⊖	d					16 00						16 07	16 20				16 30	16 33					17 00	
Watford Junction	d																							
Milton Keynes Central	d												16 50											
Rugby	d																							
Nuneaton	d																							
Tamworth Low Level	d																	17 38						
Lichfield Trent Valley	d																	17 45						
Coventry	d													16 27										
Birmingham International ✈	d													16 38										
Birmingham New Street 12	d		16 01	16 20	16 31						16 36			16 57	17 01						17 20	17 31		
Wolverhampton 7 ⛴	d		16 19	16 37	16 49						16 53			17 15	17 19						17 37	17 49		
Penkridge	d										17 03				17 29									
Stafford	a		16 35		17 00						17 09	17 22		17 29	17 35			17 58				18 00		
	d		16 35		17 01						17 09	17 23		17 30	17 36			17 59				18 01		
Stoke-on-Trent	a				17 19	17 24							17 48	17 54								18 19	18 24	
Congleton	a																							
Macclesfield	a					17 41								18 11									18 41	
Crewe 10	a		16 56	17 07							17 30				17 56						18 07			
	d		16 57	17 09							17 31				17 57						18 09			
Chester	a																							
Wrexham General	a																							
Llandudno	a																							
Bangor (Gwynedd)	a																							
Holyhead	a																							
Wilmslow	a																							
Stockport	a				17 49	17 55							18 16	18 27								18 49	18 55	
Manchester Piccadilly 10 ⛴	a				17 59	18 07							18 28	18 39								18 59	19 07	
Hartford	a		17 11												18 11									
Warrington Bank Quay	a			17 26													18 14				18 26			
	d			17 27													18 14				18 27			
Runcorn	a		17 21								17 50	17 55			18 21			18 31						
Liverpool South Parkway 7 ✈	a		17 30								17 59				18 30									
Liverpool Lime Street 10	a		17 43								18 10	18 15			18 43			18 52						
	d	16 57						17 19																
Manchester Airport ✈	d						17 00												17 29					18 00
Manchester Piccadilly 10 ⛴	d						17 15												17 46					18 16
Bolton	d						17 32												18 07					18 33
Wigan North Western	a	17 30		17 37				18 04									18 25				18 37			
	d	17 31		17 38													18 25				18 38			
Preston 8	a	17 54		17 51			17 55										18 38		18 38		18 51			18 55
Preston 8	d	17 55		17 53			17 58									18 02	18 41		18 40		18 53			18 58
Blackpool North	a	18 24																	19 10					
Lancaster 6	a			18 08			18 13									18 18	18 54				19 08			19 13
	d			18 08			18 14									18 18	18 55				19 08			19 15
Barrow-in-Furness	a															19 26								20 19
Oxenholme Lake District	a			18 22			18 28										19 08				19 22			
	d			18 23			18 28										19 08				19 24			
Windermere	a																							
Penrith North Lakes	d			18 49			18 53										19 34							
Carlisle 8	a			19 04			19 09										19 49				20 01			
	d			19 04			19 11										19 51				20 03			
Lockerbie	d						19 30																	
Carstairs	a																							
Motherwell	a						20s16																	
Glasgow Central 15	a						20 33										21 01				21 17			
Haymarket	a			20 16																				
Edinburgh 10	a			20 22																				
Perth	a																							
Dundee	a																							
Aberdeen	a																							
Inverness	a																							

A 🛒 to Preston

OVERNIGHT SLEEPERS. For sleeper trains, operated by First ScotRail, please refer to Tables 400 - 404

Table 65

Saturdays

7 July to 8 September

London and West Midlands - North West England and Scotland

Route Diagram - see first Page of Table 65

		LM	VT	VT	XC		LM	TP	VT	VT	XC	LM	XC	TP			NT	LM	TP	VT	VT	VT	VT	VT	VT
		◇1	◇1	◇1	◇1		◇1	◇1	◇1	◇1	◇1	◇1	◇1	◇1				◇1	◇1	◇1	◇1	◇1	◇1	◇1	◇1
			⊡	⊡	ᴥ			ᴥ	⊡	⊡	⊡		ᴥ							⊡	⊡	⊡	⊡	⊡	⊡
London Euston 15 ⊖	d		17 07	17 20					17 30											17 43	18 00	18 07	18 10	18 20	18 30
Watford Junction	d																								
Milton Keynes Central	d			17 50																18 13			18 41	18 50	
Rugby	d																								
Nuneaton	d		18 03																						
Tamworth Low Level	d																								
Lichfield Trent Valley	d																								
Coventry	d				17 27								18 27							18 42					
Birmingham International ✈	d				17 38								18 38							18 53					
Birmingham New Street 12	d	17 36			17 57		18 01			18 20	18 31	18 36	18 57					19 01		19 20					
Wolverhampton 7 🚊	d	17 53			18 15		18 19			18 37	18 49	18 53	19 15					19 19		19 37					
Penkridge	d	18 03					18 29					19 03						19 29							
Stafford	a	18 09	18 26		18 29		18 35				19 00	19 09	19 29					19 35				19 22			
	d	18 09	18 27		18 30		18 35				19 01	19 09	19 30					19 36				19 23			
Stoke-on-Trent	a			18 48	18 54						19 19		19 54								19 24			19 48	
Congleton	a																								
Macclesfield	a				19 11								20 11								19 41				
Crewe 10	a	18 30					18 56			19 07		19 30						19 58		20 07			19 47		
	d	18 33					18 59			19 09								19 58		20 09			19 49		
Chester	a																						20 12		
Wrexham General	a																								
Llandudno	a																								
Bangor (Gwynedd)	a																								
Holyhead	a																								
Wilmslow	a																								
Stockport	a			19 16	19 27						19 49		20 27								19 55			20 16	
Manchester Piccadilly 10 🚊	a			19 28	19 39						19 59		20 39								20 07			20 28	
Hartford	a	18 43					19 12											20 11							
Warrington Bank Quay	a								19 14	19 26										20 26					20 14
	d								19 14	19 27										20 27					20 14
Runcorn	a	18 52	18 59				19 22											20 24				19 55			
Liverpool South Parkway 7 ✈	a	19 02					19 31											20 33							
Liverpool Lime Street 10	a	19 14	19 17				19 44											20 46				20 15			
	d																19 23								
Manchester Airport ✈	d							18 29						19 00					19 29						
Manchester Piccadilly 10 🚊	d							18 46						19 16					19 46						
Bolton	d							19 07						19 33					20 07						
Wigan North Western	a								19 25	19 37							19 54			20 37					20 25
	d								19 25	19 38							19 55			20 38					20 25
Preston 8	a							19 33	19 38	19 54				19 58			20 18		20 33	↪					20 38
Preston 8	d							19 38	19 41					20 01			20 19		20 38						20 41
Blackpool North	a							20 06									20 44		21 06						
Lancaster 6	a								19 54					20 17											20 54
	d								19 55					20 17											20 55
Barrow-in-Furness	a													21 20											
Oxenholme Lake District	a								20 08																21 08
	d								20 08																21 08
Windermere	a																								
Penrith North Lakes	d								20 34																21 34
Carlisle 8	a								20 49																21 49
	d								20 51																21 51
Lockerbie	d																								
Carstairs	a																								
Motherwell	a																								22 44
Glasgow Central 15	a								22 01																23 04
Haymarket	a																								
Edinburgh 10	a																								
Perth	a																								
Dundee	a																								
Aberdeen	a																								
Inverness	a																								

OVERNIGHT SLEEPERS. For sleeper trains, operated by First ScotRail, please refer to Tables 400 - 404

London and West Midlands - North West England and Scotland

Route Diagram - see first Page of Table 65

		VT	TP	NT	VT	XC	VT	VT	VT	XC	TP	VT	LM	VT	XC	LM	XC	VT	VT	LM
		◇1	◇1		◇1	◇1	◇1	◇1	◇1	◇1	◇1	◇1	◇1	◇1	◇1	◇1	◇1	◇1	◇1	◇1
										A										
		☕			☕	☕	☕	☕	☕	🛒		☕		☕	☕		🛒	☕	☕	
London Euston 15 ⊖	d				18 33		19 00	19 07	19 20			19 30						20 11	20 20	
Watford Junction	d																			
Milton Keynes Central	d								19 50										21 05	
Rugby	d																	21 15		
Nuneaton	d							20 03											21 33	
Tamworth Low Level	d				19 38															
Lichfield Trent Valley	d				19 45															
Coventry	d									19 27										
Birmingham International ✈	d									19 38										
Birmingham New Street 12	d					19 31				19 57			20 01	20 20	20 31	20 36	20 57			21 36
Wolverhampton 7	d					19 49				20 15			20 22	20 37	20 49	20 53	21 15			21 59
Penkridge	d												20 31			21 03				22 09
Stafford	a				19 58	20 00		20 26		20 29			20 37	20 49	21 00	21 09	21 29	21 46		22 15
	d				19 59	20 01		20 27		20 30			20 38	20 50	21 01	21 09	21 30	21 46		22 16
Stoke-on-Trent	a					20 19	20 24		20 48	20 54					21 20		21 52		22 05	
Congleton	a																			
Macclesfield	a					20 36	20 41			21 11					21 38		22 10		22 21	
Crewe 10	a							20 45				21 04	20 58	21 10		21 30		22 05		22 40
	d							20 47				21 05	21 06					22 06		
Chester	a																			
Wrexham General	a																			
Llandudno	a																			
Bangor (Gwynedd)	a																			
Holyhead	a																			
Wilmslow	a																			
Stockport	a					20 49	20 55		21 16	21 27					21 53		22 26		22 35	
Manchester Piccadilly 10	a					20 59	21 07		21 28	21 39					22 04		22 39		22 51	
Hartford	a												21 19							
Warrington Bank Quay	a											21 22								
	d											21 22								
Runcorn	a				20 31			21 05					21 29					22 24		
Liverpool South Parkway 7 ✈	a												21 38							
Liverpool Lime Street 10	a				20 52			21 25					21 50					22 46		
	d			20 25																
Manchester Airport ✈	d		20 00								20 29									
Manchester Piccadilly 10	d		20 16								20 46									
Bolton	d	←	20 33								21 07									
Wigan North Western	a	20 37		20 57								21 33								
	d	20 38		20 57								21 33								
Preston 8	a	20 59	20 57	21 22							21 33	21 49								
Preston 8	d		21 02	21 24							21 38									
Blackpool North	a			21 53							22 06									
Lancaster 6	a		21 17																	
	d		21 18																	
Barrow-in-Furness	a		22 21																	
Oxenholme Lake District	a																			
	d																			
Windermere	a																			
Penrith North Lakes	d																			
Carlisle 8	a																			
	d																			
Lockerbie	d																			
Carstairs	a																			
Motherwell	a																			
Glasgow Central 15	a																			
Haymarket	a																			
Edinburgh 10	a																			
Perth	a																			
Dundee	a																			
Aberdeen	a																			
Inverness	a																			

A 🛒 to Birmingham New Street

OVERNIGHT SLEEPERS. For sleeper trains, operated by First ScotRail, please refer to Tables 400 - 404

Saturdays

7 July to 8 September

London and West Midlands - North West England and Scotland

Route Diagram - see first Page of Table 65

		XC	NT	TP	TP	VT	TP	XC	VT	LM	VT	VT
		◇1		◇1	◇1	◇1	◇1	◇1	◇1	◇1	◇1	◇1
									A		A	A
						[trolley]			[trolley]		[trolley]	[trolley]
London Euston 15 ⊖	d					20 31			22 30		23 30	23 45
Watford Junction	d					20u46						
Milton Keynes Central	d											
Rugby	d					21 36						00s42
Nuneaton	d											00s52
Tamworth Low Level	d					21 53						
Lichfield Trent Valley	d					22 00						
Coventry	d	21 27										
Birmingham International ✈	d	21 38										
Birmingham New Street 12	d	21 57						22 31		22 36		
Wolverhampton 7 ⛴	d	22 16						22 49		22 56		
Penkridge	d									23 06		
Stafford	a	22 29						23 01		23 13		01s17
	d	22 30						23 02		23 13		
Stoke-on-Trent	a	22 50						23 20	23s53		00s53	
Congleton	a											
Macclesfield	a	23 07						23 38	00s10		01s10	
Crewe 10	a					22 35				23 37		01s35
	d					22 37						
Chester	a											
Wrexham General	a											
Llandudno	a											
Bangor (Gwynedd)	a											
Holyhead	a											
Wilmslow	a											
Stockport	a	23 21						23 53	00s24		01s24	
Manchester Piccadilly 10 ⛴	a	23 32						00 10	00 37		01 37	
Hartford	a											
Warrington Bank Quay	a					22 53						
	d					22 54						
Runcorn	a											01s54
Liverpool South Parkway 7 ✈	a											
Liverpool Lime Street 10	a											02 16
	d											
Manchester Airport ✈	d			21 29	22 00		22 29					
Manchester Piccadilly 10 ⛴	d			21 46	22 16		22 46					
Bolton	d			22 07	22 33		23 07					
Wigan North Western	a					23 04						
	d					23 05						
Preston 8	a			22 36	22 54	23 19	23 33					
Preston 8	d		21 59	22 38	22 55		23 35					
Blackpool North	a			23 04			00 02					
Lancaster 6	a		22 19		23 11							
	d		22 19		23 11							
Barrow-in-Furness	a		23 24		00 15							
Oxenholme Lake District	a											
	d											
Windermere	a											
Penrith North Lakes	d											
Carlisle 8	a											
	d											
Lockerbie	d											
Carstairs	a											
Motherwell	a											
Glasgow Central 15	a											
Haymarket	a											
Edinburgh 10	a											
Perth	a											
Dundee	a											
Aberdeen	a											
Inverness	a											

A 28 July, 4 August, 11 August, 1 September, 8 September

OVERNIGHT SLEEPERS. For sleeper trains, operated by First ScotRail, please refer to Tables 400 - 404

London and West Midlands - North West England and Scotland

Route Diagram - see first Page of Table 65

		VT	TP	TP	XC	TP	SR	VT	LM		SR	TP	NT	TP	TP	LM	XC	VT		TP	LM	TP	NT
		R					R				R												
		1	◇1	◇1	◇1	◇1		◇1	◇1			◇1		◇1	◇1	1	◇1	◇1		◇1	1	◇1	
							A																
London Euston 15 ⊖	d	19p30					21p15	22p00			23p50												
Watford Junction	d						21b33				00u10												
Milton Keynes Central	d							22p31															
Rugby	d							22p54															
Nuneaton	d							23p04															
Tamworth Low Level	d							23c15															
Lichfield Trent Valley	d							23c22															
Coventry	d																						
Birmingham International ✈	d																						
Birmingham New Street 12	d				22p30				23p09								05 57						
Wolverhampton 7	d				22p48				23p36								06 16						
Penkridge	d								23p46														
Stafford	a				23p00			23c38	23p52								06 29						
	d				23p01				23p53								06 30						
Stoke-on-Trent	a				23p20												06 50						
Congleton	a																07 02						
Macclesfield	a																07 11						
Crewe 10	a							00s03	00 16														
	d						23b54						00 44			05 48		05 57			06 12		
Chester	a																						
Wrexham General	a																						
Llandudno	a																						
Bangor (Gwynedd)	a																						
Holyhead	a																						
Wilmslow	a																						
Stockport	a							00s26									07 27						
Manchester Piccadilly 10	a				00 12			00 35									07 38						
Hartford	a																						
Warrington Bank Quay	a	21p15																06 13					
	d	21p15																06 14					
Runcorn	a															06 07					06 31		
Liverpool South Parkway 7 ✈	a															06 15					06 39		
Liverpool Lime Street 10	a															06 26					06 53		
	d																						
Manchester Airport ✈	d		22p00	22p29								00 01	01 20	04 00						05 45		06 18	
Manchester Piccadilly 10	d		22p16	22p46								00 16	01a36	04 15	05 43					06 03		06 33	
Bolton	d		22p33	23p07								00s31		04s29	05 59					06 19		06 50	07 01
Wigan North Western	a	21p26	22p48															06 24					07 19
	d	21p26	22p51															06 25					
Preston 8	a	21p39	23p09	23p33								01s05		05s04	06 26			06 37		06 42		07 11	
Preston 8	d	21p41	23p13	23p35		23p51	00u52								06 37			06 40		06 44		07 14	
Blackpool North	a			00 02		00 16						01 30		05 33	07 06								
Lancaster 6	a	21p55	23p28															06 54		06 59		07 30	
	d	21p56	23p29															06 54		07 00		07 30	
Barrow-in-Furness	a		00 31																				
Oxenholme Lake District	a	22p09																07 08		07 15			
	d	22p09																07 10		07 15			
Windermere	a																						
Penrith North Lakes	d	22p35																07 35				08 07	
Carlisle 8	a	22p50									05s15							07 50		07 55		08 24	
	d	22p51																07 51		07 56		08 25	
Lockerbie	d																	08 10		08 16			
Carstairs	a										06s20												
Motherwell	a										06s56												
Glasgow Central 15	a	00 06									07 20							09 13				09 45	
Haymarket	a																			09s17			
Edinburgh 10	a										07 15									09 22			
Perth	a						05s39																
Dundee	a						06s08																
Aberdeen	a						07 36																
Inverness	a						08 38																

A Conveys a portion from Fort William, arrives at 0954

b Previous night, stops to pick up only

c Previous night, stops to set down only

OVERNIGHT SLEEPERS. For sleeper trains, operated by First ScotRail, please refer to Tables 400 - 404

Table 65

Saturdays

15 September to 20 October

London and West Midlands - North West England and Scotland

Route Diagram - see first Page of Table 65

		TP	NT	LM	LM	VT		XC	TP		LM	TP	VT	LM	NT	NT		VT	XC	VT	TP		LM	VT	VT
		◇1		◇1	◇1	◇1		◇1	◇1		◇1	◇1	◇1	◇1				◇1	◇1	◇1	◇1		◇1	◇1	◇1
						⊐		ꝏ	ꝏ			ꝏ	⊐					⊐	ꝏ	⊐	ꝏ			⊐	⊐
London Euston 15 ⊖	d												06 05							06 55				07 07	07 20
Watford Junction	d												06u20												
Milton Keynes Central	d												06 41							07 27					07 50
Rugby	d												07 03												
Nuneaton	d																								
Tamworth Low Level	d																								
Lichfield Trent Valley	d																								
Coventry	d																								
Birmingham International ✈	d																								
Birmingham New Street 12	d				06 01	06 20		06 31			06 36			07 01				07 20	07 31				07 36		
Wolverhampton 7 ⛴	d				06 18	06 37		06 49			06 54			07 18				07 37	07 49				07 53		
Penkridge	d				06 29									07 30									08 03		
Stafford	a				06 35			07 00			07 08		07 33	07 36					08 00				08 09	08 22	
	d				06 36			07 01			07 08		07 34	07 38					08 01				08 09	08 23	
Stoke-on-Trent	a							07 18											08 19	08 24					08 48
Congleton	a																								
Macclesfield	a							07 36											08 36	08 41					
Crewe 10	a				06 56	07 07					07 33		07 53	07 58				08 07					08 30	08 41	
	d			06 32	06 57	07 09					07 35		07 55	08 00				08 09					08 31	08 43	
Chester	a																								
Wrexham General	a																								
Llandudno	a																								
Bangor (Gwynedd)	a																								
Holyhead	a																								
Wilmslow	a																								
Stockport	a							07 49											08 49	08 55					09 16
Manchester Piccadilly 10 ⛴	a							07 59											08 59	09 07					09 28
Hartford	a			06 46	07 10						07 48			08 11											
Warrington Bank Quay	a					07 26							08 11					08 27							
	d					07 27							08 12					08 27							
Runcorn	a			06 59	07 20						08 02			08 24									08 50	09 00	
Liverpool South Parkway 7 ✈	a			07 08	07 30						08 11			08 33									08 59		
Liverpool Lime Street 10	a			07 22	07 42						08 24			08 46									09 12	09 21	
	d		06 57																						
Manchester Airport ✈	d								07 00			07 25									07 56				
Manchester Piccadilly 10 ⛴	d								07 15			07 45									08 15				
Bolton	d								07 31			07 59									08 32				
Wigan North Western	a		07 30			07 37							08 22					08 38							
	d		07 31			07 38							08 23			08 30		08 38							
Preston 8	a		07 54			07 51			07 57			08 22	08 36			08 54		08 51			08 58				
Preston 8	d	07 20	07 55			07 53			07 59			08 24	08 37		08 42	08 55		08 53			08 59				
Blackpool North	a		08 21						08 29							09 21					09 25				
Lancaster 6	a	07 36				08 08						08 39	08 52		09 02			09 08							
	d	07 36				08 08						08 40	08 52		09 03			09 08							
Barrow-in-Furness	a	08 39													10 07										
Oxenholme Lake District	a					08 21							09 05												
	d					08 22							09 06												
Windermere	a																								
Penrith North Lakes	d												09 32					09 45							
Carlisle 8	a					09 00						09 30	09 47		12 39			10 02							
	d					09 02						09 30	09 48					10 04							
Lockerbie	d											09 50													
Carstairs	a																								
Motherwell	a																								
Glasgow Central 15	a												11 03					11 17							
Haymarket	a					10 16						10s48													
Edinburgh 10	a					10 22						10 56													
Perth	a																								
Dundee	a																								
Aberdeen	a																								
Inverness	a																								

OVERNIGHT SLEEPERS. For sleeper trains, operated by First ScotRail, please refer to Tables 400 - 404

Table 65

Saturdays

15 September to 20 October

London and West Midlands - North West England and Scotland

Route Diagram - see first Page of Table 65

		XC		TP	VT	TP	NT	LM	VT	XC	VT	TP				LM	VT	VT	VT	XC	TP	VT	TP		NT
		◇1		◇1	◇1	◇1		◇1	◇1	◇1	◇1	◇1				◇1	◇1	◇1	◇1	◇1	◇1	◇1	◇1		
				A								A													
		🛒		🛒	□P				□P	□P	□P	🛒					□P	□P	□P	🛒	🛒	□P			
London Euston 15 ⊖	d				07 30						08 00						08 07	08 10	08 20			08 30			
Watford Junction	d																								
Milton Keynes Central	d																	08 41	08 50						
Rugby	d																								
Nuneaton	d																								
Tamworth Low Level	d																								
Lichfield Trent Valley	d																								
Coventry	d	07 27																		08 27					
Birmingham International ✈	d	07 38																		08 38					
Birmingham New Street 12	d	07 57						08 01	08 20	08 31						08 36				08 57					
Wolverhampton 7 ⛴	d	08 15						08 19	08 37	08 49						08 53				09 15					
Penkridge	d							08 29								09 03									
Stafford	a	08 29						08 35		09 00						09 09	09 22			09 29					
	d	08 30						08 36		09 01						09 09	09 23			09 30					
Stoke-on-Trent	a	08 54								09 19	09 24								09 48	09 54					
Congleton	a																								
Macclesfield	a	09 11									09 41									10 11					
Crewe 10	a							08 56	09 07							09 30		09 47							
	d							08 57	09 09							09 31		09 49							
Chester	a																	10 12							
Wrexham General	a																								
Llandudno	a																								
Bangor (Gwynedd)	a																								
Holyhead	a																								
Wilmslow	a																								
Stockport	a	09 27								09 49	09 55								10 16	10 27					
Manchester Piccadilly 10 ⛴	a	09 39								09 59	10 07								10 28	10 39					
Hartford	a							09 11																	
Warrington Bank Quay	a				09 14				09 26													10 14			
	d				09 14				09 27													10 14			
Runcorn	a							09 21								09 50	09 55								
Liverpool South Parkway 7 ✈	a							09 30								09 59									
Liverpool Lime Street 10	a							09 43								10 10	10 15								
	d						08 57																		09 57
Manchester Airport ✈	d			08 25								09 00									09 29				
Manchester Piccadilly 10 ⛴	d			08 46								09 16									09 46				
Bolton	d			09 07								09 33									10 07				
Wigan North Western	a				09 25		09 30		09 37													10 25			10 30
	d				09 25		09 31		09 38													10 25			10 31
Preston 8	a			09 30	09 38		09 54		09 51			09 55									10 33	10 38			10 54
Preston 8	d			09 32	09 41	09 45	09 55		09 53			10 08	09 58								10 38	10 41	10 45		10 55
Blackpool North	a						10 21					10 35									11 05				11 21
Lancaster 6	a			09 47	09 54	10 00			10 08				10 13									10 54	11 00		
	d			09 48	09 55	10 01			10 08				10 14									10 55	11 01		
Barrow-in-Furness	a					11 04																			
Oxenholme Lake District	a			10 04					10 22													11 08	11 17		
	d			10 05					10 24													11 08	11 18		
Windermere	a			10 26																			11 39		
Penrith North Lakes	d				10 30								10 53												
Carlisle 8	a				10 46				11 01				11 10									11 46			
	d				10 47				11 03				11 11									11 47			
Lockerbie	d												11 30												
Carstairs	a																								
Motherwell	a																								
Glasgow Central 15	a				12 01								12 32									13 01			
Haymarket	a								12 16																
Edinburgh 10	a								12 22																
Perth	a																								
Dundee	a																								
Aberdeen	a																								
Inverness	a																								

A 🛒 to Preston

OVERNIGHT SLEEPERS. For sleeper trains, operated by First ScotRail, please refer to Tables 400 - 404

Table 65

Saturdays

15 September to 20 October

London and West Midlands - North West England and Scotland

Route Diagram - see first Page of Table 65

		LM	VT	XC	TP	LM	VT	VT	VT	VT	XC	TP	VT	NT	LM	VT	XC	VT	TP	LM	VT
		◇1	◇1	◇1	◇1	◇1	◇1	◇1	◇1	◇1	◇1	◇1	◇1		◇1	◇1	◇1	◇1	◇1	◇1	◇1
																			A		
			🍽	🍽	🛒		🍽	🍽	🍽	🍽	🛒	🛒	🍽			🍽	🍽	🍽	🛒		🍽
London Euston 15 ⊖	d						08 50	09 00	09 07	09 20			09 30					10 00			10 07
Watford Junction	d						09 05														
Milton Keynes Central	d						09 25			09 50											
Rugby	d																				
Nuneaton	d																				
Tamworth Low Level	d																				
Lichfield Trent Valley	d																				
Coventry	d										09 27										
Birmingham International ✈	d										09 38										
Birmingham New Street 12	d	09 01	09 20	09 31		09 36					09 57				10 01	10 20	10 31			10 36	
Wolverhampton 7 🚌	d	09 19	09 37	09 49		09 53					10 15				10 19	10 37	10 49			10 53	
Penkridge	d					10 03														11 03	
Stafford	a	09 34		10 00		10 09			10 22		10 29				10 35		11 00			11 09	11 22
	d	09 35		10 01		10 09			10 23		10 30				10 35		11 01			11 09	11 23
Stoke-on-Trent	a			10 19				10 24		10 48	10 54						11 19	11 24			
Congleton	a																				
Macclesfield	a							10 41			11 11							11 41			
Crewe 10	a	09 56	10 07			10 30	10 32								10 56	11 07				11 30	
	d	09 57	10 09			10 31	10 43								10 57	11 09				11 31	
Chester	a						11 10														
Wrexham General	a																				
Llandudno	a																				
Bangor (Gwynedd)	a						12 19														
Holyhead	a						12 55														
Wilmslow	a																				
Stockport	a			10 49				10 55		11 16	11 27						11 49	11 55			
Manchester Piccadilly 10 🚌	a			10 59				11 07		11 28	11 39						11 59	12 07			
Hartford	a	10 10													11 11						
Warrington Bank Quay	a		10 26										11 14			11 26					
	d		10 27										11 14			11 27					
Runcorn	a	10 22				10 50			10 55						11 21					11 50	11 55
Liverpool South Parkway 7 ✈	a	10 31				10 59									11 30					11 59	
Liverpool Lime Street 10	a	10 44				11 10			11 15						11 43					12 10	12 15
	d													10 57							
Manchester Airport ✈	d				10 00							10 29							11 00		
Manchester Piccadilly 10 🚌	d				10 16							10 46							11 16		
Bolton	d				10 33							11 07							11 33		
Wigan North Western	a		10 37										11 25	11 30		11 37					
	d		10 38										11 25	11 31		11 38					
Preston 8	a		10 51		10 55							11 33	11 38	11 54		11 51			11 55		
Preston 8	d		10 53		10 58							11 38	11 41	11 55		11 53			11 58		
Blackpool North	a											12 05		12 21							
Lancaster 6	a		11 08		11 13								11 54			12 08			12 13		
	d		11 08		11 14								11 55			12 08			12 14		
Barrow-in-Furness	a																		13 11		
Oxenholme Lake District	a				11 28											12 22					
	d				11 28											12 24					
Windermere	a																				
Penrith North Lakes	d		11 45		11 53								12 30								
Carlisle 8	a		12 00		12 10								12 46			13 01					
	d		12 03		12 11								12 47			13 03					
Lockerbie	d				12 30																
Carstairs	a																				
Motherwell	a																				
Glasgow Central 15	a		13 17										14 01								
Haymarket	a				13s33											14 15					
Edinburgh 10	a				13 39											14 22					
Perth	a																				
Dundee	a																				
Aberdeen	a																				
Inverness	a																				

A 🛒 to Preston

OVERNIGHT SLEEPERS. For sleeper trains, operated by First ScotRail, please refer to Tables 400 - 404

Table 65

Saturdays

15 September to 20 October

London and West Midlands - North West England and Scotland

Route Diagram - see first Page of Table 65

		VT	VT	XC	TP		VT	NT	LM	VT	XC	VT	TP		LM		VT	VT	VT	XC	TP	TP	VT	NT	LM
		◇1	◇1	◇1	◇1		◇1		◇1	◇1	◇1	◇1	◇1		◇1		◇1	◇1	◇1	◇1	◇1	◇1	◇1		◇1
		🍽	🍽	🛒	🛒		🍽			🍽	🍽	🍽	🛒				🍽	🍽	🍽	🛒		🛒	🍽		
London Euston 15 ⊖	d	10 10	10 20				10 30					11 00					11 07	11 10	11 20				11 30		
Watford Junction	d																								
Milton Keynes Central	d	10 41	10 50															11 41	11 50						
Rugby	d																								
Nuneaton	d																								
Tamworth Low Level	d																								
Lichfield Trent Valley	d																								
Coventry	d			10 27																11 27					
Birmingham International ✈	d			10 38																11 38					
Birmingham New Street 12	d			10 57					11 01	11 20	11 31				11 36					11 57					12 01
Wolverhampton 7	d			11 15					11 19	11 37	11 49				11 53					12 15					12 19
Penkridge	d														12 03										
Stafford	a			11 29					11 35		12 00				12 09		12 22			12 29					12 35
	d			11 30					11 35		12 01				12 09		12 23			12 30					12 35
Stoke-on-Trent	a		11 48	11 54							12 19	12 24							12 48	12 54					
Congleton	a																								
Macclesfield	a			12 11								12 41								13 11					
Crewe 10	a	11 47							11 56	12 07					12 30			12 47							12 56
	d	11 49							11 57	12 09					12 31			12 49							12 57
Chester	a	12 12																13 12							
Wrexham General	a																								
Llandudno	a																								
Bangor (Gwynedd)	a																								
Holyhead	a																								
Wilmslow	a																								
Stockport	a		12 16	12 27							12 49	12 55							13 16	13 27					
Manchester Piccadilly 10	a		12 28	12 39							12 59	13 07							13 28	13 39					
Hartford	a								12 10																13 11
Warrington Bank Quay	a						12 14			12 26													13 14		
	d						12 14			12 27													13 14		
Runcorn	a								12 22						12 50		12 55								13 21
Liverpool South Parkway 7 ✈	a								12 31						12 59										13 30
Liverpool Lime Street 10	a								12 44						13 10		13 15								13 43
	d							11 57																12 57	
Manchester Airport ✈	d				11 29								12 00									12 29			
Manchester Piccadilly 10	d				11 46								12 16									12 46			
Bolton	d				12 07								12 33									13 07			
Wigan North Western	a						12 25	12 30		12 37													13 25	13 30	
	d						12 25	12 31		12 38													13 25	13 31	
Preston 8	a				12 33		12 38	12 54		12 51			12 55									13 33	13 38	13 54	
Preston 8	d				12 38		12 41	12 55		12 53			12 58								13 04	13 38	13 41	13 55	
Blackpool North	a				13 05			13 21														14 05		14 21	
Lancaster 6	a						12 54			13 08			13 13								13 19		13 54		
	d						12 55			13 08			13 14								13 20		13 55		
Barrow-in-Furness	a																								
Oxenholme Lake District	a						13 08			13 22			13 28								13 36		14 08		
	d						13 08			13 24			13 28								13 37		14 08		
Windermere	a																				13 56				
Penrith North Lakes	d												13 53												
Carlisle 8	a						13 46			14 01			14 10										14 46		
	d						13 47			14 03			14 11										14 47		
Lockerbie	d												14 30												
Carstairs	a																								
Motherwell	a																								
Glasgow Central 15	a						15 01			15 17													16 01		
Haymarket	a												15s30												
Edinburgh 10	a												15 39												
Perth	a																								
Dundee	a																								
Aberdeen	a																								
Inverness	a																								

OVERNIGHT SLEEPERS. For sleeper trains, operated by First ScotRail, please refer to Tables 400 - 404

Table 65

Saturdays

15 September to 20 October

London and West Midlands - North West England and Scotland

Route Diagram - see first Page of Table 65

		VT	XC	VT	TP	LM	VT	VT	VT	XC	TP	VT	NT	LM	VT	XC	VT	TP		LM
		◇1	◇1	◇1	◇1	◇1	◇1	◇1	◇1	◇1	◇1	◇1		◇1	◇1	◇1	◇1	◇1		◇1
		🛒	🛒	🛒	🍴		🛒	🛒	🛒	🍴	🍴	🛒			🛒	🛒	🛒	🍴		
London Euston 15 ⊖	d			12 00			12 07	12 10	12 20			12 30					13 00			
Watford Junction	d																			
Milton Keynes Central	d							12 41	12 50											
Rugby	d																			
Nuneaton	d																			
Tamworth Low Level	d																			
Lichfield Trent Valley	d																			
Coventry	d									12 27										
Birmingham International ✈	d									12 38										
Birmingham New Street 12	d	12 20	12 31			12 36				12 57				13 01	13 20	13 31				13 36
Wolverhampton 7 🚌	d	12 37	12 49			12 53				13 15				13 19	13 37	13 49				13 53
Penkridge	d					13 03														14 03
Stafford	a		13 00			13 09	13 22			13 29				13 35		14 00				14 09
	d		13 01			13 09	13 23			13 30				13 35		14 01				14 09
Stoke-on-Trent	a		13 18	13 24					13 48	13 54						14 19	14 24			
Congleton	a																			
Macclesfield	a			13 41						14 11							14 41			
Crewe 10	a	13 07				13 30		13 47						13 56	14 07					14 30
	d	13 09				13 31		13 49						13 57	14 09					14 31
Chester	a							14 12												
Wrexham General	a																			
Llandudno	a																			
Bangor (Gwynedd)	a																			
Holyhead	a																			
Wilmslow	a																			
Stockport	a		13 49	13 55					14 16	14 27						14 49	14 55			
Manchester Piccadilly 10 🚌	a		13 59	14 07					14 28	14 39						14 59	15 07			
Hartford	a													14 11						
Warrington Bank Quay	a	13 27										14 14			14 26					
	d	13 27										14 14			14 27					
Runcorn	a					13 50	13 55							14 21						14 50
Liverpool South Parkway 7 ✈	a					13 59								14 30						14 59
Liverpool Lime Street 10	a					14 10	14 15							14 43						15 10
	d												13 57							
Manchester Airport ✈	d				13 00						13 29							14 00		
Manchester Piccadilly 10 🚌	d				13 16						13 46							14 16		
Bolton	d				13 33						14 07							14 33		
Wigan North Western	a	13 38										14 25	14 30		14 37					
	d	13 38										14 25	14 31		14 38					
Preston 8	a	13 51			13 55						14 33	14 38	14 54		14 51			14 55		
Preston 8	d	13 53			13 58						14 38	14 41	14 55		14 53			14 58	15 04	
Blackpool North	a										15 05		15 21							
Lancaster 6	a	14 08			14 13							14 54			15 08			15 13	15 20	
	d	14 08			14 14							14 55			15 09			15 14	15 20	
Barrow-in-Furness	a																		16 15	
Oxenholme Lake District	a				14 28										15 22			15 28		
	d				14 28										15 24			15 28		
Windermere	a																			
Penrith North Lakes	d	14 45										15 30						15 53		
Carlisle 8	a	15 00			15 06							15 46			16 01			16 10		
	d	15 02			15 07							15 47			16 03			16 11		
Lockerbie	d				15 27													16 30		
Carstairs	a																			
Motherwell	a																			
Glasgow Central 15	a				16 30							17 01			17 17					
Haymarket	a	16 16																17s31		
Edinburgh 10	a	16 22																17 39		
Perth	a																			
Dundee	a																			
Aberdeen	a																			
Inverness	a																			

OVERNIGHT SLEEPERS. For sleeper trains, operated by First ScotRail, please refer to Tables 400 - 404

Table 65 **Saturdays**

15 September to 20 October

London and West Midlands - North West England and Scotland

Route Diagram - see first Page of Table 65

		VT	VT	VT	XC	TP	VT	NT	LM	VT	XC	VT	TP	LM	VT	VT	XC	TP	VT	NT	LM	VT
		◇1	◇1	◇1	◇1	◇1	◇1		◇1	◇1	◇1	◇1	◇1	◇1	◇1	◇1	◇1	◇1	◇1		◇1	◇1
													A									
		☕	☕	☕	🛒	🛒	☕			☕	☕	☕	🛒		☕	☕	🛒	🛒	☕			☕
London Euston 15 ⊖	d	13 07	13 10	13 20			13 30					14 00			14 07	14 20			14 30			
Watford Junction	d																					
Milton Keynes Central	d		13 41	13 50												14 50						
Rugby	d																					
Nuneaton	d																					
Tamworth Low Level	d																					
Lichfield Trent Valley	d																					
Coventry	d				13 27												14 27					
Birmingham International ✈	d				13 38												14 38					
Birmingham New Street 12	d				13 57				14 01	14 20	14 31			14 36			14 57				15 01	15 20
Wolverhampton 7 ⛴	d				14 15				14 19	14 37	14 49			14 53			15 15				15 19	15 37
Penkridge	d													15 03								
Stafford	a	14 22			14 29				14 35		15 00			15 09	15 22		15 29				15 35	
	d	14 23			14 30				14 35		15 01			15 09	15 23		15 30				15 35	
Stoke-on-Trent	a			14 48	14 54						15 19	15 24				15 48	15 54					
Congleton	a																					
Macclesfield	a				15 11							15 41					16 11					
Crewe 10	a		14 47						14 56	15 07				15 30							15 56	16 08
	d		14 49						14 57	15 09				15 31							15 57	16 09
Chester	a		15 12																			
Wrexham General	a																					
Llandudno	a																					
Bangor (Gwynedd)	a																					
Holyhead	a																					
Wilmslow	a																					
Stockport	a			15 16	15 27						15 49	15 55				16 16	16 27					
Manchester Piccadilly 10 ⛴	a			15 28	15 39						15 59	16 07				16 28	16 39					
Hartford	a								15 11												16 10	
Warrington Bank Quay	a						15 14			15 26									16 14			16 26
	d						15 14			15 27									16 14			16 27
Runcorn	a	14 55							15 21					15 50	15 55						16 22	
Liverpool South Parkway 7 ✈	a								15 30					15 59							16 31	
Liverpool Lime Street 10	a	15 15							15 43					16 10	16 15						16 44	
	d							14 57												15 57		
Manchester Airport ✈	d					14 29							15 00					15 29				
Manchester Piccadilly 10 ⛴	d					14 46							15 16					15 46				
Bolton	d					15 07							15 33					16 07				
Wigan North Western	a						15 25	15 30		15 37									16 25	16 30		16 37
	d						15 25	15 31		15 38									16 25	16 31		16 38
Preston 8	a					15 33	15 38	15 54		15 51			15 57					16 33	16 38	16 54		16 51
Preston 8	d					15 38	15 41	15 55		15 53			15 58					16 38	16 41	16 55		16 53
Blackpool North	a					16 05		16 21										17 07		17 21		
Lancaster 6	a						15 54			16 08			16 14						16 54			17 09
	d						15 55			16 08			16 15						16 55			17 10
Barrow-in-Furness	a												17 18									
Oxenholme Lake District	a						16 08															17 24
	d						16 08															17 25
Windermere	a																					
Penrith North Lakes	d									16 45									17 30			
Carlisle 8	a						16 46			17 00									17 46			18 03
	d						16 47			17 03									17 47			18 04
Lockerbie	d																					
Carstairs	a																					
Motherwell	a																					
Glasgow Central 15	a						18 01												19 01			19 17
Haymarket	a									18 14												
Edinburgh 10	a									18 22												
Perth	a																					
Dundee	a																					
Aberdeen	a																					
Inverness	a																					

A 🛒 to Preston

OVERNIGHT SLEEPERS. For sleeper trains, operated by First ScotRail, please refer to Tables 400 - 404

Table 65

Saturdays

15 September to 20 October

London and West Midlands - North West England and Scotland

Route Diagram - see first Page of Table 65

		XC	VT	TP	TP			LM	VT	VT	VT	XC	TP	VT	NT		LM	VT	XC	VT	TP	NT		LM	VT
		◇1	◇1	◇1				◇1	◇1	◇1	◇1	◇1	◇1	◇1			◇1	◇1	◇1	◇1	◇1			◇1	◇1
London Euston [1·5] ⊖	d		15 00						15 07	15 10	15 20			15 30						16 00					16 07
Watford Junction	d																								
Milton Keynes Central	d									15 41	15 50														
Rugby	d																								
Nuneaton	d																								
Tamworth Low Level	d																								
Lichfield Trent Valley	d																								
Coventry	d											15 27													
Birmingham International ✈	d											15 38													
Birmingham New Street [1·2]	d	15 31						15 36				15 57					16 01	16 20	16 31					16 36	
Wolverhampton [7] ⛴	d	15 49						15 53				16 15					16 19	16 37	16 49					16 53	
Penkridge	d							16 03																17 03	
Stafford	a	16 00						16 09	16 22			16 29					16 35		17 00					17 09	17 22
	d	16 01						16 09	16 23			16 30					16 35		17 01					17 09	17 23
Stoke-on-Trent	a	16 19	16 24								16 48	16 54							17 19	17 24					
Congleton	a																								
Macclesfield	a		16 41									17 11								17 41					
Crewe [1·0]	a							16 30		16 47							16 56	17 07						17 30	
	d							16 31		16 49							16 57	17 09						17 31	
Chester	a									17 12															
Wrexham General	a																								
Llandudno	a																								
Bangor (Gwynedd)	a																								
Holyhead	a																								
Wilmslow	a																								
Stockport	a	16 49	16 54								17 16	17 27							17 49	17 55					
Manchester Piccadilly [1·0] ⛴	a	16 59	17 07								17 28	17 39							17 59	18 07					
Hartford	a																17 11								
Warrington Bank Quay	a													17 14				17 26							
	d													17 14				17 27							
Runcorn	a							16 50	16 55								17 21							17 50	17 55
Liverpool South Parkway [7] ✈	a							16 59									17 30							17 59	
Liverpool Lime Street [1·0]	a							17 10	17 15								17 43							18 10	18 15
	d														16 57							17 19			
Manchester Airport ✈	d			16 00									16 29								17 00				
Manchester Piccadilly [1·0] ⛴	d			16 16									16 46								17 15				
Bolton	d			16 33									17 06								17 32				
Wigan North Western	a													17 25	17 30			17 37				18 04			
	d													17 25	17 31			17 38							
Preston [8]	a			16 55									17 30	17 38	17 54			17 51			17 55				
Preston [8]	d			17 00	17 04								17 32	17 41	17 55			17 53			17 58				
Blackpool North	a												18 02		18 24										
Lancaster [6]	a			17 16	17 20									17 54				18 08			18 13				
	d			17 16	17 21									17 55				18 08			18 14				
Barrow-in-Furness	a																								
Oxenholme Lake District	a			17 30	17 37									18 08				18 22			18 28				
	d			17 30	17 38									18 08				18 23			18 28				
Windermere	a				18 00																				
Penrith North Lakes	d																	18 49			18 53				
Carlisle [8]	a			18 10										18 46				19 04			19 09				
	d			18 11										18 47				19 04			19 11				
Lockerbie	d			18 30																	19 30				
Carstairs	a																								
Motherwell	a																				20s16				
Glasgow Central [1·5]	a													20 01							20 33				
Haymarket	a			19s31														20 16							
Edinburgh [1·0]	a			19 39														20 22							
Perth	a																								
Dundee	a																								
Aberdeen	a																								
Inverness	a																								

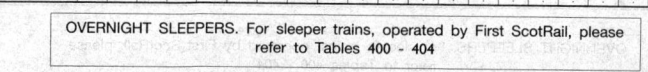

OVERNIGHT SLEEPERS. For sleeper trains, operated by First ScotRail, please refer to Tables 400 - 404

Table 65

Saturdays

15 September to 20 October

London and West Midlands - North West England and Scotland

Route Diagram - see first Page of Table 65

		VT	XC	LM	TP	VT	VT	TP	VT	XC	VT	TP	LM	VT	VT	XC	LM	TP	VT	VT	XC
		◇1	◇1	◇1	◇1	◇1	◇1	◇1	◇1	◇1	◇1	◇1	◇1	◇1	◇1	◇1	◇1	◇1	◇1	◇1	◇1
												A									
		🍴	🛒			🍴	🍴	🛒	🍴	🛒	🍴	🛒		🍴	🍴	🛒		🛒	🍴	🍴	🍴
London Euston 15 ⊖	d	16 20				16 30	16 33				17 00			17 07	17 20				17 30		
Watford Junction	d																				
Milton Keynes Central	d	16 50													17 50						
Rugby	d																				
Nuneaton	d													18 03							
Tamworth Low Level	d						17 38														
Lichfield Trent Valley	d						17 45														
Coventry	d		16 27													17 27					
Birmingham International ✈	d		16 38													17 38					
Birmingham New Street 12	d		16 57	17 01					17 20	17 31			17 36			17 57	18 01			18 20	18 31
Wolverhampton 7 ⛴	d		17 15	17 19					17 37	17 49			17 53			18 15	18 19			18 37	18 49
Penkridge	d			17 29									18 03				18 29				
Stafford	a		17 29	17 35			17 58			18 00			18 09	18 26		18 29	18 35				19 00
	d		17 30	17 36			17 59			18 01			18 09	18 27		18 30	18 35				19 01
Stoke-on-Trent	a	17 48	17 54							18 19	18 24				18 48	18 54					19 19
Congleton	a																				
Macclesfield	a		18 11								18 41					19 11					
Crewe 10	a			17 56					18 07				18 30				18 56			19 07	
	d			17 57					18 09				18 33				18 59			19 09	
Chester	a																				
Wrexham General	a																				
Llandudno	a																				
Bangor (Gwynedd)	a																				
Holyhead	a																				
Wilmslow	a																				
Stockport	a	18 16	18 27							18 49	18 55				19 16	19 27					19 49
Manchester Piccadilly 10 ⛴	a	18 28	18 39							18 59	19 07				19 28	19 39					19 59
Hartford	a			18 11									18 43				19 12				
Warrington Bank Quay	a					18 14			18 26										19 14	19 26	
	d					18 14			18 27										19 14	19 27	
Runcorn	a			18 21			18 31						18 52	18 59			19 22				
Liverpool South Parkway 7 ✈	a			18 30									19 02				19 31				
Liverpool Lime Street 10	a			18 43			18 52						19 14	19 17			19 44				
	d																				
Manchester Airport ✈	d							17 29				18 00						18 29			
Manchester Piccadilly 10 ⛴	d							17 46				18 16						18 46			
Bolton	d							18 07				18 33						19 07			
Wigan North Western	a					18 25			18 37										19 25	19 37	
	d					18 25			18 38										19 25	19 38	
Preston 8	a					18 38		18 38	18 51			18 55						19 33	19 38	19 54	
Preston 8	d				18 02	18 41		18 40	18 53			18 58						19 38	19 41		
Blackpool North	a							19 10										20 06			
Lancaster 6	a				18 18	18 54			19 08			19 13							19 54		
	d				18 18	18 55			19 08			19 15							19 55		
Barrow-in-Furness	a				19 26							20 19									
Oxenholme Lake District	a					19 08			19 22										20 08		
	d					19 08			19 24										20 08		
Windermere	a																				
Penrith North Lakes	d					19 34													20 34		
Carlisle 8	a					19 49			20 01										20 49		
	d					19 51			20 03										20 51		
Lockerbie	d																				
Carstairs	a																				
Motherwell	a																				
Glasgow Central 15	a					21 01			21 17										22 01		
Haymarket	a																				
Edinburgh 10	a																				
Perth	a																				
Dundee	a																				
Aberdeen	a																				
Inverness	a																				

A 🛒 to Preston

OVERNIGHT SLEEPERS. For sleeper trains, operated by First ScotRail, please refer to Tables 400 - 404

Table 65

Saturdays

15 September to 20 October

London and West Midlands - North West England and Scotland

Route Diagram - see first Page of Table 65

		VT	LM	TP		NT	VT		VT	VT	XC	LM	TP	VT	VT	TP			NT	VT	XC	VT	VT	VT	XC
		◇1	◇1	◇1			◇1		◇1	◇1	◇1	◇1	◇1	◇1	◇1	◇1				◇1	◇1	◇1	◇1	◇1	◇1
																									A
		☕					☕		☕	☕	🛒			☕	☕					☕	☕	☕	☕	☕	🛒
London Euston 15 ⊖	d	18 00					18 07		18 10	18 20				18 30						18 33		19 00	19 07	19 20	
Watford Junction	d																								
Milton Keynes Central	d								18 41	18 50														19 50	
Rugby	d																								
Nuneaton	d																								
Tamworth Low Level	d																						20 03		
Lichfield Trent Valley	d																			19 38					
Coventry	d										18 27									19 45					19 27
Birmingham International ✈	d										18 38														19 38
Birmingham New Street 12	d		18 36								18 57	19 01			19 20						19 31				19 57
Wolverhampton 7 ⛴	d		18 53								19 15	19 19			19 37						19 49				20 15
Penkridge	d		19 03									19 29													
Stafford	a		19 09				19 22				19 29	19 35								19 58	20 00		20 26		20 29
	d		19 09				19 23				19 30	19 36								19 59	20 01		20 27		20 30
Stoke-on-Trent	a	19 24								19 48	19 54										20 19	20 24		20 48	20 54
Congleton	a																								
Macclesfield	a	19 41									20 11										20 36	20 41			21 11
Crewe 10	a		19 30						19 47			19 58			20 07								20 45		
	d								19 49			19 58			20 09								20 47		
Chester	a								20 12																
Wrexham General	a																								
Llandudno	a																								
Bangor (Gwynedd)	a																								
Holyhead	a																								
Wilmslow	a																								
Stockport	a	19 55								20 16	20 27										20 49	20 55		21 16	21 27
Manchester Piccadilly 10 ⛴	a	20 07								20 28	20 39										20 59	21 07		21 28	21 39
Hartford	a											20 11													
Warrington Bank Quay	a													20 14	20 26										
	d													20 14	20 27										
Runcorn	a						19 55					20 24								20 31			21 05		
Liverpool South Parkway 7 ✈	a											20 33													
Liverpool Lime Street 10	a						20 15					20 46								20 52			21 25		
	d					19 23													20 25						
Manchester Airport ✈	d			19 00									19 29			20 00									
Manchester Piccadilly 10 ⛴	d			19 16									19 46			20 16									
Bolton	d			19 33									20 07			20 33									
Wigan North Western	a					19 54								20 25	20 37				20 57						
	d					19 55								20 25	20 38				20 57						
Preston 8	a			19 58		20 18							20 33	20 38	20 59	20 57			21 22						
Preston 8	d			20 01		20 19							20 38	20 41		21 02			21 24						
Blackpool North	a					20 44							21 06						21 53						
Lancaster 6	a			20 17										20 54		21 17									
	d			20 17										20 55		21 18									
Barrow-in-Furness	a			21 20												22 21									
Oxenholme Lake District	a													21 08											
	d													21 09											
Windermere	a																								
Penrith North Lakes	d													21 34											
Carlisle 8	a													21 49											
	d													21 51											
Lockerbie	d																								
Carstairs	a																								
Motherwell	a													22 44											
Glasgow Central 15	a													23 04											
Haymarket	a																								
Edinburgh 10	a																								
Perth	a																								
Dundee	a																								
Aberdeen	a																								
Inverness	a																								

A 🛒 to Birmingham New Street

OVERNIGHT SLEEPERS. For sleeper trains, operated by First ScotRail, please refer to Tables 400 - 404

Table 65

Saturdays

15 September to 20 October

London and West Midlands - North West England and Scotland

Route Diagram - see first Page of Table 65

		TP	VT		LM	VT	XC	LM	XC		VT	VT	LM		XC	NT	TP	TP		VT	TP	XC	LM		AW
		◇1	◇1		◇1	◇1	◇1	◇1	◇1		◇1	◇1	◇1		◇1		◇1	◇1		◇1	◇1	◇1	◇1		
									A																
			☕			☕	☕		🛒		☕	☕								☕					
London Euston 15 ⊖	d		19 30								20 11	20 20								20 31					
Watford Junction	d																			20u46					
Milton Keynes Central	d											21 05													
Rugby	d										21 15									21 36					
Nuneaton	d											21 33													
Tamworth Low Level	d																			21 53					
Lichfield Trent Valley	d																			22 00					
Coventry	d								20 27						21 27										
Birmingham International ✈	d								20 38						21 38										
Birmingham New Street 12	d				20 01	20 20	20 31	20 36	20 57				21 36		21 57							22 31	22 36		
Wolverhampton 7	d				20 22	20 37	20 49	20 53	21 15				21 59		22 16							22 49	22 56		
Penkridge	d				20 31			21 03					22 09										23 06		
Stafford	a				20 37	20 49	21 00	21 09	21 29		21 46		22 15		22 29							23 01	23 13		
	d				20 38	20 50	21 01	21 09	21 30		21 46		22 16		22 30							23 02	23 13		
Stoke-on-Trent	a						21 20		21 52			22 05			22 50							23 20			
Congleton	a																								
Macclesfield	a						21 38		22 11			22 21			23 07							23 38			
Crewe 10	a		21 04		20 58	21 10		21 30			22 05		22 40							22 35			23 37		
	d		21 05		21 06						22 06									22 37					23 21
Chester	a																								23 42
Wrexham General	a																								
Llandudno	a																								
Bangor (Gwynedd)	a																								
Holyhead	a																								
Wilmslow	a																								
Stockport	a						21 53		22 27			22 35			23 21							23 53			
Manchester Piccadilly 10	a						22 04		22 39			22 51			23 32							00 10			
Hartford	a				21 19																				
Warrington Bank Quay	a		21 22																	22 53					
	d		21 22																	22 54					
Runcorn	a				21 29						22 24														
Liverpool South Parkway 7 ✈	a				21 38																				
Liverpool Lime Street 10	a				21 50						22 46														
	d																								
Manchester Airport ✈	d	20 29															21 29	22 00			22 29				
Manchester Piccadilly 10	d	20 46															21 46	22 16			22 46				
Bolton	d	21 07															22 07	22 33			23 07				
Wigan North Western	a		21 33																	23 04					
	d		21 33																	23 05					
Preston 8	a	21 33	21 49														22 36	22 54		23 19	23 33				
Preston 8	d	21 38														21 59	22 38	22 55			23 35				
Blackpool North	a	22 06															23 04				00 02				
Lancaster 6	a															22 19		23 11							
	d															22 19		23 11							
Barrow-in-Furness	a															23 24		00 15							
Oxenholme Lake District	a																								
	d																								
Windermere	a																								
Penrith North Lakes	d																								
Carlisle 8	a																								
	d																								
Lockerbie	d																								
Carstairs	a																								
Motherwell	a																								
Glasgow Central 15	a																								
Haymarket	a																								
Edinburgh 10	a																								
Perth	a																								
Dundee	a																								
Aberdeen	a																								
Inverness	a																								

A 🛒 to Birmingham New Street

OVERNIGHT SLEEPERS. For sleeper trains, operated by First ScotRail, please refer to Tables 400 - 404

London and West Midlands - North West England and Scotland

Route Diagram - see first Page of Table 65

		VT	TP	TP	XC	TP	SR	VT	LM		SR	TP	NT	TP	TP	LM	XC	VT		TP	LM	TP	NT
		R					R				R												
		1	◇1	◇1	◇1	◇1		◇1	◇1			◇1		◇1	◇1	1	◇1	◇1		◇1	1	◇1	
							A																
							🛏				🛏												
		☕					☕	☕			☕							☕		🛒		🛒	
London Euston 15 ⊖	d	19p30					21p15	22p00			23p50												
Watford Junction	d						21b33				00u10												
Milton Keynes Central	d							22p31															
Rugby	d							22p54															
Nuneaton	d							23p04															
Tamworth Low Level	d							23c15															
Lichfield Trent Valley	d							23c22															
Coventry	d																						
Birmingham International ✈	d																						
Birmingham New Street 12	d				22p30				23p09								05 57						
Wolverhampton 7 🚌	d				22p48				23p36								06 16						
Penkridge	d								23p46														
Stafford	a				23p00			23c38	23p52								06 29						
	d				23p01				23p53								06 30						
Stoke-on-Trent	a				23p20												06 50						
Congleton	a																07 02						
Macclesfield	a																07 11						
Crewe 10	a							00s03	00 16														
	d						23b54						00 44			05 48		05 57			06 12		
Chester	a																						
Wrexham General	a																						
Llandudno	a																						
Bangor (Gwynedd)	a																						
Holyhead	a																						
Wilmslow	a																						
Stockport	a							00s26									07 27						
Manchester Piccadilly 10 🚌	a				00 12			00 35									07 38						
Hartford	a																						
Warrington Bank Quay	a	21p15																06 13					
	d	21p15																06 14					
Runcorn	a															06 07					06 31		
Liverpool South Parkway 7 ✈	a															06 15					06 39		
Liverpool Lime Street 10	a															06 26					06 53		
	d																						
Manchester Airport ✈	d		22p00	22p29								00 01	01 20	04 00						05 45		06 18	
Manchester Piccadilly 10 🚌	d		22p16	22p46								00 16	01a36	04 15	05 43					06 03		06 33	
Bolton	d		22p33	23p07								00s31		04s29	05 59					06 19		06 50	07 01
Wigan North Western	a	21p26	22p48															06 24					07 19
	d	21p26	22p51															06 25					
Preston 8	a	21p39	23p09	23p33								01s05		05s04	06 26			06 37		06 42		07 11	
Preston 8	d	21p41	23p13	23p35		23p51	00u52								06 37			06 40		06 44		07 14	
Blackpool North	a			00 02		00 16						01 30		05 33	07 06								
Lancaster 6	a	21p55	23p28															06 54		06 59		07 30	
	d	21p56	23p29															06 54		07 00		07 30	
Barrow-in-Furness	a		00 31																				
Oxenholme Lake District	a	22p09																07 08		07 15			
	d	22p09																07 10		07 15			
Windermere	a																						
Penrith North Lakes	d	22p35																07 35				08 07	
Carlisle 8	a	22p50									05s15							07 50		07 55		08 24	
	d	22p51																07 51		07 56		08 25	
Lockerbie	d																	08 10		08 16			
Carstairs	a										06s20												
Motherwell	a										06s56												
Glasgow Central 15	a	00 06									07 20							09 13				09 45	
Haymarket	a																			09s17			
Edinburgh 10	a									07 15										09 22			
Perth	a						05s39																
Dundee	a						06s08																
Aberdeen	a						07 36																
Inverness	a						08 38																

A Conveys a portion from Fort William, arrives at 0954

b Previous night, stops to pick up only

c Previous night, stops to set down only

OVERNIGHT SLEEPERS. For sleeper trains, operated by First ScotRail, please refer to Tables 400 - 404

London and West Midlands - North West England and Scotland

Route Diagram - see first Page of Table 65

Station		TP	NT	LM	LM	VT		XC	TP		LM	TP	VT	LM	NT	NT		VT	XC	VT	TP		LM	VT	VT
		◇1		◇1	◇1	◇1		◇1	◇1		◇1	◇1	◇1	◇1				◇1	◇1	◇1	◇1		◇1	◇1	◇1
						🍽		🛒	🛒			🛒	🍽					🍽	🛒	🍽	🛒			🍽	🍽
London Euston 15 ⊖	d												06 05							06 55				07 07	07 20
Watford Junction	d												06u20												
Milton Keynes Central	d												06 41							07 27					07 50
Rugby	d												07 03												
Nuneaton	d																								
Tamworth Low Level	d																								
Lichfield Trent Valley	d																								
Coventry	d																								
Birmingham International ✈	d																								
Birmingham New Street 12	d				06 01	06 20		06 31			06 36			07 01				07 20	07 31				07 36		
Wolverhampton 7	d				06 18	06 37		06 49			06 54			07 18				07 37	07 49				07 53		
Penkridge	d				06 29									07 30									08 03		
Stafford	a				06 35			07 00			07 08		07 33	07 36					08 00				08 09	08 22	
	d				06 36			07 01			07 08		07 34	07 38					08 01				08 09	08 23	
Stoke-on-Trent	a							07 18											08 19	08 24					08 48
Congleton	a																								
Macclesfield	a							07 36											08 36	08 41					
Crewe 10	a				06 56	07 07					07 33		07 53	07 58				08 07					08 30	08 41	
	d			06 32	06 57	07 09					07 35		07 55	08 00				08 09					08 31	08 43	
Chester	a																								
Wrexham General	a																								
Llandudno	a																								
Bangor (Gwynedd)	a																								
Holyhead	a																								
Wilmslow	a																								
Stockport	a							07 49											08 49	08 55					09 16
Manchester Piccadilly 10	a							07 59											08 59	09 07					09 28
Hartford	a			06 46	07 10						07 48			08 11											
Warrington Bank Quay	a					07 26							08 11					08 27							
	d					07 27							08 12					08 27							
Runcorn	a			06 59	07 20						08 02			08 24									08 50	09 00	
Liverpool South Parkway 7 ✈	a			07 08	07 30						08 11			08 33									08 59		
Liverpool Lime Street 10	a			07 22	07 42						08 24			08 46									09 12	09 21	
	d		06 57																						
Manchester Airport ✈	d								07 00			07 25									07 56				
Manchester Piccadilly 10	d								07 15			07 45									08 15				
Bolton	d								07 31			07 59									08 32				
Wigan North Western	a		07 30			07 37							08 22					08 38							
	d		07 31			07 38							08 23			08 30		08 38							
Preston 8	a		07 54			07 51			07 57			08 22	08 36			08 54		08 51			08 58				
Preston 8	d	07 20	07 55			07 53			07 59			08 24	08 37		08 42	08 55		08 53			08 59				
Blackpool North	a		08 21						08 29							09 21					09 25				
Lancaster 6	a	07 36				08 08						08 39	08 52		09 02			09 08							
	d	07 36				08 08						08 40	08 52		09 03			09 08							
Barrow-in-Furness	a	08 39													10 07										
Oxenholme Lake District	a					08 21							09 05												
	d					08 22							09 06												
Windermere	a																								
Penrith North Lakes	d												09 32					09 45							
Carlisle 8	a					09 00						09 30	09 47		12 39			10 02							
	d					09 02						09 30	09 48					10 04							
Lockerbie	d											09 50													
Carstairs	a																								
Motherwell	a																								
Glasgow Central 15	a												11 03					11 17							
Haymarket	a					10 16						10s48													
Edinburgh 10	a					10 22						10 56													
Perth	a																								
Dundee	a																								
Aberdeen	a																								
Inverness	a																								

OVERNIGHT SLEEPERS. For sleeper trains, operated by First ScotRail, please refer to Tables 400 - 404

Table 65

Saturdays
from 27 October

London and West Midlands - North West England and Scotland

Route Diagram - see first Page of Table 65

		XC		TP	VT	TP	NT	LM	VT	XC	VT	TP				LM	VT	VT	VT	XC	TP	VT	TP		NT
		◇1		◇1	◇1	◇1		◇1	◇1	◇1	◇1	◇1				◇1	◇1	◇1	◇1	◇1	◇1	◇1	◇1		
				A								A													
		🛒		🛒	☕				☕	☕	☕	🛒					☕	☕	☕	🛒	🛒	☕			
London Euston 15 ⊖	d				07 30						08 00						08 07	08 10	08 20			08 30			
Watford Junction	d																								
Milton Keynes Central	d																	08 41	08 50						
Rugby	d																								
Nuneaton	d																								
Tamworth Low Level	d																								
Lichfield Trent Valley	d																								
Coventry	d	07 27																		08 27					
Birmingham International ✈	d	07 38																		08 38					
Birmingham New Street 12	d	07 57						08 01	08 20	08 31						08 36				08 57					
Wolverhampton 7	d	08 15						08 19	08 37	08 49						08 53				09 15					
Penkridge	d							08 29								09 03									
Stafford	a	08 29						08 35		09 00						09 09	09 22			09 29					
	d	08 30						08 36		09 01						09 09	09 23			09 30					
Stoke-on-Trent	a	08 54								09 19	09 24								09 48	09 54					
Congleton	a																								
Macclesfield	a	09 11									09 41									10 11					
Crewe 10	a							08 56	09 07							09 30		09 47							
	d							08 57	09 09							09 31		09 49							
Chester	a																	10 12							
Wrexham General	a																								
Llandudno	a																								
Bangor (Gwynedd)	a																								
Holyhead	a																								
Wilmslow	a																								
Stockport	a	09 27								09 49	09 55								10 16	10 27					
Manchester Piccadilly 10	a	09 39								09 59	10 07								10 28	10 39					
Hartford	a							09 11																	
Warrington Bank Quay	a				09 14				09 26													10 14			
	d				09 14				09 27													10 14			
Runcorn	a							09 21								09 50	09 55								
Liverpool South Parkway 7 ✈	a							09 30								09 59									
Liverpool Lime Street 10	a							09 43								10 10	10 15								
	d						08 57																		09 57
Manchester Airport ✈	d			08 25								09 00									09 29				
Manchester Piccadilly 10	d			08 46								09 16									09 46				
Bolton	d			09 07								09 33									10 07				
Wigan North Western	a				09 25		09 30		09 37													10 25			10 30
	d				09 25		09 31		09 38													10 25			10 31
Preston 8	a			09 30	09 38		09 54		09 51			09 55									10 33	10 38			10 54
Preston 8	d			09 32	09 41	09 45	09 55		09 53			10 08	09 58								10 38	10 41	10 45		10 55
Blackpool North	a						10 21					10 35									11 05				11 21
Lancaster 6	a			09 47	09 54	10 00			10 08				10 13									10 54	11 00		
	d			09 48	09 55	10 01			10 08				10 14									10 55	11 01		
Barrow-in-Furness	a					11 04																			
Oxenholme Lake District	a			10 04					10 22													11 08	11 17		
	d			10 05					10 24													11 08	11 18		
Windermere	a			10 26																			11 39		
Penrith North Lakes	d				10 30								10 53												
Carlisle 8	a				10 46				11 01				11 10									11 46			
	d				10 47				11 03				11 11									11 47			
Lockerbie	d												11 30												
Carstairs	a																								
Motherwell	a																								
Glasgow Central 15	a				12 01								12 32									13 01			
Haymarket	a								12 16																
Edinburgh 10	a								12 22																
Perth	a																								
Dundee	a																								
Aberdeen	a																								
Inverness	a																								

A 🛒 to Preston

OVERNIGHT SLEEPERS. For sleeper trains, operated by First ScotRail, please refer to Tables 400 - 404

London and West Midlands - North West England and Scotland

Route Diagram - see first Page of Table 65

		LM	VT	XC	TP		LM	VT	VT		VT	VT	XC	TP	VT	NT	LM	VT	XC		VT	TP		LM	VT
		◇1	◇1	◇1	◇1		◇1	◇1	◇1		◇1	◇1	◇1	◇1	◇1		◇1	◇1	◇1		◇1	◇1		◇1	◇1
																						A			
			[buffet]	[buffet]	[trolley]			[buffet]	[buffet]		[buffet]	[buffet]	[trolley]	[trolley]	[buffet]			[buffet]	[buffet]		[buffet]	[trolley]			[buffet]
London Euston 15 ⊖	d							08 50	09 00		09 07	09 20			09 30						10 00				10 07
Watford Junction	d							09 05																	
Milton Keynes Central	d							09 25				09 50													
Rugby	d																								
Nuneaton	d																								
Tamworth Low Level	d																								
Lichfield Trent Valley	d																								
Coventry	d												09 27												
Birmingham International ✈	d												09 38												
Birmingham New Street 12	d	09 01	09 20	09 31			09 36						09 57				10 01	10 20	10 31					10 36	
Wolverhampton 7 ⛴	d	09 19	09 37	09 49			09 53						10 15				10 19	10 37	10 49					10 53	
Penkridge	d						10 03																	11 03	
Stafford	a	09 34		10 00			10 09				10 22		10 29				10 35		11 00					11 09	11 22
	d	09 35		10 01			10 09				10 23		10 30				10 35		11 01					11 09	11 23
Stoke-on-Trent	a			10 19					10 24			10 48	10 54						11 19		11 24				
Congleton	a																								
Macclesfield	a								10 41				11 11								11 41				
Crewe 10	a	09 56	10 07				10 30	10 32									10 56	11 07						11 30	
	d	09 57	10 09				10 31	10 43									10 57	11 09						11 31	
Chester	a							11 10																	
Wrexham General	a																								
Llandudno	a																								
Bangor (Gwynedd)	a							12 19																	
Holyhead	a							12 55																	
Wilmslow	a																								
Stockport	a			10 49					10 55			11 16	11 27						11 49		11 55				
Manchester Piccadilly 10 ⛴	a			10 59					11 07			11 28	11 39						11 59		12 07				
Hartford	a	10 10															11 11								
Warrington Bank Quay	a		10 26												11 14			11 26							
	d		10 27												11 14			11 27							
Runcorn	a	10 22					10 50				10 55						11 21							11 50	11 55
Liverpool South Parkway 7 ✈	a	10 31					10 59										11 30							11 59	
Liverpool Lime Street 10	a	10 44					11 10				11 15						11 43							12 10	12 15
	d															10 57									
Manchester Airport ✈	d				10 00									10 29								11 00			
Manchester Piccadilly 10 ⛴	d				10 16									10 46								11 16			
Bolton	d				10 33									11 07								11 33			
Wigan North Western	a		10 37												11 25	11 30		11 37							
	d		10 38												11 25	11 31		11 38							
Preston 8	a		10 51		10 55									11 33	11 38	11 54		11 51				11 55			
Preston 8	d		10 53		10 58									11 38	11 41	11 55		11 53				11 58			
Blackpool North	a													12 05		12 21									
Lancaster 6	a		11 08		11 13										11 54			12 08				12 13			
	d		11 08		11 14										11 55			12 08				12 14			
Barrow-in-Furness	a																					13 11			
Oxenholme Lake District	a				11 28													12 22							
	d				11 28													12 24							
Windermere	a																								
Penrith North Lakes	d		11 45		11 53										12 30										
Carlisle 8	a		12 00		12 10										12 46			13 01							
	d		12 03		12 11										12 47			13 03							
Lockerbie	d				12 30																				
Carstairs	a																								
Motherwell	a																								
Glasgow Central 15	a		13 17												14 01										
Haymarket	a				13s33													14 15							
Edinburgh 10	a				13 39													14 22							
Perth	a																								
Dundee	a																								
Aberdeen	a																								
Inverness	a																								

A [trolley] to Preston

OVERNIGHT SLEEPERS. For sleeper trains, operated by First ScotRail, please refer to Tables 400 - 404

Table 65

Saturdays

from 27 October

London and West Midlands - North West England and Scotland

Route Diagram - see first Page of Table 65

		VT	VT	XC	TP		VT	NT	LM	VT	XC	VT	TP		LM		VT	VT	VT	XC	TP	TP	VT	NT	LM
		◇1	◇1	◇1	◇1		◇1		◇1	◇1	◇1	◇1	◇1		◇1		◇1	◇1	◇1	◇1	◇1	◇1	◇1		◇1
London Euston 15 ⊖	d	10 10	10 20				10 30					11 00					11 07	11 10	11 20				11 30		
Watford Junction	d																								
Milton Keynes Central	d	10 41	10 50															11 41	11 50						
Rugby	d																								
Nuneaton	d																								
Tamworth Low Level	d																								
Lichfield Trent Valley	d																								
Coventry	d			10 27																11 27					
Birmingham International ✈	d			10 38																11 38					
Birmingham New Street 12	d			10 57					11 01	11 20	11 31				11 36					11 57					12 01
Wolverhampton 7	d			11 15					11 19	11 37	11 49				11 53					12 15					12 19
Penkridge	d														12 03										
Stafford	a			11 29					11 35		12 00				12 09		12 22			12 29					12 35
	d			11 30					11 35		12 01				12 09		12 23			12 30					12 35
Stoke-on-Trent	a		11 48	11 54							12 19	12 24							12 48	12 54					
Congleton	a																								
Macclesfield	a			12 11								12 41								13 11					
Crewe 10	a	11 47							11 56	12 07					12 30			12 47							12 56
	d	11 49							11 57	12 09					12 31			12 49							12 57
Chester	a	12 12																13 12							
Wrexham General	a																								
Llandudno	a																								
Bangor (Gwynedd)	a																								
Holyhead	a																								
Wilmslow	a																								
Stockport	a		12 16	12 27							12 49	12 55							13 16	13 27					
Manchester Piccadilly 10	a		12 28	12 39							12 59	13 07							13 28	13 39					
Hartford	a								12 10																13 11
Warrington Bank Quay	a						12 14			12 26													13 14		
	d						12 14			12 27													13 14		
Runcorn	a								12 22						12 50		12 55								13 21
Liverpool South Parkway 7 ✈	a								12 31						12 59										13 30
Liverpool Lime Street 10	a								12 44						13 10		13 15								13 43
	d							11 57																12 57	
Manchester Airport ✈	d				11 29								12 00									12 29			
Manchester Piccadilly 10	d				11 46								12 16									12 46			
Bolton	d				12 07								12 33									13 07			
Wigan North Western	a						12 25	12 30		12 37													13 25	13 30	
	d						12 25	12 31		12 38													13 25	13 31	
Preston 8	a				12 33		12 38	12 54		12 51			12 55									13 33	13 38	13 54	
Preston 8	d				12 38		12 41	12 55		12 53			12 58								13 04	13 38	13 41	13 55	
Blackpool North	a				13 05			13 21														14 05		14 21	
Lancaster 6	a						12 54			13 08			13 13								13 19		13 54		
	d						12 55			13 08			13 14								13 20		13 55		
Barrow-in-Furness	a																								
Oxenholme Lake District	a						13 08			13 22			13 28								13 36		14 08		
	d						13 08			13 24			13 28								13 37		14 08		
Windermere	a																				13 56				
Penrith North Lakes	d												13 53												
Carlisle 8	a						13 46			14 01			14 10										14 46		
	d						13 47			14 03			14 11										14 47		
Lockerbie	d												14 30												
Carstairs	a																								
Motherwell	a																								
Glasgow Central 15	a						15 01			15 17													16 01		
Haymarket	a												15s30												
Edinburgh 10	a												15 39												
Perth	a																								
Dundee	a																								
Aberdeen	a																								
Inverness	a																								

OVERNIGHT SLEEPERS. For sleeper trains, operated by First ScotRail, please refer to Tables 400 - 404

London and West Midlands - North West England and Scotland

Route Diagram - see first Page of Table 65

			VT	XC	VT	TP		LM	VT	VT	VT		XC	TP	VT	NT	LM	VT	XC	VT	TP				LM
			◇1	◇1	◇1	◇1		◇1	◇1	◇1	◇1		◇1	◇1	◇1		◇1	◇1	◇1	◇1	◇1				◇1
London Euston [15] ⊖	d				12 00				12 07	12 10	12 20				12 30					13 00					
Watford Junction	d																								
Milton Keynes Central	d									12 41	12 50														
Rugby	d																								
Nuneaton	d																								
Tamworth Low Level	d																								
Lichfield Trent Valley	d																								
Coventry	d												12 27												
Birmingham International ✈	d												12 38												
Birmingham New Street [12]	d		12 20	12 31				12 36					12 57				13 01	13 20	13 31						13 36
Wolverhampton [7]	d		12 37	12 49				12 53					13 15				13 19	13 37	13 49						13 53
Penkridge	d							13 03																	14 03
Stafford	a			13 00				13 09	13 22				13 29				13 35		14 00						14 09
	d			13 01				13 09	13 23				13 30				13 35		14 01						14 09
Stoke-on-Trent	a			13 18	13 24						13 48		13 54						14 19	14 24					
Congleton	a																								
Macclesfield	a				13 41								14 11							14 41					
Crewe [10]	a		13 07					13 30		13 47							13 56	14 07							14 30
	d		13 09					13 31		13 49							13 57	14 09							14 31
Chester	a									14 12															
Wrexham General	a																								
Llandudno	a																								
Bangor (Gwynedd)	a																								
Holyhead	a																								
Wilmslow	a																								
Stockport	a			13 49	13 55						14 16		14 27						14 49	14 55					
Manchester Piccadilly [10]	a			13 59	14 07						14 28		14 39						14 59	15 07					
Hartford	a																14 11								
Warrington Bank Quay	a		13 27												14 14			14 26							
	d		13 27												14 14			14 27							
Runcorn	a							13 50	13 55								14 21								14 50
Liverpool South Parkway [7] ✈	a							13 59									14 30								14 59
Liverpool Lime Street [10]	a							14 10	14 15								14 43								15 10
	d															13 57									
Manchester Airport ✈	d					13 00								13 29							14 00				
Manchester Piccadilly [10]	d					13 16								13 46							14 16				
Bolton	d					13 33								14 07							14 33				
Wigan North Western	a		13 38												14 25	14 30		14 37							
	d		13 38												14 25	14 31		14 38							
Preston [8]	a		13 51			13 55								14 33	14 38	14 54		14 51			14 55				
Preston [8]	d		13 53			13 58								14 38	14 41	14 55		14 53			14 58	15 04			
Blackpool North	a													15 05		15 21									
Lancaster [6]	a		14 08			14 13									14 54			15 08			15 13	15 20			
	d		14 08			14 14									14 55			15 09			15 14	15 20			
Barrow-in-Furness	a																					16 15			
Oxenholme Lake District	a					14 28												15 22			15 28				
	d					14 28												15 24			15 28				
Windermere	a																								
Penrith North Lakes	d		14 45												15 30						15 53				
Carlisle [8]	a		15 00			15 06									15 46			16 01			16 10				
	d		15 02			15 07									15 47			16 03			16 11				
Lockerbie	d					15 27															16 30				
Carstairs	a																								
Motherwell	a																								
Glasgow Central [15]	a					16 30									17 01			17 17							
Haymarket	a		16 16																		17s31				
Edinburgh [10]	a		16 22																		17 39				
Perth	a																								
Dundee	a																								
Aberdeen	a																								
Inverness	a																								

OVERNIGHT SLEEPERS. For sleeper trains, operated by First ScotRail, please refer to Tables 400 - 404

Table 65

Saturdays

from 27 October

London and West Midlands - North West England and Scotland

Route Diagram - see first Page of Table 65

		VT	VT	VT	XC	TP	VT	NT	LM	VT	XC	VT	TP	LM	VT	VT	XC	TP	VT	NT	LM	VT
		◇1	◇1	◇1	◇1	◇1	◇1		◇1	◇1	◇1	◇1	◇1	◇1	◇1	◇1	◇1	◇1	◇1		◇1	◇1
													A									
London Euston 15 ⊖	d	13 07	13 10	13 20			13 30					14 00			14 07	14 20			14 30			
Watford Junction	d																					
Milton Keynes Central	d		13 41	13 50												14 50						
Rugby	d																					
Nuneaton	d																					
Tamworth Low Level	d																					
Lichfield Trent Valley	d																					
Coventry	d				13 27												14 27					
Birmingham International ✈	d				13 38												14 38					
Birmingham New Street 12	d				13 57				14 01	14 20	14 31			14 36			14 57				15 01	15 20
Wolverhampton 7	d				14 15				14 19	14 37	14 49			14 53			15 15				15 19	15 37
Penkridge	d													15 03								
Stafford	a	14 22			14 29				14 35		15 00			15 09	15 22		15 29				15 35	
	d	14 23			14 30				14 35		15 01			15 09	15 23		15 30				15 35	
Stoke-on-Trent	a			14 48	14 54						15 19	15 24				15 48	15 54					
Congleton	a																					
Macclesfield	a				15 11							15 41					16 11					
Crewe 10	a		14 47						14 56	15 07				15 30							15 56	16 08
	d		14 49						14 57	15 09				15 31							15 57	16 09
Chester	a		15 12																			
Wrexham General	a																					
Llandudno	a																					
Bangor (Gwynedd)	a																					
Holyhead	a																					
Wilmslow	a																					
Stockport	a			15 16	15 27						15 49	15 55				16 16	16 27					
Manchester Piccadilly 10	a			15 28	15 39						15 59	16 07				16 28	16 39					
Hartford	a								15 11												16 10	
Warrington Bank Quay	a						15 14			15 26									16 14			16 26
	d						15 14			15 27									16 14			16 27
Runcorn	a	14 55							15 21					15 50	15 55						16 22	
Liverpool South Parkway 7 ✈	a								15 30					15 59							16 31	
Liverpool Lime Street 10	a	15 15							15 43					16 10	16 15						16 44	
	d							14 57												15 57		
Manchester Airport ✈	d					14 29							15 00					15 29				
Manchester Piccadilly 10	d					14 46							15 16					15 46				
Bolton	d					15 07							15 33					16 07				
Wigan North Western	a						15 25	15 30		15 37									16 25	16 30		16 37
	d						15 25	15 31		15 38									16 25	16 31		16 38
Preston 8	a					15 33	15 38	15 54		15 51			15 57					16 33	16 38	16 54		16 51
Preston 8	d					15 38	15 41	15 55		15 53			15 58					16 38	16 41	16 55		16 53
Blackpool North	a					16 05		16 21										17 07		17 21		
Lancaster 6	a						15 54			16 08			16 14						16 54			17 09
	d						15 55			16 08			16 15						16 55			17 10
Barrow-in-Furness	a												17 18									
Oxenholme Lake District	a						16 08															17 24
	d						16 08															17 25
Windermere	a																					
Penrith North Lakes	d									16 45									17 30			
Carlisle 8	a						16 46			17 00									17 46			18 03
	d						16 47			17 03									17 47			18 04
Lockerbie	d																					
Carstairs	a																					
Motherwell	a																					
Glasgow Central 15	a						18 01												19 01			19 17
Haymarket	a									18 14												
Edinburgh 10	a									18 22												
Perth	a																					
Dundee	a																					
Aberdeen	a																					
Inverness	a																					

A to Preston

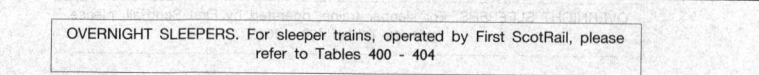

OVERNIGHT SLEEPERS. For sleeper trains, operated by First ScotRail, please refer to Tables 400 - 404

London and West Midlands - North West England and Scotland

Route Diagram - see first Page of Table 65

		XC	VT	TP				LM	VT	VT	VT	XC	TP	VT	NT		LM	VT	XC	VT	TP	NT		LM	VT
		◇1	◇1	◇1				◇1	◇1	◇1	◇1	◇1	◇1	◇1			◇1	◇1	◇1	◇1	◇1			◇1	◇1
		🛒	🛒	🍴					🛒	🛒	🛒	🍴	🍴	🛒				🛒	🛒	🛒	🍴				🛒
London Euston 15 ⊖	d		15 00						15 07	15 10	15 20			15 30						16 00					16 07
Watford Junction	d																								
Milton Keynes Central	d									15 41	15 50														
Rugby	d																								
Nuneaton	d																								
Tamworth Low Level	d																								
Lichfield Trent Valley	d																								
Coventry	d											15 27													
Birmingham International ✈	d											15 38													
Birmingham New Street 12	d	15 31						15 36				15 57					16 01	16 20	16 31					16 36	
Wolverhampton 7 🚊	d	15 49						15 53				16 15					16 19	16 37	16 49					16 53	
Penkridge	d							16 03																17 03	
Stafford	a	16 00						16 09	16 22			16 29					16 35		17 00					17 09	17 22
	d	16 01						16 09	16 23			16 30					16 35		17 01					17 09	17 23
Stoke-on-Trent	a	16 19	16 24								16 48	16 54							17 19	17 24					
Congleton	a																								
Macclesfield	a		16 41									17 11								17 41					
Crewe 10	a							16 30		16 47							16 56	17 07						17 30	
	d							16 31		16 49							16 57	17 09						17 31	
Chester	a									17 12															
Wrexham General	a																								
Llandudno	a																								
Bangor (Gwynedd)	a																								
Holyhead	a																								
Wilmslow	a																								
Stockport	a	16 49	16 54								17 16	17 27							17 49	17 55					
Manchester Piccadilly 10 🚊	a	16 59	17 07								17 28	17 39							17 59	18 07					
Hartford	a																17 11								
Warrington Bank Quay	a													17 14				17 26							
	d													17 14				17 27							
Runcorn	a							16 50	16 55								17 21							17 50	17 55
Liverpool South Parkway 7 ✈	a							16 59									17 30							17 59	
Liverpool Lime Street 10	a							17 10	17 15								17 43							18 10	18 15
	d														16 57							17 19			
Manchester Airport ✈	d			16 00									16 29								17 00				
Manchester Piccadilly 10 🚊	d			16 16									16 46								17 15				
Bolton	d			16 33									17 06								17 32				
Wigan North Western	a													17 25	17 30			17 37				18 04			
	d													17 25	17 31			17 38							
Preston 8	a			16 55									17 30	17 38	17 54			17 51			17 55				
Preston 8	d			17 00	17 04								17 32	17 41	17 55			17 53			17 58				
Blackpool North	a												18 02		18 24										
Lancaster 6	a			17 16	17 20									17 54				18 08			18 13				
	d			17 16	17 21									17 55				18 08			18 14				
Barrow-in-Furness	a																								
Oxenholme Lake District	a			17 30	17 37									18 08				18 22			18 28				
	d			17 30	17 38									18 08				18 23			18 28				
Windermere	a				18 00																				
Penrith North Lakes	d																	18 49			18 53				
Carlisle 8	a			18 10										18 46				19 04			19 09				
	d			18 11										18 47				19 04			19 11				
Lockerbie	d			18 30																	19 30				
Carstairs	a																								
Motherwell	a																				20s16				
Glasgow Central 15	a													20 01							20 33				
Haymarket	a			19s31														20 16							
Edinburgh 10	a			19 39														20 22							
Perth	a																								
Dundee	a																								
Aberdeen	a																								
Inverness	a																								

OVERNIGHT SLEEPERS. For sleeper trains, operated by First ScotRail, please refer to Tables 400 - 404

Table 65

Saturdays

from 27 October

London and West Midlands - North West England and Scotland

Route Diagram - see first Page of Table 65

		VT	XC	LM	TP	VT	VT	TP	VT	XC		VT	TP		LM	VT	VT	XC	LM	TP		VT	VT	XC
		◇1	◇1	◇1	◇1	◇1	◇1	◇1	◇1	◇1		◇1	◇1		◇1	◇1	◇1	◇1	◇1	◇1		◇1	◇1	◇1
													A											
		⊐P	⊤o			⊐P	⊐P	⊤o	⊐P	⊤o		⊐P	⊤o			⊐P	⊐P	⊤o		⊤o		⊐P	⊐P	⊐P
London Euston 15 ⊖	d	16 20				16 30	16 33					17 00				17 07	17 20					17 30		
Watford Junction	d																							
Milton Keynes Central	d	16 50															17 50							
Rugby	d																							
Nuneaton	d															18 03								
Tamworth Low Level	d						17 38																	
Lichfield Trent Valley	d						17 45																	
Coventry	d		16 27															17 27						
Birmingham International ✈	d		16 38															17 38						
Birmingham New Street 12	d		16 57	17 01					17 20	17 31					17 36			17 57	18 01				18 20	18 31
Wolverhampton 7 ⛴	d		17 15	17 19					17 37	17 49					17 53			18 15	18 19				18 37	18 49
Penkridge	d			17 29											18 03				18 29					
Stafford	a		17 29	17 35			17 58			18 00					18 09	18 26		18 29	18 35					19 00
	d		17 30	17 36			17 59			18 01					18 09	18 27		18 30	18 35					19 01
Stoke-on-Trent	a	17 48	17 54							18 19		18 24					18 48	18 54						19 19
Congleton	a																							
Macclesfield	a		18 11									18 41						19 11						
Crewe 10	a			17 56					18 07						18 30				18 56				19 07	
	d			17 57					18 09						18 33				18 59				19 09	
Chester	a																							
Wrexham General	a																							
Llandudno	a																							
Bangor (Gwynedd)	a																							
Holyhead	a																							
Wilmslow	a																							
Stockport	a	18 16	18 27							18 49		18 55					19 16	19 27						19 49
Manchester Piccadilly 10 ⛴	a	18 28	18 39							18 59		19 07					19 28	19 39						19 59
Hartford	a			18 11											18 43				19 12					
Warrington Bank Quay	a					18 14			18 26													19 14	19 26	
	d					18 14			18 27													19 14	19 27	
Runcorn	a			18 21			18 31								18 52	18 59			19 22					
Liverpool South Parkway 7 ✈	a			18 30											19 02				19 31					
Liverpool Lime Street 10	a			18 43			18 52								19 14	19 17			19 44					
	d																							
Manchester Airport ✈	d							17 29					18 00							18 29				
Manchester Piccadilly 10 ⛴	d							17 46					18 16							18 46				
Bolton	d							18 07					18 33							19 07				
Wigan North Western	a					18 25			18 37													19 25	19 37	
	d					18 25			18 38													19 25	19 38	
Preston 8	a					18 38		18 38	18 51				18 55							19 33		19 38	19 54	
Preston 8	d				18 02	18 41		18 40	18 53				18 58							19 38		19 41		
Blackpool North	a							19 10												20 06				
Lancaster 6	a				18 18	18 54			19 08				19 13									19 54		
	d				18 18	18 55			19 08				19 15									19 55		
Barrow-in-Furness	a				19 26								20 19											
Oxenholme Lake District	a					19 08			19 22													20 08		
	d					19 08			19 24													20 08		
Windermere	a																							
Penrith North Lakes	d					19 34																20 34		
Carlisle 8	a					19 49			20 01													20 49		
	d					19 51			20 03													20 51		
Lockerbie	d																							
Carstairs	a																							
Motherwell	a																							
Glasgow Central 15	a					21 01			21 17													22 01		
Haymarket	a																							
Edinburgh 10	a																							
Perth	a																							
Dundee	a																							
Aberdeen	a																							
Inverness	a																							

A ⊤o to Preston

OVERNIGHT SLEEPERS. For sleeper trains, operated by First ScotRail, please refer to Tables 400 - 404

Table 65

Saturdays
from 27 October

London and West Midlands - North West England and Scotland

Route Diagram - see first Page of Table 65

		VT	LM	TP		NT	VT		VT	VT	XC	LM	TP	VT	VT	TP			NT	VT	XC	VT	VT	VT	XC
		◇1	◇1	◇1			◇1		◇1	◇1	◇1	◇1	◇1	◇1	◇1	◇1				◇1	◇1	◇1	◇1	◇1	◇1
																									A
		🍴					🍴		🍴	🍴	🛒			🍴	🍴					🍴	🍴	🍴	🍴	🍴	🛒
London Euston 15 ⊖	d	18 00					18 07		18 10	18 20				18 30						18 33		19 00	19 07	19 20	
Watford Junction	d																								
Milton Keynes Central	d								18 41	18 50														19 50	
Rugby	d																								
Nuneaton	d																						20 03		
Tamworth Low Level	d																			19 38					
Lichfield Trent Valley	d																			19 45					
Coventry	d										18 27														19 27
Birmingham International ✈	d										18 38														19 38
Birmingham New Street 12	d		18 36								18 57	19 01			19 20						19 31				19 57
Wolverhampton 7 🚌	d		18 53								19 15	19 19			19 37						19 49				20 15
Penkridge	d		19 03									19 29													
Stafford	a		19 09				19 22				19 29	19 35								19 58	20 00		20 26		20 29
	d		19 09				19 23				19 30	19 36								19 59	20 01		20 27		20 30
Stoke-on-Trent	a	19 24								19 48	19 54										20 19	20 24		20 48	20 54
Congleton	a																								
Macclesfield	a	19 41									20 11										20 36	20 41			21 11
Crewe 10	a		19 30						19 47			19 58			20 07								20 45		
	d								19 49			19 58			20 09								20 47		
Chester	a								20 12																
Wrexham General	a																								
Llandudno	a																								
Bangor (Gwynedd)	a																								
Holyhead	a																								
Wilmslow	a																								
Stockport	a	19 55								20 16	20 27										20 49	20 55		21 16	21 27
Manchester Piccadilly 10 🚌	a	20 07								20 28	20 39										20 59	21 07		21 28	21 39
Hartford	a											20 11													
Warrington Bank Quay	a													20 14	20 26										
	d													20 14	20 27										
Runcorn	a						19 55					20 24								20 31			21 05		
Liverpool South Parkway 7 ✈	a											20 33													
Liverpool Lime Street 10	a						20 15					20 46								20 52			21 25		
	d					19 23													20 25						
Manchester Airport ✈	d			19 00									19 29			20 00									
Manchester Piccadilly 10 🚌	d			19 16									19 46			20 16									
Bolton	d			19 33									20 07			20 33									
Wigan North Western	a					19 54								20 25	20 37				20 57						
	d					19 55								20 25	20 38				20 57						
Preston 8	a			19 58		20 18							20 33	20 38	20 59	20 57			21 22						
Preston 8	d			20 01		20 19							20 38	20 41		21 02			21 24						
Blackpool North	a					20 44							21 06						21 53						
Lancaster 6	a			20 17										20 54		21 17									
	d			20 17										20 55		21 18									
Barrow-in-Furness	a			21 20												22 21									
Oxenholme Lake District	a													21 08											
	d													21 09											
Windermere	a																								
Penrith North Lakes	d													21 34											
Carlisle 8	a													21 49											
	d													21 51											
Lockerbie	d																								
Carstairs	a																								
Motherwell	a													22 44											
Glasgow Central 15	a													23 04											
Haymarket	a																								
Edinburgh 10	a																								
Perth	a																								
Dundee	a																								
Aberdeen	a																								
Inverness	a																								

A 🛒 to Birmingham New Street

OVERNIGHT SLEEPERS. For sleeper trains, operated by First ScotRail, please refer to Tables 400 - 404

Table 65

Saturdays
from 27 October

London and West Midlands - North West England and Scotland

Route Diagram - see first Page of Table 65

		TP	VT	LM	VT	XC	LM	XC	VT	VT	LM	NT	TP	TP	VT	XC	TP	XC	LM
		◇1	◇1	◇1	◇1	◇1	◇1	◇1	◇1	◇1	◇1		◇1	◇1	◇1	◇1	◇1	◇1	◇1
								A											
			(catering)		(catering)	(catering)		(trolley)	(catering)	(catering)					(catering)				
London Euston 15 ⊖	d		19 30						20 11	20 20					20 31				
Watford Junction	d														20u46				
Milton Keynes Central	d									21 05									
Rugby	d								21 15						21 36				
Nuneaton	d									21 33									
Tamworth Low Level	d														21 53				
Lichfield Trent Valley	d														22 00				
Coventry	d							20 27								21 27			
Birmingham International ✈	d							20 38								21 38			
Birmingham New Street 12	d			20 01	20 20	20 31	20 36	20 57			21 36					21 57		22 31	22 36
Wolverhampton 7 ⛴	d			20 22	20 37	20 49	20 53	21 15			21 59					22 16		22 49	22 56
Penkridge	d			20 31			21 03				22 09								23 06
Stafford	a			20 37	20 49	21 00	21 09	21 29	21 46		22 15					22 29		23 01	23 13
	d			20 38	20 50	21 01	21 09	21 30	21 46		22 16					22 30		23 02	23 13
Stoke-on-Trent	a					21 20		21 52		22 05						22 50		23 20	
Congleton	a																		
Macclesfield	a					21 38		22 11		22 21						23 07		23 38	
Crewe 10	a		21 04	20 58	21 10		21 30		22 05		22 40				22 35				23 37
	d		21 05	21 06					22 06						22 36				
Chester	a																		
Wrexham General	a																		
Llandudno	a																		
Bangor (Gwynedd)	a																		
Holyhead	a																		
Wilmslow	a																		
Stockport	a					21 53		22 27		22 35						23 21		23 53	
Manchester Piccadilly 10 ⛴	a					22 04		22 39		22 51					23 08	23 32		00 10	
Hartford	a			21 19															
Warrington Bank Quay	a		21 22																
	d		21 22																
Runcorn	a			21 29					22 24										
Liverpool South Parkway 7 ✈	a			21 38															
Liverpool Lime Street 10	a			21 50					22 46										
	d																		
Manchester Airport ✈	d	20 29											21 29	22 00			22 29		
Manchester Piccadilly 10 ⛴	d	20 46											21 46	22 16			22 46		
Bolton	d	21 07											22 07	22 33			23 07		
Wigan North Western	a		21 33																
	d		21 33																
Preston 8	a	21 33	21 49										22 36	22 54			23 33		
Preston 8	d	21 38										21 59	22 38	22 55			23 35		
Blackpool North	a	22 06											23 04				00 02		
Lancaster 6	a											22 19		23 11					
	d											22 19		23 11					
Barrow-in-Furness	a											23 24		00 15					
Oxenholme Lake District	a																		
	d																		
Windermere	a																		
Penrith North Lakes	d																		
Carlisle 8	a																		
	d																		
Lockerbie	d																		
Carstairs	a																		
Motherwell	a																		
Glasgow Central 15	a																		
Haymarket	a																		
Edinburgh 10	a																		
Perth	a																		
Dundee	a																		
Aberdeen	a																		
Inverness	a																		

A (trolley) to Birmingham New Street

OVERNIGHT SLEEPERS. For sleeper trains, operated by First ScotRail, please refer to Tables 400 - 404

Table 65

Sundays
until 24 June

London and West Midlands - North West England and Scotland

Route Diagram - see first Page of Table 65

		TP	TP	XC	TP	TP	TP	NT	TP			TP	NT	VT		NT	TP	VT	TP	VT		VT	VT	LM	XC
		◇1	◇1	◇1			◇1		◇1			◇1		◇1			◇1	◇1	◇1	◇1		◇1	◇1	◇1	◇1
					🚌	🚌																			
								✠				✠		⊡				⊡	✠	⊡		⊡	⊡		✠
London Euston 15 ⊖	d																					08 15	08 20		
Watford Junction	d																								
Milton Keynes Central	d																						09 06		
Rugby	d																								
Nuneaton	d																					09 44			
Tamworth Low Level	d																								
Lichfield Trent Valley	d																								
Coventry	d																								
Birmingham International ✈	d																								
Birmingham New Street 12	d			22p31										08 35				09 09						09 34	10 01
Wolverhampton 7 🚌	d			22p49										09 04				09 37						10 00	10 29
Penkridge	d																							10 10	
Stafford	a			23p01										09 16								10 08		10 16	10 43
	d			23p02										09 17								10 08		10 16	10 44
Stoke-on-Trent	a			23p20																			10 19		11 02
Congleton	a																								
Macclesfield	a			23p38																			10 36		11 19
Crewe 10	a													09 35				10 07				10 28		10 37	
	d													09 37				10 08		10 21		10 30		10 38	
Chester	a																								
Wrexham General	a																								
Llandudno	a																								
Bangor (Gwynedd)	a																								
Holyhead	a																								
Wilmslow	a																								
Stockport	a			23p53																			10 50		11 37
Manchester Piccadilly 10 🚌	a			00 10																			11 03		11 47
Hartford	a																							10 50	
Warrington Bank Quay	a													09 54				10 26		10 37					
	d													09 54				10 27		10 37					
Runcorn	a																					10 47		11 00	
Liverpool South Parkway 7 ✈	a																							11 09	
Liverpool Lime Street 10	a																					11 09		11 20	
	d																								
Manchester Airport ✈	d	22p00	22p29		00 05	05 30	07 55		08 47			09 00					09 30		10 00						
Manchester Piccadilly 10 🚌	d	22p16	22p46		00 30	05 55	08 11		09 03			09 16					09 46		10 16						
Bolton	d	22p33	23p07		00s55	06s20	08 30		09 23			09 33					10 05		10 33						
Wigan North Western	a													10 05				10 37		10 48					
	d													10 05				10 38		10 48					
Preston 8	a	22p54	23p33		01s30	06s55	08 57		09 50			09 57		10 22			10 33	10 51	10 57	11 02					
Preston 8	d	22p55	23p35				08 58	09 05	09 52	10 07		10 00	10 00			10 29	10 35	10 52	10 58	11 04					
Blackpool North	a		00 02		02 10	07 35	09 23		10 18							10 53	11 01								
Lancaster 6	a	23p11								10 22		10 15						11 07	11 13	11 20					
	d	23p11								10 23		10 16						11 08	11 14						
Barrow-in-Furness	a	00 15																							
Oxenholme Lake District	a									10 39		10 30						11 22	11 28						
	d									10 40		10 30						11 23	11 28						
Windermere	a									10 57															
Penrith North Lakes	d											10 55							11 53						
Carlisle 8	a							12 17				11 12	12 57					12 01	12 10						
	d											11 13						12 02	12 11						
Lockerbie	d											11 32							12 30						
Carstairs	a																								
Motherwell	a																								
Glasgow Central 15	a																	13 17	13 35						
Haymarket	a											12s32													
Edinburgh 10	a											12 39													
Perth	a																								
Dundee	a																								
Aberdeen	a																								
Inverness	a																								

OVERNIGHT SLEEPERS. For sleeper trains, operated by First ScotRail, please refer to Tables 400 - 404

Table 65

Sundays
until 24 June

London and West Midlands - North West England and Scotland

Route Diagram - see first Page of Table 65

		TP	VT	VT	VT	VT	VT	LM	XC	TP	TP	VT	VT	VT	VT	LM	XC	TP	TP	VT
		◇1	◇1	◇1	◇1	◇1	◇1	◇1	◇1	◇1	◇1	◇1	◇1	◇1	◇1	◇1	◇1	◇1	◇1	◇1
			☕	☕	☕	☕	☕		🛒			☕	☕	☕	☕		🛒	🛒		☕
London Euston 15 ⊖	d			08 45		09 15	09 20					09 45		10 15	10 20					10 45
Watford Junction	d																			
Milton Keynes Central	d			09 32			10 07					10 33			11 07					11 33
Rugby	d			10 09								11 09								12 09
Nuneaton	d					10 45								11 47						
Tamworth Low Level	d																			
Lichfield Trent Valley	d																			
Coventry	d								10 28								11 29			
Birmingham International ✈	d								10 40								11 40			
Birmingham New Street 12	d				10 09			10 35	11 01				11 09			11 33	12 01			
Wolverhampton 7	d				10 37			11 00	11 30				11 37			12 00	12 28			
Penkridge	d							11 10								12 10				
Stafford	a					11 09		11 16	11 42					12 13		12 16	12 42			
	d					11 09		11 16	11 44					12 13		12 17	12 43			
Stoke-on-Trent	a						11 20		12 03						12 24		13 02			
Congleton	a																			
Macclesfield	a						11 37		12 21						12 40		13 20			
Crewe 10	a			10 55	11 07	11 30		11 37				11 55	12 07	12 32		12 37				12 56
	d		10 42	10 57	11 09	11 32		11 38				11 57	12 09	12 34		12 38				12 58
Chester	a		11 02																	
Wrexham General	a																			
Llandudno	a																			
Bangor (Gwynedd)	a		12 09																	
Holyhead	a		12 43																	
Wilmslow	a																			
Stockport	a						11 51		12 35						12 55		13 38			
Manchester Piccadilly 10	a						12 04		12 44						13 08		13 46			
Hartford	a							11 50								12 50				
Warrington Bank Quay	a			11 14	11 26							12 14	12 26							13 15
	d			11 14	11 27							12 14	12 27							13 15
Runcorn	a					11 49		12 01						12 51		13 01				
Liverpool South Parkway 7 ✈	a							12 10								13 10				
Liverpool Lime Street 10	a					12 10		12 21						13 12		13 21				
	d																			
Manchester Airport ✈	d	10 30								11 00	11 30							12 00	12 30	
Manchester Piccadilly 10	d	10 46								11 16	11 46							12 16	12 46	
Bolton	d	11 05								11 33	12 05							12 33	13 05	
Wigan North Western	a			11 25	11 37							12 25	12 37							13 26
	d			11 25	11 38							12 25	12 38							13 26
Preston 8	a	11 33		11 38	11 51					11 57	12 33	12 38	12 51					12 57	13 33	13 40
Preston 8	d	11 35		11 40	11 53					11 58	12 35	12 40	12 53					12 58	13 35	13 42
Blackpool North	a	12 01									13 01								14 01	
Lancaster 6	a			11 54	12 08					12 13		12 54	13 08					13 13		13 56
	d			11 55	12 08					12 14		12 55	13 08					13 14		13 57
Barrow-in-Furness	a									13 17										
Oxenholme Lake District	a			12 08	12 22							13 08	13 22					13 28		14 10
	d			12 08	12 24							13 08	13 24					13 28		14 10
Windermere	a																			
Penrith North Lakes	d			12 34								13 34						13 53		14 36
Carlisle 8	a			12 49	13 01							13 49	14 01					14 10		14 51
	d			12 50	13 03							13 50	14 03					14 11		14 52
Lockerbie	d																	14 30		
Carstairs	a																			
Motherwell	a																			
Glasgow Central 15	a			14 01								15 02	15 16							16 05
Haymarket	a				14 13													15s29		
Edinburgh 10	a				14 22													15 39		
Perth	a																			
Dundee	a																			
Aberdeen	a																			
Inverness	a																			

OVERNIGHT SLEEPERS. For sleeper trains, operated by First ScotRail, please refer to Tables 400 - 404

Table 65

Sundays

until 24 June

London and West Midlands - North West England and Scotland

Route Diagram - see first Page of Table 65

		VT		VT	VT	LM	VT	VT	XC	TP				TP	VT	VT	VT	LM	VT	XC	VT	XC		TP	TP
		◇1		◇1	◇1	◇1	◇1	◇1	◇1	◇1				◇1	◇1	◇1	◇1	◇1	◇1	◇1	◇1	◇1		◇1	◇1
		☕		☕	☕		☕	☕	🛒	🛒					☕	☕	☕		☕	🛒	☕	🛒		🛒	
London Euston 15 ⊖	d			11 15	11 20		12 02	12 15							12 25	12 55			13 02		13 15				
Watford Junction	d																								
Milton Keynes Central	d			12 03	12 08			12 48													13 48				
Rugby	d																								
Nuneaton	d																								
Tamworth Low Level	d																								
Lichfield Trent Valley	d																								
Coventry	d								12 28													13 26			
Birmingham International ✈	d								12 40													13 38			
Birmingham New Street 12	d	12 09				12 28			12 58								13 10	13 28		13 31		13 58			
Wolverhampton 7 ⛴	d	12 37				12 53			13 26								13 37	13 53		14 01		14 25			
Penkridge	d					13 03												14 03							
Stafford	a			12 53		13 09	13 24		13 39									14 09	14 21			14 38			
	d			12 53		13 09	13 25		13 40									14 09	14 22			14 39			
Stoke-on-Trent	a				13 09			13 50	13 58							14 26				14 31	14 50	14 57			
Congleton	a																								
Macclesfield	a				13 26				14 16							14 42				14 49		15 14			
Crewe 10	a	13 07		13 13		13 30	13 43										14 07	14 29	14 43						
	d	13 09		13 15		13 31	13 45										14 09	14 30	14 45						
Chester	a																								
Wrexham General	a																								
Llandudno	a																								
Bangor (Gwynedd)	a																								
Holyhead	a																								
Wilmslow	a																								
Stockport	a				13 41			14 18	14 29							14 56				15 02	15 18	15 26			
Manchester Piccadilly 10 ⛴	a				13 53			14 29	14 40							15 09				15 17	15 29	15 38			
Hartford	a					13 43												14 42							
Warrington Bank Quay	a	13 26													14 16		14 26								
	d	13 27													14 16		14 27								
Runcorn	a			13 32		13 54	14 02											14 53	15 02						
Liverpool South Parkway 7 ✈	a					14 03												15 02							
Liverpool Lime Street 10	a			13 54		14 14	14 24											15 13	15 24						
	d																								
Manchester Airport ✈	d									12 58				13 30										13 58	14 30
Manchester Piccadilly 10 ⛴	d									13 16				13 46										14 16	14 46
Bolton	d									13 33				14 05										14 33	15 05
Wigan North Western	a	13 37													14 27		14 37								
	d	13 38													14 27		14 38								
Preston 8	a	13 51								13 57				14 33	14 40		14 50							14 57	15 33
Preston 8	d	13 53								14 00	14 04			14 35	14 42		14 53							15 00	15 35
Blackpool North	a													15 01											16 01
Lancaster 6	a	14 08								14 15	14 20				14 56		15 08							15 15	
	d	14 08								14 16	14 20				14 58		15 09							15 16	
Barrow-in-Furness	a										15 24														
Oxenholme Lake District	a									14 30							15 22							15 30	
	d									14 30							15 23							15 30	
Windermere	a																								
Penrith North Lakes	d	14 45								14 55					15 32									15 55	
Carlisle 8	a	15 00								15 12					15 47		16 01							16 12	
	d	15 03								15 17					15 48		16 03							16 13	
Lockerbie	d																							16 32	
Carstairs	a																								
Motherwell	a																								
Glasgow Central 15	a									16 35					17 00		17 17								
Haymarket	a	16 14																						17s30	
Edinburgh 10	a	16 22																						17 39	
Perth	a																								
Dundee	a																								
Aberdeen	a																								
Inverness	a																								

OVERNIGHT SLEEPERS. For sleeper trains, operated by First ScotRail, please refer to Tables 400 - 404

Table 65

Sundays
until 24 June

London and West Midlands - North West England and Scotland

Route Diagram - see first Page of Table 65

		VT	VT	VT	LM	VT	XC	VT	XC	TP	TP	VT	VT	VT	LM	VT	VT	XC	VT	XC
		◇1	◇1	◇1	◇1	◇1	◇1	◇1	◇1	◇1	◇1	◇1	◇1	◇1	◇1	◇1	◇1	◇1	◇1	◇1
		⊡	⊡	⊡		⊡	⊥	⊡	⊥			⊡	⊡	⊡		⊡	⊡	⊥	⊡	⊥
London Euston 15 ⊖	d	13 25	13 55			14 02		14 15				14 25	14 55			15 02	15 05		15 15	
Watford Junction	d																			
Milton Keynes Central	d							14 48									15 39		15 48	
Rugby	d																			
Nuneaton	d																			
Tamworth Low Level	d																			
Lichfield Trent Valley	d																			
Coventry	d								14 26											15 26
Birmingham International ✈	d								14 38											15 38
Birmingham New Street 12	d			14 10	14 28		14 31		14 58					15 10	15 28			15 31		15 58
Wolverhampton 7	d			14 37	14 53		15 01		15 26					15 37	15 53			16 01		16 26
Penkridge	d				15 03										16 03					
Stafford	a				15 09	15 24			15 39						16 09	16 21				16 37
	d				15 09	15 25			15 40						16 09	16 21				16 37
Stoke-on-Trent	a		15 25				15 35	15 50	15 57				16 24					16 33	16 50	16 57
Congleton	a																			
Macclesfield	a		15 42				15 57		16 14				16 42					16 54		17 14
Crewe 10	a			15 07	15 29	15 43								16 07	16 30		16 50			
	d			15 09	15 30	15 45								16 09	16 31		16 52			
Chester	a																17 14			
Wrexham General	a																			
Llandudno	a																			
Bangor (Gwynedd)	a																			
Holyhead	a																			
Wilmslow	a																			
Stockport	a		15 56				16 09	16 18	16 26				16 56					17 07	17 18	17 29
Manchester Piccadilly 10	a		16 09				16 22	16 29	16 38				17 09					17 19	17 29	17 40
Hartford	a				15 42										16 43					
Warrington Bank Quay	a	15 16		15 26								16 16		16 26						
	d	15 16		15 27								16 16		16 27						
Runcorn	a				15 53	16 02									16 54	16 57				
Liverpool South Parkway 7 ✈	a				16 02										17 03					
Liverpool Lime Street 10	a				16 13	16 24									17 14	17 16				
	d																			
Manchester Airport ✈	d									14 58	15 30									
Manchester Piccadilly 10	d									15 16	15 46									
Bolton	d									15 33	16 05									
Wigan North Western	a	15 27		15 37								16 27		16 37						
	d	15 27		15 38								16 27		16 38						
Preston 8	a	15 40		15 51						15 57	16 33	16 40		16 51						
Preston 8	d	15 42		15 53						16 00	16 35	16 42		16 53						
Blackpool North	a										17 01									
Lancaster 6	a	15 56		16 08						16 15		16 56		17 08						
	d	15 58		16 08						16 16		16 57		17 08						
Barrow-in-Furness	a									17 19										
Oxenholme Lake District	a	16 10												17 22						
	d	16 11												17 23						
Windermere	a																			
Penrith North Lakes	d			16 45								17 32								
Carlisle 8	a	16 48		17 00								17 47		18 01						
	d	16 49		17 02								17 48		18 03						
Lockerbie	d																			
Carstairs	a																			
Motherwell	a																			
Glasgow Central 15	a	18 01										19 00		19 17						
Haymarket	a			18 13																
Edinburgh 10	a			18 22																
Perth	a																			
Dundee	a																			
Aberdeen	a																			
Inverness	a																			

OVERNIGHT SLEEPERS. For sleeper trains, operated by First ScotRail, please refer to Tables 400 - 404

Table 65

Sundays
until 24 June

London and West Midlands - North West England and Scotland

Route Diagram - see first Page of Table 65

		TP		TP	VT		VT	VT	TP		LM	VT	VT	XC	VT		XC	TP	VT	VT	VT	LM	VT	VT	XC
		◇1		◇1	◇1		◇1	◇1	◇1		◇1	◇1	◇1	◇1	◇1		◇1	◇1	◇1	◇1	◇1	◇1	◇1	◇1	◇1
		⊼			⊐		⊐	⊐	⊼			⊐	⊐	⊼	⊐		⊼		⊐	⊐	⊐		⊐	⊐	⊼
London Euston 15 ⊖	d				15 25		15 55					16 02	16 05		16 15				16 25	16 55			17 02	17 05	
Watford Junction	d																								
Milton Keynes Central	d												16 39		16 48									17 39	
Rugby	d																								
Nuneaton	d																							18 10	
Tamworth Low Level	d																								
Lichfield Trent Valley	d																								
Coventry	d																16 26								
Birmingham International ✈	d																16 38								
Birmingham New Street 12	d							16 10			16 28			16 31			16 58				17 10	17 28			17 31
Wolverhampton 7 ⛴	d							16 37			16 53			17 01			17 26				17 37	17 53			18 01
Penkridge	d										17 03											18 03			
Stafford	a										17 09	17 24					17 38					18 09	18 24		
	d										17 09	17 25					17 39					18 09	18 25		
Stoke-on-Trent	a						17 25							17 34	17 50		17 57			18 25					18 30
Congleton	a																								
Macclesfield	a						17 42							17 54			18 14			18 42					18 48
Crewe 10	a							17 07			17 29		17 50								18 07	18 30		18 53	
	d							17 09			17 31		17 52								18 09	18 31		18 56	
Chester	a												18 14											19 14	
Wrexham General	a																								
Llandudno	a																								
Bangor (Gwynedd)	a																								
Holyhead	a																								
Wilmslow	a																								
Stockport	a						17 56							18 07	18 18		18 28			18 56					19 04
Manchester Piccadilly 10 ⛴	a						18 09							18 19	18 29		18 40			19 09					19 19
Hartford	a										17 42											18 43			
Warrington Bank Quay	a				17 16			17 26											18 16		18 26				
	d				17 16			17 27											18 17		18 27				
Runcorn	a										17 53	17 57										18 54	18 57		
Liverpool South Parkway 7 ✈	a										18 02											19 03			
Liverpool Lime Street 10	a										18 14	18 16										19 14	19 19		
	d																								
Manchester Airport ✈	d	15 58		16 30					16 58									17 30							
Manchester Piccadilly 10 ⛴	d	16 16		16 46					17 16									17 46							
Bolton	d	16 33		17 05					17 33									18 05							
Wigan North Western	a				17 27			17 37											18 27		18 37				
	d				17 27			17 38											18 28		18 38				
Preston 8	a	16 57		17 33	17 40			17 51	17 57									18 33	18 40		18 51				
Preston 8	d	17 00	18 07	17 35	17 42			17 53	18 00									18 35	18 42		18 53				
Blackpool North	a			18 01														19 01							
Lancaster 6	a	17 15	18 23		17 56			18 08	18 15										18 56		19 08				
	d	17 16	18 23		17 57			18 08	18 16										18 58		19 08				
Barrow-in-Furness	a																								
Oxenholme Lake District	a	17 30	18 40		18 10			18 22	18 30										19 10		19 22				
	d	17 30	18 40		18 10			18 23	18 30										19 11		19 24				
Windermere	a		19 01																						
Penrith North Lakes	d	17 55						18 49	18 55										19 36						
Carlisle 8	a	18 12			18 48			19 04	19 12										19 51		20 01				
	d	18 13			18 49			19 04	19 15										19 53		20 03				
Lockerbie	d								19 35																
Carstairs	a																								
Motherwell	a								20s22																
Glasgow Central 15	a				20 01				20 44										21 09		21 17				
Haymarket	a	19s28																							
Edinburgh 10	a	19 35						20 22																	
Perth	a																								
Dundee	a																								
Aberdeen	a																								
Inverness	a																								

OVERNIGHT SLEEPERS. For sleeper trains, operated by First ScotRail, please refer to Tables 400 - 404

Table 65

Sundays

until 24 June

London and West Midlands - North West England and Scotland

Route Diagram - see first Page of Table 65

		VT	XC	TP		TP	VT	VT	VT	TP	LM	VT	XC	VT	XC	TP	VT	VT	VT	LM	XC
		◇1	◇1	◇1		◇1	◇1	◇1	◇1	◇1	◇1	◇1	◇1	◇1	◇1	◇1	◇1	◇1	R 1	◇1	◇1
		⊡	⊼	⊼			⊡	⊡	⊡			⊡	⊼	⊡	⊼		⊡	⊡	⊡		⊼
London Euston 15 ⊖	d	17 15					17 25	17 55				18 02		18 15			18 25	18 55			
Watford Junction	d																				
Milton Keynes Central	d	17 48												18 48							
Rugby	d																				
Nuneaton	d																				
Tamworth Low Level	d																				
Lichfield Trent Valley	d																				
Coventry	d		17 26												18 26						
Birmingham International ✈	d		17 38												18 38						
Birmingham New Street 12	d		17 58						18 10		18 28		18 31		18 58				19 10	19 16	19 31
Wolverhampton 7 ⛴	d		18 26						18 37		18 54		19 01		19 26				19 37	19 45	20 01
Penkridge	d										19 04									19 54	
Stafford	a		18 36								19 10	19 24			19 38					20 00	
	d		18 36								19 10	19 25			19 39					20 01	
Stoke-on-Trent	a	18 50	18 55					19 25					19 31	19 50	19 57			20 25			20 33
Congleton	a																				
Macclesfield	a		19 14					19 42					19 49		20 14			20 42			20 56
Crewe 10	a								19 07		19 30								20 07	20 21	
	d								19 09		19 31								20 09	20 23	
Chester	a																				
Wrexham General	a																				
Llandudno	a																				
Bangor (Gwynedd)	a																				
Holyhead	a																				
Wilmslow	a																				
Stockport	a	19 18	19 28					19 56					20 02	20 18	20 29			20 56			21 09
Manchester Piccadilly 10 ⛴	a	19 29	19 40					20 09					20 18	20 29	20 40			21 09			21 20
Hartford	a										19 43									20 34	
Warrington Bank Quay	a						19 16		19 26								20 16		20 26		
	d						19 16		19 27								20 16		20 27		
Runcorn	a										19 54	19 58								20 45	
Liverpool South Parkway 7 ✈	a										20 03									20 54	
Liverpool Lime Street 10	a										20 14	20 16								21 06	
	d																				
Manchester Airport ✈	d			17 58		18 30				18 58						19 30					
Manchester Piccadilly 10 ⛴	d			18 16		18 46				19 16						19 46					
Bolton	d			18 33		19 05				19 33						20 05					
Wigan North Western	a						19 27		19 37								20 27		20 37		
	d						19 27		19 38								20 27		20 38		
Preston 8	a			18 55		19 33	19 40		19 51	19 57						20 33	20 40		20 51		
Preston 8	d			19 00	19 06	19 35	19 42		19 53	20 06						20 35	20 42		20 53		
Blackpool North	a					20 01										21 01					
Lancaster 6	a			19 15	19 22		19 56		20 08	20 23							20 56		21 08		
	d			19 16	19 22		19 57		20 08	20 24							20 57		21 08		
Barrow-in-Furness	a				20 26					21 19											
Oxenholme Lake District	a			19 30			20 10										21 10		21 22		
	d			19 30			20 10										21 11		21 24		
Windermere	a																				
Penrith North Lakes	d			19 55			20 36		20 45								21 36				
Carlisle 8	a			20 12			20 51		21 00								21 51		22 01		
	d			20 13			20 52		21 02								21 52		22 03		
Lockerbie	d			20 32															22 23		
Carstairs	a																				
Motherwell	a																22 48		23 09		
Glasgow Central 15	a						22 07										23 09		23 25		
Haymarket	a			21s30					22 15												
Edinburgh 10	a			21 39					22 21												
Perth	a																				
Dundee	a																				
Aberdeen	a																				
Inverness	a																				

OVERNIGHT SLEEPERS. For sleeper trains, operated by First ScotRail, please refer to Tables 400 - 404

Table 65

Sundays
until 24 June

London and West Midlands - North West England and Scotland

Route Diagram - see first Page of Table 65

		VT	VT	XC	VT	TP	VT	VT	VT	VT	XC	VT	XC	TP	VT	VT	LM	XC	NT	VT
		◇1	◇1	◇1	◇1	◇1	◇1	◇1	◇1	◇1	◇1	◇1	◇1	◇1	◇1	◇1	◇1	◇1		◇1
London Euston 15 ⊖	d	19 02	19 15				19 25	19 55	20 02	20 05		20 15			20 25					20 50
Watford Junction	d																			
Milton Keynes Central	d		19 48							20 38		20 48								21 37
Rugby	d																			22 01
Nuneaton	d	20 01							21 01											
Tamworth Low Level	d														21 32					
Lichfield Trent Valley	d														21 39					
Coventry	d			19 26									20 26					21 26		
Birmingham International ✈	d			19 38									20 38					21 38		
Birmingham New Street 12	d			19 58	20 10						20 31		20 58			21 12	21 41	21 59		
Wolverhampton 7	d			20 26	20 38						20 59		21 30			21 44	22 09	22 26		
Penkridge	d																22 19			
Stafford	a	20 25		20 38	20 51					21 31			21 42			21 56	22 26	22 38		
	d	20 30		20 39	20 52					21 33			21 43			21 57	22 27	22 39		
Stoke-on-Trent	a		20 50	20 56				21 25			21 33	21 50	22 03					22 58		
Congleton	a																			
Macclesfield	a			21 15				21 42			21 51		22 20					23 15		
Crewe 10	a	20 48			21 10				21 44	21 53					22 10	22 17	22 49			22 49
	d	20 50							21 46	21 55					22 13	22 18				22 51
Chester	a																			
Wrexham General	a																			
Llandudno	a																			
Bangor (Gwynedd)	a																			
Holyhead	a																			
Wilmslow	a																			
Stockport	a		21 18	21 28				21 56			22 05	22 18	22 32					23 29		
Manchester Piccadilly 10	a		21 29	21 40				22 09			22 17	22 29	22 43					23 41		
Hartford	a																			
Warrington Bank Quay	a						21 16								22 29	22 36				23 08
	d						21 16								22 30	22 36				23 08
Runcorn	a	21 07							22 03	22 12										
Liverpool South Parkway 7 ✈	a																			
Liverpool Lime Street 10	a	21 28							22 23	22 33										
	d																			
Manchester Airport ✈	d					20 30								21 30						
Manchester Piccadilly 10	d					20 46								21 46						
Bolton	d					21 05								22 05						
Wigan North Western	a						21 27								22 40	22 47				23 19
	d						21 27								22 41	22 47			23 14	23 19
Preston 8	a					21 33	21 40							22 28	22 58	23 07			23 36	23 41
Preston 8	d					21 35	21 42							22 29					23 39	
Blackpool North	a					22 01								22 55					00 05	
Lancaster 6	a						21 56													
	d						21 57													
Barrow-in-Furness	a																			
Oxenholme Lake District	a						22 10													
	d						22 11													
Windermere	a																			
Penrith North Lakes	d						22 36													
Carlisle 8	a						22 51													
	d						22 53													
Lockerbie	d																			
Carstairs	a																			
Motherwell	a																			
Glasgow Central 15	a						00 02													
Haymarket	a																			
Edinburgh 10	a																			
Perth	a																			
Dundee	a																			
Aberdeen	a																			
Inverness	a																			

OVERNIGHT SLEEPERS. For sleeper trains, operated by First ScotRail, please refer to Tables 400 - 404

Table 65

Sundays
until 24 June

London and West Midlands - North West England and Scotland

Route Diagram - see first Page of Table 65

		SR		VT	VT	VT	SR
		R		◇1	◇1	◇1	R
		A					
		(sleeper)					(sleeper)
		(catering)		(catering)	(catering)	(catering)	(catering)
London Euston 15 ⊖	d	20 55		21 21	21 25	21 51	23 27
Watford Junction	d	21u17					23u47
Milton Keynes Central	d				22 14	22 38	
Rugby	d					23 18	
Nuneaton	d			22 52		23 29	
Tamworth Low Level	d						
Lichfield Trent Valley	d						
Coventry	d						
Birmingham International (airport)	d						
Birmingham New Street 12	d						
Wolverhampton 7 (ship)	d						
Penkridge	d						
Stafford	a			23 16		23s53	
	d			23 17			
Stoke-on-Trent	a				23 29		
Congleton	a						
Macclesfield	a				23 45		
Crewe 10	a			23 43		00s21	
	d	23u39		23 45			
Chester	a						
Wrexham General	a						
Llandudno	a						
Bangor (Gwynedd)	a						
Holyhead	a						
Wilmslow	a						
Stockport	a				23 59	00s50	
Manchester Piccadilly 10 (ship)	a				00 12	01 00	
Hartford	a						
Warrington Bank Quay	a						
	d						
Runcorn	a			00 07			
Liverpool South Parkway 7 (airport)	a						
Liverpool Lime Street 10	a			00 30			
	d						
Manchester Airport (airport)	d						
Manchester Piccadilly 10 (ship)	d						
Bolton	d						
Wigan North Western	a						
	d						
Preston 8	a						
Preston 8	d	00u30					
Blackpool North	a						
Lancaster 6	a						
	d						
Barrow-in-Furness	a						
Oxenholme Lake District	a						
	d						
Windermere	a						
Penrith North Lakes	d						
Carlisle 8	a						05s04
	d						
Lockerbie	d						
Carstairs	a						06s20
Motherwell	a						06s56
Glasgow Central 15	a						07 20
Haymarket	a						
Edinburgh 10	a						07 16
Perth	a	05s39					
Dundee	a	06s08					
Aberdeen	a	07 36					
Inverness	a	08 38					

A Conveys a portion from Fort William, arrives at 0954

OVERNIGHT SLEEPERS. For sleeper trains, operated by First ScotRail, please refer to Tables 400 - 404

Table 65

Sundays

1 July to 9 September

London and West Midlands - North West England and Scotland

Route Diagram - see first Page of Table 65

		TP	TP	XC	VT	VT	VT	TP	VT	VT		VT	TP	TP	NT	TP		TP	NT	VT			NT	TP	VT
		◇1	◇1	◇1	◇1	◇1	◇1		◇1	◇1		◇1		◇1		◇1		◇1		◇1				◇1	◇1
					A	A	A		A	A		A													
					☕	☕	☕	🚌	☕	☕		☕	🚌		trolley			trolley		☕					☕
London Euston 15 ⊖	d				22p30	23p30	23p45		00ʃ30	01ʃ00		01ʃ30													
Watford Junction	d																								
Milton Keynes Central	d																								
Rugby	d						00s42			01s48															
Nuneaton	d						00s52			01s59															
Tamworth Low Level	d																								
Lichfield Trent Valley	d																								
Coventry	d																								
Birmingham International ✈	d																								
Birmingham New Street 12	d			22p31																08 45					09 20
Wolverhampton 7 ⇌	d			22p49																09 04					09 37
Penkridge	d																								
Stafford	a			23p01			01s17			02s23										09 16					
	d			23p02																09 17					
Stoke-on-Trent	a			23p20	23b53	00s53			01s53			02s53													
Congleton	a																								
Macclesfield	a			23p38	00s10	01s10			02s10			03s10													
Crewe 10	a						01s35			02s42										09 35					10 06
	d																			09 37					10 08
Chester	a																								
Wrexham General	a																								
Llandudno	a																								
Bangor (Gwynedd)	a																								
Holyhead	a																								
Wilmslow	a																								
Stockport	a			23p53	00s24	01s24			02s24			03s24													
Manchester Piccadilly 10 ⇌	a			00 10	00ʃ37	01ʃ37			02ʃ37			03ʃ39													
Hartford	a																								
Warrington Bank Quay	a																			09 54					10 26
	d																			09 54					10 26
Runcorn	a						01s54			03s01															
Liverpool South Parkway 7 ✈	a																								
Liverpool Lime Street 10	a						02ʃ16			03ʃ19															
	d																								
Manchester Airport ✈	d	22p00	22p29					00 05					05 30	07 55		08 47		09 00						09 30	
Manchester Piccadilly 10 ⇌	d	22p16	22p46					00 30					05 55	08 11		09 03		09 16						09 46	
Bolton	d	22p33	23p07					00s55					06s20	08 30		09 23		09 33						10 05	
Wigan North Western	a																			10 05					10 37
	d																			10 05					10 37
Preston 8	a	22p54	23p33					01s30					06s55	08 57		09 50		09 57		10 22				10 33	10 51
Preston 8	d	22p55	23p35											08 58	09 05	09 52	10 07	10 00	10 00				10 29	10 35	10 52
Blackpool North	a		00 02					02 10					07 35	09 23		10 18							10 53	11 01	
Lancaster 6	a	23p11															10 22	10 15							11 07
	d	23p11															10 23	10 16							11 08
Barrow-in-Furness	a	00 15																							
Oxenholme Lake District	a																10 39	10 30							11 22
	d																10 40	10 30							11 23
Windermere	a																10 57								
Penrith North Lakes	d																	10 55							
Carlisle 8	a														12 17			11 12	12 57						12 01
	d																	11 13							12 02
Lockerbie	d																	11 32							
Carstairs	a																								
Motherwell	a																								
Glasgow Central 15	a																								13 17
Haymarket	a																	12s32							
Edinburgh 10	a																	12 39							
Perth	a																								
Dundee	a																								
Aberdeen	a																								
Inverness	a																								

A 29 July, 5 August, 12 August, 2 September, 9 September

b Previous night, stops to set down only

OVERNIGHT SLEEPERS. For sleeper trains, operated by First ScotRail, please refer to Tables 400 - 404

Table 65

Sundays

1 July to 9 September

London and West Midlands - North West England and Scotland

Route Diagram - see first Page of Table 65

		TP	VT	VT	VT	LM	XC	TP	VT	VT	VT	VT	VT	LM	TP	XC	TP	VT	VT	VT
		◇1	◇1	◇1	◇1	◇1	◇1	◇1	◇1	◇1	◇1	◇1	◇1	◇1	◇1	◇1	◇1	◇1	◇1	◇1
		🛒	☕	☕	☕		🛒		☕	☕	☕	☕	☕			🛒		☕	☕	☕
London Euston 15 ⊖	d			08 15	08 20					08 45		09 15	09 20					09 45		10 15
Watford Junction	d																			
Milton Keynes Central	d				09 06					09 32			10 07					10 33		
Rugby	d									10 09								11 09		
Nuneaton	d			09 44								10 45								
Tamworth Low Level	d																			11 47
Lichfield Trent Valley	d																			
Coventry	d																			
Birmingham International ✈	d																			
Birmingham New Street 12	d					09 42	10 01				10 20			10 42		11 01			11 20	
Wolverhampton 7 🚌	d					10 00	10 19				10 37			11 00		11 19			11 37	
Penkridge	d					10 10								11 10						
Stafford	a			10 08		10 16	10 32					11 09		11 16		11 31				12 13
	d			10 08		10 17	10 33					11 09		11 17		11 32				12 13
Stoke-on-Trent	a				10 19		10 51						11 20			11 51				
Congleton	a																			
Macclesfield	a				10 36		11 08						11 37			12 09				
Crewe 10	a			10 28		10 37				10 55	11 07	11 30		11 37				11 55	12 07	12 32
	d		10 21	10 30		10 38			10 42	10 57	11 09	11 32		11 38				11 57	12 09	12 34
Chester	a								11 02											
Wrexham General	a																			
Llandudno	a																			
Bangor (Gwynedd)	a								12 09											
Holyhead	a								12 43											
Wilmslow	a																			
Stockport	a				10 50		11 22						11 51			12 22				
Manchester Piccadilly 10 🚌	a				11 03		11 31						12 04			12 40				
Hartford	a					10 50								11 50						
Warrington Bank Quay	a		10 37							11 14	11 26							12 14	12 26	
	d		10 37							11 14	11 27							12 14	12 27	
Runcorn	a			10 47		11 00						11 49		12 01						12 51
Liverpool South Parkway 7 ✈	a					11 09								12 10						
Liverpool Lime Street 10	a			11 09		11 21						12 10		12 21						13 12
	d																			
Manchester Airport ✈	d	10 00						10 30							11 00		11 30			
Manchester Piccadilly 10 🚌	d	10 16						10 46							11 16		11 46			
Bolton	d	10 33						11 05							11 33		12 05			
Wigan North Western	a		10 48							11 25	11 37							12 25	12 37	
	d		10 48							11 25	11 38							12 25	12 38	
Preston 8	a	10 57	11 02					11 33		11 38	11 51				11 57		12 33	12 38	12 51	
Preston 8	d	10 58	11 04					11 35		11 40	11 53				11 58		12 35	12 40	12 53	
Blackpool North	a							12 01									13 01			
Lancaster 6	a	11 13	11 20							11 54	12 08				12 13			12 54	13 08	
	d	11 14								11 55	12 08				12 14			12 55	13 08	
Barrow-in-Furness	a														13 17					
Oxenholme Lake District	a	11 28								12 08	12 22							13 08	13 22	
	d	11 28								12 08	12 24							13 08	13 24	
Windermere	a																			
Penrith North Lakes	d	11 53								12 34								13 34		
Carlisle 8	a	12 10								12 49	13 01							13 49	14 01	
	d	12 11								12 50	13 03							13 50	14 03	
Lockerbie	d	12 30																		
Carstairs	a																			
Motherwell	a																			
Glasgow Central 15	a	13 35								14 01								15 02	15 16	
Haymarket	a										14 13									
Edinburgh 10	a										14 22									
Perth	a																			
Dundee	a																			
Aberdeen	a																			
Inverness	a																			

OVERNIGHT SLEEPERS. For sleeper trains, operated by First ScotRail, please refer to Tables 400 - 404

Table 65

Sundays

1 July to 9 September

London and West Midlands - North West England and Scotland

Route Diagram - see first Page of Table 65

		VT		LM	TP	XC	TP		VT	VT	VT	VT		LM	VT	VT	TP		XC		TP	VT		VT	XC
		◇1		◇1	◇1	◇1	◇1		◇1	◇1	◇1	◇1		◇1	◇1	◇1	◇1		◇1		◇1	◇1		◇1	◇1
		⊡			⌶	⌶			⊡	⊡	⊡	⊡			⊡	⊡	⌶		⌶			⊡		⊡	⌶
London Euston 15 ⊖	d	10 20							10 45		11 15	11 20			12 02	12 15						12 25			
Watford Junction	d																								
Milton Keynes Central	d	11 07							11 33		12 03	12 08				12 48									
Rugby	d								12 09																
Nuneaton	d																								
Tamworth Low Level	d																								
Lichfield Trent Valley	d																								
Coventry	d																								
Birmingham International ✈	d																								
Birmingham New Street 12	d			11 42		12 01				12 20				12 35					13 01					13 20	13 31
Wolverhampton 7	d			12 00		12 19				12 37				12 53					13 19					13 37	13 49
Penkridge	d			12 10										13 03											
Stafford	a			12 16		12 32					12 53			13 09	13 24				13 33						
	d			12 17		12 33					12 53			13 09	13 25				13 34						
Stoke-on-Trent	a	12 24				12 52						13 09				13 50			13 56						14 19
Congleton	a																								
Macclesfield	a	12 40				13 10						13 26							14 14						
Crewe 10	a			12 37					12 56	13 07	13 13			13 30	13 43									14 07	
	d			12 38					12 58	13 09	13 15			13 31	13 45									14 09	
Chester	a																								
Wrexham General	a																								
Llandudno	a																								
Bangor (Gwynedd)	a																								
Holyhead	a																								
Wilmslow	a																								
Stockport	a	12 55				13 28						13 41				14 18			14 28						
Manchester Piccadilly 10	a	13 08				13 40						13 53				14 29			14 40						14 57
Hartford	a			12 50										13 43											
Warrington Bank Quay	a								13 15	13 26												14 16		14 26	
	d								13 15	13 27												14 16		14 27	
Runcorn	a			13 01							13 32			13 54	14 02										
Liverpool South Parkway 7 ✈	a			13 10										14 03											
Liverpool Lime Street 10	a			13 21							13 54			14 14	14 24										
	d																								
Manchester Airport ✈	d				12 00		12 30										13 00				13 30				
Manchester Piccadilly 10	d				12 16		12 46										13 16				13 46				
Bolton	d				12 33		13 05										13 33				14 05				
Wigan North Western	a								13 26	13 37												14 27		14 37	
	d								13 26	13 38												14 27		14 38	
Preston 8	a				12 57		13 33		13 40	13 51							13 57				14 33	14 40		14 50	
Preston 8	d				12 58		13 35		13 42	13 53							14 00	14 04			14 35	14 42		14 53	
Blackpool North	a						14 01														15 01				
Lancaster 6	a				13 13				13 56	14 08							14 15	14 20				14 56		15 08	
	d				13 14				13 57	14 08							14 16	14 20				14 58		15 09	
Barrow-in-Furness	a																	15 24							
Oxenholme Lake District	a				13 28				14 10								14 30							15 22	
	d				13 28				14 10								14 30							15 24	
Windermere	a																								
Penrith North Lakes	d				13 53				14 36	14 45							14 55					15 32			
Carlisle 8	a				14 10				14 51	15 00							15 12					15 47		16 01	
	d				14 11				14 52	15 03							15 17					15 48		16 03	
Lockerbie	d				14 30																				
Carstairs	a																								
Motherwell	a																								
Glasgow Central 15	a								16 05								16 35					17 00		17 17	
Haymarket	a				15s29					16 14															
Edinburgh 10	a				15 39					16 22															
Perth	a																								
Dundee	a																								
Aberdeen	a																								
Inverness	a																								

OVERNIGHT SLEEPERS. For sleeper trains, operated by First ScotRail, please refer to Tables 400 - 404

Table 65

Sundays
1 July to 9 September

London and West Midlands - North West England and Scotland

Route Diagram - see first Page of Table 65

		VT	LM	VT	VT	TP	XC	TP		VT		VT	XC	VT	LM	VT	VT	TP		XC	TP	VT		VT	XC
		◇1	◇1	◇1	◇1	◇1	◇1	◇1		◇1		◇1	◇1	◇1	◇1	◇1	◇1	◇1		◇1	◇1	◇1		◇1	◇1
London Euston 15 ⊖	d	12 55		13 02	13 15					13 25				13 55		14 02	14 15					14 25			
Watford Junction	d																								
Milton Keynes Central	d				13 48												14 48								
Rugby	d																								
Nuneaton	d																								
Tamworth Low Level	d																								
Lichfield Trent Valley	d																								
Coventry	d																								
Birmingham International ✈	d																								
Birmingham New Street 12	d		13 35				14 01					14 20	14 31		14 35					15 01				15 20	15 31
Wolverhampton 7	d		13 53				14 19					14 37	14 49		14 53					15 19				15 37	15 49
Penkridge	d		14 03												15 03										
Stafford	a		14 09	14 21			14 33								15 09	15 24				15 33					
	d		14 09	14 22			14 34								15 09	15 25				15 34					
Stoke-on-Trent	a	14 26			14 50		14 56						15 19	15 25			15 50			15 56					16 19
Congleton	a																								
Macclesfield	a	14 42					15 14							15 42						16 14					
Crewe 10	a		14 29	14 43								15 07			15 29	15 43								16 07	
	d		14 31	14 45								15 09			15 31	15 45								16 09	
Chester	a																								
Wrexham General	a																								
Llandudno	a																								
Bangor (Gwynedd)	a																								
Holyhead	a																								
Wilmslow	a																								
Stockport	a	14 56			15 18		15 28							15 56			16 18			16 28					
Manchester Piccadilly 10	a	15 09			15 29		15 40						15 59	16 09			16 29			16 40					16 59
Hartford	a		14 42												15 42										
Warrington Bank Quay	a									15 16		15 26										16 16		16 26	
	d									15 16		15 27										16 16		16 27	
Runcorn	a		14 53	15 02											15 53	16 02									
Liverpool South Parkway 7 ✈	a		15 02												16 02										
Liverpool Lime Street 10	a		15 14	15 24											16 14	16 24									
	d																								
Manchester Airport ✈	d					14 00		14 30										15 00			15 30				
Manchester Piccadilly 10	d					14 16		14 46										15 16			15 46				
Bolton	d					14 33		15 05										15 33			16 05				
Wigan North Western	a									15 27		15 37										16 27		16 37	
	d									15 27		15 38										16 27		16 38	
Preston 8	a					14 57		15 33		15 40		15 51						15 57			16 33	16 40		16 51	
Preston 8	d					15 00		15 35		15 42		15 53						16 00			16 35	16 42		16 53	
Blackpool North	a							16 01													17 01				
Lancaster 6	a					15 15				15 56		16 08						16 15				16 56		17 08	
	d					15 16				15 58		16 08						16 16				16 57		17 08	
Barrow-in-Furness	a																	17 19							
Oxenholme Lake District	a					15 30				16 10														17 22	
	d					15 30				16 11														17 23	
Windermere	a																								
Penrith North Lakes	d					15 55						16 45										17 32			
Carlisle 8	a					16 12				16 48		17 00										17 47		18 01	
	d					16 13				16 49		17 02										17 48		18 03	
Lockerbie	d					16 32																			
Carstairs	a																								
Motherwell	a																								
Glasgow Central 15	a									18 01												19 00		19 17	
Haymarket	a					17s30						18 13													
Edinburgh 10	a					17 39						18 22													
Perth	a																								
Dundee	a																								
Aberdeen	a																								
Inverness	a																								

OVERNIGHT SLEEPERS. For sleeper trains, operated by First ScotRail, please refer to Tables 400 - 404

Sundays

1 July to 9 September

London and West Midlands - North West England and Scotland

Route Diagram - see first Page of Table 65

		VT	LM	VT		VT	VT	XC	TP		TP	VT	VT	XC		VT	TP		LM	VT	VT	VT	XC	TP	
		◇1	◇1	◇1		◇1	◇1	◇1	◇1		◇1	◇1	◇1	◇1		◇1	◇1		◇1	◇1	◇1	◇1	◇1	◇1	
																								A	
		☕		☕		☕	☕	🛒	🛒			☕	☕	🛒		☕	🛒			☕	☕	☕	🛒	🛒	
London Euston 15 ⊖	d	14 55		15 02		15 05	15 15					15 25				15 55				16 02	16 05	16 15			
Watford Junction	d																								
Milton Keynes Central	d					15 39	15 48														16 39	16 48			
Rugby	d																								
Nuneaton	d																								
Tamworth Low Level	d																								
Lichfield Trent Valley	d																								
Coventry	d							15 26															16 26		
Birmingham International ✈	d							15 38															16 38		
Birmingham New Street 12	d		15 35					16 01					16 20	16 31					16 35				17 01		
Wolverhampton 7 🚌	d		15 53					16 19					16 37	16 49					16 53				17 19		
Penkridge	d		16 03																17 03						
Stafford	a		16 09	16 21				16 34											17 09	17 24			17 35		
	d		16 09	16 22				16 34											17 09	17 25			17 36		
Stoke-on-Trent	a	16 24					16 50	16 56						17 19		17 25						17 50	17 56		
Congleton	a																								
Macclesfield	a	16 42						17 14								17 42							18 14		
Crewe 10	a		16 30			16 50							17 07						17 30		17 50				
	d		16 31			16 52							17 09						17 31		17 52				
Chester	a					17 14															18 14				
Wrexham General	a																								
Llandudno	a																								
Bangor (Gwynedd)	a																								
Holyhead	a																								
Wilmslow	a																								
Stockport	a	16 56					17 18	17 28								17 56						18 18	18 28		
Manchester Piccadilly 10 🚌	a	17 09					17 29	17 40						17 56		18 09						18 29	18 40		
Hartford	a		16 43																17 43						
Warrington Bank Quay	a											17 16	17 26												
	d											17 16	17 27												
Runcorn	a		16 54	16 57															17 54	17 57					
Liverpool South Parkway 7 ✈	a		17 03																18 03						
Liverpool Lime Street 10	a		17 14	17 16															18 14	18 16					
	d																								
Manchester Airport ✈	d								16 00		16 30						17 00								
Manchester Piccadilly 10 🚌	d								16 16		16 46						17 16								
Bolton	d								16 33		17 05						17 33								
Wigan North Western	a											17 27	17 37												
	d											17 27	17 38												
Preston 8	a								16 57		17 33	17 40	17 51				17 57								
Preston 8	d								17 00	18 07	17 35	17 42	17 53				18 03							18 03	
Blackpool North	a										18 01														
Lancaster 6	a								17 15	18 23		17 56	18 08				18 18							18 18	
	d								17 16	18 23		17 57	18 08				18 19							18 19	
Barrow-in-Furness	a																								
Oxenholme Lake District	a								17 30	18 40		18 10	18 22				18 33							18 33	
	d								17 30	18 40		18 10	18 23				18 33							18 33	
Windermere	a									19 01															
Penrith North Lakes	d								17 55				18 49				18 58							18 58	
Carlisle 8	a								18 12			18 48	19 04				19 14							19 14	
	d								18 13			18 49	19 04				19 16							19 16	
Lockerbie	d																19 36							19 36	
Carstairs	a																								
Motherwell	a																20s22							20s22	
Glasgow Central 15	a											20 01					20 44							20 44	
Haymarket	a								19s28																
Edinburgh 10	a								19 35				20 22												
Perth	a																								
Dundee	a																								
Aberdeen	a																								
Inverness	a																								

A from 1 July until 29 July, 2 September, 9 September

OVERNIGHT SLEEPERS. For sleeper trains, operated by First ScotRail, please refer to Tables 400 - 404

Table 65

Sundays

1 July to 9 September

London and West Midlands - North West England and Scotland

Route Diagram - see first Page of Table 65

		TP	VT	VT		VT	LM	VT	VT	VT		XC	TP		TP	VT	VT	XC	VT	TP			LM	VT	VT
		◇1	◇1	◇1		◇1	◇1	◇1	◇1	◇1		◇1	◇1		◇1	◇1	◇1	◇1	◇1	◇1			◇1	◇1	◇1
			☕	☕		☕		☕	☕	☕		🛒	🛒			☕	☕		☕					☕	☕
London Euston 15 ⊖	d		16 25			16 55		17 02	17 05	17 15						17 25			17 55					18 02	18 15
Watford Junction	d																								
Milton Keynes Central	d								17 39	17 48															18 48
Rugby	d																								
Nuneaton	d								18 10																
Tamworth Low Level	d																								
Lichfield Trent Valley	d																								
Coventry	d											17 26													
Birmingham International ✈	d											17 38													
Birmingham New Street 12	d			17 20			17 35					18 01					18 20	18 31					18 35		
Wolverhampton 7	d			17 37			17 53					18 19					18 37	18 49					18 53		
Penkridge	d						18 03																19 03		
Stafford	a						18 09	18 24				18 35											19 09	19 24	
	d						18 09	18 25				18 36											19 09	19 25	
Stoke-on-Trent	a					18 25				18 50		18 55						19 19	19 25						19 50
Congleton	a																								
Macclesfield	a					18 42						19 14							19 42						
Crewe 10	a			18 07			18 30		18 53								19 07						19 29		
	d			18 09			18 31		18 56								19 09						19 31		
Chester	a								19 14																
Wrexham General	a																								
Llandudno	a																								
Bangor (Gwynedd)	a																								
Holyhead	a																								
Wilmslow	a																								
Stockport	a					18 56				19 18		19 28							19 56						20 18
Manchester Piccadilly 10	a					19 09				19 29		19 40						19 58	20 09						20 29
Hartford	a						18 43																19 42		
Warrington Bank Quay	a		18 16	18 26												19 16	19 26								
	d		18 17	18 27												19 16	19 27								
Runcorn	a						18 54	18 57															19 53	19 58	
Liverpool South Parkway 7 ✈	a						19 03																20 02		
Liverpool Lime Street 10	a						19 14	19 19															20 14	20 16	
	d																								
Manchester Airport ✈	d	17 30											18 00		18 30					19 00					
Manchester Piccadilly 10	d	17 46											18 16		18 46					19 16					
Bolton	d	18 05											18 33		19 05					19 33					
Wigan North Western	a		18 27	18 37												19 27	19 37								
	d		18 28	18 38												19 27	19 38								
Preston 8	a	18 33	18 40	18 51									18 57		19 33	19 40	19 51			19 57					
Preston 8	d	18 35	18 42	18 53									19 00	19 06	19 35	19 42	19 53			20 00					
Blackpool North	a	19 01													20 01										
Lancaster 6	a		18 56	19 08									19 15	19 22		19 56	20 08			20 15					
	d		18 58	19 08									19 16	19 22		19 57	20 08			20 16					
Barrow-in-Furness	a													20 26						21 11					
Oxenholme Lake District	a		19 10	19 22									19 30			20 10									
	d		19 11	19 24									19 30			20 10									
Windermere	a																								
Penrith North Lakes	d		19 36										19 55			20 36	20 45								
Carlisle 8	a		19 51	20 01									20 12			20 51	21 00								
	d		19 53	20 03									20 13			20 52	21 02								
Lockerbie	d												20 32												
Carstairs	a																								
Motherwell	a																								
Glasgow Central 15	a		21 09	21 17												22 07									
Haymarket	a												21s30				22 15								
Edinburgh 10	a												21 39				22 21								
Perth	a																								
Dundee	a																								
Aberdeen	a																								
Inverness	a																								

OVERNIGHT SLEEPERS. For sleeper trains, operated by First ScotRail, please refer to Tables 400 - 404

Table 65

Sundays

1 July to 9 September

London and West Midlands - North West England and Scotland

Route Diagram - see first Page of Table 65

		XC	TP	VT	VT	XC		VT		LM	VT	VT	XC	VT	TP	VT		XC	VT	VT	VT	VT	XC	TP	
					R																				
		◇1	◇1	◇1	1	◇1		◇1		◇1	◇1	◇1	◇1	◇1	◇1	◇1		◇1	◇1	◇1	◇1	◇1	◇1	◇1	
													A										A		
		✠		ⓟ	ⓟ	✠		ⓟ			ⓟ	ⓟ	✠	ⓟ		ⓟ		✠	ⓟ	ⓟ	ⓟ	ⓟ	✠		
London Euston 15 ⊖	d			18 25				18 55			19 02	19 15				19 25			19 55	20 02	20 05	20 15			
Watford Junction	d																								
Milton Keynes Central	d											19 48									20 38	20 48			
Rugby	d																								
Nuneaton	d										20 02									21 01					
Tamworth Low Level	d																								
Lichfield Trent Valley	d																								
Coventry	d	18 26											19 26										20 26		
Birmingham International ✈	d	18 38											19 38										20 38		
Birmingham New Street 12	d	19 01			19 20	19 31				19 35			20 01	20 20				20 31					21 01		
Wolverhampton 7	d	19 19			19 37	19 49				19 53			20 19	20 38				20 52					21 19		
Penkridge	d									20 03															
Stafford	a	19 37								20 09	20 26		20 36	20 51							21 31		21 36		
	d	19 38								20 09	20 30		20 37	20 52							21 33		21 37		
Stoke-on-Trent	a	19 56				20 19		20 25				20 50	20 56					21 19	21 25			21 50	21 56		
Congleton	a																								
Macclesfield	a	20 14						20 42					21 15						21 42				22 14		
Crewe 10	a				20 07					20 30	20 48			21 10						21 44	21 53				
	d				20 09					20 31	20 50									21 46	21 55				
Chester	a																								
Wrexham General	a																								
Llandudno	a																								
Bangor (Gwynedd)	a																								
Holyhead	a																								
Wilmslow	a																								
Stockport	a	20 28						20 56				21 18	21 28						21 56			22 18	22 28		
Manchester Piccadilly 10	a	20 40				21 00		21 09				21 29	21 40					21 56	22 09			22 29	22 40		
Hartford	a									20 43															
Warrington Bank Quay	a			20 16	20 26											21 16									
	d			20 16	20 27											21 16									
Runcorn	a									20 54	21 07									22 03	22 12				
Liverpool South Parkway 7 ✈	a									21 03															
Liverpool Lime Street 10	a									21 14	21 28									22 23	22 33				
	d																								
Manchester Airport ✈	d		19 30												20 30									21 30	
Manchester Piccadilly 10	d		19 46												20 46									21 46	
Bolton	d		20 05												21 05									22 05	
Wigan North Western	a			20 27	20 37											21 27									
	d			20 27	20 38											21 27									
Preston 8	a		20 33	20 40	20 51										21 33	21 40								22 28	
Preston 8	d		20 35	20 42	20 53										21 35	21 42								22 29	
Blackpool North	a		21 01												22 01									22 55	
Lancaster 6	a			20 56	21 08											21 56									
	d			20 57	21 08											21 57									
Barrow-in-Furness	a																								
Oxenholme Lake District	a			21 10	21 22											22 10									
	d			21 11	21 24											22 11									
Windermere	a																								
Penrith North Lakes	d			21 36												22 36									
Carlisle 8	a			21 51	22 01											22 51									
	d			21 52	22 03											22 53									
Lockerbie	d				22 23																				
Carstairs	a																								
Motherwell	a			22 48	23 07																				
Glasgow Central 15	a			23 09	23 22											00 02									
Haymarket	a																								
Edinburgh 10	a																								
Perth	a																								
Dundee	a																								
Aberdeen	a																								
Inverness	a																								

A ✠ to Birmingham New Street

OVERNIGHT SLEEPERS. For sleeper trains, operated by First ScotRail, please refer to Tables 400 - 404

Table 65

Sundays

1 July to 9 September

London and West Midlands - North West England and Scotland

Route Diagram - see first Page of Table 65

		VT	VT	LM	XC	NT	VT	SR	VT	VT	VT	SR	VT	VT
		◇1	◇1	◇1	◇1		◇1	B	◇1	◇1	◇1	B	◇1	◇1
								A					B	B
London Euston 15 ⊖	d	20 25					20 50	20 55	21 21	21 25	21 51	23 27	23 30	23 45
Watford Junction	d							21u17				23u47		
Milton Keynes Central	d						21 37			22 14	22 38			
Rugby	d						22 01				23 18			00s33
Nuneaton	d								22 52		23 29			00s44
Tamworth Low Level	d	21 32												
Lichfield Trent Valley	d	21 39												
Coventry	d				21 26									
Birmingham International ✈	d				21 38									
Birmingham New Street 12	d		21 20	21 35	22 01									
Wolverhampton 7	d		21 38	21 57	22 19									
Penkridge	d			22 07										
Stafford	a		21 56	22 13	22 36				23 16		23s53			01s08
	d		21 57	22 16	22 37				23 17					
Stoke-on-Trent	a				22 55					23 29			00s53	
Congleton	a													
Macclesfield	a				23 12					23 45			01s10	
Crewe 10	a	22 10	22 17	22 38			22 49		23 43		00s21			01s27
	d	22 13	22 18				22 51	23u39	23 45					
Chester	a													
Wrexham General	a													
Llandudno	a													
Bangor (Gwynedd)	a													
Holyhead	a													
Wilmslow	a													
Stockport	a				23 27					23 59	00s50		01s24	
Manchester Piccadilly 10	a				23 41					00 12	01 00		01 37	
Hartford	a													
Warrington Bank Quay	a	22 29	22 36				23 08							
	d	22 30	22 36				23 08							
Runcorn	a								00 07					01s46
Liverpool South Parkway 7 ✈	a													
Liverpool Lime Street 10	a								00 30					02 07
	d													
Manchester Airport ✈	d													
Manchester Piccadilly 10	d													
Bolton	d													
Wigan North Western	a	22 40	22 47				23 19							
	d	22 41	22 47			23 14	23 19							
Preston 8	a	22 58	23 07			23 36	23 41							
Preston 8	d					23 39		00u30						
Blackpool North	a					00 05								
Lancaster 6	a													
	d													
Barrow-in-Furness	a													
Oxenholme Lake District	a													
	d													
Windermere	a													
Penrith North Lakes	d													
Carlisle 8	a											05s04		
	d													
Lockerbie	d													
Carstairs	a											06s20		
Motherwell	a											06s56		
Glasgow Central 15	a											07 20		
Haymarket	a													
Edinburgh 10	a											07 16		
Perth	a							05s39						
Dundee	a							06s08						
Aberdeen	a							07 36						
Inverness	a							08 38						

A Conveys a portion from Fort William, arrives at 0954

B 29 July, 5 August, 12 August, 2 September, 9 September

OVERNIGHT SLEEPERS. For sleeper trains, operated by First ScotRail, please refer to Tables 400 - 404

Table 65

Sundays

16 September to 21 October

London and West Midlands - North West England and Scotland

Route Diagram - see first Page of Table 65

		TP	TP	XC	TP	TP	TP	NT	TP	TP		VT		NT	TP		VT	TP	VT	VT		VT	LM	XC	TP
		◇1	◇1	◇1			◇1		◇1	◇1		◇1			◇1		◇1	◇1	◇1	◇1		◇1	◇1	◇1	◇1
					🚌	🚌		🛒		🛒		🍽					🍽	🛒	🍽	🍽		🍽		🛒	
London Euston 15 ⊖	d																			08 15		08 20			
Watford Junction	d																								
Milton Keynes Central	d																					09 06			
Rugby	d																								
Nuneaton	d																			09 44					
Tamworth Low Level	d																								
Lichfield Trent Valley	d																								
Coventry	d																								
Birmingham International ✈	d																								
Birmingham New Street 12	d			22p31								08 45					09 20						09 42	10 01	
Wolverhampton 7	d			22p49								09 04					09 37						10 00	10 19	
Penkridge	d																						10 10		
Stafford	a			23p01								09 16								10 08			10 16	10 32	
	d			23p02								09 17								10 08			10 17	10 33	
Stoke-on-Trent	a			23p20																		10 19		10 51	
Congleton	a																								
Macclesfield	a			23p38																		10 36		11 08	
Crewe 10	a											09 35					10 07			10 28			10 37		
	d											09 37					10 08		10 21	10 30			10 38		
Chester	a																								
Wrexham General	a																								
Llandudno	a																								
Bangor (Gwynedd)	a																								
Holyhead	a																								
Wilmslow	a																								
Stockport	a			23p53																		10 50		11 22	
Manchester Piccadilly 10	a			00 10																		11 03		11 31	
Hartford	a																						10 50		
Warrington Bank Quay	a											09 54					10 26		10 37						
	d											09 54					10 27		10 37						
Runcorn	a																			10 47			11 00		
Liverpool South Parkway 7 ✈	a																						11 09		
Liverpool Lime Street 10	a																			11 09			11 21		
	d																								
Manchester Airport ✈	d	22p00	22p29		00 05	05 30	07 47		08 47	09 00					09 29			10 00							10 30
Manchester Piccadilly 10	d	22p16	22p46		00 30	05 55	08 02		09 03	09 16					09 46			10 14							10 46
Bolton	d	22p33	23p07		00s55	06s20	08 21		09 23	09 33					10 05			10 31							11 05
Wigan North Western	a											10 05					10 37		10 48						
	d											10 05					10 38		10 48						
Preston 8	a	22p54	23p33		01s30	06s55	08 48		09 50	09 57		10 22			10 33		10 51	10 57	11 02						11 33
Preston 8	d	22p55	23p35				08 49	09 05	09 52	10 00				10 29	10 35	10 41	10 52	10 58	11 04						11 35
Blackpool North	a		00 02		02 10	07 35	09 13		10 18					10 53	11 02										12 01
Lancaster 6	a	23p11								10 15						10 56	11 07	11 13	11 20						
	d	23p11								10 16						10 57	11 08	11 14							
Barrow-in-Furness	a	00 15														12 00									
Oxenholme Lake District	a									10 30							11 22	11 28							
	d									10 30							11 23	11 28							
Windermere	a																								
Penrith North Lakes	d									10 55								11 53							
Carlisle 8	a							12 17		11 12							12 01	12 10							
	d									11 13							12 02	12 11							
Lockerbie	d									11 32								12 30							
Carstairs	a																								
Motherwell	a																								
Glasgow Central 15	a																13 17	13 35							
Haymarket	a									12s32															
Edinburgh 10	a									12 39															
Perth	a																								
Dundee	a																								
Aberdeen	a																								
Inverness	a																								

OVERNIGHT SLEEPERS. For sleeper trains, operated by First ScotRail, please refer to Tables 400 - 404

Table 65

Sundays

16 September to 21 October

London and West Midlands - North West England and Scotland

Route Diagram - see first Page of Table 65

Station		VT	VT	VT	VT	VT	LM	XC	TP	VT	TP	VT	VT	VT	LM	XC	TP	TP	VT	VT
		◇1	◇1	◇1	◇1	◇1	◇1	◇1	◇1	◇1	◇1	◇1	◇1	◇1	◇1	◇1	◇1	◇1	◇1	◇1
London Euston 15	d		08 45		09 15	09 20				09 45			10 15	10 20					10 45	
Watford Junction	d																			
Milton Keynes Central	d		09 32			10 07				10 33				11 07					11 33	
Rugby	d		10 09							11 09									12 09	
Nuneaton	d				10 45								11 47							
Tamworth Low Level	d																			
Lichfield Trent Valley	d																			
Coventry	d							10 28								11 29				
Birmingham International	d							10 40								11 40				
Birmingham New Street 12	d			10 20			10 42	11 01				11 20			11 42	12 01				12 20
Wolverhampton 7	d			10 37			11 00	11 19				11 37			12 00	12 19				12 37
Penkridge	d						11 10								12 10					
Stafford	a				11 09		11 16	11 31					12 13		12 16	12 32				
	d				11 09		11 17	11 32					12 14		12 17	12 33				
Stoke-on-Trent	a					11 20		11 51						12 24		12 52				
Congleton	a																			
Macclesfield	a					11 37		12 09						12 40		13 10				
Crewe 10	a		10 55	11 07	11 30		11 37			11 55		12 07	12 32		12 37				12 56	13 07
	d	10 42	10 57	11 09	11 32		11 38			11 57		12 09	12 34		12 38				12 58	13 09
Chester	a	11 02																		
Wrexham General	a																			
Llandudno	a																			
Bangor (Gwynedd)	a	12 09																		
Holyhead	a	12 43																		
Wilmslow	a																			
Stockport	a					11 51		12 22						12 55		13 28				
Manchester Piccadilly 10	a					12 04		12 40						13 08		13 40				
Hartford	a						11 50								12 50					
Warrington Bank Quay	a		11 14	11 26						12 14		12 26							13 15	13 26
	d		11 14	11 27						12 14		12 27							13 15	13 27
Runcorn	a				11 49		12 01						12 51		13 01					
Liverpool South Parkway 7	a						12 10								13 10					
Liverpool Lime Street 10	a				12 10		12 21						13 12		13 21					
	d																			
Manchester Airport	d								11 30								12 00	12 30		
Manchester Piccadilly 10	d								11 46								12 16	12 46		
Bolton	d								12 05								12 33	13 05		
Wigan North Western	a		11 25	11 37						12 25		12 37							13 26	13 37
	d		11 25	11 38						12 25		12 38							13 26	13 38
Preston 8	a		11 38	11 51					12 33	12 38		12 51					12 57	13 33	13 40	13 51
Preston 8	d		11 40	11 53					12 35	12 40	12 48	12 53					12 58	13 35	13 42	13 53
Blackpool North	a								13 01									14 01		
Lancaster 6	a		11 54	12 08						12 54	13 03	13 08					13 13		13 56	14 08
	d		11 55	12 08						12 55	13 04	13 08					13 14		13 57	14 08
Barrow-in-Furness	a										14 07									
Oxenholme Lake District	a		12 08	12 22						13 08		13 22					13 28		14 10	
	d		12 08	12 24						13 08		13 24					13 28		14 10	
Windermere	a																			
Penrith North Lakes	d		12 34							13 34							13 53		14 36	14 45
Carlisle 8	a		12 49	13 01						13 49		14 01					14 10		14 51	15 00
	d		12 50	13 03						13 50		14 03					14 11		14 52	15 03
Lockerbie	d																14 30			
Carstairs	a																			
Motherwell	a																			
Glasgow Central 15	a		14 01							15 02		15 16							16 05	
Haymarket	a			14 13													15s29			16 14
Edinburgh 10	a			14 22													15 39			16 22
Perth	a																			
Dundee	a																			
Aberdeen	a																			
Inverness	a																			

OVERNIGHT SLEEPERS. For sleeper trains, operated by First ScotRail, please refer to Tables 400 - 404

Table 65

Sundays

16 September to 21 October

London and West Midlands - North West England and Scotland

Route Diagram - see first Page of Table 65

		VT		VT	LM	VT	VT	XC	TP	TP	VT			VT	XC	VT	LM	VT	VT	XC	TP	TP		VT
		◇1		◇1	◇1	◇1	◇1	◇1	◇1	◇1	◇1			◇1	◇1	◇1	◇1	◇1	◇1	◇1	◇1	◇1		◇1
		🍴		🍴		🍴	🍴	🛒	🛒		🍴			🍴	🛒	🍴		🍴	🍴	🛒	🛒			🍴
London Euston 15 ⊖	d	11 15		11 20		12 05	12 17				12 28					12 57		13 05	13 17					13 28
Watford Junction	d																							
Milton Keynes Central	d	12 03		12 08			12 50												13 50					
Rugby	d																							
Nuneaton	d																							
Tamworth Low Level	d																							
Lichfield Trent Valley	d																							
Coventry	d							12 28												13 26				
Birmingham International ✈	d							12 40												13 38				
Birmingham New Street 12	d				12 35			13 01						13 20	13 31		13 35			14 01				
Wolverhampton 7 ⛴	d				12 53			13 19						13 37	13 49		13 53			14 19				
Penkridge	d				13 03												14 03							
Stafford	a	12 53			13 09	13 24		13 33									14 09	14 23		14 33				
	d	12 53			13 09	13 25		13 34									14 09	14 24		14 34				
Stoke-on-Trent	a			13 09			13 50	13 56							14 19	14 26			14 50	14 55				
Congleton	a																							
Macclesfield	a			13 26				14 14								14 42				15 13				
Crewe 10	a	13 13			13 30	13 43								14 07			14 29	14 43						
	d	13 15			13 31	13 45								14 09			14 31	14 45						
Chester	a																							
Wrexham General	a																							
Llandudno	a																							
Bangor (Gwynedd)	a																							
Holyhead	a																							
Wilmslow	a																							
Stockport	a			13 41			14 18	14 28								14 56			15 18	15 27				
Manchester Piccadilly 10 ⛴	a			13 53			14 29	14 40							14 57	15 09			15 29	15 39				
Hartford	a				13 43												14 42							
Warrington Bank Quay	a										14 16			14 26										15 16
	d										14 16			14 27										15 16
Runcorn	a	13 32			13 54	14 02											14 53	15 02						
Liverpool South Parkway 7 ✈	a				14 03												15 02							
Liverpool Lime Street 10	a	13 54			14 14	14 24											15 14	15 24						
	d																							
Manchester Airport ✈	d								12 58	13 30											13 58	14 30		
Manchester Piccadilly 10 ⛴	d								13 16	13 46											14 16	14 46		
Bolton	d								13 33	14 05											14 33	15 05		
Wigan North Western	a										14 27			14 37										15 27
	d										14 27			14 38										15 27
Preston 8	a								13 57	14 33	14 40			14 50							14 57	15 33		15 40
Preston 8	d								14 00	14 35	14 42			14 53							15 00	15 35		15 42
Blackpool North	a									15 01												16 01		
Lancaster 6	a								14 15		14 56			15 08							15 15			15 56
	d								14 16		14 58			15 09							15 16			15 58
Barrow-in-Furness	a																							
Oxenholme Lake District	a								14 30					15 22							15 30			16 10
	d								14 30					15 24							15 30			16 11
Windermere	a																							
Penrith North Lakes	d								14 55		15 32										15 55			
Carlisle 8	a								15 12		15 47			16 01							16 12			16 48
	d								15 17		15 48			16 03							16 13			16 49
Lockerbie	d																				16 32			
Carstairs	a																							
Motherwell	a																							
Glasgow Central 15	a								16 35		17 00			17 17										18 01
Haymarket	a																				17s30			
Edinburgh 10	a																				17 39			
Perth	a																							
Dundee	a																							
Aberdeen	a																							
Inverness	a																							

OVERNIGHT SLEEPERS. For sleeper trains, operated by First ScotRail, please refer to Tables 400 - 404

Table 65

Sundays

16 September to 21 October

London and West Midlands - North West England and Scotland

Route Diagram - see first Page of Table 65

		VT	XC	VT	LM	VT	VT	XC		TP	TP	VT	VT	XC	VT	LM	VT	VT		VT	XC	TP	TP	VT	VT
		◇1	◇1	◇1	◇1	◇1	◇1	◇1		◇1	◇1	◇1	◇1	◇1	◇1	◇1	◇1	◇1		◇1	◇1	◇1	◇1	◇1	◇1
		🍴	🛒	🍴		🍴	🍴	🛒				🍴	🍴	🛒	🍴		🍴	🍴		🍴	🛒	🛒		🍴	🍴
London Euston 15 ⊖	d			13 57		14 05	14 17					14 28			14 57		15 05	15 08		15 17				15 28	
Watford Junction	d																								
Milton Keynes Central	d						14 50											15 42		15 50					
Rugby	d																								
Nuneaton	d																								
Tamworth Low Level	d																								
Lichfield Trent Valley	d																								
Coventry	d							14 26													15 26				
Birmingham International ✈	d							14 38													15 38				
Birmingham New Street 12	d	14 20	14 31		14 35			15 01					15 20	15 31		15 35					16 01				16 20
Wolverhampton 7	d	14 37	14 49		14 53			15 19					15 37	15 49		15 53					16 19				16 37
Penkridge	d				15 03											16 03									
Stafford	a				15 09	15 24		15 33								16 09	16 24				16 34				
	d				15 09	15 25		15 34								16 09	16 25				16 34				
Stoke-on-Trent	a		15 19	15 25			15 50	15 56						16 19	16 24					16 50	16 56				
Congleton	a																								
Macclesfield	a			15 42				16 14							16 42						17 14				
Crewe 10	a	15 07			15 29	15 43							16 07			16 30		16 50							17 07
	d	15 09			15 31	15 45							16 09			16 31		16 52							17 09
Chester	a																	17 14							
Wrexham General	a																								
Llandudno	a																								
Bangor (Gwynedd)	a																								
Holyhead	a																								
Wilmslow	a																								
Stockport	a			15 56			16 18	16 28							16 56					17 18	17 28				
Manchester Piccadilly 10	a		15 59	16 09			16 29	16 40						16 59	17 09					17 29	17 40				
Hartford	a				15 42											16 43									
Warrington Bank Quay	a	15 26										16 16	16 26											17 16	17 26
	d	15 27										16 16	16 27											17 16	17 27
Runcorn	a				15 53	16 02										16 54	16 57								
Liverpool South Parkway 7 ✈	a				16 02											17 03									
Liverpool Lime Street 10	a				16 14	16 24										17 14	17 16								
	d																								
Manchester Airport ✈	d									14 58	15 30											15 58	16 30		
Manchester Piccadilly 10	d									15 16	15 46											16 16	16 46		
Bolton	d									15 33	16 05											16 33	17 05		
Wigan North Western	a	15 37										16 27	16 37											17 27	17 37
	d	15 38										16 27	16 38											17 27	17 38
Preston 8	a	15 51								15 57	16 33	16 40	16 51									16 57	17 33	17 40	17 51
Preston 8	d	15 53								16 00	16 35	16 42	16 53									17 00	17 35	17 42	17 53
Blackpool North	a										17 01												18 01		
Lancaster 6	a	16 08								16 15		16 56	17 08									17 15		17 56	18 08
	d	16 08								16 16		16 57	17 08									17 16		17 57	18 08
Barrow-in-Furness	a									17 19															
Oxenholme Lake District	a												17 22									17 30		18 10	18 22
	d												17 23									17 30		18 10	18 23
Windermere	a																								
Penrith North Lakes	d	16 45										17 32										17 55			18 49
Carlisle 8	a	17 00										17 47	18 01									18 12		18 48	19 04
	d	17 02										17 48	18 03									18 13		18 49	19 04
Lockerbie	d																								
Carstairs	a																								
Motherwell	a																								
Glasgow Central 15	a											19 00	19 17											20 01	
Haymarket	a	18 13																				19s28			
Edinburgh 10	a	18 22																				19 35			20 22
Perth	a																								
Dundee	a																								
Aberdeen	a																								
Inverness	a																								

OVERNIGHT SLEEPERS. For sleeper trains, operated by First ScotRail, please refer to Tables 400 - 404

Table 65

Sundays

16 September to 21 October

London and West Midlands - North West England and Scotland

Route Diagram - see first Page of Table 65

		XC	VT	LM		VT	VT	VT	XC	TP	TP	VT	VT	XC		VT	LM	VT	VT	XC	TP		TP	VT
		◇1	◇1	◇1		◇1	◇1	◇1	◇1	◇1	◇1	◇1	◇1	◇1		◇1	◇1	◇1	◇1	◇1	◇1		◇1	◇1
		🛒	☕			☕	☕	☕	🛒	🛒		☕	☕	🛒		☕		☕	☕	🛒	🛒			☕
London Euston 15 ⊖	d		15 57			16 05	16 08	16 17				16 28				16 57		17 05	17 17					17 28
Watford Junction	d																							
Milton Keynes Central	d						16 42	16 50											17 50					
Rugby	d																							
Nuneaton	d																							
Tamworth Low Level	d																							
Lichfield Trent Valley	d																							
Coventry	d								16 26											17 26				
Birmingham International ✈	d								16 38											17 38				
Birmingham New Street 12	d	16 31		16 35					17 01				17 20	17 31			17 35			18 01				
Wolverhampton 7	d	16 49		16 53					17 19				17 37	17 49			17 53			18 19				
Penkridge	d			17 03													18 03							
Stafford	a			17 09		17 24			17 35								18 09	18 24		18 35				
	d			17 09		17 25			17 36								18 09	18 25		18 36				
Stoke-on-Trent	a	17 19	17 25					17 50	17 56					18 19		18 25			18 50	18 56				
Congleton	a																							
Macclesfield	a		17 42						18 14							18 42				19 15				
Crewe 10	a			17 30			17 50						18 07				18 30							
	d			17 31			17 52						18 09				18 31							
Chester	a						18 14																	
Wrexham General	a																							
Llandudno	a																							
Bangor (Gwynedd)	a																							
Holyhead	a																							
Wilmslow	a																							
Stockport	a		17 56					18 18	18 28							18 56			19 18	19 28				
Manchester Piccadilly 10 ⛴	a	17 56	18 09					18 29	18 40					18 56		19 09			19 29	19 40				
Hartford	a			17 43													18 43							
Warrington Bank Quay	a											18 16	18 26											19 16
	d											18 17	18 27											19 16
Runcorn	a			17 54		17 57											18 54	18 57						
Liverpool South Parkway 7 ✈	a			18 03													19 03							
Liverpool Lime Street 10	a			18 14		18 16											19 14	19 19						
	d																							
Manchester Airport ✈	d									16 58	17 30										17 58		18 30	
Manchester Piccadilly 10 ⛴	d									17 16	17 46										18 16		18 46	
Bolton	d									17 33	18 05										18 33		19 05	
Wigan North Western	a											18 27	18 37											19 27
	d											18 28	18 38											19 27
Preston 8	a									17 57	18 33	18 40	18 51								18 55		19 33	19 40
Preston 8	d									18 00	18 35	18 42	18 53								19 00	19 06	19 35	19 42
Blackpool North	a										19 01												20 01	
Lancaster 6	a									18 15		18 56	19 08								19 15	19 22		19 56
	d									18 16		18 58	19 08								19 16	19 22		19 57
Barrow-in-Furness	a																					20 26		
Oxenholme Lake District	a									18 30		19 10	19 22								19 30			20 10
	d									18 30		19 11	19 24								19 30			20 10
Windermere	a																							
Penrith North Lakes	d									18 56		19 36									19 55			20 36
Carlisle 8	a									19 12		19 51	20 01								20 12			20 51
	d									19 15		19 53	20 03								20 13			20 52
Lockerbie	d									19 36											20 32			
Carstairs	a																							
Motherwell	a									20s22														
Glasgow Central 15	a									20 44		21 09	21 17											22 07
Haymarket	a																				21s30			
Edinburgh 10	a																				21 39			
Perth	a																							
Dundee	a																							
Aberdeen	a																							
Inverness	a																							

OVERNIGHT SLEEPERS. For sleeper trains, operated by First ScotRail, please refer to Tables 400 - 404

Table 65

Sundays

16 September to 21 October

London and West Midlands - North West England and Scotland

Route Diagram - see first Page of Table 65

		VT	XC	VT	TP	LM	VT	VT	XC	TP	VT	VT	XC	VT	LM	VT	VT	XC	VT	TP	VT
												R									
		◇1	◇1	◇1	◇1	◇1	◇1	◇1	◇1	◇1	◇1	1	◇1	◇1	◇1	◇1	◇1	◇1	◇1	◇1	◇1
																		A			
		☕	🛒	☕			☕	☕	🛒		☕	☕	🛒	☕		☕	☕	🛒	☕		☕
London Euston 15 ⊖	d			17 57			18 05	18 17			18 28			18 57		19 05	19 17				19 28
Watford Junction	d																				
Milton Keynes Central	d							18 50									19 50				
Rugby	d																				
Nuneaton	d															20 04					
Tamworth Low Level	d																				
Lichfield Trent Valley	d																				
Coventry	d								18 26									19 26			
Birmingham International ✈	d								18 38									19 38			
Birmingham New Street 12	d	18 20	18 31			18 35			19 01			19 20	19 31		19 35			20 01	20 20		
Wolverhampton 7 ⛴	d	18 37	18 49			18 53			19 19			19 37	19 49		19 53			20 19	20 38		
Penkridge	d					19 03									20 03						
Stafford	a					19 09	19 24		19 37						20 09	20 28		20 36	20 51		
	d					19 09	19 25		19 38						20 09	20 29		20 37	20 52		
Stoke-on-Trent	a		19 19	19 25				19 50	19 56				20 19	20 25			20 50	20 56			
Congleton	a																				
Macclesfield	a			19 42					20 14					20 42				21 15			
Crewe 10	a	19 07				19 29						20 07			20 30	20 47			21 10		
	d	19 09				19 31						20 09			20 31	20 49					
Chester	a																				
Wrexham General	a																				
Llandudno	a																				
Bangor (Gwynedd)	a																				
Holyhead	a																				
Wilmslow	a																				
Stockport	a			19 56				20 18	20 28					20 56			21 18	21 28			
Manchester Piccadilly 10 ⛴	a		19 58	20 09				20 29	20 40				21 00	21 09			21 29	21 40			
Hartford	a					19 42									20 43						
Warrington Bank Quay	a	19 26									20 16	20 26									21 16
	d	19 27									20 16	20 27									21 16
Runcorn	a					19 53	19 58								20 54	21 06					
Liverpool South Parkway 7 ✈	a					20 02									21 03						
Liverpool Lime Street 10	a					20 14	20 16								21 14	21 27					
	d																				
Manchester Airport ✈	d				18 58					19 30										20 30	
Manchester Piccadilly 10 ⛴	d				19 16					19 46										20 46	
Bolton	d				19 33					20 05										21 05	
Wigan North Western	a	19 37									20 27	20 37									21 27
	d	19 38									20 27	20 38									21 27
Preston 8	a	19 51			19 57					20 33	20 40	20 51								21 33	21 40
Preston 8	d	19 53			20 06					20 35	20 42	20 53								21 35	21 42
Blackpool North	a									21 01										22 01	
Lancaster 6	a	20 07			20 23						20 56	21 08									21 56
	d	20 08			20 24						20 57	21 08									21 57
Barrow-in-Furness	a				21 19																
Oxenholme Lake District	a										21 10	21 22									22 10
	d										21 11	21 24									22 11
Windermere	a																				
Penrith North Lakes	d	20 45									21 36										22 36
Carlisle 8	a	21 00									21 51	22 01									22 51
	d	21 02									21 52	22 03									22 53
Lockerbie	d											22 23									
Carstairs	a																				
Motherwell	a										22 48	23 07									
Glasgow Central 15	a										23 09	23 22									00 02
Haymarket	a	22 15																			
Edinburgh 10	a	22 21																			
Perth	a																				
Dundee	a																				
Aberdeen	a																				
Inverness	a																				

A 🛒 to Birmingham New Street

OVERNIGHT SLEEPERS. For sleeper trains, operated by First ScotRail, please refer to Tables 400 - 404

Table 65

Sundays

16 September to 21 October

London and West Midlands - North West England and Scotland

Route Diagram - see first Page of Table 65

		XC	VT	VT	VT	VT		XC	TP		VT	VT	LM	XC	NT	VT			SR	VT	VT	VT	SR
																			🛏				🛏
		◇1	◇1	◇1	◇1	◇1		◇1	◇1		◇1	◇1	◇1	◇1		◇1				◇1	◇1	◇1	
								A											B				
																			🛏				🛏
			🍴	🍴	🍴	🍴		trolley			🍴	🍴				🍴			🍴	🍴	🍴	🍴	🍴
London Euston 15 ⊖	d		19 57	20 05	20 08	20 15					20 25					20 50			20 55	21 21	21 25	21 51	23 27
Watford Junction	d																		21u17				23u47
Milton Keynes Central	d				20 41	20 48										21 37					22 14	22 38	
Rugby	d															22 01						23 18	
Nuneaton	d			21 04																22 52		23 29	
Tamworth Low Level	d										21 32												
Lichfield Trent Valley	d										21 39												
Coventry	d							20 26						21 26									
Birmingham International ✈	d							20 38						21 38									
Birmingham New Street 12	d	20 31						21 01				21 20	21 35	22 01									
Wolverhampton 7 🚌	d	20 52						21 19				21 38	21 57	22 19									
Penkridge	d												22 07										
Stafford	a				21 31			21 36				21 56	22 13	22 36						23 16		23s53	
	d				21 33			21 37				21 57	22 16	22 37						23 17			
Stoke-on-Trent	a	21 19	21 25			21 50		21 56						22 55							23 29		
Congleton	a																						
Macclesfield	a		21 42					22 14						23 12							23 45		
Crewe 10	a			21 44	21 53						22 10	22 17	22 38			22 49				23 43		00s21	
	d			21 46	21 55						22 13	22 18				22 51			23u39	23 45			
Chester	a																						
Wrexham General	a																						
Llandudno	a																						
Bangor (Gwynedd)	a																						
Holyhead	a																						
Wilmslow	a																						
Stockport	a		21 56			22 18		22 28						23 27							23 59	00s50	
Manchester Piccadilly 10 🚌	a	21 56	22 09			22 29		22 40						23 41							00 12	01 00	
Hartford	a																						
Warrington Bank Quay	a										22 29	22 36				23 08							
	d										22 30	22 36				23 08							
Runcorn	a			22 03	22 12															00 07			
Liverpool South Parkway 7 ✈	a																						
Liverpool Lime Street 10	a			22 23	22 33															00 30			
	d																						
Manchester Airport ✈	d								21 30														
Manchester Piccadilly 10 🚌	d								21 46														
Bolton	d								22 05														
Wigan North Western	a										22 40	22 47				23 19							
	d										22 41	22 47			23 14	23 19							
Preston 8	a								22 28		22 58	23 07			23 36	23 41							
Preston 8	d								22 29						23 39				00u30				
Blackpool North	a								22 55						00 05								
Lancaster 6	a																						
	d																						
Barrow-in-Furness	a																						
Oxenholme Lake District	a																						
	d																						
Windermere	a																						
Penrith North Lakes	d																						
Carlisle 8	a																						05s04
	d																						
Lockerbie	d																						
Carstairs	a																						06s20
Motherwell	a																						06s56
Glasgow Central 15	a																						07 20
Haymarket	a																						
Edinburgh 10	a																						07 16
Perth	a																		05s39				
Dundee	a																		06s08				
Aberdeen	a																		07 36				
Inverness	a																		08 38				

A trolley to Birmingham New Street

B Conveys a portion from Fort William, arrives at 0954

OVERNIGHT SLEEPERS. For sleeper trains, operated by First ScotRail, please refer to Tables 400 - 404

Table 65

Sundays
from 28 October

London and West Midlands - North West England and Scotland

Route Diagram - see first Page of Table 65

		TP	TP	XC	TP	TP	TP	VT	TP	TP		NT		NT	TP		TP	NT	TP	VT		VT	VT	VT	LM
		◇1	◇1	◇1			◇1	◇1	◇1	◇1					◇1		◇1		◇1	◇1		◇1	◇1	◇1	◇1
					(bus)	(bus)		(catering)		(trolley)		(bus)					(trolley)	(bus)		(catering)		(catering)	(catering)	(catering)	
London Euston 15 ⊖	d																						08 15	08 20	
Watford Junction	d																								
Milton Keynes Central	d																							09 06	
Rugby	d																						09 37		
Nuneaton	d																						09 47		
Tamworth Low Level	d																								
Lichfield Trent Valley	d																								
Coventry	d																								
Birmingham International ✈	d																								
Birmingham New Street 12	d			22p31				08 45														09 20			09 42
Wolverhampton 7 ⛴	d			22p49				09 04														09 37			10 00
Penkridge	d																								10 10
Stafford	a			23p01				09 16															10 10		10 16
	d			23p02				09 17															10 11		10 17
Stoke-on-Trent	a			23p20																				10 22	
Congleton	a																								
Macclesfield	a			23p38																				10 39	
Crewe 10	a							09 35														10 06	10 30		10 37
	d																					10 11	10 32		10 38
Chester	a																								
Wrexham General	a																								
Llandudno	a																								
Bangor (Gwynedd)	a																								
Holyhead	a																								
Wilmslow	a																								
Stockport	a			23p53																				10 52	
Manchester Piccadilly 10 ⛴	a			00 10																				11 05	
Hartford	a																								10 50
Warrington Bank Quay	a																								
	d																								
Runcorn	a																						10 49		11 00
Liverpool South Parkway 7 ✈	a																								11 09
Liverpool Lime Street 10	a																						11 09		11 21
	d																								
Manchester Airport ✈	d	22p00	22p29		00 05	05 30	07 47		08 47	09 00					09 29		10 00		10 30						
Manchester Piccadilly 10 ⛴	d	22p16	22p46		00 30	05 55	08 02		09 03	09 15					09 46		10 16		10 46						
Bolton	d	22p33	23p07		00s55	06s20	08 21		09 23	09 32					10 05		10 33		11 05						
Wigan North Western	a																								
	d											09 25						10 25							
Preston 8	a	22p54	23p33		01s30	06s55	08 48		09 50	09 57		10 22			10 33		10 57	11 22	11 33			11 29			
Preston 8	d	22p55	23p35				08 49		09 52	10 00				10 29	10 35	10 41	10 58		11 35	11 40		11 53			
Blackpool North	a		00 02		02 10	07 35	09 13		10 18					10 53	11 02				12 01						
Lancaster 6	a	23p11								10 15						10 56	11 13			11 54		12 08			
	d	23p11								10 16						10 57	11 14			11 55		12 08			
Barrow-in-Furness	a	00 15														12 00									
Oxenholme Lake District	a									10 30							11 28			12 08		12 22			
	d									10 30							11 28			12 08		12 24			
Windermere	a																								
Penrith North Lakes	d									10 55							11 53			12 34					
Carlisle 8	a									11 12							12 10			12 49		13 01			
	d									11 13							12 11			12 50		13 03			
Lockerbie	d									11 32							12 30								
Carstairs	a																								
Motherwell	a																								
Glasgow Central 15	a																13 35			14 01					
Haymarket	a									12s32												14 13			
Edinburgh 10	a									12 39												14 21			
Perth	a																								
Dundee	a																								
Aberdeen	a																								
Inverness	a																								

OVERNIGHT SLEEPERS. For sleeper trains, operated by First ScotRail, please refer to Tables 400 - 404

Table 65

Sundays

from 28 October

London and West Midlands - North West England and Scotland

Route Diagram - see first Page of Table 65

Station		XC	VT		NT	TP		VT	TP	VT	VT	VT	LM	XC		TP		NT	TP	VT	VT	VT	VT	LM	XC
		◇1	◇1			◇1		◇1	◇1	◇1	◇1	◇1	◇1	◇1		◇1			◇1	◇1	◇1	◇1	◇1	◇1	◇1
					bus													bus							
		trolley	buffet					buffet		buffet	buffet	buffet		trolley		trolley				buffet	buffet	buffet	buffet		trolley
London Euston 15 ⊖	d										09 15	09 20										10 15	10 20		
Watford Junction	d																								
Milton Keynes Central	d										10 02	10 07											11 07		
Rugby	d																					11 39			
Nuneaton	d										10 45											11 50			
Tamworth Low Level	d																								
Lichfield Trent Valley	d																								
Coventry	d													10 28											11 29
Birmingham International ✈	d													10 40											11 40
Birmingham New Street 12	d	10 01								10 20			10 42	11 01							11 20			11 42	12 01
Wolverhampton 7	d	10 19								10 37			11 00	11 19							11 37			12 00	12 19
Penkridge	d												11 10											12 10	
Stafford	a	10 32									11 09		11 16	11 31								12 13		12 16	12 32
	d	10 33									11 09		11 17	11 32								12 14		12 17	12 33
Stoke-on-Trent	a	10 51										11 20		11 51									12 24		12 52
Congleton	a																								
Macclesfield	a	11 08										11 37		12 09									12 40		13 10
Crewe 10	a									11 07	11 30		11 37								12 07	12 32		12 37	
	d		10 42							11 11	11 32		11 38								12 11	12 34		12 38	
Chester	a		11 02																						
Wrexham General	a																								
Llandudno	a																								
Bangor (Gwynedd)	a		12 09																						
Holyhead	a		12 43																						
Wilmslow	a																								
Stockport	a	11 22										11 51		12 22									12 55		13 28
Manchester Piccadilly 10	a	11 31										12 04		12 34									13 08		13 40
Hartford	a												11 50											12 50	
Warrington Bank Quay	a																								
	d																								
Runcorn	a										11 49		12 01									12 51		13 01	
Liverpool South Parkway 7 ✈	a												12 10											13 10	
Liverpool Lime Street 10	a										12 10		12 21									13 12		13 21	
	d																								
Manchester Airport ✈	d					11 30										12 00			12 30						
Manchester Piccadilly 10	d					11 46										12 16			12 46						
Bolton	d					12 05										12 33			13 05						
Wigan North Western	a																								
	d				11 25													12 25							
Preston 8	a				12 22	12 33				12 44						12 57		13 22	13 33		13 26				
Preston 8	d					12 35		12 40	12 48	12 53						12 58			13 35	13 42	13 53				
Blackpool North	a					13 01													14 01						
Lancaster 6	a							12 54	13 03	13 08						13 13				13 56	14 08				
	d							12 55	13 04	13 08						13 14				13 57	14 08				
Barrow-in-Furness	a								14 07																
Oxenholme Lake District	a							13 08		13 22						13 28				14 10					
	d							13 08		13 24						13 28				14 10					
Windermere	a																								
Penrith North Lakes	d							13 34								13 53				14 36	14 45				
Carlisle 8	a							13 49		14 01						14 10				14 51	15 00				
	d							13 50		14 03						14 11				14 52	15 03				
Lockerbie	d															14 30									
Carstairs	a																								
Motherwell	a																								
Glasgow Central 15	a							15 02		15 16										16 05					
Haymarket	a															15s29					16 14				
Edinburgh 10	a															15 39					16 22				
Perth	a																								
Dundee	a																								
Aberdeen	a																								
Inverness	a																								

OVERNIGHT SLEEPERS. For sleeper trains, operated by First ScotRail, please refer to Tables 400 - 404

Table 65

Sundays
from 28 October

London and West Midlands - North West England and Scotland

Route Diagram - see first Page of Table 65

		TP	NT	TP	VT	VT	VT	VT	LM	VT	VT	XC	XC	VT	LM	VT	VT	XC	TP	NT
		◇1		◇1	◇1	◇1	◇1	◇1	◇1	◇1	◇1	◇1	◇1	◇1	◇1	◇1	◇1	◇1	◇1	
London Euston 15 ⊖	d						11 15	11 20		12 05	12 17			12 57		13 05	13 17			
Watford Junction	d																			
Milton Keynes Central	d						12 03	12 08			12 50						13 50			
Rugby	d																			
Nuneaton	d																			
Tamworth Low Level	d																			
Lichfield Trent Valley	d																			
Coventry	d											12 28						13 26		
Birmingham International ✈	d											12 40						13 38		
Birmingham New Street 12	d					12 20			12 35			13 01	13 31		13 35			14 01		
Wolverhampton 7	d					12 37			12 53			13 19	13 49		13 53			14 19		
Penkridge	d								13 03						14 03					
Stafford	a						12 53		13 09	13 24		13 33			14 09	14 23		14 33		
	d						12 53		13 09	13 25		13 34			14 09	14 24		14 34		
Stoke-on-Trent	a							13 09			13 50	13 56	14 19	14 26			14 50	14 55		
Congleton	a																			
Macclesfield	a							13 26				14 14		14 42				15 13		
Crewe 10	a					13 07	13 13		13 30	13 43					14 29	14 43				
	d					13 11	13 15		13 31	13 45					14 31	14 45				
Chester	a																			
Wrexham General	a																			
Llandudno	a																			
Bangor (Gwynedd)	a																			
Holyhead	a																			
Wilmslow	a																			
Stockport	a							13 41			14 18	14 28		14 56			15 18	15 27		
Manchester Piccadilly 10	a							13 53			14 29	14 40	14 57	15 09			15 29	15 39		
Hartford	a								13 43						14 42					
Warrington Bank Quay	a																			
	d																			
Runcorn	a						13 32		13 54	14 02					14 53	15 02				
Liverpool South Parkway 7 ✈	a								14 03						15 02					
Liverpool Lime Street 10	a						13 54		14 14	14 24					15 14	15 24				
	d																			
Manchester Airport ✈	d	12 58		13 30															13 58	
Manchester Piccadilly 10	d	13 16		13 46															14 16	
Bolton	d	13 33		14 05															14 33	
Wigan North Western	a																			
	d		13 25																	14 25
Preston 8	a	13 59	14 22	14 33		14 33													14 57	15 22
Preston 8	d	14 00		14 35	14 42	14 53													15 00	
Blackpool North	a			15 01																
Lancaster 6	a	14 15			14 56	15 08													15 15	
	d	14 16			14 58	15 09													15 16	
Barrow-in-Furness	a																			
Oxenholme Lake District	a	14 30				15 22													15 30	
	d	14 30				15 24													15 30	
Windermere	a																			
Penrith North Lakes	d	14 55			15 32														15 55	
Carlisle 8	a	15 12			15 47	16 01													16 12	
	d	15 17			15 48	16 03													16 13	
Lockerbie	d																		16 32	
Carstairs	a																			
Motherwell	a																			
Glasgow Central 15	a	16 35			17 00	17 17														
Haymarket	a																		17s30	
Edinburgh 10	a																		17 39	
Perth	a																			
Dundee	a																			
Aberdeen	a																			
Inverness	a																			

OVERNIGHT SLEEPERS. For sleeper trains, operated by First ScotRail, please refer to Tables 400 - 404

Table 65

Sundays
from 28 October

London and West Midlands - North West England and Scotland

Route Diagram - see first Page of Table 65

		TP	VT		VT	XC	LM	TP		VT	VT	VT	VT	XC	TP	VT	VT	XC		VT	LM	VT	VT	VT	XC
		◇1	◇1		◇1	◇1	◇1	◇1		◇1	◇1	◇1	◇1	◇1	◇1	◇1	◇1	◇1		◇1	◇1	◇1	◇1	◇1	◇1
London Euston 15 ⊖	d		13 28							13 45	13 57	14 05	14 17			14 28				14 57		15 05	15 08	15 17	
Watford Junction	d																								
Milton Keynes Central	d												14 50										15 42	15 50	
Rugby	d																								
Nuneaton	d																								
Tamworth Low Level	d																								
Lichfield Trent Valley	d																								
Coventry	d													14 26											15 26
Birmingham International ✈	d													14 38											15 38
Birmingham New Street 12	d				14 20	14 31	14 35							15 01			15 20	15 31			15 35				16 01
Wolverhampton 7	d				14 37	14 49	14 53							15 19			15 37	15 49			15 53				16 19
Penkridge	d						15 03														16 03				
Stafford	a						15 09					15 24		15 33							16 09	16 24			16 34
	d						15 09					15 25		15 34							16 09	16 25			16 34
Stoke-on-Trent	a					15 19					15 25		15 50	15 56				16 19		16 24				16 50	16 56
Congleton	a																								
Macclesfield	a										15 42			16 14						16 42					17 14
Crewe 10	a				15 07		15 29			15 34		15 43					16 07				16 30		16 50		
	d				15 09		15 31			15 36		15 45					16 09				16 31		16 52		
Chester	a																						17 14		
Wrexham General	a																								
Llandudno	a																								
Bangor (Gwynedd)	a																								
Holyhead	a																								
Wilmslow	a																								
Stockport	a										15 56		16 18	16 28						16 56				17 18	17 28
Manchester Piccadilly 10	a					15 59					16 09		16 29	16 40				16 59		17 09				17 29	17 40
Hartford	a						15 42														16 43				
Warrington Bank Quay	a		15 16		15 26					15 56						16 16	16 26								
	d		15 16		15 27					15 56						16 16	16 27								
Runcorn	a						15 53					16 02									16 54	16 57			
Liverpool South Parkway 7 ✈	a						16 02														17 03				
Liverpool Lime Street 10	a						16 14					16 24									17 14	17 16			
	d																								
Manchester Airport ✈	d	14 30						14 58							15 30										
Manchester Piccadilly 10	d	14 46						15 16							15 46										
Bolton	d	15 05						15 33							16 05										
Wigan North Western	a		15 27		15 37					16 07						16 27	16 37								
	d		15 27		15 38					16 07						16 27	16 38								
Preston 8	a	15 33	15 40		15 51			15 57		16 20					16 33	16 40	16 51								
Preston 8	d	15 35	15 42		15 53			16 00		16 22					16 35	16 42	16 53								
Blackpool North	a	16 01													17 01										
Lancaster 6	a		15 56		16 08			16 15		16 36						16 56	17 08								
	d		15 58		16 08			16 16		16 38						16 57	17 08								
Barrow-in-Furness	a							17 19																	
Oxenholme Lake District	a		16 10							16 50							17 22								
	d		16 11							16 51							17 23								
Windermere	a																								
Penrith North Lakes	d				16 45					17 16						17 32									
Carlisle 8	a		16 48		17 00					17 31						17 47	18 01								
	d		16 49		17 02					17 32						17 48	18 03								
Lockerbie	d																								
Carstairs	a																								
Motherwell	a																								
Glasgow Central 15	a		18 01							18 44						19 00	19 17								
Haymarket	a				18 13																				
Edinburgh 10	a				18 22																				
Perth	a																								
Dundee	a																								
Aberdeen	a																								
Inverness	a																								

OVERNIGHT SLEEPERS. For sleeper trains, operated by First ScotRail, please refer to Tables 400 - 404

Table 65

Sundays
from 28 October

London and West Midlands - North West England and Scotland

Route Diagram - see first Page of Table 65

		TP	TP	VT	VT	XC	VT	LM	VT	VT	VT	XC	TP	TP	VT	VT	XC	VT	LM	VT	VT	XC
		◇1	◇1	◇1	◇1	◇1	◇1	◇1	◇1	◇1	◇1	◇1	◇1	◇1	◇1	◇1	◇1	◇1	◇1	◇1	◇1	◇1
		⊼		☕	☕	⊼	☕		☕	☕	☕	⊼	⊼		☕	☕	⊼	☕		☕	☕	⊼
London Euston 15 ⊖	d			15 28			15 57		16 05	16 08	16 17				16 28			16 57		17 05	17 17	
Watford Junction	d																					
Milton Keynes Central	d									16 42	16 50											
Rugby	d																				17 50	
Nuneaton	d																					
Tamworth Low Level	d																					
Lichfield Trent Valley	d																					
Coventry	d											16 26										17 26
Birmingham International ✈	d											16 38										17 38
Birmingham New Street 12	d				16 20	16 31		16 35				17 01				17 20	17 31		17 35			18 01
Wolverhampton 7	d				16 37	16 49		16 53				17 19				17 37	17 49		17 53			18 19
Penkridge	d							17 03											18 03			
Stafford	a							17 09	17 24			17 35							18 09	18 24		18 35
	d							17 09	17 25			17 36							18 09	18 25		18 36
Stoke-on-Trent	a					17 19	17 25				17 50	17 56					18 19	18 25			18 50	18 56
Congleton	a																					
Macclesfield	a						17 42					18 14						18 42				19 15
Crewe 10	a				17 07			17 30		17 50						18 07			18 30			
	d				17 09			17 31		17 52						18 09			18 31			
Chester	a									18 14												
Wrexham General	a																					
Llandudno	a																					
Bangor (Gwynedd)	a																					
Holyhead	a																					
Wilmslow	a																					
Stockport	a						17 56				18 18	18 28						18 56			19 18	19 28
Manchester Piccadilly 10	a					17 56	18 09				18 29	18 40					18 56	19 09			19 29	19 40
Hartford	a							17 43											18 43			
Warrington Bank Quay	a			17 16	17 26										18 16	18 26						
	d			17 16	17 27										18 17	18 27						
Runcorn	a							17 54	17 57										18 54	18 57		
Liverpool South Parkway 7 ✈	a							18 03											19 03			
Liverpool Lime Street 10	a							18 14	18 16										19 14	19 19		
	d																					
Manchester Airport ✈	d	15 58	16 30										16 58	17 30								
Manchester Piccadilly 10	d	16 16	16 46										17 16	17 46								
Bolton	d	16 33	17 05										17 33	18 05								
Wigan North Western	a			17 27	17 37										18 27	18 37						
	d			17 27	17 38										18 28	18 38						
Preston 8	a	16 57	17 33	17 40	17 51								17 57	18 33	18 40	18 51						
Preston 8	d	17 00	17 35	17 42	17 53								18 00	18 35	18 42	18 53						
Blackpool North	a		18 01											19 01								
Lancaster 6	a	17 15		17 56	18 08								18 15		18 56	19 08						
	d	17 16		17 57	18 08								18 16		18 58	19 08						
Barrow-in-Furness	a																					
Oxenholme Lake District	a	17 30		18 10	18 22								18 30		19 10	19 22						
	d	17 30		18 10	18 23								18 30		19 11	19 24						
Windermere	a																					
Penrith North Lakes	d	17 55			18 49								18 56		19 36							
Carlisle 8	a	18 12		18 48	19 04								19 12		19 51	20 01						
	d	18 13		18 49	19 04								19 15		19 53	20 03						
Lockerbie	d												19 36									
Carstairs	a																					
Motherwell	a												20s22									
Glasgow Central 15	a			20 01									20 44		21 09	21 17						
Haymarket	a	19s28																				
Edinburgh 10	a	19 35			20 22																	
Perth	a																					
Dundee	a																					
Aberdeen	a																					
Inverness	a																					

OVERNIGHT SLEEPERS. For sleeper trains, operated by First ScotRail, please refer to Tables 400 - 404

Table 65

Sundays

from 28 October

London and West Midlands - North West England and Scotland

Route Diagram - see first Page of Table 65

		TP		TP	VT	VT	XC	VT	TP			LM	VT	VT	XC	TP	VT	VT	XC	VT			LM	VT	VT
		◇1		◇1	◇1	◇1	◇1	◇1	◇1			◇1	◇1	◇1	◇1	◇1	◇1	1	◇1	◇1			◇1	◇1	◇1
London Euston 15 ⊖	d				17 28			17 57					18 05	18 17			18 28			18 57				19 05	19 17
Watford Junction	d																								
Milton Keynes Central	d													18 50											19 50
Rugby	d																								
Nuneaton	d																							20 04	
Tamworth Low Level	d																								
Lichfield Trent Valley	d																								
Coventry	d														18 26										
Birmingham International ✈	d														18 38										
Birmingham New Street 12	d					18 20	18 31					18 35			19 01			19 20	19 31				19 35		
Wolverhampton 7	d					18 37	18 49					18 53			19 19			19 37	19 49				19 53		
Penkridge	d											19 03											20 03		
Stafford	a											19 09	19 24		19 37								20 09	20 28	
	d											19 09	19 25		19 39								20 09	20 29	
Stoke-on-Trent	a						19 19	19 25						19 50	19 56				20 19	20 25					20 50
Congleton	a																								
Macclesfield	a							19 42							20 14					20 42					
Crewe 10	a					19 07						19 29						20 07					20 30	20 47	
	d					19 09						19 31						20 09					20 31	20 49	
Chester	a																								
Wrexham General	a																								
Llandudno	a																								
Bangor (Gwynedd)	a																								
Holyhead	a																								
Wilmslow	a																								
Stockport	a							19 56						20 18	20 28					20 56					21 18
Manchester Piccadilly 10	a						19 58	20 09						20 29	20 40				21 00	21 09					21 29
Hartford	a											19 42											20 43		
Warrington Bank Quay	a				19 16	19 26											20 16	20 26							
	d				19 16	19 27											20 16	20 27							
Runcorn	a											19 53	19 58										20 54	21 06	
Liverpool South Parkway 7 ✈	a											20 02											21 03		
Liverpool Lime Street 10	a											20 14	20 16										21 14	21 27	
	d																								
Manchester Airport ✈	d	17 58		18 30					18 58							19 30									
Manchester Piccadilly 10	d	18 16		18 46					19 16							19 46									
Bolton	d	18 33		19 05					19 33							20 05									
Wigan North Western	a				19 27	19 37											20 27	20 37							
	d				19 27	19 38											20 27	20 38							
Preston 8	a	18 55		19 33	19 40	19 51			19 57							20 33	20 40	20 51							
Preston 8	d	19 00	19 06	19 35	19 42	19 53			20 06							20 35	20 42	20 53							
Blackpool North	a			20 01												21 01									
Lancaster 6	a	19 15	19 22		19 56	20 07			20 23								20 56	21 08							
	d	19 16	19 22		19 57	20 08			20 24								20 57	21 08							
Barrow-in-Furness	a		20 26						21 19																
Oxenholme Lake District	a	19 30			20 10												21 10	21 22							
	d	19 30			20 10												21 11	21 24							
Windermere	a																								
Penrith North Lakes	d	19 55			20 36	20 45											21 36								
Carlisle 8	a	20 12			20 51	21 00											21 51	22 01							
	d	20 13			20 52	21 02											21 52	22 03							
Lockerbie	d	20 32																22 23							
Carstairs	a																								
Motherwell	a																22 48	23 07							
Glasgow Central 15	a				22 07												23 09	23 22							
Haymarket	a	21s30				22 15																			
Edinburgh 10	a	21 39				22 21																			
Perth	a																								
Dundee	a																								
Aberdeen	a																								
Inverness	a																								

OVERNIGHT SLEEPERS. For sleeper trains, operated by First ScotRail, please refer to Tables 400 - 404

Table 65

Sundays

from 28 October

London and West Midlands - North West England and Scotland

Route Diagram - see first Page of Table 65

		XC	VT	TP	VT	XC		VT	VT	VT	VT	XC	TP		VT	VT		LM	XC	NT	VT		SR	VT
																							R	
		◇1	◇1	◇1	◇1	◇1		◇1	◇1	◇1	◇1	◇1	◇1		◇1	◇1		◇1	◇1		◇1			◇1
		A										A											B	
		🛒	☕		☕	🛒		☕	☕	☕	☕	🛒			☕	☕					☕		🛏 ☕	☕
London Euston 15 ⊖	d				19 28			19 57	20 05	20 08	20 15				20 25						20 50		20 55	21 21
Watford Junction	d																						21u17	
Milton Keynes Central	d									20 41	20 48										21 37			
Rugby	d																				22 01			
Nuneaton	d								21 04															22 52
Tamworth Low Level	d														21 32									
Lichfield Trent Valley	d														21 39									
Coventry	d	19 26										20 26							21 26					
Birmingham International ✈	d	19 38										20 38							21 38					
Birmingham New Street 12	d	20 01	20 20			20 31						21 01				21 20		21 35	22 01					
Wolverhampton 7 🚌	d	20 19	20 38			20 52						21 19				21 38		21 57	22 19					
Penkridge	d																	22 07						
Stafford	a	20 36	20 51							21 31		21 36				21 56		22 13	22 36					23 16
	d	20 37	20 52							21 33		21 37				21 57		22 16	22 37					23 17
Stoke-on-Trent	a	20 56				21 19		21 25			21 50	21 56							22 55					
Congleton	a																							
Macclesfield	a	21 15						21 42				22 14							23 12					
Crewe 10	a		21 10						21 44	21 53					22 10	22 17		22 38			22 49			23 43
	d								21 46	21 55					22 13	22 18					22 51		23u39	23 45
Chester	a																							
Wrexham General	a																							
Llandudno	a																							
Bangor (Gwynedd)	a																							
Holyhead	a																							
Wilmslow	a																							
Stockport	a	21 28						21 56			22 18	22 28							23 27					
Manchester Piccadilly 10 🚊	a	21 40				21 56		22 09			22 29	22 40							23 41					
Hartford	a																							
Warrington Bank Quay	a				21 16										22 29	22 36					23 08			
	d				21 16										22 30	22 36					23 08			
Runcorn	a								22 03	22 12														00 07
Liverpool South Parkway 7 ✈	a																							
Liverpool Lime Street 10	a								22 23	22 33														00 30
	d																							
Manchester Airport ✈	d			20 30									21 30											
Manchester Piccadilly 10 🚊	d			20 46									21 46											
Bolton	d			21 05									22 05											
Wigan North Western	a				21 27										22 40	22 47					23 19			
	d				21 27										22 41	22 47				23 14	23 19			
Preston 8	a			21 33	21 40								22 28		22 58	23 07				23 36	23 41			
Preston 8	d			21 35	21 42								22 29							23 39			00u30	
Blackpool North	a			22 01									22 55							00 05				
Lancaster 6	a				21 56																			
	d				21 57																			
Barrow-in-Furness	a																							
Oxenholme Lake District	a				22 10																			
	d				22 11																			
Windermere	a																							
Penrith North Lakes	d				22 36																			
Carlisle 8	a				22 51																			
	d				22 53																			
Lockerbie	d																							
Carstairs	a																							
Motherwell	a																							
Glasgow Central 15	a				00 02																			
Haymarket	a																							
Edinburgh 10	a																							
Perth	a																						05s39	
Dundee	a																						06s08	
Aberdeen	a																						07 36	
Inverness	a																						08 38	

A 🛒 to Birmingham New Street

B Conveys a portion from Fort William, arrives at 0954

OVERNIGHT SLEEPERS. For sleeper trains, operated by First ScotRail, please refer to Tables 400 - 404

Table 65

Sundays
from 28 October

London and West Midlands - North West England and Scotland

Route Diagram - see first Page of Table 65

		VT	VT	SR	
				B	
		◇1	◇1		
				⇌	
		⊡	⊡	⊡	
London Euston 15 ⊖	d	21 25	21 51	23 27	
Watford Junction	d			23u47	
Milton Keynes Central	d	22 14	22 38		
Rugby	d		23 18		
Nuneaton	d		23 29		
Tamworth Low Level	d				
Lichfield Trent Valley	d				
Coventry	d				
Birmingham International ✈	d				
Birmingham New Street 12	d				
Wolverhampton 7	d				
Penkridge	d				
Stafford	a		23s53		
	d				
Stoke-on-Trent	a	23 29			
Congleton	a				
Macclesfield	a	23 45			
Crewe 10	a		00s21		
	d				
Chester	a				
Wrexham General	a				
Llandudno	a				
Bangor (Gwynedd)	a				
Holyhead	a				
Wilmslow	a				
Stockport	a	23 59	00s50		
Manchester Piccadilly 10	a	00 12	01 00		
Hartford	a				
Warrington Bank Quay	a				
	d				
Runcorn	a				
Liverpool South Parkway 7 ✈	a				
Liverpool Lime Street 10	a				
	d				
Manchester Airport ✈	d				
Manchester Piccadilly 10	d				
Bolton	d				
Wigan North Western	a				
	d				
Preston 8	a				
Preston 8	d				
Blackpool North	a				
Lancaster 6	a				
	d				
Barrow-in-Furness	a				
Oxenholme Lake District	a				
	d				
Windermere	a				
Penrith North Lakes	d				
Carlisle 8	a			05s04	
	d				
Lockerbie	d				
Carstairs	a			06s20	
Motherwell	a				06s56
Glasgow Central 15	a				07 20
Haymarket	a				
Edinburgh 10	a			07 16	
Perth	a				
Dundee	a				
Aberdeen	a				
Inverness	a				

OVERNIGHT SLEEPERS. For sleeper trains, operated by First ScotRail, please refer to Tables 400 - 404

Table 65

Mondays to Fridays

until 29 June

Scotland and North West England - West Midlands and London

Route Diagram - see first Page of Table 65

Miles	Miles	Miles	Miles	Miles			TP MX ◇1	TP MO ◇1 A	SR MO R A	SR MO R A	LM MX ◇1	SR R B		SR MX R C		TP ◇1	AW MO D	AW MX C	TP ◇1	TP ◇1	LM 1	VT ◇1 ⊠		SR MO R E	SR MO R E
—	0	—	—	—	Inverness	d																		20p25	
—	—	0	—	—	Aberdeen	d																			21p42
—	—	71¼	—	—	Dundee	d																			23b06
—	118	—	—	—	Perth	d																		23b00	
—	130¼	187¼	—	—	**Edinburgh** 10	d			23p15			23p40		23p40											
—	131½	188½	—	—	Haymarket	d																			
0	—	—	—	—	**Glasgow Central** 15	d				23p15			23p40		23p40										
12¾	—	—	—	—	Motherwell	d				23b31			23b56		23b56										
28¾	158	—	—	—	Carstairs	d			23b47			00u16		00u16											
77	—	263½	—	—	Lockerbie	d																			
102¼	—	—	—	—	**Carlisle** 8	a																			
—	—	—	—	—		d			01u12			01u41		01u41											
120	—	—	—	—	Penrith North Lakes	d																			
—	—	—	—	—	Windermere	d																			
152¼	—	—	—	—	Oxenholme Lake District	a																			
—	—	—	—	—		d																			
—	—	—	—	—	Barrow-in-Furness	d													04 35						
171¼	—	—	—	—	Lancaster 6	a													05 28						
—	—	—	—	—		d																			
—	—	—	—	—	Blackpool North	d	22p44	23p03								03 37									
192¼	—	—	—	—	**Preston** 8	a	23p08	23p28																04s41	
—	—	—	0	—	**Preston** 8	d	23p10	23p28								04u02				05 16					
207½	—	—	—	—	Wigan North Western	a																			
—	—	—	—	—		d																			
—	—	—	—	—	Blackrod	d		23p50																	
—	—	—	—	—	Lostock	d		23p57																	
—	—	—	20	—	Bolton	a	23p34	00 02								04c31				05 42					
—	—	—	31¼	—	**Manchester Piccadilly** 10	a	23p53	00 18								04 48				06 01					
—	—	—	—	—	Manchester Airport ✈	a	00 24	00 32								05 07				06 18					
—	0	—	—	—	**Liverpool Lime Street** 10	a																			
—	—	—	—	—		d					23p34														
—	5½	—	—	—	Liverpool South Parkway ✈	d					23p45														
—	13	—	—	—	Runcorn	d					23p53														
219¼	—	—	—	—	Warrington Bank Quay	a																			
—	—	—	—	—		d																			
231½	23¾	—	—	—	Hartford	d					00 07														
—	—	—	—	0	**Manchester Piccadilly** 10	d																05 05			
—	—	—	37	5¾	Stockport	d																05 13			
—	—	—	—	—	Wilmslow	d																			
—	—	—	—	—	Holyhead	d																			
—	—	—	—	—	Bangor (Gwynedd)	d																			
—	—	—	—	—	Llandudno Junction	d																			
—	—	—	—	—	Wrexham General	d																			
—	—	—	—	—	Chester	d											04 22	04 22							
243½	35½	—	—	—	**Crewe** 10	a					00 22						04 44	04 44				05 34		05s41	
—	—	—	—	—		d											04 59	04 59			05 18	05 36			
—	—	—	49	17¾	Macclesfield	d																			
—	—	—	57	25¾	Congleton	d																			
—	—	—	68¾	37¼	**Stoke-on-Trent**	d																			
267¾	—	—	—	53½	**Stafford**	a											05 24	05 24				05 53			
—	—	—	—	—		d											05 25	05 25				05 55			
—	—	—	—	59¼	Penkridge	a																			
—	—	—	—	69¾	Wolverhampton 7	a											05 39	05 39							
—	—	—	—	82½	**Birmingham New Street** 12	a											05 59	06 01							
—	—	—	—	91	Birmingham International ✈	a																			
—	—	—	—	101½	Coventry	a																			
285	—	—	99¼	—	Lichfield Trent Valley	a															06 06				
291¼	—	—	—	—	Tamworth Low Level	a															06 13				
304¼	—	—	—	—	Nuneaton	a															06 29	06 17			
318¾	—	—	—	113	Rugby	a															06 47	06 30			
351½	—	—	—	—	Milton Keynes Central	a																06 51			
383½	—	—	—	—	Watford Junction	a			06s23			06s19		06s21											
401¼	—	—	—	—	**London Euston** 15 ⊖	a			06 46			06 43		06 45								07 28		07 50	

A from 21 May until 25 June.
B from 26 June until 29 June
C until 22 June
D also from 26 June until 29 June
E from 21 May until 25 June. Conveys portion from fort William, dep 1900
b Previous night, stops to pick up only
c Stops to pick up only

OVERNIGHT SLEEPERS. For sleeper trains, operated by First ScotRail, please refer to Tables 400 - 404

Table 65

Mondays to Fridays

until 29 June

Scotland and North West England - West Midlands and London

Route Diagram - see first Page of Table 65

		SR	SR	XC	VT	XC	VT	LM	VT	VT	XC	VT	LM	VT	VT	TP	VT	TP	VT	VT	LM		VT	LM	VT
		MX	MX	◇1	◇1	◇1	◇1	◇1	◇1	◇1	◇1	◇1	◇1	◇1	◇1	◇1	◇1	◇1	◇1	◇1	◇1		◇1	◇1	◇1
																		A							
		R	R																						
		B	B																						
Inverness	d	20p47																							
Aberdeen	d		21p42																						
Dundee	d		23b06																						
Perth	d	23b21																							
Edinburgh 10	d																								
Haymarket	d																								
Glasgow Central 15	d																								
Motherwell	d																								
Carstairs	d																								
Lockerbie	d																								
Carlisle 8	a																								
	d																								
Penrith North Lakes	d																								
Windermere	d																								
Oxenholme Lake District	a																								
	d																								
Barrow-in-Furness	d																	05 31							
Lancaster 6	a																	06 23							
	d														05 35			06 23							
Blackpool North	d															05 39									
Preston 8	a	04s32													05 52	06 03		06 42							
Preston 8	d						05 33								06 00	06 05	06 16	06 44							
Wigan North Western	a						05 44								06 11		06 27								
	d						05 45								06 11		06 27								
Blackrod	d															06 22									
Lostock	d															06 30									
Bolton	a															06 34		07 08							
Manchester Piccadilly 10	a															06 56		07 27							
Manchester Airport	a															07 17		07 47							
Liverpool Lime Street 10	a																								
	d				05 27					06 05											06 30				07 00
Liverpool South Parkway	d																				06 40				
Runcorn	d				05 43					06 21											06 48				07u15
Warrington Bank Quay	a						05 55								06 22		06 38								
	d						05 56								06 22		06 38								
Hartford	d																				07 02				
Manchester Piccadilly 10	d			05 11					05 55		06 00	06 10							06 27	06 35			06 43		
Stockport	d								06 03		06 08	06 18							06 35	06 43			06 51		
Wilmslow	d								06 11														06 59		
Holyhead	d													04 48											
Bangor (Gwynedd)	d													05 14											
Llandudno Junction	d													05 32											
Wrexham General	d																								
Chester	d													06 26											
Crewe 10	a	05s38		05 44	06 00				06 27		06 32			06 47	06 42		06 58				07 14		07 15		
	d			05 47	06 02			06 20	06 29		06 38		06 47	06 53			07 01				07 16		07 17		
Macclesfield	d											06 31							06 48	06 56					
Congleton	d																								
Stoke-on-Trent	d			06 07		←						06 48							07 06	07 12				←	
Stafford	a			06 24	06 20	06 24		06 40		06 52	06 57		07 10						07 27		07 40		07 34	07 40	
	d			06 25	06 21	06 25		06 41		06 53	06 58		07 12						07 28		07 41		07 35	07 41	
Penkridge	a			→				06 46					07 17								→			07 46	
Wolverhampton 7	a					06 39		06 57			07 12		07 28				07 31		07 43					07 57	
Birmingham New Street 12	a					06 58		07 18			07 31		07 48				07 55		08 06					08 17	
Birmingham International	a					07 13													08 19						
Coventry	a					07 24													08 30						
Lichfield Trent Valley	a						06 40			07 07															
Tamworth Low Level	a						06 46			07 14															
Nuneaton	a								07 06					07 32											
Rugby	a				06 52		07 06					07 28								07 52					
Milton Keynes Central	a				07 12																				
Watford Junction	a																		09s15						
London Euston 15	a	07 50			07 50		07 57		08 07	08 22		08 22		08 33					09 34	08 45			08 52		09 01

A from Preston

B Conveys portion from fort William, dep 1950

OVERNIGHT SLEEPERS. For sleeper trains, operated by First ScotRail, please refer to Tables 400 - 404

Scotland and North West England - West Midlands and London

Route Diagram - see first Page of Table 65

		VT	TP	XC	LM	VT	VT	VT	VT	TP	TP	XC	VT	EM	LM	VT	LM	VT	VT	TP	TP	XC	LM
		◇1	◇1	◇1	◇1	◇1	◇1	◇1	◇1	◇1	◇1	◇1	◇1	◇	◇1	◇1	◇1	◇1	◇1	◇1	◇1	◇1	◇1
								A		B													
		⊠	🛒	🛒		⊠	⊠	⊠	⊠	🛒	🛒	🛒	⊠			⊠		⊠	⊠	🛒	🛒	🛒	
Inverness	d																						
Aberdeen	d																						
Dundee	d																						
Perth	d																						
Edinburgh 10	d																			05 36			
Haymarket	d																			05u40			
Glasgow Central 15	d	04 28																	05 40				
Motherwell	d																						
Carstairs	d																						
Lockerbie	d																						
Carlisle 8	a	05 42																	06 46	06 58			
	d	05 43																	06 49	06 59			
Penrith North Lakes	d	05 57																					
Windermere	d																						
Oxenholme Lake District	a	06 20																	07 22				
	d	06 20																	07 24				
Barrow-in-Furness	d									06 20													
Lancaster 6	a	06 35								07 21									07 37	07 47			
	d	06 35							06 58	07 22									07 38	07 47			
Blackpool North	d		06 40								07 10										07 36		
Preston 8	a	06 53	07 07						07 15	07 41	07 37								07 56	08 07	08 03		
Preston 8	d	06 56	07 09						07 17	07 47									07 58	08 12			
Wigan North Western	a	07 06							07 28										08 09				
	d	07 08							07 28										08 09				
Blackrod	d																						
Lostock	d		07 30																				
Bolton	a		07 34							08 08										08 34			
Manchester Piccadilly 10	a		07 56							08 27										08 56			
Manchester Airport ✈	a		08 17							08 47										09 19			
Liverpool Lime Street 10	a																						
	d				07 04									06 47	07 34	07 48							08 04
Liverpool South Parkway ✈	d				07 14									06 57	07 44								08 15
Runcorn	d				07 22										07 52	08 04							08 24
Warrington Bank Quay	a	07 17							07 39										08 20				
	d	07 18							07 39										08 20				
Hartford	d				07 36										08 04								
Manchester Piccadilly 10	d			07 07		07 15						07 26	07 35	07 42				07 55				08 07	
Stockport	d			07 16		07 23						07 35	07 43	07a53				08 04				08 16	
Wilmslow	d																	08 11					
Holyhead	d						05 51																
Bangor (Gwynedd)	d						06 18																
Llandudno Junction	d						06 36																
Wrexham General	d							07 00															
Chester	d						07 35																
Crewe 10	a				07 48		07 54		07 58						08 19			08 27					08 47
	d				07 49		07 57		08 01						08 22			08 29					08 49
Macclesfield	d											07 49	07 56										
Congleton	d																						
Stoke-on-Trent	d			07 44		07 50						08 07	08 12				←					08 44	
Stafford	a			08 01	08 10							08 24			08 42	08 35	08 42					09 02	09 09
	d			08 02	08 10							08 25			08 43	08 36	08 43					09 03	09 10
Penkridge	a				08 16										→		08 48						09 15
Wolverhampton 7	a			08 15	08 26				08 31			08 39					08 58					09 15	09 27
Birmingham New Street 12	a			08 32	08 47				08 55			08 58					09 18					09 32	09 47
Birmingham International ✈	a											09 13											
Coventry	a											09 24											
Lichfield Trent Valley	a																						
Tamworth Low Level	a																						
Nuneaton	a												08 44										
Rugby	a						08 45																
Milton Keynes Central	a					08s46																	
Watford Junction	a												09s31										
London Euston 15 ⊖	a	09 04				09 23	09 38						09 52			09 56		10 04	10 12				

A ⊠ from Chester

B 🛒 from Preston

OVERNIGHT SLEEPERS. For sleeper trains, operated by First ScotRail, please refer to Tables 400 - 404

Scotland and North West England - West Midlands and London

Route Diagram - see first Page of Table 65

		VT	VT	VT	NT	TP	XC	VT	EM	LM	VT	LM	VT	VT	SR	XC	LM	VT	XC	VT	VT	EM
		◇1	◇1	◇1		◇1	◇1	◇1	◇	◇1	◇1	◇1	◇1	◇1		◇1	◇1	◇1	◇1	◇1	◇1	◇
						A																
		⊠	⊠	⊠		⚲	⚲	⊠			⊠		⊠	⊠		⚲		⊠	⚲	⊠	⊠	
Inverness	d																					
Aberdeen	d																					
Dundee	d																					
Perth	d																					
Edinburgh 10	d																					
Haymarket	d																					
Glasgow Central 15	d			05 50										06 30	07 05							
Motherwell	d			06 04										06 44	07 27							
Carstairs	d														07a47							
Lockerbie	d													07 25								
Carlisle 8	a			07 02										07 43								
	d			07 04										07 46								
Penrith North Lakes	d			07 19										08 00								
Windermere	d																					
Oxenholme Lake District	a			07 42										08 22								
	d			07 42										08 23								
Barrow-in-Furness	d				07 00	07 29																
Lancaster 6	a			07 56	08 04	08 26								08 37								
	d			07 57	08 05	08 27								08 38								
Blackpool North	d																					
Preston 8	a			08 15	08 30	08 45								08 56								
Preston 8	d			08 17		08 47								08 58								
Wigan North Western	a			08 28										09 09								
	d			08 28										09 09								
Blackrod	d																					
Lostock	d																					
Bolton	a					09 08																
Manchester Piccadilly 10 ⇌	a					09 27																
Manchester Airport ✈	a					09 47																
Liverpool Lime Street 10	a																					
	d								07 42	08 34	08 48						09 04					08 52
Liverpool South Parkway ✈	d								07 53	08 44							09 15					09 03
Runcorn	d									08 52	09 04						09 25					
Warrington Bank Quay	a			08 39										09 20								
	d			08 39										09 20								
Hartford	d									09 06												
Manchester Piccadilly 10 ⇌	d	08 15					08 27	08 35	08 43				08 55			09 07		09 15	09 27		09 35	09 43
Stockport	d	08 23					08 35	08 43	08a53				09 04			09 16		09 23	09 35		09 43	09a53
Wilmslow	d												09 11									
Holyhead	d		06 55																			
Bangor (Gwynedd)	d		07 22																			
Llandudno Junction	d		07 40																			
Wrexham General	d																					
Chester	d		08 35																	09 35		
Crewe 10	a		08 54	08 58						09 20			09 27				09 44			09 54		
	d		08 56	09 01						09 22			09 29				09 49			09 56		
Macclesfield	d						08 49	08 56											09 49		09 56	
Congleton	d																					
Stoke-on-Trent	d	08 50					09 07	09 12				←				09 44		09 50	10 07		10 12	
Stafford	a						09 24			09 42	09 35	09 42				10 02	10 09		10 24			
	d						09 25			09 43	09 36	09 43				10 03	10 10		10 25			
Penkridge	a									→							10 15					
Wolverhampton 7 ⇌	a			09 31			09 39					09 56				10 15	10 27		10 39			
Birmingham New Street 12	a			09 55			09 58					10 17				10 39	10 47		10 58			
Birmingham International ✈	a						10 13												11 13			
Coventry	a						10 24												11 24			
Lichfield Trent Valley	a																					
Tamworth Low Level	a																					
Nuneaton	a																					
Rugby	a																					
Milton Keynes Central	a	09 46	10 01															10 46		11 01		
Watford Junction	a																					
London Euston 15 ⊖	a	10 23	10 38					10 42			10 56		11 04	11 12				11 23		11 38	11 42	

A ⚲ from Preston

OVERNIGHT SLEEPERS. For sleeper trains, operated by First ScotRail, please refer to Tables 400 - 404

Table 65

Mondays to Fridays

until 29 June

Scotland and North West England - West Midlands and London

Route Diagram - see first Page of Table 65

Station		NT	TP	VT	TP	LM	VT	LM	VT	VT		XC	LM	NT	SR	TP	TP	VT	VT	VT		XC	VT	EM	VT FO
			◇1	◇1	◇1	◇1	◇1	◇1	◇1	◇1		◇1	◇1			◇1	◇1	◇1	◇1	◇1		◇1	◇1	◇	◇
			🛒	⊠	🛒		⊠		⊠	⊠		🛒				🛒	🛒	⊠	⊠	⊠		🛒	⊠		⊒
Inverness	d																								
Aberdeen	d																								
Dundee	d																								
Perth	d																								
Edinburgh 10	d			06 52											08 33	07 42									
Haymarket	d			06 56											08 37	07u46									
Glasgow Central 15	d				07 10					07 37										08 00					
Motherwell	d									07 52															
Carstairs	d														09a13										
Lockerbie	d				08 06																				
Carlisle 8	a			08 05	08 29					08 46						08 59				09 08					
	d			08 07	08 29					08 49						08 59				09 10					
Penrith North Lakes	d			08 22	08 45																				
Windermere	d																								
Oxenholme Lake District	a				09 09					09 22															
	d				09 11					09 23															
Barrow-in-Furness	d																								
Lancaster 6	a			08 56	09 25					09 37										09 56					
	d			08 57	09 26					09 38										09 57					
Blackpool North	d		08 44											09 37			09 43								
Preston 8	a		09 08	09 15	09 45					09 56				10 02		10 05	10 07			10 15					
Preston 8	d	09 04	09 10	09 17	09 47					09 58				10 04		10 12	(joins)			10 17					10 36
Wigan North Western	a	09 24		09 28						10 09				10 24						10 28					10 47
	d	09 24		09 28						10 09				10 24						10 28					10 47
Blackrod	d																								
Lostock	d																								
Bolton	a		09 34		10 08											10 34									
Manchester Piccadilly 10	a		09 56		10 27											10 56									
Manchester Airport ✈	a		10 17		10 47											11 17									
Liverpool Lime Street 10	a	10 02												11 02											
	d	10 16				09 34	09 48						10 04	11 16										09 52	
Liverpool South Parkway ✈	d	10a27				09 44							10 15	11a27										10 03	
Runcorn	d					09 52	10 04						10 25												
Warrington Bank Quay	a			09 39						10 20										10 39					10 58
	d			09 39						10 20										10 39					10 58
Hartford	d					10 04																			
Manchester Piccadilly 10	d								09 55			10 07						10 15				10 27	10 35	10 43	
Stockport	d								10 04			10 16						10 23				10 35	10 43	10a53	
Wilmslow	d								10 11																
Holyhead	d																		08 55						
Bangor (Gwynedd)	d																		09 22						
Llandudno Junction	d																		09 40						
Wrexham General	d																								
Chester	d																		10 35						
Crewe 10	a			09 58		10 19			10 27				10 45						10 54	10 58					
	d			10 01		10 22			10 29				10 49						10 56	11 01					
Macclesfield	d																					10 49	10 56		
Congleton	d																								
Stoke-on-Trent	d							←				10 44						10 50				11 07	11 12		
Stafford	a					10 42	10 35	10 42				11 01	11 09									11 24			
	d					10 43	10 36	10 43				11 02	11 10									11 25			
Penkridge	a					↪							11 15												
Wolverhampton 7	a			10 33				10 56				11 15	11 27							11 31		11 39			
Birmingham New Street 12	a			11 06				11 18				11 32	11 47							11 55		11 58			
Birmingham International ✈	a			11 19																		12 13			
Coventry	a			11 30																		12 24			
Lichfield Trent Valley	a																								
Tamworth Low Level	a																								
Nuneaton	a																								
Rugby	a																								
Milton Keynes Central	a																	11 46	12 01						
Watford Junction	a			12s15																					
London Euston 15 ⊖	a			12 32			11 56		12 04	12 12								12 23	12 38				12 42		12 52

OVERNIGHT SLEEPERS. For sleeper trains, operated by First ScotRail, please refer to Tables 400 - 404

Table 65

Mondays to Fridays

until 29 June

Scotland and North West England - West Midlands and London

Route Diagram - see first Page of Table 65

		TP	NT	LM	VT	LM		VT	VT	XC	LM	NT	TP	VT	VT	VT		TP	XC	VT	EM	LM	VT	LM	VT
		◇[1]		◇[1]	◇[1]	◇[1]		◇[1]	◇[1]	◇[1]	◇[1]		◇[1]	◇[1]	◇[1]	◇[1]		◇[1]	◇[1]	◇[1]	◇	◇[1]	◇[1]	◇[1]	◇[1]
		A																A							
		🛒			⊠			⊠	⊠	🛒			🛒	☕	☕	⊠		🛒	🛒	☕			☕		☕
Inverness	d																								
Aberdeen	d																								
Dundee	d																								
Perth	d																								
Edinburgh [10]	d															08 52									
Haymarket	d															08 57									
Glasgow Central [15]	d								08 40																
Motherwell	d																								
Carstairs	d																								
Lockerbie	d																								
Carlisle [8]	a								09 47							10 05									
	d								09 49							10 07									
Penrith North Lakes	d								10 03																
Windermere	d																	10 49							
Oxenholme Lake District	a															10 41		11 08							
	d															10 42		11 09							
Barrow-in-Furness	d	09 23	10 16																						
Lancaster [6]	a	10 25	11 20						10 37							10 56		11 26							
	d	10 26							10 38							10 57		11 26							
Blackpool North	d											10 37	10 44												
Preston [8]	a	10 45							10 56			11 02	11 08			11 15		11 45							
Preston [8]	d	10 47							10 58			11 04	11 10			11 17		11 47							
Wigan North Western	a								11 09			11 24				11 28									
	d								11 09			11 24				11 28									
Blackrod	d																								
Lostock	d																								
Bolton	a	11 08											11 34					12 08							
Manchester Piccadilly [10] ⛴	a	11 27											11 56					12 27							
Manchester Airport ✈	a	11 50											12 17					12 47							
Liverpool Lime Street [10]	a											12 02													
	d			10 34	10 48						11 04	12 16									10 52	11 34	11 48		
Liverpool South Parkway ✈	d			10 44							11 15	12a27									11 03	11 44			
Runcorn	d			10 52	11 04						11 25											11 52	12 04		
Warrington Bank Quay	a								11 20							11 39									
	d								11 20							11 39									
Hartford	d			11 04																		12 04			
Manchester Piccadilly [10] ⛴	d							10 55		11 07				11 15					11 27	11 35	11 43				11 55
Stockport	d							11 04		11 16				11 23					11 35	11 43	11a53				12 04
Wilmslow	d							11 11																	12 11
Holyhead	d																								
Bangor (Gwynedd)	d																								
Llandudno Junction	d																								
Wrexham General	d																								
Chester	d														11 35										
Crewe [10]	a			11 19				11 27			11 45				11 54	11 58						12 19			12 27
	d			11 22				11 29			11 49				11 56	12 01						12 22			12 29
Macclesfield	d																		11 49	11 56					
Congleton	d																								
Stoke-on-Trent	d					←				11 44				11 50					12 07	12 12				←	
Stafford	a			11 43	11 33	11 43				12 02	12 09								12 24			12 42	12 35	12 42	
	d			11 43	11 34	11 43				12 03	12 10								12 25			12 43	12 36	12 43	
Penkridge	a			→							12 15											→			
Wolverhampton [7] ⛴	a					11 57				12 15	12 27					12 31			12 39					12 56	
Birmingham New Street [12]	a					12 17				12 39	12 47					12 55			12 58					13 17	
Birmingham International ✈	a																		13 13						
Coventry	a																		13 24						
Lichfield Trent Valley	a																								
Tamworth Low Level	a																								
Nuneaton	a																								
Rugby	a																								
Milton Keynes Central	a													12 46	13 01										
Watford Junction	a																								
London Euston [15] ⊖	a				12 56			13 03	13 12					13 23	13 38					13 42			13 56		14 04

A 🛒 from Preston

OVERNIGHT SLEEPERS. For sleeper trains, operated by First ScotRail, please refer to Tables 400 - 404

Scotland and North West England - West Midlands and London

Route Diagram - see first Page of Table 65

		VT		TP	XC	LM	NT	TP FO	TP FX	VT	VT	VT		TP FO	TP	XC	VT	EM	TP FO	LM	VT	LM		VT	VT
		◇1		◇1	◇1	◇1		◇1	◇1	◇1	◇1	◇1		◇1	◇1	◇1	◇1	◇	◇1	◇1	◇1	◇1		◇1	◇1
		⊠			⊥			⊥	⊥	🍴	🍴	🍴		⊥	⊥	⊥	🍴				🍴			🍴	⊠
Inverness	d																								
Aberdeen	d																								
Dundee	d																								
Perth	d																								
Edinburgh [10]	d													09 51											
Haymarket	d													09u56											
Glasgow Central [15]	d	09 40										10 00			10 10										10 40
Motherwell	d																								
Carstairs	d																								
Lockerbie	d													11 01											
Carlisle [8]	a	10 47										11 10		11 22	11 26										11 47
	d	10 49										11 11		11 29	11 29										11 49
Penrith North Lakes	d											11 26		11 45	11 45										
Windermere	d																								
Oxenholme Lake District	a	11 22												12 09	12 09										12 22
	d	11 23												12 10	12 10										12 23
Barrow-in-Furness	d			11 25															13 25						
Lancaster [6]	a	11 37		12 18										12 26	12 26				14 18						12 37
	d	11 38		12 18										12 26	12 26										12 38
Blackpool North	d						11 37	11 44	11 44																
Preston [8]	a	11 56		12 37			12 02	12 08	12 08			12 15		12 45	12 45										12 56
Preston [8]	d	11 58					12 04	12 10	12 10			12 17		12 47	12 47										12 58
Wigan North Western	a	12 09					12 24					12 28													13 09
	d	12 09					12 24					12 28													13 09
Blackrod	d																								
Lostock	d																								
Bolton	a							12 34	12 34					13 08	13 08										
Manchester Piccadilly [10] ⇌	a							12 56	12 56					13 27	13 27										
Manchester Airport ✈	a							13 16	13 17					13 47	13 47										
Liverpool Lime Street [10]	a						13 02																		
	d					12 04	13 16											11 52		12 34	12 48				
Liverpool South Parkway ✈	d					12 15	13a27											12 03		12 44					
Runcorn	d					12 25														12 52	13 04				
Warrington Bank Quay	a	12 20										12 39													13 20
	d	12 20										12 39													13 20
Hartford	d																			13 06					
Manchester Piccadilly [10] ⇌	d				12 07					12 15						12 27	12 35	12 43						12 55	
Stockport	d				12 16					12 23						12 35	12 43	12a53						13 04	
Wilmslow	d																							13 11	
Holyhead	d																								
Bangor (Gwynedd)	d																								
Llandudno Junction	d																								
Wrexham General	d																								
Chester	d										12 35														
Crewe [10]	a					12 45					12 54	12 58								13 20				13 27	
	d					12 49					12 56	13 01								13 22				13 29	
Macclesfield	d															12 49	12 56								
Congleton	d																								
Stoke-on-Trent	d				12 44					12 50						13 07	13 12					←			
Stafford	a				13 01	13 09										13 24				13 42	13 35	13 42			
	d				13 02	13 10										13 25				13 43	13 36	13 43			
Penkridge	a					13 15														→					
Wolverhampton [7] ⇌	a				13 15	13 27						13 31				13 39						13 56			
Birmingham New Street [12]	a				13 39	13 47						13 55				13 58						14 17			
Birmingham International ✈	a															14 13									
Coventry	a															14 24									
Lichfield Trent Valley	a																								
Tamworth Low Level	a																								
Nuneaton	a																								
Rugby	a																								
Milton Keynes Central	a									13 46	14 01														
Watford Junction	a																								
London Euston [15] ⊖	a	14 12								14 23	14 38						14 42				14 56			15 04	15 12

OVERNIGHT SLEEPERS. For sleeper trains, operated by First ScotRail, please refer to Tables 400 - 404

Scotland and North West England - West Midlands and London

Route Diagram - see first Page of Table 65

		XC	LM	NT	TP	VT	VT	VT	TP	XC	VT	EM	LM	VT	LM	VT	VT	VT	XC	LM	VT	XC	VT
		◇1	◇1		◇1	◇1	◇1	◇1	◇1	◇1	◇1	◇	◇1	◇1	◇1	◇1	◇1	◇1	◇1	1	◇1	◇1	◇1
									A														
		🛒			🛒	☕	☕	☒	🛒	🛒	☕			☕		☒	☕	☕	🛒		☕	🛒	☕
Inverness	d																						
Aberdeen	d																						
Dundee	d																						
Perth	d																						
Edinburgh 10	d							10 51															
Haymarket	d							10 57															
Glasgow Central 15	d															11 40							
Motherwell	d																						
Carstairs	d																						
Lockerbie	d																						
Carlisle 8	a							12 05								12 46							
	d							12 07								12 49							
Penrith North Lakes	d															13 03							
Windermere	d								12 51														
Oxenholme Lake District	a							12 41	13 07														
	d							12 43	13 09														
Barrow-in-Furness	d																						
Lancaster 6	a							12 56	13 26														
	d							12 57	13 26									13 39					
Blackpool North	d			12 37	12 44																		
Preston 8	a			13 02	13 08			13 15	13 45							13 50		13 56					
Preston 8	d			13 04	13 10			13 17	13 47							13 53		13 59					
Wigan North Western	a			13 24				13 28										14 09					
	d			13 24				13 28										14 10					
Blackrod	d																						
Lostock	d																						
Bolton	a				13 34				14 08														
Manchester Piccadilly 10	a				13 56				14 27														
Manchester Airport	a				14 17				14 47														
Liverpool Lime Street 10	a			14 02																			
	d		13 04	14 16								12 52	13 34	13 48						14 04			
Liverpool South Parkway	d		13 15	14a27								13 03	13 44							14 15			
Runcorn	d		13 25										13 52	14 04						14 25			
Warrington Bank Quay	a							13 39										14 20					
	d							13 39										14 21					
Hartford	d												14 04										
Manchester Piccadilly 10	d	13 07				13 15				13 27	13 35	13 43					13 55		14 07		14 15	14 27	
Stockport	d	13 16				13 23				13 35	13 43	13a53					14 04		14 16		14 23	14 35	
Wilmslow	d																14 11						
Holyhead	d																						
Bangor (Gwynedd)	d						12 24																
Llandudno Junction	d						12 42																
Wrexham General	d																						
Chester	d						13 35																14 35
Crewe 10	a		13 45				13 54	13 58					14 19				14 27			14 45			14 54
	d		13 49				13 56	14 01					14 22				14 29			14 49			14 56
Macclesfield	d									13 49	13 56											14 49	
Congleton	d																						
Stoke-on-Trent	d	13 44				13 50				14 07	14 12				←				14 44		14 50	15 07	
Stafford	a	14 01	14 09							14 24			14 46	14 35	14 46				15 02	15 09		15 24	
	d	14 02	14 10							14 25			14 46	14 36	14 46				15 03	15 10		15 25	
Penkridge	a		14 15										→							15 15			
Wolverhampton 7	a	14 15	14 27					14 31		14 39					14 59				15 15	15 27		15 39	
Birmingham New Street 12	a	14 32	14 47					14 55		14 58					15 20				15 39	15 47		15 58	
Birmingham International	a									15 13												16 13	
Coventry	a									15 24												16 24	
Lichfield Trent Valley	a																						
Tamworth Low Level	a																						
Nuneaton	a																						
Rugby	a																						
Milton Keynes Central	a					14 46	15 01														15 46		16 01
Watford Junction	a																						
London Euston 15	a					15 23	15 38				15 42			15 56		16 03	16 04	16 11			16 23		16 38

A 🛒 from Preston

OVERNIGHT SLEEPERS. For sleeper trains, operated by First ScotRail, please refer to Tables 400 - 404

Scotland and North West England - West Midlands and London

Route Diagram - see first Page of Table 65

		VT	EM	NT		TP	VT	TP FX	TP	NT	LM	VT	LM	VT		VT	XC	LM	NT	TP	VT	VT	VT	TP
		◇1	◇			◇1	◇1	◇1	◇1		◇1	◇1	◇1	◇1		◇1 ⊠	◇1	◇1		◇1	◇1	◇1	◇1	◇1
Inverness	d																							
Aberdeen	d																							
Dundee	d																							
Perth	d																							
Edinburgh 10	d								12 12														12 51	
Haymarket	d								12u16														12 57	
Glasgow Central 15	d						12 00									12 40								13 09
Motherwell	d																							
Carstairs	d																							
Lockerbie	d								13 11															14 06
Carlisle 8	a						13 08		13 33							13 47							14 05	14 29
	d						13 09		13 34							13 49							14 07	14 29
Penrith North Lakes	d																						14 22	14 45
Windermere	d																							
Oxenholme Lake District	a								14 09							14 22								
	d								14 10							14 24								
Barrow-in-Furness	d							13 25		14 16														
Lancaster 6	a						13 56	14 18	14 26	15 20						14 37							14 56	15 22
	d						13 58	14 18	14 26							14 38							14 57	15 22
Blackpool North	d			13 37		13 44													14 37	14 44				
Preston 8	a			14 02		14 08	14 15	14 37	14 45							14 56			15 02	15 08			15 15	15 41
Preston 8	d			14 04		14 10	14 17		14 47							14 58			15 04	15 10			15 17	15 47
Wigan North Western	a			14 24			14 28									15 09			15 24				15 28	
	d			14 24			14 28									15 09			15 24				15 28	
Blackrod	d																							
Lostock	d																							
Bolton	a					14 34			15 08											15 34				16 08
Manchester Piccadilly 10	a					14 56			15 27											15 56				16 27
Manchester Airport ✈	a					15 17			15 47											16 17				16 47
Liverpool Lime Street 10	a			15 02															16 02					
	d		13 52	15 16							14 34	14 48						15 04	16 16					
Liverpool South Parkway ✈	d		14 03	15a27							14 44							15 15	16a27					
Runcorn	d										14 52	15 04						15 25						
Warrington Bank Quay	a						14 39									15 20							15 39	
	d						14 39									15 20							15 39	
Hartford	d										15 04													
Manchester Piccadilly 10	d	14 35	14 43											14 55			15 07				15 15			
Stockport	d	14 43	14a53											15 04			15 16				15 23			
Wilmslow	d													15 11										
Holyhead	d																					13 58		
Bangor (Gwynedd)	d																					14 25		
Llandudno Junction	d																					14 43		
Wrexham General	d																							
Chester	d																					15 35		
Crewe 10	a						14 58				15 19			15 27				15 45				15 54	15 58	
	d						15 01				15 22			15 29				15 49				15 57	16 01	
Macclesfield	d	14 56																						
Congleton	d																							
Stoke-on-Trent	d	15 12											←				15 44				15 50			
Stafford	a										15 42	15 35	15 42				16 02	16 09						
	d										15 43	15 36	15 43				16 03	16 10						
Penkridge	a										↦							16 15						
Wolverhampton 7	a						15 33						15 56				16 15	16 26					16 31	
Birmingham New Street 12	a						16 06						16 17				16 39	16 47					16 55	
Birmingham International ✈	a						16 19																	
Coventry	a						16 30																	
Lichfield Trent Valley	a																							
Tamworth Low Level	a																							
Nuneaton	a																							
Rugby	a																							
Milton Keynes Central	a																				16 46	17 01		
Watford Junction	a						17s15																	
London Euston 15 ⊖	a	16 42					17 34					16 59		17 04		17 12					17 23	17 38		

OVERNIGHT SLEEPERS. For sleeper trains, operated by First ScotRail, please refer to Tables 400 - 404

Table 65

Mondays to Fridays

until 29 June

Scotland and North West England - West Midlands and London

Route Diagram - see first Page of Table 65

		XC	VT	EM	LM	VT	LM	VT	VT	VT		TP FO	XC	LM	NT	TP	VT	VT	VT	TP FX		TP	NT	XC	VT
		◇1	◇1	◇	◇1	◇1	◇1	◇1	◇1	◇1		◇1	◇1	◇1		◇1	◇1	◇1	◇1	◇1 A		◇1		◇1	◇1
		🛒	☕			☕		⊠	☕	☕			🛒			🛒	☕	☕	☕	🛒		🛒		🛒	☕
Inverness	d																								
Aberdeen	d																								
Dundee	d																								
Perth	d																								
Edinburgh 10	d																					14 07			
Haymarket	d																					14u11			
Glasgow Central 15	d							13 40											14 00						
Motherwell	d																								
Carstairs	d																								
Lockerbie	d																					15 06			
Carlisle 8	a							14 46											15 08			15 27			
	d							14 49											15 09			15 27			
Penrith North Lakes	d																					15 43			
Windermere	d																								
Oxenholme Lake District	a							15 22											15 44			16 06			
	d							15 24											15 44			16 07			
Barrow-in-Furness	d											15 24								15 24			16 20		
Lancaster 6	a											16 18								16 18		16 21	17 26		
	d									15 39		16 18								16 18		16 22			
Blackpool North	d														15 37	15 44									
Preston 8	a							15 50		15 56		16 37			16 02	16 08			16 15	16 37		16 42			
Preston 8	d							15 53		15 59					16 04	16 10			16 17	16 47		16 47			
Wigan North Western	a									16 09					16 24				16 28						
	d									16 10					16 24				16 28						
Blackrod	d																								
Lostock	d																								
Bolton	a															16 34				17 08		17 08			
Manchester Piccadilly 10	a															16 56				17 29		17 29			
Manchester Airport ✈	a															17 17				17 48		17 48			
Liverpool Lime Street 10	a														17 05										
	d			14 52	15 34	15 48								16 04											
Liverpool South Parkway ✈	d			15 03	15 44									16 15											
Runcorn	d				15 52	16 04								16 25											
Warrington Bank Quay	a									16 20									16 39						
	d									16 21									16 39						
Hartford	d				16 04																				
Manchester Piccadilly 10	d	15 27	15 35	15 43					15 55				16 07				16 15							16 27	16 35
Stockport	d	15 35	15 43	15a53					16 04				16 16				16 23							16 35	16 43
Wilmslow	d								16 11																
Holyhead	d																								
Bangor (Gwynedd)	d																								
Llandudno Junction	d																								
Wrexham General	d																								
Chester	d																	16 35							
Crewe 10	a				16 19				16 27					16 45				16 54	16 58						
	d				16 22				16 29					16 49				16 56	17 01						
Macclesfield	d	15 49	15 56																					16 49	16 56
Congleton	d																								
Stoke-on-Trent	d	16 07	16 12				←						16 44				16 50							17 07	17 12
Stafford	a	16 24			16 46	16 35	16 46						17 02	17 10										17 24	
	d	16 25			16 46	16 36	16 46						17 03	17 10										17 25	
Penkridge	a				→									17 15											
Wolverhampton 7	a	16 39					16 59						17 15	17 27					17 31					17 39	
Birmingham New Street 12	a	16 58					17 20						17 32	17 47					17 55					17 58	
Birmingham International ✈	a	17 13																						18 13	
Coventry	a	17 24																						18 24	
Lichfield Trent Valley	a																								
Tamworth Low Level	a																								
Nuneaton	a																								
Rugby	a																								
Milton Keynes Central	a																17 46	18 01							
Watford Junction	a																								
London Euston 15 ⊖	a		17 42			17 56		18 01	18 03	18 09							18 23	18 38							18 42

A 🛒 from Preston

OVERNIGHT SLEEPERS. For sleeper trains, operated by First ScotRail, please refer to Tables 400 - 404

Scotland and North West England - West Midlands and London

Route Diagram - see first Page of Table 65

		EM	TP	LM	VT	LM		VT	VT	SR	XC	LM	NT	TP	VT	VT		VT	TP	XC	VT	EM	LM	VT	LM
																		■							
		◇	◇1	◇1	◇1	◇1		◇1	◇1		◇1	◇1		◇1	◇1	◇1		1	◇1	◇1	◇1	◇	◇1	◇1	◇1
					☕			☕	⊠		🛒			🛒	⊠	⊠		☕	🛒	🛒	⊠			⊠	
Inverness	d																								
Aberdeen	d																								
Dundee	d																								
Perth	d																								
Edinburgh 10	d																	14 51							
Haymarket	d																	14 57							
Glasgow Central 15	d								14 40	15 14															
Motherwell	d									15 34															
Carstairs	d									15a51															
Lockerbie	d																								
Carlisle 8	a								15 47									16 05							
	d								15 49									16 07							
Penrith North Lakes	d																	16 21							
Windermere	d																								
Oxenholme Lake District	a								16 22																
	d								16 24																
Barrow-in-Furness	d		17 21																						
Lancaster 6	a		18 20						16 37									16 56							
	d								16 38									16 57							
Blackpool North	d												16 35	16 40					17 20						
Preston 8	a								16 56				17 02	17 08				17 15	17 45						
Preston 8	d								16 58				17 04	17 10				17 17	17 47						
Wigan North Western	a								17 09				17 24					17 28							
	d								17 09				17 24					17 28							
Blackrod	d																								
Lostock	d																								
Bolton	a													17 34					18 08						
Manchester Piccadilly 10	a													17 56					18 27						
Manchester Airport ✈	a													18 17					18 47						
Liverpool Lime Street 10	a												18 02												
	d	15 52		16 34	16 48							17 04										16 52	17 34	17 48	
Liverpool South Parkway ✈	d	16 03		16 44								17 15										17 03	17 44		
Runcorn	d			16 52	17 04							17 25											17 52	18 04	
Warrington Bank Quay	a								17 20									17 39							
	d								17 20									17 39							
Hartford	d			17 06																			18 06		
Manchester Piccadilly 10	d	16 43						16 55			17 05				17 15					17 27	17 35	17 43			
Stockport	d	16a53						17 04			17 13				17 23					17 35	17 43	17a53			
Wilmslow	d							17 11												17 44					
Holyhead	d																								
Bangor (Gwynedd)	d																								
Llandudno Junction	d																								
Wrexham General	d																								
Chester	d															17 35									
Crewe 10	a			17 19				17 27				17 47				17 54		17 59		18 04			18 20		
	d			17 22				17 29				17 49				17 56		18 01		18 07			18 22		
Macclesfield	d										17 27										17 56				
Congleton	d																								
Stoke-on-Trent	d					←					17 44				17 50						18 12				←
Stafford	a			17 42	17 35	17 42					18 03	18 09								18 27			18 42	18 35	18 42
	d			17 43	17 36	17 43					18 04	18 10								18 28			18 43	18 36	18 43
Penkridge	a			→								18 15											→		
Wolverhampton 7	a					17 56					18 15	18 27						18 31		18 39					18 56
Birmingham New Street 12	a					18 17					18 38	18 48						18 55		18 58					19 17
Birmingham International ✈	a																			19 13					
Coventry	a																			19 24					
Lichfield Trent Valley	a																								
Tamworth Low Level	a																								
Nuneaton	a																								
Rugby	a																								
Milton Keynes Central	a				18 23										18 47	19 02									
Watford Junction	a							18s48																19s42	
London Euston 15 ⊖	a				18 59			19 08	19 13						19 23	19 39					19 43			20 02	

OVERNIGHT SLEEPERS. For sleeper trains, operated by First ScotRail, please refer to Tables 400 - 404

Scotland and North West England - West Midlands and London

Route Diagram - see first Page of Table 65

		VT		VT	XC	LM	NT	TP	VT	TP	VT	XC		VT	EM	LM	VT	VT	XC	LM	NT	VT		TP	TP
		◇1		◇1	◇1	◇1		◇1	◇1	◇1	◇1	◇1		◇1	◇	◇1	◇1	◇1	◇1	◇1		◇1		◇1	◇1
								A				B													
		⊠		⊠	🛒			🛒	🍴	🛒	⊠	🛒		⊠			⊠	⊠	🛒			⊠		🛒	
Inverness	d																								
Aberdeen	d																								
Dundee	d																								
Perth	d																								
Edinburgh [10]	d									16 12															
Haymarket	d									16u16															
Glasgow Central [15]	d								16 00													16 40			
Motherwell	d																					16 54			
Carstairs	d																								
Lockerbie	d									17 11															
Carlisle [8]	a								17 08	17 33												17 49			
	d								17 09	17 34												17 51			
Penrith North Lakes	d									17 49												18 05			
Windermere	d							17 06																	18 15
Oxenholme Lake District	a							17 25	17 44													18 27			18 34
	d							17 30	17 44													18 29			18 36
Barrow-in-Furness	d																								
Lancaster [6]	a							17 47		18 26												18 43			18 52
	d			17 36				17 48		18 26												18 44			18 52
Blackpool North	d						17 37														18 37			18 44	
Preston [8]	a			17 54			18 02	18 06	18 15	18 45											19 02	19 02		19 08	19 11
Preston [8]	d			17 56			18 04	18 08	18 17	18 47											19 04	19 05		19 10	19 16
Wigan North Western	a			18 07			18 24		18 28												19 24	19 16			
	d			18 08			18 24		18 28												19 24	19 16			
Blackrod	d																								
Lostock	d							18 30																	
Bolton	a							18 34		19 08														19 33	19 42
Manchester Piccadilly [10]	a							18 56		19 27														19 56	20 01
Manchester Airport ✈	a							19 17		19 47														20 17	20 24
Liverpool Lime Street [10]	a						19 03														20 00				
	d					18 04									17 52	18 34	18 48			19 11					
Liverpool South Parkway ✈	d					18 15									18 03	18 44				19 21					
Runcorn	d					18 24										18 52	19 04			19 29					
Warrington Bank Quay	a			18 19					18 39													19 27			
	d			18 19					18 39													19 27			
Hartford	d															19 04									
Manchester Piccadilly [10]	d	17 55			18 05						18 15	18 27		18 35	18 43			18 55	19 07						
Stockport	d	18 04			18 13						18 23	18 35		18 43	18a53			19 04	19 16						
Wilmslow	d	18 11																19 11							
Holyhead	d																								
Bangor (Gwynedd)	d																								
Llandudno Junction	d																								
Wrexham General	d																								
Chester	d																								
Crewe [10]	a	18 27				18 47			18 59							19 16	19 21	19 27		19 53					
	d	18 29				18 49			19 01							19 18	19 23	19 29		19 55					
Macclesfield	d				18 26									18 56											
Congleton	d											18 54													
Stoke-on-Trent	d				18 44						18 50	19 07		19 12					19 44						
Stafford	a				19 01	19 09						19 24				19 41	19 41		20 03	20 15					
	d				19 02	19 10						19 25				19 42	19 42		20 04	20 16					
Penkridge	a					19 15										19 47									
Wolverhampton [7]	a				19 15	19 27			19 32			19 39				19 57			20 16	20 29					
Birmingham New Street [12]	a				19 32	19 48			19 55			19 58				20 18			20 33	20 47					
Birmingham International ✈	a											20 13													
Coventry	a											20 24													
Lichfield Trent Valley	a																								
Tamworth Low Level	a																								
Nuneaton	a																								
Rugby	a																								
Milton Keynes Central	a	19 31									19 46							20 32				20 45			
Watford Junction	a																20s46								
London Euston [15] ⊖	a	20 06		20 11							20 23			20 42			21 05	21 06				21 24			

A 🛒 from Preston

B 🛒 to Birmingham New Street

OVERNIGHT SLEEPERS. For sleeper trains, operated by First ScotRail, please refer to Tables 400 - 404

Table 65

Mondays to Fridays

until 29 June

Scotland and North West England - West Midlands and London

Route Diagram - see first Page of Table 65

		VT	VT	VT	TP	SR	XC	EM		TP	LM	VT	VT	VT	XC	LM	NT	VT		TP	TP ThX	TP ThO	SR	VT	VT
		◇■	◇■	■ ■	◇■		◇■ A	◇		◇■	◇■	◇■	◇■	◇■	◇■	◇■		◇■		◇■	◇■	◇■		◇■	◇■
		🍴	🍴	🍴	⊼		⊼					🍴	🍴	🍴				🍴			⊼	⊼		🍴	⊠
Inverness	d																								
Aberdeen	d																								
Dundee	d																								
Perth	d																								
Edinburgh 10	d			16 52		17 42															18 12	18 12	18 24		
Haymarket	d			16 57		17 46															18u16	18u16	18 28		
Glasgow Central 15	d				17 06													17 40							18 40
Motherwell	d																								
Carstairs	d					18a16																	19a09		
Lockerbie	d				18 06													18 35			19 11	19 11			
Carlisle 8	a			18 05	18 28													18 52			19 34	19 34			19 47
	d			18 07	18 29													18 54			19 34	19 34			19 49
Penrith North Lakes	d				18 45													19 09			19 49	19 49			
Windermere	d																								
Oxenholme Lake District	a			18 41	19 09													19 32			20 12	20 12			20 22
	d			18 42	19 10													19 32			20 13	20 13			20 24
Barrow-in-Furness	d																								
Lancaster 6	a			18 56	19 26													19 47			20 26	20 26			20 37
	d			18 57	19 26													19 47			20 26	20 26			20 38
Blackpool North	d																19 37			19 44					
Preston 8	a			19 15	19 45												20 02	20 05		20 08	20 45	20 45			20 56
Preston 8	d			19 16	19 47									19 58			20 04	20 08		20 10	20 47	20 47			20 58
Wigan North Western	a			19 28										20 09			20 24	20 19							21 09
	d			19 29										20 09			20 24	20 19							21 09
Blackrod	d																								
Lostock	d																								
Bolton	a				20 08															20 34	21 08	21 08			
Manchester Piccadilly 10	a				20 27															20 56	21 27	21 27			
Manchester Airport ✈	a				20 47															21 17	21 46	21 47			
Liverpool Lime Street 10	a																21 00								
	d							18 52		19 22	19 34	19 48				20 04									
Liverpool South Parkway ✈	d							19 03		19 32	19 44					20 15									
Runcorn	d										19 52	20 04				20 24									
Warrington Bank Quay	a			19 39										20 20				20 30							21 20
	d			19 39										20 20				20 31							21 20
Hartford	d										20 04														
Manchester Piccadilly 10	d	19 15					19 27	19 43		20a09			19 55		20 07									20 15	
Stockport	d	19 23					19 35	19a53					20 04		20 16									20 23	
Wilmslow	d												20 11												
Holyhead	d																								
Bangor (Gwynedd)	d																								
Llandudno Junction	d																								
Wrexham General	d																								
Chester	d		19 35																						
Crewe 10	a		19 54	19 59							20 16	20 21	20 27	20 39		20 45		20 50							
	d		19 56	20 01							20 18	20 23	20 29	20 41		20 47		20 53							
Macclesfield	d	19 36					19 49																	20 36	
Congleton	d																								
Stoke-on-Trent	d	19 52					20 07								20 44									20 53	
Stafford	a						20 25				20 38		20 47		21 02	21 08		21 11							
	d						20 26				20 42		20 48		21 03	21 10		21 13							
Penkridge	a										20 47					21 15									
Wolverhampton 7	a			20 33			20 40				20 57				21 15	21 26		21 29							
Birmingham New Street 12	a			20 55			21 00				21 18				21 33	21 47		21 48							
Birmingham International ✈	a						21 13																		
Coventry	a						21 24																		
Lichfield Trent Valley	a																								
Tamworth Low Level	a																								
Nuneaton	a											21 02													
Rugby	a													21 27											
Milton Keynes Central	a	20 48	21 03										21 35	21 47										21 50	22 39
Watford Junction	a											21s48												22s11	23s14
London Euston 15 ⊖	a	21 26	21 42									22 09	22 12	22 22										22 33	23 38

A ⊼ to Birmingham New Street

OVERNIGHT SLEEPERS. For sleeper trains, operated by First ScotRail, please refer to Tables 400 - 404

until 29 June

Scotland and North West England - West Midlands and London

Route Diagram - see first Page of Table 65

		SR	XC	EM		LM	TP	VT	VT	VT	VT	TP	XC	LM		TP	VT FO	VT FX	XC FO	XC FX	EM	NT FX	TP FO	NT
			◇1	◇		◇1	◇1	◇1	◇1	◇1	◇1	◇1	◇1	◇1		◇1	◇1	◇1	◇1	◇1	◇		◇1	
																			A	B				
								☕	☕	☕	☕						☕	☕					🛒	
Inverness	d																							
Aberdeen	d																							
Dundee	d																							
Perth	d																							
Edinburgh 10	d										18 52												20 12	
Haymarket	d										18 57												20u16	
Glasgow Central 15	d	19 49															20 10	20 10						
Motherwell	d	20 06																						
Carstairs	d	20a26																20 36						
Lockerbie	d																21 05	21 05					21 11	
Carlisle 8	a										20 06						21 25	21 25					21 34	
	d										20 08						21 26	21 26					21 34	
Penrith North Lakes	d																21 40	21 41						
Windermere	d																							
Oxenholme Lake District	a										20 42						22 04	22 04					22 09	
	d										20 42						22 04	22 05					22 10	
Barrow-in-Furness	d											20 08												21 43
Lancaster 6	a										20 57	21 10					22 19	22 19					22 26	22 45
	d										20 57	21 10					22 19	22 20					22 26	22 46
Blackpool North	d						20 44									21 44						22 14		
Preston 8	a						21 08				21 15	21 29				22 08	22 36	22 37				22 41	22 45	23 11
Preston 8	d						21 10				21 17	21 31				22 10	22 40	22 40				22 43	22 47	
Wigan North Western	a										21 28	21 47					22 51	22 51				23 05		
	d										21 28	21 48					22 52	22 52						
Blackrod	d																							
Lostock	d																							
Bolton	a						21 34									22 34							23 06	
Manchester Piccadilly 10	a						21 56					22 30				22 56							23 31	
Manchester Airport ✈	a						22 17					22 47				23 17								
Liverpool Lime Street 10	a																							
	d			19 52		20 34			20 48					21 34							21 37			
Liverpool South Parkway ✈	d			20 03		20 44								21 44							21 47			
Runcorn	d					20 52			21 04					21 52										
Warrington Bank Quay	a										21 39						23 02	23 02						
	d										21 39						23 03	23 03						
Hartford	d					21 04								22 04										
Manchester Piccadilly 10	d		20 27	20 43				21 15					21 27						22 07	22 07	22 28			
Stockport	d		20 35	20a53				21 23					21 35						22 16	22 16	22a37			
Wilmslow	d																							
Holyhead	d																							
Bangor (Gwynedd)	d									20 20														
Llandudno Junction	d									20 38														
Wrexham General	d																							
Chester	d									21 35														
Crewe 10	a					21 16			21 21	21 54	21 59			22 18			23 24	23 24						
	d					21 18			21 24	21 56	22 01			22 20										
Macclesfield	d		20 49					21 36					21 49						22 29	22 29				
Congleton	d																							
Stoke-on-Trent	d		21 07					21 53					22 08						22 47	22 47				
Stafford	a		21 24			21 38			21 42				22 25	22 40					23 06	23 09				
	d		21 25			21 41			21 44				22 26	22 41					23 07	23 10				
Penkridge	a					21 46								22 46										
Wolverhampton 7	a		21 39			21 57				22 27	22 32		22 39	22 57					23 19	23 22				
Birmingham New Street 12	a		22 00			22 17				22 50	22 55		22 58	23 18					23 39	23 39				
Birmingham International ✈	a																							
Coventry	a																							
Lichfield Trent Valley	a								21 57															
Tamworth Low Level	a								22 03															
Nuneaton	a								22 16															
Rugby	a								22 30															
Milton Keynes Central	a							22 52	22 58															
Watford Junction	a							23s25	23s30															
London Euston 15 ⊖	a							23 48	23 56															

A also from 25 June until 28 June

B until 21 June

OVERNIGHT SLEEPERS. For sleeper trains, operated by First ScotRail, please refer to Tables 400 - 404

Scotland and North West England - West Midlands and London

Route Diagram - see first Page of Table 65

		LM	TP	NT	TP	LM	SR	SR	SR	SR	SR	SR	SR	SR	SR	SR
									FX	FX	FO	FO	FX	FX	FO	FO
							🛏	🛏	🛏	🛏	🛏	🛏	🛏	🛏	🛏	🛏
		◇1	◇1		◇1	◇1										
							A	A	B	B			C	C	C	C
Inverness	d												20 47		20 47	
Aberdeen	d													21 42		21 42
Dundee	d													23u06		23u06
Perth	d												23u21		23u21	
Edinburgh 10	d						23 40		23 40		23 40					
Haymarket	d															
Glasgow Central 15	d							23 40		23 40		23 40				
Motherwell	d							23b56		23b56		23b56				
Carstairs	d						00u16		00u16		00u16					
Lockerbie	d															
Carlisle 8	a															
	d						01u41		01u41		01u41					
Penrith North Lakes	d															
Windermere	d				22 45											
Oxenholme Lake District	a				23 04											
	d				23 06											
Barrow-in-Furness	d															
Lancaster 6	a				23 23											
	d			23 07	23 24											
Blackpool North	d		22 44													
Preston 8	a		23 08	23 28	23 45								04s32		04s33	
Preston 8	d		23 10													
Wigan North Western	a															
	d															
Blackrod	d															
Lostock	d															
Bolton	a		23 34													
Manchester Piccadilly 10 ⇌	a		23 53													
Manchester Airport ✈	a		00 24													
Liverpool Lime Street 10	a															
	d	22 34				23 34										
Liverpool South Parkway ✈	d	22 45				23 45										
Runcorn	d	22 54				23 53										
Warrington Bank Quay	a															
	d															
Hartford	d	23 08				00 07										
Manchester Piccadilly 10 ⇌	d															
Stockport	d															
Wilmslow	d															
Holyhead	d															
Bangor (Gwynedd)	d															
Llandudno Junction	d															
Wrexham General	d															
Chester	d															
Crewe 10	a	23 21				00 22							05s38		05s38	
	d															
Macclesfield	d															
Congleton	d															
Stoke-on-Trent	d															
Stafford	a															
	d															
Penkridge	a															
Wolverhampton 7 ⇌	a															
Birmingham New Street 12	a															
Birmingham International ✈	a															
Coventry	a															
Lichfield Trent Valley	a															
Tamworth Low Level	a															
Nuneaton	a															
Rugby	a															
Milton Keynes Central	a															
Watford Junction	a						06s19		06s21		06s27					
London Euston 15 ⊖	a						06 43		06 45		06 50		07 47		07 48	

A from 25 June until 28 June

B until 21 June

C Conveys a protion from Fort William, dep 1950

OVERNIGHT SLEEPERS. For sleeper trains, operated by First ScotRail, please refer to Tables 400 - 404

2 July to 14 September

Scotland and North West England - West Midlands and London

Route Diagram - see first Page of Table 65

		TP MX	TP MO	SR MO	SR MO	LM MX	SR MX		TP	NT	AW	TP	TP	LM	VT	SR MX	SR MX	SR MO	SR MO	XC	VT	XC	VT	LM	VT
				[R]	[R]		[R]									[R]	[R]	[R]	[R]						
		◇1	◇1			◇1			◇1			◇1	◇1	1	◇1					◇1	◇1	◇1	◇1	◇1	◇1
														A		B	B	C	C						
				🛏	🛏		🛏									🛏	🛏	🛏	🛏						
				🛏	🛏		🛏								⊠	🛏	🛏	🛏	🛏	⊤	⊠	⊤	⊠		⊠
Inverness	d															20p47		20p25							
Aberdeen	d																21p42		21p42						
Dundee	d																23b06		23b06						
Perth	d															23b21		23b00							
Edinburgh 10	d			23p15			23p40																		
Haymarket	d																								
Glasgow Central 15	d				23p15			23p40																	
Motherwell	d				23b31			23b56																	
Carstairs	d			23b47			00u16																		
Lockerbie	d																								
Carlisle 8	a																								
	d			01u12			01u41																		
Penrith North Lakes	d																								
Windermere	d																								
Oxenholme Lake District	a																								
	d																								
Barrow-in-Furness	d											04 35													
Lancaster 6	a											05 28													
	d																								
Blackpool North	d	22p44	23p03						03 37																
Preston 8	a	23p08	23p28													04s32		04s41							
Preston 8	d	23p10	23p28						04u02				05 16										05 33		
Wigan North Western	a																						05 44		
	d																						05 45		
Blackrod	d		23p50																						
Lostock	d		23p57																						
Bolton	a	23p34	00 02						04c31				05 42												
Manchester Piccadilly 10	a	23p53	00 18						04 48				06 01												
Manchester Airport ✈	a	00 24	00 32						05 07				06 18												
Liverpool Lime Street 10	a																								
	d					23p34				03 38											05 27				
Liverpool South Parkway ✈	d					23p45																			
Runcorn	d					23p53															05 43				
Warrington Bank Quay	a																						05 55		
	d																						05 56		
Hartford	d					00 07																			
Manchester Piccadilly 10	d									04a20					05 05					05 11					05 55
Stockport	d														05 13										06 03
Wilmslow	d																								06 11
Holyhead	d																								
Bangor (Gwynedd)	d																								
Llandudno Junction	d																								
Wrexham General	d																								
Chester	d										04 22														
Crewe 10	a					00 22					04 44				05 34	05s38		05s41		05 44	06 00				06 27
	d										04 59			05 18	05 36					05 47	06 02			06 20	06 29
Macclesfield	d																								
Congleton	d																								
Stoke-on-Trent	d																			06 07		←			
Stafford	a										05 24				05 53					06 24	06 20	06 24		06 40	
	d										05 25				05 55					06 25	06 21	06 25		06 41	
Penkridge	a																			→				06 46	
Wolverhampton 7	a										05 39											06 39		06 57	
Birmingham New Street 12	a										05 59											06 58		07 18	
Birmingham International ✈	a																					07 13			
Coventry	a																					07 24			
Lichfield Trent Valley	a													06 06									06 40		
Tamworth Low Level	a													06 13									06 46		
Nuneaton	a													06 29	06 17										07 06
Rugby	a													06 47	06 30						06 52		07 06		
Milton Keynes Central	a														06 51						07 12				
Watford Junction	a			06s23			06s19																		
London Euston 15 ⊖	a			06 46			06 43								07 28	07 47		07 50			07 50		07 57		08 07

A from 2 July until 7 September
B Conveys a portion from Fort William, dep 1950
C Conveys a portion from Fort William, dep 1900
b Previous night, stops to pick up only
c Stops to pick up only

OVERNIGHT SLEEPERS. For sleeper trains, operated by First ScotRail, please refer to Tables 400 - 404

Table 65

Mondays to Fridays

2 July to 14 September

Scotland and North West England - West Midlands and London

Route Diagram - see first Page of Table 65

		VT	XC	VT	LM	VT	VT	TP	VT	TP	VT	VT	LM	VT	LM	VT	VT	TP	XC	LM	VT	VT	VT
		◇1	◇1	◇1	◇1	◇1	◇1	◇1	◇1	◇1	◇1	◇1	◇1	◇1	◇1	◇1	◇1	◇1	◇1	◇1	◇1	◇1	◇1
										A													B
		⊠	🛒	⊠		⊠	⊠	🛒	⊠	🛒	⊠	⊠		⊠		⊠	⊠	🛒	🛒		⊠	⊠	⊠
Inverness	d																						
Aberdeen	d																						
Dundee	d																						
Perth	d																						
Edinburgh 10	d																						
Haymarket	d																						
Glasgow Central 15	d																04 28						
Motherwell	d																						
Carstairs	d																						
Lockerbie	d																						
Carlisle 8	a																05 42						
	d																05 43						
Penrith North Lakes	d																05 57						
Windermere	d																						
Oxenholme Lake District	a																06 20						
	d																06 20						
Barrow-in-Furness	d									05 31													
Lancaster 6	a									06 23							06 35						
	d						05 35			06 23							06 35						
Blackpool North	d							05 39										06 40					
Preston 8	a						05 52	06 03		06 42							06 53	07 07					
Preston 8	d						06 00	06 05	06 16	06 44							06 56	07 09					
Wigan North Western	a						06 11		06 27								07 06						
	d						06 11		06 27								07 08						
Blackrod	d							06 22															
Lostock	d							06 30										07 30					
Bolton	a							06 34		07 08								07 34					
Manchester Piccadilly 10	a							06 56		07 27								07 56					
Manchester Airport ✈	a							07 17		07 47								08 17					
Liverpool Lime Street 10	a																						
	d	06 05											06 30			07 00				07 04			
Liverpool South Parkway ✈	d												06 40							07 14			
Runcorn	d	06 21											06 48			07u15				07 22			
Warrington Bank Quay	a						06 22		06 38								07 17						
	d						06 22		06 38								07 18						
Hartford	d												07 02							07 36			
Manchester Piccadilly 10	d		06 00	06 10							06 27	06 35		06 43					07 07		07 15		
Stockport	d		06 08	06 18							06 35	06 43		06 51					07 16		07 23		
Wilmslow	d													06 59									
Holyhead	d					04 48																05 51	
Bangor (Gwynedd)	d					05 14																06 18	
Llandudno Junction	d					05 32																06 36	
Wrexham General	d																						07 00
Chester	d					06 26																07 35	
Crewe 10	a		06 32			06 47	06 42		06 58				07 14	07 15						07 48		07 54	
	d		06 38		06 47	06 53			07 01				07 16	07 17						07 49		07 57	
Macclesfield	d			06 31							06 48	06 56											
Congleton	d																						
Stoke-on-Trent	d			06 48							07 06	07 12			←				07 44		07 50		
Stafford	a	06 52	06 57		07 10						07 27		07 40	07 34	07 40				08 01	08 10			
	d	06 53	06 58		07 12						07 28		07 41	07 35	07 41				08 02	08 10			
Penkridge	a				07 17								→		07 46					08 16			
Wolverhampton 7	a		07 12		07 28				07 31		07 43				07 57				08 15	08 26			
Birmingham New Street 12	a		07 31		07 48				07 55		08 06				08 17				08 32	08 47			
Birmingham International ✈	a										08 19												
Coventry	a										08 30												
Lichfield Trent Valley	a	07 07																					
Tamworth Low Level	a	07 14																					
Nuneaton	a					07 32																	
Rugby	a			07 28								07 52										08 45	
Milton Keynes Central	a																				08s46		
Watford Junction	a										09s15												
London Euston 15 ⊖	a	08 22		08 22		08 33					09 34	08 45		08 52		09 01	09 04				09 23	09 38	

A 🛒 from Preston

B ⊠ from Chester

OVERNIGHT SLEEPERS. For sleeper trains, operated by First ScotRail, please refer to Tables 400 - 404

Scotland and North West England - West Midlands and London

Route Diagram - see first Page of Table 65

		VT	TP	TP		XC	VT	EM	LM	VT	LM	VT	VT	TP	TP		XC	LM	VT	VT	VT	NT	TP	XC	VT
		◇1	◇1	◇1		◇1	◇1	◇	◇1	◇1	◇1	◇1	◇1	◇1	◇1		◇1	◇1	◇1	◇1	◇1		◇1	◇1	◇1
			A																				A		
		⊠	🛒	🛒		🛒	⊠			⊠		⊠	⊠	🛒	🛒		🛒		⊠	⊠	⊠		🛒	🛒	⊠
Inverness	d																								
Aberdeen	d																								
Dundee	d																								
Perth	d																								
Edinburgh [10]	d													05 36											
Haymarket	d													05u40											
Glasgow Central [15]	d												05 40								05 50				
Motherwell	d																				06 04				
Carstairs	d																								
Lockerbie	d																								
Carlisle [8]	a												06 46	06 58							07 02				
	d												06 49	06 59							07 04				
Penrith North Lakes	d																				07 19				
Windermere	d																								
Oxenholme Lake District	a												07 22								07 42				
	d												07 24								07 42				
Barrow-in-Furness	d		06 20																			07 00	07 29		
Lancaster [6]	a		07 21										07 37	07 47							07 56	08 04	08 26		
	d	06 58	07 22										07 38	07 47							07 57	08 05	08 27		
Blackpool North	d			07 10											07 36										
Preston [8]	a	07 15	07 41	07 37									07 56	08 07	08 03						08 15	08 30	08 45		
Preston [8]	d	07 17	07 47										07 58	08 12							08 17		08 47		
Wigan North Western	a	07 28											08 09								08 28				
	d	07 28											08 09								08 28				
Blackrod	d																								
Lostock	d																								
Bolton	a		08 08											08 34									09 08		
Manchester Piccadilly [10]	a		08 27											08 56									09 27		
Manchester Airport ✈	a		08 47											09 19									09 47		
Liverpool Lime Street [10]	a																								
	d							06 47	07 34	07 48								08 04							
Liverpool South Parkway ✈	d							06 57	07 44									08 15							
Runcorn	d								07 52	08 04								08 24							
Warrington Bank Quay	a	07 39											08 20								08 39				
	d	07 39											08 20								08 39				
Hartford	d								08 04																
Manchester Piccadilly [10]	d					07 26	07 35	07 42				07 55					08 07		08 15					08 27	08 35
Stockport	d					07 35	07 43	07a53				08 04					08 16		08 23					08 35	08 43
Wilmslow	d											08 11													
Holyhead	d																			06 55					
Bangor (Gwynedd)	d																			07 22					
Llandudno Junction	d																			07 40					
Wrexham General	d																								
Chester	d																			08 35					
Crewe [10]	a	07 58							08 19			08 27						08 47		08 54	08 58				
	d	08 01							08 22			08 29						08 49		08 56	09 01				
Macclesfield	d					07 49	07 56																	08 49	08 56
Congleton	d																								
Stoke-on-Trent	d					08 07	08 12				←						08 44		08 50					09 07	09 12
Stafford	a					08 24			08 42	08 35	08 42						09 02	09 09						09 24	
	d					08 25			08 43	08 36	08 43						09 03	09 10						09 25	
Penkridge	a								→		08 48							09 15							
Wolverhampton [7]	a	08 31				08 39					08 58						09 15	09 27			09 31			09 39	
Birmingham New Street [12]	a	08 55				08 58					09 18						09 32	09 47			09 55			09 58	
Birmingham International ✈	a					09 13																		10 13	
Coventry	a					09 24																		10 24	
Lichfield Trent Valley	a																								
Tamworth Low Level	a																								
Nuneaton	a						08 44																		
Rugby	a																								
Milton Keynes Central	a																		09 46	10 01					
Watford Junction	a						09s31																		
London Euston [15] ⊖	a						09 52			09 56		10 04	10 12						10 23	10 38					10 42

A 🛒 from Preston

OVERNIGHT SLEEPERS. For sleeper trains, operated by First ScotRail, please refer to Tables 400 - 404

2 July to 14 September

Scotland and North West England - West Midlands and London

Route Diagram - see first Page of Table 65

		EM	LM	VT	LM	VT	VT	SR	XC	LM		NT	TP	VT	VT	VT	TP	XC	VT	EM		LM	VT	LM
		◇	◇1	◇1	◇1	◇1	◇1		◇1	◇1			◇1	◇1	◇1	◇1	◇1	◇1	◇1	◇		◇1	◇1	◇1
				⊠		⊠	⊠		🛒				🛒	⊠	⊠	⊠	🛒	🛒	⊠				⊠	
Inverness	d																							
Aberdeen	d																							
Dundee	d																							
Perth	d																							
Edinburgh 10	d															06 52								
Haymarket	d															06 56								
Glasgow Central 15	d						06 30	07 05									07 10							
Motherwell	d						06 44	07 27																
Carstairs	d							07a47																
Lockerbie	d						07 25										08 06							
Carlisle 8	a						07 43									08 05	08 29							
	d						07 46									08 07	08 29							
Penrith North Lakes	d						08 00									08 22	08 45							
Windermere	d																							
Oxenholme Lake District	a						08 22										09 09							
	d						08 23										09 11							
Barrow-in-Furness	d																							
Lancaster 6	a						08 37									08 56	09 25							
	d						08 38									08 57	09 26							
Blackpool North	d												08 44											
Preston 8	a						08 56						09 08			09 15	09 45							
Preston 8	d						08 58					09 04	09 10			09 17	09 47							
Wigan North Western	a						09 09					09 24				09 28								
	d						09 09					09 24				09 28								
Blackrod	d																							
Lostock	d																							
Bolton	a												09 34				10 08							
Manchester Piccadilly 10	a												09 56				10 27							
Manchester Airport ✈	a												10 17				10 47							
Liverpool Lime Street 10	a											10 02												
	d	07 42	08 34	08 48						09 04		10 16								08 52		09 34	09 48	
Liverpool South Parkway ✈	d	07 53	08 44							09 15		10a27								09 03		09 44		
Runcorn	d		08 52	09 04						09 25												09 52	10 04	
Warrington Bank Quay	a						09 20									09 39								
	d						09 20									09 39								
Hartford	d		09 06																			10 04		
Manchester Piccadilly 10	d	08 43				08 55			09 07					09 15				09 27	09 35	09 43				
Stockport	d	08a53				09 04			09 16					09 23				09 35	09 43	09a53				
Wilmslow	d					09 11																		
Holyhead	d																							
Bangor (Gwynedd)	d																							
Llandudno Junction	d																							
Wrexham General	d																							
Chester	d														09 35									
Crewe 10	a		09 20			09 27				09 44					09 54	09 58						10 19		
	d		09 22			09 29				09 49					09 56	10 01						10 22		
Macclesfield	d																	09 49	09 56					
Congleton	d																							
Stoke-on-Trent	d				←				09 44					09 50				10 07	10 12					←
Stafford	a		09 42	09 35	09 42				10 02	10 09								10 24				10 42	10 35	10 42
	d		09 43	09 36	09 43				10 03	10 10								10 25				10 43	10 36	10 43
Penkridge	a		↦							10 15												↦		
Wolverhampton 7	a				09 56				10 15	10 27						10 31		10 39						10 56
Birmingham New Street 12	a				10 17				10 39	10 47						10 55		10 58						11 18
Birmingham International ✈	a																	11 13						
Coventry	a																	11 24						
Lichfield Trent Valley	a																							
Tamworth Low Level	a																							
Nuneaton	a																							
Rugby	a																							
Milton Keynes Central	a													10 46	11 01									
Watford Junction	a																							
London Euston 15 ⊖	a			10 56		11 04	11 12							11 23	11 38				11 42				11 56	

OVERNIGHT SLEEPERS. For sleeper trains, operated by First ScotRail, please refer to Tables 400 - 404

2 July to 14 September

Scotland and North West England - West Midlands and London

Route Diagram - see first Page of Table 65

		VT	VT	XC	LM	NT	SR		TP	TP	VT	VT	VT	XC	VT	EM	VT FO		TP	NT	LM	VT	LM	VT	VT
		◇1	◇1	◇1	◇1				◇1	◇1	◇1	◇1	◇1	◇1	◇1	◇	◇		◇1 A		◇1	◇1	◇1	◇1	◇1
		⊠	⊠	🍴					🍴	🍴	⊠	⊠	⊠	🍴	⊠		▭		🍴			⊠		⊠	⊠
Inverness	d																								
Aberdeen	d																								
Dundee	d																								
Perth	d																								
Edinburgh 10	d						08 33		07 42																
Haymarket	d						08 37		07u46																
Glasgow Central 15	d		07 37										08 00												08 40
Motherwell	d		07 52																						
Carstairs	d						09a13																		
Lockerbie	d																								
Carlisle 8	a		08 46						08 59				09 08												09 47
	d		08 49						08 59				09 10												09 49
Penrith North Lakes	d																								10 03
Windermere	d																								
Oxenholme Lake District	a		09 22																						
	d		09 23																						
Barrow-in-Furness	d																		09 23	10 16					
Lancaster 6	a		09 37										09 56						10 25	11 20					10 37
	d		09 38										09 57						10 26						10 38
Blackpool North	d					09 37				09 43															
Preston 8	a		09 56			10 02			10 05	10 07			10 15						10 45						10 56
Preston 8	d		09 58			10 04			10 12				10 17				10 36		10 47						10 58
Wigan North Western	a		10 09			10 24							10 28				10 47								11 09
	d		10 09			10 24							10 28				10 47								11 09
Blackrod	d																								
Lostock	d																								
Bolton	a								10 34										11 08						
Manchester Piccadilly 10 🚊	a								10 56										11 27						
Manchester Airport ✈	a								11 17										11 50						
Liverpool Lime Street 10	a					11 02																			
	d				10 04	11 16										09 52					10 34	10 48			
Liverpool South Parkway ✈	d				10 15	11a27										10 03					10 44				
Runcorn	d				10 25																10 52	11 04			
Warrington Bank Quay	a		10 20										10 39				10 58								11 20
	d		10 20										10 39				10 58								11 20
Hartford	d																				11 04				
Manchester Piccadilly 10 🚊	d	09 55		10 07							10 15			10 27	10 35	10 43								10 55	
Stockport	d	10 04		10 16							10 23			10 35	10 43	10a53								11 04	
Wilmslow	d	10 11																						11 11	
Holyhead	d											08 55													
Bangor (Gwynedd)	d											09 22													
Llandudno Junction	d											09 40													
Wrexham General	d																								
Chester	d											10 35													
Crewe 10	a	10 27			10 45							10 54	10 58								11 19			11 27	
	d	10 29			10 49							10 56	11 01								11 22			11 29	
Macclesfield	d													10 49	10 56										
Congleton	d																								
Stoke-on-Trent	d			10 44							10 50			11 07	11 12								←		
Stafford	a			11 01	11 09									11 24							11 43	11 33	11 43		
	d			11 02	11 10									11 25							11 43	11 34	11 43		
Penkridge	a				11 15																→				
Wolverhampton 7 🚊	a			11 15	11 27								11 31	11 39									11 57		
Birmingham New Street 12	a			11 32	11 47								11 55	11 58									12 17		
Birmingham International ✈	a													12 13											
Coventry	a													12 24											
Lichfield Trent Valley	a																								
Tamworth Low Level	a																								
Nuneaton	a																								
Rugby	a																								
Milton Keynes Central	a										11 46	12 01													
Watford Junction	a																								
London Euston 15 ⊖	a	12 04	12 12								12 23	12 38			12 42		12 52					12 56		13 03	13 12

A 🍴 from Preston

OVERNIGHT SLEEPERS. For sleeper trains, operated by First ScotRail, please refer to Tables 400 - 404

2 July to 14 September

Scotland and North West England - West Midlands and London

Route Diagram - see first Page of Table 65

		XC	LM		NT	TP	VT	VT	VT	TP	XC	VT	EM		LM	VT	LM	VT	VT	TP	VT	XC	LM		NT
		◇1	◇1			◇1	◇1	◇1	◇1	◇1	◇1	◇1	◇		◇1	◇1	◇1	◇1	◇1	◇1	◇1	◇1	◇1		
										A															
		⏚				⏚	☕	☕	☒	⏚	⏚	☕				☕		☒	☒		☕	⏚			
Inverness	d																								
Aberdeen	d																								
Dundee	d																								
Perth	d																								
Edinburgh 10	d								08 52																
Haymarket	d								08 57																
Glasgow Central 15	d																	09 23	09 40						
Motherwell	d																								
Carstairs	d																								
Lockerbie	d																								
Carlisle 8	a								10 05									10 43	10 47						
	d								10 07									10 45	10 49						
Penrith North Lakes	d																								
Windermere	d									10 49															
Oxenholme Lake District	a								10 41	11 08									11 22						
	d								10 42	11 09									11 23						
Barrow-in-Furness	d																			11 25					
Lancaster 6	a								10 56	11 26								11 30		12 18					
	d								10 57	11 26								11 38		12 18					
Blackpool North	d				10 37	10 44																			11 37
Preston 8	a				11 02	11 08			11 15	11 45								11 56	11 50	12 37					12 02
Preston 8	d				11 04	11 10			11 17	11 47								11 58	11 53						12 04
Wigan North Western	a				11 24				11 28									12 09							12 24
	d				11 24				11 28									12 09							12 24
Blackrod	d																								
Lostock	d																								
Bolton	a					11 34				12 08															
Manchester Piccadilly 10 ⇌	a					11 56				12 27															
Manchester Airport ✈	a					12 17				12 47															
Liverpool Lime Street 10	a				12 02																				13 02
	d		11 04		12 16								10 52		11 34	11 48							12 04		13 16
Liverpool South Parkway ✈	d		11 15		12a27								11 03		11 44								12 15		13a27
Runcorn	d		11 25												11 52	12 04							12 25		
Warrington Bank Quay	a								11 39									12 20							
	d								11 39									12 20							
Hartford	d														12 04										
Manchester Piccadilly 10 ⇌	d	11 07					11 15				11 27	11 35	11 43								11 55	12 07			
Stockport	d	11 16					11 23				11 35	11 43	11a53								12 04	12 16			
Wilmslow	d																				12 11				
Holyhead	d																								
Bangor (Gwynedd)	d																								
Llandudno Junction	d																								
Wrexham General	d																								
Chester	d							11 35																	
Crewe 10	a		11 45					11 54	11 58						12 19						12 27		12 45		
	d		11 49					11 56	12 01						12 22						12 29		12 49		
Macclesfield	d										11 49	11 56													
Congleton	d																								
Stoke-on-Trent	d	11 44					11 50				12 07	12 12					←					12 44			
Stafford	a	12 02	12 09								12 24				12 42	12 35	12 42					13 01	13 09		
	d	12 03	12 10								12 25				12 43	12 36	12 43					13 02	13 10		
Penkridge	a		12 15												→								13 15		
Wolverhampton 7 ⇌	a	12 15	12 27						12 31		12 39						12 56					13 15	13 27		
Birmingham New Street 12	a	12 39	12 47						12 55		12 58						13 17					13 39	13 47		
Birmingham International ✈	a										13 13														
Coventry	a										13 24														
Lichfield Trent Valley	a																								
Tamworth Low Level	a																								
Nuneaton	a																								
Rugby	a																								
Milton Keynes Central	a						12 46	13 01																	
Watford Junction	a																								
London Euston 15 ⊖	a						13 23	13 38				13 42				13 56		14 12	14 03		14 04				

A ⏚ from Preston

OVERNIGHT SLEEPERS. For sleeper trains, operated by First ScotRail, please refer to Tables 400 - 404

2 July to 14 September

Scotland and North West England - West Midlands and London

Route Diagram - see first Page of Table 65

		TP	TP	VT	VT	VT	TP	TP	XC		VT	EM	TP	LM	VT	LM	VT	VT	XC		LM	VT	VT	XC	VT
		FO	FX				FO						FO												
		◇1	◇1	◇1	◇1	◇1	◇1	◇1	◇1		◇1	◇	◇1	◇1	◇1	◇1	◇1	◇1	◇1		◇1	◇1	◇1	◇1	◇1
		☕	☕	🍽	🍽	🍽	☕	☕	☕		🍽				🍽		🍽	⊠	☕			🍽	🍽	☕	🍽
Inverness	d																								
Aberdeen	d																								
Dundee	d																								
Perth	d																								
Edinburgh 10	d						09 51																		
Haymarket	d						09u56																		
Glasgow Central 15	d					10 00		10 10										10 40							
Motherwell	d																								
Carstairs	d																								
Lockerbie	d						11 01																		
Carlisle 8	a					11 10	11 22	11 26										11 47							
	d					11 11	11 29	11 29										11 49							
Penrith North Lakes	d					11 26	11 45	11 45																	
Windermere	d																								
Oxenholme Lake District	a						12 09	12 09										12 22							
	d						12 10	12 10										12 23							
Barrow-in-Furness	d												13 25												
Lancaster 6	a						12 26	12 26					14 18					12 37							
	d						12 26	12 26										12 38							
Blackpool North	d	11 44	11 44																						
Preston 8	a	12 08	12 08			12 15	12 45	12 45										12 56							
Preston 8	d	12 10	12 10			12 17	12 47	12 47										12 58							
Wigan North Western	a					12 28												13 09							
	d					12 28												13 09							
Blackrod	d																								
Lostock	d																								
Bolton	a	12 34	12 34				13 08	13 08																	
Manchester Piccadilly 10	a	12 56	12 56				13 27	13 27																	
Manchester Airport ✈	a	13 16	13 17				13 47	13 47																	
Liverpool Lime Street 10	a																								
	d											11 52		12 34	12 48						13 04				
Liverpool South Parkway ✈	d											12 03		12 44							13 15				
Runcorn	d													12 52	13 04						13 25				
Warrington Bank Quay	a					12 39												13 20							
	d					12 39												13 20							
Hartford	d													13 06											
Manchester Piccadilly 10	d			12 15					12 27		12 35	12 43					12 55		13 07			13 15		13 27	13 35
Stockport	d			12 23					12 35		12 43	12a53					13 04		13 16			13 23		13 35	13 43
Wilmslow	d																13 11								
Holyhead	d																								
Bangor (Gwynedd)	d																						12 24		
Llandudno Junction	d																						12 42		
Wrexham General	d																								
Chester	d				12 35																		13 35		
Crewe 10	a				12 54	12 58								13 20			13 27				13 45		13 54		
	d				12 56	13 01								13 22			13 29				13 49		13 56		
Macclesfield	d								12 49		12 56													13 49	13 56
Congleton	d																								
Stoke-on-Trent	d			12 50					13 07		13 12					←			13 44			13 50		14 07	14 12
Stafford	a								13 24					13 42	13 35	13 42			14 01		14 09			14 24	
	d								13 25					13 43	13 36	13 43			14 02		14 10			14 25	
Penkridge	a													↪							14 15				
Wolverhampton 7	a					13 31			13 39							13 56			14 15		14 27			14 39	
Birmingham New Street 12	a					13 55			13 58							14 17			14 32		14 47			14 58	
Birmingham International ✈	a								14 13															15 13	
Coventry	a								14 24															15 24	
Lichfield Trent Valley	a																								
Tamworth Low Level	a																								
Nuneaton	a																								
Rugby	a																								
Milton Keynes Central	a			13 46	14 01																	14 46	15 01		
Watford Junction	a																								
London Euston 15 ⊖	a			14 23	14 38						14 42				14 56		15 04	15 12				15 23	15 38		15 42

OVERNIGHT SLEEPERS. For sleeper trains, operated by First ScotRail, please refer to Tables 400 - 404

Scotland and North West England - West Midlands and London

Route Diagram - see first Page of Table 65

		EM	NT	TP	VT		TP	LM	VT	LM	VT	VT	XC	LM	NT		TP	VT	VT	VT	TP FX	TP	NT	XC	VT
		◇		◇[1]	◇[1]		◇[1]	◇[1]	◇[1]	◇[1]	◇[1]	◇[1]	◇[1]	[1]			◇[1]	◇[1]	◇[1]	◇[1]	◇[1]	◇[1]		◇[1]	◇[1]
							A																		
				[trolley]	⊠		[trolley]		[buffet]		[buffet]	⊠	[trolley]				[trolley]	[buffet]	[buffet]	[buffet]		[trolley]		[trolley]	[buffet]
Inverness	d																								
Aberdeen	d																								
Dundee	d																								
Perth	d																								
Edinburgh [10]	d				10 51																	12 12			
Haymarket	d				10 57																	12u16			
Glasgow Central [15]	d											11 40								12 00					
Motherwell	d																								
Carstairs	d																								
Lockerbie	d																					13 11			
Carlisle [8]	a				12 05							12 46								13 08		13 33			
	d				12 07							12 49								13 09		13 34			
Penrith North Lakes	d											13 03													
Windermere	d						12 51																		
Oxenholme Lake District	a				12 41		13 07															14 09			
	d				12 43		13 09															14 10			
Barrow-in-Furness	d																				13 25		14 16		
Lancaster [6]	a				12 56		13 26					13 37								13 56	14 18	14 26	15 20		
	d				12 57		13 26					13 39								13 58	14 18	14 26			
Blackpool North	d		12 37	12 44											13 37		13 44								
Preston [8]	a		13 02	13 08	13 15		13 45					13 56			14 02		14 08			14 15	14 37	14 45			
Preston [8]	d		13 04	13 10	13 17		13 47					13 59			14 04		14 10			14 17		14 47			
Wigan North Western	a		13 24		13 28							14 09			14 24					14 28					
	d		13 24		13 28							14 10			14 24					14 28					
Blackrod	d																								
Lostock	d																								
Bolton	a			13 34			14 08										14 34					15 08			
Manchester Piccadilly [10] ⇌	a			13 56			14 27										14 56					15 27			
Manchester Airport ✈	a			14 17			14 47										15 17					15 47			
Liverpool Lime Street [10]	a		14 02												15 02										
	d	12 52	14 16					13 34	13 48					14 04	15 16										
Liverpool South Parkway ✈	d	13 03	14a27					13 44						14 15	15a27										
Runcorn	d							13 52	14 04					14 25											
Warrington Bank Quay	a				13 39							14 20								14 39					
	d				13 39							14 21								14 39					
Hartford	d							14 04																	
Manchester Piccadilly [10] ⇌	d	13 43									13 55		14 07					14 15						14 27	14 35
Stockport	d	13a53									14 04		14 16					14 23						14 35	14 43
Wilmslow	d										14 11														
Holyhead	d																								
Bangor (Gwynedd)	d																								
Llandudno Junction	d																								
Wrexham General	d																								
Chester	d																		14 35						
Crewe [10]	a				13 58			14 19			14 27			14 45					14 54	14 58					
	d				14 01			14 22			14 29			14 49					14 56	15 01					
Macclesfield	d																							14 49	14 56
Congleton	d																								
Stoke-on-Trent	d									←			14 44					14 50						15 07	15 12
Stafford	a							14 46	14 35	14 46			15 02	15 09										15 24	
	d							14 46	14 36	14 46			15 03	15 10										15 25	
Penkridge	a							→						15 15											
Wolverhampton [7] ⇌	a				14 33					14 59			15 15	15 27						15 31				15 39	
Birmingham New Street [12]	a				15 06					15 20			15 39	15 47						15 55				15 58	
Birmingham International ✈	a				15 19																			16 13	
Coventry	a				15 30																			16 24	
Lichfield Trent Valley	a																								
Tamworth Low Level	a																								
Nuneaton	a																								
Rugby	a																								
Milton Keynes Central	a																	15 46	16 01						
Watford Junction	a				16s15																				
London Euston [15] ⊖	a				16 32				15 56		16 04	16 11						16 23	16 38						16 42

A [trolley] from Preston

OVERNIGHT SLEEPERS. For sleeper trains, operated by First ScotRail, please refer to Tables 400 - 404

Table 65

Mondays to Fridays

2 July to 14 September

Scotland and North West England - West Midlands and London

Route Diagram - see first Page of Table 65

		EM	LM	VT	LM	VT	VT	XC	LM	NT	TP	VT	VT	VT	VT	TP	XC	VT	EM	LM	VT	LM
		◇	◇1	◇1	◇1	◇1	◇1	◇1	◇1		◇1	◇1	◇1	◇1	◇1	◇1	◇1	◇1	◇	◇1	◇1	◇1
				☕		☕	⊠	🛒			🛒	☕	☕	☕	☕	🛒	🛒	☕			☕	
Inverness	d																					
Aberdeen	d																					
Dundee	d																					
Perth	d																					
Edinburgh 10	d														12 51							
Haymarket	d														12 57							
Glasgow Central 15	d						12 40									13 09						
Motherwell	d																					
Carstairs	d																					
Lockerbie	d															14 06						
Carlisle 8	a						13 47								14 05	14 29						
	d						13 49								14 07	14 29						
Penrith North Lakes	d														14 22	14 45						
Windermere	d																					
Oxenholme Lake District	a						14 22															
	d						14 24															
Barrow-in-Furness	d																					
Lancaster 6	a						14 37								14 56	15 22						
	d						14 38								14 57	15 22						
Blackpool North	d									14 37	14 44											
Preston 8	a						14 56			15 02	15 08				15 15	15 41						
Preston 8	d						14 58			15 04	15 10				15 17	15 47						
Wigan North Western	a						15 09			15 24					15 28							
	d						15 09			15 24					15 28							
Blackrod	d																					
Lostock	d																					
Bolton	a										15 34					16 08						
Manchester Piccadilly 10	a										15 56					16 27						
Manchester Airport ✈	a										16 17					16 47						
Liverpool Lime Street 10	a									16 02												
	d	13 52	14 34	14 48					15 04	16 16									14 52	15 34	15 48	
Liverpool South Parkway ✈	d	14 03	14 44						15 15	16a27									15 03	15 44		
Runcorn	d		14 52	15 04					15 25											15 52	16 04	
Warrington Bank Quay	a						15 20								15 39							
	d						15 20								15 39							
Hartford	d		15 04																	16 04		
Manchester Piccadilly 10	d	14 43				14 55		15 07				15 15					15 27	15 35	15 43			
Stockport	d	14a53				15 04		15 16				15 23					15 35	15 43	15a53			
Wilmslow	d					15 11																
Holyhead	d													13 58								
Bangor (Gwynedd)	d													14 25								
Llandudno Junction	d													14 43								
Wrexham General	d																					
Chester	d												15 35	15 35								
Crewe 10	a		15 19			15 27			15 45				15 54	15 54	15 58					16 19		
	d		15 22			15 29			15 49				15 56	15 57	16 01					16 22		
Macclesfield	d																15 49	15 56				
Congleton	d																					
Stoke-on-Trent	d				←			15 44				15 50					16 07	16 12				←
Stafford	a		15 42	15 35	15 42			16 02	16 09								16 24			16 46	16 35	16 46
	d		15 43	15 36	15 43			16 03	16 10								16 25			16 46	16 36	16 46
Penkridge	a		↦						16 15											↦		
Wolverhampton 7	a				15 56			16 15	16 26						16 31		16 39					16 59
Birmingham New Street 12	a				16 17			16 39	16 47						16 55		16 58					17 20
Birmingham International ✈	a																17 13					
Coventry	a																17 24					
Lichfield Trent Valley	a																					
Tamworth Low Level	a																					
Nuneaton	a																					
Rugby	a																					
Milton Keynes Central	a											16 46	17s01	17 01								
Watford Junction	a																					
London Euston 15 ⊖	a			16 59		17 04	17 12					17 23	17 38	17 38				17 42			17 56	

OVERNIGHT SLEEPERS. For sleeper trains, operated by First ScotRail, please refer to Tables 400 - 404

Table 65

Mondays to Fridays

2 July to 14 September

Scotland and North West England - West Midlands and London

Route Diagram - see first Page of Table 65

		VT	VT	VT	VT	TP	XC		LM	NT	TP	VT	VT	VT	TP	TP	NT		XC	VT	EM	TP	LM	VT	LM
						FO									FX										
		◇1	◇1	◇1	◇1	◇1	◇1		◇1		◇1	◇1	◇1	◇1	◇1	◇1			◇1	◇1	◇	◇1	◇1	◇1	◇1
		A		B	A										C										
		⊠	☕	⊠	☕		🍴				🍴	☕	☕	☕	🍴	🍴			🍴	☕				☕	
Inverness	d																								
Aberdeen	d																								
Dundee	d																								
Perth	d																								
Edinburgh 10	d															14 07									
Haymarket	d															14u11									
Glasgow Central 15	d	13 40		13 40										14 00											
Motherwell	d																								
Carstairs	d																								
Lockerbie	d															15 06									
Carlisle 8	a	14 46		14 46										15 08		15 27									
	d	14 49		14 49										15 09		15 27									
Penrith North Lakes	d															15 43									
Windermere	d																								
Oxenholme Lake District	a	15 22		15 22										15 44		16 06									
	d	15 24		15 24										15 44		16 07									
Barrow-in-Furness	d					15 24									15 24		16 20					17 21			
Lancaster 6	a			15 37		16 18									16 18	16 21	17 26					18 20			
	d			15 39	15 39	16 18									16 18	16 22									
Blackpool North	d									15 37	15 44														
Preston 8	a	15 50		15 56	15 56	16 37				16 02	16 08			16 15	16 37	16 42									
Preston 8	d	15 53		15 59	15 59					16 04	16 10			16 17	16 47	16 47									
Wigan North Western	a			16 09	16 09					16 24				16 28											
	d			16 10	16 10					16 24				16 28											
Blackrod	d																								
Lostock	d																								
Bolton	a										16 34				17 08	17 08									
Manchester Piccadilly 10	a										16 56				17 29	17 29									
Manchester Airport ✈	a										17 17				17 48	17 48									
Liverpool Lime Street 10	a									17 05															
	d								16 04												15 52		16 34	16 48	
Liverpool South Parkway ✈	d								16 15												16 03		16 44		
Runcorn	d								16 25														16 52	17 04	
Warrington Bank Quay	a			16 20	16 20									16 39											
	d			16 21	16 21									16 39											
Hartford	d																						17 06		
Manchester Piccadilly 10	d		15 55				16 07					16 15							16 27	16 35	16 43				
Stockport	d		16 04				16 16					16 23							16 35	16 43	16a53				
Wilmslow	d		16 11																						
Holyhead	d																								
Bangor (Gwynedd)	d																								
Llandudno Junction	d																								
Wrexham General	d																								
Chester	d												16 35												
Crewe 10	a		16 27						16 45				16 54	16 58									17 19		
	d		16 29						16 49				16 56	17 01									17 22		
Macclesfield	d																		16 49	16 56					
Congleton	d																								
Stoke-on-Trent	d						16 44					16 50							17 07	17 12					←
Stafford	a						17 02		17 10										17 24				17 42	17 35	17 42
	d						17 03		17 10										17 25				17 43	17 36	17 43
Penkridge	a								17 15														→		
Wolverhampton 7	a						17 15		17 27					17 31					17 39						17 56
Birmingham New Street 12	a						17 32		17 47					17 55					17 58						18 17
Birmingham International ✈	a																		18 13						
Coventry	a																		18 24						
Lichfield Trent Valley	a																								
Tamworth Low Level	a																								
Nuneaton	a																								
Rugby	a																								
Milton Keynes Central	a											17 46	18 01											18 23	
Watford Junction	a																								
London Euston 15 ⊖	a	18 01	18 03	18 09	18 09							18 23	18 38							18 42				18 59	

A not from 27 July until 10 August, from 29 August until 7 September

B from 27 July until 7 September, not from 13 August until 28 August

C 🍴 from Preston

OVERNIGHT SLEEPERS. For sleeper trains, operated by First ScotRail, please refer to Tables 400 - 404

Table 65

Mondays to Fridays

2 July to 14 September

Scotland and North West England - West Midlands and London

Route Diagram - see first Page of Table 65

		VT	VT		SR	XC	LM	NT	TP	VT	VT	VT	TP		XC	VT	EM	LM	VT	LM	VT	VT	VT		VT
		◇1	◇1			◇1	◇1		◇1	◇1	◇1	R 1	◇1		◇1	◇1	◇	◇1	◇1	◇1	◇1	◇1	◇1		◇1
																						A	B		C
		⊐	⊠			⊤			⊤	⊠	⊠	⊐	⊤		⊤	⊠			⊠		⊠	⊠	⊠		⊠
Inverness	d																								
Aberdeen	d																								
Dundee	d																								
Perth	d																								
Edinburgh 10	d											14 51													
Haymarket	d											14 57													
Glasgow Central 15	d		14 40		15 14																		15 40		15 40
Motherwell	d				15 34																				
Carstairs	d				15a51																				
Lockerbie	d																								
Carlisle 8	a		15 47									16 05											16 46		16 46
	d		15 49									16 07											16 48		16 49
Penrith North Lakes	d											16 21											17 03		17 03
Windermere	d																								
Oxenholme Lake District	a		16 22																						
	d		16 24																						
Barrow-in-Furness	d																								
Lancaster 6	a		16 37									16 56											17 37		17 37
	d		16 38									16 57										17 36	17 37		17 37
Blackpool North	d							16 35	16 40				17 20												
Preston 8	a		16 56					17 02	17 08			17 15	17 45									17 54	17 55		17 55
Preston 8	d		16 58					17 04	17 10			17 17	17 47									17 56	17 58		17 58
Wigan North Western	a		17 09					17 24				17 28										18 07	18 08		18 08
	d		17 09					17 24				17 28										18 08	18 09		18 09
Blackrod	d																								
Lostock	d																								
Bolton	a								17 34				18 08												
Manchester Piccadilly 10	a								17 56				18 27												
Manchester Airport	a								18 17				18 47												
Liverpool Lime Street 10	a							18 02																	
	d						17 04										16 52	17 34	17 48						
Liverpool South Parkway	d						17 15										17 03	17 44							
Runcorn	d						17 25											17 52	18 04						
Warrington Bank Quay	a		17 20									17 39										18 19	18 19		18 19
	d		17 20									17 39										18 19	18 20		18 20
Hartford	d																	18 06							
Manchester Piccadilly 10	d	16 55				17 05				17 15					17 27	17 35	17 43				17 55				
Stockport	d	17 04				17 13				17 23					17 35	17 43	17a53				18 04				
Wilmslow	d	17 11													17 44						18 11				
Holyhead	d																								
Bangor (Gwynedd)	d																								
Llandudno Junction	d																								
Wrexham General	d																								
Chester	d										17 35														
Crewe 10	a	17 27					17 47				17 54	17 59			18 04			18 20			18 27				
	d	17 29					17 49				17 56	18 01			18 07			18 22			18 29				
Macclesfield	d					17 27										17 56									
Congleton	d																								
Stoke-on-Trent	d					17 44				17 50						18 12				←					
Stafford	a					18 03	18 09								18 27			18 42	18 35	18 42					
	d					18 04	18 10								18 28			18 43	18 36	18 43					
Penkridge	a						18 15											→							
Wolverhampton 7	a					18 15	18 27					18 33			18 39					18 56					
Birmingham New Street 12	a					18 38	18 48					19 06			18 58					19 17					
Birmingham International	a											19 19			19 13										
Coventry	a											19 30			19 24										
Lichfield Trent Valley	a																								
Tamworth Low Level	a																								
Nuneaton	a																								
Rugby	a																								
Milton Keynes Central	a									18 47	19 01										19 31				
Watford Junction	a	18s48										20s15							19s42						
London Euston 15	a	19 08	19 13							19 23	19 38	20 34				19 42			20 02		20 06	20 11	20 11		20 11

A not from 27 July until 10 August, from 29 August until 7 September

B from 27 July until 10 August

C from 29 August until 7 September

OVERNIGHT SLEEPERS. For sleeper trains, operated by First ScotRail, please refer to Tables 400 - 404

Scotland and North West England - West Midlands and London

Route Diagram - see first Page of Table 65

		XC	LM	NT	TP	VT	TP	VT	XC		VT	EM	LM	VT	VT	XC	LM	NT	VT		TP	TP	VT	VT	VT
		◇1	◇1		◇1	◇1	◇1	◇1	◇1		◇1	◇	◇1	◇1	◇1	◇1	◇1		◇1		◇1	◇1	◇1	◇1	■ 1
					A				B																
		🛒			🛒	ℙ	🛒	☒	🛒		☒			☒	☒	🛒			☒		🛒		ℙ	ℙ	ℙ
Inverness	d																								
Aberdeen	d																								
Dundee	d																								
Perth	d																								
Edinburgh 10	d						16 12																		16 52
Haymarket	d						16u16																		16 57
Glasgow Central 15	d					16 00													16 40						
Motherwell	d																		16 54						
Carstairs	d																								
Lockerbie	d						17 11																		
Carlisle 8	a					17 08	17 33												17 49						18 05
	d					17 09	17 34												17 51						18 07
Penrith North Lakes	d						17 49												18 05						
Windermere	d				17 06																	18 15			
Oxenholme Lake District	a				17 25	17 44													18 27			18 34			18 41
	d				17 30	17 44													18 29			18 36			18 42
Barrow-in-Furness	d																								
Lancaster 6	a				17 47		18 26												18 43			18 52			18 56
	d				17 48		18 26												18 44			18 52			18 57
Blackpool North	d			17 37														18 37			18 44				
Preston 8	a			18 02	18 06	18 15	18 45											19 02	19 02		19 08	19 11			19 15
Preston 8	d			18 04	18 08	18 17	18 47											19 04	19 05		19 10	19 16			19 16
Wigan North Western	a			18 24		18 28												19 24	19 16						19 28
	d			18 24		18 28												19 24	19 16						19 29
Blackrod	d																								
Lostock	d				18 30																				
Bolton	a				18 34		19 08														19 33	19 42			
Manchester Piccadilly 10	a				18 56		19 27														19 56	20 01			
Manchester Airport ✈	a				19 17		19 47														20 17	20 24			
Liverpool Lime Street 10	a			19 03														20 00							
	d		18 04									17 52	18 34	18 48			19 11								
Liverpool South Parkway ✈	d		18 15									18 03	18 44				19 21								
Runcorn	d		18 24										18 52	19 04			19 29								
Warrington Bank Quay	a					18 39													19 27						19 39
	d					18 39													19 27						19 39
Hartford	d												19 04												
Manchester Piccadilly 10	d	18 05						18 15	18 27		18 35	18 43			18 55	19 07							19 15		
Stockport	d	18 13						18 23	18 35		18 43	18a53			19 04	19 16							19 23		
Wilmslow	d														19 11										
Holyhead	d																								
Bangor (Gwynedd)	d																								
Llandudno Junction	d																								
Wrexham General	d																								
Chester	d																							19 35	
Crewe 10	a		18 47			18 59							19 16	19 21	19 27		19 53							19 54	19 59
	d		18 49			19 01							19 18	19 23	19 29		19 55							19 56	20 01
Macclesfield	d	18 26									18 56												19 36		
Congleton	d								18 54																
Stoke-on-Trent	d	18 44						18 50	19 07		19 12					19 44							19 52		
Stafford	a	19 01	19 09						19 24				19 41	19 41		20 03	20 15								
	d	19 02	19 10						19 25				19 42	19 42		20 04	20 16								
Penkridge	a		19 15										19 47												
Wolverhampton 7	a	19 15	19 27			19 31			19 39				19 57			20 16	20 29								20 33
Birmingham New Street 12	a	19 32	19 48			19 55			19 58				20 18			20 33	20 47								20 55
Birmingham International ✈	a								20 13																
Coventry	a								20 24																
Lichfield Trent Valley	a																								
Tamworth Low Level	a																								
Nuneaton	a																								
Rugby	a																								
Milton Keynes Central	a							19 46							20 32				20 45				20 48	21 03	
Watford Junction	a													20s46											
London Euston 15 ⊖	a							20 23			20 42			21 05	21 06				21 24				21 26	21 42	

A 🛒 from Preston

B 🛒 to Birmingham New Street

OVERNIGHT SLEEPERS. For sleeper trains, operated by First ScotRail, please refer to Tables 400 - 404

Table 65

Mondays to Fridays

2 July to 14 September

Scotland and North West England - West Midlands and London

Route Diagram - see first Page of Table 65

		TP	SR	XC	EM		TP	LM	VT	VT	VT	VT	XC	LM	NT		VT	TP	TP ThX	TP ThO	SR	VT	VT	SR	XC
		◇■		◇■	◇		◇■	◇■	◇■	◇■	◇■	◇■	◇■	◇■			◇■	◇■	◇■	◇■		◇■	◇■		◇■
				A							B	C													
		🛒		🛒					🍴	🍴	🍴	🍴					🍴		🛒	🛒		🍴	⊠		
Inverness	d																								
Aberdeen	d																								
Dundee	d																								
Perth	d																								
Edinburgh 10	d		17 42																18 12	18 12	18 24				
Haymarket	d		17 46																18u16	18u16	18 28				
Glasgow Central 15	d	17 06									17 30						17 40						18 40	19 49	
Motherwell	d																							20 06	
Carstairs	d		18a16																		19a09			20a26	
Lockerbie	d	18 06															18 35		19 11	19 11					
Carlisle 8	a	18 28									18 43						18 52		19 34	19 34			19 47		
	d	18 29									18 45						18 54		19 34	19 34			19 49		
Penrith North Lakes	d	18 45									18 59						19 09		19 49	19 49					
Windermere	d																								
Oxenholme Lake District	a	19 09									19 21						19 32		20 12	20 12			20 22		
	d	19 10									19 23						19 32		20 13	20 13			20 24		
Barrow-in-Furness	d																								
Lancaster 6	a	19 26									19 36						19 47		20 26	20 26			20 37		
	d	19 26									19 37						19 47		20 26	20 26			20 38		
Blackpool North	d														19 37			19 44							
Preston 8	a	19 45									19 55				20 02		20 05	20 08	20 45	20 45			20 56		
Preston 8	d	19 47									19 58	19 58			20 04		20 08	20 10	20 47	20 47			20 58		
Wigan North Western	a										20 09	20 09			20 24		20 19						21 09		
	d										20 09	20 09			20 24		20 19						21 09		
Blackrod	d																								
Lostock	d																								
Bolton	a	20 08																20 34	21 08	21 08					
Manchester Piccadilly 10	a	20 27																20 56	21 27	21 27					
Manchester Airport ✈	a	20 47																21 17	21 46	21 47					
Liverpool Lime Street 10	a														21 00										
	d				18 52		19 22	19 34	19 48					20 04											
Liverpool South Parkway ✈	d				19 03		19 32	19 44						20 15											
Runcorn	d							19 52	20 04					20 24											
Warrington Bank Quay	a										20 20	20 20					20 30						21 20		
	d										20 20	20 20					20 31						21 20		
Hartford	d							20 04																	
Manchester Piccadilly 10	d			19 27	19 43		20a09			19 55			20 07									20 15			20 27
Stockport	d			19 35	19a53					20 04			20 16									20 23			20 35
Wilmslow	d									20 11															
Holyhead	d																								
Bangor (Gwynedd)	d																								
Llandudno Junction	d																								
Wrexham General	d																								
Chester	d																								
Crewe 10	a							20 16	20 21	20 27	20 39	20 39		20 45			20 50								
	d							20 18	20 23	20 29	20 41	20 41		20 47			20 53								
Macclesfield	d			19 49																		20 36			20 49
Congleton	d																								
Stoke-on-Trent	d			20 07									20 44									20 53			21 07
Stafford	a			20 25				20 38		20 47			21 02	21 08			21 11								21 24
	d			20 26				20 42		20 48			21 03	21 10			21 13								21 25
Penkridge	a							20 47						21 15											
Wolverhampton 7	a			20 40				20 57					21 15	21 26			21 29								21 39
Birmingham New Street 12	a			21 00				21 18					21 33	21 47			21 48								22 00
Birmingham International ✈	a			21 13																					
Coventry	a			21 24																					
Lichfield Trent Valley	a																								
Tamworth Low Level	a																								
Nuneaton	a								21 02																
Rugby	a										21 27	21 27													
Milton Keynes Central	a									21 35	21 47	21 47										21 50	22 39		
Watford Junction	a								21s48													22s11	23s14		
London Euston 15 ⊖	a								22 09	22 12	22 22	22 22										22 33	23 38		

A 🛒 to Birmingham New Street

B from 27 July until 7 September, not from 13 August until 28 August

C not from 27 July until 10 August, from 29 August until 7 September

OVERNIGHT SLEEPERS. For sleeper trains, operated by First ScotRail, please refer to Tables 400 - 404

Table 65

Mondays to Fridays

2 July to 14 September

Scotland and North West England - West Midlands and London

Route Diagram - see first Page of Table 65

		EM	LM	TP	VT	VT	VT	VT	TP	XC		LM	TP	VT	VT	XC	EM	NT	TP	NT		LM	TP	NT
														FO	FX			FX	FO					
		◇	◇1	◇1	◇1	◇1	◇1	◇1	◇1	◇1		◇1	◇1	◇1	◇1	◇1	◇		◇1			◇1	◇1	
					🍴	🍴	🍴	🍴						🍴	🍴				🍴					
Inverness	d																							
Aberdeen	d																							
Dundee	d																							
Perth	d																							
Edinburgh 10	d							18 52											20 12					
Haymarket	d							18 57											20u16					
Glasgow Central 15	d													20 10	20 10									
Motherwell	d																							
Carstairs	d														20 36									
Lockerbie	d													21 05	21 05				21 11					
Carlisle 8	a							20 06						21 25	21 25				21 34					
	d							20 08						21 26	21 26				21 34					
Penrith North Lakes	d													21 40	21 41									
Windermere	d																							
Oxenholme Lake District	a							20 42						22 04	22 04				22 09					
	d							20 42						22 04	22 05				22 10					
Barrow-in-Furness	d								20 08											21 43				
Lancaster 6	a							20 57	21 10					22 19	22 19				22 26	22 45				
	d							20 57	21 10					22 19	22 20				22 26	22 46				23 07
Blackpool North	d			20 44									21 44					22 14					22 44	
Preston 8	a			21 08				21 15	21 29				22 08	22 36	22 37			22 41	22 45	23 11			23 08	23 28
Preston 8	d			21 10				21 17	21 31				22 10	22 40	22 40			22 43	22 47				23 10	
Wigan North Western	a							21 28	21 47					22 51	22 51			23 05						
	d							21 28	21 48					22 52	22 52									
Blackrod	d																							
Lostock	d																							
Bolton	a			21 34									22 34						23 06				23 34	
Manchester Piccadilly 10	a			21 56					22 30				22 56						23 31				23 53	
Manchester Airport ✈	a			22 17					22 47				23 17										00 24	
Liverpool Lime Street 10	a																							
	d	19 52	20 34			20 48						21 34					21 37					22 34		
Liverpool South Parkway ✈	d	20 03	20 44									21 44					21 47					22 45		
Runcorn	d		20 52			21 04						21 52										22 54		
Warrington Bank Quay	a							21 39						23 02	23 02									
	d							21 39						23 03	23 03									
Hartford	d		21 04									22 04										23 08		
Manchester Piccadilly 10	d	20 43			21 15					21 27						22 07	22 28							
Stockport	d	20a53			21 23					21 35						22 16	22a37							
Wilmslow	d																							
Holyhead	d																							
Bangor (Gwynedd)	d						20 20																	
Llandudno Junction	d						20 38																	
Wrexham General	d																							
Chester	d						21 35																	
Crewe 10	a		21 16			21 21	21 54	21 59				22 18		23 24	23 24							23 21		
	d		21 18			21 24	21 56	22 01				22 20												
Macclesfield	d				21 36					21 49						22 29								
Congleton	d																							
Stoke-on-Trent	d				21 53					22 08						22 47								
Stafford	a		21 38			21 42				22 25		22 40				23 06								
	d		21 41			21 44				22 26		22 41				23 07								
Penkridge	a		21 46									22 46												
Wolverhampton 7	a		21 57				22 27	22 32		22 39		22 57				23 19								
Birmingham New Street 12	a		22 17				22 50	22 55		22 58		23 18				23 39								
Birmingham International ✈	a																							
Coventry	a																							
Lichfield Trent Valley	a					21 57																		
Tamworth Low Level	a					22 03																		
Nuneaton	a					22 16																		
Rugby	a					22 30																		
Milton Keynes Central	a				22 52	22 58																		
Watford Junction	a				23s25	23s30																		
London Euston 15 ⊖	a				23 48	23 56																		

OVERNIGHT SLEEPERS. For sleeper trains, operated by First ScotRail, please refer to Tables 400 - 404

Table 65

Mondays to Fridays

2 July to 14 September

Scotland and North West England - West Midlands and London

Route Diagram - see first Page of Table 65

		TP	LM	SR	SR	SR	SR	SR	SR	SR	SR
				FX	FX	FO	FO	FX	FX	FO	FO
		◇1	◇1	B	B	B	B	B	B	B	B
				A	A	A	A				
Inverness	d							20 47		20 47	
Aberdeen	d								21 42		21 42
Dundee	d								23u06		23u06
Perth	d							23u21		23u21	
Edinburgh 10	d			23 40		23 40					
Haymarket	d										
Glasgow Central 15	d				23 40		23 40				
Motherwell	d				23u56		23u56				
Carstairs	d			00u16		00u16					
Lockerbie	d										
Carlisle 8	a										
	d			01u41		01u41					
Penrith North Lakes	d										
Windermere	d	22 45									
Oxenholme Lake District	a	23 04									
	d	23 06									
Barrow-in-Furness	d										
Lancaster 6	a	23 23									
	d	23 24									
Blackpool North	d										
Preston 8	a	23 45						04s33		04s33	
Preston 8	d										
Wigan North Western	a										
	d										
Blackrod	d										
Lostock	d										
Bolton	a										
Manchester Piccadilly 10	a										
Manchester Airport	a										
Liverpool Lime Street 10	a										
	d		23 34								
Liverpool South Parkway	d		23 45								
Runcorn	d		23 53								
Warrington Bank Quay	a										
	d										
Hartford	d		00 07								
Manchester Piccadilly 10	d										
Stockport	d										
Wilmslow	d										
Holyhead	d										
Bangor (Gwynedd)	d										
Llandudno Junction	d										
Wrexham General	d										
Chester	d										
Crewe 10	a		00 22					05s38		05s38	
	d										
Macclesfield	d										
Congleton	d										
Stoke-on-Trent	d										
Stafford	a										
	d										
Penkridge	a										
Wolverhampton 7	a										
Birmingham New Street 12	a										
Birmingham International	a										
Coventry	a										
Lichfield Trent Valley	a										
Tamworth Low Level	a										
Nuneaton	a										
Rugby	a										
Milton Keynes Central	a										
Watford Junction	a			06s19		06s27					
London Euston 15	a			06 43		06 50		07 47		07 48	

A Conveys a protion from Fort William, dep 1950

OVERNIGHT SLEEPERS. For sleeper trains, operated by First ScotRail, please refer to Tables 400 - 404

Table 65 | **Mondays to Fridays**

from 17 September

Scotland and North West England - West Midlands and London

Route Diagram - see first Page of Table 65

		TP	TP	SR	SR	LM	SR	SR	TP	AW	TP	VT	SR	SR	SR	SR	TP	XC	VT	XC		VT	LM	VT	VT
		MX	MO	MO	MO	MX	MX	MX					MX	MX	MO	MO									
				R	R		R	R					R	R	R	R									
		◇1	◇1			◇1			◇1		◇1	◇1					◇1	◇1	◇1	◇1		◇1	◇1	◇1	◇1
				🛏	🛏		🛏	🛏				⊠	🛏	🛏	🛏	🛏			⊠			⊠		⊠	⊠
													A	A	B	B									
Inverness	d												20p47		20p25										
Aberdeen	d													21p42		21p42									
Dundee	d													23b06		23b06									
Perth	d												23b21		23b00										
Edinburgh 10	d			23p15			23p40																		
Haymarket	d																								
Glasgow Central 15	d				23p15			23p40																	
Motherwell	d				23b31			23u56																	
Carstairs	d			23b47			00u16																		
Lockerbie	d																								
Carlisle 8	a																								
	d			01u12			01u41																		
Penrith North Lakes	d																								
Windermere	d																								
Oxenholme Lake District	a																								
	d																								
Barrow-in-Furness	d										04 35														
Lancaster 6	a										05 28														
	d																								
Blackpool North	d	22p44	23p03						03 37																
Preston 8	a	23p08	23p28										04s32		04s41										
Preston 8	d	23p10	23p28						04u02								05 16					05 33			
Wigan North Western	a																					05 44			
	d																					05 45			
Blackrod	d		23p50																						
Lostock	d		23p57																						
Bolton	a	23p34	00 02						04c31								05 42								
Manchester Piccadilly 10	a	23p53	00 18						04 48								06 01								
Manchester Airport ✈	a	00 24	00 32						05 07								06 18								
Liverpool Lime Street 10	a																								
	d					23p34													05 27						06 05
Liverpool South Parkway ✈	d					23p45																			
Runcorn	d					23p53													05 43						06 21
Warrington Bank Quay	a																					05 55			
	d																					05 56			
Hartford	d					00 07																			
Manchester Piccadilly 10	d											05 05						05 11						05 55	
Stockport	d											05 13												06 03	
Wilmslow	d																							06 11	
Holyhead	d																								
Bangor (Gwynedd)	d																								
Llandudno Junction	d																								
Wrexham General	d																								
Chester	d									04 22															
Crewe 10	a					00 22				04 44		05 34	05s38		05s41			05 44	06 00					06 27	
	d									04 59		05 36						05 47	06 02				06 20	06 29	
Macclesfield	d																								
Congleton	d																								
Stoke-on-Trent	d																	06 07		←					
Stafford	a									05 24		05 53						06 24	06 20	06 24			06 40		06 52
	d									05 25		05 55						06 25	06 21	06 25			06 41		06 53
Penkridge	a																	→					06 46		
Wolverhampton 7	a									05 39										06 39			06 57		
Birmingham New Street 12	a									05 59										06 58			07 18		
Birmingham International ✈	a																			07 13					
Coventry	a																			07 24					
Lichfield Trent Valley	a																					06 40			07 07
Tamworth Low Level	a																					06 46			07 14
Nuneaton	a											06 17												07 06	
Rugby	a											06 30							06 52			07 06			
Milton Keynes Central	a											06 51							07 12						
Watford Junction	a			06s23			06s19																		
London Euston 15 ⊖	a			06 46			06 43					07 28	07 47		07 50				07 50			07 57		08 07	08 22

A Conveys a portion from Fort William, dep 1950

B Conveys a portion from Fort William, dep 1900

b Previous night, stops to pick up only

c Stops to pick up only

OVERNIGHT SLEEPERS. For sleeper trains, operated by First ScotRail, please refer to Tables 400 - 404

Scotland and North West England - West Midlands and London

Route Diagram - see first Page of Table 65

		XC	VT	LM	VT	VT		TP	VT	TP	VT	VT	LM	VT	LM	VT		VT	TP	XC	LM	VT	VT	VT	VT
		◇1	◇1	◇1	◇1	◇1		◇1	◇1	◇1	◇1	◇1	◇1	◇1	◇1	◇1		◇1	◇1	◇1	◇1	◇1	◇1	◇1	◇1
										A														B	
		⊤	⊠		⊠	⊠		⊤	⊠	⊤	⊠	⊠		⊠		⊠		⊠	⊤	⊤		⊠	⊠	⊠	⊠
Inverness	d																								
Aberdeen	d																								
Dundee	d																								
Perth	d																								
Edinburgh 10	d																								
Haymarket	d																								
Glasgow Central 15	d																	04 28							
Motherwell	d																								
Carstairs	d																								
Lockerbie	d																								
Carlisle 8	a																	05 42							
	d																	05 43							
Penrith North Lakes	d																	05 57							
Windermere	d																								
Oxenholme Lake District	a																	06 20							
	d																	06 20							
Barrow-in-Furness	d									05 31															
Lancaster 6	a									06 23								06 35							
	d					05 35				06 23								06 35							06 58
Blackpool North	d							05 39											06 40						
Preston 8	a					05 52		06 03		06 42								06 53	07 07						07 15
Preston 8	d					06 00		06 05	06 16	06 44								06 56	07 09						07 17
Wigan North Western	a					06 11			06 27									07 06							07 28
	d					06 11			06 27									07 08							07 28
Blackrod	d							06 22																	
Lostock	d							06 30											07 30						
Bolton	a							06 34		07 08									07 34						
Manchester Piccadilly 10 ⛴	a							06 56		07 27									07 56						
Manchester Airport ✈	a							07 17		07 47									08 17						
Liverpool Lime Street 10	a																								
	d												06 30			07 00					07 04				
Liverpool South Parkway ✈	d												06 40								07 14				
Runcorn	d												06 48			07u15					07 22				
Warrington Bank Quay	a					06 22			06 38									07 17							07 39
	d					06 22			06 38									07 18							07 39
Hartford	d												07 02								07 36				
Manchester Piccadilly 10 ⛴	d	06 00	06 10								06 27	06 35		06 43						07 07		07 15			
Stockport	d	06 08	06 18								06 35	06 43		06 51						07 16		07 23			
Wilmslow	d													06 59											
Holyhead	d				04 48																		05 51		
Bangor (Gwynedd)	d				05 14																		06 18		
Llandudno Junction	d				05 32																		06 36		
Wrexham General	d																							07 00	
Chester	d				06 26																		07 35		
Crewe 10	a	06 32			06 47	06 42			06 58				07 14	07 15							07 48		07 54		07 58
	d	06 38		06 47	06 53				07 01				07 16	07 17							07 49		07 57		08 01
Macclesfield	d		06 31								06 48	06 56													
Congleton	d																								
Stoke-on-Trent	d		06 48								07 06	07 12			←					07 44		07 50			
Stafford	a	06 57		07 10							07 27		07 40	07 34	07 40					08 01	08 10				
	d	06 58		07 12							07 28		07 41	07 35	07 41					08 02	08 10				
Penkridge	a			07 17									→		07 46						08 16				
Wolverhampton 7 ⛴	a	07 12		07 28					07 31		07 43				07 57					08 15	08 26				08 31
Birmingham New Street 12	a	07 31		07 48					07 55		08 06				08 17					08 32	08 47				08 55
Birmingham International ✈	a										08 19														
Coventry	a										08 30														
Lichfield Trent Valley	a																								
Tamworth Low Level	a																								
Nuneaton	a					07 32																	08 45		
Rugby	a		07 28									07 52													
Milton Keynes Central	a																					08s46			
Watford Junction	a										09s15														
London Euston 15 ⊖	a		08 22			08 33					09 34	08 45		08 52		09 01		09 04				09 23	09 38		

A ⊤ from Preston

B ⊠ from Chester

OVERNIGHT SLEEPERS. For sleeper trains, operated by First ScotRail, please refer to Tables 400 - 404

Table 65

Mondays to Fridays

from 17 September

Scotland and North West England - West Midlands and London

Route Diagram - see first Page of Table 65

		TP	TP	XC	VT	EM	LM	VT	LM	VT	VT	TP	TP	XC	LM	VT	VT	VT	NT	TP	XC	VT
		◇1	◇1	◇1	◇1	◇	◇1	◇1	◇1	◇1	◇1	◇1	◇1	◇1	◇1	◇1	◇1	◇1		◇1	◇1	◇1
		A																		A		
		⚲	⚲	⚲	⊠			⊠		⊠	⊠	⚲	⚲	⚲		⊠	⊠	⊠		⚲	⚲	⊠
Inverness	d																					
Aberdeen	d																					
Dundee	d																					
Perth	d																					
Edinburgh [10]	d											05 36										
Haymarket	d											05u40										
Glasgow Central [15]	d										05 40							05 50				
Motherwell	d																	06 04				
Carstairs	d																					
Lockerbie	d																					
Carlisle [8]	a										06 46	06 58						07 02				
	d										06 49	06 59						07 04				
Penrith North Lakes	d																	07 19				
Windermere	d																					
Oxenholme Lake District	a										07 22							07 42				
	d										07 24							07 42				
Barrow-in-Furness	d	06 20																	07 00	07 29		
Lancaster [6]	a	07 21									07 37	07 47						07 56	08 04	08 26		
	d	07 22									07 38	07 47						07 57	08 05	08 27		
Blackpool North	d		07 10										07 36									
Preston [8]	a	07 41	07 37								07 56	08 07	08 03					08 15	08 30	08 45		
Preston [8]	d	07 47									07 58	08 12						08 17		08 47		
Wigan North Western	a										08 09							08 28				
	d										08 09							08 28				
Blackrod	d																					
Lostock	d																					
Bolton	a	08 08										08 34								09 08		
Manchester Piccadilly [10] ⇌	a	08 27										08 56								09 27		
Manchester Airport ✈	a	08 47										09 19								09 47		
Liverpool Lime Street [10]	a																					
	d					06 47	07 34	07 48							08 04							
Liverpool South Parkway ✈	d					06 57	07 44								08 15							
Runcorn	d						07 52	08 04							08 24							
Warrington Bank Quay	a										08 20							08 39				
	d										08 20							08 39				
Hartford	d						08 04															
Manchester Piccadilly [10] ⇌	d			07 26	07 35	07 42				07 55				08 07		08 15					08 27	08 35
Stockport	d			07 35	07 43	07a53				08 04				08 16		08 23					08 35	08 43
Wilmslow	d									08 11												
Holyhead	d																06 55					
Bangor (Gwynedd)	d																07 22					
Llandudno Junction	d																07 40					
Wrexham General	d																					
Chester	d																08 35					
Crewe [10]	a						08 19			08 27					08 47		08 54	08 58				
	d						08 22			08 29					08 49		08 56	09 01				
Macclesfield	d			07 49	07 56																08 49	08 56
Congleton	d																					
Stoke-on-Trent	d			08 07	08 12				←					08 44		08 50					09 07	09 12
Stafford	a			08 24			08 42	08 35	08 42					09 02	09 09						09 24	
	d			08 25			08 43	08 36	08 43					09 03	09 10						09 25	
Penkridge	a						→		08 48						09 15							
Wolverhampton [7] ⇌	a			08 39					08 58					09 15	09 27			09 31			09 39	
Birmingham New Street [12]	a			08 58					09 18					09 32	09 47			09 55			09 58	
Birmingham International ✈	a			09 13																	10 13	
Coventry	a			09 24																	10 24	
Lichfield Trent Valley	a																					
Tamworth Low Level	a																					
Nuneaton	a				08 44																	
Rugby	a																					
Milton Keynes Central	a															09 46	10 01					
Watford Junction	a				09s31																	
London Euston [15] ⊖	a				09 52			09 56		10 04	10 12					10 23	10 38					10 42

A ⚲ from Preston

OVERNIGHT SLEEPERS. For sleeper trains, operated by First ScotRail, please refer to Tables 400 - 404

from 17 September

Scotland and North West England - West Midlands and London

Route Diagram - see first Page of Table 65

		EM	LM	VT	LM	VT	VT	SR	XC	LM		NT	TP	VT	VT	VT	TP	XC	VT	EM		LM	VT	LM	VT
		◇	◇1	◇1	◇1	◇1	◇1		◇1	◇1			◇1	◇1	◇1	◇1	◇1	◇1	◇1	◇		◇1	◇1	◇1	◇1
				⊠		⊠	⊠		⊤				⊤	⊠	⊠	⊠	⊤	⊤	⊠				⊠		⊠
Inverness	d																								
Aberdeen	d																								
Dundee	d																								
Perth	d																								
Edinburgh 10	d															06 52									
Haymarket	d															06 56									
Glasgow Central 15	d						06 30	07 05									07 10								
Motherwell	d						06 44	07 27																	
Carstairs	d							07a47																	
Lockerbie	d						07 25										08 06								
Carlisle 8	a						07 43									08 05	08 29								
	d						07 46									08 07	08 29								
Penrith North Lakes	d						08 00									08 22	08 45								
Windermere	d																								
Oxenholme Lake District	a						08 22										09 09								
	d						08 23										09 11								
Barrow-in-Furness	d																								
Lancaster 6	a						08 37									08 56	09 25								
	d						08 38									08 57	09 26								
Blackpool North	d												08 44												
Preston 8	a						08 56						09 08			09 15	09 45								
Preston 8	d						08 58					09 04	09 10			09 17	09 47								
Wigan North Western	a						09 09					09 24				09 28									
	d						09 09					09 24				09 28									
Blackrod	d																								
Lostock	d																								
Bolton	a												09 34				10 08								
Manchester Piccadilly 10	a												09 56				10 27								
Manchester Airport	a												10 17				10 47								
Liverpool Lime Street 10	a											10 02													
	d	07 42	08 34	08 48						09 04		10 16								08 52		09 34	09 48		
Liverpool South Parkway	d	07 53	08 44							09 15		10a27								09 03		09 44			
Runcorn	d		08 52	09 04						09 25												09 52	10 04		
Warrington Bank Quay	a						09 20									09 39									
	d						09 20									09 39									
Hartford	d		09 06																			10 04			
Manchester Piccadilly 10	d	08 43				08 55			09 07					09 15				09 27	09 35	09 43					09 55
Stockport	d	08a53				09 04			09 16					09 23				09 35	09 43	09a53					10 04
Wilmslow	d					09 11																			10 11
Holyhead	d																								
Bangor (Gwynedd)	d																								
Llandudno Junction	d																								
Wrexham General	d																								
Chester	d														09 35										
Crewe 10	a		09 20			09 27				09 44					09 54	09 58						10 19			10 27
	d		09 22			09 29				09 49					09 56	10 01						10 22			10 29
Macclesfield	d																	09 49	09 56						
Congleton	d																								
Stoke-on-Trent	d				←				09 44					09 50				10 07	10 12					←	
Stafford	a		09 42	09 35	09 42				10 02	10 09								10 24				10 42	10 35	10 42	
	d		09 43	09 36	09 43				10 03	10 10								10 25				10 43	10 36	10 43	
Penkridge	a		→							10 15												→			
Wolverhampton 7	a				09 56				10 15	10 27						10 31		10 39						10 56	
Birmingham New Street 12	a				10 17				10 39	10 47						10 55		10 58						11 18	
Birmingham International	a																	11 13							
Coventry	a																	11 24							
Lichfield Trent Valley	a																								
Tamworth Low Level	a																								
Nuneaton	a																								
Rugby	a																								
Milton Keynes Central	a													10 46	11 01										
Watford Junction	a																								
London Euston 15 ⊖	a			10 56		11 04	11 12							11 23	11 38				11 42				11 56		12 04

OVERNIGHT SLEEPERS. For sleeper trains, operated by First ScotRail, please refer to Tables 400 - 404

Table 65

Mondays to Fridays

from 17 September

Scotland and North West England - West Midlands and London

Route Diagram - see first Page of Table 65

		VT	XC	LM	NT	SR		TP	TP	VT	VT	VT	XC	VT	EM	VT FO		TP	NT	LM	VT	LM	VT	VT	XC
		◇1	◇1	◇1				◇1	◇1	◇1	◇1	◇1	◇1	◇1	◇	◇		◇1		◇1	◇1	◇1	◇1	◇1	◇1
		⊠	⊤					⊤	⊤	⊠	⊠	⊠	⊤	⊠		□		A ⊤			⊠		⊠	⊠	⊤
Inverness	d																								
Aberdeen	d																								
Dundee	d																								
Perth	d																								
Edinburgh 10	d					08 33		07 42																	
Haymarket	d					08 37		07u46																	
Glasgow Central 15	d	07 37										08 00												08 40	
Motherwell	d	07 52																							
Carstairs	d					09a13																			
Lockerbie	d																								
Carlisle 8	a	08 46						08 59				09 08												09 47	
	d	08 49						08 59				09 10												09 49	
Penrith North Lakes	d																							10 03	
Windermere	d																								
Oxenholme Lake District	a	09 22																							
	d	09 23																							
Barrow-in-Furness	d																	09 23	10 16						
Lancaster 6	a	09 37										09 56						10 25	11 20					10 37	
	d	09 38										09 57						10 26						10 38	
Blackpool North	d				09 37				09 43																
Preston 8	a	09 56			10 02			10 05	10 07			10 15						10 45						10 56	
Preston 8	d	09 58			10 04			10 12				10 17				10 36		10 47						10 58	
Wigan North Western	a	10 09			10 24							10 28				10 47								11 09	
	d	10 09			10 24							10 28				10 47								11 09	
Blackrod	d																								
Lostock	d																								
Bolton	a							10 34										11 08							
Manchester Piccadilly 10	a							10 56										11 27							
Manchester Airport ✈	a							11 17										11 50							
Liverpool Lime Street 10	a				11 02																				
	d			10 04	11 16										09 52					10 34	10 48				
Liverpool South Parkway ✈	d			10 15	11a27										10 03					10 44					
Runcorn	d			10 25																10 52	11 04				
Warrington Bank Quay	a	10 20										10 39				10 58								11 20	
	d	10 20										10 39				10 58								11 20	
Hartford	d																			11 04					
Manchester Piccadilly 10	d		10 07							10 15			10 27	10 35	10 43								10 55		11 07
Stockport	d		10 16							10 23			10 35	10 43	10a53								11 04		11 16
Wilmslow	d																						11 11		
Holyhead	d										08 55														
Bangor (Gwynedd)	d										09 22														
Llandudno Junction	d										09 40														
Wrexham General	d																								
Chester	d										10 35														
Crewe 10	a			10 45							10 54	10 58								11 19			11 27		
	d			10 49							10 56	11 01								11 22			11 29		
Macclesfield	d												10 49	10 56											
Congleton	d																								
Stoke-on-Trent	d		10 44							10 50			11 07	11 12								←			11 44
Stafford	a		11 01	11 09									11 24							11 43	11 33	11 43			12 02
	d		11 02	11 10									11 25							11 43 →	11 34	11 43			12 03
Penkridge	a			11 15																					
Wolverhampton 7	a		11 15	11 27								11 31	11 39									11 57			12 15
Birmingham New Street 12	a		11 32	11 47								11 55	11 58									12 17			12 39
Birmingham International ✈	a												12 13												
Coventry	a												12 24												
Lichfield Trent Valley	a																								
Tamworth Low Level	a																								
Nuneaton	a																								
Rugby	a																								
Milton Keynes Central	a									11 46	12 01														
Watford Junction	a																								
London Euston 15 ⊖	a	12 12								12 23	12 38			12 42		12 52					12 56		13 03	13 12	

A ⊤ from Preston

OVERNIGHT SLEEPERS. For sleeper trains, operated by First ScotRail, please refer to Tables 400 - 404

Scotland and North West England - West Midlands and London

Route Diagram - see first Page of Table 65

		LM		NT	TP	VT	VT	VT	TP	XC	VT	EM		LM	VT	LM	VT	VT	TP	XC	LM	NT		TP FO	TP FX
		◇1			◇1	◇1	◇1	◇1	◇1	◇1	◇1	◇		◇1	◇1	◇1	◇1	◇1	◇1	◇1	◇1			◇1	◇1
					⊼	⊏	⊏	⊠	A ⊼	⊼	⊏				⊏		⊏	⊠		⊼				⊼	⊼
Inverness	d																								
Aberdeen	d																								
Dundee	d																								
Perth	d																								
Edinburgh 10	d							08 52																	
Haymarket	d							08 57																	
Glasgow Central 15	d																	09 40							
Motherwell	d																								
Carstairs	d																								
Lockerbie	d																								
Carlisle 8	a							10 05										10 47							
	d							10 07										10 49							
Penrith North Lakes	d																								
Windermere	d								10 49																
Oxenholme Lake District	a							10 41	11 08									11 22							
	d							10 42	11 09									11 23							
Barrow-in-Furness	d																		11 25						
Lancaster 6	a							10 56	11 26									11 37	12 18						
	d							10 57	11 26									11 38	12 18						
Blackpool North	d			10 37	10 44																	11 37		11 44	11 44
Preston 8	a			11 02	11 08			11 15	11 45									11 56	12 37			12 02		12 08	12 08
Preston 8	d			11 04	11 10			11 17	11 47									11 58				12 04		12 10	12 10
Wigan North Western	a			11 24				11 28										12 09				12 24			
	d			11 24				11 28										12 09				12 24			
Blackrod	d																								
Lostock	d																								
Bolton	a				11 34				12 08															12 34	12 34
Manchester Piccadilly 10	a				11 56				12 27															12 56	12 56
Manchester Airport ✈	a				12 17				12 47															13 16	13 17
Liverpool Lime Street 10	a			12 02																		13 02			
	d	11 04		12 16								10 52		11 34	11 48						12 04	13 16			
Liverpool South Parkway ✈	d	11 15		12a27								11 03		11 44							12 15	13a27			
Runcorn	d	11 25												11 52	12 04						12 25				
Warrington Bank Quay	a							11 39										12 20							
	d							11 39										12 20							
Hartford	d													12 04											
Manchester Piccadilly 10	d					11 15				11 27	11 35	11 43					11 55			12 07					
Stockport	d					11 23				11 35	11 43	11a53					12 04			12 16					
Wilmslow	d																12 11								
Holyhead	d																								
Bangor (Gwynedd)	d																								
Llandudno Junction	d																								
Wrexham General	d																								
Chester	d						11 35																		
Crewe 10	a	11 45					11 54	11 58						12 19			12 27				12 45				
	d	11 49					11 56	12 01						12 22			12 29				12 49				
Macclesfield	d									11 49	11 56														
Congleton	d																								
Stoke-on-Trent	d					11 50				12 07	12 12					←				12 44					
Stafford	a	12 09								12 24				12 42	12 35	12 42				13 01	13 09				
	d	12 10								12 25				12 43	12 36	12 43				13 02	13 10				
Penkridge	a	12 15												→							13 15				
Wolverhampton 7	a	12 27						12 31		12 39						12 56				13 15	13 27				
Birmingham New Street 12	a	12 47						12 55		12 58						13 17				13 39	13 47				
Birmingham International ✈	a									13 13															
Coventry	a									13 24															
Lichfield Trent Valley	a																								
Tamworth Low Level	a																								
Nuneaton	a																								
Rugby	a																								
Milton Keynes Central	a					12 46	13 01																		
Watford Junction	a																								
London Euston 15 ⊖	a					13 23	13 38				13 42				13 56		14 04	14 12							

A ⊼ from Preston

OVERNIGHT SLEEPERS. For sleeper trains, operated by First ScotRail, please refer to Tables 400 - 404

Mondays to Fridays

from 17 September

Scotland and North West England - West Midlands and London

Route Diagram - see first Page of Table 65

		VT	VT	VT	TP FO	TP	XC	VT	EM	TP FO	LM	VT	LM	VT	VT	XC	LM	NT	TP	VT	VT	VT	TP
		◇1	◇1	◇1	◇1	◇1	◇1	◇1	◇	◇1	◇1	◇1	◇1	◇1	◇1	◇1	◇1		◇1	◇1	◇1	◇1	◇1
																							A
Inverness	d																						
Aberdeen	d																						
Dundee	d																						
Perth	d																						
Edinburgh	d				09 51																	10 51	
Haymarket	d				09u56																	10 57	
Glasgow Central	d			10 00		10 10									10 40								
Motherwell	d																						
Carstairs	d																						
Lockerbie	d				11 01																		
Carlisle	a			11 10	11 22	11 26									11 47							12 05	
	d			11 11	11 29	11 29									11 49							12 07	
Penrith North Lakes	d			11 26	11 45	11 45																	
Windermere	d																						12 51
Oxenholme Lake District	a				12 09	12 09									12 22							12 41	13 07
	d				12 10	12 10									12 23							12 43	13 09
Barrow-in-Furness	d									13 25													
Lancaster	a				12 26	12 26				14 18					12 37							12 56	13 26
	d				12 26	12 26									12 38							12 57	13 26
Blackpool North	d																	12 37	12 44				
Preston	a			12 15	12 45	12 45									12 56			13 02	13 08			13 15	13 45
Preston	d			12 17	12 47	12 47									12 58			13 04	13 10			13 17	13 47
Wigan North Western	a			12 28											13 09			13 24				13 28	
	d			12 28											13 09			13 24				13 28	
Blackrod	d																						
Lostock	d																						
Bolton	a				13 08	13 08													13 34				14 08
Manchester Piccadilly	a				13 27	13 27													13 56				14 27
Manchester Airport	a				13 47	13 47													14 17				14 47
Liverpool Lime Street	a																	14 02					
	d								11 52		12 34	12 48					13 04	14 16					
Liverpool South Parkway	d								12 03		12 44						13 15	14a27					
Runcorn	d										12 52	13 04					13 25						
Warrington Bank Quay	a			12 39											13 20							13 39	
	d			12 39											13 20							13 39	
Hartford	d										13 06												
Manchester Piccadilly	d	12 15					12 27	12 35	12 43					12 55		13 07				13 15			
Stockport	d	12 23					12 35	12 43	12a53					13 04		13 16				13 23			
Wilmslow	d													13 11									
Holyhead	d																						
Bangor (Gwynedd)	d																				12 24		
Llandudno Junction	d																				12 42		
Wrexham General	d																						
Chester	d		12 35																		13 35		
Crewe	a		12 54	12 58							13 20			13 27			13 45				13 54	13 58	
	d		12 56	13 01							13 22			13 29			13 49				13 56	14 01	
Macclesfield	d						12 49	12 56															
Congleton	d																						
Stoke-on-Trent	d	12 50					13 07	13 12					←			13 44				13 50			
Stafford	a						13 24				13 42	13 35	13 42			14 01	14 09						
	d						13 25				13 43	13 36	13 43			14 02	14 10						
Penkridge	a										→						14 15						
Wolverhampton	a			13 31			13 39						13 56			14 15	14 27					14 31	
Birmingham New Street	a			13 55			13 58						14 17			14 32	14 47					14 55	
Birmingham International	a						14 13																
Coventry	a						14 24																
Lichfield Trent Valley	a																						
Tamworth Low Level	a																						
Nuneaton	a																						
Rugby	a																						
Milton Keynes Central	a	13 46	14 01																	14 46	15 01		
Watford Junction	a																						
London Euston	a	14 23	14 38					14 42				14 56		15 04	15 12					15 23	15 38		

A from Preston

OVERNIGHT SLEEPERS. For sleeper trains, operated by First ScotRail, please refer to Tables 400 - 404

Scotland and North West England - West Midlands and London

Route Diagram - see first Page of Table 65

		XC	VT	EM		LM	VT	LM	VT	VT	VT	XC	LM	NT		TP	VT	VT	VT	TP FX	TP	NT	XC	VT	
		◇1	◇1	◇		◇1	◇1	◇1	◇1	◇1	◇1	◇1	1			◇1	◇1	◇1	◇1	◇1	◇1		◇1	◇1	
		🍴	☕				☕		☒	☕	☕	🍴				🍴	☕	☕	☕		🍴		🍴	☕	
Inverness	d																								
Aberdeen	d																								
Dundee	d																								
Perth	d																								
Edinburgh 10	d																				12 12				
Haymarket	d																				12u16				
Glasgow Central 15	d								11 40										12 00						
Motherwell	d																								
Carstairs	d																								
Lockerbie	d																				13 11				
Carlisle 8	a								12 46										13 08		13 33				
	d								12 49										13 09		13 34				
Penrith North Lakes	d								13 03																
Windermere	d																								
Oxenholme Lake District	a																				14 09				
	d																				14 10				
Barrow-in-Furness	d																			13 25		14 16			
Lancaster 6	a																		13 56	14 18	14 26	15 20			
	d										13 39								13 58	14 18	14 26				
Blackpool North	d													13 37		13 44									
Preston 8	a								13 50		13 56			14 02		14 08			14 15	14 37	14 45				
Preston 8	d								13 53		13 59			14 04		14 10			14 17		14 47				
Wigan North Western	a										14 09			14 24					14 28						
	d										14 10			14 24					14 28						
Blackrod	d																								
Lostock	d																								
Bolton	a															14 34					15 08				
Manchester Piccadilly 10 ⛴	a															14 56					15 27				
Manchester Airport ✈	a															15 17					15 47				
Liverpool Lime Street 10	a													15 02											
	d			12 52		13 34	13 48						14 04	15 16											
Liverpool South Parkway ✈	d			13 03		13 44							14 15	15a27											
Runcorn	d					13 52	14 04						14 25												
Warrington Bank Quay	a										14 20								14 39						
	d										14 21								14 39						
Hartford	d					14 04																			
Manchester Piccadilly 10 ⛴	d	13 27	13 35	13 43						13 55		14 07					14 15						14 27	14 35	
Stockport	d	13 35	13 43	13a53						14 04		14 16					14 23						14 35	14 43	
Wilmslow	d									14 11															
Holyhead	d																								
Bangor (Gwynedd)	d																								
Llandudno Junction	d																								
Wrexham General	d																								
Chester	d																	14 35							
Crewe 10	a					14 19				14 27			14 45					14 54	14 58						
	d					14 22				14 29			14 49					14 56	15 01						
Macclesfield	d	13 49	13 56																				14 49	14 56	
Congleton	d																								
Stoke-on-Trent	d	14 07	14 12					←				14 44					14 50						15 07	15 12	
Stafford	a	14 24				14 46	14 35	14 46				15 02	15 09										15 24		
	d	14 25				14 46	14 36	14 46				15 03	15 10										15 25		
Penkridge	a					↦							15 15												
Wolverhampton 7 ⛴	a	14 39						14 59				15 15	15 27						15 31				15 39		
Birmingham New Street 12	a	14 58						15 20				15 39	15 47						15 55				15 58		
Birmingham International ✈	a	15 13																					16 13		
Coventry	a	15 24																					16 24		
Lichfield Trent Valley	a																								
Tamworth Low Level	a																								
Nuneaton	a																								
Rugby	a																								
Milton Keynes Central	a																15 46	16 01							
Watford Junction	a																								
London Euston 15 ⊖	a		15 42				15 56		16 03	16 04	16 11						16 23	16 38						16 42	

OVERNIGHT SLEEPERS. For sleeper trains, operated by First ScotRail, please refer to Tables 400 - 404

Table 65

Mondays to Fridays

from 17 September

Scotland and North West England - West Midlands and London

Route Diagram - see first Page of Table 65

		EM	LM	VT	LM	VT	VT	XC	LM	NT		TP	VT	VT	VT	VT	TP	XC	VT	EM		LM	VT	LM	VT
		◇	◇1	◇1 ⊡	◇1	◇1 ⊡	◇1 ⊠	◇1 ⌶	◇1			◇1 ⌶	◇1 ⊡	◇1 ⊡	◇1 ⊡	◇1 ⊡	◇1 ⌶	◇1 ⌶	◇1 ⊡	◇		◇1	◇1 ⊡	◇1	◇1 ⊠
Inverness	d																								
Aberdeen	d																								
Dundee	d																								
Perth	d																								
Edinburgh 10	d															12 51									
Haymarket	d															12 57									
Glasgow Central 15	d						12 40										13 09								13 40
Motherwell	d																								
Carstairs	d																								
Lockerbie	d																14 06								
Carlisle 8	a						13 47									14 05	14 29								14 46
	d						13 49									14 07	14 29								14 49
Penrith North Lakes	d															14 22	14 45								
Windermere	d																								
Oxenholme Lake District	a						14 22																		15 22
	d						14 24																		15 24
Barrow-in-Furness	d																								
Lancaster 6	a						14 37									14 56	15 22								
	d						14 38									14 57	15 22								
Blackpool North	d									14 37		14 44													
Preston 8	a						14 56			15 02		15 08				15 15	15 41								15 50
Preston 8	d						14 58			15 04		15 10				15 17	15 47								15 53
Wigan North Western	a						15 09			15 24						15 28									
	d						15 09			15 24						15 28									
Blackrod	d																								
Lostock	d																								
Bolton	a											15 34					16 08								
Manchester Piccadilly 10 🚊	a											15 56					16 27								
Manchester Airport ✈	a											16 17					16 47								
Liverpool Lime Street 10	a									16 02															
	d	13 52	14 34	14 48					15 04	16 16										14 52		15 34	15 48		
Liverpool South Parkway ✈	d	14 03	14 44						15 15	16a27										15 03		15 44			
Runcorn	d		14 52	15 04					15 25													15 52	16 04		
Warrington Bank Quay	a						15 20									15 39									
	d						15 20									15 39									
Hartford	d		15 04																			16 04			
Manchester Piccadilly 10 🚊	d	14 43				14 55		15 07					15 15					15 27	15 35	15 43					
Stockport	d	14a53				15 04		15 16					15 23					15 35	15 43	15a53					
Wilmslow	d					15 11																			
Holyhead	d														13 58										
Bangor (Gwynedd)	d														14 25										
Llandudno Junction	d														14 43										
Wrexham General	d																								
Chester	d													15 35	15 35										
Crewe 10	a		15 19			15 27			15 45					15 54	15 54	15 58						16 19			
	d		15 22			15 29			15 49					15 56	15 57	16 01						16 22			
Macclesfield	d																	15 49	15 56						
Congleton	d																								
Stoke-on-Trent	d				←			15 44					15 50					16 07	16 12					←	
Stafford	a		15 42	15 35	15 42			16 02	16 09									16 24				16 46	16 35	16 46	
	d		15 43	15 36	15 43			16 03	16 10									16 25				16 46	16 36	16 46	
Penkridge	a		→						16 15													→			
Wolverhampton 7 🚊	a				15 56			16 15	16 26							16 31		16 39						16 59	
Birmingham New Street 12	a				16 17			16 39	16 47							16 55		16 58						17 20	
Birmingham International ✈	a																	17 13							
Coventry	a																	17 24							
Lichfield Trent Valley	a																								
Tamworth Low Level	a																								
Nuneaton	a																								
Rugby	a																								
Milton Keynes Central	a												16 46	17s01	17 01										
Watford Junction	a																								
London Euston 15 ⊖	a			16 59		17 04	17 12						17 23	17 38	17 38				17 42				17 56		18 01

OVERNIGHT SLEEPERS. For sleeper trains, operated by First ScotRail, please refer to Tables 400 - 404

Table 65

Mondays to Fridays

from 17 September

Scotland and North West England - West Midlands and London

Route Diagram - see first Page of Table 65

		VT	VT	TP	XC	LM		NT	TP	VT	VT	VT	TP	TP	NT	XC		VT	EM	TP	LM	VT	LM	VT	VT
				FO									FX												
		◇1	◇1	◇1	◇1	◇1			◇1	◇1	◇1	◇1	◇1	◇1		◇1		◇1	◇	◇1	◇1	◇1	◇1	◇1	◇1
													A												
		🍴	🍴		🛒				🛒	🍴	🍴	🍴	🛒	🛒		🛒		🍴				🍴		🍴	⊠
Inverness	d																								
Aberdeen	d																								
Dundee	d																								
Perth	d																								
Edinburgh 10	d													14 07											
Haymarket	d													14u11											
Glasgow Central 15	d											14 00													14 40
Motherwell	d																								
Carstairs	d																								
Lockerbie	d													15 06											
Carlisle 8	a											15 08		15 27											15 47
	d											15 09		15 27											15 49
Penrith North Lakes	d													15 43											
Windermere	d																								
Oxenholme Lake District	a											15 44		16 06											16 22
	d											15 44		16 07											16 24
Barrow-in-Furness	d			15 24									15 24		16 20					17 21					
Lancaster 6	a			16 18									16 18	16 21	17 26					18 20					16 37
	d		15 39	16 18									16 18	16 22											16 38
Blackpool North	d							15 37	15 44																
Preston 8	a		15 56	16 37				16 02	16 08			16 15	16 37	16 42											16 56
Preston 8	d		15 59					16 04	16 10			16 17	16 47	16 47											16 58
Wigan North Western	a		16 09					16 24				16 28													17 09
	d		16 10					16 24				16 28													17 09
Blackrod	d																								
Lostock	d																								
Bolton	a								16 34				17 08	17 08											
Manchester Piccadilly 10 ⇌	a								16 56				17 29	17 29											
Manchester Airport ✈	a								17 17				17 48	17 48											
Liverpool Lime Street 10	a							17 05																	
	d					16 04													15 52		16 34	16 48			
Liverpool South Parkway ✈	d					16 15													16 03		16 44				
Runcorn	d					16 25															16 52	17 04			
Warrington Bank Quay	a		16 20									16 39													17 20
	d		16 21									16 39													17 20
Hartford	d																				17 06				
Manchester Piccadilly 10 ⇌	d	15 55			16 07					16 15						16 27		16 35	16 43					16 55	
Stockport	d	16 04			16 16					16 23						16 35		16 43	16a53					17 04	
Wilmslow	d	16 11																						17 11	
Holyhead	d																								
Bangor (Gwynedd)	d																								
Llandudno Junction	d																								
Wrexham General	d																								
Chester	d										16 35														
Crewe 10	a	16 27				16 45					16 54	16 58									17 19			17 27	
	d	16 29				16 49					16 56	17 01									17 22			17 29	
Macclesfield	d															16 49		16 56							
Congleton	d																								
Stoke-on-Trent	d				16 44					16 50						17 07		17 12					←		
Stafford	a				17 02	17 10										17 24					17 42	17 35	17 42		
	d				17 03	17 10										17 25					17 43	17 36	17 43		
Penkridge	a					17 15															↦				
Wolverhampton 7 ⇌	a				17 15	17 27						17 31				17 39							17 56		
Birmingham New Street 12	a				17 32	17 47						17 55				17 58							18 17		
Birmingham International ✈	a															18 13									
Coventry	a															18 24									
Lichfield Trent Valley	a																								
Tamworth Low Level	a																								
Nuneaton	a																								
Rugby	a																								
Milton Keynes Central	a									17 46	18 01											18 23			
Watford Junction	a																							18s48	
London Euston 15 ⊖	a	18 03	18 09							18 23	18 38							18 42				18 59		19 08	19 13

A 🛒 from Preston

OVERNIGHT SLEEPERS. For sleeper trains, operated by First ScotRail, please refer to Tables 400 - 404

Table 65

Scotland and North West England - West Midlands and London

Route Diagram - see first Page of Table 65

		SR		XC	LM	NT	NT	TP	VT	VT	VT	TP		XC	VT	EM	LM	VT	LM	VT	VT	XC		LM	NT
				◇1	◇1	A	B	◇1	◇1	◇1	R 1	◇1		◇1	◇1	◇	◇1	◇1	◇1	◇1	◇1	◇1		◇1	A
				🛒				🛒	⊠	⊠	🍽	🛒		🛒	⊠			⊠		⊠	⊠	🛒			
Inverness	d																								
Aberdeen	d																								
Dundee	d																								
Perth	d																								
Edinburgh 10	d										14 51														
Haymarket	d										14 57														
Glasgow Central 15	d	15 14																							
Motherwell	d	15 34																							
Carstairs	d	15a51																							
Lockerbie	d																								
Carlisle 8	a										16 05														
	d										16 07														
Penrith North Lakes	d										16 21														
Windermere	d																								
Oxenholme Lake District	a																								
	d																								
Barrow-in-Furness	d																								
Lancaster 6	a										16 56														
	d										16 57										17 36				
Blackpool North	d					16 35	16 35	16 40				17 20													17 37
Preston 8	a					17 02	17 02	17 08			17 15	17 45									17 54				18 02
Preston 8	d					17 04	17 04	17 10			17 17	17 47									17 56				18 04
Wigan North Western	a					17 24	17 24				17 28										18 07				18 24
	d					17 24	17 24				17 28										18 08				18 24
Blackrod	d																								
Lostock	d																								
Bolton	a							17 34				18 08													
Manchester Piccadilly 10	a							17 56				18 27													
Manchester Airport ✈	a							18 17				18 47													
Liverpool Lime Street 10	a					18 02	18 04																		19 03
	d				17 04											16 52	17 34	17 48						18 04	
Liverpool South Parkway ✈	d				17 15											17 03	17 44							18 15	
Runcorn	d				17 25												17 52	18 04						18 24	
Warrington Bank Quay	a										17 39										18 19				
	d										17 39										18 19				
Hartford	d																18 06								
Manchester Piccadilly 10	d			17 05					17 15					17 27	17 35	17 43				17 55		18 05			
Stockport	d			17 13					17 23					17 35	17 43	17a53				18 04		18 13			
Wilmslow	d													17 44						18 11					
Holyhead	d																								
Bangor (Gwynedd)	d																								
Llandudno Junction	d																								
Wrexham General	d																								
Chester	d									17 35															
Crewe 10	a				17 47					17 54	17 59			18 04			18 20			18 27				18 47	
	d				17 49					17 56	18 01			18 07			18 22			18 29				18 49	
Macclesfield	d			17 27											17 56							18 26			
Congleton	d																								
Stoke-on-Trent	d			17 44					17 50						18 12				←			18 44			
Stafford	a			18 03	18 09									18 27			18 42	18 35	18 42			19 01		19 09	
	d			18 04	18 10									18 28			18 43	18 36	18 43			19 02		19 10	
Penkridge	a				18 15												→							19 15	
Wolverhampton 7	a			18 15	18 27						18 31			18 39					18 56			19 15		19 27	
Birmingham New Street 12	a			18 38	18 48						18 55			18 58					19 17			19 32		19 48	
Birmingham International ✈	a													19 13											
Coventry	a													19 24											
Lichfield Trent Valley	a																								
Tamworth Low Level	a																								
Nuneaton	a																								
Rugby	a																								
Milton Keynes Central	a								18 47	19 01										19 31					
Watford Junction	a																	19s42							
London Euston 15 ⊖	a								19 23	19 38					19 42			20 02		20 06	20 11				

A from 17 September until 28 September

B from 1 October

OVERNIGHT SLEEPERS. For sleeper trains, operated by First ScotRail, please refer to Tables 400 - 404

Scotland and North West England - West Midlands and London

Route Diagram - see first Page of Table 65

		NT	TP	VT	TP	VT	XC	VT		EM	LM	VT	VT	XC	LM	NT	NT	VT		TP	TP	VT	VT	VT	TP
			◇1	◇1	◇1	◇1	◇1	◇1		◇	◇1	◇1	◇1	◇1	◇1			◇1		◇1	◇1	◇1	◇1	■ 1	◇1
		A	B				C									D	A								
			🛒	☕	🛒	☒	🛒	☒				☒	☒	🛒				☒		🛒		☕	☕	☕	🛒
Inverness	d																								
Aberdeen	d																								
Dundee	d																								
Perth	d																								
Edinburgh 10	d				16 12																			16 52	
Haymarket	d				16u16																			16 57	
Glasgow Central 15	d			16 00														16 40							17 06
Motherwell	d																	16 54							
Carstairs	d																								
Lockerbie	d				17 11																				18 06
Carlisle 8	a			17 08	17 33													17 49						18 05	18 28
	d			17 09	17 34													17 51						18 07	18 29
Penrith North Lakes	d				17 49													18 05							18 45
Windermere	d		17 06																		18 15				
Oxenholme Lake District	a		17 25	17 44														18 27			18 34			18 41	19 09
	d		17 30	17 44														18 29			18 36			18 42	19 10
Barrow-in-Furness	d																								
Lancaster 6	a		17 47		18 26													18 43			18 52			18 56	19 26
	d		17 48		18 26													18 44			18 52			18 57	19 26
Blackpool North	d	17 37														18 37	18 37			18 44					
Preston 8	a	18 02	18 06	18 15	18 45											19 02	19 02	19 02		19 08	19 11			19 15	19 45
Preston 8	d	18 04	18 08	18 17	18 47											19 04	19 04	19 05		19 10	19 16			19 16	19 47
Wigan North Western	a	18 24		18 28												19 24	19 24	19 16						19 28	
	d	18 24		18 28												19 24	19 24	19 16						19 29	
Blackrod	d																								
Lostock	d		18 30																						
Bolton	a		18 34		19 08															19 33	19 42				20 08
Manchester Piccadilly 10	a		18 56		19 27															19 56	20 01				20 27
Manchester Airport ✈	a		19 17		19 47															20 17	20 24				20 47
Liverpool Lime Street 10	a	19 04														20 00	20 04								
	d									17 52	18 34	18 48			19 11										
Liverpool South Parkway ✈	d									18 03	18 44				19 21										
Runcorn	d										18 52	19 04			19 29										
Warrington Bank Quay	a			18 39														19 27						19 39	
	d			18 39														19 27						19 39	
Hartford	d										19 04														
Manchester Piccadilly 10	d					18 15	18 27	18 35		18 43			18 55	19 07								19 15			
Stockport	d					18 23	18 35	18 43		18a53			19 04	19 16								19 23			
Wilmslow	d												19 11												
Holyhead	d																								
Bangor (Gwynedd)	d																								
Llandudno Junction	d																								
Wrexham General	d																								
Chester	d																						19 35		
Crewe 10	a			18 59							19 16	19 21	19 27		19 53								19 54	19 59	
	d			19 01							19 18	19 23	19 29		19 55								19 56	20 01	
Macclesfield	d							18 56														19 36			
Congleton	d						18 54																		
Stoke-on-Trent	d					18 50	19 07	19 12						19 44								19 52			
Stafford	a						19 24				19 41	19 41		20 03	20 15										
	d						19 25				19 42	19 42		20 04	20 16										
Penkridge	a										19 47														
Wolverhampton 7	a			19 31			19 39				19 57			20 16	20 29									20 33	
Birmingham New Street 12	a			19 55			19 58				20 18			20 33	20 47									20 55	
Birmingham International ✈	a						20 13																		
Coventry	a						20 24																		
Lichfield Trent Valley	a																								
Tamworth Low Level	a																								
Nuneaton	a																								
Rugby	a																								
Milton Keynes Central	a					19 46							20 32					20 45				20 48	21 03		
Watford Junction	a											20s46													
London Euston 15 ⊖	a					20 23		20 42				21 05	21 06					21 24				21 26	21 42		

A from 1 October

B 🛒 from Preston

C 🛒 to Birmingham New Street

D from 17 September until 28 September

OVERNIGHT SLEEPERS. For sleeper trains, operated by First ScotRail, please refer to Tables 400 - 404

Table 65 **Mondays to Fridays**

from 17 September

Scotland and North West England - West Midlands and London

Route Diagram - see first Page of Table 65

		SR	XC	EM		TP	LM	VT	VT	VT	XC	LM	NT	NT		VT	TP	TP ThX	TP ThO	SR	VT	VT	SR	XC
			◇1	◇		◇1	◇1	◇1	◇1	◇1	◇1	◇1				◇1	◇1	◇1	◇1		◇1	◇1		◇1
			A										B	C										
			🛒					☕	☕	☕						☕		🛒	🛒		☕	⊠		
Inverness	d																							
Aberdeen	d																							
Dundee	d																							
Perth	d																							
Edinburgh 10	d	17 42																18 12	18 12	18 24				
Haymarket	d	17 46																18u16	18u16	18 28				
Glasgow Central 15	d															17 40						18 40	19 49	
Motherwell	d																						20 06	
Carstairs	d	18a16																		19a09			20a26	
Lockerbie	d															18 35		19 11	19 11					
Carlisle 8	a															18 52		19 34	19 34			19 47		
	d															18 54		19 34	19 34			19 49		
Penrith North Lakes	d															19 09		19 49	19 49					
Windermere	d																							
Oxenholme Lake District	a															19 32		20 12	20 12			20 22		
	d															19 32		20 13	20 13			20 24		
Barrow-in-Furness	d																							
Lancaster 6	a															19 47		20 26	20 26			20 37		
	d															19 47		20 26	20 26			20 38		
Blackpool North	d												19 37	19 37			19 44							
Preston 8	a												20 02	20 02		20 05	20 08	20 45	20 45			20 56		
Preston 8	d									19 58			20 04	20 04		20 08	20 10	20 47	20 47			20 58		
Wigan North Western	a									20 09			20 24	20 24		20 19						21 09		
	d									20 09			20 24	20 24		20 19						21 09		
Blackrod	d																							
Lostock	d																							
Bolton	a																20 34	21 08	21 08					
Manchester Piccadilly 10	a																20 56	21 27	21 27					
Manchester Airport ✈	a																21 17	21 46	21 47					
Liverpool Lime Street 10	a												21 00	21 04										
	d			18 52		19 22	19 34	19 48				20 04												
Liverpool South Parkway ✈	d			19 03		19 32	19 44					20 15												
Runcorn	d						19 52	20 04				20 24												
Warrington Bank Quay	a									20 20						20 30						21 20		
	d									20 20						20 31						21 20		
Hartford	d						20 04																	
Manchester Piccadilly 10	d		19 27	19 43		20a09			19 55		20 07										20 15			20 27
Stockport	d		19 35	19a53					20 04		20 16										20 23			20 35
Wilmslow	d								20 11															
Holyhead	d																							
Bangor (Gwynedd)	d																							
Llandudno Junction	d																							
Wrexham General	d																							
Chester	d																							
Crewe 10	a						20 16	20 21	20 27	20 39		20 45				20 50								
	d						20 18	20 23	20 29	20 41		20 47				20 53								
Macclesfield	d		19 49																		20 36			20 49
Congleton	d																							
Stoke-on-Trent	d		20 07								20 44										20 53			21 07
Stafford	a		20 25				20 38		20 47		21 02	21 08				21 11								21 24
	d		20 26				20 42		20 48		21 03	21 10				21 13								21 25
Penkridge	a						20 47					21 15												
Wolverhampton 7	a		20 40				20 57				21 15	21 26				21 29								21 39
Birmingham New Street 12	a		21 00				21 18				21 33	21 47				21 48								22 00
Birmingham International ✈	a		21 13																					
Coventry	a		21 24																					
Lichfield Trent Valley	a																							
Tamworth Low Level	a																							
Nuneaton	a							21 02																
Rugby	a									21 27														
Milton Keynes Central	a								21 35	21 47											21 50	22 39		
Watford Junction	a							21s48													22s11	23s14		
London Euston 15 ⊖	a							22 09	22 12	22 22											22 33	23 38		

A 🛒 to Birmingham New Street

B from 17 September until 28 September

C from 1 October

OVERNIGHT SLEEPERS. For sleeper trains, operated by First ScotRail, please refer to Tables 400 - 404

Scotland and North West England - West Midlands and London

Route Diagram - see first Page of Table 65

		EM	LM	TP	VT	VT	VT	VT	TP	XC		LM	TP	VT	VT	XC	EM	NT	TP	NT		LM	TP	NT	TP
														FO	FX			FX	FO						
		◇	◇1	◇1	◇1	◇1	◇1	◇1	◇1	◇1		◇1	◇1	◇1	◇1	◇1	◇		◇1			◇1	◇1		◇1
					☕	☕	☕	☕						☕	☕				🛒						
Inverness	d																								
Aberdeen	d																								
Dundee	d																								
Perth	d																								
Edinburgh 10	d							18 52											20 12						
Haymarket	d							18 57											20u16						
Glasgow Central 15	d													20 10	20 10										
Motherwell	d																								
Carstairs	d														20 36										
Lockerbie	d													21 05	21 05				21 11						
Carlisle 8	a							20 06						21 25	21 25				21 34						
	d							20 08						21 26	21 26				21 34						
Penrith North Lakes	d													21 40	21 41										
Windermere	d																								22 45
Oxenholme Lake District	a							20 42						22 04	22 04				22 09						23 04
	d							20 42						22 04	22 05				22 10						23 06
Barrow-in-Furness	d								20 08											21 43					
Lancaster 6	a							20 57	21 10					22 19	22 19				22 26	22 45					23 23
	d							20 57	21 10					22 19	22 20				22 26	22 46				23 07	23 24
Blackpool North	d			20 44									21 44					22 14					22 44		
Preston 8	a			21 08				21 15	21 29				22 08	22 36	22 37			22 41	22 45	23 11			23 08	23 28	23 45
Preston 8	d			21 10				21 17	21 31				22 10	22 40	22 40			22 43	22 47				23 10		
Wigan North Western	a							21 28	21 47					22 51	22 51			23 05							
	d							21 28	21 48					22 52	22 52										
Blackrod	d																								
Lostock	d																								
Bolton	a			21 34									22 34						23 06				23 34		
Manchester Piccadilly 10 ⇌	a			21 56					22 30				22 56						23 31				23 53		
Manchester Airport ✈	a			22 17					22 47				23 17										00 24		
Liverpool Lime Street 10	a																								
	d	19 52	20 34			20 48						21 34					21 37					22 34			
Liverpool South Parkway ✈	d	20 03	20 44									21 44					21 47					22 45			
Runcorn	d		20 52			21 04						21 52										22 54			
Warrington Bank Quay	a							21 39						23 02	23 02										
	d							21 39						23 03	23 03										
Hartford	d		21 04									22 04										23 08			
Manchester Piccadilly 10 ⇌	d	20 43			21 15					21 27						22 07	22 28								
Stockport	d	20a53			21 23					21 35						22 16	22a37								
Wilmslow	d																								
Holyhead	d																								
Bangor (Gwynedd)	d						20 20																		
Llandudno Junction	d						20 38																		
Wrexham General	d																								
Chester	d						21 35																		
Crewe 10	a		21 16			21 21	21 54	21 59				22 18		23 24	23 24							23 21			
	d		21 18			21 24	21 56	22 01				22 20													
Macclesfield	d				21 36					21 49						22 29									
Congleton	d																								
Stoke-on-Trent	d				21 53					22 08						22 47									
Stafford	a		21 38			21 42				22 25		22 40				23 06									
	d		21 41			21 44				22 26		22 41				23 07									
Penkridge	a		21 46									22 46													
Wolverhampton 7 ⇌	a		21 57				22 27	22 32		22 39		22 57				23 19									
Birmingham New Street 12	a		22 17				22 50	22 55		22 58		23 18				23 39									
Birmingham International ✈	a																								
Coventry	a																								
Lichfield Trent Valley	a					21 57																			
Tamworth Low Level	a					22 03																			
Nuneaton	a					22 16																			
Rugby	a					22 30																			
Milton Keynes Central	a				22 52	22 58																			
Watford Junction	a				23s25	23s30																			
London Euston 15 ⊖	a				23 48	23 56																			

OVERNIGHT SLEEPERS. For sleeper trains, operated by First ScotRail, please refer to Tables 400 - 404

Table 65

Mondays to Fridays

from 17 September

Scotland and North West England - West Midlands and London

Route Diagram - see first Page of Table 65

		LM	SR	SR	SR	SR	SR	SR	SR	SR
			FX	FX	FO	FO	FX	FX	FO	FO
		◇1	B	B	B	B	B	B	B	B
							A	A	A	A
Inverness	d						20 47		20 47	
Aberdeen	d							21 42		21 42
Dundee	d							23u06		23u06
Perth	d						23u21		23u21	
Edinburgh 10	d		23 40		23 40					
Haymarket	d									
Glasgow Central 15	d			23 40		23 40				
Motherwell	d			23u56		23u56				
Carstairs	d		00u16		00u16					
Lockerbie	d									
Carlisle 8	a									
	d		01u41		01u41					
Penrith North Lakes	d									
Windermere	d									
Oxenholme Lake District	a									
	d									
Barrow-in-Furness	d									
Lancaster 6	a									
	d									
Blackpool North	d									
Preston 8	a						04s32		04s33	
Preston 8	d									
Wigan North Western	a									
	d									
Blackrod	d									
Lostock	d									
Bolton	a									
Manchester Piccadilly 10	a									
Manchester Airport	a									
Liverpool Lime Street 10	a									
	d	23 34								
Liverpool South Parkway	d	23 45								
Runcorn	d	23 53								
Warrington Bank Quay	a									
	d									
Hartford	d	00 07								
Manchester Piccadilly 10	d									
Stockport	d									
Wilmslow	d									
Holyhead	d									
Bangor (Gwynedd)	d									
Llandudno Junction	d									
Wrexham General	d									
Chester	d									
Crewe 10	a	00 22					05s38		05s38	
	d									
Macclesfield	d									
Congleton	d									
Stoke-on-Trent	d									
Stafford	a									
	d									
Penkridge	a									
Wolverhampton 7	a									
Birmingham New Street 12	a									
Birmingham International	a									
Coventry	a									
Lichfield Trent Valley	a									
Tamworth Low Level	a									
Nuneaton	a									
Rugby	a									
Milton Keynes Central	a									
Watford Junction	a		06s19		06s27					
London Euston 15 ⊖	a		06 43		06 50		07 47		07 48	

A Conveys a portion from Fort William, dep 1950

OVERNIGHT SLEEPERS. For sleeper trains, operated by First ScotRail, please refer to Tables 400 - 404

Table 65

Saturdays

until 30 June

Scotland and North West England - West Midlands and London

Route Diagram - see first Page of Table 65

		TP	LM	SR		SR	SR	TP	NT	AW	TP	TP	XC	VT	XC	VT	LM	VT	VT	TP		XC	VT	VT	LM
				R		R	R																		
		◇1	◇1					◇1			◇1	◇1	◇1	◇1	◇1	◇1	◇1	◇1	◇1	◇1		◇1	◇1	◇1	◇1
				🛏		🛏	🛏																		
				☕		☕	☕						🛒	☕	🛒	☕		☕	☕			🛒	☕	☕	
						A	A																		
Inverness	d					20p47																			
Aberdeen	d						21p42																		
Dundee	d						23b06																		
Perth	d					23b21																			
Edinburgh 10	d			23p40																					
Haymarket	d																								
Glasgow Central 15	d				23p40																				
Motherwell	d				23u56																				
Carstairs	d			00u16																					
Lockerbie	d																								
Carlisle 8	a																								
	d			01u41																					
Penrith North Lakes	d																								
Windermere	d																								
Oxenholme Lake District	a																								
	d																								
Barrow-in-Furness	d										04 35														
Lancaster 6	a										05 28														
	d																		05 40						
Blackpool North	d	22p44						03 37												05 39					
Preston 8	a	23p08				04s33													05 55	06 03					
Preston 8	d	23p10						04u02				05 16							05 58	06 05					
Wigan North Western	a																		06 09						
	d																		06 09						
Blackrod	d																			06 22					
Lostock	d																			06 30					
Bolton	a	23p34						04c31				05 42								06 34					
Manchester Piccadilly 10	a	23p53						04 48				06 01								06 56					
Manchester Airport ✈	a	00 24						05 07				06 18								07 17					
Liverpool Lime Street 10	a																								
	d		23p34						03 38							05 47									
Liverpool South Parkway ✈	d		23p45																						
Runcorn	d		23p53													06 03									
Warrington Bank Quay	a																		06 20						
	d																		06 20						
Hartford	d		00 07																						
Manchester Piccadilly 10	d								04a14				05 11	05 25				05 55				06 00	06 10	06 35	
Stockport	d													05 34				06 03				06 08	06 18	06 43	
Wilmslow	d													05 41				06 11							
Holyhead	d																								
Bangor (Gwynedd)	d																								
Llandudno Junction	d																								
Wrexham General	d																								
Chester	d									04 22															
Crewe 10	a		00 22			05s38				04 44			05 41	05 57				06 27							
	d									04 59			05 47	06 00			06 20	06 29							06 47
Macclesfield	d																					06 21	06 31	06 56	
Congleton	d																								
Stoke-on-Trent	d												06 08		←							06 39	06 48	07 12	
Stafford	a									05 24			06 25	06 17	06 25	06 34	06 41					06 57			07 10
	d									05 25			06 26	06 19	06 26	06 35	06 41					06 58			07 12
Penkridge	a												→				06 47								07 17
Wolverhampton 7	a									05 39					06 39		06 57					07 12			07 28
Birmingham New Street 12	a									05 58					06 57		07 17					07 31			07 47
Birmingham International ✈	a														07 13										
Coventry	a														07 24										
Lichfield Trent Valley	a																						07 11		
Tamworth Low Level	a																						07 17		
Nuneaton	a															06 57									
Rugby	a													06 49										07 52	
Milton Keynes Central	a													07 11				07 31	07 37						
Watford Junction	a			06s27										07s32		07s44									
London Euston 15 ⊖	a			06 50		07 48								07 52		08 05		08 09	08 14				08 27	08 46	

A Conveys a portion from Fort William, dep 1950

b Previous night, stops to pick up only

c Stops to pick up only

OVERNIGHT SLEEPERS. For sleeper trains, operated by First ScotRail, please refer to Tables 400 - 404

Table 65

Saturdays

until 30 June

Scotland and North West England - West Midlands and London

Route Diagram - see first Page of Table 65

		VT	TP	LM	VT	LM		VT	VT	TP	XC	VT	VT	LM	VT	VT		TP	XC	VT	EM	LM	VT	LM	VT
		◇1	◇1	◇1	◇1	◇1		◇1	◇1	◇1	◇1	◇1	◇1	◇1	◇1	◇1		◇1	◇1	◇1	◇	◇1	◇1	◇1	◇1
																		A							
		🍴			🍴			🍴	🍴	🛒	🛒	🍴	🍴		🍴	🍴		🛒	🛒	🍴			🍴		🍴
Inverness	d																								
Aberdeen	d																								
Dundee	d																								
Perth	d																								
Edinburgh 10	d																								
Haymarket	d																								
Glasgow Central 15	d								04 26																
Motherwell	d																								
Carstairs	d																								
Lockerbie	d																								
Carlisle 8	a								05 43																
	d								05 44																
Penrith North Lakes	d								05 59																
Windermere	d																								
Oxenholme Lake District	a								06 21																
	d								06 22																
Barrow-in-Furness	d		05 31															06 20							
Lancaster 6	a		06 23						06 36									07 21							
	d		06 23						06 37							06 58		07 22							
Blackpool North	d									06 40															
Preston 8	a		06 42						06 55	07 07						07 15		07 41							
Preston 8	d	06 17	06 44						06 58	07 09						07 17		07 47							
Wigan North Western	a	06 28							07 09							07 28									
	d	06 28							07 10							07 28									
Blackrod	d																								
Lostock	d									07 30															
Bolton	a		07 08							07 34								08 08							
Manchester Piccadilly 10 🚊	a		07 27							07 56								08 27							
Manchester Airport ✈	a		07 47							08 17								08 47							
Liverpool Lime Street 10	a																								
	d			06 32	06 45									07 04	07 19						06 49	07 34	07 48		
Liverpool South Parkway ✈	d			06 42										07 14							06 59	07 44			
Runcorn	d			06 50	07 01									07 22	07 36							07 52	08 04		
Warrington Bank Quay	a	06 39							07 20							07 39									
	d	06 39							07 20							07 39									
Hartford	d			07 02										07 36								08 04			
Manchester Piccadilly 10 🚊	d							06 55			07 07	07 15							07 27	07 35	07 42				07 55
Stockport	d							07 04			07 16	07 23							07 35	07 43	07a53				08 04
Wilmslow	d							07 11																	08 11
Holyhead	d																								
Bangor (Gwynedd)	d																								
Llandudno Junction	d																								
Wrexham General	d																								
Chester	d												07 17												
Crewe 10	a	06 58		07 14	07 18			07 27					07 36	07 47	07 52	07 58						08 19			08 27
	d	07 01		07 16	07 20			07 29					07 39	07 49	07 55	08 01						08 22			08 29
Macclesfield	d																		07 49	07 56					
Congleton	d																								
Stoke-on-Trent	d					←					07 44	07 50							08 07	08 12				←	
Stafford	a			07 40	07 38	07 40					08 02			08 10	08 14				08 25			08 42	08 35	08 42	
	d			07 41	07 39	07 41					08 03			08 10	08 16				08 26			08 43	08 36	08 43	
Penkridge	a			→		07 46								08 16								→		08 48	
Wolverhampton 7 🚊	a	07 32				07 57					08 17			08 28		08 31			08 39					08 58	
Birmingham New Street 12	a	07 55				08 17					08 39			08 47		08 55			08 58					09 18	
Birmingham International ✈	a																		09 13						
Coventry	a																		09 24						
Lichfield Trent Valley	a														08 30										
Tamworth Low Level	a														08 36										
Nuneaton	a																								
Rugby	a																						08 58		
Milton Keynes Central	a											08 46													
Watford Junction	a																								
London Euston 15 ⊖	a				08 59			09 04	09 12			09 23	09 30		09 46					09 42			10 00		10 04

A 🛒 from Preston

OVERNIGHT SLEEPERS. For sleeper trains, operated by First ScotRail, please refer to Tables 400 - 404

Scotland and North West England - West Midlands and London

Route Diagram - see first Page of Table 65

		VT		TP	XC	LM	VT	VT	VT	TP	XC	VT		EM	LM	VT	LM	VT	VT	SR	XC	LM		NT	TP
		◇1		◇1	◇1	◇1	◇1	◇1	◇1	◇1	◇1	◇1		◇	◇1	◇1	◇1	◇1	◇1		◇1	◇1			◇1
										A															
		⊡		⌶	⌶		⊡	⊡	⊡	⌶	⌶	⊡				⊡		⊡	⊡		⌶				⌶
Inverness	d																								
Aberdeen	d																								
Dundee	d																								
Perth	d																								
Edinburgh 10	d																								
Haymarket	d																								
Glasgow Central 15	d	05 40							05 50										06 30	07 05					
Motherwell	d								06 04										06 44	07 27					
Carstairs	d																			07a47					
Lockerbie	d																		07 25						
Carlisle 8	a	06 46							07 02										07 43						
	d	06 49							07 03										07 46						
Penrith North Lakes	d								07 18										08 00						
Windermere	d																								
Oxenholme Lake District	a	07 22							07 41										08 22						
	d	07 24							07 42										08 23						
Barrow-in-Furness	d									07 29															
Lancaster 6	a	07 37							07 56	08 26									08 37						
	d	07 38							07 57	08 27									08 38						
Blackpool North	d			07 44																				08 38	08 44
Preston 8	a	07 56		08 11					08 15	08 45									08 56					09 02	09 08
Preston 8	d	07 58		08 12					08 17	08 47									08 58					09 04	09 10
Wigan North Western	a	08 09							08 28										09 09					09 24	
	d	08 09							08 28										09 09					09 24	
Blackrod	d																								
Lostock	d																								
Bolton	a			08 34						09 08															09 34
Manchester Piccadilly 10	a			08 56						09 27															09 56
Manchester Airport	a			09 19						09 47															10 17
Liverpool Lime Street 10	a																							10 02	
	d					08 04								07 42	08 34	08 48						09 04		10 16	
Liverpool South Parkway	d					08 15								07 52	08 44							09 15		10a27	
Runcorn	d					08 24									08 52	09 04						09 24			
Warrington Bank Quay	a	08 20							08 39										09 20						
	d	08 20							08 39										09 20						
Hartford	d														09 06										
Manchester Piccadilly 10	d				08 07		08 15				08 27	08 35		08 43				08 55			09 07				
Stockport	d				08 16		08 23				08 35	08 43		08a53				09 04			09 16				
Wilmslow	d																	09 11							
Holyhead	d							06 52																	
Bangor (Gwynedd)	d							07 20																	
Llandudno Junction	d							07 38																	
Wrexham General	d																								
Chester	d							08 35																	
Crewe 10	a					08 47		08 54	08 58						09 20			09 27				09 44			
	d					08 49		08 56	09 01						09 22			09 29				09 49			
Macclesfield	d										08 49	08 56													
Congleton	d																								
Stoke-on-Trent	d				08 44		08 50				09 07	09 12					←				09 44				
Stafford	a				09 02	09 09					09 25				09 42	09 35	09 42				10 02	10 10			
	d				09 03	09 10					09 26				09 43	09 36	09 43				10 03	10 10			
Penkridge	a					09 15									→							10 16			
Wolverhampton 7	a				09 15	09 27			09 31		09 39						09 56				10 15	10 27			
Birmingham New Street 12	a				09 39	09 47			09 55		09 58						10 17				10 39	10 47			
Birmingham International	a										10 13														
Coventry	a										10 24														
Lichfield Trent Valley	a																								
Tamworth Low Level	a																								
Nuneaton	a															09 58									
Rugby	a																								
Milton Keynes Central	a						09 46	10 01																	
Watford Junction	a																								
London Euston 15 ⊖	a	10 12					10 23	10 37				10 42				11 01		11 04	11 12						

A ⌶ from Preston

OVERNIGHT SLEEPERS. For sleeper trains, operated by First ScotRail, please refer to Tables 400 - 404

Table 65

Saturdays
until 30 June

Scotland and North West England - West Midlands and London

Route Diagram - see first Page of Table 65

		VT	VT	VT	TP	XC	VT	EM		LM	VT	LM	VT	VT	XC	LM	NT	TP	TP		VT	VT	VT	TP	TP
		◇1	◇1	◇1	◇1	◇1	◇1	◇		◇1	◇1	◇1	◇1	◇1	◇1	◇1		◇1	◇1		◇1	◇1	◇1	◇1	◇1
																									A
		🍴	🍴	🍴	🛒	🛒	🍴				🍴		🍴	🍴	🛒			🛒	🛒		🍴	🍴	🍴		🛒
Inverness	d																								
Aberdeen	d																								
Dundee	d																								
Perth	d																								
Edinburgh 10	d			06 52														07 42							
Haymarket	d			06 56														07u46							
Glasgow Central 15	d				07 10									07 35									08 00		
Motherwell	d													07 52											
Carstairs	d																								
Lockerbie	d				08 06																				
Carlisle 8	a			08 05	08 29									08 46				08 59					09 08		
	d			08 07	08 29									08 49				08 59					09 09		
Penrith North Lakes	d			08 22	08 45																				
Windermere	d																							09 38	
Oxenholme Lake District	a				09 09									09 22										09 57	
	d				09 11									09 23										09 58	
Barrow-in-Furness	d																								09 23
Lancaster 6	a			08 56	09 26									09 37									09 56	10 16	10 25
	d			08 57	09 26									09 38									09 57	10 16	10 26
Blackpool North	d																09 37		09 43						
Preston 8	a			09 15	09 45									09 56			10 02	10 04	10 07				10 15	10 35	10 45
Preston 8	d			09 17	09 47									09 58			10 04	10 12					10 17		10 47
Wigan North Western	a			09 28										10 09			10 24						10 28		
	d			09 28										10 09			10 24						10 28		
Blackrod	d																								
Lostock	d																								
Bolton	a				10 08													10 34							11 08
Manchester Piccadilly 10	a				10 27													10 56							11 27
Manchester Airport ✈	a				10 47													11 17							11 47
Liverpool Lime Street 10	a																11 02								
	d							08 52		09 34	09 48					10 04	11 16								
Liverpool South Parkway ✈	d							09 03		09 44						10 15	11a27								
Runcorn	d									09 52	10 04					10 25									
Warrington Bank Quay	a			09 39										10 20									10 39		
	d			09 39										10 20									10 39		
Hartford	d									10 04															
Manchester Piccadilly 10	d	09 15				09 27	09 35	09 43					09 55		10 07						10 15				
Stockport	d	09 23				09 35	09 43	09a53					10 04		10 16						10 23				
Wilmslow	d												10 11												
Holyhead	d		07 55																			08 55			
Bangor (Gwynedd)	d		08 22																			09 22			
Llandudno Junction	d		08 40																			09 40			
Wrexham General	d																								
Chester	d		09 35																			10 35			
Crewe 10	a		09 54	09 58						10 19			10 27			10 45						10 54	10 58		
	d		09 56	10 01						10 22			10 29			10 49						10 56	11 01		
Macclesfield	d					09 49	09 56																		
Congleton	d																								
Stoke-on-Trent	d	09 50				10 07	10 12					←			10 44						10 50				
Stafford	a					10 25				10 42	10 35	10 42			11 02	11 09									
	d					10 26				10 43	10 36	10 43			11 03	11 10									
Penkridge	a									→						11 15									
Wolverhampton 7	a			10 31		10 39						10 56			11 16	11 27							11 32		
Birmingham New Street 12	a			10 55		10 58						11 17			11 39	11 47							11 55		
Birmingham International ✈	a					11 13																			
Coventry	a					11 24																			
Lichfield Trent Valley	a																								
Tamworth Low Level	a																								
Nuneaton	a																								
Rugby	a																								
Milton Keynes Central	a	10 46	11 01																		11 46	12 01			
Watford Junction	a																								
London Euston 15 ⊖	a	11 23	11 38				11 42				11 56		12 04	12 12							12 23	12 38			

A 🛒 from Preston

OVERNIGHT SLEEPERS. For sleeper trains, operated by First ScotRail, please refer to Tables 400 - 404

Table 65

Saturdays

until 30 June

Scotland and North West England - West Midlands and London

Route Diagram - see first Page of Table 65

		NT	XC	VT	EM		LM	VT	LM	VT	VT	XC	LM	NT	TP		VT	VT	VT	SR	TP	XC	VT	EM	LM
			◇1	◇1	◇		◇1	◇1	◇1	◇1	◇1	◇1	◇1		◇1		◇1	◇1	◇1		◇1 A	◇1	◇1	◇	◇1
			🛒	🍴				🍴		🍴	🍴	🛒			🛒		🍴	🍴	🍴		🛒	🛒	🍴		
Inverness	d																								
Aberdeen	d																								
Dundee	d																								
Perth	d																								
Edinburgh 10	d																		08 52	09 03					
Haymarket	d																		08 57	09 07					
Glasgow Central 15	d										08 40														
Motherwell	d																								
Carstairs	d																			09a44					
Lockerbie	d																								
Carlisle 8	a										09 46								10 05						
	d										09 49								10 07						
Penrith North Lakes	d										10 03														
Windermere	d																				10 49				
Oxenholme Lake District	a																		10 41		11 08				
	d																		10 42		11 09				
Barrow-in-Furness	d	10 16																							
Lancaster 6	a	11 21									10 37								10 56		11 26				
	d										10 38								10 57		11 26				
Blackpool North	d													10 37	10 44										
Preston 8	a										10 56			11 02	11 08				11 15		11 45				
Preston 8	d										10 58			11 04	11 10				11 17		11 47				
Wigan North Western	a										11 09			11 24					11 28						
	d										11 09			11 24					11 28						
Blackrod	d																								
Lostock	d																								
Bolton	a														11 34						12 08				
Manchester Piccadilly 10 🚊	a														11 56						12 27				
Manchester Airport ✈	a														12 17						12 47				
Liverpool Lime Street 10	a													12 02											
	d				09 52		10 34	10 48					11 04	12 16										10 52	11 34
Liverpool South Parkway ✈	d				10 03		10 44						11 15	12a27										11 03	11 44
Runcorn	d						10 52	11 04					11 25												11 52
Warrington Bank Quay	a										11 20								11 39						
	d										11 20								11 39						
Hartford	d						11 04																		12 04
Manchester Piccadilly 10 🚊	d		10 27	10 35	10 43					10 55		11 07					11 15					11 27	11 35	11 43	
Stockport	d		10 35	10 43	10a53					11 04		11 16					11 23					11 35	11 43	11a53	
Wilmslow	d									11 11															
Holyhead	d																								
Bangor (Gwynedd)	d																								
Llandudno Junction	d																								
Wrexham General	d																								
Chester	d																	11 35							
Crewe 10	a						11 19			11 27			11 45					11 54	11 58						12 19
	d						11 22			11 29			11 49					11 56	12 01						12 22
Macclesfield	d		10 49	10 56																		11 49	11 56		
Congleton	d																								
Stoke-on-Trent	d		11 07	11 12					←			11 44					11 50					12 07	12 12		
Stafford	a		11 25				11 42	11 35	11 42			12 02	12 09									12 24			12 42
	d		11 26				11 43	11 36	11 43			12 03	12 10									12 25			12 43
Penkridge	a						→						12 15												→
Wolverhampton 7 🚊	a		11 39						11 56			12 16	12 27						12 31			12 39			
Birmingham New Street 12	a		11 58						12 17			12 39	12 47						12 55			12 58			
Birmingham International ✈	a		12 13																			13 13			
Coventry	a		12 24																			13 24			
Lichfield Trent Valley	a																								
Tamworth Low Level	a																								
Nuneaton	a																								
Rugby	a																								
Milton Keynes Central	a																12 46	13 01							
Watford Junction	a																								
London Euston 15 ⊖	a			12 42				12 56		13 04	13 12						13 23	13 38					13 42		

A 🛒 from Preston

OVERNIGHT SLEEPERS. For sleeper trains, operated by First ScotRail, please refer to Tables 400 - 404

Table 65

Saturdays until 30 June

Scotland and North West England - West Midlands and London

Route Diagram - see first Page of Table 65

		VT	LM	VT	VT	TP	XC	LM	NT	TP	VT	VT	VT	TP	TP	TP	TP	TP	TP	XC	VT	EM
		◇1	◇1	◇1	◇1	◇1	◇1	◇1		◇1	◇1	◇1	◇1	◇1	◇1	◇1	◇1	◇1	◇1	◇1	◇1	◇
						A								A	A	A	B	B	B			
Inverness	d																					
Aberdeen	d																					
Dundee	d																					
Perth	d																					
Edinburgh 10	d														09 51			09 51				
Haymarket	d														09u56			09u56				
Glasgow Central 15	d				09 40								10 00	10 10		10 10			10 10			
Motherwell	d																					
Carstairs	d																					
Lockerbie	d														11 01			11 01				
Carlisle 8	a				10 47								11 08	11 26	11 22	11 26		11 22	11 26			
	d				10 49								11 09	11 27	11 22	11 27		11 29				
Penrith North Lakes	d												11 24	11 43		11 43		11 45				
Windermere	d																					
Oxenholme Lake District	a				11 22									12 06		12 06		12 09				
	d				11 23									12 07		12 07		12 10				
Barrow-in-Furness	d					11 11											11 25					
Lancaster 6	a				11 37	12 04									12 14		12 18	12 26				
	d				11 38	12 04									12 15		12 18	12 26				
Blackpool North	d								11 37	11 44												
Preston 8	a				11 56	12 23			12 02	12 08			12 15	12 37	12 33	12 37	12 37	12 45				
Preston 8	d				11 58				12 04	12 10			12 17			12 47		12 47				
Wigan North Western	a				12 09				12 24				12 28									
	d				12 09				12 24				12 28									
Blackrod	d																					
Lostock	d																					
Bolton	a									12 34						13 08		13 08				
Manchester Piccadilly 10	a									12 56						13 27		13 27				
Manchester Airport ✈	a									13 17						13 47		13 47				
Liverpool Lime Street 10	a								13 02													
	d	11 48						12 04	13 16													11 52
Liverpool South Parkway ✈	d							12 15	13a27													12 03
Runcorn	d	12 04						12 25														
Warrington Bank Quay	a				12 20								12 39									
	d				12 20								12 39									
Hartford	d																					
Manchester Piccadilly 10	d			11 55			12 07				12 15									12 27	12 35	12 43
Stockport	d			12 04			12 16				12 23									12 35	12 43	12a53
Wilmslow	d			12 11																		
Holyhead	d																					
Bangor (Gwynedd)	d																					
Llandudno Junction	d																					
Wrexham General	d																					
Chester	d											12 35										
Crewe 10	a			12 27				12 45				12 54	12 58									
	d			12 29				12 49				12 57	13 01									
Macclesfield	d																			12 49	12 56	
Congleton	d																					
Stoke-on-Trent	d		←				12 44				12 50									13 07	13 12	
Stafford	a	12 35	12 42				13 02	13 09												13 25		
	d	12 36	12 43				13 03	13 10												13 26		
Penkridge	a							13 15														
Wolverhampton 7	a		12 56				13 15	13 27					13 31							13 39		
Birmingham New Street 12	a		13 17				13 39	13 47					13 55							13 58		
Birmingham International ✈	a																			14 13		
Coventry	a																			14 24		
Lichfield Trent Valley	a																					
Tamworth Low Level	a																					
Nuneaton	a																					
Rugby	a																					
Milton Keynes Central	a										13 46	14 01										
Watford Junction	a																					
London Euston 15 ⊖	a	13 56		14 04	14 12						14 23	14 38									14 42	

A 30 June

B not 30 June

OVERNIGHT SLEEPERS. For sleeper trains, operated by First ScotRail, please refer to Tables 400 - 404

Table 65

Saturdays
until 30 June

Scotland and North West England - West Midlands and London

Route Diagram - see first Page of Table 65

		LM	VT	LM	VT	VT	XC		LM	NT	TP	VT	VT	VT	VT	TP	XC		VT	EM	LM	VT	LM	VT	VT
		◇[1]	◇[1]	◇[1]	◇[1]	◇[1]	◇[1]		◇[1]		◇[1]	◇[1]	◇[1]	◇[1]	◇[1]	◇[1]	◇[1]		◇[1]	◇	◇[1]	◇[1]	◇[1]	◇[1]	◇[1]
																A									
			☕		☕	☕	🛒				🛒	☕	☕	☕	☕	🛒	🛒		☕			☕		☕	☕
Inverness	d																								
Aberdeen	d																								
Dundee	d																								
Perth	d																								
Edinburgh [10]	d														10 52										
Haymarket	d														10 57										
Glasgow Central [15]	d					10 40																			11 40
Motherwell	d																								
Carstairs	d																								
Lockerbie	d																								
Carlisle [8]	a					11 47									12 05										12 46
	d					11 49									12 07										12 49
Penrith North Lakes	d																								13 03
Windermere	d															12 51									
Oxenholme Lake District	a					12 22									12 41	13 07									
	d					12 23									12 43	13 09									
Barrow-in-Furness	d																								
Lancaster [6]	a					12 37									12 56	13 26									13 37
	d					12 38									12 57	13 26									13 38
Blackpool North	d									12 37	12 44														
Preston [8]	a					12 56				13 02	13 08				13 15	13 45									13 56
Preston [8]	d					12 58				13 04	13 10				13 17	13 47									13 58
Wigan North Western	a					13 09				13 24					13 28										14 09
	d					13 09				13 24					13 28										14 09
Blackrod	d																								
Lostock	d																								
Bolton	a										13 34					14 08									
Manchester Piccadilly [10] 🚋	a										13 56					14 27									
Manchester Airport ✈	a										14 17					14 47									
Liverpool Lime Street [10]	a									14 02															
	d	12 34	12 48						13 04	14 16										12 52	13 34	13 48			
Liverpool South Parkway ✈	d	12 44							13 15	14a27										13 03	13 44				
Runcorn	d	12 52	13 04						13 25												13 52	14 04			
Warrington Bank Quay	a					13 20									13 39										14 20
	d					13 20									13 39										14 20
Hartford	d	13 06																			14 04				
Manchester Piccadilly [10] 🚋	d				12 55		13 07					13 15					13 27		13 35	13 43				13 55	
Stockport	d				13 04		13 16					13 23					13 35		13 43	13a53				14 04	
Wilmslow	d				13 11																			14 11	
Holyhead	d												11 55												
Bangor (Gwynedd)	d												12 21												
Llandudno Junction	d												12 39												
Wrexham General	d																								
Chester	d												13 35	13 35											
Crewe [10]	a	13 20			13 27				13 45				13 54	13 54	13 58						14 19			14 27	
	d	13 22			13 29				13 49				13 56	13 56	14 01						14 22			14 29	
Macclesfield	d																13 49		13 56						
Congleton	d																								
Stoke-on-Trent	d			←			13 44					13 50					14 07		14 12				←		
Stafford	a	13 42	13 35	13 42			14 02		14 09								14 25				14 46	14 35	14 46		
	d	13 43	13 36	13 43			14 03		14 10								14 26				14 46	14 36	14 46		
Penkridge	a	↪							14 15												↪				
Wolverhampton [7] 🚋	a			13 56			14 16		14 27						14 31		14 39						14 59		
Birmingham New Street [12]	a			14 17			14 39		14 47						14 55		14 58						15 18		
Birmingham International ✈	a																15 13								
Coventry	a																15 24								
Lichfield Trent Valley	a																								
Tamworth Low Level	a																								
Nuneaton	a																								
Rugby	a																								
Milton Keynes Central	a											14 46	15 01	15 01											
Watford Junction	a																								
London Euston [15] ⊖	a		14 56		15 04	15 12						15 23	15 38	15 38					15 42			15 56		16 04	16 12

A 🛒 from Preston

OVERNIGHT SLEEPERS. For sleeper trains, operated by First ScotRail, please refer to Tables 400 - 404

Table 65

Saturdays

until 30 June

Scotland and North West England - West Midlands and London

Route Diagram - see first Page of Table 65

		XC	LM		NT	TP	VT	VT	VT	TP	TP	NT	XC		VT	EM	LM	VT	LM	VT	VT	XC	LM		NT
		◇1	◇1			◇1	◇1	◇1	◇1	◇1	◇1		◇1		◇1	◇	◇1	◇1	◇1	◇1	◇1	◇1	◇1		
										A															
		🛒				🛒	🍴	🍴	🍴	🛒	🛒		🛒		🍴			🍴		🍴	🍴	🛒			
Inverness	d																								
Aberdeen	d																								
Dundee	d																								
Perth	d																								
Edinburgh 10	d										12 08														
Haymarket	d										12u12														
Glasgow Central 15	d								12 00												12 40				
Motherwell	d																								
Carstairs	d																								
Lockerbie	d										13 07														
Carlisle 8	a								13 08		13 29										13 47				
	d								13 09		13 29										13 49				
Penrith North Lakes	d																								
Windermere	d																								
Oxenholme Lake District	a										14 06										14 22				
	d										14 07										14 24				
Barrow-in-Furness	d									13 25		14 16													
Lancaster 6	a								13 56	14 18	14 21	15 20									14 37				
	d								13 58	14 18	14 22										14 38				
Blackpool North	d				13 37	13 44																			14 37
Preston 8	a				14 02	14 08			14 15	14 37	14 41										14 56				15 02
Preston 8	d				14 04	14 10			14 17	14 47											14 58				15 04
Wigan North Western	a				14 24				14 28												15 09				15 24
	d				14 24				14 28												15 09				15 24
Blackrod	d																								
Lostock	d																								
Bolton	a					14 34				15 08															
Manchester Piccadilly 10	a					14 56				15 27															
Manchester Airport	a					15 17				15 47															
Liverpool Lime Street 10	a				15 02																				16 02
	d		14 04		15 16											13 52	14 34	14 48					15 04		16 16
Liverpool South Parkway	d		14 15		15a27											14 03	14 44						15 15		16a27
Runcorn	d		14 25														14 52	15 04					15 25		
Warrington Bank Quay	a								14 39												15 20				
	d								14 39												15 20				
Hartford	d																15 04								
Manchester Piccadilly 10	d	14 07					14 15						14 27		14 35	14 43				14 55		15 07			
Stockport	d	14 16					14 23						14 35		14 43	14a53				15 04		15 16			
Wilmslow	d																			15 11					
Holyhead	d																								
Bangor (Gwynedd)	d																								
Llandudno Junction	d																								
Wrexham General	d																								
Chester	d							14 35																	
Crewe 10	a		14 45					14 54	14 58								15 19			15 27			15 45		
	d		14 49					14 56	15 01								15 22			15 29			15 49		
Macclesfield	d												14 49		14 56										
Congleton	d																								
Stoke-on-Trent	d	14 44					14 50						15 07		15 12				←			15 44			
Stafford	a	15 02	15 09										15 25				15 42	15 35	15 42			16 02	16 09		
	d	15 03	15 10										15 26				15 43	15 36	15 43			16 03	16 10		
Penkridge	a		15 15														→						16 15		
Wolverhampton 7	a	15 16	15 27						15 31				15 39						15 56			16 16	16 27		
Birmingham New Street 12	a	15 39	15 47						15 55				15 58						16 17			16 39	16 47		
Birmingham International	a												16 13												
Coventry	a												16 24												
Lichfield Trent Valley	a																								
Tamworth Low Level	a																								
Nuneaton	a																								
Rugby	a																								
Milton Keynes Central	a						15 46	16 01																	
Watford Junction	a																								
London Euston 15	a						16 23	16 38							16 42			16 56		17 04	17 12				

A 🛒 from Preston

OVERNIGHT SLEEPERS. For sleeper trains, operated by First ScotRail, please refer to Tables 400 - 404

Table 65

Scotland and North West England - West Midlands and London

Route Diagram - see first Page of Table 65

		TP	VT	VT	VT	TP	XC	VT	EM		LM	VT	LM	VT	VT	XC	LM	NT	TP		VT	VT	VT	TP	XC
		◇1	◇1	◇1	◇1	◇1	◇1	◇1	◇		◇1	◇1	◇1	◇1	◇1	◇1	◇1		◇1		◇1	◇1	◇1	◇1	◇1
		🛒	🍴	🍴	🍴	🛒	🛒	🍴				🍴		🍴	🍴	🛒			🛒		🍴	🍴	🍴	🛒	🛒
Inverness	d																								
Aberdeen	d																								
Dundee	d																								
Perth	d																								
Edinburgh 10	d				12 52																			14 07	
Haymarket	d				12 57																			14u11	
Glasgow Central 15	d					13 09									13 40								14 00		
Motherwell	d																								
Carstairs	d																								
Lockerbie	d					14 06																		15 06	
Carlisle 8	a				14 05	14 29									14 46								15 09	15 27	
	d				14 07	14 29									14 49								15 11	15 27	
Penrith North Lakes	d				14 22	14 45																		15 43	
Windermere	d																								
Oxenholme Lake District	a					15 09									15 22								15 45	16 06	
	d					15 10									15 23								15 46	16 07	
Barrow-in-Furness	d																								
Lancaster 6	a				14 56	15 26									15 37									16 26	
	d				14 57	15 26									15 38									16 26	
Blackpool North	d	14 44																15 37	15 44						
Preston 8	a	15 08			15 15	15 45									15 56			16 02	16 08				16 15	16 45	
Preston 8	d	15 10			15 17	15 47									15 58			16 04	16 10				16 17	16 47	
Wigan North Western	a				15 28										16 09			16 24					16 28		
	d				15 28										16 09			16 24					16 28		
Blackrod	d																								
Lostock	d																								
Bolton	a	15 34				16 08													16 34					17 08	
Manchester Piccadilly 10 ⛴	a	15 56				16 27													16 56					17 27	
Manchester Airport ✈	a	16 17				16 47													17 17					17 48	
Liverpool Lime Street 10	a																	17 05							
	d								14 52		15 34	15 48					16 04								
Liverpool South Parkway ✈	d								15 03		15 44						16 15								
Runcorn	d										15 52	16 04					16 25								
Warrington Bank Quay	a				15 39										16 20								16 39		
	d				15 39										16 20								16 39		
Hartford	d										16 04														
Manchester Piccadilly 10 ⛴	d		15 15				15 27	15 35	15 43					15 55		16 07					16 15				16 27
Stockport	d		15 23				15 35	15 43	15a53					16 04		16 16					16 23				16 35
Wilmslow	d													16 11											
Holyhead	d																					14 38			
Bangor (Gwynedd)	d																					15 07			
Llandudno Junction	d																					15 27			
Wrexham General	d																								
Chester	d			15 35																		16 24			
Crewe 10	a			15 54	15 58						16 19			16 27			16 45					16 47	16 58		
	d			15 56	16 01						16 22			16 29			16 49					16 56	17 01		
Macclesfield	d						15 49	15 56																	16 49
Congleton	d																								
Stoke-on-Trent	d		15 50				16 07	16 12					←			16 44					16 50				17 07
Stafford	a						16 24				16 46	16 35	16 46			17 02	17 09								17 25
	d						16 25				16 46	16 36	16 46			17 03	17 10								17 26
Penkridge	a										→						17 15								
Wolverhampton 7 ⛴	a				16 31		16 39						16 59			17 16	17 27						17 31		17 39
Birmingham New Street 12	a				16 55		16 58						17 18			17 39	17 47						17 55		17 58
Birmingham International ✈	a						17 13																		18 13
Coventry	a						17 24																		18 24
Lichfield Trent Valley	a																								
Tamworth Low Level	a																								
Nuneaton	a																								
Rugby	a																								
Milton Keynes Central	a		16 46	17 01																	17 46	18 01			
Watford Junction	a																								
London Euston 15 ⊖	a		17 23	17 38				17 42				17 56		18 04	18 12						18 23	18 38			

OVERNIGHT SLEEPERS. For sleeper trains, operated by First ScotRail, please refer to Tables 400 - 404

Table 65

Saturdays
until 30 June

Scotland and North West England - West Midlands and London

Route Diagram - see first Page of Table 65

		VT	EM	LM	VT		LM	VT	VT	SR	XC	LM	NT	TP	VT		TP	VT	TP	XC	VT	EM	LM	VT	LM
		◇1	◇	◇1	◇1		◇1	◇1	◇1		◇1	◇1		◇1	◇1		◇1	◇1	◇1	◇1	◇1	◇	◇1	◇1	◇1
		🍴			🍴			🍴	🍴		🛒			🛒	🍴			🍴	🛒	🛒	🍴			🍴	
Inverness	d																								
Aberdeen	d																								
Dundee	d																								
Perth	d																								
Edinburgh 10	d														14 52										
Haymarket	d														14 57										
Glasgow Central 15	d								14 40	15 14															
Motherwell	d									15 34															
Carstairs	d									15a51															
Lockerbie	d																								
Carlisle 8	a								15 46						16 05										
	d								15 49						16 07										
Penrith North Lakes	d														16 22										
Windermere	d																								
Oxenholme Lake District	a								16 22																
	d								16 24																
Barrow-in-Furness	d																16 22								
Lancaster 6	a								16 37						16 56		17 19								
	d								16 38						16 57		17 20								
Blackpool North	d												16 35	16 40					17 20						
Preston 8	a								16 56				17 02	17 08	17 15		17 39		17 45						
Preston 8	d								16 58				17 04	17 10	17 17				17 47						
Wigan North Western	a								17 09				17 24		17 28										
	d								17 09				17 24		17 28										
Blackrod	d																								
Lostock	d																								
Bolton	a													17 34					18 08						
Manchester Piccadilly 10	a													17 56					18 27						
Manchester Airport ✈	a													18 17					18 47						
Liverpool Lime Street 10	a												18 02												
	d		15 52	16 34	16 48							17 04										16 52	17 34	17 48	
Liverpool South Parkway ✈	d		16 03	16 44								17 15										17 03	17 44		
Runcorn	d			16 52	17 04							17 25											17 52	18 04	
Warrington Bank Quay	a								17 20						17 39										
	d								17 20						17 39										
Hartford	d			17 06																			18 06		
Manchester Piccadilly 10	d	16 35	16 43					16 55			17 06							17 15		17 27	17 35	17 43			
Stockport	d	16 43	16a53					17 04										17 23		17 36	17 43	17a53			
Wilmslow	d							17 11																	
Holyhead	d																								
Bangor (Gwynedd)	d																								
Llandudno Junction	d																								
Wrexham General	d																								
Chester	d																								
Crewe 10	a			17 20				17 27				17 47			17 59								18 20		
	d			17 22				17 29				17 49			18 01								18 22		
Macclesfield	d	16 56									17 26										17 56				
Congleton	d																			17 54					
Stoke-on-Trent	d	17 12					←				17 44							17 50		18 08	18 12				←
Stafford	a			17 42	17 35		17 42				18 03	18 09								18 26			18 42	18 35	18 42
	d			17 43	17 36		17 43				18 04	18 10								18 27			18 43	18 36	18 43
Penkridge	a			↦								18 15											↦		
Wolverhampton 7	a						17 56				18 16	18 27			18 31					18 40					18 56
Birmingham New Street 12	a						18 17				18 38	18 47			18 55					18 58					19 17
Birmingham International ✈	a																			19 13					
Coventry	a																			19 24					
Lichfield Trent Valley	a																								
Tamworth Low Level	a																								
Nuneaton	a																								
Rugby	a																								
Milton Keynes Central	a																	18 46							
Watford Junction	a																								
London Euston 15 ⊖	a	18 42			18 56			19 04	19 12									19 23			19 42			19 56	

OVERNIGHT SLEEPERS. For sleeper trains, operated by First ScotRail, please refer to Tables 400 - 404

Table 65

Saturdays

until 30 June

Scotland and North West England - West Midlands and London

Route Diagram - see first Page of Table 65

		VT	VT	XC	LM	NT	TP	VT	TP	TP	VT	XC	VT	EM	LM	VT	LM	VT	VT	XC	LM	NT
		◇1	◇1	◇1	◇1		◇1	◇1	◇1	◇1	◇1	◇1	◇1	◇	◇1	◇1	◇1	◇1	◇1	◇1	◇1	
							A															
		⊡	⊡	⚲			⚲	⊡		⚲	⊡	⚲	⊡			⊡		⊡	⊡	⚲		
Inverness	d																					
Aberdeen	d																					
Dundee	d																					
Perth	d																					
Edinburgh 10	d									16 12												
Haymarket	d									16u16												
Glasgow Central 15	d		15 40					16 00											16 40			
Motherwell	d																		16 54			
Carstairs	d																					
Lockerbie	d									17 11												
Carlisle 8	a		16 46					17 08		17 33									17 49			
	d		16 49					17 09		17 34									17 52			
Penrith North Lakes	d		17 03							17 49												
Windermere	d						17 06															
Oxenholme Lake District	a						17 25	17 44											18 25			
	d						17 30	17 44											18 26			
Barrow-in-Furness	d								17 21													
Lancaster 6	a		17 37				17 47		18 16	18 26									18 40			
	d		17 38				17 48		18 17	18 26									18 41			
Blackpool North	d					17 37																18 37
Preston 8	a		17 56			18 02	18 06	18 15	18 36	18 45									18 59			19 00
Preston 8	d		17 58			18 04	18 08	18 17		18 47									19 01			19 04
Wigan North Western	a		18 09			18 24		18 28											19 12			19 24
	d		18 09			18 24		18 28											19 12			19 24
Blackrod	d																					
Lostock	d						18 30															
Bolton	a						18 34			19 08												
Manchester Piccadilly 10	a						18 56			19 27												
Manchester Airport ✈	a						19 17			19 50												
Liverpool Lime Street 10	a					19 02																20 02
	d				18 04									17 52	18 34	18 48					19 04	
Liverpool South Parkway ✈	d				18 15									18 03	18 44						19 14	
Runcorn	d				18 24										18 52	19 04					19 23	
Warrington Bank Quay	a		18 20					18 39											19 23			
	d		18 20					18 39											19 23			
Hartford	d														19 04							
Manchester Piccadilly 10	d	17 55		18 05							18 15	18 27	18 35	18 43				18 55		19 07		
Stockport	d	18 04		18 13							18 23	18 35	18 43	18a53				19 04		19 16		
Wilmslow	d	18 11																19 11				
Holyhead	d																					
Bangor (Gwynedd)	d																					
Llandudno Junction	d																					
Wrexham General	d																					
Chester	d																					
Crewe 10	a	18 27			18 46			18 59							19 19			19 27			19 49	
	d	18 29			18 49			19 01							19 22			19 29			19 51	
Macclesfield	d			18 26									18 56									
Congleton	d											18 54										
Stoke-on-Trent	d			18 44							18 49	19 07	19 12				←			19 44		
Stafford	a			19 02	19 09							19 25			19 42	19 35	19 42			20 02	20 11	
	d			19 03	19 10							19 25			19 43	19 36	19 43			20 03	20 12	
Penkridge	a				19 15										→		19 48					
Wolverhampton 7	a			19 16	19 27			19 31				19 39					19 59			20 16	20 28	
Birmingham New Street 12	a			19 33	19 47			19 55				19 58					20 17			20 33	20 47	
Birmingham International ✈	a											20 13										
Coventry	a											20 24										
Lichfield Trent Valley	a																					
Tamworth Low Level	a																					
Nuneaton	a																					
Rugby	a																					
Milton Keynes Central	a										19 45								20 41			
Watford Junction	a																		21s15			
London Euston 15 ⊖	a	20 04	20 15								20 24		20 59			21 15		21 18	21 38			

A ⚲ from Preston

OVERNIGHT SLEEPERS. For sleeper trains, operated by First ScotRail, please refer to Tables 400 - 404

Table 65

Saturdays
until 30 June

Scotland and North West England - West Midlands and London

Route Diagram - see first Page of Table 65

		TP	VT	TP	XC	VT	EM		LM	VT	LM	VT	NT	TP	XC	VT	TP		SR	XC	VT	EM	LM	XC	VT
		◇1	◇1	◇1	◇1	◇1	◇		◇1	◇1	◇1	◇1		◇1	◇1	◇1	◇1			◇1	◇1	◇	◇1	◇1	◇1
					A																				
			🍴	trolley	trolley	🍴				🍴		🍴				🍴	trolley				🍴				🍴
Inverness	d																								
Aberdeen	d																								
Dundee	d																								
Perth	d																								
Edinburgh [10]	d		16 52														18 12		18 24						
Haymarket	d		16 57														18u16		18 28						
Glasgow Central [15]	d			17 06								17 40				18 00									18 40
Motherwell	d																								
Carstairs	d																		19a09						
Lockerbie	d			18 06								18 32					19 11								
Carlisle [8]	a		18 06	18 28								18 50				19 08	19 34								19 46
	d		18 08	18 29								18 52				19 09	19 34								19 48
Penrith North Lakes	d			18 45								19 06					19 49								20 02
Windermere	d																								
Oxenholme Lake District	a		18 41	19 09								19 28					20 12								20 24
	d		18 42	19 10								19 29					20 13								20 25
Barrow-in-Furness	d																								
Lancaster [6]	a		18 56	19 26								19 43				19 55	20 26								20 39
	d		18 57	19 26								19 44				19 56	20 26								20 40
Blackpool North	d	18 44											19 37	19 44											
Preston [8]	a	19 08	19 15	19 45								20 02	20 02	20 08		20 15	20 45								20 58
Preston [8]	d	19 10	19 17	19 47								20 04	20 04	20 10		20 17	20 47								21 00
Wigan North Western	a		19 28									20 15	20 24			20 28									21 11
	d		19 28									20 15	20 24			20 28									21 11
Blackrod	d																								
Lostock	d																								
Bolton	a	19 34		20 08										20 34			21 08								
Manchester Piccadilly [10]	a	19 56		20 27										20 56			21 27								
Manchester Airport ✈	a	20 17		20 47										21 17			21 47								
Liverpool Lime Street [10]	a												21 02												
	d						18 52		19 34	19 48												19 52	20 34		
Liverpool South Parkway ✈	d						19 03		19 44													20 03	20 44		
Runcorn	d								19 52	20 04													20 52		
Warrington Bank Quay	a		19 39									20 26				20 39									21 22
	d		19 39									20 26				20 39									21 22
Hartford	d								20 04														21 03		
Manchester Piccadilly [10]	d				19 27	19 35	19 43								20 07					20 27	20 35	20 43		21 07	
Stockport	d				19 35	19 43	19a53								20 16					20 35	20 43	20a53			
Wilmslow	d																								
Holyhead	d																								
Bangor (Gwynedd)	d																								
Llandudno Junction	d																								
Wrexham General	d																								
Chester	d																								
Crewe [10]	a		19 59						20 16			20 45				20 59							21 16		21 41
	d		20 01						20 22			20 47				21 01							21 17		21 43
Macclesfield	d				19 49	19 56														20 49	20 56				
Congleton	d																								
Stoke-on-Trent	d				20 07	20 12					←				20 44					21 07	21 12			21 45	
Stafford	a				20 25				20 44	20 35	20 44				21 02					21 26			21 42	22 02	22 07
	d				20 26				20 45	20 36	20 45				21 03					21 27			21 42	22 03	22 08
Penkridge	a								→		20 50												21 48		
Wolverhampton [7]	a		20 32		20 39						21 01				21 15	21 31				21 39			21 58	22 14	22 22
Birmingham New Street [12]	a		20 55		20 58						21 19				21 32	21 54				21 58			22 20	22 32	22 46
Birmingham International ✈	a				21 13																				
Coventry	a				21 24																				
Lichfield Trent Valley	a																								
Tamworth Low Level	a																								
Nuneaton	a																								
Rugby	a																								
Milton Keynes Central	a					21 10						21 50									22 10				
Watford Junction	a																				22s40				
London Euston [15] ⊖	a					22 00				22 14		22 44									23 02				

A trolley to Birmingham New Street

OVERNIGHT SLEEPERS. For sleeper trains, operated by First ScotRail, please refer to Tables 400 - 404

Table 65

Saturdays
until 30 June

Scotland and North West England - West Midlands and London

Route Diagram - see first Page of Table 65

		TP	TP		VT	XC	EM	LM	EM	TP	NT	TP	LM		TP
		◇1	◇1		◇1	◇1	◇	◇1	◇	◇1		◇1	1		◇1
					🍴										
Inverness	d														
Aberdeen	d														
Dundee	d														
Perth	d														
Edinburgh 10	d				18 52										
Haymarket	d				18 57										
Glasgow Central 15	d														
Motherwell	d														
Carstairs	d														
Lockerbie	d														
Carlisle 8	a				20 06										
	d				20 08										
Penrith North Lakes	d				20 23										
Windermere	d									21 40					
Oxenholme Lake District	a				20 46					21 59					
	d				20 46					22 01					
Barrow-in-Furness	d	19 33									21 43				
Lancaster 6	a	20 34			21 00					22 17	22 45				
	d	20 35			21 01					22 17	22 46				
Blackpool North	d		20 42									21 44			22 44
Preston 8	a	20 53	21 06		21 19					22 38	23 11	22 08			23 08
Preston 8	d	21 10			21 21							22 10			23 10
Wigan North Western	a				21 32										
	d				21 32										
Blackrod	d														
Lostock	d														
Bolton	a	21 34										22 34			23 34
Manchester Piccadilly 10	a	21 56										22 56			23 53
Manchester Airport ✈	a	22 17										23 17			00 23
Liverpool Lime Street 10	a														
	d						20 52	21 34	21 37				22 04		
Liverpool South Parkway ✈	d						21 03	21 44	21 47				22 14		
Runcorn	d							21 52					22 23		
Warrington Bank Quay	a				21 43										
	d				21 43										
Hartford	d							22 04					22 34		
Manchester Piccadilly 10	d					21 27	21 43		22 31						
Stockport	d					21 36	21a52		22a41						
Wilmslow	d														
Holyhead	d														
Bangor (Gwynedd)	d														
Llandudno Junction	d														
Wrexham General	d														
Chester	d														
Crewe 10	a				22 03			22 21					22 48		
	d				22 05			22 23							
Macclesfield	d					21 50									
Congleton	d														
Stoke-on-Trent	d					22 08									
Stafford	a				22 24	22 32		22 47							
	d				22 25	22 33		22 47							
Penkridge	a							22 53							
Wolverhampton 7	a				22 39	22 45		23 03							
Birmingham New Street 12	a				22 59	23 02		23 21							
Birmingham International ✈	a														
Coventry	a														
Lichfield Trent Valley	a														
Tamworth Low Level	a														
Nuneaton	a														
Rugby	a														
Milton Keynes Central	a														
Watford Junction	a														
London Euston 15 ⊖	a														

OVERNIGHT SLEEPERS. For sleeper trains, operated by First ScotRail, please refer to Tables 400 - 404

Table 65

Saturdays

7 July to 8 September

Scotland and North West England - West Midlands and London

Route Diagram - see first Page of Table 65

		TP	LM	SR	SR	SR	SR	TP	NT	AW		TP	TP	XC	VT	XC	VT	LM	VT	VT		TP	XC	VT	VT
				B	B	B	B																		
		◇1	◇1					◇1				◇1	◇1	◇1	◇1	◇1	◇1	◇1	◇1	◇1		◇1	◇1	◇1	◇1
				🛏	🛏	🛏	🛏							⊼	🍴	⊼	🍴		🍴	🍴			⊼	🍴	🍴
						A	A																		
Inverness	d					20p47																			
Aberdeen	d						21p42																		
Dundee	d						23b06																		
Perth	d					23b21																			
Edinburgh 10	d			23p40																					
Haymarket	d																								
Glasgow Central 15	d				23p40																				
Motherwell	d				23b56																				
Carstairs	d			00u16																					
Lockerbie	d																								
Carlisle 8	a																								
	d			01u41																					
Penrith North Lakes	d																								
Windermere	d																								
Oxenholme Lake District	a																								
	d																								
Barrow-in-Furness	d											04 35													
Lancaster 6	a											05 28													
	d																								
Blackpool North	d	22p44						03 37												05 40		05 39			
Preston 8	a	23p08				04s33														05 55		06 03			
Preston 8	d	23p10						04u02					05 16							05 58		06 05			
Wigan North Western	a																			06 09					
	d																			06 09					
Blackrod	d																					06 22			
Lostock	d																					06 30			
Bolton	a	23p34						04c31					05 42									06 34			
Manchester Piccadilly 10	a	23p53						04 48					06 01									06 56			
Manchester Airport	a	00 24						05 07					06 18									07 17			
Liverpool Lime Street 10	a																								
	d		23p34						03 38								05 47								
Liverpool South Parkway	d		23p45																						
Runcorn	d		23p53														06 03								
Warrington Bank Quay	a																			06 20					
	d																			06 20					
Hartford	d		00 07																						
Manchester Piccadilly 10	d								04a14					05 11	05 25				05 55				06 00	06 10	06 35
Stockport	d														05 34				06 03				06 08	06 18	06 43
Wilmslow	d														05 41				06 11						
Holyhead	d																								
Bangor (Gwynedd)	d																								
Llandudno Junction	d																								
Wrexham General	d																								
Chester	d									04 22															
Crewe 10	a		00 22			05s38				04 44				05 41	05 57				06 27						
	d									04 59				05 47	06 00			06 20	06 29						
Macclesfield	d																						06 21	06 31	06 56
Congleton	d																								
Stoke-on-Trent	d													06 08		←							06 39	06 48	07 12
Stafford	a									05 24				06 25	06 17	06 25	06 34	06 41					06 57		
	d									05 25				06 26	06 19	06 26	06 35	06 41					06 58		
Penkridge	a													↦				06 47							
Wolverhampton 7	a									05 39						06 39		06 57					07 12		
Birmingham New Street 12	a									05 58						06 57		07 17					07 31		
Birmingham International	a															07 13									
Coventry	a															07 24									
Lichfield Trent Valley	a																							07 11	
Tamworth Low Level	a																							07 17	
Nuneaton	a																06 57								
Rugby	a														06 49										
Milton Keynes Central	a														07 11				07 31	07 37					07 52
Watford Junction	a			06s27											07s32		07s44								
London Euston 15	a			06 50		07 48									07 52		08 05		08 09	08 14				08 27	08 46

A Conveys a portion from Fort William, dep 1950 **b** Previous night, stops to pick up only **c** Stops to pick up only

OVERNIGHT SLEEPERS. For sleeper trains, operated by First ScotRail, please refer to Tables 400 - 404

Table 65

Saturdays

7 July to 8 September

Scotland and North West England - West Midlands and London

Route Diagram - see first Page of Table 65

		LM	VT	TP	LM	VT		LM	VT	VT	TP	XC	VT	VT	LM	VT		VT	TP	XC	VT	EM	LM	VT	LM
		◇1	◇1	◇1	◇1	◇1		◇1	◇1	◇1	◇1	◇1	◇1	◇1	◇1	◇1		◇1	◇1	◇1	◇1	◇	◇1	◇1	◇1
																			A						
			🛒			🛒			🛒	🛒	🍴	🍴	🛒	🛒		🛒		🛒	🍴	🍴	🛒			🛒	
Inverness	d																								
Aberdeen	d																								
Dundee	d																								
Perth	d																								
Edinburgh 10	d																								
Haymarket	d																								
Glasgow Central 15	d									04 26															
Motherwell	d																								
Carstairs	d																								
Lockerbie	d																								
Carlisle 8	a									05 43															
	d									05 44															
Penrith North Lakes	d									05 59															
Windermere	d																								
Oxenholme Lake District	a									06 21															
	d									06 22															
Barrow-in-Furness	d			05 31															06 20						
Lancaster 6	a			06 23						06 36									07 21						
	d			06 23						06 37								06 58	07 22						
Blackpool North	d										06 40														
Preston 8	a			06 42						06 55	07 07							07 15	07 41						
Preston 8	d		06 17	06 44						06 58	07 09							07 17	07 47						
Wigan North Western	a		06 28							07 09								07 28							
	d		06 28							07 10								07 28							
Blackrod	d																								
Lostock	d										07 30														
Bolton	a			07 08							07 34								08 08						
Manchester Piccadilly 10 🚊	a			07 27							07 56								08 27						
Manchester Airport ✈	a			07 47							08 17								08 47						
Liverpool Lime Street 10	a																								
	d				06 32	06 45									07 04	07 19						06 49	07 34	07 48	
Liverpool South Parkway ✈	d				06 42										07 14							06 59	07 44		
Runcorn	d				06 50	07 01									07 22	07 36							07 52	08 04	
Warrington Bank Quay	a		06 39							07 20								07 39							
	d		06 39							07 20								07 39							
Hartford	d				07 02										07 36								08 04		
Manchester Piccadilly 10 🚊	d								06 55			07 07	07 15							07 27	07 35	07 42			
Stockport	d								07 04			07 16	07 23							07 35	07 43	07a53			
Wilmslow	d								07 11																
Holyhead	d																								
Bangor (Gwynedd)	d																								
Llandudno Junction	d																								
Wrexham General	d																								
Chester	d													07 17											
Crewe 10	a		06 58		07 14	07 18			07 27					07 36	07 47	07 52		07 58					08 19		
	d	06 47	07 01		07 16	07 20			07 29					07 39	07 49	07 55		08 01					08 22		
Macclesfield	d																			07 49	07 56				
Congleton	d																								
Stoke-on-Trent	d							⟵				07 44	07 50							08 07	08 12				⟵
Stafford	a	07 10			07 40	07 38		07 40				08 02			08 10	08 14				08 25			08 42	08 35	08 42
	d	07 12			07 41	07 39		07 41				08 03			08 10	08 16				08 26			08 43	08 36	08 43
Penkridge	a	07 17			⟶			07 46							08 16								⟶		08 48
Wolverhampton 7 🚊	a	07 28	07 32					07 57				08 17			08 28			08 31		08 39					08 58
Birmingham New Street 12	a	07 47	07 55					08 17				08 39			08 47			08 55		08 58					09 18
Birmingham International ✈	a																			09 13					
Coventry	a																			09 24					
Lichfield Trent Valley	a															08 30									
Tamworth Low Level	a															08 36									
Nuneaton	a																							08 58	
Rugby	a																								
Milton Keynes Central	a												08 46												
Watford Junction	a																								
London Euston 15 ⊖	a					08 59			09 04	09 12			09 23	09 30		09 46					09 42			10 00	

A 🍴 from Preston

OVERNIGHT SLEEPERS. For sleeper trains, operated by First ScotRail, please refer to Tables 400 - 404

Table 65

Saturdays
7 July to 8 September

Scotland and North West England - West Midlands and London

Route Diagram - see first Page of Table 65

		VT		VT	TP	XC	LM	VT	VT	VT	TP	XC		VT	EM	LM	VT	LM	VT	VT	SR	XC		LM	NT
		◇1		◇1	◇1	◇1	◇1	◇1	◇1	◇1	◇1	◇1		◇1	◇	◇1	◇1	◇1	◇1	◇1		◇1		◇1	
											A														
		🍴		🍴	🛒	🛒		🍴	🍴	🍴	🛒	🛒		🍴			🍴		🍴	🍴		🛒			
Inverness	d																								
Aberdeen	d																								
Dundee	d																								
Perth	d																								
Edinburgh 10	d																								
Haymarket	d																								
Glasgow Central 15	d			05 40						05 50										06 30	07 05				
Motherwell	d									06 04										06 44	07 27				
Carstairs	d																				07a47				
Lockerbie	d																			07 25					
Carlisle 8	a			06 46						07 02										07 43					
	d			06 49						07 03										07 46					
Penrith North Lakes	d									07 18										08 00					
Windermere	d																								
Oxenholme Lake District	a			07 22						07 41										08 22					
	d			07 24						07 42										08 23					
Barrow-in-Furness	d										07 29														
Lancaster 6	a			07 37						07 56	08 26									08 37					
	d			07 38						07 57	08 27									08 38					
Blackpool North	d				07 44																				08 38
Preston 8	a			07 56	08 11					08 15	08 45									08 56					09 02
Preston 8	d			07 58	08 12					08 17	08 47									08 58					09 04
Wigan North Western	a			08 09						08 28										09 09					09 24
	d			08 09						08 28										09 09					09 24
Blackrod	d																								
Lostock	d																								
Bolton	a				08 34						09 08														
Manchester Piccadilly 10	a				08 56						09 27														
Manchester Airport ✈	a				09 19						09 47														
Liverpool Lime Street 10	a																								10 02
	d						08 04								07 42	08 34	08 48							09 04	10 16
Liverpool South Parkway ✈	d						08 15								07 52	08 44								09 15	10a27
Runcorn	d						08 24									08 52	09 04							09 24	
Warrington Bank Quay	a			08 20						08 39										09 20					
	d			08 20						08 39										09 20					
Hartford	d															09 06									
Manchester Piccadilly 10	d	07 55				08 07		08 15				08 27		08 35	08 43				08 55			09 07			
Stockport	d	08 04				08 16		08 23				08 35		08 43	08a53				09 04			09 16			
Wilmslow	d	08 11																	09 11						
Holyhead	d								06 52																
Bangor (Gwynedd)	d								07 20																
Llandudno Junction	d								07 38																
Wrexham General	d																								
Chester	d								08 35																
Crewe 10	a	08 27					08 47		08 54	08 58						09 20			09 27					09 44	
	d	08 29					08 49		08 56	09 01						09 22			09 29					09 49	
Macclesfield	d											08 49		08 56											
Congleton	d																								
Stoke-on-Trent	d					08 44		08 50				09 07		09 12				←				09 44			
Stafford	a					09 02	09 09					09 25				09 42	09 35	09 42				10 02		10 10	
	d					09 03	09 10					09 26				09 43	09 36	09 43				10 03		10 10	
Penkridge	a						09 15									→								10 16	
Wolverhampton 7	a					09 15	09 27			09 31		09 39						09 56				10 15		10 27	
Birmingham New Street 12	a					09 39	09 47			09 55		09 58						10 17				10 39		10 47	
Birmingham International ✈	a											10 13													
Coventry	a											10 24													
Lichfield Trent Valley	a																								
Tamworth Low Level	a																								
Nuneaton	a																09 58								
Rugby	a																								
Milton Keynes Central	a							09 46	10 01																
Watford Junction	a																								
London Euston 15 ⊖	a	10 04		10 12				10 23	10 37					10 42			11 01		11 04	11 12					

A 🛒 from Preston

OVERNIGHT SLEEPERS. For sleeper trains, operated by First ScotRail, please refer to Tables 400 - 404

Table 65

Saturdays

7 July to 8 September

Scotland and North West England - West Midlands and London

Route Diagram - see first Page of Table 65

		TP	VT	VT	VT	TP	XC	VT		EM	LM	VT	LM	VT	VT	XC	LM	NT		TP	TP	VT	VT	VT	TP
		◇1	◇1	◇1	◇1	◇1	◇1	◇1		◇	◇1	◇1	◇1	◇1	◇1	◇1	◇1			◇1	◇1	◇1	◇1	◇1	◇1
		trolley	shop	shop	shop	trolley	trolley	shop				shop		shop	shop	trolley				trolley	trolley	shop	shop	shop	
Inverness	d																								
Aberdeen	d																								
Dundee	d																								
Perth	d																								
Edinburgh 10	d				06 52															07 42					
Haymarket	d				06 56															07u46					
Glasgow Central 15	d					07 10									07 35									08 00	
Motherwell	d														07 52										
Carstairs	d																								
Lockerbie	d					08 06																			
Carlisle 8	a				08 05	08 29									08 46					08 59				09 08	
	d				08 07	08 29									08 49					08 59				09 09	
Penrith North Lakes	d				08 22	08 45																			
Windermere	d																								09 38
Oxenholme Lake District	a					09 09									09 22										09 57
	d					09 11									09 23										09 58
Barrow-in-Furness	d																								
Lancaster 6	a				08 56	09 26									09 37									09 56	10 16
	d				08 57	09 26									09 38									09 57	10 16
Blackpool North	d	08 44																09 37			09 43				
Preston 8	a	09 08			09 15	09 45									09 56			10 02		10 04	10 07			10 15	10 35
Preston 8	d	09 10			09 17	09 47									09 58			10 04		10 12				10 17	
Wigan North Western	a				09 28										10 09			10 24						10 28	
	d				09 28										10 09			10 24						10 28	
Blackrod	d																								
Lostock	d																								
Bolton	a	09 34				10 08														10 34					
Manchester Piccadilly 10 🚊	a	09 56				10 27														10 56					
Manchester Airport ✈	a	10 17				10 47														11 17					
Liverpool Lime Street 10	a																	11 02							
	d									08 52	09 34	09 48					10 04	11 16							
Liverpool South Parkway ✈	d									09 03	09 44						10 15	11a27							
Runcorn	d										09 52	10 04					10 25								
Warrington Bank Quay	a				09 39										10 20									10 39	
	d				09 39										10 20									10 39	
Hartford	d										10 04														
Manchester Piccadilly 10 🚊	d		09 15				09 27	09 35		09 43				09 55		10 07						10 15			
Stockport	d		09 23				09 35	09 43		09a53				10 04		10 16						10 23			
Wilmslow	d													10 11											
Holyhead	d			07 55																			08 55		
Bangor (Gwynedd)	d			08 22																			09 22		
Llandudno Junction	d			08 40																			09 40		
Wrexham General	d																								
Chester	d			09 35																			10 35		
Crewe 10	a			09 54	09 58						10 19			10 27			10 45						10 54	10 58	
	d			09 56	10 01						10 22			10 29			10 49						10 56	11 01	
Macclesfield	d						09 49	09 56																	
Congleton	d																								
Stoke-on-Trent	d		09 50				10 07	10 12					←			10 44						10 50			
Stafford	a						10 25				10 42	10 35	10 42			11 02	11 09								
	d						10 26				10 43	10 36	10 43			11 03	11 10								
Penkridge	a										→						11 15								
Wolverhampton 7 🚊	a				10 31		10 39						10 56			11 16	11 27							11 31	
Birmingham New Street 12	a				10 55		10 58						11 17			11 39	11 47							11 55	
Birmingham International ✈	a						11 13																		
Coventry	a						11 24																		
Lichfield Trent Valley	a																								
Tamworth Low Level	a																								
Nuneaton	a																								
Rugby	a																								
Milton Keynes Central	a		10 46	11 01																		11 46	12 01		
Watford Junction	a																								
London Euston 15 ⊖	a		11 23	11 38				11 42				11 56		12 04	12 12							12 23	12 38		

OVERNIGHT SLEEPERS. For sleeper trains, operated by First ScotRail, please refer to Tables 400 - 404

Table 65

Saturdays

7 July to 8 September

Scotland and North West England - West Midlands and London

Route Diagram - see first Page of Table 65

		TP	NT	XC		VT	EM	LM	VT	LM	VT	VT	XC	LM		NT	TP	VT	VT	VT	SR	TP	XC	VT
		◇1		◇1		◇1	◇	◇1	◇1	◇1	◇1	◇1	◇1	◇1			◇1	◇1	◇1	◇1		◇1	◇1	◇1
		A																				A		
		[trolley]		[trolley]		[buffet]			[buffet]		[buffet]	[buffet]	[trolley]				[trolley]	[buffet]	[buffet]	[buffet]		[trolley]	[trolley]	[buffet]
Inverness	d																							
Aberdeen	d																							
Dundee	d																							
Perth	d																							
Edinburgh 10	d																			08 52	09 03			
Haymarket	d																			08 57	09 07			
Glasgow Central 15	d											08 40												
Motherwell	d																							
Carstairs	d																				09a44			
Lockerbie	d																							
Carlisle 8	a											09 46								10 05				
	d											09 49								10 07				
Penrith North Lakes	d											10 03												
Windermere	d																					10 49		
Oxenholme Lake District	a																			10 41		11 08		
	d																			10 42		11 09		
Barrow-in-Furness	d	09 23	10 16																					
Lancaster 6	a	10 25	11 21									10 37								10 56		11 26		
	d	10 26										10 38								10 57		11 26		
Blackpool North	d															10 37	10 44							
Preston 8	a	10 45										10 56				11 02	11 08			11 15		11 45		
Preston 8	d	10 47										10 58				11 04	11 10			11 17		11 47		
Wigan North Western	a											11 09				11 24				11 28				
	d											11 09				11 24				11 28				
Blackrod	d																							
Lostock	d																							
Bolton	a	11 08															11 34					12 08		
Manchester Piccadilly 10	a	11 27															11 56					12 27		
Manchester Airport	a	11 47															12 17					12 47		
Liverpool Lime Street 10	a															12 02								
	d						09 52	10 34	10 48					11 04		12 16								
Liverpool South Parkway	d						10 03	10 44						11 15		12a27								
Runcorn	d							10 52	11 04					11 25										
Warrington Bank Quay	a											11 20								11 39				
	d											11 20								11 39				
Hartford	d							11 04																
Manchester Piccadilly 10	d			10 27		10 35	10 43				10 55		11 07					11 15					11 27	11 35
Stockport	d			10 35		10 43	10a53				11 04		11 16					11 23					11 35	11 43
Wilmslow	d										11 11													
Holyhead	d																							
Bangor (Gwynedd)	d																							
Llandudno Junction	d																							
Wrexham General	d																							
Chester	d																		11 35					
Crewe 10	a							11 19			11 27			11 45					11 54	11 58				
	d							11 22			11 29			11 49					11 56	12 01				
Macclesfield	d			10 49		10 56																	11 49	11 56
Congleton	d																							
Stoke-on-Trent	d			11 07		11 12				←			11 44					11 50					12 07	12 12
Stafford	a			11 25				11 42	11 35	11 42			12 02	12 09									12 24	
	d			11 26				11 43	11 36	11 43			12 03	12 10									12 25	
Penkridge	a							→						12 15										
Wolverhampton 7	a			11 39						11 56			12 16	12 27						12 31			12 39	
Birmingham New Street 12	a			11 58						12 17			12 39	12 47						12 55			12 58	
Birmingham International	a			12 13																			13 13	
Coventry	a			12 24																			13 24	
Lichfield Trent Valley	a																							
Tamworth Low Level	a																							
Nuneaton	a																							
Rugby	a																							
Milton Keynes Central	a																	12 46	13 01					
Watford Junction	a																							
London Euston 15 ⊖	a					12 42			12 56		13 04	13 12						13 23	13 38					13 42

A [trolley] from Preston

OVERNIGHT SLEEPERS. For sleeper trains, operated by First ScotRail, please refer to Tables 400 - 404

Saturdays

7 July to 8 September

Scotland and North West England - West Midlands and London

Route Diagram - see first Page of Table 65

		EM	LM	VT	LM	VT	VT	TP	XC	LM		NT	TP	VT	VT	VT	TP	TP	TP	TP		XC	VT	EM	LM
		◇	◇1	◇1	◇1	◇1	◇1	◇1	◇1	◇1			◇1	◇1	◇1	◇1	◇1	◇1	◇1	◇1		◇1	◇1	◇	◇1
																		A							
				🍽		🍽	🍽		🛒				🛒	🍽	🍽	🍽	🛒	🛒	🛒	🛒		🛒	🍽		
Inverness	d																								
Aberdeen	d																								
Dundee	d																								
Perth	d																								
Edinburgh 10	d																09 51	09 51							
Haymarket	d																09u56	09u56							
Glasgow Central 15	d						09 40									10 00			10 10	10 10					
Motherwell	d																								
Carstairs	d																								
Lockerbie	d																11 01	11 01							
Carlisle 8	a						10 47									11 08	11 22	11 22	11 26	11 26					
	d						10 49									11 09	11 22	11 22	11 27	11 27					
Penrith North Lakes	d															11 24			11 43	11 43					
Windermere	d																								
Oxenholme Lake District	a						11 22												12 06	12 06					
	d						11 23												12 07	12 07					
Barrow-in-Furness	d							11 11																	
Lancaster 6	a						11 37	12 04									12 14	12 14							
	d						11 38	12 04									12 15	12 15							
Blackpool North	d											11 37	11 44												
Preston 8	a						11 56	12 23				12 02	12 08			12 15	12 33	12 33	12 37	12 37					
Preston 8	d						11 58					12 04	12 10			12 17		12 47		12 47					
Wigan North Western	a						12 09					12 24				12 28									
	d						12 09					12 24				12 28									
Blackrod	d																								
Lostock	d																								
Bolton	a												12 34					13 08		13 08					
Manchester Piccadilly 10 🚊	a												12 56					13 27		13 27					
Manchester Airport ✈	a												13 17					13 47		13 47					
Liverpool Lime Street 10	a											13 02													
	d	10 52	11 34	11 48						12 04		13 16												11 52	12 34
Liverpool South Parkway ✈	d	11 03	11 44							12 15		13a27												12 03	12 44
Runcorn	d		11 52	12 04						12 25															12 52
Warrington Bank Quay	a						12 20									12 39									
	d						12 20									12 39									
Hartford	d		12 04																						13 06
Manchester Piccadilly 10 🚊	d	11 43				11 55			12 07					12 15								12 27	12 35	12 43	
Stockport	d	11a53				12 04			12 16					12 23								12 35	12 43	12a53	
Wilmslow	d					12 11																			
Holyhead	d																								
Bangor (Gwynedd)	d																								
Llandudno Junction	d																								
Wrexham General	d																								
Chester	d														12 35										
Crewe 10	a		12 19			12 27				12 45					12 54	12 58									13 20
	d		12 22			12 29				12 49					12 57	13 01									13 22
Macclesfield	d																					12 49	12 56		
Congleton	d																								
Stoke-on-Trent	d				←				12 44					12 50								13 07	13 12		
Stafford	a		12 42	12 35	12 42				13 02	13 09												13 25			13 42
	d		12 43	12 36	12 43				13 03	13 10												13 26			13 43
Penkridge	a		↦							13 15															↦
Wolverhampton 7 🚊	a				12 56				13 15	13 27						13 31						13 39			
Birmingham New Street 12	a				13 17				13 39	13 47						13 55						13 58			
Birmingham International ✈	a																					14 13			
Coventry	a																					14 24			
Lichfield Trent Valley	a																								
Tamworth Low Level	a																								
Nuneaton	a																								
Rugby	a																								
Milton Keynes Central	a													13 46	14 01										
Watford Junction	a																								
London Euston 15 ⊖	a			13 56		14 04	14 12							14 23	14 38								14 42		

A from 11 August until 8 September

OVERNIGHT SLEEPERS. For sleeper trains, operated by First ScotRail, please refer to Tables 400 - 404

Table 65

Saturdays

7 July to 8 September

Scotland and North West England - West Midlands and London

Route Diagram - see first Page of Table 65

		VT	LM	VT	VT	XC	LM	VT	VT	XC	VT	VT	EM	NT	TP	VT	TP	LM	VT	LM	VT	VT	XC
		◇1	◇1	◇1	◇1	◇1	◇1	◇1	◇1	◇1	◇1	◇1	◇		◇1	◇1	◇1	◇1	◇1	◇1	◇1	◇1	◇1
																	A						
		⊡		⊡	⊡	⚲		⊡	⊡	⚲	⊡	⊡			⚲	⊡	⚲		⊡		⊡	⊡	⚲
Inverness	d																						
Aberdeen	d																						
Dundee	d																						
Perth	d																						
Edinburgh 10	d															10 52							
Haymarket	d															10 57							
Glasgow Central 15	d				10 40																	11 40	
Motherwell	d																						
Carstairs	d																						
Lockerbie	d																						
Carlisle 8	a				11 47											12 05						12 46	
	d				11 49											12 07						12 49	
Penrith North Lakes	d																					13 03	
Windermere	d																12 51						
Oxenholme Lake District	a				12 22											12 41	13 07						
	d				12 23											12 43	13 09						
Barrow-in-Furness	d																						
Lancaster 6	a				12 37											12 56	13 26					13 37	
	d				12 38											12 57	13 26					13 38	
Blackpool North	d													12 37	12 44								
Preston 8	a				12 56									13 02	13 08	13 15	13 45					13 56	
Preston 8	d				12 58									13 04	13 10	13 17	13 47					13 58	
Wigan North Western	a				13 09									13 24		13 28						14 09	
	d				13 09									13 24		13 28						14 09	
Blackrod	d																						
Lostock	d																						
Bolton	a														13 34		14 08						
Manchester Piccadilly 10	a														13 56		14 27						
Manchester Airport ✈	a														14 17		14 47						
Liverpool Lime Street 10	a													14 02									
	d	12 48					13 04						12 52	14 16				13 34	13 48				
Liverpool South Parkway ✈	d						13 15						13 03	14a27				13 44					
Runcorn	d	13 04					13 25											13 52	14 04				
Warrington Bank Quay	a				13 20											13 39						14 20	
	d				13 20											13 39						14 20	
Hartford	d																	14 04					
Manchester Piccadilly 10	d			12 55		13 07		13 15		13 27		13 35	13 43								13 55		14 07
Stockport	d			13 04		13 16		13 23		13 35		13 43	13a53								14 04		14 16
Wilmslow	d			13 11																	14 11		
Holyhead	d								11 55														
Bangor (Gwynedd)	d								12 21														
Llandudno Junction	d								12 39														
Wrexham General	d																						
Chester	d								13 35		13 35												
Crewe 10	a			13 27			13 45		13 54		13 54					13 58		14 19			14 27		
	d			13 29			13 49		13 56		13 56					14 01		14 22			14 29		
Macclesfield	d									13 49		13 56											
Congleton	d																						
Stoke-on-Trent	d		←			13 44		13 50		14 07		14 12								←			14 44
Stafford	a	13 35	13 42			14 02	14 09			14 25								14 46	14 35	14 46			15 02
	d	13 36	13 43			14 03	14 10			14 26								14 46	14 36	14 46			15 03
Penkridge	a						14 15											→					
Wolverhampton 7	a		13 56			14 16	14 27			14 39						14 31				14 59			15 16
Birmingham New Street 12	a		14 17			14 39	14 47			14 58						15 06				15 18			15 39
Birmingham International ✈	a									15 13						15 19							
Coventry	a									15 24						15 30							
Lichfield Trent Valley	a																						
Tamworth Low Level	a																						
Nuneaton	a																						
Rugby	a																						
Milton Keynes Central	a							14 46	15 01		15 01												
Watford Junction	a															16s15							
London Euston 15 ⊖	a	14 56		15 04	15 12			15 23	15 38		15 38	15 42				16 34			15 56		16 04	16 12	

A ⚲ from Preston

OVERNIGHT SLEEPERS. For sleeper trains, operated by First ScotRail, please refer to Tables 400 - 404

Table 65

Saturdays

7 July to 8 September

Scotland and North West England - West Midlands and London

Route Diagram - see first Page of Table 65

		LM		NT	TP	VT	VT	VT	TP	TP	NT	XC		VT	EM	LM	VT	LM	VT	VT	XC	LM		NT	TP
		◇1			◇1	◇1	◇1	◇1	◇1	◇1		◇1		◇1	◇	◇1	◇1	◇1	◇1	◇1	◇1	◇1			◇1
									A																
					trolley	catering	catering	catering	trolley	trolley		trolley		catering			catering		catering	catering	trolley				trolley
Inverness	d																								
Aberdeen	d																								
Dundee	d																								
Perth	d																								
Edinburgh 10	d									12 08															
Haymarket	d									12u12															
Glasgow Central 15	d							12 00												12 40					
Motherwell	d																								
Carstairs	d																								
Lockerbie	d									13 07															
Carlisle 8	a							13 08		13 29										13 47					
	d							13 09		13 29										13 49					
Penrith North Lakes	d																								
Windermere	d																								
Oxenholme Lake District	a									14 06										14 22					
	d									14 07										14 24					
Barrow-in-Furness	d								13 25		14 16														
Lancaster 6	a							13 56	14 18	14 21	15 20									14 37					
	d							13 58	14 18	14 22										14 38					
Blackpool North	d			13 37	13 44																			14 37	14 44
Preston 8	a			14 02	14 08			14 15	14 37	14 41										14 56				15 02	15 08
Preston 8	d			14 04	14 10			14 17	14 47											14 58				15 04	15 10
Wigan North Western	a			14 24				14 28												15 09				15 24	
	d			14 24				14 28												15 09				15 24	
Blackrod	d																								
Lostock	d																								
Bolton	a				14 34				15 08																15 34
Manchester Piccadilly 10	a				14 56				15 27																15 56
Manchester Airport ✈	a				15 17				15 47																16 17
Liverpool Lime Street 10	a			15 02																				16 02	
	d	14 04		15 16											13 52	14 34	14 48					15 04		16 16	
Liverpool South Parkway ✈	d	14 15		15a27											14 03	14 44						15 15		16a27	
Runcorn	d	14 25														14 52	15 04					15 25			
Warrington Bank Quay	a							14 39												15 20					
	d							14 39												15 20					
Hartford	d															15 04									
Manchester Piccadilly 10	d					14 15						14 27		14 35	14 43				14 55		15 07				
Stockport	d					14 23						14 35		14 43	14a53				15 04		15 16				
Wilmslow	d																		15 11						
Holyhead	d																								
Bangor (Gwynedd)	d																								
Llandudno Junction	d																								
Wrexham General	d																								
Chester	d						14 35																		
Crewe 10	a	14 45					14 54	14 58								15 19			15 27			15 45			
	d	14 49					14 56	15 01								15 22			15 29			15 49			
Macclesfield	d											14 49		14 56											
Congleton	d																								
Stoke-on-Trent	d					14 50						15 07		15 12				←			15 44				
Stafford	a	15 09										15 25				15 42	15 35	15 42			16 02	16 09			
	d	15 10										15 26				15 43	15 36	15 43			16 03	16 10			
Penkridge	a	15 15														→						16 15			
Wolverhampton 7	a	15 27						15 31				15 39						15 56			16 16	16 27			
Birmingham New Street 12	a	15 47						15 55				15 58						16 17			16 39	16 47			
Birmingham International ✈	a											16 13													
Coventry	a											16 24													
Lichfield Trent Valley	a																								
Tamworth Low Level	a																								
Nuneaton	a																								
Rugby	a																								
Milton Keynes Central	a					15 46	16 01																		
Watford Junction	a																								
London Euston 15 ⊖	a					16 23	16 38							16 42			16 56		17 04	17 12					

A trolley from Preston

OVERNIGHT SLEEPERS. For sleeper trains, operated by First ScotRail, please refer to Tables 400 - 404

Table 65

Saturdays

7 July to 8 September

Scotland and North West England - West Midlands and London

Route Diagram - see first Page of Table 65

		VT	VT	VT	TP	XC	VT	EM		LM	VT	LM	VT	VT	XC	LM	NT	TP		VT	VT	VT	TP	XC	VT
		◇1	◇1	◇1	◇1	◇1	◇1	◇		◇1	◇1	◇1	◇1	◇1	◇1	◇1		◇1		◇1	◇1	◇1	◇1	◇1	◇1
		☕	☕	☕	🛒	🛒	☕				☕		☕	☕	🛒			🛒		☕	☕	☕	🛒	🛒	☕
Inverness	d																								
Aberdeen	d																								
Dundee	d																								
Perth	d																								
Edinburgh 10	d			12 52																			14 07		
Haymarket	d			12 57																			14u11		
Glasgow Central 15	d				13 09									13 40								14 00			
Motherwell	d																								
Carstairs	d																								
Lockerbie	d				14 06																		15 06		
Carlisle 8	a			14 05	14 29									14 46								15 09	15 27		
	d			14 07	14 29									14 49								15 11	15 27		
Penrith North Lakes	d			14 22	14 45																		15 43		
Windermere	d																								
Oxenholme Lake District	a				15 09									15 22								15 45	16 06		
	d				15 10									15 23								15 46	16 07		
Barrow-in-Furness	d																								
Lancaster 6	a			14 56	15 26									15 37									16 26		
	d			14 57	15 26									15 38									16 26		
Blackpool North	d																15 37	15 44							
Preston 8	a			15 15	15 45									15 56			16 02	16 08				16 15	16 45		
Preston 8	d			15 17	15 47									15 58			16 04	16 10				16 17	16 47		
Wigan North Western	a			15 28										16 09			16 24					16 28			
	d			15 28										16 09			16 24					16 28			
Blackrod	d																								
Lostock	d																								
Bolton	a				16 08													16 34					17 08		
Manchester Piccadilly 10 🚊	a				16 27													16 56					17 27		
Manchester Airport ✈	a				16 47													17 17					17 48		
Liverpool Lime Street 10	a																17 05								
	d							14 52		15 34	15 48					16 04									
Liverpool South Parkway ✈	d							15 03		15 44						16 15									
Runcorn	d									15 52	16 04					16 25									
Warrington Bank Quay	a			15 39										16 20								16 39			
	d			15 39										16 20								16 39			
Hartford	d									16 04															
Manchester Piccadilly 10 🚊	d	15 15				15 27	15 35	15 43					15 55		16 07					16 15				16 27	16 35
Stockport	d	15 23				15 35	15 43	15a53					16 04		16 16					16 23				16 35	16 43
Wilmslow	d												16 11												
Holyhead	d																				14 38				
Bangor (Gwynedd)	d																				15 07				
Llandudno Junction	d																				15 27				
Wrexham General	d																								
Chester	d		15 35																		16 24				
Crewe 10	a		15 54	15 58						16 19			16 27			16 45					16 47	16 58			
	d		15 56	16 01						16 22			16 29			16 49					16 56	17 01			
Macclesfield	d					15 49	15 56																	16 49	16 56
Congleton	d																								
Stoke-on-Trent	d	15 50				16 07	16 12					←			16 44					16 50				17 07	17 12
Stafford	a					16 24				16 46	16 35	16 46			17 02	17 09								17 25	
	d					16 25				16 46	16 36	16 46			17 03	17 10								17 26	
Penkridge	a									↦						17 15									
Wolverhampton 7 🚊	a			16 31		16 39						16 59			17 16	17 27						17 31		17 39	
Birmingham New Street 12	a			16 55		16 58						17 18			17 39	17 47						17 55		17 58	
Birmingham International ✈	a					17 13																		18 13	
Coventry	a					17 24																		18 24	
Lichfield Trent Valley	a																								
Tamworth Low Level	a																								
Nuneaton	a																								
Rugby	a																								
Milton Keynes Central	a	16 46	17 01																	17 46	18 01				
Watford Junction	a																								
London Euston 15 ⊖	a	17 23	17 38				17 42				17 56		18 04	18 12						18 23	18 38				18 42

OVERNIGHT SLEEPERS. For sleeper trains, operated by First ScotRail, please refer to Tables 400 - 404

Scotland and North West England - West Midlands and London

Route Diagram - see first Page of Table 65

		EM	LM	VT		LM	VT	VT	SR	XC	LM	VT	XC	VT		EM	NT	TP	VT	TP	TP	LM	VT	LM
		◇	◇1	◇1		◇1	◇1	◇1		◇1	◇1	◇1	◇1	◇1		◇		◇1	◇1	◇1	◇1	◇1	◇1	◇1
Inverness	d																							
Aberdeen	d																							
Dundee	d																							
Perth	d																							
Edinburgh 10	d																		14 52					
Haymarket	d																		14 57					
Glasgow Central 15	d							14 40	15 14															
Motherwell	d								15 34															
Carstairs	d								15a51															
Lockerbie	d																							
Carlisle 8	a							15 46											16 05					
	d							15 49											16 07					
Penrith North Lakes	d																		16 22					
Windermere	d																							
Oxenholme Lake District	a							16 22																
	d							16 24																
Barrow-in-Furness	d																			16 22				
Lancaster 6	a							16 37											16 56	17 19				
	d							16 38											16 57	17 20				
Blackpool North	d																16 35	16 40			17 20			
Preston 8	a							16 56									17 02	17 08	17 15	17 39	17 45			
Preston 8	d							16 58									17 04	17 10	17 17		17 47			
Wigan North Western	a							17 09									17 24		17 28					
	d							17 09									17 24		17 28					
Blackrod	d																							
Lostock	d																							
Bolton	a																	17 34			18 08			
Manchester Piccadilly 10	a																	17 56			18 27			
Manchester Airport	a																	18 17			18 47			
Liverpool Lime Street 10	a																18 02							
	d	15 52	16 34	16 48							17 04					16 52						17 34	17 48	
Liverpool South Parkway	d	16 03	16 44								17 15					17 03						17 44		
Runcorn	d		16 52	17 04							17 25											17 52	18 04	
Warrington Bank Quay	a							17 20											17 39					
	d							17 20											17 39					
Hartford	d		17 06																			18 06		
Manchester Piccadilly 10	d	16 43					16 55			17 06		17 15	17 27	17 35		17 43								
Stockport	d	16a53					17 04					17 23	17 36	17 43		17a53								
Wilmslow	d						17 11																	
Holyhead	d																							
Bangor (Gwynedd)	d																							
Llandudno Junction	d																							
Wrexham General	d																							
Chester	d																							
Crewe 10	a		17 20				17 27				17 47								17 59			18 20		
	d		17 22				17 29				17 49								18 01			18 22		
Macclesfield	d									17 26				17 56										
Congleton	d												17 54											
Stoke-on-Trent	d					←				17 44		17 50	18 08	18 12										←
Stafford	a		17 42	17 35		17 42				18 03	18 09		18 26									18 42	18 35	18 42
	d		17 43	17 36		17 43				18 04	18 10		18 27									18 43	18 36	18 43
Penkridge	a		→								18 15											→		
Wolverhampton 7	a					17 56				18 16	18 27		18 40						18 31					18 56
Birmingham New Street 12	a					18 17				18 38	18 47		18 58						19 06					19 17
Birmingham International	a												19 13						19 19					
Coventry	a												19 24						19 30					
Lichfield Trent Valley	a																							
Tamworth Low Level	a																							
Nuneaton	a																							
Rugby	a																		19 42					
Milton Keynes Central	a											18 46							20 05					
Watford Junction	a																		20s34					
London Euston 15	a			18 56			19 04	19 12				19 23		19 42					20 55				19 56	

OVERNIGHT SLEEPERS. For sleeper trains, operated by First ScotRail, please refer to Tables 400 - 404

Table 65

Saturdays

7 July to 8 September

Scotland and North West England - West Midlands and London

Route Diagram - see first Page of Table 65

		VT	VT	XC	LM	NT	TP	VT	TP	TP	VT	XC	VT	EM	LM	VT	LM	VT	VT	XC	LM	NT	TP
		◇1	◇1	◇1	◇1		◇1	◇1	◇1	◇1	◇1	◇1	◇1	◇	◇1	◇1	◇1	◇1	◇1	◇1	◇1		◇1
							A																
		🍽	🍽	🛒			🛒	🍽		🛒	🍽	🛒	🍽			🍽		🍽	🍽	🛒			
Inverness	d																						
Aberdeen	d																						
Dundee	d																						
Perth	d																						
Edinburgh 10	d									16 12													
Haymarket	d									16u16													
Glasgow Central 15	d		15 40					16 00											16 40				
Motherwell	d																		16 54				
Carstairs	d																						
Lockerbie	d									17 11													
Carlisle 8	a		16 46					17 08		17 33									17 49				
	d		16 49					17 09		17 34									17 52				
Penrith North Lakes	d		17 03							17 49													
Windermere	d						17 06																
Oxenholme Lake District	a						17 25	17 44											18 25				
	d						17 30	17 44											18 26				
Barrow-in-Furness	d								17 21														
Lancaster 6	a		17 37				17 47		18 16	18 26									18 40				
	d		17 38				17 48		18 17	18 26									18 41				
Blackpool North	d					17 37																18 37	18 44
Preston 8	a		17 56			18 02	18 06	18 15	18 36	18 45									18 59			19 00	19 08
Preston 8	d		17 58			18 04	18 08	18 17		18 47									19 01			19 04	19 10
Wigan North Western	a		18 09			18 24		18 28											19 12			19 24	
	d		18 09			18 24		18 28											19 12			19 24	
Blackrod	d																						
Lostock	d						18 30																
Bolton	a						18 34			19 08													19 34
Manchester Piccadilly 10	a						18 56			19 27													19 56
Manchester Airport ✈	a						19 17			19 50													20 17
Liverpool Lime Street 10	a					19 02																20 02	
	d				18 04									17 52	18 34	18 48					19 04		
Liverpool South Parkway ✈	d				18 15									18 03	18 44						19 14		
Runcorn	d				18 24										18 52	19 04					19 23		
Warrington Bank Quay	a		18 20					18 39											19 23				
	d		18 20					18 39											19 23				
Hartford	d														19 04								
Manchester Piccadilly 10	d	17 55		18 05							18 15	18 27	18 35	18 43				18 55		19 07			
Stockport	d	18 04		18 13							18 23	18 35	18 43	18a53				19 04		19 16			
Wilmslow	d	18 11																19 11					
Holyhead	d																						
Bangor (Gwynedd)	d																						
Llandudno Junction	d																						
Wrexham General	d																						
Chester	d																						
Crewe 10	a	18 27			18 46			18 59							19 19			19 27			19 49		
	d	18 29			18 49			19 01							19 22			19 29			19 51		
Macclesfield	d			18 26									18 56										
Congleton	d											18 54											
Stoke-on-Trent	d			18 44							18 49	19 07	19 12				←			19 44			
Stafford	a			19 02	19 09							19 25			19 42	19 35	19 42			20 02	20 11		
	d			19 03	19 10							19 25			19 43	19 36	19 43			20 03	20 12		
Penkridge	a				19 15										→		19 48						
Wolverhampton 7	a			19 16	19 27			19 31				19 39					19 59			20 16	20 28		
Birmingham New Street 12	a			19 33	19 47			19 55				19 58					20 17			20 33	20 47		
Birmingham International ✈	a											20 13											
Coventry	a											20 24											
Lichfield Trent Valley	a																						
Tamworth Low Level	a																						
Nuneaton	a																						
Rugby	a																						
Milton Keynes Central	a										19 45								20 41				
Watford Junction	a																		21s15				
London Euston 15 ⊖	a	20 04	20 15								20 24		20 59			21 15		21 18	21 38				

A 🛒 from Preston

OVERNIGHT SLEEPERS. For sleeper trains, operated by First ScotRail, please refer to Tables 400 - 404

Table 65

Saturdays

7 July to 8 September

Scotland and North West England - West Midlands and London

Route Diagram - see first Page of Table 65

		VT	TP	XC	VT	EM		LM	VT	LM	VT	NT	TP	XC	VT	TP		SR	XC	VT	EM	LM	XC	VT
		◇1	◇1	◇1	◇1	◇		◇1	◇1	◇1	◇1		◇1	◇1	◇1	◇1			◇1	◇1	◇	◇1	◇1	◇1
				A																				
		🍴	🛒	🛒	🍴				🍴		🍴				🍴	🛒				🍴				🍴
Inverness	d																							
Aberdeen	d																							
Dundee	d																							
Perth	d																							
Edinburgh 10	d	16 52														18 12		18 24						
Haymarket	d	16 57														18u16		18 28						
Glasgow Central 15	d		17 06								17 40				18 00									18 40
Motherwell	d																							
Carstairs	d																	19a09						
Lockerbie	d		18 06								18 32					19 11								
Carlisle 8	a	18 05	18 28								18 50				19 08	19 34								19 46
	d	18 07	18 29								18 52				19 09	19 34								19 48
Penrith North Lakes	d		18 45								19 06					19 49								20 02
Windermere	d																							
Oxenholme Lake District	a	18 41	19 09								19 28					20 12								20 24
	d	18 42	19 10								19 29					20 13								20 25
Barrow-in-Furness	d																							
Lancaster 6	a	18 56	19 26								19 43				19 55	20 26								20 39
	d	18 57	19 26								19 44				19 56	20 26								20 40
Blackpool North	d											19 37	19 44											
Preston 8	a	19 15	19 45								20 02	20 02	20 08		20 15	20 45								20 58
Preston 8	d	19 17	19 47								20 04	20 04	20 10		20 17	20 47								21 00
Wigan North Western	a	19 28									20 15	20 24			20 28									21 11
	d	19 28									20 15	20 24			20 28									21 11
Blackrod	d																							
Lostock	d																							
Bolton	a		20 08										20 34			21 08								
Manchester Piccadilly 10 🚊	a		20 27										20 56			21 27								
Manchester Airport ✈	a		20 47										21 17			21 47								
Liverpool Lime Street 10	a											21 02												
	d					18 52		19 34	19 48												19 52	20 34		
Liverpool South Parkway ✈	d					19 03		19 44													20 03	20 44		
Runcorn	d							19 52	20 04													20 52		
Warrington Bank Quay	a	19 39									20 26				20 39									21 22
	d	19 39									20 26				20 39									21 22
Hartford	d							20 04														21 03		
Manchester Piccadilly 10 🚊	d			19 27	19 35	19 43								20 07					20 27	20 35	20 43		21 07	
Stockport	d			19 35	19 43	19a53								20 16					20 35	20 43	20a53			
Wilmslow	d																							
Holyhead	d																							
Bangor (Gwynedd)	d																							
Llandudno Junction	d																							
Wrexham General	d																							
Chester	d																							
Crewe 10	a	19 59						20 16			20 45				20 59							21 16		21 41
	d	20 01						20 22	20u23		20 47				21 01							21 17		21 43
Macclesfield	d			19 49	19 56														20 49	20 56				
Congleton	d																							
Stoke-on-Trent	d			20 07	20 12					←				20 44					21 07	21 12			21 45	
Stafford	a			20 25				20 44	20 41	20 44				21 02					21 26			21 42	22 02	22 07
	d			20 26				20 45	20 42	20 45				21 03					21 27			21 42	22 03	22 08
Penkridge	a							→		20 50												21 48		
Wolverhampton 7 🚊	a	20 31		20 39						21 01				21 15	21 31				21 39			21 58	22 14	22 22
Birmingham New Street 12	a	20 55		20 58						21 19				21 32	21 54				21 58			22 20	22 32	22 46
Birmingham International ✈	a			21 13																				
Coventry	a			21 24																				
Lichfield Trent Valley	a																							
Tamworth Low Level	a																							
Nuneaton	a																							
Rugby	a																							
Milton Keynes Central	a				21 10						21 50									22 10				
Watford Junction	a																			22s40				
London Euston 15 ⊖	a				22 00				22 14		22 44									23 02				

A 🛒 to Birmingham New Street

OVERNIGHT SLEEPERS. For sleeper trains, operated by First ScotRail, please refer to Tables 400 - 404

Table 65

Saturdays

7 July to 8 September

Scotland and North West England - West Midlands and London

Route Diagram - see first Page of Table 65

		TP	TP	VT	XC	EM	LM	EM	TP	NT	TP	LM	TP
		◇1	◇1	◇1	◇1	◇	◇1	◇	◇1		◇1	1	◇1
				🍴									
Inverness	d												
Aberdeen	d												
Dundee	d												
Perth	d												
Edinburgh 10	d			18 52									
Haymarket	d			18 57									
Glasgow Central 15	d												
Motherwell	d												
Carstairs	d												
Lockerbie	d												
Carlisle 8	a			20 06									
	d			20 08									
Penrith North Lakes	d			20 23									
Windermere	d								21 40				
Oxenholme Lake District	a			20 46					21 59				
	d			20 46					22 01				
Barrow-in-Furness	d	19 33								21 43			
Lancaster 6	a	20 34		21 00					22 17	22 45			
	d	20 35		21 01					22 17	22 46			
Blackpool North	d		20 42								21 44		22 44
Preston 8	a	20 53	21 06	21 19					22 38	23 11	22 08		23 08
Preston 8	d	21 10		21 21							22 10		23 10
Wigan North Western	a			21 32									
	d			21 32									
Blackrod	d												
Lostock	d												
Bolton	a	21 34									22 34		23 34
Manchester Piccadilly 10 ⛴	a	21 56									22 56		23 53
Manchester Airport ✈	a	22 17									23 17		00 23
Liverpool Lime Street 10	a												
	d					20 52	21 34	21 37				22 04	
Liverpool South Parkway ✈	d					21 03	21 44	21 47				22 14	
Runcorn	d						21 52					22 23	
Warrington Bank Quay	a			21 43									
	d			21 43									
Hartford	d						22 04					22 34	
Manchester Piccadilly 10 ⛴	d				21 27	21 43		22 31					
Stockport	d				21 36	21a52		22a41					
Wilmslow	d												
Holyhead	d												
Bangor (Gwynedd)	d												
Llandudno Junction	d												
Wrexham General	d												
Chester	d												
Crewe 10	a			22 03			22 21					22 48	
	d			22 05			22 23						
Macclesfield	d				21 50								
Congleton	d												
Stoke-on-Trent	d				22 08								
Stafford	a			22 24	22 32		22 47						
	d			22 25	22 33		22 47						
Penkridge	a						22 53						
Wolverhampton 7 ⛴	a			22 39	22 45		23 03						
Birmingham New Street 12	a			22 59	23 02		23 21						
Birmingham International ✈	a												
Coventry	a												
Lichfield Trent Valley	a												
Tamworth Low Level	a												
Nuneaton	a												
Rugby	a												
Milton Keynes Central	a												
Watford Junction	a												
London Euston 15 ⊖	a												

OVERNIGHT SLEEPERS. For sleeper trains, operated by First ScotRail, please refer to Tables 400 - 404

Table 65

Saturdays

15 September to 20 October

Scotland and North West England - West Midlands and London

Route Diagram - see first Page of Table 65

		TP	LM	SR	SR	SR	SR	TP	NT	AW		TP	TP	XC	VT	XC	VT	LM	VT	VT		TP	XC	VT	VT
				R	R	R	R																		
		◇1	◇1					◇1				◇1	◇1	◇1	◇1	◇1	◇1	◇1	◇1	◇1		◇1	◇1	◇1	◇1
				🛏	🛏	🛏	🛏																		
				☕	☕	☕	☕							🛒	☕	🛒	☕		☕	☕			🛒	☕	☕
						A	A																		
Inverness	d					20p47																			
Aberdeen	d						21p42																		
Dundee	d						23b06																		
Perth	d					23b21																			
Edinburgh 10	d			23p40																					
Haymarket	d																								
Glasgow Central 15	d				23p40																				
Motherwell	d				23b56																				
Carstairs	d			00u16																					
Lockerbie	d																								
Carlisle 8	a																								
	d			01u41																					
Penrith North Lakes	d																								
Windermere	d																								
Oxenholme Lake District	a																								
	d																								
Barrow-in-Furness	d											04 35													
Lancaster 6	a											05 28													
	d																			05 40					
Blackpool North	d	22p44						03 37														05 39			
Preston 8	a	23p08				04s33														05 55		06 03			
Preston 8	d	23p10						04u02					05 16							05 58		06 05			
Wigan North Western	a																			06 09					
	d																			06 09					
Blackrod	d																					06 22			
Lostock	d																					06 30			
Bolton	a	23p34						04c31					05 42									06 34			
Manchester Piccadilly 10	a	23p53						04 48					06 01									06 56			
Manchester Airport ✈	a	00 24						05 07					06 18									07 17			
Liverpool Lime Street 10	a																								
	d		23p34						03 38								05 47								
Liverpool South Parkway ✈	d		23p45																						
Runcorn	d		23p53														06 03								
Warrington Bank Quay	a																			06 20					
	d																			06 20					
Hartford	d		00 07																						
Manchester Piccadilly 10	d								04a14					05 11	05 25				05 55				06 00	06 10	06 35
Stockport	d														05 34				06 03				06 08	06 18	06 43
Wilmslow	d														05 41				06 11						
Holyhead	d																								
Bangor (Gwynedd)	d																								
Llandudno Junction	d																								
Wrexham General	d																								
Chester	d									04 22															
Crewe 10	a		00 22			05s38				04 44				05 41	05 57				06 27						
	d									04 59				05 47	06 00			06 20	06 29						
Macclesfield	d																						06 21	06 31	06 56
Congleton	d																								
Stoke-on-Trent	d													06 08		←							06 39	06 48	07 12
Stafford	a									05 24				06 25	06 17	06 25	06 34	06 41					06 57		
	d									05 25				06 26	06 19	06 26	06 35	06 41					06 58		
Penkridge	a													→				06 47							
Wolverhampton 7	a									05 39						06 39		06 57					07 12		
Birmingham New Street 12	a									05 58						06 57		07 17					07 31		
Birmingham International ✈	a															07 13									
Coventry	a															07 24									
Lichfield Trent Valley	a																							07 11	
Tamworth Low Level	a																							07 17	
Nuneaton	a																06 57								
Rugby	a														06 49										07 52
Milton Keynes Central	a														07 11				07 31	07 37					
Watford Junction	a			06s27											07s32		07s44								
London Euston 15 ⊖	a			06 50		07 48									07 52		08 05		08 09	08 14				08 27	08 46

A Conveys a portion from Fort William, dep 1950

b Previous night, stops to pick up only

c Stops to pick up only

OVERNIGHT SLEEPERS. For sleeper trains, operated by First ScotRail, please refer to Tables 400 - 404

Table 65

Saturdays

15 September to 20 October

Scotland and North West England - West Midlands and London

Route Diagram - see first Page of Table 65

		LM	VT	TP	LM	VT		LM	VT	VT	TP	XC	VT	VT	LM	VT		VT	TP	XC	VT	EM	LM	VT	LM
		◇1	◇1	◇1	◇1	◇1		◇1	◇1	◇1	◇1	◇1	◇1	◇1	◇1	◇1		◇1	◇1	◇1	◇1	◇	◇1	◇1	◇1
																			A						
			☕			☕			☕	☕	🛒	🛒	☕	☕		☕		☕	🛒	🛒	☕			☕	
Inverness	d																								
Aberdeen	d																								
Dundee	d																								
Perth	d																								
Edinburgh 10	d																								
Haymarket	d																								
Glasgow Central 15	d									04 26															
Motherwell	d																								
Carstairs	d																								
Lockerbie	d																								
Carlisle 8	a									05 43															
	d									05 44															
Penrith North Lakes	d									05 59															
Windermere	d																								
Oxenholme Lake District	a									06 21															
	d									06 22															
Barrow-in-Furness	d			05 31															06 20						
Lancaster 6	a			06 23						06 36									07 21						
	d			06 23						06 37								06 58	07 22						
Blackpool North	d										06 40														
Preston 8	a			06 42						06 55	07 07							07 15	07 41						
Preston 8	d		06 17	06 44						06 58	07 09							07 17	07 47						
Wigan North Western	a		06 28							07 09								07 28							
	d		06 28							07 10								07 28							
Blackrod	d																								
Lostock	d										07 30														
Bolton	a			07 08							07 34								08 08						
Manchester Piccadilly 10	a			07 27							07 56								08 27						
Manchester Airport ✈	a			07 47							08 17								08 47						
Liverpool Lime Street 10	a																								
	d				06 32	06 45									07 04	07 19						06 49	07 34	07 48	
Liverpool South Parkway ✈	d				06 42										07 14							06 59	07 44		
Runcorn	d				06 50	07 01									07 22	07 36							07 52	08 04	
Warrington Bank Quay	a		06 39							07 20								07 39							
	d		06 39							07 20								07 39							
Hartford	d				07 02										07 36								08 04		
Manchester Piccadilly 10	d								06 55			07 07	07 15							07 27	07 35	07 42			
Stockport	d								07 04			07 16	07 23							07 35	07 43	07a53			
Wilmslow	d								07 11																
Holyhead	d																								
Bangor (Gwynedd)	d																								
Llandudno Junction	d																								
Wrexham General	d																								
Chester	d													07 17											
Crewe 10	a		06 58		07 14	07 18			07 27					07 36	07 47	07 52		07 58					08 19		
	d	06 47	07 01		07 16	07 20			07 29					07 39	07 49	07 55		08 01					08 22		
Macclesfield	d																			07 49	07 56				
Congleton	d																								
Stoke-on-Trent	d							←				07 44	07 50							08 07	08 12				←
Stafford	a	07 10			07 40	07 38		07 40				08 02			08 10	08 14				08 25			08 42	08 35	08 42
	d	07 12			07 41	07 39		07 41				08 03			08 10	08 16				08 26			08 43	08 36	08 43
Penkridge	a	07 17			→			07 46							08 16								→		08 48
Wolverhampton 7	a	07 28	07 32					07 57				08 16			08 28			08 31		08 39					08 58
Birmingham New Street 12	a	07 47	07 55					08 17				08 38			08 47			08 55		08 58					09 18
Birmingham International ✈	a																			09 13					
Coventry	a																			09 24					
Lichfield Trent Valley	a															08 30									
Tamworth Low Level	a															08 36									
Nuneaton	a																							08 58	
Rugby	a																								
Milton Keynes Central	a												08 46												
Watford Junction	a																								
London Euston 15 ⊖	a					08 59			09 04	09 12			09 23	09 30		09 46					09 42			10 00	

A 🛒 from Preston

OVERNIGHT SLEEPERS. For sleeper trains, operated by First ScotRail, please refer to Tables 400 - 404

Table 65

Saturdays

15 September to 20 October

Scotland and North West England - West Midlands and London

Route Diagram - see first Page of Table 65

		VT		VT	TP	XC	LM	VT	VT	VT	TP	XC		VT	EM	LM	VT	LM	VT	VT	SR	XC		LM	NT
		◇1		◇1	◇1	◇1	◇1	◇1	◇1	◇1	◇1	◇1		◇1	◇	◇1	◇1	◇1	◇1	◇1		◇1		◇1	
											A														
		⊡		⊡	🛒	🛒		⊡	⊡	⊡	🛒	🛒		⊡			⊡		⊡	⊡		🛒			
Inverness	d																								
Aberdeen	d																								
Dundee	d																								
Perth	d																								
Edinburgh 10	d																								
Haymarket	d																								
Glasgow Central 15	d			05 40						05 50										06 30	07 05				
Motherwell	d									06 04										06 44	07 27				
Carstairs	d																				07a47				
Lockerbie	d																			07 25					
Carlisle 8	a			06 46						07 02										07 43					
	d			06 49						07 03										07 46					
Penrith North Lakes	d									07 18										08 00					
Windermere	d																								
Oxenholme Lake District	a			07 22						07 41										08 22					
	d			07 24						07 42										08 23					
Barrow-in-Furness	d										07 29														
Lancaster 6	a			07 37						07 56	08 26									08 37					
	d			07 38						07 57	08 27									08 38					
Blackpool North	d				07 44																				08 38
Preston 8	a			07 56	08 11					08 15	08 45									08 56					09 02
Preston 8	d			07 58	08 12					08 17	08 47									08 58					09 04
Wigan North Western	a			08 09						08 28										09 09					09 24
	d			08 09						08 28										09 09					09 24
Blackrod	d																								
Lostock	d																								
Bolton	a				08 34						09 08														
Manchester Piccadilly 10	a				08 56						09 27														
Manchester Airport ✈	a				09 19						09 47														
Liverpool Lime Street 10	a																								10 02
	d						08 04								07 42	08 34	08 48							09 04	10 16
Liverpool South Parkway ✈	d						08 15								07 52	08 44								09 15	10a27
Runcorn	d						08 24									08 52	09 04							09 24	
Warrington Bank Quay	a			08 20						08 39										09 20					
	d			08 20						08 39										09 20					
Hartford	d															09 06									
Manchester Piccadilly 10	d	07 55				08 07		08 15				08 27		08 35	08 43				08 55			09 07			
Stockport	d	08 04				08 16		08 23				08 35		08 43	08a53				09 04			09 16			
Wilmslow	d	08 11																	09 11						
Holyhead	d								06 52																
Bangor (Gwynedd)	d								07 20																
Llandudno Junction	d								07 38																
Wrexham General	d																								
Chester	d								08 35																
Crewe 10	a	08 27					08 47		08 54	08 58						09 20			09 27					09 44	
	d	08 29					08 49		08 56	09 01						09 22			09 29					09 49	
Macclesfield	d											08 49		08 56											
Congleton	d																								
Stoke-on-Trent	d					08 44		08 50				09 07		09 12				←				09 44			
Stafford	a					09 02	09 09					09 25				09 42	09 35	09 42				10 02		10 10	
	d					09 03	09 10					09 26				09 43	09 36	09 43				10 03		10 10	
Penkridge	a						09 15									→								10 16	
Wolverhampton 7	a					09 15	09 27			09 31		09 39						09 56				10 15		10 27	
Birmingham New Street 12	a					09 39	09 47			09 55		09 58						10 17				10 39		10 47	
Birmingham International ✈	a											10 13													
Coventry	a											10 24													
Lichfield Trent Valley	a																								
Tamworth Low Level	a																								
Nuneaton	a																09 58								
Rugby	a																								
Milton Keynes Central	a							09 46	10 01																
Watford Junction	a																								
London Euston 15 ⊖	a	10 04		10 12				10 23	10 37					10 42			11 01		11 04	11 12					

A 🛒 from Preston

OVERNIGHT SLEEPERS. For sleeper trains, operated by First ScotRail, please refer to Tables 400 - 404

Scotland and North West England - West Midlands and London

Route Diagram - see first Page of Table 65

Station		TP	VT	VT	VT	TP	XC	VT		EM	LM	VT	LM	VT	VT	XC	LM	NT		TP	TP	VT	VT	VT	TP
		◇[1]	◇[1]	◇[1]	◇[1]	◇[1]	◇[1]	◇[1]		◇	◇[1]	◇[1]	◇[1]	◇[1]	◇[1]	◇[1]	◇[1]			◇[1]	◇[1]	◇[1]	◇[1]	◇[1]	◇[1]
		🛒	🍽	🍽	🍽	🛒	🛒	🍽				🍽		🍽	🍽	🛒				🛒	🛒	🍽	🍽	🍽	
Inverness	d																								
Aberdeen	d																								
Dundee	d																								
Perth	d																								
Edinburgh [10]	d				06 52																				
Haymarket	d				06 56															07u46					
Glasgow Central [15]	d					07 10									07 35									08 00	
Motherwell	d														07 52										
Carstairs	d																								
Lockerbie	d					08 06																			
Carlisle [8]	a				08 05	08 29									08 46					08 59				09 08	
	d				08 07	08 29									08 49					08 59				09 09	
Penrith North Lakes	d				08 22	08 45																			
Windermere	d																								09 38
Oxenholme Lake District	a					09 09									09 22										09 57
	d					09 11									09 23										09 58
Barrow-in-Furness	d																								
Lancaster [6]	a				08 56	09 26									09 37									09 56	10 16
	d				08 57	09 26									09 38									09 57	10 16
Blackpool North	d	08 44																09 37			09 43				
Preston [8]	a	09 08			09 15	09 45									09 56			10 02		10 04	10 07			10 15	10 35
Preston [8]	d	09 10			09 17	09 47									09 58			10 04		10 12				10 17	
Wigan North Western	a				09 28										10 09			10 24						10 28	
	d				09 28										10 09			10 24						10 28	
Blackrod	d																								
Lostock	d																								
Bolton	a	09 34				10 08														10 34					
Manchester Piccadilly [10] 🚊	a	09 56				10 27														10 56					
Manchester Airport ✈	a	10 17				10 47														11 17					
Liverpool Lime Street [10]	a																	11 02							
	d									08 52	09 34	09 48					10 04	11 16							
Liverpool South Parkway ✈	d									09 03	09 44						10 15	11a27							
Runcorn	d										09 52	10 04					10 25								
Warrington Bank Quay	a				09 39										10 20									10 39	
	d				09 39										10 20									10 39	
Hartford	d										10 04														
Manchester Piccadilly [10] 🚊	d		09 15				09 27	09 35		09 43				09 55		10 07						10 15			
Stockport	d		09 23				09 35	09 43		09a53				10 04		10 16						10 23			
Wilmslow	d													10 11											
Holyhead	d			07 55																			08 55		
Bangor (Gwynedd)	d			08 22																			09 22		
Llandudno Junction	d			08 40																			09 40		
Wrexham General	d																								
Chester	d			09 35																			10 35		
Crewe [10]	a			09 54	09 58						10 19			10 27			10 45						10 54	10 58	
	d			09 56	10 01						10 22			10 29			10 49						10 56	11 01	
Macclesfield	d						09 49	09 56																	
Congleton	d																								
Stoke-on-Trent	d		09 50				10 07	10 12					←			10 44						10 50			
Stafford	a						10 25				10 42	10 35	10 42			11 02	11 09								
	d						10 26				10 43	10 36	10 43			11 03	11 10								
Penkridge	a										→						11 15								
Wolverhampton [7] 🚊	a				10 31		10 39						10 56			11 16	11 27							11 32	
Birmingham New Street [12]	a				10 55		10 58						11 17			11 39	11 47							11 55	
Birmingham International ✈	a						11 13																		
Coventry	a						11 24																		
Lichfield Trent Valley	a																								
Tamworth Low Level	a																								
Nuneaton	a																								
Rugby	a																								
Milton Keynes Central	a		10 46	11 01																		11 46	12 01		
Watford Junction	a																								
London Euston [15] ⊖	a		11 23	11 38				11 42				11 56		12 04	12 12							12 23	12 38		

OVERNIGHT SLEEPERS. For sleeper trains, operated by First ScotRail, please refer to Tables 400 - 404

15 September to 20 October

Scotland and North West England - West Midlands and London

Route Diagram - see first Page of Table 65

		TP	NT	XC		VT	EM	LM	VT	LM	VT	VT	XC	LM		NT	TP	VT	VT	VT	SR	TP	XC	VT	
		◇1		◇1		◇1	◇	◇1	◇1	◇1	◇1	◇1	◇1	◇1			◇1	◇1	◇1	◇1		◇1	◇1	◇1	
		A																				A			
		🛒		🛒		🍽			🍽		🍽	🍽	🛒				🛒	🍽	🍽	🍽		🛒	🛒	🍽	
Inverness	d																								
Aberdeen	d																								
Dundee	d																								
Perth	d																								
Edinburgh [10]	d																			08 52	09 03				
Haymarket	d																			08 57	09 07				
Glasgow Central [15]	d											08 40													
Motherwell	d																								
Carstairs	d																				09a44				
Lockerbie	d																								
Carlisle [8]	a											09 46								10 05					
	d											09 49								10 07					
Penrith North Lakes	d											10 03													
Windermere	d																					10 49			
Oxenholme Lake District	a																			10 41		11 08			
	d																			10 42		11 09			
Barrow-in-Furness	d	09 23	10 16																						
Lancaster [6]	a	10 25	11 21									10 37								10 56		11 26			
	d	10 26										10 38								10 57		11 26			
Blackpool North	d															10 37	10 44								
Preston [8]	a	10 45										10 56				11 02	11 08			11 15		11 45			
Preston [8]	d	10 47										10 58				11 04	11 10			11 17		11 47			
Wigan North Western	a											11 09				11 24				11 28					
	d											11 09				11 24				11 28					
Blackrod	d																								
Lostock	d																								
Bolton	a	11 08															11 34					12 08			
Manchester Piccadilly [10]	a	11 27															11 56					12 27			
Manchester Airport ✈	a	11 47															12 17					12 47			
Liverpool Lime Street [10]	a															12 02									
	d						09 52	10 34	10 48					11 04		12 16									
Liverpool South Parkway ✈	d						10 03	10 44						11 15		12a27									
Runcorn	d							10 52	11 04					11 25											
Warrington Bank Quay	a											11 20								11 39					
	d											11 20								11 39					
Hartford	d							11 04																	
Manchester Piccadilly [10]	d			10 27		10 35	10 43				10 55		11 07					11 15					11 27	11 35	
Stockport	d			10 35		10 43	10a53				11 04		11 16					11 23					11 35	11 43	
Wilmslow	d										11 11														
Holyhead	d																								
Bangor (Gwynedd)	d																								
Llandudno Junction	d																								
Wrexham General	d																								
Chester	d																		11 35						
Crewe [10]	a							11 19			11 27			11 45					11 54	11 58					
	d							11 22			11 29			11 49					11 56	12 01					
Macclesfield	d			10 49		10 56																	11 49	11 56	
Congleton	d																								
Stoke-on-Trent	d			11 07		11 12				←			11 44					11 50					12 07	12 12	
Stafford	a			11 25				11 42	11 35	11 42			12 02	12 09									12 24		
	d			11 26				11 43	11 36	11 43			12 03	12 10									12 25		
Penkridge	a							→						12 15											
Wolverhampton [7]	a			11 39						11 56			12 16	12 27						12 31			12 39		
Birmingham New Street [12]	a			11 58						12 17			12 39	12 47						12 55			12 58		
Birmingham International ✈	a			12 13																			13 13		
Coventry	a			12 24																			13 24		
Lichfield Trent Valley	a																								
Tamworth Low Level	a																								
Nuneaton	a																								
Rugby	a																								
Milton Keynes Central	a																	12 46	13 01						
Watford Junction	a																								
London Euston [15] ⊖	a					12 42			12 56		13 04	13 12						13 23	13 38					13 42	

A 🛒 from Preston

OVERNIGHT SLEEPERS. For sleeper trains, operated by First ScotRail, please refer to Tables 400 - 404

Saturdays

15 September to 20 October

Scotland and North West England - West Midlands and London

Route Diagram - see first Page of Table 65

		EM	LM	VT	LM	VT	VT	TP	XC	LM		NT	TP	VT	VT	VT	TP	TP	XC	VT		EM	LM	VT	LM
		◇	◇[1]	◇[1]	◇[1]	◇[1]	◇[1]	◇[1]	◇[1]	◇[1]			◇[1]	◇[1]	◇[1]	◇[1]	◇[1]	◇[1]	◇[1]	◇[1]		◇	◇[1]	◇[1]	◇[1]
				🍴		🍴	🍴		🛒				🛒	🍴	🍴	🍴	🛒	🛒	🛒	🍴				🍴	
Inverness	d																								
Aberdeen	d																								
Dundee	d																								
Perth	d																								
Edinburgh [10]	d																09 51								
Haymarket	d																09u56								
Glasgow Central [15]	d						09 40									10 00		10 10							
Motherwell	d																								
Carstairs	d																								
Lockerbie	d																11 01								
Carlisle [8]	a						10 47									11 08	11 22	11 26							
	d						10 49									11 09	11 29								
Penrith North Lakes	d															11 24	11 45								
Windermere	d																								
Oxenholme Lake District	a						11 22										12 09								
	d						11 23										12 10								
Barrow-in-Furness	d							11 25																	
Lancaster [6]	a						11 37	12 18									12 26								
	d						11 38	12 18									12 26								
Blackpool North	d											11 37	11 44												
Preston [8]	a						11 56	12 37				12 02	12 08			12 15	12 45								
Preston [8]	d						11 58					12 04	12 10			12 17	12 47								
Wigan North Western	a						12 09					12 24				12 28									
	d						12 09					12 24				12 28									
Blackrod	d																								
Lostock	d																								
Bolton	a												12 34				13 08								
Manchester Piccadilly [10]	a												12 56				13 27								
Manchester Airport ✈	a												13 17				13 47								
Liverpool Lime Street [10]	a											13 02													
	d	10 52	11 34	11 48						12 04		13 16										11 52	12 34	12 48	
Liverpool South Parkway ✈	d	11 03	11 44							12 15		13a27										12 03	12 44		
Runcorn	d		11 52	12 04						12 25													12 52	13 04	
Warrington Bank Quay	a						12 20									12 39									
	d						12 20									12 39									
Hartford	d		12 04																				13 06		
Manchester Piccadilly [10]	d	11 43				11 55			12 07					12 15					12 27	12 35		12 43			
Stockport	d	11a53				12 04			12 16					12 23					12 35	12 43		12a53			
Wilmslow	d					12 11																			
Holyhead	d																								
Bangor (Gwynedd)	d																								
Llandudno Junction	d																								
Wrexham General	d																								
Chester	d														12 35										
Crewe [10]	a		12 19			12 27				12 45					12 54	12 58							13 20		
	d		12 22			12 29				12 49					12 57	13 01							13 22		
Macclesfield	d																		12 49	12 56					
Congleton	d																								
Stoke-on-Trent	d				←				12 44					12 50					13 07	13 12					←
Stafford	a		12 42	12 35	12 42				13 02	13 09									13 25				13 42	13 35	13 42
	d		12 43	12 36	12 43				13 03	13 10									13 26				13 43	13 36	13 43
Penkridge	a		↦							13 15													↦		
Wolverhampton [7]	a				12 56				13 15	13 27						13 31			13 39						13 56
Birmingham New Street [12]	a				13 17				13 39	13 47						13 55			13 58						14 17
Birmingham International ✈	a																		14 13						
Coventry	a																		14 24						
Lichfield Trent Valley	a																								
Tamworth Low Level	a																								
Nuneaton	a																								
Rugby	a																								
Milton Keynes Central	a													13 46	14 01										
Watford Junction	a																								
London Euston [15] ⊖	a			13 56		14 04	14 12							14 23	14 38					14 42				14 56	

OVERNIGHT SLEEPERS. For sleeper trains, operated by First ScotRail, please refer to Tables 400 - 404

Scotland and North West England - West Midlands and London

Route Diagram - see first Page of Table 65

		VT	VT	XC	LM	NT		TP	VT	VT	VT	TP	XC	VT	EM	LM		VT	LM	VT	VT	XC	LM	NT	TP
		◇1	◇1	◇1	◇1			◇1	◇1	◇1	◇1	◇1	◇1	◇1	◇	◇1		◇1	◇1	◇1	◇1	◇1	◇1		◇1
												A													
		🍽	🍽	🛒				🛒	🍽	🍽	🍽	🛒	🛒	🍽				🍽		🍽	🍽	🛒			🛒
Inverness	d																								
Aberdeen	d																								
Dundee	d																								
Perth	d																								
Edinburgh 10	d										10 52														
Haymarket	d										10 57														
Glasgow Central 15	d		10 40																		11 40				
Motherwell	d																								
Carstairs	d																								
Lockerbie	d																								
Carlisle 8	a		11 47								12 05										12 46				
	d		11 49								12 07										12 49				
Penrith North Lakes	d																				13 03				
Windermere	d											12 51													
Oxenholme Lake District	a		12 22								12 41	13 07													
	d		12 23								12 43	13 09													
Barrow-in-Furness	d																								
Lancaster 6	a		12 37								12 56	13 26									13 37				
	d		12 38								12 57	13 26									13 38				
Blackpool North	d					12 37		12 44																13 37	13 44
Preston 8	a		12 56			13 02		13 08			13 15	13 45									13 56			14 02	14 08
Preston 8	d		12 58			13 04		13 10			13 17	13 47									13 58			14 04	14 10
Wigan North Western	a		13 09			13 24					13 28										14 09			14 24	
	d		13 09			13 24					13 28										14 09			14 24	
Blackrod	d																								
Lostock	d																								
Bolton	a							13 34				14 08													14 34
Manchester Piccadilly 10 ⇌	a							13 56				14 27													14 56
Manchester Airport ✈	a							14 17				14 47													15 17
Liverpool Lime Street 10	a					14 02																		15 02	
	d				13 04	14 16									12 52	13 34		13 48					14 04	15 16	
Liverpool South Parkway ✈	d				13 15	14a27									13 03	13 44							14 15	15a27	
Runcorn	d				13 25											13 52		14 04					14 25		
Warrington Bank Quay	a		13 20								13 39										14 20				
	d		13 20								13 39										14 20				
Hartford	d															14 04									
Manchester Piccadilly 10 ⇌	d	12 55		13 07					13 15				13 27	13 35	13 43					13 55		14 07			
Stockport	d	13 04		13 16					13 23				13 35	13 43	13a53					14 04		14 16			
Wilmslow	d	13 11																		14 11					
Holyhead	d																								
Bangor (Gwynedd)	d																								
Llandudno Junction	d																								
Wrexham General	d																								
Chester	d									13 35															
Crewe 10	a	13 27			13 45					13 54	13 58					14 19				14 27			14 45		
	d	13 29			13 49					13 56	14 01					14 22				14 29			14 49		
Macclesfield	d												13 49	13 56											
Congleton	d																								
Stoke-on-Trent	d			13 44					13 50				14 07	14 12					←			14 44			
Stafford	a			14 02	14 09								14 25			14 46		14 35	14 46			15 02	15 09		
	d			14 03	14 10								14 26			14 46		14 36	14 46			15 03	15 10		
Penkridge	a				14 15											→							15 15		
Wolverhampton 7 ⇌	a			14 16	14 27						14 31		14 39						14 59			15 16	15 27		
Birmingham New Street 12	a			14 39	14 47						14 55		14 58						15 18			15 39	15 47		
Birmingham International ✈	a												15 13												
Coventry	a												15 24												
Lichfield Trent Valley	a																								
Tamworth Low Level	a																								
Nuneaton	a																								
Rugby	a																								
Milton Keynes Central	a								14 46	15 01															
Watford Junction	a																								
London Euston 15 ⊖	a	15 04	15 12						15 23	15 38				15 42				15 56		16 04	16 12				

A 🛒 from Preston

OVERNIGHT SLEEPERS. For sleeper trains, operated by First ScotRail, please refer to Tables 400 - 404

Table 65

Saturdays

15 September to 20 October

Scotland and North West England - West Midlands and London

Route Diagram - see first Page of Table 65

		VT		VT	VT	TP	TP	NT	XC	VT	EM	LM		VT	LM	VT	VT	XC	LM	NT	TP	VT		VT	VT
		◇1		◇1	◇1	◇1	◇1		◇1	◇1	◇	◇1		◇1	◇1	◇1	◇1	◇1	◇1		◇1	◇1		◇1	◇1
						A																			
		🍴		🍴	🍴	🛒	🛒		🛒	🍴				🍴		🍴	🍴	🛒			🛒	🍴		🍴	🍴
Inverness	d																								
Aberdeen	d																								
Dundee	d																								
Perth	d																								
Edinburgh 10	d						12 08																		12 52
Haymarket	d						12u12																		12 57
Glasgow Central 15	d				12 00												12 40								
Motherwell	d																								
Carstairs	d																								
Lockerbie	d						13 07																		
Carlisle 8	a				13 08		13 29										13 47								14 05
	d				13 09		13 29										13 49								14 07
Penrith North Lakes	d																								14 22
Windermere	d																								
Oxenholme Lake District	a						14 06										14 22								
	d						14 07										14 24								
Barrow-in-Furness	d					13 25		14 16																	
Lancaster 6	a				13 56	14 18	14 21	15 20									14 37								14 56
	d				13 58	14 18	14 22										14 38								14 57
Blackpool North	d																			14 37	14 44				
Preston 8	a				14 15	14 37	14 41										14 56			15 02	15 08				15 15
Preston 8	d				14 17		14 47										14 58			15 04	15 10				15 17
Wigan North Western	a				14 28												15 09			15 24					15 28
	d				14 28												15 09			15 24					15 28
Blackrod	d																								
Lostock	d																								
Bolton	a						15 08														15 34				
Manchester Piccadilly 10	a						15 27														15 56				
Manchester Airport ✈	a						15 47														16 17				
Liverpool Lime Street 10	a																			16 02					
	d										13 52	14 34		14 48					15 04	16 16					
Liverpool South Parkway ✈	d										14 03	14 44							15 15	16a27					
Runcorn	d											14 52		15 04					15 25						
Warrington Bank Quay	a				14 39												15 20								15 39
	d				14 39												15 20								15 39
Hartford	d											15 04													
Manchester Piccadilly 10	d	14 15							14 27	14 35	14 43					14 55		15 07				15 15			
Stockport	d	14 23							14 35	14 43	14a53					15 04		15 16				15 23			
Wilmslow	d															15 11									
Holyhead	d																								
Bangor (Gwynedd)	d																								
Llandudno Junction	d																								
Wrexham General	d																								
Chester	d			14 35																				15 35	
Crewe 10	a			14 54	14 58							15 19				15 27			15 45					15 54	15 58
	d			14 56	15 01							15 22				15 29			15 49					15 56	16 01
Macclesfield	d								14 49	14 56															
Congleton	d																								
Stoke-on-Trent	d	14 50							15 07	15 12					←			15 44				15 50			
Stafford	a								15 25			15 42		15 35	15 42			16 02	16 09						
	d								15 26			15 43		15 36	15 43			16 03	16 10						
Penkridge	a											→							16 15						
Wolverhampton 7	a				15 31				15 39						15 56			16 16	16 27						16 31
Birmingham New Street 12	a				15 55				15 58						16 17			16 39	16 47						16 55
Birmingham International ✈	a								16 13																
Coventry	a								16 24																
Lichfield Trent Valley	a																								
Tamworth Low Level	a																								
Nuneaton	a																								
Rugby	a																								
Milton Keynes Central	a	15 46		16 01																		16 46		17 01	
Watford Junction	a																								
London Euston 15 ⊖	a	16 23		16 38						16 42				16 56		17 04	17 12					17 23		17 38	

A 🛒 from Preston

OVERNIGHT SLEEPERS. For sleeper trains, operated by First ScotRail, please refer to Tables 400 - 404

Scotland and North West England - West Midlands and London

Route Diagram - see first Page of Table 65

		TP	XC	VT	EM	LM	VT	LM		VT	VT	XC	LM	NT	TP	VT	VT	VT		TP	XC	VT	EM	LM	VT
		◇1	◇1	◇1	◇	◇1	◇1	◇1		◇1	◇1	◇1	◇1		◇1	◇1	◇1	◇1		◇1	◇1	◇1	◇	◇1	◇1
Inverness	d																								
Aberdeen	d																								
Dundee	d																								
Perth	d																								
Edinburgh 10	d																			14 07					
Haymarket	d																			14u11					
Glasgow Central 15	d	13 09									13 40							14 00							
Motherwell	d																								
Carstairs	d																								
Lockerbie	d	14 06																		15 06					
Carlisle 8	a	14 29									14 46							15 09		15 27					
	d	14 29									14 49							15 11		15 27					
Penrith North Lakes	d	14 45																		15 43					
Windermere	d																								
Oxenholme Lake District	a	15 09									15 22							15 45		16 06					
	d	15 10									15 23							15 46		16 07					
Barrow-in-Furness	d																								
Lancaster 6	a	15 26									15 37									16 26					
	d	15 26									15 38									16 26					
Blackpool North	d													15 37	15 44										
Preston 8	a	15 45									15 56			16 02	16 08			16 15		16 45					
Preston 8	d	15 47									15 58			16 04	16 10			16 17		16 47					
Wigan North Western	a										16 09			16 24				16 28							
	d										16 09			16 24				16 28							
Blackrod	d																								
Lostock	d																								
Bolton	a	16 08													16 34					17 08					
Manchester Piccadilly 10	a	16 27													16 56					17 27					
Manchester Airport ✈	a	16 47													17 17					17 48					
Liverpool Lime Street 10	a													17 05											
	d				14 52	15 34	15 48						16 04										15 52	16 34	16 48
Liverpool South Parkway ✈	d				15 03	15 44							16 15										16 03	16 44	
Runcorn	d					15 52	16 04						16 25											16 52	17 04
Warrington Bank Quay	a										16 20							16 39							
	d										16 20							16 39							
Hartford	d					16 04																		17 06	
Manchester Piccadilly 10	d		15 27	15 35	15 43					15 55		16 07				16 15					16 27	16 35	16 43		
Stockport	d		15 35	15 43	15a53					16 04		16 16				16 23					16 35	16 43	16a53		
Wilmslow	d									16 11															
Holyhead	d																14 38								
Bangor (Gwynedd)	d																15 07								
Llandudno Junction	d																15 27								
Wrexham General	d																								
Chester	d																16 24								
Crewe 10	a					16 19				16 27			16 45				16 47	16 58						17 20	
	d					16 22				16 29			16 49				16 56	17 01						17 22	
Macclesfield	d		15 49	15 56																	16 49	16 56			
Congleton	d																								
Stoke-on-Trent	d		16 07	16 12				←				16 44				16 50					17 07	17 12			
Stafford	a		16 24			16 46	16 35	16 46				17 02	17 09								17 25			17 42	17 35
	d		16 25			16 46	16 36	16 46				17 03	17 10								17 26			17 43	17 36
Penkridge	a					→							17 15											→	
Wolverhampton 7	a		16 39					16 59				17 16	17 27					17 31			17 39				
Birmingham New Street 12	a		16 58					17 18				17 39	17 47					17 55			17 58				
Birmingham International ✈	a		17 13																		18 13				
Coventry	a		17 24																		18 24				
Lichfield Trent Valley	a																								
Tamworth Low Level	a																								
Nuneaton	a																								
Rugby	a																								
Milton Keynes Central	a															17 46	18 01								
Watford Junction	a																								
London Euston 15 ⊖	a			17 42			17 56			18 04	18 12					18 23	18 38					18 42			18 56

OVERNIGHT SLEEPERS. For sleeper trains, operated by First ScotRail, please refer to Tables 400 - 404

Table 65

Saturdays

15 September to 20 October

Scotland and North West England - West Midlands and London

Route Diagram - see first Page of Table 65

		LM	VT	VT		SR	XC	LM	NT	TP	VT	TP	VT	TP		XC	VT	EM	LM	VT	LM	VT	VT	XC
		◇1	◇1	◇1			◇1	◇1		◇1	◇1	◇1	◇1	◇1		◇1	◇1	◇	◇1	◇1	◇1	◇1	◇1	◇1
			⊏	⊏			🍴			🍴	⊏		⊏	🍴		🍴	⊏			⊏		⊏	⊏	🍴
Inverness	d																							
Aberdeen	d																							
Dundee	d																							
Perth	d																							
Edinburgh ■10	d										14 52													
Haymarket	d										14 57													
Glasgow Central ■15	d			14 40		15 14																	15 40	
Motherwell	d					15 34																		
Carstairs	d					15a51																		
Lockerbie	d																							
Carlisle ■8	a			15 46							16 05												16 46	
	d			15 49							16 07												16 49	
Penrith North Lakes	d										16 22												17 03	
Windermere	d																							
Oxenholme Lake District	a			16 22																				
	d			16 24																				
Barrow-in-Furness	d											16 22												
Lancaster ■6	a			16 37							16 56	17 19											17 37	
	d			16 38							16 57	17 20											17 38	
Blackpool North	d								16 35	16 40				17 20										
Preston ■8	a			16 56					17 02	17 08	17 15	17 39		17 45									17 56	
Preston ■8	d			16 58					17 04	17 10	17 17			17 47									17 58	
Wigan North Western	a			17 09					17 24		17 28												18 09	
	d			17 09					17 24		17 28												18 09	
Blackrod	d																							
Lostock	d																							
Bolton	a									17 34				18 08										
Manchester Piccadilly ■10	a									17 56				18 27										
Manchester Airport ✈	a									18 17				18 47										
Liverpool Lime Street ■10	a								18 02															
	d							17 04										16 52	17 34	17 48				
Liverpool South Parkway ✈	d							17 15										17 03	17 44					
Runcorn	d							17 25											17 52	18 04				
Warrington Bank Quay	a			17 20							17 39												18 20	
	d			17 20							17 39												18 20	
Hartford	d																		18 06					
Manchester Piccadilly ■10	d		16 55				17 06						17 15			17 27	17 35	17 43				17 55		18 05
Stockport	d		17 04										17 23			17 36	17 43	17a53				18 04		18 13
Wilmslow	d		17 11																			18 11		
Holyhead	d																							
Bangor (Gwynedd)	d																							
Llandudno Junction	d																							
Wrexham General	d																							
Chester	d																							
Crewe ■10	a		17 27					17 47			17 59								18 20			18 27		
	d		17 29					17 49			18 01								18 22			18 29		
Macclesfield	d						17 26										17 56							18 26
Congleton	d															17 54								
Stoke-on-Trent	d	←					17 44						17 50			18 08	18 12				←			18 44
Stafford	a	17 42					18 03	18 09								18 26			18 42	18 35	18 42			19 02
	d	17 43					18 04	18 10								18 27			18 43	18 36	18 43			19 03
Penkridge	a							18 15											→					
Wolverhampton ■7	a	17 56					18 16	18 27			18 31					18 40					18 56			19 16
Birmingham New Street ■12	a	18 17					18 38	18 47			18 55					18 58					19 17			19 33
Birmingham International ✈	a															19 13								
Coventry	a															19 24								
Lichfield Trent Valley	a																							
Tamworth Low Level	a																							
Nuneaton	a																							
Rugby	a																							
Milton Keynes Central	a												18 46											
Watford Junction	a																							
London Euston ■15 ⊖	a		19 04	19 12									19 23				19 42			19 56		20 04	20 15	

OVERNIGHT SLEEPERS. For sleeper trains, operated by First ScotRail, please refer to Tables 400 - 404

Table 65

Saturdays

15 September to 20 October

Scotland and North West England - West Midlands and London

Route Diagram - see first Page of Table 65

		LM	NT	TP	VT	TP	TP	VT	XC	VT		EM	LM	VT	LM	VT	VT	XC	LM	NT		TP	VT	TP	XC
		◇1		◇1	◇1	◇1	◇1	◇1	◇1	◇1		◇	◇1	◇1	◇1	◇1	◇1	◇1	◇1			◇1	◇1	◇1	◇1
				A 🛒	🍴		🛒	🍴	🛒	🍴				🍴		🍴	🍴	🛒					🍴	🛒	B 🛒
Inverness	d																								
Aberdeen	d																								
Dundee	d																								
Perth	d																								
Edinburgh	d						16 12																16 52		
Haymarket	d						16u16																16 57		
Glasgow Central	d				16 00												16 40							17 06	
Motherwell	d																16 54								
Carstairs	d																								
Lockerbie	d						17 11																	18 06	
Carlisle	a				17 08		17 33										17 49						18 06	18 28	
	d				17 09		17 34										17 52						18 08	18 29	
Penrith North Lakes	d						17 49																	18 45	
Windermere	d			17 06																					
Oxenholme Lake District	a			17 25	17 44												18 25						18 41	19 09	
	d			17 30	17 44												18 26						18 42	19 10	
Barrow-in-Furness	d					17 21																			
Lancaster	a			17 47		18 16	18 26										18 40						18 56	19 26	
	d			17 48		18 17	18 26										18 41						18 57	19 26	
Blackpool North	d		17 37																	18 37		18 44			
Preston	a		18 02	18 06	18 15	18 36	18 45										18 59			19 00		19 08	19 15	19 45	
Preston	d		18 04	18 08	18 17		18 47										19 01			19 04		19 10	19 17	19 47	
Wigan North Western	a		18 24		18 28												19 12			19 24			19 28		
	d		18 24		18 28												19 12			19 24			19 28		
Blackrod	d																								
Lostock	d			18 30																					
Bolton	a			18 34			19 08															19 34		20 08	
Manchester Piccadilly	a			18 56			19 27															19 56		20 27	
Manchester Airport	a			19 17			19 50															20 17		20 47	
Liverpool Lime Street	a		19 02																	20 02					
	d	18 04										17 52	18 34	18 48					19 04						
Liverpool South Parkway	d	18 15										18 03	18 44						19 14						
Runcorn	d	18 24											18 52	19 04					19 23						
Warrington Bank Quay	a				18 39												19 23						19 39		
	d				18 39												19 23						19 39		
Hartford	d												19 04												
Manchester Piccadilly	d							18 15	18 27	18 35		18 43				18 55		19 07							19 27
Stockport	d							18 23	18 35	18 43		18a53				19 04		19 16							19 35
Wilmslow	d															19 11									
Holyhead	d																								
Bangor (Gwynedd)	d																								
Llandudno Junction	d																								
Wrexham General	d																								
Chester	d																								
Crewe	a	18 46			18 59								19 19			19 27			19 49				19 59		
	d	18 49			19 01								19 22			19 29			19 51				20 01		
Macclesfield	d									18 56															19 49
Congleton	d								18 54																
Stoke-on-Trent	d							18 49	19 07	19 12					←			19 44							20 07
Stafford	a	19 09							19 25				19 42	19 35	19 42			20 02	20 11						20 25
	d	19 10							19 25				19 43	19 36	19 43			20 03	20 12						20 26
Penkridge	a	19 15											→		19 48										
Wolverhampton	a	19 27			19 31				19 39						19 59			20 16	20 28				20 32		20 39
Birmingham New Street	a	19 47			19 55				19 58						20 17			20 33	20 47				20 55		20 58
Birmingham International	a								20 13																21 13
Coventry	a								20 24																21 24
Lichfield Trent Valley	a																								
Tamworth Low Level	a																								
Nuneaton	a																								
Rugby	a																								
Milton Keynes Central	a							19 45									20 41								
Watford Junction	a																21s15								
London Euston ⊖	a							20 24		20 59				21 15		21 18	21 38								

A 🛒 from Preston

B 🛒 to Birmingham New Street

OVERNIGHT SLEEPERS. For sleeper trains, operated by First ScotRail, please refer to Tables 400 - 404

Table 65

Saturdays

15 September to 20 October

Scotland and North West England - West Midlands and London

Route Diagram - see first Page of Table 65

		VT	EM	LM	VT	LM	VT	NT	TP	XC	VT	TP	SR	XC	VT	EM	LM	XC	VT	TP	TP	VT	XC
		◇1	◇	◇1	◇1	◇1	◇1		◇1	◇1	◇1	◇1		◇1	◇1	◇	◇1	◇1	◇1	◇1	◇1	◇1	◇1
		⊏P			⊏P		⊏P				⊏P	⊥o			⊏P				⊏P			⊏P	
Inverness	d																						
Aberdeen	d																						
Dundee	d																						
Perth	d																						
Edinburgh 10	d											18 12	18 24									18 52	
Haymarket	d											18u16	18 28									18 57	
Glasgow Central 15	d						17 40				18 00								18 40				
Motherwell	d																						
Carstairs	d												19a09										
Lockerbie	d						18 32					19 11											
Carlisle 8	a						18 50				19 08	19 34							19 46			20 06	
	d						18 52				19 09	19 34							19 48			20 08	
Penrith North Lakes	d						19 06					19 49							20 02			20 23	
Windermere	d																						
Oxenholme Lake District	a						19 28					20 12							20 24			20 46	
	d						19 29					20 13							20 25			20 46	
Barrow-in-Furness	d																			19 33			
Lancaster 6	a						19 43				19 55	20 26							20 39	20 34		21 00	
	d						19 44				19 56	20 26							20 40	20 35		21 01	
Blackpool North	d							19 37	19 44												20 42		
Preston 8	a						20 02	20 02	20 08		20 15	20 45							20 58	20 53	21 06	21 19	
Preston 8	d						20 04	20 04	20 10		20 17	20 47							21 00	21 10		21 21	
Wigan North Western	a						20 15	20 24			20 28								21 11			21 32	
	d						20 15	20 24			20 28								21 11			21 32	
Blackrod	d																						
Lostock	d																						
Bolton	a								20 34			21 08								21 34			
Manchester Piccadilly 10	a								20 56			21 27								21 56			
Manchester Airport ✈	a								21 17			21 47								22 17			
Liverpool Lime Street 10	a							21 02															
	d		18 52	19 34	19 48											19 52	20 34						
Liverpool South Parkway ✈	d		19 03	19 44												20 03	20 44						
Runcorn	d			19 52	20 04												20 52						
Warrington Bank Quay	a						20 26				20 39								21 22			21 43	
	d						20 26				20 39								21 22			21 43	
Hartford	d			20 04													21 03						
Manchester Piccadilly 10	d	19 35	19 43							20 07				20 27	20 35	20 43		21 07					21 27
Stockport	d	19 43	19a53							20 16				20 35	20 43	20a53							21 36
Wilmslow	d																						
Holyhead	d																						
Bangor (Gwynedd)	d																						
Llandudno Junction	d																						
Wrexham General	d																						
Chester	d																						
Crewe 10	a			20 16			20 45				20 59						21 16		21 41			22 03	
	d			20 22			20 47				21 01						21 17		21 43			22 05	
Macclesfield	d	19 56												20 49	20 56								21 50
Congleton	d																						
Stoke-on-Trent	d	20 12				←				20 44				21 07	21 12			21 45					22 08
Stafford	a			20 44	20 35	20 44				21 02				21 26			21 42	22 02	22 07			22 24	22 32
	d			20 45	20 36	20 45				21 03				21 27			21 42	22 03	22 08			22 25	22 33
Penkridge	a			↪		20 50											21 48						
Wolverhampton 7	a					21 01				21 15	21 31			21 39			21 58	22 14	22 22			22 39	22 45
Birmingham New Street 12	a					21 19				21 32	21 54			21 58			22 20	22 32	22 46			22 59	23 02
Birmingham International ✈	a																						
Coventry	a																						
Lichfield Trent Valley	a																						
Tamworth Low Level	a																						
Nuneaton	a																						
Rugby	a																						
Milton Keynes Central	a	21 10					21 50								22 10								
Watford Junction	a														22s40								
London Euston 15 ⊖	a	22 00			22 14		22 44								23 02								

OVERNIGHT SLEEPERS. For sleeper trains, operated by First ScotRail, please refer to Tables 400 - 404

Scotland and North West England - West Midlands and London

Route Diagram - see first Page of Table 65

		EM		LM	EM	TP	NT	TP	LM	TP
		◇		◇1	◇	◇1		◇1	1	◇1
Inverness	d									
Aberdeen	d									
Dundee	d									
Perth	d									
Edinburgh 10	d									
Haymarket	d									
Glasgow Central 15	d									
Motherwell	d									
Carstairs	d									
Lockerbie	d									
Carlisle 8	a									
	d									
Penrith North Lakes	d									
Windermere	d					21 40				
Oxenholme Lake District	a					21 59				
	d					22 01				
Barrow-in-Furness	d						21 43			
Lancaster 6	a					22 17	22 45			
	d					22 17	22 46			
Blackpool North	d							21 44		22 44
Preston 8	a					22 38	23 11	22 08		23 08
Preston 8	d							22 10		23 10
Wigan North Western	a									
	d									
Blackrod	d									
Lostock	d									
Bolton	a							22 34		23 34
Manchester Piccadilly 10 🚋	a							22 56		23 53
Manchester Airport ✈	a							23 17		00 23
Liverpool Lime Street 10	a									
	d	20 52		21 34	21 37				22 04	
Liverpool South Parkway ✈	d	21 03		21 44	21 47				22 14	
Runcorn	d			21 52					22 23	
Warrington Bank Quay	a									
	d									
Hartford	d			22 04					22 34	
Manchester Piccadilly 10 🚋	d	21 43			22 31					
Stockport	d	21a52			22a41					
Wilmslow	d									
Holyhead	d									
Bangor (Gwynedd)	d									
Llandudno Junction	d									
Wrexham General	d									
Chester	d									
Crewe 10	a			22 21					22 48	
	d			22 23						
Macclesfield	d									
Congleton	d									
Stoke-on-Trent	d									
Stafford	a			22 47						
	d			22 47						
Penkridge	a			22 53						
Wolverhampton 7 🚋	a			23 03						
Birmingham New Street 12	a			23 21						
Birmingham International ✈	a									
Coventry	a									
Lichfield Trent Valley	a									
Tamworth Low Level	a									
Nuneaton	a									
Rugby	a									
Milton Keynes Central	a									
Watford Junction	a									
London Euston 15 ⊖	a									

OVERNIGHT SLEEPERS. For sleeper trains, operated by First ScotRail, please refer to Tables 400 - 404

Table 65

Saturdays
from 27 October

Scotland and North West England - West Midlands and London

Route Diagram - see first Page of Table 65

		TP	LM	SR	SR	SR	SR	TP	NT	AW		TP	TP	XC	VT	XC	VT	LM	VT	VT		TP	XC	VT	VT
				R	R	R	R																		
		◇1	◇1					◇1				◇1	◇1	◇1	◇1	◇1	◇1	◇1	◇1	◇1		◇1	◇1	◇1	◇1
				🛏	🛏	🛏	🛏																		
				🍴	🍴	🍴	🍴							🛒	🍴	🛒	🍴		🍴	🍴			🛒	🍴	🍴
						A	A																		
Inverness	d					20p47																			
Aberdeen	d						21p42																		
Dundee	d						23b06																		
Perth	d					23b21																			
Edinburgh [10]	d			23p40																					
Haymarket	d																								
Glasgow Central [15]	d				23p40																				
Motherwell	d				23b56																				
Carstairs	d			00u16																					
Lockerbie	d																								
Carlisle [8]	a																								
	d			01u41																					
Penrith North Lakes	d																								
Windermere	d																								
Oxenholme Lake District	a																								
	d																								
Barrow-in-Furness	d											04 35													
Lancaster [6]	a											05 28													
	d																			05 40					
Blackpool North	d	22p44						03 37														05 39			
Preston [8]	a	23p08				04s33														05 55		06 03			
Preston [8]	d	23p10						04u02					05 16							05 58		06 05			
Wigan North Western	a																			06 09					
	d																			06 09					
Blackrod	d																					06 22			
Lostock	d																					06 30			
Bolton	a	23p34						04c31					05 42									06 34			
Manchester Piccadilly [10] ⛴	a	23p53						04 48					06 01									06 56			
Manchester Airport ✈	a	00 24						05 07					06 18									07 17			
Liverpool Lime Street [10]	a																								
	d		23p34						03 38								05 47								
Liverpool South Parkway ✈	d		23p45																						
Runcorn	d		23p53														06 03								
Warrington Bank Quay	a																			06 20					
	d																			06 20					
Hartford	d		00 07																						
Manchester Piccadilly [10] ⛴	d								04a14					05 11	05 25				05 55				06 00	06 10	06 35
Stockport	d														05 34				06 03				06 08	06 18	06 43
Wilmslow	d														05 41				06 11						
Holyhead	d																								
Bangor (Gwynedd)	d																								
Llandudno Junction	d																								
Wrexham General	d																								
Chester	d									04 22															
Crewe [10]	a		00 22			05s38				04 44				05 41	05 57				06 27						
	d									04 59				05 47	06 00			06 20	06 29						
Macclesfield	d																						06 21	06 31	06 56
Congleton	d																								
Stoke-on-Trent	d													06 08		←							06 39	06 48	07 12
Stafford	a									05 24				06 25	06 17	06 25	06 34	06 41					06 57		
	d									05 25				06 26	06 19	06 26	06 35	06 41					06 58		
Penkridge	a													↪				06 47							
Wolverhampton [7] ⛴	a									05 39						06 39		06 57					07 12		
Birmingham New Street [12]	a									05 58						06 57		07 17					07 31		
Birmingham International ✈	a															07 13									
Coventry	a															07 24									
Lichfield Trent Valley	a																							07 11	
Tamworth Low Level	a																							07 17	
Nuneaton	a																06 57								
Rugby	a														06 49										07 52
Milton Keynes Central	a														07 11				07 31	07 37					
Watford Junction	a			06s27											07s32		07s44								
London Euston [15] ⊖	a			06 50		07 48									07 52		08 05		08 09	08 14				08 27	08 46

A Conveys a portion from Fort William, dep 1950
b Previous night, stops to pick up only
c Stops to pick up only

OVERNIGHT SLEEPERS. For sleeper trains, operated by First ScotRail, please refer to Tables 400 - 404

Table 65

Saturdays
from 27 October

Scotland and North West England - West Midlands and London

Route Diagram - see first Page of Table 65

		LM	VT	TP	LM	VT	LM	VT	VT	TP	XC	VT	VT	LM	VT	VT	TP	XC	VT	EM	LM	VT	LM
		◇1	◇1	◇1	◇1	◇1	◇1	◇1	◇1	◇1	◇1	◇1	◇1	◇1	◇1	◇1	◇1	◇1	◇1	◇	◇1	◇1	◇1
																	A						
			⊏P			⊏P		⊏P	⊏P	⊥o	⊥o	⊏P	⊏P		⊏P	⊏P	⊥o	⊥o	⊏P			⊏P	
Inverness	d																						
Aberdeen	d																						
Dundee	d																						
Perth	d																						
Edinburgh 10	d																						
Haymarket	d																						
Glasgow Central 15	d								04 26														
Motherwell	d																						
Carstairs	d																						
Lockerbie	d																						
Carlisle 8	a								05 43														
	d								05 44														
Penrith North Lakes	d								05 59														
Windermere	d																						
Oxenholme Lake District	a								06 21														
	d								06 22														
Barrow-in-Furness	d			05 31													06 20						
Lancaster 6	a			06 23					06 36								07 21						
	d			06 23					06 37							06 58	07 22						
Blackpool North	d									06 40													
Preston 8	a			06 42					06 55	07 07						07 15	07 41						
Preston 8	d		06 17	06 44					06 58	07 09						07 17	07 47						
Wigan North Western	a		06 28						07 09							07 28							
	d		06 28						07 10							07 28							
Blackrod	d																						
Lostock	d									07 30													
Bolton	a			07 08						07 34							08 08						
Manchester Piccadilly 10 ⛴	a			07 27						07 56							08 27						
Manchester Airport ✈	a			07 47						08 17							08 47						
Liverpool Lime Street 10	a																						
	d				06 32	06 45								07 04	07 19					06 49	07 34	07 48	
Liverpool South Parkway ✈	d				06 42									07 14						06 59	07 44		
Runcorn	d				06 50	07 01								07 22	07 36						07 52	08 04	
Warrington Bank Quay	a		06 39						07 20							07 39							
	d		06 39						07 20							07 39							
Hartford	d				07 02									07 36							08 04		
Manchester Piccadilly 10 ⛴	d							06 55			07 07	07 15						07 27	07 35	07 42			
Stockport	d							07 04			07 16	07 23						07 35	07 43	07a53			
Wilmslow	d							07 11															
Holyhead	d																						
Bangor (Gwynedd)	d																						
Llandudno Junction	d																						
Wrexham General	d																						
Chester	d												07 17										
Crewe 10	a		06 58		07 14	07 18		07 27					07 36	07 47	07 52	07 58					08 19		
	d	06 47	07 01		07 16	07 20		07 29					07 39	07 49	07 55	08 01					08 22		
Macclesfield	d																	07 49	07 56				
Congleton	d																						
Stoke-on-Trent	d						←				07 44	07 50						08 07	08 12				←
Stafford	a	07 10			07 40	07 38	07 40				08 02			08 10	08 14			08 25			08 42	08 35	08 42
	d	07 12			07 41	07 39	07 41				08 03			08 10	08 16			08 26			08 43	08 36	08 43
Penkridge	a	07 17			→		07 46							08 16							→		08 48
Wolverhampton 7 ⛴	a	07 28	07 32				07 57				08 16			08 28		08 31		08 39					08 58
Birmingham New Street 12	a	07 47	07 55				08 17				08 38			08 47		08 55		08 58					09 18
Birmingham International ✈	a																	09 13					
Coventry	a																	09 24					
Lichfield Trent Valley	a														08 30								
Tamworth Low Level	a														08 36								
Nuneaton	a																					08 58	
Rugby	a																						
Milton Keynes Central	a											08 46											
Watford Junction	a																						
London Euston 15 ⊖	a					08 59		09 04	09 12			09 23	09 30		09 46				09 42			10 00	

A ⊥o from Preston

OVERNIGHT SLEEPERS. For sleeper trains, operated by First ScotRail, please refer to Tables 400 - 404

Table 65

Saturdays
from 27 October

Scotland and North West England - West Midlands and London

Route Diagram - see first Page of Table 65

		VT		VT	TP	XC	LM	VT	VT	VT	TP	XC		VT	EM	LM	VT	LM	VT	VT	SR	XC		LM	NT
		◇1		◇1	◇1	◇1	◇1	◇1	◇1	◇1	◇1	◇1		◇1	◇	◇1	◇1	◇1	◇1	◇1		◇1		◇1	
											A														
		🍽		🍽	🛒	🛒		🍽	🍽	🍽	🛒	🛒		🍽			🍽		🍽	🍽		🛒			
Inverness	d																								
Aberdeen	d																								
Dundee	d																								
Perth	d																								
Edinburgh 10	d																								
Haymarket	d																								
Glasgow Central 15	d			05 40						05 50										06 30	07 05				
Motherwell	d									06 04										06 44	07 27				
Carstairs	d																				07a47				
Lockerbie	d																			07 25					
Carlisle 8	a			06 46						07 02										07 43					
	d			06 49						07 03										07 46					
Penrith North Lakes	d									07 18										08 00					
Windermere	d																								
Oxenholme Lake District	a			07 22						07 41										08 22					
	d			07 24						07 42										08 23					
Barrow-in-Furness	d										07 29														
Lancaster 6	a			07 37						07 56	08 26									08 37					
	d			07 38						07 57	08 27									08 38					
Blackpool North	d				07 44																				08 38
Preston 8	a			07 56	08 11					08 15	08 45									08 56					09 02
Preston 8	d			07 58	08 12					08 17	08 47									08 58					09 04
Wigan North Western	a			08 09						08 28										09 09					09 24
	d			08 09						08 28										09 09					09 24
Blackrod	d																								
Lostock	d																								
Bolton	a				08 34						09 08														
Manchester Piccadilly 10	a				08 56						09 27														
Manchester Airport ✈	a				09 19						09 47														
Liverpool Lime Street 10	a																								10 02
	d						08 04								07 42	08 34	08 48							09 04	10 16
Liverpool South Parkway ✈	d						08 15								07 52	08 44								09 15	10a27
Runcorn	d						08 24									08 52	09 04							09 24	
Warrington Bank Quay	a			08 20						08 39										09 20					
	d			08 20						08 39										09 20					
Hartford	d															09 06									
Manchester Piccadilly 10	d	07 55				08 07		08 15				08 27		08 35	08 43				08 55			09 07			
Stockport	d	08 04				08 16		08 23				08 35		08 43	08a53				09 04			09 16			
Wilmslow	d	08 11																	09 11						
Holyhead	d								06 52																
Bangor (Gwynedd)	d								07 20																
Llandudno Junction	d								07 38																
Wrexham General	d																								
Chester	d								08 35																
Crewe 10	a	08 27					08 47		08 54	08 58						09 20			09 27					09 44	
	d	08 29					08 49		08 56	09 01						09 22			09 29					09 49	
Macclesfield	d											08 49		08 56											
Congleton	d																								
Stoke-on-Trent	d					08 44		08 50				09 07		09 12				←				09 44			
Stafford	a					09 02	09 09					09 25				09 42	09 35	09 42				10 02		10 10	
	d					09 03	09 10					09 26				09 43	09 36	09 43				10 03		10 10	
Penkridge	a						09 15									→								10 16	
Wolverhampton 7	a					09 15	09 27			09 31		09 39						09 56				10 15		10 27	
Birmingham New Street 12	a					09 39	09 47			09 55		09 58						10 17				10 39		10 47	
Birmingham International ✈	a											10 13													
Coventry	a											10 24													
Lichfield Trent Valley	a																								
Tamworth Low Level	a																								
Nuneaton	a																09 58								
Rugby	a																								
Milton Keynes Central	a							09 46	10 01																
Watford Junction	a																								
London Euston 15 ⊖	a	10 04		10 12				10 23	10 37					10 42			11 01		11 04	11 12					

A 🛒 from Preston

OVERNIGHT SLEEPERS. For sleeper trains, operated by First ScotRail, please refer to Tables 400 - 404

Table 65

Saturdays
from 27 October

Scotland and North West England - West Midlands and London

Route Diagram - see first Page of Table 65

		TP	VT	VT	VT	TP	XC	VT		EM	LM	VT	LM	VT	VT	XC	LM	NT		TP	TP	VT	VT	VT	TP
		◇1	◇1	◇1	◇1	◇1	◇1	◇1		◇	◇1	◇1	◇1	◇1	◇1	◇1	◇1			◇1	◇1	◇1	◇1	◇1	◇1
Inverness	d																								
Aberdeen	d																								
Dundee	d																								
Perth	d																								
Edinburgh 10	d				06 52															07 42					
Haymarket	d				06 56															07u46					
Glasgow Central 15	d					07 10									07 35									08 00	
Motherwell	d														07 52										
Carstairs	d																								
Lockerbie	d					08 06																			
Carlisle 8	a				08 05	08 29									08 46					08 59				09 08	
	d				08 07	08 29									08 49					08 59				09 09	
Penrith North Lakes	d				08 22	08 45																			
Windermere	d																								09 38
Oxenholme Lake District	a					09 09									09 22										09 57
	d					09 11									09 23										09 58
Barrow-in-Furness	d																								
Lancaster 6	a				08 56	09 26									09 37									09 56	10 16
	d				08 57	09 26									09 38									09 57	10 16
Blackpool North	d	08 44																09 37			09 43				
Preston 8	a	09 08			09 15	09 45									09 56			10 02		10 04	10 07			10 15	10 35
Preston 8	d	09 10			09 17	09 47									09 58			10 04		10 12				10 17	
Wigan North Western	a				09 28										10 09			10 24						10 28	
	d				09 28										10 09			10 24						10 28	
Blackrod	d																								
Lostock	d																								
Bolton	a	09 34				10 08														10 34					
Manchester Piccadilly 10	a	09 56				10 27														10 56					
Manchester Airport ✈	a	10 17				10 47														11 17					
Liverpool Lime Street 10	a																	11 02							
	d									08 52	09 34	09 48					10 04	11 16							
Liverpool South Parkway ✈	d									09 03	09 44						10 15	11a27							
Runcorn	d										09 52	10 04					10 25								
Warrington Bank Quay	a				09 39										10 20									10 39	
	d				09 39										10 20									10 39	
Hartford	d										10 04														
Manchester Piccadilly 10	d		09 15				09 27	09 35		09 43				09 55		10 07						10 15			
Stockport	d		09 23				09 35	09 43		09a53				10 04		10 16						10 23			
Wilmslow	d													10 11											
Holyhead	d			07 55																			08 55		
Bangor (Gwynedd)	d			08 22																			09 22		
Llandudno Junction	d			08 40																			09 40		
Wrexham General	d																								
Chester	d			09 35																			10 35		
Crewe 10	a			09 54	09 58						10 19			10 27			10 45						10 54	10 58	
	d			09 56	10 01						10 22			10 29			10 49						10 56	11 01	
Macclesfield	d						09 49	09 56																	
Congleton	d																								
Stoke-on-Trent	d		09 50				10 07	10 12					←			10 44						10 50			
Stafford	a						10 25				10 42	10 35	10 42			11 02	11 09								
	d						10 26				10 43	10 36	10 43			11 03	11 10								
Penkridge	a										→						11 15								
Wolverhampton 7	a				10 31		10 39						10 56			11 16	11 27							11 32	
Birmingham New Street 12	a				10 55		10 58						11 17			11 39	11 47							11 55	
Birmingham International ✈	a						11 13																		
Coventry	a						11 24																		
Lichfield Trent Valley	a																								
Tamworth Low Level	a																								
Nuneaton	a																								
Rugby	a																								
Milton Keynes Central	a		10 46	11 01																		11 46	12 01		
Watford Junction	a																								
London Euston 15 ⊖	a		11 23	11 38				11 42				11 56		12 04	12 12							12 23	12 38		

OVERNIGHT SLEEPERS. For sleeper trains, operated by First ScotRail, please refer to Tables 400 - 404

Table 65

Saturdays

from 27 October

Scotland and North West England - West Midlands and London

Route Diagram - see first Page of Table 65

		TP	NT	XC		VT	EM	LM	VT	LM	VT	VT	XC	LM		NT	TP	VT	VT	VT	SR	TP	XC	VT
		◇1		◇1		◇1	◇	◇1	◇1	◇1	◇1	◇1	◇1	◇1			◇1	◇1	◇1	◇1		◇1	◇1	◇1
		A																				A		
		🛒		🛒		🍴			🍴		🍴	🍴	🛒				🛒	🍴	🍴	🍴		🛒	🛒	🍴
Inverness	d																							
Aberdeen	d																							
Dundee	d																							
Perth	d																							
Edinburgh 10	d																			08 52	09 03			
Haymarket	d																			08 57	09 07			
Glasgow Central 15	d											08 40												
Motherwell	d																							
Carstairs	d																				09a44			
Lockerbie	d																							
Carlisle 8	a											09 46								10 05				
	d											09 49								10 07				
Penrith North Lakes	d											10 03												
Windermere	d																					10 49		
Oxenholme Lake District	a																			10 41		11 08		
	d																			10 42		11 09		
Barrow-in-Furness	d	09 23	10 16																					
Lancaster 6	a	10 25	11 21									10 37								10 56		11 26		
	d	10 26										10 38								10 57		11 26		
Blackpool North	d															10 37	10 44							
Preston 8	a	10 45										10 56				11 02	11 08			11 15		11 45		
Preston 8	d	10 47										10 58				11 04	11 10			11 17		11 47		
Wigan North Western	a											11 09				11 24				11 28				
	d											11 09				11 24				11 28				
Blackrod	d																							
Lostock	d																							
Bolton	a	11 08															11 34					12 08		
Manchester Piccadilly 10	a	11 27															11 56					12 27		
Manchester Airport ✈	a	11 47															12 17					12 47		
Liverpool Lime Street 10	a															12 02								
	d						09 52	10 34	10 48					11 04		12 16								
Liverpool South Parkway ✈	d						10 03	10 44						11 15		12a27								
Runcorn	d							10 52	11 04					11 25										
Warrington Bank Quay	a											11 20								11 39				
	d											11 20								11 39				
Hartford	d							11 04																
Manchester Piccadilly 10	d			10 27		10 35	10 43				10 55		11 07					11 15					11 27	11 35
Stockport	d			10 35		10 43	10a53				11 04		11 16					11 23					11 35	11 43
Wilmslow	d										11 11													
Holyhead	d																							
Bangor (Gwynedd)	d																							
Llandudno Junction	d																							
Wrexham General	d																							
Chester	d																		11 35					
Crewe 10	a							11 19			11 27			11 45					11 54	11 58				
	d							11 22			11 29			11 49					11 56	12 01				
Macclesfield	d			10 49		10 56																	11 49	11 56
Congleton	d																							
Stoke-on-Trent	d			11 07		11 12				←			11 44					11 50					12 07	12 12
Stafford	a			11 25				11 42	11 35	11 42			12 02	12 09									12 24	
	d			11 26				11 43	11 36	11 43			12 03	12 10									12 25	
Penkridge	a							→						12 15										
Wolverhampton 7	a			11 39						11 56			12 16	12 27						12 31			12 39	
Birmingham New Street 12	a			11 58						12 17			12 39	12 47						12 55			12 58	
Birmingham International ✈	a			12 13																			13 13	
Coventry	a			12 24																			13 24	
Lichfield Trent Valley	a																							
Tamworth Low Level	a																							
Nuneaton	a																							
Rugby	a																							
Milton Keynes Central	a																	12 46	13 01					
Watford Junction	a																							
London Euston 15 ⊖	a					12 42			12 56		13 04	13 12						13 23	13 38					13 42

A 🛒 from Preston

OVERNIGHT SLEEPERS. For sleeper trains, operated by First ScotRail, please refer to Tables 400 - 404

Table 65

Saturdays

from 27 October

Scotland and North West England - West Midlands and London

Route Diagram - see first Page of Table 65

		EM	LM	VT	LM	VT	VT	TP	XC	LM		NT	TP	VT	VT	VT	TP	TP	XC	VT		EM	LM	VT	LM
		◇	◇■	◇■	◇■	◇■	◇■	◇■	◇■	◇■			◇■	◇■	◇■	◇■	◇■	◇■	◇■	◇■		◇	◇■	◇■	◇■
				🍴		🍴	🍴		🛒				🛒	🍴	🍴	🍴	🛒	🛒	🛒	🍴				🍴	
Inverness	d																								
Aberdeen	d																								
Dundee	d																								
Perth	d																								
Edinburgh [10]	d																09 51								
Haymarket	d																09u56								
Glasgow Central [15]	d						09 40									10 00		10 10							
Motherwell	d																								
Carstairs	d																								
Lockerbie	d																11 01								
Carlisle [8]	a						10 47									11 08	11 22	11 26							
	d						10 49									11 09	11 29								
Penrith North Lakes	d															11 24	11 45								
Windermere	d																								
Oxenholme Lake District	a						11 22										12 09								
	d						11 23										12 10								
Barrow-in-Furness	d							11 25																	
Lancaster [6]	a						11 37	12 18									12 26								
	d						11 38	12 18									12 26								
Blackpool North	d											11 37	11 44												
Preston [8]	a						11 56	12 37				12 02	12 08			12 15	12 45								
Preston [8]	d						11 58					12 04	12 10			12 17	12 47								
Wigan North Western	a						12 09					12 24				12 28									
	d						12 09					12 24				12 28									
Blackrod	d																								
Lostock	d																								
Bolton	a												12 34				13 08								
Manchester Piccadilly [10] ⛴	a												12 56				13 27								
Manchester Airport ✈	a												13 17				13 47								
Liverpool Lime Street [10]	a											13 02													
	d	10 52	11 34	11 48						12 04		13 16										11 52	12 34	12 48	
Liverpool South Parkway ✈	d	11 03	11 44							12 15		13a27										12 03	12 44		
Runcorn	d		11 52	12 04						12 25													12 52	13 04	
Warrington Bank Quay	a						12 20									12 39									
	d						12 20									12 39									
Hartford	d		12 04																				13 06		
Manchester Piccadilly [10] ⛴	d	11 43				11 55			12 07					12 15					12 27	12 35		12 43			
Stockport	d	11a53				12 04			12 16					12 23					12 35	12 43		12a53			
Wilmslow	d					12 11																			
Holyhead	d																								
Bangor (Gwynedd)	d																								
Llandudno Junction	d																								
Wrexham General	d																								
Chester	d														12 35										
Crewe [10]	a		12 19			12 27				12 45					12 54	12 58							13 20		
	d		12 22			12 29				12 49					12 57	13 01							13 22		
Macclesfield	d																		12 49	12 56					
Congleton	d																								
Stoke-on-Trent	d				←				12 44					12 50					13 07	13 12					←
Stafford	a		12 42	12 35	12 42				13 02	13 09									13 25				13 42	13 35	13 42
	d		12 43	12 36	12 43				13 03	13 10									13 26				13 43	13 36	13 43
Penkridge	a		→							13 15													→		
Wolverhampton [7] ⛴	a				12 56				13 15	13 27						13 31			13 39						13 56
Birmingham New Street [12]	a				13 17				13 39	13 47						13 55			13 58						14 17
Birmingham International ✈	a																		14 13						
Coventry	a																		14 24						
Lichfield Trent Valley	a																								
Tamworth Low Level	a																								
Nuneaton	a																								
Rugby	a																								
Milton Keynes Central	a													13 46	14 01										
Watford Junction	a																								
London Euston [15] ⊖	a			13 56		14 04	14 12							14 23	14 38					14 42				14 56	

OVERNIGHT SLEEPERS. For sleeper trains, operated by First ScotRail, please refer to Tables 400 - 404

Table 65

Saturdays

from 27 October

Scotland and North West England - West Midlands and London

Route Diagram - see first Page of Table 65

		VT	VT	XC	LM	NT		TP	VT	VT	VT	TP	XC	VT	EM	LM		VT	LM	VT	VT	XC	LM	NT	TP
		◇1	◇1	◇1	◇1			◇1	◇1	◇1	◇1	◇1	◇1	◇1	◇	◇1		◇1	◇1	◇1	◇1	◇1	◇1		◇1
												A													
		🍴	🍴	🛒				🛒	🍴	🍴	🍴	🛒	🛒	🍴				🍴		🍴	🍴	🛒			🛒
Inverness	d																								
Aberdeen	d																								
Dundee	d																								
Perth	d																								
Edinburgh 10	d										10 52														
Haymarket	d										10 57														
Glasgow Central 15	d		10 40																		11 40				
Motherwell	d																								
Carstairs	d																								
Lockerbie	d																								
Carlisle 8	a		11 47								12 05										12 46				
	d		11 49								12 07										12 49				
Penrith North Lakes	d																				13 03				
Windermere	d											12 51													
Oxenholme Lake District	a		12 22								12 41	13 07													
	d		12 23								12 43	13 09													
Barrow-in-Furness	d																								
Lancaster 6	a		12 37								12 56	13 26									13 37				
	d		12 38								12 57	13 26									13 38				
Blackpool North	d					12 37		12 44																13 37	13 44
Preston 8	a		12 56			13 02		13 08			13 15	13 45									13 56			14 02	14 08
Preston 8	d		12 58			13 04		13 10			13 17	13 47									13 58			14 04	14 10
Wigan North Western	a		13 09			13 24					13 28										14 09			14 24	
	d		13 09			13 24					13 28										14 09			14 24	
Blackrod	d																								
Lostock	d																								
Bolton	a							13 34				14 08													14 34
Manchester Piccadilly 10 🚊	a							13 56				14 27													14 56
Manchester Airport ✈	a							14 17				14 47													15 17
Liverpool Lime Street 10	a					14 02																		15 02	
	d				13 04	14 16									12 52	13 34		13 48					14 04	15 16	
Liverpool South Parkway ✈	d				13 15	14a27									13 03	13 44							14 15	15a27	
Runcorn	d				13 25											13 52		14 04					14 25		
Warrington Bank Quay	a		13 20								13 39										14 20				
	d		13 20								13 39										14 20				
Hartford	d															14 04									
Manchester Piccadilly 10 🚊	d	12 55		13 07					13 15				13 27	13 35	13 43					13 55		14 07			
Stockport	d	13 04		13 16					13 23				13 35	13 43	13a53					14 04		14 16			
Wilmslow	d	13 11																		14 11					
Holyhead	d																								
Bangor (Gwynedd)	d																								
Llandudno Junction	d																								
Wrexham General	d																								
Chester	d									13 35															
Crewe 10	a	13 27			13 45					13 54	13 58					14 19				14 27			14 45		
	d	13 29			13 49					13 56	14 01					14 22				14 29			14 49		
Macclesfield	d												13 49	13 56											
Congleton	d																								
Stoke-on-Trent	d			13 44					13 50				14 07	14 12					←			14 44			
Stafford	a			14 02	14 09								14 25			14 46		14 35	14 46			15 02	15 09		
	d			14 03	14 10								14 26			14 46		14 36	14 46			15 03	15 10		
Penkridge	a				14 15											→							15 15		
Wolverhampton 7 🚊	a			14 16	14 27						14 31		14 39						14 59			15 16	15 27		
Birmingham New Street 12	a			14 39	14 47						14 55		14 58						15 18			15 39	15 47		
Birmingham International ✈	a												15 13												
Coventry	a												15 24												
Lichfield Trent Valley	a																								
Tamworth Low Level	a																								
Nuneaton	a																								
Rugby	a																								
Milton Keynes Central	a								14 46	15 01															
Watford Junction	a																								
London Euston 15 ⊖	a	15 04	15 12						15 23	15 38				15 42				15 56		16 04	16 12				

A 🛒 from Preston

OVERNIGHT SLEEPERS. For sleeper trains, operated by First ScotRail, please refer to Tables 400 - 404

Table 65

Saturdays
from 27 October

Scotland and North West England - West Midlands and London

Route Diagram - see first Page of Table 65

		VT		VT	VT	TP	TP	NT	XC	VT	EM	LM		VT	LM	VT	VT	XC	LM	NT	TP	VT		VT	VT
		◇1		◇1	◇1	◇1	◇1		◇1	◇1	◇	◇1		◇1	◇1	◇1	◇1	◇1	◇1		◇1	◇1		◇1	◇1
						A																			
		☕		☕	☕	🛒	🛒		🛒	☕				☕		☕	☕	🛒			🛒	☕		☕	☕
Inverness	d																								
Aberdeen	d																								
Dundee	d																								
Perth	d																								
Edinburgh 10	d						12 08																		12 52
Haymarket	d						12u12																		12 57
Glasgow Central 15	d				12 00												12 40								
Motherwell	d																								
Carstairs	d																								
Lockerbie	d						13 07																		
Carlisle 8	a				13 08		13 29										13 47								14 05
	d				13 09		13 29										13 49								14 07
Penrith North Lakes	d																								14 22
Windermere	d																								
Oxenholme Lake District	a						14 06										14 22								
	d						14 07										14 24								
Barrow-in-Furness	d					13 25		14 16																	
Lancaster 6	a				13 56	14 18	14 21	15 20									14 37								14 56
	d				13 58	14 18	14 22										14 38								14 57
Blackpool North	d																			14 37	14 44				
Preston 8	a				14 15	14 37	14 41										14 56			15 02	15 08				15 15
Preston 8	d				14 17	14 47											14 58			15 04	15 10				15 17
Wigan North Western	a				14 28												15 09			15 24					15 28
	d				14 28												15 09			15 24					15 28
Blackrod	d																								
Lostock	d																								
Bolton	a					15 08															15 34				
Manchester Piccadilly 10	a					15 27															15 56				
Manchester Airport ✈	a					15 47															16 17				
Liverpool Lime Street 10	a																			16 02					
	d										13 52	14 34		14 48					15 04	16 16					
Liverpool South Parkway ✈	d										14 03	14 44							15 15	16a27					
Runcorn	d											14 52		15 04					15 25						
Warrington Bank Quay	a				14 39												15 20								15 39
	d				14 39												15 20								15 39
Hartford	d											15 04													
Manchester Piccadilly 10	d	14 15							14 27	14 35	14 43					14 55		15 07				15 15			
Stockport	d	14 23							14 35	14 43	14a53					15 04		15 16				15 23			
Wilmslow	d															15 11									
Holyhead	d																								
Bangor (Gwynedd)	d																								
Llandudno Junction	d																								
Wrexham General	d																								
Chester	d			14 35																				15 35	
Crewe 10	a			14 54	14 58							15 19				15 27			15 45					15 54	15 58
	d			14 56	15 01							15 22				15 29			15 49					15 56	16 01
Macclesfield	d								14 49	14 56															
Congleton	d																								
Stoke-on-Trent	d	14 50							15 07	15 12					←			15 44				15 50			
Stafford	a								15 25			15 42		15 35	15 42			16 02	16 09						
	d								15 26			15 43		15 36	15 43			16 03	16 10						
Penkridge	a											→							16 15						
Wolverhampton 7	a				15 31				15 39						15 56			16 16	16 27						16 31
Birmingham New Street 12	a				15 55				15 58						16 17			16 39	16 47						16 55
Birmingham International ✈	a								16 13																
Coventry	a								16 24																
Lichfield Trent Valley	a																								
Tamworth Low Level	a																								
Nuneaton	a																								
Rugby	a																								
Milton Keynes Central	a	15 46		16 01																		16 46		17 01	
Watford Junction	a																								
London Euston 15 ⊖	a	16 23		16 38						16 42				16 56		17 04	17 12					17 23		17 38	

A 🛒 from Preston

OVERNIGHT SLEEPERS. For sleeper trains, operated by First ScotRail, please refer to Tables 400 - 404

Table 65

Saturdays
from 27 October

Scotland and North West England - West Midlands and London

Route Diagram - see first Page of Table 65

		TP	XC	VT	EM	LM	VT	LM	VT	VT	XC	LM	NT	TP	VT	VT	VT	TP	XC	VT	EM	LM	VT
		◇1	◇1	◇1	◇	◇1	◇1	◇1	◇1	◇1	◇1	◇1		◇1	◇1	◇1	◇1	◇1	◇1	◇1	◇	◇1	◇1
		🛒	🛒	☕			☕		☕	☕	🛒			🛒	☕	☕	☕	🛒	🛒	☕			☕
Inverness	d																						
Aberdeen	d																						
Dundee	d																						
Perth	d																						
Edinburgh 10	d																	14 07					
Haymarket	d																	14u11					
Glasgow Central 15	d	13 09								13 40							14 00						
Motherwell	d																						
Carstairs	d																						
Lockerbie	d	14 06																15 06					
Carlisle 8	a	14 29								14 46							15 09	15 27					
	d	14 29								14 49							15 11	15 27					
Penrith North Lakes	d	14 45																15 43					
Windermere	d																						
Oxenholme Lake District	a	15 09								15 22							15 45	16 06					
	d	15 10								15 23							15 46	16 07					
Barrow-in-Furness	d																						
Lancaster 6	a	15 26								15 37								16 26					
	d	15 26								15 38								16 26					
Blackpool North	d												15 37	15 44									
Preston 8	a	15 45								15 56			16 02	16 08			16 15	16 45					
Preston 8	d	15 47								15 58			16 04	16 10			16 17	16 47					
Wigan North Western	a									16 09			16 24				16 28						
	d									16 09			16 24				16 28						
Blackrod	d																						
Lostock	d																						
Bolton	a	16 08												16 34				17 08					
Manchester Piccadilly 10	a	16 27												16 56				17 27					
Manchester Airport ✈	a	16 47												17 17				17 48					
Liverpool Lime Street 10	a												17 05										
	d				14 52	15 34	15 48					16 04									15 52	16 34	16 48
Liverpool South Parkway ✈	d				15 03	15 44						16 15									16 03	16 44	
Runcorn	d					15 52	16 04					16 25										16 52	17 04
Warrington Bank Quay	a									16 20							16 39						
	d									16 20							16 39						
Hartford	d					16 04																17 06	
Manchester Piccadilly 10	d		15 27	15 35	15 43				15 55		16 07				16 15				16 27	16 35	16 43		
Stockport	d		15 35	15 43	15a53				16 04		16 16				16 23				16 35	16 43	16a53		
Wilmslow	d								16 11														
Holyhead	d															14 38							
Bangor (Gwynedd)	d															15 07							
Llandudno Junction	d															15 27							
Wrexham General	d																						
Chester	d															16 24							
Crewe 10	a					16 19			16 27			16 45				16 47	16 58					17 20	
	d					16 22			16 29			16 49				16 56	17 01					17 22	
Macclesfield	d		15 49	15 56															16 49	16 56			
Congleton	d																						
Stoke-on-Trent	d		16 07	16 12				←			16 44				16 50				17 07	17 12			
Stafford	a		16 24			16 46	16 35	16 46			17 02	17 09							17 25			17 42	17 35
	d		16 25			16 46	16 36	16 46			17 03	17 10							17 26			17 43	17 36
Penkridge	a					↪						17 15										↪	
Wolverhampton 7	a		16 39					16 59			17 16	17 27					17 31		17 39				
Birmingham New Street 12	a		16 58					17 18			17 39	17 47					17 55		17 58				
Birmingham International ✈	a		17 13																18 13				
Coventry	a		17 24																18 24				
Lichfield Trent Valley	a																						
Tamworth Low Level	a																						
Nuneaton	a																						
Rugby	a																						
Milton Keynes Central	a														17 46	18 01							
Watford Junction	a																						
London Euston 15 ⊖	a			17 42			17 56		18 04	18 12					18 23	18 38				18 42			18 56

OVERNIGHT SLEEPERS. For sleeper trains, operated by First ScotRail, please refer to Tables 400 - 404

Table 65

Saturdays
from 27 October

Scotland and North West England - West Midlands and London

Route Diagram - see first Page of Table 65

		LM	VT	VT		SR	XC	LM	NT	TP	VT	TP	VT	TP		XC	VT	EM	LM	VT	LM	VT	VT	XC
		◇1	◇1	◇1			◇1	◇1		◇1	◇1	◇1	◇1	◇1		◇1	◇1	◇	◇1	◇1	◇1	◇1	◇1	◇1
			🍽	🍽			🛒			🛒	🍽		🍽	🛒		🛒	🍽			🍽		🍽	🍽	🛒
Inverness	d																							
Aberdeen	d																							
Dundee	d																							
Perth	d																							
Edinburgh 10	d										14 52													
Haymarket	d										14 57													
Glasgow Central 15	d			14 40		15 14																	15 40	
Motherwell	d					15 34																		
Carstairs	d					15a51																		
Lockerbie	d																							
Carlisle 8	a			15 46							16 05												16 46	
	d			15 49							16 07												16 49	
Penrith North Lakes	d										16 22												17 03	
Windermere	d																							
Oxenholme Lake District	a			16 22																				
	d			16 24																				
Barrow-in-Furness	d											16 22												
Lancaster 6	a			16 37							16 56	17 19											17 37	
	d			16 38							16 57	17 20											17 38	
Blackpool North	d								16 35	16 40				17 20										
Preston 8	a			16 56					17 02	17 08	17 15	17 39		17 45									17 56	
Preston 8	d			16 58					17 04	17 10	17 17			17 47									17 58	
Wigan North Western	a			17 09					17 24		17 28												18 09	
	d			17 09					17 24		17 28												18 09	
Blackrod	d																							
Lostock	d																							
Bolton	a									17 34				18 08										
Manchester Piccadilly 10 ⛴	a									17 56				18 27										
Manchester Airport ✈	a									18 17				18 47										
Liverpool Lime Street 10	a								18 02															
	d							17 04										16 52	17 34	17 48				
Liverpool South Parkway ✈	d							17 15										17 03	17 44					
Runcorn	d							17 25											17 52	18 04				
Warrington Bank Quay	a			17 20							17 39												18 20	
	d			17 20							17 39												18 20	
Hartford	d																		18 06					
Manchester Piccadilly 10 ⛴	d		16 55				17 06						17 15			17 27	17 35	17 43				17 55		18 05
Stockport	d		17 04										17 23			17 36	17 43	17a53				18 04		18 13
Wilmslow	d		17 11																			18 11		
Holyhead	d																							
Bangor (Gwynedd)	d																							
Llandudno Junction	d																							
Wrexham General	d																							
Chester	d																							
Crewe 10	a		17 27					17 47			17 59								18 20			18 27		
	d		17 29					17 49			18 01								18 22			18 29		
Macclesfield	d						17 26										17 56							18 26
Congleton	d															17 54								
Stoke-on-Trent	d	←					17 44						17 50			18 08	18 12				←			18 44
Stafford	a	17 42					18 03	18 09								18 26			18 42	18 35	18 42			19 02
	d	17 43					18 04	18 10								18 27			18 43	18 36	18 43			19 03
Penkridge	a							18 15											→					
Wolverhampton 7 ⛴	a	17 56					18 16	18 27			18 31					18 40					18 56			19 16
Birmingham New Street 12	a	18 17					18 38	18 47			18 55					18 58					19 17			19 33
Birmingham International ✈	a															19 13								
Coventry	a															19 24								
Lichfield Trent Valley	a																							
Tamworth Low Level	a																							
Nuneaton	a																							
Rugby	a																							
Milton Keynes Central	a												18 46											
Watford Junction	a																							
London Euston 15 ⊖	a		19 04	19 12									19 23				19 42			19 56		20 04	20 15	

OVERNIGHT SLEEPERS. For sleeper trains, operated by First ScotRail, please refer to Tables 400 - 404

Table 65

Saturdays

from 27 October

Scotland and North West England - West Midlands and London

Route Diagram - see first Page of Table 65

		LM	NT	TP	VT	TP	TP	VT	XC	VT	EM	LM	VT	LM	VT	VT	XC	LM	NT	TP	VT	TP	XC
		◇1		◇1	◇1	◇1	◇1	◇1	◇1	◇1	◇	◇1	◇1	◇1	◇1	◇1	◇1	◇1		◇1	◇1	◇1	◇1
				A																			B
				🛒	🍽		🛒	🍽	🛒	🍽			🍽		🍽	🍽	🛒				🍽	🛒	🛒
Inverness	d																						
Aberdeen	d																						
Dundee	d																						
Perth	d																						
Edinburgh 10	d						16 12														16 52		
Haymarket	d						16u16														16 57		
Glasgow Central 15	d				16 00											16 40						17 06	
Motherwell	d															16 54							
Carstairs	d																						
Lockerbie	d						17 11															18 06	
Carlisle 8	a				17 08		17 33									17 49					18 06	18 28	
	d				17 09		17 34									17 52					18 08	18 29	
Penrith North Lakes	d						17 49															18 45	
Windermere	d			17 06																			
Oxenholme Lake District	a			17 25	17 44											18 25					18 41	19 09	
	d			17 30	17 44											18 26					18 42	19 10	
Barrow-in-Furness	d					17 21																	
Lancaster 6	a			17 47		18 16	18 26									18 40					18 56	19 26	
	d			17 48		18 17	18 26									18 41					18 57	19 26	
Blackpool North	d		17 37																18 37	18 44			
Preston 8	a		18 02	18 06	18 15	18 36	18 45									18 59			19 00	19 08	19 15	19 45	
Preston 8	d		18 04	18 08	18 17		18 47									19 01			19 04	19 10	19 17	19 47	
Wigan North Western	a		18 24		18 28											19 12			19 24		19 28		
	d		18 24		18 28											19 12			19 24		19 28		
Blackrod	d																						
Lostock	d			18 30																			
Bolton	a			18 34			19 08													19 34		20 08	
Manchester Piccadilly 10 ⛴	a			18 56			19 27													19 56		20 27	
Manchester Airport ✈	a			19 17			19 50													20 17		20 47	
Liverpool Lime Street 10	a		19 02																20 02				
	d	18 04									17 52	18 34	18 48					19 04					
Liverpool South Parkway ✈	d	18 15									18 03	18 44						19 14					
Runcorn	d	18 24										18 52	19 04					19 23					
Warrington Bank Quay	a				18 39											19 23					19 39		
	d				18 39											19 23					19 39		
Hartford	d											19 04											
Manchester Piccadilly 10 ⛴	d							18 15	18 27	18 35	18 43				18 55		19 07						19 27
Stockport	d							18 23	18 35	18 43	18a53				19 04		19 16						19 35
Wilmslow	d														19 11								
Holyhead	d																						
Bangor (Gwynedd)	d																						
Llandudno Junction	d																						
Wrexham General	d																						
Chester	d																						
Crewe 10	a	18 46			18 59							19 19			19 27			19 49			19 59		
	d	18 49			19 01							19 22			19 29			19 51			20 01		
Macclesfield	d									18 56													19 49
Congleton	d								18 54														
Stoke-on-Trent	d							18 49	19 07	19 12				←			19 44						20 07
Stafford	a	19 09							19 25			19 42	19 35	19 42			20 02	20 11					20 25
	d	19 10							19 25			19 43	19 36	19 43			20 03	20 12					20 26
Penkridge	a	19 15										→		19 48									
Wolverhampton 7 ⛴	a	19 27			19 31				19 39					19 59			20 16	20 28			20 32		20 39
Birmingham New Street 12	a	19 47			19 55				19 58					20 17			20 33	20 47			20 55		20 58
Birmingham International ✈	a								20 13														21 13
Coventry	a								20 24														21 24
Lichfield Trent Valley	a																						
Tamworth Low Level	a																						
Nuneaton	a																						
Rugby	a																						
Milton Keynes Central	a							19 45								20 41							
Watford Junction	a															21s15							
London Euston 15 ⊖	a							20 24		20 59			21 15		21 18	21 38							

A 🛒 from Preston

B 🛒 to Birmingham New Street

OVERNIGHT SLEEPERS. For sleeper trains, operated by First ScotRail, please refer to Tables 400 - 404

Scotland and North West England - West Midlands and London

Route Diagram - see first Page of Table 65

		VT	EM	LM	VT	LM		VT	NT	TP	XC	VT	TP	SR	XC	VT		EM	LM	XC	VT	TP	TP	VT	XC
		◇1	◇	◇1	◇1	◇1		◇1		◇1	◇1	◇1	◇1		◇1	◇1		◇	◇1	◇1	◇1	◇1	◇1	◇1	◇1
		🍴			🍴			🍴				🍴	🛒			🍴					🍴			🍴	
Inverness	d																								
Aberdeen	d																								
Dundee	d																								
Perth	d																								
Edinburgh 10	d												18 12	18 24										18 52	
Haymarket	d												18u16	18 28										18 57	
Glasgow Central 15	d							17 40				18 00									18 40				
Motherwell	d																								
Carstairs	d													19a09											
Lockerbie	d							18 32					19 11												
Carlisle 8	a							18 50				19 08	19 34								19 46			20 06	
	d							18 52				19 09	19 34								19 48			20 08	
Penrith North Lakes	d							19 06					19 49								20 02			20 23	
Windermere	d																								
Oxenholme Lake District	a							19 28					20 12								20 24			20 46	
	d							19 29					20 13								20 25			20 46	
Barrow-in-Furness	d																					19 33			
Lancaster 6	a							19 43				19 55	20 26								20 39	20 34		21 00	
	d							19 44				19 56	20 26								20 40	20 35		21 01	
Blackpool North	d								19 37	19 44													20 42		
Preston 8	a							20 02	20 02	20 08		20 15	20 45								20 58	20 53	21 06	21 19	
Preston 8	d							20 04	20 04	20 10		20 17	20 47								21 00	21 10		21 21	
Wigan North Western	a							20 15	20 24			20 28									21 11			21 32	
	d							20 15	20 24			20 28									21 11			21 32	
Blackrod	d																								
Lostock	d																								
Bolton	a									20 34			21 08									21 34			
Manchester Piccadilly 10 🚍	a									20 56			21 27									21 56			
Manchester Airport ✈	a									21 17			21 47									22 17			
Liverpool Lime Street 10	a								21 02																
	d		18 52	19 34	19 48													19 52	20 34						
Liverpool South Parkway ✈	d		19 03	19 44														20 03	20 44						
Runcorn	d			19 52	20 04														20 52						
Warrington Bank Quay	a							20 26				20 39									21 22			21 43	
	d							20 26				20 39									21 22			21 43	
Hartford	d			20 04															21 03						
Manchester Piccadilly 10 🚍	d	19 35	19 43								20 07				20 27	20 35		20 43		21 07					21 27
Stockport	d	19 43	19a53								20 16				20 35	20 43		20a53							21 36
Wilmslow	d																								
Holyhead	d																								
Bangor (Gwynedd)	d																								
Llandudno Junction	d																								
Wrexham General	d																								
Chester	d																								
Crewe 10	a			20 16				20 45				20 59							21 16		21 41			22 03	
	d			20 22				20 47				21 01							21 17		21 43			22 05	
Macclesfield	d	19 56													20 49	20 56									21 50
Congleton	d																								
Stoke-on-Trent	d	20 12				←					20 44				21 07	21 12				21 45					22 08
Stafford	a			20 44	20 35	20 44					21 02				21 26				21 42	22 02	22 07			22 24	22 32
	d			20 45	20 36	20 45					21 03				21 27				21 42	22 03	22 08			22 25	22 33
Penkridge	a			→		20 50													21 48						
Wolverhampton 7 🚍	a					21 01					21 15	21 31			21 39				21 58	22 14	22 22			22 39	22 45
Birmingham New Street 12	a					21 19					21 32	21 54			21 58				22 20	22 32	22 46			22 59	23 02
Birmingham International ✈	a																								
Coventry	a																								
Lichfield Trent Valley	a																								
Tamworth Low Level	a																								
Nuneaton	a																								
Rugby	a																								
Milton Keynes Central	a	21 10						21 50								22 10									
Watford Junction	a															22s40									
London Euston 15 ⊖	a	22 00			22 14			22 44								23 02									

OVERNIGHT SLEEPERS. For sleeper trains, operated by First ScotRail, please refer to Tables 400 - 404

Table 65

Saturdays
from 27 October

Scotland and North West England - West Midlands and London

Route Diagram - see first Page of Table 65

Station		EM		LM	EM	TP	NT	TP	LM	TP	TP
		◇		◇1	◇	◇1		◇1	1	◇1	◇1
Inverness	d										
Aberdeen	d										
Dundee	d										
Perth	d										
Edinburgh 10	d										
Haymarket	d										
Glasgow Central 15	d										
Motherwell	d										
Carstairs	d										
Lockerbie	d										
Carlisle 8	a										
	d										
Penrith North Lakes	d										
Windermere	d					21 40					
Oxenholme Lake District	a					21 59					
	d					22 01					
Barrow-in-Furness	d						21 43				
Lancaster 6	a					22 17	22 45				
	d					22 17	22 46				
Blackpool North	d							21 44			22 44
Preston 8	a					22 38	23 11	22 08			23 07
Preston 8	d							22 10			23 09
Wigan North Western	a										
	d										
Blackrod	d										
Lostock	d										
Bolton	a							22 34			23 34
Manchester Piccadilly 10	a							22 56			23 53
Manchester Airport ✈	a							23 17			00 23
Liverpool Lime Street 10	a										
	d	20 52		21 34	21 37				22 04	22 30	
Liverpool South Parkway ✈	d	21 03		21 44	21 47				22 14	22 40	
Runcorn	d			21 52					22 23		
Warrington Bank Quay	a										
	d										
Hartford	d			22 04					22 34		
Manchester Piccadilly 10	d	21 43			22 31					23a19	
Stockport	d	21a52			22a41						
Wilmslow	d										
Holyhead	d										
Bangor (Gwynedd)	d										
Llandudno Junction	d										
Wrexham General	d										
Chester	d										
Crewe 10	a			22 21					22 48		
	d			22 23							
Macclesfield	d										
Congleton	d										
Stoke-on-Trent	d										
Stafford	a			22 47							
	d			22 47							
Penkridge	a			22 53							
Wolverhampton 7	a			23 03							
Birmingham New Street 12	a			23 21							
Birmingham International ✈	a										
Coventry	a										
Lichfield Trent Valley	a										
Tamworth Low Level	a										
Nuneaton	a										
Rugby	a										
Milton Keynes Central	a										
Watford Junction	a										
London Euston 15 ⊖	a										

OVERNIGHT SLEEPERS. For sleeper trains, operated by First ScotRail, please refer to Tables 400 - 404

Table 65

Sundays
until 24 June

Scotland and North West England - West Midlands and London

Route Diagram - see first Page of Table 65

		TP	TP	TP	TP	VT	XC	VT	VT	VT	VT	TP	XC	VT	VT	TP	LM	VT	TP	XC	VT	VT	TP
		◇1			◇1	◇1	◇1	◇1	◇1	◇1	◇1	◇1	◇1	◇1	◇1	◇1	◇1	◇1	◇1	◇1	◇1	◇1	◇1
							A						A							A			
			🚌	🚌																			
						⊡	⊡🍴	⊡	⊡	⊡	⊡		⊡🍴	⊡	⊡			⊡		⊡🍴	⊡	⊡	
Inverness	d																						
Aberdeen	d																						
Dundee	d																						
Perth	d																						
Edinburgh 10	d																						
Haymarket	d																						
Glasgow Central 15	d																						
Motherwell	d																						
Carstairs	d																						
Lockerbie	d																						
Carlisle 8	a																						
	d																						
Penrith North Lakes	d																						
Windermere	d																						
Oxenholme Lake District	a																						
	d																						
Barrow-in-Furness	d																						09 17
Lancaster 6	a																						10 17
	d																						10 21
Blackpool North	d	22p44	03 20	05 20	07 48							08 44							09 44				
Preston 8	a	23p08			08 12							09 08							10 08				10 40
Preston 8	d	23p10	04u00	06u00	08 14						09 00	09 10						10 00	10 10			10 17	10 47
Wigan North Western	a										09 10							10 10				10 28	
	d										09 11							10 11				10 28	
Blackrod	d																						
Lostock	d																						
Bolton	a	23p34	04b35	06b35	08 37							09 34							10 34				11 08
Manchester Piccadilly 10	a	23p53	05b00	07b00	08 59							09 56							10 56				11 27
Manchester Airport ✈	a	00 23	05 25	07 25	09 17							10 17							11 17				11 47
Liverpool Lime Street 10	a															09 56							
	d								08 15	08 38					09 38								
Liverpool South Parkway ✈	d																						
Runcorn	d								08 35	08 54					09 54								
Warrington Bank Quay	a										09 21							10 21				10 39	
	d										09 22							10 22				10 39	
Hartford	d																						
Manchester Piccadilly 10	d					08 05	08 10	08 20					09 07	09 20						10 06	10 20		
Stockport	d					08 14	08 19	08 28					09 16	09 27						10 16	10 29		
Wilmslow	d					08 22	08 26														10 36		
Holyhead	d																						
Bangor (Gwynedd)	d																						
Llandudno Junction	d																						
Wrexham General	d																						
Chester	d																						
Crewe 10	a					08 39	08 44		08 52	09 11	09 41				10 12			10 41			10 53	10 59	
	d					08 43	08 47		08 53	09 13	09 43				10 14		10 20	10 43			10 55	11 01	
Macclesfield	d							08 42					09 29	09 40						10 29			
Congleton	d																						
Stoke-on-Trent	d							08 59					09 46	09 57						10 47			
Stafford	a					09 01	09 06			09 31			10 09		10 32		10 41			11 04			
	d					09 02	09 07			09 32			10 10		10 33		10 41			11 05			
Penkridge	a																10 48						
Wolverhampton 7	a						09 26						10 25				10 59			11 24		11 31	
Birmingham New Street 12	a						09 58						10 56				11 25			11 56		12 04	
Birmingham International ✈	a						10 13						11 13							12 13			
Coventry	a						10 24						11 24							12 24			
Lichfield Trent Valley	a																						
Tamworth Low Level	a																						
Nuneaton	a									09 54					10 55								
Rugby	a										10 31							11 31					
Milton Keynes Central	a								10 17		11 06			11 16	11 46			12 06					
Watford Junction	a					10s35		10s41		11s16	11s43										12s35		
London Euston 15 ⊖	a					10 57		11 02	11 06	11 37	12 05			12 08	12 32			12 45			12 56		

A ⊡ from Birmingham New Street 🍴 to Birmingham New Street

b Stops to pick up only

OVERNIGHT SLEEPERS. For sleeper trains, operated by First ScotRail, please refer to Tables 400 - 404

Table 65

Sundays
until 24 June

Scotland and North West England - West Midlands and London

Route Diagram - see first Page of Table 65

		VT	VT	VT	TP	XC	VT	VT	VT	TP	VT	LM	VT	LM	VT	VT	TP	XC	VT	VT	VT	TP	VT
		◇1	◇1	◇1	◇1	◇1	◇1	◇1	◇1	◇1	◇1	◇1	◇1	◇1	◇1	◇1	◇1	◇1	◇1	◇1	◇1	◇1	◇1
						A												A					
		☕	☕	☕		☕🛒	☕	☕	☕		☕		☕		☕	☕	🛒	☕🛒	☕	☕	☕	🛒	☕
Inverness	d																						
Aberdeen	d																						
Dundee	d																						
Perth	d																						
Edinburgh 10	d																					10 10	
Haymarket	d																					10u14	
Glasgow Central 15	d															09 37							
Motherwell	d																						
Carstairs	d																						
Lockerbie	d																					11 08	
Carlisle 8	a															10 44						11 29	
	d															10 46						11 29	
Penrith North Lakes	d															11 00						11 45	
Windermere	d																						
Oxenholme Lake District	a															11 22						12 09	
	d															11 23						12 10	
Barrow-in-Furness	d									10 30													
Lancaster 6	a									11 22						11 37						12 26	
	d									11 22						11 38					12 00	12 26	
Blackpool North	d				10 44												11 44						
Preston 8	a				11 08					11 42						11 56	12 08				12 15	12 45	
Preston 8	d			10 58	11 10				11 17	11 47						11 58	12 10				12 17	12 47	
Wigan North Western	a			11 09					11 28							12 09					12 28		
	d			11 09					11 28							12 09					12 28		
Blackrod	d																						
Lostock	d																						
Bolton	a				11 34					12 08							12 34					13 08	
Manchester Piccadilly 10 ⛴	a				11 56					12 27							12 59					13 27	
Manchester Airport ✈	a				12 17					12 48							13 17					13 47	
Liverpool Lime Street 10	a																						
	d		10 38									11 34	11 48										
Liverpool South Parkway ✈	d											11 44											
Runcorn	d		10 54									11 52	12 04										
Warrington Bank Quay	a			11 20					11 39							12 20					12 39		
	d			11 20					11 39							12 20					12 39		
Hartford	d											12 04											
Manchester Piccadilly 10 ⛴	d	10 35				11 05	11 15				11 35				11 55			12 06	12 15				12 35
Stockport	d	10 42				11 14	11 23				11 43				12 05			12 15	12 23				12 44
Wilmslow	d														12 12								
Holyhead	d																			10 55			
Bangor (Gwynedd)	d																			11 22			
Llandudno Junction	d																			11 40			
Wrexham General	d																						
Chester	d							11 28												12 33			
Crewe 10	a		11 12					11 47	11 59			12 20			12 28					12 52	12 59		
	d		11 14					11 49	12 01			12 22			12 30					12 56	13 01		
Macclesfield	d	10 55				11 27					11 56							12 29					12 57
Congleton	d																						
Stoke-on-Trent	d	11 12				11 45	11 51				12 13			←				12 47	12 51				13 14
Stafford	a		11 34			12 02						12 41	12 35	12 41				13 06					
	d		11 36			12 03						12 42	12 36	12 42				13 07					
Penkridge	a											→		12 48									
Wolverhampton 7 ⛴	a					12 23			12 32					12 59				13 21			13 31		
Birmingham New Street 12	a					12 52			13 06					13 27				13 56			14 04		
Birmingham International ✈	a					13 13												14 13					
Coventry	a					13 24												14 24					
Lichfield Trent Valley	a																						
Tamworth Low Level	a																						
Nuneaton	a		11 58					12 31															
Rugby	a																						
Milton Keynes Central	a	12 20					12 50	13 03											13 49	14 02			
Watford Junction	a		12s50																				
London Euston 15 ⊖	a	12 59	13 11	13 21			13 28	13 44			13 47		14 01		14 09	14 16			14 27	14 43			14 47

A ☕ from Birmingham New Street 🛒 to Birmingham New Street

OVERNIGHT SLEEPERS. For sleeper trains, operated by First ScotRail, please refer to Tables 400 - 404

Sundays
until 24 June

Scotland and North West England - West Midlands and London

Route Diagram - see first Page of Table 65

		XC		LM	VT	LM	VT	VT	TP	XC	VT	VT		VT	VT	TP	VT	XC	EM	LM	VT	LM		VT	VT
		◇1		◇1	◇1	◇1	◇1	◇1	◇1	◇1	◇1	◇1		◇1	◇1	◇1	◇1	◇1	◇	◇1	◇1	◇1		◇1	◇1
										A															
		🛒		🍽			🍽	🍽		🍽🛒	🍽	🍽		🍽	🍽		🍽	🛒			🍽			🍽	🍽
Inverness	d																								
Aberdeen	d																								
Dundee	d																								
Perth	d																								
Edinburgh 10	d														10 52										
Haymarket	d														10 57										
Glasgow Central 15	d							10 34																	11 36
Motherwell	d							10 49																	
Carstairs	d																								
Lockerbie	d																								
Carlisle 8	a							11 44							12 05										12 47
	d							11 46							12 07										12 49
Penrith North Lakes	d							12 00																	
Windermere	d																								
Oxenholme Lake District	a							12 22							12 41										13 22
	d							12 24							12 43										13 23
Barrow-in-Furness	d															12 25									
Lancaster 6	a							12 37							12 56	13 26									13 37
	d							12 38							12 57	13 26									13 38
Blackpool North	d								12 44																
Preston 8	a							12 56	13 08						13 15	13 45									13 56
Preston 8	d							12 58	13 10						13 17	13 47									13 58
Wigan North Western	a							13 09							13 28										14 09
	d							13 09							13 28										14 09
Blackrod	d																								
Lostock	d																								
Bolton	a								13 34							14 08									
Manchester Piccadilly 10	a								13 56							14 27									
Manchester Airport	a								14 17							14 47									
Liverpool Lime Street 10	a																								
	d			12 34	12 48														12 52	13 34	13 48				
Liverpool South Parkway	d			12 44															13 03	13 44					
Runcorn	d			12 52	13 04															13 52	14 04				
Warrington Bank Quay	a							13 20							13 39										14 20
	d							13 20							13 39										14 20
Hartford	d			13 03																14 03					
Manchester Piccadilly 10	d	12 41					12 55			13 03	13 15						13 35	13 42	13 44					13 55	
Stockport	d	12 50					13 05			13 13	13 22						13 42	13 51	13a53					14 04	
Wilmslow	d						13 12																	14 11	
Holyhead	d											11 50													
Bangor (Gwynedd)	d											12 17													
Llandudno Junction	d											12 35													
Wrexham General	d																								
Chester	d											13 30		13 30											
Crewe 10	a			13 19			13 28					13 50		13 50	13 59					14 18				14 27	
	d			13 22			13 30					13 51		13 51	14 01					14 22				14 29	
Macclesfield	d	13 04								13 26							13 55	14 04							
Congleton	d																								
Stoke-on-Trent	d	13 22				←				13 44	13 50						14 12	14 22				←			
Stafford	a			13 42	13 35	13 42				14 01										14 42	14 35	14 42			
	d			13 43	13 36	13 43				14 02										14 43	14 36	14 43			
Penkridge	a			→		13 48														→		14 48			
Wolverhampton 7	a	13 52				13 59				14 20					14 32			14 53				14 59			
Birmingham New Street 12	a	14 27				14 31				14 56					15 05			15 27				15 31			
Birmingham International	a									15 13															
Coventry	a									15 24															
Lichfield Trent Valley	a																								
Tamworth Low Level	a																								
Nuneaton	a											14 31		14 31											
Rugby	a																								
Milton Keynes Central	a										14 49	15 04		15 04											
Watford Junction	a																								
London Euston 15 ⊖	a				15 01		15 09	15 15			15 27	15 45		15 45			15 47				16 01			16 09	16 15

A 🍽 from Birmingham New Street 🛒 to Birmingham New Street

OVERNIGHT SLEEPERS. For sleeper trains, operated by First ScotRail, please refer to Tables 400 - 404

Table 65

Sundays
until 24 June

Scotland and North West England - West Midlands and London

Route Diagram - see first Page of Table 65

		TP	XC	VT	VT	VT	TP	VT	XC	EM	LM	VT	LM	VT	VT	TP	XC	VT	VT	VT	TP	VT	XC
		◇1	◇1	◇1	◇1	◇1	◇1	◇1	◇1	◇	◇1	◇1	◇1	◇1	◇1	◇1	◇1	◇1	◇1	◇1	◇1	◇1	◇1
			A														A						
			⊏⊐⊼	⊏⊐	⊏⊐	⊏⊐	⊼	⊏⊐	⊼			⊏⊐		⊏⊐	⊏⊐		⊏⊐⊼	⊏⊐	⊏⊐	⊏⊐		⊏⊐	⊼
Inverness	d																						
Aberdeen	d																						
Dundee	d																						
Perth	d																						
Edinburgh 10	d						12 10													12 52			
Haymarket	d						12u14													12 56			
Glasgow Central 15	d					11 58									12 42								
Motherwell	d																						
Carstairs	d																						
Lockerbie	d						13 08																
Carlisle 8	a					13 09	13 29								13 51					14 05			
	d					13 10	13 29								13 54					14 07			
Penrith North Lakes	d						13 45													14 22			
Windermere	d																						
Oxenholme Lake District	a						14 09								14 27								
	d						14 10								14 28								
Barrow-in-Furness	d																				14 25		
Lancaster 6	a					13 56	14 26								14 42					14 56	15 26		
	d					13 58	14 26								14 43					14 57	15 26		
Blackpool North	d	13 44														14 44							
Preston 8	a	14 08				14 15	14 45								15 01	15 08				15 15	15 45		
Preston 8	d	14 10				14 17	14 47								15 03	15 10				15 17	15 47		
Wigan North Western	a					14 28									15 14					15 28			
	d					14 28									15 14					15 28			
Blackrod	d																						
Lostock	d																						
Bolton	a	14 34					15 08									15 34					16 08		
Manchester Piccadilly 10	a	14 56					15 27									15 56					16 27		
Manchester Airport ✈	a	15 17					15 47									16 17					16 46		
Liverpool Lime Street 10	a																						
	d									13 52	14 34	14 48											
Liverpool South Parkway ✈	d									14 03	14 44												
Runcorn	d										14 52	15 04											
Warrington Bank Quay	a					14 39									15 25					15 39			
	d					14 39									15 25					15 39			
Hartford	d										15 03												
Manchester Piccadilly 10	d		14 05	14 15				14 35	14 42	14 44				14 55			15 02	15 15				15 35	15 42
Stockport	d		14 14	14 22				14 42	14 51	14a53				15 04			15 11	15 22				15 42	15 51
Wilmslow	d													15 11									
Holyhead	d				12 50														13 55				
Bangor (Gwynedd)	d				13 18														14 22				
Llandudno Junction	d				13 36														14 40				
Wrexham General	d																						
Chester	d				14 33														15 33				
Crewe 10	a				14 52	14 59					15 20			15 27					15 52	15 59			
	d				14 54	15 01					15 22			15 29					15 54	16 01			
Macclesfield	d		14 27					14 55	15 04								15 24					15 55	16 04
Congleton	d																						
Stoke-on-Trent	d		14 45	14 50				15 12	15 22				←				15 45	15 50				16 12	16 23
Stafford	a		15 05								15 43	15 35	15 43				16 05						
	d		15 06								15 44	15 36	15 44				16 06						
Penkridge	a										↪		15 49										
Wolverhampton 7	a		15 19			15 31			15 53				16 00				16 21			16 32			16 53
Birmingham New Street 12	a		15 56			16 07			16 27				16 35				16 52			17 07			17 28
Birmingham International ✈	a		16 13														17 13						
Coventry	a		16 24														17 24						
Lichfield Trent Valley	a																						
Tamworth Low Level	a																						
Nuneaton	a																						
Rugby	a																						
Milton Keynes Central	a			15 49	16 04													16 49	17 03				
Watford Junction	a																						
London Euston 15 ⊖	a			16 27	16 44			16 47				17 01		17 09	17 20			17 27	17 44			17 47	

A ⊏⊐ from Birmingham New Street ⊼ to Birmingham New Street

OVERNIGHT SLEEPERS. For sleeper trains, operated by First ScotRail, please refer to Tables 400 - 404

Table 65

Sundays
until 24 June

Scotland and North West England - West Midlands and London

Route Diagram - see first Page of Table 65

		EM	LM	VT		LM	VT	VT	TP	XC	VT	VT	VT	TP		NT	VT	XC	EM	LM	VT	LM	VT	VT
		◇	◇1	◇1		◇1	◇1	◇1	◇1	◇1	◇1	◇1	◇1	◇1			◇1	◇1	◇	◇1	◇1	◇1	◇1	◇1
										A														
				⊐			⊐	⊐		⊐⊼	⊐	⊐	⊐	⊼			⊐	⊼			⊐		⊐	⊐
Inverness	d																							
Aberdeen	d																							
Dundee	d																							
Perth	d																							
Edinburgh 10	d													14 10										
Haymarket	d													14u14										
Glasgow Central 15	d							13 36					13 55											14 36
Motherwell	d																							
Carstairs	d																							
Lockerbie	d													15 08										
Carlisle 8	a							14 46					15 09	15 29										15 46
	d							14 49					15 11	15 29		15 35								15 49
Penrith North Lakes	d													15 45										
Windermere	d																							
Oxenholme Lake District	a							15 22					15 46	16 09										16 22
	d							15 23					15 46	16 10										16 23
Barrow-in-Furness	d																							
Lancaster 6	a							15 37						16 26										16 37
	d							15 38						16 26										16 38
Blackpool North	d								15 44															
Preston 8	a							15 56	16 08				16 15	16 46		18 48								16 56
Preston 8	d							15 58	16 10				16 17	16 47										16 58
Wigan North Western	a							16 09					16 28											17 09
	d							16 09					16 28											17 09
Blackrod	d																							
Lostock	d																							
Bolton	a								16 34					17 08										
Manchester Piccadilly 10 ⇌	a								16 56					17 27										
Manchester Airport ✈	a								17 17					17 47										
Liverpool Lime Street 10	a																							
	d	14 52	15 34	15 48								16 18							15 52	16 34	16 48			
Liverpool South Parkway ✈	d	15 03	15 44																16 03	16 44				
Runcorn	d		15 52	16 04								16 34								16 52	17 04			
Warrington Bank Quay	a							16 20					16 39											17 20
	d							16 20					16 39											17 20
Hartford	d		16 03																	17 03				
Manchester Piccadilly 10 ⇌	d	15 44					15 55			16 02	16 15						16 35	16 42	16 44				16 55	
Stockport	d	15a53					16 04			16 11	16 23						16 42	16 51	16a53				17 04	
Wilmslow	d						16 11																17 11	
Holyhead	d																							
Bangor (Gwynedd)	d																							
Llandudno Junction	d																							
Wrexham General	d																							
Chester	d																							
Crewe 10	a		16 18				16 27					16 51	16 59							17 18			17 27	
	d		16 22				16 29					16 54	17 01							17 22			17 29	
Macclesfield	d									16 24							16 55	17 04						
Congleton	d																							
Stoke-on-Trent	d					←				16 45	16 50						17 12	17 22				←		
Stafford	a		16 43	16 36		16 43				17 05										17 43	17 35	17 43		
	d		16 44	16 37		16 44				17 06										17 44	17 36	17 44		
Penkridge	a		→			16 49														→		17 49		
Wolverhampton 7 ⇌	a					17 00				17 20			17 32					17 53				18 00		
Birmingham New Street 12	a					17 32				17 56			18 06					18 27				18 32		
Birmingham International ✈	a									18 13														
Coventry	a									18 24														
Lichfield Trent Valley	a											17 26												
Tamworth Low Level	a																							
Nuneaton	a																							
Rugby	a																							
Milton Keynes Central	a										17 49	18 04												
Watford Junction	a																							
London Euston 15 ⊖	a			18 01			18 09	18 15			18 27	18 44					18 47				19 01		19 09	19 15

A ⊐ from Birmingham New Street ⊼ to Birmingham New Street

OVERNIGHT SLEEPERS. For sleeper trains, operated by First ScotRail, please refer to Tables 400 - 404

Sundays

until 24 June

Scotland and North West England - West Midlands and London

Route Diagram - see first Page of Table 65

		TP	XC	VT	VT	VT	TP	TP	VT	XC		EM	LM	VT	LM	VT	VT	TP	XC	VT		VT	VT	TP	NT
		◇1	◇1	◇1	◇1	◇1	◇1	◇1	◇1	◇1		◇	◇1	◇1	◇1	◇1	◇1	◇1	◇1	◇1		◇1	◇1	◇1	
			A																A						
			🍴🛒	🍴	🍴	🍴		🛒	🍴	🛒				🍴		🍴	🍴		🍴🛒	🍴		🍴	🍴	🛒	🛒
Inverness	d																								
Aberdeen	d																								
Dundee	d																								
Perth	d																								
Edinburgh 10	d					14 52																		16 10	
Haymarket	d					14 57																		16u14	
Glasgow Central 15	d							15 06									15 36						15 57		
Motherwell	d																								
Carstairs	d																								
Lockerbie	d							16 06																17 08	
Carlisle 8	a					16 05		16 26									16 46						17 08	17 29	
	d					16 07		16 26									16 49						17 09	17 29	17 41
Penrith North Lakes	d					16 22		16 42									17 03							17 45	
Windermere	d																								
Oxenholme Lake District	a							17 07															17 44	18 09	
	d							17 07															17 44	18 10	
Barrow-in-Furness	d						16 17																		
Lancaster 6	a					16 56	17 17	17 22									17 37							18 26	
	d					16 57	17 17	17 22									17 38							18 26	
Blackpool North	d	16 44																17 44							
Preston 8	a	17 08				17 15	17 37	17 41									17 56	18 08					18 13	18 45	20 47
Preston 8	d	17 10				17 17		17 47									17 58	18 10					18 16	18 47	
Wigan North Western	a					17 28											18 09						18 27		
	d					17 28											18 09						18 27		
Blackrod	d																								
Lostock	d																								
Bolton	a	17 34						18 08										18 34						19 08	
Manchester Piccadilly 10 🚢	a	17 56						18 27										18 56						19 27	
Manchester Airport ✈	a	18 17						18 45										19 17						19 47	
Liverpool Lime Street 10	a																								
	d											16 52	17 34	17 48											
Liverpool South Parkway ✈	d											17 03	17 44												
Runcorn	d												17 52	18 04											
Warrington Bank Quay	a					17 39											18 20						18 38		
	d					17 39											18 20						18 38		
Hartford	d												18 03												
Manchester Piccadilly 10 🚢	d		17 02	17 15					17 35	17 42		17 44				17 55			18 02	18 15					
Stockport	d		17 11	17 22					17 42	17 51		17a53				18 04			18 11	18 22					
Wilmslow	d															18 11									
Holyhead	d																								
Bangor (Gwynedd)	d																								
Llandudno Junction	d																								
Wrexham General	d																								
Chester	d				17 35																	18 35			
Crewe 10	a				17 53	17 59							18 20			18 27						18 53	18 58		
	d				17 55	18 01							18 22			18 29						18 55	19 00		
Macclesfield	d		17 24						17 55	18 04									18 24						
Congleton	d																								
Stoke-on-Trent	d		17 45	17 50					18 12	18 22					←				18 45	18 50					
Stafford	a		18 05										18 43	18 35	18 43				19 02						
	d		18 06										18 44	18 36	18 44				19 03						
Penkridge	a												→		18 49										
Wolverhampton 7 🚢	a		18 20			18 32				18 53					19 00				19 20				19 31		
Birmingham New Street 12	a		18 56			19 06				19 27					19 32				19 50				20 06		
Birmingham International ✈	a		19 13																20 13						
Coventry	a		19 24																20 24						
Lichfield Trent Valley	a																								
Tamworth Low Level	a																								
Nuneaton	a																								
Rugby	a																								
Milton Keynes Central	a			18 49	19 02															19 49		20 03			
Watford Junction	a																								
London Euston 15 ⊖	a			19 27	19 43				19 47					20 01		20 09	20 15			20 27		20 44			

A 🍴 from Birmingham New Street 🛒 to Birmingham New Street

OVERNIGHT SLEEPERS. For sleeper trains, operated by First ScotRail, please refer to Tables 400 - 404

Table 65

Sundays
until 24 June

Scotland and North West England - West Midlands and London

Route Diagram - see first Page of Table 65

		VT	XC	EM	LM	VT		LM	VT	VT	TP	TP	XC	VT	TP	TP		VT	LM	VT	VT	VT	XC	EM	TP
		◇1	◇1	◇	◇1	◇1		◇1	◇1	◇1	◇1	◇1	◇1	◇1	◇1	◇1		◇1	◇1	◇1	◇1	◇1	◇1	◇	◇1
													A												
		🍴	🛒			🍴			🍴	🍴			🛒	🍴		🛒		🍴		🍴	🍴	🍴			
Inverness	d																								
Aberdeen	d																								
Dundee	d																								
Perth	d																								
Edinburgh 10	d													16 52											
Haymarket	d													16 56											
Glasgow Central 15	d									16 40						17 06						17 36			
Motherwell	d									16 54															
Carstairs	d																								
Lockerbie	d																					18 32			
Carlisle 8	a									17 49				18 05		18 25						18 50			
	d									17 51				18 07		18 26						18 52			
Penrith North Lakes	d									18 05						18 42						19 06			
Windermere	d										18 01														
Oxenholme Lake District	a									18 27	18x21			18 41		19 07						19 28			
	d									18 28	18x22			18 42		19 07						19 29			
Barrow-in-Furness	d														18 17										
Lancaster 6	a									18 42	18 37			18 56	19 17	19 22						19 43			
	d									18 43	18 38			18 57	19 17	19 22						19 44			
Blackpool North	d											18 40													19 44
Preston 8	a									19 01	18 56	19 04		19 15	19 37	19 41						20 02			20 08
Preston 8	d									19 03	19 10			19 17		19 47						20 04			20 10
Wigan North Western	a									19 14				19 28								20 15			
	d									19 14				19 28								20 15			
Blackrod	d																								
Lostock	d																								
Bolton	a										19 34					20 08									20 34
Manchester Piccadilly 10	a										19 56					20 27									20 56
Manchester Airport	a										20 17					20 45									21 16
Liverpool Lime Street 10	a																								
	d			17 52	18 34	18 48													19 34		19 48			18 52	
Liverpool South Parkway	d			18 03	18 44														19 44					19 03	
Runcorn	d				18 52	19 04													19 52		20 04				
Warrington Bank Quay	a									19 25				19 39								20 26			
	d									19 25				19 39								20 26			
Hartford	d				19 03														20 03						
Manchester Piccadilly 10	d	18 35	18 42	18 44					18 55				19 02					19 15		19 35			19 42	19 44	
Stockport	d	18 42	18 51	18a53					19 04				19 11					19 22		19 41			19 51	19a53	
Wilmslow	d								19 11																
Holyhead	d																								
Bangor (Gwynedd)	d																								
Llandudno Junction	d																								
Wrexham General	d																								
Chester	d																								
Crewe 10	a				19 20				19 27					19 59					20 16		20 22	20 45			
	d				19 22				19 29					20 01					20 18		20 24	20 47			
Macclesfield	d	18 55	19 04										19 24							19 54			20 05		
Congleton	d																								
Stoke-on-Trent	d	19 12	19 22					←					19 45					19 50		20 11			20 23		
Stafford	a				19 44	19 35		19 44					20 04						20 38		20 41		20 44		
	d				19 44	19 36		19 44					20 05						20 39		20 43		20 45		
Penkridge	a				→			19 50											20 44						
Wolverhampton 7	a		19 53					20 00					20 20	20 32					20 55				20 57		
Birmingham New Street 12	a		20 27					20 32					20 50	21 06					21 32				21 27		
Birmingham International	a												21 13												
Coventry	a												21 23												
Lichfield Trent Valley	a																								
Tamworth Low Level	a																								
Nuneaton	a																								
Rugby	a																								
Milton Keynes Central	a																	20 46			21 36	21 55			
Watford Junction	a																					22s31			
London Euston 15	a	20 47				21 01			21 09	21 21								21 31		21 58	22 27	22 53			

A 🛒 to Birmingham New Street

OVERNIGHT SLEEPERS. For sleeper trains, operated by First ScotRail, please refer to Tables 400 - 404

Table 65

Sundays
until 24 June

Scotland and North West England - West Midlands and London

Route Diagram - see first Page of Table 65

		TP		NT	XC	AW	VT	EM	LM	VT	VT	VT		TP	TP	XC	VT	LM	NT	TP	VT	XC		EM	NT
		◇1			◇1	◇	◇1	◇	◇1	◇1	◇1	◇1		◇1	◇1	◇1	◇1	◇1		◇1	◇1	◇1		◇	
		🛒				🛒	☕			☕	☕	☕					☕			🛒	☕				
Inverness	d																								
Aberdeen	d																								
Dundee	d																								
Perth	d																								
Edinburgh 10	d	18 10															18 52			19 57					
Haymarket	d	18u14															18 57			20u01					
Glasgow Central 15	d											18 30									20 08				
Motherwell	d																								
Carstairs	d																								
Lockerbie	d	19 08																			21 02				
Carlisle 8	a	19 29										19 43					20 05			21 13	21 21				
	d	19 29										19 44					20 07			21 14	21 24				
Penrith North Lakes	d	19 45															20 22				21 39				
Windermere	d													20 40											
Oxenholme Lake District	a	20 09										20 19		20 59							22 02				
	d	20 10										20 19		21 01							22 03				
Barrow-in-Furness	d			20 02																					
Lancaster 6	a	20 26		21 07								20 34		21 18			20 56			22 03	22 17				
	d	20 26										20 34					20 57			22 03	22 18				
Blackpool North	d														20 44				21 50						
Preston 8	a	20 45										20 52			21 08		21 15		22 14	22 23	22 35				
Preston 8	d	20 47										20 55			21 10		21 17		22 15	22 29	22 38				
Wigan North Western	a											21 06					21 28		22 36		22 49				
	d											21 07					21 28				22 50				
Blackrod	d																								
Lostock	d																								
Bolton	a	21 08													21 34					22 50					
Manchester Piccadilly 10 ⇌	a	21 27													21 56					23 14					
Manchester Airport ✈	a	21 46													22 17					23 30					
Liverpool Lime Street 10	a																								
	d							19 52	20 34		20 48							21 34						21 21	22 01
Liverpool South Parkway ✈	d							20 03	20 44									21 44						21 31	
Runcorn	d								20 52		21 04							21 52							
Warrington Bank Quay	a											21 18					21 39				23 00				
	d											21 18					21 39				23 01				
Hartford	d								21 03									22 03							
Manchester Piccadilly 10 ⇌	d				20 07		20 20	20 44		20 55						21 07						22 07		22 11	22a50
Stockport	d				20 16		20 27	20a53		21 03						21 16						22 16		22a20	
Wilmslow	d																								
Holyhead	d					18 25																			
Bangor (Gwynedd)	d					19 04																			
Llandudno Junction	d					19 24																			
Wrexham General	d																								
Chester	d					20 27																			
Crewe 10	a					20 48			21 16		21 21	21 38					21 59	22 18			23 20				
	d					20 52			21 17		21 23	21 40					22 01	22 22							
Macclesfield	d				20 29		20 40			21 15						21 29						22 29			
Congleton	d																								
Stoke-on-Trent	d				20 47		20 57			21 33						21 47						22 47			
Stafford	a				21 08	21 16			21 37		21 42	22 01				22 06		22 42				23 04			
	d				21 08	21 16			21 38		21 43	22 02				22 06		22 45				23 05			
Penkridge	a								21 44									22 50							
Wolverhampton 7 ⇌	a				21 21	21 34			21 55			22 16				22 20	22 31	23 01				23 18			
Birmingham New Street 12	a				21 50	22 06			22 26			22 52				22 52	23 06	23 26				23 49			
Birmingham International ✈	a																								
Coventry	a																								
Lichfield Trent Valley	a										21 59														
Tamworth Low Level	a										22 05														
Nuneaton	a										22 17														
Rugby	a										22 31														
Milton Keynes Central	a						22 03			22 46	23 04														
Watford Junction	a									23s25	23s34														
London Euston 15 ⊖	a						22 56			23 49	23 54														

OVERNIGHT SLEEPERS. For sleeper trains, operated by First ScotRail, please refer to Tables 400 - 404

Table 65

Sundays
until 24 June

Scotland and North West England - West Midlands and London

Route Diagram - see first Page of Table 65

		NT	NT	TP	SR	SR	SR	SR
					R	R	R	R
				◇1				
					🛏	🛏	🛏	🛏
					⊡	⊡	⊡	⊡
							A	A
Inverness	d						20 25	
Aberdeen	d							21 42
Dundee	d							23u06
Perth	d						23u00	
Edinburgh 10	d				23 15			
Haymarket	d							
Glasgow Central 15	d					23 15		
Motherwell	d					23u31		
Carstairs	d				23u47			
Lockerbie	d							
Carlisle 8	a							
	d				01u12			
Penrith North Lakes	d							
Windermere	d							
Oxenholme Lake District	a							
	d							
Barrow-in-Furness	d							
Lancaster 6	a							
	d							
Blackpool North	d	22 44		23 03				
Preston 8	a	23 08		23 28			04s41	
Preston 8	d	23 09		23 28				
Wigan North Western	a	23 30						
	d							
Blackrod	d			23 50				
Lostock	d			23 57				
Bolton	a			00 02				
Manchester Piccadilly 10	a			00 18				
Manchester Airport ✈	a			00 32				
Liverpool Lime Street 10	a							
	d		23 01					
Liverpool South Parkway ✈	d							
Runcorn	d							
Warrington Bank Quay	a							
	d							
Hartford	d							
Manchester Piccadilly 10	d		23a50					
Stockport	d							
Wilmslow	d							
Holyhead	d							
Bangor (Gwynedd)	d							
Llandudno Junction	d							
Wrexham General	d							
Chester	d							
Crewe 10	a						05s41	
	d							
Macclesfield	d							
Congleton	d							
Stoke-on-Trent	d							
Stafford	a							
	d							
Penkridge	a							
Wolverhampton 7	a							
Birmingham New Street 12	a							
Birmingham International ✈	a							
Coventry	a							
Lichfield Trent Valley	a							
Tamworth Low Level	a							
Nuneaton	a							
Rugby	a							
Milton Keynes Central	a							
Watford Junction	a				06s23			
London Euston 15 ⊖	a				06 46		07 50	

A Conveys a portion from Fort William, dep 1900

OVERNIGHT SLEEPERS. For sleeper trains, operated by First ScotRail, please refer to Tables 400 - 404

Table 65

Sundays

1 July to 9 September

Scotland and North West England - West Midlands and London

Route Diagram - see first Page of Table 65

		TP	TP	TP	VT	VT	TP	VT	VT	VT		TP	XC	VT	VT	TP	VT	XC	VT	LM		VT	TP	VT	VT
		◇1			◇1	◇1	◇1	◇1	◇1	◇1		◇1	◇1	◇1	◇1	◇1	◇1	◇1	◇1	◇1		◇1	◇1	◇1	◇1
					A	A																			
			🚌	🚌																					
					🍴	🍴		🍴	🍴	🍴			🛒	🍴	🍴		🍴	🛒	🍴			🍴		🍴	🍴
Inverness	d																								
Aberdeen	d																								
Dundee	d																								
Perth	d																								
Edinburgh 10	d																								
Haymarket	d																								
Glasgow Central 15	d																								
Motherwell	d																								
Carstairs	d																								
Lockerbie	d																								
Carlisle 8	a																								
	d																								
Penrith North Lakes	d																								
Windermere	d																								
Oxenholme Lake District	a																								
	d																								
Barrow-in-Furness	d																								
Lancaster 6	a																								
	d																								
Blackpool North	d	22p44	03 20	05 20			07 48									08 44							09 44		
Preston 8	a	23p08					08 12									09 08							10 08		
Preston 8	d	23p10	04u00	06u00			08 14								09 00	09 10						10 00	10 10		10 17
Wigan North Western	a														09 10							10 10			10 28
	d														09 11							10 11			10 28
Blackrod	d																								
Lostock	d																								
Bolton	a	23p34	04b35	06b35			08 37									09 34							10 34		
Manchester Piccadilly 10 ⛴	a	23p53	05b00	07b00			08 59									09 56							10 56		
Manchester Airport ✈	a	00 23	05 25	07 25			09 17									10 17							11 17		
Liverpool Lime Street 10	a																								
	d					06 55				08 15		08 22		08 38					09 38						
Liverpool South Parkway ✈	d											08 32													
Runcorn	d					07 11				08 35				08 54					09 54						
Warrington Bank Quay	a														09 21							10 21			10 39
	d														09 22							10 22			10 39
Hartford	d																								
Manchester Piccadilly 10 ⛴	d				06 50			08 05	08 20			09a09	08 27				09 20	09 27						10 20	
Stockport	d				06 58			08 14	08 28				08 36				09 27	09 36						10 29	
Wilmslow	d							08 22					08 43											10 36	
Holyhead	d																								
Bangor (Gwynedd)	d																								
Llandudno Junction	d																								
Wrexham General	d																								
Chester	d																								
Crewe 10	a					07 29		08 39		08 52			09 01	09 11	09 41				10 12			10 41		10 53	10 59
	d					07 31		08 43		08 53			09 05	09 13	09 43				10 14	10 20		10 43		10 55	11 01
Macclesfield	d				07 12				08 42								09 40	09 49							
Congleton	d																								
Stoke-on-Trent	d				07 29				08 59								09 57	10 07							
Stafford	a					07 52		09 01					09 25	09 31				10 26	10 32	10 41					
	d					07 53		09 02					09 26	09 32				10 27	10 33	10 41					
Penkridge	a																			10 48					
Wolverhampton 7 ⛴	a												09 40					10 42		11 00					11 31
Birmingham New Street 12	a												09 58					10 59		11 17					11 55
Birmingham International ✈	a																								
Coventry	a																								
Lichfield Trent Valley	a																								
Tamworth Low Level	a																								
Nuneaton	a				08 00									09 54					10 55						
Rugby	a				08 16										10 31							11 31			
Milton Keynes Central	a					08 56				10 17					11 06		11 16		11 46			12 06			
Watford Junction	a					09 20		10s35	10s41					11s16	11s43									12s35	
London Euston 15 ⊖	a				09 23	09 37		10 57	11 02	11 06				11 37	12 05		12 08		12 32			12 45		12 56	

A 29 July, 5 August, 12 August, 2 September, 9 September

b Stops to pick up only

OVERNIGHT SLEEPERS. For sleeper trains, operated by First ScotRail, please refer to Tables 400 - 404

Table 65

Sundays

1 July to 9 September

Scotland and North West England - West Midlands and London

Route Diagram - see first Page of Table 65

		TP	XC	VT	VT	VT		TP	VT	VT	VT	TP	XC	VT	LM	VT		LM	VT	VT	TP	VT	VT	VT	TP
		◇1	◇1	◇1	◇1	◇1		◇1	◇1	◇1	◇1	◇1	◇1	◇1	◇1	◇1		◇1	◇1	◇1	◇1	◇1	◇1	◇1	◇1
			⊼	⊡	⊡	⊡			⊡	⊡	⊡		⊼	⊡		⊡			⊡	⊡	⊼	⊡	⊡	⊡	⊼
Inverness	d																								
Aberdeen	d																								
Dundee	d																								
Perth	d																								
Edinburgh 10	d																								10 10
Haymarket	d																								10u14
Glasgow Central 15	d																			09 37					
Motherwell	d																								
Carstairs	d																								
Lockerbie	d																								11 08
Carlisle 8	a																			10 44					11 29
	d																			10 46					11 29
Penrith North Lakes	d																			11 00					11 45
Windermere	d																								
Oxenholme Lake District	a																			11 22					12 09
	d																			11 23					12 10
Barrow-in-Furness	d	09 17										10 30													
Lancaster 6	a	10 17										11 22								11 37					12 26
	d	10 21										11 22								11 38				12 00	12 26
Blackpool North	d							10 44													11 44				
Preston 8	a	10 40						11 08				11 42								11 56	12 08			12 15	12 45
Preston 8	d	10 47				10 58		11 10			11 17	11 47								11 58	12 10			12 17	12 47
Wigan North Western	a					11 09					11 28									12 09				12 28	
	d					11 09					11 28									12 09				12 28	
Blackrod	d																								
Lostock	d																								
Bolton	a	11 08						11 34				12 08									12 34				13 08
Manchester Piccadilly 10	a	11 27						11 56				12 27									12 59				13 27
Manchester Airport	a	11 47						12 17				12 48									13 17				13 47
Liverpool Lime Street 10	a																								
	d				10 38										11 34	11 48									
Liverpool South Parkway	d														11 44										
Runcorn	d				10 54										11 52	12 04									
Warrington Bank Quay	a					11 20					11 39									12 20				12 39	
	d					11 20					11 39									12 20				12 39	
Hartford	d														12 03										
Manchester Piccadilly 10	d		10 27	10 35					11 15				11 27	11 35					11 55			12 15			
Stockport	d		10 36	10 42					11 23				11 36	11 43					12 05			12 23			
Wilmslow	d																		12 12						
Holyhead	d																						10 55		
Bangor (Gwynedd)	d																						11 22		
Llandudno Junction	d																						11 40		
Wrexham General	d																								
Chester	d									11 28													12 33		
Crewe 10	a				11 12					11 47	11 59				12 20				12 28				12 52	12 59	
	d				11 14					11 49	12 01				12 22				12 30				12 56	13 01	
Macclesfield	d		10 49	10 55									11 49	11 56											
Congleton	d																								
Stoke-on-Trent	d		11 07	11 12					11 51				12 07	12 13				←				12 51			
Stafford	a		11 27		11 34								12 24		12 41	12 35		12 41							
	d		11 28		11 36								12 25		12 42	12 36		12 42							
Penkridge	a														→			12 48							
Wolverhampton 7	a		11 41								12 32		12 40					12 59						13 31	
Birmingham New Street 12	a		12 00								12 55		12 58					13 16						13 55	
Birmingham International	a																								
Coventry	a																								
Lichfield Trent Valley	a																								
Tamworth Low Level	a																								
Nuneaton	a				11 58					12 31															
Rugby	a																								
Milton Keynes Central	a			12 20					12 50	13 03												13 49	14 02		
Watford Junction	a				12s50																				
London Euston 15	a			12 59	13 11	13 21			13 28	13 44				13 47		14 01			14 09	14 16		14 27	14 43		

OVERNIGHT SLEEPERS. For sleeper trains, operated by First ScotRail, please refer to Tables 400 - 404

Table 65

Sundays

1 July to 9 September

Scotland and North West England - West Midlands and London

Route Diagram - see first Page of Table 65

		XC		VT	LM	VT	LM	VT	VT	TP	XC	VT		VT	VT	VT	TP	XC	VT	EM	LM	VT		LM	VT
		◇1		◇1	◇1	◇1	◇1	◇1	◇1	◇1	◇1	◇1		◇1	◇1	◇1	◇1	◇1	◇1	◇	◇1	◇1		◇1	◇1
																		A							
		🛒		🍽		🍽		🍽	🍽		🛒	🍽		🍽	🍽	🍽		🍽🛒	🍽			🍽			🍽
Inverness	d																								
Aberdeen	d																								
Dundee	d																								
Perth	d																								
Edinburgh [10]	d															10 52									
Haymarket	d															10 57									
Glasgow Central [15]	d								10 34																
Motherwell	d								10 49																
Carstairs	d																								
Lockerbie	d																								
Carlisle [8]	a								11 44							12 05									
	d								11 46							12 07									
Penrith North Lakes	d								12 00																
Windermere	d																								
Oxenholme Lake District	a								12 22							12 41									
	d								12 24							12 43									
Barrow-in-Furness	d																12 25								
Lancaster [6]	a								12 37							12 56	13 26								
	d								12 38							12 57	13 26								
Blackpool North	d									12 44															
Preston [8]	a								12 56	13 08						13 15	13 45								
Preston [8]	d								12 58	13 10						13 17	13 47								
Wigan North Western	a								13 09							13 28									
	d								13 09							13 28									
Blackrod	d																								
Lostock	d																								
Bolton	a									13 34							14 08								
Manchester Piccadilly [10] ⛴	a									13 56							14 27								
Manchester Airport ✈	a									14 17							14 47								
Liverpool Lime Street [10]	a																								
	d				12 34	12 48														12 52	13 34	13 48			
Liverpool South Parkway ✈	d				12 44															13 03	13 44				
Runcorn	d				12 52	13 04															13 52	14 04			
Warrington Bank Quay	a								13 20							13 39									
	d								13 20							13 39									
Hartford	d				13 03																14 03				
Manchester Piccadilly [10] ⛴	d	12 26		12 35				12 55			13 07	13 15						13 27	13 35	13 44					13 55
Stockport	d	12 35		12 44				13 05				13 22						13 36	13 42	13a53					14 04
Wilmslow	d							13 12																	14 11
Holyhead	d													11 50											
Bangor (Gwynedd)	d													12 17											
Llandudno Junction	d													12 35											
Wrexham General	d																								
Chester	d													13 30	13 30										
Crewe [10]	a				13 19			13 28						13 50	13 50	13 59					14 18				14 27
	d				13 22			13 30						13 51	13 51	14 01					14 22				14 29
Macclesfield	d	12 49		12 57														13 49	13 55						
Congleton	d																								
Stoke-on-Trent	d	13 07		13 14			←				13 43	13 50						14 07	14 12					←	
Stafford	a	13 24			13 42	13 35	13 42											14 24			14 42	14 35		14 42	
	d	13 25			13 43	13 36	13 43											14 25			14 43	14 36		14 43	
Penkridge	a				↪		13 48														↪			14 48	
Wolverhampton [7] ⛴	a	13 40					13 59				14 13					14 32		14 40						14 59	
Birmingham New Street [12]	a	13 58					14 15				14 31					14 55		14 58						15 15	
Birmingham International ✈	a	14 13																15 13							
Coventry	a	14 24																15 24							
Lichfield Trent Valley	a																								
Tamworth Low Level	a																								
Nuneaton	a													14 31	14 31										
Rugby	a																								
Milton Keynes Central	a											14 49		15 04	15 04										
Watford Junction	a																								
London Euston [15] ⊖	a			14 47		15 01		15 09	15 15			15 27		15 45	15 45				15 47			16 01			16 09

A 🍽 from Birmingham New Street 🛒 to Birmingham New Street

OVERNIGHT SLEEPERS. For sleeper trains, operated by First ScotRail, please refer to Tables 400 - 404

Table 65

Sundays

1 July to 9 September

Scotland and North West England - West Midlands and London

Route Diagram - see first Page of Table 65

		VT	TP	XC	VT	VT	VT	TP		XC	VT	EM	LM	VT	LM	VT	VT	TP		XC	VT	VT	VT	TP	XC
		◇1	◇1	◇1	◇1	◇1	◇1	◇1		◇1	◇1	◇	◇1	◇1	◇1	◇1	◇1	◇1		◇1	◇1	◇1	◇1	◇1	◇1
										A															A
		⊏P		⫪	⊏P	⊏P	⊏P	⫪		⊏P⫪	⊏P			⊏P		⊏P	⊏P			⫪	⊏P	⊏P	⊏P		⊏P⫪
Inverness	d																								
Aberdeen	d																								
Dundee	d																								
Perth	d																								
Edinburgh 10	d							12 10															12 52		
Haymarket	d							12u14															12 56		
Glasgow Central 15	d	11 36					11 58										12 42								
Motherwell	d																								
Carstairs	d																								
Lockerbie	d							13 08																	
Carlisle 8	a	12 47					13 09	13 29									13 51						14 05		
	d	12 49					13 10	13 29									13 54						14 07		
Penrith North Lakes	d							13 45															14 22		
Windermere	d																								
Oxenholme Lake District	a	13 22						14 09									14 27								
	d	13 23						14 10									14 28								
Barrow-in-Furness	d																							14 25	
Lancaster 6	a	13 37					13 56	14 26									14 42						14 56	15 26	
	d	13 38					13 58	14 26									14 43						14 57	15 26	
Blackpool North	d		13 44															14 44							
Preston 8	a	13 56	14 08				14 15	14 45									15 01	15 08					15 15	15 45	
Preston 8	d	13 58	14 10				14 17	14 47									15 03	15 10					15 17	15 47	
Wigan North Western	a	14 09					14 28										15 14						15 28		
	d	14 09					14 28										15 14						15 28		
Blackrod	d																								
Lostock	d																								
Bolton	a		14 34					15 08										15 34						16 08	
Manchester Piccadilly 10	a		14 56					15 27										15 56						16 27	
Manchester Airport ✈	a		15 17					15 47										16 17						16 46	
Liverpool Lime Street 10	a																								
	d											13 52	14 34	14 48											
Liverpool South Parkway ✈	d											14 03	14 44												
Runcorn	d												14 52	15 04											
Warrington Bank Quay	a	14 20					14 39										15 25						15 39		
	d	14 20					14 39										15 25						15 39		
Hartford	d												15 03												
Manchester Piccadilly 10	d			14 07	14 15					14 27	14 35	14 44				14 55				15 07	15 15				15 27
Stockport	d				14 22					14 36	14 42	14a53				15 04					15 22				15 36
Wilmslow	d															15 11									
Holyhead	d					12 50																13 55			
Bangor (Gwynedd)	d					13 18																14 22			
Llandudno Junction	d					13 36																14 40			
Wrexham General	d																								
Chester	d					14 33																15 33			
Crewe 10	a					14 52	14 59						15 20			15 27						15 52	15 59		
	d					14 54	15 01						15 22			15 29						15 54	16 01		
Macclesfield	d									14 49	14 55														15 49
Congleton	d																								
Stoke-on-Trent	d			14 43	14 50					15 07	15 12				←					15 43	15 50				16 07
Stafford	a									15 24			15 42	15 35	15 42										16 24
	d									15 25			15 43	15 36	15 43										16 25
Penkridge	a												→		15 48										
Wolverhampton 7	a			15 13			15 31			15 40					15 59					16 13			16 32		16 40
Birmingham New Street 12	a			15 31			15 55			15 58					16 15					16 31			16 55		16 58
Birmingham International ✈	a									16 13															17 13
Coventry	a									16 24															17 24
Lichfield Trent Valley	a																								
Tamworth Low Level	a																								
Nuneaton	a																								
Rugby	a																								
Milton Keynes Central	a				15 49	16 04															16 49	17 03			
Watford Junction	a																								
London Euston 15 ⊖	a	16 15			16 27	16 44					16 47			17 01		17 09	17 20				17 27	17 44			

A ⊏P from Birmingham New Street ⫪ to Birmingham New Street

OVERNIGHT SLEEPERS. For sleeper trains, operated by First ScotRail, please refer to Tables 400 - 404

Table 65

Sundays

1 July to 9 September

Scotland and North West England - West Midlands and London

Route Diagram - see first Page of Table 65

		VT	EM	LM		VT	LM	VT	VT	TP	XC	VT	VT	VT		TP	NT	XC	VT	EM	LM	VT	LM	VT
		◇1	◇	◇1		◇1	◇1	◇1	◇1	◇1	◇1	◇1	◇1	◇1		◇1		◇1	◇1	◇	◇1	◇1	◇1	◇1
																		A						
		⊐				⊐		⊐	⊐		⊤	⊐	⊐	⊐		⊤		⊐⊤	⊐			⊐		⊐
Inverness	d																							
Aberdeen	d																							
Dundee	d																							
Perth	d																							
Edinburgh 10	d															14 10								
Haymarket	d															14u14								
Glasgow Central 15	d								13 36					13 55										
Motherwell	d																							
Carstairs	d																							
Lockerbie	d															15 08								
Carlisle 8	a								14 46					15 09		15 29								
	d								14 49					15 11		15 29	15 35							
Penrith North Lakes	d															15 45								
Windermere	d																							
Oxenholme Lake District	a								15 22					15 46		16 09								
	d								15 23					15 46		16 10								
Barrow-in-Furness	d																							
Lancaster 6	a								15 37							16 26								
	d								15 38							16 26								
Blackpool North	d									15 44														
Preston 8	a								15 56	16 08				16 15		16 46	18 48							
Preston 8	d								15 58	16 10				16 17		16 47								
Wigan North Western	a								16 09					16 28										
	d								16 09					16 28										
Blackrod	d																							
Lostock	d																							
Bolton	a									16 34						17 08								
Manchester Piccadilly 10	a									16 56						17 27								
Manchester Airport ✈	a									17 17						17 47								
Liverpool Lime Street 10	a																							
	d		14 52	15 34		15 48							16 18							15 52	16 34	16 48		
Liverpool South Parkway ✈	d		15 03	15 44																16 03	16 44			
Runcorn	d			15 52		16 04							16 34								16 52	17 04		
Warrington Bank Quay	a								16 20					16 39										
	d								16 20					16 39										
Hartford	d			16 03																	17 03			
Manchester Piccadilly 10	d	15 35	15 44					15 55			16 07	16 15						16 27	16 35	16 44				16 55
Stockport	d	15 42	15a53					16 04				16 23						16 36	16 42	16a53				17 04
Wilmslow	d							16 11																17 11
Holyhead	d																							
Bangor (Gwynedd)	d																							
Llandudno Junction	d																							
Wrexham General	d																							
Chester	d																							
Crewe 10	a			16 18				16 27					16 51	16 59							17 18			17 27
	d			16 22				16 29					16 54	17 01							17 22			17 29
Macclesfield	d	15 55																16 49	16 55					
Congleton	d																							
Stoke-on-Trent	d	16 12					←				16 43	16 50						17 08	17 12				←	
Stafford	a			16 42		16 36	16 42											17 25			17 42	17 35	17 42	
	d			16 43		16 37	16 43											17 26			17 43	17 36	17 43	
Penkridge	a			↦			16 48														↦		17 48	
Wolverhampton 7	a						16 59				17 13			17 31				17 40					17 59	
Birmingham New Street 12	a						17 15				17 31			17 55				17 58					18 15	
Birmingham International ✈	a																	18 13						
Coventry	a																	18 24						
Lichfield Trent Valley	a												17 26											
Tamworth Low Level	a																							
Nuneaton	a																							
Rugby	a																							
Milton Keynes Central	a											17 49	18 04											
Watford Junction	a																							
London Euston 15 ⊖	a	17 47				18 01		18 09	18 15			18 27	18 44						18 47			19 01		19 09

A ⊐ from Birmingham New Street ⊤ to Birmingham New Street

OVERNIGHT SLEEPERS. For sleeper trains, operated by First ScotRail, please refer to Tables 400 - 404

Table 65

Sundays

1 July to 9 September

Scotland and North West England - West Midlands and London

Route Diagram - see first Page of Table 65

		VT	TP	XC	VT	VT	VT	TP	TP	XC	VT	EM	LM	VT	LM	VT	VT	TP	XC	VT	VT	VT	TP
		◇1	◇1	◇1	◇1	◇1	◇1	◇1	◇1	◇1	◇1	◇	◇1	◇1	◇1	◇1	◇1	◇1	◇1	◇1	◇1	◇1	◇1
										A													
		⊏		⊤	⊏	⊏	⊏		⊤	⊏⊤	⊏			⊏		⊏	⊏		⊤	⊏	⊏	⊏	⊤
Inverness	d																						
Aberdeen	d																						
Dundee	d																						
Perth	d																						
Edinburgh 10	d						14 52																16 10
Haymarket	d						14 57																16u14
Glasgow Central 15	d	14 36							15 06								15 36					15 57	
Motherwell	d																						
Carstairs	d																						
Lockerbie	d								16 06														17 08
Carlisle 8	a	15 46					16 05		16 26								16 46					17 08	17 29
	d	15 49					16 07		16 26								16 49					17 09	17 29
Penrith North Lakes	d						16 22		16 42								17 03						17 45
Windermere	d																						
Oxenholme Lake District	a	16 22							17 07													17 44	18 09
	d	16 23							17 07													17 44	18 10
Barrow-in-Furness	d							16 17															
Lancaster 6	a	16 37					16 56	17 17	17 22								17 37						18 26
	d	16 38					16 57	17 17	17 22								17 38						18 26
Blackpool North	d		16 44															17 44					
Preston 8	a	16 56	17 08				17 15	17 37	17 41								17 56	18 08				18 13	18 45
Preston 8	d	16 58	17 10				17 17		17 47								17 58	18 10				18 17	18 47
Wigan North Western	a	17 09					17 28										18 09					18 28	
	d	17 09					17 28										18 09					18 28	
Blackrod	d																						
Lostock	d																						
Bolton	a		17 34						18 08									18 34					19 08
Manchester Piccadilly 10	a		17 56						18 27									18 56					19 27
Manchester Airport	a		18 17						18 45									19 17					19 47
Liverpool Lime Street 10	a																						
	d											16 52	17 34	17 48									
Liverpool South Parkway	d											17 03	17 44										
Runcorn	d												17 52	18 04									
Warrington Bank Quay	a	17 20					17 39										18 20					18 39	
	d	17 20					17 39										18 20					18 39	
Hartford	d												18 03										
Manchester Piccadilly 10	d			17 07	17 15					17 27	17 35	17 44				17 55			18 07	18 15			
Stockport	d				17 22					17 36	17 42	17a53				18 04				18 22			
Wilmslow	d															18 11							
Holyhead	d																						
Bangor (Gwynedd)	d																						
Llandudno Junction	d																						
Wrexham General	d																						
Chester	d					17 35															18 35		
Crewe 10	a					17 53	17 59						18 20			18 27					18 53	18 59	
	d					17 55	18 01						18 22			18 29					18 55	19 01	
Macclesfield	d									17 49	17 55												
Congleton	d																						
Stoke-on-Trent	d			17 43	17 50					18 08	18 12				←				18 43	18 50			
Stafford	a									18 25			18 42	18 35	18 42								
	d									18 26			18 43	18 36	18 43								
Penkridge	a												→		18 48								
Wolverhampton 7	a			18 13			18 32			18 40					18 59				19 13			19 31	
Birmingham New Street 12	a			18 31			18 55			18 58					19 15				19 31			19 55	
Birmingham International	a									19 13													
Coventry	a									19 24													
Lichfield Trent Valley	a																						
Tamworth Low Level	a																						
Nuneaton	a																						
Rugby	a																						
Milton Keynes Central	a				18 49	19 02														19 49	20 03		
Watford Junction	a																						
London Euston 15 ⊖	a	19 15			19 27	19 43					19 47			20 01		20 09	20 15			20 27	20 44		

A ⊏ from Birmingham New Street ⊤ to Birmingham New Street

OVERNIGHT SLEEPERS. For sleeper trains, operated by First ScotRail, please refer to Tables 400 - 404

Table 65

Sundays

1 July to 9 September

Scotland and North West England - West Midlands and London

Route Diagram - see first Page of Table 65

		NT	XC	VT	EM	LM	VT	LM	VT	VT	TP	TP	XC	VT	TP	TP	VT	XC	VT	EM	LM	VT	VT
			◇1	◇1	◇	◇1	◇1	◇1	◇1	◇1	◇1	◇1	◇1	◇1	◇1	◇1	◇1	◇1	◇1	◇	◇1	◇1	◇1
			A												B			C					
		⊤o	⊏P⊤o	⊏P			⊏P		⊏P	⊏P			⊤o	⊏P	⊤o	⊤o	⊏P	⊤o	⊏P			⊏P	⊏P
Inverness	d																						
Aberdeen	d																						
Dundee	d																						
Perth	d																						
Edinburgh 10	d													16 52									
Haymarket	d													16 56									
Glasgow Central 15	d									16 40						17 06							17 36
Motherwell	d									16 54													
Carstairs	d																						
Lockerbie	d																						18 32
Carlisle 8	a									17 49				18 05		18 25							18 50
	d	17 41								17 51				18 07		18 26							18 52
Penrith North Lakes	d									18 05						18 42							19 06
Windermere	d										18 01												
Oxenholme Lake District	a									18 27	18x21			18 41		19 07							19 28
	d									18 28	18x22			18 42		19 07							19 29
Barrow-in-Furness	d														18 17								
Lancaster 6	a									18 42	18 37			18 56	19 17	19 22							19 43
	d									18 43	18 38			18 57	19 17	19 22							19 44
Blackpool North	d											18 40											
Preston 8	a	20 47								19 01	18 56	19 04		19 15	19 37	19 41							20 02
Preston 8	d									19 03	19 10			19 17	19 47								20 04
Wigan North Western	a									19 14				19 28									20 15
	d									19 14				19 28									20 15
Blackrod	d																						
Lostock	d																						
Bolton	a										19 34				20 08								
Manchester Piccadilly 10 ⇌	a										19 56				20 27								
Manchester Airport ✈	a										20 17				20 47								
Liverpool Lime Street 10	a																						
	d				17 52	18 34	18 48													18 52	19 34	19 48	
Liverpool South Parkway ✈	d				18 03	18 44														19 03	19 44		
Runcorn	d					18 52	19 04														19 52	20 04	
Warrington Bank Quay	a									19 25				19 39									20 26
	d									19 25				19 39									20 26
Hartford	d					19 03															20 03		
Manchester Piccadilly 10 ⇌	d		18 27	18 35	18 44				18 55				19 07				19 15	19 27	19 35	19 44			
Stockport	d		18 36	18 42	18a53				19 04								19 22	19 36	19 41	19a53			
Wilmslow	d								19 11														
Holyhead	d																						
Bangor (Gwynedd)	d																						
Llandudno Junction	d																						
Wrexham General	d																						
Chester	d																						
Crewe 10	a					19 20			19 27					19 59							20 16	20 22	20 45
	d					19 22			19 29					20 01							20 18	20 24	20 47
Macclesfield	d		18 49	18 55														19 49	19 54				
Congleton	d																						
Stoke-on-Trent	d		19 07	19 12				←					19 43				19 50	20 07	20 11				
Stafford	a		19 24			19 42	19 35	19 42										20 26			20 38	20 41	
	d		19 25			19 43	19 36	19 43										20 27			20 39	20 43	
Penkridge	a					→		19 48													20 44		
Wolverhampton 7 ⇌	a		19 40					19 59					20 13	20 32				20 39			20 55		
Birmingham New Street 12	a		19 58					20 15					20 31	20 50				20 58			21 15		
Birmingham International ✈	a		20 13															21 13					
Coventry	a		20 24															21 23					
Lichfield Trent Valley	a																						
Tamworth Low Level	a																						
Nuneaton	a																						
Rugby	a																						
Milton Keynes Central	a																20 46					21 36	21 55
Watford Junction	a																						22s31
London Euston 15 ⊖	a			20 47			21 01		21 09	21 21							21 31		21 58			22 27	22 53

A ⊏P from Birmingham New Street ⊤o to Birmingham New Street

B ⊤o from Preston

C ⊤o to Birmingham New Street

OVERNIGHT SLEEPERS. For sleeper trains, operated by First ScotRail, please refer to Tables 400 - 404

Table 65

Sundays

1 July to 9 September

Scotland and North West England - West Midlands and London

Route Diagram - see first Page of Table 65

		TP	TP		NT	XC	AW	VT	EM	LM	VT	VT	VT		TP	TP	XC	VT	LM	NT	TP	VT	XC		EM
		◇1	◇1			◇1	◇	◇1	◇	◇1	◇1	◇1	◇1		◇1	◇1	◇1	◇1	◇1		◇1	◇1	◇1		◇
			🚲				🚲	☕			☕	☕	☕					☕			🚲	☕			
Inverness	d																								
Aberdeen	d																								
Dundee	d																								
Perth	d																								
Edinburgh 10	d		18 10															18 52			19 57				
Haymarket	d		18u14															18 57			20u01				
Glasgow Central 15	d												18 30									20 08			
Motherwell	d																								
Carstairs	d																								
Lockerbie	d		19 08																			21 02			
Carlisle 8	a		19 29										19 43					20 05			21 13	21 21			
	d		19 29										19 44					20 07			21 14	21 24			
Penrith North Lakes	d		19 45															20 22				21 39			
Windermere	d														20 40										
Oxenholme Lake District	a		20 09										20 19		20 59							22 02			
	d		20 10										20 19		21 01							22 03			
Barrow-in-Furness	d				20 02																				
Lancaster 6	a		20 26		21 07								20 34		21 18			20 56			22 03	22 17			
	d		20 26										20 34					20 57			22 03	22 18			
Blackpool North	d	19 44														20 44				21 50					
Preston 8	a	20 08	20 45										20 52			21 08		21 15		22 14	22 22	22 35			
Preston 8	d	20 10	20 47										20 55			21 10		21 17		22 15	22 29	22 38			
Wigan North Western	a												21 06					21 28		22 36		22 49			
	d												21 07					21 28				22 50			
Blackrod	d																								
Lostock	d																								
Bolton	a	20 34	21 08													21 34					22 50				
Manchester Piccadilly 10	a	20 56	21 27													21 56					23 14				
Manchester Airport ✈	a	21 16	21 46													22 17					23 29				
Liverpool Lime Street 10	a																								
	d								19 52	20 34		20 48							21 34						21 21
Liverpool South Parkway ✈	d								20 03	20 44									21 44						21 31
Runcorn	d									20 52		21 04							21 52						
Warrington Bank Quay	a												21 18					21 39				23 00			
	d												21 18					21 39				23 01			
Hartford	d									21 03									22 03						
Manchester Piccadilly 10	d					20 07		20 20	20 44		20 55						21 07						22 07		22 11
Stockport	d					20 16		20 27	20a53		21 03						21 16						22 16		22a20
Wilmslow	d																								
Holyhead	d						18 25																		
Bangor (Gwynedd)	d						19 04																		
Llandudno Junction	d						19 24																		
Wrexham General	d																								
Chester	d						20 27																		
Crewe 10	a						20 48			21 16		21 21	21 38					21 59	22 18			23 20			
	d						20 52			21 18		21 23	21 40					22 01	22 22						
Macclesfield	d					20 29		20 40			21 15						21 29						22 29		
Congleton	d																								
Stoke-on-Trent	d					20 47		20 57			21 33						21 47						22 47		
Stafford	a					21 08	21 16			21 39		21 42	22 01				22 06		22 42				23 04		
	d					21 09	21 16			21 39		21 43	22 02				22 06		22 45				23 05		
Penkridge	a									21 45									22 50						
Wolverhampton 7	a					21 21	21 34			21 55			22 17				22 20	22 31	23 01				23 18		
Birmingham New Street 12	a					21 39	21 52			22 16			22 38				22 39	22 55	23 17				23 36		
Birmingham International ✈	a						22 09																		
Coventry	a																								
Lichfield Trent Valley	a											21 59													
Tamworth Low Level	a											22 05													
Nuneaton	a											22 17													
Rugby	a											22 31													
Milton Keynes Central	a							22 03			22 46	23 04													
Watford Junction	a										23s25	23s34													
London Euston 15 ⊖	a							22 56			23 49	23 54													

OVERNIGHT SLEEPERS. For sleeper trains, operated by First ScotRail, please refer to Tables 400 - 404

Scotland and North West England - West Midlands and London

Route Diagram - see first Page of Table 65

Station		NT	NT	NT	TP	SR	SR	SR	SR
					◇1	R	R	R	R
								A	A
Inverness	d							20 25	
Aberdeen	d								21 42
Dundee	d								23u06
Perth	d							23u00	
Edinburgh 10	d					23 15			
Haymarket	d								
Glasgow Central 15	d						23 15		
Motherwell	d						23u31		
Carstairs	d					23u47			
Lockerbie	d								
Carlisle 8	a								
	d					01u12			
Penrith North Lakes	d								
Windermere	d								
Oxenholme Lake District	a								
	d								
Barrow-in-Furness	d								
Lancaster 6	a								
	d								
Blackpool North	d		22 44		23 03				
Preston 8	a		23 08		23 28			04s41	
Preston 8	d		23 09		23 28				
Wigan North Western	a		23 30						
	d								
Blackrod	d				23 50				
Lostock	d				23 57				
Bolton	a				00 02				
Manchester Piccadilly 10	a				00 18				
Manchester Airport ✈	a				00 32				
Liverpool Lime Street 10	a								
	d	22 01		23 01					
Liverpool South Parkway ✈	d								
Runcorn	d								
Warrington Bank Quay	a								
	d								
Hartford	d								
Manchester Piccadilly 10	d	22a50		23a50					
Stockport	d								
Wilmslow	d								
Holyhead	d								
Bangor (Gwynedd)	d								
Llandudno Junction	d								
Wrexham General	d								
Chester	d								
Crewe 10	a							05s41	
	d								
Macclesfield	d								
Congleton	d								
Stoke-on-Trent	d								
Stafford	a								
	d								
Penkridge	a								
Wolverhampton 7	a								
Birmingham New Street 12	a								
Birmingham International ✈	a								
Coventry	a								
Lichfield Trent Valley	a								
Tamworth Low Level	a								
Nuneaton	a								
Rugby	a								
Milton Keynes Central	a								
Watford Junction	a					06s23			
London Euston 15 ⊖	a					06 46		07 50	

A Conveys a portion from Fort William, dep 1900

OVERNIGHT SLEEPERS. For sleeper trains, operated by First ScotRail, please refer to Tables 400 - 404

Table 65

Sundays

16 September to 21 October

Scotland and North West England - West Midlands and London

Route Diagram - see first Page of Table 65

		TP	TP	TP	TP	VT	VT	VT	XC	VT	VT	TP	VT	XC	VT	TP	LM	VT	TP	VT	VT	TP	XC
		◇[1]			◇[1]	◇[1]	◇[1]	◇[1]	◇[1]	◇[1]	◇[1]	◇[1]	◇[1]	◇[1]	◇[1]	◇[1]	◇[1]	◇[1]	◇[1]	◇[1]	◇[1]	◇[1]	◇[1]
									A					A									A
			[bus]	[bus]		[buffet]	[buffet]	[buffet]	[buffet][restaurant]	[buffet]	[buffet]		[buffet]	[buffet][restaurant]	[buffet]			[buffet]		[buffet]	[buffet]		[buffet][restaurant]
Inverness	d																						
Aberdeen	d																						
Dundee	d																						
Perth	d																						
Edinburgh [10]	d																						
Haymarket	d																						
Glasgow Central [15]	d																						
Motherwell	d																						
Carstairs	d																						
Lockerbie	d																						
Carlisle [8]	a																						
	d																						
Penrith North Lakes	d																						
Windermere	d																						
Oxenholme Lake District	a																						
	d																						
Barrow-in-Furness	d																					09 17	
Lancaster [6]	a																					10 17	
	d																					10 21	
Blackpool North	d	22p44	03 20	05 20	07 48							08 44							09 44				
Preston [8]	a	23p08			08 12							09 08							10 08			10 40	
Preston [8]	d	23p10	04u00	06u00	08 14						09 00	09 10						10 00	10 10		10 17	10 47	
Wigan North Western	a										09 10							10 10			10 28		
	d										09 11							10 11			10 28		
Blackrod	d																						
Lostock	d																						
Bolton	a	23p34	04b35	06b35	08 37							09 34							10 34			11 08	
Manchester Piccadilly [10] [tram]	a	23p53	05b00	07b00	08 59							09 56							10 56			11 27	
Manchester Airport [plane]	a	00 23	05 25	07 25	09 17							10 17							11 17			11 47	
Liverpool Lime Street [10]	a															09 56							
	d							08 15		08 38					09 38								
Liverpool South Parkway [plane]	d																						
Runcorn	d							08 35		08 54					09 54								
Warrington Bank Quay	a										09 21							10 21			10 39		
	d										09 22							10 22			10 39		
Hartford	d																						
Manchester Piccadilly [10] [tram]	d					08 05	08 20		08 27				09 20	09 27						10 20			10 27
Stockport	d					08 14	08 28		08 36				09 27	09 36						10 29			10 36
Wilmslow	d					08 22			08 43											10 36			
Holyhead	d																						
Bangor (Gwynedd)	d																						
Llandudno Junction	d																						
Wrexham General	d																						
Chester	d																						
Crewe [10]	a					08 39		08 52	09 01	09 11	09 41				10 12			10 41		10 53	10 59		
	d					08 43		08 53	09 05	09 13	09 43				10 14		10 20	10 43		10 55	11 01		
Macclesfield	d						08 42						09 40	09 49									10 49
Congleton	d																						
Stoke-on-Trent	d						08 59						09 57	10 07									11 07
Stafford	a					09 01			09 25	09 31				10 26	10 32		10 41						11 27
	d					09 02			09 26	09 32				10 27	10 33		10 41						11 28
Penkridge	a																10 48						
Wolverhampton [7] [tram]	a								09 40					10 42			11 00				11 31		11 41
Birmingham New Street [12]	a								09 58					10 59			11 17				11 55		12 00
Birmingham International [plane]	a								10 13					11 13									12 13
Coventry	a								10 24					11 24									12 24
Lichfield Trent Valley	a																						
Tamworth Low Level	a																						
Nuneaton	a									09 54					10 55								
Rugby	a										10 31							11 31					
Milton Keynes Central	a							10 17			11 06		11 16		11 46			12 06					
Watford Junction	a					10s35	10s41			11s16	11s43									12s36			
London Euston [15] [Underground]	a					10 57	11 02	11 06		11 37	12 05		12 08		12 32			12 45		12 56			

A [buffet] from Birmingham New Street [restaurant] to Birmingham New Street

b Stops to pick up only

OVERNIGHT SLEEPERS. For sleeper trains, operated by First ScotRail, please refer to Tables 400 - 404

Table 65

Sundays

16 September to 21 October

Scotland and North West England - West Midlands and London

Route Diagram - see first Page of Table 65

		VT	VT	VT	TP	VT	VT	VT	TP	XC	VT	LM	VT	LM	VT	VT	TP	VT	VT	VT	TP	XC	VT
		◇1	◇1	◇1	◇1	◇1	◇1	◇1	◇1	◇1	◇1	◇1	◇1	◇1	◇1	◇1	◇1	◇1	◇1	◇1	◇1	◇1	◇1
										A												A	
		🛒	🛒	🛒		🛒	🛒	🛒		🛒☕	🛒		🛒		🛒	🛒	☕	🛒	🛒	🛒	☕	🛒☕	🛒
Inverness	d																						
Aberdeen	d																						
Dundee	d																						
Perth	d																						
Edinburgh 10	d																				10 10		
Haymarket	d																				10u14		
Glasgow Central 15	d															09 37							
Motherwell	d																						
Carstairs	d																						
Lockerbie	d																				11 08		
Carlisle 8	a															10 44					11 29		
	d															10 46					11 29		
Penrith North Lakes	d															11 00					11 45		
Windermere	d																						
Oxenholme Lake District	a															11 22					12 09		
	d															11 23					12 10		
Barrow-in-Furness	d								10 30														
Lancaster 6	a								11 22							11 37					12 26		
	d								11 22							11 38				12 00	12 26		
Blackpool North	d				10 44												11 44						
Preston 8	a				11 08				11 42							11 56	12 08			12 15	12 45		
Preston 8	d			10 58	11 10			11 17	11 47							11 58	12 10			12 17	12 47		
Wigan North Western	a			11 09				11 28								12 09				12 28			
	d			11 09				11 28								12 09				12 28			
Blackrod	d																						
Lostock	d																						
Bolton	a				11 34				12 08								12 34				13 08		
Manchester Piccadilly 10 ⇌	a				11 56				12 27								12 59				13 27		
Manchester Airport ✈	a				12 17				12 48								13 17				13 47		
Liverpool Lime Street 10	a																						
	d		10 38									11 34	11 48										
Liverpool South Parkway ✈	d											11 44											
Runcorn	d		10 54									11 52	12 04										
Warrington Bank Quay	a			11 20				11 39								12 20				12 39			
	d			11 20				11 39								12 20				12 39			
Hartford	d											12 03											
Manchester Piccadilly 10 ⇌	d	10 35				11 15				11 27	11 35				11 55			12 15				12 26	12 35
Stockport	d	10 42				11 23				11 36	11 43				12 05			12 23				12 35	12 44
Wilmslow	d														12 12								
Holyhead	d																		10 55				
Bangor (Gwynedd)	d																		11 22				
Llandudno Junction	d																		11 40				
Wrexham General	d																						
Chester	d						11 28												12 33				
Crewe 10	a		11 12				11 47	11 59				12 20			12 28				12 52	12 59			
	d		11 14				11 49	12 01				12 22			12 30				12 56	13 01			
Macclesfield	d	10 55								11 49	11 56											12 49	12 57
Congleton	d																						
Stoke-on-Trent	d	11 12				11 51				12 07	12 13			←				12 51				13 07	13 14
Stafford	a		11 34							12 24		12 41	12 35	12 41								13 24	
	d		11 36							12 25		12 42	12 36	12 42								13 25	
Penkridge	a											→		12 48									
Wolverhampton 7 ⇌	a							12 32		12 40				12 59						13 32		13 40	
Birmingham New Street 12	a							12 55		12 58				13 16						13 55		13 58	
Birmingham International ✈	a									13 13												14 13	
Coventry	a									13 24												14 24	
Lichfield Trent Valley	a																						
Tamworth Low Level	a																						
Nuneaton	a		11 58				12 31																
Rugby	a																						
Milton Keynes Central	a	12 20				12 50	13 03											13 46	14 02				
Watford Junction	a		12s50																				
London Euston 15 ⊖	a	12 59	13 11	13 21		13 28	13 44				13 47		14 01		14 09	14 16		14 27	14 43				14 47

A 🛒 from Birmingham New Street ☕ to Birmingham New Street

OVERNIGHT SLEEPERS. For sleeper trains, operated by First ScotRail, please refer to Tables 400 - 404

Scotland and North West England - West Midlands and London

Route Diagram - see first Page of Table 65

		LM		VT	LM	VT	VT	TP	XC	VT	VT	VT		TP	NT	XC	VT	EM	LM	VT	LM	VT		VT	TP
		◇1		◇1	◇1	◇1	◇1	◇1	◇1	◇1	◇1	◇1		◇1		◇1	◇1	◇	◇1	◇1	◇1	◇1		◇1	◇1
																A									
				☕		☕	☕		🍴	☕	☕	☕				☕🍴	☕			☕		☕		☕	
Inverness	d																								
Aberdeen	d																								
Dundee	d																								
Perth	d																								
Edinburgh 10	d											10 52													
Haymarket	d											10 57													
Glasgow Central 15	d						10 34																	11 36	
Motherwell	d						10 49																		
Carstairs	d																								
Lockerbie	d																								
Carlisle 8	a						11 44					12 05												12 47	
	d						11 46					12 07												12 49	
Penrith North Lakes	d						12 00																		
Windermere	d																								
Oxenholme Lake District	a						12 22					12 41												13 22	
	d						12 24					12 43												13 23	
Barrow-in-Furness	d													12 25	13 10										
Lancaster 6	a						12 37					12 56		13 26	14 15									13 37	
	d						12 38					12 57		13 26										13 38	
Blackpool North	d							12 44																	13 44
Preston 8	a						12 56	13 08				13 15		13 45										13 56	14 08
Preston 8	d						12 58	13 10				13 17		13 47										13 58	14 10
Wigan North Western	a						13 09					13 28												14 09	
	d						13 09					13 28												14 09	
Blackrod	d																								
Lostock	d																								
Bolton	a							13 34						14 08											14 34
Manchester Piccadilly 10	a							13 56						14 27											14 56
Manchester Airport ✈	a							14 17						14 47											15 17
Liverpool Lime Street 10	a																								
	d	12 34		12 48														12 52	13 34	13 48					
Liverpool South Parkway ✈	d	12 44																13 03	13 44						
Runcorn	d	12 52		13 04															13 52	14 04					
Warrington Bank Quay	a						13 20					13 39												14 20	
	d						13 20					13 39												14 20	
Hartford	d	13 03																	14 03						
Manchester Piccadilly 10	d					12 55			13 07	13 15						13 27	13 35	13 44				13 55			
Stockport	d					13 05				13 22						13 36	13 42	13a53				14 04			
Wilmslow	d					13 12																14 11			
Holyhead	d										11 50														
Bangor (Gwynedd)	d										12 17														
Llandudno Junction	d										12 35														
Wrexham General	d																								
Chester	d										13 30														
Crewe 10	a	13 19				13 28					13 50	13 59							14 18			14 27			
	d	13 22				13 30					13 51	14 01							14 22			14 29			
Macclesfield	d															13 49	13 55								
Congleton	d																								
Stoke-on-Trent	d				←				13 43	13 50						14 07	14 12				←				
Stafford	a	13 42		13 35	13 42											14 24			14 42	14 35	14 42				
	d	13 43		13 36	13 43											14 25			14 43	14 36	14 43				
Penkridge	a	→			13 48														→		14 48				
Wolverhampton 7	a				13 59				14 13			14 32				14 40					14 59				
Birmingham New Street 12	a				14 15				14 31			14 50				14 58					15 15				
Birmingham International ✈	a															15 13									
Coventry	a															15 24									
Lichfield Trent Valley	a																								
Tamworth Low Level	a																								
Nuneaton	a										14 31														
Rugby	a																								
Milton Keynes Central	a									14 48	15 02														
Watford Junction	a																								
London Euston 15 ⊖	a			15 01		15 05	15 12			15 26	15 43						15 47			16 01		16 05		16 12	

A ☕ from Birmingham New Street 🍴 to Birmingham New Street

OVERNIGHT SLEEPERS. For sleeper trains, operated by First ScotRail, please refer to Tables 400 - 404

Table 65

Sundays

16 September to 21 October

Scotland and North West England - West Midlands and London

Route Diagram - see first Page of Table 65

		XC	VT	VT	VT	TP	XC	VT	EM	LM	VT	LM	VT	VT	TP	XC	VT	VT	VT	TP	XC	VT	EM
		◇1	◇1	◇1	◇1	◇1	◇1	◇1	◇	◇1	◇1	◇1	◇1	◇1	◇1	◇1	◇1	◇1	◇1	◇1	◇1	◇1	◇
							A														A		
		🛒	🍴	🍴	🍴	🛒	🍴🛒	🍴			🍴		🍴	🍴		🛒	🍴	🍴	🍴		🍴🛒	🍴	
Inverness	d																						
Aberdeen	d																						
Dundee	d																						
Perth	d																						
Edinburgh 10	d					12 10													12 52				
Haymarket	d					12u14													12 56				
Glasgow Central 15	d				11 58									12 42									
Motherwell	d																						
Carstairs	d																						
Lockerbie	d					13 08																	
Carlisle 8	a				13 09	13 29								13 51					14 05				
	d				13 10	13 29								13 54					14 07				
Penrith North Lakes	d					13 45													14 22				
Windermere	d																						
Oxenholme Lake District	a					14 09								14 27									
	d					14 10								14 28									
Barrow-in-Furness	d																			14 25			
Lancaster 6	a				13 56	14 26								14 42					14 56	15 26			
	d				13 58	14 26								14 43					14 57	15 26			
Blackpool North	d														14 44								
Preston 8	a				14 15	14 45								15 01	15 08				15 15	15 45			
Preston 8	d				14 17	14 47								15 03	15 10				15 17	15 47			
Wigan North Western	a				14 28									15 14					15 28				
	d				14 28									15 14					15 28				
Blackrod	d																						
Lostock	d																						
Bolton	a					15 08									15 34					16 08			
Manchester Piccadilly 10 🚋	a					15 27									15 56					16 27			
Manchester Airport ✈	a					15 47									16 17					16 46			
Liverpool Lime Street 10	a																						
	d								13 52	14 34	14 48												14 52
Liverpool South Parkway ✈	d								14 03	14 44													15 03
Runcorn	d									14 52	15 04												
Warrington Bank Quay	a				14 39									15 25					15 39				
	d				14 39									15 25					15 39				
Hartford	d									15 03													
Manchester Piccadilly 10 🚋	d	14 07	14 15				14 27	14 35	14 44				14 55			15 07	15 15				15 27	15 35	15 44
Stockport	d		14 22				14 36	14 42	14a53				15 04				15 22				15 36	15 42	15a53
Wilmslow	d												15 11										
Holyhead	d			12 50														13 55					
Bangor (Gwynedd)	d			13 18														14 22					
Llandudno Junction	d			13 36														14 40					
Wrexham General	d																						
Chester	d			14 33														15 33					
Crewe 10	a			14 52	14 59					15 20			15 27					15 52	15 59				
	d			14 54	15 01					15 22			15 29					15 54	16 01				
Macclesfield	d						14 49	14 55													15 49	15 55	
Congleton	d																						
Stoke-on-Trent	d	14 43	14 50				15 07	15 12				←				15 43	15 50				16 07	16 12	
Stafford	a						15 24			15 42	15 35	15 42									16 24		
	d						15 25			15 43	15 36	15 43									16 25		
Penkridge	a									↪		15 48											
Wolverhampton 7 🚋	a	15 13			15 31		15 40					15 59				16 13			16 32		16 40		
Birmingham New Street 12	a	15 31			15 55		15 58					16 15				16 31			16 55		16 58		
Birmingham International ✈	a						16 13														17 13		
Coventry	a						16 24														17 24		
Lichfield Trent Valley	a																						
Tamworth Low Level	a																						
Nuneaton	a																						
Rugby	a																						
Milton Keynes Central	a		15 48	16 03													16 49	17 02					
Watford Junction	a																						
London Euston 15 ⊖	a		16 26	16 43				16 47			17 01		17 07	17 20			17 27	17 43				17 46	

A 🍴 from Birmingham New Street 🛒 to Birmingham New Street

OVERNIGHT SLEEPERS. For sleeper trains, operated by First ScotRail, please refer to Tables 400 - 404

Sundays

16 September to 21 October

Scotland and North West England - West Midlands and London

Route Diagram - see first Page of Table 65

		LM	VT	LM		VT	VT	TP	XC	VT	VT	VT	TP	XC		VT	EM	LM	VT	LM	VT	VT	TP	XC
		◇1	◇1	◇1		◇1	◇1	◇1	◇1	◇1	◇1	◇1	◇1	◇1		◇1	◇	◇1	◇1	◇1	◇1	◇1	◇1	◇1
														A										
			🍽			🍽	🍽		🛒	🍽	🍽	🍽	🛒	🍽🛒		🍽			🍽		🍽	🍽		🛒
Inverness	d																							
Aberdeen	d																							
Dundee	d																							
Perth	d																							
Edinburgh [10]	d												14 10											
Haymarket	d												14u14											
Glasgow Central [15]	d						13 36					13 55										14 36		
Motherwell	d																							
Carstairs	d																							
Lockerbie	d												15 08											
Carlisle [8]	a						14 46					15 09	15 29									15 46		
	d						14 49					15 11	15 29									15 49		
Penrith North Lakes	d												15 45											
Windermere	d																							
Oxenholme Lake District	a						15 22					15 46	16 09									16 22		
	d						15 23					15 46	16 10									16 23		
Barrow-in-Furness	d																							
Lancaster [6]	a						15 37						16 26									16 37		
	d						15 38						16 26									16 38		
Blackpool North	d							15 44															16 44	
Preston [8]	a						15 56	16 08				16 15	16 46									16 56	17 08	
Preston [8]	d						15 58	16 10				16 17	16 47									16 58	17 10	
Wigan North Western	a						16 09					16 28										17 09		
	d						16 09					16 28										17 09		
Blackrod	d																							
Lostock	d																							
Bolton	a							16 34					17 08										17 34	
Manchester Piccadilly [10] ⇌	a							16 56					17 27										17 56	
Manchester Airport ✈	a							17 17					17 47										18 17	
Liverpool Lime Street [10]	a																							
	d	15 34	15 48								16 18						15 52	16 34	16 48					
Liverpool South Parkway ✈	d	15 44															16 03	16 44						
Runcorn	d	15 52	16 04								16 34							16 52	17 04					
Warrington Bank Quay	a						16 20					16 39										17 20		
	d						16 20					16 39										17 20		
Hartford	d	16 03																17 03						
Manchester Piccadilly [10] ⇌	d					15 55			16 07	16 15				16 27		16 35	16 44				16 55			17 07
Stockport	d					16 04				16 23				16 36		16 42	16a53				17 04			
Wilmslow	d					16 11															17 11			
Holyhead	d																							
Bangor (Gwynedd)	d																							
Llandudno Junction	d																							
Wrexham General	d																							
Chester	d																							
Crewe [10]	a	16 18				16 27					16 51	16 59						17 18			17 27			
	d	16 22				16 29					16 54	17 01						17 22			17 29			
Macclesfield	d													16 49		16 55								
Congleton	d																							
Stoke-on-Trent	d			←					16 43	16 50				17 08		17 12				←				17 43
Stafford	a	16 42	16 36	16 42										17 25				17 42	17 35	17 42				
	d	16 43	16 37	16 43										17 26				17 43	17 36	17 43				
Penkridge	a	→		16 48														→		17 48				
Wolverhampton [7] ⇌	a			16 59					17 13			17 32		17 40						17 59				18 13
Birmingham New Street [12]	a			17 15					17 31			17 55		17 58						18 15				18 31
Birmingham International ✈	a													18 13										
Coventry	a													18 24										
Lichfield Trent Valley	a										17 26													
Tamworth Low Level	a																							
Nuneaton	a																							
Rugby	a																							
Milton Keynes Central	a									17 49	18 04													
Watford Junction	a																							
London Euston [15] ⊖	a		18 01			18 07	18 13			18 26	18 44					18 47			19 01		19 05	19 10		

A 🍽 from Birmingham New Street 🛒 to Birmingham New Street

OVERNIGHT SLEEPERS. For sleeper trains, operated by First ScotRail, please refer to Tables 400 - 404

Table 65

Sundays

16 September to 21 October

Scotland and North West England - West Midlands and London

Route Diagram - see first Page of Table 65

		VT	VT	VT	TP	XC	VT	EM	LM	VT	LM	VT	VT	TP	XC	VT	VT	VT	TP	NT	XC	VT	EM
		◇1	◇1	◇1	◇1	◇1	◇1	◇	◇1	◇1	◇1	◇1	◇1	◇1	◇1	◇1	◇1	◇1	◇1		◇1	◇1	◇
						A															A		
		⊏P	⊏P	⊏P	⊼o	⊏P⊼o	⊏P			⊏P		⊏P	⊏P		⊼o	⊏P	⊏P	⊏P	⊼o	⊼o	⊏P⊼o	⊏P	
Inverness	d																						
Aberdeen	d																						
Dundee	d																						
Perth	d																						
Edinburgh 10	d			14 52															16 10				
Haymarket	d			14 57															16u14				
Glasgow Central 15	d				15 06								15 36					15 57					
Motherwell	d																						
Carstairs	d																						
Lockerbie	d				16 06														17 08				
Carlisle 8	a			16 05	16 26								16 46					17 08	17 29				
	d			16 07	16 26								16 49					17 09	17 29	17 41			
Penrith North Lakes	d			16 22	16 42								17 03						17 45				
Windermere	d																						
Oxenholme Lake District	a				17 07													17 44	18 09				
	d				17 07													17 44	18 10				
Barrow-in-Furness	d																						
Lancaster 6	a			16 56	17 22								17 37						18 26				
	d			16 57	17 22								17 38						18 26				
Blackpool North	d													17 44									
Preston 8	a			17 15	17 41								17 56	18 08				18 13	18 45	20 47			
Preston 8	d			17 17	17 47								17 58	18 10				18 17	18 47				
Wigan North Western	a			17 28									18 09					18 28					
	d			17 28									18 09					18 28					
Blackrod	d																						
Lostock	d																						
Bolton	a				18 08									18 34					19 08				
Manchester Piccadilly 10	a				18 27									18 56					19 27				
Manchester Airport ✈	a				18 45									19 17					19 47				
Liverpool Lime Street 10	a																						
	d							16 52	17 34	17 48													17 52
Liverpool South Parkway ✈	d							17 03	17 44														18 03
Runcorn	d								17 52	18 04													
Warrington Bank Quay	a			17 39									18 20					18 39					
	d			17 39									18 20					18 39					
Hartford	d								18 03														
Manchester Piccadilly 10	d	17 15				17 27	17 35	17 44				17 55			18 07	18 15					18 27	18 35	18 44
Stockport	d	17 22				17 36	17 42	17a53				18 04				18 22					18 36	18 42	18a53
Wilmslow	d											18 11											
Holyhead	d																						
Bangor (Gwynedd)	d																						
Llandudno Junction	d																						
Wrexham General	d																						
Chester	d		17 35														18 35						
Crewe 10	a		17 53	17 59					18 20			18 27					18 53	18 59					
	d		17 55	18 01					18 22			18 29					18 55	19 01					
Macclesfield	d					17 49	17 55														18 49	18 55	
Congleton	d																						
Stoke-on-Trent	d	17 50				18 08	18 12				←				18 43	18 50					19 07	19 12	
Stafford	a					18 25			18 42	18 35	18 42										19 24		
	d					18 26			18 43	18 36	18 43										19 25		
Penkridge	a								→		18 48												
Wolverhampton 7	a			18 32		18 40					18 59				19 13			19 31			19 40		
Birmingham New Street 12	a			18 55		18 58					19 15				19 31			19 55			19 58		
Birmingham International ✈	a					19 13															20 13		
Coventry	a					19 24															20 24		
Lichfield Trent Valley	a																						
Tamworth Low Level	a																						
Nuneaton	a																						
Rugby	a																						
Milton Keynes Central	a	18 49	19 02													19 48	20 02						
Watford Junction	a																						
London Euston 15 ⊖	a	19 26	19 43				19 47			20 01		20 05	20 12			20 26	20 44					20 47	

A ⊏P from Birmingham New Street ⊼o to Birmingham New Street

OVERNIGHT SLEEPERS. For sleeper trains, operated by First ScotRail, please refer to Tables 400 - 404

Table 65

Sundays

16 September to 21 October

Scotland and North West England - West Midlands and London

Route Diagram - see first Page of Table 65

		LM	VT	LM	VT	VT		TP	XC	VT	TP	TP	VT	XC	VT	EM		LM	VT	VT	TP	TP	NT	XC	AW
		◇1	◇1	◇1	◇1	◇1		◇1	◇1	◇1	◇1	◇1	◇1	◇1	◇1	◇		◇1	◇1	◇1	◇1	◇1		◇1	◇
														A											
			🍽		🍽	🍽			🛒	🍽		🛒	🍽	🛒	🍽				🍽	🍽		🛒			🛒
Inverness	d																								
Aberdeen	d																								
Dundee	d																								
Perth	d																								
Edinburgh 10	d									16 52												18 10			
Haymarket	d									16 56												18u14			
Glasgow Central 15	d					16 40						17 06								17 36					
Motherwell	d					16 54																			
Carstairs	d																								
Lockerbie	d																			18 32		19 08			
Carlisle 8	a					17 49				18 05		18 25								18 50		19 29			
	d					17 51				18 07		18 26								18 52		19 29			
Penrith North Lakes	d					18 05						18 42								19 06		19 45			
Windermere	d																								
Oxenholme Lake District	a					18 27				18 41		19 07								19 28		20 09			
	d					18 28				18 42		19 07								19 29		20 10			
Barrow-in-Furness	d										18 17												20 02		
Lancaster 6	a					18 42				18 56	19 17	19 22								19 43		20 26	21 07		
	d					18 43				18 57	19 17	19 22								19 44		20 26			
Blackpool North	d							18 44													19 44				
Preston 8	a					19 01		19 08		19 15	19 37	19 41								20 02	20 08	20 45			
Preston 8	d					19 03		19 10		19 17		19 47								20 04	20 10	20 47			
Wigan North Western	a					19 14				19 28										20 15					
	d					19 14				19 28										20 15					
Blackrod	d																								
Lostock	d																								
Bolton	a							19 34				20 08									20 34	21 08			
Manchester Piccadilly 10 ⛴	a							19 56				20 27									20 56	21 27			
Manchester Airport ✈	a							20 17				20 45									21 16	21 46			
Liverpool Lime Street 10	a																								
	d	18 34	18 48													18 52		19 34	19 48						
Liverpool South Parkway ✈	d	18 44														19 03		19 44							
Runcorn	d	18 52	19 04															19 52	20 04						
Warrington Bank Quay	a					19 25				19 39										20 26					
	d					19 25				19 39										20 26					
Hartford	d	19 03																20 03							
Manchester Piccadilly 10 ⛴	d				18 55				19 07				19 15	19 27	19 35	19 44								20 07	
Stockport	d				19 04								19 22	19 36	19 41	19a53								20 16	
Wilmslow	d				19 11																				
Holyhead	d																								18 25
Bangor (Gwynedd)	d																								19 04
Llandudno Junction	d																								19 24
Wrexham General	d																								
Chester	d																								20 27
Crewe 10	a	19 20			19 27					19 59								20 16	20 22	20 45					20 48
	d	19 22			19 29					20 01								20 18	20 24	20 47					20 52
Macclesfield	d													19 49	19 54									20 29	
Congleton	d																								
Stoke-on-Trent	d			←					19 43				19 50	20 07	20 11									20 47	
Stafford	a	19 42	19 35	19 42										20 26				20 38	20 41					21 08	21 16
	d	19 43	19 36	19 43										20 27				20 39	20 43					21 09	21 16
Penkridge	a	→		19 48														20 44							
Wolverhampton 7 ⛴	a			19 59					20 13	20 32				20 39				20 55						21 21	21 34
Birmingham New Street 12	a			20 15					20 31	20 50				20 58				21 15						21 39	21 52
Birmingham International ✈	a													21 13											22 09
Coventry	a													21 23											
Lichfield Trent Valley	a																								
Tamworth Low Level	a																								
Nuneaton	a																								
Rugby	a																								
Milton Keynes Central	a												20 46						21 36	21 51					
Watford Junction	a																			22s31					
London Euston 15 ⊖	a		21 01		21 08	21 21							21 31		21 58				22 27	22 53					

A 🛒 to Birmingham New Street

OVERNIGHT SLEEPERS. For sleeper trains, operated by First ScotRail, please refer to Tables 400 - 404

Table 65

Sundays

16 September to 21 October

Scotland and North West England - West Midlands and London

Route Diagram - see first Page of Table 65

		VT		EM	LM	VT	VT	VT	TP	TP	XC	VT		LM	NT	TP	VT	XC	EM	NT	NT	NT		TP	
		◇1		◇	◇1	◇1	◇1	◇1	◇1	◇1	◇1	◇1		◇1		◇1	◇1	◇1	◇					◇1	
		☕				☕	☕	☕				☕				🛒	☕								
Inverness	d																								
Aberdeen	d																								
Dundee	d																								
Perth	d																								
Edinburgh 10	d											18 52				19 57									
Haymarket	d											18 57				20u01									
Glasgow Central 15	d							18 30									20 08								
Motherwell	d																								
Carstairs	d																								
Lockerbie	d																21 02								
Carlisle 8	a							19 43				20 05				21 13	21 21								
	d							19 44				20 07				21 14	21 24								
Penrith North Lakes	d											20 22					21 39								
Windermere	d								20 40																
Oxenholme Lake District	a							20 19	20 59								22 02								
	d							20 19	21 01								22 03								
Barrow-in-Furness	d																								
Lancaster 6	a							20 34	21 18			20 56				22 03	22 17								
	d							20 34				20 57				22 03	22 18								
Blackpool North	d									20 44					21 50						22 44			23 03	
Preston 8	a							20 52		21 08		21 15			22 14	22 23	22 35				23 08			23 28	
Preston 8	d							20 55		21 10		21 17			22 15	22 29	22 38				23 09			23 28	
Wigan North Western	a							21 06				21 28			22 36		22 49				23 30				
	d							21 07				21 28					22 50								
Blackrod	d																							23 50	
Lostock	d																							23 57	
Bolton	a									21 34						22 50								00 02	
Manchester Piccadilly 10	a									21 56						23 14								00 18	
Manchester Airport ✈	a									22 17						23 30								00 32	
Liverpool Lime Street 10	a																								
	d			19 52	20 34		20 48							21 34					21 21	22 01		23 01			
Liverpool South Parkway ✈	d			20 03	20 44									21 44					21 31						
Runcorn	d				20 52		21 04							21 52											
Warrington Bank Quay	a							21 18				21 39					23 00								
	d							21 18				21 39					23 01								
Hartford	d				21 03									22 03											
Manchester Piccadilly 10	d	20 20		20 44		20 55					21 07							22 07	22 11	22a50		23a50			
Stockport	d	20 27		20a53		21 03					21 16							22 16	22a20						
Wilmslow	d																								
Holyhead	d																								
Bangor (Gwynedd)	d																								
Llandudno Junction	d																								
Wrexham General	d																								
Chester	d																								
Crewe 10	a				21 16		21 21	21 38				21 59		22 18			23 20								
	d				21 18		21 23	21 40				22 01		22 22											
Macclesfield	d	20 40				21 15					21 29							22 29							
Congleton	d																								
Stoke-on-Trent	d	20 57				21 33					21 47							22 47							
Stafford	a				21 39		21 42	22 01			22 06			22 42				23 04							
	d				21 39		21 43	22 02			22 06			22 45				23 05							
Penkridge	a				21 45									22 50											
Wolverhampton 7	a				21 55			22 17			22 20	22 31		23 01				23 18							
Birmingham New Street 12	a				22 16			22 38			22 39	22 55		23 17				23 36							
Birmingham International ✈	a																								
Coventry	a																								
Lichfield Trent Valley	a						21 59																		
Tamworth Low Level	a						22 05																		
Nuneaton	a						22 17																		
Rugby	a						22 31																		
Milton Keynes Central	a	22 03				22 46	23 04																		
Watford Junction	a					23s25	23s34																		
London Euston 15 ⊖	a	22 56				23 49	23 54																		

OVERNIGHT SLEEPERS. For sleeper trains, operated by First ScotRail, please refer to Tables 400 - 404

Sundays

16 September to 21 October

Scotland and North West England - West Midlands and London

Route Diagram - see first Page of Table 65

		SR	SR	SR	SR
		🅱 🛏 ☕	🅱 🛏 ☕	🅱 🛏 ☕	🅱 🛏 ☕
				A	A
Inverness	d			20 25	
Aberdeen	d				21 42
Dundee	d				23u06
Perth	d			23u00	
Edinburgh 10	d	23 15			
Haymarket	d				
Glasgow Central 15	d		23 15		
Motherwell	d		23u31		
Carstairs	d	23u47			
Lockerbie	d				
Carlisle 8	a				
	d	01u12			
Penrith North Lakes	d				
Windermere	d				
Oxenholme Lake District	a				
	d				
Barrow-in-Furness	d				
Lancaster 6	a				
	d				
Blackpool North	d				
Preston 8	a			04s41	
Preston 8	d				
Wigan North Western	a				
	d				
Blackrod	d				
Lostock	d				
Bolton	a				
Manchester Piccadilly 10	a				
Manchester Airport	a				
Liverpool Lime Street 10	a				
	d				
Liverpool South Parkway	d				
Runcorn	d				
Warrington Bank Quay	a				
	d				
Hartford	d				
Manchester Piccadilly 10	d				
Stockport	d				
Wilmslow	d				
Holyhead	d				
Bangor (Gwynedd)	d				
Llandudno Junction	d				
Wrexham General	d				
Chester	d				
Crewe 10	a			05s41	
	d				
Macclesfield	d				
Congleton	d				
Stoke-on-Trent	d				
Stafford	a				
	d				
Penkridge	a				
Wolverhampton 7	a				
Birmingham New Street 12	a				
Birmingham International	a				
Coventry	a				
Lichfield Trent Valley	a				
Tamworth Low Level	a				
Nuneaton	a				
Rugby	a				
Milton Keynes Central	a				
Watford Junction	a	06s23			
London Euston 15 ⊖	a	06 46		07 50	

A Conveys a portion from Fort William, dep 1900

OVERNIGHT SLEEPERS. For sleeper trains, operated by First ScotRail, please refer to Tables 400 - 404

Table 65

Sundays

from 28 October

Scotland and North West England - West Midlands and London

Route Diagram - see first Page of Table 65

		TP	TP	TP	TP	VT	VT	VT	XC	NT	VT		TP	VT	XC	NT	VT	TP	LM	NT	VT	VT	XC	VT	VT
		◇1			◇1	◇1	◇1	◇1	◇1		◇1		◇1	◇1	◇1		◇1	◇1	◇1		◇1	◇1	◇1	◇1	◇1
									A						A								A		
			🚌	🚌						🚌						🚌				🚌					
						🍴	🍴	🍴	🍴🛒		🍴			🍴	🍴🛒		🍴				🍴	🍴	🍴🛒	🍴	🍴
Inverness	d																								
Aberdeen	d																								
Dundee	d																								
Perth	d																								
Edinburgh 10	d																								
Haymarket	d																								
Glasgow Central 15	d																								
Motherwell	d																								
Carstairs	d																								
Lockerbie	d																								
Carlisle 8	a																								
	d																								
Penrith North Lakes	d																								
Windermere	d																								
Oxenholme Lake District	a																								
	d																								
Barrow-in-Furness	d																								
Lancaster 6	a																								
	d																								
Blackpool North	d	22p44	03 20	05 20	07 48								08 44					09 44							
Preston 8	a	23p07			08 12								09 08					10 08							
Preston 8	d	23p09	04u00	06u00	08 14					08 28			09 09			09 28		10 09		10 28					
Wigan North Western	a									09 25						10 25				11 25					
	d																								
Blackrod	d																								
Lostock	d																								
Bolton	a	23p34	04b35	06b35	08 37								09 34					10 34							
Manchester Piccadilly 10	a	23p53	05b00	07b00	08 59								09 56					10 56							
Manchester Airport	a	00 23	05 25	07 25	09 17								10 17					11 17							
Liverpool Lime Street 10	a																								
	d							08 15			08 38						09 38								10 38
Liverpool South Parkway	d																								
Runcorn	d							08 35			08 54						09 54								10 54
Warrington Bank Quay	a																								
	d																								
Hartford	d																								
Manchester Piccadilly 10	d					08 05	08 20		08 27					09 20	09 27							10 20	10 27	10 35	
Stockport	d					08 14	08 28		08 36					09 27	09 36							10 29	10 36	10 42	
Wilmslow	d					08 22			08 43													10 36			
Holyhead	d																								
Bangor (Gwynedd)	d																								
Llandudno Junction	d																								
Wrexham General	d																								
Chester	d																								
Crewe 10	a					08 39		08 52	09 01		09 11						10 12					10 53			11 12
	d					08 43		08 53	09 05		09 13						10 14		10 20		10 43	10 55			11 14
Macclesfield	d						08 42							09 40	09 49								10 49	10 55	
Congleton	d																								
Stoke-on-Trent	d						08 59							09 57	10 07								11 07	11 12	
Stafford	a					09 01			09 25		09 31				10 26		10 32		10 41				11 27		11 34
	d					09 02			09 26		09 32				10 27		10 33		10 41				11 28		11 36
Penkridge	a																		10 48						
Wolverhampton 7	a								09 40						10 42				11 00				11 41		
Birmingham New Street 12	a								09 58						10 59				11 17				12 00		
Birmingham International	a								10 13						11 13								12 13		
Coventry	a								10 24						11 24								12 24		
Lichfield Trent Valley	a																								
Tamworth Low Level	a																								
Nuneaton	a										09 54						10 55								11 58
Rugby	a																				11 31				
Milton Keynes Central	a							10 17						11 16			11 46				12 06			12 20	
Watford Junction	a					10s35	10s41				11s16											12s36			12s50
London Euston 15 ⊖	a					10 57	11 02	11 06			11 37			12 08			12 32				12 45	12 56		12 59	13 11

A 🍴 from Birmingham New Street 🛒 to Birmingham New Street

b Stops to pick up only

OVERNIGHT SLEEPERS. For sleeper trains, operated by First ScotRail, please refer to Tables 400 - 404

Table 65

Sundays

from 28 October

Scotland and North West England - West Midlands and London

Route Diagram - see first Page of Table 65

		VT	VT	VT	TP	TP		XC	NT	VT	LM	VT	LM	VT	VT	VT		VT	TP	VT	TP	XC	NT	VT	LM
		◇1	◇1	◇1	◇1	◇1		◇1		◇1	◇1	◇1	◇1	◇1	◇1	◇1		◇1	◇1	◇1	◇1	◇1		◇1	◇1
								A														A			
									🚌														🚌		
		🍴	🍴	🍴				🍴🛒		🍴		🍴		🍴	🍴	🍴		🍴		🍴	🛒	🍴🛒		🍴	
Inverness	d																								
Aberdeen	d																								
Dundee	d																								
Perth	d																								
Edinburgh 10	d																								
Haymarket	d																								
Glasgow Central 15	d																			09 37					
Motherwell	d																								
Carstairs	d																								
Lockerbie	d																								
Carlisle 8	a																			10 44					
	d																			10 46					
Penrith North Lakes	d																			11 00					
Windermere	d																								
Oxenholme Lake District	a																			11 22					
	d																			11 23					
Barrow-in-Furness	d				09 17														10 30						
Lancaster 6	a				10 17														11 22	11 37					
	d				10 21														11 22	11 38					
Blackpool North	d					10 44															11 44				
Preston 8	a				10 40	11 08													11 42	11 56	12 08				
Preston 8	d			10 30	10 45	11 10			11 28									11 30	11 44		12 09		12 28		
Wigan North Western	a								13 25														13 25		
	d																								
Blackrod	d																								
Lostock	d																								
Bolton	a				11 08	11 34													12 08		12 34				
Manchester Piccadilly 10 ⛴	a			11s17	11 27	11 56												12s17	12 27		12 59				
Manchester Airport ✈	a				11 47	12 17													12 48		13 17				
Liverpool Lime Street 10	a																								
	d										11 34	11 48													12 34
Liverpool South Parkway ✈	d										11 44														12 44
Runcorn	d										11 52	12 04													12 52
Warrington Bank Quay	a																								
	d																								
Hartford	d										12 03														13 03
Manchester Piccadilly 10 ⛴	d	11 15						11 27		11 35				11 55	12 15							12 26		12 35	
Stockport	d	11 23						11 36		11 43				12 05	12 23							12 35		12 44	
Wilmslow	d													12 12											
Holyhead	d															10 55									
Bangor (Gwynedd)	d															11 22									
Llandudno Junction	d															11 40									
Wrexham General	d																								
Chester	d		11 28													12 33									
Crewe 10	a		11 47	11 48							12 20			12 28		12 52		12 48							13 19
	d		11 49	12 01							12 22			12 30		12 56		13 01							13 22
Macclesfield	d							11 49		11 56												12 49		12 57	
Congleton	d																								
Stoke-on-Trent	d	11 51						12 07		12 13			←		12 51							13 07		13 14	
Stafford	a							12 24			12 41	12 35	12 41									13 24			13 42
	d							12 25			12 42	12 36	12 42									13 25			13 43
Penkridge	a										→		12 48												→
Wolverhampton 7 ⛴	a			12 31				12 40					12 59					13 32				13 40			
Birmingham New Street 12	a			12 55				12 58					13 16					13 55				13 58			
Birmingham International ✈	a							13 13														14 13			
Coventry	a							13 24														14 24			
Lichfield Trent Valley	a																								
Tamworth Low Level	a																								
Nuneaton	a		12 31																						
Rugby	a																								
Milton Keynes Central	a	12 50	13 03												13 46	14 02									
Watford Junction	a																								
London Euston 15 ⊖	a	13 28	13 44							13 47		14 01		14 09	14 27	14 43								14 47	

A 🍴 from Birmingham New Street 🛒 to Birmingham New Street

OVERNIGHT SLEEPERS. For sleeper trains, operated by First ScotRail, please refer to Tables 400 - 404

Table 65

Sundays

from 28 October

Scotland and North West England - West Midlands and London

Route Diagram - see first Page of Table 65

		VT		LM	VT	XC	VT	VT	VT	TP	VT	TP		XC	NT	VT	EM	LM	VT	LM	VT	XC		VT	VT
		◇1		◇1	◇1	◇1	◇1	◇1	◇1	◇1	◇1	◇1		◇1		◇1	◇	◇1	◇1	◇1	◇1	◇1		◇1	◇1
														A	▭										
		⊐			⊐	⊼	⊐	⊐	⊐	⊼	⊐			⊐⊼		⊐			⊐		⊐	⊼		⊐	⊐
Inverness	d																								
Aberdeen	d																								
Dundee	d																								
Perth	d																								
Edinburgh 10	d									10 10															
Haymarket	d									10u14															
Glasgow Central 15	d										10 34														
Motherwell	d										10 49														
Carstairs	d																								
Lockerbie	d									11 08															
Carlisle 8	a									11 29	11 44														
	d									11 29	11 46														
Penrith North Lakes	d									11 45	12 00														
Windermere	d																								
Oxenholme Lake District	a									12 09	12 22														
	d									12 10	12 24														
Barrow-in-Furness	d																								
Lancaster 6	a									12 26	12 37														
	d								12 10	12 26	12 38														
Blackpool North	d											12 42													
Preston 8	a								12 27	12 45	12 56	13 06													
Preston 8	d								12 42	12 46		13 08			13 28										
Wigan North Western	a														14 25										
	d																								
Blackrod	d																								
Lostock	d																								
Bolton	a									13 09		13 34													
Manchester Piccadilly 10	a								13s17	13 28		13 56													
Manchester Airport	a									13 47		14 17													
Liverpool Lime Street 10	a																								
	d	12 48															12 52	13 34	13 48						
Liverpool South Parkway	d																13 03	13 44							
Runcorn	d	13 04																13 52	14 04						
Warrington Bank Quay	a																								
	d																								
Hartford	d																	14 03							
Manchester Piccadilly 10	d				12 55	13 07	13 15							13 27		13 35	13 44				13 55	14 07			14 15
Stockport	d				13 05		13 22							13 36		13 42	13a53				14 04				14 22
Wilmslow	d				13 12																14 11				
Holyhead	d							11 50																	
Bangor (Gwynedd)	d							12 17																	
Llandudno Junction	d							12 35																	
Wrexham General	d																								
Chester	d							13 30																	
Crewe 10	a				13 28			13 50	13 48									14 18			14 27				
	d				13 30			13 51	14 01									14 22			14 29			14 35	
Macclesfield	d													13 49		13 55									
Congleton	d																								
Stoke-on-Trent	d			←		13 43	13 50							14 07		14 12				←		14 43			14 50
Stafford	a	13 35		13 42										14 24				14 42	14 35	14 42					
	d	13 36		13 43										14 25				14 43	14 36	14 43					
Penkridge	a			13 48														→		14 48					
Wolverhampton 7	a			13 59		14 13			14 32					14 40						14 59		15 13			
Birmingham New Street 12	a			14 15		14 31			14 50					14 58						15 15		15 31			
Birmingham International	a													15 13											
Coventry	a													15 24											
Lichfield Trent Valley	a																								
Tamworth Low Level	a																								
Nuneaton	a							14 31																	
Rugby	a																								
Milton Keynes Central	a						14 48	15 02																	
Watford Junction	a																								15 48
London Euston 15 ⊖	a	15 01			15 05		15 26	15 43								15 47			16 01		16 05			16 12	16 26

A ⊐ from Birmingham New Street ⊼ to Birmingham New Street

OVERNIGHT SLEEPERS. For sleeper trains, operated by First ScotRail, please refer to Tables 400 - 404

Table 65

Sundays
from 28 October

Scotland and North West England - West Midlands and London

Route Diagram - see first Page of Table 65

		VT	VT	TP	VT	NT	TP	TP		XC	VT	EM	LM	VT	LM	VT	VT	TP		XC	VT	VT	VT	XC	VT
		◇1	◇1	◇1	◇1		◇1	◇1		◇1	◇1	◇	◇1	◇1	◇1	◇1	◇1	◇1		◇1	◇1	◇1	◇1	◇1	◇1
										A														A	
		IP	IP		IP			⊥o		IP⊥o	IP			IP		IP	IP			⊥o	IP	IP	IP	IP⊥o	IP
Inverness	d																								
Aberdeen	d																								
Dundee	d																								
Perth	d																								
Edinburgh 10	d		10 52					12 10															12 52		
Haymarket	d		10 57					12u14															12 56		
Glasgow Central 15	d				11 36												12 42								
Motherwell	d																								
Carstairs	d																								
Lockerbie	d							13 08																	
Carlisle 8	a		12 05		12 47			13 29									13 51						14 05		
	d		12 07		12 49			13 29									13 54						14 07		
Penrith North Lakes	d							13 45															14 22		
Windermere	d																								
Oxenholme Lake District	a		12 41		13 22			14 09									14 27								
	d		12 43		13 23			14 10									14 28								
Barrow-in-Furness	d			12 25		13 10																			
Lancaster 6	a		12 56	13 26	13 37	14 15		14 26									14 42						14 56		
	d		12 57	13 26	13 38			14 26									14 43						14 57		
Blackpool North	d						13 44											14 44							
Preston 8	a		13 15	13 44	13 56		14 08	14 45									15 01	15 08					15 15		
Preston 8	d		13 30	13 46			14 09	14 46									15 03	15 10					15 17		
Wigan North Western	a																15 14						15 28		
	d																15 14						15 28		
Blackrod	d																								
Lostock	d																								
Bolton	a			14 09			14 35	15 09										15 34							
Manchester Piccadilly 10 ⛴	a		14s17	14 27			14 56	15 27										15 56							
Manchester Airport ✈	a			14 47			15 17	15 47										16 17							
Liverpool Lime Street 10	a																								
	d											13 52	14 34	14 48											
Liverpool South Parkway ✈	d											14 03	14 44												
Runcorn	d												14 52	15 04											
Warrington Bank Quay	a																15 25						15 39		
	d																15 25						15 39		
Hartford	d												15 03												
Manchester Piccadilly 10 ⛴	d									14 27	14 35	14 44				14 55				15 07	15 15			15 27	15 35
Stockport	d									14 36	14 42	14a53				15 04					15 22			15 36	15 42
Wilmslow	d															15 11									
Holyhead	d	12 50																				13 55			
Bangor (Gwynedd)	d	13 18																				14 22			
Llandudno Junction	d	13 36																				14 40			
Wrexham General	d																								
Chester	d	14 33																				15 33			
Crewe 10	a	14 52	14 52										15 20			15 27						15 52	15 59		
	d	14 54	15 01										15 22			15 29						15 54	16 01		
Macclesfield	d									14 49	14 55													15 49	15 55
Congleton	d																								
Stoke-on-Trent	d									15 07	15 12				←					15 43	15 50			16 07	16 12
Stafford	a									15 24			15 42	15 35	15 42									16 24	
	d									15 25			15 43	15 36	15 43									16 25	
Penkridge	a												→		15 48										
Wolverhampton 7 ⛴	a		15 31							15 40					15 59					16 13			16 32	16 40	
Birmingham New Street 12	a		15 50							15 58					16 15					16 31			16 55	16 58	
Birmingham International ✈	a									16 13														17 13	
Coventry	a									16 24														17 24	
Lichfield Trent Valley	a																								
Tamworth Low Level	a																								
Nuneaton	a																								
Rugby	a																								
Milton Keynes Central	a	16 03																			16 49	17 02			
Watford Junction	a																								
London Euston 15 ⊖	a	16 43									16 47			17 01		17 07	17 20				17 27	17 43			17 46

A IP from Birmingham New Street ⊥o to Birmingham New Street

OVERNIGHT SLEEPERS. For sleeper trains, operated by First ScotRail, please refer to Tables 400 - 404

Table 65

Sundays
from 28 October

Scotland and North West England - West Midlands and London

Route Diagram - see first Page of Table 65

		VT	TP	EM	LM	VT	LM	VT	VT	TP	XC	VT	VT	VT	TP	XC	VT	EM	LM	VT	LM	VT
		◇1	◇1	◇	◇1	◇1	◇1	◇1	◇1	◇1	◇1	◇1	◇1	◇1	◇1	◇1	◇1	◇	◇1	◇1	◇1	◇1
																A						
		🍽				🍽		🍽	🍽		🛒	🍽	🍽	🍽	🛒	🍽🛒	🍽			🍽		🍽
Inverness	d																					
Aberdeen	d																					
Dundee	d																					
Perth	d																					
Edinburgh 10	d														14 10							
Haymarket	d														14u14							
Glasgow Central 15	d	13 05							13 36					13 55								
Motherwell	d																					
Carstairs	d																					
Lockerbie	d														15 08							
Carlisle 8	a	14 17							14 46					15 09	15 29							
	d	14 20							14 49					15 11	15 29							
Penrith North Lakes	d														15 45							
Windermere	d																					
Oxenholme Lake District	a	14 53							15 22					15 46	16 09							
	d	14 54							15 23					15 46	16 10							
Barrow-in-Furness	d		14 25																			
Lancaster 6	a		15 26						15 37						16 26							
	d		15 26						15 38						16 26							
Blackpool North	d									15 44												
Preston 8	a	15 23	15 45						15 56	16 08				16 15	16 46							
Preston 8	d	15 27	15 47						15 58	16 10				16 17	16 47							
Wigan North Western	a								16 09					16 28								
	d								16 09					16 28								
Blackrod	d																					
Lostock	d																					
Bolton	a		16 08							16 34					17 08							
Manchester Piccadilly 10	a		16 27							16 56					17 27							
Manchester Airport ✈	a		16 46							17 17					17 47							
Liverpool Lime Street 10	a																					
	d			14 52	15 34	15 48							16 18					15 52	16 34	16 48		
Liverpool South Parkway ✈	d			15 03	15 44													16 03	16 44			
Runcorn	d				15 52	16 04							16 34						16 52	17 04		
Warrington Bank Quay	a								16 20					16 39								
	d								16 20					16 39								
Hartford	d				16 03														17 03			
Manchester Piccadilly 10	d			15 44				15 55			16 07	16 15				16 27	16 35	16 44				16 55
Stockport	d			15a53				16 04				16 23				16 36	16 42	16a53				17 04
Wilmslow	d							16 11														17 11
Holyhead	d																					
Bangor (Gwynedd)	d																					
Llandudno Junction	d																					
Wrexham General	d																					
Chester	d																					
Crewe 10	a				16 18			16 27					16 51	16 59					17 18			17 27
	d				16 22			16 29					16 54	17 01					17 22			17 29
Macclesfield	d															16 49	16 55					
Congleton	d																					
Stoke-on-Trent	d						←				16 43	16 50				17 08	17 12				←	
Stafford	a				16 42	16 36	16 42									17 25			17 42	17 35	17 42	
	d				16 43	16 37	16 43									17 26			17 43	17 36	17 43	
Penkridge	a				→		16 48												→		17 48	
Wolverhampton 7	a						16 59				17 13			17 32		17 40					17 59	
Birmingham New Street 12	a						17 15				17 31			17 55		17 58					18 15	
Birmingham International ✈	a															18 13						
Coventry	a															18 24						
Lichfield Trent Valley	a												17 26									
Tamworth Low Level	a																					
Nuneaton	a																					
Rugby	a																					
Milton Keynes Central	a											17 49	18 04									
Watford Junction	a																					
London Euston 15 ⊖	a	17 53				18 01		18 07	18 13			18 26	18 44				18 47			19 01		19 05

A 🍽 from Birmingham New Street 🛒 to Birmingham New Street

OVERNIGHT SLEEPERS. For sleeper trains, operated by First ScotRail, please refer to Tables 400 - 404

Table 65

Sundays

from 28 October

Scotland and North West England - West Midlands and London

Route Diagram - see first Page of Table 65

		VT	TP	XC	VT	VT	VT	TP	XC	VT		EM	LM	VT	LM	VT	VT	TP	XC	VT		VT	VT	TP	XC
		◇1	◇1	◇1	◇1	◇1	◇1	◇1	◇1	◇1		◇	◇1	◇1	◇1	◇1	◇1	◇1	◇1	◇1		◇1	◇1	◇1	◇1
									A																A
		[R]		[T]	[R]	[R]	[R]	[T]	[R][T]	[R]				[R]		[R]	[R]		[T]	[R]		[R]	[R]	[T]	[R][T]
Inverness	d																								
Aberdeen	d																								
Dundee	d																								
Perth	d																								
Edinburgh 10	d						14 52																	16 10	
Haymarket	d						14 57																	16u14	
Glasgow Central 15	d	14 36						15 06									15 36						15 57		
Motherwell	d																								
Carstairs	d																								
Lockerbie	d							16 06																17 08	
Carlisle 8	a	15 46					16 05	16 26									16 46						17 08	17 29	
	d	15 49					16 07	16 26									16 49						17 09	17 29	
Penrith North Lakes	d						16 22	16 42									17 03							17 45	
Windermere	d																								
Oxenholme Lake District	a	16 22						17 07															17 44	18 09	
	d	16 23						17 07															17 44	18 10	
Barrow-in-Furness	d																								
Lancaster 6	a	16 37					16 56	17 22									17 37							18 26	
	d	16 38					16 57	17 22									17 38							18 26	
Blackpool North	d		16 44															17 44							
Preston 8	a	16 56	17 08				17 15	17 41									17 56	18 08					18 13	18 45	
Preston 8	d	16 58	17 10				17 17	17 47									17 58	18 10					18 17	18 47	
Wigan North Western	a	17 09					17 28										18 09						18 28		
	d	17 09					17 28										18 09						18 28		
Blackrod	d																								
Lostock	d																								
Bolton	a		17 34					18 08										18 34						19 08	
Manchester Piccadilly 10 ⇌	a		17 56					18 27										18 56						19 27	
Manchester Airport ✈	a		18 17					18 45										19 17						19 47	
Liverpool Lime Street 10	a																								
	d											16 52	17 34	17 48											
Liverpool South Parkway ✈	d											17 03	17 44												
Runcorn	d												17 52	18 04											
Warrington Bank Quay	a	17 20					17 39										18 20						18 39		
	d	17 20					17 39										18 20						18 39		
Hartford	d												18 03												
Manchester Piccadilly 10 ⇌	d			17 07	17 15				17 27	17 35		17 44				17 55			18 07	18 15					18 27
Stockport	d				17 22				17 36	17 42		17a53				18 04				18 22					18 36
Wilmslow	d															18 11									
Holyhead	d																								
Bangor (Gwynedd)	d																								
Llandudno Junction	d																								
Wrexham General	d																								
Chester	d					17 35																18 35			
Crewe 10	a					17 53	17 59						18 20			18 27						18 53	18 59		
	d					17 55	18 01						18 22			18 29						18 55	19 01		
Macclesfield	d								17 49	17 55															18 49
Congleton	d																								
Stoke-on-Trent	d			17 43	17 50				18 08	18 12					←				18 43	18 50					19 07
Stafford	a								18 25				18 42	18 35	18 42										19 24
	d								18 26				18 43	18 36	18 43										19 25
Penkridge	a												→		18 48										
Wolverhampton 7 ⇌	a			18 13			18 32		18 40						18 59				19 13				19 31		19 40
Birmingham New Street 12	a			18 31			18 55		18 58						19 15				19 31				19 55		19 58
Birmingham International ✈	a								19 13																20 13
Coventry	a								19 24																20 24
Lichfield Trent Valley	a																								
Tamworth Low Level	a																								
Nuneaton	a																								
Rugby	a																								
Milton Keynes Central	a				18 49	19 02														19 48		20 02			
Watford Junction	a																								
London Euston 15 ⊖	a	19 10			19 26	19 43				19 47				20 01		20 05	20 12			20 26		20 44			

A [R] from Birmingham New Street [T] to Birmingham New Street

OVERNIGHT SLEEPERS. For sleeper trains, operated by First ScotRail, please refer to Tables 400 - 404

Sundays
from 28 October

Scotland and North West England - West Midlands and London

Route Diagram - see first Page of Table 65

		VT	EM	LM	VT	LM		VT	VT	TP	XC	VT	TP	TP	VT	XC		VT	EM	LM	VT	VT	TP	TP	NT
		◇1	◇	◇1	◇1	◇1		◇1	◇1	◇1	◇1	◇1	◇1	◇1	◇1	◇1		◇1	◇	◇1	◇1	◇1	◇1	◇1	
																A									
		☕			☕			☕	☕		⊼	☕		⊼	☕	⊼		☕			☕	☕		⊼	
Inverness	d																								
Aberdeen	d																								
Dundee	d																								
Perth	d																								
Edinburgh 10	d											16 52												18 10	
Haymarket	d											16 56												18u14	
Glasgow Central 15	d								16 40					17 06								17 36			
Motherwell	d								16 54																
Carstairs	d																								
Lockerbie	d																					18 32		19 08	
Carlisle 8	a								17 49			18 05		18 25								18 50		19 29	
	d								17 51			18 07		18 26								18 52		19 29	
Penrith North Lakes	d								18 05					18 42								19 06		19 45	
Windermere	d																								
Oxenholme Lake District	a								18 27			18 41		19 07								19 28		20 09	
	d								18 28			18 42		19 07								19 29		20 10	
Barrow-in-Furness	d												18 17												20 02
Lancaster 6	a								18 42			18 56	19 17	19 22								19 43		20 26	21 07
	d								18 43			18 57	19 17	19 22								19 44		20 26	
Blackpool North	d									18 44													19 44		
Preston 8	a								19 01	19 08		19 15	19 37	19 41								20 02	20 08	20 45	
Preston 8	d								19 03	19 10		19 17		19 47								20 04	20 10	20 47	
Wigan North Western	a								19 14			19 28										20 15			
	d								19 14			19 28										20 15			
Blackrod	d																								
Lostock	d																								
Bolton	a									19 34				20 08									20 34	21 08	
Manchester Piccadilly 10	a									19 56				20 27									20 56	21 27	
Manchester Airport ✈	a									20 17				20 45									21 16	21 46	
Liverpool Lime Street 10	a																								
	d		17 52	18 34	18 48														18 52	19 34	19 48				
Liverpool South Parkway ✈	d		18 03	18 44															19 03	19 44					
Runcorn	d			18 52	19 04															19 52	20 04				
Warrington Bank Quay	a								19 25			19 39										20 26			
	d								19 25			19 39										20 26			
Hartford	d			19 03																20 03					
Manchester Piccadilly 10	d	18 35	18 44					18 55			19 07				19 15	19 27		19 35	19 44						
Stockport	d	18 42	18a53					19 04							19 22	19 36		19 41	19a53						
Wilmslow	d							19 11																	
Holyhead	d																								
Bangor (Gwynedd)	d																								
Llandudno Junction	d																								
Wrexham General	d																								
Chester	d																								
Crewe 10	a			19 20				19 27				19 59								20 16	20 22	20 45			
	d			19 22				19 29				20 01								20 18	20 24	20 47			
Macclesfield	d	18 55														19 49		19 54							
Congleton	d																								
Stoke-on-Trent	d	19 12				←					19 43				19 50	20 07		20 11							
Stafford	a			19 42	19 35	19 42										20 26				20 38	20 41				
	d			19 43	19 36	19 43										20 27				20 39	20 43				
Penkridge	a			→		19 48														20 44					
Wolverhampton 7	a					19 59					20 13	20 32				20 39				20 55					
Birmingham New Street 12	a					20 15					20 31	20 50				20 58				21 15					
Birmingham International ✈	a															21 13									
Coventry	a															21 23									
Lichfield Trent Valley	a																								
Tamworth Low Level	a																								
Nuneaton	a																								
Rugby	a																								
Milton Keynes Central	a														20 46						21 36	21 51			
Watford Junction	a																					22s31			
London Euston 15 ⊖	a	20 47			21 01			21 08	21 21						21 31			21 58			22 27	22 53			

A ⊼ to Birmingham New Street

OVERNIGHT SLEEPERS. For sleeper trains, operated by First ScotRail, please refer to Tables 400 - 404

Table 65

Sundays from 28 October

Scotland and North West England - West Midlands and London

Route Diagram - see first Page of Table 65

		XC		AW	VT	EM	LM	VT	VT	VT	TP	TP		XC	VT	LM	NT	TP	VT	XC	EM	NT		NT	NT
		◇1		◇	◇1	◇	◇1	◇1	◇1	◇1	◇1	◇1		◇1	◇1	◇1		◇1	◇1	◇1	◇				
				⌶	⊡			⊡	⊡	⊡					⊡			⌶	⊡						
Inverness	d																								
Aberdeen	d																								
Dundee	d																								
Perth	d																								
Edinburgh 10	d														18 52			19 57							
Haymarket	d														18 57			20u01							
Glasgow Central 15	d									18 30									20 08						
Motherwell	d																								
Carstairs	d																								
Lockerbie	d																		21 02						
Carlisle 8	a									19 43					20 05			21 13	21 21						
	d									19 44					20 07			21 14	21 24						
Penrith North Lakes	d														20 22				21 39						
Windermere	d										20 40														
Oxenholme Lake District	a									20 19	20 59								22 02						
	d									20 19	21 01								22 03						
Barrow-in-Furness	d																								
Lancaster 6	a									20 34	21 18				20 56			22 03	22 17						
	d									20 34					20 57			22 03	22 18						
Blackpool North	d											20 44					21 50							22 44	
Preston 8	a									20 52		21 08			21 15		22 14	22 23	22 35					23 08	
Preston 8	d									20 55		21 10			21 17		22 15	22 29	22 38					23 09	
Wigan North Western	a									21 06					21 28		22 36		22 49					23 30	
	d									21 07					21 28				22 50						
Blackrod	d																								
Lostock	d																								
Bolton	a											21 34						22 50							
Manchester Piccadilly 10	a											21 56						23 14							
Manchester Airport ✈	a											22 17						23 30							
Liverpool Lime Street 10	a																								
	d					19 52	20 34		20 48							21 34					21 21	22 01			23 01
Liverpool South Parkway ✈	d					20 03	20 44									21 44					21 31				
Runcorn	d						20 52		21 04							21 52									
Warrington Bank Quay	a									21 18					21 39				23 00						
	d									21 18					21 39				23 01						
Hartford	d						21 03									22 03									
Manchester Piccadilly 10	d	20 07			20 20	20 44		20 55						21 07						22 07	22 11	22a50			23a50
Stockport	d	20 16			20 27	20a53		21 03						21 16						22 16	22a20				
Wilmslow	d																								
Holyhead	d			18 25																					
Bangor (Gwynedd)	d			19 04																					
Llandudno Junction	d			19 24																					
Wrexham General	d																								
Chester	d			20 27																					
Crewe 10	a			20 48			21 16		21 21	21 38					21 59	22 18			23 20						
	d			20 52			21 18		21 23	21 40					22 01	22 22									
Macclesfield	d	20 29			20 40			21 15						21 29						22 29					
Congleton	d																								
Stoke-on-Trent	d	20 47			20 57			21 33						21 47						22 47					
Stafford	a	21 08		21 16			21 39		21 42	22 01				22 06		22 42				23 04					
	d	21 09		21 16			21 39		21 43	22 02				22 06		22 45				23 05					
Penkridge	a						21 45									22 50									
Wolverhampton 7	a	21 21		21 34			21 55			22 17				22 20	22 31	23 01				23 18					
Birmingham New Street 12	a	21 39		21 52			22 16			22 38				22 39	22 55	23 17				23 36					
Birmingham International ✈	a			22 09																					
Coventry	a																								
Lichfield Trent Valley	a								21 59																
Tamworth Low Level	a								22 05																
Nuneaton	a								22 17																
Rugby	a								22 31																
Milton Keynes Central	a				22 03			22 46	23 04																
Watford Junction	a							23s25	23s34																
London Euston 15 ⊖	a				22 56			23 49	23 54																

OVERNIGHT SLEEPERS. For sleeper trains, operated by First ScotRail, please refer to Tables 400 - 404

Table 65

Sundays
from 28 October

Scotland and North West England - West Midlands and London

Route Diagram - see first Page of Table 65

		TP	SR	SR	SR	SR
			R	R	R	R
		◇1				
			sleeper	sleeper	sleeper	sleeper
			ꟾP	ꟾP	ꟾP	ꟾP
					A	A
Inverness	d				20 25	
Aberdeen	d					21 42
Dundee	d					23u06
Perth	d				23u00	
Edinburgh 10	d		23 15			
Haymarket	d					
Glasgow Central 15	d			23 15		
Motherwell	d			23u31		
Carstairs	d		23u47			
Lockerbie	d					
Carlisle 8	a					
	d		01u12			
Penrith North Lakes	d					
Windermere	d					
Oxenholme Lake District	a					
	d					
Barrow-in-Furness	d					
Lancaster 6	a					
	d					
Blackpool North	d	23 03				
Preston 8	a	23 28			04s41	
Preston 8	d	23 28				
Wigan North Western	a					
	d					
Blackrod	d	23 50				
Lostock	d	23 57				
Bolton	a	00 02				
Manchester Piccadilly 10	a	00 18				
Manchester Airport ✈	a	00 32				
Liverpool Lime Street 10	a					
	d					
Liverpool South Parkway ✈	d					
Runcorn	d					
Warrington Bank Quay	a					
	d					
Hartford	d					
Manchester Piccadilly 10	d					
Stockport	d					
Wilmslow	d					
Holyhead	d					
Bangor (Gwynedd)	d					
Llandudno Junction	d					
Wrexham General	d					
Chester	d					
Crewe 10	a				05s41	
	d					
Macclesfield	d					
Congleton	d					
Stoke-on-Trent	d					
Stafford	a					
	d					
Penkridge	a					
Wolverhampton 7	a					
Birmingham New Street 12	a					
Birmingham International ✈	a					
Coventry	a					
Lichfield Trent Valley	a					
Tamworth Low Level	a					
Nuneaton	a					
Rugby	a					
Milton Keynes Central	a					
Watford Junction	a		06s23			
London Euston 15 ⊖	a		06 46		07 50	

A Conveys a portion from Fort William, dep 1900

OVERNIGHT SLEEPERS. For sleeper trains, operated by First ScotRail, please refer to Tables 400 - 404

London - Watford Junction, Milton Keynes Central, Northampton and West Midlands

Network Diagram - see first Page of Table 59

Miles	Miles	Miles			LM	LM	VT	LM	VT	VT	LM	LM	LM	LM	VT	VT	LM	LM	LM	LM	LM	LM	LM
					MO	MX	MO	MO	MO	MX	MX	MO	MX		MO	MX	MX	MO		MO	MX	MO	MX
					◇■	◇■	◇■	■	◇■	◇■	■	◇■	■	■	◇■	◇■	■	◇■	■	■	■	■	■
					A		A	A	A			A	B	C	A			A					
							🚌		🚌	🚌					🚌	🚌							
0	0	—	**London Euston** ■ ⊖	d	21p28	21p46	21p55	22p00	22p25	22p30	22p54	22p58	23p24	23p24	23p25	23p30	23p34	23p34	00 04	00 34	00 34	01 34	01 34
—	—	0	East Croydon ⇌	d																			
—	—	—	Clapham Junction	d																			
—	—	8¾	Imperial Wharf	d																			
—	—	9¼	West Brompton ⊖	d																			
—	—	11¼	Kensington (Olympia) ⊖	d																			
—	—	12½	Shepherd's Bush	d																			
8	—	16¾	Wembley Central ⊖	d																00 43	00 45	01 45	01 45
11½	11½	—	Harrow & Wealdstone ⊖	d	21p40			22p12			23p06	23p10					23p46	23p46	00 16	00 48	00 50	01 50	01 50
16	—	—	Bushey	d	21b45												23p51	23b51		00s53	00 55		
17½	17½	—	**Watford Junction**	a	21p47			22p18			23p12	23p16	23p39	23p43			23p54	23p54	00 22	00 56	00 57	01 56	01 56
—	—	—		d	21p48		22c09	22p19	22c39	22c45	23p12	23p17	23p40	23p43	23c40		23p54	23p55	00 23	00 58	00 58	01 57	01 57
21	—	—	Kings Langley	d	21p52						23p17	23p21					23p59	23p59		01 02	01 02		
23	—	—	Apsley	d	21p56						23p20	23p25					00 02	00 03		01 06	01 06		
24½	—	—	Hemel Hempstead	d	21p59			22p26			23p23	23p28	23p47	23p50			00 05	00 06	00 30	01 09	01 09	02 04	02 04
28	—	—	Berkhamsted	d	22p04			22p31			23p28	23p33	23p52	23p55			00 09	00 11	00 35	01 14	01 14	02 09	02 09
31¾	—	—	Tring	d				22p35			23p34	23p37					00 15	00 15	00 41	01 18	01 19	02 13	02 14
36	—	—	Cheddington	d				22p41				23p43					00 20	00 21		01 24	01 25		
40¼	—	—	Leighton Buzzard	d	22p17	22p18		22p47			23p41	23p49	00 05	00 06			00 26	00 27	00 50	01 30	01 31	02 22	02 23
46¾	—	—	Bletchley	d	22p24			22p54			23p49	23p56	00 13	00 13			00 33	00 34	00 57	01 37	01 38	02 29	02 30
49¾	49¾	—	**Milton Keynes Central** ■	a	22p32	22p32	22p42	23p02	23p11	23p28	23p55	00 04	00 21	00 19	00 11	00 27	00 41	00 42	01 05	01 45	01 46	02 37	02 38
—	—	—		d	22p32	22p32	22p44	23p03	23p12	23p29	23p55	00 05	00 21	00 20	00 12	00 28		00 43	01 05	01 46	01 47		
52½	52½	—	Wolverton	d	22p36	22p36		23p06			23p59	00 08	00 25	00 24				00 46	01 09	01 49	01 50		
65¾	—	—	**Northampton**	a	22p49	22p49		23p20			00 13	00 22	00 38	00 37				01 00	01 22	02 03	02 04		
84½	82½	—	**Rugby**	a	23p13	23p17	23p20	23p54	23p46	23p58					00s46	01 00							
—	—	—	Nuneaton	a																			
96	—	—	Coventry	a	23p25	23p29	23p31	00 05	23p57	00 10					00s57	01 13							
106¾	—	—	Birmingham International ✈	a	23p52	23p47	23p42		00 08	00 21					01s08	01 24							
115¼	—	—	**Birmingham New Street** ■	a	00 04	00 04	23p55		00 21	00 32					01s21	01 36							
120½	—	—	Sandwell & Dudley	a																			
128	—	—	Wolverhampton ■ ⇌	a			00 26		00 53	01 03					01 53	02 07							

		SN	LM	VT	LM	VT	SN	VT	LM	SN	VT	VT	LM	LM	VT	VT	LM	VT	SN	VT	LM	VT	LM
		■	◇■	◇■	◇■	◇■	■	◇■	■	■	◇■	◇■	◇■	■	◇■	◇■	◇■	◇■	■	◇■	■	◇■	◇■
				⊠		⊠		⊠			⊠	⊠			⊠	⊠		⊠		⊠		⊠	
London Euston ■ ⊖	d			05 27	05 30	05 39		06 03	06 04		06 17	06 23	06 24	06 34	06 36	06 43	06 53	06 55		07 03	07 04	07 10	07 13
East Croydon ⇌	d																						
Clapham Junction	d	05 03					05 30			05 55									06 38				
Imperial Wharf	d	05 07					05 39			06 00									06 42				
West Brompton ⊖	d	05 10					05 41			06 03									06 45				
Kensington (Olympia) ⊖	d	05 14					05 44			06 07									06 49				
Shepherd's Bush	d	05 17					05 47			06 10									06 52				
Wembley Central ⊖	d						06 02			06 24									07 07				
Harrow & Wealdstone ⊖	d	05 33			05 43		06 07		06 16	06 29				06 47					07 12		07 17		
Bushey	d																						
Watford Junction	a	05 40			05 50		06 14		06 22	06 36			06 39	06 53			07 08		07 19		07 24		
	d			05u45	05 50	06u02	06 14		06 23			06u37	06 41	06 54			07 10		07 19		07 24		
Kings Langley	d				05 55				06 27					06 58							07 29		
Apsley	d				05 59				06 31					07 02							07 32		
Hemel Hempstead	d				06 01		06 22		06 34				06 48	07 05			07 17		07 27		07 35		
Berkhamsted	d				06 06		06 26		06 39				06 53	07 10			07 22		07 32		07 40		
Tring	d				06 13		06 33		06a47				06 59	07 16					07 39		07a47		
Cheddington	d				06 18								07 05	07 21									
Leighton Buzzard	d				06 23		06 42						07 10	07 26			07 35		07 51				07 42
Bletchley	d		05 17		06 30		06 49						07 17	07 33			07 43		07 58				07 50
Milton Keynes Central ■	a		05 21	06 09	06 35	06 22	06 55				06 47		07 22	07 38		07 13	07 48	07 25	08 03			07 40	07 54
	d		05 21	06 10	06 36	06 22							07 22			07 13	07 48						07 54
Wolverton	d		05 25		06 39								07 26				07 52						07 58
Northampton	a		05 37		06 52								07 42				08 05						08 11
Rugby	a		06 02		07 17	06 44		06 51					08 04							07 51			08 38
Nuneaton	a		06 16	06 38									08 17										
Coventry	a				07 29			07 02				07 22				07 42				08 02			08 49
Birmingham International ✈	a				07 45			07 13				07 33				07 53				08 12			09 04
Birmingham New Street ■	a				08 03			07 27				07 45				08 08				08 27			09 17
Sandwell & Dudley	a											07 57											
Wolverhampton ■ ⇌	a											08 11											

A from 21 May until 25 June
B until 22 June
C from 26 June until 29 June
b Previous night, stops to set down only
c Previous night, stops to pick up only

London - Watford Junction, Milton Keynes Central, Northampton and West Midlands

Network Diagram - see first Page of Table 59

		VT	VT	LM	LM	VT	LM	LM	SN	VT	LM	VT	LM	VT	VT	LM	LM	VT	LM	LM	SN	VT	LM
		◇■	◇■	■	■	◇■	◇■	◇■	■	◇■	■	◇■	◇■	◇■	◇■	■	■	◇■	◇■	◇■	■	◇■	■
		⊠	⊠			⊠				⊠		⊠		⊠	⊠			⊠				⊠	
London Euston ■ ⊖	d	07 20	07 23	07 24	07 34	07 35	07 47	07 54		08 03	08 05	08 10	08 13	08 20	08 23	08 24	08 34	08 43	08 46	08 54		09 03	09 05
East Croydon ⇌	d																				08 07		
Clapham Junction	d								07 39												08 39		
Imperial Wharf	d								07 44												08 44		
West Brompton ⊖	d								07 47												08 47		
Kensington (Olympia) ⊖	d								07 50												08 50		
Shepherd's Bush	d								07 53												08 53		
Wembley Central ⊖	d								08 08												09 08		
Harrow & Wealdstone ⊖	d				07 46				08 13		08 21					08 36	08 46				09 13		09 17
Bushey	d										08 26						08 51						09 22
Watford Junction	a			07 40	07 52		08 01	08 11	08 20		08 29					08 43	08 54		09 00	09 09	09 20		09 25
	d		07u37	07 42	07 53		08 02	08 12	08 20		08 29				08u37	08 44	08 55		09 01	09 11	09 20		09 26
Kings Langley	d				07 58						08 34						08 59						09 30
Apsley	d				08 01						08 38						09 03						09 34
Hemel Hempstead	d			07 49	08 04			08 19	08 28		08 40					08 51	09 06			09 18	09 28		09 37
Berkhamsted	d			07 54	08 09			08 24	08 32		08 45					08 56	09 11			09 23	09 32		09 42
Tring	d			08 01	08a16				08 39		08a52					09 02	09a17				09 39		09a48
Cheddington	d			08 06												09 07							
Leighton Buzzard	d			08 11				08 37	08 48				08 42			09 12				09 36	09 48		
Bletchley	d			08 18				08 44	08 55				08 50			09 20				09 43	09 55		
Milton Keynes Central ■	a	07 50		08 23		08 05	08 25	08 49	09 01			08 40	08 54	08 50		09 26		09 13	09 24	09 48	10 01		
	d						08 31	08 50					08 54					09 13	09 25	09 49			
Wolverton	d							08 53					08 58							09 52			
Northampton	a						08 44	09 07					09 11						09 40	10 05			
Rugby	a						09 04			08 51			09 38						10 04			09 51	
Nuneaton	a						09 16												10 16				
Coventry	a		08 22							09 02			09 49		09 22			09 42				10 02	
Birmingham International ✈	a		08 33							09 13			10 04		09 33			09 53				10 13	
Birmingham New Street ■	a		08 45							09 27			10 17		09 45			10 08				10 27	
Sandwell & Dudley	a		08 57												09 57								
Wolverhampton ■ ⇌	a		09 11												10 11								

		VT	LM	VT	VT	LM	LM	VT	LM		LM	SN	VT	LM	VT	LM	VT	VT	LM	LM	VT
		◇■	◇■	◇■	◇■	■	■	◇■	◇■		◇■	■	◇■	■	◇■	◇■	◇■	◇■	■	■	◇■
		⊠		⊠	⊠			🚌					⊠		⊠		⊠	⊠			⊠
London Euston ■ ⊖	d	09 10	09 13	09 20	09 23	09 24	09 34	09 43	09 46		09 54		10 03	10 05	10 10	10 13	10 20	10 23	10 24	10 34	10 43
East Croydon ⇌	d											09 08									
Clapham Junction	d											09 39									
Imperial Wharf	d											09 44									
West Brompton ⊖	d											09 47									
Kensington (Olympia) ⊖	d											09 50									
Shepherd's Bush	d											09 53									
Wembley Central ⊖	d											10 08									
Harrow & Wealdstone ⊖	d						09 48					10 13		10 17						10 46	
Bushey	d						09 53							10 22						10 51	
Watford Junction	a					09 39	09 56		10 00		10 09	10 20		10 25					10 39	10 54	
	d				09u37	09 41	09 57		10 01		10 11	10 20		10 26				10u37	10 41	10 55	
Kings Langley	d						10 01							10 30						10 59	
Apsley	d						10 05							10 34						11 03	
Hemel Hempstead	d					09 48	10 08				10 18	10 28		10 37					10 48	11 06	
Berkhamsted	d					09 53	10 13				10 23	10 32		10 42					10 53	11 11	
Tring	d					09 59	10a19					10 39		10a48					10 59	11a17	
Cheddington	d					10 04													11 04		
Leighton Buzzard	d		09 42			10 09					10 36	10 48				10 42			11 09		
Bletchley	d		09 50			10 16					10 43	10 57				10 50			11 16		
Milton Keynes Central ■	a	09 40	09 54	09 50		10 21		10 13	10 24		10 48	11 02			10 40	10 54	10 50		11 21		11 13
	d		09 54					10 13	10 25		10 49					10 54					11 13
Wolverton	d		09 58								10 52					10 58					
Northampton	a		10 11						10 40		11 08					11 11					
Rugby	a		10 38						11 04	11 17			10 51			11 38					
Nuneaton	a								11 16												
Coventry	a		10 49		10 22			10 42		11 29			11 02			11 49		11 22			11 42
Birmingham International ✈	a		11 04		10 33			10 53		11 45			11 13			12 04		11 33			11 53
Birmingham New Street ■	a		11 16		10 45			11 06		12 01			11 27			12 16		11 45			12 08
Sandwell & Dudley	a				10 57													11 57			
Wolverhampton ■ ⇌	a				11 11			11 37										12 11			

London - Watford Junction, Milton Keynes Central, Northampton and West Midlands

Network Diagram - see first Page of Table 59

		LM		LM	SN	VT	LM	VT	LM	VT	VT	LM	LM	VT	LM		LM	SN	VT	LM	VT	LM	VT
		◇1		◇1	1	◇1 ⊐	1	◇1 ⊐	◇1	◇1 ⊐	◇1 ⊐	1	1	◇1 ⊐	◇1		◇1	1	◇1 ⊐	1	◇1 ⊐	◇1	◇1 ⊐
London Euston ⊖	d	10 46		10 54		11 03	11 04	11 10	11 13	11 20	11 23	11 24	11 34	11 43	11 46		11 54		12 03	12 04	12 10	12 13	12 20
East Croydon	d				10 10													11 11					
Clapham Junction	d				10 39													11 39					
Imperial Wharf	d				10 44													11 44					
West Brompton ⊖	d				10 47													11 47					
Kensington (Olympia) ⊖	d				10 50													11 50					
Shepherd's Bush	d				10 53													11 53					
Wembley Central ⊖	d				11 08													12 08					
Harrow & Wealdstone ⊖	d				11 13		11 17						11 46					12 13		12 17			
Bushey	d						11 22						11 51							12 22			
Watford Junction	a	11 00		11 10	11 20		11 25					11 39	11 54		12 00		12 09	12 20		12 25			
	d	11 01		11 11	11 20		11 26				11u37	11 41	11 55		12 01		12 11	12 20		12 26			
Kings Langley	d						11 30						11 59							12 30			
Apsley	d						11 34						12 03							12 34			
Hemel Hempstead	d			11 18	11 28		11 37					11 48	12 06				12 18	12 28		12 37			
Berkhamsted	d			11 23	11 32		11 42					11 53	12 11				12 23	12 32		12 42			
Tring	d				11 39		11a48					11 59	12a17					12 39		12a48			
Cheddington	d											12 04											
Leighton Buzzard	d			11 36	11 48				11 42			12 09					12 36	12 48				12 42	
Bletchley	d			11 43	11 55				11 50			12 16					12 43	12 55				12 50	
Milton Keynes Central	a	11 24		11 48	12 01			11 40	11 54	11 50		12 21		12 13	12 24		12 48	13 01			12 40	12 54	12 50
	d	11 25		11 49					11 54					12 13	12 25		12 49					12 54	
Wolverton	d			11 52					11 58								12 52					12 58	
Northampton	a	11 40		12 06					12 11						12 40		13 05					13 11	
Rugby	a	12 04	12 17			11 51			12 38						13 04	13 17			12 51			13 38	
Nuneaton	a	12 16													13 16								
Coventry	a		12 29			12 02			12 49		12 22			12 42		13 29			13 02			13 49	
Birmingham International ✈	a		12 45			12 13			13 04		12 33			12 53		13 45			13 13			14 04	
Birmingham New Street	a		13 01			12 27			13 16		12 45			13 08		14 01			13 27			14 16	
Sandwell & Dudley	a										12 57												
Wolverhampton	a										13 11												

		VT	LM	LM	VT	LM		LM	SN	VT	LM	VT	LM	VT	VT	LM	LM	VT	LM	LM	SN	VT
		◇1 ⊐	1	1	◇1 ⊐	◇1		◇1	1	◇1 ⊐	1	◇1 ⊐	◇1	◇1 ⊐	◇1 ⊐	1	1	◇1 ⊐	◇1	◇1	1	◇1 ⊐
London Euston ⊖	d	12 23	12 24	12 34	12 43	12 46		12 54		13 03	13 04	13 10	13 13	13 20	13 23	13 24	13 34	13 43	13 46	13 54		14 03
East Croydon	d								12 10												13 10	
Clapham Junction	d								12 39												13 39	
Imperial Wharf	d								12 44												13 44	
West Brompton ⊖	d								12 47												13 47	
Kensington (Olympia) ⊖	d								12 50												13 50	
Shepherd's Bush	d								12 53												13 53	
Wembley Central ⊖	d								13 08												14 08	
Harrow & Wealdstone ⊖	d			12 46					13 13		13 17						13 47				14 13	
Bushey	d			12 51							13 22						13 52					
Watford Junction	a		12 40	12 54		13 00		13 09	13 20		13 25					13 40	13 54		14 00	14 10	14 20	
	d	12u37	12 41	12 55		13 01		13 11	13 20		13 26				13u37	13 41	13 55		14 01	14 11	14 20	
Kings Langley	d			12 59							13 30						13 59					
Apsley	d			13 03							13 34						14 03					
Hemel Hempstead	d		12 48	13 06				13 18	13 28		13 37					13 48	14 06			14 18	14 28	
Berkhamsted	d		12 53	13 11				13 23	13 32		13 42					13 53	14 11			14 23	14 32	
Tring	d		12 59	13a17					13 39		13a48					13 59	14a17				14 39	
Cheddington	d		13 04													14 04						
Leighton Buzzard	d		13 09					13 36	13 48				13 42			14 09				14 36	14 48	
Bletchley	d		13 16					13 43	13 55				13 50			14 16				14 43	14 55	
Milton Keynes Central	a		13 21		13 13	13 24		13 48	14 01			13 40	13 54	13 50		14 23		14 13	14 24	14 48	15 01	
	d				13 13	13 25		13 49					13 54					14 13	14 25	14 49		
Wolverton	d							13 52					13 58							14 52		
Northampton	a					13 40		14 05					14 11						14 40	15 05		
Rugby	a					14 04	14 17			13 51			14 38						15 04			14 51
Nuneaton	a					14 16													15 16			
Coventry	a	13 22			13 42		14 29			14 02			14 49		14 22			14 42				15 02
Birmingham International ✈	a	13 33			13 53		14 45			14 13			15 04		14 33			14 53				15 13
Birmingham New Street	a	13 45			14 08		15 01			14 27			15 15		14 45			15 08				15 27
Sandwell & Dudley	a	13 57													14 57							
Wolverhampton	a	14 11													15 11							

London - Watford Junction, Milton Keynes Central, Northampton and West Midlands

Network Diagram - see first Page of Table 59

		LM	VT	LM	VT	VT	LM	LM	VT	LM	LM	SN	VT	LM	VT	LM	VT	VT	LM	LM	VT	LM	
		1	◇1 ⊐	◇1	◇1 ⊐	◇1 ⊐	1	1	1 ⊐	◇1	◇1	1	◇1 ⊐	1	◇1 ⊐	◇1	◇1 ⊐	◇1 ⊐	1	1	◇1 ⊐	◇1	
London Euston ⊖	d	14 04	14 10	14 13	14 20	14 23	14 24	14 34	14 43	14 46	14 54		15 03	15 04	15 10	15 13	15 20	15 23	15 24	15 34	15 43	15 46	
East Croydon	d											14 10											
Clapham Junction	d											14 39											
Imperial Wharf	d											14 44											
West Brompton ⊖	d											14 47											
Kensington (Olympia) ⊖	d											14 50											
Shepherd's Bush	d											14 53											
Wembley Central ⊖	d											15 08											
Harrow & Wealdstone ⊖	d	14 17						14 46				15 13		15 17						15 47			
Bushey	d	14 22						14 51						15 22						15 52			
Watford Junction	a	14 25					14 39	14 54		15 00	15 09	15 20		15 25					15 39	15 54		16 00	
	d	14 26				14u37	14 41	14 55		15 01	15 11	15 20		15 26				15u37	15 41	15 55		16 01	
Kings Langley	d	14 30						14 59						15 30						15 59			
Apsley	d	14 34						15 03						15 34						16 03			
Hemel Hempstead	d	14 37					14 48	15 06			15 18	15 28		15 37					15 48	16 06			
Berkhamsted	d	14 42					14 53	15 11			15 23	15 32		15 42					15 53	16 11			
Tring	d	14a48					14 59	15a17				15 39		15a48					15 59	16a17			
Cheddington	d						15 04												16 04				
Leighton Buzzard	d			14 42			15 09				15 36	15 48				15 42			16 09				
Bletchley	d			14 50			15 16				15 43	15 55				15 50			16 16				
Milton Keynes Central	a		14 40	14 54	14 50		15 21		15 13	15 24	15 48	16 01			15 40	15 54	15 50		16 21		16 13	16 24	
	d			14 54					15 13	15 25	15 49					15 54					16 13	16 25	
Wolverton	d			14 58							15 52					15 58							
Northampton	a			15 11						15 40	16 05					16 11						16 40	
Rugby	a			15 38						16 04			15 51			16 38						17 04	17 17
Nuneaton	a									16 16												17 16	
Coventry	a			15 49		15 22			15 42				16 02			16 49		16 22			16 42		17 29
Birmingham International ✈	a			16 04		15 33			15 53				16 13			17 04		16 33			16 53		17 45
Birmingham New Street	a			16 16		15 45			16 06				16 27			17 16		16 45			17 08		18 01
Sandwell & Dudley	a					15 57												16 57					
Wolverhampton	a					16 11			16 37									17 11					

		LM	SN	VT	LM	VT	LM	VT	VT	LM	VT	LM	VT	LM	LM	SN	VT	LM	VT	LM	LM	VT	VT
		◇1	1	◇1 ⊐	1	◇1 ⊐	◇1	◇1 ⊐	◇1 ⊐	1	◇1 ⊐	1	◇1 ⊐	◇1	1	1	◇1 ⊠	1	◇1 ⊠	◇1	1	◇1 ⊠	◇1 ⊠
London Euston ⊖	d	15 54		16 03	16 04	16 10	16 13	16 20	16 23	16 24	16 33	16 34	16 43	16 48	16 54		17 03	17 05	17 10	17 13	17 14	17 20	17 23
East Croydon	d		15 10													16 10							
Clapham Junction	d		15 39													16 39							
Imperial Wharf	d		15 44													16 44							
West Brompton ⊖	d		15 47													16 47							
Kensington (Olympia) ⊖	d		15 50													16 50							
Shepherd's Bush	d		15 53													16 53							
Wembley Central ⊖	d		16 08													17 08							
Harrow & Wealdstone ⊖	d		16 13		16 17							16 46			17 06	17 13		17 19			17 26		
Bushey	d				16 22							16 51			17 11						17 31		
Watford Junction	a	16 09	16 20		16 25					16 39		16 54			17 14	17 20		17 26			17 34		
	d	16 11	16 20		16 26				16u37	16 41		16 55			17 14	17 21		17 27			17 34		17u37
Kings Langley	d				16 30							16 59						17 31			17 39		
Apsley	d				16 34							17 03			17 20						17 42		
Hemel Hempstead	d	16 18	16 28		16 37					16 48		17 06			17 23	17 28		17 36					
Berkhamsted	d	16 23	16 32		16 42					16 53		17 11			17 28	17 33		17 41					
Tring	d		16 39		16a48					16 59		17a19			17a36	17 38		17 46			17a52		
Cheddington	d									17 04								17 51					
Leighton Buzzard	d	16 36	16 48				16 42			17 09				17 19		17 47				17 42			
Bletchley	d	16 43	16 56				16 50			17 16						17 54		18 01					
Milton Keynes Central	a	16 48	17 00				16 54			17 22				17 28		17 59		18 06		17 51			
	d	16 49					16 54						17u13	17 29					17u40	17 52			
Wolverton	d	16 52					16 58							17 33						17 56			
Northampton	a	17 05					17 13							17 46						18 10			
Rugby	a	17 38		16 51							17 21			18 17			17 51			18 38			
Nuneaton	a																		18 11				
Coventry	a	17 49		17 02					17 22				17 42	18 29			18 02			18 49			18 22
Birmingham International ✈	a	18 04		17 13					17 33				17 53	18 45			18 13			19 04			18 33
Birmingham New Street	a	18 17		17 27					17 45				18 08	19 01			18 27			19 17			18 45
Sandwell & Dudley	a								17 57														18 57
Wolverhampton	a								18 11														19 11

London - Watford Junction, Milton Keynes Central, Northampton and West Midlands

Network Diagram - see first Page of Table 59

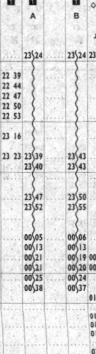

Station		LM	LM	VT	LM	LM	VT	LM	LM	SN	VT	LM	VT	LM	LM	VT	LM	VT	LM	VT	LM	LM
		1	1	◇1 ⊠	1	1	◇1 ⊠	1	1	1	◇1 ⊠	1	◇1 ⊠	1	◇1 A	◇1 ⊠	1	◇1 ⊠	◇1	◇1 ⊠	1	1
London Euston 15 ⊖	d	17 24	17 30	17 33	17 34	17 41	17 43	17 46	17 51		18 03	18 05	18 10	18 12	18 13	18 20	18 21	18 23	18 29	18 33	18 34	18 40
East Croydon	d									17 10												
Clapham Junction	d									17 39												
Imperial Wharf	d									17 44												
West Brompton ⊖	d									17 47												
Kensington (Olympia) ⊖	d									17 50												
Shepherd's Bush	d									17 53												
Wembley Central ⊖	d									18 08												
Harrow & Wealdstone ⊖	d				17 46				18 03	18 13		18 18					18 34				18 46	
Bushey	d				17 52	17 56								18 27							18 52	18 57
Watford Junction	a	17 43	17 48		17 55	18 00			18 09	18 20		18 25		18 30			18 40		18 46		18 55	19 00
	d	17 44	17 49			18 01			18 11	18 20		18 25		18 31			18 41	18u37	18 47		18 56	19 01
Kings Langley	d					18 05						18 30					18 46					19 05
Apsley	d		17 55									18 33							18 53			19 09
Hemel Hempstead	d	17 51	17 58			18 10			18 18	18 28				18 38			18 51				19 03	19 12
Berkhamsted	d	17 56				18 15			18 23	18 32				18 43					18 59			19 16
Tring	d		18 05			18a22				18 38		18 43		18a53			18 59				19 12	19a26
Cheddington	d		18 10									18 48							19 08		19 17	
Leighton Buzzard	d	18 09						18 19		18 47		18 53			18 42		19 07				19 23	
Bletchley	d	18 16	18 22						18 41	18 54		19 01							19 18		19a33	
Milton Keynes Central 10	a	18 21	18 28					18 30	18 45	19 00		19 06			18 52		19 19		19 23			
	d	18 21					18u13	18 32	18 46			19 07	18u40		18 54				19 23			
Wolverton	d	18 25						18 36	18 49			19 10			18 57				19 27			
Northampton	a	18 37						18 50	19 03			19 25			19 10				19 39			
Rugby	a	19 03		18 21				19 17			18 51				19 38				20 04	19 22		
Nuneaton	a												19 12						20 16			
Coventry	a						18 42	19 29			19 02				19 49			19 22				
Birmingham International ✈	a						18 53	19 45			19 13				20 04			19 33				
Birmingham New Street 12	a						19 08	20 01			19 27				20 16			19 45				
Sandwell & Dudley	a																	19 58				
Wolverhampton 7	a																	20 12				

Station		VT	VT FO	LM	LM	SN	VT	LM	VT	VT	VT	LM	VT	VT	LM	LM	VT	LM	LM	SN	VT	LM	VT
		◇1 ⊠	◇ ☕	◇1	1	1	▪ 1 ☕	1	▪ 1 ☕	▪ 1 ☕	▪ 1 ☕	◇1	▪ 1 ☕	▪ 1 ☕	1	1	◇1 ☕	◇1	◇1	1	◇1 ☕	1	◇1 ☕
London Euston 15 ⊖	d	18 43	18 46	18 49	18 54		19 03	19 04	19 07	19 10	19 10	19 13	19 20	19 23	19 24	19 34	19 43	19 46	19 54		20 03	20 04	20 07
East Croydon	d					18 10														19 10			
Clapham Junction	d					18 39														19 39			
Imperial Wharf	d					18 44														19 44			
West Brompton ⊖	d					18 47														19 47			
Kensington (Olympia) ⊖	d					18 50														19 50			
Shepherd's Bush	d					18 53														19 53			
Wembley Central ⊖	d					19 08														20 08			
Harrow & Wealdstone ⊖	d				19 06	19 13		19 17								19 46				20 13		20 17	
Bushey	d							19 22								19 51						20 22	
Watford Junction	a				19 12	19 20		19 25							19 40	19 54			20 09	20 20		20 25	
	d				19 13	19 21		19 26						19u37	19 42	19 55			20 11	20 20		20 26	
Kings Langley	d							19 30								19 59						20 30	
Apsley	d							19 34								20 03						20 34	
Hemel Hempstead	d				19 20	19 28		19 37							19 49	20 06			20 18	20 28		20 37	
Berkhamsted	d				19 25	19 33		19 42							19 54	20 11			20 23	20 32		20 42	
Tring	d				19 30	19 40		19a48							20 01	20a17				20 39		20a48	
Cheddington	d														20 06								
Leighton Buzzard	d			19 19	19 38	19 52						19 43			20 12			20 18	20 36	20 48			
Bletchley	d			19 25	19 46	20 01									20 19				20 43	20 55			
Milton Keynes Central 10	a	19 13		19 30	19 52	20 06					19 40	19 55	19 50		20 24		20 13	20 28	20 48	21 01			
	d	19 13		19 31								19 56					20 13	20 30	20 49				
Wolverton	d			19 35								19 59						20 33	20 52				
Northampton	a			19 49								20 11						20 47	21 05				
Rugby	a		19 38	20 17			19 51					20 38						21 17	21 38		20 51		
Nuneaton	a								20 02														21 02
Coventry	a	19 42		20 29			20 02					20 49		20 22			20 42	21 29	21 49		21 02		
Birmingham International ✈	a	19 53		20 45			20 13					21 04		20 33			20 53	21 45	22 04		21 13		
Birmingham New Street 12	a	20 06		21 01			20 27					21 16		20 45			21 06	22 01	22 17		21 25		
Sandwell & Dudley	a													20 58			21 23						
Wolverhampton 7	a	20 36												21 12			21 38				21 56		

A ◇ from Coventry

London - Watford Junction, Milton Keynes Central, Northampton and West Midlands

Network Diagram - see first Page of Table 59

Station		VT	LM	VT	LM	LM	VT	LM	LM	VT	VT	SN	LM	VT	VT	LM	SR	LM	LM	VT	LM	LM
		◇1 ☕	◇1	◇1 ☕	1	1	◇1 ☕	◇1	1	◇1 ☕	◇1 ☕	1	1	◇1 ☕	◇1 ☕	◇1	B ☕	1	1	◇1 ☕	◇1	1
London Euston 15 ⊖	d	20 10	20 13	20 23	20 24	20 34	20 43	20 46	20 54	21 00	21 03		21 04	21 07	21 10	21 13	21 15	21 24	21 34	21 43	21 46	21 54
East Croydon	d																					
Clapham Junction	d											20 39										
Imperial Wharf	d											20 44										
West Brompton ⊖	d											20 47										
Kensington (Olympia) ⊖	d											20 50										
Shepherd's Bush	d											20 53										
Wembley Central ⊖	d											21 08										
Harrow & Wealdstone ⊖	d					20 46						21 13	21 17						21 46			
Bushey	d					20 51							21 22						21 51			
Watford Junction	a				20 40	20 54			21 10			21 21	21 25					21 39	21 53			22 09
	d			20u37	20 42	20 55			21 11			21 21	21 26		21u25			21 41	21 54	21u58		22 11
Kings Langley	d					20 59							21 30						21 58			
Apsley	d					21 03							21 34						22 02			
Hemel Hempstead	d				20 49	21 06			21 18			21 28	21 36					21 48	22 05			22 18
Berkhamsted	d				20 55	21 11			21 23			21 33	21 41					21 53	22 10			22 23
Tring	d				21 00	21a17						21 39	21 48						22 16			22 27
Cheddington	d				21 05								21 53						22 22			
Leighton Buzzard	d		20 42		21 10			21 18	21 36			21 50	21 57			21 44		22 07	22 26		22 18	22 37
Bletchley	d		20 50		21 17				21 43			21 58	22a04			21 52		22 15	22 33			22 45
Milton Keynes Central 10	a	20 40	20 54		21 23		21 13	21 27	21 48	21 30	21 33	22 05		21 37		21 56		22 21	22 38	22 17	22 32	22 53
	d		20 55				21 13	21 29	21 49		21 34			21 38		21 57				22 17	22 32	22 56
Wolverton	d		20 59					21 32	21 52							22 00					22 36	22 59
Northampton	a		21 13					21 46	22 05							22 14					22 49	23 13
Rugby	a							22 17			21 56				22 02	22 38					23 17	
Nuneaton	a													22 07								
Coventry	a			21 22			21 42	22 29			22 06					22 49				22 46	23 29	
Birmingham International ✈	a			21 33			21 53	22 45			22 18					23 06				23 00	23 47	
Birmingham New Street 12	a			21 46			22 06	23 02			22 29					23 19				23 16	00 04	
Sandwell & Dudley	a			21 58			22 23				22 40									23 33		
Wolverhampton 7	a			22 12			22 38				22 56									23 47		

Station		SN	VT	LM	LM	VT	LM	LM	SN	LM	LM	VT FX	VT FO	LM	SR
		1	◇1 ☕	1	1	◇1 ☕	1	1	1	1 A	1 B	◇1 ☕	◇1 ☕	1	B ☕
London Euston 15 ⊖	d		22 00	22 04	22 24	22 30	22 34	22 54		23 24	23 24	23 30	23 30	23 34	23 50
East Croydon	d														
Clapham Junction	d	21 39							22 39						
Imperial Wharf	d	21 44							22 44						
West Brompton ⊖	d	21 47							22 47						
Kensington (Olympia) ⊖	d	21 50							22 50						
Shepherd's Bush	d	21 53							22 53						
Wembley Central ⊖	d														
Harrow & Wealdstone ⊖	d	22 16		22 17			22 49	23 06	23 16					23 46	
Bushey	d			22s22			22 54							23 51	
Watford Junction	a	22 23		22 25	22 39		22 57	23 12	23 23	23 39	23 43			23 54	
	d			22 26	22 40	22u45	22 58	23 12		23 40	23 43			23 54	
Kings Langley	d			22 30			23 02	23 17						23 59	
Apsley	d			22 33			23 06	23 20						00 02	
Hemel Hempstead	d			22 36	22 47		23 09	23 23		23 47	23 50			00 05	
Berkhamsted	d			22 40	22 52		23 14	23 28		23 52	23 55			00 09	
Tring	d			22 45			23 18	23 34						00 15	
Cheddington	d						23 24							00 20	
Leighton Buzzard	d			22 56	23 06		23 30	23 41		00 05	00 06			00 26	
Bletchley	d			23 05	23 13		23 37	23 49		00 13	00 13			00 33	
Milton Keynes Central 10	a		22 30	23 11	23 21	23 28	23 45	23 55		00 21	00 19	00 27	00 27	00 41	
	d		22 31		23 22	23 29		23 55		00 21	00 20	00 28	00 28		
Wolverton	d				23 25			23 59		00 25	00 24				
Northampton	a				23 39			00 13		00 38	00 37				
Rugby	a		22 52			23 58						01 00	01 05		
Nuneaton	a		23 03												
Coventry	a					00 10						01 13	01 18		
Birmingham International ✈	a					00 21						01 24	01 29		
Birmingham New Street 12	a					00 32						01 36	01 41		
Sandwell & Dudley	a														
Wolverhampton 7	a					01 03						02 07	02 10		

A until 22 June

B from 25 June until 29 June

London - Watford Junction, Milton Keynes Central, Northampton and West Midlands

Network Diagram - see first Page of Table 59

	LM MO ◇1	LM MX ◇1	VT MO ◇1 ⊏P	LM MO 1	VT MO ◇1 ⊏P	VT MX ◇1 ⊏P	LM MX 1	LM MO ◇1	LM MX 1	VT MO ◇1 A ⊏P	VT MX ◇1 B ⊏P	LM MX 1	LM MO ◇1	VT ◇1 C ⊏P	VT MX ◇1 D ⊏P	LM 1	VT MX ◇1 D ⊏P	VT ◇1 C ⊏P	LM MO 1	LM MX 1	LM 1 E	VT ◇1 C ⊏P
London Euston 15 ⊖ d	21p28	21p46	21p55	22p00	22p25	22p30	22p54	22p58	23p24	23p25	23p30	23p34	23p34	23p45	23p45	00 04	00 10	00 10	00 34	00 34	00 50	01 00
East Croydon d																						
Clapham Junction d																						
Imperial Wharf d																						
West Brompton ⊖ d																						
Kensington (Olympia) ⊖ d																						
Shepherd's Bush d																						
Wembley Central ⊖ d																			00 43	00 45		
Harrow & Wealdstone ⊖ d	21p40			22p12			23p06	23p10				23p46	23p46			00 16			00 48	00 50	01 03	
Bushey d	21b45											23p51	23b51						00s53	00 55		
Watford Junction a	21p47			22p18			23p12	23p16	23p43			23p54	23p54			00 22		00 24	00 56	00 57	01 09	
d	21p48		22c09	22p19	22c39	22c45	23p12	23p17	23p43	23c40		23p54	23p55			00 23		00 25	00 58	00 58	01 09	
Kings Langley d	21p52						23p17	23p21				23p59	23p59						01 02	01 02		
Apsley d	21p56						23p20	23p25				00 02	00 03						01 06	01 06		
Hemel Hempstead d	21p59			22p26			23p23	23p28	23p50			00 05	00 06			00 30			01 09	01 09	01 16	
Berkhamsted d	22p04			22p31			23p28	23p33	23p55			00 09	00 11			00 35			01 14	01 14	01 21	
Tring d				22p35			23p34	23p37				00 15	00 15			00 41			01 18	01 19	01 25	
Cheddington d				22p41				23p43				00 20	00 21						01 24	01 25		
Leighton Buzzard d	22p17	22p18		22p47			23p41	23p49	00 06			00 26	00 27			00 50			01 30	01 31	01 38	
Bletchley d	22p24			22p54			23p49	23p56	00 13			00 33	00 34			00 57			01 37	01 38	01 45	
Milton Keynes Central 10 a	22p32	22p32	22p42	23p02	23p11	23p28	23p55	00 04	00 19	00 11	00 27	00 41	00 42			01 05	00s40	00s44	01 45	01 46	01 51	
d	22p32	22p32	22p44	23p03	23p12	23p29	23p55	00 05	00 20	00 12	00 28		00 43			01 05			01 46	01 47		
Wolverton d	22p36	22p36		23p06			23p59	00 08	00 24				00 46			01 09			01 49	01 50		
Northampton a	22p49	22p49		23p20			00 13	00 22	00 37				01 00			01 22			02 03	02 04		
Rugby a	23p13	23p17	23p20	23p54	23p44	23p58				00s46	01 00			00s33	00s47		01s02	01s06				01s48
Nuneaton a														00s44	00s58							01s59
Coventry a	23p25	23p29	23p31	00 05	23p55	00 10				00s57	01 13						01s13	01s17				
Birmingham International ✈ a	23p52	23p47	23p42		00 06	00 21				01s08	01 24						01s24	01s28				
Birmingham New Street 12 a	00 04	00 04	23p54		00 19	00 32				01s21	01 36						01s39	01s43				
Sandwell & Dudley a																						
Wolverhampton 7 a			00 15		00 41	01 03				01 53	02 07						01 57	02 01				

	VT MX ◇1 D ⊏P	LM 1 F	VT 1 E ⊏P	LM 1 E	LM MO 1 A	LM MX 1 B	LM 1 E	SN 1	LM ◇1	VT ◇1 ⊠	LM ◇1	VT ◇1 ⊠	SN 1	VT ◇1 ⊠	LM 1	SN 1	VT ◇1 ⊠	VT ◇1 ⊠	LM ◇1	LM 1	VT ◇1 ⊠	VT ◇1 ⊠
London Euston 15 ⊖ d	01 00	01 04	01 10	01 34	01 34	01 34	02 00			05 27	05 30	05 39		06 03	06 04		06 17	06 23	06 24	06 34	06 36	06 43
East Croydon d																						
Clapham Junction d													05 30			05 55						
Imperial Wharf d								05 07					05 39			06 00						
West Brompton ⊖ d								05 10					05 41			06 03						
Kensington (Olympia) ⊖ d								05 14					05 44			06 07						
Shepherd's Bush d								05 17					05 47			06 10						
Wembley Central ⊖ d				01 45	01 45	01 45							06 02			06 24						
Harrow & Wealdstone ⊖ d				01 50	01 50	01 50	02 12	05 33			05 43		06 07		06 16	06 29				06 47		
Bushey d																						
Watford Junction a				01 56	01 56	01 56	02 19	05 40			05 50		06 14		06 22	06 36			06 39	06 53		
d				01 57	01 57	01 57	02 19			05u45	05 50	06u02	06 14		06 23			06u37	06 41	06 54		
Kings Langley d											05 55				06 27					06 58		
Apsley d											05 59				06 31					07 02		
Hemel Hempstead d				02 04	02 04	02 04	02 26				06 01		06 22		06 34				06 48	07 05		
Berkhamsted d				02 09	02 09	02 09	02 31				06 06		06 26		06 39				06 53	07 10		
Tring d				02 13	02 13	02 14	02 36				06 13		06 33		06a47				06 59	07 16		
Cheddington d											06 18								07 05	07 21		
Leighton Buzzard d		01 53		02 22	02 22	02 23	02 44				06 23		06 42						07 10	07 26		
Bletchley d		02 00		02 29	02 29	02 30	02 51		05 17		06 30		06 49						07 17	07 33		
Milton Keynes Central 10 a		02 04		02 33	02 37	02 38	02 58		05 21	06 09	06 35	06 22	06 55				06 47		07 22	07 38		07 13
d		02 05		02 34			02 58		05 21	06 10	06 36	06 22							07 22			07 13
Wolverton d		02 08		02 37			03 02		05 25		06 39								07 26			
Northampton a		02 24		02 53			03 20		05 37		06 52								07 42			
Rugby a	01s48		01s58						06 02		07 17	06 44		06 51					08 04			
Nuneaton a	02s05								06 16	06 38									08 17			
Coventry a			02s09								07 29			07 02				07 22				07 42
Birmingham International ✈ a			02s20								07 45			07 13				07 33				07 53
Birmingham New Street 12 a			02s34								08 03			07 27				07 45				08 08
Sandwell & Dudley a																		07 57				
Wolverhampton 7 a			02 52															08 11				

A from 2 July until 23 July, 20 August, 27 August
B not from 31 July until 10 August, from 30 August until 7 September
C 30 July, 6 August, 13 August, 3 September, 10 September
D from 31 July until 7 September, not from 14 August until 29 August
E from 30 July until 10 September, not from 14 August until 29 August
F from 27 July until 10 September, not from 14 August until 29 August
b Previous night, stops to set down only
c Previous night, stops to pick up only

London - Watford Junction, Milton Keynes Central, Northampton and West Midlands

Network Diagram - see first Page of Table 59

	LM ◇1	VT ◇1 ⊠	SN 1	VT ◇1 ⊠	LM 1	VT ◇1 ⊠	LM ◇1	VT ◇1 ⊠	VT ◇1 ⊠	LM 1	LM 1	VT ◇1 ⊠	LM ◇1	LM ◇1	SN 1	VT ◇1 A ⊠	VT ◇1 B ⊠	LM 1	VT ◇1 ⊠	LM ◇1	VT ◇1 ⊠
London Euston 15 ⊖ d	06 53	06 55		07 03	07 04	07 10	07 13	07 20	07 23	07 24	07 34	07 35	07 47	07 54		08 03	08 03	08 05	08 10	08 13	08 20
East Croydon d																					
Clapham Junction d			06 38												07 39						
Imperial Wharf d			06 42												07 44						
West Brompton ⊖ d			06 45												07 47						
Kensington (Olympia) ⊖ d			06 49												07 50						
Shepherd's Bush d			06 52												07 53						
Wembley Central ⊖ d			07 07												08 08						
Harrow & Wealdstone ⊖ d			07 12		07 17						07 46				08 13			08 21			
Bushey d																		08 26			
Watford Junction a	07 08		07 19		07 24					07 40	07 52		08 01	08 11	08 20			08 29			
d	07 10		07 19		07 24				07u37	07 42	07 53		08 02	08 12	08 20			08 29			
Kings Langley d					07 29						07 58							08 34			
Apsley d					07 32						08 01							08 38			
Hemel Hempstead d	07 17		07 27		07 35					07 49	08 04			08 19	08 28			08 40			
Berkhamsted d	07 22		07 32		07 40					07 54	08 09			08 24	08 32			08 45			
Tring d			07 39		07a47					08 01	08a16				08 39			08a52			
Cheddington d										08 06											
Leighton Buzzard d	07 35		07 51				07 42			08 11				08 37	08 48					08 42	
Bletchley d	07 43		07 58				07 50			08 18				08 44	08 55					08 50	
Milton Keynes Central 10 a	07 48	07 25	08 03			07 40	07 54	07 50		08 23		08 05	08 25	08 49	09 01				08 40	08 54	08 50
d	07 48						07 54						08 31	08 50						08 54	
Wolverton d	07 52						07 58							08 53						08 58	
Northampton a	08 05						08 11						08 44	09 07						09 11	
Rugby a				07 51			08 38						09 04			08 51	08 51			09 38	
Nuneaton a													09 16								
Coventry a				08 02			08 49		08 22							09 02	09 02			09 49	
Birmingham International ✈ a				08 12			09 04		08 33							09 12	09 13			10 04	
Birmingham New Street 12 a				08 27			09 17		08 45							09 27	09 27			10 17	
Sandwell & Dudley a									08 57												
Wolverhampton 7 a									09 11												

	VT ◇1 ⊠	LM 1	LM 1	VT ◇1 ⊠	LM ◇1	LM ◇1	SN 1	VT ◇1 ⊠	LM 1	VT ◇1 ⊠	LM ◇1	VT ◇1 ⊠	VT ◇1 ⊠	LM 1	LM 1	VT ◇1 ⊠		LM ◇1	LM ◇1	SN 1	VT ◇1 ⊠	LM 1
London Euston 15 ⊖ d	08 23	08 24	08 34	08 43	08 46	08 54		09 03	09 05	09 10	09 13	09 20	09 23	09 24	09 34	09 43		09 46	09 54		10 03	10 05
East Croydon d							08 07													09 08		
Clapham Junction d							08 39													09 39		
Imperial Wharf d							08 44													09 44		
West Brompton ⊖ d							08 47													09 47		
Kensington (Olympia) ⊖ d							08 50													09 50		
Shepherd's Bush d							08 53													09 53		
Wembley Central ⊖ d							09 08													10 08		
Harrow & Wealdstone ⊖ d		08 36	08 46				09 13		09 17						09 48					10 13		10 17
Bushey d			08 51						09 22						09 53							10 22
Watford Junction a		08 43	08 54		09 00	09 09	09 20		09 25					09 39	09 56			10 00	10 09	10 20		10 25
d	08u37	08 44	08 55		09 01	09 11	09 20		09 26				09u37	09 41	09 57			10 01	10 11	10 20		10 26
Kings Langley d			08 59						09 30						10 01							10 30
Apsley d			09 03						09 34						10 05							10 34
Hemel Hempstead d		08 51	09 06			09 18	09 28		09 37					09 48	10 08				10 18	10 28		10 37
Berkhamsted d		08 56	09 11			09 23	09 32		09 42					09 53	10 13				10 23	10 32		10 42
Tring d		09 02	09a17				09 39		09a48					09 59	10a19					10 39		10a48
Cheddington d		09 07												10 04								
Leighton Buzzard d		09 12				09 36	09 48				09 42			10 09					10 36	10 48		
Bletchley d		09 20				09 43	09 55				09 50			10 16					10 43	10 57		
Milton Keynes Central 10 a		09 26		09 13	09 24	09 48	10 01			09 40	09 54	09 50		10 21		10 13		10 24	10 48	11 02		
d				09 13	09 25	09 49					09 54					10 13		10 25	10 49			
Wolverton d						09 52					09 58								10 52			
Northampton a					09 40	10 05					10 11							10 40	11 08			
Rugby a					10 04			09 51			10 38						11 04	11 17			10 51	
Nuneaton a					10 16												11 16					
Coventry a	09 22			09 42				10 02			10 49		10 22			10 42		11 29			11 02	
Birmingham International ✈ a	09 33			09 53				10 13			11 04		10 33			10 53		11 45			11 13	
Birmingham New Street 12 a	09 45			10 08				10 27			11 16		10 45			11 08		12 01			11 27	
Sandwell & Dudley a	09 57												10 57									
Wolverhampton 7 a	10 11			10 37									11 11									

A not from 27 July until 10 August, from 29 August until 7 September
B from 27 July until 7 September, not from 13 August until 28 August

London - Watford Junction, Milton Keynes Central, Northampton and West Midlands

Network Diagram - see first Page of Table 59

		VT	LM	VT	VT	LM	LM	VT	LM		LM	SN	VT	LM	VT	LM	VT	VT	LM	LM	VT	LM	
		◇1 ⊠	◇1	◇1 ⊠	◇1 ⊠	1	1	◇1 ⊠	◇1		◇1	1	◇1 ☕	1	◇1 ☕	◇1	◇1 ☕	◇1 ☕	1	1	◇1 ☕	◇1	
London Euston 15 ⊖	d	10 10	10 13	10 20	10 23	10 24	10 34	10 43	10 46		10 54		11 03	11 04	11 10	11 13	11 20	11 23	11 24	11 34	11 43	11 46	
East Croydon	d											10 10											
Clapham Junction	d											10 39											
Imperial Wharf	d											10 44											
West Brompton ⊖	d											10 47											
Kensington (Olympia) ⊖	d											10 50											
Shepherd's Bush	d											10 53											
Wembley Central ⊖	d											11 08											
Harrow & Wealdstone ⊖	d						10 46					11 13		11 17						11 46			
Bushey	d						10 51							11 22						11 51			
Watford Junction	a					10 39	10 54		11 00		11 10	11 20		11 25					11 39	11 54		12 00	
	d				10u37	10 41	10 55		11 01		11 11	11 20		11 26				11u37	11 41	11 55		12 01	
Kings Langley	d						10 59							11 30						11 59			
Apsley	d						11 03							11 34						12 03			
Hemel Hempstead	d					10 48	11 06				11 18	11 28		11 37					11 48	12 06			
Berkhamsted	d					10 53	11 11				11 23	11 32		11 42					11 53	12 11			
Tring	d					10 59	11a17					11 39		11a48					11 59	12a17			
Cheddington	d					11 04													12 04				
Leighton Buzzard	d		10 42			11 09					11 36	11 48				11 42			12 09				
Bletchley	d		10 50			11 16					11 43	11 55				11 50			12 16				
Milton Keynes Central 10	a	10 40	10 54	10 50		11 21		11 13	11 24		11 48	12 01			11 40	11 54	11 50		12 21		12 13	12 24	
	d		10 54					11 13	11 25		11 49					11 54					12 13	12 25	
Wolverton	d		10 58								11 52					11 58							
Northampton	a		11 11						11 40		12 06					12 11						12 40	
Rugby	a		11 38						12 04	12 17			11 51			12 38						13 04	13 17
Nuneaton	a								12 16													13 16	
Coventry	a		11 49		11 22			11 42		12 29			12 02			12 49		12 22			12 42		13 29
Birmingham International ✈	a		12 04		11 33			11 53		12 45			12 13			13 04		12 33			12 53		13 45
Birmingham New Street 12	a		12 16		11 45			12 08		13 01			12 27			13 16		12 45			13 08		14 01
Sandwell & Dudley	a				11 57													12 57					
Wolverhampton 7	a				12 11													13 11					

		LM	SN	VT	LM	VT	LM	VT	VT	LM	LM	VT	LM		LM	SN	VT	LM	VT	LM	VT	VT
		◇1	1	◇1 ☕	1	◇1 ☕	◇1	◇1 ☕	◇1 ☕	1	1	◇1 ☕	◇1		◇1	1	◇1 ☕	1	◇1 ☕	◇1	◇1 ☕	◇1 ☕
London Euston 15 ⊖	d	11 54		12 03	12 04	12 10	12 13	12 20	12 23	12 24	12 34	12 43	12 46		12 54		13 03	13 04	13 10	13 13	13 20	13 23
East Croydon	d		11 11													12 10						
Clapham Junction	d		11 39													12 39						
Imperial Wharf	d		11 44													12 44						
West Brompton ⊖	d		11 47													12 47						
Kensington (Olympia) ⊖	d		11 50													12 50						
Shepherd's Bush	d		11 53													12 53						
Wembley Central ⊖	d		12 08													13 08						
Harrow & Wealdstone ⊖	d		12 13		12 17						12 46					13 13		13 17				
Bushey	d				12 22						12 51							13 22				
Watford Junction	a	12 09	12 20		12 25					12 40	12 54		13 00		13 09	13 20		13 25				
	d	12 11	12 20		12 26				12u37	12 41	12 55		13 01		13 11	13 20		13 26				13u37
Kings Langley	d				12 30						12 59							13 30				
Apsley	d				12 34						13 03							13 34				
Hemel Hempstead	d	12 18	12 28		12 37					12 48	13 06				13 18	13 28		13 37				
Berkhamsted	d	12 23	12 32		12 42					12 53	13 11				13 23	13 32		13 42				
Tring	d		12 39		12a48					12 59	13a17					13 39		13a48				
Cheddington	d									13 04												
Leighton Buzzard	d	12 36	12 48				12 42			13 09					13 36	13 48				13 42		
Bletchley	d	12 43	12 55				12 50			13 16					13 43	13 55				13 50		
Milton Keynes Central 10	a	12 48	13 01			12 40	12 54	12 50		13 21		13 13	13 24		13 48	14 01			13 40	13 54	13 50	
	d	12 49					12 54					13 13	13 25		13 49					13 54		
Wolverton	d	12 52					12 58								13 52					13 58		
Northampton	a	13 05					13 11						13 40		14 05					14 11		
Rugby	a			12 51			13 38						14 04	14 17			13 51			14 38		
Nuneaton	a												14 16									
Coventry	a			13 02			13 49		13 22			13 42		14 29			14 02			14 49		14 22
Birmingham International ✈	a			13 13			14 04		13 33			13 53		14 45			14 13			15 04		14 33
Birmingham New Street 12	a			13 27			14 16		13 45			14 08		15 01			14 27			15 15		14 45
Sandwell & Dudley	a								13 57													14 57
Wolverhampton 7	a								14 11													15 11

London - Watford Junction, Milton Keynes Central, Northampton and West Midlands

Network Diagram - see first Page of Table 59

		LM	LM	VT	LM	LM	SN	VT	LM	VT	LM	VT	VT	LM	LM	VT	LM	LM	SN	VT	LM	VT	LM
		1	1	◇1 ☕	◇1	◇1	1	◇1 ☕	1	◇1 ☕	◇1	◇1 ☕	◇1 ☕	1	1	◇1 ☕	◇1	◇1	1	◇1 ☕	1	◇1 ☕	◇1
London Euston 15 ⊖	d	13 24	13 34	13 43	13 46	13 54		14 03	14 04	14 10	14 13	14 20	14 23	14 24	14 34	14 43	14 46	14 54		15 03	15 04	15 10	15 13
East Croydon	d						13 10												14 10				
Clapham Junction	d						13 39												14 39				
Imperial Wharf	d						13 44												14 44				
West Brompton ⊖	d						13 47												14 47				
Kensington (Olympia) ⊖	d						13 50												14 50				
Shepherd's Bush	d						13 53												14 53				
Wembley Central ⊖	d						14 08												15 08				
Harrow & Wealdstone ⊖	d		13 47				14 13		14 17						14 46				15 13		15 17		
Bushey	d		13 52						14 22						14 51						15 22		
Watford Junction	a	13 40	13 54		14 00	14 10	14 20		14 25					14 39	14 54		15 00	15 09	15 20		15 25		
	d	13 41	13 55		14 01	14 11	14 20		14 26				14u37	14 41	14 55		15 01	15 11	15 20		15 26		
Kings Langley	d		13 59						14 30						14 59						15 30		
Apsley	d		14 03						14 34						15 03						15 34		
Hemel Hempstead	d	13 48	14 06			14 18	14 28		14 37					14 48	15 06			15 18	15 28		15 37		
Berkhamsted	d	13 53	14 11			14 23	14 32		14 42					14 53	15 11			15 23	15 32		15 42		
Tring	d	13 59	14a17				14 39		14a48					14 59	15a17				15 39		15a48		
Cheddington	d	14 04												15 04									
Leighton Buzzard	d	14 09				14 36	14 48				14 42			15 09				15 36	15 48				15 42
Bletchley	d	14 16				14 43	14 55				14 50			15 16				15 43	15 55				15 50
Milton Keynes Central 10	a	14 23		14 13	14 24	14 48	15 01			14 40	14 54	14 50		15 21		15 13	15 24	15 48	16 01			15 40	15 54
	d			14 13	14 25	14 49					14 54					15 13	15 25	15 49					15 54
Wolverton	d					14 52					14 58							15 52					15 58
Northampton	a				14 40	15 05					15 11						15 40	16 05					16 11
Rugby	a				15 04			14 51			15 38						16 04			15 51			16 38
Nuneaton	a				15 16												16 16						
Coventry	a			14 42				15 02			15 49		15 22			15 42				16 02			16 49
Birmingham International ✈	a			14 53				15 13			16 04		15 33			15 53				16 13			17 04
Birmingham New Street 12	a			15 08				15 27			16 16		15 45			16 08				16 27			17 16
Sandwell & Dudley	a												15 57										
Wolverhampton 7	a			15 37									16 11										

		VT	VT	LM	LM	VT	LM		LM	SN	VT	LM	VT	LM	VT	VT	LM	VT	LM	VT	LM	LM
		◇1 ☕	◇1 ☕	1	1	◇1 ☕	◇1		◇1	1	◇1 ☕	1	◇1 ☕	◇1	◇1 ☕	◇1 ☕	1	◇1 ☕	1	◇1 ☕	1 A	◇1 B
London Euston 15 ⊖	d	15 20	15 23	15 24	15 34	15 43	15 46		15 54		16 03	16 04	16 10	16 13	16 20	16 23	16 24	16 33	16 34	16 43	16 46	16 48
East Croydon	d									15 10												
Clapham Junction	d									15 39												
Imperial Wharf	d									15 44												
West Brompton ⊖	d									15 47												
Kensington (Olympia) ⊖	d									15 50												
Shepherd's Bush	d									15 53												
Wembley Central ⊖	d									16 08												
Harrow & Wealdstone ⊖	d				15 47					16 13		16 17							16 46			
Bushey	d				15 52							16 22							16 51			
Watford Junction	a			15 39	15 54		16 00		16 09	16 20		16 25					16 39		16 54			
	d		15u37	15 41	15 55		16 01		16 11	16 20		16 26				16u37	16 41		16 55			
Kings Langley	d				15 59							16 30							16 59			
Apsley	d				16 03							16 34							17 03			
Hemel Hempstead	d			15 48	16 06				16 18	16 28		16 37					16 48		17 06			
Berkhamsted	d			15 53	16 11				16 23	16 32		16 42					16 53		17 11			
Tring	d			15 59	16a17					16 39		16a48					16 59		17a19			
Cheddington	d			16 04													17 04					
Leighton Buzzard	d			16 09					16 36	16 48				16 42			17 09					17 19
Bletchley	d			16 16					16 43	16 56				16 50			17 16					
Milton Keynes Central 10	a	15 50		16 21		16 13	16 24		16 48	17 00				16 54			17 22				17 21	17 28
	d					16 13	16 25		16 49					16 54						17u13	17 23	17 29
Wolverton	d								16 52					16 58								17 33
Northampton	a						16 40		17 05					17 13							17 39	17 46
Rugby	a						17 04	17 17	17 38		16 51							17 21			18 04	18 17
Nuneaton	a						17 16														18 16	
Coventry	a		16 22			16 42		17 29	17 49		17 02					17 22				17 42		18 29
Birmingham International ✈	a		16 33			16 53		17 45	18 04		17 13					17 33				17 53		18 45
Birmingham New Street 12	a		16 45			17 08		18 01	18 17		17 27					17 45				18 08		19 01
Sandwell & Dudley	a		16 57													17 57						
Wolverhampton 7	a		17 11													18 11						

A from 10 September until 14 September

B from 2 July until 7 September

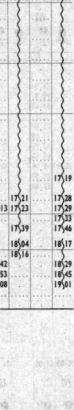

London - Watford Junction, Milton Keynes Central, Northampton and West Midlands

Network Diagram - see first Page of Table 59

	LM	LM	SN	VT	LM	VT	LM	LM	VT	VT	LM	LM	LM	VT	LM	LM	VT	LM	LM	SN	VT	LM
	1 A	1	1	◇1 ⊠	1	◇1 ⊠	◇1	1	◇1 ⊠	◇1 ⊠	1	1 A	1	◇1 ⊠	1	1	◇1 ⊠	1	1	1	◇1 ⊠	1
London Euston 15 ⊖ d	16 51	16 54		17 03	17 05	17 10	17 13	17 14	17 20	17 23	17 24	17 24	17 30	17 33	17 34	17 41	17 43	17 46	17 51		18 03	18 05
East Croydon d			16 10																	17 10		
Clapham Junction d			16 39																	17 39		
Imperial Wharf d			16 44																	17 44		
West Brompton ⊖ d			16 47																	17 47		
Kensington (Olympia) ⊖ d			16 50																	17 50		
Shepherd's Bush d			16 53																	17 53		
Wembley Central ⊖ d			17 08																	18 08		
Harrow & Wealdstone ⊖ d		17 06	17 13		17 19			17 26							17 46				18 03	18 13		18 18
Bushey d		17 11						17 31							17 52	17 56						
Watford Junction a		17 14	17 20		17 26			17 34			17 43	17 43	17 48		17 55	18 00			18 09	18 20		18 25
d		17 14	17 21		17 27			17 34		17u37	17 44	17 44	17 49			18 01			18 11	18 20		18 25
Kings Langley d					17 31			17 39								18 05						18 30
Apsley d		17 20						17 42					17 55									18 33
Hemel Hempstead d		17 23	17 28		17 36						17 51	17 51	17 58			18 10			18 18	18 28		
Berkhamsted d		17 28	17 33		17 41						17 56	17 57				18 15			18 23	18 32		
Tring d		17a36	17 38		17 46			17a52					18 05			18a22				18 38		18 43
Cheddington d					17 51								18 10									18 48
Leighton Buzzard d	17 20		17 47				17 42				18 09	18 09						18 19		18 47		18 53
Bletchley d			17 54		18 01						18 16	18 16	18 22						18 41	18 54		19 01
Milton Keynes Central 10 a	17 29		17 59		18 06		17 51				18 21	18 21	18 28					18 30	18 45	19 00		19 06
d	17 30					17u40	17 52				18 21	18 21					18u13	18 32	18 46			19 07
Wolverton d	17 34						17 56				18 25	18 25						18 36	18 49			19 10
Northampton a	17 47						18 10				18 37	18 37						18 50	19 03			19 25
Rugby a	18 17			17 51			18 38				19 03	19 05		18 21				19 17			18 51	
Nuneaton a						18 11						19 17										
Coventry a	18 29			18 02			18 49			18 22							18 42	19 29			19 02	
Birmingham International ✈ a	18 45			18 13			19 04			18 33							18 53	19 45			19 13	
Birmingham New Street 12 a	19 01			18 27			19 17			18 45							19 08	20 01			19 27	
Sandwell & Dudley a										18 57												
Wolverhampton 7 a										19 11												

	VT	LM	LM	VT	LM	VT	LM	VT	LM	LM	VT	VT FO	LM	LM	SN	VT	LM	VT	VT	LM	VT	VT
	◇1 ⊠	1	◇1 B	◇1 ⊠	1	◇1 ⊠	◇1	◇1 ⊠	1	1	◇1 ⊠	◇ 🍴	◇1	1	1	1 🍴	1	1 🍴	1 🍴	◇1	1 🍴	1 🍴
London Euston 15 ⊖ d	18 10	18 12	18 13	18 20	18 21	18 23	18 29	18 33	18 34	18 40	18 43	18 46	18 49	18 54		19 03	19 04	19 07	19 10	19 13	19 20	19 23
East Croydon d															18 10							
Clapham Junction d															18 39							
Imperial Wharf d															18 44							
West Brompton ⊖ d															18 47							
Kensington (Olympia) ⊖ d															18 50							
Shepherd's Bush d															18 53							
Wembley Central ⊖ d															19 08							
Harrow & Wealdstone ⊖ d					18 34				18 46					19 06	19 13		19 17					
Bushey d		18 27							18 52	18 57							19 22					
Watford Junction a		18 30			18 40		18 46		18 55	19 00				19 12	19 20		19 25					
d		18 31			18 41	18u37	18 47		18 56	19 01				19 13	19 21		19 26					19u37
Kings Langley d					18 46					19 05							19 30					
Apsley d							18 53			19 09							19 34					
Hemel Hempstead d		18 38			18 51				19 03	19 12				19 20	19 28		19 37					
Berkhamsted d		18 43					18 59			19 16				19 25	19 33		19 42					
Tring d		18a53			18 59				19 12	19a26				19 30	19 40		19a48					
Cheddington d							19 08		19 17													
Leighton Buzzard d			18 42		19 07				19 23				19 19	19 38	19 52					19 43		
Bletchley d							19 18		19a33				19 25	19 46	20 01							
Milton Keynes Central 10 a			18 52		19 19		19 23				19 13		19 30	19 52	20 06				19 40	19 55	19 50	
d	18u40		18 54				19 23				19 13		19 31							19 56		
Wolverton d			18 57				19 27						19 35							19 59		
Northampton a			19 10				19 39						19 49							20 11		
Rugby a			19 38				20 04	19 22				19 38	20 17			19 51				20 38		
Nuneaton a	19 12						20 16											20 02				
Coventry a			19 49			19 22					19 42		20 29			20 02				20 49		20 22
Birmingham International ✈ a			20 04			19 33					19 53		20 45			20 13				21 04		20 33
Birmingham New Street 12 a			20 16			19 45					20 06		21 01			20 27				21 16		20 45
Sandwell & Dudley a						19 58																20 58
Wolverhampton 7 a						20 12					20 36											21 12

A from 10 September until 14 September

B ◇ from Coventry

London - Watford Junction, Milton Keynes Central, Northampton and West Midlands

Network Diagram - see first Page of Table 59

	LM	LM	VT	LM	LM	SN	VT	LM	VT	VT	LM	LM	VT	LM	LM	VT	LM	LM	VT	VT	SN
	1	1	◇1 🍴	◇1	◇1	1	◇1 🍴	1	◇1 🍴	◇1 🍴	◇1	1 A	◇1 🍴	1	1	◇1 🍴	◇1	1	◇1 🍴	◇1 🍴	1
London Euston 15 ⊖ d	19 24	19 34	19 43	19 46	19 54		20 03	20 04	20 07	20 10	20 13	20 13	20 23	20 24	20 34	20 43	20 46	20 54	21 00	21 03	
East Croydon d						19 10															
Clapham Junction d						19 39															20 39
Imperial Wharf d						19 44															20 44
West Brompton ⊖ d						19 47															20 47
Kensington (Olympia) ⊖ d						19 50															20 50
Shepherd's Bush d						19 53															20 53
Wembley Central ⊖ d						20 08															21 08
Harrow & Wealdstone ⊖ d		19 46				20 13		20 17							20 46						21 13
Bushey d		19 51						20 22							20 51						
Watford Junction a	19 40	19 54			20 09	20 20		20 25						20 40	20 54			21 10			21 21
d	19 42	19 55			20 11	20 20		20 26					20u37	20 42	20 55			21 11			21 21
Kings Langley d		19 59						20 30							20 59						
Apsley d		20 03						20 34							21 03						
Hemel Hempstead d	19 49	20 06			20 18	20 28		20 37						20 49	21 06			21 18			21 28
Berkhamsted d	19 54	20 11			20 23	20 32		20 42						20 55	21 11			21 23			21 33
Tring d	20 01	20a17				20 39		20a48						21 00	21a17						21 39
Cheddington d	20 06													21 05							
Leighton Buzzard d	20 12			20 18	20 36	20 48					20 42	20 42		21 10			21 18	21 36			21 50
Bletchley d	20 19				20 43	20 55					20 50	20 50		21 17				21 43			21 58
Milton Keynes Central 10 a	20 24		20 13	20 28	20 48	21 01				20 40	20 54	20 54		21 23		21 13	21 27	21 48	21 30	21 33	22 05
d			20 13	20 30	20 49						20 55	20 55				21 13	21 29	21 49		21 34	
Wolverton d				20 33	20 52						20 59	20 59					21 32	21 52			
Northampton a				20 47	21 05						21 13	21 13					21 46	22 05			
Rugby a				21 17	21 38		20 51					21 45					22 17			21 56	
Nuneaton a									21 02			21 57									
Coventry a			20 42	21 29	21 49		21 02						21 22			21 42	22 29			22 06	
Birmingham International ✈ a			20 53	21 45	22 04		21 13						21 33			21 53	22 45			22 18	
Birmingham New Street 12 a			21 06	22 01	22 17		21 25						21 46			22 06	23 02			22 29	
Sandwell & Dudley a			21 23										21 58			22 23				22 40	
Wolverhampton 7 a			21 38				21 56						22 12			22 38				22 56	

	LM	VT	VT	LM	SR	LM	LM	VT	LM	LM	SN	VT	LM	LM	VT	LM	LM	SN	LM	VT FX	VT	LM
	1	◇1 🍴	◇1 🍴	◇1	🍴	1	1	◇1 🍴	◇1	1	1	◇1 🍴	1	1	◇1 🍴	1	1	1	1	◇1 B 🍴	◇1 C 🍴	1
London Euston 15 ⊖ d	21 04	21 07	21 10	21 13	21 15	21 24	21 34	21 43	21 46	21 54		22 00	22 04	22 24	22 30	22 34	22 54		23 24	23 30	23 30	23 34
East Croydon d																						
Clapham Junction d											21 39							22 39				
Imperial Wharf d											21 44							22 44				
West Brompton ⊖ d											21 47							22 47				
Kensington (Olympia) ⊖ d											21 50							22 50				
Shepherd's Bush d											21 53							22 53				
Wembley Central ⊖ d																						
Harrow & Wealdstone ⊖ d	21 17						21 46				22 16		22 17			22 49	23 06	23 16				23 46
Bushey d	21 22						21 51						22s22			22 54						23 51
Watford Junction a	21 25					21 39	21 53			22 09	22 23		22 25	22 39		22 57	23 12	23 23	23 43			23 54
d	21 26		21u25			21 41	21 54	21u58		22 11			22 26	22 40	22u45	22 58	23 12		23 43			23 54
Kings Langley d	21 30						21 58						22 30			23 02	23 17					23 59
Apsley d	21 34						22 02						22 33			23 06	23 20					00 02
Hemel Hempstead d	21 36					21 48	22 05			22 18			22 36	22 47		23 09	23 23		23 50			00 05
Berkhamsted d	21 41					21 53	22 10			22 23			22 40	22 52		23 14	23 28		23 55			00 09
Tring d	21 48						22 16			22 27			22 45			23 18	23 34					00 15
Cheddington d	21 53						22 22									23 24						00 20
Leighton Buzzard d	21 57			21 44		22 07	22 26		22 18	22 37			22 56	23 06		23 30	23 41		00 06			00 26
Bletchley d	22a04			21 52		22 15	22 33			22 45			23 05	23 13		23 37	23 49		00 13			00 33
Milton Keynes Central 10 a		21 37		21 56		22 21	22 38	22 17	22 32	22 53		22 30	23 11	23 21	23 28	23 45	23 55		00 19	00 27	00 27	00 41
d		21 38		21 57				22 17	22 32	22 56		22 31		23 22	23 29		23 55		00 20	00 28	00 28	
Wolverton d				22 00					22 36	22 59				23 25			23 59		00 24			
Northampton a				22 14					22 49	23 13				23 39			00 13		00 37			
Rugby a			22 02	22 38					23 17			22 52			23 58					01 00	01 05	
Nuneaton a		22 07										23 03										
Coventry a				22 49				22 46	23 29						00 10					01 13	01 18	
Birmingham International ✈ a				23 06				23 00	23 47						00 21					01 24	01 29	
Birmingham New Street 12 a				23 19				23 16	00 04						00 32					01 36	01 41	
Sandwell & Dudley a								23 33														
Wolverhampton 7 a								23 47							01 03					02 07	02 10	

A from 10 September until 14 September

B not from 30 July until 9 August, from 29 August until 6 September

C from 6 July, 13 July, 20 July, 17 August, 24 August, 14 September

Table 66

Mondays to Fridays
2 July to 14 September

London - Watford Junction, Milton Keynes Central, Northampton and West Midlands

Network Diagram - see first Page of Table 59

Station		VT A	VT B	SR
London Euston	d	23 45	23 45	23 50
East Croydon	d			
Clapham Junction	d			
Imperial Wharf	d			
West Brompton	d			
Kensington (Olympia)	d			
Shepherd's Bush	d			
Wembley Central	d			
Harrow & Wealdstone	d			
Bushey	d			
Watford Junction	a			
	d			
Kings Langley	d			
Apsley	d			
Hemel Hempstead	d			
Berkhamsted	d			
Tring	d			
Cheddington	d			
Leighton Buzzard	d			
Bletchley	d			
Milton Keynes Central	a			
	d			
Wolverton	d			
Northampton	a			
Rugby	a	00s47	00s47	
Nuneaton	a	00s58	01s02	
Coventry	a			
Birmingham International	a			
Birmingham New Street	a			
Sandwell & Dudley	a			
Wolverhampton	a			

Mondays to Fridays
from 17 September

Station		LM MO	LM MX	VT MO	LM MO	VT MO	VT MX	LM MX	LM MO	LM MX	VT MO	VT MX	LM MX	LM MO	LM	LM MO	LM MX	LM MO	LM MX	SN	LM	VT	LM
London Euston	d	21p28	21p46	21p55	22p00	22p25	22p30	22p54	22p58	23p24	23p25	23p30	23p34	23p34	00 04	00 34	00 34	01 34	01 34			05 27	05 30
East Croydon	d																						
Clapham Junction	d																			05 07			
Imperial Wharf	d																			05 10			
West Brompton	d																			05 14			
Kensington (Olympia)	d																			05 17			
Shepherd's Bush	d																						
Wembley Central	d															00 43	00 45	01 45	01 45				
Harrow & Wealdstone	d	21p40			22p12			23p06	23p10				23p46	23p46	00 16	00 48	00 50	01 50	01 50	05 33			05 43
Bushey	d	21b45											23p51	23b51		00s53	00 55						
Watford Junction	a	21p47			22p18			23p12	23p16	23p39			23p54	23p54	00 22	00 56	00 57	01 56	01 56	05 40			05 50
	d	21p48		22c09	22p19	22c39	22c45	23p12	23p17	23p40	23c39		23p54	23p55	00 23	00 58	00 58	01 57	01 57			05u45	05 50
Kings Langley	d	21p52						23p17	23p21				23p59	23p59		01 02	01 02						05 55
Apsley	d	21p56						23p20	23p25				00 02	00 03		01 06	01 06						05 59
Hemel Hempstead	d	21p59			22p26			23p23	23p28	23p47			00 05	00 06	00 30	01 09	01 09	02 04	02 04				06 01
Berkhamsted	d	22p04			22p31			23p28	23p33	23p52			00 09	00 11	00 35	01 14	01 14	02 09	02 09				06 06
Tring	d				22p35			23p34	23p37				00 15	00 15	00 41	01 18	01 19	02 13	02 14				06 13
Cheddington	d				22p41				23p43				00 20	00 21		01 24	01 25						06 18
Leighton Buzzard	d	22p17	22p18		22p47			23p41	23p49	00 05			00 26	00 27	00 50	01 30	01 31	02 22	02 23				06 23
Bletchley	d	22p24			22p54			23p49	23p56	00 13			00 33	00 34	00 57	01 37	01 38	02 29	02 30		05 17		06 30
Milton Keynes Central	a	22p32	22p32	22p42	23p02	23p11	23p28	23p55	00 04	00 21	00 11	00 27	00 41	00 42	01 05	01 45	01 46	02 37	02 38		05 21	06 09	06 35
	d	22p32	22p32	22p44	23p03	23p12	23p29	23p55	00 05	00 21	00 12	00 28		00 43	01 05	01 46	01 47				05 21	06 10	06 36
Wolverton	d	22p36	22p36		23p06			23p59	00 08	00 25				00 46	01 09	01 49	01 50				05 25		06 39
Northampton	a	22p49	22p49		23p20			00 13	00 22	00 38				01 00	01 22	02 03	02 04				05 37		06 52
Rugby	a	23p13	23p17	23p20	23p54	23p46	23p58				00s46	01 00									06 02		07 17
Nuneaton	a																				06 16	06 38	
Coventry	a	23p25	23p29	23p31	00 05	23p57	00 10				00s58	01 13											07 29
Birmingham International	a	23p52	23p47	23p42		00 08	00 21				01s09	01 24											07 45
Birmingham New Street	a	00 04	00 04	23p54		00 21	00 32				01s22	01 36											08 03
Sandwell & Dudley	a																						
Wolverhampton	a			00 15		00 43	01 03				01 53	02 07											

A FX from 30 July until 6 September, not from 13 August until 28 August

B 27 July, 3 August, 10 August, 31 August, 7 September

b Previous night, stops to set down only

c Previous night, stops to pick up only

Table 66

Mondays to Fridays
from 17 September

London - Watford Junction, Milton Keynes Central, Northampton and West Midlands

Network Diagram - see first Page of Table 59

Station		VT	SN	VT	LM	SN	VT	VT	LM	LM	VT	VT	LM	VT	SN	VT	LM	VT	LM	VT	VT	LM	LM
London Euston	d	05 39		06 03	06 04		06 17	06 23	06 24	06 34	06 36	06 43	06 53	06 55		07 03	07 04	07 10	07 13	07 20	07 23	07 24	07 34
East Croydon	d																						
Clapham Junction	d		05 30			05 55									06 38								
Imperial Wharf	d		05 39			06 00									06 42								
West Brompton	d		05 41			06 03									06 45								
Kensington (Olympia)	d		05 44			06 07									06 49								
Shepherd's Bush	d		05 47			06 10									06 52								
Wembley Central	d		06 02			06 24									07 07								
Harrow & Wealdstone	d		06 07		06 16	06 29				06 47					07 12		07 17						07 46
Bushey	d																						
Watford Junction	a		06 14		06 22	06 36			06 39	06 53			07 08		07 19		07 24					07 40	07 52
	d	06u02	06 14		06 23			06u37	06 41	06 54			07 10		07 19		07 24				07u37	07 42	07 53
Kings Langley	d				06 27					06 58							07 29						07 58
Apsley	d				06 31					07 02							07 32						08 01
Hemel Hempstead	d		06 22		06 34				06 48	07 05			07 17		07 27		07 35					07 49	08 04
Berkhamsted	d		06 26		06 39				06 53	07 10			07 22		07 32		07 40					07 54	08 09
Tring	d		06 33		06a47				06 59	07 16					07 39		07a47					08 01	08a16
Cheddington	d								07 05	07 21												08 06	
Leighton Buzzard	d		06 42						07 10	07 26			07 35		07 51				07 42			08 11	
Bletchley	d		06 49						07 17	07 33			07 43		07 58				07 50			08 18	
Milton Keynes Central	a	06 22	06 55				06 47		07 22	07 38		07 13	07 48	07 25	08 03			07 40	07 54	07 50		08 23	
	d	06 22							07 22			07 13	07 48						07 54				
Wolverton	d								07 26				07 52						07 58				
Northampton	a								07 42				08 05						08 11				
Rugby	a	06 44		06 51					08 04							07 51			08 38				
Nuneaton	a								08 17														
Coventry	a			07 02				07 22				07 42				08 02			08 49		08 22		
Birmingham International	a			07 13				07 33				07 53				08 12			09 04		08 33		
Birmingham New Street	a			07 27				07 45				08 08				08 27			09 17		08 45		
Sandwell & Dudley	a							07 57													08 57		
Wolverhampton	a							08 11													09 11		

Station		VT	LM	LM	SN	VT	LM	VT	LM	VT	VT	LM	LM	VT	LM	LM	SN	VT	LM	VT	LM	VT
London Euston	d	07 35	07 47	07 54		08 03	08 05	08 10	08 13	08 20	08 23	08 24	08 34	08 43	08 46	08 54		09 03	09 05	09 10	09 13	09 20
East Croydon	d																08 07					
Clapham Junction	d				07 39												08 39					
Imperial Wharf	d				07 44												08 44					
West Brompton	d				07 47												08 47					
Kensington (Olympia)	d				07 50												08 50					
Shepherd's Bush	d				07 53												08 53					
Wembley Central	d				08 08												09 08					
Harrow & Wealdstone	d				08 13		08 21					08 36	08 46				09 13		09 17			
Bushey	d						08 26						08 51						09 22			
Watford Junction	a		08 01	08 11	08 20		08 29					08 43	08 54		09 00	09 09	09 20		09 25			
	d		08 02	08 12	08 20		08 29				08u37	08 44	08 55		09 01	09 11	09 20		09 26			
Kings Langley	d						08 34						08 59						09 30			
Apsley	d						08 38						09 03						09 34			
Hemel Hempstead	d			08 19	08 28		08 40					08 51	09 06			09 18	09 28		09 37			
Berkhamsted	d			08 24	08 32		08 45					08 56	09 11			09 23	09 32		09 42			
Tring	d				08 39		08a52					09 02	09a17				09 39		09a48			
Cheddington	d											09 07										
Leighton Buzzard	d			08 37	08 48				08 42			09 12				09 36	09 48				09 42	
Bletchley	d			08 44	08 55				08 50			09 20				09 43	09 55				09 50	
Milton Keynes Central	a	08 05	08 25	08 49	09 01			08 40	08 54	08 50		09 26		09 13	09 24	09 48	10 01			09 40	09 54	09 50
	d		08 31	08 50					08 54					09 13	09 25	09 49					09 54	
Wolverton	d			08 53					08 58							09 52					09 58	
Northampton	a		08 44	09 07					09 11						09 40	10 05					10 11	
Rugby	a		09 04			08 51			09 38						10 04			09 51			10 38	
Nuneaton	a		09 16												10 16							
Coventry	a					09 02			09 49		09 22			09 42				10 02			10 49	
Birmingham International	a					09 12			10 04		09 33			09 53				10 13			11 04	
Birmingham New Street	a					09 27			10 17		09 45			10 08				10 27			11 16	
Sandwell & Dudley	a										09 57											
Wolverhampton	a										10 11											

London - Watford Junction, Milton Keynes Central, Northampton and West Midlands

Network Diagram - see first Page of Table 59

		VT	LM	LM	VT	LM		LM		SN	VT	LM	VT	LM	VT	VT	LM	LM		VT	LM		LM	SN	VT
		◇1 ⊠	1	1	◇1 ⊠	◇1		◇1		1	◇1 ⊠	1	◇1 ⊠	◇1	◇1 ⊠	◇1 ⊠	1	1		◇1 ⊠	◇1		◇1	1	◇1 ⊏
London Euston ⊖	d	09 23	09 24	09 34	09 43	09 46		09 54			10 03	10 05	10 10	10 13	10 20	10 23	10 24	10 34		10 43	10 46		10 54		11 03
East Croydon	d									09 08														10 10	
Clapham Junction	d									09 39														10 39	
Imperial Wharf	d									09 44														10 44	
West Brompton ⊖	d									09 47														10 47	
Kensington (Olympia) ⊖	d									09 50														10 50	
Shepherd's Bush	d									09 53														10 53	
Wembley Central ⊖	d									10 08														11 08	
Harrow & Wealdstone ⊖	d			09 48						10 13		10 17						10 46						11 13	
Bushey	d			09 53								10 22						10 51							
Watford Junction	a		09 39	09 56		10 00		10 09		10 20		10 25					10 39	10 54			11 00		11 10	11 20	
	d	09u37	09 41	09 57		10 01		10 11		10 20		10 26				10u37	10 41	10 55			11 01		11 11	11 20	
Kings Langley	d			10 01								10 30						10 59							
Apsley	d			10 05								10 34						11 03							
Hemel Hempstead	d		09 48	10 08				10 18		10 28		10 37					10 48	11 06					11 18	11 28	
Berkhamsted	d		09 53	10 13				10 23		10 32		10 42					10 53	11 11					11 23	11 32	
Tring	d		09 59	10a19						10 39		10a48					10 59	11a17						11 39	
Cheddington	d		10 04														11 04								
Leighton Buzzard	d		10 09					10 36		10 48				10 42			11 09						11 36	11 48	
Bletchley	d		10 16					10 43		10 57				10 50			11 16						11 43	11 55	
Milton Keynes Central	a		10 21		10 13	10 24		10 48		11 02			10 40	10 54	10 50		11 21			11 13	11 24		11 48	12 01	
	d				10 13	10 25		10 49						10 54						11 13	11 25		11 49		
Wolverton	d							10 52						10 58									11 52		
Northampton	a					10 40		11 08						11 11							11 40		12 06		
Rugby	a					11 04	11 17				10 51			11 38							12 04	12 17			11 51
Nuneaton	a					11 16															12 16				
Coventry	a	10 22			10 42		11 29				11 02			11 49		11 22				11 42		12 29			12 02
Birmingham International ✈	a	10 33			10 53		11 45				11 13			12 04		11 33				11 53		12 45			12 13
Birmingham New Street	a	10 45			11 08		12 01				11 27			12 16		11 45				12 08		13 01			12 27
Sandwell & Dudley	a	10 57														11 57									
Wolverhampton	a	11 11														12 11									

		LM	VT	LM		VT	VT	LM	LM	VT	LM		LM	SN		VT	LM	VT	LM	VT	VT	LM	LM	VT	
		1	◇1 ⊏	◇1		◇1 ⊏	◇1 ⊏	1	1	◇1 ⊏	◇1		◇1	1		◇1 ⊏	1	◇1 ⊏	◇1	◇1 ⊏	◇1 ⊏	1	1	◇1 ⊏	
London Euston ⊖	d	11 04	11 10	11 13		11 20	11 23	11 24	11 34	11 43	11 46		11 54			12 03	12 04	12 10	12 13	12 20	12 23	12 24	12 34	12 43	
East Croydon	d													11 11											
Clapham Junction	d													11 39											
Imperial Wharf	d													11 44											
West Brompton ⊖	d													11 47											
Kensington (Olympia) ⊖	d													11 50											
Shepherd's Bush	d													11 53											
Wembley Central ⊖	d													12 08											
Harrow & Wealdstone ⊖	d	11 17							11 46					12 13			12 17						12 46		
Bushey	d	11 22							11 51								12 22						12 51		
Watford Junction	a	11 25						11 39	11 54		12 00		12 09	12 20			12 25					12 40	12 54		
	d	11 26					11u37	11 41	11 55		12 01		12 11	12 20			12 26				12u37	12 41	12 55		
Kings Langley	d	11 30							11 59								12 30						12 59		
Apsley	d	11 34							12 03								12 34						13 03		
Hemel Hempstead	d	11 37						11 48	12 06				12 18	12 28			12 37					12 48	13 06		
Berkhamsted	d	11 42						11 53	12 11				12 23	12 32			12 42					12 53	13 11		
Tring	d	11a48						11 59	12a17					12 39			12a48					12 59	13a17		
Cheddington	d							12 04														13 04			
Leighton Buzzard	d			11 42				12 09					12 36	12 48					12 42			13 09			
Bletchley	d			11 50				12 16					12 43	12 55					12 50			13 16			
Milton Keynes Central	a		11 40	11 54		11 50		12 21		12 13	12 24		12 48	13 01				12 40	12 54	12 50		13 21		13 13	
	d			11 54						12 13	12 25		12 49						12 54					13 13	
Wolverton	d			11 58									12 52						12 58						
Northampton	a			12 11							12 40		13 05						13 11						
Rugby	a			12 38							13 04	13 17				12 51			13 38						
Nuneaton	a										13 16														
Coventry	a			12 49			12 22			12 42		13 29				13 02			13 49		13 22			13 42	
Birmingham International ✈	a			13 04			12 33			12 53		13 45				13 13			14 04		13 33			13 53	
Birmingham New Street	a			13 16			12 45			13 08		14 01				13 27			14 16		13 45			14 08	
Sandwell & Dudley	a						12 57														13 57				
Wolverhampton	a						13 11														14 11				

London - Watford Junction, Milton Keynes Central, Northampton and West Midlands

Network Diagram - see first Page of Table 59

		LM		LM	SN	VT	LM	VT	LM	VT		VT	LM	LM	VT	LM	LM	SN	VT	LM		VT	LM	VT	VT
		◇1		◇1	1	◇1 ⊏	1	◇1 ⊏	◇1	◇1 ⊏		◇1 ⊏	1	1	◇1 ⊏	◇1	◇1	1	◇1 ⊏	1		◇1 ⊏	◇1	◇1 ⊏	◇1 ⊏
London Euston ⊖	d	12 46		12 54		13 03	13 04	13 10	13 13	13 20		13 23	13 24	13 34	13 43	13 46	13 54		14 03	14 04		14 10	14 13	14 20	14 23
East Croydon	d				12 10													13 10							
Clapham Junction	d				12 39													13 39							
Imperial Wharf	d				12 44													13 44							
West Brompton ⊖	d				12 47													13 47							
Kensington (Olympia) ⊖	d				12 50													13 50							
Shepherd's Bush	d				12 53													13 53							
Wembley Central ⊖	d				13 08													14 08							
Harrow & Wealdstone ⊖	d				13 13		13 17							13 47				14 13		14 17					
Bushey	d						13 22							13 52						14 22					
Watford Junction	a	13 00		13 09	13 20		13 25						13 40	13 54		14 00	14 10	14 20		14 25					
	d	13 01		13 11	13 20		13 26					13u37	13 41	13 55		14 01	14 11	14 20		14 26					14u37
Kings Langley	d						13 30							13 59						14 30					
Apsley	d						13 34							14 03						14 34					
Hemel Hempstead	d			13 18	13 28		13 37						13 48	14 06			14 18	14 28		14 37					
Berkhamsted	d			13 23	13 32		13 42						13 53	14 11			14 23	14 32		14 42					
Tring	d				13 39		13a48						13 59	14a17				14 39		14a48					
Cheddington	d												14 04												
Leighton Buzzard	d			13 36	13 48				13 42				14 09				14 36	14 48					14 42		
Bletchley	d			13 43	13 55				13 50				14 16				14 43	14 55					14 50		
Milton Keynes Central	a	13 24		13 48	14 01			13 40	13 54	13 50			14 23		14 13	14 24	14 48	15 01				14 40	14 54	14 50	
	d	13 25		13 49					13 54						14 13	14 25	14 49						14 54		
Wolverton	d			13 52					13 58								14 52						14 58		
Northampton	a	13 40		14 05					14 11							14 40	15 05						15 11		
Rugby	a	14 04	14 17			13 51			14 38							15 04			14 51				15 38		
Nuneaton	a	14 16														15 16									
Coventry	a		14 29			14 02			14 49			14 22			14 42				15 02				15 49		15 22
Birmingham International ✈	a		14 45			14 13			15 04			14 33			14 53				15 13				16 04		15 33
Birmingham New Street	a		15 01			14 27			15 15			14 45			15 08				15 27				16 16		15 45
Sandwell & Dudley	a											14 57													15 57
Wolverhampton	a											15 11													16 11

		LM	LM	VT	LM	LM		SN	VT	LM	VT	LM	VT	VT	LM	LM		VT	LM		LM	SN	VT	LM	VT
		1	1	◇1 ⊏	◇1	◇1		1	◇1 ⊏	1	◇1 ⊏	◇1	◇1 ⊏	◇1 ⊏	1	1		◇1 ⊏	◇1		◇1	1	◇1 ⊏	1	◇1 ⊏
London Euston ⊖	d	14 24	14 34	14 43	14 46	14 54			15 03	15 04	15 10	15 13	15 20	15 23	15 24	15 34		15 43	15 46		15 54		16 03	16 04	16 10
East Croydon	d							14 10														15 10			
Clapham Junction	d							14 39														15 39			
Imperial Wharf	d							14 44														15 44			
West Brompton ⊖	d							14 47														15 47			
Kensington (Olympia) ⊖	d							14 50														15 50			
Shepherd's Bush	d							14 53														15 53			
Wembley Central ⊖	d							15 08														16 08			
Harrow & Wealdstone ⊖	d		14 46					15 13		15 17						15 47						16 13		16 17	
Bushey	d		14 51							15 22						15 52								16 22	
Watford Junction	a	14 39	14 54		15 00	15 09		15 20		15 25					15 39	15 54			16 00		16 09	16 20		16 25	
	d	14 41	14 55		15 01	15 11		15 20		15 26				15u37	15 41	15 55			16 01		16 11	16 20		16 26	
Kings Langley	d		14 59							15 30						15 59								16 30	
Apsley	d		15 03							15 34						16 03								16 34	
Hemel Hempstead	d	14 48	15 06			15 18		15 28		15 37					15 48	16 06					16 18	16 28		16 37	
Berkhamsted	d	14 53	15 11			15 23		15 32		15 42					15 53	16 11					16 23	16 32		16 42	
Tring	d	14 59	15a17					15 39		15a48					15 59	16a17						16 39		16a48	
Cheddington	d	15 04													16 04										
Leighton Buzzard	d	15 09				15 36		15 48				15 42			16 09						16 36	16 48			
Bletchley	d	15 16				15 43		15 55				15 50			16 16						16 43	16 56			
Milton Keynes Central	a	15 21		15 13	15 24	15 48		16 01			15 40	15 54	15 50		16 21			16 13	16 24		16 48	17 00			
	d			15 13	15 25	15 49						15 54						16 13	16 25		16 49				
Wolverton	d					15 52						15 58									16 52				
Northampton	a				15 40	16 05						16 11							16 40		17 05				
Rugby	a				16 04				15 51			16 38							17 04	17 17	17 38		16 51		
Nuneaton	a				16 16														17 16						
Coventry	a			15 42					16 02			16 49		16 22				16 42		17 29	17 49		17 02		
Birmingham International ✈	a			15 53					16 13			17 04		16 33				16 53		17 45	18 04		17 13		
Birmingham New Street	a			16 08					16 27			17 16		16 45				17 08		18 01	18 17		17 27		
Sandwell & Dudley	a													16 57											
Wolverhampton	a													17 11											

London - Watford Junction, Milton Keynes Central, Northampton and West Midlands

Network Diagram - see first Page of Table 59

		LM	VT	VT	LM	VT	LM	VT	LM	LM	LM	SN	VT	LM	VT	LM	LM	VT	VT	LM	LM	LM
		◇1	◇1 ⊐	◇1 ⊐	1	◇1 ⊐	1	◇1 ⊐	1	1	1	1	◇1 ⊠	1	◇1 ⊠	◇1	1	◇1 ⊠	◇1 ⊠	1	1	1
London Euston 15 ⊖	d	16 13	16 20	16 23	16 24	16 33	16 34	16 43	16 46	16 51	16 54		17 03	17 05	17 10	17 13	17 14	17 20	17 23	17 24	17 24	17 30
East Croydon ⇌	d											16 10										
Clapham Junction	d											16 39										
Imperial Wharf	d											16 44										
West Brompton ⊖	d											16 47										
Kensington (Olympia) ⊖	d											16 50										
Shepherd's Bush	d											16 53										
Wembley Central ⊖	d											17 08										
Harrow & Wealdstone ⊖	d						16 46				17 06	17 13		17 19			17 26					
Bushey	d						16 51				17 11						17 31					
Watford Junction	a				16 39		16 54				17 14	17 20		17 26			17 34			17 43	17 43	17 48
	d			16u37	16 41		16 55				17 14	17 21		17 27			17 34		17u37	17 44	17 44	17 49
Kings Langley	d						16 59							17 31			17 39					
Apsley	d						17 03				17 20						17 42					17 55
Hemel Hempstead	d				16 48		17 06				17 23	17 28		17 36						17 51	17 51	17 58
Berkhamsted	d				16 53		17 11				17 28	17 33		17 41						17 56	17 57	
Tring	d				16 59		17a19				17a36	17 38		17 46			17a52					18 05
Cheddington	d				17 04									17 51								18 10
Leighton Buzzard	d	16 42			17 09					17 20		17 47				17 42				18 09	18 09	
Bletchley	d	16 50			17 16							17 54		18 01						18 16	18 16	18 22
Milton Keynes Central 10	a	16 54			17 22				17 21	17 29		17 59		18 06		17 51				18 21	18 21	18 28
	d	16 54						17u13	17 23	17 30					17u40	17 52				18 21	18 21	
Wolverton	d	16 58								17 34						17 56				18 25	18 25	
Northampton	a	17 13							17 39	17 47						18 10				18 37	18 37	
Rugby	a					17 21			18 04	18 17			17 51			18 38				19 03	19 05	
Nuneaton	a								18 16						18 11						19 17	
Coventry	a			17 22				17 42		18 29			18 02			18 49			18 22			
Birmingham International ✈	a			17 33				17 53		18 45			18 13			19 04			18 33			
Birmingham New Street 12	a			17 45				18 08		19 01			18 27			19 17			18 45			
Sandwell & Dudley	a			17 57															18 57			
Wolverhampton 7 ⇌	a			18 11															19 11			

		VT	LM	LM	VT	LM	LM	SN	VT	LM	VT	LM	LM	VT	LM	VT	LM	VT	LM	LM	VT	VT FO	LM
		◇1 ⊠	1	1	◇1 ⊠	1	1	1	◇1 ⊠	1	◇1 ⊠	1	◇1 A	◇1 ⊠	1	◇1 ⊠	◇1	◇1 ⊠	1	1	◇1 ⊠	◇ ⊐	◇1
London Euston 15 ⊖	d	17 33	17 34	17 41	17 43	17 46	17 51		18 03	18 05	18 10	18 12	18 13	18 20	18 21	18 23	18 29	18 33	18 34	18 40	18 43	18 46	18 49
East Croydon ⇌	d							17 10															
Clapham Junction	d							17 39															
Imperial Wharf	d							17 44															
West Brompton ⊖	d							17 47															
Kensington (Olympia) ⊖	d							17 50															
Shepherd's Bush	d							17 53															
Wembley Central ⊖	d							18 08															
Harrow & Wealdstone ⊖	d		17 46				18 03	18 13		18 18					18 34				18 46				
Bushey	d		17 52	17 56								18 27							18 52	18 57			
Watford Junction	a		17 55	18 00			18 09	18 20		18 25		18 30			18 40		18 46		18 55	19 00			
	d			18 01			18 11	18 20		18 25		18 31			18 41	18u37	18 47		18 56	19 01			
Kings Langley	d			18 05						18 30					18 46					19 05			
Apsley	d									18 33							18 53			19 09			
Hemel Hempstead	d			18 10			18 18	18 28				18 38			18 51				19 03	19 12			
Berkhamsted	d			18 15			18 23	18 32				18 43					18 59			19 16			
Tring	d			18a22				18 38		18 43		18a53			18 59				19 12	19a26			
Cheddington	d									18 48							19 08		19 17				
Leighton Buzzard	d					18 19		18 47		18 53			18 42		19 07				19 23				19 19
Bletchley	d						18 41	18 54		19 01							19 18		19a33				19 25
Milton Keynes Central 10	a					18 30	18 45	19 00		19 06			18 52		19 19		19 23				19 13		19 30
	d				18u13	18 32	18 46			19 07	18u40		18 54				19 23				19 13		19 31
Wolverton	d					18 36	18 49			19 10			18 57				19 27						19 35
Northampton	a					18 50	19 03			19 25			19 10				19 39						19 49
Rugby	a	18 21				19 17			18 51				19 38				20 04	19 22				19 38	20 17
Nuneaton	a										19 12						20 16						
Coventry	a				18 42	19 29			19 02				19 49			19 22					19 42		20 29
Birmingham International ✈	a				18 53	19 45			19 13				20 04			19 33					19 53		20 45
Birmingham New Street 12	a				19 08	20 01			19 27				20 16			19 45					20 06		21 01
Sandwell & Dudley	a															19 58							
Wolverhampton 7 ⇌	a															20 12					20 36		

A ◇ from Coventry

London - Watford Junction, Milton Keynes Central, Northampton and West Midlands

Network Diagram - see first Page of Table 59

		LM	SN	VT	LM	VT	VT	LM	VT	VT	LM	LM	VT	LM	LM	SN	VT	LM	VT	VT	LM	LM
		1	1	▪ 1 ⊐	1	▪ 1 ⊐	▪ 1 ⊐	◇1	▪ 1 ⊐	▪ 1 ⊐	1	1	◇1 ⊐	◇1	◇1	1	◇1 ⊐	1	◇1 ⊐	◇1 ⊐	◇1	1
London Euston 15 ⊖	d	18 54		19 03	19 04	19 07	19 10	19 13	19 20	19 23	19 24	19 34	19 43	19 46	19 54		20 03	20 04	20 07	20 10	20 13	20 13
East Croydon ⇌	d		18 10													19 10						
Clapham Junction	d		18 39													19 39						
Imperial Wharf	d		18 44													19 44						
West Brompton ⊖	d		18 47													19 47						
Kensington (Olympia) ⊖	d		18 50													19 50						
Shepherd's Bush	d		18 53													19 53						
Wembley Central ⊖	d		19 08													20 08						
Harrow & Wealdstone ⊖	d	19 06	19 13		19 17							19 46				20 13		20 17				
Bushey	d				19 22							19 51						20 22				
Watford Junction	a	19 12	19 20		19 25						19 40	19 54			20 09	20 20		20 25				
	d	19 13	19 21		19 26					19u37	19 42	19 55			20 11	20 20		20 26				
Kings Langley	d				19 30							19 59						20 30				
Apsley	d				19 34							20 03						20 34				
Hemel Hempstead	d	19 20	19 28		19 37						19 49	20 06			20 18	20 28		20 37				
Berkhamsted	d	19 25	19 33		19 42						19 54	20 11			20 23	20 32		20 42				
Tring	d	19 30	19 40		19a48						20 01	20a17				20 39		20a48				
Cheddington	d										20 06											
Leighton Buzzard	d	19 38	19 52					19 43			20 12			20 18	20 36	20 48					20 42	20 42
Bletchley	d	19 46	20 01								20 19				20 43	20 55					20 50	20 50
Milton Keynes Central 10	a	19 52	20 06					19 55			20 24		20 13	20 28	20 48	21 01				20 40	20 54	20 54
	d							19 56					20 13	20 30	20 49						20 55	20 55
Wolverton	d							19 59						20 33	20 52						20 59	20 59
Northampton	a							20 11						20 47	21 05						21 13	21 13
Rugby	a			19 51				20 38						21 17	21 38		20 51					21 45
Nuneaton	a					20 02													21 02			21 57
Coventry	a			20 02				20 49		20 22			20 42	21 29	21 49		21 02					
Birmingham International ✈	a			20 13				21 04		20 33			20 53	21 45	22 04		21 13					
Birmingham New Street 12	a			20 27				21 16		20 45			21 06	22 01	22 17		21 25					
Sandwell & Dudley	a									20 58			21 23									
Wolverhampton 7 ⇌	a									21 12			21 38				21 56					

		VT	LM	LM	VT	LM	LM	VT	VT	SN	LM	VT	VT	LM	SR	LM	LM	VT	LM	LM	SN	VT	LM
		◇1 ⊐	1	1	◇1 ⊐	◇1	1	◇1 ⊐	◇1 ⊐	1	1	◇1 ⊐	◇1 ⊐	◇1	B 🚌 ⊐	1	1	◇1 ⊐	◇1	1	1	◇1 ⊐	1
London Euston 15 ⊖	d	20 23	20 24	20 34	20 43	20 46	20 54	21 00	21 03		21 04	21 07	21 10	21 13	21 15	21 24	21 34	21 43	21 46	21 54		22 00	22 04
East Croydon ⇌	d																						
Clapham Junction	d									20 39											21 39		
Imperial Wharf	d									20 44											21 44		
West Brompton ⊖	d									20 47											21 47		
Kensington (Olympia) ⊖	d									20 50											21 50		
Shepherd's Bush	d									20 53											21 53		
Wembley Central ⊖	d									21 08													
Harrow & Wealdstone ⊖	d			20 46						21 13	21 17						21 46				22 16		22 17
Bushey	d			20 51							21 22						21 51						22s22
Watford Junction	a		20 40	20 54			21 10			21 21	21 25					21 39	21 53			22 09	22 23		22 25
	d	20u37	20 42	20 55			21 11			21 21	21 26		21u25			21 41	21 54	21u58		22 11			22 26
Kings Langley	d			20 59							21 30						21 58						22 30
Apsley	d			21 03							21 34						22 02						22 33
Hemel Hempstead	d		20 49	21 06			21 18			21 28	21 36					21 48	22 05			22 18			22 36
Berkhamsted	d		20 55	21 11			21 23			21 33	21 41					21 53	22 10			22 23			22 40
Tring	d		21 00	21a17						21 39	21 48						22 16			22 27			22 45
Cheddington	d		21 05								21 53						22 22						
Leighton Buzzard	d		21 10			21 18	21 36			21 50	21 57			21 44		22 07	22 26		22 18	22 37			22 56
Bletchley	d		21 17				21 43			21 58	22a04			21 52		22 15	22 33			22 45			23 05
Milton Keynes Central 10	a		21 23		21 13	21 27	21 48	21 30	21 33	22 05		21 37		21 56		22 21	22 38	22 17	22 32	22 53		22 30	23 11
	d				21 13	21 29	21 49		21 34			21 38		21 57				22 17	22 32	22 56		22 31	
Wolverton	d					21 32	21 52							22 00					22 36	22 59			
Northampton	a					21 46	22 05							22 14					22 49	23 13			
Rugby	a					22 17			21 56				22 02	22 38					23 17			22 52	
Nuneaton	a											22 07										23 03	
Coventry	a	21 22			21 42	22 29			22 06					22 49				22 46	23 29				
Birmingham International ✈	a	21 33			21 53	22 45			22 18					23 06				23 00	23 47				
Birmingham New Street 12	a	21 46			22 06	23 02			22 29					23 19				23 16	00 04				
Sandwell & Dudley	a	21 58			22 23				22 40									23 33					
Wolverhampton 7 ⇌	a	22 12			22 38				22 56									23 47					

Table 66

Mondays to Fridays
from 17 September

London - Watford Junction, Milton Keynes Central, Northampton and West Midlands

Network Diagram - see first Page of Table 59

		LM	VT	LM	LM	SN	LM	VT FX	VT FO	LM	SR
		1	◇1	1	1	1	1	◇1	◇1	1	
London Euston 15 ⊖	d	22 24	22 30	22 34	22 54		23 24	23 30	23 30	23 34	23 50
East Croydon	d										
Clapham Junction	d					22 39					
Imperial Wharf	d					22 44					
West Brompton ⊖	d					22 47					
Kensington (Olympia) ⊖	d					22 50					
Shepherd's Bush	d					22 53					
Wembley Central ⊖	d										
Harrow & Wealdstone ⊖	d			22 49	23 06	23 16				23 46	
Bushey	d			22 54						23 51	
Watford Junction	a	22 39		22 57	23 12	23 23	23 39			23 54	
	d	22 40	22u45	22 58	23 12		23 40			23 54	
Kings Langley	d			23 02	23 17					23 59	
Apsley	d			23 06	23 20					00 02	
Hemel Hempstead	d	22 47		23 09	23 23		23 47			00 05	
Berkhamsted	d	22 52		23 14	23 28		23 52			00 09	
Tring	d			23 18	23 34					00 15	
Cheddington	d			23 24						00 20	
Leighton Buzzard	d	23 06		23 30	23 41		00 05			00 26	
Bletchley	d	23 13		23 37	23 49		00 13			00 33	
Milton Keynes Central 10	a	23 21	23 28	23 45	23 55		00 21	00 27	00 27	00 41	
	d	23 22	23 29		23 55		00 21	00 28	00 28		
Wolverton	d	23 25			23 59		00 25				
Northampton	a	23 39			00 13		00 38				
Rugby	a		23 58					01 00	01 05		
Nuneaton	a										
Coventry	a		00 10					01 13	01 18		
Birmingham International ✈	a		00 21					01 24	01 29		
Birmingham New Street 12	a		00 32					01 36	01 41		
Sandwell & Dudley	a										
Wolverhampton 7	a		01 03					02 07	02 10		

Saturdays
until 30 June

		LM	VT	LM	LM A	LM B	VT	LM	LM	LM	LM	SN	LM	LM	SN	VT	VT	LM	SN	VT	VT	SN	VT
		◇1	◇1	1	1	1	◇1	1	1	1	1	1	◇1	◇1	1	◇1	◇1	◇1	1	◇1	◇1	1	◇1
London Euston 15 ⊖	d	21p46	22p30	22p54	23p24	23p24	23p30	23p34	00 04	00 34	01 34			05 34		06 05	06 23	06 24		06 36	06 55		07 03
East Croydon	d																					06 10	
Clapham Junction	d											05 08			05 38				06 09			06 39	
Imperial Wharf	d											05 12			05 42				06 13			06 44	
West Brompton ⊖	d											05 15			05 45				06 16			06 47	
Kensington (Olympia) ⊖	d											05 19			05 49				06 20			06 50	
Shepherd's Bush	d											05 22			05 52				06 23			06 53	
Wembley Central ⊖	d									00 45	01 45				06 07				06 38			07 07	
Harrow & Wealdstone ⊖	d			23p06				23p46	00 16	00 50	01 50	05 40		05 46	06 12				06 43			07 12	
Bushey	d							23p51		00 55													
Watford Junction	a			23p12	23p39	23p43		23p54	00 22	00 57	01 56	05 47		05 52	06 19			06 39	06 50			07 19	
	d		22b45	23p12	23p40	23p43		23p54	00 23	00 58	01 57			05 52	06 19	06u20	06u37	06 41				07 19	
Kings Langley	d			23p17				23p59		01 02				05 57									
Apsley	d			23p20				00 02		01 06				06 01									
Hemel Hempstead	d			23p23	23p47	23p50		00 05	00 30	01 09	02 04			06 03	06 27			06 48				07 27	
Berkhamsted	d			23p28	23p52	23p55		00 09	00 35	01 14	02 09			06 08	06 31			06 53				07 32	
Tring	d			23p34				00 15	00 40	01 18	02 13			06 13	06 37			06 59				07 39	
Cheddington	d							00 20		01 24				06 18				07 05					
Leighton Buzzard	d	22p18		23p41	00 05	00 06		00 26	00 49	01 30	02 22			06 25	06 47			07 10				07 48	
Bletchley	d			23p49	00 13	00 13		00 33	00 56	01 37	02 29		05 17	06 32	06 55			07 17				07 55	
Milton Keynes Central 10	a	22p32	23p28	23p55	00 21	00 19	00 27	00 41	01 04	01 45	02 37		05 21	06 37	07 00	06 39		07 22			07 25	08 00	
	d	22p32	23p29	23p55	00 21	00 20	00 28		01 04	01 46			05 21	06 37		06 41		07 23					
Wolverton	d	22p36		23p59	00 25	00 24			01 08	01 49			05 25	06 41				07 26					
Northampton	a	22p49		00 13	00 38	00 37			01 21	02 03			05 37	06 53				07 39					
Rugby	a	23p17	23p58				01 05						06 01	07 17		07 02		08 04					07 51
Nuneaton	a												06 16					08 16					
Coventry	a	23p29	00 10				01 18							07 29			07 22						08 02
Birmingham International ✈	a	23p47	00 21				01 29							07 45			07 33						08 13
Birmingham New Street 12	a	00 04	00 32				01 41							08 01			07 45						08 27
Sandwell & Dudley	a																07 57						
Wolverhampton 7	a		01 03				02 10										08 11						

A not 30 June
B 30 June
b Previous night, stops to pick up only

Table 66

Saturdays
until 30 June

London - Watford Junction, Milton Keynes Central, Northampton and West Midlands

Network Diagram - see first Page of Table 59

		LM	VT	VT	LM	LM	VT	VT	LM	LM	SN	VT	LM	VT	VT	VT	LM	LM	VT	LM	VT	LM
		1	◇1	◇1	1	1	◇1	◇1	◇1	◇1	1	◇1	1	◇1	◇1	◇1	1	1	◇1	◇1	◇1	◇1
London Euston 15 ⊖	d	07 04	07 20	07 23	07 24	07 34	07 35	07 43	07 46	07 54		08 03	08 04	08 10	08 20	08 23	08 24	08 34	08 43	08 46	08 50	08 54
East Croydon	d										07 10											
Clapham Junction	d										07 39											
Imperial Wharf	d										07 44											
West Brompton ⊖	d										07 47											
Kensington (Olympia) ⊖	d										07 50											
Shepherd's Bush	d										07 53											
Wembley Central ⊖	d										08 07											
Harrow & Wealdstone ⊖	d	07 16				07 46					08 12		08 16					08 46				
Bushey	d	07 21											08 21					08 51				
Watford Junction	a	07 24			07 39	07 52			08 00	08 09	08 19		08 24				08 39	08 54			09 04	09 09
	d	07 24		07u37	07 42	07 53			08 01	08 11	08 19		08 25			08u37	08 41	08 55			09 05	09 11
Kings Langley	d	07 29				07 58							08 29					08 59				
Apsley	d	07 32				08 01							08 33					09 03				
Hemel Hempstead	d	07 35			07 49	08 04				08 18	08 27		08 36				08 48	09 06				09 18
Berkhamsted	d	07 40			07 54	08 09				08 23	08 31		08 41				08 53	09 11				09 23
Tring	d	07 47			08 01	08a16					08 37		08a47				08 59	09a17				
Cheddington	d	07 52			08 06												09 04					
Leighton Buzzard	d	07 57			08 11					08 36	08 47						09 09					09 36
Bletchley	d	08 04			08 18					08 43	08 55						09 16					09 43
Milton Keynes Central 10	a	08 09	07 50		08 23		08 05	08 13	08 24	08 48	09 00			08 40	08 50		09 21		09 13	09 21	09 24	09 48
	d	08 10						08 13	08 25	08 49									09 13	09 23		09 49
Wolverton	d	08 13								08 52												09 52
Northampton	a	08 26							08 41	09 05										09 39		10 05
Rugby	a	08 59							09 04	09 38		08 51								10 04 10 17		
Nuneaton	a								09 16											10 16		
Coventry	a	09 10		08 22				08 42		09 49		09 02				09 22			09 42	10 29		
Birmingham International ✈	a	09 28		08 33				08 53		10 04		09 13				09 33			09 53	10 45		
Birmingham New Street 12	a	09 42		08 45				09 08		10 16		09 27				09 45			10 08	11 01		
Sandwell & Dudley	a			08 57												09 57						
Wolverhampton 7	a			09 11												10 11						

		SN	VT	LM	LM	VT	VT	LM	LM	VT	LM	LM	SN	VT	LM	VT	LM	VT	VT	LM	LM
		1	◇1	1	◇1	◇1	◇1	1	1	◇1	◇1	1	1	◇1	1	◇1	◇1	◇1	◇1	1	1
London Euston 15 ⊖	d		09 03	09 04	09 13	09 20	09 23	09 24	09 34	09 43	09 46	09 54		10 03	10 04	10 10	10 13	10 20	10 23	10 24	10 34
East Croydon	d	08 10											09 10								
Clapham Junction	d	08 39											09 39								
Imperial Wharf	d	08 44											09 44								
West Brompton ⊖	d	08 47											09 47								
Kensington (Olympia) ⊖	d	08 50											09 50								
Shepherd's Bush	d	08 53											09 53								
Wembley Central ⊖	d	09 07											10 07								
Harrow & Wealdstone ⊖	d	09 12		09 16					09 46				10 12		10 16						10 46
Bushey	d			09 21					09 51						10 21						10 51
Watford Junction	a	09 19		09 24				09 39	09 54		10 00	10 09	10 19		10 24					10 39	10 54
	d	09 19		09 25			09u37	09 41	09 55		10 01	10 11	10 19		10 25				10u37	10 41	10 55
Kings Langley	d			09 29					09 59						10 29						10 59
Apsley	d			09 33					10 03						10 33						11 03
Hemel Hempstead	d	09 27		09 36				09 48	10 06			10 18	10 27		10 36					10 48	11 06
Berkhamsted	d	09 33		09 41				09 53	10 11			10 23	10 31		10 41					10 53	11 11
Tring	d	09 38		09a47				09 59	10a17				10 37		10a47					10 59	11a17
Cheddington	d							10 04												11 04	
Leighton Buzzard	d	09 47			09 42			10 09				10 36	10 47				10 42			11 09	
Bletchley	d	09 55			09 50			10 16				10 43	10 55				10 50			11 16	
Milton Keynes Central 10	a	10 00			09 54	09 50		10 21		10 13	10 24	10 48	11 00			10 40	10 54	10 50		11 21	
	d				09 54					10 13	10 25	10 49					10 54				
Wolverton	d				09 58							10 52					10 58				
Northampton	a				10 12						10 40	11 05					11 12				
Rugby	a		09 51		10 38						11 04 11 17			10 51			11 38				
Nuneaton	a										11 16										
Coventry	a		10 02		10 49		10 22			10 42	11 29			11 02			11 49		11 22		
Birmingham International ✈	a		10 13		11 04		10 33			10 53	11 45			11 13			12 04		11 33		
Birmingham New Street 12	a		10 27		11 16		10 45			11 08	12 01			11 27			12 16		11 45		
Sandwell & Dudley	a						10 57												11 57		
Wolverhampton 7	a						11 11												12 11		

London - Watford Junction, Milton Keynes Central, Northampton and West Midlands

Network Diagram - see first Page of Table 59

Station	VT ◇1 ☕	LM ◇1	LM ◇1	SN 1	VT ◇1 ☕	LM 1	VT ◇1 ☕	LM ◇1	VT ◇1 ☕	VT ◇1 ☕	LM 1	LM 1	VT ◇1 ☕	LM ◇1	LM ◇1	SN 1	VT ◇1 ☕	LM 1	VT ◇1 ☕	LM ◇1
London Euston ⊖ d	10 43	10 46	10 54		11 03	11 04	11 10	11 13	11 20	11 23	11 24	11 34	11 43	11 46	11 54		12 03	12 04	12 10	12 13
East Croydon d				10 10												11 10				
Clapham Junction d				10 39												11 39				
Imperial Wharf d				10 44												11 44				
West Brompton ⊖ d				10 47												11 47				
Kensington (Olympia) ⊖ d				10 50												11 50				
Shepherd's Bush d				10 53												11 53				
Wembley Central ⊖ d				11 08												12 07				
Harrow & Wealdstone ⊖ d				11 13		11 17						11 46				12 13		12 16		
Bushey d						11 22						11 51						12 21		
Watford Junction a		11 00	11 10	11 20		11 25					11 39	11 54		12 00	12 09	12 20		12 24		
Watford Junction d		11 01	11 11	11 20		11 25				11u37	11 41	11 55		12 01	12 11	12 20		12 25		
Kings Langley d						11 30						11 59						12 29		
Apsley d						11 33						12 03						12 33		
Hemel Hempstead d			11 18	11 28		11 36					11 48	12 06			12 18	12 28		12 36		
Berkhamsted d			11 23	11 33		11 41					11 53	12 11			12 23	12 32		12 41		
Tring d				11 38		11a47					11 59	12a17				12 37		12a47		
Cheddington d											12 04									
Leighton Buzzard d			11 36	11 47				11 42			12 09				12 36	12 47				12 42
Bletchley d			11 43	11 55				11 50			12 16				12 43	12 55				12 50
Milton Keynes Central a	11 13	11 24	11 48	12 00			11 40	11 54	11 50		12 21		12 13	12 24	12 48	13 00			12 40	12 54
Milton Keynes Central d	11 13	11 25	11 49					11 54					12 13	12 25	12 49					12 54
Wolverton d			11 52					11 58							12 52					12 58
Northampton a		11 41	12 05					12 12						12 41	13 05					13 12
Rugby a		12 04 / 12 17			11 51			12 38						13 04 / 13 17			12 51			13 38
Nuneaton a		12 16												13 16						
Coventry a	11 42	12 29			12 02			12 49		12 22			12 42	13 29			13 02			13 49
Birmingham International ✈ a	11 53	12 45			12 13			13 04		12 33			12 53	13 45			13 13			14 04
Birmingham New Street a	12 08	13 01			12 27			13 16		12 45			13 08	14 01			13 27			14 16
Sandwell & Dudley a										12 57										
Wolverhampton a										13 11										

Station	VT ◇1 ☕	VT ◇1 ☕	LM 1	LM 1	VT ◇1 ☕	LM ◇1	LM ◇1	SN 1	VT ◇1 ☕	LM 1	VT ◇1 ☕	LM ◇1	VT ◇1 ☕	VT ◇1 ☕	LM 1	LM 1	VT ◇1 ☕	LM ◇1	LM ◇1	SN 1
London Euston ⊖ d	12 20	12 23	12 24	12 34	12 43	12 46	12 54		13 03	13 04	13 10	13 13	13 20	13 23	13 24	13 34	13 43	13 46	13 54	
East Croydon d								12 10												13 10
Clapham Junction d								12 39												13 39
Imperial Wharf d								12 44												13 44
West Brompton ⊖ d								12 47												13 47
Kensington (Olympia) ⊖ d								12 50												13 50
Shepherd's Bush d								12 53												13 53
Wembley Central ⊖ d								13 07												14 08
Harrow & Wealdstone ⊖ d				12 46				13 12		13 16						13 46				14 13
Bushey d				12 51						13 21						13 51				
Watford Junction a			12 39	12 54		13 00	13 09	13 19		13 24					13 39	13 54		14 00	14 09	14 20
Watford Junction d		12u37	12 41	12 55		13 01	13 11	13 19		13 25				13u37	13 41	13 55		14 01	14 11	14 20
Kings Langley d				12 59						13 29						13 59				
Apsley d				13 03						13 33						14 03				
Hemel Hempstead d			12 48	13 06			13 18	13 27		13 36					13 48	14 06			14 18	14 28
Berkhamsted d			12 53	13 11			13 23	13 32		13 41					13 53	14 11			14 23	14 32
Tring d			12 59	13a17				13 37		13a47					13 59	14a17				14 37
Cheddington d			13 04												14 04					
Leighton Buzzard d			13 09				13 36	13 47				13 42			14 09				14 36	14 47
Bletchley d			13 16				13 43	13 55				13 50			14 16				14 43	14 55
Milton Keynes Central a	12 50		13 21		13 13	13 24	13 48	14 00			13 40	13 54	13 50		14 21		14 13	14 24	14 48	15 00
Milton Keynes Central d					13 13	13 25	13 49					13 54					14 13	14 25	14 49	
Wolverton d							13 52					13 58							14 52	
Northampton a						13 41	14 05					14 12						14 41	15 05	
Rugby a						14 04 / 14 17			13 51			14 38						15 04 / 15 17		
Nuneaton a						14 16												15 16		
Coventry a		13 22			13 42	14 29			14 02			14 49		14 22			14 42	15 29		
Birmingham International ✈ a		13 33			13 53	14 45			14 13			15 04		14 33			14 53	15 45		
Birmingham New Street a		13 45			14 08	15 01			14 27			15 16		14 45			15 08	16 01		
Sandwell & Dudley a		13 57												14 57						
Wolverhampton a		14 11												15 11						

London - Watford Junction, Milton Keynes Central, Northampton and West Midlands

Network Diagram - see first Page of Table 59

Station	VT ◇1 ☕	LM 1	VT ◇1 ☕	LM ◇1	VT ◇1 ☕	VT ◇1 ☕	LM 1	LM 1	VT ◇1 ☕	LM ◇1	LM ◇1	SN 1	VT ◇1 ☕	LM 1	VT ◇1 ☕	LM ◇1	VT ◇1 ☕	VT ◇1 ☕	LM 1	LM 1
London Euston ⊖ d	14 03	14 04	14 10	14 13	14 20	14 23	14 24	14 34	14 43	14 46	14 54		15 03	15 04	15 10	15 13	15 20	15 23	15 24	15 34
East Croydon d												14 10								
Clapham Junction d												14 39								
Imperial Wharf d												14 44								
West Brompton ⊖ d												14 47								
Kensington (Olympia) ⊖ d												14 50								
Shepherd's Bush d												14 53								
Wembley Central ⊖ d												15 07								
Harrow & Wealdstone ⊖ d		14 17						14 46				15 12		15 16						15 46
Bushey d		14 22						14 51						15 21						15 51
Watford Junction a		14 25					14 39	14 54		15 00	15 09	15 19		15 24					15 39	15 54
Watford Junction d		14 26				14u37	14 41	14 55		15 01	15 11	15 19		15 25				15u37	15 41	15 55
Kings Langley d		14 30						14 59						15 29						15 59
Apsley d		14 34						15 03						15 33						16 03
Hemel Hempstead d		14 37					14 48	15 06			15 18	15 27		15 36					15 48	16 06
Berkhamsted d		14 42					14 53	15 11			15 23	15 32		15 41					15 53	16 11
Tring d		14a48					14 59	15a17				15 37		15a47					15 59	16a17
Cheddington d							15 04												16 04	
Leighton Buzzard d				14 42			15 09				15 36	15 47				15 42			16 09	
Bletchley d				14 50			15 16				15 43	15 55				15 50			16 16	
Milton Keynes Central a			14 40	14 54	14 50		15 21		15 13	15 24	15 48	16 00			15 40	15 54	15 50		16 21	
Milton Keynes Central d				14 54					15 13	15 25	15 49					15 54				
Wolverton d				14 58							15 52					15 58				
Northampton a				15 12						15 41	16 05					16 12				
Rugby a	14 51			15 38						16 04 / 16 17			15 51			16 38				
Nuneaton a										16 16										
Coventry a	15 02			15 49		15 22			15 42	16 29			16 02			16 49		16 22		
Birmingham International ✈ a	15 13			16 04		15 33			15 53	16 45			16 13			17 04		16 33		
Birmingham New Street a	15 27			16 16		15 45			16 08	17 01			16 27			17 16		16 45		
Sandwell & Dudley a						15 57												16 57		
Wolverhampton a						16 11												17 11		

Station	VT ◇1 ☕	LM ◇1	LM ◇1	SN 1	VT ◇1 ☕	LM 1	VT ◇1 ☕	LM ◇1	VT ◇1 ☕	VT ◇1 ☕	LM 1	LM 1	VT ◇1 ☕	LM ◇1	LM ◇1	SN 1	VT ◇1 ☕	LM 1	VT ◇1 ☕	VT ◇1 ☕
London Euston ⊖ d	15 43	15 46	15 54		16 03	16 04	16 10	16 13	16 20	16 23	16 24	16 34	16 43	16 46	16 54		17 03	17 04	17 07	17 10
East Croydon d				15 10												16 10				
Clapham Junction d				15 39												16 39				
Imperial Wharf d				15 44												16 44				
West Brompton ⊖ d				15 47												16 47				
Kensington (Olympia) ⊖ d				15 50												16 50				
Shepherd's Bush d				15 53												16 53				
Wembley Central ⊖ d				16 07												17 07				
Harrow & Wealdstone ⊖ d				16 12		16 16						16 46				17 12		17 16		
Bushey d						16 21						16 51						17 21		
Watford Junction a		16 00	16 09	16 19		16 24					16 39	16 54		17 00	17 09	17 19		17 24		
Watford Junction d		16 01	16 11	16 19		16 25				16u37	16 41	16 55		17 01	17 11	17 19		17 25		
Kings Langley d						16 29						16 59						17 29		
Apsley d						16 33						17 03						17 33		
Hemel Hempstead d			16 18	16 27		16 36					16 48	17 06			17 18	17 27		17 36		
Berkhamsted d			16 23	16 32		16 41					16 53	17 11			17 23	17 32		17 41		
Tring d				16 37		16a47					16 59	17a17				17 37		17a47		
Cheddington d											17 04									
Leighton Buzzard d			16 36	16 47				16 42			17 09				17 36	17 47				
Bletchley d			16 43	16 55				16 50			17 16				17 43	17 55				
Milton Keynes Central a	16 13	16 24	16 48	17 00			16 40	16 54	16 50		17 21		17 13	17 24	17 48	18 00				17 40
Milton Keynes Central d	16 13	16 25	16 49					16 54					17 13	17 25	17 49					
Wolverton d			16 52					16 58							17 52					
Northampton a		16 41	17 05					17 12						17 41	18 05					
Rugby a		17 04 / 17 17			16 51			17 38						18 04 / 18 17			17 51			
Nuneaton a		17 16												18 16					18 02	
Coventry a	16 42	17 29			17 02			17 49		17 22			17 42	18 29			18 02			
Birmingham International ✈ a	16 53	17 45			17 13			18 04		17 33			17 53	18 45			18 13			
Birmingham New Street a	17 08	18 01			17 27			18 16		17 45			18 08	19 01			18 27			
Sandwell & Dudley a										17 57										
Wolverhampton a										18 11										

London - Watford Junction, Milton Keynes Central, Northampton and West Midlands

Network Diagram - see first Page of Table 59

		LM ◇1	VT ◇1	VT ◇1	LM 1	LM 1	VT ◇1	LM 1	LM ◇1	SN 1	VT ◇1	LM 1	VT ◇1	LM ◇1	VT ◇1	VT ◇1	LM 1	LM 1	VT ◇1	LM 1	LM ◇1 A
London Euston 15 ⊖	d	17 13	17 20	17 23	17 24	17 34	17 43	17 46	17 54		18 03	18 04	18 10	18 13	18 20	18 23	18 24	18 34	18 43	18 46	18 46
East Croydon	d									17 10											
Clapham Junction	d									17 39											
Imperial Wharf	d									17 44											
West Brompton ⊖	d									17 47											
Kensington (Olympia) ⊖	d									17 50											
Shepherd's Bush	d									17 53											
Wembley Central ⊖	d									18 07											
Harrow & Wealdstone ⊖	d					17 46				18 12		18 16						18 46			
Bushey	d					17 51						18 21						18 51			
Watford Junction	a				17 39	17 54		18 00	18 09	18 19		18 24					18 39	18 54		19 00	19 00
	d			17u37	17 41	17 55		18 01	18 11	18 19		18 25				18u37	18 41	18 55		19 01	19 01
Kings Langley	d					17 59						18 29						18 59			
Apsley	d					18 03						18 33						19 03			
Hemel Hempstead	d				17 48	18 06			18 18	18 27		18 36					18 48	19 06			
Berkhamsted	d				17 53	18 11			18 23	18 32		18 41					18 53	19 11			
Tring	d				17 59	18a17				18 37		18a47					18 59	19a17			
Cheddington	d				18 04												19 04				
Leighton Buzzard	d	17 42			18 09				18 36	18 47				18 42			19 09				
Bletchley	d	17 50			18 16				18 43	18 55				18 50			19 16				
Milton Keynes Central 10	a	17 54	17 50		18 21		18 13	18 24	18 48	19 00			18 40	18 54	18 50		19 21		19 13	19 24	19 24
	d	17 54					18 13	18 25	18 49					18 54					19 13	19 25	19 25
Wolverton	d	17 58							18 52					18 58							
Northampton	a	18 12						18 40	19 05					19 12						19 40	19 40
Rugby	a	18 38						19 04 / 19 17			18 51			19 38						20 04	20 17
Nuneaton	a							19 16												20 16	
Coventry	a	18 49		18 22			18 42	19 29			19 02			19 49		19 22			19 42		20 29
Birmingham International ✈	a	19 04		18 33			18 53	19 45			19 13			20 04		19 33			19 53		20 45
Birmingham New Street 12	a	19 16		18 45			19 08	20 02			19 25			20 16		19 45			20 08		21 01
Sandwell & Dudley	a			18 57							19 53					19 58					
Wolverhampton 7	a			19 11							20 08					20 12					

		LM ◇1	SN 1	VT ◇1	LM 1	VT ◇1	LM ◇1	LM 1	VT ◇1	VT ◇1	LM 1	VT ◇1	LM ◇1	SN 1	LM 1	VT ◇1	VT ◇1	VT ◇1	VT ◇1	LM ◇1	LM 1	SN 1	VT ◇1
London Euston 15 ⊖	d	18 54		19 03	19 04	19 07	19 13	19 14	19 20	19 23	19 30	19 43	19 46		20 02	20 11	20 20	20 25	20 31	20 34	20 40		21 00
East Croydon	d		18 10											19 10									
Clapham Junction	d		18 39											19 38								20 25	
Imperial Wharf	d		18 44											19 42								20 29	
West Brompton ⊖	d		18 47											19 45								20 32	
Kensington (Olympia) ⊖	d		18 50											19 48								20 36	
Shepherd's Bush	d		18 53											19 50								20 39	
Wembley Central ⊖	d		19 08																				
Harrow & Wealdstone ⊖	d		19 13		19 17						19 42			20 08							20 52	21 02	
Bushey	d				19 22						19 47										20s57		
Watford Junction	a	19 09	19 21		19 25			19 30			19 50		20 01	20 15	20 18					20 49	21 00	21 09	
	d	19 11			19 26			19 32		19u37	19 51		20 02		20 19			20u40	20u46	20 50	21 01		
Kings Langley	d				19 30						19 55		20 06								21 05		
Apsley	d				19 34						19 59		20 10								21 09		
Hemel Hempstead	d	19 18						19 39			20 02		20 13		20 26					20 57			
Berkhamsted	d	19 23			19 40			19 45			20 07		20 18		20 31					21 02			
Tring	d				19a46			19 50			20 11		20 23								21 19		
Cheddington	d							19 55					20 28							21 10			
Leighton Buzzard	d	19 36					19 42	20 00			20 20		20 35		20 42					21 15			
Bletchley	d	19 43					19 50	20 06			20a26		20 42		20 49					21 22	21 31		
Milton Keynes Central 10	a	19 48					19 54	20 12	19 50			20 20	20 49		20 54		21 03			21 30	21 39		21 43
	d	19 49					19 54					20 20	20 49				21 05			21 30			
Wolverton	d	19 52					19 58						20 53							21 34			
Northampton	a	20 05					20 12						21 07							21 51			
Rugby	a			19 51			20 42						21 38			21 15			21 34	22 17			
Nuneaton	a					20 02											21 32						
Coventry	a			20 02			20 54			20 22		20 49	21 49					21 36		22 29			
Birmingham International ✈	a			20 13			21 12			20 33		21 00	22 04					21 50		22 45			
Birmingham New Street 12	a			20 25			21 24			20 45		21 12	22 16					22 04		23 01			
Sandwell & Dudley	a			20 53						20 58								22 24					
Wolverhampton 7	a			21 08						21 12		21 38						22 38					

A 30 June. ◇ from Northampton

London - Watford Junction, Milton Keynes Central, Northampton and West Midlands

Network Diagram - see first Page of Table 59

		VT ◇1	LM ◇1	LM ◇1	VT ◇1	LM ◇1	SN 1	LM ◇1	SN 1	LM ◇1	LM ◇1
London Euston 15 ⊖	d	21 03	21 08	21 28	21 43	21 54		22 34		23 04	23 44
East Croydon	d										
Clapham Junction	d						21 39		22 39		
Imperial Wharf	d						21 44		22 44		
West Brompton ⊖	d						21 47		22 47		
Kensington (Olympia) ⊖	d						21 50		22 50		
Shepherd's Bush	d						21 53		22 53		
Wembley Central ⊖	d										
Harrow & Wealdstone ⊖	d					22 06	22 13		23 12	23 16	23 56
Bushey	d					22s11					
Watford Junction	a		21 24	21 43		22 14	22 20	22 49	23 19	23 23	00 02
	d	21u18	21 25	21 44	21u58	22 15		22 50		23 24	00 02
Kings Langley	d					22 19				23 28	00 07
Apsley	d					22 23				23 32	00 11
Hemel Hempstead	d		21 32	21 51		22 26		22 57		23 35	00 13
Berkhamsted	d		21 37	21 56		22 31		23 02		23 40	00 18
Tring	d					22 35				23 44	00 24
Cheddington	d					22 41				23 49	00 29
Leighton Buzzard	d		21 50	22 07		22 47		23 13		23 56	00 34
Bletchley	d		21 57	22 14		22 54		23 20		00 03	00 41
Milton Keynes Central 10	a	21 50	22 05	22 22	22 29	23 02		23 28		00 11	00 48
	d	21 50	22 06	22 22	22 30	23 03		23 28		00 11	00 48
Wolverton	d		22 09	22 26		23 06		23 32		00 15	00 52
Northampton	a		22 27	22 43		23 20		23 49		00 28	01 10
Rugby	a	22 11		23 17	22 51						
Nuneaton	a										
Coventry	a	22 22		23 29	23 02						
Birmingham International ✈	a	22 33		23 47	23 13						
Birmingham New Street 12	a	22 45		00 04	23 25						
Sandwell & Dudley	a	22 56			23 36						
Wolverhampton 7	a	23 10			23 50						

Saturdays
7 July to 8 September

		LM ◇1	VT ◇1	LM 1	LM 1	VT ◇1 A	LM 1	VT ◇1 B	LM 1	VT 1 B	LM 1 A	LM 1 B	LM 1 B	VT ◇1 B	VT 1 B	LM 1 B	LM 1 B	LM 1 A	LM 1 B	SN 1	LM ◇1	LM ◇1	SN 1
London Euston 15 ⊖	d	21p46	22p30	22p54	23p24	23p30	23p34	23p45	00 04	00 10	00 34	00 34	00 54	01 00	01 10	01 16	01 34	01 34	01 54			05 34	
East Croydon	d																						
Clapham Junction	d																			05 08			05 38
Imperial Wharf	d																			05 12			05 42
West Brompton ⊖	d																			05 15			05 45
Kensington (Olympia) ⊖	d																			05 19			05 49
Shepherd's Bush	d																			05 22			05 52
Wembley Central ⊖	d										00 45	00 45					01 45	01 45					06 07
Harrow & Wealdstone ⊖	d			23p06			23p46		00 16		00 50	00 50	01 07				01 50	01 50	02 06	05 40		05 46	06 12
Bushey	d						23p51				00 55	00 55											
Watford Junction	a			23p12	23p43		23p54		00 22		00 57	00 57	01 18				01 56	01 56	02 13	05 47		05 52	06 19
	d		22b45	23p12	23p43		23p54		00 23		00 58	00 58	01 20				01 57	01 57	02 13			05 52	06 19
Kings Langley	d			23p17			23p59				01 02	01 02										05 57	
Apsley	d			23p20			00 02				01 06	01 06										06 01	
Hemel Hempstead	d			23p23	23p50		00 05		00 30		01 09	01 09	01 30				02 04	02 04	02 20			06 03	06 27
Berkhamsted	d			23p28	23p55		00 09		00 35		01 14	01 14	01 34				02 09	02 09	02 25			06 08	06 31
Tring	d			23p34			00 15		00 40		01 18	01 23	01 39				02 13	02 13	02 30			06 13	06 37
Cheddington	d						00 20				01 24	01 29										06 18	
Leighton Buzzard	d	22p18		23p41	00 06		00 26		00 49		01 30	01 33	01 48			01 52	02 22	02 22	02 38			06 25	06 47
Bletchley	d			23p49	00 13		00 33		00 56		01 37	01 40	01 54			01 59	02 29	02 29	02 45		05 17	06 32	06 55
Milton Keynes Central 10	a	22p32	23p28	23p55	00 19	00 27	00 41		01 04	00s40	01 45	01 45	01 58			02 03	02 33	02 37	02 50		05 21	06 37	07 00
	d	22p32	23p29	23p55	00 20	00 28			01 04		01 46	01 46				02 03	02 34		02 50		05 21	06 37	
Wolverton	d	22p36		23p59	00 24				01 08		01 49	01 49				02 07	02 37		02 54		05 25	06 41	
Northampton	a	22p49		00 13	00 37				01 21		02 03	02 03				02 19	02 53		03 07		05 37	06 53	
Rugby	a	23p17	23p58			01 05		00s47		01s02				01s55	02s11						06 01	07 17	
Nuneaton	a							01s02						02s06							06 16		
Coventry	a	23p29	00 10			01 18				01s13					02s22							07 29	
Birmingham International ✈	a	23p47	00 21			01 29				01s24					02s33							07 45	
Birmingham New Street 12	a	00 04	00 32			01 41				01s39					02s45							08 01	
Sandwell & Dudley	a																						
Wolverhampton 7	a		01 03			02 10				01 57					03 05								

A 7 July, 14 July, 21 July, 18 August, 25 August
B 28 July, 4 August, 11 August, 1 September, 8 September
b Previous night, stops to pick up only

London - Watford Junction, Milton Keynes Central, Northampton and West Midlands

Network Diagram - see first Page of Table 59

		VT ◇1 ⊐	VT ◇1 ⊐	LM ◇1	SN 1	VT ◇1 ⊐	VT ◇1 ⊐	SN 1	VT ◇1 ⊐	LM 1	VT ◇1 ⊐	VT ◇1 ⊐	LM 1	LM 1	VT ◇1 ⊐	VT ◇1 ⊐	LM ◇1	LM ◇1	SN 1	VT ◇1 ⊐	LM 1	VT ◇1 ⊐	VT ◇1 ⊐
London Euston 15 ⊖	d	06 05	06 23	06 24		06 36	06 55		07 03	07 04	07 20	07 23	07 24	07 34	07 35	07 43	07 46	07 54		08 03	08 04	08 10	08 20
East Croydon	d							06 10											07 10				
Clapham Junction	d				06 09			06 39											07 39				
Imperial Wharf	d				06 13			06 44											07 44				
West Brompton ⊖	d				06 16			06 47											07 47				
Kensington (Olympia) ⊖	d				06 20			06 50											07 50				
Shepherd's Bush	d				06 23			06 53											07 53				
Wembley Central ⊖	d				06 38			07 07											08 07				
Harrow & Wealdstone ⊖	d				06 43			07 12		07 16				07 46					08 12		08 16		
Bushey	d									07 21											08 21		
Watford Junction	a			06 39	06 50			07 19		07 24			07 39	07 52			08 00	08 09	08 19		08 24		
	d	06u20	06u37	06 41				07 19		07 24		07u37	07 42	07 53			08 01	08 11	08 19		08 25		
Kings Langley	d									07 29				07 58							08 29		
Apsley	d									07 32				08 01							08 33		
Hemel Hempstead	d			06 48				07 27		07 35			07 49	08 04				08 18	08 27		08 36		
Berkhamsted	d			06 53				07 32		07 40			07 54	08 09				08 23	08 31		08 41		
Tring	d			06 59				07 39		07 47			08 01	08a16					08 37		08a47		
Cheddington	d			07 05						07 52			08 06										
Leighton Buzzard	d			07 10				07 48		07 57			08 11					08 36	08 47				
Bletchley	d			07 17				07 55		08 04			08 18					08 43	08 55				
Milton Keynes Central 10	a	06 39		07 22			07 25	08 00		08 09	07 50		08 23		08 05	08 13	08 24	08 48	09 00			08 40	08 50
	d	06 41		07 23						08 10						08 13	08 25	08 49					
Wolverton	d			07 26						08 13								08 52					
Northampton	a			07 39						08 26							08 41	09 05					
Rugby	a	07 02		08 04					07 51	08 59							09 04	09 38		08 51			
Nuneaton	a			08 16													09 16						
Coventry	a		07 22						08 02	09 10		08 22				08 42		09 49		09 02			
Birmingham International ✈	a		07 33						08 13	09 28		08 33				08 53		10 04		09 13			
Birmingham New Street 12	a		07 45						08 27	09 42		08 45				09 08		10 16		09 27			
Sandwell & Dudley	a		07 57									08 57											
Wolverhampton 7	a		08 11									09 11											

		VT ◇1 ⊐	LM 1	LM 1	VT ◇1 ⊐	LM ◇1		VT ◇1 ⊐	LM ◇1	SN 1	VT ◇1 ⊐	LM 1	LM ◇1	VT ◇1 ⊐	VT ◇1 ⊐	LM 1	LM 1	VT ◇1 ⊐	LM ◇1		LM 1	SN 1
London Euston 15 ⊖	d	08 23	08 24	08 34	08 43	08 46		08 50	08 54		09 03	09 04	09 13	09 20	09 23	09 24	09 34	09 43	09 46		09 54	
East Croydon	d									08 10												09 10
Clapham Junction	d									08 39												09 39
Imperial Wharf	d									08 44												09 44
West Brompton ⊖	d									08 47												09 47
Kensington (Olympia) ⊖	d									08 50												09 50
Shepherd's Bush	d									08 53												09 53
Wembley Central ⊖	d									09 07												10 07
Harrow & Wealdstone ⊖	d			08 46						09 12		09 16					09 46					10 12
Bushey	d			08 51								09 21					09 51					
Watford Junction	a		08 39	08 54				09 04	09 09	09 19		09 24				09 39	09 54		10 00		10 09	10 19
	d	08u37	08 41	08 55				09 05	09 11	09 19		09 25			09u37	09 41	09 55		10 01		10 11	10 19
Kings Langley	d			08 59								09 29					09 59					
Apsley	d			09 03								09 33					10 03					
Hemel Hempstead	d		08 48	09 06					09 18	09 27		09 36				09 48	10 06				10 18	10 27
Berkhamsted	d		08 53	09 11					09 23	09 33		09 41				09 53	10 11				10 23	10 31
Tring	d		08 59	09a17						09 38		09a47				09 59	10a17					10 37
Cheddington	d		09 04													10 04						
Leighton Buzzard	d		09 09						09 36	09 47			09 42			10 09					10 36	10 47
Bletchley	d		09 16						09 43	09 55			09 50			10 16					10 43	10 55
Milton Keynes Central 10	a		09 21		09 13	09 21		09 24	09 48	10 00			09 54	09 50		10 21		10 13	10 24		10 48	11 00
	d				09 13	09 23			09 49				09 54					10 13	10 25		10 49	
Wolverton	d								09 52				09 58								10 52	
Northampton	a					09 39			10 05				10 12						10 40		11 05	
Rugby	a					10 04	10 17				09 51		10 38						11 04	11 17		
Nuneaton	a					10 16													11 16			
Coventry	a	09 22			09 42		10 29				10 02		10 49		10 22			10 42		11 29		
Birmingham International ✈	a	09 33			09 53		10 45				10 13		11 04		10 33			10 53		11 45		
Birmingham New Street 12	a	09 45			10 08		11 01				10 27		11 16		10 45			11 08		12 01		
Sandwell & Dudley	a	09 57													10 57							
Wolverhampton 7	a	10 11			10 37										11 11							

Table 66

Saturdays

7 July to 8 September

London - Watford Junction, Milton Keynes Central, Northampton and West Midlands

Network Diagram - see first Page of Table 59

		VT ◇1 ⊐	LM 1	VT ◇1 ⊐	LM ◇1	VT ◇1 ⊐	VT ◇1 ⊐	LM 1	LM 1	VT ◇1 ⊐	LM ◇1		LM ◇1	SN 1	VT ◇1 ⊐	LM 1	VT ◇1 ⊐	LM ◇1	VT ◇1 ⊐	VT ◇1 ⊐	LM 1	LM 1	VT ◇1 ⊐
London Euston 15 ⊖	d	10 03	10 04	10 10	10 13	10 20	10 23	10 24	10 34	10 43	10 46		10 54		11 03	11 04	11 10	11 13	11 20	11 23	11 24	11 34	11 43
East Croydon	d													10 10									
Clapham Junction	d													10 39									
Imperial Wharf	d													10 44									
West Brompton ⊖	d													10 47									
Kensington (Olympia) ⊖	d													10 50									
Shepherd's Bush	d													10 53									
Wembley Central ⊖	d													11 08									
Harrow & Wealdstone ⊖	d		10 16						10 46					11 13		11 17						11 46	
Bushey	d		10 21						10 51							11 22						11 51	
Watford Junction	a		10 24					10 39	10 54		11 00		11 10	11 20		11 25					11 39	11 54	
	d		10 25				10u37	10 41	10 55		11 01		11 11	11 20		11 25				11u37	11 41	11 55	
Kings Langley	d		10 29						10 59							11 30						11 59	
Apsley	d		10 33						11 03							11 33						12 03	
Hemel Hempstead	d		10 36					10 48	11 06				11 18	11 28		11 36					11 48	12 06	
Berkhamsted	d		10 41					10 53	11 11				11 23	11 33		11 41					11 53	12 11	
Tring	d		10a47					10 59	11a17					11 38		11a47					11 59	12a17	
Cheddington	d							11 04													12 04		
Leighton Buzzard	d				10 42			11 09					11 36	11 47				11 42			12 09		
Bletchley	d				10 50			11 16					11 43	11 55				11 50			12 16		
Milton Keynes Central 10	a			10 40	10 54	10 50		11 21		11 13	11 24		11 48	12 00			11 40	11 54	11 50		12 21		12 13
	d				10 54					11 13	11 25		11 49					11 54					12 13
Wolverton	d				10 58								11 52					11 58					
Northampton	a				11 12						11 41		12 05					12 12					
Rugby	a	10 51			11 38						12 04	12 17			11 51			12 38					
Nuneaton	a										12 16												
Coventry	a	11 02			11 49		11 22			11 42		12 29			12 02			12 49		12 22			12 42
Birmingham International ✈	a	11 13			12 04		11 33			11 53		12 45			12 13			13 04		12 33			12 53
Birmingham New Street 12	a	11 27			12 16		11 45			12 08		13 01			12 27			13 16		12 45			13 08
Sandwell & Dudley	a						11 57													12 57			
Wolverhampton 7	a						12 11													13 11			

		LM ◇1		LM ◇1	SN 1	VT ◇1 ⊐	LM 1	VT ◇1 ⊐	LM ◇1	VT ◇1 ⊐	VT ◇1 ⊐	LM 1	LM 1	VT ◇1 ⊐	LM ◇1		LM ◇1	SN 1	VT ◇1 ⊐	LM 1	VT ◇1 ⊐	LM ◇1
London Euston 15 ⊖	d	11 46		11 54		12 03	12 04	12 10	12 13	12 20	12 23	12 24	12 34	12 43	12 46		12 54		13 03	13 04	13 10	13 13
East Croydon	d				11 10													12 10				
Clapham Junction	d				11 39													12 39				
Imperial Wharf	d				11 44													12 44				
West Brompton ⊖	d				11 47													12 47				
Kensington (Olympia) ⊖	d				11 50													12 50				
Shepherd's Bush	d				11 53													12 53				
Wembley Central ⊖	d				12 07													13 07				
Harrow & Wealdstone ⊖	d				12 13		12 16						12 46					13 12		13 16		
Bushey	d						12 21						12 51							13 21		
Watford Junction	a	12 00		12 09	12 20		12 24					12 39	12 54		13 00		13 09	13 19		13 24		
	d	12 01		12 11	12 20		12 25				12u37	12 41	12 55		13 01		13 11	13 19		13 25		
Kings Langley	d						12 29						12 59							13 29		
Apsley	d						12 33						13 03							13 33		
Hemel Hempstead	d			12 18	12 28		12 36					12 48	13 06				13 18	13 27		13 36		
Berkhamsted	d			12 23	12 32		12 41					12 53	13 11				13 23	13 32		13 41		
Tring	d				12 37		12a47					12 59	13a17					13 37		13a47		
Cheddington	d											13 04										
Leighton Buzzard	d			12 36	12 47				12 42			13 09					13 36	13 47				13 42
Bletchley	d			12 43	12 55				12 50			13 16					13 43	13 55				13 50
Milton Keynes Central 10	a	12 24		12 48	13 00			12 40	12 54	12 50		13 21		13 13	13 24		13 48	14 00			13 40	13 54
	d	12 25		12 49					12 54					13 13	13 25		13 49					13 54
Wolverton	d			12 52					12 58								13 52					13 58
Northampton	a	12 41		13 05					13 12						13 41		14 05					14 12
Rugby	a	13 04	13 17			12 51			13 38						14 04	14 17			13 51			14 38
Nuneaton	a	13 16													14 16							
Coventry	a		13 29			13 02			13 49		13 22			13 42		14 29			14 02			14 49
Birmingham International ✈	a		13 45			13 13			14 04		13 33			13 53		14 45			14 13			15 04
Birmingham New Street 12	a		14 01			13 27			14 16		13 45			14 08		15 01			14 27			15 16
Sandwell & Dudley	a										13 57											
Wolverhampton 7	a										14 11											

London - Watford Junction, Milton Keynes Central, Northampton and West Midlands

Network Diagram - see first Page of Table 59

		VT ◇■ ⊡	VT ◇■ ⊡	LM ■	LM ■	VT ◇■ ⊡	LM ◇■		LM ◇■	SN ■	VT ◇■ ⊡	LM ■	VT ◇■ ⊡	LM ◇■	VT ◇■ ⊡	VT ◇■ ⊡	LM ■	LM ■	VT ◇■ ⊡	LM ◇■		LM ◇■	SN ■
London Euston ■ ⊖	d	13 20	13 23	13 24	13 34	13 43	13 46		13 54		14 03	14 04	14 10	14 13	14 20	14 23	14 24	14 34	14 43	14 46		14 54	
East Croydon	d									13 10													14 10
Clapham Junction	d									13 39													14 39
Imperial Wharf	d									13 44													14 44
West Brompton ⊖	d									13 47													14 47
Kensington (Olympia) ⊖	d									13 50													14 50
Shepherd's Bush	d									13 53													14 53
Wembley Central ⊖	d									14 08													15 07
Harrow & Wealdstone ⊖	d				13 46					14 13		14 17						14 46					15 12
Bushey	d				13 51							14 22						14 51					
Watford Junction	a			13 39	13 54		14 00		14 09	14 20		14 25					14 39	14 54		15 00		15 09	15 19
	d		13u37	13 41	13 55		14 01		14 11	14 20		14 26				14u37	14 41	14 55		15 01		15 11	15 19
Kings Langley	d				13 59							14 30						14 59					
Apsley	d				14 03							14 34						15 03					
Hemel Hempstead	d			13 48	14 06				14 18	14 28		14 37					14 48	15 06				15 18	15 27
Berkhamsted	d			13 53	14 11				14 23	14 32		14 42					14 53	15 11				15 23	15 32
Tring	d			13 59	14a17					14 37		14a48					14 59	15a17					15 37
Cheddington	d			14 04													15 04						
Leighton Buzzard	d			14 09					14 36	14 47				14 42			15 09					15 36	15 47
Bletchley	d			14 16					14 43	14 55				14 50			15 16					15 43	15 55
Milton Keynes Central ■	a	13 50		14 21		14 13	14 24		14 48	15 00			14 40	14 54	14 50		15 21		15 13	15 24		15 48	16 00
	d					14 13	14 25		14 49					14 54					15 13	15 25		15 49	
Wolverton	d								14 52					14 58								15 52	
Northampton	a						14 41		15 05					15 12						15 41		16 05	
Rugby	a						15 04	15 17			14 51			15 38						16 04	16 17		
Nuneaton	a						15 16													16 16			
Coventry	a		14 22			14 42		15 29			15 02			15 49		15 22			15 42		16 29		
Birmingham International ✈	a		14 33			14 53		15 45			15 13			16 04		15 33			15 53		16 45		
Birmingham New Street ■	a		14 45			15 08		16 01			15 27			16 16		15 45			16 08		17 01		
Sandwell & Dudley	a		14 57													15 57							
Wolverhampton ■	a		15 11			15 37										16 11							

		VT ◇■ ⊡	LM ■	VT ◇■ ⊡	LM ◇■	VT ◇■ ⊡	VT ◇■ ⊡	LM ■	LM ■	VT ◇■ ⊡	LM ◇■		LM ◇■	SN ■	VT ◇■ ⊡	LM ■	VT ◇■ ⊡	LM ◇■	VT ◇■ ⊡	VT ◇■ ⊡	LM ■	LM ■	VT ◇■ ⊡
London Euston ■ ⊖	d	15 03	15 04	15 10	15 13	15 20	15 23	15 24	15 34	15 43	15 46		15 54		16 03	16 04	16 10	16 13	16 20	16 23	16 24	16 34	16 43
East Croydon	d													15 10									
Clapham Junction	d													15 39									
Imperial Wharf	d													15 44									
West Brompton ⊖	d													15 47									
Kensington (Olympia) ⊖	d													15 50									
Shepherd's Bush	d													15 53									
Wembley Central ⊖	d													16 07									
Harrow & Wealdstone ⊖	d		15 16						15 46					16 12		16 16						16 46	
Bushey	d		15 21						15 51							16 21						16 51	
Watford Junction	a		15 24					15 39	15 54		16 00		16 09	16 19		16 24					16 39	16 54	
	d		15 25				15u37	15 41	15 55		16 01		16 11	16 19		16 25				16u37	16 41	16 55	
Kings Langley	d		15 29						15 59							16 29						16 59	
Apsley	d		15 33						16 03							16 33						17 03	
Hemel Hempstead	d		15 36					15 48	16 06				16 18	16 27		16 36					16 48	17 06	
Berkhamsted	d		15 41					15 53	16 11				16 23	16 32		16 41					16 53	17 11	
Tring	d		15a47					15 59	16a17					16 37		16a47					16 59	17a17	
Cheddington	d							16 04													17 04		
Leighton Buzzard	d				15 42			16 09					16 36	16 47				16 42			17 09		
Bletchley	d				15 50			16 16					16 43	16 55				16 50			17 16		
Milton Keynes Central ■	a			15 40	15 54	15 50		16 21		16 13	16 24		16 48	17 00			16 40	16 54	16 50		17 21		17 13
	d				15 54					16 13	16 25		16 49					16 54					17 13
Wolverton	d				15 58								16 52					16 58					
Northampton	a				16 12						16 41		17 05					17 12					
Rugby	a	15 51			16 38						17 04	17 17			16 51			17 38					
Nuneaton	a										17 16												
Coventry	a	16 02			16 49		16 22			16 42		17 29			17 02			17 49		17 22			17 42
Birmingham International ✈	a	16 13			17 04		16 33			16 53		17 45			17 13			18 04		17 33			17 53
Birmingham New Street ■	a	16 27			17 16		16 45			17 08		18 01			17 27			18 16		17 45			18 08
Sandwell & Dudley	a						16 57													17 57			
Wolverhampton ■	a						17 11													18 11			

London - Watford Junction, Milton Keynes Central, Northampton and West Midlands

Network Diagram - see first Page of Table 59

		LM ◇■		LM ◇■	SN ■	VT ◇■ ⊡	LM ■	VT ◇■ ⊡	VT ◇■ ⊡	LM ◇■	VT ◇■ ⊡	VT ◇■ ⊡	LM ■	LM ■	VT ◇■ ⊡	LM ■		LM ◇■	SN ■	VT ◇■ ⊡	LM ■	VT ◇■ ⊡
London Euston ■ ⊖	d	16 46		16 54		17 03	17 04	17 07	17 10	17 13	17 20	17 23	17 24	17 34	17 43	17 46		17 54		18 03	18 04	18 10
East Croydon	d				16 10														17 10			
Clapham Junction	d				16 39														17 39			
Imperial Wharf	d				16 44														17 44			
West Brompton ⊖	d				16 47														17 47			
Kensington (Olympia) ⊖	d				16 50														17 50			
Shepherd's Bush	d				16 53														17 53			
Wembley Central ⊖	d				17 07														18 07			
Harrow & Wealdstone ⊖	d				17 12		17 16							17 46					18 12		18 16	
Bushey	d						17 21							17 51							18 21	
Watford Junction	a	17 00		17 09	17 19		17 24						17 39	17 54		18 00		18 09	18 19		18 24	
	d	17 01		17 11	17 19		17 25					17u37	17 41	17 55		18 01		18 11	18 19		18 25	
Kings Langley	d						17 29							17 59							18 29	
Apsley	d						17 33							18 03							18 33	
Hemel Hempstead	d			17 18	17 27		17 36						17 48	18 06				18 18	18 27		18 36	
Berkhamsted	d			17 23	17 32		17 41						17 53	18 11				18 23	18 32		18 41	
Tring	d				17 37		17a47						17 59	18a17					18 37		18a47	
Cheddington	d												18 04									
Leighton Buzzard	d			17 36	17 47					17 42			18 09					18 36	18 47			
Bletchley	d			17 43	17 55					17 50			18 16					18 43	18 55			
Milton Keynes Central ■	a	17 24		17 48	18 00				17 40	17 54	17 50		18 21		18 13	18 24		18 48	19 00			18 40
	d	17 25		17 49						17 54					18 13	18 25		18 49				
Wolverton	d			17 52						17 58								18 52				
Northampton	a	17 41		18 05						18 12						18 40		19 05				
Rugby	a	18 04	18 17			17 51				18 38						19 04	19 17			18 51		
Nuneaton	a	18 16						18 02								19 16						
Coventry	a		18 29			18 02				18 49		18 22			18 42		19 29			19 02		
Birmingham International ✈	a		18 45			18 13				19 04		18 33			18 53		19 45			19 13		
Birmingham New Street ■	a		19 01			18 27				19 16		18 45			19 08		20 02			19 25		
Sandwell & Dudley	a											18 57								19 53		
Wolverhampton ■	a											19 11			19 37					20 08		

		LM ◇■	VT ◇■ ⊡	VT ◇■ ⊡	LM ■	LM ■	VT ◇■ ⊡	LM ■		LM ◇■	SN ■	VT ◇■ ⊡	LM ■	VT ◇■ ⊡	LM ◇■	LM ■	VT ◇■ ⊡	VT ◇■ ⊡	LM ■	VT ◇■ ⊡	LM ◇■	SN ■	LM ■
London Euston ■ ⊖	d	18 13	18 20	18 23	18 24	18 34	18 43	18 46		18 54		19 03	19 04	19 07	19 13	19 14	19 20	19 23	19 30	19 43	19 46		20 02
East Croydon	d										18 10											19 10	
Clapham Junction	d										18 39											19 38	
Imperial Wharf	d										18 44											19 42	
West Brompton ⊖	d										18 47											19 45	
Kensington (Olympia) ⊖	d										18 50											19 48	
Shepherd's Bush	d										18 53											19 50	
Wembley Central ⊖	d										19 08												
Harrow & Wealdstone ⊖	d					18 46					19 13		19 17						19 42			20 08	
Bushey	d					18 51							19 22						19 47				
Watford Junction	a				18 39	18 54		19 00		19 09	19 21		19 25			19 30			19 50		20 01	20 15	20 18
	d			18u37	18 41	18 55		19 01		19 11			19 26			19 32		19u37	19 51		20 02		20 19
Kings Langley	d					18 59							19 30						19 55		20 06		
Apsley	d					19 03							19 34						19 59		20 10		
Hemel Hempstead	d				18 48	19 06				19 18						19 39			20 02		20 13		20 26
Berkhamsted	d				18 53	19 11				19 23			19 40			19 45			20 07		20 18		20 31
Tring	d				18 59	19a17							19a46			19 50			20 11		20 23		
Cheddington	d				19 04											19 55					20 28		
Leighton Buzzard	d	18 42			19 09					19 36					19 42	20 00			20 20		20 35		20 42
Bletchley	d	18 50			19 16					19 43					19 50	20 06			20a26		20 42		20 49
Milton Keynes Central ■	a	18 54	18 50		19 21		19 13	19 24		19 48					19 54	20 12	19 50			20 20	20 49		20 54
	d	18 54					19 13	19 25		19 49					19 54					20 20	20 49		
Wolverton	d	18 58								19 52					19 58						20 53		
Northampton	a	19 12						19 40		20 05					20 12						21 07		
Rugby	a	19 38						20 04	20 17			19 51			20 42						21 38		
Nuneaton	a							20 16						20 02									
Coventry	a	19 49		19 22			19 42		20 29			20 02			20 54			20 22		20 49	21 49		
Birmingham International ✈	a	20 04		19 33			19 53		20 45			20 13			21 12			20 33		21 00	22 04		
Birmingham New Street ■	a	20 16		19 45			20 08		21 01			20 25			21 24			20 45		21 12	22 16		
Sandwell & Dudley	a			19 58								20 53						20 58					
Wolverhampton ■	a			20 12								21 08						21 12		21 38			

Table 66

London - Watford Junction, Milton Keynes Central, Northampton and West Midlands

Network Diagram - see first Page of Table 59

		VT	VT	VT	VT	LM	LM	SN	VT	VT	LM	LM	VT	LM	SN	LM	SN	LM	VT	LM	VT
		◇1	◇1	◇1	◇1	◇1	1	1	◇1	◇1	◇1	◇1	◇1	◇1	1	◇1	1	◇1	1 A	◇1	◇1 A
London Euston 15 ⊖	d	20 11	20 20	20 25	20 31	20 34	20 40		21 00	21 03	21 08	21 28	21 43	21 54		22 34		23 04	23 10	23 44	23 45
East Croydon	d																				
Clapham Junction	d							20 25							21 39		22 39				
Imperial Wharf	d							20 29							21 44		22 44				
West Brompton ⊖	d							20 32							21 47		22 47				
Kensington (Olympia) ⊖	d							20 36							21 50		22 50				
Shepherd's Bush	d							20 39							21 53		22 53				
Wembley Central ⊖	d																				
Harrow & Wealdstone ⊖	d						20 52	21 02						22 06	22 13		23 12	23 16		23 56	
Bushey	d						20s57							22s11							
Watford Junction	a					20 49	21 00	21 09			21 24	21 43		22 14	22 20	22 49	23 19	23 23		00 02	
	d			20u40	20u46	20 50	21 01			21u18	21 25	21 44	21u58	22 15		22 50		23 24		00 02	
Kings Langley	d						21 05							22 19				23 28		00 07	
Apsley	d						21 09							22 23				23 32		00 11	
Hemel Hempstead	d					20 57					21 32	21 51		22 26		22 57		23 35		00 13	
Berkhamsted	d					21 02					21 37	21 56		22 31		23 02		23 40		00 18	
Tring	d						21 19							22 35				23 44		00 24	
Cheddington	d					21 10								22 41				23 49		00 29	
Leighton Buzzard	d					21 15					21 50	22 07		22 47		23 13		23 56		00 34	
Bletchley	d					21 22	21 31				21 57	22 14		22 54		23 20		00 03		00 41	
Milton Keynes Central 10	a		21 03			21 30	21 39		21 43	21 50	22 05	22 22	22 29	23 02		23 28		00 11		00 48	
	d		21 05			21 30				21 50	22 06	22 22	22 30	23 03		23 28		00 11		00 48	
Wolverton	d					21 34					22 09	22 26		23 06		23 32		00 15		00 52	
Northampton	a					21 51					22 27	22 43		23 20		23 49		00 28		01 10	
Rugby	a	21 15			21 34	22 17				22 11		23 17	22 51						23s58		00s42
Nuneaton	a		21 32																		00s52
Coventry	a			21 36		22 29				22 22		23 29	23 02						00s09		
Birmingham International ✈	a			21 50		22 45				22 33		23 47	23 13						00s20		
Birmingham New Street 12	a			22 04		23 01				22 45		00 04	23 25						00 34		
Sandwell & Dudley	a			22 24						22 56			23 36								
Wolverhampton 7	a			22 38						23 10			23 50								

		LM	VT	LM	LM	LM	VT	LM	LM	LM	LM	SN	LM	LM	SN	VT	VT	LM	SN	VT	VT	SN	VT
		◇1	◇1	1	1 B	1 C	◇1	1	1	1	1	1	◇1	◇1	1	◇1	◇1	◇1	1	◇1	◇1	1	◇1
London Euston 15 ⊖	d	21p46	22p30	22p54	23p24	23p24	23p30	23p34	00 04	00 34	01 34			05 34		06 05	06 23	06 24		06 36	06 55		07 03
East Croydon	d																					06 10	
Clapham Junction	d											05 08			05 38				06 09			06 39	
Imperial Wharf	d											05 12			05 42				06 13			06 44	
West Brompton ⊖	d											05 15			05 45				06 16			06 47	
Kensington (Olympia) ⊖	d											05 19			05 49				06 20			06 50	
Shepherd's Bush	d											05 22			05 52				06 23			06 53	
Wembley Central ⊖	d									00 45	01 45				06 07				06 38			07 07	
Harrow & Wealdstone ⊖	d			23p06				23p46	00 16	00 50	01 50	05 40		05 46	06 12				06 43			07 12	
Bushey	d							23p51		00 55													
Watford Junction	a			23p12	23p39	23p43		23p54	00 22	00 57	01 56	05 47		05 52	06 19			06 39	06 50			07 19	
	d		22b45	23p12	23p40	23p43		23p54	00 23	00 58	01 57			05 52	06 19	06u20	06u37	06 41				07 19	
Kings Langley	d			23p17				23p59		01 02				05 57									
Apsley	d			23p20				00 02		01 06				06 01									
Hemel Hempstead	d			23p23	23p47	23p50		00 05	00 30	01 09	02 04			06 03	06 27			06 48				07 27	
Berkhamsted	d			23p28	23p52	23p55		00 09	00 35	01 14	02 09			06 08	06 31			06 53				07 32	
Tring	d			23p34				00 15	00 40	01 18	02 13			06 13	06 37			06 59				07 39	
Cheddington	d							00 20		01 24				06 18				07 05					
Leighton Buzzard	d	22p18		23p41	00 05	00 06		00 26	00 49	01 30	02 22			06 25	06 47			07 10				07 48	
Bletchley	d			23p49	00 13	00 13		00 33	00 56	01 37	02 29		05 17	06 32	06 55			07 17				07 55	
Milton Keynes Central 10	a	22p32	23p28	23p55	00 21	00 19	00 27	00 41	01 04	01 45	02 37		05 21	06 37	07 00	06 39		07 22			07 25	08 00	
	d	22p32	23p29	23p55	00 21	00 20	00 28		01 04	01 46			05 21	06 37		06 41		07 23					
Wolverton	d	22p36		23p59	00 25	00 24			01 08	01 49			05 25	06 41				07 26					
Northampton	a	22p49		00 13	00 38	00 37			01 21	02 03			05 37	06 53				07 39					
Rugby	a	23p17	23p58				01 05						06 01	07 17		07 02		08 04					07 51
Nuneaton	a												06 16					08 16					
Coventry	a	23p29	00 10				01 18							07 29			07 22						08 02
Birmingham International ✈	a	23p47	00 21				01 29							07 45			07 33						08 13
Birmingham New Street 12	a	00 04	00 32				01 41							08 01			07 45						08 27
Sandwell & Dudley	a																07 57						
Wolverhampton 7	a		01 03				02 10										08 11						

A 28 July, 4 August, 11 August, 1 September, 8 September
B not 15 September
C 15 September
b Previous night, stops to pick up only

Table 66

London - Watford Junction, Milton Keynes Central, Northampton and West Midlands

Network Diagram - see first Page of Table 59

		LM	VT	VT	LM	LM	VT	VT	LM	LM	SN	VT	LM	VT	VT	VT	LM	LM	VT	LM		VT	LM
		1	◇1	◇1	1	1	◇1	◇1	◇1	◇1	1	◇1	1	◇1	◇1	◇1	1	1	◇1	◇1		◇1	◇1
London Euston 15 ⊖	d	07 04	07 20	07 23	07 24	07 34	07 35	07 43	07 46	07 54		08 03	08 04	08 10	08 20	08 23	08 24	08 34	08 43	08 46		08 50	08 54
East Croydon	d										07 10												
Clapham Junction	d										07 39												
Imperial Wharf	d										07 44												
West Brompton ⊖	d										07 47												
Kensington (Olympia) ⊖	d										07 50												
Shepherd's Bush	d										07 53												
Wembley Central ⊖	d										08 07												
Harrow & Wealdstone ⊖	d	07 16				07 46					08 12		08 16					08 46					
Bushey	d	07 21											08 21					08 51					
Watford Junction	a	07 24			07 39	07 52			08 00	08 09	08 19		08 24				08 39	08 54				09 04	09 09
	d	07 24		07u37	07 42	07 53			08 01	08 11	08 19		08 25			08u37	08 41	08 55				09 05	09 11
Kings Langley	d	07 29				07 58							08 29					08 59					
Apsley	d	07 32				08 01							08 33					09 03					
Hemel Hempstead	d	07 35			07 49	08 04				08 18	08 27		08 36				08 48	09 06					09 18
Berkhamsted	d	07 40			07 54	08 09				08 23	08 31		08 41				08 53	09 11					09 23
Tring	d	07 47			08 01	08a16					08 37		08a47				08 59	09a17					
Cheddington	d	07 52			08 06												09 04						
Leighton Buzzard	d	07 57			08 11					08 36	08 47						09 09						09 36
Bletchley	d	08 04			08 18					08 43	08 55						09 16						09 43
Milton Keynes Central 10	a	08 09	07 50		08 23		08 05	08 13	08 24	08 48	09 00			08 40	08 50		09 21		09 13	09 21		09 24	09 48
	d	08 10						08 13	08 25	08 49									09 13	09 23			09 49
Wolverton	d	08 13								08 52													09 52
Northampton	a	08 26							08 41	09 05										09 39			10 05
Rugby	a	08 59							09 04	09 38		08 51								10 04	10 17		
Nuneaton	a								09 16											10 16			
Coventry	a	09 10		08 22				08 42		09 49		09 02				09 22			09 42		10 29		
Birmingham International ✈	a	09 28		08 33				08 53		10 04		09 13				09 33			09 53		10 45		
Birmingham New Street 12	a	09 42		08 45				09 08		10 16		09 27				09 45			10 08		11 01		
Sandwell & Dudley	a			08 57												09 57							
Wolverhampton 7	a			09 11												10 11							

		SN	VT	LM	LM	VT	VT	LM	LM	VT	LM		LM	SN	VT	LM	VT	LM	VT	VT	LM	LM
		1	◇1	1	◇1	◇1	◇1	1	1	◇1	◇1		1	1	◇1	1	◇1	◇1	◇1	◇1	1	1
London Euston 15 ⊖	d		09 03	09 04	09 13	09 20	09 23	09 24	09 34	09 43	09 46		09 54		10 03	10 04	10 10	10 13	10 20	10 23	10 24	10 34
East Croydon	d	08 10												09 10								
Clapham Junction	d	08 39												09 39								
Imperial Wharf	d	08 44												09 44								
West Brompton ⊖	d	08 47												09 47								
Kensington (Olympia) ⊖	d	08 50												09 50								
Shepherd's Bush	d	08 53												09 53								
Wembley Central ⊖	d	09 07												10 07								
Harrow & Wealdstone ⊖	d	09 12		09 16					09 46					10 12		10 16						10 46
Bushey	d			09 21					09 51							10 21						10 51
Watford Junction	a	09 19		09 24				09 39	09 54		10 00		10 09	10 19		10 24					10 39	10 54
	d	09 19		09 25			09u37	09 41	09 55		10 01		10 11	10 19		10 25				10u37	10 41	10 55
Kings Langley	d			09 29					09 59							10 29						10 59
Apsley	d			09 33					10 03							10 33						11 03
Hemel Hempstead	d	09 27		09 36				09 48	10 06				10 18	10 27		10 36					10 48	11 06
Berkhamsted	d	09 33		09 41				09 53	10 11				10 23	10 31		10 41					10 53	11 11
Tring	d	09 38		09a47				09 59	10a17					10 37		10a47					10 59	11a17
Cheddington	d							10 04													11 04	
Leighton Buzzard	d	09 47			09 42			10 09					10 36	10 47				10 42			11 09	
Bletchley	d	09 55			09 50			10 16					10 43	10 55				10 50			11 16	
Milton Keynes Central 10	a	10 00			09 54	09 50		10 21		10 13	10 24		10 48	11 00			10 40	10 54	10 50		11 21	
	d				09 54					10 13	10 25		10 49					10 54				
Wolverton	d				09 58								10 52					10 58				
Northampton	a				10 12						10 40		11 05					11 12				
Rugby	a		09 51		10 38						11 04	11 17			10 51			11 38				
Nuneaton	a										11 16											
Coventry	a		10 02		10 49		10 22			10 42		11 29			11 02			11 49		11 22		
Birmingham International ✈	a		10 13		11 04		10 33			10 53		11 45			11 13			12 04		11 33		
Birmingham New Street 12	a		10 27		11 16		10 45			11 08		12 01			11 27			12 16		11 45		
Sandwell & Dudley	a						10 57													11 57		
Wolverhampton 7	a						11 11													12 11		

London - Watford Junction, Milton Keynes Central, Northampton and West Midlands

Network Diagram - see first Page of Table 59

		VT	LM		LM	SN	VT	LM	VT	LM	VT	VT	LM	LM	VT	LM		LM	SN	VT	LM	VT	LM
		◇1	◇1		◇1	1	◇1	1	◇1	◇1	◇1	◇1	1	1	◇1	◇1		◇1	1	◇1	1	◇1	◇1
London Euston	d	10 43	10 46		10 54		11 03	11 04	11 10	11 13	11 20	11 23	11 24	11 34	11 43	11 46		11 54		12 03	12 04	12 10	12 13
East Croydon	d					10 10													11 10				
Clapham Junction	d					10 39													11 39				
Imperial Wharf	d					10 44													11 44				
West Brompton	d					10 47													11 47				
Kensington (Olympia)	d					10 50													11 50				
Shepherd's Bush	d					10 53													11 53				
Wembley Central	d					11 08													12 07				
Harrow & Wealdstone	d					11 13		11 17						11 46					12 13		12 16		
Bushey	d							11 22						11 51							12 21		
Watford Junction	a		11 00		11 10	11 20		11 25					11 39	11 54		12 00		12 09	12 20		12 24		
	d		11 01		11 11	11 20		11 25				11u37	11 41	11 55		12 01		12 11	12 20		12 25		
Kings Langley	d							11 30						11 59							12 29		
Apsley	d							11 33						12 03							12 33		
Hemel Hempstead	d				11 18	11 28		11 36					11 48	12 06				12 18	12 28		12 36		
Berkhamsted	d				11 23	11 33		11 41					11 53	12 11				12 23	12 32		12 41		
Tring	d					11 38		11a47					11 59	12a17					12 37		12a47		
Cheddington	d												12 04										
Leighton Buzzard	d				11 36	11 47				11 42			12 09					12 36	12 47				12 42
Bletchley	d				11 43	11 55				11 50			12 16					12 43	12 55				12 50
Milton Keynes Central	a	11 13	11 24		11 48	12 00			11 40	11 54	11 50		12 21		12 13	12 24		12 48	13 00			12 40	12 54
	d	11 13	11 25		11 49					11 54					12 13	12 25		12 49					12 54
Wolverton	d				11 52					11 58								12 52					12 58
Northampton	a		11 41		12 05					12 12						12 41		13 05					13 12
Rugby	a		12 04	12 17			11 51			12 38						13 04	13 17			12 51			13 38
Nuneaton	a		12 16													13 16							
Coventry	a	11 42		12 29			12 02			12 49		12 22			12 42		13 29			13 02			13 49
Birmingham International	a	11 53		12 45			12 13			13 04		12 33			12 53		13 45			13 13			14 04
Birmingham New Street	a	12 08		13 01			12 27			13 16		12 45			13 08		14 01			13 27			14 16
Sandwell & Dudley	a											12 57											
Wolverhampton	a											13 11											

		VT	VT	LM	LM	VT	LM		LM	SN	VT	LM	VT	LM	VT	VT	LM	LM	VT	LM		LM	SN
		◇1	◇1	1	1	◇1	◇1		◇1	1	◇1	1	◇1	◇1	◇1	◇1	1	1	◇1	◇1		◇1	1
London Euston	d	12 20	12 23	12 24	12 34	12 43	12 46		12 54		13 03	13 04	13 10	13 13	13 20	13 23	13 24	13 34	13 43	13 46		13 54	
East Croydon	d									12 10													13 10
Clapham Junction	d									12 39													13 39
Imperial Wharf	d									12 44													13 44
West Brompton	d									12 47													13 47
Kensington (Olympia)	d									12 50													13 50
Shepherd's Bush	d									12 53													13 53
Wembley Central	d									13 07													14 08
Harrow & Wealdstone	d				12 46					13 12		13 16						13 46					14 13
Bushey	d				12 51							13 21						13 51					
Watford Junction	a			12 39	12 54		13 00		13 09	13 19		13 24					13 39	13 54		14 00		14 09	14 20
	d		12u37	12 41	12 55		13 01		13 11	13 19		13 25				13u37	13 41	13 55		14 01		14 11	14 20
Kings Langley	d				12 59							13 29						13 59					
Apsley	d				13 03							13 33						14 03					
Hemel Hempstead	d			12 48	13 06				13 18	13 27		13 36					13 48	14 06				14 18	14 28
Berkhamsted	d			12 53	13 11				13 23	13 32		13 41					13 53	14 11				14 23	14 32
Tring	d			12 59	13a17					13 37		13a47					13 59	14a17					14 37
Cheddington	d			13 04													14 04						
Leighton Buzzard	d			13 09					13 36	13 47				13 42			14 09					14 36	14 47
Bletchley	d			13 16					13 43	13 55				13 50			14 16					14 43	14 55
Milton Keynes Central	a	12 50		13 21		13 13	13 24		13 48	14 00			13 40	13 54	13 50		14 21		14 13	14 24		14 48	15 00
	d					13 13	13 25		13 49					13 54					14 13	14 25		14 49	
Wolverton	d								13 52					13 58								14 52	
Northampton	a						13 41		14 05					14 12						14 41		15 05	
Rugby	a						14 04	14 17			13 51			14 38						15 04	15 17		
Nuneaton	a						14 16													15 16			
Coventry	a		13 22			13 42		14 29			14 02			14 49		14 22			14 42		15 29		
Birmingham International	a		13 33			13 53		14 45			14 13			15 04		14 33			14 53		15 45		
Birmingham New Street	a		13 45			14 08		15 01			14 27			15 16		14 45			15 08		16 01		
Sandwell & Dudley	a		13 57													14 57							
Wolverhampton	a		14 11													15 11							

Table 66

Saturdays
from 15 September

London - Watford Junction, Milton Keynes Central, Northampton and West Midlands

Network Diagram - see first Page of Table 59

		VT	LM	VT	LM	VT	VT	LM	LM	VT	LM		LM	SN	VT	LM	VT	LM	VT	VT	LM	LM
		◇1	1	◇1	◇1	◇1	◇1	1	1	◇1	◇1		◇1	1	◇1	1	◇1	◇1	◇1	◇1	1	1
London Euston	d	14 03	14 04	14 10	14 13	14 20	14 23	14 24	14 34	14 43	14 46		14 54		15 03	15 04	15 10	15 13	15 20	15 23	15 24	15 34
East Croydon	d													14 10								
Clapham Junction	d													14 39								
Imperial Wharf	d													14 44								
West Brompton	d													14 47								
Kensington (Olympia)	d													14 50								
Shepherd's Bush	d													14 53								
Wembley Central	d													15 07								
Harrow & Wealdstone	d		14 17						14 46					15 12		15 16						15 46
Bushey	d		14 22						14 51							15 21						15 51
Watford Junction	a		14 25					14 39	14 54		15 00		15 09	15 19		15 24					15 39	15 54
	d		14 26				14u37	14 41	14 55		15 01		15 11	15 19		15 25				15u37	15 41	15 55
Kings Langley	d		14 30						14 59							15 29						15 59
Apsley	d		14 34						15 03							15 33						16 03
Hemel Hempstead	d		14 37					14 48	15 06				15 18	15 27		15 36					15 48	16 06
Berkhamsted	d		14 42					14 53	15 11				15 23	15 32		15 41					15 53	16 11
Tring	d		14a48					14 59	15a17					15 37		15a47					15 59	16a17
Cheddington	d							15 04													16 04	
Leighton Buzzard	d				14 42			15 09					15 36	15 47				15 42			16 09	
Bletchley	d				14 50			15 16					15 43	15 55				15 50			16 16	
Milton Keynes Central	a			14 40	14 54	14 50		15 21		15 13	15 24		15 48	16 00			15 40	15 54	15 50		16 21	
	d				14 54					15 13	15 25		15 49					15 54				
Wolverton	d				14 58								15 52					15 58				
Northampton	a				15 12						15 41		16 05					16 12				
Rugby	a	14 51			15 38						16 04	16 17			15 51			16 38				
Nuneaton	a										16 16											
Coventry	a	15 02			15 49		15 22			15 42		16 29			16 02			16 49		16 22		
Birmingham International	a	15 13			16 04		15 33			15 53		16 45			16 13			17 04		16 33		
Birmingham New Street	a	15 27			16 16		15 45			16 08		17 01			16 27			17 16		16 45		
Sandwell & Dudley	a						15 57													16 57		
Wolverhampton	a						16 11													17 11		

		VT	LM		LM	SN	VT	LM	VT	LM	VT	VT	LM	LM	VT	LM		LM	SN	VT	LM	VT	VT
		◇1	◇1		◇1	1	◇1	1	◇1	◇1	◇1	◇1	1	1	◇1	◇1		◇1	1	◇1	1	◇1	◇1
London Euston	d	15 43	15 46		15 54		16 03	16 04	16 10	16 13	16 20	16 23	16 24	16 34	16 43	16 46		16 54		17 03	17 04	17 07	17 10
East Croydon	d					15 10													16 10				
Clapham Junction	d					15 39													16 39				
Imperial Wharf	d					15 44													16 44				
West Brompton	d					15 47													16 47				
Kensington (Olympia)	d					15 50													16 50				
Shepherd's Bush	d					15 53													16 53				
Wembley Central	d					16 07													17 07				
Harrow & Wealdstone	d					16 12		16 16						16 46					17 12		17 16		
Bushey	d							16 21						16 51							17 21		
Watford Junction	a		16 00		16 09	16 19		16 24					16 39	16 54		17 00		17 09	17 19		17 24		
	d		16 01		16 11	16 19		16 25				16u37	16 41	16 55		17 01		17 11	17 19		17 25		
Kings Langley	d							16 29						16 59							17 29		
Apsley	d							16 33						17 03							17 33		
Hemel Hempstead	d				16 18	16 27		16 36					16 48	17 06				17 18	17 27		17 36		
Berkhamsted	d				16 23	16 32		16 41					16 53	17 11				17 23	17 32		17 41		
Tring	d					16 37		16a47					16 59	17a17					17 37		17a47		
Cheddington	d												17 04										
Leighton Buzzard	d				16 36	16 47				16 42			17 09					17 36	17 47				
Bletchley	d				16 43	16 55				16 50			17 16					17 43	17 55				
Milton Keynes Central	a	16 13	16 24		16 48	17 00			16 40	16 54	16 50		17 21		17 13	17 24		17 48	18 00				17 40
	d	16 13	16 25		16 49					16 54					17 13	17 25		17 49					
Wolverton	d				16 52					16 58								17 52					
Northampton	a		16 41		17 05					17 12						17 41		18 05					
Rugby	a		17 04	17 17			16 51			17 38						18 04	18 17			17 51			
Nuneaton	a		17 16													18 16						18 02	
Coventry	a	16 42		17 29			17 02			17 49		17 22			17 42		18 29			18 02			
Birmingham International	a	16 53		17 45			17 13			18 04		17 33			17 53		18 45			18 13			
Birmingham New Street	a	17 08		18 01			17 27			18 16		17 45			18 08		19 01			18 27			
Sandwell & Dudley	a											17 57											
Wolverhampton	a											18 11											

Table 66

Saturdays from 15 September

London - Watford Junction, Milton Keynes Central, Northampton and West Midlands

Network Diagram - see first Page of Table 59

		LM	VT	VT	LM	LM	VT	LM		LM	SN	VT	LM	VT	LM	VT	VT	LM	LM	VT	LM	
		◇1	◇1	◇1	1	1	◇1	1		◇1	1	◇1	1	◇1	◇1	◇1	◇1	1	1	◇1	1	
			🍴	🍴			🍴					🍴		🍴		🍴	🍴			🍴		
London Euston 15 ⊖	d	17 13	17 20	17 23	17 24	17 34	17 43	17 46		17 54		18 03	18 04	18 10	18 13	18 20	18 23	18 24	18 34	18 43	18 46	
East Croydon	d										17 10											
Clapham Junction	d										17 39											
Imperial Wharf	d										17 44											
West Brompton ⊖	d										17 47											
Kensington (Olympia) ⊖	d										17 50											
Shepherd's Bush	d										17 53											
Wembley Central ⊖	d										18 07											
Harrow & Wealdstone ⊖	d					17 46					18 12		18 16						18 46			
Bushey	d					17 51							18 21						18 51			
Watford Junction	a				17 39	17 54		18 00		18 09	18 19		18 24					18 39	18 54		19 00	
	d			17u37	17 41	17 55		18 01		18 11	18 19		18 25				18u37	18 41	18 55		19 01	
Kings Langley	d					17 59							18 29						18 59			
Apsley	d					18 03							18 33						19 03			
Hemel Hempstead	d				17 48	18 06				18 18	18 27		18 36					18 48	19 06			
Berkhamsted	d				17 53	18 11				18 23	18 32		18 41					18 53	19 11			
Tring	d				17 59	18a17					18 37		18a47					18 59	19a17			
Cheddington	d				18 04													19 04				
Leighton Buzzard	d	17 42			18 09					18 36	18 47				18 42			19 09				
Bletchley	d	17 50			18 16					18 43	18 55				18 50			19 16				
Milton Keynes Central 10	a	17 54	17 50		18 21		18 13	18 24		18 48	19 00			18 40	18 54	18 50		19 21		19 13	19 24	
	d	17 54					18 13	18 25		18 49					18 54					19 13	19 25	
Wolverton	d	17 58								18 52					18 58							
Northampton	a	18 12						18 40		19 05					19 12						19 40	
Rugby	a	18 38						19 04	19 17			18 51			19 38						20 04	20 17
Nuneaton	a							19 16													20 16	
Coventry	a	18 49		18 22			18 42		19 29			19 02			19 49		19 22			19 42		20 29
Birmingham International ✈	a	19 04		18 33			18 53		19 45			19 13			20 04		19 33			19 53		20 45
Birmingham New Street 12	a	19 16		18 45			19 08		20 02			19 25			20 16		19 45			20 08		21 01
Sandwell & Dudley	a			18 57								19 53					19 58					
Wolverhampton 7	a			19 11								20 08					20 12					

		LM	SN	VT	LM	VT	LM	LM	VT	VT	LM	VT	LM	SN	LM	VT	VT	VT	VT	LM	LM	SN	VT
		◇1	1	◇1	1	◇1	◇1	1	◇1	◇1	1	◇1	◇1	1	1	◇1	◇1	◇1	◇1	◇1	1	1	◇1
				🍴		🍴			🍴	🍴		🍴				🍴	🍴	🍴	🍴				🍴
London Euston 15 ⊖	d	18 54		19 03	19 04	19 07	19 13	19 14	19 20	19 23	19 30	19 43	19 46		20 02	20 11	20 20	20 25	20 31	20 34	20 40		21 00
East Croydon	d		18 10											19 10									
Clapham Junction	d		18 39											19 38								20 25	
Imperial Wharf	d		18 44											19 42								20 29	
West Brompton ⊖	d		18 47											19 45								20 32	
Kensington (Olympia) ⊖	d		18 50											19 48								20 36	
Shepherd's Bush	d		18 53											19 50								20 39	
Wembley Central ⊖	d		19 08																				
Harrow & Wealdstone ⊖	d		19 13		19 17						19 42			20 08							20 52	21 02	
Bushey	d				19 22						19 47										20s57		
Watford Junction	a	19 09	19 21		19 25			19 30			19 50		20 01	20 15	20 18					20 49	21 00	21 09	
	d	19 11			19 26			19 32		19u37	19 51		20 02		20 19			20u40	20u46	20 50	21 01		
Kings Langley	d				19 30						19 55		20 06								21 05		
Apsley	d				19 34						19 59		20 10								21 09		
Hemel Hempstead	d	19 18						19 39			20 02		20 13		20 26					20 57			
Berkhamsted	d	19 23			19 40			19 45			20 07		20 18		20 31					21 02			
Tring	d				19a46			19 50			20 11		20 23								21 19		
Cheddington	d							19 55					20 28							21 10			
Leighton Buzzard	d	19 36					19 42	20 00			20 20		20 35		20 42					21 15			
Bletchley	d	19 43					19 50	20 06			20a26		20 42		20 49					21 22	21 31		
Milton Keynes Central 10	a	19 48					19 54	20 12	19 50			20 20	20 49		20 54		21 03			21 30	21 39		21 43
	d	19 49					19 54					20 20	20 49				21 05			21 30			
Wolverton	d	19 52					19 58						20 53							21 34			
Northampton	a	20 05					20 12						21 07							21 51			
Rugby	a			19 51			20 42						21 38			21 15			21 34	22 17			
Nuneaton	a					20 02											21 32						
Coventry	a			20 02			20 54			20 22		20 49	21 49					21 36		22 29			
Birmingham International ✈	a			20 13			21 12			20 33		21 00	22 04					21 50		22 45			
Birmingham New Street 12	a			20 25			21 24			20 45		21 12	22 16					22 04		23 01			
Sandwell & Dudley	a			20 53						20 58								22 24					
Wolverhampton 7	a			21 08						21 12		21 38						22 38					

Table 66

Saturdays from 15 September

London - Watford Junction, Milton Keynes Central, Northampton and West Midlands

Network Diagram - see first Page of Table 59

		VT	LM	LM	VT	LM	SN	LM	SN	LM	LM
		◇1	◇1	◇1	◇1	◇1	1	◇1	1	◇1	◇1
		🍴			🍴						
London Euston 15 ⊖	d	21 03	21 08	21 28	21 43	21 54		22 34		23 04	23 44
East Croydon	d										
Clapham Junction	d						21 39		22 39		
Imperial Wharf	d						21 44		22 44		
West Brompton ⊖	d						21 47		22 47		
Kensington (Olympia) ⊖	d						21 50		22 50		
Shepherd's Bush	d						21 53		22 53		
Wembley Central ⊖	d										
Harrow & Wealdstone ⊖	d					22 06	22 13		23 12	23 16	23 56
Bushey	d					22s11					
Watford Junction	a		21 24	21 43		22 14	22 20	22 49	23 19	23 23	00 02
	d	21u18	21 25	21 44	21u58	22 15		22 50		23 24	00 02
Kings Langley	d					22 19				23 28	00 07
Apsley	d					22 23				23 32	00 11
Hemel Hempstead	d		21 32	21 51		22 26		22 57		23 35	00 13
Berkhamsted	d		21 37	21 56		22 31		23 02		23 40	00 18
Tring	d					22 35				23 44	00 24
Cheddington	d					22 41				23 49	00 29
Leighton Buzzard	d		21 50	22 07		22 47		23 13		23 56	00 34
Bletchley	d		21 57	22 14		22 54		23 20		00 03	00 41
Milton Keynes Central 10	a	21 50	22 05	22 22	22 29	23 02		23 28		00 11	00 48
	d	21 50	22 06	22 22	22 30	23 03		23 28		00 11	00 48
Wolverton	d		22 09	22 26		23 06		23 32		00 15	00 52
Northampton	a		22 27	22 43		23 20		23 49		00 28	01 10
Rugby	a	22 11		23 17	22 51						
Nuneaton	a										
Coventry	a	22 22		23 29	23 02						
Birmingham International ✈	a	22 33		23 47	23 13						
Birmingham New Street 12	a	22 45		00 04	23 25						
Sandwell & Dudley	a	22 56			23 36						
Wolverhampton 7	a	23 10			23 50						

Sundays until 24 June

		LM	LM	LM	LM	LM	LM	LM	LM	LM	VT	VT	VT	LM	SN	VT	VT	LM	VT	VT	LM	SN	VT
		◇1	◇1	◇1	◇1			◇1	◇1	◇1	◇1	◇1	◇1	◇1	1	◇1	◇1	◇1	◇1	◇1	◇1	1	◇1
						🚌	🚌				🍴	🍴	🍴			🍴	🍴		🍴	🍴			🍴
London Euston 15 ⊖	d	21p28	23p04	23p44	00 15			06 53	07 23	07 50	08 10	08 15	08 20	08 23		08 45	08 50	08 53	09 15	09 20	09 23		09 45
East Croydon	d																						
Clapham Junction	d														08 15							09 15	
Imperial Wharf	d														08 19							09 19	
West Brompton ⊖	d														08 22							09 22	
Kensington (Olympia) ⊖	d														08 26							09 26	
Shepherd's Bush	d														08 29							09 29	
Wembley Central ⊖	d				00 24																		
Harrow & Wealdstone ⊖	d		23p16	23p56	00 29			07 05	07 35	08 02				08 35	08 48			09 05			09 35	09 48	
Bushey	d								07s40												09s40		
Watford Junction	a	21p43	23p23	00 02	00 35			07 11	07 43	08 08				08 41	08 56			09 11			09 42	09 58	
	d	21p44	23p24	00 02	00 35	02 50	02 55	07 12	07 44	08 08				08 42			09u05	09 12			09 43		
Kings Langley	d		23p28	00 07	00 40		03 11		07 48					08 46							09 47		
Apsley	d		23p32	00 11	00 44		03 22		07 52					08 50							09 51		
Hemel Hempstead	d	21p51	23p35	00 13	00 46	03 16	03 28	07 19	07 55	08 15				08 53				09 19			09 54		
Berkhamsted	d	21p56	23p40	00 18	00 51		03 39	07 24	08 00	08 20				08 58				09 24			09 59		
Tring	d		23p44	00 24	00 56		03 55	07 28		08 25								09 28					
Cheddington	d		23p49	00 29	01 01		04 16	07 34		08 30								09 34					
Leighton Buzzard	d	22p07	23p56	00 34	01 06	03 53	04 37	07 40	08 13	08 37				09 11				09 40			10 12		
Bletchley	d	22p14	00 03	00 41	01 13	04 19	05 03	07 47	08 20	08 44				09 18				09 47			10 19		
Milton Keynes Central 10	a	22p22	00 11	00 48	01 19	04 34	05 18	07 55	08 28	08 50	08 55		09 05	09 26		09 31	09 37	09 55		10 06	10 27		10 32
	d	22p22	00 11	00 48	01 19			07 56	08 28	08 51				09 26		09 32	09 38	09 56			10 27		10 33
Wolverton	d	22p26	00 15	00 52	01 23			07 59	08 32	08 54				09 30				09 59			10 31		
Northampton	a	22p43	00 28	01 10	01 36			08 13	08 45	09 09				09 43				10 13			10 44		
Rugby	a	23p17								09 52				10 22		10 07	10 12				11 22		11 07
Nuneaton	a											09 43							10 44				
Coventry	a	23p29								10 03				10 33			10 23				11 33		
Birmingham International ✈	a	23p47								10 13				10 51			10 34				11 51		
Birmingham New Street 12	a	00 04								10 30				11 03			10 47				12 03		
Sandwell & Dudley	a																						
Wolverhampton 7	a																11 19						

London - Watford Junction, Milton Keynes Central, Northampton and West Midlands

Network Diagram - see first Page of Table 59

		VT ◇1 ☕	LM 1	LM ◇1	VT ◇1 ☕	VT ◇1 ☕	LM ◇1	LM ◇1	SN 1	VT ◇1 ☕	VT ◇1 ☕	LM ◇1	VT ◇1 ☕	VT ◇1 ☕	LM ◇1	SN 1	VT ◇1 ☕	LM ◇1	LM 1	VT ◇1 ☕	VT ◇1 ☕	SN 1	LM ◇1
London Euston [15] ⊖	d	09 50	09 54	10 01	10 15	10 20	10 24	10 28		10 45	10 50	10 53	11 15	11 20	11 24		11 45	11 53	12 14	12 15	12 18		12 34
East Croydon 🚊	d																						
Clapham Junction	d								10 15							11 15						12 05	
Imperial Wharf	d								10 19							11 19						12 09	
West Brompton ⊖	d								10 22							11 22						12 12	
Kensington (Olympia) ⊖	d								10 26							11 26						12 16	
Shepherd's Bush	d								10 29							11 29						12 19	
Wembley Central ⊖	d																						
Harrow & Wealdstone ⊖	d			10 13				10 40	10 48			11 05			11 36	11 48		12 05	12 26			12 36	
Bushey	d											11s10						12s10	12 31				
Watford Junction	a		10 09	10 19			10 39	10 46	10 56			11 13			11 42	11 56		12 13	12 34			12 44	12 49
	d	10u05	10 10	10 19			10 40	10 46			11u04	11 14			11 42		12u02	12 14	12 34		12u32		12 50
Kings Langley	d							10 51							11 47				12 39				
Apsley	d							10 55							11 51				12 43				
Hemel Hempstead	d		10 17	10 26			10 47	10 57				11 21			11 53			12 21	12 45				12 57
Berkhamsted	d		10 22	10 31			10 52	11 02				11 26			11 58			12 26	12 50				13 02
Tring	d			10 36								11 30						12 30	12a57				
Cheddington	d			10 41								11 36						12 36					
Leighton Buzzard	d		10 35	10 47			11 05	11 15				11 42			12 12			12 42					13 15
Bletchley	d		10 42				11 12					11 49			12 19			12 49					13 22
Milton Keynes Central [10]	a	10 38	10 50	11 00		11 06	11 20	11 27		11 32	11 37	11 57	12 02	12 08	12 27		12 26	12 57		12 48			13 27
	d	10 39	10 50	11 00			11 20	11 28		11 33	11 39	11 58			12 28		12 27	12 58					13 28
Wolverton	d			11 04				11 32				12 01			12 32			13 01					13 31
Northampton	a		11 06	11 17			11 35	11 45				12 15			12 45			13 15					13 44
Rugby	a	11 13	11 30				12 02	12 20		12 07	12 13				13 14		12 46						14 13
Nuneaton	a		11 42		11 46		12 16																
Coventry	a	11 25						12 31			12 24				13 28		12 56				13 20		14 28
Birmingham International ✈	a	11 36						12 49			12 35				13 46		13 07				13 31		14 46
Birmingham New Street [12]	a	11 49						13 01			12 48				13 58		13 22				13 44		14 58
Sandwell & Dudley	a																						
Wolverhampton [7] 🚊	a	12 21									13 19										14 16		

		VT ◇1 ☕	LM ◇1	LM 1	VT ◇1 ☕	LM 1	VT ◇1 ☕	VT ◇1 ☕	SN 1	LM ◇1	VT ◇1 ☕	LM ◇1	LM 1	VT ◇1 ☕	LM 1	VT ◇1 ☕	VT ◇1 ☕	SN 1	LM ◇1	VT ◇1 ☕	LM ◇1	LM 1
London Euston [15] ⊖	d	12 38	12 50	12 54	12 58	13 14	13 15	13 18		13 34	13 38	13 50	13 54	13 58	14 14	14 15	14 18		14 34	14 38	14 50	14 54
East Croydon 🚊	d																					
Clapham Junction	d								13 05									14 05				
Imperial Wharf	d								13 09									14 09				
West Brompton ⊖	d								13 12									14 12				
Kensington (Olympia) ⊖	d								13 16									14 16				
Shepherd's Bush	d								13 19									14 19				
Wembley Central ⊖	d																					
Harrow & Wealdstone ⊖	d			13 06		13 26			13 36				14 06		14 26			14 36				15 06
Bushey	d					13 31									14 31							
Watford Junction	a		13 06	13 12		13 34			13 44	13 49		14 06	14 12		14 34			14 44	14 49		15 06	15 12
	d		13 06	13 13		13 34		13u32		13 50		14 06	14 13		14 34		14u32		14 50		15 06	15 13
Kings Langley	d					13 39									14 39							
Apsley	d					13 43									14 43							
Hemel Hempstead	d			13 20		13 45				13 57			14 20		14 45				14 57			15 20
Berkhamsted	d			13 25		13 50				14 02			14 25		14 50				15 02			15 25
Tring	d			13 29		13a57							14 29		14a57							15 29
Cheddington	d			13 35									14 35									15 35
Leighton Buzzard	d		13 26	13 41						14 15		14 26	14 41						15 15		15 26	15 41
Bletchley	d			13 48						14 22			14 48						15 22			15 48
Milton Keynes Central [10]	a	13 11	13 36	13 54			13 48			14 27	14 11	14 36	14 54			14 48			15 27	15 11	15 36	15 54
	d	13 11	13 36							14 28	14 11	14 36							15 28	15 11	15 36	
Wolverton	d									14 31									15 31			
Northampton	a		13 54							14 44		14 54							15 46		15 54	
Rugby	a		14 24		13 49					15 13		15 24		14 49					16 13		16 24	
Nuneaton	a		14 39									15 39									16 39	
Coventry	a	13 40			14 00			14 20		15 28	14 40			15 00			15 20		16 28	15 40		
Birmingham International ✈	a	13 51			14 11			14 31		15 46	14 51			15 11			15 31		16 46	15 51		
Birmingham New Street [12]	a	14 05			14 25			14 44		15 58	15 05			15 25			15 44		16 58	16 05		
Sandwell & Dudley	a																					
Wolverhampton [7] 🚊	a							15 18									16 16					

London - Watford Junction, Milton Keynes Central, Northampton and West Midlands

Network Diagram - see first Page of Table 59

		VT ◇1 ☕	VT ◇1 ☕	LM 1	VT ◇1 ☕	VT ◇1 ☕	SN 1	LM ◇1	VT ◇1 A ☕	LM ◇1	LM 1	VT ◇1 ☕	VT ◇1 ☕	LM 1	VT ◇1 ☕	VT ◇1 ☕	SN 1	LM ◇1	VT ◇1 ☕	LM ◇1	LM 1	VT ◇1 ☕	VT ◇1 ☕
London Euston [15] ⊖	d	14 58	15 05	15 14	15 15	15 18		15 34	15 38	15 50	15 54	15 58	16 05	16 14	16 15	16 18		16 34	16 38	16 50	16 54	16 58	17 05
East Croydon 🚊	d																						
Clapham Junction	d						15 05										16 05						
Imperial Wharf	d						15 09										16 09						
West Brompton ⊖	d						15 12										16 12						
Kensington (Olympia) ⊖	d						15 16										16 16						
Shepherd's Bush	d						15 19										16 19						
Wembley Central ⊖	d																						
Harrow & Wealdstone ⊖	d			15 26			15 36				16 06			16 26			16 36				17 06		
Bushey	d			15 31										16 31									
Watford Junction	a			15 34			15 44	15 49		16 06	16 12			16 34			16 44	16 49		17 06	17 12		
	d			15 34		15u32		15 50		16 06	16 13			16 34		16u32		16 50		17 06	17 13		
Kings Langley	d			15 39										16 39									
Apsley	d			15 43										16 43									
Hemel Hempstead	d			15 45				15 57			16 20			16 45				16 57			17 20		
Berkhamsted	d			15 50				16 02			16 25			16 50				17 02			17 25		
Tring	d			15a57							16 29			16a57							17 29		
Cheddington	d										16 35										17 35		
Leighton Buzzard	d							16 15		16 26	16 41							17 15		17 26	17 41		
Bletchley	d							16 22			16 48							17 22			17 48		
Milton Keynes Central [10]	a		15 38		15 48			16 27	16 11	16 36	16 54		16 38		16 48			17 27	17 11	17 36	17 54		17 38
	d							16 28	16 11	16 36								17 28	17 11	17 36			17 39
Wolverton	d							16 31										17 31					
Northampton	a							16 44		16 54								17 44		17 54			
Rugby	a	15 49						17 13		17 24		16 49						18 13		18 24		17 49	
Nuneaton	a									17 39										18 40			18 09
Coventry	a	16 00				16 20		17 28	16 40			17 00				17 20		18 28	17 40			18 00	
Birmingham International ✈	a	16 11				16 31		17 46	16 51			17 11				17 31		18 46	17 51			18 11	
Birmingham New Street [12]	a	16 25				16 44		17 58	17 05			17 25				17 44		18 58	18 05			18 25	
Sandwell & Dudley	a																						
Wolverhampton [7] 🚊	a					17 16										18 16							

		LM 1	VT ◇1 ☕	VT ◇1 ☕	SN 1	LM ◇1	VT ◇1 ☕	LM ◇1	LM 1	VT ◇1 ☕	VT ◇1 ☕	LM 1	VT ◇1 ☕	VT ◇1 ☕	SN 1	LM ◇1	VT ◇1 ☕	LM ◇1	LM 1	VT ◇1 ☕	VT ◇1 ☕	VT ◇1 ☕
London Euston [15] ⊖	d	17 14	17 15	17 18		17 34	17 38	17 50	17 54	17 58	18 05	18 14	18 15	18 18		18 34	18 38	18 50	18 54	18 58	19 02	19 05
East Croydon 🚊	d																					
Clapham Junction	d				17 05										18 05							
Imperial Wharf	d				17 09										18 09							
West Brompton ⊖	d				17 12										18 12							
Kensington (Olympia) ⊖	d				17 16										18 16							
Shepherd's Bush	d				17 19										18 19							
Wembley Central ⊖	d																					
Harrow & Wealdstone ⊖	d	17 26			17 36				18 06			18 26			18 36				19 06			
Bushey	d	17 31										18 31										
Watford Junction	a	17 34			17 44	17 49		18 06	18 12			18 34			18 44	18 49		19 06	19 12			
	d	17 34		17u32		17 50		18 06	18 13			18 34		18u32		18 50		19 06	19 13			
Kings Langley	d	17 39										18 39										
Apsley	d	17 43										18 43										
Hemel Hempstead	d	17 45				17 57			18 20			18 45				18 57			19 20			
Berkhamsted	d	17 50				18 02			18 25			18 50				19 02			19 25			
Tring	d	17a57							18 29			18a57							19 29			
Cheddington	d								18 35										19 35			
Leighton Buzzard	d					18 15		18 26	18 41							19 15		19 26	19 41			
Bletchley	d					18 22			18 48							19 22			19 48			
Milton Keynes Central [10]	a		17 48			18 27	18 11	18 36	18 54		18 38		18 48			19 27	19 11	19 36	19 54			19 38
	d					18 28	18 11	18 36								19 28	19 11	19 36				
Wolverton	d					18 31										19 31						
Northampton	a					18 44		18 54								19 44		19 54				
Rugby	a					19 13		19 24		18 49						20 13		20 24		19 49		
Nuneaton	a							19 39										20 40			20 00	
Coventry	a			18 20		19 28	18 40			19 00				19 20		20 28	19 40			20 00		
Birmingham International ✈	a			18 31		19 46	18 51			19 11				19 31		20 46	19 51			20 11		
Birmingham New Street [12]	a			18 44		19 58	19 05			19 24				19 44		20 58	20 05			20 23		
Sandwell & Dudley	a																					
Wolverhampton [7] 🚊	a			19 16						19 55				20 16						20 55		

A 20 May, 27 May, 3 June

Table 66

Sundays
until 24 June

London - Watford Junction, Milton Keynes Central, Northampton and West Midlands

Network Diagram - see first Page of Table 59

Station		LM	VT	VT	SN	LM	VT	LM	LM	VT		VT	VT	LM	VT	VT	SN	LM	VT	VT		VT	SR	LM	VT
		1	◇1	◇1	1	◇1	◇1	◇1	1	◇1		◇1	◇1	1	◇1	◇1	1	◇1	◇1	◇1		◇1	B	◇1	◇1
London Euston 15 ⊖	d	19 14	19 15	19 18		19 34	19 38	19 50	19 54	19 58		20 02	20 05	20 14	20 15	20 18		20 34	20 38	20 50		20 54	20 55	21 02	21 21
East Croydon	d																								
Clapham Junction	d				19 05												20 05								
Imperial Wharf	d				19 09												20 09								
West Brompton ⊖	d				19 12												20 12								
Kensington (Olympia) ⊖	d				19 16												20 16								
Shepherd's Bush	d				19 19												20 19								
Wembley Central ⊖	d																								
Harrow & Wealdstone ⊖	d	19 26			19 36				20 06					20 26			20 36								
Bushey	d	19 31												20 31											
Watford Junction	a	19 34			19 43	19 50		20 06	20 12					20 34			20 44	20 49						21 22	
	d	19 34		19u32		19 51		20 06	20 13					20 34		20u32		20 50				21u08		21 23	
Kings Langley	d	19 39												20 39											
Apsley	d	19 43												20 43											
Hemel Hempstead	d	19 45				19 58			20 20					20 45				20 57						21 30	
Berkhamsted	d	19 50				20 03			20 25					20 50				21 03						21 35	
Tring	d	19a57							20 29					20a57										21 39	
Cheddington	d								20 35															21 45	
Leighton Buzzard	d					20 15		20 26	20 41									21 16						21 49	
Bletchley	d					20 22			20 48									21 23						21 56	
Milton Keynes Central 10	a		19 48			20 27	20 11	20 36	20 54				20 38		20 48			21 28	21 16	21 35		21 40		22 04	
	d					20 28	20 11	20 36										21 29	21 16	21 37		21 42		22 05	
Wolverton	d					20 31												21 32						22 08	
Northampton	a					20 44		20 54										21 45						22 22	
Rugby	a					21 13		21 21		20 49								22 14		21 59		22 04			
Nuneaton	a							21 35				21 00													22 51
Coventry	a			20 20		21 27	20 40			21 00						21 20		22 27	21 46			22 15			
Birmingham International ✈	a			20 31		21 46	20 51			21 11						21 31		22 46	21 57			22 26			
Birmingham New Street 12	a			20 44		21 58	21 04			21 24						21 44		22 58	22 09			22 39			
Sandwell & Dudley	a																								
Wolverhampton 7	a			21 16			21 36			21 56						22 16			22 44			23 14			

Station		VT	LM	SN	VT	VT		LM	VT	LM	SN	LM	VT	SR	LM
		◇1	◇1	1	◇1	◇1		1	◇1	◇1	1	◇1	◇1	B	◇1
London Euston 15 ⊖	d	21 25	21 28		21 51	21 55		22 00	22 25	22 28		22 58	23 25	23 27	23 34
East Croydon	d														
Clapham Junction	d			21 15							22 15				
Imperial Wharf	d			21 19							22 19				
West Brompton ⊖	d			21 22							22 22				
Kensington (Olympia) ⊖	d			21 26							22 26				
Shepherd's Bush	d			21 29							22 29				
Wembley Central ⊖	d														
Harrow & Wealdstone ⊖	d		21 40	21 47				22 12		22 40	22 48	23 10			23 46
Bushey	d		21s45							22s45					23s51
Watford Junction	a		21 47	21 54				22 18		22 48	22 56	23 16			23 54
	d		21 48			22u09		22 19	22u39	22 49		23 17	23u40		23 55
Kings Langley	d		21 52							22 53		23 21			23 59
Apsley	d		21 56							22 57		23 25			00 03
Hemel Hempstead	d		21 59					22 26		23 00		23 28			00 06
Berkhamsted	d		22 04					22 31		23 05		23 33			00 11
Tring	d							22 35				23 37			00 15
Cheddington	d							22 41				23 43			00 21
Leighton Buzzard	d		22 17					22 47		23 18		23 49			00 27
Bletchley	d		22 24					22 54		23 25		23 56			00 34
Milton Keynes Central 10	a	22 13	22 32		22 36	22 42		23 02	23 11	23 33		00 04	00 11		00 42
	d		22 32		22 38	22 44		23 03	23 12	23 33		00 05	00 12		00 43
Wolverton	d		22 36					23 06		23 37		00 08			00 46
Northampton	a		22 49					23 20		23 50		00 22			01 00
Rugby	a		23 13		23 16	23 20		23 54	23 46				00s46		
Nuneaton	a				23 28										
Coventry	a		23 25			23 31		00 05	23 57				00s57		
Birmingham International ✈	a		23 52			23 42			00 08				01s08		
Birmingham New Street 12	a		00 04			23 55			00 21				01s21		
Sandwell & Dudley	a														
Wolverhampton 7	a					00 26			00 53				01 53		

Table 66

Sundays
1 July to 9 September

London - Watford Junction, Milton Keynes Central, Northampton and West Midlands

Network Diagram - see first Page of Table 59

Station		LM	LM	VT	LM	VT	VT	LM	LM	VT		LM	VT	LM	LM	LM	LM	LM	LM	LM		VT	VT	VT	LM
		◇1	◇1	1	◇1	◇1	◇1	◇1	◇1	◇1		◇1	1	◇1	◇1	🚌	🚌	◇1	◇1	◇1		◇1	◇1	◇1	◇1
				A		A	A		A	A		A	A	A	A										
London Euston 15 ⊖	d	21p28	23p04	23p10	23p44	23p45	00 10	00 15	00 54	01 00		01 04	01 10	01 34	01 54			07 00	07 23	07 50		08 10	08 15	08 20	08 23
East Croydon	d																								
Clapham Junction	d																								
Imperial Wharf	d																								
West Brompton ⊖	d																								
Kensington (Olympia) ⊖	d																								
Shepherd's Bush	d																								
Wembley Central ⊖	d							00 24						01 44											
Harrow & Wealdstone ⊖	d		23p16		23p56			00 29	01 06					01 48	02 06			07 12	07 35	08 02					08 35
Bushey	d																		07s40						
Watford Junction	a	21p43	23p23		00 02			00 35	01 12					01 54	02 12			07 18	07 43	08 08					08 41
	d	21p44	23p24		00 02			00 35	01 12					01 55	02 12	02 50	02 55	07 18	07 44	08 08					08 42
Kings Langley	d		23p28		00 07			00 40									03 11		07 48						08 46
Apsley	d		23p32		00 11			00 44									03 22		07 52						08 50
Hemel Hempstead	d	21p51	23p35		00 13			00 46	01 19					02 02	02 19	03 16	03 28	07 25	07 55	08 15					08 53
Berkhamsted	d	21p56	23p40		00 18			00 51	01 24					02 07	02 24		03 39	07 30	08 00	08 20					08 58
Tring	d		23p44		00 24			00 56	01 29					02 11	02 29		03 55	07 35		08 25					
Cheddington	d		23p49		00 29			01 01									04 16	07 40		08 30					
Leighton Buzzard	d	22p07	23p56		00 34			01 06	01 36			01 41		02 18	02 36	03 53	04 37	07 47	08 13	08 37					09 11
Bletchley	d	22p14	00 03		00 41			01 13	01 43			01 49		02 25	02 43	04 19	05 03	07 54	08 20	08 44					09 18
Milton Keynes Central 10	a	22p22	00 11		00 48		00s40	01 19	01 49			01 55		02 31	02 49	04 34	05 18	08 00	08 28	08 50		08 55		09 05	09 26
	d	22p22	00 11		00 48			01 19	01 49			01 56		02 32	02 49			08 00	08 28	08 51					09 26
Wolverton	d	22p26	00 15		00 52			01 23	01 53			01 59		02 35	02 53			08 04	08 32	08 54					09 30
Northampton	a	22p43	00 28		01 10			01 36	02 06			02 15		02 49	03 06			08 17	08 45	09 09					09 43
Rugby	a	23p17		23b58		00s42	01s02			01s48			01s58							09 52					10 22
Nuneaton	a					00s52				01s59													09 43		
Coventry	a	23p29		00s09			01s13						02s09							10 03					10 33
Birmingham International ✈	a	23p47		00s20			01s24						02s20							10 13					10 51
Birmingham New Street 12	a	00 04		00 34			01s39						02s34							10 30					11 03
Sandwell & Dudley	a																								
Wolverhampton 7	a						01 57						02 52												

Station		SN	VT	VT	LM	VT		VT	LM	SN	VT	VT	LM	LM	VT	VT		LM	LM	SN	VT	VT	LM	VT	VT
		1	◇1	◇1	◇1	◇1		◇1	◇1	1	◇1	◇1	1	◇1	◇1	◇1		◇1	◇1	1	◇1	◇1	◇1	◇1	◇1
London Euston 15 ⊖	d		08 45	08 50	08 53	09 15		09 20	09 23		09 45	09 50	09 54	10 01	10 15	10 20		10 24	10 28		10 45	10 50	10 53	11 15	11 20
East Croydon	d																								
Clapham Junction	d	08 15								09 15										10 15					
Imperial Wharf	d	08 19								09 19										10 19					
West Brompton ⊖	d	08 22								09 22										10 22					
Kensington (Olympia) ⊖	d	08 26								09 26										10 26					
Shepherd's Bush	d	08 29								09 29										10 29					
Wembley Central ⊖	d																								
Harrow & Wealdstone ⊖	d	08 48			09 05				09 35	09 48				10 13					10 40	10 48			11 05		
Bushey	d								09s40														11s10		
Watford Junction	a	08 56			09 11				09 42	09 58			10 09	10 19				10 39	10 46	10 56			11 13		
	d			09u05	09 12				09 43			10u06	10 10	10 19				10 40	10 46			11u04	11 14		
Kings Langley	d								09 47										10 51						
Apsley	d								09 51										10 55						
Hemel Hempstead	d				09 19				09 54				10 17	10 26				10 47	10 57				11 21		
Berkhamsted	d				09 24				09 59				10 22	10 31				10 52	11 02				11 26		
Tring	d				09 28									10 36									11 30		
Cheddington	d				09 34									10 41									11 36		
Leighton Buzzard	d				09 40				10 12				10 35	10 47				11 05	11 15				11 42		
Bletchley	d				09 47				10 19				10 42					11 12					11 49		
Milton Keynes Central 10	a		09 31	09 37	09 55			10 06	10 27		10 32	10 38	10 50	11 00		11 06		11 20	11 27		11 32	11 37	11 57	12 02	12 08
	d		09 32	09 38	09 56				10 27		10 33	10 39	10 50	11 00				11 20	11 28		11 33	11 39	11 58		
Wolverton	d				09 59				10 31					11 04					11 32				12 01		
Northampton	a				10 13				10 44				11 06	11 17				11 35	11 45				12 15		
Rugby	a		10 07	10 12					11 22		11 07	11 13	11 30					12 02	12 20		12 07	12 13			
Nuneaton	a					10 44							11 42		11 46			12 16							
Coventry	a			10 23					11 33			11 25							12 31			12 24			
Birmingham International ✈	a			10 34					11 51			11 36							12 49			12 35			
Birmingham New Street 12	a			10 47					12 03			11 49							13 01			12 48			
Sandwell & Dudley	a			10 59								12 01										13 00			
Wolverhampton 7	a			11 13								12 15										13 14			

A 29 July, 5 August, 12 August, 2 September, 9 September

b Previous night, stops to set down only

London - Watford Junction, Milton Keynes Central, Northampton and West Midlands

Network Diagram - see first Page of Table 59

		LM ◇1		SN 1	VT ◇1 ⊡	LM ◇1	LM 1	VT ◇1 ⊡	VT ◇1 ⊡	SN 1	LM ◇1	VT ◇1 ⊡		LM ◇1	LM 1	VT ◇1 ⊡	LM 1	VT ◇1 ⊡	VT ◇1 ⊡	SN 1	LM ◇1	VT ◇1 ⊡		LM ◇1	LM 1
London Euston 15 ⊖	d	11 24			11 45	11 53	12 14	12 15	12 18		12 34	12 38		12 50	12 54	12 58	13 14	13 15	13 18		13 34	13 38		13 50	13 54
East Croydon	d																								
Clapham Junction	d			11 15						12 05										13 05					
Imperial Wharf	d			11 19						12 09										13 09					
West Brompton ⊖	d			11 22						12 12										13 12					
Kensington (Olympia) ⊖	d			11 26						12 16										13 16					
Shepherd's Bush	d			11 29						12 19										13 19					
Wembley Central ⊖	d																								
Harrow & Wealdstone ⊖	d	11 36		11 48		12 05	12 26			12 36					13 06		13 26			13 36					14 06
Bushey	d					12s10	12 31										13 31								
Watford Junction	a	11 42		11 56		12 13	12 34			12 44	12 49			13 06	13 12		13 34			13 44	13 49			14 06	14 12
	d	11 42			12u02	12 14	12 34		12u32		12 50			13 06	13 13		13 34		13u32		13 50			14 06	14 13
Kings Langley	d	11 47					12 39										13 39								
Apsley	d	11 51					12 43										13 43								
Hemel Hempstead	d	11 53				12 21	12 45				12 57				13 20		13 45				13 57				14 20
Berkhamsted	d	11 58				12 26	12 50				13 02				13 25		13 50				14 02				14 25
Tring	d					12 30	12a57								13 29		13a57								14 29
Cheddington	d					12 36									13 35										14 35
Leighton Buzzard	d	12 12				12 42					13 15			13 26	13 41						14 15			14 26	14 41
Bletchley	d	12 19				12 49					13 22				13 48						14 22				14 48
Milton Keynes Central 10	a	12 27			12 26	12 57		12 48			13 27	13 11		13 36	13 54			13 48			14 27	14 11		14 36	14 54
	d	12 28			12 27	12 58					13 28	13 11		13 36							14 28	14 11		14 36	
Wolverton	d	12 32				13 01					13 31										14 31				
Northampton	a	12 45				13 15					13 44			13 54							14 44			14 54	
Rugby	a	13 14			12 46						14 13			14 24		13 49					15 13			15 24	
Nuneaton	a													14 39										15 39	
Coventry	a	13 28			12 56				13 20		14 28	13 40				14 00			14 20		15 28	14 40			
Birmingham International ✈	a	13 46			13 07				13 31		14 46	13 51				14 11			14 31		15 46	14 51			
Birmingham New Street 12	a	13 58			13 22				13 44		14 58	14 05				14 25			14 44		15 58	15 05			
Sandwell & Dudley	a								13 56										14 56						
Wolverhampton 7	a								14 10										15 10						

		VT ◇1 ⊡	LM 1	VT ◇1 ⊡	VT ◇1 ⊡	SN 1	LM ◇1	VT ◇1 ⊡		LM 1	VT ◇1 ⊡	VT ◇1 ⊡	LM 1	VT ◇1 ⊡	VT ◇1 ⊡	SN 1	LM ◇1	VT ◇1 ⊡		LM ◇1	LM 1	VT ◇1 ⊡	VT ◇1 ⊡	LM 1	VT ◇1 ⊡
London Euston 15 ⊖	d	13 58	14 14	14 15	14 18		14 34	14 38		14 54	14 58	15 05	15 14	15 15	15 18		15 34	15 38		15 50	15 54	15 58	16 05	16 14	16 15
East Croydon	d																								
Clapham Junction	d					14 05										15 05									
Imperial Wharf	d					14 09										15 09									
West Brompton ⊖	d					14 12										15 12									
Kensington (Olympia) ⊖	d					14 16										15 16									
Shepherd's Bush	d					14 19										15 19									
Wembley Central ⊖	d																								
Harrow & Wealdstone ⊖	d		14 26			14 36				15 06			15 26			15 36					16 06			16 26	
Bushey	d		14 31										15 31											16 31	
Watford Junction	a		14 34			14 44	14 49			15 12			15 34			15 44	15 49			16 06	16 12			16 34	
	d		14 34		14u32		14 50			15 13			15 34		15u32		15 50			16 06	16 13			16 34	
Kings Langley	d		14 39										15 39											16 39	
Apsley	d		14 43										15 43											16 43	
Hemel Hempstead	d		14 45				14 57			15 20			15 45				15 57				16 20			16 45	
Berkhamsted	d		14 50				15 02			15 25			15 50				16 02				16 25			16 50	
Tring	d		14a57							15 29			15a57								16 29			16a57	
Cheddington	d									15 35											16 35				
Leighton Buzzard	d						15 15			15 41							16 15			16 26	16 41				
Bletchley	d						15 22			15 48							16 22				16 48				
Milton Keynes Central 10	a			14 48			15 27	15 11		15 54		15 38		15 48			16 27	16 11		16 36	16 54		16 38		16 48
	d						15 28	15 11									16 28	16 11		16 36					
Wolverton	d						15 31										16 31								
Northampton	a						15 46										16 44			16 54					
Rugby	a	14 49					16 13				15 49						17 13			17 24		16 49			
Nuneaton	a																			17 39					
Coventry	a	15 00			15 20		16 28	15 40			15 59				16 20		17 28	16 40				17 00			
Birmingham International ✈	a	15 11			15 31		16 46	15 51			16 10				16 31		17 46	16 51				17 11			
Birmingham New Street 12	a	15 25			15 44		16 58	16 05			16 24				16 44		17 58	17 05				17 25			
Sandwell & Dudley	a				15 56										16 56										
Wolverhampton 7	a				16 10										17 10										

London - Watford Junction, Milton Keynes Central, Northampton and West Midlands

Network Diagram - see first Page of Table 59

		VT ◇1 ⊡	SN 1	LM ◇1		VT ◇1 ⊡	LM ◇1	LM 1	VT ◇1 ⊡	VT ◇1 ⊡	LM 1	VT ◇1 ⊡	VT ◇1 ⊡	SN 1		LM ◇1	VT ◇1 ⊡	LM ◇1	LM 1	VT ◇1 ⊡	VT ◇1 ⊡	LM 1	VT ◇1 ⊡	VT ◇1 ⊡	
London Euston 15 ⊖	d	16 18		16 34		16 38	16 50	16 54	16 58	17 05	17 14	17 15	17 18			17 34	17 38	17 50	17 54	17 58	18 05	18 14	18 15	18 18	
East Croydon	d																								
Clapham Junction	d		16 05											17 05											
Imperial Wharf	d		16 09											17 09											
West Brompton ⊖	d		16 12											17 12											
Kensington (Olympia) ⊖	d		16 16											17 16											
Shepherd's Bush	d		16 19											17 19											
Wembley Central ⊖	d																								
Harrow & Wealdstone ⊖	d		16 36					17 06			17 26			17 36					18 06			18 26			
Bushey	d										17 31											18 31			
Watford Junction	a		16 44	16 49			17 06	17 12			17 34			17 44		17 49		18 06	18 12			18 34			
	d	16u32		16 50			17 06	17 13			17 34		17u32			17 50		18 06	18 13			18 34		18u32	
Kings Langley	d										17 39											18 39			
Apsley	d										17 43											18 43			
Hemel Hempstead	d			16 57				17 20			17 45					17 57			18 20			18 45			
Berkhamsted	d			17 02				17 25			17 50					18 02			18 25			18 50			
Tring	d							17 29			17a57								18 29			18a57			
Cheddington	d							17 35											18 35						
Leighton Buzzard	d			17 15			17 26	17 41								18 15		18 26	18 41						
Bletchley	d			17 22				17 48								18 22			18 48						
Milton Keynes Central 10	a			17 27		17 11	17 36	17 54		17 38		17 48				18 27	18 11	18 36	18 54		18 38		18 48		
	d			17 28		17 11	17 36			17 39						18 28	18 11	18 36							
Wolverton	d			17 31												18 31									
Northampton	a			17 44			17 54									18 44		18 54							
Rugby	a			18 13			18 24		17 49							19 13		19 24		18 49					
Nuneaton	a						18 40			18 09								19 39							
Coventry	a	17 20		18 28		17 40			18 00				18 20			19 28	18 40			19 00				19 20	
Birmingham International ✈	a	17 31		18 46		17 51			18 11				18 31			19 46	18 51			19 11				19 31	
Birmingham New Street 12	a	17 44		18 58		18 05			18 25				18 44			19 58	19 05			19 24				19 44	
Sandwell & Dudley	a	17 56											18 56							19 48				19 56	
Wolverhampton 7	a	18 10											19 10							20 02				20 10	

		SN 1	LM ◇1	VT ◇1 ⊡	LM ◇1	LM 1	VT ◇1 ⊡	VT ◇1 ⊡	VT ◇1 ⊡	LM 1		VT ◇1 ⊡	VT ◇1 ⊡	SN 1	LM ◇1	VT ◇1 ⊡	LM ◇1	LM 1	VT ◇1 ⊡	VT ◇1 ⊡		VT ◇1 ⊡	LM 1	VT ◇1 ⊡	VT ◇1 ⊡
London Euston 15 ⊖	d		18 34	18 38	18 50	18 54	18 58	19 02	19 05	19 14		19 15	19 18		19 34	19 38	19 50	19 54	19 58	20 02		20 05	20 14	20 15	20 18
East Croydon	d																								
Clapham Junction	d	18 05												19 05											
Imperial Wharf	d	18 09												19 09											
West Brompton ⊖	d	18 12												19 12											
Kensington (Olympia) ⊖	d	18 16												19 16											
Shepherd's Bush	d	18 19												19 19											
Wembley Central ⊖	d																								
Harrow & Wealdstone ⊖	d	18 36				19 06				19 26				19 36				20 06					20 26		
Bushey	d									19 31													20 31		
Watford Junction	a	18 44	18 49		19 06	19 12				19 34				19 43	19 50		20 06	20 12					20 34		
	d		18 50		19 06	19 13				19 34			19u32		19 51		20 06	20 13					20 34		20u32
Kings Langley	d									19 39													20 39		
Apsley	d									19 43													20 43		
Hemel Hempstead	d		18 57			19 20				19 45					19 58			20 20					20 45		
Berkhamsted	d		19 02			19 25				19 50					20 03			20 25					20 50		
Tring	d					19 29				19a57								20 29					20a57		
Cheddington	d					19 35												20 35							
Leighton Buzzard	d		19 15		19 26	19 41									20 15		20 26	20 41							
Bletchley	d		19 22			19 48									20 22			20 48							
Milton Keynes Central 10	a		19 27	19 11	19 36	19 54			19 38			19 48			20 27	20 11	20 36	20 54				20 38		20 48	
	d		19 28	19 11	19 36										20 28	20 11	20 36								
Wolverton	d		19 31												20 31										
Northampton	a		19 44		19 54										20 44		20 54								
Rugby	a		20 13		20 24		19 49								21 13		21 21		20 49						
Nuneaton	a				20 40			20 01									21 35			21 00					
Coventry	a		20 28	19 40			19 59						20 20		21 27	20 40			21 00						21 20
Birmingham International ✈	a		20 46	19 51			20 10						20 31		21 46	20 51			21 11						21 31
Birmingham New Street 12	a		20 58	20 05			20 22						20 44		21 58	21 04			21 24						21 44
Sandwell & Dudley	a						20 35						20 56			21 15			21 36						21 56
Wolverhampton 7	a						20 46						21 10			21 31			21 51						22 10

Table 66

Sundays
1 July to 9 September

London - Watford Junction, Milton Keynes Central, Northampton and West Midlands

Network Diagram - see first Page of Table 59

	SN	LM	VT	VT	VT	SR	LM	VT	VT	LM	SN	VT	VT	LM	VT	LM	SN	LM	VT	SR	LM	VT
	1	◇1	◇1	◇1	◇1	B	◇1	◇1	◇1	◇1	1	◇1	◇1	1	◇1	◇1	1	◇1	◇1	B	◇1	◇1
																			A			B
			🍴	🍴	🍴	🛏 🍴		🍴	🍴			🍴	🍴		🍴				🍴	🛏 🍴		🍴
London Euston 15 ⊖ d		20 34	20 38	20 50	20 54	20 55	21 02	21 21	21 25	21 28		21 51	21 55	22 00	22 25	22 28		22 58	23 25	23 27	23 34	23 45
East Croydon d																						
Clapham Junction d	20 05										21 15						22 15					
Imperial Wharf d	20 09										21 19						22 19					
West Brompton ⊖ d	20 12										21 22						22 22					
Kensington (Olympia) ⊖ d	20 16										21 26						22 26					
Shepherd's Bush d	20 19										21 29						22 29					
Wembley Central ⊖ d																						
Harrow & Wealdstone ⊖ d	20 36									21 40	21 47			22 12		22 40	22 48	23 10			23 46	
Bushey d										21s45						22s45					23s51	
Watford Junction a	20 44	20 49					21 22			21 47	21 54			22 18		22 48	22 56	23 16			23 54	
d		20 50			21u10		21 23			21 48			22u09	22 19	22u39	22 49		23 17	23u40		23 55	
Kings Langley d										21 52						22 53		23 21			23 59	
Apsley d										21 56						22 57		23 25			00 03	
Hemel Hempstead d		20 57					21 30			21 59				22 26		23 00		23 28			00 06	
Berkhamsted d		21 03					21 35			22 04				22 31		23 05		23 33			00 11	
Tring d							21 39							22 35				23 37			00 15	
Cheddington d							21 45							22 41				23 43			00 21	
Leighton Buzzard d		21 16					21 49			22 17				22 47		23 18		23 49			00 27	
Bletchley d		21 23					21 56			22 24				22 54		23 25		23 56			00 34	
Milton Keynes Central 10 a		21 28	21 16	21 35	21 41		22 04		22 13	22 32		22 36	22 42	23 02	23 11	23 33		00 04	00 11		00 42	
d		21 29	21 16	21 37	21 43		22 05			22 32		22 38	22 44	23 03	23 12	23 33		00 05	00 12		00 43	
Wolverton d		21 32					22 08			22 36				23 06		23 37		00 08			00 46	
Northampton a		21 45					22 22			22 49				23 20		23 50		00 22			01 00	
Rugby a		22 14		21 59	22 05					23 13		23 16	23 20	23 54	23 44				00s46			00s33
Nuneaton a								22 51				23 28										00s44
Coventry a		22 27	21 46		22 16					23 25			23 31	00 05	23 55				00s57			
Birmingham International ✈ a		22 46	21 57		22 27					23 52			23 42		00 06				01s08			
Birmingham New Street 12 a		22 58	22 09		22 39					00 04			23 54		00 19				01s21			
Sandwell & Dudley a			22 24		22 52																	
Wolverhampton 7 ⇌ a			22 38		23 06								00 15		00 41				01 53			

Sundays
from 16 September

	LM	LM	LM	LM	LM	LM	LM	LM	LM	VT	VT	VT	VT	LM	SN	VT	VT	LM	VT	VT	VT	LM
	◇1	◇1	◇1	◇1	🚌	🚌	◇1	◇1	◇1	◇1	◇1	◇1	◇1	◇1	1	◇1	◇1	◇1	◇1	◇1	◇1	◇1
											C	D				C			C	D		
										🍴	🍴	🍴	🍴			🍴	🍴		🍴	🍴	🍴	
London Euston 15 ⊖ d	21p28	23p04	23p44	00 15			06 53	07 23	07 50	08 10	08 15	08 15	08 20	08 23		08 45	08 50	08 53	09 15	09 15	09 20	09 23
East Croydon d																						
Clapham Junction d															08 15							
Imperial Wharf d															08 19							
West Brompton ⊖ d															08 22							
Kensington (Olympia) ⊖ d															08 26							
Shepherd's Bush d															08 29							
Wembley Central ⊖ d				00 24																		
Harrow & Wealdstone ⊖ d		23p16	23p56	00 29			07 05	07 35	08 02					08 35	08 48			09 05				09 35
Bushey d								07s40														09s40
Watford Junction a	21p43	23p23	00 02	00 35			07 11	07 43	08 08					08 41	08 56			09 11				09 42
d	21p44	23p24	00 02	00 35	02 50	02 55	07 12	07 44	08 08					08 42			09u05	09 12				09 43
Kings Langley d		23p28	00 07	00 40		03 11		07 48						08 46								09 47
Apsley d		23p32	00 11	00 44		03 22		07 52						08 50								09 51
Hemel Hempstead d	21p51	23p35	00 13	00 46	03 16	03 28	07 19	07 55	08 15					08 53				09 19				09 54
Berkhamsted d	21p56	23p40	00 18	00 51		03 39	07 24	08 00	08 20					08 58				09 24				09 59
Tring d		23p44	00 24	00 56		03 55	07 28		08 25									09 28				
Cheddington d		23p49	00 29	01 01		04 16	07 34		08 30									09 34				
Leighton Buzzard d	22p07	23p56	00 34	01 06	03 53	04 37	07 40	08 13	08 37					09 11				09 40				10 12
Bletchley d	22p14	00 03	00 41	01 13	04 19	05 03	07 47	08 20	08 44					09 18				09 47				10 19
Milton Keynes Central 10 a	22p22	00 11	00 48	01 19	04 34	05 18	07 55	08 28	08 50	08 55			09 05	09 26		09 31	09 37	09 55	10 00		10 06	10 27
d	22p22	00 11	00 48	01 19			07 56	08 28	08 51					09 26		09 32	09 38	09 56	10 02			10 27
Wolverton d	22p26	00 15	00 52	01 23			07 59	08 32	08 54					09 30				09 59				10 31
Northampton a	22p43	00 28	01 10	01 36			08 13	08 45	09 09					09 43				10 13				10 44
Rugby a	23p17								09 52			09 35		10 22		10 07	10 12					11 22
Nuneaton a											09 43	09 46							10 44	10 44		
Coventry a	23p29								10 03					10 33			10 23					11 33
Birmingham International ✈ a	23p47								10 13					10 51			10 34					11 51
Birmingham New Street 12 a	00 04								10 30					11 03			10 47					12 03
Sandwell & Dudley a																	10 59					
Wolverhampton 7 ⇌ a																	11 13					

A from 1 July until 22 July, 19 August, 26 August
B 29 July, 5 August, 12 August, 2 September, 9 September
C from 16 September until 21 October
D from 28 October

Table 66

Sundays
from 16 September

London - Watford Junction, Milton Keynes Central, Northampton and West Midlands

Network Diagram - see first Page of Table 59

	SN	VT	VT	LM	LM	VT	VT	VT	LM	LM	SN	VT	VT	LM	VT	VT	LM	SN	VT	LM	LM	VT
	1	◇1	◇1	1	◇1	◇1	◇1	◇1	◇1	◇1	1	◇1	◇1	◇1	◇1	◇1	◇1	1	◇1	◇1	1	◇1
		A				A	B					A										
		🍴	🍴			🍴	🍴	🍴				🍴	🍴		🍴	🍴			🍴			🍴
London Euston 15 ⊖ d		09 45	09 50	09 54	10 01	10 15	10 15	10 20	10 24	10 28		10 45	10 50	10 53	11 15	11 20	11 24		11 45	11 53	12 14	12 17
East Croydon d																						
Clapham Junction d	09 15										10 15							11 15				
Imperial Wharf d	09 19										10 19							11 19				
West Brompton ⊖ d	09 22										10 22							11 22				
Kensington (Olympia) ⊖ d	09 26										10 26							11 26				
Shepherd's Bush d	09 29										10 29							11 29				
Wembley Central ⊖ d																						
Harrow & Wealdstone ⊖ d	09 48				10 13					10 40	10 48			11 05			11 36	11 48		12 05	12 26	
Bushey d														11s10						12s10	12 31	
Watford Junction a	09 58			10 09	10 19				10 39	10 46	10 56			11 13			11 42	11 56		12 13	12 34	
d			10u06	10 10	10 19				10 40	10 46			11u04	11 14			11 42		12u03	12 14	12 34	
Kings Langley d										10 51							11 47				12 39	
Apsley d										10 55							11 51				12 43	
Hemel Hempstead d				10 17	10 26				10 47	10 57				11 21			11 53			12 21	12 45	
Berkhamsted d				10 22	10 31				10 52	11 02				11 26			11 58			12 26	12 50	
Tring d					10 36									11 30						12 30	12a57	
Cheddington d					10 41									11 36						12 36		
Leighton Buzzard d				10 35	10 47				11 05	11 15				11 42			12 12			12 42		
Bletchley d				10 42					11 12					11 49			12 19			12 49		
Milton Keynes Central 10 a		10 32	10 38	10 50	11 00			11 06	11 20	11 27		11 32	11 37	11 57	12 02	12 08	12 27		12 26	12 57		12 50
d		10 33	10 39	10 50	11 00				11 20	11 28		11 33	11 39	11 58			12 28		12 27	12 58		
Wolverton d					11 04					11 32				12 01			12 32			13 01		
Northampton a				11 06	11 17				11 35	11 45				12 15			12 45			13 15		
Rugby a		11 07	11 13	11 30			11 38		12 02	12 20		12 07	12 13				13 14		12 46			
Nuneaton a				11 42		11 46	11 48		12 16													
Coventry a			11 25							12 31			12 24				13 28		12 56			
Birmingham International ✈ a			11 36							12 49			12 35				13 46		13 07			
Birmingham New Street 12 a			11 49							13 01			12 48				13 58		13 22			
Sandwell & Dudley a			12 01										13 00									
Wolverhampton 7 ⇌ a			12 15										13 14									

	VT	SN	LM	VT	LM	LM	VT	LM	VT	VT	SN	LM	VT	LM	LM	VT	LM	VT	VT	SN	LM
	◇1	1	◇1	◇1	◇1	1	◇1	1	◇1	◇1	1	◇1	◇1	◇1	1	◇1	1	◇1	◇1	1	◇1
	🍴			🍴			🍴		🍴	🍴			🍴			🍴		🍴	🍴		
London Euston 15 ⊖ d	12 20		12 34	12 40	12 50	12 54	13 00	13 14	13 17	13 20		13 34	13 40	13 50	13 54	14 00	14 14	14 17	14 20		14 34
East Croydon d																					
Clapham Junction d		12 05									13 05									14 05	
Imperial Wharf d		12 09									13 09									14 09	
West Brompton ⊖ d		12 12									13 12									14 12	
Kensington (Olympia) ⊖ d		12 16									13 16									14 16	
Shepherd's Bush d		12 19									13 19									14 19	
Wembley Central ⊖ d																					
Harrow & Wealdstone ⊖ d		12 36				13 06		13 26			13 36				14 06		14 26			14 36	
Bushey d								13 31									14 31				
Watford Junction a		12 44	12 49		13 06	13 12		13 34			13 44	13 49		14 06	14 12		14 34			14 44	14 49
d	12u34		12 50		13 06	13 13		13 34		13u34		13 50		14 06	14 13		14 34		14u34		14 50
Kings Langley d								13 39									14 39				
Apsley d								13 43									14 43				
Hemel Hempstead d			12 57			13 20		13 45				13 57			14 20		14 45				14 57
Berkhamsted d			13 02			13 25		13 50				14 02			14 25		14 50				15 02
Tring d						13 29		13a57							14 29		14a57				
Cheddington d						13 35									14 35						
Leighton Buzzard d			13 15		13 26	13 41						14 15		14 26	14 41						15 15
Bletchley d			13 22			13 48						14 22			14 48						15 22
Milton Keynes Central 10 a			13 27	13 13	13 36	13 54			13 50			14 27	14 13	14 36	14 54			14 50			15 27
d			13 28	13 13	13 36							14 28	14 13	14 36							15 28
Wolverton d			13 31									14 31									15 31
Northampton a			13 44		13 54							14 44		14 54							15 46
Rugby a			14 13		14 24		13 51					15 13		15 24		14 51					16 13
Nuneaton a					14 39									15 39							
Coventry a	13 22		14 28	13 42			14 02			14 21		15 28	14 42			15 02			15 21		16 28
Birmingham International ✈ a	13 33		14 46	13 53			14 13			14 32		15 46	14 53			15 13			15 32		16 46
Birmingham New Street 12 a	13 44		14 58	14 05			14 25			14 44		15 58	15 05			15 25			15 44		16 58
Sandwell & Dudley a	13 56									14 56									15 56		
Wolverhampton 7 ⇌ a	14 10									15 10									16 10		

A from 16 September until 21 October
B from 28 October

London - Watford Junction, Milton Keynes Central, Northampton and West Midlands

Network Diagram - see first Page of Table 59

		VT	LM	VT	VT	LM	VT	VT	SN	LM	VT	LM	LM	VT	VT	LM	VT	VT	SN	LM	VT	LM	LM
		◇1 ☕	1	◇1 ☕	◇1 ☕	1	◇1 ☕	◇1 ☕	1	◇1	◇1 ☕	◇1	1	◇1 ☕	◇1 ☕	1	◇1 ☕	◇1 ☕	1	◇1	◇1 ☕	◇1	1
London Euston 15 ⊖	d	14 40	14 54	15 00	15 08	15 14	15 17	15 20		15 34	15 40	15 50	15 54	16 00	16 08	16 14	16 17	16 20		16 34	16 40	16 50	16 54
East Croydon	d																						
Clapham Junction	d								15 05										16 05				
Imperial Wharf	d								15 09										16 09				
West Brompton ⊖	d								15 12										16 12				
Kensington (Olympia) ⊖	d								15 16										16 16				
Shepherd's Bush	d								15 19										16 19				
Wembley Central ⊖	d																						
Harrow & Wealdstone ⊖	d		15 06			15 26			15 36				16 06			16 26			16 36				17 06
Bushey	d					15 31										16 31							
Watford Junction	a		15 12			15 34			15 44	15 49		16 06	16 12			16 34			16 44	16 49		17 06	17 12
	d		15 13			15 34		15u34		15 50		16 06	16 13			16 34		16u34		16 50		17 06	17 13
Kings Langley	d					15 39										16 39							
Apsley	d					15 43										16 43							
Hemel Hempstead	d		15 20			15 45				15 57			16 20			16 45				16 57			17 20
Berkhamsted	d		15 25			15 50				16 02			16 25			16 50				17 02			17 25
Tring	d		15 29			15a57							16 29			16a57							17 29
Cheddington	d		15 35										16 35										17 35
Leighton Buzzard	d		15 41							16 15		16 26	16 41							17 15		17 26	17 41
Bletchley	d		15 48							16 22			16 48							17 22			17 48
Milton Keynes Central 10	a	15 13	15 54		15 41		15 50			16 27	16 13	16 36	16 54		16 41		16 50			17 27	17 13	17 36	17 54
	d	15 13								16 28	16 13	16 36								17 28	17 13	17 36	
Wolverton	d									16 31										17 31			
Northampton	a									16 44		16 54								17 44		17 54	
Rugby	a			15 51						17 13		17 24		16 51						18 13		18 24	
Nuneaton	a											17 39										18 40	
Coventry	a	15 42		16 02				16 21		17 28	16 42			17 02				17 21		18 28	17 42		
Birmingham International ✈	a	15 53		16 13				16 32		17 46	16 53			17 13				17 32		18 46	17 53		
Birmingham New Street 12	a	16 05		16 25				16 44		17 58	17 05			17 25				17 44		18 58	18 05		
Sandwell & Dudley	a							16 56										17 56					
Wolverhampton 7	a							17 10										18 10					

		VT	VT	LM	VT	VT	SN	LM	VT	LM	LM	VT	VT	LM	VT	VT	SN	LM	VT	LM	LM	VT
		◇1 ☕	◇1 ☕	1	◇1 ☕	◇1 ☕	1	◇1	◇1 ☕	◇1	1	◇1 ☕	◇1 ☕	1	◇1 ☕	◇1 ☕	1	◇1	◇1 ☕	◇1	1	◇1 ☕
London Euston 15 ⊖	d	17 00	17 08	17 14	17 17	17 20		17 34	17 40	17 50	17 54	18 00	18 08	18 14	18 17	18 20		18 34	18 40	18 50	18 54	19 00
East Croydon	d																					
Clapham Junction	d						17 05										18 05					
Imperial Wharf	d						17 09										18 09					
West Brompton ⊖	d						17 12										18 12					
Kensington (Olympia) ⊖	d						17 16										18 16					
Shepherd's Bush	d						17 19										18 19					
Wembley Central ⊖	d																					
Harrow & Wealdstone ⊖	d			17 26			17 36				18 06			18 26			18 36				19 06	
Bushey	d			17 31										18 31								
Watford Junction	a			17 34			17 44	17 49		18 06	18 12			18 34			18 44	18 49		19 06	19 12	
	d			17 34		17u34		17 50		18 06	18 13			18 34		18u34		18 50		19 06	19 13	
Kings Langley	d			17 39										18 39								
Apsley	d			17 43										18 43								
Hemel Hempstead	d			17 45				17 57			18 20			18 45				18 57			19 20	
Berkhamsted	d			17 50				18 02			18 25			18 50				19 02			19 25	
Tring	d			17a57							18 29			18a57							19 29	
Cheddington	d										18 35										19 35	
Leighton Buzzard	d							18 15		18 26	18 41							19 15		19 26	19 41	
Bletchley	d							18 22			18 48							19 22			19 48	
Milton Keynes Central 10	a		17 41		17 50			18 27	18 13	18 36	18 54		18 41		18 50			19 27	19 13	19 36	19 54	
	d		17 42					18 28	18 13	18 36								19 28	19 13	19 36		
Wolverton	d							18 31										19 31				
Northampton	a							18 44		18 54								19 44		19 54		
Rugby	a	17 51						19 13		19 24		18 50						20 13		20 24		19 51
Nuneaton	a		18 12							19 39										20 39		
Coventry	a	18 02				18 21		19 28	18 42			19 01				19 21		20 28	19 42			20 01
Birmingham International ✈	a	18 13				18 32		19 46	18 53			19 12				19 32		20 46	19 53			20 12
Birmingham New Street 12	a	18 25				18 44		19 58	19 05			19 24				19 44		20 58	20 05			20 23
Sandwell & Dudley	a					18 56						19 48				19 56						20 35
Wolverhampton 7	a					19 10						20 02				20 10						20 46

London - Watford Junction, Milton Keynes Central, Northampton and West Midlands

Network Diagram - see first Page of Table 59

		VT	VT	LM	VT	VT	SN	LM	VT	LM	LM	VT	VT	VT	LM	VT	VT	SN	LM	VT	VT	VT	SR
		◇1 ☕	◇1 ☕	1	◇1 ☕	◇1 ☕	1	◇1	◇1 ☕	◇1	1	◇1 ☕	◇1 ☕	◇1 ☕	1	◇1 ☕	◇1 ☕	1	◇1	◇1 ☕	◇1 ☕	◇1 ☕	B ☕
London Euston 15 ⊖	d	19 05	19 08	19 14	19 17	19 20		19 34	19 40	19 50	19 54	20 00	20 05	20 08	20 14	20 15	20 18		20 34	20 38	20 50	20 54	20 55
East Croydon	d																						
Clapham Junction	d						19 05											20 05					
Imperial Wharf	d						19 09											20 09					
West Brompton ⊖	d						19 12											20 12					
Kensington (Olympia) ⊖	d						19 16											20 16					
Shepherd's Bush	d						19 19											20 19					
Wembley Central ⊖	d																						
Harrow & Wealdstone ⊖	d			19 26			19 36				20 06				20 26			20 36					
Bushey	d			19 31											20 31								
Watford Junction	a			19 34			19 43	19 50		20 06	20 12				20 34			20 44	20 49				
	d			19 34		19u34		19 51		20 06	20 13				20 34		20u32		20 50			21u10	
Kings Langley	d			19 39											20 39								
Apsley	d			19 43											20 43								
Hemel Hempstead	d			19 45				19 58			20 20				20 45				20 57				
Berkhamsted	d			19 50				20 03			20 25				20 50				21 03				
Tring	d			19a57							20 29				20a57								
Cheddington	d										20 35												
Leighton Buzzard	d							20 15		20 26	20 41								21 16				
Bletchley	d							20 22			20 48								21 23				
Milton Keynes Central 10	a		19 41		19 50			20 27	20 13	20 36	20 54			20 41		20 48			21 28	21 16	21 35	21 41	
	d							20 28	20 13	20 36									21 29	21 16	21 37	21 43	
Wolverton	d							20 31											21 32				
Northampton	a							20 44		20 54									21 45				
Rugby	a							21 13		21 21		20 51							22 14		21 59	22 05	
Nuneaton	a	20 03								21 35			21 03										
Coventry	a					20 21		21 27	20 42			21 02					21 20		22 27	21 46		22 16	
Birmingham International ✈	a					20 32		21 46	20 53			21 13					21 31		22 46	21 57		22 27	
Birmingham New Street 12	a					20 44		21 58	21 04			21 24					21 44		22 58	22 09		22 39	
Sandwell & Dudley	a					20 56			21 15			21 36					21 56			22 24		22 52	
Wolverhampton 7	a					21 10			21 31			21 51					22 10			22 38		23 06	

		LM	VT	VT	LM	SN	VT	VT	LM	VT	LM	SN	LM	VT	SR	LM
		◇1	◇1 ☕	◇1 ☕	◇1	1	◇1 ☕	◇1 ☕	1	◇1 ☕	◇1	1	◇1	◇1 ☕	B ☕	◇1
London Euston 15 ⊖	d	21 02	21 21	21 25	21 28		21 51	21 55	22 00	22 25	22 28		22 58	23 25	23 27	23 34
East Croydon	d															
Clapham Junction	d					21 15						22 15				
Imperial Wharf	d					21 19						22 19				
West Brompton ⊖	d					21 22						22 22				
Kensington (Olympia) ⊖	d					21 26						22 26				
Shepherd's Bush	d					21 29						22 29				
Wembley Central ⊖	d															
Harrow & Wealdstone ⊖	d				21 40	21 47			22 12		22 40	22 48	23 10			23 46
Bushey	d				21s45						22s45					23s51
Watford Junction	a	21 22			21 47	21 54			22 18		22 48	22 56	23 16			23 54
	d	21 23			21 48			22u09	22 19	22u39	22 49		23 17	23u39		23 55
Kings Langley	d				21 52						22 53		23 21			23 59
Apsley	d				21 56						22 57		23 25			00 03
Hemel Hempstead	d	21 30			21 59				22 26		23 00		23 28			00 06
Berkhamsted	d	21 35			22 04				22 31		23 05		23 33			00 11
Tring	d	21 39							22 35				23 37			00 15
Cheddington	d	21 45							22 41				23 43			00 21
Leighton Buzzard	d	21 49			22 17				22 47		23 18		23 49			00 27
Bletchley	d	21 56			22 24				22 54		23 25		23 56			00 34
Milton Keynes Central 10	a	22 04		22 13	22 32		22 36	22 42	23 02	23 11	23 33		00 04	00 11		00 42
	d	22 05			22 32		22 38	22 44	23 03	23 12	23 33		00 05	00 12		00 43
Wolverton	d	22 08			22 36				23 06		23 37		00 08			00 46
Northampton	a	22 22			22 49				23 20		23 50		00 22			01 00
Rugby	a				23 13		23 16	23 20	23 54	23 46				00s46		
Nuneaton	a		22 51				23 28									
Coventry	a				23 25			23 31	00 05	23 57				00s58		
Birmingham International ✈	a				23 52			23 42		00 08				01s09		
Birmingham New Street 12	a				00 04			23 54		00 21				01s22		
Sandwell & Dudley	a															
Wolverhampton 7	a							00 15		00 43				01 53		

West Midlands, Northampton, Milton Keynes Central and Watford Junction - London

Network Diagram - see first Page of Table 59

Miles	Miles	Miles	Station		SN MX	SN A	SN MX	LM MX	VT MX	LM A	VT A	LM TO	LM B	VT A	VT C	VT D	LM	LM	LM	SN	LM	LM	SR B C
0	—	—	Wolverhampton	d					21p45		21p50			22p33	22p45	22p45							
7½	—	—	Sandwell & Dudley	d					21p56						22p55	22p55							
12¾	—	—	**Birmingham New Street**	d				21p33	22p10		22p30			23p00	23p10	23p10							
21¼	—	—	Birmingham International	d				21p45	22p22		22p40			23p10	23p20	23p20							
32	—	—	Coventry	d				22p01	22p32		22p51			23p21	23p31	23p31							
—	—	—	Nuneaton	d																			
43½	0	—	**Rugby**	d				22p12	22p43		23p04			23p34	23p44	23p44							
62¼	—	—	**Northampton**	d				22p55		23p00		23p30	23p46	23b54	00s05	00s05		04 15	04 48		05 05		
75¼	30	—	Wolverton	d				23p07		23p12		23p46	00 02					04 27	05 00		05 17		
78¾	32¾	—	**Milton Keynes Central**	a				23p12	23b05	23p15	23p36	23p50	00 05	00s11	00s23	00s23		04 30	05 03		05 20		
—	—	—		d	22p11			23p13		23p16	23p37	23p50	00 06				03 30	04 31	05 04		05 21		
81¼	—	—	Bletchley	d	22p15			23p18		23p21		23p55	00 11				03 35	04 36	05 09		05 26	05 38	
87¾	—	—	Leighton Buzzard	d	22p22			23p24		23p27		00 02	00 17				03 41	04 42	05 15		05 33	05 45	
92	—	—	Cheddington	d				23p29		23p32		00 08	00 24						05 20			05 50	
96¼	—	—	Tring	d	22p34			23p38		23p41		00 14	00 30				03 53	04 54	05 29			05 56	
100	—	—	Berkhamsted	d	22p39			23p43		23p45		00 18	00 34				03 58	04 59	05 34		05 47	06 01	
103½	—	—	Hemel Hempstead	d	22p43			23p47		23p49		00 22	00 39				04 02	05 03	05 38		05 52	06 05	
105	—	—	Apsley	d				23p50											05 41			06 08	
107	—	—	Kings Langley	d				23p53											05 44			06 11	
110½	65	—	**Watford Junction**	a	22p52			23p58	23b37	23p56	00s06	00 29	00 46	00s41	00s52	00s52	04 09	05 10	05 49		05 59	06 16	
—	—	—		d	22p53	23p17	23p29	23p58		23p57		00 30	00 47				04 10	05 11	05 50	05 54	06 01	06 17	
112	—	—	Bushey	d				00 01		23p59													
116½	71	—	Harrow & Wealdstone	d	23p00	23p23	23p35	00 06		00 05		00 36	00 53				04 16	05 17	05 56	06 00		06 23	
119¾	—	0	Wembley Central	d								00 40	00 57				04 20	05 21		06 05			
—	—	4¼	Shepherd's Bush	a	23p21	23p45	23p53													06 19			
—	—	5½	Kensington (Olympia)	a	23p23	23p47	23p56													06 21			
—	—	7½	West Brompton	a	23p26	23p50	23p59													06 24			
—	—	8	Imperial Wharf	a	23p28	23p53	00 02													06 27			
—	—	—	Clapham Junction	d	23p40	00 05	00a07													06a32			
—	—	16¾	East Croydon	a	00 01	00 22																	
128	82½	—	**London Euston**	a				00 21	00 04	00 19	00 27	00 53	01 09	01 01	01 13	01 15	04 35	05 35	06 12		06 19	06 40	06 43

Station		SR B D	SR B A	LM	LM	LM	VT	LM	SN	LM	VT	LM	LM	LM	LM	VT	VT	VT	VT	SN	LM	VT	LM
Wolverhampton	d						05 00				05 24							05 45	06 04				
Sandwell & Dudley	d										05 34							05 56	06 15				
Birmingham New Street	d						05 29				05 50							06 10	06 30		05 53		
Birmingham International	d						05 40				06 00							06 20	06 40		06 05		
Coventry	d						05 51				06 11							06 31	06 51		06 21		
Nuneaton	d																06 18						
Rugby	d				05 20		06 03								06 13	06 20	06 32				06 32	06 53	
Northampton	d				05 45					06 17					06 38	06 42					07 00		
Wolverton	d				05 57					06 29					06 50						07 12		
Milton Keynes Central	a				06 00		06 22			06 33	06 38				06 53		06 51	06 59			07 15	07 12	
	d			05 54	06 02	06 20	06 23			06 34	06 38			06 48	06 55		06 52	06 59		07 01	07 17	07 14	
Bletchley	d			05 59	06 07	06 25				06 39		06 34		06 53	07 00					07 05			07 13
Leighton Buzzard	d			06 05	06 14	06 31				06 46		06 41		06 59	07 07					07 13	07 26		
Cheddington	d					06 37								07 05									
Tring	d					06 42		06 24				06 52	07 00	07 11						07 22			07 28
Berkhamsted	d			06 17		06 47		06 28				06 56	07 05	07 16						07 26			07 32
Hemel Hempstead	d			06 22		06 52		06 33				07 01	07 09	07 20						07 31			07 37
Apsley	d							06 36				07 04		07 24									
Kings Langley	d							06 39				07 07		07 27									
Watford Junction	a			06 29	06 31	06 59	06s43	06 44		07 04		07 12	07 18	07 31					07s36	07 38			07 44
	d			06 30	06 33	07 00		06 45	06 53	07 05		07 12	07 18	07 32						07 38			07 45
Bushey	d							06 48				07 15	07 22	07 34									
Harrow & Wealdstone	d					07 06		06 53	06 59			07 20		07 40						07 45			
Wembley Central	d								07 04											07 49			
Shepherd's Bush	a								07 19											08 04			
Kensington (Olympia)	a								07 21											08 06			
West Brompton	a								07 24											08 09			
Imperial Wharf	a								07 27											08 12			
Clapham Junction	d								07a32											08 36			
East Croydon	a																			09 04			
London Euston	a	06 45	06 46	06 49	06 50	07 20	07 02	07 07		07 22	07 13	07 34	07 40	07 54	07 40	07 30	07 28	07 34	07 53		08 02	07 50	08 05

A MO from 21 May until 25 June
B WThFO
C from 26 June until 29 June
D MX until 22 June
b Previous night, stops to set down only

West Midlands, Northampton, Milton Keynes Central and Watford Junction - London

Network Diagram - see first Page of Table 59

Station		LM	LM	LM	VT	LM	LM	LM	LM	VT	VT	VT	VT	VT	LM	VT	LM	LM	SN	LM	VT	VT	LM
Wolverhampton	d				06 27								06 45			07 04							
Sandwell & Dudley	d				06 37								06 56			07 15							
Birmingham New Street	d				06 50								07 10			07 30				06 53			
Birmingham International	d				07 00								07 20							07 05		07 41	
Coventry	d				07 11								07 31							07 21		07 52	
Nuneaton	d										07 07			07 33									
Rugby	d								07 02	07 08		07 29								07 32	07 55		
Northampton	d			07 13					07 32						07 39					08 05			08 25
Wolverton	d			07 25											07 51					08 17			08 37
Milton Keynes Central	a			07 29	07s40				07 46						07 54					08 21			08 41
	d		07 21	07 30					07 46						07 55		07 59		08 13	08 21			08 41
Bletchley	d		07 26			07 39			07 51								08 04		08 17	08 27			08 46
Leighton Buzzard	d		07 33	07 39		07 46			07 58						08 05		08 11		08 24	08 34			08 53
Cheddington	d		07 38						08 04														
Tring	d		07 45					08 04	08 10									08 25	08 34				
Berkhamsted	d		07 49			07 59			08 15									08 29	08 39				
Hemel Hempstead	d		07 54			08 03			08 19								08 28	08 34	08 43				
Apsley	d		07 57					08 13										08 37					
Kings Langley	d		08 00					08 16										08 40					
Watford Junction	a		08 05			08 10		08 20	08 26								08 35	08 45	08 51				
	d	07 55	08 05			08 11	08 15	08 22	08 28								08 36	08 46	08 51				
Bushey	d	07 59					08 19											08 48					
Harrow & Wealdstone	d	08 05				08 17	08 24	08 29	08 34									08 54	08 58				
Wembley Central	d																		09 05				
Shepherd's Bush	a																		09 18				
Kensington (Olympia)	a																		09 20				
West Brompton	a																		09 23				
Imperial Wharf	a																		09 26				
Clapham Junction	d																		09 34				
East Croydon	a																		09 57				
London Euston	a	08 18	08 24	08 11	08 14	08 33	08 38	08 42	08 49	07 57	08 07	08 22	08 30	08 33	08 39	08 42	08 55	09 08		09 10	08 45	08 49	09 27

Station		LM	VT	LM	LM	LM	VT	VT	VT	LM	SN	VT	LM	VT	LM	VT	VT	LM	LM	VT	LM	LM
Wolverhampton	d		07 45														08 45					
Sandwell & Dudley	d		07 56														08 56					
Birmingham New Street	d		08 10				07 50					08 30	07 53				09 10				08 33	
Birmingham International	d		08 20				08 00					08 40	08 05				09 20				08 45	
Coventry	d		08 31				08 11					08 51	08 21				09 31				09 01	
Nuneaton	d					08 02			08 46													09 02
Rugby	d					08 20	08 23						08 32	08 46							09 12	09 20
Northampton	d					08 47							09 05		09 25						09 50	
Wolverton	d												09 17		09 37							
Milton Keynes Central	a					09 01						09 18	09 20		09 41						10 04	
	d				08 47	09 01					09 13	09 19	09 22		09 41	09 47			09 47	10 02	10 05	
Bletchley	d				08 52						09 17		09 27		09 46				09 52			
Leighton Buzzard	d				08 58						09 24		09 33		09 53				09 58			
Cheddington	d				09 04														10 04			
Tring	d	08 48		09 01	09 10					09 26	09 34							09 56	10 10			
Berkhamsted	d	08 53		09 05	09 15					09 30	09 39		09 46					10 00	10 15			
Hemel Hempstead	d	08 57		09 10	09 19					09 35	09 43		09 51					10 05	10 19			
Apsley	d			09 13						09 38								10 08				
Kings Langley	d			09 16						09 41								10 11				
Watford Junction	a	09 04	09s15	09 20	09 26	09 27			09s31	09 46	09 51		09 58				10s15	10 16	10 26		10 30	
	d	09 05		09 21	09 27	09 28				09 46	09 51		09 59					10 16	10 27		10 31	
Bushey	d	09 08		09 23						09 49								10 19				
Harrow & Wealdstone	d	09 13		09 28	09 33					09 54	09 58							10 24				
Wembley Central	d										10 05											
Shepherd's Bush	a										10 21											
Kensington (Olympia)	a										10 23											
West Brompton	a										10 26											
Imperial Wharf	a										10 29											
Clapham Junction	d										10 34											
East Croydon	a										10 57											
London Euston	a	09 27	09 34	09 42	09 47	09 44	09 13	09 23	09 52	10 08		09 54	10 18	09 38	10 27	10 23	10 32	10 38	10 46	10 38	10 49	

West Midlands, Northampton, Milton Keynes Central and Watford Junction - London

Network Diagram - see first Page of Table 59

		VT ◇■ ⊠	LM ■	SN ■	VT ◇■ ⊠	LM ◇■	LM ◇■	VT ◇■ ⊠	VT ◇■ ⊠	LM ■	LM ■	VT ◇■ ⊠	LM ◇■ A	LM ◇■	VT ◇■ ⊠	LM ■	SN ■	VT ◇■ ⊠	LM ◇■	LM ◇■	VT ◇■ ⊠	VT ◇■ ⊠	LM ■
Wolverhampton ⑦	d								09 45													10 45	
Sandwell & Dudley	d								09 56													10 56	
Birmingham New Street	d	08 50			09 30	08 53	09 13		10 10				09 33		09 50			10 30	09 53	10 13		11 10	
Birmingham International	d	09 00			09 40	09 05	09 29		10 20				09 45		09 59			10 40	10 05	10 29		11 20	
Coventry	d	09 11			09 51	09 21	09 48		10 31				10 01		10 10			10 51	10 21	10 48		11 31	
Nuneaton	d													10 02									
Rugby	d	09 23				09 32	09 59						10 12	10 20	10 24				10 32	10 59			
Northampton	d					10 05	10 25						10 50						11 05	11 25			
Wolverton	d					10 17	10 37												11 17	11 37			
Milton Keynes Central	a				10 18	10 20	10 41						11 04					11 18	11 20	11 41			
	d			10 13	10 19	10 22	10 41	10 47			10 47	11 02	11 05				11 13	11 19	11 22	11 41	11 47		
Bletchley	d			10 17		10 27	10 46				10 52						11 17		11 27	11 46			
Leighton Buzzard	d			10 24		10 33	10 53				10 58						11 24		11 33	11 53			
Cheddington	d										11 04												
Tring	d		10 26	10 34						10 56	11 10					11 26	11 34						11 56
Berkhamsted	d		10 30	10 39		10 46				11 00	11 15					11 30	11 39		11 46				12 00
Hemel Hempstead	d		10 35	10 43		10 51				11 05	11 19					11 35	11 43		11 51				12 05
Apsley	d		10 38							11 08						11 38							12 08
Kings Langley	d		10 41							11 11						11 41							12 11
Watford Junction	a		10 46	10 51		10 58			11s15	11 16	11 26		11 30			11 46	11 51		11 58			12s15	12 16
	d		10 46	10 51		10 59				11 16	11 27		11 31			11 46	11 51		11 59				12 16
Bushey	d		10 49							11 19						11 49							12 19
Harrow & Wealdstone	⊖ d		10 54	10 59						11 24						11 54	11 59						12 24
Wembley Central	⊖ d			11 04													12 04						
Shepherd's Bush	a			11 19													12 19						
Kensington (Olympia)	⊖ a			11 21													12 21						
West Brompton	⊖ a			11 23													12 24						
Imperial Wharf	a			11 26													12 27						
Clapham Junction	d			11 34													12 34						
East Croydon	a			11 57													12 57						
London Euston	⊖ a	10 14	11 08		10 54	11 17	11 27	11 23	11 32	11 38	11 46	11 38	11 49		11 15	12 08		11 54	12 17	12 27	12 23	12 32	12 38

		LM ■	VT ◇■ ⊠	LM ◇■	VT ◇■ ⊠	LM ■	SN ■	VT ◇■ ☕	LM ◇■	LM ◇■	VT ◇■ ☕	VT ◇■ ☕	LM ■	LM ■	VT ◇■ ☕	LM ◇■	LM ◇■	VT ◇■ ☕	LM ■	SN ■	VT ◇■ ☕	LM ◇■
Wolverhampton ⑦	d											11 45										
Sandwell & Dudley	d											11 56										
Birmingham New Street	d				10 50			11 30	10 53	11 13		12 10				11 33		11 50			12 30	11 53
Birmingham International	d				11 00			11 40	11 05	11 29		12 20				11 45		12 00			12 40	12 05
Coventry	d				11 11			11 51	11 21	11 48		12 31				12 01		12 11			12 51	12 21
Nuneaton	d			11 02													12 02					
Rugby	d			11 20	11 24				11 32	11 59						12 12	12 20	12 24				12 32
Northampton	d			11 50					12 05	12 25						12 50						13 05
Wolverton	d								12 17	12 37												13 17
Milton Keynes Central	a			12 04				12 18	12 20	12 41						13 04					13 18	13 20
	d	11 47	12 02	12 05			12 13	12 19	12 22	12 41	12 46			12 47	13 02	13 05				13 13	13 19	13 22
Bletchley	d	11 52					12 17		12 27	12 46				12 52						13 17		13 27
Leighton Buzzard	d	11 58					12 24		12 33	12 53				12 58						13 24		13 33
Cheddington	d	12 04												13 04								
Tring	d	12 10				12 26	12 34						12 56	13 10					13 26	13 34		
Berkhamsted	d	12 15				12 30	12 39		12 46				13 00	13 15					13 30	13 39		13 46
Hemel Hempstead	d	12 19				12 35	12 43		12 51				13 05	13 19					13 35	13 43		13 51
Apsley	d					12 38							13 08						13 38			
Kings Langley	d					12 41							13 11						13 41			
Watford Junction	a	12 26		12 30		12 46	12 51		12 58			13s15	13 16	13 26		13 30			13 46	13 51		13 58
	d	12 27		12 31		12 46	12 51		12 59				13 16	13 27		13 31			13 46	13 51		13 59
Bushey	d					12 49							13 19						13 49			
Harrow & Wealdstone	⊖ d					12 54	12 59						13 24						13 54	13 59		
Wembley Central	⊖ d						13 04													14 04		
Shepherd's Bush	a						13 19													14 19		
Kensington (Olympia)	⊖ a						13 21													14 21		
West Brompton	⊖ a						13 24													14 24		
Imperial Wharf	a						13 27													14 27		
Clapham Junction	d						13 34													14 34		
East Croydon	a						13 57													14 57		
London Euston	⊖ a	12 45	12 38	12 49	12 14	13 08		12 54	13 17	13 27	13 23	13 32	13 38	13 45	13 38	13 49		13 14	14 08		13 54	14 17

A ◇ from Northampton

West Midlands, Northampton, Milton Keynes Central and Watford Junction - London

Network Diagram - see first Page of Table 59

		LM ◇■	VT ◇■ ☕	VT ◇■ ☕	LM ■	LM ■	VT ◇■ ☕	LM ◇■ A	LM ◇■	VT ◇■ ☕	LM ■	SN ■	VT ◇■ ☕	LM ◇■	LM ◇■	VT ◇■ ☕	VT ◇■ ☕	LM ■	LM ■	VT ◇■ ☕	LM ◇■ A	LM ◇■	VT ◇■ ☕
Wolverhampton ⑦	d			12 45													13 45						
Sandwell & Dudley	d			12 56													13 56						
Birmingham New Street	d	12 13		13 10				12 33		12 50			13 30	12 53	13 13		14 10				13 33		13 50
Birmingham International	d	12 29		13 20				12 45		13 00			13 40	13 05	13 29		14 20				13 45		14 00
Coventry	d	12 48		13 31				13 01		13 11			13 51	13 21	13 48		14 31				14 01		14 11
Nuneaton	d								13 02													14 02	
Rugby	d	13 00						13 12	13 20	13 24				13 32	13 59						14 12	14 20	14 24
Northampton	d	13 25						13 50						14 05	14 25						14 50		
Wolverton	d	13 37												14 17	14 37								
Milton Keynes Central	a	13 41						14 04					14 18	14 20	14 41						15 04		
	d	13 41	13 47			13 47	14 02	14 05				14 13	14 19	14 22	14 41	14 47			14 47	15 02	15 05		
Bletchley	d	13 46				13 52						14 17		14 27	14 46				14 52				
Leighton Buzzard	d	13 53				13 58						14 24		14 33	14 53				14 58				
Cheddington	d					14 04													15 04				
Tring	d				13 56	14 10					14 26	14 34						14 56	15 10				
Berkhamsted	d				14 00	14 15					14 30	14 39		14 46				15 00	15 15				
Hemel Hempstead	d				14 05	14 19					14 35	14 43		14 51				15 05	15 19				
Apsley	d				14 08						14 38							15 08					
Kings Langley	d				14 11						14 41							15 11					
Watford Junction	a			14s14	14 16	14 26		14 30			14 46	14 51		14 58			15s15	15 16	15 26		15 30		
	d				14 16	14 27		14 31			14 46	14 51		14 59				15 16	15 27		15 31		
Bushey	d				14 19						14 49							15 19					
Harrow & Wealdstone	⊖ d				14 24						14 54	14 59						15 24					
Wembley Central	⊖ d											15 04											
Shepherd's Bush	a											15 22											
Kensington (Olympia)	⊖ a											15 24											
West Brompton	⊖ a											15 26											
Imperial Wharf	a											15 29											
Clapham Junction	d											15 34											
East Croydon	a											15 57											
London Euston	⊖ a	14 27	14 23	14 32	14 38	14 45	14 38	14 49		14 14	15 08		14 54	15 17	15 27	15 23	15 32	15 38	15 45	15 38	15 49		15 14

		LM ■	SN ■	VT ◇■ ☕	LM ◇■	LM ◇■	VT ◇■ ☕	VT ◇■ ☕	LM ■	LM ■	VT ◇■ ☕	LM ◇■ A	LM ◇■	VT ◇■ ☕	LM ■	SN ■	VT ◇■ ☕	LM ◇■	LM ◇■	VT ◇■ ☕	VT ◇■ ☕	LM ■	LM ■
Wolverhampton ⑦	d							14 45													15 45		
Sandwell & Dudley	d							14 56													15 56		
Birmingham New Street	d			14 30	13 53	14 13		15 10				14 33		14 50			15 30	14 53	15 13		16 10		
Birmingham International	d			14 40	14 05	14 29		15 20				14 45		15 00			15 40	15 05	15 29		16 20		
Coventry	d			14 51	14 21	14 48		15 31				15 01		15 11			15 51	15 21	15 48		16 31		
Nuneaton	d												15 02										
Rugby	d				14 32	14 59						15 12	15 20	15 24				15 32	15 59				
Northampton	d				15 05	15 25						15 50						16 05	16 25				
Wolverton	d				15 17	15 37												16 17	16 37				
Milton Keynes Central	a			15 18	15 20	15 41						16 04					16 18	16 20	16 41				
	d		15 13	15 19	15 22	15 41	15 47			15 47	16 02	16 05				16 13	16 19	16 22	16 41	16 47			16 47
Bletchley	d		15 17		15 27	15 46				15 52						16 17		16 27	16 46				16 52
Leighton Buzzard	d		15 24		15 33	15 53				15 58						16 24		16 33	16 53				16 58
Cheddington	d									16 04													17 04
Tring	d	15 26	15 34						15 56	16 10					16 26	16 34						16 56	17 10
Berkhamsted	d	15 30	15 39		15 46				16 00	16 15					16 30	16 39		16 46				17 00	17 15
Hemel Hempstead	d	15 35	15 43		15 51				16 05	16 19					16 35	16 43		16 51				17 05	17 19
Apsley	d	15 38							16 08						16 38							17 08	
Kings Langley	d	15 41							16 11						16 41							17 11	
Watford Junction	a	15 46	15 51		15 58			16s15	16 16	16 26		16 30			16 46	16 51		16 58			17s15	17 16	17 26
	d	15 46	15 51		15 59				16 16	16 27		16 31			16 46	16 51		16 59				17 16	17 27
Bushey	d	15 49							16 19						16 49							17 19	
Harrow & Wealdstone	⊖ d	15 54	15 59						16 24						16 54	16 59						17 24	
Wembley Central	⊖ d		16 05													17 05							
Shepherd's Bush	a		16 19													17 19							
Kensington (Olympia)	⊖ a		16 21													17 21							
West Brompton	⊖ a		16 24													17 24							
Imperial Wharf	a		16 27													17 27							
Clapham Junction	d		16 34													17 33							
East Croydon	a		16 58													17 59							
London Euston	⊖ a	16 08		15 54	16 17	16 27	16 23	16 32	16 38	16 45	16 38	16 49		16 14	17 08		16 57	17 18	17 27	17 23	17 34	17 38	17 47

A ◇ from Northampton

West Midlands, Northampton, Milton Keynes Central and Watford Junction - London

Network Diagram - see first Page of Table 59

Station		VT ◇1 ⎍	LM ◇1 A	LM ◇1	VT ◇1 ⎍	LM 1	SN 1	VT ◇1 ⎍	LM ◇1	LM 1	VT ◇1 ⎍	VT ◇1 ⎍	LM 1	LM 1	VT ◇1 ⎍	LM FX ◇1 A	LM ◇1	VT ◇1 ⎍	LM 1	SN 1	VT ◇1 ⊠	LM ◇1
Wolverhampton 7	d											16 45										
Sandwell & Dudley	d											16 56										
Birmingham New Street 12	d		15 33		15 50			16 30	15 53			17 10				16 33		16 50			17 30	16 53
Birmingham International ✈	d		15 45		16 00			16 40	16 05			17 20				16 45		17 00			17 40	17 05
Coventry	d		16 01		16 11			16 51	16 21			17 31				17 01		17 11			17 51	17 21
Nuneaton	d			16 02													17 02					
Rugby	d		16 12	16 20	16 24				16 32							17 12	17 20	17 24				17 32
Northampton	d			16 50					17 05	17 25						17 50	17 50					18 05
Wolverton	d								17 17	17 37												18 17
Milton Keynes Central 10	a			17 04				17 18	17 20	17 41						18 04	18 04				18 18	18 20
	d	17 02		17 05			17 13	17 19	17 22	17 41	17 47			17 47	18 02	18 05	18 05			18 13	18 19	18 22
Bletchley	d						17 17		17 27	17 46				17 52						18 17		18 27
Leighton Buzzard	d						17 24		17 33	17 53				17 58						18 24		18 33
Cheddington	d													18 04								
Tring	d					17 26	17 34						17 59	18 10					18 27	18 34		
Berkhamsted	d					17 30	17 39		17 46				18 03	18 15					18 31	18 39		18 46
Hemel Hempstead	d					17 35	17 43		17 51				18 08	18 19					18 36	18 43		18 51
Apsley	d					17 38							18 11						18 39			
Kings Langley	d					17 41							18 14						18 42			
Watford Junction	a			17 30		17 46	17 51		17 59			18s15	18 19	18 26		18 31	18 31		18 46	18 51		18 58
	d			17 31		17 46	17 51		17 59				18 19	18 27		18 31	18 31		18 47	18 51		18 59
Bushey	d					17 49							18 22						18 49			
Harrow & Wealdstone ⊖	d					17 54	17 59						18 27						18 54	18 59		
Wembley Central ⊖	d						18 05													19 05		
Shepherd's Bush	a						18 19													19 18		
Kensington (Olympia) ⊖	a						18 21													19 20		
West Brompton ⊖	a						18 24													19 23		
Imperial Wharf	a						18 27													19 25		
Clapham Junction	d						18 34													19a30		
East Croydon ⇌	a						19 02															
London Euston 15 ⊖	a	17 38		17 49	17 14	18 10		17 54	18 18	18 27	18 23	18 34	18 41	18 45	18 38	18 49	18 49	18 14	19 09		18 54	19 18

Station		VT ◇1 ⎍	VT ◇1 ⎍	LM 1	VT ◇1 ⊠	LM 1	LM 1	VT ◇1 ⊠	VT ◇1 ⊠	LM ◇1	VT ◇1 ⊠	LM 1	SN 1	VT ◇1 ⊠	VT ◇1 ⊠	LM ◇1	VT ◇1 ⊠	LM ◇1	VT ◇1 ⊠	VT ◇1 ⊠	LM 1	LM 1
Wolverhampton 7	d				17 45															18 45		
Sandwell & Dudley	d				17 56															18 56		
Birmingham New Street 12	d			17 13	18 10						17 50			18 30		17 53				19 10		
Birmingham International ✈	d			17 25	18 20						18 00			18 40		18 05				19 20		
Coventry	d			17 40	18 31						18 11			18 51		18 21				19 31		
Nuneaton	d									18 02												
Rugby	d			17 51						18 20	18 24					18 32						
Northampton	d			18 25						18 50						19 05		19 25				
Wolverton	d			18 37												19 17		19 37				
Milton Keynes Central 10	a			18 41						19 04				19 18		19 20		19 41				
	d	18 24		18 41			18 47	18 48	19 03	19 05			19 15	19 19		19 22	19 32	19 41	19 47			19 47
Bletchley	d			18 46			18 52						19 19			19 27		19 46				19 52
Leighton Buzzard	d			18 53			18 58						19 26			19 33		19 53				19 58
Cheddington	d						19 06															20 04
Tring	d					19 00	19 12					19 29	19 36								19 56	20 10
Berkhamsted	d					19 04	19 17					19 33	19 41			19 46					20 00	20 15
Hemel Hempstead	d					19 09	19 21					19 38	19 45			19 51					20 05	20 19
Apsley	d					19 12						19 41									20 08	
Kings Langley	d					19 15						19 44									20 11	
Watford Junction	a				19s16	19 20	19 28			19 30		19 49	19 54			19 59				20s15	20 16	20 26
	d					19 20	19 29			19 31		19 49	19 54			19 59					20 16	20 27
Bushey	d					19 23						19 52									20 19	
Harrow & Wealdstone ⊖	d					19 28						19 57	20 01								20 24	
Wembley Central ⊖	d												20 06									
Shepherd's Bush	a												20 21									
Kensington (Olympia) ⊖	a												20 23									
West Brompton ⊖	a												20 25									
Imperial Wharf	a												20 28									
Clapham Junction	d												20a33									
East Croydon ⇌	a																					
London Euston 15 ⊖	a	18 59	19 08	19 29	19 34	19 42	19 47	19 23	19 39	19 50	19 14	20 11		19 54	20 02	20 19	20 06	20 27	20 23	20 34	20 38	20 51

A ◇ from Northampton

West Midlands, Northampton, Milton Keynes Central and Watford Junction - London

Network Diagram - see first Page of Table 59

Station		LM ◇1 A	LM ◇1	VT ◇1 ⊠	LM 1	SN 1	VT ◇1 ⎍	VT ◇1 ⊠	LM ◇1	VT ◇1 ⊠	VT ◇1 ⎍	LM ◇1	VT ◇1 ⊠	LM 1	LM 1	VT ◇1 ⎍	VT ◇1 ⎍	VT ◇1 ⎍	LM 1	VT ◇1 ⎍	SN 1	LM ◇1
Wolverhampton 7	d																19 45					
Sandwell & Dudley	d																19 56					
Birmingham New Street 12	d	18 33		18 50			19 30		18 53		19 50						20 10					19 53
Birmingham International ✈	d	18 45		19 00			19 40		19 05		20 00						20 20					20 05
Coventry	d	19 01		19 11			19 51		19 21		20 11						20 31					20 21
Nuneaton	d		19 02																	21 03		
Rugby	d	19 12	19 20	19 24					19 32		20 23											20 32
Northampton	d		19 51						20 05			20 25										21 05
Wolverton	d								20 17			20 37										21 17
Milton Keynes Central 10	a		20 05				20 18		20 20			20 41					20 58					21 20
	d		20 09			20 13	20 19		20 22	20 33		20 41	20 46		20 47	20 50	20 59	21 04			21 13	21 22
Bletchley	d					20 17			20 27			20 46			20 52						21 17	21 27
Leighton Buzzard	d					20 24			20 33			20 53			20 58						21 24	21 33
Cheddington	d														21 06							
Tring	d				20 26	20 34								20 56	21 11				21 26		21 34	
Berkhamsted	d				20 30	20 39			20 46					21 00	21 16				21 30		21 39	21 46
Hemel Hempstead	d				20 35	20 43			20 51					21 05	21 20				21 35		21 43	21 51
Apsley	d				20 38									21 08					21 38			
Kings Langley	d				20 41									21 11					21 41			
Watford Junction	a		20 31		20 46	20 51			20 58					21 16	21 27		21s19		21 46	21s48	21 51	21 58
	d		20 32		20 46	20 51			20 59					21 16	21 27				21 46		21 51	21 59
Bushey	d				20 49									21 19					21 49			
Harrow & Wealdstone ⊖	d				20 54	20 59								21 24					21 54		21 59	
Wembley Central ⊖	d					21 04																
Shepherd's Bush	a					21 22															22 23	
Kensington (Olympia) ⊖	a					21 24															22 25	
West Brompton ⊖	a					21 27															22 27	
Imperial Wharf	a					21 29															22 30	
Clapham Junction	d					21a34															22a34	
East Croydon ⇌	a																					
London Euston 15 ⊖	a		20 49	20 14	21 08		20 54	21 05	21 17	21 06	21 14	21 29	21 24	21 38	21 46	21 26	21 38	21 42	22 08	22 09		22 20

Station		VT ◇1 ⎍	LM 1	VT ◇1 ⎍	VT ◇1 ⎍	VT ◇1 ⎍	LM 1	VT ◇1 ⎍	SN 1	LM 1	SN 1	LM ◇1	VT ◇1 ⊠	VT ◇1 ⎍	SN 1	LM ◇1	VT ◇1 ⎍	VT ◇1 ⎍	LM MO 1	LM MX 1	VT ◇1 B ⎍	VT ◇1 C ⎍
Wolverhampton 7	d							20 47										21 45			22 45	22 45
Sandwell & Dudley	d							20 57										21 56			22 55	22 55
Birmingham New Street 12	d			20 50				21 10				20 53				21 33		22 10			23 10	23 10
Birmingham International ✈	d			21 00				21 20				21 05				21 45		22 22			23 20	23 20
Coventry	d			21 11				21 31				21 21				22 01		22 32			23 31	23 31
Nuneaton	d		21 02														22 17					
Rugby	d		21 20	21 23	21 28							21 32				22 12	22 34	22 43			23 44	23 44
Northampton	d		21 50				21 37					22 05				22 55			23 30	23 46	00s05	00s05
Wolverton	d						21 49					22 17				23 07			23 46	00 02		
Milton Keynes Central 10	a		22 04		21 47		21 52	21 58				22 20				23 12	22 58	23s05	23 50	00 05	00s23	00s23
	d	21 36	22 05		21 49	21 52	21 53	21 59		22 05	22 11	22 22	22 41	22 53		23 13	22 59		23 50	00 06		
Bletchley	d						21 58			22 10	22 15	22 27				23 18			23 55	00 11		
Leighton Buzzard	d						22 04			22 17	22 22	22 33				23 24			00 02	00 17		
Cheddington	d						22 10			22 23						23 29			00 08	00 24		
Tring	d						22 16			22 28	22 34					23 38			00 14	00 30		
Berkhamsted	d						22 20			22 33	22 39	22 48				23 43			00 18	00 34		
Hemel Hempstead	d						22 25			22 37	22 43	22 53				23 47			00 22	00 39		
Apsley	d									22 41						23 50						
Kings Langley	d									22 44						23 53						
Watford Junction	a		22 35			22s11	22 32	22s20		22 48	22 52	23 00	23s14	23s25		23 58	23s30	23s37	00 29	00 46	00s52	00s52
	d		22 36				22 33		22 27	22 49	22 53	23 01			23 29	23 58			00 30	00 47		
Bushey	d									22 51						00 01						
Harrow & Wealdstone ⊖	d								22 33	22 57	23 00				23 35	00 06			00 36	00 53		
Wembley Central ⊖	d																		00 40	00 57		
Shepherd's Bush	a								22 49		23 21				23 53							
Kensington (Olympia) ⊖	a								22 51		23 23				23 56							
West Brompton ⊖	a								22 54		23 26				23 59							
Imperial Wharf	a								22 56		23 28				00 02							
Clapham Junction	d								23a01		23 40				00a07							
East Croydon ⇌	a										00 01											
London Euston 15 ⊖	a	22 12	22 56	22 12	22 22	22 33	22 52	22 43		23 12		23 21	23 38	23 48		00 21	23 56	00 04	00 53	01 09	01 13	01 15

A ◇ from Northampton

B from 25 June until 29 June

C until 22 June

West Midlands, Northampton, Milton Keynes Central and Watford Junction - London

Network Diagram - see first Page of Table 59

		SN MX	SN MO	SN MX	LM MX	VT MX	LM MO	VT MO	LM TO	LM WThFO	VT MO	VT MX	LM	LM	LM	SN	LM	LM	SR MX	SR MO	LM	LM	LM
		1	1	1	◇1	◇1	◇1	◇1	1	1	◇1	◇1	1	1	1	1	1	1			1	1	1
Wolverhampton 7 ⇌	d					21p45		22p05			22p37	22p45											
Sandwell & Dudley	d					21p56		22p15			22p47	22p55											
Birmingham New Street 12	d				21p33	22p10		22p30			23p00	23p10											
Birmingham International ✈	d				21p45	22p22		22p40			23p10	23p20											
Coventry	d				22p01	22p32		22p51			23p21	23p31											
Nuneaton	d																						
Rugby	d				22p12	22p43		23p04			23p34	23p44										05 20	
Northampton	d				22p55		23p00		23p30	23p46	23b53	00s05		04 15	04 48		05 05					05 45	
Wolverton	d				23p07		23p12		23p46	00 02				04 27	05 00		05 17					05 57	
Milton Keynes Central 10	a				23p12	23b05	23p15	23p36	23p50	00 05	00s13	00s23		04 30	05 03		05 20					06 00	
	d	22p11			23p13		23p16	23p37	23p50	00 06			03 30	04 31	05 04		05 21				05 54	06 02	06 20
Bletchley	d	22p15			23p18		23p21		23p55	00 11			03 35	04 36	05 09		05 26	05 38			05 59	06 07	06 25
Leighton Buzzard	d	22p22			23p24		23p27		00 02	00 17			03 41	04 42	05 15		05 33	05 45			06 05	06 14	06 31
Cheddington	d				23p29		23p32		00 08	00 24					05 20			05 50					06 37
Tring	d	22p34			23p38		23p41		00 14	00 30			03 53	04 54	05 29			05 56					06 42
Berkhamsted	d	22p39			23p43		23p45		00 18	00 34			03 58	04 59	05 34		05 47	06 01			06 17		06 47
Hemel Hempstead	d	22p43			23p47		23p49		00 22	00 39			04 02	05 03	05 38		05 52	06 05			06 22		06 52
Apsley	d				23p50										05 41			06 08					
Kings Langley	d				23p53										05 44			06 11					
Watford Junction	a	22p52			23p58	23b37	23p56	00s06	00 29	00 46	00s42	00s52	04 09	05 10	05 49		05 59	06 16			06 29	06 31	06 59
	d	22p53	23p17	23p29	23p58		23p57		00 30	00 47			04 10	05 11	05 50	05 54	06 01	06 17			06 30	06 33	07 00
Bushey	d				00 01		23p59																
Harrow & Wealdstone ⊖	d	23p00	23p23	23p35	00 06		00 05		00 36	00 53			04 16	05 17	05 56	06 00		06 23					07 06
Wembley Central ⊖	d								00 40	00 57			04 20	05 21		06 05							
Shepherd's Bush	a	23p21	23p45	23p53												06 19							
Kensington (Olympia) ⊖	a	23p23	23p47	23p56												06 21							
West Brompton ⊖	a	23p26	23p50	23p59												06 24							
Imperial Wharf	a	23p28	23p53	00 02												06 27							
Clapham Junction	d	23p40	00 05	00a07												06a32							
East Croydon ⇌	a	00 01	00 22																				
London Euston 15 ⊖	a				00 21	00 04	00 19	00 27	00 53	01 09	01 04	01 13	04 35	05 35	06 12		06 19	06 40	06 43	06 46	06 49	06 50	07 20

		VT	LM	SN	LM	VT	LM	LM	LM	LM	VT	VT	VT	VT	SN	LM	LM	VT	LM	LM	LM	LM	VT
		◇1	1	1		◇1	1	1	1	1	◇1	◇1	◇1	◇1	1	◇1	1	◇1	1	1	1	1	◇1
																	B					C	
		⊠				⊠					⊠	⊠	⊠	⊠				⊠					⊠
Wolverhampton 7 ⇌	d	05 00				05 24							05 45	06 04									06 27
Sandwell & Dudley	d					05 34							05 56	06 15									06 37
Birmingham New Street 12	d	05 29				05 50							06 10	06 30		05 53							06 50
Birmingham International ✈	d	05 40				06 00							06 20	06 40		06 05							07 00
Coventry	d	05 51				06 11							06 31	06 51		06 21							07 11
Nuneaton	d											06 18					06 29						
Rugby	d	06 03								06 13	06 20	06 32				06 32	06 45	06 53					
Northampton	d				06 17					06 38	06 42					07 00	07 13					07 13	
Wolverton	d				06 29					06 50						07 12	07 25					07 25	
Milton Keynes Central 10	a	06 22			06 33	06 38				06 53		06 51	06 59			07 15	07 29	07 12				07 29	07s40
	d	06 23			06 34	06 38			06 48	06 55		06 52	06 59		07 01	07 17	07 30	07 14			07 21	07 30	
Bletchley	d				06 39		06 34		06 53	07 00					07 05				07 13		07 26		
Leighton Buzzard	d				06 46		06 41		06 59	07 07					07 13	07 26	07 39				07 33	07 39	
Cheddington	d								07 05												07 38		
Tring	d		06 24				06 52	07 00	07 11						07 22				07 28		07 45		
Berkhamsted	d		06 28				06 56	07 05	07 16						07 26				07 32		07 49		
Hemel Hempstead	d		06 33				07 01	07 09	07 20						07 31				07 37		07 54		
Apsley	d		06 36				07 04		07 24												07 57		
Kings Langley	d		06 39				07 07		07 27												08 00		
Watford Junction	a	06s43	06 44		07 04		07 12	07 18	07 31					07s36	07 38				07 44		08 05		
	d		06 45	06 53	07 05		07 12	07 18	07 32						07 38				07 45	07 55	08 05		
Bushey	d		06 48				07 15	07 22	07 34											07 59			
Harrow & Wealdstone ⊖	d		06 53	06 59			07 20		07 40						07 45					08 05			
Wembley Central ⊖	d			07 04											07 49								
Shepherd's Bush	a			07 19											08 04								
Kensington (Olympia) ⊖	a			07 21											08 06								
West Brompton ⊖	a			07 24											08 09								
Imperial Wharf	a			07 27											08 12								
Clapham Junction	d			07a32											08 36								
East Croydon ⇌	a														09 04								
London Euston 15 ⊖	a	07 02	07 07		07 22	07 13	07 34	07 40	07 54	07 40	07 30	07 28	07 34	07 53		08 02	08 11	07 50	08 05	08 18	08 24	08 11	08 14

B from 10 September until 14 September

C from 2 July until 7 September

b Previous night, stops to set down only

West Midlands, Northampton, Milton Keynes Central and Watford Junction - London

Network Diagram - see first Page of Table 59

		LM	LM	LM	LM	VT	VT	LM	LM	VT	VT	VT	LM	VT	LM	LM	SN	LM	VT	VT	LM	LM
		1	1	1	1	◇1	◇1	1	1	◇1	◇1	◇1	1	◇1	1	1	1	◇1	◇1	◇1	◇1	1
					A			B	B				A									
						⊠	⊠			⊠	⊠	⊠		⊠					⊠	⊠		
Wolverhampton 7 ⇌	d										06 45			07 04								
Sandwell & Dudley	d										06 56			07 15								
Birmingham New Street 12	d								06 33		07 10			07 30				06 53				
Birmingham International ✈	d								06 45		07 20							07 05		07 41		
Coventry	d								07 01		07 31							07 21		07 52		
Nuneaton	d						07 07					07 33										
Rugby	d				07 02	07 08			07 12	07 29								07 32	07 55			
Northampton	d				07 32			07 32	07 39				07 39					08 05			08 25	
Wolverton	d								07 51				07 51					08 17			08 37	
Milton Keynes Central 10	a				07 46			07 46	07 54				07 54					08 21			08 41	
	d				07 46			07 46	07 55				07 55		07 59		08 13	08 21			08 41	
Bletchley	d	07 39			07 51			07 51							08 04		08 17	08 27			08 46	
Leighton Buzzard	d	07 46			07 58			07 58	08 05				08 05		08 11		08 24	08 34			08 53	
Cheddington	d				08 04			08 04														
Tring	d			08 04	08 10			08 10								08 25	08 34					08 48
Berkhamsted	d	07 59			08 15			08 15								08 29	08 39					08 53
Hemel Hempstead	d	08 03			08 19			08 19							08 28	08 34	08 43					08 57
Apsley	d			08 13												08 37						
Kings Langley	d			08 16												08 40						
Watford Junction	a	08 10		08 20	08 26			08 26							08 35	08 45	08 51					09 04
	d	08 11	08 15	08 22	08 28			08 28							08 36	08 46	08 51					09 05
Bushey	d		08 19													08 48						09 08
Harrow & Wealdstone ⊖	d	08 17	08 24	08 29	08 34			08 34								08 54	08 58					09 13
Wembley Central ⊖	d																09 05					
Shepherd's Bush	a																09 18					
Kensington (Olympia) ⊖	a																09 20					
West Brompton ⊖	a																09 23					
Imperial Wharf	a																09 26					
Clapham Junction	d																09 34					
East Croydon ⇌	a																09 57					
London Euston 15 ⊖	a	08 33	08 38	08 42	08 49	07 57	08 07	08 49	08 39	08 22	08 30	08 33	08 39	08 42	08 55	09 08		09 10	08 45	08 49	09 27	09 27

		VT	LM	LM	LM	VT	VT	VT	LM	SN	VT	LM	VT	LM	VT	VT	LM	LM	VT	LM	LM	VT	LM
		◇1	1	1	◇1	◇1	◇1	◇1	1	1	◇1	◇1	◇1	◇1	◇1	◇1	1	1	◇1	◇1	◇1	◇1	1
		⊠				⊠	⊠	⊠			⊠		⊠		⊠	⊠			⊠			⊠	
Wolverhampton 7 ⇌	d	07 45														08 45							
Sandwell & Dudley	d	07 56														08 56							
Birmingham New Street 12	d	08 10				07 50					08 30	07 53				09 10				08 33		08 50	
Birmingham International ✈	d	08 20				08 00					08 40	08 05				09 20				08 45		09 00	
Coventry	d	08 31				08 11					08 51	08 21				09 31				09 01		09 11	
Nuneaton	d				08 02			08 46													09 02		
Rugby	d				08 20	08 23						08 32	08 46							09 12	09 20	09 23	
Northampton	d				08 47							09 05		09 25						09 50			
Wolverton	d											09 17		09 37									
Milton Keynes Central 10	a				09 01						09 18	09 20		09 41						10 04			
	d			08 47	09 01					09 13	09 19	09 22		09 41	09 47			09 47	10 02	10 05			
Bletchley	d			08 52						09 17		09 27		09 46				09 52					
Leighton Buzzard	d			08 58						09 24		09 33		09 53				09 58					
Cheddington	d			09 04														10 04					
Tring	d		09 01	09 10					09 26	09 34							09 56	10 10					10 26
Berkhamsted	d		09 05	09 15					09 30	09 39		09 46					10 00	10 15					10 30
Hemel Hempstead	d		09 10	09 19					09 35	09 43		09 51					10 05	10 19					10 35
Apsley	d		09 13						09 38								10 08						10 38
Kings Langley	d		09 16						09 41								10 11						10 41
Watford Junction	a	09s15	09 20	09 26	09 27			09s31	09 46	09 51		09 58				10s15	10 16	10 26		10 30			10 46
	d		09 21	09 27	09 28				09 46	09 51		09 59					10 16	10 27		10 31			10 46
Bushey	d		09 23						09 49								10 19						10 49
Harrow & Wealdstone ⊖	d		09 28	09 33					09 54	09 58							10 24						10 54
Wembley Central ⊖	d									10 05													
Shepherd's Bush	a									10 21													
Kensington (Olympia) ⊖	a									10 23													
West Brompton ⊖	a									10 26													
Imperial Wharf	a									10 29													
Clapham Junction	d									10 34													
East Croydon ⇌	a									10 57													
London Euston 15 ⊖	a	09 34	09 42	09 47	09 44	09 13	09 23	09 52	10 08		09 54	10 18	09 38	10 27	10 23	10 32	10 38	10 46	10 38	10 49		10 14	11 08

A from 2 July until 7 September

B from 10 September until 14 September

West Midlands, Northampton, Milton Keynes Central and Watford Junction - London

Network Diagram - see first Page of Table 59

		SN	VT	LM	LM	VT	VT	LM	LM	VT	LM	LM	VT	LM	SN	VT	LM	LM	VT	VT	LM	LM
		■	◇■ ⊠	◇■	◇■	◇■ ⊠	◇■ ⊠	■	■	◇■ ⊠	◇■ A	◇■	◇■ ⊠	■	■	◇■ ⊠	◇■	◇■	◇■ ⊠	◇■ ⊠	■	■
Wolverhampton 7 ⇌	d						09 45													10 45		
Sandwell & Dudley	d						09 56													10 56		
Birmingham New Street 12	d		09 30	08 53	09 13		10 10				09 33		09 50			10 30	09 53	10 13		11 10		
Birmingham International ✈	d		09 40	09 05	09 29		10 20				09 45		10 00			10 40	10 05	10 29		11 20		
Coventry	d		09 51	09 21	09 48		10 31				10 01		10 11			10 51	10 21	10 48		11 31		
Nuneaton	d											10 02										
Rugby	d			09 32	09 59						10 12	10 20	10 24				10 32	10 59				
Northampton	d			10 05	10 25						10 50						11 05	11 25				
Wolverton	d			10 17	10 37												11 17	11 37				
Milton Keynes Central 10	a		10 18	10 20	10 41						11 04					11 18	11 20	11 41				
	d	10 13	10 19	10 22	10 41	10 47			10 47	11 02	11 05				11 13	11 19	11 22	11 41	11 47			11 47
Bletchley	d	10 17		10 27	10 46				10 52						11 17		11 27	11 46				11 52
Leighton Buzzard	d	10 24		10 33	10 53				10 58						11 24		11 33	11 53				11 58
Cheddington	d								11 04													12 04
Tring	d	10 34						10 56	11 10					11 26	11 34						11 56	12 10
Berkhamsted	d	10 39		10 46				11 00	11 15					11 30	11 39		11 46				12 00	12 15
Hemel Hempstead	d	10 43		10 51				11 05	11 19					11 35	11 43		11 51				12 05	12 19
Apsley	d							11 08						11 38							12 08	
Kings Langley	d							11 11						11 41							12 11	
Watford Junction	a	10 51		10 58			11s15	11 16	11 26		11 30			11 46	11 51		11 58			12s15	12 16	12 26
	d	10 51		10 59				11 16	11 27		11 31			11 46	11 51		11 59				12 16	12 27
Bushey	d							11 19						11 49							12 19	
Harrow & Wealdstone ⊖	d	10 59						11 24						11 54	11 59						12 24	
Wembley Central ⊖	d	11 04													12 04							
Shepherd's Bush	a	11 19													12 19							
Kensington (Olympia) ⊖	a	11 21													12 21							
West Brompton ⊖	a	11 23													12 24							
Imperial Wharf	a	11 26													12 27							
Clapham Junction	d	11 34													12 34							
East Croydon ⇌	a	11 57													12 57							
London Euston 15 ⊖	a		10 54	11 17	11 27	11 23	11 32	11 38	11 46	11 38	11 49		11 14	12 08		11 54	12 17	12 27	12 23	12 32	12 38	12 45

		VT	LM	VT	LM	SN	VT	LM	LM	VT	VT	LM	LM	VT	LM	LM	VT	LM	SN	VT	LM	LM	VT
		◇■ ⊠	◇■	◇■ ⊠	■	■	◇■ 🛒	◇■	◇■	◇■ 🛒	◇■ 🛒	■	■	◇■ 🛒	◇■	◇■	◇■ 🛒	■	■	◇■ 🛒	◇■	◇■	◇■ 🛒
Wolverhampton 7 ⇌	d										11 45												
Sandwell & Dudley	d										11 56												
Birmingham New Street 12	d			10 50			11 30	10 53	11 13		12 10				11 33		11 50			12 30	11 53	12 13	
Birmingham International ✈	d			11 00			11 40	11 05	11 29		12 20				11 45		12 00			12 40	12 05	12 29	
Coventry	d			11 11			11 51	11 21	11 48		12 31				12 01		12 11			12 51	12 21	12 48	
Nuneaton	d		11 02													12 02							
Rugby	d		11 20	11 24				11 32	11 59						12 12	12 20	12 24				12 32	13 00	
Northampton	d		11 50					12 05	12 25						12 50						13 05	13 25	
Wolverton	d							12 17	12 37												13 17	13 37	
Milton Keynes Central 10	a		12 04				12 18	12 20	12 41						13 04					13 18	13 20	13 41	
	d	12 02	12 05			12 13	12 19	12 22	12 41	12 46			12 47	13 02	13 05				13 13	13 19	13 22	13 41	13 47
Bletchley	d					12 17		12 27	12 46				12 52						13 17		13 27	13 46	
Leighton Buzzard	d					12 24		12 33	12 53				12 58						13 24		13 33	13 53	
Cheddington	d												13 04										
Tring	d				12 26	12 34						12 56	13 10					13 26	13 34				
Berkhamsted	d				12 30	12 39		12 46				13 00	13 15					13 30	13 39		13 46		
Hemel Hempstead	d				12 35	12 43		12 51				13 05	13 19					13 35	13 43		13 51		
Apsley	d				12 38							13 08						13 38					
Kings Langley	d				12 41							13 11						13 41					
Watford Junction	a		12 30		12 46	12 51		12 58			13s15	13 16	13 26		13 30			13 46	13 51		13 58		
	d		12 31		12 46	12 51		12 59				13 16	13 27		13 31			13 46	13 51		13 59		
Bushey	d				12 49							13 19						13 49					
Harrow & Wealdstone ⊖	d				12 54	12 59						13 24						13 54	13 59				
Wembley Central ⊖	d					13 04													14 04				
Shepherd's Bush	a					13 19													14 19				
Kensington (Olympia) ⊖	a					13 21													14 21				
West Brompton ⊖	a					13 24													14 24				
Imperial Wharf	a					13 27													14 27				
Clapham Junction	d					13 34													14 34				
East Croydon ⇌	a					13 57													14 57				
London Euston 15 ⊖	a	12 38	12 49	12 14	13 08		12 54	13 17	13 27	13 23	13 32	13 38	13 45	13 38	13 49		13 14	14 08		13 54	14 17	14 27	14 23

A ◇ from Northampton

West Midlands, Northampton, Milton Keynes Central and Watford Junction - London

Network Diagram - see first Page of Table 59

		VT	LM	LM	VT	LM	LM	VT	LM	SN	VT	LM	LM	VT	VT	LM	LM	VT	LM	LM	VT	LM	SN
		◇■ 🛒	■	■	◇■ 🛒	◇■ A	◇■	◇■ 🛒	■	■	◇■ 🛒	◇■	◇■	◇■ 🛒	◇■ 🛒	■	■	◇■ 🛒	◇■ A	◇■	◇■ 🛒	■	■
Wolverhampton 7 ⇌	d	12 45													13 45								
Sandwell & Dudley	d	12 56													13 56								
Birmingham New Street 12	d	13 10				12 33		12 50			13 30	12 53	13 13		14 10				13 33		13 50		
Birmingham International ✈	d	13 20				12 45		13 00			13 40	13 05	13 29		14 20				13 45		14 00		
Coventry	d	13 31				13 01		13 11			13 51	13 21	13 48		14 31				14 01		14 11		
Nuneaton	d						13 02													14 02			
Rugby	d					13 12	13 20	13 24				13 32	13 59						14 12	14 20	14 24		
Northampton	d					13 50						14 05	14 25						14 50				
Wolverton	d											14 17	14 37										
Milton Keynes Central 10	a					14 04					14 18	14 20	14 41						15 04				
	d			13 47	14 02	14 05				14 13	14 19	14 22	14 41	14 47			14 47	15 02	15 05				15 13
Bletchley	d			13 52						14 17		14 27	14 46				14 52						15 17
Leighton Buzzard	d			13 58						14 24		14 33	14 53				14 58						15 24
Cheddington	d			14 04													15 04						
Tring	d		13 56	14 10					14 26	14 34						14 56	15 10					15 26	15 34
Berkhamsted	d		14 00	14 15					14 30	14 39		14 46				15 00	15 15					15 30	15 39
Hemel Hempstead	d		14 05	14 19					14 35	14 43		14 51				15 05	15 19					15 35	15 43
Apsley	d		14 08						14 38							15 08						15 38	
Kings Langley	d		14 11						14 41							15 11						15 41	
Watford Junction	a	14s14	14 16	14 26		14 30			14 46	14 51		14 58			15s15	15 16	15 26		15 30			15 46	15 51
	d		14 16	14 27		14 31			14 46	14 51		14 59				15 16	15 27		15 31			15 46	15 51
Bushey	d		14 19						14 49							15 19						15 49	
Harrow & Wealdstone ⊖	d		14 24						14 54	14 59						15 24						15 54	15 59
Wembley Central ⊖	d									15 04													16 05
Shepherd's Bush	a									15 22													16 19
Kensington (Olympia) ⊖	a									15 24													16 21
West Brompton ⊖	a									15 26													16 24
Imperial Wharf	a									15 29													16 27
Clapham Junction	d									15 34													16 34
East Croydon ⇌	a									15 57													16 58
London Euston 15 ⊖	a	14 32	14 38	14 45	14 38	14 49		14 14	15 08		14 54	15 17	15 27	15 23	15 32	15 38	15 45	15 38	15 49		15 14	16 08	

		VT	LM	LM	VT	VT	LM	LM	VT	LM	LM	VT	LM	SN	VT	LM	LM	VT	VT	LM	LM	VT
		◇■ 🛒	◇■	◇■	◇■ 🛒	◇■ ⊠	■	■	◇■ 🛒	◇■ A	◇■	◇■ 🛒	■	■	◇■ 🛒	◇■	◇■	◇■ 🛒	◇■ 🛒	■	■	◇■ 🛒
Wolverhampton 7 ⇌	d					14 45													15 45			
Sandwell & Dudley	d					14 56													15 56			
Birmingham New Street 12	d	14 30	13 53	14 13		15 10				14 33		14 50			15 30	14 53	15 13		16 10			
Birmingham International ✈	d	14 40	14 05	14 29		15 20				14 45		15 00			15 40	15 05	15 29		16 20			
Coventry	d	14 51	14 21	14 48		15 31				15 01		15 11			15 51	15 21	15 48		16 31			
Nuneaton	d										15 02											
Rugby	d		14 32	14 59						15 12	15 20	15 24				15 32	15 59					
Northampton	d		15 05	15 25						15 50						16 05	16 25					
Wolverton	d		15 17	15 37												16 17	16 37					
Milton Keynes Central 10	a	15 18	15 20	15 41						16 04					16 18	16 20	16 41					
	d	15 19	15 22	15 41	15 47			15 47	16 02	16 05				16 13	16 19	16 22	16 41	16 47			16 47	17 02
Bletchley	d		15 27	15 46				15 52						16 17		16 27	16 46				16 52	
Leighton Buzzard	d		15 33	15 53				15 58						16 24		16 33	16 53				16 58	
Cheddington	d							16 04													17 04	
Tring	d						15 56	16 10					16 26	16 34						16 56	17 10	
Berkhamsted	d		15 46				16 00	16 15					16 30	16 39		16 46				17 00	17 15	
Hemel Hempstead	d		15 51				16 05	16 19					16 35	16 43		16 51				17 05	17 19	
Apsley	d						16 08						16 38							17 08		
Kings Langley	d						16 11						16 41							17 11		
Watford Junction	a		15 58			16s15	16 16	16 26		16 30			16 46	16 51		16 58			17s15	17 16	17 26	
	d		15 59				16 16	16 27		16 31			16 46	16 51		16 59				17 16	17 27	
Bushey	d						16 19						16 49							17 19		
Harrow & Wealdstone ⊖	d						16 24						16 54	16 59						17 24		
Wembley Central ⊖	d													17 05								
Shepherd's Bush	a													17 19								
Kensington (Olympia) ⊖	a													17 21								
West Brompton ⊖	a													17 24								
Imperial Wharf	a													17 27								
Clapham Junction	d													17 33								
East Croydon ⇌	a													17 59								
London Euston 15 ⊖	a	15 54	16 17	16 27	16 23	16 32	16 38	16 45	16 38	16 49		16 14	17 08		16 57	17 18	17 27	17 23	17 34	17 38	17 47	17 38

A ◇ from Northampton

2 July to 14 September

West Midlands, Northampton, Milton Keynes Central and Watford Junction - London

Network Diagram - see first Page of Table 59

Station		LM	LM	VT	VT	LM	SN	VT	LM		LM	VT	VT	LM	LM	VT	LM FX	LM	VT		LM	SN	VT	LM	VT
		◇■ A	◇■	◇■ ☕	◇■ ☕	■	■	◇■ ☕	◇■		■	◇■ ☕	◇■ ☕	■	■	◇■ ☕	◇■ A	◇■	◇■ ☕		■	■	◇■ ⊠	◇■	◇■ ☕
Wolverhampton 7	d												16 45												
Sandwell & Dudley	d												16 56												
Birmingham New Street 12	d	15 33		15 50				16 30	15 53				17 10				16 33		16 50				17 30	16 53	
Birmingham International ✈	d	15 45		16 00				16 40	16 05				17 20				16 45		17 00				17 40	17 05	
Coventry	d	16 01		16 11				16 51	16 21				17 31				17 01		17 11				17 51	17 21	
Nuneaton	d		16 02															17 02							
Rugby	d	16 12	16 20	16 24					16 32								17 12	17 20	17 24					17 32	
Northampton	d	16 50							17 05		17 25						17 50	17 50						18 05	
Wolverton	d								17 17		17 37													18 17	
Milton Keynes Central 10	a	17 04						17 18	17 20		17 41						18 04	18 04					18 18	18 20	
	d	17 05					17 13	17 19	17 22		17 41	17 47			17 47	18 02	18 05	18 05				18 13	18 19	18 22	18 24
Bletchley	d						17 17		17 27		17 46				17 52							18 17		18 27	
Leighton Buzzard	d						17 24		17 33		17 53				17 58							18 24		18 33	
Cheddington	d														18 04										
Tring	d					17 26	17 34							17 59	18 10						18 27	18 34			
Berkhamsted	d					17 30	17 39		17 46					18 03	18 15						18 31	18 39		18 46	
Hemel Hempstead	d					17 35	17 43		17 51					18 08	18 19						18 36	18 43		18 51	
Apsley	d					17 38								18 11							18 39				
Kings Langley	d					17 41								18 14							18 42				
Watford Junction	a	17 30				17 46	17 51		17 59				18s15	18 19	18 26		18 31	18 31			18 46	18 51		18 58	
	d	17 31				17 46	17 51		17 59					18 19	18 27		18 31	18 31			18 47	18 51		18 59	
Bushey	d					17 49								18 22							18 49				
Harrow & Wealdstone ⊖	d					17 54	17 59							18 27							18 54	18 59			
Wembley Central ⊖	d						18 05															19 05			
Shepherd's Bush	a						18 19															19 18			
Kensington (Olympia) ⊖	a						18 21															19 20			
West Brompton ⊖	a						18 24															19 23			
Imperial Wharf	a						18 27															19 25			
Clapham Junction	d						18 34															19a30			
East Croydon	a						19 02																		
London Euston 15 ⊖	a	17 49		17 14	17 38	18 10		17 54	18 18		18 27	18 23	18 34	18 41	18 45	18 38	18 49	18 49	18 14		19 09		18 54	19 18	18 59

Station		VT	LM	VT	LM		LM	VT	VT	LM	VT	LM	SN	VT	VT		LM	VT	LM	VT	VT	LM	LM	LM	LM
		◇■ ☕	■	◇■ ⊠	■		■	◇■ ⊠	◇■ ⊠	◇■	◇■ ⊠	■	■	◇■ ⊠	◇■ ⊠		◇■	◇■ ⊠	◇■	◇■ ⊠	■ ■ ☕	■	■	◇■ A	◇■
Wolverhampton 7	d			17 45																	18 45				
Sandwell & Dudley	d			17 56																	18 56				
Birmingham New Street 12	d		17 13	18 10							17 50			18 30			17 53				19 10			18 33	
Birmingham International ✈	d		17 25	18 20							18 00			18 40			18 05				19 20			18 45	
Coventry	d		17 40	18 31							18 11			18 51			18 21				19 31			19 01	
Nuneaton	d									18 02															19 02
Rugby	d		17 51							18 20	18 24						18 32							19 12	19 20
Northampton	d		18 25							18 50							19 05		19 25					19 51	
Wolverton	d		18 37														19 17		19 37						
Milton Keynes Central 10	a		18 41							19 04				19 18			19 20		19 41					20 05	
	d		18 41				18 47	18 48	19 02	19 05			19 15	19 19			19 22	19 32	19 41	19 47			19 47	20 09	
Bletchley	d		18 46				18 52						19 19				19 27		19 46				19 52		
Leighton Buzzard	d		18 53				18 58						19 26				19 33		19 53				19 58		
Cheddington	d						19 06																20 04		
Tring	d				19 00		19 12					19 29	19 36									19 56	20 10		
Berkhamsted	d				19 04		19 17					19 33	19 41				19 46					20 00	20 15		
Hemel Hempstead	d				19 09		19 21					19 38	19 45				19 51					20 05	20 19		
Apsley	d				19 12							19 41										20 08			
Kings Langley	d				19 15							19 44										20 11			
Watford Junction	a			19s16	19 20		19 28			19 30		19 49	19 54				19 59				20s15	20 16	20 26	20 31	
	d				19 20		19 29			19 31		19 49	19 54				19 59					20 16	20 27	20 32	
Bushey	d				19 23							19 52										20 19			
Harrow & Wealdstone ⊖	d				19 28							19 57	20 01									20 24			
Wembley Central ⊖	d												20 06												
Shepherd's Bush	a												20 21												
Kensington (Olympia) ⊖	a												20 23												
West Brompton ⊖	a												20 25												
Imperial Wharf	a												20 28												
Clapham Junction	d												20a33												
East Croydon	a																								
London Euston 15 ⊖	a	19 08	19 29	19 34	19 42		19 47	19 23	19 38	19 50	19 14	20 11		19 54	20 02		20 19	20 06	20 27	20 23	20 34	20 38	20 51	20 49	

A ◇ from Northampton

2 July to 14 September

West Midlands, Northampton, Milton Keynes Central and Watford Junction - London

Network Diagram - see first Page of Table 59

Station			VT	LM	SN	VT	VT	LM	VT	VT	LM		VT	LM	LM	VT	VT	VT	LM	VT	SN		LM	VT	LM
			◇■ ⊠	■	■	◇■ ☕	◇■ ⊠	◇■	◇■ ⊠	◇■ ☕	◇■		◇■ ⊠	■	■	◇■ ☕	◇■ ☕	◇■ ☕	■	◇■ ☕	■		◇■	◇■ ☕	■
Wolverhampton 7	d																19 45								
Sandwell & Dudley	d																19 56								
Birmingham New Street 12	d		18 50			19 30		18 53		19 50							20 10						19 53		
Birmingham International ✈	d		19 00			19 40		19 05		20 00							20 20						20 05		
Coventry	d		19 11			19 51		19 21		20 11							20 31						20 21		
Nuneaton	d																			21 03					21 02
Rugby	d		19 24					19 32		20 23													20 32		21 20
Northampton	d							20 05			20 25												21 05		21 50
Wolverton	d							20 17			20 37												21 17		
Milton Keynes Central 10	a					20 18		20 20			20 41						20 58						21 20		22 04
	d				20 13	20 19		20 22	20 33		20 41		20 46		20 47	20 50	20 59	21 04			21 13		21 22	21 36	22 05
Bletchley	d				20 17			20 27			20 46				20 52						21 17		21 27		
Leighton Buzzard	d				20 24			20 33			20 53				20 58						21 24		21 33		
Cheddington	d														21 06										
Tring	d			20 26	20 34									20 56	21 11				21 26		21 34				
Berkhamsted	d			20 30	20 39			20 46						21 00	21 16				21 30		21 39		21 46		
Hemel Hempstead	d			20 35	20 43			20 51						21 05	21 20				21 35		21 43		21 51		
Apsley	d			20 38										21 08					21 38						
Kings Langley	d			20 41										21 11					21 41						
Watford Junction	a			20 46	20 51			20 58						21 16	21 27		21s19		21 46	21s48	21 51		21 58		22 35
	d			20 46	20 51			20 59						21 16	21 27				21 46		21 51		21 59		22 36
Bushey	d			20 49										21 19					21 49						
Harrow & Wealdstone ⊖	d			20 54	20 59									21 24					21 54		21 59				
Wembley Central ⊖	d				21 04																				
Shepherd's Bush	a				21 22																22 23				
Kensington (Olympia) ⊖	a				21 24																22 25				
West Brompton ⊖	a				21 27																22 27				
Imperial Wharf	a				21 29																22 30				
Clapham Junction	d				21a34																22a34				
East Croydon	a																								
London Euston 15 ⊖	a		20 14	21 08		20 54	21 05	21 17	21 06	21 14	21 29		21 24	21 38	21 46	21 26	21 38	21 42	22 08	22 09			22 20	22 12	22 56

Station		VT	VT	VT	LM	VT	SN		LM	SN	LM	VT	VT	SN	LM	VT	VT		LM MO	LM MX	VT			
		◇■ ☕	◇■ ☕	◇■ ☕	■	◇■ ☕	■		■	■	◇■	◇■ ⊠	◇■ ☕	■	◇■	◇■ ☕	◇■ ☕		■	■	◇■ ☕			
Wolverhampton 7	d					20 47											21 45				22 45			
Sandwell & Dudley	d					20 57											21 56				22 55			
Birmingham New Street 12	d	20 50				21 10					20 53				21 33		22 10				23 10			
Birmingham International ✈	d	21 00				21 20					21 05				21 45		22 22				23 20			
Coventry	d	21 11				21 31					21 21				22 01		22 32				23 31			
Nuneaton	d															22 17								
Rugby	d	21 23	21 28								21 32				22 12	22 34	22 43				23 44			
Northampton	d				21 37						22 05				22 55				23 30	23 46	00s05			
Wolverton	d				21 49						22 17				23 07				23 46	00 02				
Milton Keynes Central 10	a		21 47		21 52	21 58					22 20				23 12	22 58	23s05		23 50	00 05	00s23			
	d		21 49	21 52	21 53	21 59			22 05	22 11	22 22	22 41	22 53		23 13	22 59			23 50	00 06				
Bletchley	d				21 58				22 10	22 15	22 27				23 18				23 55	00 11				
Leighton Buzzard	d				22 04				22 17	22 22	22 33				23 24				00 02	00 17				
Cheddington	d				22 10				22 23						23 29				00 08	00 24				
Tring	d				22 16				22 28	22 34					23 38				00 14	00 30				
Berkhamsted	d				22 20				22 33	22 39	22 48				23 43				00 18	00 34				
Hemel Hempstead	d				22 25				22 37	22 43	22 53				23 47				00 22	00 39				
Apsley	d								22 41						23 50									
Kings Langley	d								22 44						23 53									
Watford Junction	a			22s11	22 32	22s20			22 48	22 52	23 00	23s14	23s25		23 58	23s30	23s37		00 29	00 46	00s52			
	d				22 33		22 27		22 49	22 53	23 01			23 29	23 58				00 30	00 47				
Bushey	d								22 51						00 01									
Harrow & Wealdstone ⊖	d						22 33		22 57	23 00				23 35	00 06				00 36	00 53				
Wembley Central ⊖	d																		00 40	00 57				
Shepherd's Bush	a						22 49			23 21				23 53										
Kensington (Olympia) ⊖	a						22 51			23 23				23 56										
West Brompton ⊖	a						22 54			23 26				23 59										
Imperial Wharf	a						22 56			23 28				00 02										
Clapham Junction	d						23a01			23 40				00a07										
East Croydon	a									00 01														
London Euston 15 ⊖	a	22 12	22 22	22 33	22 52	22 43			23 12		23 21	23 38	23 48		00 21	23 56	00 04		00 53	01 09	01 13			

West Midlands, Northampton, Milton Keynes Central and Watford Junction - London

Network Diagram - see first Page of Table 59

		SN	SN	SN	LM	VT	LM	VT	LM	LM	VT	VT	LM	LM	LM	SN	LM	LM	SR	SR	LM	LM	LM
		MX	MO	MX	MX	MX	MO	MO	TO	WTh FO	MO	MX							MX	MO			
		1	1	1	◇1	◇1	◇1	◇1	1	1	◇1	◇1	1	1	1	1	1	1	B	B	1	1	1
Wolverhampton 7	d					21p45		22p05			22p37	22p45											
Sandwell & Dudley	d					21p56		22p15			22p47	22p55											
Birmingham New Street 12	d				21p33	22p10		22p30			23p00	23p10											
Birmingham International	d				21p45	22p22		22p40			23p10	23p20											
Coventry	d				22p01	22p32		22p51			23p21	23p31											
Nuneaton	d																						
Rugby	d				22p12	22p43		23p04			23p34	23p44										05 20	
Northampton	d				22p55		23p00		23p30	23p46	23b53	00s05		04 15	04 48		05 05					05 45	
Wolverton	d				23p07		23p12		23p46	00 02				04 27	05 00		05 17					05 57	
Milton Keynes Central 10	a				23p12	23b05	23p15	23p36	23p50	00 05	00s12	00s23		04 30	05 03		05 20					06 00	
	d	22p11			23p13		23p16	23p37	23p50	00 06			03 30	04 31	05 04		05 21				05 54	06 02	06 20
Bletchley	d	22p15			23p18		23p21		23p55	00 11			03 35	04 36	05 09		05 26	05 38			05 59	06 07	06 25
Leighton Buzzard	d	22p22			23p24		23p27		00 02	00 17			03 41	04 42	05 15		05 33	05 45			06 05	06 14	06 31
Cheddington	d				23p29		23p32		00 08	00 24					05 20			05 50					06 37
Tring	d	22p34			23p38		23p41		00 14	00 30			03 53	04 54	05 29			05 56					06 42
Berkhamsted	d	22p39			23p43		23p45		00 18	00 34			03 58	04 59	05 34		05 47	06 01			06 17		06 47
Hemel Hempstead	d	22p43			23p47		23p49		00 22	00 39			04 02	05 03	05 38		05 52	06 05			06 22		06 52
Apsley	d				23p50										05 41			06 08					
Kings Langley	d				23p53										05 44			06 11					
Watford Junction	a	22p52			23p58	23b37	23p56	00s06	00 29	00 46	00s42	00s52	04 09	05 10	05 49		05 59	06 16			06 29	06 31	06 59
	d	22p53	23p17	23p29	23p58		23p57		00 30	00 47			04 10	05 11	05 50	05 54	06 01	06 17			06 30	06 33	07 00
Bushey	d				00 01		23p59																
Harrow & Wealdstone	d	23p00	23p23	23p35	00 06		00 05		00 36	00 53			04 16	05 17	05 56	06 00		06 23					07 06
Wembley Central	d								00 40	00 57			04 20	05 21		06 05							
Shepherd's Bush	a	23p21	23p45	23p53												06 19							
Kensington (Olympia)	a	23p23	23p47	23p56												06 21							
West Brompton	a	23p26	23p50	23p59												06 24							
Imperial Wharf	a	23p28	23p53	00 02												06 27							
Clapham Junction	d	23p40	00 05	00a07												06a32							
East Croydon	a	00 01	00 22																				
London Euston 15	a				00 21	00 04	00 19	00 27	00 53	01 09	01 04	01 15	04 35	05 35	06 12		06 19	06 40	06 43	06 46	06 49	06 50	07 20

		VT	LM	SN	LM	VT	LM	LM	LM	LM	VT	VT	VT	VT	SN	LM	LM	VT	VT	LM	VT	LM	LM
		◇1 ⊠	1	1		◇1 ⊠	1	1	1	1	◇1 ⊠	◇1 ⊠	◇1 ⊠	◇1 ⊠	1	◇1	1	◇1 ⊠	◇1 ⊠	1	◇1 ⊠	1	1
Wolverhampton 7	d	05 00				05 24							05 45	06 04									
Sandwell & Dudley	d					05 34							05 56	06 15									
Birmingham New Street 12	d	05 29				05 50							06 10	06 30		05 53							
Birmingham International	d	05 40				06 00							06 20	06 40		06 05							
Coventry	d	05 51				06 11							06 31	06 51		06 21							
Nuneaton	d											06 18					06 29				07 07		
Rugby	d	06 03								06 13	06 20	06 32				06 32	06 45	06 53	07 08				
Northampton	d				06 17					06 38	06 42					07 00	07 13						
Wolverton	d				06 29					06 50						07 12	07 25						
Milton Keynes Central 10	a	06 22			06 33	06 38				06 53		06 51	06 59			07 15	07 29	07 12					
	d	06 23			06 34	06 38			06 48	06 55		06 52	06 59		07 01	07 17	07 30	07 14					07 21
Bletchley	d				06 39		06 34		06 53	07 00					07 05					07 13			07 26
Leighton Buzzard	d				06 46		06 41		06 59	07 07					07 13	07 26	07 39						07 33
Cheddington	d								07 05														07 38
Tring	d		06 24				06 52	07 00	07 11						07 22					07 28			07 45
Berkhamsted	d		06 28				06 56	07 05	07 16						07 26					07 32			07 49
Hemel Hempstead	d		06 33				07 01	07 09	07 20						07 31					07 37			07 54
Apsley	d		06 36				07 04		07 24														07 57
Kings Langley	d		06 39				07 07		07 27														08 00
Watford Junction	a	06s43	06 44		07 04		07 12	07 18	07 31					07s36	07 38					07 44			08 05
	d		06 45	06 53	07 05		07 12	07 18	07 32						07 38					07 45		07 55	08 05
Bushey	d		06 48				07 15	07 22	07 34													07 59	
Harrow & Wealdstone	d		06 53	06 59			07 20		07 40						07 45							08 05	
Wembley Central	d			07 04											07 49								
Shepherd's Bush	a			07 19											08 04								
Kensington (Olympia)	a			07 21											08 06								
West Brompton	a			07 24											08 09								
Imperial Wharf	a			07 27											08 12								
Clapham Junction	d			07a32											08 36								
East Croydon	a														09 04								
London Euston 15	a	07 02	07 07		07 22	07 13	07 34	07 40	07 54	07 40	07 30	07 28	07 34	07 53		08 02	08 11	07 50	07 57	08 05	08 07	08 18	08 24

b Previous night, stops to set down only

Table 66

Mondays to Fridays
from 17 September

West Midlands, Northampton, Milton Keynes Central and Watford Junction - London

Network Diagram - see first Page of Table 59

		VT	LM	LM	LM	LM	LM	VT	VT	VT	VT	LM	LM	SN	LM	VT	VT	LM	LM	VT	LM	LM
		◇1 ⊠	1	1	1	1	1	◇1 ⊠	◇1 ⊠	◇1 ⊠	◇1 ⊠	1	1	1	◇1	◇1 ⊠	◇1 ⊠	◇1	1	◇1 ⊠	1	1
Wolverhampton 7	d	06 27							06 45		07 04									07 45		
Sandwell & Dudley	d	06 37							06 56		07 15									07 56		
Birmingham New Street 12	d	06 50					06 33		07 10		07 30				06 53					08 10		
Birmingham International	d	07 00					06 45		07 20						07 05		07 41			08 20		
Coventry	d	07 11					07 01		07 31						07 21		07 52			08 31		
Nuneaton	d									07 33												
Rugby	d						07 12	07 29							07 32	07 55						
Northampton	d					07 32	07 39								08 05			08 25				
Wolverton	d						07 51								08 17			08 37				
Milton Keynes Central 10	a	07s40				07 46	07 54								08 21			08 41				
	d					07 46	07 55					07 59		08 13	08 21			08 41				08 47
Bletchley	d		07 39			07 51						08 04		08 17	08 27			08 46				08 52
Leighton Buzzard	d		07 46			07 58	08 05					08 11		08 24	08 34			08 53				08 58
Cheddington	d					08 04																09 04
Tring	d				08 04	08 10							08 25	08 34					08 48		09 01	09 10
Berkhamsted	d		07 59			08 15							08 29	08 39					08 53		09 05	09 15
Hemel Hempstead	d		08 03			08 19						08 28	08 34	08 43					08 57		09 10	09 19
Apsley	d				08 13								08 37								09 13	
Kings Langley	d				08 16								08 40								09 16	
Watford Junction	a		08 10		08 20	08 26						08 35	08 45	08 51					09 04	09s15	09 20	09 26
	d		08 11	08 15	08 22	08 28						08 36	08 46	08 51					09 05		09 21	09 27
Bushey	d			08 19									08 48						09 08		09 23	
Harrow & Wealdstone	d		08 17	08 24	08 29	08 34							08 54	08 58					09 13		09 28	09 33
Wembley Central	d													09 05								
Shepherd's Bush	a													09 18								
Kensington (Olympia)	a													09 20								
West Brompton	a													09 23								
Imperial Wharf	a													09 26								
Clapham Junction	d													09 34								
East Croydon	a													09 57								
London Euston 15	a	08 14	08 33	08 38	08 42	08 49	08 39	08 22	08 30	08 33	08 42	08 55	09 08		09 10	08 45	08 49	09 27	09 27	09 34	09 42	09 47

		LM	VT	VT	VT	LM	SN	VT	LM	VT	LM	VT	VT	LM	LM	VT	LM	LM	VT	LM	SN	VT	LM
		◇1	◇1 ⊠	◇1 ⊠	◇1 ⊠	1	1	◇1 ⊠	◇1	◇1 ⊠	◇1	◇1 ⊠	◇1 ⊠	1	1	◇1 ⊠	◇1	◇1	◇1 ⊠	1	1	◇1 ⊠	◇1
Wolverhampton 7	d												08 45										
Sandwell & Dudley	d												08 56										
Birmingham New Street 12	d		07 50					08 30	07 53				09 10				08 33		08 50			09 30	08 53
Birmingham International	d		08 00					08 40	08 05				09 20				08 45		09 00			09 40	09 05
Coventry	d		08 11					08 51	08 21				09 31				09 01		09 11			09 51	09 21
Nuneaton	d	08 02			08 46													09 02					
Rugby	d	08 20	08 23						08 32	08 46							09 12	09 20	09 23				09 32
Northampton	d	08 47							09 05		09 25						09 50 (both columns)						10 05
Wolverton	d								09 17		09 37												10 17
Milton Keynes Central 10	a	09 01						09 18	09 20		09 41						10 04					10 18	10 20
	d	09 01					09 13	09 19	09 22		09 41	09 47			09 47	10 02	10 05				10 13	10 19	10 22
Bletchley	d						09 17		09 27		09 46				09 52						10 17		10 27
Leighton Buzzard	d						09 24		09 33		09 53				09 58						10 24		10 33
Cheddington	d														10 04								
Tring	d					09 26	09 34							09 56	10 10					10 26	10 34		
Berkhamsted	d					09 30	09 39		09 46					10 00	10 15					10 30	10 39		10 46
Hemel Hempstead	d					09 35	09 43		09 51					10 05	10 19					10 35	10 43		10 51
Apsley	d					09 38								10 08						10 38			
Kings Langley	d					09 41								10 11						10 41			
Watford Junction	a	09 27			09s31	09 46	09 51		09 58				10s15	10 16	10 26		10 30			10 46	10 51		10 58
	d	09 28				09 46	09 51		09 59					10 16	10 27		10 31			10 46	10 51		10 59
Bushey	d					09 49								10 19						10 49			
Harrow & Wealdstone	d					09 54	09 58							10 24						10 54	10 59		
Wembley Central	d						10 05														11 04		
Shepherd's Bush	a						10 21														11 19		
Kensington (Olympia)	a						10 23														11 21		
West Brompton	a						10 26														11 23		
Imperial Wharf	a						10 29														11 26		
Clapham Junction	d						10 34														11 34		
East Croydon	a						10 57														11 57		
London Euston 15	a	09 44	09 13	09 23	09 52	10 08		09 54	10 18	09 38	10 27	10 23	10 32	10 38	10 46	10 38	10 49		10 14	11 08		10 54	11 17

West Midlands, Northampton, Milton Keynes Central and Watford Junction - London

Network Diagram - see first Page of Table 59

	LM	VT	VT	LM	LM	VT	LM	LM	VT	LM	SN	VT	LM	LM	VT	VT	LM	LM	VT	LM	VT	LM
	◇1	◇1 ⊠	◇1 ⊠	1	1	◇1 ⊠	◇1 A	◇1	◇1 ⊠	1	1	◇1 ⊠	◇1	◇1	◇1 ⊠	◇1 ⊠	1	1	◇1 ⊠	◇1	◇1 ⊠	1
Wolverhampton 7 d			09 45													10 45						
Sandwell & Dudley d			09 56													10 56						
Birmingham New Street 12 d	09 13		10 10				09 33		09 50			10 30	09 53	10 13		11 10					10 50	
Birmingham International d	09 29		10 20				09 45		10 00			10 40	10 05	10 29		11 20					11 00	
Coventry d	09 48		10 31				10 01		10 11			10 51	10 21	10 48		11 31					11 11	
Nuneaton d								10 02												11 02		
Rugby d	09 59						10 12	10 20	10 24				10 32	10 59						11 20	11 24	
Northampton d	10 25						10 50						11 05	11 25						11 50		
Wolverton d	10 37												11 17	11 37								
Milton Keynes Central 10 a	10 41						11 04					11 18	11 20	11 41						12 04		
d	10 41	10 47			10 47	11 02	11 05				11 13	11 19	11 22	11 41	11 47			11 47	12 02	12 05		
Bletchley d	10 46				10 52						11 17		11 27	11 46				11 52				
Leighton Buzzard d	10 53				10 58						11 24		11 33	11 53				11 58				
Cheddington d					11 04													12 04				
Tring d				10 56	11 10					11 26	11 34						11 56	12 10				12 26
Berkhamsted d				11 00	11 15					11 30	11 39		11 46				12 00	12 15				12 30
Hemel Hempstead d				11 05	11 19					11 35	11 43		11 51				12 05	12 19				12 35
Apsley d				11 08						11 38							12 08					12 38
Kings Langley d				11 11						11 41							12 11					12 41
Watford Junction a			11s15	11 16	11 26		11 30			11 46	11 51		11 58			12s15	12 16	12 26		12 30		12 46
d				11 16	11 27		11 31			11 46	11 51		11 59				12 16	12 27		12 31		12 46
Bushey d				11 19						11 49							12 19					12 49
Harrow & Wealdstone ⊖ d				11 24						11 54	11 59						12 24					12 54
Wembley Central ⊖ d											12 04											
Shepherd's Bush a											12 19											
Kensington (Olympia) ⊖ a											12 21											
West Brompton ⊖ a											12 24											
Imperial Wharf a											12 27											
Clapham Junction d											12 34											
East Croydon a											12 57											
London Euston 15 ⊖ a	11 27	11 23	11 32	11 38	11 46	11 38	11 49		11 14	12 08		11 54	12 17	12 27	12 23	12 32	12 38	12 45	12 38	12 49	12 14	13 08

	SN	VT	LM	LM	VT	VT	LM	LM	VT	LM	LM	VT	LM	SN	VT	LM	LM	VT	VT	LM	LM
	1	◇1 ☕	◇1	◇1	◇1 ☕	◇1 ☕	1	1	◇1 ☕	◇1	◇1	◇1 ☕	1	1	◇1 ☕	◇1	◇1	◇1 ☕	◇1 ☕	1	1
Wolverhampton 7 d						11 45													12 45		
Sandwell & Dudley d						11 56													12 56		
Birmingham New Street 12 d		11 30	10 53	11 13		12 10				11 33		11 50			12 30	11 53	12 13		13 10		
Birmingham International d		11 40	11 05	11 29		12 20				11 45		12 00			12 40	12 05	12 29		13 20		
Coventry d		11 51	11 21	11 48		12 31				12 01		12 11			12 51	12 21	12 48		13 31		
Nuneaton d											12 02										
Rugby d			11 32	11 59						12 12	12 20	12 24				12 32	13 00				
Northampton d			12 05	12 25						12 50						13 05	13 25				
Wolverton d			12 17	12 37												13 17	13 37				
Milton Keynes Central 10 a		12 18	12 20	12 41						13 04					13 18	13 20	13 41				
d	12 13	12 19	12 22	12 41	12 46			12 47	13 02	13 05				13 13	13 19	13 22	13 41	13 47			13 47
Bletchley d	12 17		12 27	12 46				12 52						13 17		13 27	13 46				13 52
Leighton Buzzard d	12 24		12 33	12 53				12 58						13 24		13 33	13 53				13 58
Cheddington d								13 04													14 04
Tring d	12 34						12 56	13 10					13 26	13 34						13 56	14 10
Berkhamsted d	12 39		12 46				13 00	13 15					13 30	13 39		13 46				14 00	14 15
Hemel Hempstead d	12 43		12 51				13 05	13 19					13 35	13 43		13 51				14 05	14 19
Apsley d							13 08						13 38							14 08	
Kings Langley d							13 11						13 41							14 11	
Watford Junction a	12 51		12 58			13s15	13 16	13 26		13 30			13 46	13 51		13 58			14s14	14 16	14 26
d	12 51		12 59				13 16	13 27		13 31			13 46	13 51		13 59				14 16	14 27
Bushey d							13 19						13 49							14 19	
Harrow & Wealdstone ⊖ d	12 59						13 24						13 54	13 59						14 24	
Wembley Central ⊖ d	13 04													14 04							
Shepherd's Bush a	13 19													14 19							
Kensington (Olympia) ⊖ a	13 21													14 21							
West Brompton ⊖ a	13 24													14 24							
Imperial Wharf a	13 27													14 27							
Clapham Junction d	13 34													14 34							
East Croydon a	13 57													14 57							
London Euston 15 ⊖ a		12 54	13 17	13 27	13 23	13 32	13 38	13 45	13 38	13 49		13 14	14 08		13 54	14 17	14 27	14 23	14 32	14 38	14 45

A ◇ from Northampton

West Midlands, Northampton, Milton Keynes Central and Watford Junction - London

Network Diagram - see first Page of Table 59

	VT	LM	LM	VT	LM	SN	VT	LM	LM	VT	VT	LM	LM	VT	LM	LM	VT	LM	SN	VT	LM	LM
	◇1 ☕	◇1 A	◇1	◇1 ☕	1	1	◇1 ☕	◇1	◇1	◇1 ☕	◇1 ☕	1	1	◇1 ☕	◇1 A	◇1	◇1 ☕	1	1	◇1 ☕	◇1	◇1
Wolverhampton 7 d											13 45											
Sandwell & Dudley d											13 56											
Birmingham New Street 12 d		12 33		12 50			13 30	12 53	13 13		14 10				13 33		13 50			14 30	13 53	14 13
Birmingham International d		12 45		13 00			13 40	13 05	13 29		14 20				13 45		14 00			14 40	14 05	14 29
Coventry d		13 01		13 11			13 51	13 21	13 48		14 31				14 01		14 11			14 51	14 21	14 48
Nuneaton d			13 02													14 02						
Rugby d		13 12	13 20	13 24				13 32	13 59						14 12	14 20	14 24				14 32	14 59
Northampton d		13 50						14 05	14 25						14 50						15 05	15 25
Wolverton d								14 17	14 37												15 17	15 37
Milton Keynes Central 10 a		14 04					14 18	14 20	14 41						15 04					15 18	15 20	15 41
d	14 02	14 05				14 13	14 19	14 22	14 41	14 47			14 47	15 02	15 05				15 13	15 19	15 22	15 41
Bletchley d						14 17		14 27	14 46				14 52						15 17		15 27	15 46
Leighton Buzzard d						14 24		14 33	14 53				14 58						15 24		15 33	15 53
Cheddington d													15 04									
Tring d					14 26	14 34						14 56	15 10					15 26	15 34			
Berkhamsted d					14 30	14 39		14 46				15 00	15 15					15 30	15 39		15 46	
Hemel Hempstead d					14 35	14 43		14 51				15 05	15 19					15 35	15 43		15 51	
Apsley d					14 38							15 08						15 38				
Kings Langley d					14 41							15 11						15 41				
Watford Junction a		14 30			14 46	14 51		14 58			15s15	15 16	15 26		15 30			15 46	15 51		15 58	
d		14 31			14 46	14 51		14 59				15 16	15 27		15 31			15 46	15 51		15 59	
Bushey d					14 49							15 19						15 49				
Harrow & Wealdstone ⊖ d					14 54	14 59						15 24						15 54	15 59			
Wembley Central ⊖ d						15 04													16 05			
Shepherd's Bush a						15 22													16 19			
Kensington (Olympia) ⊖ a						15 24													16 21			
West Brompton ⊖ a						15 26													16 24			
Imperial Wharf a						15 29													16 27			
Clapham Junction d						15 34													16 34			
East Croydon a						15 57													16 58			
London Euston 15 ⊖ a	14 38	14 49		14 14	15 08		14 54	15 17	15 27	15 23	15 32	15 38	15 45	15 38	15 49		15 14	16 08		15 54	16 17	16 27

	VT	VT	LM	LM	VT	LM	LM	VT	LM	SN	VT	LM	LM	VT	VT	LM	LM	VT	LM	LM	VT
	◇1 ☕	◇1 ☕	1	1	◇1 ☕	◇1 A	◇1	◇1 ☕	1	1	◇1 ☕	◇1	◇1	◇1 ☕	◇1 ☕	1	1	◇1 ☕	◇1 A	◇1	◇1 ☕
Wolverhampton 7 d		14 45													15 45						
Sandwell & Dudley d		14 56													15 56						
Birmingham New Street 12 d		15 10				14 33		14 50			15 30	14 53	15 13		16 10				15 33		15 50
Birmingham International d		15 20				14 45		15 00			15 40	15 05	15 29		16 20				15 45		16 00
Coventry d		15 31				15 01		15 11			15 51	15 21	15 48		16 31				16 01		16 11
Nuneaton d							15 02													16 02	
Rugby d						15 12	15 20	15 24				15 32	15 59						16 12	16 20	16 24
Northampton d						15 50						16 05	16 25						16 50		
Wolverton d												16 17	16 37								
Milton Keynes Central 10 a						16 04					16 18	16 20	16 41						17 04		
d	15 47			15 47	16 02	16 05				16 13	16 19	16 22	16 41	16 47			16 47	17 02	17 05		
Bletchley d				15 52						16 17		16 27	16 46				16 52				
Leighton Buzzard d				15 58						16 24		16 33	16 53				16 58				
Cheddington d				16 04													17 04				
Tring d			15 56	16 10					16 26	16 34						16 56	17 10				
Berkhamsted d			16 00	16 15					16 30	16 39		16 46				17 00	17 15				
Hemel Hempstead d			16 05	16 19					16 35	16 43		16 51				17 05	17 19				
Apsley d			16 08						16 38							17 08					
Kings Langley d			16 11						16 41							17 11					
Watford Junction a		16s15	16 16	16 26		16 30			16 46	16 51		16 58			17s15	17 16	17 26		17 30		
d			16 16	16 27		16 31			16 46	16 51		16 59				17 16	17 27		17 31		
Bushey d			16 19						16 49							17 19					
Harrow & Wealdstone ⊖ d			16 24						16 54	16 59						17 24					
Wembley Central ⊖ d										17 05											
Shepherd's Bush a										17 19											
Kensington (Olympia) ⊖ a										17 21											
West Brompton ⊖ a										17 24											
Imperial Wharf a										17 27											
Clapham Junction d										17 33											
East Croydon a										17 59											
London Euston 15 ⊖ a	16 23	16 32	16 38	16 45	16 38	16 49		16 14	17 08		16 57	17 18	17 27	17 23	17 34	17 38	17 47	17 38	17 49		17 14

A ◇ from Northampton

Table 66

Mondays to Fridays
from 17 September

West Midlands, Northampton, Milton Keynes Central and Watford Junction - London

Network Diagram - see first Page of Table 59

Station		VT	LM	SN	VT	LM	LM	VT	VT	LM		LM	VT	LM FX	LM	VT	LM	SN	VT	LM		VT	VT	LM	VT
		◇1 🍴	1	1	◇1 🍴	◇1	1	◇1 🍴	◇1 🍴	1		1	◇1 🍴	◇1 A	◇1	◇1 🍴	1	1	◇1 ⊠	◇1		◇1 🍴	◇1 🍴	1	◇1 ⊠
Wolverhampton 7	d								16 45																17 45
Sandwell & Dudley	d								16 56																17 56
Birmingham New Street 12	d				16 30	15 53			17 10					16 33		16 50			17 30	16 53				17 13	18 10
Birmingham International ✈	d				16 40	16 05			17 20					16 45		17 00			17 40	17 05				17 25	18 20
Coventry	d				16 51	16 21			17 31					17 01		17 11			17 51	17 21				17 40	18 31
Nuneaton	d														17 02										
Rugby	d					16 32								17 12	17 20	17 24				17 32				17 51	
Northampton	d					17 05	17 25							17 50	17 50					18 05				18 25	
Wolverton	d					17 17	17 37													18 17				18 37	
Milton Keynes Central 10	a				17 18	17 20	17 41							18 04	18 04				18 18	18 20				18 41	
	d			17 13	17 19	17 22	17 41	17 47				17 47	18 02	18 05	18 05			18 13	18 19	18 22		18 24		18 41	
Bletchley	d			17 17		17 27	17 46					17 52						18 17		18 27				18 46	
Leighton Buzzard	d			17 24		17 33	17 53					17 58						18 24		18 33				18 53	
Cheddington	d											18 04													
Tring	d		17 26	17 34						17 59		18 10					18 27	18 34							
Berkhamsted	d		17 30	17 39		17 46				18 03		18 15					18 31	18 39		18 46					
Hemel Hempstead	d		17 35	17 43		17 51				18 08		18 19					18 36	18 43		18 51					
Apsley	d		17 38							18 11							18 39								
Kings Langley	d		17 41							18 14							18 42								
Watford Junction	a		17 46	17 51		17 59			18s15	18 19		18 26		18 31	18 31		18 46	18 51		18 58					19s16
	d		17 46	17 51		17 59				18 19		18 27		18 31	18 31		18 47	18 51		18 59					
Bushey	d		17 49							18 22							18 49								
Harrow & Wealdstone ⊖	d		17 54	17 59						18 27							18 54	18 59							
Wembley Central ⊖	d			18 05														19 05							
Shepherd's Bush	a			18 19														19 18							
Kensington (Olympia) ⊖	a			18 21														19 20							
West Brompton ⊖	a			18 24														19 23							
Imperial Wharf	a			18 27														19 25							
Clapham Junction	d			18 34														19a30							
East Croydon	a			19 02																					
London Euston 15 ⊖	a	17 38	18 10		17 54	18 18	18 27	18 23	18 34	18 41		18 45	18 38	18 49	18 49	18 14	19 09		18 54	19 18		18 59	19 08	19 29	19 34

Station		LM	LM	VT	VT	LM		VT	LM	SN	VT	VT	LM	VT	LM	VT		VT	LM	LM	LM	LM	VT	LM	SN
		1	1	◇1 ⊠	◇1 ⊠	◇1		◇1 ⊠	1	1	◇1 ⊠	◇1 ⊠	◇1	◇1 ⊠	◇1	◇1 ⊠		◇1 ⊠	1	1	◇1 A	◇1	◇1 ⊠	1	1
Wolverhampton 7	d																	18 45							
Sandwell & Dudley	d																	18 56							
Birmingham New Street 12	d							17 50			18 30		17 53					19 10			18 33		18 50		
Birmingham International ✈	d							18 00			18 40		18 05					19 20			18 45		19 00		
Coventry	d							18 11			18 51		18 21					19 31			19 01		19 11		
Nuneaton	d					18 02																19 02			
Rugby	d					18 20		18 24					18 32								19 12	19 20	19 24		
Northampton	d					18 50							19 05		19 25							19 51			
Wolverton	d												19 17		19 37										
Milton Keynes Central 10	a					19 04					19 18		19 20		19 41							20 05			
	d		18 47	18 48	19 02	19 05				19 15	19 19		19 22	19 32	19 41	19 47				19 47		20 09			20 13
Bletchley	d		18 52							19 19			19 27		19 46					19 52					20 17
Leighton Buzzard	d		18 58							19 26			19 33		19 53					19 58					20 24
Cheddington	d		19 06																	20 04					
Tring	d	19 00	19 12						19 29	19 36									19 56	20 10				20 26	20 34
Berkhamsted	d	19 04	19 17						19 33	19 41			19 46						20 00	20 15				20 30	20 39
Hemel Hempstead	d	19 09	19 21						19 38	19 45			19 51						20 05	20 19				20 35	20 43
Apsley	d	19 12							19 41										20 08					20 38	
Kings Langley	d	19 15							19 44										20 11					20 41	
Watford Junction	a	19 20	19 28			19 30			19 49	19 54			19 59					20s15	20 16	20 26		20 31		20 46	20 51
	d	19 20	19 29			19 31			19 49	19 54			19 59						20 16	20 27		20 32		20 46	20 51
Bushey	d	19 23							19 52										20 19					20 49	
Harrow & Wealdstone ⊖	d	19 28							19 57	20 01									20 24					20 54	20 59
Wembley Central ⊖	d									20 06															21 04
Shepherd's Bush	a									20 21															21 22
Kensington (Olympia) ⊖	a									20 23															21 24
West Brompton ⊖	a									20 25															21 27
Imperial Wharf	a									20 28															21 29
Clapham Junction	d									20a33															21a34
East Croydon	a																								
London Euston 15 ⊖	a	19 42	19 47	19 23	19 38	19 50		19 14	20 11		19 54	20 02	20 19	20 06	20 27	20 23		20 34	20 38	20 51		20 49	20 14	21 08	

A ◇ from Northampton

Table 66

Mondays to Fridays
from 17 September

West Midlands, Northampton, Milton Keynes Central and Watford Junction - London

Network Diagram - see first Page of Table 59

Station		VT		VT	LM	VT	VT	LM	VT	LM	LM	VT		VT	VT	LM	VT	SN	LM	VT	LM	VT		VT	VT
		◇1 🍴		◇1 ⊠	◇1	◇1 ⊠	◇1 🍴	◇1	◇1 ⊠	1	1	◇1 🍴		◇1 🍴	◇1 🍴	1	◇1 🍴	1	◇1	◇1 🍴	1	◇1 🍴		◇1 🍴	◇1 🍴
Wolverhampton 7	d													19 45											
Sandwell & Dudley	d													19 56											
Birmingham New Street 12	d	19 30			18 53		19 50							20 10					19 53			20 50			
Birmingham International ✈	d	19 40			19 05		20 00							20 20					20 05			21 00			
Coventry	d	19 51			19 21		20 11							20 31					20 21			21 11			
Nuneaton	d																21 03				21 02				
Rugby	d				19 32		20 23												20 32		21 20	21 23		21 28	
Northampton	d				20 05			20 25											21 05		21 50				
Wolverton	d				20 17			20 37											21 17						
Milton Keynes Central 10	a	20 18			20 20			20 41						20 58					21 20		22 04			21 47	
	d	20 19			20 22	20 33		20 41	20 46		20 47	20 50		20 59	21 04			21 13	21 22	21 36	22 05			21 49	21 52
Bletchley	d				20 27			20 46			20 52							21 17	21 27						
Leighton Buzzard	d				20 33			20 53			20 58							21 24	21 33						
Cheddington	d										21 06														
Tring	d									20 56	21 11					21 26		21 34							
Berkhamsted	d				20 46					21 00	21 16					21 30		21 39	21 46						
Hemel Hempstead	d				20 51					21 05	21 20					21 35		21 43	21 51						
Apsley	d									21 08						21 38									
Kings Langley	d									21 11						21 41									
Watford Junction	a				20 58					21 16	21 27			21s19		21 46	21s48	21 51	21 58		22 35				22s11
	d				20 59					21 16	21 27					21 46		21 51	21 59		22 36				
Bushey	d									21 19						21 49									
Harrow & Wealdstone ⊖	d									21 24						21 54		21 59							
Wembley Central ⊖	d																								
Shepherd's Bush	a																	22 23							
Kensington (Olympia) ⊖	a																	22 25							
West Brompton ⊖	a																	22 27							
Imperial Wharf	a																	22 30							
Clapham Junction	d																	22a34							
East Croydon	a																								
London Euston 15 ⊖	a	20 54		21 05	21 17	21 06	21 14	21 29	21 24	21 38	21 46	21 26		21 38	21 42	22 08	22 09		22 20	22 12	22 56	22 12		22 22	22 33

Station		LM	VT	SN	LM	SN	LM	VT		VT	SN	LM	VT	VT	LM MO	LM MX	VT
		1	◇1 🍴	1	1	1	◇1	◇1 ⊠		◇1 🍴	1	◇1	◇1 🍴	◇1 🍴	1	1	◇1 🍴
Wolverhampton 7	d		20 47											21 45			22 45
Sandwell & Dudley	d		20 57											21 56			22 55
Birmingham New Street 12	d		21 10				20 53					21 33		22 10			23 10
Birmingham International ✈	d		21 20				21 05					21 45		22 22			23 20
Coventry	d		21 31				21 21					22 01		22 32			23 31
Nuneaton	d												22 17				
Rugby	d						21 32					22 12	22 34	22 43			23 44
Northampton	d	21 37					22 05					22 55			23 30	23 46	00s05
Wolverton	d	21 49					22 17					23 07			23 46	00 02	
Milton Keynes Central 10	a	21 52	21 58				22 20					23 12	22 58	23s05	23 50	00 05	00s23
	d	21 53	21 59		22 05	22 11	22 22	22 41		22 53		23 13	22 59		23 50	00 06	
Bletchley	d	21 58			22 10	22 15	22 27					23 18			23 55	00 11	
Leighton Buzzard	d	22 04			22 17	22 22	22 33					23 24			00 02	00 17	
Cheddington	d	22 10			22 23							23 29			00 08	00 24	
Tring	d	22 16			22 28	22 34						23 38			00 14	00 30	
Berkhamsted	d	22 20			22 33	22 39	22 48					23 43			00 18	00 34	
Hemel Hempstead	d	22 25			22 37	22 43	22 53					23 47			00 22	00 39	
Apsley	d				22 41							23 50					
Kings Langley	d				22 44							23 53					
Watford Junction	a	22 32	22s20		22 48	22 52	23 00	23s14		23s25		23 58	23s30	23s37	00 29	00 46	00s52
	d	22 33		22 27	22 49	22 53	23 01				23 29	23 58			00 30	00 47	
Bushey	d				22 51							00 01					
Harrow & Wealdstone ⊖	d			22 33	22 57	23 00					23 35	00 06			00 36	00 53	
Wembley Central ⊖	d														00 40	00 57	
Shepherd's Bush	a			22 49		23 21					23 53						
Kensington (Olympia) ⊖	a			22 51		23 23					23 56						
West Brompton ⊖	a			22 54		23 26					23 59						
Imperial Wharf	a			22 56		23 28					00 02						
Clapham Junction	d			23a01		23 40					00a07						
East Croydon	a					00 01											
London Euston 15 ⊖	a	22 52	22 43		23 12		23 21	23 38		23 48		00 21	23 56	00 04	00 53	01 09	01 15

West Midlands, Northampton, Milton Keynes Central and Watford Junction - London

Network Diagram - see first Page of Table 59

		SN	SN	LM	VT	LM	VT	VT	LM	LM	SN	LM	SR	LM	VT	SN	LM	LM	LM	VT	VT	VT	VT
		1	1	◇1	◇1	1	◇1	◇1	1	1	1	◇1	R	1	◇1	1	◇1	1	1	◇1	◇1	◇1	◇1
							A	B															
					☕		☕	☕					🚌 ☕		☕					☕	☕	☕	☕
Wolverhampton 7	d				21p45		22p45	22p45												05 45		06 06	
Sandwell & Dudley	d				21p56		22p55	22p55												05 56		06 17	
Birmingham New Street 12	d			21p33	22p10		23p10	23p10							05 50					06 10		06 30	
Birmingham International	d			21p45	22p22		23p20	23p20							06 00					06 20		06 40	
Coventry	d			22p01	22p32		23p31	23p31							06 10					06 31		06 51	
Nuneaton	d																						06 59
Rugby	d			22p12	22p43		23p44	23p44							06 24						06 51		
Northampton	d			22p55		23p46	00s05	00s05				05 16					06 05						
Wolverton	d			23p07		00 02						05 28					06 17						
Milton Keynes Central 10	a			23p12	23b05	00 05	00s23	00s23				05 31					06 20			06 58	07 11		
	d	22p11		23p13		00 06			03 40	04 35		05 32					06 22		06 47	06 59	07 12		
Bletchley	d	22p15		23p18		00 11			03 45	04 40		05 37		06 10			06 27	06 40	06 52				
Leighton Buzzard	d	22p22		23p24		00 17			03 51	04 46		05 43		06 17			06 33	06 47	06 58				
Cheddington	d			23p29		00 24						05 49							07 04				
Tring	d	22p34		23p38		00 30			04 03	04 58		05 55		06 26			06 43	06 56	07 10				
Berkhamsted	d	22p39		23p43		00 34			04 08	05 03		06 00		06 31			06 47	07 01	07 15				
Hemel Hempstead	d	22p43		23p47		00 39			04 12	05 07		06 04		06 35			06 52	07 05	07 19				
Apsley	d			23p50								06 07		06 38				07 08					
Kings Langley	d			23p53								06 10		06 41				07 11					
Watford Junction	a	22p52		23p58	23b37	00 46	00s52	00s52	04 19	05 14		06 15		06 46			06 59	07 16	07 26	07s19	07s32	07s36	07s44
	d	22p53	23p29	23p58		00 47			04 20	05 15	05 52	06 16		06 47		06 55	07 01	07 17	07 27				
Bushey	d			00 01								06 18		06 49				07 20					
Harrow & Wealdstone	d	23p00	23p35	00 06		00 53			04 26	05 21	05 58	06 24		06 55		07 01		07 25					
Wembley Central	d					00 57			04 34	05 25						07 06							
Shepherd's Bush	a	23p21	23p53								06 20					07 19							
Kensington (Olympia)	a	23p23	23p56								06 22					07 21							
West Brompton	a	23p26	23p59								06 25					07 24							
Imperial Wharf	a	23p28	00 02								06 28					07 27							
Clapham Junction	d	23p40	00a07								06 34					07 34							
East Croydon	a	00 01									06 57					07 57							
London Euston 15	a			00 21	00 04	01 09	01 13	01 15	04 46	05 41		06 38	06 50	07 09	07 16		07 20	07 39	07 45	07 38	07 52	07 55	08 05

		LM	SN	LM	VT	VT	VT	VT	LM	LM	LM	LM	SN	VT	LM	VT	LM	VT	LM	VT	LM	LM	LM
		1	1	◇1	◇1	◇1	◇1	◇1	1	1	◇1	1	1	◇1	◇1	◇1	◇1	◇1	1	◇1	1	◇1	◇1
					☕	☕	☕	☕						☕		☕		☕		☕			
Wolverhampton 7	d					06 27		06 45						07 04						07 45			
Sandwell & Dudley	d					06 37		06 56						07 15						07 56			
Birmingham New Street 12	d					06 50		07 10						07 30	06 53		07 13			08 10		07 33	
Birmingham International	d					07 00		07 20						07 40	07 05		07 29			08 20		07 45	
Coventry	d					07 11		07 31						07 52	07 21		07 48			08 31		08 01	
Nuneaton	d																						08 02
Rugby	d					07 23									07 32	07 54	07 59					08 12	08 20
Northampton	d			07 05							07 33				08 05		08 25					08 50	
Wolverton	d			07 17							07 45				08 17		08 37						
Milton Keynes Central 10	a			07 20							07 49			08 18	08 20		08 41					09 04	
	d		07 13	07 22	07 32		07 38			07 44	07 49		08 13	08 19	08 22		08 41	08 47			08 47	09 05	
Bletchley	d	07 10	07 17	07 27						07 49	07 54		08 17		08 27		08 46				08 52		
Leighton Buzzard	d	07 17	07 24	07 33						07 55	08 01		08 24		08 33		08 53				08 58		
Cheddington	d									08 01											09 04		
Tring	d	07 26	07 34						07 56	08 07		08 26	08 34						08 56		09 10		
Berkhamsted	d	07 31	07 39	07 46					08 00	08 11		08 30	08 39		08 46				09 00		09 15		
Hemel Hempstead	d	07 35	07 43	07 51					08 05	08 16		08 35	08 43		08 51				09 05		09 19		
Apsley	d	07 38							08 08			08 38							09 08				
Kings Langley	d	07 41							08 11			08 41							09 11				
Watford Junction	a	07 46	07 51	07 58				08s15	08 16	08 23	08 20	08 46	08 51		08 58				09 16	09s17	09 26	09 33	
	d	07 47	07 52	07 59					08 16	08 24	08 20	08 46	08 52		08 59				09 16		09 27	09 34	
Bushey	d	07 49							08 19			08 49							09 19				
Harrow & Wealdstone	d	07 55	07 59						08 24			08 54	08 59						09 24				
Wembley Central	d		08 04										09 04										
Shepherd's Bush	a		08 19										09 19										
Kensington (Olympia)	a		08 21										09 21										
West Brompton	a		08 24										09 24										
Imperial Wharf	a		08 27										09 27										
Clapham Junction	d		08 34										09 34										
East Croydon	a		08 57										09 57										
London Euston 15	a	08 09		08 17	08 09	08 14	08 14	08 34	08 38	08 42	08 38	09 08		08 54	09 17	08 46	09 27	09 23	09 38	09 35	09 45	09 50	

A 30 June

B not 30 June

b Previous night, stops to set down only

West Midlands, Northampton, Milton Keynes Central and Watford Junction - London

Network Diagram - see first Page of Table 59

		VT	LM	SN	VT	VT	LM	LM	VT	VT	LM	LM	VT	LM	LM	VT	LM	SN	VT	VT	LM	LM
		◇1	1	1	◇1	◇1	◇1	◇1	◇1	◇1	1	1	◇1	◇1	◇1	◇1	1	1	◇1	◇1	◇1	◇1
		☕			☕	☕			☕	☕			☕			☕			☕	☕		
Wolverhampton 7	d				08 06					08 45												
Sandwell & Dudley	d									08 56												
Birmingham New Street 12	d	07 50			08 30		07 53	08 13		09 10				08 33		08 50			09 30		08 53	09 13
Birmingham International	d	08 00			08 40		08 05	08 29		09 20				08 45		09 00			09 40		09 05	09 29
Coventry	d	08 11			08 51		08 21	08 48		09 31				09 01		09 11			09 51		09 21	09 48
Nuneaton	d					08 59									09 02					09 59		
Rugby	d	08 23					08 32	08 59						09 12	09 20	09 23					09 32	09 59
Northampton	d						09 05	09 25						09 50							10 05	10 25
Wolverton	d						09 17	09 37													10 17	10 37
Milton Keynes Central 10	a				09 18		09 20	09 41						10 04					10 18		10 20	10 41
	d			09 13	09 19		09 22	09 41	09 47			09 47	10 02	10 05				10 13	10 19		10 22	10 41
Bletchley	d			09 17			09 27	09 46				09 52						10 17			10 27	10 46
Leighton Buzzard	d			09 24			09 33	09 53				09 58						10 24			10 33	10 53
Cheddington	d											10 04										
Tring	d		09 26	09 34							09 56	10 10					10 26	10 34				
Berkhamsted	d		09 30	09 39			09 46				10 00	10 15					10 30	10 39			10 46	
Hemel Hempstead	d		09 35	09 43			09 51				10 05	10 19					10 35	10 43			10 51	
Apsley	d		09 38								10 08						10 38					
Kings Langley	d		09 41								10 11						10 41					
Watford Junction	a		09 46	09 51			09 58			10s15	10 16	10 26		10 30			10 46	10 51			10 58	
	d		09 46	09 52			09 59				10 16	10 27		10 31			10 46	10 52			10 59	
Bushey	d		09 49								10 19						10 49					
Harrow & Wealdstone	d		09 54	09 59							10 24						10 54	10 59				
Wembley Central	d			10 04														11 04				
Shepherd's Bush	a			10 19														11 19				
Kensington (Olympia)	a			10 21														11 21				
West Brompton	a			10 24														11 24				
Imperial Wharf	a			10 27														11 27				
Clapham Junction	d			10 34														11 34				
East Croydon	a			10 57														11 57				
London Euston 15	a	09 14	10 08		09 55	10 00	10 17	10 27	10 23	10 34	10 38	10 45	10 37	10 49		10 14	11 08		10 54	11 01	11 17	11 27

		VT	VT	LM	LM	VT	LM	LM	VT	LM	SN	VT	LM	LM	VT	VT	LM	LM	VT	LM	LM	VT	LM
		◇1	◇1	1	1	◇1	◇1	◇1	◇1	1	1	◇1	◇1	◇1	◇1	◇1	1	1	◇1	◇1	◇1	◇1	1
		☕	☕			☕			☕			☕			☕	☕			☕			☕	
Wolverhampton 7	d		09 45													10 45							
Sandwell & Dudley	d		09 56													10 56							
Birmingham New Street 12	d		10 10				09 33		09 50			10 30	09 53	10 13		11 10				10 33		10 50	
Birmingham International	d		10 20				09 45		10 00			10 40	10 05	10 29		11 20				10 45		11 00	
Coventry	d		10 31				10 01		10 11			10 51	10 21	10 48		11 31				11 01		11 11	
Nuneaton	d							10 02													11 02		
Rugby	d						10 12	10 20	10 23				10 32	10 59						11 12	11 20	11 23	
Northampton	d						10 50						11 05	11 25						11 50			
Wolverton	d												11 17	11 37									
Milton Keynes Central 10	a						11 04					11 18	11 20	11 41						12 04			
	d	10 47			10 47	11 02	11 05				11 13	11 20	11 22	11 41	11 47			11 47	12 02	12 05			
Bletchley	d				10 52						11 17		11 27	11 46				11 52					
Leighton Buzzard	d				10 58						11 24		11 33	11 53				11 58					
Cheddington	d				11 04													12 04					
Tring	d			10 56	11 10					11 26	11 34						11 56	12 10					12 26
Berkhamsted	d			11 00	11 15					11 30	11 39		11 46				12 00	12 15					12 30
Hemel Hempstead	d			11 05	11 19					11 35	11 43		11 51				12 05	12 19					12 35
Apsley	d			11 08						11 38							12 08						12 38
Kings Langley	d			11 11						11 41							12 11						12 41
Watford Junction	a		11s15	11 16	11 26		11 30			11 46	11 51		11 58			12s15	12 16	12 26		12 30			12 46
	d			11 16	11 27		11 31			11 46	11 52		11 59				12 16	12 27		12 31			12 46
Bushey	d			11 19						11 49							12 19						12 49
Harrow & Wealdstone	d			11 24						11 54	11 59						12 24						12 54
Wembley Central	d										12 04												
Shepherd's Bush	a										12 19												
Kensington (Olympia)	a										12 21												
West Brompton	a										12 24												
Imperial Wharf	a										12 27												
Clapham Junction	d										12 34												
East Croydon	a										12 57												
London Euston 15	a	11 23	11 34	11 38	11 45	11 38	11 49		11 14	12 08		11 54	12 17	12 27	12 23	12 34	12 38	12 45	12 38	12 49		12 14	13 08

Table 66

Saturdays until 30 June

West Midlands, Northampton, Milton Keynes Central and Watford Junction - London

Network Diagram - see first Page of Table 59

	SN	VT	LM	LM	VT	VT	LM	LM	VT	LM	LM	VT	LM	SN	VT	LM	LM	VT	VT	LM	LM
	1	◇1 ☕	◇1	◇1	◇1 ☕	◇1 ☕	1	1	◇1 ☕	◇1	◇1	◇1 ☕	1	1	◇1 ☕	◇1	◇1	◇1 ☕	◇1 ☕	1	1
Wolverhampton 7 d						11 45													12 45		
Sandwell & Dudley d						11 56													12 56		
Birmingham New Street 12 d		11 30	10 53	11 13		12 10				11 33		11 50			12 30	11 53	12 13		13 10		
Birmingham International d		11 40	11 05	11 29		12 20				11 45		12 00			12 40	12 05	12 29		13 20		
Coventry d		11 51	11 21	11 48		12 31				12 01		12 11			12 51	12 21	12 48		13 31		
Nuneaton d											12 02										
Rugby d			11 32	11 59						12 12	12 20	12 23				12 32	12 59				
Northampton d			12 05	12 25						12 50						13 05	13 25				
Wolverton d			12 17	12 37												13 17	13 37				
Milton Keynes Central 10 a		12 18	12 20	12 41						13 04					13 18	13 20	13 41				
d	12 13	12 19	12 22	12 41	12 47			12 47	13 02	13 05				13 13	13 19	13 22	13 41	13 47			13 47
Bletchley d	12 17		12 27	12 46				12 52						13 17		13 27	13 46				13 52
Leighton Buzzard d	12 24		12 33	12 53				12 58						13 24		13 33	13 53				13 58
Cheddington d								13 04													14 04
Tring d	12 34						12 56	13 10					13 26	13 34						13 56	14 10
Berkhamsted d	12 39		12 46				13 00	13 15					13 30	13 39		13 46				14 00	14 15
Hemel Hempstead d	12 43		12 51				13 05	13 19					13 35	13 43		13 51				14 05	14 19
Apsley d							13 08						13 38							14 08	
Kings Langley d							13 11						13 41							14 11	
Watford Junction a	12 51		12 58			13s15	13 16	13 26		13 30			13 46	13 51		13 58			14s15	14 16	14 26
d	12 52		12 59				13 16	13 27		13 31			13 46	13 52		13 59				14 16	14 27
Bushey d							13 19						13 49							14 19	
Harrow & Wealdstone ⊖ d	12 59						13 24						13 54	13 59						14 24	
Wembley Central ⊖ d	13 04													14 04							
Shepherd's Bush a	13 19													14 19							
Kensington (Olympia) ⊖ a	13 21													14 21							
West Brompton ⊖ a	13 24													14 24							
Imperial Wharf a	13 27													14 27							
Clapham Junction d	13 34													14 34							
East Croydon a	13 57													14 57							
London Euston 15 ⊖ a		12 54	13 17	13 27	13 23	13 34	13 38	13 47	13 38	13 49		13 14	14 08		13 54	14 17	14 27	14 23	14 34	14 38	14 45

	VT	LM	LM	VT	LM	SN	VT	LM	LM	VT	VT	LM	LM	VT	LM	LM	VT	LM	SN	VT	LM	LM
	◇1 ☕	◇1	◇1	◇1 ☕	1	1	◇1 ☕	◇1	◇1	◇1 ☕	◇1 ☕	1	1	◇1 ☕	◇1	◇1	◇1 ☕	1	1	◇1 ☕	◇1	◇1
Wolverhampton 7 d											13 45											
Sandwell & Dudley d											13 56											
Birmingham New Street 12 d		12 33		12 50			13 30	12 53	13 13		14 10				13 33		13 50			14 30	13 53	14 13
Birmingham International d		12 45		13 00			13 40	13 05	13 29		14 20				13 45		14 00			14 40	14 05	14 29
Coventry d		13 01		13 11			13 51	13 21	13 48		14 31				14 01		14 11			14 51	14 21	14 48
Nuneaton d			13 02													14 02						
Rugby d		13 12	13 20	13 23				13 32	13 59						14 12	14 20	14 23				14 32	14 59
Northampton d		13 50						14 05	14 25						14 50						15 05	15 25
Wolverton d								14 17	14 37												15 17	15 37
Milton Keynes Central 10 a		14 04					14 18	14 20	14 41						15 04					15 18	15 20	15 41
d	14 02	14 05				14 13	14 19	14 22	14 41	14 47			14 47	15 02	15 05				15 13	15 19	15 22	15 41
Bletchley d						14 17		14 27	14 46				14 52						15 17		15 27	15 46
Leighton Buzzard d						14 24		14 33	14 53				14 58						15 24		15 33	15 53
Cheddington d													15 04									
Tring d					14 26	14 34						14 56	15 10					15 26	15 34			
Berkhamsted d					14 30	14 39		14 46				15 00	15 15					15 30	15 39		15 46	
Hemel Hempstead d					14 35	14 43		14 51				15 05	15 19					15 35	15 43		15 51	
Apsley d					14 38							15 08						15 38				
Kings Langley d					14 41							15 11						15 41				
Watford Junction a		14 30			14 46	14 51		14 58			15s15	15 16	15 26		15 30			15 46	15 51		15 58	
d		14 31			14 46	14 52		14 59				15 16	15 27		15 31			15 46	15 52		15 59	
Bushey d					14 49							15 19						15 49				
Harrow & Wealdstone ⊖ d					14 54	14 59						15 24						15 54	15 59			
Wembley Central ⊖ d						15 04													16 04			
Shepherd's Bush a						15 19													16 19			
Kensington (Olympia) ⊖ a						15 21													16 21			
West Brompton ⊖ a						15 24													16 24			
Imperial Wharf a						15 27													16 27			
Clapham Junction d						15 34													16 34			
East Croydon a						15 57													16 57			
London Euston 15 ⊖ a	14 38	14 49		14 14	15 08		14 54	15 18	15 27	15 23	15 34	15 38	15 45	15 38	15 49		15 14	16 08		15 54	16 18	16 27

Table 66

Saturdays until 30 June

West Midlands, Northampton, Milton Keynes Central and Watford Junction - London

Network Diagram - see first Page of Table 59

	VT	VT	LM	LM	VT	LM	LM	VT	LM	SN	VT	LM	LM	VT	VT	LM	LM	VT	LM	LM	VT	LM
	◇1 ☕	◇1 ☕	1	1	◇1 ☕	◇1	◇1	◇1 ☕	1	1	◇1 ☕	◇1	◇1	◇1 ☕	◇1 ☕	1	1	◇1 ☕	◇1	◇1	◇1 ☕	1
Wolverhampton 7 d		14 45													15 45							
Sandwell & Dudley d		14 56													15 56							
Birmingham New Street 12 d		15 10				14 33		14 50			15 30	14 53	15 13		16 10				15 33		15 50	
Birmingham International d		15 20				14 45		15 00			15 40	15 05	15 29		16 20				15 45		16 00	
Coventry d		15 31				15 01		15 11			15 51	15 21	15 48		16 31				16 01		16 11	
Nuneaton d							15 02													16 02		
Rugby d						15 12	15 20	15 23				15 32	15 59						16 12	16 20	16 23	
Northampton d						15 50						16 05	16 25						16 50			
Wolverton d												16 17	16 37									
Milton Keynes Central 10 a						16 04					16 18	16 20	16 41						17 04			
d	15 47			15 47	16 02	16 05				16 13	16 19	16 22	16 41	16 47			16 47	17 02	17 05			
Bletchley d				15 52						16 17		16 27	16 46				16 52					
Leighton Buzzard d				15 58						16 24		16 33	16 53				16 58					
Cheddington d				16 04													17 04					
Tring d			15 56	16 10					16 26	16 34						16 56	17 10					17 26
Berkhamsted d			16 00	16 15					16 30	16 39		16 46				17 00	17 15					17 30
Hemel Hempstead d			16 05	16 19					16 35	16 43		16 51				17 05	17 19					17 35
Apsley d			16 08						16 38							17 08						17 38
Kings Langley d			16 11						16 41							17 11						17 41
Watford Junction a		16s15	16 16	16 26		16 30			16 46	16 51		16 58			17s15	17 16	17 26		17 30			17 46
d			16 16	16 27		16 31			16 46	16 52		16 59				17 16	17 27		17 31			17 46
Bushey d			16 19						16 49							17 19						17 49
Harrow & Wealdstone ⊖ d			16 24						16 54	16 59						17 24						17 54
Wembley Central ⊖ d										17 04												
Shepherd's Bush a										17 19												
Kensington (Olympia) ⊖ a										17 21												
West Brompton ⊖ a										17 24												
Imperial Wharf a										17 27												
Clapham Junction d										17 34												
East Croydon a										17 57												
London Euston 15 ⊖ a	16 23	16 34	16 38	16 45	16 38	16 49		16 14	17 08		16 54	17 17	17 27	17 23	17 34	17 38	17 45	17 38	17 49		17 14	18 08

	SN	VT	LM	LM	VT	VT	LM	LM	VT	LM	LM	VT	LM	SN	VT	LM	VT	VT	LM	LM
	1	◇1 ☕	◇1	◇1	◇1 ☕	◇1 ☕	1	1	◇1 ☕	◇1	◇1	◇1 ☕	1	1	◇1 ☕	◇1	◇1 ☕	◇1 ☕	1	◇1
Wolverhampton 7 d						16 45												17 45		
Sandwell & Dudley d						16 56												17 56		
Birmingham New Street 12 d		16 30	15 53	16 13		17 10				16 33		16 50			17 30	16 53		18 10		17 13
Birmingham International d		16 40	16 05	16 29		17 20				16 45		17 00			17 40	17 05		18 20		17 30
Coventry d		16 51	16 21	16 48		17 31				17 01		17 11			17 51	17 21		18 31		17 48
Nuneaton d											17 02									
Rugby d			16 32	16 59						17 12	17 20	17 23				17 32				17 59
Northampton d			17 05	17 25						17 50						18 05				18 31
Wolverton d			17 17	17 37												18 17				18 43
Milton Keynes Central 10 a		17 18	17 20	17 41						18 05					18 18	18 20				18 46
d	17 13	17 19	17 22	17 41	17 47			17 47	18 02	18 05				18 13	18 19	18 22	18 47			18 47
Bletchley d	17 17		17 27	17 46				17 52						18 17		18 27				18 52
Leighton Buzzard d	17 24		17 33	17 53				17 58						18 24		18 33				18 58
Cheddington d								18 04												19 04
Tring d	17 34						17 56	18 10					18 26	18 34					18 56	19 10
Berkhamsted d	17 39		17 46				18 00	18 15					18 30	18 39		18 46			19 00	19 15
Hemel Hempstead d	17 43		17 51				18 05	18 19					18 35	18 43		18 51			19 05	19 19
Apsley d							18 08						18 38						19 08	
Kings Langley d							18 11						18 41						19 11	
Watford Junction a	17 51		17 58			18s15	18 16	18 26		18 31			18 46	18 51		18 58		19s15	19 16	19 26
d	17 52		17 59				18 16	18 27		18 31			18 46	18 52		18 59			19 16	19 27
Bushey d							18 19						18 49						19 19	
Harrow & Wealdstone ⊖ d	17 59						18 24						18 54	18 59					19 24	
Wembley Central ⊖ d	18 04													19 04						
Shepherd's Bush a	18 19													19 19						
Kensington (Olympia) ⊖ a	18 21													19 21						
West Brompton ⊖ a	18 24													19 24						
Imperial Wharf a	18 27													19 27						
Clapham Junction d	18 34													19 34						
East Croydon a	18 57													19 57						
London Euston 15 ⊖ a		17 52	18 17	18 27	18 23	18 34	18 38	18 45	18 38	18 49		18 14	19 08		18 54	19 17	19 23	19 34	19 38	19 45

West Midlands, Northampton, Milton Keynes Central and Watford Junction - London

Network Diagram - see first Page of Table 59

		LM	LM	VT	SN	LM	SN	VT	LM	LM	LM	VT	VT	LM	VT	SN	VT	LM	LM	LM	VT	VT	SN
		◇1	◇1	◇1	1	1	1	◇1	◇1	1	◇1	◇1	◇1	◇1	◇1	1	◇1	◇1	1	◇1	◇1	◇1	1
Wolverhampton [7]	d														18 45						19 45		
Sandwell & Dudley	d														18 56						19 56		
Birmingham New Street [12]	d	17 33		17 50				18 30	17 53		18 13	18 50		18 53	19 10			19 13		19 53	20 10		
Birmingham International	d	17 45		18 00				18 40	18 05		18 29	19 00		19 05	19 20			19 29		20 05	20 20		
Coventry	d	18 01		18 11				18 51	18 21		18 48	19 11		19 21	19 31			19 48		20 21	20 31		
Nuneaton	d		18 02																				
Rugby	d	18 12	18 20	18 23					18 32		18 59	19 23		19 32	19 44			19 59		20 32	20 43		
Northampton	d	18 50							19 05		19 31			20 00				20 32		21 00			
Wolverton	d								19 17		19 43			20 12						21 12			
Milton Keynes Central [10]	a	19 04						19 18	19 20		19 46			20 15	20 05			20 47		21 15	21 04		
	d	19 05					19 13	19 19	19 22		19 47		19 46	20 16	20 07		20 43	20 47	20 50	21 16	21 05	21 11	
Bletchley	d						19 17		19 27		19 52			20 21					20 55				
Leighton Buzzard	d						19 24		19 33		19 58			20 27				20 56					
Cheddington	d										20 04							21 03					
Tring	d					19 24	19 34			19 58	20 10							21 08	21 12				
Berkhamsted	d					19 28	19 39		19 46	20 02	20 15								21 17	21 38			
Hemel Hempstead	d					19 33	19 43		19 51	20 07	20 19							21 15	21 21	21 42			
Apsley	d					19 36				20 10								21 18					
Kings Langley	d					19 39				20 13								21 21					
Watford Junction	a	19 30				19 44	19 50		19 58	20 18	20 26			20 50	20s34		21s15	21 26	21 30	21 49	21s34		
	d	19 31			19 31	19 44	19 51		20 03	20 19	20 27			20 51		20 43		21 27	21 30	21 51			21 43
Bushey	d					19 47													21s33				
Harrow & Wealdstone ⊖	d				19 38	19 52	19 58			20 25						20 50			21 38				21 50
Wembley Central ⊖	d				19 43																		
Shepherd's Bush	a				19 57		20 19									21 07							22 07
Kensington (Olympia) ⊖	a				19 59		20 21									21 09							22 09
West Brompton ⊖	a				20 02		20 24									21 12							22 12
Imperial Wharf	a				20 05		20 27									21 15							22 15
Clapham Junction	d				20a10		20 34									21a20							22a20
East Croydon	a						20 59																
London Euston [15] ⊖	a	19 49		19 14		20 06		19 54	20 21	20 39	20 45	20 15	20 24	21 09	20 55		21 38	21 45	21 52	22 11	21 56	22 00	

		LM	VT	LM	VT	VT	SN	VT	SN	LM	LM
		◇1	◇1	◇1	◇1	◇1	1	◇1	1	◇1	◇1
Wolverhampton [7]	d				20 45			21 07			
Sandwell & Dudley	d				20 56			21 17			
Birmingham New Street [12]	d			20 53	21 10			21 30		21 53	
Birmingham International	d			21 05	21 20			21 40		22 05	
Coventry	d			21 21	21 31			21 51		22 21	
Nuneaton	d										
Rugby	d			21 32	21 43			22 03		22 32	
Northampton	d	21 20		22 05						22 55	23 30
Wolverton	d			22 17						23 07	23 42
Milton Keynes Central [10]	a	21 34		22 20	22 04			22 28		23 10	23 45
	d	21 34	21 52	22 21	22 05	22 11		22 29		23 11	23 46
Bletchley	d	21 39		22 26						23 16	23 51
Leighton Buzzard	d	21 46		22 32						23 22	23 57
Cheddington	d	21 51		22 37						23 27	
Tring	d	21 58		22 44						23 36	
Berkhamsted	d	22 02		22 49						23 41	
Hemel Hempstead	d	22 07		22 53						23 45	
Apsley	d	22 10		22 56						23 49	
Kings Langley	d	22 13		23 00						23 52	
Watford Junction	a	22 18		23 06	22s34	22s40		23s11		23 56	00 19
	d	22 19		23 07			22 48		23 25	23 57	00 20
Bushey	d										
Harrow & Wealdstone ⊖	d			23 13			22 55		23 31	00 03	
Wembley Central ⊖	d										
Shepherd's Bush	a						23 14		23 48		
Kensington (Olympia) ⊖	a						23 16		23 51		
West Brompton ⊖	a						23 19		23 54		
Imperial Wharf	a						23 21		23 57		
Clapham Junction	d						23a26		00a02		
East Croydon	a										
London Euston [15] ⊖	a	22 37	22 44	23 27	22 55	23 02		23 30		00 17	00 40

West Midlands, Northampton, Milton Keynes Central and Watford Junction - London

Network Diagram - see first Page of Table 59

		SN	SN	LM	VT	LM	VT	LM	LM	SN	LM	SR	LM	VT	SN	LM	LM	LM	VT	VT	VT	VT	LM
		1	1	◇1	◇1	1	◇1	1	1	1	◇1	B	1	◇1	1	◇1	1	1	◇1	◇1	◇1	◇1	1
Wolverhampton [7]	d				21p45		22p45												05 45		06 06		
Sandwell & Dudley	d				21p56		22p55												05 56		06 17		
Birmingham New Street [12]	d			21p33	22p10		23p10							05 50					06 10		06 30		
Birmingham International	d			21p45	22p22		23p20							06 00					06 20		06 40		
Coventry	d			22p01	22p32		23p31							06 10					06 31		06 51		
Nuneaton	d																					06 59	
Rugby	d			22p12	22p43		23p44							06 24						06 51			
Northampton	d			22p55		23p46	00s05				05 16					06 05							
Wolverton	d			23p07		00 02					05 28					06 17							
Milton Keynes Central [10]	a			23p12	23b05	00 05	00s23				05 31					06 20			06 58	07 11			
	d	22p11		23p13		00 06		03 40	04 35		05 32					06 22		06 47	06 59	07 12			
Bletchley	d	22p15		23p18		00 11		03 45	04 40		05 37		06 10			06 27	06 40	06 52					07 10
Leighton Buzzard	d	22p22		23p24		00 17		03 51	04 46		05 43		06 17			06 33	06 47	06 58					07 17
Cheddington	d			23p29		00 24					05 49							07 04					
Tring	d	22p34		23p38		00 30		04 03	04 58		05 55		06 26			06 43	06 56	07 10					07 26
Berkhamsted	d	22p39		23p43		00 34		04 08	05 03		06 00		06 31			06 47	07 01	07 15					07 31
Hemel Hempstead	d	22p43		23p47		00 39		04 12	05 07		06 04		06 35			06 52	07 05	07 19					07 35
Apsley	d			23p50							06 07		06 38				07 08						07 38
Kings Langley	d			23p53							06 10		06 41				07 11						07 41
Watford Junction	a	22p52		23p58	23b37	00 46	00s52	04 19	05 14		06 15		06 46			06 59	07 16	07 26	07s19	07s32	07s36	07s44	07 46
	d	22p53	23p29	23p58		00 47		04 20	05 15	05 52	06 16		06 47		06 55	07 01	07 17	07 27					07 47
Bushey	d			00 01							06 18		06 49				07 20						07 49
Harrow & Wealdstone ⊖	d	23p00	23p35	00 06		00 53		04 26	05 21	05 58	06 24		06 55		07 01		07 25						07 55
Wembley Central ⊖	d					00 57		04 34	05 25						07 06								
Shepherd's Bush	a	23p21	23p53							06 20					07 19								
Kensington (Olympia) ⊖	a	23p23	23p56							06 22					07 21								
West Brompton ⊖	a	23p26	23p59							06 25					07 24								
Imperial Wharf	a	23p28	00 02							06 28					07 27								
Clapham Junction	d	23p40	00a07							06 34					07 34								
East Croydon	a	00 01								06 57					07 57								
London Euston [15] ⊖	a			00 21	00 04	01 09	01 13	04 46	05 41		06 38	06 50	07 09	07 16		07 20	07 39	07 45	07 38	07 52	07 55	08 05	08 09

		SN	LM	VT	VT	VT	VT	LM	LM	LM	LM	SN	VT	LM	VT	LM	VT	LM	VT	LM	LM	LM	VT
		1	◇1	◇1	◇1	◇1	◇1	1	1	◇1	1	1	◇1	◇1	◇1	◇1	◇1	1	◇1	1	◇1	◇1	◇1
Wolverhampton [7]	d				06 27		06 45						07 04						07 45				
Sandwell & Dudley	d				06 37		06 56						07 15						07 56				
Birmingham New Street [12]	d				06 50		07 10						07 30	06 53		07 13			08 10		07 33		07 50
Birmingham International	d				07 00		07 20						07 40	07 05		07 29			08 20		07 45		08 00
Coventry	d				07 11		07 31						07 51	07 21		07 48			08 31		08 01		08 11
Nuneaton	d																					08 02	
Rugby	d				07 23									07 32	07 54	07 59					08 12	08 20	08 23
Northampton	d		07 05							07 33				08 05		08 25					08 50		
Wolverton	d		07 17							07 45				08 17		08 37							
Milton Keynes Central [10]	a		07 20							07 49			08 18	08 20		08 41					09 04		
	d	07 13	07 22	07 32		07 38			07 44	07 49		08 13	08 19	08 22		08 41	08 47			08 47	09 05		
Bletchley	d	07 17	07 27						07 49	07 54		08 17		08 27		08 46				08 52			
Leighton Buzzard	d	07 24	07 33						07 55	08 01		08 24		08 33		08 53				08 58			
Cheddington	d								08 01											09 04			
Tring	d	07 34						07 56	08 07		08 26	08 34						08 56		09 10			
Berkhamsted	d	07 39	07 46					08 00	08 11		08 30	08 39		08 46				09 00		09 15			
Hemel Hempstead	d	07 43	07 51					08 05	08 16		08 35	08 43		08 51				09 05		09 19			
Apsley	d							08 08			08 38							09 08					
Kings Langley	d							08 11			08 41							09 11					
Watford Junction	a	07 51	07 58				08s15	08 16	08 23	08 20	08 46	08 51		08 58				09 16	09s17	09 26	09 33		
	d	07 52	07 59					08 16	08 24	08 20	08 46	08 52		08 59				09 16		09 27	09 34		
Bushey	d							08 19			08 49							09 19					
Harrow & Wealdstone ⊖	d	07 59						08 24			08 54	08 59						09 24					
Wembley Central ⊖	d	08 04										09 04											
Shepherd's Bush	a	08 19										09 19											
Kensington (Olympia) ⊖	a	08 21										09 21											
West Brompton ⊖	a	08 24										09 24											
Imperial Wharf	a	08 27										09 27											
Clapham Junction	d	08 34										09 34											
East Croydon	a	08 57										09 57											
London Euston [15] ⊖	a		08 17	08 09	08 14	08 14	08 34	08 38	08 42	08 38	09 08		08 54	09 17	08 46	09 27	09 23	09 38	09 35	09 45	09 50		09 14

b Previous night, stops to set down only

West Midlands, Northampton, Milton Keynes Central and Watford Junction - London

Network Diagram - see first Page of Table 59

Station	LM 1	SN 1	VT ◇1 ⊡	VT ◇1 ⊡	LM ◇1	LM ◇1	VT ◇1 ⊡	VT ◇1 ⊡	LM 1	LM 1	VT ◇1 ⊡	LM ◇1	LM ◇1	VT ◇1 ⊡	LM 1	SN 1	VT ◇1 ⊡	VT ◇1 ⊡	LM ◇1	LM ◇1	VT ◇1 ⊡
Wolverhampton 7 d			08 06					08 45													
Sandwell & Dudley d								08 56													
Birmingham New Street 12 d			08 30		07 53	08 13		09 10				08 33		08 50			09 30		08 53	09 13	
Birmingham International ✈ d			08 40		08 05	08 29		09 20				08 45		09 00			09 40		09 05	09 29	
Coventry d			08 51		08 21	08 48		09 31				09 01		09 11			09 51		09 21	09 48	
Nuneaton d				08 59									09 02					09 59			
Rugby d					08 32	08 59						09 12	09 20	09 23					09 32	09 59	
Northampton d					09 05	09 25						09 50							10 05	10 25	
Wolverton d					09 17	09 37													10 17	10 37	
Milton Keynes Central 10 a			09 18		09 20	09 41						10 04					10 18		10 20	10 41	
d		09 13	09 19		09 22	09 41	09 47			09 47	10 02	10 05				10 13	10 19		10 22	10 41	10 47
Bletchley d		09 17			09 27	09 46				09 52						10 17			10 27	10 46	
Leighton Buzzard d		09 24			09 33	09 53				09 58						10 24			10 33	10 53	
Cheddington d										10 04											
Tring d	09 26	09 34							09 56	10 10					10 26	10 34					
Berkhamsted d	09 30	09 39			09 46				10 00	10 15					10 30	10 39			10 46		
Hemel Hempstead d	09 35	09 43			09 51				10 05	10 19					10 35	10 43			10 51		
Apsley d	09 38								10 08						10 38						
Kings Langley d	09 41								10 11						10 41						
Watford Junction a	09 46	09 51			09 58			10s15	10 16	10 26		10 30			10 46	10 51			10 58		
d	09 46	09 52			09 59				10 16	10 27		10 31			10 46	10 52			10 59		
Bushey d	09 49								10 19						10 49						
Harrow & Wealdstone ⊖ d	09 54	09 59							10 24						10 54	10 59					
Wembley Central ⊖ d		10 04														11 04					
Shepherd's Bush a		10 19														11 19					
Kensington (Olympia) ⊖ a		10 21														11 21					
West Brompton ⊖ a		10 24														11 24					
Imperial Wharf a		10 27														11 27					
Clapham Junction d		10 34														11 34					
East Croydon a		10 57														11 57					
London Euston 15 ⊖ a	10 08		09 55	10 00	10 17	10 27	10 23	10 34	10 38	10 45	10 37	10 49		10 14	11 08		10 54	11 01	11 17	11 27	11 23

Station	VT ◇1 ⊡	LM 1	LM 1	VT ◇1 ⊡	LM ◇1	LM ◇1	VT ◇1 ⊡	LM 1	SN 1	VT ◇1 ⊡	LM ◇1	LM ◇1	VT ◇1 ⊡	VT ◇1 ⊡	LM 1	LM 1	VT ◇1 ⊡	LM ◇1	LM ◇1	VT ◇1 ⊡	LM 1	SN 1
Wolverhampton 7 d	09 45													10 45								
Sandwell & Dudley d	09 56													10 56								
Birmingham New Street 12 d	10 10				09 33		09 50			10 30	09 53	10 13		11 10				10 33		10 50		
Birmingham International ✈ d	10 20				09 45		10 00			10 40	10 05	10 29		11 20				10 45		11 00		
Coventry d	10 31				10 01		10 11			10 51	10 21	10 48		11 31				11 01		11 11		
Nuneaton d						10 02													11 02			
Rugby d					10 12	10 20	10 23				10 32	10 59						11 12	11 20	11 23		
Northampton d					10 50						11 05	11 25						11 50				
Wolverton d											11 17	11 37										
Milton Keynes Central 10 a					11 04					11 18	11 20	11 41						12 04				
d			10 47	11 02	11 05				11 13	11 19	11 22	11 41	11 47			11 47	12 02	12 05				12 13
Bletchley d			10 52						11 17		11 27	11 46				11 52						12 17
Leighton Buzzard d			10 58						11 24		11 33	11 53				11 58						12 24
Cheddington d			11 04													12 04						
Tring d		10 56	11 10					11 26	11 34						11 56	12 10					12 26	12 34
Berkhamsted d		11 00	11 15					11 30	11 39		11 46				12 00	12 15					12 30	12 39
Hemel Hempstead d		11 05	11 19					11 35	11 43		11 51				12 05	12 19					12 35	12 43
Apsley d		11 08						11 38							12 08						12 38	
Kings Langley d		11 11						11 41							12 11						12 41	
Watford Junction a	11s15	11 16	11 26		11 30			11 46	11 51		11 58			12s15	12 16	12 26		12 30			12 46	12 51
d		11 16	11 27		11 31			11 46	11 52		11 59				12 16	12 27		12 31			12 46	12 52
Bushey d		11 19						11 49							12 19						12 49	
Harrow & Wealdstone ⊖ d		11 24						11 54	11 59						12 24						12 54	12 59
Wembley Central ⊖ d									12 04													13 04
Shepherd's Bush a									12 19													13 19
Kensington (Olympia) ⊖ a									12 21													13 21
West Brompton ⊖ a									12 24													13 24
Imperial Wharf a									12 27													13 27
Clapham Junction d									12 34													13 34
East Croydon a									12 57													13 57
London Euston 15 ⊖ a	11 34	11 38	11 45	11 38	11 49		11 14	12 08		11 54	12 17	12 27	12 23	12 34	12 38	12 45	12 38	12 49		12 14	13 08	

Table 66

Saturdays

7 July to 8 September

West Midlands, Northampton, Milton Keynes Central and Watford Junction - London

Network Diagram - see first Page of Table 59

Station	VT ◇1 ⊡	LM ◇1	LM ◇1	VT ◇1 ⊡	VT ◇1 ⊡	LM 1	LM 1	VT ◇1 ⊡	LM ◇1	LM ◇1	VT ◇1 ⊡	LM 1	SN 1	VT ◇1 ⊡	LM ◇1	LM ◇1	VT ◇1 ⊡	VT ◇1 ⊡	LM 1	LM 1	VT ◇1 ⊡
Wolverhampton 7 d					11 45													12 45			
Sandwell & Dudley d					11 56													12 56			
Birmingham New Street 12 d	11 30	10 53	11 13		12 10				11 33		11 50			12 30	11 53	12 13		13 10			
Birmingham International ✈ d	11 40	11 05	11 29		12 20				11 45		12 00			12 40	12 05	12 29		13 20			
Coventry d	11 51	11 21	11 48		12 31				12 01		12 11			12 51	12 21	12 48		13 31			
Nuneaton d										12 02											
Rugby d		11 32	11 59						12 12	12 20	12 23				12 32	12 59					
Northampton d		12 05	12 25						12 50						13 05	13 25					
Wolverton d		12 17	12 37												13 17	13 37					
Milton Keynes Central 10 a	12 18	12 20	12 41						13 04					13 18	13 20	13 41					
d	12 19	12 22	12 41	12 47			12 47	13 02	13 05				13 13	13 19	13 22	13 41	13 47			13 47	14 02
Bletchley d		12 27	12 46				12 52						13 17		13 27	13 46				13 52	
Leighton Buzzard d		12 33	12 53				12 58						13 24		13 33	13 53				13 58	
Cheddington d							13 04													14 04	
Tring d						12 56	13 10					13 26	13 34						13 56	14 10	
Berkhamsted d		12 46				13 00	13 15					13 30	13 39		13 46				14 00	14 15	
Hemel Hempstead d		12 51				13 05	13 19					13 35	13 43		13 51				14 05	14 19	
Apsley d						13 08						13 38							14 08		
Kings Langley d						13 11						13 41							14 11		
Watford Junction a		12 58			13s15	13 16	13 26		13 30			13 46	13 51		13 58			14s15	14 16	14 26	
d		12 59				13 16	13 27		13 31			13 46	13 52		13 59				14 16	14 27	
Bushey d						13 19						13 49							14 19		
Harrow & Wealdstone ⊖ d						13 24						13 54	13 59						14 24		
Wembley Central ⊖ d													14 04								
Shepherd's Bush a													14 19								
Kensington (Olympia) ⊖ a													14 21								
West Brompton ⊖ a													14 24								
Imperial Wharf a													14 27								
Clapham Junction d													14 34								
East Croydon a													14 57								
London Euston 15 ⊖ a	12 54	13 17	13 27	13 23	13 34	13 38	13 47	13 38	13 49		13 14	14 08		13 54	14 17	14 27	14 23	14 34	14 38	14 45	14 38

Station	LM ◇1	LM ◇1	VT ◇1 ⊡	LM 1	SN 1	VT ◇1 ⊡	LM ◇1	LM ◇1	VT ◇1 ⊡	VT ◇1 ⊡	LM 1	LM 1	VT ◇1 ⊡	LM ◇1	LM ◇1	VT ◇1 ⊡	LM 1	SN 1	VT ◇1 ⊡	LM ◇1	LM ◇1	VT ◇1 ⊡
Wolverhampton 7 d										13 45												
Sandwell & Dudley d										13 56												
Birmingham New Street 12 d	12 33		12 50			13 30	12 53	13 13		14 10				13 33		13 50			14 30	13 53	14 13	
Birmingham International ✈ d	12 45		13 00			13 40	13 05	13 29		14 20				13 45		14 00			14 40	14 05	14 29	
Coventry d	13 01		13 11			13 51	13 21	13 48		14 31				14 01		14 11			14 51	14 21	14 48	
Nuneaton d		13 02													14 02							
Rugby d	13 12	13 20	13 23				13 32	13 59						14 12	14 20	14 23				14 32	14 59	
Northampton d	13 50						14 05	14 25						14 50						15 05	15 25	
Wolverton d							14 17	14 37												15 17	15 37	
Milton Keynes Central 10 a	14 04					14 18	14 20	14 41						15 04					15 18	15 20	15 41	
d	14 05				14 13	14 19	14 22	14 41	14 47			14 47	15 02	15 05				15 13	15 19	15 22	15 41	15 47
Bletchley d					14 17		14 27	14 46				14 52						15 17		15 27	15 46	
Leighton Buzzard d					14 24		14 33	14 53				14 58						15 24		15 33	15 53	
Cheddington d												15 04										
Tring d				14 26	14 34						14 56	15 10					15 26	15 34				
Berkhamsted d				14 30	14 39		14 46				15 00	15 15					15 30	15 39		15 46		
Hemel Hempstead d				14 35	14 43		14 51				15 05	15 19					15 35	15 43		15 51		
Apsley d				14 38							15 08						15 38					
Kings Langley d				14 41							15 11						15 41					
Watford Junction a	14 30			14 46	14 51		14 58			15s15	15 16	15 26		15 30			15 46	15 51		15 58		
d	14 31			14 46	14 52		14 59				15 16	15 27		15 31			15 46	15 52		15 59		
Bushey d				14 49							15 19						15 49					
Harrow & Wealdstone ⊖ d				14 54	14 59						15 24						15 54	15 59				
Wembley Central ⊖ d					15 04													16 04				
Shepherd's Bush a					15 19													16 19				
Kensington (Olympia) ⊖ a					15 21													16 21				
West Brompton ⊖ a					15 24													16 24				
Imperial Wharf a					15 27													16 27				
Clapham Junction d					15 34													16 34				
East Croydon a					15 57													16 57				
London Euston 15 ⊖ a	14 49		14 14	15 08		14 54	15 18	15 27	15 23	15 34	15 38	15 45	15 38	15 49		15 14	16 08		15 54	16 18	16 27	16 23

7 July to 8 September

West Midlands, Northampton, Milton Keynes Central and Watford Junction - London

Network Diagram - see first Page of Table 59

		VT	LM	LM	VT	LM	LM		VT	LM	SN	VT	LM	LM	VT	VT	LM		LM	VT	LM	LM	VT	LM	SN
		◇1 ☕	1	1	◇1 ☕	◇1	◇1		◇1 ☕	1	1	◇1 ☕	◇1	◇1	◇1 ☕	◇1 ☕	1		1	◇1 ☕	◇1	◇1	◇1 ☕	1	1
Wolverhampton 7	d	14 45														15 45									
Sandwell & Dudley	d	14 56														15 56									
Birmingham New Street 12	d	15 10				14 33			14 50			15 30	14 53	15 13		16 10					15 33		15 50		
Birmingham International ✈	d	15 20				14 45			15 00			15 40	15 05	15 29		16 20					15 45		16 00		
Coventry	d	15 31				15 01			15 11			15 51	15 21	15 48		16 31					16 01		16 11		
Nuneaton	d						15 02															16 02			
Rugby	d					15 12	15 20		15 23				15 32	15 59							16 12	16 20	16 23		
Northampton	d					15 50							16 05	16 25							16 50				
Wolverton	d												16 17	16 37											
Milton Keynes Central 10	a					16 04						16 18	16 20	16 41							17 04				
	d			15 47	16 02	16 05					16 13	16 19	16 22	16 41	16 47				16 47	17 02	17 05				17 13
Bletchley	d			15 52							16 17		16 27	16 46					16 52						17 17
Leighton Buzzard	d			15 58							16 24		16 33	16 53					16 58						17 24
Cheddington	d			16 04															17 04						
Tring	d		15 56	16 10						16 26	16 34						16 56		17 10					17 26	17 34
Berkhamsted	d		16 00	16 15						16 30	16 39		16 46				17 00		17 15					17 30	17 39
Hemel Hempstead	d		16 05	16 19						16 35	16 43		16 51				17 05		17 19					17 35	17 43
Apsley	d		16 08							16 38							17 08							17 38	
Kings Langley	d		16 11							16 41							17 11							17 41	
Watford Junction	a	16s15	16 16	16 26		16 30				16 46	16 51		16 58			17s15	17 16		17 26		17 30			17 46	17 51
	d		16 16	16 27		16 31				16 46	16 52		16 59				17 16		17 27		17 31			17 46	17 52
Bushey	d		16 19							16 49							17 19							17 49	
Harrow & Wealdstone ⊖	d		16 24							16 54	16 59						17 24							17 54	17 59
Wembley Central ⊖	d										17 04														18 04
Shepherd's Bush	a										17 19														18 19
Kensington (Olympia) ⊖	a										17 21														18 21
West Brompton ⊖	a										17 24														18 24
Imperial Wharf	a										17 27														18 27
Clapham Junction	d										17 34														18 34
East Croydon	a										17 57														18 57
London Euston 15 ⊖	a	16 34	16 38	16 45	16 38	16 49			16 14	17 08		16 54	17 17	17 27	17 23	17 34	17 38		17 45	17 38	17 49		17 14	18 08	

		VT	LM		LM	VT	VT	LM	LM	VT	LM	LM	VT		LM	SN	VT	LM	VT	VT	LM	LM	LM	LM
		◇1 ☕	◇1		◇1	◇1 ☕	◇1 ☕	1	1	◇1 ☕	◇1	◇1	◇1 ☕		1	1	◇1 ☕	◇1	◇1 ☕	◇1 ☕	1	◇1	◇1	◇1
Wolverhampton 7	d						16 45													17 45				
Sandwell & Dudley	d						16 56													17 56				
Birmingham New Street 12	d	16 30	15 53		16 13		17 10				16 33		16 50				17 30	16 53		18 10		17 13	17 33	
Birmingham International ✈	d	16 40	16 05		16 29		17 20				16 45		17 00				17 40	17 05		18 20		17 30	17 45	
Coventry	d	16 51	16 21		16 48		17 31				17 01		17 11				17 51	17 21		18 31		17 48	18 01	
Nuneaton	d											17 02												18 02
Rugby	d		16 32		16 59						17 12	17 20	17 23					17 32				17 59	18 12	18 20
Northampton	d		17 05		17 25						17 50							18 05				18 31	18 50	
Wolverton	d		17 17		17 37													18 17				18 43		
Milton Keynes Central 10	a	17 18	17 20		17 41						18 05						18 18	18 20				18 46	19 04	
	d	17 19	17 22		17 41	17 47			17 47	18 02	18 05					18 13	18 19	18 22	18 47			18 47	19 05	
Bletchley	d		17 27		17 46				17 52							18 17		18 27				18 52		
Leighton Buzzard	d		17 33		17 53				17 58							18 24		18 33				18 58		
Cheddington	d								18 04													19 04		
Tring	d							17 56	18 10						18 26	18 34					18 56	19 10		
Berkhamsted	d		17 46					18 00	18 15						18 30	18 39		18 46			19 00	19 15		
Hemel Hempstead	d		17 51					18 05	18 19						18 35	18 43		18 51			19 05	19 19		
Apsley	d							18 08							18 38						19 08			
Kings Langley	d							18 11							18 41						19 11			
Watford Junction	a		17 58				18s15	18 16	18 26		18 31				18 46	18 51		18 58		19s15	19 16	19 26	19 30	
	d		17 59					18 16	18 27		18 31				18 46	18 52		18 59			19 16	19 27	19 31	
Bushey	d							18 19							18 49						19 19			
Harrow & Wealdstone ⊖	d							18 24							18 54	18 59					19 24			
Wembley Central ⊖	d															19 04								
Shepherd's Bush	a															19 19								
Kensington (Olympia) ⊖	a															19 21								
West Brompton ⊖	a															19 24								
Imperial Wharf	a															19 27								
Clapham Junction	d															19 34								
East Croydon	a															19 57								
London Euston 15 ⊖	a	17 52	18 17		18 27	18 23	18 34	18 38	18 45	18 38	18 49		18 14		19 08		18 54	19 17	19 23	19 34	19 38	19 45	19 49	

7 July to 8 September

West Midlands, Northampton, Milton Keynes Central and Watford Junction - London

Network Diagram - see first Page of Table 59

		VT	SN	LM	SN	VT	LM	LM	LM	VT		VT	LM	VT	SN	VT	LM	LM	LM	VT		VT	SN	LM	VT
		◇1 ☕	1	1	1	◇1 ☕	◇1	1	◇1	◇1 ☕		◇1 ☕	◇1	◇1 ☕	1	◇1 ☕	◇1	1	◇1	◇1 ☕		◇1 ☕	1	◇1	◇1 ☕
Wolverhampton 7	d													18 45						19 45					
Sandwell & Dudley	d													18 56						19 56					
Birmingham New Street 12	d	17 50				18 30	17 53		18 13	18 50			18 53	19 10			19 13		19 53	20 10					
Birmingham International ✈	d	18 00				18 40	18 05		18 29	19 00			19 05	19 20			19 29		20 05	20 20					
Coventry	d	18 11				18 51	18 21		18 48	19 11			19 21	19 31			19 48		20 21	20 31					
Nuneaton	d																								
Rugby	d	18 23					18 32		18 59	19 23			19 32	19 44			19 59		20 32	20 43					
Northampton	d						19 05		19 31				20 00				20 32		21 00					21 20	
Wolverton	d						19 17		19 43				20 12						21 12						
Milton Keynes Central 10	a					19 18	19 20		19 46				20 15	20 05			20 47		21 15	21 04				21 34	
	d				19 13	19 19	19 22		19 47			19 46	20 16	20 07		20 43	20 47	20 50	21 16	21 05		21 11		21 34	21 52
Bletchley	d				19 17		19 27		19 52				20 21					20 55						21 39	
Leighton Buzzard	d				19 24		19 33		19 58				20 27				20 56							21 46	
Cheddington	d								20 04								21 03							21 51	
Tring	d			19 24	19 34			19 58	20 10								21 08	21 12						21 58	
Berkhamsted	d			19 28	19 39		19 46	20 02	20 15									21 17	21 38					22 02	
Hemel Hempstead	d			19 33	19 43		19 51	20 07	20 19								21 15	21 21	21 42					22 07	
Apsley	d			19 36				20 10									21 18							22 10	
Kings Langley	d			19 39				20 13									21 21							22 13	
Watford Junction	a			19 44	19 50		19 58	20 18	20 26				20 50	20s34		21s15	21 26	21 30	21 49	21s34				22 18	
	d		19 31	19 44	19 51		20 03	20 19	20 27				20 51		20 43		21 27	21 30	21 51				21 43	22 19	
Bushey	d			19 47														21s33							
Harrow & Wealdstone ⊖	d		19 38	19 52	19 58			20 25							20 50			21 38					21 50		
Wembley Central ⊖	d		19 43																						
Shepherd's Bush	a		19 57		20 19										21 07								22 07		
Kensington (Olympia) ⊖	a		19 59		20 21										21 09								22 09		
West Brompton ⊖	a		20 02		20 24										21 12								22 12		
Imperial Wharf	a		20 05		20 27										21 15								22 15		
Clapham Junction	d		20a10		20 34										21a20								22a20		
East Croydon	a				20 59																				
London Euston 15 ⊖	a	19 14		20 06		19 54	20 21	20 39	20 45	20 15		20 24	21 09	20 55		21 38	21 45	21 52	22 11	21 56		22 00		22 37	22 44

		LM	VT	VT	SN	VT		SN	LM	LM
		◇1	◇1 ☕	◇1 ☕	1	◇1 ☕		1	◇1	◇1
Wolverhampton 7	d		20 45			21 07				
Sandwell & Dudley	d		20 56			21 17				
Birmingham New Street 12	d	20 53	21 10			21 30			21 53	
Birmingham International ✈	d	21 05	21 20			21 40			22 05	
Coventry	d	21 21	21 31			21 51			22 21	
Nuneaton	d									
Rugby	d	21 32	21 43			22 03			22 32	
Northampton	d	22 05							22 55	23 30
Wolverton	d	22 17							23 07	23 42
Milton Keynes Central 10	a	22 20	22 04			22 28			23 10	23 45
	d	22 21	22 05	22 11		22 29			23 11	23 46
Bletchley	d	22 26							23 16	23 51
Leighton Buzzard	d	22 32							23 22	23 57
Cheddington	d	22 37							23 27	
Tring	d	22 44							23 36	
Berkhamsted	d	22 49							23 41	
Hemel Hempstead	d	22 53							23 45	
Apsley	d	22 56							23 49	
Kings Langley	d	23 00							23 52	
Watford Junction	a	23 06	22s34	22s40		23s11			23 56	00 19
	d	23 07			22 48			23 25	23 57	00 20
Bushey	d									
Harrow & Wealdstone ⊖	d	23 13			22 55			23 31	00 03	
Wembley Central ⊖	d									
Shepherd's Bush	a				23 14			23 48		
Kensington (Olympia) ⊖	a				23 16			23 51		
West Brompton ⊖	a				23 19			23 54		
Imperial Wharf	a				23 21			23 57		
Clapham Junction	d				23a26			00a02		
East Croydon	a									
London Euston 15 ⊖	a	23 27	22 55	23 02		23 30			00 17	00 40

Table 66

Saturdays from 15 September

West Midlands, Northampton, Milton Keynes Central and Watford Junction - London

Network Diagram - see first Page of Table 59

	SN	SN	LM	VT	LM	VT	VT	LM	LM	SN	LM	SR	LM	VT	SN	LM	LM	LM	VT	VT	VT	VT
						A	B															
Wolverhampton d				21p45		22p45	22p45												05 45		06 06	
Sandwell & Dudley d				21p56		22p55	22p55												05 56		06 17	
Birmingham New Street d			21p33	22p10		23p10	23p10							05 50					06 10		06 30	
Birmingham International d			21p45	22p22		23p20	23p20							06 00					06 20		06 40	
Coventry d			22p01	22p32		23p31	23p31							06 10					06 31		06 51	
Nuneaton d																						06 59
Rugby d			22p12	22p43		23p44	23p44							06 24						06 51		
Northampton d			22p55		23p46	00s05	00s05				05 16					06 05						
Wolverton d			23p07		00 02						05 28					06 17						
Milton Keynes Central a			23p12	23b05	00 05	00s23	00s23				05 31					06 20			06 58	07 11		
d	22p11		23p13		00 06			03 40	04 35		05 32					06 22		06 47	06 59	07 12		
Bletchley d	22p15		23p18		00 11			03 45	04 40		05 37		06 10			06 27	06 40	06 52				
Leighton Buzzard d	22p22		23p24		00 17			03 51	04 46		05 43		06 17			06 33	06 47	06 58				
Cheddington d			23p29		00 24						05 49							07 04				
Tring d	22p34		23p38		00 30			04 03	04 58		05 55		06 26			06 43	06 56	07 10				
Berkhamsted d	22p39		23p43		00 34			04 08	05 03		06 00		06 31			06 47	07 01	07 15				
Hemel Hempstead d	22p43		23p47		00 39			04 12	05 07		06 04		06 35			06 52	07 05	07 19				
Apsley d			23p50								06 07		06 38				07 08					
Kings Langley d			23p53								06 10		06 41				07 11					
Watford Junction a	22p52		23p58	23b37	00 46	00s52	00s52	04 19	05 14		06 15		06 46			06 59	07 16	07 26	07s19	07s32	07s36	07s44
d	22p53	23p29	23p58		00 47			04 20	05 15	05 52	06 16		06 47		06 55	07 01	07 17	07 27				
Bushey d			00 01								06 18		06 49				07 20					
Harrow & Wealdstone d	23p00	23p35	00 06		00 53			04 26	05 21	05 58	06 24		06 55		07 01		07 25					
Wembley Central d					00 57			04 34	05 25						07 06							
Shepherd's Bush a	23p21	23p53								06 20					07 19							
Kensington (Olympia) a	23p23	23p56								06 22					07 21							
West Brompton a	23p26	23p59								06 25					07 24							
Imperial Wharf a	23p28	00 02								06 28					07 27							
Clapham Junction d	23p40	00a07								06 34					07 34							
East Croydon a	00 01									06 57					07 57							
London Euston a			00 21	00 04	01 09	01 13	01 15	04 46	05 41		06 38	06 50	07 09	07 16		07 20	07 39	07 45	07 38	07 52	07 55	08 05

	LM	SN	LM	VT	VT	VT	VT	LM	LM	LM	LM	SN	VT	LM	VT	LM	VT	LM	VT	LM	LM	LM
Wolverhampton d					06 27		06 45						07 04						07 45			
Sandwell & Dudley d					06 37		06 56						07 15						07 56			
Birmingham New Street d					06 50		07 10						07 30	06 53		07 13			08 10		07 33	
Birmingham International d					07 00		07 20						07 40	07 05		07 29			08 20		07 45	
Coventry d					07 11		07 31						07 52	07 21		07 48			08 31		08 01	
Nuneaton d																						08 02
Rugby d					07 23									07 32	07 54	07 59					08 12	08 20
Northampton d			07 05							07 33				08 05		08 25						08 50
Wolverton d			07 17							07 45				08 17		08 37						
Milton Keynes Central a			07 20							07 49			08 18	08 20		08 41						09 04
d		07 13	07 22	07 32		07 38			07 44	07 49		08 13	08 19	08 22		08 41	08 47			08 47		09 05
Bletchley d	07 10	07 17	07 27						07 49	07 54		08 17		08 27		08 46				08 52		
Leighton Buzzard d	07 17	07 24	07 33						07 55	08 01		08 24		08 33		08 53				08 58		
Cheddington d									08 01											09 04		
Tring d	07 26	07 34						07 56	08 07		08 26	08 34						08 56		09 10		
Berkhamsted d	07 31	07 39	07 46					08 00	08 11		08 30	08 39		08 46				09 00		09 15		
Hemel Hempstead d	07 35	07 43	07 51					08 05	08 16		08 35	08 43		08 51				09 05		09 19		
Apsley d	07 38							08 08			08 38							09 08				
Kings Langley d	07 41							08 11			08 41							09 11				
Watford Junction a	07 46	07 51	07 58				08s15	08 16	08 23	08 20	08 46	08 51		08 58				09 16	09s17	09 26		09 33
d	07 47	07 52	07 59					08 16	08 24	08 20	08 46	08 52		08 59				09 16		09 27		09 34
Bushey d	07 49							08 19			08 49							09 19				
Harrow & Wealdstone d	07 55	07 59						08 24			08 54	08 59						09 24				
Wembley Central d		08 04										09 04										
Shepherd's Bush a		08 19										09 19										
Kensington (Olympia) a		08 21										09 21										
West Brompton a		08 24										09 24										
Imperial Wharf a		08 27										09 27										
Clapham Junction d		08 34										09 34										
East Croydon a		08 57										09 57										
London Euston a	08 09		08 17	08 09	08 14	08 14	08 34	08 38	08 42	08 38	09 08		08 54	09 17	08 46	09 27	09 23	09 38	09 35	09 45		09 50

A 15 September

B not 15 September

b Previous night, stops to set down only

Table 66

Saturdays from 15 September

West Midlands, Northampton, Milton Keynes Central and Watford Junction - London

Network Diagram - see first Page of Table 59

	VT	LM	SN	VT	VT	LM	LM	VT	VT	LM	LM	VT	LM	LM	VT	LM	SN	VT	VT	LM	LM
Wolverhampton d				08 06					08 45												
Sandwell & Dudley d									08 56												
Birmingham New Street d	07 50			08 30		07 53	08 13		09 10				08 33		08 50			09 30		08 53	09 13
Birmingham International d	08 00			08 40		08 05	08 29		09 20				08 45		09 00			09 40		09 05	09 29
Coventry d	08 11			08 51		08 21	08 48		09 31				09 01		09 11			09 51		09 21	09 48
Nuneaton d					08 59									09 02					09 59		
Rugby d	08 23					08 32	08 59						09 12	09 20	09 23					09 32	09 59
Northampton d						09 05	09 25							09 50						10 05	10 25
Wolverton d						09 17	09 37													10 17	10 37
Milton Keynes Central a				09 18		09 20	09 41							10 04				10 18		10 20	10 41
d			09 13	09 19		09 22	09 41	09 47			09 47	10 02		10 05			10 13	10 19		10 22	10 41
Bletchley d			09 17			09 27	09 46				09 52						10 17			10 27	10 46
Leighton Buzzard d			09 24			09 33	09 53				09 58						10 24			10 33	10 53
Cheddington d											10 04										
Tring d		09 26	09 34							09 56	10 10					10 26	10 34				
Berkhamsted d		09 30	09 39			09 46				10 00	10 15					10 30	10 39			10 46	
Hemel Hempstead d		09 35	09 43			09 51				10 05	10 19					10 35	10 43			10 51	
Apsley d		09 38								10 08						10 38					
Kings Langley d		09 41								10 11						10 41					
Watford Junction a		09 46	09 51			09 58			10s15	10 16	10 26			10 30		10 46	10 51			10 58	
d		09 46	09 52			09 59				10 16	10 27			10 31		10 46	10 52			10 59	
Bushey d		09 49								10 19						10 49					
Harrow & Wealdstone d		09 54	09 59							10 24						10 54	10 59				
Wembley Central d			10 04														11 04				
Shepherd's Bush a			10 19														11 19				
Kensington (Olympia) a			10 21														11 21				
West Brompton a			10 24														11 24				
Imperial Wharf a			10 27														11 27				
Clapham Junction d			10 34														11 34				
East Croydon a			10 57														11 57				
London Euston a	09 14	10 08		09 55	10 00	10 17	10 27	10 23	10 34	10 38	10 45	10 37		10 49	10 14	11 08		10 54	11 01	11 17	11 27

	VT	VT	LM	LM	VT	LM	LM	VT	LM	SN	VT	LM	LM	VT	VT	LM	LM	VT	LM	LM	VT	LM
Wolverhampton d		09 45													10 45							
Sandwell & Dudley d		09 56													10 56							
Birmingham New Street d		10 10				09 33		09 50			10 30	09 53	10 13		11 10				10 33		10 50	
Birmingham International d		10 20				09 45		10 00			10 40	10 05	10 29		11 20				10 45		11 00	
Coventry d		10 31				10 01		10 11			10 51	10 21	10 48		11 31				11 01		11 11	
Nuneaton d							10 02													11 02		
Rugby d						10 12	10 20	10 23				10 32	10 59						11 12	11 20	11 23	
Northampton d							10 50					11 05	11 25							11 50		
Wolverton d												11 17	11 37									
Milton Keynes Central a							11 04				11 18	11 20	11 41							12 04		
d	10 47			10 47	11 02		11 05			11 13	11 19	11 22	11 41	11 47			11 47	12 02		12 05		
Bletchley d				10 52						11 17		11 27	11 46				11 52					
Leighton Buzzard d				10 58						11 24		11 33	11 53				11 58					
Cheddington d				11 04													12 04					
Tring d			10 56	11 10					11 26	11 34						11 56	12 10					12 26
Berkhamsted d			11 00	11 15					11 30	11 39		11 46				12 00	12 15					12 30
Hemel Hempstead d			11 05	11 19					11 35	11 43		11 51				12 05	12 19					12 35
Apsley d			11 08						11 38							12 08						12 38
Kings Langley d			11 11						11 41							12 11						12 41
Watford Junction a		11s15	11 16	11 26			11 30		11 46	11 51		11 58			12s15	12 16	12 26			12 30		12 46
d			11 16	11 27			11 31		11 46	11 52		11 59				12 16	12 27			12 31		12 46
Bushey d			11 19						11 49							12 19						12 49
Harrow & Wealdstone d			11 24						11 54	11 59						12 24						12 54
Wembley Central d										12 04												
Shepherd's Bush a										12 19												
Kensington (Olympia) a										12 21												
West Brompton a										12 24												
Imperial Wharf a										12 27												
Clapham Junction d										12 34												
East Croydon a										12 57												
London Euston a	11 23	11 34	11 38	11 45	11 38		11 49	11 14	12 08		11 54	12 17	12 27	12 23	12 34	12 38	12 45	12 38		12 49	12 14	13 08

West Midlands, Northampton, Milton Keynes Central and Watford Junction - London

Network Diagram - see first Page of Table 59

		SN	VT	LM	LM	VT	VT	LM	LM	VT	LM	LM	VT	LM	SN	VT	LM	LM	VT	VT	LM	LM
		1	◇1 ☕	◇1	◇1	◇1 ☕	◇1 ☕	1	1	◇1 ☕	◇1	◇1	◇1 ☕	1	1	◇1 ☕	◇1	◇1	◇1 ☕	◇1 ☕	1	1
Wolverhampton 7	d						11 45													12 45		
Sandwell & Dudley	d						11 56													12 56		
Birmingham New Street 12	d		11 30	10 53	11 13		12 10				11 33		11 50			12 30	11 53	12 13		13 10		
Birmingham International	d		11 40	11 05	11 29		12 20				11 45		12 00			12 40	12 05	12 29		13 20		
Coventry	d		11 51	11 21	11 48		12 31				12 01		12 11			12 51	12 21	12 48		13 31		
Nuneaton	d											12 02										
Rugby	d			11 32	11 59						12 12	12 20	12 23				12 32	12 59				
Northampton	d			12 05	12 25						12 50						13 05	13 25				
Wolverton	d			12 17	12 37												13 17	13 37				
Milton Keynes Central 10	a		12 18	12 20	12 41						13 04					13 18	13 20	13 41				
	d	12 13	12 19	12 22	12 41	12 47			12 47	13 02	13 05				13 13	13 19	13 22	13 41	13 47			13 47
Bletchley	d	12 17		12 27	12 46				12 52						13 17		13 27	13 46				13 52
Leighton Buzzard	d	12 24		12 33	12 53				12 58						13 24		13 33	13 53				13 58
Cheddington	d								13 04													14 04
Tring	d	12 34						12 56	13 10					13 26	13 34						13 56	14 10
Berkhamsted	d	12 39		12 46				13 00	13 15					13 30	13 39		13 46				14 00	14 15
Hemel Hempstead	d	12 43		12 51				13 05	13 19					13 35	13 43		13 51				14 05	14 19
Apsley	d							13 08						13 38							14 08	
Kings Langley	d							13 11						13 41							14 11	
Watford Junction	a	12 51		12 58			13s15	13 16	13 26		13 30			13 46	13 51		13 58			14s15	14 16	14 26
	d	12 52		12 59				13 16	13 27		13 31			13 46	13 52		13 59				14 16	14 27
Bushey	d							13 19						13 49							14 19	
Harrow & Wealdstone ⊖	d	12 59						13 24						13 54	13 59						14 24	
Wembley Central ⊖	d	13 04													14 04							
Shepherd's Bush	a	13 19													14 19							
Kensington (Olympia) ⊖	a	13 21													14 21							
West Brompton ⊖	a	13 24													14 24							
Imperial Wharf	a	13 27													14 27							
Clapham Junction	d	13 34													14 34							
East Croydon	a	13 57													14 57							
London Euston 15 ⊖	a		12 54	13 17	13 27	13 23	13 34	13 38	13 47	13 38	13 49		13 14	14 08		13 54	14 17	14 27	14 23	14 34	14 38	14 45

		VT	LM	LM	VT	LM	SN	VT	LM	LM	VT	VT	LM	LM	VT	LM	LM	VT	LM	SN	VT	LM	LM
		◇1 ☕	◇1	◇1	◇1 ☕	1	1	◇1 ☕	◇1	◇1	◇1 ☕	◇1 ☕	1	1	◇1 ☕	◇1	◇1	◇1 ☕	1	1	◇1 ☕	◇1	◇1
Wolverhampton 7	d											13 45											
Sandwell & Dudley	d											13 56											
Birmingham New Street 12	d		12 33		12 50			13 30	12 53	13 13		14 10				13 33		13 50			14 30	13 53	14 13
Birmingham International	d		12 45		13 00			13 40	13 05	13 29		14 20				13 45		14 00			14 40	14 05	14 29
Coventry	d		13 01		13 11			13 51	13 21	13 48		14 31				14 01		14 11			14 51	14 21	14 48
Nuneaton	d			13 02													14 02						
Rugby	d		13 12	13 20	13 23				13 32	13 59						14 12	14 20	14 23				14 32	14 59
Northampton	d		13 50						14 05	14 25						14 50						15 05	15 25
Wolverton	d								14 17	14 37												15 17	15 37
Milton Keynes Central 10	a		14 04					14 18	14 20	14 41						15 04					15 18	15 20	15 41
	d	14 02	14 05				14 13	14 19	14 22	14 41	14 47			14 47	15 02	15 05				15 13	15 19	15 22	15 41
Bletchley	d						14 17		14 27	14 46				14 52						15 17		15 27	15 46
Leighton Buzzard	d						14 24		14 33	14 53				14 58						15 24		15 33	15 53
Cheddington	d													15 04									
Tring	d					14 26	14 34						14 56	15 10					15 26	15 34			
Berkhamsted	d					14 30	14 39		14 46				15 00	15 15					15 30	15 39		15 46	
Hemel Hempstead	d					14 35	14 43		14 51				15 05	15 19					15 35	15 43		15 51	
Apsley	d					14 38							15 08						15 38				
Kings Langley	d					14 41							15 11						15 41				
Watford Junction	a		14 30			14 46	14 51		14 58			15s15	15 16	15 26		15 30			15 46	15 51		15 58	
	d		14 31			14 46	14 52		14 59				15 16	15 27		15 31			15 46	15 52		15 59	
Bushey	d					14 49							15 19						15 49				
Harrow & Wealdstone ⊖	d					14 54	14 59						15 24						15 54	15 59			
Wembley Central ⊖	d						15 04													16 04			
Shepherd's Bush	a						15 19													16 19			
Kensington (Olympia) ⊖	a						15 21													16 21			
West Brompton ⊖	a						15 24													16 24			
Imperial Wharf	a						15 27													16 27			
Clapham Junction	d						15 34													16 34			
East Croydon	a						15 57													16 57			
London Euston 15 ⊖	a	14 38	14 49		14 14	15 08		14 54	15 18	15 27	15 23	15 34	15 38	15 45	15 38	15 49		15 14	16 08		15 54	16 18	16 27

Table 59
Saturdays
from 15 September

West Midlands, Northampton, Milton Keynes Central and Watford Junction - London

Network Diagram - see first Page of Table 59

		VT	VT	LM	LM	VT	LM	LM	VT	LM	SN	VT	LM	LM	VT	VT	LM	LM	VT	LM	LM	VT	LM
		◇1 ☕	◇1 ☕	1	1	◇1 ☕	◇1	◇1	◇1 ☕	1	1	◇1 ☕	◇1	◇1	◇1 ☕	◇1 ☕	1	1	◇1 ☕	◇1	◇1	◇1 ☕	1
Wolverhampton 7	d		14 45													15 45							
Sandwell & Dudley	d		14 56													15 56							
Birmingham New Street 12	d		15 10				14 33		14 50			15 30	14 53	15 13		16 10				15 33		15 50	
Birmingham International	d		15 20				14 45		15 00			15 40	15 05	15 29		16 20				15 45		16 00	
Coventry	d		15 31				15 01		15 11			15 51	15 21	15 48		16 31				16 01		16 11	
Nuneaton	d							15 02													16 02		
Rugby	d						15 12	15 20	15 23				15 32	15 59						16 12	16 20	16 23	
Northampton	d						15 50						16 05	16 25						16 50			
Wolverton	d												16 17	16 37									
Milton Keynes Central 10	a						16 04					16 18	16 20	16 41						17 04			
	d	15 47			15 47	16 02	16 05				16 13	16 19	16 22	16 41	16 47			16 47	17 02	17 05			
Bletchley	d				15 52						16 17		16 27	16 46				16 52					
Leighton Buzzard	d				15 58						16 24		16 33	16 53				16 58					
Cheddington	d				16 04													17 04					
Tring	d			15 56	16 10					16 26	16 34						16 56	17 10					17 26
Berkhamsted	d			16 00	16 15					16 30	16 39		16 46				17 00	17 15					17 30
Hemel Hempstead	d			16 05	16 19					16 35	16 43		16 51				17 05	17 19					17 35
Apsley	d			16 08						16 38							17 08						17 38
Kings Langley	d			16 11						16 41							17 11						17 41
Watford Junction	a		16s15	16 16	16 26		16 30			16 46	16 51		16 58			17s15	17 16	17 26		17 30			17 46
	d			16 16	16 27		16 31			16 46	16 52		16 59				17 16	17 27		17 31			17 46
Bushey	d			16 19						16 49							17 19						17 49
Harrow & Wealdstone ⊖	d			16 24						16 54	16 59						17 24						17 54
Wembley Central ⊖	d										17 04												
Shepherd's Bush	a										17 19												
Kensington (Olympia) ⊖	a										17 21												
West Brompton ⊖	a										17 24												
Imperial Wharf	a										17 27												
Clapham Junction	d										17 34												
East Croydon	a										17 57												
London Euston 15 ⊖	a	16 23	16 34	16 38	16 45	16 38	16 49		16 14	17 08		16 54	17 17	17 27	17 23	17 34	17 38	17 45	17 38	17 49		17 14	18 08

		SN	VT	LM	LM	VT	VT	LM	LM	VT	LM	LM	VT	LM	SN	VT	LM	VT	VT	LM	LM
		1	◇1 ☕	◇1	◇1	◇1 ☕	◇1 ☕	1	1	◇1 ☕	◇1	◇1	◇1 ☕	1	1	◇1 ☕	◇1	◇1 ☕	◇1 ☕	1	◇1
Wolverhampton 7	d						16 45												17 45		
Sandwell & Dudley	d						16 56												17 56		
Birmingham New Street 12	d		16 30	15 53	16 13		17 10				16 33		16 50			17 30	16 53		18 10		17 13
Birmingham International	d		16 40	16 05	16 29		17 20				16 45		17 00			17 40	17 05		18 20		17 30
Coventry	d		16 51	16 21	16 48		17 31				17 01		17 11			17 51	17 21		18 31		17 48
Nuneaton	d											17 02									
Rugby	d			16 32	16 59						17 12	17 20	17 23				17 32				17 59
Northampton	d			17 05	17 25						17 50						18 05				18 31
Wolverton	d			17 17	17 37												18 17				18 43
Milton Keynes Central 10	a		17 18	17 20	17 41						18 05					18 18	18 20				18 46
	d	17 13	17 19	17 22	17 41	17 47			17 47	18 02	18 05				18 13	18 19	18 22	18 47			18 47
Bletchley	d	17 17		17 27	17 46				17 52						18 17		18 27				18 52
Leighton Buzzard	d	17 24		17 33	17 53				17 58						18 24		18 33				18 58
Cheddington	d								18 04												19 04
Tring	d	17 34						17 56	18 10					18 26	18 34					18 56	19 10
Berkhamsted	d	17 39		17 46				18 00	18 15					18 30	18 39		18 46			19 00	19 15
Hemel Hempstead	d	17 43		17 51				18 05	18 19					18 35	18 43		18 51			19 05	19 19
Apsley	d							18 08						18 38						19 08	
Kings Langley	d							18 11						18 41						19 11	
Watford Junction	a	17 51		17 58			18s15	18 16	18 26		18 31			18 46	18 51		18 58		19s15	19 16	19 26
	d	17 52		17 59				18 16	18 27		18 31			18 46	18 52		18 59			19 16	19 27
Bushey	d							18 19						18 49						19 19	
Harrow & Wealdstone ⊖	d	17 59						18 24						18 54	18 59					19 24	
Wembley Central ⊖	d	18 04													19 04						
Shepherd's Bush	a	18 19													19 19						
Kensington (Olympia) ⊖	a	18 21													19 21						
West Brompton ⊖	a	18 24													19 24						
Imperial Wharf	a	18 27													19 27						
Clapham Junction	d	18 34													19 34						
East Croydon	a	18 57													19 57						
London Euston 15 ⊖	a		17 52	18 17	18 27	18 23	18 34	18 38	18 45	18 38	18 49		18 14	19 08		18 54	19 17	19 23	19 34	19 38	19 45

Table 66

Saturdays from 15 September

West Midlands, Northampton, Milton Keynes Central and Watford Junction - London

Network Diagram - see first Page of Table 59

		LM	LM	VT	SN	LM	SN	VT	LM	LM		LM	VT	VT	LM	VT	SN	VT	LM	LM		LM	VT	VT	SN
		◇1	◇1	◇1	1	1	1	◇1	◇1	1		◇1	◇1	◇1	◇1	◇1	1	◇1	◇1	1		◇1	◇1	◇1	1
				☕				☕					☕	☕		☕		☕					☕	☕	
Wolverhampton 7 ⇌	d															18 45							19 45		
Sandwell & Dudley	d															18 56							19 56		
Birmingham New Street 12	d	17 33		17 50				18 30	17 53			18 13	18 50		18 53	19 10			19 13			19 53	20 10		
Birmingham International ✈	d	17 45		18 00				18 40	18 05			18 29	19 00		19 05	19 20			19 29			20 05	20 20		
Coventry	d	18 01		18 11				18 51	18 21			18 48	19 11		19 21	19 31			19 48			20 21	20 31		
Nuneaton	d		18 02																						
Rugby	d	18 12	18 20	18 23					18 32			18 59	19 23		19 32	19 44			19 59			20 32	20 43		
Northampton	d		18 50						19 05			19 31			20 00				20 32			21 00			
Wolverton	d								19 17			19 43			20 12							21 12			
Milton Keynes Central 10	a		19 04					19 18	19 20			19 46			20 15	20 05			20 47			21 15	21 04		
	d		19 05				19 13	19 19	19 22			19 47		19 46	20 16	20 07		20 43	20 47	20 50		21 16	21 05	21 11	
Bletchley	d						19 17		19 27			19 52			20 21					20 55					
Leighton Buzzard	d						19 24		19 33			19 58			20 27				20 56						
Cheddington	d											20 04							21 03						
Tring	d					19 24	19 34			19 58		20 10							21 08	21 12					
Berkhamsted	d					19 28	19 39		19 46	20 02		20 15								21 17		21 38			
Hemel Hempstead	d					19 33	19 43		19 51	20 07		20 19							21 15	21 21		21 42			
Apsley	d					19 36				20 10									21 18						
Kings Langley	d					19 39				20 13									21 21						
Watford Junction	a		19 30			19 44	19 50		19 58	20 18		20 26			20 50	20s34		21s15	21 26	21 30		21 49	21s34		
	d		19 31		19 31	19 44	19 51		20 03	20 19		20 27			20 51		20 43		21 27	21 30		21 51			21 43
Bushey	d					19 47														21s33					
Harrow & Wealdstone ⊖	d				19 38	19 52	19 58			20 25							20 50			21 38					21 50
Wembley Central ⊖	d				19 43																				
Shepherd's Bush	a				19 57		20 19										21 07								22 07
Kensington (Olympia) ⊖	a				19 59		20 21										21 09								22 09
West Brompton ⊖	a				20 02		20 24										21 12								22 12
Imperial Wharf	a				20 05		20 27										21 15								22 15
Clapham Junction	d				20a10		20 34										21a20								22a20
East Croydon ⇌	a						20 59																		
London Euston 15 ⊖	a		19 49	19 14		20 06		19 54	20 21	20 39		20 45	20 15	20 24	21 09	20 55		21 38	21 45	21 52		22 11	21 56	22 00	

		LM	VT	LM	VT	VT		SN	VT	SN	LM	LM
		◇1	◇1	◇1	◇1	◇1		1	◇1	1	◇1	◇1
			☕		☕	☕			☕			
Wolverhampton 7 ⇌	d				20 45				21 07			
Sandwell & Dudley	d				20 56				21 17			
Birmingham New Street 12	d			20 53	21 10				21 30		21 53	
Birmingham International ✈	d			21 05	21 20				21 40		22 05	
Coventry	d			21 21	21 31				21 51		22 21	
Nuneaton	d											
Rugby	d			21 32	21 43				22 03		22 32	
Northampton	d	21 20		22 05							22 55	23 30
Wolverton	d			22 17							23 07	23 42
Milton Keynes Central 10	a	21 34		22 20	22 04				22 28		23 10	23 45
	d	21 34	21 52	22 21	22 05	22 11			22 29		23 11	23 46
Bletchley	d	21 39		22 26							23 16	23 51
Leighton Buzzard	d	21 46		22 32							23 22	23 57
Cheddington	d	21 51		22 37							23 27	
Tring	d	21 58		22 44							23 36	
Berkhamsted	d	22 02		22 49							23 41	
Hemel Hempstead	d	22 07		22 53							23 45	
Apsley	d	22 10		22 56							23 49	
Kings Langley	d	22 13		23 00							23 52	
Watford Junction	a	22 18		23 06	22s34	22s40			23s11		23 56	00 19
	d	22 19		23 07				22 48		23 25	23 57	00 20
Bushey	d											
Harrow & Wealdstone ⊖	d			23 13				22 55		23 31	00 03	
Wembley Central ⊖	d											
Shepherd's Bush	a							23 14		23 48		
Kensington (Olympia) ⊖	a							23 16		23 51		
West Brompton ⊖	a							23 19		23 54		
Imperial Wharf	a							23 21		23 57		
Clapham Junction	d							23a26		00a02		
East Croydon ⇌	a											
London Euston 15 ⊖	a	22 37	22 44	23 27	22 55	23 02			23 30		00 17	00 40

Table 66

Sundays until 24 June

West Midlands, Northampton, Milton Keynes Central and Watford Junction - London

Network Diagram - see first Page of Table 59

		LM	LM	LM	LM	LM	LM	LM	SN	LM		LM	VT	SN	LM	VT	VT	VT	LM	LM		VT	VT	SN	VT
		◇1	◇1	1		1	1	◇1	1	◇1		◇1	◇1	1	◇1	◇1	◇1	◇1	◇1	◇1		◇1	◇1	1	◇1
					🚌								☕			☕	☕	☕				☕	☕		☕
Wolverhampton 7 ⇌	d												08 03									09 01			
Sandwell & Dudley	d																								
Birmingham New Street 12	d	21p53											08 30							09 14		09 30			
Birmingham International ✈	d	22p05											08 40							09 25		09 40			
Coventry	d	22p21											08 51							09 44		09 51			
Nuneaton	d																						09 55		
Rugby	d	22p32											09 04							09 55		10 04			10 33
Northampton	d	22p55	23p30		06 20			07 53		08 23		08 53			09 31				10 08	10 37					
Wolverton	d	23p07	23p42		06 52			08 05		08 37		09 05			09 43				10 20	10 51					
Milton Keynes Central 10	a	23p10	23p45		07 00			08 08		08 40		09 08	09 37		09 46				10 23	10 54		10 37			11 06
	d	23p11	23p46	06 42		07 11	07 40	08 09		08 41		09 09	09 39		09 47			10 19	10 24	10 55		10 39			11 08
Bletchley	d	23p16	23p51	06 47		07 16	07 45	08 14		08 46		09 14			09 52				10 29	11 00					
Leighton Buzzard	d	23p22	23p57	06 53		07 22	07 51	08 20		08 52		09 20			09 58				10 35	11 06					
Cheddington	d	23p27				07 27		08 25				09 25							10 44						
Tring	d	23p36				07 36		08 34				09 34							10 49						
Berkhamsted	d	23p41		07 08		07 41	08 06	08 39		09 07		09 38			10 13				10 54	11 21					
Hemel Hempstead	d	23p45		07 13		07 45	08 11	08 43		09 12		09 42			10 18				10 58	11 26					
Apsley	d	23p49		07 16			08 14			09 15					10 21					11 29					
Kings Langley	d	23p52		07 19			08 17			09 18					10 24					11 32					
Watford Junction	a	23p56	00 19	07 24		07 52	08 22	08 50		09 23		09 49	10s07		10 29				11 05	11 37		11s11	11s16		11s43
	d	23p57	00 20	07 24		07 53	08 22	08 53	09 17	09 23		09 53		10 17	10 29				11 05	11 37				11 22	
Bushey	d						08 25			09 26					10 32					11 40					
Harrow & Wealdstone ⊖	d	00 03		07 30		07 59	08 30	08 59	09 23	09 31		09 59		10 23	10 37				11 11	11 45				11 28	
Wembley Central ⊖	d																								
Shepherd's Bush	a								09 45					10 45										11 45	
Kensington (Olympia) ⊖	a								09 47					10 47										11 47	
West Brompton ⊖	a								09 50					10 50										11 50	
Imperial Wharf	a								09 53					10 53										11 53	
Clapham Junction	d								09a58					10a58										11a58	
East Croydon ⇌	a																								
London Euston 15 ⊖	a	00 17	00 40	07 44		08 13	08 44	09 13		09 45		10 13	10 28		10 51	10 57	11 02	11 06	11 25	11 59		11 31	11 37		12 05

		VT	LM	LM	VT	VT		SN	LM	VT	LM	VT	VT	LM	VT	LM		VT	VT	VT	VT	SN	LM	VT	LM
		◇1	◇1	◇1	◇1	◇1		1	◇1	◇1	1	◇1	◇1	1	◇1	◇1		◇1	◇1	◇1	◇1	1	◇1	◇1	1
		☕			☕	☕				☕		☕	☕		☕			☕	☕	☕	☕			☕	
Wolverhampton 7 ⇌	d				09 51													10 51		11 42					
Sandwell & Dudley	d																								
Birmingham New Street 12	d			10 14	10 30											11 14		11 30		12 10				11 50	
Birmingham International ✈	d			10 25	10 40											11 25		11 40		12 20				12 00	
Coventry	d			10 44	10 51											11 44		11 51		12 31				12 11	
Nuneaton	d					10 56			10 54				11 59								12 32		11 58		
Rugby	d			10 55	11 04				11 14	11 33						11 55		12 05					12 20	12 25	
Northampton	d		11 08	11 25					11 48							12 25							12 50		
Wolverton	d		11 20	11 37												12 37									
Milton Keynes Central 10	a		11 23	11 42	11 37	11 46			12 02	12 06						12 40		12 24			13 03		13 04		
	d	11 17	11 24	11 42	11 39	11 47			12 03	12 07				12 12	12 22	12 41		12 26	12 52		13 04		13 06		
Bletchley	d		11 29	11 47							11 56			12 17		12 46									
Leighton Buzzard	d		11 35	11 54					12 11		12 02			12 23		12 52							13 15		
Cheddington	d		11 40								12 08			12 29											
Tring	d		11 49								12 14			12 35											13 15
Berkhamsted	d		11 53	12 06							12 19			12 39		13 05									13 19
Hemel Hempstead	d		11 58	12 10							12 23			12 44		13 10									13 24
Apsley	d										12 26														13 27
Kings Langley	d										12 29														13 30
Watford Junction	a		12 06	12 17	12s07				12 32		12 34		12s50	12 52		13 17				13s18			13 35		13 35
	d		12 06	12 18				12 22	12 32		12 34			12 52		13 17						13 22	13 35		13 35
Bushey	d										12 37														13 38
Harrow & Wealdstone ⊖	d		12 12	12 24				12 29			12 42			12 58		13 23						13 28			13 43
Wembley Central ⊖	d																								
Shepherd's Bush	a							12 45														13 45			
Kensington (Olympia) ⊖	a							12 47														13 47			
West Brompton ⊖	a							12 50														13 50			
Imperial Wharf	a							12 53														13 53			
Clapham Junction	d							12a58														13a58			
East Croydon ⇌	a																								
London Euston 15 ⊖	a	12 08	12 25	12 37	12 27	12 32			12 50	12 45	12 56	12 56	13 11	13 11	12 59	13 37		13 03	13 28	13 37	13 44		13 53	13 19	13 57

West Midlands, Northampton, Milton Keynes Central and Watford Junction - London

Network Diagram - see first Page of Table 59

		LM	VT	VT	LM	VT	VT	SN	LM	VT	LM	LM	VT	VT	LM	VT	SN	LM	VT	VT	LM	LM
Wolverhampton	d			12 42										13 42								
Sandwell & Dudley	d																					
Birmingham New Street	d		12 30	13 10	12 14					12 50			13 30	14 10	13 14				13 50			
Birmingham International	d		12 39	13 20	12 25					13 00			13 39	14 20	13 25				14 01			
Coventry	d		12 51	13 31	12 44					13 11			13 51	14 31	13 44				14 11			
Nuneaton	d								12 58									13 58		14 32		
Rugby	d				12 55				13 20	13 25					13 55			14 20	14 26			
Northampton	d				13 25				13 50						14 25			14 50				
Wolverton	d				13 37										14 37							
Milton Keynes Central	a		13 18		13 40				14 04				14 18		14 40			15 04		15 04		
	d	13 12	13 19		13 41	13 51	14 03		14 06			14 12	14 19		14 41	14 51		15 06		15 05		15 12
Bletchley	d	13 17			13 46							14 17			14 46							15 17
Leighton Buzzard	d	13 23			13 52				14 15			14 23			14 52			15 15				15 23
Cheddington	d	13 29										14 29										15 29
Tring	d	13 35									14 15	14 35									15 15	15 35
Berkhamsted	d	13 39			14 05						14 19	14 39			15 05						15 19	15 39
Hemel Hempstead	d	13 44			14 10						14 24	14 44			15 10						15 24	15 44
Apsley	d										14 27										15 27	
Kings Langley	d										14 30										15 30	
Watford Junction	a	13 52		14s16	14 17				14 35		14 35	14 52		15s16	15 17			15 35			15 35	15 52
	d	13 52			14 17			14 22	14 36		14 35	14 52			15 17		15 22	15 35			15 35	15 52
Bushey	d										14 38										15 38	
Harrow & Wealdstone	d	13 58			14 23			14 28			14 43	14 58			15 23		15 28				15 43	15 58
Wembley Central	d																					
Shepherd's Bush	a							14 45									15 45					
Kensington (Olympia)	a							14 47									15 47					
West Brompton	a							14 50									15 50					
Imperial Wharf	a							14 53									15 53					
Clapham Junction	d							14a58									15a58					
East Croydon	a																					
London Euston	a	14 11	13 57	14 37	14 37	14 27	14 43		14 53	14 17	14 57	15 11	14 57	15 37	15 37	15 27		15 53	15 17	15 45	15 57	16 11

		VT	VT	LM	VT	SN	LM	VT	VT	LM	LM	VT	VT	LM	VT	SN	LM	VT	VT	LM	LM	VT	VT
Wolverhampton	d		14 42										15 43										16 42
Sandwell & Dudley	d																						
Birmingham New Street	d	14 30	15 10	14 14				14 50				15 30	16 10	15 14				15 50				16 30	17 10
Birmingham International	d	14 39	15 20	14 25				15 01				15 39	16 20	15 25				16 01				16 39	17 20
Coventry	d	14 51	15 31	14 44				15 11				15 51	16 31	15 44				16 11				16 51	17 31
Nuneaton	d						14 58										15 58						
Rugby	d			14 55			15 20	15 26						15 55			16 20	16 24					
Northampton	d			15 25			15 50							16 25			16 50						
Wolverton	d			15 37										16 37									
Milton Keynes Central	a	15 18		15 40			16 04					16 18		16 40			17 04					17 18	
	d	15 19		15 41	15 51		16 06		16 05		16 12	16 19		16 41	16 51		17 06		17 04		17 12	17 19	
Bletchley	d			15 46							16 17			16 46							17 17		
Leighton Buzzard	d			15 52			16 15				16 23			16 52			17 15				17 23		
Cheddington	d										16 29										17 29		
Tring	d									16 15	16 35									17 15	17 35		
Berkhamsted	d			16 05						16 19	16 39			17 05						17 19	17 39		
Hemel Hempstead	d			16 10						16 24	16 44			17 10						17 24	17 44		
Apsley	d									16 27										17 27			
Kings Langley	d									16 30										17 30			
Watford Junction	a		16s16	16 17			16 35			16 35	16 52		17s16	17 17			17 35			17 35	17 52		18s16
	d			16 17		16 22	16 35			16 35	16 52			17 17		17 22	17 35			17 35	17 52		
Bushey	d									16 38										17 38			
Harrow & Wealdstone	d			16 23		16 28				16 43	16 58			17 23		17 28				17 43	17 58		
Wembley Central	d																						
Shepherd's Bush	a					16 45										17 45							
Kensington (Olympia)	a					16 47										17 47							
West Brompton	a					16 50										17 50							
Imperial Wharf	a					16 53										17 53							
Clapham Junction	d					16a58										17a58							
East Croydon	a																						
London Euston	a	15 57	16 37	16 37	16 27		16 53	16 17	16 44	16 57	17 11	16 57	17 37	17 37	17 27		17 53	17 17	17 44	17 57	18 11	17 57	18 37

West Midlands, Northampton, Milton Keynes Central and Watford Junction - London

Network Diagram - see first Page of Table 59

		LM	VT	SN	LM	VT	VT	LM	LM	VT	VT	LM	VT	VT	SN	LM	VT	LM	LM	VT	VT	LM
Wolverhampton	d										17 43										18 43	
Sandwell & Dudley	d																					
Birmingham New Street	d	16 14				16 50				17 30	18 10	17 14					17 50			18 30	19 10	18 14
Birmingham International	d	16 25				17 01				17 39	18 20	17 25					18 01			18 39	19 20	18 25
Coventry	d	16 44				17 11				17 51	18 31	17 44					18 11			18 51	19 31	18 44
Nuneaton	d				16 58											18 03						
Rugby	d	16 55			17 20	17 26						17 55				18 20	18 26					18 55
Northampton	d	17 25			17 50							18 25				18 50						19 25
Wolverton	d	17 37										18 37										19 37
Milton Keynes Central	a	17 40			18 04					18 18		18 40				19 04				19 18		19 40
	d	17 41	17 51		18 06		18 05		18 12	18 19		18 41	18 51	19 03		19 06			19 12	19 19		19 41
Bletchley	d	17 46							18 17			18 46							19 17			19 46
Leighton Buzzard	d	17 52			18 15				18 23			18 52				19 15			19 23			19 52
Cheddington	d								18 29										19 29			
Tring	d							18 15	18 35									19 15	19 35			
Berkhamsted	d	18 05						18 19	18 39			19 05						19 19	19 39			20 05
Hemel Hempstead	d	18 10						18 24	18 44			19 10						19 24	19 44			20 10
Apsley	d							18 27										19 27				
Kings Langley	d							18 30										19 30				
Watford Junction	a	18 17			18 35			18 35	18 52		19s16	19 17				19 35		19 35	19 52		20s16	20 17
	d	18 17		18 22	18 35			18 35	18 52			19 17			19 22	19 35		19 35	19 52			20 17
Bushey	d							18 38										19 38				
Harrow & Wealdstone	d	18 23		18 28				18 43	18 58			19 23			19 28			19 43	19 58			20 23
Wembley Central	d																					
Shepherd's Bush	a			18 45											19 45							
Kensington (Olympia)	a			18 47											19 47							
West Brompton	a			18 50											19 50							
Imperial Wharf	a			18 53											19 53							
Clapham Junction	d			18a58											19a58							
East Croydon	a																					
London Euston	a	18 37	18 27		18 53	18 17	18 44	18 57	19 11	18 57	19 37	19 37	19 27	19 43		19 53	19 17	19 57	20 11	19 57	20 37	20 37

		VT	VT	SN	LM	VT	LM	LM	VT	SN	LM	VT	VT	LM	LM	LM	VT	VT	SN	VT	VT	LM	LM
Wolverhampton	d												19 43										
Sandwell & Dudley	d																						
Birmingham New Street	d					18 50			19 30		19 14		20 10			20 14	20 30						21 14
Birmingham International	d					19 01			19 39		19 25		20 20			20 25	20 40						21 25
Coventry	d					19 11			19 51		19 44		20 31			20 43	20 51						21 44
Nuneaton	d				18 58									20 03								20 57	
Rugby	d				19 20	19 26					19 55			20 19		20 55	21 05					21 19	21 55
Northampton	d				19 50						20 25			20 50		21 25						21 54	22 25
Wolverton	d				20 02						20 37			21 02		21 38						22 06	22 37
Milton Keynes Central	a				20 06				20 18		20 40			21 05		21 42	21 26					22 09	22 40
	d	19 51	20 04		20 06			20 12	20 19		20 41	20 48		21 06	21 15	21 42	21 28	21 38		21 57	22 04	22 10	22 41
Bletchley	d							20 17			20 46				21 20	21 47						22 15	22 46
Leighton Buzzard	d				20 15			20 23			20 52			21 14	21 26	21 54						22 21	22 52
Cheddington	d							20 28							21 31							22 26	
Tring	d						20 15	20 37							21 39							22 35	
Berkhamsted	d						20 19	20 42			21 07				21 43	22 09						22 40	23 05
Hemel Hempstead	d						20 24	20 46			21 11				21 48	22 13						22 44	23 10
Apsley	d						20 27				21 14					22 16							23 13
Kings Langley	d						20 30				21 17					22 19							23 16
Watford Junction	a				20 35		20 35	20 53			21 22		21s28	21 35	21 57	22 23	22s02			22s31		22 51	23 20
	d			20 22	20 35		20 35	20 54		21 17	21 22			21 36	21 58	22 24			22 17			22 52	23 21
Bushey	d						20 38								22 00							22 54	
Harrow & Wealdstone	d			20 28			20 43	21 00		21 23	21 28				22 05	22 30			22 23			23 00	23 27
Wembley Central	d																						
Shepherd's Bush	a			20 45						21 45									22 45				
Kensington (Olympia)	a			20 47						21 47									22 47				
West Brompton	a			20 50						21 50									22 50				
Imperial Wharf	a			20 53						21 53									22 53				
Clapham Junction	d			20a58						21a58									22a58				
East Croydon	a																						
London Euston	a	20 27	20 44		20 53	20 17	20 59	21 14	20 57		21 42	21 31	21 49	21 54	22 19	22 44	22 23	22 27		22 53	22 56	23 14	23 41

Table 66

Sundays until 24 June

West Midlands, Northampton, Milton Keynes Central and Watford Junction - London

Network Diagram - see first Page of Table 59

	VT	SN	VT	VT	LM	VT	VT
	◇1	1	◇1	◇1	◇1	◇1	◇1
Wolverhampton 7 d	20 50					21 50	22 33
Sandwell & Dudley d							
Birmingham New Street 12 d	21 30					22 30	23 00
Birmingham International d	21 40					22 40	23 10
Coventry d	21 51					22 51	23 21
Nuneaton d				22 18			
Rugby d	22 04			22 32		23 04	23 34
Northampton d					23 00		23s54
Wolverton d					23 12		
Milton Keynes Central 10 a	22 35			23 04	23 15	23 36	00s11
d	22 37		22 48	23 05	23 16	23 37	
Bletchley d					23 21		
Leighton Buzzard d					23 27		
Cheddington d					23 32		
Tring d					23 41		
Berkhamsted d					23 45		
Hemel Hempstead d					23 49		
Apsley d							
Kings Langley d							
Watford Junction a	23s05		23s25	23s34	23 56	00s06	00s41
d		23 17			23 57		
Bushey d					23 59		
Harrow & Wealdstone ⊖ d		23 23			00 05		
Wembley Central ⊖ d							
Shepherd's Bush a		23 45					
Kensington (Olympia) ⊖ a		23 47					
West Brompton ⊖ a		23 50					
Imperial Wharf a		23 53					
Clapham Junction d		00 05					
East Croydon a		00 22					
London Euston 15 ⊖ a	23 25		23 49	23 54	00 19	00 27	01 01

Sundays 1 July to 9 September

	LM	LM	LM	LM	LM	LM	LM	LM	LM	VT	VT	SN	LM	VT	LM	VT	SN	LM	VT	VT	VT	LM
	◇1	◇1	1 A	◇1 A	1	🚌	1	1	◇1	◇1 A	◇1 A	1	◇1	◇1 A	◇1	◇1	1	◇1	◇1	◇1	◇1	◇1
Wolverhampton 7 d										07 05						08 05						
Sandwell & Dudley d										07 15						08 15						
Birmingham New Street 12 d	21p53									07 30						08 30						
Birmingham International d	22p05									07 40						08 40						
Coventry d	22p21									07 51						08 51						
Nuneaton d											08 02											
Rugby d	22p32									08 03	08 18					09 04						
Northampton d	22p55	23p30		06 15		06 20			07 53				08 23		08 53			09 31				10 08
Wolverton d	23p07	23p42		06 29		06 52			08 05				08 37		09 05			09 43				10 20
Milton Keynes Central 10 a	23p10	23p45		06 32		07 00			08 08	08 33			08 40		09 08	09 37		09 46				10 23
d	23p11	23p46	06 15	06 33	06 42		07 11	07 40	08 09	08 34			08 41	08 57	09 09	09 39		09 47			10 19	10 24
Bletchley d	23p16	23p51	06 20	06 38	06 47		07 16	07 45	08 14				08 46		09 14			09 52				10 29
Leighton Buzzard d	23p22	23p57	06 26	06 44	06 53		07 22	07 51	08 20				08 52		09 20			09 58				10 35
Cheddington d	23p27		06 31				07 27		08 25						09 25							10 44
Tring d	23p36						07 36		08 34						09 34							10 49
Berkhamsted d	23p41		06 43	06 59	07 08		07 41	08 06	08 39				09 07		09 38			10 13				10 54
Hemel Hempstead d	23p45		06 47	07 03	07 13		07 45	08 11	08 43				09 12		09 42			10 18				10 58
Apsley d	23p49				07 16			08 14					09 15					10 21				
Kings Langley d	23p52				07 19			08 17					09 18					10 24				
Watford Junction a	23p56	00 19	06 54	07 10	07 24		07 52	08 22	08 50	08 59			09 23	09 20	09 49	10s07		10 29				11 05
d	23p57	00 20	06 55	07 11	07 24		07 53	08 22	08 53	09 00		09 17	09 23	09 21	09 53		10 17	10 29				11 05
Bushey d								08 25					09 26					10 32				
Harrow & Wealdstone ⊖ d	00 03		07 01		07 30		07 59	08 30	08 59			09 23	09 31		09 59		10 23	10 37				11 11
Wembley Central ⊖ d																						
Shepherd's Bush a												09 45					10 45					
Kensington (Olympia) ⊖ a												09 47					10 47					
West Brompton ⊖ a												09 50					10 50					
Imperial Wharf a												09 53					10 53					
Clapham Junction d												09a58					10a58					
East Croydon a																						
London Euston 15 ⊖ a	00 17	00 40	07 15	07 29	07 44		08 13	08 44	09 13	09 16	09 23		09 45	09 37	10 13	10 28		10 51	10 57	11 02	11 06	11 25

A 29 July, 5 August, 12 August, 2 September, 9 September

Table 66

Sundays 1 July to 9 September

West Midlands, Northampton, Milton Keynes Central and Watford Junction - London

Network Diagram - see first Page of Table 59

	LM	VT	VT	SN	VT	VT	LM	LM	VT	VT	SN	LM	VT	LM	VT	VT	LM	VT	LM	VT	VT	VT
	◇1	◇1	◇1	1	◇1	◇1	◇1	◇1	◇1	◇1	1	◇1	◇1	1	◇1	◇1	1	◇1	◇1	◇1	◇1	◇1
Wolverhampton 7 d		09 05							10 05											11 05		11 45
Sandwell & Dudley d		09 15							10 15											11 15		11 57
Birmingham New Street 12 d	09 14	09 30						10 14	10 30										11 14	11 30		12 10
Birmingham International d	09 25	09 40						10 25	10 40										11 25	11 40		12 20
Coventry d	09 44	09 51						10 44	10 51										11 44	11 51		12 31
Nuneaton d			09 55							10 56		10 54				11 59						
Rugby d	09 55	10 04			10 33			10 55	11 04			11 14	11 33						11 55	12 05		
Northampton d	10 37						11 08	11 25				11 48							12 25			
Wolverton d	10 51						11 20	11 37											12 37			
Milton Keynes Central 10 a	10 54	10 37			11 06		11 23	11 42	11 37	11 46		12 02	12 06						12 40	12 24		
d	10 55	10 39			11 08	11 17	11 24	11 42	11 39	11 47		12 03	12 07				12 12	12 22	12 41	12 26	12 52	
Bletchley d	11 00						11 29	11 47						11 56			12 17		12 46			
Leighton Buzzard d	11 06						11 35	11 54				12 11		12 02			12 23		12 52			
Cheddington d							11 40							12 08			12 29					
Tring d							11 49							12 14			12 35					
Berkhamsted d	11 21						11 53	12 06						12 19			12 39		13 05			
Hemel Hempstead d	11 26						11 58	12 10						12 23			12 44		13 10			
Apsley d	11 29													12 26								
Kings Langley d	11 32													12 29								
Watford Junction a	11 37	11s11	11s16		11s43		12 06	12 17	12s07			12 32		12 34		12s50	12 52		13 17			13s18
d	11 37			11 22			12 06	12 18			12 22	12 32		12 34			12 52		13 17			
Bushey d	11 40													12 37								
Harrow & Wealdstone ⊖ d	11 45			11 28			12 12	12 24			12 29			12 42			12 58		13 23			
Wembley Central ⊖ d																						
Shepherd's Bush a				11 45							12 45											
Kensington (Olympia) ⊖ a				11 47							12 47											
West Brompton ⊖ a				11 50							12 50											
Imperial Wharf a				11 53							12 53											
Clapham Junction d				11a58							12a58											
East Croydon a																						
London Euston 15 ⊖ a	11 59	11 31	11 37		12 05	12 08	12 25	12 37	12 27	12 32		12 50	12 45	12 56	12 56	13 11	13 11	12 59	13 37	13 04	13 28	13 37

	VT	SN	LM	VT	LM	LM	VT	VT	LM	VT	VT	SN	LM	VT	LM	LM	VT	VT	LM	VT	SN
	◇1	1	◇1	◇1	1	1	◇1	◇1	◇1	◇1	◇1	1	◇1	◇1	1	1	◇1	◇1	◇1	◇1	1
Wolverhampton 7 d								12 45										13 45			
Sandwell & Dudley d								12 55										13 56			
Birmingham New Street 12 d				11 50			12 30	13 10	12 14					12 50			13 30	14 10	13 14		
Birmingham International d				12 00			12 39	13 20	12 25					13 00			13 39	14 20	13 25		
Coventry d				12 11			12 51	13 31	12 44					13 11			13 51	14 31	13 44		
Nuneaton d	12 32		11 58										12 58								
Rugby d			12 20	12 25					12 55				13 20	13 25					13 55		
Northampton d			12 50						13 25				13 50						14 25		
Wolverton d									13 37										14 37		
Milton Keynes Central 10 a	13 03		13 04				13 18		13 40				14 04				14 18		14 40		
d	13 04		13 06			13 12	13 19		13 41	13 51	14 03		14 06			14 12	14 19		14 41	14 51	
Bletchley d						13 17			13 46							14 17			14 46		
Leighton Buzzard d			13 15			13 23			13 52				14 15			14 23			14 52		
Cheddington d						13 29										14 29					
Tring d					13 15	13 35									14 15	14 35					
Berkhamsted d					13 19	13 39			14 05						14 19	14 39			15 05		
Hemel Hempstead d					13 24	13 44			14 10						14 24	14 44			15 10		
Apsley d					13 27										14 27						
Kings Langley d					13 30										14 30						
Watford Junction a			13 35		13 35	13 52		14s16	14 17				14 35		14 35	14 52		15s16	15 17		
d		13 22	13 35		13 35	13 52			14 17			14 22	14 36		14 35	14 52			15 17		15 22
Bushey d					13 38										14 38						
Harrow & Wealdstone ⊖ d		13 28			13 43	13 58			14 23			14 28			14 43	14 58			15 23		15 28
Wembley Central ⊖ d																					
Shepherd's Bush a		13 45										14 45									15 45
Kensington (Olympia) ⊖ a		13 47										14 47									15 47
West Brompton ⊖ a		13 50										14 50									15 50
Imperial Wharf a		13 53										14 53									15 53
Clapham Junction d		13a58										14a58									15a58
East Croydon a																					
London Euston 15 ⊖ a	13 44		13 53	13 19	13 57	14 11	13 57	14 37	14 37	14 27	14 43		14 53	14 18	14 57	15 11	14 57	15 37	15 37	15 27	

West Midlands, Northampton, Milton Keynes Central and Watford Junction - London

Network Diagram - see first Page of Table 59

		LM	VT	VT	LM	LM	VT	VT		LM	VT	SN	LM	VT	VT	LM	LM	VT		VT	LM	VT	SN	LM	VT
		◇1	◇1	◇1	1	1	◇1	◇1		◇1	◇1	1	◇1	◇1	◇1	1	1	◇1		◇1	◇1	◇1	1	◇1	◇1
Wolverhampton 7	d							14 45												15 45					
Sandwell & Dudley	d							14 56												15 56					
Birmingham New Street 12	d		13 50				14 30	15 10		14 14				14 50				15 30		16 10	15 14				15 50
Birmingham International	d		14 01				14 39	15 20		14 25				15 01				15 39		16 20	15 25				16 01
Coventry	d		14 11				14 51	15 31		14 44				15 11				15 51		16 31	15 44				16 11
Nuneaton	d	13 58		14 32									14 58											15 58	
Rugby	d	14 20	14 26							14 55			15 20	15 26							15 55			16 20	16 24
Northampton	d	14 50								15 25			15 50								16 25			16 50	
Wolverton	d									15 37											16 37				
Milton Keynes Central 10	a	15 04		15 04			15 18			15 40			16 04					16 18			16 40			17 04	
	d	15 06		15 05		15 12	15 19			15 41	15 51		16 06		16 05		16 12	16 19			16 41	16 51		17 06	
Bletchley	d					15 17				15 46							16 17				16 46				
Leighton Buzzard	d	15 15				15 23				15 52			16 15				16 23				16 52			17 15	
Cheddington	d					15 29											16 29								
Tring	d				15 15	15 35										16 15	16 35								
Berkhamsted	d				15 19	15 39				16 05						16 19	16 39				17 05				
Hemel Hempstead	d				15 24	15 44				16 10						16 24	16 44				17 10				
Apsley	d				15 27											16 27									
Kings Langley	d				15 30											16 30									
Watford Junction	a	15 35			15 35	15 52		16s16		16 17			16 35			16 35	16 52			17s16	17 17			17 35	
	d	15 35			15 35	15 52				16 17		16 22	16 35			16 35	16 52				17 17		17 22	17 35	
Bushey	d				15 38											16 38									
Harrow & Wealdstone	d				15 43	15 58				16 23		16 28				16 43	16 58				17 23		17 28		
Wembley Central	d																								
Shepherd's Bush	a											16 45											17 45		
Kensington (Olympia)	a											16 47											17 47		
West Brompton	a											16 50											17 50		
Imperial Wharf	a											16 53											17 53		
Clapham Junction	d											16a58											17a58		
East Croydon	a																								
London Euston 15	a	15 53	15 17	15 45	15 57	16 11	15 57	16 37		16 37	16 27		16 53	16 17	16 44	16 57	17 11	16 57		17 37	17 37	17 27		17 53	17 17

		VT	LM	LM		VT	VT	LM	VT	SN	LM	VT	VT	LM		LM	VT	VT	LM	VT	VT	SN	LM	VT
		◇1	1	1		◇1	◇1	◇1	◇1	1	◇1	◇1	◇1	1		1	◇1	◇1	◇1	◇1	◇1	1	◇1	◇1
Wolverhampton 7	d						16 45											17 45						
Sandwell & Dudley	d						16 56											17 56						
Birmingham New Street 12	d					16 30	17 10	16 14				16 50					17 30	18 10	17 14					17 50
Birmingham International	d					16 39	17 20	16 25				17 01					17 39	18 20	17 25					18 01
Coventry	d					16 51	17 31	16 44				17 11					17 51	18 31	17 44					18 11
Nuneaton	d										16 58												18 03	
Rugby	d							16 55			17 20	17 26							17 55				18 20	18 26
Northampton	d							17 25			17 50								18 25				18 50	
Wolverton	d							17 37											18 37					
Milton Keynes Central 10	a					17 18		17 40			18 04						18 18		18 40				19 04	
	d	17 04		17 12		17 19		17 41	17 51		18 06		18 05			18 12	18 19		18 41	18 51	19 03		19 06	
Bletchley	d			17 17				17 46								18 17			18 46					
Leighton Buzzard	d			17 23				17 52			18 15					18 23			18 52				19 15	
Cheddington	d			17 29												18 29								
Tring	d		17 15	17 35										18 15		18 35								
Berkhamsted	d		17 19	17 39				18 05						18 19		18 39			19 05					
Hemel Hempstead	d		17 24	17 44				18 10						18 24		18 44			19 10					
Apsley	d		17 27											18 27										
Kings Langley	d		17 30											18 30										
Watford Junction	a		17 35	17 52			18s16	18 17			18 35			18 35		18 52		19s16	19 17				19 35	
	d		17 35	17 52				18 17		18 22	18 35			18 35		18 52			19 17			19 22	19 35	
Bushey	d		17 38											18 38										
Harrow & Wealdstone	d		17 43	17 58				18 23		18 28				18 43		18 58			19 23			19 28		
Wembley Central	d																							
Shepherd's Bush	a									18 45												19 45		
Kensington (Olympia)	a									18 47												19 47		
West Brompton	a									18 50												19 50		
Imperial Wharf	a									18 53												19 53		
Clapham Junction	d									18a58												19a58		
East Croydon	a																							
London Euston 15	a	17 44	17 57	18 11		17 57	18 37	18 37	18 27		18 53	18 18	18 44	18 57		19 11	18 57	19 37	19 37	19 27	19 43		19 53	19 17

West Midlands, Northampton, Milton Keynes Central and Watford Junction - London

Network Diagram - see first Page of Table 59

		LM	LM	VT	VT	LM	VT	VT	SN	LM		VT	LM	LM	VT	SN	LM	VT	VT	LM		LM	LM	VT	VT
		1	1	◇1	◇1	◇1	◇1	◇1	1	◇1		◇1	1	1	◇1	1	◇1	◇1	◇1	◇1		1	◇1	◇1	◇1
Wolverhampton 7	d				18 45														19 45						
Sandwell & Dudley	d				18 56														19 58						
Birmingham New Street 12	d			18 30	19 10	18 14						18 50			19 30		19 14		20 10				20 14	20 30	
Birmingham International	d			18 39	19 20	18 25						19 01			19 39		19 25		20 20				20 25	20 40	
Coventry	d			18 51	19 31	18 44						19 11			19 51		19 44		20 31				20 43	20 51	
Nuneaton	d									18 58										20 03					
Rugby	d					18 55				19 20		19 26					19 55			20 19			20 55	21 05	
Northampton	d					19 25				19 50							20 25			20 50			21 25		
Wolverton	d					19 37				20 02							20 37			21 02			21 38		
Milton Keynes Central 10	a			19 18		19 40				20 06					20 18		20 40			21 05			21 42	21 26	
	d		19 12	19 19		19 41	19 51	20 04		20 06				20 12	20 19		20 41	20 48		21 06		21 15	21 42	21 28	21 38
Bletchley	d		19 17			19 46								20 17			20 46					21 20	21 47		
Leighton Buzzard	d		19 23			19 52				20 15				20 23			20 52			21 14		21 26	21 54		
Cheddington	d		19 29											20 28								21 31			
Tring	d	19 15	19 35										20 15	20 37								21 39			
Berkhamsted	d	19 19	19 39			20 05							20 19	20 42			21 07					21 43	22 09		
Hemel Hempstead	d	19 24	19 44			20 10							20 24	20 46			21 11					21 48	22 13		
Apsley	d	19 27											20 27				21 14						22 16		
Kings Langley	d	19 30											20 30				21 17						22 19		
Watford Junction	a	19 35	19 52		20s16	20 17				20 35			20 35	20 53			21 22		21s26	21 35		21 57	22 23	22s02	
	d	19 35	19 52			20 17			20 22	20 35			20 35	20 54		21 17	21 22			21 36		21 58	22 24		
Bushey	d	19 38											20 38									22 00			
Harrow & Wealdstone	d	19 43	19 58			20 23			20 28				20 43	21 00		21 23	21 28					22 05	22 30		
Wembley Central	d																								
Shepherd's Bush	a								20 45							21 45									
Kensington (Olympia)	a								20 47							21 47									
West Brompton	a								20 50							21 50									
Imperial Wharf	a								20 53							21 53									
Clapham Junction	d								20a58							21a58									
East Croydon	a																								
London Euston 15	a	19 57	20 11	19 57	20 37	20 37	20 27	20 44		20 53		20 17	20 59	21 14	20 57		21 42	21 31	21 47	21 54		22 19	22 44	22 23	22 27

		SN	VT	VT	LM	LM		VT	SN	VT	VT	LM	VT	VT
		1	◇1	◇1	◇1	◇1		◇1	1	◇1	◇1	◇1	◇1	◇1
Wolverhampton 7	d							21 05					22 05	22 37
Sandwell & Dudley	d							21 17					22 15	22 47
Birmingham New Street 12	d					21 14		21 30					22 30	23 00
Birmingham International	d					21 25		21 40					22 40	23 10
Coventry	d					21 44		21 51					22 51	23 21
Nuneaton	d				20 57						22 18			
Rugby	d				21 19	21 55		22 04			22 32		23 04	23 34
Northampton	d				21 54	22 25						23 00		23s53
Wolverton	d				22 06	22 37						23 12		
Milton Keynes Central 10	a				22 09	22 40		22 35			23 04	23 15	23 36	00s13
	d		21 57	22 04	22 10	22 41		22 37		22 48	23 05	23 16	23 37	
Bletchley	d				22 15	22 46						23 21		
Leighton Buzzard	d				22 21	22 52						23 27		
Cheddington	d				22 26							23 32		
Tring	d				22 35							23 41		
Berkhamsted	d				22 40	23 05						23 45		
Hemel Hempstead	d				22 44	23 10						23 49		
Apsley	d					23 13								
Kings Langley	d					23 16								
Watford Junction	a		22s31		22 51	23 20		23s05		23s25	23s34	23 56	00s06	00s42
	d	22 17			22 52	23 21			23 17			23 57		
Bushey	d				22 54							23 59		
Harrow & Wealdstone	d	22 23			23 00	23 27			23 23			00 05		
Wembley Central	d													
Shepherd's Bush	a	22 45							23 45					
Kensington (Olympia)	a	22 47							23 47					
West Brompton	a	22 50							23 50					
Imperial Wharf	a	22 53							23 53					
Clapham Junction	d	22a58							00 05					
East Croydon	a								00 22					
London Euston 15	a		22 53	22 56	23 14	23 41		23 25		23 49	23 54	00 19	00 27	01 04

Sundays
from 16 September

West Midlands, Northampton, Milton Keynes Central and Watford Junction - London

Network Diagram - see first Page of Table 59

		LM	LM	LM	LM	LM	LM	LM	SN	LM	LM	VT	SN	LM	VT	VT	VT	LM	LM	VT	VT	SN	VT
		◇1	◇1	1	🚌	1	1	◇1	1	◇1	◇1	◇1	1	◇1	◇1	◇1	◇1	◇1	◇1	◇1	◇1	1	◇1 A
												☕			☕	☕	☕			☕	☕		☕
Wolverhampton 7	d											08 05								09 05			
Sandwell & Dudley	d											08 15								09 15			
Birmingham New Street 12	d	21p53										08 30							09 14	09 30			
Birmingham International	d	22p05										08 40							09 25	09 40			
Coventry	d	22p21										08 51							09 44	09 51			
Nuneaton	d																				09 55		
Rugby	d	22p32										09 04							09 55	10 04			10 33
Northampton	d	22p55	23p30		06 20			07 53		08 23	08 53			09 31				10 08	10 37				
Wolverton	d	23p07	23p42		06 52			08 05		08 37	09 05			09 43				10 20	10 51				
Milton Keynes Central 10	a	23p10	23p45		07 00			08 08		08 40	09 08	09 37		09 46				10 23	10 54	10 37			11 06
	d	23p11	23p46	06 42		07 11	07 40	08 09		08 41	09 09	09 39		09 47			10 19	10 24	10 55	10 39			11 08
Bletchley	d	23p16	23p51	06 47		07 16	07 45	08 14		08 46	09 14			09 52				10 29	11 00				
Leighton Buzzard	d	23p22	23p57	06 53		07 22	07 51	08 20		08 52	09 20			09 58				10 35	11 06				
Cheddington	d	23p27				07 27		08 25			09 25							10 44					
Tring	d	23p36				07 36		08 34			09 34							10 49					
Berkhamsted	d	23p41		07 08		07 41	08 06	08 39		09 07	09 38			10 13				10 54	11 21				
Hemel Hempstead	d	23p45		07 13		07 45	08 11	08 43		09 12	09 42			10 18				10 58	11 26				
Apsley	d	23p49		07 16			08 14			09 15				10 21					11 29				
Kings Langley	d	23p52		07 19			08 17			09 18				10 24					11 32				
Watford Junction	a	23p56	00 19	07 24		07 52	08 22	08 50		09 23	09 49	10s07		10 29				11 05	11 37	11s11	11s16		11s43
	d	23p57	00 20	07 24		07 53	08 22	08 53	09 17	09 23	09 53		10 17	10 29				11 05	11 37			11 22	
Bushey	d						08 25			09 26				10 32					11 40				
Harrow & Wealdstone ⊖	d	00 03		07 30		07 59	08 30	08 59	09 23	09 31	09 59		10 23	10 37				11 11	11 45			11 28	
Wembley Central ⊖	d																						
Shepherd's Bush	a								09 45				10 45									11 45	
Kensington (Olympia) ⊖	a								09 47				10 47									11 47	
West Brompton ⊖	a								09 50				10 50									11 50	
Imperial Wharf	a								09 53				10 53									11 53	
Clapham Junction	d								09a58				10a58									11a58	
East Croydon	a																						
London Euston 15 ⊖	a	00 17	00 40	07 44		08 13	08 44	09 13		09 45	10 13	10 28		10 51	10 57	11 02	11 06	11 25	11 59	11 31	11 37		12 05

		VT	LM	LM	VT	VT	SN	LM	VT	LM	VT	VT	LM	VT	LM	VT	VT	VT	VT	SN	LM	VT	LM
		◇1	◇1	◇1	◇1	◇1	1	◇1	◇1	1	◇1	◇1	1	◇1	◇1	◇1	◇1	◇1	◇1	1	◇1	◇1	1
		☕			☕	☕			☕		☕	☕		☕		☕	☕	☕	☕			☕	
Wolverhampton 7	d				10 05											11 05		11 45					
Sandwell & Dudley	d				10 15											11 15		11 57					
Birmingham New Street 12	d			10 14	10 30										11 14	11 30		12 10				11 50	
Birmingham International	d			10 25	10 40										11 25	11 40		12 20				12 00	
Coventry	d			10 44	10 51										11 44	11 51		12 31				12 11	
Nuneaton	d					10 56		10 54				11 59							12 32		11 58		
Rugby	d			10 55	11 04			11 14	11 33						11 55	12 05					12 20	12 25	
Northampton	d		11 08	11 25				11 48							12 25						12 50		
Wolverton	d		11 20	11 37											12 37								
Milton Keynes Central 10	a		11 23	11 42	11 37	11 46		12 02	12 06						12 40	12 24			13 03		13 04		
	d	11 17	11 24	11 42	11 39	11 47		12 03	12 07				12 12	12 22	12 41	12 26	12 52		13 04		13 06		
Bletchley	d		11 29	11 47						11 56			12 17		12 46								
Leighton Buzzard	d		11 35	11 54				12 11		12 02			12 23		12 52						13 15		
Cheddington	d		11 40							12 08			12 29										
Tring	d		11 49							12 14			12 35										13 15
Berkhamsted	d		11 53	12 06						12 19			12 39		13 05								13 19
Hemel Hempstead	d		11 58	12 10						12 23			12 44		13 10								13 24
Apsley	d									12 26													13 27
Kings Langley	d									12 29													13 30
Watford Junction	a		12 06	12 17	12s07			12 32		12 34		12s50	12 52		13 17			13s18			13 35		13 35
	d		12 06	12 18			12 22	12 32		12 34			12 52		13 17					13 22	13 35		13 35
Bushey	d									12 37													13 38
Harrow & Wealdstone ⊖	d		12 12	12 24			12 29			12 42			12 58		13 23					13 28			13 43
Wembley Central ⊖	d																						
Shepherd's Bush	a						12 45													13 45			
Kensington (Olympia) ⊖	a						12 47													13 47			
West Brompton ⊖	a						12 50													13 50			
Imperial Wharf	a						12 53													13 53			
Clapham Junction	d						12a58													13a58			
East Croydon	a																						
London Euston 15 ⊖	a	12 08	12 25	12 37	12 27	12 32		12 50	12 45	12 56	12 56	13 11	13 11	12 59	13 37	13 04	13 28	13 37	13 44		13 53	13 19	13 57

A from 16 September until 21 October

Sundays
from 16 September

West Midlands, Northampton, Milton Keynes Central and Watford Junction - London

Network Diagram - see first Page of Table 59

		LM	VT	VT	LM	VT	VT	SN	LM	VT	LM	LM	VT	VT	LM	VT	VT	SN	LM	VT	LM	LM
		1	◇1	◇1	◇1	◇1	◇1	1	◇1	◇1	1	1	◇1	◇1	◇1	◇1	◇1	1	◇1	◇1	1	1
			☕	☕		☕	☕			☕			☕	☕		☕	☕			☕		
Wolverhampton 7	d			12 45										13 45								
Sandwell & Dudley	d			12 55										13 56								
Birmingham New Street 12	d		12 30	13 10	12 14					12 50			13 30	14 10	13 14					13 50		
Birmingham International	d		12 39	13 20	12 25					13 00			13 39	14 20	13 25					14 01		
Coventry	d		12 51	13 31	12 44					13 11			13 51	14 31	13 44					14 11		
Nuneaton	d								12 58								14 32		13 58			
Rugby	d				12 55				13 20	13 25					13 55				14 20	14 26		
Northampton	d				13 25				13 50						14 25				14 50			
Wolverton	d				13 37										14 37							
Milton Keynes Central 10	a		13 18		13 40				14 04				14 18		14 40		15 02		15 04			
	d	13 12	13 19		13 41	13 48	14 03		14 06			14 12	14 19		14 41	14 50	15 03		15 06			15 12
Bletchley	d	13 17			13 46							14 17			14 46							15 17
Leighton Buzzard	d	13 23			13 52				14 15			14 23			14 52				15 15			15 23
Cheddington	d	13 29										14 29										15 29
Tring	d	13 35									14 15	14 35									15 15	15 35
Berkhamsted	d	13 39			14 05						14 19	14 39			15 05						15 19	15 39
Hemel Hempstead	d	13 44			14 10						14 24	14 44			15 10						15 24	15 44
Apsley	d										14 27										15 27	
Kings Langley	d										14 30										15 30	
Watford Junction	a	13 52		14s16	14 17				14 35		14 35	14 52		15s16	15 17				15 35		15 35	15 52
	d	13 52			14 17			14 22	14 36		14 35	14 52			15 17			15 22	15 35		15 35	15 52
Bushey	d										14 38										15 38	
Harrow & Wealdstone ⊖	d	13 58			14 23			14 28			14 43	14 58			15 23			15 28			15 43	15 58
Wembley Central ⊖	d																					
Shepherd's Bush	a							14 45										15 45				
Kensington (Olympia) ⊖	a							14 47										15 47				
West Brompton ⊖	a							14 50										15 50				
Imperial Wharf	a							14 53										15 53				
Clapham Junction	d							14a58										15a58				
East Croydon	a																					
London Euston 15 ⊖	a	14 11	13 57	14 37	14 37	14 27	14 43		14 53	14 17	14 57	15 11	14 57	15 37	15 37	15 26	15 43		15 53	15 17	15 57	16 11

		VT	VT	LM	VT	SN	LM	VT	VT	LM	LM	VT	VT	LM	VT	VT	SN	LM	LM	LM	VT	LM	VT
		◇1	◇1	◇1	◇1	1	◇1	◇1	◇1	1	1	◇1	◇1	◇1	◇1	◇1	1	◇1 A	1	◇1 B	◇1	1	◇1
		☕	☕		☕			☕	☕			☕	☕		☕	☕					☕		☕
Wolverhampton 7	d		14 45										15 45										
Sandwell & Dudley	d		14 56										15 56										
Birmingham New Street 12	d	14 30	15 10	14 14				14 50				15 30	16 10	15 14							15 50		16 30
Birmingham International	d	14 39	15 20	14 25				15 01				15 39	16 20	15 25							16 01		16 39
Coventry	d	14 51	15 31	14 44				15 11				15 51	16 31	15 44							16 11		16 51
Nuneaton	d						14 58											15 58		15 58			
Rugby	d			14 55			15 20	15 26						15 55				16 20		16 20	16 24		
Northampton	d			15 25			15 50							16 25				16 50		16 50			
Wolverton	d			15 37										16 37									
Milton Keynes Central 10	a	15 18		15 40			16 04					16 18		16 40				17 04		17 04			17 18
	d	15 19		15 41	15 50		16 06		16 04		16 12	16 19		16 41	16 51	17 03		17 06		17 06		17 12	17 19
Bletchley	d			15 46							16 17			16 46								17 17	
Leighton Buzzard	d			15 52			16 15				16 23			16 52				17 15		17 15		17 23	
Cheddington	d										16 29											17 29	
Tring	d									16 15	16 35								17 15			17 35	
Berkhamsted	d			16 05						16 19	16 39			17 05					17 19			17 39	
Hemel Hempstead	d			16 10						16 24	16 44			17 10					17 24			17 44	
Apsley	d									16 27									17 27				
Kings Langley	d									16 30									17 30				
Watford Junction	a		16s16	16 17			16 35			16 35	16 52		17s16	17 17				17 35	17 35	17 37		17 52	
	d			16 17		16 22	16 35			16 35	16 52			17 17			17 22	17 35	17 35	17 37		17 52	
Bushey	d									16 38									17 38				
Harrow & Wealdstone ⊖	d			16 23		16 28				16 43	16 58			17 23			17 28		17 43			17 58	
Wembley Central ⊖	d																						
Shepherd's Bush	a					16 45											17 45						
Kensington (Olympia) ⊖	a					16 47											17 47						
West Brompton ⊖	a					16 50											17 50						
Imperial Wharf	a					16 53											17 53						
Clapham Junction	d					16a58											17a58						
East Croydon	a																						
London Euston 15 ⊖	a	15 57	16 37	16 37	16 26		16 53	16 17	16 43	16 57	17 11	16 57	17 37	17 37	17 27	17 43		17 53	17 57	17 53	17 17	18 11	17 57

A from 16 September until 21 October

B from 28 October

Table 66

Sundays
from 16 September

West Midlands, Northampton, Milton Keynes Central and Watford Junction - London

Network Diagram - see first Page of Table 59

		VT	LM	VT	SN	LM	VT	VT	LM	LM	VT	VT	LM	VT	VT	SN	LM	VT	LM	LM	VT	VT
		◇1	◇1	◇1	1	◇1	◇1	◇1	1	1	◇1	◇1	◇1	◇1	◇1	1	◇1	◇1	1	1	◇1	◇1
		🍴		🍴			🍴	🍴			🍴	🍴		🍴	🍴			🍴			🍴	🍴
Wolverhampton 7 ⇌	d	16 45										17 45										18 45
Sandwell & Dudley	d	16 56										17 56										18 56
Birmingham New Street 12	d	17 10	16 14				16 50				17 30	18 10	17 14					17 50			18 30	19 10
Birmingham International ✈	d	17 20	16 25				17 01				17 39	18 20	17 25					18 01			18 39	19 20
Coventry	d	17 31	16 44				17 11				17 51	18 31	17 44					18 11			18 51	19 31
Nuneaton	d					16 58											18 03					
Rugby	d		16 55			17 20	17 26						17 55				18 20	18 26				
Northampton	d		17 25			17 50							18 25				18 50					
Wolverton	d		17 37										18 37									
Milton Keynes Central 10	a		17 40			18 04					18 18		18 40				19 04				19 18	
	d		17 41	17 50		18 06		18 05		18 12	18 19		18 41	18 50	19 03		19 06			19 12	19 19	
Bletchley	d		17 46							18 17			18 46							19 17		
Leighton Buzzard	d		17 52			18 15				18 23			18 52				19 15			19 23		
Cheddington	d									18 29										19 29		
Tring	d								18 15	18 35									19 15	19 35		
Berkhamsted	d		18 05						18 19	18 39			19 05						19 19	19 39		
Hemel Hempstead	d		18 10						18 24	18 44			19 10						19 24	19 44		
Apsley	d								18 27										19 27			
Kings Langley	d								18 30										19 30			
Watford Junction	a	18s16	18 17			18 35			18 35	18 52		19s16	19 17				19 35		19 35	19 52		20s16
	d		18 17		18 22	18 35			18 35	18 52			19 17			19 22	19 35		19 35	19 52		
Bushey	d								18 38										19 38			
Harrow & Wealdstone ⊖	d		18 23		18 28				18 43	18 58			19 23			19 28			19 43	19 58		
Wembley Central ⊖	d																					
Shepherd's Bush	a				18 45											19 45						
Kensington (Olympia) ⊖	a				18 47											19 47						
West Brompton ⊖	a				18 50											19 50						
Imperial Wharf	a				18 53											19 53						
Clapham Junction	d				18a58											19a58						
East Croydon ⇌	a																					
London Euston 15 ⊖	a	18 37	18 37	18 26		18 53	18 17	18 44	18 57	19 11	18 57	19 37	19 37	19 26	19 43		19 53	19 17	19 57	20 11	19 57	20 37

		LM	VT	VT	SN	LM	VT	LM	LM	VT	SN	LM	VT	VT	LM	LM	LM	VT	VT	SN	VT	VT	LM
		◇1	◇1	◇1	1	◇1	◇1	1	1	◇1	1	◇1	◇1	◇1	◇1	1	◇1	◇1	◇1	1	◇1	◇1	◇1
			🍴	🍴			🍴			🍴			🍴	🍴				🍴	🍴		🍴	🍴	
Wolverhampton 7 ⇌	d													19 45									
Sandwell & Dudley	d													19 58									
Birmingham New Street 12	d	18 14					18 50			19 30		19 14		20 10			20 14	20 30					
Birmingham International ✈	d	18 25					19 01			19 39		19 25		20 20			20 25	20 40					
Coventry	d	18 44					19 11			19 51		19 44		20 31			20 43	20 51					
Nuneaton	d					18 58									20 03								20 57
Rugby	d	18 55				19 20	19 26					19 55			20 19		20 55	21 05					21 19
Northampton	d	19 25				19 50						20 25			20 50		21 25						21 54
Wolverton	d	19 37				20 02						20 37			21 02		21 38						22 06
Milton Keynes Central 10	a	19 40				20 06				20 18		20 40			21 05		21 42	21 26					22 09
	d	19 41	19 50	20 03		20 06			20 12	20 19		20 41	20 48		21 06	21 15	21 42	21 28	21 38		21 53	22 04	22 10
Bletchley	d	19 46							20 17			20 46				21 20	21 47						22 15
Leighton Buzzard	d	19 52				20 15			20 23			20 52			21 14	21 26	21 54						22 21
Cheddington	d								20 28							21 31							22 26
Tring	d							20 15	20 37							21 39							22 35
Berkhamsted	d	20 05						20 19	20 42			21 07				21 43	22 09						22 40
Hemel Hempstead	d	20 10						20 24	20 46			21 11				21 48	22 13						22 44
Apsley	d							20 27				21 14					22 16						
Kings Langley	d							20 30				21 17					22 19						
Watford Junction	a	20 17				20 35		20 35	20 53			21 22		21s26	21 35	21 57	22 23	22s02			22s31		22 51
	d	20 17			20 22	20 35		20 35	20 54		21 17	21 22			21 36	21 58	22 24			22 17			22 52
Bushey	d							20 38								22 00							22 54
Harrow & Wealdstone ⊖	d	20 23			20 28			20 43	21 00		21 23	21 28				22 05	22 30			22 23			23 00
Wembley Central ⊖	d																						
Shepherd's Bush	a				20 45						21 45									22 45			
Kensington (Olympia) ⊖	a				20 47						21 47									22 47			
West Brompton ⊖	a				20 50						21 50									22 50			
Imperial Wharf	a				20 53						21 53									22 53			
Clapham Junction	d				20a58						21a58									22a58			
East Croydon ⇌	a																						
London Euston 15 ⊖	a	20 37	20 26	20 44		20 53	20 17	20 59	21 14	20 57		21 42	21 31	21 47	21 54	22 19	22 44	22 23	22 27		22 53	22 56	23 14

Table 66

Sundays
from 16 September

West Midlands, Northampton, Milton Keynes Central and Watford Junction - London

Network Diagram - see first Page of Table 59

		LM	VT	SN	VT	VT	LM	VT	VT
		◇1	◇1	1	◇1	◇1	◇1	◇1	◇1
			🍴		🍴	🍴		🍴	🍴
Wolverhampton 7 ⇌	d		21 05					22 05	22 37
Sandwell & Dudley	d		21 17					22 15	22 47
Birmingham New Street 12	d	21 14	21 30					22 30	23 00
Birmingham International ✈	d	21 25	21 40					22 40	23 10
Coventry	d	21 44	21 51					22 51	23 21
Nuneaton	d					22 18			
Rugby	d	21 55	22 04			22 32		23 04	23 34
Northampton	d	22 25					23 00		23s53
Wolverton	d	22 37					23 12		
Milton Keynes Central 10	a	22 40	22 35			23 04	23 15	23 36	00s12
	d	22 41	22 37		22 48	23 05	23 16	23 37	
Bletchley	d	22 46					23 21		
Leighton Buzzard	d	22 52					23 27		
Cheddington	d						23 32		
Tring	d						23 41		
Berkhamsted	d	23 05					23 45		
Hemel Hempstead	d	23 10					23 49		
Apsley	d	23 13							
Kings Langley	d	23 16							
Watford Junction	a	23 20	23s05		23s25	23s34	23 56	00s06	00s42
	d	23 21		23 17			23 57		
Bushey	d						23 59		
Harrow & Wealdstone ⊖	d	23 27		23 23			00 05		
Wembley Central ⊖	d								
Shepherd's Bush	a			23 45					
Kensington (Olympia) ⊖	a			23 47					
West Brompton ⊖	a			23 50					
Imperial Wharf	a			23 53					
Clapham Junction	d			00 05					
East Croydon ⇌	a			00 22					
London Euston 15 ⊖	a	23 41	23 25		23 49	23 54	00 19	00 27	01 04

Network Diagram for Tables 67, 68, 69, 70

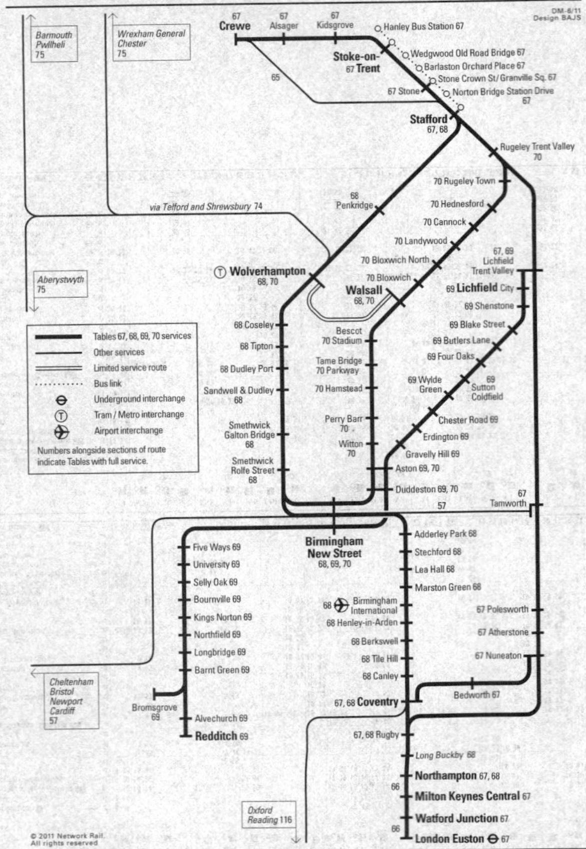

Table 67

Mondays to Fridays
until 29 June

London - Stoke-on-Trent and Crewe
Coventry - Nuneaton

Network Diagram - see first Page of Table 67

Miles	Miles	Miles			VT	VT	LM	VT	VT	XC	LM	XC	LM		LM	VT	VT	LM	LM	XC	LM	LM	LM		XC
					MO	MX	MX	MO																	
					◇1	◇1	◇1	◇1	◇1	◇1	1	◇1	◇1			◇1	◇1		◇1	◇1	◇1	◇1			◇1
					A			A																	
					🛏	🛏		🛏	⊠			⊼				⊠	⊠	🚌		⊼					⊼
0	—	—	**London Euston** ⊖	d	21p51	22p00										05 27	05 39								
17½	—	—	Watford Junction	d	⌇											05u45	06u02								
49¾	—	—	Milton Keynes Central	d	22p38	22p31							05 21			06 10	06 22								
65¾	—	—	Northampton	d	⌇								05 42									06 41			
84½	—	—	Rugby	d	23p18	22p54							06 05				06 45					07 01			
—	—	0	**Coventry**	d	⌇										06 12								07 06		
—	—	6¼	Bedworth	d	⌇										06 23								07 17		
99	—	10	Nuneaton	a	23p28	23p03							06 16		06 30	06 38						07 13	07 27		
—	—	—		d	23p29	23p04							06 17			06 39						07 15			
104	—	—	Atherstone	d	⌇								06 23									07 21			
108	—	—	Polesworth	d	⌇																	07 26			
111½	—	—	Tamworth	d	⌇	23b15							06 31									07 31			
117¾	—	—	Lichfield Trent Valley	d	⌇	23b22							06 37									07 37			
125¾	—	—	Rugeley Trent Valley	d	⌇			←					06 44									07 43			
135½	0	—	**Stafford**	d	23b53	23b38	23p53	23b53	06 02	06 30	06 36	06 55	06 58			07 03			07 08	07 30	07 36	07 54			08 01
—	—	—	Norton Bridge Station Drv	d	↦			⌇																	
144½	—	—	Stone	d				⌇					07 18									08 05			
—	—	—	Stone Crown Street	d				⌇										07 05							
—	—	—	Stone Granville Square	a				⌇																	
—	—	—	Barlaston Orchard Place	d				⌇										07 15							
—	—	—	Wedgwood Old Road Bridge	d				⌇										07 17							
151¾	—	—	**Stoke-on-Trent**	d				⌇		06a50		07a13	07 26					07 38				08 13			08a19
—	—	—	Hanley Bus Station	a				⌇										07 45							
159	—	—	Kidsgrove	d				⌇					07 34									08 21			
161¾	—	—	Alsager	d				⌇					07 39									08 26			
167¾	24½	—	**Crewe**	a		00s03	00 16	00s21	06 21		06 56		07 49			07 22	07 30		07 33	07 50	07 56	08 38			

		LM	LM	LM	VT	VT	VT	LM	XC		LM	LM	VT	XC	LM	LM	LM	VT	VT		XC	LM	LM	VT	XC
		◇1		◇1	◇1	◇1	◇1		◇1			◇1	◇1	◇1	◇1		◇1	◇1	◇1		◇1		◇1	◇1	◇1
			🚌		⊠	⊠	⊠	🚌	⊼				⊠	⊼		🚌		⊠	⊠		⊼			⊠	⊼
London Euston ⊖	d			06 24	06 36	07 07	07 10						07 35				07 47	08 07	08 10					08 40	
Watford Junction	d			06 41	06u51												08 02								
Milton Keynes Central	d			07 22			07 41						08 06				08 31		08 41						
Northampton	d			07 45													08 45								
Rugby	d			08 04													09 04								
Coventry	d								07 27		08 04										08 27	09 06			
Bedworth	d										08 15											09 17			
Nuneaton	a			08 17							08 23						09 16					09 25			
	d			08 17													09 17								
Atherstone	d			08 23													09 23								
Polesworth	d																								
Tamworth	d			08 31													09 31								
Lichfield Trent Valley	d			08 37													09 37								
Rugeley Trent Valley	d			08 43													09 43								
Stafford	d	08 09		08 54		08a22		08 25	08 30			08 36		09 01	09 09		09 54	09a22			09 30		09 35		10 01
Norton Bridge Station Drv	d							08 40																	
Stone	d			09 05													10 05								
Stone Crown Street	d		08 15													09 20									
Stone Granville Square	a							09 02																	
Barlaston Orchard Place	d		08 25													09 30									
Wedgwood Old Road Bridge	d		08 27													09 32									
Stoke-on-Trent	d		08 48	09 13					08a54					09a19		09 48	10 13				09a54				10a19
Hanley Bus Station	a		08 55													09 55									
Kidsgrove	d			09 21													10 21								
Alsager	d			09 26													10 26								
Crewe	a	08 30		09 38	08 10		08 47					08 56	09 10		09 30		10 38		09 47				09 56	10 10	

A from 21 May until 25 June

b Previous night, stops to set down only

Table 67

Mondays to Fridays
until 29 June

London - Stoke-on-Trent and Crewe
Coventry - Nuneaton

Network Diagram - see first Page of Table 67

		LM	LM	LM	VT		VT	LM	XC	LM	VT	LM	XC	LM	VT		LM	LM	VT	VT	XC	LM	VT	LM	XC
		◇1	bus	◇1	◇1 ⊠		◇1 ⊠	bus	◇1 ⌶	◇1	◇1 ⊠		◇1 ⌶	◇1	◇1 ⊡		bus	◇1	◇1 ⊠	◇1 ⊠	◇1 ⌶	◇1	◇1 ⊠		◇1 ⌶
London Euston 15 ⊖	d			08 46	09 07		09 10				09 40				09 43			09 46	10 07	10 10			10 40		
Watford Junction	d			09 01														10 01							
Milton Keynes Central	d			09 25			09 41								10 13			10 25		10 41					
Northampton	d			09 45														10 45							
Rugby	d			10 04														11 04							
Coventry	d								09 27			10 42			10 42						10 27			11 42	
Bedworth	d											10 53												11 53	
Nuneaton	a			10 16								11 00						11 16						12 00	
	d			10 17														11 17							
Atherstone	d			10 23														11 23							
Polesworth	d																								
Tamworth	d			10 31														11 31							
Lichfield Trent Valley	d			10 37														11 37							
Rugeley Trent Valley	d			10 43														11 43							
Stafford	d	10 09		10 54	10a22			10 25	10 30	10 35			11 01	11 09				11 54	11a22		11 30	11 35			12 01
Norton Bridge Station Drv	d							10 40																	
Stone	d			11 05														12 05							
Stone Crown Street	d		10 20														11 20								
Stone Granville Square	a							11 02																	
Barlaston Orchard Place	d		10 30														11 30								
Wedgwood Old Road Bridge	d		10 32														11 32								
Stoke-on-Trent	d		10 48	11 13					10a54				11a19				11 48	12 13			11a54				12a19
Hanley Bus Station	a		10 55														11 55								
Kidsgrove	d			11 21														12 21							
Alsager	d			11 26														12 26							
Crewe	a	10 30		11 38			10 47			10 56	11 10			11 30	12 07					11 47		11 56	12 10		

			LM	LM	LM	VT	VT	XC	LM	VT	LM		LM	XC	LM	LM	LM	VT	VT	XC	LM		VT	LM	XC
			◇1	bus	◇1	◇1 ⊡	◇1 ⊡	◇1 ⌶	◇1	◇1 ⊡	bus			◇1 ⌶	◇1	bus	◇1	◇1 ⊡	◇1 ⊡	◇1 ⌶	◇1		◇1 ⊡		◇1 ⌶
London Euston 15 ⊖	d				10 46	11 07	11 10			11 40							11 46	12 07	12 10				12 40		
Watford Junction	d				11 01												12 01								
Milton Keynes Central	d				11 25		11 41										12 25		12 41						
Northampton	d				11 45												12 45								
Rugby	d				12 04												13 04								
Coventry	d							11 27					12 42							12 27				13 42	
Bedworth	d												12 53											13 53	
Nuneaton	a				12 16								13 00				13 16							14 00	
	d				12 17												13 17								
Atherstone	d				12 23												13 23								
Polesworth	d																								
Tamworth	d				12 31												13 31								
Lichfield Trent Valley	d				12 37												13 37								
Rugeley Trent Valley	d				12 43												13 43								
Stafford	d		12 09		12 54	12a22		12 30	12 35		12 35			13 01	13 09		13 54	13a22		13 30	13 35				14 01
Norton Bridge Station Drv	d										12 59														
Stone	d				13 05												14 05								
Stone Crown Street	d			12 20												13 20									
Stone Granville Square	a										13 39														
Barlaston Orchard Place	d			12 30												13 30									
Wedgwood Old Road Bridge	d			12 32												13 32									
Stoke-on-Trent	d			12 48	13 13			12a54						13a19		13 48	14 13			13a54					14a19
Hanley Bus Station	a			12 55												13 55									
Kidsgrove	d				13 21												14 21								
Alsager	d				13 26												14 26								
Crewe	a		12 30		13 38		12 47		12 56	13 10					13 30		14 38		13 47		13 56		14 10		

		LM	LM	LM	LM	VT	VT		XC	LM	VT FO	VT	LM	XC	LM	LM	LM		VT	VT	XC	LM	VT	LM	XC
		◇1	bus	bus	◇1	◇1 ⊡	◇1 ⊡		◇1 ⌶	◇1	◇ ⊡	◇1 ⊡		◇1 ⌶	◇1	bus	◇1		◇1 ⊡	◇1 ⊡	◇1 ⌶	◇1	◇1 ⊡		◇1 ⌶
London Euston 15 ⊖	d				12 46	13 07	13 10				13 33	13 40					13 46		14 07	14 10			14 40		
Watford Junction	d				13 01												14 01								
Milton Keynes Central	d				13 25		13 41										14 25			14 41					
Northampton	d				13 45												14 45								
Rugby	d				14 04												15 04								
Coventry	d								13 27				14 42								14 27			15 42	
Bedworth	d												14 53											15 53	
Nuneaton	a				14 16								15 00				15 16							16 00	
	d				14 17												15 17								
Atherstone	d				14 23												15 23								
Polesworth	d																								
Tamworth	d				14 31												15 31								
Lichfield Trent Valley	d				14 37												15 37								
Rugeley Trent Valley	d				14 43												15 43								
Stafford	d	14 09	14 18		14 54	14a22			14 30	14 35				15 01	15 09		15 54		15a22		15 30	15 35			16 02
Norton Bridge Station Drv	d		14 42																						
Stone	d				15 05												16 05								
Stone Crown Street	d			14 20												15 20									
Stone Granville Square	a		14 54																						
Barlaston Orchard Place	d			14 30												15 30									
Wedgwood Old Road Bridge	d			14 32												15 32									
Stoke-on-Trent	d			14 48	15 13				14a54					15a19		15 48	16 13				15a54				16a20
Hanley Bus Station	a			14 55												15 55									
Kidsgrove	d				15 21												16 21								
Alsager	d				15 26												16 26								
Crewe	a	14 30			15 38		14 47			14 56	15 16	15 10			15 30		16 38			15 47		15 56	16 11		

Table 67

Mondays to Fridays
until 29 June

London - Stoke-on-Trent and Crewe
Coventry - Nuneaton

Network Diagram - see first Page of Table 67

		LM	VT		LM	LM	LM	VT	VT	XC	LM	VT	LM		XC	LM	LM	LM	VT	VT	XC	LM	LM		VT
		◇1	■ 1 ⊡		bus	bus	◇1	◇1 ⊡	◇1 ⊡	◇1 ⌶	◇1	◇1 ⊡			◇1 ⌶	◇1	bus	◇1	◇1 ⊡	◇1 ⊡	◇1 ⌶	◇1	bus		◇1 ⊡
London Euston 15 ⊖	d		14 43				14 46	15 07	15 10			15 40						15 46	16 07	16 10					16 33
Watford Junction	d						15 01											16 01							
Milton Keynes Central	d		15 13				15 25		15 41									16 25		16u40					
Northampton	d						15 45											16 45							
Rugby	d						16 04											17 04							17 22
Coventry	d		15 42							15 27			16 42								16 27				
Bedworth	d												16 53												
Nuneaton	a						16 16						17 00					17 16							
	d						16 17											17 17							
Atherstone	d						16 23											17 23							
Polesworth	d																								
Tamworth	d						16 31											17 31							
Lichfield Trent Valley	d						16 37											17 37							
Rugeley Trent Valley	d						16 43											17 43							
Stafford	d	16 09			16 18		16 54	16a22		16 31	16 35				17 01	17 09		18 20	17a22		17 30	17 36	17 40		17 56
Norton Bridge Station Drv	d				16a42													→					18a04		
Stone	d						17 05																		
Stone Crown Street	d					16 20											17 20								
Stone Granville Square	a																								
Barlaston Orchard Place	d					16 30											17 30								
Wedgwood Old Road Bridge	d					16 32											17 32								
Stoke-on-Trent	d					16 48	17 13			16a54					17a19		17 48				17a54				
Hanley Bus Station	a					16 55											17 55								
Kidsgrove	d						17 21																		
Alsager	d						17 26																		
Crewe	a	16 30	17 07				17 38		16 47		16 56	17 10				17 30				17 47		17 56			18 16

		VT	XC	LM	LM	VT	LM	XC	LM		VT	LM	VT	VT	LM	XC	LM	VT	XC		LM	VT	LM	LM	LM
		◇1 ⊡	◇1 ⌶	◇1	◇1	◇1 ⊠	bus	◇1 ⌶			◇1 ⊠	◇1	◇1 ⊠	◇1 ⊠	bus	◇1 ⌶	◇1	◇1 ⊠	◇1 ⌶			◇1 ⊠	◇1		◇1
London Euston 15 ⊖	d	16 40				17 07					17 10		17 33	17 40				18 07				18 10			18 29
Watford Junction	d																								18 47
Milton Keynes Central	d										17u40											18u40			19 23
Northampton	d																								19 45
Rugby	d												18 23												20 04
Coventry	d							17 27	17 42										18 27		18 42			19 43	
Bedworth	d								17 53												18 53			19 54	
Nuneaton	a								18 00		18 11										19 00	19 12		20 01	20 16
	d										18 12											19 13			20 17
Atherstone	d																								20 23
Polesworth	d																								
Tamworth	d																								20 31
Lichfield Trent Valley	d																								→
Rugeley Trent Valley	d				←																				
Stafford	d		18 02	18 09	18 20	18 24		18 30				18 35	18 55			19 01	19 09	19 24	19 29				19 36		
Norton Bridge Station Drv	d																								
Stone	d				18 31																				
Stone Crown Street	d						18 20								18 45										
Stone Granville Square	a																								
Barlaston Orchard Place	d						18 30								18 55										
Wedgwood Old Road Bridge	d						18 32								18 57										
Stoke-on-Trent	d		18a20		18 43		18 48	18a54							19 13	19a19			19a54						
Hanley Bus Station	a						19 00								19 20										
Kidsgrove	d				18 51																				
Alsager	d				18 56																				
Crewe	a	18 10		18 30	19 05	18 42					18 53	19 00	19 14	19 10			19 30	19 42				19 53	20 01		

Table 67

London - Stoke-on-Trent and Crewe
Coventry - Nuneaton

Mondays to Fridays
until 29 June

Network Diagram - see first Page of Table 67

	VT	VT	XC	LM	VT	VT ThFO	VT	VT	XC	VT	LM	VT	LM	LM	VT	VT	XC	VT	VT	LM	XC
	◇1 ⊠	◇1 ⊠	◇1 ⊤	◇1	◇1 ⊠	◇ ☕	■ 1 ☕	■ 1 ☕	◇1	◇1 ⊠	◇1	◇1 ☕		◇1	◇1 ☕	◇1 ☕	◇1	◇1 ☕	◇1 ☕	◇1	◇1
London Euston 15 ⊖ d	18 33	18 40			18 43	18 57	19 07	19 10				19 40			20 07	20 10		20 40			
Watford Junction d																					
Milton Keynes Central d					19 13			19u40								20 40					
Northampton d																					
Rugby d	19 23																				
Coventry d					19 42				19 27				20 42				20 27				21 27
Bedworth d													20 53								
Nuneaton a							20 02						21 00		21 02						
d							20 03								21 03						
Atherstone d																					
Polesworth d											←										
Tamworth d											20 31	20 43									
Lichfield Trent Valley d											20 37	20 50									
Rugeley Trent Valley d										←	20 43										
Stafford d	19 56		20 01	20 09	20 52		20a26		20 30	20 52		21 04		21 09	21a27		21 32		21 55	22 09	22 30
Norton Bridge Station Drv d					→																
Stone d																					
Stone Crown Street d																					
Stone Granville Square a																					
Barlaston Orchard Place d																					
Wedgwood Old Road Bridge d																					
Stoke-on-Trent d			20a19						20a54		21 05						21a54				22a53
Hanley Bus Station a																					
Kidsgrove d											21 14										
Alsager d											21 18										
Crewe a	20 15	20 11		20 30		20s33		20 48		21 15	21 27	21 21		21 30		21 48		22 12	22 17	22 30	

	LM	VT FO	VT FX	VT FO	VT FX	XC	LM	AW FO	AW FX	VT	LM
		◇1 B ☕	◇1 C ☕	◇1 B ☕	◇1 C ☕	◇1	◇1	◇ B	◇ C	◇1 ☕	◇1
London Euston 15 ⊖ d		21 07	21 07	21 10	21 10					22 00	
Watford Junction d				21u25	21u25						
Milton Keynes Central d		21 38	21 38							22 31	
Northampton d											
Rugby d				22 04	22 04					22 54	
Coventry d	21 42										
Bedworth d	21 53										
Nuneaton a	22 02	22 07	22 07							23 03	
d		22 08	22 08							23 04	
Atherstone d											
Polesworth d											
Tamworth d										23s15	
Lichfield Trent Valley d										23s22	
Rugeley Trent Valley d											
Stafford d				22 34	22 34	23 01	23 13	23 30	23 30	23s38	23 53
Norton Bridge Station Drv d											
Stone d											
Stone Crown Street d											
Stone Granville Square a											
Barlaston Orchard Place d											
Wedgwood Old Road Bridge d											
Stoke-on-Trent d						23a21					
Hanley Bus Station a											
Kidsgrove d											
Alsager d											
Crewe a		22 46	22 49	22 53	22 56		23 43	23 55	23 56	00s03	00 16

B also from 25 June until 28 June

C until 21 June

Table 67

London - Stoke-on-Trent and Crewe
Coventry - Nuneaton

Mondays to Fridays
2 July to 14 September

Network Diagram - see first Page of Table 67

	VT MO	VT MX	LM MX	VT MO	VT	VT MX	VT	VT MX	VT	XC	LM	XC	LM	LM	VT	VT	LM	LM	XC	LM	LM	LM
	◇1 ☕	◇1 ☕	◇1	◇1 ☕	◇1 A ☕	◇1 B ☕	◇1 A ☕	◇1 B ☕	◇1 ⊠	◇1	1	◇1 ⊤	◇1		◇1 ⊠	◇1 ⊠	🚌	◇1	◇1 ⊤	◇1	◇1	
London Euston 15 ⊖ d	21p51	22p00			23p45	23p45	01 00	01 00							05 27	05 39						
Watford Junction d															05u45	06u02						
Milton Keynes Central d	22p38	22p31											05 21		06 10	06 22						
Northampton d													05 42								06 41	
Rugby d	23p18	22p54			00s33	00s47	01s48	01s48					06 05			06 45					07 01	
Coventry d														06 12								07 06
Bedworth d														06 23								07 17
Nuneaton a	23p28	23p03			00s44	00s58	01s59	02s05					06 16	06 30	06 38						07 13	07 27
d	23p29	23p04											06 17		06 39						07 15	
Atherstone d													06 23								07 21	
Polesworth d																					07 26	
Tamworth d		23b15											06 31								07 31	
Lichfield Trent Valley d		23b22											06 37								07 37	
Rugeley Trent Valley d				←									06 44								07 43	
Stafford d	23b53	23b38	23p53	23b53	01s08	01s22	02s23	02s29	06 02	06 30	06 36	06 55	06 58		07 03			07 08	07 30	07 36	07 54	
Norton Bridge Station Drv d	→																					
Stone d													07 18								08 05	
Stone Crown Street d																	07 05					
Stone Granville Square a																						
Barlaston Orchard Place d																	07 15					
Wedgwood Old Road Bridge d																	07 17					
Stoke-on-Trent d										06a50		07a13	07 26				07 38				08 13	
Hanley Bus Station a																	07 45					
Kidsgrove d													07 34								08 21	
Alsager d													07 39								08 26	
Crewe a		00s03	00 16	00s21	01s27	01s41	02s42	02s50	06 21		06 56		07 49		07 22	07 30		07 33	07 50	07 56	08 38	

	XC	LM	LM	LM	VT	VT	VT	LM	XC	LM	LM	VT	XC	LM	LM	LM	VT	VT	XC	LM	LM	VT
	◇1 ⊤	◇1	🚌	◇1	◇1 ⊠	◇1 ⊠	◇1 ⊠	🚌	◇1 ⊤		◇1	◇1 ⊠	◇1 ⊤	◇1	🚌	◇1	◇1 ⊠	◇1 ⊠	◇1 ⊤		◇1	◇1 ⊠
London Euston 15 ⊖ d				06 24	06 36	07 07	07 10					07 35				07 47	08 07	08 10				08 40
Watford Junction d				06 41	06u51											08 02						
Milton Keynes Central d				07 22			07 41					08 06				08 31		08 41				
Northampton d				07 45												08 45						
Rugby d				08 04												09 04						
Coventry d									07 27	08 04									08 27	09 06		
Bedworth d										08 15										09 17		
Nuneaton a				08 17						08 23						09 16				09 25		
d				08 17												09 17						
Atherstone d				08 23												09 23						
Polesworth d																						
Tamworth d				08 31												09 31						
Lichfield Trent Valley d				08 37												09 37						
Rugeley Trent Valley d				08 43												09 43						
Stafford d	08 01	08 09		08 54		08a22		08 25	08 30		08 36		09 01	09 09		09 54	09a22		09 30		09 35	
Norton Bridge Station Drv d								08 40														
Stone d				09 05												10 05						
Stone Crown Street d			08 15												09 20							
Stone Granville Square a								09 02														
Barlaston Orchard Place d			08 25												09 30							
Wedgwood Old Road Bridge d			08 27												09 32							
Stoke-on-Trent d	08a19		08 48	09 13					08a54				09a19		09 48	10 13			09a54			
Hanley Bus Station a			08 55												09 55							
Kidsgrove d				09 21												10 21						
Alsager d				09 26												10 26						
Crewe a		08 30		09 38	08 10		08 47				08 56	09 10		09 30		10 38		09 47			09 56	10 10

A 30 July, 6 August, 13 August, 3 September, 10 September

B from 31 July until 7 September, not from 14 August until 29 August

b Previous night, stops to set down only

London - Stoke-on-Trent and Crewe
Coventry - Nuneaton

Network Diagram - see first Page of Table 67

		XC		LM	VT	LM	LM	VT	VT	VT	LM	XC		LM	VT	LM	XC	LM	LM	LM	VT	VT		XC	LM
		◇1		◇1	◇1		◇1	◇1	◇1	◇1		◇1		◇1	◇1		◇1	◇1		◇1	◇1	◇1		◇1	◇1
		⌶			⊠	🚌		⊠	⊠	⊠	🚌	⌶			⊠		⌶		🚌		⊠	⊠		⌶	
London Euston 15 ⊖	d				08 43		08 46	09 07	09 10	09 10					09 40					09 46	10 07	10 10			
Watford Junction	d						09 01													10 01					
Milton Keynes Central	d				09 13		09 25		09 40	09 41										10 25		10 41			
Northampton	d						09 45													10 45					
Rugby	d						10 04													11 04					
Coventry	d				09 42							09 27				10 42								10 27	
Bedworth	d															10 53									
Nuneaton	a						10 16									11 00				11 16					
	d						10 17													11 17					
Atherstone	d						10 23													11 23					
Polesworth	d																								
Tamworth	d						10 31													11 31					
Lichfield Trent Valley	d						10 37													11 37					
Rugeley Trent Valley	d						10 43													11 43					
Stafford	d	10 01		10 09			10 54	10a22			10 25	10 30		10 35			11 01	11 09		11 54	11a22			11 30	11 35
Norton Bridge Station Drv	d										10 40														
Stone	d						11 05													12 05					
Stone Crown Street	d					10 20													11 20						
Stone Granville Square	a										11 02														
Barlaston Orchard Place	d					10 30													11 30						
Wedgwood Old Road Bridge	d					10 32													11 32						
Stoke-on-Trent	d	10a19				10 48	11 13					10a54					11a19		11 48	12 13				11a54	
Hanley Bus Station	a					10 55													11 55						
Kidsgrove	d						11 21													12 21					
Alsager	d						11 26													12 26					
Crewe	a			10 30	11 07		11 38		10 47	10 47				10 56	11 10			11 30		12 38		11 47			11 56

		VT	LM	XC	LM	LM	LM	VT		VT	XC	LM	VT	LM	LM	XC	LM	LM		LM	VT	VT	XC	LM	VT
		◇1		◇1	◇1		◇1	◇1		◇1	◇1	◇1	◇1			◇1	◇1			◇1	◇1	◇1	◇1	◇1	◇1
		⊠		⌶		🚌		☕		☕	⌶		☕	🚌		⌶		🚌			☕	☕	⌶		☕
London Euston 15 ⊖	d	10 40					10 46	11 07		11 10			11 40							11 46	12 07	12 10			12 40
Watford Junction	d						11 01													12 01					
Milton Keynes Central	d						11 25			11 41										12 25		12 41			
Northampton	d						11 45													12 45					
Rugby	d						12 04													13 04					
Coventry	d		11 42								11 27				12 42								12 27		
Bedworth	d		11 53												12 53										
Nuneaton	a		12 00				12 16								13 00					13 16					
	d						12 17													13 17					
Atherstone	d						12 23													13 23					
Polesworth	d																								
Tamworth	d						12 31													13 31					
Lichfield Trent Valley	d						12 37													13 37					
Rugeley Trent Valley	d						12 43													13 43					
Stafford	d			12 01	12 09		12 54	12a22			12 30	12 35		12 35		13 01	13 09			13 54	13a22		13 30	13 35	
Norton Bridge Station Drv	d													12 59											
Stone	d						13 05													14 05					
Stone Crown Street	d					12 20												13 20							
Stone Granville Square	a													13 39											
Barlaston Orchard Place	d					12 30												13 30							
Wedgwood Old Road Bridge	d					12 32												13 32							
Stoke-on-Trent	d			12a19		12 48	13 13				12a54					13a19		13 48		14 13			13a54		
Hanley Bus Station	a					12 55												13 55							
Kidsgrove	d						13 21													14 21					
Alsager	d						13 26													14 26					
Crewe	a	12 10			12 30		13 38			12 47		12 56	13 10				13 30			14 38		13 47		13 56	14 10

London - Stoke-on-Trent and Crewe
Coventry - Nuneaton

Network Diagram - see first Page of Table 67

		LM	XC	LM		LM	LM	LM	VT	VT	XC	LM	VT	VT		LM	XC	LM	VT	LM	LM	VT	VT	XC	
			◇1	◇1				◇1	◇1	◇1	◇1	◇1	◇	◇1			◇1	◇1	◇1		◇1	◇1	◇1	◇1	
													A												
			⌶			🚌	🚌		☕	☕	⌶		☕	☕			⌶		☕	🚌		☕	☕	⌶	
London Euston 15 ⊖	d							12 46	13 07	13 10			13 33	13 40					13 43		13 46	14 07	14 10		
Watford Junction	d							13 01													14 01				
Milton Keynes Central	d							13 25		13 41									14 13		14 25		14 41		
Northampton	d							13 45													14 45				
Rugby	d							14 04													15 04				
Coventry	d	13 42									13 27					14 42			14 42					14 27	
Bedworth	d	13 53														14 53									
Nuneaton	a	14 00						14 16								15 00					15 16				
	d							14 17													15 17				
Atherstone	d							14 23													15 23				
Polesworth	d																								
Tamworth	d							14 31													15 31				
Lichfield Trent Valley	d							14 37													15 37				
Rugeley Trent Valley	d							14 43													15 43				
Stafford	d		14 01	14 09		14 18		14 54	14a22		14 30	14 35					15 01	15 09			15 54	15a22		15 30	
Norton Bridge Station Drv	d					14 42																			
Stone	d							15 05													16 05				
Stone Crown Street	d						14 20													15 20					
Stone Granville Square	a					14 54																			
Barlaston Orchard Place	d						14 30													15 30					
Wedgwood Old Road Bridge	d						14 32													15 32					
Stoke-on-Trent	d		14a19				14 48	15 13			14a54						15a19			15 48	16 13			15a54	
Hanley Bus Station	a						14 55													15 55					
Kidsgrove	d							15 21													16 21				
Alsager	d							15 26													16 26				
Crewe	a			14 30				15 38		14 47		14 56	15 16	15 10				15 30	16 07		16 38		15 47		

		LM	VT	LM	XC	LM	LM	LM	LM	VT		VT	XC	LM	VT	LM	XC	LM	LM	LM		VT	VT	XC	LM
		◇1	◇1		◇1	◇1			◇1	◇1		◇1	◇1	◇1	◇1		◇1	◇1		◇1		◇1	◇1	◇1	◇1
			☕		⌶		🚌	🚌		☕		☕	⌶		☕		⌶		🚌			☕	☕	⌶	
London Euston 15 ⊖	d		14 40						14 46	15 07		15 10			15 40					15 46		16 07	16 10		
Watford Junction	d								15 01											16 01					
Milton Keynes Central	d								15 25			15 41								16 25			16u40		
Northampton	d								15 45											16 45					
Rugby	d								16 04											17 04					
Coventry	d			15 42									15 27			16 42								16 27	
Bedworth	d			15 53												16 53									
Nuneaton	a			16 00					16 16							17 00				17 16					
	d								16 17											17 17					
Atherstone	d								16 23											17 23					
Polesworth	d																								
Tamworth	d								16 31											17 31					
Lichfield Trent Valley	d								16 37											17 37					
Rugeley Trent Valley	d								16 43											17 43					
Stafford	d	15 35			16 02	16 09	16 18		16 54	16a22			16 31	16 35			17 01	17 09		18 20		17a22		17 30	17 36
Norton Bridge Station Drv	d						16a42													→					
Stone	d								17 05																
Stone Crown Street	d							16 20											17 20						
Stone Granville Square	a																								
Barlaston Orchard Place	d							16 30											17 30						
Wedgwood Old Road Bridge	d							16 32											17 32						
Stoke-on-Trent	d				16a20			16 48	17 13				16a54				17a19		17 48					17a54	
Hanley Bus Station	a							16 55											17 55						
Kidsgrove	d								17 21																
Alsager	d								17 26																
Crewe	a	15 56	16 11			16 30			17 38			16 47		16 56	17 10			17 30					17 47		17 56

A 6 July, 13 July, 20 July, 17 August, 24 August, September

Table 67

Mondays to Fridays
2 July to 14 September

London - Stoke-on-Trent and Crewe
Coventry - Nuneaton

Network Diagram - see first Page of Table 67

		LM	VT	VT	LM	XC	LM	LM	LM	LM	VT	VT	XC	LM	LM	LM	LM	VT	VT	XC	LM	LM	VT
		🚌	◇■ ⊐	◇■ ⊐		◇■ ⌶	◇■	◇■	🚌	■ A	◇■ ⊠	◇■ ⊠	◇■ ⌶	◇■		🚌	■ A	◇■ ⊠	◇■ ⊠	◇■ ⌶	◇■	■ A	◇■ ⊠
London Euston ⊖	d		16 33	16 40						16 46	17 07	17 10					17 24	17 33	17 40				18 07
Watford Junction	d																17 44						
Milton Keynes Central	d									17 23		17u40					18 21						
Northampton	d									17 45							18 43						
Rugby	d		17 22							18 04							19 05	18 23					
Coventry	d				17 42								17 27		18 42								
Bedworth	d				17 53										18 53								
Nuneaton	a				18 00					18 16		18 11			19 00		19 17						
	d									18 22		18 12					19 20						
Atherstone	d									18 28							19 26						
Polesworth	d																						
Tamworth	d									18 36							19 35						
Lichfield Trent Valley	d									18 42							19 41						
Rugeley Trent Valley	d							←		18 49							19 48					←	
Stafford	d	17 40	17 56			18 02	18 09	18 20		19 13	18 24		18 30	18 35				18 55		19 01	19 09	19 13	19 24
Norton Bridge Station Drv	d	18a04								→													
Stone	d							18 31														19 31	
Stone Crown Street	d								18 20							18 45							
Stone Granville Square	a																						
Barlaston Orchard Place	d								18 30							18 55							
Wedgwood Old Road Bridge	d								18 32							18 57							
Stoke-on-Trent	d					18a20		18 43	18 48				18a54			19 13	20 13			19a19		19 43	
Hanley Bus Station	a								19 00							19 20							
Kidsgrove	d							18 51									20 21					19 51	
Alsager	d							18 56									20 25					19 56	
Crewe	a		18 16	18 10			18 30	19 05			18 42	18 53		19 00			→	19 14	19 10		19 30	20 05	19 42

		VT	XC	LM	LM	LM	LM	VT	VT	XC	LM	VT	VT ThFO	LM	VT	VT	XC	VT	LM	LM	VT
		◇■ ⊠	◇■ ⌶	◇■		◇■ B	◇■ A	◇■ ⊠	◇■ ⊠	◇■ ⌶	◇■	◇■ ⊠	◇ C ⊐	■ A	■ ⊐	■ ⊐	◇■	◇■ ⊠	◇■ B	◇■ A	◇■ ⊐
London Euston ⊖	d	18 10				18 29	18 29	18 33	18 40			18 43	18 57		19 07	19 10					19 40
Watford Junction	d					18 47	18 47														
Milton Keynes Central	d	18u40				19 23	19 23					19 13				19 40					
Northampton	d					19 45	19 45														
Rugby	d					20 04	20 04	19 23													
Coventry	d		18 27		19 43							19 42					19 27				
Bedworth	d				19 54																
Nuneaton	a	19 12			20 01	20 16	20 16								20 02						
	d	19 13				20 17	20 17								20 03						
Atherstone	d					20 23	20 23														
Polesworth	d																		←	←	
Tamworth	d					20 31	20 31												20 31	20 31	20 43
Lichfield Trent Valley	d					→	→												20 37	20 37	20 50
Rugeley Trent Valley	d																	←	20 43	20 43	
Stafford	d		19 29	19 36				19 56		20 01	20 09	20 52			20a26		20 30	20 52		20 54	21 04
Norton Bridge Station Drv	d											→									
Stone	d																			21 05	
Stone Crown Street	d																				
Stone Granville Square	a																				
Barlaston Orchard Place	d																				
Wedgwood Old Road Bridge	d																				
Stoke-on-Trent	d		19a54							20a19							20a54		21 05	21 13	
Hanley Bus Station	a																				
Kidsgrove	d													←					21 14	21 21	
Alsager	d													20 25					21 18	21 26	
Crewe	a	19 53		20 01				20 15	20 11		20 30		20s33	20 37		20 48		21 15	21 27	21 36	21 21

A from 10 September until 14 September
B from 2 July until 7 September

Table 67

Mondays to Fridays
2 July to 14 September

London - Stoke-on-Trent and Crewe
Coventry - Nuneaton

Network Diagram - see first Page of Table 67

		LM	LM	VT	VT	XC	LM	VT	VT	LM	XC	LM	VT	VT	LM	XC	LM	AW	VT	LM	VT FX	VT
			◇■	◇■ ⊐	◇■ ⊐	◇■	■ A	◇■ ⊐	◇■ ⊐	◇■	◇■		◇■ ⊐	◇■ ⊐	■ A	◇■	◇■	◇	◇■ ⊐	◇■	◇■ B ⊐	◇■ C ⊐
London Euston ⊖	d			20 07	20 10		20 13	20 40					21 07	21 10					22 00		23 45	23 45
Watford Junction	d													21u25								
Milton Keynes Central	d				20 40		20 55						21 38						22 31			
Northampton	d						21 24															
Rugby	d						21 45							22 04					22 54		00s47	00s47
Coventry	d	20 42				20 27					21 27	21 42										
Bedworth	d	20 53										21 53										
Nuneaton	a	21 00		21 02			21 57					22 02	22 07						23 03		00s58	01s02
	d			21 03			22 01						22 08						23 04			
Atherstone	d						22 07															
Polesworth	d																					
Tamworth	d						22 15												23s15			
Lichfield Trent Valley	d						22 21												23s22			
Rugeley Trent Valley	d						22 28								←							
Stafford	d		21 09	21a27		21 32	22 41		21 55	22 09	22 30			22 34	22 41	23 01	23 13	23 30	23s38	23 53	01s22	01s31
Norton Bridge Station Drv	d						→															
Stone	d																					
Stone Crown Street	d																					
Stone Granville Square	a																					
Barlaston Orchard Place	d																					
Wedgwood Old Road Bridge	d																					
Stoke-on-Trent	d					21a54					22a53					23a20						
Hanley Bus Station	a																					
Kidsgrove	d																					
Alsager	d																					
Crewe	a		21 30		21 48			22 12	22 17	22 30			22 46	22 53	23 04		23 43	23 55	00s03	00 16	01s41	01s55

Mondays to Fridays
from 17 September

		VT MO	VT MX	LM MX	VT MO	VT	XC	LM	XC	LM	LM	VT	VT	LM	LM	XC	LM	LM	LM	XC	LM	LM	LM
		◇■ ⊐	◇■ ⊐	◇■	◇■ ⊐	◇■ ⊠	◇■	■	◇■ ⌶	◇■		◇■ ⊠	◇■ ⊠	🚌	◇■	◇■ ⌶	◇■	◇■		◇■ ⌶	◇■	🚌	◇■
London Euston ⊖	d	21p51	22p00									05 27	05 39										06 24
Watford Junction	d											05u45	06u02										06 41
Milton Keynes Central	d	22p38	22p31							05 21		06 10	06 22										07 22
Northampton	d									05 42								06 41					07 45
Rugby	d	23p18	22p54							06 05			06 45					07 01					08 04
Coventry	d										06 12								07 06				
Bedworth	d										06 23								07 17				
Nuneaton	a	23p28	23p03							06 16	06 30	06 38						07 13	07 27				08 17
	d	23p29	23p04							06 17		06 39						07 15					08 17
Atherstone	d									06 23								07 21					08 23
Polesworth	d																	07 26					
Tamworth	d		23b15							06 31								07 31					08 31
Lichfield Trent Valley	d		23b22							06 37								07 37					08 37
Rugeley Trent Valley	d				←					06 44								07 43					08 43
Stafford	d	23b53	23b38	23p53	23b53	06 02	06 30	06 36	06 55	06 58		07 03			07 08	07 30	07 36	07 54		08 01	08 09		08 54
Norton Bridge Station Drv	d	→																					
Stone	d									07 18								08 05					09 05
Stone Crown Street	d													07 05								08 15	
Stone Granville Square	a																						
Barlaston Orchard Place	d													07 15								08 25	
Wedgwood Old Road Bridge	d													07 17								08 27	
Stoke-on-Trent	d						06a50		07a13	07 26				07 38				08 13		08a19		08 48	09 13
Hanley Bus Station	a													07 45								08 55	
Kidsgrove	d									07 34								08 21					09 21
Alsager	d									07 39								08 26					09 26
Crewe	a		00s03	00 16	00s21	06 21		06 56		07 49		07 22	07 30		07 33	07 50	07 56	08 38			08 30		09 38

A from 10 September until 14 September
B from 30 July until 6 September, not from 13 August until 28 August
C 27 July, 3 August, 10 August, 31 August, 7 September
b Previous night, stops to set down only

Table 67

Mondays to Fridays
from 17 September

London - Stoke-on-Trent and Crewe
Coventry - Nuneaton

Network Diagram - see first Page of Table 67

		VT	VT	VT	LM	XC		LM	LM	VT	XC	LM	LM	LM	VT	VT		XC	LM	LM	VT	XC	LM	LM	LM
		◇1 ⊠	◇1 ⊠	◇1 ⊠	🚌	◇1 ⌶			◇1	◇1 ⊠	◇1 ⌶	◇1	🚌	◇1	◇1 ⊠	◇1 ⊠		◇1 ⌶		◇1	◇1 ⊠	◇1 ⌶	◇1	🚌	◇1
London Euston ⊖	d	06 36	07 07	07 10						07 35				07 47	08 07	08 10					08 40				08 46
Watford Junction	d	06u51												08 02											09 01
Milton Keynes Central	d			07 41						08 06				08 31		08 41									09 25
Northampton	d													08 45											09 45
Rugby	d													09 04											10 04
Coventry	d					07 27		08 04										08 27	09 06						
Bedworth	d							08 15											09 17						
Nuneaton	a							08 23						09 16					09 25						10 16
	d													09 17											10 17
Atherstone	d													09 23											10 23
Polesworth	d																								
Tamworth	d													09 31											10 31
Lichfield Trent Valley	d													09 37											10 37
Rugeley Trent Valley	d													09 43											10 43
Stafford	d		08a22		08 25	08 30			08 36		09 01	09 09		09 54	09a22			09 30		09 35		10 01	10 09		10 54
Norton Bridge Station Drv	d				08 40																				
Stone	d													10 05											11 05
Stone Crown Street	d												09 20											10 20	
Stone Granville Square	a				09 02																				
Barlaston Orchard Place	d												09 30											10 30	
Wedgwood Old Road Bridge	d												09 32											10 32	
Stoke-on-Trent	d					08a54					09a19		09 48	10 13				09a54				10a19		10 48	11 13
Hanley Bus Station	a												09 55											10 55	
Kidsgrove	d													10 21											11 21
Alsager	d													10 26											11 26
Crewe	a	08 10		08 47					08 56	09 10		09 30		10 38		09 47				09 56	10 10		10 30		11 38

		VT		VT	VT	LM	XC	LM	VT	LM	XC	LM		LM	LM	VT	VT	XC	LM	VT	LM	XC		LM	LM
		◇1 ⊠		◇1 ⊠	◇1 ⊠	🚌	◇1 ⌶	◇1	◇1 ⊠		◇1 ⌶	◇1		🚌	◇1	◇1 ⊠	◇1 ⊠	◇1 ⌶	◇1	◇1 ⊠		◇1 ⌶		◇1	🚌
London Euston ⊖	d	09 07		09 10	09 10				09 40						09 46	10 07	10 10			10 40					
Watford Junction	d														10 01										
Milton Keynes Central	d			09 40	09 41										10 25		10 41								
Northampton	d														10 45										
Rugby	d														11 04										
Coventry	d						09 27			10 42								10 27			11 42				
Bedworth	d									10 53											11 53				
Nuneaton	a									11 00					11 16						12 00				
	d														11 17										
Atherstone	d														11 23										
Polesworth	d																								
Tamworth	d														11 31										
Lichfield Trent Valley	d														11 37										
Rugeley Trent Valley	d														11 43										
Stafford	d	10a22				10 25	10 30	10 35			11 01	11 09			11 54	11a22		11 30	11 35			12 01		12 09	
Norton Bridge Station Drv	d					10 40																			
Stone	d														12 05										
Stone Crown Street	d													11 20											12 20
Stone Granville Square	a					11 02																			
Barlaston Orchard Place	d													11 30											12 30
Wedgwood Old Road Bridge	d													11 32											12 32
Stoke-on-Trent	d						10a54				11a19			11 48	12 13			11a54				12a19			12 48
Hanley Bus Station	a													11 55											12 55
Kidsgrove	d														12 21										
Alsager	d														12 26										
Crewe	a			10 47	10 47			10 56	11 10			11 30			12 38		11 47		11 56	12 10				12 30	

		LM	VT	VT	XC	LM	VT	LM		LM	XC	LM	LM	LM	VT	VT	XC	LM		VT	LM	XC	LM	LM	LM
		◇1	◇1 ⊒	◇1 ⊒	◇1 ⌶	◇1	◇1 ⊒	🚌			◇1 ⌶	◇1	🚌	◇1	◇1 ⊒	◇1 ⊒	◇1 ⌶	◇1		◇1 ⊒		◇1 ⌶	◇1	🚌	🚌
London Euston ⊖	d	10 46	11 07	11 10			11 40							11 46	12 07	12 10				12 40					
Watford Junction	d	11 01												12 01											
Milton Keynes Central	d	11 25		11 41										12 25		12 41									
Northampton	d	11 45												12 45											
Rugby	d	12 04												13 04											
Coventry	d				11 27					12 42							12 27				13 42				
Bedworth	d									12 53											13 53				
Nuneaton	a	12 16								13 00				13 16							14 00				
	d	12 17												13 17											
Atherstone	d	12 23												13 23											
Polesworth	d																								
Tamworth	d	12 31												13 31											
Lichfield Trent Valley	d	12 37												13 37											
Rugeley Trent Valley	d	12 43												13 43											
Stafford	d	12 54	12a22		12 30	12 35		12 35			13 01	13 09		13 54	13a22		13 30	13 35				14 01	14 09	14 18	
Norton Bridge Station Drv	d							12 59																14 42	
Stone	d	13 05												14 05											
Stone Crown Street	d												13 20												14 20
Stone Granville Square	a							13 39																14 54	
Barlaston Orchard Place	d												13 30												14 30
Wedgwood Old Road Bridge	d												13 32												14 32
Stoke-on-Trent	d	13 13			12a54						13a19		13 48	14 13			13a54					14a19			14 48
Hanley Bus Station	a												13 55												14 55
Kidsgrove	d	13 21												14 21											
Alsager	d	13 26												14 26											
Crewe	a	13 38		12 47		12 56	13 10					13 30		14 38		13 47		13 56		14 10			14 30		

Table 67

Mondays to Fridays
from 17 September

London - Stoke-on-Trent and Crewe
Coventry - Nuneaton

Network Diagram - see first Page of Table 67

		LM	VT	VT		XC	LM	VT FO	VT	LM	XC	LM	LM	LM		VT	VT	XC	LM	VT	LM	XC	LM	LM
		◇1	◇1 ⊒	◇1 ⊒		◇1 ⌶	◇1	◇ ⊒	◇1 ⊒		◇1 ⌶	◇1	🚌	◇1		◇1 ⊒	◇1 ⊒	◇1 ⌶	◇1	◇1 ⊒		◇1 ⌶	◇1	🚌
London Euston ⊖	d	12 46	13 07	13 10				13 33	13 40					13 46		14 07	14 10			14 40				
Watford Junction	d	13 01												14 01										
Milton Keynes Central	d	13 25		13 41										14 25			14 41							
Northampton	d	13 45												14 45										
Rugby	d	14 04												15 04										
Coventry	d					13 27				14 42								14 27			15 42			
Bedworth	d									14 53											15 53			
Nuneaton	a	14 16								15 00				15 16							16 00			
	d	14 17												15 17										
Atherstone	d	14 23												15 23										
Polesworth	d																							
Tamworth	d	14 31												15 31										
Lichfield Trent Valley	d	14 37												15 37										
Rugeley Trent Valley	d	14 43												15 43										
Stafford	d	14 54	14a22			14 30	14 35				15 01	15 09		15 54		15a22		15 30	15 35			16 02	16 09	16 18
Norton Bridge Station Drv	d																							16a42
Stone	d	15 05												16 05										
Stone Crown Street	d												15 20											
Stone Granville Square	a																							
Barlaston Orchard Place	d												15 30											
Wedgwood Old Road Bridge	d												15 32											
Stoke-on-Trent	d	15 13				14a54					15a19		15 48	16 13				15a54				16a20		
Hanley Bus Station	a												15 55											
Kidsgrove	d	15 21												16 21										
Alsager	d	15 26												16 26										
Crewe	a	15 38		14 47			14 56	15 16	15 10			15 30		16 38			15 47		15 56	16 11			16 30	

		LM	LM	VT	VT	XC	LM	VT	LM	XC		LM	LM	LM	VT	VT	XC	LM	LM	VT		VT	LM	XC	LM
		🚌	◇1	◇1 ⊒	◇1 ⊒	◇1 ⌶	◇1	◇1 ⊒		◇1 ⌶		◇1	🚌	◇1	◇1 ⊒	◇1 ⊒	◇1 ⌶	◇1	🚌	◇1 ⊒		◇1 ⊒		◇1 ⌶	◇1
London Euston ⊖	d		14 46	15 07	15 10			15 40						15 46	16 07	16 10				16 33		16 40			
Watford Junction	d		15 01											16 01											
Milton Keynes Central	d		15 25		15 41									16 25		16u40									
Northampton	d		15 45											16 45											
Rugby	d		16 04											17 04						17 22					
Coventry	d					15 27			16 42								16 27						17 42		
Bedworth	d								16 53														17 53		
Nuneaton	a		16 16						17 00					17 16									18 00		
	d		16 17											17 17											
Atherstone	d		16 23											17 23											
Polesworth	d																								
Tamworth	d		16 31											17 31											
Lichfield Trent Valley	d		16 37											17 37											
Rugeley Trent Valley	d		16 43											17 43											
Stafford	d		16 54	16a22		16 31	16 35			17 01		17 09		18 20	17a22		17 30	17 36	17 40	17 56				18 02	18 09
Norton Bridge Station Drv	d													→					18a04						
Stone	d		17 05																						
Stone Crown Street	d	16 20											17 20												
Stone Granville Square	a																								
Barlaston Orchard Place	d	16 30											17 30												
Wedgwood Old Road Bridge	d	16 32											17 32												
Stoke-on-Trent	d	16 48	17 13			16a54				17a19			17 48				17a54							18a20	
Hanley Bus Station	a	16 55											17 55												
Kidsgrove	d		17 21																						
Alsager	d		17 26																						
Crewe	a		17 38		16 47		16 56	17 10				17 30				17 47		17 56		18 16		18 10			18 30

		LM	LM	LM	VT	VT		XC	LM	LM	LM	LM	VT	VT	XC	LM		LM	VT	VT	XC	LM	LM	LM	VT
		◇1	🚌	1	◇1 ⊠	◇1 ⊠		◇1 ⌶	◇1		🚌	1	◇1 ⊠	◇1 ⊠	◇1 ⌶	◇1		1	◇1 ⊠	◇1 ⊠	◇1 ⌶	◇1		◇1	◇1 ⊠
London Euston ⊖	d			16 46	17 07	17 10						17 24	17 33	17 40					18 07	18 10				18 29	18 33
Watford Junction	d											17 44												18 47	
Milton Keynes Central	d			17 23		17u40						18 21								18u40				19 23	
Northampton	d			17 45								18 43												19 45	
Rugby	d			18 04								19 05	18 23											20 04	19 23
Coventry	d							17 27		18 42											18 27		19 43		
Bedworth	d									18 53													19 54		
Nuneaton	a			18 16		18 11				19 00		19 17								19 12			20 01	20 16	
	d			18 22		18 12						19 20								19 13				20 17	
Atherstone	d			18 28								19 26												20 23	
Polesworth	d																								
Tamworth	d			18 36								19 35												20 31	
Lichfield Trent Valley	d			18 42								19 41												→	
Rugeley Trent Valley	d	←		18 49								19 48						←							
Stafford	d	18 20		19 13	18 24			18 30	18 35				18 55		19 01	19 09		19 13	19 24		19 29	19 36			19 56
Norton Bridge Station Drv	d			→																					
Stone	d	18 31																19 31							
Stone Crown Street	d		18 20								18 45														
Stone Granville Square	a																								
Barlaston Orchard Place	d		18 30								18 55														
Wedgwood Old Road Bridge	d		18 32								18 57														
Stoke-on-Trent	d	18 43	18 48					18a54			19 13	20 13			19a19			19 43			19a54				
Hanley Bus Station	a		19 00								19 20														
Kidsgrove	d	18 51										20 21						19 51							
Alsager	d	18 56										20 25						19 56							
Crewe	a	19 05			18 42	18 53			19 00			→	19 14	19 10		19 30		20 05	19 42	19 53		20 01			20 15

Mondays to Fridays

from 17 September

London - Stoke-on-Trent and Crewe
Coventry - Nuneaton

Network Diagram - see first Page of Table 67

	VT	XC	LM	VT	VT ThFO	LM	VT	VT	XC	VT	LM	VT	LM	LM	VT	VT	XC	LM	VT	VT
	◇1 ⊠	◇1 H	◇1	◇1 ⊠	◇ ☕	1	1 ☕	1 ☕	◇1	◇1 ⊠	◇1	◇1 ☕		◇1	◇1 ☕	◇1 ☕	◇1	1	◇1 ☕	◇1 ☕
London Euston ⊖ d	18 40			18 43	18 57		19 07	19 10				19 40			20 07	20 10		20 13	20 40	
Watford Junction d																				
Milton Keynes Central d				19 13				19u40								20 40		20 55		
Northampton d																		21 24		
Rugby d																		21 45		
Coventry d				19 42					19 27				20 42				20 27			
Bedworth d													20 53							
Nuneaton a							20 02						21 00		21 02			21 57		
Nuneaton d							20 03								21 03			22 01		
Atherstone d																		22 07		
Polesworth d											←									
Tamworth d											20 31	20 43						22 15		
Lichfield Trent Valley d											20 37	20 50						22 21		
Rugeley Trent Valley d										←	20 43							22 28		
Stafford d		20 01	20 09	20 52			20a26		20 30	20 52	20 54	21 04		21 09	21a27		21 32	22 41		21 55
Norton Bridge Station Drv d				→														→		
Stone d											21 05									
Stone Crown Street d																				
Stone Granville Square a																				
Barlaston Orchard Place d																				
Wedgwood Old Road Bridge d																				
Stoke-on-Trent d		20a19							20a54		21 13						21a54			
Hanley Bus Station a																				
Kidsgrove d						←					21 21									
Alsager d						20 25					21 26									
Crewe a	20 11		20 30		20s33	20 37		20 48		21 15	21 36	21 21		21 30		21 48			22 12	22 17

	LM	XC	LM	VT	VT	LM	XC	LM	AW	VT	LM
	◇1	◇1		◇1 ☕	◇1 ☕	1	◇1	◇1	◇	◇1 ☕	◇1
London Euston ⊖ d				21 07	21 10					22 00	
Watford Junction d					21u25						
Milton Keynes Central d				21 38						22 31	
Northampton d											
Rugby d					22 04					22 54	
Coventry d		21 27	21 42								
Bedworth d			21 53								
Nuneaton a			22 02	22 07						23 03	
Nuneaton d				22 08						23 04	
Atherstone d											
Polesworth d											
Tamworth d										23s15	
Lichfield Trent Valley d										23s22	
Rugeley Trent Valley d						←					
Stafford d	22 09	22 30			22 34	22 41	23 01	23 13	23 30	23s38	23 53
Norton Bridge Station Drv d											
Stone d											
Stone Crown Street d											
Stone Granville Square a											
Barlaston Orchard Place d											
Wedgwood Old Road Bridge d											
Stoke-on-Trent d		22a53					23a20				
Hanley Bus Station a											
Kidsgrove d											
Alsager d											
Crewe a	22 30			22 46	22 53	23 04		23 43	23 55	00s03	00 16

Saturdays

until 30 June

London - Stoke-on-Trent and Crewe
Coventry - Nuneaton

Network Diagram - see first Page of Table 67

	VT	LM	VT	XC	LM	LM	LM	XC	LM	LM	XC	VT	LM	LM	LM	XC	LM	LM	VT	LM	VT	LM
	◇1 ☕	◇1	◇1 ☕	◇1	◇1	◇1		◇1 H	◇1	🚌	◇1 H	◇1 ☕	◇1	◇1		◇1 H	🚌	◇1	◇1 ☕	◇1	◇1 ☕	🚌
London Euston ⊖ d	22p00											06 05						06 24	06 36		07 07	
Watford Junction d												06u20						06 41	06u51			
Milton Keynes Central d	22p31					05 21						06 41						07 23				
Northampton d						05 42								06 38				07 45				
Rugby d	22p54					06 05						07 03		06 58				08 04				
Coventry d							06 16								07 16							
Bedworth d							06 27								07 27							
Nuneaton a	23p03					06 16	06 34							07 09	07 35			08 16				
Nuneaton d	23p04					06 17								07 15				08 17				
Atherstone d						06 23								07 21				08 23				
Polesworth d														07 26								
Tamworth d	23b15					06 31								07 31				08 31				
Lichfield Trent Valley d	23b22					06 37								07 37				08 37				
Rugeley Trent Valley d						06 44								07 43				08 43				
Stafford d	23b38	23p53	06 01	06 30	06 36	06 54		07 01	07 08		07 30	07 34	07 38	07 54		08 01		08 54		08 09	08 23	08 25
Norton Bridge Station Drv d																		→				08 40
Stone d						07 05								08 05								
Stone Crown Street d										07 20							08 20					
Stone Granville Square a																						09 02
Barlaston Orchard Place d										07 28							08 28					
Wedgwood Old Road Bridge d										07 30							08 30					
Stoke-on-Trent d				06a50		07 13		07a18		07 41				08 13		08a19	08 41					
Hanley Bus Station a										07 47							08 47					
Kidsgrove d						07 21								08 21								
Alsager d						07 26								08 26								
Crewe a	00s03	00 16	06 20		06 56	07 36			07 33		07 50	07 53	07 58	08 37					08 10	08 30	08 41	

	XC	LM	VT	LM	LM	XC	LM	LM	LM	VT	VT	XC	LM	VT	LM	XC	LM	LM	LM	VT	VT	LM
	◇1 H	◇1	◇1 ☕	◇1		◇1 ☕	◇1	🚌	◇1	◇1 ☕	◇1 ☕	◇1 H	◇1	◇1 ☕		◇1 ☕	◇1	🚌	◇1	◇1 ☕	◇1 ☕	🚌
London Euston ⊖ d			07 35						07 46	08 07	08 10			08 40					08 46	08 50	09 07	
Watford Junction d									08 01											09 05		
Milton Keynes Central d			08 06						08 25		08 41								09 23	09 25		
Northampton d									08 45										09 45			
Rugby d									09 04										10 04			
Coventry d	07 27				08 42							08 27			09 42							
Bedworth d					08 53										09 53							
Nuneaton a					09 00				09 16						10 00				10 16			
Nuneaton d									09 17										10 17			
Atherstone d									09 23										10 23			
Polesworth d																						
Tamworth d									09 31										10 31			
Lichfield Trent Valley d									09 37										10 37			
Rugeley Trent Valley d				←					09 43										10 43			
Stafford d	08 30	08 36		08 54		09 01	09 09		09 54	09a22		09 30	09 35			10 01	10 09		10 54		10a22	10 25
Norton Bridge Station Drv d																						10 40
Stone d				09 05					10 05										11 05			
Stone Crown Street d								09 20										10 20				
Stone Granville Square a																						11 02
Barlaston Orchard Place d								09 28										10 28				
Wedgwood Old Road Bridge d								09 30										10 30				
Stoke-on-Trent d	08a54			09 13		09a19		09 41	10 13			09a54				10a19		10 41	11 13			
Hanley Bus Station a								09 47										10 47				
Kidsgrove d				09 21					10 21										11 21			
Alsager d				09 26					10 26										11 26			
Crewe a		08 56	09 10	09 38			09 30		10 38		09 47		09 56	10 10			10 30		11 38	10 32		

	XC	LM	VT	LM	XC	LM	LM	LM	VT	VT	XC	LM	VT	LM	XC	LM	LM	LM	VT	VT	XC
	◇1 H	◇1	◇1 ☕		◇1 ☕	◇1	🚌	◇1	◇1 ☕	◇1 ☕	◇1 H	◇1	◇1 ☕		◇1 ☕	◇1	🚌	◇1	◇1 ☕	◇1 ☕	◇1 H
London Euston ⊖ d			09 40					09 46	10 07	10 10			10 40					10 46	11 07	11 10	
Watford Junction d								10 01										11 01			
Milton Keynes Central d								10 25		10 41								11 25		11 41	
Northampton d								10 45										11 45			
Rugby d								11 04										12 04			
Coventry d	09 27			10 42							10 27			11 42							11 27
Bedworth d				10 53										11 53							
Nuneaton a				11 00				11 16						12 00				12 16			
Nuneaton d								11 17										12 17			
Atherstone d								11 23										12 23			
Polesworth d																					
Tamworth d								11 31										12 31			
Lichfield Trent Valley d								11 37										12 37			
Rugeley Trent Valley d								11 43										12 43			
Stafford d	10 30	10 35			11 01	11 09		11 54	11a22		11 30	11 35			12 01	12 09		12 54	12a22		12 30
Norton Bridge Station Drv d																					
Stone d								12 05										13 05			
Stone Crown Street d							11 20										12 20				
Stone Granville Square a																					
Barlaston Orchard Place d							11 28										12 28				
Wedgwood Old Road Bridge d							11 30										12 30				
Stoke-on-Trent d	10a54				11a19		11 41	12 13			11a54				12a19		12 41	13 13			12a54
Hanley Bus Station a							11 47										12 47				
Kidsgrove d								12 21										13 21			
Alsager d								12 26										13 26			
Crewe a		10 56	11 10			11 30		12 38		11 47		11 56	12 10			12 30		13 38		12 47	

b Previous night, stops to set down only

London - Stoke-on-Trent and Crewe
Coventry - Nuneaton

Network Diagram - see first Page of Table 67

		LM ◇1	VT ◇1 ⊡	LM 🚌	LM	XC ◇1 ⊡	LM ◇1	LM 🚌		LM ◇1	VT ◇1 ⊡	VT ◇1 ⊡	XC ◇1 ⊼	LM ◇1	VT ◇1 ⊡	LM	XC ◇1 ⊡	LM ◇1		LM 🚌	LM 🚌	LM ◇1	VT ◇1 ⊡	VT ◇1 ⊡	XC ◇1 ⊼
London Euston 15 ⊖	d		11 40							11 46	12 07	12 10			12 40							12 46	13 07	13 10	
Watford Junction	d									12 01												13 01			
Milton Keynes Central	d									12 25		12 41										13 25		13 41	
Northampton	d									12 45												13 45			
Rugby	d									13 04												14 04			
Coventry	d				12 42								12 27			13 42									13 27
Bedworth	d				12 53											13 53									
Nuneaton	a				13 00					13 16						14 00						14 16			
	d									13 17												14 17			
Atherstone	d									13 23												14 23			
Polesworth	d																								
Tamworth	d									13 31												14 31			
Lichfield Trent Valley	d									13 37												14 37			
Rugeley Trent Valley	d									13 43												14 43			
Stafford	d	12 35		12 35		13 01	13 09			13 54	13a22		13 30	13 35			14 01	14 09		14 18		14 54	14a22		14 30
Norton Bridge Station Drv	d			12 59																14 42					
Stone	d									14 05												15 05			
Stone Crown Street	d							13 20													14 20				
Stone Granville Square	a			13 39																14 54					
Barlaston Orchard Place	d							13 28													14 28				
Wedgwood Old Road Bridge	d							13 30													14 30				
Stoke-on-Trent	d					13a18		13 41		14 13			13a54				14a19				14 41	15 13			14a54
Hanley Bus Station	a							13 47													14 47				
Kidsgrove	d									14 21												15 21			
Alsager	d									14 26												15 26			
Crewe	a	12 56	13 10				13 30			14 38		13 47		13 56	14 10			14 30				15 38		14 47	

		LM ◇1	VT ◇1 ⊡	LM		XC ◇1 ⊡	LM ◇1	LM 🚌	LM ◇1	VT ◇1 ⊡	VT ◇1 ⊡	XC ◇1 ⊼	LM ◇1	VT ◇1 ⊡		LM	XC ◇1 ⊡	LM ◇1	LM 🚌	LM 🚌	LM ◇1	VT ◇1 ⊡	VT ◇1 ⊡	XC ◇1 ⊼
London Euston 15 ⊖	d		13 40						13 46	14 07	14 10			14 40							14 46	15 07	15 10	
Watford Junction	d								14 01												15 01			
Milton Keynes Central	d								14 25		14 41										15 25		15 41	
Northampton	d								14 45												15 45			
Rugby	d								15 04												16 04			
Coventry	d			14 42								14 27				15 42								15 27
Bedworth	d			14 53												15 53								
Nuneaton	a			15 00					15 16							16 00					16 16			
	d								15 17												16 17			
Atherstone	d								15 23												16 23			
Polesworth	d																							
Tamworth	d								15 31												16 31			
Lichfield Trent Valley	d								15 37												16 37			
Rugeley Trent Valley	d								15 43												16 43			
Stafford	d	14 35				15 01	15 09		15 54	15a22		15 30	15 35				16 01	16 09	16 18		16 54	16a22		16 30
Norton Bridge Station Drv	d																		16a42					
Stone	d								16 05												17 05			
Stone Crown Street	d							15 20												16 20				
Stone Granville Square	a																							
Barlaston Orchard Place	d							15 28												16 28				
Wedgwood Old Road Bridge	d							15 30												16 30				
Stoke-on-Trent	d					15a19		15 41	16 13			15a54					16a18			16 41	17 13			16a54
Hanley Bus Station	a							15 47												16 47				
Kidsgrove	d								16 21												17 21			
Alsager	d								16 26												17 26			
Crewe	a	14 56	15 10				15 30		16 38		15 47		15 56	16 10				16 30			17 38		16 47	

		LM ◇1	VT ◇1 ⊡	LM	XC ◇1 ⊡	LM ◇1	LM 🚌	LM ◇1	VT ◇1 ⊡	VT ◇1 ⊡		XC ◇1 ⊼	LM ◇1	LM 🚌	VT ◇1 ⊡	VT ◇1 ⊡	LM	XC ◇1 ⊼	LM ◇1	LM ◇1		VT ◇1 ⊡	VT ◇1 ⊡	XC ◇1 ⊼	LM ◇1
London Euston 15 ⊖	d		15 40					15 46	16 07	16 10					16 33	16 40				16 46		17 07	17 10		
Watford Junction	d							16 01												17 01					
Milton Keynes Central	d							16 25		16 41										17 25			17 41		
Northampton	d							16 45												17 45					
Rugby	d							17 04												18 04					
Coventry	d			16 42								16 27					17 42							17 27	
Bedworth	d			16 53													17 53								
Nuneaton	a			17 00				17 16									18 00			18 16		18 02			
	d							17 17												18 17		18 03			
Atherstone	d							17 23												18 23					
Polesworth	d																								
Tamworth	d							17 31							17 38					18 31					
Lichfield Trent Valley	d							17 37							17 45					18 37					
Rugeley Trent Valley	d							17 43												18 43					
Stafford	d	16 35			17 01	17 09		18 20	17a22			17 30	17 36	17 40	17a58			18 01	18 09	18 54		18a26		18 30	18 35
Norton Bridge Station Drv	d													18a04											
Stone	d							18 31												19 05					
Stone Crown Street	d						17 20																		
Stone Granville Square	a																								
Barlaston Orchard Place	d						17 28																		
Wedgwood Old Road Bridge	d						17 30																		
Stoke-on-Trent	d				17a19		17 41	18 41				17a54						18a19		19 13				18a54	
Hanley Bus Station	a						17 47																		
Kidsgrove	d							18 49												19 21					
Alsager	d							18 54												19 26					
Crewe	a	16 56	17 10			17 30		19 05		17 47			17 56			18 10			18 30	19 36			18 48		18 56

London - Stoke-on-Trent and Crewe
Coventry - Nuneaton

Network Diagram - see first Page of Table 67

		VT ◇1 ⊡	LM	LM 🚌	XC ◇1 ⊡	LM ◇1		LM 1	VT ◇1 ⊡	VT ◇1 ⊡	XC ◇1 ⊼	LM ◇1	VT ◇1 ⊡	VT ◇1 ⊡	XC ◇1 ⊡	LM 1		VT ◇1 ⊡	XC ◇1	LM	LM ◇1	VT ◇1 ⊡	VT ◇1 ⊡	VT ◇1 ⊡	LM 1
London Euston 15 ⊖	d	17 40						17 46	18 07	18 10			18 33	18 40		18 46		19 07				19 30		19 40	
Watford Junction	d							18 01								19 01									
Milton Keynes Central	d							18 25		18 41						19 25									
Northampton	d							18 45								19 45									
Rugby	d							19 04								20 04									
Coventry	d		18 42								18 27								19 27	20 15					
Bedworth	d		18 53																	20 26					
Nuneaton	a		19 00					19 16								20 16		20 02		20 34					
	d							19 17								20 17		20 03							
Atherstone	d							19 23								20 23									
Polesworth	d																								
Tamworth	d							19 31					19 38			20 31									
Lichfield Trent Valley	d							19 37					19 45			20 37									
Rugeley Trent Valley	d							19 43								20 43									←
Stafford	d				19 01	19 09		19 54	19a22		19 30	19 36	19a58		20 01	20 55		20 27	20 30		20 38		20 50		20 55
Norton Bridge Station Drv	d															→									
Stone	d							20 05																	21 07
Stone Crown Street	d			18 45																					
Stone Granville Square	a																								
Barlaston Orchard Place	d			18 53																					
Wedgwood Old Road Bridge	d			18 55																					
Stoke-on-Trent	d			19 06	19a19			20 13			19a54				20a19				20a54						21 15
Hanley Bus Station	a			19 12																					
Kidsgrove	d							20 21																	21 23
Alsager	d							20 26																	21 28
Crewe	a	19 10				19 30		20 36		19 47		19 58		20 10				20 45			20 58	21 04	21 10	21 18	21 38

		XC ◇1 ⊡		LM ◇1	XC ◇1 ⊼	VT ◇1 ⊡	VT ◇1 ⊡	VT ◇1 ⊡	LM ◇1	XC ◇1	VT ◇1 ⊡	LM		XC ◇1	LM ◇1
London Euston 15 ⊖	d					20 11	20 20	20 31			21 00				
Watford Junction	d							20u46							
Milton Keynes Central	d						21 05				21 45				
Northampton	d														
Rugby	d					21 15		21 36							
Coventry	d									21 27		21 45			
Bedworth	d											21 56			
Nuneaton	a						21 32					22 03			
	d						21 33								
Atherstone	d														
Polesworth	d														
Tamworth	d							21 53							
Lichfield Trent Valley	d							22 00							
Rugeley Trent Valley	d														
Stafford	d	21 01		21 09	21 30	21 46			22 16	22 30	22 34			23 02	23 13
Norton Bridge Station Drv	d														
Stone	d														
Stone Crown Street	d														
Stone Granville Square	a														
Barlaston Orchard Place	d														
Wedgwood Old Road Bridge	d														
Stoke-on-Trent	d	21a20			21a52		22a05			22a50				23a20	
Hanley Bus Station	a														
Kidsgrove	d														
Alsager	d														
Crewe	a			21 30		22 05		22 35	22 40		22 58				23 37

London - Stoke-on-Trent and Crewe
Coventry - Nuneaton

Network Diagram - see first Page of Table 67

		VT	LM	VT	VT	VT	XC	LM	LM	LM	XC	LM	LM	XC	VT	LM	LM	LM	XC	LM	LM	VT	LM
		◇1	◇1	◇1	◇1	◇1	◇1	◇1	◇1		◇1	◇1	🚌	◇1	◇1	◇1	◇1		◇1	🚌	◇1	◇1	◇1
				A	A																		
London Euston ⊖	d	22p00		23p45	01 00										06 05						06 24	06 36	
Watford Junction	d														06u20						06 41	06u51	
Milton Keynes Central	d	22p31							05 21						06 41						07 23		
Northampton	d								05 42								06 38				07 45		
Rugby	d	22p54		00s47	01s55				06 05						07 03		06 58				08 04		
Coventry	d									06 16								07 16					
Bedworth	d									06 27								07 27					
Nuneaton	a	23p03		01s02	02s06				06 16	06 34							07 09	07 35			08 16		
	d	23p04							06 17								07 15				08 17		
Atherstone	d								06 23								07 21				08 23		
Polesworth	d																07 26						
Tamworth	d	23b15							06 31								07 31				08 31		
Lichfield Trent Valley	d	23b22							06 37								07 37				08 37		
Rugeley Trent Valley	d								06 44								07 43				08 43		
Stafford	d	23b38	23p53	01s31	02s31	06 01	06 30	06 36	06 54		07 01	07 08		07 30	07 34	07 38	07 54		08 01		08 54		08 09
Norton Bridge Station Drv	d																				→		
Stone	d								07 05								08 05						
Stone Crown Street	d												07 20							08 20			
Stone Granville Square	a																						
Barlaston Orchard Place	d												07 28							08 28			
Wedgwood Old Road Bridge	d												07 30							08 30			
Stoke-on-Trent	d						06a50		07 13		07a18		07 41				08 13		08a19	08 41			
Hanley Bus Station	a												07 47							08 47			
Kidsgrove	d								07 21								08 21						
Alsager	d								07 26								08 26						
Crewe	a	00s03	00 16	01s55	03s00	06 20		06 56	07 36			07 33		07 50	07 53	07 58	08 37					08 10	08 30

		VT	LM	XC	LM	VT	LM	LM	XC	LM	LM	LM	VT	VT	XC	LM	VT	LM	XC	LM	VT	LM	LM
		◇1	🚌	◇1	◇1	◇1	◇1		◇1	◇1	🚌	◇1	◇1	◇1	◇1	◇1	◇1		◇1	◇1	◇1	🚌	◇1
London Euston ⊖	d	07 07				07 35						07 46	08 07	08 10			08 40				08 43		08 46
Watford Junction	d											08 01											
Milton Keynes Central	d					08 06						08 25		08 41							09 13		09 23
Northampton	d											08 45											09 45
Rugby	d											09 04											10 04
Coventry	d			07 27				08 42							08 27			09 42			09 42		
Bedworth	d							08 53										09 53					
Nuneaton	a							09 00				09 16						10 00					10 16
	d											09 17											10 17
Atherstone	d											09 23											10 23
Polesworth	d																						
Tamworth	d											09 31											10 31
Lichfield Trent Valley	d											09 37											10 37
Rugeley Trent Valley	d						←					09 43											10 43
Stafford	d	08 23	08 25	08 30	08 36		08 54		09 01	09 09		09 54	09a22		09 30	09 35			10 01	10 09			10 54
Norton Bridge Station Drv	d		08 40																				
Stone	d						09 05					10 05											11 05
Stone Crown Street	d										09 20											10 20	
Stone Granville Square	a		09 02																				
Barlaston Orchard Place	d										09 28											10 28	
Wedgwood Old Road Bridge	d										09 30											10 30	
Stoke-on-Trent	d			08a54			09 13		09a19		09 41	10 13			09a54				10a19			10 41	11 13
Hanley Bus Station	a										09 47											10 47	
Kidsgrove	d						09 21					10 21											11 21
Alsager	d						09 26					10 26											11 26
Crewe	a	08 41			08 56	09 10	09 38			09 30		10 38		09 47		09 56	10 10			10 30	11 07		11 38

A 28 July, 4 August, 11 August, 1 September, 8 September

b Previous night, stops to set down only

Table 67

Saturdays
7 July to 8 September

London - Stoke-on-Trent and Crewe
Coventry - Nuneaton

Network Diagram - see first Page of Table 67

		VT	VT	LM	XC	LM	VT	LM	XC	LM	LM	LM	VT	VT	XC	LM	VT	LM	XC	LM	LM	LM
		◇1	◇1	🚌	◇1	◇1	◇1		◇1	◇1	🚌	◇1	◇1	◇1	◇1	◇1	◇1		◇1	◇1	🚌	◇1
London Euston ⊖	d	08 50	09 07				09 40					09 46	10 07	10 10			10 40					10 46
Watford Junction	d	09 05										10 01										11 01
Milton Keynes Central	d	09 25										10 25		10 41								11 25
Northampton	d											10 45										11 45
Rugby	d											11 04										12 04
Coventry	d				09 27			10 42							10 27			11 42				
Bedworth	d							10 53										11 53				
Nuneaton	a							11 00				11 16						12 00				12 16
	d											11 17										12 17
Atherstone	d											11 23										12 23
Polesworth	d																					
Tamworth	d											11 31										12 31
Lichfield Trent Valley	d											11 37										12 37
Rugeley Trent Valley	d											11 43										12 43
Stafford	d		10a22	10 25	10 30	10 35			11 01	11 09		11 54	11a22		11 30	11 35			12 01	12 09		12 54
Norton Bridge Station Drv	d			10 40																		
Stone	d											12 05										13 05
Stone Crown Street	d										11 20										12 20	
Stone Granville Square	a			11 02																		
Barlaston Orchard Place	d										11 28										12 28	
Wedgwood Old Road Bridge	d										11 30										12 30	
Stoke-on-Trent	d				10a54				11a19		11 41	12 13			11a54				12a19		12 41	13 13
Hanley Bus Station	a										11 47										12 47	
Kidsgrove	d											12 21										13 21
Alsager	d											12 26										13 26
Crewe	a	10 32				10 56	11 10			11 30		12 38		11 47		11 56	12 10			12 30		13 38

		VT	VT	XC	LM	VT	LM	LM	XC	LM	LM	LM	VT	VT	XC	LM	VT	LM	XC	LM	LM	LM	LM
		◇1	◇1	◇1	◇1	◇1	🚌		◇1	◇1	🚌	◇1	◇1	◇1	◇1	◇1	◇1		◇1	◇1	🚌	🚌	◇1
London Euston ⊖	d	11 07	11 10			11 40						11 46	12 07	12 10			12 40						12 46
Watford Junction	d											12 01											13 01
Milton Keynes Central	d		11 41									12 25		12 41									13 25
Northampton	d											12 45											13 45
Rugby	d											13 04											14 04
Coventry	d			11 27				12 42							12 27			13 42					
Bedworth	d							12 53										13 53					
Nuneaton	a							13 00				13 16						14 00					14 16
	d											13 17											14 17
Atherstone	d											13 23											14 23
Polesworth	d																						
Tamworth	d											13 31											14 31
Lichfield Trent Valley	d											13 37											14 37
Rugeley Trent Valley	d											13 43											14 43
Stafford	d	12a22		12 30	12 35		12 35		13 01	13 09		13 54	13a22		13 30	13 35			14 01	14 09	14 18		14 54
Norton Bridge Station Drv	d						12 59														14 42		
Stone	d											14 05											15 05
Stone Crown Street	d										13 20											14 20	
Stone Granville Square	a						13 39														14 54		
Barlaston Orchard Place	d										13 28											14 28	
Wedgwood Old Road Bridge	d										13 30											14 30	
Stoke-on-Trent	d			12a54					13a18		13 41	14 13			13a54				14a19			14 41	15 13
Hanley Bus Station	a										13 47											14 47	
Kidsgrove	d											14 21											15 21
Alsager	d											14 26											15 26
Crewe	a		12 47		12 56	13 10				13 30		14 38		13 47		13 56	14 10			14 30			15 38

		VT	VT	XC	LM	VT	LM	XC	LM	VT	LM	LM	VT	VT	XC	LM	VT	LM	XC	LM	LM	LM
		◇1	◇1	◇1	◇1	◇1		◇1	◇1	◇1	🚌	◇1	◇1	◇1	◇1	◇1	◇1		◇1	◇1	🚌	🚌
London Euston ⊖	d	13 07	13 10			13 40				13 43		13 46	14 07	14 10			14 40					
Watford Junction	d											14 01										
Milton Keynes Central	d		13 41							14 13		14 25		14 41								
Northampton	d											14 45										
Rugby	d											15 04										
Coventry	d			13 27			14 42			14 42					14 27			15 42				
Bedworth	d						14 53											15 53				
Nuneaton	a						15 00					15 16						16 00				
	d											15 17										
Atherstone	d											15 23										
Polesworth	d																					
Tamworth	d											15 31										
Lichfield Trent Valley	d											15 37										
Rugeley Trent Valley	d											15 43										
Stafford	d	14a22		14 30	14 35			15 01	15 09			15 54	15a22		15 30	15 35			16 01	16 09	16 18	
Norton Bridge Station Drv	d																				16a42	
Stone	d											16 05										
Stone Crown Street	d										15 20											16 20
Stone Granville Square	a																					
Barlaston Orchard Place	d										15 28											16 28
Wedgwood Old Road Bridge	d										15 30											16 30
Stoke-on-Trent	d			14a54				15a19			15 41	16 13			15a54				16a18			16 41
Hanley Bus Station	a										15 47											16 47
Kidsgrove	d											16 21										
Alsager	d											16 26										
Crewe	a		14 47		14 56	15 10			15 30	16 08		16 38		15 47		15 56	16 10			16 30		

Table 67

Saturdays
7 July to 8 September

London - Stoke-on-Trent and Crewe
Coventry - Nuneaton

Network Diagram - see first Page of Table 67

		LM	VT	VT	XC	LM	VT	LM	XC	LM	LM	LM	VT	VT	XC	LM	LM	VT	VT	LM	XC	LM	LM
		◇1	◇1	◇1	◇1	◇1	◇1		◇1	◇1		◇1	◇1	◇1	◇1	◇1		◇1	◇1		◇1	◇1	◇1
			☕	☕	🛒		☕		☕		🚌		☕	☕	🛒		🚌	☕	☕		🛒		
London Euston 15 ⊖	d	14 46	15 07	15 10			15 40					15 46	16 07	16 10				16 33	16 40				16 46
Watford Junction	d	15 01										16 01											17 01
Milton Keynes Central	d	15 25		15 41								16 25		16 41									17 25
Northampton	d	15 45										16 45											17 45
Rugby	d	16 04										17 04											18 04
Coventry	d				15 27			16 42							16 27					17 42			
Bedworth	d							16 53												17 53			
Nuneaton	a	16 16						17 00				17 16								18 00			18 16
	d	16 17										17 17											18 17
Atherstone	d	16 23										17 23											18 23
Polesworth	d																						
Tamworth	d	16 31										17 31						17 38					18 31
Lichfield Trent Valley	d	16 37										17 37						17 45					18 37
Rugeley Trent Valley	d	16 43										17 43											18 43
Stafford	d	16 54	16a22		16 30	16 35			17 01	17 09		18 20	17a22		17 30	17 36	17 40	17a58			18 01	18 09	18 54
Norton Bridge Station Drv	d																18a04						
Stone	d	17 05										18 31											19 05
Stone Crown Street	d										17 20												
Stone Granville Square	a																						
Barlaston Orchard Place	d										17 28												
Wedgwood Old Road Bridge	d										17 30												
Stoke-on-Trent	d	17 13			16a54				17a19		17 41	18 41			17a54						18a19		19 13
Hanley Bus Station	a										17 47												
Kidsgrove	d	17 21										18 49											19 21
Alsager	d	17 26										18 54											19 26
Crewe	a	17 38		16 47		16 56	17 10			17 30		19 05		17 47		17 56			18 10			18 30	19 36

		VT	VT	XC	LM	VT	LM	LM	XC	LM	VT	LM	VT	VT	XC	LM	VT	VT	XC	LM	VT	XC	LM
		◇1	◇1	◇1	◇1	◇1			◇1	◇1	◇1	1	◇1	◇1	◇1	◇1	◇1	◇1	◇1	1	◇1	◇1	
		☕	☕	🛒		☕		🚌	☕		☕		☕	☕	🛒		☕	☕	☕		☕		
London Euston 15 ⊖	d	17 07	17 10			17 40					17 43	17 46	18 07	18 10			18 33	18 40		18 46	19 07		
Watford Junction	d											18 01								19 01			
Milton Keynes Central	d		17 41								18 13	18 25		18 41						19 25			
Northampton	d											18 45								19 45			
Rugby	d											19 04								20 04			
Coventry	d			17 27			18 42				18 42				18 27							19 27	20 15
Bedworth	d						18 53																20 26
Nuneaton	a	18 02					19 00					19 16								20 16	20 02		20 34
	d	18 03										19 17								20 17	20 03		
Atherstone	d											19 23								20 23			
Polesworth	d																						
Tamworth	d											19 31					19 38			20 31			
Lichfield Trent Valley	d											19 37					19 45			20 37			
Rugeley Trent Valley	d											19 43								20 43			
Stafford	d	18a26		18 30	18 35				19 01	19 09		19 54	19a22		19 30	19 36	19a58		20 01	20 55	20 27	20 30	
Norton Bridge Station Drv	d																			→			
Stone	d											20 05											
Stone Crown Street	d							18 45															
Stone Granville Square	a																						
Barlaston Orchard Place	d							18 53															
Wedgwood Old Road Bridge	d							18 55															
Stoke-on-Trent	d			18a54				19 06	19a19			20 13			19a54				20a19			20a54	
Hanley Bus Station	a							19 12															
Kidsgrove	d											20 21											
Alsager	d											20 26											
Crewe	a		18 48		18 56	19 10				19 30	20 07	20 36		19 47		19 58		20 10			20 45		

Table 67

Saturdays
7 July to 8 September

London - Stoke-on-Trent and Crewe
Coventry - Nuneaton

Network Diagram - see first Page of Table 67

		LM	VT	VT	VT	LM	XC	LM	XC	VT	VT	VT	LM	XC	VT	LM	XC	LM	VT
		◇1	◇1	◇1	◇1	1	◇1	◇1	◇1	◇1	◇1	◇1	◇1	◇1	◇1		◇1	◇1	◇1
																			A
			☕	☕	☕		☕		🛒	☕	☕	☕			☕				☕
London Euston 15 ⊖	d		19 30		19 40					20 11	20 20	20 31			21 00				23 45
Watford Junction	d											20u46							
Milton Keynes Central	d										21 05				21 45				
Northampton	d																		
Rugby	d									21 15		21 36							00s42
Coventry	d													21 27		21 45			
Bedworth	d															21 56			
Nuneaton	a										21 32					22 03			00s52
	d										21 33								
Atherstone	d																		
Polesworth	d																		
Tamworth	d											21 53							
Lichfield Trent Valley	d											22 00							
Rugeley Trent Valley	d					←													
Stafford	d	20 38		20 50		20 55	21 01	21 09	21 30	21 46			22 16	22 30	22 34		23 02	23 13	01s17
Norton Bridge Station Drv	d																		
Stone	d					21 07													
Stone Crown Street	d																		
Stone Granville Square	a																		
Barlaston Orchard Place	d																		
Wedgwood Old Road Bridge	d																		
Stoke-on-Trent	d					21 15	21a20		21a52		22a05			22a50			23a20		
Hanley Bus Station	a																		
Kidsgrove	d					21 23													
Alsager	d					21 28													
Crewe	a	20 58	21 04	21 10	21 18	21 38		21 30		22 05		22 35	22 40		22 58			23 37	01s35

Saturdays
from 15 September

		VT	LM	VT	XC	LM	LM	LM	XC	LM	LM	XC	VT	LM	LM	LM	XC	LM	LM	VT	LM	VT	LM
		◇1	◇1	◇1	◇1	◇1	◇1		◇1	◇1		◇1	◇1	◇1	◇1		◇1		◇1	◇1	◇1	◇1	
		☕		☕					🛒		🚌	🛒	☕				🛒	🚌		☕		☕	🚌
London Euston 15 ⊖	d	22p00											06 05						06 24	06 36		07 07	
Watford Junction	d												06u20						06 41	06u51			
Milton Keynes Central	d	22p31					05 21						06 41						07 23				
Northampton	d						05 42								06 38				07 45				
Rugby	d	22p54					06 05						07 03		06 58				08 04				
Coventry	d							06 16								07 16							
Bedworth	d							06 27								07 27							
Nuneaton	a	23p03					06 16	06 34							07 09	07 35			08 16				
	d	23p04					06 17								07 15				08 17				
Atherstone	d						06 23								07 21				08 23				
Polesworth	d														07 26								
Tamworth	d	23b15					06 31								07 31				08 31				
Lichfield Trent Valley	d	23b22					06 37								07 37				08 37				
Rugeley Trent Valley	d						06 44								07 43				08 43				
Stafford	d	23b38	23p53	06 01	06 30	06 36	06 54		07 01	07 08		07 30	07 34	07 38	07 54		08 01		08 54		08 09	08 23	08 25
Norton Bridge Station Drv	d																		→				08 40
Stone	d						07 05								08 05								
Stone Crown Street	d										07 20							08 20					
Stone Granville Square	a																						09 02
Barlaston Orchard Place	d										07 28							08 28					
Wedgwood Old Road Bridge	d										07 30							08 30					
Stoke-on-Trent	d				06a50		07 13		07a18		07 41				08 13		08a19	08 41					
Hanley Bus Station	a										07 47							08 47					
Kidsgrove	d						07 21								08 21								
Alsager	d						07 26								08 26								
Crewe	a	00s03	00 16	06 20		06 56	07 36			07 33		07 50	07 53	07 58	08 37					08 10	08 30	08 41	

A 28 July, 4 August, 11 August, 1 September, 8 September

b Previous night, stops to set down only

London - Stoke-on-Trent and Crewe
Coventry - Nuneaton

Network Diagram - see first Page of Table 67

		XC	LM	VT	LM	LM		XC	LM	LM	LM	VT	VT	XC	LM	VT		LM	XC	LM	LM	LM	VT	VT	LM
		◇■	◇■	◇■	◇■			◇■	◇■	🚌	◇■	◇■	◇■	◇■	◇■	◇■			◇■	◇■	🚌	◇■	◇■	◇■	🚌
London Euston ⊖	d			07 35							07 46	08 07	08 10			08 40						08 46	08 50	09 07	
Watford Junction	d										08 01												09 05		
Milton Keynes Central	d			08 06							08 25		08 41									09 23	09 25		
Northampton	d										08 45											09 45			
Rugby	d										09 04											10 04			
Coventry	d	07 27				08 42								08 27				09 42							
Bedworth	d					08 53												09 53							
Nuneaton	a					09 00					09 16							10 00				10 16			
	d										09 17											10 17			
Atherstone	d										09 23											10 23			
Polesworth	d																								
Tamworth	d										09 31											10 31			
Lichfield Trent Valley	d										09 37											10 37			
Rugeley Trent Valley	d				←						09 43											10 43			
Stafford	d	08 30	08 36		08 54			09 01	09 09		09 54	09a22		09 30	09 35				10 01	10 09		10 54		10a22	10 25
Norton Bridge Station Drv	d																								10 40
Stone	d				09 05						10 05											11 05			
Stone Crown Street	d									09 20											10 20				
Stone Granville Square	a																								11 02
Barlaston Orchard Place	d									09 28											10 28				
Wedgwood Old Road Bridge	d									09 30											10 30				
Stoke-on-Trent	d	08a54			09 13			09a19		09 41	10 13			09a54					10a19		10 41	11 13			
Hanley Bus Station	a									09 47											10 47				
Kidsgrove	d				09 21						10 21											11 21			
Alsager	d				09 26						10 26											11 26			
Crewe	a		08 56	09 10	09 38				09 30		10 38		09 47		09 56	10 10				10 30		11 38	10 32		

		XC		LM	VT	LM	XC	LM	LM	LM	VT	VT		XC	LM	VT	LM	XC	LM	LM	LM	VT		VT	XC
		◇■		◇■	◇■		◇■	◇■	🚌	◇■	◇■	◇■		◇■	◇■	◇■		◇■	◇■	🚌	◇■	◇■		◇■	◇■
London Euston ⊖	d				09 40					09 46	10 07	10 10				10 40					10 46	11 07		11 10	
Watford Junction	d									10 01											11 01				
Milton Keynes Central	d									10 25		10 41									11 25			11 41	
Northampton	d									10 45											11 45				
Rugby	d									11 04											12 04				
Coventry	d	09 27				10 42								10 27			11 42								11 27
Bedworth	d					10 53											11 53								
Nuneaton	a					11 00				11 16							12 00				12 16				
	d									11 17											12 17				
Atherstone	d									11 23											12 23				
Polesworth	d																								
Tamworth	d									11 31											12 31				
Lichfield Trent Valley	d									11 37											12 37				
Rugeley Trent Valley	d									11 43											12 43				
Stafford	d	10 30		10 35			11 01	11 09		11 54	11a22			11 30	11 35			12 01	12 09		12 54	12a22			12 30
Norton Bridge Station Drv	d																								
Stone	d									12 05											13 05				
Stone Crown Street	d								11 20											12 20					
Stone Granville Square	a																								
Barlaston Orchard Place	d								11 28											12 28					
Wedgwood Old Road Bridge	d								11 30											12 30					
Stoke-on-Trent	d	10a54					11a19		11 41	12 13				11a54				12a19		12 41	13 13				12a54
Hanley Bus Station	a								11 47											12 47					
Kidsgrove	d									12 21											13 21				
Alsager	d									12 26											13 26				
Crewe	a			10 56	11 10			11 30		12 38		11 47			11 56	12 10			12 30		13 38			12 47	

		LM	VT	LM	LM	XC	LM	LM		LM	VT	VT	XC	LM	VT	LM	XC	LM		LM	LM	LM	VT	VT	XC
		◇■	◇■	🚌		◇■	◇■	🚌		◇■	◇■	◇■	◇■	◇■	◇■		◇■	◇■		🚌	🚌	◇■	◇■	◇■	◇■
London Euston ⊖	d		11 40							11 46	12 07	12 10			12 40							12 46	13 07	13 10	
Watford Junction	d									12 01												13 01			
Milton Keynes Central	d									12 25		12 41										13 25		13 41	
Northampton	d									12 45												13 45			
Rugby	d									13 04												14 04			
Coventry	d				12 42								12 27			13 42									13 27
Bedworth	d				12 53											13 53									
Nuneaton	a				13 00					13 16						14 00						14 16			
	d									13 17												14 17			
Atherstone	d									13 23												14 23			
Polesworth	d																								
Tamworth	d									13 31												14 31			
Lichfield Trent Valley	d									13 37												14 37			
Rugeley Trent Valley	d									13 43												14 43			
Stafford	d	12 35		12 35		13 01	13 09			13 54	13a22		13 30	13 35			14 01	14 09		14 18		14 54	14a22		14 30
Norton Bridge Station Drv	d			12 59																14 42					
Stone	d									14 05												15 05			
Stone Crown Street	d							13 20													14 20				
Stone Granville Square	a			13 39																14 54					
Barlaston Orchard Place	d							13 28													14 28				
Wedgwood Old Road Bridge	d							13 30													14 30				
Stoke-on-Trent	d					13a18		13 41		14 13			13a54				14a19				14 41	15 13			14a54
Hanley Bus Station	a							13 47													14 47				
Kidsgrove	d									14 21												15 21			
Alsager	d									14 26												15 26			
Crewe	a	12 56	13 10				13 30			14 38		13 47		13 56	14 10			14 30				15 38		14 47	

Table 67

Saturdays
from 15 September

London - Stoke-on-Trent and Crewe
Coventry - Nuneaton

Network Diagram - see first Page of Table 67

		LM	VT	LM		XC	LM	LM	LM	VT	VT	XC	LM	VT		LM	XC	LM	LM	LM	LM	VT	VT	XC	
		◇■	◇■			◇■	◇■	🚌	◇■	◇■	◇■	◇■	◇■	◇■			◇■	◇■	🚌	🚌	◇■	◇■	◇■	◇■	
London Euston ⊖	d		13 40						13 46	14 07	14 10			14 40							14 46	15 07	15 10		
Watford Junction	d								14 01												15 01				
Milton Keynes Central	d								14 25		14 41										15 25		15 41		
Northampton	d								14 45												15 45				
Rugby	d								15 04												16 04				
Coventry	d			14 42								14 27				15 42								15 27	
Bedworth	d			14 53												15 53									
Nuneaton	a			15 00					15 16							16 00					16 16				
	d								15 17												16 17				
Atherstone	d								15 23												16 23				
Polesworth	d																								
Tamworth	d								15 31												16 31				
Lichfield Trent Valley	d								15 37												16 37				
Rugeley Trent Valley	d								15 43												16 43				
Stafford	d	14 35				15 01	15 09		15 54	15a22		15 30	15 35				16 01	16 09	16 18		16 54	16a22		16 30	
Norton Bridge Station Drv	d																		16a42						
Stone	d								16 05												17 05				
Stone Crown Street	d							15 20												16 20					
Stone Granville Square	a																								
Barlaston Orchard Place	d							15 28												16 28					
Wedgwood Old Road Bridge	d							15 30												16 30					
Stoke-on-Trent	d					15a19		15 41	16 13			15a54					16a19			16 41	17 13			16a54	
Hanley Bus Station	a							15 47												16 47					
Kidsgrove	d								16 21												17 21				
Alsager	d								16 26												17 26				
Crewe	a	14 56	15 10				15 30		16 38		15 47		15 56	16 10				16 30			17 38		16 47		

		LM	VT	LM	XC	LM	LM	LM	VT	VT		XC	LM	LM	VT	VT	LM	XC	LM	LM		VT	VT	XC	LM
		◇■	◇■		◇■	◇■	🚌	◇■	◇■	◇■		◇■	◇■	🚌	◇■	◇■		◇■	◇■	◇■		◇■	◇■	◇■	◇■
London Euston ⊖	d		15 40					15 46	16 07	16 10					16 33	16 40				16 46		17 07	17 10		
Watford Junction	d							16 01												17 01					
Milton Keynes Central	d							16 25		16 41										17 25			17 41		
Northampton	d							16 45												17 45					
Rugby	d							17 04												18 04					
Coventry	d			16 42								16 27					17 42							17 27	
Bedworth	d			16 53													17 53								
Nuneaton	a			17 00				17 16									18 00			18 16		18 02			
	d							17 17												18 17		18 03			
Atherstone	d							17 23												18 23					
Polesworth	d																								
Tamworth	d							17 31							17 38					18 31					
Lichfield Trent Valley	d							17 37							17 45					18 37					
Rugeley Trent Valley	d							17 43												18 43					
Stafford	d	16 35			17 01	17 09		18 20	17a22			17 30	17 36	17 40	17a58			18 01	18 09	18 54		18a26		18 30	18 35
Norton Bridge Station Drv	d													18a04											
Stone	d							18 31												19 05					
Stone Crown Street	d						17 20																		
Stone Granville Square	a																								
Barlaston Orchard Place	d						17 28																		
Wedgwood Old Road Bridge	d						17 30																		
Stoke-on-Trent	d				17a19		17 41	18 41				17a54						18a19		19 13				18a54	
Hanley Bus Station	a						17 47																		
Kidsgrove	d							18 49												19 21					
Alsager	d							18 54												19 26					
Crewe	a	16 56	17 10			17 30		19 05		17 47			17 56			18 10			18 30	19 36			18 48		18 56

		VT	LM	LM	XC	LM		LM	VT	VT	XC	LM	VT	VT	XC	LM		VT	XC	LM	LM	VT	VT	VT	LM
		◇■		🚌	◇■	◇■		■	◇■	◇■	◇■	◇■	◇■	◇■	◇■	■		◇■	◇■		◇■	◇■	◇■	◇■	■
London Euston ⊖	d	17 40						17 46	18 07	18 10			18 33	18 40		18 46		19 07				19 30		19 40	
Watford Junction	d							18 01								19 01									
Milton Keynes Central	d							18 25		18 41						19 25									
Northampton	d							18 45								19 45									
Rugby	d							19 04								20 04									
Coventry	d		18 42								18 27								19 27	20 15					
Bedworth	d		18 53																	20 26					
Nuneaton	a		19 00					19 16								20 16		20 02		20 34					
	d							19 17								20 17		20 03							
Atherstone	d							19 23								20 23									
Polesworth	d																								
Tamworth	d							19 31					19 38			20 31									
Lichfield Trent Valley	d							19 37					19 45			20 37									
Rugeley Trent Valley	d							19 43								20 43									←
Stafford	d				19 01	19 09		19 54	19a22		19 30	19 36	19a58		20 01	20 55		20 27	20 30		20 38		20 50		20 55
Norton Bridge Station Drv	d															→									
Stone	d							20 05																	21 07
Stone Crown Street	d			18 45																					
Stone Granville Square	a																								
Barlaston Orchard Place	d			18 53																					
Wedgwood Old Road Bridge	d			18 55																					
Stoke-on-Trent	d			19 06	19a19			20 13			19a54				20a19				20a54						21 15
Hanley Bus Station	a			19 12																					
Kidsgrove	d							20 21																	21 23
Alsager	d							20 26																	21 28
Crewe	a	19 10				19 30		20 36		19 47		19 58		20 10				20 45			20 58	21 04	21 10	21 18	21 38

Table 67

Saturdays from 15 September

London - Stoke-on-Trent and Crewe
Coventry - Nuneaton

Network Diagram - see first Page of Table 67

Station		XC	LM	XC	VT	VT	VT	LM	XC	VT	LM	XC	LM
London Euston ⊖	d				20 11	20 20	20 31			21 00			
Watford Junction	d						20u46						
Milton Keynes Central	d					21 05				21 45			
Northampton	d												
Rugby	d				21 15		21 36						
Coventry	d			20 27					21 27		21 45		
Bedworth	d										21 56		
Nuneaton	a					21 32					22 03		
	d					21 33							
Atherstone	d												
Polesworth	d												
Tamworth	d						21 53						
Lichfield Trent Valley	d						22 00						
Rugeley Trent Valley	d												
Stafford	d	21 01	21 09	21 30	21 46			22 16	22 30	22 34		23 02	23 13
Norton Bridge Station Drv	d												
Stone	d												
Stone Crown Street	d												
Stone Granville Square	a												
Barlaston Orchard Place	d												
Wedgwood Old Road Bridge	d												
Stoke-on-Trent	d	21a20		21a52		22a05			22a50			23a20	
Hanley Bus Station	a												
Kidsgrove	d												
Alsager	d												
Crewe	a		21 30		22 05		22 35	22 40		22 58			23 37

Sundays until 24 June

Station		VT	XC	VT	VT	LM	VT	XC	LM	VT	LM	VT	XC	LM	VT	LM	LM	LM	VT	LM	XC	VT	LM
London Euston ⊖	d			08 10	08 15		08 45			09 15		09 45		09 54	10 15			10 24	10 45			11 15	
Watford Junction	d													10 10				10 40					
Milton Keynes Central	d			08 56			09 32					10 33		10 50				11 20	11 33			12 03	
Northampton	d								09 40					11 08				11 40					
Rugby	d						10 09		10 02			11 09		11 30				12 03	12 09				
Coventry	d												10 28			11 55					11 29		
Bedworth	d															12 06							
Nuneaton	a				09 43				10 15	10 44				11 42	11 46	12 13		12 16					
	d				09 44				10 16	10 45				11 43	11 47			12 17					
Atherstone	d								10 22					11 49				12 23					
Polesworth	d																						
Tamworth	d								10 30					11 57				12 31					
Lichfield Trent Valley	d								10 36					12 03				12 37					
Rugeley Trent Valley	d								10 42					12 09				12 43		←			←
Stafford	d	09 17	09 33		10 08	10 16		10 44	10 57	11 09	11 16		11 44	12 22	12 13		12 17	13 00		12 22	12 43	12 53	13 00
Norton Bridge Station Drv	d													→				→					
Stone	d								11 07											12 32			13 10
Stone Crown Street	d																						
Stone Granville Square	a																						
Barlaston Orchard Place	d																						
Wedgwood Old Road Bridge	d																						
Stoke-on-Trent	d							11a02	11 16				12a03							12 40	13a02		13 20
Hanley Bus Station	a																						
Kidsgrove	d								11 24											12 48			13 28
Alsager	d								11 28											12 53			13 32
Crewe	a	09 35	09 54	10 17	10 28	10 37	10 55		11 43	11 30	11 37	11 55			12 32		12 37		12 56	13 03		13 13	13 43

Station		LM	VT	XC	VT	LM	LM	LM	LM	VT	XC	VT	LM	LM	LM	LM	VT	XC	VT	LM	LM	LM	LM
London Euston ⊖	d		12 02		12 35				12 50	13 02		13 35				13 50	14 02		14 35				14 50
Watford Junction	d								13 06							14 06							15 06
Milton Keynes Central	d								13 36							14 36							15 36
Northampton	d						13 02		14 02							15 02							16 02
Rugby	d						13 25		14 26							15 26							16 26
Coventry	d			12 28				13 46			13 26		14 46					14 26		15 46			
Bedworth	d							13 57					14 57							15 57			
Nuneaton	a						13 40	14 04	14 39				15 04			15 39				16 04			16 39
	d						13 41		14 40							15 40							16 40
Atherstone	d						13 47		14 46							15 46							16 46
Polesworth	d																						
Tamworth	d						13 55		14 54							15 54							16 54
Lichfield Trent Valley	d						14 01		15 00							16 00							17 00
Rugeley Trent Valley	d						14 07		15 07						←	16 07						←	17 07
Stafford	d	13 09	13 25	13 40		14 09	14 18		15 18	14 22	14 39			15 09	15 18	16 18	15 25	15 40			16 09	16 18	17 18
Norton Bridge Station Drv	d								→							→							
Stone	d						14 28								15 30							16 29	17 29
Stone Crown Street	d																						
Stone Granville Square	a																						
Barlaston Orchard Place	d																						
Wedgwood Old Road Bridge	d																						
Stoke-on-Trent	d			13a58			14 37				14a57				15 41			15a57				16 40	17 40
Hanley Bus Station	a																						
Kidsgrove	d						14 45								15 50							16 48	17 48
Alsager	d						14 50								15 54							16 53	17 53
Crewe	a	13 30	13 43		14 12	14 29	15 00			14 43		15 12		15 29	16 04		15 43		16 12		16 30	17 03	18 03

Table 67

Sundays until 24 June

London - Stoke-on-Trent and Crewe
Coventry - Nuneaton

Network Diagram - see first Page of Table 67

Station		VT	VT	XC	VT	LM	LM	LM	VT	VT	XC	VT	LM	LM	LM	VT	VT	XC	VT	LM	LM	VT
London Euston ⊖	d	15 02	15 05		15 35			15 50	16 02	16 05		16 35			16 50	17 02	17 05		17 35		17 50	18 02
Watford Junction	d							16 06							17 06						18 06	
Milton Keynes Central	d		15 39					16 36		16 39					17 36		17 39				18 36	
Northampton	d							17 02							18 02						19 02	
Rugby	d							17 26							18 29						19 26	
Coventry	d			15 26		16 46					16 26		17 46					17 26				
Bedworth	d					16 57							17 57									
Nuneaton	a					17 04		17 39					18 04		18 40		18 09				19 39	
	d							17 40							18 41		18 10				19 40	
Atherstone	d							17 46							18 47						19 46	
Polesworth	d																					
Tamworth	d							17 54							18 55						19 54	
Lichfield Trent Valley	d							18 00							19 01						20 00	
Rugeley Trent Valley	d							18 07							19 08						20 07	
Stafford	d	16a21		16 37			17 09	18 18	17a24		17 39			18 09	19 18	18a24		18 36		19 10	20 18	19a24
Norton Bridge Station Drv	d																					
Stone	d							18 28							19 29						20 29	
Stone Crown Street	d																					
Stone Granville Square	a																					
Barlaston Orchard Place	d																					
Wedgwood Old Road Bridge	d																					
Stoke-on-Trent	d			16a57				18 43			17a57				19 44			18a55			20 41	
Hanley Bus Station	a																					
Kidsgrove	d							18 51							19 52						20 50	
Alsager	d							18 55							19 56						20 54	
Crewe	a		16 50		17 12		17 29	19 05		17 50		18 12		18 30	20 06		18 53		19 12	19 30	21 05	

Station		VT	XC	VT	LM	LM	VT	VT	XC	LM	VT	VT	LM	VT	LM	VT	VT	XC	VT	VT	VT	LM
London Euston ⊖	d	18 05		18 35		18 50	19 02	19 05				19 35	19 50	20 02		20 05	20 25			20 35	20 50	
Watford Junction	d					19 06							20 06									
Milton Keynes Central	d	18 39				19 36		19 39					20 36			20 38					21 37	
Northampton	d					20 02							20 59									
Rugby	d					20 28							21 24								22 01	
Coventry	d		18 26						19 26	19 46								20 26				
Bedworth	d									19 57												
Nuneaton	a					20 40	20 00			20 04			21 35	21 00								
	d					20 40	20 01						21 36	21 01								
Atherstone	d					20 46							21 42									
Polesworth	d																					←
Tamworth	d					20 54							21 50				21 32					21 50
Lichfield Trent Valley	d					21 00							→				21 39					21 56
Rugeley Trent Valley	d					21 07									←							22 03
Stafford	d		19 39		20 01	21 18	20 30		20 39		20 52				21 18	21 33		21 43	21 57	22 00		22 19
Norton Bridge Station Drv	d					→																
Stone	d														21 29							22 31
Stone Crown Street	d																					
Stone Granville Square	a																					
Barlaston Orchard Place	d																					
Wedgwood Old Road Bridge	d																					
Stoke-on-Trent	d		19a57						20a56						21 43			22a03				22 43
Hanley Bus Station	a																					
Kidsgrove	d														21 52							22 51
Alsager	d														21 57							22 55
Crewe	a	19 50		20 12	20 21		20 48	20 53			21 10	21 13		21 44	22 08	21 53	22 10		22 17	22 20	22 49	23 05

Station		LM	XC	LM	VT	AW	VT
London Euston ⊖	d				21 21		21 51
Watford Junction	d						
Milton Keynes Central	d						22 38
Northampton	d						
Rugby	d						23 18
Coventry	d		21 26	21 35			
Bedworth	d			21 46			
Nuneaton	a			21 53	22 51		23 28
	d				22 52		23 29
Atherstone	d						
Polesworth	d						
Tamworth	d						
Lichfield Trent Valley	d						
Rugeley Trent Valley	d						
Stafford	d	22 27	22 39		23 17	23 31	23s53
Norton Bridge Station Drv	d						
Stone	d						
Stone Crown Street	d						
Stone Granville Square	a						
Barlaston Orchard Place	d						
Wedgwood Old Road Bridge	d						
Stoke-on-Trent	d		22a58				
Hanley Bus Station	a						
Kidsgrove	d						
Alsager	d						
Crewe	a	22 49			23 43	23 55	00s21

1 July to 9 September

London - Stoke-on-Trent and Crewe
Coventry - Nuneaton

Network Diagram - see first Page of Table 67

		VT	VT	VT	XC	VT	VT	LM	VT	XC	LM	VT	LM	VT	XC	LM	VT	LM	LM	LM	VT	LM	XC
		◇1	◇1	◇1	◇1	◇1	◇1	◇1	◇1	◇1	1	◇1	◇1	◇1	◇1	1	◇1		◇1	◇1	◇1	1	◇1
		A	A																				
London Euston ⊖	d	23p45	01 00			08 10	08 15		08 45			09 15		09 45		09 54	10 15			10 24	10 45		
Watford Junction	d															10 10				10 40			
Milton Keynes Central	d					08 56			09 32					10 33		10 50				11 20	11 33		
Northampton	d										09 40					11 08				11 40			
Rugby	d	00s42	01s48						10 09		10 02			11 09		11 30				12 03	12 09		
Coventry	d																	11 55					
Bedworth	d																	12 06					
Nuneaton	a	00s52	01s59				09 43				10 15	10 44				11 42	11 46	12 13		12 16			
	d						09 44				10 16	10 45				11 43	11 47			12 17			
Atherstone	d										10 22					11 49				12 23			
Polesworth	d																						
Tamworth	d										10 30					11 57				12 31			
Lichfield Trent Valley	d										10 36					12 03				12 37			
Rugeley Trent Valley	d										10 42					12 09				12 43		←	
Stafford	d	01s17	02s23	09 17	09 33		10 08	10 17		10 33	10 57	11 09	11 17		11 32	12 22 →	12 13		12 17	13 00 →		12 22	12 33
Norton Bridge Station Drv	d																						
Stone	d										11 07											12 32	
Stone Crown Street	d																						
Stone Granville Square	a																						
Barlaston Orchard Place	d																						
Wedgwood Old Road Bridge	d																						
Stoke-on-Trent	d									10a51	11 16				11a51							12 40	12a52
Hanley Bus Station	a																						
Kidsgrove	d										11 24											12 48	
Alsager	d										11 28											12 53	
Crewe	a	01s35	02s42	09 35	09 54	10 17	10 28	10 37	10 55		11 43	11 30	11 37	11 55			12 32		12 37		12 56	13 03	

		VT	LM	LM	VT	VT	XC	LM	LM	LM	LM	VT	VT	XC	LM	LM	LM	LM	VT	VT	XC	LM	LM
		◇1	◇1	◇1	◇1	◇1	◇1	◇1	◇1		◇1	◇1	◇1	◇1		◇1	◇1	◇1	◇1	◇1	◇1	◇1	◇1
London Euston ⊖	d	11 15			12 02	12 35					12 50	13 02	13 35					13 50	14 02	14 35			
Watford Junction	d										13 06							14 06					
Milton Keynes Central	d	12 03									13 36							14 36					
Northampton	d								13 02		14 02							15 02					
Rugby	d								13 25		14 26							15 26					
Coventry	d									13 46					14 46								
Bedworth	d									13 57					14 57								
Nuneaton	a								13 40	14 04	14 39				15 04			15 39					
	d								13 41		14 40							15 40					
Atherstone	d								13 47		14 46							15 46					
Polesworth	d																						
Tamworth	d								13 55		14 54							15 54					
Lichfield Trent Valley	d								14 01		15 00							16 00					
Rugeley Trent Valley	d		←						14 07		15 07						←	16 07					←
Stafford	d	12 53	13 00	13 09	13 25		13 34	14 09	14 18		15 18 →	14 22		14 34		15 09	15 18	16 18 →	15 25		15 34	16 09	16 18
Norton Bridge Station Drv	d																						
Stone	d		13 10						14 28								15 29						16 29
Stone Crown Street	d																						
Stone Granville Square	a																						
Barlaston Orchard Place	d																						
Wedgwood Old Road Bridge	d																						
Stoke-on-Trent	d		13 20				13a56		14 37					14a56			15 41				15a56		16 40
Hanley Bus Station	a																						
Kidsgrove	d		13 28						14 45								15 50						16 48
Alsager	d		13 32						14 50								15 54						16 53
Crewe	a	13 13	13 43	13 30	13 43	14 12		14 29	15 00			14 43	15 12			15 29	16 04		15 43	16 12		16 30	17 03

		VT	VT	XC	VT	LM	LM	LM	LM	VT	VT	XC	VT	LM	LM	LM	VT	VT	XC	VT	LM	LM
		◇1	◇1	◇1	◇1			◇1	◇1	◇1	◇1	◇1	◇1		◇1	◇1	◇1	◇1	◇1	◇1	◇1	◇1
London Euston ⊖	d	15 02	15 05		15 35				15 50	16 02	16 05		16 35			16 50	17 02	17 05		17 35		17 50
Watford Junction	d								16 06							17 06						18 06
Milton Keynes Central	d		15 39						16 36		16 39					17 36		17 39				18 36
Northampton	d								17 02							18 02						19 02
Rugby	d								17 26							18 29						19 26
Coventry	d			15 26		15 46	16 46					16 26		17 46					17 26			
Bedworth	d					15 57	16 57							17 57								
Nuneaton	a					16 04	17 04		17 39					18 04		18 40		18 09				19 39
	d								17 40							18 41		18 10				19 40
Atherstone	d								17 46							18 47						19 46
Polesworth	d																					
Tamworth	d								17 54							18 55						19 54
Lichfield Trent Valley	d								18 00							19 01						20 00
Rugeley Trent Valley	d								18 07							19 08						20 07
Stafford	d	16a21		16 34				17 09	18 18	17a24		17 36			18 09	19 18	18a24		18 36		19 09	20 18
Norton Bridge Station Drv	d																					
Stone	d								18 28							19 29						20 29
Stone Crown Street	d																					
Stone Granville Square	a																					
Barlaston Orchard Place	d																					
Wedgwood Old Road Bridge	d																					
Stoke-on-Trent	d			16a56					18 43			17a56				19 44			18a55			20 41
Hanley Bus Station	a																					
Kidsgrove	d								18 51							19 52						20 50
Alsager	d								18 55							19 56						20 54
Crewe	a		16 50		17 12			17 30	19 05		17 50		18 12		18 30	20 06		18 53		19 12	19 29	21 05

A 29 July, 5 August, 12 August, 2 September, 9 September

1 July to 9 September

London - Stoke-on-Trent and Crewe
Coventry - Nuneaton

Network Diagram - see first Page of Table 67

		VT	VT	XC	VT	LM	LM	VT	VT	XC	LM	VT	VT	LM	VT	LM	VT	VT	XC	VT	VT	LM	VT
		◇1	◇1	◇1	◇1	◇1	◇1	◇1	◇1	◇1		◇1	◇1	◇1	◇1	◇1	◇1	◇1	◇1	◇1	◇1	◇1	◇1
London Euston ⊖	d	18 02	18 05		18 35		18 50	19 02	19 05				19 35	19 50	20 02		20 05	20 25			20 35		20 50
Watford Junction	d						19 06							20 06									
Milton Keynes Central	d		18 39				19 36		19 39					20 36			20 38						21 37
Northampton	d						20 02							20 59									
Rugby	d						20 28							21 24									22 01
Coventry	d			18 26						19 26	19 46								20 26				
Bedworth	d										19 57												
Nuneaton	a						20 40	20 01			20 04			21 35	21 00								
	d						20 40	20 02						21 36	21 01								
Atherstone	d						20 46							21 42									
Polesworth	d																						
Tamworth	d						20 54							21 50 →				21 32					
Lichfield Trent Valley	d						21 00											21 39					
Rugeley Trent Valley	d						21 07									←							
Stafford	d	19a24		19 38		20 09	21 18 →	20 30		20 37		20 52				21 18	21 33		21 37	21 57	22 00	22 16	
Norton Bridge Station Drv	d																						
Stone	d															21 29							
Stone Crown Street	d																						
Stone Granville Square	a																						
Barlaston Orchard Place	d																						
Wedgwood Old Road Bridge	d																						
Stoke-on-Trent	d			19a56						20a56						21 43			21a56				
Hanley Bus Station	a																						
Kidsgrove	d															21 52							
Alsager	d															21 57							
Crewe	a		19 50		20 12	20 30		20 48	20 53			21 10	21 13		21 44	22 08	21 53	22 10		22 17	22 20	22 38	22 49

		LM	XC	LM	VT	AW	VT	VT
		◇1	◇1		◇1	◇	◇1	◇1
								A
London Euston ⊖	d				21 21		21 51	23 45
Watford Junction	d							
Milton Keynes Central	d						22 38	
Northampton	d							
Rugby	d						23 18	00s33
Coventry	d		21 26	21 35				
Bedworth	d			21 46				
Nuneaton	a			21 53	22 51		23 28	00s44
	d				22 52		23 29	
Atherstone	d							
Polesworth	d	←						
Tamworth	d	21 50						
Lichfield Trent Valley	d	21 56						
Rugeley Trent Valley	d	22 03						
Stafford	d	22 19	22 37		23 17	23 31	23s53	01s08
Norton Bridge Station Drv	d							
Stone	d	22 31						
Stone Crown Street	d							
Stone Granville Square	a							
Barlaston Orchard Place	d							
Wedgwood Old Road Bridge	d							
Stoke-on-Trent	d	22 43	22a55					
Hanley Bus Station	a							
Kidsgrove	d	22 51						
Alsager	d	22 55						
Crewe	a	23 05			23 43	23 55	00s21	01s27

A 29 July, 5 August, 12 August, 2 September, 9 September

London - Stoke-on-Trent and Crewe
Coventry - Nuneaton

Network Diagram - see first Page of Table 67

		VT	XC	VT	VT	LM	VT	XC	LM	VT	LM	VT	XC	LM	VT	LM	LM	LM	VT	LM	XC	VT	LM
		◇1	◇1	◇1	◇1	◇1	◇1	◇1	1	◇1	◇1	◇1	◇1	1	◇1		◇1	◇1	◇1	1	◇1	◇1	◇1
London Euston 15 ⊖	d			08 10	08 15		08 45			09 15		09 45		09 54	10 15			10 24	10 45			11 15	
Watford Junction	d													10 10				10 40					
Milton Keynes Central	d			08 56			09 32					10 33		10 50				11 20	11 33			12 03	
Northampton	d								09 40					11 08				11 40					
Rugby	d						10 09		10 02			11 09		11 30				12 03	12 09				
Coventry	d												10 28			11 55					11 29		
Bedworth	d															12 06							
Nuneaton	a				09 43				10 15	10 44				11 42	11 46	12 13		12 16					
	d				09 44				10 16	10 45				11 43	11 47			12 17					
Atherstone	d								10 22					11 49				12 23					
Polesworth	d																						
Tamworth	d								10 30					11 57				12 31					
Lichfield Trent Valley	d								10 36					12 03				12 37					
Rugeley Trent Valley	d								10 42					12 09				12 43		←			←
Stafford	d	09 17	09 33		10 08	10 17		10 33	10 57	11 09	11 17		11 32	12 22	12 14		12 17	13 00		12 22	12 33	12 53	13 00
Norton Bridge Station Drv	d													→				→					
Stone	d								11 07											12 32			13 10
Stone Crown Street	d																						
Stone Granville Square	a																						
Barlaston Orchard Place	d																						
Wedgwood Old Road Bridge	d																						
Stoke-on-Trent	d							10a51	11 16				11a51							12 40	12a52		13 20
Hanley Bus Station	a																						
Kidsgrove	d								11 24											12 48			13 28
Alsager	d								11 28											12 53			13 32
Crewe	a	09 35	09 54	10 17	10 28	10 37	10 55		11 43	11 30	11 37	11 55			12 32		12 37		12 56	13 03		13 13	13 43

		LM	VT	XC	VT	LM	LM	LM	LM	VT	XC	VT	LM	LM	LM	LM	VT	XC	VT	LM	LM	VT	VT
		◇1	◇1	◇1	◇1	◇1	◇1		◇1	◇1	◇1	◇1		◇1	◇1	◇1	◇1	◇1	◇1	◇1	◇1	◇1	◇1
London Euston 15 ⊖	d		12 05		12 37				12 50	13 05		13 37				13 50	14 05		14 37			15 05	15 08
Watford Junction	d								13 06							14 06							
Milton Keynes Central	d								13 36							14 36							15 42
Northampton	d						13 02		14 02							15 02							
Rugby	d						13 25		14 26							15 26							
Coventry	d			12 28				13 46			13 26		14 46					14 26					
Bedworth	d							13 57					14 57										
Nuneaton	a						13 40	14 04	14 39				15 04			15 39							
	d						13 41		14 40							15 40							
Atherstone	d						13 47		14 46							15 46							
Polesworth	d																						
Tamworth	d						13 55		14 54							15 54							
Lichfield Trent Valley	d						14 01		15 00							16 00							
Rugeley Trent Valley	d						14 07		15 07						←	16 07					←		
Stafford	d	13 09	13 25	13 34		14 09	14 18		15 18	14 24	14 34			15 09	15 18	16 18	15 25	15 34		16 09	16 18	16a24	
Norton Bridge Station Drv	d								→							→							
Stone	d						14 28								15 29						16 29		
Stone Crown Street	d																						
Stone Granville Square	a																						
Barlaston Orchard Place	d																						
Wedgwood Old Road Bridge	d																						
Stoke-on-Trent	d			13a56			14 37				14a55				15 41			15a56			16 40		
Hanley Bus Station	a																						
Kidsgrove	d						14 45								15 50						16 48		
Alsager	d						14 50								15 54						16 53		
Crewe	a	13 30	13 43		14 12	14 29	15 00			14 43		15 12		15 29	16 04		15 43		16 12	16 30	17 03		16 50

		XC	VT	LM	LM	LM	LM	VT	VT	XC	VT	LM	LM	LM	VT	VT	XC	VT	LM	LM	VT	VT
		◇1	◇1			◇1	◇1	◇1	◇1	◇1	◇1		◇1	◇1	◇1	◇1	◇1	◇1	◇1	◇1	◇1	◇1
London Euston 15 ⊖	d		15 37				15 50	16 05	16 08		16 37			16 50	17 05	17 08		17 37		17 50	18 05	18 08
Watford Junction	d						16 06							17 06						18 06		
Milton Keynes Central	d						16 36		16 42					17 36		17 42				18 36		18 42
Northampton	d						17 02							18 02						19 02		
Rugby	d						17 26							18 29						19 26		
Coventry	d	15 26		15 46	16 46					16 26		17 46					17 26					
Bedworth	d			15 57	16 57							17 57										
Nuneaton	a			16 04	17 04		17 39					18 04		18 40		18 12				19 39		
	d						17 40							18 41		18 13				19 40		
Atherstone	d						17 46							18 47						19 46		
Polesworth	d																					
Tamworth	d						17 54							18 55						19 54		
Lichfield Trent Valley	d						18 00							19 01						20 00		
Rugeley Trent Valley	d						18 07							19 08						20 07		
Stafford	d	16 34				17 09	18 18	17a24		17 36			18 09	19 18	18a24		18 36		19 09	20 18	19a24	
Norton Bridge Station Drv	d																					
Stone	d						18 28							19 29						20 29		
Stone Crown Street	d																					
Stone Granville Square	a																					
Barlaston Orchard Place	d																					
Wedgwood Old Road Bridge	d																					
Stoke-on-Trent	d	16a56					18 43			17a56				19 44			18a56			20 41		
Hanley Bus Station	a																					
Kidsgrove	d						18 51							19 52						20 50		
Alsager	d						18 55							19 56						20 54		
Crewe	a		17 12			17 30	19 05		17 50		18 12		18 30	20 06		18 53		19 12	19 29	21 05		19 50

Table 67

Sundays
16 September to 21 October

London - Stoke-on-Trent and Crewe
Coventry - Nuneaton

Network Diagram - see first Page of Table 67

		XC	VT	LM	LM	LM	VT	VT	XC	VT	VT	LM	VT	LM	VT	VT	XC	VT	VT	LM	VT	LM
		◇1	◇1		◇1	◇1	◇1	◇1	◇1	◇1	◇1	◇1	◇1	◇1	◇1	◇1	◇1	◇1	◇1	◇1	◇1	◇1
London Euston 15 ⊖	d		18 37			18 50	19 05	19 08			19 37	19 50	20 05		20 08	20 25			20 35		20 50	
Watford Junction	d					19 06						20 06										
Milton Keynes Central	d					19 36		19 42				20 36			20 41						21 37	
Northampton	d					20 02						20 59										
Rugby	d					20 27						21 24									22 01	
Coventry	d	18 26		19 46					19 26								20 26					
Bedworth	d			19 57																		
Nuneaton	a			20 04		20 39	20 03					21 35	21 03									
	d					20 39	20 04					21 36	21 04									
Atherstone	d					20 45						21 42										
Polesworth	d																					←
Tamworth	d					20 53						21 50				21 32						21 50
Lichfield Trent Valley	d					20 59						→				21 39						21 56
Rugeley Trent Valley	d					21 06								←								22 03
Stafford	d	19 38			20 09	21 18	20 29		20 37	20 52				21 18	21 33		21 37	21 57	22 00	22 16		22 19
Norton Bridge Station Drv	d					→																
Stone	d													21 29								22 31
Stone Crown Street	d																					
Stone Granville Square	a																					
Barlaston Orchard Place	d																					
Wedgwood Old Road Bridge	d																					
Stoke-on-Trent	d	19a56							20a56					21 43			21a56					22 43
Hanley Bus Station	a																					
Kidsgrove	d													21 52								22 51
Alsager	d													21 57								22 55
Crewe	a		20 12		20 30		20 47	20 50		21 10	21 13		21 44	22 08	21 53	22 10		22 17	22 20	22 38	22 49	23 05

		XC	LM	VT	AW	VT
		◇1		◇1	◇	◇1
London Euston 15 ⊖	d			21 21		21 51
Watford Junction	d					
Milton Keynes Central	d					22 38
Northampton	d					
Rugby	d					23 18
Coventry	d	21 26	21 35			
Bedworth	d		21 46			
Nuneaton	a		21 53	22 51		23 28
	d			22 52		23 29
Atherstone	d					
Polesworth	d					
Tamworth	d					
Lichfield Trent Valley	d					
Rugeley Trent Valley	d					
Stafford	d	22 37		23 17	23 31	23s53
Norton Bridge Station Drv	d					
Stone	d					
Stone Crown Street	d					
Stone Granville Square	a					
Barlaston Orchard Place	d					
Wedgwood Old Road Bridge	d					
Stoke-on-Trent	d	22a55				
Hanley Bus Station	a					
Kidsgrove	d					
Alsager	d					
Crewe	a			23 43	23 55	00s21

Table 67

London - Stoke-on-Trent and Crewe
Coventry - Nuneaton

Sundays
from 28 October

Network Diagram - see first Page of Table 67

		VT	XC	VT	VT	LM	XC	LM	VT	LM		XC	LM	VT	LM	LM	XC	LM	LM	VT		LM	LM	VT	XC
		◇1	◇1	◇1	◇1	◇1	◇1	1	◇1	◇1		◇1	1	◇1	◇1	1	◇1		◇1	◇1		◇1	◇1	◇1	◇1
		☕	🛒	☕	☕		🛒		☕			🛒		☕			🛒			☕				☕	🛒
London Euston 15 ⊖	d			08 10	08 15				09 15				09 54	10 15					10 24	11 15				12 05	
Watford Junction	d												10 10						10 40						
Milton Keynes Central	d			08 56					10 02				10 50						11 20	12 03					
Northampton	d							09 40					11 08						11 40						
Rugby	d				09 37			10 02					11 30	11 39					12 03						
Coventry	d											10 28					11 29	11 55							12 28
Bedworth	d																	12 06							
Nuneaton	a				09 46			10 15	10 44				11 42	11 48				12 13	12 16						
	d				09 47			10 16	10 45				11 43	11 50					12 17						
Atherstone	d							10 22					11 49						12 23						
Polesworth	d																								
Tamworth	d							10 30					11 57						12 31						
Lichfield Trent Valley	d							10 36					12 03						12 37						
Rugeley Trent Valley	d							10 42					12 09			←			12 43			←			
Stafford	d	09 17	09 33		10 11	10 17	10 33	10 57	11 09	11 17		11 32	12 22	12 14	12 17	12 22	12 33		13 00	12 53		13 00	13 09	13 25	13 34
Norton Bridge Station Drv	d												→						→						
Stone	d							11 07								12 32						13 10			
Stone Crown Street	d																								
Stone Granville Square	a																								
Barlaston Orchard Place	d																								
Wedgwood Old Road Bridge	d																								
Stoke-on-Trent	d						10a51	11 16				11a51				12 40	12a52					13 20			13a56
Hanley Bus Station	a																								
Kidsgrove	d							11 24								12 48						13 28			
Alsager	d							11 28								12 53						13 32			
Crewe	a	09 35	09 54	10 17	10 30	10 37		11 43	11 30	11 37				12 32	12 37	13 03				13 13		13 43	13 30	13 43	

		VT	LM	LM	LM	LM		VT	XC	VT	LM	LM	VT	LM	LM	VT		XC	VT	LM	LM	VT	VT	XC	VT
		◇1	◇1	◇1		◇1		◇1	◇1	◇1		◇1	◇1	◇1	◇1	◇1		◇1	◇1	◇1	◇1	◇1	◇1	◇1	◇1
		☕						☕	🛒	☕			☕			☕		🛒	☕			☕	☕	🛒	☕
London Euston 15 ⊖	d	12 37				12 50		13 05		13 37			13 45		13 50	14 05			14 37			15 05	15 08		15 37
Watford Junction	d					13 06									14 06										
Milton Keynes Central	d					13 36									14 36								15 42		
Northampton	d			13 02		14 02									15 02										
Rugby	d			13 25		14 26									15 26										
Coventry	d				13 46				13 26		14 46							14 26						15 26	
Bedworth	d				13 57						14 57														
Nuneaton	a			13 40	14 04	14 39					15 04				15 39										
	d			13 41		14 40									15 40										
Atherstone	d			13 47		14 46									15 46										
Polesworth	d																								
Tamworth	d			13 55		14 54									15 54										
Lichfield Trent Valley	d			14 01		15 00									16 00										
Rugeley Trent Valley	d			14 07		15 07								←	16 07						←				
Stafford	d		14 09	14 18		15 18		14 24	14 34			15 09		15 18	16 18	15 25		15 34		16 09	16 18	16a24		16 34	
Norton Bridge Station Drv	d					→									→										
Stone	d			14 28										15 29							16 29				
Stone Crown Street	d																								
Stone Granville Square	a																								
Barlaston Orchard Place	d																								
Wedgwood Old Road Bridge	d																								
Stoke-on-Trent	d			14 37					14a55					15 41				15a56			16 40			16a56	
Hanley Bus Station	a																								
Kidsgrove	d			14 45										15 50							16 48				
Alsager	d			14 50										15 54							16 53				
Crewe	a	14 12	14 29	15 00				14 43		15 12		15 29	15 34	16 04		15 43			16 12	16 30	17 03		16 50		17 12

		LM		LM	LM	LM	VT	VT	XC	VT	LM	LM		LM	VT	VT	XC	VT	LM	LM	VT	VT		XC	VT
					◇1	◇1	◇1	◇1	◇1	◇1		◇1		◇1	◇1	◇1	◇1	◇1	◇1	◇1	◇1	◇1		◇1	◇1
							☕	☕	🛒	☕					☕	☕	🛒	☕			☕	☕		🛒	☕
London Euston 15 ⊖	d					15 50	16 05	16 08		16 37				16 50	17 05	17 08		17 37		17 50	18 05	18 08			18 37
Watford Junction	d					16 06								17 06						18 06					
Milton Keynes Central	d					16 36		16 42						17 36		17 42				18 36		18 42			
Northampton	d					17 02								18 02						19 02					
Rugby	d					17 26								18 29						19 26					
Coventry	d	15 46		16 46					16 26		17 46						17 26							18 26	
Bedworth	d	15 57		16 57							17 57														
Nuneaton	a	16 04		17 04		17 39					18 04			18 40		18 12				19 39					
	d					17 40								18 41		18 13				19 40					
Atherstone	d					17 46								18 47						19 46					
Polesworth	d																								
Tamworth	d					17 54								18 55						19 54					
Lichfield Trent Valley	d					18 00								19 01						20 00					
Rugeley Trent Valley	d					18 07								19 08						20 07					
Stafford	d				17 09	18 18	17a24		17 36			18 09		19 18	18a24		18 36		19 09	20 18	19a24			19 39	
Norton Bridge Station Drv	d																								
Stone	d					18 28								19 29						20 29					
Stone Crown Street	d																								
Stone Granville Square	a																								
Barlaston Orchard Place	d																								
Wedgwood Old Road Bridge	d																								
Stoke-on-Trent	d					18 43			17a56					19 44			18a56			20 41				19a56	
Hanley Bus Station	a																								
Kidsgrove	d					18 51								19 52						20 50					
Alsager	d					18 55								19 56						20 54					
Crewe	a				17 30	19 05		17 50		18 12		18 30		20 06		18 53		19 12	19 29	21 05		19 50			20 12

Table 67

London - Stoke-on-Trent and Crewe
Coventry - Nuneaton

Sundays
from 28 October

Network Diagram - see first Page of Table 67

		LM	LM	LM	VT	VT	XC	VT		VT	LM	VT	LM	VT	VT	XC	VT	VT		LM	VT	LM		XC	LM
			◇1	◇1	◇1	◇1	◇1	◇1		◇1	◇1	◇1	◇1	◇1	◇1	◇1	◇1	◇1		◇1	◇1	◇1		◇1	
					☕	☕		☕		☕		☕		☕	☕		☕	☕			☕				
London Euston 15 ⊖	d			18 50	19 05	19 08				19 37	19 50	20 05		20 08	20 25			20 35			20 50				
Watford Junction	d			19 06							20 06														
Milton Keynes Central	d			19 36		19 42					20 36			20 41							21 37				
Northampton	d			20 02							20 59														
Rugby	d			20 27							21 24										22 01				
Coventry	d	19 46					19 26									20 26								21 26	21 35
Bedworth	d	19 57																							21 46
Nuneaton	a	20 04		20 39	20 03						21 35	21 03													21 53
	d			20 39	20 04						21 36	21 04													
Atherstone	d			20 45							21 42														
Polesworth	d																					←			
Tamworth	d			20 53							21 50				21 32							21 50			
Lichfield Trent Valley	d			20 59							→				21 39							21 56			
Rugeley Trent Valley	d			21 06									←									22 03			
Stafford	d		20 09	21 18	20 29		20 37	20 52					21 18	21 33		21 37	21 57	22 00		22 16		22 19		22 37	
Norton Bridge Station Drv	d			→																					
Stone	d												21 29									22 31			
Stone Crown Street	d																								
Stone Granville Square	a																								
Barlaston Orchard Place	d																								
Wedgwood Old Road Bridge	d																								
Stoke-on-Trent	d						20a56						21 43			21a56						22 43		22a55	
Hanley Bus Station	a																								
Kidsgrove	d												21 52									22 51			
Alsager	d												21 57									22 55			
Crewe	a		20 30		20 47	20 50		21 10		21 13		21 44	22 08	21 53	22 10		22 17	22 20		22 38	22 49	23 05			

		VT	AW	VT
		◇1	◇	◇1
		☕		☕
London Euston 15 ⊖	d	21 21		21 51
Watford Junction	d			
Milton Keynes Central	d			22 38
Northampton	d			
Rugby	d			23 18
Coventry	d			
Bedworth	d			
Nuneaton	a	22 51		23 28
	d	22 52		23 29
Atherstone	d			
Polesworth	d			
Tamworth	d			
Lichfield Trent Valley	d			
Rugeley Trent Valley	d			
Stafford	d	23 17	23 31	23s53
Norton Bridge Station Drv	d			
Stone	d			
Stone Crown Street	d			
Stone Granville Square	a			
Barlaston Orchard Place	d			
Wedgwood Old Road Bridge	d			
Stoke-on-Trent	d			
Hanley Bus Station	a			
Kidsgrove	d			
Alsager	d			
Crewe	a	23 43	23 55	00s21

until 29 June

Crewe and Stoke-on-Trent - London
Nuneaton - Coventry

Network Diagram - see first Page of Table 67

Miles	Miles	Miles			AW	LM	VT	LM	XC	VT	XC	LM	VT	LM	VT	LM	XC	LM	VT	LM	VT
						1	◇1		◇1	◇1	◇1	◇1	◇1		◇1	◇1	◇1	◇1	◇1		◇1
							⊠		⊥	⊠	⊥		⊠	🚌	⊠		⊥		⊠		⊠
0	0	—	**Crewe**	d	04 59	05 18	05 36		05 47	06 02		06 20	06 29			06 35	06 38	06 47	06 53		
6½	—	—	Alsager	d												06 44					
8¾	—	—	Kidsgrove	d												06 48					
—	—	—	Hanley Bus Station	d										06 45							
16	—	—	**Stoke-on-Trent**	d					06 07					06 51		06 58					07 06
—	—	—	Wedgwood Old Road Bridge	d										07 06							
—	—	—	Barlaston Orchard Place	d										07 10							
—	—	—	Stone Granville Square	d										07a20							
23¼	—	—	Stone	d												07 06					
—	—	—	Norton Bridge Station Drv	d							←										
32¼	24½	—	**Stafford**	d	05a24		05 55		06 25	06 21	06 25	06a40			06 53	07 22	06a57	07a10			07 28
42	—	—	Rugeley Trent Valley	d		06 00			→							07 33					
50	—	—	Lichfield Trent Valley	d		06 07									07 08	07 40					
56¼	—	—	Tamworth	d		06 14									07 15	07 47					
59¾	—	—	Polesworth	d																	
63¾	—	—	Atherstone	d		06 23										07 56					
68¾	—	0	Nuneaton	a		06 29	06 17						07 06			08 02			07 32		
—	—	—		d		06 30	06 18	06 37					07 07			08 02			07 33	07 37	
—	—	3¾	Bedworth	d				06 44												07 44	
—	—	10	**Coventry**	a				06 56			07 24									07 57	08 30
83¼	—	—	Rugby	a		06 47	06 30			06 52						08 17					
102	—	—	Northampton	a												08 41					
118	—	—	Milton Keynes Central	a			06 51			07 12						09 01					
150¼	—	—	Watford Junction	a												09 27					09s15
167¾	—	—	**London Euston** [15] ⊖	a			07 28			07 50			08 07		08 22	09 44			08 33		09 34

		LM	VT	XC	LM	LM	LM	LM	LM	VT	XC	VT	VT	LM	VT	XC	LM	LM	LM	VT	LM	LM	XC
		◇1	◇1	◇1		◇1	◇1			◇1	◇1	◇1	◇1	◇1	◇1	◇1		◇1	◇1	◇1	◇1		◇1
			⊠	⊥				🚌	🚌	⊠	⊥	⊠	⊠		⊠	⊥				⊠		🚌	⊥
Crewe	d	07 16	07 17			07 33	07 49			07 57				08 22	08 29			08 33	08 49	08 56			
Alsager	d					07 41												08 41					
Kidsgrove	d					07 46												08 46					
Hanley Bus Station	d							07 50														09 00	
Stoke-on-Trent	d			07 44		07 54		08 01			08 07	08 12				08 44		08 54				09 06	09 07
Wedgwood Old Road Bridge	d							08 10														09 21	
Barlaston Orchard Place	d							08 11														09 25	
Stone Granville Square	d							08a25														09a35	
Stone	d					08 02												09 02					
Norton Bridge Station Drv	d								07 52														
Stafford	d	07a40	07 35	08a01		08 21	08a10		08a22		08 25		08 36	08a42		09a02		09 21	09a09				09 25
Rugeley Trent Valley	d					08 33												09 33					
Lichfield Trent Valley	d					08 40												09 40					
Tamworth	d					08 47												09 47					
Polesworth	d																						
Atherstone	d					08 56												09 56					
Nuneaton	a					09 02						08 44						10 02					
	d				08 28	09 02						08 46					09 30	10 02					
Bedworth	d				08 35												09 37						
Coventry	a				08 47						09 24						09 56						10 24
Rugby	a					09 17				08 45								10 17					
Northampton	a					09 39												10 39			←		
Milton Keynes Central	a					10 04												11 04		10 01	10 04		
Watford Junction	a					→						09s31						→			10 30		
London Euston [15] ⊖	a		08 52							09 38		09 52	09 56		10 04					10 38	10 49		

Table 67

Mondays to Fridays

until 29 June

Crewe and Stoke-on-Trent - London
Nuneaton - Coventry

Network Diagram - see first Page of Table 67

		VT	LM	VT	XC	LM	LM	LM	VT	LM	LM	XC	VT	VT	LM	VT	XC	LM	LM	LM	VT	LM	LM
		◇1	◇1	◇1	◇1	◇1	◇1		◇1	◇1		◇1	◇1	◇1	◇1	◇1	◇1		◇1	◇1	◇1	◇1	
		⊠		⊠	⊥			🚌	⊠		🚌	⊥	⊠	⊠		⊠	⊥				⊠		🚌
Crewe	d		09 22	09 29		09 33	09 49		09 56					10 01	10 22	10 29			10 33	10 49	10 56		
Alsager	d					09 41													10 41				
Kidsgrove	d					09 46													10 46				
Hanley Bus Station	d										10 00												11 00
Stoke-on-Trent	d				09 44	09 54					10 06	10 07					10 44		10 54				11 06
Wedgwood Old Road Bridge	d										10 21												11 21
Barlaston Orchard Place	d										10 25												11 25
Stone Granville Square	d										10a35												11a35
Stone	d					10 02													11 02				
Norton Bridge Station Drv	d							09 52															
Stafford	d	09 36	09a42		10a02	10 21	10a09	10a22				10 25	10 36		10a42		11a01		11 21	11a09			
Rugeley Trent Valley	d					10 33													11 33				
Lichfield Trent Valley	d					10 40													11 40				
Tamworth	d					10 47													11 47				
Polesworth	d																						
Atherstone	d					10 56													11 56				
Nuneaton	a					11 02													12 02				
	d					11 02												11 15	12 02				
Bedworth	d																	11 22					
Coventry	a											11 24		11 30				11 34					
Rugby	a					11 17													12 17				
Northampton	a					11 42				←									12 43			←	
Milton Keynes Central	a					12 04			11 01	11 04									13 04		12 01	12 04	
Watford Junction	a					→				11 30				12s15					→			12 30	
London Euston [15] ⊖	a	10 56		11 04					11 38	11 49			11 56	12 32		12 04					12 38	12 49	

		XC	VT	LM	VT	XC	LM	LM	LM	VT	LM	LM	XC	LM	VT	LM	VT	XC	LM	LM	LM	VT
		◇1	◇1	◇1	◇1	◇1		◇1	◇1	◇1	◇1		◇1		◇1	◇1	◇1	◇1		◇1	◇1	◇1
		⊥	⊠		⊠	⊥				⊓		🚌	⊥	🚌	⊓		⊓	⊥				⊓
Crewe	d			11 22	11 29			11 33	11 49	11 56						12 22	12 29			12 33	12 49	12 56
Alsager	d							11 41												12 41		
Kidsgrove	d							11 46												12 46		
Hanley Bus Station	d											12 00										
Stoke-on-Trent	d	11 07				11 44		11 54				12 06	12 07					12 44		12 54		
Wedgwood Old Road Bridge	d											12 21										
Barlaston Orchard Place	d											12 25										
Stone Granville Square	d											12a35		11 39								
Stone	d							12 02												13 02		
Norton Bridge Station Drv	d													12 02								
Stafford	d	11 25	11 34	11a43		12a02		12 21	12a09				12 25	12a32	12 36	12a42		13a01		13 21	13a09	
Rugeley Trent Valley	d							12 33												13 33		
Lichfield Trent Valley	d							12 40												13 40		
Tamworth	d							12 47												13 47		
Polesworth	d																					
Atherstone	d							12 56												13 56		
Nuneaton	a							13 02												14 02		
	d						12 15	13 02											13 15	14 02		
Bedworth	d						12 22												13 22			
Coventry	a	12 24					12 34						13 24						13 34			
Rugby	a							13 17												14 17		
Northampton	a							13 40			←									14 42		
Milton Keynes Central	a							14 04		13 01	13 04									15 04		14 01
Watford Junction	a							→			13 30									→		
London Euston [15] ⊖	a		12 56		13 03					13 38	13 49				13 56		14 04					14 38

		LM	LM	XC	VT	LM	VT	XC	LM	LM	LM	LM	VT	LM	LM	XC	VT	LM	VT	XC	LM	LM	LM
		◇1		◇1	◇1	◇1	◇1	◇1		◇1	◇1		◇1	◇1		◇1	◇1	◇1	◇1	◇1		◇1	1
			🚌	⊥	⊓		⊓	⊥				🚌	⊓		🚌	⊥	⊓		⊓	⊥			
Crewe	d					13 22	13 29			13 33	13 49		13 56					14 22	14 29			14 33	14 49
Alsager	d									13 41												14 41	
Kidsgrove	d									13 46												14 46	
Hanley Bus Station	d		13 00												14 00								
Stoke-on-Trent	d		13 06	13 07				13 44		13 54					14 06	14 07				14 44		14 54	
Wedgwood Old Road Bridge	d		13 21												14 21								
Barlaston Orchard Place	d		13 25												14 25								
Stone Granville Square	d		13a35									13 39			14a35								
Stone	d									14 02												15 02	
Norton Bridge Station Drv	d											13 54											
Stafford	d			13 25	13 36	13a42		14a01		14 21	14a09	14a15				14 25	14 36	14a46		15a02		15 21	15a09
Rugeley Trent Valley	d									14 33												15 33	
Lichfield Trent Valley	d									14 40												15 40	
Tamworth	d									14 47												15 47	
Polesworth	d																						
Atherstone	d									14 56												15 56	
Nuneaton	a									15 02												16 02	
	d								14 15	15 02											15 15	16 02	
Bedworth	d								14 22												15 22		
Coventry	a			14 24					14 34							15 24					15 34		
Rugby	a									15 17												16 17	
Northampton	a	←								15 42				←								16 43	
Milton Keynes Central	a	14 04								16 04			15 01	15 04								17 04	
Watford Junction	a	14 30								→				15 30								→	
London Euston [15] ⊖	a	14 49			14 56		15 04						15 38	15 49			15 56		16 04				

Crewe and Stoke-on-Trent - London
Nuneaton - Coventry

Network Diagram - see first Page of Table 67

		VT	LM	LM	XC	VT	VT	LM	VT	XC	LM	LM	LM	LM	VT	LM	LM	XC	VT	LM	VT	XC
		◇1 ⊡	◇1	🚌	◇1 ⊼	◇1 ⊡	◇1 ⊡	◇1	◇1 ⊡	◇1 ⊼		◇1	◇1	🚌	◇1 ⊡	◇1	🚌	◇1 ⊼	◇1 ⊡	◇1	◇1 ⊡	◇1 ⊼
Crewe	d	14 56					15 01	15 22	15 29			15 33	15 49		15 57					16 22	16 29	
Alsager	d											15 41										
Kidsgrove	d											15 46										
Hanley Bus Station	d			15 00													16 00					
Stoke-on-Trent	d			15 06	15 07					15 44		15 54					16 06	16 07				16 44
Wedgwood Old Road Bridge	d			15 21													16 21					
Barlaston Orchard Place	d			15 25													16 25					
Stone Granville Square	d			15a35										15 29			16a35					
Stone	d											16 02										
Norton Bridge Station Drv	d													15 52								
Stafford	d				15 25	15 36		15a42		16a02		16 21	16a09	16a13				16 25	16 36	16a46		17a02
Rugeley Trent Valley	d											16 33										
Lichfield Trent Valley	d											16 40										
Tamworth	d											16 47										
Polesworth	d																					
Atherstone	d											16 56										
Nuneaton	a											17 02										
	d										16 13	17 02										
Bedworth	d										16 20											
Coventry	a				16 24		16 30				16 34							17 24				
Rugby	a											17 17										
Northampton	a		←									17 39				←						
Milton Keynes Central	a	16 01	16 04									18 04			17 01	17 04						
Watford Junction	a		16 30				17s15					→				17 30						
London Euston 15 ⊖	a	16 38	16 49			16 59	17 34		17 04						17 38	17 49			17 56		18 03	

		LM	LM	LM	VT	LM	LM	XC	VT	LM	VT	XC	LM	LM	LM	VT	LM	LM	XC	VT	LM	VT	LM
			◇1	◇1	◇1 ⊡	◇1	🚌	◇1 ⊼	◇1 ⊡	◇1	◇1 ⊡	◇1 ⊼		◇1	◇1	◇1 ⊠	◇1	🚌	◇1 ⊼	◇1 ⊠	◇1	◇1 ⊠	◇1
Crewe	d		16 33	16 49	16 56					17 22	17 29			17 33	17 49	17 56			18 07		18 22	18 29	
Alsager	d		16 41											17 41									
Kidsgrove	d		16 46											17 46									
Hanley Bus Station	d						17 00											18 00					
Stoke-on-Trent	d		16 54				17 06	17 07				17 44		17 54				18 06					
Wedgwood Old Road Bridge	d						17 21											18 21					
Barlaston Orchard Place	d						17 25											18 25					
Stone Granville Square	d						17a35											18a33					
Stone	d		17 02											18 02									
Norton Bridge Station Drv	d																						
Stafford	d		17 21	17a10				17 25	17 36	17a42		18a03		18 21	18a09				18 28	18 36	18a42		
Rugeley Trent Valley	d		17 33											18 33									
Lichfield Trent Valley	d		17 40											18 40									
Tamworth	d		17 47											18 47									
Polesworth	d																						
Atherstone	d		17 56											18 56									
Nuneaton	a		18 02											19 02									
	d	17 15	18 02										18 10	19 02									
Bedworth	d	17 22											18 17										
Coventry	a	17 34						18 24					18 34						19 24				
Rugby	a		18 17											19 18									
Northampton	a		18 39			←								19 45			←						←
Milton Keynes Central	a		19 04		18 01	18 04			18 23					20 05		19 02	19 04					19 31	20 05
Watford Junction	a		→			18 31					18s48			→			19 30			19s42			20 31
London Euston 15 ⊖	a				18 38	18 49			18 59		19 08					19 39	19 50			20 02		20 06	20 49

		XC	LM	LM	LM	XC	LM	VT	VT	XC	LM	LM	LM	VT	XC	LM	VT	VT	VT	LM	XC	LM	VT
		◇1 ⊼		◇1	◇1	◇1 A ⊼	◇1	◇1 ⊠	◇1 ⊠	◇1 ⊼		■1	◇1	◇1 ⊡	◇1 A ⊼	◇1	◇1 ⊡	◇1 ⊡	◇1 ⊡	■1	◇1	◇1	◇1 ⊡
Crewe	d			18 33	18 49		19 18	19 23	19 29			19 33	19 55	19 56		20 18	20 23	20 29	20 41			20 47	20 53
Alsager	d			18 41								19 41											
Kidsgrove	d			18 46								19 46											
Hanley Bus Station	d																						
Stoke-on-Trent	d	18 44		18 54		19 07				19 44		19 54			20 07						20 44		
Wedgwood Old Road Bridge	d																						
Barlaston Orchard Place	d																						
Stone Granville Square	d																						
Stone	d			19 02								20 02											
Norton Bridge Station Drv	d																						
Stafford	d	19a01		19 21	19a09	19 25	19a41	19 42		20a03		20 21	20a15		20 26	20a38		20 48			21a02	21a08	21a11
Rugeley Trent Valley	d			19 33								20 33											
Lichfield Trent Valley	d			19 40								20 40											
Tamworth	d			19 47								20 47											
Polesworth	d																						
Atherstone	d			19 56								20 56											
Nuneaton	a			20 02								21 02					21 02						
	d		19 15	20 02							20 15	21 02					21 03						
Bedworth	d		19 22								20 22												
Coventry	a		19 38			20 24					20 34				21 24								
Rugby	a			20 17								21 17							21 27				
Northampton	a			20 43								21 39								←			
Milton Keynes Central	a								20 32			22 04		21 03				21 35	21 47	22 04			
Watford Junction	a							20s46				→					21s48			22 35			
London Euston 15 ⊖	a							21 05	21 06					21 42			22 09	22 12	22 22	22 56			

A ⊼ to Stafford

Crewe and Stoke-on-Trent - London
Nuneaton - Coventry

Network Diagram - see first Page of Table 67

		XC	LM	LM	VT	XC	LM	LM	XC
		◇1		◇1	◇1 ⊡	◇1	◇1		◇1
Crewe	d			21 18	21 24		22 20		
Alsager	d								
Kidsgrove	d								
Hanley Bus Station	d								
Stoke-on-Trent	d	21 07				22 08			22 47
Wedgwood Old Road Bridge	d								
Barlaston Orchard Place	d								
Stone Granville Square	d								
Stone	d								
Norton Bridge Station Drv	d								
Stafford	d	21a24		21a38	21 44	22a25	22a40		23a06
Rugeley Trent Valley	d								
Lichfield Trent Valley	d				21 58				
Tamworth	d				22 05				
Polesworth	d								
Atherstone	d								
Nuneaton	a				22 16				
	d		21 15		22 17			22 20	
Bedworth	d		21 22					22 27	
Coventry	a		21 34					22 39	
Rugby	a				22 30				
Northampton	a								
Milton Keynes Central	a				22 58				
Watford Junction	a				23s30				
London Euston 15 ⊖	a				23 56				

Mondays to Fridays
2 July to 14 September

		AW	LM	LM	VT	LM	XC	VT	XC	LM	VT	LM	LM	VT	LM	XC	LM	VT	LM	VT	LM
			■1 A	■1	◇1 ⊠		◇1 ⊼	◇1 ⊠	◇1 ⊼	◇1	◇1 ⊠	■1 A	🚌	◇1 ⊠	◇1	◇1 ⊼	◇1	◇1 ⊠		◇1 ⊠	◇1
Crewe	d	04 59	05 18	05 18	05 36		05 47	06 02		06 20	06 29				06 35	06 38	06 47	06 53			07 16
Alsager	d														06 44						
Kidsgrove	d														06 48						
Hanley Bus Station	d												06 45								
Stoke-on-Trent	d						06 07						06 51		06 58					07 06	
Wedgwood Old Road Bridge	d												07 06								
Barlaston Orchard Place	d												07 10								
Stone Granville Square	d												07a20								
Stone	d														07 06						
Norton Bridge Station Drv	d								←												
Stafford	d	05a24			05 55		06 25	06 21	06 25	06a40				06 53	07 22	06a57	07a10			07 28	07a40
Rugeley Trent Valley	d		06 00	06 00			→								07 33						
Lichfield Trent Valley	d		06 07	06 07										07 08	07 40						
Tamworth	d		06 14	06 14										07 15	07 47						
Polesworth	d																				
Atherstone	d		06 23	06 23											07 56						
Nuneaton	a		06 29	06 29	06 17						07 06				08 02			07 32			
	d		06 29	06 30	06 18	06 37					07 07				08 02			07 33	07 37		
Bedworth	d					06 44													07 44		
Coventry	a					06 56			07 24										07 57	08 30	
Rugby	a		06 44	06 47	06 30			06 52							08 17						
Northampton	a		07 06									←			08 41						
Milton Keynes Central	a		07 29		06 51			07 12				07 29			09 01						
Watford Junction	a		→												09 27					09s15	
London Euston 15 ⊖	a				07 28			07 50			08 07	08 11		08 22	09 44			08 33		09 34	

A from 10 September until 14 September

Crewe and Stoke-on-Trent - London Nuneaton - Coventry

Network Diagram - see first Page of Table 67

		VT	XC	LM	LM	LM	LM	LM	VT	XC	VT	VT	LM	VT	XC	LM	LM	LM	VT	LM	LM	XC	VT
		◇1	◇1		◇1	◇1			◇1	◇1	◇1	◇1	◇1	◇1	◇1		◇1	◇1	◇1	◇1		◇1	◇1
		⊠	⌶				bus	bus	⊠	⌶	⊠	⊠		⊠	⌶				⊠		bus	⌶	⊠
Crewe	d	07 17			07 33	07 49			07 57				08 22	08 29			08 33	08 49	08 56				
Alsager	d				07 41												08 41						
Kidsgrove	d				07 46												08 46						
Hanley Bus Station	d						07 50														09 00		
Stoke-on-Trent	d		07 44		07 54		08 01			08 07	08 12				08 44		08 54				09 06	09 07	
Wedgwood Old Road Bridge	d						08 10														09 21		
Barlaston Orchard Place	d						08 11														09 25		
Stone Granville Square	d						08a25														09a35		
Stone	d				08 02												09 02						
Norton Bridge Station Drv	d							07 52															
Stafford	d	07 35	08a01		08 21	08a10		08a22		08 25		08 36	08a42		09a02		09 21	09a09				09 25	09 36
Rugeley Trent Valley	d				08 33												09 33						
Lichfield Trent Valley	d				08 40												09 40						
Tamworth	d				08 47												09 47						
Polesworth	d																						
Atherstone	d				08 56												09 56						
Nuneaton	a				09 02						08 44						10 02						
	d			08 28	09 02						08 46					09 30	10 02						
Bedworth	d			08 35												09 37							
Coventry	a			08 47						09 24						09 56						10 24	
Rugby	a				09 17				08 45								10 17						
Northampton	a				09 39												10 39			←			
Milton Keynes Central	a				10 04												11 04		10 01	10 04			
Watford Junction	a				→						09s31						→			10 30			
London Euston ⊖	a	08 52							09 38		09 52	09 56		10 04					10 38	10 49			10 56

		LM	VT	XC	LM	LM	LM	VT	LM	LM	XC	VT	LM	VT	XC	LM	LM	LM	VT	LM	LM	XC
		◇1	◇1	◇1	◇1	◇1		◇1	◇1		◇1	◇1	◇1	◇1	◇1		◇1	◇1	◇1	◇1		◇1
			⊠	⌶			bus	⊠		bus	⌶	⊠		⊠	⌶				⊠		bus	⌶
Crewe	d	09 22	09 29		09 33	09 49		09 56					10 22	10 29			10 33	10 49	10 56			
Alsager	d				09 41												10 41					
Kidsgrove	d				09 46												10 46					
Hanley Bus Station	d									10 00											11 00	
Stoke-on-Trent	d			09 44	09 54					10 06	10 07				10 44		10 54				11 06	11 07
Wedgwood Old Road Bridge	d									10 21											11 21	
Barlaston Orchard Place	d									10 25											11 25	
Stone Granville Square	d									10a35											11a35	
Stone	d				10 02												11 02					
Norton Bridge Station Drv	d						09 52															
Stafford	d	09a42		10a02	10 21	10a09	10a22				10 25	10 36	10a42		11a01		11 21	11a09				11 25
Rugeley Trent Valley	d				10 33												11 33					
Lichfield Trent Valley	d				10 40												11 40					
Tamworth	d				10 47												11 47					
Polesworth	d																					
Atherstone	d				10 56												11 56					
Nuneaton	a				11 02												12 02					
	d				11 02											11 15	12 02					
Bedworth	d															11 22						
Coventry	a										11 24					11 34						12 24
Rugby	a				11 17												12 17					
Northampton	a				11 42				←								12 43			←		
Milton Keynes Central	a				12 04			11 01	11 04								13 04		12 01	12 04		
Watford Junction	a				→				11 30								→			12 30		
London Euston ⊖	a		11 04					11 38	11 49			11 56		12 04					12 38	12 49		

		VT	LM	VT	XC	LM	LM	LM	VT	LM	LM	XC	LM	VT	LM	VT	XC	LM	LM	LM	VT	LM	LM
		◇1	◇1	◇1	◇1		◇1	◇1	◇1	◇1		◇1		◇1	◇1	◇1	◇1		◇1	◇1	◇1	◇1	
		⊠		⊠	⌶				⊐		bus	⌶	bus	⊐		⊐	⌶				⊐		bus
Crewe	d		11 22	11 29			11 33	11 49	11 56						12 22	12 29			12 33	12 49	12 56		
Alsager	d						11 41												12 41				
Kidsgrove	d						11 46												12 46				
Hanley Bus Station	d										12 00												13 00
Stoke-on-Trent	d				11 44		11 54				12 06	12 07					12 44		12 54				13 06
Wedgwood Old Road Bridge	d										12 21												13 21
Barlaston Orchard Place	d										12 25												13 25
Stone Granville Square	d										12a35		11 39										13a35
Stone	d						12 02												13 02				
Norton Bridge Station Drv	d												12 02										
Stafford	d	11 34	11a43		12a02		12 21	12a09				12 25	12a32	12 36	12a42		13a01		13 21	13a09			
Rugeley Trent Valley	d						12 33												13 33				
Lichfield Trent Valley	d						12 40												13 40				
Tamworth	d						12 47												13 47				
Polesworth	d																						
Atherstone	d						12 56												13 56				
Nuneaton	a						13 02												14 02				
	d					12 15	13 02											13 15	14 02				
Bedworth	d					12 22												13 22					
Coventry	a					12 34						13 24						13 34					
Rugby	a						13 17												14 17				
Northampton	a						13 40			←									14 42			←	
Milton Keynes Central	a						14 04		13 01	13 04									15 04		14 01	14 04	
Watford Junction	a						→			13 30									→			14 30	
London Euston ⊖	a	12 56		13 03					13 38	13 49				13 56		14 04					14 38	14 49	

Table 67

Mondays to Fridays
2 July to 14 September

Crewe and Stoke-on-Trent - London Nuneaton - Coventry

Network Diagram - see first Page of Table 67

		XC	VT	LM	VT	XC	LM	LM	LM	LM	VT	LM	LM	XC	VT	VT	LM	VT	XC	LM	LM	LM
		◇1	◇1	◇1	◇1	◇1		◇1	◇1		◇1	◇1		◇1	◇1	◇1	◇1	◇1	◇1		◇1	1
		⌶	⊐		⊐	⌶				bus	⊐		bus	⌶	⊐	⊠		⊐	⌶			
Crewe	d			13 22	13 29			13 33	13 49		13 56					14 01	14 22	14 29			14 33	14 49
Alsager	d							13 41													14 41	
Kidsgrove	d							13 46													14 46	
Hanley Bus Station	d												14 00									
Stoke-on-Trent	d	13 07				13 44		13 54					14 06	14 07					14 44		14 54	
Wedgwood Old Road Bridge	d												14 21									
Barlaston Orchard Place	d												14 25									
Stone Granville Square	d									13 39			14a35									
Stone	d							14 02													15 02	
Norton Bridge Station Drv	d									13 54												
Stafford	d	13 25	13 36	13a42		14a01		14 21	14a09	14a15				14 25	14 36		14a46		15a02		15 21	15a09
Rugeley Trent Valley	d							14 33													15 33	
Lichfield Trent Valley	d							14 40													15 40	
Tamworth	d							14 47													15 47	
Polesworth	d																					
Atherstone	d							14 56													15 56	
Nuneaton	a							15 02													16 02	
	d						14 15	15 02												15 15	16 02	
Bedworth	d						14 22													15 22		
Coventry	a	14 24					14 34							15 24		15 30				15 34		
Rugby	a							15 17													16 17	
Northampton	a							15 42				←									16 43	
Milton Keynes Central	a							16 04			15 01	15 04									17 04	
Watford Junction	a							→				15 30				16s15					→	
London Euston ⊖	a		14 56		15 04						15 38	15 49			15 56	16 32		16 04				

		VT	LM	LM	XC	VT	LM	VT	XC	LM	LM	LM	LM	VT	VT	LM	LM	XC	VT	LM	VT	XC	LM
		◇1	◇1		◇1	◇1	◇1	◇1	◇1		◇1	◇1		◇1	◇1	◇1		◇1	◇1	◇1	◇1	◇1	
		⊐		bus	⌶	⊐		⊐	⌶				bus	⊐	⊐		bus	⌶	⊐		⊐	⌶	
Crewe	d	14 56					15 22	15 29			15 33	15 49		15 56	15 57					16 22	16 29		
Alsager	d										15 41												
Kidsgrove	d										15 46												
Hanley Bus Station	d			15 00													16 00						
Stoke-on-Trent	d			15 06	15 07				15 44		15 54						16 06	16 07				16 44	
Wedgwood Old Road Bridge	d			15 21													16 21						
Barlaston Orchard Place	d			15 25													16 25						
Stone Granville Square	d			15a35									15 29				16a35						
Stone	d										16 02												
Norton Bridge Station Drv	d												15 52										
Stafford	d				15 25	15 36	15a42		16a02		16 21	16a09	16a13					16 25	16 36	16a46		17a02	
Rugeley Trent Valley	d										16 33												
Lichfield Trent Valley	d										16 40												
Tamworth	d										16 47												
Polesworth	d																						
Atherstone	d										16 56												
Nuneaton	a										17 02												
	d									16 13	17 02												17 15
Bedworth	d									16 20													17 22
Coventry	a				16 24					16 34								17 24					17 34
Rugby	a										17 17												
Northampton	a		←								17 39					←							
Milton Keynes Central	a	16 01	16 04								18 04			17s01	17 01	17 04							
Watford Junction	a		16 30								→					17 30							
London Euston ⊖	a	16 38	16 49			16 59		17 04						17 38	17 38	17 49			17 56		18 03		

		LM	LM	VT	LM	LM	XC	VT	LM	VT	XC	LM	LM	LM	VT	LM	LM	VT	XC	VT	LM	VT	LM
		◇1	◇1	◇1	◇1		◇1	◇1	◇1	◇1	◇1		◇1	◇1	◇1	◇1		1	◇1	◇1	◇1	◇1	◇1
				⊐		bus	⌶	⊐		⊐	⌶				⊠		bus	⊐	⌶	⊠		⊠	
Crewe	d	16 33	16 49	16 56					17 22	17 29			17 33	17 49	17 56			18 01	18 07		18 22	18 29	
Alsager	d	16 41											17 41										
Kidsgrove	d	16 46											17 46										
Hanley Bus Station	d					17 00											18 00						
Stoke-on-Trent	d	16 54				17 06	17 07				17 44		17 54				18 06						
Wedgwood Old Road Bridge	d					17 21											18 21						
Barlaston Orchard Place	d					17 25											18 25						
Stone Granville Square	d					17a35											18a33						
Stone	d	17 02											18 02										
Norton Bridge Station Drv	d																						
Stafford	d	17 21	17a10				17 25	17 36	17a42		18a03		18 21	18a09					18 28	18 36	18a42		
Rugeley Trent Valley	d	17 33											18 33										
Lichfield Trent Valley	d	17 40											18 40										
Tamworth	d	17 47											18 47										
Polesworth	d																						
Atherstone	d	17 56											18 56										
Nuneaton	a	18 02											19 02										
	d	18 02										18 10	19 02										
Bedworth	d											18 17											
Coventry	a						18 24					18 34						19 30	19 24				
Rugby	a	18 17											19 18										
Northampton	a	18 39			←								19 45			←							←
Milton Keynes Central	a	19 04		18 01	18 04			18 23					20 05		19 01	19 04						19 31	20 05
Watford Junction	a	→			18 31					18s48			→			19 30		20s15		19s42			20 31
London Euston ⊖	a			18 38	18 49			18 59		19 08					19 38	19 50		20 34		20 02		20 06	20 49

2 July to 14 September

Crewe and Stoke-on-Trent - London
Nuneaton - Coventry

Network Diagram - see first Page of Table 67

		XC	LM	LM	LM	XC	LM	VT	VT	XC	LM	LM	LM	LM	VT	XC	LM	VT	VT	XC	LM	LM
		◇1 🛒		◇1	◇1	◇1 A 🛒	◇1	◇1 ⊠	◇1 ⊠	◇1 🛒		1 B	1	◇1	◇1 🍴	◇1 A 🛒	◇1	◇1 🍴	◇1 🍴	◇1		1 B
Crewe	d			18 33	18 49		19 18	19 23	19 29			19 33	19 33	19 55	19 56		20 18	20 23	20 29			20 39
Alsager	d			18 41								19 41	19 41									20 48
Kidsgrove	d			18 46								19 46	19 46									20 52
Hanley Bus Station	d																					
Stoke-on-Trent	d	18 44		18 54		19 07				19 44		19 54	19 54			20 07				20 44		21 01
Wedgwood Old Road Bridge	d																					
Barlaston Orchard Place	d																					
Stone Granville Square	d																					
Stone	d			19 02								20 02	20 02									21 09
Norton Bridge Station Drv	d																					
Stafford	d	19a01		19 21	19a09	19 25	19a41	19 42		20a03		20 21	20 21	20a15		20 26	20a38		20 48	21a02		21 27
Rugeley Trent Valley	d			19 33								20 33	20 33									21 36
Lichfield Trent Valley	d			19 40								20 40	20 40									21 43
Tamworth	d			19 47								20 47	20 47									21 50
Polesworth	d																					
Atherstone	d			19 56								20 56	20 56									21 59
Nuneaton	a			20 02								21 02	21 02					21 02				22 05
	d		19 15	20 02							20 15	21 02	21 02					21 03			21 15	22 05
Bedworth	d		19 22								20 22										21 22	
Coventry	a		19 38			20 24					20 34					21 24					21 34	
Rugby	a			20 17								21 17	21 17									22 20
Northampton	a			20 43								21 39	21 39									22 41
Milton Keynes Central	a								20 32				22 04		21 03				21 35			
Watford Junction	a							20s46					→					21s48				
London Euston 15	⊖ a							21 05	21 06						21 42			22 09	22 12			

		VT	LM	LM	VT	XC	LM	VT	XC	LM	LM	XC
		◇1 🍴	1	◇1	◇1 🍴	◇1	◇1	◇1 🍴	◇1	◇1		◇1
Crewe	d	20 41		20 47	20 53		21 18	21 24		22 20		
Alsager	d											
Kidsgrove	d											
Hanley Bus Station	d											
Stoke-on-Trent	d					21 07			22 08			22 47
Wedgwood Old Road Bridge	d											
Barlaston Orchard Place	d											
Stone Granville Square	d											
Stone	d											
Norton Bridge Station Drv	d											
Stafford	d			21a08	21a11	21a24	21a38	21 44	22a25	22a40		23a06
Rugeley Trent Valley	d											
Lichfield Trent Valley	d							21 58				
Tamworth	d							22 05				
Polesworth	d											
Atherstone	d											
Nuneaton	a							22 16				
	d							22 17			22 20	
Bedworth	d										22 27	
Coventry	a										22 39	
Rugby	a	21 27						22 30				
Northampton	a		←									
Milton Keynes Central	a	21 47	22 04					22 58				
Watford Junction	a		22 35					23s30				
London Euston 15	⊖ a	22 22	22 56					23 56				

A 🛒 to Stafford

B from 10 September until 14 September

from 17 September

Crewe and Stoke-on-Trent - London
Nuneaton - Coventry

Network Diagram - see first Page of Table 67

		AW	LM	LM	VT	LM	XC	VT	XC	LM	VT	LM	LM	VT	LM	XC	LM	VT	LM	VT	LM
			1	1	◇1 ⊠		◇1 🛒	◇1 ⊠	◇1 🛒	◇1	◇1 ⊠	1	🚌	◇1 ⊠	◇1	◇1 🛒	◇1	◇1 ⊠		◇1 ⊠	◇1
Crewe	d	04 59	05 18	05 18	05 36		05 47	06 02		06 20	06 29				06 35	06 38	06 47	06 53			07 16
Alsager	d														06 44						
Kidsgrove	d														06 48						
Hanley Bus Station	d												06 45								
Stoke-on-Trent	d						06 07						06 51		06 58					07 06	
Wedgwood Old Road Bridge	d												07 06								
Barlaston Orchard Place	d												07 10								
Stone Granville Square	d												07a20								
Stone	d														07 06						
Norton Bridge Station Drv	d								←												
Stafford	d	05a24			05 55		06 25	06 21	06 25	06a40				06 53	07 22	06a57	07a10			07 28	07a40
Rugeley Trent Valley	d		06 00	06 00			→								07 33						
Lichfield Trent Valley	d		06 07	06 07										07 08	07 40						
Tamworth	d		06 14	06 14										07 15	07 47						
Polesworth	d																				
Atherstone	d		06 23	06 23											07 56						
Nuneaton	a		06 29	06 29	06 17						07 06				08 02			07 32			
	d		06 29	06 30	06 18	06 37					07 07				08 02			07 33	07 37		
Bedworth	d					06 44													07 44		
Coventry	a					06 56			07 24										07 57	08 30	
Rugby	a		06 44	06 47	06 30			06 52							08 17						
Northampton	a		07 06									←			08 41						
Milton Keynes Central	a		07 29		06 51			07 12				07 29			09 01						
Watford Junction	a		→												09 27					09s15	
London Euston 15	⊖ a				07 28			07 50			08 07	08 11		08 22	09 44			08 33		09 34	

		VT	XC	LM	LM	LM	LM	LM	VT	XC	VT	VT	LM	VT	XC	LM	LM	LM	VT	LM	LM	XC	VT
		◇1 ⊠	◇1 🛒		◇1	◇1	🚌	🚌	◇1 ⊠	◇1 🛒	◇1 ⊠	◇1 ⊠	◇1	◇1 ⊠	◇1 🛒		◇1	◇1	◇1 ⊠	◇1	🚌	◇1 🛒	◇1 ⊠
Crewe	d	07 17			07 33	07 49			07 57				08 22	08 29			08 33	08 49	08 56				
Alsager	d				07 41												08 41						
Kidsgrove	d				07 46												08 46						
Hanley Bus Station	d						07 50														09 00		
Stoke-on-Trent	d		07 44		07 54		08 01			08 07	08 12				08 44		08 54				09 06	09 07	
Wedgwood Old Road Bridge	d						08 10														09 21		
Barlaston Orchard Place	d						08 11														09 25		
Stone Granville Square	d						08a25														09a35		
Stone	d				08 02												09 02						
Norton Bridge Station Drv	d							07 52															
Stafford	d	07 35	08a01		08 21	08a10		08a22		08 25		08 36	08a42		09a02		09 21	09a09				09 25	09 36
Rugeley Trent Valley	d				08 33												09 33						
Lichfield Trent Valley	d				08 40												09 40						
Tamworth	d				08 47												09 47						
Polesworth	d																						
Atherstone	d				08 56												09 56						
Nuneaton	a				09 02						08 44						10 02						
	d			08 28	09 02						08 46					09 30	10 02						
Bedworth	d			08 35												09 37							
Coventry	a			08 47						09 24						09 56						10 24	
Rugby	a				09 17				08 45								10 17						
Northampton	a				09 39												10 39			←			
Milton Keynes Central	a				10 04												11 04		10 01	10 04			
Watford Junction	a				→						09s31						→			10 30			
London Euston 15	⊖ a	08 52							09 38		09 52	09 56		10 04					10 38	10 49			10 56

		LM	VT	XC	LM	LM	LM	VT	LM	LM	XC	VT	LM	VT	XC	LM	LM	LM	VT	LM	LM	XC
		◇1	◇1 ⊠	◇1 🛒	◇1	◇1	🚌	◇1 ⊠	◇1	🚌	◇1 🛒	◇1 ⊠	◇1	◇1 ⊠	◇1 🛒		◇1	◇1	◇1 ⊠	◇1	🚌	◇1 🛒
Crewe	d	09 22	09 29		09 33	09 49		09 56					10 22	10 29			10 33	10 49	10 56			
Alsager	d				09 41												10 41					
Kidsgrove	d				09 46												10 46					
Hanley Bus Station	d									10 00											11 00	
Stoke-on-Trent	d			09 44	09 54					10 06	10 07				10 44		10 54				11 06	11 07
Wedgwood Old Road Bridge	d									10 21											11 21	
Barlaston Orchard Place	d									10 25											11 25	
Stone Granville Square	d									10a35											11a35	
Stone	d				10 02												11 02					
Norton Bridge Station Drv	d						09 52															
Stafford	d	09a42		10a02	10 21	10a09	10a22				10 25	10 36	10a42		11a01		11 21	11a09				11 25
Rugeley Trent Valley	d				10 33												11 33					
Lichfield Trent Valley	d				10 40												11 40					
Tamworth	d				10 47												11 47					
Polesworth	d																					
Atherstone	d				10 56												11 56					
Nuneaton	a				11 02												12 02					
	d				11 02											11 15	12 02					
Bedworth	d															11 22						
Coventry	a										11 24					11 34						12 24
Rugby	a				11 17												12 17					
Northampton	a				11 42				←								12 43			←		
Milton Keynes Central	a				12 04			11 01	11 04								13 04		12 01	12 04		
Watford Junction	a				→				11 30								→			12 30		
London Euston 15	⊖ a		11 04					11 38	11 49			11 56		12 04					12 38	12 49		

Crewe and Stoke-on-Trent - London
Nuneaton - Coventry

Network Diagram - see first Page of Table 67

		VT	LM	VT	XC	LM	LM	LM		VT	LM	LM	XC	LM	VT	LM	VT	XC		LM	LM	LM	VT	LM	LM
		◇1 ⊠	◇1	◇1 ⊠	◇1 ⌶		◇1	◇1		◇1 ☕	◇1	🚌	◇1 ⌶	🚌	◇1 ☕	◇1	◇1 ☕	◇1 ⌶			◇1	◇1	◇1 ☕	◇1	🚌
Crewe	d		11 22	11 29			11 33	11 49		11 56						12 22	12 29				12 33	12 49	12 56		
Alsager	d						11 41														12 41				
Kidsgrove	d						11 46														12 46				
Hanley Bus Station	d											12 00													13 00
Stoke-on-Trent	d				11 44		11 54					12 06	12 07					12 44			12 54				13 06
Wedgwood Old Road Bridge	d											12 21													13 21
Barlaston Orchard Place	d											12 25													13 25
Stone Granville Square	d											12a35		11 39											13a35
Stone	d						12 02														13 02				
Norton Bridge Station Drv	d													12 02											
Stafford	d	11 34	11a43		12a02		12 21	12a09					12 25	12a32	12 36	12a42		13a01			13 21	13a09			
Rugeley Trent Valley	d						12 33														13 33				
Lichfield Trent Valley	d						12 40														13 40				
Tamworth	d						12 47														13 47				
Polesworth	d																								
Atherstone	d						12 56														13 56				
Nuneaton	a						13 02														14 02				
	d					12 15	13 02													13 15	14 02				
Bedworth	d					12 22														13 22					
Coventry	a					12 34							13 24							13 34					
Rugby	a						13 17														14 17				
Northampton	a						13 40				←										14 42			←	
Milton Keynes Central	a						14 04			13 01	13 04										15 04		14 01	14 04	
Watford Junction	a						→				13 30										→			14 30	
London Euston 15 ⊖	a	12 56		13 03						13 38	13 49				13 56		14 04						14 38	14 49	

		XC	VT	LM		VT	XC	LM	LM	LM	LM	VT	LM	LM		XC	VT	LM	VT	XC	LM	LM	LM	VT	
		◇1 ⌶	◇1 ☕	◇1		◇1 ☕	◇1 ⌶		◇1	◇1	🚌	◇1 ☕	◇1	🚌		◇1 ⌶	◇1 ☕	◇1	◇1 ☕	◇1 ⌶		◇1	1	◇1 ☕	
Crewe	d			13 22		13 29			13 33	13 49		13 56						14 22	14 29			14 33	14 49	14 56	
Alsager	d								13 41													14 41			
Kidsgrove	d								13 46													14 46			
Hanley Bus Station	d													14 00											
Stoke-on-Trent	d	13 07					13 44		13 54					14 06		14 07				14 44		14 54			
Wedgwood Old Road Bridge	d													14 21											
Barlaston Orchard Place	d													14 25											
Stone Granville Square	d										13 39			14a35											
Stone	d								14 02													15 02			
Norton Bridge Station Drv	d										13 54														
Stafford	d	13 25	13 36	13a42			14a01		14 21	14a09	14a15					14 25	14 36	14a46		15a02		15 21	15a09		
Rugeley Trent Valley	d								14 33													15 33			
Lichfield Trent Valley	d								14 40													15 40			
Tamworth	d								14 47													15 47			
Polesworth	d																								
Atherstone	d								14 56													15 56			
Nuneaton	a								15 02													16 02			
	d							14 15	15 02												15 15	16 02			
Bedworth	d							14 22													15 22				
Coventry	a	14 24						14 34								15 24					15 34				
Rugby	a								15 17													16 17			
Northampton	a								15 42				←									16 43			
Milton Keynes Central	a								16 04			15 01	15 04									17 04		16 01	
Watford Junction	a								→				15 30									→			
London Euston 15 ⊖	a		14 56			15 04						15 38	15 49				15 56		16 04					16 38	

		LM	LM	XC	VT	LM	VT	XC	LM	LM		LM	LM	VT	VT	LM	LM	XC	VT	LM		VT	XC	LM	LM
		◇1	🚌	◇1 ⌶	◇1 ☕	◇1	◇1 ☕	◇1 ⌶		◇1		◇1	🚌	◇1 ☕	◇1 ☕	◇1	🚌	◇1 ⌶	◇1 ☕	◇1		◇1 ☕	◇1 ⌶		◇1
Crewe	d					15 22	15 29			15 33		15 49		15 56	15 57					16 22		16 29			16 33
Alsager	d									15 41															16 41
Kidsgrove	d									15 46															16 46
Hanley Bus Station	d		15 00														16 00								
Stoke-on-Trent	d		15 06	15 07				15 44		15 54							16 06	16 07					16 44		16 54
Wedgwood Old Road Bridge	d		15 21														16 21								
Barlaston Orchard Place	d		15 25														16 25								
Stone Granville Square	d		15a35										15 29				16a35								
Stone	d									16 02															17 02
Norton Bridge Station Drv	d												15 52												
Stafford	d			15 25	15 36	15a42		16a02		16 21		16a09	16a13					16 25	16 36	16a46			17a02		17 21
Rugeley Trent Valley	d									16 33															17 33
Lichfield Trent Valley	d									16 40															17 40
Tamworth	d									16 47															17 47
Polesworth	d																								
Atherstone	d									16 56															17 56
Nuneaton	a									17 02															18 02
	d								16 13	17 02														17 15	18 02
Bedworth	d								16 20															17 22	
Coventry	a			16 24					16 34									17 24						17 34	
Rugby	a									17 17															18 17
Northampton	a	←								17 39						←									18 39
Milton Keynes Central	a	16 04								18 04				17s01	17 01	17 04									19 04
Watford Junction	a	16 30								→						17 30									→
London Euston 15 ⊖	a	16 49			16 59		17 04							17 38	17 38	17 49			17 56			18 03			

Table 67

Mondays to Fridays

from 17 September

Crewe and Stoke-on-Trent - London
Nuneaton - Coventry

Network Diagram - see first Page of Table 67

		LM	VT	LM	LM	XC		VT	LM	VT	XC	LM	LM	LM	VT	LM		LM	XC	VT	LM	VT	LM	XC	LM
		◇1	◇1 ☕	◇1	🚌	◇1 ⌶		◇1 ☕	◇1	◇1 ☕	◇1 ⌶		◇1	◇1	◇1 ⊠	◇1		🚌	◇1 ⌶	◇1 ⊠	◇1	◇1 ⊠	◇1	◇1 ⌶	
Crewe	d	16 49	16 56						17 22	17 29			17 33	17 49	17 56				18 07		18 22	18 29			
Alsager	d												17 41												
Kidsgrove	d												17 46												
Hanley Bus Station	d				17 00													18 00							
Stoke-on-Trent	d				17 06	17 07					17 44		17 54					18 06						18 44	
Wedgwood Old Road Bridge	d				17 21													18 21							
Barlaston Orchard Place	d				17 25													18 25							
Stone Granville Square	d				17a35													18a33							
Stone	d												18 02												
Norton Bridge Station Drv	d																								
Stafford	d	17a10				17 25		17 36	17a42		18a03		18 21	18a09					18 28	18 36	18a42			19a01	
Rugeley Trent Valley	d												18 33												
Lichfield Trent Valley	d												18 40												
Tamworth	d												18 47												
Polesworth	d																								
Atherstone	d												18 56												
Nuneaton	a												19 02												
	d											18 10	19 02												19 15
Bedworth	d											18 17													19 22
Coventry	a					18 24						18 34							19 24						19 38
Rugby	a												19 18												
Northampton	a			←									19 45			←							←		
Milton Keynes Central	a		18 01	18 04				18 23					20 05		19 01	19 04						19 31	20 05		
Watford Junction	a			18 31						18s48			→			19 30				19s42			20 31		
London Euston 15 ⊖	a		18 38	18 49				18 59		19 08					19 38	19 50				20 02		20 06	20 49		

		LM		LM	XC	LM	VT	VT	XC	LM	LM	LM		LM	VT	XC	LM	VT	VT	XC	LM	LM		VT	LM
		◇1		◇1	◇1 A ⌶	◇1	◇1 ⊠	◇1 ⊠	◇1 ⌶		1	1		◇1	◇1 ☕	◇1 A ⌶	◇1	◇1 ☕	◇1 ☕	◇1		1		◇1 ☕	1
Crewe	d	18 33		18 49		19 18	19 23	19 29			19 33	19 33		19 55	19 56		20 18	20 23	20 29			20 39		20 41	
Alsager	d	18 41									19 41	19 41										20 48			
Kidsgrove	d	18 46									19 46	19 46										20 52			
Hanley Bus Station	d																								
Stoke-on-Trent	d	18 54			19 07				19 44		19 54	19 54				20 07				20 44		21 01			
Wedgwood Old Road Bridge	d																								
Barlaston Orchard Place	d																								
Stone Granville Square	d																								
Stone	d	19 02									20 02	20 02										21 09			
Norton Bridge Station Drv	d																								
Stafford	d	19 21		19a09	19 25	19a41	19 42		20a03		20 21	20 21		20a15		20 26	20a38		20 48	21a02		21 27			
Rugeley Trent Valley	d	19 33									20 33	20 33										21 36			
Lichfield Trent Valley	d	19 40									20 40	20 40										21 43			
Tamworth	d	19 47									20 47	20 47										21 50			
Polesworth	d																								
Atherstone	d	19 56									20 56	20 56										21 59			
Nuneaton	a	20 02									21 02	21 02						21 02				22 05			
	d	20 02								20 15	21 02	21 02						21 03			21 15	22 05			
Bedworth	d									20 22											21 22				
Coventry	a				20 24					20 34						21 24					21 34				
Rugby	a	20 17									21 17	21 17										22 20		21 27	
Northampton	a	20 43									21 39	21 39										22 41			←
Milton Keynes Central	a							20 32				22 04			21 03				21 35					21 47	22 04
Watford Junction	a						20s46					→						21s48							22 35
London Euston 15 ⊖	a						21 05	21 06							21 42			22 09	22 12					22 22	22 56

		LM	VT	XC	LM	VT	XC	LM		LM	XC
		◇1	◇1 ☕	◇1	◇1	◇1 ☕	◇1	◇1			◇1
Crewe	d	20 47	20 53		21 18	21 24		22 20			
Alsager	d										
Kidsgrove	d										
Hanley Bus Station	d										
Stoke-on-Trent	d			21 07			22 08				22 47
Wedgwood Old Road Bridge	d										
Barlaston Orchard Place	d										
Stone Granville Square	d										
Stone	d										
Norton Bridge Station Drv	d										
Stafford	d	21a08	21a11	21a24	21a38	21 44	22a25	22a40			23a06
Rugeley Trent Valley	d										
Lichfield Trent Valley	d					21 58					
Tamworth	d					22 05					
Polesworth	d										
Atherstone	d										
Nuneaton	a					22 16					
	d					22 17				22 20	
Bedworth	d									22 27	
Coventry	a									22 39	
Rugby	a					22 30					
Northampton	a										
Milton Keynes Central	a					22 58					
Watford Junction	a					23s30					
London Euston 15 ⊖	a					23 56					

A ⌶ to Stafford

Crewe and Stoke-on-Trent - London
Nuneaton - Coventry

Network Diagram - see first Page of Table 67

		AW	LM	XC	VT	XC	VT	LM	VT	XC	LM	LM	LM	VT	VT	XC	LM	LM	LM	VT	LM	VT
				◇1	◇1	◇1	◇1	◇1	◇1	◇1	◇1	◇1	◇1	◇1	◇1	◇1	🚌		◇1	◇1	◇1	◇1
Crewe	d	04 59		05 47	06 00			06 20	06 29		06 38	06 47	07 16	07 20	07 29				07 38	07 39	07 49	07 55
Alsager	d										06 47								07 47			
Kidsgrove	d										06 51								07 51			
Hanley Bus Station	d																07 50					
Stoke-on-Trent	d			06 08						06 39	07 00					07 44	07 56		08 00			
Wedgwood Old Road Bridge	d																08 05					
Barlaston Orchard Place	d																08 06					
Stone Granville Square	d																08a12					
Stone	d										07 08								08 08			
Norton Bridge Station Drv	d					←																
Stafford	d	05a24		06 26	06 19	06 26	06 35	06a41		06a57	07 24	07a10	07a40	07 39		08a02			08 23		08a10	08 16
Rugeley Trent Valley	d			→							07 33								→			
Lichfield Trent Valley	d										07 40											08 31
Tamworth	d										07 47											08 37
Polesworth	d																					
Atherstone	d										07 56											
Nuneaton	a						06 57				08 02											
	d		06 47				06 59				08 02							08 14				
Bedworth	d		06 54															08 21				
Coventry	a		07 06			07 24												08 33				
Rugby	a				06 49						08 17											
Northampton	a										08 40											
Milton Keynes Central	a				07 11				07 31		09 04											
Watford Junction	a				07s32		07s44				09 33											
London Euston 15 ⊖	a				07 52		08 05		08 09		09 50			08 59	09 04					09 30		09 46

		LM	LM	XC	VT	LM	VT	XC	LM	LM	LM	LM	VT	LM	XC	VT	LM	VT	XC	LM	LM	LM	LM
		◇1	🚌	◇1	◇1	◇1	◇1	◇1		◇1	◇1	🚌	◇1	◇1	◇1	◇1	◇1	◇1	◇1		◇1	◇1	🚌
Crewe	d					08 22	08 29			08 33	08 49		08 56				09 22	09 29			09 33	09 49	
Alsager	d									08 41											09 41		
Kidsgrove	d									08 46											09 46		
Hanley Bus Station	d											08 50											09 50
Stoke-on-Trent	d			08 07				08 44		08 54		08 56			09 07				09 44		09 54		09 56
Wedgwood Old Road Bridge	d											09 05											10 05
Barlaston Orchard Place	d											09 06											10 06
Stone Granville Square	d											09a12											10a12
Stone	d									09 02											10 02		
Norton Bridge Station Drv	d	←	07 52																				
Stafford	d	08 23	08a22	08 26	08 36	08a42		09a02		09 21	09a09				09 26	09 36	09a42		10a02		10 21	10a10	
Rugeley Trent Valley	d	08 33								09 33											10 33		
Lichfield Trent Valley	d	08 40								09 40											10 40		
Tamworth	d	08 47								09 47											10 47		
Polesworth	d																						
Atherstone	d	08 56								09 56											10 56		
Nuneaton	a	09 02			08 58					10 02						09 58					11 02		
	d	09 02			08 59				09 15	10 02						09 59				10 15	11 02		
Bedworth	d								09 22											10 22			
Coventry	a			09 24					09 34						10 24					10 34			
Rugby	a	09 17								10 17											11 17		
Northampton	a	09 41								10 39				←							11 39		
Milton Keynes Central	a	10 04								11 04			10 01	10 04							12 04		
Watford Junction	a	→								→				10 30							→		
London Euston 15 ⊖	a				10 00		10 04						10 37	10 49		11 01		11 04					

		LM	VT	LM	XC	VT	LM	VT	XC	LM	LM	LM	LM	VT	LM	XC	VT	LM	VT	XC	LM	LM
		🚌	◇1	◇1	◇1	◇1	◇1	◇1	◇1		◇1	◇1	🚌	◇1	◇1	◇1	◇1	◇1	◇1	◇1		◇1
Crewe	d		09 56				10 22	10 29			10 33	10 49		10 56				11 22	11 29			11 33
Alsager	d										10 41											11 41
Kidsgrove	d										10 46											11 46
Hanley Bus Station	d												10 50									
Stoke-on-Trent	d				10 07				10 44		10 54		10 56			11 07				11 44		11 54
Wedgwood Old Road Bridge	d												11 05									
Barlaston Orchard Place	d												11 06									
Stone Granville Square	d												11a12									
Stone	d										11 02											12 02
Norton Bridge Station Drv	d	09 52																				
Stafford	d	10a22			10 26	10 36	10a42		11a02		11 21	11a09				11 26	11 36	11a42		12a02		12 21
Rugeley Trent Valley	d										11 33											12 33
Lichfield Trent Valley	d										11 40											12 40
Tamworth	d										11 47											12 47
Polesworth	d																					
Atherstone	d										11 56											12 56
Nuneaton	a										12 02											13 02
	d									11 15	12 02										12 15	13 02
Bedworth	d									11 22											12 22	
Coventry	a				11 24					11 34						12 24					12 34	
Rugby	a										12 17											13 17
Northampton	a			←							12 39				←							13 39
Milton Keynes Central	a		11 01	11 04							13 04			12 01	12 04							14 04
Watford Junction	a			11 30							→				12 30							→
London Euston 15 ⊖	a		11 38	11 49		11 56		12 04						12 38	12 49		12 56		13 04			

Table 67

Saturdays
until 30 June

Crewe and Stoke-on-Trent - London
Nuneaton - Coventry

Network Diagram - see first Page of Table 67

		LM	LM	VT	LM	XC	LM	VT	LM	VT	XC	LM	LM	LM	LM	VT	LM	XC	VT	LM	VT	XC	LM
		◇1	🚌	◇1	◇1	◇1	🚌	◇1	◇1	◇1	◇1		◇1	◇1	🚌	◇1	◇1	◇1	◇1	◇1	◇1	◇1	
Crewe	d	11 49		11 56					12 22	12 29			12 33	12 49		12 57				13 22	13 29		
Alsager	d												12 41										
Kidsgrove	d												12 46										
Hanley Bus Station	d		11 50												12 50								
Stoke-on-Trent	d		11 56			12 07					12 44		12 54		12 56			13 07				13 44	
Wedgwood Old Road Bridge	d		12 05												13 05								
Barlaston Orchard Place	d		12 06												13 06								
Stone Granville Square	d		12a12				11 39								13a12								
Stone	d												13 02										
Norton Bridge Station Drv	d						12 02																
Stafford	d	12a09				12 25	12a32	12 36	12a42		13a02		13 21	13a09				13 26	13 36	13a42		14a02	
Rugeley Trent Valley	d												13 33										
Lichfield Trent Valley	d												13 40										
Tamworth	d												13 47										
Polesworth	d																						
Atherstone	d												13 56										
Nuneaton	a												14 02										
	d											13 15	14 02										14 15
Bedworth	d											13 22											14 22
Coventry	a					13 24						13 34						14 24					14 34
Rugby	a												14 17										
Northampton	a				←								14 39				←						
Milton Keynes Central	a			13 01	13 04								15 04			14 01	14 04						
Watford Junction	a				13 30								→				14 30						
London Euston 15 ⊖	a			13 38	13 49			13 56		14 04						14 38	14 49		14 56		15 04		

		LM	LM	LM	LM	VT	LM	XC	VT	LM	VT	XC	LM	LM	LM	LM	VT	LM	XC	VT	LM	VT
		◇1	◇1	🚌	🚌	◇1	◇1	◇1	◇1	◇1	◇1	◇1		◇1	◇1	🚌	◇1	◇1	◇1	◇1	◇1	◇1
Crewe	d	13 33	13 49			13 56				14 22	14 29			14 33	14 49		14 56				15 22	15 29
Alsager	d	13 41												14 41								
Kidsgrove	d	13 46												14 46								
Hanley Bus Station	d				13 50											14 50						
Stoke-on-Trent	d	13 54			13 56			14 07				14 44		14 54		14 56			15 07			
Wedgwood Old Road Bridge	d				14 05											15 05						
Barlaston Orchard Place	d				14 06											15 06						
Stone Granville Square	d			13 39	14a12											15a12						
Stone	d	14 02												15 02								
Norton Bridge Station Drv	d			13 54																		
Stafford	d	14 21	14a09	14a15				14 26	14 36	14a46		15a02		15 21	15a09				15 26	15 36	15a42	
Rugeley Trent Valley	d	14 33												15 33								
Lichfield Trent Valley	d	14 40												15 40								
Tamworth	d	14 47												15 47								
Polesworth	d																					
Atherstone	d	14 56												15 56								
Nuneaton	a	15 02												16 02								
	d	15 02											15 15	16 02								
Bedworth	d												15 22									
Coventry	a							15 24					15 34						16 24			
Rugby	a	15 17												16 17								
Northampton	a	15 39					←							16 39				←				
Milton Keynes Central	a	16 04				15 01	15 04							17 04			16 01	16 04				
Watford Junction	a	→					15 30							→				16 30				
London Euston 15 ⊖	a					15 38	15 49		15 56		16 04						16 38	16 49		16 56		17 04

		XC	LM	LM	LM	LM	LM	VT	LM	XC	VT	LM	VT	XC	LM	LM	LM	LM	VT	LM	XC	VT	LM
		◇1		◇1	◇1	🚌	🚌	◇1	◇1	◇1	◇1	◇1	◇1	◇1		◇1	◇1	🚌	◇1	◇1	◇1	◇1	◇1
Crewe	d			15 33	15 49			15 56				16 22	16 29			16 33	16 49		16 56				17 22
Alsager	d			15 41												16 41							
Kidsgrove	d			15 46												16 46							
Hanley Bus Station	d						15 50											16 50					
Stoke-on-Trent	d	15 44		15 54			15 56			16 07				16 44		16 54		16 56			17 07		
Wedgwood Old Road Bridge	d						16 05											17 05					
Barlaston Orchard Place	d						16 06											17 06					
Stone Granville Square	d					15 29	16a12											17a12					
Stone	d			16 02												17 02							
Norton Bridge Station Drv	d					15 52																	
Stafford	d	16a02		16 21	16a09	16a13				16 25	16 36	16a46		17a02		17 21	17a09				17 26	17 36	17a42
Rugeley Trent Valley	d			16 33												17 33							
Lichfield Trent Valley	d			16 40												17 40							
Tamworth	d			16 47												17 47							
Polesworth	d																						
Atherstone	d			16 56												17 56							
Nuneaton	a			17 02												18 02							
	d		16 15	17 02											17 15	18 02							
Bedworth	d		16 22												17 22								
Coventry	a		16 34							17 24					17 34						18 24		
Rugby	a			17 17												18 17							
Northampton	a			17 39					←							18 39				←			
Milton Keynes Central	a			18 05				17 01	17 04							19 04			18 01	18 05			
Watford Junction	a			→					17 30							→				18 31			
London Euston 15 ⊖	a							17 38	17 49		17 56		18 04						18 38	18 49		18 56	

Saturdays
until 30 June

Crewe and Stoke-on-Trent - London
Nuneaton - Coventry

Network Diagram - see first Page of Table 67

		VT	LM	XC	LM	LM		LM	LM	XC	VT	LM	VT	XC	LM	LM		LM	XC	VT	LM	VT	XC	LM	XC
		◇■ ☕	◇■	◇■ 🛒		◇■		◇■	🚌	◇■ 🛒	◇■ ☕	◇■	◇■ ☕	◇■ 🛒		◇■		◇■	◇■ 🛒	◇■ ☕	◇■	◇■ ☕	◇■ 🛒	◇■	◇■ A 🛒
Crewe	d	17 29				17 33		17 49				18 22	18 29			18 33		18 49			19 22	19 29		19 51	
Alsager	d					17 41										18 41									
Kidsgrove	d					17 46										18 46									
Hanley Bus Station	d								17 50																
Stoke-on-Trent	d			17 44		17 54			17 56	18 08				18 44		18 54			19 07				19 44		20 07
Wedgwood Old Road Bridge	d								18 05																
Barlaston Orchard Place	d								18 06																
Stone Granville Square	d								18a12																
Stone	d					18 02										19 02									
Norton Bridge Station Drv	d																								
Stafford	d			18a03		18 21		18a09		18 27	18 36	18a42		19a02		19 21		19a09	19 25	19 36	19a42		20a02	20a11	20 26
Rugeley Trent Valley	d					18 33										19 33									
Lichfield Trent Valley	d					18 40										19 40									
Tamworth	d					18 47										19 47									
Polesworth	d																								
Atherstone	d					18 56										19 56									
Nuneaton	a					19 02										20 02									
	d				18 15	19 02									19 46	20 02									
Bedworth	d				18 22										19 53										
Coventry	a				18 34					19 24					20 05				20 24						21 24
Rugby	a					19 17										20 17									
Northampton	a		←			19 43										20 40									
Milton Keynes Central	a		19 04																						
Watford Junction	a		19 30																						
London Euston ⊖	a	19 04	19 49								19 56		20 04							21 15		21 18			

		VT		LM	XC	VT	XC	LM	LM	XC	VT	VT		XC	LM	LM
		◇■ ☕		◇■	◇■	◇■ ☕	◇■		◇■	◇■	◇■ ☕	◇■ ☕		◇■		◇■
Crewe	d			20 22		20 47			21 17		21 43	22 05				22 23
Alsager	d															
Kidsgrove	d															
Hanley Bus Station	d															
Stoke-on-Trent	d				20 44		21 07			21 45				22 08		
Wedgwood Old Road Bridge	d															
Barlaston Orchard Place	d															
Stone Granville Square	d															
Stone	d															
Norton Bridge Station Drv	d															
Stafford	d	20 36		20a44	21a02		21a26		21a42	22a02	22a07	22a24		22a32		22a47
Rugeley Trent Valley	d															
Lichfield Trent Valley	d															
Tamworth	d															
Polesworth	d															
Atherstone	d															
Nuneaton	a															
	d							21 15							22 15	
Bedworth	d							21 22							22 22	
Coventry	a							21 34							22 34	
Rugby	a															
Northampton	a															
Milton Keynes Central	a					21 50										
Watford Junction	a															
London Euston ⊖	a	22 14				22 44										

A 🛒 to Stafford

Table 67

Saturdays
7 July to 8 September

Crewe and Stoke-on-Trent - London
Nuneaton - Coventry

Network Diagram - see first Page of Table 67

		AW	LM		XC	VT	XC	VT	LM	VT		XC	LM	LM	LM	VT	VT	XC	LM	LM		LM	VT	LM	VT
					◇■ 🛒	◇■ ☕	◇■ 🛒	◇■ ☕	◇■	◇■ ☕		◇■ 🛒	◇■	◇■	◇■	◇■ ☕	◇■ ☕	◇■ 🛒	🚌			◇■	◇■ ☕	◇■	◇■ ☕
Crewe	d	04 59			05 47	06 00			06 20	06 29			06 38	06 47	07 16	07 20	07 29					07 38	07 39	07 49	07 55
Alsager	d												06 47									07 47			
Kidsgrove	d												06 51									07 51			
Hanley Bus Station	d																		07 50						
Stoke-on-Trent	d				06 08							06 39	07 00					07 44	07 56			08 00			
Wedgwood Old Road Bridge	d																		08 05						
Barlaston Orchard Place	d																		08 06						
Stone Granville Square	d																		08a12						
Stone	d												07 08									08 08			
Norton Bridge Station Drv	d						←																		
Stafford	d	05a24			06 26	06 19	06 26	06 35	06a41			06a57	07 24	07a10	07a40	07 39		08a02				08 23		08a10	08 16
Rugeley Trent Valley	d				→								07 33									→			
Lichfield Trent Valley	d												07 40												08 31
Tamworth	d												07 47												08 37
Polesworth	d																								
Atherstone	d												07 56												
Nuneaton	a							06 57					08 02												
	d		06 47					06 59					08 02							08 14					
Bedworth	d		06 54																	08 21					
Coventry	a		07 06				07 24													08 33					
Rugby	a					06 49							08 17												
Northampton	a												08 40												
Milton Keynes Central	a					07 11				07 31			09 04												
Watford Junction	a					07s32		07s44					09 33												
London Euston ⊖	a					07 52		08 05		08 09			09 50			08 59	09 04						09 30		09 46

		LM	LM	XC	VT	LM		VT	XC	LM	LM	LM	LM	VT	LM	XC		VT	LM	VT	XC	LM	LM	LM	LM
		◇■	🚌	◇■ 🛒	◇■ ☕	◇■		◇■ ☕	◇■ 🛒		◇■	◇■	🚌	◇■ ☕	◇■	◇■ 🛒		◇■ ☕	◇■	◇■ ☕	◇■ 🛒		◇■	◇■	🚌
Crewe	d					08 22		08 29			08 33	08 49		08 56					09 22	09 29			09 33	09 49	
Alsager	d										08 41												09 41		
Kidsgrove	d										08 46												09 46		
Hanley Bus Station	d												08 50												09 50
Stoke-on-Trent	d			08 07					08 44		08 54		08 56			09 07					09 44		09 54		09 56
Wedgwood Old Road Bridge	d												09 05												10 05
Barlaston Orchard Place	d												09 06												10 06
Stone Granville Square	d												09a12												10a12
Stone	d										09 02												10 02		
Norton Bridge Station Drv	d	←	07 52																						
Stafford	d	08 23	08a22	08 26	08 36	08a42			09a02		09 21	09a09				09 26		09 36	09a42		10a02		10 21	10a10	
Rugeley Trent Valley	d	08 33									09 33												10 33		
Lichfield Trent Valley	d	08 40									09 40												10 40		
Tamworth	d	08 47									09 47												10 47		
Polesworth	d																								
Atherstone	d	08 56									09 56												10 56		
Nuneaton	a	09 02			08 58						10 02							09 58					11 02		
	d	09 02			08 59					09 15	10 02							09 59				10 15	11 02		
Bedworth	d									09 22												10 22			
Coventry	a			09 24						09 34						10 24						10 34			
Rugby	a	09 17									10 17												11 17		
Northampton	a	09 41									10 39				←								11 39		
Milton Keynes Central	a	10 04									11 04			10 01	10 04								12 04		
Watford Junction	a	→									→				10 30								→		
London Euston ⊖	a				10 00			10 04						10 37	10 49			11 01		11 04					

		LM		VT	LM	XC	VT	LM	VT	XC	LM	LM		LM	LM	VT	LM	XC	VT	LM	VT	XC		LM	LM
		🚌		◇■ ☕	◇■	◇■ 🛒	◇■ ☕	◇■	◇■ ☕	◇■ 🛒		◇■		◇■	🚌	◇■ ☕	◇■	◇■ 🛒	◇■ ☕	◇■	◇■ ☕	◇■ 🛒			◇■
Crewe	d			09 56				10 22	10 29			10 33		10 49		10 56				11 22	11 29				11 33
Alsager	d											10 41													11 41
Kidsgrove	d											10 46													11 46
Hanley Bus Station	d														10 50										
Stoke-on-Trent	d					10 07				10 44		10 54			10 56			11 07				11 44			11 54
Wedgwood Old Road Bridge	d														11 05										
Barlaston Orchard Place	d														11 06										
Stone Granville Square	d														11a12										
Stone	d											11 02													12 02
Norton Bridge Station Drv	d	09 52																							
Stafford	d	10a22				10 26	10 36	10a42		11a02		11 21		11a09				11 26	11 36	11a42		12a02			12 21
Rugeley Trent Valley	d											11 33													12 33
Lichfield Trent Valley	d											11 40													12 40
Tamworth	d											11 47													12 47
Polesworth	d																								
Atherstone	d											11 56													12 56
Nuneaton	a											12 02													13 02
	d										11 15	12 02												12 15	13 02
Bedworth	d										11 22													12 22	
Coventry	a					11 24					11 34							12 24						12 34	
Rugby	a											12 17													13 17
Northampton	a				←							12 39					←								13 39
Milton Keynes Central	a			11 01	11 04							13 04				12 01	12 04								14 04
Watford Junction	a				11 30							→					12 30								→
London Euston ⊖	a			11 38	11 49		11 56		12 04							12 38	12 49		12 56		13 04				

Table 67

Saturdays
7 July to 8 September

Crewe and Stoke-on-Trent - London
Nuneaton - Coventry

Network Diagram - see first Page of Table 67

		LM	LM	VT	LM	XC	LM	VT		LM	VT	XC	LM	LM	LM	LM	VT	LM		XC	VT	LM	VT	XC	LM
		◇1	🚌	◇1 🍴	◇1	◇1 🛒	🚌	◇1 🍴		◇1	◇1 🍴	◇1 🛒		◇1	◇1	🚌	◇1 🍴	◇1		◇1 🛒	◇1 🍴	◇1	◇1 🍴	◇1 🛒	
Crewe	d	11 49		11 56						12 22	12 29			12 33	12 49		12 57					13 22	13 29		
Alsager	d													12 41											
Kidsgrove	d													12 46											
Hanley Bus Station	d		11 50													12 50									
Stoke-on-Trent	d		11 56			12 07						12 44		12 54		12 56				13 07				13 44	
Wedgwood Old Road Bridge	d		12 05													13 05									
Barlaston Orchard Place	d		12 06													13 06									
Stone Granville Square	d		12a12				11 39									13a12									
Stone	d													13 02											
Norton Bridge Station Drv	d						12 02																		
Stafford	d	12a09				12 25	12a32	12 36		12a42		13a02		13 21	13a09					13 26	13 36	13a42		14a02	
Rugeley Trent Valley	d													13 33											
Lichfield Trent Valley	d													13 40											
Tamworth	d													13 47											
Polesworth	d																								
Atherstone	d													13 56											
Nuneaton	a													14 02											
	d												13 15	14 02											14 15
Bedworth	d												13 22												14 22
Coventry	a					13 24							13 34							14 24					14 34
Rugby	a													14 17											
Northampton	a				←									14 39				←							
Milton Keynes Central	a			13 01	13 04									15 04			14 01	14 04							
Watford Junction	a				13 30									→				14 30							
London Euston ⊖	a			13 38	13 49			13 56			14 04						14 38	14 49			14 56		15 04		

		LM	LM	LM		LM	VT	LM	XC	VT	VT	LM	VT	XC		LM	LM	LM	LM	VT	LM	XC	VT	LM	
		◇1	◇1	🚌		🚌	◇1 🍴	◇1	◇1 🛒	◇1 🍴	◇1 🍴	◇1	◇1 🍴	◇1 🛒			◇1	◇1	🚌	◇1 🍴	◇1	◇1 🛒	◇1 🍴	◇1	
Crewe	d	13 33	13 49				13 56				14 01	14 22	14 29				14 33	14 49		14 56				15 22	
Alsager	d	13 41															14 41								
Kidsgrove	d	13 46															14 46								
Hanley Bus Station	d					13 50													14 50						
Stoke-on-Trent	d	13 54				13 56			14 07					14 44			14 54		14 56			15 07			
Wedgwood Old Road Bridge	d					14 05													15 05						
Barlaston Orchard Place	d					14 06													15 06						
Stone Granville Square	d			13 39		14a12													15a12						
Stone	d	14 02															15 02								
Norton Bridge Station Drv	d			13 54																					
Stafford	d	14 21	14a09	14a15					14 26	14 36		14a46		15a02			15 21	15a09				15 26	15 36	15a42	
Rugeley Trent Valley	d	14 33															15 33								
Lichfield Trent Valley	d	14 40															15 40								
Tamworth	d	14 47															15 47								
Polesworth	d																								
Atherstone	d	14 56															15 56								
Nuneaton	a	15 02															16 02								
	d	15 02														15 15	16 02								
Bedworth	d															15 22									
Coventry	a								15 24		15 30					15 34						16 24			
Rugby	a	15 17															16 17								
Northampton	a	15 39						←									16 39				←				
Milton Keynes Central	a	16 04					15 01	15 04									17 04			16 01	16 04				
Watford Junction	a	→						15 30			16s15						→				16 30				
London Euston ⊖	a						15 38	15 49		15 56	16 34		16 04							16 38	16 49		16 56		

		VT	XC	LM	LM	LM	LM	LM	VT	LM		XC	VT	LM	VT	XC	LM	LM	LM	LM		VT	LM	XC	VT
		◇1 🍴	◇1 🛒		◇1	◇1	🚌	🚌	◇1 🍴	◇1		◇1 🛒	◇1 🍴	◇1	◇1 🍴	◇1 🛒		◇1	◇1	🚌		◇1 🍴	◇1	◇1 🛒	◇1 🍴
Crewe	d	15 29			15 33	15 49			15 56					16 22	16 29			16 33	16 49			16 56			
Alsager	d				15 41													16 41							
Kidsgrove	d				15 46													16 46							
Hanley Bus Station	d							15 50												16 50					
Stoke-on-Trent	d		15 44		15 54			15 56				16 07				16 44		16 54		16 56				17 07	
Wedgwood Old Road Bridge	d							16 05												17 05					
Barlaston Orchard Place	d							16 06												17 06					
Stone Granville Square	d						15 29	16a12												17a12					
Stone	d				16 02													17 02							
Norton Bridge Station Drv	d						15 52																		
Stafford	d		16a02		16 21	16a09	16a13					16 25	16 36	16a46		17a02		17 21	17a09					17 26	17 36
Rugeley Trent Valley	d				16 33													17 33							
Lichfield Trent Valley	d				16 40													17 40							
Tamworth	d				16 47													17 47							
Polesworth	d																								
Atherstone	d				16 56													17 56							
Nuneaton	a				17 02													18 02							
	d			16 15	17 02												17 15	18 02							
Bedworth	d			16 22													17 22								
Coventry	a			16 34								17 24					17 34							18 24	
Rugby	a				17 17													18 17							
Northampton	a				17 39					←								18 39					←		
Milton Keynes Central	a				18 05				17 01	17 04								19 04				18 01	18 05		
Watford Junction	a				→					17 30								→					18 31		
London Euston ⊖	a	17 04							17 38	17 49			17 56		18 04							18 38	18 49		18 56

Table 67

Saturdays
7 July to 8 September

Crewe and Stoke-on-Trent - London
Nuneaton - Coventry

Network Diagram - see first Page of Table 67

		LM	VT	LM	XC	LM		LM	LM	LM	XC	VT	VT	LM	VT	XC		LM	LM	LM	XC	VT	LM	VT	XC
		◇1	◇1 🍴	◇1	◇1 🛒			◇1	◇1	🚌	◇1 🛒	◇1 🍴	◇1 🍴	◇1	◇1 🍴	◇1 🛒			◇1	◇1	◇1 🛒	◇1 🍴	◇1	◇1 🍴	◇1 🛒
Crewe	d	17 22	17 29					17 33	17 49				18 01	18 22	18 29				18 33	18 49			19 22	19 29	
Alsager	d							17 41											18 41						
Kidsgrove	d							17 46											18 46						
Hanley Bus Station	d									17 50															
Stoke-on-Trent	d				17 44			17 54		17 56	18 08					18 44			18 54		19 07				19 44
Wedgwood Old Road Bridge	d									18 05															
Barlaston Orchard Place	d									18 06															
Stone Granville Square	d									18a12															
Stone	d							18 02											19 02						
Norton Bridge Station Drv	d																								
Stafford	d	17a42			18a03			18 21	18a09		18 27	18 36		18a42		19a02			19 21	19a09	19 25	19 36	19a42		20a02
Rugeley Trent Valley	d							18 33											19 33						
Lichfield Trent Valley	d							18 40											19 40						
Tamworth	d							18 47											19 47						
Polesworth	d																								
Atherstone	d							18 56											19 56						
Nuneaton	a							19 02											20 02						
	d					18 15		19 02										19 46	20 02						
Bedworth	d					18 22												19 53							
Coventry	a					18 34					19 24		19 30					20 05			20 24				
Rugby	a							19 17					19 42						20 17						
Northampton	a			←				19 43											20 40						
Milton Keynes Central	a			19 04									20 05												
Watford Junction	a			19 30									20s34												
London Euston ⊖	a		19 04	19 49								19 56	20 55		20 04							21 15		21 18	

		LM		XC	LM	VT	XC	VT	XC	LM	LM	XC		VT	VT	XC	LM	LM
		◇1		◇1 A 🛒	◇1	◇1 🍴	◇1	◇1 🍴	◇1		◇1	◇1		◇1 🍴	◇1 🍴	◇1		◇1
Crewe	d	19 51			20 22	20u23		20 47			21 17			21 43	22 05			22 23
Alsager	d																	
Kidsgrove	d																	
Hanley Bus Station	d																	
Stoke-on-Trent	d			20 07			20 44		21 07			21 45				22 08		
Wedgwood Old Road Bridge	d																	
Barlaston Orchard Place	d																	
Stone Granville Square	d																	
Stone	d																	
Norton Bridge Station Drv	d																	
Stafford	d	20a11		20 26	20a44	20 42	21a02		21a26		21a42	22a02		22a07	22a24	22a32		22a47
Rugeley Trent Valley	d																	
Lichfield Trent Valley	d																	
Tamworth	d																	
Polesworth	d																	
Atherstone	d																	
Nuneaton	a																	
	d									21 15							22 15	
Bedworth	d									21 22							22 22	
Coventry	a			21 24						21 34							22 34	
Rugby	a																	
Northampton	a																	
Milton Keynes Central	a							21 50										
Watford Junction	a																	
London Euston ⊖	a					22 14		22 44										

A 🛒 to Stafford

Crewe and Stoke-on-Trent - London
Nuneaton - Coventry

Network Diagram - see first Page of Table 67

		AW	LM		XC	VT	XC	VT	LM	VT		XC	LM	LM	LM	VT	VT	XC	LM	LM		LM	VT	LM	VT
					◇1	◇1	◇1	◇1	◇1	◇1		◇1	◇1	◇1	◇1	◇1	◇1	◇1				◇1	◇1	◇1	◇1
Crewe	d	04 59			05 47	06 00			06 20	06 29			06 38	06 47	07 16	07 20	07 29					07 38	07 39	07 49	07 55
Alsager	d												06 47									07 47			
Kidsgrove	d												06 51									07 51			
Hanley Bus Station	d																		07 50						
Stoke-on-Trent	d				06 08							06 39	07 00					07 44	07 56			08 00			
Wedgwood Old Road Bridge	d																		08 05						
Barlaston Orchard Place	d																		08 06						
Stone Granville Square	d																		08a12						
Stone	d												07 08									08 08			
Norton Bridge Station Drv	d						←																		
Stafford	d	05a24			06 26	06 19	06 26	06 35	06a41			06a57	07 24	07a10	07a40	07 39		08a02				08 23		08a10	08 16
Rugeley Trent Valley	d				→								07 33									→			
Lichfield Trent Valley	d												07 40												08 31
Tamworth	d												07 47												08 37
Polesworth	d																								
Atherstone	d												07 56												
Nuneaton	a							06 57					08 02												
	d		06 47					06 59					08 02							08 14					
Bedworth	d		06 54																	08 21					
Coventry	a		07 06				07 24													08 33					
Rugby	a					06 49							08 17												
Northampton	a												08 40												
Milton Keynes Central	a					07 11				07 31			09 04												
Watford Junction	a					07s32		07s44					09 33												
London Euston 15 ⊖	a					07 52		08 05		08 09			09 50			08 59	09 04						09 30		09 46

		LM	LM	XC	VT	LM		VT	XC	LM	LM	LM	LM	VT	LM	XC		VT	LM	VT	XC	LM	LM	LM	LM
		◇1		◇1	◇1	◇1		◇1	◇1		◇1	◇1		◇1	◇1	◇1		◇1	◇1	◇1	◇1		◇1	◇1	
Crewe	d					08 22		08 29			08 33	08 49		08 56					09 22	09 29			09 33	09 49	
Alsager	d										08 41												09 41		
Kidsgrove	d										08 46												09 46		
Hanley Bus Station	d												08 50												09 50
Stoke-on-Trent	d			08 07					08 44		08 54		08 56			09 07					09 44		09 54		09 56
Wedgwood Old Road Bridge	d												09 05												10 05
Barlaston Orchard Place	d												09 06												10 06
Stone Granville Square	d												09a12												10a12
Stone	d										09 02												10 02		
Norton Bridge Station Drv	d	←	07 52																						
Stafford	d	08 23	08a22	08 26	08 36	08a42			09a02		09 21	09a09				09 26		09 36	09a42		10a02		10 21	10a10	
Rugeley Trent Valley	d	08 33									09 33												10 33		
Lichfield Trent Valley	d	08 40									09 40												10 40		
Tamworth	d	08 47									09 47												10 47		
Polesworth	d																								
Atherstone	d	08 56									09 56												10 56		
Nuneaton	a	09 02			08 58						10 02							09 58					11 02		
	d	09 02			08 59					09 15	10 02							09 59				10 15	11 02		
Bedworth	d									09 22												10 22			
Coventry	a			09 24						09 34						10 24						10 34			
Rugby	a	09 17									10 17												11 17		
Northampton	a	09 41									10 39				←								11 39		
Milton Keynes Central	a	10 04									11 04			10 01	10 04								12 04		
Watford Junction	a	→									→				10 30								→		
London Euston 15 ⊖	a				10 00			10 04						10 37	10 49			11 01		11 04					

		LM		VT	LM	XC	VT	LM	VT	XC	LM	LM		LM	LM	VT	LM	XC	VT	LM	VT	XC		LM	LM
				◇1	◇1	◇1	◇1	◇1	◇1	◇1		◇1		◇1		◇1	◇1	◇1	◇1	◇1	◇1	◇1			◇1
Crewe	d			09 56				10 22	10 29			10 33		10 49		10 56				11 22	11 29				11 33
Alsager	d											10 41													11 41
Kidsgrove	d											10 46													11 46
Hanley Bus Station	d														10 50										
Stoke-on-Trent	d					10 07				10 44		10 54			10 56			11 07				11 44			11 54
Wedgwood Old Road Bridge	d														11 05										
Barlaston Orchard Place	d														11 06										
Stone Granville Square	d														11a12										
Stone	d											11 02													12 02
Norton Bridge Station Drv	d	09 52																							
Stafford	d	10a22				10 26	10 36	10a42		11a02		11 21		11a09				11 26	11 36	11a42		12a02			12 21
Rugeley Trent Valley	d											11 33													12 33
Lichfield Trent Valley	d											11 40													12 40
Tamworth	d											11 47													12 47
Polesworth	d																								
Atherstone	d											11 56													12 56
Nuneaton	a											12 02													13 02
	d										11 15	12 02												12 15	13 02
Bedworth	d										11 22													12 22	
Coventry	a					11 24					11 34							12 24						12 34	
Rugby	a											12 17													13 17
Northampton	a				←							12 39					←								13 39
Milton Keynes Central	a			11 01	11 04							13 04				12 01	12 04								14 04
Watford Junction	a				11 30							→					12 30								→
London Euston 15 ⊖	a			11 38	11 49		11 56		12 04							12 38	12 49		12 56		13 04				

Crewe and Stoke-on-Trent - London
Nuneaton - Coventry

Network Diagram - see first Page of Table 67

		LM	LM	VT	LM	XC	LM	VT		LM	VT	XC	LM	LM	LM	LM	VT	LM		XC	VT	LM	VT	XC	LM
		◇1		◇1	◇1	◇1		◇1		◇1	◇1	◇1		◇1	◇1		◇1	◇1		◇1	◇1	◇1	◇1	◇1	
Crewe	d	11 49		11 56						12 22	12 29			12 33	12 49		12 57					13 22	13 29		
Alsager	d													12 41											
Kidsgrove	d													12 46											
Hanley Bus Station	d		11 50													12 50									
Stoke-on-Trent	d		11 56			12 07						12 44		12 54		12 56				13 07				13 44	
Wedgwood Old Road Bridge	d		12 05													13 05									
Barlaston Orchard Place	d		12 06													13 06									
Stone Granville Square	d		12a12				11 39									13a12									
Stone	d													13 02											
Norton Bridge Station Drv	d						12 02																		
Stafford	d	12a09				12 25	12a32	12 36		12a42		13a02		13 21	13a09					13 26	13 36	13a42		14a02	
Rugeley Trent Valley	d													13 33											
Lichfield Trent Valley	d													13 40											
Tamworth	d													13 47											
Polesworth	d																								
Atherstone	d													13 56											
Nuneaton	a													14 02											
	d												13 15	14 02											14 15
Bedworth	d												13 22												14 22
Coventry	a					13 24							13 34							14 24					14 34
Rugby	a													14 17											
Northampton	a				←									14 39				←							
Milton Keynes Central	a			13 01	13 04									15 04			14 01	14 04							
Watford Junction	a				13 30									→				14 30							
London Euston 15 ⊖	a			13 38	13 49			13 56			14 04						14 38	14 49			14 56		15 04		

		LM	LM	LM		LM	VT	LM	XC	VT	LM	VT	XC	LM		LM	LM	LM	VT	LM	XC	VT	LM	VT	
		◇1	◇1				◇1	◇1	◇1	◇1	◇1	◇1	◇1			◇1	◇1		◇1	◇1	◇1	◇1	◇1	◇1	
Crewe	d	13 33	13 49				13 56				14 22	14 29				14 33	14 49		14 56				15 22	15 29	
Alsager	d	13 41														14 41									
Kidsgrove	d	13 46														14 46									
Hanley Bus Station	d					13 50												14 50							
Stoke-on-Trent	d	13 54				13 56			14 07				14 44			14 54		14 56			15 07				
Wedgwood Old Road Bridge	d					14 05												15 05							
Barlaston Orchard Place	d					14 06												15 06							
Stone Granville Square	d			13 39		14a12												15a12							
Stone	d	14 02														15 02									
Norton Bridge Station Drv	d			13 54																					
Stafford	d	14 21	14a09	14a15					14 26	14 36	14a46		15a02			15 21	15a09				15 26	15 36	15a42		
Rugeley Trent Valley	d	14 33														15 33									
Lichfield Trent Valley	d	14 40														15 40									
Tamworth	d	14 47														15 47									
Polesworth	d																								
Atherstone	d	14 56														15 56									
Nuneaton	a	15 02														16 02									
	d	15 02												15 15		16 02									
Bedworth	d													15 22											
Coventry	a								15 24					15 34							16 24				
Rugby	a	15 17														16 17									
Northampton	a	15 39						←								16 39				←					
Milton Keynes Central	a	16 04					15 01	15 04								17 04			16 01	16 04					
Watford Junction	a	→						15 30								→				16 30					
London Euston 15 ⊖	a						15 38	15 49		15 56		16 04							16 38	16 49		16 56		17 04	

		XC	LM	LM	LM	LM	LM	VT	LM	XC		VT	LM	VT	XC	LM	LM	LM	LM	VT		LM	XC	VT	LM
		◇1		◇1	◇1			◇1	◇1	◇1		◇1	◇1	◇1	◇1		◇1	◇1		◇1		◇1	◇1	◇1	◇1
Crewe	d			15 33	15 49			15 56					16 22	16 29			16 33	16 49		16 56					17 22
Alsager	d			15 41													16 41								
Kidsgrove	d			15 46													16 46								
Hanley Bus Station	d						15 50												16 50						
Stoke-on-Trent	d	15 44		15 54			15 56			16 07					16 44		16 54		16 56				17 07		
Wedgwood Old Road Bridge	d						16 05												17 05						
Barlaston Orchard Place	d						16 06												17 06						
Stone Granville Square	d					15 29	16a12												17a12						
Stone	d			16 02													17 02								
Norton Bridge Station Drv	d					15 52																			
Stafford	d	16a02		16 21	16a09	16a13				16 25		16 36	16a46		17a02		17 21	17a09					17 26	17 36	17a42
Rugeley Trent Valley	d			16 33													17 33								
Lichfield Trent Valley	d			16 40													17 40								
Tamworth	d			16 47													17 47								
Polesworth	d																								
Atherstone	d			16 56													17 56								
Nuneaton	a			17 02													18 02								
	d		16 15	17 02												17 15	18 02								
Bedworth	d		16 22													17 22									
Coventry	a		16 34							17 24						17 34							18 24		
Rugby	a			17 17													18 17								
Northampton	a			17 39					←								18 39					←			
Milton Keynes Central	a			18 05				17 01	17 04								19 04			18 01		18 05			
Watford Junction	a			→					17 30								→					18 31			
London Euston 15 ⊖	a							17 38	17 49			17 56		18 04						18 38		18 49		18 56	

Table 67

Saturdays
from 15 September

Crewe and Stoke-on-Trent - London
Nuneaton - Coventry

Network Diagram - see first Page of Table 67

		VT ◇1 ⌂	LM ◇1	XC ◇1 ⌶	LM	LM ◇1	LM ◇1	LM ═	XC ◇1 ⌶	VT ◇1 ⌂	LM ◇1	VT ◇1 ⌂	XC ◇1 ⌶	LM	LM ◇1	LM ◇1	XC ◇1 ⌶	VT ◇1 ⌂	LM ◇1	VT ◇1 ⌂	XC ◇1 ⌶	LM 1	LM ◇1
Crewe	d	17 29				17 33	17 49				18 22	18 29			18 33	18 49			19 22	19 29		19 33	19 51
Alsager	d					17 41									18 41							19 41	
Kidsgrove	d					17 46									18 46							19 46	
Hanley Bus Station	d							17 50															
Stoke-on-Trent	d			17 44		17 54		17 56	18 08				18 44		18 54		19 07				19 44	19 54	
Wedgwood Old Road Bridge	d							18 05															
Barlaston Orchard Place	d							18 06															
Stone Granville Square	d							18a12															
Stone	d					18 02									19 02							20 02	
Norton Bridge Station Drv	d																						
Stafford	d			18a03		18 21	18a09		18 27	18 36	18a42		19a02		19 21	19a09	19 25	19 36	19a42		20a02	20 21	20a11
Rugeley Trent Valley	d					18 33									19 33							20 33	
Lichfield Trent Valley	d					18 40									19 40							20 40	
Tamworth	d					18 47									19 47							20 47	
Polesworth	d																						
Atherstone	d					18 56									19 56							20 56	
Nuneaton	a					19 02									20 02							21 02	
	d				18 15	19 02								19 46	20 02							21 02	
Bedworth	d				18 22									19 53									
Coventry	a				18 34				19 24					20 05			20 24						
Rugby	a					19 17									20 17							21 17	
Northampton	a		←			19 43									20 40							21 40	
Milton Keynes Central	a		19 04																				
Watford Junction	a		19 30																				
London Euston 15 ⊖	a	19 04	19 49							19 56		20 04						21 15		21 18			

		XC ◇1 A ⌶	VT ◇1 ⌂	LM ◇1	XC ◇1	VT ◇1 ⌂	XC ◇1	LM	LM ◇1	XC ◇1	VT ◇1 ⌂	VT ◇1 ⌂	XC ◇1	LM	LM ◇1
Crewe	d			20 22		20 47			21 17		21 43	22 05			22 23
Alsager	d														
Kidsgrove	d														
Hanley Bus Station	d														
Stoke-on-Trent	d	20 07			20 44		21 07			21 45			22 08		
Wedgwood Old Road Bridge	d														
Barlaston Orchard Place	d														
Stone Granville Square	d														
Stone	d														
Norton Bridge Station Drv	d														
Stafford	d	20 26	20 36	20a44	21a02		21a26		21a42	22a02	22a07	22a24	22a32		22a47
Rugeley Trent Valley	d														
Lichfield Trent Valley	d														
Tamworth	d														
Polesworth	d														
Atherstone	d														
Nuneaton	a														
	d							21 15						22 15	
Bedworth	d							21 22						22 22	
Coventry	a	21 24						21 34						22 34	
Rugby	a														
Northampton	a														
Milton Keynes Central	a					21 50									
Watford Junction	a														
London Euston 15 ⊖	a		22 14			22 44									

A ⌶ to Stafford

Table 67

Sundays
until 24 June

Crewe and Stoke-on-Trent - London
Nuneaton - Coventry

Network Diagram - see first Page of Table 67

		VT ◇1 ⌂	XC ◇1 A ⌶	VT ◇1 ⌂	VT ◇1 ⌂	XC ◇1 A ⌶	LM ◇1	VT ◇1 ⌂	VT ◇1 ⌂	LM ◇1	LM ◇1	XC ◇1 A ⌶	LM ◇1	VT ◇1 ⌂	VT ◇1 ⌂	VT ◇1 ⌂	LM	XC ◇1 A ⌶	LM ◇1	VT ◇1 ⌂	LM ◇1	VT ◇1 ⌂	LM ◇1
Crewe	d	08 43	08 47	08 53	09 13		09 30	09 43	10 14		10 20		10 38	10 43	10 55	11 14			11 38	11 49			12 22
Alsager	d						09 38						10 46						11 46				
Kidsgrove	d						09 43						10 50						11 50				
Hanley Bus Station	d																						
Stoke-on-Trent	d					09 46	09 51					10 47	10 59					11 45	11 59				
Wedgwood Old Road Bridge	d																						
Barlaston Orchard Place	d																						
Stone Granville Square	d																						
Stone	d						10 00						11 07						12 07				
Norton Bridge Station Drv	d																						
Stafford	d	09 02	09 07		09 32	10 10	10 15		10 33		10a41	11 05	11 19			11 36		12 03	12 19			12 36	12a41
Rugeley Trent Valley	d						10 24						11 28						12 28				
Lichfield Trent Valley	d						10 31						11 35						12 35				
Tamworth	d						10 38						11 42						12 42				
Polesworth	d																						
Atherstone	d						10 47						11 51						12 51				
Nuneaton	a				09 54		10 53		10 55				11 57			11 58			12 57	12 31			
	d				09 55		10 54		10 56				11 58			11 59	12 30		12 58	12 32			
Bedworth	d																12 36						
Coventry	a		10 24			11 24						12 24					12 54	13 24					
Rugby	a						11 14	10 31					12 13	11 31					13 13				
Northampton	a						11 36			←			12 41						13 41		←		
Milton Keynes Central	a			10 17			12 02	11 06	11 46	12 02			13 04	12 06					14 04	13 03	13 04		
Watford Junction	a	10s35			11s16		→	11s43		12 32			→		12s35	12s50			→		13 35		
London Euston 15 ⊖	a	10 57		11 06	11 37			12 05	12 32	12 50				12 45	12 56	13 11				13 44	13 53	14 01	

		VT ◇1 ⌂	XC ◇1 A ⌶	LM ◇1	VT ◇1 ⌂	LM ◇1	VT ◇1 ⌂	LM ◇1	VT ◇1 ⌂	LM	XC ◇1 A ⌶	LM ◇1	VT ◇1 ⌂	LM ◇1	VT ◇1 ⌂	LM ◇1	VT ◇1 ⌂	LM	XC ◇1 A ⌶	LM ◇1	VT ◇1 ⌂	LM ◇1	VT ◇1 ⌂
Crewe	d	12 30		12 38	12 56			13 22	13 30			13 38	13 51			14 22	14 29			14 33	14 54		
Alsager	d			12 46								13 47								14 41			
Kidsgrove	d			12 50								13 51								14 45			
Hanley Bus Station	d																						
Stoke-on-Trent	d		12 47	12 59							13 44	13 59							14 45	14 55			
Wedgwood Old Road Bridge	d																						
Barlaston Orchard Place	d																						
Stone Granville Square	d																						
Stone	d			13 07								14 07								15 03			
Norton Bridge Station Drv	d																						
Stafford	d		13 07	13 19			13 36	13a42			14 02	14 19			14 36	14a42			15 06	15 20			15 36
Rugeley Trent Valley	d			13 28								14 28								15 28			
Lichfield Trent Valley	d			13 35								14 35								15 35			
Tamworth	d			13 42								14 42								15 42			
Polesworth	d																						
Atherstone	d			13 51								14 51								15 52			
Nuneaton	a			13 58								14 57	14 31							15 58			
	d			13 58						14 11		14 58	14 32					15 11		15 58			
Bedworth	d									14 17								15 17					
Coventry	a		14 24							14 34	15 24							15 34	16 24				
Rugby	a			14 14								15 13								16 13			
Northampton	a			14 41		←						15 41		←						16 41		←	
Milton Keynes Central	a			15 04	14 02	14 04						16 04	15 04	15 04						17 04	16 04	16 04	
Watford Junction	a			→		14 35						→		15 35						→		16 35	
London Euston 15 ⊖	a	14 09			14 43	14 53	15 01		15 09				15 45	15 53	16 01		16 09				16 44	16 53	17 01

		LM ◇1	VT ◇1 ⌂	LM	XC ◇1 A ⌶	LM ◇1	VT ◇1 ⌂	LM ◇1	VT ◇1 ⌂	LM ◇1	VT ◇1 ⌂	LM	XC ◇1 A ⌶	LM ◇1	VT ◇1 ⌂	LM ◇1	VT ◇1 ⌂	LM ◇1	VT ◇1 ⌂	LM	XC ◇1 A ⌶	LM ◇1
Crewe	d	15 22	15 29			15 38	15 54			16 22	16 29			16 33	16 54			17 22	17 29			17 38
Alsager	d					15 46								16 41								17 46
Kidsgrove	d					15 50								16 45								17 50
Hanley Bus Station	d																					
Stoke-on-Trent	d				15 45	15 59							16 45	16 54							17 45	17 59
Wedgwood Old Road Bridge	d																					
Barlaston Orchard Place	d																					
Stone Granville Square	d																					
Stone	d					16 07								17 02								18 07
Norton Bridge Station Drv	d																					
Stafford	d	15a43			16 06	16 19			16 37	16a43			17 06	17 21			17 36	17a43			18 06	18 19
Rugeley Trent Valley	d					16 28								17 33								18 28
Lichfield Trent Valley	d					16 35								17 40	17 27							18 35
Tamworth	d					16 42								17 47								18 42
Polesworth	d																					
Atherstone	d					16 51								17 56								18 51
Nuneaton	a					16 57								18 02								18 57
	d			16 11		16 58						17 11		18 03						18 11		18 58
Bedworth	d			16 17								17 17								18 17		
Coventry	a			16 34	17 24							17 34	18 24							18 34	19 24	
Rugby	a					17 13								18 18								19 13
Northampton	a					17 41		←						18 41		←						19 41
Milton Keynes Central	a					18 04	17 03	17 04						19 04	18 04	18 04						20 06
Watford Junction	a					→		17 35						→		18 35						→
London Euston 15 ⊖	a		17 09				17 44	17 53	18 01		18 09				18 44	18 53	19 01		19 09			

A ⌶ to Stafford

Crewe and Stoke-on-Trent - London
Nuneaton - Coventry

Sundays
until 24 June

Network Diagram - see first Page of Table 67

		VT ◇1 ☕	LM ◇1	VT ◇1 ☕	LM ◇1	VT ◇1 ☕	XC ◇1 A 🍴	LM ◇1	VT ◇1 ☕	LM ◇1	VT ◇1 ☕	LM ◇1	VT ◇1 ☕	LM ◇1	LM	XC ◇1 A 🍴	LM ◇1	LM ◇1	VT ◇1 ☕	XC ◇1	XC ◇1	LM	LM ◇1
Crewe	d	17 55			18 22	18 29		18 37	18 55			19 22	19 29				19 38	20 18	20 24				20 41
Alsager	d							18 45									19 46						20 49
Kidsgrove	d							18 49									19 50						20 53
Hanley Bus Station	d																						
Stoke-on-Trent	d						18 45	18 58								19 45	19 59			20 23	20 47		21 04
Wedgwood Old Road Bridge	d																						
Barlaston Orchard Place	d																						
Stone Granville Square	d																						
Stone	d							19 06									20 07						21 12
Norton Bridge Station Drv	d																						
Stafford	d			18 36	18a43		19 03	19 22			19 36	19a44				20 05	20 18	20a38	20 43	20a44	21a08		21 24
Rugeley Trent Valley	d							19 33									20 27						21 33
Lichfield Trent Valley	d							19 40									20 34						21 40
Tamworth	d							19 47									20 41						21 47
Polesworth	d																						
Atherstone	d							19 56									20 50						21 56
Nuneaton	a							20 02									20 56						22 02
	d							20 03							20 11		20 57					22 00	22 03
Bedworth	d														20 17							22 06	
Coventry	a						20 24								20 34	21 23						22 21	
Rugby	a							20 18									21 12						22 18
Northampton	a		←					20 40		←				←			21 40						22 43
Milton Keynes Central	a	19 02	19 04					21 05	20 03	20 06				21 05			22 09		21 36				
Watford Junction	a		19 35					→		20 35				21 35			→						
London Euston 15 ⊖	a	19 43	19 53	20 01		20 09			20 44	20 53	21 01		21 09	21 54					22 27				

		VT ◇1 ☕	LM ◇1	AW ◇ 🍴	LM ◇1	VT ◇1 ☕	VT ◇1 ☕	XC ◇1	LM ◇1	XC ◇1
Crewe	d	20 47		20 52	21 17	21 23	21 40		22 22	
Alsager	d									
Kidsgrove	d									
Hanley Bus Station	d									
Stoke-on-Trent	d							21 47		22 47
Wedgwood Old Road Bridge	d									
Barlaston Orchard Place	d									
Stone Granville Square	d									
Stone	d									
Norton Bridge Station Drv	d									
Stafford	d			21a16	21a37	21 43	22a01	22a06	22a42	23a04
Rugeley Trent Valley	d									
Lichfield Trent Valley	d					22 00				
Tamworth	d					22 06				
Polesworth	d									
Atherstone	d									
Nuneaton	a					22 17				
	d					22 18				
Bedworth	d									
Coventry	a									
Rugby	a					22 31				
Northampton	a		←							
Milton Keynes Central	a	21 55	22 09			23 04				
Watford Junction	a	22s31	22 51			23s34				
London Euston 15 ⊖	a	22 53	23 14			23 54				

A 🍴 to Stafford

Crewe and Stoke-on-Trent - London
Nuneaton - Coventry

Sundays
1 July to 9 September

Network Diagram - see first Page of Table 67

		VT ◇1 A ☕	VT ◇1 A ☕	VT ◇1 ☕	VT ◇1 ☕	XC ◇1 🍴	VT ◇1 ☕	LM ◇1	VT ◇1 ☕	XC ◇1 🍴	VT ◇1 ☕	LM ◇1	LM ◇1	LM ◇1	VT ◇1 ☕	VT ◇1 ☕	XC ◇1 🍴	VT ◇1 ☕	LM	LM ◇1	VT ◇1 ☕	LM ◇1	XC ◇1 🍴
Crewe	d		07 31	08 43	08 53	09 05	09 13	09 30	09 43		10 14		10 20	10 38	10 43	10 55		11 14		11 38	11 49		
Alsager	d							09 38						10 46						11 46			
Kidsgrove	d							09 43						10 50						11 50			
Hanley Bus Station	d																						
Stoke-on-Trent	d	07 29						09 51		10 07				10 59			11 07			11 59			12 07
Wedgwood Old Road Bridge	d																						
Barlaston Orchard Place	d																						
Stone Granville Square	d																						
Stone	d							10 00						11 07						12 07			
Norton Bridge Station Drv	d																						
Stafford	d		07 53	09 02		09a25	09 32	10 15		10a26	10 33		10a41	11 19			11a27	11 36		12 19			12a24
Rugeley Trent Valley	d							10 24						11 28						12 28			
Lichfield Trent Valley	d							10 31						11 35						12 35			
Tamworth	d							10 38						11 42						12 42			
Polesworth	d																						
Atherstone	d							10 47						11 51						12 51			
Nuneaton	a	08 00					09 54	10 53			10 55			11 57				11 58		12 57	12 31		
	d	08 02					09 55	10 54			10 56			11 58				11 59	12 30	12 58	12 32		
Bedworth	d																		12 36				
Coventry	a																		12 54				
Rugby	a	08 16						11 14	10 31					12 13	11 31					13 13			
Northampton	a							11 36				←		12 41						13 41		←	
Milton Keynes Central	a		08 56		10 17			12 02	11 06		11 46	12 02		13 04	12 06					14 04	13 03	13 04	
Watford Junction	a		09 20	10s35			11s16	→	11s43			12 32		→		12s35		12s50		→		13 35	
London Euston 15 ⊖	a	09 23	09 37	10 57	11 06		11 37		12 05		12 32	12 50			12 45	12 56		13 11			13 44	13 53	

		VT ◇1 ☕	LM ◇1	VT ◇1 ☕	LM ◇1	VT ◇1 ☕	LM ◇1	XC ◇1 🍴	VT ◇1 ☕	LM ◇1	VT ◇1 ☕	LM	LM ◇1	VT ◇1 ☕	LM ◇1	XC ◇1 B 🍴	VT ◇1 ☕	LM ◇1	VT ◇1 ☕	LM	LM ◇1	VT ◇1 ☕	LM ◇1
Crewe	d		12 22	12 30	12 38	12 56				13 22	13 30		13 38	13 51				14 22	14 29		14 33	14 54	
Alsager	d				12 46								13 47								14 41		
Kidsgrove	d				12 50								13 51								14 45		
Hanley Bus Station	d																						
Stoke-on-Trent	d				12 59			13 07					13 59			14 07					14 55		
Wedgwood Old Road Bridge	d																						
Barlaston Orchard Place	d																						
Stone Granville Square	d																						
Stone	d				13 07								14 07								15 03		
Norton Bridge Station Drv	d																						
Stafford	d	12 36	12a41		13 19			13 25	13 36	13a42			14 19			14 25	14 36	14a42			15 20		
Rugeley Trent Valley	d				13 28								14 28								15 28		
Lichfield Trent Valley	d				13 35								14 35								15 35		
Tamworth	d				13 42								14 42								15 42		
Polesworth	d																						
Atherstone	d				13 51								14 51								15 52		
Nuneaton	a				13 58								14 57	14 31							15 58		
	d				13 58							14 11	14 58	14 32						15 11	15 58		
Bedworth	d											14 17								15 17			
Coventry	a							14 24				14 34				15 24				15 34			
Rugby	a				14 14								15 13								16 13		
Northampton	a				14 41		←						15 41		←						16 41		←
Milton Keynes Central	a				15 04	14 02	14 04						16 04	15 04	15 04						17 04	16 04	16 04
Watford Junction	a				→		14 35						→		15 35						→		16 35
London Euston 15 ⊖	a	14 01		14 09		14 43	14 53		15 01		15 09			15 45	15 53		16 01		16 09			16 44	16 53

		XC ◇1 B 🍴	VT ◇1 ☕	LM ◇1	VT ◇1 ☕	LM	LM ◇1	VT ◇1 ☕	LM ◇1	XC ◇1 B 🍴	VT ◇1 ☕	LM ◇1	VT ◇1 ☕	LM	LM ◇1	VT ◇1 ☕	LM ◇1	XC ◇1 B 🍴	VT ◇1 ☕	LM ◇1	VT ◇1 ☕	LM
Crewe	d			15 22	15 29		15 38	15 54				16 22	16 29		16 33	16 54				17 22	17 29	
Alsager	d						15 46								16 41							
Kidsgrove	d						15 50								16 45							
Hanley Bus Station	d																					
Stoke-on-Trent	d	15 07					15 59			16 07					16 54			17 08				
Wedgwood Old Road Bridge	d																					
Barlaston Orchard Place	d																					
Stone Granville Square	d																					
Stone	d						16 07								17 02							
Norton Bridge Station Drv	d																					
Stafford	d	15 25	15 36	15a42			16 19			16 25	16 37	16a42			17 21			17 26	17 36	17a42		
Rugeley Trent Valley	d						16 28								17 33							
Lichfield Trent Valley	d						16 35								17 40	17 27						
Tamworth	d						16 42								17 47							
Polesworth	d																					
Atherstone	d						16 51								17 56							
Nuneaton	a						16 57								18 02							
	d					16 11	16 58							17 11	18 03							18 11
Bedworth	d					16 17								17 17								18 17
Coventry	a	16 24				16 34				17 24				17 34				18 24				18 34
Rugby	a						17 13								18 18							
Northampton	a						17 41		←						18 41		←					
Milton Keynes Central	a						18 04	17 03	17 04						19 04	18 04	18 04					
Watford Junction	a						→		17 35						→		18 35					
London Euston 15 ⊖	a		17 01		17 09			17 44	17 53		18 01		18 09			18 44	18 53		19 01		19 09	

A 29 July, 5 August, 12 August, 2 September, 9 September

B 🍴 to Stafford

Table 67

Sundays

1 July to 9 September

Crewe and Stoke-on-Trent - London
Nuneaton - Coventry

Network Diagram - see first Page of Table 67

		LM	VT	LM	XC	VT	LM	VT		LM	VT	LM	XC	VT	LM	VT	LM	LM		LM	XC	LM	VT	XC	LM
		◇1	◇1	◇1	◇1	◇1	◇1	◇1		◇1	◇1	◇1	◇1	◇1	◇1	◇1	◇1			◇1	◇1	◇1	◇1	◇1	
			🛒		A 🍴	🛒		🛒			🛒		A 🍴	🛒		🛒					A 🍴		🛒		
Crewe	d	17 38	17 55				18 22	18 29		18 37	18 55				19 22	19 29				19 38		20 18	20 24		
Alsager	d	17 46								18 45										19 46					
Kidsgrove	d	17 50								18 49										19 50					
Hanley Bus Station	d																								
Stoke-on-Trent	d	17 59			18 08					18 58			19 07							19 59	20 07			20 47	
Wedgwood Old Road Bridge	d																								
Barlaston Orchard Place	d																								
Stone Granville Square	d																								
Stone	d	18 07								19 06										20 07					
Norton Bridge Station Drv	d																								
Stafford	d	18 19			18 26	18 36	18a42			19 22			19 25	19 36	19a42					20 18	20 27	20a38	20 43	21a08	
Rugeley Trent Valley	d	18 28								19 33										20 27					
Lichfield Trent Valley	d	18 35								19 40										20 34					
Tamworth	d	18 42								19 47										20 41					
Polesworth	d																								
Atherstone	d	18 51								19 56										20 50					
Nuneaton	a	18 57								20 02										20 56					
	d	18 58								20 03								20 11		20 57					22 00
Bedworth	d																	20 17							22 06
Coventry	a				19 24								20 24					20 34			21 23				22 21
Rugby	a	19 13								20 18										21 12					
Northampton	a	19 41		←						20 40		←					←			21 40					
Milton Keynes Central	a	20 06	19 02	19 04						21 05	20 03	20 06					21 05			22 09			21 36		
Watford Junction	a	→		19 35						→		20 35					21 35			→					
London Euston 15 ⊖	a		19 43	19 53		20 01		20 09			20 44	20 53		21 01		21 09	21 54						22 27		

		LM	VT	LM		AW	LM	VT	VT	XC	LM	XC
		◇1	◇1	◇1		◇	◇1	◇1	◇1	◇1	◇1	◇1
			🛒			🍴		🛒	🛒			
Crewe	d	20 41	20 47			20 52	21 18	21 23	21 40		22 22	
Alsager	d	20 49										
Kidsgrove	d	20 53										
Hanley Bus Station	d											
Stoke-on-Trent	d	21 04								21 47		22 47
Wedgwood Old Road Bridge	d											
Barlaston Orchard Place	d											
Stone Granville Square	d											
Stone	d	21 12										
Norton Bridge Station Drv	d											
Stafford	d	21 24				21a16	21a39	21 43	22a01	22a06	22a42	23a04
Rugeley Trent Valley	d	21 33										
Lichfield Trent Valley	d	21 40						22 00				
Tamworth	d	21 47						22 06				
Polesworth	d											
Atherstone	d	21 56										
Nuneaton	a	22 02						22 17				
	d	22 03						22 18				
Bedworth	d											
Coventry	a											
Rugby	a	22 18						22 31				
Northampton	a	22 43		←								
Milton Keynes Central	a		21 55	22 09				23 04				
Watford Junction	a		22s31	22 51				23s34				
London Euston 15 ⊖	a		22 53	23 14				23 54				

Sundays

16 September to 21 October

		VT	VT	XC	VT	LM	VT	XC	VT	LM		LM	LM	VT	VT	XC	VT	LM	LM	VT		LM	XC	VT	LM
		◇1	◇1	◇1	◇1	◇1	◇1	◇1	◇1	◇1		◇1	◇1	◇1	◇1	◇1	◇1		◇1	◇1		◇1	◇1	◇1	◇1
		🛒	🛒	A 🍴	🛒		🛒	A 🍴	🛒					🛒	🛒	A 🍴	🛒			🛒			A 🍴	🛒	
Crewe	d	08 43	08 53	09 05	09 13	09 30	09 43		10 14			10 20	10 38	10 43	10 55		11 14		11 38	11 49					12 22
Alsager	d					09 38							10 46						11 46						
Kidsgrove	d					09 43							10 50						11 50						
Hanley Bus Station	d																								
Stoke-on-Trent	d					09 51		10 07					10 59			11 07			11 59				12 07		
Wedgwood Old Road Bridge	d																								
Barlaston Orchard Place	d																								
Stone Granville Square	d																								
Stone	d					10 00							11 07						12 07						
Norton Bridge Station Drv	d																								
Stafford	d	09 02		09 26	09 32	10 15		10 27	10 33			10a41	11 19			11 28	11 36		12 19				12 25	12 36	12a41
Rugeley Trent Valley	d					10 24							11 28						12 28						
Lichfield Trent Valley	d					10 31							11 35						12 35						
Tamworth	d					10 38							11 42						12 42						
Polesworth	d																								
Atherstone	d					10 47							11 51						12 51						
Nuneaton	a				09 54	10 53			10 55				11 57				11 58		12 57	12 31					
	d				09 55	10 54			10 56				11 58				11 59	12 30	12 58	12 32					
Bedworth	d																	12 36							
Coventry	a			10 24				11 24								12 24		12 54					13 24		
Rugby	a					11 14	10 31						12 13	11 31					13 13						
Northampton	a					11 36				←			12 41						13 41			←			
Milton Keynes Central	a		10 17			12 02	11 06		11 46	12 02			13 04	12 06					14 04	13 03		13 04			
Watford Junction	a	10s35			11s16	→	11s43			12 32			→		12s36		12s50		→			13 35			
London Euston 15 ⊖	a	10 57	11 06		11 37		12 05		12 32	12 50				12 45	12 56		13 11			13 44		13 53		14 01	

A 🍴 to Stafford

Table 67

Sundays

16 September to 21 October

Crewe and Stoke-on-Trent - London
Nuneaton - Coventry

Network Diagram - see first Page of Table 67

		VT	LM	VT	LM	XC		VT	LM	VT	LM	LM	VT	LM	XC	VT		LM	VT	LM	LM	VT	LM	XC	VT
		◇1	◇1	◇1	◇1	◇1		◇1	◇1	◇1		◇1	◇1	◇1	◇1	◇1		◇1	◇1		◇1	◇1	◇1	◇1	◇1
		🛒		🛒		A 🍴		🛒		🛒			🛒		A 🍴	🛒			🛒			🛒		A 🍴	🛒
Crewe	d	12 30	12 38	12 56					13 22	13 30		13 38	13 51					14 22	14 29		14 33	14 54			
Alsager	d		12 46									13 47									14 41				
Kidsgrove	d		12 50									13 51									14 45				
Hanley Bus Station	d																								
Stoke-on-Trent	d		12 59			13 07						13 59			14 07						14 55			15 07	
Wedgwood Old Road Bridge	d																								
Barlaston Orchard Place	d																								
Stone Granville Square	d																								
Stone	d		13 07									14 07									15 03				
Norton Bridge Station Drv	d																								
Stafford	d		13 19			13 25		13 36	13a42			14 19			14 25	14 36		14a42			15 20			15 25	15 36
Rugeley Trent Valley	d		13 28									14 28									15 28				
Lichfield Trent Valley	d		13 35									14 35									15 35				
Tamworth	d		13 42									14 42									15 42				
Polesworth	d																								
Atherstone	d		13 51									14 51									15 52				
Nuneaton	a		13 58									14 57	14 31								15 58				
	d		13 58								14 11	14 58	14 32							15 11	15 58				
Bedworth	d										14 17									15 17					
Coventry	a					14 24					14 34				15 24					15 34				16 24	
Rugby	a		14 14									15 13									16 13				
Northampton	a		14 41		←							15 41		←							16 41		←		
Milton Keynes Central	a		15 04	14 02	14 04							16 04	15 02	15 04							17 04	16 03	16 04		
Watford Junction	a		→		14 35							→		15 35							→		16 35		
London Euston 15 ⊖	a	14 09		14 43	14 53			15 01		15 05			15 43	15 53		16 01			16 05			16 43	16 53		17 01

		LM		VT	LM	LM	VT	LM	XC	VT	LM	VT		LM	LM	VT	LM	XC	VT	LM	VT	LM		LM	VT
		◇1		◇1		◇1	◇1	◇1	◇1	◇1	◇1	◇1			◇1	◇1	◇1	◇1	◇1	◇1	◇1			◇1	◇1
				🛒			🛒		A 🍴	🛒		🛒				🛒		A 🍴	🛒		🛒				🛒
Crewe	d	15 22		15 29		15 38	15 54				16 22	16 29			16 33	16 54				17 22	17 29			17 38	17 55
Alsager	d					15 46									16 41									17 46	
Kidsgrove	d					15 50									16 45									17 50	
Hanley Bus Station	d																								
Stoke-on-Trent	d					15 59			16 07						16 54			17 08						17 59	
Wedgwood Old Road Bridge	d																								
Barlaston Orchard Place	d																								
Stone Granville Square	d																								
Stone	d					16 07									17 02									18 07	
Norton Bridge Station Drv	d																								
Stafford	d	15a42				16 19			16 25	16 37	16a42				17 21			17 26	17 36	17a42				18 19	
Rugeley Trent Valley	d					16 28									17 33									18 28	
Lichfield Trent Valley	d					16 35									17 40	17 27								18 35	
Tamworth	d					16 42									17 47									18 42	
Polesworth	d																								
Atherstone	d					16 51									17 56									18 51	
Nuneaton	a					16 57									18 02									18 57	
	d				16 11	16 58								17 11	18 03							18 11		18 58	
Bedworth	d				16 17									17 17								18 17			
Coventry	a				16 34				17 24					17 34				18 24				18 34			
Rugby	a					17 13									18 18									19 13	
Northampton	a					17 41		←							18 41		←							19 41	
Milton Keynes Central	a					18 04	17 02	17 04							19 04	18 04	18 04							20 06	19 02
Watford Junction	a					→		17 35							→		18 35							→	
London Euston 15 ⊖	a			17 07			17 43	17 53		18 01		18 07				18 44	18 53		19 01		19 05				19 43

		LM	XC	VT	LM	VT	LM	VT		LM	XC	VT	LM	VT	LM	LM	LM	XC		LM	VT	XC	LM	LM	VT
		◇1	◇1	◇1	◇1	◇1	◇1	◇1		◇1	◇1	◇1	◇1	◇1	◇1		◇1	◇1		◇1	◇1	◇1		◇1	◇1
			A 🍴	🛒		🛒		🛒			A 🍴	🛒		🛒				A 🍴			🛒				🛒
Crewe	d				18 22	18 29	18 37	18 55					19 22	19 29			19 38			20 18	20 24			20 41	20 47
Alsager	d						18 45										19 46							20 49	
Kidsgrove	d						18 49										19 50							20 53	
Hanley Bus Station	d																								
Stoke-on-Trent	d		18 08				18 58				19 07						19 59	20 07				20 47		21 04	
Wedgwood Old Road Bridge	d																								
Barlaston Orchard Place	d																								
Stone Granville Square	d																								
Stone	d						19 06										20 07							21 12	
Norton Bridge Station Drv	d																								
Stafford	d		18 26	18 36	18a42		19 22				19 25	19 36	19a42				20 18	20 27		20a38	20 43	21a08		21 24	
Rugeley Trent Valley	d						19 33										20 27							21 33	
Lichfield Trent Valley	d						19 40										20 34							21 40	
Tamworth	d						19 47										20 41							21 47	
Polesworth	d																								
Atherstone	d						19 56										20 50							21 56	
Nuneaton	a						20 02										20 56							22 02	
	d						20 03									20 11	20 57						22 00	22 03	
Bedworth	d															20 17							22 06		
Coventry	a		19 24								20 24					20 34		21 23					22 21		
Rugby	a						20 18										21 12							22 18	
Northampton	a	←					20 40			←					←		21 40							22 43	
Milton Keynes Central	a	19 04					21 05	20 02		20 06					21 05		22 09				21 36				21 51
Watford Junction	a	19 35					→			20 35					21 35		→								22s31
London Euston 15 ⊖	a	19 53		20 01		20 05		20 44		20 53		21 01		21 08	21 54						22 27				22 53

A 🍴 to Stafford

Table 67

Sundays
16 September to 21 October

Crewe and Stoke-on-Trent - London
Nuneaton - Coventry

Network Diagram - see first Page of Table 67

		LM ◇1	AW ◇ 🚌	LM ◇1		VT ◇1 🍴	VT ◇1 🍴	XC ◇1	LM ◇1	XC ◇1
Crewe	d		20 52	21 18		21 23	21 40		22 22	
Alsager	d									
Kidsgrove	d									
Hanley Bus Station	d									
Stoke-on-Trent	d							21 47		22 47
Wedgwood Old Road Bridge	d									
Barlaston Orchard Place	d									
Stone Granville Square	d									
Stone	d									
Norton Bridge Station Drv	d									
Stafford	d		21a16	21a39		21 43	22a01	22a06	22a42	23a04
Rugeley Trent Valley	d									
Lichfield Trent Valley	d					22 00				
Tamworth	d					22 06				
Polesworth	d									
Atherstone	d									
Nuneaton	a					22 17				
	d					22 18				
Bedworth	d									
Coventry	a									
Rugby	a					22 31				
Northampton	a	←								
Milton Keynes Central	a	22 09				23 04				
Watford Junction	a	22 51				23s34				
London Euston ⊖	a	23 14				23 54				

Sundays
from 28 October

		VT ◇1 🍴	VT ◇1 🍴	XC ◇1 A 🚌	VT ◇1 🍴	LM ◇1	XC ◇1 A 🚌	VT ◇1 🍴	LM ◇1	LM ◇1		LM ◇1	VT ◇1 🍴	VT ◇1 🍴	XC ◇1 A 🚌	VT ◇1 🍴	LM	LM ◇1	VT ◇1 🍴	LM ◇1		XC ◇1 A 🚌	VT ◇1 🍴	LM ◇1	VT ◇1 🍴
Crewe	d	08 43	08 53	09 05	09 13	09 30		10 14		10 20		10 38	10 43	10 55		11 14		11 38	11 49					12 22	12 30
Alsager	d					09 38						10 46						11 46							
Kidsgrove	d					09 43						10 50						11 50							
Hanley Bus Station	d																								
Stoke-on-Trent	d					09 51	10 07					10 59			11 07			11 59				12 07			
Wedgwood Old Road Bridge	d																								
Barlaston Orchard Place	d																								
Stone Granville Square	d																								
Stone	d					10 00						11 07						12 07							
Norton Bridge Station Drv	d																								
Stafford	d	09 02		09 26	09 32	10 15	10 27	10 33		10a41		11 19			11 28	11 36		12 19				12 25	12 36	12a41	
Rugeley Trent Valley	d					10 24						11 28						12 28							
Lichfield Trent Valley	d					10 31						11 35						12 35							
Tamworth	d					10 38						11 42						12 42							
Polesworth	d																								
Atherstone	d					10 47						11 51						12 51							
Nuneaton	a				09 54	10 53		10 55				11 57				11 58		12 57	12 31						
	d				09 55	10 54		10 56				11 58				11 59	12 30	12 58	12 32						
Bedworth	d																12 36								
Coventry	a			10 24			11 24								12 24		12 54					13 24			
Rugby	a					11 14						12 13	11 31					13 13							
Northampton	a					11 36			←			12 41						13 41		←					
Milton Keynes Central	a		10 17			12 02		11 46	12 02			13 04	12 06					14 04	13 03	13 04					
Watford Junction	a	10s35			11s16	→			12 32			→		12s36		12s50		→		13 35					
London Euston ⊖	a	10 57	11 06		11 37			12 32	12 50				12 45	12 56		13 11			13 44	13 53			14 01		14 09

		LM ◇1	VT ◇1 🍴	LM ◇1	XC ◇1 A 🚌	VT ◇1 🍴		LM ◇1	VT ◇1 🍴	LM	LM ◇1	VT ◇1 🍴	LM ◇1	XC ◇1 A 🚌	VT ◇1 🍴	LM ◇1		VT ◇1 🍴	LM	LM ◇1	VT ◇1 🍴	VT ◇1 🍴	LM ◇1	XC ◇1 A 🚌	VT ◇1 🍴
Crewe	d	12 38	12 56					13 22	13 30		13 38	13 51				14 22		14 29		14 33	14 35	14 54			
Alsager	d	12 46									13 47									14 41					
Kidsgrove	d	12 50									13 51									14 45					
Hanley Bus Station	d																								
Stoke-on-Trent	d	12 59			13 07						13 59			14 07						14 55				15 07	
Wedgwood Old Road Bridge	d																								
Barlaston Orchard Place	d																								
Stone Granville Square	d																								
Stone	d	13 07									14 07									15 03					
Norton Bridge Station Drv	d																								
Stafford	d	13 19			13 25	13 36		13a42			14 19			14 25	14 36	14a42				15 20				15 25	15 36
Rugeley Trent Valley	d	13 28									14 28									15 28					
Lichfield Trent Valley	d	13 35									14 35									15 35					
Tamworth	d	13 42									14 42									15 42					
Polesworth	d																								
Atherstone	d	13 51									14 51									15 52					
Nuneaton	a	13 58									14 57	14 31								15 58					
	d	13 58								14 11	14 58	14 32							15 11	15 58					
Bedworth	d									14 17									15 17						
Coventry	a				14 24					14 34				15 24					15 34					16 24	
Rugby	a	14 14									15 13									16 13					
Northampton	a	14 41		←							15 41		←							16 41			←		
Milton Keynes Central	a	15 04	14 02	14 04							16 04	15 02	15 04							17 04		16 03	16 04		
Watford Junction	a	→		14 35							→		15 35							→			16 35		
London Euston ⊖	a		14 43	14 53		15 01			15 05			15 43	15 53		16 01			16 05			16 12	16 43	16 53		17 01

A 🚌 to Stafford

Table 67

Sundays
from 28 October

Crewe and Stoke-on-Trent - London
Nuneaton - Coventry

Network Diagram - see first Page of Table 67

		LM ◇1		VT ◇1 🍴	LM	LM ◇1	VT ◇1 🍴	LM ◇1	XC ◇1 A 🚌	VT ◇1 🍴	LM ◇1	VT ◇1 🍴		LM	LM ◇1	VT ◇1 🍴	LM ◇1	XC ◇1 A 🚌	VT ◇1 🍴	LM ◇1	VT ◇1 🍴	LM		LM ◇1	VT ◇1 🍴
Crewe	d	15 22		15 29		15 38	15 54				16 22	16 29			16 33	16 54				17 22	17 29			17 38	17 55
Alsager	d					15 46									16 41									17 46	
Kidsgrove	d					15 50									16 45									17 50	
Hanley Bus Station	d																								
Stoke-on-Trent	d					15 59			16 07						16 54			17 08						17 59	
Wedgwood Old Road Bridge	d																								
Barlaston Orchard Place	d																								
Stone Granville Square	d																								
Stone	d					16 07									17 02									18 07	
Norton Bridge Station Drv	d																								
Stafford	d	15a42				16 19			16 25	16 37	16a42				17 21			17 26	17 36	17a42				18 19	
Rugeley Trent Valley	d					16 28									17 33									18 28	
Lichfield Trent Valley	d					16 35									17 40	17 27								18 35	
Tamworth	d					16 42									17 47									18 42	
Polesworth	d																								
Atherstone	d					16 51									17 56									18 51	
Nuneaton	a					16 57									18 02									18 57	
	d				16 11	16 58								17 11	18 03							18 11		18 58	
Bedworth	d				16 17									17 17								18 17			
Coventry	a				16 34				17 24					17 34				18 24				18 34			
Rugby	a					17 13									18 18									19 13	
Northampton	a					17 41		←							18 41		←							19 41	
Milton Keynes Central	a					18 04	17 02	17 04							19 04	18 04	18 04							20 06	19 02
Watford Junction	a					→		17 37							→		18 35							→	
London Euston ⊖	a			17 07			17 43	17 53		18 01		18 07				18 44	18 53		19 01		19 05				19 43

		LM ◇1	XC ◇1 A 🚌	VT ◇1 🍴	LM ◇1	VT ◇1 🍴	LM ◇1	VT ◇1 🍴		LM ◇1	XC ◇1 A 🚌	VT ◇1 🍴	LM ◇1	VT ◇1 🍴	LM ◇1	LM	LM ◇1	XC ◇1 A 🚌		LM ◇1	VT ◇1 🍴	XC ◇1	LM	LM ◇1	VT ◇1 🍴
Crewe	d				18 22	18 29	18 37	18 55					19 22	19 29			19 38			20 18	20 24			20 41	20 47
Alsager	d						18 45										19 46							20 49	
Kidsgrove	d						18 49										19 50							20 53	
Hanley Bus Station	d																								
Stoke-on-Trent	d		18 08				18 58				19 07						19 59	20 07				20 47		21 04	
Wedgwood Old Road Bridge	d																								
Barlaston Orchard Place	d																								
Stone Granville Square	d																								
Stone	d						19 06										20 07							21 12	
Norton Bridge Station Drv	d																								
Stafford	d		18 26	18 36	18a42		19 22				19 25	19 36	19a42				20 18	20 27		20a38	20 43	21a08		21 24	
Rugeley Trent Valley	d						19 33										20 27							21 33	
Lichfield Trent Valley	d						19 40										20 34							21 40	
Tamworth	d						19 47										20 41							21 47	
Polesworth	d																								
Atherstone	d						19 56										20 50							21 56	
Nuneaton	a						20 02										20 56							22 02	
	d						20 03									20 11	20 57						22 00	22 03	
Bedworth	d															20 17							22 06		
Coventry	a		19 24								20 24					20 34		21 23					22 21		
Rugby	a						20 18										21 12							22 18	
Northampton	a	←					20 40			←					←		21 40							22 43	
Milton Keynes Central	a	19 04					21 05	20 02		20 06					21 05		22 09				21 36				21 51
Watford Junction	a	19 35					→			20 35					21 35		→								22s31
London Euston ⊖	a	19 53		20 01		20 05		20 44		20 53		21 01		21 08	21 54						22 27				22 53

		LM ◇1	AW ◇ 🚌	LM ◇1		VT ◇1 🍴	VT ◇1 🍴	XC ◇1	LM ◇1	XC ◇1
Crewe	d		20 52	21 18		21 23	21 40		22 22	
Alsager	d									
Kidsgrove	d									
Hanley Bus Station	d									
Stoke-on-Trent	d							21 47		22 47
Wedgwood Old Road Bridge	d									
Barlaston Orchard Place	d									
Stone Granville Square	d									
Stone	d									
Norton Bridge Station Drv	d									
Stafford	d		21a16	21a39		21 43	22a01	22a06	22a42	23a04
Rugeley Trent Valley	d									
Lichfield Trent Valley	d					22 00				
Tamworth	d					22 06				
Polesworth	d									
Atherstone	d									
Nuneaton	a					22 17				
	d					22 18				
Bedworth	d									
Coventry	a									
Rugby	a					22 31				
Northampton	a	←								
Milton Keynes Central	a	22 09				23 04				
Watford Junction	a	22 51				23s34				
London Euston ⊖	a	23 14				23 54				

A 🚌 to Stafford

Northampton - Coventry - Birmingham - Wolverhampton - Stafford

Network Diagram - see first Page of Table 67

Miles			LM MO	AW TThO	AW WFO	LM MO	LM MX	VT MO	VT MO	LM MO	XC	VT MX	VT MO	VT MX	VT	LM	XC	LM	LM	LM	VT	XC	LM
						◇■	◇■	◇■	◇■	■		◇■	◇■	◇■	◇■		◇■	■		◇■	◇■	◇■	◇■
			A 🚌			A		A ⊏	A ⊏	A	C 🚌	⊏	A ⊏	⊏	⊠						⊠	⊤	
—	London Euston ⊖	d				21p28	21p46	21p55	22p25	22p00		22p30	23p25	23p30									
0	**Northampton**	d				22p51	22p55			23p32										05 16			05 42
9½	Long Buckby	d				23p02	23p06			23p43										05 27			
18¾	Rugby	d				23p13	23p17	23p21	23p48	23p54		00 01	00s46	01 00						05 38			06 05
32¼	**Coventry**	a				23p25	23p29	23p31	23p57	00 05		00 10	00s57	01 13						05 49			
—		d				23p35	23p30	23p31	23p58			00 10		01 13						05 50			
34	Canley	d				23p38	23p33																
36	Tile Hill	d				23p42	23p37													05 55			
38	Berkswell	d				23p45	23p40																
41¼	Hampton-in-Arden	d				23p49	23p44													06 01			
43	**Birmingham International** ✈	a				23p52	23p47	23p42	00 08		00 10	00 21	01s08	01 24						06 04			
—		d				23p53	23p48	23p42	00 09			00 21		01 24						06 05			
45	Marston Green	d				23p56	23p51													06 08			
46½	Lea Hall	d					23p54																
47¾	Stechford	d					23p57																
49½	Adderley Park	d																					
51½	**Birmingham New Street**	a				00 04	00 04	23p55	00 21			00 32	01s21	01 36						06 16			
—		d	23p00	23p32	23p32			23p58	00 25			00 35		01 37	05 30	05 51	05 57	06 01	06 06		06 19	06 22	
54¾	Smethwick Rolfe Street	d	23p11																06 12				
55½	Smethwick Galton Bridge ■	d	23p16															06 08	06 14				
56¾	Sandwell & Dudley	d	23p23													05 59			06 17				
57¾	Dudley Port	d	23p32																06 20				
58½	Tipton	d	23p41																06 22				
60	Coseley	d	23p50																06 25				
64¼	**Wolverhampton** ■	a	00 03	00 01	00 02			00 26	00 53			01 03	01 53	02 07	05 47	06 09	06 14	06 19	06 31		06 35	06 39	
—		d													05 48		06 16	06 19				06 40	
74¼	Penkridge	d																06 29					
79½	**Stafford**	a													06 01		06 29	06 35				06 53	06 58

		AW	LM	LM	LM	LM	XC	LM	LM	LM	LM	VT	AW	VT	LM	LM	XC	LM	LM	VT	XC	LM	LM
		◇		◇■		■	◇■	◇■	◇■		◇■	◇■	◇	◇■	◇■		◇■	◇■		◇■	◇■	◇■	◇■
		⊤					⊤					⊠	⊤	⊠			⊤			⊠	⊤		
London Euston ⊖	d													06 03						06 23			05 30
Northampton	d							05 55			06 16				06 41								06 55
Long Buckby	d							06 06			06 27												07 06
Rugby	d							06 17			06 38			06 51	07 01								07 17
Coventry	a							06 29			06 49			07 02						07 22			07 29
	d					06 10		06 30			06 50			07 02					07 07	07 22	07 27		07 30
Canley	d					06 13		06 33											07 09				07 33
Tile Hill	d					06 17		06 37			06 55								07 13				07 37
Berkswell	d					06 20		06 40											07 16				07 40
Hampton-in-Arden	d					06 24					07 01								07 20				
Birmingham International ✈	a					06 27		06 45			07 04			07 13					07 23	07 33	07 37		07 45
	d		06 17			06 28		06 46			07 05		07 09	07 13				07 17	07 24	07 33	07 38		07 46
Marston Green	d					06 31		06 49			07 08								07 27				07 49
Lea Hall	d		06 22					06 52										07 22					07 52
Stechford	d		06 25					06 55										07 25					07 55
Adderley Park	d		06 28															07 28					07 58
Birmingham New Street	a		06 33			06 39		07 01			07 16		07 20	07 27				07 32	07 36	07 45	07 48		08 03
	d	06 24		06 36	06 38		06 57		07 01	07 08		07 20	07 24			07 27	07 31	07 36	07 38	07 49	07 57	08 01	
Smethwick Rolfe Street	d				06 44					07 14									07 44				
Smethwick Galton Bridge ■	d	06 30			06 46				07 08	07 16			07 30						07 46			08 08	
Sandwell & Dudley	d				06 49					07 19									07 49	07 58			
Dudley Port	d				06 52					07 22									07 52				
Tipton	d				06 54					07 24									07 54				
Coseley	d				06 57					07 27								07 46	07 57				
Wolverhampton ■	a	06 42		06 52	07 03		07 14		07 19	07 33		07 36	07 41			07 45	07 48	07 53	08 03	08 11	08 14	08 19	
	d			06 53			07 15		07 19								07 49	07 53			08 15	08 19	
Penkridge	d								07 29									08 03				08 29	
Stafford	a			07 08			07 29		07 36						07 53		08 00	08 09			08 29	08 35	

A from 21 May until 25 June

C from 26 June until 29 June

Northampton - Coventry - Birmingham - Wolverhampton - Stafford

Network Diagram - see first Page of Table 67

		LM	VT	LM	LM	VT	AW	VT	LM	XC	LM	LM	LM	LM	VT	XC	LM	LM	LM	LM	LM	VT
			◇■		◇■	◇■	◇	◇■	◇■	◇■		◇■		■	◇■	◇■	◇■	◇■			◇■	◇■
			⊠			⊠	⊤	⊠		⊤					⊠	⊤						⊠
London Euston ⊖	d		06 43					07 03	06 24						07 23						07 13	
Northampton	d				07 16				07 45								07 55				08 16	
Long Buckby	d				07 27												08 06				08 27	
Rugby	d				07 38			07 51	08 04								08 17				08 38	
Coventry	a		07 42		07 49			08 02							08 22		08 29				08 49	
	d		07 42		07 50			08 02						08 11	08 22	08 27	08 30				08 50	
Canley	d													08 14			08 33					
Tile Hill	d				07 55									08 18			08 37				08 55	
Berkswell	d													08 21			08 40					
Hampton-in-Arden	d				08 01									08 25							09 01	
Birmingham International ✈	a		07 53		08 04			08 12						08 28	08 33	08 37	08 45				09 04	
	d		07 53		08 05		08 09	08 13			08 17			08 29	08 33	08 38	08 46				09 05	
Marston Green	d				08 08						08 20			08 32			08 49				09 08	
Lea Hall	d										08 23						08 52					
Stechford	d										08 26						08 55					
Adderley Park	d										08 29											
Birmingham New Street	a		08 08		08 16		08 20	08 27			08 33			08 42	08 45	08 48	09 01				09 17	
	d	08 05		08 08		08 20	08 24			08 31		08 36	08 38		08 49	08 57		09 01	09 05	09 08		09 20
Smethwick Rolfe Street	d			08 14									08 44							09 14		
Smethwick Galton Bridge ■	d			08 16			08 30						08 46					09 08		09 16		
Sandwell & Dudley	d	08 13		08 19									08 49		08 58				09 13	09 19		
Dudley Port	d			08 22									08 52							09 22		
Tipton	d			08 24									08 54							09 24		
Coseley	d			08 27								08 46	08 57							09 27		
Wolverhampton ■	a	08 24		08 33		08 37	08 42			08 48		08 53	09 03		09 11	09 14		09 19	09 24	09 33		09 37
	d									08 49		08 53				09 15		09 19				
Penkridge	d											09 03										
Stafford	a								08 53	09 00		09 09				09 29		09 34				

		AW	VT	LM	XC	LM	LM	LM	LM	VT	XC	LM	LM	LM	VT	LM	LM	VT	AW	LM	VT	LM	XC
		◇	◇■	◇■	◇■		◇■		■	◇■	◇■	◇■	◇■		◇■		◇■	◇■	◇	■	◇■	◇■	◇■
		⊤	⊠		⊤					⊠	⊤				⊠			⊠	⊤		⊠		⊤
London Euston ⊖	d		08 03	07 47						08 23					08 43		08 13				09 03	08 46	
Northampton	d			08 45								08 55					09 16			09 25		09 45	
Long Buckby	d											09 06					09 27			09 36			
Rugby	d		08 51	09 04								09 17					09 38			09 47	09 51	10 04	
Coventry	a		09 02							09 22		09 29			09 42		09 49			09 58	10 02		
	d		09 02						09 11	09 22	09 27	09 30			09 42		09 50			10 11	10 02		
Canley	d								09 14			09 33								10 14			
Tile Hill	d								09 18			09 37					09 55			10 18			
Berkswell	d								09 21			09 40								10 21			
Hampton-in-Arden	d								09 25								10 01			10 25			
Birmingham International ✈	a		09 13						09 28	09 33	09 37	09 45			09 53		10 04			10 28	10 13		
	d	09 09	09 13			09 17			09 29	09 33	09 38	09 46			09 53		10 05		10 09	10 29	10 13		
Marston Green	d								09 32			09 49					10 08			10 32			
Lea Hall	d					09 22						09 52											
Stechford	d					09 25						09 55											
Adderley Park	d					09 28																	
Birmingham New Street	a	09 20	09 27			09 33			09 42	09 45	09 48	10 01			10 08		10 17		10 19	10 42	10 27		
	d	09 24			09 31		09 36	09 38		09 49	09 57		10 01	10 05		10 08		10 20	10 24				10 31
Smethwick Rolfe Street	d							09 44								10 14							
Smethwick Galton Bridge ■	d	09 30						09 46					10 08			10 16			10 30				
Sandwell & Dudley	d							09 49		09 58				10 13		10 19							
Dudley Port	d							09 52								10 22							
Tipton	d							09 54								10 24							
Coseley	d						09 46	09 57								10 27							
Wolverhampton ■	a	09 43			09 48		09 53	10 03		10 11	10 14		10 19	10 24		10 33		10 37	10 42				10 48
	d				09 49		09 53				10 15		10 19										10 49
Penkridge	d						10 03																
Stafford	a			09 53	10 00		10 09				10 29		10 34									10 53	11 00

until 29 June

Northampton - Coventry - Birmingham - Wolverhampton - Stafford

Network Diagram - see first Page of Table 67

		LM	LM ◇1	LM	VT ◇1 ⊠		XC ◇1 工	LM 1	LM ◇1	LM	LM	VT ◇1 ⊡	LM ◇1	AW ◇ 工	LM 1		VT ◇1 ⊠	XC ◇1 工	LM	LM ◇1	LM	VT ◇1 ⊠	XC ◇1 工		LM ◇1
London Euston 15 ⊖	d				09 23							09 43	09 13				10 03					10 23			09 46
Northampton	d							09 55					10 16		10 25									10 45	10 55
Long Buckby	d							10 06					10 27		10 36										11 06
Rugby	d							10 17					10 38		10 47		10 51							11 04	11 17
Coventry	a				10 22			10 29				10 42	10 49		10 58		11 02					11 22			11 29
	d				10 22		10 27	10 30				10 42	10 50		11 11		11 02					11 22	11 27		11 30
Canley	d							10 33							11 14										11 33
Tile Hill	d							10 37					10 55		11 18										11 37
Berkswell	d							10 40							11 21										11 40
Hampton-in-Arden	d												11 01		11 25										
Birmingham International ✈	a				10 33		10 37	10 45				10 53	11 04		11 28		11 13					11 33	11 37		11 45
	d	10 17			10 33		10 38	10 46				10 53	11 05	11 09	11 29		11 13		11 17			11 33	11 38		11 46
Marston Green	d							10 49					11 08		11 32										11 49
Lea Hall	d	10 21						10 52											11 21						11 52
Stechford	d	10 24						10 55											11 24						11 55
Adderley Park	d	10 27																	11 27						
Birmingham New Street 12	a	10 33			10 45		10 48	11 01				11 06	11 16	11 20	11 42		11 27		11 33			11 45	11 48		12 01
	d		10 36	10 38	10 49		10 57		11 01	11 05	11 08	11 20		11 24				11 31		11 36	11 38	11 49	11 57		
Smethwick Rolfe Street	d			10 44							11 14										11 44				
Smethwick Galton Bridge 7	d			10 46					11 08		11 16			11 30							11 46				
Sandwell & Dudley	d			10 49	10 58					11 13	11 19										11 49	11 58			
Dudley Port	d			10 52							11 22										11 52				
Tipton	d			10 54							11 24										11 54				
Coseley	d		10 46	10 57							11 27									11 46	11 57				
Wolverhampton 7 🚢	a		10 53	11 03	11 11		11 14		11 19	11 24	11 33	11 37		11 42				11 48		11 53	12 03	12 11	12 14		
	d		10 53				11 15		11 19									11 49		11 53			12 15		
Penkridge	d		11 03																	12 03					
Stafford	a		11 09				11 28		11 34									12 00		12 09			12 29	11 53	

			LM ◇1	LM	VT ◇1 ⊠	LM	LM ◇1	VT ◇1 ⊡	AW ◇ 工	LM 1	VT ◇1 ⊡		XC ◇1 工	LM	LM ◇1	LM	VT ◇1 ⊡	XC ◇1 工		LM ◇1	LM ◇1		LM	VT ◇1 ⊡	LM
London Euston 15 ⊖	d				10 43		10 13				11 03						11 23			10 46				11 43	
Northampton	d						11 16			11 25									11 45	11 55					
Long Buckby	d						11 27			11 36										12 06					
Rugby	d						11 38			11 47	11 51								12 04	12 17					
Coventry	a				11 42		11 49			11 58	12 02						12 22			12 29				12 42	
	d				11 42		11 50			12 11	12 02						12 22	12 27		12 30				12 42	
Canley	d									12 14										12 33					
Tile Hill	d						11 55			12 18										12 37					
Berkswell	d									12 21										12 40					
Hampton-in-Arden	d						12 01			12 25															
Birmingham International ✈	a				11 53		12 04			12 28	12 13						12 33	12 37		12 45				12 53	
	d				11 53		12 05		12 09	12 29	12 13			12 17			12 33	12 38		12 46				12 53	
Marston Green	d						12 08			12 32										12 49					
Lea Hall	d													12 21						12 52					
Stechford	d													12 24						12 55					
Adderley Park	d													12 27											
Birmingham New Street 12	a				12 08		12 16		12 20	12 42	12 27			12 33			12 45	12 48		13 01				13 08	
	d		12 01	12 05		12 08		12 20	12 24				12 31		12 36	12 38	12 49	12 57			13 01		13 05		13 08
Smethwick Rolfe Street	d					12 14										12 44									13 14
Smethwick Galton Bridge 7	d		12 08			12 16			12 30							12 46					13 08				13 16
Sandwell & Dudley	d			12 13		12 19										12 49	12 58						13 13		13 19
Dudley Port	d					12 22										12 52									13 22
Tipton	d					12 24										12 54									13 24
Coseley	d					12 27									12 46	12 57									13 27
Wolverhampton 7 🚢	a		12 19	12 24		12 33		12 37	12 42				12 48		12 53	13 03	13 11	13 14			13 19		13 24		13 33
	d		12 19										12 49		12 53			13 15			13 19				
Penkridge	d														13 03										
Stafford	a		12 34										13 00		13 09			13 29	12 53		13 34				

until 29 June

Northampton - Coventry - Birmingham - Wolverhampton - Stafford

Network Diagram - see first Page of Table 67

		LM ◇1	VT ◇1 ⊡	AW ◇ 工	LM 1	VT ◇1 ⊡	XC ◇1 工		LM	LM ◇1	LM	VT ◇1 ⊡	XC ◇1 工		LM ◇1	LM ◇1	LM		VT ◇1 ⊡	LM	LM ◇1	VT ◇1 ⊡	AW ◇ 工	LM 1	VT ◇1 ⊡
London Euston 15 ⊖	d	11 13				12 03						12 23			11 46				12 43		12 13				13 03
Northampton	d	12 16			12 25									12 45	12 55						13 16			13 25	
Long Buckby	d	12 27			12 36										13 06						13 27			13 36	
Rugby	d	12 38			12 47	12 51								13 04	13 17						13 38			13 47	13 51
Coventry	a	12 49			12 58	13 02						13 22			13 29				13 42		13 49			13 58	14 02
	d	12 50			13 11	13 02						13 22	13 27		13 30				13 42		13 50			14 11	14 02
Canley	d				13 14										13 33									14 14	
Tile Hill	d	12 55			13 18										13 37						13 55			14 18	
Berkswell	d				13 21										13 40									14 21	
Hampton-in-Arden	d	13 01			13 25																14 01			14 25	
Birmingham International ✈	a	13 04			13 28	13 13						13 33	13 37		13 45				13 53		14 04			14 28	14 13
	d	13 05		13 09	13 29	13 13			13 17			13 33	13 38		13 46				13 53		14 05		14 09	14 29	14 13
Marston Green	d	13 08			13 32										13 49						14 08			14 32	
Lea Hall	d								13 21						13 52										
Stechford	d								13 24						13 55										
Adderley Park	d								13 27																
Birmingham New Street 12	a	13 16		13 22	13 42	13 27			13 33			13 45	13 48		14 01				14 08		14 16		14 20	14 42	14 27
	d		13 20	13 24			13 31			13 36	13 38	13 49	13 57			14 01	14 05			14 08		14 20	14 24		
Smethwick Rolfe Street	d										13 44									14 14					
Smethwick Galton Bridge 7	d			13 30							13 46					14 08				14 16			14 30		
Sandwell & Dudley	d										13 49	13 58					14 13			14 19					
Dudley Port	d										13 52									14 22					
Tipton	d										13 54									14 24					
Coseley	d									13 46	13 57									14 27					
Wolverhampton 7 🚢	a		13 37	13 42			13 48			13 53	14 03	14 11	14 14			14 19	14 24			14 33		14 37	14 42		
	d						13 49			13 53			14 15			14 19									
Penkridge	d									14 03															
Stafford	a						14 00			14 09			14 29	13 53		14 34									

		XC ◇1 工	LM		LM ◇1	LM	VT ◇1 ⊡	XC ◇1 工		LM ◇1	LM ◇1	LM	VT ◇1 ⊡		LM	LM ◇1	VT ◇1 ⊡	AW ◇ 工	LM 1	VT ◇1 ⊡	LM ◇1	XC ◇1 工	LM		LM ◇1
London Euston 15 ⊖	d						13 23			12 46			13 43			13 13				14 03	13 46				
Northampton	d								13 45	13 55						14 16			14 25		14 45				
Long Buckby	d									14 06						14 27			14 36						
Rugby	d								14 04	14 17						14 38			14 47	14 51	15 04				
Coventry	a						14 22			14 29			14 42			14 49			14 58	15 02					
	d						14 22	14 27		14 30			14 42			14 50			15 11	15 02					
Canley	d									14 33									15 14						
Tile Hill	d									14 37						14 55			15 18						
Berkswell	d									14 40									15 21						
Hampton-in-Arden	d															15 01			15 25						
Birmingham International ✈	a						14 33	14 37		14 45			14 53			15 04			15 28	15 13					
	d		14 17				14 33	14 38		14 46			14 53			15 05		15 09	15 29	15 13			15 17		
Marston Green	d									14 49						15 08			15 32						
Lea Hall	d		14 21							14 52													15 21		
Stechford	d		14 24							14 55													15 24		
Adderley Park	d		14 27																				15 27		
Birmingham New Street 12	a		14 33				14 45	14 48		15 01			15 08			15 15		15 19	15 42	15 27			15 33		
	d	14 31			14 36	14 38	14 49	14 57			15 01	15 05			15 08		15 20	15 26				15 31			15 36
Smethwick Rolfe Street	d					14 44									15 14										
Smethwick Galton Bridge 7	d					14 46					15 08				15 16			15 32							
Sandwell & Dudley	d					14 49	14 58					15 13			15 19										
Dudley Port	d					14 52									15 22										
Tipton	d					14 54									15 24										
Coseley	d				14 46	14 57									15 27										15 46
Wolverhampton 7 🚢	a	14 48			14 53	15 03	15 11	15 14			15 19	15 24			15 33		15 37	15 44				15 49			15 53
	d	14 49			14 53			15 15			15 19											15 50			15 53
Penkridge	d				15 03																				16 03
Stafford	a	15 00			15 09			15 29	14 53		15 34										15 53	16 01			16 09

Northampton - Coventry - Birmingham - Wolverhampton - Stafford

Network Diagram - see first Page of Table 67

		LM	VT	XC	LM	LM	LM	LM	VT	LM	AW	VT	XC	LM	LM	LM	LM	LM	VT	XC	LM	LM	LM
			◇1 ⊏	◇1 ⌶	◇1	1			■ 1 ⊏	◇1	■ ⌶	◇1 ⊏	◇1 ⌶		◇1		1	◇1	◇1 ⊏	◇1 ⌶	◇1	1	
London Euston 15 ⊖	d		14 23						14 43	14 13		15 03						14 46	15 23				
Northampton	d					14 55				15 16							15 35	15 45				15 55	
Long Buckby	d					15 06				15 27							15 46					16 06	
Rugby	d					15 17				15 38		15 51					15 59	16 04				16 17	
Coventry	a		15 22			15 29			15 42	15 49		16 02					16 10		16 22			16 29	
	d		15 22	15 27		15 30			15 42	15 50		16 02					16 11		16 22	16 27		16 30	
Canley	d					15 33											16 14					16 33	
Tile Hill	d					15 37				15 55							16 18					16 37	
Berkswell	d					15 40											16 21					16 40	
Hampton-in-Arden	d									16 01							16 25						
Birmingham International ✈	a		15 33	15 37		15 45			15 53	16 04		16 13					16 28		16 33	16 37		16 45	
	d		15 33	15 38		15 46			15 53	16 05	16 09	16 13		16 17			16 29		16 33	16 38		16 46	
Marston Green	d					15 49				16 08							16 32					16 49	
Lea Hall	d					15 52								16 21								16 52	
Stechford	d					15 55								16 24								16 55	
Adderley Park	d													16 27									
Birmingham New Street 12	a		15 45	15 48		16 02			16 06	16 16	16 20	16 27		16 33			16 42		16 45	16 48		17 02	
	d	15 38	15 49	15 57	16 01		16 05	16 08	16 20		16 24		16 31		16 36	16 38			16 49	16 57	17 01		17 05
Smethwick Rolfe Street	d	15 44						16 14								16 44							
Smethwick Galton Bridge 7	d	15 46			16 08			16 16			16 30					16 46					17 08		
Sandwell & Dudley	d	15 49	15 58				16 13	16 19								16 49			16 58				17 13
Dudley Port	d	15 52						16 22								16 53							
Tipton	d	15 54						16 24								16 55							
Coseley	d	15 57						16 27							16 46	16 58							
Wolverhampton 7 ⇌	a	16 03	16 11	16 14	16 19		16 24	16 33	16 37		16 42		16 48		16 53	17 04			17 11	17 14	17 19		17 24
	d			16 15	16 19								16 49		16 53					17 15	17 19		
Penkridge	d														17 03						17 29		
Stafford	a			16 30	16 34								17 00		17 09			16 54		17 29	17 35		

		VT	LM	LM	VT	AW	VT	XC	LM	LM	LM	LM	LM	VT	XC	LM		LM	LM	VT	LM	LM	VT
		◇1 ⊏		◇1	■ 1 ⊏	◇ ⌶	◇1 ⊏	◇1 ⌶		◇1		1		◇1 ⊏	◇1 ⌶	◇1		◇1		◇1 ⊏		◇1	◇1 ⊏
London Euston 15 ⊖	d	15 43		15 13			16 03							16 23		15 46				16 43		15 54	
Northampton	d			16 16												16 45	16 55					17 16	
Long Buckby	d			16 27													17 06					17 27	
Rugby	d			16 38			16 51									17 04	17 17					17 38	
Coventry	a	16 42		16 49			17 02							17 22			17 29			17 42		17 49	
	d	16 42		16 50			17 02					17 11		17 22	17 27		17 30			17 42		17 50	
Canley	d											17 14					17 33						
Tile Hill	d			16 55								17 18					17 37					17 55	
Berkswell	d											17 21					17 40						
Hampton-in-Arden	d			17 01								17 25										18 01	
Birmingham International ✈	a	16 53		17 04			17 13					17 28		17 33	17 37		17 45			17 53		18 04	
	d	16 53		17 05		17 09	17 13		17 17			17 29		17 33	17 38		17 46			17 53		18 05	
Marston Green	d			17 08								17 32					17 49					18 08	
Lea Hall	d								17 21								17 52						
Stechford	d								17 24								17 55						
Adderley Park	d								17 27														
Birmingham New Street 12	a	17 08		17 16		17 19	17 27		17 33			17 42		17 45	17 48		18 01			18 08		18 17	
	d		17 08		17 20	17 26		17 31		17 36	17 38		17 46	17 49	17 57			18 01	18 05		18 08		18 20
Smethwick Rolfe Street	d		17 14								17 44										18 14		
Smethwick Galton Bridge 7	d		17 16			17 32					17 46							18 08			18 16		
Sandwell & Dudley	d		17 19								17 49			17 58					18 13		18 19		
Dudley Port	d		17 22								17 52		17 56								18 22		
Tipton	d		17 24								17 54		17 58								18 24		
Coseley	d		17 27							17 46	17 57										18 27		
Wolverhampton 7 ⇌	a		17 33		17 37	17 44		17 49		17 53	18 03		18 06	18 11	18 14			18 19	18 24		18 33		18 37
	d							17 50		17 53					18 15			18 19					
Penkridge	d									18 02								18 29					
Stafford	a							18 01		18 09					18 29	18 01		18 35					

		AW	VT	XC	LM	LM	LM	LM	VT	XC	LM	LM	LM	VT	LM	LM	VT	AW	VT	LM	XC	LM
		◇ ⌶	◇1 ⊠	◇1 ⌶		◇1		1	◇1 ⊠	◇1 ⌶	◇1	◇1		◇1 ⊠		◇1	◇1 ⊏	◇ ⌶	◇1 ⊠	1	◇1 ⌶	
London Euston 15 ⊖	d		17 03						17 23		16 48			17 43		17 13			18 03	17 24		
Northampton	d										17 55					18 16				18 40		
Long Buckby	d										18 06					18 27				18 51		
Rugby	d		17 51								18 17					18 38			18 51	19a03		
Coventry	a		18 02						18 22		18 29			18 42		18 49			19 02			
	d		18 02					18 11	18 22	18 27	18 30			18 42		18 50			19 02			
Canley	d							18 14			18 33											
Tile Hill	d							18 18			18 37					18 55						
Berkswell	d							18 21			18 40											
Hampton-in-Arden	d							18 25								19 01						
Birmingham International ✈	a		18 13					18 28	18 33	18 37	18 45			18 53		19 04			19 13			
	d	18 09	18 13		18 17			18 29	18 33	18 38	18 46			18 53		19 05		19 09	19 13			19 17
Marston Green	d							18 32			18 49					19 08						
Lea Hall	d				18 21						18 52											19 21
Stechford	d				18 24						18 55											19 24
Adderley Park	d				18 27																	19 27
Birmingham New Street 12	a	18 20	18 27		18 33			18 42	18 45	18 48	19 01			19 08		19 17		19 20	19 27			19 33
	d	18 24		18 31		18 36	18 38		18 49	18 57		19 01	19 05		19 08		19 20	19 24			19 31	
Smethwick Rolfe Street	d						18 44								19 14							
Smethwick Galton Bridge 7	d	18 30					18 46					19 08			19 16			19 30				
Sandwell & Dudley	d						18 49		18 58				19 13		19 19							
Dudley Port	d						18 52								19 22							
Tipton	d						18 54								19 24							
Coseley	d					18 46	18 57								19 27							
Wolverhampton 7 ⇌	a	18 42		18 48		18 53	19 03		19 11	19 14		19 19	19 24		19 33		19 37	19 42			19 48	
	d			18 49		18 53				19 15		19 19									19 49	
Penkridge	d					19 03						19 29										
Stafford	a			19 00		19 09				19 27		19 36									20 00	

		LM	LM	LM	VT	XC	LM	LM	LM	VT	LM	AW	VT	LM	XC	LM	LM	LM	LM	VT	XC	LM	LM
		◇1		1	◇1 ⊠	◇1 A ⌶	1			◇1 ⊠	◇1 B	◇	■ 1 ⊏	◇1	◇1		◇1		1	■ 1 ⊏	◇1 A ⌶	◇1	
London Euston 15 ⊖	d				18 23		17 46			18 43	18 13		19 03	18 29						19 23		18 49	
Northampton	d						18 55				19 16			19 45								19 55	
Long Buckby	d						19 06				19 27											20 06	
Rugby	d						19 17				19 38		19 51	20a04								20 17	
Coventry	a				19 22		19 29			19 42	19 49		20 02							20 22		20 29	
	d			19 11	19 22	19 27	19 30			19 42	19 50		20 02						20 11	20 22	20 27	20 30	
Canley	d			19 14			19 33												20 14			20 33	
Tile Hill	d			19 18			19 37				19 55								20 18			20 37	
Berkswell	d			19 21			19 40												20 21			20 40	
Hampton-in-Arden	d			19 25							20 01								20 25				
Birmingham International ✈	a			19 28	19 33	19 37	19 45			19 53	20 04		20 13						20 28	20 33	20 37	20 45	
	d			19 29	19 33	19 38	19 46			19 53	20 05	20 09	20 13			20 17			20 29	20 33	20 38	20 46	
Marston Green	d			19 32			19 49				20 08								20 32			20 49	
Lea Hall	d						19 52									20 21						20 52	
Stechford	d						19 55									20 24						20 55	
Adderley Park	d															20 27							
Birmingham New Street 12	a			19 42	19 45	19 48	20 01			20 06	20 16	20 20	20 27			20 33			20 42	20 45	20 48	21 01	
	d	19 36	19 38		19 50	19 57		20 05	20 08	20 20		20 24			20 31		20 36	20 38		20 50	20 57		21 05
Smethwick Rolfe Street	d		19 44						20 14									20 44					
Smethwick Galton Bridge 7	d		19 46						20 16			20 30						20 46					
Sandwell & Dudley	d		19 49		19 59			20 13	20 19									20 49		20 59			21 13
Dudley Port	d		19 52						20 22									20 52					
Tipton	d		19 54						20 24									20 54					
Coseley	d	19 46	19 57						20 27								20 46	20 57					
Wolverhampton 7 ⇌	a	19 53	20 03		20 12	20 14		20 24	20 33	20 36		20 42			20 48		20 53	21 04		21 12	21 14		21 24
	d	19 53				20 16				20 36							20 53				21 16		
Penkridge	d	20 03															21 03						
Stafford	a	20 09				20 29				20 49							21 09				21 31		

A ⌶ to Birmingham New Street

B ◇ from Coventry

Table 68

Mondays to Fridays
until 29 June

Northampton - Coventry - Birmingham - Wolverhampton - Stafford

Network Diagram - see first Page of Table 67

		LM	VT		LM	VT	AW	VT	LM	LM	LM	LM	VT		XC	LM	LM	VT	LM	LM	XC	VT	LM		LM
			◇■		◇■	◇■	◇	◇■		◇■		■	◇■		◇■	◇■		◇■	◇■		◇■	◇■	◇■		
			☕			☕		☕					☕					☕				☕			
London Euston ■ ⊖	d		19 43		19 13			20 03					20 23			19 46		20 43	19 54			21 03			
Northampton	d				20 16											20 55			21 16						
Long Buckby	d				20 27											21 06			21 27						
Rugby	d				20 38			20 51								21 17			21 38			21 57			
Coventry	a		20 42		20 49			21 02					21 22			21 29		21 42	21 49			22 06			
	d		20 42		20 50			21 02				21 11	21 22		21 27	21 30		21 42	21 50			22 07			
Canley	d											21 14				21 33									
Tile Hill	d				20 55							21 18				21 37			21 55						
Berkswell	d											21 21				21 40									
Hampton-in-Arden	d				21 01							21 25							22 01						
Birmingham International ✈	a		20 53		21 04			21 13				21 28	21 33		21 37	21 45		21 53	22 04			22 18			
	d		20 53		21 05		21 09	21 13	21 17			21 29	21 33		21 38	21 46		21 53	22 05			22 18			22 22
Marston Green	d				21 08							21 32				21 49			22 08						
Lea Hall	d								21 21							21 52									22 26
Stechford	d								21 24							21 55									22 29
Adderley Park	d								21 27																22 32
Birmingham New Street ■	a		21 06		21 16		21 19	21 25	21 33			21 42	21 46		21 48	22 01		22 06	22 17			22 29			22 38
	d	21 08	21 13			21 20	21 24	21 28		21 36	21 38		21 50		21 57		22 08	22 13		22 21	22 30	22 32	22 36		
Smethwick Rolfe Street	d	21 14									21 44						22 14								
Smethwick Galton Bridge ■	d	21 16					21 30				21 46						22 16						22 43		
Sandwell & Dudley	d	21 19	21 24								21 49		21 59				22 19	22 24		22 29		22 41			
Dudley Port	d	21 22									21 52						22 22								
Tipton	d	21 24									21 54						22 24								
Coseley	d	21 27								21 46	21 57						22 27						22 50		
Wolverhampton ■ 🚌	a	21 33	21 38			21 40	21 42	21 56		21 53	22 03		22 12		22 14		22 33	22 38		22 41	22 47	22 56	22 57		
	d					21 41				21 53					22 16						22 48		22 57		
Penkridge	d									22 03													23 07		
Stafford	a					21 53				22 09					22 29						23 00		23 13		

		LM	LM	XC	AW	LM	LM	VT	LM		AW MW FO	AW TThO	XC	LM	VT	VT FX	VT FO
			■	◇■	◇	◇■	◇■	◇■	◇■				◇■	◇■	◇■	◇■	◇■
				A									A				
								☕							☕	☕	☕
London Euston ■ ⊖	d					20 46		21 43	21 13					21 46	22 30	23 30	23 30
Northampton	d					21 55			22 16					22 55			
Long Buckby	d					22 06			22 27					23 06			
Rugby	d					22 17			22 38					23 17	00 01	01 00	01 05
Coventry	a					22 29		22 46	22 49					23 29	00 10	01 13	01 18
	d		22 11	22 24		22 30		22 46	22 50				23 27	23 30	00 10	01 13	01 18
Canley	d		22 14			22 33								23 33			
Tile Hill	d		22 18			22 37			22 55					23 37			
Berkswell	d		22 21			22 40								23 40			
Hampton-in-Arden	d		22 25						23 01					23 44			
Birmingham International ✈	a		22 28	22 33		22 45		23 00	23 06				23 36	23 47	00 21	01 24	01 29
	d		22 29	22 34		22 46		23 01	23 07				23 37	23 48	00 21	01 24	01 29
Marston Green	d		22 32			22 49			23 10					23 51			
Lea Hall	d					22 52								23 54			
Stechford	d					22 55								23 57			
Adderley Park	d																
Birmingham New Street ■	a		22 42	22 45		23 02		23 16	23 19				23 57	00 04	00 32	01 36	01 41
	d	22 38			22 55		23 09	23 20			23 32	23 32			00 35	01 37	01 42
Smethwick Rolfe Street	d	22 44					23 15										
Smethwick Galton Bridge ■	d	22 46					23 17										
Sandwell & Dudley	d	22 49					23 20	23 34									
Dudley Port	d	22 52					23 24										
Tipton	d	22 54					23 26										
Coseley	d	22 57					23 29										
Wolverhampton ■ 🚌	a	23 03			23 11		23 35	23 47			00 01	00 02			01 03	02 07	02 10
	d				23 13		23 36										
Penkridge	d						23 46										
Stafford	a				23 30		23 52										

A until 22 June

Table 68

Mondays to Fridays
2 July to 14 September

Northampton - Coventry - Birmingham - Wolverhampton - Stafford

Network Diagram - see first Page of Table 67

		AW TThO	AW WFO	LM MO	LM MX	VT MO	VT MO	LM MO	XC MX	VT MX		VT MO	VT MX	VT	VT	VT	VT	LM	XC	LM		LM	LM	VT	XC
				◇■	◇■	◇■	◇■	■		◇■		◇■	◇■	◇■	◇■	■	◇■		◇■	■			◇■	◇■	◇■
												B	C	D	E	F									
						☕	☕		🚌	☕		☕	☕	☕	☕	☕	⊠							⊠	🍴
London Euston ■ ⊖	d			21p28	21p46	21p55	22p25	22p00		22p30		23p25	23p30	00 10	00 10	01 10									
Northampton	d			22p51	22p55			23p32															05 16		
Long Buckby	d			23p02	23p06			23p43															05 27		
Rugby	d			23p13	23p17	23p21	23p46	23p54		00 01		00s46	01 00	01s02	01s06	01s58							05 38		
Coventry	a			23p25	23p29	23p31	23p55	00 05		00 10		00s57	01 13	01s13	01s17	02s09							05 49		
	d			23p35	23p30	23p31	23p56			00 10			01 13										05 50		
Canley	d			23p38	23p33																				
Tile Hill	d			23p42	23p37																		05 55		
Berkswell	d			23p45	23p40																				
Hampton-in-Arden	d			23p49	23p44																		06 01		
Birmingham International ✈	a			23p52	23p47	23p42	00 06		00 10	00 21		01s08	01 24	01s24	01s28	02s20							06 04		
	d			23p53	23p48	23p42	00 07			00 21			01 24										06 05		
Marston Green	d			23p56	23p51																		06 08		
Lea Hall	d				23p54																				
Stechford	d				23p57																				
Adderley Park	d																								
Birmingham New Street ■	a			00 04	00 04	23p54	00 19			00 32		01s21	01 36	01s39	01s43	02s34							06 16		
	d	23p32	23p32			23p57	00 22			00 35			01 37				05 30	05 51	05 57	06 01		06 06		06 19	06 22
Smethwick Rolfe Street	d																					06 12			
Smethwick Galton Bridge ■	d																			06 08		06 14			
Sandwell & Dudley	d																	05 59				06 17			
Dudley Port	d																					06 20			
Tipton	d																					06 22			
Coseley	d																					06 25			
Wolverhampton ■ 🚌	a	00 01	00 02			00 15	00 41			01 03		01 53	02 07	01 57	02 01	02 52	05 47	06 09	06 14	06 19		06 31		06 35	06 39
	d																05 48		06 16	06 19					06 40
Penkridge	d																			06 29					
Stafford	a																06 01		06 29	06 35					06 53

		LM	AW	LM	LM	LM		LM	XC	LM	LM	LM	LM	VT	AW	VT		LM	LM	XC	LM	LM	VT	XC	LM
		◇■	◇		◇■			■	◇■	◇■	◇■		◇■	◇■	◇	◇■		◇■		◇■	◇■		◇■	◇■	◇■
			🍴						🍴					⊠	🍴	⊠				🍴			⊠	🍴	
London Euston ■ ⊖	d															06 03							06 23		
Northampton	d	05 42								05 55			06 16					06 41							
Long Buckby	d									06 06			06 27												
Rugby	d	06 05								06 17			06 38			06 51		07 01							
Coventry	a									06 29			06 49			07 02							07 22		
	d							06 10		06 30			06 50			07 02						07 07	07 22	07 27	
Canley	d							06 13		06 33												07 09			
Tile Hill	d							06 17		06 37			06 55									07 13			
Berkswell	d							06 20		06 40												07 16			
Hampton-in-Arden	d							06 24					07 01									07 20			
Birmingham International ✈	a							06 27		06 45			07 04			07 13						07 23	07 33	07 37	
	d			06 17				06 28		06 46			07 05		07 09	07 13					07 17	07 24	07 33	07 38	
Marston Green	d							06 31		06 49			07 08									07 27			
Lea Hall	d			06 22						06 52											07 22				
Stechford	d			06 25						06 55											07 25				
Adderley Park	d			06 28																	07 28				
Birmingham New Street ■	a			06 33				06 39		07 01			07 16		07 20	07 27					07 32	07 36	07 45	07 48	
	d		06 24		06 36	06 38			06 57		07 01	07 08		07 20	07 24				07 27	07 31	07 36	07 38	07 49	07 57	08 01
Smethwick Rolfe Street	d					06 44						07 14										07 44			
Smethwick Galton Bridge ■	d		06 30			06 46					07 08	07 16			07 30							07 46			08 08
Sandwell & Dudley	d					06 49						07 19										07 49	07 58		
Dudley Port	d					06 52						07 22										07 52			
Tipton	d					06 54						07 24										07 54			
Coseley	d					06 57						07 27									07 46	07 57			
Wolverhampton ■ 🚌	a		06 42		06 52	07 03			07 14		07 19	07 33		07 36	07 41				07 45	07 48	07 53	08 03	08 11	08 14	08 19
	d				06 53				07 15		07 19									07 49	07 53			08 15	08 19
Penkridge	d										07 29										08 03				08 29
Stafford	a	06 58			07 08				07 29		07 36							07 53		08 00	08 09			08 29	08 35

B from 2 July until 23 July, 20 August, 27 August
C not from 31 July until 10 August, from 30 August until 7 September
D MX from 31 July until 7 September, not from 14 August until 29 August
E 30 July, 6 August, 13 August, 3 September, 10 September
F from 30 July until 10 September, not from 14 August until 29 August

Northampton - Coventry - Birmingham - Wolverhampton - Stafford

Network Diagram - see first Page of Table 67

Station		LM		LM	VT	LM	LM	VT	AW	VT	LM	XC	
		◇■			◇■ ⊠		◇■	◇■ ⊠	◇ ⊤	◇■ ⊠	◇■	◇■ ⊤	
London Euston 15 ⊖	d	05 30			06 43					07 03	06 24		
Northampton	d	06 55					07 16				07 45		
Long Buckby	d	07 06					07 27						
Rugby	d	07 17					07 38			07 51	08 04		
Coventry	a	07 29			07 42		07 49			08 02			
	d	07 30			07 42		07 50			08 02			
Canley	d	07 33											
Tile Hill	d	07 37					07 55						
Berkswell	d	07 40											
Hampton-in-Arden	d						08 01						
Birmingham International ✈	a	07 45			07 53		08 04			08 12			
	d	07 46			07 53		08 05		08 09	08 13			
Marston Green	d	07 49					08 08						
Lea Hall	d	07 52											
Stechford	d	07 55											
Adderley Park	d	07 58											
Birmingham New Street 12	a	08 03			08 08		08 16		08 20	08 27			
	d			08 05		08 08		08 20	08 24			08 31	
Smethwick Rolfe Street	d					08 14							
Smethwick Galton Bridge 7	d					08 16			08 30				
Sandwell & Dudley	d			08 13		08 19							
Dudley Port	d					08 22							
Tipton	d					08 24							
Coseley	d					08 27							
Wolverhampton 7 ⇌	a			08 24		08 33		08 37	08 42			08 48	
	d											08 49	
Penkridge	d												
Stafford	a										08 53	09 00	

Station		LM	LM	LM	LM	VT	XC	LM	LM	LM		LM	LM
			◇■		■	◇■ ⊠	◇■ ⊤	◇■	◇■				◇■
London Euston 15 ⊖	d					07 23							07 13
Northampton	d							07 55					08 16
Long Buckby	d							08 06					08 27
Rugby	d							08 17					08 38
Coventry	a					08 22		08 29					08 49
	d				08 11	08 22	08 27	08 30					08 50
Canley	d				08 14			08 33					
Tile Hill	d				08 18			08 37					08 55
Berkswell	d				08 21			08 40					
Hampton-in-Arden	d				08 25								09 01
Birmingham International ✈	a				08 28	08 33	08 37	08 45					09 04
	d	08 17			08 29	08 33	08 38	08 46					09 05
Marston Green	d	08 20			08 32			08 49					09 08
Lea Hall	d	08 23						08 52					
Stechford	d	08 26						08 55					
Adderley Park	d	08 29											
Birmingham New Street 12	a	08 33			08 42	08 45	08 48	09 01					09 17
	d		08 36	08 38		08 49	08 57		09 01	09 05		09 08	
Smethwick Rolfe Street	d			08 44								09 14	
Smethwick Galton Bridge 7	d			08 46					09 08			09 16	
Sandwell & Dudley	d			08 49		08 58				09 13		09 19	
Dudley Port	d			08 52								09 22	
Tipton	d			08 54								09 24	
Coseley	d		08 46	08 57								09 27	
Wolverhampton 7 ⇌	a		08 53	09 03		09 11	09 14		09 19	09 24		09 33	
	d		08 53				09 15		09 19				
Penkridge	d		09 03										
Stafford	a		09 09				09 29		09 34				

Station		VT	AW	VT	VT	LM	XC	LM		LM	LM	LM	VT
		◇■ ⊠	◇ ⊤	◇■ A ⊠	◇■ B ⊠	◇■	◇■ ⊤			◇■		■	◇■ ⊠
London Euston 15 ⊖	d			08 03	08 03	07 47							08 23
Northampton	d					08 45							
Long Buckby	d												
Rugby	d			08 51	08 51	09 04							
Coventry	a			09 02	09 02								09 22
	d			09 02	09 02							09 11	09 22
Canley	d											09 14	
Tile Hill	d											09 18	
Berkswell	d											09 21	
Hampton-in-Arden	d											09 25	
Birmingham International ✈	a			09 12	09 13							09 28	09 33
	d		09 09	09 13	09 13			09 17				09 29	09 33
Marston Green	d											09 32	
Lea Hall	d							09 22					
Stechford	d							09 25					
Adderley Park	d							09 28					
Birmingham New Street 12	a		09 20	09 27	09 27			09 33				09 42	09 45
	d	09 20	09 24				09 31			09 36	09 38		09 49
Smethwick Rolfe Street	d										09 44		
Smethwick Galton Bridge 7	d		09 30								09 46		
Sandwell & Dudley	d										09 49		09 58
Dudley Port	d										09 52		
Tipton	d										09 54		
Coseley	d									09 46	09 57		
Wolverhampton 7 ⇌	a	09 37	09 43				09 48			09 53	10 03		10 11
	d						09 49			09 53			
Penkridge	d									10 03			
Stafford	a					09 53	10 00			10 09			

Station		XC	LM	LM	LM	LM		VT	LM	AW	LM	VT	LM
		◇■ ⊤	◇■	◇■				◇■ ⊠	◇■	◇ ⊤	■	◇■ ⊠	◇■
London Euston 15 ⊖	d							08 43	08 13			09 03	08 46
Northampton	d		08 55						09 16		09 25		09 45
Long Buckby	d		09 06						09 27		09 36		
Rugby	d		09 17						09 38		09 47	09 51	10 04
Coventry	a		09 29					09 42	09 49		09 58	10 02	
	d	09 27	09 30					09 42	09 50		10 11	10 02	
Canley	d		09 33								10 14		
Tile Hill	d		09 37						09 55		10 18		
Berkswell	d		09 40								10 21		
Hampton-in-Arden	d								10 01		10 25		
Birmingham International ✈	a	09 37	09 45					09 53	10 04		10 28	10 13	
	d	09 38	09 46					09 53	10 05	10 09	10 29	10 13	
Marston Green	d		09 49						10 08		10 32		
Lea Hall	d		09 52										
Stechford	d		09 55										
Adderley Park	d												
Birmingham New Street 12	a	09 48	10 01					10 08	10 17	10 19	10 42	10 27	
	d	09 57		10 01	10 05	10 08		10 20		10 24			
Smethwick Rolfe Street	d					10 14							
Smethwick Galton Bridge 7	d			10 08		10 16				10 30			
Sandwell & Dudley	d				10 13	10 19							
Dudley Port	d					10 22							
Tipton	d					10 24							
Coseley	d					10 27							
Wolverhampton 7 ⇌	a	10 14		10 19	10 24	10 33		10 37		10 42			
	d	10 15		10 19									
Penkridge	d												
Stafford	a	10 29		10 34									10 53

A not from 27 July until 10 August, from 29 August until 7 September

B from 27 July until 7 September, not from 13 August until 28 August

Northampton - Coventry - Birmingham - Wolverhampton - Stafford

Network Diagram - see first Page of Table 67

Station		XC	LM	LM		LM	VT	XC	LM	LM	LM	VT	LM
		◇■ ⊤		◇■			◇■ ⊠	◇■ ⊤	■	◇■		◇■ ⊠	
London Euston 15 ⊖	d						09 23					09 43	
Northampton	d								09 55				
Long Buckby	d								10 06				
Rugby	d								10 17				
Coventry	a						10 22		10 29			10 42	
	d						10 22	10 27	10 30			10 42	
Canley	d								10 33				
Tile Hill	d								10 37				
Berkswell	d								10 40				
Hampton-in-Arden	d												
Birmingham International ✈	a						10 33	10 37	10 45			10 53	
	d		10 17				10 33	10 38	10 46			10 53	
Marston Green	d								10 49				
Lea Hall	d		10 21						10 52				
Stechford	d		10 24						10 55				
Adderley Park	d		10 27										
Birmingham New Street 12	a		10 33				10 45	10 48	11 01			11 08	
	d	10 31		10 36		10 38	10 49	10 57		11 01	11 05		11 08
Smethwick Rolfe Street	d					10 44							11 14
Smethwick Galton Bridge 7	d					10 46				11 08			11 16
Sandwell & Dudley	d					10 49	10 58				11 13		11 19
Dudley Port	d					10 52							11 22
Tipton	d					10 54							11 24
Coseley	d			10 46		10 57							11 27
Wolverhampton 7 ⇌	a	10 48		10 53		11 03	11 11	11 14		11 19	11 24		11 33
	d	10 49		10 53				11 15		11 19			
Penkridge	d			11 03									
Stafford	a	11 00		11 09				11 28		11 34			

Station		LM		VT	AW	LM	VT	XC	LM	LM	LM	VT	
		◇■		◇■ ⊏	◇ ⊤	■	◇■ ⊠	◇■ ⊤		◇■		◇■ ⊠	
London Euston 15 ⊖	d	09 13					10 03					10 23	
Northampton	d	10 16				10 25							
Long Buckby	d	10 27				10 36							
Rugby	d	10 38				10 47	10 51						
Coventry	a	10 49				10 58	11 02					11 22	
	d	10 50				11 11	11 02					11 22	
Canley	d					11 14							
Tile Hill	d	10 55				11 18							
Berkswell	d					11 21							
Hampton-in-Arden	d	11 01				11 25							
Birmingham International ✈	a	11 04				11 28	11 13					11 33	
	d	11 05			11 09	11 29	11 13		11 17			11 33	
Marston Green	d	11 08				11 32							
Lea Hall	d								11 21				
Stechford	d								11 24				
Adderley Park	d								11 27				
Birmingham New Street 12	a	11 16			11 20	11 42	11 27		11 33			11 45	
	d			11 20	11 24			11 31		11 36	11 38	11 49	
Smethwick Rolfe Street	d										11 44		
Smethwick Galton Bridge 7	d				11 30						11 46		
Sandwell & Dudley	d										11 49	11 58	
Dudley Port	d										11 52		
Tipton	d										11 54		
Coseley	d									11 46	11 57		
Wolverhampton 7 ⇌	a			11 37	11 42			11 48		11 53	12 03	12 11	
	d							11 49		11 53			
Penkridge	d									12 03			
Stafford	a							12 00		12 09			

Station		XC	LM		LM	LM	VT	LM	LM	VT		AW	LM
		◇■ ⊤	◇■		◇■		◇■ ⊠		◇■	◇■ ⊏		◇ ⊤	■
London Euston 15 ⊖	d		09 46				10 43		10 13				
Northampton	d		10 45	10 55					11 16				11 25
Long Buckby	d			11 06					11 27				11 36
Rugby	d		11 04	11 17					11 38				11 47
Coventry	a			11 29			11 42		11 49				11 58
	d	11 27		11 30			11 42		11 50				12 11
Canley	d			11 33									12 14
Tile Hill	d			11 37					11 55				12 18
Berkswell	d			11 40									12 21
Hampton-in-Arden	d								12 01				12 25
Birmingham International ✈	a	11 37		11 45			11 53		12 04				12 28
	d	11 38		11 46			11 53		12 05			12 09	12 29
Marston Green	d			11 49					12 08				12 32
Lea Hall	d			11 52									
Stechford	d			11 55									
Adderley Park	d												
Birmingham New Street 12	a	11 48		12 01			12 08		12 16			12 20	12 42
	d	11 57			12 01	12 05		12 08		12 20		12 24	
Smethwick Rolfe Street	d							12 14					
Smethwick Galton Bridge 7	d				12 08			12 16				12 30	
Sandwell & Dudley	d					12 13		12 19					
Dudley Port	d							12 22					
Tipton	d							12 24					
Coseley	d							12 27					
Wolverhampton 7 ⇌	a	12 14			12 19	12 24		12 33		12 37		12 42	
	d	12 15			12 19								
Penkridge	d												
Stafford	a	12 29	11 53		12 34								

Station		VT	XC	LM	LM	LM	VT	XC		LM		LM	LM
		◇■ ⊏	◇■ ⊤		◇■		◇■ ⊏	◇■ ⊤		◇■		◇■	
London Euston 15 ⊖	d	11 03					11 23			10 46			
Northampton	d									11 45	11 55		
Long Buckby	d										12 06		
Rugby	d	11 51								12 04	12 17		
Coventry	a	12 02					12 22				12 29		
	d	12 02					12 22	12 27			12 30		
Canley	d										12 33		
Tile Hill	d										12 37		
Berkswell	d										12 40		
Hampton-in-Arden	d												
Birmingham International ✈	a	12 13					12 33	12 37			12 45		
	d	12 13		12 17			12 33	12 38			12 46		
Marston Green	d										12 49		
Lea Hall	d			12 21							12 52		
Stechford	d			12 24							12 55		
Adderley Park	d			12 27									
Birmingham New Street 12	a	12 27		12 33			12 45	12 48			13 01		
	d		12 31		12 36	12 38	12 49	12 57				13 01	13 05
Smethwick Rolfe Street	d					12 44							
Smethwick Galton Bridge 7	d					12 46						13 08	
Sandwell & Dudley	d					12 49	12 58						13 13
Dudley Port	d					12 52							
Tipton	d					12 54							
Coseley	d				12 46	12 57							
Wolverhampton 7 ⇌	a		12 48		12 53	13 03	13 11	13 14				13 19	13 24
	d		12 49		12 53			13 15				13 19	
Penkridge	d				13 03								
Stafford	a		13 00		13 09			13 29		12 53		13 34	

Northampton - Coventry - Birmingham - Wolverhampton - Stafford

2 July to 14 September

Network Diagram - see first Page of Table 67

Station		VT	LM	LM	VT	AW		LM	VT	XC	LM	LM	LM	VT	XC	LM			LM	LM	VT	LM	LM	VT	AW
		◇1 ⊡		◇1	◇1 ⊡	◇ ℶ		1	◇1 ⊡	◇1 ℶ		◇1		◇1 ⊡	◇1 ℶ	◇1			◇1		◇1 ⊡		◇1	◇1 ⊡	◇ ℶ
London Euston ⊖	d	11 43		11 13					12 03					12 23		11 46					12 43		12 13		
Northampton	d			12 16				12 25								12 45	12 55						13 16		
Long Buckby	d			12 27				12 36									13 06						13 27		
Rugby	d			12 38				12 47	12 51							13 04	13 17						13 38		
Coventry	a	12 42		12 49				12 58	13 02					13 22			13 29				13 42		13 49		
	d	12 42		12 50				13 11	13 02					13 22	13 27		13 30				13 42		13 50		
Canley	d							13 14									13 33								
Tile Hill	d			12 55				13 18									13 37						13 55		
Berkswell	d							13 21									13 40								
Hampton-in-Arden	d			13 01				13 25															14 01		
Birmingham International ✈	a	12 53		13 04				13 28	13 13					13 33	13 37		13 45				13 53		14 04		
	d	12 53		13 05		13 09		13 29	13 13		13 17			13 33	13 38		13 46				13 53		14 05		14 09
Marston Green	d			13 08				13 32									13 49						14 08		
Lea Hall	d										13 21						13 52								
Stechford	d										13 24						13 55								
Adderley Park	d										13 27														
Birmingham New Street	a	13 08		13 16		13 22		13 42	13 27		13 33			13 45	13 48		14 01				14 08		14 16		14 20
	d		13 08		13 20	13 24				13 31		13 36	13 38	13 49	13 57				14 01	14 05		14 08		14 20	14 24
Smethwick Rolfe Street	d		13 14										13 44									14 14			
Smethwick Galton Bridge	d		13 16			13 30							13 46						14 08			14 16			14 30
Sandwell & Dudley	d		13 19										13 49	13 58						14 13		14 19			
Dudley Port	d		13 22										13 52									14 22			
Tipton	d		13 24										13 54									14 24			
Coseley	d		13 27									13 46	13 57									14 27			
Wolverhampton	a		13 33		13 37	13 42				13 48		13 53	14 03	14 11	14 14				14 19	14 24		14 33		14 37	14 42
	d									13 49		13 53			14 15				14 19						
Penkridge	d											14 03													
Stafford	a									14 00		14 09			14 29	13 53			14 34						

Station		LM	VT		XC	LM	LM	LM	VT	XC	LM		LM		LM	LM	VT	LM	AW	LM	VT	LM	XC		LM
		1	◇1 ⊡		◇1 ℶ		◇1		◇1 ⊡	◇1 ℶ	◇1		◇1				◇1 ⊡	◇1	◇ ℶ	1	◇1 ⊡	◇1	◇1 ℶ		
London Euston ⊖	d		13 03						13 23		12 46						13 43	13 13			14 03	13 46			
Northampton	d	13 25									13 45	13 55						14 16		14 25		14 45			
Long Buckby	d	13 36										14 06						14 27		14 36					
Rugby	d	13 47	13 51								14 04	14 17						14 38		14 47	14 51	15 04			
Coventry	a	13 58	14 02						14 22			14 29					14 42	14 49		14 58	15 02				
	d	14 11	14 02						14 22	14 27		14 30					14 42	14 50		15 11	15 02				
Canley	d	14 14										14 33								15 14					
Tile Hill	d	14 18										14 37						14 55		15 18					
Berkswell	d	14 21										14 40								15 21					
Hampton-in-Arden	d	14 25																15 01		15 25					
Birmingham International ✈	a	14 28	14 13						14 33	14 37		14 45					14 53	15 04		15 28	15 13				
	d	14 29	14 13			14 17			14 33	14 38		14 46					14 53	15 05	15 09	15 29	15 13				15 17
Marston Green	d	14 32										14 49						15 08		15 32					
Lea Hall	d					14 21						14 52													15 21
Stechford	d					14 24						14 55													15 24
Adderley Park	d					14 27																			15 27
Birmingham New Street	a	14 42	14 27			14 33			14 45	14 48		15 01					15 08	15 15	15 19	15 42	15 27				15 33
	d				14 31		14 36	14 38	14 49	14 57			15 01		15 05	15 08	15 20		15 26				15 31		
Smethwick Rolfe Street	d							14 44								15 14									
Smethwick Galton Bridge	d							14 46					15 08			15 16			15 32						
Sandwell & Dudley	d							14 49	14 58						15 13	15 19									
Dudley Port	d							14 52								15 22									
Tipton	d							14 54								15 24									
Coseley	d						14 46	14 57								15 27									
Wolverhampton	a				14 48		14 53	15 03	15 11	15 14			15 19		15 24	15 33	15 37		15 44				15 49		
	d				14 49		14 53			15 15			15 19										15 50		
Penkridge	d						15 03																		
Stafford	a				15 00		15 09			15 29	14 53		15 34									15 53	16 01		

Northampton - Coventry - Birmingham - Wolverhampton - Stafford

2 July to 14 September

Network Diagram - see first Page of Table 67

Station		LM	LM	VT	XC	LM	LM	LM	VT		LM	LM	VT	AW	VT	XC	LM	LM	LM		LM	LM	VT	XC	LM
		◇1		◇1 ⊡	◇1 ℶ	◇1	1		◇1 ⊡			◇1	■ 1 ⊡	■ ℶ	◇1 ⊡	◇1 ℶ		◇1			1	◇1	◇1 ⊡	◇1 ℶ	◇1
London Euston ⊖	d			14 23					14 43			14 13			15 03							14 46	15 23		
Northampton	d						14 55					15 16									15 35	15 45			
Long Buckby	d						15 06					15 27									15 46				
Rugby	d						15 17					15 38			15 51						15 59	16 04			
Coventry	a			15 22			15 29		15 42			15 49			16 02						16 10		16 22		
	d			15 22	15 27		15 30		15 42			15 50			16 02						16 11		16 22	16 27	
Canley	d						15 33														16 14				
Tile Hill	d						15 37					15 55									16 18				
Berkswell	d						15 40														16 21				
Hampton-in-Arden	d											16 01									16 25				
Birmingham International ✈	a			15 33	15 37		15 45		15 53			16 04			16 13						16 28		16 33	16 37	
	d			15 33	15 38		15 46		15 53			16 05		16 09	16 13		16 17				16 29		16 33	16 38	
Marston Green	d						15 49					16 08									16 32				
Lea Hall	d						15 52										16 21								
Stechford	d						15 55										16 24								
Adderley Park	d																16 27								
Birmingham New Street	a			15 45	15 48		16 02		16 08			16 16		16 20	16 27		16 33				16 42		16 45	16 48	
	d	15 36	15 38	15 49	15 57	16 01		16 05			16 08		16 20	16 24		16 31		16 36	16 38				16 49	16 57	17 01
Smethwick Rolfe Street	d		15 44								16 14								16 44						
Smethwick Galton Bridge	d		15 46			16 08					16 16			16 30					16 46						17 08
Sandwell & Dudley	d		15 49	15 58				16 13			16 19								16 49				16 58		
Dudley Port	d		15 52								16 22								16 53						
Tipton	d		15 54								16 24								16 55						
Coseley	d	15 46	15 57								16 27							16 46	16 58						
Wolverhampton	a	15 53	16 03	16 11	16 14	16 19		16 24			16 33		16 37	16 42		16 48		16 53	17 04				17 11	17 14	17 19
	d	15 53			16 15	16 19										16 49		16 53						17 15	17 19
Penkridge	d	16 03																17 03							17 29
Stafford	a	16 09			16 30	16 34										17 00		17 09				16 54		17 29	17 35

Station		LM	LM	VT	LM		LM	VT	AW	VT	XC	LM	LM	LM	LM		LM	VT	XC	LM		LM	LM	VT	LM
		1		◇1 ⊡			◇1	■ 1 ⊡	◇ ℶ	◇1 ⊡	◇1 ℶ		◇1		1			◇1 ⊡	◇1 ℶ	◇1		◇1		◇1 ⊡	
London Euston ⊖	d			15 43			15 13			16 03								16 23		15 46				16 43	
Northampton	d	15 55					16 16													16 45	16 55				
Long Buckby	d	16 06					16 27														17 06				
Rugby	d	16 17					16 38			16 51										17 04	17 17				
Coventry	a	16 29		16 42			16 49			17 02								17 22			17 29			17 42	
	d	16 30		16 42			16 50			17 02					17 11			17 22	17 27		17 30			17 42	
Canley	d	16 33													17 14						17 33				
Tile Hill	d	16 37					16 55								17 18						17 37				
Berkswell	d	16 40													17 21						17 40				
Hampton-in-Arden	d						17 01								17 25										
Birmingham International ✈	a	16 45		16 53			17 04			17 13					17 28			17 33	17 37		17 45			17 53	
	d	16 46		16 53			17 05		17 09	17 13		17 17			17 29			17 33	17 38		17 46			17 53	
Marston Green	d	16 49					17 08								17 32						17 49				
Lea Hall	d	16 52										17 21									17 52				
Stechford	d	16 55										17 24									17 55				
Adderley Park	d											17 27													
Birmingham New Street	a	17 02		17 08			17 16		17 19	17 27		17 33			17 42			17 45	17 48		18 01			18 08	
	d		17 05		17 08			17 20	17 26		17 31		17 36	17 38			17 46	17 49	17 57			18 01	18 05		18 08
Smethwick Rolfe Street	d				17 14									17 44											18 14
Smethwick Galton Bridge	d				17 16				17 32					17 46								18 08			18 16
Sandwell & Dudley	d		17 13		17 19									17 49				17 58					18 13		18 19
Dudley Port	d				17 22									17 52			17 56								18 22
Tipton	d				17 24									17 54			17 58								18 24
Coseley	d				17 27								17 46	17 57											18 27
Wolverhampton	a		17 24		17 33			17 37	17 44		17 49		17 53	18 03			18 06	18 11	18 14			18 19	18 24		18 33
	d										17 50		17 53						18 15			18 19			
Penkridge	d												18 02									18 29			
Stafford	a										18 01		18 09						18 29	18 01		18 35			

Table 68

Mondays to Fridays

2 July to 14 September

Northampton - Coventry - Birmingham - Wolverhampton - Stafford

Network Diagram - see first Page of Table 67

		LM ◇1	VT ◇1 ⊐	AW ◇ ⊤	VT ◇1 ⊠	XC ◇1 ⊤	LM 1 A	LM	LM ◇1	LM	LM 1	VT ◇1 ⊠	XC ◇1 ⊤	LM ◇1 B	LM 1 A	LM ◇1	LM	VT ◇1 ⊠	LM	LM ◇1	VT ◇1 ⊐	AW ◇ ⊤
London Euston 15 ⊖	d	15 54			17 03		16 46					17 23		16 48	16 51			17 43		17 13		
Northampton	d	17 16					17 45							17 55	17 55					18 16		
Long Buckby	d	17 27												18 06	18 06					18 27		
Rugby	d	17 38			17 51		18 04							18 17	18 17					18 38		
Coventry	a	17 49			18 02							18 22		18 29	18 29			18 42		18 49		
	d	17 50			18 02						18 11	18 22	18 27	18 30	18 30			18 42		18 50		
Canley	d										18 14			18 33	18 33							
Tile Hill	d	17 55									18 18			18 37	18 37					18 55		
Berkswell	d										18 21			18 40	18 40							
Hampton-in-Arden	d	18 01									18 25									19 01		
Birmingham International ✈	a	18 04			18 13						18 28	18 33	18 37	18 45	18 45			18 53		19 04		
	d	18 05		18 09	18 13			18 17			18 29	18 33	18 38	18 46	18 46			18 53		19 05		19 09
Marston Green	d	18 08									18 32			18 49	18 49					19 08		
Lea Hall	d							18 21						18 52	18 52							
Stechford	d							18 24						18 55	18 55							
Adderley Park	d							18 27														
Birmingham New Street 12	a	18 17		18 20	18 27			18 33			18 42	18 45	18 48	19 01	19 01			19 08		19 17		19 20
	d		18 20	18 24		18 31			18 36	18 38		18 49	18 57			19 01	19 05		19 08		19 20	19 24
Smethwick Rolfe Street	d									18 44									19 14			
Smethwick Galton Bridge 7	d			18 30						18 46						19 08			19 16			19 30
Sandwell & Dudley	d									18 49		18 58					19 13		19 19			
Dudley Port	d									18 52									19 22			
Tipton	d									18 54									19 24			
Coseley	d								18 46	18 57									19 27			
Wolverhampton 7	a		18 37	18 42		18 48			18 53	19 03		19 11	19 14			19 19	19 24		19 33		19 37	19 42
	d					18 49			18 53				19 15			19 19						
Penkridge	d								19 03							19 29						
Stafford	a					19 00	19 01		19 09				19 27			19 36						

		VT ◇1 ⊠	LM 1	LM 1 A	XC ◇1 ⊤	LM	LM ◇1	LM	LM 1	VT ◇1 ⊠	XC ◇1 C ⊤	LM 1	LM	LM	VT ◇1 ⊠	LM ◇1 D	AW ◇	VT ■ 1 ⊐	LM ◇1 B	LM ◇1 A	XC ◇1	LM	LM ◇1
London Euston 15 ⊖	d	18 03	17 24	17 24						18 23		17 46			18 43	18 13		19 03	18 29	18 29			
Northampton	d		18 40	18 43								18 55				19 16			19 45	19 45			
Long Buckby	d		18 51	18 54								19 06				19 27							
Rugby	d	18 51	19a03	19a05								19 17				19 38		19 51	20a04	20 04			
Coventry	a	19 02								19 22		19 29			19 42	19 49		20 02					
	d	19 02							19 11	19 22	19 27	19 30			19 42	19 50		20 02					
Canley	d								19 14			19 33											
Tile Hill	d								19 18			19 37				19 55							
Berkswell	d								19 21			19 40											
Hampton-in-Arden	d								19 25							20 01							
Birmingham International ✈	a	19 13							19 28	19 33	19 37	19 45			19 53	20 04		20 13					
	d	19 13				19 17			19 29	19 33	19 38	19 46			19 53	20 05	20 09	20 13				20 17	
Marston Green	d								19 32			19 49				20 08							
Lea Hall	d					19 21						19 52										20 21	
Stechford	d					19 24						19 55										20 24	
Adderley Park	d					19 27																20 27	
Birmingham New Street 12	a	19 27				19 33			19 42	19 45	19 48	20 01			20 06	20 16	20 20	20 27				20 33	
	d				19 31		19 36	19 38		19 50	19 57		20 05	20 08	20 20		20 24				20 31		20 36
Smethwick Rolfe Street	d							19 44						20 14									
Smethwick Galton Bridge 7	d							19 46						20 16			20 30						
Sandwell & Dudley	d							19 49		19 59			20 13	20 19									
Dudley Port	d							19 52						20 22									
Tipton	d							19 54						20 24									
Coseley	d						19 46	19 57						20 27									20 46
Wolverhampton 7	a				19 48		19 53	20 03		20 12	20 14		20 24	20 33	20 36		20 42				20 48		20 53
	d				19 49		19 53				20 16				20 36								20 53
Penkridge	d						20 03																21 03
Stafford	a				20 00		20 09				20 29				20 49					20 53			21 09

A from 10 September until 14 September
B from 2 July until 7 September
C ⊤ to Birmingham New Street
D ◇ from Coventry

Table 68

Mondays to Fridays

2 July to 14 September

Northampton - Coventry - Birmingham - Wolverhampton - Stafford

Network Diagram - see first Page of Table 67

		LM	LM 1	VT ■ 1 ⊐	XC ◇1 A ⊤	LM ◇1	LM	LM	VT ◇1 ⊐	LM ◇1	VT ◇1 ⊐	AW ◇	VT ◇1 ⊐	LM	LM ◇1	LM	LM 1	VT ◇1 ⊐	XC ◇1	LM ◇1	LM	VT ◇1 ⊐
London Euston 15 ⊖	d			19 23		18 49			19 43	19 13			20 03					20 23		19 46		20 43
Northampton	d					19 55				20 16										20 55		
Long Buckby	d					20 06				20 27										21 06		
Rugby	d					20 17				20 38			20 51							21 17		
Coventry	a			20 22		20 29			20 42	20 49			21 02					21 22		21 29		21 42
	d		20 11	20 22	20 27	20 30			20 42	20 50			21 02				21 11	21 22	21 27	21 30		21 42
Canley	d		20 14			20 33											21 14			21 33		
Tile Hill	d		20 18			20 37				20 55							21 18			21 37		
Berkswell	d		20 21			20 40											21 21			21 40		
Hampton-in-Arden	d		20 25							21 01							21 25					
Birmingham International ✈	a		20 28	20 33	20 37	20 45			20 53	21 04			21 13				21 28	21 33	21 37	21 45		21 53
	d		20 29	20 33	20 38	20 46			20 53	21 05		21 09	21 13	21 17			21 29	21 33	21 38	21 46		21 53
Marston Green	d		20 32			20 49				21 08							21 32			21 49		
Lea Hall	d					20 52								21 21						21 52		
Stechford	d					20 55								21 24						21 55		
Adderley Park	d													21 27								
Birmingham New Street 12	a		20 42	20 45	20 48	21 01			21 06	21 16		21 19	21 25	21 33			21 42	21 46	21 48	22 01		22 06
	d	20 38		20 50	20 57		21 05	21 08	21 13		21 20	21 24	21 28		21 36	21 38		21 50	21 57		22 08	22 13
Smethwick Rolfe Street	d	20 44						21 14								21 44					22 14	
Smethwick Galton Bridge 7	d	20 46						21 16				21 30				21 46					22 16	
Sandwell & Dudley	d	20 49		20 59			21 13	21 19	21 24							21 49		21 59			22 19	22 24
Dudley Port	d	20 52						21 22								21 52					22 22	
Tipton	d	20 54						21 24								21 54					22 24	
Coseley	d	20 57						21 27							21 46	21 57					22 27	
Wolverhampton 7	a	21 04		21 12	21 14		21 24	21 33	21 38		21 40	21 42	21 56		21 53	22 03		22 12	22 14		22 33	22 38
	d				21 16						21 41				21 53				22 16			
Penkridge	d														22 03							
Stafford	a				21 31						21 53				22 09				22 29			

		LM ◇1	LM 1 B	LM	XC ◇1	VT ◇1 ⊐	LM ◇1	LM	LM	LM 1	AW ◇	LM ◇1	LM ◇1	VT ◇1 ⊐	LM ◇1	AW MWFO	AW TThO	LM ◇1	VT ◇1 ⊐	VT FX ◇1 E ⊐	VT ◇1 F ⊐
London Euston 15 ⊖	d	19 54	20 13			21 03						20 46		21 43	21 13			21 46	22 30	23 30	23 30
Northampton	d	21 16	21 24									21 55			22 16			22 55			
Long Buckby	d	21 27										22 06			22 27			23 06			
Rugby	d	21 38	21 45			21 57						22 17			22 38			23 17	00 01	01 00	01 05
Coventry	a	21 49				22 06						22 29		22 46	22 49			23 29	00 10	01 13	01 18
	d	21 50				22 07				22 11		22 30		22 46	22 50			23 30	00 10	01 13	01 18
Canley	d									22 14		22 33						23 33			
Tile Hill	d	21 55								22 18		22 37			22 55			23 37			
Berkswell	d									22 21		22 40						23 40			
Hampton-in-Arden	d	22 01								22 25					23 01			23 44			
Birmingham International ✈	a	22 04				22 18				22 28		22 45		23 00	23 06			23 47	00 21	01 24	01 29
	d	22 05				22 18		22 22		22 29		22 46		23 01	23 07			23 48	00 21	01 24	01 29
Marston Green	d	22 08								22 32		22 49			23 10			23 51			
Lea Hall	d							22 26				22 52						23 54			
Stechford	d							22 29				22 55						23 57			
Adderley Park	d							22 32													
Birmingham New Street 12	a	22 17				22 29		22 38		22 42		23 02		23 16	23 19			00 04	00 32	01 36	01 41
	d			22 21	22 30	22 32	22 36		22 38		22 55		23 09	23 20		23 32	23 32		00 35	01 37	01 42
Smethwick Rolfe Street	d								22 44				23 15								
Smethwick Galton Bridge 7	d						22 43		22 46				23 17								
Sandwell & Dudley	d			22 29		22 41			22 49				23 20	23 34							
Dudley Port	d								22 52				23 24								
Tipton	d								22 54				23 26								
Coseley	d						22 50		22 57				23 29								
Wolverhampton 7	a			22 41	22 47	22 56	22 57		23 03		23 11		23 35	23 47		00 01	00 02		01 03	02 07	02 10
	d				22 48		22 57				23 13		23 36								
Penkridge	d						23 07						23 46								
Stafford	a		22 39		23 00		23 13				23 30		23 52								

A ⊤ to Birmingham New Street
B from 10 September until 14 September
E not from 30 July until 9 August, from 29 August until 6 September
F 6 July, 13 July, 20 July, 17 August, 24 August, August, 14 September

Northampton - Coventry - Birmingham - Wolverhampton - Stafford

Network Diagram - see first Page of Table 67

Station		AW TThO	AW WFO	LM MO	LM MX	VT MO	VT MO	LM MO	VT MX	VT MO	VT MX	VT	LM	XC	LM	LM	LM	VT	XC	LM	AW	LM	LM
London Euston ⊖	d			21p28	21p46	21p55	22p25	22p00	22p30	23p25	23p30												
Northampton	d			22p51	22p55			23p32									05 16			05 42			
Long Buckby	d			23p02	23p06			23p43									05 27						
Rugby	d			23p13	23p17	23p21	23p48	23p54	00 01	00s46	01 00						05 38			06 05			
Coventry	a			23p25	23p29	23p31	23p57	00 05	00 10	00s58	01 13						05 49						
	d			23p35	23p30	23p31	23p58		00 10		01 13						05 50						
Canley	d			23p38	23p33																		
Tile Hill	d			23p42	23p37												05 55						
Berkswell	d			23p45	23p40																		
Hampton-in-Arden	d			23p49	23p44												06 01						
Birmingham International ✈	a			23p52	23p47	23p42	00 08		00 21	01s09	01 24						06 04						
	d			23p53	23p48	23p42	00 09		00 21		01 24						06 05					06 17	
Marston Green	d			23p56	23p51												06 08						
Lea Hall	d				23p54																	06 22	
Stechford	d				23p57																	06 25	
Adderley Park	d																					06 28	
Birmingham New Street	a			00 04	00 04	23p54	00 21		00 32	01s22	01 36						06 16					06 33	
	d	23p32	23p32			23p57	00 24		00 35		01 37	05 30	05 51	05 57	06 01	06 06		06 19	06 22		06 24		06 36
Smethwick Rolfe Street	d															06 12							
Smethwick Galton Bridge	d														06 08	06 14					06 30		
Sandwell & Dudley	d												05 59			06 17							
Dudley Port	d															06 20							
Tipton	d															06 22							
Coseley	d															06 25							
Wolverhampton	a	00 01	00 02			00 15	00 43		01 03	01 53	02 07	05 47	06 09	06 14	06 19	06 31		06 35	06 39		06 42		06 52
	d											05 48		06 16	06 19				06 40				06 53
Penkridge	d														06 29								
Stafford	a											06 01		06 29	06 35				06 53	06 58			07 08

Station		LM	LM	XC	LM	LM	LM	LM	VT	AW	VT	LM	LM	XC	LM	LM	VT	XC	LM	LM	LM	VT	LM
London Euston ⊖	d										06 03						06 23			05 30		06 43	
Northampton	d				05 55			06 16				06 41								06 55			
Long Buckby	d				06 06			06 27												07 06			
Rugby	d				06 17			06 38			06 51	07 01								07 17			
Coventry	a				06 29			06 49			07 02						07 22			07 29		07 42	
	d		06 10		06 30			06 50			07 02					07 07	07 22	07 27		07 30		07 42	
Canley	d		06 13		06 33											07 09				07 33			
Tile Hill	d		06 17		06 37			06 55								07 13				07 37			
Berkswell	d		06 20		06 40											07 16				07 40			
Hampton-in-Arden	d		06 24					07 01								07 20							
Birmingham International ✈	a		06 27		06 45			07 04			07 13					07 23	07 33	07 37		07 45		07 53	
	d		06 28		06 46			07 05		07 09	07 13				07 17	07 24	07 33	07 38		07 46		07 53	
Marston Green	d		06 31		06 49			07 08								07 27				07 49			
Lea Hall	d				06 52										07 22					07 52			
Stechford	d				06 55										07 25					07 55			
Adderley Park	d														07 28					07 58			
Birmingham New Street	a		06 39		07 01			07 16		07 20	07 27				07 32	07 36	07 45	07 48		08 03		08 08	
	d	06 38		06 57		07 01	07 08		07 20	07 24			07 27	07 31	07 36	07 38	07 49	07 57	08 01		08 05		08 08
Smethwick Rolfe Street	d	06 44					07 14									07 44							08 14
Smethwick Galton Bridge	d	06 46				07 08	07 16			07 30						07 46			08 08				08 16
Sandwell & Dudley	d	06 49					07 19									07 49	07 58				08 13		08 19
Dudley Port	d	06 52					07 22									07 52							08 22
Tipton	d	06 54					07 24									07 54							08 24
Coseley	d	06 57					07 27								07 46	07 57							08 27
Wolverhampton	a	07 03		07 14		07 19	07 33		07 36	07 41			07 45	07 48	07 53	08 03	08 11	08 14	08 19		08 24		08 33
	d			07 15		07 19								07 49	07 53			08 15	08 19				
Penkridge	d					07 29									08 03				08 29				
Stafford	a			07 29		07 36						07 53		08 00	08 09			08 29	08 35				

Northampton - Coventry - Birmingham - Wolverhampton - Stafford

Network Diagram - see first Page of Table 67

Station		LM	VT	AW	VT	LM	XC	LM	LM	LM	LM	VT	XC	LM	LM	LM	LM	LM	VT	AW	VT	LM
London Euston ⊖	d				07 03	06 24						07 23						07 13			08 03	07 47
Northampton	d	07 16				07 45								07 55				08 16				08 45
Long Buckby	d	07 27												08 06				08 27				
Rugby	d	07 38			07 51	08 04								08 17				08 38			08 51	09 04
Coventry	a	07 49			08 02							08 22		08 29				08 49			09 02	
	d	07 50			08 02						08 11	08 22	08 27	08 30				08 50			09 02	
Canley	d										08 14			08 33								
Tile Hill	d	07 55									08 18			08 37				08 55				
Berkswell	d										08 21			08 40								
Hampton-in-Arden	d	08 01									08 25							09 01				
Birmingham International ✈	a	08 04			08 12						08 28	08 33	08 37	08 45				09 04			09 12	
	d	08 05		08 09	08 13			08 17			08 29	08 33	08 38	08 46				09 05		09 09	09 13	
Marston Green	d	08 08						08 20			08 32			08 49				09 08				
Lea Hall	d							08 23						08 52								
Stechford	d							08 26						08 55								
Adderley Park	d							08 29														
Birmingham New Street	a	08 16		08 20	08 27			08 33			08 42	08 45	08 48	09 01				09 17		09 20	09 27	
	d		08 20	08 24			08 31		08 36	08 38		08 49	08 57		09 01	09 05	09 08		09 20	09 24		
Smethwick Rolfe Street	d									08 44							09 14					
Smethwick Galton Bridge	d			08 30						08 46					09 08		09 16			09 30		
Sandwell & Dudley	d									08 49		08 58				09 13	09 19					
Dudley Port	d									08 52							09 22					
Tipton	d									08 54							09 24					
Coseley	d								08 46	08 57							09 27					
Wolverhampton	a		08 37	08 42			08 48		08 53	09 03		09 11	09 14		09 19	09 24	09 33		09 37	09 43		
	d						08 49		08 53				09 15		09 19							
Penkridge	d								09 03													
Stafford	a					08 53	09 00		09 09				09 29		09 34							09 53

Station		XC	LM	LM	LM	LM	VT	XC	LM	LM	LM	VT	LM	LM	VT	AW	LM	VT	LM	XC	LM	LM	LM
London Euston ⊖	d						08 23					08 43		08 13				09 03	08 46				
Northampton	d								08 55					09 16			09 25		09 45				
Long Buckby	d								09 06					09 27			09 36						
Rugby	d								09 17					09 38			09 47	09 51	10 04				
Coventry	a						09 22		09 29			09 42		09 49			09 58	10 02					
	d					09 11	09 22	09 27	09 30			09 42		09 50			10 11	10 02					
Canley	d					09 14			09 33								10 14						
Tile Hill	d					09 18			09 37					09 55			10 18						
Berkswell	d					09 21			09 40								10 21						
Hampton-in-Arden	d					09 25								10 01			10 25						
Birmingham International ✈	a					09 28	09 33	09 37	09 45			09 53		10 04			10 28	10 13					
	d		09 17			09 29	09 33	09 38	09 46			09 53		10 05		10 09	10 29	10 13			10 17		
Marston Green	d					09 32			09 49					10 08			10 32						
Lea Hall	d		09 22						09 52												10 21		
Stechford	d		09 25						09 55												10 24		
Adderley Park	d		09 28																		10 27		
Birmingham New Street	a		09 33			09 42	09 45	09 48	10 01			10 08		10 17		10 19	10 42	10 27			10 33		
	d	09 31		09 36	09 38		09 49	09 57		10 01	10 05		10 08		10 20	10 24				10 31		10 36	10 38
Smethwick Rolfe Street	d				09 44								10 14										10 44
Smethwick Galton Bridge	d				09 46					10 08			10 16			10 30							10 46
Sandwell & Dudley	d				09 49		09 58				10 13		10 19										10 49
Dudley Port	d				09 52								10 22										10 52
Tipton	d				09 54								10 24										10 54
Coseley	d			09 46	09 57								10 27									10 46	10 57
Wolverhampton	a	09 48		09 53	10 03		10 11	10 14		10 19	10 24		10 33		10 37	10 42				10 48		10 53	11 03
	d	09 49		09 53				10 15		10 19										10 49		10 53	
Penkridge	d			10 03																		11 03	
Stafford	a	10 00		10 09				10 29		10 34									10 53	11 00		11 09	

Table 68

Mondays to Fridays
from 17 September

Northampton - Coventry - Birmingham - Wolverhampton - Stafford

Network Diagram - see first Page of Table 67

		VT ◇1 ⊠	XC ◇1 🛒	LM 1	LM ◇1	LM	VT ◇1 ⊠	LM	LM ◇1	VT ◇1 ☕	AW ◇ 🛒	LM 1	VT ◇1 ⊠	XC ◇1 🛒	LM	LM ◇1	LM	VT ◇1 ⊠	XC ◇1 🛒	LM ◇1		LM ◇1
London Euston 15 ⊖	d	09 23					09 43		09 13				10 03					10 23		09 46		
Northampton	d			09 55					10 16			10 25								10 45	10 55	
Long Buckby	d			10 06					10 27			10 36									11 06	
Rugby	d			10 17					10 38			10 47	10 51							11 04	11 17	
Coventry	a	10 22		10 29			10 42		10 49			10 58	11 02					11 22			11 29	
	d	10 22	10 27	10 30			10 42		10 50			11 11	11 02					11 22	11 27		11 30	
Canley	d			10 33								11 14									11 33	
Tile Hill	d			10 37					10 55			11 18									11 37	
Berkswell	d			10 40								11 21									11 40	
Hampton-in-Arden	d								11 01			11 25										
Birmingham International ✈	a	10 33	10 37	10 45			10 53		11 04			11 28	11 13					11 33	11 37		11 45	
	d	10 33	10 38	10 46			10 53		11 05		11 09	11 29	11 13		11 17			11 33	11 38		11 46	
Marston Green	d			10 49					11 08			11 32									11 49	
Lea Hall	d			10 52											11 21						11 52	
Stechford	d			10 55											11 24						11 55	
Adderley Park	d														11 27							
Birmingham New Street 12	a	10 45	10 48	11 01			11 08		11 16		11 20	11 42	11 27		11 33			11 45	11 48		12 01	
	d	10 49	10 57		11 01	11 05		11 08		11 20	11 24			11 31		11 36	11 38	11 49	11 57			12 01
Smethwick Rolfe Street	d							11 14									11 44					
Smethwick Galton Bridge 7	d				11 08			11 16			11 30						11 46					12 08
Sandwell & Dudley	d	10 58				11 13		11 19									11 49	11 58				
Dudley Port	d							11 22									11 52					
Tipton	d							11 24									11 54					
Coseley	d							11 27								11 46	11 57					
Wolverhampton 7	a	11 11	11 14		11 19	11 24		11 33		11 37	11 42			11 48		11 53	12 03	12 11	12 14			12 19
	d		11 15		11 19									11 49		11 53			12 15			12 19
Penkridge	d															12 03						
Stafford	a		11 28		11 34									12 00		12 09			12 29	11 53		12 34

		LM	VT ◇1 ⊠	LM	LM ◇1	VT ◇1 ☕	AW ◇ 🛒	LM 1	VT ◇1 ☕	XC ◇1 🛒	LM	LM ◇1	LM	VT ◇1 ☕	XC ◇1 🛒	LM ◇1		LM ◇1	LM	VT ◇1 ☕	LM	LM ◇1	VT ◇1 ☕
London Euston 15 ⊖	d		10 43		10 13				11 03					11 23		10 46				11 43		11 13	
Northampton	d				11 16			11 25								11 45	11 55					12 16	
Long Buckby	d				11 27			11 36									12 06					12 27	
Rugby	d				11 38			11 47	11 51							12 04	12 17					12 38	
Coventry	a		11 42		11 49			11 58	12 02					12 22			12 29			12 42		12 49	
	d		11 42		11 50			12 11	12 02					12 22	12 27		12 30			12 42		12 50	
Canley	d							12 14									12 33						
Tile Hill	d				11 55			12 18									12 37					12 55	
Berkswell	d							12 21									12 40						
Hampton-in-Arden	d				12 01			12 25														13 01	
Birmingham International ✈	a		11 53		12 04			12 28	12 13					12 33	12 37		12 45			12 53		13 04	
	d		11 53		12 05		12 09	12 29	12 13		12 17			12 33	12 38		12 46			12 53		13 05	
Marston Green	d				12 08			12 32									12 49					13 08	
Lea Hall	d										12 21						12 52						
Stechford	d										12 24						12 55						
Adderley Park	d										12 27												
Birmingham New Street 12	a		12 08		12 16		12 20	12 42	12 27		12 33			12 45	12 48		13 01			13 08		13 16	
	d	12 05		12 08		12 20	12 24			12 31		12 36	12 38	12 49	12 57			13 01	13 05		13 08		13 20
Smethwick Rolfe Street	d			12 14									12 44								13 14		
Smethwick Galton Bridge 7	d			12 16			12 30						12 46					13 08			13 16		
Sandwell & Dudley	d	12 13		12 19									12 49	12 58					13 13		13 19		
Dudley Port	d			12 22									12 52								13 22		
Tipton	d			12 24									12 54								13 24		
Coseley	d			12 27								12 46	12 57								13 27		
Wolverhampton 7	a	12 24		12 33		12 37	12 42			12 48		12 53	13 03	13 11	13 14			13 19	13 24		13 33		13 37
	d									12 49		12 53			13 15			13 19					
Penkridge	d											13 03											
Stafford	a									13 00		13 09			13 29	12 53		13 34					

Table 68

Mondays to Fridays
from 17 September

Northampton - Coventry - Birmingham - Wolverhampton - Stafford

Network Diagram - see first Page of Table 67

		AW ◇ 🛒	LM 1	VT ◇1 ☕	XC ◇1 🛒	LM	LM ◇1	LM	VT ◇1 ☕	XC ◇1 🛒	LM ◇1		LM ◇1	LM	VT ◇1 ☕	LM	LM ◇1	VT ◇1 ☕	AW ◇ 🛒	LM 1	VT ◇1 ☕	XC ◇1 🛒	LM
London Euston 15 ⊖	d			12 03					12 23		11 46				12 43		12 13				13 03		
Northampton	d		12 25								12 45	12 55					13 16			13 25			
Long Buckby	d		12 36									13 06					13 27			13 36			
Rugby	d		12 47	12 51							13 04	13 17					13 38			13 47	13 51		
Coventry	a		12 58	13 02					13 22			13 29			13 42		13 49			13 58	14 02		
	d		13 11	13 02					13 22	13 27		13 30			13 42		13 50			14 11	14 02		
Canley	d		13 14									13 33								14 14			
Tile Hill	d		13 18									13 37					13 55			14 18			
Berkswell	d		13 21									13 40								14 21			
Hampton-in-Arden	d		13 25														14 01			14 25			
Birmingham International ✈	a		13 28	13 13					13 33	13 37		13 45			13 53		14 04			14 28	14 13		
	d	13 09	13 29	13 13		13 17			13 33	13 38		13 46			13 53		14 05		14 09	14 29	14 13		14 17
Marston Green	d		13 32									13 49					14 08			14 32			
Lea Hall	d					13 21						13 52											14 21
Stechford	d					13 24						13 55											14 24
Adderley Park	d					13 27																	14 27
Birmingham New Street 12	a	13 22	13 42	13 27		13 33			13 45	13 48		14 01			14 08		14 16		14 20	14 42	14 27		14 33
	d	13 24			13 31		13 36	13 38	13 49	13 57			14 01	14 05		14 08		14 20	14 24			14 31	
Smethwick Rolfe Street	d							13 44								14 14							
Smethwick Galton Bridge 7	d	13 30						13 46					14 08			14 16			14 30				
Sandwell & Dudley	d							13 49	13 58					14 13		14 19							
Dudley Port	d							13 52								14 22							
Tipton	d							13 54								14 24							
Coseley	d						13 46	13 57								14 27							
Wolverhampton 7	a	13 42			13 48		13 53	14 03	14 11	14 14			14 19	14 24		14 33		14 37	14 42			14 48	
	d				13 49		13 53			14 15			14 19									14 49	
Penkridge	d						14 03																
Stafford	a				14 00		14 09			14 29	13 53		14 34									15 00	

		LM ◇1	LM	VT ◇1 ☕	XC ◇1 🛒	LM ◇1		LM ◇1	LM	VT ◇1 ☕	LM	LM ◇1	VT ◇1 ☕	AW ◇ 🛒	LM 1	VT ◇1 ☕	LM ◇1	XC ◇1 🛒	LM	LM ◇1	LM	VT ◇1 ☕
London Euston 15 ⊖	d			13 23		12 46				13 43		13 13				14 03	13 46					14 23
Northampton	d					13 45	13 55					14 16			14 25		14 45					
Long Buckby	d						14 06					14 27			14 36							
Rugby	d					14 04	14 17					14 38			14 47	14 51	15 04					
Coventry	a			14 22			14 29			14 42		14 49			14 58	15 02						15 22
	d			14 22	14 27		14 30			14 42		14 50			15 11	15 02						15 22
Canley	d						14 33								15 14							
Tile Hill	d						14 37					14 55			15 18							
Berkswell	d						14 40								15 21							
Hampton-in-Arden	d											15 01			15 25							
Birmingham International ✈	a			14 33	14 37		14 45			14 53		15 04			15 28	15 13						15 33
	d			14 33	14 38		14 46			14 53		15 05		15 09	15 29	15 13			15 17			15 33
Marston Green	d						14 49					15 08			15 32							
Lea Hall	d						14 52												15 21			
Stechford	d						14 55												15 24			
Adderley Park	d																		15 27			
Birmingham New Street 12	a			14 45	14 48		15 01			15 08		15 15		15 19	15 42	15 27			15 33			15 45
	d	14 36	14 38	14 49	14 57			15 01	15 05		15 08		15 20	15 26				15 31		15 36	15 38	15 49
Smethwick Rolfe Street	d		14 44								15 14										15 44	
Smethwick Galton Bridge 7	d		14 46					15 08			15 16			15 32							15 46	
Sandwell & Dudley	d		14 49	14 58					15 13		15 19										15 49	15 58
Dudley Port	d		14 52								15 22										15 52	
Tipton	d		14 54								15 24										15 54	
Coseley	d	14 46	14 57								15 27									15 46	15 57	
Wolverhampton 7	a	14 53	15 03	15 11	15 14			15 19	15 24		15 33		15 37	15 44				15 49		15 53	16 03	16 11
	d	14 53			15 15			15 19										15 50		15 53		
Penkridge	d	15 03																		16 03		
Stafford	a	15 09			15 29	14 53		15 34									15 53	16 01		16 09		

from 17 September

Northampton - Coventry - Birmingham - Wolverhampton - Stafford

Network Diagram - see first Page of Table 67

		XC	LM	LM	LM	VT	LM	LM	VT	AW	VT	XC	LM	LM	LM	LM	LM	VT	XC	LM	LM	LM	VT
		◇■ ⌶	◇■	■		◇■ ⊡		◇■	■ ⊡	■ ⌶	◇■ ⊡	◇■ ⌶		◇■		■	◇■	◇■ ⊡	◇■ ⌶	◇■	■		◇■ ⊡
London Euston ■ ⊖	d					14 43		14 13			15 03						14 46	15 23					15 43
Northampton	d			14 55				15 16								15 35	15 45				15 55		
Long Buckby	d			15 06				15 27								15 46					16 06		
Rugby	d			15 17				15 38			15 51					15 59	16 04				16 17		
Coventry	a			15 29		15 42		15 49			16 02					16 10		16 22			16 29		16 42
	d	15 27		15 30		15 42		15 50			16 02					16 11		16 22	16 27		16 30		16 42
Canley	d			15 33												16 14					16 33		
Tile Hill	d			15 37				15 55								16 18					16 37		
Berkswell	d			15 40												16 21					16 40		
Hampton-in-Arden	d							16 01								16 25							
Birmingham International ✈	a	15 37		15 45		15 53		16 04			16 13					16 28		16 33	16 37		16 45		16 53
	d	15 38		15 46		15 53		16 05		16 09	16 13		16 17			16 29		16 33	16 38		16 46		16 53
Marston Green	d			15 49				16 08								16 32					16 49		
Lea Hall	d			15 52									16 21								16 52		
Stechford	d			15 55									16 24								16 55		
Adderley Park	d												16 27										
Birmingham New Street ■	a	15 48		16 02		16 08		16 16		16 20	16 27		16 33			16 42		16 45	16 48		17 02		17 08
	d	15 57	16 01		16 05		16 08		16 20	16 24		16 31		16 36	16 38			16 49	16 57	17 01		17 05	
Smethwick Rolfe Street	d						16 14								16 44								
Smethwick Galton Bridge ■	d		16 08				16 16			16 30					16 46					17 08			
Sandwell & Dudley	d				16 13		16 19								16 49			16 58				17 13	
Dudley Port	d						16 22								16 53								
Tipton	d						16 24								16 55								
Coseley	d						16 27							16 46	16 58								
Wolverhampton ■	a	16 14	16 19		16 24		16 33		16 37	16 42		16 48		16 53	17 04			17 11	17 14	17 19		17 24	
	d	16 15	16 19									16 49		16 53					17 15	17 19			
Penkridge	d													17 03						17 29			
Stafford	a	16 30	16 34									17 00		17 09			16 54		17 29	17 35			

		LM	LM	VT	AW	VT	XC	LM	LM	LM	LM	LM	VT	XC	LM	LM	LM	LM	VT	LM	LM	VT
			◇■	■ ⊡	◇ ⌶	◇■ ⊡	◇■ ⌶		◇■		■		◇■ ⊡	◇■ ⌶	◇■		◇■		◇■ ⊡		◇■	◇■ ⊡
London Euston ■ ⊖	d		15 13			16 03							16 23		15 46				16 43		15 54	
Northampton	d		16 16												16 45	16 55					17 16	
Long Buckby	d		16 27													17 06					17 27	
Rugby	d		16 38			16 51									17 04	17 17					17 38	
Coventry	a		16 49			17 02							17 22			17 29			17 42		17 49	
	d		16 50			17 02					17 11		17 22	17 27		17 30			17 42		17 50	
Canley	d										17 14					17 33						
Tile Hill	d		16 55								17 18					17 37					17 55	
Berkswell	d										17 21					17 40						
Hampton-in-Arden	d		17 01								17 25										18 01	
Birmingham International ✈	a		17 04			17 13					17 28		17 33	17 37		17 45			17 53		18 04	
	d		17 05		17 09	17 13		17 17			17 29		17 33	17 38		17 46			17 53		18 05	
Marston Green	d		17 08								17 32					17 49					18 08	
Lea Hall	d							17 21								17 52						
Stechford	d							17 24								17 55						
Adderley Park	d							17 27														
Birmingham New Street ■	a		17 16		17 19	17 27		17 33			17 42		17 45	17 48		18 01			18 08		18 17	
	d	17 08		17 20	17 26		17 31		17 36	17 38		17 46	17 49	17 57			18 01	18 05		18 08		18 20
Smethwick Rolfe Street	d	17 14								17 44										18 14		
Smethwick Galton Bridge ■	d	17 16			17 32					17 46							18 08			18 16		
Sandwell & Dudley	d	17 19								17 49			17 58					18 13		18 19		
Dudley Port	d	17 22								17 52		17 56								18 22		
Tipton	d	17 24								17 54		17 58								18 24		
Coseley	d	17 27							17 46	17 57										18 27		
Wolverhampton ■	a	17 33		17 37	17 44		17 49		17 53	18 03		18 06	18 11	18 14			18 19	18 24		18 33		18 37
	d						17 50		17 53					18 15			18 19					
Penkridge	d								18 02								18 29					
Stafford	a						18 01		18 09					18 29	18 01		18 35					

from 17 September

Northampton - Coventry - Birmingham - Wolverhampton - Stafford

Network Diagram - see first Page of Table 67

		AW	VT	XC	LM	LM	LM	LM	LM	VT	XC	LM	LM	LM	VT	LM	LM	VT	AW	VT	LM	LM	XC
		◇ ⌶	◇■ ⊠	◇■ ⌶	■		◇■		■	◇■ ⊠	◇■ ⌶	■	◇■		◇■ ⊠		◇■	◇■ ⊡	◇ ⌶	◇■ ⊠	■	■	◇■ ⌶
London Euston ■ ⊖	d		17 03		16 46					17 23		16 51			17 43		17 13			18 03	17 24	17 24	
Northampton	d				17 45							17 55					18 16				18 40	18 43	
Long Buckby	d											18 06					18 27				18 51	18 54	
Rugby	d		17 51		18 04							18 17					18 38			18 51	19a03	19a05	
Coventry	a		18 02							18 22		18 29			18 42		18 49			19 02			
	d		18 02						18 11	18 22	18 27	18 30			18 42		18 50			19 02			
Canley	d								18 14			18 33											
Tile Hill	d								18 18			18 37					18 55						
Berkswell	d								18 21			18 40											
Hampton-in-Arden	d								18 25								19 01						
Birmingham International ✈	a		18 13						18 28	18 33	18 37	18 45			18 53		19 04			19 13			
	d	18 09	18 13			18 17			18 29	18 33	18 38	18 46			18 53		19 05		19 09	19 13			
Marston Green	d								18 32			18 49					19 08						
Lea Hall	d					18 21						18 52											
Stechford	d					18 24						18 55											
Adderley Park	d					18 27																	
Birmingham New Street ■	a	18 20	18 27			18 33			18 42	18 45	18 48	19 01			19 08		19 17		19 20	19 27			
	d	18 24		18 31			18 36	18 38		18 49	18 57		19 01	19 05		19 08		19 20	19 24				19 31
Smethwick Rolfe Street	d							18 44								19 14							
Smethwick Galton Bridge ■	d	18 30						18 46					19 08			19 16			19 30				
Sandwell & Dudley	d							18 49		18 58				19 13		19 19							
Dudley Port	d							18 52								19 22							
Tipton	d							18 54								19 24							
Coseley	d						18 46	18 57								19 27							
Wolverhampton ■	a	18 42		18 48			18 53	19 03		19 11	19 14		19 19	19 24		19 33		19 37	19 42				19 48
	d			18 49			18 53				19 15		19 19										19 49
Penkridge	d						19 03						19 29										
Stafford	a			19 00	19 01		19 09				19 27		19 36										20 00

		LM	LM	LM	LM	VT	XC	LM	LM	LM	VT	LM	AW	VT	LM	XC	LM	LM	LM	LM	VT	XC	LM
			◇■		■	◇■ ⊠	◇■ A ⌶	■			◇■ ⊠	◇■ B	◇	■ ⊡	◇■	◇■		◇■		■	■ ⊡	◇■ A ⌶	◇■
London Euston ■ ⊖	d					18 23		17 46			18 43	18 13		19 03	18 29						19 23		18 49
Northampton	d							18 55				19 16			19 45								19 55
Long Buckby	d							19 06				19 27											20 06
Rugby	d							19 17				19 38		19 51	20 04								20 17
Coventry	a					19 22		19 29			19 42	19 49		20 02							20 22		20 29
	d				19 11	19 22	19 27	19 30			19 42	19 50		20 02						20 11	20 22	20 27	20 30
Canley	d				19 14			19 33												20 14			20 33
Tile Hill	d				19 18			19 37				19 55								20 18			20 37
Berkswell	d				19 21			19 40												20 21			20 40
Hampton-in-Arden	d				19 25							20 01								20 25			
Birmingham International ✈	a				19 28	19 33	19 37	19 45			19 53	20 04		20 13						20 28	20 33	20 37	20 45
	d	19 17			19 29	19 33	19 38	19 46			19 53	20 05	20 09	20 13			20 17			20 29	20 33	20 38	20 46
Marston Green	d				19 32			19 49				20 08								20 32			20 49
Lea Hall	d	19 21						19 52									20 21						20 52
Stechford	d	19 24						19 55									20 24						20 55
Adderley Park	d	19 27															20 27						
Birmingham New Street ■	a	19 33			19 42	19 45	19 48	20 01			20 06	20 16	20 20	20 27			20 33			20 42	20 45	20 48	21 01
	d		19 36	19 38		19 50	19 57		20 05	20 08	20 20		20 24			20 31		20 36	20 38		20 50	20 57	
Smethwick Rolfe Street	d			19 44						20 14									20 44				
Smethwick Galton Bridge ■	d			19 46						20 16			20 30						20 46				
Sandwell & Dudley	d			19 49		19 59			20 13	20 19									20 49		20 59		
Dudley Port	d			19 52						20 22									20 52				
Tipton	d			19 54						20 24									20 54				
Coseley	d		19 46	19 57						20 27								20 46	20 57				
Wolverhampton ■	a		19 53	20 03		20 12	20 14		20 24	20 33	20 36		20 42			20 48		20 53	21 04		21 12	21 14	
	d		19 53				20 16				20 36							20 53				21 16	
Penkridge	d		20 03															21 03					
Stafford	a		20 09				20 29				20 49				20 53			21 09				21 31	

A ⌶ to Birmingham New Street

B ◇ from Coventry

Table 68

Mondays to Fridays
from 17 September

Northampton - Coventry - Birmingham - Wolverhampton - Stafford

Network Diagram - see first Page of Table 67

		LM	LM	VT ◇1 ⊏	LM ◇1	VT ◇1 ⊏	AW ◇	VT ◇1 ⊏	LM	LM ◇1	LM	LM 1	VT ◇1 ⊏	XC ◇1	LM ◇1	LM	VT ◇1 ⊏	LM ◇1	LM 1	LM	XC ◇1	VT ◇1 ⊏
London Euston 15 ⊖	d			19 43	19 13			20 03					20 23		19 46		20 43	19 54	20 13			21 03
Northampton	d				20 16										20 55			21 16	21 24			
Long Buckby	d				20 27										21 06			21 27				
Rugby	d				20 38			20 51							21 17			21 38	21 45			21 57
Coventry	a			20 42	20 49			21 02					21 22		21 29		21 42	21 49				22 06
	d			20 42	20 50			21 02				21 11	21 22	21 27	21 30		21 42	21 50				22 07
Canley	d											21 14			21 33							
Tile Hill	d				20 55							21 18			21 37			21 55				
Berkswell	d											21 21			21 40							
Hampton-in-Arden	d				21 01							21 25						22 01				
Birmingham International ✈	a			20 53	21 04			21 13				21 28	21 33	21 37	21 45		21 53	22 04				22 18
	d			20 53	21 05		21 09	21 13	21 17			21 29	21 33	21 38	21 46		21 53	22 05				22 18
Marston Green	d				21 08							21 32			21 49			22 08				
Lea Hall	d								21 21						21 52							
Stechford	d								21 24						21 55							
Adderley Park	d								21 27													
Birmingham New Street 12	a			21 06	21 16		21 19	21 25	21 33			21 42	21 46	21 48	22 01		22 06	22 17				22 29
	d	21 05	21 08	21 13		21 20	21 24	21 28		21 36	21 38		21 50	21 57		22 08	22 13			22 21	22 30	22 32
Smethwick Rolfe Street	d		21 14								21 44					22 14						
Smethwick Galton Bridge 7	d		21 16				21 30				21 46					22 16						
Sandwell & Dudley	d	21 13	21 19	21 24							21 49		21 59			22 19	22 24			22 29		22 41
Dudley Port	d		21 22								21 52					22 22						
Tipton	d		21 24								21 54					22 24						
Coseley	d		21 27							21 46	21 57					22 27						
Wolverhampton 7	a	21 24	21 33	21 38		21 40	21 42	21 56		21 53	22 03		22 12	22 14		22 33	22 38			22 41	22 47	22 56
	d					21 41				21 53				22 16							22 48	
Penkridge	d									22 03												
Stafford	a					21 53				22 09				22 29					22 39		23 00	

		LM ◇1	LM	LM	LM 1	XC ◇1	AW ◇	LM ◇1	LM ◇1	VT ◇1 ⊏	LM ◇1	AW MWFO	AW TThO	XC ◇1	LM ◇1	VT ◇1 ⊏	VT FX ◇1 ⊏	VT FO ◇1 ⊏
London Euston 15 ⊖	d							20 46		21 43	21 13				21 46	22 30	23 30	23 30
Northampton	d							21 55			22 16				22 55			
Long Buckby	d							22 06			22 27				23 06			
Rugby	d							22 17			22 38				23 17	00 01	01 00	01 05
Coventry	a							22 29		22 46	22 49				23 29	00 10	01 13	01 18
	d				22 11	22 24		22 30		22 46	22 50			23 27	23 30	00 10	01 13	01 18
Canley	d				22 14			22 33							23 33			
Tile Hill	d				22 18			22 37			22 55				23 37			
Berkswell	d				22 21			22 40							23 40			
Hampton-in-Arden	d				22 25						23 01				23 44			
Birmingham International ✈	a				22 28	22 33		22 45		23 00	23 06			23 36	23 47	00 21	01 24	01 29
	d		22 22		22 29	22 34		22 46		23 01	23 07			23 37	23 48	00 21	01 24	01 29
Marston Green	d				22 32			22 49			23 10				23 51			
Lea Hall	d		22 26					22 52							23 54			
Stechford	d		22 29					22 55							23 57			
Adderley Park	d		22 32															
Birmingham New Street 12	a		22 38		22 42	22 45		23 02		23 16	23 19			23 57	00 04	00 32	01 36	01 41
	d	22 36		22 38			22 55		23 09	23 20		23 32	23 32			00 35	01 37	01 42
Smethwick Rolfe Street	d			22 44					23 15									
Smethwick Galton Bridge 7	d	22 43		22 46					23 17									
Sandwell & Dudley	d			22 49					23 20	23 34								
Dudley Port	d			22 52					23 24									
Tipton	d			22 54					23 26									
Coseley	d	22 50		22 57					23 29									
Wolverhampton 7	a	22 57		23 03			23 11		23 35	23 47		00 01	00 02			01 03	02 07	02 10
	d	22 57					23 13		23 36									
Penkridge	d	23 07							23 46									
Stafford	a	23 13					23 30		23 52									

Table 68

Saturdays
until 30 June

Northampton - Coventry - Birmingham - Wolverhampton - Stafford

Network Diagram - see first Page of Table 67

		AW	LM ◇1	XC A 🚌	VT ◇1 ⊏	VT ◇1 ⊏	VT ◇1 ⊏	XC ◇1	LM ◇1	LM ◇1	LM	VT ◇1 ⊏	AW ◇ ⊼	XC ◇1 ⊼	LM	LM ◇1	LM	LM 1	XC ◇1 ⊼	LM ◇1	LM ◇1	LM	LM
London Euston 15 ⊖	d		21p46		22p30	23p30																	
Northampton	d		22p55							05 42										05 55			
Long Buckby	d		23p06																	06 06			
Rugby	d		23p17		00 01	01 05				06 05										06 17			
Coventry	a		23p29		00 10	01 18														06 29			
	d		23p30		00 10	01 18												06 10		06 30			
Canley	d		23p33															06 13		06 33			
Tile Hill	d		23p37															06 17		06 37			
Berkswell	d		23p40															06 20		06 40			
Hampton-in-Arden	d		23p44															06 24					
Birmingham International ✈	a		23p47	00 10	00 21	01 29												06 27		06 45			
	d		23p48		00 21	01 29									06 17			06 28		06 46			
Marston Green	d		23p51															06 31		06 49			
Lea Hall	d		23p54												06 21					06 52			
Stechford	d		23p57												06 24					06 55			
Adderley Park	d														06 27								
Birmingham New Street 12	a		00 04		00 32	01 41									06 32			06 39		07 01			
	d	23p32			00 35	01 42	05 30	05 57	06 01		06 08	06 20	06 24	06 31		06 36	06 38		06 57		07 01	07 05	07 08
Smethwick Rolfe Street	d										06 14						06 44						07 14
Smethwick Galton Bridge 7	d								06 07		06 16		06 30				06 46				07 07		07 16
Sandwell & Dudley	d										06 19						06 49					07 13	07 19
Dudley Port	d										06 22						06 52						07 22
Tipton	d										06 24						06 54						07 24
Coseley	d										06 27						06 57						07 27
Wolverhampton 7	a	00 01			01 03	02 10	05 47	06 14	06 18		06 33	06 37	06 42	06 48		06 54	07 03		07 14		07 18	07 24	07 33
	d						05 48	06 16	06 18					06 49		06 54			07 15		07 18		
Penkridge	d								06 29												07 30		
Stafford	a						06 00	06 29	06 35	06 54				07 00		07 08			07 29		07 36		

		LM ◇1	LM ◇1	VT ◇1 ⊏	AW ◇ ⊼	XC ◇1 ⊼	LM	LM ◇1	LM	LM 1	VT ◇1 ⊏	XC ◇1 ⊼	LM ◇1	LM ◇1	LM	LM	LM ◇1	VT ◇1 ⊏	AW ◇ ⊼	VT ◇1 ⊏	XC ◇1 ⊏	LM	LM ◇1
London Euston 15 ⊖	d										06 23		05 34							07 03			
Northampton	d	06 16	06 38										06 55				07 16						
Long Buckby	d	06 27											07 06				07 27						
Rugby	d	06 38	06 58										07 17				07 38			07 51			
Coventry	a	06 49									07 22		07 29				07 49			08 02			
	d	06 50								07 10	07 22	07 27	07 30				07 50			08 02			
Canley	d									07 13			07 33										
Tile Hill	d	06 55								07 17			07 37				07 55						
Berkswell	d									07 20			07 40										
Hampton-in-Arden	d	07 01								07 24							08 01						
Birmingham International ✈	a	07 04								07 27	07 33	07 37	07 45				08 04			08 13			
	d	07 05			07 09		07 17			07 28	07 33	07 38	07 46				08 05		08 09	08 13		08 17	
Marston Green	d	07 08								07 31			07 49				08 08						
Lea Hall	d						07 21						07 52									08 21	
Stechford	d						07 24						07 55									08 24	
Adderley Park	d						07 27															08 27	
Birmingham New Street 12	a	07 16			07 19		07 32			07 42	07 45	07 48	08 01				08 16		08 20	08 27		08 32	
	d			07 20	07 23	07 31		07 36	07 38		07 49	07 57		08 01	08 05	08 08		08 20	08 24		08 31		08 36
Smethwick Rolfe Street	d								07 44							08 14							
Smethwick Galton Bridge 7	d				07 29				07 46					08 08		08 16			08 30				
Sandwell & Dudley	d								07 49		07 58				08 13	08 19							
Dudley Port	d								07 52							08 22							
Tipton	d								07 54							08 24							
Coseley	d							07 46	07 57							08 27							08 46
Wolverhampton 7	a			07 37	07 40	07 48		07 53	08 03		08 11	08 14		08 19	08 24	08 33		08 37	08 42		08 48		08 53
	d					07 49		07 53				08 15		08 19							08 49		08 53
Penkridge	d							08 03						08 29									09 03
Stafford	a		07 53			08 00		08 09				08 29		08 35							09 00		09 09

A 30 June

Northampton - Coventry - Birmingham - Wolverhampton - Stafford

Network Diagram - see first Page of Table 67

		LM		LM ■	LM ◇■	VT ◇■	XC ◇■	LM ◇■	LM ◇■	LM	VT ◇■	LM		LM ◇■	VT ◇■	AW ◇	VT ◇■	XC ◇■	LM	LM ◇■	LM	LM ■		LM ◇■	VT ◇■
London Euston ⊖	d				06 24	07 23					07 43						08 03					07 04		07 46	08 23
Northampton	d			07 37	07 45			07 55						08 16								08 37		08 45	
Long Buckby	d			07 48				08 06						08 27								08 48			
Rugby	d			07 59	08 04			08 17						08 38			08 51					08 59		09 04	
Coventry	a			08 10		08 22		08 29			08 42			08 49			09 02					09 10			09 22
	d			08 11		08 22	08 27	08 30			08 42			08 50			09 02					09 11			09 22
Canley	d			08 14				08 33														09 14			
Tile Hill	d			08 18				08 37						08 55								09 18			
Berkswell	d			08 21				08 40														09 21			
Hampton-in-Arden	d			08 25										09 01								09 25			
Birmingham International ✈	a			08 28		08 33	08 37	08 45			08 53			09 04			09 13					09 28			09 33
	d			08 29		08 33	08 38	08 46			08 53			09 05		09 09	09 13		09 17			09 29			09 33
Marston Green	d			08 32				08 49						09 08								09 32			
Lea Hall	d							08 52											09 21						
Stechford	d							08 55											09 24						
Adderley Park	d																		09 27						
Birmingham New Street	a			08 42		08 45	08 48	09 01			09 08			09 16		09 20	09 27		09 32			09 42			09 45
	d	08 38				08 49	08 57		09 01	09 05		09 08			09 20	09 24		09 31		09 36	09 38				09 49
Smethwick Rolfe Street	d	08 44										09 14									09 44				
Smethwick Galton Bridge ■	d	08 46							09 08			09 16				09 30					09 46				
Sandwell & Dudley	d	08 49				08 58				09 13		09 19									09 49				09 58
Dudley Port	d	08 52										09 22									09 52				
Tipton	d	08 54										09 24									09 54				
Coseley	d	08 57										09 27								09 46	09 57				
Wolverhampton ■	a	09 03				09 11	09 14		09 19	09 24		09 33			09 37	09 43		09 48		09 53	10 03				10 11
	d						09 15		09 19									09 49		09 53					
Penkridge	d																			10 03					
Stafford	a				08 53		09 29		09 34									10 00		10 09				09 53	

		XC ◇■	LM ◇■	LM ◇■	LM	VT ◇■	LM	LM ◇■		VT ◇■	AW ◇	VT ◇■	XC ◇■	LM	LM ◇■	LM	LM ■	VT ◇■		XC ◇■	LM ◇■		LM ◇■	LM	VT ◇■
London Euston ⊖	d					08 43		07 54				09 03						09 23			08 46				09 43
Northampton	d		08 55					09 16									09 37				09 45	09 55			
Long Buckby	d		09 06					09 27									09 48					10 06			
Rugby	d		09 17					09 38				09 51					09 59				10 04	10 17			
Coventry	a		09 29			09 42		09 49				10 02					10 10	10 22				10 29			10 42
	d	09 27	09 30			09 42		09 50				10 02					10 11	10 22		10 27		10 30			10 42
Canley	d		09 33														10 14					10 33			
Tile Hill	d		09 37					09 55									10 18					10 37			
Berkswell	d		09 40														10 21					10 40			
Hampton-in-Arden	d							10 01									10 25								
Birmingham International ✈	a	09 37	09 45			09 53		10 04				10 13					10 28	10 33		10 37		10 45			10 53
	d	09 38	09 46			09 53		10 05			10 09	10 13		10 17			10 29	10 33		10 38		10 46			10 53
Marston Green	d		09 49					10 08									10 32					10 49			
Lea Hall	d		09 52											10 21								10 52			
Stechford	d		09 55											10 24								10 55			
Adderley Park	d													10 27											
Birmingham New Street	a	09 48	10 01			10 08		10 16			10 19	10 27		10 32			10 42	10 45		10 48		11 01			11 08
	d	09 57		10 01	10 05		10 08			10 20	10 24		10 31		10 36	10 38		10 49		10 57			11 01	11 05	
Smethwick Rolfe Street	d						10 14									10 44									
Smethwick Galton Bridge ■	d			10 08			10 16				10 30					10 46							11 08		
Sandwell & Dudley	d				10 13		10 19									10 49		10 58						11 13	
Dudley Port	d						10 22									10 52									
Tipton	d						10 24									10 54									
Coseley	d						10 27								10 46	10 57									
Wolverhampton ■	a	10 14		10 19	10 24		10 33			10 37	10 42		10 48		10 53	11 03		11 11		11 14			11 19	11 24	
	d	10 15		10 19									10 49		10 53					11 15			11 19		
Penkridge	d														11 03										
Stafford	a	10 29		10 35									11 00		11 09					11 29	10 53		11 35		

Northampton - Coventry - Birmingham - Wolverhampton - Stafford

Network Diagram - see first Page of Table 67

		LM	LM ◇■	VT ◇■		AW ◇	LM ■	VT ◇■	XC ◇■	LM	LM ◇■	LM	VT ◇■	XC ◇■		LM ◇■		LM ◇■	LM	VT ◇■	LM	LM ◇■	VT ◇■	AW ◇	
London Euston ⊖	d		09 13					10 03					10 23			09 46				10 43		10 13			
Northampton	d		10 16				10 25									10 45	10 55					11 16			
Long Buckby	d		10 27				10 36										11 06					11 27			
Rugby	d		10 38				10 48	10 51								11 04	11 17					11 38			
Coventry	a		10 49				10 59	11 02					11 22				11 29			11 42		11 49			
	d		10 50				11 11	11 02					11 22	11 27			11 30			11 42		11 50			
Canley	d						11 14										11 33								
Tile Hill	d		10 55				11 18										11 37					11 55			
Berkswell	d						11 21										11 40								
Hampton-in-Arden	d		11 01				11 25															12 01			
Birmingham International ✈	a		11 04				11 28	11 13					11 33	11 37			11 45			11 53		12 04			
	d		11 05			11 09	11 29	11 13		11 17			11 33	11 38			11 46			11 53		12 05		12 09	
Marston Green	d		11 08				11 32										11 49					12 08			
Lea Hall	d									11 21							11 52								
Stechford	d									11 24							11 55								
Adderley Park	d									11 27															
Birmingham New Street	a		11 16			11 20	11 42	11 27		11 32			11 45	11 48			12 01			12 08		12 16		12 20	
	d	11 08		11 20		11 24			11 31		11 36	11 38	11 49	11 57				12 01	12 05		12 08		12 20	12 24	
Smethwick Rolfe Street	d	11 14										11 44									12 14				
Smethwick Galton Bridge ■	d	11 16				11 30						11 46						12 08			12 16			12 30	
Sandwell & Dudley	d	11 19										11 49	11 58						12 13		12 19				
Dudley Port	d	11 22										11 52									12 22				
Tipton	d	11 24										11 54									12 24				
Coseley	d	11 27									11 46	11 57									12 27				
Wolverhampton ■	a	11 33		11 37		11 42			11 48		11 53	12 03	12 11	12 14				12 19	12 24		12 33		12 37	12 42	
	d								11 49		11 53			12 15				12 19							
Penkridge	d										12 03														
Stafford	a								12 00		12 09			12 29		11 53		12 35							

		LM ■	VT ◇■	XC ◇■	LM	LM ◇■	LM	VT ◇■	XC ◇■	LM ◇■			LM ◇■	LM	VT ◇■	LM	LM ◇■	VT ◇■	AW ◇	LM ■	VT ◇■		XC ◇■	LM	LM ◇■
London Euston ⊖	d		11 03					11 23		10 46					11 43		11 13				12 03				
Northampton	d	11 25								11 45	11 55						12 16			12 25					
Long Buckby	d	11 36									12 06						12 27			12 36					
Rugby	d	11 47	11 51							12 04	12 17						12 38			12 47	12 51				
Coventry	a	11 58	12 02					12 22			12 29				12 42		12 49			12 58	13 02				
	d	12 11	12 02					12 22	12 27		12 30				12 42		12 50			13 11	13 02				
Canley	d	12 14									12 33									13 14					
Tile Hill	d	12 18									12 37						12 55			13 18					
Berkswell	d	12 21									12 40									13 21					
Hampton-in-Arden	d	12 25															13 01			13 25					
Birmingham International ✈	a	12 28	12 13					12 33	12 37		12 45				12 53		13 04			13 28	13 13				
	d	12 29	12 13		12 17			12 33	12 38		12 46				12 53		13 05		13 09	13 29	13 13			13 17	
Marston Green	d	12 32									12 49						13 08			13 32					
Lea Hall	d				12 21						12 52													13 21	
Stechford	d				12 24						12 55													13 24	
Adderley Park	d				12 27																			13 27	
Birmingham New Street	a	12 42	12 27		12 32			12 45	12 48		13 01				13 08		13 16		13 21	13 42	13 27			13 32	
	d			12 31		12 36	12 38	12 49	12 57				13 01	13 05		13 08		13 20	13 24				13 31		13 36
Smethwick Rolfe Street	d						12 44									13 14									
Smethwick Galton Bridge ■	d						12 46						13 08			13 16			13 30						
Sandwell & Dudley	d						12 49	12 58						13 13		13 19									
Dudley Port	d						12 52									13 22									
Tipton	d						12 54									13 24									
Coseley	d					12 46	12 57									13 27									13 46
Wolverhampton ■	a			12 48		12 53	13 03	13 11	13 14				13 19	13 24		13 33		13 37	13 42				13 48		13 53
	d			12 49		12 53			13 15				13 19										13 49		13 53
Penkridge	d					13 03																			14 03
Stafford	a			13 00		13 09			13 29	12 53			13 35										14 00		14 09

Table 68

Northampton - Coventry - Birmingham - Wolverhampton - Stafford

Network Diagram - see first Page of Table 67

		LM	VT	XC	LM		LM	LM	VT	LM	LM	VT	AW	LM	VT	XC	LM	LM	LM	VT	XC	LM	
			◇1 ⊏⊐	◇1 ⊼	◇1		◇1		◇1 ⊏⊐		◇1	◇1 ⊏⊐	◇ ⊼	1	◇1 ⊏⊐	◇1 ⊏⊐		◇1		◇1 ⊏⊐	◇1 ⊼	◇1	
London Euston 15 ⊖	d		12 23		11 46				12 43		12 13				13 03					13 23		12 46	
Northampton	d				12 45	12 55					13 16			13 25								13 45	13 55
Long Buckby	d					13 06					13 27			13 36									14 06
Rugby	d				13 04	13 17					13 38			13 47	13 51							14 04	14 17
Coventry	a		13 22			13 29			13 42		13 49			13 58	14 02					14 22			14 29
	d		13 22	13 27		13 30			13 42		13 50			14 11	14 02					14 22	14 27		14 30
Canley	d					13 33								14 14									14 33
Tile Hill	d					13 37					13 55			14 18									14 37
Berkswell	d					13 40								14 21									14 40
Hampton-in-Arden	d										14 01			14 25									
Birmingham International ✈	a		13 33	13 37		13 45			13 53		14 04			14 28	14 13					14 33	14 37		14 45
	d		13 33	13 38		13 46			13 53		14 05		14 09	14 29	14 13		14 17			14 33	14 38		14 46
Marston Green	d					13 49					14 08			14 32									14 49
Lea Hall	d					13 52											14 21						14 52
Stechford	d					13 55											14 24						14 55
Adderley Park	d																14 27						
Birmingham New Street 12	a		13 45	13 48		14 01			14 08		14 16		14 19	14 42	14 27		14 32			14 45	14 48		15 01
	d	13 38	13 49	13 57			14 01	14 05		14 08		14 20	14 24			14 31		14 36	14 38	14 49	14 57		
Smethwick Rolfe Street	d	13 44								14 14									14 44				
Smethwick Galton Bridge 7	d	13 46					14 08			14 16			14 30						14 46				
Sandwell & Dudley	d	13 49	13 58					14 13		14 19									14 49	14 58			
Dudley Port	d	13 52								14 22									14 52				
Tipton	d	13 54								14 24									14 54				
Coseley	d	13 57								14 27								14 46	14 57				
Wolverhampton 7 ⇌	a	14 03	14 11	14 14			14 19	14 24		14 33		14 37	14 42			14 48		14 53	15 03	15 11	15 14		
	d			14 15			14 19									14 49		14 53			15 15		
Penkridge	d																	15 03					
Stafford	a			14 29	13 53		14 35									15 00		15 09			15 29	14 53	

		LM	LM	VT	LM	LM	VT	AW	LM	VT	XC	LM	LM	LM	VT	XC	LM		LM	LM	VT	LM
		◇1		◇1 ⊏⊐		◇1	◇1 ⊏⊐	◇ ⊼	1	◇1 ⊏⊐	◇1 ⊏⊐		◇1		◇1 ⊏⊐	◇1 ⊼	◇1		◇1		◇1 ⊏⊐	
London Euston 15 ⊖	d			13 43		13 13				14 03					14 23		13 46				14 43	
Northampton	d					14 16			14 25								14 45	14 55				
Long Buckby	d					14 27			14 36									15 06				
Rugby	d					14 38			14 47	14 51							15 04	15 17				
Coventry	a			14 42		14 49			14 58	15 02					15 22			15 29			15 42	
	d			14 42		14 50			15 11	15 02					15 22	15 27		15 30			15 42	
Canley	d								15 14									15 33				
Tile Hill	d					14 55			15 18									15 37				
Berkswell	d								15 21									15 40				
Hampton-in-Arden	d					15 01			15 25													
Birmingham International ✈	a			14 53		15 04			15 28	15 13					15 33	15 37		15 45			15 53	
	d			14 53		15 05		15 09	15 29	15 13		15 17			15 33	15 38		15 46			15 53	
Marston Green	d					15 08			15 32									15 49				
Lea Hall	d											15 21						15 52				
Stechford	d											15 24						15 55				
Adderley Park	d											15 27										
Birmingham New Street 12	a			15 08		15 16		15 20	15 42	15 27		15 32			15 45	15 48		16 01			16 08	
	d	15 01	15 05		15 08		15 20	15 24			15 31		15 36	15 38	15 49	15 57			16 01	16 05		16 08
Smethwick Rolfe Street	d				15 14									15 44								16 14
Smethwick Galton Bridge 7	d	15 08			15 16			15 30						15 46					16 08			16 16
Sandwell & Dudley	d		15 13		15 19									15 49	15 58					16 13		16 19
Dudley Port	d				15 22									15 52								16 22
Tipton	d				15 24									15 54								16 24
Coseley	d				15 27								15 46	15 57								16 27
Wolverhampton 7 ⇌	a	15 19	15 24		15 33		15 37	15 42			15 48		15 53	16 03	16 11	16 14			16 19	16 24		16 33
	d	15 19									15 49		15 53			16 15			16 19			
Penkridge	d												16 03									
Stafford	a	15 35									16 00		16 09			16 29	15 53		16 35			

Table 68

Northampton - Coventry - Birmingham - Wolverhampton - Stafford

Network Diagram - see first Page of Table 67

		LM	VT	AW	LM	VT	XC	LM	LM	LM	VT	XC	LM		LM	LM	VT	LM	LM	VT	AW	LM	VT
		◇1	◇1 ⊏⊐	■ ⊼	1	◇1 ⊏⊐	◇1 ⊏⊐		◇1		◇1 ⊏⊐	◇1 ⊼	◇1		◇1		◇1 ⊏⊐		◇1	◇1 ⊏⊐	◇ ⊼	1	◇1 ⊏⊐
London Euston 15 ⊖	d	14 13				15 03					15 23		14 46				15 43		15 13				16 03
Northampton	d	15 16			15 25								15 45	15 55					16 16			16 25	
Long Buckby	d	15 27			15 36									16 06					16 27			16 36	
Rugby	d	15 38			15 47	15 51							16 04	16 17					16 38			16 47	16 51
Coventry	a	15 49			15 58	16 02					16 22			16 29			16 42		16 49			16 58	17 02
	d	15 50			16 11	16 02					16 22	16 27		16 30			16 42		16 50			17 11	17 02
Canley	d				16 14									16 33								17 14	
Tile Hill	d	15 55			16 18									16 37					16 55			17 18	
Berkswell	d				16 21									16 40								17 21	
Hampton-in-Arden	d	16 01			16 25														17 01			17 25	
Birmingham International ✈	a	16 04			16 28	16 13					16 33	16 37		16 45			16 53		17 04			17 28	17 13
	d	16 05		16 09	16 29	16 13		16 17			16 33	16 38		16 46			16 53		17 05		17 09	17 29	17 13
Marston Green	d	16 08			16 32									16 49					17 08			17 32	
Lea Hall	d							16 21						16 52									
Stechford	d							16 24						16 55									
Adderley Park	d							16 27															
Birmingham New Street 12	a	16 16		16 20	16 42	16 27		16 32			16 45	16 48		17 01			17 08		17 16		17 20	17 42	17 27
	d		16 20	16 24			16 31		16 36	16 38	16 49	16 57			17 01	17 05		17 08		17 20	17 24		
Smethwick Rolfe Street	d									16 44								17 14					
Smethwick Galton Bridge 7	d			16 30						16 46					17 08			17 16			17 31		
Sandwell & Dudley	d									16 49	16 58					17 13		17 19					
Dudley Port	d									16 52								17 22					
Tipton	d									16 54								17 24					
Coseley	d								16 46	16 57								17 27					
Wolverhampton 7 ⇌	a		16 37	16 42			16 48		16 53	17 04	17 11	17 14			17 19	17 24		17 33		17 37	17 42		
	d						16 49		16 53			17 15			17 19								
Penkridge	d								17 03						17 29								
Stafford	a						17 00		17 09			17 29	16 53		17 35								

		XC	LM	LM	LM		VT	XC	LM		LM	LM	VT	LM	LM	VT	AW	LM	VT	XC	LM	LM	LM	VT
		◇1 ⊼		◇1			◇1 ⊏⊐	◇1 ⊼	◇1		◇1		◇1 ⊏⊐		◇1	◇1 ⊏⊐	◇ ⊼	1	◇1 ⊏⊐	◇1 ⊏⊐		◇1		◇1 ⊏⊐
London Euston 15 ⊖	d						16 23		15 46				16 43		16 13				17 03					17 23
Northampton	d								16 45	16 55					17 16			17 25						
Long Buckby	d									17 06					17 27			17 36						
Rugby	d								17 04	17 17					17 38			17 47	17 51					
Coventry	a						17 22			17 29			17 42		17 49			17 58	18 02					18 22
	d						17 22	17 27		17 30			17 42		17 50			18 11	18 02					18 22
Canley	d									17 33								18 14						
Tile Hill	d									17 37					17 55			18 18						
Berkswell	d									17 40								18 21						
Hampton-in-Arden	d														18 01			18 25						
Birmingham International ✈	a						17 33	17 37		17 45			17 53		18 04			18 28	18 13					18 33
	d		17 17				17 33	17 38		17 46			17 53		18 05		18 09	18 29	18 13		18 17			18 33
Marston Green	d									17 49					18 08			18 32						
Lea Hall	d		17 21							17 52											18 21			
Stechford	d		17 24							17 55											18 24			
Adderley Park	d		17 27																		18 27			
Birmingham New Street 12	a		17 32				17 45	17 48		18 01			18 08		18 16		18 20	18 42	18 27		18 32			18 45
	d	17 31		17 36	17 38		17 49	17 57			18 01	18 05		18 08		18 20	18 24			18 31		18 36	18 38	18 49
Smethwick Rolfe Street	d				17 44									18 14									18 44	
Smethwick Galton Bridge 7	d				17 46						18 08			18 16			18 30						18 46	
Sandwell & Dudley	d				17 49	17 58						18 13		18 19									18 49	18 58
Dudley Port	d				17 52									18 22									18 52	
Tipton	d				17 54									18 24									18 54	
Coseley	d			17 46	17 57									18 27								18 46	18 57	
Wolverhampton 7 ⇌	a	17 48		17 53	18 03		18 11	18 14			18 19	18 24		18 33		18 37	18 42			18 48		18 53	19 03	19 11
	d	17 49		17 53				18 15			18 19									18 49		18 53		
Penkridge	d			18 03							18 29											19 03		
Stafford	a	18 00		18 09				18 29	18 04		18 35									19 00		19 09		

Northampton - Coventry - Birmingham - Wolverhampton - Stafford

Network Diagram - see first Page of Table 67

		XC	LM	LM	LM	LM	VT	LM	LM	VT	AW	XC	LM	VT	LM	LM	VT	XC	LM	LM	LM	LM
		◇1	◇1		◇1		◇1		◇1	◇1	◇	◇1	1	◇1			◇1	◇1	◇1	1		
																		A				
		🛒					☕			☕	🛒	☕		☕			☕	🛒				
London Euston 15 ⊖	d		16 46				17 43		17 13					18 03			18 23			17 46		
Northampton	d		17 45	17 55					18 16				18 25							18 45	18 55	
Long Buckby	d			18 06					18 27				18 36								19 06	
Rugby	d		18 04	18 17					18 38				18 47	18 51						19 04	19 17	
Coventry	a			18 29			18 42		18 49				18 58	19 02			19 22				19 29	
	d	18 27		18 30			18 42		18 50				19 11	19 02			19 22	19 27			19 30	
Canley	d			18 33									19 14								19 33	
Tile Hill	d			18 37					18 55				19 18								19 37	
Berkswell	d			18 40									19 21								19 40	
Hampton-in-Arden	d								19 01				19 25									
Birmingham International ✈	a	18 37		18 45			18 53		19 04				19 28	19 13			19 33	19 37			19 45	
	d	18 38		18 46			18 53		19 05		19 09		19 29	19 13	19 17		19 33	19 38			19 46	
Marston Green	d			18 49					19 08				19 32								19 49	
Lea Hall	d			18 52											19 21						19 52	
Stechford	d			18 55											19 24						19 55	
Adderley Park	d														19 27							
Birmingham New Street 12	a	18 48		19 01			19 08		19 16		19 20		19 42	19 25	19 32		19 45	19 48			20 02	
	d	18 57			19 01	19 05		19 08		19 20	19 24	19 31		19 42		19 38	19 50	19 57	20 01			20 05
Smethwick Rolfe Street	d							19 14								19 44						
Smethwick Galton Bridge 7	d				19 08			19 16			19 30					19 46			20 08			
Sandwell & Dudley	d					19 13		19 19						19 54		19 49	19 59					20 13
Dudley Port	d							19 22								19 52						
Tipton	d							19 24								19 54						
Coseley	d							19 27								19 57						
Wolverhampton 7	a	19 14			19 19	19 24		19 33		19 37	19 42	19 48		20 08		20 03	20 12	20 14	20 20			20 24
	d	19 15			19 19							19 49						20 15	20 22			
Penkridge	d				19 29														20 31			
Stafford	a	19 29	18 53		19 35							20 00						20 29	20 37	19 53		

		VT	LM	LM	VT	AW	XC	VT	LM	LM	LM	LM	LM	VT	XC	XC	LM	LM	LM	LM	VT	AW	LM
		◇1		◇1	◇1	◇	◇1	◇1		◇1		1	1	◇1	◇1	◇1	◇1	◇1			◇1	◇	◇1
																	B						
		☕			☕		☕	☕						☕	🛒	🛒					☕		
London Euston 15 ⊖	d	18 43		18 13				19 03					18 46	19 23			18 46				19 43		19 13
Northampton	d			19 16								19 37	19 45				19 55	19 55					20 20
Long Buckby	d			19 27								19 48					20 06	20 06					20 31
Rugby	d			19 38				19 51				19 59	20 04				20 17	20 17					20 43
Coventry	a	19 42		19 49				20 02				20 10		20 22			20 29	20 29			20 49		20 54
	d	19 42		19 50				20 02				20 11		20 22	20 27		20 30	20 30			20 49		20 55
Canley	d											20 14					20 33	20 33					20 58
Tile Hill	d			19 55								20 18					20 37	20 37					21 02
Berkswell	d											20 21					20 40	20 40					21 05
Hampton-in-Arden	d			20 01								20 25											21 09
Birmingham International ✈	a	19 53		20 04				20 13				20 28		20 33	20 37		20 45	20 45			21 00		21 12
	d	19 53		20 05		20 09		20 13	20 17			20 29		20 33	20 38		20 46	20 46			21 00	21 09	21 13
Marston Green	d			20 08								20 32					20 49	20 49					21 16
Lea Hall	d								20 21								20 52	20 52					
Stechford	d								20 24								20 55	20 55					
Adderley Park	d								20 27														
Birmingham New Street 12	a	20 08		20 16		20 20		20 25	20 32			20 42		20 45	20 48		21 01	21 01			21 12	21 19	21 24
	d		20 08		20 20	20 24	20 31	20 42		20 36	20 38			20 50		20 57			21 05	21 08	21 16	21 24	
Smethwick Rolfe Street	d		20 14								20 44									21 14			
Smethwick Galton Bridge 7	d		20 16			20 30					20 46									21 16		21 30	
Sandwell & Dudley	d		20 19					20 54			20 49			20 59					21 13	21 19			
Dudley Port	d		20 22								20 52									21 22			
Tipton	d		20 24								20 54									21 24			
Coseley	d		20 27							20 46	20 57									21 27			
Wolverhampton 7	a		20 33		20 37	20 42	20 48	21 08		20 53	21 03			21 12		21 14			21 24	21 33	21 38	21 42	
	d				20 37		20 49			20 53						21 15							
Penkridge	d									21 03													
Stafford	a				20 49		21 00			21 09			20 54			21 29							

A 🛒 to Birmingham New Street

B 30 June. ◇ from Northampton

Northampton - Coventry - Birmingham - Wolverhampton - Stafford

Network Diagram - see first Page of Table 67

		LM	LM	LM	LM	XC	LM	LM	LM	VT	LM	XC	XC	LM	LM	LM	LM	VT	XC	AW	LM	LM
			◇1		1	◇1	◇1			◇1	◇1	◇1	◇1		◇1		1	◇1	◇1		◇1	
								A														
										☕								☕				
London Euston 15 ⊖	d									20 25	19 46							21 03			20 34	
Northampton	d						20 55				21 16										21 55	
Long Buckby	d						21 06				21 27										22 06	
Rugby	d						21 17				21 38							22 12			22 17	
Coventry	a						21 29			21 36	21 49							22 22			22 29	
	d				21 11	21 27	21 30			21 36	21 50	21 56					22 11	22 23	22 27		22 30	
Canley	d				21 14		21 33										22 14				22 33	
Tile Hill	d				21 18		21 37				21 55						22 18				22 37	
Berkswell	d				21 21		21 40										22 21				22 40	
Hampton-in-Arden	d				21 25						22 01						22 25					
Birmingham International ✈	a				21 28	21 37	21 45			21 50	22 04	22 10					22 28	22 33	22 36		22 45	
	d	21 17			21 29	21 38	21 46			21 50	22 05	22 11		22 21			22 29	22 34	22 38		22 46	
Marston Green	d				21 32		21 49				22 08						22 32				22 49	
Lea Hall	d	21 21					21 52							22 25							22 52	
Stechford	d	21 24					21 55							22 28							22 55	
Adderley Park	d	21 27												22 31								
Birmingham New Street 12	a	21 32			21 42	21 48	22 01			22 04	22 16	22 21		22 36			22 42	22 45	22 48		23 01	
	d		21 36	21 38		21 57		22 05	22 08	22 16			22 31		22 36	22 38		22 48		22 55		23 08
Smethwick Rolfe Street	d			21 44					22 14							22 44						23 14
Smethwick Galton Bridge 7	d			21 46					22 16						22 42	22 46						23 16
Sandwell & Dudley	d			21 49				22 13	22 19	22 25						22 49		22 57				23 19
Dudley Port	d			21 52					22 22							22 52						23 22
Tipton	d			21 54					22 24							22 54						23 24
Coseley	d		21 46	21 57					22 27						22 48	22 57						23 27
Wolverhampton 7	a		21 53	22 03		22 14		22 24	22 33	22 38			22 48		22 55	23 03		23 10		23 12		23 33
	d		21 59			22 16							22 49		22 56							
Penkridge	d		22 09												23 06							
Stafford	a		22 15			22 29							23 01		23 13							

		LM	VT	AW	LM
		◇1	◇1		◇1
			☕		
London Euston 15 ⊖	d		21 43		21 28
Northampton	d	22 16			22 55
Long Buckby	d	22 27			23 06
Rugby	d	22 38	22 53		23 17
Coventry	a	22 49	23 02		23 29
	d	22 50	23 02		23 30
Canley	d				23 33
Tile Hill	d	22 55			23 37
Berkswell	d				23 40
Hampton-in-Arden	d	23 01			23 44
Birmingham International ✈	a	23 04	23 13		23 47
	d	23 05	23 13		23 48
Marston Green	d	23 08			23 51
Lea Hall	d				23 54
Stechford	d				23 57
Adderley Park	d				
Birmingham New Street 12	a	23 16	23 25		00 04
	d		23 28	23 35	
Smethwick Rolfe Street	d				
Smethwick Galton Bridge 7	d				
Sandwell & Dudley	d		23 37		
Dudley Port	d				
Tipton	d				
Coseley	d				
Wolverhampton 7	a		23 50	23 53	
	d				
Penkridge	d				
Stafford	a				

A not 30 June

Table 68

Saturdays
7 July to 8 September

Northampton - Coventry - Birmingham - Wolverhampton - Stafford

Network Diagram - see first Page of Table 67

		AW	LM	XC	VT	VT	VT	VT	VT	XC		LM	LM	LM	VT	AW	XC	LM	LM	LM		LM	XC	LM	LM
						A	B	A																	
London Euston	d		21p46		22p30	00 10	23p30	01 10																	
Northampton	d		22p55										05 42											05 55	
Long Buckby	d		23p06																					06 06	
Rugby	d		23p17		00 01	01s02	01 05	02s11					06 05											06 17	
Coventry	a		23p29		00 10	01s13	01 18	02s22																06 29	
	d		23p30		00 10		01 18															06 10		06 30	
Canley	d		23p33																			06 13		06 33	
Tile Hill	d		23p37																			06 17		06 37	
Berkswell	d		23p40																			06 20		06 40	
Hampton-in-Arden	d		23p44																			06 24			
Birmingham International	a		23p47	00 10	00 21	01s24	01 29	02s33														06 27		06 45	
	d		23p48		00 21		01 29											06 17				06 28		06 46	
Marston Green	d		23p51																			06 31		06 49	
Lea Hall	d		23p54															06 21						06 52	
Stechford	d		23p57															06 24						06 55	
Adderley Park	d																	06 27							
Birmingham New Street	a		00 04		00 32	01s39	01 41	02s45										06 32				06 39		07 01	
	d	23p32			00 35		01 42		05 30	05 57		06 01		06 08	06 20	06 24	06 31		06 36	06 38			06 57		07 01
Smethwick Rolfe Street	d													06 14						06 44					
Smethwick Galton Bridge	d											06 07		06 16		06 30				06 46					07 07
Sandwell & Dudley	d													06 19						06 49					
Dudley Port	d													06 22						06 52					
Tipton	d													06 24						06 54					
Coseley	d													06 27						06 57					
Wolverhampton	a	00 01			01 03	01 57	02 10	03 05	05 47	06 14		06 18		06 33	06 37	06 42	06 48		06 54	07 03			07 14		07 18
	d								05 48	06 16		06 18					06 49		06 54				07 15		07 18
Penkridge	d											06 29													07 30
Stafford	a								06 00	06 29		06 35	06 54				07 00		07 08				07 29		07 36

		LM	LM	LM	LM	VT		AW	XC	LM	LM	LM	LM	VT	XC	LM		LM	LM	LM	LM	VT	AW	VT	XC
London Euston	d													06 23		05 34								07 03	
Northampton	d			06 16	06 38											06 55					07 16				
Long Buckby	d			06 27												07 06					07 27				
Rugby	d			06 38	06 58											07 17					07 38			07 51	
Coventry	a			06 49										07 22		07 29					07 49			08 02	
	d			06 50									07 10	07 22	07 27	07 30					07 50			08 02	
Canley	d												07 13			07 33									
Tile Hill	d			06 55									07 17			07 37					07 55				
Berkswell	d												07 20			07 40									
Hampton-in-Arden	d			07 01									07 24								08 01				
Birmingham International	a			07 04									07 27	07 33	07 37	07 45					08 04			08 13	
	d			07 05				07 09		07 17			07 28	07 33	07 38	07 46					08 05		08 09	08 13	
Marston Green	d			07 08									07 31			07 49					08 08				
Lea Hall	d									07 21						07 52									
Stechford	d									07 24						07 55									
Adderley Park	d									07 27															
Birmingham New Street	a			07 16				07 19		07 32			07 42	07 45	07 48	08 01					08 16		08 20	08 27	
	d	07 05	07 08			07 20		07 23	07 31		07 36	07 38		07 49	07 57			08 01	08 05	08 08		08 20	08 24		08 31
Smethwick Rolfe Street	d		07 14									07 44								08 14					
Smethwick Galton Bridge	d		07 16					07 29				07 46						08 08		08 16			08 30		
Sandwell & Dudley	d	07 13	07 19									07 49		07 58					08 13	08 19					
Dudley Port	d		07 22									07 52								08 22					
Tipton	d		07 24									07 54								08 24					
Coseley	d		07 27								07 46	07 57								08 27					
Wolverhampton	a	07 24	07 33			07 37		07 40	07 48		07 53	08 03		08 11	08 14			08 19	08 24	08 33		08 37	08 42		08 48
	d								07 49		07 53				08 15			08 19							08 49
Penkridge	d										08 03							08 29							
Stafford	a				07 53				08 00		08 09				08 29			08 35							09 00

A from 28 July until 11 August, then from 1 September B from 7 July until 21 July, 18 August, 25 August

Table 68

Saturdays
7 July to 8 September

Northampton - Coventry - Birmingham - Wolverhampton - Stafford

Network Diagram - see first Page of Table 67

		LM		LM	LM	LM	LM	VT	XC	LM	LM	LM		VT	LM	LM	VT	AW	VT	XC	LM	LM		LM	LM
London Euston	d						06 24	07 23						07 43					08 03						07 04
Northampton	d					07 37	07 45			07 55						08 16									08 37
Long Buckby	d					07 48				08 06						08 27									08 48
Rugby	d					07 59	08 04			08 17						08 38			08 51						08 59
Coventry	a					08 10		08 22		08 29				08 42		08 49			09 02						09 10
	d					08 11		08 22	08 27	08 30				08 42		08 50			09 02						09 11
Canley	d					08 14				08 33															09 14
Tile Hill	d					08 18				08 37						08 55									09 18
Berkswell	d					08 21				08 40															09 21
Hampton-in-Arden	d					08 25										09 01									09 25
Birmingham International	a					08 28		08 33	08 37	08 45				08 53		09 04			09 13						09 28
	d	08 17				08 29		08 33	08 38	08 46				08 53		09 05		09 09	09 13		09 17				09 29
Marston Green	d					08 32				08 49						09 08									09 32
Lea Hall	d	08 21								08 52											09 21				
Stechford	d	08 24								08 55											09 24				
Adderley Park	d	08 27																			09 27				
Birmingham New Street	a	08 32				08 42		08 45	08 48	09 01				09 08		09 16		09 20	09 27		09 32				09 42
	d			08 36	08 38			08 49	08 57		09 01	09 05			09 08		09 20	09 24		09 31		09 36		09 38	
Smethwick Rolfe Street	d				08 44										09 14									09 44	
Smethwick Galton Bridge	d				08 46						09 08				09 16			09 30						09 46	
Sandwell & Dudley	d				08 49			08 58				09 13			09 19									09 49	
Dudley Port	d				08 52										09 22									09 52	
Tipton	d				08 54										09 24									09 54	
Coseley	d			08 46	08 57										09 27							09 46		09 57	
Wolverhampton	a			08 53	09 03			09 11	09 14		09 19	09 24			09 33		09 37	09 43		09 48		09 53		10 03	
	d			08 53					09 15		09 19									09 49		09 53			
Penkridge	d			09 03																		10 03			
Stafford	a			09 09			08 53		09 29		09 34									10 00		10 09			

		LM	VT	XC	LM	LM	LM	LM		VT	LM	AW	VT	XC	LM	LM	LM	LM		VT	XC	LM		LM	LM
London Euston	d	07 46	08 23							08 43	07 54		09 03							09 23		08 46			
Northampton	d	08 45			08 55						09 16							09 37				09 45	09 55		
Long Buckby	d				09 06						09 27							09 48					10 06		
Rugby	d	09 04			09 17						09 38		09 51					09 59				10 04	10 17		
Coventry	a		09 22		09 29					09 42	09 49		10 02					10 10		10 22			10 29		
	d		09 22	09 27	09 30					09 42	09 50		10 02					10 11		10 22	10 27		10 30		
Canley	d				09 33													10 14					10 33		
Tile Hill	d				09 37						09 55							10 18					10 37		
Berkswell	d				09 40													10 21					10 40		
Hampton-in-Arden	d										10 01							10 25							
Birmingham International	a		09 33	09 37	09 45					09 53	10 04		10 13					10 28		10 33	10 37		10 45		
	d		09 33	09 38	09 46					09 53	10 05	10 09	10 13		10 17			10 29		10 33	10 38		10 46		
Marston Green	d				09 49						10 08							10 32					10 49		
Lea Hall	d				09 52										10 21								10 52		
Stechford	d				09 55										10 24								10 55		
Adderley Park	d														10 27										
Birmingham New Street	a		09 45	09 48	10 01					10 08	10 16	10 19	10 27		10 32			10 42		10 45	10 48		11 01		
	d		09 49	09 57		10 01	10 05	10 08		10 20		10 24		10 31		10 36	10 38			10 49	10 57			11 01	11 05
Smethwick Rolfe Street	d							10 14									10 44								
Smethwick Galton Bridge	d					10 08		10 16				10 30					10 46							11 08	
Sandwell & Dudley	d		09 58				10 13	10 19									10 49			10 58					11 13
Dudley Port	d							10 22									10 52								
Tipton	d							10 24									10 54								
Coseley	d							10 27								10 46	10 57								
Wolverhampton	a		10 11	10 14		10 19	10 24	10 33		10 37		10 42		10 48		10 53	11 03			11 11	11 14			11 19	11 24
	d			10 15		10 19								10 49		10 53					11 15			11 19	
Penkridge	d															11 03									
Stafford	a	09 53		10 29		10 35								11 00		11 09					11 29	10 53		11 35	

Northampton - Coventry - Birmingham - Wolverhampton - Stafford

Network Diagram - see first Page of Table 67

		VT ◇1	LM	LM ◇1	VT ◇1	AW ◇	LM 1	VT ◇1	XC ◇1	LM	LM ◇1	LM	VT ◇1	XC ◇1	LM ◇1	LM ◇1	LM ◇1	LM	VT ◇1	LM	LM ◇1	VT ◇1
London Euston 15 ⊖	d	09 43		09 13				10 03					10 23			09 46			10 43		10 13	
Northampton	d			10 16			10 25								10 45	10 55					11 16	
Long Buckby	d			10 27			10 36									11 06					11 27	
Rugby	d			10 38			10 48	10 51							11 04	11 17					11 38	
Coventry	a	10 42		10 49			10 59	11 02					11 22			11 29			11 42		11 49	
	d	10 42		10 50			11 11	11 02					11 22	11 27		11 30			11 42		11 50	
Canley	d						11 14									11 33						
Tile Hill	d			10 55			11 18									11 37					11 55	
Berkswell	d						11 21									11 40						
Hampton-in-Arden	d			11 01			11 25														12 01	
Birmingham International ✈	a	10 53		11 04			11 28	11 13					11 33	11 37		11 45			11 53		12 04	
	d	10 53		11 05		11 09	11 29	11 13		11 17			11 33	11 38		11 46			11 53		12 05	
Marston Green	d			11 08			11 32									11 49					12 08	
Lea Hall	d									11 21						11 52						
Stechford	d									11 24						11 55						
Adderley Park	d									11 27												
Birmingham New Street 12	a	11 08		11 16		11 20	11 42	11 27		11 32			11 45	11 48		12 01			12 08		12 16	
	d		11 08		11 20	11 24			11 31		11 36	11 38	11 49	11 57			12 01	12 05		12 08		12 20
Smethwick Rolfe Street	d		11 14									11 44								12 14		
Smethwick Galton Bridge 7	d		11 16			11 30						11 46					12 08			12 16		
Sandwell & Dudley	d		11 19									11 49	11 58					12 13		12 19		
Dudley Port	d		11 22									11 52								12 22		
Tipton	d		11 24									11 54								12 24		
Coseley	d		11 27								11 46	11 57								12 27		
Wolverhampton 7	a		11 33		11 37	11 42			11 48		11 53	12 03	12 11	12 14			12 19	12 24		12 33		12 37
	d								11 49		11 53			12 15			12 19					
Penkridge	d										12 03											
Stafford	a								12 00		12 09			12 29	11 53		12 35					

		AW ◇	LM 1	VT ◇1	XC ◇1	LM	LM ◇1	LM	VT ◇1	XC ◇1	LM ◇1	LM ◇1	LM ◇1	LM	VT ◇1	LM	LM ◇1	VT ◇1	AW ◇	LM 1	VT ◇1	XC ◇1	LM
London Euston 15 ⊖	d			11 03					11 23			10 46			11 43		11 13				12 03		
Northampton	d		11 25								11 45	11 55					12 16			12 25			
Long Buckby	d		11 36									12 06					12 27			12 36			
Rugby	d		11 47	11 51							12 04	12 17					12 38			12 47	12 51		
Coventry	a		11 58	12 02					12 22			12 29			12 42		12 49			12 58	13 02		
	d		12 11	12 02					12 22	12 27		12 30			12 42		12 50			13 11	13 02		
Canley	d		12 14									12 33								13 14			
Tile Hill	d		12 18									12 37					12 55			13 18			
Berkswell	d		12 21									12 40								13 21			
Hampton-in-Arden	d		12 25														13 01			13 25			
Birmingham International ✈	a		12 28	12 13					12 33	12 37		12 45			12 53		13 04			13 28	13 13		
	d	12 09	12 29	12 13		12 17			12 33	12 38		12 46			12 53		13 05		13 09	13 29	13 13		13 17
Marston Green	d		12 32									12 49					13 08			13 32			
Lea Hall	d					12 21						12 52											13 21
Stechford	d					12 24						12 55											13 24
Adderley Park	d					12 27																	13 27
Birmingham New Street 12	a	12 20	12 42	12 27		12 32			12 45	12 48		13 01			13 08		13 16		13 21	13 42	13 27		13 32
	d	12 24			12 31		12 36	12 38	12 49	12 57			13 01	13 05		13 08		13 20	13 24			13 31	
Smethwick Rolfe Street	d							12 44								13 14							
Smethwick Galton Bridge 7	d	12 30						12 46					13 08			13 16			13 30				
Sandwell & Dudley	d							12 49	12 58					13 13		13 19							
Dudley Port	d							12 52								13 22							
Tipton	d							12 54								13 24							
Coseley	d						12 46	12 57								13 27							
Wolverhampton 7	a	12 42			12 48		12 53	13 03	13 11	13 14			13 19	13 24		13 33		13 37	13 42			13 48	
	d				12 49		12 53			13 15			13 19									13 49	
Penkridge	d						13 03																
Stafford	a				13 00		13 09			13 29	12 53		13 35									14 00	

Northampton - Coventry - Birmingham - Wolverhampton - Stafford

Network Diagram - see first Page of Table 67

		LM ◇1	LM	VT ◇1	XC ◇1	LM ◇1	LM ◇1	LM ◇1	LM	VT ◇1	LM	LM ◇1	VT ◇1	AW ◇	LM 1	VT ◇1	XC ◇1	LM	LM ◇1	LM	VT ◇1	XC ◇1
London Euston 15 ⊖	d			12 23			11 46			12 43		12 13				13 03					13 23	
Northampton	d					12 45	12 55					13 16			13 25							
Long Buckby	d						13 06					13 27			13 36							
Rugby	d					13 04	13 17					13 38			13 47	13 51						
Coventry	a			13 22			13 29			13 42		13 49			13 58	14 02					14 22	
	d			13 22	13 27		13 30			13 42		13 50			14 11	14 02					14 22	14 27
Canley	d						13 33								14 14							
Tile Hill	d						13 37					13 55			14 18							
Berkswell	d						13 40								14 21							
Hampton-in-Arden	d											14 01			14 25							
Birmingham International ✈	a			13 33	13 37		13 45			13 53		14 04			14 28	14 13					14 33	14 37
	d			13 33	13 38		13 46			13 53		14 05		14 09	14 29	14 13		14 17			14 33	14 38
Marston Green	d						13 49					14 08			14 32							
Lea Hall	d						13 52											14 21				
Stechford	d						13 55											14 24				
Adderley Park	d																	14 27				
Birmingham New Street 12	a			13 45	13 48		14 01			14 08		14 16		14 19	14 42	14 27		14 32			14 45	14 48
	d	13 36	13 38	13 49	13 57			14 01	14 05		14 08		14 20	14 24			14 31		14 36	14 38	14 49	14 57
Smethwick Rolfe Street	d		13 44								14 14									14 44		
Smethwick Galton Bridge 7	d		13 46					14 08			14 16			14 30						14 46		
Sandwell & Dudley	d		13 49	13 58					14 13		14 19									14 49	14 58	
Dudley Port	d		13 52								14 22									14 52		
Tipton	d		13 54								14 24									14 54		
Coseley	d	13 46	13 57								14 27								14 46	14 57		
Wolverhampton 7	a	13 53	14 03	14 11	14 14			14 19	14 24		14 33		14 37	14 42			14 48		14 53	15 03	15 11	15 14
	d	13 53			14 15			14 19									14 49		14 53			15 15
Penkridge	d	14 03																	15 03			
Stafford	a	14 09			14 29	13 53		14 35									15 00		15 09			15 29

		LM ◇1	LM ◇1	LM ◇1	LM	LM	VT ◇1	LM ◇1	AW ◇	LM 1	VT ◇1	XC ◇1	LM	LM ◇1	LM	VT ◇1	XC ◇1	LM ◇1	LM ◇1	LM ◇1	LM	VT ◇1
London Euston 15 ⊖	d		12 46				13 43	13 13			14 03					14 23			13 46			14 43
Northampton	d	13 45	13 55					14 16		14 25								14 45	14 55			
Long Buckby	d		14 06					14 27		14 36									15 06			
Rugby	d	14 04	14 17					14 38		14 47	14 51							15 04	15 17			
Coventry	a		14 29				14 42	14 49		14 58	15 02					15 22			15 29			15 42
	d		14 30				14 42	14 50		15 11	15 02					15 22	15 27		15 30			15 42
Canley	d		14 33							15 14									15 33			
Tile Hill	d		14 37					14 55		15 18									15 37			
Berkswell	d		14 40							15 21									15 40			
Hampton-in-Arden	d							15 01		15 25												
Birmingham International ✈	a		14 45				14 53	15 04		15 28	15 13					15 33	15 37		15 45			15 53
	d		14 46				14 53	15 05	15 09	15 29	15 13		15 17			15 33	15 38		15 46			15 53
Marston Green	d		14 49					15 08		15 32									15 49			
Lea Hall	d		14 52										15 21						15 52			
Stechford	d		14 55										15 24						15 55			
Adderley Park	d												15 27									
Birmingham New Street 12	a		15 01				15 08	15 16	15 20	15 42	15 27		15 32			15 45	15 48		16 01			16 08
	d			15 01	15 05	15 08	15 20		15 24			15 31		15 36	15 38	15 49	15 57			16 01	16 05	
Smethwick Rolfe Street	d					15 14									15 44							
Smethwick Galton Bridge 7	d			15 08		15 16			15 30						15 46					16 08		
Sandwell & Dudley	d				15 13	15 19									15 49	15 58					16 13	
Dudley Port	d					15 22									15 52							
Tipton	d					15 24									15 54							
Coseley	d					15 27								15 46	15 57							
Wolverhampton 7	a			15 19	15 24	15 33	15 37		15 42			15 48		15 53	16 03	16 11	16 14			16 19	16 24	
	d			15 19								15 49		15 53			16 15			16 19		
Penkridge	d													16 03								
Stafford	a	14 53		15 35								16 00		16 09			16 29	15 53		16 35		

Table 68

Saturdays

7 July to 8 September

Northampton - Coventry - Birmingham - Wolverhampton - Stafford

Network Diagram - see first Page of Table 67

		LM	LM	VT	AW	LM	VT	XC	LM	LM	LM	VT	XC	LM		LM	LM	VT	LM	LM	VT	AW	LM
			◇■	◇■ ⊡	■ ⌶	■	◇■ ⊡	◇■ ⊡		◇■		◇■ ⊡	◇■ ⌶	◇■		◇■		◇■ ⊡		◇■	◇■ ⊡	◇ ⌶	■
London Euston ⊖	d		14 13				15 03					15 23		14 46				15 43		15 13			
Northampton	d		15 16			15 25								15 45	15 55					16 16			16 25
Long Buckby	d		15 27			15 36									16 06					16 27			16 36
Rugby	d		15 38			15 47	15 51							16 04	16 17					16 38			16 47
Coventry	a		15 49			15 58	16 02					16 22			16 29			16 42		16 49			16 58
	d		15 50			16 11	16 02					16 22	16 27		16 30			16 42		16 50			17 11
Canley	d					16 14									16 33								17 14
Tile Hill	d		15 55			16 18									16 37					16 55			17 18
Berkswell	d					16 21									16 40								17 21
Hampton-in-Arden	d		16 01			16 25														17 01			17 25
Birmingham International ✈	a		16 04			16 28	16 13					16 33	16 37		16 45			16 53		17 04			17 28
	d		16 05		16 09	16 29	16 13		16 17			16 33	16 38		16 46			16 53		17 05		17 09	17 29
Marston Green	d		16 08			16 32									16 49					17 08			17 32
Lea Hall	d								16 21						16 52								
Stechford	d								16 24						16 55								
Adderley Park	d								16 27														
Birmingham New Street ■	a		16 16		16 20	16 42	16 27		16 32			16 45	16 48		17 01			17 08		17 16		17 20	17 42
	d	16 08		16 20	16 24			16 31		16 36	16 38	16 49	16 57			17 01	17 05		17 08		17 20	17 24	
Smethwick Rolfe Street	d	16 14									16 44								17 14				
Smethwick Galton Bridge ■	d	16 16			16 30						16 46					17 08			17 16			17 31	
Sandwell & Dudley	d	16 19									16 49	16 58					17 13		17 19				
Dudley Port	d	16 22									16 52								17 22				
Tipton	d	16 24									16 54								17 24				
Coseley	d	16 27								16 46	16 57								17 27				
Wolverhampton ■ ⛴	a	16 33		16 37	16 42			16 48		16 53	17 04	17 11	17 14			17 19	17 24		17 33		17 37	17 42	
	d							16 49		16 53			17 15			17 19							
Penkridge	d									17 03						17 29							
Stafford	a							17 00		17 09			17 29	16 53		17 35							

		VT	XC	LM	LM	LM	VT	XC	LM		LM	LM	VT	LM	LM	VT	AW	LM	VT	XC	LM	LM	LM
		◇■ ⊡	◇■ ⌶		◇■		◇■ ⊡	◇■ ⌶	◇■		◇■		◇■ ⊡		◇■	◇■ ⊡	◇ ⌶	■	◇■ ⊡	◇■ ⊡		◇■	
London Euston ⊖	d	16 03					16 23		15 46				16 43		16 13				17 03				
Northampton	d								16 45	16 55					17 16			17 25					
Long Buckby	d									17 06					17 27			17 36					
Rugby	d	16 51							17 04	17 17					17 38			17 47	17 51				
Coventry	a	17 02					17 22			17 29			17 42		17 49			17 58	18 02				
	d	17 02					17 22	17 27		17 30			17 42		17 50			18 11	18 02				
Canley	d									17 33								18 14					
Tile Hill	d									17 37					17 55			18 18					
Berkswell	d									17 40								18 21					
Hampton-in-Arden	d														18 01			18 25					
Birmingham International ✈	a	17 13					17 33	17 37		17 45			17 53		18 04			18 28	18 13				
	d	17 13		17 17			17 33	17 38		17 46			17 53		18 05		18 09	18 29	18 13		18 17		
Marston Green	d									17 49					18 08			18 32					
Lea Hall	d			17 21						17 52											18 21		
Stechford	d			17 24						17 55											18 24		
Adderley Park	d			17 27																	18 27		
Birmingham New Street ■	a	17 27		17 32			17 45	17 48		18 01			18 08		18 16		18 20	18 42	18 27		18 32		
	d		17 31		17 36	17 38	17 49	17 57			18 01	18 05		18 08		18 20	18 24			18 31		18 36	18 38
Smethwick Rolfe Street	d					17 44								18 14									18 44
Smethwick Galton Bridge ■	d					17 46					18 08			18 16			18 30						18 46
Sandwell & Dudley	d					17 49	17 58					18 13		18 19									18 49
Dudley Port	d					17 52								18 22									18 52
Tipton	d					17 54								18 24									18 54
Coseley	d				17 46	17 57								18 27								18 46	18 57
Wolverhampton ■ ⛴	a		17 48		17 53	18 03	18 11	18 14			18 19	18 24		18 33		18 37	18 42			18 48		18 53	19 03
	d		17 49		17 53			18 15			18 19									18 49		18 53	
Penkridge	d				18 03						18 29											19 03	
Stafford	a		18 00		18 09			18 29	18 04		18 35									19 00		19 09	

Table 68

Saturdays

7 July to 8 September

Northampton - Coventry - Birmingham - Wolverhampton - Stafford

Network Diagram - see first Page of Table 67

		VT	XC	LM		LM	LM	LM	VT	LM	AW	XC	LM	VT	LM	LM	VT	XC	LM	LM		LM
		◇■ ⊡	◇■ ⌶	◇■		◇■			◇■ ⊡	◇■	◇ ⌶	◇■ ⊡	■	◇■ ⊡			◇■ ⊡	◇■ A ⌶	◇■	■		
London Euston ⊖	d	17 23		16 46					17 43	17 13				18 03			18 23			17 46		
Northampton	d			17 45	17 55					18 16			18 25							18 45	18 55	
Long Buckby	d				18 06					18 27			18 36								19 06	
Rugby	d			18 04	18 17					18 38			18 47	18 51						19 04	19 17	
Coventry	a	18 22			18 29				18 42	18 49			18 58	19 02			19 22				19 29	
	d	18 22	18 27		18 30				18 42	18 50			19 11	19 02			19 22	19 27			19 30	
Canley	d				18 33								19 14								19 33	
Tile Hill	d				18 37					18 55			19 18								19 37	
Berkswell	d				18 40								19 21								19 40	
Hampton-in-Arden	d									19 01			19 25									
Birmingham International ✈	a	18 33	18 37		18 45				18 53	19 04			19 28	19 13			19 33	19 37			19 45	
	d	18 33	18 38		18 46				18 53	19 05	19 09		19 29	19 13	19 17		19 33	19 38			19 46	
Marston Green	d				18 49					19 08			19 32								19 49	
Lea Hall	d				18 52										19 21						19 52	
Stechford	d				18 55										19 24						19 55	
Adderley Park	d														19 27							
Birmingham New Street ■	a	18 45	18 48		19 01				19 08	19 16	19 20		19 42	19 25	19 32		19 45	19 48			20 02	
	d	18 49	18 57			19 01	19 05	19 08	19 20		19 24	19 31		19 42		19 38	19 50	19 57	20 01			20 05
Smethwick Rolfe Street	d							19 14								19 44						
Smethwick Galton Bridge ■	d					19 08		19 16			19 30					19 46			20 08			
Sandwell & Dudley	d	18 58					19 13	19 19						19 54		19 49	19 59					20 13
Dudley Port	d							19 22								19 52						
Tipton	d							19 24								19 54						
Coseley	d							19 27								19 57						
Wolverhampton ■ ⛴	a	19 11	19 14			19 19	19 24	19 33	19 37		19 42	19 48		20 08		20 03	20 12	20 14	20 20			20 24
	d		19 15			19 19						19 49						20 15	20 22			
Penkridge	d					19 29													20 31			
Stafford	a		19 29	18 53		19 35						20 00						20 29	20 37	19 53		

		VT	LM	LM	VT	AW	XC	VT	LM	LM	LM	LM	VT	XC	XC	LM		LM	LM	VT	AW	LM	LM
		◇■ ⊡		◇■	◇■ ⊡	◇	◇■ ⊡	◇■ ⊡		◇■		■	◇■ ⊡	◇■ ⌶	◇■ ⌶	■				◇■ ⊡	◇	◇■	
London Euston ⊖	d	18 43		18 13				19 03					19 23			18 46				19 43		19 13	
Northampton	d			19 16								19 37				19 45	19 55					20 20	
Long Buckby	d			19 27								19 48					20 06					20 31	
Rugby	d			19 38				19 51				19 59				20 04	20 17					20 43	
Coventry	a	19 42		19 49				20 02				20 10	20 22				20 29			20 49		20 54	
	d	19 42		19 50				20 02				20 11	20 22	20 27			20 30			20 49		20 55	
Canley	d											20 14					20 33					20 58	
Tile Hill	d			19 55								20 18					20 37					21 02	
Berkswell	d											20 21					20 40					21 05	
Hampton-in-Arden	d			20 01								20 25										21 09	
Birmingham International ✈	a	19 53		20 04				20 13				20 28	20 33	20 37			20 45			21 00		21 12	
	d	19 53		20 05		20 09		20 13	20 17			20 29	20 33	20 38			20 46			21 00	21 09	21 13	21 17
Marston Green	d			20 08								20 32					20 49					21 16	
Lea Hall	d								20 21								20 52						21 21
Stechford	d								20 24								20 55						21 24
Adderley Park	d								20 27														21 27
Birmingham New Street ■	a	20 08		20 16		20 20		20 25	20 32			20 42	20 45	20 48			21 01			21 12	21 19	21 24	21 32
	d		20 08		20 20	20 24	20 31	20 42		20 36	20 38		20 50		20 57			21 05	21 08	21 16	21 24		
Smethwick Rolfe Street	d		20 14								20 44								21 14				
Smethwick Galton Bridge ■	d		20 16			20 30					20 46								21 16		21 30		
Sandwell & Dudley	d		20 19					20 54			20 49		20 59					21 13	21 19				
Dudley Port	d		20 22								20 52								21 22				
Tipton	d		20 24								20 54								21 24				
Coseley	d		20 27							20 46	20 57								21 27				
Wolverhampton ■ ⛴	a		20 33		20 37	20 42	20 48	21 08		20 53	21 03		21 12		21 14			21 24	21 33	21 38	21 42		
	d				20 37		20 49			20 53					21 15								
Penkridge	d									21 03													
Stafford	a				20 49		21 00			21 09					21 29	20 54							

A ⌶ to Birmingham New Street

Table 68

Saturdays
7 July to 8 September

Northampton - Coventry - Birmingham - Wolverhampton - Stafford

Network Diagram - see first Page of Table 67

Station		LM	LM	LM	XC	LM	LM	VT	LM	XC	XC	LM	LM	LM	LM	VT	XC	AW	LM	LM	LM	VT	AW
		◇1		1	◇1	◇1		◇1 ⊏	◇1	◇1	◇1		◇1		1	◇1 ⊏	◇1		◇1		◇1	◇1 ⊏	
London Euston 15 ⊖	d							20 25	19 46							21 03			20 34			21 43	
Northampton	d					20 55			21 16										21 55		22 16		
Long Buckby	d					21 06			21 27										22 06		22 27		
Rugby	d					21 17			21 38							22 12			22 17		22 38	22 53	
Coventry	a					21 29		21 36	21 49							22 22			22 29		22 49	23 02	
	d			21 11	21 27	21 30		21 36	21 50	21 56					22 11	22 23	22 27		22 30		22 50	23 02	
Canley	d			21 14		21 33									22 14				22 33				
Tile Hill	d			21 18		21 37			21 55						22 18				22 37		22 55		
Berkswell	d			21 21		21 40									22 21				22 40				
Hampton-in-Arden	d			21 25					22 01						22 25						23 01		
Birmingham International ✈	a			21 28	21 37	21 45		21 50	22 04	22 10					22 28	22 33	22 36		22 45		23 04	23 13	
	d			21 29	21 38	21 46		21 50	22 05	22 11		22 21			22 29	22 34	22 38		22 46		23 05	23 13	
Marston Green	d			21 32		21 49			22 08						22 32				22 49		23 08		
Lea Hall	d					21 52						22 25							22 52				
Stechford	d					21 55						22 28							22 55				
Adderley Park	d											22 31											
Birmingham New Street 12	a			21 42	21 48	22 01		22 04	22 16	22 21		22 36			22 42	22 45	22 48		23 01		23 16	23 25	
	d	21 36	21 38		21 57		22 08	22 16			22 31		22 36	22 38		22 48		22 55		23 08		23 28	23 35
Smethwick Rolfe Street	d		21 44				22 14							22 44						23 14			
Smethwick Galton Bridge 7	d		21 46				22 16						22 42	22 46						23 16			
Sandwell & Dudley	d		21 49				22 19	22 25						22 49		22 57				23 19		23 37	
Dudley Port	d		21 52				22 22							22 52						23 22			
Tipton	d		21 54				22 24							22 54						23 24			
Coseley	d	21 46	21 57				22 27						22 48	22 57						23 27			
Wolverhampton 7	a	21 53	22 03		22 14		22 33	22 38			22 48		22 55	23 03		23 10		23 12		23 33		23 50	23 53
	d	21 59			22 16						22 49		22 56										
Penkridge	d	22 09											23 06										
Stafford	a	22 15			22 29						23 01		23 13										

Station		LM	VT
		◇1	8 1 A ⊏
London Euston 15 ⊖	d	21 28	23 10
Northampton	d	22 55	⌇
Long Buckby	d	23 06	⌇
Rugby	d	23 17	23s58
Coventry	a	23 29	00s09
	d	23 30	⌇
Canley	d	23 33	⌇
Tile Hill	d	23 37	⌇
Berkswell	d	23 40	⌇
Hampton-in-Arden	d	23 44	⌇
Birmingham International ✈	a	23 47	00s20
	d	23 48	⌇
Marston Green	d	23 51	⌇
Lea Hall	d	23 54	⌇
Stechford	d	23 57	⌇
Adderley Park	d		⌇
Birmingham New Street 12	a	00 04	00 34
	d		
Smethwick Rolfe Street	d		
Smethwick Galton Bridge 7	d		
Sandwell & Dudley	d		
Dudley Port	d		
Tipton	d		
Coseley	d		
Wolverhampton 7	a		
	d		
Penkridge	d		
Stafford	a		

A from 28 Jul until 11 August, then from 1 September

Table 68

Saturdays
from 15 September

Northampton - Coventry - Birmingham - Wolverhampton - Stafford

Network Diagram - see first Page of Table 67

Station		AW	LM	VT	VT	VT	XC	LM	LM	LM	VT	AW	XC	LM	LM	LM	LM	XC	LM	LM	LM	LM
			◇1	◇1 ⊏	◇1 ⊏	◇1 ⊏	◇1	◇1	◇1		◇1 ⊏	◇ ⌶	◇1 ⌶		◇1		1	◇1 ⌶	◇1	◇1		
London Euston 15 ⊖	d		21p46	22p30	23p30																	
Northampton	d		22p55						05 42										05 55			
Long Buckby	d		23p06																06 06			
Rugby	d		23p17	00 01	01 05				06 05										06 17			
Coventry	a		23p29	00 10	01 18														06 29			
	d		23p30	00 10	01 18												06 10		06 30			
Canley	d		23p33														06 13		06 33			
Tile Hill	d		23p37														06 17		06 37			
Berkswell	d		23p40														06 20		06 40			
Hampton-in-Arden	d		23p44														06 24					
Birmingham International ✈	a		23p47	00 21	01 29												06 27		06 45			
	d		23p48	00 21	01 29									06 17			06 28		06 46			
Marston Green	d		23p51														06 31		06 49			
Lea Hall	d		23p54											06 21					06 52			
Stechford	d		23p57											06 24					06 55			
Adderley Park	d													06 27								
Birmingham New Street 12	a		00 04	00 32	01 41									06 32			06 39		07 01			
	d	23p32		00 35	01 42	05 30	05 57	06 01		06 08	06 20	06 24	06 31		06 36	06 38		06 57		07 01	07 05	07 08
Smethwick Rolfe Street	d									06 14						06 44						07 14
Smethwick Galton Bridge 7	d							06 07		06 16		06 30				06 46				07 07		07 16
Sandwell & Dudley	d									06 19						06 49					07 13	07 19
Dudley Port	d									06 22						06 52						07 22
Tipton	d									06 24						06 54						07 24
Coseley	d									06 27						06 57						07 27
Wolverhampton 7	a	00 01		01 03	02 10	05 47	06 14	06 18		06 33	06 37	06 42	06 48		06 54	07 03		07 14		07 18	07 24	07 33
	d					05 48	06 16	06 18					06 49		06 54			07 15		07 18		
Penkridge	d							06 29												07 30		
Stafford	a					06 00	06 29	06 35	06 54				07 00		07 08			07 29		07 36		

Station		LM	LM	VT	AW	XC	LM	LM	LM	LM	VT	XC	LM	LM	LM	LM	LM	VT	AW	VT	XC	LM	LM
		◇1	◇1	◇1 ⊏	◇ ⌶	◇1 ⌶		◇1		1	◇1 ⊏	◇1 ⌶	◇1	◇1			◇1	◇1 ⊏	◇ ⌶	◇1 ⊏	◇1 ⊏		◇1
London Euston 15 ⊖	d										06 23		05 34							07 03			
Northampton	d	06 16	06 38										06 55				07 16						
Long Buckby	d	06 27											07 06				07 27						
Rugby	d	06 38	06 58										07 17				07 38			07 51			
Coventry	a	06 49									07 22		07 29				07 49			08 02			
	d	06 50								07 10	07 22	07 27	07 30				07 50			08 02			
Canley	d									07 13			07 33										
Tile Hill	d	06 55								07 17			07 37				07 55						
Berkswell	d									07 20			07 40										
Hampton-in-Arden	d	07 01								07 24							08 01						
Birmingham International ✈	a	07 04								07 27	07 33	07 37	07 45				08 04			08 13			
	d	07 05			07 09		07 17			07 28	07 33	07 38	07 46				08 05		08 09	08 13		08 17	
Marston Green	d	07 08								07 31			07 49				08 08						
Lea Hall	d						07 21						07 52									08 21	
Stechford	d						07 24						07 55									08 24	
Adderley Park	d						07 27															08 27	
Birmingham New Street 12	a	07 16			07 19		07 32			07 42	07 45	07 48	08 01				08 16		08 20	08 27		08 32	
	d			07 20	07 23	07 31		07 36	07 38		07 49	07 57		08 01	08 05	08 08		08 20	08 24		08 31		08 36
Smethwick Rolfe Street	d								07 44							08 14							
Smethwick Galton Bridge 7	d				07 29				07 46					08 08		08 16			08 30				
Sandwell & Dudley	d								07 49		07 58				08 13	08 19							
Dudley Port	d								07 52							08 22							
Tipton	d								07 54							08 24							
Coseley	d							07 46	07 57							08 27							08 46
Wolverhampton 7	a			07 37	07 40	07 48		07 53	08 03		08 11	08 14		08 19	08 24	08 33		08 37	08 42		08 48		08 53
	d					07 49		07 53				08 15		08 19							08 49		08 53
Penkridge	d							08 03						08 29									09 03
Stafford	a		07 53			08 00		08 09				08 29		08 35							09 00		09 09

Northampton - Coventry - Birmingham - Wolverhampton - Stafford

Network Diagram - see first Page of Table 67

	LM	LM ■	LM ◇■	VT ◇■	XC ◇■	LM ◇■	LM ◇■	LM	VT ◇■	LM	LM ◇■	VT ◇■	AW ◇	VT ◇■	XC ◇■	LM	LM ◇■	LM	LM ■	LM ◇■	VT ◇■
London Euston ⊖ d			06 24	07 23					07 43					08 03					07 04	07 46	08 23
Northampton d		07 37	07 45			07 55					08 16								08 37	08 45	
Long Buckby d		07 48				08 06					08 27								08 48		
Rugby d		07 59	08 04			08 17					08 38			08 51					08 59	09 04	
Coventry a		08 10		08 22		08 29			08 42		08 49			09 02					09 10		09 22
d		08 11		08 22	08 27	08 30			08 42		08 50			09 02					09 11		09 22
Canley d		08 14				08 33													09 14		
Tile Hill d		08 18				08 37					08 55								09 18		
Berkswell d		08 21				08 40													09 21		
Hampton-in-Arden d		08 25									09 01								09 25		
Birmingham International ✈ a		08 28		08 33	08 37	08 45			08 53		09 04			09 13					09 28		09 33
d		08 29		08 33	08 38	08 46			08 53		09 05		09 09	09 13		09 17			09 29		09 33
Marston Green d		08 32				08 49					09 08								09 32		
Lea Hall d						08 52										09 21					
Stechford d						08 55										09 24					
Adderley Park d																09 27					
Birmingham New Street a		08 42		08 45	08 48	09 01			09 08		09 16		09 20	09 27		09 32			09 42		09 45
d	08 38			08 49	08 57		09 01	09 05		09 08		09 20	09 24		09 31		09 36	09 38			09 49
Smethwick Rolfe Street d	08 44									09 14								09 44			
Smethwick Galton Bridge d	08 46						09 08			09 16			09 30					09 46			
Sandwell & Dudley d	08 49			08 58				09 13		09 19								09 49			09 58
Dudley Port d	08 52									09 22								09 52			
Tipton d	08 54									09 24								09 54			
Coseley d	08 57									09 27							09 46	09 57			
Wolverhampton a	09 03			09 11	09 14		09 19	09 24		09 33		09 37	09 43		09 48		09 53	10 03			10 11
d					09 15		09 19								09 49		09 53				
Penkridge d																	10 03				
Stafford a			08 53		09 29		09 34								10 00		10 09			09 53	

	XC ◇■	LM ◇■	LM ◇■	LM	VT ◇■	LM	LM ◇■	VT ◇■	AW ◇	VT ◇■	XC ◇■	LM	LM ◇■	LM	LM ■	VT ◇■	XC ◇■	LM ◇■		LM ◇■	LM	VT ◇■
London Euston ⊖ d					08 43		07 54			09 03						09 23		08 46				09 43
Northampton d		08 55					09 16								09 37			09 45	09 55			
Long Buckby d		09 06					09 27								09 48				10 06			
Rugby d		09 17					09 38			09 51					09 59			10 04	10 17			
Coventry a		09 29			09 42		09 49			10 02					10 10	10 22			10 29			10 42
d	09 27	09 30			09 42		09 50			10 02					10 11	10 22	10 27		10 30			10 42
Canley d		09 33													10 14				10 33			
Tile Hill d		09 37					09 55								10 18				10 37			
Berkswell d		09 40													10 21				10 40			
Hampton-in-Arden d							10 01								10 25							
Birmingham International ✈ a	09 37	09 45			09 53		10 04			10 13					10 28	10 33	10 37		10 45			10 53
d	09 38	09 46			09 53		10 05		10 09	10 13		10 17			10 29	10 33	10 38		10 46			10 53
Marston Green d		09 49					10 08								10 32				10 49			
Lea Hall d		09 52										10 21							10 52			
Stechford d		09 55										10 24							10 55			
Adderley Park d												10 27										
Birmingham New Street a	09 48	10 01			10 08		10 16		10 19	10 27		10 32			10 42	10 45	10 48		11 01			11 08
d	09 57		10 01	10 05		10 08		10 20	10 24		10 31		10 36	10 38		10 49	10 57			11 01	11 05	
Smethwick Rolfe Street d						10 14								10 44								
Smethwick Galton Bridge d			10 08			10 16			10 30					10 46						11 08		
Sandwell & Dudley d				10 13		10 19								10 49		10 58					11 13	
Dudley Port d						10 22								10 52								
Tipton d						10 24								10 54								
Coseley d						10 27							10 46	10 57								
Wolverhampton a	10 14		10 19	10 24		10 33		10 37	10 42		10 48		10 53	11 03		11 11	11 14			11 19	11 24	
d	10 15		10 19								10 49		10 53				11 15			11 19		
Penkridge d													11 03									
Stafford a	10 29		10 35								11 00		11 09				11 29	10 53		11 35		

Table 68

Saturdays
from 15 September

Northampton - Coventry - Birmingham - Wolverhampton - Stafford

Network Diagram - see first Page of Table 67

	LM	LM ◇■	VT ◇■	AW ◇	LM ■	VT ◇■	XC ◇■	LM	LM ◇■	LM	VT ◇■	XC ◇■	LM ◇■		LM ◇■	LM	VT ◇■	LM	LM ◇■	VT ◇■	AW ◇
London Euston ⊖ d		09 13				10 03					10 23		09 46				10 43		10 13		
Northampton d		10 16			10 25								10 45	10 55					11 16		
Long Buckby d		10 27			10 36									11 06					11 27		
Rugby d		10 38			10 48	10 51							11 04	11 17					11 38		
Coventry a		10 49			10 59	11 02					11 22			11 29			11 42		11 49		
d		10 50			11 11	11 02					11 22	11 27		11 30			11 42		11 50		
Canley d					11 14									11 33							
Tile Hill d		10 55			11 18									11 37					11 55		
Berkswell d					11 21									11 40							
Hampton-in-Arden d		11 01			11 25														12 01		
Birmingham International ✈ a		11 04			11 28	11 13					11 33	11 37		11 45			11 53		12 04		
d		11 05		11 09	11 29	11 13		11 17			11 33	11 38		11 46			11 53		12 05		12 09
Marston Green d		11 08			11 32									11 49					12 08		
Lea Hall d								11 21						11 52							
Stechford d								11 24						11 55							
Adderley Park d								11 27													
Birmingham New Street a		11 16		11 20	11 42	11 27		11 32			11 45	11 48		12 01			12 08		12 16		12 20
d	11 08		11 20	11 24			11 31		11 36	11 38	11 49	11 57			12 01	12 05		12 08		12 20	12 24
Smethwick Rolfe Street d	11 14									11 44								12 14			
Smethwick Galton Bridge d	11 16			11 30						11 46					12 08			12 16			12 30
Sandwell & Dudley d	11 19									11 49	11 58					12 13		12 19			
Dudley Port d	11 22									11 52								12 22			
Tipton d	11 24									11 54								12 24			
Coseley d	11 27								11 46	11 57								12 27			
Wolverhampton a	11 33		11 37	11 42			11 48		11 53	12 03	12 11	12 14			12 19	12 24		12 33		12 37	12 42
d							11 49		11 53			12 15			12 19						
Penkridge d									12 03												
Stafford a							12 00		12 09			12 29	11 53		12 35						

	LM ■	VT ◇■	XC ◇■	LM	LM ◇■	LM	VT ◇■	XC ◇■	LM ◇■		LM ◇■	LM	VT ◇■	LM	LM ◇■	VT ◇■	AW ◇	LM ■	VT ◇■	XC ◇■	LM	LM ◇■
London Euston ⊖ d		11 03					11 23		10 46				11 43		11 13				12 03			
Northampton d	11 25								11 45	11 55					12 16			12 25				
Long Buckby d	11 36									12 06					12 27			12 36				
Rugby d	11 47	11 51							12 04	12 17					12 38			12 47	12 51			
Coventry a	11 58	12 02					12 22			12 29			12 42		12 49			12 58	13 02			
d	12 11	12 02					12 22	12 27		12 30			12 42		12 50			13 11	13 02			
Canley d	12 14									12 33								13 14				
Tile Hill d	12 18									12 37					12 55			13 18				
Berkswell d	12 21									12 40								13 21				
Hampton-in-Arden d	12 25														13 01			13 25				
Birmingham International ✈ a	12 28	12 13					12 33	12 37		12 45			12 53		13 04			13 28	13 13			
d	12 29	12 13		12 17			12 33	12 38		12 46			12 53		13 05		13 09	13 29	13 13		13 17	
Marston Green d	12 32									12 49					13 08			13 32				
Lea Hall d				12 21						12 52											13 21	
Stechford d				12 24						12 55											13 24	
Adderley Park d				12 27																	13 27	
Birmingham New Street a	12 42	12 27		12 32			12 45	12 48		13 01			13 08		13 16		13 21	13 42	13 27		13 32	
d			12 31		12 36	12 38	12 49	12 57			13 01	13 05		13 08		13 20	13 24			13 31		13 36
Smethwick Rolfe Street d						12 44								13 14								
Smethwick Galton Bridge d						12 46					13 08			13 16			13 30					
Sandwell & Dudley d						12 49	12 58					13 13		13 19								
Dudley Port d						12 52								13 22								
Tipton d						12 54								13 24								
Coseley d					12 46	12 57								13 27								13 46
Wolverhampton a			12 48		12 53	13 03	13 11	13 14			13 19	13 24		13 33		13 37	13 42			13 48		13 53
d			12 49		12 53			13 15			13 19									13 49		13 53
Penkridge d					13 03																	14 03
Stafford a			13 00		13 09			13 29	12 53		13 35									14 00		14 09

Saturdays from 15 September

Northampton - Coventry - Birmingham - Wolverhampton - Stafford

Network Diagram - see first Page of Table 67

		LM	VT	XC	LM		LM		LM	VT	LM	LM	VT	AW	LM	VT	XC		LM	LM	LM	VT	XC	LM	
			◇1	◇1	◇1		◇1			◇1		◇1	◇1	◇	1	◇1	◇1			◇1		◇1	◇1	◇1	
London Euston ⊖	d		12 23		11 46					12 43		12 13				13 03						13 23		12 46	
Northampton	d				12 45	12 55						13 16			13 25									13 45	13 55
Long Buckby	d					13 06						13 27			13 36										14 06
Rugby	d				13 04	13 17						13 38			13 47	13 51								14 04	14 17
Coventry	a		13 22			13 29				13 42		13 49			13 58	14 02						14 22			14 29
	d		13 22	13 27		13 30				13 42		13 50			14 11	14 02						14 22	14 27		14 30
Canley	d					13 33									14 14										14 33
Tile Hill	d					13 37						13 55			14 18										14 37
Berkswell	d					13 40									14 21										14 40
Hampton-in-Arden	d											14 01			14 25										
Birmingham International ✈	a		13 33	13 37		13 45				13 53		14 04			14 28	14 13						14 33	14 37		14 45
	d		13 33	13 38		13 46				13 53		14 05		14 09	14 29	14 13			14 17			14 33	14 38		14 46
Marston Green	d					13 49						14 08			14 32										14 49
Lea Hall	d					13 52													14 21						14 52
Stechford	d					13 55													14 24						14 55
Adderley Park	d																		14 27						
Birmingham New Street	a		13 45	13 48		14 01				14 08		14 16		14 19	14 42	14 27			14 32			14 45	14 48		15 01
	d	13 38	13 49	13 57			14 01		14 05		14 08		14 20	14 24			14 31			14 36	14 38	14 49	14 57		
Smethwick Rolfe Street	d	13 44									14 14										14 44				
Smethwick Galton Bridge	d	13 46					14 08				14 16			14 30							14 46				
Sandwell & Dudley	d	13 49	13 58						14 13		14 19										14 49	14 58			
Dudley Port	d	13 52									14 22										14 52				
Tipton	d	13 54									14 24										14 54				
Coseley	d	13 57									14 27									14 46	14 57				
Wolverhampton	a	14 03	14 11	14 14			14 19		14 24		14 33		14 37	14 42			14 48			14 53	15 03	15 11	15 14		
	d			14 15			14 19										14 49			14 53			15 15		
Penkridge	d																			15 03					
Stafford	a			14 29	13 53		14 35										15 00			15 09			15 29	14 53	

		LM	LM		VT	LM	LM	VT	AW	LM	VT	XC	LM		LM	LM	VT	XC	LM		LM	LM	VT		LM
		◇1			◇1		◇1	◇1	◇	1	◇1	◇1			◇1		◇1	◇1	◇1		◇1		◇1		
London Euston ⊖	d				13 43		13 13				14 03						14 23		13 46				14 43		
Northampton	d						14 16			14 25									14 45	14 55					
Long Buckby	d						14 27			14 36										15 06					
Rugby	d						14 38			14 47	14 51								15 04	15 17					
Coventry	a				14 42		14 49			14 58	15 02						15 22			15 29			15 42		
	d				14 42		14 50			15 11	15 02						15 22	15 27		15 30			15 42		
Canley	d									15 14										15 33					
Tile Hill	d						14 55			15 18										15 37					
Berkswell	d									15 21										15 40					
Hampton-in-Arden	d						15 01			15 25															
Birmingham International ✈	a				14 53		15 04			15 28	15 13						15 33	15 37		15 45			15 53		
	d				14 53		15 05		15 09	15 29	15 13		15 17				15 33	15 38		15 46			15 53		
Marston Green	d						15 08			15 32										15 49					
Lea Hall	d												15 21							15 52					
Stechford	d												15 24							15 55					
Adderley Park	d												15 27												
Birmingham New Street	a				15 08		15 16		15 20	15 42	15 27		15 32				15 45	15 48		16 01			16 08		
	d	15 01	15 05			15 08		15 20	15 24			15 31			15 36	15 38	15 49	15 57			16 01	16 05			16 08
Smethwick Rolfe Street	d					15 14										15 44									16 14
Smethwick Galton Bridge	d	15 08				15 16			15 30							15 46					16 08				16 16
Sandwell & Dudley	d		15 13			15 19										15 49	15 58					16 13			16 19
Dudley Port	d					15 22										15 52									16 22
Tipton	d					15 24										15 54									16 24
Coseley	d					15 27									15 46	15 57									16 27
Wolverhampton	a	15 19	15 24			15 33		15 37	15 42			15 48			15 53	16 03	16 11	16 14			16 19	16 24			16 33
	d	15 19										15 49			15 53			16 15			16 19				
Penkridge	d														16 03										
Stafford	a	15 35										16 00			16 09			16 29	15 53		16 35				

Table 68

Saturdays from 15 September

Northampton - Coventry - Birmingham - Wolverhampton - Stafford

Network Diagram - see first Page of Table 67

		LM	VT	AW	LM	VT	XC	LM	LM		LM	VT	XC	LM		LM	LM	VT	LM		LM	VT	AW	LM	VT
		◇1	◇1	1	1	◇1	◇1		◇1			◇1	◇1	◇1		◇1		◇1			◇1	◇1	◇	1	◇1
London Euston ⊖	d	14 13				15 03						15 23		14 46				15 43			15 13				16 03
Northampton	d	15 16			15 25									15 45	15 55						16 16			16 25	
Long Buckby	d	15 27			15 36										16 06						16 27			16 36	
Rugby	d	15 38			15 47	15 51								16 04	16 17						16 38			16 47	16 51
Coventry	a	15 49			15 58	16 02						16 22			16 29			16 42			16 49			16 58	17 02
	d	15 50			16 11	16 02						16 22	16 27		16 30			16 42			16 50			17 11	17 02
Canley	d				16 14										16 33									17 14	
Tile Hill	d	15 55			16 18										16 37						16 55			17 18	
Berkswell	d				16 21										16 40									17 21	
Hampton-in-Arden	d	16 01			16 25																17 01			17 25	
Birmingham International ✈	a	16 04			16 28	16 13						16 33	16 37		16 45			16 53			17 04			17 28	17 13
	d	16 05		16 09	16 29	16 13		16 17				16 33	16 38		16 46			16 53			17 05		17 09	17 29	17 13
Marston Green	d	16 08			16 32										16 49						17 08			17 32	
Lea Hall	d							16 21							16 52										
Stechford	d							16 24							16 55										
Adderley Park	d							16 27																	
Birmingham New Street	a	16 16		16 20	16 42	16 27		16 32				16 45	16 48		17 01			17 08			17 16		17 20	17 42	17 27
	d		16 20	16 24			16 31		16 36		16 38	16 49	16 57			17 01	17 05		17 08			17 20	17 24		
Smethwick Rolfe Street	d										16 44								17 14						
Smethwick Galton Bridge	d			16 30							16 46					17 08			17 16				17 31		
Sandwell & Dudley	d										16 49	16 58					17 13		17 19						
Dudley Port	d										16 52								17 22						
Tipton	d										16 54								17 24						
Coseley	d								16 46		16 57								17 27						
Wolverhampton	a		16 37	16 42			16 48		16 53		17 04	17 11	17 14			17 19	17 24		17 33			17 37	17 42		
	d						16 49		16 53				17 15			17 19									
Penkridge	d								17 03							17 29									
Stafford	a						17 00		17 09				17 29	16 53		17 35									

		XC	LM	LM	LM		VT	XC	LM		LM	LM	VT	LM	LM		VT	AW	LM	VT	XC	LM	LM	LM	VT
		◇1		◇1			◇1	◇1	◇1		◇1		◇1		◇1		◇1	◇	1	◇1	◇1		◇1		◇1
London Euston ⊖	d						16 23		15 46				16 43		16 13					17 03					17 23
Northampton	d								16 45	16 55					17 16				17 25						
Long Buckby	d									17 06					17 27				17 36						
Rugby	d								17 04	17 17					17 38				17 47	17 51					
Coventry	a						17 22			17 29			17 42		17 49				17 58	18 02					18 22
	d						17 22	17 27		17 30			17 42		17 50				18 11	18 02					18 22
Canley	d									17 33									18 14						
Tile Hill	d									17 37					17 55				18 18						
Berkswell	d									17 40									18 21						
Hampton-in-Arden	d														18 01				18 25						
Birmingham International ✈	a						17 33	17 37		17 45			17 53		18 04				18 28	18 13					18 33
	d		17 17				17 33	17 38		17 46			17 53		18 05			18 09	18 29	18 13		18 17			18 33
Marston Green	d									17 49					18 08				18 32						
Lea Hall	d		17 21							17 52												18 21			
Stechford	d		17 24							17 55												18 24			
Adderley Park	d		17 27																			18 27			
Birmingham New Street	a		17 32				17 45	17 48		18 01			18 08		18 16			18 20	18 42	18 27		18 32			18 45
	d	17 31		17 36	17 38		17 49	17 57			18 01	18 05		18 08			18 20	18 24			18 31		18 36	18 38	18 49
Smethwick Rolfe Street	d				17 44									18 14										18 44	
Smethwick Galton Bridge	d				17 46						18 08			18 16				18 30						18 46	
Sandwell & Dudley	d				17 49		17 58					18 13		18 19										18 49	18 58
Dudley Port	d				17 52									18 22										18 52	
Tipton	d				17 54									18 24										18 54	
Coseley	d			17 46	17 57									18 27									18 46	18 57	
Wolverhampton	a	17 48		17 53	18 03		18 11	18 14			18 19	18 24		18 33			18 37	18 42			18 48		18 53	19 03	19 11
	d	17 49		17 53				18 15			18 19										18 49		18 53		
Penkridge	d			18 03							18 29												19 03		
Stafford	a	18 00		18 09				18 29	18 04		18 35										19 00		19 09		

Table 68

Saturdays
from 15 September

Northampton - Coventry - Birmingham - Wolverhampton - Stafford

Network Diagram - see first Page of Table 67

		XC ◇■ 🛒	LM ◇■		LM ◇■	LM	VT ◇■ 🍴	LM	LM ◇■	VT ◇■ 🍴	AW ◇ 🛒	XC ◇■ 🍴	LM ■	VT ◇■ 🍴	LM	LM	VT ◇■ 🍴	XC ◇■ A 🛒	LM ◇■	LM ■		LM
London Euston ⊖	d		16 46				17 43		17 13					18 03			18 23			17 46		
Northampton	d		17 45	17 55					18 16				18 25							18 45	18 55	
Long Buckby	d			18 06					18 27				18 36								19 06	
Rugby	d		18 04	18 17					18 38				18 47	18 51						19 04	19 17	
Coventry	a			18 29			18 42		18 49				18 58	19 02			19 22				19 29	
	d	18 27		18 30			18 42		18 50				19 11	19 02			19 22	19 27			19 30	
Canley	d			18 33									19 14								19 33	
Tile Hill	d			18 37					18 55				19 18								19 37	
Berkswell	d			18 40									19 21								19 40	
Hampton-in-Arden	d								19 01				19 25									
Birmingham International ✈	a	18 37		18 45			18 53		19 04				19 28	19 13			19 33	19 37			19 45	
	d	18 38		18 46			18 53		19 05		19 09		19 29	19 13	19 17		19 33	19 38			19 46	
Marston Green	d			18 49					19 08				19 32								19 49	
Lea Hall	d			18 52											19 21						19 52	
Stechford	d			18 55											19 24						19 55	
Adderley Park	d														19 27							
Birmingham New Street	a	18 48		19 01			19 08		19 16		19 20		19 42	19 25	19 32		19 45	19 48			20 02	
	d	18 57			19 01	19 05		19 08		19 20	19 24	19 31		19 42		19 38	19 50	19 57	20 01			20 05
Smethwick Rolfe Street	d							19 14								19 44						
Smethwick Galton Bridge	d				19 08			19 16			19 30					19 46			20 08			
Sandwell & Dudley	d					19 13		19 19						19 54		19 49	19 59					20 13
Dudley Port	d							19 22								19 52						
Tipton	d							19 24								19 54						
Coseley	d							19 27								19 57						
Wolverhampton	a	19 14			19 19	19 24		19 33		19 37	19 42	19 48		20 08		20 03	20 12	20 14	20 20			20 24
	d	19 15			19 19							19 49						20 15	20 22			
Penkridge	d				19 29														20 31			
Stafford	a	19 29	18 53		19 35							20 00						20 29	20 37	19 53		

		VT ◇■ 🍴	LM	LM ◇■	VT ◇■ 🍴	AW ◇	XC ◇■ 🍴	VT ◇■ 🍴	LM	LM ◇■	LM	LM ■	VT ◇■ 🍴	XC ◇■ A 🛒	LM ■		LM	LM	VT ◇■ 🍴	AW ◇	LM ◇■	LM	LM ◇■
London Euston ⊖	d	18 43		18 13				19 03					19 23		18 46				19 43		19 13		
Northampton	d			19 16								19 37			19 45	19 55					20 20		
Long Buckby	d			19 27								19 48				20 06					20 31		
Rugby	d			19 38				19 51				19 59			20 04	20 17					20 43		
Coventry	a	19 42		19 49				20 02				20 10	20 22			20 29			20 49		20 54		
	d	19 42		19 50				20 02				20 11	20 22	20 27		20 30			20 49		20 55		
Canley	d											20 14				20 33					20 58		
Tile Hill	d			19 55								20 18				20 37					21 02		
Berkswell	d											20 21				20 40					21 05		
Hampton-in-Arden	d			20 01								20 25									21 09		
Birmingham International ✈	a	19 53		20 04				20 13				20 28	20 33	20 37		20 45			21 00		21 12		
	d	19 53		20 05		20 09		20 13	20 17			20 29	20 33	20 38		20 46			21 00	21 09	21 13	21 17	
Marston Green	d			20 08								20 32				20 49					21 16		
Lea Hall	d								20 21							20 52						21 21	
Stechford	d								20 24							20 55						21 24	
Adderley Park	d								20 27													21 27	
Birmingham New Street	a	20 08		20 16		20 20		20 25	20 32			20 42	20 45	20 48		21 01			21 12	21 19	21 24	21 32	
	d		20 08		20 20	20 24	20 31	20 42		20 36	20 38		20 50	20 57			21 05	21 08	21 16	21 24			21 36
Smethwick Rolfe Street	d		20 14								20 44							21 14					
Smethwick Galton Bridge	d		20 16			20 30					20 46							21 16		21 30			
Sandwell & Dudley	d		20 19					20 54			20 49		20 59				21 13	21 19					
Dudley Port	d		20 22								20 52							21 22					
Tipton	d		20 24								20 54							21 24					
Coseley	d		20 27							20 46	20 57							21 27					21 46
Wolverhampton	a		20 33		20 37	20 42	20 48	21 08		20 53	21 03		21 12	21 14			21 24	21 33	21 38	21 42			21 53
	d				20 37		20 49			20 53				21 15									21 59
Penkridge	d									21 03													22 09
Stafford	a				20 49		21 00			21 09				21 29	20 54								22 15

A 🛒 to Birmingham New Street

Table 68

Saturdays
from 15 September

Northampton - Coventry - Birmingham - Wolverhampton - Stafford

Network Diagram - see first Page of Table 67

		LM	LM ■	XC ◇■	LM ◇■	LM A	LM	VT ◇■ 🍴	LM ◇■	XC ◇■	XC ◇■	LM	LM ◇■	LM	LM ■	VT ◇■ 🍴	XC ◇■	AW	LM ◇■	LM	LM ◇■	VT ◇■ 🍴
London Euston ⊖	d							20 25	19 46							21 03			20 34			21 43
Northampton	d				20 55				21 16										21 55		22 16	
Long Buckby	d				21 06				21 27										22 06		22 27	
Rugby	d				21 17				21 38							22 12			22 17		22 38	22 53
Coventry	a				21 29			21 36	21 49							22 22			22 29		22 49	23 02
	d		21 11	21 27	21 30			21 36	21 50	21 56					22 11	22 23	22 27		22 30		22 50	23 02
Canley	d		21 14		21 33										22 14				22 33			
Tile Hill	d		21 18		21 37				21 55						22 18				22 37		22 55	
Berkswell	d		21 21		21 40										22 21				22 40			
Hampton-in-Arden	d		21 25						22 01						22 25						23 01	
Birmingham International ✈	a		21 28	21 37	21 45			21 50	22 04	22 10					22 28	22 33	22 36		22 45		23 04	23 13
	d		21 29	21 38	21 46			21 50	22 05	22 11		22 21			22 29	22 34	22 38		22 46		23 05	23 13
Marston Green	d		21 32		21 49				22 08						22 32				22 49		23 08	
Lea Hall	d				21 52							22 25							22 52			
Stechford	d				21 55							22 28							22 55			
Adderley Park	d											22 31										
Birmingham New Street	a		21 42	21 48	22 01			22 04	22 16	22 21		22 36			22 42	22 45	22 48		23 01		23 16	23 25
	d	21 38		21 57		22 05	22 08	22 16			22 31		22 36	22 38		22 48		22 55		23 08		23 28
Smethwick Rolfe Street	d	21 44					22 14							22 44						23 14		
Smethwick Galton Bridge	d	21 46					22 16						22 42	22 46						23 16		
Sandwell & Dudley	d	21 49				22 13	22 19	22 25						22 49		22 57				23 19		23 37
Dudley Port	d	21 52					22 22							22 52						23 22		
Tipton	d	21 54					22 24							22 54						23 24		
Coseley	d	21 57					22 27						22 48	22 57						23 27		
Wolverhampton	a	22 03		22 14		22 24	22 33	22 38			22 48		22 55	23 03		23 10		23 12		23 33		23 50
	d			22 16							22 49		22 56									
Penkridge	d												23 06									
Stafford	a			22 29							23 01		23 13									

		AW	LM ◇■
London Euston ⊖	d		21 28
Northampton	d		22 55
Long Buckby	d		23 06
Rugby	d		23 17
Coventry	a		23 29
	d		23 30
Canley	d		23 33
Tile Hill	d		23 37
Berkswell	d		23 40
Hampton-in-Arden	d		23 44
Birmingham International ✈	a		23 47
	d		23 48
Marston Green	d		23 51
Lea Hall	d		23 54
Stechford	d		23 57
Adderley Park	d		
Birmingham New Street	a		00 04
	d	23 35	
Smethwick Rolfe Street	d		
Smethwick Galton Bridge	d		
Sandwell & Dudley	d		
Dudley Port	d		
Tipton	d		
Coseley	d		
Wolverhampton	a	23 53	
	d		
Penkridge	d		
Stafford	a		

A 8 December

Table 68

Sundays until 24 June

Northampton - Coventry - Birmingham - Wolverhampton - Stafford

Network Diagram - see first Page of Table 67

		LM	LM	VT	XC	LM	VT	LM	LM	LM		LM	AW	XC	VT	LM	LM	LM	LM	LM		VT	AW	XC	LM
		◇1	🚌	◇1	◇1	1	◇1	1	🚌	◇1		1		◇1	◇1	◇1	1	🚌	◇1	1		◇1	◇	◇1	◇1
London Euston	d	21p28														07 50						08 50			08 23
Northampton	d	22p55														09 30	09 40								10 00
Long Buckby	d	23p06														09 41	09 51								10 11
Rugby	d	23p17														09 52	10 02					10 14			10 22
Coventry	a	23p29														10 03						10 23			10 33
	d	23p30				08 37						09 07				10 04				10 08		10 24		10 28	10 34
Canley	d	23p33				08 40						09 10								10 11					10 37
Tile Hill	d	23p37				08 44						09 14								10 15					10 41
Berkswell	d	23p40				08 47						09 17								10 18					10 44
Hampton-in-Arden	d	23p44				08 51						09 21								10 22					10 48
Birmingham International	a	23p47				08 54						09 24				10 13				10 26		10 34		10 38	10 51
	d	23p48				08 55		09 03				09 25				10 13				10 26		10 35		10 40	10 52
Marston Green	d	23p51				08 58		09 06				09 28				10 16				10 29					10 55
Lea Hall	d	23p54						09 09								10 20									
Stechford	d	23p57						09 12								10 22									
Adderley Park	d							09 15								10 26									
Birmingham New Street	a	00 04				09 06		09 20				09 36				10 30				10 38		10 47		10 50	11 03
	d		08 30	08 35	08 50		09 09		09 30	09 34			09 52	10 01	10 09			10 30	10 35			10 51	10 57	11 01	
Smethwick Rolfe Street	d		08 41						09 41									10 41							
Smethwick Galton Bridge	d		08 46						09 46									10 46							
Sandwell & Dudley	d		08 53						09 53									10 53							
Dudley Port	d		09 02						10 02									11 02							
Tipton	d		09 11						10 11									11 11							
Coseley	d		09 20						10 20									11 20							
Wolverhampton	a		09 33	09 02	09 18		09 36		10 33	10 00			10 21	10 28	10 36			11 33	10 59			11 19	11 26	11 29	
	d			09 04	09 19					10 00				10 29					11 00					11 30	
Penkridge	d									10 10									11 10						
Stafford	a			09 16	09 32					10 16				10 43			10 56		11 16					11 42	

		VT	LM	LM	LM	VT		XC	LM	LM	LM	VT	AW	LM	LM	LM		VT	XC	LM	AW	VT	VT	LM	LM
		◇1	🚌	◇1	1	◇1		◇1	◇1	1	◇1	◇1	◇	◇1	🚌	1		◇1	◇1	◇1	◇	◇1	◇1	◇1	🚌
London Euston	d					09 50			09 23	09 54	10 24							10 50		10 28			11 45		
Northampton	d								11 00	11 08	11 40									11 58					
Long Buckby	d								11 11	11 19	11 51									12 09					
Rugby	d					11 15			11 22	11 30	12 03							12 14		12 20			12 48		
Coventry	a					11 25			11 33									12 24		12 31			12 56		
	d				11 08	11 25		11 29	11 34							12 08		12 25	12 28	12 32			12 57		
Canley	d								11 37											12 35					
Tile Hill	d								11 41											12 39					
Berkswell	d								11 44											12 42					
Hampton-in-Arden	d								11 48											12 46					
Birmingham International	a				11 18	11 36		11 38	11 51							12 17		12 35	12 38	12 49			13 07		
	d				11 18	11 36		11 40	11 52							12 18		12 36	12 40	12 50			13 08		
Marston Green	d				11 21				11 55							12 21				12 53					
Lea Hall	d				11 24											12 24									
Stechford	d				11 27											12 27									
Adderley Park	d				11 30											12 30									
Birmingham New Street	a				11 37	11 49		11 50	12 03							12 37		12 48	12 50	13 01			13 22		
	d	11 09	11 30	11 33		11 52		12 01				12 09	12 12	12 28	12 30			12 52	12 58		13 02	13 10		13 28	13 30
Smethwick Rolfe Street	d		11 41												12 41										13 41
Smethwick Galton Bridge	d		11 46												12 46										13 46
Sandwell & Dudley	d		11 53												12 53										13 53
Dudley Port	d		12 02												13 02										14 02
Tipton	d		12 11												13 11										14 11
Coseley	d		12 20												13 20										14 20
Wolverhampton	a	11 36	12 33	11 59		12 21		12 28				12 37	12 41	12 52	13 33			13 19	13 25		13 31	13 37		13 52	14 33
	d			12 00				12 28						12 53					13 26					13 53	
Penkridge	d			12 10										13 03										14 03	
Stafford	a			12 16				12 42		12 19	12 59			13 09					13 39					14 09	

Table 68

Sundays until 24 June

Northampton - Coventry - Birmingham - Wolverhampton - Stafford

Network Diagram - see first Page of Table 67

		XC		LM	VT	XC	LM	LM	AW	VT	VT	VT		LM	LM	XC	LM	VT	XC	LM	LM	AW		VT	VT
		◇1		1	◇1	◇1	◇1	◇1	◇	◇1	◇1	◇1		◇1	🚌	◇1	1	◇1	◇1	◇1	◇1	◇		◇1	◇1
London Euston	d				12 18		11 24			12 38		12 58						13 18		12 34	12 50			13 38	
Northampton	d						12 51	13 02												13 51	14 02				
Long Buckby	d						13 02	13 13												14 02	14 13				
Rugby	d						13 15	13 25				13 49								14 15	14 26				
Coventry	a				13 20		13 28			13 40		14 00						14 20		14 28				14 40	
	d			13 10	13 21	13 26	13 29			13 40		14 00					14 10	14 20	14 26	14 29				14 40	
Canley	d						13 32													14 32					
Tile Hill	d			13 15			13 36										14 15			14 36					
Berkswell	d						13 39													14 39					
Hampton-in-Arden	d						13 43													14 43					
Birmingham International	a			13 22	13 31	13 37	13 46			13 51		14 11					14 22	14 31	14 35	14 46				14 51	
	d			13 22	13 32	13 38	13 47			13 51		14 11					14 22	14 31	14 38	14 47				14 51	
Marston Green	d			13 25			13 50										14 25			14 50					
Lea Hall	d			13 29													14 29								
Stechford	d			13 31													14 31								
Adderley Park	d			13 35													14 35								
Birmingham New Street	a			13 40	13 44	13 48	13 58			14 05		14 25					14 40	14 44	14 48	14 58				15 05	
	d	13 31			13 48	13 58			14 03		14 10			14 28	14 30	14 31		14 48	14 58			15 02			15 10
Smethwick Rolfe Street	d														14 41										
Smethwick Galton Bridge	d														14 46										
Sandwell & Dudley	d														14 53										
Dudley Port	d														15 02										
Tipton	d														15 11										
Coseley	d														15 20										
Wolverhampton	a	14 00			14 16	14 24			14 32		14 37			14 53	15 33	15 00		15 18	15 25			15 31			15 37
	d					14 25								14 53					15 26						
Penkridge	d													15 03											
Stafford	a					14 38		14 17						15 09					15 39		15 17				

		VT	LM	LM	XC	LM	VT	XC		LM	LM	AW	VT	VT	VT	LM	LM	XC		LM	VT	XC	LM	LM	AW
		◇1	◇1	🚌	◇1	1	◇1	◇1		◇1	◇1	◇	◇1	◇1	◇1	◇1	🚌	◇1		1	◇1	◇1	◇1	◇1	◇
London Euston	d	13 58					14 18			13 34	13 50		14 38		14 58						15 18		14 34	14 50	
Northampton	d									14 51	15 02												15 51	16 02	
Long Buckby	d									15 02	15 13												16 02	16 13	
Rugby	d	14 49								15 15	15 26				15 49								16 16	16 26	
Coventry	a	15 00					15 20			15 28			15 40		16 00						16 20		16 28		
	d	15 00				15 10	15 20	15 26		15 29			15 40		16 00					16 10	16 20	16 26	16 29		
Canley	d									15 32													16 32		
Tile Hill	d					15 15				15 36										16 15			16 36		
Berkswell	d									15 39													16 39		
Hampton-in-Arden	d									15 43													16 43		
Birmingham International	a	15 11				15 22	15 31	15 35		15 46			15 51		16 11					16 22	16 31	16 35	16 46		
	d	15 11				15 22	15 31	15 38		15 47			15 51		16 11					16 22	16 31	16 38	16 47		
Marston Green	d					15 25				15 50										16 25			16 50		
Lea Hall	d					15 29														16 29					
Stechford	d					15 31														16 31					
Adderley Park	d					15 35														16 35					
Birmingham New Street	a	15 25				15 40	15 44	15 48		15 58			16 05		16 25					16 41	16 44	16 48	16 58		
	d		15 28	15 30	15 31		15 48	15 58				16 02		16 10		16 28	16 30	16 31			16 48	16 58			17 02
Smethwick Rolfe Street	d			15 41													16 41								
Smethwick Galton Bridge	d			15 46													16 46								
Sandwell & Dudley	d			15 53													16 53								
Dudley Port	d			16 02													17 02								
Tipton	d			16 11													17 11								
Coseley	d			16 20													17 20								
Wolverhampton	a		15 53	16 33	16 00		16 16	16 25				16 31		16 37		16 53	17 33	16 59			17 16	17 25			17 31
	d		15 53					16 26								16 53						17 26			
Penkridge	d		16 03													17 03									
Stafford	a		16 09					16 37			16 16					17 09						17 38		17 16	

Sundays
until 24 June

Northampton - Coventry - Birmingham - Wolverhampton - Stafford

Network Diagram - see first Page of Table 67

	VT	VT	VT		LM	LM	XC	LM	VT	XC	LM	LM	AW		VT	VT	VT	LM	LM	XC	LM	VT	XC
	◇■	◇■	◇■		◇■		◇■	■	◇■	◇■	◇■	◇■	◇		◇■	◇■	◇■	◇■		◇■	■	◇■	◇■
	A																						
London Euston ⊖ d	15 38		15 58						16 18		15 34	15 50			16 38		16 58					17 18	
Northampton d											16 51	17 02											
Long Buckby d											17 02	17 13											
Rugby d			16 49								17 15	17 26					17 49						
Coventry a	16 40		17 00						17 20		17 28				17 40		18 00					18 20	
Coventry d	16 40		17 00					17 10	17 20	17 26	17 29				17 40		18 00				18 10	18 20	18 26
Canley d											17 32												
Tile Hill d								17 15			17 36										18 15		
Berkswell d											17 39												
Hampton-in-Arden d											17 43												
Birmingham International a	16 51		17 11					17 22	17 31	17 35	17 46				17 51		18 11				18 22	18 31	18 35
d	16 51		17 11					17 22	17 31	17 38	17 47				17 51		18 11				18 22	18 31	18 38
Marston Green d								17 25			17 50										18 25		
Lea Hall d								17 29													18 29		
Stechford d								17 31													18 31		
Adderley Park d								17 35													18 35		
Birmingham New Street a	17 05		17 25					17 41	17 44	17 48	17 58				18 05		18 25				18 41	18 44	18 48
d		17 10			17 28	17 30	17 31		17 48	17 58			18 02			18 10		18 28	18 30	18 31		18 48	18 58
Smethwick Rolfe Street d						17 41													18 41				
Smethwick Galton Bridge ■ d						17 46													18 46				
Sandwell & Dudley d						17 53													18 53				
Dudley Port d						18 02													19 02				
Tipton d						18 11													19 11				
Coseley d						18 20													19 20				
Wolverhampton ■ a		17 37			17 53	18 33	17 59		18 16	18 25			18 33			18 37		18 54	19 33	19 00		19 16	19 25
d					17 53					18 26								18 54					19 26
Penkridge d					18 03													19 04					
Stafford a					18 09					18 36		18 16						19 10					19 38

	LM	LM	AW	VT	VT	LM	VT	LM	XC		LM	VT	XC	LM	LM	AW	VT	VT	XC		VT	LM	XC	LM
	◇■	◇■	◇	◇■	■	◇■	◇■		◇■		■	◇■	◇■	◇■	◇■	◇	◇■	◇■	◇■		◇■		◇■	■
London Euston ⊖ d	16 34	16 50		17 38			17 58					18 18		17 34	17 50		18 38				18 58			
Northampton d	17 51	18 02												18 51	19 02									
Long Buckby d	18 02	18 13												19 02	19 13									
Rugby d	18 15	18 29					18 49							19 15	19 26						19 49			
Coventry a	18 28			18 40			19 00					19 20		19 28			19 40				20 00			
Coventry d	18 29			18 40			19 01				19 10	19 20	19 26	19 29			19 40		19 54		20 00			20 10
Canley d	18 32													19 32										
Tile Hill d	18 36										19 15			19 36										20 15
Berkswell d	18 39													19 39										
Hampton-in-Arden d	18 43													19 43										
Birmingham International a	18 46			18 51			19 11				19 22	19 31	19 35	19 46			19 51		20 03		20 11			20 22
d	18 47			18 51			19 12				19 22	19 31	19 38	19 47			19 51		20 04		20 11			20 22
Marston Green d	18 50										19 25			19 50										20 25
Lea Hall d											19 29													20 29
Stechford d											19 31													20 31
Adderley Park d											19 35													20 35
Birmingham New Street a	18 58			19 05			19 24				19 40	19 44	19 48	19 58			20 05		20 15		20 23			20 41
d			19 02		19 10	19 16	19 28	19 30	19 31			19 48	19 58			20 02		20 10			20 26	20 30	20 31	
Smethwick Rolfe Street d								19 41														20 41		
Smethwick Galton Bridge ■ d								19 46														20 46		
Sandwell & Dudley d								19 53														20 53		
Dudley Port d								20 02														21 02		
Tipton d								20 11														21 11		
Coseley d								20 20														21 20		
Wolverhampton ■ a			19 31		19 37	19 42	19 55	20 33	20 00			20 16	20 25			20 31		20 37			20 55	21 33	20 58	
d						19 45							20 26					20 38						
Penkridge d						19 54																		
Stafford a		19 17				20 00							20 38		20 16			20 51						

A until 3 June

Sundays
until 24 June

Northampton - Coventry - Birmingham - Wolverhampton - Stafford

Network Diagram - see first Page of Table 67

	VT	XC	LM	LM	AW		VT	VT	XC	VT	LM	LM	LM	VT	XC		LM	LM	AW	VT	XC	LM	AW	LM
	◇■	◇■	◇■	◇■	◇		◇■	◇■	◇■	◇■		■	◇■	◇■	◇■		◇■	◇■		◇■	◇■		◇	■
London Euston ⊖ d	19 18		18 34	18 50			19 38			19 58				20 18			19 34	19 50		20 38				
Northampton d			19 51	20 02													20 51	20 59						
Long Buckby d			20 02	20 13													21 02	21 10						
Rugby d			20 15	20 28						20 49							21 15	21 24						
Coventry a	20 20		20 28				20 40			21 00				21 20			21 27			21 46				
Coventry d	20 20	20 26	20 29				20 40		20 54	21 00		21 10		21 20	21 26		21 29			21 46	21 53			22 08
Canley d			20 32														21 32							
Tile Hill d			20 36									21 15					21 36							
Berkswell d			20 39														21 39							
Hampton-in-Arden d			20 43														21 43							
Birmingham International a	20 31	20 35	20 46				20 51		21 03	21 11		21 22		21 31	21 35		21 46			21 57	22 02			22 17
d	20 31	20 38	20 47				20 51		21 04	21 11		21 22		21 31	21 38		21 47			21 57	22 03			22 18
Marston Green d			20 50									21 25					21 50							22 21
Lea Hall d												21 29												22 24
Stechford d												21 31												22 27
Adderley Park d												21 35												22 30
Birmingham New Street a	20 44	20 48	20 58				21 04		21 15	21 24		21 40		21 44	21 48		21 58			22 09	22 14			22 36
d	20 48	20 58			21 01		21 07	21 12		21 28	21 30		21 41	21 48	21 59				22 08	22 13		22 30	22 32	
Smethwick Rolfe Street d											21 41											22 41		
Smethwick Galton Bridge ■ d											21 46											22 46		
Sandwell & Dudley d											21 53											22 53		
Dudley Port d											22 02											23 02		
Tipton d											22 11											23 11		
Coseley d											22 20											23 20		
Wolverhampton ■ a	21 16	21 25			21 30		21 36	21 38		21 56	22 33		22 09	22 16	22 25				22 38	22 44		23 33	23 02	
d		21 30						21 44					22 09		22 26								23 15	
Penkridge d													22 19											
Stafford a		21 42		21 17				21 56					22 26		22 38			22 16					23 30	

	VT		XC	LM	LM	AW	XC	LM	LM	VT	VT		LM	VT
	◇■		◇■	◇■			◇■	■	◇■	◇■	◇■		■	◇■
London Euston ⊖ d	20 54			20 34					21 28	21 55	22 25		22 00	23 25
Northampton d				21 52					22 51				23 32	
Long Buckby d				22 03					23 02				23 43	
Rugby d	22 06			22 15					23 13	23 21	23 48		23 54	00s46
Coventry a	22 15			22 27					23 25	23 31	23 57		00 05	00s57
Coventry d	22 16		22 23	22 29			22 53	23 08	23 35	23 31	23 58			
Canley d				22 32					23 38					
Tile Hill d				22 36					23 42					
Berkswell d				22 39					23 45					
Hampton-in-Arden d				22 43					23 49					
Birmingham International a	22 26		22 32	22 46			23 02	23 17	23 52	23 42	00 08			01s08
d	22 27		22 33	22 47			23 03	23 18	23 53	23 42	00 09			
Marston Green d				22 50				23 21	23 56					
Lea Hall d								23 24						
Stechford d								23 27						
Adderley Park d								23 30						
Birmingham New Street a	22 39		22 42	22 58			23 13	23 36	00 04	23 55	00 21			01s21
d	22 44				23 00	23 11				23 58	00 25			
Smethwick Rolfe Street d					23 11									
Smethwick Galton Bridge ■ d					23 16									
Sandwell & Dudley d					23 23									
Dudley Port d					23 32									
Tipton d					23 41									
Coseley d					23 50									
Wolverhampton ■ a	23 14				00 03	23 40				00 26	00 53			01 53
d														
Penkridge d														
Stafford a														

1 July to 9 September

Northampton - Coventry - Birmingham - Wolverhampton - Stafford

Network Diagram - see first Page of Table 67

	LM ◇■	VT ■ ■ A ☕	VT ◇■ A ☕	VT ■ ■ A ☕	VT ◇■ ☕	XC ◇■ 🛒	LM ■	LM	LM ■		VT ◇■ ☕	LM ■	LM ◇■	XC ◇■ 🛒	AW	VT ◇■ ☕	LM	LM ◇■	LM ■		LM ■	LM ◇■	VT ◇■ ☕	XC ◇■ 🛒
London Euston ⊖ d	21p28	23p10	00 10	01 10														07 50					08 50	
Northampton d	22p55																	09 30	09 40					
Long Buckby d	23p06																	09 41	09 51					
Rugby d	23p17	23b58	01s02	01s58														09 52	10 02				10 14	
Coventry a	23p29	00s09	01s13	02s09														10 03					10 23	
d	23p30						08 37					09 07						10 04			10 08		10 24	
Canley d	23p33						08 40					09 10									10 11			
Tile Hill d	23p37						08 44					09 14									10 15			
Berkswell d	23p40						08 47					09 17									10 18			
Hampton-in-Arden d	23p44						08 51					09 21									10 22			
Birmingham International ✈ a	23p47	00s20	01s24	02s20			08 54					09 24						10 13			10 26		10 34	
d	23p48						08 55		09 03			09 25			09 51			10 13			10 26		10 35	
Marston Green d	23p51						08 58		09 06			09 28						10 16			10 29			
Lea Hall d	23p54								09 09									10 20						
Stechford d	23p57								09 12									10 22						
Adderley Park d									09 15									10 26						
Birmingham New Street a	00 04	00 34	01s39	02s34			09 06		09 20			09 36			10 02			10 30			10 38		10 47	
d					08 45	09 01		09 09			09 20		09 42	10 01	10 05	10 20	10 23					10 42	10 51	11 01
Smethwick Rolfe Street d								09 15									10 29							
Smethwick Galton Bridge d								09 17									10 31							
Sandwell & Dudley d								09 19									10 33						11 00	
Dudley Port d								09 22									10 36							
Tipton d								09 24									10 38							
Coseley d								09 27									10 41							
Wolverhampton a			01 57	02 52	09 02	09 18		09 32			09 37		09 59	10 18	10 21	10 37	10 46					10 59	11 13	11 18
d					09 04	09 19							10 00	10 19								11 00		11 19
Penkridge d													10 10									11 10		
Stafford a					09 16	09 32							10 16	10 32					10 56			11 16		11 31

	AW ◇	LM ◇■	LM	VT ◇■ ☕	LM ■		LM ◇■	VT ◇■ ☕	XC ◇■ 🛒	LM ◇■	LM ■	LM ◇■	LM	VT ◇■ ☕	AW ◇ 🛒		LM ◇■	LM ■	VT ◇■ ☕	LM ◇■	XC ◇■ 🛒	LM	VT ◇■ ☕	VT ◇■ ☕
London Euston ⊖ d		08 23						09 50		09 23	09 54	10 24							10 50	10 28				11 45
Northampton d		10 00								11 00	11 08	11 40								11 58				
Long Buckby d		10 11								11 11	11 19	11 51								12 09				
Rugby d		10 22						11 15		11 22	11 30	12 03							12 14	12 20				12 48
Coventry a		10 33						11 25		11 33									12 24	12 31				12 56
d		10 34			11 08			11 25		11 34								12 08	12 25	12 32				12 57
Canley d		10 37								11 37										12 35				
Tile Hill d		10 41								11 41										12 39				
Berkswell d		10 44								11 44										12 42				
Hampton-in-Arden d		10 48								11 48										12 46				
Birmingham International ✈ a		10 51			11 18			11 36		11 51								12 17	12 35	12 49				13 07
d	10 48	10 52			11 18			11 36		11 52					12 08			12 18	12 36	12 50				13 08
Marston Green d		10 55			11 21					11 55								12 21		12 53				
Lea Hall d					11 24													12 24						
Stechford d					11 27													12 27						
Adderley Park d					11 30													12 30						
Birmingham New Street a	10 58	11 03			11 37			11 49		12 03					12 18			12 37	12 48	13 01				13 22
d	11 05		11 09	11 20			11 42	11 52	12 01				12 09	12 20	12 24		12 35		12 52		13 01	13 09	13 20	
Smethwick Rolfe Street d			11 15										12 15									13 15		
Smethwick Galton Bridge d			11 17										12 17									13 17		
Sandwell & Dudley d			11 19					12 02					12 19						13 01			13 19		
Dudley Port d			11 22										12 22									13 22		
Tipton d			11 24										12 24									13 24		
Coseley d			11 27										12 27									13 27		
Wolverhampton a	11 26		11 32	11 37			11 59	12 15	12 19				12 32	12 37	12 42		12 52		13 14		13 18	13 32	13 37	
d							12 00		12 19								12 53				13 19			
Penkridge d							12 10										13 03							
Stafford a							12 16		12 32		12 19	12 59					13 09				13 33			

A from 29 July to 12 August, then from 2 September   b Previous night, stops to set down only

1 July to 9 September

Northampton - Coventry - Birmingham - Wolverhampton - Stafford

Network Diagram - see first Page of Table 67

	AW ◇ 🛒		XC ◇■ 🛒	LM ◇■	LM ■	VT ◇■ ☕	LM ◇■	LM ◇■	XC ◇■ 🛒	VT ◇■ ☕	LM		VT ◇■ ☕	AW ◇ 🛒	VT ◇■ ☕	XC ◇■ 🛒	LM ◇■	LM ■	VT ◇■ ☕	LM ◇■	LM ◇■		XC ◇■ 🛒	VT ◇■ ☕
London Euston ⊖ d						12 18	11 24			12 38					12 58				13 18	12 34	12 50			13 38
Northampton d							12 51	13 02												13 51	14 02			
Long Buckby d							13 02	13 13												14 02	14 13			
Rugby d							13 15	13 25							13 49					14 15	14 26			
Coventry a						13 20	13 28			13 40					14 00				14 20	14 28				14 40
d					13 10	13 21	13 29			13 40					14 00			14 10	14 20	14 29				14 40
Canley d							13 32													14 32				
Tile Hill d					13 15		13 36											14 15		14 36				
Berkswell d							13 39													14 39				
Hampton-in-Arden d							13 43													14 43				
Birmingham International ✈ a					13 22	13 31	13 46			13 51					14 11			14 22	14 31	14 46				14 51
d	13 12				13 22	13 32	13 47			13 51				14 07	14 11			14 22	14 31	14 47				14 51
Marston Green d					13 25		13 50											14 25		14 50				
Lea Hall d					13 29													14 29						
Stechford d					13 31													14 31						
Adderley Park d					13 35													14 35						
Birmingham New Street a	13 21				13 40	13 44	13 58			14 05				14 18	14 25			14 40	14 44	14 58				15 05
d	13 24		13 31	13 35		13 48			14 01		14 09		14 20	14 24		14 31	14 35		14 48				15 01	
Smethwick Rolfe Street d											14 15													
Smethwick Galton Bridge d											14 17													
Sandwell & Dudley d						13 57					14 19								14 57					
Dudley Port d											14 22													
Tipton d											14 24													
Coseley d											14 27													
Wolverhampton a	13 41		13 48	13 52		14 10			14 18		14 32		14 37	14 42		14 48	14 52		15 10				15 18	
d				13 53					14 19								14 53						15 19	
Penkridge d				14 03													15 03							
Stafford a				14 09				14 17	14 33								15 09				15 17		15 33	

	LM	VT ◇■ ☕	AW ◇ 🛒	VT ◇■ ☕	XC ◇■ 🛒	LM ◇■	LM ■		VT ◇■ ☕	XC ◇■ 🛒	LM ◇■	LM ◇■	VT ◇■ ☕	LM	VT ◇■ ☕	AW ◇ 🛒	VT ◇■ ☕		XC ◇■ 🛒	LM ◇■	LM ■	VT ◇■ ☕	XC ◇■ 🛒	LM ◇■
London Euston ⊖ d				13 58					14 18		13 34	13 50	14 38				14 58					15 18		14 34
Northampton d											14 51	15 02												15 51
Long Buckby d											15 02	15 13												16 02
Rugby d				14 49							15 15	15 26					15 49							16 16
Coventry a				15 00					15 20		15 28		15 40				15 59					16 20		16 28
d				15 00			15 10		15 20	15 26	15 29		15 40				15 59				16 10	16 20	16 26	16 29
Canley d											15 32													16 32
Tile Hill d							15 15				15 36										16 15			16 36
Berkswell d											15 39													16 39
Hampton-in-Arden d											15 43													16 43
Birmingham International ✈ a				15 11			15 22		15 31	15 35	15 46		15 51				16 10				16 22	16 31	16 35	16 46
d			15 07	15 11			15 22		15 31	15 38	15 47		15 51			16 07	16 10				16 22	16 31	16 38	16 47
Marston Green d							15 25				15 50										16 25			16 50
Lea Hall d							15 29														16 29			
Stechford d							15 31														16 31			
Adderley Park d							15 35														16 35			
Birmingham New Street a			15 18	15 25			15 40		15 44	15 48	15 58		16 05			16 18	16 24				16 41	16 44	16 48	16 58
d	15 09	15 20	15 24		15 31	15 35			15 48	16 01				16 09	16 20	16 24			16 31	16 35		16 48	17 01	
Smethwick Rolfe Street d	15 15													16 15										
Smethwick Galton Bridge d	15 17													16 17										
Sandwell & Dudley d	15 19								15 57					16 19								16 57		
Dudley Port d	15 22													16 22										
Tipton d	15 24													16 24										
Coseley d	15 27													16 27										
Wolverhampton a	15 32	15 37	15 42		15 48	15 52			16 10	16 18				16 32	16 37	16 42			16 48	16 52		17 10	17 18	
d						15 53				16 19										16 53			17 19	
Penkridge d						16 03														17 03				
Stafford a						16 09				16 34		16 16								17 09			17 35	

Table 68

Sundays

1 July to 9 September

Northampton - Coventry - Birmingham - Wolverhampton - Stafford

Network Diagram - see first Page of Table 67

Station		VT	LM	VT	AW	VT	LM	LM	VT	XC	LM	LM	VT	LM	VT	AW	VT	XC	LM	LM	VT	XC
		◇1 ☕		◇1 ☕	◇ 🍴	◇1 ☕	◇1	1	◇1 ☕	◇1 🍴	◇1	◇1	◇1 ☕		◇1 ☕	◇ 🍴	◇1 ☕	◇1	◇1	1	◇1 ☕	◇1 🍴
London Euston ⊖	d	15 38				15 58			16 18		15 34	15 50	16 38				16 58				17 18	
Northampton	d										16 51	17 02										
Long Buckby	d										17 02	17 13										
Rugby	d					16 49					17 15	17 26					17 49					
Coventry	a	16 40				17 00			17 20		17 28		17 40				18 00				18 20	
	d	16 40				17 00		17 10	17 20	17 26	17 29		17 40				18 00			18 10	18 20	18 26
Canley	d										17 32											
Tile Hill	d							17 15			17 36									18 15		
Berkswell	d										17 39											
Hampton-in-Arden	d										17 43											
Birmingham International ✈	a	16 51				17 11		17 22	17 31	17 35	17 46		17 51				18 11			18 22	18 31	18 35
	d	16 51			17 07	17 11		17 22	17 31	17 38	17 47		17 51			18 07	18 11			18 22	18 31	18 38
Marston Green	d							17 25			17 50									18 25		
Lea Hall	d							17 29												18 29		
Stechford	d							17 31												18 31		
Adderley Park	d							17 35												18 35		
Birmingham New Street	a	17 05			17 18	17 25		17 41	17 44	17 48	17 58		18 05			18 18	18 25			18 41	18 44	18 48
	d		17 09	17 20	17 24		17 35		17 48	18 01				18 09	18 20	18 24		18 31	18 35		18 48	19 01
Smethwick Rolfe Street	d		17 15											18 15								
Smethwick Galton Bridge 7	d		17 17											18 17								
Sandwell & Dudley	d		17 19						17 57					18 19							18 57	
Dudley Port	d		17 22											18 22								
Tipton	d		17 24											18 24								
Coseley	d		17 27											18 27								
Wolverhampton 7	a		17 32	17 37	17 42		17 52		18 10	18 18				18 32	18 37	18 42		18 48	18 52		19 10	19 18
	d						17 53			18 19									18 53			19 19
Penkridge	d						18 03												19 03			
Stafford	a						18 09			18 35		18 16							19 09			19 37

Station		LM	LM	VT	LM	VT	AW	XC	LM	VT	LM	VT	XC	LM	LM	VT	LM	XC	VT	AW	VT	XC	LM
		◇1	◇1	◇1 ☕		1 ☕	◇ 🍴	◇1 🍴	◇1	◇1 ☕	1	◇1 ☕	◇1 A 🍴	◇1	◇1	◇1 ☕		◇1 🍴	◇1 ☕	◇	◇1 ☕	◇1 🍴	1
London Euston ⊖	d	16 34	16 50	17 38						17 58		18 18		17 34	17 50	18 38					18 58		
Northampton	d	17 51	18 02											18 51	19 02								
Long Buckby	d	18 02	18 13											19 02	19 13								
Rugby	d	18 15	18 29							18 49				19 15	19 26						19 49		
Coventry	a	18 28		18 40						19 00		19 20		19 28		19 40					19 59		
	d	18 29		18 40						19 01	19 10	19 20	19 26	19 29		19 40		19 54			19 59		20 10
Canley	d	18 32												19 32									
Tile Hill	d	18 36									19 15			19 36									20 15
Berkswell	d	18 39												19 39									
Hampton-in-Arden	d	18 43												19 43									
Birmingham International ✈	a	18 46		18 51						19 11	19 22	19 31	19 35	19 46		19 51		20 03			20 10		20 22
	d	18 47		18 51			19 07			19 12	19 22	19 31	19 38	19 47		19 51		20 04		20 07	20 10		20 22
Marston Green	d	18 50									19 25			19 50									20 25
Lea Hall	d										19 29												20 29
Stechford	d										19 31												20 31
Adderley Park	d										19 35												20 35
Birmingham New Street	a	18 58		19 05			19 18			19 24	19 40	19 44	19 48	19 58		20 05		20 15		20 18	20 22		20 41
	d				19 09	19 20	19 24	19 31	19 35	19 39		19 48	20 01				20 09		20 20	20 24	20 26	20 31	
Smethwick Rolfe Street	d				19 15												20 15						
Smethwick Galton Bridge 7	d				19 17												20 17						
Sandwell & Dudley	d				19 19					19 49		19 57					20 19				20 36		
Dudley Port	d				19 22												20 22						
Tipton	d				19 24												20 24						
Coseley	d				19 27												20 27						
Wolverhampton 7	a				19 32	19 37	19 42	19 48	19 52	20 02		20 10	20 18				20 32		20 36	20 42	20 46	20 50	
	d								19 53				20 19						20 38				
Penkridge	d								20 03														
Stafford	a		19 17						20 09				20 36		20 16				20 51				

A 🍴 to Birmingham New Street

Table 68

Sundays

1 July to 9 September

Northampton - Coventry - Birmingham - Wolverhampton - Stafford

Network Diagram - see first Page of Table 67

Station		VT	XC	LM	LM	VT	LM	XC	VT	AW	VT	LM	LM	VT	XC	LM	LM	LM	VT	XC	AW	LM	VT
		◇1 ☕	◇1 A 🍴	◇1	◇1	◇1 ☕		◇1 🍴	◇1 ☕	◇	◇1 ☕	◇1	1	◇1 ☕	◇1	◇1	◇1		◇1 ☕	◇1		1	◇1 ☕
London Euston ⊖	d	19 18		18 34	18 50	19 38					19 58			20 18		19 34	19 50		20 38				20 54
Northampton	d			19 51	20 02											20 51	20 59						
Long Buckby	d			20 02	20 13											21 02	21 10						
Rugby	d			20 15	20 28						20 49					21 15	21 24						22 07
Coventry	a	20 20		20 28		20 40					21 00			21 20		21 27			21 46				22 16
	d	20 20	20 26	20 29		20 40		20 54			21 00		21 10	21 20	21 26	21 29			21 46	21 53		22 08	22 16
Canley	d			20 32												21 32							
Tile Hill	d			20 36									21 15			21 36							
Berkswell	d			20 39												21 39							
Hampton-in-Arden	d			20 43												21 43							
Birmingham International ✈	a	20 31	20 35	20 46		20 51		21 03			21 11		21 22	21 31	21 35	21 46			21 57	22 02		22 17	22 27
	d	20 31	20 38	20 47		20 51		21 04		21 07	21 11		21 22	21 31	21 38	21 47			21 57	22 03	22 11	22 18	22 27
Marston Green	d			20 50									21 25			21 50						22 21	
Lea Hall	d												21 29									22 24	
Stechford	d												21 31									22 27	
Adderley Park	d												21 35									22 30	
Birmingham New Street	a	20 44	20 48	20 58		21 04		21 15		21 18	21 24		21 40	21 44	21 48	21 58			22 09	22 14	22 21	22 36	22 39
	d	20 48	21 01			21 07	21 09		21 20	21 24	21 28	21 35		21 48	22 01			22 09	22 16		22 24		22 44
Smethwick Rolfe Street	d						21 15											22 15					
Smethwick Galton Bridge 7	d						21 17											22 17					
Sandwell & Dudley	d	20 57				21 16	21 19				21 37			21 57				22 19	22 25				22 53
Dudley Port	d						21 22											22 22					
Tipton	d						21 24											22 24					
Coseley	d						21 27											22 27					
Wolverhampton 7	a	21 10	21 18			21 31	21 33		21 38	21 42	21 51	21 56		22 10	22 18			22 32	22 38		22 41		23 06
	d		21 19						21 38			21 57			22 19								
Penkridge	d											22 07											
Stafford	a		21 36		21 17				21 56			22 13			22 36		22 16						

Station		XC	AW	LM	LM	XC	AW	LM	LM	VT	VT	LM	VT
		◇1	◇	◇1		◇1		1	◇1	◇1 ☕	◇1 ☕	1	◇1 B ☕
London Euston ⊖	d			20 34					21 28	21 55	22 25	22 00	23 25
Northampton	d			21 52					22 51			23 32	
Long Buckby	d			22 03					23 02			23 43	
Rugby	d			22 15					23 13	23 21	23 46	23 54	00s46
Coventry	a			22 27					23 25	23 31	23 55	00 05	00s57
	d	22 23		22 29		22 53		23 08	23 35	23 31	23 56		
Canley	d			22 32					23 38				
Tile Hill	d			22 36					23 42				
Berkswell	d			22 39					23 45				
Hampton-in-Arden	d			22 43					23 49				
Birmingham International ✈	a	22 32		22 46		23 02		23 17	23 52	23 42	00 06		01s08
	d	22 33	22 40	22 47		23 03	23 08	23 18	23 53	23 42	00 07		
Marston Green	d			22 50				23 21	23 56				
Lea Hall	d							23 24					
Stechford	d							23 27					
Adderley Park	d							23 30					
Birmingham New Street	a	22 42	22 50	22 58		23 13	23 19	23 36	00 04	23 54	00 19		01s21
	d		22 55		23 09		23 24			23 57	00 22		
Smethwick Rolfe Street	d				23 15								
Smethwick Galton Bridge 7	d				23 17								
Sandwell & Dudley	d				23 19								
Dudley Port	d				23 22								
Tipton	d				23 24								
Coseley	d				23 27								
Wolverhampton 7	a		23 13		23 32		23 40			00 15	00 41		01 53
	d		23 15										
Penkridge	d												
Stafford	a		23 30										

A 🍴 to Birmingham New Street

B from 1 July until 22 July, 19 August, 26 August

Table 68

Sundays from 16 September

Northampton - Coventry - Birmingham - Wolverhampton - Stafford

Network Diagram - see first Page of Table 67

Station		LM	VT	XC	LM	LM	LM	VT	LM	LM		XC	AW	VT	LM	LM	LM	LM	LM	VT		XC	AW	LM	LM
London Euston ⊖	d	21p28														07 50				08 50				08 23	
Northampton	d	22p55														09 30	09 40							10 00	
Long Buckby	d	23p06														09 41	09 51							10 11	
Rugby	d	23p17														09 52	10 02			10 14				10 22	
Coventry	a	23p29														10 03				10 23				10 33	
	d	23p30			08 37				09 07							10 04		10 08		10 24		10 28		10 34	
Canley	d	23p33			08 40				09 10									10 11						10 37	
Tile Hill	d	23p37			08 44				09 14									10 15						10 41	
Berkswell	d	23p40			08 47				09 17									10 18						10 44	
Hampton-in-Arden	d	23p44			08 51				09 21									10 22						10 48	
Birmingham International ✈	a	23p47			08 54				09 24							10 13		10 26		10 34		10 38		10 51	
	d	23p48			08 55		09 03		09 25				09 51			10 13		10 26		10 35		10 40	10 48	10 52	
Marston Green	d	23p51			08 58		09 06		09 28							10 16		10 29						10 55	
Lea Hall	d	23p54					09 09									10 20									
Stechford	d	23p57					09 12									10 22									
Adderley Park	d						09 15									10 26									
Birmingham New Street	a	00 04			09 06		09 20		09 36				10 02			10 30		10 38		10 47		10 50	10 58	11 03	
	d		08 45	09 01		09 09		09 20		09 42		10 01	10 05	10 20	10 23				10 42	10 51		11 01	11 05		11 09
Smethwick Rolfe Street	d					09 15									10 29										11 15
Smethwick Galton Bridge	d					09 17									10 31										11 17
Sandwell & Dudley	d					09 19									10 33					11 00					11 19
Dudley Port	d					09 22									10 36										11 22
Tipton	d					09 24									10 38										11 24
Coseley	d					09 27									10 41										11 27
Wolverhampton	a		09 02	09 18		09 32		09 37		09 59		10 18	10 21	10 37	10 46				10 59	11 13		11 18	11 26		11 32
	d		09 04	09 19						10 00		10 19							11 00			11 19			
Penkridge	d									10 10									11 10						
Stafford	a		09 16	09 32						10 16		10 32					10 56		11 16			11 31			

Station		VT	LM	LM	VT	XC		LM	LM A	LM B	LM	LM	VT	AW	LM	LM		VT	XC	LM	LM	VT A	VT	AW	XC
London Euston ⊖	d				09 50			09 23	09 54	09 54	10 24							10 50		10 28			11 45		
Northampton	d							11 00	11 08	11 08	11 40									11 58					
Long Buckby	d							11 11	11 19	11 19	11 51									12 09					
Rugby	d				11 15			11 22	11 30	11 30	12 03							12 14		12 20			12 48		
Coventry	a				11 25			11 33										12 24		12 31			12 56		
	d		11 08		11 25	11 29		11 34								12 08		12 25	12 28	12 32			12 57		
Canley	d							11 37												12 35					
Tile Hill	d							11 41												12 39					
Berkswell	d							11 44												12 42					
Hampton-in-Arden	d							11 48												12 46					
Birmingham International ✈	a		11 18		11 36	11 38		11 51								12 17		12 35	12 38	12 49			13 07		
	d		11 18		11 36	11 40		11 52						12 08		12 18		12 36	12 40	12 50			13 08	13 12	
Marston Green	d		11 21					11 55								12 21				12 53					
Lea Hall	d		11 24													12 24									
Stechford	d		11 27													12 27									
Adderley Park	d		11 30													12 30									
Birmingham New Street	a		11 37		11 49	11 51		12 03						12 18		12 37		12 48	12 50	13 01			13 22	13 21	
	d	11 20		11 42	11 52	12 01						12 09	12 20	12 24	12 35			12 52	13 01		13 09	13 20		13 24	13 31
Smethwick Rolfe Street	d											12 15									13 15				
Smethwick Galton Bridge	d											12 17									13 17				
Sandwell & Dudley	d				12 02							12 19						13 01			13 19				
Dudley Port	d											12 22									13 22				
Tipton	d											12 24									13 24				
Coseley	d											12 27									13 27				
Wolverhampton	a	11 37		11 59	12 15	12 19						12 32	12 37	12 42	12 52			13 14	13 18		13 32	13 37		13 41	13 48
	d			12 00		12 19									12 53				13 19						
Penkridge	d			12 10											13 03										
Stafford	a			12 16		12 32			12 19	12 21	12 59				13 09				13 33						

A from 16 September until 21 October

B from 28 October

Table 68

Sundays from 16 September

Northampton - Coventry - Birmingham - Wolverhampton - Stafford

Network Diagram - see first Page of Table 67

Station		LM		LM	VT	XC	LM	VT	LM	LM	VT	AW		VT	XC	LM	LM	VT	XC	LM	LM	VT		LM	VT
London Euston ⊖	d				12 20		11 24	12 40						13 00				13 20		12 34	12 50	13 40			
Northampton	d						12 51		13 02											13 51	14 02				
Long Buckby	d						13 02		13 13											14 02	14 13				
Rugby	d						13 15		13 25					13 51						14 15	14 26				
Coventry	a				13 22		13 28	13 42						14 02				14 21		14 28		14 42			
	d			13 10	13 22	13 26	13 29	13 42						14 02			14 10	14 22	14 26	14 29		14 42			
Canley	d						13 32													14 32					
Tile Hill	d			13 15			13 36										14 15			14 36					
Berkswell	d						13 39													14 39					
Hampton-in-Arden	d						13 43													14 43					
Birmingham International ✈	a			13 22	13 33	13 36	13 46	13 53						14 13			14 22	14 32	14 35	14 46		14 53			
	d			13 22	13 33	13 38	13 47	13 53				14 07		14 13			14 22	14 33	14 38	14 47		14 53			
Marston Green	d			13 25			13 50										14 25			14 50					
Lea Hall	d			13 29													14 29								
Stechford	d			13 31													14 31								
Adderley Park	d			13 35													14 35								
Birmingham New Street	a			13 40	13 44	13 48	13 58	14 05				14 18		14 25			14 40	14 44	14 48	14 58		15 05			
	d	13 35			13 48	14 01				14 09	14 20	14 24			14 31	14 35		14 48	15 01					15 09	15 20
Smethwick Rolfe Street	d									14 15														15 15	
Smethwick Galton Bridge	d									14 17														15 17	
Sandwell & Dudley	d				13 57					14 19								14 57						15 19	
Dudley Port	d									14 22														15 22	
Tipton	d									14 24														15 24	
Coseley	d									14 27														15 27	
Wolverhampton	a	13 52			14 10	14 18				14 32	14 37	14 42			14 48	14 52		15 10	15 18					15 32	15 37
	d	13 53				14 19										14 53			15 19						
Penkridge	d	14 03														15 03									
Stafford	a	14 09				14 33			14 17							15 09			15 33		15 17				

Station		AW	VT	XC	LM	LM	VT	XC		LM	LM	VT	LM	VT	AW	VT	XC	LM		LM	VT	XC	LM	VT	LM
London Euston ⊖	d		14 00				14 20			13 34	13 50	14 40				15 00					15 20		14 34	15 40	
Northampton	d									14 51	15 02												15 51		
Long Buckby	d									15 02	15 13												16 02		
Rugby	d		14 51							15 15	15 26					15 51							16 16		
Coventry	a		15 02				15 21			15 28		15 42				16 02					16 21		16 28	16 42	
	d		15 02			15 10	15 22	15 26		15 29		15 42				16 02				16 10	16 22	16 26	16 29	16 42	
Canley	d									15 32													16 32		
Tile Hill	d					15 15				15 36										16 15			16 36		
Berkswell	d									15 39													16 39		
Hampton-in-Arden	d									15 43													16 43		
Birmingham International ✈	a		15 13			15 22	15 32	15 35		15 46		15 53				16 13				16 22	16 32	16 35	16 46	16 53	
	d	15 07	15 13			15 22	15 33	15 38		15 47		15 53			16 07	16 13				16 22	16 33	16 38	16 47	16 53	
Marston Green	d					15 25				15 50										16 25			16 50		
Lea Hall	d					15 29														16 29					
Stechford	d					15 31														16 31					
Adderley Park	d					15 35														16 35					
Birmingham New Street	a	15 18	15 25			15 40	15 44	15 48		15 58		16 05			16 18	16 25				16 41	16 44	16 48	16 58	17 05	
	d	15 24		15 31	15 35		15 48	16 01					16 09	16 20	16 24		16 31	16 35			16 48	17 01			17 09
Smethwick Rolfe Street	d												16 15												17 15
Smethwick Galton Bridge	d												16 17												17 17
Sandwell & Dudley	d						15 57						16 19								16 57				17 19
Dudley Port	d												16 22												17 22
Tipton	d												16 24												17 24
Coseley	d												16 27												17 27
Wolverhampton	a	15 42		15 48	15 52		16 10	16 18					16 32	16 37	16 42		16 48	16 52			17 10	17 18			17 32
	d				15 53			16 19										16 53				17 19			
Penkridge	d				16 03													17 03							
Stafford	a				16 09			16 34			16 16							17 09				17 35			

Table 68

Sundays
from 16 September

Northampton - Coventry - Birmingham - Wolverhampton - Stafford

Network Diagram - see first Page of Table 67

		VT	AW	VT	XC	LM	LM	VT	XC	LM	LM	VT	LM	VT	AW	VT	XC	XC	LM	LM	VT	XC
		◇■	◇	◇■	◇■	◇■	■	◇■	◇■	◇■	◇■	◇■		◇■	◇	◇■	◇■	◇■	◇■	■	◇■	◇■
																	A	B				
		⊡	✕	⊡	✕			⊡	✕			⊡		⊡	✕	⊡		✕			⊡	✕
London Euston ⊖	d			16 00				16 20		15 34	15 50	16 40				17 00					17 20	
Northampton	d									16 51	17 02											
Long Buckby	d									17 02	17 13											
Rugby	d			16 51						17 15	17 26					17 51						
Coventry	a			17 02				17 21		17 28		17 42				18 02					18 21	
	d			17 02			17 10	17 22	17 26	17 29		17 42				18 02				18 10	18 22	18 26
Canley	d									17 32												
Tile Hill	d						17 15			17 36										18 15		
Berkswell	d									17 39												
Hampton-in-Arden	d									17 43												
Birmingham International ✈	a			17 13			17 22	17 32	17 35	17 46		17 53				18 13				18 22	18 32	18 35
	d		17 07	17 13			17 22	17 33	17 38	17 47		17 53			18 07	18 13				18 22	18 33	18 38
Marston Green	d						17 25			17 50										18 25		
Lea Hall	d						17 29													18 29		
Stechford	d						17 31													18 31		
Adderley Park	d						17 35													18 35		
Birmingham New Street	a		17 18	17 25			17 41	17 44	17 48	17 58		18 05			18 18	18 25				18 41	18 44	18 48
	d	17 20	17 24		17 31	17 35		17 48	18 01				18 09	18 20	18 24		18 31	18 31	18 35		18 48	19 01
Smethwick Rolfe Street	d												18 15									
Smethwick Galton Bridge	d												18 17									
Sandwell & Dudley	d							17 57					18 19								18 57	
Dudley Port	d												18 22									
Tipton	d												18 24									
Coseley	d												18 27									
Wolverhampton	a	17 37	17 42		17 48	17 52		18 10	18 18				18 32	18 37	18 42		18 48	18 48	18 52		19 10	19 18
	d					17 53			18 19										18 53			19 19
Penkridge	d					18 03													19 03			
Stafford	a					18 09			18 35		18 16								19 09			19 37

		LM	LM	VT	LM	VT	AW	XC	LM	VT	LM	VT	XC	LM	LM	VT	LM	XC	VT	AW	VT	XC	XC
		◇■	◇■	◇■		■ ■	◇	◇■	◇■	◇■	■	◇■	◇■	◇■	◇■	◇■		◇■	◇■	◇	◇■	◇■	◇■
													C									A	B
				⊡		⊡	✕	✕		⊡		⊡	✕			⊡		✕	⊡		⊡	✕	
London Euston ⊖	d	16 34	16 50	17 40						18 00		18 20		17 34	17 50	18 40					19 00		
Northampton	d	17 51	18 02											18 51	19 02								
Long Buckby	d	18 02	18 13											19 02	19 13								
Rugby	d	18 15	18 29							18 50				19 15	19 26						19 51		
Coventry	a	18 28		18 42						19 01		19 21		19 28		19 42					20 01		
	d	18 29		18 42						19 01	19 10	19 22	19 26	19 29		19 42		19 54			20 02		
Canley	d	18 32												19 32									
Tile Hill	d	18 36									19 15			19 36									
Berkswell	d	18 39												19 39									
Hampton-in-Arden	d	18 43												19 43									
Birmingham International ✈	a	18 46		18 53						19 12	19 22	19 32	19 35	19 46		19 53		20 03			20 12		
	d	18 47		18 53			19 07			19 12	19 22	19 33	19 38	19 47		19 53		20 04		20 07	20 12		
Marston Green	d	18 50									19 25			19 50									
Lea Hall	d										19 29												
Stechford	d										19 31												
Adderley Park	d										19 35												
Birmingham New Street	a	18 58		19 05			19 18			19 24	19 40	19 44	19 48	19 58		20 05		20 15		20 18	20 23		
	d				19 09	19 20	19 24	19 31	19 35	19 39		19 48	20 01				20 09		20 20	20 24	20 26	20 31	20 31
Smethwick Rolfe Street	d				19 15												20 15						
Smethwick Galton Bridge	d				19 17												20 17						
Sandwell & Dudley	d				19 19					19 49		19 57					20 19				20 36		
Dudley Port	d				19 22												20 22						
Tipton	d				19 24												20 24						
Coseley	d				19 27												20 27						
Wolverhampton	a				19 32	19 37	19 42	19 48	19 52	20 02		20 10	20 18				20 32		20 36	20 42	20 46	20 50	20 50
	d								19 53				20 19						20 38				
Penkridge	d								20 03														
Stafford	a		19 17						20 09				20 36		20 16				20 51				

A from 28 October

B from 16 September until 21 October

C ✕ to Birmingham New Street

Table 68

Sundays
from 16 September

Northampton - Coventry - Birmingham - Wolverhampton - Stafford

Network Diagram - see first Page of Table 67

		LM	VT	XC	LM	LM	VT	LM	XC	VT	AW	VT	LM	LM	VT	XC	LM	LM	LM	VT	XC	AW	LM
		■	◇■	◇■	◇■	◇■	◇■		◇■	◇■	◇	◇■	◇■	■	◇■	◇■	◇■	◇■		◇■	◇■		■
				A																			
			⊡	✕			⊡		✕	⊡		⊡			⊡					⊡			
London Euston ⊖	d		19 20		18 34	18 50	19 40					20 00			20 18		19 34	19 50		20 38			
Northampton	d				19 51	20 02											20 51	20 59					
Long Buckby	d				20 02	20 13											21 02	21 10					
Rugby	d				20 15	20 27						20 51					21 15	21 24					
Coventry	a		20 21		20 28		20 42					21 02			21 20		21 27			21 46			
	d	20 10	20 22	20 26	20 29		20 42		20 54			21 02		21 10	21 20	21 26	21 29			21 46	21 53		22 08
Canley	d				20 32												21 32						
Tile Hill	d	20 15			20 36									21 15			21 36						
Berkswell	d				20 39												21 39						
Hampton-in-Arden	d				20 43												21 43						
Birmingham International ✈	a	20 22	20 32	20 35	20 46		20 53		21 03			21 13		21 22	21 31	21 35	21 46			21 57	22 02		22 17
	d	20 22	20 33	20 38	20 47		20 53		21 04		21 07	21 13		21 22	21 31	21 38	21 47			21 57	22 03	22 11	22 18
Marston Green	d	20 25			20 50									21 25			21 50						22 21
Lea Hall	d	20 29												21 29									22 24
Stechford	d	20 31												21 31									22 27
Adderley Park	d	20 35												21 35									22 30
Birmingham New Street	a	20 41	20 44	20 48	20 58		21 04		21 15		21 18	21 24		21 40	21 44	21 48	21 58			22 09	22 14	22 21	22 36
	d		20 48	21 01			21 07	21 09		21 20	21 24	21 28	21 35		21 48	22 01			22 09	22 16		22 24	
Smethwick Rolfe Street	d							21 15											22 15				
Smethwick Galton Bridge	d							21 17											22 17				
Sandwell & Dudley	d		20 57				21 16	21 19				21 37			21 57				22 19	22 25			
Dudley Port	d							21 22											22 22				
Tipton	d							21 24											22 24				
Coseley	d							21 27											22 27				
Wolverhampton	a		21 10	21 18			21 31	21 33		21 38	21 42	21 51	21 56		22 10	22 18			22 32	22 38		22 41	
	d			21 19						21 38			21 57			22 19							
Penkridge	d												22 07										
Stafford	a			21 36		21 17				21 56			22 13			22 36		22 16					

		VT	XC	AW	LM	LM	XC	AW	LM	LM	VT	VT	LM	VT
		◇■	◇■	◇	◇■		◇■		■	◇■	◇■	◇■	■	◇■
		⊡									⊡	⊡		⊡
London Euston ⊖	d	20 54			20 34					21 28	21 55	22 25	22 00	23 25
Northampton	d				21 52					22 51			23 32	
Long Buckby	d				22 03					23 02			23 43	
Rugby	d	22 07			22 15					23 13	23 21	23 48	23 54	00s46
Coventry	a	22 16			22 27					23 25	23 31	23 57	00 05	00s58
	d	22 16	22 23		22 29		22 54		23 08	23 35	23 31	23 58		
Canley	d				22 32					23 38				
Tile Hill	d				22 36					23 42				
Berkswell	d				22 39					23 45				
Hampton-in-Arden	d				22 43					23 49				
Birmingham International ✈	a	22 27	22 32		22 46		23 03		23 17	23 52	23 42	00 08		01s09
	d	22 27	22 33	22 40	22 47		23 04	23 08	23 18	23 53	23 42	00 09		
Marston Green	d				22 50				23 21	23 56				
Lea Hall	d								23 24					
Stechford	d								23 27					
Adderley Park	d								23 30					
Birmingham New Street	a	22 39	22 42	22 50	22 58		23 14	23 19	23 36	00 04	23 54	00 21		01s22
	d	22 44		22 55		23 09		23 24			23 57	00 24		
Smethwick Rolfe Street	d					23 15								
Smethwick Galton Bridge	d					23 17								
Sandwell & Dudley	d	22 53				23 19								
Dudley Port	d					23 22								
Tipton	d					23 24								
Coseley	d					23 27								
Wolverhampton	a	23 06		23 13		23 32		23 40			00 15	00 43		01 53
	d			23 15										
Penkridge	d													
Stafford	a			23 30										

A ✕ to Birmingham New Street

until 29 June

Stafford - Wolverhampton - Birmingham - Coventry - Northampton

Network Diagram - see first Page of Table 67

Miles			LM MX ◇■	VT MX ◇■ 🚌	VT MO ◇■ A 🚌	VT MO ◇■ A 🚌	VT ◇■ B 🚌	VT MX ◇■ C 🚌	LM MX ■	LM ■	VT ◇■ ⊠	VT ◇■ ⊠	LM ■	VT ◇■ ⊠	LM ◇■	AW MO D	AW MX C	XC ◇■ ⚲	VT ◇■ ⊠	LM ■	AW	VT ◇■ ⊠	LM
—	**Stafford**	d														05 25	05 25						
0	Penkridge	d																					
9½	**Wolverhampton** ■	a														05 39	05 39						
—		d		21p45	21p50	22p33	22p45	22p45			05 00	05 24				05 40	05 40		05 45		05 59	06 04	06 15
18¾	Coseley	d																					
32¼	Tipton	d																					
34	Dudley Port	d																					
36	Sandwell & Dudley	d		21p56			22p55	22p55				05 34							05 56			06 15	
38	Smethwick Galton Bridge ■	d																			06 10		
41¼	Smethwick Rolfe Street	d																					
43	**Birmingham New Street** ■	a		22p06	22p15	22p56	23p06	23p06			05 26	05 43				05 59	06 01		06 06		06 15	06 24	06 32
—		d	21p33	22p10	22p30	23p00	23p10	23p10	23p53		05 29	05 50			05 53			06 04	06 10	06 13	06 36	06 30	
45	Adderley Park	d																			→		
46½	Stechford	d																		06 20			
47¾	Lea Hall	d																		06 23			
49½	Marston Green	d	21p41						00 01						06 01					06 26			
51½	**Birmingham International** ✈	a	21p45	22p21	22p39	23p09	23p19	23p19	00 04		05 38	05 59			06 05			06 13	06 19	06 29		06 39	
—		d	21p45	22p22	22p40	23p10	23p20	23p20	00 05		05 40	06 00			06 05			06 14	06 20	06 29		06 40	
54¾	Hampton-in-Arden	d	21p48																	06 32			
55½	Berkswell	d													06 11					06 37			
56¾	Tile Hill	d	21p55												06 14					06 40			
57¾	Canley	d													06 17					06 44			
58½	**Coventry**	a	22p00	22p31	22p50	23p20	23p30	23p30	00 15		05 50	06 10			06 20			06 24	06 30	06 47		06 49	
—		d	22p01	22p32	22p51	23p21	23p31	23p31			05 51	06 11			06 21				06 31			06 51	
60	Rugby	d	22p12	22p43	23p04	23p34	23p44	23p44		05 20	06 03		06 13	06 20	06 32								
64¼	Long Buckby	d	22p22							05 30			06 23		06 42								
74¼	**Northampton**	a	22p34			23b54	00s05	00s05		05 42			06 35	06 39	06 54								
79½	London Euston ■ ⊖	a	00 21	00 04	00 27	01 01	01 13	01 15		06 50	07 02	07 13	07 40	07 30	08 02				07 34			07 53	

		LM ■	LM ■	AW	LM	LM ■	VT ◇■ ⊠	LM ◇■	XC ◇■ ⚲	VT ◇■ ⊠	LM ■	LM	LM ◇■	VT ◇■ ⊠	VT ◇■ ⊠	AW	XC ◇■ ⚲	LM ◇■	LM	LM	LM ◇■	LM ◇■	VT ◇■ ⊠
Stafford	d								06 25				06 41				06 58				07 12	07 22	
Penkridge	d												06 47								07 18		
Wolverhampton ■	a								06 39				06 57				07 12				07 28		
	d					06 19	06 27		06 41	06 45		06 49	06 59	07 04		07 10	07 15			07 19	07 28		
Coseley	d					06 24						06 54	07 04							07 24			
Tipton	d					06 26						06 57								07 26			
Dudley Port	d					06 28						06 59								07 28			
Sandwell & Dudley	d					06 32	06 37			06 56		07 03		07 15						07 32			
Smethwick Galton Bridge ■	d					06 34						07 06				07 21				07 34	07 40		
Smethwick Rolfe Street	d			←		06 36						07 09								07 36			
Birmingham New Street ■	a			06 15		06 43	06 46		06 58	07 06		07 15	07 18	07 24		07 26	07 31			07 44	07 48		
	d		06 33	06 36	06 39		06 50	06 53	07 04	07 10	07 13			07 30		07 36		07 33	07 39				07 50
Adderley Park	d				06 44														07 44				
Stechford	d				06 47						07 20								07 47				
Lea Hall	d				06 50						07 23								07 50				
Marston Green	d		06 41					07 01			07 26							07 41					
Birmingham International ✈	a		06 45	06 50	06 55		06 59	07 05	07 13	07 19	07 29					07 50		07 45	07 55				07 59
	d		06 45				07 00	07 05	07 14	07 20	07 29				07 41			07 45					08 00
Hampton-in-Arden	d		06 48					07 08										07 48					
Berkswell	d							07 13			07 35												
Tile Hill	d		06 55								07 38							07 55					
Canley	d							07 18										07 58					
Coventry	a		07 00				07 10	07 21	07 24	07 30	07 43				07 51			08 02					08 10
	d		07 01				07 11	07 21		07 31					07 52			08 03					08 11
Rugby	d	07 02	07 12					07 32										08 14				08 20	08 23
Long Buckby	d	07 12	07 21					07 42										08 24					
Northampton	a	07 25	07 33					07 54										08 37				08 41	
London Euston ■ ⊖	a	08 49					08 14	09 10		08 30				08 42	08 49							09 44	09 13

A from 21 May until 25 June
B from 26 June until 29 June
C until 22 June
D also from 26 June until 29 June
b Previous night, stops to set down only

until 29 June

Stafford - Wolverhampton - Birmingham - Coventry - Northampton

Network Diagram - see first Page of Table 67

		LM ◇■	VT ◇■ ⊠	LM	LM	XC ◇■ ⚲	VT ◇■ ⊠	LM ■	LM	LM ◇■	LM	VT ◇■ ⊠	AW ◇ ⚲	XC ◇■ ⚲	LM	LM	LM ◇■	LM ◇■	LM ◇■	VT ◇■ ⊠	LM ◇■	VT ◇■ ⊠
Stafford	d						07 28			07 41				08 02			08 10		08 21			
Penkridge	d									07 47							08 16					
Wolverhampton ■	a						07 43			07 57				08 15			08 26					
	d		07 32	07 35	07 39		07 45		07 49	07 57	08 04		08 09	08 16		08 19	08 28					08 32
Coseley	d				07 44				07 54	08 03						08 24						
Tipton	d				07 47				07 57							08 26						
Dudley Port	d				07 49				07 59							08 28						
Sandwell & Dudley	d			07 45			07 56		08 02							08 32						
Smethwick Galton Bridge ■	d				07 53				08 05				08 21			08 34	08 40					
Smethwick Rolfe Street	d				07 55				08 07							08 36						
Birmingham New Street ■	a		07 55	07 54	08 03		08 06		08 14	08 17	08 20		08 26	08 32		08 44	08 47					08 55
	d	07 53				08 04	08 10	08 13				08 30	08 36		08 39			08 33		08 50	08 53	
Adderley Park	d														08 44							
Stechford	d							08 20							08 47							
Lea Hall	d							08 23							08 50							
Marston Green	d	08 01						08 26										08 41			09 01	
Birmingham International ✈	a	08 05				08 13	08 19	08 29				08 39	08 50		08 55			08 45		08 59	09 05	
	d	08 05				08 14	08 20	08 29				08 40						08 45		09 00	09 05	
Hampton-in-Arden	d							08 32										08 48				
Berkswell	d	08 11						08 37													09 11	
Tile Hill	d	08 14						08 40										08 55			09 14	
Canley	d	08 17						08 44													09 17	
Coventry	a	08 20				08 24	08 30	08 47				08 49						09 00		09 10	09 20	
	d	08 21					08 31					08 51						09 01		09 11	09 21	
Rugby	d	08 32																09 12	09 20	09 23	09 32	
Long Buckby	d	08 42																09 22			09 42	
Northampton	a	08 56																09 34	09 39		09 54	
London Euston ■ ⊖	a	10 18					09 34					09 54						10 49		10 14	11 17	

		LM	XC ◇■ ⚲	VT ◇■ ⊠	LM ◇■	LM	LM ◇■	VT ◇■ ⊠	AW ◇ ⚲	XC ◇■ ⚲	LM	LM	LM ◇■	LM ◇■ A	LM ◇■	VT ◇■ ⊠	LM ◇■	VT ◇■ ⊠	LM	XC ◇■ ⚲	VT ◇■ ⊠	LM ◇■	LM
Stafford	d		08 25				08 43			09 03			09 10		09 21					09 25			
Penkridge	d						08 48						09 16										
Wolverhampton ■	a		08 39				08 58			09 15			09 27							09 39			
	d	08 37	08 41	08 45		08 49	08 58		09 10	09 16		09 19	09 28					09 32	09 37	09 41	09 45		09 49
Coseley	d					08 54	09 04					09 24											09 54
Tipton	d					08 56						09 26											09 56
Dudley Port	d					08 58						09 28											09 58
Sandwell & Dudley	d	08 46		08 56		09 02						09 32							09 46		09 56		10 02
Smethwick Galton Bridge ■	d					09 04			09 21			09 34	09 40										10 04
Smethwick Rolfe Street	d					09 06						09 36											10 06
Birmingham New Street ■	a	08 55	08 58	09 06		09 14	09 18		09 26	09 32		09 44	09 47					09 55	09 55	09 58	10 06		10 14
	d		09 04	09 10	09 13			09 30	09 36		09 39			09 33		09 50	09 53			10 04	10 10	10 13	
Adderley Park	d										09 44												
Stechford	d				09 20						09 47											10 20	
Lea Hall	d				09 23						09 50											10 23	
Marston Green	d				09 26									09 41			10 01					10 26	
Birmingham International ✈	a		09 13	09 19	09 29			09 39	09 50		09 55			09 45		09 59	10 05			10 13	10 19	10 29	
	d		09 14	09 20	09 29			09 40						09 45		09 59	10 05			10 14	10 20	10 29	
Hampton-in-Arden	d				09 32									09 48								10 32	
Berkswell	d				09 37												10 11					10 37	
Tile Hill	d				09 40									09 55			10 14					10 40	
Canley	d				09 44												10 17					10 44	
Coventry	a		09 24	09 30	09 47			09 49						10 00		10 09	10 20			10 24	10 30	10 47	
	d			09 31	09 48			09 51						10 01		10 10	10 21				10 31	10 48	
Rugby	d				09 59									10 12	10 20	10 24	10 32					10 59	
Long Buckby	d				10 09									10 22			10 42					11 09	
Northampton	a				10 21									10 34	10 39		10 54					11 21	
London Euston ■ ⊖	a			10 32	11 27			10 54						11 49		11 15	12 17				11 32	12 27	

A ◇ from Northampton

Stafford - Wolverhampton - Birmingham - Coventry - Northampton

Network Diagram - see first Page of Table 67

	LM	VT	LM	AW		XC	LM	LM	LM	LM	VT	LM	LM	XC		VT	LM	LM	LM	VT	AW	XC	LM	LM
	◇■	◇■	■	◇		◇■			◇■	◇■	◇■	◇■		◇■		◇■	◇■		◇■	◇■	◇	◇■		
		⊠		⌶		⌶					⊠			⌶		⊠				R	⌶	⌶		
Stafford d	09 43					10 03			10 10	10 21				10 25					10 43			11 02		
Penkridge d									10 16															
Wolverhampton ■ a	09 56					10 15			10 27					10 39					10 56			11 15		
d	09 57			10 08		10 17		10 19	10 28				10 37	10 41		10 45		10 49	10 57		11 09	11 16		11 19
Coseley d	10 03							10 24										10 54	11 03					11 24
Tipton d								10 26										10 56						11 26
Dudley Port d								10 28										10 58						11 28
Sandwell & Dudley d								10 32					10 46			10 56		11 02						11 32
Smethwick Galton Bridge ■ d				10 19				10 34	10 40									11 04			11 20			11 34
Smethwick Rolfe Street d								10 36										11 06						11 36
Birmingham New Street ■ a	10 17			10 25		10 39		10 44	10 47				10 55	10 58		11 06		11 14	11 18		11 26	11 32		11 44
d		10 30	10 33	10 36			10 39				10 50	10 53		11 04		11 10	11 13			11 30	11 36		11 39	
Adderley Park d							10 44																11 44	
Stechford d							10 47										11 20						11 47	
Lea Hall d							10 50										11 23						11 50	
Marston Green d			10 41									11 01					11 26							
Birmingham International ✈ a		10 39	10 45	10 50			10 55				10 59	11 05		11 13		11 19	11 29			11 39	11 50		11 55	
d		10 40	10 45								11 00	11 05		11 14		11 20	11 29			11 40				
Hampton-in-Arden d			10 48														11 32							
Berkswell d												11 11					11 37							
Tile Hill d			10 55									11 14					11 40							
Canley d												11 17					11 44							
Coventry a		10 49	11 00								11 10	11 20		11 24		11 30	11 47			11 49				
d		10 51	11 01								11 11	11 21				11 31	11 48			11 51				
Rugby d			11 12							11 20	11 24	11 32					11 59							
Long Buckby d			11 22									11 42					12 09							
Northampton a			11 35							11 42		11 54					12 21							
London Euston ■ ⊖ a		11 54								12 49	12 14	13 17				12 32	13 27			12 54				

		LM	LM	LM	VT	LM	VT	LM	XC	VT		LM	LM	LM	VT	AW	XC	LM	LM	LM		LM	LM	VT
		◇■	◇■	◇■	◇■	◇■	◇■		◇■	◇■		◇■		◇■	◇■	◇	◇■			◇■		◇■ A	◇■	◇■
					R		⊠		⌶	R					R	⌶	⌶							R
Stafford d		11 10		11 21					11 25					11 43			12 03			12 10			12 21	
Penkridge d		11 16																		12 16				
Wolverhampton ■ a		11 27							11 39					11 57			12 15			12 27				
d		11 28					11 32	11 37	11 41	11 45			11 49	11 57		12 09	12 17		12 19	12 28				
Coseley d													11 54	12 03					12 24					
Tipton d													11 56						12 26					
Dudley Port d													11 58						12 28					
Sandwell & Dudley d								11 46		11 56			12 02						12 32					
Smethwick Galton Bridge ■ d		11 40											12 04			12 20			12 34	12 40				
Smethwick Rolfe Street d													12 06						12 36					
Birmingham New Street ■ a		11 47					11 55	11 55	11 58	12 06			12 14	12 17		12 26	12 39		12 44	12 47				
d			11 33		11 50	11 53			12 04	12 10		12 13			12 30	12 36		12 39				12 33		12 50
Adderley Park d																		12 44						
Stechford d												12 20						12 47						
Lea Hall d												12 23						12 50						
Marston Green d			11 41			12 01						12 26										12 41		
Birmingham International ✈ a			11 45		11 59	12 05			12 13	12 19		12 29			12 39	12 50		12 55				12 45		12 59
d			11 45		12 00	12 05			12 14	12 20		12 29			12 40							12 45		13 00
Hampton-in-Arden d			11 48									12 32										12 48		
Berkswell d						12 11						12 37												
Tile Hill d			11 55			12 14						12 40										12 55		
Canley d						12 17						12 44												
Coventry a			12 00		12 10	12 20			12 24	12 30		12 47			12 49							13 00		13 10
d			12 01		12 11	12 21				12 31		12 48			12 51							13 01		13 11
Rugby d			12 12	12 20	12 24	12 32						13 00										13 12	13 20	13 24
Long Buckby d			12 22			12 42						13 10										13 22		
Northampton a			12 34	12 43		12 58						13 22										13 34	13 40	
London Euston ■ ⊖ a			13 49		13 14	14 17				13 32		14 27			13 54							14 49		14 14

A ◇ from Northampton

Table 68

Mondays to Fridays

until 29 June

Stafford - Wolverhampton - Birmingham - Coventry - Northampton

Network Diagram - see first Page of Table 67

	LM	VT	LM	XC	VT	LM		LM	LM	VT	AW	XC	LM	LM	LM	LM	LM		VT	LM	VT	LM	XC	VT
	◇■	◇■		◇■	◇■	◇■			◇■	◇■	◇	◇■			◇■	◇■ A	◇■		◇■	◇■	◇■		◇■	◇■
		⊠		⌶	R					R	⌶	⌶							R		R		⌶	R
Stafford d				12 25					12 43			13 02			13 10		13 21						13 25	
Penkridge d															13 16									
Wolverhampton ■ a				12 39					12 56			13 15			13 27								13 39	
d		12 32	12 37	12 41	12 45			12 49	12 57		13 09	13 16		13 19	13 28						13 32	13 37	13 41	13 45
Coseley d								12 54	13 03					13 24										
Tipton d								12 56						13 26										
Dudley Port d								12 58						13 28										
Sandwell & Dudley d			12 46		12 56			13 02						13 32								13 46		13 56
Smethwick Galton Bridge ■ d								13 04			13 21			13 34	13 40									
Smethwick Rolfe Street d								13 06						13 36										
Birmingham New Street ■ a		12 55	12 55	12 58	13 06			13 14	13 17		13 26	13 39		13 44	13 47						13 55	13 55	13 58	14 06
d	12 53			13 04	13 10	13 13				13 30	13 36		13 39			13 33			13 50	13 53			14 04	14 10
Adderley Park d													13 44											
Stechford d						13 20							13 47											
Lea Hall d						13 23							13 50											
Marston Green d	13 01					13 26										13 41				14 01				
Birmingham International ✈ a	13 05			13 13	13 19	13 29				13 39	13 50		13 55			13 45			13 59	14 05			14 13	14 19
d	13 05			13 14	13 20	13 29				13 40						13 45			14 00	14 05			14 14	14 20
Hampton-in-Arden d						13 32										13 48								
Berkswell d	13 11					13 37														14 11				
Tile Hill d	13 14					13 40										13 55				14 14				
Canley d	13 17					13 44														14 17				
Coventry a	13 20			13 24	13 30	13 47				13 49						14 00			14 10	14 20			14 24	14 30
d	13 21				13 31	13 48				13 51						14 01			14 11	14 21				14 31
Rugby d	13 32					13 59										14 12	14 20		14 24	14 32				
Long Buckby d	13 42					14 09										14 22				14 42				
Northampton a	13 54					14 21										14 35	14 42			14 54				
London Euston ■ ⊖ a	15 17				14 32	15 27				14 54						15 49			15 14	16 17				15 32

	LM	LM	LM		VT	AW	XC	LM	LM	LM	LM	LM	VT		LM	VT	LM	XC	VT	LM	LM	LM	VT	
	◇■		◇■		◇■	◇	◇■			◇■	◇■ A	◇■	◇■		◇■	◇■		◇■	◇■	◇■		◇■	◇■	
					R	⌶	⌶						R			⊠		⌶	R				R	
Stafford d			13 43				14 02			14 10		14 21						14 25				14 46		
Penkridge d										14 16														
Wolverhampton ■ a			13 56				14 15			14 27								14 39				14 59		
d		13 49	13 57			14 08	14 16		14 19	14 28						14 32	14 37	14 41	14 45		14 49	14 59		
Coseley d		13 54	14 03						14 24												14 54	15 05		
Tipton d		13 56							14 26												14 56			
Dudley Port d		13 58							14 28												14 58			
Sandwell & Dudley d		14 02							14 32								14 46		14 56		15 02			
Smethwick Galton Bridge ■ d		14 04				14 20			14 34	14 40											15 04			
Smethwick Rolfe Street d		14 06							14 36												15 06			
Birmingham New Street ■ a		14 14	14 17			14 26	14 32		14 44	14 47						14 55	14 55	14 58	15 06		15 14	15 20		
d	14 13				14 30	14 36		14 39			14 33		14 50		14 53			15 04	15 10	15 13			15 30	
Adderley Park d								14 44																
Stechford d	14 20							14 47												15 20				
Lea Hall d	14 23							14 50												15 23				
Marston Green d	14 26										14 41				15 01					15 26				
Birmingham International ✈ a	14 29				14 39	14 50		14 55			14 45		14 59		15 05			15 13	15 19	15 29			15 39	
d	14 29				14 40						14 45		15 00		15 05			15 14	15 20	15 29			15 40	
Hampton-in-Arden d	14 32										14 48									15 32				
Berkswell d	14 37														15 11					15 37				
Tile Hill d	14 40										14 55				15 14					15 40				
Canley d	14 44														15 17					15 44				
Coventry a	14 47				14 49						15 00		15 10		15 20			15 24	15 30	15 47			15 49	
d	14 48				14 51						15 01		15 11		15 21				15 31	15 48			15 51	
Rugby d	14 59										15 12	15 20	15 24		15 32					15 59				
Long Buckby d	15 09										15 22				15 42									
Northampton a	15 21										15 34	15 42			15 54					16 18				
London Euston ■ ⊖ a	16 27				15 54						16 49		16 14		17 18				16 32	17 27			16 57	

A ◇ from Northampton

Stafford - Wolverhampton - Birmingham - Coventry - Northampton

Network Diagram - see first Page of Table 67

		AW	XC	LM	LM	LM	LM	LM	VT	LM	LM	XC	VT	LM	LM	LM	VT	LM	LM FX	AW	XC	LM	LM
		◇ ⊼	◇■ ⊼			■	◇■ A	◇■	◇■ 🍴	◇■		◇■ ⊼	◇■ 🍴	■		◇■	◇■ 🍴	■	◇■ A	◇ ⊼	◇■ ⊼		
Stafford	d		15 03			15 10		15 21				15 25				15 43					16 03		
Penkridge	d					15 16																	
Wolverhampton [7] ⇌	a		15 15			15 27						15 39				15 56					16 15		
	d	15 10	15 17		15 19	15 28					15 37	15 41	15 45		15 49	15 57				16 09	16 17		16 19
Coseley	d				15 24										15 54	16 03							16 24
Tipton	d				15 26										15 56								16 26
Dudley Port	d				15 28										15 58								16 28
Sandwell & Dudley	d				15 32						15 46		15 56		16 02								16 32
Smethwick Galton Bridge [7]	d	15 21			15 34	15 40									16 04					16 20			16 34
Smethwick Rolfe Street	d				15 36										16 06								16 36
Birmingham New Street [12]	a	15 27	15 39		15 44	15 47					15 55	15 58	16 06		16 14	16 17				16 27	16 39		16 45
	d	15 36		15 39			15 33		15 50	15 53		16 04	16 10	16 13			16 30	16 33	16 33	16 36		16 39	
Adderley Park	d			15 44																		16 44	
Stechford	d			15 47										16 20								16 47	
Lea Hall	d			15 50										16 23								16 50	
Marston Green	d						15 41			16 01				16 26				16 41	16 41				
Birmingham International ✈	a	15 50		15 55			15 45		15 59	16 05		16 13	16 19	16 29			16 39	16 45	16 45	16 50		16 55	
	d						15 45		16 00	16 05		16 14	16 20	16 29			16 40	16 45	16 45				
Hampton-in-Arden	d						15 48							16 32				16 48	16 48				
Berkswell	d									16 11				16 37									
Tile Hill	d						15 55			16 14				16 40				16 55	16 55				
Canley	d									16 17				16 44									
Coventry	a						16 00		16 10	16 20		16 24	16 30	16 47			16 49	17 00	17 00				
	d						16 01		16 11	16 21			16 31				16 51	17 01	17 01				
Rugby	d						16 12	16 20	16 24	16 32								17 12	17 12				
Long Buckby	d						16 22			16 42								17 22	17 22				
Northampton	a						16 34	16 43		16 54								17 34	17 34				
London Euston [15] ⊖	a						17 49		17 14	18 18			17 34				17 54		18 49				

		LM	LM	VT	LM	VT	LM	XC	VT	LM	LM	LM	LM	VT	AW	XC	LM	LM	LM	LM	LM	VT	LM
		◇■	◇■	◇■ 🍴	◇■	◇■ 🍴		◇■ ⊼	◇■ 🍴	■		■	◇■	◇■ ⊠	◇ ⊼	◇■ ⊼	◇■			◇■	◇■	◇■ ⊠	◇■
Stafford	d	16 10	16 21					16 25					16 46			17 03				17 10	17 21		
Penkridge	d	16 16																		17 16			
Wolverhampton [7] ⇌	a	16 26						16 39					16 59			17 15				17 27			
	d	16 28				16 32	16 37	16 41	16 45		16 49		16 59		17 09	17 16			17 19	17 28			
Coseley	d										16 54		17 05						17 24				
Tipton	d										16 56								17 26				
Dudley Port	d										16 58								17 28				
Sandwell & Dudley	d						16 46		16 56		17 02								17 32				
Smethwick Galton Bridge [7]	d	16 40									17 04				17 22				17 34	17 40			
Smethwick Rolfe Street	d										17 06								17 36				
Birmingham New Street [12]	a	16 47				16 55	16 55	16 58	17 06		17 14		17 20		17 28	17 32			17 44	17 47			
	d			16 50	16 53			17 04	17 10	17 13		17 16		17 30	17 36		17 33	17 39				17 50	17 53
Adderley Park	d											17 21						17 44					
Stechford	d									17 20								17 47					
Lea Hall	d											17 25						17 50					
Marston Green	d				17 01							17 28					17 41						18 01
Birmingham International ✈	a			16 59	17 05			17 13	17 19	17 25		17 32		17 39	17 49		17 45	17 55				17 59	18 05
	d			17 00	17 05			17 14	17 20	17 25		17 32		17 40			17 45					18 00	18 05
Hampton-in-Arden	d											17 35					17 48						
Berkswell	d				17 11							17 40											18 11
Tile Hill	d				17 14					17 32							17 55						18 14
Canley	d				17 17					17 36													18 17
Coventry	a			17 10	17 20			17 24	17 30	17 40		17 47		17 49			18 00					18 10	18 20
	d			17 11	17 21				17 31	17 40				17 51			18 01					18 11	18 21
Rugby	d		17 20	17 24	17 32					17 51							18 12				18 20	18 24	18 32
Long Buckby	d				17 42					18 01							18 22						18 42
Northampton	a		17 39		17 54					18 13							18 34				18 39		18 54
London Euston [15] ⊖	a		18 49	18 14	19 18				18 34	19 29				18 54							19 50	19 14	20 19

A ◇ from Northampton

Table 68

Mondays to Fridays
until 29 June

Stafford - Wolverhampton - Birmingham - Coventry - Northampton

Network Diagram - see first Page of Table 67

		VT	LM	XC	VT	LM	LM	LM	VT	AW	XC	LM	LM	LM	LM	LM	VT	LM	VT	LM	XC	VT
		◇■ 🍴		◇■ ⊼	◇■ ⊠	■		◇■	◇■ ⊠	◇ ⊼	◇■ ⊼			◇■	◇■ A	◇■	◇■ ⊠	◇■	■ 🍴		◇■ ⊼	◇■ ⊠
Stafford	d			17 25				17 43			18 04			18 10		18 21					18 28	
Penkridge	d													18 16								
Wolverhampton [7] ⇌	a			17 39				17 56			18 15			18 27							18 39	
	d	17 32	17 37	17 41	17 45		17 49	17 57		18 09	18 16		18 19	18 28					18 32	18 37	18 41	18 45
Coseley	d						17 54	18 03					18 24									
Tipton	d						17 56						18 26									
Dudley Port	d						17 58						18 28									
Sandwell & Dudley	d		17 46		17 56		18 02						18 32							18 46		18 56
Smethwick Galton Bridge [7]	d						18 04			18 20			18 34	18 40								
Smethwick Rolfe Street	d						18 06						18 36									
Birmingham New Street [12]	a	17 55	17 55	17 58	18 06		18 14	18 17		18 26	18 38		18 44	18 48					18 55	18 55	18 58	19 06
	d			18 04	18 10	18 13			18 30	18 36		18 39			18 33		18 50	18 53			19 04	19 10
Adderley Park	d											18 44										
Stechford	d					18 20						18 47										
Lea Hall	d					18 23						18 50										
Marston Green	d					18 26									18 41			19 01				
Birmingham International ✈	a			18 13	18 19	18 29			18 39	18 50		18 55			18 45		18 59	19 05			19 13	19 19
	d			18 14	18 20	18 29			18 40						18 45		19 00	19 05			19 14	19 20
Hampton-in-Arden	d					18 32									18 48							
Berkswell	d					18 37												19 11				
Tile Hill	d					18 40									18 55			19 14				
Canley	d					18 44												19 17				
Coventry	a			18 24	18 30	18 47			18 49						19 00		19 10	19 20			19 24	19 30
	d				18 31				18 51						19 01		19 11	19 21				19 31
Rugby	d														19 12	19 20	19 24	19 32				
Long Buckby	d														19 22			19 42				
Northampton	a														19 34	19 45		19 55				
London Euston [15] ⊖	a				19 34				19 54						20 49		20 14	21 17				20 34

		LM	LM	LM	VT	AW	XC	LM	LM	LM	LM	LM	VT	LM	VT	LM	XC	VT	LM	LM	LM	LM	AW
		■		◇■	◇■ 🍴	◇ ⊼	◇■ ⊼	◇■			◇■	◇■	◇■ 🍴	◇■	◇■ 🍴		◇■ B ⊼	◇■ 🍴	■		◇■	◇■	◇ ⊼
Stafford	d			18 43			19 02				19 10	19 21					19 25				19 42		
Penkridge	d										19 16										19 47		
Wolverhampton [7] ⇌	a			18 56			19 15				19 27						19 39				19 57		
	d		18 49	18 57		19 09	19 16			19 19	19 28				19 33	19 37	19 41	19 45		19 49	19 57		20 11
Coseley	d		18 54	19 03						19 24										19 54	20 03		
Tipton	d		18 56							19 26										19 56			
Dudley Port	d		18 58							19 28										19 58			
Sandwell & Dudley	d		19 02							19 32						19 46		19 56		20 02			
Smethwick Galton Bridge [7]	d		19 04			19 20				19 34	19 40									20 04			20 22
Smethwick Rolfe Street	d		19 06							19 36										20 06			
Birmingham New Street [12]	a		19 14	19 17		19 26	19 32			19 44	19 48				19 55	19 55	19 58	20 06		20 14	20 18		20 27
	d	19 13			19 30	19 36		19 33	19 39				19 50	19 53			20 04	20 10	20 13			20 33	20 36
Adderley Park	d								19 44														
Stechford	d	19 20							19 47										20 20				
Lea Hall	d	19 23							19 50										20 23				
Marston Green	d	19 26						19 41						20 01					20 26			20 41	
Birmingham International ✈	a	19 29			19 39	19 50		19 45	19 55				19 59	20 05			20 13	20 19	20 29			20 45	20 50
	d	19 29			19 40			19 45					20 00	20 05			20 14	20 20	20 29			20 45	
Hampton-in-Arden	d	19 32						19 48											20 32			20 48	
Berkswell	d	19 37												20 11					20 37				
Tile Hill	d	19 40						19 55						20 14					20 40			20 55	
Canley	d	19 44												20 17					20 44				
Coventry	a	19 47			19 49			20 00					20 10	20 20			20 24	20 30	20 47			21 00	
	d				19 51			20 01					20 11	20 21				20 31				21 01	
Rugby	d							20 12				20 20	20 23	20 32								21 12	
Long Buckby	d							20 22						20 42								21 22	
Northampton	a							20 37				20 43		20 54								21 34	
London Euston [15] ⊖	a				20 54								21 14	22 20				21 38					

A ◇ from Northampton

B ⊼ to Birmingham New Street

Table 68

Mondays to Fridays
until 29 June

Stafford - Wolverhampton - Birmingham - Coventry - Northampton

Network Diagram - see first Page of Table 67

		XC	LM	LM		LM	LM	VT	LM	VT	LM	XC	VT	LM		LM	LM	XC	LM	LM	LM	LM	VT	LM
		◇❶				◇❶	❶	◇❶	◇❶	■ ❶		◇❶	◇❶	❶			◇❶	◇❶	◇❶			◇❶	◇❶	❶
												A												
		⌶						▭		▭		⌶	▭										▭	
Stafford	d	20 04				20 16	20 21					20 26					20 42	21 03				21 10	21 13	
Penkridge	d																20 47					21 16		
Wolverhampton ❼ ⇌	a	20 16				20 29						20 40					20 57	21 15				21 26	21 29	
	d	20 17		20 19		20 29				20 34	20 38	20 43	20 47			20 49	20 57	21 16			21 19	21 28	21 32	
Coseley	d			20 24												20 54	21 03				21 24			
Tipton	d			20 26												20 56					21 26			
Dudley Port	d			20 28												20 58					21 28			
Sandwell & Dudley	d			20 32							20 47		20 57			21 02					21 32			
Smethwick Galton Bridge ❼	d			20 34		20 41										21 04					21 34	21 40		
Smethwick Rolfe Street	d			20 36												21 06					21 36			
Birmingham New Street 12	a	20 33		20 44		20 47				20 55	20 56	21 00	21 06			21 14	21 18	21 33			21 44	21 47	21 48	
	d		20 39					20 50	20 53			21 04	21 10	21 13					21 33	21 39				21 53
Adderley Park	d		20 44																	21 44				
Stechford	d		20 47											21 20						21 48				
Lea Hall	d		20 50											21 23						21 50				
Marston Green	d								21 01					21 26					21 41					22 01
Birmingham International ✈	a		20 55					20 59	21 05			21 13	21 19	21 29					21 45	21 55				22 05
	d							21 00	21 05			21 14	21 20	21 29					21 45					22 05
Hampton-in-Arden	d													21 32					21 48					
Berkswell	d								21 11					21 37										22 11
Tile Hill	d								21 14					21 40					21 55					22 14
Canley	d								21 17					21 44										22 17
Coventry	a							21 10	21 20			21 24	21 30	21 53					22 00					22 20
	d							21 11	21 21				21 31						22 01					22 21
Rugby	d						21 20	21 23	21 32										22 12					22 32
Long Buckby	d								21 42										22 22					22 42
Northampton	a						21 39		21 54										22 34					22 58
London Euston 15 ⊖	a						22 56	22 12	23 21				22 43						00 21					

		LM	XC	XC	VT	LM	LM	LM	AW	LM		LM	VT	LM	VT	LM	XC	VT	VT	LM		LM	AW MW FO	AW TThO	LM
			◇❶	◇❶	◇❶	❶		◇❶	◇	❶			◇❶	❶	◇❶		◇❶	◇❶	◇❶	❶			◇	◇	◇❶
				B														C	B				D	E	
					▭								▭		▭			▭	▭						
Stafford	d		21 25					21 41									22 26								22 41
Penkridge	d							21 47																	22 47
Wolverhampton ❼ ⇌	a		21 39					21 57									22 39								22 57
	d	21 37	21 41		21 45		21 49	21 57	22 09			22 19	22 28		22 32	22 37	22 41	22 45	22 45			22 49	22 55	22 55	22 57
Coseley	d						21 54	22 03				22 24										22 54			23 03
Tipton	d						21 56					22 26										22 56			
Dudley Port	d						21 58					22 28										22 58			
Sandwell & Dudley	d	21 46			21 56		22 02					22 32				22 46		22 55	22 55			23 02			
Smethwick Galton Bridge ❼	d						22 04		22 20			22 34										23 04			
Smethwick Rolfe Street	d						22 06					22 36										23 06			
Birmingham New Street 12	a	21 55	22 00		22 06		22 14	22 17	22 33			22 44	22 50		22 55	22 55	22 58	23 06	23 06			23 14	23 27	23 28	23 18
	d			22 04	22 10	22 13				22 33				22 53				23 10	23 10	23 13					
Adderley Park	d																			23 18					
Stechford	d					22 20														23 21					
Lea Hall	d					22 23														23 24					
Marston Green	d					22 26				22 41				23 01						23 27					
Birmingham International ✈	a			22 13	22 21	22 29				22 45				23 05				23 19	23 19	23 30					
	d			22 14	22 22	22 29				22 45				23 05				23 20	23 20	23 30					
Hampton-in-Arden	d					22 32				22 48										23 33					
Berkswell	d					22 37								23 11						23 38					
Tile Hill	d					22 40				22 55				23 14						23 41					
Canley	d					22 44								23 17						23 45					
Coventry	a			22 24	22 31	22 47				23 00				23 20				23 30	23 30	23 48					
	d				22 32									23 21				23 31	23 31						
Rugby	d				22 43									23 32				23 44	23 44						
Long Buckby	d													23 42											
Northampton	a													23 54				00s05	00s05						
London Euston 15 ⊖	a				00 04													01 13	01 15						

A ⌶ to Birmingham New Street
B until 22 June
C from 25 June until 29 June

Table 68

Mondays to Fridays
until 29 June

Stafford - Wolverhampton - Birmingham - Coventry - Northampton

Network Diagram - see first Page of Table 67

		XC FO	XC FX	LM
		◇❶	◇❶	❶
		A	B	
Stafford	d	23 07	23 10	
Penkridge	d			
Wolverhampton ❼ ⇌	a	23 19	23 22	
	d	23 21	23 23	
Coseley	d			
Tipton	d			
Dudley Port	d			
Sandwell & Dudley	d			
Smethwick Galton Bridge ❼	d			
Smethwick Rolfe Street	d			
Birmingham New Street 12	a	23 39	23 39	
	d			23 53
Adderley Park	d			
Stechford	d			
Lea Hall	d			
Marston Green	d			00 01
Birmingham International ✈	a			00 04
	d			00 05
Hampton-in-Arden	d			
Berkswell	d			
Tile Hill	d			
Canley	d			
Coventry	a			00 15
	d			
Rugby	d			
Long Buckby	d			
Northampton	a			
London Euston 15 ⊖	a			

Mondays to Fridays
2 July to 14 September

		LM MX	VT MX	VT MO	VT MO	VT MX	LM MX	LM	VT	VT		LM	VT	LM	AW	XC	VT	LM	AW	VT		LM	LM	LM	LM
		◇❶	◇❶	◇❶	◇❶	◇❶	❶	❶	◇❶	◇❶		❶	◇❶	◇❶		◇❶	◇❶	❶		◇❶			❶	❶	❶
																							C	D	
			▭	▭	▭	▭			⊠	⊠			⊠			⌶	⊠			⊠					
Stafford	d														05 25										
Penkridge	d																								
Wolverhampton ❼ ⇌	a														05 39										
	d		21p45	22p05	22p37	22p45			05 00	05 24					05 40		05 45		05 59	06 04		06 15			
Coseley	d																								
Tipton	d																								
Dudley Port	d																								
Sandwell & Dudley	d		21p56	22p15	22p47	22p55				05 34							05 56			06 15					
Smethwick Galton Bridge ❼	d																		06 10						
Smethwick Rolfe Street	d																								
Birmingham New Street 12	a		22p06	22p24	22p56	23p06			05 26	05 43					05 59		06 06		06 15	06 24		06 32			
	d	21p33	22p10	22p30	23p00	23p10	23p53		05 29	05 50				05 53		06 04	06 10	06 13	06 36	06 30					06 33
Adderley Park	d																		→						
Stechford	d																	06 20							
Lea Hall	d																	06 23							
Marston Green	d	21p41					00 01							06 01				06 26							06 41
Birmingham International ✈	a	21p45	22p21	22p39	23p09	23p19	00 04		05 38	05 59				06 05		06 13	06 19	06 29		06 39					06 45
	d	21p45	22p22	22p40	23p10	23p20	00 05		05 40	06 00				06 05		06 14	06 20	06 29		06 40					06 45
Hampton-in-Arden	d	21p48																06 32							06 48
Berkswell	d													06 11				06 37							
Tile Hill	d	21p55												06 14				06 40							06 55
Canley	d													06 17				06 44							
Coventry	a	22p00	22p31	22p50	23p20	23p30	00 15		05 50	06 10				06 20		06 24	06 30	06 47		06 49					07 00
	d	22p01	22p32	22p51	23p21	23p31			05 51	06 11				06 21			06 31			06 51					07 01
Rugby	d	22p12	22p43	23p04	23p34	23p44		05 20	06 03			06 13	06 20	06 32									06 45	07 02	07 12
Long Buckby	d	22p22						05 30				06 23		06 42									06 54	07 12	07 21
Northampton	a	22p34			23b53	00s05		05 42				06 35	06 39	06 54									07 06	07 25	07 33
London Euston 15 ⊖	a	00 21	00 04	00 27	01 04	01 13		06 50	07 02	07 13		07 40	07 30	08 02			07 34			07 53			08 11	08 49	

A also from 25 June until 28 June
B until 21 June
C from 10 September until 14 September
D from 2 July until 7 September
b Previous night, stops to set down only

2 July to 14 September

Stafford - Wolverhampton - Birmingham - Coventry - Northampton

Network Diagram - see first Page of Table 67

	LM ■ A	AW	LM	LM ■	VT ◇■ ⊠	LM ◇■	XC ◇■ ⌶	VT ◇■ ⊠	LM ■	LM	LM ◇■	VT ◇■ ⊠	VT ◇■ ⊠	AW	XC ◇■ ⌶	LM ◇■	LM	LM	LM ◇■	LM ◇■	VT ◇■ ⊠	LM ◇■
Stafford d							06 25				06 41				06 58				07 12	07 22		
Penkridge d											06 47								07 18			
Wolverhampton ■ a							06 39				06 57				07 12				07 28			
Wolverhampton d				06 19	06 27		06 41	06 45		06 49	06 59	07 04		07 10	07 15			07 19	07 28			
Coseley d				06 24						06 54	07 04							07 24				
Tipton d				06 26						06 57								07 26				
Dudley Port d				06 28						06 59								07 28				
Sandwell & Dudley d				06 32	06 37			06 56		07 03		07 15						07 32				
Smethwick Galton Bridge ■ d				06 34						07 06				07 21				07 34	07 40			
Smethwick Rolfe Street d		←		06 36						07 09								07 36				
Birmingham New Street ■ a		06 15		06 43	06 46		06 58	07 06		07 15	07 18	07 24		07 26	07 31			07 44	07 48			
Birmingham New Street d	06 33	06 36	06 39		06 50	06 53	07 04	07 10	07 13			07 30		07 36		07 33	07 39				07 50	07 53
Adderley Park d			06 44														07 44					
Stechford d			06 47						07 20								07 47					
Lea Hall d			06 50						07 23								07 50					
Marston Green d	06 41					07 01			07 26							07 41						08 01
Birmingham International ✈ a	06 45	06 50	06 55		06 59	07 05	07 13	07 19	07 29					07 50		07 45	07 55				07 59	08 05
Birmingham International d	06 45				07 00	07 05	07 14	07 20	07 29				07 41			07 45					08 00	08 05
Hampton-in-Arden d	06 48					07 08										07 48						
Berkswell d						07 13			07 35													08 11
Tile Hill d	06 55								07 38							07 55						08 14
Canley d						07 18										07 58						08 17
Coventry a	07 00				07 10	07 21	07 24	07 30	07 43				07 51			08 02					08 10	08 20
Coventry d	07 01				07 11	07 21		07 31					07 52			08 03					08 11	08 21
Rugby d	07 12					07 32										08 14				08 20	08 23	08 32
Long Buckby d	07 21					07 42										08 24						08 42
Northampton a	07 33					07 54										08 37				08 41		08 56
London Euston ■ ⊖ a	08 39				08 14	09 10		08 30				08 42	08 49							09 44	09 13	10 18

	VT ◇■ ⊠	LM	LM	XC ◇■ ⌶	VT ◇■ ⊠	LM ■	LM	LM ◇■	LM	VT ◇■ ⊠	AW ◇ ⌶	XC ◇■ ⌶	LM	LM	LM ◇■	LM ◇■	LM ◇■	VT ◇■ ⊠	LM ◇■	VT ◇■ ⊠	LM
Stafford d					07 28			07 41				08 02			08 10		08 21				
Penkridge d								07 47							08 16						
Wolverhampton ■ a					07 43			07 57				08 15			08 26						
Wolverhampton d	07 32	07 35	07 39		07 45		07 49	07 57	08 04		08 09	08 16		08 19	08 28					08 32	08 37
Coseley d			07 44				07 54	08 03						08 24							
Tipton d			07 47				07 57							08 26							
Dudley Port d			07 49				07 59							08 28							
Sandwell & Dudley d		07 45			07 56		08 02							08 32							
Smethwick Galton Bridge ■ d			07 53				08 05				08 21			08 34	08 40						08 46
Smethwick Rolfe Street d			07 55				08 07							08 36							
Birmingham New Street ■ a	07 55	07 54	08 03		08 06		08 14	08 17	08 20		08 26	08 32		08 44	08 47					08 55	08 55
Birmingham New Street d				08 04	08 10	08 13				08 30	08 36		08 39			08 33		08 50	08 53		
Adderley Park d													08 44								
Stechford d						08 20							08 47								
Lea Hall d						08 23							08 50								
Marston Green d						08 26										08 41			09 01		
Birmingham International ✈ a				08 13	08 19	08 29				08 39	08 50		08 55			08 45		08 59	09 05		
Birmingham International d				08 14	08 20	08 29				08 40						08 45		09 00	09 05		
Hampton-in-Arden d						08 32										08 48					
Berkswell d						08 37													09 11		
Tile Hill d						08 40										08 55			09 14		
Canley d						08 44													09 17		
Coventry a				08 24	08 30	08 47				08 49						09 00		09 10	09 20		
Coventry d					08 31					08 51						09 01		09 11	09 21		
Rugby d																09 12	09 20	09 23	09 32		
Long Buckby d																09 22			09 42		
Northampton a																09 34	09 39		09 54		
London Euston ■ ⊖ a					09 34					09 54						10 49		10 14	11 17		

A from 10 September until 14 September

2 July to 14 September

Stafford - Wolverhampton - Birmingham - Coventry - Northampton

Network Diagram - see first Page of Table 67

	XC ◇■ ⌶	VT ◇■ ⊠	LM ◇■	LM	LM ◇■	VT ◇■ ⊠	AW ◇ ⌶	XC ◇■ ⌶	LM	LM	LM ◇■	LM ◇■ A	LM ◇■	VT ◇■ B ⊠	VT ◇■ C ⊠	LM ◇■	VT ◇■ ⊠	LM	XC ◇■ ⌶	VT ◇■ ⊠	LM ◇■	LM
Stafford d	08 25				08 43			09 03			09 10		09 21						09 25			
Penkridge d					08 48						09 16											
Wolverhampton ■ a	08 39				08 58			09 15			09 27								09 39			
Wolverhampton d	08 41	08 45		08 49	08 58		09 10	09 16		09 19	09 28						09 32	09 37	09 41	09 45		09 49
Coseley d				08 54	09 04					09 24												09 54
Tipton d				08 56						09 26												09 56
Dudley Port d				08 58						09 28												09 58
Sandwell & Dudley d		08 56		09 02						09 32								09 46		09 56		10 02
Smethwick Galton Bridge ■ d				09 04			09 21			09 34	09 40											10 04
Smethwick Rolfe Street d				09 06						09 36												10 06
Birmingham New Street ■ a	08 58	09 06		09 14	09 18		09 26	09 32		09 44	09 47						09 55	09 55	09 58	10 06		10 14
Birmingham New Street d	09 04	09 10	09 13			09 30	09 36		09 39			09 33		09 50	09 50	09 53			10 04	10 10	10 13	
Adderley Park d									09 44													
Stechford d			09 20						09 47												10 20	
Lea Hall d			09 23						09 50												10 23	
Marston Green d			09 26									09 41				10 01					10 26	
Birmingham International ✈ a	09 13	09 19	09 29			09 39	09 50		09 55			09 45		09 59	09 59	10 05			10 13	10 19	10 29	
Birmingham International d	09 14	09 20	09 29			09 40						09 45		10 00	10 00	10 05			10 14	10 20	10 29	
Hampton-in-Arden d			09 32									09 48									10 32	
Berkswell d			09 37													10 11					10 37	
Tile Hill d			09 40									09 55				10 14					10 40	
Canley d			09 44													10 17					10 44	
Coventry a	09 24	09 30	09 47			09 49						10 00		10 11	10 10	10 20			10 24	10 30	10 47	
Coventry d		09 31	09 48			09 51						10 01		10 11	10 11	10 21				10 31	10 48	
Rugby d			09 59									10 12	10 20	10 24	10 24	10 32					10 59	
Long Buckby d			10 09									10 22				10 42					11 09	
Northampton a			10 21									10 34	10 39			10 54					11 21	
London Euston ■ ⊖ a		10 32	11 27			10 54						11 49		11 14	11 14	12 17				11 32	12 27	

	LM ◇■	VT ◇■ ⊠	LM ■	AW ◇ ⌶	XC ◇■ ⌶	LM	LM	LM ◇■	LM ◇■	VT ◇■ ⊠	LM ◇■	VT ◇■ ⊠	LM	XC ◇■ ⌶	VT ◇■ ⊠	LM ◇■	LM	LM ◇■	VT ◇■	AW ◇ ⌶	XC ◇■ ⌶
Stafford d	09 43				10 03			10 10	10 21					10 25				10 43			11 02
Penkridge d								10 16													
Wolverhampton ■ a	09 56				10 15			10 27						10 39				10 56			11 15
Wolverhampton d	09 57			10 08	10 17		10 19	10 28				10 32	10 37	10 41	10 45		10 49	10 57		11 09	11 16
Coseley d	10 03						10 24										10 54	11 03			
Tipton d							10 26										10 56				
Dudley Port d							10 28										10 58				
Sandwell & Dudley d							10 32						10 46		10 56		11 02				
Smethwick Galton Bridge ■ d				10 19			10 34	10 40									11 04			11 20	
Smethwick Rolfe Street d							10 36										11 06				
Birmingham New Street ■ a	10 17			10 25	10 39		10 44	10 47				10 55	10 55	10 58	11 06		11 14	11 18		11 26	11 32
Birmingham New Street d		10 30	10 33	10 36		10 39				10 50	10 53			11 04	11 10	11 13			11 30	11 36	
Adderley Park d						10 44															
Stechford d						10 47										11 20					
Lea Hall d						10 50										11 23					
Marston Green d			10 41								11 01					11 26					
Birmingham International ✈ a		10 39	10 45	10 50		10 55				10 59	11 05			11 13	11 19	11 29			11 39	11 50	
Birmingham International d		10 40	10 45							11 00	11 05			11 14	11 20	11 29			11 40		
Hampton-in-Arden d			10 48													11 32					
Berkswell d											11 11					11 37					
Tile Hill d			10 55								11 14					11 40					
Canley d											11 17					11 44					
Coventry a		10 49	11 00							11 10	11 20			11 24	11 30	11 47			11 49		
Coventry d		10 51	11 01							11 11	11 21				11 31	11 48			11 51		
Rugby d			11 12						11 20	11 24	11 32					11 59					
Long Buckby d			11 22								11 42					12 09					
Northampton a			11 35						11 42		11 54					12 21					
London Euston ■ ⊖ a		11 54							12 49	12 14	13 17				12 32	13 27			12 54		

A ◇ from Northampton

B from 27 July until 7 September, not from 13 August until 28 August

C not from 27 July until 10 August, from 29 August until 7 September

2 July to 14 September

Stafford - Wolverhampton - Birmingham - Coventry - Northampton

Network Diagram - see first Page of Table 67

		LM	LM	LM	LM	LM	VT	LM	VT	LM		XC	VT	LM	LM	LM	VT	AW	XC	LM		LM	LM	LM	LM
				◇1	◇1	◇1	◇1	◇1	◇1			◇1	◇1	◇1		◇1	◇1	◇	◇1				◇1	◇1	◇1
																								A	
							⊏		⊠			⊼	⊏				⊏	⊼	⊼						
Stafford	d			11 10		11 21						11 25				11 43			12 03				12 10		12 21
Penkridge	d			11 16																			12 16		
Wolverhampton 7 ⇌	a			11 27								11 39				11 57			12 15				12 27		
	d		11 19	11 28					11 32	11 37		11 41	11 45		11 49	11 57		12 09	12 17			12 19	12 28		
Coseley	d		11 24												11 54	12 03						12 24			
Tipton	d		11 26												11 56							12 26			
Dudley Port	d		11 28												11 58							12 28			
Sandwell & Dudley	d		11 32							11 46			11 56		12 02							12 32			
Smethwick Galton Bridge 7	d		11 34	11 40											12 04			12 20				12 34	12 40		
Smethwick Rolfe Street	d		11 36												12 06							12 36			
Birmingham New Street 12	a		11 44	11 47					11 55	11 55		11 58	12 06		12 14	12 17		12 26	12 39			12 44	12 47		
	d	11 39			11 33		11 50	11 53				12 04	12 10	12 13			12 30	12 36		12 39				12 33	
Adderley Park	d	11 44																		12 44					
Stechford	d	11 47												12 20						12 47					
Lea Hall	d	11 50												12 23						12 50					
Marston Green	d				11 41			12 01						12 26										12 41	
Birmingham International ✈	a	11 55			11 45		11 59	12 05				12 13	12 19	12 29			12 39	12 50		12 55				12 45	
	d				11 45		12 00	12 05				12 14	12 20	12 29			12 40							12 45	
Hampton-in-Arden	d				11 48									12 32										12 48	
Berkswell	d							12 11						12 37											
Tile Hill	d				11 55			12 14						12 40										12 55	
Canley	d							12 17						12 44											
Coventry	a				12 00		12 10	12 20				12 24	12 30	12 47			12 49							13 00	
	d				12 01		12 11	12 21					12 31	12 48			12 51							13 01	
Rugby	d				12 12	12 20	12 24	12 32						13 00										13 12	13 20
Long Buckby	d				12 22			12 42						13 10										13 22	
Northampton	a				12 34	12 43		12 58						13 22										13 34	13 40
London Euston 15 ⊖	a				13 49		13 14	14 17					13 32	14 27			13 54							14 49	

		VT	LM	VT	LM	XC		VT	LM	LM	LM	VT	AW	XC	LM	LM		LM	LM	LM	VT	LM	VT	LM	XC
		◇1	◇1	◇1		◇1		◇1	◇1		◇1	◇1	◇	◇1				◇1	◇1	◇1	◇1	◇1	◇1		◇1
																			A						
		⊏		⊠		⊼		⊏				⊏	⊼	⊼							⊏		⊏		⊼
Stafford	d					12 25					12 43			13 02				13 10		13 21					13 25
Penkridge	d																	13 16							
Wolverhampton 7 ⇌	a					12 39					12 56			13 15				13 27							13 39
	d			12 32	12 37	12 41		12 45		12 49	12 57		13 09	13 16		13 19		13 28					13 32	13 37	13 41
Coseley	d									12 54	13 03					13 24									
Tipton	d									12 56						13 26									
Dudley Port	d									12 58						13 28									
Sandwell & Dudley	d				12 46			12 56		13 02						13 32								13 46	
Smethwick Galton Bridge 7	d									13 04			13 21			13 34		13 40							
Smethwick Rolfe Street	d									13 06						13 36									
Birmingham New Street 12	a			12 55	12 55	12 58		13 06		13 14	13 17		13 26	13 39		13 44		13 47					13 55	13 55	13 58
	d	12 50	12 53			13 04		13 10	13 13			13 30	13 36		13 39				13 33		13 50	13 53			14 04
Adderley Park	d														13 44										
Stechford	d								13 20						13 47										
Lea Hall	d								13 23						13 50										
Marston Green	d		13 01						13 26										13 41			14 01			
Birmingham International ✈	a	12 59	13 05			13 13		13 19	13 29			13 39	13 50		13 55				13 45		13 59	14 05			14 13
	d	13 00	13 05			13 14		13 20	13 29			13 40							13 45		14 00	14 05			14 14
Hampton-in-Arden	d								13 32										13 48						
Berkswell	d		13 11						13 37													14 11			
Tile Hill	d		13 14						13 40										13 55			14 14			
Canley	d		13 17						13 44													14 17			
Coventry	a	13 10	13 20			13 24		13 30	13 47			13 49							14 00		14 10	14 20			14 24
	d	13 11	13 21					13 31	13 48			13 51							14 01		14 11	14 21			
Rugby	d	13 24	13 32						13 59										14 12	14 20	14 24	14 32			
Long Buckby	d		13 42						14 09										14 22			14 42			
Northampton	a		13 54						14 21										14 35	14 42		14 54			
London Euston 15 ⊖	a	14 14	15 17					14 32	15 27			14 54							15 49		15 14	16 17			

A ◇ from Northampton

2 July to 14 September

Stafford - Wolverhampton - Birmingham - Coventry - Northampton

Network Diagram - see first Page of Table 67

		VT		LM	LM	LM	VT	AW	XC	LM	LM	LM		LM	LM	VT	LM	LM	XC	VT	LM	LM		LM	VT
		◇1		◇1		◇1	◇1	◇	◇1			◇1		◇1	◇1	◇1	◇1		◇1	◇1	◇1			◇1	◇1
														A											
		⊏					⊏	⊼	⊼							⊏			⊼	⊠					⊏
Stafford	d					13 43			14 02			14 10			14 21				14 25					14 46	
Penkridge	d											14 16													
Wolverhampton 7 ⇌	a					13 56			14 15			14 27							14 39					14 59	
	d	13 45			13 49	13 57		14 08	14 16		14 19	14 28						14 37	14 41	14 45		14 49		14 59	
Coseley	d				13 54	14 03					14 24											14 54		15 05	
Tipton	d				13 56						14 26											14 56			
Dudley Port	d				13 58						14 28											14 58			
Sandwell & Dudley	d	13 56			14 02						14 32							14 46		14 56		15 02			
Smethwick Galton Bridge 7	d				14 04			14 20			14 34	14 40										15 04			
Smethwick Rolfe Street	d				14 06						14 36											15 06			
Birmingham New Street 12	a	14 06			14 14	14 17		14 26	14 32		14 44	14 47						14 55	14 58	15 06		15 14		15 20	
	d	14 10		14 13			14 30	14 36		14 39				14 33		14 50	14 53		15 04	15 10	15 13				15 30
Adderley Park	d									14 44															
Stechford	d			14 20						14 47											15 20				
Lea Hall	d			14 23						14 50											15 23				
Marston Green	d			14 26										14 41			15 01				15 26				
Birmingham International ✈	a	14 19		14 29			14 39	14 50		14 55				14 45		14 59	15 05		15 13	15 19	15 29				15 39
	d	14 20		14 29			14 40							14 45		15 00	15 05		15 14	15 20	15 29				15 40
Hampton-in-Arden	d			14 32										14 48							15 32				
Berkswell	d			14 37													15 11				15 37				
Tile Hill	d			14 40										14 55			15 14				15 40				
Canley	d			14 44													15 17				15 44				
Coventry	a	14 30		14 47			14 49							15 00		15 10	15 20		15 24	15 30	15 47				15 49
	d	14 31		14 48			14 51							15 01		15 11	15 21			15 31	15 48				15 51
Rugby	d			14 59										15 12	15 20	15 24	15 32				15 59				
Long Buckby	d			15 09										15 22			15 42								
Northampton	a			15 21										15 34	15 42		15 54				16 18				
London Euston 15 ⊖	a	15 32		16 27			15 54							16 49		16 14	17 18			16 32	17 27				16 57

		AW	XC	LM	LM	LM	LM	LM		VT	LM	VT	LM	XC	VT	LM	LM	LM		VT	LM	LM FX	AW	XC	LM
		◇	◇1			1	◇1	◇1		◇1	◇1	◇1		◇1	◇1	1		◇1		◇1	1	◇1	◇	◇1	
							A															A			
		⊼	⊼							⊏		⊏		⊼	⊏					⊏			⊼	⊼	
Stafford	d		15 03			15 10		15 21						15 25				15 43						16 03	
Penkridge	d					15 16																			
Wolverhampton 7 ⇌	a		15 15			15 27								15 39				15 56						16 15	
	d	15 10	15 17		15 19	15 28						15 32	15 37	15 41	15 45		15 49	15 57					16 09	16 17	
Coseley	d				15 24												15 54	16 03							
Tipton	d				15 26												15 56								
Dudley Port	d				15 28												15 58								
Sandwell & Dudley	d				15 32								15 46		15 56		16 02								
Smethwick Galton Bridge 7	d	15 21			15 34	15 40											16 04						16 20		
Smethwick Rolfe Street	d				15 36												16 06								
Birmingham New Street 12	a	15 27	15 39		15 44	15 47						15 55	15 55	15 58	16 06		16 14	16 17					16 27	16 39	
	d	15 36		15 39			15 33			15 50	15 53			16 04	16 10	16 13				16 30	16 33	16 33	16 36		16 39
Adderley Park	d			15 44																					16 44
Stechford	d			15 47												16 20									16 47
Lea Hall	d			15 50												16 23									16 50
Marston Green	d						15 41				16 01					16 26					16 41	16 41			
Birmingham International ✈	a	15 50		15 55			15 45			15 59	16 05			16 13	16 19	16 29				16 39	16 45	16 45	16 50		16 55
	d						15 45			16 00	16 05			16 14	16 20	16 29				16 40	16 45	16 45			
Hampton-in-Arden	d						15 48									16 32					16 48	16 48			
Berkswell	d										16 11					16 37									
Tile Hill	d						15 55				16 14					16 40					16 55	16 55			
Canley	d										16 17					16 44									
Coventry	a						16 00			16 10	16 20			16 24	16 30	16 47				16 49	17 00	17 00			
	d						16 01			16 11	16 21				16 31					16 51	17 01	17 01			
Rugby	d						16 12	16 20		16 24	16 32										17 12	17 12			
Long Buckby	d						16 22				16 42										17 22	17 22			
Northampton	a						16 34	16 43			16 54										17 34	17 34			
London Euston 15 ⊖	a						17 49			17 14	18 18				17 34					17 54		18 49			

A ◇ from Northampton

Stafford - Wolverhampton - Birmingham - Coventry - Northampton

Network Diagram - see first Page of Table 67

		LM	LM	LM	VT	LM	VT	LM	XC	VT	LM	LM	LM	LM	VT	AW	XC	LM	LM	LM	LM	LM
			◇1	◇1	◇1 ⊐	◇1	◇1 ⊐		◇1 ⌶	◇1 ⊐	1		1	◇1	◇1 ⊠	◇ ⌶	◇1 ⌶	◇1			◇1	◇1
Stafford	d		16 10	16 21					16 25					16 46			17 03				17 10	17 21
Penkridge	d		16 16																		17 16	
Wolverhampton 7	a		16 26						16 39					16 59			17 15				17 27	
	d	16 19	16 28				16 32	16 37	16 41	16 45		16 49		16 59		17 09	17 16			17 19	17 28	
Coseley	d	16 24										16 54		17 05						17 24		
Tipton	d	16 26										16 56								17 26		
Dudley Port	d	16 28										16 58								17 28		
Sandwell & Dudley	d	16 32						16 46		16 56		17 02								17 32		
Smethwick Galton Bridge 7	d	16 34	16 40									17 04				17 22				17 34	17 40	
Smethwick Rolfe Street	d	16 36										17 06								17 36		
Birmingham New Street 12	a	16 45	16 47				16 55	16 55	16 58	17 06		17 14		17 20		17 28	17 32			17 44	17 47	
	d				16 50	16 53			17 04	17 10	17 13		17 16		17 30	17 36		17 33	17 39			
Adderley Park	d												17 21						17 44			
Stechford	d										17 20								17 47			
Lea Hall	d												17 25						17 50			
Marston Green	d					17 01							17 28					17 41				
Birmingham International ✈	a				16 59	17 05			17 13	17 19	17 25		17 32		17 39	17 49		17 45	17 55			
	d				17 00	17 05			17 14	17 20	17 25		17 32		17 40			17 45				
Hampton-in-Arden	d												17 35					17 48				
Berkswell	d					17 11							17 40									
Tile Hill	d					17 14					17 32							17 55				
Canley	d					17 17					17 36											
Coventry	a				17 10	17 20			17 24	17 30	17 40		17 47		17 49			18 00				
	d				17 11	17 21				17 31	17 40				17 51			18 01				
Rugby	d			17 20	17 24	17 32					17 51							18 12				18 20
Long Buckby	d					17 42					18 01							18 22				
Northampton	a			17 39		17 54					18 13							18 34				18 39
London Euston 15 ⊖	a			18 49	18 14	19 18				18 34	19 29				18 54							19 50

		VT	LM	VT	LM	XC	VT	LM	LM	LM	VT	AW	XC	LM	LM	LM	LM	LM	VT	LM	LM	XC	VT
		◇1 ⊠	◇1	◇1 ⊐		◇1 ⌶	◇1 ⊠	1		◇1	◇1 ⊠	◇ ⌶	◇1 ⌶			◇1	◇1 A	◇1	◇1 ⊠	◇1		◇1 ⌶	■ 1 ⊐
Stafford	d					17 25				17 43			18 04			18 10		18 21				18 28	
Penkridge	d															18 16							
Wolverhampton 7	a					17 39				17 56			18 15			18 27						18 39	
	d			17 32	17 37	17 41	17 45		17 49	17 57		18 09	18 16		18 19	18 28					18 37	18 41	18 45
Coseley	d								17 54	18 03					18 24								
Tipton	d								17 56						18 26								
Dudley Port	d								17 58						18 28								
Sandwell & Dudley	d				17 46		17 56		18 02						18 32						18 46		18 56
Smethwick Galton Bridge 7	d								18 04			18 20			18 34	18 40							
Smethwick Rolfe Street	d								18 06						18 36								
Birmingham New Street 12	a			17 55	17 55	17 58	18 06		18 14	18 17		18 26	18 38		18 44	18 48					18 55	18 58	19 06
	d	17 50	17 53			18 04	18 10	18 13			18 30	18 36		18 39			18 33		18 50	18 53		19 04	19 10
Adderley Park	d													18 44									
Stechford	d							18 20						18 47									
Lea Hall	d							18 23						18 50									
Marston Green	d		18 01					18 26									18 41			19 01			
Birmingham International ✈	a	17 59	18 05			18 13	18 19	18 29			18 39	18 50		18 55			18 45		18 59	19 05		19 13	19 19
	d	18 00	18 05			18 14	18 20	18 29			18 40						18 45		19 00	19 05		19 14	19 20
Hampton-in-Arden	d							18 32									18 48						
Berkswell	d		18 11					18 37												19 11			
Tile Hill	d		18 14					18 40									18 55			19 14			
Canley	d		18 17					18 44												19 17			
Coventry	a	18 10	18 20			18 24	18 30	18 47			18 49						19 00		19 10	19 20		19 24	19 30
	d	18 11	18 21				18 31				18 51						19 01		19 11	19 21			19 31
Rugby	d	18 24	18 32														19 12	19 20	19 24	19 32			
Long Buckby	d		18 42														19 22			19 42			
Northampton	a		18 54														19 34	19 45		19 55			
London Euston 15 ⊖	a	19 14	20 19				19 34				19 54						20 49		20 14	21 17			20 34

A ◇ from Northampton

Table 68 | Mondays to Fridays
2 July to 14 September

Stafford - Wolverhampton - Birmingham - Coventry - Northampton

Network Diagram - see first Page of Table 67

		LM	LM	LM	VT	AW	XC	LM	LM	LM	LM	LM	VT	LM	VT	LM	XC	VT	LM	LM	LM	LM	AW
		1		◇1	◇1 ⊐	◇ ⌶	◇1 ⌶	◇1			◇1	◇1	◇1 ⊐	◇1	◇1 ⊐		◇1 A ⌶	◇1 ⊐	1		◇1	◇1	◇ ⌶
Stafford	d			18 43			19 02				19 10	19 21					19 25				19 42		
Penkridge	d										19 16										19 47		
Wolverhampton 7	a			18 56			19 15				19 27						19 39				19 57		
	d		18 49	18 57		19 09	19 16			19 19	19 28				19 32	19 37	19 41	19 45		19 49	19 57		20 11
Coseley	d		18 54	19 03						19 24										19 54	20 03		
Tipton	d		18 56							19 26										19 56			
Dudley Port	d		18 58							19 28										19 58			
Sandwell & Dudley	d		19 02							19 32						19 46		19 56		20 02			
Smethwick Galton Bridge 7	d		19 04			19 20				19 34	19 40									20 04			20 22
Smethwick Rolfe Street	d		19 06							19 36										20 06			
Birmingham New Street 12	a		19 14	19 17		19 26	19 32			19 44	19 48				19 55	19 55	19 58	20 06		20 14	20 18		20 27
	d	19 13			19 30	19 36		19 33	19 39				19 50	19 53			20 04	20 10	20 13			20 33	20 36
Adderley Park	d								19 44														
Stechford	d	19 20							19 47										20 20				
Lea Hall	d	19 23							19 50										20 23				
Marston Green	d	19 26						19 41						20 01					20 26			20 41	
Birmingham International ✈	a	19 29			19 39	19 50		19 45	19 55				19 59	20 05			20 13	20 19	20 29			20 45	20 50
	d	19 29			19 40			19 45					20 00	20 05			20 14	20 20	20 29			20 45	
Hampton-in-Arden	d	19 32						19 48											20 32			20 48	
Berkswell	d	19 37												20 11					20 37				
Tile Hill	d	19 40						19 55						20 14					20 40			20 55	
Canley	d	19 44												20 17					20 44				
Coventry	a	19 47			19 49			20 00					20 10	20 20			20 24	20 30	20 47			21 00	
	d				19 51			20 01					20 11	20 21				20 31				21 01	
Rugby	d							20 12				20 20	20 23	20 32								21 12	
Long Buckby	d							20 22						20 42								21 22	
Northampton	a							20 37				20 43		20 54								21 34	
London Euston 15 ⊖	a				20 54								21 14	22 20				21 38					

		XC	LM	LM	LM	LM	LM	VT	LM	VT	LM	XC	VT	LM	LM	LM	XC	LM	LM	LM	LM	VT
		◇1 ⌶			◇1	1 B	1	◇1 ⊐	◇1	■ 1 ⊐		◇1 A ⌶	◇1 ⊐	1		◇1	◇1	◇1			◇1	◇1 ⊐
Stafford	d	20 04			20 16	20 21	20 21					20 26				20 42	21 03				21 10	21 13
Penkridge	d															20 47					21 16	
Wolverhampton 7	a	20 16			20 29							20 40				20 57	21 15				21 26	21 29
	d	20 17		20 19	20 29					20 34	20 38	20 43	20 47		20 49	20 57	21 16			21 19	21 28	21 32
Coseley	d			20 24											20 54	21 03				21 24		
Tipton	d			20 26											20 56					21 26		
Dudley Port	d			20 28											20 58					21 28		
Sandwell & Dudley	d			20 32							20 47		20 57		21 02					21 32		
Smethwick Galton Bridge 7	d			20 34	20 41										21 04					21 34	21 40	
Smethwick Rolfe Street	d			20 36											21 06					21 36		
Birmingham New Street 12	a	20 33		20 44	20 47					20 55	20 56	21 00	21 06		21 14	21 18	21 33			21 44	21 47	21 48
	d		20 39					20 50	20 53			21 04	21 10	21 13				21 33	21 39			
Adderley Park	d		20 44																21 44			
Stechford	d		20 47											21 20					21 48			
Lea Hall	d		20 50											21 23					21 50			
Marston Green	d								21 01					21 26				21 41				
Birmingham International ✈	a		20 55					20 59	21 05			21 13	21 19	21 29				21 45	21 55			
	d							21 00	21 05			21 14	21 20	21 29				21 45				
Hampton-in-Arden	d													21 32				21 48				
Berkswell	d								21 11					21 37								
Tile Hill	d								21 14					21 40				21 55				
Canley	d								21 17					21 44								
Coventry	a							21 10	21 20			21 24	21 30	21 53				22 00				
	d							21 11	21 21				21 31					22 01				
Rugby	d					21 20	21 20	21 23	21 32									22 12				
Long Buckby	d								21 42									22 22				
Northampton	a					21 39	21 39		21 54									22 34				
London Euston 15 ⊖	a						22 56	22 12	23 21				22 43					00 21				

A ⌶ to Birmingham New Street

B from 10 September until 14 September

2 July to 14 September

Stafford - Wolverhampton - Birmingham - Coventry - Northampton

Network Diagram - see first Page of Table 67

		LM	LM	LM	XC	VT	LM	LM	LM	AW	LM	LM	VT	LM	VT	LM	XC	VT	LM	LM	AW MW FO	AW TThO	LM
		■ A	■		◇■	◇■	■		◇■	◇	■		◇■	■	◇■		◇■	◇■	■		◇	◇	◇■
Stafford	d	21 27			21 25				21 41								22 26						22 41
Penkridge	d								21 47														22 47
Wolverhampton	a				21 39				21 57								22 39						22 57
	d			21 37	21 41	21 45		21 49	21 57	22 09		22 19	22 28		22 32	22 37	22 41	22 45		22 49	22 55	22 55	22 57
Coseley	d							21 54	22 03			22 24								22 54			23 03
Tipton	d							21 56				22 26								22 56			
Dudley Port	d							21 58				22 28								22 58			
Sandwell & Dudley	d			21 46		21 56		22 02				22 32				22 46		22 55		23 02			
Smethwick Galton Bridge	d							22 04		22 20		22 34								23 04			
Smethwick Rolfe Street	d							22 06				22 36								23 06			
Birmingham New Street	a			21 55	22 00	22 06		22 14	22 17	22 33		22 44	22 50		22 55	22 55	22 58	23 06		23 14	23 27	23 28	23 18
	d		21 53			22 10	22 13				22 33			22 53				23 10	23 13				
Adderley Park	d																		23 18				
Stechford	d						22 20												23 21				
Lea Hall	d						22 23												23 24				
Marston Green	d		22 01				22 26				22 41			23 01					23 27				
Birmingham International	a		22 05			22 21	22 29				22 45			23 05				23 19	23 30				
	d		22 05			22 22	22 29				22 45			23 05				23 20	23 30				
Hampton-in-Arden	d						22 32				22 48								23 33				
Berkswell	d		22 11				22 37							23 11					23 38				
Tile Hill	d		22 14				22 40				22 55			23 14					23 41				
Canley	d		22 17				22 44							23 17					23 45				
Coventry	a		22 20			22 31	22 47				23 00			23 20				23 30	23 48				
	d		22 21			22 32								23 21				23 31					
Rugby	d	22 21	22 32			22 43								23 32				23 44					
Long Buckby	d		22 42											23 42									
Northampton	a	22 41	22 58											23 54				00s05					
London Euston	a					00 04												01 13					

		XC	LM
		◇■	■
Stafford	d	23 07	
Penkridge	d		
Wolverhampton	a	23 19	
	d	23 21	
Coseley	d		
Tipton	d		
Dudley Port	d		
Sandwell & Dudley	d		
Smethwick Galton Bridge	d		
Smethwick Rolfe Street	d		
Birmingham New Street	a	23 39	
	d		23 53
Adderley Park	d		
Stechford	d		
Lea Hall	d		
Marston Green	d		00 01
Birmingham International	a		00 04
	d		00 05
Hampton-in-Arden	d		
Berkswell	d		
Tile Hill	d		
Canley	d		
Coventry	a		00 15
	d		
Rugby	d		
Long Buckby	d		
Northampton	a		
London Euston	a		

A from 10 September until 14 September

from 17 September

Stafford - Wolverhampton - Birmingham - Coventry - Northampton

Network Diagram - see first Page of Table 67

		LM MX	VT MX	VT MO	VT MO	VT MX	LM MX	LM	VT	VT	LM	VT	LM	AW	XC	VT	LM	AW	VT	LM	LM	LM	LM
		◇■	◇■	◇■	◇■	◇■	■	■	◇■ ⊠	◇■ ⊠	■	◇■ ⊠	◇■		◇■	◇■ ⊠	■		◇■ ⊠		■	■	■
Stafford	d													05 25									
Penkridge	d																						
Wolverhampton	a													05 39									
	d		21p45	22p05	22p37	22p45			05 00	05 24				05 40		05 45		05 59	06 04	06 15			
Coseley	d																						
Tipton	d																						
Dudley Port	d																						
Sandwell & Dudley	d		21p56	22p15	22p47	22p55				05 34						05 56			06 15				
Smethwick Galton Bridge	d																	06 10					
Smethwick Rolfe Street	d																						
Birmingham New Street	a		22p06	22p24	22p56	23p06			05 26	05 43				05 59		06 06		06 15	06 24	06 32			
	d	21p33	22p10	22p30	23p00	23p10	23p53		05 29	05 50			05 53		06 04	06 10	06 13	06 36	06 30			06 33	06 33
Adderley Park	d																	→					
Stechford	d																06 20						
Lea Hall	d																06 23						
Marston Green	d	21p41					00 01						06 01				06 26					06 41	06 41
Birmingham International	a	21p45	22p21	22p39	23p09	23p19	00 04		05 38	05 59			06 05		06 13	06 19	06 29		06 39			06 45	06 45
	d	21p45	22p22	22p40	23p10	23p20	00 05		05 40	06 00			06 05		06 14	06 20	06 29		06 40			06 45	06 45
Hampton-in-Arden	d	21p48															06 32					06 48	06 48
Berkswell	d												06 11				06 37						
Tile Hill	d	21p55											06 14				06 40					06 55	06 55
Canley	d												06 17				06 44						
Coventry	a	22p00	22p31	22p50	23p20	23p30	00 15		05 50	06 10			06 20		06 24	06 30	06 47		06 49			07 00	07 00
	d	22p01	22p32	22p51	23p21	23p31			05 51	06 11			06 21			06 31			06 51			07 01	07 01
Rugby	d	22p12	22p43	23p04	23p34	23p44		05 20	06 03		06 13	06 20	06 32								06 45	07 12	07 12
Long Buckby	d	22p22						05 30			06 23		06 42								06 54	07 21	07 21
Northampton	a	22p34			23b53	00s05		05 42			06 35	06 39	06 54								07 06	07 33	07 33
London Euston	a	00 21	00 04	00 27	01 04	01 15		06 50	07 02	07 13	07 40	07 30	08 02			07 34			07 53		08 11		08 39

		AW	LM	LM	VT	LM	XC	VT	LM	LM	LM	VT	VT	AW	XC	LM	LM	LM	LM	LM	VT	LM	VT
				■	◇■ ⊠	◇■	◇■	◇■ ⊠	■		◇■	◇■ ⊠	◇■ ⊠		◇■	◇■		A	◇■	◇■	◇■ ⊠	◇■	◇■ ⊠
Stafford	d						06 25				06 41				06 58				07 12	07 22			
Penkridge	d										06 47								07 18				
Wolverhampton	a						06 39				06 57				07 12				07 28				
	d			06 19	06 27		06 41	06 45		06 49	06 59	07 04		07 10	07 15			07 19	07 28				07 32
Coseley	d			06 24						06 54	07 04							07 24					
Tipton	d			06 26						06 57								07 26					
Dudley Port	d			06 28						06 59								07 28					
Sandwell & Dudley	d			06 32	06 37			06 56		07 03		07 15						07 32					
Smethwick Galton Bridge	d			06 34						07 06				07 21				07 34	07 40				
Smethwick Rolfe Street	d	←		06 36						07 09								07 36					
Birmingham New Street	a	06 15		06 43	06 46		06 58	07 06		07 15	07 18	07 24		07 26	07 31			07 44	07 48				07 55
	d	06 36	06 39		06 50	06 53	07 04	07 10	07 13			07 30		07 36		07 33	07 39				07 50	07 53	
Adderley Park	d		06 44														07 44						
Stechford	d		06 47						07 20								07 47						
Lea Hall	d		06 50						07 23								07 50						
Marston Green	d					07 01			07 26							07 41						08 01	
Birmingham International	a	06 50	06 55		06 59	07 05	07 13	07 19	07 29					07 50		07 45	07 55				07 59	08 05	
	d				07 00	07 05	07 14	07 20	07 29				07 41			07 45					08 00	08 05	
Hampton-in-Arden	d					07 08										07 48							
Berkswell	d					07 13			07 35													08 11	
Tile Hill	d								07 38							07 55						08 14	
Canley	d					07 18										07 58						08 17	
Coventry	a				07 10	07 21	07 24	07 30	07 43				07 51			08 02					08 10	08 20	
	d				07 11	07 21		07 31					07 52			08 03					08 11	08 21	
Rugby	d					07 32										08 14				08 20	08 23	08 32	
Long Buckby	d					07 42										08 24						08 42	
Northampton	a					07 54										08 37				08 41		08 56	
London Euston	a				08 14	09 10		08 30				08 42	08 49							09 44	09 13	10 18	

A from 17 September until 19 October

b Previous night, stops to set down only

Stafford - Wolverhampton - Birmingham - Coventry - Northampton

Network Diagram - see first Page of Table 67

Station		LM		LM	XC	VT	LM	LM	LM	LM	VT	AW		XC	LM	LM	LM	LM	LM	VT	LM	VT		LM	XC
					◇■ ⊼	◇■ ⊠	■		◇■		◇■ ⊠	◇ ⊼		◇■ ⊼			◇■	◇■	◇■	◇■ ⊠	◇■	◇■ ⊠			◇■ ⊼
Stafford	d					07 28			07 41					08 02			08 10		08 21						08 25
Penkridge	d								07 47								08 16								
Wolverhampton 7	a					07 43			07 57					08 15			08 26								08 39
	d	07 35		07 39		07 45		07 49	07 57	08 04		08 09		08 16		08 19	08 28					08 32		08 37	08 41
Coseley	d			07 44				07 54	08 03							08 24									
Tipton	d			07 47				07 57								08 26									
Dudley Port	d			07 49				07 59								08 28									
Sandwell & Dudley	d	07 45				07 56		08 02								08 32								08 46	
Smethwick Galton Bridge 7	d			07 53				08 05				08 21				08 34	08 40								
Smethwick Rolfe Street	d			07 55				08 07								08 36									
Birmingham New Street 12	a	07 54		08 03		08 06		08 14	08 17	08 20		08 26		08 32		08 44	08 47					08 55		08 55	08 58
	d				08 04	08 10	08 13				08 30	08 36			08 39			08 33		08 50	08 53				09 04
Adderley Park	d														08 44										
Stechford	d						08 20								08 47										
Lea Hall	d						08 23								08 50										
Marston Green	d						08 26											08 41			09 01				
Birmingham International ✈	a				08 13	08 19	08 29				08 39	08 50			08 55			08 45		08 59	09 05				09 13
	d				08 14	08 20	08 29				08 40							08 45		09 00	09 05				09 14
Hampton-in-Arden	d						08 32											08 48							
Berkswell	d						08 37														09 11				
Tile Hill	d						08 40											08 55			09 14				
Canley	d						08 44														09 17				
Coventry	a				08 24	08 30	08 47				08 49							09 00		09 10	09 20				09 24
	d					08 31					08 51							09 01		09 11	09 21				
Rugby	d																	09 12	09 20	09 23	09 32				
Long Buckby	d																	09 22			09 42				
Northampton	a																	09 34	09 39		09 54				
London Euston 15 ⊖	a					09 34					09 54							10 49		10 14	11 17				

Station		VT	LM	LM	LM	VT	AW	XC		LM	LM	LM	LM	LM	VT	LM	VT	LM		XC	VT	LM	LM	LM	VT
		◇■ ⊠	◇■		◇■	◇■ ⊠	◇ ⊼	◇■ ⊼				◇■	◇■ A	◇■	◇■ ⊠	◇■	◇■ ⊠			◇■ ⊼	◇■ ⊠	◇■		◇■	◇■ ⊠
Stafford	d				08 43			09 03				09 10		09 21						09 25				09 43	
Penkridge	d				08 48							09 16													
Wolverhampton 7	a				08 58			09 15				09 27								09 39				09 56	
	d	08 45		08 49	08 58		09 10	09 16			09 19	09 28					09 32	09 37		09 41	09 45		09 49	09 57	
Coseley	d			08 54	09 04						09 24												09 54	10 03	
Tipton	d			08 56							09 26												09 56		
Dudley Port	d			08 58							09 28												09 58		
Sandwell & Dudley	d	08 56		09 02							09 32							09 46			09 56		10 02		
Smethwick Galton Bridge 7	d			09 04			09 21				09 34	09 40											10 04		
Smethwick Rolfe Street	d			09 06							09 36												10 06		
Birmingham New Street 12	a	09 06		09 14	09 18		09 26	09 32			09 44	09 47					09 55	09 55		09 58	10 06		10 14	10 17	
	d	09 10	09 13			09 30	09 36			09 39			09 33		09 50	09 53				10 04	10 10	10 13			10 30
Adderley Park	d									09 44															
Stechford	d		09 20							09 47												10 20			
Lea Hall	d		09 23							09 50												10 23			
Marston Green	d		09 26										09 41			10 01						10 26			
Birmingham International ✈	a	09 19	09 29			09 39	09 50			09 55			09 45		09 59	10 05				10 13	10 19	10 29			10 39
	d	09 20	09 29			09 40							09 45		10 00	10 05				10 14	10 20	10 29			10 40
Hampton-in-Arden	d		09 32										09 48									10 32			
Berkswell	d		09 37													10 11						10 37			
Tile Hill	d		09 40										09 55			10 14						10 40			
Canley	d		09 44													10 17						10 44			
Coventry	a	09 30	09 47			09 49							10 00		10 10	10 20				10 24	10 30	10 47			10 49
	d	09 31	09 48			09 51							10 01		10 11	10 21					10 31	10 48			10 51
Rugby	d		09 59										10 12	10 20	10 24	10 32						10 59			
Long Buckby	d		10 09										10 22			10 42						11 09			
Northampton	a		10 21										10 34	10 39		10 54						11 21			
London Euston 15 ⊖	a	10 32	11 27			10 54							11 49		11 14	12 17					11 32	12 27			11 54

A ◇ from Northampton

Table 68

Mondays to Fridays
from 17 September

Stafford - Wolverhampton - Birmingham - Coventry - Northampton

Network Diagram - see first Page of Table 67

Station		LM	AW	XC		LM	LM	LM	LM	VT	LM	VT	LM	XC		VT	LM	LM	LM	VT	AW	XC	LM	LM	
		■	◇ ⊼	◇■ ⊼				◇■	◇■	◇■ ⊠	◇■	◇■ ⊠		◇■ ⊼		◇■ ⊠	◇■		◇■	◇■ ⊡	◇ ⊼	◇■ ⊼			
Stafford	d			10 03				10 10	10 21					10 25					10 43			11 02			
Penkridge	d							10 16																	
Wolverhampton 7	a			10 15				10 27						10 39					10 56			11 15			
	d		10 08	10 17			10 19	10 28				10 32	10 37	10 41		10 45		10 49	10 57		11 09	11 16		11 19	
Coseley	d						10 24											10 54	11 03					11 24	
Tipton	d						10 26											10 56						11 26	
Dudley Port	d						10 28											10 58						11 28	
Sandwell & Dudley	d						10 32						10 46			10 56		11 02						11 32	
Smethwick Galton Bridge 7	d		10 19				10 34	10 40										11 04			11 20			11 34	
Smethwick Rolfe Street	d						10 36											11 06						11 36	
Birmingham New Street 12	a		10 25	10 39			10 44	10 47				10 55	10 55	10 58		11 06		11 14	11 18		11 26	11 32		11 44	
	d	10 33	10 36			10 39				10 50	10 53			11 04		11 10	11 13			11 30	11 36		11 39		
Adderley Park	d					10 44																	11 44		
Stechford	d					10 47											11 20						11 47		
Lea Hall	d					10 50											11 23						11 50		
Marston Green	d	10 41									11 01						11 26								
Birmingham International ✈	a	10 45	10 50			10 55				10 59	11 05			11 13		11 19	11 29			11 39	11 50		11 55		
	d	10 45								11 00	11 05			11 14		11 20	11 29			11 40					
Hampton-in-Arden	d	10 48															11 32								
Berkswell	d										11 11						11 37								
Tile Hill	d	10 55									11 14						11 40								
Canley	d										11 17						11 44								
Coventry	a	11 00								11 10	11 20			11 24		11 30	11 47			11 49					
	d	11 01								11 11	11 21					11 31	11 48			11 51					
Rugby	d	11 12							11 20	11 24	11 32						11 59								
Long Buckby	d	11 22									11 42						12 09								
Northampton	a	11 35							11 42		11 54						12 21								
London Euston 15 ⊖	a								12 49	12 14	13 17					12 32	13 27			12 54					

Station		LM	LM	LM	VT	LM	VT	LM	XC	VT		LM	LM	LM	VT	AW	XC	LM	LM	LM		LM	LM	VT	LM
		◇■	◇■	◇■	◇■ ⊡	◇■	◇■ ⊠		◇■ ⊼	◇■ ⊡		◇■		◇■	◇■ ⊡	◇ ⊼	◇■ ⊼			◇■		◇■ A	◇■	◇■ ⊡	◇■
Stafford	d	11 10		11 21					11 25					11 43			12 03			12 10			12 21		
Penkridge	d	11 16																		12 16					
Wolverhampton 7	a	11 27							11 39					11 57			12 15			12 27					
	d	11 28					11 32	11 37	11 41	11 45			11 49	11 57		12 09	12 17		12 19	12 28					
Coseley	d												11 54	12 03					12 24						
Tipton	d												11 56						12 26						
Dudley Port	d												11 58						12 28						
Sandwell & Dudley	d							11 46		11 56			12 02						12 32						
Smethwick Galton Bridge 7	d	11 40											12 04			12 20			12 34	12 40					
Smethwick Rolfe Street	d												12 06						12 36						
Birmingham New Street 12	a	11 47					11 55	11 55	11 58	12 06			12 14	12 17		12 26	12 39		12 44	12 47					
	d		11 33		11 50	11 53			12 04	12 10		12 13			12 30	12 36		12 39				12 33		12 50	12 53
Adderley Park	d																	12 44							
Stechford	d											12 20						12 47							
Lea Hall	d											12 23						12 50							
Marston Green	d		11 41			12 01						12 26										12 41			13 01
Birmingham International ✈	a		11 45		11 59	12 05			12 13	12 19		12 29			12 39	12 50		12 55				12 45		12 59	13 05
	d		11 45		12 00	12 05			12 14	12 20		12 29			12 40							12 45		13 00	13 05
Hampton-in-Arden	d		11 48									12 32										12 48			
Berkswell	d					12 11						12 37													13 11
Tile Hill	d		11 55			12 14						12 40										12 55			13 14
Canley	d					12 17						12 44													13 17
Coventry	a		12 00		12 10	12 20			12 24	12 30		12 47			12 49							13 00		13 10	13 20
	d		12 01		12 11	12 21				12 31		12 48			12 51							13 01		13 11	13 21
Rugby	d		12 12	12 20	12 24	12 32						13 00										13 12	13 20	13 24	13 32
Long Buckby	d		12 22			12 42						13 10										13 22			13 42
Northampton	a		12 34	12 43		12 58						13 22										13 34	13 40		13 54
London Euston 15 ⊖	a		13 49		13 14	14 17				13 32		14 27			13 54							14 49		14 14	15 17

A ◇ from Northampton

Table 68

Mondays to Fridays
from 17 September

Stafford - Wolverhampton - Birmingham - Coventry - Northampton

Network Diagram - see first Page of Table 67

		VT	LM	XC	VT	LM		LM	LM	VT	AW	XC	LM	LM	LM	LM	LM		VT	LM	VT	LM	XC	VT	LM
		◇1		◇1	◇1	◇1			◇1	◇1	◇	◇1			◇1	◇1	◇1		◇1	◇1	◇1		◇1	◇1	◇1
																A									
		⊠		H	⊏					⊏	H	H							⊏		⊏		H	⊏	
Stafford	d			12 25					12 43			13 02			13 10		13 21						13 25		
Penkridge	d														13 16										
Wolverhampton 7 ⇌	a			12 39					12 56			13 15			13 27								13 39		
	d	12 32	12 37	12 41	12 45			12 49	12 57		13 09	13 16		13 19	13 28					13 32	13 37	13 41	13 45		
Coseley	d							12 54	13 03					13 24											
Tipton	d							12 56						13 26											
Dudley Port	d							12 58						13 28											
Sandwell & Dudley	d		12 46		12 56			13 02						13 32							13 46		13 56		
Smethwick Galton Bridge 7	d							13 04			13 21			13 34	13 40										
Smethwick Rolfe Street	d							13 06						13 36											
Birmingham New Street 12	a	12 55	12 55	12 58	13 06			13 14	13 17		13 26	13 39		13 44	13 47					13 55	13 55	13 58	14 06		
	d			13 04	13 10	13 13				13 30	13 36		13 39			13 33			13 50	13 53			14 04	14 10	14 13
Adderley Park	d												13 44												
Stechford	d					13 20							13 47												14 20
Lea Hall	d					13 23							13 50												14 23
Marston Green	d					13 26										13 41				14 01					14 26
Birmingham International ✈	a			13 13	13 19	13 29				13 39	13 50		13 55			13 45			13 59	14 05			14 13	14 19	14 29
	d			13 14	13 20	13 29				13 40						13 45			14 00	14 05			14 14	14 20	14 29
Hampton-in-Arden	d					13 32										13 48									14 32
Berkswell	d					13 37														14 11					14 37
Tile Hill	d					13 40										13 55				14 14					14 40
Canley	d					13 44														14 17					14 44
Coventry	a			13 24	13 30	13 47				13 49						14 00			14 10	14 20			14 24	14 30	14 47
	d				13 31	13 48				13 51						14 01			14 11	14 21				14 31	14 48
Rugby	d					13 59										14 12	14 20		14 24	14 32					14 59
Long Buckby	d					14 09										14 22				14 42					15 09
Northampton	a					14 21										14 35	14 42			14 54					15 21
London Euston 15 ⊖	a				14 32	15 27				14 54						15 49			15 14	16 17				15 32	16 27

		LM	LM		VT	AW	XC	LM	LM	LM	LM	LM	VT		LM	VT	LM	XC	VT	LM	LM	LM	VT		AW
			◇1		◇1	◇	◇1			◇1	◇1	◇1	◇1		◇1	◇1		◇1	◇1	◇1		◇1	◇1		◇
											A														
					⊏	H	H						⊏			⊠		H	⊏				⊏		H
Stafford	d		13 43				14 02			14 10		14 21						14 25				14 46			
Penkridge	d									14 16															
Wolverhampton 7 ⇌	a		13 56				14 15			14 27								14 39				14 59			
	d	13 49	13 57			14 08	14 16		14 19	14 28						14 32	14 37	14 41	14 45		14 49	14 59			15 10
Coseley	d	13 54	14 03						14 24												14 54	15 05			
Tipton	d	13 56							14 26												14 56				
Dudley Port	d	13 58							14 28												14 58				
Sandwell & Dudley	d	14 02							14 32								14 46		14 56		15 02				
Smethwick Galton Bridge 7	d	14 04				14 20			14 34	14 40											15 04				15 21
Smethwick Rolfe Street	d	14 06							14 36												15 06				
Birmingham New Street 12	a	14 14	14 17			14 26	14 32		14 44	14 47						14 55	14 55	14 58	15 06		15 14	15 20			15 27
	d				14 30	14 36		14 39			14 33		14 50		14 53			15 04	15 10	15 13			15 30		15 36
Adderley Park	d							14 44																	
Stechford	d							14 47												15 20					
Lea Hall	d							14 50												15 23					
Marston Green	d										14 41				15 01					15 26					
Birmingham International ✈	a				14 39	14 50		14 55			14 45		14 59		15 05			15 13	15 19	15 29			15 39		15 50
	d				14 40						14 45		15 00		15 05			15 14	15 20	15 29			15 40		
Hampton-in-Arden	d										14 48									15 32					
Berkswell	d														15 11					15 37					
Tile Hill	d										14 55				15 14					15 40					
Canley	d														15 17					15 44					
Coventry	a				14 49						15 00		15 10		15 20			15 24	15 30	15 47			15 49		
	d				14 51						15 01		15 11		15 21				15 31	15 48			15 51		
Rugby	d										15 12	15 20	15 24		15 32					15 59					
Long Buckby	d										15 22				15 42										
Northampton	a										15 34	15 42			15 54					16 18					
London Euston 15 ⊖	a				15 54						16 49		16 14		17 18				16 32	17 27			16 57		

A ◇ from Northampton

Table 68

Mondays to Fridays
from 17 September

Stafford - Wolverhampton - Birmingham - Coventry - Northampton

Network Diagram - see first Page of Table 67

		XC	LM	LM	LM	LM	LM	VT	LM		VT	LM	XC	VT	LM	LM	LM	VT	LM		LM FX	AW	XC	LM	LM
		◇1			1	◇1	◇1	◇1	◇1		◇1	◇1	◇1	◇1	1		◇1	◇1	1		◇1	◇	◇1		
						A															A				
		H						⊏			⊏		H	⊏				⊏				H	H		
Stafford	d	15 03			15 10		15 21						15 25				15 43						16 03		
Penkridge	d				15 16																				
Wolverhampton 7 ⇌	a	15 15			15 27								15 39				15 56						16 15		
	d	15 17		15 19	15 28						15 32	15 37	15 41	15 45		15 49	15 57					16 09	16 17		16 19
Coseley	d			15 24												15 54	16 03								16 24
Tipton	d			15 26												15 56									16 26
Dudley Port	d			15 28												15 58									16 28
Sandwell & Dudley	d			15 32								15 46		15 56		16 02									16 32
Smethwick Galton Bridge 7	d			15 34	15 40											16 04						16 20			16 34
Smethwick Rolfe Street	d			15 36												16 06									16 36
Birmingham New Street 12	a	15 39		15 44	15 47						15 55	15 55	15 58	16 06		16 14	16 17					16 27	16 39		16 45
	d		15 39			15 33		15 50	15 53				16 04	16 10	16 13			16 30	16 33		16 33	16 36		16 39	
Adderley Park	d		15 44																					16 44	
Stechford	d		15 47												16 20									16 47	
Lea Hall	d		15 50												16 23									16 50	
Marston Green	d					15 41			16 01						16 26				16 41		16 41				
Birmingham International ✈	a		15 55			15 45		15 59	16 05				16 13	16 19	16 29			16 39	16 45		16 45	16 50		16 55	
	d					15 45		16 00	16 05				16 14	16 20	16 29			16 40	16 45		16 45				
Hampton-in-Arden	d					15 48									16 32				16 48		16 48				
Berkswell	d								16 11						16 37										
Tile Hill	d					15 55			16 14						16 40				16 55		16 55				
Canley	d								16 17						16 44										
Coventry	a					16 00		16 10	16 20				16 24	16 30	16 47			16 49	17 00		17 00				
	d					16 01		16 11	16 21					16 31				16 51	17 01		17 01				
Rugby	d					16 12	16 20	16 24	16 32										17 12		17 12				
Long Buckby	d					16 22			16 42										17 22		17 22				
Northampton	a					16 34	16 43		16 54										17 34		17 34				
London Euston 15 ⊖	a					17 49		17 14	18 18					17 34				17 54			18 49				

		LM	LM	VT	LM		VT	LM	XC	VT	LM	LM	LM	LM	VT		AW	XC	LM	LM	LM	LM	LM	VT	LM
		◇1	◇1	◇1	◇1		◇1		◇1	◇1	1		1	◇1	◇1		◇	◇1	◇1			◇1	◇1	◇1	◇1
				⊏			⊏		H	⊏					⊠		H	H						⊠	
Stafford	d	16 10	16 21						16 25					16 46				17 03				17 10	17 21		
Penkridge	d	16 16																				17 16			
Wolverhampton 7 ⇌	a	16 26							16 39					16 59				17 15				17 27			
	d	16 28					16 32	16 37	16 41	16 45		16 49		16 59			17 09	17 16			17 19	17 28			
Coseley	d											16 54		17 05							17 24				
Tipton	d											16 56									17 26				
Dudley Port	d											16 58									17 28				
Sandwell & Dudley	d							16 46		16 56		17 02									17 32				
Smethwick Galton Bridge 7	d	16 40										17 04					17 22				17 34	17 40			
Smethwick Rolfe Street	d											17 06									17 36				
Birmingham New Street 12	a	16 47					16 55	16 55	16 58	17 06		17 14		17 20			17 28	17 32			17 44	17 47			
	d			16 50	16 53				17 04	17 10	17 13		17 16		17 30		17 36		17 33	17 39				17 50	17 53
Adderley Park	d												17 21							17 44					
Stechford	d										17 20									17 47					
Lea Hall	d												17 25							17 50					
Marston Green	d				17 01								17 28						17 41						18 01
Birmingham International ✈	a			16 59	17 05				17 13	17 19	17 25		17 32		17 39		17 49		17 45	17 55				17 59	18 05
	d			17 00	17 05				17 14	17 20	17 25		17 32		17 40				17 45					18 00	18 05
Hampton-in-Arden	d												17 35						17 48						
Berkswell	d				17 11								17 40												18 11
Tile Hill	d				17 14						17 32								17 55						18 14
Canley	d				17 17						17 36														18 17
Coventry	a			17 10	17 20				17 24	17 30	17 40		17 47		17 49				18 00					18 10	18 20
	d			17 11	17 21					17 31	17 40				17 51				18 01					18 11	18 21
Rugby	d		17 20	17 24	17 32						17 51								18 12				18 20	18 24	18 32
Long Buckby	d				17 42						18 01								18 22						18 42
Northampton	a		17 39		17 54						18 13								18 34				18 39		18 54
London Euston 15 ⊖	a		18 49	18 14	19 18					18 34	19 29				18 54								19 50	19 14	20 19

A ◇ from Northampton

Table 68

Stafford - Wolverhampton - Birmingham - Coventry - Northampton

Mondays to Fridays from 17 September

Network Diagram - see first Page of Table 67

	VT	LM	XC	VT	LM	LM	LM	VT	AW	XC	LM	LM	LM	LM	LM	VT	LM	VT	LM	XC	VT
	◇1 ☕		◇1 🛒	◇1 ⊠	1		◇1	◇1 ⊠	◇ 🛒	◇1 🛒			◇1	◇1 A	◇1	◇1 ⊠	◇1	1 ☕		◇1 🛒	◇1 ⊠
Stafford d			17 25				17 43			18 04			18 10		18 21					18 28	
Penkridge d													18 16								
Wolverhampton 7 a			17 39				17 56			18 15			18 27							18 39	
Wolverhampton 7 d	17 32	17 37	17 41	17 45		17 49	17 57		18 09	18 16		18 19	18 28					18 32	18 37	18 41	18 45
Coseley d						17 54	18 03					18 24									
Tipton d						17 56						18 26									
Dudley Port d						17 58						18 28									
Sandwell & Dudley d		17 46		17 56		18 02						18 32							18 46		18 56
Smethwick Galton Bridge 7 d						18 04			18 20			18 34	18 40								
Smethwick Rolfe Street d						18 06						18 36									
Birmingham New Street 12 a	17 55	17 55	17 58	18 06		18 14	18 17		18 26	18 38		18 44	18 48					18 55	18 55	18 58	19 06
d			18 04	18 10	18 13			18 30	18 36		18 39			18 33		18 50	18 53			19 04	19 10
Adderley Park d											18 44										
Stechford d					18 20						18 47										
Lea Hall d					18 23						18 50										
Marston Green d					18 26									18 41			19 01				
Birmingham International ✈ a			18 13	18 19	18 29			18 39	18 50		18 55			18 45		18 59	19 05			19 13	19 19
d			18 14	18 20	18 29			18 40						18 45		19 00	19 05			19 14	19 20
Hampton-in-Arden d					18 32									18 48							
Berkswell d					18 37												19 11				
Tile Hill d					18 40									18 55			19 14				
Canley d					18 44												19 17				
Coventry a			18 24	18 30	18 47			18 49						19 00		19 10	19 20			19 24	19 30
d				18 31				18 51						19 01		19 11	19 21				19 31
Rugby d														19 12	19 20	19 24	19 32				
Long Buckby d														19 22			19 42				
Northampton a														19 34	19 45		19 55				
London Euston 15 ⊖ a				19 34				19 54						20 49		20 14	21 17				20 34

	LM	LM	LM	VT	AW	XC	LM	LM	LM	LM	LM	VT	LM	VT	LM	XC	VT	LM	LM	LM	LM	AW
	1		◇1	◇1 ☕	◇ 🛒	◇1 🛒	◇1			◇1	◇1	◇1 ☕	◇1	◇1 ☕		◇1 B 🛒	◇1 ☕	1		◇1	◇1	◇ 🛒
Stafford d			18 43			19 02				19 10	19 21					19 25				19 42		
Penkridge d										19 16										19 47		
Wolverhampton 7 a			18 56			19 15				19 27						19 39				19 57		
Wolverhampton 7 d		18 49	18 57		19 09	19 16			19 19	19 28				19 32	19 37	19 41	19 45		19 49	19 57		20 11
Coseley d		18 54	19 03						19 24										19 54	20 03		
Tipton d		18 56							19 26										19 56			
Dudley Port d		18 58							19 28										19 58			
Sandwell & Dudley d		19 02							19 32						19 46		19 56		20 02			
Smethwick Galton Bridge 7 d		19 04			19 20				19 34	19 40									20 04			20 22
Smethwick Rolfe Street d		19 06							19 36										20 06			
Birmingham New Street 12 a		19 14	19 17		19 26	19 32			19 44	19 48				19 55	19 55	19 58	20 06		20 14	20 18		20 27
d	19 13			19 30	19 36		19 33	19 39				19 50	19 53			20 04	20 10	20 13			20 33	20 36
Adderley Park d								19 44														
Stechford d	19 20							19 47										20 20				
Lea Hall d	19 23							19 50										20 23				
Marston Green d	19 26						19 41						20 01					20 26			20 41	
Birmingham International ✈ a	19 29			19 39	19 50		19 45	19 55				19 59	20 05			20 13	20 19	20 29			20 45	20 50
d	19 29			19 40			19 45					20 00	20 05			20 14	20 20	20 29			20 45	
Hampton-in-Arden d	19 32						19 48											20 32			20 48	
Berkswell d	19 37												20 11					20 37				
Tile Hill d	19 40						19 55						20 14					20 40			20 55	
Canley d	19 44												20 17					20 44				
Coventry a	19 47			19 49			20 00					20 10	20 20			20 24	20 30	20 47			21 00	
d				19 51			20 01					20 11	20 21				20 31				21 01	
Rugby d							20 12				20 20	20 23	20 32								21 12	
Long Buckby d							20 22						20 42								21 22	
Northampton a							20 37				20 43		20 54								21 34	
London Euston 15 ⊖ a				20 54								21 14	22 20				21 38					

A ◇ from Northampton

B 🛒 to Birmingham New Street

Table 68

Stafford - Wolverhampton - Birmingham - Coventry - Northampton

Mondays to Fridays from 17 September

Network Diagram - see first Page of Table 67

	XC	LM	LM	LM	LM	LM	VT	LM	VT	LM	XC	VT	LM	LM	LM	XC	LM	LM	LM	LM	VT
	◇1 🛒			◇1	1	1	◇1 ☕	◇1	1 ☕		◇1 A 🛒	◇1 ☕	1		◇1	◇1	◇1			◇1	◇1 ☕
Stafford d	20 04			20 16	20 21	20 21					20 26				20 42	21 03				21 10	21 13
Penkridge d															20 47					21 16	
Wolverhampton 7 a	20 16			20 29							20 40				20 57	21 15				21 26	21 29
Wolverhampton 7 d	20 17		20 19	20 29					20 34	20 38	20 43	20 47		20 49	20 57	21 16			21 19	21 28	21 32
Coseley d			20 24											20 54	21 03				21 24		
Tipton d			20 26											20 56					21 26		
Dudley Port d			20 28											20 58					21 28		
Sandwell & Dudley d			20 32							20 47		20 57		21 02					21 32		
Smethwick Galton Bridge 7 d			20 34	20 41										21 04					21 34	21 40	
Smethwick Rolfe Street d			20 36											21 06					21 36		
Birmingham New Street 12 a	20 33		20 44	20 47					20 55	20 56	21 00	21 06		21 14	21 18	21 33			21 44	21 47	21 48
d		20 39					20 50	20 53			21 04	21 10	21 13				21 33	21 39			
Adderley Park d		20 44																21 44			
Stechford d		20 47											21 20					21 48			
Lea Hall d		20 50											21 23					21 50			
Marston Green d								21 01					21 26				21 41				
Birmingham International ✈ a		20 55					20 59	21 05			21 13	21 19	21 29				21 45	21 55			
d							21 00	21 05			21 14	21 20	21 29				21 45				
Hampton-in-Arden d													21 32				21 48				
Berkswell d								21 11					21 37								
Tile Hill d								21 14					21 40				21 55				
Canley d								21 17					21 44								
Coventry a							21 10	21 20			21 24	21 30	21 53				22 00				
d							21 11	21 21				21 31					22 01				
Rugby d					21 20	21 20	21 23	21 32									22 12				
Long Buckby d								21 42									22 22				
Northampton a					21 39	21 39		21 54									22 34				
London Euston 15 ⊖ a						22 56	22 12	23 21				22 43					00 21				

	LM	LM	LM	XC	XC	VT	LM	LM	LM	AW	LM	LM	VT	LM	VT	LM	XC	VT	LM	LM	AW MWFO	AW TThO
	1	1		◇1	◇1	◇1 ☕	1		◇1	◇	1		◇1 ☕	1	◇1 ☕		◇1	◇1 ☕	1		◇ B	◇ C
Stafford d	21 27			21 25					21 41								22 26					
Penkridge d									21 47													
Wolverhampton 7 a				21 39					21 57								22 39					
Wolverhampton 7 d			21 37	21 41		21 45		21 49	21 57	22 09		22 19	22 28		22 32	22 37	22 41	22 45		22 49	22 55	22 55
Coseley d								21 54	22 03			22 24								22 54		
Tipton d								21 56				22 26								22 56		
Dudley Port d								21 58				22 28								22 58		
Sandwell & Dudley d			21 46			21 56		22 02				22 32				22 46		22 55		23 02		
Smethwick Galton Bridge 7 d								22 04		22 20		22 34								23 04		
Smethwick Rolfe Street d								22 06				22 36								23 06		
Birmingham New Street 12 a			21 55	22 00		22 06		22 14	22 17	22 33		22 44	22 50		22 55	22 55	22 58	23 06		23 14	23 27	23 28
d		21 53			22 04	22 10	22 13				22 33			22 53				23 10	23 13			
Adderley Park d																			23 18			
Stechford d							22 20												23 21			
Lea Hall d							22 23												23 24			
Marston Green d		22 01					22 26				22 41			23 01					23 27			
Birmingham International ✈ a		22 05			22 13	22 21	22 29				22 45			23 05				23 19	23 30			
d		22 05			22 14	22 22	22 29				22 45			23 05				23 20	23 30			
Hampton-in-Arden d							22 32				22 48								23 33			
Berkswell d		22 11					22 37							23 11					23 38			
Tile Hill d		22 14					22 40				22 55			23 14					23 41			
Canley d		22 17					22 44							23 17					23 45			
Coventry a		22 20			22 24	22 31	22 47				23 00			23 20				23 30	23 48			
d		22 21				22 32								23 21				23 31				
Rugby d	22 21	22 32				22 43								23 32				23 44				
Long Buckby d		22 42												23 42								
Northampton a	22 41	22 58												23 54				00s05				
London Euston 15 ⊖ a						00 04												01 15				

A 🛒 to Birmingham New Street

Table 68

Mondays to Fridays
from 17 September

Stafford - Wolverhampton - Birmingham - Coventry - Northampton

Network Diagram - see first Page of Table 67

Station		LM ◇1	XC ◇1	LM 1
Stafford	d	22 41	23 07	
Penkridge	d	22 47		
Wolverhampton 7	a	22 57	23 19	
	d	22 57	23 21	
Coseley	d	23 03		
Tipton	d			
Dudley Port	d			
Sandwell & Dudley	d			
Smethwick Galton Bridge 7	d			
Smethwick Rolfe Street	d			
Birmingham New Street 12	a	23 18	23 39	
	d			23 53
Adderley Park	d			
Stechford	d			
Lea Hall	d			
Marston Green	d			00 01
Birmingham International	a			00 04
	d			00 05
Hampton-in-Arden	d			
Berkswell	d			
Tile Hill	d			
Canley	d			
Coventry	a			00 15
	d			
Rugby	d			
Long Buckby	d			
Northampton	a			
London Euston 15	a			

Saturdays
until 30 June

Station		LM ◇1	VT ◇1	VT ◇1 A	VT ◇1 B	LM 1	VT ◇1	AW	XC ◇1	VT ◇1	LM 1	AW	VT ◇1	LM ◇1	AW	LM	LM	VT ◇1	LM ◇1	XC ◇1	VT ◇1	LM ◇1	LM
Stafford	d							05 25												06 26			
Penkridge	d																						
Wolverhampton 7	a							05 39												06 39			
	d		21p45	22p45	22p45			05 40		05 45		06 03	06 06				06 19	06 27		06 41	06 45		06 49
Coseley	d																06 24						06 54
Tipton	d																06 26						06 56
Dudley Port	d																06 28						06 58
Sandwell & Dudley	d		21p56	22p55	22p55					05 56			06 17				06 32	06 37			06 56		07 02
Smethwick Galton Bridge 7	d											06 14					06 34						07 04
Smethwick Rolfe Street	d																06 36						07 06
Birmingham New Street 12	a		22p06	23p06	23p06			05 58		06 06		06 20	06 26		← 06 20		06 44	06 47		06 57	07 06		07 14
	d	21p33	22p10	23p10	23p10	23p53	05 50		06 04	06 10	06 13	06 36 →	06 30	06 33	06 36	06 39		06 50	06 53	07 04	07 10	07 13	
Adderley Park	d															06 44							
Stechford	d										06 20					06 47						07 20	
Lea Hall	d										06 23					06 50						07 23	
Marston Green	d	21p41				00 01					06 26			06 41					07 01			07 26	
Birmingham International	a	21p45	22p21	23p19	23p19	00 04	05 59		06 13	06 19	06 29		06 39	06 45	06 50	06 54		06 59	07 05	07 13	07 19	07 29	
	d	21p45	22p22	23p20	23p20	00 05	06 00		06 14	06 20	06 29		06 40	06 45				07 00	07 05	07 14	07 20	07 29	
Hampton-in-Arden	d	21p48									06 32			06 48								07 32	
Berkswell	d										06 37								07 11			07 37	
Tile Hill	d	21p55									06 40			06 55					07 14			07 40	
Canley	d										06 44								07 17			07 44	
Coventry	a	22p00	22p31	23p30	23p30	00 15	06 10		06 24	06 30	06 47		06 50	07 00				07 10	07 20	07 24	07 30	07 47	
	d	22p01	22p32	23p31	23p31		06 10			06 31			06 51	07 01				07 11	07 21		07 31	07 48	
Rugby	d	22p12	22p43	23p44	23p44		06 24							07 12				07 23	07 32			07 59	
Long Buckby	d	22p22												07 22					07 42			08 09	
Northampton	a	22p34		00s05	00s05									07 34					07 54			08 21	
London Euston 15	a	00 21	00 04	01 13	01 15		07 16			07 38			07 55					08 14	09 17		08 34	09 27	

A 30 June

B not 30 June

Table 68

Saturdays
until 30 June

Stafford - Wolverhampton - Birmingham - Coventry - Northampton

Network Diagram - see first Page of Table 67

Station		LM ◇1	VT ◇1	AW	XC ◇1	LM	LM	LM ◇1	LM ◇1	LM ◇1	VT ◇1	LM ◇1	VT ◇1	LM	XC ◇1	VT ◇1	LM ◇1	LM	LM ◇1	VT ◇1	AW ◇	XC ◇1	LM
Stafford	d	06 41			06 58			07 12		07 24									07 41			08 03	
Penkridge	d	06 47						07 18											07 47				
Wolverhampton 7	a	06 57			07 12			07 28											07 57			08 17	
	d	06 57	07 04	07 10	07 15		07 19	07 28					07 32	07 37		07 45		07 49	07 57	08 06	08 09	08 18	
Coseley	d	07 03					07 24											07 54	08 03				
Tipton	d						07 26											07 56					
Dudley Port	d						07 28											07 58					
Sandwell & Dudley	d		07 15				07 32							07 46		07 56		08 02					
Smethwick Galton Bridge 7	d			07 21			07 34	07 40										08 04			08 21		
Smethwick Rolfe Street	d						07 36											08 06					
Birmingham New Street 12	a	07 17	07 24	07 26	07 31		07 44	07 47					07 55	07 55		08 06		08 14	08 17	08 24	08 26	08 39	
	d		07 30	07 36		07 39			07 33		07 50	07 53			08 04	08 10	08 13			08 30	08 36		08 39
Adderley Park	d					07 44																	08 44
Stechford	d					07 47											08 20						08 47
Lea Hall	d					07 50											08 23						08 50
Marston Green	d								07 41			08 01					08 26						
Birmingham International	a		07 39	07 50		07 54			07 45		07 59	08 05			08 13	08 19	08 29			08 39	08 50		08 54
	d		07 40						07 45		08 00	08 05			08 14	08 20	08 29			08 40			
Hampton-in-Arden	d								07 48								08 32						
Berkswell	d											08 11					08 37						
Tile Hill	d								07 55			08 14					08 40						
Canley	d											08 17					08 44						
Coventry	a		07 50						08 00		08 10	08 20			08 24	08 30	08 47			08 49			
	d		07 52						08 01		08 11	08 21				08 31	08 48			08 51			
Rugby	d								08 12	08 20	08 23	08 32					08 59						
Long Buckby	d								08 22			08 42					09 09						
Northampton	a								08 34	08 40		08 54					09 21						
London Euston 15	a		08 54							09 50	09 14	10 17				09 35	10 27			09 55			

Station		LM	LM ◇1	LM ◇1	LM ◇1	VT ◇1	LM ◇1	VT ◇1	LM	XC ◇1	VT ◇1	LM ◇1	LM	LM ◇1	VT ◇1	AW ◇	XC ◇1	LM	LM	LM ◇1	LM ◇1	LM ◇1
Stafford	d		08 10		08 23					08 26				08 43			09 03			09 10		09 21
Penkridge	d		08 16											08 48						09 16		
Wolverhampton 7	a		08 28							08 39				08 58			09 15			09 27		
	d	08 19	08 28					08 32	08 37	08 41	08 45		08 49	08 59		09 10	09 17		09 19	09 28		
Coseley	d	08 24											08 54	09 04					09 24			
Tipton	d	08 26											08 56						09 26			
Dudley Port	d	08 28											08 58						09 28			
Sandwell & Dudley	d	08 32							08 46		08 56		09 02						09 32			
Smethwick Galton Bridge 7	d	08 34	08 40										09 04			09 22			09 34	09 40		
Smethwick Rolfe Street	d	08 36											09 06						09 36			
Birmingham New Street 12	a	08 44	08 47					08 55	08 55	08 58	09 05		09 14	09 18		09 26	09 39		09 44	09 47		
	d			08 33		08 50	08 53			09 04	09 10	09 13			09 30	09 36		09 39			09 33	
Adderley Park	d																	09 44				
Stechford	d											09 20						09 47				
Lea Hall	d											09 23						09 50				
Marston Green	d			08 41			09 01					09 26									09 41	
Birmingham International	a			08 45		08 59	09 05			09 13	09 19	09 29			09 39	09 50		09 54			09 45	
	d			08 45		09 00	09 05			09 14	09 20	09 29			09 40						09 45	
Hampton-in-Arden	d			08 48								09 32									09 48	
Berkswell	d						09 11					09 37										
Tile Hill	d			08 55			09 14					09 40									09 55	
Canley	d						09 17					09 44										
Coventry	a			09 00		09 10	09 20			09 24	09 30	09 47			09 49						10 00	
	d			09 01		09 11	09 21				09 31	09 48			09 51						10 01	
Rugby	d			09 12	09 20	09 23	09 32					09 59									10 12	10 20
Long Buckby	d			09 22			09 42					10 09									10 22	
Northampton	a			09 34	09 41		09 58					10 21									10 34	10 39
London Euston 15	a				10 49	10 14	11 17				10 34	11 27			10 54							11 49

Stafford - Wolverhampton - Birmingham - Coventry - Northampton

Network Diagram - see first Page of Table 67

		VT	LM	VT	LM	XC	VT	LM	LM	LM	VT	AW	XC	LM	LM	LM	LM	LM	VT	LM	VT	LM	XC
Stafford	d					09 26				09 43			10 03			10 10		10 21					10 26
Penkridge	d															10 16							
Wolverhampton 7	a					09 39				09 56			10 15			10 27							10 39
	d			09 32	09 37	09 41	09 45		09 49	09 57		10 09	10 17		10 19	10 28					10 32	10 37	10 41
Coseley	d								09 54	10 03					10 24								
Tipton	d								09 56						10 26								
Dudley Port	d								09 58						10 28								
Sandwell & Dudley	d				09 46		09 56		10 02						10 32							10 46	
Smethwick Galton Bridge 7	d								10 04			10 20			10 34	10 40							
Smethwick Rolfe Street	d								10 06						10 36								
Birmingham New Street 12	a			09 55	09 55	09 58	10 06		10 14	10 17		10 26	10 39		10 44	10 47					10 55	10 55	10 58
	d	09 50	09 53			10 04	10 10	10 13			10 30	10 36		10 39			10 33		10 50	10 53			11 04
Adderley Park	d													10 44									
Stechford	d							10 20						10 47									
Lea Hall	d							10 23						10 50									
Marston Green	d		10 01					10 26									10 41			11 01			
Birmingham International	a	09 59	10 05			10 13	10 19	10 29			10 39	10 50		10 54			10 45		10 59	11 05			11 13
	d	10 00	10 05			10 14	10 20	10 29			10 40						10 45		11 00	11 05			11 14
Hampton-in-Arden	d							10 32									10 48						
Berkswell	d		10 11					10 37												11 11			
Tile Hill	d		10 14					10 40									10 55			11 14			
Canley	d		10 17					10 44												11 17			
Coventry	a	10 10	10 20			10 24	10 30	10 47			10 49						11 00		11 10	11 20			11 24
	d	10 11	10 21				10 31	10 48			10 51						11 01		11 11	11 21			
Rugby	d	10 23	10 32					10 59									11 12	11 20	11 23	11 32			
Long Buckby	d		10 42					11 09									11 22			11 42			
Northampton	a		10 54					11 21									11 34	11 39		11 54			
London Euston 15 ⊖	a	11 14	12 17				11 34	12 27			11 54						12 49		12 14	13 17			

		VT	LM	LM	LM	VT	AW	XC	LM	LM	LM	LM	LM	VT	LM	VT	LM	XC	VT	LM	LM	LM	VT
Stafford	d				10 43			11 03			11 10		11 21					11 26				11 43	
Penkridge	d										11 16												
Wolverhampton 7	a				10 56			11 16			11 27							11 39				11 56	
	d	10 45		10 49	10 57		11 10	11 17		11 19	11 28					11 33	11 37	11 41	11 45		11 49	11 57	
Coseley	d			10 54	11 03					11 24											11 54	12 03	
Tipton	d			10 56						11 26											11 56		
Dudley Port	d			10 58						11 28											11 58		
Sandwell & Dudley	d	10 56		11 02						11 32							11 46		11 56		12 02		
Smethwick Galton Bridge 7	d			11 04			11 21			11 34	11 40										12 04		
Smethwick Rolfe Street	d			11 06						11 36											12 06		
Birmingham New Street 12	a	11 06		11 14	11 17		11 27	11 39		11 44	11 47					11 55	11 55	11 58	12 06		12 14	12 17	
	d	11 10	11 13			11 30	11 36		11 39			11 33		11 50	11 53			12 04	12 10	12 13			12 30
Adderley Park	d								11 44														
Stechford	d		11 20						11 47											12 20			
Lea Hall	d		11 23						11 50											12 23			
Marston Green	d		11 26									11 41			12 01					12 26			
Birmingham International	a	11 19	11 29			11 39	11 50		11 54			11 45		11 59	12 05			12 13	12 19	12 29			12 39
	d	11 20	11 29			11 40						11 45		12 00	12 05			12 14	12 20	12 29			12 40
Hampton-in-Arden	d		11 32									11 48								12 32			
Berkswell	d		11 37												12 11					12 37			
Tile Hill	d		11 40									11 55			12 14					12 40			
Canley	d		11 44												12 17					12 44			
Coventry	a	11 30	11 47			11 49						12 00		12 10	12 20			12 24	12 30	12 47			12 49
	d	11 31	11 48			11 51						12 01		12 11	12 21				12 31	12 48			12 51
Rugby	d		11 59									12 12	12 20	12 23	12 32					12 59			
Long Buckby	d		12 09									12 22			12 42					13 09			
Northampton	a		12 21									12 34	12 39		12 54					13 21			
London Euston 15 ⊖	a	12 34	13 27			12 54						13 49		13 14	14 17				13 34	14 27			13 54

		AW	XC	LM	LM	LM	LM	LM	VT	LM	VT	LM	XC	VT	LM	LM	LM	VT	AW	XC	LM	LM
Stafford	d		12 03			12 10		12 21					12 25				12 43			13 03		
Penkridge	d					12 16																
Wolverhampton 7	a		12 16			12 27							12 39				12 56			13 15		
	d	12 09	12 17		12 19	12 28					12 32	12 37	12 41	12 45		12 49	12 57		13 09	13 16		13 19
Coseley	d				12 24											12 54	13 03					13 24
Tipton	d				12 26											12 56						13 26
Dudley Port	d				12 28											12 58						13 28
Sandwell & Dudley	d				12 32							12 46		12 56		13 02						13 32
Smethwick Galton Bridge 7	d	12 20			12 34	12 40										13 04			13 21			13 34
Smethwick Rolfe Street	d				12 36											13 06						13 36
Birmingham New Street 12	a	12 26	12 39		12 44	12 47					12 55	12 55	12 58	13 06		13 14	13 17		13 27	13 39		13 44
	d	12 36		12 39			12 33		12 50	12 53			13 04	13 10	13 13			13 30	13 36		13 39	
Adderley Park	d			12 44																	13 44	
Stechford	d			12 47											13 20						13 47	
Lea Hall	d			12 50											13 23						13 50	
Marston Green	d						12 41			13 01					13 26							
Birmingham International	a	12 50		12 54			12 45		12 59	13 05			13 13	13 19	13 29			13 39	13 50		13 54	
	d						12 45		13 00	13 05			13 14	13 20	13 29			13 40				
Hampton-in-Arden	d						12 48								13 32							
Berkswell	d									13 11					13 37							
Tile Hill	d						12 55			13 14					13 40							
Canley	d									13 17					13 44							
Coventry	a						13 00		13 10	13 20			13 24	13 30	13 47			13 49				
	d						13 01		13 11	13 21				13 31	13 48			13 51				
Rugby	d						13 12	13 20	13 23	13 32					13 59							
Long Buckby	d						13 22			13 42					14 09							
Northampton	a						13 34	13 39		13 54					14 21							
London Euston 15 ⊖	a						14 49		14 14	15 18				14 34	15 27			14 54				

		LM	LM	LM	VT	LM	VT	LM	XC	VT	LM	LM	LM	VT	AW	XC	LM	LM	LM	LM	LM	VT	LM
Stafford	d	13 10		13 21					13 26				13 43			14 03			14 10		14 21		
Penkridge	d	13 16																	14 16				
Wolverhampton 7	a	13 27							13 39				13 56			14 16			14 27				
	d	13 28					13 32	13 37	13 41	13 45		13 49	13 57		14 09	14 17		14 19	14 28				
Coseley	d											13 54	14 03					14 24					
Tipton	d											13 56						14 26					
Dudley Port	d											13 58						14 28					
Sandwell & Dudley	d							13 46		13 56		14 02						14 32					
Smethwick Galton Bridge 7	d	13 40										14 04			14 20			14 34	14 40				
Smethwick Rolfe Street	d											14 06						14 36					
Birmingham New Street 12	a	13 47					13 55	13 55	13 58	14 06		14 14	14 17		14 26	14 39		14 44	14 47				
	d		13 33		13 50	13 53			14 04	14 10	14 13			14 30	14 36		14 39			14 33		14 50	14 53
Adderley Park	d																14 44						
Stechford	d										14 20						14 47						
Lea Hall	d										14 23						14 50						
Marston Green	d		13 41			14 01					14 26									14 41			15 01
Birmingham International	a		13 45		13 59	14 05			14 13	14 19	14 29			14 39	14 50		14 54			14 45		14 59	15 05
	d		13 45		14 00	14 05			14 14	14 20	14 29			14 40						14 45		15 00	15 05
Hampton-in-Arden	d		13 48								14 32									14 48			
Berkswell	d					14 11					14 37												15 11
Tile Hill	d		13 55			14 14					14 40									14 55			15 14
Canley	d					14 17					14 44												15 17
Coventry	a		14 00		14 10	14 20			14 24	14 30	14 47			14 49						15 00		15 10	15 20
	d		14 01		14 11	14 21				14 31	14 48			14 51						15 01		15 11	15 21
Rugby	d		14 12	14 20	14 23	14 32					14 59									15 12	15 20	15 23	15 32
Long Buckby	d		14 22			14 42					15 09									15 22			15 42
Northampton	a		14 34	14 39		14 54					15 21									15 34	15 39		15 54
London Euston 15 ⊖	a		15 49		15 14	16 18				15 34	16 27			15 54						16 49		16 14	17 17

Stafford - Wolverhampton - Birmingham - Coventry - Northampton

Network Diagram - see first Page of Table 67

		VT	LM	XC	VT	LM	LM	LM	VT	AW	XC	LM	LM	LM	LM	LM	VT	LM	VT	LM	XC	VT
Stafford	d			14 26				14 46			15 03			15 10		15 21					15 26	
Penkridge	d													15 16								
Wolverhampton	a			14 39				14 59			15 16			15 27							15 39	
	d	14 32	14 37	14 41	14 45		14 49	14 59		15 10	15 17		15 19	15 28					15 32	15 37	15 41	15 45
Coseley	d						14 54	15 05					15 24									
Tipton	d						14 56						15 26									
Dudley Port	d						14 58						15 28									
Sandwell & Dudley	d		14 46		14 56		15 02						15 32							15 46		15 56
Smethwick Galton Bridge	d						15 04			15 21			15 34	15 40								
Smethwick Rolfe Street	d						15 06						15 36									
Birmingham New Street	a	14 55	14 55	14 58	15 06		15 14	15 18		15 27	15 39		15 44	15 47					15 55	15 55	15 58	16 06
	d			15 04	15 10	15 13			15 30	15 36		15 39			15 33		15 50	15 53			16 04	16 10
Adderley Park	d											15 44										
Stechford	d					15 20						15 47										
Lea Hall	d					15 23						15 50										
Marston Green	d					15 26									15 41			16 01				
Birmingham International	a			15 13	15 19	15 29			15 39	15 50		15 54			15 45		15 59	16 05			16 13	16 19
	d			15 14	15 20	15 29			15 40						15 45		16 00	16 05			16 14	16 20
Hampton-in-Arden	d					15 32									15 48							
Berkswell	d					15 37												16 11				
Tile Hill	d					15 40									15 55			16 14				
Canley	d					15 44												16 17				
Coventry	a			15 24	15 30	15 47			15 49						16 00		16 10	16 20			16 24	16 30
	d				15 31	15 48			15 51						16 01		16 11	16 21				16 31
Rugby	d					15 59									16 12	16 20	16 23	16 32				
Long Buckby	d					16 09									16 22			16 42				
Northampton	a					16 21									16 34	16 39		16 54				
London Euston	a				16 34	17 27			16 54						17 49		17 14	18 17				17 34

		LM	LM	LM	VT	AW	XC	LM	LM	LM	LM	LM	VT	LM	VT	LM	XC	VT	LM	LM	LM	VT	AW
Stafford	d			15 43			16 03			16 10		16 21					16 25				16 46		
Penkridge	d									16 16													
Wolverhampton	a			15 56			16 16			16 27							16 39				16 59		
	d		15 49	15 57		16 09	16 17		16 19	16 28					16 32	16 37	16 41	16 45		16 49	16 59		17 09
Coseley	d		15 54	16 03					16 24											16 54	17 05		
Tipton	d		15 56						16 26											16 56			
Dudley Port	d		15 58						16 28											16 58			
Sandwell & Dudley	d		16 02						16 32							16 46		16 56		17 02			
Smethwick Galton Bridge	d		16 04			16 20			16 34	16 40										17 04			17 22
Smethwick Rolfe Street	d		16 06						16 36											17 06			
Birmingham New Street	a		16 14	16 17		16 26	16 39		16 44	16 47					16 55	16 55	16 58	17 06		17 14	17 18		17 28
	d	16 13			16 30	16 36		16 39			16 33		16 50	16 53			17 04	17 10	17 13			17 30	17 37
Adderley Park	d							16 44											17 17				
Stechford	d	16 20						16 47											17 21				
Lea Hall	d	16 23						16 50											17 23				
Marston Green	d	16 26									16 41			17 01					17 26				
Birmingham International	a	16 29			16 39	16 50		16 54			16 45		16 59	17 05			17 13	17 19	17 29			17 39	17 50
	d	16 29			16 40						16 45		17 00	17 05			17 14	17 20	17 30			17 40	
Hampton-in-Arden	d	16 32									16 48								17 33				
Berkswell	d	16 37												17 11					17 38				
Tile Hill	d	16 40									16 55			17 14					17 41				
Canley	d	16 44												17 17					17 44				
Coventry	a	16 47			16 49						17 00		17 10	17 20			17 24	17 30	17 47			17 49	
	d	16 48			16 51						17 01		17 11	17 21				17 31	17 48			17 51	
Rugby	d	16 59									17 12	17 20	17 23	17 32					17 59				
Long Buckby	d	17 09									17 22			17 42					18 09				
Northampton	a	17 21									17 34	17 39		17 54					18 21				
London Euston	a	18 27			17 52						18 49		18 14	19 17				18 34	19 45			18 54	

Table 68

Saturdays
until 30 June

Stafford - Wolverhampton - Birmingham - Coventry - Northampton

Network Diagram - see first Page of Table 67

		XC	LM	LM	LM	LM	LM	VT	LM	VT	LM	XC	VT	LM	LM	LM	VT	LM	AW	XC	LM	LM	LM
Stafford	d	17 03			17 10		17 21					17 26				17 43				18 04			18 10
Penkridge	d				17 16																		18 16
Wolverhampton	a	17 16			17 27							17 39				17 56				18 16			18 27
	d	17 17		17 19	17 28					17 32	17 37	17 41	17 45		17 49	17 57			18 09	18 17		18 19	18 28
Coseley	d			17 24											17 54	18 03						18 24	
Tipton	d			17 26											17 56							18 26	
Dudley Port	d			17 28											17 58							18 28	
Sandwell & Dudley	d			17 32							17 46		17 56		18 02							18 32	
Smethwick Galton Bridge	d			17 34	17 40										18 04				18 20			18 34	18 40
Smethwick Rolfe Street	d			17 36											18 06							18 36	
Birmingham New Street	a	17 39		17 44	17 47					17 55	17 55	17 58	18 06		18 14	18 17			18 26	18 38		18 44	18 47
	d		17 39			17 33		17 50	17 53			18 04	18 10	18 13			18 30	18 33	18 36		18 39		
Adderley Park	d		17 44																		18 44		
Stechford	d		17 47											18 20							18 47		
Lea Hall	d		17 50											18 23							18 50		
Marston Green	d					17 41			18 01					18 26				18 41					
Birmingham International	a		17 54			17 45		17 59	18 05			18 13	18 19	18 29			18 39	18 45	18 50		18 54		
	d					17 45		18 00	18 05			18 14	18 20	18 29			18 40	18 45					
Hampton-in-Arden	d					17 48								18 32				18 48					
Berkswell	d								18 11					18 37									
Tile Hill	d					17 55			18 14					18 40				18 55					
Canley	d								18 17					18 44									
Coventry	a					18 00		18 10	18 20			18 24	18 30	18 47			18 49	19 00					
	d					18 01		18 11	18 21				18 31	18 48			18 51	19 01					
Rugby	d					18 12	18 20	18 23	18 32					18 59				19 12					
Long Buckby	d					18 22			18 42					19 09				19 22					
Northampton	a					18 34	18 39		18 54					19 21				19 40					
London Euston	a					19 49		19 14	20 21				19 34	20 45			19 54						

		LM	VT	LM	VT	LM	XC	VT	LM	LM	LM	LM	AW	XC	LM	LM	LM	LM	LM	VT	LM	XC
Stafford	d	18 21					18 27				18 43			19 03			19 10	19 21				19 25
Penkridge	d																19 16					
Wolverhampton	a						18 40				18 56			19 16			19 27					19 39
	d				18 32	18 37	18 41	18 45		18 49	18 57		19 09	19 17		19 19	19 28			19 32	19 37	19 41
Coseley	d									18 54	19 03					19 24						
Tipton	d									18 56						19 26						
Dudley Port	d									18 58						19 28						
Sandwell & Dudley	d					18 46		18 56		19 02						19 32					19 46	
Smethwick Galton Bridge	d									19 04			19 20			19 34	19 40					
Smethwick Rolfe Street	d									19 06						19 36						
Birmingham New Street	a				18 55	18 55	18 58	19 06		19 14	19 17		19 26	19 33		19 44	19 47			19 55	19 55	19 58
	d		18 50	18 53			19 04	19 10	19 13			19 33	19 36		19 39				19 53			20 04
Adderley Park	d														19 44							
Stechford	d								19 20						19 47							
Lea Hall	d								19 23						19 50							
Marston Green	d			19 01					19 26			19 41							20 01			
Birmingham International	a		18 59	19 05			19 13	19 19	19 29			19 45	19 50		19 54				20 05			20 13
	d		19 00	19 05			19 14	19 20	19 29			19 45							20 05			20 14
Hampton-in-Arden	d								19 32			19 48										
Berkswell	d			19 11					19 37										20 11			
Tile Hill	d			19 14					19 40			19 55							20 14			
Canley	d			19 17					19 44										20 17			
Coventry	a		19 10	19 20			19 24	19 30	19 47			20 00							20 20			20 24
	d		19 11	19 21				19 31	19 48			20 01							20 21			
Rugby	d	19 20	19 23	19 32				19 44	19 59			20 12						20 20	20 32			
Long Buckby	d			19 42					20 09			20 22							20 42			
Northampton	a	19 43		19 54					20 21			20 34						20 40	20 54			
London Euston	a		20 15	21 09				20 55	21 45										22 11			

Saturdays until 30 June

Stafford - Wolverhampton - Birmingham - Coventry - Northampton

Network Diagram - see first Page of Table 67

		VT	LM	LM	LM	LM	AW		XC	LM	LM	LM	LM	VT	LM	XC	VT		LM	LM	LM	VT	XC	LM	LM
		◇1 ☕	1		◇1	◇1	◇ 🛒		◇1 🛒			◇1	◇1	◇1 ☕		◇1 A 🛒	◇1 ☕		1		◇1	◇1 ☕	◇1	◇1	
Stafford	d				19 43				20 03			20 12				20 26					20 45		21 03		
Penkridge	d				19 49																20 51				
Wolverhampton 7	a				19 59				20 16			20 28				20 39					21 01		21 15		
	d	19 45		19 49	19 59		20 10		20 17		20 19	20 28		20 33	20 37	20 41	20 45			20 49	21 01	21 07	21 16		
Coseley	d			19 54	20 04						20 24									20 54	21 06				
Tipton	d			19 56							20 26									20 56					
Dudley Port	d			19 58							20 28									20 58					
Sandwell & Dudley	d	19 56		20 02							20 32				20 46		20 56			21 02		21 17			
Smethwick Galton Bridge 7	d			20 04			20 21				20 34	20 40								21 04					
Smethwick Rolfe Street	d			20 06							20 36									21 06					
Birmingham New Street 12	a	20 06		20 14	20 17		20 26		20 33		20 44	20 47		20 55	20 57	20 58	21 06			21 14	21 19	21 26	21 32		
	d	20 10	20 13			20 33	20 36			20 39			20 53			21 04	21 10		21 13			21 30		21 33	21 39
Adderley Park	d									20 44															21 44
Stechford	d		20 20							20 47									21 20						21 47
Lea Hall	d		20 23							20 50									21 23						21 50
Marston Green	d		20 26			20 41							21 01						21 26					21 41	
Birmingham International ✈	a	20 19	20 29			20 45	20 49			20 54			21 05			21 13	21 19		21 29			21 39		21 45	21 54
	d	20 20	20 29			20 45							21 05			21 14	21 20		21 29			21 40		21 45	
Hampton-in-Arden	d		20 32			20 48													21 32					21 48	
Berkswell	d		20 37										21 11						21 37						
Tile Hill	d		20 40			20 55							21 14						21 40					21 55	
Canley	d		20 44										21 17						21 44						
Coventry	a	20 30	20 47			21 00							21 20			21 24	21 30		21 47			21 50		22 00	
	d	20 31				21 01							21 21				21 31					21 51		22 01	
Rugby	d	20 43				21 12							21 32				21 43					22 03		22 12	
Long Buckby	d					21 22							21 42											22 22	
Northampton	a					21 34							21 54											22 34	
London Euston 15 ⊖	a	21 56											23 27				22 55					23 30			

		LM	LM		VT	LM	XC	LM	LM	LM	AW	XC	LM		LM	VT	LM	LM	VT	XC	LM	LM	LM		AW
			◇1		◇1 ☕		◇1	1		◇1	◇	◇1	1			◇1 ☕	◇1		◇1 ☕	◇1	1		◇1		◇
Stafford	d						21 27			21 42		22 03				22 08			22 25	22 33			22 47		
Penkridge	d									21 48													22 53		
Wolverhampton 7	a						21 39			21 58		22 14				22 22			22 39	22 45			23 03		
	d	21 19			21 33	21 37	21 41		21 49	21 58	22 08	22 16			22 19	22 23		22 37	22 40	22 46		22 49	23 03		23 08
Coseley	d	21 24							21 54	22 04					22 24							22 54	23 09		
Tipton	d	21 26							21 56						22 26							22 56			
Dudley Port	d	21 28							21 58						22 28							22 58			
Sandwell & Dudley	d	21 32				21 46			22 02						22 32			22 46				23 02			
Smethwick Galton Bridge 7	d	21 34							22 04		22 19				22 34							23 04			
Smethwick Rolfe Street	d	21 36							22 06						22 36							23 06			
Birmingham New Street 12	a	21 44			21 54	21 55	21 58		22 14	22 20	22 32	22 32			22 44	22 46		22 55	22 59	23 02		23 14	23 21		23 28
	d		21 53					22 13					22 33				22 53				23 13				
Adderley Park	d																				23 18				
Stechford	d							22 20													23 21				
Lea Hall	d							22 23													23 24				
Marston Green	d		22 01					22 26					22 41				23 01				23 27				
Birmingham International ✈	a		22 05					22 29					22 45				23 05				23 30				
	d		22 05					22 29					22 45				23 05				23 30				
Hampton-in-Arden	d							22 32					22 48								23 33				
Berkswell	d		22 11					22 37									23 11				23 38				
Tile Hill	d		22 14					22 40					22 55				23 14				23 41				
Canley	d		22 17					22 44									23 17				23 45				
Coventry	a		22 20					22 47					23 00				23 20				23 48				
	d		22 21														23 21								
Rugby	d		22 32														23 32								
Long Buckby	d		22 41														23 42								
Northampton	a		22 53														23 55								
London Euston 15 ⊖	a		00 17																						

A 🛒 to Birmingham New Street

Saturdays 7 July to 8 September

Stafford - Wolverhampton - Birmingham - Coventry - Northampton

Network Diagram - see first Page of Table 67

		LM	VT	VT	LM	VT	AW	XC	VT	LM		AW	VT	LM	AW	LM	LM	VT	LM	XC		VT	LM	LM	LM
		◇1	◇1 ☕	◇1 ☕	1	◇1 ☕		◇1 🛒	◇1 ☕	1			◇1 ☕	◇1				◇1 ☕	◇1	◇1 🛒		◇1 ☕	◇1		◇1
Stafford	d						05 25													06 26					06 41
Penkridge	d																								06 47
Wolverhampton 7	a						05 39													06 39					06 57
	d		21p45	22p45			05 40		05 45			06 03	06 06				06 19	06 27		06 41		06 45		06 49	06 57
Coseley	d																06 24							06 54	07 03
Tipton	d																06 26							06 56	
Dudley Port	d																06 28							06 58	
Sandwell & Dudley	d		21p56	22p55					05 56				06 17				06 32	06 37				06 56		07 02	
Smethwick Galton Bridge 7	d											06 14					06 34							07 04	
Smethwick Rolfe Street	d														←		06 36							07 06	
Birmingham New Street 12	a		22p06	23p06			05 58		06 06			06 20	06 26		06 20		06 44	06 47		06 57		07 06		07 14	07 17
	d	21p33	22p10	23p10	23p53	05 50		06 04	06 10	06 13		06 36	06 30	06 33	06 36	06 39		06 50	06 53	07 04		07 10	07 13		
Adderley Park	d											→				06 44									
Stechford	d									06 20						06 47							07 20		
Lea Hall	d									06 23						06 50							07 23		
Marston Green	d	21p41			00 01					06 26				06 41					07 01				07 26		
Birmingham International ✈	a	21p45	22p21	23p19	00 04	05 59		06 13	06 19	06 29			06 39	06 45	06 50	06 54		06 59	07 05	07 13		07 19	07 29		
	d	21p45	22p22	23p20	00 05	06 00		06 14	06 20	06 29			06 40	06 45				07 00	07 05	07 14		07 20	07 29		
Hampton-in-Arden	d	21p48								06 32				06 48									07 32		
Berkswell	d									06 37									07 11				07 37		
Tile Hill	d	21p55								06 40				06 55					07 14				07 40		
Canley	d									06 44									07 17				07 44		
Coventry	a	22p00	22p31	23p30	00 15	06 10		06 24	06 30	06 47			06 50	07 00				07 10	07 20	07 24		07 30	07 47		
	d	22p01	22p32	23p31		06 10			06 31				06 51	07 01				07 11	07 21			07 31	07 48		
Rugby	d	22p12	22p43	23p44		06 24								07 12				07 23	07 32				07 59		
Long Buckby	d	22p22												07 22					07 42				08 09		
Northampton	a	22p34		00s05										07 34					07 54				08 21		
London Euston 15 ⊖	a	00 21	00 04	01 13		07 16			07 38				07 55					08 14	09 17			08 34	09 27		

		VT	AW	XC	LM	LM		LM	LM	LM	VT	LM	VT	LM	XC	VT		LM	LM	LM	VT	AW	XC	LM	LM
		◇1 ☕	🛒	◇1 🛒				◇1	◇1	◇1	◇1 ☕	◇1	◇1 ☕		◇1 🛒	◇1 ☕		◇1		◇1	◇1 ☕	◇ 🛒	◇1 🛒		
Stafford	d			06 58				07 12		07 24										07 41			08 03		
Penkridge	d							07 18												07 47					
Wolverhampton 7	a			07 12				07 28												07 57			08 17		
	d	07 04	07 10	07 15		07 19		07 28					07 32	07 37		07 45			07 49	07 57	08 06	08 09	08 18		08 19
Coseley	d					07 24													07 54	08 03					08 24
Tipton	d					07 26													07 56						08 26
Dudley Port	d					07 28													07 58						08 28
Sandwell & Dudley	d	07 15				07 32								07 46		07 56			08 02						08 32
Smethwick Galton Bridge 7	d		07 21			07 34		07 40											08 04			08 21			08 34
Smethwick Rolfe Street	d					07 36													08 06						08 36
Birmingham New Street 12	a	07 24	07 26	07 31		07 44		07 47					07 55	07 55		08 06			08 14	08 17	08 24	08 26	08 39		08 44
	d	07 30	07 36		07 39				07 33		07 50	07 53			08 04	08 10		08 13			08 30	08 36		08 39	
Adderley Park	d				07 44																			08 44	
Stechford	d				07 47													08 20						08 47	
Lea Hall	d				07 50													08 23						08 50	
Marston Green	d								07 41			08 01						08 26							
Birmingham International ✈	a	07 39	07 50		07 54				07 45		07 59	08 05			08 13	08 19		08 29			08 39	08 50		08 54	
	d	07 40							07 45		08 00	08 05			08 14	08 20		08 29			08 40				
Hampton-in-Arden	d								07 48									08 32							
Berkswell	d											08 11						08 37							
Tile Hill	d								07 55			08 14						08 40							
Canley	d											08 17						08 44							
Coventry	a	07 49							08 00		08 10	08 20			08 24	08 30		08 47			08 49				
	d	07 51							08 01		08 11	08 21				08 31		08 48			08 51				
Rugby	d								08 12	08 20	08 23	08 32						08 59							
Long Buckby	d								08 22			08 42						09 09							
Northampton	a								08 34	08 40		08 54						09 21							
London Euston 15 ⊖	a	08 54							09 50		09 14	10 17				09 35		10 27			09 55				

7 July to 8 September

Stafford - Wolverhampton - Birmingham - Coventry - Northampton

Network Diagram - see first Page of Table 67

		LM	LM	LM	VT	LM	VT	LM	XC	VT	LM	LM	LM	VT	AW	XC	LM	LM	LM	LM	LM	VT
		◇1	◇1	◇1	◇1	◇1	◇1		◇1	◇1	◇1		◇1	◇1	◇	◇1			◇1	◇1	◇1	◇1
Stafford	d	08 10		08 23					08 26				08 43			09 03			09 10		09 21	
Penkridge	d	08 16											08 48						09 16			
Wolverhampton 7	a	08 28							08 39				08 58			09 15			09 27			
	d	08 28					08 32	08 37	08 41	08 45		08 49	08 59		09 10	09 17		09 19	09 28			
Coseley	d											08 54	09 04					09 24				
Tipton	d											08 56						09 26				
Dudley Port	d											08 58						09 28				
Sandwell & Dudley	d							08 46		08 56		09 02						09 32				
Smethwick Galton Bridge 7	d	08 40										09 04			09 22			09 34	09 40			
Smethwick Rolfe Street	d											09 06						09 36				
Birmingham New Street 12	a	08 47					08 55	08 55	08 58	09 05		09 14	09 18		09 26	09 39		09 44	09 47			
	d		08 33		08 50	08 53			09 04	09 10	09 13			09 30	09 36		09 39			09 33		09 50
Adderley Park	d																09 44					
Stechford	d										09 20						09 47					
Lea Hall	d										09 23						09 50					
Marston Green	d		08 41			09 01					09 26									09 41		
Birmingham International ✈	a		08 45		08 59	09 05			09 13	09 19	09 29			09 39	09 50		09 54			09 45		09 59
	d		08 45		09 00	09 05			09 14	09 20	09 29			09 40						09 45		10 00
Hampton-in-Arden	d		08 48								09 32									09 48		
Berkswell	d					09 11					09 37											
Tile Hill	d		08 55			09 14					09 40									09 55		
Canley	d					09 17					09 44											
Coventry	a		09 00		09 10	09 20			09 24	09 30	09 47			09 49						10 00		10 10
	d		09 01		09 11	09 21				09 31	09 48			09 51						10 01		10 11
Rugby	d		09 12	09 20	09 23	09 32					09 59									10 12	10 20	10 23
Long Buckby	d		09 22			09 42					10 09									10 22		
Northampton	a		09 34	09 41		09 58					10 21									10 34	10 39	
London Euston 15 ⊖	a		10 49		10 14	11 17				10 34	11 27			10 54						11 49		11 14

		LM	VT	LM	XC	VT	LM	LM	LM	VT	AW	XC	LM	LM	LM	LM	LM	VT	LM	VT	LM	XC	VT
		◇1	◇1		◇1	◇1	◇1		◇1	◇1	◇	◇1			◇1	◇1	◇1	◇1	◇1	◇1		◇1	◇1
Stafford	d				09 26				09 43			10 03			10 10		10 21					10 26	
Penkridge	d														10 16								
Wolverhampton 7	a				09 39				09 56			10 15			10 27							10 39	
	d		09 32	09 37	09 41	09 45		09 49	09 57		10 09	10 17		10 19	10 28					10 32	10 37	10 41	10 45
Coseley	d							09 54	10 03					10 24									
Tipton	d							09 56						10 26									
Dudley Port	d							09 58						10 28									
Sandwell & Dudley	d			09 46		09 56		10 02						10 32							10 46		10 56
Smethwick Galton Bridge 7	d							10 04			10 20			10 34	10 40								
Smethwick Rolfe Street	d							10 06						10 36									
Birmingham New Street 12	a		09 55	09 55	09 58	10 06		10 14	10 17		10 26	10 39		10 44	10 47					10 55	10 55	10 58	11 06
	d	09 53			10 04	10 10	10 13			10 30	10 36		10 39			10 33		10 50	10 53			11 04	11 10
Adderley Park	d												10 44										
Stechford	d						10 20						10 47										
Lea Hall	d						10 23						10 50										
Marston Green	d	10 01					10 26									10 41			11 01				
Birmingham International ✈	a	10 05			10 13	10 19	10 29			10 39	10 50		10 54			10 45		10 59	11 05			11 13	11 19
	d	10 05			10 14	10 20	10 29			10 40						10 45		11 00	11 05			11 14	11 20
Hampton-in-Arden	d						10 32									10 48							
Berkswell	d	10 11					10 37												11 11				
Tile Hill	d	10 14					10 40									10 55			11 14				
Canley	d	10 17					10 44												11 17				
Coventry	a	10 20			10 24	10 30	10 47			10 49						11 00		11 10	11 20			11 24	11 30
	d	10 21				10 31	10 48			10 51						11 01		11 11	11 21				11 31
Rugby	d	10 32					10 59									11 12	11 20	11 23	11 32				
Long Buckby	d	10 42					11 09									11 22			11 42				
Northampton	a	10 54					11 21									11 34	11 39		11 54				
London Euston 15 ⊖	a	12 17				11 34	12 27			11 54						12 49		12 14	13 17				12 34

Table 68

Saturdays

7 July to 8 September

Stafford - Wolverhampton - Birmingham - Coventry - Northampton

Network Diagram - see first Page of Table 67

		LM	LM	LM	VT	AW	XC	LM	LM	LM	LM	LM	VT	LM	VT	LM	XC	VT	LM	LM	LM	VT	AW
		◇1		◇1	◇1	◇	◇1			◇1	◇1	◇1	◇1	◇1	◇1		◇1	◇1	◇1		◇1	◇1	◇
Stafford	d			10 43			11 03			11 10		11 21					11 26				11 43		
Penkridge	d									11 16													
Wolverhampton 7	a			10 56			11 16			11 27							11 39				11 56		
	d		10 49	10 57		11 10	11 17		11 19	11 28					11 32	11 37	11 41	11 45		11 49	11 57		12 09
Coseley	d		10 54	11 03					11 24											11 54	12 03		
Tipton	d		10 56						11 26											11 56			
Dudley Port	d		10 58						11 28											11 58			
Sandwell & Dudley	d		11 02						11 32							11 46		11 56		12 02			
Smethwick Galton Bridge 7	d		11 04			11 21			11 34	11 40										12 04			12 20
Smethwick Rolfe Street	d		11 06						11 36											12 06			
Birmingham New Street 12	a		11 14	11 17		11 27	11 39		11 44	11 47					11 55	11 55	11 58	12 06		12 14	12 17		12 26
	d	11 13			11 30	11 36		11 39			11 33		11 50	11 53			12 04	12 10	12 13			12 30	12 36
Adderley Park	d							11 44															
Stechford	d	11 20						11 47											12 20				
Lea Hall	d	11 23						11 50											12 23				
Marston Green	d	11 26									11 41			12 01					12 26				
Birmingham International ✈	a	11 29			11 39	11 50		11 54			11 45		11 59	12 05			12 13	12 19	12 29			12 39	12 50
	d	11 29			11 40						11 45		12 00	12 05			12 14	12 20	12 29			12 40	
Hampton-in-Arden	d	11 32									11 48								12 32				
Berkswell	d	11 37												12 11					12 37				
Tile Hill	d	11 40									11 55			12 14					12 40				
Canley	d	11 44												12 17					12 44				
Coventry	a	11 47			11 49						12 00		12 10	12 20			12 24	12 30	12 47			12 49	
	d	11 48			11 51						12 01		12 11	12 21				12 31	12 48			12 51	
Rugby	d	11 59									12 12	12 20	12 23	12 32					12 59				
Long Buckby	d	12 09									12 22			12 42					13 09				
Northampton	a	12 21									12 34	12 39		12 54					13 21				
London Euston 15 ⊖	a	13 27			12 54						13 49		13 14	14 17				13 34	14 27			13 54	

		XC	LM	LM	LM	LM	LM	VT	LM	VT	LM	XC	VT	LM	LM	LM	VT	AW	XC	LM	LM	LM
		◇1			◇1	◇1	◇1	◇1	◇1	◇1		◇1	◇1	◇1		◇1	◇1		◇1			◇1
Stafford	d	12 03			12 10		12 21					12 25				12 43			13 03			13 10
Penkridge	d				12 16																	13 16
Wolverhampton 7	a	12 16			12 27							12 39				12 56			13 15			13 27
	d	12 17		12 19	12 28					12 32	12 37	12 41	12 45		12 49	12 57		13 09	13 16		13 19	13 28
Coseley	d			12 24											12 54	13 03					13 24	
Tipton	d			12 26											12 56						13 26	
Dudley Port	d			12 28											12 58						13 28	
Sandwell & Dudley	d			12 32							12 46		12 56		13 02						13 32	
Smethwick Galton Bridge 7	d			12 34	12 40										13 04			13 21			13 34	13 40
Smethwick Rolfe Street	d			12 36											13 06						13 36	
Birmingham New Street 12	a	12 39		12 44	12 47					12 55	12 55	12 58	13 06		13 14	13 17		13 27	13 39		13 44	13 47
	d		12 39			12 33		12 50	12 53			13 04	13 10	13 13			13 30	13 36		13 39		
Adderley Park	d		12 44																	13 44		
Stechford	d		12 47											13 20						13 47		
Lea Hall	d		12 50											13 23						13 50		
Marston Green	d					12 41			13 01					13 26								
Birmingham International ✈	a		12 54			12 45		12 59	13 05			13 13	13 19	13 29			13 39	13 50		13 54		
	d					12 45		13 00	13 05			13 14	13 20	13 29			13 40					
Hampton-in-Arden	d					12 48								13 32								
Berkswell	d								13 11					13 37								
Tile Hill	d					12 55			13 14					13 40								
Canley	d								13 17					13 44								
Coventry	a					13 00		13 10	13 20			13 24	13 30	13 47			13 49					
	d					13 01		13 11	13 21				13 31	13 48			13 51					
Rugby	d					13 12	13 20	13 23	13 32					13 59								
Long Buckby	d					13 22			13 42					14 09								
Northampton	a					13 34	13 39		13 54					14 21								
London Euston 15 ⊖	a					14 49		14 14	15 18				14 34	15 27			14 54					

7 July to 8 September

Stafford - Wolverhampton - Birmingham - Coventry - Northampton

Network Diagram - see first Page of Table 67

		LM	LM	VT	LM	VT	LM		XC	VT	LM	LM	LM	VT	AW	XC	LM		LM	LM	LM	LM	VT	LM	LM
		◇1	◇1	◇1	◇1	◇1			◇1	◇1	◇1		◇1	◇1	◇	◇1				◇1	◇1	◇1	◇1	◇1	
Stafford	d		13 21						13 26				13 43			14 03				14 10		14 21			
Penkridge	d																			14 16					
Wolverhampton 7	a								13 39				13 56			14 16				14 27					
	d					13 32	13 37		13 41	13 45		13 49	13 57		14 09	14 17			14 19	14 28					14 37
Coseley	d											13 54	14 03						14 24						
Tipton	d											13 56							14 26						
Dudley Port	d											13 58							14 28						
Sandwell & Dudley	d						13 46			13 56		14 02							14 32						14 46
Smethwick Galton Bridge 7	d											14 04			14 20				14 34	14 40					
Smethwick Rolfe Street	d											14 06							14 36						
Birmingham New Street 12	a					13 55	13 55		13 58	14 06		14 14	14 17		14 26	14 39			14 44	14 47					14 55
	d	13 33		13 50	13 53				14 04	14 10	14 13			14 30	14 36		14 39				14 33		14 50	14 53	
Adderley Park	d																14 44								
Stechford	d										14 20						14 47								
Lea Hall	d										14 23						14 50								
Marston Green	d	13 41			14 01						14 26										14 41			15 01	
Birmingham International ✈	a	13 45		13 59	14 05				14 13	14 19	14 29			14 39	14 50		14 54				14 45		14 59	15 05	
	d	13 45		14 00	14 05				14 14	14 20	14 29			14 40							14 45		15 00	15 05	
Hampton-in-Arden	d	13 48									14 32										14 48				
Berkswell	d				14 11						14 37													15 11	
Tile Hill	d	13 55			14 14						14 40										14 55			15 14	
Canley	d				14 17						14 44													15 17	
Coventry	a	14 00		14 10	14 20				14 24	14 30	14 47			14 49							15 00		15 10	15 20	
	d	14 01		14 11	14 21					14 31	14 48			14 51							15 01		15 11	15 21	
Rugby	d	14 12	14 20	14 23	14 32						14 59										15 12	15 20	15 23	15 32	
Long Buckby	d	14 22			14 42						15 09										15 22			15 42	
Northampton	a	14 34	14 39		14 54						15 21										15 34	15 39		15 54	
London Euston 15 ⊖	a	15 49		15 14	16 18					15 34	16 27			15 54							16 49		16 14	17 17	

		XC	VT		LM	LM	LM	VT	AW	XC	LM	LM	LM		LM	LM	VT	LM	VT	LM	XC	VT	LM		LM
		◇1	◇1		◇1		◇1	◇1	◇	◇1			◇1		◇1	◇1	◇1	◇1	◇1		◇1	◇1	◇1		
Stafford	d	14 26					14 46			15 03			15 10			15 21					15 26				
Penkridge	d												15 16												
Wolverhampton 7	a	14 39					14 59			15 16			15 27								15 39				
	d	14 41	14 45			14 49	14 59		15 10	15 17		15 19	15 28						15 32	15 37	15 41	15 45			15 49
Coseley	d					14 54	15 05					15 24													15 54
Tipton	d					14 56						15 26													15 56
Dudley Port	d					14 58						15 28													15 58
Sandwell & Dudley	d		14 56			15 02						15 32								15 46		15 56			16 02
Smethwick Galton Bridge 7	d					15 04			15 21			15 34	15 40												16 04
Smethwick Rolfe Street	d					15 06						15 36													16 06
Birmingham New Street 12	a	14 58	15 06			15 14	15 18		15 27	15 39		15 44	15 47						15 55	15 55	15 58	16 06			16 14
	d	15 04	15 10		15 13			15 30	15 36		15 39				15 33		15 50	15 53			16 04	16 10	16 13		
Adderley Park	d										15 44														
Stechford	d				15 20						15 47												16 20		
Lea Hall	d				15 23						15 50												16 23		
Marston Green	d				15 26										15 41			16 01					16 26		
Birmingham International ✈	a	15 13	15 19		15 29			15 39	15 50		15 54				15 45		15 59	16 05			16 13	16 19	16 29		
	d	15 14	15 20		15 29			15 40							15 45		16 00	16 05			16 14	16 20	16 29		
Hampton-in-Arden	d				15 32										15 48								16 32		
Berkswell	d				15 37													16 11					16 37		
Tile Hill	d				15 40										15 55			16 14					16 40		
Canley	d				15 44													16 17					16 44		
Coventry	a	15 24	15 30		15 47			15 49							16 00		16 10	16 20			16 24	16 30	16 47		
	d		15 31		15 48			15 51							16 01		16 11	16 21				16 31	16 48		
Rugby	d				15 59										16 12	16 20	16 23	16 32					16 59		
Long Buckby	d				16 09										16 22			16 42					17 09		
Northampton	a				16 21										16 34	16 39		16 54					17 21		
London Euston 15 ⊖	a		16 34		17 27			16 54							17 49		17 14	18 17				17 34	18 27		

Table 68

Saturdays

7 July to 8 September

Stafford - Wolverhampton - Birmingham - Coventry - Northampton

Network Diagram - see first Page of Table 67

		LM	VT	AW	XC	LM	LM	LM	LM	LM		VT	LM	VT	LM	XC	VT	LM	LM	LM		VT	AW	XC	LM
		◇1	◇1	◇	◇1			◇1	◇1	◇1		◇1	◇1	◇1		◇1	◇1	◇1		◇1		◇1	◇	◇1	
Stafford	d	15 43			16 03			16 10		16 21						16 25				16 46				17 03	
Penkridge	d							16 16																	
Wolverhampton 7	a	15 56			16 16			16 27								16 39				16 59				17 16	
	d	15 57		16 09	16 17		16 19	16 28						16 32	16 37	16 41	16 45		16 49	16 59			17 09	17 17	
Coseley	d	16 03					16 24												16 54	17 05					
Tipton	d						16 26												16 56						
Dudley Port	d						16 28												16 58						
Sandwell & Dudley	d						16 32								16 46		16 56		17 02						
Smethwick Galton Bridge 7	d			16 20			16 34	16 40											17 04				17 22		
Smethwick Rolfe Street	d						16 36												17 06						
Birmingham New Street 12	a	16 17		16 26	16 39		16 44	16 47						16 55	16 55	16 58	17 06		17 14	17 18			17 28	17 39	
	d		16 30	16 36		16 39			16 33			16 50	16 53			17 04	17 10	17 13				17 30	17 37		17 39
Adderley Park	d					16 44												17 17							17 44
Stechford	d					16 47												17 21							17 47
Lea Hall	d					16 50												17 23							17 50
Marston Green	d								16 41				17 01					17 26							
Birmingham International ✈	a		16 39	16 50		16 54			16 45			16 59	17 05			17 13	17 19	17 29				17 39	17 50		17 54
	d		16 40						16 45			17 00	17 05			17 14	17 20	17 30				17 40			
Hampton-in-Arden	d								16 48									17 33							
Berkswell	d												17 11					17 38							
Tile Hill	d								16 55				17 14					17 41							
Canley	d												17 17					17 44							
Coventry	a		16 49						17 00			17 10	17 20			17 24	17 30	17 47				17 49			
	d		16 51						17 01			17 11	17 21				17 31	17 48				17 51			
Rugby	d								17 12	17 20		17 23	17 32					17 59							
Long Buckby	d								17 22				17 42					18 09							
Northampton	a								17 34	17 39			17 54					18 21							
London Euston 15 ⊖	a		17 52						18 49			18 14	19 17				18 34	19 45				18 54			

		LM	LM	LM	LM	VT		LM	VT	LM	XC	VT	LM	LM	LM	VT		LM	AW	XC	LM	LM	LM	LM	VT
			◇1	◇1	◇1	◇1		◇1	◇1		◇1	◇1	◇1		◇1	◇1		◇1	◇	◇1			◇1	◇1	◇1
Stafford	d		17 10		17 21						17 26				17 43					18 04			18 10	18 21	
Penkridge	d		17 16																				18 16		
Wolverhampton 7	a		17 27								17 39				17 56					18 16			18 27		
	d	17 19	17 28						17 32	17 37	17 41	17 45		17 49	17 57				18 09	18 17		18 19	18 28		
Coseley	d	17 24												17 54	18 03							18 24			
Tipton	d	17 26												17 56								18 26			
Dudley Port	d	17 28												17 58								18 28			
Sandwell & Dudley	d	17 32								17 46		17 56		18 02								18 32			
Smethwick Galton Bridge 7	d	17 34	17 40											18 04					18 20			18 34	18 40		
Smethwick Rolfe Street	d	17 36												18 06								18 36			
Birmingham New Street 12	a	17 44	17 47						17 55	17 55	17 58	18 06		18 14	18 17				18 26	18 38		18 44	18 47		
	d			17 33		17 50		17 53			18 04	18 10	18 13			18 30		18 33	18 36		18 39				18 50
Adderley Park	d																				18 44				
Stechford	d												18 20								18 47				
Lea Hall	d												18 23								18 50				
Marston Green	d			17 41				18 01					18 26					18 41							
Birmingham International ✈	a			17 45		17 59		18 05			18 13	18 19	18 29			18 39		18 45	18 50		18 54				18 59
	d			17 45		18 00		18 05			18 14	18 20	18 29			18 40		18 45							19 00
Hampton-in-Arden	d			17 48									18 32					18 48							
Berkswell	d							18 11					18 37												
Tile Hill	d			17 55				18 14					18 40					18 55							
Canley	d							18 17					18 44												
Coventry	a			18 00		18 10		18 20			18 24	18 30	18 47			18 49		19 00							19 10
	d			18 01		18 11		18 21				18 31	18 48			18 51		19 01							19 11
Rugby	d			18 12	18 20	18 23		18 32					18 59					19 12						19 20	19 23
Long Buckby	d			18 22				18 42					19 09					19 22							
Northampton	a			18 34	18 39			18 54					19 21					19 40						19 43	
London Euston 15 ⊖	a			19 49		19 14		20 21				19 34	20 45			19 54									20 15

Table 68

Saturdays
7 July to 8 September

Stafford - Wolverhampton - Birmingham - Coventry - Northampton

Network Diagram - see first Page of Table 67

		LM	LM	XC	VT	LM	LM	LM	LM	AW	XC	LM	LM	LM	LM	LM	VT	LM	XC	VT	LM	LM
		◇1		◇1 ✕	◇1 ⊐	◇1		◇1	◇1	◇ ✕	◇1 ✕			◇1	◇1	◇1	◇1 ⊐		◇1 ✕	◇1 ⊐	1	
Stafford	d			18 27				18 43			19 03			19 10	19 21				19 25			
Penkridge	d													19 16								
Wolverhampton 7 ⇌	a			18 40				18 56			19 16			19 27					19 39			
	d		18 37	18 41	18 45		18 49	18 57		19 09	19 17		19 19	19 28			19 32	19 37	19 41	19 45		19 49
Coseley	d						18 54	19 03					19 24									19 54
Tipton	d						18 56						19 26									19 56
Dudley Port	d						18 58						19 28									19 58
Sandwell & Dudley	d		18 46		18 56		19 02						19 32					19 46		19 56		20 02
Smethwick Galton Bridge 7	d						19 04			19 20			19 34	19 40								20 04
Smethwick Rolfe Street	d						19 06						19 36									20 06
Birmingham New Street 12	a		18 55	18 58	19 06		19 14	19 17		19 26	19 33		19 44	19 47			19 55	19 55	19 58	20 06		20 14
	d	18 53		19 04	19 10	19 13			19 33	19 36		19 39				19 53			20 04	20 10	20 13	
Adderley Park	d											19 44										
Stechford	d					19 20						19 47									20 20	
Lea Hall	d					19 23						19 50									20 23	
Marston Green	d	19 01				19 26			19 41							20 01					20 26	
Birmingham International ✈	a	19 05		19 13	19 19	19 29			19 45	19 50		19 54				20 05			20 13	20 19	20 29	
	d	19 05		19 14	19 20	19 29			19 45							20 05			20 14	20 20	20 29	
Hampton-in-Arden	d					19 32			19 48												20 32	
Berkswell	d	19 11				19 37										20 11					20 37	
Tile Hill	d	19 14				19 40			19 55							20 14					20 40	
Canley	d	19 17				19 44										20 17					20 44	
Coventry	a	19 20		19 24	19 30	19 47			20 00							20 20			20 24	20 30	20 47	
	d	19 21			19 31	19 48			20 01							20 21				20 31		
Rugby	d	19 32			19 44	19 59			20 12						20 20	20 32				20 43		
Long Buckby	d	19 42				20 09			20 22							20 42						
Northampton	a	19 54				20 21			20 34						20 40	20 54						
London Euston 15 ⊖	a	21 09			20 55	21 45										22 11				21 56		

		LM	LM	AW	XC	LM	LM	LM	LM	VT	LM	XC	VT	LM	LM	LM	VT	XC	LM	LM	LM	LM	VT
		◇1	◇1	◇ ✕	◇1 ✕			◇1	◇1	◇1 ⊐		◇1 A ✕	◇1 ⊐	1		◇1	◇1 ⊐	◇1	◇1			◇1	◇1 ⊐
Stafford	d	19 43			20 03			20 12				20 26				20 45		21 03					
Penkridge	d	19 49														20 51							
Wolverhampton 7 ⇌	a	19 59			20 16			20 28				20 39				21 01		21 15					
	d	19 59		20 10	20 17		20 19	20 28		20 32	20 37	20 41	20 45		20 49	21 01	21 07	21 16			21 19		21 33
Coseley	d	20 04					20 24								20 54	21 06					21 24		
Tipton	d						20 26								20 56						21 26		
Dudley Port	d						20 28								20 58						21 28		
Sandwell & Dudley	d						20 32				20 46		20 56		21 02		21 17				21 32		
Smethwick Galton Bridge 7	d			20 21			20 34	20 40							21 04						21 34		
Smethwick Rolfe Street	d						20 36								21 06						21 36		
Birmingham New Street 12	a	20 17		20 26	20 33		20 44	20 47		20 55	20 57	20 58	21 06		21 14	21 19	21 26	21 32			21 44		21 54
	d		20 33	20 36		20 39			20 53			21 04	21 10	21 13			21 30		21 33	21 39		21 53	
Adderley Park	d					20 44														21 44			
Stechford	d					20 47								21 20						21 47			
Lea Hall	d					20 50								21 23						21 50			
Marston Green	d		20 41						21 01					21 26					21 41			22 01	
Birmingham International ✈	a		20 45	20 49		20 54			21 05			21 13	21 19	21 29			21 39		21 45	21 54		22 05	
	d		20 45						21 05			21 14	21 20	21 29			21 40		21 45			22 05	
Hampton-in-Arden	d		20 48											21 32					21 48				
Berkswell	d								21 11					21 37								22 11	
Tile Hill	d		20 55						21 14					21 40					21 55			22 14	
Canley	d								21 17					21 44								22 17	
Coventry	a		21 00						21 20			21 24	21 30	21 47			21 50		22 00			22 20	
	d		21 01						21 21				21 31				21 51		22 01			22 21	
Rugby	d		21 12						21 32				21 43				22 03		22 12			22 32	
Long Buckby	d		21 22						21 42										22 22			22 41	
Northampton	a		21 34						21 54										22 34			22 53	
London Euston 15 ⊖	a								23 27				22 55				23 30					00 17	

A ✕ to Birmingham New Street

Table 68

Saturdays
7 July to 8 September

Stafford - Wolverhampton - Birmingham - Coventry - Northampton

Network Diagram - see first Page of Table 67

		LM	XC	LM	LM	LM	AW	XC	LM	LM	VT	LM	LM	VT	XC	LM	LM	LM	AW
			◇1	1		◇1	◇	◇1	1		◇1 ⊐	◇1		◇1 ⊐	◇1	1		◇1	◇
Stafford	d		21 27			21 42		22 03			22 08			22 25	22 33			22 47	
Penkridge	d					21 48												22 53	
Wolverhampton 7 ⇌	a		21 39			21 58		22 14			22 22			22 39	22 45			23 03	
	d	21 37	21 41		21 49	21 58	22 08	22 16		22 19	22 23		22 37	22 40	22 46		22 49	23 03	23 08
Coseley	d				21 54	22 04				22 24							22 54	23 09	
Tipton	d				21 56					22 26							22 56		
Dudley Port	d				21 58					22 28							22 58		
Sandwell & Dudley	d	21 46			22 02					22 32			22 46				23 02		
Smethwick Galton Bridge 7	d				22 04		22 19			22 34							23 04		
Smethwick Rolfe Street	d				22 06					22 36							23 06		
Birmingham New Street 12	a	21 55	21 58		22 14	22 20	22 32	22 32		22 44	22 46		22 55	22 59	23 02		23 14	23 21	23 28
	d			22 13					22 33			22 53				23 13			
Adderley Park	d															23 18			
Stechford	d			22 20												23 21			
Lea Hall	d			22 23												23 24			
Marston Green	d			22 26					22 41			23 01				23 27			
Birmingham International ✈	a			22 29					22 45			23 05				23 30			
	d			22 29					22 45			23 05				23 30			
Hampton-in-Arden	d			22 32					22 48							23 33			
Berkswell	d			22 37								23 11				23 38			
Tile Hill	d			22 40					22 55			23 14				23 41			
Canley	d			22 44								23 17				23 45			
Coventry	a			22 47					23 00			23 20				23 48			
	d											23 21							
Rugby	d											23 32							
Long Buckby	d											23 42							
Northampton	a											23 55							
London Euston 15 ⊖	a																		

Saturdays
from 15 September

		LM	VT	VT	VT	LM	VT	AW	XC	VT	LM	AW	VT	LM	AW	LM	LM	VT	LM	XC	VT	LM	LM
		◇1	◇1 ⊐	◇1 A ⊐	◇1 B ⊐	1	◇1 ⊐		◇1 ✕	◇1 ⊐	1		◇1 ⊐	◇1				◇1 ⊐	◇1	◇1 ✕	◇1 ⊐	◇1	
Stafford	d							05 25												06 26			
Penkridge	d																						
Wolverhampton 7 ⇌	a							05 39												06 39			
	d		21p45	22p45	22p45			05 40		05 45		06 03	06 06				06 19	06 27		06 41	06 45		06 49
Coseley	d			⌇	⌇												06 24						06 54
Tipton	d			⌇	⌇												06 26						06 56
Dudley Port	d			⌇	⌇												06 28						06 58
Sandwell & Dudley	d		21p56	22p55	22p55					05 56			06 17				06 32	06 37			06 56		07 02
Smethwick Galton Bridge 7	d			⌇	⌇							06 14					06 34						07 04
Smethwick Rolfe Street	d			⌇	⌇										←		06 36						07 06
Birmingham New Street 12	a		22p06	23p06	23p06			05 58		06 06		06 20	06 26		06 20		06 44	06 47		06 57	07 06		07 14
	d	21p33	22p10	23p10	23p10	23p53	05 50		06 04	06 10	06 13	06 36	06 30	06 33	06 36	06 39		06 50	06 53	07 04	07 10	07 13	
Adderley Park	d			⌇	⌇							→				06 44							
Stechford	d			⌇	⌇						06 20					06 47						07 20	
Lea Hall	d			⌇	⌇						06 23					06 50						07 23	
Marston Green	d	21p41		⌇	⌇	00 01					06 26			06 41					07 01			07 26	
Birmingham International ✈	a	21p45	22p21	23p19	23p19	00 04	05 59		06 13	06 19	06 29		06 39	06 45	06 50	06 54		06 59	07 05	07 13	07 19	07 29	
	d	21p45	22p22	23p20	23p20	00 05	06 00		06 14	06 20	06 29		06 40	06 45				07 00	07 05	07 14	07 20	07 29	
Hampton-in-Arden	d	21p48		⌇	⌇						06 32			06 48								07 32	
Berkswell	d			⌇	⌇						06 37								07 11			07 37	
Tile Hill	d	21p55		⌇	⌇						06 40			06 55					07 14			07 40	
Canley	d			⌇	⌇						06 44								07 17			07 44	
Coventry	a	22p00	22p31	23p30	23p30	00 15	06 10		06 24	06 30	06 47		06 50	07 00				07 10	07 20	07 24	07 30	07 47	
	d	22p01	22p32	23p31	23p31		06 10			06 31			06 51	07 01				07 11	07 21		07 31	07 48	
Rugby	d	22p12	22p43	23p44	23p44		06 24							07 12				07 23	07 32			07 59	
Long Buckby	d	22p22		⌇	⌇									07 22					07 42			08 09	
Northampton	a	22p34		00s05	00s05									07 34					07 54			08 21	
London Euston 15 ⊖	a	00 21	00 04	01 13	01 15		07 16			07 38			07 55					08 14	09 17		08 34	09 27	

A 15 September

B not 15 September

Table 68

Saturdays
from 15 September

Stafford - Wolverhampton - Birmingham - Coventry - Northampton

Network Diagram - see first Page of Table 67

		LM	VT	AW	XC	LM		LM	LM	LM	LM	VT	LM	VT	LM	XC		VT	LM	LM	LM	VT	AW	XC	LM
		◇1	◇1		◇1				◇1	◇1	◇1	◇1	◇1	◇1		◇1		◇1	◇1		◇1	◇1	◇	◇1	
Stafford	d	06 41			06 58				07 12		07 24										07 41			08 03	
Penkridge	d	06 47							07 18												07 47				
Wolverhampton 7	a	06 57			07 12				07 28												07 57			08 16	
	d	06 57	07 04	07 10	07 15			07 19	07 28					07 32	07 37			07 45		07 49	07 57	08 06	08 09	08 18	
Coseley	d	07 03						07 24												07 54	08 03				
Tipton	d							07 26												07 56					
Dudley Port	d							07 28												07 58					
Sandwell & Dudley	d		07 15					07 32							07 46			07 56		08 02					
Smethwick Galton Bridge 7	d			07 21				07 34	07 40											08 04			08 21		
Smethwick Rolfe Street	d							07 36												08 06					
Birmingham New Street 12	a	07 17	07 24	07 26	07 31			07 44	07 47					07 55	07 55			08 06		08 14	08 17	08 23	08 26	08 38	
	d		07 30	07 36		07 39				07 33		07 50	07 53			08 04		08 10	08 13			08 30	08 36		08 39
Adderley Park	d					07 44																			08 44
Stechford	d					07 47													08 20						08 47
Lea Hall	d					07 50													08 23						08 50
Marston Green	d									07 41			08 01						08 26						
Birmingham International	a		07 39	07 50		07 54				07 45		07 59	08 05			08 13		08 19	08 29			08 39	08 50		08 54
	d		07 40							07 45		08 00	08 05			08 14		08 20	08 29			08 40			
Hampton-in-Arden	d									07 48									08 32						
Berkswell	d												08 11						08 37						
Tile Hill	d									07 55			08 14						08 40						
Canley	d												08 17						08 44						
Coventry	a		07 50							08 00		08 10	08 20			08 24		08 30	08 47			08 49			
	d		07 52							08 01		08 11	08 21					08 31	08 48			08 51			
Rugby	d									08 12	08 20	08 23	08 32						08 59						
Long Buckby	d									08 22			08 42						09 09						
Northampton	a									08 34	08 40		08 54						09 21						
London Euston 15	a		08 54							09 50		09 14	10 17					09 35	10 27			09 55			

		LM		LM	LM	LM	VT	LM	VT	LM	XC	VT		LM	LM	LM	VT	AW	XC	LM	LM	LM		LM	LM
				◇1	◇1	◇1	◇1	◇1	◇1		◇1	◇1		◇1		◇1	◇1	◇	◇1			◇1		◇1	◇1
Stafford	d			08 10		08 23					08 26					08 43			09 03			09 10			09 21
Penkridge	d			08 16												08 48						09 16			
Wolverhampton 7	a			08 28							08 39					08 58			09 15			09 27			
	d	08 19		08 28					08 32	08 37	08 41	08 45			08 49	08 59		09 10	09 17		09 19	09 28			
Coseley	d	08 24													08 54	09 04					09 24				
Tipton	d	08 26													08 56						09 26				
Dudley Port	d	08 28													08 58						09 28				
Sandwell & Dudley	d	08 32								08 46		08 56			09 02						09 32				
Smethwick Galton Bridge 7	d	08 34		08 40											09 04			09 22			09 34	09 40			
Smethwick Rolfe Street	d	08 36													09 06						09 36				
Birmingham New Street 12	a	08 44		08 47					08 55	08 55	08 58	09 05			09 14	09 18		09 26	09 39		09 44	09 47			
	d				08 33		08 50	08 53			09 04	09 10		09 13			09 30	09 36		09 39				09 33	
Adderley Park	d																			09 44					
Stechford	d													09 20						09 47					
Lea Hall	d													09 23						09 50					
Marston Green	d				08 41			09 01						09 26										09 41	
Birmingham International	a				08 45		08 59	09 05			09 13	09 19		09 29			09 39	09 50		09 54				09 45	
	d				08 45		09 00	09 05			09 14	09 20		09 29			09 40							09 45	
Hampton-in-Arden	d				08 48									09 32										09 48	
Berkswell	d							09 11						09 37											
Tile Hill	d				08 55			09 14						09 40										09 55	
Canley	d							09 17						09 44											
Coventry	a				09 00		09 10	09 20			09 24	09 30		09 47			09 49							10 00	
	d				09 01		09 11	09 21				09 31		09 48			09 51							10 01	
Rugby	d				09 12	09 20	09 23	09 32						09 59										10 12	10 20
Long Buckby	d				09 22			09 42						10 09										10 22	
Northampton	a				09 34	09 41		09 58						10 21										10 34	10 39
London Euston 15	a				10 49		10 14	11 17				10 34		11 27			10 54							11 49	

Table 68

Saturdays
from 15 September

Stafford - Wolverhampton - Birmingham - Coventry - Northampton

Network Diagram - see first Page of Table 67

		VT	LM	VT	LM	XC	VT	LM		LM	LM	VT	AW	XC	LM	LM	LM	LM	LM		VT	LM	VT	LM	XC
		◇1	◇1	◇1		◇1	◇1	◇1			◇1	◇1	◇	◇1			◇1	◇1	◇1		◇1	◇1	◇1		◇1
Stafford	d					09 26					09 43			10 03			10 10		10 21						10 26
Penkridge	d																10 16								
Wolverhampton 7	a					09 39					09 56			10 15			10 27								10 39
	d			09 32	09 37	09 41	09 45			09 49	09 57		10 09	10 17		10 19	10 28						10 32	10 37	10 41
Coseley	d									09 54	10 03					10 24									
Tipton	d									09 56						10 26									
Dudley Port	d									09 58						10 28									
Sandwell & Dudley	d				09 46		09 56			10 02						10 32								10 46	
Smethwick Galton Bridge 7	d									10 04			10 20			10 34	10 40								
Smethwick Rolfe Street	d									10 06						10 36									
Birmingham New Street 12	a			09 55	09 55	09 58	10 06			10 14	10 17		10 26	10 39		10 44	10 47						10 55	10 55	10 58
	d	09 50	09 53			10 04	10 10	10 13				10 30	10 36		10 39			10 33			10 50	10 53			11 04
Adderley Park	d														10 44										
Stechford	d							10 20							10 47										
Lea Hall	d							10 23							10 50										
Marston Green	d		10 01					10 26										10 41				11 01			
Birmingham International	a	09 59	10 05			10 13	10 19	10 29				10 39	10 50		10 54			10 45			10 59	11 05			11 13
	d	10 00	10 05			10 14	10 20	10 29				10 40						10 45			11 00	11 05			11 14
Hampton-in-Arden	d							10 32										10 48							
Berkswell	d		10 11					10 37														11 11			
Tile Hill	d		10 14					10 40										10 55				11 14			
Canley	d		10 17					10 44														11 17			
Coventry	a	10 10	10 20			10 24	10 30	10 47				10 49						11 00			11 10	11 20			11 24
	d	10 11	10 21				10 31	10 48				10 51						11 01			11 11	11 21			
Rugby	d	10 23	10 32					10 59										11 12	11 20		11 23	11 32			
Long Buckby	d		10 42					11 09										11 22				11 42			
Northampton	a		10 54					11 21										11 34	11 39			11 54			
London Euston 15	a	11 14	12 17				11 34	12 27				11 54						12 49			12 14	13 17			

		VT	LM	LM	LM		VT	AW	XC	LM	LM	LM	LM	LM	VT		LM	VT	LM	XC	VT	LM	LM	LM	VT
		◇1	◇1		◇1		◇1	◇	◇1			◇1	◇1	◇1	◇1		◇1	◇1		◇1	◇1	◇1		◇1	◇1
Stafford	d				10 43				11 03			11 10		11 21						11 26				11 43	
Penkridge	d											11 16													
Wolverhampton 7	a				10 56				11 16			11 27								11 39				11 56	
	d	10 45		10 49	10 57			11 10	11 17		11 19	11 28						11 33	11 37	11 41	11 45		11 49	11 57	
Coseley	d			10 54	11 03						11 24												11 54	12 03	
Tipton	d			10 56							11 26												11 56		
Dudley Port	d			10 58							11 28												11 58		
Sandwell & Dudley	d	10 56		11 02							11 32								11 46		11 56		12 02		
Smethwick Galton Bridge 7	d			11 04				11 21			11 34	11 40											12 04		
Smethwick Rolfe Street	d			11 06							11 36												12 06		
Birmingham New Street 12	a	11 06		11 14	11 17			11 27	11 39		11 44	11 47						11 55	11 55	11 58	12 06		12 14	12 17	
	d	11 10	11 13				11 30	11 36		11 39			11 33		11 50		11 53			12 04	12 10	12 13			12 30
Adderley Park	d									11 44															
Stechford	d		11 20							11 47												12 20			
Lea Hall	d		11 23							11 50												12 23			
Marston Green	d		11 26										11 41				12 01					12 26			
Birmingham International	a	11 19	11 29				11 39	11 50		11 54			11 45		11 59		12 05			12 13	12 19	12 29			12 39
	d	11 20	11 29				11 40						11 45		12 00		12 05			12 14	12 20	12 29			12 40
Hampton-in-Arden	d		11 32										11 48									12 32			
Berkswell	d		11 37														12 11					12 37			
Tile Hill	d		11 40										11 55				12 14					12 40			
Canley	d		11 44														12 17					12 44			
Coventry	a	11 30	11 47				11 49						12 00		12 10		12 20			12 24	12 30	12 47			12 49
	d	11 31	11 48				11 51						12 01		12 11		12 21				12 31	12 48			12 51
Rugby	d		11 59										12 12	12 20	12 23		12 32					12 59			
Long Buckby	d		12 09										12 22				12 42					13 09			
Northampton	a		12 21										12 34	12 39			12 54					13 21			
London Euston 15	a	12 34	13 27				12 54						13 49		13 14		14 17				13 34	14 27			13 54

Table 68

Saturdays
from 15 September

Stafford - Wolverhampton - Birmingham - Coventry - Northampton

Network Diagram - see first Page of Table 67

		AW	XC	LM	LM	LM	LM	LM	VT	LM	VT	LM	XC	VT	LM	LM	LM	VT	AW	XC	LM	LM
		◇	◇■			◇■	◇■	◇■	◇■	◇■	◇■		◇■	◇■	◇■		◇■	◇■		◇■		
Stafford	d		12 03			12 10		12 21					12 25				12 43			13 03		
Penkridge	d					12 16																
Wolverhampton ■	a		12 16			12 27							12 39				12 56			13 15		
	d	12 09	12 17		12 19	12 28					12 32	12 37	12 41	12 45		12 49	12 57		13 09	13 16		13 19
Coseley	d				12 24											12 54	13 03					13 24
Tipton	d				12 26											12 56						13 26
Dudley Port	d				12 28											12 58						13 28
Sandwell & Dudley	d				12 32							12 46		12 56		13 02						13 32
Smethwick Galton Bridge ■	d	12 20			12 34	12 40										13 04			13 21			13 34
Smethwick Rolfe Street	d				12 36											13 06						13 36
Birmingham New Street ■	a	12 26	12 39		12 44	12 47					12 55	12 55	12 58	13 06		13 14	13 17		13 27	13 39		13 44
	d	12 36		12 39			12 33		12 50	12 53			13 04	13 10	13 13			13 30	13 36		13 39	
Adderley Park	d			12 44																	13 44	
Stechford	d			12 47											13 20						13 47	
Lea Hall	d			12 50											13 23						13 50	
Marston Green	d						12 41			13 01					13 26							
Birmingham International	a	12 50		12 54			12 45		12 59	13 05			13 13	13 19	13 29			13 39	13 50		13 54	
	d						12 45		13 00	13 05			13 14	13 20	13 29			13 40				
Hampton-in-Arden	d						12 48								13 32							
Berkswell	d									13 11					13 37							
Tile Hill	d						12 55			13 14					13 40							
Canley	d									13 17					13 44							
Coventry	a						13 00		13 10	13 20			13 24	13 30	13 47			13 49				
	d						13 01		13 11	13 21				13 31	13 48			13 51				
Rugby	d						13 12	13 20	13 23	13 32					13 59							
Long Buckby	d						13 22			13 42					14 09							
Northampton	a						13 34	13 39		13 54					14 21							
London Euston ■ ⊖	a						14 49		14 14	15 18				14 34	15 27			14 54				

		LM	LM	LM	VT	LM	VT	LM	XC	VT	LM	LM	LM	VT	AW	XC	LM	LM	LM	LM	LM	VT	LM
		◇■	◇■	◇■	◇■	◇■	◇■		◇■	◇■	◇■		◇■	◇■	◇	◇■			◇■	◇■	◇■	◇■	◇■
Stafford	d	13 10		13 21					13 26				13 43			14 03			14 10		14 21		
Penkridge	d	13 16																	14 16				
Wolverhampton ■	a	13 27							13 39				13 56			14 16			14 27				
	d	13 28					13 32	13 37	13 41	13 45		13 49	13 57		14 09	14 17		14 19	14 28				
Coseley	d											13 54	14 03					14 24					
Tipton	d											13 56						14 26					
Dudley Port	d											13 58						14 28					
Sandwell & Dudley	d							13 46		13 56		14 02						14 32					
Smethwick Galton Bridge ■	d	13 40										14 04			14 20			14 34	14 40				
Smethwick Rolfe Street	d											14 06						14 36					
Birmingham New Street ■	a	13 47					13 55	13 55	13 58	14 06		14 14	14 17		14 26	14 39		14 44	14 47				
	d		13 33		13 50	13 53			14 04	14 10	14 13			14 30	14 36		14 39			14 33		14 50	14 53
Adderley Park	d																14 44						
Stechford	d										14 20						14 47						
Lea Hall	d										14 23						14 50						
Marston Green	d		13 41			14 01					14 26									14 41			15 01
Birmingham International	a		13 45		13 59	14 05			14 13	14 19	14 29			14 39	14 50		14 54			14 45		14 59	15 05
	d		13 45		14 00	14 05			14 14	14 20	14 29			14 40						14 45		15 00	15 05
Hampton-in-Arden	d		13 48								14 32									14 48			
Berkswell	d					14 11					14 37												15 11
Tile Hill	d		13 55			14 14					14 40									14 55			15 14
Canley	d					14 17					14 44												15 17
Coventry	a		14 00		14 10	14 20			14 24	14 30	14 47			14 49						15 00		15 10	15 20
	d		14 01		14 11	14 21				14 31	14 48			14 51						15 01		15 11	15 21
Rugby	d		14 12	14 20	14 23	14 32					14 59									15 12	15 20	15 23	15 32
Long Buckby	d		14 22			14 42					15 09									15 22			15 42
Northampton	a		14 34	14 39		14 54					15 21									15 34	15 39		15 54
London Euston ■ ⊖	a		15 49		15 14	16 18				15 34	16 27			15 54						16 49		16 14	17 17

Table 68

Saturdays
from 15 September

Stafford - Wolverhampton - Birmingham - Coventry - Northampton

Network Diagram - see first Page of Table 67

		VT	LM	XC	VT	LM	LM	LM	VT	AW	XC	LM	LM	LM	LM	LM	VT	LM	VT	LM	XC	VT
		◇■		◇■	◇■	◇■		◇■	◇■	◇	◇■			◇■	◇■	◇■	◇■	◇■	◇■		◇■	◇■
Stafford	d			14 26				14 46			15 03			15 10		15 21					15 26	
Penkridge	d													15 16								
Wolverhampton ■	a			14 39				14 59			15 16			15 27							15 39	
	d	14 32	14 37	14 41	14 45		14 49	14 59		15 10	15 17		15 19	15 28					15 32	15 37	15 41	15 45
Coseley	d						14 54	15 05					15 24									
Tipton	d						14 56						15 26									
Dudley Port	d						14 58						15 28									
Sandwell & Dudley	d		14 46		14 56		15 02						15 32							15 46		15 56
Smethwick Galton Bridge ■	d						15 04			15 21			15 34	15 40								
Smethwick Rolfe Street	d						15 06						15 36									
Birmingham New Street ■	a	14 55	14 55	14 58	15 06		15 14	15 18		15 27	15 39		15 44	15 47					15 55	15 55	15 58	16 06
	d			15 04	15 10	15 13			15 30	15 36		15 39			15 33		15 50	15 53			16 04	16 10
Adderley Park	d											15 44										
Stechford	d					15 20						15 47										
Lea Hall	d					15 23						15 50										
Marston Green	d					15 26									15 41			16 01				
Birmingham International	a			15 13	15 19	15 29			15 39	15 50		15 54			15 45		15 59	16 05			16 13	16 19
	d			15 14	15 20	15 29			15 40						15 45		16 00	16 05			16 14	16 20
Hampton-in-Arden	d					15 32									15 48							
Berkswell	d					15 37												16 11				
Tile Hill	d					15 40									15 55			16 14				
Canley	d					15 44												16 17				
Coventry	a			15 24	15 30	15 47			15 49						16 00		16 10	16 20			16 24	16 30
	d				15 31	15 48			15 51						16 01		16 11	16 21				16 31
Rugby	d					15 59									16 12	16 20	16 23	16 32				
Long Buckby	d					16 09									16 22			16 42				
Northampton	a					16 21									16 34	16 39		16 54				
London Euston ■ ⊖	a				16 34	17 27			16 54						17 49		17 14	18 17				17 34

		LM	LM	LM	VT	AW	XC	LM	LM	LM	LM	LM	VT	LM	VT	LM	XC	VT	LM	LM	LM	VT	AW
		◇■		◇■	◇■	◇	◇■			◇■	◇■	◇■	◇■	◇■	◇■		◇■	◇■	◇■		◇■	◇■	◇
Stafford	d			15 43			16 03			16 10		16 21					16 25				16 46		
Penkridge	d									16 16													
Wolverhampton ■	a			15 56			16 16			16 27							16 39				16 59		
	d		15 49	15 57		16 09	16 17		16 19	16 28					16 32	16 37	16 41	16 45		16 49	16 59		17 09
Coseley	d		15 54	16 03					16 24											16 54	17 05		
Tipton	d		15 56						16 26											16 56			
Dudley Port	d		15 58						16 28											16 58			
Sandwell & Dudley	d		16 02						16 32							16 46		16 56		17 02			
Smethwick Galton Bridge ■	d		16 04			16 20			16 34	16 40										17 04			17 22
Smethwick Rolfe Street	d		16 06						16 36											17 06			
Birmingham New Street ■	a		16 14	16 17		16 26	16 39		16 44	16 47					16 55	16 55	16 58	17 06		17 14	17 18		17 28
	d	16 13			16 30	16 36		16 39			16 33		16 50	16 53			17 04	17 10	17 13			17 30	17 37
Adderley Park	d							16 44											17 17				
Stechford	d	16 20						16 47											17 21				
Lea Hall	d	16 23						16 50											17 23				
Marston Green	d	16 26									16 41			17 01					17 26				
Birmingham International	a	16 29			16 39	16 50		16 54			16 45		16 59	17 05			17 13	17 19	17 29			17 39	17 50
	d	16 29			16 40						16 45		17 00	17 05			17 14	17 20	17 30			17 40	
Hampton-in-Arden	d	16 32									16 48								17 33				
Berkswell	d	16 37												17 11					17 38				
Tile Hill	d	16 40									16 55			17 14					17 41				
Canley	d	16 44												17 17					17 44				
Coventry	a	16 47			16 49						17 00		17 10	17 20			17 24	17 30	17 47			17 49	
	d	16 48			16 51						17 01		17 11	17 21				17 31	17 48			17 51	
Rugby	d	16 59									17 12	17 20	17 23	17 32					17 59				
Long Buckby	d	17 09									17 22			17 42					18 09				
Northampton	a	17 21									17 34	17 39		17 54					18 21				
London Euston ■ ⊖	a	18 27			17 52						18 49		18 14	19 17				18 34	19 45			18 54	

Stafford - Wolverhampton - Birmingham - Coventry - Northampton

Network Diagram - see first Page of Table 67

		XC	LM	LM	LM	LM	LM	VT	LM	VT	LM	XC	VT	LM	LM	LM	VT	LM	AW	XC	LM	LM	LM
		◇■ ⊼			◇■	◇■	◇■	◇■ ⊏	◇■	◇■ ⊏		◇■ ⊼	◇■ ⊏	◇■		◇■	◇■ ⊏	◇■	◇ ⊼	◇■ ⊼			◇■
Stafford	d	17 03			17 10		17 21					17 26				17 43				18 04			18 10
Penkridge	d				17 16																		18 16
Wolverhampton ■	a	17 16			17 27							17 39				17 56				18 16			18 27
	d	17 17		17 19	17 28					17 32	17 37	17 41	17 45		17 49	17 57			18 09	18 17		18 19	18 28
Coseley	d			17 24											17 54	18 03						18 24	
Tipton	d			17 26											17 56							18 26	
Dudley Port	d			17 28											17 58							18 28	
Sandwell & Dudley	d			17 32							17 46		17 56		18 02							18 32	
Smethwick Galton Bridge ■	d			17 34	17 40										18 04				18 20			18 34	18 40
Smethwick Rolfe Street	d			17 36											18 06							18 36	
Birmingham New Street ■	a	17 39		17 44	17 47					17 55	17 55	17 58	18 06		18 14	18 17			18 26	18 38		18 44	18 47
	d		17 39			17 33		17 50	17 53			18 04	18 10	18 13			18 30	18 33	18 36		18 39		
Adderley Park	d		17 44																		18 44		
Stechford	d		17 47											18 20							18 47		
Lea Hall	d		17 50											18 23							18 50		
Marston Green	d					17 41			18 01					18 26				18 41					
Birmingham International ✈	a		17 54			17 45		17 59	18 05			18 13	18 19	18 29			18 39	18 45	18 50		18 54		
	d					17 45		18 00	18 05			18 14	18 20	18 29			18 40	18 45					
Hampton-in-Arden	d					17 48								18 32				18 48					
Berkswell	d								18 11					18 37									
Tile Hill	d					17 55			18 14					18 40				18 55					
Canley	d								18 17					18 44									
Coventry	a					18 00		18 10	18 20			18 24	18 30	18 47			18 49	19 00					
	d					18 01		18 11	18 21				18 31	18 48			18 51	19 01					
Rugby	d					18 12	18 20	18 23	18 32					18 59				19 12					
Long Buckby	d					18 22			18 42					19 09				19 22					
Northampton	a					18 34	18 39		18 54					19 21				19 40					
London Euston ■ ⊖	a					19 49		19 14	20 21				19 34	20 45			19 54						

(London Euston 19 49 is printed bracketed under both of the two LM columns that arrive at Northampton at 18 34 and 18 39.)

		LM	VT	LM	VT	LM	XC	VT	LM	LM	LM	LM	AW	XC	LM	LM	LM	LM	LM	VT	LM	XC
		◇■	◇■ ⊏	◇■	◇■ ⊏		◇■ ⊼	◇■ ⊏	◇■		◇■	◇■	◇ ⊼	◇■ ⊼			◇■	◇■	◇■	◇■ ⊏		◇■ ⊼
Stafford	d	18 21					18 27				18 43			19 03			19 10	19 21				19 25
Penkridge	d																19 16					
Wolverhampton ■	a						18 40				18 56			19 16			19 27					19 39
	d				18 32	18 37	18 41	18 45		18 49	18 57		19 09	19 17		19 19	19 28			19 32	19 37	19 41
Coseley	d									18 54	19 03					19 24						
Tipton	d									18 56						19 26						
Dudley Port	d									18 58						19 28						
Sandwell & Dudley	d					18 46		18 56		19 02						19 32					19 46	
Smethwick Galton Bridge ■	d									19 04			19 20			19 34	19 40					
Smethwick Rolfe Street	d									19 06						19 36						
Birmingham New Street ■	a				18 55	18 55	18 58	19 06		19 14	19 17		19 26	19 33		19 44	19 47			19 55	19 55	19 58
	d		18 50	18 53			19 04	19 10	19 13			19 33	19 36		19 39				19 53			20 04
Adderley Park	d														19 44							
Stechford	d								19 20						19 47							
Lea Hall	d								19 23						19 50							
Marston Green	d			19 01					19 26			19 41							20 01			
Birmingham International ✈	a		18 59	19 05			19 13	19 19	19 29			19 45	19 50		19 54				20 05			20 13
	d		19 00	19 05			19 14	19 20	19 29			19 45							20 05			20 14
Hampton-in-Arden	d								19 32			19 48										
Berkswell	d			19 11					19 37										20 11			
Tile Hill	d			19 14					19 40			19 55							20 14			
Canley	d			19 17					19 44										20 17			
Coventry	a		19 10	19 20			19 24	19 30	19 47			20 00							20 20			20 24
	d		19 11	19 21				19 31	19 48			20 01							20 21			
Rugby	d	19 20	19 23	19 32				19 44	19 59			20 12						20 20	20 32			
Long Buckby	d			19 42					20 09			20 22							20 42			
Northampton	a	19 43		19 54					20 21			20 34						20 40	20 54			
London Euston ■ ⊖	a		20 15	21 09				20 55	21 45										22 11			

Table 68

Saturdays
from 15 September

Stafford - Wolverhampton - Birmingham - Coventry - Northampton

Network Diagram - see first Page of Table 67

		VT	LM	LM	LM	LM	AW	XC	LM	LM	LM	LM	LM	VT	LM	XC	VT	LM	LM	LM	VT	XC	LM
		◇■ ⊏	■		◇■	◇■	◇ ⊼	◇■ ⊼			◇■	■	◇■	◇■ ⊏		◇■ A ⊼	◇■ ⊏	■		◇■	◇■ ⊏	◇■	◇■
Stafford	d				19 43			20 03			20 12	20 21				20 26				20 45		21 03	
Penkridge	d				19 49															20 51			
Wolverhampton ■	a				19 59			20 16			20 28					20 39				21 01		21 15	
	d	19 45		19 49	19 59		20 10	20 17		20 19	20 28			20 33	20 37	20 41	20 45		20 49	21 01	21 07	21 16	
Coseley	d			19 54	20 04					20 24									20 54	21 06			
Tipton	d			19 56						20 26									20 56				
Dudley Port	d			19 58						20 28									20 58				
Sandwell & Dudley	d	19 56		20 02						20 32					20 46		20 56		21 02		21 17		
Smethwick Galton Bridge ■	d			20 04			20 21			20 34	20 40								21 04				
Smethwick Rolfe Street	d			20 06						20 36									21 06				
Birmingham New Street ■	a	20 06		20 14	20 17		20 26	20 33		20 44	20 47			20 55	20 57	20 58	21 06		21 14	21 19	21 26	21 32	
	d	20 10	20 13			20 33	20 36		20 39				20 53			21 04	21 10	21 13			21 30		21 33
Adderley Park	d								20 44														
Stechford	d		20 20						20 47									21 20					
Lea Hall	d		20 23						20 50									21 23					
Marston Green	d		20 26			20 41							21 01					21 26					21 41
Birmingham International ✈	a	20 19	20 29			20 45	20 49		20 54				21 05			21 13	21 19	21 29			21 39		21 45
	d	20 20	20 29			20 45							21 05			21 14	21 20	21 29			21 40		21 45
Hampton-in-Arden	d		20 32			20 48												21 32					21 48
Berkswell	d		20 37										21 11					21 37					
Tile Hill	d		20 40			20 55							21 14					21 40					21 55
Canley	d		20 44										21 17					21 44					
Coventry	a	20 30	20 47			21 00							21 20			21 24	21 30	21 47			21 50		22 00
	d	20 31				21 01							21 21				21 31				21 51		22 01
Rugby	d	20 43				21 12						21 20	21 32				21 43				22 03		22 12
Long Buckby	d					21 22							21 42										22 22
Northampton	a					21 34						21 40	21 54										22 34
London Euston ■ ⊖	a	21 56											23 27				22 55				23 30		

		LM	LM	LM	VT	LM	XC	LM	LM	LM	AW	XC	LM	LM	VT	LM	LM	VT	XC	LM	LM	LM
				◇■	◇■ ⊏		◇■	■		◇■	◇	◇■	■		◇■ ⊏	◇■		◇■ ⊏	◇■	■		◇■
Stafford	d						21 27			21 42		22 03			22 08			22 25	22 33			22 47
Penkridge	d									21 48												22 53
Wolverhampton ■	a						21 39			21 58		22 14			22 22			22 39	22 45			23 03
	d		21 19		21 33	21 37	21 41		21 49	21 58	22 08	22 16		22 19	22 23		22 37	22 40	22 46		22 49	23 03
Coseley	d		21 24						21 54	22 04				22 24							22 54	23 09
Tipton	d		21 26						21 56					22 26							22 56	
Dudley Port	d		21 28						21 58					22 28							22 58	
Sandwell & Dudley	d		21 32			21 46			22 02					22 32			22 46				23 02	
Smethwick Galton Bridge ■	d		21 34						22 04		22 19			22 34							23 04	
Smethwick Rolfe Street	d		21 36						22 06					22 36							23 06	
Birmingham New Street ■	a		21 44		21 54	21 55	21 58		22 14	22 20	22 32	22 32		22 44	22 46		22 55	22 59	23 02		23 14	23 21
	d	21 39		21 53				22 13					22 33			22 53				23 13		
Adderley Park	d	21 44																		23 18		
Stechford	d	21 47						22 20												23 21		
Lea Hall	d	21 50						22 23												23 24		
Marston Green	d			22 01				22 26					22 41			23 01				23 27		
Birmingham International ✈	a	21 54		22 05				22 29					22 45			23 05				23 30		
	d			22 05				22 29					22 45			23 05				23 30		
Hampton-in-Arden	d							22 32					22 48							23 33		
Berkswell	d			22 11				22 37								23 11				23 38		
Tile Hill	d			22 14				22 40					22 55			23 14				23 41		
Canley	d			22 17				22 44								23 17				23 45		
Coventry	a			22 20				22 47					23 00			23 20				23 48		
	d			22 21												23 21						
Rugby	d			22 32												23 32						
Long Buckby	d			22 41												23 42						
Northampton	a			22 53												23 55						
London Euston ■ ⊖	a			00 17																		

A ⊼ to Birmingham New Street

Stafford - Wolverhampton - Birmingham - Coventry - Northampton

Saturdays from 15 September

Network Diagram - see first Page of Table 67

		AW
		◇
Stafford	d	
Penkridge	d	
Wolverhampton 7	a	
	d	23 08
Coseley	d	
Tipton	d	
Dudley Port	d	
Sandwell & Dudley	d	
Smethwick Galton Bridge 7	d	
Smethwick Rolfe Street	d	
Birmingham New Street 12	a	23 28
	d	
Adderley Park	d	
Stechford	d	
Lea Hall	d	
Marston Green	d	
Birmingham International	a	
	d	
Hampton-in-Arden	d	
Berkswell	d	
Tile Hill	d	
Canley	d	
Coventry	a	
	d	
Rugby	d	
Long Buckby	d	
Northampton	a	
London Euston 15 ⊖	a	

Sundays until 24 June

		LM	LM	VT	LM	LM	XC	LM	LM	VT	AW	LM	XC	LM	LM	VT	AW	LM	XC	LM	LM	LM	VT
		◇1		◇1	1	1	◇1	◇1		◇1		1	◇1 A	◇1		◇1		1	◇1 A	◇1	◇1		◇1
			🚌	⊐			⊥		🚌	⊐			⊐⊥		🚌	⊐			⊐⊥			🚌	⊐
Stafford	d												09 07						10 10	10 15			
Penkridge	d																						
Wolverhampton 7	a												09 26						10 25				
	d		07 46	08 03					08 46	09 01	09 04		09 27		09 46	09 51	09 59		10 26			10 46	10 51
Coseley	d		07 57						08 57						09 57							10 57	
Tipton	d		08 06						09 06						10 06							11 06	
Dudley Port	d		08 14						09 14						10 14							11 14	
Sandwell & Dudley	d		08 23						09 23						10 23							11 23	
Smethwick Galton Bridge 7	d		08 29						09 29						10 29							11 29	
Smethwick Rolfe Street	d		08 33						09 33						10 33							11 33	
Birmingham New Street 12	a		08 48	08 27					09 48	09 24	09 34		09 58		10 48	10 20	10 28		10 56			11 48	11 20
	d	21p53		08 30	08 34	08 38	09 04	09 14		09 30		09 34	10 04	10 14		10 30		10 34	11 04		11 14		11 30
Adderley Park	d					08 42						09 38						10 38					
Stechford	d					08 46						09 42						10 42					
Lea Hall	d					08 48						09 44						10 44					
Marston Green	d	22p01			08 42	08 52		09 22				09 48		10 22				10 48			11 22		
Birmingham International	a	22p05		08 39	08 45	08 55	09 13	09 25		09 39		09 51	10 13	10 25		10 39		10 52	11 13		11 25		11 39
	d	22p05		08 40	08 45		09 14	09 25		09 40		09 51	10 14	10 25		10 40		10 52	11 14		11 25		11 40
Hampton-in-Arden	d							09 28						10 28							11 28		
Berkswell	d	22p11			08 51			09 33						10 33							11 33		
Tile Hill	d	22p14			08 54			09 36						10 36							11 36		
Canley	d	22p17			08 57			09 40						10 40							11 40		
Coventry	a	22p20		08 50	09 00		09 24	09 44		09 50		10 01	10 24	10 44		10 50		11 03	11 24		11 44		11 50
	d	22p21		08 51				09 44		09 51				10 44		10 51					11 44		11 51
Rugby	d	22p32		09 04				09 55		10 04				10 55		11 04				11 14	11 55		12 05
Long Buckby	d	22p41						10 05						11 05						11 24	12 05		
Northampton	a	22p53						10 17						11 17						11 36	12 17		
London Euston 15 ⊖	a	00 17		10 28				11 59		11 31				12 37		12 27				12 50	13 37		13 03

A ⊐ from Birmingham New Street ⊥ to Birmingham New Street

Stafford - Wolverhampton - Birmingham - Coventry - Northampton

Sundays until 24 June

Network Diagram - see first Page of Table 67

		LM	AW	LM	LM	VT	XC	VT	VT	LM	VT	LM	LM	LM	AW	VT	XC	VT	VT	LM	LM	LM	VT
		◇1	◇	◇1	1	◇1	◇1 A	◇1	◇1	◇1	◇1	◇1	1		◇	◇1	◇1 A	◇1	◇1	◇1		◇1	◇1
						⊐	⊐⊥	⊐	⊐		⊐			🚌	⊥	⊐	⊐⊥	⊐	⊐		🚌		⊐
Stafford	d	10 41		11 19			11 05					12 19					12 03					12 42	
Penkridge	d	10 49																				12 49	
Wolverhampton 7	a	10 59					11 24										12 23					12 59	
	d	10 59	11 02				11 25	11 32	11 42					11 46	12 17		12 24	12 32	12 42		12 46	12 59	
Coseley	d													11 57							12 57		
Tipton	d													12 06							13 06		
Dudley Port	d													12 14							13 14		
Sandwell & Dudley	d													12 23							13 23		
Smethwick Galton Bridge 7	d													12 29							13 29		
Smethwick Rolfe Street	d													12 33							13 33		
Birmingham New Street 12	a	11 25	11 32				11 56	12 04	12 06					12 48	12 49		12 52	13 06	13 06		13 48	13 27	
	d				11 34	11 50	12 04		12 10	12 14	12 30		12 34			12 50	13 04		13 10	13 14			13 30
Adderley Park	d				11 38								12 38										
Stechford	d				11 42								12 42										
Lea Hall	d				11 44								12 44										
Marston Green	d				11 48					12 22			12 48							13 22			
Birmingham International	a				11 51	11 59	12 13		12 19	12 25	12 38		12 51			12 59	13 13		13 19	13 25			13 38
	d				11 51	12 00	12 14		12 20	12 25	12 39		12 51			13 00	13 14		13 20	13 25			13 39
Hampton-in-Arden	d									12 28										13 28			
Berkswell	d									12 33										13 33			
Tile Hill	d									12 36			12 58							13 36			
Canley	d									12 40										13 40			
Coventry	a				12 01	12 10	12 24		12 30	12 44	12 49		13 04			13 10	13 24		13 30	13 44			13 49
	d					12 11			12 31	12 44	12 51					13 11			13 31	13 44			13 51
Rugby	d			12 20		12 25				12 55		13 20				13 25				13 55			
Long Buckby	d			12 29						13 05		13 29								14 05			
Northampton	a			12 41						13 17		13 41								14 17			
London Euston 15 ⊖	a			13 53		13 19			13 37	14 37	13 57	14 53				14 17			14 37	15 37			14 57

		LM	LM	AW	VT	XC	VT	VT	LM	LM	XC	VT	LM	LM	LM	AW	VT	XC	VT	VT	LM	LM
		◇1	1	◇	◇1	◇1 A	◇1	◇1	◇1		◇1	◇1	◇1	◇1	1	◇	◇1	◇1 A	◇1	◇1	◇1	
				⊥	⊐	⊐⊥	⊐	⊐		🚌	⊥	⊐				⊥	⊐	⊐⊥	⊐	⊐		🚌
Stafford	d	13 19				13 07							13 43	14 19				14 02				
Penkridge	d												13 49									
Wolverhampton 7	a					13 21							13 59					14 20				
	d			13 09		13 22	13 32	13 42		13 46	13 53		13 59			14 08		14 21	14 33	14 42		14 46
Coseley	d									13 57												14 57
Tipton	d									14 06												15 06
Dudley Port	d									14 14												15 14
Sandwell & Dudley	d									14 23												15 23
Smethwick Galton Bridge 7	d									14 29												15 29
Smethwick Rolfe Street	d									14 33												15 33
Birmingham New Street 12	a			13 42		13 56	14 04	14 06		14 48	14 27		14 31			14 40		14 56	15 05	15 06		15 48
	d		13 34		13 50	14 04		14 10	14 14			14 30			14 34		14 50	15 04		15 10	15 14	
Adderley Park	d		13 38												14 38							
Stechford	d		13 42												14 42							
Lea Hall	d		13 44												14 44							
Marston Green	d		13 48						14 22						14 48						15 22	
Birmingham International	a		13 51		13 59	14 13		14 19	14 25			14 38			14 51		14 59	15 13		15 19	15 25	
	d		13 51		14 01	14 14		14 20	14 25			14 39			14 51		15 01	15 14		15 20	15 25	
Hampton-in-Arden	d								14 28												15 28	
Berkswell	d								14 33												15 33	
Tile Hill	d		13 58						14 36						14 58						15 36	
Canley	d								14 40												15 40	
Coventry	a		14 04		14 11	14 24		14 30	14 44			14 49			15 04		15 11	15 24		15 30	15 44	
	d				14 11			14 31	14 44			14 51					15 11			15 31	15 44	
Rugby	d	14 20			14 26				14 55					15 20			15 26				15 55	
Long Buckby	d	14 29							15 05					15 29							16 05	
Northampton	a	14 41							15 17					15 41							16 17	
London Euston 15 ⊖	a	15 53			15 17			15 37	16 37			15 57		16 53			16 17			16 37	17 37	

A ⊐ from Birmingham New Street ⊥ to Birmingham New Street

Table 68

Sundays until 24 June

Stafford - Wolverhampton - Birmingham - Coventry - Northampton

Network Diagram - see first Page of Table 67

	XC	VT	LM	LM	LM	AW	VT	XC	VT	VT	LM	LM	XC	VT	LM	LM	AW	LM	VT	XC	VT	VT
	◇1 ⌶	◇1 ⊐	◇1	◇1	1	◇	◇1 ⊐	◇1 A ⊐⌶	◇1 ⊐	◇1 ⊐	◇1	🚌	◇1 ⌶	◇1 ⊐	1	◇1	◇ ⌶	◇1	◇1 ⊐	◇1 A ⊐⌶	◇1 ⊐	◇1 ⊐
Stafford d			14 43	15 20				15 06								15 44		16 19		16 06		
Penkridge d			14 49													15 50						
Wolverhampton 7 ⇌ a			14 59					15 19								16 00				16 21		
d	14 54		14 59			15 09		15 20	15 32	15 43		15 46	15 54			16 00	16 09			16 22	16 32	16 42
Coseley d												15 57										
Tipton d												16 06										
Dudley Port d												16 14										
Sandwell & Dudley d												16 23										
Smethwick Galton Bridge 7 d												16 29										
Smethwick Rolfe Street d												16 33										
Birmingham New Street 12 a	15 27		15 31			15 40		15 56	16 07	16 06		16 48	16 27			16 35	16 41			16 52	17 07	17 06
d		15 30			15 34		15 50	16 04		16 10	16 14			16 30	16 34				16 50	17 04		17 10
Adderley Park d					15 38										16 38							
Stechford d					15 42										16 42							
Lea Hall d					15 44										16 44							
Marston Green d					15 48						16 22				16 48							
Birmingham International ✈ a		15 38			15 51		15 59	16 13		16 19	16 25			16 38	16 51				16 59	17 13		17 19
d		15 39			15 51		16 01	16 14		16 20	16 25			16 39	16 51				17 01	17 14		17 20
Hampton-in-Arden d											16 28											
Berkswell d											16 33											
Tile Hill d					15 58						16 36				16 58							
Canley d											16 40											
Coventry a		15 49			16 04		16 11	16 24		16 30	16 44			16 49	17 05				17 11	17 24		17 30
d		15 51					16 11			16 31	16 44			16 51					17 11			17 31
Rugby d				16 20			16 24				16 55							17 20	17 26			
Long Buckby d				16 29							17 05							17 29				
Northampton a				16 41							17 17							17 41				
London Euston 15 ⊖ a		16 57		17 53			17 17			17 37	18 37			17 57				18 53	18 17			18 37

	LM	LM	XC	VT	LM	LM	LM	VT	AW	XC	VT	VT	LM	LM	XC	VT	LM	LM	LM	AW	VT
	◇1	🚌	◇1 ⌶	◇1 ⊐	◇1	◇1	1	◇1 ⊐	◇ ⌶	◇1 A ⊐⌶	◇1 ⊐	◇1 ⊐	◇1	🚌	◇1 ⌶	◇1 ⊐	◇1	◇1	1	◇ ⌶	◇1 ⊐
Stafford d					16 44	17 21				17 06							17 44	18 19			
Penkridge d					16 50												17 50				
Wolverhampton 7 ⇌ a					17 00					17 20							18 00				
d		16 46	16 54		17 00				17 19	17 24	17 33	17 43		17 46	17 54		18 00			18 09	
Coseley d		16 57												17 57							
Tipton d		17 06												18 06							
Dudley Port d		17 14												18 14							
Sandwell & Dudley d		17 23												18 23							
Smethwick Galton Bridge 7 d		17 29												18 29							
Smethwick Rolfe Street d		17 33												18 33							
Birmingham New Street 12 a		17 48	17 28		17 32				17 53	17 56	18 06	18 06		18 48	18 27		18 32			18 41	
d	17 14			17 30			17 34	17 50		18 04		18 10	18 14			18 30			18 34		18 50
Adderley Park d							17 38												18 38		
Stechford d							17 42												18 42		
Lea Hall d							17 44												18 44		
Marston Green d	17 22						17 48						18 22						18 48		
Birmingham International ✈ a	17 25			17 38			17 51	17 59		18 13		18 19	18 25			18 38			18 51		18 59
d	17 25			17 39			17 51	18 01		18 14		18 20	18 25			18 39			18 51		19 01
Hampton-in-Arden d	17 28												18 28								
Berkswell d	17 33												18 33								
Tile Hill d	17 36						17 58						18 36						18 58		
Canley d	17 40												18 40								
Coventry a	17 44			17 49			18 05	18 11		18 24		18 30	18 44			18 49			19 05		19 11
d	17 44			17 51				18 11				18 31	18 44			18 51					19 11
Rugby d	17 55					18 20		18 26					18 55					19 20			19 26
Long Buckby d	18 05					18 29							19 05					19 29			
Northampton a	18 17					18 41							19 17					19 41			
London Euston 15 ⊖ a	19 37			18 57		19 53		19 17				19 37	20 37			19 57		20 53			20 17

A ⊐ from Birmingham New Street ⌶ to Birmingham New Street

Table 68

Sundays until 24 June

Stafford - Wolverhampton - Birmingham - Coventry - Northampton

Network Diagram - see first Page of Table 67

	XC	VT	VT	LM	LM	XC	VT	LM	LM	AW	XC	VT	VT	LM	LM	LM	XC	VT	LM	LM	AW	XC
	◇1 A ⊐⌶	◇1 ⊐	◇1 ⊐	◇1	🚌	◇1 ⌶	◇1 ⊐	◇1	1	◇	◇1 A ⊐⌶	◇1 ⊐	◇1 ⊐	◇1	◇1	🚌	◇1 ⌶	◇1 ⊐	◇1	1	◇ ⌶	◇1 B ⌶
Stafford d	18 06							18 44			19 03			19 22					19 44			20 05
Penkridge d								18 50											19 50			
Wolverhampton 7 ⇌ a	18 20							19 00			19 20								20 00			20 20
d	18 21	18 33	18 43		18 46	18 54		19 00		19 09	19 21	19 32	19 43			19 46	19 54		20 01		20 08	20 21
Coseley d					18 57											19 57						
Tipton d					19 06											20 06						
Dudley Port d					19 14											20 14						
Sandwell & Dudley d					19 23											20 23						
Smethwick Galton Bridge 7 d					19 29											20 29						
Smethwick Rolfe Street d					19 33											20 33						
Birmingham New Street 12 a	18 56	19 06	19 06		19 48	19 27		19 32		19 39	19 50	20 06	20 06			20 48	20 27		20 32		20 40	20 50
d	19 04		19 10	19 14			19 30		19 34		20 04		20 10		20 14			20 30		20 34		21 04
Adderley Park d									19 38											20 38		
Stechford d									19 42											20 42		
Lea Hall d									19 44											20 44		
Marston Green d				19 22					19 48						20 22					20 48		
Birmingham International ✈ a	19 13		19 19	19 25			19 38		19 51		20 13		20 19		20 25			20 39		20 51		21 13
d	19 14		19 20	19 25			19 39		19 51		20 14		20 20		20 25			20 40		20 51		21 14
Hampton-in-Arden d				19 28											20 28							
Berkswell d				19 33											20 33							
Tile Hill d				19 36					19 58						20 36					20 58		
Canley d				19 40											20 40							
Coventry a	19 24		19 30	19 44			19 49		20 05		20 24		20 30		20 43			20 50		21 04		21 23
d			19 31	19 44			19 51						20 31		20 43			20 51				
Rugby d				19 55										20 19	20 55			21 05				
Long Buckby d				20 05										20 28	21 05							
Northampton a				20 17										20 40	21 17							
London Euston 15 ⊖ a			20 37	21 42			20 57						21 49	21 54	22 44			22 23				

	LM	VT	LM	LM	VT	XC	LM	LM	AW	XC	AW	LM	LM	LM	VT	LM	LM	AW	VT	LM	XC	VT
	◇1	◇1 ⊐	◇1	🚌	◇1 ⊐	◇1	◇1	1		◇1	◇ ⌶	◇1	◇1	🚌	◇1 ⊐	◇1	1	◇	◇1 ⊐	🚌	◇1	◇1 ⊐
Stafford d	20 18					20 45	20 39			21 08	21 16	21 24				21 38			22 02		22 06	
Penkridge d							20 45									21 45						
Wolverhampton 7 ⇌ a						20 57	20 55			21 21	21 34					21 55			22 16		22 20	
d		20 33		20 46	20 50	20 58	21 03		21 12	21 22	21 35			21 46	21 50	22 01		22 08	22 16	22 16	22 22	22 33
Coseley d				20 57										21 57						22 27		
Tipton d				21 06										22 06						22 36		
Dudley Port d				21 14										22 14						22 44		
Sandwell & Dudley d				21 23										22 23						22 53		
Smethwick Galton Bridge 7 d				21 29										22 29						22 59		
Smethwick Rolfe Street d				21 33										22 33						23 03		
Birmingham New Street 12 a		21 06		21 48	21 15	21 27	21 32		21 41	21 50	22 06			22 48	22 15	22 26		22 37	22 52	23 18	22 52	22 56
d			21 14		21 30			21 34					22 14		22 30		22 34					23 00
Adderley Park d								21 38									22 38					
Stechford d								21 42									22 42					
Lea Hall d								21 44									22 45					
Marston Green d			21 22					21 48					22 22				22 48					
Birmingham International ✈ a			21 25		21 39			21 51					22 25		22 39		22 51					23 09
d			21 25		21 40			21 51					22 25		22 40		22 52					23 10
Hampton-in-Arden d			21 28										22 28									
Berkswell d			21 33										22 33									
Tile Hill d			21 36										22 36									
Canley d			21 40										22 40									
Coventry a			21 44		21 50			22 01					22 44		22 50		23 01					23 20
d			21 44		21 51								22 44		22 51							23 21
Rugby d	21 19		21 55		22 04							22 20	22 55		23 04							23 34
Long Buckby d	21 28		22 05									22 29	23 05									
Northampton a	21 40		22 17									22 43	23 17									23s54
London Euston 15 ⊖ a	23 14		23 41		23 25										00 27							01 01

A ⊐ from Birmingham New Street ⌶ to Birmingham New Street

B ⌶ to Birmingham New Street

Table 68

Stafford - Wolverhampton - Birmingham - Coventry - Northampton

Network Diagram - see first Page of Table 67

		VT	LM	LM	XC
		◇1 ⊏	1	◇1	◇1
Stafford	d			22 45	23 05
Penkridge	d			22 51	
Wolverhampton 7	a			23 01	23 18
	d	22 35		23 01	23 20
Coseley	d				
Tipton	d				
Dudley Port	d				
Sandwell & Dudley	d				
Smethwick Galton Bridge 7	d				
Smethwick Rolfe Street	d				
Birmingham New Street 12	a	23 06		23 26	23 49
	d		23 14		
Adderley Park	d		23 19		
Stechford	d		23 22		
Lea Hall	d		23 25		
Marston Green	d		23 28		
Birmingham International	a		23 31		
	d		23 32		
Hampton-in-Arden	d		23 35		
Berkswell	d		23 40		
Tile Hill	d		23 43		
Canley	d		23 46		
Coventry	a		23 50		
	d				
Rugby	d				
Long Buckby	d				
Northampton	a				
London Euston 15	a				

		LM	VT	VT	LM	LM	LM	LM	AW	VT	LM	LM	XC	LM	AW	VT	LM	LM	LM	XC	LM	AW	LM
		◇1	◇1 A ⊏	◇1 ⊏	1	1		◇1		◇1 ⊏	1		◇1 ⊼	◇1		◇1 ⊏	◇1	1		◇1 ⊼	◇1	◇	◇1
Stafford	d												09 26				10 15			10 27			10 41
Penkridge	d																						10 49
Wolverhampton 7	a												09 40							10 42			11 00
	d		07 05	08 05			08 22		09 00	09 05		09 22	09 41		09 59	10 05			10 22	10 43		10 57	11 01
Coseley	d						08 27					09 27							10 27				
Tipton	d						08 29					09 29							10 29				
Dudley Port	d						08 31					09 31							10 31				
Sandwell & Dudley	d		07 15	08 15			08 35			09 15		09 35				10 15			10 35				
Smethwick Galton Bridge 7	d						08 37					09 37							10 37				
Smethwick Rolfe Street	d						08 39					09 39							10 39				
Birmingham New Street 12	a		07 24	08 24			08 46		09 15	09 24		09 46	09 58		10 14	10 24			10 46	10 59		11 13	11 17
	d	21p53	07 30	08 30	08 34	08 38		09 14	09 20	09 30	09 34			10 14	10 20	10 30		10 34			11 14	11 19	
Adderley Park	d					08 42					09 38							10 38					
Stechford	d					08 46					09 42							10 42					
Lea Hall	d					08 48					09 44							10 44					
Marston Green	d	22p01			08 42	08 52		09 22			09 48			10 22				10 48			11 22		
Birmingham International	a	22p05	07 40	08 39	08 45	08 55		09 25	09 31	09 39	09 51			10 25	10 32	10 39		10 52			11 25	11 31	
	d	22p05	07 40	08 40	08 45			09 25		09 40	09 51			10 25		10 40		10 52			11 25		
Hampton-in-Arden	d							09 28						10 28							11 28		
Berkswell	d	22p11			08 51			09 33						10 33							11 33		
Tile Hill	d	22p14			08 54			09 36						10 36							11 36		
Canley	d	22p17			08 57			09 40						10 40							11 40		
Coventry	a	22p20	07 50	08 50	09 00			09 44		09 50	10 01			10 44		10 50		11 03			11 44		
	d	22p21	07 51	08 51				09 44		09 51				10 44		10 51					11 44		
Rugby	d	22p32	08 03	09 04				09 55		10 04				10 55		11 04	11 14				11 55		
Long Buckby	d	22p41						10 05						11 05			11 24				12 05		
Northampton	a	22p53						10 17						11 17			11 36				12 17		
London Euston 15	a	00 17	09 16	10 28				11 59		11 31				12 37		12 27	12 50				13 37		

A from 29 July until 12 August, then from 2 September

Table 68

Stafford - Wolverhampton - Birmingham - Coventry - Northampton

Network Diagram - see first Page of Table 67

		VT	LM	LM	LM	VT	VT	XC	VT	LM	VT	LM	LM	AW	LM	VT	VT	XC	VT	LM	LM	VT	LM
		◇1 ⊏	◇1	1		◇1 ⊏	◇1 ⊏	◇1 ⊼	◇1 ⊏	◇1	◇1 ⊏	◇1	1	◇ ⊼		◇1 ⊏	◇1 ⊏	◇1 ⊼	◇1 ⊏	◇1	◇1	◇1 ⊏	◇1
Stafford	d		11 19					11 28				12 19						12 25			12 42		13 19
Penkridge	d																				12 49		
Wolverhampton 7	a							11 41										12 40			12 59		
	d	11 05			11 22		11 32	11 42	11 45					12 17	12 22		12 32	12 41	12 45		13 00		
Coseley	d				11 27										12 27								
Tipton	d				11 29										12 29								
Dudley Port	d				11 31										12 31								
Sandwell & Dudley	d	11 15			11 35				11 57						12 35				12 55				
Smethwick Galton Bridge 7	d				11 37										12 37								
Smethwick Rolfe Street	d				11 39										12 39								
Birmingham New Street 12	a	11 26			11 48		11 55	12 00	12 06					12 32	12 46		12 55	12 58	13 06		13 16		
	d	11 30		11 34		11 50			12 10	12 14	12 30		12 34	12 37		12 50			13 10	13 14		13 30	
Adderley Park	d			11 38									12 38										
Stechford	d			11 42									12 42										
Lea Hall	d			11 44									12 44										
Marston Green	d			11 48						12 22			12 48							13 22			
Birmingham International	a	11 39		11 51		11 59			12 19	12 25	12 38		12 51	12 56		12 59			13 19	13 25		13 38	
	d	11 40		11 51		12 00			12 20	12 25	12 39		12 51			13 00			13 20	13 25		13 39	
Hampton-in-Arden	d									12 28										13 28			
Berkswell	d									12 33										13 33			
Tile Hill	d									12 36			12 58							13 36			
Canley	d									12 40										13 40			
Coventry	a	11 50		12 01		12 10			12 30	12 44	12 49		13 04			13 10			13 30	13 44		13 49	
	d	11 51				12 11			12 31	12 44	12 51					13 11			13 31	13 44		13 51	
Rugby	d	12 05	12 20			12 25				12 55		13 20				13 25				13 55			14 20
Long Buckby	d		12 29							13 05		13 29								14 05			14 29
Northampton	a		12 41							13 17		13 41								14 17			14 41
London Euston 15	a	13 04	13 53			13 19			13 37	14 37	13 57	14 53				14 18			14 37	15 37		14 57	15 53

		LM	AW	LM	VT	VT	XC	VT	LM	LM	VT	AW	XC	LM	LM	LM	VT	VT	XC	VT	LM	LM
		1	◇ ⊼		◇1 ⊏	◇1 ⊏	◇1 ⊼	◇1 ⊏	◇1	◇1	◇1 ⊏	◇ ⊼	◇1 ⊼	◇1	1		◇1 ⊏	◇1 ⊏	◇1 A ⊏⊼	◇1 ⊏	◇1	◇1
Stafford	d						13 25			13 43				14 19					14 25			14 43
Penkridge	d									13 49												14 49
Wolverhampton 7	a						13 40			13 59									14 40			14 59
	d		13 08	13 22		13 32	13 41	13 45		13 59		14 08	14 15			14 22		14 33	14 41	14 45		14 59
Coseley	d			13 27												14 27						
Tipton	d			13 29												14 29						
Dudley Port	d			13 31												14 31						
Sandwell & Dudley	d			13 35				13 56								14 35				14 56		
Smethwick Galton Bridge 7	d			13 37												14 37						
Smethwick Rolfe Street	d			13 39												14 39						
Birmingham New Street 12	a		13 23	13 46		13 55	13 58	14 06		14 15		14 23	14 31			14 46		14 55	14 58	15 06		15 15
	d	13 34	13 36		13 50		14 04	14 10	14 14		14 30	14 36			14 34		14 50		15 04	15 10	15 14	
Adderley Park	d	13 38													14 38							
Stechford	d	13 42													14 42							
Lea Hall	d	13 44													14 44							
Marston Green	d	13 48							14 22						14 48						15 22	
Birmingham International	a	13 51	13 55		13 59		14 13	14 19	14 25		14 38	14 55			14 51		14 59		15 13	15 19	15 25	
	d	13 51			14 01		14 14	14 20	14 25		14 39				14 51		15 01		15 14	15 20	15 25	
Hampton-in-Arden	d								14 28												15 28	
Berkswell	d								14 33												15 33	
Tile Hill	d	13 58							14 36						14 58						15 36	
Canley	d								14 40												15 40	
Coventry	a	14 04			14 11		14 24	14 30	14 44		14 49				15 04		15 11		15 24	15 30	15 44	
	d				14 11			14 31	14 44		14 51						15 11			15 31	15 44	
Rugby	d				14 26				14 55					15 20			15 26				15 55	
Long Buckby	d								15 05					15 29							16 05	
Northampton	a								15 17					15 41							16 17	
London Euston 15	a				15 17			15 37	16 37		15 57			16 53			16 17			16 37	17 37	

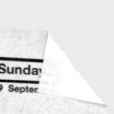

A ⊏ from Birmingham New Street ⊼ to Birmingham New Street

Table 68

Sundays

1 July to 9 September

Stafford - Wolverhampton - Birmingham - Coventry - Northampton

Network Diagram - see first Page of Table 67

		VT	AW	XC	LM	LM	LM	VT	VT	XC	VT	LM	LM	VT	AW	XC	LM	LM	LM	VT	VT	XC	VT
										A												A	
Stafford	d				15 20					15 25			15 43				16 19					16 25	
Penkridge	d												15 49										
Wolverhampton	a									15 40			15 59									16 40	
	d		15 09	15 15			15 22		15 32	15 41	15 45		15 59		16 09	16 15			16 22		16 32	16 41	16 45
Coseley	d						15 27												16 27				
Tipton	d						15 29												16 29				
Dudley Port	d						15 31												16 31				
Sandwell & Dudley	d						15 35				15 56								16 35				16 56
Smethwick Galton Bridge	d						15 37												16 37				
Smethwick Rolfe Street	d						15 39												16 39				
Birmingham New Street	a		15 24	15 31			15 46		15 55	15 58	16 06		16 15		16 24	16 31			16 46		16 55	16 58	17 06
	d	15 30	15 36			15 34		15 50		16 04	16 10	16 14		16 30	16 35			16 34		16 50		17 04	17 10
Adderley Park	d					15 38												16 38					
Stechford	d					15 42												16 42					
Lea Hall	d					15 44												16 44					
Marston Green	d					15 48						16 22						16 48					
Birmingham International	a	15 38	15 55			15 51		15 59		16 13	16 19	16 25		16 38	16 55			16 51		16 59		17 13	17 19
	d	15 39				15 51		16 01		16 14	16 20	16 25		16 39				16 51		17 01		17 14	17 20
Hampton-in-Arden	d											16 28											
Berkswell	d											16 33											
Tile Hill	d					15 58						16 36						16 58					
Canley	d											16 40											
Coventry	a	15 49				16 04		16 11		16 24	16 30	16 44		16 49				17 05		17 11		17 24	17 30
	d	15 51						16 11			16 31	16 44		16 51						17 11			17 31
Rugby	d				16 20			16 24				16 55					17 20			17 26			
Long Buckby	d				16 29							17 05					17 29						
Northampton	a				16 41							17 17					17 41						
London Euston	a	16 57			17 53			17 17			17 37	18 37		17 57			18 53			18 18			18 37

		LM	LM	VT	XC	LM	LM	AW	LM	VT	VT	XC	VT	LM	LM	VT	AW	XC	LM	LM	LM	VT
												A										
Stafford	d		16 43			17 21						17 26			17 43				18 19			
Penkridge	d		16 49												17 49							
Wolverhampton	a		16 59									17 40			17 59							
	d		16 59		17 15			17 19	17 22		17 32	17 41	17 45		17 59		18 09	18 15			18 22	
Coseley	d								17 27												18 27	
Tipton	d								17 29												18 29	
Dudley Port	d								17 31												18 31	
Sandwell & Dudley	d								17 35				17 56								18 35	
Smethwick Galton Bridge	d								17 37												18 37	
Smethwick Rolfe Street	d								17 39												18 39	
Birmingham New Street	a		17 15		17 31			17 35	17 46		17 55	17 58	18 06		18 15		18 27	18 31			18 46	
	d	17 14		17 30			17 34	17 38		17 50		18 04	18 10	18 14		18 30	18 36			18 34		18 50
Adderley Park	d						17 38													18 38		
Stechford	d						17 42													18 42		
Lea Hall	d						17 44													18 44		
Marston Green	d	17 22					17 48							18 22						18 48		
Birmingham International	a	17 25		17 38			17 51	17 56		17 59		18 13	18 19	18 25		18 38	18 55			18 51		18 59
	d	17 25		17 39			17 51			18 01		18 14	18 20	18 25		18 39				18 51		19 01
Hampton-in-Arden	d	17 28												18 28								
Berkswell	d	17 33												18 33								
Tile Hill	d	17 36					17 58							18 36						18 58		
Canley	d	17 40												18 40								
Coventry	a	17 44		17 49			18 05			18 11		18 24	18 30	18 44		18 49				19 05		19 11
	d	17 44		17 51						18 11			18 31	18 44		18 51						19 11
Rugby	d	17 55				18 20				18 26				18 55					19 20			19 26
Long Buckby	d	18 05				18 29								19 05					19 29			
Northampton	a	18 17				18 41								19 17					19 41			
London Euston	a	19 37		18 57		19 53				19 17			19 37	20 37		19 57			20 53			20 17

A from Birmingham New Street, to Birmingham New Street

Table 68

Sundays

1 July to 9 September

Stafford - Wolverhampton - Birmingham - Coventry - Northampton

Network Diagram - see first Page of Table 67

		VT	XC	VT	LM	LM	VT	AW	XC	LM	LM	LM	VT	XC	VT	LM	LM	VT	AW	XC	LM	LM	LM
			A											A									
Stafford	d		18 26			18 43				19 22				19 25			19 43				20 18		
Penkridge	d					18 49											19 49						
Wolverhampton	a		18 40			18 59								19 40			19 59						
	d	18 33	18 41	18 45		18 59		19 08	19 15			19 22	19 32	19 41	19 45		19 59		20 08	20 15			20 22
Coseley	d											19 27											20 27
Tipton	d											19 29											20 29
Dudley Port	d											19 31											20 31
Sandwell & Dudley	d			18 56								19 35			19 58								20 35
Smethwick Galton Bridge	d											19 37											20 37
Smethwick Rolfe Street	d											19 39											20 39
Birmingham New Street	a	18 55	18 58	19 06		19 15		19 26	19 31			19 46	19 55	19 58	20 07		20 15		20 23	20 31			20 46
	d		19 04	19 10	19 14		19 30	19 36			19 34			20 04	20 10	20 14		20 30	20 36			20 34	
Adderley Park	d										19 38											20 38	
Stechford	d										19 42											20 42	
Lea Hall	d										19 44											20 44	
Marston Green	d				19 22						19 48					20 22						20 48	
Birmingham International	a		19 13	19 19	19 25		19 38	19 55			19 51			20 13	20 19	20 25		20 39	20 55			20 51	
	d		19 14	19 20	19 25		19 39				19 51			20 14	20 20	20 25		20 40				20 51	
Hampton-in-Arden	d				19 28											20 28							
Berkswell	d				19 33											20 33							
Tile Hill	d				19 36						19 58					20 36						20 58	
Canley	d				19 40											20 40							
Coventry	a		19 24	19 30	19 44		19 49				20 05			20 24	20 30	20 43		20 50				21 04	
	d			19 31	19 44		19 51								20 31	20 43		20 51					
Rugby	d				19 55					20 19						20 55		21 05			21 19		
Long Buckby	d				20 05					20 28						21 05					21 28		
Northampton	a				20 17					20 40						21 17					21 40		
London Euston	a			20 37	21 42		20 57			21 54					21 47	22 44		22 23			23 14		

		VT	XC	LM	LM	VT	LM	AW	XC	LM	AW	LM	LM	LM	VT	LM	AW	VT	XC	LM	VT	VT	LM
			B																				
Stafford	d		20 27		20 39				21 09		21 16	21 24		21 39				22 02	22 06				
Penkridge	d				20 45									21 45									
Wolverhampton	a		20 39		20 55				21 21		21 34			21 55				22 17	22 20				
	d	20 33	20 41		20 59	21 05		21 12	21 22	21 25	21 35			22 00	22 05		22 08	22 18	22 22	22 25	22 32	22 37	
Coseley	d									21 30										22 30			
Tipton	d									21 32										22 32			
Dudley Port	d									21 34										22 34			
Sandwell & Dudley	d					21 17				21 38					22 15					22 38		22 47	
Smethwick Galton Bridge	d									21 40										22 40			
Smethwick Rolfe Street	d									21 42										22 42			
Birmingham New Street	a	20 50	20 58		21 15	21 26		21 29	21 39	21 49	21 52			22 16	22 24		22 27	22 38	22 39	22 49	22 55	22 56	
	d		21 04	21 14		21 30	21 34	21 37			21 55		22 14		22 30	22 34	22 40					23 00	23 14
Adderley Park	d						21 38									22 38							23 19
Stechford	d						21 42									22 42							23 22
Lea Hall	d						21 44									22 45							23 25
Marston Green	d			21 22			21 48						22 22			22 48							23 28
Birmingham International	a		21 13	21 25		21 39	21 51	21 56			22 09		22 25		22 39	22 51	22 55					23 09	23 31
	d		21 14	21 25		21 40	21 51						22 25		22 40	22 52						23 10	23 32
Hampton-in-Arden	d			21 28									22 28										23 35
Berkswell	d			21 33									22 33										23 40
Tile Hill	d			21 36									22 36										23 43
Canley	d			21 40									22 40										23 46
Coventry	a		21 23	21 44		21 50	22 01						22 44		22 50	23 01						23 20	23 50
	d			21 44		21 51							22 44		22 51							23 21	
Rugby	d			21 55		22 04						22 20	22 55		23 04							23 34	
Long Buckby	d			22 05								22 29	23 05										
Northampton	a			22 17								22 43	23 17									23s53	
London Euston	a			23 41		23 25									00 27							01 04	

A from Birmingham New Street, to Birmingham New Street

B to Birmingham New Street

Table 68

Sundays
1 July to 9 September

Stafford - Wolverhampton - Birmingham - Coventry - Northampton

Network Diagram - see first Page of Table 67

		LM	XC
Stafford	d	22 45	23 05
Penkridge	d	22 51	
Wolverhampton	a	23 01	23 18
	d	23 01	23 19
Coseley	d		
Tipton	d		
Dudley Port	d		
Sandwell & Dudley	d		
Smethwick Galton Bridge	d		
Smethwick Rolfe Street	d		
Birmingham New Street	a	23 17	23 36
	d		
Adderley Park	d		
Stechford	d		
Lea Hall	d		
Marston Green	d		
Birmingham International	a		
	d		
Hampton-in-Arden	d		
Berkswell	d		
Tile Hill	d		
Canley	d		
Coventry	a		
	d		
Rugby	d		
Long Buckby	d		
Northampton	a		
London Euston	a		

Sundays
from 16 September

		LM	VT	LM	LM	LM	XC	LM	AW	VT		LM	LM
Stafford	d												
Penkridge	d												
Wolverhampton	a												
	d		08 05			08 22			09 00	09 05			09 22
Coseley	d					08 27							09 27
Tipton	d					08 29							09 29
Dudley Port	d					08 31							09 31
Sandwell & Dudley	d		08 15			08 35				09 15			09 35
Smethwick Galton Bridge	d					08 37							09 37
Smethwick Rolfe Street	d					08 39							09 39
Birmingham New Street	a		08 24			08 46			09 15	09 24			09 46
	d	21p53	08 30	08 34	08 38		09 04	09 14	09 20	09 30		09 34	
Adderley Park	d				08 42							09 38	
Stechford	d				08 46							09 42	
Lea Hall	d				08 48							09 44	
Marston Green	d	22p01		08 42	08 52			09 22				09 48	
Birmingham International	a	22p05	08 39	08 45	08 55		09 13	09 25	09 31	09 39		09 51	
	d	22p05	08 40	08 45			09 14	09 25		09 40		09 51	
Hampton-in-Arden	d							09 28					
Berkswell	d	22p11		08 51				09 33					
Tile Hill	d	22p14		08 54				09 36					
Canley	d	22p17		08 57				09 40					
Coventry	a	22p20	08 50	09 00			09 24	09 44		09 50		10 01	
	d	22p21	08 51					09 44		09 51			
Rugby	d	22p32	09 04					09 55		10 04			
Long Buckby	d	22p41						10 05					
Northampton	a	22p53						10 17					
London Euston	a	00 17	10 28					11 59		11 31			

		XC A	LM	AW	VT	LM	LM	LM		XC A	LM	AW	LM
Stafford	d	09 26				10 15				10 27			10 41
Penkridge	d												10 49
Wolverhampton	a	09 40								10 42			11 00
	d	09 41		09 59	10 05			10 22		10 43		10 57	11 01
Coseley	d							10 27					
Tipton	d							10 29					
Dudley Port	d							10 31					
Sandwell & Dudley	d				10 15			10 35					
Smethwick Galton Bridge	d							10 37					
Smethwick Rolfe Street	d							10 39					
Birmingham New Street	a	09 58		10 14	10 24			10 46		10 59		11 13	11 17
	d	10 04	10 14	10 20	10 30		10 34			11 04	11 14	11 19	
Adderley Park	d						10 38						
Stechford	d						10 42						
Lea Hall	d						10 44						
Marston Green	d		10 22				10 48				11 22		
Birmingham International	a	10 13	10 25	10 32	10 39		10 52			11 13	11 25	11 31	
	d	10 14	10 25		10 40		10 52			11 14	11 25		
Hampton-in-Arden	d		10 28								11 28		
Berkswell	d		10 33								11 33		
Tile Hill	d		10 36								11 36		
Canley	d		10 40								11 40		
Coventry	a	10 24	10 44		10 50		11 03			11 24	11 44		
	d		10 44		10 51						11 44		
Rugby	d		10 55		11 04	11 14					11 55		
Long Buckby	d		11 05			11 24					12 05		
Northampton	a		11 17			11 36					12 17		
London Euston	a		12 37		12 27	12 50					13 37		

A from Birmingham New Street to Birmingham New Street

Table 68

Sundays
from 16 September

Stafford - Wolverhampton - Birmingham - Coventry - Northampton

Network Diagram - see first Page of Table 67

		VT	LM	LM	LM	VT		VT A	XC B	VT	LM	VT	LM
Stafford	d		11 19						11 28				12 19
Penkridge	d												
Wolverhampton	a								11 41				
	d	11 05			11 22			11 32	11 42	11 45			
Coseley	d				11 27								
Tipton	d				11 29								
Dudley Port	d				11 31								
Sandwell & Dudley	d	11 15			11 35					11 57			
Smethwick Galton Bridge	d				11 37								
Smethwick Rolfe Street	d				11 39								
Birmingham New Street	a	11 26			11 48			11 55	12 00	12 06			
	d	11 30		11 34		11 50			12 04	12 10	12 14	12 30	
Adderley Park	d			11 38									
Stechford	d			11 42									
Lea Hall	d			11 44									
Marston Green	d			11 48							12 22		
Birmingham International	a	11 39		11 51		11 59			12 13	12 19	12 25	12 38	
	d	11 40		11 51		12 00			12 14	12 20	12 25	12 39	
Hampton-in-Arden	d										12 28		
Berkswell	d										12 33		
Tile Hill	d										12 36		
Canley	d										12 40		
Coventry	a	11 50		12 01		12 10			12 24	12 30	12 44	12 49	
	d	11 51				12 11				12 31	12 44	12 51	
Rugby	d	12 05	12 20			12 25					12 55		13 20
Long Buckby	d		12 29								13 05		13 29
Northampton	a		12 41								13 17		13 41
London Euston	a	13 04	13 53			13 19				13 37	14 37	13 57	14 53

		LM	AW	LM		VT	VT	XC B	VT	LM	LM	VT	LM
Stafford	d							12 25			12 42		13 19
Penkridge	d										12 49		
Wolverhampton	a							12 40			12 59		
	d		12 17	12 22			12 32	12 41	12 45		13 00		
Coseley	d			12 27									
Tipton	d			12 29									
Dudley Port	d			12 31									
Sandwell & Dudley	d			12 35					12 55				
Smethwick Galton Bridge	d			12 37									
Smethwick Rolfe Street	d			12 39									
Birmingham New Street	a		12 32	12 46			12 55	12 58	13 06		13 16		
	d	12 34	12 37			12 50		13 04	13 10	13 14		13 30	
Adderley Park	d	12 38											
Stechford	d	12 42											
Lea Hall	d	12 44											
Marston Green	d	12 48								13 22			
Birmingham International	a	12 51	12 56			12 59		13 13	13 19	13 25		13 38	
	d	12 51				13 00		13 14	13 20	13 25		13 39	
Hampton-in-Arden	d									13 28			
Berkswell	d									13 33			
Tile Hill	d	12 58								13 36			
Canley	d									13 40			
Coventry	a	13 04				13 10		13 24	13 30	13 44		13 49	
	d					13 11			13 31	13 44		13 51	
Rugby	d					13 25				13 55			14 20
Long Buckby	d									14 05			14 29
Northampton	a									14 17			14 41
London Euston	a					14 17			14 37	15 37		14 57	15 53

		LM		AW	LM	VT	VT	XC B	VT	LM	LM	VT	
Stafford	d							13 25			13 43		
Penkridge	d										13 49		
Wolverhampton	a							13 40			13 59		
	d			13 08	13 22		13 32	13 41	13 45		13 59		
Coseley	d				13 27								
Tipton	d				13 29								
Dudley Port	d				13 31								
Sandwell & Dudley	d				13 35				13 56				
Smethwick Galton Bridge	d				13 37								
Smethwick Rolfe Street	d				13 39								
Birmingham New Street	a			13 23	13 46		13 55	13 58	14 06		14 15		
	d	13 34		13 36		13 50		14 04	14 10	14 14		14 30	
Adderley Park	d	13 38											
Stechford	d	13 42											
Lea Hall	d	13 44											
Marston Green	d	13 48								14 22			
Birmingham International	a	13 51		13 55		13 59		14 13	14 19	14 25		14 38	
	d	13 51				14 01		14 14	14 20	14 25		14 39	
Hampton-in-Arden	d									14 28			
Berkswell	d									14 33			
Tile Hill	d	13 58								14 36			
Canley	d									14 40			
Coventry	a	14 04				14 11		14 24	14 30	14 44		14 49	
	d					14 11			14 31	14 44		14 51	
Rugby	d					14 26				14 55			
Long Buckby	d									15 05			
Northampton	a									15 17			
London Euston	a					15 17			15 37	16 37		15 57	

		AW	XC	LM	LM	LM	VT	VT	XC B	VT		LM	LM
Stafford	d			14 19					14 25				14 43
Penkridge	d												14 49
Wolverhampton	a								14 40				14 59
	d	14 08	14 15			14 22	14 33		14 41	14 45			14 59
Coseley	d					14 27							
Tipton	d					14 29							
Dudley Port	d					14 31							
Sandwell & Dudley	d					14 35				14 56			
Smethwick Galton Bridge	d					14 37							
Smethwick Rolfe Street	d					14 39							
Birmingham New Street	a	14 23	14 31			14 46	14 50		14 58	15 06			15 15
	d	14 36			14 34			14 50	15 04	15 10		15 14	
Adderley Park	d				14 38								
Stechford	d				14 42								
Lea Hall	d				14 44								
Marston Green	d				14 48							15 22	
Birmingham International	a	14 55			14 51			14 59	15 13	15 19		15 25	
	d				14 51			15 01	15 14	15 20		15 25	
Hampton-in-Arden	d											15 28	
Berkswell	d											15 33	
Tile Hill	d				14 58							15 36	
Canley	d											15 40	
Coventry	a				15 04			15 11	15 24	15 30		15 44	
	d							15 11		15 31		15 44	
Rugby	d			15 20				15 26				15 55	
Long Buckby	d			15 29								16 05	
Northampton	a			15 41								16 17	
London Euston	a			16 53				16 17		16 37		17 37	

A from 16 September until 21 October

B from Birmingham New Street to Birmingham New Street

Stafford - Wolverhampton - Birmingham - Coventry - Northampton

Network Diagram - see first Page of Table 67

		VT	AW	XC	LM	LM	LM	VT	VT	VT	XC	VT	LM	LM	VT	AW	XC	LM	LM	LM	VT	VT	XC
		◇1	◇	◇1	◇1	1		◇1	◇1	◇1	◇1	◇1	◇1	◇1	◇1	◇	◇1	◇1	1		◇1	◇1	◇1
								A		B	C												C
		☕		ᴨ				☕	☕	☕	☕ᴨ	☕			☕	ᴨ	ᴨ				☕	☕	☕ᴨ
Stafford	d				15 20						15 25			15 43				16 19					16 25
Penkridge	d													15 49									
Wolverhampton 7	a										15 40			15 59									16 40
	d		15 09	15 15			15 22	15 32		15 32	15 41	15 45		15 59		16 09	16 15			16 22		16 32	16 41
Coseley	d						15 27													16 27			
Tipton	d						15 29													16 29			
Dudley Port	d						15 31													16 31			
Sandwell & Dudley	d						15 35					15 56								16 35			
Smethwick Galton Bridge 7	d						15 37													16 37			
Smethwick Rolfe Street	d						15 39													16 39			
Birmingham New Street 12	a		15 24	15 31			15 46	15 50		15 55	15 58	16 06		16 15		16 24	16 31			16 46		16 55	16 58
	d	15 30	15 36			15 34			15 50		16 04	16 10	16 14		16 30	16 35			16 34		16 50		17 04
Adderley Park	d					15 38													16 38				
Stechford	d					15 42													16 42				
Lea Hall	d					15 44													16 44				
Marston Green	d					15 48							16 22						16 48				
Birmingham International ✈	a	15 38	15 55			15 51			15 59		16 13	16 19	16 25		16 38	16 55			16 51		16 59		17 13
	d	15 39				15 51			16 01		16 14	16 20	16 25		16 39				16 51		17 01		17 14
Hampton-in-Arden	d												16 28										
Berkswell	d												16 33										
Tile Hill	d					15 58							16 36						16 58				
Canley	d												16 40										
Coventry	a	15 49				16 04			16 11		16 24	16 30	16 44		16 49				17 05		17 11		17 24
	d	15 51							16 11			16 31	16 44		16 51						17 11		
Rugby	d				16 20				16 24				16 55					17 20			17 26		
Long Buckby	d				16 29								17 05					17 29					
Northampton	a				16 41								17 17					17 41					
London Euston 15 ⊖	a	16 57			17 53				17 17			17 37	18 37		17 57			18 53			18 17		

		VT	LM	LM	VT	XC	LM	LM	AW	LM	VT	VT	XC	VT	LM	LM	VT	AW	XC	LM	LM	LM
		◇1	◇1	◇1	◇1	◇1	◇1	1	◇		◇1	◇1	◇1	◇1	◇1	◇1	◇1	◇	◇1	◇1	1	
													C									
		☕			☕	ᴨ			ᴨ		☕	☕	☕ᴨ	☕			☕	ᴨ	ᴨ			
Stafford	d			16 43			17 21						17 26			17 43				18 19		
Penkridge	d			16 49												17 49						
Wolverhampton 7	a			16 59									17 40			17 59						
	d	16 45		16 59		17 15			17 19	17 22		17 33	17 41	17 45		17 59		18 09	18 15			18 22
Coseley	d									17 27												18 27
Tipton	d									17 29												18 29
Dudley Port	d									17 31												18 31
Sandwell & Dudley	d	16 56								17 35				17 56								18 35
Smethwick Galton Bridge 7	d									17 37												18 37
Smethwick Rolfe Street	d									17 39												18 39
Birmingham New Street 12	a	17 06		17 15		17 31			17 35	17 46		17 55	17 58	18 06		18 15		18 27	18 31			18 46
	d	17 10	17 14		17 30			17 34	17 38		17 50		18 04	18 10	18 14		18 30	18 36			18 34	
Adderley Park	d							17 38													18 38	
Stechford	d							17 42													18 42	
Lea Hall	d							17 44													18 44	
Marston Green	d		17 22					17 48							18 22						18 48	
Birmingham International ✈	a	17 19	17 25		17 38			17 51	17 56		17 59		18 13	18 19	18 25		18 38	18 55			18 51	
	d	17 20	17 25		17 39			17 51			18 01		18 14	18 20	18 25		18 39				18 51	
Hampton-in-Arden	d		17 28												18 28							
Berkswell	d		17 33												18 33							
Tile Hill	d		17 36					17 58							18 36						18 58	
Canley	d		17 40												18 40							
Coventry	a	17 30	17 44		17 49			18 05			18 11		18 24	18 30	18 44		18 49				19 05	
	d	17 31	17 44		17 51						18 11			18 31	18 44		18 51					
Rugby	d		17 55				18 20				18 26				18 55					19 20		
Long Buckby	d		18 05				18 29								19 05					19 29		
Northampton	a		18 17				18 41								19 17					19 41		
London Euston 15 ⊖	a	18 37	19 37		18 57		19 53				19 17			19 37	20 37		19 57			20 53		

A from 28 October
B from 16 September until 21 October
C ☕ from Birmingham New Street ᴨ to Birmingham New Street

Table 68

Sundays
from 16 September

Stafford - Wolverhampton - Birmingham - Coventry - Northampton

Network Diagram - see first Page of Table 67

		VT	VT	XC	VT	LM	LM	VT	AW	XC	LM	LM	LM	VT	XC	VT	LM	LM	VT	AW	XC	LM	LM
		◇1	◇1	◇1	◇1	◇1	◇1	◇1	◇	◇1	◇1	1		◇1	◇1	◇1	◇1	◇1	◇1	◇	◇1	◇1	1
				A											A								
		☕	☕	☕ᴨ	☕			☕		ᴨ				☕	☕ᴨ	☕			☕	ᴨ	ᴨ		
Stafford	d			18 26			18 43				19 22				19 25			19 43				20 18	
Penkridge	d						18 49											19 49					
Wolverhampton 7	a			18 40			18 59								19 40			19 59					
	d		18 33	18 41	18 45		18 59		19 08	19 15			19 22	19 32	19 41	19 45		19 59		20 08	20 15		
Coseley	d												19 27										
Tipton	d												19 29										
Dudley Port	d												19 31										
Sandwell & Dudley	d				18 56								19 35			19 58							
Smethwick Galton Bridge 7	d												19 37										
Smethwick Rolfe Street	d												19 39										
Birmingham New Street 12	a		18 55	18 58	19 06		19 15		19 26	19 31			19 46	19 55	19 58	20 07		20 15		20 23	20 31		
	d	18 50		19 04	19 10	19 14		19 30	19 36			19 34			20 04	20 10	20 14		20 30	20 36			20 34
Adderley Park	d											19 38											20 38
Stechford	d											19 42											20 42
Lea Hall	d											19 44											20 44
Marston Green	d					19 22						19 48					20 22						20 48
Birmingham International ✈	a	18 59		19 13	19 19	19 25		19 38	19 55			19 51			20 13	20 19	20 25		20 39	20 55			20 51
	d	19 01		19 14	19 20	19 25		19 39				19 51			20 14	20 20	20 25		20 40				20 51
Hampton-in-Arden	d					19 28											20 28						
Berkswell	d					19 33											20 33						
Tile Hill	d					19 36						19 58					20 36						20 58
Canley	d					19 40											20 40						
Coventry	a	19 11		19 24	19 30	19 44		19 49				20 05			20 24	20 30	20 43		20 50				21 04
	d	19 11			19 31	19 44		19 51								20 31	20 43		20 51				
Rugby	d	19 26				19 55					20 19						20 55		21 05			21 19	
Long Buckby	d					20 05					20 28						21 05					21 28	
Northampton	a					20 17					20 40						21 17					21 40	
London Euston 15 ⊖	a	20 17			20 37	21 42		20 57			21 54					21 47	22 44		22 23			23 14	

		LM	VT	XC	LM	LM	VT	LM	AW	XC	LM	AW	LM	LM	LM	VT	LM	AW	VT	XC	LM	VT	VT
			◇1	◇1	◇1	◇1	◇1	1		◇1		◇	◇1	◇1	◇1	◇1	1	◇	◇1	◇1		◇1	◇1
				B																			
			☕	ᴨ			☕					ᴨ				☕			☕			☕	☕
Stafford	d			20 27		20 39				21 09		21 16	21 24		21 39				22 02	22 06			
Penkridge	d					20 45									21 45								
Wolverhampton 7	a			20 39		20 55				21 21		21 34			21 55				22 17	22 20			
	d	20 22	20 33	20 41		20 59	21 05		21 12	21 22	21 25	21 35			22 00	22 05		22 08	22 18	22 22	22 25	22 32	22 37
Coseley	d	20 27									21 30										22 30		
Tipton	d	20 29									21 32										22 32		
Dudley Port	d	20 31									21 34										22 34		
Sandwell & Dudley	d	20 35					21 17				21 38					22 15					22 38		22 47
Smethwick Galton Bridge 7	d	20 37									21 40										22 40		
Smethwick Rolfe Street	d	20 39									21 42										22 42		
Birmingham New Street 12	a	20 46	20 50	20 58		21 15	21 26		21 29	21 39	21 49	21 52			22 16	22 24		22 27	22 38	22 39	22 49	22 55	22 56
	d			21 04	21 14		21 30	21 34	21 37			21 55		22 14		22 30	22 34	22 40					23 00
Adderley Park	d							21 38									22 38						
Stechford	d							21 42									22 42						
Lea Hall	d							21 44									22 45						
Marston Green	d				21 22			21 48						22 22			22 48						
Birmingham International ✈	a			21 13	21 25		21 39	21 51	21 56			22 09		22 25		22 39	22 51	22 55					23 09
	d			21 14	21 25		21 40	21 51						22 25		22 40	22 52						23 10
Hampton-in-Arden	d				21 28									22 28									
Berkswell	d				21 33									22 33									
Tile Hill	d				21 36									22 36									
Canley	d				21 40									22 40									
Coventry	a			21 23	21 44		21 50	22 01						22 44		22 50	23 01						23 20
	d				21 44		21 51							22 44		22 51							23 21
Rugby	d				21 55		22 04						22 20	22 55		23 04							23 34
Long Buckby	d				22 05								22 29	23 05									
Northampton	a				22 17								22 43	23 17									23s53
London Euston 15 ⊖	a				23 41		23 25									00 27							01 04

A ☕ from Birmingham New Street ᴨ to Birmingham New Street
B ᴨ to Birmingham New Street

Table 68

Sundays
from 16 September

Stafford - Wolverhampton - Birmingham - Coventry - Northampton

Network Diagram - see first Page of Table 67

		LM 1		LM ◇1	XC ◇1
Stafford	d			22 45	23 05
Penkridge	d			22 51	
Wolverhampton 7 ⇌	a			23 01	23 18
	d			23 01	23 19
Coseley	d				
Tipton	d				
Dudley Port	d				
Sandwell & Dudley	d				
Smethwick Galton Bridge 7	d				
Smethwick Rolfe Street	d				
Birmingham New Street 12	a			23 17	23 36
	d	23 14			
Adderley Park	d	23 19			
Stechford	d	23 22			
Lea Hall	d	23 25			
Marston Green	d	23 28			
Birmingham International ✈	a	23 31			
	d	23 32			
Hampton-in-Arden	d	23 35			
Berkswell	d	23 40			
Tile Hill	d	23 43			
Canley	d	23 46			
Coventry	a	23 50			
	d				
Rugby	d				
Long Buckby	d				
Northampton	a				
London Euston 15 ⊖	a				

Table 69

Mondays to Fridays
until 19 October

Lichfield - Birmingham - Longbridge and Redditch

Network Diagram - see first Page of Table 67

Miles	Miles			LM	LM	LM	LM	LM	LM	LM	LM	LM	LM	LM	LM	XC ◇1	LM	LM	LM	LM	LM	LM	LM
0	—	**Lichfield Trent Valley**	d							06 09		06 20					06 50		07 10		07 20		07 38
1¼	—	**Lichfield City**	d							06 12		06 24			06 45		06 54		07 13		07 24		07 42
4¼	—	Shenstone	d							06 17					06 50				07 18				07 47
6¾	—	Blake Street	d					06 03		06 21		06 32			06 54		07 02		07 22		07 32		07 51
8½	—	Butlers Lane	d					06 05		06 23		06 34			06 56		07 04		07 24		07 34		07 53
9½	—	Four Oaks	d					06 08	06 17	06 26		06 37	06 47		06 59		07 07	07 17	07 27		07 37	07 47	07 56
11	—	Sutton Coldfield	d					06 11	06 20	06 30		06 40	06 50		07 02		07 10	07 20	07 31		07 40	07 50	08 00
12	—	Wylde Green	d					06 14	06 23	06 32		06 43	06 53		07 05		07 13	07 23	07 33		07 43	07 53	08 03
12¾	—	Chester Road	d					06 16	06 25	06 35		06 45	06 55		07 07		07 15	07 25	07 36		07 45	07 55	08 05
13¾	—	Erdington	d					06 17	06 27	06 36		06 47	06 57		07 09		07 17	07 27	07 37		07 47	07 57	08 07
14½	—	Gravelly Hill	d					06 20	06 29	06 39		06 49	06 59		07 11		07 19	07 29	07 40		07 49	07 59	08 10
15¾	—	Aston	d					06 23	06 33	06 42		06 53	07 03		07 14		07 23	07 33	07 43		07 53	08 03	08 13
17	—	Duddeston	d					06 26	06 35	06 45			07 05					07 35	07 46			08 05	08 16
18½	0	**Birmingham New Street** 12	a					06 31	06 40	06 49		06 59	07 10		07 21		07 30	07 42	07 51		08 01	08 10	08 21
—	—		d	05 53	06 03	06 13	06 23	06 33	06 43	06 53	06 59	07 03	07 13	07 19	07 23	07 30	07 33	07 43	07 53	07 59	08 03	08 13	08 23
19½	—	Five Ways	d	05 56	06 06	06 16	06 26	06 36	06 46	06 56		07 06	07 16		07 26		07 36	07 46	07 56		08 06	08 16	08 26
20	1½	University	d	06 00	06 10	06 20	06 30	06 40	06 50	07 00	07 05	07 10	07 20	07 25	07 30	07a36	07 40	07 50	08 00	08 05	08 10	08 20	08 30
20¾	—	Selly Oak	d	06 03	06 13	06 23	06 33	06 43	06 53	07 03		07 13	07 23		07 33		07 43	07 53	08 03		08 13	08 23	08 33
21¾	—	Bournville	d	06 05	06 15	06 25	06 35	06 45	06 55	07 05		07 15	07 25		07 35		07 45	07 55	08 05		08 15	08 25	08 35
22¾	—	Kings Norton	d	06 07	06 17	06 27	06 37	06 47	06 57	07 07		07 17	07 27		07 37		07 47	07 57	08 07		08 17	08 27	08 37
24¼	—	Northfield	d	06 10	06 20	06 30	06 40	06 50	07 00	07 10		07 20	07 30		07 40		07 50	08 00	08 10		08 20	08 30	08 40
25¼	—	Longbridge	d	06a14	06a24	06 34	06a44	06a54	07 04	07a14		07a24	07 34		07a44		07a54	08 04	08a14		08a24	08 34	08a44
28	9½	Barnt Green	d			06 39			07 09				07 39	07 41				08 09		08 18		08 39	
29¾	—	Alvechurch	d			06 43			07 13				07 43					08 13				08 43	
33	—	**Redditch**	a			06 52			07 22				07 52					08 22				08 52	
—	13	Bromsgrove	a								07 21			07 46						08 22			

		XC ◇1	LM	LM	LM	LM	LM	LM	LM	LM	XC ◇1	LM	LM	LM	LM	LM	LM	LM	XC ◇1	LM	LM	LM	LM
Lichfield Trent Valley	d		07 50				08 11			08 41		08 50				09 20				09 50			
Lichfield City	d		07 54		08 10		08 15	08 26		08 44		08 54			09 13	09 24		09 43		09 54			10 13
Shenstone	d						08 20			08 49					09 18			09 48					10 18
Blake Street	d		08 01				08 23	08 33		08 53		09 02			09 22	09 32		09 52		10 02			10 22
Butlers Lane	d		08 03				08 25	08 35		08 55		09 04			09 24	09 34		09 54		10 04			10 24
Four Oaks	d		08 06	08 15	08 20		08 28	08 38	08 47	08 58		09 07	09 17		09 27	09 37	09 47	09 57		10 07	10 17		10 27
Sutton Coldfield	d		08 10	08 18	08 23		08 32	08 42	08 50	09 02		09 10	09 20		09 30	09 40	09 50	10 00		10 10	10 20		10 30
Wylde Green	d		08 13	08 21	08 26		08 34	08 44	08 53	09 04		09 13	09 23		09 33	09 43	09 53	10 03		10 13	10 23		10 33
Chester Road	d		08 15	08 23	08 28		08 37	08 47	08 55	09 07		09 15	09 25		09 35	09 45	09 55	10 05		10 15	10 25		10 35
Erdington	d		08 17	08 25	08 29		08 38	08 48	08 57	09 08		09 17	09 27		09 37	09 47	09 57	10 07		10 17	10 27		10 37
Gravelly Hill	d		08 20		08 32		08 41	08 51	08 59	09 11		09 19	09 29		09 39	09 49	09 59	10 09		10 19	10 29		10 39
Aston	d		08 23		08 35		08 44	08 54	09 03	09 14		09 23	09 33		09 43	09 53	10 03	10 13		10 23	10 33		10 43
Duddeston	d				08 37		08 47	08 57	09 05				09 35				10 05				10 35		
Birmingham New Street 12	a		08 31	08 36	08 42		08 51	09 01	09 11	09 20		09 30	09 41		09 50	10 00	10 10	10 21		10 30	10 41		10 50
	d	08 30	08 33		08 43	08 49	08 53	09 03	09 13	09 23	09 30	09 33	09 43	09 49	09 53	10 03	10 13	10 23	10 30	10 33	10 43	10 49	10 53
Five Ways	d		08 36		08 46		08 56	09 06	09 16	09 26		09 36	09 46		09 56	10 06	10 16	10 26		10 36	10 46		10 56
University	d	08a36	08 40		08 50	08 55	09 00	09 10	09 20	09 30	09a36	09 41	09 50	09 55	10 00	10 10	10 20	10 30	10a36	10 40	10 50	10 55	11 00
Selly Oak	d		08 43		08 53		09 03	09 13	09 23	09 33		09 43	09 53		10 03	10 13	10 23	10 33		10 43	10 53		11 03
Bournville	d		08 45		08 55		09 05	09 15	09 25	09 35		09 45	09 55		10 05	10 15	10 25	10 35		10 45	10 55		11 05
Kings Norton	d		08 47		08 57		09 07	09 17	09 27	09 37		09 47	09 57		10 07	10 17	10 27	10 37		10 47	10 57		11 07
Northfield	d		08 50		09 00		09 10	09 20	09 30	09 40		09 50	10 00		10 10	10 20	10 30	10 40		10 50	11 00		11 10
Longbridge	d		08a54		09 06		09a14	09a24	09 34	09a44		09a54	10 06		10a14	10a24	10 34	10a44		10a54	11 06		11a14
Barnt Green	d				09 10				09 39				10 10				10 39				11 10		
Alvechurch	d				09 15				09 43				10 15				10 43				11 15		
Redditch	a				09 22				09 52				10 22				10 52				11 22		
Bromsgrove	a					09 09								10 09								11 09	

		LM	LM	LM	XC ◇1	LM	LM	LM	LM	LM	LM	LM	XC ◇1	LM	LM	LM	LM	LM	LM	LM	XC ◇1	LM
Lichfield Trent Valley	d	10 20				10 50				11 20				11 50				12 20				12 50
Lichfield City	d	10 24		10 43		10 54			11 13	11 24		11 43		11 54			12 13	12 24		12 43		12 54
Shenstone	d			10 48					11 18			11 48					12 18			12 48		
Blake Street	d	10 32		10 52		11 02			11 22	11 32		11 52		12 02			12 22	12 32		12 52		13 02
Butlers Lane	d	10 34		10 54		11 04			11 24	11 34		11 54		12 04			12 24	12 34		12 54		13 04
Four Oaks	d	10 37	10 47	10 57		11 07	11 17		11 27	11 37	11 47	11 57		12 07	12 17		12 27	12 37	12 47	12 57		13 07
Sutton Coldfield	d	10 40	10 50	11 00		11 10	11 20		11 30	11 40	11 50	12 00		12 10	12 20		12 30	12 40	12 50	13 00		13 10
Wylde Green	d	10 43	10 53	11 03		11 13	11 23		11 33	11 43	11 53	12 03		12 13	12 23		12 33	12 43	12 53	13 03		13 13
Chester Road	d	10 45	10 55	11 05		11 15	11 25		11 35	11 45	11 55	12 05		12 15	12 25		12 35	12 45	12 55	13 05		13 15
Erdington	d	10 47	10 57	11 07		11 17	11 27		11 37	11 47	11 57	12 07		12 17	12 27		12 37	12 47	12 57	13 07		13 17
Gravelly Hill	d	10 49	10 59	11 09		11 19	11 29		11 39	11 49	11 59	12 09		12 19	12 29		12 39	12 49	12 59	13 09		13 19
Aston	d	10 53	11 03	11 13		11 23	11 33		11 43	11 53	12 03	12 13		12 23	12 33		12 43	12 53	13 03	13 13		13 23
Duddeston	d		11 05				11 35				12 05				12 35				13 05			
Birmingham New Street 12	a	11 00	11 10	11 21		11 30	11 41		11 50	12 00	12 10	12 21		12 30	12 41		12 50	13 00	13 10	13 21		13 31
	d	11 03	11 13	11 23	11 30	11 33	11 43	11 49	11 53	12 03	12 13	12 23	12 30	12 33	12 43	12 49	12 53	13 03	13 13	13 23	13 30	13 33
Five Ways	d	11 06	11 16	11 26		11 36	11 46		11 56	12 06	12 16	12 26		12 36	12 46		12 56	13 06	13 16	13 26		13 36
University	d	11 10	11 20	11 30	11a36	11 40	11 50	11 55	12 00	12 10	12 20	12 30	12a36	12 40	12 50	12 55	13 00	13 10	13 20	13 30	13a36	13 40
Selly Oak	d	11 13	11 23	11 33		11 43	11 53		12 03	12 13	12 23	12 33		12 43	12 53		13 03	13 13	13 23	13 33		13 43
Bournville	d	11 15	11 25	11 35		11 45	11 55		12 05	12 15	12 25	12 35		12 45	12 55		13 05	13 15	13 25	13 35		13 45
Kings Norton	d	11 17	11 27	11 37		11 47	11 57		12 07	12 17	12 27	12 37		12 47	12 57		13 07	13 17	13 27	13 37		13 47
Northfield	d	11 20	11 30	11 40		11 50	12 00		12 10	12 20	12 30	12 40		12 50	13 00		13 10	13 20	13 30	13 40		13 50
Longbridge	d	11a24	11 34	11a44		11a54	12 06		12a14	12a24	12 34	12a44		12a54	13 06		13a14	13a24	13 34	13a44		13a54
Barnt Green	d		11 39				12 10				12 39				13 10				13 39			
Alvechurch	d		11 43				12 15				12 43				13 15				13 43			
Redditch	a		11 52				12 22				12 52				13 22				13 52			
Bromsgrove	a							12 09								13 09						

until 19 October

Lichfield - Birmingham - Longbridge and Redditch

Network Diagram - see first Page of Table 67

		LM	LM	LM	LM	LM	LM	XC ◇1	LM	LM		LM	LM	LM	LM	LM	XC ◇1	LM	LM	LM		LM	LM	LM	LM
Lichfield Trent Valley	d				13 20				13 50					14 20				14 50					15 20		
Lichfield City	d			13 13	13 24		13 43		13 54				14 13	14 24		14 43		14 54				15 13	15 24		
Shenstone	d			13 18			13 48						14 18			14 48						15 18			
Blake Street	d			13 22	13 32		13 52		14 02				14 22	14 32		14 52		15 02				15 22	15 32		
Butlers Lane	d			13 24	13 34		13 54		14 04				14 24	14 34		14 54		15 04				15 24	15 34		
Four Oaks	d	13 17		13 27	13 37	13 47	13 57		14 07	14 17			14 27	14 37	14 47	14 57		15 07	15 17			15 27	15 37	15 47	
Sutton Coldfield	d	13 20		13 30	13 40	13 50	14 00		14 10	14 20			14 30	14 40	14 50	15 00		15 10	15 20			15 30	15 40	15 50	
Wylde Green	d	13 23		13 33	13 43	13 53	14 03		14 13	14 23			14 33	14 43	14 53	15 03		15 13	15 23			15 33	15 43	15 53	
Chester Road	d	13 25		13 35	13 45	13 55	14 05		14 15	14 25			14 35	14 45	14 55	15 05		15 15	15 25			15 35	15 45	15 55	
Erdington	d	13 27		13 37	13 47	13 57	14 07		14 17	14 27			14 37	14 47	14 57	15 07		15 17	15 27			15 37	15 47	15 57	
Gravelly Hill	d	13 29		13 39	13 49	13 59	14 09		14 19	14 29			14 39	14 49	14 59	15 09		15 19	15 29			15 39	15 49	15 59	
Aston	d	13 33		13 43	13 53	14 03	14 13		14 23	14 33			14 43	14 53	15 03	15 13		15 23	15 33			15 43	15 53	16 03	
Duddeston	d	13 35				14 05				14 35					15 05				15 35					16 05	
Birmingham New Street 12	a	13 41		13 50	14 00	14 10	14 21		14 30	14 41			14 50	15 00	15 10	15 21		15 30	15 42			15 50	16 01	16 10	
	d	13 43	13 49	13 53	14 03	14 13	14 23	14 30	14 33	14 43		14 49	14 53	15 03	15 13	15 23	15 30	15 33	15 43	15 49		15 53	16 03	16 13	16 19
Five Ways	d	13 46		13 56	14 06	14 16	14 26		14 36	14 46			14 56	15 06	15 16	15 26		15 36	15 46			15 56	16 06	16 16	
University	d	13 50	13 55	14 00	14 10	14 20	14 30	14a36	14 40	14 50		14 55	15 00	15 10	15 20	15 30	15a36	15 40	15 50	15 55		16 00	16 10	16 20	16 25
Selly Oak	d	13 53		14 03	14 13	14 23	14 33		14 43	14 53			15 03	15 13	15 23	15 33		15 43	15 53			16 03	16 13	16 23	
Bournville	d	13 55		14 05	14 15	14 25	14 35		14 45	14 55			15 05	15 15	15 25	15 35		15 45	15 55			16 05	16 15	16 25	
Kings Norton	d	13 57		14 07	14 17	14 27	14 37		14 47	14 57			15 07	15 17	15 27	15 37		15 47	15 57			16 07	16 17	16 27	
Northfield	d	14 00		14 10	14 20	14 30	14 40		14 50	15 00			15 10	15 20	15 30	15 40		15 50	16 00			16 10	16 20	16 30	
Longbridge	d	14 06		14a14	14a24	14 34	14a44		14a54	15 06			15a14	15a24	15 34	15a44		15a54	16 06			16a14	16a24	16 36	
Barnt Green	d	14 10				14 39				15 10					15 39				16 10					16 40	
Alvechurch	d	14 15				14 43				15 15					15 43				16 15					16 45	
Redditch	a	14 22				14 52				15 22					15 52				16 22					16 52	
Bromsgrove	a		14 09									15 09								16 09					16 40

		LM	XC ◇1	LM	LM	LM		LM	LM	LM	LM	LM	XC ◇1	LM	LM	LM		LM	LM	LM	LM	LM	LM	XC ◇1	LM
Lichfield Trent Valley	d			15 50					16 20					16 50						17 20			17 40		17 50
Lichfield City	d	15 43		15 54				16 13	16 24			16 43		16 54	17 05					17 24			17 44		17 54
Shenstone	d	15 48		15 59				16 18				16 48								17 29			17 49		
Blake Street	d	15 52		16 03				16 22	16 32			16 52		17 02	17 13					17 33			17 53		18 02
Butlers Lane	d	15 54		16 05				16 24	16 34			16 54		17 04	17 15					17 35			17 55		18 04
Four Oaks	d	15 57		16 08	16 17			16 27	16 37	16 47		16 57		17 07	17 18			17 28		17 38	17 47		17 58		18 07
Sutton Coldfield	d	16 00		16 11	16 20			16 30	16 40	16 50		17 00		17 10	17 21			17 31		17 41	17 50		18 01		18 10
Wylde Green	d	16 03		16 14	16 23			16 33	16 43	16 53		17 03		17 13	17 24			17 34		17 44	17 53		18 04		18 13
Chester Road	d	16 05		16 16	16 25			16 35	16 45	16 55		17 05		17 15	17 26			17 36		17 46	17 55		18 06		18 15
Erdington	d	16 07		16 18	16 27			16 37	16 47	16 57		17 07		17 17	17 28			17 38		17 48	17 57		18 08		18 17
Gravelly Hill	d	16 09		16 20	16 29			16 39	16 49	16 59		17 09		17 19	17 30			17 40		17 50	17 59		18 10		18 19
Aston	d	16 13		16 24	16 33			16 43	16 53	17 03		17 13		17 23	17 34			17 44		17 54	18 04		18 14		18 23
Duddeston	d				16 35					17 05					17 36						18 06				
Birmingham New Street 12	a	16 21		16 31	16 41			16 50	17 00	17 12		17 21		17 30	17 41			17 51		18 01	18 12		18 21		18 31
	d	16 23	16 30	16 33	16 43	16 49		16 53	17 03	17 13	17 19	17 23	17 30	17 33	17 43	17 49		17 53	17 59	18 03	18 13	18 19	18 23	18 30	18 33
Five Ways	d	16 26		16 36	16 46			16 56	17 06	17 16		17 26		17 36	17 46			17 56		18 06	18 16		18 26		18 36
University	d	16 30	16a36	16 40	16 50	16 55		17 00	17 10	17 20	17 25	17 31	17 36	17 40	17 50	17a55		18 00	18 05	18 10	18 20	18 25	18 30	18 36	18 40
Selly Oak	d	16 33		16 43	16 53			17 03	17 13	17 23		17 33		17 43	17 53			18 03		18 13	18 23		18 33		18 43
Bournville	d	16 35		16 45	16 55			17 05	17 15	17 25		17 35		17 45	17 55			18 05		18 15	18 25		18 35		18 45
Kings Norton	d	16 37		16 47	16 57			17 07	17 17	17 27		17 37		17 47	17 57			18 07		18 17	18 27		18 37		18 47
Northfield	d	16 40		16 50	17 00			17 10	17 20	17 30		17 40		17 50	18 00			18 10		18 20	18 30		18 40		18 50
Longbridge	d	16a44		16a54	17 06			17a14	17a24	17 36		17a44		17a54	18 06			18a14		18a24	18 34		18a44		18a54
Barnt Green	d				17 10					17 40					18 10						18 39				
Alvechurch	d				17 15					17 44					18 15						18 43				
Redditch	a				17 22					17 52					18 22						18 52				
Bromsgrove	a					17 09					17 40		17 51						18 21			18 44		18 49	

		LM		LM	LM	LM	LM	LM	XC ◇1	LM	LM	LM		LM	LM	LM	LM	XC ◇1	LM	LM	LM	LM		LM	LM
Lichfield Trent Valley	d			18 10	18 20					18 50					19 20				20 00			20 30			21 00
Lichfield City	d			18 14	18 24			18 43		18 54				19 13	19 24		19 43		20 04			20 34			21 04
Shenstone	d			18 19				18 48						19 18			19 48		20 09			20 39			21 09
Blake Street	d			18 23	18 32			18 52		19 02				19 22	19 32		19 52		20 13			20 43			21 13
Butlers Lane	d			18 25	18 34			18 54		19 04				19 24	19 34		19 54		20 15			20 45			21 15
Four Oaks	d	18 17		18 28	18 37	18 47		18 57		19 07	19 17			19 27	19 37	19 50	19 57		20 18			20 48			21 18
Sutton Coldfield	d	18 20		18 31	18 40	18 50		19 00		19 10	19 20			19 30	19 40	19 53	20 00		20 21			20 51			21 21
Wylde Green	d	18 23		18 34	18 43	18 53		19 03		19 13	19 23			19 33	19 43	19 56	20 03		20 24			20 54			21 24
Chester Road	d	18 25		18 36	18 45	18 55		19 05		19 15	19 25			19 35	19 45	19 58	20 05		20 26			20 56			21 26
Erdington	d	18 27		18 38	18 47	18 57		19 07		19 17	19 27			19 37	19 47	20 00	20 07		20 28			20 58			21 28
Gravelly Hill	d	18 29		18 40	18 49	18 59		19 09		19 19	19 29			19 39	19 49	20 02	20 09		20 30			21 00			21 30
Aston	d	18 33		18 44	18 53	19 03		19 13		19 23	19 33			19 43	19 53	20 06	20 13		20 33			21 03			21 33
Duddeston	d	18 35				19 05					19 35				19 55				20 36			21 06			21 36
Birmingham New Street 12	a	18 40		18 50	19 00	19 11		19 21		19 31	19 41			19 50	20 02	20 13	20 20		20 40			21 12			21 41
	d	18 43		18 53	19 03	19 13	19 19	19 23	19 30	19 33	19 43	19 49		19 53		20 13	20 23	20 30	20 43	20 53	20 59	21 13		21 23	21 43
Five Ways	d	18 46		18 56	19 06	19 16		19 26		19 36	19 46			19 56		20 16	20 26		20 46	20 56		21 16		21 26	21 46
University	d	18 50		19 00	19 10	19 20	19 25	19 30	19a36	19 40	19 50	19 55		20 00		20 20	20 30	20a36	20 50	21 00	21 05	21 20		21 30	21 50
Selly Oak	d	18 53		19 03	19 13	19 23		19 33		19 43	19 53			20 03		20 23	20 33		20 53	21 03		21 23		21 33	21 53
Bournville	d	18 55		19 05	19 15	19 25		19 35		19 45	19 55			20 05		20 25	20 35		20 55	21 05		21 25		21 35	21 55
Kings Norton	d	18 57		19 07	19 17	19 27		19 37		19 47	19 57			20 07		20 27	20 37		20 57	21 07		21 27		21 37	21 57
Northfield	d	19 00		19 10	19 20	19 30		19 40		19 50	20 00			20 10		20 30	20 40		21 00	21 10		21 30		21 40	22 00
Longbridge	d	19 04		19a14	19a24	19 34		19a44		19a54	20 06			20a14		20 34	20a44		21 04	21a14		21 34		21a44	22 04
Barnt Green	d	19 09				19 39					20 10					20 39			21 09			21 39			22 09
Alvechurch	d	19 13				19 44					20 15					20 43			21 13			21 43			22 13
Redditch	a	19 22				19 52					20 22					20 52			21 22			21 52			22 22
Bromsgrove	a						19 40					20 10									21 19				

until 19 October

Lichfield - Birmingham - Longbridge and Redditch

Network Diagram - see first Page of Table 67

		LM	LM	LM	LM	LM	LM	LM		LM	LM	LM
Lichfield Trent Valley	d			21 30		22 00				22 30	22 56	
Lichfield City	d			21 34		22 04				22 34	23 00	
Shenstone	d			21 39		22 09				22 39	23 05	
Blake Street	d			21 43		22 13				22 43	23 09	23 36
Butlers Lane	d			21 45		22 15				22 45	23 11	23 38
Four Oaks	d			21 48		22 18				22 48	23 14	23 41
Sutton Coldfield	d			21 51		22 21				22 51	23 17	23 44
Wylde Green	d			21 54		22 24				22 54	23 20	
Chester Road	d			21 56		22 26				22 56		
Erdington	d			21 58		22 28				22 58		
Gravelly Hill	d			22 00		22 30				23 00		
Aston	d			22 03		22 33				23 03		
Duddeston	d			22 06		22 36				23 06		
Birmingham New Street 12	a			22 12		22 41				23 11	23 31	23 59
	d	21 53	22 00	22 13	22 23	22 43	22 53	23 00		23 13	23 33	
Five Ways	d	21 56		22 16	22 26	22 46	22 56			23 16	23 36	
University	d	22 00	22 06	22 20	22 30	22 50	23 00	23 06		23 20	23 40	
Selly Oak	d	22 03		22 23	22 33	22 53	23 03			23 23	23 43	
Bournville	d	22 05		22 25	22 35	22 55	23 05			23 25	23 45	
Kings Norton	d	22 07		22 27	22 37	22 57	23 07			23 27	23 47	
Northfield	d	22 10		22 30	22 40	23 00	23 10			23 30	23 50	
Longbridge	d	22a14		22 34	22a44	23 04	23a14			23 34	23a54	
Barnt Green	d			22 39		23 09				23 39		
Alvechurch	d			22 43		23 13				23 43		
Redditch	a			22 52		23 22				23 52		
Bromsgrove	a		22 19					23 19				

Mondays to Fridays

from 22 October

		LM	LM	LM	LM	LM	LM	LM	LM	LM		XC ◇1	LM	LM	LM	LM	LM	LM	LM	XC ◇1		LM	LM	LM	LM
Lichfield Trent Valley	d							06 17					06 47				07 17					07 47			
Lichfield City	d					06 09		06 20					06 50	07 03			07 20	07 33				07 50	08 03		
Shenstone	d					06 14		06 26					06 56				07 26					07 56			
Blake Street	d				06 00	06 18		06 30					07 00	07 11			07 30	07 41				08 00	08 11		
Butlers Lane	d				06 02	06 21		06 32					07 02	07 13			07 32	07 43				08 02	08 13		
Four Oaks	d				06 05	06 24		06 35		06 54			07 05	07 16	07 24		07 35	07 46	07 54			08 05	08 16		08 24
Sutton Coldfield	d				06 09	06 27		06 39		06 57			07 09	07 20	07 27		07 39	07 50	07 57			08 09	08 20		08 27
Wylde Green	d				06 12	06 30		06 42		07 00			07 12	07 23	07 30		07 42	07 53	08 00			08 12	08 23		08 30
Chester Road	d				06 14	06 33		06 44		07 03			07 14	07 25	07 33		07 44	07 55	08 03			08 14	08 25		08 33
Erdington	d				06 16	06 35		06 46		07 05			07 16	07 27	07 35		07 46	07 57	08 05			08 16	08 27		08 35
Gravelly Hill	d				06 19	06 38		06 49		07 08			07 19	07 30	07 38		07 49	08 00	08 08			08 19	08 30		08 38
Aston	d				06 23	06 41		06 53		07 11			07 23	07 34	07 41		07 53	08 04	08 11			08 23	08 34		08 41
Duddeston	d				06 25	06 43				07 13				07 36	07 43			08 06	08 13				08 37		08 43
Birmingham New Street 12	a				06 30	06 49		07 00		07 20			07 30	07 41	07 51		08 01	08 12	08 21			08 31	08 41		08 51
	d	05 53	06 03	06 23	06 33	06 53	06 59	07 03	07 19	07 23		07 30	07 33	07 43	07 53	07 59	08 03	08 13	08 23	08 30		08 33	08 43	08 49	08 53
Five Ways	d	05 56	06 06	06 26	06 36	06 56		07 06		07 26			07 36	07 46	07 56		08 06	08 16	08 26			08 36	08 46		08 56
University	d	06 00	06 10	06 30	06 40	07 00	07 05	07 10	07 25	07 30		07a36	07 40	07 50	08 00	08 05	08 10	08 20	08 30	08a36		08 40	08 50	08 55	09 00
Selly Oak	d	06 04	06 13	06 33	06 43	07 03		07 13		07 33			07 43	07 53	08 03		08 13	08 23	08 33			08 43	08 53		09 03
Bournville	d	06 06	06 15	06 35	06 45	07 05		07 15		07 35			07 45	07 55	08 05		08 15	08 25	08 35			08 45	08 55		09 05
Kings Norton	d	06 09	06 18	06 38	06 48	07 08		07 18		07 38			07 48	07 58	08 08		08 18	08 28	08 38			08 48	08 58		09 08
Northfield	d	06 12	06 21	06 41	06 51	07 11		07 21		07 41			07 51	08 01	08 11		08 21	08 31	08 41			08 51	09 01		09 11
Longbridge	d	06a17	06 26	06a46	06 58	07a16		07 26		07a46			07 58	08a06	08a16		08 26	08a37	08a46			08 58	09a06		09a16
Barnt Green	d		06 39		07 09			07 39	07 41				08 09			08 18	08 39					09 09			
Alvechurch	d		06 43		07 13			07 43					08 13				08 43					09 13			
Redditch	a		06 52		07 22			07 52					08 22				08 52					09 22			
Bromsgrove	a						07 21		07 46							08 22								09 09	

		LM	LM	LM	XC ◇1	LM		LM	LM	LM	LM	LM	LM	XC ◇1	LM	LM		LM	LM	LM	XC ◇1	LM	LM	LM	LM
Lichfield Trent Valley	d	08 17				08 47		08 58			09 17	09 28			09 47				10 17			10 47			11 17
Lichfield City	d	08 20	08 32			08 50		09 01			09 20	09 31			09 50				10 20			10 50			11 20
Shenstone	d	08 26	08 37			08 56		09 07			09 26	09 37			09 56				10 26			10 56			11 26
Blake Street	d	08 30	08 41			09 00		09 11			09 30	09 41			10 00				10 30			11 00			11 30
Butlers Lane	d	08 32	08 44			09 02		09 13			09 32	09 43			10 02				10 32			11 02			11 32
Four Oaks	d	08 35	08 47	08 54		09 05		09 16		09 24	09 35	09 46	09 54		10 05			10 24	10 35	10 54		11 05		11 24	11 35
Sutton Coldfield	d	08 39	08 50	08 57		09 09		09 20		09 27	09 39	09 50	09 57		10 09			10 27	10 39	10 57		11 09		11 27	11 39
Wylde Green	d	08 42	08 53	09 00		09 12		09 23		09 30	09 42	09 53	10 00		10 12			10 30	10 42	11 00		11 12		11 30	11 42
Chester Road	d	08 44	08 56	09 03		09 14		09 25		09 33	09 44	09 55	10 03		10 14			10 33	10 44	11 03		11 14		11 33	11 44
Erdington	d	08 46	08 58	09 05		09 16		09 27		09 35	09 46	09 57	10 05		10 16			10 35	10 46	11 05		11 16		11 35	11 46
Gravelly Hill	d	08 49	09 01	09 08		09 19		09 30		09 38	09 49	10 00	10 08		10 19			10 38	10 49	11 08		11 19		11 38	11 49
Aston	d	08 53	09 04	09 11		09 23		09 34		09 41	09 53	10 04	10 11		10 23			10 41	10 53	11 11		11 23		11 41	11 53
Duddeston	d			09 13						09 43			10 13					10 43		11 13				11 43	
Birmingham New Street 12	a	09 01	09 11	09 19		09 31		09 42		09 51	10 01	10 11	10 21		10 31			10 51	11 01	11 21		11 31		11 51	12 01
	d	09 03	09 13	09 23	09 30	09 33			09 49	09 53	10 03	10 13	10 23	10 30	10 33	10 49		10 53	11 03	11 23	11 30	11 33	11 49	11 53	12 03
Five Ways	d	09 06	09 16	09 26		09 36				09 56	10 06	10 16	10 26		10 36			10 56	11 06	11 26		11 36		11 56	12 06
University	d	09 10	09 20	09 30	09a36	09 40			09 55	10 00	10 10	10 20	10 30	10a36	10 40	10 55		11 00	11 10	11 30	11a36	11 40	11 55	12 00	12 10
Selly Oak	d	09 13	09 23	09 33		09 43				10 03	10 13	10 23	10 33		10 43			11 03	11 13	11 33		11 43		12 03	12 13
Bournville	d	09 15	09 25	09 35		09 45				10 05	10 15	10 25	10 35		10 45			11 05	11 15	11 35		11 45		12 05	12 15
Kings Norton	d	09 18	09 28	09 38		09 48				10 08	10 18	10 28	10 38		10 48			11 08	11 18	11 38		11 48		12 08	12 18
Northfield	d	09 21	09 31	09 41		09 51				10 11	10 21	10 31	10 41		10 51			11 11	11 21	11 41		11 51		12 11	12 21
Longbridge	d	09 26	09a37	09a46		09 58				10a16	10 26	10a37	10a46		10 58			11a16	11 26	11a46		11 58		12a16	12 26
Barnt Green	d	09 39				10 09					10 39				11 09				11 39			12 09			12 39
Alvechurch	d	09 43				10 13					10 43				11 13				11 43			12 13			12 43
Redditch	a	09 52				10 22					10 52				11 22				11 52			12 22			12 52
Bromsgrove	a								10 09							11 09							12 09		

Lichfield - Birmingham - Longbridge and Redditch

Network Diagram - see first Page of Table 67

		LM		XC ◇1 ⊼	LM	LM	LM	LM	LM	XC ◇1 ⊼	LM	LM		LM	LM	LM	XC ◇1 ⊼	LM	LM	LM	LM	LM		XC ◇1 ⊼	LM
Lichfield Trent Valley	d				11 47			12 17			12 47				13 17			13 47			14 17				14 47
Lichfield City	d				11 50			12 20			12 50				13 20			13 50			14 20				14 50
Shenstone	d				11 56			12 26			12 56				13 26			13 56			14 26				14 56
Blake Street	d				12 00			12 30			13 00				13 30			14 00			14 30				15 00
Butlers Lane	d				12 02			12 32			13 02				13 32			14 02			14 32				15 02
Four Oaks	d	11 54			12 05		12 24	12 35	12 54		13 05			13 24	13 35	13 54		14 05		14 24	14 35	14 54			15 05
Sutton Coldfield	d	11 57			12 09		12 27	12 39	12 57		13 09			13 27	13 39	13 57		14 09		14 27	14 39	14 57			15 09
Wylde Green	d	12 00			12 12		12 30	12 42	13 00		13 12			13 30	13 42	14 00		14 12		14 30	14 42	15 00			15 12
Chester Road	d	12 03			12 14		12 33	12 44	13 03		13 14			13 33	13 44	14 03		14 14		14 33	14 44	15 03			15 14
Erdington	d	12 05			12 16		12 35	12 46	13 05		13 16			13 35	13 46	14 05		14 16		14 35	14 46	15 05			15 16
Gravelly Hill	d	12 08			12 19		12 38	12 49	13 08		13 19			13 38	13 49	14 08		14 19		14 38	14 49	15 08			15 19
Aston	d	12 11			12 23		12 41	12 53	13 11		13 23			13 41	13 53	14 11		14 23		14 41	14 53	15 11			15 23
Duddeston	d	12 13					12 43		13 13					13 43		14 13				14 43		15 13			
Birmingham New Street 12	a	12 21			12 31		12 51	13 01	13 21		13 31			13 51	14 01	14 21		14 31		14 51	15 01	15 21			15 31
	d	12 23		12 30	12 33	12 49	12 53	13 03	13 23	13 30	13 33	13 49		13 53	14 03	14 23	14 30	14 33	14 49	14 53	15 03	15 23		15 30	15 33
Five Ways	d	12 26			12 36		12 56	13 06	13 26		13 36			13 56	14 06	14 26		14 36		14 56	15 06	15 26			15 36
University	d	12 30		12a36	12 40	12 55	13 00	13 10	13 30	13a36	13 40	13 55		14 00	14 10	14 30	14a36	14 40	14 55	15 00	15 10	15 30		15a36	15 40
Selly Oak	d	12 33			12 43		13 03	13 13	13 33		13 43			14 03	14 13	14 33		14 43		15 03	15 13	15 33			15 43
Bournville	d	12 35			12 45		13 05	13 15	13 35		13 45			14 05	14 15	14 35		14 45		15 05	15 15	15 35			15 45
Kings Norton	d	12 38			12 48		13 08	13 18	13 38		13 48			14 08	14 18	14 38		14 48		15 08	15 18	15 38			15 48
Northfield	d	12 41			12 51		13 11	13 21	13 41		13 51			14 11	14 21	14 41		14 51		15 11	15 21	15 41			15 51
Longbridge	d	12a46			12 58		13a16	13 26	13a46		13 58			14a16	14 26	14a46		14 58		15a16	15 26	15a46			15 58
Barnt Green	d				13 09			13 39			14 09				14 39			15 09			15 39				16 09
Alvechurch	d				13 13			13 43			14 13				14 43			15 13			15 43				16 13
Redditch	a				13 22			13 52			14 22				14 52			15 22			15 52				16 22
Bromsgrove	a					13 09						14 09							15 09						

		LM	LM	LM	LM	LM	LM	LM		XC ◇1	LM	LM	LM	LM	LM	LM	LM	LM		XC ◇1	LM	LM	LM	LM	LM
Lichfield Trent Valley	d				15 17						15 47				16 17						16 47				
Lichfield City	d				15 20						15 50				16 20						16 50				
Shenstone	d				15 26						15 56				16 26						16 56				
Blake Street	d				15 30			15 49			16 00				16 30						17 00				
Butlers Lane	d				15 32			15 51			16 02				16 32						17 02				
Four Oaks	d			15 24	15 35	15 44		15 54			16 05			16 24	16 35			16 54			17 05			17 24	
Sutton Coldfield	d			15 27	15 39	15 47		15 57			16 09			16 27	16 39			16 57			17 09			17 27	
Wylde Green	d			15 30	15 42	15 50		16 00			16 12			16 30	16 42			17 00			17 12			17 30	
Chester Road	d			15 33	15 44	15 53		16 03			16 14			16 33	16 44			17 03			17 14			17 33	
Erdington	d			15 35	15 46	15 55		16 05			16 16			16 35	16 46			17 05			17 16			17 35	
Gravelly Hill	d			15 38	15 49	15 58		16 08			16 19			16 38	16 49			17 08			17 19			17 38	
Aston	d			15 41	15 53	16 01		16 11			16 23			16 41	16 53			17 11			17 23			17 41	
Duddeston	d			15 43		16 04		16 13						16 43				17 13						17 43	
Birmingham New Street 12	a			15 51	16 01	16 11		16 21			16 31			16 51	17 01			17 21			17 31			17 51	
	d	15 43	15 49	15 53	16 03	16 13	16 19	16 23		16 30	16 33	16 43	16 49	16 53	17 03	17 13	17 19	17 23		17 30	17 33	17 43	17 49	17 53	17 59
Five Ways	d	15 46		15 56	16 06	16 16		16 26			16 36	16 46		16 56	17 06	17 16		17 26			17 36	17 46		17 56	
University	d	15 50	15 55	16 00	16 10	16 20	16 25	16 30		16a36	16 40	16 50	16 55	17 00	17 10	17 20	17 25	17 30		17 36	17 40	17 50	17a55	18 00	18 05
Selly Oak	d	15 53		16 03	16 13	16 23		16 33			16 43	16 53		17 03	17 13	17 23		17 33			17 43	17 54		18 03	
Bournville	d	15 55		16 05	16 15	16 25		16 35			16 45	16 55		17 05	17 15	17 25		17 35			17 45	17 56		18 05	
Kings Norton	d	15 58		16 08	16 18	16 28		16 38			16 48	16 58		17 08	17 18	17 28		17 38			17 48	17 59		18 08	
Northfield	d	16 01		16 11	16 21	16 31		16 41			16 51	17 01		17 11	17 21	17 31		17 41			17 51	18 02		18 11	
Longbridge	d	16a06		16a16	16 26	16a36		16a46			16 58	17a06		17a16	17 26	17a37		17a46			17 58	18a06		18a16	
Barnt Green	d				16 39						17 09				17 39						18 09				
Alvechurch	d				16 43						17 13				17 43						18 13				
Redditch	a				16 52						17 22				17 52						18 22				
Bromsgrove	a		16 09				16 40						17 09				17 40			17 51					18 21

		LM	LM	LM		XC ◇1	LM	LM	LM	LM	LM	XC ◇1	LM	LM		LM	LM	LM	XC ◇1	LM	LM	LM	LM	LM	
Lichfield Trent Valley	d	17 17					17 47		18 17								19 17			19 57			20 27		
Lichfield City	d	17 20					17 50		18 20								19 20			20 00			20 30		
Shenstone	d	17 26					17 56		18 26								19 26			20 06			20 36		
Blake Street	d	17 30					18 00		18 30								19 30			20 10			20 40		
Butlers Lane	d	17 32					18 02		18 32								19 32			20 12			20 42		
Four Oaks	d	17 35		17 54			18 05	18 24	18 35		18 54		19 16				19 35	19 54		20 15			20 45		
Sutton Coldfield	d	17 39		17 57			18 09	18 27	18 39		18 57		19 19				19 39	19 57		20 19			20 49		
Wylde Green	d	17 42		18 00			18 12	18 30	18 42		19 00		19 22				19 42	20 00		20 22			20 52		
Chester Road	d	17 44		18 03			18 14	18 33	18 44		19 03		19 25				19 44	20 03		20 24			20 54		
Erdington	d	17 46		18 05			18 16	18 35	18 46		19 05		19 27				19 46	20 05		20 26			20 56		
Gravelly Hill	d	17 49		18 08			18 19	18 38	18 49		19 08		19 30				19 49	20 08		20 29			20 59		
Aston	d	17 53		18 11			18 23	18 41	18 53		19 11		19 33				19 53	20 11		20 33			21 03		
Duddeston	d			18 13				18 43			19 13		19 35				19 55			20 35			21 05		
Birmingham New Street 12	a	18 01		18 21			18 31	18 51	19 01		19 21		19 41				20 01	20 21		20 41			21 11		
	d	18 04	18 19	18 23		18 30	18 33	18 53	19 03	19 19	19 23	19 30	19 43	19 49		19 53	20 13	20 23	20 30	20 43	20 53	20 59	21 13	21 23	
Five Ways	d	18 07		18 26			18 36	18 56	19 06		19 26		19 46			19 56	20 16	20 26		20 46	20 56		21 16	21 26	
University	d	18 11	18 25	18 30		18 36	18 40	19 00	19 10	19 25	19 30	19a36	19 50	19 55		20 00	20 20	20 30	20a36	20 50	21 00	21 05	21 20	21 30	
Selly Oak	d	18 14		18 33			18 43	19 03	19 13		19 33		19 53			20 03	20 23	20 33		20 53	21 03		21 23	21 33	
Bournville	d	18 16		18 35			18 45	19 05	19 15		19 35		19 55			20 05	20 25	20 35		20 55	21 05		21 25	21 35	
Kings Norton	d	18 19		18 38			18 48	19 08	19 18		19 38		19 58			20 08	20 28	20 39		20 58	21 08		21 28	21 38	
Northfield	d	18 22		18 41			18 51	19 11	19 21		19 41		20 01			20 11	20 31	20 42		21 01	21 11		21 31	21 41	
Longbridge	d	18 27		18a46			18 58	19a16	19 26		19a46		20 05			20a16	20 35	20a46		21 05	21a16		21 35	21a46	
Barnt Green	d	18 40					19 09		19 39				20 09				20 39			21 09			21 39		
Alvechurch	d	18 44					19 13		19 43				20 14				20 44			21 14			21 44		
Redditch	a	18 52					19 22		19 52				20 22				20 52			21 22			21 52		
Bromsgrove	a		18 44			18 49				19 40				20 10								21 19			

Table 69

Mondays to Fridays

from 22 October

Lichfield - Birmingham - Longbridge and Redditch

Network Diagram - see first Page of Table 67

		LM	LM	LM	LM	LM	LM	LM	LM	LM		LM
Lichfield Trent Valley	d	20 57			21 27		21 57			22 27		22 55
Lichfield City	d	21 00			21 30		22 00			22 30		22 58
Shenstone	d	21 06			21 36		22 06			22 36		23 04
Blake Street	d	21 10			21 40		22 10			22 40		23 08
Butlers Lane	d	21 12			21 42		22 12			22 42		23 10
Four Oaks	d	21 15			21 45		22 15			22 45		23 13
Sutton Coldfield	d	21 19			21 49		22 19			22 49		23 17
Wylde Green	d	21 22			21 52		22 22			22 52		23 20
Chester Road	d	21 24			21 54		22 24			22 54		
Erdington	d	21 26			21 56		22 26			22 56		
Gravelly Hill	d	21 29			21 59		22 29			22 59		
Aston	d	21 33			22 03		22 33			23 03		
Duddeston	d	21 35			22 05		22 35			23 05		
Birmingham New Street 12	a	21 41			22 13		22 41			23 11		23 31
	d	21 43	21 53	22 00	22 13	22 23	22 43	22 53	23 00	23 13		23 33
Five Ways	d	21 46	21 56		22 16	22 26	22 46	22 56		23 16		23 36
University	d	21 50	22 00	22 06	22 20	22 30	22 50	23 00	23 06	23 20		23 40
Selly Oak	d	21 53	22 03		22 23	22 33	22 53	23 03		23 23		23 43
Bournville	d	21 55	22 05		22 25	22 35	22 55	23 05		23 25		23 45
Kings Norton	d	21 58	22 08		22 28	22 38	22 58	23 08		23 28		23 48
Northfield	d	22 01	22 11		22 31	22 41	23 01	23 11		23 31		23 51
Longbridge	d	22 05	22a16		22 35	22a46	23 05	23a16		23 35		23a56
Barnt Green	d	22 09			22 39		23 09			23 39		
Alvechurch	d	22 14			22 44		23 14			23 44		
Redditch	a	22 22			22 52		23 22			23 53		
Bromsgrove	a			22 19					23 19			

Saturdays

until 20 October

		XC ◇1	LM	LM	LM	LM	LM	LM	LM	LM		LM	LM	LM	XC ◇1 ⊼	LM	LM	LM	LM	LM		LM	LM	XC ◇1 ⊼	LM
Lichfield Trent Valley	d											06 20				06 50				07 20					07 50
Lichfield City	d											06 24	06 38			06 54	07 07			07 24			07 43		07 54
Shenstone	d											06 29				06 59				07 29			07 48		
Blake Street	d						06 03					06 33				07 03				07 33			07 52		08 02
Butlers Lane	d						06 05					06 35				07 05				07 35			07 54		08 04
Four Oaks	d						06 08					06 38	06 48			07 08	07 17			07 38		07 47	07 57		08 07
Sutton Coldfield	d						06 11					06 41	06 51			07 11	07 20			07 41		07 50	08 00		08 10
Wylde Green	d						06 14					06 44	06 54			07 14	07 23			07 44		07 53	08 03		08 13
Chester Road	d						06 16					06 46	06 56			07 16	07 25			07 46		07 55	08 05		08 15
Erdington	d						06 17					06 48	06 58			07 18	07 27			07 47		07 57	08 07		08 17
Gravelly Hill	d						06 20					06 50	07 00			07 20	07 29			07 50		07 59	08 09		08 19
Aston	d						06 23					06 53	07 04			07 23	07 33			07 53		08 03	08 13		08 23
Duddeston	d						06 26					06 56	07 06			07 26	07 35					08 05			
Birmingham New Street 12	a						06 31					07 00	07 11			07 31	07 40			08 00		08 11	08 21		08 31
	d	05 42	05 53	06 03	06 13	06 23	06 33	06 43	06 49	06 53		07 03	07 13	07 23	07 30	07 33	07 43	07 49	07 53	08 03		08 13	08 23	08 30	08 33
Five Ways	d		05 56	06 06	06 16	06 26	06 36	06 46		06 56		07 06	07 16	07 26		07 36	07 46		07 56	08 06		08 16	08 26		08 36
University	d		06 00	06 10	06 20	06 30	06 40	06 50	06 55	07 00		07 10	07 20	07 30	07a36	07 40	07 50	07 55	08 00	08 10		08 20	08 30	08a36	08 40
Selly Oak	d		06 03	06 13	06 23	06 33	06 43	06 53		07 03		07 13	07 23	07 33		07 43	07 53		08 03	08 13		08 23	08 33		08 43
Bournville	d		06 05	06 15	06 25	06 35	06 45	06 55		07 05		07 15	07 25	07 35		07 45	07 55		08 05	08 15		08 25	08 35		08 45
Kings Norton	d		06 07	06 17	06 27	06 37	06 47	06 57		07 07		07 17	07 27	07 37		07 47	07 57		08 07	08 17		08 27	08 37		08 47
Northfield	d		06 10	06 20	06 30	06 40	06 50	07 00		07 10		07 20	07 30	07 40		07 50	08 00		08 10	08 20		08 30	08 40		08 50
Longbridge	d		06a14	06a24	06 34	06a44	06a54	07 06		07a14		07a24	07 34	07a44		07a54	08 06		08a14	08a24		08 34	08a44		08a54
Barnt Green	d				06 39			07 10					07 39				08 10					08 39			
Alvechurch	d				06 43			07 15					07 43				08 15					08 43			
Redditch	a				06 52			07 22					07 52				08 22					08 52			
Bromsgrove	a	06 03							07 09									08 09							

		LM	LM	LM	LM	LM		LM	XC ◇1 ⊼	LM	LM	LM	LM	LM	LM	LM		XC ◇1 ⊼	LM	LM	LM	LM	LM	LM	LM
Lichfield Trent Valley	d				08 20					08 50				09 20					09 50				10 20		
Lichfield City	d			08 13	08 24			08 43		08 54			09 13	09 24		09 43			09 54			10 13	10 24		10 43
Shenstone	d			08 18				08 48					09 18			09 48						10 18			10 48
Blake Street	d			08 22	08 32			08 52		09 02			09 22	09 32		09 52			10 02			10 22	10 32		10 52
Butlers Lane	d			08 24	08 34			08 54		09 04			09 24	09 34		09 54			10 04			10 24	10 34		10 54
Four Oaks	d	08 17		08 27	08 37	08 47		08 57		09 07	09 17		09 27	09 37	09 47	09 57			10 07	10 17		10 27	10 37	10 47	10 57
Sutton Coldfield	d	08 20		08 30	08 40	08 50		09 00		09 10	09 20		09 30	09 40	09 50	10 00			10 10	10 20		10 30	10 40	10 50	11 00
Wylde Green	d	08 23		08 33	08 43	08 53		09 03		09 13	09 23		09 33	09 43	09 53	10 03			10 13	10 23		10 33	10 43	10 53	11 03
Chester Road	d	08 25		08 35	08 45	08 55		09 05		09 15	09 25		09 35	09 45	09 55	10 05			10 15	10 25		10 35	10 45	10 55	11 05
Erdington	d	08 27		08 37	08 47	08 57		09 07		09 17	09 27		09 37	09 47	09 57	10 07			10 17	10 27		10 37	10 47	10 57	11 07
Gravelly Hill	d	08 29		08 39	08 49	08 59		09 09		09 19	09 29		09 39	09 49	09 59	10 09			10 19	10 29		10 39	10 49	10 59	11 09
Aston	d	08 33		08 43	08 53	09 03		09 13		09 23	09 33		09 43	09 53	10 03	10 13			10 23	10 33		10 43	10 53	11 03	11 13
Duddeston	d	08 35				09 05					09 35				10 05					10 35				11 05	
Birmingham New Street 12	a	08 41		08 50	09 00	09 10		09 21		09 31	09 41		09 50	10 00	10 10	10 21			10 31	10 41		10 50	11 00	11 10	11 21
	d	08 43	08 49	08 53	09 03	09 13		09 23	09 30	09 33	09 43	09 49	09 53	10 03	10 13	10 23		10 30	10 33	10 43	10 49	10 53	11 03	11 13	11 23
Five Ways	d	08 46		08 56	09 06	09 16		09 26		09 36	09 46		09 56	10 06	10 16	10 26			10 36	10 46		10 56	11 06	11 16	11 26
University	d	08 50	08 55	09 00	09 10	09 20		09 30	09a36	09 40	09 50	09 55	10 00	10 10	10 20	10 30		10a36	10 40	10 50	10 55	11 00	11 10	11 20	11 30
Selly Oak	d	08 53		09 03	09 13	09 23		09 33		09 43	09 53		10 03	10 13	10 23	10 33			10 43	10 53		11 03	11 13	11 23	11 33
Bournville	d	08 55		09 05	09 15	09 25		09 35		09 45	09 55		10 05	10 15	10 25	10 35			10 45	10 55		11 05	11 15	11 25	11 35
Kings Norton	d	08 57		09 07	09 17	09 27		09 37		09 47	09 57		10 07	10 17	10 27	10 37			10 47	10 57		11 07	11 17	11 27	11 37
Northfield	d	09 00		09 10	09 20	09 30		09 40		09 50	10 00		10 10	10 20	10 30	10 40			10 50	11 00		11 10	11 20	11 30	11 40
Longbridge	d	09 06		09a14	09a24	09 34		09a44		09a54	10 06		10a14	10a24	10 34	10a44			10a54	11 06		11a14	11a24	11 34	11a44
Barnt Green	d	09 10				09 39					10 10				10 39					11 10				11 39	
Alvechurch	d	09 15				09 43					10 15				10 43					11 15				11 43	
Redditch	a	09 22				09 52					10 22				10 52					11 22				11 52	
Bromsgrove	a		09 09									10 09									11 10				

Lichfield - Birmingham - Longbridge and Redditch

Saturdays until 20 October

Network Diagram - see first Page of Table 67

		XC ◇1		LM	LM	LM	LM	LM	LM	LM	XC ◇1	LM		LM	LM	LM	LM	LM	LM	XC ◇1	LM	LM		LM	LM
Lichfield Trent Valley	d			10 50				11 20				11 50					12 20				12 50				
Lichfield City	d			10 54			11 13	11 24		11 43		11 54				12 13	12 24		12 43		12 54				13 13
Shenstone	d						11 18			11 48						12 18			12 48						13 18
Blake Street	d			11 02			11 22	11 32		11 52		12 02				12 22	12 32		12 52		13 02				13 22
Butlers Lane	d			11 04			11 24	11 34		11 54		12 04				12 24	12 34		12 54		13 04				13 24
Four Oaks	d			11 07	11 17		11 27	11 37	11 47	11 57		12 07		12 17		12 27	12 37	12 47	12 57		13 07	13 17			13 27
Sutton Coldfield	d			11 10	11 20		11 30	11 40	11 50	12 00		12 10		12 20		12 30	12 40	12 50	13 00		13 10	13 20			13 30
Wylde Green	d			11 13	11 23		11 33	11 43	11 53	12 03		12 13		12 23		12 33	12 43	12 53	13 03		13 13	13 23			13 33
Chester Road	d			11 15	11 25		11 35	11 45	11 55	12 05		12 15		12 25		12 35	12 45	12 55	13 05		13 15	13 25			13 35
Erdington	d			11 17	11 27		11 37	11 47	11 57	12 07		12 17		12 27		12 37	12 47	12 57	13 07		13 17	13 27			13 37
Gravelly Hill	d			11 19	11 29		11 39	11 49	11 59	12 09		12 19		12 29		12 39	12 49	12 59	13 09		13 19	13 29			13 39
Aston	d			11 23	11 33		11 43	11 53	12 03	12 13		12 23		12 33		12 43	12 53	13 03	13 13		13 23	13 33			13 43
Duddeston	d				11 35				12 05					12 35				13 05				13 35			
Birmingham New Street	a			11 30	11 41		11 50	12 00	12 10	12 21		12 30		12 41		12 50	13 00	13 10	13 21		13 30	13 41			13 50
	d	11 30		11 33	11 43	11 49	11 53	12 03	12 13	12 23	12 30	12 33		12 43	12 49	12 53	13 03	13 13	13 23	13 30	13 33	13 43		13 49	13 53
Five Ways	d			11 36	11 46		11 56	12 06	12 16	12 26		12 36		12 46		12 56	13 06	13 16	13 26		13 36	13 46			13 56
University	d	11a36		11 40	11 50	11 55	12 00	12 10	12 20	12 30	12a36	12 40		12 50	12 55	13 00	13 10	13 20	13 30	13a36	13 40	13 50		13 55	14 00
Selly Oak	d			11 43	11 53		12 03	12 13	12 23	12 33		12 43		12 53		13 03	13 13	13 23	13 33		13 43	13 53			14 03
Bournville	d			11 45	11 55		12 05	12 15	12 25	12 35		12 45		12 55		13 05	13 15	13 25	13 35		13 45	13 55			14 05
Kings Norton	d			11 47	11 57		12 07	12 17	12 27	12 37		12 47		12 57		13 07	13 17	13 27	13 37		13 47	13 57			14 07
Northfield	d			11 50	12 00		12 10	12 20	12 30	12 40		12 50		13 00		13 10	13 20	13 30	13 40		13 50	14 00			14 10
Longbridge	d			11a54	12 06		12a14	12a24	12 34	12a44		12a54		13 06		13a14	13a24	13 34	13a44		13a54	14 06			14a14
Barnt Green	d				12 10				12 39					13 10				13 39				14 10			
Alvechurch	d				12 15				12 43					13 15				13 43				14 15			
Redditch	a				12 22				12 52					13 22				13 52				14 22			
Bromsgrove	a					12 09									13 09									14 10	

		LM	LM	LM	XC ◇1	LM	LM	LM		LM	LM	LM	LM	XC ◇1	LM	LM	LM	LM		LM	LM	LM	LM	XC ◇1	LM
Lichfield Trent Valley	d	13 20				13 50					14 20				14 50					15 20					15 50
Lichfield City	d	13 24		13 43		13 54				14 13	14 24		14 43		14 54			15 13		15 24			15 43		15 54
Shenstone	d			13 48						14 18			14 48					15 18					15 48		
Blake Street	d	13 32		13 52		14 02				14 22	14 32		14 52		15 02			15 22		15 32			15 52		16 02
Butlers Lane	d	13 34		13 54		14 04				14 24	14 34		14 54		15 04			15 24		15 34			15 54		16 04
Four Oaks	d	13 37	13 47	13 57		14 07	14 17			14 27	14 37	14 47	14 57		15 07	15 17		15 27		15 37	15 47		15 57		16 07
Sutton Coldfield	d	13 40	13 50	14 00		14 10	14 20			14 30	14 40	14 50	15 00		15 10	15 20		15 30		15 40	15 50		16 00		16 10
Wylde Green	d	13 43	13 53	14 03		14 13	14 23			14 33	14 43	14 53	15 03		15 13	15 23		15 33		15 43	15 53		16 03		16 13
Chester Road	d	13 45	13 55	14 05		14 15	14 25			14 35	14 45	14 55	15 05		15 15	15 25		15 35		15 45	15 55		16 05		16 15
Erdington	d	13 47	13 57	14 07		14 17	14 27			14 37	14 47	14 57	15 07		15 17	15 27		15 37		15 47	15 57		16 07		16 17
Gravelly Hill	d	13 49	13 59	14 09		14 19	14 29			14 39	14 49	14 59	15 09		15 19	15 29		15 39		15 49	15 59		16 09		16 19
Aston	d	13 53	14 03	14 13		14 23	14 33			14 43	14 53	15 03	15 13		15 23	15 33		15 43		15 53	16 03		16 13		16 23
Duddeston	d		14 05				14 35					15 05				15 35					16 05				
Birmingham New Street	a	14 00	14 10	14 21		14 30	14 41			14 50	15 00	15 10	15 20		15 30	15 41		15 50		16 00	16 10		16 21		16 30
	d	14 03	14 13	14 23	14 30	14 33	14 43	14 49		14 53	15 03	15 13	15 23	15 30	15 33	15 43	15 49	15 53		16 03	16 13	16 19	16 23	16 30	16 33
Five Ways	d	14 06	14 16	14 26		14 36	14 46			14 56	15 06	15 16	15 26		15 36	15 46		15 56		16 06	16 16		16 26		16 36
University	d	14 10	14 20	14 30	14a36	14 40	14 50	14 55		15 00	15 10	15 20	15 30	15a36	15 40	15 50	15 55	16 00		16 10	16 20		16 30	16a36	16 40
Selly Oak	d	14 13	14 23	14 33		14 43	14 53			15 03	15 13	15 23	15 33		15 43	15 53		16 03		16 13	16 23		16 33		16 43
Bournville	d	14 15	14 25	14 35		14 45	14 55			15 05	15 15	15 25	15 35		15 45	15 55		16 05		16 15	16 25		16 35		16 45
Kings Norton	d	14 17	14 27	14 37		14 47	14 57			15 07	15 17	15 27	15 37		15 47	15 57		16 07		16 17	16 27		16 37		16 47
Northfield	d	14 20	14 30	14 40		14 50	15 00			15 10	15 20	15 30	15 40		15 50	16 00		16 10		16 20	16 30		16 40		16 50
Longbridge	d	14a24	14 34	14a44		14a54	15 06			15a14	15a24	15 34	15a44		15a54	16 06		16a14		16a24	16 36		16a44		16a54
Barnt Green	d		14 39				15 10					15 39				16 10					16 40				
Alvechurch	d		14 43				15 15					15 43				16 15					16 45				
Redditch	a		14 52				15 22					15 52				16 22					16 52				
Bromsgrove	a							15 09									16 09					16 43			

		LM	LM	LM		LM	LM	LM	LM	XC ◇1	LM	LM	LM	LM		LM	LM	LM	XC ◇1	LM	LM	LM	LM	LM	
Lichfield Trent Valley	d					16 20					16 50					17 20				17 50				18 20	
Lichfield City	d			16 13		16 24			16 43		16 54			17 13		17 24		17 43		17 54			18 13	18 24	
Shenstone	d			16 18					16 48					17 18				17 48					18 18		
Blake Street	d			16 22		16 32			16 52		17 02			17 22		17 32		17 52		18 02			18 22	18 32	
Butlers Lane	d			16 24		16 34			16 54		17 04			17 24		17 34		17 54		18 04			18 24	18 34	
Four Oaks	d	16 17		16 27		16 37	16 47		16 57		17 07	17 17		17 27		17 37	17 47	17 57		18 07	18 17		18 27	18 37	
Sutton Coldfield	d	16 20		16 30		16 40	16 50		17 00		17 10	17 20		17 30		17 40	17 50	18 00		18 10	18 20		18 30	18 40	
Wylde Green	d	16 23		16 33		16 43	16 53		17 03		17 13	17 23		17 33		17 43	17 53	18 03		18 13	18 23		18 33	18 43	
Chester Road	d	16 25		16 35		16 45	16 55		17 05		17 15	17 25		17 35		17 45	17 55	18 05		18 15	18 25		18 35	18 45	
Erdington	d	16 27		16 37		16 47	16 57		17 07		17 17	17 27		17 37		17 47	17 57	18 07		18 17	18 27		18 37	18 47	
Gravelly Hill	d	16 29		16 39		16 49	16 59		17 09		17 19	17 29		17 39		17 49	17 59	18 09		18 19	18 29		18 39	18 49	
Aston	d	16 33		16 43		16 53	17 03		17 13		17 23	17 33		17 43		17 53	18 03	18 13		18 23	18 33		18 43	18 53	
Duddeston	d	16 35					17 05					17 35					18 05				18 35				
Birmingham New Street	a	16 41		16 50		17 00	17 10		17 21		17 30	17 41		17 50		18 00	18 10	18 21		18 30	18 41		18 50	19 00	
	d	16 43	16 49	16 53		17 03	17 13	17 19	17 23	17 30	17 33	17 43	17 49	17 53		18 03	18 13	18 23	18 30	18 33	18 43	18 49	18 53	19 03	
Five Ways	d	16 46		16 56		17 06	17 16		17 26		17 36	17 46		17 56		18 06	18 16	18 26		18 36	18 46		18 56	19 06	
University	d	16 50	16 55	17 00		17 10	17 20		17 30	17 36	17 40	17 50	17 55	18 00		18 10	18 20	18 30	18a36	18 40	18 50	18 55	19 00	19 10	
Selly Oak	d	16 53		17 03		17 13	17 23		17 33		17 43	17 53		18 03		18 13	18 23	18 33		18 43	18 53		19 03	19 13	
Bournville	d	16 55		17 05		17 15	17 25		17 35		17 45	17 55		18 05		18 15	18 25	18 35		18 45	18 55		19 05	19 15	
Kings Norton	d	16 57		17 07		17 17	17 27		17 37		17 47	17 57		18 07		18 17	18 27	18 37		18 47	18 57		19 07	19 17	
Northfield	d	17 00		17 10		17 20	17 30		17 40		17 50	18 00		18 10		18 20	18 30	18 40		18 50	19 00		19 10	19 20	
Longbridge	d	17 06		17a14		17a24	17 36		17a44		17a54	18 06		18a14		18a24	18 34	18a44		18a54	19 06		19a14	19a24	
Barnt Green	d	17 10					17 40					18 10					18 39				19 10				
Alvechurch	d	17 15					17 45					18 15					18 43				19 15				
Redditch	a	17 22					17 52					18 22					18 52				19 22				
Bromsgrove	a		17 10					17 40		17 49			18 09									19 09			

Lichfield - Birmingham - Longbridge and Redditch

Saturdays until 20 October

Network Diagram - see first Page of Table 67

		LM	LM	LM	XC ◇1	LM	LM	LM	LM	LM		LM	XC ◇1	LM	LM	LM	LM	LM	LM	LM		LM	LM	LM	LM
Lichfield Trent Valley	d					18 50			19 20					20 00			20 30		21 00			21 30		22 00	
Lichfield City	d			18 43		18 54		19 13	19 24			19 43		20 04			20 34		21 04			21 34		22 04	
Shenstone	d			18 48				19 18				19 48		20 09			20 39		21 09			21 39		22 09	
Blake Street	d			18 52		19 02		19 22	19 32			19 52		20 13			20 43		21 13			21 43		22 13	
Butlers Lane	d			18 54		19 04		19 24	19 34			19 54		20 15			20 45		21 15			21 45		22 15	
Four Oaks	d	18 47		18 57		19 07	19 17	19 27	19 37	19 50		19 57		20 18			20 48		21 18			21 48		22 18	
Sutton Coldfield	d	18 50		19 00		19 10	19 20	19 30	19 40	19 53		20 00		20 21			20 51		21 21			21 51		22 21	
Wylde Green	d	18 53		19 03		19 13	19 23	19 33	19 43	19 56		20 03		20 24			20 54		21 24			21 54		22 24	
Chester Road	d	18 55		19 05		19 15	19 25	19 35	19 45	19 58		20 05		20 26			20 56		21 26			21 56		22 26	
Erdington	d	18 57		19 07		19 17	19 27	19 37	19 47	20 00		20 07		20 28			20 58		21 28			21 58		22 28	
Gravelly Hill	d	18 59		19 09		19 19	19 29	19 39	19 49	20 02		20 09		20 30			21 00		21 30			22 00		22 30	
Aston	d	19 03		19 13		19 23	19 33	19 43	19 53	20 06		20 13		20 33			21 03		21 33			22 03		22 33	
Duddeston	d	19 05					19 35		19 55					20 36			21 06		21 36			22 06		22 36	
Birmingham New Street	a	19 10		19 21		19 30	19 41	19 50	20 02	20 13		20 20		20 41			21 12		21 41			22 11		22 41	
	d	19 13	19 19	19 23	19 30	19 33	19 43	19 53		20 13		20 23	20 30	20 43	20 53	20 59	21 13	21 23	21 43	21 53		22 13	22 23	22 43	22 53
Five Ways	d	19 16		19 26		19 36	19 46	19 56		20 16		20 26		20 46	20 56		21 16	21 26	21 46	21 56		22 16	22 26	22 46	22 56
University	d	19 20	19 25	19 30	19a36	19 40	19 50	20 00		20 20		20 30	20a36	20 50	21 00	21 05	21 20	21 30	21 50	22 00		22 20	22 30	22 50	23 00
Selly Oak	d	19 23		19 33		19 43	19 53	20 03		20 23		20 33		20 53	21 03		21 23	21 33	21 53	22 03		22 23	22 33	22 53	23 03
Bournville	d	19 25		19 35		19 45	19 55	20 05		20 25		20 35		20 55	21 05		21 25	21 35	21 55	22 05		22 25	22 35	22 55	23 05
Kings Norton	d	19 27		19 37		19 47	19 57	20 07		20 27		20 37		20 57	21 07		21 27	21 37	21 57	22 07		22 27	22 37	22 57	23 07
Northfield	d	19 30		19 40		19 50	20 00	20 10		20 30		20 40		21 00	21 10		21 30	21 40	22 00	22 10		22 30	22 40	23 00	23 10
Longbridge	d	19 36		19a44		19a54	20 04	20a14		20 34		20a44		21 04	21a14		21 34	21a44	22 04	22a14		22 34	22a44	23 04	23a14
Barnt Green	d	19 40					20 09			20 39				21 09			21 39		22 09			22 39		23 09	
Alvechurch	d	19 45					20 13			20 43				21 13			21 43		22 13			22 43		23 13	
Redditch	a	19 52					20 22			20 52				21 22			21 52		22 22			22 52		23 22	
Bromsgrove	a		19 39													21 19									

		LM	LM	LM
Lichfield Trent Valley	d	22 30	22 56	
Lichfield City	d	22 34	23 00	
Shenstone	d	22 39	23 05	
Blake Street	d	22 43	23 09	23 36
Butlers Lane	d	22 45	23 11	23 38
Four Oaks	d	22 48	23 14	23 41
Sutton Coldfield	d	22 51	23 17	23 44
Wylde Green	d	22 54	23 20	
Chester Road	d	22 56		
Erdington	d	22 58		
Gravelly Hill	d	23 00		
Aston	d	23 03		
Duddeston	d	23 06		
Birmingham New Street	a	23 11	23 31	23 59
	d	23 13	23 33	
Five Ways	d	23 16	23 36	
University	d	23 20	23 40	
Selly Oak	d	23 23	23 43	
Bournville	d	23 25	23 45	
Kings Norton	d	23 27	23 47	
Northfield	d	23 30	23 50	
Longbridge	d	23 34	23a54	
Barnt Green	d	23 39		
Alvechurch	d	23 43		
Redditch	a	23 53		
Bromsgrove	a			

Saturdays from 27 October

		XC ◇1	LM	LM	LM	LM	LM	LM	LM	LM		LM	LM	LM	XC ◇1	LM	LM	LM	LM	LM		LM	LM	XC ◇1	LM
Lichfield Trent Valley	d											06 20				06 50				07 20					07 50
Lichfield City	d											06 24	06 38			06 54	07 07			07 24			07 43		07 54
Shenstone	d											06 29				06 59				07 29			07 48		
Blake Street	d						06 03					06 33				07 03				07 33			07 52		08 02
Butlers Lane	d						06 05					06 35				07 05				07 35			07 54		08 04
Four Oaks	d						06 08					06 38	06 48			07 08	07 17			07 38		07 47	07 57		08 07
Sutton Coldfield	d						06 11					06 41	06 51			07 11	07 20			07 41		07 50	08 00		08 10
Wylde Green	d						06 14					06 44	06 54			07 14	07 23			07 44		07 53	08 03		08 13
Chester Road	d						06 16					06 46	06 56			07 16	07 25			07 46		07 55	08 05		08 15
Erdington	d						06 17					06 48	06 58			07 18	07 27			07 47		07 57	08 07		08 17
Gravelly Hill	d						06 20					06 50	07 00			07 20	07 29			07 50		07 59	08 09		08 19
Aston	d						06 23					06 53	07 04			07 23	07 33			07 53		08 03	08 13		08 23
Duddeston	d						06 26					06 56	07 06			07 26	07 35					08 05			
Birmingham New Street	a						06 31					07 00	07 11			07 31	07 40			08 00		08 11	08 21		08 31
	d	05 42	05 53	06 03	06 13	06 23	06 33	06 43	06 49	06 53		07 03	07 13	07 23	07 30	07 33	07 43	07 49	07 53	08 03		08 13	08 23	08 30	08 33
Five Ways	d		05 56	06 06	06 16	06 26	06 36	06 46		06 56		07 06	07 16	07 26		07 36	07 46		07 56	08 06		08 16	08 26		08 36
University	d		06 00	06 10	06 20	06 30	06 40	06 50	06 55	07 00		07 10	07 20	07 30	07a36	07 40	07 50	07 55	08 00	08 10		08 20	08 30	08a36	08 40
Selly Oak	d		06 03	06 13	06 23	06 33	06 43	06 53		07 03		07 13	07 23	07 33		07 43	07 53		08 03	08 13		08 23	08 33		08 43
Bournville	d		06 05	06 15	06 25	06 35	06 45	06 55		07 05		07 15	07 25	07 35		07 45	07 55		08 05	08 15		08 25	08 35		08 45
Kings Norton	d		06 07	06 17	06 27	06 37	06 47	06 57		07 07		07 17	07 27	07 37		07 47	07 57		08 07	08 17		08 27	08 37		08 47
Northfield	d		06 10	06 20	06 30	06 40	06 50	07 00		07 10		07 20	07 30	07 40		07 50	08 00		08 10	08 20		08 30	08 40		08 50
Longbridge	d		06a14	06a24	06 34	06a44	06a54	07 06		07a14		07a24	07 34	07a44		07a54	08 06		08a14	08a24		08 34	08a44		08a54
Barnt Green	d				06 39			07 10					07 39				08 10					08 39			
Alvechurch	d				06 43			07 15					07 43				08 15					08 43			
Redditch	a				06 52			07 22					07 52				08 22					08 52			
Bromsgrove	a	06 03							07 09									08 09							

Lichfield - Birmingham - Longbridge and Redditch

Network Diagram - see first Page of Table 67

		LM	LM	LM	LM	LM	LM	XC ◇1	LM	LM	LM	LM	LM	LM	LM	XC ◇1	LM	LM	LM	LM	LM	LM	LM
Lichfield Trent Valley	d				08 20				08 50				09 20				09 50				10 20		
Lichfield City	d			08 13	08 24		08 43		08 54			09 13	09 24		09 43		09 54			10 13	10 24		10 43
Shenstone	d			08 18			08 48					09 18			09 48					10 18			10 48
Blake Street	d			08 22	08 32		08 52		09 02			09 22	09 32		09 52		10 02			10 22	10 32		10 52
Butlers Lane	d			08 24	08 34		08 54		09 04			09 24	09 34		09 54		10 04			10 24	10 34		10 54
Four Oaks	d	08 17		08 27	08 37	08 47	08 57		09 07	09 17		09 27	09 37	09 47	09 57		10 07	10 17		10 27	10 37	10 47	10 57
Sutton Coldfield	d	08 20		08 30	08 40	08 50	09 00		09 10	09 20		09 30	09 40	09 50	10 00		10 10	10 20		10 30	10 40	10 50	11 00
Wylde Green	d	08 23		08 33	08 43	08 53	09 03		09 13	09 23		09 33	09 43	09 53	10 03		10 13	10 23		10 33	10 43	10 53	11 03
Chester Road	d	08 25		08 35	08 45	08 55	09 05		09 15	09 25		09 35	09 45	09 55	10 05		10 15	10 25		10 35	10 45	10 55	11 05
Erdington	d	08 27		08 37	08 47	08 57	09 07		09 17	09 27		09 37	09 47	09 57	10 07		10 17	10 27		10 37	10 47	10 57	11 07
Gravelly Hill	d	08 29		08 39	08 49	08 59	09 09		09 19	09 29		09 39	09 49	09 59	10 09		10 19	10 29		10 39	10 49	10 59	11 09
Aston	d	08 33		08 43	08 53	09 03	09 13		09 23	09 33		09 43	09 53	10 03	10 13		10 23	10 33		10 43	10 53	11 03	11 13
Duddeston	d	08 35				09 05				09 35				10 05				10 35				11 05	
Birmingham New Street 12	a	08 41		08 50	09 00	09 10	09 21		09 31	09 41		09 50	10 00	10 10	10 21		10 31	10 41		10 50	11 00	11 10	11 21
	d	08 43	08 49	08 53	09 03	09 13	09 23	09 30	09 33	09 43	09 49	09 53	10 03	10 13	10 23	10 30	10 33	10 43	10 49	10 53	11 03	11 13	11 23
Five Ways	d	08 46		08 56	09 06	09 16	09 26		09 36	09 46		09 56	10 06	10 16	10 26		10 36	10 46		10 56	11 06	11 16	11 26
University	d	08 50	08 55	09 00	09 10	09 20	09 30	09a36	09 40	09 50	09 55	10 00	10 10	10 20	10 30	10a36	10 40	10 50	10 55	11 00	11 10	11 20	11 30
Selly Oak	d	08 53		09 03	09 13	09 23	09 33		09 43	09 53		10 03	10 13	10 23	10 33		10 43	10 53		11 03	11 13	11 23	11 33
Bournville	d	08 55		09 05	09 15	09 25	09 35		09 45	09 55		10 05	10 15	10 25	10 35		10 45	10 55		11 05	11 15	11 25	11 35
Kings Norton	d	08 57		09 07	09 17	09 27	09 37		09 47	09 57		10 07	10 17	10 27	10 37		10 47	10 57		11 07	11 17	11 27	11 37
Northfield	d	09 00		09 10	09 20	09 30	09 40		09 50	10 00		10 10	10 20	10 30	10 40		10 50	11 00		11 10	11 20	11 30	11 40
Longbridge	d	09 06		09a14	09a24	09 34	09a44		09a54	10 06		10a14	10a24	10 34	10a44		10a54	11 06		11a14	11a24	11 34	11a44
Barnt Green	d	09 10				09 39				10 10				10 39				11 10				11 39	
Alvechurch	d	09 15				09 43				10 15				10 43				11 15				11 43	
Redditch	a	09 22				09 52				10 22				10 52				11 22				11 52	
Bromsgrove	a		09 09								10 09								11 10				

		XC ◇1	LM	LM	LM	LM	LM	LM	LM	XC ◇1	LM	LM	LM	LM	LM	LM	LM	XC ◇1	LM	LM	LM	LM
Lichfield Trent Valley	d		10 50				11 20				11 50				12 20				12 50			
Lichfield City	d		10 54			11 13	11 24		11 43		11 54			12 13	12 24		12 43		12 54			13 13
Shenstone	d					11 18			11 48					12 18			12 48					13 18
Blake Street	d		11 02			11 22	11 32		11 52		12 02			12 22	12 32		12 52		13 02			13 22
Butlers Lane	d		11 04			11 24	11 34		11 54		12 04			12 24	12 34		12 54		13 04			13 24
Four Oaks	d		11 07	11 17		11 27	11 37	11 47	11 57		12 07	12 17		12 27	12 37	12 47	12 57		13 07	13 17		13 27
Sutton Coldfield	d		11 10	11 20		11 30	11 40	11 50	12 00		12 10	12 20		12 30	12 40	12 50	13 00		13 10	13 20		13 30
Wylde Green	d		11 13	11 23		11 33	11 43	11 53	12 03		12 13	12 23		12 33	12 43	12 53	13 03		13 13	13 23		13 33
Chester Road	d		11 15	11 25		11 35	11 45	11 55	12 05		12 15	12 25		12 35	12 45	12 55	13 05		13 15	13 25		13 35
Erdington	d		11 17	11 27		11 37	11 47	11 57	12 07		12 17	12 27		12 37	12 47	12 57	13 07		13 17	13 27		13 37
Gravelly Hill	d		11 19	11 29		11 39	11 49	11 59	12 09		12 19	12 29		12 39	12 49	12 59	13 09		13 19	13 29		13 39
Aston	d		11 23	11 33		11 43	11 53	12 03	12 13		12 23	12 33		12 43	12 53	13 03	13 13		13 23	13 33		13 43
Duddeston	d			11 35				12 05				12 35				13 05				13 35		
Birmingham New Street 12	a		11 30	11 41		11 50	12 00	12 10	12 21		12 30	12 41		12 50	13 00	13 10	13 21		13 30	13 41		13 50
	d	11 30	11 33	11 43	11 49	11 53	12 03	12 13	12 23	12 30	12 33	12 43	12 49	12 53	13 03	13 13	13 23	13 30	13 33	13 43	13 49	13 53
Five Ways	d		11 36	11 46		11 56	12 06	12 16	12 26		12 36	12 46		12 56	13 06	13 16	13 26		13 36	13 46		13 56
University	d	11a36	11 40	11 50	11 55	12 00	12 10	12 20	12 30	12a36	12 40	12 50	12 55	13 00	13 10	13 20	13 30	13a36	13 40	13 50	13 55	14 00
Selly Oak	d		11 43	11 53		12 03	12 13	12 23	12 33		12 43	12 53		13 03	13 13	13 23	13 33		13 43	13 53		14 03
Bournville	d		11 45	11 55		12 05	12 15	12 25	12 35		12 45	12 55		13 05	13 15	13 25	13 35		13 45	13 55		14 05
Kings Norton	d		11 47	11 57		12 07	12 17	12 27	12 37		12 47	12 57		13 07	13 17	13 27	13 37		13 47	13 57		14 07
Northfield	d		11 50	12 00		12 10	12 20	12 30	12 40		12 50	13 00		13 10	13 20	13 30	13 40		13 50	14 00		14 10
Longbridge	d		11a54	12 06		12a14	12a24	12 34	12a44		12a54	13 06		13a14	13a24	13 34	13a44		13a54	14 06		14a14
Barnt Green	d			12 10				12 39				13 10				13 39				14 10		
Alvechurch	d			12 15				12 43				13 15				13 43				14 15		
Redditch	a			12 22				12 52				13 22				13 52				14 22		
Bromsgrove	a				12 09								13 09								14 10	

		LM	LM	LM	XC ◇1	LM	LM	LM	LM	LM	LM	LM	XC ◇1	LM	LM	LM	LM	LM	LM	LM	LM	XC ◇1	LM
Lichfield Trent Valley	d	13 20				13 50				14 20				14 50				15 20					15 50
Lichfield City	d	13 24		13 43		13 54			14 13	14 24		14 43		14 54			15 13	15 24			15 43		15 54
Shenstone	d			13 48					14 18			14 48					15 18				15 48		
Blake Street	d	13 32		13 52		14 02			14 22	14 32		14 52		15 02			15 22	15 32			15 52		16 02
Butlers Lane	d	13 34		13 54		14 04			14 24	14 34		14 54		15 04			15 24	15 34			15 54		16 04
Four Oaks	d	13 37	13 47	13 57		14 07	14 17		14 27	14 37	14 47	14 57		15 07	15 17		15 27	15 37	15 47		15 57		16 07
Sutton Coldfield	d	13 40	13 50	14 00		14 10	14 20		14 30	14 40	14 50	15 00		15 10	15 20		15 30	15 40	15 50		16 00		16 10
Wylde Green	d	13 43	13 53	14 03		14 13	14 23		14 33	14 43	14 53	15 03		15 13	15 23		15 33	15 43	15 53		16 03		16 13
Chester Road	d	13 45	13 55	14 05		14 15	14 25		14 35	14 45	14 55	15 05		15 15	15 25		15 35	15 45	15 55		16 05		16 15
Erdington	d	13 47	13 57	14 07		14 17	14 27		14 37	14 47	14 57	15 07		15 17	15 27		15 37	15 47	15 57		16 07		16 17
Gravelly Hill	d	13 49	13 59	14 09		14 19	14 29		14 39	14 49	14 59	15 09		15 19	15 29		15 39	15 49	15 59		16 09		16 19
Aston	d	13 53	14 03	14 13		14 23	14 33		14 43	14 53	15 03	15 13		15 23	15 33		15 43	15 53	16 03		16 13		16 23
Duddeston	d		14 05				14 35				15 05				15 35				16 05				
Birmingham New Street 12	a	14 00	14 10	14 21		14 30	14 41		14 50	15 00	15 10	15 20		15 30	15 41		15 50	16 00	16 10		16 21		16 30
	d	14 03	14 13	14 23	14 30	14 33	14 43	14 49	14 53	15 03	15 13	15 23	15 30	15 33	15 43	15 49	15 53	16 03	16 13	16 19	16 23	16 30	16 33
Five Ways	d	14 06	14 16	14 26		14 36	14 46		14 56	15 06	15 16	15 26		15 36	15 46		15 56	16 06	16 16		16 26		16 36
University	d	14 10	14 20	14 30	14a36	14 40	14 50	14 55	15 00	15 10	15 20	15 30	15a36	15 40	15 50	15 55	16 00	16 10	16 20		16 30	16a36	16 40
Selly Oak	d	14 13	14 23	14 33		14 43	14 53		15 03	15 13	15 23	15 33		15 43	15 53		16 03	16 13	16 23		16 33		16 43
Bournville	d	14 15	14 25	14 35		14 45	14 55		15 05	15 15	15 25	15 35		15 45	15 55		16 05	16 15	16 25		16 35		16 45
Kings Norton	d	14 17	14 27	14 37		14 47	14 57		15 07	15 17	15 27	15 37		15 47	15 57		16 07	16 17	16 27		16 37		16 47
Northfield	d	14 20	14 30	14 40		14 50	15 00		15 10	15 20	15 30	15 40		15 50	16 00		16 10	16 20	16 30		16 40		16 50
Longbridge	d	14a24	14 34	14a44		14a54	15 06		15a14	15a24	15 34	15a44		15a54	16 06		16a14	16a24	16 36		16a44		16a54
Barnt Green	d		14 39				15 10				15 39				16 10				16 40				
Alvechurch	d		14 43				15 15				15 43				16 15				16 45				
Redditch	a		14 52				15 22				15 52				16 22				16 52				
Bromsgrove	a							15 09								16 09				16 43			

Lichfield - Birmingham - Longbridge and Redditch

Network Diagram - see first Page of Table 67

		LM	LM	LM	LM	LM	LM	LM	XC ◇1	LM	LM	LM	LM	LM	LM	LM	XC ◇1	LM	LM	LM	LM	LM
Lichfield Trent Valley	d				16 20					16 50				17 20				17 50				18 20
Lichfield City	d			16 13	16 24			16 43		16 54			17 13	17 24		17 43		17 54			18 13	18 24
Shenstone	d			16 18				16 48					17 18			17 48					18 18	
Blake Street	d			16 22	16 32			16 52		17 02			17 22	17 32		17 52		18 02			18 22	18 32
Butlers Lane	d			16 24	16 34			16 54		17 04			17 24	17 34		17 54		18 04			18 24	18 34
Four Oaks	d	16 17		16 27	16 37	16 47		16 57		17 07	17 17		17 27	17 37	17 47	17 57		18 07	18 17		18 27	18 37
Sutton Coldfield	d	16 20		16 30	16 40	16 50		17 00		17 10	17 20		17 30	17 40	17 50	18 00		18 10	18 20		18 30	18 40
Wylde Green	d	16 23		16 33	16 43	16 53		17 03		17 13	17 23		17 33	17 43	17 53	18 03		18 13	18 23		18 33	18 43
Chester Road	d	16 25		16 35	16 45	16 55		17 05		17 15	17 25		17 35	17 45	17 55	18 05		18 15	18 25		18 35	18 45
Erdington	d	16 27		16 37	16 47	16 57		17 07		17 17	17 27		17 37	17 47	17 57	18 07		18 17	18 27		18 37	18 47
Gravelly Hill	d	16 29		16 39	16 49	16 59		17 09		17 19	17 29		17 39	17 49	17 59	18 09		18 19	18 29		18 39	18 49
Aston	d	16 33		16 43	16 53	17 03		17 13		17 23	17 33		17 43	17 53	18 03	18 13		18 23	18 33		18 43	18 53
Duddeston	d	16 35				17 05					17 35				18 05				18 35			
Birmingham New Street 12	a	16 41		16 50	17 00	17 10		17 21		17 30	17 41		17 50	18 00	18 10	18 21		18 30	18 41		18 50	19 00
	d	16 43	16 49	16 53	17 03	17 13	17 19	17 23	17 30	17 33	17 43	17 49	17 53	18 03	18 13	18 23	18 30	18 33	18 43	18 49	18 53	19 03
Five Ways	d	16 46		16 56	17 06	17 16		17 26		17 36	17 46		17 56	18 06	18 16	18 26		18 36	18 46		18 56	19 06
University	d	16 50	16 55	17 00	17 10	17 20		17 30	17 36	17 40	17 50	17 55	18 00	18 10	18 20	18 30	18a36	18 40	18 50	18 55	19 00	19 10
Selly Oak	d	16 53		17 03	17 13	17 23		17 33		17 43	17 53		18 03	18 13	18 23	18 33		18 43	18 53		19 03	19 13
Bournville	d	16 55		17 05	17 15	17 25		17 35		17 45	17 55		18 05	18 15	18 25	18 35		18 45	18 55		19 05	19 15
Kings Norton	d	16 57		17 07	17 17	17 27		17 37		17 47	17 57		18 07	18 17	18 27	18 37		18 47	18 57		19 07	19 17
Northfield	d	17 00		17 10	17 20	17 30		17 40		17 50	18 00		18 10	18 20	18 30	18 40		18 50	19 00		19 10	19 20
Longbridge	d	17 06		17a14	17a24	17 36		17a44		17a54	18 06		18a14	18a24	18 34	18a44		18a54	19 06		19a14	19a24
Barnt Green	d	17 10				17 40					18 10				18 39				19 10			
Alvechurch	d	17 15				17 45					18 15				18 43				19 15			
Redditch	a	17 22				17 52					18 22				18 52				19 22			
Bromsgrove	a		17 10				17 40		17 49			18 09								19 09		

		LM	LM	LM	XC ◇1	LM	LM	LM	LM	LM	LM	XC ◇1	LM	LM	LM	LM	LM	LM	LM	LM	LM	LM	LM
Lichfield Trent Valley	d					18 50			19 20				20 00			20 30		21 00		21 30		22 00	
Lichfield City	d			18 43		18 54		19 13	19 24		19 43		20 04			20 34		21 04		21 34		22 04	
Shenstone	d			18 48				19 18			19 48		20 09			20 39		21 09		21 39		22 09	
Blake Street	d			18 52		19 02		19 22	19 32		19 52		20 13			20 43		21 13		21 43		22 13	
Butlers Lane	d			18 54		19 04		19 24	19 34		19 54		20 15			20 45		21 15		21 45		22 15	
Four Oaks	d	18 47		18 57		19 07	19 17	19 27	19 37	19 50	19 57		20 18			20 48		21 18		21 48		22 18	
Sutton Coldfield	d	18 50		19 00		19 10	19 20	19 30	19 40	19 53	20 00		20 21			20 51		21 21		21 51		22 21	
Wylde Green	d	18 53		19 03		19 13	19 23	19 33	19 43	19 56	20 03		20 24			20 54		21 24		21 54		22 24	
Chester Road	d	18 55		19 05		19 15	19 25	19 35	19 45	19 58	20 05		20 26			20 56		21 26		21 56		22 26	
Erdington	d	18 57		19 07		19 17	19 27	19 37	19 47	20 00	20 07		20 28			20 58		21 28		21 58		22 28	
Gravelly Hill	d	18 59		19 09		19 19	19 29	19 39	19 49	20 02	20 09		20 30			21 00		21 30		22 00		22 30	
Aston	d	19 03		19 13		19 23	19 33	19 43	19 53	20 06	20 13		20 33			21 03		21 33		22 03		22 33	
Duddeston	d	19 05					19 35		19 55				20 36			21 06		21 36		22 06		22 36	
Birmingham New Street 12	a	19 10		19 21		19 30	19 41	19 50	20 02	20 13	20 20		20 41			21 12		21 41		22 11		22 41	
	d	19 13	19 19	19 23	19 30	19 33	19 43	19 53		20 13	20 23	20 30	20 43	20 53	20 59	21 13	21 23	21 43	21 53	22 13	22 23	22 43	22 53
Five Ways	d	19 16		19 26		19 36	19 46	19 56		20 16	20 26		20 46	20 56		21 16	21 26	21 46	21 56	22 16	22 26	22 46	22 56
University	d	19 20	19 25	19 30	19a36	19 40	19 50	20 00		20 20	20 30	20a36	20 50	21 00	21 05	21 20	21 30	21 50	22 00	22 20	22 30	22 50	23 00
Selly Oak	d	19 23		19 33		19 43	19 53	20 03		20 23	20 33		20 53	21 03		21 23	21 33	21 53	22 03	22 23	22 33	22 53	23 03
Bournville	d	19 25		19 35		19 45	19 55	20 05		20 25	20 35		20 55	21 05		21 25	21 35	21 55	22 05	22 25	22 35	22 55	23 05
Kings Norton	d	19 27		19 37		19 47	19 57	20 07		20 27	20 37		20 57	21 07		21 27	21 37	21 57	22 07	22 27	22 37	22 57	23 07
Northfield	d	19 30		19 40		19 50	20 00	20 10		20 30	20 40		21 00	21 10		21 30	21 40	22 00	22 10	22 30	22 40	23 00	23 10
Longbridge	d	19 36		19a44		19a54	20 04	20a14		20 34	20a44		21 04	21a14		21 34	21a44	22 04	22a14	22 34	22a44	23 04	23a14
Barnt Green	d	19 40					20 09			20 39			21 09			21 39		22 09		22 39		23 09	
Alvechurch	d	19 45					20 13			20 43			21 13			21 43		22 13		22 43		23 13	
Redditch	a	19 52					20 22			20 52			21 22			21 52		22 22		22 52		23 22	
Bromsgrove	a		19 39												21 19								

		LM	LM	LM
Lichfield Trent Valley	d	22 30	22 56	
Lichfield City	d	22 34	23 00	
Shenstone	d	22 39	23 05	
Blake Street	d	22 43	23 09	23 36
Butlers Lane	d	22 45	23 11	23 38
Four Oaks	d	22 48	23 14	23 41
Sutton Coldfield	d	22 51	23 17	23 44
Wylde Green	d	22 54	23 20	
Chester Road	d	22 56		
Erdington	d	22 58		
Gravelly Hill	d	23 00		
Aston	d	23 03		
Duddeston	d	23 06		
Birmingham New Street 12	a	23 11	23 31	23 59
	d	23 13	23 33	
Five Ways	d	23 16	23 36	
University	d	23 20	23 40	
Selly Oak	d	23 23	23 43	
Bournville	d	23 25	23 45	
Kings Norton	d	23 27	23 47	
Northfield	d	23 30	23 50	
Longbridge	d	23 34	23a54	
Barnt Green	d	23 39		
Alvechurch	d	23 43		
Redditch	a	23 53		
Bromsgrove	a			

Lichfield - Birmingham - Longbridge and Redditch

Network Diagram - see first Page of Table 67

		LM	LM	LM	XC ◇1 A	LM	LM	XC ◇1 B	LM	XC ◇1 C	LM D	LM	XC ◇1 A	LM D	LM D	LM	XC ◇1 A	LM	LM E	XC ◇1	LM	LM F	XC ◇1
Lichfield Trent Valley	d					09 31	10 01		10 31		11 01	11 31		12 01	12 31			13 01	13 31		14 01	14 31	
Lichfield City	d					09 35	10 05		10 35		11 05	11 35		12 05	12 35			13 05	13 35		14 05	14 35	
Shenstone	d					09 40	10 10		10 40		11 10	11 40		12 10	12 40			13 10	13 40		14 10	14 40	
Blake Street	d					09 44	10 14		10 44		11 14	11 44		12 14	12 44			13 14	13 44		14 14	14 44	
Butlers Lane	d					09 46	10 16		10 46		11 16	11 46		12 16	12 46			13 16	13 46		14 16	14 46	
Four Oaks	d			09 19		09 49	10 19		10 49		11 19	11 49		12 19	12 49			13 19	13 49		14 19	14 49	
Sutton Coldfield	d			09 22		09 52	10 22		10 52		11 22	11 52		12 22	12 52			13 22	13 52		14 22	14 52	
Wylde Green	d			09 25		09 55	10 25		10 55		11 25	11 55		12 25	12 55			13 25	13 55		14 25	14 55	
Chester Road	d			09 27		09 57	10 27		10 57		11 27	11 57		12 27	12 57			13 27	13 57		14 27	14 57	
Erdington	d			09 29		09 59	10 29		10 59		11 29	11 59		12 29	12 59			13 29	13 59		14 29	14 59	
Gravelly Hill	d			09 31		10 01	10 31		11 01		11 31	12 01		12 31	13 01			13 31	14 01		14 31	15 01	
Aston	d			09 35		10 05	10 35		11 05		11 35	12 05		12 35	13 05			13 35	14 05		14 35	15 05	
Duddeston	d			09 37		10 07	10 37		11 07		11 37	12 07		12 38	13 07			13 37	14 07		14 37	15 07	
Birmingham New Street	a			09 42		10 12	10 42		11 12		11 42	12 12		12 42	13 12			13 42	14 12		14 42	15 12	
	d	08 55	09 15	09 45	10 12	10 15	10 45	11 12	11 15	11 30	11 45	12 15	12 30	12 45	13 15	13 24	13 30	13 45	14 15	14 30	14 45	15 15	15 30
Five Ways	d		09 19	09 49		10 19	10 49		11 19		11 49	12 19		12 49	13 19			13 49	14 19		14 49	15 19	
University	d	09 01	09 23	09 53	10a18	10 23	10 53	11a18	11 23	11a36	11 53	12 23	12a36	12 53	13 23		13a36	13 53	14 23	14a36	14 53	15 23	15a36
Selly Oak	d		09 25	09 55		10 25	10 55		11 25		11 55	12 25		12 55	13 25			13 55	14 25		14 55	15 25	
Bournville	d		09 27	09 57		10 27	10 57		11 27		11 57	12 27		12 57	13 27			13 57	14 27		14 57	15 27	
Kings Norton	d		09 30	10 00		10 30	11 00		11 30		12 00	12 30		13 00	13 30			14 00	14 30		15 00	15 30	
Northfield	d		09 33	10 03		10 33	11 03		11 33		12 03	12 33		13 03	13 33			14 03	14 33		15 03	15 33	
Longbridge	d	09 09	09 36	10 06		10 36	11 06		11 36		12 06	12 36		13 06	13 36			14 06	14 36		15 06	15 36	
Barnt Green	d		09 40	10 10		10 40	11 10		11 40		12 10	12 40		13 10	13 40			14 10	14 40		15 10	15 40	
Alvechurch	d		09 45	10 15		10 45	11 15		11 45		12 15	12 45		13 15	13 45			14 15	14 45		15 15	15 45	
Redditch	a	09 24	09 53	10 23		10 53	11 23		11 53		12 23	12 53		13 23	13 53			14 23	14 53		15 23	15 53	
Bromsgrove	a															13 41							

		LM F	LM	LM F	XC ◇1	LM F	LM F	XC ◇1	LM G	LM	LM F	XC ◇1 H	LM G	LM	LM G	XC ◇1 I	LM G	LM	LM G	LM	LM F	LM F	LM F
Lichfield Trent Valley	d	15 01		15 31		16 01	16 31		17 01		17 31		18 01		18 31		19 01	19 31	20 01		20 31	21 01	21 31
Lichfield City	d	15 05		15 35		16 05	16 35		17 05		17 35		18 05		18 35		19 05	19 35	20 05		20 35	21 05	21 35
Shenstone	d	15 10		15 40		16 10	16 40		17 10		17 40		18 10		18 40		19 10	19 40	20 10		20 40	21 10	21 40
Blake Street	d	15 14		15 44		16 14	16 44		17 14		17 44		18 14		18 44		19 14	19 44	20 14		20 44	21 14	21 44
Butlers Lane	d	15 16		15 46		16 16	16 46		17 16		17 46		18 16		18 46		19 16	19 46	20 16		20 46	21 16	21 46
Four Oaks	d	15 19		15 49		16 19	16 49		17 19		17 49		18 19		18 49		19 19	19 49	20 19		20 49	21 19	21 49
Sutton Coldfield	d	15 22		15 52		16 22	16 52		17 22		17 52		18 22		18 52		19 22	19 52	20 22		20 52	21 22	21 52
Wylde Green	d	15 25		15 55		16 25	16 55		17 25		17 55		18 25		18 55		19 25	19 55	20 25		20 55	21 25	21 55
Chester Road	d	15 27		15 57		16 27	16 57		17 27		17 57		18 27		18 57		19 27	19 57	20 27		20 57	21 27	21 57
Erdington	d	15 29		15 59		16 29	16 59		17 29		17 59		18 29		18 59		19 29	19 59	20 29		20 59	21 29	21 59
Gravelly Hill	d	15 31		16 01		16 31	17 01		17 31		18 01		18 31		19 01		19 31	20 01	20 31		21 01	21 31	22 01
Aston	d	15 35		16 05		16 35	17 05		17 35		18 05		18 35		19 05		19 35	20 05	20 35		21 05	21 35	22 05
Duddeston	d	15 37		16 07		16 37	17 07		17 37		18 07		18 37		19 07		19 37	20 07	20 37		21 07	21 37	22 07
Birmingham New Street	a	15 42		16 12		16 42	17 12		17 42		18 12		18 42		19 12		19 42	20 12	20 42		21 12	21 42	22 12
	d	15 45	16 00	16 15	16 30	16 45	17 15	17 30	17 45	18 00	18 15	18 30	18 45	19 00	19 15	19 30	19 45	20 15	20 45	21 00	21 15	21 45	22 15
Five Ways	d	15 49		16 19		16 49	17 19		17 49		18 19		18 49		19 19		19 49	20 19	20 49		21 19	21 49	22 19
University	d	15 53		16 23	16a36	16 53	17 23	17a36	17 53		18 23	18a36	18 53		19 23	19a36	19 53	20 23	20 53		21 23	21 53	22 23
Selly Oak	d	15 55		16 25		16 55	17 25		17 55		18 25		18 55		19 25		19 55	20 25	20 55		21 25	21 55	22 25
Bournville	d	15 57		16 27		16 57	17 27		17 57		18 27		18 57		19 27		19 57	20 27	20 57		21 27	21 57	22 27
Kings Norton	d	16 00		16 30		17 00	17 30		18 00		18 30		19 00		19 30		20 00	20 30	21 00		21 30	22 00	22 30
Northfield	d	16 03		16 33		17 03	17 33		18 03		18 33		19 03		19 33		20 03	20 33	21 03		21 33	22 03	22 33
Longbridge	d	16 06		16 36		17 06	17 36		18 06		18 36		19 06		19 36		20 06	20 36	21 06		21 36	22 06	22 36
Barnt Green	d	16 10		16 40		17 10	17 40		18 10		18 40		19 10		19 40		20 10	20 40	21 10		21 40	22 10	22 40
Alvechurch	d	16 15		16 45		17 15	17 45		18 15		18 45		19 15		19 45		20 15	20 45	21 15		21 45	22 15	22 45
Redditch	a	16 23		16 53		17 23	17 53		18 23		18 53		19 23		19 53		20 23	20 53	21 23		21 53	22 23	22 53
Bromsgrove	a		16 20							18 20				19 21						21 19			

A until 21 October
B until 24 June, from 16 September until 21 October
C from 1 July until 9 September
D until 24 June
E until 27 May
F until 3 June
G until 3 June, from 1 July
H until 9 September
I until 24 June, from 16 September

Lichfield - Birmingham - Longbridge and Redditch

Network Diagram - see first Page of Table 67

		LM	LM A	LM
Lichfield Trent Valley	d	22 01	22 31	23 01
Lichfield City	d	22 05	22 35	23 05
Shenstone	d	22 10	22 40	23 10
Blake Street	d	22 14	22 44	23 14
Butlers Lane	d	22 16	22 46	23 16
Four Oaks	d	22 19	22 49	23 19
Sutton Coldfield	d	22 22	22 52	23 22
Wylde Green	d	22 25	22 55	23 25
Chester Road	d	22 27	22 57	
Erdington	d	22 29	22 59	
Gravelly Hill	d	22 31	23 01	
Aston	d	22 35	23 05	
Duddeston	d	22 37	23 07	
Birmingham New Street	a	22 43	23 12	23 40
	d	22 45	23 15	
Five Ways	d	22 49	23 19	
University	d	22 53	23 23	
Selly Oak	d	22 55	23 25	
Bournville	d	22 57	23 27	
Kings Norton	d	23 00	23 30	
Northfield	d	23 03	23 33	
Longbridge	d	23 06	23 36	
Barnt Green	d	23 10	23 40	
Alvechurch	d	23 15	23 45	
Redditch	a	23 23	23 53	
Bromsgrove	a			

A until 3 June

Table 69

Mondays to Fridays
until 19 October

Redditch and Longbridge - Birmingham - Lichfield

Network Diagram - see first Page of Table 67

Miles	Miles			LM	LM	LM	LM	LM	LM	LM	LM	LM	LM	LM	LM	LM	LM	LM	LM	LM	LM	XC	LM
																						◇1	
—	0	Bromsgrove	d					06 22			06 44					07 24						07 49	
0	—	**Redditch**	d							06 27				06 57					07 27				
3¼	—	Alvechurch	d							06 32				07 02					07 32				
5	3½	Barnt Green	d							06 38				07 08					07 38				
7¾	—	Longbridge	d			06 12	06 22		06 32	06 43		06 52	07 03	07 12	07 22			07 32	07 42		07 52		08 02
8¾	—	Northfield	d			06 14	06 24		06 34	06 45		06 54	07 04	07 14	07 24			07 34	07 44		07 54		08 04
10¼	—	Kings Norton	d			06 17	06 27		06 37	06 48		06 57	07 07	07 17	07 27			07 37	07 47		07 57		08 07
11¼	—	Bournville	d			06 19	06 29		06 39	06 50		06 59	07 09	07 19	07 29			07 39	07 49		07 59		08 09
12¼	—	Selly Oak	d			06 22	06 32		06 42	06 53		07 02	07 12	07 22	07 32			07 42	07 52		08 02		08 12
13	11½	University	d			06 25	06 35	06 39	06 45	06 56	06 59	07 05	07 15	07 25	07 35	07 39		07 45	07 55	07 59	08 05	08 09	08 15
13½	—	Five Ways	d			06 29	06 39		06 49	07 00		07 09	07 19	07 29	07 39			07 49	07 59		08 09		08 19
14½	13	**Birmingham New Street** 12	a			06 33	06 42	06 45	06 52	07 03	07 07	07 13	07 22	07 34	07 42	07 46		07 52	08 03	08 09	08 12	08 16	08 22
—	—		d	06 03	06 25	06 35	06 46		06 55	07 06		07 15	07 25	07 35	07 45		07 47	07 55	08 05		08 15		08 25
16	—	Duddeston	d	06 07	06 29					07 10			07 29				07 52	07 59					08 29
17¼	—	Aston	d	06 10	06 32	06 41	06 52		07 00	07 13		07 21	07 32	07 41			07 54	08 02	08 11		08 21		08 32
18½	—	Gravelly Hill	d	06 13	06 35	06 44	06 55		07 03	07 16		07 24	07 35	07 44			07 57	08 05	08 14		08 24		08 35
19¼	—	Erdington	d	06 16	06 38	06 46	06 57		07 06	07 18		07 26	07 38	07 46			08 00	08 08	08 16		08 26		08 38
20¼	—	Chester Road	d	06 18	06 40	06 48	06 59		07 08	07 20		07 28	07 40	07 48			08 02	08 10	08 18		08 28		08 40
21	—	Wylde Green	d	06 20	06 42	06 50	07 01		07 10	07 22		07 30	07 42	07 50			08 04	08 12	08 20		08 30		08 42
22	—	Sutton Coldfield	d	06 23	06 45	06 54	07 05		07 13	07 25		07 34	07 45	07 53	07 59		08 07	08 15	08 24		08 34		08 45
23½	—	Four Oaks	d	06 26	06 48	06 58	07a12		07 16	07 29		07a41	07 48		08 03		08a12	08 18	08 28		08a41		08 48
24½	—	Butlers Lane	d	06 28	06 50	07 00			07 18	07 31			07 50		08 05			08 20	08 30				08 50
26¼	—	Blake Street	d	06 31	06 53	07 02			07 21	07 33			07 53		08 07			08 23	08 32				08 53
28¾	—	Shenstone	d	06 35	06 57				07 25				07 57		08 11			08 27	08 36				08 57
31¾	—	**Lichfield City**	d	06a41	07 02	07 11			07 30	07 41			08 02	08a08	08a17			08 32	08 41				09a02
33	—	**Lichfield Trent Valley**	a		07 06	07 16			07 34	07 47			08 06					08 36	08 46				

		LM	LM	LM	XC	LM	LM	LM	LM	LM	LM	LM	LM	XC	LM	LM	LM	LM	LM	LM	LM	XC	LM
					◇1									◇1 🛒								◇1 🛒	
Bromsgrove	d				08 24			08 42				09 11						09 54					
Redditch	d	07 57					08 27				08 57					09 27				09 57			
Alvechurch	d	08 02					08 32				09 02					09 32				10 02			
Barnt Green	d	08 08					08 38				09 08					09 38				10 08			
Longbridge	d	08 12		08 22		08 32	08 42		08 52	09 02	09 12		09 22		09 32	09 42	09 52		10 02	10 12	10 22		10 32
Northfield	d	08 14		08 24		08 34	08 44		08 54	09 04	09 14		09 24		09 34	09 44	09 54		10 04	10 14	10 24		10 34
Kings Norton	d	08 17		08 27		08 37	08 47		08 57	09 07	09 17		09 27		09 37	09 47	09 57		10 07	10 17	10 27		10 37
Bournville	d	08 19		08 29		08 39	08 49		08 59	09 09	09 19		09 29		09 39	09 49	09 59		10 09	10 19	10 29		10 39
Selly Oak	d	08 22		08 32		08 42	08 52		09 02	09 12	09 22		09 32		09 42	09 52	10 02		10 12	10 22	10 32		10 42
University	d	08 25	08 29	08 35	08 39	08 45	08 55	08 59	09 05	09 15	09 25	09 30	09 35	09 39	09 45	09 55	10 05	10 09	10 15	10 25	10 35	10 39	10 45
Five Ways	d	08 29		08 39		08 49	08 59		09 09	09 19	09 29		09 39		09 49	09 59	10 09		10 19	10 29	10 39		10 49
Birmingham New Street 12	a	08 33	08 37	08 42	08 45	08 52	09 03	09 07	09 13	09 22	09 33	09 43	09 42	09 45	09 52	10 03	10 12	10 24	10 22	10 33	10 42	10 45	10 52
	d	08 35		08 45		08 55	09 05		09 14	09 24	09 35		09 45		09 55	10 05	10 15		10 25	10 35	10 45		10 55
Duddeston	d					08 59				09 28					09 59				10 29				10 59
Aston	d	08 41		08 51		09 02	09 11		09 19	09 31	09 41		09 51		10 02	10 11	10 21		10 32	10 41	10 51		11 02
Gravelly Hill	d	08 44		08 54		09 05	09 14		09 22	09 34	09 44		09 54		10 05	10 14	10 24		10 35	10 44	10 54		11 05
Erdington	d	08 46		08 56		09 08	09 16		09 25	09 38	09 46		09 56		10 08	10 16	10 26		10 38	10 46	10 56		11 08
Chester Road	d	08 48		08 58		09 10	09 18		09 26	09 40	09 48		09 58		10 10	10 18	10 28		10 40	10 48	10 58		11 10
Wylde Green	d	08 50		09 00		09 12	09 20		09 28	09 42	09 50		10 00		10 12	10 20	10 30		10 42	10 50	11 00		11 12
Sutton Coldfield	d	08 54		09 04		09 15	09 24		09 32	09 45	09 54		10 04		10 15	10 24	10 34		10 45	10 54	11 04		11 15
Four Oaks	d	08 58		09a11		09 18	09 28		09a39	09 48	09 58		10a11		10 18	10 28	10a41		10 48	10 58	11a11		11 18
Butlers Lane	d	09 00				09 20	09 30			09 50	10 00				10 20	10 30			10 50	11 00			11 20
Blake Street	d	09 02				09 23	09 32			09 53	10 02				10 23	10 32			10 53	11 02			11 23
Shenstone	d					09 27				09 57					10 27				10 57				11 27
Lichfield City	d	09 11				09a34	09 41			10a02	10 11				10a32	10 41			11a02	11 11			11a32
Lichfield Trent Valley	a	09 15					09 45				10 15					10 45				11 15			

		LM	LM	LM	LM	LM	LM	XC	LM	LM	LM	LM	LM	LM	LM	XC	LM	LM	LM	LM	LM	LM
								◇1 🛒								◇1 🛒						
Bromsgrove	d		10 42								11 42								12 42			
Redditch	d	10 27				10 57				11 27				11 57				12 27				12 57
Alvechurch	d	10 32				11 02				11 32				12 02				12 32				13 02
Barnt Green	d	10 38				11 08				11 38				12 08				12 38				13 08
Longbridge	d	10 42		10 52	11 02	11 12	11 22		11 32	11 42		11 52	12 02	12 12	12 22		12 32	12 42		12 52	13 02	13 12
Northfield	d	10 44		10 54	11 04	11 14	11 24		11 34	11 44		11 54	12 04	12 14	12 24		12 34	12 44		12 54	13 04	13 14
Kings Norton	d	10 47		10 57	11 07	11 17	11 27		11 37	11 47		11 57	12 07	12 17	12 27		12 37	12 47		12 57	13 07	13 17
Bournville	d	10 49		10 59	11 09	11 19	11 29		11 39	11 49		11 59	12 09	12 19	12 29		12 39	12 49		12 59	13 09	13 19
Selly Oak	d	10 52		11 02	11 12	11 22	11 32		11 42	11 52		12 02	12 12	12 22	12 32		12 42	12 52		13 02	13 12	13 22
University	d	10 55	10 59	11 05	11 15	11 25	11 35	11 39	11 45	11 55	11 59	12 05	12 15	12 25	12 35	12 39	12 45	12 55	12 59	13 05	13 15	13 25
Five Ways	d	10 59		11 09	11 19	11 29	11 39		11 49	11 59		12 09	12 19	12 29	12 39		12 49	12 59		13 09	13 19	13 29
Birmingham New Street 12	a	11 02	11 13	11 12	11 22	11 33	11 42	11 45	11 52	12 03	12 11	12 12	12 22	12 33	12 42	12 45	12 52	13 03	13 13	13 12	13 22	13 33
	d	11 05		11 15	11 25	11 35	11 45		11 55	12 05		12 15	12 25	12 35	12 45		12 55	13 05		13 15	13 25	13 35
Duddeston	d				11 29				11 59				12 29				12 59				13 29	
Aston	d	11 11		11 21	11 32	11 41	11 51		12 02	12 11		12 21	12 32	12 41	12 51		13 02	13 11		13 21	13 32	13 41
Gravelly Hill	d	11 14		11 24	11 35	11 44	11 54		12 05	12 14		12 24	12 35	12 44	12 54		13 05	13 14		13 24	13 35	13 44
Erdington	d	11 16		11 26	11 38	11 46	11 56		12 08	12 16		12 26	12 38	12 46	12 56		13 08	13 16		13 26	13 38	13 46
Chester Road	d	11 18		11 28	11 40	11 48	11 58		12 10	12 18		12 28	12 40	12 48	12 58		13 10	13 18		13 28	13 40	13 48
Wylde Green	d	11 20		11 30	11 42	11 50	12 00		12 12	12 20		12 30	12 42	12 50	13 00		13 12	13 20		13 30	13 42	13 50
Sutton Coldfield	d	11 24		11 34	11 45	11 54	12 04		12 15	12 24		12 34	12 45	12 54	13 04		13 15	13 24		13 34	13 45	13 54
Four Oaks	d	11 28		11a41	11 48	11 58	12a11		12 18	12 28		12a41	12 48	12 58	13a11		13 18	13 28		13a41	13 48	13 58
Butlers Lane	d	11 30			11 50	12 00			12 20	12 30			12 50	13 00			13 20	13 30			13 50	14 00
Blake Street	d	11 32			11 53	12 02			12 23	12 32			12 53	13 02			13 23	13 32			13 53	14 02
Shenstone	d				11 57				12 27				12 57				13 27				13 57	
Lichfield City	d	11 41			12a02	12 11			12a32	12 41			13a02	13 11			13a32	13 41			14a02	14 11
Lichfield Trent Valley	a	11 45				12 15				12 45				13 15				13 45				14 15

Table 69

Mondays to Fridays
until 19 October

Redditch and Longbridge - Birmingham - Lichfield

Network Diagram - see first Page of Table 67

		LM	XC	LM	LM	LM	LM	LM	LM	LM	XC	LM	LM	LM	LM	LM	LM	LM	XC	LM	LM	LM	LM
			◇1 🛒								◇1 🛒								◇1 🛒				
Bromsgrove	d					13 42								14 42								15 42	
Redditch	d				13 27				13 57				14 27				14 57				15 27		
Alvechurch	d				13 32				14 02				14 32				15 02				15 32		
Barnt Green	d				13 38				14 08				14 38				15 08				15 38		
Longbridge	d	13 22		13 32	13 42		13 52	14 02	14 12	14 22		14 32	14 42		14 52	15 02	15 12	15 22		15 32	15 42		15 52
Northfield	d	13 24		13 34	13 44		13 54	14 04	14 14	14 24		14 34	14 44		14 54	15 04	15 14	15 24		15 34	15 44		15 54
Kings Norton	d	13 27		13 37	13 47		13 57	14 07	14 17	14 27		14 37	14 47		14 57	15 07	15 17	15 27		15 37	15 47		15 57
Bournville	d	13 29		13 39	13 49		13 59	14 09	14 19	14 29		14 39	14 49		14 59	15 09	15 19	15 29		15 39	15 49		15 59
Selly Oak	d	13 32		13 42	13 52		14 02	14 12	14 22	14 32		14 42	14 52		15 02	15 12	15 22	15 32		15 42	15 52		16 02
University	d	13 35	13 39	13 45	13 55	13 59	14 05	14 15	14 25	14 35	14 39	14 45	14 55	14 59	15 05	15 15	15 25	15 35	15 39	15 45	15 55	15 59	16 05
Five Ways	d	13 39		13 49	13 59		14 09	14 19	14 29	14 39		14 49	14 59		15 09	15 19	15 29	15 39		15 49	15 59		16 09
Birmingham New Street 12	a	13 42	13 45	13 52	14 03	14 12	14 12	14 22	14 33	14 42	14 45	14 52	15 03	15 13	15 12	15 22	15 33	15 42	15 45	15 53	16 03	16 13	16 12
	d	13 45		13 55	14 05		14 15	14 25	14 35	14 45		14 55	15 05		15 15	15 25	15 35	15 45		15 55	16 05		16 15
Duddeston	d			13 59				14 29				14 59				15 29				15 59			
Aston	d	13 51		14 02	14 11		14 21	14 32	14 41	14 51		15 02	15 11		15 21	15 32	15 41	15 51		16 02	16 11		16 21
Gravelly Hill	d	13 54		14 05	14 14		14 24	14 35	14 44	14 54		15 05	15 14		15 24	15 35	15 44	15 54		16 05	16 14		16 24
Erdington	d	13 56		14 08	14 16		14 26	14 38	14 46	14 56		15 08	15 16		15 26	15 38	15 46	15 56		16 08	16 16		16 26
Chester Road	d	13 58		14 10	14 18		14 28	14 40	14 48	14 58		15 10	15 18		15 28	15 40	15 48	15 58		16 10	16 18		16 28
Wylde Green	d	14 00		14 12	14 20		14 30	14 42	14 50	15 00		15 12	15 20		15 30	15 42	15 50	16 00		16 12	16 20		16 30
Sutton Coldfield	d	14 04		14 15	14 24		14 34	14 45	14 54	15 04		15 15	15 24		15 34	15 45	15 54	16 04		16 15	16 24		16 34
Four Oaks	d	14a11		14 18	14 28		14a41	14 48	14 58	15a11		15 18	15 28		15a41	15 48	15 58	16a11		16 18	16 28		16a41
Butlers Lane	d			14 20	14 30			14 50	15 00			15 20	15 30			15 50	16 00			16 20	16 30		
Blake Street	d			14 23	14 32			14 53	15 02			15 23	15 32			15 53	16 02			16 23	16 32		
Shenstone	d			14 27				14 57				15 27				15 57				16 27			
Lichfield City	d			14a32	14 41			15a02	15 11			15a32	15 41			16a02	16 11			16a32	16 41		
Lichfield Trent Valley	a				14 45				15 15				15 45				16 15				16 45		

		LM	LM	LM	XC	LM	LM	LM	LM	LM	LM	LM	XC	LM	LM	LM	LM	LM	LM	LM	XC	LM	LM
					◇1 🛒								◇1								◇1		
Bromsgrove	d							16 42								17 42							
Redditch	d		15 57				16 27				16 57				17 27				17 57				18 27
Alvechurch	d		16 02				16 32				17 02				17 32				18 02				18 32
Barnt Green	d		16 08				16 38	16 49			17 08				17 38				18 08				18 38
Longbridge	d	16 02	16 12	16 22		16 32	16 42		16 52	17 02	17 12	17 22		17 32	17 42		17 52	18 02	18 12	18 22		18 32	18 42
Northfield	d	16 04	16 14	16 24		16 34	16 44		16 54	17 04	17 14	17 24		17 34	17 44		17 54	18 04	18 14	18 24		18 34	18 44
Kings Norton	d	16 07	16 17	16 27		16 37	16 47		16 57	17 07	17 17	17 27		17 37	17 47		17 57	18 07	18 17	18 27		18 37	18 47
Bournville	d	16 09	16 19	16 29		16 39	16 49		16 59	17 09	17 19	17 29		17 39	17 49		17 59	18 09	18 19	18 29		18 39	18 49
Selly Oak	d	16 12	16 22	16 32		16 42	16 52		17 02	17 12	17 22	17 32		17 42	17 52		18 02	18 12	18 22	18 32		18 42	18 52
University	d	16 15	16 25	16 35	16 39	16 45	16 55	16 59	17 05	17 15	17 25	17 35	17 39	17 45	17 55	17 59	18 05	18 15	18 25	18 35	18 39	18 45	18 55
Five Ways	d	16 19	16 29	16 39		16 49	16 59		17 09	17 19	17 29	17 39		17 49	17 59		18 09	18 19	18 29	18 39		18 49	18 59
Birmingham New Street 12	a	16 22	16 32	16 42	16 45	16 53	17 03	17 13	17 12	17 23	17 33	17 42	17 45	17 53	18 03	18 11	18 12	18 23	18 33	18 42	18 45	18 53	19 03
	d	16 25	16 35	16 45		16 55	17 05		17 15	17 25	17 35	17 45		17 55	18 05		18 15	18 25	18 35	18 45		18 55	19 05
Duddeston	d	16 29				16 59				17 29				17 59				18 29				18 59	
Aston	d	16 32	16 41	16 51		17 02	17 11		17 21	17 32	17 41	17 51		18 02	18 11		18 21	18 32	18 41	18 51		19 02	19 11
Gravelly Hill	d	16 35	16 44	16 54		17 05	17 14		17 24	17 35	17 44	17 54		18 05	18 14		18 24	18 35	18 44	18 54		19 05	19 14
Erdington	d	16 38	16 46	16 56		17 08	17 16		17 26	17 38	17 46	17 56		18 08	18 16		18 26	18 38	18 46	18 56		19 08	19 16
Chester Road	d	16 39	16 48	16 58		17 10	17 18		17 28	17 40	17 48	17 58		18 10	18 18		18 28	18 40	18 48	18 58		19 10	19 18
Wylde Green	d	16 41	16 50	17 00		17 12	17 20		17 30	17 42	17 50	18 00		18 12	18 20		18 30	18 42	18 50	19 00		19 12	19 20
Sutton Coldfield	d	16 44	16 54	17 04		17 15	17 24		17 34	17 45	17 54	18 04		18 15	18 24		18 34	18 45	18 54	19 04		19 15	19 24
Four Oaks	d	16 48	16 58	17a11		17 18	17 28		17a41	17 48	17 58	18a11		18 18	18 28		18a41	18 48	18 58	19a11		19 18	19 28
Butlers Lane	d	16 50	17 00			17 20	17 30			17 50	18 00			18 20	18 30			18 50	19 00			19 20	19 30
Blake Street	d	16 52	17 02			17 23	17 32			17 53	18 02			18 23	18 32			18 53	19 02			19 23	19 32
Shenstone	d	16 56				17 27	17 36			17 57	18 06			18 27				18 57				19 27	
Lichfield City	d	17a02	17 11			17 32	17 41			18 02	18 11			18a32	18 41			19a02	19 11			19a32	19 41
Lichfield Trent Valley	a		17 15			17 36	17 46			18 06	18 16				18 45				19 15				19 45

		LM	LM	LM	LM	LM	XC	LM	LM	LM	LM	LM	LM	XC	LM	LM	LM	LM	LM	LM	XC	LM
							◇1 🛒							◇1							◇1	
Bromsgrove	d	18 43									19 46							20 55				
Redditch	d				18 57				19 27				19 57			20 27			20 57			21 27
Alvechurch	d				19 02				19 32				20 02			20 32			21 02			21 32
Barnt Green	d	18 49			19 08				19 38				20 08			20 38			21 08			21 38
Longbridge	d		18 52	19 02	19 12	19 22		19 32	19 42	19 52		20 02	20 12		20 30	20 42	20 57		21 12	21 27		21 42
Northfield	d		18 54	19 04	19 14	19 24		19 34	19 44	19 54		20 04	20 14		20 32	20 44	20 59		21 14	21 29		21 44
Kings Norton	d		18 57	19 07	19 17	19 27		19 37	19 47	19 57		20 07	20 17		20 35	20 47	21 02		21 17	21 32		21 47
Bournville	d		18 59	19 09	19 19	19 29		19 39	19 49	19 59		20 09	20 19		20 37	20 49	21 04		21 19	21 34		21 49
Selly Oak	d		19 02	19 12	19 22	19 32		19 42	19 52	20 02		20 12	20 22		20 40	20 52	21 07		21 22	21 37		21 52
University	d	18 59	19 05	19 15	19 25	19 35	19 39	19 45	19 55	20 05	20 09	20 15	20 25	20 39	20 42	20 55	21 10	21 14	21 25	21 40	21 45	21 55
Five Ways	d		19 09	19 19	19 29	19 39		19 49	19 59	20 09		20 19	20 29		20 46	20 59	21 14		21 29	21 44		21 59
Birmingham New Street 12	a	19 12	19 12	19 22	19 33	19 42	19 45	19 52	20 03	20 12	20 20	20 23	20 33	20 45	20 50	21 02	21 17	21 20	21 33	21 47	21 51	22 03
	d		19 15		19 35				20 05				20 35			21 05			21 35			22 05
Duddeston	d				19 39				20 09				20 39			21 09			21 39			22 09
Aston	d		19 21		19 42				20 12				20 42			21 12			21 42			22 12
Gravelly Hill	d		19 24		19 45				20 15				20 45			21 15			21 45			22 15
Erdington	d		19 26		19 48				20 18				20 48			21 18			21 48			22 18
Chester Road	d		19 28		19 50				20 20				20 50			21 20			21 50			22 20
Wylde Green	d		19 30		19 52				20 22				20 52			21 22			21 52			22 22
Sutton Coldfield	d		19 34		19 55				20 25				20 55			21 25			21 55			22 25
Four Oaks	d		19a41		19 58				20 28				20 58			21 28			21 58			22 28
Butlers Lane	d				20 00				20 30				21 00			21 30			22 00			22 30
Blake Street	d				20 03				20 33				21 03			21 33			22 03			22 33
Shenstone	d				20 07				20 37				21 07			21 37			22 07			22 37
Lichfield City	d				20 12				20 42				21 12			21 42			22 12			22 42
Lichfield Trent Valley	a				20 16				20 46				21 16			21 46			22 16			22 46

Redditch and Longbridge - Birmingham - Lichfield

Network Diagram - see first Page of Table 67

		LM	LM	LM	LM	LM	LM	LM		LM
Bromsgrove	d				22 28					
Redditch	d		21 57			22 27		22 57		
Alvechurch	d		22 02			22 32		23 02		
Barnt Green	d		22 08			22 38		23 08		
Longbridge	d	21 57	22 12	22 27		22 42	22 52	23 12		23 30
Northfield	d	21 59	22 14	22 29		22 44	22 54	23 14		23 32
Kings Norton	d	22 02	22 17	22 32		22 47	22 57	23 17		23 35
Bournville	d	22 04	22 19	22 34		22 49	22 59	23 19		23 37
Selly Oak	d	22 07	22 22	22 37		22 52	23 02	23 22		23 40
University	d	22 10	22 25	22 40	22 44	22 55	23 05	23 25		23 43
Five Ways	d	22 14	22 29	22 44		22 59	23 09	23 29		23 47
Birmingham New Street 12	a	22 17	22 33	22 47	22 50	23 03	23 12	23 36		23 50
	d		22 35	22 55			23 15			
Duddeston	d		22 39	22 59			23 19			
Aston	d		22 42	23 02			23 22			
Gravelly Hill	d		22 45	23 05			23 25			
Erdington	d		22 48	23 08			23 28			
Chester Road	d		22 50	23 10			23 30			
Wylde Green	d		22 52	23 12			23 32			
Sutton Coldfield	d		22 55	23 15			23 35			
Four Oaks	d		22 58	23 18			23 38			
Butlers Lane	d		23 00	23 20			23 40			
Blake Street	d		23 03	23a24			23 43			
Shenstone	d		23 07				23 47			
Lichfield City	d		23 12				23a52			
Lichfield Trent Valley	a		23 16							

Mondays to Fridays from 22 October

		LM	LM	LM	LM	LM	LM	LM	LM	LM		LM	LM	LM	LM	LM	LM	XC ◇1	LM	LM		LM	LM	XC ◇1	LM
Bromsgrove	d				06 22		06 44					07 24						07 49						08 24	
Redditch	d			05 57				06 27		06 57							07 27						07 57		
Alvechurch	d			06 02				06 32		07 02							07 32						08 02		
Barnt Green	d			06 13				06 40		07 09							07 44						08 14		
Longbridge	d		06 02	06 22		06 32		06 52	07 02	07 22			07 32		07 42		07 52		08 02	08 12			08 22		08 32
Northfield	d		06 04	06 24		06 34		06 54	07 04	07 24			07 34		07 44		07 54		08 04	08 14			08 24		08 34
Kings Norton	d		06 07	06 27		06 37		06 57	07 07	07 27			07 37		07 47		07 57		08 07	08 17			08 27		08 37
Bournville	d		06 09	06 29		06 39		07 00	07 09	07 29			07 39		07 49		07 59		08 09	08 19			08 29		08 39
Selly Oak	d		06 12	06 32		06 42		07 02	07 12	07 32			07 42		07 52		08 02		08 12	08 22			08 32		08 42
University	d		06 15	06 35	06 39	06 45	06 59	07 05	07 15	07 35		07 39	07 44		07 55	07 59	08 05	08 09	08 15	08 25		08 29	08 35	08 39	08 45
Five Ways	d		06 19	06 39		06 49		07 09	07 19	07 39			07 48		07 59		08 09		08 19	08 29			08 39		08 49
Birmingham New Street 12	a		06 22	06 42	06 45	06 52	07 07	07 15	07 22	07 42		07 46	07 51		08 03	08 09	08 12	08 16	08 22	08 33		08 37	08 42	08 45	08 52
	d	06 01	06 25	06 45		06 55		07 15	07 25	07 45			07 55	08 00	08 05		08 15		08 25	08 35			08 45		08 55
Duddeston	d	06 05	06 29			06 59			07 29					08 04					08 29						08 59
Aston	d	06 08	06 32	06 51		07 02		07 22	07 32	07 51				08 07	08 11		08 21		08 32	08 41			08 51		09 02
Gravelly Hill	d	06 11	06 35	06 54		07 06		07 25	07 36	07 54				08 11	08 14		08 24		08 36	08 44			08 54		09 06
Erdington	d	06 14	06 38	06 57		07 09		07 28	07 39	07 57				08 14	08 17		08 27		08 39	08 47			08 57		09 09
Chester Road	d	06 16	06 40	06 59		07 11		07 30	07 41	07 59				08 16	08 19		08 29		08 41	08 49			08 59		09 11
Wylde Green	d	06 18	06 43	07 02		07 13		07 32	07 43	08 02				08 18	08 22		08 32		08 43	08 52			09 02		09 13
Sutton Coldfield	d	06 21	06 46	07 05		07 16		07 35	07 46	08 05			08 08	08 21	08 25		08 35		08 46	08 55			09 05		09 16
Four Oaks	d	06 24	06 49	07a13		07 20		07a43	07 50	08a13			08 11	08 25	08 28		08a43		08 50	08 58			09a13		09 20
Butlers Lane	d	06 26	06 52			07 22			07 52					08 27	08 31				08 52	09 01					09 22
Blake Street	d	06 29	06 54			07 25			07 55					08 30	08 33				08 55	09 03					09 25
Shenstone	d	06 33	06 59			07 29			07 59					08 34	08 38				08 59						09 29
Lichfield City	d	06 38	07 04			07 34			08 04				08a21	08 39	08 47				09 04	09 16					09 34
Lichfield Trent Valley	a	06 44	07 10			07 40			08 10					08 44	08 55				09 10	09 25					09 40

		LM	LM	LM	LM	LM		LM	LM	XC ◇1	LM	LM	LM	LM	LM	LM		XC ◇1	LM	LM	LM	LM	LM	XC ◇1	LM
Bromsgrove	d		08 42					09 11						09 54						10 42					
Redditch	d			08 27					08 57				09 27			09 57					10 27		10 57		
Alvechurch	d			08 32					09 02				09 32			10 02					10 32		11 02		
Barnt Green	d			08 39					09 09				09 47			10 09					10 39		11 09		
Longbridge	d	08 42		08 52	09 02	09 12			09 22		09 32	09 42	09 52		10 02	10 22			10 32		10 52	11 02	11 22		11 32
Northfield	d	08 44		08 54	09 04	09 14			09 24		09 34	09 44	09 54		10 04	10 24			10 34		10 54	11 04	11 24		11 34
Kings Norton	d	08 47		08 57	09 07	09 17			09 27		09 37	09 47	09 57		10 07	10 27			10 37		10 57	11 07	11 27		11 37
Bournville	d	08 49		08 59	09 09	09 19			09 29		09 39	09 49	09 59		10 09	10 29			10 39		10 59	11 09	11 29		11 39
Selly Oak	d	08 52		09 02	09 12	09 22			09 32		09 42	09 52	10 02		10 12	10 32			10 42		11 02	11 12	11 32		11 42
University	d	08 55	08 59	09 05	09 15	09 25		09 30	09 35	09 39	09 45	09 55	10 05	10 09	10 15	10 35		10 39	10 45	10 59	11 05	11 15	11 35	11 39	11 45
Five Ways	d	08 59		09 09	09 19	09 29			09 39		09 49	09 59	10 09		10 19	10 39			10 49		11 09	11 19	11 39		11 49
Birmingham New Street 12	a	09 03	09 07	09 12	09 22	09 32		09 43	09 42	09 45	09 52	10 03	10 12	10 24	10 22	10 42		10 45	10 52	11 13	11 12	11 22	11 42	11 45	11 52
	d	09 05		09 15	09 25	09 35			09 45		09 55	10 05	10 15		10 25	10 45			10 55		11 15	11 25	11 45		11 56
Duddeston	d				09 29						09 59				10 29				10 59			11 29			11 59
Aston	d	09 11		09 21	09 32	09 41			09 51		10 02	10 11	10 21		10 32	10 51			11 02		11 21	11 32	11 51		12 02
Gravelly Hill	d	09 14		09 24	09 36	09 44			09 54		10 06	10 14	10 24		10 36	10 54			11 05		11 24	11 36	11 54		12 06
Erdington	d	09 17		09 27	09 39	09 47			09 57		10 09	10 17	10 27		10 39	10 57			11 09		11 27	11 39	11 57		12 09
Chester Road	d	09 19		09 29	09 41	09 49			09 59		10 11	10 19	10 29		10 41	10 59			11 11		11 29	11 41	11 59		12 11
Wylde Green	d	09 22		09 32	09 43	09 52			10 02		10 13	10 22	10 32		10 43	11 02			11 13		11 32	11 43	12 02		12 13
Sutton Coldfield	d	09 25		09 35	09 46	09 55			10 05		10 16	10 25	10 35		10 46	11 05			11 16		11 35	11 46	12 05		12 16
Four Oaks	d	09 28		09a43	09 50	09 58			10a13		10 20	10 28	10 38		10a53	11a13			11 20		11a43	11 50	12a13		12 20
Butlers Lane	d	09 31			09 52	10 01					10 22	10 31	10 41						11 22			11 52			12 22
Blake Street	d	09 33			09 55	10 03					10 25	10 33	10 43						11 25			11 55			12 25
Shenstone	d				09 59						10 29		10 48						11 29			11 59			12 29
Lichfield City	d	09a45			10 04	10a15					10 34	10a45	10 57						11 34			12 04			12 34
Lichfield Trent Valley	a				10 10						10 40		11 02						11 40			12 10			12 40

Redditch and Longbridge - Birmingham - Lichfield

Network Diagram - see first Page of Table 67

		LM		LM	LM	LM	XC ◇1	LM	LM	LM	LM	LM		XC ◇1	LM	LM	LM	LM	LM	XC ◇1	LM	LM		LM	LM
Bromsgrove	d	11 42							12 42							13 42						14 42			
Redditch	d			11 27		11 57				12 27		12 57					13 27		13 57					14 27	
Alvechurch	d			11 32		12 02				12 32		13 02					13 32		14 02					14 32	
Barnt Green	d			11 39		12 09				12 39		13 09					13 39		14 09					14 39	
Longbridge	d			11 52	12 02	12 22		12 32		12 52	13 02	13 22			13 32		13 52	14 02	14 22		14 32			14 52	15 02
Northfield	d			11 54	12 04	12 24		12 34		12 54	13 04	13 24			13 34		13 54	14 04	14 24		14 34			14 54	15 04
Kings Norton	d			11 57	12 07	12 27		12 37		12 57	13 07	13 27			13 37		13 57	14 07	14 27		14 37			14 57	15 07
Bournville	d			11 59	12 09	12 29		12 39		12 59	13 09	13 29			13 39		13 59	14 09	14 29		14 39			14 59	15 09
Selly Oak	d			12 02	12 12	12 32		12 42		13 02	13 12	13 32			13 42		14 02	14 12	14 32		14 42			15 02	15 12
University	d	11 59		12 05	12 15	12 35	12 39	12 45	12 59	13 05	13 15	13 35		13 39	13 45	13 59	14 05	14 15	14 35	14 39	14 45	14 59		15 05	15 15
Five Ways	d			12 09	12 19	12 39		12 49		13 09	13 19	13 39			13 49		14 09	14 19	14 39		14 49			15 09	15 19
Birmingham New Street 12	a	12 11		12 12	12 22	12 42	12 45	12 52	13 13	13 12	13 22	13 42		13 45	13 52	14 12	14 12	14 22	14 42	14 45	14 52	15 13		15 12	15 22
	d			12 15	12 25	12 45		12 55		13 15	13 25	13 45			13 55		14 15	14 25	14 45		14 55			15 15	15 25
Duddeston	d				12 29			12 59			13 29				13 59			14 29			14 59				15 29
Aston	d			12 21	12 32	12 51		13 02		13 21	13 32	13 51			14 02		14 21	14 32	14 51		15 02			15 21	15 32
Gravelly Hill	d			12 24	12 36	12 54		13 06		13 24	13 36	13 54			14 06		14 24	14 36	14 54		15 06			15 24	15 36
Erdington	d			12 27	12 39	12 57		13 09		13 27	13 39	13 57			14 09		14 27	14 39	14 57		15 09			15 27	15 39
Chester Road	d			12 29	12 41	12 59		13 11		13 29	13 41	13 59			14 11		14 29	14 41	14 59		15 11			15 29	15 41
Wylde Green	d			12 32	12 43	13 02		13 13		13 32	13 43	14 02			14 13		14 32	14 43	15 02		15 13			15 32	15 43
Sutton Coldfield	d			12 35	12 46	13 05		13 16		13 35	13 46	14 05			14 16		14 35	14 46	15 05		15 16			15 35	15 46
Four Oaks	d			12a43	12 50	13a13		13 20		13a43	13 50	14a13			14 20		14a43	14 50	15a13		15 20			15 38	15 50
Butlers Lane	d				12 52			13 22			13 52				14 22			14 52			15 22			15 41	15 52
Blake Street	d				12 55			13 25			13 55				14 25			14 55			15 25			15a46	15 55
Shenstone	d				12 59			13 29			13 59				14 29			14 59			15 29				15 59
Lichfield City	d				13 04			13 34			14 04				14 34			15 04			15 34				16 04
Lichfield Trent Valley	a				13 10			13 40			14 10				14 40			15 10			15 40				16 10

		LM	LM	XC ◇1	LM	LM	LM	LM		LM	LM	XC ◇1	LM	LM	LM	LM	LM	LM		LM	XC ◇1	LM	LM	LM	LM
Bromsgrove	d					15 42										16 42								17 42	
Redditch	d		14 57				15 27				15 57				16 27					16 57					17 27
Alvechurch	d		15 02				15 32				16 02				16 32					17 02					17 32
Barnt Green	d		15 16				15 39				16 09				16 39	16 49				17 17					17 44
Longbridge	d	15 12	15 22		15 32		15 52	16 02		16 12	16 22		16 32		16 53		17 02			17 22		17 32			17 52
Northfield	d	15 14	15 24		15 34		15 54	16 04		16 14	16 24		16 34		16 55		17 04			17 24		17 34			17 54
Kings Norton	d	15 17	15 27		15 37		15 57	16 07		16 17	16 27		16 37		16 58		17 07			17 27		17 37			17 57
Bournville	d	15 19	15 29		15 39		15 59	16 09		16 19	16 29		16 39		17 00		17 09			17 29		17 39			17 59
Selly Oak	d	15 22	15 32		15 42		16 02	16 12		16 22	16 32		16 42		17 03		17 12			17 32		17 42			18 02
University	d	15 25	15 35	15 39	15 45	15 59	16 05	16 15		16 25	16 35	16 39	16 45	16 55	17 06	16 59	17 15	17 25		17 35	17 39	17 45	17 55	17 59	18 05
Five Ways	d	15 29	15 39		15 49		16 09	16 19		16 29	16 39		16 49	16 58	17 10		17 19	17 28		17 39		17 49	17 58		18 09
Birmingham New Street 12	a	15 32	15 42	15 45	15 52	16 13	16 12	16 22		16 33	16 42	16 45	16 52	17 02	17 13	17 13	17 22	17 32		17 42	17 45	17 52	18 02	18 11	18 12
	d	15 35	15 45		15 55		16 15	16 25		16 35	16 45		16 55	17 05	17 16		17 25	17 35		17 45		17 55	18 05		18 15
Duddeston	d				15 59			16 29					16 59				17 29					17 59			
Aston	d	15 41	15 51		16 02		16 21	16 32		16 41	16 51		17 02	17 11	17 22		17 32	17 41		17 51		18 02	18 11		18 21
Gravelly Hill	d	15 44	15 54		16 06		16 24	16 36		16 44	16 54		17 06	17 14	17 25		17 36	17 44		17 54		18 06	18 14		18 24
Erdington	d	15 47	15 57		16 09		16 27	16 39		16 47	16 57		17 09	17 17	17 28		17 39	17 47		17 57		18 09	18 17		18 27
Chester Road	d	15 49	15 59		16 11		16 29	16 41		16 49	16 59		17 11	17 19	17 30		17 41	17 49		17 59		18 11	18 19		18 29
Wylde Green	d	15 52	16 02		16 13		16 32	16 43		16 52	17 02		17 13	17 22	17 33		17 43	17 52		18 02		18 13	18 22		18 32
Sutton Coldfield	d	15 55	16 05		16 16		16 35	16 46		16 55	17 05		17 16	17 25	17 36		17 46	17 55		18 05		18 16	18 25		18 35
Four Oaks	d	15 58	16a13		16 20		16a43	16 50		16 58	17a13		17 20	17 28	17a43		17 50	17 58		18a13		18 20	18 28		18a43
Butlers Lane	d	16 01			16 22			16 52		17 01			17 22	17 31			17 52	18 01				18 22	18 31		
Blake Street	d	16 03			16 25			16 55		17a08			17 25	17 33			17 55	18 03				18 25	18 33		
Shenstone	d	16 08			16 29			16 59					17 29	17 38			17 59	18 08				18 29	18 38		
Lichfield City	d	16a15			16 34			17 04					17 34	17 49			18 04	18 19				18 34	18 49		
Lichfield Trent Valley	a				16 40			17 10					17 40	17 53			18 10	18 23				18 40	18 53		

		LM	LM	XC ◇1		LM	LM	LM	LM	LM	XC ◇1	LM	LM	LM		LM	LM	XC ◇1	LM	LM	LM	LM	LM	XC ◇1	
Bromsgrove	d						18 43							19 46								20 55			
Redditch	d		17 57					18 27		18 57			19 27				19 57			20 27			20 57		
Alvechurch	d		18 02					18 32		19 02			19 32				20 02			20 32			21 02		
Barnt Green	d		18 09				18 49	18 39		19 08			19 38				20 08			20 38			21 08		
Longbridge	d	18 02	18 22			18 32		18 52	19 02	19 12		19 32	19 42			20 02	20 12		20 30	20 42	20 57		21 12		
Northfield	d	18 04	18 24			18 34		18 54	19 04	19 14		19 34	19 44			20 04	20 14		20 32	20 44	20 59		21 14		
Kings Norton	d	18 07	18 27			18 37		18 58	19 07	19 17		19 37	19 47			20 07	20 17		20 35	20 47	21 02		21 17		
Bournville	d	18 09	18 29			18 39		19 00	19 09	19 19		19 39	19 49			20 09	20 19		20 37	20 49	21 04		21 19		
Selly Oak	d	18 12	18 32			18 42		19 03	19 12	19 22		19 42	19 52			20 12	20 22		20 40	20 52	21 07		21 22		
University	d	18 15	18 35	18 39		18 45	18 59	19 06	19 15	19 25	19 39	19 45	19 55	20 09		20 15	20 25	20 39	20 43	20 55	21 10	21 14	21 25	21 45	
Five Ways	d	18 19	18 39			18 49		19 10	19 19	19 29		19 49	19 59			20 19	20 29		20 47	20 59	21 14		21 29		
Birmingham New Street 12	a	18 22	18 42	18 45		18 52	19 12	19 13	19 22	19 32	19 45	19 55	20 03	20 20		20 25	20 33	20 45	20 53	21 02	21 20	21 20	21 33	21 51	
	d	18 25	18 45			18 55		19 16	19 25	19 35			20 05				20 35			21 05			21 35		
Duddeston	d	18 29				18 59				19 39			20 09				20 39			21 09			21 39		
Aston	d	18 32	18 51			19 02		19 22	19 31	19 42			20 12				20 42			21 12			21 42		
Gravelly Hill	d	18 36	18 54			19 06		19 25	19 34	19 46			20 16				20 46			21 16			21 46		
Erdington	d	18 39	18 57			19 09		19 28	19 37	19 49			20 19				20 49			21 19			21 49		
Chester Road	d	18 41	18 59			19 11		19 30	19 39	19 51			20 21				20 51			21 21			21 51		
Wylde Green	d	18 43	19 02			19 13		19 33	19 42	19 53			20 23				20 53			21 23			21 53		
Sutton Coldfield	d	18 46	19 05			19 16		19 36	19 45	19 56			20 26				20 56			21 26			21 56		
Four Oaks	d	18 50	19a13			19 20		19a43	19 48	20 00			20 30				21 00			21 30			22 00		
Butlers Lane	d	18 52				19 22			19 51	20 02			20 32				21 02			21 32			22 02		
Blake Street	d	18 55				19 25			19 53	20 05			20 35				21 05			21 35			22 05		
Shenstone	d	18 59				19 29			19 58	20 09			20 39				21 09			21 39			22 09		
Lichfield City	d	19 04				19 34			20 03	20 14			20 44				21 14			21 44			22 14		
Lichfield Trent Valley	a	19 10				19 40			20 10	20 20			20 50				21 20			21 50			22 20		

Mondays to Fridays
from 22 October

Redditch and Longbridge - Birmingham - Lichfield

Network Diagram - see first Page of Table 67

		LM	LM	LM	LM	LM	LM	LM	LM	LM	LM
Bromsgrove	d						22 28				
Redditch	d		21 27		21 57			22 27		22 57	
Alvechurch	d		21 32		22 02			22 32		23 02	
Barnt Green	d		21 38		22 08			22 38		23 08	
Longbridge	d	21 30	21 42	22 00	22 12	22 27		22 45	22 53	23 12	23 30
Northfield	d	21 32	21 44	22 02	22 14	22 29		22 47	22 55	23 14	23 32
Kings Norton	d	21 35	21 47	22 05	22 17	22 32		22 50	22 58	23 17	23 35
Bournville	d	21 37	21 49	22 07	22 19	22 34		22 52	23 00	23 19	23 37
Selly Oak	d	21 40	21 52	22 10	22 22	22 37		22 55	23 03	23 22	23 40
University	d	21 43	21 55	22 13	22 25	22 40	22 44	22 58	23 06	23 25	23 43
Five Ways	d	21 47	21 59	22 17	22 29	22 44		23 02	23 10	23 29	23 47
Birmingham New Street 12	a	21 53	22 02	22 23	22 33	22 47	22 50	23 06	23 13	23 34	23 53
	d		22 05		22 35	22 55			23 15		
Duddeston	d		22 09		22 39	22 59			23 19		
Aston	d		22 12		22 42	23 02			23 22		
Gravelly Hill	d		22 16		22 46	23 06			23 26		
Erdington	d		22 19		22 49	23 09			23 29		
Chester Road	d		22 21		22 51	23 11			23 31		
Wylde Green	d		22 23		22 53	23 13			23 33		
Sutton Coldfield	d		22 26		22 56	23 16			23 36		
Four Oaks	d		22 30		23 00	23 20			23 40		
Butlers Lane	d		22 32		23 02	23 22			23 42		
Blake Street	d		22 35		23 05	23a28			23 45		
Shenstone	d		22 39		23 09				23 49		
Lichfield City	d		22 44		23 14				23a57		
Lichfield Trent Valley	a		22 50		23 20						

Saturdays
until 20 October

		LM	LM	LM	LM	LM	LM	LM	LM	LM	LM	LM	LM	LM	XC ◇1	LM	LM	LM	LM	LM	XC ◇1	LM	LM
Bromsgrove	d								06 51						07 44		07 52						
Redditch	d						06 27				06 57			07 27					07 57				08 27
Alvechurch	d						06 32				07 02			07 32					08 02				08 32
Barnt Green	d						06 38				07 08			07 38					08 08				08 38
Longbridge	d			06 12	06 22	06 32	06 42	06 52		07 02	07 12	07 22	07 32	07 42		07 52		08 02	08 12	08 22		08 32	08 42
Northfield	d			06 14	06 24	06 34	06 44	06 54		07 04	07 14	07 24	07 34	07 44		07 54		08 04	08 14	08 24		08 34	08 44
Kings Norton	d			06 17	06 27	06 37	06 47	06 57		07 07	07 17	07 27	07 37	07 47		07 57		08 07	08 17	08 27		08 37	08 47
Bournville	d			06 19	06 29	06 39	06 49	06 59		07 09	07 19	07 29	07 39	07 49		07 59		08 09	08 19	08 29		08 39	08 49
Selly Oak	d			06 22	06 32	06 42	06 52	07 02		07 12	07 22	07 32	07 42	07 52		08 02		08 12	08 22	08 32		08 42	08 52
University	d			06 25	06 35	06 45	06 55	07 05	07 09	07 15	07 25	07 35	07 45	07 55	08 00	08 05	08 09	08 15	08 25	08 35	08 39	08 45	08 55
Five Ways	d			06 29	06 39	06 49	06 59	07 09		07 19	07 29	07 39	07 49	07 59		08 09		08 19	08 29	08 39		08 49	08 59
Birmingham New Street 12	a			06 33	06 43	06 53	07 02	07 13	07 16	07 23	07 33	07 43	07 53	08 03	08 08	08 13	08 16	08 23	08 33	08 43	08 45	08 52	09 03
	d	05 57	06 25	06 35		06 55	07 05	07 15		07 25	07 35	07 45	07 55	08 05		08 15		08 25	08 35	08 45		08 55	09 05
Duddeston	d	06 01	06 29			06 59				07 29			07 59					08 29				08 59	
Aston	d	06 04	06 32			07 02	07 11	07 21		07 32	07 41	07 51	08 02	08 11		08 21		08 32	08 41	08 51		09 02	09 11
Gravelly Hill	d	06 07	06 35			07 05	07 14	07 24		07 35	07 44	07 54	08 05	08 14		08 24		08 35	08 44	08 54		09 05	09 14
Erdington	d	06 10	06 38	06 44		07 08	07 16	07 26		07 38	07 46	07 56	08 08	08 16		08 26		08 38	08 46	08 56		09 08	09 16
Chester Road	d	06 12	06 40	06 46		07 10	07 18	07 28		07 40	07 48	07 58	08 10	08 18		08 28		08 40	08 48	08 58		09 10	09 18
Wylde Green	d	06 14	06 42	06 48		07 12	07 20	07 30		07 42	07 50	08 00	08 12	08 20		08 30		08 42	08 50	09 00		09 12	09 20
Sutton Coldfield	d	06 17	06 45	06 52		07 15	07 24	07 34		07 45	07 54	08 04	08 15	08 24		08 34		08 45	08 54	09 04		09 15	09 24
Four Oaks	d	06 20	06 48	06 55		07 18	07 28	07a41		07 48	07 58	08a11	08 18	08 28		08a41		08 48	08 58	09a11		09 18	09 28
Butlers Lane	d	06 22	06 50	06 57		07 20	07 30			07 50	08 00		08 20	08 30				08 50	09 00			09 20	09 30
Blake Street	d	06 24	06 53	07 00		07 23	07 32			07 53	08 02		08 23	08 32				08 53	09 02			09 23	09 32
Shenstone	d	06 28	06 57			07 27				07 57			08 27	08 36				08 57				09 27	
Lichfield City	d	06a34	07a02	07 08		07a32	07 41			08a02	08 11		08a32	08 41				09a02	09 11			09a32	09 41
Lichfield Trent Valley	a			07 12			07 44				08 15			08 45					09 15				09 45

		LM	LM	LM	LM	LM	XC ◇1	LM	LM	LM	LM	LM	LM	LM	LM	XC ◇1	LM	LM	LM	LM	LM	LM	LM
Bromsgrove	d	08 42								09 42				10 13					10 42				11 15
Redditch	d				08 57				09 27				09 57					10 27				10 57	
Alvechurch	d				09 02				09 32				10 02					10 32				11 02	
Barnt Green	d				09 08				09 38				10 08					10 38				11 08	
Longbridge	d		08 52	09 02	09 12	09 22		09 32	09 42		09 52	10 02	10 12		10 22		10 32	10 42		10 52	11 02	11 12	
Northfield	d		08 54	09 04	09 14	09 24		09 34	09 44		09 54	10 04	10 14		10 24		10 34	10 44		10 54	11 04	11 14	
Kings Norton	d		08 57	09 07	09 17	09 27		09 37	09 47		09 57	10 07	10 17		10 27		10 37	10 47		10 57	11 07	11 17	
Bournville	d		08 59	09 09	09 19	09 29		09 39	09 49		09 59	10 09	10 19		10 29		10 39	10 49		10 59	11 09	11 19	
Selly Oak	d		09 02	09 12	09 22	09 32		09 42	09 52		10 02	10 12	10 22		10 32		10 42	10 52		11 02	11 12	11 22	
University	d	08 59	09 05	09 15	09 25	09 35	09 39	09 45	09 55	09 59	10 05	10 15	10 25		10 35	10 39	10 45	10 55	10 59	11 05	11 15	11 25	
Five Ways	d		09 09	09 19	09 29	09 39		09 49	09 59		10 09	10 19	10 29		10 39		10 49	10 59		11 09	11 19	11 29	
Birmingham New Street 12	a	09 11	09 13	09 23	09 33	09 43	09 45	09 52	10 03	10 11	10 13	10 23	10 33	10 41	10 43	10 45	10 53	11 03	11 11	11 13	11 23	11 33	11 38
	d		09 15	09 25	09 35	09 45		09 55	10 05		10 15	10 25	10 35		10 45		10 55	11 05		11 15	11 25	11 35	
Duddeston	d			09 29				09 59				10 29					10 59				11 29		
Aston	d		09 21	09 32	09 41	09 51		10 02	10 11		10 21	10 32	10 41		10 51		11 02	11 11		11 21	11 32	11 41	
Gravelly Hill	d		09 24	09 35	09 44	09 54		10 05	10 14		10 24	10 35	10 44		10 54		11 05	11 14		11 24	11 35	11 44	
Erdington	d		09 26	09 38	09 46	09 56		10 08	10 16		10 26	10 38	10 46		10 56		11 08	11 16		11 26	11 38	11 46	
Chester Road	d		09 28	09 40	09 48	09 58		10 10	10 18		10 28	10 40	10 48		10 58		11 10	11 18		11 28	11 40	11 48	
Wylde Green	d		09 30	09 42	09 50	10 00		10 12	10 20		10 30	10 42	10 50		11 00		11 12	11 20		11 30	11 42	11 50	
Sutton Coldfield	d		09 34	09 45	09 54	10 04		10 15	10 24		10 34	10 45	10 54		11 04		11 15	11 24		11 34	11 45	11 54	
Four Oaks	d		09a41	09 48	09 58	10a11		10 18	10 28		10a41	10 48	10 58		11a11		11 18	11 28		11a41	11 48	11 58	
Butlers Lane	d			09 50	10 00			10 20	10 30			10 50	11 00				11 20	11 30			11 50	12 00	
Blake Street	d			09 53	10 02			10 23	10 32			10 53	11 02				11 23	11 32			11 53	12 02	
Shenstone	d			09 57				10 27				10 57					11 27				11 57		
Lichfield City	d			10a02	10 11			10a32	10 41			11a02	11 11				11a32	11 41			12a02	12 11	
Lichfield Trent Valley	a				10 15				10 45				11 15					11 45				12 15	

Saturdays
until 20 October

Redditch and Longbridge - Birmingham - Lichfield

Network Diagram - see first Page of Table 67

		LM	XC ◇1	LM	LM	LM	LM	LM	LM	LM	XC ◇1	LM	LM	LM	LM	LM	LM	LM	XC ◇1	LM	LM	LM
Bromsgrove	d					11 42								12 42								13 42
Redditch	d				11 27				11 57				12 27				12 57				13 27	
Alvechurch	d				11 32				12 02				12 32				13 02				13 32	
Barnt Green	d				11 38				12 08				12 38				13 08				13 38	
Longbridge	d	11 22		11 32	11 42		11 52	12 02	12 12	12 22		12 32	12 42		12 52	13 02	13 12	13 22		13 32	13 42	
Northfield	d	11 24		11 34	11 44		11 54	12 04	12 14	12 24		12 34	12 44		12 54	13 04	13 14	13 24		13 34	13 44	
Kings Norton	d	11 27		11 37	11 47		11 57	12 07	12 17	12 27		12 37	12 47		12 57	13 07	13 17	13 27		13 37	13 47	
Bournville	d	11 29		11 39	11 49		11 59	12 09	12 19	12 29		12 39	12 49		12 59	13 09	13 19	13 29		13 39	13 49	
Selly Oak	d	11 32		11 42	11 52		12 02	12 12	12 22	12 32		12 42	12 52		13 02	13 12	13 22	13 32		13 42	13 52	
University	d	11 35	11 39	11 45	11 55	11 59	12 05	12 15	12 25	12 35	12 39	12 45	12 55	12 59	13 05	13 15	13 25	13 35	13 39	13 45	13 55	13 59
Five Ways	d	11 39		11 49	11 59		12 09	12 19	12 29	12 39		12 49	12 59		13 09	13 19	13 29	13 39		13 49	13 59	
Birmingham New Street 12	a	11 43	11 45	11 53	12 03	12 11	12 13	12 23	12 33	12 43	12 45	12 53	13 03	13 11	13 13	13 23	13 33	13 43	13 45	13 53	14 03	14 11
	d	11 45		11 55	12 05		12 15	12 25	12 35	12 45		12 55	13 05		13 15	13 25	13 35	13 45		13 55	14 05	
Duddeston	d			11 59				12 29				12 59				13 29				13 59		
Aston	d	11 51		12 02	12 11		12 21	12 32	12 41	12 51		13 02	13 11		13 21	13 32	13 41	13 51		14 02	14 11	
Gravelly Hill	d	11 54		12 05	12 14		12 24	12 35	12 44	12 54		13 05	13 14		13 24	13 35	13 44	13 54		14 05	14 14	
Erdington	d	11 56		12 08	12 16		12 26	12 38	12 46	12 56		13 08	13 16		13 26	13 38	13 46	13 56		14 08	14 16	
Chester Road	d	11 58		12 10	12 18		12 28	12 40	12 48	12 58		13 10	13 18		13 28	13 40	13 48	13 58		14 10	14 18	
Wylde Green	d	12 00		12 12	12 20		12 30	12 42	12 50	13 00		13 12	13 20		13 30	13 42	13 50	14 00		14 12	14 20	
Sutton Coldfield	d	12 04		12 15	12 24		12 34	12 45	12 54	13 04		13 15	13 24		13 34	13 45	13 54	14 04		14 15	14 24	
Four Oaks	d	12a11		12 18	12 28		12a41	12 48	12 58	13a11		13 18	13 28		13a41	13 48	13 58	14a11		14 18	14 28	
Butlers Lane	d			12 20	12 30			12 50	13 00			13 20	13 30			13 50	14 00			14 20	14 30	
Blake Street	d			12 23	12 32			12 53	13 02			13 23	13 32			13 53	14 02			14 23	14 32	
Shenstone	d			12 27				12 57				13 27				13 57				14 27		
Lichfield City	d			12a32	12 41			13a02	13 11			13a32	13 41			14a02	14 11			14a32	14 41	
Lichfield Trent Valley	a				12 45				13 15				13 45				14 15				14 45	

		LM	LM	LM	LM	XC ◇1	LM	LM	LM	LM	LM	LM	LM	XC ◇1	LM	LM	LM	LM	LM	LM	LM	LM	XC ◇1
Bromsgrove	d								14 42								15 42				16 12		
Redditch	d			13 57				14 27				14 57				15 27				15 57			
Alvechurch	d			14 02				14 32				15 02				15 32				16 02			
Barnt Green	d			14 08				14 38				15 08				15 38				16 08			
Longbridge	d	13 52	14 02	14 12	14 22		14 32	14 42		14 52	15 02	15 12	15 22		15 32	15 42		15 52	16 02	16 12		16 22	
Northfield	d	13 54	14 04	14 14	14 24		14 34	14 44		14 54	15 04	15 14	15 24		15 34	15 44		15 54	16 04	16 14		16 24	
Kings Norton	d	13 57	14 07	14 17	14 27		14 37	14 47		14 57	15 07	15 17	15 27		15 37	15 47		15 57	16 07	16 17		16 27	
Bournville	d	13 59	14 09	14 19	14 29		14 39	14 49		14 59	15 09	15 19	15 29		15 39	15 49		15 59	16 09	16 19		16 29	
Selly Oak	d	14 02	14 12	14 22	14 32		14 42	14 52		15 02	15 12	15 22	15 32		15 42	15 52		16 02	16 12	16 22		16 32	
University	d	14 05	14 15	14 25	14 35	14 39	14 45	14 55	14 59	15 05	15 15	15 25	15 35	15 39	15 45	15 55	15 59	16 05	16 15	16 25		16 35	16 39
Five Ways	d	14 09	14 19	14 29	14 39		14 49	14 59		15 09	15 19	15 29	15 39		15 49	15 59		16 09	16 19	16 29		16 39	
Birmingham New Street 12	a	14 13	14 23	14 33	14 43	14 45	14 53	15 03	15 11	15 13	15 23	15 33	15 43	15 45	15 53	16 03	16 11	16 13	16 23	16 33	16 45	16 43	16 45
	d	14 15	14 25	14 35	14 45		14 55	15 05		15 15	15 25	15 35	15 45		15 55	16 05		16 15	16 25	16 35		16 45	
Duddeston	d		14 29				14 59				15 29				15 59				16 29				
Aston	d	14 21	14 32	14 41	14 51		15 02	15 11		15 21	15 32	15 41	15 51		16 02	16 11		16 21	16 32	16 41		16 51	
Gravelly Hill	d	14 24	14 35	14 44	14 54		15 05	15 14		15 24	15 35	15 44	15 54		16 05	16 14		16 24	16 35	16 44		16 54	
Erdington	d	14 26	14 38	14 46	14 56		15 08	15 16		15 26	15 38	15 46	15 56		16 08	16 16		16 26	16 38	16 46		16 56	
Chester Road	d	14 28	14 40	14 48	14 58		15 10	15 18		15 28	15 40	15 48	15 58		16 10	16 18		16 28	16 40	16 48		16 58	
Wylde Green	d	14 30	14 42	14 50	15 00		15 12	15 20		15 30	15 42	15 50	16 00		16 12	16 20		16 30	16 42	16 50		17 00	
Sutton Coldfield	d	14 34	14 45	14 54	15 04		15 15	15 24		15 34	15 45	15 54	16 04		16 15	16 24		16 34	16 45	16 54		17 04	
Four Oaks	d	14a41	14 48	14 58	15a11		15 18	15 28		15a41	15 48	15 58	16a11		16 18	16 28		16a41	16 48	16 58		17a11	
Butlers Lane	d		14 50	15 00			15 20	15 30			15 50	16 00			16 20	16 30			16 50	17 00			
Blake Street	d		14 53	15 02			15 23	15 32			15 53	16 02			16 23	16 32			16 53	17 02			
Shenstone	d		14 57				15 27				15 57				16 27				16 57				
Lichfield City	d		15a02	15 11			15a32	15 41			16a02	16 11			16a32	16 41			17a02	17 11			
Lichfield Trent Valley	a			15 15				15 45				16 15				16 45				17 15			

		LM	LM	LM	LM	LM	LM	LM	XC ◇1	LM	LM	LM	LM	LM	LM	LM	XC ◇1	LM	LM	LM	LM	LM
Bromsgrove	d			16 42								17 44								18 42		
Redditch	d		16 27				16 57				17 27				17 57				18 27			
Alvechurch	d		16 32				17 02				17 32				18 02				18 32			
Barnt Green	d		16 38				17 08				17 38				18 08				18 38			
Longbridge	d	16 32	16 42		16 52	17 02	17 12	17 22		17 32	17 42		17 52	18 02	18 12	18 22		18 32	18 42		18 52	19 02
Northfield	d	16 34	16 44		16 54	17 04	17 14	17 24		17 34	17 44		17 54	18 04	18 14	18 24		18 34	18 44		18 54	19 04
Kings Norton	d	16 37	16 47		16 57	17 07	17 17	17 27		17 37	17 47		17 57	18 07	18 17	18 27		18 37	18 47		18 57	19 07
Bournville	d	16 39	16 49		16 59	17 09	17 19	17 29		17 39	17 49		17 59	18 09	18 19	18 29		18 39	18 49		18 59	19 09
Selly Oak	d	16 42	16 52		17 02	17 12	17 22	17 32		17 42	17 52		18 02	18 12	18 22	18 32		18 42	18 52		19 02	19 12
University	d	16 45	16 55	16 59	17 05	17 15	17 25	17 35	17 39	17 45	17 55	17 59	18 05	18 15	18 25	18 35	18 39	18 45	18 55	18 59	19 05	19 15
Five Ways	d	16 49	16 59		17 09	17 19	17 29	17 39		17 49	17 59		18 09	18 19	18 29	18 39		18 49	18 59		19 09	19 19
Birmingham New Street 12	a	16 53	17 03	17 11	17 13	17 23	17 33	17 43	17 45	17 53	18 03	18 11	18 13	18 23	18 33	18 43	18 45	18 53	19 03	19 11	19 13	19 23
	d	16 55	17 05		17 15	17 25	17 35	17 45		17 55	18 05		18 15	18 25	18 35	18 45		18 55	19 05		19 15	
Duddeston	d	16 59				17 29				17 59				18 29				18 59				
Aston	d	17 02	17 11		17 21	17 32	17 41	17 51		18 02	18 11		18 21	18 32	18 41	18 51		19 02	19 11		19 21	
Gravelly Hill	d	17 05	17 14		17 24	17 35	17 44	17 54		18 05	18 14		18 24	18 35	18 44	18 54		19 05	19 14		19 24	
Erdington	d	17 08	17 16		17 26	17 38	17 46	17 56		18 08	18 16		18 26	18 38	18 46	18 56		19 08	19 16		19 26	
Chester Road	d	17 10	17 18		17 28	17 40	17 48	17 58		18 10	18 18		18 28	18 40	18 48	18 58		19 10	19 18		19 28	
Wylde Green	d	17 12	17 20		17 30	17 42	17 50	18 00		18 12	18 20		18 30	18 42	18 50	19 00		19 12	19 20		19 30	
Sutton Coldfield	d	17 15	17 24		17 34	17 45	17 54	18 04		18 15	18 24		18 34	18 45	18 54	19 04		19 15	19 24		19 34	
Four Oaks	d	17 18	17 28		17a41	17 48	17 58	18a11		18 18	18 28		18a41	18 48	18 58	19a11		19 18	19 28		19a41	
Butlers Lane	d	17 20	17 30			17 50	18 00			18 20	18 30			18 50	19 00			19 20	19 30			
Blake Street	d	17 23	17 32			17 53	18 02			18 23	18 32			18 53	19 02			19 23	19 32			
Shenstone	d	17 27				17 57				18 27				18 57				19 27				
Lichfield City	d	17a32	17 41			18a02	18 11			18a32	18 41			19a02	19 11			19a32	19 41			
Lichfield Trent Valley	a		17 45				18 15				18 45				19 15				19 45			

Saturdays
until 20 October

Redditch and Longbridge - Birmingham - Lichfield

Network Diagram - see first Page of Table 67

	LM	LM	XC ◇1	LM	LM	LM	LM	LM	XC ◇1	LM	LM	LM	LM	LM	LM	LM	XC ◇1	LM	LM	XC ◇1	LM	LM
Bromsgrove d													20 59				21 44					
Redditch d	18 57				19 27			19 57			20 27			20 57		21 27			21 57			22 27
Alvechurch d	19 02				19 32			20 02			20 32			21 02		21 32			22 02			22 32
Barnt Green d	19 08				19 38			20 08			20 38			21 08		21 38			22 08			22 38
Longbridge d	19 12	19 22		19 32	19 42	19 52	20 02	20 12		20 30	20 42	20 57		21 12	21 27	21 42		21 57	22 12		22 27	22 42
Northfield d	19 14	19 24		19 34	19 44	19 54	20 04	20 14		20 32	20 44	20 59		21 14	21 29	21 44		21 59	22 14		22 29	22 44
Kings Norton d	19 17	19 27		19 37	19 47	19 57	20 07	20 17		20 35	20 47	21 02		21 17	21 32	21 47		22 02	22 17		22 32	22 47
Bournville d	19 19	19 29		19 39	19 49	19 59	20 09	20 19		20 37	20 49	21 04		21 19	21 34	21 49		22 04	22 19		22 34	22 49
Selly Oak d	19 22	19 32		19 42	19 52	20 02	20 12	20 22		20 40	20 52	21 07		21 22	21 37	21 52		22 07	22 22		22 37	22 52
University d	19 25	19 35	19 39	19 45	19 55	20 05	20 15	20 25	20 34	20 42	20 55	21 10	21 14	21 25	21 40	21 55	22 01	22 10	22 25	22 36	22 40	22 55
Five Ways d	19 29	19 39		19 49	19 59	20 09	20 19	20 29		20 46	20 59	21 14		21 29	21 44	21 59		22 14	22 29		22 44	22 59
Birmingham New Street a	19 33	19 43	19 45	19 53	20 03	20 13	20 23	20 33	20 40	20 51	21 03	21 18	21 21	21 33	21 48	22 03	22 07	22 18	22 33	22 42	22 48	23 03
d	19 35				20 05			20 35			21 05			21 35		22 05			22 35		22 55	
Duddeston d	19 39				20 09			20 39			21 09			21 39		22 09			22 39		22 59	
Aston d	19 42				20 12			20 42			21 12			21 42		22 12			22 42		23 02	
Gravelly Hill d	19 45				20 15			20 45			21 15			21 45		22 15			22 45		23 05	
Erdington d	19 48				20 18			20 48			21 18			21 48		22 18			22 48		23 08	
Chester Road d	19 50				20 20			20 50			21 20			21 50		22 20			22 50		23 10	
Wylde Green d	19 52				20 22			20 52			21 22			21 52		22 22			22 52		23 12	
Sutton Coldfield d	19 55				20 25			20 55			21 25			21 55		22 25			22 55		23 15	
Four Oaks d	19 58				20 28			20 58			21 28			21 58		22 28			22 58		23 18	
Butlers Lane d	20 00				20 30			21 00			21 30			22 00		22 30			23 00		23 20	
Blake Street d	20 03				20 33			21 03			21 33			22 03		22 33			23 03		23a24	
Shenstone d	20 07				20 37			21 07			21 37			22 07		22 37			23 07			
Lichfield City d	20 12				20 42			21 12			21 42			22 12		22 42			23 12			
Lichfield Trent Valley a	20 16				20 46			21 16			21 46			22 16		22 46			23 16			

	LM	LM	LM
Bromsgrove d			
Redditch d		22 57	
Alvechurch d		23 02	
Barnt Green d		23 08	
Longbridge d	22 52	23 12	23 30
Northfield d	22 54	23 14	23 32
Kings Norton d	22 57	23 17	23 35
Bournville d	22 59	23 19	23 37
Selly Oak d	23 02	23 22	23 40
University d	23 05	23 25	23 43
Five Ways d	23 09	23 29	23 47
Birmingham New Street a	23 13	23 33	23 51
d	23 15		
Duddeston d	23 19		
Aston d	23 22		
Gravelly Hill d	23 25		
Erdington d	23 28		
Chester Road d	23 30		
Wylde Green d	23 32		
Sutton Coldfield d	23 35		
Four Oaks d	23 38		
Butlers Lane d	23 40		
Blake Street d	23 43		
Shenstone d	23 47		
Lichfield City d	23a52		
Lichfield Trent Valley a			

Saturdays
from 27 October

	LM	LM	LM	LM	LM	LM	LM	LM	LM	LM	LM	LM	LM	XC ◇1	LM	LM	LM	LM	LM	XC ◇1	LM	LM
Bromsgrove d								06 51						07 44		07 52						
Redditch d						06 27				06 57			07 27					07 57				08 27
Alvechurch d						06 32				07 02			07 32					08 02				08 32
Barnt Green d						06 38				07 08			07 38					08 08				08 38
Longbridge d			06 12	06 22	06 32	06 42	06 52		07 02	07 12	07 22	07 32	07 42		07 52		08 02	08 12	08 22		08 32	08 42
Northfield d			06 14	06 24	06 34	06 44	06 54		07 04	07 14	07 24	07 34	07 44		07 54		08 04	08 14	08 24		08 34	08 44
Kings Norton d			06 17	06 27	06 37	06 47	06 57		07 07	07 17	07 27	07 37	07 47		07 57		08 07	08 17	08 27		08 37	08 47
Bournville d			06 19	06 29	06 39	06 49	06 59		07 09	07 19	07 29	07 39	07 49		07 59		08 09	08 19	08 29		08 39	08 49
Selly Oak d			06 22	06 32	06 42	06 52	07 02		07 12	07 22	07 32	07 42	07 52		08 02		08 12	08 22	08 32		08 42	08 52
University d			06 25	06 35	06 45	06 55	07 05	07 09	07 15	07 25	07 35	07 45	07 55	08 00	08 05	08 09	08 15	08 25	08 35	08 39	08 45	08 55
Five Ways d			06 29	06 39	06 49	06 59	07 09		07 19	07 29	07 39	07 49	07 59		08 09		08 19	08 29	08 39		08 49	08 59
Birmingham New Street a			06 33	06 43	06 53	07 02	07 13	07 16	07 23	07 33	07 43	07 53	08 03	08 08	08 13	08 16	08 23	08 33	08 43	08 45	08 52	09 03
d	05 57	06 25	06 35		06 55	07 05	07 15		07 25	07 35	07 45	07 55	08 05		08 15		08 25	08 35	08 45		08 55	09 05
Duddeston d	06 01	06 29			06 59				07 29			07 59					08 29				08 59	
Aston d	06 04	06 32			07 02	07 11	07 21		07 32	07 41	07 51	08 02	08 11		08 21		08 32	08 41	08 51		09 02	09 11
Gravelly Hill d	06 07	06 35			07 05	07 14	07 24		07 35	07 44	07 54	08 05	08 14		08 24		08 35	08 44	08 54		09 05	09 14
Erdington d	06 10	06 38	06 44		07 08	07 16	07 26		07 38	07 46	07 56	08 08	08 16		08 26		08 38	08 46	08 56		09 08	09 16
Chester Road d	06 12	06 40	06 46		07 10	07 18	07 28		07 40	07 48	07 58	08 10	08 18		08 28		08 40	08 48	08 58		09 10	09 18
Wylde Green d	06 14	06 42	06 48		07 12	07 20	07 30		07 42	07 50	08 00	08 12	08 20		08 30		08 42	08 50	09 00		09 12	09 20
Sutton Coldfield d	06 17	06 45	06 52		07 15	07 24	07 34		07 45	07 54	08 04	08 15	08 24		08 34		08 45	08 54	09 04		09 15	09 24
Four Oaks d	06 20	06 48	06 55		07 18	07 28	07a41		07 48	07 58	08a11	08 18	08 28		08a41		08 48	08 58	09a11		09 18	09 28
Butlers Lane d	06 22	06 50	06 57		07 20	07 30			07 50	08 00		08 20	08 30				08 50	09 00			09 20	09 30
Blake Street d	06 24	06 53	07 00		07 23	07 32			07 53	08 02		08 23	08 32				08 53	09 02			09 23	09 32
Shenstone d	06 28	06 57			07 27				07 57			08 27	08 36				08 57				09 27	
Lichfield City d	06a34	07a02	07 08		07a32	07 41			08a02	08 11		08a32	08 41				09a02	09 11			09a32	09 41
Lichfield Trent Valley a			07 12			07 44				08 15			08 45					09 15				09 45

Table 69

Saturdays
from 27 October

Redditch and Longbridge - Birmingham - Lichfield

Network Diagram - see first Page of Table 67

	LM	LM	LM	LM	LM	XC ◇1	LM	LM	LM	LM	LM	LM	LM	LM	XC ◇1	LM	LM	LM	LM	LM	LM	LM
Bromsgrove d	08 42								09 42				10 13					10 42				11 15
Redditch d				08 57				09 27				09 57					10 27				10 57	
Alvechurch d				09 02				09 32				10 02					10 32				11 02	
Barnt Green d				09 08				09 38				10 08					10 38				11 08	
Longbridge d		08 52	09 02	09 12	09 22		09 32	09 42		09 52	10 02	10 12		10 22		10 32	10 42		10 52	11 02	11 12	
Northfield d		08 54	09 04	09 14	09 24		09 34	09 44		09 54	10 04	10 14		10 24		10 34	10 44		10 54	11 04	11 14	
Kings Norton d		08 57	09 07	09 17	09 27		09 37	09 47		09 57	10 07	10 17		10 27		10 37	10 47		10 57	11 07	11 17	
Bournville d		08 59	09 09	09 19	09 29		09 39	09 49		09 59	10 09	10 19		10 29		10 39	10 49		10 59	11 09	11 19	
Selly Oak d		09 02	09 12	09 22	09 32		09 42	09 52		10 02	10 12	10 22		10 32		10 42	10 52		11 02	11 12	11 22	
University d	08 59	09 05	09 15	09 25	09 35	09 39	09 45	09 55	09 59	10 05	10 15	10 25		10 35	10 39	10 45	10 55	10 59	11 05	11 15	11 25	
Five Ways d		09 09	09 19	09 29	09 39		09 49	09 59		10 09	10 19	10 29		10 39		10 49	10 59		11 09	11 19	11 29	
Birmingham New Street a	09 11	09 13	09 23	09 33	09 43	09 45	09 52	10 03	10 11	10 13	10 23	10 33	10 41	10 43	10 45	10 53	11 03	11 11	11 13	11 23	11 33	11 38
d		09 15	09 25	09 35	09 45		09 55	10 05		10 15	10 25	10 35		10 45		10 55	11 05		11 15	11 25	11 35	
Duddeston d			09 29				09 59				10 29					10 59				11 29		
Aston d		09 21	09 32	09 41	09 51		10 02	10 11		10 21	10 32	10 41		10 51		11 02	11 11		11 21	11 32	11 41	
Gravelly Hill d		09 24	09 35	09 44	09 54		10 05	10 14		10 24	10 35	10 44		10 54		11 05	11 14		11 24	11 35	11 44	
Erdington d		09 26	09 38	09 46	09 56		10 08	10 16		10 26	10 38	10 46		10 56		11 08	11 16		11 26	11 38	11 46	
Chester Road d		09 28	09 40	09 48	09 58		10 10	10 18		10 28	10 40	10 48		10 58		11 10	11 18		11 28	11 40	11 48	
Wylde Green d		09 30	09 42	09 50	10 00		10 12	10 20		10 30	10 42	10 50		11 00		11 12	11 20		11 30	11 42	11 50	
Sutton Coldfield d		09 34	09 45	09 54	10 04		10 15	10 24		10 34	10 45	10 54		11 04		11 15	11 24		11 34	11 45	11 54	
Four Oaks d		09a41	09 48	09 58	10a11		10 18	10 28		10a41	10 48	10 58		11a11		11 18	11 28		11a41	11 48	11 58	
Butlers Lane d			09 50	10 00			10 20	10 30			10 50	11 00				11 20	11 30			11 50	12 00	
Blake Street d			09 53	10 02			10 23	10 32			10 53	11 02				11 23	11 32			11 53	12 02	
Shenstone d			09 57				10 27				10 57					11 27				11 57		
Lichfield City d			10a02	10 11			10a32	10 41			11a02	11 11				11a32	11 41			12a02	12 11	
Lichfield Trent Valley a				10 15				10 45				11 15					11 45				12 15	

	LM	XC ◇1	LM	LM	LM	LM	LM	LM	LM	XC ◇1	LM	LM	LM	LM	LM	LM	LM	XC ◇1	LM	LM	LM
Bromsgrove d					11 42								12 42								13 42
Redditch d				11 27				11 57				12 27				12 57				13 27	
Alvechurch d				11 32				12 02				12 32				13 02				13 32	
Barnt Green d				11 38				12 08				12 38				13 08				13 38	
Longbridge d	11 22		11 32	11 42		11 52	12 02	12 12	12 22		12 32	12 42		12 52	13 02	13 12	13 22		13 32	13 42	
Northfield d	11 24		11 34	11 44		11 54	12 04	12 14	12 24		12 34	12 44		12 54	13 04	13 14	13 24		13 34	13 44	
Kings Norton d	11 27		11 37	11 47		11 57	12 07	12 17	12 27		12 37	12 47		12 57	13 07	13 17	13 27		13 37	13 47	
Bournville d	11 29		11 39	11 49		11 59	12 09	12 19	12 29		12 39	12 49		12 59	13 09	13 19	13 29		13 39	13 49	
Selly Oak d	11 32		11 42	11 52		12 02	12 12	12 22	12 32		12 42	12 52		13 02	13 12	13 22	13 32		13 42	13 52	
University d	11 35	11 39	11 45	11 55	11 59	12 05	12 15	12 25	12 35	12 39	12 45	12 55	12 59	13 05	13 15	13 25	13 35	13 39	13 45	13 55	13 59
Five Ways d	11 39		11 49	11 59		12 09	12 19	12 29	12 39		12 49	12 59		13 09	13 19	13 29	13 39		13 49	13 59	
Birmingham New Street a	11 43	11 45	11 53	12 03	12 11	12 13	12 23	12 33	12 43	12 45	12 53	13 03	13 11	13 13	13 23	13 33	13 43	13 45	13 53	14 03	14 11
d	11 45		11 55	12 05		12 15	12 25	12 35	12 45		12 55	13 05		13 15	13 25	13 35	13 45		13 55	14 05	
Duddeston d			11 59				12 29				12 59				13 29				13 59		
Aston d	11 51		12 02	12 11		12 21	12 32	12 41	12 51		13 02	13 11		13 21	13 32	13 41	13 51		14 02	14 11	
Gravelly Hill d	11 54		12 05	12 14		12 24	12 35	12 44	12 54		13 05	13 14		13 24	13 35	13 44	13 54		14 05	14 14	
Erdington d	11 56		12 08	12 16		12 26	12 38	12 46	12 56		13 08	13 16		13 26	13 38	13 46	13 56		14 08	14 16	
Chester Road d	11 58		12 10	12 18		12 28	12 40	12 48	12 58		13 10	13 18		13 28	13 40	13 48	13 58		14 10	14 18	
Wylde Green d	12 00		12 12	12 20		12 30	12 42	12 50	13 00		13 12	13 20		13 30	13 42	13 50	14 00		14 12	14 20	
Sutton Coldfield d	12 04		12 15	12 24		12 34	12 45	12 54	13 04		13 15	13 24		13 34	13 45	13 54	14 04		14 15	14 24	
Four Oaks d	12a11		12 18	12 28		12a41	12 48	12 58	13a11		13 18	13 28		13a41	13 48	13 58	14a11		14 18	14 28	
Butlers Lane d			12 20	12 30			12 50	13 00			13 20	13 30			13 50	14 00			14 20	14 30	
Blake Street d			12 23	12 32			12 53	13 02			13 23	13 32			13 53	14 02			14 23	14 32	
Shenstone d			12 27				12 57				13 27				13 57				14 27		
Lichfield City d			12a32	12 41			13a02	13 11			13a32	13 41			14a02	14 11			14a32	14 41	
Lichfield Trent Valley a				12 45				13 15				13 45				14 15				14 45	

	LM	LM	LM	LM	XC ◇1	LM	LM	LM	LM	LM	LM	LM	XC ◇1	LM	LM	LM	LM	LM	LM	LM	LM	XC ◇1
Bromsgrove d								14 42								15 42				16 12		
Redditch d			13 57				14 27				14 57				15 27				15 57			
Alvechurch d			14 02				14 32				15 02				15 32				16 02			
Barnt Green d			14 08				14 38				15 08				15 38				16 08			
Longbridge d	13 52	14 02	14 12	14 22		14 32	14 42		14 52	15 02	15 12	15 22		15 32	15 42		15 52	16 02	16 12		16 22	
Northfield d	13 54	14 04	14 14	14 24		14 34	14 44		14 54	15 04	15 14	15 24		15 34	15 44		15 54	16 04	16 14		16 24	
Kings Norton d	13 57	14 07	14 17	14 27		14 37	14 47		14 57	15 07	15 17	15 27		15 37	15 47		15 57	16 07	16 17		16 27	
Bournville d	13 59	14 09	14 19	14 29		14 39	14 49		14 59	15 09	15 19	15 29		15 39	15 49		15 59	16 09	16 19		16 29	
Selly Oak d	14 02	14 12	14 22	14 32		14 42	14 52		15 02	15 12	15 22	15 32		15 42	15 52		16 02	16 12	16 22		16 32	
University d	14 05	14 15	14 25	14 35	14 39	14 45	14 55	14 59	15 05	15 15	15 25	15 35	15 39	15 45	15 55	15 59	16 05	16 15	16 25		16 35	16 39
Five Ways d	14 09	14 19	14 29	14 39		14 49	14 59		15 09	15 19	15 29	15 39		15 49	15 59		16 09	16 19	16 29		16 39	
Birmingham New Street a	14 13	14 23	14 33	14 43	14 45	14 53	15 03	15 11	15 13	15 23	15 33	15 43	15 45	15 53	16 03	16 11	16 13	16 23	16 33	16 45	16 43	16 45
d	14 15	14 25	14 35	14 45		14 55	15 05		15 15	15 25	15 35	15 45		15 55	16 05		16 15	16 25	16 35		16 45	
Duddeston d		14 29				14 59				15 29				15 59				16 29				
Aston d	14 21	14 32	14 41	14 51		15 02	15 11		15 21	15 32	15 41	15 51		16 02	16 11		16 21	16 32	16 41		16 51	
Gravelly Hill d	14 24	14 35	14 44	14 54		15 05	15 14		15 24	15 35	15 44	15 54		16 05	16 14		16 24	16 35	16 44		16 54	
Erdington d	14 26	14 38	14 46	14 56		15 08	15 16		15 26	15 38	15 46	15 56		16 08	16 16		16 26	16 38	16 46		16 56	
Chester Road d	14 28	14 40	14 48	14 58		15 10	15 18		15 28	15 40	15 48	15 58		16 10	16 18		16 28	16 40	16 48		16 58	
Wylde Green d	14 30	14 42	14 50	15 00		15 12	15 20		15 30	15 42	15 50	16 00		16 12	16 20		16 30	16 42	16 50		17 00	
Sutton Coldfield d	14 34	14 45	14 54	15 04		15 15	15 24		15 34	15 45	15 54	16 04		16 15	16 24		16 34	16 45	16 54		17 04	
Four Oaks d	14a41	14 48	14 58	15a11		15 18	15 28		15a41	15 48	15 58	16a11		16 18	16 28		16a41	16 48	16 58		17a11	
Butlers Lane d		14 50	15 00			15 20	15 30			15 50	16 00			16 20	16 30			16 50	17 00			
Blake Street d		14 53	15 02			15 23	15 32			15 53	16 02			16 23	16 32			16 53	17 02			
Shenstone d		14 57				15 27				15 57				16 27				16 57				
Lichfield City d		15a02	15 11			15a32	15 41			16a02	16 11			16a32	16 41			17a02	17 11			
Lichfield Trent Valley a			15 15				15 45				16 15				16 45				17 15			

Table 69

Saturdays from 27 October

Redditch and Longbridge - Birmingham - Lichfield

Network Diagram - see first Page of Table 67

		LM	LM	LM	LM	LM	LM	LM	XC ◇1	LM	LM	LM	LM	LM	LM	LM	XC ◇1	LM	LM	LM	LM	LM
Bromsgrove	d			16 42								17 44								18 42		
Redditch	d		16 27				16 57				17 27				17 57				18 27			
Alvechurch	d		16 32				17 02				17 32				18 02				18 32			
Barnt Green	d		16 38				17 08				17 38				18 08				18 38			
Longbridge	d	16 32	16 42		16 52	17 02	17 12	17 22		17 32	17 42		17 52	18 02	18 12	18 22		18 32	18 42		18 52	19 02
Northfield	d	16 34	16 44		16 54	17 04	17 14	17 24		17 34	17 44		17 54	18 04	18 14	18 24		18 34	18 44		18 54	19 04
Kings Norton	d	16 37	16 47		16 57	17 07	17 17	17 27		17 37	17 47		17 57	18 07	18 17	18 27		18 37	18 47		18 57	19 07
Bournville	d	16 39	16 49		16 59	17 09	17 19	17 29		17 39	17 49		17 59	18 09	18 19	18 29		18 39	18 49		18 59	19 09
Selly Oak	d	16 42	16 52		17 02	17 12	17 22	17 32		17 42	17 52		18 02	18 12	18 22	18 32		18 42	18 52		19 02	19 12
University	d	16 45	16 55	16 59	17 05	17 15	17 25	17 35	17 39	17 45	17 55	17 59	18 05	18 15	18 25	18 35	18 39	18 45	18 55	18 59	19 05	19 15
Five Ways	d	16 49	16 59		17 09	17 19	17 29	17 39		17 49	17 59		18 09	18 19	18 29	18 39		18 49	18 59		19 09	19 19
Birmingham New Street 12	a	16 53	17 03	17 11	17 13	17 23	17 33	17 43	17 45	17 53	18 03	18 11	18 13	18 23	18 33	18 43	18 45	18 53	19 03	19 11	19 13	19 23
	d	16 55	17 05		17 15	17 25	17 35	17 45		17 55	18 05		18 15	18 25	18 35	18 45		18 55	19 05		19 15	
Duddeston	d	16 59				17 29				17 59				18 29				18 59				
Aston	d	17 02	17 11		17 21	17 32	17 41	17 51		18 02	18 11		18 21	18 32	18 41	18 51		19 02	19 11		19 21	
Gravelly Hill	d	17 05	17 14		17 24	17 35	17 44	17 54		18 05	18 14		18 24	18 35	18 44	18 54		19 05	19 14		19 24	
Erdington	d	17 08	17 16		17 26	17 38	17 46	17 56		18 08	18 16		18 26	18 38	18 46	18 56		19 08	19 16		19 26	
Chester Road	d	17 10	17 18		17 28	17 40	17 48	17 58		18 10	18 18		18 28	18 40	18 48	18 58		19 10	19 18		19 28	
Wylde Green	d	17 12	17 20		17 30	17 42	17 50	18 00		18 12	18 20		18 30	18 42	18 50	19 00		19 12	19 20		19 30	
Sutton Coldfield	d	17 15	17 24		17 34	17 45	17 54	18 04		18 15	18 24		18 34	18 45	18 54	19 04		19 15	19 24		19 34	
Four Oaks	d	17 18	17 28		17a41	17 48	17 58	18a11		18 18	18 28		18a41	18 48	18 58	19a11		19 18	19 28		19a41	
Butlers Lane	d	17 20	17 30			17 50	18 00			18 20	18 30			18 50	19 00			19 20	19 30			
Blake Street	d	17 23	17 32			17 53	18 02			18 23	18 32			18 53	19 02			19 23	19 32			
Shenstone	d	17 27				17 57				18 27				18 57				19 27				
Lichfield City	d	17a32	17 41			18a02	18 11			18a32	18 41			19a02	19 11			19a32	19 41			
Lichfield Trent Valley	a		17 45				18 15				18 45				19 15				19 45			

		LM	LM	XC ◇1 ✕	LM	LM	LM	LM	LM	XC ◇1	LM	LM	LM	LM	LM	LM	LM	XC ◇1	LM	XC ◇1	LM	LM	LM
Bromsgrove	d													20 59				21 44					
Redditch	d	18 57				19 27			19 57			20 27			20 57		21 27					22 27	22 57
Alvechurch	d	19 02				19 32			20 02			20 32			21 02		21 32					22 32	23 02
Barnt Green	d	19 08				19 38			20 08			20 38			21 08		21 38					22 38	23 08
Longbridge	d	19 12	19 22		19 32	19 42	19 52	20 02	20 12		20 30	20 42	20 57		21 12	21 27	21 42		21 57		22 27	22 42	23 12
Northfield	d	19 14	19 24		19 34	19 44	19 54	20 04	20 14		20 32	20 44	20 59		21 14	21 29	21 44		21 59		22 29	22 44	23 14
Kings Norton	d	19 17	19 27		19 37	19 47	19 57	20 07	20 17		20 35	20 47	21 02		21 17	21 32	21 47		22 02		22 32	22 47	23 17
Bournville	d	19 19	19 29		19 39	19 49	19 59	20 09	20 19		20 37	20 49	21 04		21 19	21 34	21 49		22 04		22 34	22 49	23 19
Selly Oak	d	19 22	19 32		19 42	19 52	20 02	20 12	20 22		20 40	20 52	21 07		21 22	21 37	21 52		22 07		22 37	22 52	23 22
University	d	19 25	19 35	19 39	19 45	19 55	20 05	20 15	20 25	20 34	20 42	20 55	21 10	21 14	21 25	21 40	21 55	22 01	22 10	22 36	22 40	22 55	23 25
Five Ways	d	19 29	19 39		19 49	19 59	20 09	20 19	20 29		20 46	20 59	21 14		21 29	21 44	21 59		22 14		22 44	22 59	23 29
Birmingham New Street 12	a	19 33	19 43	19 45	19 53	20 03	20 13	20 23	20 33	20 40	20 51	21 03	21 18	21 21	21 33	21 48	22 03	22 07	22 18	22 42	22 48	23 03	23 33
	d	19 35				20 05			20 35			21 05			21 35		22 05				22 55		
Duddeston	d	19 39				20 09			20 39			21 09			21 39		22 09				22 59		
Aston	d	19 42				20 12			20 42			21 12			21 42		22 12				23 02		
Gravelly Hill	d	19 45				20 15			20 45			21 15			21 45		22 15				23 05		
Erdington	d	19 48				20 18			20 48			21 18			21 48		22 18				23 08		
Chester Road	d	19 50				20 20			20 50			21 20			21 50		22 20				23 10		
Wylde Green	d	19 52				20 22			20 52			21 22			21 52		22 22				23 12		
Sutton Coldfield	d	19 55				20 25			20 55			21 25			21 55		22 25				23 15		
Four Oaks	d	19 58				20 28			20 58			21 28			21 58		22 28				23 18		
Butlers Lane	d	20 00				20 30			21 00			21 30			22 00		22 30				23 20		
Blake Street	d	20 03				20 33			21 03			21 33			22 03		22 33				23a24		
Shenstone	d	20 07				20 37			21 07			21 37			22 07		22 37						
Lichfield City	d	20 12				20 42			21 12			21 42			22 12		22 42						
Lichfield Trent Valley	a	20 16				20 46			21 16			21 46			22 16		22 46						

		LM
Bromsgrove	d	
Redditch	d	
Alvechurch	d	
Barnt Green	d	
Longbridge	d	23 30
Northfield	d	23 32
Kings Norton	d	23 35
Bournville	d	23 37
Selly Oak	d	23 40
University	d	23 43
Five Ways	d	23 47
Birmingham New Street 12	a	23 51
	d	
Duddeston	d	
Aston	d	
Gravelly Hill	d	
Erdington	d	
Chester Road	d	
Wylde Green	d	
Sutton Coldfield	d	
Four Oaks	d	
Butlers Lane	d	
Blake Street	d	
Shenstone	d	
Lichfield City	d	
Lichfield Trent Valley	a	

Table 69

Sundays

Redditch and Longbridge - Birmingham - Lichfield

Network Diagram - see first Page of Table 67

		LM	LM	LM	LM	LM	LM	LM	LM	XC ◇1 A ✕	LM	LM	XC ◇1 A ✕	LM	LM	XC ◇1 A ✕	LM	LM	LM	XC ◇1 A ✕	LM	LM	XC ◇1 ✕
Bromsgrove	d																		15 10				
Redditch	d			09 27	09 57	10 27	10 57	11 27	11 57		12 27	12 57		13 27	13 57		14 27	14 57			15 27	15 57	
Alvechurch	d			09 32	10 02	10 32	11 02	11 32	12 02		12 32	13 02		13 32	14 02		14 32	15 02			15 32	16 02	
Barnt Green	d			09 38	10 08	10 38	11 08	11 38	12 08		12 38	13 08		13 38	14 08		14 38	15 08			15 38	16 08	
Longbridge	d			09 43	10 13	10 43	11 13	11 43	12 13		12 43	13 13		13 43	14 13		14 43	15 13			15 43	16 13	
Northfield	d			09 45	10 15	10 45	11 15	11 45	12 15		12 45	13 15		13 45	14 15		14 45	15 15			15 45	16 15	
Kings Norton	d			09 48	10 18	10 48	11 18	11 48	12 18		12 48	13 18		13 48	14 18		14 48	15 18			15 48	16 18	
Bournville	d			09 51	10 21	10 51	11 21	11 51	12 21		12 51	13 21		13 51	14 21		14 51	15 21			15 51	16 21	
Selly Oak	d			09 53	10 23	10 53	11 23	11 53	12 23		12 53	13 23		13 53	14 23		14 53	15 23			15 53	16 23	
University	d			09 56	10 26	10 56	11 26	11 56	12 26	12 39	12 56	13 26	13 35	13 56	14 26	14 38	14 56	15 26		15 35	15 56	16 26	16 35
Five Ways	d			10 00	10 30	11 00	11 30	12 00	12 30		13 00	13 30		14 00	14 30		15 00	15 30			16 00	16 30	
Birmingham New Street 12	a			10 03	10 33	11 03	11 33	12 03	12 33	12 45	13 03	13 34	13 41	14 03	14 33	14 45	15 03	15 33	15 37	15 41	16 03	16 33	16 41
	d	09 06	09 36	10 06	10 36	11 06	11 36	12 06	12 36		13 06	13 36		14 06	14 36		15 06	15 36			16 06	16 36	
Duddeston	d	09 10	09 40	10 10	10 40	11 10	11 40	12 10	12 40		13 10	13 40		14 10	14 40		15 10	15 40			16 10	16 40	
Aston	d	09 13	09 43	10 13	10 43	11 13	11 43	12 13	12 43		13 13	13 43		14 13	14 43		15 13	15 43			16 13	16 43	
Gravelly Hill	d	09 16	09 46	10 16	10 46	11 16	11 46	12 16	12 46		13 16	13 46		14 16	14 46		15 16	15 46			16 16	16 46	
Erdington	d	09 19	09 49	10 19	10 49	11 19	11 49	12 19	12 49		13 19	13 49		14 19	14 49		15 19	15 49			16 19	16 49	
Chester Road	d	09 21	09 51	10 21	10 51	11 21	11 51	12 21	12 51		13 21	13 51		14 21	14 51		15 21	15 51			16 21	16 51	
Wylde Green	d	09 23	09 53	10 23	10 53	11 23	11 53	12 23	12 53		13 23	13 53		14 23	14 53		15 23	15 53			16 23	16 53	
Sutton Coldfield	d	09 26	09 56	10 26	10 56	11 26	11 56	12 26	12 56		13 26	13 56		14 26	14 56		15 26	15 56			16 26	16 56	
Four Oaks	d	09 29	09 59	10 29	10 59	11 29	11 59	12 29	12 59		13 29	13 59		14 29	14 59		15 29	15 59			16 29	16 59	
Butlers Lane	d	09 31	10 01	10 31	11 01	11 31	12 01	12 31	13 01		13 31	14 01		14 31	15 01		15 31	16 01			16 31	17 01	
Blake Street	d	09 34	10 04	10 34	11 04	11 34	12 04	12 34	13 04		13 34	14 04		14 34	15 04		15 34	16 04			16 34	17 04	
Shenstone	d	09 38	10 08	10 38	11 08	11 38	12 08	12 38	13 08		13 38	14 08		14 38	15 08		15 38	16 08			16 38	17 08	
Lichfield City	d	09 43	10 13	10 43	11 13	11 43	12 13	12 43	13 13		13 43	14 13		14 43	15 13		15 43	16 13			16 43	17 13	
Lichfield Trent Valley	a	09 47	10 17	10 47	11 17	11 47	12 17	12 47	13 17		13 47	14 17		14 47	15 17		15 47	16 17			16 47	17 17	

		LM	LM	LM	XC ◇1 B	LM	LM	LM	XC ◇1	LM	LM	XC ◇1	LM	LM	LM	XC ◇1	LM	LM	LM	XC ◇1	LM C	LM	XC ◇1 C
Bromsgrove	d		16 51				17 53								20 10				21 09				
Redditch	d	16 27		16 57		17 27		17 57		18 27	18 57		19 27	19 57			20 27	20 57			21 27	21 57	
Alvechurch	d	16 32		17 02		17 32		18 02		18 32	19 02		19 32	20 02			20 32	21 02			21 32	22 02	
Barnt Green	d	16 38		17 08		17 38		18 08		18 38	19 08		19 38	20 08			20 38	21 08			21 38	22 08	
Longbridge	d	16 43		17 13		17 43		18 13		18 43	19 13		19 43	20 13			20 43	21 13			21 43	22 13	
Northfield	d	16 45		17 15		17 45		18 15		18 45	19 15		19 45	20 15			20 45	21 15			21 45	22 15	
Kings Norton	d	16 48		17 18		17 48		18 18		18 48	19 18		19 48	20 18			20 48	21 18			21 48	22 18	
Bournville	d	16 51		17 21		17 51		18 21		18 51	19 21		19 51	20 21			20 51	21 21			21 51	22 21	
Selly Oak	d	16 53		17 23		17 53		18 23		18 53	19 23		19 53	20 23			20 53	21 23			21 53	22 23	
University	d	16 56		17 26	17 35	17 56		18 26	18 35	18 56	19 26	19 35	19 56	20 26		20 38	20 56	21 26		21 38	21 56	22 26	22 36
Five Ways	d	17 00		17 30		18 00		18 30		19 00	19 30		20 00	20 30			21 00	21 30			22 00	22 30	
Birmingham New Street 12	a	17 03	17 17	17 33	17 41	18 03	18 15	18 33	18 41	19 03	19 33	19 41	20 03	20 33	20 36	20 44	21 03	21 33	21 42	21 44	22 03	22 33	22 42
	d	17 06		17 36		18 06		18 36		19 06	19 36		20 06	20 36			21 06	21 36			22 06	22 36	
Duddeston	d	17 10		17 40		18 10		18 40		19 10	19 40		20 10	20 40			21 10	21 40			22 10	22 40	
Aston	d	17 13		17 43		18 13		18 43		19 13	19 43		20 13	20 43			21 13	21 43			22 13	22 43	
Gravelly Hill	d	17 16		17 46		18 16		18 46		19 16	19 46		20 16	20 46			21 16	21 46			22 16	22 46	
Erdington	d	17 19		17 49		18 19		18 49		19 19	19 49		20 19	20 49			21 19	21 49			22 19	22 49	
Chester Road	d	17 21		17 51		18 21		18 51		19 21	19 51		20 21	20 51			21 21	21 51			22 21	22 51	
Wylde Green	d	17 23		17 53		18 23		18 53		19 23	19 53		20 23	20 53			21 23	21 53			22 23	22 53	
Sutton Coldfield	d	17 26		17 56		18 26		18 56		19 26	19 56		20 26	20 56			21 26	21 56			22 26	22 56	
Four Oaks	d	17 29		17 59		18 29		18 59		19 29	19 59		20 29	20 59			21 29	21 59			22 29	22 59	
Butlers Lane	d	17 31		18 01		18 31		19 01		19 31	20 01		20 31	21 01			21 31	22 01			22 31	23 01	
Blake Street	d	17 34		18 04		18 34		19 04		19 34	20 04		20 34	21 04			21 34	22 04			22 34	23 04	
Shenstone	d	17 38		18 08		18 38		19 08		19 38	20 08		20 38	21 08			21 38	22 08			22 38	23 08	
Lichfield City	d	17 43		18 13		18 43		19 13		19 43	20 13		20 43	21 13			21 43	22 13			22 43	23 13	
Lichfield Trent Valley	a	17 47		18 17		18 47		19 17		19 47	20 17		20 47	21 18			21 47	22 17			22 47	23 17	

		LM	LM
Bromsgrove	d		
Redditch	d	22 27	22 57
Alvechurch	d	22 32	23 02
Barnt Green	d	22 38	23 08
Longbridge	d	22 43	23 13
Northfield	d	22 45	23 15
Kings Norton	d	22 48	23 18
Bournville	d	22 51	23 21
Selly Oak	d	22 53	23 23
University	d	22 56	23 26
Five Ways	d	23 00	23 30
Birmingham New Street 12	a	23 03	23 33
	d	23 06	
Duddeston	d	23 10	
Aston	d	23 13	
Gravelly Hill	d	23 16	
Erdington	d	23 19	
Chester Road	d	23 21	
Wylde Green	d	23 23	
Sutton Coldfield	d	23 26	
Four Oaks	d	23 29	
Butlers Lane	d	23 31	
Blake Street	d	23 34	
Shenstone	d	23 38	
Lichfield City	d	23 43	
Lichfield Trent Valley	a	23 47	

A until 21 October B until 24 June, from 16 September C until 24 June

Birmingham - Walsall and Rugeley

Network Diagram - see first Page of Table 67

Miles			LM MX	LM	LM	LM ◇1	LM	LM 1	LM	LM ◇1	LM	LM A	LM	LM	LM	LM	LM	LM	LM	LM	LM	LM	LM
—	Wolverhampton 7	d						06 19						07 49		08 19		08 49		09 19		09 49	
0	**Birmingham New Street 12**	d	23p18	05 33	05 56	06 21	06 39	06 46	07 07	07 21	07 39	07 59	08 07	08 17	08 39	08 47	09 07	09 17	09 39	09 47	10 07	10 17	10 39
1½	Duddeston	d	23p23		06 00	06 25		06 51		07 25		08 03		08 22		08 52		09 22		09 52		10 22	
2¾	Aston	d	23p26		06 03	06 28		06 54		07 28		08 06		08 25		08 55		09 25		09 55		10 25	
3½	Witton	d	23p28		06 05	06 30		06 56		07 30		08 08		08 27		08 57		09 27		09 57		10 27	
4¼	Perry Barr	d	23p31		06 07	06 33		06 58		07 33		08 10		08 29		08 59		09 29		09 59		10 29	
5¾	Hamstead	d	23p34	05 41	06 10	06 36		07 00		07 36		08 13		08 31		09 01		09 31		10 01		10 31	
8½	Tame Bridge Parkway	d	23p39	05 45	06 15	06 41	06 51	07 04		07 41	07 50	08 18	08 20	08 35	08 50	09 05	09 20	09 35	09 50	10 05	10 20	10 35	10 50
9½	Bescot Stadium	d	23p41	05 48	06 18	06 43		07 07		07 43		08 21		08 38		09 08		09 38		10 08		10 38	
10¾	**Walsall**	a	23p47	05 55	06 23	06 48	06 58	07 13	07 26	07 48	07 59	08 25	08 29	08 44	08 59	09 14	09 29	09 44	09 59	10 14	10 35	10 46	10 59
—		d	23p47		06 24		06 59		07 27		08 00		08 30		09 00		09 30		10 00				11 00
14	Bloxwich	d	23p54		06 31		07 06		07 34		08 07				09 07				10 07				11 07
14½	Bloxwich North	d	23p57		06 33		07 08		07 36		08 09				09 09				10 09				11 09
16¾	Landywood	d	00 01		06 37		07 12		07 41		08 13				09 13				10 13				11 13
18¾	Cannock	d	00 06		06 42		07 16		07 45		08 18		08 44		09 18		09 44		10 18				11 18
20¾	Hednesford	d	00a12		06 47		07 21		07 49		08 23		08 49		09 23		09 49		10 23				11 23
24¾	Rugeley Town	d			06 55		07 29		07 57		08 31		08 57		09 31		09 57		10 31				11 31
26¼	**Rugeley Trent Valley**	a			07 00		07 35		08 04		08 36		09 04		09 36		10 04		10 36				11 36

		LM	LM	LM	LM	LM	LM	LM	LM	LM	LM	LM	LM	LM	LM	LM	LM	LM	LM	LM	LM	LM	LM
Wolverhampton 7	d	10 19		10 49		11 19		11 49		12 19		12 49		13 19		13 49		14 19		14 49		15 19	
Birmingham New Street 12	d	10 47	11 07	11 17	11 39	11 47	12 07	12 17	12 39	12 47	13 07	13 17	13 39	13 47	14 07	14 17	14 39	14 47	15 07	15 17	15 39	15 47	16 07
Duddeston	d	10 52		11 22		11 52		12 22		12 52		13 22		13 52		14 22		14 52		15 22		15 52	
Aston	d	10 55		11 25		11 55		12 25		12 55		13 25		13 55		14 25		14 55		15 25		15 55	
Witton	d	10 57		11 27		11 57		12 27		12 57		13 27		13 57		14 27		14 57		15 27		15 57	
Perry Barr	d	10 59		11 29		11 59		12 29		12 59		13 29		13 59		14 29		14 59		15 29		15 59	
Hamstead	d	11 01		11 31		12 01		12 31		13 01		13 31		14 01		14 31		15 01		15 31		16 01	
Tame Bridge Parkway	d	11 05	11 20	11 35	11 50	12 05	12 20	12 35	12 50	13 05	13 20	13 35	13 50	14 05	14 20	14 35	14 50	15 05	15 20	15 35	15 50	16 05	16 20
Bescot Stadium	d	11 08		11 38		12 08		12 38		13 08		13 38		14 08		14 38		15 08		15 38		16 08	
Walsall	a	11 14	11 35	11 44	11 59	12 14	12 34	12 44	12 59	13 14	13 35	13 44	13 59	14 14	14 35	14 44	14 59	15 14	15 35	15 44	15 59	16 14	16 29
	d				12 00				13 00				14 00				15 00				16 00		16 31
Bloxwich	d				12 07				13 07				14 07				15 07				16 07		16 38
Bloxwich North	d				12 09				13 09				14 09				15 09				16 09		16 40
Landywood	d				12 13				13 13				14 13				15 13				16 13		16 45
Cannock	d				12 18				13 18				14 18				15 18				16 18		16 49
Hednesford	d				12 23				13 23				14 23				15 23				16 23		16 54
Rugeley Town	d				12 31				13 31				14 31				15 31				16 31		17 02
Rugeley Trent Valley	a				12 36				13 36				14 36				15 36				16 36		17 08

		LM	LM	LM	LM	LM	LM	LM	LM	LM	LM	LM	LM	LM	LM	LM	LM	LM	LM	LM	LM
Wolverhampton 7	d	15 49		16 19		16 49		17 19		17 49		18 19		19 19							
Birmingham New Street 12	d	16 17	16 39	16 47	17 07	17 17	17 42	17 47	18 12	18 17	18 39	18 47	19 17	19 47	20 17	20 47	21 17	21 47	22 17	22 47	23 18
Duddeston	d	16 22		16 52		17 22		17 52		18 22		18 52	19 22	19 52		20 52		21 52		22 52	23 23
Aston	d	16 25		16 55		17 25		17 55		18 25		18 55	19 25	19 55		20 55		21 55		22 55	23 26
Witton	d	16 27		16 57		17 27		17 57		18 27		18 57	19 27	19 57		20 57		21 57		22 57	23 28
Perry Barr	d	16 29		16 59		17 29		17 59		18 29		18 59	19 29	19 59		20 59		21 59		22 59	23 31
Hamstead	d	16 31		17 01		17 31		18 01		18 31		19 01	19 32	20 01		21 01		22 01		23 01	23 34
Tame Bridge Parkway	d	16 35	16 50	17 05	17 20	17 35	17 54	18 05	18 23	18 35	18 50	19 05	19 37	20 05	20 30	21 05	21 30	22 05	22 30	23 05	23 39
Bescot Stadium	d	16 38		17 08		17 38		18 08		18 38		19 08	19 40	20 08		21 08		22 08		23 10	23 41
Walsall	a	16 44	16 59	17 14	17 29	17 44	18 01	18 14	18 30	18 44	18 59	19 15	19 45	20 14	20 38	21 14	21 38	22 14	22 38	23 14	23 47
	d		17 00		17 30		18 02		18 31		19 00		19 46		20 39		21 39		22 39		23 47
Bloxwich	d		17 07		17 37		18 09		18 38		19 07		19 53		20 46		21 46		22 46		23 54
Bloxwich North	d		17 09		17 39		18 11		18 40		19 09		19 56		20 49		21 49		22 49		23 57
Landywood	d		17 13		17 43		18 15		18 44		19 13		20 00		20 53		21 53		22 53		00 01
Cannock	d		17 18		17 48		18 20		18 48		19 18		20 05		20 57		21 57		22 57		00 06
Hednesford	d		17 23		17 53		18 25		18 53		19 23		20 10		21 02		22 02		23 02		00a12
Rugeley Town	d		17 31		18 01		18 33		19 01		19 31		20 18		21 10		22 10		23 10		
Rugeley Trent Valley	a		17 36		18 06		18 38		19 07		19 36		20 22		21 15		22 15		23 15		

Saturdays

		LM	LM	LM	LM	LM	LM	LM	LM	LM	LM	LM	LM	LM	LM	LM	LM	LM	LM	LM	LM	LM	LM
Wolverhampton 7	d					06 49		07 19		07 49		08 19		08 49		09 19		09 49		10 19		10 49	
Birmingham New Street 12	d	23p18	06 02	06 27	07 00	07 17	07 39	07 47	08 07	08 17	08 39	08 47	09 07	09 17	09 39	09 47	10 07	10 17	10 39	10 47	11 07	11 17	11 39
Duddeston	d	23p23	06 06	06 32		07 22		07 52		08 22		08 52		09 22		09 52		10 22		10 52		11 22	
Aston	d	23p26	06 09	06 35	07 06	07 25		07 55		08 25		08 55		09 25		09 55		10 25		10 55		11 25	
Witton	d	23p28	06 11	06 37		07 27		07 57		08 27		08 57		09 27		09 57		10 27		10 57		11 27	
Perry Barr	d	23p31	06 13	06 40	07 09	07 29		07 59		08 29		08 59		09 29		09 59		10 29		10 59		11 29	
Hamstead	d	23p34	06 16	06 43	07 12	07 31		08 01		08 31		09 01		09 31		10 01		10 31		11 01		11 31	
Tame Bridge Parkway	d	23p39	06 21	06 48	07 17	07 35	07 50	08 05	08 20	08 35	08 50	09 05	09 20	09 35	09 50	10 05	10 20	10 35	10 50	11 05	11 20	11 35	11 50
Bescot Stadium	d	23p41	06 24	06 50		07 38		08 08		08 38		09 08		09 38		10 08		10 38		11 08		11 38	
Walsall	a	23p47	06 29	06 56	07 25	07 44	07 57	08 14	08 29	08 44	08 59	09 14	09 29	09 44	09 59	10 14	10 29	10 44	10 59	11 14	11 29	11 44	11 59
	d	23p47	06 30	06 57	07 26		07 57		08 30		09 00		09 30		10 00		10 30		11 00		11 30		12 00
Bloxwich	d	23p54	06 37	07 04	07 33		08 04				09 07				10 07				11 07				12 07
Bloxwich North	d	23p57	06 39	07 06	07 35		08 06				09 09				10 09				11 09				12 09
Landywood	d	00 01	06 43	07 10	07 39		08 10				09 13				10 13				11 13				12 13
Cannock	d	00 06	06 48	07 15	07 44		08 15		08 44		09 18		09 44		10 18		10 44		11 18		11 44		12 18
Hednesford	d	00a12	06a53	07 20	07 49		08 20		08 49		09 23		09 49		10 23		10 49		11 23		11 49		12 23
Rugeley Town	d			07 28	07 57		08 28		08 57		09 31		09 57		10 31		10 57		11 31		11 57		12 31
Rugeley Trent Valley	a			07 32	08 04		08 35		09 04		09 36		10 04		10 36		11 04		11 36		12 04		12 36

A until 19 October

For connections to Stafford please refer to Table 67

Birmingham - Walsall and Rugeley

Network Diagram - see first Page of Table 67

		LM	LM	LM	LM	LM	LM	LM	LM	LM	LM	LM	LM	LM	LM	LM	LM	LM	LM	LM	LM	LM	LM
Wolverhampton 7	d	11 19		11 49		12 19		12 49		13 19		13 49		14 19		14 49		15 19		15 49		16 19	
Birmingham New Street 12	d	11 47	12 07	12 17	12 39	12 47	13 07	13 17	13 39	13 47	14 07	14 17	14 39	14 47	15 07	15 17	15 39	15 47	16 07	16 17	16 39	16 47	17 07
Duddeston	d	11 52		12 22		12 52		13 22		13 52		14 22		14 52		15 22		15 52		16 22		16 52	
Aston	d	11 55		12 25		12 55		13 25		13 55		14 25		14 55		15 25		15 55		16 25		16 55	
Witton	d	11 57		12 27		12 57		13 27		13 57		14 27		14 57		15 27		15 57		16 27		16 57	
Perry Barr	d	11 59		12 29		12 59		13 29		13 59		14 29		14 59		15 29		15 59		16 29		16 59	
Hamstead	d	12 01		12 31		13 01		13 31		14 01		14 31		15 01		15 31		16 01		16 31		17 01	
Tame Bridge Parkway	d	12 05	12 20	12 35	12 50	13 05	13 20	13 35	13 50	14 05	14 20	14 35	14 50	15 05	15 20	15 35	15 50	16 05	16 20	16 35	16 50	17 05	17 20
Bescot Stadium	d	12 08		12 38		13 08		13 38		14 08		14 38		15 08		15 38		16 08		16 38		17 08	
Walsall	a	12 14	12 29	12 44	12 59	13 14	13 29	13 44	13 59	14 14	14 29	14 44	14 59	15 14	15 29	15 46	15 59	16 14	16 29	16 44	16 59	17 14	17 29
	d		12 30		13 00		13 30		14 00		14 30		15 00		15 30		16 00		16 30		17 00		17 30
Bloxwich	d				13 07				14 07				15 07				16 07				17 07		17 37
Bloxwich North	d				13 09				14 09				15 09				16 09				17 09		17 39
Landywood	d				13 13				14 13				15 13				16 13				17 13		17 43
Cannock	d		12 44		13 18		13 44		14 18		14 44		15 18		15 44		16 18		16 44		17 18		17 48
Hednesford	d		12 49		13 23		13 49		14 23		14 49		15 23		15 49		16 23		16 49		17 23		17 53
Rugeley Town	d		12 57		13 31		13 57		14 31		14 57		15 31		15 57		16 31		16 57		17 31		18 01
Rugeley Trent Valley	a		13 04		13 36		14 04		14 36		15 04		15 36		16 04		16 36		17 04		17 36		18 06

		LM	LM	LM	LM	LM	LM	LM	LM	LM	LM	LM	LM	LM	LM	LM	LM
Wolverhampton 7	d	16 49		17 19		17 49		18 19		19 19							
Birmingham New Street 12	d	17 17	17 39	17 47	18 07	18 17	18 39	18 47	19 17	19 47	20 17	20 47	21 17	21 47	22 17	22 47	23 18
Duddeston	d	17 22		17 52		18 22		18 52	19 22	19 52		20 52		21 52		22 52	23 23
Aston	d	17 25		17 55		18 25		18 55	19 25	19 55		20 55		21 55		22 55	23 26
Witton	d	17 27		17 57		18 27		18 57	19 27	19 57		20 57		21 57		22 57	23 28
Perry Barr	d	17 29		17 59		18 29		18 59	19 29	19 59		20 59		21 59		22 59	23 31
Hamstead	d	17 31		18 01		18 31		19 01	19 32	20 01		21 01		22 01		23 01	23 34
Tame Bridge Parkway	d	17 35	17 50	18 05	18 20	18 35	18 50	19 05	19 37	20 05	20 31	21 05	21 31	22 05	22 31	23 05	23 39
Bescot Stadium	d	17 38		18 08		18 38		19 08	19 40	20 08		21 08		22 08		23 08	23 41
Walsall	a	17 44	17 59	18 14	18 29	18 44	18 59	19 14	19 45	20 14	20 38	21 14	21 38	22 14	22 38	23 14	23 47
	d		18 00		18 30		19 00		19 46		20 39		21 39		22 39		23 47
Bloxwich	d		18 07		18 37		19 07		19 53		20 46		21 46		22 46		23 54
Bloxwich North	d		18 09		18 39		19 09		19 56		20 49		21 49		22 49		23 57
Landywood	d		18 13		18 43		19 13		20 00		20 53		21 53		22 53		00 01
Cannock	d		18 18		18 48		19 18		20 05		20 57		21 57		22 57		00 06
Hednesford	d		18 23		18 53		19 23		20 10		21 02		22 02		23 02		00a12
Rugeley Town	d		18 31		19 01		19 31		20 18		21 10		22 10		23 10		
Rugeley Trent Valley	a		18 36		19 06		19 36		20 22		21 15		22 15		23 15		

Sundays

		LM	LM	LM	LM	LM	LM	LM	LM	LM A	LM	LM	LM	LM	LM	LM	LM	LM	LM	LM	LM	LM	LM
Wolverhampton 7	d																						
Birmingham New Street 12	d	23p18	09 17	09 40	10 17	10 40	11 17	11 40	12 17	12 40	13 17	13 40	14 17	14 40	15 17	15 40	16 17	16 40	17 17	17 40	18 17	18 40	19 17
Duddeston	d	23p23	09 21		10 21		11 21		12 21		13 21		14 21		15 21		16 21		17 21		18 21		19 21
Aston	d	23p26	09 24		10 24		11 24		12 24		13 24		14 24		15 24		16 24		17 24		18 24		19 24
Witton	d	23p28	09 26		10 26		11 26		12 26		13 26		14 26		15 26		16 26		17 26		18 26		19 26
Perry Barr	d	23p31	09 29		10 29		11 29		12 29		13 29		14 29		15 29		16 29		17 29		18 29		19 29
Hamstead	d	23p34	09 32		10 32		11 32		12 32		13 32		14 32		15 32		16 32		17 32		18 32		19 32
Tame Bridge Parkway	d	23p39	09 37	09 52	10 37	10 52	11 37	11 52	12 37	12 52	13 37	13 52	14 37	14 52	15 37	15 52	16 37	16 52	17 37	17 52	18 37	18 52	19 37
Bescot Stadium	d	23p41	09 39		10 39		11 39		12 39		13 39		14 39		15 39		16 39		17 39		18 39		19 39
Walsall	a	23p47	09 44	10 00	10 44	11 00	11 44	12 00	12 44	13 00	13 44	14 00	14 44	15 00	15 44	16 00	16 44	17 00	17 44	18 00	18 44	19 00	19 44
	d	23p47		10 01		11 01		12 01		13 01		14 01		15 01		16 01		17 01		18 01		19 01	
Bloxwich	d	23p54		10 08		11 08		12 08		13 08		14 08		15 08		16 08		17 08		18 08		19 08	
Bloxwich North	d	23p57		10 10		11 10		12 10		13 10		14 10		15 10		16 10		17 10		18 10		19 10	
Landywood	d	00 01		10 15		11 15		12 15		13 15		14 15		15 15		16 15		17 15		18 15		19 15	
Cannock	d	00 06		10 19		11 19		12 19		13 19		14 19		15 19		16 19		17 19		18 19		19 19	
Hednesford	d	00a12		10 24		11 24		12 24		13 24		14 24		15 24		16 24		17 24		18 24		19 24	
Rugeley Town	d			10 32		11 32		12 32		13 32		14 32		15 32		16 32		17 32		18 32		19 32	
Rugeley Trent Valley	a			10 37		11 37		12 37		13 37		14 37		15 37		16 37		17 37		18 37		19 37	

		LM	LM	LM	LM	LM A	LM	LM	LM
Wolverhampton 7	d								
Birmingham New Street 12	d	19 40	20 17	20 40	21 17	21 40	22 17	22 40	23 17
Duddeston	d		20 21		21 21		22 21		23 21
Aston	d		20 24		21 24		22 24		23 24
Witton	d		20 26		21 26		22 26		23 26
Perry Barr	d		20 29		21 29		22 29		23 29
Hamstead	d		20 32		21 32		22 32		23 32
Tame Bridge Parkway	d	19 52	20 37	20 52	21 37	21 52	22 37	22 52	23 37
Bescot Stadium	d		20 39		21 39		22 39		23 39
Walsall	a	20 00	20 44	21 00	21 44	22 00	22 44	23 00	23 44
	d	20 01		21 01		22 01		23 01	
Bloxwich	d	20 08		21 08		22 08		23 08	
Bloxwich North	d	20 10		21 10		22 10		23 10	
Landywood	d	20 15		21 15		22 15		23 15	
Cannock	d	20 19		21 19		22 19		23 19	
Hednesford	d	20 24		21 24		22 24		23 24	
Rugeley Town	d	20 32		21 32		22 32		23 32	
Rugeley Trent Valley	a	20 37		21 37		22 37		23 37	

A until 24 June

For connections to Stafford please refer to Table 67

Rugeley and Walsall - Birmingham

Network Diagram - see first Page of Table 67

Miles			LM MX	LM	LM	LM	LM	LM ◇■	LM	LM A	LM B	LM	LM	LM	LM	LM	LM	LM	LM	LM	LM	LM	LM
0	**Rugeley Trent Valley**	d			05 55		06 39		07 04			07 40		08 06		08 42		09 06		09 42		10 06	
1½	Rugeley Town	d			05 59		06 43		07 08			07 44		08 10		08 46		09 10		09 46		10 10	
5½	Hednesford	d			06 07		06 51		07 16			07 52		08 18		08 54		09 18		09 54		10 18	
7½	Cannock	d			06 11		06 55		07 20			07 56		08 22		08 58		09 22		09 58		10 22	
9½	Landywood	d			06 14		06 58		07 23			07 59		08 25				09 25				10 25	
11¾	Bloxwich North	d			06 19		07 03		07 27			08 04		08 30				09 30				10 30	
12¼	Bloxwich	d			06 21		07 05		07 29			08 06		08 32				09 32				10 32	
15½	**Walsall**	a			06 28		07 12		07 37			08 13		08 39		09 12		09 39		10 12		10 39	
—		d	23p40	06 01	06 29	07 01	07 13	07 30	07 37	08 01	08 01	08 14	08 30	08 40	09 01	09 13	09 30	09 40	10 01	10 13	10 31	10 40	11 01
16¾	Bescot Stadium	d	23p44	06 04	06 34	07 04		07 34		08 04	08 04		08 34		09 04		09 34		10 04		10 34		11 04
17¾	Tame Bridge Parkway	d	23p47	06 07	06 37	07 07	07 19	07 37	07 43	08 07	08 07	08 20	08 37	08 47	09 07	09 19	09 37	09 46	10 07	10 19	10 37	10 46	11 07
20½	Hamstead	d	23p51	06 11	06 41	07 11		07 41		08 11	08 11		08 41		09 11		09 41		10 11		10 41		11 11
22	Perry Barr	d	23p55	06 14	06 44	07 14		07 44		08 14	08 14		08 44		09 14		09 44		10 14		10 44		11 14
22¾	Witton	d	23p57	06 16	06 46	07 16		07 47		08 16	08 16		08 46		09 16		09 46		10 16		10 46		11 16
23½	Aston	d	00 01	06 19	06 49	07 19		07 49		08 19	08 19		08 49		09 19		09 49		10 19		10 48		11 19
24¾	Duddeston	d	00 04	06 21	06 52	07 21		07 52		08 21	08 21		08 52		09 21		09 51		10 21		10 51		11 21
26¼	**Birmingham New Street** ■	a	00 08	06 28	06 57	07 28	07 36	07 57	08 00	08 28	08 28	08 37	08 58	09 03	09 28	09 36	09 58	10 03	10 28	10 36	10 59	11 03	11 28
—	Wolverhampton ■	a		07 03				08 19			09 03				10 03				11 03		11 33		12 03

		LM	LM	LM	LM	LM	LM	LM	LM	LM	LM	LM	LM	LM	LM	LM	LM	LM	LM	LM	LM	LM	LM
Rugeley Trent Valley	d			11 06				12 06				13 06				14 06				15 06			
Rugeley Town	d			11 10				12 10				13 10				14 10				15 10			
Hednesford	d			11 18				12 18				13 18				14 18				15 18			
Cannock	d			11 22				12 22				13 22				14 22				15 22			
Landywood	d			11 25				12 25				13 25				14 25				15 25			
Bloxwich North	d			11 30				12 30				13 30				14 30				15 30			
Bloxwich	d			11 32				12 32				13 32				14 32				15 32			
Walsall	a			11 39				12 39				13 39				14 39				15 39			
	d	11 10	11 31	11 40	12 01	12 10	12 31	12 40	13 01	13 10	13 31	13 40	14 01	14 10	14 31	14 40	15 01	15 10	15 31	15 40	16 01	16 10	16 31
Bescot Stadium	d		11 34		12 04		12 34		13 04		13 34		14 04		14 34		15 04		15 34		16 04		16 34
Tame Bridge Parkway	d	11 19	11 37	11 46	12 07	12 19	12 37	12 46	13 07	13 19	13 37	13 46	14 07	14 19	14 37	14 46	15 07	15 19	15 37	15 46	16 07	16 19	16 37
Hamstead	d		11 41		12 11		12 41		13 11		13 41		14 11		14 41		15 11		15 41		16 11		16 41
Perry Barr	d		11 44		12 14		12 44		13 14		13 44		14 14		14 44		15 14		15 44		16 14		16 44
Witton	d		11 46		12 16		12 46		13 16		13 46		14 16		14 46		15 16		15 46		16 16		16 46
Aston	d		11 49		12 19		12 50		13 19		13 49		14 19		14 49		15 19		15 49		16 19		16 49
Duddeston	d		11 51		12 21		12 52		13 21		13 51		14 21		14 51		15 21		15 51		16 21		16 51
Birmingham New Street ■	a	11 36	11 58	12 03	12 28	12 36	12 58	13 03	13 28	13 36	13 59	14 03	14 28	14 36	14 58	15 03	15 28	15 36	15 58	16 03	16 30	16 36	16 58
Wolverhampton ■	a		12 33		13 03		13 33		14 03		14 33		15 03		15 33		16 03		16 33		17 04		17 33

		LM	LM	LM	LM	LM	LM	LM	LM	LM	LM	LM	LM	LM	LM	LM	LM	LM	LM	LM	LM	LM
Rugeley Trent Valley	d	16 06		16 42		17 13		17 42		18 12		18 46		19 10	19 42		20 35		21 40		22 33	
Rugeley Town	d	16 10		16 46		17 17		17 46		18 16		18 50		19 14	19 46		20 39		21 44		22 37	
Hednesford	d	16 18		16 54		17 25		17 54		18 24		18 58		19 22	19 54		20 47		21 52		22 45	
Cannock	d	16 22		16 58		17 29		17 58		18 28		19 02		19 26	19 58		20 51		21 56		22 49	
Landywood	d	16 25				17 32				18 31				19 29	20 01		20 54		21 59		22 53	
Bloxwich North	d	16 30				17 37				18 36				19 34	20 06		20 59		22 04		22 58	
Bloxwich	d	16 32				17 39				18 38				19 36	20 08		21 01		22 06		23 00	
Walsall	a	16 39		17 12		17 46		18 12		18 45		19 16		19 43	20 15		21 08		22 16		23 07	
	d	16 40	17 01	17 13	17 31	17 47	18 01	18 13	18 31	18 46	19 01	19 18	19 36	19 44	20 16	20 40	21 10	21 40	22 17	22 40	23 10	23 40
Bescot Stadium	d		17 04		17 34		18 04		18 34		19 04	19 23		19 48		20 44		21 44		22 44		23 44
Tame Bridge Parkway	d	16 46	17 07	17 19	17 37	17 53	18 07	18 19	18 37	18 52	19 07	19 26		19 51	20 22	20 47	21 16	21 47	22 23	22 47	23 16	23 47
Hamstead	d		17 11		17 41		18 11		18 41		19 11	19 30		19 55		20 51		21 51		22 51		23 51
Perry Barr	d		17 14		17 44		18 14		18 44		19 14	19 33		19 59		20 55		21 55		22 55		23 55
Witton	d		17 16		17 46		18 16		18 46		19 16	19 36		20 01		20 57		21 57		22 57		23 57
Aston	d		17 19		17 49		18 19		18 49		19 19	19 39		20 04		21 00		22 00		23 00		00 01
Duddeston	d		17 21		17 51		18 21		18 51		19 21	19 42		20 07		21 03		22 03		23 03		00 04
Birmingham New Street ■	a	17 03	17 29	17 36	17 58	18 10	18 28	18 36	18 58	19 09	19 28	19 46		20 11	20 39	21 09	21 35	22 09	22 39	23 09	23 33	00 08
Wolverhampton ■	a		18 03		18 33		19 03		19 33		20 03		19 50									

Saturdays

		LM	LM	LM	LM	LM	LM	LM	LM	LM	LM	LM	LM	LM	LM	LM	LM	LM	LM	LM	LM	LM	LM
Rugeley Trent Valley	d				06 26				07 39		08 06		08 42		09 06		09 42		10 06		10 42		11 06
Rugeley Town	d				06 30				07 43		08 10		08 46		09 10		09 46		10 10		10 46		11 10
Hednesford	d				06 38	06 58			07 51		08 18		08 54		09 18		09 54		10 18		10 54		11 18
Cannock	d				06 42	07 02			07 55		08 22		08 58		09 22		09 58		10 22		10 58		11 22
Landywood	d				06 45	07 05			07 58		08 25				09 25				10 25				11 25
Bloxwich North	d				06 50	07 10			08 03		08 30				09 30				10 30				11 30
Bloxwich	d				06 52	07 12			08 05		08 32				09 32				10 32				11 32
Walsall	a				06 59	07 19			08 12		08 39		09 12		09 39		10 12		10 39		11 12		11 39
	d	23p40	06 01	06 31	07 00	07 20	07 31	08 01	08 13	08 31	08 40	09 01	09 13	09 31	09 40	10 01	10 13	10 31	10 40	11 01	11 13	11 31	11 40
Bescot Stadium	d	23p44	06 04	06 34	07 04		07 34	08 04		08 34		09 04		09 34		10 04		10 34		11 04		11 34	
Tame Bridge Parkway	d	23p47	06 07	06 37	07 07	07 26	07 37	08 07	08 19	08 37	08 46	09 07	09 19	09 37	09 46	10 07	10 19	10 37	10 46	11 07	11 19	11 37	11 46
Hamstead	d	23p51	06 11	06 41	07 12		07 41	08 11		08 41		09 11		09 41		10 11		10 41		11 11		11 41	
Perry Barr	d	23p55	06 14	06 44	07 15		07 44	08 14		08 44		09 14		09 44		10 14		10 44		11 14		11 44	
Witton	d	23p57	06 16	06 46	07 17		07 46	08 16		08 46		09 16		09 46		10 16		10 46		11 16		11 46	
Aston	d	00 01	06 19	06 49	07 20		07 49	08 19		08 49		09 19		09 49		10 19		10 49		11 19		11 49	
Duddeston	d	00 04	06 21	06 51	07 23		07 51	08 21		08 51		09 21		09 51		10 21		10 51		11 21		11 51	
Birmingham New Street ■	a	00 08	06 28	06 58	07 28	07 44	07 58	08 28	08 36	08 58	09 03	09 29	09 36	09 58	10 03	10 29	10 36	10 58	11 03	11 28	11 36	11 58	12 03
Wolverhampton ■	a		07 03	07 33			08 33	09 03		09 33		10 03		10 33		11 03		11 33		12 03		12 33	

A until 19 October

B from 22 October

For connections from Stafford please refer to Table 67

Rugeley and Walsall - Birmingham

Network Diagram - see first Page of Table 67

		LM	LM	LM	LM	LM	LM	LM	LM	LM	LM	LM	LM	LM	LM	LM	LM	LM	LM	LM	LM	LM	LM
Rugeley Trent Valley	d		11 42		12 06		12 42		13 06		13 42		14 06		14 42		15 06		15 42		16 06		16 42
Rugeley Town	d		11 46		12 10		12 46		13 10		13 46		14 10		14 46		15 10		15 46		16 10		16 46
Hednesford	d		11 54		12 18		12 54		13 18		13 54		14 18		14 54		15 18		15 54		16 18		16 54
Cannock	d		11 58		12 22		12 58		13 22		13 58		14 22		14 58		15 22		15 58		16 22		16 58
Landywood	d				12 25				13 25				14 25				15 25				16 25		
Bloxwich North	d				12 30				13 30				14 30				15 30				16 30		
Bloxwich	d				12 32				13 32				14 32				15 32				16 32		
Walsall	a		12 12		12 39		13 12		13 39		14 12		14 39		15 12		15 39		16 12		16 39		17 12
	d	12 01	12 13	12 31	12 40	13 01	13 13	13 31	13 40	14 01	14 13	14 31	14 40	15 01	15 13	15 31	15 40	16 01	16 13	16 31	16 40	17 01	17 13
Bescot Stadium	d	12 04		12 34		13 04		13 34		14 04		14 34		15 04		15 34		16 04		16 34		17 04	
Tame Bridge Parkway	d	12 07	12 19	12 37	12 46	13 07	13 19	13 37	13 46	14 07	14 19	14 37	14 46	15 07	15 19	15 37	15 46	16 07	16 19	16 37	16 46	17 07	17 19
Hamstead	d	12 11		12 41		13 11		13 41		14 11		14 41		15 11		15 41		16 11		16 41		17 11	
Perry Barr	d	12 14		12 44		13 14		13 44		14 14		14 44		15 14		15 44		16 14		16 44		17 14	
Witton	d	12 16		12 46		13 16		13 46		14 16		14 46		15 16		15 46		16 16		16 46		17 16	
Aston	d	12 19		12 49		13 19		13 49		14 19		14 49		15 19		15 49		16 19		16 49		17 19	
Duddeston	d	12 21		12 51		13 21		13 51		14 21		14 51		15 21		15 51		16 21		16 51		17 21	
Birmingham New Street ■	a	12 28	12 36	12 58	13 03	13 28	13 36	13 58	14 03	14 28	14 36	14 58	15 03	15 28	15 36	15 58	16 03	16 28	16 36	16 58	17 03	17 28	17 36
Wolverhampton ■	a	13 03		13 33		14 03		14 33		15 03		15 33		16 03		16 33		17 04		17 33		18 03	

		LM	LM	LM	LM	LM	LM	LM	LM	LM	LM	LM	LM	LM	LM	LM	LM	LM
Rugeley Trent Valley	d		17 06		17 42		18 12		18 45	19 10	19 42		20 39		21 35		22 35	
Rugeley Town	d		17 10		17 46		18 16		18 49	19 14	19 46		20 43		21 39		22 39	
Hednesford	d		17 18		17 54		18 24		18 57	19 21	19 54		20 51		21 47		22 47	
Cannock	d		17 22		17 58		18 28		19 01	19 25	19 58		20 55		21 51		22 51	
Landywood	d		17 25				18 31			19 29	20 01		20 58		21 54		22 54	
Bloxwich North	d		17 30				18 36			19 33	20 06		21 03		21 59		22 59	
Bloxwich	d		17 32				18 38			19 35	20 08		21 05		22 01		23 01	
Walsall	a		17 39		18 12		18 45		19 15	19 43	20 15		21 12		22 08		23 08	
	d	17 31	17 40	18 01	18 13	18 31	18 46	19 01	19 18	19 43	20 16	20 40	21 13	21 40	22 10	22 40	23 10	23 40
Bescot Stadium	d	17 34		18 04		18 34		19 04	19 23	19 48		20 44		21 44		22 44		23 44
Tame Bridge Parkway	d	17 37	17 46	18 07	18 19	18 37	18 52	19 07	19 26	19 51	20 22	20 47	21 19	21 47	22 16	22 47	23 16	23 47
Hamstead	d	17 41		18 11		18 41		19 11	19 30	19 55		20 51		21 51		22 51		23 51
Perry Barr	d	17 44		18 14		18 44		19 14	19 33	19 58		20 55		21 55		22 55		23 55
Witton	d	17 46		18 16		18 46		19 16	19 36	20 01		20 57		21 57		22 57		23 57
Aston	d	17 49		18 19		18 49		19 19	19 39	20 03		21 00		22 00		23 00		00 01
Duddeston	d	17 51		18 21		18 51		19 21	19 42	20 06		21 03		22 03		23 03		00 04
Birmingham New Street ■	a	17 58	18 03	18 28	18 36	18 58	19 09	19 28	19 46	20 12	20 39	21 09	21 36	22 09	22 33	23 09	23 34	00 09
Wolverhampton ■	a	18 33		19 03		19 33		20 03										

Sundays

		LM	LM	LM	LM	LM	LM	LM	LM	LM	LM	LM	LM	LM	LM	LM	LM	LM	LM	LM	LM A	LM B	LM
Rugeley Trent Valley	d			09 48		10 48		11 48		12 48		13 48		14 48		15 48		16 48		17 48			18 48
Rugeley Town	d			09 52		10 52		11 52		12 52		13 52		14 52		15 52		16 52		17 52			18 52
Hednesford	d			10 00		11 00		12 00		13 00		14 00		15 00		16 00		17 00		18 00			19 00
Cannock	d			10 04		11 04		12 04		13 04		14 04		15 04		16 04		17 04		18 04			19 04
Landywood	d			10 07		11 07		12 07		13 07		14 07		15 07		16 07		17 07		18 07			19 07
Bloxwich North	d			10 12		11 12		12 12		13 12		14 12		15 12		16 12		17 12		18 12			19 12
Bloxwich	d			10 14		11 14		12 14		13 14		14 14		15 14		16 14		17 14		18 14			19 14
Walsall	a			10 21		11 21		12 21		13 21		14 21		15 21		16 21		17 21		18 21			19 21
	d	23p40	10 00	10 23	11 00	11 23	12 00	12 23	13 00	13 23	14 00	14 23	15 00	15 23	16 00	16 23	17 00	17 23	18 00	18 23	19 00	19 00	19 23
Bescot Stadium	d	23p44	10 04		11 04		12 04		13 04		14 04		15 04		16 04		17 04		18 04		19 04	19 04	
Tame Bridge Parkway	d	23p47	10 07	10 29	11 07	11 29	12 07	12 29	13 07	13 29	14 07	14 29	15 07	15 29	16 07	16 29	17 07	17 29	18 07	18 29	19 07	19 07	19 29
Hamstead	d	23p51	10 11		11 11		12 11		13 11		14 11		15 11		16 11		17 11		18 11		19 11	19 11	
Perry Barr	d	23p55	10 14		11 14		12 14		13 14		14 14		15 14		16 14		17 14		18 14		19 14	19 14	
Witton	d	23p57	10 17		11 17		12 17		13 17		14 17		15 17		16 17		17 17		18 17		19 17	19 17	
Aston	d	00 01	10 20		11 20		12 20		13 20		14 20		15 20		16 20		17 20		18 20		19 20	19 20	
Duddeston	d	00 04	10 23		11 23		12 23		13 23		14 23		15 23		16 23		17 23		18 23		19 23	19 23	
Birmingham New Street ■	a	00 09	10 27	10 46	11 27	11 46	12 27	12 46	13 27	13 46	14 27	14 46	15 30	15 46	16 30	16 46	17 30	17 46	18 28	18 46	19 27	19 30	19 47
Wolverhampton ■	a																						

		LM	LM	LM C	LM	LM	LM	LM	LM
Rugeley Trent Valley	d		19 48		20 48		21 48		22 48
Rugeley Town	d		19 52		20 52		21 52		22 52
Hednesford	d		20 00		21 00		22 00		23 00
Cannock	d		20 04		21 04		22 04		23 04
Landywood	d		20 07		21 07		22 07		23 07
Bloxwich North	d		20 12		21 12		22 12		23 12
Bloxwich	d		20 14		21 14		22 14		23 14
Walsall	a		20 21		21 21		22 21		23 21
	d	20 00	20 23	21 00	21 23	22 00	22 23	23 00	23 23
Bescot Stadium	d	20 04		21 04		22 04		23 04	
Tame Bridge Parkway	d	20 07	20 29	21 07	21 29	22 07	22 29	23 07	23 29
Hamstead	d	20 11		21 11		22 11		23 11	
Perry Barr	d	20 14		21 14		22 14		23 14	
Witton	d	20 17		21 17		22 17		23 17	
Aston	d	20 20		21 20		22 20		23 20	
Duddeston	d	20 23		21 23		22 23		23 23	
Birmingham New Street ■	a	20 29	20 46	21 27	21 46	22 27	22 48	23 27	23 46
Wolverhampton ■	a								

A until 24 June

B from 1 July

C until 24 June, from 16 September

For connections from Stafford please refer to Table 67

Network Diagram for Tables 71, 72

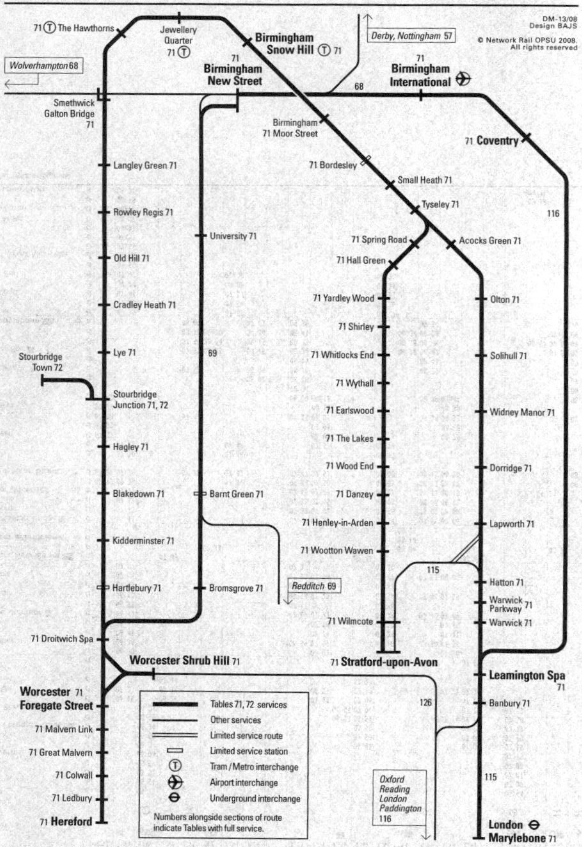

Hereford, Worcester and Stourbridge - Birmingham - Leamington Spa, Marylebone and Stratford-upon-Avon

Network Diagram - see first Page of Table 71

Miles	Miles	Miles	Station		CH MX	CH	CH	LM	XC	CH	CH	LM	GW	LM	CH	XC	LM	LM	CH	CH	CH	XC	LM
							◇		◇1		◇		◇1			◇1			◇	◇	◇	◇1	
0	—	—	**Hereford** [7]	d																			
13¾	—	—	Ledbury	a																			
—	—	—		d																			
18	—	—	Colwall	d																			
20¾	—	—	**Great Malvern**	a																			
—	—	—		d									05 18				05 52						
22	—	—	Malvern Link	d									05 21				05 55						
28¾	0	—	**Worcester Foregate Street** [7]	a									05 31				06 02						
—	—	—		d									05 32				06 04						
29½	—	—	**Worcester Shrub Hill** [7]	a									05 36										
—	—	—		d								05 30											
34¼	5½	—	Droitwich Spa	d								05 38					06 13						
40½	—	—	Bromsgrove	d													06 22						
44	—	—	Barnt Green	d																			
52	—	—	University	d													06 39						
—	11	—	Hartlebury	d																			
—	14¼	—	**Kidderminster**	d								05 48									06 10		
—	17¾	—	Blakedown	d																			
—	19½	—	Hagley	d																			
—	21½	—	**Stourbridge Junction** [2]	d								05 57									06 18		06 24
—	22¾	—	Lye	d								06 01											06 28
—	24	—	Cradley Heath	d								06 04									06 24		06 31
—	25½	—	Old Hill	d								06 08											06 35
—	26¾	—	Rowley Regis	d								06 12									06 30		06 39
—	28½	0	Langley Green	d								06 15											06 42
54½	—	6¾	**Birmingham New Street** [10]	a													06 45						
—	—	—		d					06 04							06 33						07 04	
—	—	—	**Birmingham International** ✈	d					06 14													07 14	
—	—	—	**Coventry**	d					06 25													07 25	
—	29½	—	Smethwick Galton Bridge [7]	d								06 18									06 35		06 46
—	30¼	—	The Hawthorns	d								06 21									06 38		06 48
—	32¾	—	Jewellery Quarter	d								06 25											06 52
—	33½	—	**Birmingham Snow Hill**	a								06 28									06 45		06 55
—	—	—		d	23p30			05 55				06 29		06 35				06 40			06 46		07 02
—	34	—	**Birmingham Moor Street**	d	23p33		05 46	05 58			06 19	06 32		06 38				06 43		06 55	06 59		07 05
—	34¾	—	Bordesley	d																			
—	35¾	9¼	Small Heath	d				06 02						06 42				06 47					07 09
—	36¾	10¼	Tyseley	d	23p38			06 04				06 36		06 45				06 49					07 11
—	—	11¼	Acocks Green	d	23p41			06 07						06 48									07 14
—	—	12¾	Olton	d	23p44			06 10						06 50									07 17
—	—	14	Solihull	d	23p48		05 54	06 13			06 29			06 54						07 03	07 08		07 20
—	—	15½	Widney Manor	d	23p51			06 17						06 58									07 24
—	—	17½	Dorridge	d	23p55		05 59	06 21			06 35			07a03							07 13		07 28
—	—	20	Lapworth	d	23p59			06 25															07 32
—	—	24¼	Hatton	d	00 05					06 31											07 20		07 38
—	—	27	Warwick Parkway	d	00 10	05 40	06 09				06 45								07 08	07 16	07 25		07 42
—	—	28¼	Warwick	d	00 13		06 12			06 38									07 11		07 29		07 45
—	—	30¼	**Leamington Spa** [8]	a	00 17	05 45	06 17		06 36	06 45	06 50					06 58			07 17		07 33	07 37	07 51
—	—	—		d	00 18	05 45	06 17		06 38		06 52				06 52	07 00			07 23		07 33	07 38	
—	—	—	Banbury	d	00a39	06 03	06 36		06a56		07 11					07a21			07 40		07 51	07a54	
—	—	—	**London Marylebone** [10] ⊖	a		07 10	07 38				08 06								08 48	08 25	09 08		
—	37¾	—	Spring Road	d								06 39						06 52					
—	38¼	—	Hall Green	d								06 42						06 55					
—	39½	—	Yardley Wood	d								06 45						06 58					
—	40¾	—	Shirley	d								06 48						07 01					
—	41¾	—	Whitlocks End	d								06 51						07 04					
—	42¾	—	Wythall	d								06 53						07 06					
—	43¾	—	Earlswood (West Midlands)	d														07 09					
—	44½	—	The Lakes	d														07x11					
—	45¾	—	Wood End	d														07x13					
—	47½	—	Danzey	d														07x17					
—	50¼	—	Henley-in-Arden	d								07 04						07 22					
—	52¼	—	Wootton Wawen	d														07x24					
—	56	—	Wilmcote	d				06 42							07 21			07 30					
—	58¾	—	**Stratford-upon-Avon**	a				06 48				07 16			07 27			07 36					

Hereford, Worcester and Stourbridge - Birmingham - Leamington Spa, Marylebone and Stratford-upon-Avon

Network Diagram - see first Page of Table 71

		LM	LM	GW ◇■ Ø	LM	CH ◇ ⌶	XC ◇■	LM	CH ◇		CH ◇	LM	GW ■	LM	LM	XC ◇■ ⌶	CH ◇ ⌶	LM	LM		GW ◇■ A Ø	CH ◇	XC ◇■ ⌶	CH ◇ ⌶	LM
Hereford ■	d			05 35																	06 44				
Ledbury	a			05 51																	07 00				
	d			05 52																	07 01				
Colwall	d			05 59																	07 08				
Great Malvern	a			06 04																	07 13				
	d			06 04										06 47					07 04		07 15				
Malvern Link	d			06 08										06 50					07 07		07 19				
Worcester Foregate Street ■	a			06 19										06 58					07 15		07 29				
	d			06 19									06 53	06 59				07 14	07 17		07 30				
Worcester Shrub Hill ■	a			06 21									06 55	07 01					07 19		07 33				
	d		06 15		06 28							06 47		07 06					07 25						
Droitwich Spa	d		06 23		06 35							06 55		07 14				07 23	07 34						
Bromsgrove	d				06 44									07 24											
Barnt Green	d																								
University	d				06 59									07 39					07 59						
Hartlebury	d		06 30									07 02						07 30							
Kidderminster	d		06 36								06 59	07 09			07 18		07 30	07 36							
Blakedown	d		06 41									07 14			07 24			07 41							
Hagley	d		06 44									07 18			07 28			07 45							
Stourbridge Junction ■	d		06 49								07 07	07 22			07 32		07 40	07 49							07 55
Lye	d		06 53								07 11				07 36										07 59
Cradley Heath	d		06 56								07 14	07 28			07 39		07 46	07 55							08 02
Old Hill	d		07 00								07 18				07 43										08 06
Rowley Regis	d		07 04								07 22	07 34			07 47		07 53	08 00							08 10
Langley Green	d		07 07								07 25				07 50										08 13
Birmingham New Street ■	a				07 07									07 46					08 09						
	d						07 33									08 04							08 33		
Birmingham International ✈	d															08 14									
Coventry	d															08 25									
Smethwick Galton Bridge ■	d		07 11								07 29	07 39			07 54		07 59	08 06							08 16
The Hawthorns	d		07 13								07 32	07 42			07 56		08 02	08 08							08 19
Jewellery Quarter	d		07 17								07 36	07 46			08 00		08 06	08 12							08 23
Birmingham Snow Hill	a		07 22								07 40	07 49			08 03		08 11	08 15							08 26
	d	07 19	07 23					07 39			07 44	07 50			08 05		08 12	08 17						08 22	08 27
Birmingham Moor Street	d	07 22	07 26			07 33		07 42			07 47	07 53			08 08		08 15	08 20						08 25	08 30
Bordesley	d																								
Small Heath	d		07 30					07 46							08 12										
Tyseley	d		07 32					07 48				07 57			08 14										
Acocks Green	d	07 27										08 00						08 25							
Olton	d	07 30										08 03						08 28							
Solihull	d	07 34				07 41					07 55	08 07					08 24	08 32						08 37	
Widney Manor	d	07 37										08 10						08 35							
Dorridge	d	07a42									08 00	08a16					08 29	08a41						08 50	
Lapworth	d										08 04													08 54	
Hatton	d								08 02		08 10													09 00	
Warwick Parkway	d					07 53			08 09		08 16						08 39								
Warwick	d										08 19						08 43							09 05	
Leamington Spa ■	a					07 58	08 03		08 15		08 24					08 36	08 47						08 59	09 09	
	d					07 58	08 04		08 15		08 25					08 38	08 48					08 51	09 00	09 10	
Banbury	d					08 16	08a20		08 34		08 43					08a54	09 08						09a18	09 29	
London Marylebone ■ ⊖	a					09 09			09 42		09 58						09 59							10 28	
Spring Road	d		07 35					07 51							08 17										08 36
Hall Green	d		07 38					07 54							08 20										08 39
Yardley Wood	d		07 41					07 57							08 23										08 42
Shirley	d		07 44					08 00							08 26										08 45
Whitlocks End	d		07 47					08a02							08a28										08 48
Wythall	d		07 50																						08 50
Earlswood (West Midlands)	d		07 52																						08 53
The Lakes	d		07x55																						08x55
Wood End	d		07x57																						08x58
Danzey	d		08x01																						09x01
Henley-in-Arden	d		08 07																						09 07
Wootton Wawen	d		08x10																						09x10
Wilmcote	d		08 15																			09 18			09 15
Stratford-upon-Avon	a		08 21																			09 31			09 21

A The Cathedrals Express

Hereford, Worcester and Stourbridge - Birmingham - Leamington Spa, Marylebone and Stratford-upon-Avon

Network Diagram - see first Page of Table 71

		LM	LM	LM	CH ◇ ⌶		LM	LM	XC ◇■ ⌶	LM	GW ◇■ ⌶	CH ◇ ⌶	LM	LM	LM		LM	XC ◇■ ⌶	LM	GW	CH ◇ ⌶	LM	LM	CH ◇	CH ◇
Hereford ■	d		07 10							07 34															
Ledbury	a		07 25							07 49															
	d		07 26							07 50															
Colwall	d		07 32							07 56															
Great Malvern	a		07 37							08 00															
	d		07 39							08 05									08 38	08 50					
Malvern Link	d		07 42							08 08									08 41	08 53					
Worcester Foregate Street ■	a		07 50							08 16									08 49	09 03					
	d		07 51					08 04		08 24	08 26						08 38		08 52	09 03			09 06		
Worcester Shrub Hill ■	a		07 53								08 28						08 40			09 06					
	d	07 35	07 57														08 44								
Droitwich Spa	d	07 43	08 05					08 13		08 33							08 52		09 01				09 15		
Bromsgrove	d									08 42									09 11						
Barnt Green	d																								
University	d		08 29							08 59									09 30						
Hartlebury	d																								
Kidderminster	d	07 54			08 09			08 23							08 57		09 06						09 26		
Blakedown	d	07 59			08 14			08 28							09 02		09 11						09 31		
Hagley	d	08 03			08 18			08 32							09 05		09 15						09 35		
Stourbridge Junction ■	d	08 07		08 14	08 22			08 36					08 45	08 54	09 09		09 19					09 25	09 39		
Lye	d			08 18				08 40						08 58								09 29			
Cradley Heath	d	08 13		08 21	08 28			08 43					08 51	09 01	09 15		09 24					09 32	09 44		
Old Hill	d			08 25				08 47						09 05								09 36			
Rowley Regis	d	08 19		08 29	08 34			08 51					08 57	09 09	09 21		09 30					09 39	09 50		
Langley Green	d			08 32				08 54						09 12								09 42			
Birmingham New Street ■	a		08 37							09 07									09 43						
	d								09 04									09 33							
Birmingham International ✈	d								09 14																
Coventry	d								09 25																
Smethwick Galton Bridge ■	d	08 25		08 36	08 40			08 57					09 02	09 15	09 26		09 36					09 46	09 56		
The Hawthorns	d	08 28		08 38	08 42			08 59					09 05	09 17	09 29		09 38					09 48	09 58		
Jewellery Quarter	d	08 32		08 42	08 47			09 03					09 09	09 21	09 33		09 42					09 52	10 02		
Birmingham Snow Hill	a	08 35		08 45	08 51			09 06					09 15	09 25	09 36		09 45					09 55	10 05		
	d	08 37		08 47	08 52		08 57	09 07				09 12	09 17	09 27	09 37		09 47					09 57	10 07		
Birmingham Moor Street	d	08 40		08 50	08 55		09 00	09 10				09 15	09 20	09 30	09 40		09 50				09 55	10 00	10 10		
Bordesley	d																								
Small Heath	d	08 44						09 14							09 44								10 14		
Tyseley	d	08 47						09 16							09 46								10 16		
Acocks Green	d	08 50					09 05						09 25		09 49							10 05			
Olton	d	08 53					09 08						09 28		09 52							10 08			
Solihull	d	08 57			09 03		09 12					09 23	09 32		09 56						10 03	10 12			
Widney Manor	d	09 00					09 15						09 35		09 59							10 15			
Dorridge	d	09a05					09a22					09 28	09a41		10a04							10a22			
Lapworth	d											09 32													
Hatton	d																							10 15	
Warwick Parkway	d				09 15							09 40									10 15				
Warwick	d											09 44												10 23	
Leamington Spa ■	a								09 36			09 49						09 58			10 20			10 27	
	d								09 38			09 49						10 00			10 21			10 27	10 33
Banbury	d								09a54			10 07						10a17			10 38			10 48	
London Marylebone ■ ⊖	a				10 29							11 15									11 31			12 00	
Spring Road	d			08 56				09 19						09 36			09 56						10 19		
Hall Green	d			08 59				09 22						09 39			09 59						10 22		
Yardley Wood	d			09 02				09 25						09 42			10 02						10 25		
Shirley	d			09 05				09 28						09 45			10 05						10 28		
Whitlocks End	d			09a07				09a30						09 48			10a07						10a30		
Wythall	d													09 50											
Earlswood (West Midlands)	d													09 53											
The Lakes	d													09x55											
Wood End	d													09x58											
Danzey	d													10x01											
Henley-in-Arden	d													10 07											
Wootton Wawen	d													10x10											
Wilmcote	d													10 15											
Stratford-upon-Avon	a													10 21											11 09

Hereford, Worcester and Stourbridge - Birmingham - Leamington Spa, Marylebone and Stratford-upon-Avon

Network Diagram - see first Page of Table 71

		XC	LM	CH	LM	LM	LM	LM	GW	XC	CH	LM	LM	XC	CH	LM	LM	LM	CH	XC	CH	LM
		◇1 ✕		◇ ✕					◇1 ✕	◇1 ✕	◇ ✕			◇1 ✕	◇ ✕				◇	◇1 ✕		
Hereford 7	d		08 49														09 40					
Ledbury	a		09 05														09 56					
	d		09 08														09 58					
Colwall	d		09 14														10 04					
Great Malvern	a		09 18														10 08					
	d		09 19						09 54								10 10					
Malvern Link	d		09 22						09 56								10 13					
Worcester Foregate Street 7	a		09 30						10 05								10 22					
	d		09 31						10 05							10 16	10 24					
Worcester Shrub Hill 7	a		09 33						10 08													
	d		09 37					09 47														
Droitwich Spa	d		09 45					09 55								10 25	10 33					
Bromsgrove	d		09 54														10 42					
Barnt Green	d																					
University	d		10 09														10 59					
Hartlebury	d																					
Kidderminster	d				09 36		09 58	10 06					10 26			10 36						10 56
Blakedown	d				09 41			10 11								10 41						
Hagley	d				09 45			10 15								10 45						
Stourbridge Junction 2	d				09 49	09 55	10 09	10 19				10 25	10 39			10 49		10 55				11 09
Lye	d					09 59						10 29						10 59				
Cradley Heath	d				09 54	10 02	10 14	10 24				10 32	10 44			10 54		11 02				11 14
Old Hill	d					10 06						10 36						11 06				
Rowley Regis	d				10 00	10 10	10 20	10 30				10 40	10 50			11 00		11 10				11 20
Langley Green	d					10 13						10 43						11 13				
Birmingham New Street 12	a		10 24														11 13					
	d	10 04								10 33				11 04						11 33		
Birmingham International ✈	d	10 14												11 14								
Coventry	d	10 25												11 25								
Smethwick Galton Bridge 7	d				10 06	10 16	10 26	10 36				10 46	10 56			11 06		11 16				11 26
The Hawthorns	d				10 08	10 18	10 28	10 38				10 48	10 58			11 08		11 18				11 28
Jewellery Quarter	d				10 12	10 22	10 32	10 42				10 52	11 02			11 12		11 22				11 32
Birmingham Snow Hill	a				10 15	10 25	10 35	10 45				10 55	11 05			11 15		11 25				11 35
	d			10 12	10 17	10 27	10 37	10 47				10 57	11 07		11 12	11 17		11 27				11 37
Birmingham Moor Street	d			10 15	10 20	10 30	10 40	10 50			10 55	11 00	11 10		11 15	11 20		11 30			11 33	11 40
Bordesley	d																					
Small Heath	d						10 44						11 14									11 44
Tyseley	d						10 46						11 16									11 46
Acocks Green	d				10 25		10 49					11 05				11 25						11 49
Olton	d				10 28		10 52					11 08				11 28						11 52
Solihull	d			10 23	10 32		10 56				11 04	11 12			11 23	11 32					11 42	11 56
Widney Manor	d				10 35		10 59					11 15				11 35						11 59
Dorridge	d			10 28	10a41		11a04					11a21			11 28	11a41					11 50	12a04
Lapworth	d																				11 54	
Hatton	d																		11 38		12 00	
Warwick Parkway	d			10 39							11 15				11 39						12 05	
Warwick	d			10 42											11 42				11 46		12 08	
Leamington Spa 8	a	10 36		10 46						10 58	11 21			11 36	11 46				11 50	11 59	12 16	
	d	10 38		10 47						11 00	11 21			11 38	11 47				11 51	12 00		
Banbury	d	10a54		11 05						11a17	11 39			11a54	12 04				12 11	12a17		
London Marylebone 10 ⊖	a			12 09							12 31				13 07				13 30			
Spring Road	d					10 36		10 56					11 19					11 36				
Hall Green	d					10 39		10 59					11 22					11 39				
Yardley Wood	d					10 42		11 02					11 25					11 42				
Shirley	d					10 45		11 05					11 28					11 45				
Whitlocks End	d					10 48		11a07					11a30					11 48				
Wythall	d					10 50												11 50				
Earlswood (West Midlands)	d					10 53												11 53				
The Lakes	d					10x55												11x55				
Wood End	d					10x58												11x58				
Danzey	d					11x01												12x01				
Henley-in-Arden	d					11 07												12 07				
Wootton Wawen	d					11x10												12x10				
Wilmcote	d					11 15												12 15				
Stratford-upon-Avon	a					11 21												12 21				

Hereford, Worcester and Stourbridge - Birmingham - Leamington Spa, Marylebone and Stratford-upon-Avon

Network Diagram - see first Page of Table 71

		LM	GW	CH	CH	LM	LM	XC	CH	LM	LM	LM	LM	LM	GW	XC	CH	LM	LM	XC	CH	CH	LM
			■	◇	◇ ✕			◇1 ✕	◇						◇1 ✕	◇1 ✕	◇			◇1 ✕		◇	
Hereford 7	d										10 40												
Ledbury	a										10 56												
	d										10 58												
Colwall	d										11 04												
Great Malvern	a										11 08												
	d		10 50								11 10			11 34									
Malvern Link	d		10 53								11 13			11 36									
Worcester Foregate Street 7	a		11 03								11 22			11 45									
	d		11 03							11 16	11 24			11 46	12 06								12 16
Worcester Shrub Hill 7	a		11 06												12 08								
	d	10 47																					
Droitwich Spa	d	10 55								11 25	11 33			11 55									12 25
Bromsgrove	d										11 42												
Barnt Green	d																						
University	d										11 59												
Hartlebury	d																						
Kidderminster	d	11 06					11 26			11 36			11 56	12 06					12 26				12 36
Blakedown	d	11 11								11 41				12 11									12 41
Hagley	d	11 14								11 44				12 14									12 44
Stourbridge Junction 2	d	11 19				11 25	11 39			11 49		11 55	12 09	12 19				12 25	12 39				12 49
Lye	d					11 29						11 59						12 29					
Cradley Heath	d	11 24				11 32	11 44			11 54		12 02	12 14	12 24				12 32	12 44				12 54
Old Hill	d					11 36						12 06						12 36					
Rowley Regis	d	11 30				11 40	11 50			12 00		12 10	12 20	12 30				12 40	12 50				13 00
Langley Green	d					11 43						12 13						12 43					
Birmingham New Street 12	a										12 11												
	d							12 04								12 33				13 04			
Birmingham International ✈	d							12 14												13 14			
Coventry	d							12 25												13 25			
Smethwick Galton Bridge 7	d	11 36				11 46	11 56			12 06		12 16	12 26	12 36				12 46	12 56				13 06
The Hawthorns	d	11 38				11 48	11 58			12 08		12 18	12 28	12 38				12 48	12 58				13 08
Jewellery Quarter	d	11 42				11 52	12 02			12 12		12 22	12 32	12 42				12 52	13 02				13 12
Birmingham Snow Hill	a	11 45				11 55	12 05			12 15		12 25	12 35	12 45				12 55	13 05				13 15
	d	11 47				11 57	12 07		12 12	12 17		12 27	12 37	12 47				12 57	13 07			13 12	13 17
Birmingham Moor Street	d	11 50			11 55	12 00	12 10		12 15	12 20		12 30	12 40	12 50			12 55	13 00	13 10			13 15	13 20
Bordesley	d																						
Small Heath	d						12 14						12 44						13 14				
Tyseley	d						12 16						12 46						13 16				
Acocks Green	d					12 05				12 25			12 49					13 05					13 25
Olton	d					12 08				12 28			12 52					13 08					13 28
Solihull	d				12 03	12 12			12 23	12 32			12 56				13 03	13 12				13 23	13 32
Widney Manor	d					12 15				12 35			12 59					13 15					13 35
Dorridge	d					12a22			12 28	12a41			13a04					13a21				13 28	13a41
Lapworth	d																						
Hatton	d																				13 27		
Warwick Parkway	d				12 15				12 39								13 15					13 39	
Warwick	d								12 42												13 35	13 42	
Leamington Spa 8	a				12 20			12 36	12 46							12 58	13 20			13 36	13 41	13 46	
	d			12 19	12 20			12 38	12 47							13 00	13 20			13 38		13 47	
Banbury	d				12 38			12a54	13 04							13a20	13 39			13a54		14 04	
London Marylebone 10 ⊖	a				13 31				14 09								14 31					15 07	
Spring Road	d	11 56					12 19					12 36		12 56					13 19				
Hall Green	d	11 59					12 22					12 39		12 59					13 22				
Yardley Wood	d	12 02					12 25					12 42		13 02					13 25				
Shirley	d	12 05					12 28					12 45		13 05					13 28				
Whitlocks End	d	12a07					12a30					12 48		13a07					13a30				
Wythall	d											12 50											
Earlswood (West Midlands)	d											12 53											
The Lakes	d											12x55											
Wood End	d											12x58											
Danzey	d											13x01											
Henley-in-Arden	d											13 07											
Wootton Wawen	d											13x10											
Wilmcote	d											13 15											
Stratford-upon-Avon	a			12 54								13 21											

Hereford, Worcester and Stourbridge - Birmingham - Leamington Spa, Marylebone and Stratford-upon-Avon

Network Diagram - see first Page of Table 71

		LM	LM		XC	CH	LM	LM	GW	CH	LM	LM	CH		XC	CH	LM	LM	LM	LM	LM	GW	XC		CH
					◇■ H				◇	◇			◇		◇■ H	◇						◇■	◇■ H		◇
Hereford ■	d	11 40																12 40				13 14			
Ledbury	a	11 56																12 56				13 30			
	d	11 58																12 58				13 31			
Colwall	d	12 04																13 04				13 39			
Great Malvern	a	12 09																13 08				13 44			
	d	12 10							12 50									13 10				13 44			
Malvern Link	d	12 13							12 53									13 13				13 49			
Worcester Foregate Street ■	a	12 22							13 03									13 21				13 58			
	d	12 24						12 46	13 03									13 24			13 46	13 59			
Worcester Shrub Hill ■	a								13 06													14 03			
	d																13 17								
Droitwich Spa	d	12 33						12 55									13 25	13 33			13 55				
Bromsgrove	d	12 42																13 42							
Barnt Green	d																								
University	d	12 59																13 59							
Hartlebury	d																								
Kidderminster	d						12 56	13 06									13 36			13 56	14 06				
Blakedown	d							13 11									13 41				14 11				
Hagley	d							13 14									13 44				14 14				
Stourbridge Junction ■	d		12 55				13 09	13 19			13 25	13 39					13 49		13 55	14 09	14 19				
Lye	d		12 59								13 29								13 59						
Cradley Heath	d		13 02				13 14	13 24			13 32	13 44					13 54		14 02	14 14	14 24				
Old Hill	d		13 06								13 36								14 06						
Rowley Regis	d		13 10				13 20	13 30			13 40	13 50					14 00		14 10	14 20	14 30				
Langley Green	d		13 13								13 43								14 13						
Birmingham New Street ■	a	13 13																14 12							
	d				13 33										14 04								14 33		
Birmingham International ✈	d														14 14										
Coventry	d														14 25										
Smethwick Galton Bridge ■	d		13 16				13 26	13 36			13 46	13 56					14 06		14 16	14 26	14 36				
The Hawthorns	d		13 18				13 28	13 38			13 48	13 58					14 08		14 18	14 28	14 38				
Jewellery Quarter	d		13 22				13 32	13 42			13 52	14 02					14 12		14 22	14 32	14 42				
Birmingham Snow Hill	a		13 25				13 35	13 45			13 55	14 05					14 15		14 25	14 35	14 45				
	d		13 27				13 37	13 47			13 57	14 07				14 12	14 17		14 27	14 37	14 47				
Birmingham Moor Street	d		13 30			13 33	13 40	13 50		13 55	14 00	14 10				14 15	14 20		14 30	14 40	14 50				14 55
Bordesley	d																								
Small Heath	d						13 44					14 14								14 44					
Tyseley	d						13 46					14 16								14 46					
Acocks Green	d						13 49				14 05						14 25			14 49					
Olton	d						13 52				14 08						14 28			14 52					
Solihull	d					13 42	13 56			14 03	14 12					14 23	14 32			14 56					15 03
Widney Manor	d						13 59				14 15						14 35			14 59					
Dorridge	d					13 50	14a04				14a22					14 28	14a41			15a04					
Lapworth	d					13 54																			
Hatton	d					14 00																			
Warwick Parkway	d					14 05				14 15						14 39									15 15
Warwick	d					14 08										14 42									
Leamington Spa ■	a				13 59	14 16				14 21					14 36	14 46							14 58		15 20
	d				14 00					14 21			14 32		14 38	14 47							15 00		15 20
Banbury	d				14a17					14 39					14a54	15 04							15a17		15 39
London Marylebone ■ ⊖	a									15 31						16 11									16 32
Spring Road	d		13 36					13 56				14 19							14 36		14 56				
Hall Green	d		13 39					13 59				14 22							14 39		14 59				
Yardley Wood	d		13 42					14 02				14 25							14 42		15 02				
Shirley	d		13 45					14 05				14 28							14 45		15 05				
Whitlocks End	d		13 48					14a07				14a30							14 48		15a07				
Wythall	d		13 50																14 50						
Earlswood (West Midlands)	d		13 53																14 53						
The Lakes	d		13x55																14x55						
Wood End	d		13x58																14x58						
Danzey	d		14x01																15x01						
Henley-in-Arden	d		14 07																15 07						
Wootton Wawen	d		14x10																15x10						
Wilmcote	d		14 15										15 00						15 15						
Stratford-upon-Avon	a		14 21										15 07						15 21						

Hereford, Worcester and Stourbridge - Birmingham - Leamington Spa, Marylebone and Stratford-upon-Avon

Network Diagram - see first Page of Table 71

		LM	LM	XC	CH	LM	LM	GW	LM		CH	XC	CH	LM	LM	GW	CH	LM	LM		CH	XC	CH	LM	LM
				◇■ H	◇			◇■ H			◇	◇■ H				◇	◇ H				◇	◇■ H	◇		
Hereford ■	d						13 43																		14 40
Ledbury	a						14 00																		14 56
	d						14 00																		14 58
Colwall	d						14 06																		15 04
Great Malvern	a						14 11																		15 08
	d					14 00	14 11	14 26								14 50									15 10
Malvern Link	d					14 02	14 14	14 28								14 53									15 13
Worcester Foregate Street ■	a					14 10	14 23	14 38								15 03									15 22
	d					14 16	14 24	14 38								15 03								15 16	15 24
Worcester Shrub Hill ■	a							14 41								15 06									
	d														14 47										
Droitwich Spa	d					14 25	14 33								14 55									15 25	15 33
Bromsgrove	d						14 42																		15 42
Barnt Green	d																								
University	d						14 59																		15 59
Hartlebury	d																								
Kidderminster	d		14 26			14 36								14 56	15 06				15 26					15 36	
Blakedown	d					14 41									15 11				15 31					15 41	
Hagley	d					14 44									15 14				15 34					15 44	
Stourbridge Junction ■	d	14 25	14 39			14 49			14 55					15 09	15 19			15 25	15 39					15 49	
Lye	d	14 29							14 59									15 29							
Cradley Heath	d	14 32	14 44			14 54			15 02					15 14	15 24			15 32	15 44					15 54	
Old Hill	d	14 36							15 06									15 36							
Rowley Regis	d	14 40	14 50			15 00			15 10					15 20	15 30			15 40	15 50					16 00	
Langley Green	d	14 43							15 13									15 43							
Birmingham New Street ■	a						15 13																		16 13
	d			15 04								15 33										16 04			
Birmingham International ✈	d			15 14																		16 14			
Coventry	d			15 25																		16 25			
Smethwick Galton Bridge ■	d	14 46	14 56			15 06			15 16					15 26	15 36			15 46	15 56					16 06	
The Hawthorns	d	14 48	14 58			15 08			15 18					15 28	15 38			15 48	15 58					16 08	
Jewellery Quarter	d	14 52	15 02			15 12			15 22					15 32	15 42			15 52	16 02					16 12	
Birmingham Snow Hill	a	14 55	15 05			15 15			15 25					15 35	15 45			15 55	16 05					16 15	
	d	14 57	15 07		15 12	15 17			15 26					15 37	15 47			15 57	16 07				16 12	16 17	
Birmingham Moor Street	d	15 00	15 10		15 15	15 20			15 29				15 33	15 40	15 50		15 55	16 00	16 10				16 15	16 20	
Bordesley	d																								
Small Heath	d		15 14											15 44					16 14						
Tyseley	d		15 16											15 46					16 16						
Acocks Green	d	15 05				15 25								15 49				16 05						16 25	
Olton	d	15 08				15 28								15 52				16 08						16 28	
Solihull	d	15 12			15 23	15 32							15 42	15 56			16 04	16 12					16 23	16 32	
Widney Manor	d	15 15				15 35								15 59				16 15						16 35	
Dorridge	d	15a21			15 28	15a41							15 50	16a04				16a22					16 28	16a41	
Lapworth	d												15 54												
Hatton	d										15 42		16 00												
Warwick Parkway	d				15 39								16 05				16 17						16 39		
Warwick	d				15 42						15 49		16 08										16 42		
Leamington Spa ■	a			15 36	15 46						15 55	15 58	16 18				16 23					16 36	16 46		
	d			15 38	15 47							16 00					16 24				16 35	16 38	16 47		
Banbury	d			15a54	16 04							16a17					16 42					16a54	17 06		
London Marylebone ■ ⊖	a				17 11												17 46						18 19		
Spring Road	d		15 19						15 35						15 56				16 19						
Hall Green	d		15 22						15 38						15 59				16 22						
Yardley Wood	d		15 25						15 41						16 02				16 25						
Shirley	d		15 28						15 44						16 05				16 28						
Whitlocks End	d		15a30						15 47						16a07				16a30						
Wythall	d								15 49																
Earlswood (West Midlands)	d								15 52																
The Lakes	d								15x54																
Wood End	d								15x56																
Danzey	d								15x59																
Henley-in-Arden	d								16 04																
Wootton Wawen	d								16x07																
Wilmcote	d								16 12												17 03				
Stratford-upon-Avon	a								16 21												17 14				

Hereford, Worcester and Stourbridge - Birmingham - Leamington Spa, Marylebone and Stratford-upon-Avon

Network Diagram - see first Page of Table 71

		GW 1	LM	LM	LM		GW ◇1	XC ◇1	CH ◇	LM	LM	XC ◇1	CH ◇	CH	LM		LM	LM	LM	XC ◇1	CH ◇	LM	LM	LM	GW
Hereford	d						15 14											15 40							
Ledbury	a						15 30											15 56							
	d						15 31											15 58							
Colwall	d						15 38											16 04							
Great Malvern	a						15 43											16 09							
	d	15 22			15 30		15 44											16 10							16 48
Malvern Link	d				15 32		15 48											16 13							16 51
Worcester Foregate Street	a	15 30			15 40		15 58											16 21							17 01
	d	15 34			15 41		15 59								16 07			16 24					16 34	16 47	17 02
Worcester Shrub Hill	a	15 36			15 43		16 02																16 36		17 04
	d				15 47												16 17						16 40		
Droitwich Spa	d				15 55										16 16		16 25	16 33					16 48	16 56	
Bromsgrove	d																	16 42							
Barnt Green	d																	16 49							
University	d																	16 59							
Hartlebury	d														16 23										
Kidderminster	d			15 56	16 06						16 23				16 30		16 37					16 53	16 59	17 06	
Blakedown	d				16 11						16 28				16 35		16 43						17 04	17 11	
Hagley	d				16 14						16 31				16 39		16 47						17 08	17 15	
Stourbridge Junction	d		15 55	16 09	16 19					16 25	16 35				16 44		16 51		16 55			17 06	17 13	17 19	
Lye	d		15 59							16 29									16 59						
Cradley Heath	d		16 02	16 14	16 24					16 32	16 41				16 50		16 57		17 02			17 12	17 19	17 24	
Old Hill	d		16 06							16 36									17 06						
Rowley Regis	d		16 10	16 20	16 30					16 40	16 47				16 55		17 03		17 10			17 17	17 24	17 30	
Langley Green	d		16 13							16 43									17 13						
Birmingham New Street	a																	17 13							
	d							16 33				17 04								17 33					
Birmingham International	d											17 14													
Coventry	d											17 25													
Smethwick Galton Bridge	d		16 16	16 26	16 36					16 46	16 52				17 01		17 08		17 16			17 23	17 30	17 36	
The Hawthorns	d		16 18	16 28	16 38					16 48	16 55				17 03		17 11		17 19			17 25	17 32	17 38	
Jewellery Quarter	d		16 22	16 32	16 42					16 52	16 59				17 07		17 15		17 22			17 29	17 36	17 42	
Birmingham Snow Hill	a		16 25	16 35	16 45					16 55	17 02				17 10		17 18		17 25			17 32	17 39	17 45	
	d		16 27	16 37	16 47				16 52	16 57	17 03			17 10	17 14		17 22		17 27			17 35	17 42	17 47	
Birmingham Moor Street	d		16 30	16 40	16 50				16 55	17 00	17 06		17 10	17 13	17 17		17 25		17 30			17 38	17 45	17 50	
Bordesley	d																								
Small Heath	d			16 44	16 54										17 21							17 42	17 49	17 54	
Tyseley	d		16 34	16 46	16 56					17 04					17 23				17 34			17 45	17 51	17 56	
Acocks Green	d			16 49						17 07							17 30					17 48	17 54		
Olton	d			16 52						17 10							17 33					17 50	17 57		
Solihull	d			16 56					17 03	17 14			17 19	17 23			17 37					17 54	18 01		
Widney Manor	d			16 59						17 17				17 26			17 40					17 58	18 04		
Dorridge	d			17a04						17a22			17 25	17 30			17a46					18 02	18a09		
Lapworth	d													17 35								18 06			
Hatton	d													17 41							18 01	18 12			
Warwick Parkway	d								17 15				17 35	17 46								18 16			
Warwick	d								17 18				17 38	17 49							18 08	18 19			
Leamington Spa	a							16 58	17 22			17 36	17 42	17 59						17 59	18 12	18 24			
	d							17 00	17 23			17 38	17 43							18 00	18 12				
Banbury	d							17a17	17 42			17a54	18 02							18a18	18 31				
London Marylebone	a								18 46				19 09								19 39				
Spring Road	d		16 37		16 59						17 12				17 26				17 37					17 59	
Hall Green	d		16 40		17 02						17 15				17 29				17 40					18 02	
Yardley Wood	d		16 43		17 05						17 18				17 32				17 43					18 05	
Shirley	d		16 46		17 08						17 21				17 35				17 46					18 08	
Whitlocks End	d		16 49		17a10						17 24				17a37				17 49					18 11	
Wythall	d		16 51								17 26								17 51					18 13	
Earlswood (West Midlands)	d		16 54																17 54					18 16	
The Lakes	d		16x56																17x56					18x18	
Wood End	d		16x59																17x59					18x21	
Danzey	d		17x02																18x02					18x24	
Henley-in-Arden	d		17 07								17 37								18 08					18 30	
Wootton Wawen	d		17x10																18x11					18x33	
Wilmcote	d		17 16																18 16					18 38	
Stratford-upon-Avon	a		17 22								17 51								18 23					18 45	

Hereford, Worcester and Stourbridge - Birmingham - Leamington Spa, Marylebone and Stratford-upon-Avon

Network Diagram - see first Page of Table 71

			CH ◇	XC ◇1	CH ◇	LM	LM	CH ◇	LM	LM	GW ◇1		LM	LM	XC ◇1	CH ◇	LM	LM	XC ◇1	LM	CH ◇		CH	LM	LM
Hereford	d									16 40										17 40					
Ledbury	a									16 56										17 56					
	d									16 58										18 01					
Colwall	d									17 04										18 07					
Great Malvern	a									17 08										18 11					
	d									17 10			17 41							18 12					
Malvern Link	d									17 13			17 44							18 15					
Worcester Foregate Street	a									17 21			17 52							18 23					
	d								17 16	17 24	17 28		17 53					17 56		18 24					
Worcester Shrub Hill	a										17 30		17 55												
	d																								
Droitwich Spa	d								17 25	17 33								18 05		18 33					
Bromsgrove	d									17 42										18 43					
Barnt Green	d																			18 49					
University	d									17 59										18 59					
Hartlebury	d								17 32																
Kidderminster	d						17 27		17 38								18 00	18 16						18 38	
Blakedown	d						17 32		17 43								18 05							18 43	
Hagley	d						17 35		17 46								18 09							18 46	
Stourbridge Junction	d					17 25	17 39		17 50					17 55			18 13	18 25						18 50	
Lye	d					17 29								17 59				18 29						18 54	
Cradley Heath	d					17 32	17 45		17 56					18 02			18 19	18 32						18 57	
Old Hill	d					17 36								18 06				18 36						19 01	
Rowley Regis	d					17 40	17 51		18 02					18 10			18 25	18 40						19 05	
Langley Green	d					17 43								18 13				18 43						19 08	
Birmingham New Street	a									18 11										19 12					
	d			18 04											18 33				19 04						
Birmingham International	d			18 14															19 14						
Coventry	d			18 25															19 25						
Smethwick Galton Bridge	d					17 46	17 56		18 08					18 16			18 30	18 46						19 11	
The Hawthorns	d					17 48	17 58		18 10					18 19			18 33	18 48						19 14	
Jewellery Quarter	d					17 52	18 02		18 14					18 23			18 37	18 52						19 18	
Birmingham Snow Hill	a					17 55	18 05		18 17					18 26			18 41	18 55						19 21	
	d		17 52			17 57	18 07	18 12	18 22					18 27		18 40	18 45	18 57						19 22	19 27
Birmingham Moor Street	d		17 55			18 00	18 10	18 15	18 25					18 30		18 43	18 48	19 00					19 17	19 25	19 30
Bordesley	d																								
Small Heath	d					18 04	18 14							18 34			18 52	19 04							19 34
Tyseley	d					18 06	18 16							18 36			18 54	19 06							19 36
Acocks Green	d					18 09			18 30								18 57							19 30	
Olton	d					18 12			18 33								19 00							19 33	
Solihull	d		18 04			18 16		18 24	18 37							18 52	19 04						19 26	19 37	
Widney Manor	d					18 19			18 40								19 07							19 40	
Dorridge	d		18 11			18 23		18 29	18a45							18 57	19 11						19 31	19a47	
Lapworth	d					18 27		18 33									19 15						19 35		
Hatton	d					18 33		18 39									19 21				19 37		19 41		
Warwick Parkway	d		18 21			18 38		18 44								19 06							19 46		
Warwick	d					18 41		18 47									19 27				19 44		19 49		
Leamington Spa	a		18 27	18 36		18 47		18 52							18 58	19 11	19 32		19 37		19 48		19 57		
	d		18 28	18 38	18 36			18 53							19 00	19 12			19 38		19 49				
Banbury	d		18 46	18a54				19 13							19a17	19 34			19a54		20 08				
London Marylebone	a		19 56					20 28								20 44					21 22				
Spring Road	d						18 19							18 39				19 09							19 39
Hall Green	d						18 22							18 42				19 12							19 42
Yardley Wood	d						18 25							18 45				19 15							19 45
Shirley	d						18 28							18 48				19 18							19 48
Whitlocks End	d						18a30							18 51				19a20							19 51
Wythall	d													18 53											19 53
Earlswood (West Midlands)	d													18 56											19 56
The Lakes	d													18x58											19x58
Wood End	d													19x00											20x00
Danzey	d													19x03											20x03
Henley-in-Arden	d													19 08											20 08
Wootton Wawen	d													19x10											20x10
Wilmcote	d				19 01									19 16											20 16
Stratford-upon-Avon	a				19 12									19 22											20 23

Hereford, Worcester and Stourbridge - Birmingham - Leamington Spa, Marylebone and Stratford-upon-Avon

Network Diagram - see first Page of Table 71

		LM	XC	CH	LM	GW	GW	CH	LM	XC	LM	XC	CH	LM	GW	LM	XC	LM	CH	LM	GW	GW	LM
			◇■	◇		◇■				◇■		◇■	◇		◇■ A		◇■		◇		◇■		
Hereford ■	d										18 48							19 50					20 54
Ledbury	a										19 03							20 06					21 10
	d										19 04							20 10					21 14
Colwall	d										19 10							20 16					21 20
Great Malvern	a										19 14							20 20					21 24
	d						18 50				19 15				19 44			20 21				21 15	21 25
Malvern Link	d						18 53				19 18				19 46			20 24				21 18	21 28
Worcester Foregate Street ■	a						19 03				19 26				19 54			20 32				21 27	21 36
	d				18 46	18 49	19 03				19 28			19 46	19 54			20 37			20 59	21 28	21 37
Worcester Shrub Hill ■	a					18 52	19 06								19 57						21 02	21 31	21 39
	d	18 37																		20 52			
Droitwich Spa	d	18 45			18 55						19 37			19 55				20 46		21 00			
Bromsgrove	d										19 46							20 55					
Barnt Green	d																						
University	d										20 09							21 14					
Hartlebury	d				19 02																		
Kidderminster	d	18 55			19 10									20 10						21 10			
Blakedown	d	19 00			19 15									20 15						21 15			
Hagley	d	19 04			19 19									20 19						21 19			
Stourbridge Junction ■	d	19 09			19 25				19 55					20 25		20 55				21 25			
Lye	d				19 29				19 59					20 29		20 59				21 29			
Cradley Heath	d	19 14			19 32				20 02					20 32		21 02				21 32			
Old Hill	d				19 36				20 06					20 36		21 06				21 36			
Rowley Regis	d	19 20			19 40				20 10					20 40		21 10				21 40			
Langley Green	d				19 43				20 13					20 43		21 13				21 43			
Birmingham New Street ■	a										20 20							21 20					
	d		19 33							20 04		20 33					21 04						
Birmingham International ✈	d									20 14							21 14						
Coventry	d									20 25							21 25						
Smethwick Galton Bridge ■	d	19 26			19 46				20 16					20 46		21 16				21 46			
The Hawthorns	d	19 28			19 48				20 18					20 48		21 18				21 48			
Jewellery Quarter	d	19 32			19 52				20 22					20 52		21 22				21 52			
Birmingham Snow Hill	a	19 35			19 55				20 25					20 55		21 25				21 55			
	d	19 37		19 48	19 57				20 27				20 37	20 57		21 27			21 42	21 57			
Birmingham Moor Street	d	19a39		19 51	20 00				20 30				20 40	21 00		21 30			21 45	22 00			
Bordesley	d																						
Small Heath	d				20 04				20 34					21 04		21 34				22 04			
Tyseley	d				20 06				20 36					21 06		21 36				22 06			
Acocks Green	d				20 09									21 09						22 09			
Olton	d				20 12									21 12						22 12			
Solihull	d			19 59	20 16								20 48	21 16					21 53	22 16			
Widney Manor	d				20 19									21 19						22 19			
Dorridge	d			20 04	20a24								20 53	21a24					21 58	22a24			
Lapworth	d												20 57										
Hatton	d												21 03										
Warwick Parkway	d			20 14									21 08						22 08				
Warwick	d			20 17									21 11						22 11				
Leamington Spa ■	a		20 04	20 21						20 36		20 58	21 16				21 36		22 16				
	d		20 05	20 22				20 22		20 38		21 00	21 16				21 38		22 17				
Banbury	d		20a22	20 42						20a54		21a17	21 34				21a54		22 34				
London Marylebone ■ ⊖	a			21 53									22 53						23 50				
Spring Road	d								20 39							21 39							
Hall Green	d								20 42							21 42							
Yardley Wood	d								20 45							21 45							
Shirley	d								20 48							21 48							
Whitlocks End	d								20 51							21a50							
Wythall	d								20 53														
Earlswood (West Midlands)	d								20 56														
The Lakes	d								20x58														
Wood End	d								21x00														
Danzey	d								21x03														
Henley-in-Arden	d								21 08														
Wootton Wawen	d								21x10														
Wilmcote	d							20 53	21 16														
Stratford-upon-Avon	a							21 04	21 23														

A until 14 September

Hereford, Worcester and Stourbridge - Birmingham - Leamington Spa, Marylebone and Stratford-upon-Avon

Network Diagram - see first Page of Table 71

		CH	XC	CH	XC	XC	CH	LM	CH	LM	LM	LM	GW	LM	CH
			◇■ A		B	◇■ B							◇■		
Hereford ■	d										21 29		21 51	23 00	
Ledbury	a										21 44		22 07	23 15	
	d										21 45		22 09	23 16	
Colwall	d										21 51		22 17	23 22	
Great Malvern	a										21 55		22 22	23 26	
	d										21 56		22 22	23 27	
Malvern Link	d										21 59			23 30	
Worcester Foregate Street ■	a										22 07		22 33	23 38	
	d										22 10	22 17	22 34	23 39	
Worcester Shrub Hill ■	a											22 19	22 38	23 44	
	d									21 52		22 27			
Droitwich Spa	d									22 00	22 19	22 35			
Bromsgrove	d										22 28				
Barnt Green	d														
University	d										22 44				
Hartlebury	d														
Kidderminster	d									22 10		22 45			
Blakedown	d									22 15					
Hagley	d									22 19					
Stourbridge Junction ■	d							21 55		22 25		22 55			
Lye	d							21 59		22 29		22 59			
Cradley Heath	d							22 02		22 32		23 02			
Old Hill	d							22 06		22 36		23 06			
Rowley Regis	d							22 10		22 40		23 10			
Langley Green	d							22 13		22 43		23 13			
Birmingham New Street ■	a										22 50				
	d		22 04			22 04									
Birmingham International ✈	d		22 14												
Coventry	d		22 25		22 25										
Smethwick Galton Bridge ■	d							22 16		22 46		23 16			
The Hawthorns	d							22 18		22 48		23 18			
Jewellery Quarter	d							22 22		22 52		23 22			
Birmingham Snow Hill	a							22 25		22 55		23 24			
	d						22 15	22 27		22 57		23 25			23 30
Birmingham Moor Street	d						22 18	22 30		23 00		23 28			23 33
Bordesley	d														
Small Heath	d							22 34		23 04		23 32			
Tyseley	d						22 23	22 36		23 06		23 34			23 38
Acocks Green	d						22 26			23 09					23 41
Olton	d						22 29			23 12					23 44
Solihull	d						22 33			23 16					23 48
Widney Manor	d						22 36			23 19					23 51
Dorridge	d						22 40			23 23					23 55
Lapworth	d						22 44			23 27					23 59
Hatton	d	22 17					22 49			23 33					00 05
Warwick Parkway	d						22 54			23 38					00 10
Warwick	d	22 24					22 58		23 34	23 41					00 13
Leamington Spa ■	a	22 30	22 37		22 45	22 51	23 02		23 38	23 46					00 17
	d		22 38	22 40		22 53	23 03		23 38						00 18
Banbury	d		22a54			23a15	23a24		23a57						00a39
London Marylebone ■ ⊖	a														
Spring Road	d							22 39				23 37			
Hall Green	d							22 42				23 40			
Yardley Wood	d							22 45				23 43			
Shirley	d							22 48				23 46			
Whitlocks End	d							22a50				23a48			
Wythall	d														
Earlswood (West Midlands)	d														
The Lakes	d														
Wood End	d														
Danzey	d														
Henley-in-Arden	d														
Wootton Wawen	d														
Wilmcote	d														
Stratford-upon-Avon	a			23 12											

A until 22 June, from 17 September B from 25 June until 14 September

Hereford, Worcester and Stourbridge - Birmingham - Leamington Spa, Marylebone and Stratford-upon-Avon

Network Diagram - see first Page of Table 71

		CH	XC	CH	XC	CH	LM	LM	GW	XC	CH	LM
			◇■ ✠	◇	◇■	◇			◇■ ⊡	◇■ ✠	◇	
Hereford ■	d											
Ledbury	a											
	d											
Colwall	d											
Great Malvern	a											
	d								05 56			
Malvern Link	d								05 59			
Worcester Foregate Street ■	a								06 08			
	d								06 09			
Worcester Shrub Hill ■	a								06 11			
	d						05 44	06 07				
Droitwich Spa	d						05 52	06 15				
Bromsgrove	d											
Barnt Green	d											
University	d											
Hartlebury	d											
Kidderminster	d						06 02				06 37	
Blakedown	d						06 07					
Hagley	d						06 11					
Stourbridge Junction ■	d						06 15				06 45	
Lye	d						06 19					
Cradley Heath	d						06 22				06 51	
Old Hill	d						06 26					
Rowley Regis	d						06 30				06 57	
Langley Green	d						06 33					
Birmingham New Street ■	a							06 48				
	d		06 04		06 33					07 04		
Birmingham International ✈	d		06 14							07 14		
Coventry	d		06 25							07 25		
Smethwick Galton Bridge ■	d						06 36				07 03	
The Hawthorns	d						06 38				07 05	
Jewellery Quarter	d						06 42					
Birmingham Snow Hill	a						06 45				07 11	
	d	23p30					06 51				07 12	07 20
Birmingham Moor Street	d	23p33		06 15		06 44	06 54				07 15	07 23
Bordesley	d											
Small Heath	d						06 58					07 27
Tyseley	d	23p38					07 00					07 29
Acocks Green	d	23p41					07 03					
Olton	d	23p44					07 06					
Solihull	d	23p48		06 24		06 53	07 10				07 24	
Widney Manor	d	23p51					07 13					
Dorridge	d	23p55		06 29		06 58	07a18				07 29	
Lapworth	d	23p59		06 33								
Hatton	d	00 05		06 39								
Warwick Parkway	d	00 10		06 44		07 07					07 39	
Warwick	d	00 13		06 47							07 42	
Leamington Spa ■	a	00 17	06 36	06 52	06 58	07 13				07 36	07 46	
	d	00 18	06 38	06 52	07 00	07 14				07 38	07 47	
Banbury	d	00a39	06a54	07 10	07a17	07 31				07a54	08 05	
London Marylebone ■ ⊖	a			08 22		08 32					09 12	
Spring Road	d											07 32
Hall Green	d											07 35
Yardley Wood	d											07 38
Shirley	d											07 41
Whitlocks End	d											07 44
Wythall	d											07 46
Earlswood (West Midlands)	d											07 49
The Lakes	d											07x51
Wood End	d											07x54
Danzey	d											07x57
Henley-in-Arden	d											08 03
Wootton Wawen	d											08x06
Wilmcote	d											08 11
Stratford-upon-Avon	a											08 17

		XC	CH	LM	LM	CH	LM	GW	CH	CH	XC	LM
		◇■ ✠				◇		◇■ ⊡	◇		◇■ ✠	
Hereford ■	d							06 17				
Ledbury	a							06 33				
	d							06 34				
Colwall	d							06 41				
Great Malvern	a							06 46				
	d				06 21			06 49				
Malvern Link	d				06 24			06 53				
Worcester Foregate Street ■	a				06 31			07 02				
	d				06 33			07 04				
Worcester Shrub Hill ■	a							07 07				
	d			06 25			07 01					07 35
Droitwich Spa	d			06 33	06 42		07 09					07 43
Bromsgrove	d				06 51							07 52
Barnt Green	d											
University	d				07 09							08 09
Hartlebury	d			06 40			07 16					
Kidderminster	d			06 46		07 14	07 22					
Blakedown	d			06 51			07 27					
Hagley	d			06 54			07 30					
Stourbridge Junction ■	d			07 02		07 22	07 35					
Lye	d			07 06			07 39					
Cradley Heath	d			07 09		07 28	07 42					
Old Hill	d			07 13			07 46					
Rowley Regis	d			07 17		07 34	07 50					
Langley Green	d			07 20			07 53					
Birmingham New Street ■	a				07 16							08 16
	d	07 33									08 04	
Birmingham International ✈	d										08 14	
Coventry	d										08 25	
Smethwick Galton Bridge ■	d			07 23		07 40	07 56					
The Hawthorns	d			07 25		07 42	07 58					
Jewellery Quarter	d			07 29			08 02					
Birmingham Snow Hill	a			07 32		07 50	08 05					
	d			07 37		07 52	08 07					
Birmingham Moor Street	d		07 33	07 40		07 55	08 10					
Bordesley	d											
Small Heath	d						08 14					
Tyseley	d						08 16					
Acocks Green	d			07 45								
Olton	d			07 48								
Solihull	d		07 42	07 52		08 04						
Widney Manor	d			07 55								
Dorridge	d		07 50	08a01								
Lapworth	d		07 54									
Hatton	d		08 00						08 17			
Warwick Parkway	d		08 05			08 18						
Warwick	d		08 08						08 24			
Leamington Spa ■	a	07 58	08 17			08 23			08 28		08 36	
	d	08 00				08 24			08 29	08 28	08 38	
Banbury	d	08a17				08 44			08 49		08a54	
London Marylebone ■ ⊖	a					09 39			10 12			
Spring Road	d						08 19					
Hall Green	d						08 22					
Yardley Wood	d						08 25					
Shirley	d						08 28					
Whitlocks End	d						08a30					
Wythall	d											
Earlswood (West Midlands)	d											
The Lakes	d											
Wood End	d											
Danzey	d											
Henley-in-Arden	d											
Wootton Wawen	d											
Wilmcote	d									08 58		
Stratford-upon-Avon	a									09 09		

Hereford, Worcester and Stourbridge - Birmingham - Leamington Spa, Marylebone and Stratford-upon-Avon

Network Diagram - see first Page of Table 71

		CH	LM	LM	LM	LM	GW	XC	CH	LM	LM	XC
		◇					◇■ Ø	◇■ ✠	◇			◇■ ✠
Hereford ■	d						07 10					
Ledbury	a						07 28					
	d						07 30					
Colwall	d						07 37					
Great Malvern	a						07 42					
	d					07 32	07 43					
Malvern Link	d					07 35	07 46					
Worcester Foregate Street ■	a					07 43	07 58					
	d					07 46	07 59					
Worcester Shrub Hill ■	a						08 02					
	d											
Droitwich Spa	d					07 55						
Bromsgrove	d											
Barnt Green	d											
University	d											
Hartlebury	d											
Kidderminster	d			07 46		08 06			08 13			
Blakedown	d			07 51		08 11						
Hagley	d			07 54		08 14						
Stourbridge Junction ■	d			07 59	08 05	08 19			08 26		08 35	
Lye	d				08 09						08 39	
Cradley Heath	d			08 04	08 12	08 24			08 32		08 42	
Old Hill	d				08 16						08 46	
Rowley Regis	d			08 10	08 20	08 30			08 37		08 50	
Langley Green	d				08 23						08 53	
Birmingham New Street ■	a											
	d							08 33				09 04
Birmingham International ✈	d											09 14
Coventry	d											09 25
Smethwick Galton Bridge ■	d			08 16	08 26	08 36			08 43		08 56	
The Hawthorns	d			08 18	08 28	08 38			08 45		08 58	
Jewellery Quarter	d			08 22	08 32	08 42					09 02	
Birmingham Snow Hill	a			08 25	08 35	08 45			08 51		09 05	
	d		08 17	08 27	08 37	08 47			08 52	08 57	09 07	
Birmingham Moor Street	d	08 15	08 20	08 30	08 40	08 50			08 55	09 00	09 10	
Bordesley	d											
Small Heath	d				08 44						09 14	
Tyseley	d				08 46						09 16	
Acocks Green	d		08 25		08 49					09 05		
Olton	d		08 28		08 52					09 08		
Solihull	d	08 25	08 32		08 56				09 05	09 12		
Widney Manor	d		08 35		08 59					09 15		
Dorridge	d	08 30	08a41		09a04					09a21		
Lapworth	d											
Hatton	d											
Warwick Parkway	d	08 39							09 19			
Warwick	d	08 43										
Leamington Spa ■	a	08 47						08 58	09 24			09 36
	d	08 48						09 00	09 24			09 38
Banbury	d	09 10						09a17	09 45			09a54
London Marylebone ■ ⊖	a	10 16							10 42			
Spring Road	d			08 36		08 56					09 19	
Hall Green	d			08 39		08 59					09 22	
Yardley Wood	d			08 42		09 02					09 25	
Shirley	d			08 45		09 05					09 28	
Whitlocks End	d			08 48		09a08					09a30	
Wythall	d			08 50								
Earlswood (West Midlands)	d			08 53								
The Lakes	d			08x55								
Wood End	d			08x58								
Danzey	d			09x01								
Henley-in-Arden	d			09 07								
Wootton Wawen	d			09x10								
Wilmcote	d			09 15								
Stratford-upon-Avon	a			09 21								

		CH	LM	LM	GW	LM	CH	XC	CH	CH	LM	LM
		◇			◇■ ⊡		◇	◇■ ✠	◇			
Hereford ■	d			07 40								
Ledbury	a			07 56								
	d			07 58								
Colwall	d			08 04								
Great Malvern	a			08 08								
	d			08 10	08 43							
Malvern Link	d			08 13	08 47							
Worcester Foregate Street ■	a			08 21	08 56							
	d			08 24	08 58							
Worcester Shrub Hill ■	a				09 01							
	d		08 15									
Droitwich Spa	d		08 23	08 33								
Bromsgrove	d			08 42								
Barnt Green	d											
University	d			08 59								
Hartlebury	d		08 30									
Kidderminster	d		08 36									
Blakedown	d		08 41									
Hagley	d		08 44									
Stourbridge Junction ■	d		08 49			08 55					09 09	
Lye	d					08 59						
Cradley Heath	d		08 54			09 02					09 14	
Old Hill	d					09 06						
Rowley Regis	d		09 00			09 10					09 20	
Langley Green	d					09 13						
Birmingham New Street ■	a			09 11								
	d							09 33				
Birmingham International ✈	d											
Coventry	d											
Smethwick Galton Bridge ■	d		09 06			09 16					09 26	
The Hawthorns	d		09 08			09 18					09 28	
Jewellery Quarter	d		09 12			09 22					09 32	
Birmingham Snow Hill	a		09 15			09 25					09 35	
	d	09 12	09 17			09 27					09 37	09 47
Birmingham Moor Street	d	09 15	09 20			09 30				09 33	09 40	09 50
Bordesley	d											
Small Heath	d										09 44	
Tyseley	d										09 46	
Acocks Green	d		09 25								09 49	
Olton	d		09 28								09 52	
Solihull	d	09 23	09 32							09 42	09 56	
Widney Manor	d		09 35								09 59	
Dorridge	d	09 28	09a41							09 50	10a04	
Lapworth	d									09 54		
Hatton	d						09 41			10 00		
Warwick Parkway	d	09 38								10 05		
Warwick	d	09 41					09 48			10 08		
Leamington Spa ■	a	09 46					09 53	09 58		10 20		
	d	09 47					09 54	10 00	10 08			
Banbury	d	10 05					10 14	10a17				
London Marylebone ■ ⊖	a	11 12					11 42					
Spring Road	d					09 36						09 56
Hall Green	d					09 39						09 59
Yardley Wood	d					09 42						10 02
Shirley	d					09 45						10 05
Whitlocks End	d					09 48						10a08
Wythall	d					09 50						
Earlswood (West Midlands)	d					09 53						
The Lakes	d					09x55						
Wood End	d					09x58						
Danzey	d					10x01						
Henley-in-Arden	d					10 07						
Wootton Wawen	d					10x10						
Wilmcote	d					10 15						
Stratford-upon-Avon	a					10 21			10 40			

Table 71

Saturdays

Hereford, Worcester and Stourbridge - Birmingham - Leamington Spa, Marylebone and Stratford-upon-Avon

Network Diagram - see first Page of Table 71

		CH		LM	LM	XC	CH	LM	LM	LM	LM	LM		XC	LM	GW	CH	LM	LM	XC	CH	LM		LM	LM
		◇				◇1	◇							◇1		◇1	◇			◇1	◇				
						H								H		H				H					
Hereford ■	d								08 40															09 40	
Ledbury	a								08 56															09 56	
	d								08 58															09 58	
Colwall	d								09 04															10 04	
Great Malvern	a								09 09															10 08	
	d							09 00	09 10							09 51								10 10	
Malvern Link	d							09 03	09 13							09 54								10 13	
Worcester Foregate Street ■	a							09 11	09 22							10 02								10 21	
	d			08 56				09 16	09 24							10 04						10 16		10 24	
Worcester Shrub Hill ■	a															10 06									
	d											09 47			09 56										
Droitwich Spa	d			09 05				09 25	09 33			09 55			10 04							10 25		10 33	
Bromsgrove	d								09 42						10 13									10 42	
Barnt Green	d																								
University	d								09 59															10 59	
Hartlebury	d																								
Kidderminster	d	09 03		09 16	09 26			09 36			09 56	10 06							10 26			10 36			
Blakedown	d	09 08			09 31			09 41				10 11										10 41			
Hagley	d	09 12			09 34			09 44				10 14										10 44			
Stourbridge Junction ■	d	09 16		09 25	09 39			09 49		09 55	10 09	10 19						10 25	10 39			10 49			10 55
Lye	d			09 29						09 59								10 29							10 59
Cradley Heath	d	09 22		09 32	09 44			09 54		10 02	10 14	10 24						10 32	10 44			10 54			11 02
Old Hill	d			09 36						10 06								10 36							11 06
Rowley Regis	d	09 28		09 40	09 50			10 00		10 10	10 20	10 30						10 40	10 50			11 00			11 10
Langley Green	d			09 43						10 13								10 43							11 13
Birmingham New Street ■	a								10 11						10 41									11 11	
	d					10 04								10 33						11 04					
Birmingham International ✈	d					10 14														11 14					
Coventry	d					10 25														11 25					
Smethwick Galton Bridge ■	d	09 33		09 46	09 56			10 06		10 16	10 26	10 36						10 46	10 56			11 06			11 16
The Hawthorns	d	09 36		09 48	09 58			10 08		10 18	10 28	10 38						10 48	10 58			11 08			11 18
Jewellery Quarter	d			09 52	10 02			10 12		10 22	10 32	10 42						10 52	11 02			11 12			11 22
Birmingham Snow Hill	a	09 42		09 55	10 05			10 15		10 25	10 35	10 45						10 55	11 05			11 15			11 25
	d	09 52		09 57	10 07		10 12	10 17		10 27	10 37	10 47						10 57	11 07		11 12	11 17			11 27
Birmingham Moor Street	d	09 55		10 00	10 10		10 15	10 20		10 30	10 40	10 50					10 55	11 00	11 10		11 15	11 20			11 30
Bordesley	d																								
Small Heath	d				10 14						10 44								11 14						
Tyseley	d				10 16						10 46								11 16						
Acocks Green	d			10 05				10 25			10 49							11 05				11 25			
Olton	d			10 08				10 28			10 52							11 08				11 28			
Solihull	d	10 05		10 12			10 24	10 32			10 56						11 03	11 12			11 23	11 32			
Widney Manor	d			10 15				10 35			10 59							11 15				11 35			
Dorridge	d			10a22			10 30	10a41			11a04							11a22			11 28	11a41			
Lapworth	d																								
Hatton	d																								
Warwick Parkway	d	10 19					10 39										11 15				11 38				
Warwick	d						10 43														11 41				
Leamington Spa ■	a	10 24				10 36	10 48							10 58			11 20			11 36	11 46				
	d	10 25				10 38	10 48							11 00			11 20			11 38	11 47				
Banbury	d	10 46				10a54	11 08							11a17			11 40			11a54	12 04				
London Marylebone ■ ⊖	a	11 46					12 16										12 46				13 16				
Spring Road	d				10 19					10 36		10 56							11 19						11 36
Hall Green	d				10 22					10 39		10 59							11 22						11 39
Yardley Wood	d				10 25					10 42		11 02							11 25						11 42
Shirley	d				10 28					10 45		11 05							11 28						11 45
Whitlocks End	d				10a30					10 48		11a08							11a30						11 48
Wythall	d									10 50															11 50
Earlswood (West Midlands)	d									10 53															11 53
The Lakes	d									10x55															11x55
Wood End	d									10x58															11x58
Danzey	d									11x01															12x01
Henley-in-Arden	d									11 07															12 07
Wootton Wawen	d									11x10															12x10
Wilmcote	d									11 15															12 15
Stratford-upon-Avon	a									11 21															12 21

Table 71

Saturdays

Hereford, Worcester and Stourbridge - Birmingham - Leamington Spa, Marylebone and Stratford-upon-Avon

Network Diagram - see first Page of Table 71

		XC	CH	CH	CH	LM	LM	GW		GW	CH	LM	LM	XC	CH	LM	LM	LM		LM	LM	XC	CH	LM	LM
								■																	
		◇1	◇	◇						◇1	◇			◇1	◇							◇1	◇		
		H								H				H								H			
Hereford ■	d																10 40								
Ledbury	a																10 56								
	d																10 58								
Colwall	d																11 04								
Great Malvern	a																11 08								
	d							10 46		10 58							11 10				11 35				
Malvern Link	d							10 48		11 01							11 13				11 37				
Worcester Foregate Street ■	a							10 56		11 09							11 21				11 45				
	d							10 57		11 11							11 24				11 46				
Worcester Shrub Hill ■	a							11 00		11 13															
	d						10 47									11 17									
Droitwich Spa	d						10 55									11 25	11 33				11 55				
Bromsgrove	d																11 42								
Barnt Green	d																								
University	d																11 59								
Hartlebury	d																								
Kidderminster	d					10 56	11 06						11 26			11 36				11 56	12 06				12 26
Blakedown	d						11 11									11 41					12 11				
Hagley	d						11 14									11 44					12 14				
Stourbridge Junction ■	d					11 09	11 19					11 25	11 39			11 49		11 55		12 09	12 19			12 25	12 39
Lye	d											11 29						11 59						12 29	
Cradley Heath	d					11 14	11 24					11 32	11 44			11 54		12 02		12 14	12 24			12 32	12 44
Old Hill	d											11 36						12 06						12 36	
Rowley Regis	d					11 20	11 30					11 40	11 50			12 00		12 10		12 20	12 30			12 40	12 50
Langley Green	d											11 43						12 13						12 43	
Birmingham New Street ■	a																12 11								
	d	11 33												12 04								12 33			
Birmingham International ✈	d													12 14											
Coventry	d													12 25											
Smethwick Galton Bridge ■	d					11 26	11 36					11 46	11 56			12 06		12 16		12 26	12 36			12 46	12 56
The Hawthorns	d					11 28	11 38					11 48	11 58			12 08		12 18		12 28	12 38			12 48	12 58
Jewellery Quarter	d					11 32	11 42					11 52	12 02			12 12		12 22		12 32	12 42			12 52	13 02
Birmingham Snow Hill	a					11 35	11 45					11 55	12 05			12 15		12 25		12 35	12 45			12 55	13 05
	d					11 37	11 47					11 57	12 07		12 12	12 17		12 27		12 37	12 47			12 57	13 07
Birmingham Moor Street	d				11 33	11 40	11 50				11 55	12 00	12 10		12 15	12 20		12 30		12 40	12 50		12 55	13 00	13 10
Bordesley	d																								
Small Heath	d					11 44							12 14							12 44					13 14
Tyseley	d					11 46							12 16							12 46					13 16
Acocks Green	d					11 49						12 05				12 25				12 49				13 05	
Olton	d					11 52						12 08				12 28				12 52				13 08	
Solihull	d				11 42	11 56					12 04	12 12			12 23	12 32				12 56			13 05	13 12	
Widney Manor	d					11 59						12 15				12 35				12 59				13 15	
Dorridge	d				11 50	12a04						12a22			12 28	12a41				13a04				13a21	
Lapworth	d				11 54																				
Hatton	d		11 57		12 00																				
Warwick Parkway	d				12 05						12 20				12 38								13 18		
Warwick	d		12 04		12 08										12 41										
Leamington Spa ■	a	11 58	12 08		12 20						12 25			12 36	12 46							12 59	13 23		
	d	12 00	12 08	12 17							12 26			12 38	12 47							13 02	13 24		
Banbury	d	12a17	12 26								12 46			12a54	13 08							13a19	13 44		
London Marylebone ■ ⊖	a		13 43								13 46				14 16								14 42		
Spring Road	d						11 56						12 19					12 36			12 56				13 19
Hall Green	d						11 59						12 22					12 39			12 59				13 22
Yardley Wood	d						12 02						12 25					12 42			13 02				13 25
Shirley	d						12 05						12 28					12 45			13 05				13 28
Whitlocks End	d						12a08						12a30					12 48			13a08				13a30
Wythall	d																	12 50							
Earlswood (West Midlands)	d																	12 53							
The Lakes	d																	12x55							
Wood End	d																	12x58							
Danzey	d																	13x01							
Henley-in-Arden	d																	13 07							
Wootton Wawen	d																	13x10							
Wilmcote	d			12 43														13 15							
Stratford-upon-Avon	a			12 53														13 21							

Hereford, Worcester and Stourbridge - Birmingham - Leamington Spa, Marylebone and Stratford-upon-Avon

Network Diagram - see first Page of Table 71

		XC	CH	LM	LM	GW	LM	CH	XC	CH	LM	LM	GW	CH	CH	LM	LM	XC	CH	LM	LM	LM
		◇1	◇			◇		◇	◇1				◇1	◇	◇			◇1	◇			
Hereford 7	d				11 40								12 13								12 40	
Ledbury	a				11 56								12 30								12 56	
	d				11 58								12 31								12 58	
Colwall	d				12 04								12 38								13 04	
Great Malvern	a				12 08								12 43								13 08	
	d				12 10								12 44								13 10	
Malvern Link	d				12 13								12 48								13 13	
Worcester Foregate Street 7	a				12 21								12 58								13 21	
	d			12 16	12 24	12 40						12 46	12 59								13 24	
Worcester Shrub Hill 7	a					12 42							13 02									
	d																			13 17		
Droitwich Spa	d			12 25	12 33							12 55								13 25	13 33	
Bromsgrove	d				12 42																13 42	
Barnt Green	d																					
University	d				12 59																13 59	
Hartlebury	d																					
Kidderminster	d			12 36							12 56	13 06					13 26			13 36		
Blakedown	d			12 41								13 11								13 41		
Hagley	d			12 44								13 14								13 44		
Stourbridge Junction 2	d			12 49			12 55				13 09	13 19				13 25	13 39			13 49		13 55
Lye	d						12 59									13 29						13 59
Cradley Heath	d			12 54			13 02				13 14	13 24				13 32	13 44			13 54		14 02
Old Hill	d						13 06									13 36						14 06
Rowley Regis	d			13 00			13 10				13 20	13 30				13 40	13 50			14 00		14 10
Langley Green	d						13 13									13 43						14 13
Birmingham New Street 12	a				13 11																14 11	
	d	13 04							13 33									14 04				
Birmingham International ✈	d	13 14																14 14				
Coventry	d	13 25																14 25				
Smethwick Galton Bridge 7	d			13 06			13 16				13 26	13 36				13 46	13 56			14 06		14 16
The Hawthorns	d			13 08			13 18				13 28	13 38				13 48	13 58			14 08		14 18
Jewellery Quarter	d			13 12			13 22				13 32	13 42				13 52	14 02			14 12		14 22
Birmingham Snow Hill	a			13 15			13 25				13 35	13 45				13 55	14 05			14 15		14 25
	d		13 12	13 17			13 27				13 37	13 47				13 57	14 07		14 12	14 17		14 27
Birmingham Moor Street	d		13 15	13 20			13 30			13 33	13 40	13 50			13 55	14 00	14 10		14 15	14 20		14 30
Bordesley	d																					
Small Heath	d										13 44						14 14					
Tyseley	d										13 46						14 16					
Acocks Green	d			13 25							13 49					14 05				14 25		
Olton	d			13 28							13 52					14 08				14 28		
Solihull	d		13 23	13 32						13 42	13 56				14 03	14 12			14 23	14 32		
Widney Manor	d			13 35							13 59					14 15				14 35		
Dorridge	d		13 28	13a41						13 50	14a04					14a22			14 28	14a41		
Lapworth	d									13 54												
Hatton	d							13 41		14 00												
Warwick Parkway	d		13 38							14 05					14 15				14 38			
Warwick	d		13 41					13 48		14 08									14 41			
Leamington Spa 5	a	13 36	13 46					13 53	13 58	14 16					14 21			14 36	14 46			
	d	13 38	13 47					13 54	14 00					14 17	14 21			14 38	14 47			
Banbury	d	13a54	14 08					14 13	14a17						14 42			14a54	15 08			
London Marylebone 10 ⊖	a		15 16					15 39							15 42				16 16			
Spring Road	d						13 36					13 56					14 19					14 36
Hall Green	d						13 39					13 59					14 22					14 39
Yardley Wood	d						13 42					14 02					14 25					14 42
Shirley	d						13 45					14 05					14 28					14 45
Whitlocks End	d						13 48					14a08					14a30					14 48
Wythall	d						13 50															14 50
Earlswood (West Midlands)	d						13 53															14 53
The Lakes	d						13x55															14x55
Wood End	d						13x58															14x58
Danzey	d						14x01															15x01
Henley-in-Arden	d						14 07															15 07
Wootton Wawen	d						14x10															15x10
Wilmcote	d						14 15															15 15
Stratford-upon-Avon	a						14 21							14 50								15 21

Hereford, Worcester and Stourbridge - Birmingham - Leamington Spa, Marylebone and Stratford-upon-Avon

Network Diagram - see first Page of Table 71

		LM	LM	XC	CH	LM	LM	XC	CH	LM	LM	LM	CH	XC	CH	LM	LM	GW	GW	CH	CH	LM	LM
				◇1	◇			◇1	◇				◇	◇1				◇1	◇	◇	◇		
Hereford 7	d										13 40												
Ledbury	a										13 56												
	d										13 58												
Colwall	d										14 04												
Great Malvern	a										14 08												
	d		13 35								14 10							14 34	14 50				
Malvern Link	d		13 37								14 13							14 37	14 52				
Worcester Foregate Street 7	a		13 45								14 21							14 55	15 02				
	d		13 46							14 16	14 24							14 57	15 02				
Worcester Shrub Hill 7	a																	14 59	15 06				
	d																14 43						
Droitwich Spa	d		13 55							14 25	14 33						14 55						
Bromsgrove	d										14 42												
Barnt Green	d																						
University	d										14 59												
Hartlebury	d																						
Kidderminster	d	13 56	14 06				14 26			14 36						14 56	15 06						15 26
Blakedown	d		14 11							14 41							15 11						15 31
Hagley	d		14 14							14 44							15 14						15 34
Stourbridge Junction 2	d	14 09	14 19			14 25	14 39			14 49		14 55				15 09	15 19					15 25	15 39
Lye	d					14 29						14 59										15 29	
Cradley Heath	d	14 14	14 24			14 32	14 44			14 54		15 02				15 14	15 24					15 32	15 44
Old Hill	d					14 36						15 06										15 36	
Rowley Regis	d	14 20	14 30			14 40	14 50			15 00		15 10				15 20	15 30					15 40	15 50
Langley Green	d					14 43						15 13										15 43	
Birmingham New Street 12	a										15 11												
	d			14 33				15 04						15 33									
Birmingham International ✈	d							15 14															
Coventry	d							15 25															
Smethwick Galton Bridge 7	d	14 26	14 36			14 46	14 56			15 06		15 16				15 26	15 36					15 46	15 56
The Hawthorns	d	14 28	14 38			14 48	14 58			15 08		15 18				15 28	15 38					15 48	15 58
Jewellery Quarter	d	14 32	14 42			14 52	15 02			15 12		15 22				15 32	15 42					15 52	16 02
Birmingham Snow Hill	a	14 35	14 45			14 55	15 05			15 15		15 25				15 35	15 45					15 55	16 05
	d	14 37	14 47			14 57	15 07		15 12	15 17		15 27				15 37	15 47					15 57	16 07
Birmingham Moor Street	d	14 40	14 50		14 55	15 00	15 10		15 15	15 20		15 30			15 33	15 40	15 50				15 55	16 00	16 10
Bordesley	d																						
Small Heath	d	14 44					15 14									15 44							16 14
Tyseley	d	14 46					15 16									15 46							16 16
Acocks Green	d	14 49				15 05				15 25						15 49						16 05	
Olton	d	14 52				15 08				15 28						15 52						16 08	
Solihull	d	14 56			15 03	15 12			15 23	15 32					15 42	15 56					16 03	16 12	
Widney Manor	d	14 59				15 15				15 35						15 59						16 15	
Dorridge	d	15a04				15a21			15 28	15a41					15 50	16a04						16a21	
Lapworth	d														15 54								
Hatton	d												15 42		16 00								
Warwick Parkway	d				15 15				15 38						16 05						16 15		
Warwick	d								15 41				15 49		16 08								
Leamington Spa 5	a			14 58	15 21			15 36	15 46				15 54	16 00	16 16						16 21		
	d			15 00	15 21			15 38	15 47				15 55	16 02						16 17	16 21		
Banbury	d			15a19	15 41			15a54	16 07				16 15	16a18							16 44		
London Marylebone 10 ⊖	a				16 46				17 16				17 41								17 46		
Spring Road	d		14 56				15 19					15 36					15 56						16 19
Hall Green	d		14 59				15 22					15 39					15 59						16 22
Yardley Wood	d		15 02				15 25					15 42					16 02						16 25
Shirley	d		15 05				15 28					15 45					16 05						16 28
Whitlocks End	d		15a08				15a30					15 48					16a08						16a30
Wythall	d											15 50											
Earlswood (West Midlands)	d											15 53											
The Lakes	d											15x55											
Wood End	d											15x58											
Danzey	d											16x01											
Henley-in-Arden	d											16 07											
Wootton Wawen	d											16x10											
Wilmcote	d											16 15								16 45			
Stratford-upon-Avon	a											16 21								16 55			

Table 71

Saturdays

Hereford, Worcester and Stourbridge - Birmingham - Leamington Spa, Marylebone and Stratford-upon-Avon

Network Diagram - see first Page of Table 71

Station		XC	CH	LM	LM	LM	LM	LM	XC	LM	GW	CH	LM	LM	XC	CH	LM	LM	LM	XC	CH	CH	LM
		◇■	◇						◇■		◇■	◇			◇■	◇				◇■	◇		
Hereford ■	d				14 40						15 13							15 40					
Ledbury	a				14 56						15 30							15 56					
	d				14 58						15 31							15 58					
Colwall	d				15 04						15 38							16 04					
Great Malvern	a				15 08						15 43							16 08					
	d				15 10			15 30			15 44							16 10					
Malvern Link	d				15 13			15 32			15 48							16 13					
Worcester Foregate Street ■	a				15 21			15 40			15 58							16 21					
	d			15 16	15 24			15 46			15 59						16 15	16 24					
Worcester Shrub Hill ■	a										16 02												
	d									15 54													
Droitwich Spa	d			15 25	15 33			15 55		16 02							16 24	16 33					
Bromsgrove	d				15 42					16 12								16 42					
Barnt Green	d																						
University	d				15 59													16 59					
Hartlebury	d																16 31						
Kidderminster	d			15 36			15 56	16 06						16 26			16 37						16 56
Blakedown	d			15 41				16 11						16 31			16 42						
Hagley	d			15 44				16 14						16 34			16 45						
Stourbridge Junction ■	d			15 49		15 55	16 09	16 19					16 25	16 39			16 49		16 55				17 09
Lye	d					15 59							16 29						16 59				
Cradley Heath	d			15 54		16 02	16 14	16 24					16 32	16 44			16 54		17 02				17 14
Old Hill	d					16 06							16 36						17 06				
Rowley Regis	d			16 00		16 10	16 20	16 30					16 40	16 50			17 00		17 10				17 20
Langley Green	d					16 13							16 43						17 13				
Birmingham New Street ■	a				16 11					16 45								17 11					
	d	16 04							16 33						17 04					17 33			
Birmingham International ✈	d	16 14													17 14								
Coventry	d	16 25													17 25								
Smethwick Galton Bridge ■	d			16 06		16 16	16 26	16 36					16 46	16 56			17 06		17 16				17 26
The Hawthorns	d			16 08		16 18	16 28	16 38					16 48	16 58			17 08		17 18				17 28
Jewellery Quarter	d			16 12		16 22	16 32	16 42					16 52	17 02			17 12		17 22				17 32
Birmingham Snow Hill	a			16 15		16 25	16 35	16 45					16 55	17 05			17 16		17 25				17 35
	d		16 12	16 17		16 27	16 37	16 47					16 57	17 07		17 12	17 17		17 27				17 37
Birmingham Moor Street	d		16 15	16 20		16 30	16 40	16 50				16 55	17 00	17 10		17 15	17 20		17 30			17 33	17 40
Bordesley	d																						
Small Heath	d						16 44	16 54						17 14									17 44
Tyseley	d					16 34	16 46	16 56					17 04	17 16					17 34				17 46
Acocks Green	d			16 25			16 49						17 07				17 25						17 49
Olton	d			16 28			16 52						17 10				17 28						17 52
Solihull	d		16 23	16 32			16 56					17 03	17 14			17 23	17 32					17 42	17 56
Widney Manor	d			16 35			16 59						17 17				17 35						17 59
Dorridge	d		16 28	16a41			17a04						17a22			17 28	17a41					17 50	18a04
Lapworth	d																					17 54	
Hatton	d																					18 00	
Warwick Parkway	d		16 38									17 15				17 38						18 05	
Warwick	d		16 41													17 41					18 02	18 08	
Leamington Spa ■	a	16 36	16 46						16 59			17 21			17 36	17 46				18 00	18 06	18 19	
	d	16 38	16 47						17 00			17 21			17 38	17 47				18 02	18 06		
Banbury	d	16a54	17 07						17a17			17 43			17a54	18 06				18a18	18 24		
London Marylebone ■ ⊖	a		18 16									18 46				19 16					19 22		
Spring Road	d					16 37		16 59						17 19					17 37				
Hall Green	d					16 40		17 02						17 22					17 40				
Yardley Wood	d					16 43		17 05						17 25					17 43				
Shirley	d					16 46		17 08						17 28					17 46				
Whitlocks End	d					16 49		17a11						17 31					17a49				
Wythall	d					16 51								17 33									
Earlswood (West Midlands)	d					16 54								17 36									
The Lakes	d					16x56								17x38									
Wood End	d					16x59								17x41									
Danzey	d					17x02								17x44									
Henley-in-Arden	d					17 07								17 49									
Wootton Wawen	d					17x10								17x52									
Wilmcote	d					17 16								17 58									
Stratford-upon-Avon	a					17 22								18 04									

Table 71

Saturdays

Hereford, Worcester and Stourbridge - Birmingham - Leamington Spa, Marylebone and Stratford-upon-Avon

Network Diagram - see first Page of Table 71

Station		LM	GW	GW	CH	CH	LM	LM	LM	LM	XC	LM	XC	CH	LM	GW	LM	LM	LM	XC	LM	GW
			◇■		◇	◇					◇■		◇■	◇		◇■				◇■		◇■
Hereford ■	d											16 40									17 40	
Ledbury	a											16 56									17 56	
	d											16 58									17 58	
Colwall	d											17 04									18 04	
Great Malvern	a											17 08									18 08	
	d		16 34	16 50								17 10				17 49		18 00			18 10	18 35
Malvern Link	d		16 37	16 52								17 13				17 52		18 02			18 13	18 38
Worcester Foregate Street ■	a		16 54	17 04								17 21				18 00		18 10			18 21	18 46
	d	16 46	16 55	17 04								17 24			17 48	18 02		18 11			18 24	18 48
Worcester Shrub Hill ■	a		16 58	17 07												18 04		18 13				18 50
	d								17 15									18 17				
Droitwich Spa	d	16 55							17 23			17 35			17 57			18 25			18 33	
Bromsgrove	d											17 44									18 42	
Barnt Green	d																					
University	d											17 59									18 59	
Hartlebury	d								17 30													
Kidderminster	d	17 06						17 26	17 36						18 07			18 36				
Blakedown	d	17 11						17 31	17 41						18 12			18 41				
Hagley	d	17 14						17 34	17 44						18 16			18 44				
Stourbridge Junction ■	d	17 19					17 25	17 39	17 49	17 55					18 20		18 27	18 49	18 55			
Lye	d						17 29			17 59							18 30		18 59			
Cradley Heath	d	17 24					17 32	17 44	17 54	18 02					18 25		18 33	18 54	19 02			
Old Hill	d						17 36			18 06							18 37		19 06			
Rowley Regis	d	17 30					17 40	17 50	18 00	18 10					18 31		18 41	19 00	19 10			
Langley Green	d						17 43			18 13							18 44		19 13			
Birmingham New Street ■	a											18 11									19 11	
	d										18 04		18 33							19 04		
Birmingham International ✈	d										18 14									19 14		
Coventry	d										18 25									19 25		
Smethwick Galton Bridge ■	d	17 36					17 46	17 56	18 06	18 16					18 37		18 47	19 06	19 16			
The Hawthorns	d	17 38					17 48	17 58	18 08	18 18					18 39		18 50	19 08	19 18			
Jewellery Quarter	d	17 42					17 52	18 02	18 12	18 22					18 43		18 53	19 12	19 22			
Birmingham Snow Hill	a	17 45					17 55	18 05	18 15	18 25					18 46		18 56	19 15	19 25			
	d	17 47				17 52	17 57	18 07	18 17	18 27				18 42	18 47		18 57	19 17	19 27			
Birmingham Moor Street	d	17 50				17 55	18 00	18 10	18 20	18 30				18 45	18 50		19 00	19 20	19 30			
Bordesley	d																					
Small Heath	d	17 54						18 14	18 24						18 54		19 04	19 24	19 34			
Tyseley	d	17 56						18 16	18 26						18 56		19 06	19 26	19 36			
Acocks Green	d						18 05		18 29						18 59			19 29				
Olton	d						18 08		18 32						19 02			19 32				
Solihull	d					18 03	18 12		18 36					18 53	19 06			19 36				
Widney Manor	d						18 15		18 39						19 09			19 39				
Dorridge	d						18a22		18a44					18 58	19a14			19a44				
Lapworth	d																					
Hatton	d																					
Warwick Parkway	d					18 15								19 08								
Warwick	d					18 18								19 11								
Leamington Spa ■	a					18 23					18 36		18 58	19 16						19 36		
	d				18 19	18 24					18 38		19 00	19 17						19 38		
Banbury	d					18 46					18a54		19a17	19 34						19a54		
London Marylebone ■ ⊖	a					19 49								20 42								
Spring Road	d	17 59						18 19		18 36							19 09		19 39			
Hall Green	d	18 02						18 22		18 39							19 12		19 42			
Yardley Wood	d	18 05						18 25		18 42							19 15		19 45			
Shirley	d	18 08						18 28		18 45							19 18		19 48			
Whitlocks End	d	18 11						18a30		18 48							19a21		19 51			
Wythall	d	18 13								18 50									19 53			
Earlswood (West Midlands)	d	18 16								18 53									19 56			
The Lakes	d	18x18								18x55									19x58			
Wood End	d	18x21								18x58									20x00			
Danzey	d	18x24								19x01									20x03			
Henley-in-Arden	d	18 30								19 07									20 08			
Wootton Wawen	d	18x33								19x10									20x10			
Wilmcote	d	18 38			18 47					19 15									20 16			
Stratford-upon-Avon	a	18 45			18 59					19 21									20 23			

Hereford, Worcester and Stourbridge - Birmingham - Leamington Spa, Marylebone and Stratford-upon-Avon

Network Diagram - see first Page of Table 71

		CH ◇	XC ◇[1] ⌶	CH ◇	LM	GW	CH ◇	LM	XC ◇[1] ⌶	XC ◇[1] ⌶	CH ◇	LM	GW ◇[1]	XC ◇[1]	LM	CH	CH ◇	LM	LM	GW ◇[1]	GW	CH	LM
Hereford [7]	d											19 11			20 00					20 20			
Ledbury	a											19 27			20 15					20 36			
	d											19 28			20 16					20 40			
Colwall	d											19 34			20 22					20 47			
Great Malvern	a											19 39			20 26					20 52			
	d					18 50						19 39			20 28					20 53	21 15		
Malvern Link	d					18 52						19 42			20 31					20 57	21 17		
Worcester Foregate Street [7]	a					19 03						19 51			20 39					21 09	21 27		
	d				18 51	19 03						19 51	20 02		20 41					21 11	21 27		
Worcester Shrub Hill [7]	a					19 06							20 05							21 14	21 30		
	d																		20 52				
Droitwich Spa	d				19 00							20 00			20 50				21 00				
Bromsgrove	d														20 59								
Barnt Green	d																						
University	d														21 14								
Hartlebury	d				19 07																		
Kidderminster	d				19 13			19 40				20 10							21 10				
Blakedown	d				19 18			19 45				20 15							21 15				
Hagley	d				19 21			19 49				20 19							21 19				
Stourbridge Junction [2]	d				19 25			19 55				20 25						20 55	21 25				21 55
Lye	d				19 29			19 59				20 29						20 59	21 29				21 59
Cradley Heath	d				19 32			20 02				20 32						21 02	21 32				22 02
Old Hill	d				19 36			20 06				20 36						21 06	21 36				22 06
Rowley Regis	d				19 40			20 10				20 40						21 10	21 40				22 10
Langley Green	d				19 43			20 13				20 43						21 13	21 43				22 13
Birmingham New Street [12]	a														21 21								
	d		19 33						20 04	20 33				21 04									
Birmingham International ✈	d								20 14					21 14									
Coventry	d								20 25					21 25									
Smethwick Galton Bridge [7]	d				19 46			20 16				20 46						21 16	21 46				22 16
The Hawthorns 🚋	d				19 48			20 18				20 48						21 18	21 48				22 18
Jewellery Quarter 🚋	d				19 52			20 22				20 52						21 22	21 52				22 22
Birmingham Snow Hill 🚋	a				19 55			20 25				20 55						21 25	21 55				22 25
	d			19 42	19 57			20 27			20 42	20 57					21 20	21 27	21 57			22 15	22 27
Birmingham Moor Street	d			19 45	20 00			20 30			20 45	21 00					21 23	21 30	22 00			22 18	22 30
Bordesley	d																						
Small Heath	d				20 04			20 34				21 04						21 34	22 04				22 34
Tyseley	d				20 06			20 36				21 06						21 36	22 06			22 23	22 36
Acocks Green	d				20 09							21 09							22 09			22 26	
Olton	d				20 12							21 12							22 12			22 29	
Solihull	d			19 53	20 16						20 53	21 16					21 31		22 16			22 33	
Widney Manor	d				20 19							21 19					21 34		22 19			22 36	
Dorridge	d			19 58	20a24						20 58	21a24					21 38		22a24			22 40	
Lapworth	d			20 03							21 03						21 43					22 44	
Hatton	d	19 36		20 09							21 09						21 49					22 49	
Warwick Parkway	d	19 43		20 14							21 14						21 54					22 54	
Warwick	d	19 46		20 17							21 17					21 37	21 57					22 58	
Leamington Spa [8]	a	19 51	20 01	20 22					20 36	20 58	21 21			21 36		21 48	22 02					23 03	
	d	19 52	20 03	20 23			20 28		20 38	21 00	21 21			21 38			22 03					23 03	
Banbury	d	20 11	20a19	20 46					20a54	21a19	21 39			21a54			22 20					23a24	
London Marylebone [10] ⊖	a	21 46		21 57							22 58						23 37						
Spring Road	d							20 39										21 39					22 39
Hall Green	d							20 42										21 42					22 42
Yardley Wood	d							20 45										21 45					22 45
Shirley	d							20 48										21 48					22 48
Whitlocks End	d							20 51										21a50					22a50
Wythall	d							20 53															
Earlswood (West Midlands)	d							20 56															
The Lakes	d							20x58															
Wood End	d							21x00															
Danzey	d							21x03															
Henley-in-Arden	d							21 08															
Wootton Wawen	d							21x10															
Wilmcote	d						20 56	21 16															
Stratford-upon-Avon	a						21 06	21 23															

Hereford, Worcester and Stourbridge - Birmingham - Leamington Spa, Marylebone and Stratford-upon-Avon

Network Diagram - see first Page of Table 71

		LM	LM	LM	LM	GW [1]	LM
Hereford [7]	d		21 35				22 50
Ledbury	a		21 50				23 05
	d		21 51				23 06
Colwall	d		21 57				23 12
Great Malvern	a		22 02				23 16
	d	21 30	22 05			22 41	23 17
Malvern Link	d	21 32	22 08			22 44	23 20
Worcester Foregate Street [7]	a	21 41	22 17			22 51	23 27
	d	21 42	22 18			22 53	23 28
Worcester Shrub Hill [7]	a	21 44	22 20			22 55	23 34
	d	21 52			22 47		
Droitwich Spa	d	22 00			22 55		
Bromsgrove	d						
Barnt Green	d						
University	d						
Hartlebury	d						
Kidderminster	d	22 10			23 05		
Blakedown	d	22 15			23 10		
Hagley	d	22 19			23 14		
Stourbridge Junction [2]	d	22 25		22 55	23 18		
Lye	d	22 29		22 59			
Cradley Heath	d	22 32		23 02			
Old Hill	d	22 36		23 06			
Rowley Regis	d	22 40		23 10			
Langley Green	d	22 43		23 13			
Birmingham New Street [12]	a						
	d						
Birmingham International ✈	d						
Coventry	d						
Smethwick Galton Bridge [7]	d	22 46		23 16			
The Hawthorns 🚋	d	22 48		23 18			
Jewellery Quarter 🚋	d	22 52		23 22			
Birmingham Snow Hill 🚋	a	22 55		23 25	23 36		
	d	22 57		23 27	23 37		
Birmingham Moor Street	d	23 00		23 30	23 40		
Bordesley	d						
Small Heath	d	23 04		23 34	23 44		
Tyseley	d	23 06		23 36	23 46		
Acocks Green	d	23 09			23 49		
Olton	d	23 12			23 52		
Solihull	d	23 16			23 56		
Widney Manor	d	23 19			23 59		
Dorridge	d	23a24			00 03		
Lapworth	d				00 07		
Hatton	d				00 13		
Warwick Parkway	d				00 18		
Warwick	d				00 21		
Leamington Spa [8]	a				00 26		
	d						
Banbury	d						
London Marylebone [10] ⊖	a						
Spring Road	d			23 39			
Hall Green	d			23 42			
Yardley Wood	d			23 45			
Shirley	d			23 48			
Whitlocks End	d			23a50			
Wythall	d						
Earlswood (West Midlands)	d						
The Lakes	d						
Wood End	d						
Danzey	d						
Henley-in-Arden	d						
Wootton Wawen	d						
Wilmcote	d						
Stratford-upon-Avon	a						

Sundays until 24 June

Hereford, Worcester and Stourbridge - Birmingham - Leamington Spa, Marylebone and Stratford-upon-Avon

Network Diagram - see first Page of Table 71

		LM	CH	XC	CH	LM	CH	CH	XC	CH		LM	GW	CH	LM	CH	XC	CH	LM	XC		CH	LM	CH	XC
			◇	◇1 ✕	◇			◇	◇1 🛒	◇			◇1	◇			◇1 🛒	◇		◇1 ✕		◇		◇	◇1 🛒
Hereford	d																								
Ledbury	a																								
	d																								
Colwall	d																								
Great Malvern	a																								
	d											09 03	09 20						10 02						
Malvern Link	d											09 06	09 23						10 04						
Worcester Foregate Street	a											09 15	09 30						10 12						
	d											09 15	09 31						10 16						
Worcester Shrub Hill	a											09 18	09 33						10 18						
	d	22p47										09 23							10 22						
Droitwich Spa	d	22p55										09 32							10 30						
Bromsgrove	d																								
Barnt Green	d																								
University	d																								
Hartlebury	d																								
Kidderminster	d	23p05										09 42			10 08				10 40						
Blakedown	d	23p10										09 47			10 13										
Hagley	d	23p14										09 51			10 17				10 47						
Stourbridge Junction	d	23p18										09 55			10 22				10 52				11 22		
Lye	d														10 25								11 25		
Cradley Heath	d											10 01			10 29				10 58				11 29		
Old Hill	d														10 33								11 33		
Rowley Regis	d											10 06			10 36				11 03				11 36		
Langley Green	d														10 39								11 39		
Birmingham New Street	a																								
	d			09 04					10 04								11 04			11 33					12 04
Birmingham International ✈	d			09 14					10 14								11 14								12 14
Coventry	d			09 25					10 25								11 25								12 25
Smethwick Galton Bridge	d											10 12			10 43				11 09				11 43		
The Hawthorns	d											10 15			10 45				11 12				11 45		
Jewellery Quarter	d											10 18			10 49				11 15				11 49		
Birmingham Snow Hill	a	23p36										10 20			10 52				11 17				11 52		
	d	23p37				09 19	09 40					10 22		10 40	10 53				11 19			11 40	11 53		
Birmingham Moor Street	d	23p40	08 55		09 13	09 22	09 43			10 13		10 25		10 43	10 56			11 13	11 22			11 43	11 56		
Bordesley	d																								
Small Heath	d	23p44																							
Tyseley	d	23p46				09 26						10 29							11 26						
Acocks Green	d	23p49													11 02								12 02		
Olton	d	23p52													11 04								12 04		
Solihull	d	23p56	09 04		09 22		09 52			10 22				10 52	11 08			11 22				11 52	12 08		
Widney Manor	d	23p59													11 11								12 11		
Dorridge	d	00 03	09 09		09 27		09 57			10 27				10 57	11a17			11 27				11 57	12a17		
Lapworth	d	00 07												11 02											
Hatton	d	00 13						10 15						11 08										12 15	
Warwick Parkway	d	00 18	09 18		09 37		10 08			10 37				11 13				11 37				12 08			
Warwick	d	00 21	09 22		09 41			10 23		10 41								11 41						12 23	
Leamington Spa	a	00 26	09 26	09 36	09 45		10 15	10 27	10 36	10 45				11 18			11 36	11 45		11 59		12 15		12 27	12 36
	d		09 27	09 38	09 46		10 16	10 27	10 38	10 46				11 18		11 20	11 38	11 46		12 00		12 16		12 27	12 38
Banbury	d		09 45	09a54	10 06		10 34	10 47	10a54	11 06				11 36			11a54	12 06		12a17		12 34		12 47	12a54
London Marylebone ⊖	a		10 46		11 14		11 47	12 11		12 14				12 47				13 14				13 47		14 11	
Spring Road	d					09 29						10 32							11 29						
Hall Green	d					09 32						10 35							11 32						
Yardley Wood	d					09 35						10 38							11 35						
Shirley	d					09 38						10 41							11 38						
Whitlocks End	d					09 41						10 44							11 41						
Wythall	d					09 43						10 46							11 43						
Earlswood (West Midlands)	d																								
The Lakes	d					09x46						10x49							11x46						
Wood End	d																								
Danzey	d																								
Henley-in-Arden	d					09 54						10 57							11 54						
Wootton Wawen	d																								
Wilmcote	d					10 04						11 05				11 43			12 02						
Stratford-upon-Avon	a					10 09						11 12				11 54			12 09						

Table 71

Sundays until 24 June

Hereford, Worcester and Stourbridge - Birmingham - Leamington Spa, Marylebone and Stratford-upon-Avon

Network Diagram - see first Page of Table 71

		CH	LM	GW	XC	CH		LM	CH	XC	CH	LM	XC	CH	LM	CH		XC	CH	LM	GW	XC	CH	LM	CH
				◇1	◇1 ✕	◇			◇	◇1 🛒	◇		◇1 ✕	◇		◇		◇1 🛒	◇		◇1	◇1 ✕	◇		◇
Hereford	d																								
Ledbury	a																								
	d																								
Colwall	d																								
Great Malvern	a																								
	d		10 56	11 15								12 04									13 15				
Malvern Link	d		10 58	11 18								12 06									13 18				
Worcester Foregate Street	a		11 06	11 26								12 15									13 25				
	d		11 20	11 27								12 16								13 20	13 26				
Worcester Shrub Hill	a			11 29								12 18									13 29				
	d											12 24													
Droitwich Spa	d		11 29									12 32								13 29					
Bromsgrove	d																								
Barnt Green	d																								
University	d																								
Hartlebury	d																								
Kidderminster	d		11 39									12 42								13 39					
Blakedown	d											12 47													
Hagley	d		11 46									12 51								13 46					
Stourbridge Junction	d		11 52					12 22				12 55			13 22					13 52				14 22	
Lye	d							12 25							13 25									14 25	
Cradley Heath	d		11 58					12 29				13 01			13 29					13 58				14 29	
Old Hill	d							12 33							13 33									14 33	
Rowley Regis	d		12 03					12 36				13 06			13 36					14 03				14 36	
Langley Green	d							12 39							13 39									14 39	
Birmingham New Street	a																								
	d				12 33					13 04			13 33					14 04				14 33			
Birmingham International ✈	d									13 14								14 14							
Coventry	d									13 25								14 25							
Smethwick Galton Bridge	d		12 08					12 43				13 11			13 43					14 08				14 43	
The Hawthorns	d		12 11					12 45				13 14			13 45					14 11				14 45	
Jewellery Quarter	d		12 14					12 49				13 17			13 49					14 14				14 49	
Birmingham Snow Hill	a		12 17					12 52				13 20			13 52					14 17				14 52	
	d		12 19			12 40		12 53				13 22		13 40	13 53					14 19			14 40	14 53	
Birmingham Moor Street	d	12 13	12 22			12 43		12 56			13 13	13 25		13 43	13 56				14 13	14 22			14 43	14 56	
Bordesley	d																								
Small Heath	d																								
Tyseley	d		12 26									13 29								14 26					
Acocks Green	d							13 02							14 02									15 02	
Olton	d							13 04							14 04									15 04	
Solihull	d	12 22				12 52		13 08			13 22			13 52	14 08				14 22				14 52	15 08	
Widney Manor	d							13 11							14 11									15 11	
Dorridge	d	12 27				12 57		13a18			13 27			13 57	14a17				14 27				14 57	15a17	
Lapworth	d													14 02											
Hatton	d													14 08		14 15									
Warwick Parkway	d	12 37				13 08					13 37			14 13					14 37				15 08		
Warwick	d	12 41									13 41					14 23			14 41						
Leamington Spa	a	12 45			12 59	13 15				13 36	13 45		13 59	14 18		14 27		14 36	14 45			14 59	15 15		
	d	12 46			13 00	13 16			13 20	13 38	13 46		14 00	14 18		14 27		14 38	14 46			15 00	15 16		15 20
Banbury	d	13 06			13a17	13 34				13a54	14 06		14a17	14 36		14 47		14a54	15 06			15a18	15 34		
London Marylebone ⊖	a	14 14				14 47					15 14			15 48		16 11			16 14				16 47		
Spring Road	d		12 29									13 32								14 29					
Hall Green	d		12 32									13 35								14 32					
Yardley Wood	d		12 35									13 38								14 35					
Shirley	d		12 38									13 41								14 38					
Whitlocks End	d		12 41									13 44								14 40					
Wythall	d		12 43									13 46								14 43					
Earlswood (West Midlands)	d																								
The Lakes	d		12x46									13x49								14x46					
Wood End	d																								
Danzey	d																								
Henley-in-Arden	d		12 54									13 57								14 53					
Wootton Wawen	d																								
Wilmcote	d		13 02						13 43			14 05								15 01					15 43
Stratford-upon-Avon	a		13 09						13 54			14 12								15 07					15 54

Sundays until 24 June

Hereford, Worcester and Stourbridge - Birmingham - Leamington Spa, Marylebone and Stratford-upon-Avon

Network Diagram - see first Page of Table 71

		XC	CH	LM	GW	XC	LM	CH	LM	CH	XC	CH	LM	GW	LM	XC	CH	LM	CH	XC	LM	CH
		◇■	◇		◇■	◇■		◇		◇	◇■	◇		◇■		◇■	◇		◇	◇■		◇
		☕			☕	🍴					☕			☕		🍴				☕		
Hereford ■	d				13 32									14 32							15 30	
Ledbury	a				13 49									14 49							15 47	
	d				13 50									14 55							15 51	
Colwall	d				13 57									15 02							15 58	
Great Malvern	a				14 02									15 07							16 02	
	d				14 11		14 35							15 08							16 03	
Malvern Link	d				14 15		14 37							15 12							16 05	
Worcester Foregate Street ■	a				14 24		14 45							15 21							16 14	
	d			14 20	14 26		14 45						15 20	15 23							16 15	
Worcester Shrub Hill ■	a				14 29		14 48							15 26							16 18	
	d						14 53								15 46						16 33	
Droitwich Spa	d			14 29			15 01						15 29		15 54						16 41	
Bromsgrove	d						15 10														16 51	
Barnt Green	d																					
University	d																					
Hartlebury	d																					
Kidderminster	d			14 39									15 40		16 04							
Blakedown	d			14 44																		
Hagley	d			14 48									15 47		16 11							
Stourbridge Junction ■	d			14 52					15 22				15 52		16 16			16 22				
Lye	d								15 25									16 25				
Cradley Heath	d			14 58					15 29				15 58					16 29				
Old Hill	d								15 33									16 33				
Rowley Regis	d			15 03					15 36				16 03					16 36				
Langley Green	d								15 39									16 39				
Birmingham New Street ■	a						15 37														17 17	
	d	15 04				15 33					16 04					16 33				17 04		
Birmingham International ✈	d	15 14									16 14									17 14		
Coventry	d	15 25									16 25									17 25		
Smethwick Galton Bridge ■	d			15 08					15 43				16 08		16 29			16 43				
The Hawthorns	d			15 11					15 45				16 11					16 45				
Jewellery Quarter	d			15 14					15 49				16 14					16 49				
Birmingham Snow Hill	a			15 17					15 52				16 17		16 35			16 52				
	d			15 19				15 40	15 53				16 19		16 45		16 40	16 53				
Birmingham Moor Street	d		15 13	15 22				15 43	15 56			16 13	16 22		16a47		16 43	16 56				17 13
Bordesley	d																					
Small Heath	d																					
Tyseley	d			15 26									16 26									
Acocks Green	d								16 02									17 02				
Olton	d								16 04									17 04				
Solihull	d		15 22					15 52	16 08			16 22					16 52	17 08				17 22
Widney Manor	d								16 11									17 11				
Dorridge	d		15 27					15 57	16a17			16 27					16 57	17a17				17 27
Lapworth	d							16 02														
Hatton	d							16 08		16 15												
Warwick Parkway	d		15 37					16 13				16 37					17 08					17 37
Warwick	d		15 41							16 23		16 41										17 41
Leamington Spa ■	a	15 36	15 45			15 59		16 18		16 27	16 36	16 45				16 59	17 15			17 36		17 45
	d	15 38	15 46			16 00		16 18		16 27	16 38	16 46				17 00	17 16		17 20	17 38		17 46
Banbury	d	15a54	16 06			16a17		16 36		16 47	16a54	17 06				17a17	17 34			17a54		18 06
London Marylebone ■ ⊖	a		17 14					17 48		18 11		18 14					18 47					19 14
Spring Road	d			15 29									16 29									
Hall Green	d			15 32									16 32									
Yardley Wood	d			15 35									16 35									
Shirley	d			15 38									16 38									
Whitlocks End	d			15 41									16 41									
Wythall	d			15 43									16 43									
Earlswood (West Midlands)	d																					
The Lakes	d			15x46									16x46									
Wood End	d																					
Danzey	d																					
Henley-in-Arden	d			15 54									16 55									
Wootton Wawen	d																					
Wilmcote	d			16 02									17 03						17 43			
Stratford-upon-Avon	a			16 09									17 10						17 54			

Sundays until 24 June

Hereford, Worcester and Stourbridge - Birmingham - Leamington Spa, Marylebone and Stratford-upon-Avon

Network Diagram - see first Page of Table 71

		LM	GW	XC	CH	LM	CH	XC	CH	LM	LM	XC	CH	CH	XC	CH	LM	GW	GW	XC	CH	XC	CH
			◇■	◇■			◇	◇■	◇			◇■	◇	◇	◇■	◇		◇■	◇■	◇■	◇	◇■	◇
			☕	🍴				☕				🍴			☕				☕	🍴		☕	
Hereford ■	d		16 35																18 30				
Ledbury	a		16 51																18 47				
	d		16 52																18 48				
Colwall	d		17 00																18 55				
Great Malvern	a		17 04																19 00				
	d		17 05								17 17								19 11				
Malvern Link	d		17 09								17 20								19 14				
Worcester Foregate Street ■	a		17 20								17 28								19 23				
	d	16 20	17 22							17 20	17 28						18 20	18 25	19 29				
Worcester Shrub Hill ■	a		17 26								17 31							18 26	19 31				
	d										17 36												
Droitwich Spa	d	16 29								17 29	17 44						18 29						
Bromsgrove	d										17 53												
Barnt Green	d																						
University	d																						
Hartlebury	d																						
Kidderminster	d	16 39								17 39							18 39						
Blakedown	d									17 44													
Hagley	d	16 46								17 48							18 46						
Stourbridge Junction ■	d	16 52				17 22				17 52							18 52						
Lye	d					17 25																	
Cradley Heath	d	16 58				17 29				17 58							18 58						
Old Hill	d					17 33																	
Rowley Regis	d	17 03				17 36				18 03							19 03						
Langley Green	d					17 39																	
Birmingham New Street ■	a										18 15												
	d			17 33				18 04				18 33			19 04					19 33		20 04	
Birmingham International ✈	d							18 14							19 14							20 14	
Coventry	d							18 25							19 25							20 25	
Smethwick Galton Bridge ■	d	17 08				17 43				18 08							19 08						
The Hawthorns	d	17 11				17 45				18 11							19 11						
Jewellery Quarter	d	17 14				17 49				18 14							19 14						
Birmingham Snow Hill	a	17 17				17 53				18 17							19 19						
	d	17 19			17 40	17 53				18 19			18 40			19 15	19 21						20 15
Birmingham Moor Street	d	17 22			17 43	17 56			18 13	18 22			18 43			19 18	19a23						20 18
Bordesley	d																						
Small Heath	d																						
Tyseley	d	17 26								18 26													
Acocks Green	d					18 02																	
Olton	d					18 04																	
Solihull	d				17 52	18 08			18 22				18 52			19 26							20 27
Widney Manor	d					18 11										19 30							20 30
Dorridge	d				17 57	18a17			18 27				18 57			19 34							20 34
Lapworth	d				18 02											19 38							
Hatton	d				18 08		18 15									19 44					20 15		
Warwick Parkway	d				18 13				18 37				19 08			19 49							20 46
Warwick	d						18 23		18 41							19 52					20 23		20 49
Leamington Spa ■	a			18 00	18 18		18 27	18 36	18 45			18 59	19 15		19 36	19 56				19 59	20 27	20 36	20 53
	d			18 01	18 18		18 27	18 38	18 46			19 00	19 16	19 20	19 38	19 57				20 00	20 27	20 38	20 54
Banbury	d			18a19	18 36		18 47	18a54	19 06			19a17	19 34		19a54	20 15				20a18	20 47	20a54	21 13
London Marylebone ■ ⊖	a				19 48		20 11		20 14				20 47			21 50					21 58		22 52
Spring Road	d	17 29								18 29													
Hall Green	d	17 32								18 32													
Yardley Wood	d	17 35								18 35													
Shirley	d	17 38								18 38													
Whitlocks End	d	17 41								18 41													
Wythall	d	17 43								18 43													
Earlswood (West Midlands)	d																						
The Lakes	d	17x46								18x46													
Wood End	d																						
Danzey	d																						
Henley-in-Arden	d	17 54								18 54													
Wootton Wawen	d																						
Wilmcote	d	18 02								19 02				19 43									
Stratford-upon-Avon	a	18 09								19 09				19 54									

Table 71

Sundays
until 24 June

Hereford, Worcester and Stourbridge - Birmingham - Leamington Spa, Marylebone and Stratford-upon-Avon

Network Diagram - see first Page of Table 71

		LM	XC	LM		GW	XC	CH	LM	LM	LM	LM	LM
			◇1			◇1	◇1	◇					
Hereford	d									20 05			22 40
Ledbury	a									20 21			22 56
	d									20 22			22 56
Colwall	d									20 28			23 03
Great Malvern	a									20 33			23 07
	d					20 15				20 33		22 10	23 08
Malvern Link	d					20 18				20 36		22 13	23 10
Worcester Foregate Street	a					20 25				20 44		22 22	23 19
	d					20 26				20 45		22 23	23 22
Worcester Shrub Hill	a					20 29				20 47		22 25	23 24
	d	19 38		19 53					20 34	20 52	21 25	22 29	
Droitwich Spa	d	19 46		20 01					20 42	21 00	21 33	22 37	
Bromsgrove	d			20 10						21 09			
Barnt Green	d												
University	d												
Hartlebury	d												
Kidderminster	d	19 56							20 52		21 43	22 47	
Blakedown	d												
Hagley	d	20 03							20 59		21 50	22 54	
Stourbridge Junction	d	20 07							21 03		21 54	22 58	
Lye	d												
Cradley Heath	d	20 13							21 08		21 59	23 04	
Old Hill	d												
Rowley Regis	d	20 19							21 14		22 05	23 09	
Langley Green	d												
Birmingham New Street	a			20 36						21 42			
	d		20 33				21 04						
Birmingham International	d						21 14						
Coventry	d						21 24						
Smethwick Galton Bridge	d	20 24							21 19		22 10	23 14	
The Hawthorns	d	20 26							21 21		22 12	23 17	
Jewellery Quarter	d	20 30							21 25		22 16	23 20	
Birmingham Snow Hill	a	20 33							21 28		22 19	23 24	
	d	20 33						21 15	21 28		22 20		
Birmingham Moor Street	d	20a36						21 18	21a31		22a22		
Bordesley	d												
Small Heath	d												
Tyseley	d												
Acocks Green	d												
Olton	d												
Solihull	d							21 26					
Widney Manor	d							21 30					
Dorridge	d							21 34					
Lapworth	d												
Hatton	d												
Warwick Parkway	d							21 46					
Warwick	d							21 49					
Leamington Spa	a		20 58				21 34	21 53					
	d		21 00					21 54					
Banbury	d		21a17					22 15					
London Marylebone	a							23 52					
Spring Road	d												
Hall Green	d												
Yardley Wood	d												
Shirley	d												
Whitlocks End	d												
Wythall	d												
Earlswood (West Midlands)	d												
The Lakes	d												
Wood End	d												
Danzey	d												
Henley-in-Arden	d												
Wootton Wawen	d												
Wilmcote	d												
Stratford-upon-Avon	a												

Table 71

Sundays
1 July to 9 September

Hereford, Worcester and Stourbridge - Birmingham - Leamington Spa, Marylebone and Stratford-upon-Avon

Network Diagram - see first Page of Table 71

		LM	CH	CH	XC	XC	CH	LM	CH	CH		XC	XC	CH	LM	GW	CH	LM	CH	XC		XC	CH	LM	XC
			◇	◇	◇1		◇			◇			◇1	◇		◇1	◇			◇1			◇		◇1
			A																						
Hereford	d																								
Ledbury	a																								
	d																								
Colwall	d																								
Great Malvern	a																								
	d														09 03	09 20								10 02	
Malvern Link	d														09 06	09 23								10 04	
Worcester Foregate Street	a														09 15	09 30								10 12	
	d														09 15	09 31								10 16	
Worcester Shrub Hill	a														09 18	09 33								10 18	
	d	22p47													09 23									10 22	
Droitwich Spa	d	22p55													09 32									10 30	
Bromsgrove	d																								
Barnt Green	d																								
University	d																								
Hartlebury	d																								
Kidderminster	d	23p05													09 42			10 08						10 40	
Blakedown	d	23p10													09 47			10 13							
Hagley	d	23p14													09 51			10 17						10 47	
Stourbridge Junction	d	23p18													09 55			10 22						10 52	
Lye	d																	10 25							
Cradley Heath	d														10 01			10 29						10 58	
Old Hill	d																	10 33							
Rowley Regis	d														10 06			10 36						11 03	
Langley Green	d																	10 39							
Birmingham New Street	a																								
	d				09 04								10 04							11 04					11 33
Birmingham International	d																								
Coventry	d					09 05						10 05										11 05			
Smethwick Galton Bridge	d														10 12			10 43						11 09	
The Hawthorns	d														10 15			10 45						11 12	
Jewellery Quarter	d														10 18			10 49						11 15	
Birmingham Snow Hill	a	23p36													10 20			10 52						11 17	
	d	23p37	07 40					09 19	09 40						10 22		10 40	10 53						11 19	
Birmingham Moor Street	d	23p40	07 43	08 55			09 13	09 22	09 43					10 13	10 25		10 43	10 56					11 13	11 22	
Bordesley	d																								
Small Heath	d	23p44																							
Tyseley	d	23p46						09 26							10 29									11 26	
Acocks Green	d	23p49																11 02							
Olton	d	23p52																11 04							
Solihull	d	23p56	07 51	09 04			09 22		09 52					10 22			10 52	11 08					11 22		
Widney Manor	d	23p59																11 11							
Dorridge	d	00 03	07 56	09 09			09 27		09 57					10 27			10 57	11a17					11 27		
Lapworth	d	00 07															11 02								
Hatton	d	00 13								10 15							11 08								
Warwick Parkway	d	00 18	08 06	09 18			09 37		10 08					10 37			11 13						11 37		
Warwick	d	00 21	08 09	09 22			09 41			10 23				10 41									11 41		
Leamington Spa	a	00 26	08 14	09 26	09 30	09 30	09 45		10 15	10 27		10 30	10 33	10 45			11 18			11 29		11 30	11 45		11 59
	d		08 15	09 27	09 38		09 46		10 16	10 27			10 38	10 46			11 18		11 20	11 38			11 46		12 00
Banbury	d		08 33	09 45	09a54		10 06		10 34	10 47			10a54	11 06			11 36			11a54			12 06		12a17
London Marylebone	a		09 47	10 46			11 14		11 47	12 11				12 14			12 47						13 14		
Spring Road	d							09 29							10 32									11 29	
Hall Green	d							09 32							10 35									11 32	
Yardley Wood	d							09 35							10 38									11 35	
Shirley	d							09 38							10 41									11 38	
Whitlocks End	d							09 41							10 44									11 41	
Wythall	d							09 43							10 46									11 43	
Earlswood (West Midlands)	d																								
The Lakes	d							09x46							10x49									11x46	
Wood End	d																								
Danzey	d																								
Henley-in-Arden	d							09 54							10 57									11 54	
Wootton Wawen	d																								
Wilmcote	d							10 04							11 05				11 43					12 02	
Stratford-upon-Avon	a							10 09							11 12				11 54					12 09	

A from 29 July until 12 August

Hereford, Worcester and Stourbridge - Birmingham - Leamington Spa, Marylebone and Stratford-upon-Avon

Network Diagram - see first Page of Table 71

		CH	LM	CH	XC	XC	CH	LM	GW	XC	CH	LM	CH	XC	XC	CH	LM	XC	CH	LM	CH	XC	CH
		◇		◇		◇1			◇1	◇1	◇		◇	◇1		◇		◇1	◇		◇	◇1	◇
					bus	trolley				trolley				trolley	bus			trolley				trolley	
Hereford	d																						
Ledbury	a																						
	d																						
Colwall	d																						
Great Malvern	a																						
	d							10 56	11 15								12 04						
Malvern Link	d							10 58	11 18								12 06						
Worcester Foregate Street	a							11 06	11 26								12 15						
	d							11 20	11 27								12 16						
Worcester Shrub Hill	a								11 29								12 18						
	d																12 24						
Droitwich Spa	d							11 29									12 32						
Bromsgrove	d																						
Barnt Green	d																						
University	d																						
Hartlebury	d																						
Kidderminster	d							11 39									12 42						
Blakedown	d																12 47						
Hagley	d							11 46									12 51						
Stourbridge Junction	d		11 22					11 52				12 22					12 55			13 22			
Lye	d		11 25									12 25								13 25			
Cradley Heath	d		11 29					11 58				12 29					13 01			13 29			
Old Hill	d		11 33									12 33								13 33			
Rowley Regis	d		11 36					12 03				12 36					13 06			13 36			
Langley Green	d		11 39									12 39								13 39			
Birmingham New Street	a																						
	d					12 04				12 33				13 04				13 33				14 04	
Birmingham International ✈	d																					14 14	
Coventry	d				12 05										13 05							14 25	
Smethwick Galton Bridge	d		11 43					12 08				12 43					13 11			13 43			
The Hawthorns	d		11 45					12 11				12 45					13 14			13 45			
Jewellery Quarter	d		11 49					12 14				12 49					13 17			13 49			
Birmingham Snow Hill	a		11 52					12 17				12 52					13 20			13 52			
	d	11 40	11 53					12 19			12 40	12 53					13 22		13 40	13 53			
Birmingham Moor Street	d	11 43	11 56				12 13	12 22			12 43	12 56				13 13	13 25		13 43	13 56			14 13
Bordesley	d																						
Small Heath	d																						
Tyseley	d							12 26									13 29						
Acocks Green	d		12 02									13 02								14 02			
Olton	d		12 04									13 04								14 04			
Solihull	d	11 52	12 08				12 22				12 52	13 08				13 22			13 52	14 08			14 22
Widney Manor	d		12 11									13 11								14 11			
Dorridge	d	11 57	12a17				12 27				12 57	13a18				13 27			13 57	14a17			14 27
Lapworth	d																		14 02				
Hatton	d			12 15															14 08		14 15		
Warwick Parkway	d	12 08					12 37				13 08					13 37			14 13				14 37
Warwick	d			12 23			12 41									13 41					14 23		14 41
Leamington Spa	a	12 15		12 27	12 30	12 33	12 45			12 59	13 15			13 29	13 30	13 45		13 59	14 18		14 27	14 36	14 45
	d	12 16		12 27		12 38	12 46			13 00	13 16		13 20	13 38		13 46		14 00	14 18		14 27	14 38	14 46
Banbury	d	12 34		12 47		12a54	13 06			13a17	13 34			13a54		14 06		14a17	14 36		14 47	14a54	15 06
London Marylebone ⊖	a	13 47		14 11			14 14				14 47					15 14			15 48		16 11		16 14
Spring Road	d							12 29									13 32						
Hall Green	d							12 32									13 35						
Yardley Wood	d							12 35									13 38						
Shirley	d							12 38									13 41						
Whitlocks End	d							12 41									13 44						
Wythall	d							12 43									13 46						
Earlswood (West Midlands)	d																						
The Lakes	d							12x46									13x49						
Wood End	d																						
Danzey	d																						
Henley-in-Arden	d							12 54									13 57						
Wootton Wawen	d																						
Wilmcote	d							13 02					13 43				14 05						
Stratford-upon-Avon	a							13 09					13 54				14 12						

Hereford, Worcester and Stourbridge - Birmingham - Leamington Spa, Marylebone and Stratford-upon-Avon

Network Diagram - see first Page of Table 71

		LM	GW	CH	LM	CH	XC	CH	LM	GW	XC	LM	CH	LM	CH	XC	CH	LM	GW	LM	XC	CH
			◇1	◇		◇	◇1	◇		◇1	◇1		◇		◇	◇1	◇		◇1		◇1	◇
							seat			seat	trolley					seat			seat		trolley	
Hereford	d									13 32									14 32			
Ledbury	a									13 49									14 49			
	d									13 50									14 55			
Colwall	d									13 57									15 02			
Great Malvern	a									14 02									15 07			
	d		13 15							14 11		14 35							15 08			
Malvern Link	d		13 18							14 15		14 37							15 12			
Worcester Foregate Street	a		13 25							14 24		14 45							15 21			
	d	13 20	13 26						14 20	14 26		14 45						15 20	15 23			
Worcester Shrub Hill	a		13 29							14 29		14 48							15 26			
	d											14 53								15 46		
Droitwich Spa	d	13 29							14 29			15 01						15 29		15 54		
Bromsgrove	d											15 10										
Barnt Green	d																					
University	d																					
Hartlebury	d																					
Kidderminster	d	13 39							14 39									15 40		16 04		
Blakedown	d								14 44													
Hagley	d	13 46							14 48									15 47		16 11		
Stourbridge Junction	d	13 52			14 22				14 52					15 22				15 52		16 16		
Lye	d				14 25									15 25								
Cradley Heath	d	13 58			14 29				14 58					15 29				15 58				
Old Hill	d				14 33									15 33								
Rowley Regis	d	14 03			14 36				15 03					15 36				16 03				
Langley Green	d				14 39									15 39								
Birmingham New Street	a											15 37										
	d						15 04				15 33					16 04					16 33	
Birmingham International ✈	d						15 14									16 14						
Coventry	d						15 25									16 25						
Smethwick Galton Bridge	d	14 08			14 43				15 08					15 43				16 08		16 29		
The Hawthorns	d	14 11			14 45				15 11					15 45				16 11				
Jewellery Quarter	d	14 14			14 49				15 14					15 49				16 14				
Birmingham Snow Hill	a	14 17			14 52				15 17					15 52				16 17		16 35		
	d	14 19		14 40	14 53				15 19				15 40	15 53				16 19		16 45		16 40
Birmingham Moor Street	d	14 22		14 43	14 56			15 13	15 22				15 43	15 56			16 13	16 22		16a47		16 43
Bordesley	d																					
Small Heath	d																					
Tyseley	d	14 26							15 26									16 26				
Acocks Green	d				15 02									16 02								
Olton	d				15 04									16 04								
Solihull	d			14 52	15 08			15 22					15 52	16 08			16 22					16 52
Widney Manor	d				15 11									16 11								
Dorridge	d			14 57	15a17			15 27					15 57	16a17			16 27					16 57
Lapworth	d												16 02									
Hatton	d												16 08		16 15							
Warwick Parkway	d			15 08				15 37					16 13				16 37					17 08
Warwick	d							15 41							16 23		16 41					
Leamington Spa	a			15 15			15 36	15 45			15 59		16 18		16 27	16 36	16 45				16 59	17 15
	d			15 16		15 20	15 38	15 46			16 00		16 18		16 27	16 38	16 46				17 00	17 16
Banbury	d			15 34			15a54	16 06			16a17		16 36		16 47	16a54	17 06				17a17	17 34
London Marylebone ⊖	a			16 47				17 14					17 48		18 11		18 14					18 47
Spring Road	d	14 29							15 29									16 29				
Hall Green	d	14 32							15 32									16 32				
Yardley Wood	d	14 35							15 35									16 35				
Shirley	d	14 38							15 38									16 38				
Whitlocks End	d	14 40							15 41									16 41				
Wythall	d	14 43							15 43									16 43				
Earlswood (West Midlands)	d																					
The Lakes	d	14x46							15x46									16x46				
Wood End	d																					
Danzey	d																					
Henley-in-Arden	d	14 53							15 54									16 55				
Wootton Wawen	d																					
Wilmcote	d	15 01				15 43			16 02									17 03				
Stratford-upon-Avon	a	15 07				15 54			16 09									17 10				

1 July to 9 September

Hereford, Worcester and Stourbridge - Birmingham - Leamington Spa, Marylebone and Stratford-upon-Avon

Network Diagram - see first Page of Table 71

		LM	CH	XC	LM	CH	LM	GW		XC	CH	LM	CH	XC	CH	LM	LM	XC		CH	CH	XC	CH	LM	GW
			◇	◇■		◇		◇■		◇■			◇	◇■	◇			◇■		◇	◇	◇■	◇		◇■
Hereford ■	d				15 30			16 35																	
Ledbury	a				15 47			16 51																	
	d				15 51			16 52																	
Colwall	d				15 58			17 00																	
Great Malvern	a				16 02			17 04																	
	d				16 03			17 05									17 17								
Malvern Link	d				16 05			17 09									17 20								
Worcester Foregate Street ■	a				16 14			17 20									17 28								
	d				16 15		16 20	17 22								17 20	17 28							18 20	18 25
Worcester Shrub Hill ■	a				16 18			17 27									17 31								18 26
	d				16 33												17 36								
Droitwich Spa	d				16 41		16 29									17 29	17 44							18 29	
Bromsgrove	d				16 51												17 53								
Barnt Green	d																								
University	d																								
Hartlebury	d																								
Kidderminster	d						16 39									17 39								18 39	
Blakedown	d															17 44									
Hagley	d						16 46									17 48								18 46	
Stourbridge Junction ■	d	16 22					16 52					17 22				17 52								18 52	
Lye	d	16 25										17 25													
Cradley Heath	d	16 29					16 58					17 29				17 58								18 58	
Old Hill	d	16 33										17 33													
Rowley Regis	d	16 36					17 03					17 36				18 03								19 03	
Langley Green	d	16 39										17 39													
Birmingham New Street ■	a				17 17												18 15								
	d			17 04						17 33				18 04				18 33				19 04			
Birmingham International ✈	d			17 14										18 14								19 14			
Coventry	d			17 25										18 25								19 25			
Smethwick Galton Bridge ■	d	16 43					17 08					17 43				18 08								19 08	
The Hawthorns	d	16 45					17 11					17 45				18 11								19 11	
Jewellery Quarter	d	16 49					17 14					17 49				18 14								19 14	
Birmingham Snow Hill	a	16 52					17 17					17 53				18 17								19 19	
	d	16 53					17 19				17 40	17 53				18 19				18 40			19 15	19 21	
Birmingham Moor Street	d	16 56				17 13	17 22				17 43	17 56			18 13	18 22				18 43			19 18	19a23	
Bordesley	d																								
Small Heath	d																								
Tyseley	d						17 26									18 26									
Acocks Green	d	17 02										18 02													
Olton	d	17 04										18 04													
Solihull	d	17 08				17 22					17 52	18 08			18 22					18 52			19 26		
Widney Manor	d	17 11										18 11											19 30		
Dorridge	d	17a17				17 27					17 57	18a17			18 27					18 57			19 34		
Lapworth	d										18 02												19 38		
Hatton	d										18 08		18 15										19 44		
Warwick Parkway	d					17 37					18 13				18 37					19 08			19 49		
Warwick	d					17 41							18 23		18 41								19 52		
Leamington Spa ■	a			17 36		17 45				18 00	18 18		18 27	18 36	18 45			18 59		19 15		19 36	19 56		
	d		17 20	17 38		17 46				18 01	18 18		18 27	18 38	18 46			19 00		19 16	19 20	19 38	19 57		
Banbury	d			17a54		18 06				18a19	18 36		18 47	18a54	19 06			19a17		19 34		19a54	20 15		
London Marylebone ■ ⊖	a					19 14					19 48		20 11		20 14					20 47			21 50		
Spring Road	d						17 29									18 29									
Hall Green	d						17 32									18 32									
Yardley Wood	d						17 35									18 35									
Shirley	d						17 38									18 38									
Whitlocks End	d						17 41									18 41									
Wythall	d						17 43									18 43									
Earlswood (West Midlands)	d																								
The Lakes	d						17x46									18x46									
Wood End	d																								
Danzey	d																								
Henley-in-Arden	d						17 54									18 54									
Wootton Wawen	d																								
Wilmcote	d		17 43				18 02									19 02					19 43				
Stratford-upon-Avon	a		17 54				18 09									19 09					19 54				

1 July to 9 September

Hereford, Worcester and Stourbridge - Birmingham - Leamington Spa, Marylebone and Stratford-upon-Avon

Network Diagram - see first Page of Table 71

		GW	XC	CH		XC	CH	LM	XC	LM	GW	XC	CH	LM		LM	LM	LM	LM
		◇■	◇■	◇		◇■	◇		◇■		◇■	◇■	◇						
Hereford ■	d	18 30														20 05			22 40
Ledbury	a	18 47														20 21			22 56
	d	18 48														20 22			22 56
Colwall	d	18 55														20 28			23 03
Great Malvern	a	19 00														20 33			23 07
	d	19 11									20 15					20 33		22 10	23 08
Malvern Link	d	19 14									20 18					20 36		22 13	23 10
Worcester Foregate Street ■	a	19 23									20 25					20 44		22 22	23 19
	d	19 29									20 26					20 45		22 23	23 22
Worcester Shrub Hill ■	a	19 31									20 29					20 47		22 25	23 24
	d							19 38		19 53				20 34		20 52	21 25	22 29	
Droitwich Spa	d							19 46		20 01				20 42		21 00	21 33	22 37	
Bromsgrove	d									20 10						21 09			
Barnt Green	d																		
University	d																		
Hartlebury	d																		
Kidderminster	d							19 56						20 52			21 43	22 47	
Blakedown	d																		
Hagley	d							20 03						20 59			21 50	22 54	
Stourbridge Junction ■	d							20 07						21 03			21 54	22 58	
Lye	d																		
Cradley Heath	d							20 13						21 08			21 59	23 04	
Old Hill	d																		
Rowley Regis	d							20 19						21 14			22 05	23 09	
Langley Green	d																		
Birmingham New Street ■	a									20 36						21 42			
	d		19 33			20 04			20 33			21 04							
Birmingham International ✈	d					20 14						21 14							
Coventry	d					20 25						21 24							
Smethwick Galton Bridge ■	d							20 24						21 19			22 10	23 14	
The Hawthorns	d							20 26						21 21			22 12	23 17	
Jewellery Quarter	d							20 30						21 25			22 16	23 20	
Birmingham Snow Hill	a							20 33						21 28			22 19	23 24	
	d						20 15	20 33					21 15	21 28			22 20		
Birmingham Moor Street	d						20 18	20a36					21 18	21a31			22a22		
Bordesley	d																		
Small Heath	d																		
Tyseley	d																		
Acocks Green	d																		
Olton	d																		
Solihull	d						20 26						21 26						
Widney Manor	d						20 30						21 30						
Dorridge	d						20 34						21 34						
Lapworth	d																		
Hatton	d			20 15															
Warwick Parkway	d						20 46						21 46						
Warwick	d			20 23			20 49						21 49						
Leamington Spa ■	a		19 59	20 27		20 36	20 53		20 58			21 34	21 53						
	d		20 00	20 27		20 38	20 54		21 00				21 54						
Banbury	d		20a18	20 47		20a54	21 13		21a17				22 15						
London Marylebone ■ ⊖	a			21 58			22 52						23 52						
Spring Road	d																		
Hall Green	d																		
Yardley Wood	d																		
Shirley	d																		
Whitlocks End	d																		
Wythall	d																		
Earlswood (West Midlands)	d																		
The Lakes	d																		
Wood End	d																		
Danzey	d																		
Henley-in-Arden	d																		
Wootton Wawen	d																		
Wilmcote	d																		
Stratford-upon-Avon	a																		

Table 71

Sundays from 16 September

Hereford, Worcester and Stourbridge - Birmingham - Leamington Spa, Marylebone and Stratford-upon-Avon

Network Diagram - see first Page of Table 71

		LM	CH	XC	CH	LM	CH	CH	XC	CH	LM	GW	CH	LM	CH	XC	CH	LM	CH	LM	CH	XC	CH
			◇	◇1	◇			◇	◇1	◇		◇1	◇			◇1	◇		◇		◇	◇1	
Hereford 7	d																						
Ledbury	a																						
	d																						
Colwall	d																						
Great Malvern	a																						
	d										09 03	09 20						10 02					
Malvern Link	d										09 06	09 23						10 04					
Worcester Foregate Street 7	a										09 15	09 30						10 12					
	d										09 15	09 31						10 16					
Worcester Shrub Hill 7	a										09 18	09 33						10 18					
	d	22p47									09 23							10 22					
Droitwich Spa	d	22p55									09 32							10 30					
Bromsgrove	d																						
Barnt Green	d																						
University	d																						
Hartlebury	d																						
Kidderminster	d	23p05									09 42			10 08				10 40					
Blakedown	d	23p10									09 47			10 13									
Hagley	d	23p14									09 51			10 17				10 47					
Stourbridge Junction 2	d	23p18									09 55			10 22				10 52		11 22			
Lye	d													10 25						11 25			
Cradley Heath	d										10 01			10 29				10 58		11 29			
Old Hill	d													10 33						11 33			
Rowley Regis	d										10 06			10 36				11 03		11 36			
Langley Green	d													10 39						11 39			
Birmingham New Street 12	a																						
	d			09 04					10 04							11 04						12 04	
Birmingham International ✈	d			09 14					10 14							11 14						12 14	
Coventry	d			09 25					10 25							11 25						12 25	
Smethwick Galton Bridge 7	d										10 12			10 43				11 09		11 43			
The Hawthorns	d										10 15			10 45				11 12		11 45			
Jewellery Quarter	d										10 18			10 49				11 15		11 49			
Birmingham Snow Hill	a	23p36									10 20			10 52				11 17		11 52			
	d	23p37				09 19	09 40				10 22		10 40	10 53				11 19	11 40	11 53			
Birmingham Moor Street	d	23p40	08 55		09 13	09 22	09 43			10 13	10 25		10 43	10 56			11 13	11 22	11 43	11 56			12 13
Bordesley	d																						
Small Heath	d	23p44																					
Tyseley	d	23p46				09 26					10 29							11 26					
Acocks Green	d	23p49												11 02						12 02			
Olton	d	23p52												11 04						12 04			
Solihull	d	23p56	09 04		09 22		09 52			10 22			10 52	11 08			11 22		11 52	12 08			12 22
Widney Manor	d	23p59												11 11						12 11			
Dorridge	d	00 03	09 09		09 27		09 57			10 27			10 57	11a17			11 27		11 57	12a17			12 27
Lapworth	d	00 07											11 02										
Hatton	d	00 13						10 15					11 08								12 15		
Warwick Parkway	d	00 18	09 18		09 37		10 08			10 37			11 13				11 37		12 08				12 37
Warwick	d	00 21	09 22		09 41			10 23		10 41							11 41				12 23		12 41
Leamington Spa 8	a	00 26	09 26	09 36	09 45		10 15	10 27	10 36	10 45			11 18			11 36	11 45		12 15		12 27	12 36	12 45
	d		09 27	09 38	09 46		10 16	10 27	10 38	10 46			11 18		11 20	11 38	11 46		12 16		12 27	12 38	12 46
Banbury	d		09 45	09a54	10 06		10 34	10 47	10a54	11 06			11 36			11a54	12 06		12 34		12 47	12a54	13 06
London Marylebone 10 ⊖	a		10 46		11 14		11 47	12 11		12 14			12 47				13 14		13 47		14 11		14 14
Spring Road	d					09 29					10 32							11 29					
Hall Green	d					09 32					10 35							11 32					
Yardley Wood	d					09 35					10 38							11 35					
Shirley	d					09 38					10 41							11 38					
Whitlocks End	d					09 41					10 44							11 41					
Wythall	d					09 43					10 46							11 43					
Earlswood (West Midlands)	d																						
The Lakes	d					09x46					10x49							11x46					
Wood End	d																						
Danzey	d																						
Henley-in-Arden	d					09 54					10 57							11 54					
Wootton Wawen	d																						
Wilmcote	d					10 04					11 05				11 43			12 02					
Stratford-upon-Avon	a					10 09					11 12				11 54			12 09					

Table 71

Sundays from 16 September

Hereford, Worcester and Stourbridge - Birmingham - Leamington Spa, Marylebone and Stratford-upon-Avon

Network Diagram - see first Page of Table 71

		LM	GW	XC	CH	LM	CH	XC	CH	LM	XC	CH	LM	CH	XC	CH	LM	GW	XC	CH	LM	CH	XC
			◇1	◇1	◇		◇	◇1	◇		◇1	◇		◇	◇1	◇		◇1	◇1	◇		◇	◇1
Hereford 7	d																						
Ledbury	a																						
	d																						
Colwall	d																						
Great Malvern	a																						
	d	10 56	11 15							12 04								13 15					
Malvern Link	d	10 58	11 18							12 06								13 18					
Worcester Foregate Street 7	a	11 06	11 26							12 15								13 25					
	d	11 20	11 27							12 16							13 20	13 26					
Worcester Shrub Hill 7	a		11 29							12 18								13 29					
	d									12 24													
Droitwich Spa	d	11 29								12 32							13 29						
Bromsgrove	d																						
Barnt Green	d																						
University	d																						
Hartlebury	d																						
Kidderminster	d	11 39								12 42							13 39						
Blakedown	d									12 47													
Hagley	d	11 46								12 51							13 46						
Stourbridge Junction 2	d	11 52				12 22				12 55			13 22				13 52				14 22		
Lye	d					12 25							13 25								14 25		
Cradley Heath	d	11 58				12 29				13 01			13 29				13 58				14 29		
Old Hill	d					12 33							13 33								14 33		
Rowley Regis	d	12 03				12 36				13 06			13 36				14 03				14 36		
Langley Green	d					12 39							13 39								14 39		
Birmingham New Street 12	a																						
	d			12 33				13 04			13 33				14 04				14 33				15 04
Birmingham International ✈	d							13 14							14 14								15 14
Coventry	d							13 25							14 25								15 25
Smethwick Galton Bridge 7	d	12 08				12 43				13 11			13 43				14 08				14 43		
The Hawthorns	d	12 11				12 45				13 14			13 45				14 11				14 45		
Jewellery Quarter	d	12 14				12 49				13 17			13 49				14 14				14 49		
Birmingham Snow Hill	a	12 17				12 52				13 20			13 52				14 17				14 52		
	d	12 19			12 40	12 53				13 22		13 40	13 53				14 19			14 40	14 53		
Birmingham Moor Street	d	12 22			12 43	12 56			13 13	13 25		13 43	13 56			14 13	14 22			14 43	14 56		
Bordesley	d																						
Small Heath	d																						
Tyseley	d	12 26								13 29							14 26						
Acocks Green	d					13 02							14 02								15 02		
Olton	d					13 04							14 04								15 04		
Solihull	d				12 52	13 08			13 22			13 52	14 08			14 22				14 52	15 08		
Widney Manor	d					13 11							14 11								15 11		
Dorridge	d				12 57	13a18			13 27			13 57	14a17			14 27				14 57	15a17		
Lapworth	d											14 02											
Hatton	d											14 08		14 15									
Warwick Parkway	d				13 08				13 37			14 13				14 37				15 08			
Warwick	d								13 41					14 23		14 41							
Leamington Spa 8	a			12 59	13 15			13 36	13 45		13 59	14 18		14 27	14 36	14 45			14 59	15 15			15 36
	d			13 00	13 16		13 20	13 38	13 46		14 00	14 18		14 27	14 38	14 46			15 00	15 16		15 20	15 38
Banbury	d			13a17	13 34			13a54	14 06		14a17	14 36		14 47	14a54	15 06			15a18	15 34			15a54
London Marylebone 10 ⊖	a				14 47				15 14			15 48		16 11		16 14				16 47			
Spring Road	d	12 29								13 32							14 29						
Hall Green	d	12 32								13 35							14 32						
Yardley Wood	d	12 35								13 38							14 35						
Shirley	d	12 38								13 41							14 38						
Whitlocks End	d	12 41								13 44							14 40						
Wythall	d	12 43								13 46							14 43						
Earlswood (West Midlands)	d																						
The Lakes	d	12x46								13x49							14x46						
Wood End	d																						
Danzey	d																						
Henley-in-Arden	d	12 54								13 57							14 53						
Wootton Wawen	d																						
Wilmcote	d	13 02					13 43			14 05							15 01					15 43	
Stratford-upon-Avon	a	13 09					13 54			14 12							15 07					15 54	

Table 71

Sundays
from 16 September

Hereford, Worcester and Stourbridge - Birmingham - Leamington Spa, Marylebone and Stratford-upon-Avon

Network Diagram - see first Page of Table 71

		CH	LM	GW	XC	LM	CH	LM	CH	XC	CH	LM	GW	LM	XC	CH	LM	CH	XC	LM	CH	LM
		◇		◇1	◇1		◇		◇	◇1	◇		◇1		◇1	◇		◇	◇1		◇	
				⊐	⊼					⊐			⊐		⊼				⊐			
Hereford	d			13 32									14 32							15 30		
Ledbury	a			13 49									14 49							15 47		
	d			13 50									14 55							15 51		
Colwall	d			13 57									15 02							15 58		
Great Malvern	a			14 02									15 07							16 02		
	d			14 11		14 35							15 08							16 03		
Malvern Link	d			14 15		14 37							15 12							16 05		
Worcester Foregate Street	a			14 24		14 45							15 21							16 14		
	d		14 20	14 26		14 45						15 20	15 23							16 15		16 20
Worcester Shrub Hill	a			14 29		14 48							15 26							16 18		
	d					14 53								15 46						16 33		
Droitwich Spa	d		14 29			15 01						15 29		15 54						16 41		16 29
Bromsgrove	d					15 10														16 51		
Barnt Green	d																					
University	d																					
Hartlebury	d																					
Kidderminster	d		14 39									15 40		16 04								16 39
Blakedown	d		14 44																			
Hagley	d		14 48									15 47		16 11								16 46
Stourbridge Junction	d		14 52					15 22				15 52		16 16			16 22					16 52
Lye	d							15 25									16 25					
Cradley Heath	d		14 58					15 29				15 58					16 29					16 58
Old Hill	d							15 33									16 33					
Rowley Regis	d		15 03					15 36				16 03					16 36					17 03
Langley Green	d							15 39									16 39					
Birmingham New Street	a					15 37														17 17		
	d				15 33					16 04					16 33				17 04			
Birmingham International ✈	d									16 14									17 14			
Coventry	d									16 25									17 25			
Smethwick Galton Bridge	d		15 08					15 43				16 08		16 29			16 43					17 08
The Hawthorns	d		15 11					15 45				16 11					16 45					17 11
Jewellery Quarter	d		15 14					15 49				16 14					16 49					17 14
Birmingham Snow Hill	a		15 17					15 52				16 17		16 35			16 52					17 17
	d		15 19				15 40	15 53				16 19		16 45		16 40	16 53					17 19
Birmingham Moor Street	d	15 13	15 22				15 43	15 56			16 13	16 22		16a47		16 43	16 56				17 13	17 22
Bordesley	d																					
Small Heath	d																					
Tyseley	d		15 26									16 26										17 26
Acocks Green	d							16 02									17 02					
Olton	d							16 04									17 04					
Solihull	d	15 22					15 52	16 08			16 22					16 52	17 08				17 22	
Widney Manor	d							16 11									17 11					
Dorridge	d	15 27					15 57	16a17			16 27					16 57	17a17				17 27	
Lapworth	d						16 02															
Hatton	d						16 08		16 15													
Warwick Parkway	d	15 37					16 13				16 37					17 08					17 37	
Warwick	d	15 41							16 23		16 41										17 41	
Leamington Spa	a	15 45			15 59		16 18		16 27	16 36	16 45				16 59	17 15			17 36		17 45	
	d	15 46			16 00		16 18		16 27	16 38	16 46				17 00	17 16		17 20	17 38		17 46	
Banbury	d	16 06			16a17		16 36		16 47	16a54	17 06				17a17	17 34			17a54		18 06	
London Marylebone ⊖	a	17 14					17 48		18 11		18 14					18 47					19 14	
Spring Road	d		15 29									16 29										17 29
Hall Green	d		15 32									16 32										17 32
Yardley Wood	d		15 35									16 35										17 35
Shirley	d		15 38									16 38										17 38
Whitlocks End	d		15 41									16 41										17 41
Wythall	d		15 43									16 43										17 43
Earlswood (West Midlands)	d																					
The Lakes	d		15x46									16x46										17x46
Wood End	d																					
Danzey	d																					
Henley-in-Arden	d		15 54									16 55										17 54
Wootton Wawen	d																					
Wilmcote	d		16 02									17 03						17 43				18 02
Stratford-upon-Avon	a		16 09									17 10						17 54				18 09

Table 71

Sundays
from 16 September

Hereford, Worcester and Stourbridge - Birmingham - Leamington Spa, Marylebone and Stratford-upon-Avon

Network Diagram - see first Page of Table 71

		GW	XC	CH	LM	CH	XC	CH	LM	LM	XC	CH	CH	XC	CH	LM	GW	GW	XC	CH	XC	CH	LM
		◇1	◇1			◇	◇1	◇			◇1	◇	◇	◇1	◇		◇1	◇1	◇1	◇	◇1	◇	
		⊐	⊼				⊐				⊼			⊐					⊼		⊐		
Hereford	d	16 35																18 30					
Ledbury	a	16 51																18 47					
	d	16 52																18 48					
Colwall	d	17 00																18 55					
Great Malvern	a	17 04																19 00					
	d	17 05								17 17								19 11					
Malvern Link	d	17 09								17 20								19 14					
Worcester Foregate Street	a	17 20								17 28								19 23					
	d	17 22							17 20	17 28						18 20	18 25	19 29					
Worcester Shrub Hill	a	17 26								17 31							18 26	19 31					
	d									17 36													19 38
Droitwich Spa	d								17 29	17 44						18 29							19 46
Bromsgrove	d									17 53													
Barnt Green	d																						
University	d																						
Hartlebury	d																						
Kidderminster	d								17 39							18 39							19 56
Blakedown	d								17 44														
Hagley	d								17 48							18 46							20 03
Stourbridge Junction	d				17 22				17 52							18 52							20 07
Lye	d				17 25																		
Cradley Heath	d				17 29				17 58							18 58							20 13
Old Hill	d				17 33																		
Rowley Regis	d				17 36				18 03							19 03							20 19
Langley Green	d				17 39																		
Birmingham New Street	a									18 15													
	d		17 33				18 04				18 33			19 04					19 33		20 04		
Birmingham International ✈	d						18 14							19 14							20 14		
Coventry	d						18 25							19 25							20 25		
Smethwick Galton Bridge	d				17 43				18 08							19 08							20 24
The Hawthorns	d				17 45				18 11							19 11							20 26
Jewellery Quarter	d				17 49				18 14							19 14							20 30
Birmingham Snow Hill	a				17 53				18 17							19 19							20 33
	d			17 40	17 53				18 19			18 40			19 15	19 21						20 15	20 33
Birmingham Moor Street	d			17 43	17 56			18 13	18 22			18 43			19 18	19a23						20 18	20a36
Bordesley	d																						
Small Heath	d																						
Tyseley	d								18 26														
Acocks Green	d				18 02																		
Olton	d				18 04																		
Solihull	d			17 52	18 08			18 22				18 52			19 26							20 26	
Widney Manor	d				18 11										19 30							20 30	
Dorridge	d			17 57	18a17			18 27				18 57			19 34							20 34	
Lapworth	d			18 02											19 38								
Hatton	d			18 08		18 15									19 44					20 15			
Warwick Parkway	d			18 13				18 37				19 08			19 49							20 46	
Warwick	d					18 23		18 41							19 52					20 23		20 49	
Leamington Spa	a		18 00	18 18		18 27	18 36	18 45			18 59	19 15		19 36	19 56				19 59	20 27	20 36	20 53	
	d		18 01	18 18		18 27	18 38	18 46			19 00	19 16	19 20	19 38	19 57				20 00	20 27	20 38	20 54	
Banbury	d		18a19	18 36		18 47	18a54	19 06			19a17	19 34		19a54	20 15				20a18	20 47	20a54	21 13	
London Marylebone ⊖	a			19 48		20 11		20 14				20 47			21 50					21 58		22 52	
Spring Road	d								18 29														
Hall Green	d								18 32														
Yardley Wood	d								18 35														
Shirley	d								18 38														
Whitlocks End	d								18 41														
Wythall	d								18 43														
Earlswood (West Midlands)	d																						
The Lakes	d								18x46														
Wood End	d																						
Danzey	d																						
Henley-in-Arden	d								18 54														
Wootton Wawen	d																						
Wilmcote	d								19 02				19 43										
Stratford-upon-Avon	a								19 09				19 54										

Sundays
from 16 September

Hereford, Worcester and Stourbridge - Birmingham - Leamington Spa, Marylebone and Stratford-upon-Avon

Network Diagram - see first Page of Table 71

		XC	LM	GW	XC	CH	LM	LM	LM	LM	LM
		◇■ ✠		◇■	◇■	◇					
Hereford ■	d							20 05			22 40
Ledbury	a							20 21			22 56
	d							20 22			22 56
Colwall	d							20 28			23 03
Great Malvern	a							20 33			23 07
	d			20 15				20 33		22 10	23 08
Malvern Link	d			20 18				20 36		22 13	23 10
Worcester Foregate Street ■	a			20 25				20 44		22 22	23 19
	d			20 26				20 45		22 23	23 22
Worcester Shrub Hill ■	a			20 29				20 47		22 25	23 24
	d		19 53				20 34	20 52	21 25	22 29	
Droitwich Spa	d		20 01				20 42	21 00	21 33	22 37	
Bromsgrove	d		20 10					21 09			
Barnt Green	d										
University	d										
Hartlebury	d										
Kidderminster	d						20 52		21 43	22 47	
Blakedown	d										
Hagley	d						20 59		21 50	22 54	
Stourbridge Junction ■	d						21 03		21 54	22 58	
Lye	d										
Cradley Heath	d						21 08		21 59	23 04	
Old Hill	d										
Rowley Regis	d						21 14		22 05	23 09	
Langley Green	d										
Birmingham New Street ■	a		20 36					21 42			
	d	20 33			21 04						
Birmingham International ✈	d				21 14						
Coventry	d				21 24						
Smethwick Galton Bridge ■	d						21 19		22 10	23 14	
The Hawthorns	d						21 21		22 12	23 17	
Jewellery Quarter	d						21 25		22 16	23 20	
Birmingham Snow Hill	a						21 28		22 19	23 24	
	d					21 15	21 28		22 20		
Birmingham Moor Street	d					21 18	21a31		22a22		
Bordesley	d										
Small Heath	d										
Tyseley	d										
Acocks Green	d										
Olton	d										
Solihull	d					21 26					
Widney Manor	d					21 30					
Dorridge	d					21 34					
Lapworth	d										
Hatton	d										
Warwick Parkway	d					21 46					
Warwick	d					21 49					
Leamington Spa ■	a	20 58			21 34	21 53					
	d	21 00				21 54					
Banbury	d	21a17				22 15					
London Marylebone ■ ⊖	a					23 52					
Spring Road	d										
Hall Green	d										
Yardley Wood	d										
Shirley	d										
Whitlocks End	d										
Wythall	d										
Earlswood (West Midlands)	d										
The Lakes	d										
Wood End	d										
Danzey	d										
Henley-in-Arden	d										
Wootton Wawen	d										
Wilmcote	d										
Stratford-upon-Avon	a										

Mondays to Fridays

Stratford-upon-Avon, Marylebone and Leamington Spa - Birmingham - Stourbridge, Worcester and Hereford

Network Diagram - see first Page of Table 71

Miles	Miles	Miles			LM MX	XC MX	CH MX	CH MX	CH	LM	GW	LM	LM		LM	LM	CH	LM	GW	LM	GW	LM	CH		LM
						A 🚌	◇	◇	◇ B		■						◇				◇■ ✠				
—	0	—	**Stratford-upon-Avon**	d																			06 10		06 27
—	2¾	—	Wilmcote	d																			06 16		06 32
—	6½	—	Wootton Wawen	d																					06x37
—	8¼	—	Henley-in-Arden	d																					06 41
—	11¼	—	Danzey	d																					06x46
—	13	—	Wood End	d																					06x50
—	14¼	—	The Lakes	d																					06x53
—	15	—	Earlswood (West Midlands)	d																					06 55
—	16	—	Wythall	d																					06 58
—	17	—	Whitlocks End	d												06 28		06 46							07 00
—	18	—	Shirley	d												06 31		06 52							07 03
—	19¼	—	Yardley Wood	d												06 34		06 55							07 06
—	20½	—	Hall Green	d												06 37		06 58							07 09
—	21	—	Spring Road	d												06 39		07 00							07 11
—	—	—	**London Marylebone** ■ ⊖	d			22p37	23p07	01 30																
—	—	—	Banbury	d			23p39	00 03	02 36								06 07								
—	—	0	**Leamington Spa** ■	a			23p56	00 20	02 54								06 24						06 45		
—	—	—		d		23p20	23p56	00 21	02 54				05 47				06 25					06 29			
—	—	2	Warwick	d			23p59	00 25	02 59				05 51				06 29					06 33			
—	—	3¼	Warwick Parkway	d			00 04	00 29	03 02				05 55				06 33					06 37			
—	—	6	Hatton	d									06 00									06 42			
—	—	10¼	Lapworth	d									06 06									06 48			
—	—	12¾	Dorridge	d	22p33		00 14		03 12			05 40	06 11				06 44					06 53			
—	—	14¾	Widney Manor	d	22p37							05 45	06 14									06 56			
—	—	16¼	Solihull	d	22p41		00 19	00 41				05 48	06 18				06 49					07 00			
—	—	18	Olton	d	22p44							05 52	06 21									07 03			
—	—	19	Acocks Green	d	22p47							05 54	06 24									07 06			
—	22	20	Tyseley	d	22p50							05 57	06 27			06 42		07 03				07 09			07 14
—	23	21	Small Heath	d	22p52							06 00	06 29			06 44		07 05				07 11			07 17
—	24	—	Bordesley	d																					
—	24¾	—	**Birmingham Moor Street**	d	22p56		00a33	00a55	03 23			06 04	06 33			06 48	07a03	07 09				07 16			07 22
—	25¼	—	**Birmingham Snow Hill**	a	22p59				03 32			06 06	06 37			06 51		07 12				07 19			07 24
—	—	—		d	23p00							06 08				06 53		07 13				07 23			
—	26	—	Jewellery Quarter	d	23p02							06 10				06 55		07 15				07 25			
—	28½	—	The Hawthorns	d	23p07							06 15				07 00		07 20				07 30			
—	29¼	29	Smethwick Galton Bridge ■	d	23p10							06 17				07 03		07 23				07 33			
—	—	—	**Coventry**	a		23b40																			
—	—	—	**Birmingham International** ✈	a		00 10																			
0	—	24	**Birmingham New Street** ■	a																					
—	—	—		d											06 59					07 19					
—	30½	30¼	Langley Green	d	23p13							06 20				07 06						07 36			
—	32¼	—	Rowley Regis	d	23p16							06 24				07 09		07 28				07 39			
—	33½	—	Old Hill	d	23p19							06 27				07 12						07 42			
—	34¾	—	Cradley Heath	d	23p23							06 30				07 16		07 33				07 46			
—	36¼	—	Lye	d	23p26							06 33				07 19						07 49			
—	37¼	—	**Stourbridge Junction** ■	d	23p30							06 37				07 23		07a39				07 53			
—	39¼	—	Hagley	d	23p33							06 40				07 26						07 56			
—	41	—	Blakedown	d	23p36							06 43				07 29						07 59			
—	44¼	—	**Kidderminster**	d	23p41							06 48				07 34						08 04			
—	47¾	—	Hartlebury	d												07 39						08 09			
2½	—	—	University	d											07 05					07 25					
10½	—	—	Barnt Green	d																07 41					
13	—	—	Bromsgrove	d											07 22					07 46					
19¼	53½	—	Droitwich Spa	d	23p52							06 59			07 32	07 46				07 56		08 17			
25	—	—	**Worcester Shrub Hill** ■	a	00 01															08 03		08 25			
—	—	—		d						06 00	06 33								07 55	08 07	08 14	08 29			
25¾	58¾	—	**Worcester Foregate Street** ■	a						06 02	06 39	07 09			07 42	07 57			07 58	08 09	08 17	08 31			
—	—	—		d						06 03					07 43				07 58	08 11					
32½	—	—	Malvern Link	d						06 12					07 53				08 07	08 20					
33¾	—	—	**Great Malvern**	a						06 15					07 56				08 12	08 22					
—	—	—		d						06 15					07 59										
36½	—	—	Colwall	d						06 20					08 04										
40¾	—	—	Ledbury	a						06 27					08 11										
—	—	—		d						06 29					08 12										
54½	—	—	**Hereford** ■	a						06 50					08 32										

A from 26 June until 14 September

B from 30 July until 13 August

b Previous night, stops to set down only

Stratford-upon-Avon, Marylebone and Leamington Spa - Birmingham - Stourbridge, Worcester and Hereford

Network Diagram - see first Page of Table 71

Station		CH	LM	LM	LM	LM	XC	CH	CH	LM	XC	LM	LM	LM	GW	LM	LM	LM	XC	CH	LM	CH	LM
							◇1 ⊼	◇			◇1 ⊼				1 ⊼				◇1 ⊼	◇		◇ ⊼	
Stratford-upon-Avon	d				06 52			06 47		07 23						07 42				07 35			
Wilmcote	d				06 57											07 47				07 41			
Wootton Wawen	d				07x02											07x52							
Henley-in-Arden	d				07 06					07 34						07 57							
Danzey	d				07x11											08x02							
Wood End	d				07x15											08x06							
The Lakes	d				07x18											08x08							
Earlswood (West Midlands)	d				07 20					07 42						08 11							
Wythall	d				07 23					07 44						08 14							
Whitlocks End	d				07 26					07 47			08 07			08 16					08 35		
Shirley	d				07 29					07 50			08 10			08 20					08 38		
Yardley Wood	d				07 32					07 53			08 13			08 23					08 41		
Hall Green	d				07 36					07 57			08 16			08 27					08 44		
Spring Road	d				07 38					07 59			08 18			08 29					08 46		
London Marylebone 10 ⊖	d																					07 00	
Banbury	d						06 54		07 02		07 26								07 54			08 07	
Leamington Spa 8	a						07 10	07 17	07 21		07 42								08 11	08 15		08 24	
	d	06 52				07 08	07 12		07 22		07 43			07 46				08 00	08 12			08 25	
Warwick	d	06 56				07 12			07 26					07 50				08 04				08 30	
Warwick Parkway	d	06 59				07 16			07 30					07 54				08 08				08 33	
Hatton	d	07a06				07 21			07 35					07 59				08 13					
Lapworth	d					07 28								08 05				08 19					
Dorridge	d		07 09			07 34			07 43			07 56		08 10			08 20	08 25				08 43	
Widney Manor	d		07 14			07 37			07 47			08 01		08 14			08 24	08 28					
Solihull	d		07 17			07 41			07 51			08 04		08 17			08 28	08 32				08 49	
Olton	d		07 21			07 44			07 55			08 08		08 21			08 32	08 36					
Acocks Green	d		07 23			07 47						08 11		08 24			08 35	08 38					
Tyseley	d		07 26		07 41	07 50						08 14	08 21	08 27		08 32	08 38	08 42			08 49		
Small Heath	d		07 29		07 43	07 53							08 24	08 29		08 35		08 45			08 51		
Bordesley	d																						
Birmingham Moor Street	d		07 33		07 47	07 57			08 02	08 06		08 19	08 28	08 33		08 39	08 42	08 49			08 55	08 59	
Birmingham Snow Hill ⇌	a		07 35		07 52	07 59			08 10	08 10		08 21	08 30	08 37		08 41	08 47	08 51			08 58	09 07	
	d		07 37		07 53	08 03				08 13		08 23	08 33			08 43		08 53			09 03		
Jewellery Quarter ⇌	d		07 39		07 55	08 05				08 15		08 25	08 35			08 45		08 55			09 05		
The Hawthorns ⇌	d		07 44		08 00	08 10				08 20		08 30	08 40			08 50		09 00			09 10		
Smethwick Galton Bridge 7	d		07 47		08 03	08 13				08 23		08 33	08 43			08 53		09 03			09 13		
Coventry	a						07 22												08 23				
Birmingham International ✈	a						07 37												08 37				
Birmingham New Street 12	a						07 48				08 15								08 48				
	d			07 59																			08 49
Langley Green	d		07 50			08 16							08 46								09 16		
Rowley Regis	d		07 53		08 08	08 19				08 28		08 38	08 49			08 58		09 08			09 19		
Old Hill	d		07 56			08 22							08 52								09 22		
Cradley Heath	d		08 00		08 13	08 26				08 33		08 43	08 56			09 03		09 13			09 26		
Lye	d		08 03			08 29							08 59								09 29		
Stourbridge Junction 2	d		08a07		08 19	08 33				08a39		08a49	09 03			09 09		09a19			09 33		
Hagley	d				08 23	08 36										09 12							
Blakedown	d				08 26	08 39										09 15							
Kidderminster	d				08 31	08a45							09a12			09 20					09a42		
Hartlebury	d				08 36																		
University	d			08 05																			08 55
Barnt Green	d			08 18																			
Bromsgrove	d			08 23																			09 10
Droitwich Spa	d			08 32	08 44											09 31							09 20
Worcester Shrub Hill 7	a															09 40							
	d														09 15								
Worcester Foregate Street 7	a			08 41	08 59										09 18								09 28
	d			08 42											09 18								09 32
Malvern Link	d			08 52											09 27								09 42
Great Malvern	a			08 54											09 32								09 44
	d			08 55																			09 45
Colwall	d			09 00																			09 50
Ledbury	a			09 07																			09 57
	d			09 08																			09 59
Hereford 7	a			09 28																			10 17

Stratford-upon-Avon, Marylebone and Leamington Spa - Birmingham - Stourbridge, Worcester and Hereford

Network Diagram - see first Page of Table 71

Station		XC	CH	LM	LM	LM	LM	CH	XC	GW	LM	LM	LM	CH	XC	LM	GW	LM	CH	LM	LM	LM	GW
		◇1 ⊼	◇					◇	◇1 ⊼					◇	◇1 ⊼		◇1 ⊡		◇ ⊼				◇1 ⊼
Stratford-upon-Avon	d				08 26															09 26			
Wilmcote	d				08 31															09 31			
Wootton Wawen	d				08x36															09x36			
Henley-in-Arden	d				08 41															09 41			
Danzey	d				08x46															09x46			
Wood End	d				08x50															09x50			
The Lakes	d				08x52															09x52			
Earlswood (West Midlands)	d				08 55															09 55			
Wythall	d				08 57															09 57			
Whitlocks End	d				09 00							09 19				09 39				10 00			
Shirley	d				09 03							09 22				09 42				10 03			
Yardley Wood	d				09 06							09 25				09 45				10 06			
Hall Green	d				09 09							09 28				09 48				10 09			
Spring Road	d				09 11							09 30				09 50				10 11			
London Marylebone 10 ⊖	d		07 08					07 33						08 03					08 37				
Banbury	d	08 27	08 32					08 38	08 54					09 05	09 26				09 30				
Leamington Spa 8	a	08 43	08 51					08 56	09 10					09 22	09 42				09 47				
	d	08 44	08 51					08 56	09 12					09 22	09 43				09 47				
Warwick	d		08 56					09 01						09 27									
Warwick Parkway	d							09 04						09 30					09 53				
Hatton	d		09a03					09 09															
Lapworth	d							09 15															
Dorridge	d			08 46			09 10	09 20					09 28	09 40				09 46			10 09		
Widney Manor	d			08 50			09 14						09 32					09 50			10 13		
Solihull	d			08 54			09 18	09 25					09 36	09 46				09 54	10 05		10 17		
Olton	d			08 57			09 21						09 39					09 57			10 20		
Acocks Green	d			09 00			09 24						09 42					10 00			10 23		
Tyseley	d			09 03								09 33						10 03					
Small Heath	d			09 05								09 35						10 05					
Bordesley	d																						
Birmingham Moor Street	d			09 09	09 18		09 31	09a39				09 39	09 48	09 55		09 59		10 09	10a17	10 18	10 29		
Birmingham Snow Hill ⇌	a			09 12	09 21		09 34					09 42	09 51	10 05		10 02		10 12		10 21	10 32		
	d			09 13	09 23	09 33						09 43	09 53			10 03		10 13		10 23	10 33		
Jewellery Quarter ⇌	d			09 15	09 25	09 35						09 45	09 55			10 05		10 15		10 25	10 35		
The Hawthorns ⇌	d			09 20	09 30	09 40						09 50	10 00			10 10		10 20		10 30	10 40		
Smethwick Galton Bridge 7	d			09 23	09 33	09 43						09 53	10 03			10 13		10 23		10 33	10 43		
Coventry	a								09 22														
Birmingham International ✈	a								09 37														
Birmingham New Street 12	a	09 18							09 48						10 18								
	d										09 49											10 49	
Langley Green	d					09 46										10 16					10 46		
Rowley Regis	d			09 28	09 38	09 49						09 58	10 08			10 19		10 28		10 38	10 49		
Old Hill	d					09 52										10 22					10 52		
Cradley Heath	d			09 33	09 43	09 56						10 03	10 13			10 26		10 33		10 43	10 56		
Lye	d					09 59										10 29					10 59		
Stourbridge Junction 2	d			09 39	09a49	10 03						10 09	10a19			10 33		10 39		10a49	11 03		
Hagley	d			09 42								10 12						10 42					
Blakedown	d			09 45								10 15						10 45					
Kidderminster	d			09 50		10a13						10 20				10a43		10 50			11a13		
Hartlebury	d																						
University	d										09 55											10 55	
Barnt Green	d																						
Bromsgrove	d										10 10											11 10	
Droitwich Spa	d			10 01							10 20	10 31						11 01				11 20	
Worcester Shrub Hill 7	a																						
	d									10 15							10 45						11 35
Worcester Foregate Street 7	a			10 10						10 17	10 30	10 40					10 48	11 10				11 30	11 40
	d									10 18	10 32	10 42					10 49					11 32	
Malvern Link	d									10 27	10 42	10 52					11 03					11 42	
Great Malvern	a									10 32	10 44	10 55					11 06					11 44	
	d										10 45						11 07					11 45	
Colwall	d										10 50						11 14					11 50	
Ledbury	a										10 57						11 22					11 57	
	d										10 59						11 24					11 59	
Hereford 7	a										11 19						11 42					12 19	

Table 71

Mondays to Fridays

Stratford-upon-Avon, Marylebone and Leamington Spa - Birmingham - Stourbridge, Worcester and Hereford

Network Diagram - see first Page of Table 71

		LM	CH	XC	LM	CH	CH	CH	XC	LM	LM	LM	CH	XC	LM	GW	LM	LM	LM	CH	XC	CH
			◇	◇1 ⊼		◇ ⊼	◇	◇	◇1 ⊼				◇ ⊼	◇1 ⊼		◇				◇ ⊼	◇1 ⊼	◇
Stratford-upon-Avon	d						09 55					10 26										11 20
Wilmcote	d						10 00					10 31										11 25
Wootton Wawen	d											10x36										
Henley-in-Arden	d											10 41										
Danzey	d											10x46										
Wood End	d											10x50										
The Lakes	d											10x52										
Earlswood (West Midlands)	d											10 55										
Wythall	d											10 57										
Whitlocks End	d	10 19								10 39		11 00						11 19				
Shirley	d	10 22								10 42		11 03						11 22				
Yardley Wood	d	10 25								10 45		11 06						11 25				
Hall Green	d	10 28								10 48		11 09						11 28				
Spring Road	d	10 30								10 50		11 11						11 30				
London Marylebone 10 ⊖	d					09 07		09 10					09 37							10 07		
Banbury	d			09 54		10 05		10 15	10 25				10 30	10 54						11 05	11 25	
Leamington Spa 8	a			10 11		10 22	10 27	10 32	10 41				10 48	11 10						11 22	11 41	11 50
	d		09 55	10 12		10 23		10 33	10 42				10 48	11 12						11 23	11 43	
Warwick	d		09 59			10 27		10a37												11 27		
Warwick Parkway	d		10 03			10 31							10 54							11 31		
Hatton	d		10 08																			
Lapworth	d		10 14																			
Dorridge	d		10 19		10 28	10 41					10 46				11 09				11 28	11 41		
Widney Manor	d				10 32						10 50				11 13				11 32			
Solihull	d		10 24		10 36	10 46					10 54		11 06		11 17				11 36	11 46		
Olton	d				10 39						10 57				11 20				11 39			
Acocks Green	d				10 42						11 00				11 23				11 42			
Tyseley	d	10 33									11 03							11 33				
Small Heath	d	10 35									11 05							11 35				
Bordesley	d																					
Birmingham Moor Street	d	10 39	10a40		10 48	10 55				10 59	11 09	11 19	11a19		11 29			11 39	11 48	11 55		
Birmingham Snow Hill ⇌	a	10 42			10 51	11 04				11 02	11 12	11 22			11 32			11 42	11 51	12 04		
	d	10 43			10 53					11 03	11 13	11 23			11 33			11 43	11 53			
Jewellery Quarter ⇌	d	10 45			10 55					11 05	11 15	11 25			11 35			11 45	11 55			
The Hawthorns ⇌	d	10 50			11 00					11 10	11 20	11 30			11 40			11 50	12 00			
Smethwick Galton Bridge 7	d	10 53			11 03					11 13	11 23	11 33			11 43			11 53	12 03			
Coventry	a			10 23										11 22								
Birmingham International ✈	a			10 37										11 37								
Birmingham New Street 12	a			10 48					11 18					11 48							12 18	
	d																11 49					
Langley Green	d									11 16					11 46							
Rowley Regis	d	10 58			11 08					11 19	11 28	11 38			11 49			11 58	12 08			
Old Hill	d									11 22					11 52							
Cradley Heath	d	11 03			11 13					11 26	11 33	11 43			11 56			12 03	12 13			
Lye	d									11 29					11 59							
Stourbridge Junction 2	d	11 09			11a19					11 33	11 39	11a49			12 03			12 09	12a19			
Hagley	d	11 12									11 42							12 12				
Blakedown	d	11 15									11 45							12 15				
Kidderminster	d	11 20								11a43	11 50				12a13			12 20				
Hartlebury	d																					
University	d																11 55					
Barnt Green	d																					
Bromsgrove	d																12 10					
Droitwich Spa	d	11 31									12 01						12 20	12 31				
Worcester Shrub Hill 7	a	11 39																				
	d															12 15						
Worcester Foregate Street 7	a										12 10					12 17	12 30	12 40				
	d															12 18	12 32					
Malvern Link	d															12 27	12 42					
Great Malvern	a															12 34	12 44					
	d																12 45					
Colwall	d																12 50					
Ledbury	a																12 57					
	d																12 59					
Hereford 7	a																13 19					

Table 71

Mondays to Fridays

Stratford-upon-Avon, Marylebone and Leamington Spa - Birmingham - Stourbridge, Worcester and Hereford

Network Diagram - see first Page of Table 71

		LM	GW	LM	LM	CH	LM	LM	LM	CH	XC	CH	LM	CH	XC	LM	GW	LM	LM	CH	XC	LM	GW
			◇1 ⊏⊐			◇ ⊼				◇	◇1 ⊼	◇		◇ ⊼	◇1 ⊼		◇1 ⊼			◇ ⊼	◇1 ⊼		◇
Stratford-upon-Avon	d				11 26														12 26				
Wilmcote	d				11 31														12 31				
Wootton Wawen	d				11x36														12x36				
Henley-in-Arden	d				11 41														12 41				
Danzey	d				11x46														12x46				
Wood End	d				11x50														12x50				
The Lakes	d				11x52														12x52				
Earlswood (West Midlands)	d				11 55														12 55				
Wythall	d				11 57														12 57				
Whitlocks End	d	11 39			12 00				12 19							12 39			13 00				
Shirley	d	11 42			12 03				12 22							12 42			13 03				
Yardley Wood	d	11 45			12 06				12 25							12 45			13 06				
Hall Green	d	11 48			12 09				12 28							12 48			13 09				
Spring Road	d	11 50			12 11				12 30							12 50			13 11				
London Marylebone 10 ⊖	d					10 37						10 40		11 07						11 37			
Banbury	d					11 33					11 54	12 00		12 05	12 25					12 29	12 54		
Leamington Spa 8	a					11 50					12 11	12 18		12 22	12 42					12 46	13 10		
	d					11 50				11 55	12 12	12 19		12 23	12 43					12 47	13 12		
Warwick	d									11 59		12 23		12 27									
Warwick Parkway	d					11 56				12 03				12 31						12 52			
Hatton	d									12 08		12a31											
Lapworth	d									12 14													
Dorridge	d			11 46			12 09			12 19			12 28	12 41				12 46				13 09	
Widney Manor	d			11 50			12 13						12 32					12 50				13 13	
Solihull	d			11 54		12 08	12 17			12 24			12 36	12 46				12 54		13 05		13 17	
Olton	d			11 57			12 20						12 39					12 57				13 20	
Acocks Green	d			12 00			12 23						12 42					13 00				13 23	
Tyseley	d			12 03					12 33									13 03					
Small Heath	d			12 05					12 35									13 05					
Bordesley	d																						
Birmingham Moor Street	d	11 59		12 09	12 18	12a25	12 29		12 39	12a40			12 48	12 55		12 59		13 09	13 18	13a19		13 29	
Birmingham Snow Hill ⇌	a	12 02		12 12	12 22		12 32		12 42				12 51	13 04		13 02		13 12	13 21			13 32	
	d	12 03		12 13	12 23		12 33		12 43				12 53			13 03		13 13	13 23			13 33	
Jewellery Quarter ⇌	d	12 05		12 15	12 25		12 35		12 45				12 55			13 05		13 15	13 25			13 35	
The Hawthorns ⇌	d	12 10		12 20	12 30		12 40		12 50				13 00			13 10		13 20	13 30			13 40	
Smethwick Galton Bridge 7	d	12 13		12 23	12 33		12 43		12 53				13 03			13 13		13 23	13 33			13 43	
Coventry	a										12 24										13 22		
Birmingham International ✈	a										12 37										13 37		
Birmingham New Street 12	a										12 48				13 18						13 48		
	d							12 49															
Langley Green	d	12 16					12 46									13 16						13 46	
Rowley Regis	d	12 19		12 28	12 38		12 49		12 58				13 08			13 19		13 28	13 38			13 49	
Old Hill	d	12 22					12 52									13 22						13 52	
Cradley Heath	d	12 26		12 33	12 43		12 56		13 03				13 13			13 26		13 33	13 43			13 56	
Lye	d	12 29					12 59									13 29						13 59	
Stourbridge Junction 2	d	12 33		12 39	12a49		13 03		13 09				13a19			13a33		13 44	13a49			14 03	
Hagley	d			12 42					13 12									13 47					
Blakedown	d			12 45					13 15									13 50					
Kidderminster	d	12a43		12 50			13a13		13 20									13 55				14a13	
Hartlebury	d																						
University	d							12 55															
Barnt Green	d																						
Bromsgrove	d							13 10															
Droitwich Spa	d			13 01				13 20	13 31									14 06					
Worcester Shrub Hill 7	a																	14 14					
	d		12 45														13 32						14 15
Worcester Foregate Street 7	a		12 48	13 10				13 30	13 40								13 35						14 18
	d		12 49	13 11				13 32									13 43						14 18
Malvern Link	d		12 58	13 20				13 42									13 51						14 27
Great Malvern	a		13 02	13 24				13 44									13 56						14 37
	d		13 09					13 45															
Colwall	d		13 16					13 50															
Ledbury	a		13 24					13 58															
	d		13 31					14 00															
Hereford 7	a		13 48					14 21															

Stratford-upon-Avon, Marylebone and Leamington Spa - Birmingham - Stourbridge, Worcester and Hereford

Network Diagram - see first Page of Table 71

		LM	LM	LM	CH	CH	XC	LM	GW	LM	LM	CH	LM	CH	XC	LM	LM	LM	CH	CH	XC	LM
					◇ ⌶		◇1 ⌶		◇1 ⌶			◇ ⌶		◇	◇1 ⌶				◇ ⌶	◇	◇1 ⌶	
Stratford-upon-Avon	d					13 06					13 26											
Wilmcote	d					13 11					13 31											
Wootton Wawen	d										13x36											
Henley-in-Arden	d										13 41											
Danzey	d										13x46											
Wood End	d										13x50											
The Lakes	d										13x52											
Earlswood (West Midlands)	d										13 55											
Wythall	d										13 57											
Whitlocks End	d		13 19					13 39			14 00						14 19					14 39
Shirley	d		13 22					13 42			14 03						14 22					14 42
Yardley Wood	d		13 25					13 45			14 06						14 25					14 45
Hall Green	d		13 28					13 48			14 09						14 28					14 48
Spring Road	d		13 30					13 50			14 11						14 30					14 50
London Marylebone ⊖	d				12 07							12 37							13 07			
Banbury	d				13 05		13 25					13 29			13 54				14 05		14 26	
Leamington Spa	a				13 22	13 41	13 42					13 46			14 10				14 22		14 41	
	d				13 23		13 43					13 47		13 52	14 12				14 23	14 32	14 42	
Warwick	d				13 27									13 57					14 27	14 37		
Warwick Parkway	d				13 31							13 52		14 01					14 31			
Hatton	d													14 06						14a44		
Lapworth	d													14 12								
Dorridge	d			13 28	13 41					13 46			14 09	14 17				14 28	14 41			
Widney Manor	d			13 32						13 50			14 13					14 32				
Solihull	d			13 36	13 46					13 54		14 05	14 17	14 23				14 36	14 46			
Olton	d			13 39						13 57			14 20					14 39				
Acocks Green	d			13 42						14 00			14 23					14 42				
Tyseley	d		13 33							14 03							14 33					
Small Heath	d		13 35							14 05							14 35					
Bordesley	d																					
Birmingham Moor Street	d		13 39	13 48	13 55			13 58		14 09	14 18	14a19	14 29	14a39			14 39	14 48	14 55			14 59
Birmingham Snow Hill ⇌	a		13 42	13 51	14 04			14 02		14 12	14 21		14 32				14 42	14 51	15 04			15 02
	d		13 43	13 53				14 03		14 13	14 23		14 33				14 43	14 53				15 03
Jewellery Quarter ⇌	d		13 45	13 55				14 05		14 15	14 25		14 35				14 45	14 55				15 05
The Hawthorns ⇌	d		13 50	14 00				14 10		14 20	14 30		14 40				14 50	15 00				15 10
Smethwick Galton Bridge	d		13 53	14 03				14 13		14 23	14 33		14 43				14 53	15 03				15 13
Coventry	a														14 22							
Birmingham International ✈	a														14 37							
Birmingham New Street	a						14 18								14 48						15 18	
	d	13 49														14 49						
Langley Green	d							14 16					14 46									15 16
Rowley Regis	d		13 58	14 08				14 19		14 28	14 38		14 49				14 58	15 08				15 19
Old Hill	d							14 22					14 52									15 22
Cradley Heath	d		14 03	14 13				14 26		14 33	14 43		14 56				15 03	15 13				15 26
Lye	d							14 29					14 59									15 29
Stourbridge Junction	d		14 09	14a19				14 33		14 39	14a49		15 03				15 09	15a19				15 33
Hagley	d		14 12							14 42							15 12					15 37
Blakedown	d		14 15							14 45							15 15					
Kidderminster	d		14 20					14a43		14 50			15a13				15 20					15a44
Hartlebury	d																					
University	d	13 55														14 55						
Barnt Green	d																					
Bromsgrove	d	14 10														15 10						
Droitwich Spa	d	14 20	14 31							15 01						15 20	15 31					
Worcester Shrub Hill	a		14 39																			
	d		14 43						14 49													
Worcester Foregate Street	a	14 30	14 45						14 51	15 10						15 30	15 40					
	d	14 32	14 46						14 53							15 32						
Malvern Link	d	14 42	14 54						15 06							15 42						
Great Malvern	a	14 44	14 58						15 09							15 44						
	d	14 45														15 45						
Colwall	d	14 50														15 50						
Ledbury	a	14 57														15 57						
	d	14 59														15 59						
Hereford	a	15 19														16 19						

Stratford-upon-Avon, Marylebone and Leamington Spa - Birmingham - Stourbridge, Worcester and Hereford

Network Diagram - see first Page of Table 71

		LM	LM	CH	XC	LM	GW	LM	LM	LM	CH	XC	LM	GW	LM	LM	CH	CH	LM	LM	LM	LM	LM
				◇	◇1 ⌶		◇				◇ ⌶	◇1 ⌶		◇1			◇ ⌶	◇					
Stratford-upon-Avon	d		14 26															15 20	15 26				
Wilmcote	d		14 31															15 25	15 31				
Wootton Wawen	d		14x36																15x36				
Henley-in-Arden	d		14 41																15 41				
Danzey	d		14x46																15x46				
Wood End	d		14x50																15x50				
The Lakes	d		14x52																15x52				
Earlswood (West Midlands)	d		14 55																15 55				
Wythall	d		14 57																15 57				
Whitlocks End	d		15 00						15 19				15 39						16 00			16 18	
Shirley	d		15 03						15 22				15 42						16 03			16 21	
Yardley Wood	d		15 06						15 25				15 45						16 06			16 24	
Hall Green	d		15 09						15 28				15 48						16 09			16 27	
Spring Road	d		15 11						15 30				15 50						16 11			16 29	
London Marylebone ⊖	d			13 37							14 07						14 37						
Banbury	d			14 30	14 54						15 05	15 25					15 29						
Leamington Spa	a			14 47	15 11						15 22	15 42					15 46	15 55					
	d			14 47	15 12						15 23	15 43					15 47						
Warwick	d										15 27												
Warwick Parkway	d			14 53							15 31						15 52						
Hatton	d																						
Lapworth	d																						
Dorridge	d	14 46				15 09				15 28	15 41					15 46				16 09			16 27
Widney Manor	d	14 50				15 13				15 32						15 50				16 13			16 31
Solihull	d	14 54		15 05		15 17				15 36	15 46					15 54	16 05			16 17			16 35
Olton	d	14 57				15 20				15 39						15 57				16 20			16 38
Acocks Green	d	15 00				15 23				15 42						16 00				16 23			16 41
Tyseley	d	15 03							15 33							16 03						16 32	16 44
Small Heath	d	15 05							15 35							16 05						16 34	
Bordesley	d																						
Birmingham Moor Street	d	15 09	15 18	15a19		15 29			15 39	15 48	15 55		15 59			16 09	16 13		16 18	16 29		16 38	16 49
Birmingham Snow Hill ⇌	a	15 12	15 21			15 32			15 42	15 51	16 04		16 02			16 12	16 21		16 21	16 32		16 41	16 51
	d	15 13	15 23			15 33			15 43	15 53			16 03			16 13			16 23	16 33		16 43	16 53
Jewellery Quarter ⇌	d	15 15	15 25			15 35			15 45	15 55			16 05			16 15			16 25	16 35		16 46	16 55
The Hawthorns ⇌	d	15 20	15 30			15 40			15 50	16 00			16 10			16 20			16 30	16 40		16 51	17 00
Smethwick Galton Bridge	d	15 23	15 33			15 43			15 53	16 03			16 13			16 23			16 33	16 43		16 54	17 03
Coventry	a				15 24																		
Birmingham International ✈	a				15 37																		
Birmingham New Street	a				15 48							16 18											
	d							15 49							16 19						16 49		
Langley Green	d					15 46							16 16							16 46			
Rowley Regis	d	15 28	15 38			15 49			15 58	16 08			16 19			16 28			16 38	16 49		16 59	17 08
Old Hill	d					15 52							16 22							16 52			
Cradley Heath	d	15 33	15 43			15 56			16 03	16 13			16 26			16 33			16 43	16 56		17 05	17 13
Lye	d					15 59							16 29							16 59			
Stourbridge Junction	d	15 39	15a49			16 03			16 09	16a19			16 33			16 39			16a49	17 03		17 11	17a19
Hagley	d	15 43				16 06			16 12							16 42				17 06		17 15	
Blakedown	d	15 46							16 15							16 45				17 09		17 19	
Kidderminster	d	15 51				16a14			16 20				16a43			16 50				17a15		17 24	
Hartlebury	d																					17 29	
University	d							15 55							16 25						16 55		
Barnt Green	d																						
Bromsgrove	d							16 10							16 41						17 10		
Droitwich Spa	d	16 03						16 20	16 31						16 51	17 01					17 20	17 37	
Worcester Shrub Hill	a	16 11													16 58						17 27		
	d						16 15							16 40	17 06						17 32		
Worcester Foregate Street	a						16 18	16 30	16 40					16 43	17 08	17 10					17 34	17 47	
	d						16 18	16 32							17 09						17 35		
Malvern Link	d						16 27	16 42							17 18						17 44		
Great Malvern	a						16 33	16 44							17 21						17 46		
	d							16 45													17 47		
Colwall	d							16 50													17 52		
Ledbury	a							16 57													17 59		
	d							16 59													18 00		
Hereford	a							17 19													18 22		

Stratford-upon-Avon, Marylebone and Leamington Spa - Birmingham - Stourbridge, Worcester and Hereford

Network Diagram - see first Page of Table 71

		CH	XC	LM	CH	CH	XC	LM	LM	LM	CH	XC	GW	LM	LM	LM	LM	LM	CH	XC	LM	CH	LM
		◇	◇■ ⊼		◇	◇	◇■ ⊼				◇	◇■ ⊼							◇	◇■ ⊼		◇	
Stratford-upon-Avon	d									16 23													17 26
Wilmcote	d									16 28													17 31
Wootton Wawen	d									16x33													17x36
Henley-in-Arden	d									16 38													17 41
Danzey	d									16x43													17x46
Wood End	d									16x47													17x50
The Lakes	d									16x49													17x52
Earlswood (West Midlands)	d									16 52													17 55
Wythall	d									16 55													17 57
Whitlocks End	d			16 39						16 58						17 18					17 42		18 00
Shirley	d			16 42						17 01						17 21					17 44		18 03
Yardley Wood	d			16 45						17 04						17 24					17 47		18 06
Hall Green	d			16 48						17 07						17 27					17 50		18 09
Spring Road	d			16 50						17 09						17 29					17 52		18 11
London Marylebone ■ ⊖	d				15 07	15 10					15 37								16 07			16 30	
Banbury	d		15 54		16 06	16 17	16 26				16 33	16 54							17 02	17 28			
Leamington Spa ■	a		16 10		16 23	16 34	16 43				16 49	17 11							17 20	17 47			
	d	16 07	16 12		16 23	16 35	16 44				16 50	17 12							17 20	17 48			
Warwick	d	16 13			16 28	16 39													17 25				
Warwick Parkway	d	16 16			16 31						16 55								17 29			17 39	
Hatton	d	16 22				16a47																	
Lapworth	d	16 28																					
Dorridge	d	16 33			16 41				16 46						17 09			17 27	17 39				
Widney Manor	d								16 50						17 13			17 31					
Solihull	d	16 41			16 47				16 54		17 08				17 17			17 35	17 44			17 51	
Olton	d								16 57						17 20			17 38					
Acocks Green	d								17 00						17 23			17 41					
Tyseley	d			16 53					17 03							17 32		17 44					
Small Heath	d								17 05							17 34		17 46					
Bordesley	d																						
Birmingham Moor Street	d	16 53		16 59	17a01				17 09	17 16	17 18				17 29	17 38		17 50	17 56		17 59	18 04	18 18
Birmingham Snow Hill ⇌	a	17 01		17 02					17 12	17 19	17 27				17 32	17 41		17 53	18 03		18 02	18 12	18 21
	d			17 03					17 13	17 20					17 33	17 43		17 54			18 03		18 23
Jewellery Quarter ⇌	d			17 05					17 16	17 23					17 36	17 45		17 57			18 05		18 25
The Hawthorns ⇌	d			17 10					17 21	17 27					17 41	17 50		18 02			18 10		18 30
Smethwick Galton Bridge ■	d			17 13					17 24	17 30					17 44	17 53		18 05			18 13		18 33
Coventry	a		16 22									17 23											
Birmingham International ✈	a		16 37									17 37											
Birmingham New Street ■	a		16 48				17 18					17 48								18 18			
	d							17 19						17 49			17 59						
Langley Green	d			17 16						17 33						17 56					18 16		
Rowley Regis	d			17 19					17 30	17 37					17 50	17 59		18 10			18 19		18 38
Old Hill	d			17 22						17 40						18 02					18 22		
Cradley Heath	d			17 26					17 35	17 43					17 55	18 06		18 15			18 26		18 43
Lye	d			17 29						17 46						18 09					18 29		
Stourbridge Junction ■	d			17 33					17 42	17a51					18 01	18 13		18 21			18 33		18 50
Hagley	d			17 37					17 46						18 05	18 17		18 25			18 37		18 54
Blakedown	d			17 40					17 49						18 08	18 20		18 28			18 40		18 57
Kidderminster	d			17a45					17 54						18 13	18a26		18 33			18a45		19a02
Hartlebury	d														18 18			18 38					
University	d							17 25						17 55			18 05						
Barnt Green	d																						
Bromsgrove	d							17 40									18 21						
Droitwich Spa	d							17 52	18 05					18 17	18 26		18 34	18 49					
Worcester Shrub Hill ■	a							17 59	18 18					18 25			18 42	18 58					
	d							18 04					18 18	18 32			18 53						
Worcester Foregate Street ■	a							18 06					18 21	18 34	18 36		18 55						
	d							18 07					18 21	18 35			18 56						
Malvern Link	d							18 16					18 29	18 44			19 05						
Great Malvern	a							18 18					18 36	18 47			19 08						
	d							18 19						18 49									
Colwall	d							18 24						18 54									
Ledbury	a							18 31						19 02									
	d							18 31						19 04									
Hereford ■	a							18 51						19 24									

Stratford-upon-Avon, Marylebone and Leamington Spa - Birmingham - Stourbridge, Worcester and Hereford

Network Diagram - see first Page of Table 71

		LM	CH	GW	LM	GW	LM	LM	LM	CH	CH	XC	CH	CH	XC	LM	LM	GW	LM	CH	LM	CH
			◇	■ A		◇■ ⊏				◇	◇	◇■ ⊼	◇	◇	◇■ ⊼					◇		◇ ⊼
Stratford-upon-Avon	d						17 58				17 40					18 26					18 50	
Wilmcote	d										17 46					18 31					18 55	
Wootton Wawen	d															18x36					19x00	
Henley-in-Arden	d						18 08									18 40					19 04	
Danzey	d															18x45						
Wood End	d															18x49						
The Lakes	d															18x51						
Earlswood (West Midlands)	d															18 54						
Wythall	d															18 56						
Whitlocks End	d								18 36							18 59					19 15	
Shirley	d						18 21		18 39							19 02					19 18	
Yardley Wood	d						18 24		18 42							19 05					19 21	
Hall Green	d						18 27		18 45							19 08					19 24	
Spring Road	d						18 29		18 47							19 10					19 26	
London Marylebone ■ ⊖	d		16 46										17 07	17 10						17 37		18 07
Banbury	d		17 43									17 54	18 04	18 19	18 26					18 37		
Leamington Spa ■	a		18 00								18 12	18 11	18 21	18 36	18 45					18 54		
	d		18 01							18 08		18 12	18 21	18 36	18 46					18 54		
Warwick	d									18 13				18 41						18 59		
Warwick Parkway	d		18 07							18 17			18 27							19 02		19 20
Hatton	d									18 22				18a48								
Lapworth	d									18 28												
Dorridge	d	18 03	18 19					18 23		18 32			18 39						18 59	19 12		
Widney Manor	d	18 08						18 27											19 03			
Solihull	d	18 11	18 25					18 31		18 38			18 45						19 07	19 18		19 32
Olton	d	18 15						18 34											19 10			
Acocks Green	d	18 17						18 37											19 13			
Tyseley	d	18 20					18 32	18 40	18 50										19 16			
Small Heath	d	18 23					18 34	18 42											19 18			
Bordesley	d																					
Birmingham Moor Street	d	18 27	18a36				18 38	18 46	18 55	18a55			19 02			19 17			19 22	19 28	19 33	19 41
Birmingham Snow Hill ⇌	a	18 29					18 41	18 49	18 57				19 04			19 20			19 25	19 36	19 36	19 43
	d	18 33					18 43		18 59				19 10						19 27		19 40	19 50
Jewellery Quarter ⇌	d	18 35					18 45		19 01										19 29		19 42	
The Hawthorns ⇌	d	18 40					18 50		19 06				19 16						19 34		19 47	
Smethwick Galton Bridge ■	d	18 43					18 53		19 09				19 19						19 37		19 50	
Coventry	a											18 22										
Birmingham International ✈	a											18 37										
Birmingham New Street ■	a											18 48			19 18							
	d				18 19												19 19					
Langley Green	d	18 46							19 12										19 40			
Rowley Regis	d	18 49					18 58		19 15				19 24						19 43		19 55	20 02
Old Hill	d	18 52							19 18										19 46			
Cradley Heath	d	18 56					19 04		19 22				19 29						19 50		20 00	
Lye	d	18 59							19 25										19 53			
Stourbridge Junction ■	d	19a03					19 10		19a29				19 36						19 57		20a06	20 14
Hagley	d						19 13												20 00			
Blakedown	d						19 16												20 03			
Kidderminster	d						19 21						19a49						20 08			20a30
Hartlebury	d																					
University	d				18 25												19 25					
Barnt Green	d																					
Bromsgrove	d				18 45												19 41					
Droitwich Spa	d				18 57		19 32										19 52		20 19			
Worcester Shrub Hill ■	a				19 10												19 59		20 27			
	d			19 09		19 35											20 10	20 20				
Worcester Foregate Street ■	a			19 11		19 38	19 41										20 12	20 22				
	d			19 12		19 39											20 13	20 25				
Malvern Link	d			19 21		19 48											20 22	20 34				
Great Malvern	a			19 24		19 52											20 24	20 40				
	d					19 52											20 25					
Colwall	d					19 58											20 30					
Ledbury	a					20 06											20 37					
	d					20 09											20 38					
Hereford ■	a					20 27											21 02					

A until 14 September

Stratford-upon-Avon, Marylebone and Leamington Spa - Birmingham - Stourbridge, Worcester and Hereford

Network Diagram - see first Page of Table 71

		LM	LM	GW	LM	XC	CH	CH	LM	XC	CH	CH	XC	CH	LM	GW	LM	CH	LM	XC	CH	XC	GW
				◇1 A ⊡		◇1 ⌶	◇	◇		◇1 ⌶	◇	◇	◇1 ⌶			◇1 ⊡		◇		◇1	◇	◇1	◇1
Stratford-upon-Avon	d							19 20	19 26										20 26				
Wilmcote	d							19 25	19 31										20 31				
Wootton Wawen	d								19x36										20x36				
Henley-in-Arden	d								19 40										20 40				
Danzey	d								19x44										20x44				
Wood End	d								19x48										20x48				
The Lakes	d								19x50										20x50				
Earlswood (West Midlands)	d								19 53										20 53				
Wythall	d								19 55										20 55				
Whitlocks End	d	19 25							19 58										20 58				
Shirley	d	19 27							20 01										21 01				
Yardley Wood	d	19 30							20 04										21 04				
Hall Green	d	19 33							20 07										21 07				
Spring Road	d	19 35							20 09										21 09				
London Marylebone 10 ⊖	d						18 10				18 37			18 44				19 15			19 37		
Banbury	d					18 54	19 05			19 31	19 36		19 54	20 01				20 13		20 28	20 39	20 54	
Leamington Spa 8	a					19 10	19 23	19 48		19 49	19 53		20 10	20 21				20 30		20 45	20 56	21 10	
	d				19 02	19 12	19 23			19 50	19 53	20 05	20 12	20 22				20 31		20 46	20 57	21 12	
Warwick	d				19 06		19 28				19 58			20 27							21 01		
Warwick Parkway	d				19 10		19 32				20 01	20 11						20 36			21 05		
Hatton	d				19 15							20 16		20a35									
Lapworth	d				19 21							20 22											
Dorridge	d				19 30		19 43				20 12	20 26					20 29	20 46			21 15		
Widney Manor	d				19 34												20 33						
Solihull	d				19 38		19 48				20 18	20 32					20 36	20 52			21 20		
Olton	d				19 41												20 40						
Acocks Green	d				19 44												20 42						
Tyseley	d	19 38			19 47												20 45						
Small Heath	d	19 40			19 49												20 48						
Bordesley	d																						
Birmingham Moor Street	d	19 44			19 53		19 59		20 16		20 27	20a47					20 52	21 00	21 16		21 29		
Birmingham Snow Hill ⇌	a	19 47			19 56		20 11		20 19		20 37						20 54	21 04	21 19		21 37		
	d				19 58				20 20								20 55	21 05	21 20				
Jewellery Quarter ⇌	d				20 00				20 22								20 58		21 22				
The Hawthorns ⇌	d				20 05				20 27								21 02	21 11	21 27				
Smethwick Galton Bridge 7	d				20 08				20 30								21 05	21 14	21 30				
Coventry	a					19 22							20 22									21 22	
Birmingham International ✈	a					19 37							20 37									21 37	
Birmingham New Street 12	a					19 48				20 18			20 48							21 22		21 48	
	d		19 49												20 59								
Langley Green	d				20 11				20 33								21 08		21 33				
Rowley Regis	d				20 14				20 36								21 11	21 20	21 36				
Old Hill	d				20 17				20 39								21 14		21 39				
Cradley Heath	d				20 21				20 43								21 17	21 25	21 43				
Lye	d				20 24				20 46								21 20		21 46				
Stourbridge Junction 2	d				20 28				20a51								21 24	21 33	21a50				
Hagley	d				20 31												21 28						
Blakedown	d				20 34												21 31						
Kidderminster	d				20 39												21 36	21a49					
Hartlebury	d																						
University	d		19 55												21 05								
Barnt Green	d																						
Bromsgrove	d		20 10												21 20								
Droitwich Spa	d		20 26		20 50										21 30		21 47						
Worcester Shrub Hill 7	a		20 34		20 59												21 57						
	d			20 42												21 47	22 03						22 41
Worcester Foregate Street 7	a			20 45											21 38	21 50	22 05						22 44
	d			20 46											21 41	21 51							22 45
Malvern Link	d			20 55											21 51	22 02							22 53
Great Malvern	a			20 58											21 53	22 06							22 59
	d			20 59											21 54	22 19							
Colwall	d			21 05											21 59	22 26							
Ledbury	a			21 12											22 06	22 33							
	d			21 14											22 09	22 35							
Hereford 7	a			21 33											22 29	22 54							

A The Cathedrals Express

Stratford-upon-Avon, Marylebone and Leamington Spa - Birmingham - Stourbridge, Worcester and Hereford

Network Diagram - see first Page of Table 71

		LM	LM	CH	XC	LM	LM	CH	XC	XC	CH	LM	LM	CH	CH	LM	CH	XC	XC	XC	CH	CH		CH
				◇	◇1			◇	◇1 A	◇1 B				◇			◇	◇1 B	◇1 A	B 🚌	◇			◇
Stratford-upon-Avon	d					21 36					22 00											23 15		
Wilmcote	d										22 05													
Wootton Wawen	d																							
Henley-in-Arden	d																							
Danzey	d																							
Wood End	d																							
The Lakes	d																							
Earlswood (West Midlands)	d																							
Wythall	d																							
Whitlocks End	d						21 55									22 55								
Shirley	d						21 57									22 57								
Yardley Wood	d						22 00									23 00								
Hall Green	d						22 03									23 03								
Spring Road	d						22 05									23 05								
London Marylebone 10 ⊖	d			20 10				20 37						21 07			21 37				22 07		22 37	23 07
Banbury	d			21 06	21 33			21 45	21 54	21 54				22 13			22 43	22 54	22 54		23 04		23 39	00 03
Leamington Spa 8	a			21 24	21 51			22 04	22 10	22 10	22 30			22 30			23 00	23 12	23 12		23 22	23 38	23 56	00 20
	d			21 24	21 52			22 04	22 12	22 12				22 30	22 40		23 00	23 13	23 13	23 20	23 23		23 56	00 21
Warwick	d							22 09						22 34	22a45		23 05				23 27		23 59	00 25
Warwick Parkway	d			21 30				22 12						22 37			23 09				23 31		00 04	00 29
Hatton	d													22 42										
Lapworth	d													22 48										
Dorridge	d		21 31	21 40				22 22					22 33	22 53			23 19				23 41		00 14	
Widney Manor	d		21 35										22 37	22 56										
Solihull	d		21 38	21 45				22 28					22 41	23 00			23 24				23 46		00 19	00 41
Olton	d		21 42										22 44											
Acocks Green	d		21 44										22 47											
Tyseley	d		21 47				22 08						22 50			23 08								
Small Heath	d		21 50				22 11						22 52			23 10								
Bordesley	d																							
Birmingham Moor Street	d		21 54	21 58		22 08	22 14	22a42					22 56	23 09		23 14	23a39				23a59		00a33	00a55
Birmingham Snow Hill ⇌	a		21 56	22 00		22 10	22 17						22 59	23 12		23 17								
	d		21 57	22 10			22 20						23 00	23 22										
Jewellery Quarter ⇌	d		22 00				22 22						23 02	23 24										
The Hawthorns ⇌	d		22 04	22 16			22 27						23 07	23 29										
Smethwick Galton Bridge 7	d		22 07	22 19			22 30						23 10	23 32										
Coventry	a								22 22										23 25	23s40				
Birmingham International ✈	a								22 33										23 36	00 10				
Birmingham New Street 12	a				22 17				22 45	22 45								23 49	23 57					
	d	22 00										23 00												
Langley Green	d		22 10				22 33						23 13	23 35										
Rowley Regis	d		22 13	22 24			22 36						23 16	23 38										
Old Hill	d		22 16				22 39						23 19	23 41										
Cradley Heath	d		22 19	22 29			22 43						23 23	23 45										
Lye	d		22 22				22 46						23 26	23 48										
Stourbridge Junction 2	d		22 26	22 36			22a50						23 30	23a52										
Hagley	d		22 30										23 33											
Blakedown	d		22 33										23 36											
Kidderminster	d		22 38	22a50									23 41											
Hartlebury	d																							
University	d	22 06										23 06												
Barnt Green	d																							
Bromsgrove	d	22 20										23 19												
Droitwich Spa	d	22 34	22 49									23 29	23 52											
Worcester Shrub Hill 7	a	22 47	22 57									23 37	00 01											
	d		23 05																					
Worcester Foregate Street 7	a		23 07																					
	d		23 08																					
Malvern Link	d		23 16																					
Great Malvern	a		23 19																					
	d																							
Colwall	d																							
Ledbury	a																							
	d																							
Hereford 7	a																							

A until 22 June, from 17 September

B from 25 June until 14 September

Stratford-upon-Avon, Marylebone and Leamington Spa - Birmingham - Stourbridge, Worcester and Hereford

Network Diagram - see first Page of Table 71

		LM	XC	CH	CH	CH	CH	LM	LM	LM	GW	LM	LM	XC	LM	LM	GW	LM	LM	CH	XC	LM	LM
			A	◇	◇	◇	◇ B				◇1			◇1			◇1				◇1		
Stratford-upon-Avon	d																		07 00				07 44
Wilmcote	d																		07 05				07 49
Wootton Wawen	d																		07x10				07x54
Henley-in-Arden	d																		07 14				07 59
Danzey	d																		07x19				08x04
Wood End	d																		07x23				08x08
The Lakes	d																		07x26				08x10
Earlswood (West Midlands)	d																		07 28				08 13
Wythall	d																		07 31				08 15
Whitlocks End	d														07 03				07 33				08 18
Shirley	d														07 05				07 36				08 21
Yardley Wood	d														07 08				07 39				08 24
Hall Green	d														07 11				07 42				08 27
Spring Road	d														07 13				07 44				08 29
London Marylebone 10 ⊖	d			22p37	23p07	00 05	01 30																
Banbury	d			23p39	00 03	01 19	02 36							06 56						07 02	07 33		
Leamington Spa 8	a			23p56	00 20	01 50	02 54							07 12						07 20	07 50		
	d		23p20	23p56	00 21		02 54						06 26	07 14						07 21	07 51		
Warwick	d			23p59	00 25		02 59						06 30							07 25			
Warwick Parkway	d			00 04	00 29		03 02						06 34							07 29			
Hatton	d												06 39							07 34			
Lapworth	d												06 45										
Dorridge	d	22p33		00 14			03 12						06 50					07 25		07 42		08 05	
Widney Manor	d	22p37											06 53					07 29				08 09	
Solihull	d	22p41		00 19	00 41								06 57					07 33		07 48		08 13	
Olton	d	22p44											07 00					07 36				08 16	
Acocks Green	d	22p47											07 03					07 39				08 19	
Tyseley	d	22p50											07 06		07 16			07 42	07 47			08 22	08 32
Small Heath	d	22p52											07 08		07 19			07 44	07 50				08 34
Bordesley	d																						
Birmingham Moor Street	d	22p56		00a33	00a55		03 23			06 31		07 01	07 12		07 23			07 48	07 55	08a03		08 27	08 38
Birmingham Snow Hill	a	22p59					03 32			06 33		07 03	07 15		07 25			07 51	07 57			08 29	08 42
	d	23p00								06 35		07 05			07 28			07 53	08 03			08 30	08 43
Jewellery Quarter	d	23p02								06 37		07 07			07 30			07 55	08 05			08 33	08 45
The Hawthorns	d	23p07								06 42		07 12			07 35			08 00	08 10			08 37	08 50
Smethwick Galton Bridge 7	d	23p10								06 45		07 15			07 38			08 03	08 13			08 40	08 53
Coventry	a		23b40											07 24									
Birmingham International ✈	a		00 10											07 37									
Birmingham New Street 12	a													07 48							08 17		
	d								06 49							07 49							
Langley Green	d	23p13								06 48		07 18			07 41				08 16			08 43	
Rowley Regis	d	23p16								06 51		07 21			07 44			08 08	08 19			08 47	08 58
Old Hill	d	23p19								06 54		07 24			07 47				08 22			08 50	
Cradley Heath	d	23p23								06 57		07 27			07 51			08 12	08 26			08 53	09 02
Lye	d	23p26								07 00		07 30			07 54				08 29			08 56	
Stourbridge Junction 2	d	23p30								07 04		07 35			07a58			08 18	08a33			09a00	09a08
Hagley	d	23p33								07 08		07 38						08 21					
Blakedown	d	23p36								07 11		07 41						08 24					
Kidderminster	d	23p41								07 16		07 46						08 29					
Hartlebury	d									07 21													
University	d								06 55							07 55							
Barnt Green	d																						
Bromsgrove	d								07 10							08 10							
Droitwich Spa	d	23p52							07 20	07 28		07 57				08 20		08 40					
Worcester Shrub Hill 7	a	00 01								07 39		08 07											
	d							06 30			07 46	08 11					08 41						
Worcester Foregate Street 7	a							06 32	07 30		07 48	08 13				08 30	08 44	08 49					
	d							06 33	07 32		07 50	08 14				08 32	08 45						
Malvern Link	d							06 42	07 42		07 59	08 23				08 42	08 54						
Great Malvern	a							06 44	07 44		08 03	08 26				08 44	09 00						
	d							06 45	07 45							08 45							
Colwall	d							06 50	07 50							08 50							
Ledbury	a							06 57	07 57							08 57							
	d							06 58	07 59							08 59							
Hereford 7	a							07 14	08 19							09 19							

A from 30 June until 15 September
B from 28 July until 11 August
b Previous night, stops to set down only

Stratford-upon-Avon, Marylebone and Leamington Spa - Birmingham - Stourbridge, Worcester and Hereford

Network Diagram - see first Page of Table 71

		LM	GW	LM	XC	LM	CH	CH	CH	LM	CH	LM	XC	XC	LM	GW	LM	LM	LM	LM	CH	XC	CH
			◇1		◇1		◇	◇			◇		◇1	◇1							◇	◇1	◇
Stratford-upon-Avon	d							08 00				08 26											09 19
Wilmcote	d											08 31											09 25
Wootton Wawen	d											08x36											
Henley-in-Arden	d											08 41											
Danzey	d											08x46											
Wood End	d											08x50											
The Lakes	d											08x52											
Earlswood (West Midlands)	d											08 55											
Wythall	d											08 57											
Whitlocks End	d					08 35						09 00						09 19		09 39			
Shirley	d					08 38						09 03						09 22		09 42			
Yardley Wood	d					08 41						09 06						09 25		09 45			
Hall Green	d					08 44						09 09						09 28		09 48			
Spring Road	d					08 46						09 11						09 30		09 50			
London Marylebone 10 ⊖	d						07 00														08 00		
Banbury	d				07 54		08 03		08 08				08 33	08 54							09 06	09 24	
Leamington Spa 8	a				08 10		08 21	08 28	08 27				08 49	09 10							09 24	09 41	09 53
	d			07 56	08 12		08 21		08 28		08 41		08 50	09 12							09 25	09 42	
Warwick	d			08 00			08 26		08 32												09 29		
Warwick Parkway	d			08 04			08 29		08 36		08 47										09 33		
Hatton	d			08 09					08a43														
Lapworth	d			08 15			08 37																
Dorridge	d			08 21			08 42			08 46					09 09				09 28		09 43		
Widney Manor	d			08 24						08 50					09 13				09 32				
Solihull	d			08 28			08 48			08 54	09 00				09 17				09 36		09 48		
Olton	d			08 31						08 57					09 20				09 39				
Acocks Green	d			08 34						09 00					09 23				09 42				
Tyseley	d			08 37		08 49				09 03								09 33					
Small Heath	d			08 39		08 51				09 05								09 35					
Bordesley	d																						
Birmingham Moor Street	d			08 43		08 55	09 00			09 09	09a15	09 18			09 29			09 39	09 48	09 58	10 02		
Birmingham Snow Hill	a			08 47		08 58	09 07			09 12		09 20			09 32			09 42	09 51	10 00	10 09		
	d			08 53		09 03				09 13		09 23			09 33			09 43	09 53	10 03			
Jewellery Quarter	d			08 55		09 05				09 15		09 25			09 35			09 45	09 55	10 05			
The Hawthorns	d			09 00		09 10				09 20		09 30			09 40			09 50	10 00	10 10			
Smethwick Galton Bridge 7	d			09 03		09 13				09 23		09 33			09 43			09 53	10 03	10 13			
Coventry	a				08 22									09 22									
Birmingham International ✈	a				08 37									09 37									
Birmingham New Street 12	a				08 48								09 18	09 48								10 18	
	d	08 49															09 49						
Langley Green	d					09 16									09 46					10 16			
Rowley Regis	d			09 08		09 19				09 28		09 38			09 49			09 58	10 08	10 19			
Old Hill	d					09 22									09 52					10 22			
Cradley Heath	d			09 13		09 26				09 33		09 43			09 56			10 03	10 13	10 26			
Lye	d					09 29									09 59					10 29			
Stourbridge Junction 2	d			09 19		09 33				09 39		09a49			10 03			10 09	10a19	10 33			
Hagley	d			09 22						09 42								10 12					
Blakedown	d			09 25						09 45								10 15					
Kidderminster	d			09 30		09a42				09 50					10a12			10 20		10a42			
Hartlebury	d																						
University	d	08 55															09 55						
Barnt Green	d																						
Bromsgrove	d	09 10															10 10						
Droitwich Spa	d	09 20		09 41						10 01							10 20	10 31					
Worcester Shrub Hill 7	a			09 49														10 39					
	d		09 41													10 15							
Worcester Foregate Street 7	a	09 30	09 44							10 10						10 17	10 30						
	d	09 32	09 45													10 18	10 32						
Malvern Link	d	09 42	09 54													10 27	10 42						
Great Malvern	a	09 44	10 00													10 32	10 44						
	d	09 45															10 45						
Colwall	d	09 50															10 50						
Ledbury	a	09 57															10 57						
	d	09 59															10 59						
Hereford 7	a	10 19															11 19						

Table 71

Saturdays

Stratford-upon-Avon, Marylebone and Leamington Spa - Birmingham - Stourbridge, Worcester and Hereford

Network Diagram - see first Page of Table 71

Station		GW ◇1	LM	LM	LM	CH ◇	CH ◇	XC ◇1	LM	LM	LM	CH ◇	XC ◇1	LM	LM	CH ◇	LM	LM	CH ◇	XC ◇1	GW ◇	LM
Stratford-upon-Avon	d			09 26													10 26					
Wilmcote	d			09 31													10 31					
Wootton Wawen	d			09x36													10x36					
Henley-in-Arden	d			09 41													10 41					
Danzey	d			09x46													10x46					
Wood End	d			09x50													10x50					
The Lakes	d			09x52													10x52					
Earlswood (West Midlands)	d			09 55													10 55					
Wythall	d			09 57													10 57					
Whitlocks End	d			10 00						10 19				10 39			11 00					
Shirley	d			10 03						10 22				10 42			11 03					
Yardley Wood	d			10 06						10 25				10 45			11 06					
Hall Green	d			10 09						10 28				10 48			11 09					
Spring Road	d			10 11						10 30				10 50			11 11					
London Marylebone ⊖	d					08 23	08 54					09 00				09 30						
Banbury	d					09 35	09 51	09 54				10 04	10 24			10 28				10 54		
Leamington Spa	a					09 53	10 08	10 12				10 22	10 41			10 45				11 10		
	d					09 54	10 08	10 13				10 23	10 42			10 46			10 53	11 12		
Warwick	d					09 58	10a13					10 27							10 58			
Warwick Parkway	d					10 02						10 31				10 51			11 01			
Hatton	d					10 07													11 07			
Lapworth	d					10 12													11 12			
Dorridge	d		09 46		10 09	10 17					10 28	10 41			10 46			11 09	11 17			
Widney Manor	d		09 50		10 13						10 32				10 50			11 13				
Solihull	d		09 54		10 17	10 23					10 36	10 46			10 54	11 04		11 17	11 22			
Olton	d		09 57		10 20						10 39				10 57			11 20				
Acocks Green	d		10 00		10 23						10 42				11 00			11 23				
Tyseley	d		10 03							10 33					11 03							
Small Heath	d		10 05							10 35					11 05							
Bordesley	d																					
Birmingham Moor Street	d		10 09	10 18	10 29	10a35				10 39	10 48	10 55		10 57	11 09	11a17	11 18	11 29	11a37			
Birmingham Snow Hill	a		10 12	10 21	10 32					10 42	10 51	11 02		11 01	11 12		11 21	11 32				
	d		10 13	10 23	10 33					10 43	10 53			11 03	11 13		11 23	11 33				
Jewellery Quarter	d		10 15	10 25	10 35					10 45	10 55			11 05	11 15		11 25	11 35				
The Hawthorns	d		10 20	10 30	10 40					10 50	11 00			11 10	11 20		11 30	11 40				
Smethwick Galton Bridge	d		10 23	10 33	10 43					10 53	11 03			11 13	11 23		11 33	11 43				
Coventry	a							10 22												11 22		
Birmingham International	a							10 37												11 37		
Birmingham New Street	a							10 48					11 18							11 48		
	d								10 49													11 49
Langley Green	d				10 46									11 16				11 46				
Rowley Regis	d		10 28	10 38	10 49					10 58	11 08			11 19	11 28		11 38	11 49				
Old Hill	d				10 52									11 22				11 52				
Cradley Heath	d		10 33	10 43	10 56					11 03	11 13			11 26	11 33		11 43	11 56				
Lye	d				10 59									11 29				11 59				
Stourbridge Junction	d		10 39	10a49	11 03					11 09	11a19			11 33	11 39		11a49	12 03				
Hagley	d		10 42							11 12					11 42							
Blakedown	d		10 45							11 15					11 45							
Kidderminster	d		10 50		11a12					11 20				11a42	11 50			12a12				
Hartlebury	d																					
University	d								10 55													11 55
Barnt Green	d																					
Bromsgrove	d								11 10													12 10
Droitwich Spa	d		11 01						11 20	11 31					12 01							12 20
Worcester Shrub Hill	a									11 39												
	d	10 46																			12 16	
Worcester Foregate Street	a	10 48	11 10						11 30						12 10						12 18	12 30
	d	10 50	11 11						11 32													12 32
Malvern Link	d	10 58	11 19						11 42													12 42
Great Malvern	a	11 05	11 22						11 44													12 44
	d	11 06							11 45													12 45
Colwall	d	11 12							11 50													12 50
Ledbury	a	11 20							11 57													12 57
	d	11 22							11 59													12 59
Hereford	a	11 41							12 19													13 19

Table 71

Saturdays

Stratford-upon-Avon, Marylebone and Leamington Spa - Birmingham - Stourbridge, Worcester and Hereford

Network Diagram - see first Page of Table 71

Station		LM	LM	CH ◇	XC ◇1	LM	GW ◇1	LM	CH ◇	LM	CH ◇	XC ◇1	CH ◇	LM	LM	LM	LM	CH ◇	XC ◇1	LM	GW ◇1	LM	CH ◇
Stratford-upon-Avon	d									11 26	11 34												
Wilmcote	d									11 31	11 41												
Wootton Wawen	d									11x36													
Henley-in-Arden	d									11 41													
Danzey	d									11x46													
Wood End	d									11x50													
The Lakes	d									11x52													
Earlswood (West Midlands)	d									11 55													
Wythall	d									11 57													
Whitlocks End	d	11 19				11 39				12 00						12 19				12 39			
Shirley	d	11 22				11 42				12 03						12 22				12 42			
Yardley Wood	d	11 25				11 45				12 06						12 25				12 45			
Hall Green	d	11 28				11 48				12 09						12 28				12 48			
Spring Road	d	11 30				11 50				12 11						12 30				12 50			
London Marylebone ⊖	d			10 00					10 30				10 33					11 00					11 30
Banbury	d			11 04	11 24				11 28			11 54	11 58					12 04	12 24				12 28
Leamington Spa	a			11 22	11 41				11 45		12 08	12 10	12 16					12 21	12 41				12 45
	d			11 22	11 42				11 46			12 12	12 17					12 22	12 42				12 46
Warwick	d			11 26									12 21					12 26					
Warwick Parkway	d			11 30					11 51									12 30					12 51
Hatton	d												12a29										
Lapworth	d																						
Dorridge	d		11 28	11 40				11 46						12 09			12 28	12 40				12 46	
Widney Manor	d		11 32					11 50						12 13			12 32					12 50	
Solihull	d		11 36	11 45				11 54	12 05					12 17			12 36	12 45				12 54	13 04
Olton	d		11 39					11 57						12 20			12 39					12 57	
Acocks Green	d		11 42					12 00						12 23			12 42					13 00	
Tyseley	d	11 33						12 03								12 33						13 03	
Small Heath	d	11 35						12 05								12 35						13 05	
Bordesley	d																						
Birmingham Moor Street	d	11 39	11 48	11 55		11 57		12 09	12a17	12 18				12 29		12 39	12 48	12 55		12 57		13 09	13a17
Birmingham Snow Hill	a	11 42	11 51	12 02		12 01		12 12		12 21				12 32		12 42	12 51	13 02		13 01		13 12	
	d	11 43	11 53			12 03		12 13		12 23				12 33		12 43	12 53			13 03		13 13	
Jewellery Quarter	d	11 45	11 55			12 05		12 15		12 25				12 35		12 45	12 55			13 05		13 15	
The Hawthorns	d	11 50	12 00			12 10		12 20		12 30				12 40		12 50	13 00			13 10		13 20	
Smethwick Galton Bridge	d	11 53	12 03			12 13		12 23		12 33				12 43		12 53	13 03			13 13		13 23	
Coventry	a											12 22											
Birmingham International	a											12 37											
Birmingham New Street	a				12 18							12 48							13 18				
	d														12 49								
Langley Green	d					12 16								12 46						13 16			
Rowley Regis	d	11 58	12 08			12 19		12 28		12 38				12 49		12 58	13 08			13 19		13 28	
Old Hill	d					12 22								12 52						13 22			
Cradley Heath	d	12 03	12 13			12 26		12 33		12 43				12 56		13 03	13 13			13 26		13 33	
Lye	d					12 29								12 59						13 29			
Stourbridge Junction	d	12 09	12a19			12 33		12 39		12a49				13 03		13 09	13a19			13 33		13 39	
Hagley	d	12 12						12 42								13 12						13 42	
Blakedown	d	12 15						12 45								13 15						13 45	
Kidderminster	d	12 20				12a42		12 50						13a12		13 20				13a42		13 50	
Hartlebury	d																						
University	d														12 55								
Barnt Green	d																						
Bromsgrove	d														13 10								
Droitwich Spa	d	12 31						13 01							13 20	13 31						14 01	
Worcester Shrub Hill	a															13 39							
	d						12 45														13 41		
Worcester Foregate Street	a	12 40					12 47	13 10							13 30						13 44	14 10	
	d						12 49	13 11							13 32						13 45		
Malvern Link	d						12 57	13 19							13 42						13 54		
Great Malvern	a						13 02	13 22							13 44						14 00		
	d						13 06								13 45								
Colwall	d						13 13								13 50								
Ledbury	a						13 21								13 57								
	d						13 23								13 59								
Hereford	a						13 40								14 19								

Table 71

Saturdays

Stratford-upon-Avon, Marylebone and Leamington Spa - Birmingham - Stourbridge, Worcester and Hereford

Network Diagram - see first Page of Table 71

		LM	LM	CH		XC	GW	LM	LM	LM	CH	XC	LM	LM		CH	CH	LM	XC	CH	LM	LM	LM	LM
				◇		◇■	◇				◇	◇■				◇	◇		◇■	◇				
Stratford-upon-Avon	d	12 26															13 19	13 26						
Wilmcote	d	12 31															13 25	13 31						
Wootton Wawen	d	12x36																13x36						
Henley-in-Arden	d	12 41																13 41						
Danzey	d	12x46																13x46						
Wood End	d	12x50																13x50						
The Lakes	d	12x52																13x52						
Earlswood (West Midlands)	d	12 55																13 55						
Wythall	d	12 57																13 57						
Whitlocks End	d	13 00							13 19				13 39					14 00					14 19	
Shirley	d	13 03							13 22				13 42					14 03					14 22	
Yardley Wood	d	13 06							13 25				13 45					14 06					14 25	
Hall Green	d	13 09							13 28				13 48					14 09					14 28	
Spring Road	d	13 11							13 30				13 50					14 11					14 30	
London Marylebone ⊖	d										12 00					12 30				12 37				
Banbury	d					12 54					13 04	13 24				13 28			13 54	13 58				
Leamington Spa	a					13 10					13 22	13 41				13 45	13 53		14 10	14 17				
	d			12 53		13 12					13 22	13 42				13 46			14 12	14 17				
Warwick	d			12 58							13 26									14 22				
Warwick Parkway	d			13 01							13 30					13 51								
Hatton	d			13 07																14a29				
Lapworth	d			13 12																				
Dorridge	d		13 09	13 18						13 28	13 40			13 46							14 09			14 28
Widney Manor	d		13 13							13 32				13 50							14 13			14 32
Solihull	d		13 17	13 23						13 36	13 45			13 54		14 04					14 17			14 36
Olton	d		13 20							13 39				13 57							14 20			14 39
Acocks Green	d		13 23							13 42				14 00							14 23			14 42
Tyseley	d								13 33					14 03									14 33	
Small Heath	d								13 35					14 05									14 35	
Bordesley	d								13 37															
Birmingham Moor Street	d	13 18	13 29	13a37					13 40	13 48	13 55		13 57	14 09		14a17		14 18			14 29		14 39	14 48
Birmingham Snow Hill	a	13 21	13 32						13 43	13 51	14 02		14 01	14 12				14 21			14 32		14 42	14 51
	d	13 23	13 33						13 43	13 53			14 03	14 13				14 23			14 33		14 43	14 53
Jewellery Quarter	d	13 25	13 35						13 45	13 55			14 05	14 15				14 25			14 35		14 45	14 55
The Hawthorns	d	13 30	13 40						13 50	14 00			14 10	14 20				14 30			14 40		14 50	15 00
Smethwick Galton Bridge	d	13 33	13 43						13 53	14 03			14 13	14 23				14 33			14 43		14 53	15 03
Coventry	a					13 22													14 22					
Birmingham International ✈	a					13 37													14 37					
Birmingham New Street	a					13 48						14 18							14 48					
	d							13 49														14 49		
Langley Green	d		13 46										14 16								14 46			
Rowley Regis	d	13 38	13 49						13 58	14 08			14 19	14 28				14 38			14 49		14 58	15 08
Old Hill	d		13 52										14 22								14 52			
Cradley Heath	d	13 43	13 56						14 03	14 13			14 26	14 33				14 43			14 56		15 03	15 13
Lye	d		13 59										14 29								14 59			
Stourbridge Junction	d	13a49	14 03						14 09	14a19			14 33	14 39				14a49			15 03		15 09	15a19
Hagley	d								14 12					14 42									15 12	
Blakedown	d								14 15					14 45									15 15	
Kidderminster	d		14a12						14 20				14a42	14 50							15a12		15 20	
Hartlebury	d																							
University	d							13 55														14 55		
Barnt Green	d																							
Bromsgrove	d							14 10														15 10		
Droitwich Spa	d							14 20	14 31					15 01								15 20	15 31	
Worcester Shrub Hill	a								14 40														15 39	
	d						14 15		14 46															
Worcester Foregate Street	a						14 18	14 30	14 48					15 10								15 30		
	d						14 18	14 32	14 49													15 32		
Malvern Link	d						14 27	14 42	14 57													15 42		
Great Malvern	a						14 31	14 44	15 00													15 44		
	d							14 45														15 45		
Colwall	d							14 50														15 50		
Ledbury	a							14 57														15 57		
	d							14 59														15 59		
Hereford	a							15 19														16 17		

Table 71

Saturdays

Stratford-upon-Avon, Marylebone and Leamington Spa - Birmingham - Stourbridge, Worcester and Hereford

Network Diagram - see first Page of Table 71

		CH	XC	LM	GW	LM	CH	LM	LM	CH		XC	GW	LM	LM	LM	CH	XC	LM	GW		LM	CH	CH	LM
		◇	◇■		◇■		◇			◇		◇■	◇				◇	◇■		◇■			◇	◇	
Stratford-upon-Avon	d							14 26																15 19	15 26
Wilmcote	d							14 31																15 25	15 31
Wootton Wawen	d							14x36																	15x36
Henley-in-Arden	d							14 41																	15 41
Danzey	d							14x46																	15x46
Wood End	d							14x50																	15x50
The Lakes	d							14x52																	15x52
Earlswood (West Midlands)	d							14 55																	15 55
Wythall	d							14 57																	15 57
Whitlocks End	d			14 39				15 00							15 19				15 39						16 00
Shirley	d			14 42				15 03							15 22				15 42						16 03
Yardley Wood	d			14 45				15 06							15 25				15 45						16 06
Hall Green	d			14 48				15 09							15 28				15 48						16 09
Spring Road	d			14 50				15 11							15 30				15 50						16 11
London Marylebone ⊖	d	13 00					13 30										14 00						14 30		
Banbury	d	14 04	14 24				14 28					14 54					15 04	15 24					15 28		
Leamington Spa	a	14 21	14 41				14 45					15 10					15 22	15 41					15 45	15 54	
	d	14 22	14 42				14 46			14 53		15 12					15 22	15 42					15 46		
Warwick	d	14 26								14 58							15 26								
Warwick Parkway	d	14 30					14 51			15 01							15 30						15 51		
Hatton	d									15 07															
Lapworth	d									15 12															
Dorridge	d	14 40				14 46			15 09	15 18						15 28	15 40					15 46			
Widney Manor	d					14 50			15 13							15 32						15 50			
Solihull	d	14 45				14 54	15 04		15 17	15 23						15 36	15 45					15 54	16 04		
Olton	d					14 57			15 20							15 39						15 57			
Acocks Green	d					15 00			15 23							15 42						16 00			
Tyseley	d					15 03									15 33							16 03			
Small Heath	d					15 05									15 35							16 05			
Bordesley	d																								
Birmingham Moor Street	d	14 55		14 57		15 09	15a17	15 18	15 29	15a37					15 39	15 48	15 55		15 57			16 09	16a17		16 18
Birmingham Snow Hill	a	15 02		15 01		15 12		15 21	15 32						15 42	15 51	16 02		16 01			16 12			16 21
	d			15 03		15 13		15 23	15 33						15 43	15 53			16 03			16 13			16 23
Jewellery Quarter	d			15 05		15 15		15 25	15 35						15 45	15 55			16 05			16 15			16 25
The Hawthorns	d			15 10		15 20		15 30	15 40						15 50	16 00			16 10			16 20			16 30
Smethwick Galton Bridge	d			15 13		15 23		15 33	15 43						15 53	16 03			16 13			16 23			16 33
Coventry	a											15 22													
Birmingham International ✈	a											15 37													
Birmingham New Street	a		15 18									15 48						16 18							
	d													15 49											
Langley Green	d			15 16					15 46										16 16						
Rowley Regis	d			15 19		15 28		15 38	15 49						15 58	16 08			16 19			16 28			16 38
Old Hill	d			15 22					15 52										16 22						
Cradley Heath	d			15 26		15 33		15 43	15 56						16 03	16 13			16 26			16 33			16 43
Lye	d			15 29					15 59										16 29						
Stourbridge Junction	d			15 33		15 39		15a49	16 03						16 09	16a19			16 33			16 39			16a49
Hagley	d					15 42									16 12							16 42			
Blakedown	d					15 45									16 15							16 45			
Kidderminster	d			15a42		15 50			16a12						16 20				16a42			16 50			
Hartlebury	d																								
University	d													15 55											
Barnt Green	d																								
Bromsgrove	d													16 10											
Droitwich Spa	d					16 01								16 20	16 31							17 01			
Worcester Shrub Hill	a																								
	d				15 41								16 15							16 41					
Worcester Foregate Street	a				15 44	16 10							16 17	16 30	16 40					16 44		17 10			
	d				15 45								16 18	16 32						16 47		17 11			
Malvern Link	d				15 54								16 26	16 42						16 56		17 20			
Great Malvern	a				16 00								16 32	16 44						17 00		17 23			
	d													16 45											
Colwall	d													16 50											
Ledbury	a													16 57											
	d													16 59											
Hereford	a													17 19											

Stratford-upon-Avon, Marylebone and Leamington Spa - Birmingham - Stourbridge, Worcester and Hereford

Network Diagram - see first Page of Table 71

		XC	CH	LM	LM	LM	LM	CH	XC	LM	GW	LM	LM	CH	LM	LM	CH	XC	GW	LM	LM	LM	CH
		◇■	◇					◇	◇■		◇■			◇			◇	◇■					◇
Stratford-upon-Avon	d														16 26								
Wilmcote	d														16 31								
Wootton Wawen	d														16x36								
Henley-in-Arden	d														16 41								
Danzey	d														16x46								
Wood End	d														16x50								
The Lakes	d														16x52								
Earlswood (West Midlands)	d														16 55								
Wythall	d														16 57								
Whitlocks End	d					16 19				16 39					17 00						17 19		
Shirley	d					16 22				16 42					17 03						17 22		
Yardley Wood	d					16 25				16 45					17 06						17 25		
Hall Green	d					16 28				16 48					17 09						17 28		
Spring Road	d					16 30				16 50					17 11						17 30		
London Marylebone ■ ⊖	d		14 33					15 00						15 30									16 00
Banbury	d	15 54	15 58					16 04	16 24					16 28				16 54					17 04
Leamington Spa ■	a	16 10	16 17					16 22	16 41					16 45				17 10					17 22
	d	16 12	16 17					16 23	16 42					16 46			16 53	17 12					17 22
Warwick	d		16 22					16 27									16 58						17 26
Warwick Parkway	d							16 31						16 51			17 01						17 30
Hatton	d		16a29														17 07						
Lapworth	d																17 12						
Dorridge	d			16 09			16 27	16 41					16 46			17 09	17 17					17 27	17 40
Widney Manor	d			16 13			16 31						16 50			17 13						17 31	
Solihull	d			16 17			16 35	16 46					16 54	17 04		17 17	17 22					17 35	17 45
Olton	d			16 20			16 38						16 57			17 20						17 38	
Acocks Green	d			16 23			16 41						17 00			17 23						17 41	
Tyseley	d					16 33	16 44			16 53			17 03								17 33	17 44	
Small Heath	d					16 35							17 05								17 35		
Bordesley	d																						
Birmingham Moor Street	d			16 29		16 39	16 49	16 55		16 58			17 09	17a17	17 18	17 29	17 33				17 39	17 49	17 55
Birmingham Snow Hill	a			16 32		16 42	16 51	17 02		17 01			17 12		17 21	17 32	17 41				17 42	17 51	18 02
	d			16 33		16 43	16 53			17 03			17 13		17 23	17 33					17 43	17 53	
Jewellery Quarter	d			16 35		16 45	16 55			17 05			17 15		17 25	17 35					17 45	17 55	
The Hawthorns	d			16 40		16 50	17 00			17 10			17 20		17 30	17 40					17 50	18 00	
Smethwick Galton Bridge ■	d			16 43		16 53	17 03			17 13			17 23		17 33	17 43					17 53	18 03	
Coventry	a	16 22																17 22					
Birmingham International	a	16 37																17 37					
Birmingham New Street ■	a	16 48							17 18									17 48					
	d				16 49							17 19								17 49			
Langley Green	d			16 46						17 16						17 46						18 06	
Rowley Regis	d			16 49		16 58	17 08			17 19			17 28		17 38	17 49					17 58	18 09	
Old Hill	d			16 52						17 22						17 52						18 12	
Cradley Heath	d			16 56		17 03	17 13			17 26			17 33		17 43	17 56					18 03	18 16	
Lye	d			16 59						17 29						17 59						18 19	
Stourbridge Junction ■	d			17 03		17 11	17a19			17 33			17 39		17a49	18 03					18 10	18a23	
Hagley	d			17 06		17 14							17 42			18 06					18 13		
Blakedown	d			17 09		17 17							17 45			18 09					18 16		
Kidderminster	d			17a15		17 22				17a42			17 50			18a15					18 21		
Hartlebury	d					17 27							17 55								18 26		
University	d				16 55															17 55			
Barnt Green	d																						
Bromsgrove	d				17 10							17 40								18 10			
Droitwich Spa	d				17 20	17 35						17 50	18 03							18 20	18 34		
Worcester Shrub Hill ■	a											17 58	18 12							18 27			
	d										17 41								18 19	18 31			
Worcester Foregate Street ■	a				17 29	17 43					17 44								18 21	18 33	18 43		
	d				17 32						17 45								18 22	18 34			
Malvern Link	d				17 42						17 54								18 30	18 44			
Great Malvern	a				17 45						18 00								18 36	18 46			
	d				17 45															18 47			
Colwall	d				17 50															18 52			
Ledbury	a				17 57															18 59			
	d				17 59															19 00			
Hereford ■	a				18 16															19 20			

Stratford-upon-Avon, Marylebone and Leamington Spa - Birmingham - Stourbridge, Worcester and Hereford

Network Diagram - see first Page of Table 71

		XC	LM	CH	GW	LM	CH	XC	CH	LM	LM	LM	GW	LM	CH	LM	XC	CH	LM	GW	GW	LM
		◇■		◇	◇■		◇	◇■	◇				◇■		◇		◇■	◇		◇		
																				A	B	
Stratford-upon-Avon	d					17 26	17 40									18 08						
Wilmcote	d					17 31										18 13						
Wootton Wawen	d					17x36										18x18						
Henley-in-Arden	d					17 41										18 23						
Danzey	d					17x46										18x28						
Wood End	d					17x50										18x32						
The Lakes	d					17x52										18x34						
Earlswood (West Midlands)	d					17 55										18 37						
Wythall	d					17 57										18 39						
Whitlocks End	d					18 00					18 19					18 42						
Shirley	d					18 03					18 22					18 45						
Yardley Wood	d					18 06					18 25					18 48						
Hall Green	d					18 09					18 28					18 51						
Spring Road	d					18 11					18 30					18 53						
London Marylebone ■ ⊖	d			16 30					16 33						17 00			17 30				
Banbury	d	17 24		17 28				17 54	18 00						18 04		18 24	18 28				
Leamington Spa ■	a	17 41		17 45			18 06	18 10	18 18						18 23		18 41	18 45				
	d	17 42		17 46				18 12	18 19						18 24		18 42	18 46				
Warwick	d								18 23						18 28							
Warwick Parkway	d			17 51											18 32			18 51				
Hatton	d								18a31													
Lapworth	d																					
Dorridge	d		17 46							18 09				18 28	18 43							19 01
Widney Manor	d		17 50							18 13				18 32								19 05
Solihull	d		17 54	18 04						18 17				18 36	18 49			19 05				19 09
Olton	d		17 57							18 20				18 39								19 12
Acocks Green	d		18 00							18 23				18 42								19 15
Tyseley	d		18 03								18 33			18 45		18 56						19 18
Small Heath	d		18 05								18 35			18 47		18 58						19 20
Bordesley	d																					
Birmingham Moor Street	d		18 09	18a17		18 18				18 29	18 39			18 51	18 57	19 02		19a17				19 24
Birmingham Snow Hill	a		18 12			18 21				18 32	18 42			18 54	19 05	19 06						19 27
	d		18 13			18 23				18 33				18 58								19 28
Jewellery Quarter	d		18 15			18 25				18 35				19 00								19 30
The Hawthorns	d		18 20			18 30				18 40				19 05								19 35
Smethwick Galton Bridge ■	d		18 23			18 33				18 43				19 08								19 38
Coventry	a							18 22														
Birmingham International	a							18 37														
Birmingham New Street ■	a	18 18						18 48									19 18					
	d											18 49							19 19			
Langley Green	d		18 26							18 46				19 11								19 41
Rowley Regis	d		18 29			18 38				18 49				19 14								19 44
Old Hill	d		18 32							18 52				19 17								19 47
Cradley Heath	d		18 36			18 43				18 56				19 21								19 51
Lye	d		18 39							18 59				19 24								19 54
Stourbridge Junction ■	d		18a43			18 49				19 03				19 28								19 58
Hagley	d					18 52				19 06				19 31								20 01
Blakedown	d					18 55				19 09				19 34								20 04
Kidderminster	d					19 00				19a15				19 39								20 09
Hartlebury	d					19 05																
University	d											18 55							19 25			
Barnt Green	d																					
Bromsgrove	d											19 10							19 40			
Droitwich Spa	d					19 13						19 20		19 50					19 57			20 20
Worcester Shrub Hill ■	a											19 27		19 58								20 30
	d				18 53							19 35	19 42							20 20	20 20	
Worcester Foregate Street ■	a				18 55	19 22						19 37	19 44						20 05	20 22	20 22	
	d				18 57	19 23						19 38							20 06	20 25	20 25	
Malvern Link	d				19 05	19 32						19 48							20 16	20 34	20 34	
Great Malvern	a				19 09	19 35						19 50							20 18	20 40	20 40	
	d				19 09														20 25			
Colwall	d				19 15														20 30			
Ledbury	a				19 23														20 38			
	d				19 29														20 39			
Hereford ■	a				19 45														21 02			

A until 8 September

B from 15 September

Stratford-upon-Avon, Marylebone and Leamington Spa - Birmingham - Stourbridge, Worcester and Hereford

Network Diagram - see first Page of Table 71

		CH	LM	XC	GW	LM	CH	XC		LM	CH	CH	XC	LM	LM	CH	CH	LM		XC	CH	XC	GW	LM	CH
		◇		◇1 ✠	◇1 ⊟		◇	◇1 ✠			◇	◇	◇1 ✠			◇	◇			◇1	◇	◇1	◇1		◇
Stratford-upon-Avon	d		18 49							19 26		19 16						20 26							
Wilmcote	d		18 54							19 31		19 22						20 31							
Wootton Wawen	d		18x59							19x36								20x36							
Henley-in-Arden	d		19 03							19 40								20 40							
Danzey	d		19x08							19x44								20x44							
Wood End	d		19x12							19x48								20x48							
The Lakes	d		19x14							19x50								20x50							
Earlswood (West Midlands)	d		19 17							19 53								20 53							
Wythall	d		19 19							19 55								20 55							
Whitlocks End	d		19 22							19 58								20 58							
Shirley	d		19 25							20 01								21 01							
Yardley Wood	d		19 28							20 04								21 04							
Hall Green	d		19 31							20 07								21 07							
Spring Road	d		19 33							20 09								21 09							
London Marylebone 15 ⊖	d						18 00				18 30					19 00	18 33				19 30				20 00
Banbury	d			18 54			19 04	19 24			19 28		19 54			20 04	20 09			20 29	20 33	20 54			21 04
Leamington Spa 8	a			19 10			19 22	19 41			19 45	19 51	20 10			20 21	20 28			20 45	20 51	21 10			21 21
	d	18 55		19 12			19 23	19 42			19 46		20 12			20 22	20 28			20 46	20 52	21 12			21 22
Warwick	d	19 00					19 27									20 26	20 33								21 26
Warwick Parkway	d	19 03					19 31				19 51					20 30					20 57				21 30
Hatton	d	19 09														20 35	20a40								
Lapworth	d	19 14														20 40									
Dorridge	d	19 20				19 28	19 42								20 28	20 45								21 28	21 40
Widney Manor	d					19 32									20 32									21 32	
Solihull	d	19 25				19 36	19 47				20 04				20 36	20 51					21 09			21 36	21 45
Olton	d					19 39									20 39									21 39	
Acocks Green	d					19 42									20 42									21 42	
Tyseley	d		19 36			19 45									20 45									21 45	
Small Heath	d		19 39			19 47									20 47									21 47	
Bordesley	d																								
Birmingham Moor Street	d	19a39	19 43			19 51	19 56			20 16	20a17				20 51	21 00		21 16			21a22			21 51	21 56
Birmingham Snow Hill ⇌	a		19 46			19 54	20 04			20 19					20 54	21 08		21 19						21 54	22 03
	d					19 55				20 20					20 55			21 20						21 55	
Jewellery Quarter ⇌	d					19 57				20 22					20 57			21 22						21 57	
The Hawthorns ⇌	d					20 02				20 27					21 02			21 27						22 02	
Smethwick Galton Bridge 7	d					20 05				20 30					21 05			21 30						22 05	
Coventry	a			19 22									20 22									21 22			
Birmingham International ✈	a			19 37									20 37									21 37			
Birmingham New Street 12	a			19 48				20 18					20 48							21 18		21 48			
	d													20 59											
Langley Green	d					20 08				20 33					21 08			21 33						22 08	
Rowley Regis	d					20 11				20 36					21 11			21 36						22 11	
Old Hill	d					20 14				20 39					21 14			21 39						22 14	
Cradley Heath	d					20 18				20 43					21 18			21 43						22 18	
Lye	d					20 21				20 46					21 21			21 46						22 21	
Stourbridge Junction 2	d					20 25				20a50					21 25			21a50						22 25	
Hagley	d					20 28									21 28									22 28	
Blakedown	d					20 31									21 31									22 31	
Kidderminster	d					20 36									21 36									22 36	
Hartlebury	d																								
University	d													21 05											
Barnt Green	d																								
Bromsgrove	d													21 20											
Droitwich Spa	d					20 47								21 30	21 47									22 47	
Worcester Shrub Hill 7	a					20 55								21 37	21 55									22 55	
	d				20 46	20 59								21 47									22 04	23 00	
Worcester Foregate Street 7	a				20 48	21 01								21 49									22 06	23 02	
	d				20 50	21 02								21 50									22 08	23 03	
Malvern Link	d				20 58	21 11								21 59									22 17	23 11	
Great Malvern	a				21 02	21 14								22 01									22 22	23 14	
	d				21 02									22 02											
Colwall	d				21 08									22 07											
Ledbury	a				21 16									22 14											
	d				21 18									22 15											
Hereford 7	a				21 34									22 35											

Stratford-upon-Avon, Marylebone and Leamington Spa - Birmingham - Stourbridge, Worcester and Hereford

Network Diagram - see first Page of Table 71

		XC	CH	LM		CH	XC	LM	CH	XC	LM	CH
		◇1				◇	◇1		◇	◇1 ✠		◇
Stratford-upon-Avon	d		21 16									
Wilmcote	d											
Wootton Wawen	d											
Henley-in-Arden	d											
Danzey	d											
Wood End	d											
The Lakes	d											
Earlswood (West Midlands)	d											
Wythall	d											
Whitlocks End	d			21 55							22 57	
Shirley	d			21 58							23 00	
Yardley Wood	d			22 01							23 03	
Hall Green	d			22 04							23 06	
Spring Road	d			22 06							23 08	
London Marylebone 15 ⊖	d								21 00			22 10
Banbury	d	21 25					21 54		22 08	22 29		23 05
Leamington Spa 8	a	21 44	21 48				22 10		22 26	22 45		23 23
	d	21 45				21 53	22 12		22 26	22 46		23 24
Warwick	d					21 58			22 31			23 28
Warwick Parkway	d					22 01			22 34			23 32
Hatton	d					22 06						
Lapworth	d					22 12						
Dorridge	d					22 17		22 33	22 44			23 42
Widney Manor	d							22 37				23 46
Solihull	d					22 22		22 41	22 50			23 49
Olton	d							22 44				
Acocks Green	d							22 47				
Tyseley	d			22 09				22 50			23 11	
Small Heath	d			22 11				22 52			23 13	
Bordesley	d											
Birmingham Moor Street	d			22 15		22a37		22 56	23 01		23 17	00a01
Birmingham Snow Hill ⇌	a			22 18				22 59	23 09		23 20	
	d			22 20				23 00			23 23	
Jewellery Quarter ⇌	d			22 22				23 02			23 25	
The Hawthorns ⇌	d			22 27				23 07			23 30	
Smethwick Galton Bridge 7	d			22 30				23 10			23 33	
Coventry	a	21 55					22 22					
Birmingham International ✈	a	22 10					22 36					
Birmingham New Street 12	a	22 21					22 48			23 16		
	d											
Langley Green	d			22 33				23 13			23 36	
Rowley Regis	d			22 36				23 16			23 39	
Old Hill	d			22 39				23 19			23 42	
Cradley Heath	d			22 43				23 23			23 46	
Lye	d			22 46				23 26			23 49	
Stourbridge Junction 2	d			22a50				23 30			23a52	
Hagley	d							23 33				
Blakedown	d							23 36				
Kidderminster	d							23 41				
Hartlebury	d											
University	d											
Barnt Green	d											
Bromsgrove	d											
Droitwich Spa	d							23 52				
Worcester Shrub Hill 7	a							00 01				
	d											
Worcester Foregate Street 7	a											
	d											
Malvern Link	d											
Great Malvern	a											
	d											
Colwall	d											
Ledbury	a											
	d											
Hereford 7	a											

Table 71

Sundays until 24 June

Stratford-upon-Avon, Marylebone and Leamington Spa - Birmingham - Stourbridge, Worcester and Hereford

Network Diagram - see first Page of Table 71

		LM	LM	GW	LM	CH	XC	CH	LM	CH	XC	CH	GW	LM	LM	CH	GW	LM	CH	XC	CH	LM	CH
				◇1		◇	◇1 ✠	◇		◇	◇1 ✠		◇1 ⊡			◇	◇1 ⊡		◇	◇1 ✠	◇		
Stratford-upon-Avon	d				09 30			10 00						10 30				11 30			12 00		
Wilmcote	d				09 35			10 05						10 35				11 35			12 05		
Wootton Wawen	d																						
Henley-in-Arden	d				09 42									10 42				11 42					
Danzey	d																						
Wood End	d																						
The Lakes	d				09x49									10x49				11x49					
Earlswood (West Midlands)	d																						
Wythall	d				09 53									10 53				11 53					
Whitlocks End	d				09 55									10 55				11 55					
Shirley	d				09 59									10 59				11 59					
Yardley Wood	d				10 02									11 02				12 02					
Hall Green	d				10 05									11 05				12 05					
Spring Road	d				10 07									11 07				12 07					
London Marylebone 10 ⊖	d					08 15				09 00		09 36				10 00			10 33				11 00
Banbury	d					09 28	09 54			10 11	10 54	11 01				11 11			11 29	11 54			12 11
Leamington Spa 8	a					09 45	10 11	10 27		10 28	11 11	11 20				11 28			11 46	12 11	12 27		12 28
	d					09 45	10 12			10 28	11 12	11 20				11 28			11 47	12 12			12 28
Warwick	d					09 50				10 33		11 25				11 33							12 33
Warwick Parkway	d					09 53				10 36						11 36			11 53				12 36
Hatton	d					09 59						11a32				11 42							
Lapworth	d					10 05										11 48							
Dorridge	d	22p33				10 10			10 25	10 47					11 25	11 53			12 03			12 25	12 47
Widney Manor	d	22p37							10 29						11 29							12 29	
Solihull	d	22p41				10 15			10 32	10 53					11 32	11 58			12 09			12 32	12 53
Olton	d	22p44							10 36						11 36							12 36	
Acocks Green	d	22p47							10 38						11 38							12 38	
Tyseley	d	22p50			10 10									11 10				12 10					
Small Heath	d	22p52																					
Bordesley	d																						
Birmingham Moor Street	d	22p56	09 26		10 17	10 24			10 45	11 03				11 17	11 45	12 07		12 17	12a25			12 45	13 02
Birmingham Snow Hill ⇌	a	22p59	09 28		10 19	10 31			10 47	11 10				11 19	11 47	12 14		12 19				12 47	13 09
	d	23p00	09 30		10 20				10 48					11 20	11 48			12 20				12 48	
Jewellery Quarter ⇌	d	23p02	09 32		10 22				10 51					11 22	11 51			12 22				12 51	
The Hawthorns ⇌	d	23p07	09 37		10 27				10 55					11 27	11 55			12 27				12 55	
Smethwick Galton Bridge 7	d	23p10	09 39		10 29				10 58					11 29	11 58			12 29				12 58	
Coventry	a						10 22				11 22									12 22			
Birmingham International ✈	a						10 38				11 38									12 38			
Birmingham New Street 12	a						10 50				11 50									12 50			
	d																						
Langley Green	d	23p13							11 01						12 01							13 01	
Rowley Regis	d	23p16	09 44		10 34				11 04					11 34	12 04			12 34				13 04	
Old Hill	d	23p19							11 07						12 07							13 07	
Cradley Heath	d	23p23	09 49		10 39				11 10					11 39	12 10			12 39				13 10	
Lye	d	23p26							11 13						12 13							13 13	
Stourbridge Junction 2	d	23p30	09 54		10 45				11a17					11 45	12a17			12 45				13a17	
Hagley	d	23p33	09 58		10 48									11 49				12 48					
Blakedown	d	23p36												11 52				12 51					
Kidderminster	d	23p41	10 04		10 55									11 57				12 56					
Hartlebury	d																						
University	d																						
Barnt Green	d																						
Bromsgrove	d																						
Droitwich Spa	d	23p52	10 15		11 06									12 08				13 08					
Worcester Shrub Hill 7	a	00 01	10 23		11 14									12 16				13 15					
	d		10 27	10 32	11 32								12 06				13 09	13 31					
Worcester Foregate Street 7	a		10 29	10 34	11 34								12 09				13 12	13 33					
	d		10 30	10 36	11 35								12 10				13 13	13 34					
Malvern Link	d		10 38	10 47	11 43								12 19				13 22	13 42					
Great Malvern	a		10 41	10 50	11 46								12 22				13 26	13 45					
	d												12 23				13 27						
Colwall	d												12 29				13 33						
Ledbury	a												12 36				13 41						
	d												12 38				13 49						
Hereford 7	a												12 54				14 06						

Table 71

Sundays until 24 June

Stratford-upon-Avon, Marylebone and Leamington Spa - Birmingham - Stourbridge, Worcester and Hereford

Network Diagram - see first Page of Table 71

		LM	CH	LM	XC	CH	LM	CH	XC	GW	LM	CH	XC	CH	LM	CH	XC	LM	CH	XC	CH	LM	CH
			◇		◇1 ✠	◇		◇	◇1 ✠	◇1 ⊡			◇1 ✠	◇			◇1 ✠		◇	◇1 ✠	◇		◇
Stratford-upon-Avon	d	12 30									13 30			14 00				14 30					
Wilmcote	d	12 35									13 35			14 05				14 35					
Wootton Wawen	d																						
Henley-in-Arden	d	12 42									13 42							14 42					
Danzey	d																						
Wood End	d																						
The Lakes	d	12x49									13x49							14x49					
Earlswood (West Midlands)	d																						
Wythall	d	12 53									13 53							14 53					
Whitlocks End	d	12 55									13 55							14 55					
Shirley	d	12 59									13 59							14 59					
Yardley Wood	d	13 02									14 02							15 02					
Hall Green	d	13 05									14 05							15 05					
Spring Road	d	13 07									14 07							15 07					
London Marylebone 10 ⊖	d		11 33			11 36		12 00				12 33				13 00			13 33		13 36		14 00
Banbury	d		12 29		12 54	13 01		13 11	13 35			13 40	13 54			14 11	14 24		14 31	14 54	15 01		15 11
Leamington Spa 8	a		12 46		13 11	13 20		13 28	13 50			13 59	14 11	14 27		14 28	14 40		14 48	15 11	15 20		15 28
	d		12 47		13 12	13 20		13 28	13 52			14 00	14 12			14 28	14 42		14 49	15 12	15 20		15 28
Warwick	d					13 25		13 33								14 33					15 25		15 33
Warwick Parkway	d		12 53					13 36				14 06				14 36			14 55				15 36
Hatton	d					13a32		13 42													15a32		
Lapworth	d							13 48															
Dorridge	d		13 03				13 25	13 53				14 16			14 25	14 47			15 05			15 25	15 47
Widney Manor	d						13 29								14 29							15 29	
Solihull	d		13 09				13 32	13 58				14 22			14 32	14 53			15 11			15 32	15 53
Olton	d						13 36								14 36							15 36	
Acocks Green	d						13 38								14 38							15 38	
Tyseley	d	13 10									14 10							15 10					
Small Heath	d																						
Bordesley	d																						
Birmingham Moor Street	d	13 15	13a25				13 45	14 07			14 17	14a37			14 45	15 02		15 15	15a26			15 45	16 02
Birmingham Snow Hill ⇌	a	13 18					13 48	14 14			14 19				14 47	15 09		15 19				15 48	16 09
	d	13 20					13 48				14 20				14 48			15 20				15 48	
Jewellery Quarter ⇌	d	13 22					13 51				14 22				14 51			15 22				15 51	
The Hawthorns ⇌	d	13 27					13 55				14 27				14 55			15 27				15 55	
Smethwick Galton Bridge 7	d	13 29					13 58				14 29				14 58			15 29				15 58	
Coventry	a				13 22								14 22							15 22			
Birmingham International ✈	a				13 37								14 35							15 35			
Birmingham New Street 12	a				13 48				14 19				14 48				15 09			15 48			
	d			13 24																			
Langley Green	d						14 01								15 01							16 01	
Rowley Regis	d	13 34					14 04				14 34				15 04			15 34				16 04	
Old Hill	d						14 07								15 07							16 07	
Cradley Heath	d	13 39					14 10				14 39				15 10			15 39				16 10	
Lye	d						14 13								15 13							16 13	
Stourbridge Junction 2	d	13 45					14a18				14 45				15a17			15 45				16a18	
Hagley	d	13 49									14 48							15 48					
Blakedown	d										14 51												
Kidderminster	d	13 55									14 56							15 54					
Hartlebury	d																						
University	d																						
Barnt Green	d																						
Bromsgrove	d			13 42																			
Droitwich Spa	d	14 07		13 52							15 08							16 06					
Worcester Shrub Hill 7	a			13 59																			
	d			14 14						15 10													
Worcester Foregate Street 7	a	14 15		14 16						15 12	15 16							16 14					
	d			14 17						15 13													
Malvern Link	d			14 25						15 23													
Great Malvern	a			14 28						15 26													
	d			14 29						15 27													
Colwall	d			14 34						15 33													
Ledbury	a			14 41						15 41													
	d			14 49						15 48													
Hereford 7	a			15 10						16 05													

Table 71

Sundays
until 24 June

Stratford-upon-Avon, Marylebone and Leamington Spa - Birmingham - Stourbridge, Worcester and Hereford

Network Diagram - see first Page of Table 71

		LM		XC	GW	LM	CH	XC	LM	LM	CH	CH		XC	GW	LM	CH	XC	CH	LM	CH	LM		XC	GW
				◇1 ⊼	◇1		◇	◇1 ⊼			◇	◇		◇1 ⊼	◇1		◇	◇1 ⊼	◇		■			◇1 ⊼	◇1
Stratford-upon-Avon	d					15 30						16 00				16 30									
Wilmcote	d					15 35						16 05				16 35									
Wootton Wawen	d																								
Henley-in-Arden	d					15 42										16 42									
Danzey	d															16x47									
Wood End	d																								
The Lakes	d					15x49										16x51									
Earlswood (West Midlands)	d																								
Wythall	d					15 53										16 55									
Whitlocks End	d					15 55										16 57									
Shirley	d					15 59										17 00									
Yardley Wood	d					16 02										17 03									
Hall Green	d					16 05										17 06									
Spring Road	d					16 07										17 08									
London Marylebone 10 ⊖	d						14 33				15 00						15 33		15 36		16 00				
Banbury	d			15 25			15 31	15 54			16 09			16 25			16 31	16 54	17 01		17 11			17 25	
Leamington Spa 8	a			15 41			15 48	16 11			16 26	16 27		16 41			16 48	17 11	17 20		17 28			17 41	
	d			15 43			15 49	16 12			16 26			16 43			16 49	17 12	17 20		17 28			17 43	
Warwick	d										16 31								17 25		17 33				
Warwick Parkway	d						15 55				16 34						16 55				17 36				
Hatton	d						16 00												17a32						
Lapworth	d						16 05																		
Dorridge	d						16 10		16 25		16 45						17 05			17 25	17 47				
Widney Manor	d								16 29											17 29					
Solihull	d						16 17		16 32		16 51						17 11			17 32	17 53				
Olton	d								16 36											17 36					
Acocks Green	d								16 38											17 38					
Tyseley	d					16 10										17 11									
Small Heath	d																								
Bordesley	d																								
Birmingham Moor Street	d					16 15	16a31		16 45	17 02	17 05					17 17	17a26			17 45	18 02				
Birmingham Snow Hill ⇌	a					16 19			16 48	17 04	17 13					17 20				17 48	18 09				
	d					16 20			16 48	17 06						17 21				17 48					
Jewellery Quarter ⇌	d					16 22			16 51							17 24				17 51					
The Hawthorns ⇌	d					16 27			16 55							17 28				17 55					
Smethwick Galton Bridge 7	d					16 29			16 58							17 31				17 58					
Coventry	a							16 22										17 22							
Birmingham International ✈	a							16 35										17 35							
Birmingham New Street 12	a			16 12				16 48						17 12				17 48						18 09	
	d	16 00																				18 00			
Langley Green	d								17 01											18 01					
Rowley Regis	d					16 34			17 04							17 35				18 04					
Old Hill	d								17 07											18 07					
Cradley Heath	d					16 39			17 10							17 40				18 10					
Lye	d								17 13											18 13					
Stourbridge Junction 2	d					16 45			17a18	17 27						17 46				18a19					
Hagley	d					16 48				17 30						17 50									
Blakedown	d																								
Kidderminster	d					16 54				17 36						17 56									
Hartlebury	d																								
University	d																								
Barnt Green	d																								
Bromsgrove	d	16 21																				18 21			
Droitwich Spa	d	16 30				17 06				17 48						18 07						18 30			
Worcester Shrub Hill 7	a	16 38														18 15						18 38			
	d	16 45			17 10										18 08							18 43			19 10
Worcester Foregate Street 7	a	16 47			17 12	17 14				18 01					18 10							18 45			19 13
	d	16 48			17 13																	18 46			19 14
Malvern Link	d	16 57			17 22																	18 55			19 23
Great Malvern	a	17 01			17 26																	18 58			19 27
	d				17 26																	18 58			
Colwall	d				17 32																	19 03			
Ledbury	a				17 41																	19 10			
	d				17 42																	19 10			
Hereford 7	a				17 58																	19 31			

Table 71

Sundays
until 24 June

Stratford-upon-Avon, Marylebone and Leamington Spa - Birmingham - Stourbridge, Worcester and Hereford

Network Diagram - see first Page of Table 71

		LM	CH	XC	CH	CH	LM	XC		GW	LM	CH	XC	CH	CH	XC	LM	CH		XC	CH	CH	LM	XC	CH
			◇	◇1 ⊼	◇	◇		◇1 ⊼		◇1		◇	◇1 ⊼	◇	◇	◇1 ⊼		◇		◇1 ⊼	◇	◇		◇1 ⊼	◇
Stratford-upon-Avon	d	17 30			18 00						18 30						19 30				20 00				
Wilmcote	d	17 35			18 05						18 35						19 35				20 05				
Wootton Wawen	d																								
Henley-in-Arden	d	17 42									18 42						19 42								
Danzey	d																								
Wood End	d																								
The Lakes	d	17x49									18x49						19x49								
Earlswood (West Midlands)	d																								
Wythall	d	17 53									18 53						19 53								
Whitlocks End	d	17 55									18 55						19 55								
Shirley	d	17 59									18 59						19 59								
Yardley Wood	d	18 02									19 02						20 02								
Hall Green	d	18 05									19 05						20 05								
Spring Road	d	18 07									19 07						20 07								
London Marylebone 10 ⊖	d		16 33			17 00						17 33		17 36	18 00			18 33				19 00			19 33
Banbury	d		17 31	17 54		18 11		18 25				18 31	18 54	19 01	19 11	19 25		19 31		19 54		20 11		20 25	20 31
Leamington Spa 8	a		17 48	18 11	18 27	18 28		18 41				18 48	19 11	19 20	19 28	19 41		19 48		20 11	20 27	20 28		20 41	20 48
	d		17 49	18 12		18 28		18 43				18 49	19 12	19 20	19 28	19 43		19 49		20 12		20 28		20 43	20 49
Warwick	d					18 33								19 25	19 33							20 33			
Warwick Parkway	d		17 55			18 36						18 55			19 36			19 55				20 36			20 55
Hatton	d		18 00											19a32				20 00							
Lapworth	d		18 05															20 05							
Dorridge	d		18 10			18 47						19 05			19 47			20 10				20 47			21 05
Widney Manor	d					18 51									19 51							20 51			
Solihull	d		18 17			18 56						19 11			19 56			20 17				20 56			21 11
Olton	d																								
Acocks Green	d																								
Tyseley	d	18 10									19 10						20 10								
Small Heath	d																								
Bordesley	d																								
Birmingham Moor Street	d	18 15	18a31			19 05					19 15	19a25			20 05		20 15	20a31				21 05			21a25
Birmingham Snow Hill ⇌	a	18 19				19 12					19 18				20 12		20 18					21 12			
	d	18 20									19 20						20 20								
Jewellery Quarter ⇌	d	18 22									19 22						20 22								
The Hawthorns ⇌	d	18 27									19 27						20 27								
Smethwick Galton Bridge 7	d	18 29									19 29						20 29								
Coventry	a			18 22									19 22			19 53				20 22				20 53	
Birmingham International ✈	a			18 35									19 35			20 03				20 35				21 03	
Birmingham New Street 12	a			18 48				19 11					19 48			20 15				20 48				21 15	
	d						19 00																21 00		
Langley Green	d																								
Rowley Regis	d	18 34									19 34						20 34								
Old Hill	d																								
Cradley Heath	d	18 39									19 39						20 39								
Lye	d																								
Stourbridge Junction 2	d	18 45									19 45						20 45								
Hagley	d	18 49									19 48						20 49								
Blakedown	d	18 52																							
Kidderminster	d	18 57									19 55						20 57								
Hartlebury	d																								
University	d																								
Barnt Green	d																								
Bromsgrove	d						19 21																21 20		
Droitwich Spa	d	19 08					19 31				20 08						21 09						21 30		
Worcester Shrub Hill 7	a	19 16					19 41				20 16						21 16						21 37		
	d									20 12							21 22						21 42		
Worcester Foregate Street 7	a									20 16							21 24						21 44		
	d									20 17							21 25						21 45		
Malvern Link	d									20 26							21 34						21 54		
Great Malvern	a									20 29							21 37						21 57		
	d									20 32													21 57		
Colwall	d									20 38													22 02		
Ledbury	a									20 45													22 09		
	d									20 47													22 10		
Hereford 7	a									21 03													22 30		

Table 71

Sundays
until 24 June

Stratford-upon-Avon, Marylebone and Leamington Spa - Birmingham - Stourbridge, Worcester and Hereford

Network Diagram - see first Page of Table 71

		XC	GW	LM	CH	LM	XC	CH	XC	LM	CH	XC	CH
		◇■	◇■		◇		◇■	◇	◇■		◇	◇■	◇
Stratford-upon-Avon	d												
Wilmcote	d												
Wootton Wawen	d												
Henley-in-Arden	d												
Danzey	d												
Wood End	d												
The Lakes	d												
Earlswood (West Midlands)	d												
Wythall	d												
Whitlocks End	d												
Shirley	d												
Yardley Wood	d												
Hall Green	d												
Spring Road	d												
London Marylebone ⊖	d				20 00			20 33			21 00		22 00
Banbury	d	20 54			21 11		21 24	21 44	21 54		22 11	22 24	22 55
Leamington Spa	a	21 11			21 28		21 41	22 01	22 11		22 28	22 40	23 12
	d	21 12			21 28		21 42	22 01	22 12		22 28	22 42	23 13
Warwick	d				21 33						22 33		23 17
Warwick Parkway	d				21 36			22 07			22 36		23 21
Hatton	d										22 42		
Lapworth	d										22 48		
Dorridge	d				21 47			22 17			22 53		23 31
Widney Manor	d				21 51						22 57		
Solihull	d				21 56			22 23			23 01		23 37
Olton	d												
Acocks Green	d												
Tyseley	d												
Small Heath	d												
Bordesley	d												
Birmingham Moor Street	d			21 36	22 05			22a37		22 52	23 10		23 47
Birmingham Snow Hill	a			21 38	22 12					22 54	23 17		23 54
	d			21 45						22 55			
Jewellery Quarter	d			21 47						22 57			
The Hawthorns	d			21 52						23 02			
Smethwick Galton Bridge	d			21 54						23 04			
Coventry	a	21 22					21 52		22 22			22 52	
Birmingham International	a	21 35					22 02		22 32			23 02	
Birmingham New Street	a	21 48					22 14		22 42			23 13	
	d					22 05							
Langley Green	d												
Rowley Regis	d			21 59						23 09			
Old Hill	d												
Cradley Heath	d			22 03						23 14			
Lye	d												
Stourbridge Junction	d			22 09						23 19			
Hagley	d			22 12						23 23			
Blakedown	d												
Kidderminster	d			22 18						23 29			
Hartlebury	d												
University	d												
Barnt Green	d												
Bromsgrove	d												
Droitwich Spa	d			22 30		22 39				23 40			
Worcester Shrub Hill	a			22 37		22 48				23 48			
	d		22 11	22 41									
Worcester Foregate Street	a		22 13	22 43									
	d		22 15	22 44									
Malvern Link	d		22 24	22 52									
Great Malvern	a		22 27	22 55									
	d												
Colwall	d												
Ledbury	a												
	d												
Hereford	a												

Table 71

Sundays
1 July to 9 September

Stratford-upon-Avon, Marylebone and Leamington Spa - Birmingham - Stourbridge, Worcester and Hereford

Network Diagram - see first Page of Table 71

		LM	CH	LM	GW	LM	CH	XC	XC	CH
			◇ A		◇■		◇	◇■		◇
Stratford-upon-Avon	d					09 30				10 00
Wilmcote	d					09 35				10 05
Wootton Wawen	d									
Henley-in-Arden	d					09 42				
Danzey	d									
Wood End	d									
The Lakes	d					09x49				
Earlswood (West Midlands)	d									
Wythall	d					09 53				
Whitlocks End	d					09 55				
Shirley	d					09 59				
Yardley Wood	d					10 02				
Hall Green	d					10 05				
Spring Road	d					10 07				
London Marylebone ⊖	d		01 30				08 15			
Banbury	d		02 36				09 28	09 54		
Leamington Spa	a		02 54				09 45	10 11		10 27
	d		02 54				09 45	10 12	10 20	
Warwick	d		02 59				09 50			
Warwick Parkway	d		03 02				09 53			
Hatton	d						09 59			
Lapworth	d						10 05			
Dorridge	d	22p33	03 12				10 10			
Widney Manor	d	22p37								
Solihull	d	22p41					10 15			
Olton	d	22p44								
Acocks Green	d	22p47								
Tyseley	d	22p50				10 10				
Small Heath	d	22p52								
Bordesley	d									
Birmingham Moor Street	d	22p56	03 23	09 26		10 17	10 24			
Birmingham Snow Hill	a	22p59	03 32	09 28		10 19	10 31			
	d	23p00		09 30		10 20				
Jewellery Quarter	d	23p02		09 32		10 22				
The Hawthorns	d	23p07		09 37		10 27				
Smethwick Galton Bridge	d	23p10		09 39		10 29				
Coventry	a								10 45	
Birmingham International	a									
Birmingham New Street	a							10 55		
	d									
Langley Green	d	23p13								
Rowley Regis	d	23p16		09 44		10 34				
Old Hill	d	23p19								
Cradley Heath	d	23p23		09 49		10 39				
Lye	d	23p26								
Stourbridge Junction	d	23p30		09 54		10 45				
Hagley	d	23p33		09 58		10 48				
Blakedown	d	23p36								
Kidderminster	d	23p41		10 04		10 55				
Hartlebury	d									
University	d									
Barnt Green	d									
Bromsgrove	d									
Droitwich Spa	d	23p52		10 15		11 06				
Worcester Shrub Hill	a	00 01		10 23		11 14				
	d			10 27	10 33	11 32				
Worcester Foregate Street	a			10 29	10 35	11 34				
	d			10 30	10 37	11 35				
Malvern Link	d			10 38	10 48	11 43				
Great Malvern	a			10 41	10 50	11 46				
	d									
Colwall	d									
Ledbury	a									
	d									
Hereford	a									

		LM	CH	XC	CH	XC	GW	LM	LM	CH	GW	LM	CH	XC
			◇	◇■			◇■			◇	◇■		◇	◇■
Stratford-upon-Avon	d							10 30				11 30		
Wilmcote	d							10 35				11 35		
Wootton Wawen	d													
Henley-in-Arden	d							10 42				11 42		
Danzey	d													
Wood End	d													
The Lakes	d							10x49				11x49		
Earlswood (West Midlands)	d													
Wythall	d							10 53				11 53		
Whitlocks End	d							10 55				11 55		
Shirley	d							10 59				11 59		
Yardley Wood	d							11 02				12 02		
Hall Green	d							11 05				12 05		
Spring Road	d							11 07				12 07		
London Marylebone ⊖	d		09 00		09 36					10 00			10 33	
Banbury	d		10 11	10 54	11 01					11 11			11 29	11 54
Leamington Spa	a		10 28	11 11	11 20					11 28			11 46	12 11
	d		10 28	11 12	11 20	11 20				11 28			11 47	12 12
Warwick	d		10 33		11 25					11 33				
Warwick Parkway	d		10 36							11 36			11 53	
Hatton	d				11a32					11 42				
Lapworth	d									11 48				
Dorridge	d	10 25	10 47						11 25	11 53			12 03	
Widney Manor	d	10 29							11 29					
Solihull	d	10 32	10 53						11 32	11 58			12 09	
Olton	d	10 36							11 36					
Acocks Green	d	10 38							11 38					
Tyseley	d							11 10				12 10		
Small Heath	d													
Bordesley	d													
Birmingham Moor Street	d	10 45	11 03					11 17	11 45	12 07		12 17	12a25	
Birmingham Snow Hill	a	10 47	11 10					11 19	11 47	12 14		12 19		
	d	10 48						11 20	11 48			12 20		
Jewellery Quarter	d	10 51						11 22	11 51			12 22		
The Hawthorns	d	10 55						11 27	11 55			12 27		
Smethwick Galton Bridge	d	10 58						11 29	11 58			12 29		
Coventry	a					11 45								
Birmingham International	a													
Birmingham New Street	a			11 54										12 54
	d													
Langley Green	d	11 01							12 01					
Rowley Regis	d	11 04						11 34	12 04			12 34		
Old Hill	d	11 07							12 07					
Cradley Heath	d	11 10						11 39	12 10			12 39		
Lye	d	11 13							12 13					
Stourbridge Junction	d	11a17						11 45	12a17			12 45		
Hagley	d							11 49				12 48		
Blakedown	d							11 52				12 51		
Kidderminster	d							11 57				12 56		
Hartlebury	d													
University	d													
Barnt Green	d													
Bromsgrove	d													
Droitwich Spa	d							12 08				13 08		
Worcester Shrub Hill	a							12 16				13 15		
	d						12 06				13 10	13 31		
Worcester Foregate Street	a						12 09				13 12	13 33		
	d						12 10				13 13	13 34		
Malvern Link	d						12 19				13 23	13 42		
Great Malvern	a						12 22				13 26	13 45		
	d						12 23				13 27			
Colwall	d						12 29				13 33			
Ledbury	a						12 36				13 41			
	d						12 38				13 49			
Hereford	a						12 54				14 06			

A from 29 July until 12 August

Table 71

Sundays

1 July to 9 September

Stratford-upon-Avon, Marylebone and Leamington Spa - Birmingham - Stourbridge, Worcester and Hereford

Network Diagram - see first Page of Table 71

		XC	CH	LM	CH	LM	CH	LM	XC	CH	XC	LM	CH	XC	GW	LM	CH	XC	XC	CH	LM	CH	XC
		(bus)	◇				◇		◇1 (trolley)	◇	(bus)		◇	◇1 (trolley)	◇1 (restaurant)			◇1 (trolley)	(bus)	◇			◇1 (trolley)
Stratford-upon-Avon	d		12 00			12 30										13 30				14 00			
Wilmcote	d		12 05			12 35										13 35				14 05			
Wootton Wawen	d																						
Henley-in-Arden	d					12 42										13 42							
Danzey	d																						
Wood End	d																						
The Lakes	d					12x49										13x49							
Earlswood (West Midlands)	d																						
Wythall	d					12 53										13 53							
Whitlocks End	d					12 55										13 55							
Shirley	d					12 59										13 59							
Yardley Wood	d					13 02										14 02							
Hall Green	d					13 05										14 05							
Spring Road	d					13 07										14 07							
London Marylebone ⊖	d				11 00		11 33			11 36			12 00				12 33					13 00	
Banbury	d				12 11		12 29		12 54	13 01			13 11	13 35			13 40	13 54				14 11	14 24
Leamington Spa	a		12 27		12 28		12 46		13 11	13 20			13 28	13 50			13 59	14 11		14 27		14 28	14 40
	d	12 20			12 28		12 47		13 12	13 20	13 20		13 28	13 52			14 00	14 12	14 20			14 28	14 42
Warwick	d				12 33					13 25			13 33									14 33	
Warwick Parkway	d				12 36		12 53						13 36				14 06					14 36	
Hatton	d									13a32			13 42										
Lapworth	d												13 48										
Dorridge	d			12 25	12 47		13 03					13 25	13 53				14 16				14 25	14 47	
Widney Manor	d			12 29								13 29									14 29		
Solihull	d			12 32	12 53		13 09					13 32	13 58				14 22				14 32	14 53	
Olton	d			12 36								13 36									14 36		
Acocks Green	d			12 38								13 38									14 38		
Tyseley	d					13 10										14 10							
Small Heath	d																						
Bordesley	d																						
Birmingham Moor Street	d			12 45	13 02	13 15	13a25					13 45	14 07			14 17	14a37				14 45	15 02	
Birmingham Snow Hill	a			12 47	13 09	13 18						13 48	14 14			14 19					14 47	15 09	
	d			12 48		13 20						13 48				14 20					14 48		
Jewellery Quarter	d			12 51		13 22						13 51				14 22					14 51		
The Hawthorns	d			12 55		13 27						13 55				14 27					14 55		
Smethwick Galton Bridge	d			12 58		13 29						13 58				14 29					14 58		
Coventry	a	12 45									13 45								14 45				
Birmingham International	a																						
Birmingham New Street	a								13 54					14 19				14 54					15 09
	d							13 24															
Langley Green	d			13 01								14 01									15 01		
Rowley Regis	d			13 04		13 34						14 04				14 34					15 04		
Old Hill	d			13 07								14 07									15 07		
Cradley Heath	d			13 10		13 39						14 10				14 39					15 10		
Lye	d			13 13								14 13									15 13		
Stourbridge Junction	d			13a17		13 45						14a18				14 45					15a17		
Hagley	d					13 49										14 48							
Blakedown	d															14 51							
Kidderminster	d					13 55										14 56							
Hartlebury	d																						
University	d																						
Barnt Green	d																						
Bromsgrove	d							13 42															
Droitwich Spa	d					14 07		13 52								15 08							
Worcester Shrub Hill	a							13 59															
	d							14 14							15 10								
Worcester Foregate Street	a					14 15		14 16							15 12	15 16							
	d							14 17							15 13								
Malvern Link	d							14 25							15 23								
Great Malvern	a							14 28							15 26								
	d							14 29							15 27								
Colwall	d							14 34							15 33								
Ledbury	a							14 41							15 41								
	d							14 49							15 48								
Hereford	a							15 10							16 05								

Table 71

Sundays

1 July to 9 September

Stratford-upon-Avon, Marylebone and Leamington Spa - Birmingham - Stourbridge, Worcester and Hereford

Network Diagram - see first Page of Table 71

		LM	CH	XC	CH	LM	CH	LM	XC	GW	LM	CH	XC	LM	LM	CH	CH	XC	GW	LM	CH	XC
			◇	◇1 (trolley)	◇		◇		◇1 (trolley)	◇1		◇	◇1 (trolley)			◇	◇	◇1 (trolley)	◇1		◇	◇1 (trolley)
Stratford-upon-Avon	d	14 30									15 30						16 00			16 30		
Wilmcote	d	14 35									15 35						16 05			16 35		
Wootton Wawen	d																					
Henley-in-Arden	d	14 42									15 42									16 42		
Danzey	d																			16x47		
Wood End	d																					
The Lakes	d	14x49									15x49									16x51		
Earlswood (West Midlands)	d																					
Wythall	d	14 53									15 53									16 55		
Whitlocks End	d	14 55									15 55									16 57		
Shirley	d	14 59									15 59									17 00		
Yardley Wood	d	15 02									16 02									17 03		
Hall Green	d	15 05									16 05									17 06		
Spring Road	d	15 07									16 07									17 08		
London Marylebone ⊖	d		13 33		13 36		14 00					14 33				15 00					15 33	
Banbury	d		14 31	14 54	15 01		15 11		15 25			15 31	15 54			16 09		16 25			16 31	16 54
Leamington Spa	a		14 48	15 11	15 20		15 28		15 41			15 48	16 11			16 26	16 27	16 41			16 48	17 11
	d		14 49	15 12	15 20		15 28		15 43			15 49	16 12			16 26		16 43			16 49	17 12
Warwick	d				15 25		15 33									16 31						
Warwick Parkway	d		14 55				15 36					15 55				16 34					16 55	
Hatton	d				15a32							16 00										
Lapworth	d											16 05										
Dorridge	d		15 05			15 25	15 47					16 10		16 25		16 45					17 05	
Widney Manor	d					15 29								16 29								
Solihull	d		15 11			15 32	15 53					16 17		16 32		16 51					17 11	
Olton	d					15 36								16 36								
Acocks Green	d					15 38								16 38								
Tyseley	d	15 10									16 10									17 11		
Small Heath	d																					
Bordesley	d																					
Birmingham Moor Street	d	15 15	15a26			15 45	16 02				16 15	16a31		16 45	17 02	17 05				17 17	17a26	
Birmingham Snow Hill	a	15 19				15 48	16 09				16 19			16 48	17 04	17 13				17 20		
	d	15 20				15 48					16 20			16 48	17 06					17 21		
Jewellery Quarter	d	15 22				15 51					16 22			16 51						17 24		
The Hawthorns	d	15 27				15 55					16 27			16 55						17 28		
Smethwick Galton Bridge	d	15 29				15 58					16 29			16 58						17 31		
Coventry	a			15 22									16 22									17 22
Birmingham International	a			15 35									16 35									17 35
Birmingham New Street	a			15 48					16 12				16 48					17 12				17 48
	d							16 00														
Langley Green	d					16 01								17 01								
Rowley Regis	d	15 34				16 04					16 34			17 04						17 35		
Old Hill	d					16 07								17 07								
Cradley Heath	d	15 39				16 10					16 39			17 10						17 40		
Lye	d					16 13								17 13								
Stourbridge Junction	d	15 45				16a18					16 45			17a18	17 27					17 46		
Hagley	d	15 48									16 48				17 30					17 50		
Blakedown	d																					
Kidderminster	d	15 54									16 54				17 36					17 56		
Hartlebury	d																					
University	d																					
Barnt Green	d																					
Bromsgrove	d							16 21														
Droitwich Spa	d	16 06						16 30			17 06				17 48					18 07		
Worcester Shrub Hill	a							16 38												18 15		
	d							16 45		17 10									18 08			
Worcester Foregate Street	a	16 14						16 47		17 12	17 14				18 01				18 10			
	d							16 48		17 13												
Malvern Link	d							16 57		17 23												
Great Malvern	a							17 01		17 26												
	d									17 27												
Colwall	d									17 33												
Ledbury	a									17 41												
	d									17 42												
Hereford	a									17 58												

Table 71

Sundays
1 July to 9 September

Stratford-upon-Avon, Marylebone and Leamington Spa - Birmingham - Stourbridge, Worcester and Hereford

Network Diagram - see first Page of Table 71

		CH	LM	CH	LM	XC	GW	LM		CH	XC	CH	CH	LM	XC	GW	LM	CH		XC	CH	CH	XC	LM	CH
		◇		■		◇1 ✠	◇1 ⊡			◇	◇1 ✠	◇	◇		◇1 ✠	◇1 ⊡		◇		◇1 ✠	◇	◇	◇1 ✠		◇
Stratford-upon-Avon	d							17 30				18 00					18 30							19 30	
Wilmcote	d							17 35				18 05					18 35							19 35	
Wootton Wawen	d																								
Henley-in-Arden	d							17 42									18 42							19 42	
Danzey	d																								
Wood End	d																								
The Lakes	d							17x49									18x49							19x49	
Earlswood (West Midlands)	d																								
Wythall	d							17 53									18 53							19 53	
Whitlocks End	d							17 55									18 55							19 55	
Shirley	d							17 59									18 59							19 59	
Yardley Wood	d							18 02									19 02							20 02	
Hall Green	d							18 05									19 05							20 05	
Spring Road	d							18 07									19 07							20 07	
London Marylebone 10 ⊖	d	15 36		16 00						16 33			17 00					17 33			17 36	18 00			18 33
Banbury	d	17 01		17 11		17 25				17 31	17 54		18 11		18 25			18 31		18 54	19 01	19 11	19 25		19 31
Leamington Spa 8	a	17 20		17 28		17 41				17 48	18 11	18 27	18 28		18 41			18 48		19 11	19 20	19 28	19 41		19 48
	d	17 20		17 28		17 43				17 49	18 12		18 28		18 43			18 49		19 12	19 20	19 28	19 43		19 49
Warwick	d	17 25		17 33									18 33								19 25	19 33			
Warwick Parkway	d			17 36						17 55			18 36					18 55				19 36			19 55
Hatton	d	17a32								18 00											19a32				20 00
Lapworth	d									18 05															20 05
Dorridge	d		17 25	17 47						18 10			18 47					19 05				19 47			20 10
Widney Manor	d		17 29										18 51									19 51			
Solihull	d		17 32	17 53						18 17			18 56					19 11				19 56			20 17
Olton	d		17 36																						
Acocks Green	d		17 38																						
Tyseley	d							18 10									19 10							20 10	
Small Heath	d																								
Bordesley	d																								
Birmingham Moor Street	d		17 45	18 02				18 15		18a31			19 05				19 15	19a25				20 05		20 15	20a31
Birmingham Snow Hill ⇌	a		17 48	18 09				18 19					19 12				19 18					20 12		20 18	
	d		17 48					18 20									19 20							20 20	
Jewellery Quarter ⇌	d		17 51					18 22									19 22							20 22	
The Hawthorns ⇌	d		17 55					18 27									19 27							20 27	
Smethwick Galton Bridge 7	d		17 58					18 29									19 29							20 29	
Coventry	a										18 22									19 22			19 53		
Birmingham International ✈	a										18 35									19 35			20 03		
Birmingham New Street 12	a					18 09					18 48				19 11					19 48			20 15		
	d				18 00									19 00											
Langley Green	d		18 01																						
Rowley Regis	d		18 04					18 34									19 34							20 34	
Old Hill	d		18 07																						
Cradley Heath	d		18 10					18 39									19 39							20 39	
Lye	d		18 13																						
Stourbridge Junction 2	d		18a19					18 45									19 45							20 45	
Hagley	d							18 49									19 48							20 49	
Blakedown	d							18 52																	
Kidderminster	d							18 57									19 55							20 57	
Hartlebury	d																								
University	d																								
Barnt Green	d																								
Bromsgrove	d				18 21									19 21											
Droitwich Spa	d				18 30			19 08						19 31			20 08							21 09	
Worcester Shrub Hill 7	a				18 38			19 16						19 41			20 16							21 16	
	d				18 43		19 10									20 12								21 22	
Worcester Foregate Street 7	a				18 45		19 13									20 16								21 24	
	d				18 46		19 14									20 16								21 25	
Malvern Link	d				18 55		19 23									20 25								21 34	
Great Malvern	a				18 58		19 26									20 29								21 37	
	d				18 58											20 32									
Colwall	d				19 03											20 38									
Ledbury	a				19 10											20 45									
	d				19 10											20 47									
Hereford 7	a				19 31											21 03									

Table 71

Sundays
1 July to 9 September

Stratford-upon-Avon, Marylebone and Leamington Spa - Birmingham - Stourbridge, Worcester and Hereford

Network Diagram - see first Page of Table 71

		XC	CH	CH		LM	XC	CH	XC	GW	LM	CH	LM	XC		CH	XC	LM	CH	XC	CH
		◇1 ✠	◇	◇			◇1 ✠	◇	◇1	◇1 ⊡		◇		◇1		◇	◇1		◇	◇1	◇
Stratford-upon-Avon	d		20 00																		
Wilmcote	d		20 05																		
Wootton Wawen	d																				
Henley-in-Arden	d																				
Danzey	d																				
Wood End	d																				
The Lakes	d																				
Earlswood (West Midlands)	d																				
Wythall	d																				
Whitlocks End	d																				
Shirley	d																				
Yardley Wood	d																				
Hall Green	d																				
Spring Road	d																				
London Marylebone 10 ⊖	d			19 00				19 33				20 00				20 33			21 00		22 00
Banbury	d	19 54		20 11			20 25	20 31	20 54			21 11		21 24		21 44	21 54		22 11	22 24	22 55
Leamington Spa 8	a	20 11	20 27	20 28			20 41	20 48	21 11			21 28		21 41		22 01	22 11		22 28	22 40	23 12
	d	20 12		20 28			20 43	20 49	21 12			21 28		21 42		22 01	22 12		22 28	22 42	23 13
Warwick	d			20 33								21 33							22 33		23 17
Warwick Parkway	d			20 36				20 55				21 36				22 07			22 36		23 21
Hatton	d																		22 42		
Lapworth	d																		22 48		
Dorridge	d			20 47				21 05				21 47				22 17			22 53		23 31
Widney Manor	d			20 51								21 51							22 57		
Solihull	d			20 56				21 11				21 56				22 23			23 01		23 37
Olton	d																				
Acocks Green	d																				
Tyseley	d																				
Small Heath	d																				
Bordesley	d																				
Birmingham Moor Street	d			21 05				21a25			21 36	22 05				22a37		22 52	23 10		23 47
Birmingham Snow Hill ⇌	a			21 12							21 38	22 12						22 54	23 17		23 54
	d										21 45							22 55			
Jewellery Quarter ⇌	d										21 47							22 57			
The Hawthorns ⇌	d										21 52							23 02			
Smethwick Galton Bridge 7	d										21 54							23 04			
Coventry	a	20 22					20 53		21 22					21 52			22 22			22 52	
Birmingham International ✈	a	20 35					21 03		21 35					22 02			22 32			23 02	
Birmingham New Street 12	a	20 48					21 15		21 48					22 14			22 42			23 13	
	d					21 00							22 05								
Langley Green	d																				
Rowley Regis	d										21 59							23 09			
Old Hill	d																				
Cradley Heath	d										22 03							23 14			
Lye	d																				
Stourbridge Junction 2	d										22 09							23 19			
Hagley	d										22 12							23 23			
Blakedown	d																				
Kidderminster	d										22 18							23 29			
Hartlebury	d																				
University	d																				
Barnt Green	d																				
Bromsgrove	d					21 20															
Droitwich Spa	d					21 30					22 30		22 39					23 40			
Worcester Shrub Hill 7	a					21 37					22 37		22 48					23 48			
	d					21 42				22 11	22 41										
Worcester Foregate Street 7	a					21 44				22 13	22 43										
	d					21 45				22 15	22 44										
Malvern Link	d					21 54				22 24	22 52										
Great Malvern	a					21 57				22 27	22 55										
	d					21 57															
Colwall	d					22 02															
Ledbury	a					22 09															
	d					22 10															
Hereford 7	a					22 30															

Table 71

Sundays
from 16 September

Stratford-upon-Avon, Marylebone and Leamington Spa - Birmingham - Stourbridge, Worcester and Hereford

Network Diagram - see first Page of Table 71

		LM	LM	GW	LM	CH	XC	CH	LM	CH	XC	CH	GW	LM	LM	CH	GW	LM	CH	XC	CH	LM	CH
				◇1		◇	◇1	◇		◇	◇1		◇1			◇	◇1		◇	◇1	◇		
Stratford-upon-Avon	d				09 30			10 00						10 30				11 30			12 00		
Wilmcote	d				09 35			10 05						10 35				11 35			12 05		
Wootton Wawen	d																						
Henley-in-Arden	d				09 42									10 42				11 42					
Danzey	d																						
Wood End	d																						
The Lakes	d				09x49									10x49				11x49					
Earlswood (West Midlands)	d																						
Wythall	d				09 53									10 53				11 53					
Whitlocks End	d				09 55									10 55				11 55					
Shirley	d				09 59									10 59				11 59					
Yardley Wood	d				10 02									11 02				12 02					
Hall Green	d				10 05									11 05				12 05					
Spring Road	d				10 07									11 07				12 07					
London Marylebone 10 ⊖	d					08 15				09 00		09 36				10 00			10 33				11 00
Banbury	d					09 28	09 54			10 11	10 54	11 01				11 11			11 29	11 54			12 11
Leamington Spa 8	a					09 45	10 11	10 27		10 28	11 11	11 20				11 28			11 46	12 11	12 27		12 28
	d					09 45	10 12			10 28	11 12	11 20				11 28			11 47	12 12			12 28
Warwick	d					09 50				10 33		11 25				11 33							12 33
Warwick Parkway	d					09 53				10 36						11 36			11 53				12 36
Hatton	d					09 59						11a32				11 42							
Lapworth	d					10 05										11 48							
Dorridge	d	22p33				10 10			10 25	10 47					11 25	11 53			12 03			12 25	12 47
Widney Manor	d	22p37							10 29						11 29							12 29	
Solihull	d	22p41				10 15			10 32	10 53					11 32	11 58			12 09			12 32	12 53
Olton	d	22p44							10 36						11 36							12 36	
Acocks Green	d	22p47							10 38						11 38							12 38	
Tyseley	d	22p50			10 10									11 10				12 10					
Small Heath	d	22p52																					
Bordesley	d																						
Birmingham Moor Street	d	22p56	09 26		10 17	10 24			10 45	11 03				11 17	11 45	12 07		12 17	12a25			12 45	13 02
Birmingham Snow Hill ⇌	a	22p59	09 28		10 19	10 31			10 47	11 10				11 19	11 47	12 14		12 19				12 47	13 09
	d	23p00	09 30		10 20				10 48					11 20	11 48			12 20				12 48	
Jewellery Quarter ⇌	d	23p02	09 32		10 22				10 51					11 22	11 51			12 22				12 51	
The Hawthorns ⇌	d	23p07	09 37		10 27				10 55					11 27	11 55			12 27				12 55	
Smethwick Galton Bridge 7	d	23p10	09 39		10 29				10 58					11 29	11 58			12 29				12 58	
Coventry	a						10 22				11 22									12 22			
Birmingham International ✈	a						10 38				11 38									12 38			
Birmingham New Street 12	a						10 50				11 51									12 50			
	d																						
Langley Green	d	23p13							11 01						12 01							13 01	
Rowley Regis	d	23p16	09 44		10 34				11 04					11 34	12 04			12 34				13 04	
Old Hill	d	23p19							11 07						12 07							13 07	
Cradley Heath	d	23p23	09 49		10 39				11 10					11 39	12 10			12 39				13 10	
Lye	d	23p26							11 13						12 13							13 13	
Stourbridge Junction 2	d	23p30	09 54		10 45				11a17					11 45	12a17			12 45				13a17	
Hagley	d	23p33	09 58		10 48									11 49				12 48					
Blakedown	d	23p36												11 52				12 51					
Kidderminster	d	23p41	10 04		10 55									11 57				12 56					
Hartlebury	d																						
University	d																						
Barnt Green	d																						
Bromsgrove	d																						
Droitwich Spa	d	23p52	10 15		11 06									12 08				13 08					
Worcester Shrub Hill 7	a	00 01	10 23		11 14									12 16				13 15					
	d		10 27	10 32	11 32								12 06				13 09	13 31					
Worcester Foregate Street 7	a		10 29	10 34	11 34								12 09				13 12	13 33					
	d		10 30	10 36	11 35								12 10				13 13	13 34					
Malvern Link	d		10 38	10 47	11 43								12 19				13 22	13 42					
Great Malvern	a		10 41	10 50	11 46								12 22				13 26	13 45					
	d												12 23				13 27						
Colwall	d												12 29				13 33						
Ledbury	a												12 36				13 41						
	d												12 38				13 49						
Hereford 7	a												12 54				14 06						

Table 71

Sundays
from 16 September

Stratford-upon-Avon, Marylebone and Leamington Spa - Birmingham - Stourbridge, Worcester and Hereford

Network Diagram - see first Page of Table 71

		LM	CH	LM	XC	CH	LM	CH	XC	GW	LM	CH	XC	CH	LM	CH	XC	LM	CH	XC	CH	LM	CH
			◇		◇1	◇		◇	◇1	◇1			◇1	◇			◇1		◇	◇1	◇		◇
Stratford-upon-Avon	d	12 30									13 30			14 00				14 30					
Wilmcote	d	12 35									13 35			14 05				14 35					
Wootton Wawen	d																						
Henley-in-Arden	d	12 42									13 42							14 42					
Danzey	d																						
Wood End	d																						
The Lakes	d	12x49									13x49							14x49					
Earlswood (West Midlands)	d																						
Wythall	d	12 53									13 53							14 53					
Whitlocks End	d	12 55									13 55							14 55					
Shirley	d	12 59									13 59							14 59					
Yardley Wood	d	13 02									14 02							15 02					
Hall Green	d	13 05									14 05							15 05					
Spring Road	d	13 07									14 07							15 07					
London Marylebone 10 ⊖	d		11 33			11 36		12 00				12 33				13 00			13 33		13 36		14 00
Banbury	d		12 29		12 53	13 01		13 11	13 35			13 40	13 54			14 11	14 24		14 31	14 54	15 01		15 11
Leamington Spa 8	a		12 46		13 11	13 20		13 28	13 50			13 59	14 11	14 27		14 28	14 40		14 48	15 11	15 20		15 28
	d		12 47		13 12	13 20		13 28	13 52			14 00	14 12			14 28	14 42		14 49	15 12	15 20		15 28
Warwick	d					13 25		13 33								14 33					15 25		15 33
Warwick Parkway	d		12 53					13 36				14 06				14 36			14 55				15 36
Hatton	d					13a32		13 42													15a32		
Lapworth	d							13 48															
Dorridge	d		13 03				13 25	13 53				14 16			14 25	14 47			15 05			15 25	15 47
Widney Manor	d						13 29								14 29							15 29	
Solihull	d		13 09				13 32	13 58				14 22			14 32	14 53			15 11			15 32	15 53
Olton	d						13 36								14 36							15 36	
Acocks Green	d						13 38								14 38							15 38	
Tyseley	d	13 10									14 10							15 10					
Small Heath	d																						
Bordesley	d																						
Birmingham Moor Street	d	13 15	13a25				13 45	14 07			14 17	14a37			14 45	15 02		15 15	15a26			15 45	16 02
Birmingham Snow Hill ⇌	a	13 18					13 48	14 14			14 19				14 47	15 09		15 19				15 48	16 09
	d	13 20					13 48				14 20				14 48			15 20				15 48	
Jewellery Quarter ⇌	d	13 22					13 51				14 22				14 51			15 22				15 51	
The Hawthorns ⇌	d	13 27					13 55				14 27				14 55			15 27				15 55	
Smethwick Galton Bridge 7	d	13 29					13 58				14 29				14 58			15 29				15 58	
Coventry	a				13 22								14 22							15 22			
Birmingham International ✈	a				13 36								14 35							15 35			
Birmingham New Street 12	a				13 48				14 19				14 48				15 09			15 48			
	d			13 24																			
Langley Green	d						14 01								15 01							16 01	
Rowley Regis	d	13 34					14 04				14 34				15 04			15 34				16 04	
Old Hill	d						14 07								15 07							16 07	
Cradley Heath	d	13 39					14 10				14 39				15 10			15 39				16 10	
Lye	d						14 13								15 13							16 13	
Stourbridge Junction 2	d	13 45					14a18				14 45				15a17			15 45				16a18	
Hagley	d	13 49									14 48							15 48					
Blakedown	d										14 51												
Kidderminster	d	13 55									14 56							15 54					
Hartlebury	d																						
University	d																						
Barnt Green	d																						
Bromsgrove	d			13 42																			
Droitwich Spa	d	14 07		13 52							15 08							16 06					
Worcester Shrub Hill 7	a			13 59																			
	d			14 14						15 10													
Worcester Foregate Street 7	a	14 15		14 16						15 12	15 16							16 14					
	d			14 17						15 13													
Malvern Link	d			14 25						15 23													
Great Malvern	a			14 28						15 26													
	d			14 29						15 27													
Colwall	d			14 34						15 33													
Ledbury	a			14 41						15 41													
	d			14 49						15 48													
Hereford 7	a			15 10						16 05													

Table 71

Sundays
from 16 September

Stratford-upon-Avon, Marylebone and Leamington Spa - Birmingham - Stourbridge, Worcester and Hereford

Network Diagram - see first Page of Table 71

		LM		XC	GW	LM	CH	XC	LM	LM	CH	CH		XC	GW	LM	CH	XC	CH	LM	CH	LM		XC	GW
				◇■ H	◇■		◇	◇■ H			◇	◇		◇■ H	◇■		◇	◇■ H	◇		■			◇■ H	◇■
Stratford-upon-Avon	d					15 30						16 00				16 30									
Wilmcote	d					15 35						16 05				16 35									
Wootton Wawen	d																								
Henley-in-Arden	d					15 42										16 42									
Danzey	d															16x47									
Wood End	d																								
The Lakes	d					15x49										16x51									
Earlswood (West Midlands)	d																								
Wythall	d					15 53										16 55									
Whitlocks End	d					15 55										16 57									
Shirley	d					15 59										17 00									
Yardley Wood	d					16 02										17 03									
Hall Green	d					16 05										17 06									
Spring Road	d					16 07										17 08									
London Marylebone ■ ⊖	d						14 33				15 00						15 33		15 36		16 00				
Banbury	d			15 25			15 31	15 54			16 09			16 25			16 31	16 54	17 01		17 11			17 25	
Leamington Spa ■	a			15 41			15 48	16 11			16 26	16 27		16 41			16 48	17 11	17 20		17 28			17 41	
	d			15 43			15 49	16 12			16 26			16 43			16 49	17 12	17 20		17 28			17 43	
Warwick	d										16 31								17 25		17 33				
Warwick Parkway	d						15 55				16 34						16 55				17 36				
Hatton	d						16 00												17a32						
Lapworth	d						16 05																		
Dorridge	d						16 10		16 25		16 45						17 05			17 25	17 47				
Widney Manor	d								16 29											17 29					
Solihull	d						16 17		16 32		16 51						17 11			17 32	17 53				
Olton	d								16 36											17 36					
Acocks Green	d								16 38											17 38					
Tyseley	d					16 10										17 11									
Small Heath	d																								
Bordesley	d																								
Birmingham Moor Street	d					16 15	16a31		16 45	17 02	17 05					17 17	17a26			17 45	18 02				
Birmingham Snow Hill ⇌	a					16 19			16 48	17 04	17 13					17 20				17 48	18 09				
	d					16 20			16 48	17 06						17 21				17 48					
Jewellery Quarter ⇌	d					16 22			16 51							17 24				17 51					
The Hawthorns ⇌	d					16 27			16 55							17 28				17 55					
Smethwick Galton Bridge ■	d					16 29			16 58							17 31				17 58					
Coventry	a							16 22										17 22							
Birmingham International ✈	a							16 35										17 35							
Birmingham New Street ■	a			16 12				16 48						17 12				17 48						18 09	
	d	16 00																				18 00			
Langley Green	d								17 01											18 01					
Rowley Regis	d					16 34			17 04							17 35				18 04					
Old Hill	d								17 07											18 07					
Cradley Heath	d					16 39			17 10							17 40				18 10					
Lye	d								17 13											18 13					
Stourbridge Junction ■	d					16 45			17a18	17 27						17 46				18a19					
Hagley	d					16 48				17 30						17 50									
Blakedown	d																								
Kidderminster	d					16 54				17 36						17 56									
Hartlebury	d																								
University	d																								
Barnt Green	d																								
Bromsgrove	d	16 21																				18 21			
Droitwich Spa	d	16 30				17 06				17 48						18 07						18 30			
Worcester Shrub Hill ■	a	16 38														18 15						18 38			
	d	16 45			17 10										18 08							18 43			19 10
Worcester Foregate Street ■	a	16 47			17 12	17 14				18 01					18 10							18 45			19 13
	d	16 48			17 13																	18 46			19 14
Malvern Link	d	16 57			17 23																	18 55			19 23
Great Malvern	a	17 01			17 26																	18 58			19 27
	d				17 27																	18 58			
Colwall	d				17 33																	19 03			
Ledbury	a				17 41																	19 10			
	d				17 42																	19 10			
Hereford ■	a				17 58																	19 31			

Table 71

Sundays
from 16 September

Stratford-upon-Avon, Marylebone and Leamington Spa - Birmingham - Stourbridge, Worcester and Hereford

Network Diagram - see first Page of Table 71

		LM	CH	XC	CH	CH	LM	XC		GW	LM	CH	XC	CH	CH	XC	LM	CH		XC	CH	CH	LM	XC	CH
			◇	◇■ H	◇	◇		◇■ H		◇■		◇	◇■ H	◇	◇	◇■ H		◇		◇■ H	◇	◇		◇■ H	◇
Stratford-upon-Avon	d	17 30			18 00						18 30						19 30				20 00				
Wilmcote	d	17 35			18 05						18 35						19 35				20 05				
Wootton Wawen	d																								
Henley-in-Arden	d	17 42									18 42						19 42								
Danzey	d																								
Wood End	d																								
The Lakes	d	17x49									18x49						19x49								
Earlswood (West Midlands)	d																								
Wythall	d	17 53									18 53						19 53								
Whitlocks End	d	17 55									18 55						19 55								
Shirley	d	17 59									18 59						19 59								
Yardley Wood	d	18 02									19 02						20 02								
Hall Green	d	18 05									19 05						20 05								
Spring Road	d	18 07									19 07						20 07								
London Marylebone ■ ⊖	d		16 33			17 00						17 33		17 36	18 00			18 33				19 00			19 33
Banbury	d		17 31	17 54		18 11		18 25				18 31	18 54	19 01	19 11	19 25		19 31		19 54		20 11		20 25	20 31
Leamington Spa ■	a		17 48	18 11	18 27	18 28		18 41				18 48	19 11	19 20	19 28	19 41		19 48		20 11	20 27	20 28		20 41	20 48
	d		17 49	18 12		18 28		18 43				18 49	19 12	19 20	19 28	19 43		19 49		20 12		20 28		20 43	20 49
Warwick	d					18 33								19 25	19 33							20 33			
Warwick Parkway	d		17 55			18 36						18 55			19 36			19 55				20 36			20 55
Hatton	d		18 00											19a32				20 00							
Lapworth	d		18 05															20 05							
Dorridge	d		18 10			18 47						19 05			19 47			20 10				20 47			21 05
Widney Manor	d					18 51									19 51							20 51			
Solihull	d		18 17			18 56						19 11			19 56			20 17				20 56			21 11
Olton	d																								
Acocks Green	d																								
Tyseley	d	18 10									19 10						20 10								
Small Heath	d																								
Bordesley	d																								
Birmingham Moor Street	d	18 15	18a31			19 05					19 15	19a25			20 05		20 15	20a31				21 05			21a25
Birmingham Snow Hill ⇌	a	18 19				19 12					19 18				20 12		20 18					21 12			
	d	18 20									19 20						20 20								
Jewellery Quarter ⇌	d	18 22									19 22						20 22								
The Hawthorns ⇌	d	18 27									19 27						20 27								
Smethwick Galton Bridge ■	d	18 29									19 29						20 29								
Coventry	a			18 22									19 22			19 53				20 22				20 53	
Birmingham International ✈	a			18 35									19 35			20 03				20 35				21 03	
Birmingham New Street ■	a			18 48				19 11					19 48			20 15				20 48				21 15	
	d						19 00																21 00		
Langley Green	d																								
Rowley Regis	d	18 34									19 34						20 34								
Old Hill	d																								
Cradley Heath	d	18 39									19 39						20 39								
Lye	d																								
Stourbridge Junction ■	d	18 45									19 45						20 45								
Hagley	d	18 49									19 48						20 49								
Blakedown	d	18 52																							
Kidderminster	d	18 57									19 55						20 57								
Hartlebury	d																								
University	d																								
Barnt Green	d																								
Bromsgrove	d						19 21																21 20		
Droitwich Spa	d	19 08					19 31				20 08						21 09						21 30		
Worcester Shrub Hill ■	a	19 16					19 41				20 16						21 16						21 37		
	d									20 12							21 22						21 42		
Worcester Foregate Street ■	a									20 16							21 24						21 44		
	d									20 16							21 25						21 45		
Malvern Link	d									20 25							21 34						21 54		
Great Malvern	a									20 29							21 37						21 57		
	d									20 32													21 57		
Colwall	d									20 38													22 02		
Ledbury	a									20 45													22 09		
	d									20 47													22 10		
Hereford ■	a									21 03													22 30		

Sundays
from 16 September

Stratford-upon-Avon, Marylebone and Leamington Spa - Birmingham - Stourbridge, Worcester and Hereford

Network Diagram - see first Page of Table 71

		XC ◇■	GW ◇■	LM	CH ◇	LM	XC ◇■	CH ◇	XC ◇■	LM	CH ◇	XC ◇■	CH ◇
Stratford-upon-Avon	d												
Wilmcote	d												
Wootton Wawen	d												
Henley-in-Arden	d												
Danzey	d												
Wood End	d												
The Lakes	d												
Earlswood (West Midlands)	d												
Wythall	d												
Whitlocks End	d												
Shirley	d												
Yardley Wood	d												
Hall Green	d												
Spring Road	d												
London Marylebone ⊖	d				20 00			20 33			21 00		22 00
Banbury	d	20 54			21 11		21 24	21 44	21 54		22 11	22 26	22 55
Leamington Spa	a	21 11			21 28		21 41	22 01	22 11		22 28	22 42	23 12
	d	21 12			21 28		21 42	22 01	22 12		22 28	22 43	23 13
Warwick	d				21 33						22 33		23 17
Warwick Parkway	d				21 36			22 07			22 36		23 21
Hatton	d										22 42		
Lapworth	d										22 48		
Dorridge	d				21 47			22 17			22 53		23 31
Widney Manor	d				21 51						22 57		
Solihull	d				21 56			22 23			23 01		23 37
Olton	d												
Acocks Green	d												
Tyseley	d												
Small Heath	d												
Bordesley	d												
Birmingham Moor Street	d			21 36	22 05			22a37		22 52	23 10		23 47
Birmingham Snow Hill	a			21 38	22 12					22 54	23 17		23 54
	d			21 45						22 55			
Jewellery Quarter	d			21 47						22 57			
The Hawthorns	d			21 52						23 02			
Smethwick Galton Bridge	d			21 54						23 04			
Coventry	a	21 22					21 52		22 22			22 53	
Birmingham International	a	21 35					22 02		22 32			23 03	
Birmingham New Street	a	21 48					22 14		22 42			23 14	
	d					22 05							
Langley Green	d												
Rowley Regis	d			21 59						23 09			
Old Hill	d												
Cradley Heath	d			22 03						23 14			
Lye	d												
Stourbridge Junction	d			22 09						23 19			
Hagley	d			22 12						23 23			
Blakedown	d												
Kidderminster	d			22 18						23 29			
Hartlebury	d												
University	d												
Barnt Green	d												
Bromsgrove	d												
Droitwich Spa	d			22 30		22 39				23 40			
Worcester Shrub Hill	a			22 37		22 48				23 48			
	d		22 11	22 41									
Worcester Foregate Street	a		22 13	22 43									
	d		22 15	22 44									
Malvern Link	d		22 24	22 52									
Great Malvern	a		22 27	22 55									
	d												
Colwall	d												
Ledbury	a												
	d												
Hereford	a												

Mondays to Saturdays

Stourbridge Junction - Stourbridge Town

Network Diagram - see first Page of Table 71

Miles			LM SX	LM	LM SX	LM	LM SX	LM SX	LM	LM SX	LM	LM	LM	LM	LM	LM	LM	LM	LM	LM	LM	LM
0	Stourbridge Junction	d	05 47	05 58	06 08	06 19	06 29	06 39	06 49	06 59	07 09	07 19	07 29	07 39	07 49	07 59	08 09	08 19	08 29	08 39	08 49	08 59
0¾	Stourbridge Town	a	05 50	06 01	06 11	06 22	06 32	06 42	06 52	07 02	07 12	07 22	07 32	07 42	07 52	08 02	08 12	08 22	08 32	08 42	08 52	09 02

		LM	LM	LM	LM	LM	LM	LM	LM	LM	LM	LM	LM	LM	LM	LM	LM	LM	LM	LM	LM	LM
Stourbridge Junction	d	09 09	09 19	09 29	09 39	09 49	09 59	10 09	10 19	10 29	10 39	10 49	10 59	11 09	11 19	11 29	11 39	11 49	11 59	12 09	12 19	12 29
Stourbridge Town	a	09 12	09 22	09 32	09 42	09 52	10 02	10 12	10 22	10 32	10 42	10 52	11 02	11 12	11 22	11 32	11 42	11 52	12 02	12 12	12 22	12 32

		LM	LM	LM	LM	LM	LM	LM	LM	LM	LM	LM	LM	LM	LM	LM	LM	LM	LM	LM	LM
Stourbridge Junction	d	12 39	12 49	12 59	13 09	13 19	13 29	13 39	13 49	13 59	14 09	14 19	14 29	14 39	14 49	14 59	15 09	15 19	15 29	15 39	15 49
Stourbridge Town	a	12 42	12 52	13 02	13 12	13 22	13 32	13 42	13 52	14 02	14 12	14 22	14 32	14 42	14 52	15 02	15 12	15 22	15 32	15 42	15 52

		LM	LM	LM	LM	LM	LM	LM	LM	LM	LM	LM	LM	LM	LM	LM	LM	LM	LM	LM	LM	LM
Stourbridge Junction	d	15 59	16 09	16 19	16 29	16 39	16 49	16 59	17 09	17 19	17 29	17 39	17 49	17 59	18 09	18 19	18 29	18 39	18 49	18 59	19 09	19 19
Stourbridge Town	a	16 02	16 12	16 22	16 32	16 42	16 52	17 02	17 12	17 22	17 32	17 42	17 52	18 02	18 12	18 22	18 32	18 42	18 52	19 02	19 12	19 22

		LM	LM	LM	LM	LM	LM	LM	LM	LM	LM	LM	LM	LM	LM	LM	LM	LM	LM	LM	LM
Stourbridge Junction	d	19 29	19 39	19 49	19 59	20 09	20 19	20 29	20 39	20 49	20 59	21 09	21 19	21 29	21 39	21 49	21 59	22 09	22 19	22 29	22 39
Stourbridge Town	a	19 32	19 42	19 52	20 02	20 12	20 22	20 32	20 42	20 52	21 02	21 12	21 22	21 32	21 42	21 52	22 02	22 12	22 22	22 32	22 42

		LM	LM	LM	LM	LM
Stourbridge Junction	d	22 50	23 00	23 15	23 30	23 54
Stourbridge Town	a	22 53	23 03	23 18	23 33	23 57

Sundays

		LM	LM	LM	LM	LM	LM	LM	LM	LM	LM	LM	LM	LM	LM	LM	LM	LM	LM	LM	LM	LM
Stourbridge Junction	d	09 43	10 00	10 11	10 21	10 41	10 54	11 11	11 21	11 41	11 54	12 11	12 21	12 41	12 54	13 11	13 21	13 41	13 54	14 11	14 21	14 41
Stourbridge Town	a	09 46	10 03	10 14	10 24	10 44	10 57	11 14	11 24	11 44	11 57	12 14	12 24	12 44	12 57	13 14	13 24	13 44	13 57	14 14	14 24	14 44

		LM	LM	LM	LM	LM	LM	LM	LM	LM	LM	LM	LM	LM	LM	LM	LM	LM	LM	LM	LM
Stourbridge Junction	d	14 54	15 11	15 21	15 41	15 54	16 11	16 21	16 41	16 54	17 11	17 21	17 41	17 54	18 11	18 21	18 41	18 54	19 11	19 21	19 47
Stourbridge Town	a	14 57	15 14	15 24	15 44	15 57	16 14	16 24	16 44	16 57	17 14	17 24	17 44	17 57	18 14	18 24	18 44	18 57	19 14	19 24	19 50

Mondays to Saturdays

Stourbridge Town - Stourbridge Junction

Network Diagram - see first Page of Table 71

Miles			LM MX	LM SX	LM SX	LM SO	LM SX	LM SX	LM SX	LM SO	LM SX	LM	LM SX	LM	LM	LM	LM	LM	LM	LM	LM	LM
0	Stourbridge Town	d	23p59	05 52	06 03	06 10	06 13	06 24	06 34	06 40	06 44	06 54	07 04	07 14	07 24	07 34	07 44	07 54	08 04	08 14	08 24	08 34
0¾	Stourbridge Junction	a	00 02	05 55	06 06	06 13	06 16	06 27	06 37	06 43	06 47	06 57	07 07	07 17	07 27	07 37	07 47	07 57	08 07	08 17	08 27	08 37

		LM	LM	LM	LM	LM	LM	LM	LM	LM	LM	LM	LM	LM	LM	LM	LM	LM	LM	LM	LM	LM
Stourbridge Town	d	08 44	08 54	09 04	09 14	09 24	09 34	09 44	09 54	10 04	10 14	10 24	10 34	10 44	10 54	11 04	11 14	11 24	11 34	11 44	11 54	12 04
Stourbridge Junction	a	08 47	08 57	09 07	09 17	09 27	09 37	09 47	09 57	10 07	10 17	10 27	10 37	10 47	10 57	11 07	11 17	11 27	11 37	11 47	11 57	12 07

		LM	LM	LM	LM	LM	LM	LM	LM	LM	LM	LM	LM	LM	LM	LM	LM	LM	LM	LM	LM
Stourbridge Town	d	12 14	12 24	12 34	12 44	12 54	13 04	13 14	13 24	13 34	13 44	13 54	14 04	14 14	14 24	14 34	14 44	14 54	15 04	15 14	15 24
Stourbridge Junction	a	12 17	12 27	12 37	12 47	12 57	13 07	13 17	13 27	13 37	13 47	13 57	14 07	14 17	14 27	14 37	14 47	14 57	15 07	15 17	15 27

		LM	LM	LM	LM	LM	LM	LM	LM	LM	LM	LM	LM	LM	LM	LM	LM	LM	LM	LM	LM	LM
Stourbridge Town	d	15 34	15 44	15 54	16 04	16 14	16 24	16 34	16 44	16 54	17 04	17 14	17 24	17 34	17 44	17 54	18 04	18 14	18 24	18 34	18 44	18 54
Stourbridge Junction	a	15 37	15 47	15 57	16 07	16 17	16 27	16 37	16 47	16 57	17 07	17 17	17 27	17 37	17 47	17 57	18 07	18 17	18 27	18 37	18 47	18 57

		LM	LM	LM	LM	LM	LM	LM	LM	LM	LM	LM	LM	LM	LM	LM	LM	LM	LM	LM	LM
Stourbridge Town	d	19 04	19 14	19 24	19 34	19 44	19 54	20 04	20 14	20 24	20 34	20 44	20 54	21 04	21 14	21 24	21 34	21 44	21 54	22 04	22 14
Stourbridge Junction	a	19 07	19 17	19 27	19 37	19 47	19 57	20 07	20 17	20 27	20 37	20 47	20 57	21 07	21 17	21 27	21 37	21 47	21 57	22 07	22 17

		LM	LM	LM	LM	LM	LM	LM	LM
Stourbridge Town	d	22 24	22 34	22 44	22 55	23 05	23 20	23 35	23 59
Stourbridge Junction	a	22 27	22 37	22 47	22 58	23 08	23 23	23 38	00 02

Sundays

		LM	LM	LM	LM	LM	LM	LM	LM	LM	LM	LM	LM	LM	LM	LM	LM	LM	LM	LM	LM	LM
Stourbridge Town	d	23p59	09 49	10 05	10 16	10 36	10 46	11 00	11 16	11 36	11 46	12 00	12 16	12 36	12 46	13 00	13 16	13 36	13 46	14 00	14 16	14 36
Stourbridge Junction	a	00 02	09 52	10 08	10 19	10 39	10 49	11 03	11 19	11 39	11 49	12 03	12 19	12 39	12 49	13 03	13 19	13 39	13 49	14 03	14 19	14 39

		LM	LM	LM	LM	LM	LM	LM	LM	LM	LM	LM	LM	LM	LM	LM	LM	LM	LM	LM	LM	LM
Stourbridge Town	d	14 46	15 00	15 16	15 36	15 46	16 00	16 16	16 36	16 46	17 00	17 16	17 36	17 46	18 00	18 16	18 36	18 46	19 00	19 16	19 36	19 55
Stourbridge Junction	a	14 49	15 03	15 19	15 39	15 49	16 03	16 19	16 39	16 49	17 03	17 19	17 39	17 49	18 03	18 19	18 39	18 49	19 03	19 19	19 39	19 58

Network Diagram for Tables 74, 75

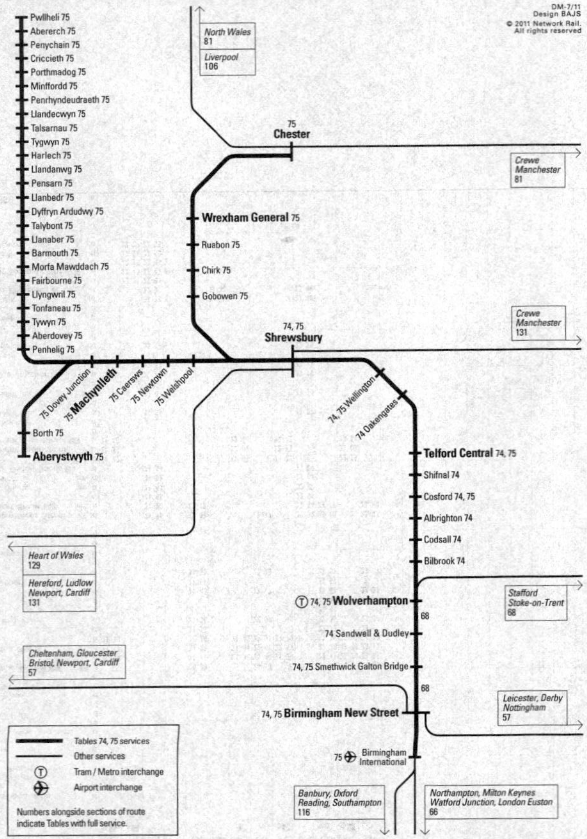

Table 74

Mondays to Fridays

Birmingham - Shrewsbury

Network Diagram - see first Page of Table 67

Miles			AW MO	AW MO	AW MX	AW MX	LM	AW	LM	AW	LM		LM	AW	LM	AW	LM	AW	LM	AW	LM		AW	LM	AW
								◇		◇				◇		◇		◇		◇			◇		◇
			A	B				C		D				E		D		E		D			E		D
0	**Birmingham New Street**	d	23p11	23p24	23p32		05 51	06 24		07 24	07 27		08 05	08 24	09 05	09 24	10 05	10 24	11 05	11 24	12 05		12 24	13 05	13 24
4	Smethwick Galton Bridge	d						06 30		07 30				08 30		09 30		10 30		11 30			12 30		13 30
5¼	Sandwell & Dudley	d					05 59						08 13		09 13		10 13		11 13		12 13			13 13	
13	**Wolverhampton** ⇌	d	23p46	23p46	00 02	00 20	06 13	06 43	06 48	07 42	07 46		08 25	08 43	09 25	09 43	10 25	10 43	11 25	11 43	12 25		12 43	13 25	13 43
17	Bilbrook	d	23p52	23p52	00 08		06 19		06 53		07 52		08 31		09 31		10 31		11 31		12 31			13 31	
17½	Codsall	d	23p54	23p54	00 11		06 21		06 56		07 55		08 33		09 33		10 33		11 33		12 33			13 33	
20¾	Albrighton	d	23p59	23p59	00 15		06 26		07 00		07 59		08 38		09 38		10 38		11 38		12 38			13 38	
22¼	Cosford	d	00 02	00 02	00 19		06 29		07 04		08 03		08 41		09 41		10 41		11 41		12 41			13 41	
25½	Shifnal	d	00 07	00 07	00 24		06 34		07 09		08 07		08 46		09 46		10 46		11 46		12 46			13 46	
28½	Telford Central	d	00 13	00 13	00 29	00 36	06 40	06 59	07 15	07 59	08 13		08 52	08 59	09 52	09 59	10 52	10 59	11 52	11 59	12 52		12 59	13 52	13 59
29½	Oakengates	d	00 15	00 15	00 31		06 42		07 17		08 16		08 54		09 54		10 54		11 54		12 54			13 54	
32½	Wellington (Shropshire)	d	00 20	00 20	00 36	00 43	06 47	07 06	07 23	08 05	08 22		08 59	09 06	09 59	10 06	10 59	11 06	11 59	12 06	12 59		13 06	13 59	14 06
43	**Shrewsbury**	a	00 35	00 35	00 52	01 02	07 00	07 18	07 37	08 19	08 36		09 15	09 19	10 15	10 19	11 15	11 19	12 15	12 19	13 15		13 19	14 15	14 19

		LM	AW	LM	AW	LM	AW		LM	AW	LM	LM	AW	LM	AW	LM	AW		LM	AW	LM	AW
							■															
			◇		◇					◇			◇		◇		◇			◇		
			E		D		E			D			E		F		E			G		
Birmingham New Street	d	14 05	14 24	15 05	15 26	16 05	16 24		17 05	17 26	17 46	18 05	18 24	19 05	19 24	20 05	20 24		21 05	21 24	22 21	23 32
Smethwick Galton Bridge	d		14 30		15 32		16 30			17 32			18 30		19 30		20 30			21 30		
Sandwell & Dudley	d	14 13		15 13		16 13			17 13			18 13		19 13		20 13			21 13		22 29	
Wolverhampton ⇌	d	14 25	14 43	15 25	15 44	16 25	16 43		17 25	17 44	18 07	18 25	18 43	19 25	19 43	20 25	20 43		21 25	21 43	22 43	00 02
Bilbrook	d	14 31		15 31		16 31			17 31		18 13	18 31		19 31		20 31			21 31		22 49	00 08
Codsall	d	14 33		15 33		16 33			17 33		18 15	18 33		19 33		20 33			21 33		22 51	00 11
Albrighton	d	14 38		15 38		16 38			17 38		18 20	18 38		19 38		20 38			21 38		22 56	00 15
Cosford	d	14 41		15 41		16 41			17 41		18 23	18 41		19 41		20 41			21 41		22 59	00 19
Shifnal	d	14 46		15 46		16 46			17 46		18 28	18 46		19 46		20 46			21 46		23 04	00 24
Telford Central	d	14 52	14 59	15 52	16 01	16 52	16 59		17 52	18 01	18 33	18 52	18 59	19 52	19 59	20 52	20 59		21 52	21 59	23 10	00 29
Oakengates	d	14 54		15 54		16 54			17 54		18 35	18 54		19 54		20 54			21 54		23 12	00 31
Wellington (Shropshire)	d	14 59	15 06	15 59	16 07	16 59	17 06		17 59	18 07	18 41	18 59	19 06	19 59	20 06	20 59	21 06		21 59	22 07	23 17	00 36
Shrewsbury	a	15 15	15 19	16 15	16 20	17 15	17 19		18 15	18 20	18 56	19 15	19 19	20 15	20 19	21 15	21 19		22 14	22 19	23 30	00 52

Saturdays

		AW	AW	AW	LM	AW	LM	AW	LM	AW		LM	AW	LM	AW	LM	AW	LM	AW	LM		AW	LM	AW	LM
				◇		◇		◇		◇			◇		◇		◇		◇			◇		◇	
				C		D		E		D			E		D		E		D			E		D	
Birmingham New Street	d	23p32		06 24	07 05	07 23	08 05	08 24	09 05	09 24		10 05	10 24	11 05	11 24	12 05	12 24	13 05	13 24	14 05		14 24	15 05	15 24	16 05
Smethwick Galton Bridge	d			06 30		07 29		08 30		09 30			10 30		11 30		12 30		13 30			14 30		15 30	
Sandwell & Dudley	d				07 13		08 13		09 13			10 13		11 13		12 13		13 13		14 13			15 13		16 13
Wolverhampton ⇌	d	00 02	00 20	06 42	07 25	07 41	08 25	08 43	09 25	09 43		10 25	10 43	11 25	11 43	12 25	12 43	13 25	13 43	14 25		14 43	15 25	15 43	16 25
Bilbrook	d	00 08			07 31		08 31		09 31			10 31		11 31		12 31		13 31		14 31			15 31		16 31
Codsall	d	00 11			07 33		08 33		09 33			10 33		11 33		12 33		13 33		14 33			15 33		16 33
Albrighton	d	00 15			07 38		08 38		09 38			10 38		11 38		12 38		13 38		14 38			15 38		16 38
Cosford	d	00 19			07 41		08 41		09 41			10 41		11 41		12 41		13 41		14 41			15 41		16 41
Shifnal	d	00 24			07 46		08 46		09 46			10 46		11 46		12 46		13 46		14 46			15 46		16 46
Telford Central	d	00 29	00 36	06 59	07 52	07 58	08 52	08 59	09 52	09 59		10 52	10 59	11 52	11 59	12 52	12 59	13 52	13 59	14 52		14 59	15 52	15 59	16 52
Oakengates	d	00 31			07 54		08 54		09 54			10 54		11 54		12 54		13 54		14 54			15 54		16 54
Wellington (Shropshire)	d	00 36	00 43	07 05	07 59	08 04	08 59	09 06	09 59	10 06		10 59	11 06	11 59	12 06	12 59	13 06	13 59	14 06	14 59		15 06	15 59	16 06	16 59
Shrewsbury	a	00 52	01 00	07 18	08 15	08 18	09 15	09 19	10 15	10 19		11 15	11 19	12 15	12 19	13 15	13 19	14 15	14 19	15 15		15 19	16 15	16 19	17 15

		AW	LM	AW	LM	AW		LM	AW	LM	AW	LM	AW	LM	AW	AW
		■														
				◇		◇			◇		◇		◇			
		E		D		E			F		E		F	H	I	
Birmingham New Street	d	16 24	17 05	17 24	18 05	18 24		19 05	19 24	20 05	20 24	21 05	21 24	22 05	22 55	23 35
Smethwick Galton Bridge	d	16 30		17 31		18 30			19 30		20 30		21 30			
Sandwell & Dudley	d		17 13		18 13			19 13		20 13		21 13		22 13		
Wolverhampton ⇌	d	16 43	17 25	17 43	18 25	18 43		19 25	19 43	20 25	20 43	21 25	21 42	22 25	23 13	23 54
Bilbrook	d		17 31		18 31			19 31		20 31		21 31		22 31		00 01
Codsall	d		17 33		18 33			19 33		20 33		21 33		22 33		00 04
Albrighton	d		17 38		18 38			19 38		20 38		21 38		22 38		00 08
Cosford	d		17 41		18 41			19 41		20 41		21 41		22 41		00 12
Shifnal	d		17 46		18 46			19 46		20 46		21 46		22 46		00 17
Telford Central	d	16 59	17 52	17 59	18 52	18 59		19 52	19 59	20 52	21 02	21 52	21 59	22 52	23 29	00 22
Oakengates	d		17 54		18 54			19 54		20 54		21 54		22 54		00 25
Wellington (Shropshire)	d	17 06	17 59	18 06	18 59	19 06		19 59	20 06	20 59	21 09	21 59	22 05	22 59	23 36	00 30
Shrewsbury	a	17 19	18 15	18 19	19 15	19 19		20 15	20 19	21 15	21 23	22 14	22 22	23 15	23 49	00 43

A from 21 May until 25 June
B from 2 July. From Birmingham International
C To Aberystwyth
D From Birmingham International to Holyhead
E From Birmingham International to Aberystwyth
F From Birmingham International to Chester
G From Birmingham International to Manchester Piccadilly
H until 23 June, 8 December
I To Crewe

Table 74

Sundays until 24 June

Birmingham - Shrewsbury

Network Diagram - see first Page of Table 67

		AW	AW	AW	AW	AW	AW	AW	AW	AW	AW	AW	AW	AW	AW	AW	AW	AW	AW	AW	AW	AW
						◇ A	◇ B ⌶		◇ A ⌶	◇ B ⌶		◇ A ⌶	◇ B ⌶		◇ C ⌶	◇ B ⌶		◇ A ⌶	◇ B	◇ A		
Birmingham New Street	d	23p35		09 52		10 57	12 12		13 02	14 03		15 02	16 02		17 02	18 02		19 02	20 02	21 01	22 08	23 11
Smethwick Galton Bridge	d																					
Sandwell & Dudley	d																					
Wolverhampton [7]	d	23p54	00 18	10 22	11 06	11 27	12 42	13 06	13 42	14 43	15 06	15 43	16 43	17 06	17 43	18 43	19 06	19 43	20 43	21 43	22 42	23 46
Bilbrook	d	00 01		10 28	11 12	11 33		13 12			15 12			17 12			19 12			21 49	22 48	23 52
Codsall	d	00 04		10 31	11 15	11 35		13 15			15 15			17 15			19 15			21 51	22 50	23 54
Albrighton	d	00 08		10 35	11 19	11 40		13 19			15 19			17 19			19 19			21 56	22 55	23 59
Cosford	d	00 12		10 39	11 23	11 43		13 23			15 23			17 23			19 23			21 59	22 58	00 02
Shifnal	d	00 17		10 44	11 28	11 48		13 28			15 28			17 28			19 28			22 04	23 03	00 07
Telford Central	d	00 22	00 36	10 49	11 34	11 54	12 59	13 34	13 58	14 59	15 34	15 59	16 59	17 34	17 59	18 59	19 34	19 59	20 59	22 10	23 09	00 13
Oakengates	d	00 25		10 51	11 37	11 56		13 37			15 37			17 37			19 37			22 12	23 11	00 15
Wellington (Shropshire)	d	00 30	00 43	10 57	11 43	12 01	13 05	13 43	14 04	15 06	15 43	16 06	17 06	17 43	18 05	19 06	19 43	20 06	21 06	22 17	23 16	00 20
Shrewsbury	a	00 43	00 59	11 10	11 58	12 15	13 18	13 58	14 18	15 19	15 58	16 26	17 19	17 59	18 19	19 19	19 58	20 19	21 19	22 30	23 32	00 35

Sundays from 1 July

		AW	AW	AW	AW	AW	AW	AW	AW	AW	AW	AW	AW	AW	AW	AW	AW	AW	AW	AW	AW	AW
				D		◇ E	◇ F ⌶		◇ E ⌶	◇ F ⌶		◇ E ⌶	◇ F ⌶		◇ G ⌶	◇ F ⌶		◇ E ⌶	◇ F	◇ E	D	D
Birmingham New Street	d	23p35		10 05		11 05	12 24		13 24	14 24		15 24	16 24		17 24	18 24		19 24	20 24	21 24	22 24	23 24
Smethwick Galton Bridge	d																					
Sandwell & Dudley	d																					
Wolverhampton [7]	d	23p54	00 18	10 22	11 06	11 27	12 42	13 06	13 42	14 43	15 06	15 43	16 43	17 06	17 43	18 43	19 06	19 43	20 43	21 43	22 42	23 46
Bilbrook	d	00 01		10 28	11 12	11 33		13 12			15 12			17 12			19 12			21 49	22 48	23 52
Codsall	d	00 04		10 31	11 15	11 35		13 15			15 15			17 15			19 15			21 51	22 50	23 54
Albrighton	d	00 08		10 35	11 19	11 40		13 19			15 19			17 19			19 19			21 56	22 55	23 59
Cosford	d	00 12		10 39	11 23	11 43		13 23			15 23			17 23			19 23			21 59	22 58	00 02
Shifnal	d	00 17		10 44	11 28	11 48		13 28			15 28			17 28			19 28			22 04	23 03	00 07
Telford Central	d	00 22	00 36	10 49	11 34	11 54	12 59	13 34	13 58	14 59	15 34	15 59	16 59	17 34	17 59	18 59	19 34	19 59	20 59	22 10	23 09	00 13
Oakengates	d	00 25		10 51	11 37	11 56		13 37			15 37			17 37			19 37			22 12	23 11	00 15
Wellington (Shropshire)	d	00 30	00 43	10 57	11 43	12 01	13 05	13 43	14 04	15 06	15 43	16 06	17 06	17 43	18 05	19 06	19 43	20 06	21 06	22 17	23 16	00 20
Shrewsbury	a	00 43	00 59	11 10	11 58	12 15	13 18	13 58	14 18	15 19	15 58	16 26	17 19	17 59	18 19	19 19	19 58	20 19	21 19	22 30	23 32	00 35

A To Chester
B To Aberystwyth
C To Holyhead
D From Birmingham International
E From Birmingham International to Chester
F From Birmingham International to Aberystwyth
G From Birmingham International to Holyhead

Table 74

Mondays to Fridays

Shrewsbury - Birmingham

Network Diagram - see first Page of Table 67

Miles			AW MX	AW	LM	LM	AW	LM	LM	AW	LM	AW	LM	AW	LM	AW	LM	AW	LM	AW	LM	AW	LM
			◇ A	B			B			◇ C ⌶		◇ D ⌶		◇ E ⌶		◇ D ⌶		◇ F ⌶		◇ D ⌶		◇ F ⌶	
0	**Shrewsbury**	d	23p26	05 20	05 26	05 58	06 31	06 55	07 14	07 31	07 47	08 31	08 47	09 31	09 47	10 32	10 47	11 31	11 47	12 31	12 47	13 31	13 47
10½	Wellington (Shropshire)	d	23p40	05 33	05 40	06 12	06 44	07 09	07 28	07 44	08 01	08 44	09 01	09 44	10 01	10 46	11 01	11 44	12 01	12 44	13 01	13 44	14 01
13½	Oakengates	d	23p44		05 44	06 16			07 32		08 05		09 05		10 05		11 05		12 05		13 05		14 05
14½	Telford Central	d	23p47	05 40	05 47	06 19	06 51	07 15	07 35	07 51	08 08	08 51	09 08	09 51	10 08	10 52	11 08	11 51	12 08	12 52	13 08	13 51	14 08
17½	Shifnal	d	23p52		05 52	06 24			07 40		08 13		09 13		10 13		11 13		12 13		13 13		14 13
20¾	Cosford	d	23p57		05 57	06 29			07 45		08 18		09 18		10 18		11 18		12 18		13 18		14 18
22¼	Albrighton	d	00 01		06 00	06 33			07 48		08 22		09 22		10 22		11 22		12 22		13 22		14 22
25½	Codsall	d	00 06		06 06	06 38			07 54		08 27		09 27		10 27		11 27		12 27		13 27		14 27
26	Bilbrook	d	00 08		06 08	06 40			07 56		08 29		09 29		10 29		11 29		12 29		13 29		14 29
30	**Wolverhampton [7]**	a	00 17	05 57	06 15	06 47	07 09	07 34	08 03	08 09	08 36	09 09	09 36	10 08	10 36	11 09	11 36	12 09	12 36	13 08	13 36	14 08	14 36
37¾	Sandwell & Dudley	a				07 03		07 45			08 46		09 46		10 46		11 46		12 46		13 46		14 46
39	Smethwick Galton Bridge	a		06 10		07 06	07 21			08 20		09 21		10 19		11 20		12 20		13 21		14 20	
43	**Birmingham New Street [12]**	a		06 15	06 32	07 15	07 26	07 54	08 20	08 26	08 55	09 26	09 55	10 25	10 55	11 26	11 55	12 26	12 55	13 26	13 55	14 26	14 55

		AW	LM	AW	LM	AW	LM	AW	LM	AW	LM	AW	LM	LM	AW	LM	AW MWFO	AW TThO	AW
		◇ D ⌶		◇ F ⌶		◇ D ⌶		◇ F ⌶		◇ D ⌶		◇ C ⌶			◇ G		◇ H	◇ I	◇ A
Shrewsbury	d	14 31	14 47	15 31	15 47	16 33	16 47	17 31	17 47	18 31	18 47	19 33	19 47	20 47	21 33	21 47	22 18	22 18	23 26
Wellington (Shropshire)	d	14 44	15 01	15 44	16 01	16 46	17 01	17 44	18 01	18 44	19 01	19 46	20 01	21 01	21 46	22 01	22 32	22 32	23 40
Oakengates	d		15 05		16 05		17 05		18 05		19 05		20 05	21 05		22 05			23 44
Telford Central	d	14 52	15 08	15 51	16 08	16 53	17 08	17 51	18 08	18 51	19 08	19 53	20 08	21 08	21 53	22 08	22 38	22 38	23 47
Shifnal	d		15 13		16 13		17 13		18 13		19 13		20 13	21 13		22 13			23 52
Cosford	d		15 18		16 18		17 18		18 18		19 18		20 18	21 18		22 18			23 57
Albrighton	d		15 22		16 22		17 22		18 22		19 22		20 22	21 22		22 22			00 01
Codsall	d		15 27		16 27		17 27		18 27		19 27		20 27	21 27		22 27			00 06
Bilbrook	d		15 29		16 29		17 29		18 29		19 29		20 29	21 29		22 29			00 08
Wolverhampton [7]	a	15 09	15 36	16 09	16 36	17 09	17 36	18 09	18 36	19 09	19 36	20 11	20 36	21 36	22 09	22 36	22 55	22 55	00 17
Sandwell & Dudley	a		15 46		16 46		17 46		18 46		19 46		20 47	21 46		22 46			
Smethwick Galton Bridge	a	15 21		16 20		17 22		18 20		19 20		20 22			22 20				
Birmingham New Street [12]	a	15 27	15 55	16 27	16 55	17 28	17 55	18 26	18 55	19 26	19 55	20 27	20 56	21 55	22 33	22 55	23 27	23 28	

Saturdays

		AW	AW	AW	LM	AW	LM	AW	LM	AW	LM	AW	LM	AW	LM	AW	LM	AW	LM	AW	LM	AW	LM
		◇ A	B	B ⌶		◇ C ⌶		◇ D ⌶		◇ E ⌶		◇ D ⌶		◇ F ⌶		D		◇ F ⌶		◇ D ⌶		◇ F ⌶	
Shrewsbury	d	23p26	05 24	06 31	06 47	07 31	07 47	08 31	08 47	09 31	09 47	10 32	10 47	11 31	11 47	12 31	12 47	13 31	13 47	14 31	14 47	15 31	15 47
Wellington (Shropshire)	d	23p40	05 37	06 44	07 01	07 44	08 01	08 44	09 01	09 44	10 01	10 45	11 01	11 44	12 01	12 44	13 01	13 44	14 01	14 44	15 01	15 44	16 01
Oakengates	d	23p44			07 05		08 05		09 05		10 05		11 05		12 05		13 05		14 05		15 05		16 05
Telford Central	d	23p47	05 44	06 51	07 08	07 51	08 08	08 51	09 08	09 51	10 08	10 52	11 08	11 51	12 08	12 52	13 08	13 51	14 08	14 52	15 08	15 51	16 08
Shifnal	d	23p52			07 13		08 13		09 13		10 13		11 13		12 13		13 13		14 13		15 13		16 13
Cosford	d	23p57			07 18		08 18		09 18		10 18		11 18		12 18		13 18		14 18		15 18		16 18
Albrighton	d	00 01			07 22		08 22		09 22		10 22		11 22		12 22		13 22		14 22		15 22		16 22
Codsall	d	00 06			07 27		08 27		09 27		10 27		11 27		12 27		13 27		14 27		15 27		16 27
Bilbrook	d	00 08			07 29		08 29		09 29		10 29		11 29		12 29		13 29		14 29		15 29		16 29
Wolverhampton [7]	a	00 17	06 02	07 09	07 36	08 09	08 36	09 09	09 36	10 09	10 36	11 10	11 36	12 09	12 36	13 08	13 36	14 09	14 36	15 09	15 36	16 09	16 36
Sandwell & Dudley	a				07 46		08 46		09 46		10 46		11 46		12 46		13 46		14 46		15 46		16 46
Smethwick Galton Bridge	a		06 14	07 21		08 20		09 22		10 20		11 21		12 20		13 21		14 20		15 21		16 20	
Birmingham New Street [12]	a		06 20	07 26	07 55	08 26	08 55	09 26	09 55	10 26	10 55	11 27	11 55	12 26	12 55	13 27	13 55	14 26	14 55	15 27	15 55	16 26	16 55

		AW	LM	AW	LM	AW	LM	AW	LM	LM	AW	LM	AW	AW
		◇ D ⌶		◇ F ⌶		◇ D ⌶		◇ C ⌶			◇ G		◇ J	◇ A
Shrewsbury	d	16 33	16 47	17 31	17 47	18 31	18 47	19 33	19 47	20 47	21 33	21 47	22 31	23 26
Wellington (Shropshire)	d	16 46	17 01	17 44	18 01	18 44	19 01	19 46	20 01	21 01	21 46	22 01	22 45	23 40
Oakengates	d		17 05		18 05		19 05		20 05	21 05		22 05		23 44
Telford Central	d	16 53	17 08	17 51	18 08	18 51	19 08	19 53	20 08	21 08	21 53	22 08	22 51	23 47
Shifnal	d		17 13		18 13		19 13		20 13	21 13		22 13		23 52
Cosford	d		17 18		18 18		19 18		20 18	21 18		22 18		23 57
Albrighton	d		17 22		18 22		19 22		20 22	21 22		22 22		00 02
Codsall	d		17 27		18 27		19 27		20 27	21 27		22 27		00 07
Bilbrook	d		17 29		18 29		19 29		20 29	21 29		22 29		00 09
Wolverhampton [7]	a	17 09	17 36	18 09	18 36	19 09	19 36	20 10	20 36	21 36	22 08	22 36	23 07	00 16
Sandwell & Dudley	a		17 46		18 46		19 46		20 46	21 46		22 45		
Smethwick Galton Bridge	a	17 22		18 20		19 20		20 21			22 19			
Birmingham New Street [12]	a	17 28	17 55	18 26	18 55	19 26	19 55	20 26	20 57	21 55	22 32	22 55	23 28	

A From Chester
B To Birmingham International
C From Aberystwyth to Birmingham International
D From Holyhead to Birmingham International
E From Barmouth to Birmingham International
F From Pwllheli to Birmingham International
G From Aberystwyth
H From Holyhead
I From Holyhead
J From Holyhead

Table 74

Shrewsbury - Birmingham

Sundays until 24 June

Network Diagram - see first Page of Table 67

		AW	AW	AW	AW	AW	AW	AW	AW	AW	AW	AW	AW	AW	AW	AW	AW	AW	AW	AW	AW	AW
		◇ A				◇ A	◇ B 🍴		◇ A 🍴	◇ B 🍴		◇ A	◇ C 🍴		◇ A 🍴	◇ C 🍴		◇ A	◇ B 🍴	A	◇ B	◇ D
Shrewsbury	d	23p26	08 10	09 09	09 55	10 20	11 40	12 10	12 31	13 31	14 10	14 31	15 33	16 10	16 40	17 33	18 10	18 31	19 31	20 23	21 31	22 23
Wellington (Shropshire)	d	23p40	08 24	09 23	10 09	10 34	11 54	12 24	12 45	13 45	14 23	14 45	15 47	16 23	16 54	17 47	18 23	18 45	19 45	20 37	21 45	22 37
Oakengates	d	23p44	08 28	09 27	10 14			12 29			14 29			16 29			18 29			20 41		22 43
Telford Central	d	23p47	08 31	09 30	10 17	10 40	12 00	12 32	12 51	13 51	14 32	14 51	15 53	16 32	17 00	17 53	18 32	18 51	19 51	20 44	21 51	22 45
Shifnal	d	23p52	08 36	09 35	10 22			12 37			14 37			16 37			18 37			20 49		22 51
Cosford	d	23p57	08 41	09 40	10 28			12 43			14 43			16 43			18 43			20 54		22 56
Albrighton	d	00 02	08 44	09 43	10 31			12 46			14 46			16 46			18 46			20 57		22 59
Codsall	d	00 07	08 50	09 48	10 37			12 52			14 52			16 52			18 52			21 02		23 05
Bilbrook	d	00 09	08 52	09 50	10 39			12 55			14 54			16 54			18 54			21 04		23 07
Wolverhampton 7	a	00 16	08 59	09 57	10 50	10 56	12 16	13 03	13 07	14 07	15 03	15 07	16 09	17 03	17 15	18 09	19 03	19 07	20 07	21 11	22 07	23 13
Sandwell & Dudley	a																					
Smethwick Galton Bridge	a																					
Birmingham New Street 12	a		09 34	10 28		11 32	12 49		13 42	14 40		15 40	16 41		17 53	18 41		19 39	20 40	21 41	22 37	

Sundays from 1 July

		AW	AW	AW	AW	AW	AW	AW	AW	AW	AW	AW	AW	AW	AW	AW	AW	AW	AW	AW	AW	AW	AW
		◇ A	E	E		◇ F	◇ G 🍴		◇ F 🍴	◇ G 🍴		◇ F	◇ G 🍴		◇ F 🍴	◇ G 🍴		◇ F	◇ H 🍴	◇ I 🍴	F	◇ G	◇ D
Shrewsbury	d	23p26	08 10	09 09	09 55	10 20	11 40	12 10	12 31	13 31	14 10	14 31	15 33	16 10	16 40	17 33	18 10	18 31	19 30	19 31	20 23	21 31	22 23
Wellington (Shropshire)	d	23p40	08 24	09 23	10 09	10 34	11 54	12 24	12 45	13 45	14 23	14 45	15 47	16 23	16 54	17 47	18 23	18 45	19 45	19 45	20 37	21 45	22 37
Oakengates	d	23p44	08 28	09 27	10 14			12 29			14 29			16 29			18 29				20 41		22 43
Telford Central	d	23p47	08 31	09 30	10 17	10 40	12 00	12 32	12 51	13 51	14 32	14 51	15 53	16 32	17 00	17 53	18 32	18 51	19 51	19 51	20 44	21 51	22 45
Shifnal	d	23p52	08 36	09 35	10 22			12 37			14 37			16 37			18 37				20 49		22 51
Cosford	d	23p57	08 41	09 40	10 28			12 43			14 43			16 43			18 43				20 54		22 56
Albrighton	d	00 02	08 44	09 43	10 31			12 46			14 46			16 46			18 46				20 57		22 59
Codsall	d	00 07	08 50	09 48	10 37			12 52			14 52			16 52			18 52				21 02		23 05
Bilbrook	d	00 09	08 52	09 50	10 39			12 55			14 54			16 54			18 54				21 04		23 07
Wolverhampton 7	a	00 16	08 59	09 57	10 50	10 56	12 16	13 03	13 07	14 07	15 03	15 07	16 09	17 03	17 15	18 09	19 03	19 07	20 07	20 07	21 11	22 07	23 13
Sandwell & Dudley	a																						
Smethwick Galton Bridge	a																						
Birmingham New Street 12	a		09 15	10 14		11 13	12 32		13 23	14 23		15 24	16 24		17 35	18 27		19 26	20 23	20 23	21 29	22 27	

A From Chester
B From Aberystwyth
C From Pwllheli
D From Holyhead
E To Birmingham International
F From Chester to Birmingham International
G From Aberystwyth to Birmingham International
H from 16 September. From Aberystwyth to Birmingham International
I from 1 July until 9 September. From Aberystwyth to Birmingham International

Table 75

Mondays to Fridays

Birmingham and Shrewsbury - Chester, Aberystwyth, Barmouth and Pwllheli

Network Diagram - see first Page of Table 67

Miles	Miles	Miles			AW MX	AW	AW	AW	AW	AW	AW	AW	VT	AW	AW	AW	AW	AW	AW	AW	AW	AW	AW
							◇		◇			◇	◇ 1	◇ 🍴		◇ 🍴	◇ 🍴	◇ 🍴	◇	◇ 🍴	◇ 🍴	◇ 🍴	◇
—	—	—	Birmingham International ✈	d													07 09			08 09	09 09		
0	—	—	**Birmingham New Street** 12	d												06 24	07 24			08 24	09 24		
—	—	—	Tame Bridge Parkway	d																			
—	—	—	Smethwick Galton Bridge 4	d												06 30	07 30			08 30	09 30		
12¾	—	—	**Wolverhampton** 7	d												06 43	07 42			08 43	09 43		
22	—	—	Cosford	d																			
28¼	—	—	Telford Central	d												06 59	07 59			08 59	09 59		
32¼	—	—	Wellington (Shropshire)	d												07 06	08 05			09 06	10 06		
42¾	—	—	**Shrewsbury**	a												07 18	08 19			09 19	10 19		
—	—	—	Cardiff Central 7	d										05 10				07 21				09 21	
—	—	0	**Shrewsbury**	d	23p37			05 20		06 10				07 24		07 27	08 21	09 24		09 27	10 23	11 24	
—	—	17¾	Gobowen	d	23p57			05 39		06 30				07 43			08 40	09 43			10 42	11 43	
—	—	20¾	Chirk	d	00 03			05 45		06 35				07 48			08 46	09 48			10 48	11 48	
—	—	25	Ruabon	d	00 09			05 51		06 42				07 54			08 52	09 54			10 54	11 54	
—	—	30	Wrexham General	a	00 14			05 57		06 49				08 01			08 59	10 01			11 00	12 01	
—	—	—		d	00 15			06 04					07 00	08 02			09 00	10 02			11 01	12 02	
—	—	42	**Chester**	a	00 35			06 24					07 16	08 19			09 17	10 19			11 19	12 19	
62½	—	—	Welshpool	d												07 49				09 49			
76½	—	—	Newtown (Powys)	d												08 04				10 04			
82	—	—	Caersws	d												08 13				10 13			
103¾	0	—	**Machynlleth** 4	a												08 46				10 46			
—	—	—		d		04 35	05 13		05 30		06 35	06 47			08 07	08 48			08 57	10 48			10 54
107¾	4	—	Dovey Junction	d		04x42	05x20		05x46		06x42	06x54			08x14	08x55			09x04	10x55			11x01
116	—	—	Borth	d		04 53					06 53				08 25	09 06				11 06			
124¼	—	—	**Aberystwyth**	a		05 12					07 10				08 44	09 25				11 25			
—	9	—	Penhelig	d			05x28		05x54			07x02							09x12				11x09
—	10	—	Aberdovey	d			05 33		05 59			07 06							09 16				11 14
—	13½	—	Tywyn	a			05 39		06 08			07 16							09 26				11 23
—	—	—		d			05 40		06 11			07 16							09 29				11 23
—	16	—	Tonfanau	d			05x43		06x15			07x20							09x33				11x27
—	20	—	Llwyngwril	d			05x50		06x21			07x26							09x39				11x33
—	22¾	—	Fairbourne	d			05 58		06 29			07 34							09 47				11 42
—	23¾	—	Morfa Mawddach	d			05x59		06x31			07x36							09 49				11x43
—	25½	—	**Barmouth**	a			06 09		06 45			07 45							09 58				11 52
—	—	—		d			06 10					07 47							10 01				11 55
—	26¾	—	Llanaber	d			06x13					07x49							10x03				11x57
—	29¼	—	Talybont	d								07x53							10x07				12x01
—	30¼	—	Dyffryn Ardudwy	d								07x56							10x10				12x04
—	32½	—	Llanbedr	d								08x00							10x14				12x08
—	33¼	—	Pensarn	d								08x02							10x16				12x10
—	34	—	Llandanwg	d								08x04							10x18				12x12
—	35¾	—	Harlech	a			06 29					08 10							10 25				12 19
—	—	—		d			06 29					08 25							10 25				12 21
—	38½	—	Tygwyn	d								08x29							10x29				12x24
—	39¼	—	Talsarnau	d								08x31							10x31				12x27
—	40½	—	Llandecwyn	d								08x34							10x34				12x30
—	41¼	—	Penrhyndeudraeth	d								08 38							10 38				12 34
—	42½	—	Minffordd	d								08 42							10 42				12 37
—	44½	—	Porthmadog	a			06 46					08 49							10 49				12 45
—	—	—		d			06 54					08 50							10 50				12 45
—	49½	—	Criccieth	d			07 01					08 57							10 57				12 53
—	54	—	Penychain	d			07x07					09x02							11x02				12x58
—	55½	—	Abererch	d								09x05							11x05				13x01
—	57½	—	**Pwllheli**	a			07 14					09 12							11 12				13 10

For connections from London Euston please refer to Table 66

For connections from Manchester Piccadilly and Crewe please refer to Table 131

Birmingham and Shrewsbury - Chester, Aberystwyth, Barmouth and Pwllheli

Network Diagram - see first Page of Table 67

		AW ◇ A 🛒		AW ◇ 🛒	AW ◇ 🛒	AW ◇ A 🛒		AW ◇ 🛒	AW ◇ 🛒	AW ◇ A 🛒		AW ◇ 🛒	AW ■ 🛒	AW ◇ A 🛒		AW ◇ 🛒	AW ■ 🛒	AW ◇ 🛒	AW ■ 🛒	AW ◇ 🛒
Birmingham International ✈	d	10 09		11 09		12 09		13 09		14 09		15 09		16 09		17 09		18 09		19 09
Birmingham New Street 12	d	10 24		11 24		12 24		13 24		14 24		15 26		16 24		17 26		18 24		19 24
Tame Bridge Parkway	d																			
Smethwick Galton Bridge 4	d	10 30		11 30		12 30		13 30		14 30		15 32		16 30		17 32		18 30		19 30
Wolverhampton 7 ⛴	d	10 43		11 43		12 43		13 43		14 43		15 44		16 43		17 44		18 43		19 43
Cosford	d																			
Telford Central	d	10 59		11 59		12 59		13 59		14 59		16 01		16 59		18 01		18 59		19 59
Wellington (Shropshire)	d	11 06		12 06		13 06		14 06		15 06		16 07		17 06		18 07		19 06		20 06
Shrewsbury	a	11 19		12 19		13 19		14 19		15 19		16 20		17 19		18 20		19 19		20 19
Cardiff Central 7	d				11 21				13 21				15 21				17 21		18 18	
Shrewsbury	d	11 27		12 22	13 24	13 27		14 22	15 24	15 27		16 24	17 24	17 27		18 24	19 24	19 30	20 05	20 24
Gobowen	d			12 42	13 43			14 42	15 43			16 43	17 43			18 43	19 43		20 24	20 43
Chirk	d			12 47	13 48			14 47	15 48			16 49	17 48			18 49	19 48			20 49
Ruabon	d			12 54	13 54			14 54	15 54			16 55	17 54			18 55	19 54		20 34	20 55
Wrexham General	a			13 00	14 01			15 00	16 01			17 01	18 01			19 01	20 01		20 42	21 01
	d			13 00	14 02			15 00	16 02			17 02	18 02			19 02	20 02		20 43	21 02
Chester	a			13 19	14 19			15 20	16 20			17 22	18 20			19 20	20 20		20 58	21 19
Welshpool	d	11 49				13 49				15 49				17 49				19 52		
Newtown (Powys)	d	12 04				14 04				16 04				18 04				20 07		
Caersws	d	12 13				14 13				16 13				18 13				20 16		
Machynlleth 4	a	12 46				14 46				16 46				18 46				20 47		
	d	12 48	12 55			14 48	14 56			16 48	16 58			18 48	18 59			20 49		
Dovey Junction 4	d	12x55	13x02			14x55	15x03			16x55	17x05			18x55	19x06			20x56		
Borth	d	13 06				15 06				17 06				19 06				21 07		
Aberystwyth	a	13 25				15 25				17 25				19 25				21 25		
Penhelig	d		13x10				15x11				17x13				19x14					
Aberdovey	d		13 14				15 15				17 17				19 19					
Tywyn	a		13 24				15 25				17 27				19 28					
	d		13 24				15 25				17 28				19 30					
Tonfanau	d		13x28				15x29				17x31				19x33					
Llwyngwril	d		13x34				15x35				17x38				19x40					
Fairbourne	d		13 42				15 43				17 46				19 48					
Morfa Mawddach	d		13x44				15x45				17x47				19x49					
Barmouth	a		13 53				15 54				17 57				20 03					
	d		13 56				15 57				17 59									
Llanaber	d		13x58				16x00				18x03									
Talybont	d		14x02				16x03				18x06									
Dyffryn Ardudwy	d		14x05				16x06				18x09									
Llanbedr	d		14x09				16x10				18x13									
Pensarn	d		14x11				16x12				18x15									
Llandanwg	d		14x13				16x14				18x17									
Harlech	a		14 20				16 21				18 23									
	d		14 31				16 29				18 33									
Tygwyn	d		14x35				16x32				18x36									
Talsarnau	d		14x37				16x35				18x39									
Llandecwyn	d		14x40				16x38				18x42									
Penrhyndeudraeth	d		14 44				16 42				18 46									
Minffordd	d		14 48				16 45				18 49									
Porthmadog	a		14 55				16 52				18 56									
	d		14 56				16 53				18 57									
Criccieth	d		15 03				17 00				19 04									
Penychain	d		15x08				17x05				19x09									
Abererch	d		15x11				17x08				19x12									
Pwllheli	a		15 21				17 17				19 21									

A 🛒 to Machynlleth

For connections from London Euston please refer to Table 66

For connections from Manchester Piccadilly and Crewe please refer to Table 131

Birmingham and Shrewsbury - Chester, Aberystwyth, Barmouth and Pwllheli

Network Diagram - see first Page of Table 67

		AW ◇	AW ◇	AW ◇	AW ◇	AW
Birmingham International ✈	d			20 09	21 09	
Birmingham New Street 12	d			20 24	21 24	
Tame Bridge Parkway	d					
Smethwick Galton Bridge 4	d			20 30	21 30	
Wolverhampton 7 ⛴	d			20 43	21 43	
Cosford	d					
Telford Central	d			20 59	21 59	
Wellington (Shropshire)	d			21 06	22 07	
Shrewsbury	a			21 19	22 19	
Cardiff Central 7	d	19 34				
Shrewsbury	d	21 39		21 42	22 24	23 37
Gobowen	d	21 58			22 43	23 57
Chirk	d	22 03			22 49	00 03
Ruabon	d	22 09			22 55	00 09
Wrexham General	a	22 13			23 01	00 14
	d	22 14			23 01	00 15
Chester	a	22 34			23 19	00 35
Welshpool	d			22 04		
Newtown (Powys)	d			22 20		
Caersws	d			22 29		
Machynlleth 4	a			23 00		
	d		21 20	23 07		
Dovey Junction 4	d		21x27	23x14		
Borth	d			23 25		
Aberystwyth	a			23 44		
Penhelig	d		21x35			
Aberdovey	d		21 39			
Tywyn	a		21 49			
	d		21 49			
Tonfanau	d		21x53			
Llwyngwril	d		21x59			
Fairbourne	d		22 07			
Morfa Mawddach	d		22x09			
Barmouth	a		22 18			
	d		22 21			
Llanaber	d		22x23			
Talybont	d		22x27			
Dyffryn Ardudwy	d		22x30			
Llanbedr	d		22x34			
Pensarn	d		22x36			
Llandanwg	d		22x38			
Harlech	a		22 45			
	d		22 45			
Tygwyn	d		22x49			
Talsarnau	d		22x51			
Llandecwyn	d		22x54			
Penrhyndeudraeth	d		22 58			
Minffordd	d		23 02			
Porthmadog	a		23 09			
	d		23 10			
Criccieth	d		23 17			
Penychain	d		23x22			
Abererch	d		23x25			
Pwllheli	a		23 32			

For connections from London Euston please refer to Table 66

For connections from Manchester Piccadilly and Crewe please refer to Table 131

Birmingham and Shrewsbury - Chester, Aberystwyth, Barmouth and Pwllheli

Network Diagram - see first Page of Table 67

		AW	AW	AW	AW	AW	AW	AW	AW	AW	AW	AW	AW	AW	AW	AW		AW	AW	AW		AW	AW
				◇		◇	🚌	◇ 🚌		◇	◇ A 🚌	◇ B 🚌	◇ 🚌	◇ 🚌	◇	◇ 🚌		◇ 🚌	◇ 🚌	◇ 🚌		◇ 🚌	◇ 🚌
Birmingham International ✈	d												07 09			08 09		09 09		10 09		11 09	
Birmingham New Street 12	d										06 24	06 24	07 23			08 24		09 24		10 24		11 24	
Tame Bridge Parkway	d																						
Smethwick Galton Bridge 4	d										06 30	06 30	07 29			08 30		09 30		10 30		11 30	
Wolverhampton 7 ⇌	d										06 42	06 42	07 41			08 43		09 43		10 43		11 43	
Cosford	d																						
Telford Central	d										06 59	06 59	07 58			08 59		09 59		10 59		11 59	
Wellington (Shropshire)	d										07 05	07 05	08 04			09 06		10 06		11 06		12 06	
Shrewsbury	a										07 18	07 18	08 18			09 19		10 19		11 19		12 19	
Cardiff Central 7	d							05 20						07 21					09 21				11 21
Shrewsbury	d	23p37			05 20		06 10	07 24			07 26	07 27	08 21	09 24		09 27		10 23	11 24	11 27		12 22	13 24
Gobowen	d	23p57			05 39		06 30	07 43					08 40	09 43				10 42	11 43			12 42	13 43
Chirk	d	00 03			05 45		06 35	07 48					08 46	09 48				10 48	11 48			12 47	13 48
Ruabon	d	00 09			05 51		06 42	07 54					08 52	09 54				10 54	11 54			12 54	13 54
Wrexham General	a	00 14			05 57		06 48	08 00					08 59	10 01				11 00	12 01			13 00	14 01
	d	00 15			05 58		06 50	08 01					09 00	10 02				11 01	12 02			13 00	14 02
Chester	a	00 35			06 16		07 08	08 18					09 17	10 19				11 19	12 19			13 18	14 19
Welshpool	d										07 49	07 49				09 49				11 49			
Newtown (Powys)	d										08 04	08 04				10 04				12 04			
Caersws	d										08 13	08 13				10 13				12 13			
Machynlleth 4	a										08 46	08 46				10 46				12 46			
	d		04 35	05 13		05 30			06 35	06 47	08 48	08 48			08 57	10 48	10 54			12 48	12 55		
Dovey Junction 4	d		04x42	05x20		05x46			06x42	06x54	08x55	08x55			09x04	10x55	11x01			12x55	13x02		
Borth	d		04 53						06 53		09 06	09 06				11 06				13 06			
Aberystwyth	a		05 12						07 10		09 25	09 25				11 25				13 25			
Penhelig	d			05x28		05x54				07x02					09x12		11x09				13x10		
Aberdovey	d			05 33		05 59				07 06					09 16		11 14				13 14		
Tywyn	a			05 39		06 08				07 16					09 26		11 23				13 24		
	d			05 40		06 11				07 16					09 29		11 23				13 24		
Tonfanau	d			05x43		06x15				07x20					09x33		11x27				13x28		
Llwyngwril	d			05x50		06x21				07x26					09x39		11x33				13x34		
Fairbourne	d			05 58		06 29				07 34					09 47		11 42				13 42		
Morfa Mawddach	d			05x59		06x31				07x36					09 49		11x43				13x44		
Barmouth	a			06 09		06 45				07 45					09 58		11 52				13 53		
	d			06 10						07 47					10 01		11 55				13 56		
Llanaber	d			06x13						07x49					10x03		11x57				13x58		
Talybont	d									07x53					10x07		12x01				14x02		
Dyffryn Ardudwy	d									07x56					10x10		12x04				14x05		
Llanbedr	d									08x00					10x14		12x08				14x09		
Pensarn	d									08x02					10x16		12x10				14x11		
Llandanwg	d									08x04					10x18		12x12				14x13		
Harlech	a			06 29						08 10					10 25		12 19				14 20		
	d			06 29						08 25					10 25		12 21				14 31		
Tygwyn	d									08x29					10x29		12x24				14x35		
Talsarnau	d									08x31					10x31		12x27				14x37		
Llandecwyn	d									08x34					10x34		12x30				14x40		
Penrhyndeudraeth	d									08 38					10 38		12 34				14 44		
Minffordd	d									08 42					10 42		12 37				14 48		
Porthmadog	a			06 46						08 49					10 49		12 45				14 55		
	d			06 54						08 50					10 50		12 45				14 56		
Criccieth	d			07 01						08 57					10 57		12 53				15 03		
Penychain	d			07x07						09x02					11x02		12x58				15x08		
Abererch	d									09x05					11x05		13x01				15x11		
Pwllheli	a			07 14						09 12					11 12		13 10				15 21		

A from 15 September

B until 8 September

For connections from London Euston please refer to Table 66

For connections from Manchester Piccadilly and Crewe please refer to Table 131

Birmingham and Shrewsbury - Chester, Aberystwyth, Barmouth and Pwllheli

Network Diagram - see first Page of Table 67

		AW		AW	AW	AW		AW	AW	AW	AW	AW	AW	AW	AW	AW	AW	AW	AW	AW
		◇ A 🚌		◇ 🚌	◇ 🚌	◇ 🚌		◇ 🚌	■ 🚌	■ 🚌	◇ 🚌		■ B 🚌	◇ 🚌	◇ 🚌	◇	◇	◇	◇	
Birmingham International ✈	d	12 09		13 09		14 09		15 09		16 09	17 09			18 09	19 09			20 09	21 09	
Birmingham New Street 12	d	12 24		13 24		14 24		15 24		16 24	17 24			18 24	19 24			20 24	21 24	
Tame Bridge Parkway	d																			
Smethwick Galton Bridge 4	d	12 30		13 30		14 30		15 30		16 30	17 31			18 30	19 30			20 30	21 30	
Wolverhampton 7 ⇌	d	12 43		13 43		14 43		15 43		16 43	17 43			18 43	19 43			20 43	21 42	
Cosford	d																			
Telford Central	d	12 59		13 59		14 59		15 59		16 59	17 59			18 59	19 59			21 02	21 59	
Wellington (Shropshire)	d	13 06		14 06		15 06		16 06		17 06	18 06			19 06	20 06			21 09	22 05	
Shrewsbury	a	13 19		14 19		15 19		16 19		17 19	18 19			19 19	20 19			21 23	22 22	
Cardiff Central 7	d				13 21				15 21				17 21			19 34				
Shrewsbury	d	13 27		14 22	15 24	15 27		16 22	17 24	17 27	18 22		19 24	19 30	20 24	21 37		21 42	22 24	23 33
Gobowen	d			14 42	15 43			16 42	17 43		18 42		19 43		20 43	21 56			22 43	23 52
Chirk	d			14 47	15 48			16 47	17 48		18 47		19 48		20 49	22 01			22 49	23 58
Ruabon	d			14 54	15 54			16 54	17 54		18 54		19 54		20 55	22 07			22 55	00 04
Wrexham General	a			15 00	16 01			17 00	18 01		19 01		20 01		21 01	22 13			23 01	00 10
	d			15 00	16 02			17 02	18 02		19 02	19 46	20 02		21 02	22 13			23 02	00 14
Chester	a			15 20	16 22			17 19	18 19		19 20	20 04	20 19		21 21	22 31			23 21	00 33
Welshpool	d	13 49				15 49				17 49				19 52				22 04		
Newtown (Powys)	d	14 04				16 04				18 04				20 07				22 20		
Caersws	d	14 13				16 13				18 13				20 16				22 29		
Machynlleth 4	a	14 46				16 46				18 46				20 47				22 59		
	d	14 48	14 56			16 48	16 58			18 48				20 49			21 20	23 04		
Dovey Junction 4	d	14x55	15x03			16x55	17x05			18x55				20x56			21x27	23x11		
Borth	d	15 06				17 06				19 06				21 07				23 22		
Aberystwyth	a	15 25				17 25				19 25				21 25				23 41		
Penhelig	d		15x11				17x13										21x35			
Aberdovey	d		15 15				17 17										21 39			
Tywyn	a		15 25				17 27										21 49			
	d		15 25				17 28										21 49			
Tonfanau	d		15x29				17x31										21x53			
Llwyngwril	d		15x35				17x38										21x59			
Fairbourne	d		15 43				17 46										22 07			
Morfa Mawddach	d		15x45				17x47										22x09			
Barmouth	a		15 54				17 57										22 18			
	d		15 57				17 59										22 21			
Llanaber	d		16x00				18x03										22x23			
Talybont	d		16x03				18x06										22x27			
Dyffryn Ardudwy	d		16x06				18x09										22x30			
Llanbedr	d		16x10				18x13										22x34			
Pensarn	d		16x12				18x15										22x36			
Llandanwg	d		16x14				18x17										22x38			
Harlech	a		16 21				18 23										22 45			
	d		16 29				18 33										22 45			
Tygwyn	d		16x32				18x36										22x49			
Talsarnau	d		16x35				18x39										22x51			
Llandecwyn	d		16x38				18x42										22x54			
Penrhyndeudraeth	d		16 42				18 46										22 58			
Minffordd	d		16 45				18 49										23 02			
Porthmadog	a		16 52				18 56										23 09			
	d		16 53				18 57										23 10			
Criccieth	d		17 00				19 04										23 17			
Penychain	d		17x05				19x09										23x22			
Abererch	d		17x08				19x12										23x25			
Pwllheli	a		17 17				19 21										23 32			

A 🚌 to Machynlleth

B 🚌 from Shrewsbury

For connections from London Euston please refer to Table 66

For connections from Manchester Piccadilly and Crewe please refer to Table 131

Birmingham and Shrewsbury - Chester, Aberystwyth, Barmouth and Pwllheli

Network Diagram - see first Page of Table 67

		AW	AW	AW	AW	AW	AW	AW	AW	AW	AW	AW	AW	AW	AW	AW		AW	AW	AW	AW	AW	AW
				◇	◇	H		◇		◇ H	◇ H	■	◇	◇ H	◇ H	◇ H		■ ◇ A H	◇ H	◇ H	◇ H	◇	
Birmingham International ✈	d																						
Birmingham New Street	d							10 57		12 12	13 02			14 03	15 02	16 02			17 02	18 02	19 02	20 02	
Tame Bridge Parkway	d																						
Smethwick Galton Bridge	d																						
Wolverhampton	d							11 27		12 42	13 42			14 43	15 43	16 43			17 43	18 43	19 43	20 43	
Cosford	d							11 43															
Telford Central	d							11 54		12 59	13 58			14 59	15 59	16 59			17 59	18 59	19 59	20 59	
Wellington (Shropshire)	d							12 01		13 05	14 04			15 06	16 06	17 06			18 05	19 06	20 06	21 06	
Shrewsbury	a							12 15		13 18	14 18			15 19	16 26	17 19			18 19	19 19	20 19	21 19	
Cardiff Central	d											13 22						15 22					
Shrewsbury	d	23p33		08 45		10 16		12 17		13 27	14 20	15 22		15 27	16 27	17 27		17 30	18 20	19 27	20 22	21 30	
Gobowen	d	23p52				10 35		12 37			14 39	15 42			16 47			17 49	18 40		20 42		
Chirk	d	23p58				10 41		12 42			14 45	15 47			16 52			17 55	18 45		20 47		
Ruabon	d	00 04				10 47		12 49			14 51	15 54			16 59			18 01	18 51		20 54		
Wrexham General	a	00 10				10 53		12 55			14 57	16 00			17 05			18 07	18 57		21 00		
	d	00 14				10 54		12 56			14 58	16 00			17 05			18 08	18 58		21 01		22 35
Chester	a	00 33				11 12		13 20			15 18	16 18			17 26			18 25	19 16		21 20		22 53
Welshpool	d			09 07						13 49				15 49		17 49				19 49		21 52	
Newtown (Powys)	d			09 23						14 04				16 04		18 04				20 04		22 07	
Caersws	d			09 32						14 13				16 13		18 13				20 13		22 16	
Machynlleth	a			10 02						14 46				16 46		18 46				20 46		22 47	
	d		08 50	10 05	10 10		10 50		12 35	14 48			15 00	16 48		18 48	18 55			20 48		22 49	
Dovey Junction	d		08x57	10x12	10x17		10x57		12x42	14x55			15x07	16x55		18x55	19x02			20x55		22x56	
Borth	d		09 08	10 22			11 08		12 53	15 06				17 06		19 06				21 06		23 07	
Aberystwyth	a		09 25	10 41			11 27		13 10	15 25				17 25		19 25				21 25		23 26	
Penhelig	d				10x25								15x15				19x10						
Aberdovey	d				10 30								15 20				19 14						
Tywyn	a				10 36								15 26				19 20						
	d				10 36								15 31				19 21						
Tonfanau	d				10x40								15x34				19x24						
Llwyngwril	d				10x47								15x41				19x31						
Fairbourne	d				10 55								15 49				19 39						
Morfa Mawddach	d				10 56								15 51				19x41						
Barmouth	a				11 03								15 58				19 48						
	d				11 05								15 59				19 49						
Llanaber	d				11x08								16x02				19x53						
Talybont	d				11x12								16x06				19x56						
Dyffryn Ardudwy	d				11x15								16x10				20x00						
Llanbedr	d				11x19								16x14				20x04						
Pensarn	d				11x22								16x16				20x07						
Llandanwg	d				11x24								16x18				20x09						
Harlech	a				11 30								16 25				20 15						
	d				11 33								16 25				20 18						
Tygwyn	d				11x36								16x29				20x21						
Talsarnau	d				11x39								16x32				20x24						
Llandecwyn	d				11x42								16x36				20x27						
Penrhyndeudraeth	d				11 46								16 39				20 31						
Minffordd	d				11 50								16 42				20 35						
Porthmadog	a				11 55								16 47				20 40						
	d				11 58								16 48				20 41						
Criccieth	d				12 05								16 55				20 48						
Penychain	d				12x11								17x01				20x53						
Abererch	d				12x14								17x04				20x57						
Pwllheli	a				12 24								17 14				21 07						

A ◇ from Shrewsbury ■ to Shrewsbury

For connections from London Euston please refer to Table 66

For connections from Manchester Piccadilly and Crewe please refer to Table 131

Birmingham and Shrewsbury - Chester, Aberystwyth, Barmouth and Pwllheli

Network Diagram - see first Page of Table 67

		AW	AW	AW	AW	AW	AW	AW	AW	AW	AW	AW	AW	AW	AW	AW		AW	AW	AW	AW	AW	AW
				◇	◇	H		◇		◇ H	◇ H	■	◇	◇ H	◇ H	◇ H		■ ◇ A H	◇ H	◇ H	◇ H	◇	
Birmingham International ✈	d							10 48		12 08	13 12			14 07	15 07	16 07			17 07	18 07	19 07	20 07	
Birmingham New Street	d							11 05		12 24	13 24			14 24	15 24	16 24			17 24	18 24	19 24	20 24	
Tame Bridge Parkway	d																						
Smethwick Galton Bridge	d																						
Wolverhampton	d							11 27		12 42	13 42			14 43	15 43	16 43			17 43	18 43	19 43	20 43	
Cosford	d							11 43															
Telford Central	d							11 54		12 59	13 58			14 59	15 59	16 59			17 59	18 59	19 59	20 59	
Wellington (Shropshire)	d							12 01		13 05	14 04			15 06	16 06	17 06			18 05	19 06	20 06	21 06	
Shrewsbury	a							12 15		13 18	14 18			15 19	16 26	17 19			18 19	19 19	20 19	21 19	
Cardiff Central	d											13 22						15 22					
Shrewsbury	d	23p33		08 45		10 16		12 17		13 27	14 20	15 22		15 27	16 27	17 27		17 30	18 20	19 27	20 22	21 30	
Gobowen	d	23p52				10 35		12 37			14 39	15 42			16 47			17 49	18 40		20 42		
Chirk	d	23p58				10 41		12 42			14 45	15 47			16 52			17 55	18 45		20 47		
Ruabon	d	00 04				10 47		12 49			14 51	15 54			16 59			18 01	18 51		20 54		
Wrexham General	a	00 10				10 53		12 55			14 57	16 00			17 05			18 07	18 57		21 00		
	d	00 14				10 54		12 56			14 58	16 00			17 05			18 08	18 58		21 01		22 35
Chester	a	00 33				11 12		13 20			15 18	16 18			17 26			18 25	19 16		21 20		22 53
Welshpool	d			09 07						13 49				15 49		17 49				19 49		21 52	
Newtown (Powys)	d			09 23						14 04				16 04		18 04				20 04		22 07	
Caersws	d			09 32						14 13				16 13		18 13				20 13		22 16	
Machynlleth	a			10 02						14 46				16 46		18 46				20 46		22 47	
	d		08 50	10 05	10 10		10 50		12 35	14 48			15 00	16 48		18 48	18 55			20 48		22 49	
Dovey Junction	d		08x57	10x12	10x17		10x57		12x42	14x55			15x07	16x55		18x55	19x02			20x55		22x56	
Borth	d		09 08	10 22			11 08		12 53	15 06				17 06		19 06				21 06		23 07	
Aberystwyth	a		09 25	10 41			11 27		13 10	15 25				17 25		19 25				21 25		23 26	
Penhelig	d				10x25								15x15				19x10						
Aberdovey	d				10 30								15 20				19 14						
Tywyn	a				10 36								15 26				19 20						
	d				10 36								15 31				19 21						
Tonfanau	d				10x40								15x34				19x24						
Llwyngwril	d				10x47								15x41				19x31						
Fairbourne	d				10 55								15 49				19 39						
Morfa Mawddach	d				10 56								15 51				19x41						
Barmouth	a				11 03								15 58				19 48						
	d				11 05								15 59				19 49						
Llanaber	d				11x08								16x02				19x53						
Talybont	d				11x12								16x06				19x56						
Dyffryn Ardudwy	d				11x15								16x10				20x00						
Llanbedr	d				11x19								16x14				20x04						
Pensarn	d				11x22								16x16				20x07						
Llandanwg	d				11x24								16x18				20x09						
Harlech	a				11 30								16 25				20 15						
	d				11 33								16 25				20 18						
Tygwyn	d				11x36								16x29				20x21						
Talsarnau	d				11x39								16x32				20x24						
Llandecwyn	d				11x42								16x36				20x27						
Penrhyndeudraeth	d				11 46								16 39				20 31						
Minffordd	d				11 50								16 42				20 35						
Porthmadog	a				11 55								16 47				20 40						
	d				11 58								16 48				20 41						
Criccieth	d				12 05								16 55				20 48						
Penychain	d				12x11								17x01				20x53						
Abererch	d				12x14								17x04				20x57						
Pwllheli	a				12 24								17 14				21 07						

A ◇ from Shrewsbury ■ to Shrewsbury

For connections from London Euston please refer to Table 66

For connections from Manchester Piccadilly and Crewe please refer to Table 131

Table 75

Sundays
from 16 September

Birmingham and Shrewsbury - Chester, Aberystwyth, Barmouth and Pwllheli

Network Diagram - see first Page of Table 67

		AW	AW	AW	AW	AW	AW	AW	AW	AW	AW	AW	AW		AW	AW	AW	AW	AW	AW
										■					■					
						◇	◇	◇	◇		◇	◇	◇		◇	◇	◇	◇	◇	
															A					
				⊼				⊼	⊼		⊼	⊼	⊼		⊼	⊼	⊼	⊼		
Birmingham International	d						10 48	12 08	13 12		14 07	15 07	16 07			17 07	18 07	19 07	20 07	
Birmingham New Street	d						11 05	12 24	13 24		14 24	15 24	16 24			17 24	18 24	19 24	20 24	
Tame Bridge Parkway	d																			
Smethwick Galton Bridge	d																			
Wolverhampton	d						11 27	12 42	13 42		14 43	15 43	16 43			17 43	18 43	19 43	20 43	
Cosford	d						11 43													
Telford Central	d						11 54	12 59	13 58		14 59	15 59	16 59			17 59	18 59	19 59	20 59	
Wellington (Shropshire)	d						12 01	13 05	14 04		15 06	16 06	17 06			18 05	19 06	20 06	21 06	
Shrewsbury	a						12 15	13 18	14 18		15 19	16 26	17 19			18 19	19 19	20 19	21 19	
Cardiff Central	d									13 22					15 22					
Shrewsbury	d	23p33		10 16		11 27	12 17	13 27	14 20	15 22	15 27	16 27	17 27		17 30	18 20	19 27	20 22	21 30	
Gobowen	d	23p52		10 35			12 37		14 39	15 42		16 47			17 49	18 40		20 42		
Chirk	d	23p58		10 41			12 42		14 45	15 47		16 52			17 55	18 45		20 47		
Ruabon	d	00 04		10 47			12 49		14 51	15 54		16 59			18 01	18 51		20 54		
Wrexham General	a	00 10		10 53			12 55		14 57	16 00		17 05			18 07	18 57		21 00		
	d	00 14		10 54			12 56		14 58	16 00		17 05			18 08	18 58		21 01		22 35
Chester	a	00 33		11 12			13 20		15 18	16 18		17 26			18 25	19 16		21 20		22 53
Welshpool	d					11 49		13 49			15 49		17 49				19 49		21 52	
Newtown (Powys)	d					12 05		14 04			16 04		18 04				20 04		22 07	
Caersws	d					12 14		14 13			16 13		18 13				20 13		22 16	
Machynlleth	a					12 46		14 46			16 46		18 46				20 46		22 47	
	d		08 50		10 50	12 48		14 48			16 48		18 48	18 55			20 48		22 49	
Dovey Junction	d		08x57		10x57	12x55		14x55			16x55		18x55	19x02			20x55		22x56	
Borth	d		09 08		11 08	13 06		15 06			17 06		19 06				21 06		23 07	
Aberystwyth	a		09 25		11 27	13 23		15 25			17 25		19 25				21 25		23 26	
Penhelig	d													19x10						
Aberdovey	d													19 14						
Tywyn	a													19 20						
	d													19 21						
Tonfanau	d													19x24						
Llwyngwril	d													19x31						
Fairbourne	d													19 39						
Morfa Mawddach	d													19x41						
Barmouth	a													19 48						
	d													19 49						
Llanaber	d													19x53						
Talybont	d													19x56						
Dyffryn Ardudwy	d													20x00						
Llanbedr	d													20x04						
Pensarn	d													20x07						
Llandanwg	d													20x09						
Harlech	a													20 15						
	d													20 18						
Tygwyn	d													20x21						
Talsarnau	d													20x24						
Llandecwyn	d													20x27						
Penrhyndeudraeth	d													20 31						
Minffordd	d													20 35						
Porthmadog	a													20 40						
	d													20 41						
Criccieth	d													20 48						
Penychain	d													20x53						
Abererch	d													20x57						
Pwllheli	a													21 07						

A ◇ from Shrewsbury ■ to Shrewsbury

For connections from London Euston please refer to Table 66

For connections from Manchester Piccadilly and Crewe please refer to Table 131

Table 75

Mondays to Fridays

Pwllheli, Barmouth, Aberystwyth and Chester - Shrewsbury and Birmingham

Network Diagram - see first Page of Table 67

Miles	Miles	Miles			AW MX	AW MO	AW MX	AW	AW	AW	AW	AW	AW	AW	AW	AW	AW	AW	AW	AW	AW	AW	AW
																	■						■
					◇			◇	◇		◇	◇	◇	◇	◇	◇			◇	◇	◇	◇	
						A								B				C		B			
									⊼		⊼	⊼	⊼	⊼	⊼		⊼		⊼	⊼	⊼	⊼	⊼
—	0	—	**Pwllheli**	d												06 29				07 20			
—	1¾	—	Abererch	d												06x32				07x23			
—	3¼	—	Penychain	d												06x35				07x26			
—	7¾	—	Criccieth	d												06 43				07 34			
—	12¾	—	Porthmadog	a												06 51				07 41			
—	—	—		d												06 53				07 43			
—	15	—	Minffordd	d												06 57				07 47			
—	16¼	—	Penrhyndeudraeth	d												07 01				07 51			
—	17	—	Llandecwyn	d												07x03				07x53			
—	18¾	—	Talsarnau	d												07x05				07x56			
—	19	—	Tygwyn	d												07x08				07x58			
—	21½	—	Harlech	a												07 15				08 06			
—	—	—		d												07 17				08 25			
—	23½	—	Llandanwg	d												07x21				08x29			
—	24¼	—	Pensarn	d												07x23				08x30			
—	30½	—	Llanbedr	d												07x25				08x33			
—	27	—	Dyffryn Ardudwy	d												07x29				08x37			
—	28¼	—	Talybont	d												07x32				08x40			
—	25	—	Llanaber	d												07x37				08x44			
—	32	—	**Barmouth**	a												07 41				08 49			
—	—	—		d										06 46		07 47				08 52			
—	33¾	—	Morfa Mawddach	d										06x50		07x51				08x56			
—	34¾	—	Fairbourne	d										06 54		07 55				09 00			
—	37¼	—	Llwyngwril	d										07x00		08x01				09x06			
—	41½	—	Tonfanau	d										07x07		08x08				09x13			
—	44¼	—	Tywyn	a										07 13		08 12				09 19			
—	—	—		d										07 17		08 16				09 27			
—	47½	—	Aberdovey	d										07 23		08 22				09 33			
—	48½	—	Penhelig	d										07x25		08x24				09x35			
0	—	—	**Aberystwyth**	d		23p30	23p53		05 14						07 30						09 30		
8¼	—	—	Borth	d		23p43	00 06		05 27						07 43						09 43		
16½	53½	—	Dovey Junction	d		23b54	00x17		05x38					07x38	07x54	08x37				09x47	09x54		
20½	57½	—	**Machynlleth**	a		00 04	00 24		05 45					07 46	08 03	08 47				09 55	10 03		
—	—	—		d					05 47					08 07						10 07			
42¼	—	—	Caersws	d					06 11					08 33						10 33			
47¾	—	—	Newtown (Powys)	d					06 25					08 46						10 46			
61¾	—	—	Welshpool	d					06 41					09 01						11 01			
—	—	0	**Chester**	d	22p28			05 15		05 45	06 18	07 19	08 19				09 26	09 26	10 20			11 29	12 19
—	12	—	Wrexham General	a	22p44			05 31		06 03	06 35	07 35	08 34				09 42	09 42	10 35			11 44	12 34
—	—	—		d	22p44			05 31			06 38	07 44	08 34				09 42	09 42	10 36			11 45	12 34
—	—	17	Ruabon	d	22p51			05 38			06 45	07 51	08 41				09 49	09 49	10 42			11 52	12 41
—	—	21¼	Chirk	d	22p57			05 44			06 51	07 57	08 47				09 56	09 56	10 48			11 59	12 48
—	—	24¼	Gobowen	d	23p03			05 50			06 57	08 03	08 53				10 01	10 01	10 54			12 04	12 53
81½	—	42	**Shrewsbury**	a	23p22			06 10	07 11		07 17	08 23	09 13	09 26			10 22	10 22	11 14	11 26		12 27	13 14
—	—	—	Cardiff Central	a				08 17			09 23		11 15				12 08		13 22				15 19
—	—	—	**Shrewsbury**	d	23p26				07 31			08 31		09 31						11 31		12 31	
92	—	—	Wellington (Shropshire)	d	23p40				07 44			08 44		09 44						11 44		12 44	
96	—	—	Telford Central	d	23p47				07 51			08 51		09 51						11 51		12 52	
122¾	—	—	Cosford	d	23p57																		
111½	—	—	**Wolverhampton**	a	00 17				08 09			09 09		10 08						12 09		13 08	
120¾	—	—	Smethwick Galton Bdg L.L.	a					08 20			09 21		10 19						12 20		13 21	
—	—	—	Tame Bridge Parkway	d																			
124¾	—	—	**Birmingham New Street**	a					08 26			09 26		10 25						12 26		13 26	
—	—	—	Birmingham International	a					08 50			09 50		10 50						12 50		13 50	

A from 21 May
B ⊼ from Machynlleth
C 4 June, 27 August
b Previous night, stops on request

For connections to Crewe and Manchester Piccadilly please refer to Table 131

For connections to London Euston please refer to Table 66

Pwllheli, Barmouth, Aberystwyth and Chester - Shrewsbury and Birmingham

Network Diagram - see first Page of Table 67

		AW	AW	AW	AW	AW	AW	AW	AW	AW	AW	AW	AW	AW	AW	AW	AW	AW	VT	AW	AW MW FO	AW TThO	AW
		◇ A 🚲	◇ 🚲	◇ 🚲	◇ 🚲	◇ A 🚲	◇ 🚲	◇ 🚲	◇ 🚲	◇ A 🚲	◇ 🚲	◇	◇ 🚲	◇ 🚲	◇ 🚲	◇	◇ 🚲	◇	◇ 1		◇	◇	
Pwllheli	d	09 34				11 30				13 38		15 37				17 45							
Abererch	d	09x37				11x33				13x41		15x40				17x48							
Penychain	d	09x40				11x36				13x44		15x43				17x51							
Criccieth	d	09 48				11 44				13 52		15 51				17 59							
Porthmadog	a	09 56				11 52				14 00		15 59				18 07							
	d	09 58				11 54				14 02		16 01				18 09							
Minffordd	d	10 02				11 58				14 06		16 05				18 13							
Penrhyndeudraeth	d	10 06				12 02				14 10		16 09				18 17							
Llandecwyn	d	10x08				12x04				14x12		16x11				18x19							
Talsarnau	d	10x10				12x06				14x14		16x13				18x21							
Tygwyn	d	10x13				12x09				14x17		16x16				18x24							
Harlech	a	10 21				12 16				14 24		16 23				18 31							
	d	10 25				12 22				14 28		16 29				18 33							
Llandanwg	d	10x29				12x26				14x32		16x34				18x38							
Pensarn	d	10x31				12x28				14x34		16x35				18x40							
Llanbedr	d	10x33				12x30				14x36		16x37				18x41							
Dyffryn Ardudwy	d	10x37				12x34				14x40		16x41				18x45							
Talybont	d	10x40				12x37				14x43		16x44				18x48							
Llanaber	d	10x45				12x42				14x48		16x49				18x53							
Barmouth	a	10 49				12 46				14 52		16 53				18 57							
	d	10 52				12 50				14 55		16 56				19 00							
Morfa Mawddach	d	10x56				12x54				14x59		17x00				19x04							
Fairbourne	d	11 00				12 58				15 03		17 04				19 08							
Llwyngwril	d	11x06				13x04				15x09		17x10				19x14							
Tonfanau	d	11x13				13x11				15x16		17x17				19x21							
Tywyn	a	11 19				13 17				15 23		17 23				19 27							
	d	11 24				13 25				15 26		17 28				19 29							
Aberdovey	d	11 30				13 31				15 32		17 34				19 35							
Penhelig	d	11x32				13x33				15x35		17x36				19x37							
Aberystwyth	d		11 30				13 30				15 30				17 30			19 30					21 36
Borth	d		11 43				13 43				15 43				17 43			19 43					21 49
Dovey Junction 4	d	11x45	11x55			13x46	13x54			15x46	15x54	17x49			17x54	19x50		19x54					22x00
Machynlleth 4	a	11 55	12 03			13 55	14 03			15 54	16 03	17 59			18 03	20 00		20 03					22 07
	d	12 07				14 07				16 07					18 07			20 07					
Caersws	d	12 33				14 33				16 33					18 33			20 34					
Newtown (Powys)	d	12 46				14 46				16 46					18 46			20 48					
Welshpool	d	13 01				15 01				17 01					19 01			21 04					
Chester	d			13 30	14 19			15 30	16 19				17 24	18 18			19 28		20 22		21 21	21 21	
Wrexham General	a			13 46	14 34			15 46	16 35				17 39	18 36			19 44		20 38		21 37	21 37	
	d			13 46	14 34			15 46	16 35				17 40	18 36			19 44			20 49	21 37	21 37	
Ruabon	d			13 53	14 41			15 53	16 42				17 47	18 43			19 51			20 57	21 44	21 44	
Chirk	d			14 00	14 47			16 00	16 48				17 54	18 49			19 57			21 03	21 50	21 50	
Gobowen	d			14 05	14 53			16 05	16 54				17 59	18 55			20 03			21 08	21 56	21 56	
Shrewsbury	a	13 26		14 27	15 13	15 26		16 28	17 14	17 27			18 24	19 15	19 26		20 26	21 28		21 28	22 16	22 16	
Cardiff Central 7	a				17 15				19 21					21 19									
Shrewsbury	d	13 31		14 31		15 31		16 33		17 31			18 31		19 33			21 33			22 18	22 18	
Wellington (Shropshire)	d	13 44		14 44		15 44		16 46		17 44			18 44		19 46			21 46			22 32	22 32	
Telford Central	d	13 51		14 52		15 51		16 53		17 51			18 51		19 53			21 53			22 38	22 38	
Cosford	d																						
Wolverhampton 7	a	14 08		15 09		16 09		17 09		18 09			19 09		20 11			22 09			22 55	22 55	
Smethwick Galton Bdg L.L.	a	14 20		15 21		16 20		17 22		18 20			19 20		20 22			22 20					
Tame Bridge Parkway	d																						
Birmingham New Street 12	a	14 26		15 27		16 27		17 28		18 26			19 26		20 27			22 33			23 27	23 28	
Birmingham International ✈	a	14 50		15 50		16 50		17 49		18 50			19 50		20 50								

A 🚲 from Machynlleth

For connections to Crewe and Manchester Piccadilly please refer to Table 131

For connections to London Euston please refer to Table 66

Pwllheli, Barmouth, Aberystwyth and Chester - Shrewsbury and Birmingham

Network Diagram - see first Page of Table 67

		AW	AW FO	AW	AW
		◇		◇	
Pwllheli	d	20 05			
Abererch	d	20x08			
Penychain	d	20x11			
Criccieth	d	20 19			
Porthmadog	a	20 27			
	d	20 29			
Minffordd	d	20 33			
Penrhyndeudraeth	d	20 37			
Llandecwyn	d	20x39			
Talsarnau	d	20x41			
Tygwyn	d	20x44			
Harlech	a	20 51			
	d	20 53			
Llandanwg	d	20x57			
Pensarn	d	20x59			
Llanbedr	d	21x01			
Dyffryn Ardudwy	d	21x05			
Talybont	d	21x08			
Llanaber	d	21x13			
Barmouth	a	21 18			
	d	21 20	22 22		
Morfa Mawddach	d	21x24	22x26		
Fairbourne	d	21 28	22 30		
Llwyngwril	d	21x34	22x36		
Tonfanau	d	21x41	22x43		
Tywyn	a	21 48	22 47		
	d	21 50	22 49		
Aberdovey	d	21 56	22 55		
Penhelig	d	21x59	22x57		
Aberystwyth	d				23 53
Borth	d				00 06
Dovey Junction 4	d	22x11	23x14		00x17
Machynlleth 4	a	22 22	23 21		00 24
	d				
Caersws	d				
Newtown (Powys)	d				
Welshpool	d				
Chester	d			22 28	
Wrexham General	a			22 44	
	d			22 44	
Ruabon	d			22 51	
Chirk	d			22 57	
Gobowen	d			23 03	
Shrewsbury	a			23 22	
Cardiff Central 7	a				
Shrewsbury	d			23 26	
Wellington (Shropshire)	d			23 40	
Telford Central	d			23 47	
Cosford	d			23 57	
Wolverhampton 7	a			00 17	
Smethwick Galton Bdg L.L.	a				
Tame Bridge Parkway	d				
Birmingham New Street 12	a				
Birmingham International ✈	a				

For connections to Crewe and Manchester Piccadilly please refer to Table 131

For connections to London Euston please refer to Table 66

Table 75

Saturdays

Pwllheli, Barmouth, Aberystwyth and Chester - Shrewsbury and Birmingham

Network Diagram - see first Page of Table 67

		AW ◇	AW	AW ◇ ⚒	AW	AW ◇ ⚒	AW ◇ ⚒	AW ◇ ⚒	AW ◇ A ⚒	AW ◇ ⚒	AW ◇	AW ◇ ⚒	AW ◇ ⚒	AW ◇ A ⚒	AW ◇ ⚒	AW	AW ■ ⚒	AW ◇ A ⚒	AW ◇ ⚒	AW ◇ ⚒	AW ◇ ⚒	AW ◇ A ⚒	AW ◇ ⚒
Pwllheli	d										06 29			07 20				09 34				11 30	
Abererch	d										06x32			07x23				09x37				11x33	
Penychain	d										06x35			07x26				09x40				11x36	
Criccieth	d										06 43			07 34				09 48				11 44	
Porthmadog	a										06 51			07 41				09 56				11 52	
	d										06 53			07 43				09 58				11 54	
Minffordd	d										06 57			07 47				10 02				11 58	
Penrhyndeudraeth	d										07 01			07 51				10 06				12 02	
Llandecwyn	d										07x03			07x53				10x08				12x04	
Talsarnau	d										07x05			07x56				10x10				12x06	
Tygwyn	d										07x08			07x58				10x13				12x09	
Harlech	a										07 15			08 06				10 21				12 16	
	d										07 17			08 25				10 25				12 22	
Llandanwg	d										07x21			08x29				10x29				12x26	
Pensarn	d										07x23			08x30				10x31				12x28	
Llanbedr	d										07x25			08x33				10x33				12x30	
Dyffryn Ardudwy	d										07x29			08x37				10x37				12x34	
Talybont	d										07x32			08x40				10x40				12x37	
Llanaber	d										07x37			08x44				10x45				12x42	
Barmouth	a										07 41			08 49				10 49				12 46	
	d								06 46		07 47			08 52				10 52				12 50	
Morfa Mawddach	d								06x50		07x51			08x56				10x56				12x54	
Fairbourne	d								06 54		07 55			09 00				11 00				12 58	
Llwyngwril	d								07x00		08x01			09x06				11x06				13x04	
Tonfanau	d								07x07		08x08			09x13				11x13				13x11	
Tywyn	a								07 13		08 12			09 19				11 19				13 17	
	d								07 17		08 16			09 27				11 24				13 25	
Aberdovey	d								07 23		08 22			09 33				11 30				13 31	
Penhelig	d								07x25		08x24			09x35				11x32				13x33	
Aberystwyth	d		23p53	05 14						07 30					09 30				11 30				13 30
Borth	d		00 06	05 27						07 43					09 43				11 43				13 43
Dovey Junction 4	d		00x17	05x38					07x38	07x54	08x37			09x47	09x54			11 45	11x54			13x46	13x54
Machynlleth 4	a		00 24	05 45					07 46	08 03	08 47			09 55	10 03			11 55	12 03			13 55	14 03
	d			05 47						08 07					10 07				12 07				14 07
Caersws	d			06 11						08 33					10 33				12 33				14 33
Newtown (Powys)	d			06 25						08 46					10 46				12 46				14 46
Welshpool	d			06 41						09 01					11 01				13 01				15 01
Chester	d	22p28			05 37	06 12	07 21	08 19				09 20	10 19			11 29	12 19			13 30	14 19		
Wrexham General	a	22p44			05 55	06 35	07 37	08 34				09 36	10 34			11 44	12 34			13 46	14 34		
	d	22p44				06 38	07 37	08 34				09 36	10 35			11 45	12 34			13 46	14 34		
Ruabon	d	22p51				06 45	07 44	08 41				09 43	10 42			11 52	12 41			13 53	14 41		
Chirk	d	22p57				06 51	07 51	08 47				09 50	10 48			11 59	12 47			14 00	14 47		
Gobowen	d	23p03				06 57	07 56	08 53				09 55	10 54			12 04	12 53			14 05	14 53		
Shrewsbury	a	23p22		07 11		07 17	08 20	09 13		09 25		10 29	11 14		11 25	12 27	13 13		13 25	14 27	15 13		15 25
Cardiff Central 7	a					09 22		11 15					13 15				15 26				17 08		
Shrewsbury	d	23p26		07 31			08 31			09 31		10 32			11 31	12 31			13 31	14 31			15 31
Wellington (Shropshire)	d	23p40		07 44			08 44			09 44		10 45			11 44	12 44			13 44	14 44			15 44
Telford Central	d	23p47		07 51			08 51			09 51		10 52			11 51	12 52			13 51	14 52			15 51
Cosford	d	23p57																					
Wolverhampton 7 ⇌	a	00 17		08 09			09 09			10 09		11 10			12 09	13 08			14 09	15 09			16 09
Smethwick Galton Bdg L.L.	a			08 20			09 22			10 20		11 21			12 20	13 21			14 20	15 21			16 20
Tame Bridge Parkway	d																						
Birmingham New Street 12	a			08 26			09 26			10 26		11 27			12 26	13 26			14 26	15 27			16 26
Birmingham International ✈	a			08 50			09 50			10 50		11 50			12 50	13 50			14 50	15 50			16 50

A ⚒ from Machynlleth

For connections to Crewe and Manchester Piccadilly please refer to Table 131

For connections to London Euston please refer to Table 66

Table 75

Saturdays

Pwllheli, Barmouth, Aberystwyth and Chester - Shrewsbury and Birmingham

Network Diagram - see first Page of Table 67

		AW ◇ ⚒	AW ◇ ⚒	AW ◇ A ⚒	AW ◇ ⚒	AW ◇	AW ◇ ⚒	AW ◇ ⚒	AW ◇ ⚒	AW ◇	AW ◇ ⚒	AW	AW ◇	AW ◇	AW	AW ◇	AW ◇	AW
Pwllheli	d			13 38		15 37				17 45						20 05		
Abererch	d			13x41		15x40				17x48						20x08		
Penychain	d			13x44		15x43				17x51						20x11		
Criccieth	d			13 52		15 51				17 59						20 19		
Porthmadog	a			14 00		15 59				18 07						20 27		
	d			14 02		16 01				18 09						20 29		
Minffordd	d			14 06		16 05				18 13						20 33		
Penrhyndeudraeth	d			14 10		16 09				18 17						20 37		
Llandecwyn	d			14x12		16x11				18x19						20x39		
Talsarnau	d			14x14		16x13				18x21						20x41		
Tygwyn	d			14x17		16x16				18x24						20x44		
Harlech	a			14 24		16 23				18 31						20 51		
	d			14 28		16 29				18 33						20 53		
Llandanwg	d			14x32		16x34				18x38						20x58		
Pensarn	d			14x34		16x35				18x40						21x00		
Llanbedr	d			14x36		16x37				18x41						21x01		
Dyffryn Ardudwy	d			14x40		16x41				18x45						21x05		
Talybont	d			14x43		16x44				18x48						21x08		
Llanaber	d			14x48		16x49				18x53						21x13		
Barmouth	a			14 52		16 53				18 57						21 18		
	d			14 55		16 56				19 00						21 20		
Morfa Mawddach	d			14x59		17x00				19x04						21x24		
Fairbourne	d			15 03		17 04				19 08						21 28		
Llwyngwril	d			15x09		17x10				19x14						21x34		
Tonfanau	d			15x16		17x17				19x21						21x41		
Tywyn	a			15 23		17 23				19 27						21 48		
	d			15 26		17 28				19 29						21 50		
Aberdovey	d			15 32		17 34				19 35						21 56		
Penhelig	d			15x35		17x36				19x37						21x59		
Aberystwyth	d				15 30				17 30				19 30		21 36			23 46
Borth	d				15 43				17 43				19 43		21 49			23 59
Dovey Junction 4	d			15x46	15x54	17x49			17x54	19x50			19x54		22x00	22x11		00x10
Machynlleth 4	a			15 54	16 03	17 59			18 03	20 00			20 03		22 07	22 22		00 17
	d				16 07				18 07				20 07					
Caersws	d				16 33				18 33				20 34					
Newtown (Powys)	d				16 46				18 46				20 48					
Welshpool	d				17 01				19 01				21 04					
Chester	d	15 30	16 19				17 28	18 20			19 28	20 27		21 20			22 28	
Wrexham General	a	15 46	16 35				17 44	18 35			19 44	20 43		21 36			22 44	
	d	15 46	16 35				17 44	18 36			19 44	20 43		21 37			22 44	
Ruabon	d	15 53	16 42				17 51	18 42			19 51	20 51		21 44			22 51	
Chirk	d	16 00	16 48				17 58	18 49			19 57	20 57		21 51			22 57	
Gobowen	d	16 05	16 54				18 03	18 54			20 03	21 02		21 57			23 03	
Shrewsbury	a	16 28	17 14		17 25		18 24	19 15	19 25		20 26	21 22	21 28	22 17			23 23	
Cardiff Central 7	a		19 16					21 21										
Shrewsbury	d	16 33			17 31		18 31		19 33				21 33	22 31			23 26	
Wellington (Shropshire)	d	16 46			17 44		18 44		19 46				21 46	22 45			23 40	
Telford Central	d	16 53			17 51		18 51		19 53				21 53	22 51			23 47	
Cosford	d																23 57	
Wolverhampton 7 ⇌	a	17 09			18 09		19 09		20 10				22 08	23 07			00 16	
Smethwick Galton Bdg L.L.	a	17 22			18 20		19 20		20 21				22 19					
Tame Bridge Parkway	d																	
Birmingham New Street 12	a	17 28			18 26		19 26		20 26				22 32	23 28				
Birmingham International ✈	a	17 49			18 50		19 50		20 49									

A ⚒ from Machynlleth

For connections to Crewe and Manchester Piccadilly please refer to Table 131

For connections to London Euston please refer to Table 66

Table 75

Sundays until 24 June

Pwllheli, Barmouth, Aberystwyth and Chester - Shrewsbury and Birmingham

Network Diagram - see first Page of Table 67

		AW	AW	AW	AW	AW	AW	AW	AW	AW	AW	AW	AW	AW	AW	AW	AW	AW	AW	AW	AW	AW	AW	AW	AW
		◇			◇	◇ ⌶	◇ ⌶	◇ ⌶	◇ ⌶	◇	◇ A ⌶	◇ ⌶	◇ ⌶	◇ A ⌶	◇ ⌶	◇	■ ⌶	◇ ⌶	◇		◇	◇			
Pwllheli	d										11 28			13 48					17 36						
Abererch	d										11x32			13x51					17x40						
Penychain	d										11x35			13x54					17x44						
Criccieth	d										11 41			14 02					17 50						
Porthmadog	a										11 50			14 10					17 59						
	d										11 57			14 12					18 00						
Minffordd	d										12 02			14 16					18 05						
Penrhyndeudraeth	d										12 06			14 20					18 09						
Llandecwyn	d										12x09			14x22					18x12						
Talsarnau	d										12x11			14x24					18x14						
Tygwyn	d										12x13			14x27					18x16						
Harlech	a										12 18			14 32					18 21						
	d										12 19			14 34					18 22						
Llandanwg	d										12x25			14x38					18x28						
Pensarn	d										12x28			14x40					18x30						
Llanbedr	d										12x30			14x42					18x32						
Dyffryn Ardudwy	d										12x34			14x46					18x36						
Talybont	d										12x37			14x49					18x39						
Llanaber	d										12x42			14x54					18x45						
Barmouth	a										12 45			14 59					18 48						
	d										12 48			15 01					18 50						
Morfa Mawddach	d										12x53			15x05					18x55						
Fairbourne	d										12 56			15 09					18 57						
Llwyngwril	d										13x04			15x15					19x05						
Tonfanau	d										13x11			15x22					19x12						
Tywyn	a										13 16			15 27					19 19						
	d										13 16			15 28					19 22						
Aberdovey	d										13 22			15 35					19 28						
Penhelig	d										13x26			15x37					19x32						
Aberystwyth	d		23p46			09 30			11 30			13 30			15 30			17 30			19 30		21 30		23 30
Borth	d		23p59			09 43			11 43			13 43			15 43			17 43			19 43		21 43		23 43
Dovey Junction 4	d		00x10			09x54			11x54		13x36	13x54		15x49	15x54			17x54	19x42		19x54		21x54		23x54
Machynlleth 4	a		00 17			10 03			12 03		13 45	14 03		15 59	16 03			18 03	19 52		20 03		22 04		00 04
	d					10 07			12 07			14 07			16 07			18 07			20 07				
Caersws	d					10 29			12 29			14 33			16 33			18 33			20 33				
Newtown (Powys)	d					10 45			12 46			14 46			16 46			18 46			20 46				
Welshpool	d					11 01			13 01			15 01			17 01			19 01			21 01				
Chester	d	22p28		08 08	09 22		11 31	12 21		13 31			15 31			17 31	18 24			19 26		21 26		22 04	
Wrexham General	a	22p44		08 26	09 38		11 47	12 38		13 47			15 47			17 47	18 40			19 42		21 42		22 22	
	d	22p44			09 38		11 48	12 38		13 48			15 48			17 48	18 41			19 42		21 44			
Ruabon	d	22p51			09 45		11 55	12 45		13 55			15 55			17 55	18 47			19 49		21 51			
Chirk	d	22p57			09 52		12 01	12 52		14 01			16 01			18 01	18 54			19 55		21 57			
Gobowen	d	23p03			09 57		12 07	12 57		14 07			16 07			18 07	18 59			20 01		22 02			
Shrewsbury	a	23p23			10 18	11 25	12 27	13 18	13 25	14 27		15 25	16 27		17 27	18 27	19 20	19 25		20 21	21 25	22 22			
Cardiff Central 7	a							15 28									21 36								
Shrewsbury	d	23p26			10 20	11 40	12 31		13 31	14 31		15 33	16 40		17 33	18 31		19 31		20 23	21 31	22 23			
Wellington (Shropshire)	d	23p40			10 34	11 54	12 45		13 45	14 45		15 47	16 54		17 47	18 45		19 45		20 37	21 45	22 37			
Telford Central	d	23p47			10 40	12 00	12 51		13 51	14 51		15 53	17 00		17 53	18 51		19 51		20 44	21 51	22 45			
Cosford	d	23p57																		20 54		22 56			
Wolverhampton 7 ⇌	a	00 16			10 56	12 16	13 07		14 07	15 07		16 09	17 15		18 09	19 07		20 07		21 11	22 07	23 13			
Smethwick Galton Bdg L.L.	a																								
Tame Bridge Parkway	d																								
Birmingham New Street 12	a				11 32	12 49	13 42		14 40	15 40		16 41	17 53		18 41	19 39		20 40		21 41	22 37				
Birmingham International ✈	a																								

A ⌶ from Machynlleth

For connections to Crewe and Manchester Piccadilly please refer to Table 131

For connections to London Euston please refer to Table 66

Table 75

Sundays 1 July to 9 September

Pwllheli, Barmouth, Aberystwyth and Chester - Shrewsbury and Birmingham

Network Diagram - see first Page of Table 67

		AW	AW	AW	AW	AW	AW	AW	AW	AW		AW	AW		AW	AW	AW	AW	AW	AW	AW	AW	AW	AW	AW
		◇			◇	◇ ⌶	◇ ⌶	◇ ⌶	◇ ⌶	A ◇ ⌶		◇	A ◇ ⌶		◇ ⌶	◇	■ ⌶	◇ ⌶	◇		◇	◇			
Pwllheli	d									11 28			13 48						17 36						
Abererch	d									11x32			13x51						17x40						
Penychain	d									11x35			13x54						17x44						
Criccieth	d									11 41			14 02						17 50						
Porthmadog	a									11 50			14 10						17 59						
	d									11 57			14 12						18 00						
Minffordd	d									12 02			14 16						18 05						
Penrhyndeudraeth	d									12 06			14 20						18 09						
Llandecwyn	d									12x09			14x22						18x12						
Talsarnau	d									12x11			14x24						18x14						
Tygwyn	d									12x13			14x27						18x16						
Harlech	a									12 18			14 32						18 21						
	d									12 19			14 34						18 22						
Llandanwg	d									12x25			14x38						18x28						
Pensarn	d									12x28			14x40						18x30						
Llanbedr	d									12x30			14x42						18x32						
Dyffryn Ardudwy	d									12x34			14x46						18x36						
Talybont	d									12x37			14x49						18x39						
Llanaber	d									12x42			14x54						18x45						
Barmouth	a									12 45			14 59						18 48						
	d									12 48			15 01						18 50						
Morfa Mawddach	d									12x53			15x05						18x55						
Fairbourne	d									12 56			15 09						18 57						
Llwyngwril	d									13x04			15x15						19x05						
Tonfanau	d									13x11			15x22						19x12						
Tywyn	a									13 16			15 27						19 19						
	d									13 16			15 28						19 22						
Aberdovey	d									13 22			15 35						19 28						
Penhelig	d									13x26			15x37						19x32						
Aberystwyth	d		23p46			09 30			11 30		13 30			15 30				17 30			19 30		21 30		23 30
Borth	d		23p59			09 43			11 43		13 43			15 43				17 43			19 43		21 43		23 43
Dovey Junction 4	d		00x10			09x54			11x54	13x36	13x54		15x49	15x54				17x54	19x42		19x54		21x54		23x54
Machynlleth 4	a		00 17			10 03			12 03	13 45	14 03		15 59	16 03				18 03	19 52		20 03		22 04		00 04
	d					10 07			12 07		14 07			16 07				18 07			20 07				
Caersws	d					10 29			12 29		14 33			16 33				18 33			20 33				
Newtown (Powys)	d					10 45			12 46		14 46			16 46				18 46			20 46				
Welshpool	d					11 01			13 01		15 01			17 01				19 01			21 01				
Chester	d	22p28		08 08	09 22		11 31	12 21				13 31			15 31	17 31	18 24			19 26		21 26		22 04	
Wrexham General	a	22p44		08 26	09 38		11 47	12 38				13 47			15 47	17 47	18 40			19 42		21 42		22 22	
	d	22p44			09 38		11 48	12 38				13 48			15 48	17 48	18 41			19 42		21 44			
Ruabon	d	22p51			09 45		11 55	12 45				13 55			15 55	17 55	18 47			19 49		21 51			
Chirk	d	22p57			09 52		12 01	12 52				14 01			16 01	18 01	18 54			19 55		21 57			
Gobowen	d	23p03			09 57		12 07	12 57				14 07			16 07	18 07	18 59			20 01		22 02			
Shrewsbury	a	23p23			10 18	11 25	12 27	13 18	13 25		15 25	14 27		17 27	16 27	18 27	19 20	19 25		20 21	21 25	22 22			
Cardiff Central 7	a							15 28									21 36								
Shrewsbury	d	23p26			10 20	11 40	12 31		13 31		15 33	14 31		17 33	16 40	18 31		19 31		20 23	21 31	22 23			
Wellington (Shropshire)	d	23p40			10 34	11 54	12 45		13 45		15 47	14 45		17 47	16 54	18 45		19 45		20 37	21 45	22 37			
Telford Central	d	23p47			10 40	12 00	12 51		13 51		15 53	14 51		17 53	17 00	18 51		19 51		20 44	21 51	22 45			
Cosford	d	23p57																		20 54		22 56			
Wolverhampton 7 ⇌	a	00 16			10 56	12 16	13 07		14 07		16 09	15 07		18 09	17 15	19 07		20 07		21 11	22 07	23 13			
Smethwick Galton Bdg L.L.	a																								
Tame Bridge Parkway	d																								
Birmingham New Street 12	a				11 13	12 32	13 23		14 23		16 41	15 24		18 41	17 35	19 26		20 23		21 29	22 27				
Birmingham International ✈	a				11 31	12 56	13 55		14 55			15 55			17 56	19 55		20 55		21 56	22 55				

A ⌶ from Machynlleth

For connections to Crewe and Manchester Piccadilly please refer to Table 131

For connections to London Euston please refer to Table 66

Sundays
from 16 September

Pwllheli, Barmouth, Aberystwyth and Chester - Shrewsbury and Birmingham

Network Diagram - see first Page of Table 67

		AW	AW	AW	AW	AW	AW	AW	AW	AW	AW	AW A		AW		AW	AW ■	AW	AW	AW		AW	AW	AW	AW
		◇			◇	◇ ⌶	◇ ⌶	◇ ⌶	◇ ⌶	◇	◇ ⌶	◇ ⌶		◇ ⌶		◇	⌶	◇ ⌶		◇		◇			
Pwllheli	d											13 48													
Abererch	d											13x51													
Penychain	d											13x54													
Criccieth	d											14 02													
Porthmadog	a											14 10													
	d											14 12													
Minffordd	d											14 16													
Penrhyndeudraeth	d											14 20													
Llandecwyn	d											14x22													
Talsarnau	d											14x24													
Tygwyn	d											14x27													
Harlech	a											14 32													
	d											14 34													
Llandanwg	d											14x38													
Pensarn	d											14x40													
Llanbedr	d											14x42													
Dyffryn Ardudwy	d											14x46													
Talybont	d											14x49													
Llanaber	d											14x54													
Barmouth	a											14 59													
	d											15 01													
Morfa Mawddach	d											15x05													
Fairbourne	d											15 09													
Llwyngwril	d											15x15													
Tonfanau	d											15x22													
Tywyn	a											15 27													
	d											15 28													
Aberdovey	d											15 35													
Penhelig	d											15x37													
Aberystwyth	d		23p46			09 30			11 30		13 30		15 30					17 30		19 30			21 30		23 30
Borth	d		23p59			09 43			11 43		13 43		15 43					17 43		19 43			21 43		23 43
Dovey Junction 4	d		00x10			09x54			11x54		13x54	15x49	15x54					17x54		19x54			21x54		23x54
Machynlleth 4	a		00 17			10 03			12 03		14 03	15 59	16 03					18 03		20 03			22 04		00 04
	d					10 07			12 07		14 07	16 07						18 07		20 07					
Caersws	d					10 29			12 29		14 33	16 33						18 33		20 33					
Newtown (Powys)	d					10 45			12 46		14 46	16 46						18 46		20 46					
Welshpool	d					11 01			13 01		15 01	17 01						19 01		21 01					
Chester	d	22p28		08 08	09 22		11 31	12 21		13 31				15 31		17 31	18 24		19 26			21 26		22 04	
Wrexham General	a	22p44		08 26	09 38		11 47	12 38		13 47				15 47		17 47	18 40		19 42			21 42		22 22	
	d	22p44			09 38		11 48	12 38		13 48				15 48		17 48	18 41		19 42			21 44			
Ruabon	d	22p51			09 45		11 55	12 45		13 55				15 55		17 55	18 47		19 49			21 51			
Chirk	d	22p57			09 52		12 01	12 52		14 01				16 01		18 01	18 54		19 55			21 57			
Gobowen	d	23p03			09 57		12 07	12 57		14 07				16 07		18 07	18 59		20 01			22 02			
Shrewsbury	a	23p23			10 18	11 25	12 27	13 18	13 25	14 27	15 25	17 27		16 27		18 27	19 19	19 24	20 21	21 25		22 22			
Cardiff Central 7	a							15 28									21 36								
Shrewsbury	d	23p26			10 20	11 40	12 31		13 31	14 31	15 33	17 33		16 40		18 31		19 30	20 23	21 31		22 23			
Wellington (Shropshire)	d	23p40			10 34	11 54	12 45		13 45	14 45	15 47	17 47		16 54		18 45		19 45	20 37	21 45		22 37			
Telford Central	d	23p47			10 40	12 00	12 51		13 51	14 51	15 53	17 53		17 00		18 51		19 51	20 44	21 51		22 45			
Cosford	d	23p57																	20 54			22 56			
Wolverhampton 7 ⇌	a	00 16			10 56	12 16	13 07		14 07	15 07	16 09	18 09		17 15		19 07		20 07	21 11	22 07		23 13			
Smethwick Galton Bdg L.L.	a																								
Tame Bridge Parkway	d																								
Birmingham New Street 12	a				11 13	12 32	13 23		14 23	15 24	16 24	18 41		17 35		19 26		20 23	21 29	22 27					
Birmingham International ✈	a				11 31	12 56	13 55		14 55	15 55	16 55			17 56		19 55		20 55	21 56	22 55					

A ⌶ from Machynlleth

For connections to Crewe and Manchester Piccadilly please refer to Table 131

For connections to London Euston please refer to Table 66

Network Diagram for Tables 78, 79, 84, 85, 86

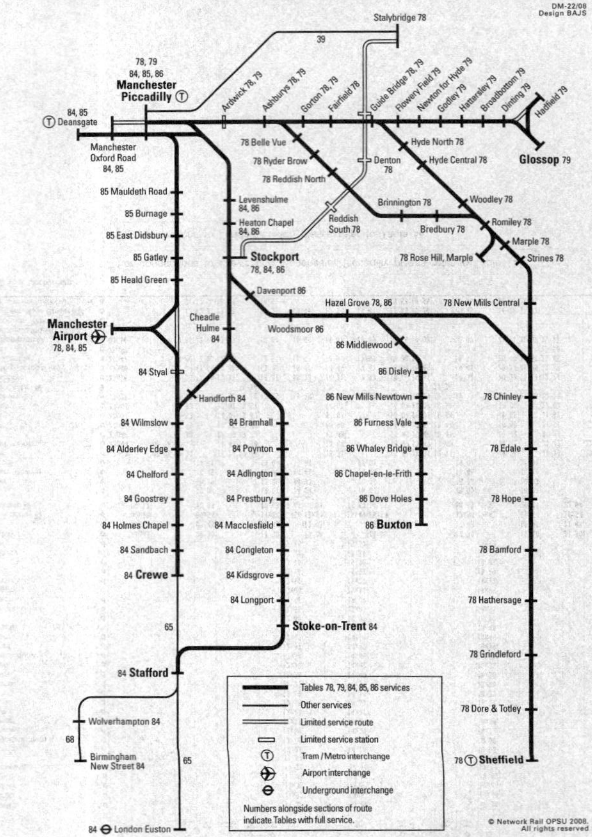

until 28 September

Manchester Airport and Manchester Romiley, Marple, Chinley and Sheffield

Network Diagram - see first Page of Table 78

Miles	Miles	Miles	Station		TP MO	TP MX	TP	NT	NT	NT	NT	NT	NT	NT	NT	NT	NT	NT	TP	NT	NT	NT	EM
					◇1 A	◇1	◇1 B		C	D		E		C		C	G	C	◇1 B	E			◇ H
—	—	—	Manchester Airport 85 ✈	d	22p55	23p52	05 15												06 55				
0	0	—	Manchester Piccadilly 10	a	23p09	00 09	05 33												07 13				
—	—	—		d	23p20	00 15	05 44	05 50	06 16	06 24	06 30		06 41	06 46	06 57	07 03	07 08	07 18	07 20		07 23	07 39	07 42
0½	0½	—	Ardwick	d																			
1½	1½	—	Ashburys	d					06 20				06 45	06 50		07 07	07 12	07 22			07 27		
2½	—	—	Belle Vue	d									06 47								07 29		
2¾	—	—	Ryder Brow	d									06 49								07 31		
3¾	—	—	Reddish North	d									06 52				07 17				07 34		
5½	—	—	Brinnington	d									06 55				07 20				07 37		
6½	—	—	Bredbury	d									06 58				07 23				07 40		
—	2½	—	Gorton	d					06 22					06 52		07 09		07 24					
—	3½	—	Fairfield	d						06 31												07 46	
—	4¾	—	Guide Bridge	a					06 26	06 34				06 56		07 13		07 28				07 49	
—	—	—		d						06 34												07 49	
—	6½	—	Hyde North	d						06 38												07 53	
—	7¾	—	Hyde Central	d						06 40												07 55	
—	9¼	—	Woodley	d						06 43		←										07 58	
7½	10½	—	Romiley	d						06 47	06 44	06 47	07 02		07 09		07 26				07 43	08 02	
—	12½	—	Rose Hill Marple	a						→		06 53										08 08	
9	—	—	Marple	d							06 47		07 05		07 13		07 30				07a48		
11¼	—	—	Strines	d																			
12¾	—	—	New Mills Central	a							06 55		07 12		07 20		07 35						
—	—	—		d													07 39						
—	—	—	Stockport 86	d	23p28		05 52	06 00											07 28				07 54
—	—	0	Hazel Grove 86	d				06 07															
16½	—	8½	Chinley	d				06 18									07 47						
22	—	—	Edale	d				06 26									07 55						
27¼	—	—	Hope (Derbyshire)	d				06 32									08 01						
29	—	—	Bamford	d				06 35									08 04						
30¾	—	—	Hathersage	d				06 39									08 09						
32¼	—	—	Grindleford	d				06 42									08 11			←			
37¾	—	—	Dore & Totley	d				06 51									08 22		08 03	08 22			08 28
42	—	—	Sheffield 7	a	00 15	01 06	06 49	07 01									→		08 10	08 32			08 34

Station		NT	NT	NT	NT	NT	NT	NT	TP	NT	NT	EM	NT	NT	NT	NT	NT	NT	NT	TP	NT	EM	NT
		C			C	D		E	◇1 B	C		◇ H		C	D		E	C		◇1 B		◇ H	
Manchester Airport 85 ✈	d								07 53											08 55			
Manchester Piccadilly 10	a								08 12											09 13			
	d	07 48	07 52	08 04	08 07	08 12	08 15		08 20	08 29	08 37	08 43	08 45	08 48	09 00	09 05		09 15	09 18	09 20	09 36	09 43	09 45
Ardwick	d																						
Ashburys	d	07 52		08 08	08 11					08 33				08 52		09 09		09 19	09 23				
Belle Vue	d			08 10															09 26				
Ryder Brow	d			08 12															09 28				
Reddish North	d			08 15									08 52			09 14							09 52
Brinnington	d			08 18									08 56			09 17							09 56
Bredbury	d			08 21									08 59			09 20							09 59
Gorton	d	07 54			08 13					08 35				08 54				09 21					
Fairfield	d					08 20									09 07						09 43		
Guide Bridge	a	07 58			08 17	08 23				08 39				08 58	09 10			09 25			09 46		
	d					08 23									09 11						09 46		
Hyde North	d					08 28									09 17						09 50		
Hyde Central	d					08 30									09 20						09 52		
Woodley	d					08 33		←							09 23		←				09 55		
Romiley	d		08 05	08 24		08 37	08 29	08 37					09 02		09 26	09 23	09 26		09 35		09 59		10 02
Rose Hill Marple	a			08 30		→		08 45							→		09 33				10 05		
Marple	d		08 08				08a33				08 52		09 06			09a28			09a40				10 06
Strines	d										08 56												10 10
New Mills Central	a		08 15								09 01		09 11										10 15
	d												09 11										
Stockport 86	d								08 28			08 54								09 28		09 54	
Hazel Grove 86	d																						
Chinley	d												09 19										
Edale	d												09 28										
Hope (Derbyshire)	d												09 34										
Bamford	d												09 37										
Hathersage	d												09 40										
Grindleford	d												09 44										
Dore & Totley	d												09 57										
Sheffield 7	a								09 08			09 35	10 07							10 08		10 35	

A from 21 May until 24 September
B To Cleethorpes
C To Hadfield
D To Rose Hill Marple
E From Manchester Piccadilly
G To Sheffield
H From Liverpool Lime Street to Norwich

until 28 September

Manchester Airport and Manchester Romiley, Marple, Chinley and Sheffield

Network Diagram - see first Page of Table 78

Station		NT	NT	NT	NT	TP	NT	EM	NT	NT	NT	NT	TP	NT	NT	EM	NT	NT	NT	NT	TP	NT	NT
		A		A		◇1 B		◇ C		A		A	◇1 B			◇ C		A		A	◇1 B		
Manchester Airport 85 ✈	d					09 55							10 55								11 55		
Manchester Piccadilly 10	a					10 13							11 13								12 13		
	d	09 48	10 03	10 15	10 18	10 20	10 36	10 43	10 45	10 48	11 03	11 18	11 20	11 23	11 36	11 43	11 45	11 48	12 03	12 18	12 20	12 23	12 36
Ardwick	d																						
Ashburys	d	09 52	10 07	10 19						10 52	11 07	11 22						11 52	12 07	12 22			
Belle Vue	d		10 09								11 09								12 09				
Ryder Brow	d		10 11								11 11								12 11				
Reddish North	d		10 14						10 52		11 14						11 52		12 14				
Brinnington	d		10 17						10 56		11 17						11 56		12 17				
Bredbury	d		10 20						10 59		11 20						11 59		12 20				
Gorton	d	09 54		10 21						10 54		11 24						11 54		12 24			
Fairfield	d						10 43								11 43								12 43
Guide Bridge	a	09 58		10 25			10 46			10 58		11 28			11 46			11 58		12 28			12 46
	d						10 46								11 46								12 46
Hyde North	d						10 50								11 50								12 50
Hyde Central	d						10 52								11 52								12 52
Woodley	d						10 55								11 55								12 55
Romiley	d		10 23		10 37		10 59		11 02		11 23			11 37	11 59		12 02		12 23			12 37	12 59
Rose Hill Marple	a				10 42		11 05							11 43	12 05							12 43	13 05
Marple	d		10 27						11 06		11 27						12 06		12 27				
Strines	d																12 10						
New Mills Central	a		10 34						11 11		11 34						12 15		12 34				
	d								11 11														
Stockport 86	d					10 28		10 54					11 28			11 54					12 28		
Hazel Grove 86	d																						
Chinley	d								11 19														
Edale	d								11 28														
Hope (Derbyshire)	d								11 34														
Bamford	d								11 37														
Hathersage	d								11 40														
Grindleford	d								11 44														
Dore & Totley	d								11 53														
Sheffield 7	a					11 08		11 34	12 03				12 08			12 35					13 08		

Station		EM	NT	NT	NT	NT	TP	NT	NT	EM	NT	NT	NT	NT	TP	NT	NT	EM	NT	NT	NT	NT
		◇ C		A		A	◇1 B			◇ C		A		A	◇1 B			◇ C		A		A
Manchester Airport 85 ✈	d						12 55								13 55							
Manchester Piccadilly 10	a						13 13								14 13							
	d	12 43	12 45	12 48	13 03	13 18	13 20	13 23	13 36	13 43	13 45	13 48	14 03	14 18	14 20	14 23	14 36	14 43	14 45	14 48	15 03	15 18
Ardwick	d																					
Ashburys	d			12 52	13 07	13 22						13 52	14 07	14 22						14 52	15 07	15 22
Belle Vue	d				13 09								14 09								15 09	
Ryder Brow	d				13 11								14 11								15 11	
Reddish North	d		12 52		13 14						13 52		14 14						14 52		15 14	
Brinnington	d		12 56		13 17						13 56		14 17						14 56		15 17	
Bredbury	d		12 59		13 20						13 59		14 20						14 59		15 20	
Gorton	d			12 54		13 24						13 54		14 24						14 54		15 24
Fairfield	d								13 43								14 43					
Guide Bridge	a			12 58		13 28			13 46			13 58		14 28			14 46			14 58		15 28
	d								13 46								14 46					
Hyde North	d								13 50								14 50					
Hyde Central	d								13 52								14 52					
Woodley	d								13 55								14 55					
Romiley	d		13 02		13 23			13 37	13 59		14 02		14 23			14 37	14 59		15 02		15 23	
Rose Hill Marple	a							13 43	14 05							14 43	15 05					
Marple	d		13 06		13 27						14 06		14 27						15 06		15 27	
Strines	d										14 10											
New Mills Central	a		13 11		13 34						14 15		14 34						15 11		15 34	
	d		13 11																15 11			
Stockport 86	d	12 54					13 28			13 54					14 28			14 54				
Hazel Grove 86	d																					
Chinley	d		13 19																15 19			
Edale	d		13 28																15 28			
Hope (Derbyshire)	d		13 34																15 34			
Bamford	d		13 37																15 37			
Hathersage	d		13 40																15 40			
Grindleford	d		13 44																15 44			
Dore & Totley	d		13 57																15 58			
Sheffield 7	a	13 35	14 04				14 08			14 35					15 08			15 35	16 04			

A To Hadfield
B To Cleethorpes
C From Liverpool Lime Street to Norwich

Manchester Airport and Manchester Romiley, Marple, Chinley and Sheffield

Network Diagram - see first Page of Table 78

		TP	NT	NT	EM	NT	NT	NT	NT	NT	TP	NT	NT	EM	NT	NT	NT	NT	NT	NT	TP	NT	NT
		◇1 A			◇ B		E			E	◇1 A		E	◇ B			E		E		◇1 A		
Manchester Airport 85 ✈	d	14 55									15 55										16 55		
Manchester Piccadilly 10	a	15 13									16 13										17 13		
	d	15 20	15 23	15 36	15 43	15 45	15 48	16 03	16 06	16 15	16 20	16 23	16 36	16 43	16 45	16 48	16 59	17 03	17 15	17 18	17 20	17 21	17 32
Ardwick	d																	17 07					
Ashburys	d						15 52	16 07		16 19			16 40		16 49	16 52	17 03	17 09	17 19				17 36
Belle Vue	d							16 09										17 12					17 38
Ryder Brow	d							16 11										17 14					17 40
Reddish North	d					15 52		16 14				16 30			16 54			17 16					17 43
Brinnington	d					15 56		16 17				16 34			16 57			17 20					17 46
Bredbury	d					15 59		16 20				16 37			17 00			17 23		17 30			17 49
Gorton	d						15 54			16 21			16 42				17 05		17 21				
Fairfield	d			15 43					16 13							16 56							
Guide Bridge	a			15 46			15 58		16 16	16 25			16 46			16 59	17 10		17 25			17 30	
	d			15 46					16 16							16 59						17 30	
Hyde North	d			15 50					16 20							17 03						17 34	
Hyde Central	d			15 52					16 22							17 05						17 36	
Woodley	d			15 55					16 25							17 08						17 39	
Romiley	d		15 37	15 59		16 02		16 23	16 29			16 40			17 03	17 13		17 27		17 33		17 43	17 53
Rose Hill Marple	a		15 43	16 05					16 36							17 20						17 49	
Marple	d					16 06		16 27				16a44			17 07			17a31		17 38			17 57
Strines	d					16 10									17 11								18 01
New Mills Central	a					16 13		16 34							17 15					17 43			18 04
	d					16 13									17 15								
Stockport 86	d	15 28			15 54						16 28			16 54							17 28		
Hazel Grove 86	d																						
Chinley	d					16 21								17 09	17 21								
Edale	d					16 30									17 30								
Hope (Derbyshire)	d					16 36									17 36								
Bamford	d					16 39									17 39								
Hathersage	d					16 42									17 42								
Grindleford	d					16 46									17 46								
Dore & Totley	d					16 54								17 31	17 56						18 03		
Sheffield 7	a	16 08			16 34	17 03					17 08			17 40	18 04						18 10		

		NT	EM	NT	NT	NT	NT	NT	TP	NT	NT	EM	NT	NT	NT	TP	NT	NT	EM	NT	NT	TP
		E	◇ D		E			E	◇1 A			◇ B		E		◇1 A	E		◇ D		E	◇1
Manchester Airport 85 ✈	d								17 55							18 55						19 55
Manchester Piccadilly 10	a								18 13							19 13						20 13
	d	17 37	17 43	17 48	17 59	18 03	18 06	18 15	18 20	18 22	18 36	18 43	18 45	18 48	19 00	19 18	19 18	19 23	19 43	19 45	19 48	20 20
Ardwick	d						18 09															
Ashburys	d	17 41			18 03	18 07	18 11	18 19						18 52	19 04		19 22			19 49	19 52	
Belle Vue	d					18 09									19 06					19 51		
Ryder Brow	d					18 11									19 08					19 53		
Reddish North	d			17 55		18 14				18 30			18 52		19 11					19 56		
Brinnington	d			17 59		18 17							18 56		19 14					19 59		
Bredbury	d			18 02		18 20				18 36			18 59		19 17					20 02		
Gorton	d	17 43			18 05			18 21						18 54			19 24				19 54	
Fairfield	d						18 15				18 43											
Guide Bridge	a	17 47			18 09		18 18	18 25			18 46			18 58			19 28				19 58	
	d						18 18				18 46											
Hyde North	d						18 22				18 50											
Hyde Central	d						18 25				18 52											
Woodley	d						18 28				18 55											
Romiley	d			18 05		18 23	18 31			18 39	18 59		19 02		19 20			19 38		20 05		
Rose Hill Marple	a						18 37				19 05											
Marple	d			18 08		18a28				18 42			19 06		19a25			19a43		20 09		
Strines	d									18 46										20 13		
New Mills Central	a			18 14						18 52			19 11							20 18		
	d			18 14									19 11									
Stockport 86	d		17 54						18 28			18 54				19 26			19 54			20 28
Hazel Grove 86	d																					
Chinley	d		18 09	18 20									19 19									
Edale	d			18 30									19 28									
Hope (Derbyshire)	d			18 36									19 34									
Bamford	d			18 39									19 37									
Hathersage	d			18 42									19 40									
Grindleford	d			18 46									19 44									
Dore & Totley	d		18 34	18 56					19 03				19 52			20 01						21 03
Sheffield 7	a		18 41	19 06					19 09			19 33	20 02			20 08			20 36			21 11

A To Cleethorpes
B From Liverpool Lime Street to Norwich
D From Liverpool Lime Street to Nottingham
E To Hadfield

Manchester Airport and Manchester Romiley, Marple, Chinley and Sheffield

Network Diagram - see first Page of Table 78

		NT	EM	NT	NT	TP	NT	NT	TP	EM	NT	NT	NT	NT	TP
			◇ A		B	◇1 C		B	◇1	◇ A		B		D	◇1
Manchester Airport 85 ✈	d					20 47			21 47						23 52
Manchester Piccadilly 10	a					21 13			22 13						00 09
	d	20 36	20 43	20 45	20 48	21 20	21 45	21 48	22 20	22 28	22 45	22 48	23 24	23 27	00 15
Ardwick	d														
Ashburys	d				20 52		21 49	21 52			22 49	22 52	23 28	23 31	
Belle Vue	d						21 51				22 51		23 30		
Ryder Brow	d						21 53				22 53		23 32		
Reddish North	d			20 52			21 56				22 56		23 35		
Brinnington	d			20 56			21 59				22 59		23 38		
Bredbury	d			20 59			22 02				23 02		23 41		
Gorton	d				20 54			21 54				22 54		23 33	
Fairfield	d	20 43													
Guide Bridge	a	20 46			20 58			21 58				22 58		23 37	
	d	20 46													
Hyde North	d	20 50													
Hyde Central	d	20 52													
Woodley	d	20 55													
Romiley	d	20 59		21 02			22 05				23 05		23 44		
Rose Hill Marple	a	21 05													
Marple	d			21 06			22 09				23 09		23 48		
Strines	d						22 13				23 13		23 52		
New Mills Central	a			21 11			22 18				23 18		23 57		
	d			21 11											
Stockport 86	d		20 54			21 28			22 28	22 37					
Hazel Grove 86	d														
Chinley	d			21 19						22 53					
Edale	d			21 28						23 02					
Hope (Derbyshire)	d			21 34						23 08					
Bamford	d			21 37						23 11					
Hathersage	d			21 41						23 15					
Grindleford	d			21 44						23 19					
Dore & Totley	d			21 52						23 28					
Sheffield 7	a		21 35	22 05		22 08			23 16	23 35					01 06

Mondays to Fridays
from 1 October

		TP	TP	TP	NT	NT	NT	NT	NT	NT	NT	NT	NT	NT	NT	TP	NT	NT	NT	EM	NT	NT	NT
		MO ◇1	MX ◇1	◇1 C		B	F		G		B		B	H	B	◇1 C	G			◇ I	B		
Manchester Airport 85 ✈	d	22p55	23p52	05 15												06 55							
Manchester Piccadilly 10	a	23p09	00 09	05 33												07 13							
	d	23p20	00 15	05 44	05 50	06 13	06 24	06 30		06 41	06 46	06 57	07 03	07 08	07 18	07 20		07 23	07 39	07 42	07 47	07 52	08 04
Ardwick	d																						
Ashburys	d					06 17				06 45			07 07	07 12	07 22			07 27					08 08
Belle Vue	d									06 47								07 29					08 10
Ryder Brow	d									06 49								07 31					08 12
Reddish North	d									06 52				07 17				07 34					08 15
Brinnington	d									06 55				07 20				07 37					08 18
Bredbury	d									06 58				07 23				07 40					08 21
Gorton	d					06 19							07 09		07 24								
Fairfield	d						06 31												07 46				
Guide Bridge	a					06 23	06 34				06 54		07 13		07 28				07 49		07 55		
	d						06 34												07 49				
Hyde North	d						06 38												07 53				
Hyde Central	d						06 40												07 55				
Woodley	d						06 43		←										07 58				
Romiley	d						06 47	06 44	06 47	07 02		07 09		07 26				07 43	08 02			08 05	08 24
Rose Hill Marple	a						→		06 53										08 08				08 30
Marple	d							06 47		07 05		07 13		07 30				07a48				08 08	
Strines	d																						
New Mills Central	a							06 55		07 12		07 20		07 35								08 15	
	d													07 39									
Stockport 86	d	23p28		05 52	06 00											07 28				07 54			
Hazel Grove 86	d				06 07																		
Chinley	d				06 18									07 47									
Edale	d				06 26									07 55									
Hope (Derbyshire)	d				06 32									08 01									
Bamford	d				06 35									08 04									
Hathersage	d				06 39									08 09									
Grindleford	d				06 42									08 11			←						
Dore & Totley	d				06 51									08 22		08 03	08 22			08 28			
Sheffield 7	a	00 15	01 06	06 49	07 01									→		08 10	08 32			08 34			

A From Liverpool Lime Street to Nottingham
B To Hadfield
C To Cleethorpes
D To Glossop
F To Rose Hill Marple
G From Manchester Piccadilly
H To Sheffield
I From Liverpool Lime Street to Norwich

Manchester Airport and Manchester Romiley, Marple, Chinley and Sheffield

Network Diagram - see first Page of Table 78

Station	NT A	NT B	NT	NT C	TP ◇1 D	NT A	NT	EM ◇ E	NT	NT A	NT B	NT	NT C	NT A	NT	TP ◇1 D	NT	EM ◇ E	NT	NT A	NT	NT A
Manchester Airport 85 ✈ d					07 53											08 55						
Manchester Piccadilly 10 a					08 12											09 13						
d	08 07	08 12	08 15		08 20	08 29	08 37	08 43	08 45	08 48	09 00	09 05		09 15	09 18	09 20	09 36	09 43	09 45	09 48	10 03	10 15
Ardwick d																						
Ashburys d	08 11									08 52		09 09		09 19	09 23					09 52	10 07	10 19
Belle Vue d															09 26						10 09	
Ryder Brow d															09 28						10 11	
Reddish North d									08 52			09 14							09 52		10 14	
Brinnington d									08 56			09 17							09 56		10 17	
Bredbury d									08 59			09 20							09 59		10 20	
Gorton d	08 13									08 54				09 21						09 54		10 21
Fairfield d		08 20									09 07						09 43					
Guide Bridge a	08 17	08 23				08 37				08 58	09 10			09 25			09 46			09 58		10 25
d		08 23									09 11						09 46					
Hyde North d		08 28									09 17						09 50					
Hyde Central d		08 30									09 20						09 52					
Woodley d		08 33		←							09 23		←				09 55					
Romiley d		08 37	08 29	08 37					09 02		09 26	09 23	09 26		09 35		09 59		10 02		10 23	
Rose Hill Marple a		→		08 45							→		09 33				10 05					
Marple d			08a33				08 52		09 06			09a28			09a40				10 06		10 27	
Strines d							08 56												10 10			
New Mills Central a							09 01		09 11										10 15		10 34	
d									09 11													
Stockport 86 d					08 28			08 54								09 28		09 54				
Hazel Grove 86 d																						
Chinley d									09 19													
Edale d									09 28													
Hope (Derbyshire) d									09 34													
Bamford d									09 37													
Hathersage d									09 40													
Grindleford d									09 44													
Dore & Totley d									09 57													
Sheffield 7 a					09 08			09 35	10 07							10 08		10 35				

Station	NT	TP ◇1 D	NT	EM ◇ E	NT	NT A	NT	NT A	TP ◇1 D	NT	NT	EM ◇ E	NT	NT A	NT	NT A	TP ◇1 D	NT	NT	EM ◇ E	NT
Manchester Airport 85 ✈ d		09 55							10 55								11 55				
Manchester Piccadilly 10 a		10 13							11 13								12 13				
d	10 18	10 20	10 36	10 43	10 45	10 48	11 03	11 18	11 20	11 23	11 36	11 43	11 45	11 48	12 03	12 18	12 20	12 23	12 36	12 43	12 45
Ardwick d																					
Ashburys d						10 52	11 07	11 22						11 52	12 07	12 22					
Belle Vue d							11 09								12 09						
Ryder Brow d							11 11								12 11						
Reddish North d					10 52		11 14						11 52		12 14						12 52
Brinnington d					10 56		11 17						11 56		12 17						12 56
Bredbury d					10 59		11 20						11 59		12 20						12 59
Gorton d						10 54		11 24						11 54		12 24					
Fairfield d			10 43								11 43								12 43		
Guide Bridge a			10 46			10 58		11 28			11 46			11 58		12 28			12 46		
d			10 46								11 46								12 46		
Hyde North d			10 50								11 50								12 50		
Hyde Central d			10 52								11 52								12 52		
Woodley d			10 55								11 55								12 55		
Romiley d	10 37		10 59		11 02		11 23			11 37	11 59		12 02		12 23			12 37	12 59		13 02
Rose Hill Marple a	10 42		11 05							11 43	12 05							12 43	13 05		
Marple d					11 06		11 27						12 06		12 27						13 06
Strines d													12 10								
New Mills Central a					11 11		11 34						12 15		12 34						13 11
d					11 11																13 11
Stockport 86 d		10 28		10 54					11 28			11 54					12 28			12 54	
Hazel Grove 86 d																					
Chinley d					11 19																13 19
Edale d					11 28																13 28
Hope (Derbyshire) d					11 34																13 34
Bamford d					11 37																13 37
Hathersage d					11 40																13 40
Grindleford d					11 44																13 44
Dore & Totley d					11 53																13 57
Sheffield 7 a		11 08		11 34	12 03				12 08			12 35					13 08			13 35	14 04

A To Hadfield
B To Rose Hill Marple
C From Manchester Piccadilly
D To Cleethorpes
E From Liverpool Lime Street to Norwich

Table 78 — Mondays to Fridays from 1 October

Manchester Airport and Manchester Romiley, Marple, Chinley and Sheffield

Network Diagram - see first Page of Table 78

Station	NT A	NT	NT A	TP ◇1 B	NT	NT	EM ◇ C	NT	NT A	NT	NT A	TP ◇1 B	NT	NT	EM ◇ C	NT	NT A	NT	NT A	TP ◇1 B	NT	NT
Manchester Airport 85 ✈ d				12 55								13 55								14 55		
Manchester Piccadilly 10 a				13 13								14 13								15 13		
d	12 48	13 03	13 18	13 20	13 23	13 36	13 43	13 45	13 48	14 03	14 18	14 20	14 23	14 36	14 43	14 45	14 48	15 03	15 18	15 20	15 23	15 36
Ardwick d																						
Ashburys d	12 52	13 07	13 22						13 52	14 07	14 22						14 52	15 07	15 22			
Belle Vue d		13 09								14 09								15 09				
Ryder Brow d		13 11								14 11								15 11				
Reddish North d		13 14						13 52		14 14						14 52		15 14				
Brinnington d		13 17						13 56		14 17						14 56		15 17				
Bredbury d		13 20						13 59		14 20						14 59		15 20				
Gorton d	12 54		13 24						13 54		14 24						14 54		15 24			
Fairfield d						13 43								14 43								15 43
Guide Bridge a	12 58		13 28			13 46			13 58		14 28			14 46			14 58		15 28			15 46
d						13 46								14 46								15 46
Hyde North d						13 50								14 50								15 50
Hyde Central d						13 52								14 52								15 52
Woodley d						13 55								14 55								15 55
Romiley d		13 23			13 37	13 59		14 02		14 23			14 37	14 59		15 02		15 23			15 37	15 59
Rose Hill Marple a					13 43	14 05							14 43	15 05							15 43	16 05
Marple d		13 27						14 06		14 27						15 06		15 27				
Strines d								14 10														
New Mills Central a		13 34						14 15		14 34						15 11		15 34				
d																15 11						
Stockport 86 d				13 28			13 54					14 28			14 54					15 28		
Hazel Grove 86 d																						
Chinley d																15 19						
Edale d																15 28						
Hope (Derbyshire) d																15 34						
Bamford d																15 37						
Hathersage d																15 40						
Grindleford d																15 44						
Dore & Totley d																15 58						
Sheffield 7 a				14 08			14 35					15 08			15 35	16 04				16 08		

Station	EM ◇ C	NT	NT A	NT	NT	NT A	TP ◇1 B	NT	NT A	EM ◇ C	NT	NT	NT A	NT	NT A	NT	TP ◇1 B	NT	NT	NT A	EM ◇ D
Manchester Airport 85 ✈ d							15 55										16 55				
Manchester Piccadilly 10 a							16 13										17 13				
d	15 43	15 45	15 48	16 03	16 06	16 15	16 20	16 23	16 36	16 43	16 45	16 48	16 59	17 03	17 15	17 18	17 20	17 21	17 32	17 37	17 43
Ardwick d														17 07							
Ashburys d			15 52	16 07		16 19			16 40		16 49	16 52	17 03	17 09	17 19				17 36	17 41	
Belle Vue d				16 09										17 12					17 38		
Ryder Brow d				16 11										17 14					17 40		
Reddish North d		15 52		16 14				16 30			16 54			17 16					17 43		
Brinnington d		15 56		16 17				16 34			16 57			17 20					17 46		
Bredbury d		15 59		16 20				16 37			17 00			17 23		17 30			17 49		
Gorton d			15 54			16 21			16 42				17 05		17 21					17 43	
Fairfield d					16 13							16 56									
Guide Bridge a			15 58		16 16	16 25			16 46			16 59	17 10		17 25			17 30		17 47	
d					16 16							16 59						17 30			
Hyde North d					16 20							17 03						17 34			
Hyde Central d					16 22							17 05						17 36			
Woodley d					16 25							17 08						17 39			
Romiley d		16 02		16 23	16 29			16 40			17 03	17 13		17 27		17 33		17 43	17 53		
Rose Hill Marple a					16 36							17 20						17 49			
Marple d		16 06		16 27				16a44			17 07			17a31		17 38			17 57		
Strines d		16 10									17 11								18 01		
New Mills Central a		16 13		16 34							17 15					17 43			18 04		
d		16 13									17 15										
Stockport 86 d	15 54						16 28			16 54							17 28				17 54
Hazel Grove 86 d																					
Chinley d		16 21								17 09	17 21										18 09
Edale d		16 30									17 30										
Hope (Derbyshire) d		16 36									17 36										
Bamford d		16 39									17 39										
Hathersage d		16 42									17 42										
Grindleford d		16 46									17 46										
Dore & Totley d		16 54								17 31	17 56						18 03				18 34
Sheffield 7 a	16 34	17 03					17 08			17 40	18 04						18 10				18 41

A To Hadfield
B To Cleethorpes
C From Liverpool Lime Street to Norwich
D From Liverpool Lime Street to Nottingham

from 1 October

Manchester Airport and Manchester Romiley, Marple, Chinley and Sheffield

Network Diagram - see first Page of Table 78

	NT	NT B	NT	NT	NT B	TP ◇1 C	NT	NT	EM ◇ D	NT	NT B	NT	TP ◇1 C	NT B	NT	EM ◇ E	NT	NT B	TP ◇1	NT	EM ◇ E	NT
Manchester Airport 85 ✈ d						17 55							18 55						19 55			
Manchester Piccadilly 10 a						18 13							19 13						20 13			
d	17 48	17 59	18 03	18 06	18 15	18 20	18 22	18 36	18 43	18 45	18 48	19 00	19 18	19 18	19 23	19 43	19 45	19 48	20 20	20 36	20 43	20 45
Ardwick d				18 09																		
Ashburys d		18 03	18 07	18 11	18 19						18 52	19 04		19 22			19 49	19 52				
Belle Vue d			18 09									19 06					19 51					
Ryder Brow d			18 11									19 08					19 53					
Reddish North d	17 55		18 14				18 30			18 52		19 11					19 56					20 52
Brinnington d	17 59		18 17							18 56		19 14					19 59					20 56
Bredbury d	18 02		18 20				18 36			18 59		19 17					20 02					20 59
Gorton d		18 05			18 21						18 54			19 24				19 54				
Fairfield d				18 15				18 43												20 43		
Guide Bridge a		18 09		18 18	18 25			18 46			18 58			19 28				19 58		20 46		
d				18 18				18 46												20 46		
Hyde North d				18 22				18 50												20 50		
Hyde Central d				18 25				18 52												20 52		
Woodley d				18 28				18 55												20 55		
Romiley d	18 05		18 23	18 31			18 39	18 59		19 02		19 20			19 38		20 05			20 59		21 02
Rose Hill Marple a				18 37				19 05												21 05		
Marple d	18 08		18a28				18 42			19 06		19a25			19a43		20 09					21 06
Strines d							18 46										20 13					
New Mills Central a	18 14						18 52			19 11							20 18					21 11
d	18 14									19 11												21 11
Stockport 86 d						18 28			18 54				19 26			19 54			20 28		20 54	
Hazel Grove 86 d																						
Chinley d	18 20									19 19												21 19
Edale d	18 30									19 28												21 28
Hope (Derbyshire) d	18 36									19 34												21 34
Bamford d	18 39									19 37												21 37
Hathersage d	18 42									19 40												21 41
Grindleford d	18 46									19 44												21 44
Dore & Totley d	18 56					19 03				19 52			20 01						21 03			21 52
Sheffield 7 a	19 06					19 09			19 33	20 02			20 08			20 36			21 11		21 35	22 05

	NT B	TP ◇1 C	NT	NT B	TP ◇1	EM ◇ E	NT	NT B	NT	NT F	TP ◇1
Manchester Airport 85 ✈ d		20 47			21 47						23 52
Manchester Piccadilly 10 a		21 13			22 13						00 09
d	20 48	21 20	21 45	21 48	22 20	22 28	22 45	22 48	23 24	23 27	00 15
Ardwick d											
Ashburys d	20 52		21 49	21 52			22 49	22 52	23 28	23 31	
Belle Vue d			21 51				22 51		23 30		
Ryder Brow d			21 53				22 53		23 32		
Reddish North d			21 56				22 56		23 35		
Brinnington d			21 59				22 59		23 38		
Bredbury d			22 02				23 02		23 41		
Gorton d	20 54			21 54				22 54		23 33	
Fairfield d											
Guide Bridge a	20 58			21 58				22 58		23 37	
d											
Hyde North d											
Hyde Central d											
Woodley d											
Romiley d			22 05				23 05		23 44		
Rose Hill Marple a											
Marple d			22 09				23 09		23 48		
Strines d			22 13				23 13		23 52		
New Mills Central a			22 18				23 18		23 57		
d											
Stockport 86 d		21 28			22 28	22 37					
Hazel Grove 86 d											
Chinley d						22 53					
Edale d						23 02					
Hope (Derbyshire) d						23 08					
Bamford d						23 11					
Hathersage d						23 15					
Grindleford d						23 19					
Dore & Totley d						23 28					
Sheffield 7 a		22 08			23 16	23 35					01 06

B To Hadfield
C To Cleethorpes
D From Liverpool Lime Street to Norwich
E From Liverpool Lime Street to Nottingham
F To Glossop

Manchester Airport and Manchester Romiley, Marple, Chinley and Sheffield

Network Diagram - see first Page of Table 78

	TP ◇1	TP ◇1 A	NT	NT B	NT	NT B	NT	NT B	TP ◇1 A	NT	EM ◇ C	NT	NT B	NT	NT B	TP ◇1 A	NT	NT	EM ◇ C	NT	NT B	NT
Manchester Airport 85 ✈ d	23p52	05 20							06 55							07 53						
Manchester Piccadilly 10 a	00 09	05 35							07 13							08 12						
d	00 15	05 44	05 50	06 16	06 35	06 48	07 03	07 18	07 20	07 39	07 42	07 44	07 48	08 03	08 15	08 20	08 23	08 36	08 43	08 45	08 48	09 03
Ardwick d																						
Ashburys d				06 20	06 39	06 52	07 07	07 22					07 52	08 07	08 19						08 52	09 07
Belle Vue d					06 41		07 09							08 09								09 09
Ryder Brow d					06 43		07 11							08 11								09 11
Reddish North d					06 46		07 14					07 52		08 14						08 52		09 14
Brinnington d					06 49		07 17					07 56		08 17						08 56		09 17
Bredbury d					06 52		07 20					07 59		08 20						08 59		09 20
Gorton d				06 22		06 54		07 24					07 54		08 21						08 54	
Fairfield d										07 46								08 43				
Guide Bridge a				06 26		06 58		07 28		07 49			07 58		08 25			08 46			08 58	
d										07 49								08 46				
Hyde North d										07 53								08 50				
Hyde Central d										07 55								08 52				
Woodley d										07 58								08 55				
Romiley d					06 55		07 23			08 02		08 02		08 23			08 37	08 59		09 02		09 23
Rose Hill Marple a										08 10								09 05				
Marple d					06 59		07a28					08 06		08a28			08a43			09 06		09a28
Strines d																				09 10		
New Mills Central a					07 04							08 11								09 13		
d					07 04							08 11								09 13		
Stockport 86 d		05 52	06 00						07 28		07 54					08 28			08 54			
Hazel Grove 86 d			06 07																			
Chinley d			06 18		07 12							08 19								09 21		
Edale d			06 26		07 21							08 28								09 30		
Hope (Derbyshire) d			06 32		07 27							08 34								09 36		
Bamford d			06 35		07 30							08 37								09 39		
Hathersage d			06 39		07 33							08 40								09 42		
Grindleford d			06 42		07 37							08 44								09 46		
Dore & Totley d			06 51		07 47				08 03		08 28	08 53								09 57		
Sheffield 7 a	01 06	06 49	07 01		07 57				08 10		08 34	09 03				09 08			09 35	10 06		

	NT B	TP ◇1 A	NT	NT	EM ◇ C	NT	NT B	NT	NT B	TP ◇1 A	NT	NT	EM ◇ C	NT	NT B	NT	NT B	TP ◇1 A	NT	NT	EM ◇ C	NT
Manchester Airport 85 ✈ d		08 55								09 55								10 55				
Manchester Piccadilly 10 a		09 13								10 13								11 13				
d	09 18	09 20	09 23	09 36	09 43	09 45	09 48	10 03	10 18	10 20	10 23	10 36	10 43	10 45	10 48	11 03	11 18	11 20	11 23	11 36	11 43	11 45
Ardwick d																						
Ashburys d	09 22						09 52	10 07	10 22						10 52	11 07	11 22					
Belle Vue d								10 09								11 09						
Ryder Brow d								10 11								11 11						
Reddish North d						09 52		10 14						10 52		11 14						11 52
Brinnington d						09 56		10 17						10 56		11 17						11 56
Bredbury d						09 59		10 20						10 59		11 20						11 59
Gorton d	09 24						09 54		10 24						10 54		11 24					
Fairfield d				09 43								10 43								11 43		
Guide Bridge a	09 28			09 46			09 58		10 28			10 46			10 58		11 28			11 46		
d				09 46								10 46								11 46		
Hyde North d				09 50								10 50								11 50		
Hyde Central d				09 52								10 52								11 52		
Woodley d				09 55								10 55								11 55		
Romiley d			09 37	09 59		10 02		10 23			10 37	10 59		11 02		11 23			11 37	11 59		12 02
Rose Hill Marple a				10 05							10 43	11 05							11 43	12 05		
Marple d			09a43			10 06		10a28						11 06		11a28						12 06
Strines d						10 10																12 10
New Mills Central a						10 13								11 11								12 13
d						10 13								11 11								12 13
Stockport 86 d		09 28			09 54					10 28			10 54					11 28			11 54	
Hazel Grove 86 d																						
Chinley d						10 21								11 19								12 21
Edale d						10 30								11 28								12 30
Hope (Derbyshire) d						10 36								11 34								12 36
Bamford d						10 39								11 37								12 39
Hathersage d						10 42								11 40								12 42
Grindleford d						10 46								11 44								12 46
Dore & Totley d						10 57								11 57								12 54
Sheffield 7 a		10 08			10 35	11 04				11 08			11 35	12 04				12 08			12 35	13 03

A To Cleethorpes
B To Hadfield
C From Liverpool Lime Street to Norwich

Manchester Airport and Manchester Romiley, Marple, Chinley and Sheffield

Network Diagram - see first Page of Table 78

	NT	NT	NT	TP	NT	NT	EM	NT	NT	NT	NT	TP	NT	NT	EM	NT	NT	NT	NT	TP	NT
				◇1			◇					◇1			◇					◇1	
	A		A	B 🍴			C		A		A	B 🍴			C		A		A	B 🍴	
Manchester Airport 85 ✈ d				11 55								12 55								13 55	
Manchester Piccadilly 10 a				12 13								13 13								14 13	
d	11 48	12 03	12 18	12 20	12 23	12 36	12 43	12 45	12 48	13 03	13 18	13 20	13 23	13 36	13 43	13 45	13 48	14 03	14 18	14 20	14 23
Ardwick d																					
Ashburys d	11 52	12 07	12 22						12 52	13 07	13 22						13 52	14 07	14 22		
Belle Vue d		12 09								13 09								14 09			
Ryder Brow d		12 11								13 11								14 11			
Reddish North d		12 14						12 52		13 14						13 52		14 14			
Brinnington d		12 17						12 56		13 17						13 56		14 17			
Bredbury d		12 20						12 59		13 20						13 59		14 20			
Gorton d	11 54		12 24						12 54		13 24						13 54		14 24		
Fairfield d						12 43								13 43							
Guide Bridge a	11 58		12 28			12 46			12 58		13 28			13 46			13 58		14 28		
d						12 46								13 46							
Hyde North d						12 50								13 50							
Hyde Central d						12 52								13 52							
Woodley d						12 55								13 55							
Romiley d		12 23			12 37	12 59		13 02		13 23			13 37	13 59		14 02		14 23			14 37
Rose Hill Marple a					12 43	13 05							13 43	14 05							14 43
Marple d		12a28						13 06		13a28						14 06		14a28			
Strines d																14 10					
New Mills Central a								13 11								14 13					
d								13 11								14 13					
Stockport 86 d				12 28			12 54					13 28			13 54					14 28	
Hazel Grove 86 d																					
Chinley d								13 19								14 21					
Edale d								13 28								14 30					
Hope (Derbyshire) d								13 34								14 36					
Bamford d								13 37								14 39					
Hathersage d								13 40								14 42					
Grindleford d								13 44								14 46					
Dore & Totley d								13 57								14 57					
Sheffield 7 a				13 08			13 35	14 04				14 08			14 35	15 04				15 08	

	NT	EM	NT	NT	NT	NT	TP	NT	NT	EM	NT	NT	NT	NT	TP	NT	NT	EM	NT	NT	NT	NT
		◇					◇1			◇					◇1			◇				
		C		A		A	B 🍴			C		A		A	B 🍴			C		A		A
Manchester Airport 85 ✈ d							14 55								15 55							
Manchester Piccadilly 10 a							15 13								16 13							
d	14 36	14 43	14 45	14 48	15 03	15 18	15 20	15 23	15 36	15 43	15 45	15 48	16 02	16 18	16 20	16 23	16 36	16 43	16 45	16 48	17 02	17 18
Ardwick d																						
Ashburys d				14 52	15 07	15 22						15 52	16 06	16 22						16 52	17 06	17 22
Belle Vue d					15 09								16 08								17 08	
Ryder Brow d					15 11								16 10								17 10	
Reddish North d			14 52		15 14						15 52		16 13						16 52		17 13	
Brinnington d			14 56		15 17						15 56		16 16						16 56		17 16	
Bredbury d			14 59		15 20						15 59		16 19						16 59		17 19	
Gorton d				14 54		15 24						15 54		16 24						16 54		17 24
Fairfield d	14 43								15 43								16 43					
Guide Bridge a	14 46			14 58		15 28			15 46			15 58		16 28			16 46			16 58		17 28
d	14 46								15 46								16 46					
Hyde North d	14 50								15 50								16 50					
Hyde Central d	14 52								15 52								16 52					
Woodley d	14 55								15 55								16 55					
Romiley d	14 59		15 02		15 23			15 37	15 59		16 02		16 22			16 37	16 59		17 02		17 22	
Rose Hill Marple a	15 05							15 43	16 05							16 43	17 05					
Marple d			15 06		15a28						16 06		16a27						17 06		17a27	
Strines d											16 10											
New Mills Central a			15 11								16 13								17 11			
d			15 11								16 13								17 11			
Stockport 86 d		14 54					15 28			15 54					16 28			16 54				
Hazel Grove 86 d																						
Chinley d			15 19								16 21							17 09	17 19			
Edale d			15 28								16 30								17 28			
Hope (Derbyshire) d			15 34								16 36								17 34			
Bamford d			15 37								16 39								17 37			
Hathersage d			15 40								16 42								17 40			
Grindleford d			15 44								16 46								17 44			
Dore & Totley d			15 57								16 57							17 30	17 52			
Sheffield 7 a		15 36	16 04				16 08			16 35	17 04				17 08			17 37	18 01			

A To Hadfield
B To Cleethorpes
C From Liverpool Lime Street to Norwich

Manchester Airport and Manchester Romiley, Marple, Chinley and Sheffield

Network Diagram - see first Page of Table 78

	TP	NT	NT	EM	NT	NT	NT	NT	TP	NT	NT	EM	NT	NT	TP	NT	EM	NT	NT	TP	NT
	◇1			◇					◇1			◇			◇1		◇			◇1	
	A 🍴			B		C		C	A 🍴			D		C	A		B		C		
Manchester Airport 85 ✈ d	16 55								17 55						18 55					19 55	
Manchester Piccadilly 10 a	17 13								18 13						19 13					20 13	
d	17 20	17 23	17 36	17 43	17 45	17 48	18 03	18 18	18 20	18 23	18 36	18 43	18 45	18 48	19 18	19 23	19 43	19 45	19 48	20 20	20 36
Ardwick d																					
Ashburys d						17 52	18 07	18 22						18 52		19 28		19 49	19 52		
Belle Vue d							18 09									19 31		19 51			
Ryder Brow d							18 11									19 33		19 53			
Reddish North d					17 52		18 14						18 52			19 35		19 56			
Brinnington d					17 56		18 17						18 56			19 39		19 59			
Bredbury d					17 59		18 20						18 59			19 42		20 02			
Gorton d						17 54		18 24						18 54					19 54		
Fairfield d			17 43								18 43										20 43
Guide Bridge a			17 46			17 58		18 28			18 46			18 58					19 58		20 46
d			17 46								18 46										20 46
Hyde North d			17 50								18 50										20 50
Hyde Central d			17 52								18 52										20 52
Woodley d			17 55								18 55										20 55
Romiley d		17 37	17 59		18 02		18 23			18 37	18 59		19 02			19 45		20 05			20 59
Rose Hill Marple a			18 05								19 05										21 05
Marple d		17a43			18 06		18a28			18a43			19 06			19a49		20 09			
Strines d					18 10													20 13			
New Mills Central a					18 13								19 11					20 18			
d					18 13								19 11								
Stockport 86 d	17 28			17 54					18 28			18 54			19 26		19 54			20 28	
Hazel Grove 86 d																					
Chinley d				18 08	18 21								19 19								
Edale d					18 30								19 28								
Hope (Derbyshire) d					18 36								19 34								
Bamford d					18 39								19 37								
Hathersage d					18 42								19 40								
Grindleford d					18 46								19 44								
Dore & Totley d	18 03				18 54				19 03				19 57		20 01					21 03	
Sheffield 7 a	18 10			18 35	19 03				19 09			19 35	20 04		20 08		20 35			21 14	

	EM	NT	NT	TP	EM	NT	NT	TP	EM	NT	NT	NT	NT
	◇			◇1	◇			◇1	◇				
	B		C	A	B		C		B		C		E
Manchester Airport 85 ✈ d				20 47				21 47					
Manchester Piccadilly 10 a				21 13				22 13					
d	20 43	20 45	20 48	21 20	21 43	21 45	21 48	22 20	22 31	22 45	22 48	23 24	23 27
Ardwick d													
Ashburys d			20 52			21 49	21 52			22 49	22 52	23 28	23 31
Belle Vue d						21 51				22 51		23 30	
Ryder Brow d						21 53				22 53		23 32	
Reddish North d		20 52				21 56				22 56		23 35	
Brinnington d		20 56				21 59				22 59		23 38	
Bredbury d		20 59				22 02				23 02		23 41	
Gorton d			20 54				21 54				22 54		23 33
Fairfield d													
Guide Bridge a			20 58				21 58				22 58		23 37
d													
Hyde North d													
Hyde Central d													
Woodley d													
Romiley d		21 02				22 05				23 05		23 44	
Rose Hill Marple a													
Marple d		21 06				22 09				23 09		23 48	
Strines d						22 13				23 13		23 52	
New Mills Central a		21 11				22 18				23 18		23 57	
d		21 11											
Stockport 86 d	20 54			21 28	21 52			22 28	22 42				
Hazel Grove 86 d													
Chinley d		21 19							22 57				
Edale d		21 28							23 05				
Hope (Derbyshire) d		21 34							23 11				
Bamford d		21 37							23 15				
Hathersage d		21 40							23 19				
Grindleford d		21 44							23 23				
Dore & Totley d		21 53							23 32				
Sheffield 7 a	21 34	22 03		22 08	22 31			23 16	23 39				

A To Cleethorpes
B From Liverpool Lime Street to Nottingham
C To Hadfield
D From Liverpool Lime Street to Norwich
E To Glossop

Table 78

Manchester Airport and Manchester Romiley, Marple, Chinley and Sheffield

Sundays until 9 September

Network Diagram - see first Page of Table 78

		NT	NT	TP ◇1	NT A	NT	NT A	NT A	NT	NT A	TP ◇1 B	NT A	NT	NT A	NT A	TP ◇1 C	EM ◇ D	NT A	NT A	TP ◇1 E	TP ◇1 F	EM ◇ G	NT
Manchester Airport 85 ✈	d			08 40							10 44									12 55	12 55		
Manchester Piccadilly 10 ⇌	a			08 54							10 58									13 09	13 09		
	d	07 45	08 22	08 58	09 18	09 22	09 48	10 18	10 45	10 48	11 18	11 18	11 45	11 48	12 18	12 20	12 44	12 48	13 18	13 20	13 20	13 44	13 45
Ardwick	d																						
Ashburys	d				09 22		09 52	10 22		10 52		11 22		11 52	12 22			12 53	13 22				
Belle Vue	d																						
Ryder Brow	d																						
Reddish North	d	07 52	08 29			09 29			10 52				11 52										13 52
Brinnington	d	07 56	08 33			09 33			10 56				11 56										13 56
Bredbury	d	07 59	08 36			09 36			10 59				11 59										13 59
Gorton	d				09 24		09 54	10 24		10 54		11 24		11 54	12 24			12 55	13 24				
Fairfield	d																						
Guide Bridge	a				09 28		09 58	10 28		10 58		11 28		11 58	12 28			12 59	13 28				
	d																						
Hyde North	d																						
Hyde Central	d																						
Woodley	d																						
Romiley	d	08 02	08 39			09 39			11 02				12 02										14 02
Rose Hill Marple	a																						
Marple	d	08 06	08 43			09 43			11 06				12 06										14 06
Strines	d	08 10	08 47			09 47			11 10				12 10										14 10
New Mills Central	a	08 14	08 51			09 51			11 14				12 14										14 14
	d	08 14	08 51			09 51			11 14				12 14										14 14
Stockport 86	d			09 07							11 27					12 28	12 55			13 28	13 29	13 54	
Hazel Grove 86	d																						
Chinley	d	08 23	09 00			09 59			11 23				12 23										14 23
Edale	d	08 32	09 09			10 08			11 32				12 32										14 32
Hope (Derbyshire)	d	08 38	09 15			10 14			11 38				12 38										14 38
Bamford	d	08 41	09 18			10 17			11 41				12 41										14 41
Hathersage	d	08 45	09 22			10 20			11 45				12 45										14 45
Grindleford	d	08 48	09 25			10 24			11 48				12 48										14 48
Dore & Totley	d	08 57	09 34			10 34			11 57				12 57										14 57
Sheffield 7 ⇌	a	09 06	09 42	09 45		10 43			12 06		12 09		13 06			13 08	13 37			14 08	14 08	14 39	15 06

		NT A	NT A	TP ◇1 B	EM ◇ G	NT	NT A	NT A	TP ◇1 B	EM ◇ G	NT	NT A	NT A	TP ◇1 B	EM ◇ G	NT	NT A	NT A	TP ◇1 B	EM ◇ H	NT	NT A	NT A
Manchester Airport 85 ✈	d			13 55					14 55					15 55					16 55				
Manchester Piccadilly 10 ⇌	a			14 09					15 09					16 09					17 09				
	d	13 48	14 18	14 20	14 44	14 45	14 48	15 18	15 20	15 44	15 45	15 48	16 18	16 20	16 44	16 45	16 48	17 18	17 20	17 44	17 45	17 48	18 18
Ardwick	d																						
Ashburys	d	13 52	14 22				14 52	15 22				15 52	16 22				16 52	17 22				17 52	18 22
Belle Vue	d																						
Ryder Brow	d																						
Reddish North	d					14 52					15 52					16 52					17 52		
Brinnington	d					14 56					15 56					16 56					17 56		
Bredbury	d					14 59					15 59					16 59					17 59		
Gorton	d	13 54	14 24				14 54	15 24				15 54	16 24				16 54	17 24				17 54	18 24
Fairfield	d																						
Guide Bridge	a	13 58	14 28				14 58	15 28				15 58	16 28				16 58	17 28				17 58	18 28
	d																						
Hyde North	d																						
Hyde Central	d																						
Woodley	d																						
Romiley	d					15 02					16 02					17 02					18 02		
Rose Hill Marple	a																						
Marple	d					15 06					16 06					17 06					18 06		
Strines	d					15 10					16 10					17 10					18 10		
New Mills Central	a					15 14					16 14					17 14					18 14		
	d					15 14					16 14					17 14					18 14		
Stockport 86	d			14 28	14 54				15 28	15 54				16 28	16 54				17 28	17 54			
Hazel Grove 86	d																						
Chinley	d					15 23					16 23					17 23					18 23		
Edale	d					15 32					16 32					17 32					18 32		
Hope (Derbyshire)	d					15 38					16 38					17 38					18 38		
Bamford	d					15 41					16 41					17 41					18 41		
Hathersage	d					15 45					16 45					17 45					18 45		
Grindleford	d					15 48					16 48					17 48					18 48		
Dore & Totley	d					15 57					16 57					17 57					18 57		
Sheffield 7 ⇌	a			15 08	15 37	16 05			16 09	16 36	17 06			17 08	17 36	18 06			18 08	18 37	19 06		

A To Hadfield
B To Cleethorpes
C To Doncaster
D To Norwich
E from 1 July until 9 September. To Cleethorpes
F until 24 June. To Cleethorpes
G From Liverpool Lime Street to Norwich
H From Liverpool Lime Street to Nottingham

Table 78

Manchester Airport and Manchester Romiley, Marple, Chinley and Sheffield

Sundays until 9 September

Network Diagram - see first Page of Table 78

		TP ◇1 A	EM ◇ B	NT C	NT C	TP ◇1 A	EM ◇ D	NT	NT C	TP ◇1 A	EM ◇ D	NT C	TP ◇1	EM ◇ D	TP ◇1	NT	TP ◇1
Manchester Airport 85 ✈	d	17 55				18 55				19 55			20 55		21 55		22 55
Manchester Piccadilly 10 ⇌	a	18 09				19 09				20 09			21 09		22 09		23 09
	d	18 20	18 44	18 48	19 18	19 20	19 44	19 45	19 48	20 18	20 44	20 48	21 20	22 11	22 15	22 20	23 20
Ardwick	d																
Ashburys	d			18 52	19 22				19 52			20 52					
Belle Vue	d																
Ryder Brow	d																
Reddish North	d							19 52								22 27	
Brinnington	d							19 56								22 31	
Bredbury	d							19 59								22 34	
Gorton	d			18 54	19 24				19 54			20 54					
Fairfield	d																
Guide Bridge	a			18 58	19 28				19 58			20 58					
	d																
Hyde North	d																
Hyde Central	d																
Woodley	d																
Romiley	d							20 02								22 37	
Rose Hill Marple	a																
Marple	d							20 06								22 40	
Strines	d							20 10								22 44	
New Mills Central	a							20 14								22 49	
	d							20 14									
Stockport 86	d	18 28	18 54			19 28	19 54			20 27	20 54		21 28	22 28	22 23		23 28
Hazel Grove 86	d																
Chinley	d							20 23						22 43			
Edale	d							20 32						22 51			
Hope (Derbyshire)	d							20 38						22 57			
Bamford	d							20 41						23 00			
Hathersage	d							20 45						23 03			
Grindleford	d							20 48						23 07			
Dore & Totley	d							20 57						23 17			
Sheffield 7 ⇌	a	19 08	19 34			20 08	20 34	21 06		21 08	21 36		22 12	23 25	23 04		00 15

Sundays from 16 September

		NT	TP ◇1	NT C	NT	NT C	NT C	NT C	TP ◇1 A	NT C	NT	NT C	NT C	TP ◇1 E	EM ◇ F	NT C	NT C	TP ◇1 A	EM ◇ B	NT	NT C	NT C	TP ◇1 A
Manchester Airport 85 ✈	d		08 40						10 44									12 55					13 55
Manchester Piccadilly 10 ⇌	a		08 54						10 58									13 09					14 09
	d	07 45	08 58	09 18	09 22	09 30	10 18	10 48	11 18	11 18	11 45	11 48	12 18	12 18	12 44	12 48	13 18	13 20	13 44	13 45	13 48	14 18	14 20
Ardwick	d																						
Ashburys	d			09 22		09 34	10 22	10 52		11 22		11 52	12 22			12 53	13 22				13 52	14 22	
Belle Vue	d																						
Ryder Brow	d																						
Reddish North	d	07 52			09 29						11 52									13 52			
Brinnington	d	07 56			09 33						11 56									13 56			
Bredbury	d	07 59			09 36						11 59									13 59			
Gorton	d			09 24		09 36	10 24	10 54		11 24		11 54	12 24			12 55	13 24				13 54	14 24	
Fairfield	d																						
Guide Bridge	a			09 28		09 40	10 28	10 58		11 28		11 58	12 28			12 59	13 28				13 58	14 28	
	d																						
Hyde North	d																						
Hyde Central	d																						
Woodley	d																						
Romiley	d	08 02			09 39						12 02									14 02			
Rose Hill Marple	a																						
Marple	d	08 06			09 43						12 06									14 06			
Strines	d	08 10			09 47						12 10									14 10			
New Mills Central	a	08 14			09 51						12 14									14 14			
	d	08 14			09 51						12 14									14 14			
Stockport 86	d		09 07						11 27					12 28	12 55			13 28	13 54				14 28
Hazel Grove 86	d																						
Chinley	d	08 23			09 59						12 23									14 23			
Edale	d	08 32			10 08						12 32									14 32			
Hope (Derbyshire)	d	08 38			10 14						12 38									14 38			
Bamford	d	08 41			10 17						12 41									14 41			
Hathersage	d	08 45			10 20						12 45									14 45			
Grindleford	d	08 48			10 24						12 48									14 48			
Dore & Totley	d	08 57			10 34						12 57									14 57			
Sheffield 7 ⇌	a	09 06	09 45		10 43				12 09		13 06			13 08	13 37			14 08	14 39	15 06			15 08

A To Cleethorpes
B From Liverpool Lime Street to Norwich
C To Hadfield
D From Liverpool Lime Street to Nottingham
E To Doncaster
F To Norwich

Sundays from 16 September

Manchester Airport and Manchester Romiley, Marple, Chinley and Sheffield

Network Diagram - see first Page of Table 78

		EM ◇ A	NT B	NT B	TP ◇1 C	EM ◇ A		NT	NT B	NT B	TP ◇1 C	EM ◇ A	NT B	NT B	TP ◇1 C	EM ◇ D		NT	NT B	NT B	TP ◇1 C	EM ◇ A	NT B	NT B	TP ◇1 C
Manchester Airport 85 ✈	d				14 55						15 55				16 55						17 55				18 55
Manchester Piccadilly 10	a				15 09						16 09				17 09						18 09				19 09
	d	14 44	14 48	15 18	15 20	15 44		15 45	15 48	16 18	16 20	16 44	16 48	17 18	17 20	17 44		17 45	17 48	18 18	18 20	18 44	18 48	19 18	19 20
Ardwick	d																								
Ashburys	d		14 52	15 22					15 52	16 22			16 52	17 22					17 52	18 22			18 52	19 22	
Belle Vue	d																								
Ryder Brow	d																								
Reddish North	d							15 52										17 52							
Brinnington	d							15 56										17 56							
Bredbury	d							15 59										17 59							
Gorton	d		14 54	15 24					15 54	16 24			16 54	17 24					17 54	18 24			18 54	19 24	
Fairfield	d																								
Guide Bridge	a		14 58	15 28					15 58	16 28			16 58	17 28					17 58	18 28			18 58	19 28	
	d																								
Hyde North	d																								
Hyde Central	d																								
Woodley	d																								
Romiley	d							16 02										18 02							
Rose Hill Marple	a																								
Marple	d							16 06										18 06							
Strines	d							16 10										18 10							
New Mills Central	a							16 14										18 14							
	d							16 14										18 14							
Stockport 86	d	14 54			15 28	15 54					16 28	16 54			17 28	17 54					18 28	18 54			19 28
Hazel Grove 86	d																								
Chinley	d							16 23										18 23							
Edale	d							16 32										18 32							
Hope (Derbyshire)	d							16 38										18 38							
Bamford	d							16 41										18 41							
Hathersage	d							16 45										18 45							
Grindleford	d							16 48										18 48							
Dore & Totley	d							16 57										18 57							
Sheffield 7	a	15 37			16 09	16 36		17 06			17 08	17 36			18 08	18 37		19 06			19 08	19 34			20 08

		EM ◇ D		NT	NT B	TP ◇1 C	EM ◇ D	NT B	TP ◇1	EM ◇ D	TP ◇1	NT		TP ◇1
Manchester Airport 85 ✈	d					19 55			20 55		21 55			22 55
Manchester Piccadilly 10	a					20 09			21 09		22 09			23 09
	d	19 44		19 45	19 48	20 18	20 44	20 48	21 20	22 11	22 15	22 20		23 20
Ardwick	d													
Ashburys	d				19 52			20 52						
Belle Vue	d													
Ryder Brow	d													
Reddish North	d			19 52								22 27		
Brinnington	d			19 56								22 31		
Bredbury	d			19 59								22 34		
Gorton	d				19 54			20 54						
Fairfield	d													
Guide Bridge	a				19 58			20 58						
	d													
Hyde North	d													
Hyde Central	d													
Woodley	d													
Romiley	d			20 02								22 37		
Rose Hill Marple	a													
Marple	d			20 06								22 40		
Strines	d			20 10								22 44		
New Mills Central	a			20 14								22 49		
	d			20 14										
Stockport 86	d	19 54				20 27	20 54		21 28	22 28	22 23			23 28
Hazel Grove 86	d													
Chinley	d			20 23						22 43				
Edale	d			20 32						22 51				
Hope (Derbyshire)	d			20 38						22 57				
Bamford	d			20 41						23 00				
Hathersage	d			20 45						23 03				
Grindleford	d			20 48						23 07				
Dore & Totley	d			20 57						23 17				
Sheffield 7	a	20 34		21 06		21 08	21 36		22 12	23 25	23 04			00 15

A From Liverpool Lime Street to Norwich
B To Hadfield
C To Cleethorpes
D From Liverpool Lime Street to Nottingham

Mondays to Fridays until 28 September

Sheffield, Chinley, Marple and Romiley Manchester and Manchester Airport

Network Diagram - see first Page of Table 78

Miles	Miles	Miles			NT MX	NT MX	TP ◇1	TP ◇1	NT A	NT	TP ◇1 B	NT	NT		NT A	EM ◇ C	NT	NT A	NT	NT	TP ◇1 D	NT A	NT		NT
0	—	—	**Sheffield** 7	d	22p47		03 45	05 11			06 11					06 20					07 09				
4¼	—	—	Dore & Totley	d	22p54											06 27					07 15				
9¾	—	—	Grindleford	d	23p01											06 35									
11¼	—	—	Hathersage	d	23p05											06 39									
13	—	—	Bamford	d	23p08											06 43									
14¾	—	—	Hope (Derbyshire)	d	23p12											06 47									
20	—	—	Edale	d	23p19											06 55									
25½	—	0	**Chinley**	d	23p27											07 03									
—	—	8½	Hazel Grove 86	a																					
—	—	—	Stockport 86	a	23p47			05 53			06 53					07 22					07 53				
29¼	—	—	New Mills Central	d		23p30				06 13			06 36				07 01			07 23					07 39
30¾	—	—	Strines	d		23p33				06 16			06 39				07 04			07 26					07 42
33	—	—	**Marple**	d		23p36				06 19			06 42				07 07			07 29					07 45
—	0	—	**Rose Hill Marple**	d								06 32							07 16				07 41		
34¼	2	—	**Romiley**	d		23p40				06 23		06 37	06 46				07 12		07 21	07 33			07 46		07 49
—	3¼	—	Woodley	d								06 40							07 24				07 49		
—	4¾	—	Hyde Central	d								06 43							07 27				07 52		
—	6	—	Hyde North	d								06 46							07 30				07 55		
—	7¾	—	Guide Bridge	d					06 27			06 50			06 57			07 27	07 34			07 47	07 59		
—	9	—	Fairfield	d								06 53							07 37				08 02		
—	10	—	Gorton	d					06 30						07 00			07 30				07 50			
35½	—	—	Bredbury	d		23p43				06 26			06 49				07 15			07 36					07 52
36½	—	—	Brinnington	d		23p45				06 28			06 52				07 17			07 39					07 55
38¼	—	—	Reddish North	d		23p48				06 31			06 55				07 20			07 43					07 58
39¼	—	—	Ryder Brow	d		23p51				06 34			06 58				07 24			07 45					
39½	—	—	Belle Vue	d		23p52				06 36			07 00				07 26			07 47					
40½	11	—	Ashburys	d		23p55			06 33	06 39			07 03		07 06		07 29	07 33		07 50		07 53			
41½	12	—	Ardwick	d														07 36							
42	12½	8¾	**Manchester Piccadilly** 10	a	00 02	00 03	04 40	06 05	06 42	06 47	07 02	07 03	07 12		07 15	07 34	07 36	07 43	07 47	07 56	08 02	08 03	08 12		08 09
—	—	—	**Manchester Airport** 85 ✈	a			05 00	06 29			07 29										08 26				

		NT A	NT	NT	EM ◇ C	NT A	NT	NT	NT		TP ◇1 D	NT A	NT	NT A	NT	NT	NT FO E	EM ◇ C	NT A	NT	TP ◇1 D	NT A	NT	NT	NT
Sheffield 7	d			07 12	07 35						08 05							08 42			09 11				09 14
Dore & Totley	d			07 19	07 42						08 11														09 21
Grindleford	d			07 29																					09 29
Hathersage	d			07 32																					09 32
Bamford	d			07 36																					09 36
Hope (Derbyshire)	d			07 39																					09 39
Edale	d			07 47																					09 47
Chinley	d			07 55	08 03						08 32														09 55
Hazel Grove 86	a				08 16																				
Stockport 86	a				08 24						08 53						09d22	09 25			09 53				
New Mills Central	d			08 02				08 22								09 04									10 01
Strines	d							08 25								09 07									10 04
Marple	d		07 59	08 09				08 29					08 48			09 10				09 35			09 52		10 07
Rose Hill Marple	d						08 15		08 35						08 59									09 55	
Romiley	d		08 03	08 13			08 20	08 33	08 40				08 51		09 04	09 14				09 38			09 56	10 00	10 11
Woodley	d						08 23								09 07									10 03	
Hyde Central	d						08 26								09 10									10 06	
Hyde North	d						08 29								09 13									10 09	
Guide Bridge	d	08 10				08 27	08 33					08 49		09 12	09 17		09a42		09 28			09 58		10 13	
Fairfield	d						08 36								09 20									10 16	
Gorton	d	08 13				08 31						08 52		09 15					09 31			10 01			
Bredbury	d		08 06					08 36	08 43				08 54			09 17				09 41					10 14
Brinnington	d		08 09					08 39	08 45				08 57			09 19				09 44					10 16
Reddish North	d		08 12					08 43	08 48				09 00			09 22				09 47					10 19
Ryder Brow	d		08 15										09 03										10 03		
Belle Vue	d		08 16										09 04										10 05		
Ashburys	d	08 16	08 20			08 34		08 48				08 56	09 07	09 18					09 34			10 04	10 07		
Ardwick	d		08 22						08 54																
Manchester Piccadilly 10	a	08 25	08 30	08 33	08 36	08 43	08 47	08 55	09 00		09 02	09 04	09 15	09 27	09 30	09 34		09 36	09 42	09 57	10 02	10 12	10 15	10 26	10 32
Manchester Airport 85 ✈	a										09 33										10 26				

A From Hadfield
B From Doncaster
C From Nottingham to Liverpool Lime Street
D From Cleethorpes
E To Stalybridge arr. 09.48. Also stops at Reddish South 09x26 and Denton 09x31

Sheffield, Chinley, Marple and Romiley Manchester and Manchester Airport

Network Diagram - see first Page of Table 78

	EM ◇ A	NT B	NT	NT		TP ◇1 C	NT B	NT	NT	EM ◇ A	NT B	NT	NT	TP ◇1 C		NT B	NT	NT	EM ◇ A	NT B	NT	NT	TP ◇1 C	NT B
Sheffield 7 d	09 42					10 11			10 14	10 42				11 11					11 42				12 11	
Dore & Totley d									10 21															
Grindleford d									10 29															
Hathersage d									10 32															
Bamford d									10 36															
Hope (Derbyshire) d									10 39															
Edale d									10 47															
Chinley d									10 55															
Hazel Grove 86 a																								
Stockport 86 a	10 25					10 53				11 25				11 53					12 25				12 53	
New Mills Central d				10 30					11 01				11 30					12 01				12 30		
Strines d																		12 04						
Marple d				10 35					11 07				11 35					12 07				12 35		
Rose Hill Marple d			10 30					10 51				11 30					11 51				12 30			
Romiley d			10 35	10 38				10 56	11 11			11 35	11 38				11 56	12 11			12 35	12 38		
Woodley d			10 38									11 38									12 38			
Hyde Central d			10 41									11 41									12 41			
Hyde North d			10 44									11 44									12 44			
Guide Bridge d		10 28	10 48				10 58				11 28	11 48				11 58				12 28	12 48			12 58
Fairfield d			10 51									11 51									12 51			
Gorton d		10 31					11 01				11 31					12 01				12 31				13 01
Bredbury d				10 41					11 14				11 41					12 14				12 41		
Brinnington d				10 44					11 16				11 44					12 16				12 44		
Reddish North d				10 47					11 19				11 47					12 19				12 47		
Ryder Brow d								11 03									12 03							
Belle Vue d								11 05									12 05							
Ashburys d		10 34					11 04	11 07			11 34					12 04	12 07			12 34				13 04
Ardwick d																								
Manchester Piccadilly 10 a	10 36	10 42	11 02	10 57		11 02	11 12	11 15	11 32	11 36	11 42	12 02	11 57	12 02		12 12	12 15	12 32	12 36	12 42	13 02	12 57	13 02	13 12
Manchester Airport 85 ✈ a						11 26								12 26									13 26	

		NT	NT	EM ◇ A	NT B	NT	NT	TP ◇1 C	NT B	NT		NT	EM ◇ A	NT B	NT	NT	TP ◇1 C	NT B	NT	NT		EM ◇ A	NT B	NT
Sheffield 7 d			12 14	12 42				13 11					13 42				14 11			14 14		14 42		
Dore & Totley d			12 21																	14 21				
Grindleford d			12 29																	14 29				
Hathersage d			12 32																	14 32				
Bamford d			12 36																	14 36				
Hope (Derbyshire) d			12 39																	14 39				
Edale d			12 47																	14 47				
Chinley d			12 55																	14 55				
Hazel Grove 86 a																								
Stockport 86 a				13 25				13 53					14 25				14 53					15 25		
New Mills Central d			13 01				13 30					14 01				14 30				15 01				
Strines d												14 04												
Marple d			13 07				13 35					14 07				14 35				15 07				
Rose Hill Marple d		12 51				13 30				13 51					14 30				14 51					15 30
Romiley d		12 56	13 11			13 35	13 38			13 56		14 11			14 35	14 38			14 56	15 11				15 35
Woodley d						13 38									14 38									15 38
Hyde Central d						13 41									14 41									15 41
Hyde North d						13 44									14 44									15 44
Guide Bridge d					13 28	13 48			13 58					14 28	14 48			14 58					15 28	15 48
Fairfield d						13 51									14 51									15 51
Gorton d					13 31				14 01					14 31				15 01					15 31	
Bredbury d			13 14				13 41					14 14				14 41				15 14				
Brinnington d			13 16				13 44					14 16				14 44				15 16				
Reddish North d			13 19				13 47					14 19				14 47				15 19				
Ryder Brow d		13 03								14 03									15 03					
Belle Vue d		13 05								14 05									15 05					
Ashburys d		13 07			13 34				14 04	14 07				14 34				15 04	15 07				15 34	
Ardwick d																								
Manchester Piccadilly 10 a		13 15	13 32	13 36	13 42	14 02	13 57	14 02	14 12	14 15		14 32	14 36	14 42	15 02	14 57	15 02	15 12	15 15	15 32		15 36	15 42	16 02
Manchester Airport 85 ✈ a								14 26									15 26							

A From Norwich to Liverpool Lime Street
B From Hadfield
C From Cleethorpes

Sheffield, Chinley, Marple and Romiley Manchester and Manchester Airport

Network Diagram - see first Page of Table 78

	NT	TP ◇1 A	NT B	NT	NT	EM ◇ C		NT B	NT	TP ◇1 A	NT B	NT	NT	NT	NT B	EM ◇ C		NT	NT	NT B	TP ◇1 A	NT	NT B	NT
Sheffield 7 d		15 11				15 42				16 11				16 14		16 42					17 11			
Dore & Totley d														16 21										
Grindleford d														16 29										
Hathersage d														16 32										
Bamford d														16 36										
Hope (Derbyshire) d														16 39										
Edale d														16 47										
Chinley d														16 55										
Hazel Grove 86 a																								
Stockport 86 a		15 53				16 25				16 53						17 25					17 53			
New Mills Central d	15 30				16 01							16 37		17 01										17 48
Strines d					16 04																			
Marple d	15 35				16 07							16 42	16 52	17 06								17 38		17 53
Rose Hill Marple d				15 51					16 26									17 10	17 27					
Romiley d	15 38			15 56	16 11				16 31			16 45	16 56	17 10				17 15	17 32			17 41		17 57
Woodley d												16 49						17 18						
Hyde Central d												16 52						17 21						
Hyde North d												16 54						17 24						
Guide Bridge d			15 58					16 28			16 49	16 58			17 15			17 28		17 42			17 58	
Fairfield d																		17 31						
Gorton d			16 01					16 31			16 52				17 18					17 45			18 01	
Bredbury d	15 41				16 14				16 34					17 13								17 44		
Brinnington d	15 44				16 16				16 37													17 47		
Reddish North d	15 47				16 19				16 40				17 02									17 50		
Ryder Brow d				16 03					16 42				17 04									17 52		
Belle Vue d				16 05					16 44													17 54		
Ashburys d			16 04	16 07				16 34	16 47		16 55	17 03	17 07		17 24					17 48		17 57	18 04	18 07
Ardwick d																								
Manchester Piccadilly 10 a	15 57	16 02	16 12	16 15	16 32	16 36		16 42	16 56	17 02	17 05	17 10	17 16	17 29	17 33	17 37		17 42	17 48	17 57	18 02	18 03	18 12	18 13
Manchester Airport 85 ✈ a		16 26								17 32											18 26			

	NT	NT B		EM ◇ C	NT	NT	TP ◇1 A	NT B	NT	NT B	NT	EM ◇ C		NT B	TP ◇1 A	NT	NT	NT B	NT	EM ◇ C	NT B	TP ThFO ◇1 E		TP MTWO ◇1 E
Sheffield 7 d	17 14			17 40			18 11				18 14	18 43			19 11				19 14	19 42		20 11		20 11
Dore & Totley d	17 21										18 21								19 21					
Grindleford d	17 28										18 28								19 29					
Hathersage d	17 31										18 32								19 32					
Bamford d	17 35																		19 36					
Hope (Derbyshire) d	17 38										18 38								19 39					
Edale d	17 46										18 45								19 47					
Chinley d	17 54										18 53								19 55					
Hazel Grove 86 a																								
Stockport 86 a				18 25			18 53					19 25			19 53					20 25		20 53		20 53
New Mills Central d	18 00										19 00								20 01					
Strines d	18 03										19 03													
Marple d	18 06					18 35					19 07						19 37		20 07					
Rose Hill Marple d					18 11				18 44							19 30								
Romiley d	18 10				18 16	18 38			18 49		19 11					19 35	19 40		20 11					
Woodley d					18 19											19 38								
Hyde Central d					18 22											19 41								
Hyde North d					18 25											19 44								
Guide Bridge d		18 17			18 29			18 46		19 01				19 28		19 48		19 58			20 28			
Fairfield d					18 32											19 51								
Gorton d		18 20						18 49		19 04				19 31				20 01			20 31			
Bredbury d	18 13					18 41			18 52		19 14						19 43		20 14					
Brinnington d						18 44			18 54		19 17						19 46		20 16					
Reddish North d						18 47			18 58		19 20						19 49		20 19					
Ryder Brow d									19 00								19 51							
Belle Vue d									19 02								19 53							
Ashburys d		18 23						18 54	19 05	19 08				19 34			19 56	20 04			20 34			
Ardwick d																								
Manchester Piccadilly 10 a	18 30	18 34		18 36	18 41	18 57	19 02	19 03	19 12	19 15	19 33	19 36		19 42	20 02	20 02	20 05	20 12	20 32	20 36	20 42	21 02		21 02
Manchester Airport 85 ✈ a							19 28								20 39							21 36		21 38

A From Cleethorpes
B From Hadfield
C From Norwich to Liverpool Lime Street
E From Cleethorpes

until 28 September

Sheffield, Chinley, Marple and Romiley Manchester and Manchester Airport

Network Diagram - see first Page of Table 78

		NT	NT A	EM ◇ B	NT	NT	NT A	TP ◇1 C	NT	NT A	NT	NT
Sheffield 7	d			20 32		20 35		22 11			22 47	
Dore & Totley	d					20 43					22 54	
Grindleford	d					20 50					23 01	
Hathersage	d					20 53					23 05	
Bamford	d					20 57					23 08	
Hope (Derbyshire)	d					21 00					23 12	
Edale	d					21 08					23 19	
Chinley	d					21 16					23 27	
Hazel Grove 86	a											
Stockport 86	a			21 20				22 53			23 47	
New Mills Central	d	20 30				21 30			22 30			23 30
Strines	d	20 33							22 33			23 33
Marple	d	20 36				21 36			22 36			23 36
Rose Hill Marple	d				21 12							
Romiley	d	20 40			21 17	21 40			22 40			23 40
Woodley	d				21 20							
Hyde Central	d				21 23							
Hyde North	d				21 26							
Guide Bridge	d		20 58		21 30		21 58			22 58		
Fairfield	d				21 33							
Gorton	d		21 01				22 01			23 01		
Bredbury	d	20 43				21 43			22 43			23 43
Brinnington	d	20 45				21 45			22 45			23 45
Reddish North	d	20 48				21 48			22 48			23 48
Ryder Brow	d	20 51				21 51			22 51			23 51
Belle Vue	d	20 52				21 52			22 52			23 52
Ashburys	d	20 55	21 04			21 55	22 04		22 55	23 04		23 55
Ardwick	d											
Manchester Piccadilly 10	a	21 03	21 12	21 32	21 42	22 05	22 12	23 02	23 03	23 12	00 02	00 03
Manchester Airport 85	a							23 26				

Mondays to Fridays

from 1 October

		NT MX	NT MX	TP ◇1	TP ◇1	NT A	NT	TP ◇1 D	NT	NT	NT A	EM ◇ E	NT	NT A	NT	NT	TP ◇1 C	NT A	NT	NT	NT A	NT	NT
Sheffield 7	d	22p47		03 45	05 11			06 11				06 20					07 09						07 12
Dore & Totley	d	22p54										06 27					07 15						07 19
Grindleford	d	23p01										06 35											07 29
Hathersage	d	23p05										06 39											07 32
Bamford	d	23p08										06 43											07 36
Hope (Derbyshire)	d	23p12										06 47											07 39
Edale	d	23p19										06 55											07 47
Chinley	d	23p27										07 03											07 55
Hazel Grove 86	a																						
Stockport 86	a	23p47			05 53			06 53				07 22					07 53						
New Mills Central	d		23p30				06 10			06 33			06 58			07 20				07 36			08 02
Strines	d		23p33				06 13			06 36			07 01			07 23				07 39			
Marple	d		23p36				06 16			06 39			07 04			07 26				07 42		07 59	08 09
Rose Hill Marple	d								06 30						07 16				07 41				
Romiley	d		23p40				06 20		06 37	06 43			07 09		07 21	07 30			07 46	07 49		08 03	08 13
Woodley	d								06 40						07 24				07 49				
Hyde Central	d								06 43						07 27				07 52				
Hyde North	d								06 46						07 30				07 55				
Guide Bridge	d					06 27			06 50		06 57			07 28	07 34			07 47	07 59		08 10		
Fairfield	d								06 53						07 37				08 02				
Gorton	d					06 30					07 00			07 31				07 50			08 13		
Bredbury	d		23p43				06 23			06 46			07 12			07 33				07 52		08 06	
Brinnington	d		23p45				06 25			06 49			07 14			07 36				07 55		08 09	
Reddish North	d		23p48				06 28			06 52			07 17			07 40				07 58		08 12	
Ryder Brow	d		23p51				06 31			06 55			07 21			07 42						08 15	
Belle Vue	d		23p52				06 33			06 57			07 23			07 44						08 16	
Ashburys	d		23p55			06 33	06 39			07 03	07 06		07 29	07 34		07 50		07 53			08 16	08 20	
Ardwick	d													07 38								08 22	
Manchester Piccadilly 10	a	00 02	00 03	04 40	06 05	06 42	06 47	07 02	07 03	07 12	07 15	07 34	07 36	07 44	07 47	07 56	08 02	08 03	08 12	08 09	08 25	08 30	08 33
Manchester Airport 85	a			05 00	06 29			07 29									08 26						

A From Hadfield
B From Norwich
C From Cleethorpes
D From Doncaster
E From Nottingham to Liverpool Lime Street

from 1 October

Sheffield, Chinley, Marple and Romiley Manchester and Manchester Airport

Network Diagram - see first Page of Table 78

		EM ◇ A	NT B	NT	NT	NT	TP ◇1 C	NT B	NT	NT B	NT	NT	NT FO E	EM ◇ A	NT B	NT	TP ◇1 C	NT B	NT	NT	NT	EM ◇ D	NT B	NT
Sheffield 7	d	07 35					08 05							08 42			09 11				09 14	09 42		
Dore & Totley	d	07 42					08 11														09 21			
Grindleford	d																				09 29			
Hathersage	d																				09 32			
Bamford	d																				09 36			
Hope (Derbyshire)	d																				09 39			
Edale	d																				09 47			
Chinley	d	08 03					08 32														09 55			
Hazel Grove 86	a	08 16																						
Stockport 86	a	08 24					08 53						09d22	09 25			09 53					10 25		
New Mills Central	d				08 22							09 04									10 01			
Strines	d				08 25							09 07									10 04			
Marple	d				08 29				08 48			09 10				09 35			09 52		10 07			
Rose Hill Marple	d			08 15		08 35					08 59									09 55				10 30
Romiley	d			08 20	08 33	08 40			08 51		09 04	09 14				09 38			09 56	10 00	10 11			10 35
Woodley	d			08 23							09 07									10 03				10 38
Hyde Central	d			08 26							09 10									10 06				10 41
Hyde North	d			08 29							09 13									10 09				10 44
Guide Bridge	d		08 27	08 33				08 49		09 12	09 17		09a42		09 28			09 58		10 13			10 28	10 48
Fairfield	d			08 36							09 20									10 16				10 51
Gorton	d		08 31					08 52		09 15					09 31			10 01					10 31	
Bredbury	d				08 36	08 43			08 54			09 17				09 41					10 14			
Brinnington	d				08 39	08 45			08 57			09 19				09 44					10 16			
Reddish North	d				08 43	08 48			09 00			09 22				09 47					10 19			
Ryder Brow	d								09 03										10 03					
Belle Vue	d								09 04										10 05					
Ashburys	d		08 34		08 48			08 56	09 07	09 18					09 34			10 04	10 07				10 34	
Ardwick	d					08 54																		
Manchester Piccadilly 10	a	08 36	08 43	08 47	08 55	09 00	09 02	09 04	09 15	09 27	09 30	09 34		09 36	09 42	09 57	10 02	10 11	10 15	10 26	10 32	10 36	10 41	11 02
Manchester Airport 85	a						09 33										10 26							

		NT	TP ◇1 C	NT B	NT	NT	EM ◇ D	NT B	NT	NT	TP ◇1 C	NT B	NT	NT	EM ◇ D	NT B	NT	NT	TP ◇1 C	NT B	NT	NT
Sheffield 7	d		10 11			10 14	10 42				11 11				11 42				12 11			12 14
Dore & Totley	d					10 21																12 21
Grindleford	d					10 29																12 29
Hathersage	d					10 32																12 32
Bamford	d					10 36																12 36
Hope (Derbyshire)	d					10 39																12 39
Edale	d					10 47																12 47
Chinley	d					10 55																12 55
Hazel Grove 86	a																					
Stockport 86	a		10 53				11 25				11 53				12 25				12 53			
New Mills Central	d	10 30				11 01				11 30				12 01				12 30				13 01
Strines	d													12 04								
Marple	d	10 35				11 07				11 35				12 07				12 35				13 07
Rose Hill Marple	d				10 51				11 30				11 51				12 30				12 51	
Romiley	d	10 38			10 56	11 11			11 35	11 38			11 56	12 11			12 35	12 38			12 56	13 11
Woodley	d								11 38								12 38					
Hyde Central	d								11 41								12 41					
Hyde North	d								11 44								12 44					
Guide Bridge	d			10 58				11 28	11 48			11 58				12 28	12 48			12 58		
Fairfield	d								11 51								12 51					
Gorton	d			11 01				11 31				12 01				12 31				13 01		
Bredbury	d	10 41				11 14				11 41				12 14				12 41				13 14
Brinnington	d	10 44				11 16				11 44				12 16				12 44				13 16
Reddish North	d	10 47				11 19				11 47				12 19				12 47				13 19
Ryder Brow	d				11 03								12 03								13 03	
Belle Vue	d				11 05								12 05								13 05	
Ashburys	d			11 04	11 07			11 34				12 04	12 07			12 34				13 04	13 07	
Ardwick	d																					
Manchester Piccadilly 10	a	10 57	11 02	11 11	11 15	11 32	11 36	11 41	12 02	11 57	12 02	12 11	12 15	12 32	12 36	12 41	13 02	12 57	13 02	13 11	13 15	13 32
Manchester Airport 85	a		11 26								12 26								13 26			

A From Nottingham to Liverpool Lime Street
B From Hadfield
C From Cleethorpes
D From Norwich to Liverpool Lime Street
E To Stalybridge arr. 09.48. Also stops at Reddish South 09x26 and Denton 09x31

Sheffield, Chinley, Marple and Romiley Manchester and Manchester Airport

Network Diagram - see first Page of Table 78

	EM	NT	NT	NT	TP	NT	NT		NT	EM	NT	NT	NT	TP	NT	NT	NT		EM	NT	NT	NT	TP	NT
	◇				◇■					◇				◇■					◇				◇■	
	A	B			C ✕	B				A	B			C ✕	B				A	B			C ✕	B
Sheffield 7 ⇌ d	12 42				13 11					13 42				14 11			14 14		14 42				15 11	
Dore & Totley d																	14 21							
Grindleford d																	14 29							
Hathersage d																	14 32							
Bamford d																	14 36							
Hope (Derbyshire) d																	14 39							
Edale d																	14 47							
Chinley d																	14 55							
Hazel Grove 86 a																								
Stockport 86 a	13 25				13 53					14 25				14 53					15 25				15 53	
New Mills Central d				13 30					14 01				14 30				15 01					15 30		
Strines d									14 04															
Marple d				13 35					14 07				14 35				15 07					15 35		
Rose Hill Marple d			13 30				13 51					14 30				14 51					15 30			
Romiley d			13 35	13 38			13 56		14 11			14 35	14 38			14 56	15 11				15 35	15 38		
Woodley d			13 38									14 38									15 38			
Hyde Central d			13 41									14 41									15 41			
Hyde North d			13 44									14 44									15 44			
Guide Bridge d		13 28	13 48			13 58					14 28	14 48			14 58					15 28	15 48			15 58
Fairfield d			13 51									14 51									15 51			
Gorton d		13 31				14 01					14 31				15 01					15 31				16 01
Bredbury d				13 41					14 14				14 41				15 14					15 41		
Brinnington d				13 44					14 16				14 44				15 16					15 44		
Reddish North d				13 47					14 19				14 47				15 19					15 47		
Ryder Brow d							14 03									15 03								
Belle Vue d							14 05									15 05								
Ashburys d		13 34				14 04	14 07				14 34				15 04	15 07				15 34				16 04
Ardwick d																								
Manchester Piccadilly 10 ⇌ a	13 36	13 41	14 02	13 57	14 02	14 11	14 15		14 32	14 36	14 41	15 02	14 57	15 02	15 11	15 15	15 32		15 36	15 41	16 02	15 57	16 02	16 11
Manchester Airport 85 ✈ a					14 26									15 26									16 26	

	NT	NT	EM		NT	NT	TP	NT	NT	NT	NT	NT	EM		NT	NT	NT	TP	NT	NT	NT	NT	NT
			◇				◇■						◇					◇■					
			A		B		C ✕	B				B	A				B	C ✕		B			B
Sheffield 7 ⇌ d			15 42				16 11				16 14		16 42					17 11				17 14	
Dore & Totley d											16 21											17 21	
Grindleford d											16 29											17 28	
Hathersage d											16 32											17 31	
Bamford d											16 36											17 35	
Hope (Derbyshire) d											16 39											17 38	
Edale d											16 47											17 46	
Chinley d											16 55											17 54	
Hazel Grove 86 a																							
Stockport 86 a			16 25				16 53						17 25					17 53					
New Mills Central d		16 01							16 37		17 01										17 48	18 00	
Strines d		16 04																				18 03	
Marple d		16 07							16 42	16 52	17 06								17 38		17 53	18 06	
Rose Hill Marple d	15 51					16 26									17 10	17 27							
Romiley d	15 56	16 11				16 31			16 45	16 56	17 10				17 15	17 32			17 41		17 57	18 10	
Woodley d									16 49						17 18								
Hyde Central d									16 52						17 21								
Hyde North d									16 54						17 24								
Guide Bridge d					16 28			16 49	16 58			17 17			17 28		17 42			18 00			18 17
Fairfield d															17 31								
Gorton d					16 31			16 52				17 20					17 45						18 20
Bredbury d		16 14				16 34					17 13								17 44			18 13	
Brinnington d		16 16				16 37													17 47				
Reddish North d		16 19				16 40				17 02									17 50				
Ryder Brow d	16 03					16 42				17 04									17 52				
Belle Vue d	16 05					16 44													17 54				
Ashburys d	16 07				16 34	16 47		16 55	17 03	17 07		17 24					17 48		17 57		18 07		18 23
Ardwick d																							
Manchester Piccadilly 10 ⇌ a	16 15	16 32	16 36		16 41	16 56	17 02	17 05	17 10	17 16	17 29	17 33	17 37		17 42	17 48	17 57	18 02	18 03	18 12	18 13	18 30	18 34
Manchester Airport 85 ✈ a							17 32											18 26					

A From Norwich to Liverpool Lime Street
B From Hadfield
C From Cleethorpes

Sheffield, Chinley, Marple and Romiley Manchester and Manchester Airport

Network Diagram - see first Page of Table 78

	EM	NT	NT	TP	NT	NT	NT	NT	EM		NT	TP	NT	NT	NT	NT	EM	NT	TP ThFO		TP MTWO	NT	NT	EM
	◇			◇■					◇			◇■					◇		◇■		◇■			◇
	A			B ✕	D		D		A		D	B ✕			D		A	D	B		B		D	G
Sheffield 7 ⇌ d	17 40			18 11				18 14	18 43			19 11				19 14	19 42		20 11		20 11			20 32
Dore & Totley d								18 21								19 21								
Grindleford d								18 28								19 29								
Hathersage d								18 32								19 32								
Bamford d																19 36								
Hope (Derbyshire) d								18 38								19 39								
Edale d								18 45								19 47								
Chinley d								18 53								19 55								
Hazel Grove 86 a																								
Stockport 86 a	18 25			18 53					19 25			19 53					20 25		20 53		20 53			21 20
New Mills Central d								19 00								20 01						20 30		
Strines d								19 03														20 33		
Marple d			18 35					19 07						19 37		20 07						20 36		
Rose Hill Marple d		18 11				18 44							19 30											
Romiley d		18 16	18 38			18 49		19 11					19 35	19 40		20 11						20 40		
Woodley d		18 19											19 38											
Hyde Central d		18 22											19 41											
Hyde North d		18 25											19 44											
Guide Bridge d		18 29			18 46		19 01				19 28		19 48		19 58			20 28					20 58	
Fairfield d		18 32											19 51											
Gorton d					18 49		19 04				19 31				20 01			20 31					21 01	
Bredbury d			18 41			18 52		19 14						19 43		20 14						20 43		
Brinnington d			18 44			18 54		19 17						19 46		20 16						20 45		
Reddish North d			18 47			18 58		19 20						19 49		20 19						20 48		
Ryder Brow d						19 00								19 51								20 51		
Belle Vue d						19 02								19 53								20 52		
Ashburys d					18 54	19 05	19 08				19 34			19 56	20 04			20 34				20 55	21 04	
Ardwick d																								
Manchester Piccadilly 10 ⇌ a	18 36	18 41	18 57	19 02	19 03	19 12	19 15	19 33	19 36		19 42	20 02	20 02	20 05	20 12	20 32	20 36	20 42	21 02		21 02	21 03	21 12	21 32
Manchester Airport 85 ✈ a				19 28								20 39							21 36		21 38			

	NT	NT	NT	TP	NT		NT	NT	NT
				◇■					
			D	B			D		
Sheffield 7 ⇌ d		20 35		22 11				22 47	
Dore & Totley d		20 43						22 54	
Grindleford d		20 50						23 01	
Hathersage d		20 53						23 05	
Bamford d		20 57						23 08	
Hope (Derbyshire) d		21 00						23 12	
Edale d		21 08						23 19	
Chinley d		21 16						23 27	
Hazel Grove 86 a									
Stockport 86 a				22 53				23 47	
New Mills Central d		21 30			22 30				23 30
Strines d					22 33				23 33
Marple d		21 36			22 36				23 36
Rose Hill Marple d	21 12								
Romiley d	21 17	21 40			22 40				23 40
Woodley d	21 20								
Hyde Central d	21 23								
Hyde North d	21 26								
Guide Bridge d	21 30		21 58				22 58		
Fairfield d	21 33								
Gorton d			22 01				23 01		
Bredbury d		21 43			22 43				23 43
Brinnington d		21 45			22 45				23 45
Reddish North d		21 48			22 48				23 48
Ryder Brow d		21 51			22 51				23 51
Belle Vue d		21 52			22 52				23 52
Ashburys d		21 55	22 04		22 55		23 04		23 55
Ardwick d									
Manchester Piccadilly 10 ⇌ a	21 42	22 05	22 12	23 02	23 03		23 12	00 02	00 03
Manchester Airport 85 ✈ a				23 26					

A From Norwich to Liverpool Lime Street
B From Cleethorpes
D From Hadfield
G From Norwich

Sheffield, Chinley, Marple and Romiley Manchester and Manchester Airport

Network Diagram - see first Page of Table 78

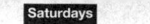

		NT	NT	TP	TP	TP	NT	EM	NT	NT	NT	NT	TP	NT	NT	EM	NT	NT	NT	TP	NT	NT	NT
				◇1	◇1	◇1 A	B	◇ C		B			◇1 D	B		◇ C	B			◇1 D	B		
Sheffield 7 ⇌	d	22p47		03 45	05 11	06 11		06 20					07 09		07 12	07 35				08 05			08 14
Dore & Totley	d	22p54						06 27					07 15		07 19	07 42				08 11			08 21
Grindleford	d	23p01						06 35							07 29								08 29
Hathersage	d	23p05						06 39							07 32								08 32
Bamford	d	23p08						06 43							07 36								08 36
Hope (Derbyshire)	d	23p12						06 47							07 39								08 39
Edale	d	23p19						06 55							07 47								08 47
Chinley	d	23p27						07 03							07 55	08 03				08 32			08 55
Hazel Grove 86	a															08 16							
Stockport 86	a	23p47			05 53	06 53		07 22					07 53			08 24				08 53			
New Mills Central	d		23p30						06 58						08 01								09 01
Strines	d		23p33						07 01						08 04								09 04
Marple	d		23p36						07 04			07 35			08 07				08 35			08 52	09 07
Rose Hill Marple	d										07 30							08 30					
Romiley	d		23p40						07 12		07 35	07 38			08 12			08 35	08 38			08 56	09 11
Woodley	d										07 38							08 38					
Hyde Central	d										07 41							08 41					
Hyde North	d										07 44							08 44					
Guide Bridge	d						06 57			07 28	07 48			07 58			08 28	08 48			08 58		
Fairfield	d										07 51							08 51					
Gorton	d						07 00			07 31				08 01			08 31				09 01		
Bredbury	d		23p43						07 15			07 41			08 15				08 41				09 14
Brinnington	d		23p45						07 17			07 44			08 16				08 44				09 16
Reddish North	d		23p48						07 20			07 47			08 19				08 47				09 19
Ryder Brow	d		23p51						07 24													09 03	
Belle Vue	d		23p52						07 26													09 05	
Ashburys	d		23p55				07 03		07 29	07 34				08 04			08 34				09 04	09 07	
Ardwick	d																						
Manchester Piccadilly 10 ⇌	a	00 02	00 03	04 40	06 05	07 02	07 12	07 34	07 36	07 42	08 02	07 59	08 02	08 12	08 32	08 36	08 42	09 02	08 57	09 02	09 12	09 15	09 32
Manchester Airport 85 ✈	a			05 00	06 29	07 29							08 26							09 26			

		EM	NT	NT	NT	TP	NT	NT	NT	EM	NT	NT	NT	TP	NT	NT	NT	EM	NT	NT	NT	TP	NT
		◇ C	B			◇1 D	B			◇ E	B			◇1 D	B			◇ E	B			◇1 D	B
Sheffield 7 ⇌	d	08 42				09 11			09 14	09 42				10 11			10 14	10 42				11 11	
Dore & Totley	d								09 21								10 21						
Grindleford	d								09 29								10 29						
Hathersage	d								09 32								10 32						
Bamford	d								09 36								10 36						
Hope (Derbyshire)	d								09 39								10 39						
Edale	d								09 47								10 47						
Chinley	d								09 55								10 55						
Hazel Grove 86	a																						
Stockport 86	a	09 25				09 53				10 25				10 53				11 25				11 53	
New Mills Central	d								10 01								11 01						
Strines	d								10 04														
Marple	d				09 35			09 52	10 07				10 35				11 07				11 35		
Rose Hill Marple	d			09 30								10 30				10 51				11 30			
Romiley	d			09 35	09 38			09 56	10 11			10 35	10 38			10 56	11 11			11 35	11 38		
Woodley	d			09 38								10 38								11 38			
Hyde Central	d			09 41								10 41								11 41			
Hyde North	d			09 44								10 44								11 44			
Guide Bridge	d		09 28	09 48			09 58				10 28	10 48			10 58				11 28	11 48			11 58
Fairfield	d			09 51								10 51								11 51			
Gorton	d		09 31				10 01				10 31				11 01				11 31				12 01
Bredbury	d				09 41				10 14				10 41				11 14				11 41		
Brinnington	d				09 44				10 16				10 44				11 16				11 44		
Reddish North	d				09 47				10 19				10 47				11 19				11 47		
Ryder Brow	d							10 03								11 03							
Belle Vue	d							10 05								11 05							
Ashburys	d		09 34				10 04	10 07			10 34				11 04	11 07			11 34				12 04
Ardwick	d																						
Manchester Piccadilly 10 ⇌	a	09 36	09 42	10 02	09 57	10 02	10 12	10 15	10 32	10 36	10 42	11 02	10 57	11 02	11 12	11 15	11 32	11 36	11 42	12 02	11 57	12 02	12 12
Manchester Airport 85 ✈	a					10 26								11 26								12 26	

A From Doncaster
B From Hadfield
C From Nottingham to Liverpool Lime Street
D From Cleethorpes
E From Norwich to Liverpool Lime Street

Sheffield, Chinley, Marple and Romiley Manchester and Manchester Airport

Network Diagram - see first Page of Table 78

		NT	NT	EM	NT	NT	NT	TP	NT	NT	NT	EM	NT	NT	NT	TP	NT	NT	NT	EM	NT	NT
				◇ A	B			◇1 C	B			◇ A	B			◇1 C	B			◇ A	B	
Sheffield 7 ⇌	d		11 14	11 42				12 11			12 14	12 42				13 11			13 14	13 42		
Dore & Totley	d		11 21								12 21								13 21			
Grindleford	d		11 29								12 29								13 29			
Hathersage	d		11 32								12 32								13 32			
Bamford	d		11 36								12 36								13 36			
Hope (Derbyshire)	d		11 39								12 39								13 39			
Edale	d		11 47								12 47								13 47			
Chinley	d		11 55								12 55								13 55			
Hazel Grove 86	a																					
Stockport 86	a			12 25				12 53				13 25				13 53				14 25		
New Mills Central	d		12 01								13 01								14 01			
Strines	d		12 04																14 04			
Marple	d		12 07				12 35				13 07				13 35				14 07			
Rose Hill Marple	d	11 51				12 30				12 51				13 30				13 51				14 30
Romiley	d	11 56	12 11			12 35	12 38			12 56	13 11			13 35	13 38			13 56	14 11			14 35
Woodley	d					12 38								13 38								14 38
Hyde Central	d					12 41								13 41								14 41
Hyde North	d					12 44								13 44								14 44
Guide Bridge	d				12 28	12 48			12 58				13 28	13 48			13 58				14 28	14 48
Fairfield	d					12 51								13 51								14 51
Gorton	d				12 31				13 01				13 31				14 01				14 31	
Bredbury	d		12 14				12 41				13 14				13 41				14 14			
Brinnington	d		12 16				12 44				13 16				13 44				14 16			
Reddish North	d		12 19				12 47				13 19				13 47				14 19			
Ryder Brow	d	12 03								13 03								14 03				
Belle Vue	d	12 05								13 05								14 05				
Ashburys	d	12 07			12 34				13 04	13 07			13 34				14 04	14 07			14 34	
Ardwick	d																					
Manchester Piccadilly 10 ⇌	a	12 15	12 32	12 36	12 42	13 02	12 57	13 02	13 12	13 15	13 32	13 36	13 42	14 02	13 57	14 02	14 12	14 15	14 32	14 36	14 42	15 02
Manchester Airport 85 ✈	a							13 26								14 26						

		NT	TP	NT	NT	NT	EM	NT	NT	NT	TP	NT	NT	NT	EM	NT	NT	NT	TP	NT	NT	NT	EM
			◇1 C	B			◇ A	B			◇1 C	B			◇ A	B			◇1 C	B			◇ A
Sheffield 7 ⇌	d		14 11			14 14	14 42				15 11			15 14	15 42				16 11			16 14	16 42
Dore & Totley	d					14 21								15 21								16 21	
Grindleford	d					14 29								15 29								16 29	
Hathersage	d					14 32								15 32								16 32	
Bamford	d					14 36								15 36								16 36	
Hope (Derbyshire)	d					14 39								15 39								16 39	
Edale	d					14 47								15 47								16 47	
Chinley	d					14 55								15 55								16 55	
Hazel Grove 86	a																						
Stockport 86	a		14 53				15 25				15 53				16 25				16 53				17 25
New Mills Central	d					15 01								16 01								17 01	
Strines	d													16 04									
Marple	d	14 35				15 07				15 35				16 07				16 34				17 07	
Rose Hill Marple	d				14 51				15 30				15 51				16 30				16 51		
Romiley	d	14 38			14 56	15 11			15 35	15 38			15 56	16 11			16 35	16 38			16 56	17 11	
Woodley	d								15 38								16 38						
Hyde Central	d								15 41								16 41						
Hyde North	d								15 44								16 44						
Guide Bridge	d			14 58				15 28	15 48			15 58				16 28	16 48			16 58			
Fairfield	d								15 51								16 51						
Gorton	d			15 01				15 31				16 01				16 31				17 01			
Bredbury	d	14 41				15 14				15 41				16 14				16 41				17 14	
Brinnington	d	14 44				15 16				15 44				16 16				16 43				17 16	
Reddish North	d	14 47				15 19				15 47				16 19				16 46				17 19	
Ryder Brow	d				15 03								16 03								17 03		
Belle Vue	d				15 05								16 05								17 05		
Ashburys	d			15 04	15 07			15 34				16 04	16 07			16 34				17 04	17 07		
Ardwick	d																						
Manchester Piccadilly 10 ⇌	a	14 57	15 02	15 12	15 15	15 32	15 36	15 42	16 02	15 57	16 02	16 12	16 15	16 33	16 36	16 42	17 02	16 56	17 02	17 12	17 15	17 32	17 37
Manchester Airport 85 ✈	a		15 26								16 26								17 32				

A From Norwich to Liverpool Lime Street
B From Hadfield
C From Cleethorpes

Table 78

Sheffield, Chinley, Marple and Romiley Manchester and Manchester Airport

Network Diagram - see first Page of Table 78

	NT	NT	NT	TP	NT	NT	NT	EM	NT	NT	NT	TP	NT	NT	NT	EM	NT	TP	NT	NT	NT
				◇■				◇				◇■				◇		◇■			
	A			B	A			C	A			B	A			C	A	B		A	
Sheffield d				17 11			17 14	17 40				18 11			18 14	18 42		19 11			
Dore & Totley d							17 21								18 21						
Grindleford d							17 29								18 28						
Hathersage d							17 32								18 32						
Bamford d							17 36								18 35						
Hope (Derbyshire) d							17 39								18 39						
Edale d							17 47								18 46						
Chinley d							17 55								18 54						
Hazel Grove 86 a																					
Stockport 86 a				17 53				18 25				18 53				19 25		19 53			
New Mills Central d							18 01								19 01						
Strines d							18 04								19 04						
Marple d			17 34			17 52	18 07				18 35			18 52	19 07						19 56
Rose Hill Marple d		17 30								18 30									19 30		
Romiley d		17 35	17 38			17 56	18 11			18 35	18 38			18 56	19 11				19 35		19 59
Woodley d		17 38								18 38									19 38		
Hyde Central d		17 41								18 41									19 41		
Hyde North d		17 44								18 44									19 44		
Guide Bridge d	17 28	17 48			17 58				18 28	18 48			18 58				19 28		19 48	19 58	
Fairfield d		17 51								18 51									19 51		
Gorton d	17 31				18 01				18 31				19 01				19 31			20 01	
Bredbury d			17 41				18 14				18 41				19 14						20 02
Brinnington d			17 43				18 16				18 44				19 16						20 05
Reddish North d			17 46				18 19				18 47				19 19						20 08
Ryder Brow d						18 03								19 03							20 10
Belle Vue d						18 05								19 05							20 12
Ashburys d	17 34				18 04	18 07			18 34				19 04	19 07			19 34			20 04	20 15
Ardwick d																					
Manchester Piccadilly a	17 42	18 02	17 56	18 02	18 12	18 15	18 32	18 36	18 42	19 02	18 57	19 02	19 12	19 15	19 32	19 36	19 42	20 02	20 02	20 12	20 22
Manchester Airport 85 a				18 26								19 28						20 36			

	NT	EM	TP	NT	NT	EM	NT	NT	NT	NT	NT	NT	NT
		◇	◇■			◇							
		C	B		A	D			A		A		
Sheffield d	19 14	19 42	20 11			20 31		20 35				22 24	
Dore & Totley d	19 21							20 42				22 31	
Grindleford d	19 29							20 50				22 38	
Hathersage d	19 32							20 53				22 41	
Bamford d	19 36							20 57				22 45	
Hope (Derbyshire) d	19 39							21 00				22 48	
Edale d	19 47							21 08				22 56	
Chinley d	19 55							21 16				23 04	
Hazel Grove 86 a													
Stockport 86 a		20 25	20 53			21 20						23 21	
New Mills Central d	20 01			20 30				21 30		22 30			23 30
Strines d				20 33						22 33			23 33
Marple d	20 07			20 36				21 36		22 36			23 36
Rose Hill Marple d							21 12						
Romiley d	20 11			20 40			21 17	21 40		22 40			23 40
Woodley d							21 20						
Hyde Central d							21 23						
Hyde North d							21 26						
Guide Bridge d					20 58		21 30		21 58		22 58		
Fairfield d							21 33						
Gorton d					21 01				22 01		23 01		
Bredbury d	20 14			20 43				21 43		22 43			23 43
Brinnington d	20 16			20 45				21 45		22 45			23 45
Reddish North d	20 19			20 48				21 48		22 48			23 48
Ryder Brow d				20 51				21 51		22 51			23 51
Belle Vue d				20 52				21 52		22 52			23 52
Ashburys d				20 55	21 04			21 55	22 04	22 55	23 04		23 55
Ardwick d													
Manchester Piccadilly a	20 32	20 36	21 02	21 03	21 12	21 32	21 42	22 05	22 12	23 03	23 12	23 43	00 03
Manchester Airport 85 a			21 36										

A From Hadfield
B From Cleethorpes
C From Norwich to Liverpool Lime Street
D From Norwich

Table 78

Sheffield, Chinley, Marple and Romiley Manchester and Manchester Airport

Network Diagram - see first Page of Table 78

	NT	TP	TP	NT	NT	TP	NT	NT	EM	NT	TP	NT	NT	EM	NT	TP	NT	NT	EM	NT	TP	NT
		◇■	◇■			◇■			◇		◇■			◇		◇■			◇		◇■	
			A		B		B		C	B	D	B		C	B	D	B		C	B	D	B
Sheffield d		07 50	09 10	09 20		10 10		10 20	10 41		11 10		11 14	11 38		12 10		12 13	12 41		13 10	
Dore & Totley d				09 27				10 27	10 48				11 21					12 21				
Grindleford d				09 34				10 34					11 29					12 28				
Hathersage d				09 38				10 38					11 32					12 32				
Bamford d				09 41				10 41					11 36					12 35				
Hope (Derbyshire) d				09 45				10 45					11 39					12 39				
Edale d				09 52				10 52					11 47					12 46				
Chinley d				10 00				11 00					11 55					12 54				
Hazel Grove 86 a																						
Stockport 86 a		08 31	09 53			10 53			11 25		11 53			12 25		12 53			13 25		13 53	
New Mills Central d	23p30			10 07				11 07					12 01					13 01				
Strines d	23p33			10 10				11 10					12 04					13 04				
Marple d	23p36			10 13				11 13					12 07					13 07				
Rose Hill Marple d																						
Romiley d	23p40			10 17				11 17					12 11					13 11				
Woodley d																						
Hyde Central d																						
Hyde North d																						
Guide Bridge d					10 28		10 58			11 28		11 58			12 28		12 58			13 28		13 58
Fairfield d																						
Gorton d					10 31		11 01			11 31		12 01			12 31		13 01			13 31		14 01
Bredbury d	23p43			10 20				11 20					12 14					13 14				
Brinnington d	23p45			10 22				11 22					12 16					13 16				
Reddish North d	23p48			10 25				11 25					12 19					13 19				
Ryder Brow d	23p51																					
Belle Vue d	23p52																					
Ashburys d	23p55				10 34		11 04			11 34		12 04			12 34		13 04			13 34		14 04
Ardwick d																						
Manchester Piccadilly a	00 03	08 42	10 04	10 37	10 42	11 06	11 12	11 38	11 37	11 42	12 06	12 12	12 31	12 35	12 42	13 06	13 12	13 31	13 37	13 42	14 06	14 12
Manchester Airport 85 a		09 07									12 27					13 27					14 27	

	NT	EM	NT	TP	NT	EM	NT	TP	NT	NT	EM	NT	TP	NT	NT	EM	NT	TP	NT	NT	EM	NT
		◇		◇■		◇		◇■			◇		◇■			◇		◇■			◇	
		E	B	F	B	E	B	D	B		C	B	D	B		C	B	D	B		E	B
Sheffield d	13 13	13 38		14 11		14 39		15 11		15 14	15 38		16 11		16 15	16 44		17 11		17 14	17 44	
Dore & Totley d	13 20									15 21					16 23					17 21		
Grindleford d	13 28									15 29					16 30					17 29		
Hathersage d	13 31									15 32					16 33					17 32		
Bamford d	13 35									15 36					16 37					17 36		
Hope (Derbyshire) d	13 38									15 39					16 40					17 39		
Edale d	13 46									15 47					16 48					17 47		
Chinley d	13 54									15 55					16 56					17 55		
Hazel Grove 86 a																						
Stockport 86 a		14 25		14 53		15 25		15 53			16 25		16 53			17 28		17 53			18 25	
New Mills Central d	14 00									16 01					17 02					18 01		
Strines d	14 03									16 04					17 05					18 04		
Marple d	14 07									16 07					17 08					18 07		
Rose Hill Marple d																						
Romiley d	14 10									16 11					17 12					18 11		
Woodley d																						
Hyde Central d																						
Hyde North d																						
Guide Bridge d			14 28		14 58		15 28		15 58			16 28		16 58			17 28		17 58			18 28
Fairfield d																						
Gorton d			14 31		15 01		15 31		16 01			16 31		17 01			17 31		18 01			18 31
Bredbury d	14 13									16 14					17 15					18 14		
Brinnington d	14 16									16 16					17 17					18 16		
Reddish North d	14 19									16 19					17 20					18 19		
Ryder Brow d																						
Belle Vue d																						
Ashburys d			14 34		15 04		15 34		16 04			16 34		17 04			17 34		18 04			18 34
Ardwick d																						
Manchester Piccadilly a	14 31	14 37	14 42	15 06	15 12	15 37	15 42	16 06	16 12	16 31	16 37	16 42	17 06	17 12	17 32	17 37	17 42	18 06	18 12	18 31	18 37	18 42
Manchester Airport 85 a				15 28				16 34					17 27					18 27				

A From Meadowhall
B From Hadfield
C From Nottingham to Liverpool Lime Street
D From Cleethorpes
E From Norwich to Liverpool Lime Street
F From Doncaster

Sundays
until 9 September

Sheffield, Chinley, Marple and Romiley Manchester and Manchester Airport

Network Diagram - see first Page of Table 78

		TP ◇■ A	NT B	NT	EM ◇ C	NT B	TP ◇■ A	NT B	NT	EM ◇ D	NT B	TP ◇■ A	NT B	EM ◇ D	TP ◇■ A	NT B	NT	NT
Sheffield ■	d	18 11		18 15	18 37		19 11		19 14	19 35		20 11		20 35	21 11		22 17	
Dore & Totley	d			18 22					19 21								22 24	
Grindleford	d			18 30					19 29								22 32	
Hathersage	d			18 33					19 32								22 35	
Bamford	d			18 37					19 36								22 39	
Hope (Derbyshire)	d			18 40					19 39								22 42	
Edale	d			18 48					19 47								22 50	
Chinley	d			18 56					19 55								22 58	
Hazel Grove 86	a																	
Stockport 86	a	18 53			19 25		19 53			20 25		20 53		21 24	21 53		23 16	
New Mills Central	d			19 02					20 01									23 01
Strines	d			19 05					20 04									23 04
Marple	d			19 08					20 07									23 07
Rose Hill Marple	d																	
Romiley	d			19 12					20 11									23 11
Woodley	d																	
Hyde Central	d																	
Hyde North	d																	
Guide Bridge	d		18 58			19 28		19 58			20 28		20 58			21 58		
Fairfield	d																	
Gorton	d		19 01			19 31		20 01			20 31		21 01			22 01		
Bredbury	d			19 15					20 14									23 14
Brinnington	d			19 17					20 16									23 16
Reddish North	d			19 20					20 19									23 19
Ryder Brow	d																	
Belle Vue	d																	
Ashburys	d		19 04			19 34		20 04			20 34		21 04			22 04		
Ardwick	d																	
Manchester Piccadilly ■	a	19 06	19 12	19 36	19 37	19 42	20 09	20 12	20 32	20 38	20 42	21 06	21 12	21 36	22 06	22 12	23 29	23 31
Manchester Airport 85 ✈	a	19 27					20 30					21 27			22 27			

Sundays
from 16 September

		NT	TP ◇■	TP ◇■ E	NT	NT B	TP ◇■	NT B	EM ◇ F	NT B	TP ◇■ A	NT B	NT	EM ◇ F	NT B	TP ◇■ A	NT B	EM ◇ F	NT B	TP ◇■ A	NT B	NT	EM ◇ F
Sheffield ■	d		07 50	09 10	09 20		10 10		10 41		11 10		11 14	11 38		12 10		12 41		13 10		13 13	13 38
Dore & Totley	d				09 27				10 48				11 21									13 20	
Grindleford	d				09 34								11 29									13 28	
Hathersage	d				09 38								11 32									13 31	
Bamford	d				09 41								11 36									13 35	
Hope (Derbyshire)	d				09 45								11 39									13 38	
Edale	d				09 52								11 47									13 46	
Chinley	d				10 00								11 55									13 54	
Hazel Grove 86	a																						
Stockport 86	a		08 31	09 53					11 25		11 53			12 25		12 50		13 25		13 53			14 25
New Mills Central	d	23p30			10 07								12 01									14 00	
Strines	d	23p33			10 10								12 04									14 03	
Marple	d	23p36			10 13								12 07									14 07	
Rose Hill Marple	d																						
Romiley	d	23p40			10 17								12 11									14 10	
Woodley	d																						
Hyde Central	d																						
Hyde North	d																						
Guide Bridge	d					10 28		10 58		11 28		11 58			12 28		12 58		13 28		13 58		
Fairfield	d																						
Gorton	d					10 31		11 01		11 31		12 01			12 31		13 01		13 31		14 01		
Bredbury	d	23p43			10 20								12 14									14 13	
Brinnington	d	23p45			10 22								12 16									14 16	
Reddish North	d	23p48			10 25								12 19									14 19	
Ryder Brow	d	23p51																					
Belle Vue	d	23p52																					
Ashburys	d	23p55				10 34		11 04		11 34		12 04			12 34		13 04		13 34		14 04		
Ardwick	d																						
Manchester Piccadilly ■	a	00 03	08 42	10 01	10 37	10 42	11 04	11 12	11 37	11 42	12 06	12 12	12 31	12 37	12 42	13 03	13 12	13 37	13 42	14 06	14 12	14 31	14 37
Manchester Airport 85 ✈	a		09 07								12 34					13 27				14 34			

A From Cleethorpes
B From Hadfield
C From Norwich to Liverpool Lime Street
D From Norwich
E From Meadowhall
F From Nottingham to Liverpool Lime Stree

Sundays
from 16 September

Sheffield, Chinley, Marple and Romiley Manchester and Manchester Airport

Network Diagram - see first Page of Table 78

		NT A	TP ◇■ B	NT A	EM ◇ C	NT A	TP ◇■ D	NT A	NT	EM ◇ E	NT A	TP ◇■ D	NT A	EM ◇ E	NT A	TP ◇■ D	NT A	NT	EM ◇ C	NT A	TP ◇■ D	NT A	EM ◇ C
Sheffield ■	d		14 11		14 39		15 11		15 14	15 38		16 11		16 44		17 11		17 14	17 44		18 11		18 37
Dore & Totley	d								15 21									17 21					
Grindleford	d								15 29									17 29					
Hathersage	d								15 32									17 32					
Bamford	d								15 36									17 36					
Hope (Derbyshire)	d								15 39									17 39					
Edale	d								15 47									17 47					
Chinley	d								15 55									17 55					
Hazel Grove 86	a																						
Stockport 86	a		14 53		15 25		15 53			16 25		16 53		17 28		17 53			18 25		18 53		19 25
New Mills Central	d								16 01									18 01					
Strines	d								16 04									18 04					
Marple	d								16 07									18 07					
Rose Hill Marple	d																						
Romiley	d								16 11									18 11					
Woodley	d																						
Hyde Central	d																						
Hyde North	d																						
Guide Bridge	d	14 28		14 58		15 28		15 58			16 28		16 58		17 28		17 58			18 28		18 58	
Fairfield	d																						
Gorton	d	14 31		15 01		15 31		16 01			16 31		17 01		17 31		18 01			18 31		19 01	
Bredbury	d								16 14									18 14					
Brinnington	d								16 16									18 16					
Reddish North	d								16 19									18 19					
Ryder Brow	d																						
Belle Vue	d																						
Ashburys	d	14 34		15 04		15 34		16 04			16 34		17 04		17 34		18 04			18 34		19 04	
Ardwick	d																						
Manchester Piccadilly ■	a	14 42	15 06	15 12	15 37	15 42	16 06	16 12	16 31	16 37	16 42	17 06	17 12	17 37	17 42	18 06	18 12	18 31	18 37	18 42	19 06	19 12	19 37
Manchester Airport 85 ✈	a		15 34				16 34					17 27				18 27					19 27		

		NT A	TP ◇■ D	NT A	NT	EM ◇ F	NT A	TP ◇■ D	NT A	EM ◇ F	TP ◇■ D	NT A	NT	NT
Sheffield ■	d		19 11		19 14	19 35		20 11		20 35	21 11		22 17	
Dore & Totley	d				19 21								22 24	
Grindleford	d				19 29								22 32	
Hathersage	d				19 32								22 35	
Bamford	d				19 36								22 39	
Hope (Derbyshire)	d				19 39								22 42	
Edale	d				19 47								22 50	
Chinley	d				19 55								22 58	
Hazel Grove 86	a													
Stockport 86	a		19 53			20 25		20 53		21 24	21 53		23 16	
New Mills Central	d				20 01									23 01
Strines	d				20 04									23 04
Marple	d				20 07									23 07
Rose Hill Marple	d													
Romiley	d				20 11									23 11
Woodley	d													
Hyde Central	d													
Hyde North	d													
Guide Bridge	d	19 28		19 58			20 28		20 58			21 58		
Fairfield	d													
Gorton	d	19 31		20 01			20 31		21 01			22 01		
Bredbury	d				20 14									23 14
Brinnington	d				20 16									23 16
Reddish North	d				20 19									23 19
Ryder Brow	d													
Belle Vue	d													
Ashburys	d	19 34		20 04			20 34		21 04			22 04		
Ardwick	d													
Manchester Piccadilly ■	a	19 42	20 09	20 12	20 32	20 38	20 42	21 06	21 12	21 36	22 06	22 12	23 29	23 31
Manchester Airport 85 ✈	a		20 30					21 27			22 27			

A From Hadfield
B From Doncaster
C From Norwich to Liverpool Lime Street
D From Cleethorpes
E From Nottingham to Liverpool Lime Street
F From Norwich

Table 79

Manchester - Glossop and Hadfield

Mondays to Fridays
until 28 September

Network Diagram - see first Page of Table 78

Miles	Miles			NT	NT	NT	NT	NT	NT	NT	NT	NT	NT	NT	NT		NT	NT	NT	NT	NT	NT
0	—	**Manchester Picc.** 10 78 ⇌	d	06 16	06 46	07 03	07 18	07 48	08 07	08 29	08 48	09 15	09 48	10 15	10 48	and every 30 minutes until	15 48	16 15	16 36	16 59	17 15	17 37
0½	—	Ardwick 78	d																			
1½	—	Ashburys 78	d	06 20	06 50	07 07	07 22	07 52	08 11	08 33	08 52	09 19	09 52	10 19	10 52		15 52	16 19	16 40	17 03	17 19	17 41
2½	—	Gorton 78	d	06 22	06 52	07 09	07 24	07 54	08 13	08 35	08 54	09 21	09 54	10 21	10 54		15 54	16 21	16 42	17 05	17 21	17 43
4¾	—	Guide Bridge 78	d	06 26	06 56	07 13	07 28	07 58	08 17	08 39	08 58	09 25	09 58	10 25	10 58		15 58	16 25	16 46	17 10	17 25	17 47
6¾	—	Flowery Field	d	06 29	06 59	07 16	07 31	08 01	08 20	08 42	09 01	09 28	10 01	10 28	11 01		16 01	16 28	16 49	17 13	17 28	17 50
7½	—	Newton for Hyde	d	06 31	07 01	07 18	07 33	08 03	08 22	08 44	09 03	09 30	10 03	10 30	11 03		16 03	16 30	16 51	17 15	17 30	17 52
8½	—	Godley	d	06 33	07 03	07 20	07 35	08 05	08 24	08 46	09 05	09 32	10 05	10 32	11 05		16 05	16 32	16 53	17 17	17 32	17 54
9	—	Hattersley	d	06 35	07 05	07 22	07 37	08 07	08 26	08 48	09 07	09 34	10 07	10 34	11 07		16 07	16 34	16 55	17 19	17 34	17 56
10	—	Broadbottom	d	06 37	07 07	07 24	07 39	08 09	08 28	08 50	09 09	09 36	10 09	10 36	11 09		16 09	16 36	16 57	17 21	17 36	17 59
12¼	0	Dinting 3	d	06 45	07 15	07 35	07 45	08 14	08 34	08 56	09 16	09 46	10 16	10 46	11 16		16 16	16 42	17 03	17 27	17 42	18 05
13¼	—	**Glossop**	a	06 48	07 25	07 45	08 03	08 26	08 46	09 06	09 19	09 49	10 19	10 49	11 19		16 19	16 45	17 06	17 31	17 45	18 08
—	—		d	06 51							09 22	09 52	10 22	10 52	11 22		16 22	16 48	17 09	17 33	17 48	18 11
15	0¾	**Hadfield**	a	06 59	07 17	07 37	07 47	08 17	08 38	08 58	09 29	09 59	10 29	10 59	11 29		16 29	16 54	17 15	17 40	17 54	18 17

		NT	NT	NT	NT	NT		NT	NT
Manchester Picc. 10 78 ⇌	d	17 59	18 15	18 48	19 18	19 48	and hourly until	22 48	23 27
Ardwick 78	d								
Ashburys 78	d	18 03	18 19	18 52	19 22	19 52		22 52	23 31
Gorton 78	d	18 05	18 21	18 54	19 24	19 54		22 54	23 33
Guide Bridge 78	d	18 10	18 25	18 58	19 28	19 58		22 58	23 37
Flowery Field	d	18 13	18 28	19 01	19 31	20 01		23 01	23 40
Newton for Hyde	d	18 15	18 30	19 03	19 33	20 03		23 03	23 42
Godley	d	18 17	18 32	19 05	19 35	20 05		23 05	23 44
Hattersley	d	18 19	18 34	19 07	19 37	20 07		23 07	23 46
Broadbottom	d	18 21	18 36	19 09	19 39	20 09		23 09	23 48
Dinting 3	d	18 27	18 42	19 16	19 46	20 16		23 16	23 54
Glossop	a	18 30	18 45	19 19	19 49	20 19		23 19	00 05
	d	18 33	18 48	19 22	19 52	20 22		23 22	
Hadfield	a	18 39	18 54	19 29	19 59	20 29		23 29	23 56

Mondays to Fridays
from 1 October

		NT	NT	NT	NT	NT	NT	NT	NT	NT	NT	NT	NT	NT	NT	NT		NT	NT	NT	NT	NT
Manchester Picc. 10 78 ⇌	d	06 13	06 46	07 03	07 18	07 47	08 07	08 29	08 48	09 15	09 48	10 15	10 48	11 18	11 48	12 18	and every 30 minutes until	15 18	15 48	16 15	16 36	16 59
Ardwick 78	d																					
Ashburys 78	d	06 17		07 07	07 22		08 11		08 52	09 19	09 52	10 19	10 52	11 22	11 52	12 22		15 22	15 52	16 19	16 40	17 03
Gorton 78	d	06 19		07 09	07 24		08 13		08 54	09 21	09 54	10 21	10 54	11 24	11 54	12 24		15 24	15 54	16 21	16 42	17 05
Guide Bridge 78	d	06 23	06 54	07 13	07 28	07 55	08 17	08 37	08 58	09 25	09 58	10 25	10 58	11 28	11 58	12 28		15 28	15 58	16 25	16 46	17 10
Flowery Field	d	06 26	06 57	07 16	07 31	07 58	08 20		09 01	09 28	10 01	10 28	11 01	11 31	12 01	12 31		15 31	16 01	16 28	16 49	17 13
Newton for Hyde	d	06 28	06 59	07 18	07 33	08 00	08 22		09 03	09 30	10 03	10 30	11 03	11 33	12 03	12 33		15 33	16 03	16 30	16 51	17 15
Godley	d	06 30		07 20	07 35	08 02	08 24		09 05	09 32	10 05	10 32	11 05	11 35	12 05	12 35		15 35	16 05	16 32	16 53	17 17
Hattersley	d	06 32	07 02	07 22	07 37	08 04	08 26		09 07	09 34	10 07	10 34	11 07	11 37	12 07	12 37		15 37	16 07	16 34	16 55	17 19
Broadbottom	d	06 34	07 04	07 24	07 39	08 06	08 28		09 09	09 36	10 09	10 36	11 09	11 39	12 09	12 39		15 39	16 09	16 36	16 57	17 21
Dinting 3	d	06 44	07 10	07 30	07 50	08 11	08 34	08 48	09 16	09 46	10 16	10 46	11 16	11 46	12 16	12 46		15 46	16 16	16 42	17 03	17 27
Glossop	a	07 00	07 20	07 40	08 00	08 22	08 44	09 00	09 29	09 59	10 29	10 59	11 29	11 59	12 29	12 49		15 49	16 19	16 45	17 06	17 30
	d															12 54		15 54	16 22	16 48	17 09	17 33
Hadfield	a	06 48	07 12	07 32	07 52	08 14	08 36	08 51	09 19	09 49	10 19	10 49	11 19	11 49	12 19	13 01		16 01	16 29	16 54	17 15	17 39

		NT	NT	NT	NT	NT	NT	NT		NT	NT
Manchester Picc. 10 78 ⇌	d	17 15	17 37	17 59	18 15	18 48	19 18	19 48	and hourly until	22 48	23 27
Ardwick 78	d										
Ashburys 78	d	17 19	17 41	18 03	18 19	18 52	19 22	19 52		22 52	23 31
Gorton 78	d	17 21	17 43	18 05	18 21	18 54	19 24	19 54		22 54	23 33
Guide Bridge 78	d	17 25	17 47	18 10	18 25	18 58	19 28	19 58		22 58	23 37
Flowery Field	d	17 28	17 50	18 13	18 28	19 01	19 31	20 01		23 01	23 40
Newton for Hyde	d	17 30	17 52	18 15	18 30	19 03	19 33	20 03		23 03	23 42
Godley	d	17 32	17 54	18 17	18 32	19 05	19 35	20 05		23 05	23 44
Hattersley	d	17 34	17 56	18 19	18 34	19 07	19 37	20 07		23 07	23 46
Broadbottom	d	17 36	17 58	18 21	18 36	19 09	19 39	20 09		23 09	23 48
Dinting 3	d	17 42	18 05	18 28	18 42	19 16	19 46	20 16		23 16	23 54
Glossop	a	17 45	18 08	18 31	18 45	19 19	19 49	20 19		23 19	00 05
	d	17 48	18 11	18 34	18 48	19 22	19 52	20 22		23 22	
Hadfield	a	17 54	18 18	18 40	18 54	19 29	19 59	20 29		23 29	23 56

Saturdays

		NT	NT	NT	NT	NT	NT		NT	NT		NT	NT
Manchester Picc. 10 78 ⇌	d	06 16	06 48	07 18	07 48	08 15	08 48	and every 30 minutes until	18 48	19 48	and hourly until	22 48	23 27
Ardwick 78	d												
Ashburys 78	d	06 20	06 52	07 22	07 52	08 19	08 52		18 52	19 52		22 52	23 31
Gorton 78	d	06 22	06 54	07 24	07 54	08 21	08 54		18 54	19 54		22 54	23 33
Guide Bridge 78	d	06 26	06 58	07 28	07 58	08 25	08 58		18 58	19 58		22 58	23 37
Flowery Field	d	06 29	07 01	07 31	08 01	08 28	09 01		19 01	20 01		23 01	23 40
Newton for Hyde	d	06 31	07 03	07 33	08 03	08 30	09 03		19 03	20 03		23 03	23 42
Godley	d	06 33	07 05	07 35	08 05	08 32	09 05		19 05	20 05		23 05	23 44
Hattersley	d	06 35	07 07	07 37	08 07	08 34	09 07		19 07	20 07		23 07	23 46
Broadbottom	d	06 37	07 09	07 39	08 09	08 36	09 09		19 09	20 09		23 09	23 48
Dinting 3	d	06 45	07 16	07 46	08 16	08 46	09 16		19 16	20 16		23 16	23 54
Glossop	a	06 48	07 19	07 49	08 19	08 49	09 19		19 19	20 19		23 19	
	d	06 51	07 22	07 52	08 22	08 52	09 22		19 22	20 22		23 22	
Hadfield	a	06 59	07 29	07 59	08 29	08 59	09 29		19 29	20 29		23 29	23 56

Table 79

Manchester - Glossop and Hadfield

Sundays
until 9 September

Network Diagram - see first Page of Table 78

		NT		NT	NT
Manchester Picc. 10 78 ⇌	d	09 18	and every 30 minutes until	19 48	20 48
Ardwick 78	d				
Ashburys 78	d	09 22		19 52	20 52
Gorton 78	d	09 24		19 54	20 54
Guide Bridge 78	d	09 28		19 58	20 58
Flowery Field	d	09 31		20 01	21 01
Newton for Hyde	d	09 33		20 03	21 03
Godley	d	09 35		20 05	21 05
Hattersley	d	09 37		20 07	21 07
Broadbottom	d	09 39		20 09	21 09
Dinting 3	d	09 46		20 16	21 16
Glossop	a	09 49		20 19	21 19
	d	09 52		20 22	21 22
Hadfield	a	09 58		20 28	21 28

Sundays
from 16 September

		NT	NT	NT		NT	NT
Manchester Picc. 10 78 ⇌	d	09 18	09 30	10 18	and every 30 minutes until	19 48	20 48
Ardwick 78	d						
Ashburys 78	d	09 22	09 34	10 22		19 52	20 52
Gorton 78	d	09 24	09 36	10 24		19 54	20 54
Guide Bridge 78	d	09 28	09 58	10 28		19 58	20 58
Flowery Field	d	09 31	10 01	10 31		20 01	21 01
Newton for Hyde	d	09 33	10 03	10 33		20 03	21 03
Godley	d	09 35	10 05	10 35		20 05	21 05
Hattersley	d	09 37	10 07	10 37		20 07	21 07
Broadbottom	d	09 39	10 09	10 39		20 09	21 09
Dinting 3	d	09 46	10 16	10 46		20 16	21 16
Glossop	a	09 49	10 19	10 49		20 19	21 19
	d	09 52	10 22	10 52		20 22	21 22
Hadfield	a	09 58	10 28	10 58		20 28	21 28

Hadfield and Glossop - Manchester

Mondays to Fridays

until 28 September

Network Diagram - see first Page of Table 78

Miles	Miles			NT MX	NT	NT	NT	NT	NT	NT	NT	NT	NT		NT	NT	NT	NT	NT	NT	NT	NT
0	0	**Hadfield**	d	23p59	06 00	06 30	07 00	07 20	07 40	07 58	08 21	08 41	09 01		16 01	16 31	16 57	17 22	17 44	17 59	18 28	18 43
1¼	—	**Glossop**	a	00 05	06 05	06 35	07 05	07 25	07 45	08 03	08 26	08 46	09 06		16 06							
—	—		d		06 08	06 38	07 08	07 28	07 48	08 06	08 29	08 49	09 09		16 09							
2¼	0¾	Dinting 3	d		06 11	06 41	07 11	07 31	07 51	08 09	08 32	08 52	09 12		16 12	16 33	16 59	17 24	17 46	18 01	18 30	18 45
5	—	Broadbottom	d		06 15	06 45	07 15	07 35	07 56	08 13	08 37	08 57	09 16	and	16 16	16 37	17 03	17 28	17 50	18 05	18 34	18 49
6	—	Hattersley	d		06 18	06 48	07 18	07 38	07 59	08 16	08 40	08 59	09 19	every 30	16 19	16 40	17 06	17 31		18 08	18 37	18 52
6½	—	Godley	d		06 20	06 50	07 20	07 40	08 01	08 18	08 42	09 02	09 21	minutes	16 21	16 42	17 08	17 33		18 10	18 39	18 54
7½	—	Newton for Hyde	d		06 22	06 52	07 22	07 42	08 03	08 21	08 44	09 04	09 23	until	16 23	16 44	17 10	17 36	17 54	18 12	18 41	18 56
8¼	—	Flowery Field	d		06 24	06 54	07 24	07 44	08 06	08 23	08 46	09 07	09 25		16 25	16 46	17 12	17 38		18 14	18 43	18 58
10¼	—	Guide Bridge 78	a		06 27	06 57	07 27	07 47	08 10	08 26	08 49	09 11	09 28		16 28	16 49	17 15	17 42	17 58	18 17	18 46	19 01
12½	—	Gorton 78	a		06 30	07 00	07 30	07 50	08 13	08 30	08 52	09 15	09 31		16 31	16 52	17 18	17 45	18 01	18 20	18 49	19 04
13½	—	Ashburys 78	a		06 33	07 06	07 33	07 53	08 16	08 34	08 56	09 18	09 34		16 34	16 55	17 24	17 48	18 04	18 23	18 54	19 08
14½	—	Ardwick 78	a				07 35															
15	—	**Manchester Picc.** 10 78	a		06 42	07 15	07 43	08 03	08 25	08 43	09 04	09 27	09 42		16 42	17 05	17 33	17 57	18 12	18 34	19 03	19 15

		NT		NT	NT	NT	NT
Hadfield	d	19 01		20 31	21 31	22 31	23 59
Glossop	a	19 06		20 36	21 36	22 36	00 05
	d	19 09		20 39	21 39	22 39	
Dinting 3	d	19 12		20 42	21 42	22 42	
Broadbottom	d	19 16	and	20 46	21 46	22 46	
Hattersley	d	19 19	every 30	20 49	21 49	22 49	
Godley	d	19 21	minutes	20 51	21 51	22 51	
Newton for Hyde	d	19 23	until	20 53	21 53	22 53	
Flowery Field	d	19 25		20 55	21 55	22 55	
Guide Bridge 78	a	19 28		20 58	21 58	22 58	
Gorton 78	a	19 31		21 01	22 01	23 01	
Ashburys 78	a	19 34		21 04	22 04	23 04	
Ardwick 78	a						
Manchester Picc. 10 78	a	19 42		21 12	22 12	23 12	

Mondays to Fridays

from 1 October

		NT MX	NT	NT	NT	NT	NT	NT	NT	NT	NT	NT		NT	NT		NT	NT	NT	NT	NT
Hadfield	d	23p59	05 55	06 25	06 55	07 15	07 35	07 55	08 17	08 39	08 55	09 24		12 24	13 05		16 05	16 31	16 57	17 18	17 44
Glossop	a	00 05	06 00	06 30	07 00	07 20	07 40	08 00	08 22	08 44	09 00	09 29		12 29							
	d		06 03	06 33	07 03	07 23	07 43	08 03	08 25	08 50	09 03	09 34		12 34							
Dinting 3	d		06 06	06 36	07 06	07 26	07 46	08 06	08 28	08 54	09 07	09 37	and	12 37	13 07	and	16 07	16 33	16 59	17 20	17 46
Broadbottom	d		06 10	06 40	07 10	07 30	07 51	08 10	08 32	08 58	09 11	09 41	every 30	12 41	13 11	every 30	16 11	16 37	17 03	17 24	17 50
Hattersley	d		06 13	06 43	07 13	07 33	07 54	08 13	08 35	09 00	09 14	09 44	minutes	12 44	13 14	minutes	16 14	16 40	17 06	17 27	
Godley	d		06 15	06 45	07 15	07 35	07 56	08 15	08 37	09 02	09 16	09 46	until	12 46	13 16	until	16 16	16 42	17 08	17 29	
Newton for Hyde	d		06 17	06 47	07 17	07 37	07 58	08 18	08 39	09 04	09 19	09 48		12 48	13 18		16 18	16 44	17 10	17 32	17 54
Flowery Field	d		06 19	06 49	07 20	07 39	08 01	08 20	08 41	09 06	09 21	09 50		12 50	13 20		16 20	16 46	17 12	17 34	
Guide Bridge 78	a		06 27	06 57	07 28	07 47	08 10	08 26	08 49	09 11	09 28	09 58		12 58	13 28		16 28	16 49	17 17	17 42	18 00
Gorton 78	a		06 30	07 00	07 30	07 50	08 13	08 30	08 52	09 15	09 31	10 01		13 01	13 31		16 31	16 52	17 20	17 45	
Ashburys 78	a		06 33	07 06	07 34	07 53	08 16	08 34	08 56	09 18	09 34	10 04		13 04	13 34		16 34	16 55	17 24	17 48	
Ardwick 78	a				07 36																
Manchester Picc. 10 78	a		06 42	07 15	07 44	08 03	08 25	08 43	09 04	09 27	09 42	10 11		13 11	13 41		16 41	17 05	17 33	17 57	18 12

		NT	NT	NT	NT		NT	NT	NT	NT
Hadfield	d	17 56	18 22	18 43	19 01		20 31	21 31	22 31	23 59
Glossop	a				19 06		20 36	21 36	22 36	00 05
	d				19 09		20 39	21 39	22 39	
Dinting 3	d	17 59	18 24	18 45	19 12		20 42	21 42	22 42	
Broadbottom	d	18 03	18 28	18 49	19 16	and	20 46	21 46	22 46	
Hattersley	d	18 05	18 31	18 52	19 19	every 30	20 49	21 49	22 49	
Godley	d	18 07	18 33	18 54	19 21	minutes	20 51	21 51	22 51	
Newton for Hyde	d	18 09	18 35	18 56	19 23	until	20 53	21 53	22 53	
Flowery Field	d	18 11	18 37	18 58	19 25		20 55	21 55	22 55	
Guide Bridge 78	a	18 17	18 46	19 01	19 28		20 58	21 58	22 58	
Gorton 78	a	18 20	18 49	19 04	19 31		21 01	22 01	23 01	
Ashburys 78	a	18 23	18 54	19 08	19 34		21 04	22 04	23 04	
Ardwick 78	a									
Manchester Picc. 10 78	a	18 34	19 03	19 15	19 42		21 12	22 12	23 12	

Saturdays

		NT	NT	NT		NT	NT	NT	NT	NT
Hadfield	d	23p59	06 30	07 01		19 31	20 31	21 31	22 31	23 59
Glossop	a	00 05	06 35	07 06		19 36	20 36	21 36	22 36	00 05
	d		06 38	07 09		19 39	20 39	21 39	22 39	
Dinting 3	d		06 41	07 12		19 42	20 42	21 42	22 42	
Broadbottom	d		06 45	07 16	and	19 46	20 46	21 46	22 46	
Hattersley	d		06 48	07 19	every 30	19 49	20 49	21 49	22 49	
Godley	d		06 50	07 21	minutes	19 51	20 51	21 51	22 51	
Newton for Hyde	d		06 52	07 23	until	19 53	20 53	21 53	22 53	
Flowery Field	d		06 54	07 25		19 55	20 55	21 55	22 55	
Guide Bridge 78	a		06 57	07 28		19 58	20 58	21 58	22 58	
Gorton 78	a		07 00	07 31		20 01	21 01	22 01	23 01	
Ashburys 78	a		07 03	07 34		20 04	21 04	22 04	23 04	
Ardwick 78	a									
Manchester Picc. 10 78	a		07 12	07 42		20 12	21 12	22 12	23 12	

Hadfield and Glossop - Manchester

Sundays

until 9 September

Network Diagram - see first Page of Table 78

		NT	NT		NT	NT
Hadfield	d	23p59	10 01		20 31	21 31
Glossop	a	00 05	10 06		20 36	21 36
	d		10 09		20 39	21 39
Dinting 3	d		10 12		20 42	21 42
Broadbottom	d		10 16	and	20 46	21 46
Hattersley	d		10 19	every 30	20 49	21 49
Godley	d		10 21	minutes	20 51	21 51
Newton for Hyde	d		10 23	until	20 53	21 53
Flowery Field	d		10 25		20 55	21 55
Guide Bridge 78	a		10 28		20 58	21 58
Gorton 78	a		10 31		21 01	22 01
Ashburys 78	a		10 34		21 04	22 04
Ardwick 78	a					
Manchester Picc. 10 78	a		10 42		21 12	22 12

Sundays

from 16 September

		NT	NT		NT	NT
Hadfield	d	23p59	10 01		20 31	21 31
Glossop	a	00 05	10 06		20 36	21 36
	d		10 09		20 39	21 39
Dinting 3	d		10 12		20 42	21 42
Broadbottom	d		10 16	and	20 46	21 46
Hattersley	d		10 19	every 30	20 49	21 49
Godley	d		10 21	minutes	20 51	21 51
Newton for Hyde	d		10 23	until	20 53	21 53
Flowery Field	d		10 25		20 55	21 55
Guide Bridge 78	a		10 28		20 58	21 58
Gorton 78	a		10 31		21 01	22 01
Ashburys 78	a		10 34		21 04	22 04
Ardwick 78	a					
Manchester Picc. 10 78	a		10 42		21 12	22 12

Network Diagram for Tables 81, 102

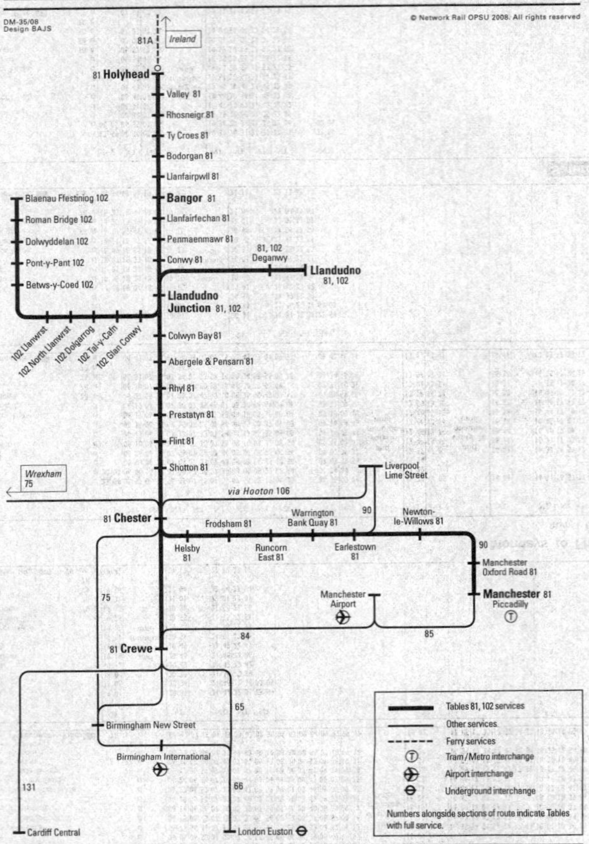

Crewe and Manchester - Chester and North Wales

Network Diagram - see first Page of Table 81

Miles	Miles		AW	AW	AW	AW	AW	AW	AW	AW	AW	NT	AW	AW	AW	NT	AW	AW	AW	VT	AW		AW	NT
			MX	MX	MO	MO		MX	MO	MX	MO		MO	MX	MO	MX								
				◇	◇ A	A	◇ B	◇ C	◇ A		A		A	◇	◇ A					◇■	◇		◇	
—	—	London Euston ⊖65 d																						
—	—	Birmingham New Street 65 d					22p55	22p55	22p32											05 30				
—	—	Manchester Airport 84,85 ✈ d																			05 33			
—	—	Cardiff Central 131 d		19p34										20p53	21p04									
0	—	**Crewe** d			22p29	23p38	23p57	23p57	00 01					00 02	00 10					06 23			06 54	
—	0	**Manchester Pic'dilly** 90 d									22p14		23p20			23p17					05 50			06 18
—	0½	**Manchester Oxford Road** 90 d									22p19										05 53			
—	16¼	Newton-le-Willows 90 d									22p49										06 12			
—	18	Earlestown 90 d									22p59										06 15			
—	22	Warrington Bank Quay 90 d								23p55	23p24	05 49									06 26			
—	27	Runcorn East d								00 02	23p44										06 33			
—	30¼	Frodsham d								00 06	23p59										06 37			
—	32¾	Helsby d								00 10	00 04	06 03									06 41			
—	—	Liverpool Lime Street 106 d																						
21	40¼	**Chester** a		22p34	22p52	00 01	00 18	00 19	00 22	00 22	00 24		00 25	00 27	00 33	00 40				06 43	06 53		07 14	07 45
—	—	d	22p04	22p56	23p00		00 40	00 40	00 38											06 44	06 55		07 23	
29	—	Shotton d	22p13	23p05	23p09																07 04			
33½	—	Flint d	22p19	23p11	23p15		00 53	00 53	00 51											06 57	07 10		07 36	
47½	—	Prestatyn d	22p32	23p24	23p28		01 06	01 06	01 04											07 10	07 23		07 49	
51	—	Rhyl d	22p38	23p30	23p34		01 12	01 12	01 10											07 16	07 29		07 55	
55¼	—	Abergele & Pensarn d	22p44	23p36																	07 35			
61½	—	Colwyn Bay d	22p52	23p44	23p45		01 23	01 23	01 21											07 26	07 43		08 06	
65½	0	**Llandudno Junction** a	22p57	23p49	23p50		01 28	01 28	01 27											07 32	07 48		08 11	
—	—	d	22p59	23p52	23p51		01 29	01 29	01 28								06 13	06 51	07 31	07 33	07 50		08 12	
—	1¼	Deganwy d															06x16	06x54	07x34		07x54			
—	3	**Llandudno** a															06 23	07 01	07 41		08 06			
66½	—	Conwy d	23b01	23b54	23b53																		08x14	
70¾	—	Penmaenmawr d	23b07	23b59	00x01																		08x20	
73¾	—	Llanfairfechan d	23b11	00x04	00x03																		08x24	
80¾	—	**Bangor (Gwynedd)** a	23p19	00 12	00 11		01 45	01 45	01 44											07 49			08 32	
—	—	d	23p21	00 14	00 14		01 45	01 45	01 44											07 49			08 37	
84½	—	Llanfairpwll d	23b27																				08x43	
93½	—	Bodorgan d	23b37																				08x53	
96¼	—	Ty Croes d	23b42																				08x57	
98	—	Rhosneigr d	23b45																				09x00	
102	—	Valley d	23b50																				09x06	
105½	—	**Holyhead** a	00 05	00 48	00 49		02 15	02 15	02 20											08 23			09 20	

	AW	AW	AW	AW	NT	AW	AW		AW	VT	AW	AW	NT	AW	AW	AW	VT		AW	NT	AW	AW	AW	VT
			◇	◇					◇	◇■	◇ D	◇ E				◇	◇■		◇				◇	◇■
London Euston ⊖65 d										07 10							08 10							09 10
Birmingham New Street 65 d												07 24												
Manchester Airport 84,85 ✈ d																								
Cardiff Central 131 d				05 10															07 21					
Crewe d	07 23					08 23				08 49				09 23			09 49				10 23			10 49
Manchester Pic'dilly 90 d			06 50		07 17				07 50				08 17			08 50				09 17			09 50	
Manchester Oxford Road 90 d			06 53						07 53							08 53							09 53	
Newton-le-Willows 90 d			07 12						08 12							09 12							10 12	
Earlestown 90 d			07 15						08 15							09 15							10 15	
Warrington Bank Quay 90 d			07 22						08 24							09 26							10 26	
Runcorn East d			07 29						08 31							09 33							10 33	
Frodsham d			07 34						08 36							09 37							10 37	
Helsby d			07 38						08 41							09 41							10 41	
Liverpool Lime Street 106 d																								
Chester a	07 46		07 50	08 19	08 45	08 46			08 53	09 12		09 17	09 45	09 46		09 53	10 09		10 19	10 45	10 46		10 53	11 09
d			07 55	08 22					08 55			09 23				09 55	10 16		10 24				10 55	11 16
Shotton d			08 04						09 04							10 04							11 04	
Flint d			08 10	08 36					09 10			09 36				10 10	10 29		10 39				11 10	
Prestatyn d			08 23	08 49					09 23			09 49				10 23	10 42		10 52				11 23	
Rhyl d			08 29	08 55					09 29			09 55				10 29	10 48		10 58				11 29	11 43
Abergele & Pensarn d			08 35						09 35							10 35							11 35	
Colwyn Bay d			08 43	09 06					09 43			10 06				10 43	10 59		11 09				11 43	11 54
Llandudno Junction a			08 48	09 11					09 48			10 11				10 48	11 04		11 14				11 48	12 00
d		08 28	08 50	09 12			09 28		09 50		10 03	10 12			10 28	10 50	11 06		11 15			11 26	11 50	12 01
Deganwy d		08x31	08x54				09x31		09x54		10x06				10x31	10x54						11x29	11x54	
Llandudno a		08 38	09 06				09 38		10 06		10 13				10 38	11 06						11 36	12 06	
Conwy d				09x14															11x17					
Penmaenmawr d				09x20															11x23					
Llanfairfechan d				09x24															11x27					
Bangor (Gwynedd) a				09 32								10 28					11 27		11 37					12 16
d				09 35								10 29							11 40					12 17
Llanfairpwll d												10x35												
Bodorgan d				09x49																				
Ty Croes d				09x53																				
Rhosneigr d				09x56																				
Valley d												10x53												
Holyhead a				10 14								11 07							12 14					12 50

A from 21 May until 25 June
B from 26 June until 29 June
C until 22 June
D From Blaenau Ffestiniog
E From Birmingham International
b Previous night, stops on request

Crewe and Manchester - Chester and North Wales

Network Diagram - see first Page of Table 81

	AW	NT	AW		AW	AW	VT	AW	AW	NT	AW	AW	AW		VT	AW	NT	AW	AW	AW	VT	AW	NT	
	◇ A 🛒					◇ 🛒	◇1 ⊠	◇ B	◇ 🛒				◇ 🛒		◇1 ☕	◇ A 🛒				◇ 🛒	◇1 ☕	◇ 🛒		
London Euston [15] ⊖65 d							10 10								11 10						12 10			
Birmingham New Street [12] 65 d	09 24															11 24								
Manchester Airport 84,85 ✈ d																								
Cardiff Central [7] 131 d									09 21													11 21		
Crewe [10] d			11 23				11 49				12 23				12 49			13 23			13 49			
Manchester Pic'dilly [10] 90 ⇌ d		10 17				10 50				11 17			11 50				12 17			12 50			13 17	
Manchester Oxford Road 90 d						10 53							11 53							12 53				
Newton-le-Willows 90 d						11 12							12 12							13 12				
Earlestown [8] 90 d						11 15							12 15							13 15				
Warrington Bank Quay 90 d						11 26							12 26							13 26				
Runcorn East d						11 33							12 33							13 33				
Frodsham d						11 37							12 37							13 37				
Helsby d						11 41							12 41							13 41				
Liverpool Lime Street [10] 106 d																								
Chester a	11 19	11 43	11 46			11 53	12 12		12 19	12 45	12 46		12 53		13 12	13 19	13 45	13 46		13 53	14 12	14 19	14 45	
d	11 22					11 55			12 23				12 55			13 24				13 55		14 23		
Shotton d						12 04							13 04							14 04				
Flint d	11 38					12 10			12 36				13 10			13 37				14 10		14 36		
Prestatyn d	11 51					12 23			12 49				13 23			13 50				14 23		14 49		
Rhyl d	11 57					12 29			12 55				13 29			13 56				14 29		14 55		
Abergele & Pensarn d						12 35							13 35							14 35				
Colwyn Bay d	12 08					12 43			13 06				13 43			14 07				14 43		15 06		
Llandudno Junction a	12 13					12 48			13 11				13 48			14 12				14 48		15 11		
d	12 14				12 28	12 50		13 03	13 12			13 28	13 50			14 13			14 28	14 50		15 12		
Deganwy d					12x31	12x54		13x06				13x31	13x54						14x31	14x54				
Llandudno a					12 38	13 06		13 13				13 38	14 06						14 38	15 06				
Conwy d	12x16															14x15								
Penmaenmawr d	12x22															14x21								
Llanfairfechan d	12x26															14x25								
Bangor (Gwynedd) a	12 34								13 28							14 33						15 28		
d	12 37								13 29							14 36						15 30		
Llanfairpwll d	12x43								13x36													15x38		
Bodorgan d	12x53								13x46													15x48		
Ty Croes d	12x57								13x50													15x52		
Rhosneigr d	13x00								13x53													15x55		
Valley d	13x06								13x58													16x01		
Holyhead a	13 18								14 13							15 08						16 15		

	AW	AW	VT	AW	AW	NT	AW	AW	VT		AW	NT	AW	AW	VT	AW	NT	AW	AW		AW	AW	VT	AW
		◇ 🛒	◇1 ☕	◇ B	◇ A 🛒			◇ 🛒	◇1 ☕		◇ 🛒			◇ 🛒	◇1 ☕	◇ A 🛒					◇ B	◇ 🛒	◇1 ☕	[2] 🛒
London Euston [15] ⊖65 d			13 10						14 10						15 10								16 10	
Birmingham New Street [12] 65 d					13 24											15 26								
Manchester Airport 84,85 ✈ d																								
Cardiff Central [7] 131 d											13 21													15 21
Crewe [10] d	14 23		14 49				15 23		15 49				16 23		16 49			17 23					17 49	
Manchester Pic'dilly [10] 90 ⇌ d		13 50				14 17		14 50				15 17		15 50			16 17					16 50		
Manchester Oxford Road 90 d		13 53						14 53						15 53								16 53		
Newton-le-Willows 90 d		14 12						15 12						16 12								17 12		
Earlestown [8] 90 d		14 15						15 15						16 15								17 15		
Warrington Bank Quay 90 d		14 26						15 26						16 26								17 26		
Runcorn East d		14 33						15 33						16 33								17 33		
Frodsham d		14 37						15 37						16 37								17 37		
Helsby d		14 41						15 41						16 41								17 41		
Liverpool Lime Street [10] 106 d																								
Chester a	14 46	14 53	15 12		15 20	15 45	15 46	15 53	16 12		16 20	16 45	16 46	16 54	17 12	17 22	17 45	17 46				17 53	18 08	18 20
d		14 55			15 22			15 55			16 25			16 55		17 27						17 55	18 10	18 24
Shotton d		15 04						16 04						17 04		17 36						18 04		
Flint d		15 10			15 37			16 10			16 38			17 10		17 42						18 10	18 23	18 37
Prestatyn d		15 23			15 50			16 23			16 51			17 23		17 55						18 23	18 36	18 50
Rhyl d		15 29			15 56			16 29			16 57			17 29		18 01						18 29	18 42	18 56
Abergele & Pensarn d		15 35						16 35						17 35		18 07						18 35		
Colwyn Bay d		15 43			16 07			16 43			17 08			17 43		18 15						18 43	18 53	19 07
Llandudno Junction a		15 48			16 12			16 48			17 13			17 49		18 20						18 48	18 58	19 12
d		15 50		16 04	16 14			16 50			17 13			17 50		18 22			18 26		18 41	18 50	19 00	19 13
Deganwy d		15x54		16x07				16x54						17x54					18x29		18x44	18x54		
Llandudno a		16 06		16 17				17 06						18 06					18 36		18 54	19 06		
Conwy d					16x16						17x15					18x24								
Penmaenmawr d					16x22						17x21					18x30								
Llanfairfechan d					16x26						17x25					18x34								
Bangor (Gwynedd) a					16 34						17 33					18 42							19 21	19 33
d					16 36						17 36					18 44								19 35
Llanfairpwll d											17x42													19x41
Bodorgan d											17x52													19x51
Ty Croes d											17x56													19x55
Rhosneigr d											17x59													19x58
Valley d											18x05													20x04
Holyhead a					17 11						18 19					19 16								20 18

A From Birmingham International

B From Blaenau Ffestiniog

Table 81

Mondays to Fridays

until 29 June

Crewe and Manchester - Chester and North Wales

Network Diagram - see first Page of Table 81

	AW	NT	AW	AW	AW		AW	VT	VT	AW	NT	AW	AW	VT	AW		VT	AW	NT	AW	AW	AW	AW	VT
	🛒				◇ 🛒		[2] 1 ⊠	◇1 ⊠	◇1 ⊠	◇ A 🛒			🛒	◇1 B ⊠			◇1 ⊠	[2] 🛒				◇ C	[2] 🛒	[2] 1 ☕
London Euston [15] ⊖65 d								17 10	17 10					18 10			18 10							19 10
Birmingham New Street [12] 65 d										17 26														
Manchester Airport 84,85 ✈ d																								
Cardiff Central [7] 131 d							16 15											17 21					18 18	
Crewe [10] d			18 23				18 43	18 56	18 56			19 23		19 56			19 56			20 23				20 50
Manchester Pic'dilly [10] 90 ⇌ d	17 19	17 09			17 50						18 17		18 50						19 17		19 50			
Manchester Oxford Road 90 d	17 22				17 53								18 53								19 53			
Newton-le-Willows 90 d	17 40				18 12								19 12								20 12			
Earlestown [8] 90 d	17 44				18 15								19 16								20 15			
Warrington Bank Quay 90 d	17 53				18 24								19 26								20 26			
Runcorn East d	18 00				18 31								19 33								20 33			
Frodsham d	18 05				18 36								19 37								20 37			
Helsby d	18 09				18 40								19 41								20 41			
Liverpool Lime Street [10] 106 d																								
Chester a	18 23	18 32	18 46		18 53		19 06	19 15	19 15	19 20	19 45	19 46	19 53	20 15			20 15	20 20	20 45	20 46	20 53		20 58	21 10
d					18 55		19 07		19 21	19 32							20 26	20 32					21 03	
Shotton d					19 04					19 41								20 41						
Flint d					19 10		19 21		19 35	19 47								20 47						
Prestatyn d					19 23				19 48	20 00								21 02						
Rhyl d					19 29		19 39		19 54	20 06							20 53	21 08					21 30	
Abergele & Pensarn d					19 35					20 12														
Colwyn Bay d					19 43				20 05	20 20							21 04	21 18					21 41	
Llandudno Junction a					19 48		19 52		20 10	20 25							21 09	21 24					21 46	
d				19 28	19 50		19 53		20 12	20 27					20 30		21 10	21 26				21 32	21 49	
Deganwy d				19x31	19x54										20x33							21x35		
Llandudno a				19 38	20 06										20 40							21 46		
Conwy d										20x29														
Penmaenmawr d										20x35														
Llanfairfechan d										20x39														
Bangor (Gwynedd) a							20 09		20 27	20 47							21 25	21 41					22 04	
d							20 11		20 28	20 49							21 27	21 43					22 06	
Llanfairpwll d										20x55								21x49						
Bodorgan d										21x05								21x59						
Ty Croes d										21x10								22x03						
Rhosneigr d										21x13								22x06						
Valley d										21x18								22x12						
Holyhead a							20 49		20 59	21 31							21 59	22 25					22 36	

	VT		AW	AW	NT	AW	AW	VT	AW	AW	NT		AW	AW	AW	AW FO	AW FX	AW	NT	AW FX	AW FO		AW FO	AW FX
	[2] 1 ☕		◇ A 🛒					◇1 ☕		◇					◇ D								◇ E	◇ F
London Euston [15] ⊖65 d	19 10							20 10																
Birmingham New Street [12] 65 d			19 24												21 24								22 55	22 55
Manchester Airport 84,85 ✈ d						20 32								21 32										
Cardiff Central [7] 131 d										19 34														
Crewe [10] d	20 50			21 00			21 36	21 50					22 23					23 23					23 57	23 57
Manchester Pic'dilly [10] 90 ⇌ d					20 17	20 50					21 17			21 50		22 12			22 17	22 45	23 14			
Manchester Oxford Road 90 d						20 53								21 53		22 29					23 17			
Newton-le-Willows 90 d						21 12								22 12		22 47					23 36			
Earlestown [8] 90 d						21 15								22 15		22 50					23 39			
Warrington Bank Quay 90 d						21 24								22 24		22 59	22 59				23 48			
Runcorn East d						21 33								22 31		23 06	23 06				23 55			
Frodsham d						21 37								22 35		23 10	23 10				23 59			
Helsby d						21 41								22 39		23 14	23 14				00 03			
Liverpool Lime Street [10] 106 d																								
Chester a	21 10		21 19	21 23	21 45	21 55	21 59	22 15		22 34	22 45		22 45	22 51	23 19	23 26	23 26	23 44	23 45	23 49	00 15		00 18	00 19
d	21 17								22 04	22 56													00 40	00 40
Shotton d									22 13	23 05														
Flint d	21 30								22 19	23 11													00 53	00 53
Prestatyn d	21 43								22 32	23 24													01 06	01 06
Rhyl d	21 50								22 38	23 30													01 12	01 12
Abergele & Pensarn d									22 44	23 36														
Colwyn Bay d	22 01								22 52	23 44													01 23	01 23
Llandudno Junction a	22 06								22 57	23 49													01 28	01 28
d	22 07								22 59	23 52													01 29	01 29
Deganwy d																								
Llandudno a																								
Conwy d									23x01	23x54														
Penmaenmawr d									23x07	23x59														
Llanfairfechan d									23x11	00x04														
Bangor (Gwynedd) a	22 22								23 19	00 12													01 45	01 45
d	22 24								23 21	00 14													01 45	01 45
Llanfairpwll d									23x27															
Bodorgan d									23x37															
Ty Croes d									23x42															
Rhosneigr d									23x45															
Valley d									23x50															
Holyhead a	22 56								00 05	00 48													02 15	02 15

A From Birmingham International

B To Wrexham General

C From Blaenau Ffestiniog

D From Birmingham International to Manchester Piccadilly

E also from 25 June until 28 June

F until 21 June

Table 81

Mondays to Fridays

until 29 June

Crewe and Manchester - Chester and North Wales

Network Diagram - see first Page of Table 81

	AW FX	AW ◇	NT
London Euston 15 ⊖65 d			
Birmingham New Street 12 65 d			
Manchester Airport 84,85 ✈ d			
Cardiff Central 7 131 d		20 53	
Crewe 10 d		00 02	
Manchester Pic'dilly 10 90 d			23 17
Manchester Oxford Road 90 d			
Newton-le-Willows 90 d			
Earlestown 8 90 d			
Warrington Bank Quay 90 d	23 55		
Runcorn East d	00 02		
Frodsham d	00 06		
Helsby d	00 10		
Liverpool Lime Street 10 106 d			
Chester a	00 22	00 27	00 40
Chester d			
Shotton d			
Flint d			
Prestatyn d			
Rhyl d			
Abergele & Pensarn d			
Colwyn Bay d			
Llandudno Junction a			
Llandudno Junction d			
Deganwy d			
Llandudno a			
Conwy d			
Penmaenmawr d			
Llanfairfechan d			
Bangor (Gwynedd) a			
Bangor (Gwynedd) d			
Llanfairpwll d			
Bodorgan d			
Ty Croes d			
Rhosneigr d			
Valley d			
Holyhead a			

Mondays to Fridays

2 July to 28 September

	AW MX	AW MX ◇	AW MO ◇	AW MO	AW MX ◇	AW MO ◇ A	AW MX	AW MO ▬	AW MO	AW MX ◇	AW MO ◇	NT MX	AW ■ B	AW ■ C	AW ■ D	AW	AW	AW	NT	VT ◇1 ⊠	AW ◇ ✠	AW ◇ ✠	NT
London Euston 15 ⊖65 d																				05 30			
Birmingham New Street 12 65 d					22p55	22p55																	
Manchester Airport 84,85 ✈ d																					05 33		
Cardiff Central 7 131 d		19p34								20p53	21p04		22p31	22p31	22p31								
Crewe 10 d			22p29	23p38	23p57	00 01				00 02	00 10		01 34	01 49	01 50					06 23		06 54	
Manchester Pic'dilly 10 90 d								22p14	23p20			23p17									05 50		06 18
Manchester Oxford Road 90 d								22p19													05 53		
Newton-le-Willows 90 d								22p49													06 12		
Earlestown 8 90 d								22p59													06 15		
Warrington Bank Quay 90 d							23p55	23p24											05 49		06 26		
Runcorn East d							00 02	23p44													06 33		
Frodsham d							00 06	23p59													06 37		
Helsby d							00 10	00 04											06 03		06 41		
Liverpool Lime Street 10 106 d																							
Chester a		22p34	22p52	00 01	00 18	00 22	00 22	00 24	00 25	00 27	00 33	00 40	01 58	02 14	02 14					06 43	06 53	07 14	07 45
Chester d	22p04	22p56	23p00		00 40	00 38							02 01	02 16	02 17					06 44	06 55	07 23	
Shotton d	22p13	23p05	23p09																		07 04		
Flint d	22p19	23p11	23p15		00 53	00 51														06 57	07 10	07 36	
Prestatyn d	22p32	23p24	23p28		01 06	01 04														07 10	07 23	07 49	
Rhyl d	22p38	23p30	23p34		01 12	01 10							02 28	02 44	02 44					07 16	07 29	07 55	
Abergele & Pensarn d	22p44	23p36																			07 35		
Colwyn Bay d	22p52	23p44	23p45		01 23	01 21														07 26	07 43	08 06	
Llandudno Junction a	22p57	23p49	23p50		01 28	01 27							02 41	02 57	02 57					07 32	07 48	08 11	
Llandudno Junction d	22p59	23p52	23p51		01 29	01 28							02 43	02 58	02 59	06 13	06 51	07 31		07 33	07 50	08 12	
Deganwy d																06x16	06x54	07x34			07x54		
Llandudno a																06 23	07 01	07 41			08 06		
Conwy d	23b01	23b54	23b53																			08x14	
Penmaenmawr d	23b07	23b59	00x01																			08x20	
Llanfairfechan d	23b11	00x04	00x03																			08x24	
Bangor (Gwynedd) a	23p19	00 12	00 11		01 45	01 44							02 59	03 14	03 15					07 49		08 32	
Bangor (Gwynedd) d	23p21	00 14	00 14		01 45	01 44							03 00	03 16	03 16					07 49		08 37	
Llanfairpwll d	23b27																					08x43	
Bodorgan d	23b37																					08x53	
Ty Croes d	23b42																					08x57	
Rhosneigr d	23b45																					09x00	
Valley d	23b50																					09x06	
Holyhead a	00 05	00 48	00 49		02 15	02 20							03 33	03 49	03 49					08 23		09 20	

A From Birmingham International
B 2 August
C 26 July
D 27 July
b Previous night, stops on request

Table 81

Mondays to Fridays

2 July to 28 September

Crewe and Manchester - Chester and North Wales

Network Diagram - see first Page of Table 81

	AW	AW	AW ◇ ✠	AW ◇ ✠	NT	AW	AW	AW ◇ ✠	VT ◇1 ⊠	AW ◇ A	AW ◇ B ✠	NT	AW	AW	AW ◇ ✠	VT ◇1 ⊠	AW ◇ ✠	NT	AW	AW	AW ◇ ✠	VT ◇1 ⊠
London Euston 15 ⊖65 d									07 10							08 10						09 10
Birmingham New Street 12 65 d											07 24											
Manchester Airport 84,85 ✈ d																						
Cardiff Central 7 131 d				05 10													07 21					
Crewe 10 d	07 23					08 23			08 49				09 23			09 49			10 23			10 49
Manchester Pic'dilly 10 90 d			06 50		07 17			07 50				08 17			08 50			09 17			09 50	
Manchester Oxford Road 90 d			06 53					07 53							08 53						09 53	
Newton-le-Willows 90 d			07 12					08 12							09 12						10 12	
Earlestown 8 90 d			07 15					08 15							09 15						10 15	
Warrington Bank Quay 90 d			07 22					08 24							09 26						10 26	
Runcorn East d			07 29					08 31							09 33						10 33	
Frodsham d			07 34					08 36							09 37						10 37	
Helsby d			07 38					08 41							09 41						10 41	
Liverpool Lime Street 10 106 d																						
Chester a	07 46		07 50	08 19	08 45	08 46		08 53	09 12		09 17	09 45	09 46		09 53	10 09	10 19	10 45	10 46		10 53	11 09
Chester d			07 55	08 22				08 55			09 23				09 55	10 16	10 24				10 55	
Shotton d			08 04					09 04							10 04						11 04	
Flint d			08 10	08 36				09 10			09 36				10 10	10 29	10 39				11 10	
Prestatyn d			08 23	08 49				09 23			09 49				10 23	10 42	10 52				11 23	
Rhyl d			08 29	08 55				09 29			09 55				10 29	10 48	10 58				11 29	
Abergele & Pensarn d			08 35					09 35							10 35						11 35	
Colwyn Bay d			08 43	09 06				09 43			10 06				10 43	10 59	11 09				11 43	
Llandudno Junction a			08 48	09 11				09 48			10 11				10 48	11 04	11 14				11 48	
Llandudno Junction d		08 28	08 50	09 12			09 28	09 50		10 03	10 12			10 28	10 50	11 06	11 15			11 26	11 50	
Deganwy d		08x31	08x54				09x31	09x54		10x06				10x31	10x54					11x29	11x54	
Llandudno a		08 38	09 06				09 38	10 06		10 13				10 38	11 06					11 36	12 06	
Conwy d				09x14													11x17					
Penmaenmawr d				09x20													11x23					
Llanfairfechan d				09x24													11x27					
Bangor (Gwynedd) a				09 32							10 28					11 27	11 37					
Bangor (Gwynedd) d				09 35							10 29						11 40					
Llanfairpwll d											10x35											
Bodorgan d				09x49																		
Ty Croes d				09x53																		
Rhosneigr d				09x56																		
Valley d											10x53											
Holyhead a				10 14							11 07						12 14					

	VT ◇1 ⊠	AW ◇ B ✠	NT	AW	AW	AW ◇ ✠	VT ◇1 ⊠	AW ◇ A	AW ◇ ✠	NT	AW	AW	AW ◇ ✠	VT ◇1 ⊓	AW ◇ B ✠	NT	AW	AW	AW ◇ ✠	VT ◇1 ⊓	AW ◇ ✠
London Euston 15 ⊖65 d	09 10						10 10							11 10						12 10	
Birmingham New Street 12 65 d		09 24													11 24						
Manchester Airport 84,85 ✈ d																					
Cardiff Central 7 131 d									09 21												11 21
Crewe 10 d	10 49			11 23			11 49				12 23			12 49			13 23			13 49	
Manchester Pic'dilly 10 90 d			10 17			10 50				11 17			11 50			12 17			12 50		
Manchester Oxford Road 90 d						10 53							11 53						12 53		
Newton-le-Willows 90 d						11 12							12 12						13 12		
Earlestown 8 90 d						11 15							12 15						13 15		
Warrington Bank Quay 90 d						11 26							12 26						13 26		
Runcorn East d						11 33							12 33						13 33		
Frodsham d						11 37							12 37						13 37		
Helsby d						11 41							12 41						13 41		
Liverpool Lime Street 10 106 d																					
Chester a	11 09	11 19	11 43	11 46		11 53	12 12		12 19	12 45	12 46		12 53	13 12	13 19	13 45	13 46		13 53	14 12	14 19
Chester d	11 16	11 22				11 55			12 23				12 55		13 24				13 55		14 23
Shotton d						12 04							13 04						14 04		
Flint d		11 38				12 10			12 36				13 10		13 37				14 10		14 36
Prestatyn d		11 51				12 23			12 49				13 23		13 50				14 23		14 49
Rhyl d	11 43	11 57				12 29			12 55				13 29		13 56				14 29		14 55
Abergele & Pensarn d						12 35							13 35						14 35		
Colwyn Bay d	11 54	12 08				12 43			13 06				13 43		14 07				14 43		15 06
Llandudno Junction a	12 00	12 13				12 48			13 11				13 48		14 12				14 48		15 11
Llandudno Junction d	12 01	12 14			12 28	12 50		13 03	13 12			13 28	13 50		14 13			14 28	14 50		15 12
Deganwy d					12x31	12x54		13x06				13x31	13x54					14x31	14x54		
Llandudno a					12 38	13 06		13 13				13 38	14 06					14 38	15 06		
Conwy d		12x16													14x15						
Penmaenmawr d		12x22													14x21						
Llanfairfechan d		12x26													14x25						
Bangor (Gwynedd) a	12 16	12 34							13 28						14 33						15 28
Bangor (Gwynedd) d	12 17	12 37							13 29						14 36						15 30
Llanfairpwll d		12x43							13x36												15x38
Bodorgan d		12x53							13x46												15x48
Ty Croes d		12x57							13x50												15x52
Rhosneigr d		13x00							13x53												15x55
Valley d		13x06							13x58												16x01
Holyhead a	12 50	13 18							14 13						15 08						16 15

A From Blaenau Ffestiniog
B From Birmingham International

Table 81

Mondays to Fridays

2 July to 28 September

Crewe and Manchester - Chester and North Wales

Network Diagram - see first Page of Table 81

	NT	AW	AW	VT	AW	AW	NT	AW	AW	VT	AW	NT	AW	AW	VT	AW	NT	AW	AW	AW	AW	VT
			◇	◇■1	◇	◇			◇	◇■1	◇			◇	◇■1	◇				◇	◇	◇■1
					A	B										B				A		
			⊼	☕		⊼			⊼	☕	⊼			⊼	☕	⊼					⊼	☕
London Euston ⊖65 d				13 10						14 10					15 10							16 10
Birmingham New Street 65 d						13 24										15 26						
Manchester Airport 84,85 ✈ d																						
Cardiff Central 131 d											13 21											
Crewe d		14 23		14 49				15 23		15 49			16 23		16 49			17 23				17 49
Manchester Pic'dilly 90 d	13 17		13 50				14 17		14 50			15 17		15 50			16 17				16 50	
Manchester Oxford Road 90 d			13 53						14 53					15 53							16 53	
Newton-le-Willows 90 d			14 12						15 12					16 12							17 12	
Earlestown 90 d			14 15						15 15					16 15							17 15	
Warrington Bank Quay 90 d			14 26						15 26					16 26							17 26	
Runcorn East d			14 33						15 33					16 33							17 33	
Frodsham d			14 37						15 37					16 37							17 37	
Helsby d			14 41						15 41					16 41							17 41	
Liverpool Lime Street 106 d																						
Chester a	14 45	14 46	14 53	15 12		15 20	15 45	15 46	15 53	16 12	16 20	16 45	16 46	16 54	17 12	17 22	17 45	17 46			17 53	18 08
d			14 55			15 22			15 55		16 25			16 55		17 27					17 55	18 10
Shotton d			15 04						16 04					17 04		17 36					18 04	
Flint d			15 10			15 37			16 10		16 38			17 10		17 42					18 10	18 23
Prestatyn d			15 23			15 50			16 23		16 51			17 23		17 55					18 23	18 36
Rhyl d			15 29			15 56			16 29		16 57			17 29		18 01					18 29	18 42
Abergele & Pensarn d			15 35						16 35					17 35		18 07					18 35	
Colwyn Bay d			15 43			16 07			16 43		17 08			17 43		18 15					18 43	18 53
Llandudno Junction a			15 48			16 12			16 48		17 13			17 49		18 20					18 48	18 58
d			15 50		16 04	16 14			16 50		17 13			17 50		18 22			18 26	18 41	18 50	19 00
Deganwy d			15x54		16x07				16x54					17x54					18x29	18x44	18x54	
Llandudno a			16 06		16 17				17 06					18 06					18 36	18 54	19 06	
Conwy d						16x16					17x15					18x24						
Penmaenmawr d						16x22					17x21					18x30						
Llanfairfechan d						16x26					17x25					18x34						
Bangor (Gwynedd) a						16 34					17 33					18 42						19 21
d						16 36					17 36					18 44						
Llanfairpwll d											17x42											
Bodorgan d											17x52											
Ty Croes d											17x56											
Rhosneigr d											17x59											
Valley d											18x05											
Holyhead a						17 11					18 19					19 16						

	AW	AW	NT	AW	AW	AW	AW	VT	VT	AW	NT	AW	AW	VT	AW	VT	AW	NT	AW	AW	AW
	■						■ ■1										■				
						◇		◇■1	◇■1	◇				◇■1		◇■1					◇
										B				C							A
	⊼	⊼				⊼	⊠	⊠	⊠	⊼			⊼	⊠		⊠	⊼				
London Euston ⊖65 d								17 10	17 10					18 10		18 10					
Birmingham New Street 65 d										17 26											
Manchester Airport 84,85 ✈ d																					
Cardiff Central 131 d	15 21						16 15										17 21				
Crewe d				18 23			18 43	18 56	18 56			19 23		19 56		19 56			20 23		
Manchester Pic'dilly 90 d		17 19	17 09			17 50					18 17		18 50					19 17		19 50	
Manchester Oxford Road 90 d		17 22				17 53							18 53							19 53	
Newton-le-Willows 90 d		17 40				18 12							19 12							20 12	
Earlestown 90 d		17 44				18 15							19 16							20 15	
Warrington Bank Quay 90 d		17 53				18 24							19 26							20 26	
Runcorn East d		18 00				18 31							19 33							20 33	
Frodsham d		18 05				18 36							19 37							20 37	
Helsby d		18 09				18 40							19 41							20 41	
Liverpool Lime Street 106 d																					
Chester a	18 20	18 23	18 32	18 46		18 53	19 06	19 15	19 15	19 20	19 45	19 46	19 53	20 15		20 15	20 20	20 45	20 46	20 53	
d	18 24					18 55	19 07		19 21	19 32						20 26	20 32				
Shotton d						19 04				19 41							20 41				
Flint d	18 37					19 10	19 21		19 35	19 47							20 47				
Prestatyn d	18 50					19 23			19 48	20 00							21 02				
Rhyl d	18 56					19 29	19 39		19 54	20 06						20 53	21 08				
Abergele & Pensarn d						19 35				20 12											
Colwyn Bay d	19 07					19 43			20 05	20 20						21 04	21 18				
Llandudno Junction a	19 12					19 48	19 52		20 10	20 25						21 09	21 24				
d	19 13				19 28	19 50	19 53		20 12	20 27					20 30	21 10	21 26				21 32
Deganwy d					19x31	19x54									20x33						21x35
Llandudno a					19 38	20 06									20 40						21 46
Conwy d										20x29											
Penmaenmawr d										20x35											
Llanfairfechan d										20x39											
Bangor (Gwynedd) a	19 33						20 09		20 27	20 47						21 25	21 41				
d	19 35						20 11		20 28	20 49						21 27	21 43				
Llanfairpwll d	19x41									20x55							21x49				
Bodorgan d	19x51									21x05							21x59				
Ty Croes d	19x55									21x10							22x03				
Rhosneigr d	19x58									21x13							22x06				
Valley d	20x04									21x18							22x12				
Holyhead a	20 18						20 49		20 59	21 31						21 59	22 25				

A From Blaenau Ffestiniog

B From Birmingham International

C To Wrexham General

Table 81

Mondays to Fridays

2 July to 28 September

Crewe and Manchester - Chester and North Wales

Network Diagram - see first Page of Table 81

	AW	VT	AW	AW	NT	AW	AW	VT	AW	AW	NT	AW	AW	AW	AW FO	AW FX	AW	NT	AW FX	AW FO	AW	AW FX
	■	■																				
		■1	◇					◇■1		◇				◇							◇	
			A											B								
	⊼	☕	⊼					☕														
London Euston ⊖65 d		19 10						20 10														
Birmingham New Street 65 d			19 24											21 24							22 55	
Manchester Airport 84,85 ✈ d						20 32							21 32									
Cardiff Central 131 d	18 18									19 34												
Crewe d		20 50		21 00			21 36	21 50				22 23					23 23				23 57	
Manchester Pic'dilly 90 d					20 17	20 50					21 17		21 50		22 12			22 17	22 45	23 14		
Manchester Oxford Road 90 d						20 53							21 53		22 29					23 17		
Newton-le-Willows 90 d						21 12							22 12		22 47					23 36		
Earlestown 90 d						21 15							22 15		22 50					23 39		
Warrington Bank Quay 90 d						21 24							22 24		22 59	22 59				23 48		23 55
Runcorn East d						21 33							22 31		23 06	23 06				23 55		00 02
Frodsham d						21 37							22 35		23 10	23 10				23 59		00 06
Helsby d						21 41							22 39		23 14	23 14				00 03		00 10
Liverpool Lime Street 106 d																						
Chester a	20 58	21 10	21 19	21 23	21 45	21 55	21 59	22 15		22 34	22 45	22 45	22 51	23 19	23 26	23 26	23 44	23 45	23 49	00 15	00 18	00 22
d	21 03	21 17							22 04	22 56											00 40	
Shotton d									22 13	23 05												
Flint d		21 30							22 19	23 11											00 53	
Prestatyn d		21 43							22 32	23 24											01 06	
Rhyl d	21 30	21 50							22 38	23 30											01 12	
Abergele & Pensarn d									22 44	23 36												
Colwyn Bay d	21 41	22 01							22 52	23 44											01 23	
Llandudno Junction a	21 46	22 06							22 57	23 49											01 28	
d	21 49	22 07							22 59	23 52											01 29	
Deganwy d																						
Llandudno a																						
Conwy d									23x01	23x54												
Penmaenmawr d									23x07	23x59												
Llanfairfechan d									23x11	00x04												
Bangor (Gwynedd) a	22 04	22 22							23 19	00 12											01 45	
d	22 06	22 24							23 21	00 14											01 45	
Llanfairpwll d									23x27													
Bodorgan d									23x37													
Ty Croes d									23x42													
Rhosneigr d									23x45													
Valley d									23x50													
Holyhead a	22 36	22 56							00 05	00 48											02 15	

	AW	NT	NT FO	AW	AW	AW	AW	AW
				■	■	■	■	■
	◇							
		C	D	E	F	G	H	I
London Euston ⊖65 d								
Birmingham New Street 65 d								
Manchester Airport 84,85 ✈ d								
Cardiff Central 131 d	20 53			22 31	22 31	22 31	22 31	22 31
Crewe d	00 02			01 33	01 33	01 34	01 49	01 50
Manchester Pic'dilly 90 d		23 17	23 17					
Manchester Oxford Road 90 d								
Newton-le-Willows 90 d								
Earlestown 90 d								
Warrington Bank Quay 90 d								
Runcorn East d								
Frodsham d								
Helsby d								
Liverpool Lime Street 106 d								
Chester a	00 27	00 40	00 43	01 57	01 57	01 58	02 14	02 14
d				02 00	02 00	02 01	02 16	02 17
Shotton d								
Flint d								
Prestatyn d								
Rhyl d				02 27	02 27	02 28	02 44	02 44
Abergele & Pensarn d								
Colwyn Bay d								
Llandudno Junction a				02 40	02 40	02 41	02 57	02 57
d				02 42	02 42	02 43	02 58	02 59
Deganwy d								
Llandudno a								
Conwy d								
Penmaenmawr d								
Llanfairfechan d								
Bangor (Gwynedd) a				02 58	02 58	02 59	03 14	03 15
d				02 59	02 59	03 00	03 16	03 16
Llanfairpwll d								
Bodorgan d								
Ty Croes d								
Rhosneigr d								
Valley d								
Holyhead a				03 32	03 37	03 33	03 49	03 49

A From Birmingham International

B From Birmingham International to Manchester Piccadilly

C from 2 July until 9 August, FX from 13 August until 27 September

D from 10 August until 28 September

E 3 August

F 10 August

G 1 August

H 25 July

I 26 July

Crewe and Manchester - Chester and North Wales

Network Diagram - see first Page of Table 81

	AW MX	AW MX	AW MO	AW MO	AW MX	AW MO	AW MX	AW MO	AW MO	NT	AW MX	AW MO	NT MX	AW	AW	AW	VT	AW	AW		NT	AW	AW	AW
		◇	◇		◇	◇ A		🚌			◇	◇					◇1 ⊠	◇ ⌶	◇ ⌶					◇ ⌶
London Euston ⊖65 d																	05 30							
Birmingham New Street 65 d					22p55	22p55												05 33						
Manchester Airport 84,85 ✈ d																								
Cardiff Central 131 d		19p34									20p53	21p04												
Crewe d			22p29	23p38	23p57	00 01					00 02	00 10					06 23		06 54			07 23		
Manchester Pic'dilly 90 d								22p14	23p20				23p17					05 50			06 18			06 50
Manchester Oxford Road 90 d								22p19										05 53						06 53
Newton-le-Willows 90 d								22p49										06 12						07 12
Earlestown 90 d								22p59										06 15						07 15
Warrington Bank Quay 90 d							23p55	23p24		05 49								06 26						07 22
Runcorn East d							00 02	23p44										06 33						07 29
Frodsham d							00 06	23p59										06 37						07 34
Helsby d							00 10	00 04		06 03								06 41						07 38
Liverpool Lime Street 106 d																								
Chester a		22p34	22p52	00 01	00 18	00 22	00 22	00 24	00 25		00 27	00 33	00 42				06 43	06 53	07 14		07 46	07 46		07 50
d	22p04	22p56	23p00		00 40	00 38											06 44	06 55	07 23					07 55
Shotton d	22p13	23p05	23p09															07 04						08 04
Flint d	22p19	23p11	23p15		00 53	00 51											06 57	07 10	07 36					08 10
Prestatyn d	22p32	23p24	23p28		01 06	01 04											07 10	07 23	07 49					08 23
Rhyl d	22p38	23p30	23p34		01 12	01 10											07 16	07 29	07 55					08 29
Abergele & Pensarn d	22p44	23p36																07 35						08 35
Colwyn Bay d	22p52	23p44	23p45		01 23	01 21											07 26	07 43	08 06					08 43
Llandudno Junction a	22p57	23p49	23p50		01 28	01 27											07 32	07 48	08 11					08 48
d	22p59	23p52	23p51		01 29	01 28								06 13	06 51	07 31	07 33	07 50	08 12				08 28	08 50
Deganwy d														06x16	06x54	07x34		07x54					08x31	08x54
Llandudno a														06 23	07 01	07 41		08 06					08 38	09 06
Conwy d	23b01	23b54	23b53																08x14					
Penmaenmawr d	23b07	23b59	00x01																08x20					
Llanfairfechan d	23b11	00x04	00x03																08x24					
Bangor (Gwynedd) a	23p19	00 12	00 11		01 45	01 44											07 49		08 32					
d	23p21	00 14	00 14		01 45	01 44											07 49		08 37					
Llanfairpwll d	23b27																		08x43					
Bodorgan d	23b37																		08x53					
Ty Croes d	23b42																		08x57					
Rhosneigr d	23b45																		09x00					
Valley d	23b50																		09x06					
Holyhead a	00 05	00 48	00 49		02 15	02 20											08 23		09 20					

	AW	NT	AW	AW	AW		VT	AW	AW	NT	AW	AW	AW	VT	AW		NT	AW	AW	AW	VT	VT	AW	NT
	◇ ⌶				◇ ⌶		◇1 ⊠	◇ B	◇ A ⌶				◇ ⌶	◇1 ⊠	◇ ⌶					◇ ⌶	◇1 ⊠	◇1 ⊠	◇ A ⌶	
London Euston ⊖65 d							07 10							08 10							09 10	09 10		
Birmingham New Street 65 d									07 24														09 24	
Manchester Airport 84,85 ✈ d															07 21									
Cardiff Central 131 d	05 10																							
Crewe d			08 23				08 49				09 23			09 49				10 23			10 49	10 49		
Manchester Pic'dilly 90 d		07 17			07 50					08 17			08 50				09 17			09 50				10 17
Manchester Oxford Road 90 d					07 53								08 53							09 53				
Newton-le-Willows 90 d					08 12								09 12							10 12				
Earlestown 90 d					08 15								09 15							10 15				
Warrington Bank Quay 90 d					08 24								09 26							10 26				
Runcorn East d					08 31								09 33							10 33				
Frodsham d					08 36								09 37							10 37				
Helsby d					08 41								09 41							10 41				
Liverpool Lime Street 106 d																								
Chester a	08 19	08 46	08 46		08 53		09 12		09 17	09 45	09 46		09 53	10 09	10 19		10 44	10 46		10 53	11 09	11 09	11 19	11 44
d	08 22				08 55				09 23				09 55	10 16	10 24					10 55		11 16	11 22	
Shotton d					09 04								10 04							11 04				
Flint d	08 36				09 10				09 36				10 10	10 29	10 39					11 10			11 38	
Prestatyn d	08 49				09 23				09 49				10 23	10 42	10 52					11 23			11 51	
Rhyl d	08 55				09 29				09 55				10 29	10 48	10 58					11 29		11 43	11 57	
Abergele & Pensarn d					09 35								10 35							11 35				
Colwyn Bay d	09 06				09 43				10 06				10 43	10 59	11 09					11 43		11 54	12 08	
Llandudno Junction a	09 11				09 48				10 11				10 48	11 04	11 14					11 48		12 00	12 13	
d	09 12			09 28	09 50			10 03	10 12			10 28	10 50	11 06	11 15				11 26	11 50		12 01	12 14	
Deganwy d				09x31	09x54			10x06				10x31	10x54						11x29	11x54				
Llandudno a				09 38	10 06			10 13				10 38	11 06						11 36	12 06				
Conwy d	09x14														11x17								12x16	
Penmaenmawr d	09x20														11x23								12x22	
Llanfairfechan d	09x24														11x27								12x26	
Bangor (Gwynedd) a	09 32								10 28					11 27	11 37							12 16	12 34	
d	09 35								10 29						11 40							12 17	12 37	
Llanfairpwll d									10x35														12x43	
Bodorgan d	09x49																						12x53	
Ty Croes d	09x53																						12x57	
Rhosneigr d	09x56																						13x00	
Valley d									10x53														13x06	
Holyhead a	10 14								11 07						12 14							12 50	13 18	

A From Birmingham International   B From Blaenau Ffestiniog   b Previous night, stops on request

Crewe and Manchester - Chester and North Wales

Network Diagram - see first Page of Table 81

	AW		AW	AW	VT	AW	AW	NT	AW	AW	AW		VT	AW	NT	AW	AW	AW	VT	AW	NT		AW	AW
				◇ ⌶	◇1 ⊠	◇ A	◇ ⌶				◇ ⌶		◇1 ⊐	◇ B ⌶				◇ ⌶	◇1 ⊐	◇ ⌶				◇ ⌶
London Euston ⊖65 d					10 10								11 10						12 10					
Birmingham New Street 65 d														11 24										
Manchester Airport 84,85 ✈ d																								
Cardiff Central 131 d							09 21													11 21				
Crewe d	11 23				11 49				12 23				12 49			13 23			13 49				14 23	
Manchester Pic'dilly 90 d				10 50				11 17			11 50				12 17			12 50			13 17			13 50
Manchester Oxford Road 90 d				10 53							11 53							12 53						13 53
Newton-le-Willows 90 d				11 12							12 12							13 12						14 12
Earlestown 90 d				11 15							12 15							13 15						14 15
Warrington Bank Quay 90 d				11 26							12 26							13 26						14 26
Runcorn East d				11 33							12 33							13 33						14 33
Frodsham d				11 37							12 37							13 37						14 37
Helsby d				11 41							12 41							13 41						14 41
Liverpool Lime Street 106 d																								
Chester a	11 46			11 53	12 12		12 19	12 44	12 46		12 53		13 12	13 19	13 44	13 46		13 53	14 12	14 19	14 44		14 46	14 53
d				11 55			12 23				12 55			13 24				13 55		14 23				14 55
Shotton d				12 04							13 04							14 04						15 04
Flint d				12 10			12 36				13 10			13 37				14 10		14 36				15 10
Prestatyn d				12 23			12 49				13 23			13 50				14 23		14 49				15 23
Rhyl d				12 29			12 55				13 29			13 56				14 29		14 55				15 29
Abergele & Pensarn d				12 35							13 35							14 35						15 35
Colwyn Bay d				12 43			13 06				13 43			14 07				14 43		15 06				15 43
Llandudno Junction a				12 48			13 11				13 48			14 12				14 48		15 11				15 48
d			12 28	12 50		13 03	13 12			13 28	13 50			14 13			14 28	14 50		15 12				15 50
Deganwy d			12x31	12x54		13x06				13x31	13x54						14x31	14x54						15x54
Llandudno a			12 38	13 06		13 13				13 38	14 06						14 38	15 06						16 06
Conwy d														14x15										
Penmaenmawr d														14x21										
Llanfairfechan d														14x25										
Bangor (Gwynedd) a							13 28							14 33						15 28				
d							13 29							14 36						15 30				
Llanfairpwll d							13x36													15x38				
Bodorgan d							13x46													15x48				
Ty Croes d							13x50													15x52				
Rhosneigr d							13x53													15x55				
Valley d							13x58													16x01				
Holyhead a							14 13							15 08						16 15				

	VT	AW	AW	NT	AW	AW	VT		AW	NT	AW	AW	VT	AW	NT	AW	AW		AW	AW	VT	AW	AW	NT
	◇1 ⊐	◇ A	◇ B ⌶			◇ ⌶	◇1 ⊐		◇ ⌶			◇ ⌶	◇1 ⊐	◇ B ⌶					◇ A	◇ ⌶	◇1 ⊐	■ ⌶	⌶	
London Euston ⊖65 d	13 10						14 10						15 10								16 10			
Birmingham New Street 65 d			13 24											15 26										
Manchester Airport 84,85 ✈ d																								
Cardiff Central 131 d									13 21													15 21		
Crewe d	14 49				15 23		15 49				16 23		16 49			17 23					17 49			
Manchester Pic'dilly 90 d				14 17		14 50				15 17		15 50			16 17					16 50			17 19	17 09
Manchester Oxford Road 90 d						14 53						15 53								16 53			17 22	
Newton-le-Willows 90 d						15 12						16 12								17 12			17 40	
Earlestown 90 d						15 15						16 15								17 15			17 44	
Warrington Bank Quay 90 d						15 26						16 26								17 26			17 53	
Runcorn East d						15 33						16 33								17 33			18 00	
Frodsham d						15 37						16 37								17 37			18 05	
Helsby d						15 41						16 41								17 41			18 09	
Liverpool Lime Street 106 d																								
Chester a	15 12		15 20	15 44	15 46	15 53	16 12		16 20	16 44	16 46	16 54	17 12	17 22	17 44	17 46				17 53	18 08	18 20	18 23	18 34
d			15 22			15 55			16 25			16 55		17 27						17 55	18 10	18 24		
Shotton d						16 04						17 04		17 36						18 04				
Flint d			15 37			16 10			16 38			17 10		17 42						18 10	18 23	18 37		
Prestatyn d			15 50			16 23			16 51			17 23		17 55						18 23	18 36	18 50		
Rhyl d			15 56			16 29			16 57			17 29		18 01						18 29	18 42	18 56		
Abergele & Pensarn d						16 35						17 35		18 07						18 35				
Colwyn Bay d			16 07			16 43			17 08			17 43		18 15						18 43	18 53	19 07		
Llandudno Junction a			16 12			16 48			17 13			17 49		18 20						18 48	18 58	19 12		
d		16 04	16 14			16 50			17 13			17 50		18 22			18 26		18 41	18 50	19 00	19 13		
Deganwy d		16x07				16x54						17x54					18x29		18x44	18x54				
Llandudno a		16 17				17 06						18 06					18 36		18 54	19 06				
Conwy d			16x16						17x15					18x24										
Penmaenmawr d			16x22						17x21					18x30										
Llanfairfechan d			16x26						17x25					18x34										
Bangor (Gwynedd) a			16 34						17 33					18 42							19 21	19 33		
d			16 36						17 36					18 44								19 35		
Llanfairpwll d									17x42													19x41		
Bodorgan d									17x52													19x51		
Ty Croes d									17x56													19x55		
Rhosneigr d									17x59													19x58		
Valley d									18x05													20x04		
Holyhead a			17 11						18 19					19 16								20 18		

A From Blaenau Ffestiniog   B From Birmingham International

Crewe and Manchester - Chester and North Wales

Mondays to Fridays
from 1 October

Network Diagram - see first Page of Table 81

	AW	AW	AW	AW	VT	VT	AW	NT	AW	AW	VT	AW	VT	AW	NT	AW	AW	AW	AW	VT	AW
			◇ 🍴	1 ⊠	◇1 ⊠	◇1 ⊠	◇ A 🍴			🍴	◇1 B ⊠		◇1 ⊠	🍴				◇ C	🍴	1 ☕	◇ A 🍴
London Euston 15 ⊖65 d					17 10	17 10					18 10		18 10							19 10	
Birmingham New Street 12 65 d							17 26														19 24
Manchester Airport 84,85 ✈ d																					
Cardiff Central 7 131 d				16 15										17 21					18 18		
Crewe 10 d	18 23			18 43	18 56	18 56			19 23		19 56		19 56			20 23				20 50	
Manchester Pic'dilly 10 90 d			17 50					18 17		18 50					19 17		19 50				
Manchester Oxford Road 90 d			17 53							18 53							19 53				
Newton-le-Willows 90 d			18 12							19 12							20 12				
Earlestown 8 90 d			18 15							19 16							20 15				
Warrington Bank Quay 90 d			18 24							19 26							20 26				
Runcorn East d			18 31							19 33							20 33				
Frodsham d			18 36							19 37							20 37				
Helsby d			18 40							19 41							20 41				
Liverpool Lime Street 10 106 d																					
Chester a	18 46		18 53	19 06	19 15	19 15	19 20	19 44	19 46	19 53	20 15		20 15	20 20	20 44	20 46	20 53		20 58	21 10	21 19
d			18 55	19 07		19 21	19 32						20 26	20 32					21 03	21 17	
Shotton d			19 04				19 41							20 41							
Flint d			19 10	19 21		19 35	19 47							20 47						21 30	
Prestatyn d			19 23			19 48	20 00							21 02						21 43	
Rhyl d			19 29	19 39		19 54	20 06						20 53	21 08					21 30	21 50	
Abergele & Pensarn d			19 35				20 12														
Colwyn Bay d			19 43			20 05	20 20						21 04	21 18					21 41	22 01	
Llandudno Junction a			19 48	19 52		20 10	20 25						21 09	21 24					21 46	22 06	
d		19 28	19 50	19 53		20 12	20 27					20 30	21 10	21 26				21 32	21 49	22 07	
Deganwy d		19x31	19x54									20x33						21x35			
Llandudno a		19 38	20 06									20 40						21 46			
Conwy d							20x29														
Penmaenmawr d							20x35														
Llanfairfechan d							20x39														
Bangor (Gwynedd) a				20 09		20 27	20 47						21 25	21 41					22 04	22 22	
d				20 11		20 28	20 49						21 27	21 43					22 06	22 24	
Llanfairpwll d							20x55							21x49							
Bodorgan d							21x05							21x59							
Ty Croes d							21x10							22x03							
Rhosneigr d							21x13							22x06							
Valley d							21x18							22x12							
Holyhead a				20 49		20 59	21 31						21 59	22 25					22 36	22 56	

	AW	NT	AW	AW	VT	AW	AW	NT	AW	AW	AW	AW FO	AW FX	NT FO	AW	NT FX	AW FX	AW FO	AW	AW FX	AW	NT
					◇1 ☕		◇				◇ D								◇		◇	
London Euston 15 ⊖65 d					20 10																	
Birmingham New Street 12 65 d											21 24								22 55			
Manchester Airport 84,85 ✈ d			20 32							21 32												
Cardiff Central 7 131 d							19 34														20 53	
Crewe 10 d	21 00			21 36	21 50				22 23						23 23				23 57		00 02	
Manchester Pic'dilly 10 90 d		20 17	20 50					21 17		21 50		22 12		22 17		22 17	22 45	23 14				23 17
Manchester Oxford Road 90 d			20 53							21 53		22 29						23 17				
Newton-le-Willows 90 d			21 12							22 12		22 47						23 36				
Earlestown 8 90 d			21 15							22 15		22 50						23 39				
Warrington Bank Quay 90 d			21 24							22 24		22 59	22 59					23 48		23 55		
Runcorn East d			21 33							22 31		23 06	23 06					23 55		00 02		
Frodsham d			21 37							22 35		23 10	23 10					23 59		00 06		
Helsby d			21 41							22 39		23 14	23 14					00 03		00 10		
Liverpool Lime Street 10 106 d																						
Chester a	21 23	21 44	21 55	21 59	22 15		22 34	22 44	22 45	22 51	23 19	23 26	23 26	23 44	23 44	23 46	23 49	00 15	00 18	00 22	00 27	00 42
d						22 04	22 56												00 40			
Shotton d						22 13	23 05															
Flint d						22 19	23 11												00 53			
Prestatyn d						22 32	23 24												01 06			
Rhyl d						22 38	23 30												01 12			
Abergele & Pensarn d						22 44	23 36															
Colwyn Bay d						22 52	23 44												01 23			
Llandudno Junction a						22 57	23 49												01 28			
d						22 59	23 52												01 29			
Deganwy d																						
Llandudno a																						
Conwy d						23x01	23x54															
Penmaenmawr d						23x07	23x59															
Llanfairfechan d						23x11	00x04															
Bangor (Gwynedd) a						23 19	00 12												01 45			
d						23 21	00 14												01 45			
Llanfairpwll d						23x27																
Bodorgan d						23x37																
Ty Croes d						23x42																
Rhosneigr d						23x45																
Valley d						23x50																
Holyhead a						00 05	00 48												02 15			

A From Birmingham International
B To Wrexham General
C From Blaenau Ffestiniog
D From Birmingham International to Manchester Piccadilly

Crewe and Manchester - Chester and North Wales

Saturdays
until 30 June

Network Diagram - see first Page of Table 81

	AW	AW	AW	AW	AW	NT	AW	AW	AW	AW	VT	AW	AW	NT	AW	AW	AW	AW	NT	AW	AW	AW
		◇		◇	◇						◇1 ☕	◇ 🍴	◇ 🍴				◇ 🍴	◇ 🍴				◇ 🍴
London Euston 15 ⊖65 d																						
Birmingham New Street 12 65 d				22p55							05 30											
Manchester Airport 84,85 ✈ d												05 33										
Cardiff Central 7 131 d		19p34			20p53													05 20				
Crewe 10 d				23p57	00 02						06 23		07 03		07 23					08 23		
Manchester Pic'dilly 10 90 d			23p14			23p17	00 28					05 50		06 17			06 50		07 17			07 50
Manchester Oxford Road 90 d			23p17									05 53					06 53					07 53
Newton-le-Willows 90 d			23p36									06 12					07 12					08 12
Earlestown 8 90 d			23p39									06 15					07 15					08 15
Warrington Bank Quay 90 d			23p48									06 26					07 22					08 24
Runcorn East d			23p55									06 33					07 29					08 31
Frodsham d			23p59									06 37					07 34					08 35
Helsby d			00 03									06 41					07 38					08 39
Liverpool Lime Street 10 106 d																						
Chester a		22p34	00 15	00 18	00 27	00 40	01 31				06 43	06 53	07 23	07 45	07 46		07 50	08 18	08 45	08 46		08 51
d	22p04	22p56		00 40							06 44	06 55	07 25				07 55	08 22				08 55
Shotton d	22p13	23p05										07 04					08 04					09 04
Flint d	22p19	23p11		00 53							06 57	07 10	07 39				08 10	08 36				09 10
Prestatyn d	22p32	23p24		01 06							07 10	07 23	07 52				08 23	08 49				09 23
Rhyl d	22p38	23p30		01 12							07 16	07 29	07 58				08 29	08 55				09 29
Abergele & Pensarn d	22p44	23p36										07 35					08 35					09 35
Colwyn Bay d	22p52	23p44		01 23							07 27	07 43	08 09				08 43	09 06				09 43
Llandudno Junction a	22p57	23p49		01 28							07 33	07 48	08 14				08 48	09 11				09 48
d	22p59	23p52		01 29				06 13	06 51	07 31	07 33	07 50	08 15			08 28	08 50	09 12			09 28	09 50
Deganwy d								06x16	06x54	07x34		07x54				08x31	08x54				09x31	09x54
Llandudno a								06 23	07 01	07 41		08 06				08 38	09 06				09 38	10 06
Conwy d	23b01	23b54											08x17					09x14				
Penmaenmawr d	23b07	23b59											08x23					09x20				
Llanfairfechan d	23b11	00x04											08x27					09x24				
Bangor (Gwynedd) a	23p19	00 12		01 45							07 49		08 35					09 32				
d	23p21	00 14		01 45							07 50		08 38					09 35				
Llanfairpwll d	23b27												08x44									
Bodorgan d	23b37												08x54					09x49				
Ty Croes d	23b42												08x58					09x53				
Rhosneigr d	23b45												09x01					09x56				
Valley d	23b50												09x07									
Holyhead a	00 05	00 48		02 15							08 23		09 21					10 14				

	AW	AW	NT	AW	AW	AW	VT	AW	NT	AW	AW	AW	VT	AW	NT	AW	AW	AW	VT	AW	AW	NT
	◇ A	◇ B 🍴				◇ 🍴	◇1 ☕	◇ 🍴				◇ 🍴	◇1 ☕	◇ B 🍴				◇ 🍴	◇1 ☕	◇ A	◇ 🍴	
London Euston 15 ⊖65 d							08 10						08 50						10 10			
Birmingham New Street 12 65 d		07 23												09 24								
Manchester Airport 84,85 ✈ d																						
Cardiff Central 7 131 d								07 21													09 21	
Crewe 10 d				09 23			09 49			10 23			10 43			11 23			11 49			
Manchester Pic'dilly 10 90 d			08 17			08 50			09 17			09 50			10 17			10 50				11 17
Manchester Oxford Road 90 d						08 53						09 53						10 53				
Newton-le-Willows 90 d						09 12						10 12						11 12				
Earlestown 8 90 d						09 15						10 15						11 15				
Warrington Bank Quay 90 d						09 26						10 26						11 26				
Runcorn East d						09 33						10 33						11 33				
Frodsham d						09 37						10 37						11 37				
Helsby d						09 41						10 41						11 41				
Liverpool Lime Street 10 106 d																						
Chester a		09 17	09 45	09 46		09 53	10 12	10 19	10 45	10 46		10 53	11 10	11 19	11 45	11 46		11 53	12 12		12 19	12 45
d		09 24				09 55		10 23				10 55	11 12	11 24				11 55			12 23	
Shotton d						10 04						11 04						12 04				
Flint d		09 37				10 10		10 36				11 10		11 39				12 10			12 36	
Prestatyn d		09 50				10 23		10 49				11 23		11 52				12 23			12 49	
Rhyl d		09 56				10 29		10 55				11 29	11 41	11 58				12 29			12 55	
Abergele & Pensarn d						10 35						11 35						12 35				
Colwyn Bay d		10 07				10 43		11 06				11 43	11 54	12 09				12 43			13 06	
Llandudno Junction a		10 12				10 48		11 11				11 48	12 00	12 14				12 48			13 11	
d	10 00	10 13			10 28	10 50		11 12			11 26	11 50	12 01	12 15			12 28	12 50		13 00	13 12	
Deganwy d	10x03				10x31	10x54					11x29	11x54					12x31	12x54		13x03		
Llandudno a	10 13				10 38	11 06					11 36	12 06					12 38	13 06		13 13		
Conwy d								11x14						12x17								
Penmaenmawr d								11x20						12x23								
Llanfairfechan d								11x24						12x27								
Bangor (Gwynedd) a		10 29						11 32					12 19	12 35							13 28	
d		10 30						11 35					12 20	12 38							13 29	
Llanfairpwll d		10x36												12x44							13x36	
Bodorgan d														12x54							13x46	
Ty Croes d														12x58							13x50	
Rhosneigr d														13x01							13x53	
Valley d		10x54												13x07							13x58	
Holyhead a		11 05						12 09					12 55	13 18							14 13	

A From Blaenau Ffestiniog
B From Birmingham International
b Previous night, stops on request

Crewe and Manchester - Chester and North Wales

Network Diagram - see first Page of Table 81

		AW		AW	AW	VT	AW	NT	AW	AW	AW	VT		AW	NT	AW	AW	AW	VT	AW	AW	NT		AW	AW
					◇ ✕	◇■ ⊡	◇ A ✕				◇ ✕	◇■ ⊡		◇ ✕				◇ ✕	◇■ ⊡	◇ B	◇ A ✕				
London Euston ⊖65	d					11 10						12 10							13 10						
Birmingham New Street 65	d						11 24														13 24				
Manchester Airport 84,85 ✈	d																								
Cardiff Central 131	d													11 21											
Crewe	d	12 23				12 49			13 23			13 49				14 23			14 49					15 23	
Manchester Pic'dilly 90	d				11 50			12 17			12 50				13 17			13 50				14 17			
Manchester Oxford Road 90	d				11 53						12 53							13 53							
Newton-le-Willows 90	d				12 12						13 12							14 12							
Earlestown 90	d				12 15						13 15							14 15							
Warrington Bank Quay 90	d				12 26						13 26							14 26							
Runcorn East	d				12 33						13 33							14 33							
Frodsham	d				12 37						13 37							14 37							
Helsby	d				12 41						13 41							14 41							
Liverpool Lime Street 106	d																								
Chester	a	12 46			12 53	13 12	13 18	13 45	13 46		13 53	14 12		14 19	14 45	14 46		14 53	15 12		15 20	15 45		15 46	
	d				12 55		13 22				13 55			14 23				14 55			15 22				
Shotton	d				13 04						14 04							15 04							
Flint	d				13 10		13 36				14 10			14 36				15 10			15 37				
Prestatyn	d				13 23		13 49				14 23			14 49				15 23			15 50				
Rhyl	d				13 29		13 55				14 29			14 55				15 29			15 56				
Abergele & Pensarn	d				13 35						14 35							15 35							
Colwyn Bay	d				13 43		14 06				14 43			15 06				15 43			16 07				
Llandudno Junction	a				13 48		14 11				14 48			15 11				15 48			16 12				
	d			13 28	13 50		14 12			14 28	14 50			15 12			15 30	15 50		16 00	16 14				16 26
Deganwy	d			13x31	13x54					14x31	14x54						15x33	15 54		16x03					16x29
Llandudno	a			13 38	14 06					14 38	15 06						15 40	16 06		16 13					16 36
Conwy	d						14x14														16x16				
Penmaenmawr	d						14x20														16x22				
Llanfairfechan	d						14x24														16x26				
Bangor (Gwynedd)	a						14 32							15 28							16 35				
	d						14 35							15 29							16 36				
Llanfairpwll	d													15x36											
Bodorgan	d													15x46											
Ty Croes	d													15x50											
Rhosneigr	d													15x53											
Valley	d													15x58											
Holyhead	a						15 08							16 13							17 11				

		AW	VT	AW	NT	AW	AW	AW		VT	AW	NT	AW	AW	AW	AW	VT	AW		NT	AW	AW	AW	VT	AW
		◇ ✕	◇■ ⊡	◇ ✕				◇ ✕		◇■ ⊡	◇ A ✕				◇ B	◇ ✕	◇■ ⊡	■ ✕					◇ ✕	◇■ ⊡	◇ A ✕
London Euston ⊖65	d		14 10							15 10							16 10							17 10	
Birmingham New Street 65	d										15 24														17 24
Manchester Airport 84,85 ✈	d																								
Cardiff Central 131	d			13 21														15 21							
Crewe	d		15 49			16 23				16 49			17 23				17 49				18 23			18 50	
Manchester Pic'dilly 90	d	14 50			15 17			15 50				16 17				16 50				17 17			17 50		
Manchester Oxford Road 90	d	14 53						15 53								16 53							17 53		
Newton-le-Willows 90	d	15 12						16 12								17 12							18 12		
Earlestown 90	d	15 15						16 15								17 15							18 15		
Warrington Bank Quay 90	d	15 26						16 26								17 26							18 25		
Runcorn East	d	15 33						16 33								17 33							18 32		
Frodsham	d	15 37						16 37								17 37							18 37		
Helsby	d	15 41						16 41								17 41							18 42		
Liverpool Lime Street 106	d																								
Chester	a	15 53	16 10	16 22	16 45	16 46		16 53		17 12	17 19	17 45	17 46			17 53	18 09	18 19		18 45	18 46		18 54	19 10	19 20
	d	15 55	16 12	16 26				16 55			17 24					17 55	18 16	18 24					18 55	19 17	19 32
Shotton	d	16 04						17 04			17 33					18 04							19 04		19 41
Flint	d	16 10	16 25	16 39				17 10			17 39					18 10	18 29	18 39					19 10	19 30	19 47
Prestatyn	d	16 23	16 38	16 52				17 23			17 52					18 23	18 42	18 52					19 23	19 43	20 00
Rhyl	d	16 29	16 45	16 58				17 29			17 58					18 29	18 49	18 58					19 29	19 50	20 06
Abergele & Pensarn	d	16 35						17 35			18 04					18 35							19 35		20 12
Colwyn Bay	d	16 43	16 56	17 09				17 43			18 12					18 43	19 00	19 09					19 43	20 01	20 20
Llandudno Junction	a	16 48	17 01	17 14				17 48			18 17					18 48	19 05	19 14					19 48	20 06	20 25
	d	16 50	17 02	17 14			17 28	17 50			18 19			18 26	18 41	18 50	19 06	19 15				19 28	19 50	20 07	20 27
Deganwy	d	16x54					17x31	17x54						18x29	18x44	18x54						19x31	19x54		
Llandudno	a	17 06					17 38	18 06						18 36	18 54	19 06						19 38	20 06		
Conwy	d			17x16							18x21														20x29
Penmaenmawr	d			17x22							18x27														20x35
Llanfairfechan	d			17x26							18x31														20x39
Bangor (Gwynedd)	a		17 17	17 34							18 39						19 21	19 32						20 22	20 47
	d		17 19	17 37							18 41						19 23	19 33						20 24	20 49
Llanfairpwll	d			17x43														19x40							20x55
Bodorgan	d			17x53														19x51							21x05
Ty Croes	d			17x57														19x55							21x10
Rhosneigr	d			18x00														19x58							21x13
Valley	d			18x06														20x04							21x18
Holyhead	a		17 51	18 20							19 13						19 55	20 18						20 56	21 31

A From Birmingham International

B From Blaenau Ffestiniog

Crewe and Manchester - Chester and North Wales

Network Diagram - see first Page of Table 81

		NT	AW	AW		VT	AW	AW	NT	AW	AW	AW	AW	AW		NT	AW	AW	AW	NT	AW	AW	AW	AW	
				✕		◇■ ⊡		■ A ✕				◇ B ✕	◇ C	◇					◇				◇ B		
London Euston ⊖65	d					18 10																			
Birmingham New Street 65	d											19 24											21 24		
Manchester Airport 84,85 ✈	d																20 32								
Cardiff Central 131	d							17 21											19 34						
Crewe	d		19 23			19 49				20 23				21 00				21 36			22 23				
Manchester Pic'dilly 90	d	18 17		18 50					19 17		19 50					20 17	20 50			21 17		21 50		22 26	
Manchester Oxford Road 90	d			18 53							19 53						20 53					21 53		22 29	
Newton-le-Willows 90	d			19 12							20 12						21 12					22 12		22 47	
Earlestown 90	d			19 16							20 15						21 15					22 15		22 50	
Warrington Bank Quay 90	d			19 27							20 30						21 27					22 24		22 59	
Runcorn East	d			19 34							20 37						21 34					22 31		23 06	
Frodsham	d			19 38							20 41						21 38					22 35		23 10	
Helsby	d			19 42							20 45						21 42					22 39		23 14	
Liverpool Lime Street 106	d																								
Chester	a	19 45	19 46	19 54		20 12		20 19	20 45	20 46	20 57	21 21		21 21		21 45	21 57	21 59	22 31	22 45	22 45	22 53	23 21	23 26	
	d							20 32						21 26					22 36						
Shotton	d							20 41						21 35					22 45						
Flint	d							20 47						21 41					22 51						
Prestatyn	d							21 00						21 54					23 05						
Rhyl	d							21 06						22 00					23 11						
Abergele & Pensarn	d													22 06					23 17						
Colwyn Bay	d							21 17						22 14					23 25						
Llandudno Junction	a							21 24						22 19					23 38						
	d						20 30	21 26					21 32	22 21											
Deganwy	d						20x33						21x35												
Llandudno	a						20 40						21 46												
Conwy	d													22 23											
Penmaenmawr	d													22 29											
Llanfairfechan	d													22 33											
Bangor (Gwynedd)	a							21 41						22 41											
	d							21 43						22 43											
Llanfairpwll	d							21x49																	
Bodorgan	d							21x59																	
Ty Croes	d							22x03																	
Rhosneigr	d							22x06																	
Valley	d							22x12																	
Holyhead	a							22 25						23 18											

		AW	NT	AW	AW	NT	AW
					◇		🚌
London Euston ⊖65	d						
Birmingham New Street 65	d						
Manchester Airport 84,85 ✈	d						
Cardiff Central 131	d				20 55		
Crewe	d	23 21			23 58		
Manchester Pic'dilly 90	d		22 17	23 14		23 17	
Manchester Oxford Road 90	d			23 17			
Newton-le-Willows 90	d			23 36			
Earlestown 90	d			23 39			
Warrington Bank Quay 90	d			23 48			
Runcorn East	d			23 55			
Frodsham	d			23 59			
Helsby	d			00 03			
Liverpool Lime Street 106	d						
Chester	a	23 42	23 45	00 15	00 24	00 43	
	d						
Shotton	d						
Flint	d						
Prestatyn	d						
Rhyl	d						
Abergele & Pensarn	d						
Colwyn Bay	d						
Llandudno Junction	a						
	d						23 48
Deganwy	d						
Llandudno	a						
Conwy	d						
Penmaenmawr	d						
Llanfairfechan	d						
Bangor (Gwynedd)	a						00 38
	d						00 38
Llanfairpwll	d						
Bodorgan	d						
Ty Croes	d						
Rhosneigr	d						
Valley	d						
Holyhead	a						02 02

A ✕ from Chester

B From Birmingham International

C From Blaenau Ffestiniog

Crewe and Manchester - Chester and North Wales

Network Diagram - see first Page of Table 81

	AW	AW ◇	AW	AW ◇	AW ◇	NT A	NT B	AW	AW ■ C	AW ■ D	AW	AW	AW	VT ◇1 ⊏	AW ◇ ⊥	AW ◇ ⊥	NT	AW	AW	AW ◇ ⊥	AW ◇ ⊥	NT
London Euston 15 ⊖65 d																						
Birmingham New Street 12 65 d				22p55										05 30								
Manchester Airport 84,85 ✈ d															05 33							
Cardiff Central 7 131 d		19p34			20p53				22p31	22p31											05 20	
Crewe 10 d				23p57	00 02				01 33	01 33				06 23		07 03		07 23				
Manchester Pic'dilly 10 90 ⛴ d			23p14			23p17	23p17	00 28							05 50		06 17			06 50		07 17
Manchester Oxford Road 90 d			23p17												05 53					06 53		
Newton-le-Willows 90 d			23p36												06 12					07 12		
Earlestown 8 90 d			23p39												06 15					07 15		
Warrington Bank Quay 90 d			23p48												06 26					07 22		
Runcorn East d			23p55												06 33					07 29		
Frodsham d			23p59												06 37					07 34		
Helsby d			00 03												06 41					07 38		
Liverpool Lime Street 10 106 d																						
Chester a		22p34	00 15	00 18	00 27	00 40	00 43	01 31	01 57	01 57				06 43	06 53	07 23	07 45	07 46		07 50	08 18	08 45
d	22p04	22p56		00 40					02 00	02 00				06 44	06 55	07 25				07 55	08 22	
Shotton d	22p13	23p05													07 04					08 04		
Flint d	22p19	23p11		00 53										06 57	07 10	07 39				08 10	08 36	
Prestatyn d	22p32	23p24		01 06										07 10	07 23	07 52				08 23	08 49	
Rhyl d	22p38	23p30		01 12					02 27	02 27				07 16	07 29	07 58				08 29	08 55	
Abergele & Pensarn d	22p44	23p36													07 35					08 35		
Colwyn Bay d	22p52	23p44		01 23										07 27	07 43	08 09				08 43	09 06	
Llandudno Junction a	22p57	23p49		01 28					02 40	02 40				07 33	07 48	08 14				08 48	09 11	
d	22p59	23p52		01 29					02 42	02 42	06 13	06 51	07 31	07 33	07 50	08 15			08 28	08 50	09 12	
Deganwy d											06x16	06x54	07x34		07x54				08x31	08x54		
Llandudno a											06 23	07 01	07 41		08 06				08 38	09 06		
Conwy d	23b01	23b54														08x17					09x14	
Penmaenmawr d	23b07	23b59														08x23					09x20	
Llanfairfechan d	23b11	00x04														08x27					09x24	
Bangor (Gwynedd) a	23p19	00 12		01 45					02 58	02 58				07 49		08 35					09 32	
d	23p21	00 14		01 45					02 59	02 59				07 50		08 38					09 35	
Llanfairpwll d	23b27															08x44						
Bodorgan d	23b37															08x54						
Ty Croes d	23b42															08x58					09x49	
Rhosneigr d	23b45															09x01					09x53	
Valley d	23b50															09x07					09x56	
Holyhead a	00 05	00 48		02 15					03 32	03 37				08 23		09 21					10 14	

	AW	AW	AW ◇ ⊥	AW ◇ E	AW ◇ F ⊥	NT	AW	AW	AW ◇ ⊥	VT ◇1 ⊏	AW ◇ ⊥	NT	AW	AW	AW ◇ ⊥	VT ◇1 ⊏	AW ◇ F ⊥	NT	AW	AW	AW ◇ ⊥	VT ◇1 ⊏
London Euston 15 ⊖65 d										08 10						08 50						10 10
Birmingham New Street 12 65 d					07 23												09 24					
Manchester Airport 84,85 ✈ d																						
Cardiff Central 7 131 d											07 21											
Crewe 10 d	08 23						09 23			09 49			10 23			10 43			11 23			11 49
Manchester Pic'dilly 10 90 ⛴ d			07 50			08 17			08 50			09 17			09 50			10 17			10 50	
Manchester Oxford Road 90 d			07 53						08 53						09 53						10 53	
Newton-le-Willows 90 d			08 12						09 12						10 12						11 12	
Earlestown 8 90 d			08 15						09 15						10 15						11 15	
Warrington Bank Quay 90 d			08 24						09 26						10 26						11 26	
Runcorn East d			08 31						09 33						10 33						11 33	
Frodsham d			08 35						09 37						10 37						11 37	
Helsby d			08 39						09 41						10 41						11 41	
Liverpool Lime Street 10 106 d																						
Chester a	08 46		08 51		09 17	09 45	09 46		09 53	10 12	10 19	10 45	10 46		10 53	11 10	11 19	11 45	11 46		11 53	12 12
d			08 55		09 24				09 55		10 23				10 55	11 12	11 24				11 55	
Shotton d			09 04						10 04						11 04						12 04	
Flint d			09 10		09 37				10 10		10 36				11 10		11 39				12 10	
Prestatyn d			09 23		09 50				10 23		10 49				11 23		11 52				12 23	
Rhyl d			09 29		09 56				10 29		10 55				11 29	11 41	11 58				12 29	
Abergele & Pensarn d			09 35						10 35						11 35						12 35	
Colwyn Bay d			09 43		10 07				10 43		11 06				11 43	11 54	12 09				12 43	
Llandudno Junction a			09 48		10 12				10 48		11 11				11 48	12 00	12 14				12 48	
d		09 28	09 50	10 00	10 13			10 28	10 50		11 12			11 26	11 50	12 01	12 15			12 28	12 50	
Deganwy d		09x31	09x54	10x03				10x31	10x54					11x29	11x54					12x31	12x54	
Llandudno a		09 38	10 06	10 13				10 38	11 06					11 36	12 06					12 38	13 06	
Conwy d											11x14						12x17					
Penmaenmawr d											11x20						12x23					
Llanfairfechan d											11x24						12x27					
Bangor (Gwynedd) a					10 29						11 32					12 19	12 35					
d					10 30						11 35					12 20	12 38					
Llanfairpwll d					10x36												12x44					
Bodorgan d																	12x54					
Ty Croes d																	12x58					
Rhosneigr d																	13x01					
Valley d					10x54												13x07					
Holyhead a					11 05						12 09					12 55	13 18					

A from 7 July until 4 August
B from 11 August until 29 September
C 4 August
D 11 August
E From Blaenau Ffestiniog
F From Birmingham International
b Previous night, stops on request

Crewe and Manchester - Chester and North Wales

Network Diagram - see first Page of Table 81

	AW ◇ A	AW ◇ ⊥	NT	AW	AW	AW ◇ ⊥	VT ◇1 ⊏	AW ◇ B ⊥	NT	AW	AW	AW ◇ ⊥	VT ◇1 ⊏	AW ◇ ⊥	NT	AW	AW	AW ◇ ⊥	VT ◇1 ⊏	AW ◇ A	AW ◇ B ⊥
London Euston 15 ⊖65 d							11 10						12 10						13 10		
Birmingham New Street 12 65 d								11 24													13 24
Manchester Airport 84,85 ✈ d																					
Cardiff Central 7 131 d		09 21												11 21							
Crewe 10 d				12 23			12 49			13 23			13 49			14 23			14 49		
Manchester Pic'dilly 10 90 ⛴ d			11 17			11 50			12 17			12 50			13 17			13 50			
Manchester Oxford Road 90 d						11 53						12 53						13 53			
Newton-le-Willows 90 d						12 12						13 12						14 12			
Earlestown 8 90 d						12 15						13 15						14 15			
Warrington Bank Quay 90 d						12 26						13 26						14 26			
Runcorn East d						12 33						13 33						14 33			
Frodsham d						12 37						13 37						14 37			
Helsby d						12 41						13 41						14 41			
Liverpool Lime Street 10 106 d																					
Chester a		12 19	12 45	12 46		12 53	13 12	13 18	13 45	13 46		13 53	14 12	14 19	14 45	14 46		14 53	15 12		15 20
d		12 23				12 55		13 22				13 55		14 23				14 55			15 22
Shotton d						13 04						14 04						15 04			
Flint d		12 36				13 10		13 36				14 10		14 36				15 10			15 37
Prestatyn d		12 49				13 23		13 49				14 23		14 49				15 23			15 50
Rhyl d		12 55				13 29		13 55				14 29		14 55				15 29			15 56
Abergele & Pensarn d						13 35						14 35						15 35			
Colwyn Bay d		13 06				13 43		14 06				14 43		15 06				15 43			16 07
Llandudno Junction a		13 11				13 48		14 11				14 48		15 11				15 48			16 12
d	13 00	13 12			13 28	13 50		14 12			14 28	14 50		15 12			15 30	15 50		16 00	16 14
Deganwy d	13x03				13x31	13x54					14x31	14x54					15x33	15 54		16x03	
Llandudno a	13 13				13 38	14 06					14 38	15 06					15 40	16 06		16 13	
Conwy d								14x14													16x16
Penmaenmawr d								14x20													16x22
Llanfairfechan d								14x24													16x26
Bangor (Gwynedd) a		13 28						14 32						15 28							16 35
d		13 29						14 35						15 29							16 36
Llanfairpwll d		13x36												15x36							
Bodorgan d		13x46												15x46							
Ty Croes d		13x50												15x50							
Rhosneigr d		13x53												15x53							
Valley d		13x58												15x58							
Holyhead a		14 13						15 08						16 13							17 11

	NT	AW	AW	AW ◇ ⊥	VT ◇1 ⊏	AW ◇ ⊥	NT	AW	AW	AW ◇ ⊥	VT ◇1 ⊏	AW ◇ B ⊥	NT	AW	AW	AW ◇ A	AW ◇ ⊥	VT ◇1 ⊏	AW ■ ⊥	NT	AW	AW
London Euston 15 ⊖65 d					14 10						15 10							16 10				
Birmingham New Street 12 65 d												15 24										
Manchester Airport 84,85 ✈ d																						
Cardiff Central 7 131 d						13 21													15 21			
Crewe 10 d		15 23			15 49			16 23			16 49			17 23				17 49			18 23	
Manchester Pic'dilly 10 90 ⛴ d	14 17			14 50			15 17			15 50			16 17				16 50			17 17		
Manchester Oxford Road 90 d				14 53						15 53							16 53					
Newton-le-Willows 90 d				15 12						16 12							17 12					
Earlestown 8 90 d				15 15						16 15							17 15					
Warrington Bank Quay 90 d				15 26						16 26							17 26					
Runcorn East d				15 33						16 33							17 33					
Frodsham d				15 37						16 37							17 37					
Helsby d				15 41						16 41							17 41					
Liverpool Lime Street 10 106 d																						
Chester a	15 45	15 46		15 53	16 10	16 22	16 45	16 46		16 53	17 12	17 19	17 45	17 46			17 53	18 09	18 19	18 45	18 46	
d				15 55	16 12	16 26				16 55		17 24					17 55	18 16	18 24			
Shotton d				16 04						17 04		17 33					18 04					
Flint d				16 10	16 25	16 39				17 10		17 39					18 10	18 29	18 39			
Prestatyn d				16 23	16 38	16 52				17 23		17 52					18 23	18 42	18 52			
Rhyl d				16 29	16 45	16 58				17 29		17 58					18 29	18 49	18 58			
Abergele & Pensarn d				16 35						17 35		18 04					18 35					
Colwyn Bay d				16 43	16 56	17 09				17 43		18 12					18 43	19 00	19 09			
Llandudno Junction a				16 48	17 01	17 14				17 48		18 17					18 48	19 05	19 14			
d			16 26	16 50	17 02	17 14			17 28	17 50		18 19			18 26	18 41	18 50	19 06	19 15			19 28
Deganwy d			16x29	16x54					17x31	17x54					18x29	18x44	18x54					19x31
Llandudno a			16 36	17 06					17 38	18 06					18 36	18 54	19 06					19 38
Conwy d						17x16						18x21										
Penmaenmawr d						17x22						18x27										
Llanfairfechan d						17x26						18x31										
Bangor (Gwynedd) a					17 17	17 34						18 39						19 21	19 32			
d					17 19	17 37						18 41						19 23	19 33			
Llanfairpwll d						17x43													19x40			
Bodorgan d						17x53													19x51			
Ty Croes d						17x57													19x55			
Rhosneigr d						18x00													19x58			
Valley d						18x06													20x04			
Holyhead a					17 51	18 20						19 13						19 55	20 18			

A From Blaenau Ffestiniog
B From Birmingham International

Table 81

Saturdays 7 July to 29 September

Crewe and Manchester - Chester and North Wales

Network Diagram - see first Page of Table 81

	AW	VT	AW		NT	AW	AW	VT	AW	AW	NT	AW	AW		AW	AW	AW	NT	AW	AW	AW	NT	AW
	◇ ✣	◇1 ⊓	◇ A ✣				✣	◇1 ⊓		■ B ✣					◇ A ✣	◇ C	◇				◇		
London Euston [15] ⊖65 d		17 10						18 10															
Birmingham New Street [12] 65 d			17 24												19 24								
Manchester Airport 84,85 ✈ d																			20 32				
Cardiff Central [7] 131 d										17 21											19 34		
Crewe [10] d		18 50				19 23		19 49				20 23					21 00			21 36			22 23
Manchester Pic'dilly [10] 90 ⛴ d	17 50				18 17		18 50				19 17		19 50					20 17	20 50			21 17	
Manchester Oxford Road 90 d	17 53						18 53						19 53						20 53				
Newton-le-Willows 90 d	18 12						19 12						20 12						21 12				
Earlestown [8] 90 d	18 15						19 16						20 15						21 15				
Warrington Bank Quay 90 d	18 25						19 27						20 30						21 27				
Runcorn East d	18 32						19 34						20 37						21 34				
Frodsham d	18 37						19 38						20 41						21 38				
Helsby d	18 42						19 42						20 45						21 42				
Liverpool Lime Street [10] 106 d																							
Chester a	18 54	19 10	19 20		19 45	19 46	19 54	20 12		20 19	20 45	20 46	20 57		21 21		21 21	21 45	21 57	21 59	22 31	22 45	22 45
d	18 55	19 17	19 32							20 32							21 26				22 36		
Shotton d	19 04		19 41							20 41							21 35				22 45		
Flint d	19 10	19 30	19 47							20 47							21 41				22 51		
Prestatyn d	19 23	19 43	20 00							21 00							21 54				23 05		
Rhyl d	19 29	19 50	20 06							21 06							22 00				23 11		
Abergele & Pensarn d	19 35		20 12														22 06				23 17		
Colwyn Bay d	19 43	20 01	20 20							21 17							22 14				23 25		
Llandudno Junction a	19 48	20 06	20 25							21 24							22 19				23 38		
d	19 50	20 07	20 27						20 30	21 26						21 32	22 21						
Deganwy d	19x54								20x33							21x35							
Llandudno a	20 06								20 40							21 46							
Conwy d			20x29														22 23						
Penmaenmawr d			20x35														22 29						
Llanfairfechan d			20x39														22 33						
Bangor (Gwynedd) a		20 22	20 47							21 41							22 41						
d		20 24	20 49							21 43							22 43						
Llanfairpwll d			20x55							21x49													
Bodorgan d			21x05							21x59													
Ty Croes d			21x10							22x03													
Rhosneigr d			21x13							22x06													
Valley d			21x18							22x12													
Holyhead a		20 56	21 31							22 25							23 18						

	AW	AW	AW	AW	NT	AW	AW	AW	AW		NT	AW
		◇ A					◇	🚌	■ D			■ E
London Euston [15] ⊖65 d												
Birmingham New Street [12] 65 d		21 24										
Manchester Airport 84,85 ✈ d												
Cardiff Central [7] 131 d							20 55		21 20			22 20
Crewe [10] d				23 21			23 58		00 15			01 20
Manchester Pic'dilly [10] 90 ⛴ d	21 50		22 26		22 17	23 14					23 17	
Manchester Oxford Road 90 d	21 53		22 29			23 17						
Newton-le-Willows 90 d	22 12		22 47			23 36						
Earlestown [8] 90 d	22 15		22 50			23 39						
Warrington Bank Quay 90 d	22 24		22 59			23 48						
Runcorn East d	22 31		23 06			23 55						
Frodsham d	22 35		23 10			23 59						
Helsby d	22 39		23 14			00 03						
Liverpool Lime Street [10] 106 d												
Chester a	22 53	23 21	23 26	23 42	23 45	00 15	00 24		00 40		00 43	01 44
d									00 42			01 46
Shotton d												
Flint d												
Prestatyn d												
Rhyl d									01 10			02 13
Abergele & Pensarn d												
Colwyn Bay d												
Llandudno Junction a									01 23			02 26
d								23 48	01 24			02 28
Deganwy d												
Llandudno a												
Conwy d												
Penmaenmawr d												
Llanfairfechan d												
Bangor (Gwynedd) a								00 38	01 40			02 44
d								00 38	01 42			02 45
Llanfairpwll d												
Bodorgan d												
Ty Croes d												
Rhosneigr d												
Valley d												
Holyhead a								02 02	02 20			03 23

A From Birmingham International
B ✣ from Chester
C From Blaenau Ffestiniog
D 28 July
E 4 August

Table 81

Saturdays from 6 October

Crewe and Manchester - Chester and North Wales

Network Diagram - see first Page of Table 81

	AW	AW	AW	AW	AW	NT	AW	AW	AW		AW	VT	AW	AW	AW	NT	AW	AW	AW		AW	NT	AW	AW
		◇		◇	◇							◇1 ⊓	◇ ✣	◇ ✣				◇ ✣	◇ ✣					◇ ✣
London Euston [15] ⊖65 d																								
Birmingham New Street [12] 65 d				22p55								05 30												
Manchester Airport 84,85 ✈ d													05 33											
Cardiff Central [7] 131 d		19p34			20p53														05 20					
Crewe [10] d				23p57	00 02							06 23		07 03	07 23						08 23			
Manchester Pic'dilly [10] 90 ⛴ d			23p14			23p17	00 28						05 50			06 17		06 50				07 17		07 50
Manchester Oxford Road 90 d			23p17										05 53					06 53						07 53
Newton-le-Willows 90 d			23p36										06 12					07 12						08 12
Earlestown [8] 90 d			23p39										06 15					07 15						08 15
Warrington Bank Quay 90 d			23p48										06 26					07 22						08 24
Runcorn East d			23p55										06 33					07 29						08 31
Frodsham d			23p59										06 37					07 34						08 35
Helsby d			00 03										06 41					07 38						08 39
Liverpool Lime Street [10] 106 d																								
Chester a		22p34	00 15	00 18	00 27	00 42	01 31					06 43	06 53	07 23	07 46	07 47		07 50	08 18		08 46	08 47		08 51
d	22p04	22p56		00 40								06 44	06 55	07 25				07 55	08 22					08 55
Shotton d	22p13	23p05											07 04					08 04						09 04
Flint d	22p19	23p11		00 53								06 57	07 10	07 39				08 10	08 36					09 10
Prestatyn d	22p32	23p24		01 06								07 10	07 23	07 52				08 23	08 49					09 23
Rhyl d	22p38	23p30		01 12								07 16	07 29	07 58				08 29	08 55					09 29
Abergele & Pensarn d	22p44	23p36											07 35					08 35						09 35
Colwyn Bay d	22p52	23p44		01 23								07 27	07 43	08 09				08 43	09 06					09 43
Llandudno Junction a	22p57	23p49		01 28								07 33	07 48	08 14				08 48	09 11					09 48
d	22p59	23p52		01 29				06 13	06 51		07 31	07 33	07 50	08 15			08 28	08 50	09 12				09 28	09 50
Deganwy d								06x16	06x54		07x34		07x54				08x31	08x54					09x31	09x54
Llandudno a								06 23	07 01		07 41		08 06				08 38	09 06					09 38	10 06
Conwy d	23b01	23b54												08x17					09x14					
Penmaenmawr d	23b07	23b59												08x23					09x20					
Llanfairfechan d	23b11	00x04												08x27					09x24					
Bangor (Gwynedd) a	23p19	00 12		01 45								07 49		08 35					09 32					
d	23p21	00 14		01 45								07 50		08 38					09 35					
Llanfairpwll d	23b27													08x44										
Bodorgan d	23b37													08x54					09x49					
Ty Croes d	23b42													08x58					09x53					
Rhosneigr d	23b45													09x01					09x56					
Valley d	23b50													09x07										
Holyhead a	00 05	00 48		02 15								08 23		09 21					10 14					

	AW	AW	AW	NT	AW		AW	VT	AW	AW	NT	AW	AW	VT	AW		AW	NT	AW	AW	VT	AW	AW	AW
	◇ A	◇ B ✣					◇ ✣	◇1 ⊓	◇ ✣				◇ ✣	◇1 ⊓	◇ B ✣					◇ ✣	◇1 ⊓	◇ A	◇ ✣	
London Euston [15] ⊖65 d								08 10						08 50							10 10			
Birmingham New Street [12] 65 d		07 23													09 24									
Manchester Airport 84,85 ✈ d																								
Cardiff Central [7] 131 d									07 21														09 21	
Crewe [10] d			09 23					09 49		10 23				10 43			11 23				11 49			12 23
Manchester Pic'dilly [10] 90 ⛴ d				08 17			08 50				09 17		09 50					10 17		10 50				
Manchester Oxford Road 90 d							08 53						09 53							10 53				
Newton-le-Willows 90 d							09 12						10 12							11 12				
Earlestown [8] 90 d							09 15						10 15							11 15				
Warrington Bank Quay 90 d							09 26						10 26							11 26				
Runcorn East d							09 33						10 33							11 33				
Frodsham d							09 37						10 37							11 37				
Helsby d							09 41						10 41							11 41				
Liverpool Lime Street [10] 106 d																								
Chester a		09 17	09 46	09 47			09 53	10 12	10 19	10 46	10 47		10 53	11 10	11 19		11 46	11 47		11 53	12 12		12 19	12 46
d		09 24					09 55		10 23				10 55	11 12	11 24					11 55			12 23	
Shotton d							10 04						11 04							12 04				
Flint d		09 37					10 10		10 36				11 10		11 39					12 10			12 36	
Prestatyn d		09 50					10 23		10 49				11 23		11 52					12 23			12 49	
Rhyl d		09 56					10 29		10 55				11 29	11 41	11 58					12 29			12 55	
Abergele & Pensarn d							10 35						11 35							12 35				
Colwyn Bay d		10 07					10 43		11 06				11 43	11 54	12 09					12 43			13 06	
Llandudno Junction a		10 12					10 48		11 11				11 48	12 00	12 14					12 48			13 11	
d	10 00	10 13			10 28		10 50		11 12			11 26	11 50	12 01	12 15				12 28	12 50		13 00	13 12	
Deganwy d	10x03				10x31		10x54					11x29	11x54						12x31	12x54		13x03		
Llandudno a	10 13				10 38		11 06					11 36	12 06						12 38	13 06		13 13		
Conwy d									11x14						12x17									
Penmaenmawr d									11x20						12x23									
Llanfairfechan d									11x24						12x27									
Bangor (Gwynedd) a		10 29							11 32					12 19	12 35								13 28	
d		10 30							11 35					12 20	12 38								13 29	
Llanfairpwll d		10x36													12x44								13x36	
Bodorgan d															12x54								13x46	
Ty Croes d															12x58								13x50	
Rhosneigr d															13x01								13x53	
Valley d		10x54													13x07								13x58	
Holyhead a		11 05							12 09					12 55	13 18								14 13	

A From Blaenau Ffestiniog
B From Birmingham International
b Previous night, stops on request

Saturdays from 6 October

Crewe and Manchester - Chester and North Wales

Network Diagram - see first Page of Table 81

Station		NT	AW	AW ◇ ⚒	VT ◇1 ⊡	AW ◇ A ⚒	AW	NT	AW	AW ◇ ⚒	VT ◇1 ⊡	AW ◇ ⚒	AW	NT	AW	AW ◇ ⚒	VT ◇1 ⊡	AW ◇ B	AW ◇ A ⚒	AW	NT	AW
London Euston 15 ⊖65	d				11 10						12 10						13 10					
Birmingham New Street 12 65	d					11 24													13 24			
Manchester Airport 84,85 ✈	d																					
Cardiff Central 7 131	d											11 21										
Crewe 10	d				12 49		13 23				13 49		14 23				14 49			15 23		
Manchester Pic'dilly 10 90	d	11 17		11 50				12 17		12 50				13 17		13 50					14 17	
Manchester Oxford Road 90	d			11 53						12 53						13 53						
Newton-le-Willows 90	d			12 12						13 12						14 12						
Earlestown 8 90	d			12 15						13 15						14 15						
Warrington Bank Quay 90	d			12 26						13 26						14 26						
Runcorn East	d			12 33						13 33						14 33						
Frodsham	d			12 37						13 37						14 37						
Helsby	d			12 41						13 41						14 41						
Liverpool Lime Street 10 106	d																					
Chester	a	12 47		12 53	13 12	13 18	13 46	13 47		13 53	14 12	14 19	14 46	14 47		14 53	15 12		15 20	15 46	15 47	
	d			12 55		13 22				13 55		14 23				14 55			15 22			
Shotton	d			13 04						14 04						15 04						
Flint	d			13 10		13 36				14 10		14 36				15 10			15 37			
Prestatyn	d			13 23		13 49				14 23		14 49				15 23			15 50			
Rhyl	d			13 29		13 55				14 29		14 55				15 29			15 56			
Abergele & Pensarn	d			13 35						14 35						15 35						
Colwyn Bay	d			13 43		14 06				14 43		15 06				15 43			16 07			
Llandudno Junction	a			13 48		14 11				14 48		15 11				15 48			16 12			
	d		13 28	13 50		14 12			14 28	14 50		15 12			15 30	15 50		16 00	16 14			16 26
Deganwy	d		13x31	13x54					14x31	14x54					15x33	15 54		16x03				16x29
Llandudno	a		13 38	14 06					14 38	15 06					15 40	16 06		16 13				16 36
Conwy	d					14x14													16x16			
Penmaenmawr	d					14x20													16x22			
Llanfairfechan	d					14x24													16x26			
Bangor (Gwynedd)	a					14 32						15 28							16 35			
	d					14 35						15 29							16 36			
Llanfairpwll	d											15x36										
Bodorgan	d											15x46										
Ty Croes	d											15x50										
Rhosneigr	d											15x53										
Valley	d											15x58										
Holyhead	a					15 08						16 13							17 11			

Station		AW ◇ ⚒	VT ◇1 ⊡	AW ◇ ⚒	AW	NT	AW	AW ◇ ⚒	VT ◇1 ⊡	AW ◇ A ⚒	AW	NT	AW	AW ◇ B	AW ◇ ⚒	VT ◇1 ⊡	AW ■ ⚒	AW	NT	AW	AW ◇ ⚒	VT ◇1 ⊡	AW ◇ A ⚒
London Euston 15 ⊖65	d		14 10						15 10							16 10						17 10	
Birmingham New Street 12 65	d									15 24													17 24
Manchester Airport 84,85 ✈	d																						
Cardiff Central 7 131	d			13 21													15 21						
Crewe 10	d		15 49		16 23				16 49		17 23					17 49		18 23				18 50	
Manchester Pic'dilly 10 90	d	14 50				15 17		15 50				16 17			16 50				17 17		17 50		
Manchester Oxford Road 90	d	14 53						15 53							16 53						17 53		
Newton-le-Willows 90	d	15 12						16 12							17 12						18 12		
Earlestown 8 90	d	15 15						16 15							17 15						18 15		
Warrington Bank Quay 90	d	15 26						16 26							17 26						18 25		
Runcorn East	d	15 33						16 33							17 33						18 32		
Frodsham	d	15 37						16 37							17 37						18 37		
Helsby	d	15 41						16 41							17 41						18 42		
Liverpool Lime Street 10 106	d																						
Chester	a	15 53	16 10	16 22	16 46	16 47		16 53	17 12	17 19	17 46	17 47			17 53	18 09	18 19	18 46	18 47		18 54	19 10	19 20
	d	15 55	16 12	16 26				16 55		17 24					17 55	18 16	18 24				18 55	19 17	19 32
Shotton	d	16 04						17 04		17 33					18 04						19 04		19 41
Flint	d	16 10	16 25	16 39				17 10		17 39					18 10	18 29	18 39				19 10	19 30	19 47
Prestatyn	d	16 23	16 38	16 52				17 23		17 52					18 23	18 42	18 52				19 23	19 43	20 00
Rhyl	d	16 29	16 45	16 58				17 29		17 58					18 29	18 49	18 58				19 29	19 50	20 06
Abergele & Pensarn	d	16 35						17 35		18 04					18 35						19 35		20 12
Colwyn Bay	d	16 43	16 56	17 09				17 43		18 12					18 43	19 00	19 09				19 43	20 01	20 20
Llandudno Junction	a	16 48	17 01	17 14				17 48		18 17					18 48	19 05	19 14				19 48	20 06	20 25
	d	16 50	17 02	17 14			17 28	17 50		18 19			18 26	18 41	18 50	19 06	19 15			19 28	19 50	20 07	20 27
Deganwy	d	16x54					17x31	17x54					18x29	18x44	18x54					19x31	19x54		
Llandudno	a	17 06					17 38	18 06					18 36	18 54	19 06					19 38	20 06		
Conwy	d			17x16						18x21													20x29
Penmaenmawr	d			17x22						18x27													20x35
Llanfairfechan	d			17x26						18x31													20x39
Bangor (Gwynedd)	a		17 17	17 34						18 39						19 21	19 32					20 22	20 47
	d		17 19	17 37						18 41						19 23	19 33					20 24	20 49
Llanfairpwll	d			17x43													19x40						20x55
Bodorgan	d			17x53													19x51						21x05
Ty Croes	d			17x57													19x55						21x10
Rhosneigr	d			18x00													19x58						21x13
Valley	d			18x06													20x04						21x18
Holyhead	a		17 51	18 20						19 13						19 55	20 18					20 56	21 31

A From Birmingham International

B From Blaenau Ffestiniog

Table 81

Saturdays from 6 October

Crewe and Manchester - Chester and North Wales

Network Diagram - see first Page of Table 81

Station		AW	NT	AW ⚒	VT ◇1 ⊡	AW	AW ■ A ⚒	AW	NT	AW	AW ◇ B ⚒	AW ◇ C	AW ◇	NT	AW	AW	AW ◇	AW	NT	AW	AW ◇ B	AW D
London Euston 15 ⊖65	d				18 10																	
Birmingham New Street 12 65	d										19 24										21 24	
Manchester Airport 84,85 ✈	d														20 32							
Cardiff Central 7 131	d						17 21										19 34					
Crewe 10	d	19 23			19 49			20 23					21 00			21 36		22 23				
Manchester Pic'dilly 10 90	d		18 17	18 50					19 17	19 50				20 17	20 50				21 17	21 50		22 26
Manchester Oxford Road 90	d			18 53						19 53					20 53					21 53		22 29
Newton-le-Willows 90	d			19 12						20 12					21 12					22 12		22 47
Earlestown 8 90	d			19 16						20 15					21 15					22 15		22 50
Warrington Bank Quay 90	d			19 27						20 30					21 27					22 24		22 59
Runcorn East	d			19 34						20 37					21 34					22 31		23 06
Frodsham	d			19 38						20 41					21 38					22 35		23 10
Helsby	d			19 42						20 45					21 42					22 39		23 14
Liverpool Lime Street 10 106	d																					
Chester	a	19 46	19 47	19 54	20 12		20 19	20 46	20 47	20 57	21 21		21 21	21 47	21 57	21 59	22 31	22 45	22 47	22 53	23 21	23 26
	d						20 32						21 26				22 36					
Shotton	d						20 41						21 35				22 45					
Flint	d						20 47						21 41				22 51					
Prestatyn	d						21 00						21 54				23 05					
Rhyl	d						21 06						22 00				23 11					
Abergele & Pensarn	d												22 06				23 17					
Colwyn Bay	d						21 17						22 14				23 25					
Llandudno Junction	a						21 24						22 19				23 38					
	d					20 30	21 26					21 32	22 21									
Deganwy	d					20x33						21x35										
Llandudno	a					20 40						21 46										
Conwy	d												22 23									
Penmaenmawr	d												22 29									
Llanfairfechan	d												22 33									
Bangor (Gwynedd)	a						21 41						22 41									
	d						21 43						22 43									
Llanfairpwll	d						21x49															
Bodorgan	d						21x59															
Ty Croes	d						22x03															
Rhosneigr	d						22x06															
Valley	d						22x12															
Holyhead	a						22 25						23 18									

Station		AW	AW E	NT	AW D	AW E	AW ◇	AW E 🚌	NT	AW E 🚌	AW 🚌
London Euston 15 ⊖65	d										
Birmingham New Street 12 65	d										
Manchester Airport 84,85 ✈	d										
Cardiff Central 7 131	d						20 55				
Crewe 10	d	23 21					23 58				
Manchester Pic'dilly 10 90	d		22 26	22 17	23 14	23 14		22 26	23 17	23 14	
Manchester Oxford Road 90	d				23 17			22 31		23 19	
Newton-le-Willows 90	d				23 36			23 01		23 49	
Earlestown 8 90	d				23 39			23 11		23 59	
Warrington Bank Quay 90	d				23 48			23 36		00 24	
Runcorn East	d				23 55			23 56		00 44	
Frodsham	d				23 59			00 11		00 59	
Helsby	d				00 03			00 16		01 04	
Liverpool Lime Street 10 106	d										
Chester	a	23 42	23 46	23 47	00 15	00 17	00 24	00 36	00 45	01 24	
	d										
Shotton	d										
Flint	d										
Prestatyn	d										
Rhyl	d										
Abergele & Pensarn	d										
Colwyn Bay	d										
Llandudno Junction	a										
	d										23 48
Deganwy	d										
Llandudno	a										
Conwy	d										
Penmaenmawr	d										
Llanfairfechan	d										
Bangor (Gwynedd)	a										00 38
	d										00 38
Llanfairpwll	d										
Bodorgan	d										
Ty Croes	d										
Rhosneigr	d										
Valley	d										
Holyhead	a										02 02

A ⚒ from Chester

B From Birmingham International

C From Blaenau Ffestiniog

D 6 October, 13 October, 20 October

E from 27 October

Table 81

Sundays
until 24 June

Crewe and Manchester - Chester and North Wales

Network Diagram - see first Page of Table 81

		AW	AW	NT	AW	AW	AW	AW	AW	AW	AW	NT	AW	AW	AW	VT	AW	AW	AW	AW	AW	AW	NT
			◇		🚌	◇	◇	🚌		◇		A				◇■ 🍽			◇ B	◇			C
London Euston [15] ⊖65	d																						
Birmingham New Street [12] 65	d																						
Manchester Airport 84,85 ✈	d																						
Cardiff Central [7] 131	d		20p55																				
Crewe [10]	d		23p58				08 27			09 27	09 57					10 42	10 57			11 27		11 57	
Manchester Pic'dilly [10] 90 ⛴	d	23p14		23p17				07 28				09 22	09 56								10 55		11 22
Manchester Oxford Road 90	d	23p17						07 33					09 59								10 59		
Newton-le-Willows 90	d	23p36						08 03					10 18								11 20		
Earlestown [8] 90	d	23p39						08 13					10 21								11 23		
Warrington Bank Quay 90	d	23p48						08 38					10 28								11 30		
Runcorn East	d	23p55						08 58					10 35								11 37		
Frodsham	d	23p59						09 13					10 40								11 41		
Helsby	d	00 03						09 18					10 44								11 45		
Liverpool Lime Street [10] 106	d																						
Chester	a	00 15	00 24	00 43			08 49	09 38		09 49	10 20	10 46	10 59			11 02	11 22			11 50	11 57	12 20	12 43
	d					06 20	09 02			09 50						11 07				12 03			
Shotton	d									09 59										12 12			
Flint	d					06 33	09 15			10 05										12 18			
Prestatyn	d					06 47	09 28			10 19						11 30				12 31			
Rhyl	d					06 53	09 34			10 25						11 37				12 37			
Abergele & Pensarn	d									10 31													
Colwyn Bay	d					07 03	09 45			10 39						11 48				12 48			
Llandudno Junction	a					07 08	09 49			10 44						11 53				12 53			
	d				23p48	07 10	09 54		10 00	10 45				10 50	11 25	11 54		12 00	12 42	12 54			
Deganwy	d								10x03					10x53	11x28			12x03	12x45				
Llandudno	a								10 10					11 00	11 35			12 10	12 55				
Conwy	d				23p56					10x47													
Penmaenmawr	d				00 08					10x53													
Llanfairfechan	d				00 23					10x57													
Bangor (Gwynedd)	a				00 38	07 25	10 11			11 05						12 09				13 10			
	d				00 38	07 26	10 12			11 08						12 11				13 11			
Llanfairpwll	d				00 47					11x14													
Bodorgan	d				00 57					11x24													
Ty Croes	d				01 07					11x28													
Rhosneigr	d				01 27					11x31													
Valley	d				01 52					11x37													
Holyhead	a				02 02	08 00	10 48			11 51						12 43				13 42			

		AW	AW	AW	AW	AW	AW	AW	AW	AW	AW	NT	AW	AW	AW	AW	AW	AW	AW	AW	AW	AW	AW
				◇ 🍴	🍴	◇			◇ 🍴	🍴		C			◇ 🍴	🍴	◇ 🍴				◇	🍴	
London Euston [15] ⊖65	d																						
Birmingham New Street [12] 65	d					10 57											13 02						
Manchester Airport 84,85 ✈	d																						
Cardiff Central [7] 131	d																						
Crewe [10]	d			12 27			12 57		13 27		13 57				14 27			14 57			15 27		
Manchester Pic'dilly [10] 90 ⛴	d				11 56					12 56		13 22				13 56						14 56	
Manchester Oxford Road 90	d				11 59					12 59						13 59						14 59	
Newton-le-Willows 90	d				12 18					13 18						14 18						15 18	
Earlestown [8] 90	d				12 21					13 21						14 21						15 21	
Warrington Bank Quay 90	d				12 28					13 29						14 28						15 29	
Runcorn East	d				12 35					13 36						14 35						15 36	
Frodsham	d				12 39					13 40						14 39						15 40	
Helsby	d				12 43					13 44						14 43						15 44	
Liverpool Lime Street [10] 106	d																						
Chester	a			12 52	12 55	13 20	13 20		13 51	13 56	14 20	14 46			14 51	14 55	15 18	15 20			15 49	15 56	
	d			13 02					14 02						15 02						16 02		
Shotton	d			13 11					14 11						15 11						16 11		
Flint	d			13 17					14 17						15 17						16 17		
Prestatyn	d			13 30					14 30						15 30						16 30		
Rhyl	d			13 36					14 36						15 36						16 36		
Abergele & Pensarn	d			13 42					14 42						15 42						16 42		
Colwyn Bay	d			13 50					14 50						15 50						16 50		
Llandudno Junction	a			13 55					14 55						15 55						16 55		
	d	12 58	13 39	13 57				14 02	14 57				15 00	15 30	15 57				16 04	16 39	16 57		17 05
Deganwy	d	13x01	13x43					14x05					15x03	15x33					16x07	16x42			17x08
Llandudno	a	13 08	13 49					14 12					15 10	15 40					16 14	16 49			17 15
Conwy	d			13x59											15x59								
Penmaenmawr	d			14x05											16x05								
Llanfairfechan	d			14x09											16x09								
Bangor (Gwynedd)	a			14 17					15 12						16 17						17 12		
	d			14 19					15 14						16 19						17 14		
Llanfairpwll	d								15x20												17x20		
Bodorgan	d								15x30												17x30		
Ty Croes	d								15x34												17x34		
Rhosneigr	d								15x37												17x37		
Valley	d								15x43												17x43		
Holyhead	a			14 53					15 57						16 53						17 57		

A From Wigan Wallgate
B From Blaenau Ffestiniog
C From Southport

Table 81

Sundays
until 24 June

Crewe and Manchester - Chester and North Wales

Network Diagram - see first Page of Table 81

		AW	AW	NT	AW	AW	AW	VT	AW	AW	AW	VT	AW	AW	NT	AW	AW	VT	VT	AW	AW	AW
		■		A		◇	🍴	◇■ 🍽	◇ 🍴	◇		◇■ 🍽	◇ B	◇ C 🍴	A	◇	🍴	◇■ 🍽	◇■ 🍽	◇ 🍴		
London Euston [15] ⊖65	d							15 05				16 05						17 05	17 05			
Birmingham New Street [12] 65	d								15 02											17 02		
Manchester Airport 84,85 ✈	d																					
Cardiff Central [7] 131	d	13 22												15 22								
Crewe [10]	d		15 57			16 27		16 52		17 27		17 52				18 27		18 56	18 56		19 24	
Manchester Pic'dilly [10] 90 ⛴	d			15 22			15 56				16 56				17 22		17 56					18 56
Manchester Oxford Road 90	d						15 59				16 59						17 59					18 59
Newton-le-Willows 90	d						16 18				17 18						18 18					19 18
Earlestown [8] 90	d						16 21				17 21						18 21					19 21
Warrington Bank Quay 90	d						16 28				17 28						18 28					19 29
Runcorn East	d						16 35				17 35						18 35					19 36
Frodsham	d						16 39				17 39						18 39					19 40
Helsby	d						16 43				17 43						18 43					19 44
Liverpool Lime Street [10] 106	d																					
Chester	a	16 18	16 20	16 46		16 49	16 55	17 14	17 26	17 50	17 55	18 14		18 25	18 46	18 49	18 55	19 14	19 14	19 16	19 45	19 56
	d	16 36				17 02								18 29		18 52			19 22	19 38		
Shotton	d	16 45				17 11								18 38		19 01				19 47		
Flint	d	16 51				17 17								18 44		19 07			19 35	19 53		
Prestatyn	d	17 04				17 30								18 57		19 21			19 48	20 06		
Rhyl	d	17 10				17 36								19 03		19 27			19 55	20 12		
Abergele & Pensarn	d	17 16				17 42								19 09		19 33				20 18		
Colwyn Bay	d	17 24				17 50								19 17		19 41			20 06	20 26		
Llandudno Junction	a	17 29				17 55								19 22		19 46			20 11	20 31		
	d	17 31			17 40	17 57							18 31	19 24		19 47			20 12	20 33		
Deganwy	d				17x43								18x34									
Llandudno	a				17 50								18 44									
Conwy	d	17x33				17x59								19x26		19x49				20x35		
Penmaenmawr	d	17x39				18x05								19x32		19x55				20x41		
Llanfairfechan	d	17x43				18x09								19x36		19x59				20x45		
Bangor (Gwynedd)	a	17 51				18 17								19 44		20 07			20 27	20 53		
	d	17 54				18 19								19 45		20 09			20 29	20 55		
Llanfairpwll	d	18x00																				
Bodorgan	d	18x10																				
Ty Croes	d	18x14																				
Rhosneigr	d	18x17																				
Valley	d	18x23																				
Holyhead	a	18 37				18 54								20 18		20 44			20 59	21 30		

		VT	NT	AW	AW	VT	AW	AW	AW	AW	NT	AW	AW	AW	AW	AW	AW	AW	AW	AW
		◇■ 🍽	A			◇■ 🍽	◇ 🍴	◇			A		◇	◇			◇	🚌		◇
London Euston [15] ⊖65	d	18 05				19 05														
Birmingham New Street [12] 65	d						19 02							21 01			22 32			
Manchester Airport 84,85 ✈	d																			
Cardiff Central [7] 131	d																			21 04
Crewe [10]	d	19 52		20 27		20 55		21 27		21 57			22 29	23 06		23 38	00 01			00 10
Manchester Pic'dilly [10] 90 ⛴	d		19 22		19 56				20 56		21 22	21 50			22 52			22 14	23 20	
Manchester Oxford Road 90	d				19 59				20 59									22 19		
Newton-le-Willows 90	d				20 18				21 18									22 49		
Earlestown [8] 90	d				20 21				21 21									22 59		
Warrington Bank Quay 90	d				20 30				21 28									23 24		
Runcorn East	d				20 37				21 35									23 44		
Frodsham	d				20 41				21 39									23 59		
Helsby	d				20 45				21 43									00 04		
Liverpool Lime Street [10] 106	d																			
Chester	a	20 11	20 46	20 50	20 57	21 14	21 20	21 50	21 55	22 20	22 46	22 52	22 52	23 31	23 54	00 01	00 22	00 24	00 25	00 33
	d	20 18				21 17		22 00					23 00				00 38			
Shotton	d							22 09					23 09							
Flint	d	20 31				21 30		22 15					23 15				00 51			
Prestatyn	d	20 44				21 43		22 28					23 28				01 04			
Rhyl	d	20 51				21 50		22 34					23 34				01 10			
Abergele & Pensarn	d							22 40												
Colwyn Bay	d	21 02				22 01		22 48					23 45				01 21			
Llandudno Junction	a	21 07				22 06		22 53					23 50				01 27			
	d	21 08				22 07		22 55					23 51				01 28			
Deganwy	d																			
Llandudno	a																			
Conwy	d												23x53							
Penmaenmawr	d												00x01							
Llanfairfechan	d												00x03							
Bangor (Gwynedd)	a	21 23				22 22		23 10					00 11				01 44			
	d	21 25				22 24		23 12					00 14				01 44			
Llanfairpwll	d							23x18												
Bodorgan	d							23x28												
Ty Croes	d							23x32												
Rhosneigr	d							23x35												
Valley	d							23x41												
Holyhead	a	21 57				22 56		23 55					00 49				02 20			

A From Southport
B From Blaenau Ffestiniog
C ◇ from Chester

Crewe and Manchester - Chester and North Wales

Network Diagram - see first Page of Table 81

	AW	AW	AW	AW	NT	AW	AW	AW	AW		AW	AW	AW	NT	AW	AW	AW	VT	AW		AW	AW	AW	AW
		◇		A		B	◇	◇				◇		C				◇1				◇ D	◇	
London Euston 15 ⊖65 d																								
Birmingham New Street 12 65 d																								
Manchester Airport 84,85 ✈ d																								
Cardiff Central 7 131 d		20p55		21p20		22p20																		
Crewe 10 d		23p58		00 15		01 20		08 27				09 27	09 57					10 42	10 57				11 27	
Manchester Pic'dilly 10 90 ⇌ d	23p14				23p17				07 28					09 22	09 56									10 55
Manchester Oxford Road 90 d	23p17								07 33						09 59									10 59
Newton-le-Willows 90 d	23p36								08 03						10 18									11 20
Earlestown 8 90 d	23p39								08 13						10 21									11 23
Warrington Bank Quay 90 d	23p48								08 38						10 28									11 30
Runcorn East d	23p55								08 58						10 35									11 37
Frodsham d	23p59								09 13						10 40									11 41
Helsby d	00 03								09 18						10 44									11 45
Liverpool Lime Street 10 106 d																								
Chester a	00 15	00 24		00 40	00 43	01 44		08 49	09 38			09 49	10 20	10 46	10 59			11 02	11 22				11 50	11 57
d				00 42		01 46	06 20	09 02				09 50						11 07					12 03	
Shotton d												09 59											12 12	
Flint d							06 33	09 15				10 05											12 18	
Prestatyn d							06 47	09 28				10 19						11 30					12 31	
Rhyl d				01 10		02 13	06 53	09 34				10 25						11 37					12 37	
Abergele & Pensarn d												10 31												
Colwyn Bay d							07 03	09 45				10 39						11 48					12 48	
Llandudno Junction a				01 23		02 26	07 08	09 49				10 44						11 53					12 53	
d			23p48	01 24		02 28	07 10	09 54			10 00	10 45				10 50	11 25	11 54			12 00	12 42	12 54	
Deganwy d											10x03					10x53	11x28				12x03	12x45		
Llandudno a											10 10					11 00	11 35				12 10	12 55		
Conwy d			23p56									10x47												
Penmaenmawr d			00 08									10x53												
Llanfairfechan d			00 23									10x57												
Bangor (Gwynedd) a			00 38	01 40		02 44	07 25	10 11				11 05						12 09					13 10	
d			00 38	01 42		02 45	07 26	10 12				11 08						12 11					13 11	
Llanfairpwll d			00 47									11x14												
Bodorgan d			00 57									11x24												
Ty Croes d			01 07									11x28												
Rhosneigr d			01 27									11x31												
Valley d			01 52									11x37												
Holyhead a			02 02	02 20		03 23	08 00	10 48				11 51						12 43					13 42	

	AW	NT	AW	AW	AW		AW	AW	AW	AW	AW	AW	AW	NT	AW		AW	AW	AW	AW	AW	AW	AW	AW
		E			◇			◇ F			◇			E				◇		◇ F				◇
London Euston 15 ⊖65 d																								
Birmingham New Street 12 65 d								11 05												13 24				
Manchester Airport 84,85 ✈ d																								
Cardiff Central 7 131 d																								
Crewe 10 d	11 57				12 27				12 57		13 27		13 57					14 27			14 57			15 27
Manchester Pic'dilly 10 90 ⇌ d		11 22					11 56					12 56		13 22					13 56					
Manchester Oxford Road 90 d							11 59					12 59							13 59					
Newton-le-Willows 90 d							12 18					13 18							14 18					
Earlestown 8 90 d							12 21					13 21							14 21					
Warrington Bank Quay 90 d							12 28					13 29							14 28					
Runcorn East d							12 35					13 36							14 35					
Frodsham d							12 39					13 40							14 39					
Helsby d							12 43					13 44							14 43					
Liverpool Lime Street 10 106 d																								
Chester a	12 20	12 43			12 52		12 55	13 20	13 20		13 51	13 56	14 20	14 46				14 51	14 55	15 18	15 20			15 49
d					13 02						14 02							15 02						16 02
Shotton d					13 11						14 11							15 11						16 11
Flint d					13 17						14 17							15 17						16 17
Prestatyn d					13 30						14 30							15 30						16 30
Rhyl d					13 36						14 36							15 36						16 36
Abergele & Pensarn d					13 42						14 42							15 42						16 42
Colwyn Bay d					13 50						14 50							15 50						16 50
Llandudno Junction a					13 55						14 55							15 55						16 55
d			12 58	13 39	13 57					14 02	14 57				15 00		15 30	15 57				16 04	16 39	16 57
Deganwy d			13x01	13x43						14x05					15x03		15x33					16x07	16x42	
Llandudno a			13 08	13 49						14 12					15 10		15 40					16 14	16 49	
Conwy d					13x59													15x59						
Penmaenmawr d					14x05													16x05						
Llanfairfechan d					14x09													16x09						
Bangor (Gwynedd) a					14 17						15 12							16 17						17 12
d					14 19						15 14							16 19						17 14
Llanfairpwll d											15x20													17x20
Bodorgan d											15x30													17x30
Ty Croes d											15x34													17x34
Rhosneigr d											15x37													17x37
Valley d											15x43													17x43
Holyhead a					14 53						15 57							16 53						17 57

A 29 July
B 5 August
C From Wigan Wallgate
D From Blaenau Ffestiniog
E From Southport
F From Birmingham International

Crewe and Manchester - Chester and North Wales

Network Diagram - see first Page of Table 81

	AW		AW	AW	AW	NT	AW	AW	AW	VT	AW		AW	AW	VT	AW	AW	NT	AW	AW	VT		VT	AW
						A		◇		◇1	◇ B		◇		◇1	◇ C	◇ D	A	◇		◇1		◇1	◇ B
London Euston 15 ⊖65 d										15 05					16 05						17 05		17 05	
Birmingham New Street 12 65 d											15 24													17 24
Manchester Airport 84,85 ✈ d																								
Cardiff Central 7 131 d				13 22													15 22							
Crewe 10 d					15 57			16 27		16 52			17 27		17 52				18 27		18 56		18 56	
Manchester Pic'dilly 10 90 ⇌ d	14 56					15 22			15 56					16 56				17 22		17 56				
Manchester Oxford Road 90 d	14 59								15 59					16 59						17 59				
Newton-le-Willows 90 d	15 18								16 18					17 18						18 18				
Earlestown 8 90 d	15 21								16 21					17 21						18 21				
Warrington Bank Quay 90 d	15 29								16 28					17 28						18 28				
Runcorn East d	15 36								16 35					17 35						18 35				
Frodsham d	15 40								16 39					17 39						18 39				
Helsby d	15 44								16 43					17 43						18 43				
Liverpool Lime Street 10 106 d																								
Chester a	15 56			16 18	16 20	16 46		16 49	16 55	17 14	17 26		17 50	17 55	18 14		18 25	18 46	18 49	18 55	19 14		19 14	19 16
d				16 36				17 02									18 29		18 52				19 22	19 38
Shotton d				16 45				17 11									18 38		19 01					19 47
Flint d				16 51				17 17									18 44		19 07				19 35	19 53
Prestatyn d				17 04				17 30									18 57		19 21				19 48	20 06
Rhyl d				17 10				17 36									19 03		19 27				19 55	20 12
Abergele & Pensarn d				17 16				17 42									19 09		19 33					20 18
Colwyn Bay d				17 24				17 50									19 17		19 41				20 06	20 26
Llandudno Junction a				17 29				17 55									19 22		19 46				20 11	20 31
d			17 05	17 31			17 40	17 57								18 31	19 24		19 47				20 12	20 33
Deganwy d			17x08				17x43									18x34								
Llandudno a			17 15				17 50									18 44								
Conwy d				17x33				17x59									19x26		19x49					20x35
Penmaenmawr d				17x39				18x05									19x32		19x55					20x41
Llanfairfechan d				17x43				18x09									19x36		19x59					20x45
Bangor (Gwynedd) a				17 51				18 17									19 44		20 07				20 27	20 53
d				17 54				18 19									19 45		20 09				20 29	20 55
Llanfairpwll d				18x00																				
Bodorgan d				18x10																				
Ty Croes d				18x14																				
Rhosneigr d				18x17																				
Valley d				18x23																				
Holyhead a				18 37				18 54									20 18		20 44				20 59	21 30

	AW	AW	VT	NT	AW	AW	VT		AW	AW	AW	AW	NT	AW	AW	AW	AW		AW	AW	AW	AW	AW
			◇1	A			◇1		◇ B	◇			A		◇	◇ B				◇ B			◇
London Euston 15 ⊖65 d			18 05				19 05																
Birmingham New Street 12 65 d									19 24							21 24				22 55			
Manchester Airport 84,85 ✈ d																							
Cardiff Central 7 131 d																							21 04
Crewe 10 d	19 24		19 52		20 27		20 55			21 27		21 57			22 29	23 06			23 38	00 01			00 10
Manchester Pic'dilly 10 90 ⇌ d		18 56		19 22		19 56					20 56		21 22	21 50			22 52				22 14	23 20	
Manchester Oxford Road 90 d		18 59				19 59					20 59										22 19		
Newton-le-Willows 90 d		19 18				20 18					21 18										22 49		
Earlestown 8 90 d		19 21				20 21					21 21										22 59		
Warrington Bank Quay 90 d		19 29				20 30					21 28										23 24		
Runcorn East d		19 36				20 37					21 35										23 44		
Frodsham d		19 40				20 41					21 39										23 59		
Helsby d		19 44				20 45					21 43										00 04		
Liverpool Lime Street 10 106 d																							
Chester a	19 45	19 56	20 11	20 48	20 50	20 57	21 14		21 20	21 50	21 55	22 20	22 46	22 52	22 52	23 31	23 54		00 01	00 22	00 24	00 25	00 33
d			20 18				21 17			22 00					23 00					00 38			
Shotton d										22 09					23 09								
Flint d			20 31				21 30			22 15					23 15					00 51			
Prestatyn d			20 44				21 43			22 28					23 28					01 04			
Rhyl d			20 51				21 50			22 34					23 34					01 10			
Abergele & Pensarn d										22 40													
Colwyn Bay d			21 02				22 01			22 48					23 45					01 21			
Llandudno Junction a			21 07				22 06			22 53					23 50					01 27			
d			21 08				22 07			22 55					23 51					01 28			
Deganwy d																							
Llandudno a																							
Conwy d															23x53								
Penmaenmawr d															00x01								
Llanfairfechan d															00x03								
Bangor (Gwynedd) a			21 23				22 22			23 10					00 11					01 44			
d			21 25				22 24			23 12					00 14					01 44			
Llanfairpwll d										23x18													
Bodorgan d										23x28													
Ty Croes d										23x32													
Rhosneigr d										23x35													
Valley d										23x41													
Holyhead a			21 57				22 56			23 55					00 49					02 20			

A From Southport
B From Birmingham International
C From Blaenau Ffestiniog
D ◇ from Chester

Table 81

Sundays

16 September to 30 September

Crewe and Manchester - Chester and North Wales

Network Diagram - see first Page of Table 81

	AW	AW ◇	NT	AW 🚌	AW 🚌	AW ◇	AW	NT A	AW	VT ◇1 🍴	AW	AW ◇	AW	AW	NT B	AW ◇ ☕	AW ☕	AW	AW ◇ C	AW ◇ ☕	AW ☕	AW
London Euston 15 ⊖65 d																						
Birmingham New Street 12 65 d																			11 05			
Manchester Airport 84,85 ✈ d																						
Cardiff Central 7 131 d		20p55																				
Crewe 10 d		23p58				09 24	10 07			10 42	11 05	11 27		11 57		12 27		12 54		13 27		13 57
Manchester Pic'dilly 10 90 ⇌ d	23p14		23p17		07 28			09 22	09 56				10 55		11 22		11 56				12 56	
Manchester Oxford Road 90 d	23p17				07 33				09 59				10 59				11 59				12 59	
Newton-le-Willows 90 d	23p36				08 03				10 18				11 20				12 18				13 18	
Earlestown 8 90 d	23p39				08 13				10 21				11 23				12 21				13 21	
Warrington Bank Quay 90 d	23p48				08 38				10 28				11 30				12 28				13 29	
Runcorn East d	23p55				08 58				10 35				11 37				12 35				13 36	
Frodsham d	23p59				09 13				10 40				11 41				12 39				13 40	
Helsby d	00 03				09 18				10 44				11 45				12 43				13 44	
Liverpool Lime Street 10 106 d																						
Chester a	00 15	00 24	00 43		09 38	09 46	10 30	10 46	10 59	11 02	11 30	11 50	11 57	12 20	12 43	12 52	12 55	13 19	13 20	13 51	13 56	14 20
d						09 48				11 07		12 03				13 02				14 02		
Shotton d						09 57						12 12				13 11				14 11		
Flint d						10 03						12 18				13 17				14 17		
Prestatyn d						10 16				11 30		12 31				13 30				14 30		
Rhyl d						10 22				11 37		12 37				13 36				14 36		
Abergele & Pensarn d						10 28										13 42				14 42		
Colwyn Bay d						10 36				11 48		12 48				13 50				14 50		
Llandudno Junction a						10 41				11 53		12 53				13 55				14 55		
d				23p48		10 43				11 54		12 54				13 57				14 57		
Deganwy d																						
Llandudno a																						
Conwy d				23p56		10x45										13x59						
Penmaenmawr d				00 08		10x51										14x05						
Llanfairfechan d				00 23		10x55										14x09						
Bangor (Gwynedd) a				00 38		11 03				12 09		13 10				14 17				15 12		
d				00 38		11 05				12 11		13 11				14 19				15 14		
Llanfairpwll d				00 47		11x12														15x20		
Bodorgan d				00 57		11x22														15x30		
Ty Croes d				01 07		11x26														15x34		
Rhosneigr d				01 27		11x29														15x37		
Valley d				01 52		11x34														15x43		
Holyhead a				02 02		11 49				12 43		13 42				14 53				15 57		

	NT B	AW ◇ ☕	AW ☕	AW ◇ C ☕	AW	AW ◇	AW ☕	AW ■	NT B	AW ◇	AW ☕	VT ◇1 🍴	AW ◇ C ☕	AW ◇	AW	VT ◇1 🍴	AW ◇ D ☕	NT B	AW ◇	AW ☕	VT ◇1 🍴	AW ◇ C ☕
London Euston 15 ⊖65 d												15 08				16 08					17 08	
Birmingham New Street 12 65 d				13 24									15 24									17 24
Manchester Airport 84,85 ✈ d																	15 22					
Cardiff Central 7 131 d								13 22														
Crewe 10 d		14 27			14 57	15 27				16 27		16 52		17 27		17 52			18 27		18 56	
Manchester Pic'dilly 10 90 ⇌ d	13 22		13 56				14 56		15 22		15 56				16 56			17 22		17 56		
Manchester Oxford Road 90 d			13 59				14 59				15 59				16 59					17 59		
Newton-le-Willows 90 d			14 18				15 18				16 18				17 18					18 18		
Earlestown 8 90 d			14 21				15 21				16 21				17 21					18 21		
Warrington Bank Quay 90 d			14 28				15 29				16 28				17 28					18 28		
Runcorn East d			14 35				15 36				16 35				17 35					18 35		
Frodsham d			14 39				15 40				16 39				17 39					18 39		
Helsby d			14 43				15 44				16 43				17 43					18 43		
Liverpool Lime Street 10 106 d																						
Chester a	14 46	14 51	14 55	15 18	15 20	15 49	15 56	16 18	16 46	16 49	16 55	17 14	17 26	17 49	17 55	18 14	18 25	18 46	18 49	18 55	19 14	19 16
d		15 02				16 02		16 36		17 02				18 02			18 29		18 52		19 22	19 38
Shotton d		15 11				16 11		16 45		17 11				18 11			18 38		19 01			19 47
Flint d		15 17				16 17		16 51		17 17				18 17			18 44		19 07		19 35	19 53
Prestatyn d		15 30				16 30		17 04		17 30				18 30			18 57		19 21		19 48	20 06
Rhyl d		15 36				16 36		17 10		17 36				18 36			19 03		19 27		19 55	20 12
Abergele & Pensarn d		15 42				16 42		17 16		17 42				18 42			19 09		19 33			20 18
Colwyn Bay d		15 50				16 50		17 24		17 50				18 50			19 17		19 41		20 06	20 26
Llandudno Junction a		15 55				16 55		17 29		17 55				18 55			19 22		19 46		20 11	20 31
d		15 57				16 57		17 31		17 57				18 57			19 24		19 47		20 12	20 33
Deganwy d																						
Llandudno a																						
Conwy d		15x59						17x33		17x59							19x26		19x49			20x35
Penmaenmawr d		16x05						17x39		18x05							19x32		19x55			20x41
Llanfairfechan d		16x09						17x43		18x09							19x36		19x59			20x45
Bangor (Gwynedd) a		16 17				17 12		17 52		18 17				19 12			19 44		20 07		20 27	20 53
d		16 19				17 14		17 54		18 19				19 14			19 45		20 09		20 29	20 55
Llanfairpwll d						17x20		18x00						19x20								
Bodorgan d						17x30		18x10						19x30								
Ty Croes d						17x34		18x14						19x34								
Rhosneigr d						17x37		18x17						19x37								
Valley d						17x43		18x23						19x43								
Holyhead a		16 53				17 57		18 37		18 54				19 54			20 18		20 44		20 59	21 30

A From Wigan Wallgate
B From Southport
C From Birmingham International
D ◇ from Chester

Table 81

Sundays

16 September to 30 September

Crewe and Manchester - Chester and North Wales

Network Diagram - see first Page of Table 81

	AW	AW	VT ◇1 🍴	NT A	AW	AW	VT ◇1 🍴	AW ◇ B ☕	AW ◇	AW	AW	NT A	AW	AW ◇	AW ◇ B	AW	AW	AW ◇ B	AW 🚌	AW	AW ◇
London Euston 15 ⊖65 d			18 08				19 08														
Birmingham New Street 12 65 d								19 24							21 24			22 55			
Manchester Airport 84,85 ✈ d																					
Cardiff Central 7 131 d																					21 04
Crewe 10 d	19 24		19 52		20 27		20 55		21 27		22 03			22 29	23 06		23 38	00 01			00 10
Manchester Pic'dilly 10 90 ⇌ d		18 56		19 22		19 56				20 56		21 22	21 50			22 52			22 14	23 20	
Manchester Oxford Road 90 d		18 59				19 59				20 59									22 19		
Newton-le-Willows 90 d		19 18				20 18				21 18									22 49		
Earlestown 8 90 d		19 21				20 21				21 21									22 59		
Warrington Bank Quay 90 d		19 29				20 30				21 28									23 24		
Runcorn East d		19 36				20 37				21 35									23 44		
Frodsham d		19 40				20 41				21 39									23 59		
Helsby d		19 44				20 45				21 43									00 04		
Liverpool Lime Street 10 106 d																					
Chester a	19 45	19 56	20 11	20 43	20 50	20 57	21 14	21 20	21 50	21 55	22 26	22 46	22 52	22 52	23 31	23 54	00 01	00 22	00 24	00 25	00 33
d			20 18				21 17		22 00					23 00				00 38			
Shotton d									22 09					23 09							
Flint d			20 31				21 30		22 15					23 15				00 51			
Prestatyn d			20 44				21 43		22 28					23 28				01 04			
Rhyl d			20 51				21 50		22 34					23 34				01 10			
Abergele & Pensarn d									22 40												
Colwyn Bay d			21 02				22 01		22 48					23 45				01 21			
Llandudno Junction a			21 07				22 06		22 53					23 50				01 27			
d			21 08				22 07		22 55					23 51				01 28			
Deganwy d																					
Llandudno a																					
Conwy d														23x53							
Penmaenmawr d														00x01							
Llanfairfechan d														00x03							
Bangor (Gwynedd) a			21 23				22 22		23 10					00 11				01 44			
d			21 25				22 24		23 12					00 14				01 44			
Llanfairpwll d									23x18												
Bodorgan d									23x28												
Ty Croes d									23x32												
Rhosneigr d									23x35												
Valley d									23x41												
Holyhead a			21 54				22 56		23 55					00 49				02 20			

Sundays

from 7 October

	AW C	AW D	AW ◇	AW D 🚌	NT	AW D 🚌	AW 🚌	AW 🚌	AW ◇	AW	NT E	AW D	AW D 🚌	AW C	VT ◇1 🍴	AW	AW ◇	AW D 🚌	AW C	AW D	AW	NT A
London Euston 15 ⊖65 d																						
Birmingham New Street 12 65 d																						
Manchester Airport 84,85 ✈ d																						
Cardiff Central 7 131 d			20p55																			
Crewe 10 d			23p58						09 24	10 07					10 42	11 05	11 27				11 57	
Manchester Pic'dilly 10 90 ⇌ d	23p14	23p14		22p26	23p17	23p14		07 28			09 22	09 56	08 49	09 56				09 47	10 55	10 50		11 21
Manchester Oxford Road 90 d	23p17			22p31		23p19		07 33					08 54	09 59				09 52	10 59			
Newton-le-Willows 90 d	23p36			23p01		23p49		08 03					09 24	10 18				10 22	11 20			
Earlestown 8 90 d	23p39			23p11		23p59		08 13					09 34	10 21				10 32	11 23			
Warrington Bank Quay 90 d	23p48			23p36		00 24		08 38					09 59	10 28				10 57	11 30			
Runcorn East d	23p55			23p56		00 44		08 58					10 19	10 35				11 17	11 37			
Frodsham d	23p59			00 11		00 59		09 13					10 34	10 40				11 32	11 41			
Helsby d	00 03			00 16		01 04		09 18					10 39	10 44				11 37	11 45			
Liverpool Lime Street 10 106 d																						
Chester a	00 15	00 17	00 24	00 36	00 45	01 24		09 38	09 46	10 30	10 46	10 58	10 59	10 59	11 02	11 30	11 50	11 57	11 57	11 58	12 20	12 46
d									09 48						11 07		12 03					
Shotton d									09 57								12 12					
Flint d									10 03								12 18					
Prestatyn d									10 16						11 30		12 31					
Rhyl d									10 22						11 37		12 37					
Abergele & Pensarn d									10 28													
Colwyn Bay d									10 36						11 48		12 48					
Llandudno Junction a									10 41						11 53		12 53					
d							23p48		10 43						11 54		12 54					
Deganwy d																						
Llandudno a																						
Conwy d							23p56		10x45													
Penmaenmawr d							00 08		10x51													
Llanfairfechan d							00 23		10x55													
Bangor (Gwynedd) a							00 38		11 03						12 09		13 10					
d							00 38		11 05						12 11		13 11					
Llanfairpwll d							00 47		11x12													
Bodorgan d							00 57		11x22													
Ty Croes d							01 07		11x26													
Rhosneigr d							01 27		11x29													
Valley d							01 52		11x34													
Holyhead a							02 02		11 49						12 43		13 42					

A From Southport
B From Birmingham International
C 7 October, 14 October, 21 October
D from 28 October
E From Wigan Wallgate

Sundays from 7 October

Crewe and Manchester - Chester and North Wales

Network Diagram - see first Page of Table 81

	AW	AW	AW	AW	AW	AW	AW	AW	AW	AW	AW	NT	AW	AW	AW	AW	AW	AW	AW	AW	AW	NT
	◇ 🛒	A 🚌	A 🛒	B 🛒		◇ C	◇ 🛒	A 🛒	A 🚌	B 🛒		D	◇ 🛒	A 🛒	A 🚌	B 🛒	◇ C 🛒		◇	🛒	■	D
London Euston ⊖65 d																						
Birmingham New Street 65 d						11 05											13 24					
Manchester Airport 84,85 ✈ d																						
Cardiff Central 131 d																					13 22	
Crewe d	12 27				12 54		13 27				13 57		14 27					14 57	15 27			
Manchester Pic'dilly 90 d		10 45	11 48	11 56				12 50	11 45	12 56		13 22		13 49	12 45	13 56				14 56		15 22
Manchester Oxford Road 90 d		10 50		11 59					11 50	12 59					12 50	13 59				14 59		
Newton-le-Willows 90 d		11 20		12 18					12 20	13 18					13 20	14 18				15 18		
Earlestown 90 d		11 30		12 21					12 30	13 21					13 30	14 21				15 21		
Warrington Bank Quay 90 d		11 55		12 28					12 55	13 29					13 55	14 28				15 29		
Runcorn East d		12 15		12 35					13 15	13 36					14 15	14 35				15 36		
Frodsham d		12 30		12 39					13 30	13 40					14 30	14 39				15 40		
Helsby d		12 35		12 43					13 35	13 44					14 35	14 43				15 44		
Liverpool Lime Street 106 d																						
Chester a	12 52	12 55	12 55	12 55	13 19	13 20	13 51	13 53	13 55	13 56	14 20	14 46	14 51	14 52	14 55	14 55	15 18	15 20	15 49	15 56	16 18	16 46
d	13 02						14 02						15 02						16 02		16 36	
Shotton d	13 11						14 11						15 11						16 11		16 45	
Flint d	13 17						14 17						15 17						16 17		16 51	
Prestatyn d	13 30						14 30						15 30						16 30		17 04	
Rhyl d	13 36						14 36						15 36						16 36		17 10	
Abergele & Pensarn d	13 42						14 42						15 42						16 42		17 16	
Colwyn Bay d	13 50						14 50						15 50						16 50		17 24	
Llandudno Junction a	13 55						14 55						15 55						16 55		17 29	
d	13 57						14 57						15 57						16 57		17 31	
Deganwy d																						
Llandudno a																						
Conwy d	13x59												15x59								17x33	
Penmaenmawr d	14x05												16x05								17x39	
Llanfairfechan d	14x09												16x09								17x43	
Bangor (Gwynedd) a	14 17						15 12						16 17						17 12		17 52	
d	14 19						15 14						16 19						17 14		17 54	
Llanfairpwll d							15x20												17x20		18x00	
Bodorgan d							15x30												17x30		18x10	
Ty Croes d							15x34												17x34		18x14	
Rhosneigr d							15x37												17x37		18x17	
Valley d							15x43												17x43		18x23	
Holyhead a	14 53						15 57						16 53						17 57		18 37	

	AW	AW	VT	AW	AW	AW	VT	AW	NT	AW	AW	VT	AW	AW	AW	VT	NT	AW	AW	VT	AW
	◇	🛒	◇ [1] ⊐	◇ C 🛒	◇		◇ [1] ⊐	◇ E 🛒	D	◇	🛒	◇ [1] ⊐	◇ C 🛒			◇ [1] ⊐	D			◇ [1] ⊐	◇ C 🛒
London Euston ⊖65 d			15 08				16 08					17 08				18 08				19 08	
Birmingham New Street 65 d				15 24									17 24								19 24
Manchester Airport 84,85 ✈ d																					
Cardiff Central 131 d								15 22													
Crewe d	16 27		16 52		17 27		17 52			18 27		18 56		19 24		19 52		20 27		20 55	
Manchester Pic'dilly 90 d		15 56				16 56			17 22		17 56				18 56		19 22		19 56		
Manchester Oxford Road 90 d		15 59				16 59					17 59				18 59				19 59		
Newton-le-Willows 90 d		16 18				17 18					18 18				19 18				20 18		
Earlestown 90 d		16 21				17 21					18 21				19 21				20 21		
Warrington Bank Quay 90 d		16 28				17 28					18 28				19 29				20 30		
Runcorn East d		16 35				17 35					18 35				19 36				20 37		
Frodsham d		16 39				17 39					18 39				19 40				20 41		
Helsby d		16 43				17 43					18 43				19 44				20 45		
Liverpool Lime Street 106 d																					
Chester a	16 49	16 55	17 14	17 26	17 49	17 55	18 14	18 25	18 46	18 49	18 55	19 14	19 16	19 45	19 56	20 11	20 48	20 50	20 57	21 14	21 20
d	17 02				18 02			18 29		18 52		19 22	19 38			20 18				21 17	
Shotton d	17 11				18 11			18 38		19 01			19 47								
Flint d	17 17				18 17			18 44		19 07		19 35	19 53			20 31				21 30	
Prestatyn d	17 30				18 30			18 57		19 21		19 48	20 06			20 44				21 43	
Rhyl d	17 36				18 36			19 03		19 27		19 55	20 12			20 51				21 50	
Abergele & Pensarn d	17 42				18 42			19 09		19 33			20 18								
Colwyn Bay d	17 50				18 50			19 17		19 41		20 06	20 26			21 02				22 01	
Llandudno Junction a	17 55				18 55			19 22		19 46		20 11	20 31			21 07				22 06	
d	17 57				18 57			19 24		19 47		20 12	20 33			21 08				22 07	
Deganwy d																					
Llandudno a																					
Conwy d	17x59							19x26		19x49			20x35								
Penmaenmawr d	18x05							19x32		19x55			20x41								
Llanfairfechan d	18x09							19x36		19x59			20x45								
Bangor (Gwynedd) a	18 17				19 12			19 44		20 07		20 27	20 53			21 23				22 22	
d	18 19				19 14			19 45		20 09		20 29	20 55			21 25				22 24	
Llanfairpwll d					19x20																
Bodorgan d					19x30																
Ty Croes d					19x34																
Rhosneigr d					19x37																
Valley d					19x43																
Holyhead a	18 54				19 54			20 18		20 44		20 59	21 30			21 54				22 56	

A from 28 October
B 7 October, 14 October, 21 October
C From Birmingham International
D From Southport
E ◇ from Chester

Sundays from 7 October

Crewe and Manchester - Chester and North Wales

Network Diagram - see first Page of Table 81

	AW	AW	AW	NT	AW	AW	AW	AW	AW	AW	AW	AW	AW
	◇			A		◇	◇ B			◇ B	🚌		◇
London Euston ⊖65 d													
Birmingham New Street 65 d							21 24			22 55			
Manchester Airport 84,85 ✈ d													
Cardiff Central 131 d													21 04
Crewe d	21 27		22 03			22 29	23 06		23 38	00 01			00 10
Manchester Pic'dilly 90 d		20 56		21 22	21 50			22 52			22 14	23 20	
Manchester Oxford Road 90 d		20 59									22 19		
Newton-le-Willows 90 d		21 18									22 49		
Earlestown 90 d		21 21									22 59		
Warrington Bank Quay 90 d		21 28									23 24		
Runcorn East d		21 35									23 44		
Frodsham d		21 39									23 59		
Helsby d		21 43									00 04		
Liverpool Lime Street 106 d													
Chester a	21 50	21 55	22 26	22 48	22 52	22 52	23 31	23 54	00 01	00 22	00 24	00 25	00 33
d	22 00					23 00				00 38			
Shotton d	22 09					23 09							
Flint d	22 15					23 15				00 51			
Prestatyn d	22 28					23 28				01 04			
Rhyl d	22 34					23 34				01 10			
Abergele & Pensarn d	22 40												
Colwyn Bay d	22 48					23 45				01 21			
Llandudno Junction a	22 53					23 50				01 27			
d	22 55					23 51				01 28			
Deganwy d													
Llandudno a													
Conwy d						23x53							
Penmaenmawr d						00x01							
Llanfairfechan d						00x03							
Bangor (Gwynedd) a	23 10					00 11				01 44			
d	23 12					00 14				01 44			
Llanfairpwll d	23x18												
Bodorgan d	23x28												
Ty Croes d	23x32												
Rhosneigr d	23x35												
Valley d	23x41												
Holyhead a	23 55					00 49				02 20			

A From Southport
B From Birmingham International

North Wales and Chester - Manchester and Crewe

Network Diagram - see first Page of Table 81

Miles	Miles			AW	NT	AW	AW	AW	AW	AW	AW	AW	AW	NT	AW	VT	AW	AW	NT	AW	AW	NT	AW	VT
				MO	MX		MO	MX																
				A ⇌			B	C		◇ D					◇ ⌶	◇1 ⊠	◇			◇ E ⌶	◇1 ⊠		⌶	◇1 ⊠
0	—	**Holyhead**	d												04 25	04 48				05 11	05 32			05 51
3½	—	Valley	d												04x31									
7½	—	Rhosneigr	d																					
9¼	—	Ty Croes	d																					
12	—	Bodorgan	d																					
21	—	Llanfairpwll	d												04x48									
24¾	—	**Bangor (Gwynedd)**	a												04 55	05 14				05 38	06 00			06 17
—	—		d												04 57	05 14				05 40	06 02			06 18
32¼	—	Llanfairfechan	d																	05x47				
34¾	—	Penmaenmawr	d																	05x51				
39	—	Conwy	d																	05x57				
—	0	**Llandudno**	d																					
—	1¾	Deganwy	d																					
40	3	**Llandudno Junction**	a												05 13	05 32				06 01	06 19			06 35
—	—		d								04 38				05 15	05 32	05 46			06 07	06 21			06 36
44	—	Colwyn Bay	d								04 44				05 21	05 38	05 52			06 13				06 42
50¼	—	Abergele & Pensarn	d								04 51													
54½	—	Rhyl	d								04 57				05 31	05 49	06 02			06 23	06 36			06 53
58	—	Prestatyn	d								05 02				05 37		06 08			06 29				06 58
72	—	Flint	d								05 16				05 50		06 21			06 42	06 52			07 12
76¼	—	Shotton	d								05 22						06 27			06 48				
84¼	0	**Chester**	a								05 33				06 05	06 17	06 38			07 00	07 07			07 26
—	—		d	22p09	22p48	03 36	04 22	04 22	04 55	05 15	05 37	05 38	05 50	06 05	06 18	06 26	06 40	06 43	06 59	07 19	07 08		07 12	07 35
—	—	Liverpool Lime Street 10 106	a																					
—	7½	Helsby	d	22p29								05 47					06 49					07 03	07 21	
—	10	Frodsham	d	22p34								05 51					06 53					07 08	07 25	
—	13¼	Runcorn East	d	22p49								05 56					06 59					07 14	07 31	
—	18¼	Warrington Bank Quay 90	a	23p09								06 05					07 06					07 23	07 38	
—	22¼	Earlestown 8 90	a	23p34								06 12					07 14						07 46	
—	24	Newton-le-Willows 90	a	23p44								06 15					07 17						07 49	
—	39¾	**Manchester Oxford Road** 90	a	00 14								06 35					07 41						08 09	
—	40¼	**Manchester Pic'dilly** 10 90 ⇌	a	00 19	00 18	04 43						06 45		07 31			07 50		08 32				08 18	
105½	—	**Crewe** 10	a				04 44	04 44	05 20		05 58		06 15			06 47		07 04			07 32			07 54
—	—	Cardiff Central 7 131	a							08 17					09 23						09 58			
—	—	Manchester Airport 84,85 ✈	a			05 09																		
—	—	Birmingham New Street 12 65	a				05 59	06 01												09 26				
—	—	London Euston 15 ⊖65	a													08 33								09 38

		VT	AW	AW	AW	NT	AW	VT	AW	AW	AW	NT	AW	AW	VT	AW	AW	AW	NT	AW	VT	AW	AW
		◇1 F ⊠	◇ ⌶				◇ ⌶	◇1 ⊠	◇ ⌶				◇ E ⌶	■ ⌶	◇1 ⊠	◇ ⌶				◇ ⌶	◇1 ⊠	◇ ⌶	
Holyhead	d						06 28	06 55					07 15	07 51						08 05	08 55		
Valley	d						06x34						07x21							08x11			
Rhosneigr	d						06x40						07x26							08x17			
Ty Croes	d						06x43						07x30							08x20			
Bodorgan	d						06x48						07x34							08x25			
Llanfairpwll	d						06x57						07x44							08x34			
Bangor (Gwynedd)	a						07 05	07 21					07 52	08 17						08 42	09 21		
	d						07 06	07 22					08 02	08 21						09 02	09 22		
Llanfairfechan	d												08x09							09x09			
Penmaenmawr	d												08x13							09x13			
Conwy	d												08x19							09x19			
Llandudno	d		06 34	07 08					07 45	08 08						08 45	09 08					09 45	10 08
Deganwy	d		06x38	07x12					07x49	08x12						08x49	09x12					09x49	10x12
Llandudno Junction	a		06 42	07 18			07 22	07 39	07 53	08 18			08 23	08 38		08 53	09 18			09 23	09 39	09 53	10 18
	d		06 44				07 24	07 40	07 54				08 25	08 39		08 54				09 25	09 40	09 54	
Colwyn Bay	d		06 50				07 30	07 47	08 00				08 31	08 45		09 00				09 31	09 47	10 00	
Abergele & Pensarn	d		06 57						08 07							09 07						10 07	
Rhyl	d		07 03				07 40	07 58	08 13				08 41	08 56		09 13				09 41	09 58	10 13	
Prestatyn	d		07 08				07 46	08 04	08 19				08 47			09 19				09 47	10 04	10 19	
Flint	d		07 21				07 59	08 17	08 32				09 00			09 32				10 00	10 17	10 32	
Shotton	d		07 27						08 38							09 38						10 38	
Chester	a		07 38				08 14	08 31	08 50				09 15	09 23		09 50				10 15	10 31	10 50	
	d	07 35	07 40		07 55	08 07	08 19	08 35	08 52		08 55	09 07	09 19	09 26	09 35	09 52		09 55	10 07	10 20	10 35	10 52	
Liverpool Lime Street 10 106	a																						
Helsby	d		07 49						09 01							10 01						11 01	
Frodsham	d		07 53						09 05							10 05						11 05	
Runcorn East	d		07 59						09 11							10 11						11 11	
Warrington Bank Quay 90	a		08 06						09 18							10 18						11 18	
Earlestown 8 90	a		08 15						09 26							10 26						11 26	
Newton-le-Willows 90	a		08 18						09 29							10 29						11 29	
Manchester Oxford Road 90	a		08 41						09 48							10 48						11 48	
Manchester Pic'dilly 10 90 ⇌	a		08 50			09 36			09 57			10 36				10 57			11 36			11 57	
Crewe 10	a	07 54			08 18			08 54			09 18		09 40		09 54			10 18			10 54		
Cardiff Central 7 131	a						11 15							12 08						13 22			
Manchester Airport 84,85 ✈	a																						
Birmingham New Street 12 65	a												11 26										
London Euston 15 ⊖65	a	09 38						10 38							11 38						12 38		

A from 21 May until 25 June
B also from 26 June until 29 June
C until 22 June
D To Maesteg
E To Birmingham International
F From Wrexham General

North Wales and Chester - Manchester and Crewe

Network Diagram - see first Page of Table 81

		AW	NT	AW	AW	VT	AW	AW	AW	NT	AW	VT	AW	AW	AW	NT	AW	VT	AW	AW	AW	NT
				◇ A ⌶	◇ B	◇1 ⊟	◇ ⌶				■ ⌶	◇1 ⊟	◇ ⌶				◇ A ⌶	◇1 ⊟	◇ ⌶			
Holyhead	d			09 23							10 33						11 23					
Valley	d			09x29							10x39						11x29					
Rhosneigr	d			09x34													11x34					
Ty Croes	d			09x38													11x38					
Bodorgan	d			09x42													11x42					
Llanfairpwll	d			09x52							10x56						11x52					
Bangor (Gwynedd)	a			10 00							11 03						12 00					
	d			10 02							11 05						12 02	12 24				
Llanfairfechan	d			10x09													12x09					
Penmaenmawr	d			10x13													12x13					
Conwy	d			10x19													12x19					
Llandudno	d				10 22		10 44	11 08					11 44	12 08					12 44	13 08		
Deganwy	d				10x26		10x48	11x12					11x48	12x12					12x48	13x12		
Llandudno Junction	a			10 23	10 32		10 52	11 18			11 21		11 52	12 18			12 23	12 40	12 52	13 18		
	d			10 25			10 53				11 25		11 53				12 25	12 42	12 53			
Colwyn Bay	d			10 31			10 59				11 31		11 59				12 31	12 48	12 59			
Abergele & Pensarn	d						11 06						12 06						13 06			
Rhyl	d			10 41			11 12				11 41		12 12				12 41	12 59	13 12			
Prestatyn	d			10 47			11 18				11 47		12 18				12 47	13 05	13 18			
Flint	d			11 00			11 31				12 00		12 31				13 00	13 18	13 31			
Shotton	d						11 37						12 37						13 37			
Chester	a			11 15			11 49				12 14		12 49				13 15	13 32	13 49			
	d	10 55	11 07	11 21		11 35	11 50		11 55	12 07	12 19	12 35	12 50		12 55	13 07	13 21	13 35	13 50		13 55	14 07
Liverpool Lime Street 10 106	a																					
Helsby	d						12 00						13 00						14 00			
Frodsham	d						12 04						13 04						14 04			
Runcorn East	d						12 09						13 09						14 09			
Warrington Bank Quay 90	a						12 18						13 18						14 18			
Earlestown 8 90	a						12 26						13 26						14 26			
Newton-le-Willows 90	a						12 29						13 29						14 29			
Manchester Oxford Road 90	a						12 48						13 48						14 48			
Manchester Pic'dilly 10 90 ⇌	a		12 36				12 57			13 36			13 57			14 36			14 57			15 36
Crewe 10	a	11 18				11 54			12 18			12 54			13 18			13 54			14 18	
Cardiff Central 7 131	a										15 19											
Manchester Airport 84,85 ✈	a																					
Birmingham New Street 12 65	a			13 26													15 27					
London Euston 15 ⊖65	a					13 38						14 38						15 38				

		AW	AW	VT	AW	AW	AW	NT	AW	VT	AW	AW	NT	NT	AW	AW	VT	AW	NT	AW	AW	AW	AW	VT	AW
		◇ C ⌶	◇ B	◇1 ⊟	◇ ⌶				◇ A ⌶	◇1 ⊟	◇ ⌶				◇ ⌶	◇ ⌶	◇1 ⊟			◇ ⌶	⌶	◇ A ⌶	◇ B	◇1 ⊠	
Holyhead	d	12 39							13 23	13 58						14 34						15 44			
Valley	d								13x29													15x50			
Rhosneigr	d								13x34													15x55			
Ty Croes	d								13x38													15x59			
Bodorgan	d								13x42													16x03			
Llanfairpwll	d								13x52													16x13			
Bangor (Gwynedd)	a	13 05							14 00	14 24						15 01						16 21			
	d	13 07							14 02	14 25						15 04						16 23			
Llanfairfechan	d								14x09							15x11						16x30			
Penmaenmawr	d								14x13							15x15						16x34			
Conwy	d								14x19							15x21						16x40			
Llandudno	d		13 22		13 44	14 08					14 40				15 08					16 06			16 20		
Deganwy	d		13x26		13x48	14x12					14x44				15x12					16x10			16x24		
Llandudno Junction	a	13 23	13 32		13 52	14 18			14 23	14 42	14 48				15 16	15 26				16 14		16 44	16 28		
	d	13 25			13 53				14 25	14 43	14 49				15 17	15 27				16 15	16 25	16 46			
Colwyn Bay	d	13 31			13 59				14 31	14 50	14 55				15 23	15 33				16 21	16 33				
Abergele & Pensarn	d				14 06						15 02				15 30					16 28					
Rhyl	d	13 41			14 12				14 41	15 00	15 08				15 36	15 44				16 34	16 44				
Prestatyn	d	13 47			14 18				14 47		15 14				15 42	15 49				16 39	16 50				
Flint	d	14 00			14 31				15 00		15 27				15 55	16 03				16 53	17 03				
Shotton	d				14 37						15 33				16 01					16 59					
Chester	a	14 14			14 49				15 15	15 27	15 44				16 13	16 15				17 10	17 19	17 25			
	d	14 19		14 35	14 50		14 55	15 07	15 20	15 35	15 46	15 55	16 07		16 22	16 19	16 35	16 55	17 07	17 19		17 30		17 35	17 55
Liverpool Lime Street 10 106	a																								
Helsby	d				15 00						15 55			16 14	16 31					17 28					
Frodsham	d				15 04						15 59			16 19	16 35					17 33					
Runcorn East	d				15 09						16 04			16 25	16 41					17 38					
Warrington Bank Quay 90	a				15 18						16 12			16 34	16 51					17 49					
Earlestown 8 90	a				15 26						16 26				16 59					17 57					
Newton-le-Willows 90	a				15 29						16 29				17 01					17 59					
Manchester Oxford Road 90	a				15 48						16 48				17 21					18 19					
Manchester Pic'dilly 10 90 ⇌	a				15 57			16 36			16 57		17 36		17 30				18 36	18 28					
Crewe 10	a			14 54			15 18			15 54		16 18					16 54	17 18						17 54	18 18
Cardiff Central 7 131	a	17 15														19 21									
Manchester Airport 84,85 ✈	a																								
Birmingham New Street 12 65	a								17 28													19 26			
London Euston 15 ⊖65	a			16 38						17 38							18 38							19 39	

A To Birmingham International
B To Blaenau Ffestiniog
C To Maesteg

until 29 June

North Wales and Chester - Manchester and Crewe

Network Diagram - see first Page of Table 81

		NT	AW	AW	AW	AW	AW	AW	NT	VT	AW	AW	AW	AW	NT	AW	AW	AW	AW	NT	AW MWFO	AW TThO	VT
			◇	◇		◇ A				◇1	◇	◇ B				◇	◇				◇	◇	◇1
Holyhead	d			16 38		17 30										18 23					19 21	19 21	
Valley	d					17x36										18x29					19x27	19x27	
Rhosneigr	d					17x41										18x34					19x32	19x32	
Ty Croes	d					17x45										18x38					19x36	19x36	
Bodorgan	d					17x49										18x42					19x40	19x40	
Llanfairpwll	d					17x59										18x52					19x50	19x50	
Bangor (Gwynedd)	a			17 04		18 07										19 00					19 58	19 58	
	d			17 06		18 09										19 02					20 00	20 00	20 20
Llanfairfechan	d					18x16										19x09					20x07	20x07	
Penmaenmawr	d					18x20										19x13					20x11	20x11	
Conwy	d					18x26										19x19					20x17	20x17	
Llandudno	d		17 05		18 08						18 44	19 03	19 08				19 42	20 08					
Deganwy	d		17x09		18x12						18x48	19x07	19x12				19x46	20x12					
Llandudno Junction	a		17 13	17 23	18 18	18 30					18 52	19 11	19 18			19 23	19 50	20 18			20 21	20 21	20 36
	d		17 14	17 25		18 32					18 53					19 25	19 51				20 23	20 23	20 38
Colwyn Bay	d		17 20	17 31		18 38					18 59					19 31	19 57				20 29	20 29	20 44
Abergele & Pensarn	d		17 27								19 06						20 04						
Rhyl	d		17 33	17 41		18 48					19 12					19 41	20 10				20 39	20 39	20 55
Prestatyn	d		17 38	17 47		18 54					19 18					19 47	20 16				20 45	20 45	21 01
Flint	d		17 52	18 01		19 07					19 31					20 00	20 29				20 58	20 58	21 14
Shotton	d		17 58								19 37						20 35						
Chester	a		18 11	18 16		19 24					19 49					20 15	20 47				21 15	21 15	21 28
	d	18 07	18 16	18 18			18 49	18 55	19 07	19 35	19 50			19 55	20 07	20 17	20 50		20 55	21 07	21 21	21 21	21 35
Liverpool Lime Street [10] 106	a																						
Helsby	d		18 25				18 59				20 00						20 59						
Frodsham	d		18 30				19 03				20 04						21 03						
Runcorn East	d		18 35				19 08				20 09						21 09						
Warrington Bank Quay 90	a		18 45				19 18				20 18						21 18						
Earlestown [8] 90	a		18 57				19 26				20 26						21 26						
Newton-le-Willows 90	a		18 59				19 29				20 29						21 29						
Manchester Oxford Road 90	a		19 21				19 48				20 48						21 48						
Manchester Pic'dilly [10] 90	a	19 35	19 29				19 52		20 35		20 52				21 35		21 57			22 35			
Crewe [10]	a							19 18		19 54				20 18		20 41			21 18				21 54
Cardiff Central [7] 131	a			21 19																			
Manchester Airport 84,85 ✈	a						20 18				21 18												
Birmingham New Street [12] 65	a																				23 27	23 28	22 50
London Euston [15] ⊖65	a									21 42													

		AW	AW FX	AW FO	AW	NT	AW	AW FO	AW FX
					◇			◇ E	◇ E
Holyhead	d				20 37				
Valley	d								
Rhosneigr	d								
Ty Croes	d								
Bodorgan	d								
Llanfairpwll	d								
Bangor (Gwynedd)	a				21 04				
	d				21 06				
Llanfairfechan	d				21x13				
Penmaenmawr	d				21x17				
Conwy	d				21x23				
Llandudno	d	20 43					21 45		
Deganwy	d	20x47					21x49		
Llandudno Junction	a	20 51			21 27		21 53		
	d	20 52			21 29		21 55		
Colwyn Bay	d	20 58			21 35		22 01		
Abergele & Pensarn	d	21 05			21 42		22 09		
Rhyl	d	21 11			21 48		22 16		
Prestatyn	d	21 17			21 53		22 22		
Flint	d	21 30			22 07		22 37		
Shotton	d	21 36			22 13		22 44		
Chester	a	21 47			22 23		22 55		
	d		21 52	21 52	22 26	22 48	23 01	23 22	23 22
Liverpool Lime Street [10] 106	a								
Helsby	d		22 01	22 01				23 31	23 31
Frodsham	d		22 05	22 05				23 35	23 36
Runcorn East	d		22 11	22 11				23 41	23 41
Warrington Bank Quay 90	a		22 18	22 18				23 49	23 50
Earlestown [8] 90	a			22 26				23 56	
Newton-le-Willows 90	a			22 29				23 59	
Manchester Oxford Road 90	a			22 50					
Manchester Pic'dilly [10] 90	a			22 58		00 18		00 28	
Crewe [10]	a				22 50		23 26		
Cardiff Central [7] 131	a								
Manchester Airport 84,85 ✈	a								
Birmingham New Street [12] 65	a								
London Euston [15] ⊖65	a								

A To Shrewsbury

B To Blaenau Ffestiniog

E From Birmingham International

2 July to 28 September

North Wales and Chester - Manchester and Crewe

Network Diagram - see first Page of Table 81

		AW MO	NT MX	AW	AW	AW	AW	AW	AW	AW	NT	AW	VT	AW	AW	NT	AW	AW	NT	AW	VT	VT	AW	AW
							◇ A					◇	◇1	◇			◇ B	◇1			◇1	◇1 C	◇	
Holyhead	d											04 25	04 48				05 11	05 32			05 51			
Valley	d											04x31												
Rhosneigr	d																							
Ty Croes	d																							
Bodorgan	d																							
Llanfairpwll	d											04x48												
Bangor (Gwynedd)	a											04 55	05 14				05 38	06 00			06 17			
	d											04 57	05 14				05 40	06 02			06 18			
Llanfairfechan	d																05x47							
Penmaenmawr	d																05x51							
Conwy	d																05x57							
Llandudno	d																						06 34	07 08
Deganwy	d																						06x38	07x12
Llandudno Junction	a											05 13	05 32				06 01	06 19			06 35		06 42	07 18
	d							04 38				05 15	05 32	05 46			06 07	06 21			06 36		06 44	
Colwyn Bay	d							04 44				05 21	05 38	05 52			06 13				06 42		06 50	
Abergele & Pensarn	d							04 51															06 57	
Rhyl	d							04 57				05 31	05 49	06 02			06 23	06 36			06 53		07 03	
Prestatyn	d							05 02				05 37		06 08			06 29				06 58		07 08	
Flint	d							05 16				05 50		06 21			06 42	06 52			07 12		07 21	
Shotton	d							05 22						06 27			06 48						07 27	
Chester	a							05 33				06 05	06 17	06 38			07 00	07 07			07 26		07 38	
	d	22p09	22p48	03 36	04 22	04 55	05 15	05 37	05 38	05 50	06 05	06 18	06 26	06 40	06 43	06 59	07 19	07 08		07 12	07 35	07 35	07 40	
Liverpool Lime Street [10] 106	a																							
Helsby	d	22p29							05 47					06 49					07 03	07 21			07 49	
Frodsham	d	22p34							05 51					06 53					07 08	07 25			07 53	
Runcorn East	d	22p49							05 56					06 59					07 14	07 31			07 59	
Warrington Bank Quay 90	a	23p09							06 05					07 06					07 23	07 38			08 06	
Earlestown [8] 90	a	23p34							06 12					07 14						07 46			08 15	
Newton-le-Willows 90	a	23p44							06 15					07 17						07 49			08 18	
Manchester Oxford Road 90	a	00 14							06 35					07 41						08 09			08 41	
Manchester Pic'dilly [10] 90	a	00 19	00 18	04 43					06 45		07 31			07 50		08 32				08 18			08 50	
Crewe [10]	a				04 44	05 20		05 58		06 15			06 47		07 04			07 32			07 54	07 54		
Cardiff Central [7] 131	a						08 17					09 23						09 58						
Manchester Airport 84,85 ✈	a			05 09																				
Birmingham New Street [12] 65	a				05 59												09 26							
London Euston [15] ⊖65	a												08 33								09 38	09 38		

		AW	NT	AW	VT	AW	AW	AW	NT	AW	AW	VT	AW	AW	AW	NT	AW	VT	AW	AW	AW	NT	AW
				◇	◇1	◇				◇ B		◇1	◇				◇	◇1	◇				◇ B
Holyhead	d			06 28	06 55					07 15	07 51						08 05	08 55					09 23
Valley	d			06x34						07x21							08x11						09x29
Rhosneigr	d			06x40						07x26							08x17						09x34
Ty Croes	d			06x43						07x30							08x20						09x38
Bodorgan	d			06x48						07x34							08x25						09x42
Llanfairpwll	d			06x57						07x44							08x34						09x52
Bangor (Gwynedd)	a			07 05	07 21					07 52	08 17						08 42	09 21					10 00
	d			07 06	07 22					08 02	08 21						09 02	09 22					10 02
Llanfairfechan	d									08x09							09x09						10x09
Penmaenmawr	d									08x13							09x13						10x13
Conwy	d									08x19							09x19						10x19
Llandudno	d					07 45	08 08						08 45	09 08					09 45	10 08			
Deganwy	d					07x49	08x12						08x49	09x12					09x49	10x12			
Llandudno Junction	a			07 22	07 39	07 53	08 18			08 23	08 38		08 53	09 18			09 23	09 39	09 53	10 18			10 23
	d			07 24	07 40	07 54				08 25	08 39		08 54				09 25	09 40	09 54				10 25
Colwyn Bay	d			07 30	07 47	08 00				08 31	08 45		09 00				09 31	09 47	10 00				10 31
Abergele & Pensarn	d					08 07							09 07						10 07				
Rhyl	d			07 40	07 58	08 13				08 41	08 56		09 13				09 41	09 58	10 13				10 41
Prestatyn	d			07 46	08 04	08 19				08 47			09 19				09 47	10 04	10 19				10 47
Flint	d			07 59	08 17	08 32				09 00			09 32				10 00	10 17	10 32				11 00
Shotton	d					08 38							09 38						10 38				
Chester	a			08 14	08 31	08 50				09 15	09 23		09 50				10 15	10 31	10 50				11 15
	d	07 55	08 07	08 19	08 35	08 52		08 55	09 07	09 19	09 26	09 35	09 52		09 55	10 07	10 20	10 35	10 52		10 55	11 07	11 21
Liverpool Lime Street [10] 106	a																						
Helsby	d					09 01							10 01						11 01				
Frodsham	d					09 05							10 05						11 05				
Runcorn East	d					09 11							10 11						11 11				
Warrington Bank Quay 90	a					09 18							10 18						11 18				
Earlestown [8] 90	a					09 26							10 26						11 26				
Newton-le-Willows 90	a					09 29							10 29						11 29				
Manchester Oxford Road 90	a					09 48							10 48						11 48				
Manchester Pic'dilly [10] 90	a		09 36			09 57			10 36				10 57			11 36			11 57			12 36	
Crewe [10]	a	08 18			08 54			09 18		09 40		09 54			10 18			10 54			11 18		
Cardiff Central [7] 131	a			11 15							12 08						13 22						
Manchester Airport 84,85 ✈	a																						
Birmingham New Street [12] 65	a									11 26													13 26
London Euston [15] ⊖65	a				10 38							11 38						12 38					

A To Maesteg

B To Birmingham International

C From Wrexham General

North Wales and Chester - Manchester and Crewe

Network Diagram - see first Page of Table 81

	AW		VT	AW	AW	AW	NT	AW	VT	AW	AW		AW	NT	AW	VT	AW	AW	AW	NT	AW		AW	VT
	◇ A		◇■ ☕	◇ H				■ H	◇■ ☕	◇ H					◇ B H	◇■ ☕	◇ H				◇ C H		◇ A	◇■ ☕
Holyhead d								10 33							11 23						12 39			
Valley d								10x39							11x29									
Rhosneigr d															11x34									
Ty Croes d															11x38									
Bodorgan d															11x42									
Llanfairpwll d								10x56							11x52									
Bangor (Gwynedd) a								11 03							12 00						13 05			
d								11 05							12 02	12 24					13 07			
Llanfairfechan d															12x09									
Penmaenmawr d															12x13									
Conwy d															12x19									
Llandudno d	10 22			10 44	11 08					11 44	12 08						12 44	13 08					13 22	
Deganwy d	10x26			10x48	11x12					11x48	12x12						12x48	13x12					13x26	
Llandudno Junction a	10 32			10 52	11 18			11 21		11 52	12 18				12 23	12 40	12 52	13 18			13 23		13 32	
d				10 53				11 25		11 53					12 25	12 42	12 53				13 25			
Colwyn Bay d				10 59				11 31		11 59					12 31	12 48	12 59				13 31			
Abergele & Pensarn d				11 06						12 06							13 06							
Rhyl d				11 12				11 41		12 12					12 41	12 59	13 12				13 41			
Prestatyn d				11 18				11 47		12 18					12 47	13 05	13 18				13 47			
Flint d				11 31				12 00		12 31					13 00	13 18	13 31				14 00			
Shotton d				11 37						12 37							13 37							
Chester a				11 49				12 14		12 49					13 15	13 32	13 49				14 14			
d			11 35	11 50		11 55	12 07	12 19	12 35	12 50			12 55	13 07	13 21	13 35	13 50		13 55	14 07	14 19			14 35
Liverpool Lime Street 106 a																								
Helsby d				12 00						13 00							14 00							
Frodsham d				12 04						13 04							14 04							
Runcorn East d				12 09						13 09							14 09							
Warrington Bank Quay 90 a				12 18						13 18							14 18							
Earlestown 90 a				12 26						13 26							14 26							
Newton-le-Willows 90 a				12 29						13 29							14 29							
Manchester Oxford Road 90 a				12 48						13 48							14 48							
Manchester Pic'dilly 90 a				12 57			13 36			13 57				14 36			14 57			15 36				
Crewe a			11 54			12 18			12 54				13 18			13 54			14 18					14 54
Cardiff Central 131 a								15 19													17 15			
Manchester Airport 84,85 a																								
Birmingham New Street 65 a															15 27									
London Euston ⊖65 a			13 38						14 38							15 38								16 38

	AW	AW	AW	NT	AW	VT	VT	AW	AW	NT	NT	AW	AW	VT	AW	NT	AW		AW	AW	VT	AW	NT	AW
	◇ H				◇ B H	◇■ ☕	◇■ ☕	◇ H				◇ H	◇ H	◇■ ☕			◇ H		◇ B H	◇ A	◇■ ⊠			◇ H
Holyhead d					13 23	13 58							14 34						15 23					
Valley d					13x29														15x29					
Rhosneigr d					13x34														15x34					
Ty Croes d					13x38														15x38					
Bodorgan d					13x42														15x42					
Llanfairpwll d					13x52														15x52					
Bangor (Gwynedd) a					14 00	14 24							15 01						16 00					
d					14 02	14 25							15 04						16 02					
Llanfairfechan d					14x09								15x11						16x09					
Penmaenmawr d					14x13								15x15						16x13					
Conwy d					14x19								15x21						16x19					
Llandudno d	13 44	14 08						14 40				15 08					16 06			16 20				17 05
Deganwy d	13x48	14x12						14x44				15x12					16x10			16x24				17x09
Llandudno Junction a	13 52	14 18			14 23	14 42		14 48				15 16	15 26				16 14		16 23	16 28				17 13
d	13 53				14 25	14 43		14 49				15 17	15 27				16 15		16 25					17 14
Colwyn Bay d	13 59				14 31	14 50		14 55				15 23	15 33				16 21		16 34					17 20
Abergele & Pensarn d	14 06							15 02				15 30					16 28							17 27
Rhyl d	14 12				14 41	15 00		15 08				15 36	15 44				16 34		16 44					17 33
Prestatyn d	14 18				14 47			15 14				15 42	15 49				16 39		16 50					17 38
Flint d	14 31				15 00			15 27				15 55	16 03				16 53		17 03					17 52
Shotton d	14 37							15 33				16 01					16 59							17 58
Chester a	14 49				15 15	15 27		15 44				16 13	16 15				17 10		17 17					18 11
d	14 50		14 55	15 07	15 20	15 35	15 35	15 46	15 55	16 07		16 22	16 19	16 35	16 55	17 07	17 19		17 24		17 35	17 55	18 07	18 16
Liverpool Lime Street 106 a																								
Helsby d	15 00							15 55			16 14	16 31					17 28							18 25
Frodsham d	15 04							15 59			16 19	16 35					17 33							18 30
Runcorn East d	15 09							16 04			16 25	16 41					17 38							18 35
Warrington Bank Quay 90 a	15 18							16 12			16 34	16 51					17 49							18 45
Earlestown 90 a	15 26							16 26				16 59					17 57							18 57
Newton-le-Willows 90 a	15 29							16 29				17 01					17 59							18 59
Manchester Oxford Road 90 a	15 48							16 48				17 21					18 19							19 21
Manchester Pic'dilly 90 a	15 57			16 36				16 57		17 36		17 30				18 36	18 28						19 35	19 29
Crewe a			15 18			15 54	15 54		16 18					16 54	17 18						17 54	18 18		
Cardiff Central 131 a													19 21											
Manchester Airport 84,85 a																								
Birmingham New Street 65 a					17 28														19 26					
London Euston ⊖65 a						17 38	17 38							18 38							19 38			

A To Blaenau Ffestiniog

B To Birmingham International

C To Maesteg

North Wales and Chester - Manchester and Crewe

Network Diagram - see first Page of Table 81

	AW	AW	AW		AW	AW	NT	VT	AW	AW	AW	AW	NT		AW	AW	AW	AW	NT	AW MWFO	AW TThO	VT	AW	
	◇ H		◇ A H					◇■ ☕	◇ H	◇ B					◇ H	◇				◇	◇	◇■ ☕		
Holyhead d	16 38		17 30												18 23					19 21	19 21			
Valley d			17x36												18x29					19x27	19x27			
Rhosneigr d			17x41												18x34					19x32	19x32			
Ty Croes d			17x45												18x38					19x36	19x36			
Bodorgan d			17x49												18x42					19x40	19x40			
Llanfairpwll d			17x59												18x52					19x50	19x50			
Bangor (Gwynedd) a	17 04		18 07												19 00					19 58	19 58			
d	17 06		18 09												19 02					20 00	20 00	20 20		
Llanfairfechan d			18x16												19x09					20x07	20x07			
Penmaenmawr d			18x20												19x13					20x11	20x11			
Conwy d			18x26												19x19					20x17	20x17			
Llandudno d		18 08							18 44	19 03	19 08					19 42	20 08						20 43	
Deganwy d		18x12							18x48	19x07	19x12					19x46	20x12						20x47	
Llandudno Junction a	17 23	18 18	18 30						18 52	19 11	19 18				19 23	19 50	20 18			20 21	20 21	20 36	20 51	
d	17 25		18 32						18 53						19 25	19 51				20 23	20 23	20 38	20 52	
Colwyn Bay d	17 31		18 38						18 59						19 31	19 57				20 29	20 29	20 44	20 58	
Abergele & Pensarn d									19 06							20 04							21 05	
Rhyl d	17 41		18 48						19 12						19 41	20 10				20 39	20 39	20 55	21 11	
Prestatyn d	17 47		18 54						19 18						19 47	20 16				20 45	20 45	21 01	21 17	
Flint d	18 01		19 07						19 31						20 00	20 29				20 58	20 58	21 14	21 30	
Shotton d									19 37							20 35							21 36	
Chester a	18 16		19 24						19 49						20 15	20 47				21 15	21 15	21 28	21 47	
d	18 18				18 49	18 55	19 07	19 35	19 50			19 55	20 07		20 17	20 50		20 55	21 07	21 21	21 21	21 35		
Liverpool Lime Street 106 a																								
Helsby d					18 59				20 00							20 59								
Frodsham d					19 03				20 04							21 03								
Runcorn East d					19 08				20 09							21 09								
Warrington Bank Quay 90 a					19 18				20 18							21 18								
Earlestown 90 a					19 26				20 26							21 26								
Newton-le-Willows 90 a					19 29				20 29							21 29								
Manchester Oxford Road 90 a					19 48				20 48							21 48								
Manchester Pic'dilly 90 a					19 52		20 35		20 52				21 35			21 57			22 35					
Crewe a						19 18		19 54				20 18			20 41			21 18				21 54		
Cardiff Central 131 a	21 19																							
Manchester Airport 84,85 a					20 18				21 18															
Birmingham New Street 65 a																				23 27	23 28	22 50		
London Euston ⊖65 a								21 42																

	AW FX	AW FO	AW	NT	AW	AW FO	AW FX
			◇			◇ E	◇ E
Holyhead d			20 37				
Valley d							
Rhosneigr d							
Ty Croes d							
Bodorgan d							
Llanfairpwll d							
Bangor (Gwynedd) a			21 04				
d			21 06				
Llanfairfechan d			21x13				
Penmaenmawr d			21x17				
Conwy d			21x23				
Llandudno d					21 45		
Deganwy d					21x49		
Llandudno Junction a			21 27		21 53		
d			21 29		21 55		
Colwyn Bay d			21 35		22 01		
Abergele & Pensarn d			21 42		22 09		
Rhyl d			21 48		22 16		
Prestatyn d			21 53		22 22		
Flint d			22 07		22 37		
Shotton d			22 13		22 44		
Chester a			22 23		22 55		
d	21 52	21 52	22 26	22 48	23 01	23 22	23 22
Liverpool Lime Street 106 a							
Helsby d	22 01	22 01				23 31	23 31
Frodsham d	22 05	22 05				23 35	23 36
Runcorn East d	22 11	22 11				23 41	23 41
Warrington Bank Quay 90 a	22 18	22 18				23 49	23 50
Earlestown 90 a		22 26				23 56	
Newton-le-Willows 90 a		22 29				23 59	
Manchester Oxford Road 90 a		22 50					
Manchester Pic'dilly 90 a		22 58		00 18		00 28	
Crewe a			22 50		23 26		
Cardiff Central 131 a							
Manchester Airport 84,85 a							
Birmingham New Street 65 a							
London Euston ⊖65 a							

A To Shrewsbury

B To Blaenau Ffestiniog

E From Birmingham International

North Wales and Chester - Manchester and Crewe

Network Diagram - see first Page of Table 81

	AW MO	NT MX	AW	AW	AW	AW	AW	AW	AW		NT	AW	VT	AW	AW	NT	AW	AW	NT	AW	VT	VT	AW	AW
	▬					◇ A						◇ ⌶	◇1 ⊠	◇			◇ B ⌶	◇1 ⊠		⌶	◇1 ⊠	◇1 C ⊠	◇ ⌶	
Holyhead d												04 25	04 48				05 11	05 32			05 51			
Valley d												04x31												
Rhosneigr d																								
Ty Croes d																								
Bodorgan d																								
Llanfairpwll d												04x48												
Bangor (Gwynedd) a												04 55	05 14				05 38	06 00			06 17			
d												04 57	05 14				05 40	06 02			06 18			
Llanfairfechan d																	05x47							
Penmaenmawr d																	05x51							
Conwy d																	05x57							
Llandudno d																							06 34	07 08
Deganwy d																							06x38	07x12
Llandudno Junction a												05 13	05 32				06 01	06 19			06 35		06 42	07 18
d							04 38					05 15	05 32	05 46			06 07	06 21			06 36		06 44	
Colwyn Bay d							04 44					05 21	05 38	05 52			06 13				06 42		06 50	
Abergele & Pensarn d							04 51																06 57	
Rhyl d							04 57					05 31	05 49	06 02			06 23	06 36			06 53		07 03	
Prestatyn d							05 02					05 37		06 08			06 29				06 58		07 08	
Flint d							05 16					05 50		06 21			06 42	06 52			07 12		07 21	
Shotton d							05 22							06 27			06 48						07 27	
Chester a							05 33					06 05	06 17	06 38			07 00	07 07			07 26		07 38	
d	22p09	22p44	03 36	04 22	04 55	05 15	05 37	05 38	05 50		06 01	06 18	06 26	06 40	06 43	06 59	07 19	07 08		07 12	07 35	07 35	07 40	
Liverpool Lime Street 10 106 a																								
Helsby d	22p29							05 47						06 49					07 03	07 21			07 49	
Frodsham d	22p34							05 51						06 53					07 08	07 25			07 53	
Runcorn East d	22p49							05 56						06 59					07 14	07 31			07 59	
Warrington Bank Quay 90 a	23p09							06 05						07 06					07 23	07 38			08 06	
Earlestown 8 90 a	23p34							06 12						07 14						07 46			08 15	
Newton-le-Willows 90 a	23p44							06 15						07 17						07 49			08 18	
Manchester Oxford Road 90 a	00 14							06 35						07 41						08 09			08 41	
Manchester Pic'dilly 10 90 a	00 19	00 18	04 43					06 45			07 31			07 50		08 32				08 18			08 50	
Crewe 10 a				04 44	05 20		05 58		06 15				06 47		07 04			07 32			07 54	07 54		
Cardiff Central 7 131 a						08 17						09 23						09 58						
Manchester Airport 84,85 a			05 09																					
Birmingham New Street 12 65 a				05 59													09 26							
London Euston 15 ⊖65 a													08 33								09 38	09 38		

	AW	NT	AW	VT	AW		AW	AW	NT	AW	AW	VT	AW	AW	AW		NT	AW	VT	AW	AW	AW	NT	AW
			◇ ⌶	◇1 ⊠	◇ ⌶					◇ B ⌶	■ ⌶	◇1 ⊠	◇ ⌶					◇ ⌶	◇1 ⊠	◇ ⌶				◇ B ⌶
Holyhead d			06 28	06 55						07 15	07 51							08 05	08 55					09 23
Valley d			06x34							07x21								08x11						09x29
Rhosneigr d			06x40							07x26								08x17						09x34
Ty Croes d			06x43							07x30								08x20						09x38
Bodorgan d			06x48							07x34								08x25						09x42
Llanfairpwll d			06x57							07x44								08x34						09x52
Bangor (Gwynedd) a			07 05	07 21						07 52	08 17							08 42	09 21					10 00
d			07 06	07 22						08 02	08 21							09 02	09 22					10 02
Llanfairfechan d										08x09								09x09						10x09
Penmaenmawr d										08x13								09x13						10x13
Conwy d										08x19								09x19						10x19
Llandudno d					07 45		08 08						08 45	09 08						09 45	10 08			
Deganwy d					07x49		08x12						08x49	09x12						09x49	10x12			
Llandudno Junction a			07 22	07 39	07 53		08 18			08 23	08 38		08 53	09 18				09 23	09 39	09 53	10 18			10 23
d			07 24	07 40	07 54					08 25	08 39		08 54					09 25	09 40	09 54				10 25
Colwyn Bay d			07 30	07 47	08 00					08 31	08 45		09 00					09 31	09 47	10 00				10 31
Abergele & Pensarn d					08 07								09 07							10 07				
Rhyl d			07 40	07 58	08 13					08 41	08 56		09 13					09 41	09 58	10 13				10 41
Prestatyn d			07 46	08 04	08 19					08 47			09 19					09 47	10 04	10 19				10 47
Flint d			07 59	08 17	08 32					09 00			09 32					10 00	10 17	10 32				11 00
Shotton d					08 38								09 38							10 38				
Chester a			08 14	08 31	08 50					09 15	09 23		09 50					10 15	10 31	10 50				11 15
d	07 55	08 03	08 19	08 35	08 52			08 55	09 03	09 19	09 26	09 35	09 52		09 55		10 03	10 20	10 35	10 52		10 55	11 03	11 21
Liverpool Lime Street 10 106 a																								
Helsby d					09 01								10 01							11 01				
Frodsham d					09 05								10 05							11 05				
Runcorn East d					09 11								10 11							11 11				
Warrington Bank Quay 90 a					09 18								10 18							11 18				
Earlestown 8 90 a					09 26								10 26							11 26				
Newton-le-Willows 90 a					09 29								10 29							11 29				
Manchester Oxford Road 90 a					09 48								10 48							11 48				
Manchester Pic'dilly 10 90 a		09 36			09 57				10 36				10 57				11 36			11 57			12 36	
Crewe 10 a	08 18			08 54				09 18		09 40		09 54			10 18				10 54			11 18		
Cardiff Central 7 131 a			11 15								12 08							13 22						
Manchester Airport 84,85 a																								
Birmingham New Street 12 65 a										11 26														13 26
London Euston 15 ⊖65 a				10 38								11 38							12 38					

A To Maesteg

B To Birmingham International

C From Wrexham General

North Wales and Chester - Manchester and Crewe

Network Diagram - see first Page of Table 81

	AW		VT	AW	AW	AW	NT	AW	VT	AW	AW		AW	NT	AW	VT	AW	AW	AW	NT	AW		AW	VT
	◇ A		◇1 ◻	◇ ⌶				■ ⌶	◇1 ◻	◇ ⌶					◇ B ⌶	◇1 ◻	◇ ⌶				◇ C ⌶		◇ A	◇1 ◻
Holyhead d								10 33							11 23						12 39			
Valley d								10x39							11x29									
Rhosneigr d															11x34									
Ty Croes d															11x38									
Bodorgan d															11x42									
Llanfairpwll d								10x56							11x52									
Bangor (Gwynedd) a								11 03							12 00						13 05			
d								11 05							12 02	12 24					13 07			
Llanfairfechan d															12x09									
Penmaenmawr d															12x13									
Conwy d															12x19									
Llandudno d	10 22			10 44	11 08					11 44	12 08						12 44	13 08					13 22	
Deganwy d	10x26			10x48	11x12					11x48	12x12						12x48	13x12					13x26	
Llandudno Junction a	10 32			10 52	11 18			11 21		11 52	12 18				12 23	12 40	12 52	13 18			13 23		13 32	
d				10 53				11 25		11 53					12 25	12 42	12 53				13 25			
Colwyn Bay d				10 59				11 31		11 59					12 31	12 48	12 59				13 31			
Abergele & Pensarn d				11 06						12 06							13 06							
Rhyl d				11 12				11 41		12 12					12 41	12 59	13 12				13 41			
Prestatyn d				11 18				11 47		12 18					12 47	13 05	13 18				13 47			
Flint d				11 31				12 00		12 31					13 00	13 18	13 31				14 00			
Shotton d				11 37						12 37							13 37							
Chester a				11 49				12 14		12 49					13 15	13 32	13 49				14 14			
d			11 35	11 50		11 55	12 03	12 19	12 35	12 50			12 55	13 03	13 21	13 35	13 50		13 55	14 03	14 19			14 35
Liverpool Lime Street 10 106 a																								
Helsby d				12 00						13 00							14 00							
Frodsham d				12 04						13 04							14 04							
Runcorn East d				12 09						13 09							14 09							
Warrington Bank Quay 90 a				12 18						13 18							14 18							
Earlestown 8 90 a				12 26						13 26							14 26							
Newton-le-Willows 90 a				12 29						13 29							14 29							
Manchester Oxford Road 90 a				12 48						13 48							14 48							
Manchester Pic'dilly 10 90 a				12 57			13 36			13 57				14 36			14 57			15 36				
Crewe 10 a			11 54			12 18			12 54				13 18			13 54			14 18					14 54
Cardiff Central 7 131 a								15 19													17 15			
Manchester Airport 84,85 a																								
Birmingham New Street 12 65 a															15 27									
London Euston 15 ⊖65 a			13 38						14 38							15 38								16 38

	AW	AW	AW	NT	AW	VT	VT		AW	AW	NT	NT	AW	AW	VT	AW	NT	AW	AW	AW	VT	AW	NT	AW
	◇ ⌶				◇ B ⌶	◇1 ◻	◇1 ◻		◇ ⌶				◇ ⌶	◇ ⌶	◇1 ◻			◇ ⌶	◇ B ⌶	◇ A	◇1 ⊠			◇ ⌶
Holyhead d					13 23	13 58								14 34					15 23					
Valley d					13x29														15x29					
Rhosneigr d					13x34														15x34					
Ty Croes d					13x38														15x38					
Bodorgan d					13x42														15x42					
Llanfairpwll d					13x52														15x52					
Bangor (Gwynedd) a					14 00	14 24								15 01					16 00					
d					14 02	14 25								15 04					16 02					
Llanfairfechan d					14x09									15x11					16x09					
Penmaenmawr d					14x13									15x15					16x13					
Conwy d					14x19									15x21					16x19					
Llandudno d	13 44	14 08							14 40				15 08					16 06		16 20				17 05
Deganwy d	13x48	14x12							14x44				15x12					16x10		16x24				17x09
Llandudno Junction a	13 52	14 18			14 23	14 42			14 48				15 16	15 26				16 14	16 23	16 28				17 13
d	13 53				14 25	14 43			14 49				15 17	15 27				16 15	16 25					17 14
Colwyn Bay d	13 59				14 31	14 50			14 55				15 23	15 33				16 21	16 34					17 20
Abergele & Pensarn d	14 06								15 02				15 30					16 28						17 27
Rhyl d	14 12				14 41	15 00			15 08				15 36	15 44				16 34	16 44					17 33
Prestatyn d	14 18				14 47				15 14				15 42	15 49				16 39	16 50					17 38
Flint d	14 31				15 00				15 27				15 55	16 03				16 53	17 03					17 52
Shotton d	14 37								15 33				16 01					16 59						17 58
Chester a	14 49				15 15	15 27			15 44				16 13	16 15				17 10	17 17					18 11
d	14 50		14 55	15 03	15 20	15 35	15 35		15 46	15 55	16 03		16 22	16 19	16 35	16 55	17 03	17 19	17 24		17 35	17 55	18 03	18 16
Liverpool Lime Street 10 106 a																								
Helsby d	15 00								15 55			16 14	16 31					17 28						18 25
Frodsham d	15 04								15 59			16 19	16 35					17 33						18 30
Runcorn East d	15 09								16 04			16 25	16 41					17 38						18 35
Warrington Bank Quay 90 a	15 18								16 12			16 34	16 51					17 49						18 45
Earlestown 8 90 a	15 26								16 26				16 59					17 57						18 57
Newton-le-Willows 90 a	15 29								16 29				17 01					17 59						18 59
Manchester Oxford Road 90 a	15 48								16 48				17 21					18 19						19 21
Manchester Pic'dilly 10 90 a	15 57			16 36					16 57		17 36		17 30				18 36	18 28					19 35	19 29
Crewe 10 a			15 18			15 54	15 54			16 18					16 54	17 18					17 54	18 18		
Cardiff Central 7 131 a														19 21										
Manchester Airport 84,85 a																								
Birmingham New Street 12 65 a					17 28														19 26					
London Euston 15 ⊖65 a						17 38	17 38								18 38						19 38			

A To Blaenau Ffestiniog

B To Birmingham International

C To Maesteg

Mondays to Fridays
from 1 October

North Wales and Chester - Manchester and Crewe

Network Diagram - see first Page of Table 81

	AW ◇ ✕	AW	AW ◇ A ✕	AW	AW	NT	VT ◇1 ⊡	AW ◇ ✕	AW B ◇ B	AW	AW	NT	AW ◇ ✕	AW ◇	AW	AW	NT	AW MT WO ◇	AW TThO ◇	VT ◇1 ⊡	AW
Holyhead d	16 38		17 30										18 23					19 21	19 21		
Valley d			17x36										18x29					19x27	19x27		
Rhosneigr d			17x41										18x34					19x32	19x32		
Ty Croes d			17x45										18x38					19x36	19x36		
Bodorgan d			17x49										18x42					19x40	19x40		
Llanfairpwll d			17x59										18x52					19x50	19x50		
Bangor (Gwynedd) a	17 04		18 07										19 00					19 58	19 58		
d	17 06		18 09										19 02					20 00	20 00	20 20	
Llanfairfechan d			18x16										19x09					20x07	20x07		
Penmaenmawr d			18x20										19x13					20x11	20x11		
Conwy d			18x26										19x19					20x17	20x17		
Llandudno d		18 08						18 44	19 03	19 08				19 42	20 08						20 43
Deganwy d		18x12						18x48	19x07	19x12				19x46	20x12						20x47
Llandudno Junction a	17 23	18 18	18 30					18 52	19 11	19 18			19 23	19 50	20 18			20 21	20 21	20 36	20 51
d	17 25		18 32					18 53					19 25	19 51				20 23	20 23	20 38	20 52
Colwyn Bay d	17 31		18 38					18 59					19 31	19 57				20 29	20 29	20 44	20 58
Abergele & Pensarn d								19 06						20 04							21 05
Rhyl d	17 41		18 48					19 12					19 41	20 10				20 39	20 39	20 55	21 11
Prestatyn d	17 47		18 54					19 18					19 47	20 16				20 45	20 45	21 01	21 17
Flint d	18 01		19 07					19 31					20 00	20 29				20 58	20 58	21 14	21 30
Shotton d								19 37						20 35							21 36
Chester a	18 16		19 24					19 49					20 15	20 47				21 15	21 15	21 28	21 47
d	18 18			18 49	18 55	19 03	19 35	19 50			19 55	20 03	20 17	20 50		20 55	21 03	21 21	21 21	21 35	
Liverpool Lime Street 10 106 a																					
Helsby d				18 59				20 00						20 59							
Frodsham d				19 03				20 04						21 03							
Runcorn East d				19 08				20 09						21 09							
Warrington Bank Quay 90 a				19 18				20 18						21 18							
Earlestown 8 90 a				19 26				20 26						21 26							
Newton-le-Willows 90 a				19 29				20 29						21 29							
Manchester Oxford Road 90 a				19 48				20 48						21 48							
Manchester Pic'dilly 10 90 ⇌ a				19 52		20 35		20 52				21 35		21 57			22 35				
Crewe 10 a					19 18		19 54				20 18		20 41			21 18				21 54	
Cardiff Central 7 131 a	21 19																				
Manchester Airport 84,85 ✈ a				20 18				21 18													
Birmingham New Street 12 65 a																		23 27	23 28	22 50	
London Euston 15 ⊖65 a							21 42														

	AW FX	AW FO	AW ◇	NT	AW	AW FO ◇ E	AW FX ◇ E
Holyhead d			20 37				
Valley d							
Rhosneigr d							
Ty Croes d							
Bodorgan d							
Llanfairpwll d							
Bangor (Gwynedd) a			21 04				
d			21 06				
Llanfairfechan d			21x13				
Penmaenmawr d			21x17				
Conwy d			21x23				
Llandudno d					21 45		
Deganwy d					21x49		
Llandudno Junction a			21 27		21 53		
d			21 29		21 55		
Colwyn Bay d			21 35		22 01		
Abergele & Pensarn d			21 42		22 09		
Rhyl d			21 48		22 16		
Prestatyn d			21 53		22 22		
Flint d			22 07		22 37		
Shotton d			22 13		22 44		
Chester a			22 23		22 55		
d	21 52	21 52	22 26	22 44	23 01	23 22	23 22
Liverpool Lime Street 10 106 a							
Helsby d	22 01	22 01				23 31	23 31
Frodsham d	22 05	22 05				23 35	23 36
Runcorn East d	22 11	22 11				23 41	23 41
Warrington Bank Quay 90 a	22 18	22 18				23 49	23 50
Earlestown 8 90 a		22 26				23 56	
Newton-le-Willows 90 a		22 29				23 59	
Manchester Oxford Road 90 a		22 50					
Manchester Pic'dilly 10 90 ⇌ a		22 58		00 18		00 28	
Crewe 10 a			22 50		23 26		
Cardiff Central 7 131 a							
Manchester Airport 84,85 ✈ a							
Birmingham New Street 12 65 a							
London Euston 15 ⊖65 a							

A To Shrewsbury
B To Blaenau Ffestiniog
E From Birmingham International

Saturdays
until 30 June

North Wales and Chester - Manchester and Crewe

Network Diagram - see first Page of Table 81

	NT	AW ◇ A	AW	AW	AW	AW	AW	AW	NT	AW ◇ ✕	AW ◇	AW	NT	AW B ✕	VT ◇1 ⊡	AW ◇ C ✕	AW ✕	AW	AW	NT	AW ◇ ✕	VT ◇1 ⊡
Holyhead d											04 25					05 22					06 35	06 52
Valley d											04x31					05x28					06x41	
Rhosneigr d																05x33						
Ty Croes d																05x37						
Bodorgan d																05x41						
Llanfairpwll d											04x48					05x51					06x58	
Bangor (Gwynedd) a											04 55					05 59					07 05	07 18
d											04 57					06 01					07 07	07 20
Llanfairfechan d																06x08						
Penmaenmawr d																06x12						
Conwy d																06x18						
Llandudno d																	06 34	07 08				
Deganwy d																	06x38	07x12				
Llandudno Junction a											05 13					06 22	06 42	07 18			07 23	07 36
d						04 38					05 15	05 37				06 24	06 44				07 25	07 38
Colwyn Bay d						04 44					05 21	05 43				06 30	06 50				07 31	07 44
Abergele & Pensarn d						04 51						05 50					06 57					
Rhyl d						04 57					05 31	05 56				06 40	07 03				07 41	07 55
Prestatyn d						05 02					05 37	06 01				06 46	07 08				07 47	08 01
Flint d						05 16					05 50	06 15				06 59	07 21				08 00	08 15
Shotton d						05 22						06 21					07 27					
Chester a						05 33					06 04	06 33				07 15	07 38				08 14	08 28
d	22p48	23p22	03 36	04 22	04 55	05 37	05 38	05 51	06 05	06 12	06 13	06 35	07 03	07 12	07 17	07 21	07 40		07 55	08 07	08 19	08 35
Liverpool Lime Street 10 106 a																						
Helsby d		23p31					05 47				06 22			07 21			07 49					
Frodsham d		23p35					05 51				06 26			07 25			07 53					
Runcorn East d		23p41					05 56				06 32			07 31			07 59					
Warrington Bank Quay 90 a		23p49					06 05				06 39			07 38			08 06					
Earlestown 8 90 a		23p56					06 12				06 47			07 46			08 15					
Newton-le-Willows 90 a		23p59					06 15				06 50			07 49			08 18					
Manchester Oxford Road 90 a							06 35				07 09			08 09			08 41					
Manchester Pic'dilly 10 90 ⇌ a	00 18	00 28	04 44				06 45		07 31		07 18		08 32	08 18			08 45			09 36		
Crewe 10 a				04 44	05 20	05 58		06 15				06 59			07 36				08 18			08 54
Cardiff Central 7 131 a										09 22											11 15	
Manchester Airport 84,85 ✈ a			05 19																			
Birmingham New Street 12 65 a				05 58												09 26						
London Euston 15 ⊖65 a															09 30							10 37

	AW ✕	AW	AW	NT	AW ◇ C ✕	VT ◇1 ⊡	AW ✕	AW	AW	NT	AW ◇ ✕	VT ◇1 ⊡	AW ◇ ✕	AW	AW	NT	AW C	AW ◇ D	VT ◇1 ⊡	AW ◇ ✕	AW	AW
Holyhead d					07 15	07 55					08 20	08 55					09 23					
Valley d					07x21						08x26						09x29					
Rhosneigr d					07x26						08x32						09x34					
Ty Croes d					07x30						08x35						09x38					
Bodorgan d					07x34						08x40						09x42					
Llanfairpwll d					07x44						08x49						09x52					
Bangor (Gwynedd) a					07 52	08 21					08 57	09 21					10 00					
d					08 02	08 22					09 02	09 22					10 02					
Llanfairfechan d					08x09						09x09						10x09					
Penmaenmawr d					08x13						09x13						10x13					
Conwy d					08x19						09x19						10x19					
Llandudno d	07 45	08 08					08 45	09 08					09 45	10 08				10 22		10 44	11 08	
Deganwy d	07x49	08x12					08x49	09x12					09x49	10x12				10x26		10x48	11x12	
Llandudno Junction a	07 53	08 18			08 23	08 39	08 53	09 18			09 23	09 39	09 53	10 18			10 23	10 32		10 52	11 18	
d	07 54				08 25	08 40	08 54				09 25	09 40	09 54				10 25			10 53		
Colwyn Bay d	08 00				08 31	08 47	09 00				09 31	09 47	10 00				10 31			10 59		
Abergele & Pensarn d	08 07						09 07						10 07							11 06		
Rhyl d	08 13				08 41	08 58	09 13				09 41	09 58	10 13				10 41			11 12		
Prestatyn d	08 19				08 47	09 04	09 19				09 47	10 03	10 19				10 47			11 18		
Flint d	08 32				09 00	09 17	09 32				10 00		10 32				11 00			11 31		
Shotton d	08 38						09 38						10 38							11 37		
Chester a	08 50				09 15	09 31	09 50				10 14	10 28	10 50				11 16			11 49		
d	08 52		08 55	09 07	09 20	09 35	09 52		09 55	10 07	10 19	10 35	10 52		10 55	11 07	11 21		11 35	11 50		11 55
Liverpool Lime Street 10 106 a																						
Helsby d	09 01						10 01						11 01							12 00		
Frodsham d	09 05						10 05						11 05							12 04		
Runcorn East d	09 11						10 11						11 11							12 09		
Warrington Bank Quay 90 a	09 18						10 18						11 18							12 18		
Earlestown 8 90 a	09 26						10 26						11 26							12 26		
Newton-le-Willows 90 a	09 29						10 29						11 29							12 29		
Manchester Oxford Road 90 a	09 48						10 48						11 48							12 48		
Manchester Pic'dilly 10 90 ⇌ a	09 52			10 36			10 52			11 36			11 52			12 36				12 52		
Crewe 10 a			09 18			09 54			10 18			10 54			11 18				11 54			12 18
Cardiff Central 7 131 a											13 15											
Manchester Airport 84,85 ✈ a																						
Birmingham New Street 12 65 a					11 27												13 27					
London Euston 15 ⊖65 a						11 38						12 38							13 38			

A From Birmingham International
B From Shrewsbury
C To Birmingham International
D To Blaenau Ffestiniog

Table 81

North Wales and Chester - Manchester and Crewe

Saturdays until 30 June

Network Diagram - see first Page of Table 81

		NT		AW	VT	AW	AW	AW	NT	AW	VT	VT		AW	AW	AW	NT	AW	AW	VT	AW	AW		AW	NT
				■ ⌶	◇■ ⊡	◇ ⌶				◇ A ⌶	◇■ ⊡	◇■ ⊡		◇ ⌶				◇ B ⌶	◇ C	◇■ ⊡	◇ ⌶				
Holyhead	d			10 33						11 23	11 55							12 38							
Valley	d			10x39						11x29															
Rhosneigr	d									11x34															
Ty Croes	d									11x38															
Bodorgan	d									11x42															
Llanfairpwll	d			10x56						11x52															
Bangor (Gwynedd)	a			11 03						12 00	12 20							13 05							
	d			11 05						12 02	12 21							13 07							
Llanfairfechan	d									12x09															
Penmaenmawr	d									12x13															
Conwy	d									12x19															
Llandudno	d					11 44	12 08							12 44	13 08				13 22		13 44	14 08			
Deganwy	d					11x48	12x12							12x48	13x12				13x26		13x48	14x12			
Llandudno Junction	a			11 21		11 52	12 18			12 23	12 38			12 52	13 18			13 23	13 32		13 52	14 18			
	d			11 25		11 53				12 25	12 39			12 53				13 25			13 53				
Colwyn Bay	d			11 31		11 59				12 31	12 46			12 59				13 31			13 59				
Abergele & Pensarn	d					12 06								13 06							14 06				
Rhyl	d			11 41		12 12				12 41	12 57			13 12				13 41			14 12				
Prestatyn	d			11 47		12 18				12 47				13 18				13 47			14 18				
Flint	d			12 00		12 31				13 00				13 31				14 00			14 31				
Shotton	d					12 37								13 37							14 37				
Chester	a			12 14		12 49				13 15	13 24			13 49				14 14			14 49				
	d	12 07		12 19	12 35	12 50		12 55	13 07	13 20	13 35	13 35		13 50		13 55	14 07	14 19		14 35	14 50			14 55	15 07
Liverpool Lime Street [10] 106	a																								
Helsby	d					13 00								14 00							15 00				
Frodsham	d					13 04								14 04							15 04				
Runcorn East	d					13 09								14 09							15 09				
Warrington Bank Quay 90	a					13 18								14 18							15 18				
Earlestown [8] 90	a					13 26								14 26							15 26				
Newton-le-Willows 90	a					13 29								14 29							15 29				
Manchester Oxford Road 90	a					13 48								14 48							15 48				
Manchester Pic'dilly [10] 90 ⇌	a	13 36				13 52			14 36					14 57			15 36				15 52				16 36
Crewe [10]	a				12 54			13 18			13 54	13 54				14 18				14 54				15 18	
Cardiff Central [7] 131	a			15 26														17 08							
Manchester Airport 84,85 ✈	a																								
Birmingham New Street [12] 65	a									15 27															
London Euston [15] ⊖65	a				14 38						15 38	15 38								16 38					

		AW	VT	AW	AW	NT	AW	AW		VT	AW	AW	AW	NT	AW	AW	VT	AW		AW	AW	NT	AW	AW	AW
		◇ A ⌶	◇■ ⊡	◇ ⌶			◇ ⌶			◇■ ⊡	◇ ⌶				◇ A ⌶	◇ C	◇■ ⊡	◇ ⌶					◇ ⌶	◇ ⌶	
Holyhead	d	13 23					14 23			14 38					15 23								16 38		
Valley	d	13x29													15x29										
Rhosneigr	d	13x34													15x34										
Ty Croes	d	13x38													15x38										
Bodorgan	d	13x42													15x42										
Llanfairpwll	d	13x52													15x52										
Bangor (Gwynedd)	a	14 00					14 52			15 06					16 00								17 05		
	d	14 02					14 53			15 07					16 02								17 07		
Llanfairfechan	d	14x09					15x00								16x09										
Penmaenmawr	d	14x13					15x04								16x13										
Conwy	d	14x19					15x10								16x19										
Llandudno	d			14 42				15 08			15 44	16 08				16 20		16 44		17 08				17 44	18 08
Deganwy	d			14x46				15x12			15x48	16x12				16x24		16x48		17x12				17x48	18x12
Llandudno Junction	a	14 23		14 50			15 15	15 18		15 25	15 52	16 18			16 23	16 30		16 52		17 18			17 23	17 52	18 18
	d	14 25		14 51			15 16			15 27	15 53				16 25			16 53					17 25	17 53	
Colwyn Bay	d	14 31		14 57			15 22			15 35	15 59				16 31			16 59					17 31	17 59	
Abergele & Pensarn	d			15 04							16 06							17 06						18 06	
Rhyl	d	14 41		15 10			15 33			15 48	16 12				16 41			17 12					17 41	18 12	
Prestatyn	d	14 47		15 16			15 38				16 18				16 47			17 18					17 47	18 18	
Flint	d	15 00		15 29			15 52				16 31				17 00			17 31					18 00	18 31	
Shotton	d			15 35							16 37							17 37						18 37	
Chester	a	15 17		15 46			16 05			16 18	16 49				17 15			17 49					18 15	18 49	
	d	15 20	15 35	15 48	15 55	16 07	16 19			16 24	16 50		16 55	17 07	17 28		17 35	17 50			17 55	18 07	18 20	18 50	
Liverpool Lime Street [10] 106	a																								
Helsby	d			15 57							17 00							18 00						19 00	
Frodsham	d			16 02							17 04							18 04						19 04	
Runcorn East	d			16 07							17 09							18 09						19 09	
Warrington Bank Quay 90	a			16 16							17 18							18 18						19 18	
Earlestown [8] 90	a			16 26							17 26							18 26						19 26	
Newton-le-Willows 90	a			16 29							17 29							18 29						19 29	
Manchester Oxford Road 90	a			16 48							17 48							18 48						19 48	
Manchester Pic'dilly [10] 90 ⇌	a			16 57		17 36					17 57			18 36				18 57				19 35		19 52	
Crewe [10]	a		15 54		16 18					16 47			17 18				17 54				18 18				
Cardiff Central [7] 131	a						19 16																21 21		
Manchester Airport 84,85 ✈	a																							20 13	
Birmingham New Street [12] 65	a	17 28													19 26										
London Euston [15] ⊖65	a		17 38							18 38															

A To Birmingham International
B To Maesteg
C To Blaenau Ffestiniog

Table 81

North Wales and Chester - Manchester and Crewe

Saturdays until 30 June

Network Diagram - see first Page of Table 81

		AW	NT	AW		AW	AW	AW	AW	NT	AW	VT	AW	AW		AW	AW	AW	NT	AW	AW	NT	AW	AW
				◇ A ⌶		◇ ⌶	◇ B				⌶	◇ ⊡	◇				◇				◇			
Holyhead	d			17 30							18 23						19 21				20 37			
Valley	d			17x36							18x29						19x27							
Rhosneigr	d			17x41							18x34						19x32							
Ty Croes	d			17x45							18x38						19x36							
Bodorgan	d			17x49							18x42						19x40							
Llanfairpwll	d			17x59							18x52						19x50							
Bangor (Gwynedd)	a			18 07							19 00						19 58				21 05			
	d			18 09							19 02						20 00				21 06			
Llanfairfechan	d			18x16							19x09						20x07				21x13			
Penmaenmawr	d			18x20							19x13						20x11				21x17			
Conwy	d			18x26							19x19						20x17				21x23			
Llandudno	d					18 44	19 03	19 08					19 42	20 08				20 43					21 45	
Deganwy	d					18x48	19x07	19x12					19x46	20x12				20x47					21x49	
Llandudno Junction	a			18 30		18 52	19 11	19 18			19 23		19 50	20 18			20 21	20 51			21 28		21 53	
	d			18 32		18 53					19 25		19 51				20 23	20 52			21 29		21 55	
Colwyn Bay	d			18 38		18 59					19 31		19 57				20 29	20 58			21 35		22 01	
Abergele & Pensarn	d					19 06							20 04					21 05			21 42		22 09	
Rhyl	d			18 48		19 12					19 41		20 10				20 39	21 11			21 48		22 16	
Prestatyn	d			18 54		19 18					19 47		20 16				20 45	21 17			21 54		22 22	
Flint	d			19 07		19 31					20 00		20 29				20 58	21 30			22 07		22 37	
Shotton	d					19 37							20 35					21 36			22 13		22 44	
Chester	a			19 24		19 49					20 15		20 47				21 15	21 47			22 23		22 55	
	d	18 55	19 07	19 35		19 50			19 55	20 07	20 17	20 35	20 50			20 55	21 20		21 33	21 52	22 26	22 49	23 01	23 22
Liverpool Lime Street [10] 106	a																							
Helsby	d					20 00							20 59							22 01				23 31
Frodsham	d					20 04							21 03							22 05				23 35
Runcorn East	d					20 09							21 09							22 11				23 41
Warrington Bank Quay 90	a					20 18							21 16							22 19				23 50
Earlestown [8] 90	a					20 26							21 26							22 26				23 58
Newton-le-Willows 90	a					20 29							21 29							22 30				00 01
Manchester Oxford Road 90	a					20 48							21 48							22 50				
Manchester Pic'dilly [10] 90 ⇌	a		20 35			20 57				21 35			21 57						23 00	22 58		00 15		00 26
Crewe [10]	a	19 18		20 00					20 18		20 41	20 54				21 18					22 50		23 26	
Cardiff Central [7] 131	a																							
Manchester Airport 84,85 ✈	a																							
Birmingham New Street [12] 65	a																23 28							
London Euston [15] ⊖65	a																							

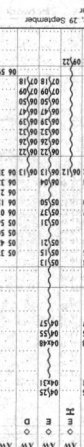

Saturdays 7 July to 29 September

		NT	AW	AW	AW	AW	AW	AW	AW	NT		AW	AW	AW	AW	AW	NT	AW	VT	AW		AW	AW	AW	NT
			◇ C									◇ D ⌶	◇ E ⌶	◇ E	◇ D			F ⌶	◇■ ⊡	◇ G ⌶		⌶			
Holyhead	d											04⌇25		04⌇25						05 22					
Valley	d											04x31		04x31						05x28					
Rhosneigr	d											⌇		⌇						05x33					
Ty Croes	d											⌇		⌇						05x37					
Bodorgan	d											⌇		⌇						05x41					
Llanfairpwll	d											04x48		04x48						05x51					
Bangor (Gwynedd)	a											04⌇55		04⌇55						05 59					
	d											04⌇57		04⌇57						06 01					
Llanfairfechan	d											⌇		⌇						06x08					
Penmaenmawr	d											⌇		⌇						06x12					
Conwy	d											⌇		⌇						06x18					
Llandudno	d											⌇		⌇								06 34	07 08		
Deganwy	d											⌇		⌇								06x38	07x12		
Llandudno Junction	a											05⌇13		05⌇13						06 22		06 42	07 18		
	d						04 38					05⌇15		05⌇15		05 37				06 24		06 44			
Colwyn Bay	d						04 44					05⌇21		05⌇21		05 43				06 30		06 50			
Abergele & Pensarn	d						04 51					⌇		⌇		05 50						06 57			
Rhyl	d						04 57					05⌇31		05⌇31		05 56				06 40		07 03			
Prestatyn	d						05 02					05⌇37		05⌇37		06 01				06 46		07 08			
Flint	d						05 16					05⌇50		05⌇50		06 15				06 59		07 21			
Shotton	d						05 22					⌇		⌇		06 21						07 27			
Chester	a						05 33					06⌇04		06⌇04		06 33				07 15		07 38			
	d	22p48	23p22	03 36	04 22	04 55	05 37	05 38	05 51	06 05		06⌇12	06⌇12	06⌇13	06⌇13	06 35	07 03	07 12	07 17	07 21		07 40		07 55	08 07
Liverpool Lime Street [10] 106	a											⌇	⌇	⌇	⌇										
Helsby	d		23p31					05 47				⌇	⌇	06⌇22	06⌇22			07 21				07 49			
Frodsham	d		23p35					05 51				⌇	⌇	06⌇26	06⌇26			07 25				07 53			
Runcorn East	d		23p41					05 56				⌇	⌇	06⌇32	06⌇32			07 31				07 59			
Warrington Bank Quay 90	a		23p49					06 05				⌇	⌇	06⌇39	06⌇39			07 38				08 06			
Earlestown [8] 90	a		23p56					06 12				⌇	⌇	06⌇47	06⌇47			07 46				08 15			
Newton-le-Willows 90	a		23p59					06 15				⌇	⌇	06⌇50	06⌇50			07 49				08 18			
Manchester Oxford Road 90	a							06 35				⌇	⌇	07⌇09	07⌇09			08 09				08 41			
Manchester Pic'dilly [10] 90 ⇌	a	00 18	00 28	04 44				06 45		07 31		⌇	⌇	07⌇18	07⌇18		08 32	08 18				08 45			09 36
Crewe [10]	a				04 44	05 20	05 58		06 15			⌇	⌇			06 59			07 36					08 18	
Cardiff Central [7] 131	a											09⌇22	09⌇22												
Manchester Airport 84,85 ✈	a			05 19																					
Birmingham New Street [12] 65	a				05 58															09 26					
London Euston [15] ⊖65	a																		09 30						

A ⌶ to Chester ◇ to Chester
B To Blaenau Ffestiniog
C From Birmingham International
D 15 September, 22 September, 29 September
E from 7 July until 8 September
F From Shrewsbury
G To Birmingham International

North Wales and Chester - Manchester and Crewe

Network Diagram - see first Page of Table 81

	AW ◇ ⌶	VT ◇1 ⊡	AW ⌶	AW	AW	NT	AW ◇ A ⌶	VT ◇1 ⊡	AW ⌶	AW	AW	NT	AW ◇ ⌶	VT ◇1 ⊡	AW ◇ ⌶	AW	AW	NT	AW A	AW ◇ B	VT ◇1 ⊡	AW ◇ ⌶
Holyhead d	06 35	06 52					07 15	07 55					08 20	08 55					09 23			
Valley d	06x41						07x21						08x26						09x29			
Rhosneigr d							07x26						08x32						09x34			
Ty Croes d							07x30						08x35						09x38			
Bodorgan d							07x34						08x40						09x42			
Llanfairpwll d	06x58						07x44						08x49						09x52			
Bangor (Gwynedd) a	07 05	07 18					07 52	08 21					08 57	09 21					10 00			
d	07 07	07 20					08 02	08 22					09 02	09 22					10 02			
Llanfairfechan d							08x09						09x09						10x09			
Penmaenmawr d							08x13						09x13						10x13			
Conwy d							08x19						09x19						10x19			
Llandudno d			07 45	08 08					08 45	09 08					09 45	10 08				10 22		10 44
Deganwy d			07x49	08x12					08x49	09x12					09x49	10x12				10x26		10x48
Llandudno Junction a	07 23	07 36	07 53	08 18			08 23	08 39	08 53	09 18			09 23	09 39	09 53	10 18			10 23	10 32		10 52
d	07 25	07 38	07 54				08 25	08 40	08 54				09 25	09 40	09 54				10 25			10 53
Colwyn Bay d	07 31	07 44	08 00				08 31	08 47	09 00				09 31	09 47	10 00				10 31			10 59
Abergele & Pensarn d			08 07						09 07						10 07							11 06
Rhyl d	07 41	07 55	08 13				08 41	08 58	09 13				09 41	09 58	10 13				10 41			11 12
Prestatyn d	07 47	08 01	08 19				08 47	09 04	09 19				09 47	10 03	10 19				10 47			11 18
Flint d	08 00	08 15	08 32				09 00	09 17	09 32				10 00		10 32				11 00			11 31
Shotton d			08 38						09 38						10 38							11 37
Chester a	08 14	08 28	08 50				09 15	09 31	09 50				10 14	10 28	10 50				11 16			11 49
d	08 19	08 35	08 52		08 55	09 07	09 20	09 35	09 52		09 55	10 07	10 19	10 35	10 52		10 55	11 07	11 21		11 35	11 50
Liverpool Lime Street ■10 106 a																						
Helsby d			09 01						10 01						11 01							12 00
Frodsham d			09 05						10 05						11 05							12 04
Runcorn East d			09 11						10 11						11 11							12 09
Warrington Bank Quay 90 a			09 18						10 18						11 18							12 18
Earlestown ■8 90 a			09 26						10 26						11 26							12 26
Newton-le-Willows 90 a			09 29						10 29						11 29							12 29
Manchester Oxford Road 90 a			09 48						10 48						11 48							12 48
Manchester Pic'dilly ■10 90 ⇌ a			09 52			10 36			10 52			11 36			11 52			12 36				12 52
Crewe ■10 a		08 54			09 18			09 54			10 18			10 54			11 18				11 54	
Cardiff Central ■7 131 a	11 15												13 15									
Manchester Airport 84,85 ✈ a																						
Birmingham New Street ■12 65 a							11 27												13 27			
London Euston ■15 ⊖65 a		10 37						11 38						12 38							13 38	

	AW	AW	NT	AW ■ ⌶	VT ◇1 ⊡	AW ◇ ⌶	AW	AW	NT	AW ◇ A ⌶	VT ◇1 C ⊡	VT ◇1 ⊡	AW ◇ ⌶	AW	AW	NT	AW ◇ D ⌶	AW ◇ B	VT ◇1 ⊡	AW ◇ ⌶	AW
Holyhead d				10 33						11 23	11 55						12 38				
Valley d				10x39						11x29											
Rhosneigr d										11x34											
Ty Croes d										11x38											
Bodorgan d										11x42											
Llanfairpwll d				10x56						11x52											
Bangor (Gwynedd) a				11 03						12 00	12 20						13 05				
d				11 05						12 02	12 21						13 07				
Llanfairfechan d										12x09											
Penmaenmawr d										12x13											
Conwy d										12x19											
Llandudno d	11 08					11 44	12 08						12 44	13 08				13 22		13 44	14 08
Deganwy d	11x12					11x48	12x12						12x48	13x12				13x26		13x48	14x12
Llandudno Junction a	11 18			11 21		11 52	12 18			12 23	12 38		12 52	13 18			13 23	13 32		13 52	14 18
d				11 25		11 53				12 25	12 39		12 53				13 25			13 53	
Colwyn Bay d				11 31		11 59				12 31	12 46		12 59				13 31			13 59	
Abergele & Pensarn d						12 06							13 06							14 06	
Rhyl d				11 41		12 12				12 41	12 57		13 12				13 41			14 12	
Prestatyn d				11 47		12 18				12 47			13 18				13 47			14 18	
Flint d				12 00		12 31				13 00			13 31				14 00			14 31	
Shotton d						12 37							13 37							14 37	
Chester a				12 14		12 49				13 15	13 24		13 49				14 14			14 49	
d		11 55	12 07	12 19	12 35	12 50		12 55	13 07	13 20	13 35	13 35	13 50		13 55	14 07	14 19		14 35	14 50	
Liverpool Lime Street ■10 106 a																					
Helsby d						13 00							14 00							15 00	
Frodsham d						13 04							14 04							15 04	
Runcorn East d						13 09							14 09							15 09	
Warrington Bank Quay 90 a						13 18							14 18							15 18	
Earlestown ■8 90 a						13 26							14 26							15 26	
Newton-le-Willows 90 a						13 29							14 29							15 29	
Manchester Oxford Road 90 a						13 48							14 48							15 48	
Manchester Pic'dilly ■10 90 ⇌ a			13 36			13 52			14 36				14 57			15 36				15 52	
Crewe ■10 a		12 18			12 54			13 18			13 54	13 54			14 18				14 54		
Cardiff Central ■7 131 a				15 26													17 08				
Manchester Airport 84,85 ✈ a																					
Birmingham New Street ■12 65 a										15 27											
London Euston ■15 ⊖65 a					14 38						15 38	15 38							16 38		

A To Birmingham International
B To Blaenau Ffestiniog
C from 7 July until 8 September
D To Maesteg

North Wales and Chester - Manchester and Crewe

Network Diagram - see first Page of Table 81

	AW	NT	AW ◇ A ⌶	VT ◇1 ⊡	AW ◇ ⌶	AW	NT	AW ◇ ⌶	AW	VT ◇1 ⊡	AW ◇ ⌶	AW	AW	NT	AW ◇ A ⌶	AW ◇ B	VT ◇1 ⊡	AW ◇ ⌶	AW	AW	NT	AW ◇ ⌶
Holyhead d			13 23					14 23		14 38					15 23							16 38
Valley d			13x29												15x29							
Rhosneigr d			13x34												15x34							
Ty Croes d			13x38												15x38							
Bodorgan d			13x42												15x42							
Llanfairpwll d			13x52												15x52							
Bangor (Gwynedd) a			14 00					14 52		15 06					16 00							17 05
d			14 02					14 53		15 07					16 02							17 07
Llanfairfechan d			14x09					15x00							16x09							
Penmaenmawr d			14x13					15x04							16x13							
Conwy d			14x19					15x10							16x19							
Llandudno d					14 42				15 08		15 44	16 08				16 20		16 44	17 08			
Deganwy d					14x46				15x12		15x48	16x12				16x24		16x48	17x12			
Llandudno Junction a			14 23		14 50			15 15	15 18	15 25	15 52	16 18			16 23	16 30		16 52	17 18			17 23
d			14 25		14 51			15 16		15 27	15 53				16 25			16 53				17 25
Colwyn Bay d			14 31		14 57			15 22		15 35	15 59				16 31			16 59				17 31
Abergele & Pensarn d					15 04						16 06							17 06				
Rhyl d			14 41		15 10			15 33		15 48	16 12				16 41			17 12				17 41
Prestatyn d			14 47		15 16			15 38			16 18				16 47			17 18				17 47
Flint d			15 00		15 29			15 52			16 31				17 00			17 31				18 00
Shotton d					15 35						16 37							17 37				
Chester a			15 17		15 46			16 05		16 18	16 49				17 15			17 49				18 15
d	14 55	15 07	15 20	15 35	15 48	15 55	16 07	16 19		16 24	16 50		16 55	17 07	17 28		17 35	17 50		17 55	18 07	18 20
Liverpool Lime Street ■10 106 a																						
Helsby d					15 57						17 00							18 00				
Frodsham d					16 02						17 04							18 04				
Runcorn East d					16 07						17 09							18 09				
Warrington Bank Quay 90 a					16 16						17 18							18 18				
Earlestown ■8 90 a					16 26						17 26							18 26				
Newton-le-Willows 90 a					16 29						17 29							18 29				
Manchester Oxford Road 90 a					16 48						17 48							18 48				
Manchester Pic'dilly ■10 90 ⇌ a		16 36			16 57		17 36				17 57			18 36				18 57			19 35	
Crewe ■10 a	15 18			15 54		16 18				16 47			17 18				17 54			18 18		
Cardiff Central ■7 131 a								19 16														21 21
Manchester Airport 84,85 ✈ a																						
Birmingham New Street ■12 65 a			17 28												19 26							
London Euston ■15 ⊖65 a				17 38						18 38												

	AW ◇ ⌶	AW	AW ◇ C ⌶	AW	NT	AW ◇ D ⌶	AW ◇ ⌶	AW ◇ B	AW	AW	NT	AW ⌶	VT ◇ ⊡	AW ◇	AW	AW	AW ◇	AW	NT	AW	AW ◇
Holyhead d			17 30			17 30						18 23					19 21				20 37
Valley d			17x36			17x36						18x29					19x27				
Rhosneigr d			17x41			17x41						18x34					19x32				
Ty Croes d			17x45			17x45						18x38					19x36				
Bodorgan d			17x49			17x49						18x42					19x40				
Llanfairpwll d			17x59			17x59						18x52					19x50				
Bangor (Gwynedd) a			18 07			18 07						19 00					19 58				21 05
d			18 09			18 09						19 02					20 00				21 06
Llanfairfechan d			18x16			18x16						19x09					20x07				21x13
Penmaenmawr d			18x20			18x20						19x13					20x11				21x17
Conwy d			18x26			18x26						19x19					20x17				21x23
Llandudno d	17 44	18 08					18 44	19 03	19 08					19 42	20 08			20 43			
Deganwy d	17x48	18x12					18x48	19x07	19x12					19x46	20x12			20x47			
Llandudno Junction a	17 52	18 18	18 30			18 30	18 52	19 11	19 18			19 23		19 50	20 18		20 21	20 51			21 28
d	17 53		18 32			18 32	18 53					19 25		19 51			20 23	20 52			21 29
Colwyn Bay d	17 59		18 38			18 38	18 59					19 31		19 57			20 29	20 58			21 35
Abergele & Pensarn d	18 06						19 06							20 04				21 05			21 42
Rhyl d	18 12		18 48			18 48	19 12					19 41		20 10			20 39	21 11			21 48
Prestatyn d	18 18		18 54			18 54	19 18					19 47		20 16			20 45	21 17			21 54
Flint d	18 31		19 07			19 07	19 31					20 00		20 29			20 58	21 30			22 07
Shotton d	18 37						19 37							20 35				21 36			22 13
Chester a	18 49		19 24			19 24	19 49					20 15		20 47			21 15	21 47			22 23
d	18 50			18 55	19 07	19 35	19 50			19 55	20 07	20 17	20 35	20 50		20 55	21 20		21 33	21 52	22 26
Liverpool Lime Street ■10 106 a																					
Helsby d	19 00						20 00							20 59						22 01	
Frodsham d	19 04						20 04							21 03						22 05	
Runcorn East d	19 09						20 09							21 09						22 11	
Warrington Bank Quay 90 a	19 18						20 18							21 16						22 19	
Earlestown ■8 90 a	19 26						20 26							21 26						22 26	
Newton-le-Willows 90 a	19 29						20 29							21 29						22 30	
Manchester Oxford Road 90 a	19 48						20 48							21 48						22 50	
Manchester Pic'dilly ■10 90 ⇌ a	19 52				20 35		20 57				21 35			21 57					23 00	22 58	
Crewe ■10 a				19 18		20 00				20 18		20 41	20 54			21 18					22 50
Cardiff Central ■7 131 a																					
Manchester Airport 84,85 ✈ a	20 13																				
Birmingham New Street ■12 65 a																	23 28				
London Euston ■15 ⊖65 a																					

A To Birmingham International
B To Blaenau Ffestiniog
C To Shrewsbury
D from 7 July until 8 September. ⌶ to Chester ◇ to Chester

Table 81

North Wales and Chester - Manchester and Crewe

Saturdays
7 July to 29 September

Network Diagram - see first Page of Table 81

	NT	AW	AW
Holyhead d			
Valley d			
Rhosneigr d			
Ty Croes d			
Bodorgan d			
Llanfairpwll d			
Bangor (Gwynedd) a			
d			
Llanfairfechan d			
Penmaenmawr d			
Conwy d			
Llandudno d		21 45	
Deganwy d		21x49	
Llandudno Junction a		21 53	
d		21 55	
Colwyn Bay d		22 01	
Abergele & Pensarn d		22 09	
Rhyl d		22 16	
Prestatyn d		22 22	
Flint d		22 37	
Shotton d		22 44	
Chester a		22 55	
d	22 49	23 01	23 22
Liverpool Lime Street ■ 106 a			
Helsby d			23 31
Frodsham d			23 35
Runcorn East d			23 41
Warrington Bank Quay 90 a			23 50
Earlestown ■ 90 a			23 58
Newton-le-Willows 90 a			00 01
Manchester Oxford Road 90 a			
Manchester Pic'dilly ■ 90 a	00 15		00 26
Crewe ■ a		23 26	
Cardiff Central ■ 131 a			
Manchester Airport 84,85 ✈ a			
Birmingham New Street ■ 65 a			
London Euston ■ ⊖65 a			

Saturdays
from 6 October

	NT	AW ◇ A	AW	AW	AW	AW	AW	AW	NT	AW ◇ 🍴	AW ◇	AW	NT	AW B 🍴	VT ◇■ ☕	AW ◇ C 🍴	AW 🍴	AW	AW	NT	AW ◇ 🍴	VT ◇■ ☕
Holyhead d										04 25						05 22					06 35	06 52
Valley d										04x31						05x28					06x41	
Rhosneigr d																05x33						
Ty Croes d																05x37						
Bodorgan d																05x41						
Llanfairpwll d										04x48						05x51					06x58	
Bangor (Gwynedd) a										04 55						05 59					07 05	07 18
d										04 57						06 01					07 07	07 20
Llanfairfechan d																06x08						
Penmaenmawr d																06x12						
Conwy d																06x18						
Llandudno d																	06 34	07 08				
Deganwy d																	06x38	07x12				
Llandudno Junction a										05 13						06 22	06 42	07 18			07 23	07 36
d						04 38				05 15		05 37				06 24	06 44				07 25	07 38
Colwyn Bay d						04 44				05 21		05 43				06 30	06 50				07 31	07 44
Abergele & Pensarn d						04 51						05 50					06 57					
Rhyl d						04 57				05 31		05 56				06 40	07 03				07 41	07 55
Prestatyn d						05 02				05 37		06 01				06 46	07 08				07 47	08 01
Flint d						05 16				05 50		06 15				06 59	07 21				08 00	08 15
Shotton d						05 22						06 21					07 27					
Chester a						05 33				06 04		06 33				07 15	07 38				08 14	08 28
d	22p44	23p22	03 36	04 22	04 55	05 37	05 38	05 51	06 01	06 12	06 13	06 35	06 59	07 12	07 17	07 21	07 40		07 55	08 03	08 19	08 35
Liverpool Lime Street ■ 106 a																						
Helsby d		23p31					05 47				06 22			07 21			07 49					
Frodsham d		23p35					05 51				06 26			07 25			07 53					
Runcorn East d		23p41					05 56				06 32			07 31			07 59					
Warrington Bank Quay 90 a		23p49					06 05				06 39			07 38			08 06					
Earlestown ■ 90 a		23p56					06 12				06 47			07 46			08 15					
Newton-le-Willows 90 a		23p59					06 15				06 50			07 49			08 18					
Manchester Oxford Road 90 a							06 35				07 09			08 09			08 41					
Manchester Pic'dilly ■ 90 a	00 18	00 28	04 44				06 45		07 31		07 18		08 32	08 18			08 45			09 36		
Crewe ■ a				04 44	05 20	05 58		06 15				06 59			07 36				08 18			08 54
Cardiff Central ■ 131 a										09 22												
Manchester Airport 84,85 ✈ a			05 19																		11 15	
Birmingham New Street ■ 65 a				05 58												09 26						
London Euston ■ ⊖65 a															09 30							10 37

A From Birmingham International
B From Shrewsbury
C To Birmingham International

Table 81

North Wales and Chester - Manchester and Crewe

Saturdays
from 6 October

Network Diagram - see first Page of Table 81

	AW 🍴	AW	AW	NT	AW ◇ A 🍴	VT ◇■ ☕	AW 🍴	AW	AW	NT	AW ◇ 🍴	VT ◇■ ☕	AW ◇ 🍴	AW	AW	NT	AW A	AW ◇ B	VT ◇■ ☕	AW ◇ 🍴	AW	AW
Holyhead d					07 15	07 55					08 20	08 55					09 23					
Valley d					07x21						08x26						09x29					
Rhosneigr d					07x26						08x32						09x34					
Ty Croes d					07x30						08x35						09x38					
Bodorgan d					07x34						08x40						09x42					
Llanfairpwll d					07x44						08x49						09x52					
Bangor (Gwynedd) a					07 52	08 21					08 57	09 21					10 00					
d					08 02	08 22					09 02	09 22					10 02					
Llanfairfechan d					08x09						09x09						10x09					
Penmaenmawr d					08x13						09x13						10x13					
Conwy d					08x19						09x19						10x19					
Llandudno d	07 45	08 08					08 45	09 08					09 45	10 08				10 22		10 44	11 08	
Deganwy d	07x49	08x12					08x49	09x12					09x49	10x12				10x26		10x48	11x12	
Llandudno Junction a	07 53	08 18			08 23	08 39	08 53	09 18			09 23	09 39	09 53	10 18			10 23	10 32		10 52	11 18	
d	07 54				08 25	08 40	08 54				09 25	09 40	09 54				10 25			10 53		
Colwyn Bay d	08 00				08 31	08 47	09 00				09 31	09 47	10 00				10 31			10 59		
Abergele & Pensarn d	08 07						09 07						10 07							11 06		
Rhyl d	08 13				08 41	08 58	09 13				09 41	09 58	10 13				10 41			11 12		
Prestatyn d	08 19				08 47	09 04	09 19				09 47	10 03	10 19				10 47			11 18		
Flint d	08 32				09 00	09 17	09 32				10 00		10 32				11 00			11 31		
Shotton d	08 38						09 38						10 38							11 37		
Chester a	08 50				09 15	09 31	09 50				10 14	10 28	10 50				11 16			11 49		
d	08 52		08 55	09 03	09 20	09 35	09 52		09 55	10 03	10 19	10 35	10 52		10 55	11 03	11 21		11 35	11 50		11 55
Liverpool Lime Street ■ 106 a																						
Helsby d	09 01						10 01						11 01							12 00		
Frodsham d	09 05						10 05						11 05							12 04		
Runcorn East d	09 11						10 11						11 11							12 09		
Warrington Bank Quay 90 a	09 18						10 18						11 18							12 18		
Earlestown ■ 90 a	09 26						10 26						11 26							12 26		
Newton-le-Willows 90 a	09 29						10 29						11 29							12 29		
Manchester Oxford Road 90 a	09 48						10 48						11 48							12 48		
Manchester Pic'dilly ■ 90 a	09 52			10 36			10 52			11 36			11 52			12 36				12 52		
Crewe ■ a			09 18			09 54			10 18			10 54			11 18				11 54			12 18
Cardiff Central ■ 131 a											13 15											
Manchester Airport 84,85 ✈ a																						
Birmingham New Street ■ 65 a					11 27												13 27					
London Euston ■ ⊖65 a						11 38						12 38							13 38			

	NT	AW ■ 🍴	VT ◇■ ☕	AW ◇ 🍴	AW	AW	NT	AW ◇ A 🍴	VT ◇■ ☕	AW ◇ 🍴	AW	AW	NT	AW ◇ C 🍴	AW ◇ B	VT ◇■ ☕	AW ◇ 🍴	AW	AW	NT	AW ◇ A 🍴
Holyhead d		10 33						11 23						12 38							13 23
Valley d		10x39						11x29													13x29
Rhosneigr d								11x34													13x34
Ty Croes d								11x38													13x38
Bodorgan d								11x42													13x42
Llanfairpwll d		10x56						11x52													13x52
Bangor (Gwynedd) a		11 03						12 00						13 05							14 00
d		11 05						12 02						13 07							14 02
Llanfairfechan d								12x09													14x09
Penmaenmawr d								12x13													14x13
Conwy d								12x19													14x19
Llandudno d				11 44	12 08					12 44	13 08				13 22		13 44	14 08			
Deganwy d				11x48	12x12					12x48	13x12				13x26		13x48	14x12			
Llandudno Junction a		11 21		11 52	12 18			12 23		12 52	13 18			13 23	13 32		13 52	14 18			14 23
d		11 25		11 53				12 25		12 53				13 25			13 53				14 25
Colwyn Bay d		11 31		11 59				12 31		12 59				13 31			13 59				14 31
Abergele & Pensarn d				12 06						13 06							14 06				
Rhyl d		11 41		12 12				12 41		13 12				13 41			14 12				14 41
Prestatyn d		11 47		12 18				12 47		13 18				13 47			14 18				14 47
Flint d		12 00		12 31				13 00		13 31				14 00			14 31				15 00
Shotton d				12 37						13 37							14 37				
Chester a		12 14		12 49				13 15		13 49				14 14			14 49				15 17
d	12 03	12 19	12 35	12 50		12 55	13 03	13 20	13 35	13 50		13 55	14 03	14 19		14 35	14 50		14 55	15 03	15 20
Liverpool Lime Street ■ 106 a																					
Helsby d				13 00						14 00							15 00				
Frodsham d				13 04						14 04							15 04				
Runcorn East d				13 09						14 09							15 09				
Warrington Bank Quay 90 a				13 18						14 18							15 18				
Earlestown ■ 90 a				13 26						14 26							15 26				
Newton-le-Willows 90 a				13 29						14 29							15 29				
Manchester Oxford Road 90 a				13 48						14 48							15 48				
Manchester Pic'dilly ■ 90 a	13 36			13 52			14 36			14 57			15 36				15 52			16 36	
Crewe ■ a			12 54			13 18			13 54			14 18				14 54			15 18		
Cardiff Central ■ 131 a		15 26												17 08							
Manchester Airport 84,85 ✈ a																					
Birmingham New Street ■ 65 a								15 27													17 28
London Euston ■ ⊖65 a			14 38						15 38							16 38					

A To Birmingham International
B To Blaenau Ffestiniog
C To Maesteg

Table 81

Saturdays from 6 October

North Wales and Chester - Manchester and Crewe

Network Diagram - see first Page of Table 81

	VT ◇■	AW ◇	AW	NT	AW ◇	AW	VT ◇■		AW ◇	AW	AW	NT	AW ◇ A	AW ◇ B	VT ◇■	AW ◇	AW		AW	NT	AW ◇	AW ◇	AW	AW ◇ C
Holyhead d					14 23		14 38						15 23								16 38			17 30
Valley d													15x29											17x36
Rhosneigr d													15x34											17x41
Ty Croes d													15x38											17x45
Bodorgan d													15x42											17x49
Llanfairpwll d													15x52											17x59
Bangor (Gwynedd) a					14 52		15 06						16 00								17 05			18 07
d					14 53		15 07						16 02								17 07			18 09
Llanfairfechan d					15x00								16x09											18x16
Penmaenmawr d					15x04								16x13											18x20
Conwy d					15x10								16x19											18x26
Llandudno d		14 42				15 08			15 44	16 08				16 20		16 44	17 08					17 44	18 08	
Deganwy d		14x46				15x12			15x48	16x12				16x24		16x48	17x12					17x48	18x12	
Llandudno Junction a		14 50			15 15	15 18	15 25		15 52	16 18			16 23	16 30		16 52	17 18				17 23	17 52	18 18	18 30
d		14 51			15 16		15 27		15 53				16 25			16 53					17 25	17 53		18 32
Colwyn Bay d		14 57			15 22		15 35		15 59				16 31			16 59					17 31	17 59		18 38
Abergele & Pensarn d		15 04							16 06							17 06						18 06		
Rhyl d		15 10			15 33		15 48		16 12				16 41			17 12					17 41	18 12		18 48
Prestatyn d		15 16			15 38				16 18				16 47			17 18					17 47	18 18		18 54
Flint d		15 29			15 52				16 31				17 00			17 31					18 00	18 31		19 07
Shotton d		15 35							16 37							17 37						18 37		
Chester a		15 46			16 05		16 18		16 49				17 15			17 49					18 15	18 49		19 24
d	15 35	15 48	15 55	16 03	16 19		16 24		16 50		16 55	17 03	17 28		17 35	17 50			17 55	18 03	18 20	18 50		
Liverpool Lime Street ■ 106 a																								
Helsby d		15 57							17 00							18 00						19 00		
Frodsham d		16 02							17 04							18 04						19 04		
Runcorn East d		16 07							17 09							18 09						19 09		
Warrington Bank Quay 90 a		16 16							17 18							18 18						19 18		
Earlestown ■ 90 a		16 26							17 26							18 26						19 26		
Newton-le-Willows 90 a		16 29							17 29							18 29						19 29		
Manchester Oxford Road 90 a		16 48							17 48							18 48						19 48		
Manchester Pic'dilly ■ 90 ⇌ a		16 57		17 36					17 57			18 36				18 57				19 35		19 52		
Crewe ■ a	15 54		16 18				16 47				17 18				17 54				18 18					
Cardiff Central ■ 131 a					19 16																21 21			
Manchester Airport 84,85 ✈ a																						20 13		
Birmingham New Street ■ 65 a													19 26											
London Euston ■ ⊖65 a	17 38						18 38																	

	AW	NT	AW ◇		AW ◇ B	AW	AW	NT	AW	VT ◇	AW ◇	AW	AW		AW ◇	AW	NT	AW	AW ◇	NT	AW	AW D	AW E	
Holyhead d									18 23						19 21				20 37					
Valley d									18x29						19x27									
Rhosneigr d									18x34						19x32									
Ty Croes d									18x38						19x36									
Bodorgan d									18x42						19x40									
Llanfairpwll d									18x52						19x50									
Bangor (Gwynedd) a									19 00						19 58				21 05					
d									19 02						20 00				21 06					
Llanfairfechan d									19x09						20x07				21x13					
Penmaenmawr d									19x13						20x11				21x17					
Conwy d									19x19						20x17				21x23					
Llandudno d			18 44		19 03	19 08					19 42	20 08				20 43					21 45			
Deganwy d			18x48		19x07	19x12					19x46	20x12				20x47					21x49			
Llandudno Junction a			18 52		19 11	19 18			19 23		19 50	20 18			20 21	20 51			21 28		21 53			
d			18 53						19 25		19 51				20 23	20 52			21 29		21 55			
Colwyn Bay d			18 59						19 31		19 57				20 29	20 58			21 35		22 01			
Abergele & Pensarn d			19 06								20 04					21 05			21 42		22 09			
Rhyl d			19 12						19 41		20 10				20 39	21 11			21 48		22 16			
Prestatyn d			19 18						19 47		20 16				20 45	21 17			21 54		22 22			
Flint d			19 31						20 00		20 29				20 58	21 30			22 07		22 37			
Shotton d			19 37								20 35					21 36			22 13		22 44			
Chester a			19 49						20 15		20 47				21 15	21 47			22 23		22 55			
d	18 55	19 03	19 50				19 55	20 03	20 17	20 35	20 50		20 55		21 20		21 33	21 52	22 26	22 45	23 01	23 22	23 22	
Liverpool Lime Street ■ 106 a																								
Helsby d			20 00								20 59							22 01				23 31		
Frodsham d			20 04								21 03							22 05				23 35		
Runcorn East d			20 09								21 09							22 11				23 41		
Warrington Bank Quay 90 a			20 18								21 16							22 19				23 50		
Earlestown ■ 90 a			20 26								21 26							22 26				23 58		
Newton-le-Willows 90 a			20 29								21 29							22 30				00 01		
Manchester Oxford Road 90 a			20 48								21 48							22 50						
Manchester Pic'dilly ■ 90 ⇌ a		20 35	20 57					21 35			21 57						23 00	22 58		00 15		00 26	00 29	
Crewe ■ a	19 18						20 18		20 41	20 54			21 18						22 50		23 26			
Cardiff Central ■ 131 a																								
Manchester Airport 84,85 ✈ a																								
Birmingham New Street ■ 65 a															23 28									
London Euston ■ ⊖65 a																								

A To Birmingham International
B To Blaenau Ffestiniog
C To Shrewsbury
D 6 October, 13 October, 20 October
E from 27 October

Table 81

Saturdays from 6 October

North Wales and Chester - Manchester and Crewe

Network Diagram - see first Page of Table 81

	AW A ⇌
Holyhead d	
Valley d	
Rhosneigr d	
Ty Croes d	
Bodorgan d	
Llanfairpwll d	
Bangor (Gwynedd) a	
d	
Llanfairfechan d	
Penmaenmawr d	
Conwy d	
Llandudno d	
Deganwy d	
Llandudno Junction a	
d	
Colwyn Bay d	
Abergele & Pensarn d	
Rhyl d	
Prestatyn d	
Flint d	
Shotton d	
Chester a	
d	23 22
Liverpool Lime Street ■ 106 a	
Helsby d	23 42
Frodsham d	23 47
Runcorn East d	00 02
Warrington Bank Quay 90 a	00 22
Earlestown ■ 90 a	00 47
Newton-le-Willows 90 a	00 57
Manchester Oxford Road 90 a	
Manchester Pic'dilly ■ 90 ⇌ a	01 32
Crewe ■ a	
Cardiff Central ■ 131 a	
Manchester Airport 84,85 ✈ a	
Birmingham New Street ■ 65 a	
London Euston ■ ⊖65 a	

Sundays until 24 June

	NT	AW	AW	AW	AW	AW ◇	NT B	AW ◇	AW		AW ◇	AW	AW	AW ◇	AW ◇ C	AW	AW	NT B	VT ◇■		AW ◇	AW	AW	AW ◇
Holyhead d						07 16					07 50			08 45										10 20
Valley d											07x56													10x26
Rhosneigr d											08x02													10x31
Ty Croes d											08x05													10x35
Bodorgan d											08x10													10x39
Llanfairpwll d											08x19													10x49
Bangor (Gwynedd) a						07 42					08 27			09 12										10 57
d						07 43					08 28			09 13										10 59
Llanfairfechan d											08x35													11x06
Penmaenmawr d											08x39													11x10
Conwy d											08x45													11x16
Llandudno d															10 22		11 07							
Deganwy d															10x26		11x11							
Llandudno Junction a						07 58					08 50			09 29	10 30		11 17							11 20
d						08 00					08 51			09 35										11 22
Colwyn Bay d						08 07					08 57			09 41										11 28
Abergele & Pensarn d						08 14								09 48										11 35
Rhyl d						08 20					09 08			09 54										11 41
Prestatyn d						08 25								09 59										11 46
Flint d						08 39								10 13										12 00
Shotton d						08 45					09 28			10 19										12 06
Chester a						08 56					09 39			10 30										12 18
d	22p49	23p22	07 56	08 27	08 41	08 57	08 58	09 22	09 27		09 42	09 57	10 36	10 39		10 57		11 07	11 28		11 31	11 36	11 57	12 21
Liverpool Lime Street ■ 106 a																								
Helsby d		23p31			08 50						09 51		10 45									11 45		
Frodsham d		23p35			08 54						09 55		10 49									11 49		
Runcorn East d		23p41			08 59						10 00		10 54									11 54		
Warrington Bank Quay 90 a		23p50			09 10						10 09		11 03									12 03		
Earlestown ■ 90 a		23p58			09 16						10 19		11 10									12 10		
Newton-le-Willows 90 a		00 01			09 19						10 22		11 13									12 13		
Manchester Oxford Road 90 a					09 39						10 41		11 32									12 32		
Manchester Pic'dilly ■ 90 ⇌ a	00 15	00 26			09 48		10 22				10 50		11 41					12 31				12 41		
Crewe ■ a			08 20	08 51		09 22			09 50			10 20		11 03		11 20			11 47				12 20	
Cardiff Central ■ 131 a																								15 28
Manchester Airport 84,85 ✈ a																								
Birmingham New Street ■ 65 a								11 32													13 42			
London Euston ■ ⊖65 a																			13 44					

A from 27 October
B To Southport
C To Blaenau Ffestiniog

Table 81

Sundays until 24 June

North Wales and Chester - Manchester and Crewe

Network Diagram - see first Page of Table 81

		AW	VT ◇■	AW	AW	AW		AW	NT A	VT ◇■	AW	VT ◇■	AW ◇	AW	AW	VT ◇■		AW ◇ B	AW	AW	AW	AW	NT A	AW ◇	VT ◇■
Holyhead	d		10 55							11 50						12 50									13 55
Valley	d																								
Rhosneigr	d																								
Ty Croes	d																								
Bodorgan	d																								
Llanfairpwll	d																								
Bangor (Gwynedd)	a		11 21							12 16						13 16									14 21
	d		11 22							12 17						13 18									14 22
Llanfairfechan	d																								
Penmaenmawr	d																								
Conwy	d																								
Llandudno	d			11 40	12 18						13 19							13 30	13 50	14 20					
Deganwy	d			11x44	12x22						13x23							13x34	13x54	14x24					
Llandudno Junction	a		11 39	11 50	12 28					12 34	13 29					13 34		13 38	14 00	14 30					14 39
	d		11 40							12 35						13 36									14 40
Colwyn Bay	d		11 47							12 42						13 42									14 46
Abergele & Pensarn	d																								
Rhyl	d		11 58							12 53						13 53									14 57
Prestatyn	d		12 03							12 59						13 59									15 03
Flint	d		12 17													14 13									
Shotton	d																								
Chester	a		12 30							13 24						14 26									15 31
	d	12 24	12 33			12 36		12 57	13 07	13 30		13 30	13 31	13 36	13 57	14 33					14 36	14 57	15 07	15 31	15 33
Liverpool Lime Street 106	a																								
Helsby	d					12 45								13 45							14 45				
Frodsham	d					12 49								13 49							14 49				
Runcorn East	d					12 54								13 54							14 54				
Warrington Bank Quay 90	a					13 03								14 03							15 03				
Earlestown 90	a					13 10								14 10							15 10				
Newton-le-Willows 90	a					13 13								14 13							15 13				
Manchester Oxford Road 90	a					13 32								14 32							15 32				
Manchester Pic'dilly 90	a					13 41			14 33					14 41							15 41		16 33		
Crewe	a	12 47	12 52					13 20		13 50		13 50			14 20	14 52						15 20			15 52
Cardiff Central 131	a																								
Manchester Airport 84,85	a																								
Birmingham New Street 65	a												15 40											17 53	
London Euston ⊖65	a		14 43							15 45		15 45				16 44									17 44

		AW		AW	AW	AW	AW ◇	AW	AW	AW	NT A	AW ◇		VT ◇■	AW ◇	AW	AW	AW ■	AW	AW	VT ◇■	AW		AW	NT A
Holyhead	d						14 30								15 40			16 25							
Valley	d						14x36											16x31							
Rhosneigr	d						14x42											16x36							
Ty Croes	d						14x45											16x40							
Bodorgan	d						14x50											16x44							
Llanfairpwll	d						14x59											16x54							
Bangor (Gwynedd)	a						15 07								16 06			17 02							
	d						15 08								16 08			17 04							
Llanfairfechan	d														16x15										
Penmaenmawr	d														16x19										
Conwy	d														16x25										
Llandudno	d	15 11						15 45	16 16							16 52			17 20	18 05					
Deganwy	d	15x15						15x49	16x20							16x56			17x24	18x09					
Llandudno Junction	a	15 21					15 25	15 55	16 26						16 29	17 02		17 20	17 30	18 15					
	d						15 26								16 35			17 25							
Colwyn Bay	d						15 32								16 41			17 31							
Abergele & Pensarn	d						15 39								16 48			17 38							
Rhyl	d						15 45								16 54			17 44							
Prestatyn	d						15 51								16 59			17 49							
Flint	d						16 04								17 13			18 03							
Shotton	d						16 10								17 19			18 11							
Chester	a						16 21								17 31			18 21							
	d			15 36	15 57	16 27	16 36			16 57	17 07	17 31		17 35	17 36		17 59	18 24			18 35	18 36		18 57	19 07
Liverpool Lime Street 106	a																								
Helsby	d			15 45			16 45								17 45							18 45			
Frodsham	d			15 49			16 49								17 49							18 49			
Runcorn East	d			15 54			16 54								17 54							18 54			
Warrington Bank Quay 90	a			16 03			17 03								18 03							19 03			
Earlestown 90	a			16 10			17 10								18 10							19 10			
Newton-le-Willows 90	a			16 13			17 13								18 13							19 13			
Manchester Oxford Road 90	a			16 32			17 32								18 32							19 32			
Manchester Pic'dilly 90	a			16 41			17 41				18 33				18 41							19 41			20 33
Crewe	a				16 20	16 51				17 20				17 53			18 22				18 53			19 19	
Cardiff Central 131	a																	21 36							
Manchester Airport 84,85	a																								
Birmingham New Street 65	a											19 39													
London Euston ⊖65	a													19 43							20 44				

A To Southport

B To Blaenau Ffestiniog

Table 81

Sundays until 24 June

North Wales and Chester - Manchester and Crewe

Network Diagram - see first Page of Table 81

		AW ◇	AW	AW	VT ◇	AW	AW	AW ◇		AW ◇ A	AW	VT ◇	AW	NT B	AW	AW	AW	AW		AW	AW ◇	AW ◇	AW C		
Holyhead	d	17 30						18 25		19 15											20 35	21 40			
Valley	d							18x31		19x21											20x41				
Rhosneigr	d							18x36		19x26											20x46				
Ty Croes	d							18x40		19x30											20x50				
Bodorgan	d							18x44		19x34											20x54				
Llanfairpwll	d							18x54		19x44											21x04				
Bangor (Gwynedd)	a	17 57						19 02		19 52											21 12	22 07			
	d	17 59						19 04		19 54											21 14	22 09			
Llanfairfechan	d	18x06								20x01											21x21				
Penmaenmawr	d	18x10								20x05											21x25				
Conwy	d	18x16								20x11											21x31				
Llandudno	d		18 55																						
Deganwy	d		18x59																						
Llandudno Junction	a	18 20	19 05					19 20		20 15											21 35	22 25			
	d	18 24						19 24		20 21											21 37	22 27			
Colwyn Bay	d	18 30						19 30		20 27											21 43	22 33			
Abergele & Pensarn	d	18 37						19 37		20 34											21 50				
Rhyl	d	18 43						19 43		20 40											21 56	22 43			
Prestatyn	d	18 48						19 48		20 46											22 01	22 49			
Flint	d	19 02						20 02		21 00											22 15	23 02			
Shotton	d	19 10						20 10		21 06											22 21				
Chester	a	19 21						20 19		21 21											22 32	23 16			
	d	19 22		19 26	19 35	19 36	19 57	20 27			20 36	20 37	20 57	21 07	21 27	21 36	21 57	22 09		22 09	22 35		23 00		
Liverpool Lime Street 106	a																								
Helsby	d					19 45					20 45									22 29					
Frodsham	d					19 49					20 49									22 34					
Runcorn East	d					19 54					20 54									22 49					
Warrington Bank Quay 90	a					20 03					21 03									23 09					
Earlestown 90	a					20 10					21 10									23 34					
Newton-le-Willows 90	a					20 13					21 13									23 44					
Manchester Oxford Road 90	a					20 32					21 32									00 14					
Manchester Pic'dilly 90	a					20 41					21 41			22 33		22 43		23 18		00 19					
Crewe	a	19 47			19 54		20 20	20 48				20 56	21 20		21 50		22 20				22 59		23 21		
Cardiff Central 131	a																								
Manchester Airport 84,85	a																								
Birmingham New Street 65	a			21 41				22 06																	
London Euston ⊖65	a																								

Sundays 1 July to 9 September

		NT	AW	AW	AW	AW	AW ◇	NT D	AW ◇ E	AW		AW ◇	AW	AW	AW ◇	AW ◇ F	AW	AW	NT D	VT ◇■		AW ◇ E	AW	AW	AW ◇
Holyhead	d						07 16					07 50			08 45										10 20
Valley	d											07x56													10x26
Rhosneigr	d											08x02													10x31
Ty Croes	d											08x05													10x35
Bodorgan	d											08x10													10x39
Llanfairpwll	d											08x19													10x49
Bangor (Gwynedd)	a						07 42					08 27			09 12										10 57
	d						07 43					08 28			09 13										10 59
Llanfairfechan	d											08x35													11x06
Penmaenmawr	d											08x39													11x10
Conwy	d											08x45													11x16
Llandudno	d															10 22		11 07							
Deganwy	d															10x26		11x11							
Llandudno Junction	a						07 58					08 50			09 29	10 30		11 17							11 20
	d						08 00					08 51			09 35										11 22
Colwyn Bay	d						08 07					08 57			09 41										11 28
Abergele & Pensarn	d						08 14								09 48										11 35
Rhyl	d						08 20					09 08			09 54										11 41
Prestatyn	d						08 25								09 59										11 46
Flint	d						08 39								10 13										12 00
Shotton	d						08 45					09 28			10 19										12 06
Chester	a						08 56					09 39			10 30										12 18
	d	22p49	23p22	07 56	08 27	08 41	08 57	08 58	09 22	09 27		09 42	09 57	10 36	10 39		10 57		11 07	11 28		11 31	11 36	11 57	12 21
Liverpool Lime Street 106	a																								
Helsby	d		23p31			08 50						09 51		10 45									11 45		
Frodsham	d		23p35			08 54						09 55		10 49									11 49		
Runcorn East	d		23p41			08 59						10 00		10 54									11 54		
Warrington Bank Quay 90	a		23p50			09 10						10 09		11 03									12 03		
Earlestown 90	a		23p58			09 16						10 19		11 10									12 10		
Newton-le-Willows 90	a		00 01			09 19						10 22		11 13									12 13		
Manchester Oxford Road 90	a					09 39						10 41		11 32									12 32		
Manchester Pic'dilly 90	a	00 15	00 26			09 48		10 22				10 50		11 41					12 31				12 41		
Crewe	a			08 20	08 51		09 22			09 50			10 20		11 03		11 20			11 47				12 20	
Cardiff Central 131	a																								15 28
Manchester Airport 84,85	a																								
Birmingham New Street 65	a								11 13													13 23			
London Euston ⊖65	a																			13 44					

A To Wolverhampton

B To Wigan Wallgate

C To Shrewsbury

D To Southport

E To Birmingham International

F To Blaenau Ffestiniog

Table 81

North Wales and Chester - Manchester and Crewe

Sundays

1 July to 9 September

Network Diagram - see first Page of Table 81

	AW	VT	AW	AW	AW	AW	NT	VT	AW	VT	AW	AW	AW	VT	AW	AW	AW	AW	AW	NT	AW	VT
		◇1 🍴			🛒		A	◇1 🍴		◇1 🍴	◇ B	🛒		◇1 🍴	◇ C			🛒		A	◇ B 🛒	◇1 🍴
Holyhead d		10 55						11 50						12 50								13 55
Valley d																						
Rhosneigr d																						
Ty Croes d																						
Bodorgan d																						
Llanfairpwll d																						
Bangor (Gwynedd) a		11 21						12 16						13 16								14 21
d		11 22						12 17						13 18								14 22
Llanfairfechan d																						
Penmaenmawr d																						
Conwy d																						
Llandudno d			11 40	12 18					13 19						13 30	13 50	14 20					
Deganwy d			11x44	12x22					13x23						13x34	13x54	14x24					
Llandudno Junction a		11 39	11 50	12 28				12 34	13 29					13 34	13 38	14 00	14 30					14 39
d		11 40						12 35						13 36								14 40
Colwyn Bay d		11 47						12 42						13 42								14 46
Abergele & Pensarn d																						
Rhyl d		11 58						12 53						13 53								14 57
Prestatyn d		12 03						12 59						13 59								15 03
Flint d		12 17												14 13								
Shotton d																						
Chester a		12 30						13 24						14 26								15 31
d	12 24	12 33			12 36	12 57	13 07	13 30		13 30	13 31	13 36	13 57	14 33				14 36	14 57	15 07	15 31	15 33
Liverpool Lime Street 10 106 a																						
Helsby d					12 45							13 45						14 45				
Frodsham d					12 49							13 49						14 49				
Runcorn East d					12 54							13 54						14 54				
Warrington Bank Quay 90 a					13 03							14 03						15 03				
Earlestown 8 90 a					13 10							14 10						15 10				
Newton-le-Willows 90 a					13 13							14 13						15 13				
Manchester Oxford Road 90 a					13 32							14 32						15 32				
Manchester Pic'dilly 10 90 ⇌ a					13 41		14 33					14 41						15 41		16 33		
Crewe 10 a	12 47	12 52				13 20		13 50		13 50			14 20	14 52					15 20			15 52
Cardiff Central 7 131 a																						
Manchester Airport 84,85 ✈ a																						
Birmingham New Street 12 65 a											15 24										17 35	
London Euston 15 ⊖65 a		14 43						15 45		15 45				16 44								17 44

	AW	AW	AW	AW	AW	AW	AW	AW	NT	AW	VT	AW	AW	AW	AW	AW	AW	VT	AW	AW	NT
					◇ 🛒				A	◇ B	◇1 🍴	◇ 🛒			■ 🛒			◇1 🍴			A
Holyhead d					14 30							15 40			16 25						
Valley d					14x36										16x31						
Rhosneigr d					14x42										16x36						
Ty Croes d					14x45										16x40						
Bodorgan d					14x50										16x44						
Llanfairpwll d					14x59										16x54						
Bangor (Gwynedd) a					15 07							16 06			17 02						
d					15 08							16 08			17 04						
Llanfairfechan d												16x15									
Penmaenmawr d												16x19									
Conwy d												16x25									
Llandudno d	15 11					15 45	16 16						16 52			17 20	18 05				
Deganwy d	15x15					15x49	16x20						16x56			17x24	18x09				
Llandudno Junction a	15 21				15 25	15 55	16 26					16 29	17 02		17 20	17 30	18 15				
d					15 26							16 35			17 25						
Colwyn Bay d					15 32							16 41			17 31						
Abergele & Pensarn d					15 39							16 48			17 38						
Rhyl d					15 45							16 54			17 44						
Prestatyn d					15 51							16 59			17 49						
Flint d					16 04							17 13			18 03						
Shotton d					16 10							17 19			18 11						
Chester a					16 21							17 31			18 21						
d		15 36	15 57	16 27	16 36			16 57	17 07	17 31	17 35	17 36		17 59	18 24			18 35	18 36	18 57	19 07
Liverpool Lime Street 10 106 a																					
Helsby d		15 45			16 45							17 45							18 45		
Frodsham d		15 49			16 49							17 49							18 49		
Runcorn East d		15 54			16 54							17 54							18 54		
Warrington Bank Quay 90 a		16 03			17 03							18 03							19 03		
Earlestown 8 90 a		16 10			17 10							18 10							19 10		
Newton-le-Willows 90 a		16 13			17 13							18 13							19 13		
Manchester Oxford Road 90 a		16 32			17 32							18 32							19 32		
Manchester Pic'dilly 10 90 ⇌ a		16 41			17 41				18 33			18 41							19 41		20 33
Crewe 10 a			16 20	16 51				17 20			17 53			18 22				18 53		19 19	
Cardiff Central 7 131 a															21 36						
Manchester Airport 84,85 ✈ a																					
Birmingham New Street 12 65 a										19 26											
London Euston 15 ⊖65 a											19 43							20 44			

A To Southport
B To Birmingham International
C To Blaenau Ffestiniog

Table 81

North Wales and Chester - Manchester and Crewe

Sundays

1 July to 9 September

Network Diagram - see first Page of Table 81

	AW	AW	AW	VT	AW	AW	AW	AW	AW	VT	AW	NT	AW	AW	AW	AW	AW	AW	AW	AW
	◇		A	◇ 🍴			◇ A 🛒	◇ B		◇ 🍴		C					🚌	◇	◇	D
Holyhead d	17 30						18 25	19 15										20 35	21 40	
Valley d							18x31	19x21										20x41		
Rhosneigr d							18x36	19x26										20x46		
Ty Croes d							18x40	19x30										20x50		
Bodorgan d							18x44	19x34										20x54		
Llanfairpwll d							18x54	19x44										21x04		
Bangor (Gwynedd) a	17 57						19 02	19 52										21 12	22 07	
d	17 59						19 04	19 54										21 14	22 09	
Llanfairfechan d	18x06							20x01										21x21		
Penmaenmawr d	18x10							20x05										21x25		
Conwy d	18x16							20x11										21x31		
Llandudno d		18 55																		
Deganwy d		18x59																		
Llandudno Junction a	18 20	19 05					19 20	20 15										21 35	22 25	
d	18 24						19 24	20 21										21 37	22 27	
Colwyn Bay d	18 30						19 30	20 27										21 43	22 33	
Abergele & Pensarn d	18 37						19 37	20 34										21 50		
Rhyl d	18 43						19 43	20 40										21 56	22 43	
Prestatyn d	18 48						19 48	20 46										22 01	22 49	
Flint d	19 02						20 02	21 00										22 15	23 02	
Shotton d	19 10						20 10	21 06										22 21		
Chester a	19 21						20 19	21 21										22 32	23 16	
d	19 22		19 26	19 35	19 36	19 57	20 27		20 36	20 37	20 57	21 07	21 27	21 36	21 57	22 09	22 09	22 35		23 00
Liverpool Lime Street 10 106 a																				
Helsby d					19 45				20 45								22 29			
Frodsham d					19 49				20 49								22 34			
Runcorn East d					19 54				20 54								22 49			
Warrington Bank Quay 90 a					20 03				21 03								23 09			
Earlestown 8 90 a					20 10				21 10								23 34			
Newton-le-Willows 90 a					20 13				21 13								23 44			
Manchester Oxford Road 90 a					20 32				21 32								00 14			
Manchester Pic'dilly 10 90 ⇌ a					20 41				21 41			22 33		22 43		23 18	00 19			
Crewe 10 a	19 47			19 54		20 20	20 48			20 56	21 20		21 50		22 20			22 59		23 21
Cardiff Central 7 131 a																				
Manchester Airport 84,85 ✈ a																				
Birmingham New Street 12 65 a			21 29				21 52													
London Euston 15 ⊖65 a																				

Sundays

16 September to 30 September

	NT	AW	AW	AW	NT	AW	AW	AW	AW	AW	NT	VT	AW	AW	AW	AW	VT	AW	NT	AW	VT	AW
					E	◇ A		◇	🛒	◇	E	◇1 🍴	◇ A 🛒	🛒	◇ 🛒		◇1 🍴	🛒	E		◇1 🍴	◇ A
Holyhead d										08 45					10 20		10 55				11 50	
Valley d															10x26							
Rhosneigr d															10x31							
Ty Croes d															10x35							
Bodorgan d															10x39							
Llanfairpwll d															10x49							
Bangor (Gwynedd) a										09 12					10 57		11 21				12 16	
d										09 13					10 59		11 22				12 17	
Llanfairfechan d															11x06							
Penmaenmawr d															11x10							
Conwy d															11x16							
Llandudno d																						
Deganwy d																						
Llandudno Junction a										09 29					11 20		11 39				12 34	
d										09 35					11 22		11 40				12 35	
Colwyn Bay d										09 41					11 28		11 47				12 42	
Abergele & Pensarn d										09 48					11 35							
Rhyl d										09 54					11 41		11 58				12 53	
Prestatyn d										09 59					11 46		12 03				12 59	
Flint d										10 13					12 00		12 17					
Shotton d										10 19					12 06							
Chester a										10 30					12 18		12 30				13 24	
d	22p49	23p22	08 40	08 41	08 58	09 22	09 39	09 42	10 36	10 39	11 07	11 28	11 31	11 36	12 21	12 24	12 33	12 36	13 07	13 20	13 30	13 31
Liverpool Lime Street 10 106 a																						
Helsby d		23p31		08 50				09 51	10 45					11 45				12 45				
Frodsham d		23p35		08 54				09 55	10 49					11 49				12 49				
Runcorn East d		23p41		08 59				10 00	10 54					11 54				12 54				
Warrington Bank Quay 90 a		23p50		09 10				10 09	11 03					12 03				13 03				
Earlestown 8 90 a		23p58		09 16				10 19	11 10					12 10				13 10				
Newton-le-Willows 90 a		00 01		09 19				10 22	11 13					12 13				13 13				
Manchester Oxford Road 90 a				09 39				10 41	11 32					12 32				13 32				
Manchester Pic'dilly 10 90 ⇌ a	00 15	00 26		09 48	10 22			10 50	11 41		12 31			12 41				13 41	14 33			
Crewe 10 a			09 03				10 02			11 03		11 47				12 47	12 52			13 43	13 50	
Cardiff Central 7 131 a															15 28							
Manchester Airport 84,85 ✈ a																						
Birmingham New Street 12 65 a						11 13							13 23									15 24
London Euston 15 ⊖65 a												13 44					14 43				15 43	

A To Birmingham International
B To Wolverhampton
C To Wigan Wallgate
D To Shrewsbury
E To Southport

Sundays
16 September to 30 September

North Wales and Chester - Manchester and Crewe

Network Diagram - see first Page of Table 81

		AW	AW	VT	AW	NT	AW	VT	AW	AW	AW	NT	AW	AW	VT	AW	AW	VT	AW	AW	NT	AW	AW
		⊼		◇1 ⊡	⊼		◇ ⊼	◇1 ⊡			◇ ⊼		◇	◇	◇1 ⊡	◇	■ ⊼	◇1 ⊡				◇	
						A	B					A		B							A		B
Holyhead	d			12 50				13 55			14 30		15 30				16 25					17 30	
Valley	d										14x36						16x31						
Rhosneigr	d										14x42						16x36						
Ty Croes	d										14x45						16x40						
Bodorgan	d										14x50						16x44						
Llanfairpwll	d										14x59						16x54						
Bangor (Gwynedd)	a			13 16				14 21			15 07		15 56				17 02					17 57	
	d			13 18				14 22			15 08		15 58				17 04					17 59	
Llanfairfechan	d												16x05									18x06	
Penmaenmawr	d												16x09									18x10	
Conwy	d												16x15									18x16	
Llandudno	d																						
Deganwy	d																						
Llandudno Junction	a			13 34				14 39			15 25		16 19				17 20					18 20	
	d			13 36				14 40			15 26		16 25				17 25					18 24	
Colwyn Bay	d			13 42				14 46			15 32		16 31				17 31					18 30	
Abergele & Pensarn	d										15 39		16 38				17 38					18 37	
Rhyl	d			13 53				14 57			15 45		16 44				17 44					18 43	
Prestatyn	d			13 59				15 03			15 51		16 49				17 49					18 48	
Flint	d			14 13							16 04		17 03				18 03					19 02	
Shotton	d										16 10		17 09				18 11					19 10	
Chester	a			14 26				15 31			16 21		17 20				18 21					19 21	
	d	13 36	14 20	14 33	14 36	15 07	15 31	15 33	15 36	16 27	16 36	17 07	17 22	17 31	17 35	17 36	18 24	18 35	18 36	18 57	19 07	19 22	19 26
Liverpool Lime Street [10] 106	a																						
Helsby	d	13 45			14 45				15 45		16 45					17 45			18 45				
Frodsham	d	13 49			14 49				15 49		16 49					17 49			18 49				
Runcorn East	d	13 54			14 54				15 54		16 54					17 54			18 54				
Warrington Bank Quay 90	a	14 03			15 03				16 03		17 03					18 03			19 03				
Earlestown [8] 90	a	14 10			15 10				16 10		17 10					18 10			19 10				
Newton-le-Willows 90	a	14 13			15 13				16 13		17 13					18 13			19 13				
Manchester Oxford Road 90	a	14 32			15 32				16 32		17 32					18 32			19 32				
Manchester Pic'dilly [10] 90 ⇌	a	14 41			15 41	16 33			16 41		17 41	18 33				18 41			19 41		20 33		
Crewe [10]	a		14 43	14 52				15 52		16 51			17 44		17 53			18 53		19 19		19 47	
Cardiff Central [7] 131	a																21 36						
Manchester Airport 84,85 ✈	a																						
Birmingham New Street [12] 65	a						17 35							19 26									21 29
London Euston [15] ⊖65	a			16 43				17 43							19 43			20 44					

		VT	AW	AW	AW	AW	VT	AW	NT	AW	AW	AW	AW	AW	AW	AW	AW
		◇ ⊡			◇ ⊼		◇ ⊡			◇				═	◇	◇	
					B				C								D
Holyhead	d				18 25					19 40					20 35	21 40	
Valley	d				18x31										20x41		
Rhosneigr	d				18x36										20x46		
Ty Croes	d				18x40										20x50		
Bodorgan	d				18x44										20x54		
Llanfairpwll	d				18x54										21x04		
Bangor (Gwynedd)	a				19 02					20 07					21 12	22 07	
	d				19 04					20 09					21 14	22 09	
Llanfairfechan	d									20x16					21x21		
Penmaenmawr	d									20x20					21x25		
Conwy	d									20x26					21x31		
Llandudno	d																
Deganwy	d																
Llandudno Junction	a				19 20					20 30					21 35	22 25	
	d				19 24					20 37					21 37	22 27	
Colwyn Bay	d				19 30					20 43					21 43	22 33	
Abergele & Pensarn	d				19 37					20 50					21 50		
Rhyl	d				19 43					20 56					21 56	22 43	
Prestatyn	d				19 48					21 01					22 01	22 49	
Flint	d				20 02					21 15					22 15	23 02	
Shotton	d				20 10					21 21					22 21		
Chester	a				20 19					21 33					22 32	23 16	
	d	19 35	19 36	19 50	20 27	20 36	20 37	20 50	21 07	21 35	21 36	21 50	22 09	22 09	22 35		23 00
Liverpool Lime Street [10] 106	a																
Helsby	d		19 45			20 45								22 29			
Frodsham	d		19 49			20 49								22 34			
Runcorn East	d		19 54			20 54								22 49			
Warrington Bank Quay 90	a		20 03			21 03								23 09			
Earlestown [8] 90	a		20 10			21 10								23 34			
Newton-le-Willows 90	a		20 13			21 13								23 44			
Manchester Oxford Road 90	a		20 32			21 32								00 14			
Manchester Pic'dilly [10] 90 ⇌	a		20 41			21 41			22 33		22 43		23 18	00 19			
Crewe [10]	a	19 54		20 13	20 48		20 56	21 13		21 59		22 13			22 59		23 21
Cardiff Central [7] 131	a																
Manchester Airport 84,85 ✈	a																
Birmingham New Street [12] 65	a				21 52												
London Euston [15] ⊖65	a																

A To Southport
B To Birmingham International
C To Wigan Wallgate
D To Shrewsbury

Sundays
from 7 October

North Wales and Chester - Manchester and Crewe

Network Diagram - see first Page of Table 81

		NT	AW	AW	AW	AW	AW	AW	AW	NT	AW	AW	AW	AW	AW	AW	AW	AW	AW	NT	VT	AW	AW
					═				═		◇		◇		═	⊼		◇	═		◇1 ⊡	◇ ⊼	⊼
			A	B	B		A	B	B	C	D		A	B	B	A	B		B	C		D	A
Holyhead	d																	08 45					
Valley	d																						
Rhosneigr	d																						
Ty Croes	d																						
Bodorgan	d																						
Llanfairpwll	d																						
Bangor (Gwynedd)	a																	09 12					
	d																	09 13					
Llanfairfechan	d																						
Penmaenmawr	d																						
Conwy	d																						
Llandudno	d																						
Deganwy	d																						
Llandudno Junction	a																	09 29					
	d																	09 35					
Colwyn Bay	d																	09 41					
Abergele & Pensarn	d																	09 48					
Rhyl	d																	09 54					
Prestatyn	d																	09 59					
Flint	d																	10 13					
Shotton	d																	10 19					
Chester	a																	10 30					
	d	22p45	23p22	23p22	23p22	08 40	08 41	08 41	08 41	08 54	09 22	09 39	09 42	09 42	09 49	10 36	10 36	10 39	10 40	11 03	11 28	11 31	11 36
Liverpool Lime Street [10] 106	a																						
Helsby	d		23p31		23p42		08 50		09 01				09 51		10 09	10 45			11 00				11 45
Frodsham	d		23p35		23p47		08 54		09 06				09 55		10 14	10 49			11 05				11 49
Runcorn East	d		23p41		00 02		08 59		09 21				10 00		10 29	10 54			11 20				11 54
Warrington Bank Quay 90	a		23p50		00 22		09 10		09 41				10 09		10 49	11 03			11 40				12 03
Earlestown [8] 90	a		23p58		00 47		09 16		10 06				10 19		11 14	11 10			12 05				12 10
Newton-le-Willows 90	a		00 01		00 57		09 19		10 16				10 22		11 24	11 13			12 15				12 13
Manchester Oxford Road 90	a						09 39		10 46				10 41		11 54	11 32			12 45				12 32
Manchester Pic'dilly [10] 90 ⇌	a	00 15	00 26	00 29	01 32		09 48	09 50	10 51	10 22			10 50	10 51	11 59	11 41	11 46		12 50	12 31			12 41
Crewe [10]	a					09 03						10 02						11 03			11 47		
Cardiff Central [7] 131	a																						
Manchester Airport 84,85 ✈	a																						
Birmingham New Street [12] 65	a										11 13											13 23	
London Euston [15] ⊖65	a																				13 44		

		AW	AW	AW	AW	VT	AW	AW	AW	NT	AW	VT	AW	AW	AW	AW	AW	VT	AW	NT	AW	VT	AW
			═	◇ ⊼		◇1 ⊡	⊼		═			◇1 ⊡	◇	⊼	═			◇1 ⊡	⊼		◇ ⊼	◇1 ⊡	
		B	B				A	B	B	C			D	A	B	B				C	D		
Holyhead	d			10 20		10 55						11 50						12 50				13 55	
Valley	d			10x26																			
Rhosneigr	d			10x31																			
Ty Croes	d			10x35																			
Bodorgan	d			10x39																			
Llanfairpwll	d			10x49																			
Bangor (Gwynedd)	a			10 57		11 21						12 16						13 16				14 21	
	d			10 59		11 22						12 17						13 18				14 22	
Llanfairfechan	d			11x06																			
Penmaenmawr	d			11x10																			
Conwy	d			11x16																			
Llandudno	d																						
Deganwy	d																						
Llandudno Junction	a			11 20		11 39						12 34						13 34				14 39	
	d			11 22		11 40						12 35						13 36				14 40	
Colwyn Bay	d			11 28		11 47						12 42						13 42				14 46	
Abergele & Pensarn	d			11 35																			
Rhyl	d			11 41		11 58						12 53						13 53				14 57	
Prestatyn	d			11 46		12 03						12 59						13 59				15 03	
Flint	d			12 00		12 17												14 13					
Shotton	d			12 06																			
Chester	a			12 18		12 30						13 24						14 26				15 31	
	d	11 36	11 36	12 21	12 24	12 33	12 36	12 36	12 36	13 03	13 20	13 30	13 31	13 36	13 36	13 36	14 20	14 33	14 36	15 03	15 31	15 33	15 36
Liverpool Lime Street [10] 106	a																						
Helsby	d		11 56				12 45		12 56					13 45	13 56				14 45				15 45
Frodsham	d		12 01				12 49		13 01					13 49	14 01				14 49				15 49
Runcorn East	d		12 16				12 54		13 16					13 54	14 16				14 54				15 54
Warrington Bank Quay 90	a		12 36				13 03		13 36					14 03	14 36				15 03				16 03
Earlestown [8] 90	a		13 01				13 10		14 01					14 10					15 10				16 10
Newton-le-Willows 90	a		13 11				13 13		14 11					14 13					15 13				16 13
Manchester Oxford Road 90	a		13 41				13 32		14 41					14 32					15 32				16 32
Manchester Pic'dilly [10] 90 ⇌	a	12 51	13 46				13 41	13 47	14 46	14 33				14 41		14 47			15 41	16 33			16 41
Crewe [10]	a				12 47	12 52					13 43	13 50					14 43	14 52				15 52	
Cardiff Central [7] 131	a			15 28																			
Manchester Airport 84,85 ✈	a																						
Birmingham New Street [12] 65	a												15 24								17 35		
London Euston [15] ⊖65	a					14 43						15 43						16 43				17 43	

A 7 October, 14 October, 21 October
B from 28 October
C To Southport
D To Birmingham International

Table 81

Sundays
from 7 October

North Wales and Chester - Manchester and Crewe

Network Diagram - see first Page of Table 81

		AW	AW	NT	AW	AW	VT	AW	AW	VT	AW	AW	NT	AW	AW	VT	AW	AW	AW	AW	VT	AW
									■													
			◇		◇	◇	◇[1]	◇		◇[1]				◇		◇			◇		◇	
				A		B							A		B				B			
			✠				⊐		✠	⊐						⊐			✠		⊐	
Holyhead	d		14 30		15 30				16 25					17 30					18 25			
Valley	d		14x36						16x31										18x31			
Rhosneigr	d		14x42						16x36										18x36			
Ty Croes	d		14x45						16x40										18x40			
Bodorgan	d		14x50						16x44										18x44			
Llanfairpwll	d		14x59						16x54										18x54			
Bangor (Gwynedd)	a		15 07		15 56				17 02					17 57					19 02			
	d		15 08		15 58				17 04					17 59					19 04			
Llanfairfechan	d				16x05									18x06								
Penmaenmawr	d				16x09									18x10								
Conwy	d				16x15									18x16								
Llandudno	d																					
Deganwy	d																					
Llandudno Junction	a		15 25		16 19				17 20					18 20					19 20			
	d		15 26		16 25				17 25					18 24					19 24			
Colwyn Bay	d		15 32		16 31				17 31					18 30					19 30			
Abergele & Pensarn	d		15 39		16 38				17 38					18 37					19 37			
Rhyl	d		15 45		16 44				17 44					18 43					19 43			
Prestatyn	d		15 51		16 49				17 49					18 48					19 48			
Flint	d		16 04		17 03				18 03					19 02					20 02			
Shotton	d		16 10		17 09				18 11					19 10					20 10			
Chester	a		16 21		17 20				18 21					19 21					20 19			
	d	16 27	16 36	17 03	17 22	17 31	17 35	17 36	18 24	18 35	18 36	18 57	19 03	19 22	19 26	19 35	19 36	19 50	20 27	20 36	20 37	20 50
Liverpool Lime Street [10] 106	a																					
Helsby	d		16 45					17 45			18 45						19 45			20 45		
Frodsham	d		16 49					17 49			18 49						19 49			20 49		
Runcorn East	d		16 54					17 54			18 54						19 54			20 54		
Warrington Bank Quay 90	a		17 03					18 03			19 03						20 03			21 03		
Earlestown [8] 90	a		17 10					18 10			19 10						20 10			21 10		
Newton-le-Willows 90	a		17 13					18 13			19 13						20 13			21 13		
Manchester Oxford Road 90	a		17 32					18 32			19 32						20 32			21 32		
Manchester Pic'dilly [10] 90 ⇌	a		17 41	18 33				18 41			19 41		20 33				20 41			21 41		
Crewe [10]	a	16 51			17 44		17 53			18 53		19 19		19 47		19 54		20 13	20 48		20 56	21 13
Cardiff Central [7] 131	a								21 36													
Manchester Airport 84,85 ✈	a																					
Birmingham New Street [12] 65	a					19 26									21 29				21 52			
London Euston [15] ⊖65	a						19 43			20 44												

		NT	AW	AW	AW	AW	AW	AW	AW	AW
			◇					◇	◇	
		C								D
							🚌			
Holyhead	d		19 40					20 35	21 40	
Valley	d							20x41		
Rhosneigr	d							20x46		
Ty Croes	d							20x50		
Bodorgan	d							20x54		
Llanfairpwll	d							21x04		
Bangor (Gwynedd)	a		20 07					21 12	22 07	
	d		20 09					21 14	22 09	
Llanfairfechan	d		20x16					21x21		
Penmaenmawr	d		20x20					21x25		
Conwy	d		20x26					21x31		
Llandudno	d									
Deganwy	d									
Llandudno Junction	a		20 30					21 35	22 25	
	d		20 37					21 37	22 27	
Colwyn Bay	d		20 43					21 43	22 33	
Abergele & Pensarn	d		20 50					21 50		
Rhyl	d		20 56					21 56	22 43	
Prestatyn	d		21 01					22 01	22 49	
Flint	d		21 15					22 15	23 02	
Shotton	d		21 21					22 21		
Chester	a		21 33					22 32	23 16	
	d	21 03	21 35	21 36	21 50	22 09	22 09	22 35		23 00
Liverpool Lime Street [10] 106	a									
Helsby	d						22 29			
Frodsham	d						22 34			
Runcorn East	d						22 49			
Warrington Bank Quay 90	a						23 09			
Earlestown [8] 90	a						23 34			
Newton-le-Willows 90	a						23 44			
Manchester Oxford Road 90	a						00 14			
Manchester Pic'dilly [10] 90 ⇌	a	22 33		22 43		23 18	00 19			
Crewe [10]	a		21 59		22 13			22 59		23 21
Cardiff Central [7] 131	a									
Manchester Airport 84,85 ✈	a									
Birmingham New Street [12] 65	a									
London Euston [15] ⊖65	a									

A To Southport
B To Birmingham International
C To Wigan Wallgate
D To Shrewsbury

Table 81A

Holyhead - Dublin

		AW	AW	AW	AW	AW
		[B]	[B]	[B]	[B]	[B]
			A			
Holyhead	⛴ d	02 40	10 00	11 50	14 10	17 15
Dun Laoghaire	⛴ a		11 39			
Dublin Ferryport §	⛴ a	05 55		13 39	17 25	19 15

§ Bus connections to/from city centre and railway stations
A until 11 September

Table 81A

Dublin - Holyhead

		AW	AW	AW	AW	AW	AW	AW
		A			SX	SO		
		[B]	[B]	[B]	[B]	[B]	[B]	[B]
		A						
Dublin Ferryport §	⛴ d	20p55	08 45	08 05			14 30	20 55
Dun Laoghaire	⛴ d				13 15	13 15		
Holyhead	⛴ a	00 20	10 34	11 30	14 54	15 05	16 30	00 20

§ Bus connections to/from city centre and railway stations
A not 14 May
B until 11 September
C until 8 September

Network Diagram for Tables 82, 83, 94

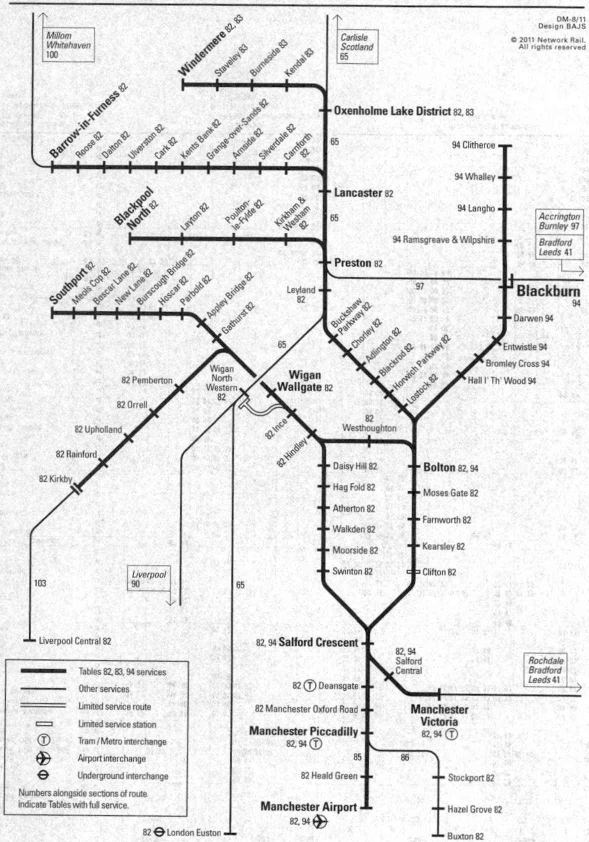

Manchester - Bolton - Wigan, Kirkby, Southport, Preston, Blackpool North and Barrow-in-Furness

Network Diagram - see first Page of Table 82

Miles	Miles	Miles	Miles	Miles	Station	Table		TP MX ◇1	TP MO ◇1 A	TP MX ◇1	NT MX	NT MX	TP ◇1			TP ◇1			NT D	NT E	TP 1	TP ◇1	TP ◇1 F		NT G	NT
0	0	0	—	—	**Manchester Airport**	85	d	22p00	22p30	22p29			00 01			04 00			04 38				05 45			
1½	1½	1½	—	—	Heald Green	85	d			22p33													05 49			
—	—	—	—	—	Buxton	86	d																			
—	—	—	—	—	Hazel Grove	86	d																			
—	—	—	—	—	Stockport	84	d																			
9¾	9¾	9¾	—	—	**Manchester Piccadilly** 10		d	22p16	22p46	22p46			00 16			04 15			04a51			05 46	06 03			
10¼	10¼	10¼	—	—	**Manchester Oxford Road**		d	22p19	22p49	22p49													06 06			
10½	10½	10½	—	—	Deansgate		d		22p51	22p51																
—	—	—	—	—	Rochdale	41	d																			
—	—	—	0	—	**Manchester Victoria**		d				23p20	23p23													05 55	06 00
—	—	—	0¾	—	Salford Central		d																			
12	12	12	1¾	—	**Salford Crescent**		a		22p54	22p56	23p25	23p31										05 51			05 59	06 04
—	—	—	—	—			d		22p55	22p56	23p26	23p32										05 52			06 00	06 05
—	—	—	5¾	—	Swinton		d				23p33															
—	—	—	6½	—	Moorside		d				23p35															
—	—	—	8¼	—	Walkden		d				23p39															
—	—	—	11¾	—	Atherton		d				23p44															
—	—	—	13	—	Hag Fold		d				23p47															
—	—	—	13¾	—	Daisy Hill		d				23p50															
18	18	18	—	—	Kearsley		d																			
18¾	18	18¾	—	—	Farnworth		d																			
19¾	19¾	19¾	—	—	Moses Gate		d																			
21	21	21	—	—	**Bolton**		a	22p32	23p05	23p06		23p42	00s31			04s29							06 19		06 11	06 15
—	—	—	—	—			d	22p33	23p05	23p07		23p42											06 19			06 15
—	—	25½	—	—	Westhoughton		d																			06 23
—	—	28	15¾	—	Hindley		d				23p54															06 27
—	—	29½	17¼	0	Ince		d				23p57															
—	—	—	—	0¾	Wigan North Western		a	22p48								04 44						06 15				
—	—	30½	18¼	—	**Wigan Wallgate**		a				00 04															06 32
—	—	—	—	—			d																			06 34
—	—	—	20	—	Pemberton		d																			06 38
—	—	—	22	—	Orrell		d																			06 42
—	—	—	23¼	—	Upholland		d																			06 45
—	—	—	25¼	—	Rainford		d																			06 49
—	—	—	30½	—	**Kirkby**		a																			07 01
—	—	33¼	—	—	Gathurst		d																			
—	—	35	—	—	Appley Bridge		d																			
—	—	37¼	—	—	Parbold		d																			
—	—	38¾	—	—	Hoscar		d																			
—	—	40¾	—	—	Burscough Bridge		d																			
—	—	41½	—	—	New Lane		d																			
—	—	43½	—	—	Bescar Lane		d																			
—	—	46¾	—	—	Meols Cop		d																			
—	—	48	—	—	**Southport**		a																			
24	24	—	—	—	Lostock		d		23p10			23p47														
26	26	—	—	—	Horwich Parkway		d		23p14	23p13		23p51														
27½	27½	—	—	—	Blackrod		d		23p17			23p54														
29½	29½	—	—	—	Adlington (Lancashire)		d		23p20			23p58														
33½	33½	—	—	—	Chorley		d		23p25	23p21		00 03											06 31			
36	36	—	—	—	Buckshaw Parkway		d		23p28	23p24		00 07														
37	37	—	—	—	Leyland		d		23p36			00 14										06 27				
41	41	—	—	—	**Preston** 8	65,97	a	23p09	23p42	23p33		00 19	01s05			05s04						06 35	06 42			
—	—	—	—	—			d	23p13	23p47	23p35		00 21								05 22		06 37	06 44			
48¾	—	—	—	—	Kirkham & Wesham	97	a		23p56			00 30										06 46				
55¼	—	—	—	—	Poulton-le-Fylde	97	a		00 05	23p52		00 38										06 56				
57¼	—	—	—	—	Layton	97	a					00 43										06 59				
58½	—	—	—	—	**Blackpool North**	97	a		00 14	00 02		00 50	01 30			05 33						07 06				
—	62	—	—	—	**Lancaster** 6	65	a	23p28												05 42			06 59			
—	—	—	—	—			d	23p29												05 42	05 46		07 00			
—	81	—	—	—	Oxenholme Lake District	65	a														06 21		07 15			
—	91	—	—	—	Windermere	83	a														06 41					
—	68	—	—	—	Carnforth		d	23p37												05 52						
—	71¾	—	—	—	Silverdale		d	23p43												05 58						
—	74	—	—	—	Arnside		d	23p47												06 03						
—	77¼	—	—	—	Grange-over-Sands		d	23p53												06 09						
—	79½	—	—	—	Kents Bank		d	23p56												06 12						
—	81½	—	—	—	Cark		d	00 01												06 17						
—	87½	—	—	—	Ulverston		d	00 09												06 25						
—	90¾	—	—	—	Dalton		d	00 17												06 33						
—	95	—	—	—	Roose		d	00 23												06 39						
—	96¾	—	—	—	**Barrow-in-Furness**		a	00 31												06 47						

A from 21 May until 24 September
C To Scarborough
D To Liverpool Lime Street
E To Carlisle
F To Edinburgh
G To Clitheroe

Manchester - Bolton - Wigan, Kirkby, Southport, Preston, Blackpool North and Barrow-in-Furness

Network Diagram - see first Page of Table 82

	NT	TP ◇1 A	NT	NT	NT	NT B	TP ◇1 C	NT D	TP ◇1	NT E	NT	NT F	TP ◇1	NT	NT G	NT	NT	TP ◇1 H	NT I	NT J	NT
Manchester Airport 85 ✈ d		06 18											07 00					07 25			
Heald Green 85 d																		07 30			
Buxton 86 d						05 59											06 23				06 50
Hazel Grove 86 d						06 33											07 00				07 27
Stockport 84 d						06 41											07 10				07 37
Manchester Piccadilly 10 ⇌ d		06 33				06 54	07 07						07 15				07 27	07 45			07 54
Manchester Oxford Road d		06 36				06 57	07a09						07 18				07 30				07 57
Deansgate ⇌ d						06 59											07 32				07 59
Rochdale 41 d																					
Manchester Victoria ⇌ d	06 17		06 38		06 45					07 01	07 06			07 17	07 23	07 27			07 47		
Salford Central d			06 40		06 48					07 04	07 09			07 19	07 26	07 30			07 50		
Salford Crescent a	06 23		06 44		06 51	07 03				07 07	07 12			07 24	07 29	07 33	07 37		07 53		08 04
d	06 24		06 45		06 52	07 03				07 08	07 13			07 25	07 30	07 33	07 37		07 53		08 04
Swinton d					06 58					07 14									08 00		
Moorside d										07 17									08 02		
Walkden d					07 03					07 20						07 42			08 06		
Atherton d					07 08					07 26						07 48			08 11		
Hag Fold d										07 28									08 14		
Daisy Hill d					07 12					07 31						07 51			08 17		
Kearsley d			06 52														07 45				
Farnworth d			06 54														07 47				
Moses Gate d			06 57														07 49				
Bolton a	06 34	06 50	07 00			07 16					07 23		07 31	07 35	07 41		07 53	07 59			08 14
d	06 34	06 50	07 01								07 23		07 31	07 35			07 53	07 59			08 15
Westhoughton d											07 31	←					08 01				
Hindley d					07 16					07 39	07 35	07 39							08 21		
Ince d										→		07 42									
Wigan North Western a			07 19														08 16				
Wigan Wallgate a					07 21						07 40	07 45				08 03			08 26		
d				06 40	07 23						07 41	07 46							08 28		
Pemberton d												07 50									
Orrell d												07 54									
Upholland d												07 58									
Rainford d												08 01									
Kirkby a												08 13									
Gathurst d				06 44	07 27						07 46								08 32		
Appley Bridge d				06 48	07 31						07 49								08 36		
Parbold d				06 52	07 35						07 53										
Hoscar d				06 55							07 56										
Burscough Bridge d				06 58	07 39						07 59								08 42		
New Lane d				07 00							08 02										
Bescar Lane d				07 04							08 05										
Meols Cop d				07 09	07 47						08 10										
Southport a				07 18	07 56						08 20								08 59		
Lostock d	06 39													07 42							08 20
Horwich Parkway d	06 43												07 38	07 46							08 24
Blackrod d	06 46													07 49							
Adlington (Lancashire) d	06 50													07 53							08 29
Chorley d	06 55												07 46	07 58				08 11			08 34
Buckshaw Parkway d	06 59													08 01							08 37
Leyland d	07 06													08 08							08 43
Preston 8 65,97 a	07 11	07 11											07 57	08 14				08 22			08 50
d	07 13	07 14							07 20				07 59	08 15				08 24		08 38	08 51
Kirkham & Wesham 97 a	07 22												08 08	08 25							
Poulton-le-Fylde 97 a	07 30												08 18	08 33							
Layton 97 a	07 34												08 22	08 37							
Blackpool North 97 a	07 41												08 29	08 44							09 17
Lancaster 6 65 a		07 30							07 36									08 39		08 58	
d								07 10	07 36									08 40		08 58	
Oxenholme Lake District 65 a																		08 54			
Windermere 83 a																					
Carnforth d								07a19	07 45											09 08	
Silverdale d									07 51											09 14	
Arnside d									07 55											09 19	
Grange-over-Sands d									08 00											09 25	
Kents Bank d									08 04											09 28	
Cark d									08 08											09 33	
Ulverston d									08 16											09 42	
Dalton d									08 24											09 50	
Roose d									08 30											09 56	
Barrow-in-Furness a									08 39											10 04	

A To Glasgow Central
B To Clitheroe
C To Liverpool Lime Street
D To Leeds
E To Kirkby
F From Manchester Victoria
G To Blackburn
H To Edinburgh
I From Huddersfield
J To Carlisle

Manchester - Bolton - Wigan, Kirkby, Southport, Preston, Blackpool North and Barrow-in-Furness

Network Diagram - see first Page of Table 82

	NT A	TP ◇1 B	NT	NT C	NT	NT D	TP ◇1	NT	NT	EM ◇ E	NT F	NT G	NT	TP ◇1	NT	NT A	NT		TP ◇1 H	NT	NT	NT
Manchester Airport 85 ✈ d							07 56		08 01					08 25					09 00			09 03
Heald Green 85 d									08 05					08 29								
Buxton 86 d																						
Hazel Grove 86 d										08 17					08 32							
Stockport 84 d										08 24					08 41							
Manchester Piccadilly 10 ⇌ d		08 07					08 15		08 22	08 37				08 46	08 54				09 16			09 22
Manchester Oxford Road d		08a09					08 19		08 26	08a40				08 49	08 58				09 19			09 26
Deansgate ⇌ d									08 28					08 51	09 00							09 28
Rochdale 41 d												08 00										
Manchester Victoria ⇌ d	08 00			08 03	08 11			08 22			08 29	08 33	08 46			09 00	09 07			09 10	09 22	
Salford Central d	08 03			08 08	08 13			08 25			08 32	08 36	08 49			09 03	09 10			09 13	09 25	
Salford Crescent a	08 07			08 12	08 17			08 29	08 33		08 37	08 39	08 52	08 56	09 04	09 07	09 13			09 16	09 29	09 33
d	08 08			08 13	08 17			08 30	08 34		08 37	08 40	08 53	08 56	09 04	09 08	09 13			09 17	09 30	09 34
Swinton d				08 19									08 59							09 23		
Moorside d				08 22																09 26		
Walkden d				08 25									09 04							09 29		
Atherton d				08 31									09 09							09 35		
Hag Fold d				08 33																09 37		
Daisy Hill d				08 36									09 13							09 40		
Kearsley d												08 47										
Farnworth d												08 49										
Moses Gate d												08 52										
Bolton a	08 19				08 27		08 32	08 40	08 44		08 49	08 55		09 06	09 14	09 19	09 23		09 32		09 40	09 45
d					08 28		08 32	08 40	08 45			08 56		09 07	09 15		09 24		09 33		09 40	09 45
Westhoughton d					08 35	←			08 53								09 31					09 53
Hindley d				08 43	08 39	08 43							09 17				09 35			09 45		09 57
Ince d				→	08 42	08 46														09 48		
Wigan North Western a																						
Wigan Wallgate a					08 45	08 49			09 00			09 14	09 22				09 44			09 51		10 02
d					08 47	08 51			09 05				09 24							09 52		10 03
Pemberton d						08 55														09 56		
Orrell d						08 59														10 00		
Upholland d						09 02														10 04		
Rainford d						09 06														10 07		
Kirkby a						09 18														10 19		
Gathurst d					08 51								09 28									
Appley Bridge d					08 55				09 11				09 32									10 10
Parbold d					08 59				09 15				09 36									10 14
Hoscar d													09 39									
Burscough Bridge d					09 03				09 20				09 42									10 18
New Lane d													09 44									
Bescar Lane d													09 48									
Meols Cop d					09 11								09 53									
Southport a					09 20				09 36				10 02									10 35
Lostock d								08 45							09 20						09 45	
Horwich Parkway d							08 39	08 49						09 13	09 24						09 49	
Blackrod d								08 52													09 52	
Adlington (Lancashire) d								08 56													09 56	
Chorley d							08 47	09 01						09 21	09 32				09 44		10 01	
Buckshaw Parkway d								09 05						09 24	09 35						10 05	
Leyland d								09 12							09 42						10 12	
Preston 8 65,97 a							08 58	09 17						09 33	09 50				09 55		10 17	
d							08 59	09 19						09 38				09 58	10 07		10 19	
Kirkham & Wesham 97 a								09 28													10 28	
Poulton-le-Fylde 97 a							09 16	09 36						09 56							10 36	
Layton 97 a								09 43													10 43	
Blackpool North 97 a							09 25	09 50						10 05							10 51	
Lancaster 6 65 a																		10 13	10 22			
d			09 39																10 23			
Oxenholme Lake District 65 a																						
Windermere 83 a																						
Carnforth d			09 49																10 32			
Silverdale d			09 56																			
Arnside d			10 00																10 41			
Grange-over-Sands d			10 06																10 46			
Kents Bank d			10 10																			
Cark d			10 14																			
Ulverston d			10 23																10 59			
Dalton d			10 31																			
Roose d			10 37																			
Barrow-in-Furness a			10 47																11 17			

A To Clitheroe
B From Hull to Liverpool Lime Street
C To Kirkby
D From Manchester Victoria
E From Nottingham to Liverpool Lime Street
F To Blackburn
G From Todmorden
H To Glasgow Central

Table 82

Mondays to Fridays
until 28 September

Manchester - Bolton - Wigan, Kirkby, Southport, Preston, Blackpool North and Barrow-in-Furness

Network Diagram - see first Page of Table 82

	NT	NT		NT	TP	NT	NT	NT	TP	NT	NT		NT	NT	NT	TP	NT	NT	NT	NT	NT		TP
					◇1				◇1							◇1							◇1
				A			B		C									B					D
					🛒				🛒							🛒							🛒
Manchester Airport 85 ✈ d					09 29				10 00				10 03			10 29							11 00
Heald Green 85 d					09 33											10 33							
Buxton 86 d																							
Hazel Grove 86 d						09 32											10 33						
Stockport 84 d						09 41											10 41						
Manchester Piccadilly 10 ⇌ d					09 46	09 54			10 16				10 22			10 46	10 54						11 16
Manchester Oxford Road d					09 49	09 58			10 19				10 26			10 49	10 58						11 19
Deansgate ⇌ d					09 51	10 00							10 28			10 51	11 00						
Rochdale 41 d	09 04													10 05									
Manchester Victoria ⇌ d	09 33	09 46					10 00	10 07		10 10	10 22			10 33	10 46			11 00	11 07	11 10			
Salford Central d	09 36	09 49					10 03	10 10		10 13	10 25			10 36	10 49			11 03	11 10	11 13			
Salford Crescent a	09 39	09 52			09 56	10 04	10 07	10 13		10 16	10 29		10 33	10 39	10 52	10 56	11 04	11 07	11 13	11 16			
d	09 40	09 53			09 56	10 04	10 08	10 13		10 17	10 30		10 34	10 40	10 53	10 56	11 04	11 08	11 13	11 17			
Swinton d		09 59								10 23					10 59					11 23			
Moorside d										10 26										11 26			
Walkden d		10 04								10 29					11 04					11 29			
Atherton d		10 09								10 35					11 09					11 35			
Hag Fold d										10 37										11 37			
Daisy Hill d		10 13								10 40					11 13					11 40			
Kearsley d	09 47													10 47									
Farnworth d	09 49													10 49									
Moses Gate d	09 52													10 52									
Bolton a	09 55				10 06	10 14	10 19	10 23	10 32		10 40		10 45	10 55		11 06	11 14	11 19	11 23				11 32
d	09 56				10 07	10 15		10 24	10 33		10 40		10 45	10 56		11 07	11 15		11 24				11 33
Westhoughton d								10 31					10 53						11 31				
Hindley d		10 17						10 35		10 45			10 57		11 17				11 35	11 45			
Ince d										10 48										11 48			
Wigan North Western a																							
Wigan Wallgate a	10 13	10 22						10 44		10 51			11 02	11 13	11 22				11 44	11 51			
d		10 24								10 52			11 03		11 24					11 52			
Pemberton d										10 56										11 56			
Orrell d										11 00										12 00			
Upholland d										11 04										12 04			
Rainford d										11 07										12 07			
Kirkby a										11 19										12 19			
Gathurst d		10 28													11 28								
Appley Bridge d		10 32											11 10		11 32								
Parbold d		10 36											11 14		11 36								
Hoscar d															11 39								
Burscough Bridge d		10 40											11 18		11 42								
New Lane d															11 44								
Bescar Lane d															11 48								
Meols Cop d		10 48													11 53								
Southport a		10 57											11 35		12 02								
Lostock d						10 20					10 45						11 20						
Horwich Parkway d					10 13	10 24					10 49					11 13	11 24						
Blackrod d											10 52												
Adlington (Lancashire) d											10 56												
Chorley d					10 21	10 32			10 44		11 01					11 21	11 32						11 44
Buckshaw Parkway d					10 24	10 35					11 05					11 24	11 35						
Leyland d						10 42					11 12						11 42						
Preston 8 65,97 a					10 33	10 51			10 55		11 17					11 33	11 50						11 57
d					10 38 10 45				10 58		11 19					11 38							11 58
Kirkham & Wesham 97 a											11 28												
Poulton-le-Fylde 97 a					10 56						11 36					11 56							
Layton 97 a											11 43												
Blackpool North 97 a					11 05						11 50					12 05							
Lancaster 6 65 a					11 00				11 13														12 13
d				10 49	11 01				11 14												11 32		12 14
Oxenholme Lake District 65 a					11 17				11 28														
Windermere 83 a					11 39																		
Carnforth d				10a58																	11 42		12 23
Silverdale d																					11 48		
Arnside d																					11 53		12 32
Grange-over-Sands d																					11 59		12 38
Kents Bank d																					12 02		
Cark d																					12 07		
Ulverston d																					12 15		12 50
Dalton d																					12 23		
Roose d																					12 29		
Barrow-in-Furness a																					12 39		13 11

A From Morecambe to Leeds
B To Clitheroe
C To Edinburgh
D 🛒 to Preston

Table 82

Mondays to Fridays
until 28 September

Manchester - Bolton - Wigan, Kirkby, Southport, Preston, Blackpool North and Barrow-in-Furness

Network Diagram - see first Page of Table 82

	NT	NT	NT	NT	TP	NT	NT	NT		TP	NT	TP	NT	NT	NT	NT	TP	NT		NT	NT	TP	NT	NT
					◇1					◇1		◇1					◇1					◇1		
							A			B										A		C		
					🛒					🛒							🛒					🛒		
Manchester Airport 85 ✈ d		11 03			11 29					12 00				12 03			12 29					13 00		
Heald Green 85 d					11 33												12 33							
Buxton 86 d																								
Hazel Grove 86 d						11 33												12 33						
Stockport 84 d						11 41												12 41						
Manchester Piccadilly 10 ⇌ d		11 22			11 46	11 54				12 16				12 22			12 46	12 54				13 16		
Manchester Oxford Road d		11 26			11 49	11 58				12 19				12 26			12 49	12 58				13 19		
Deansgate ⇌ d		11 28			11 51	12 00								12 28			12 51	13 00						
Rochdale 41 d			11 04												12 04									
Manchester Victoria ⇌ d	11 22		11 33	11 46			12 00	12 07			12 10		12 22		12 33	12 46				13 00	13 07		13 10	
Salford Central d	11 25		11 36	11 49			12 03	12 10			12 13		12 25		12 36	12 49				13 03	13 10		13 13	
Salford Crescent a	11 29	11 33	11 39	11 52	11 56	12 04	12 07	12 13			12 16		12 29	12 33	12 39	12 52	12 56	13 04		13 07	13 13		13 16	
d	11 30	11 34	11 40	11 53	11 56	12 04	12 08	12 13			12 17		12 30	12 34	12 40	12 53	12 56	13 04		13 08	13 13		13 17	
Swinton d				11 59							12 23					12 59							13 23	
Moorside d											12 26												13 26	
Walkden d				12 04							12 29					13 04							13 29	
Atherton d				12 09							12 35					13 09							13 35	
Hag Fold d											12 37												13 37	
Daisy Hill d				12 13							12 40					13 13							13 40	
Kearsley d			11 47												12 47									
Farnworth d			11 49												12 49									
Moses Gate d			11 52												12 52									
Bolton a	11 40	11 45	11 55		12 06	12 14	12 19	12 23		12 32			12 40	12 45	12 55		13 06	13 14		13 19	13 23	13 32		
d	11 40	11 45	11 56		12 07	12 15		12 24		12 33			12 40	12 45	12 56		13 07	13 15			13 24	13 33		
Westhoughton d		11 53						12 31						12 53							13 31			
Hindley d		11 57		12 17				12 35			12 45			12 57		13 17					13 35		13 45	
Ince d											12 48												13 48	
Wigan North Western a																								
Wigan Wallgate a		12 02	12 13	12 22				12 44			12 51			13 02	13 13	13 22					13 44		13 51	
d		12 03		12 24							12 52			13 03		13 24							13 52	
Pemberton d											12 56												13 56	
Orrell d											13 00												14 00	
Upholland d											13 04												14 04	
Rainford d											13 07												14 07	
Kirkby a											13 19												14 19	
Gathurst d				12 28												13 28								
Appley Bridge d		12 10		12 32										13 10		13 32								
Parbold d		12 14		12 36										13 14		13 36								
Hoscar d																13 39								
Burscough Bridge d		12 18		12 41										13 18		13 42								
New Lane d																13 44								
Bescar Lane d																13 48								
Meols Cop d				12 49												13 53								
Southport a		12 35		12 59										13 35		14 02								
Lostock d	11 45					12 20							12 45					13 20						
Horwich Parkway d	11 49				12 13	12 24							12 49				13 13	13 24						
Blackrod d	11 52												12 52											
Adlington (Lancashire) d	11 56												12 56											
Chorley d	12 01				12 21	12 32				12 44			13 01				13 21	13 32				13 44		
Buckshaw Parkway d	12 05				12 24	12 35							13 05				13 24	13 35						
Leyland d	12 12					12 42							13 12					13 42						
Preston 8 65,97 a	12 17				12 33	12 50				12 55			13 17				13 33	13 50				13 55		
d	12 19				12 38					12 58		13 04	13 19				13 38					13 58		
Kirkham & Wesham 97 a	12 28												13 28											
Poulton-le-Fylde 97 a	12 36				12 56								13 36				13 56							
Layton 97 a	12 43												13 43											
Blackpool North 97 a	12 50				13 05								13 50				14 05							
Lancaster 6 65 a										13 13		13 19										14 13		
d										13 14		13 20												13 32
Oxenholme Lake District 65 a										13 28		13 36												
Windermere 83 a												13 56												
Carnforth d																								13 42
Silverdale d																								13 48
Arnside d																								13 52
Grange-over-Sands d																								13 58
Kents Bank d																								14 02
Cark d																								14 06
Ulverston d																								14 15
Dalton d																								14 23
Roose d																								14 29
Barrow-in-Furness a																								14 39

A To Clitheroe
B To Edinburgh
C To Glasgow Central

Manchester - Bolton - Wigan, Kirkby, Southport, Preston, Blackpool North and Barrow-in-Furness

Network Diagram - see first Page of Table 82

		NT A	TP FX ◇1 B ✠	NT	NT	NT	NT	TP ◇1 ✠	NT	NT C	NT	NT	TP FO ◇1	TP ◇1 D ✠	NT	NT	NT	NT	TP ◇1 ✠	NT	NT C	NT	NT
Manchester Airport	85 ✈ d		13 00		13 03			13 29						14 00		14 03			14 29				
Heald Green	85 d							13 33											14 33				
Buxton	86 d																						
Hazel Grove	86 d								13 33											14 33			
Stockport	84 d								13 41											14 41			
Manchester Piccadilly 10	⇌ d		13 16		13 22			13 46	13 54					14 16		14 22			14 46	14 54			
Manchester Oxford Road	d		13 19		13 26			13 49	13 58					14 19		14 26			14 49	14 58			
Deansgate	⇌ d				13 28			13 51	14 00							14 28			14 51	15 00			
Rochdale	41 d					13 04											14 04						
Manchester Victoria	⇌ d			13 22		13 33	13 46			14 00	14 07	14 10			14 22		14 33	14 46			15 00	15 07	15 10
Salford Central	d			13 25		13 36	13 49			14 03	14 10	14 13			14 25		14 36	14 49			15 03	15 10	15 13
Salford Crescent	a			13 29	13 33	13 39	13 52	13 56	14 04	14 07	14 13	14 16			14 29	14 33	14 39	14 52	14 56	15 04	15 07	15 13	15 16
	d			13 30	13 34	13 40	13 53	13 56	14 04	14 08	14 13	14 17			14 30	14 34	14 40	14 53	14 56	15 04	15 08	15 13	15 17
Swinton	d						13 59					14 23						14 59					15 23
Moorside	d											14 26											15 26
Walkden	d						14 04					14 29						15 04					15 29
Atherton	d						14 09					14 35						15 09					15 35
Hag Fold	d											14 37											15 37
Daisy Hill	d						14 13					14 40						15 13					15 40
Kearsley	d					13 47											14 47						
Farnworth	d					13 49											14 49						
Moses Gate	d					13 52											14 52						
Bolton	a		13 32	13 40	13 45	13 55		14 06	14 14	14 19	14 23			14 32	14 40	14 45	14 55		15 06	15 14	15 19	15 23	
	d		13 33	13 40	13 45	13 56		14 07	14 15		14 24			14 33	14 40	14 45	14 56		15 07	15 15		15 24	
Westhoughton	d				13 53						14 31					14 53						15 31	
Hindley	d				13 57		14 17				14 35	14 45				14 57		15 17				15 35	15 45
Ince	d											14 48											15 48
Wigan North Western	a																						
Wigan Wallgate	a				14 02	14 13	14 22				14 44	14 51				15 02	15 13	15 22				15 44	15 51
	d				14 03		14 24					14 52				15 03		15 24					15 58
Pemberton	d											14 56											16 02
Orrell	d											15 00											16 06
Upholland	d											15 04											16 09
Rainford	d											15 07											16 13
Kirkby	a											15 19											16 25
Gathurst	d						14 28											15 28					
Appley Bridge	d				14 10		14 32									15 10		15 32					
Parbold	d				14 14		14 36									15 14		15 36					
Hoscar	d																						
Burscough Bridge	d				14 18		14 41									15 18		15 40					
New Lane	d																						
Bescar Lane	d																						
Meols Cop	d						14 49											15 48					
Southport	a				14 35		14 59									15 35		15 57					
Lostock	d			13 45					14 20						14 45					15 20			
Horwich Parkway	d			13 49				14 13	14 24						14 49				15 13	15 24			
Blackrod	d			13 52											14 52								
Adlington (Lancashire)	d			13 56											14 56								
Chorley	d		13 44	14 01				14 21	14 32					14 44	15 01				15 21	15 32			
Buckshaw Parkway	d			14 05				14 24	14 35						15 05				15 24	15 36			
Leyland	d			14 12					14 42						15 12					15 42			
Preston 8	65,97 a		13 55	14 17				14 33	14 50					14 55	15 17				15 33	15 50			
	d		14 04	14 19				14 38						14 58	15 19				15 38				
Kirkham & Wesham	97 a			14 28											15 28								
Poulton-le-Fylde	97 a			14 36				14 56							15 36				15 56				
Layton	97 a			14 43											15 43								
Blackpool North	97 a			14 51				15 05							15 50				16 05				
Lancaster 8	65 a		14 19											15 13									
	d	13 48	14 20										14 20	15 14									
Oxenholme Lake District	65 a													15 28									
Windermere	83 a																						
Carnforth	d	13a58	14 28										14 28										
Silverdale	d																						
Arnside	d		14 37										14 37										
Grange-over-Sands	d		14 42										14 42										
Kents Bank	d																						
Cark	d																						
Ulverston	d		14 55										14 55										
Dalton	d																						
Roose	d																						
Barrow-in-Furness	a		15 15										15 15										

A From Heysham Port to Leeds
B ✠ to Preston
C To Clitheroe
D To Edinburgh

Table 82

Mondays to Fridays
until 28 September

Manchester - Bolton - Wigan, Kirkby, Southport, Preston, Blackpool North and Barrow-in-Furness

Network Diagram - see first Page of Table 82

		NT A	TP ◇1 B ✠	NT	NT	NT	NT C	NT	TP ◇1 ✠	NT	NT	NT	NT D	TP ◇1 E ✠	NT F	TP FX ◇1 B ✠	TP ◇1	NT	NT C	NT	NT	NT
Manchester Airport	85 ✈ d		15 00		15 03				15 29					16 00		16 00				16 03		
Heald Green	85 d								15 33													
Buxton	86 d																				15 27	
Hazel Grove	86 d									15 33											16 04	
Stockport	84 d									15 41											16 12	
Manchester Piccadilly 10	⇌ d		15 16		15 22				15 46	15 54				16 16		16 16				16 22	16 27	
Manchester Oxford Road	d		15 19		15 26				15 49	15 58				16 19		16 19				16 26	16 30	
Deansgate	⇌ d				15 28				15 51	16 00										16 28	16 33	
Rochdale	41 d					15 04																16 04
Manchester Victoria	⇌ d			15 22		15 33	15 40	15 46			16 07	16 10						16 20	16 23			16 36
Salford Central	d			15 25		15 36	15 43	15 49			16 10	16 13						16 23	16 26			16 39
Salford Crescent	a			15 29	15 33	15 39	15 46	15 52	15 56	16 04	16 13	16 16						16 26	16 30	16 34	16 38	16 42
	d			15 30	15 34	15 40	15 47	15 53	15 56	16 04	16 13	16 17						16 27	16 31	16 34	16 38	16 43
Swinton	d							15 59				16 23										
Moorside	d											16 26										
Walkden	d							16 04				16 29										
Atherton	d							16 09				16 35										
Hag Fold	d											16 37										
Daisy Hill	d							16 13				16 40										
Kearsley	d					15 47																16 50
Farnworth	d					15 49																16 52
Moses Gate	d					15 52					16 21											16 55
Bolton	a		15 32	15 40	15 45	15 55	15 59		16 06	16 19	16 25			16 32		16 32		16 37	16 42	16 45	16 48	16 58
	d		15 33	15 40	15 45	15 56			16 07		16 25			16 33		16 33		16 37		16 45	16 49	16 59
Westhoughton	d				15 53						16 33									16 53		17 06
Hindley	d				15 57			16 17			16 37	16 45								16 57		17 10
Ince	d											16 48										
Wigan North Western	a																					
Wigan Wallgate	a				16 02	16 13		16 22			16 46	16 51								17 02		17 19
	d				16 03			16 24				16 52								17 03		
Pemberton	d											16 56										
Orrell	d											17 00										
Upholland	d											17 04										
Rainford	d											17 07										
Kirkby	a											17 19										
Gathurst	d				16 08			16 28												17 08		
Appley Bridge	d				16 11			16 32												17 11		
Parbold	d				16 15			16 36												17 15		
Hoscar	d				16 18																	
Burscough Bridge	d				16 21			16 40												17 20		
New Lane	d				16 24																	
Bescar Lane	d				16 27																	
Meols Cop	d				16 32			16 48												17 27		
Southport	a				16 42			16 57												17 37		
Lostock	d			15 45					16 12									16 43			16 54	
Horwich Parkway	d			15 49					16 15									16 47			16 58	
Blackrod	d			15 52														16 51			17 01	
Adlington (Lancashire)	d			15 56														16 55			17 05	
Chorley	d		15 44	16 01					16 23					16 44		16 44		17 00			17 10	
Buckshaw Parkway	d			16 05					16 26									17 04			17 13	
Leyland	d			16 12														17 11			17 21	
Preston 8	65,97 a		15 57	16 19					16 35					16 55		16 55		17 19			17 26	
	d		15 58						16 38					17 00		17 04	17 04	17 21			17 28	
Kirkham & Wesham	97 a								16 47									17 30				
Poulton-le-Fylde	97 a								16 57									17 38				
Layton	97 a								17 00									17 43				
Blackpool North	97 a								17 07									17 50				
Lancaster 8	65 a		16 14											17 15		17 23	17 23				17 48	
	d	15 34	16 15										16 55	17 16	17 19	17 25	17 25				17 48	
Oxenholme Lake District	65 a													17 30		17 43	17 43					
Windermere	83 a															18 08	18 08					
Carnforth	d	15 44	16 23										17 05		17 28						18 00	
Silverdale	d	15 51	16 29										17 12		17 35						18 06	
Arnside	d	15 55	16 33										17 16		17 40						18 11	
Grange-over-Sands	d	16 01	16 39										17 22		17 46						18 19	
Kents Bank	d	16 05	16 42										17 26		17 49						18 23	
Cark	d	16 09	16 47										17 30		17 54						18 27	
Ulverston	d	16 17	16 55										17 39		18 02						18 36	
Dalton	d	16 26	17 03										17 48		18 10						18 44	
Roose	d	16 32	17 09										17 54		18 17						18 50	
Barrow-in-Furness	a	16 39	17 18										18 02		18 25						18 59	

A To Carlisle
B ✠ to Preston
C To Clitheroe
D To Millom
E To Edinburgh
F From Morecambe

Manchester - Bolton - Wigan, Kirkby, Southport, Preston, Blackpool North and Barrow-in-Furness

Network Diagram - see first Page of Table 82

		TP ◇**1** 🛒	NT	NT	NT A	TP ◇**1** B 🛒		NT C	NT	NT	NT D	NT	NT	NT	NT	NT	TP ◇**1** 🛒	NT	NT A	NT	TP ◇**1** E	TP ◇**1** F 🛒	
Manchester Airport 85 ✈	d	16 29				17 00						17 03					17 29					18 00	
Heald Green 85	d	16 33															17 33						
Buxton 86	d												16 30					16 59					
Hazel Grove 86	d			16 30									17 04					17 33					
Stockport 84	d			16 41									17 12					17 41					
Manchester Piccadilly 10 ⇌	d	16 46		16 54		17 15						17 22	17 27				17 46	17 54				18 16	
Manchester Oxford Road	d	16 49		16 58		17 18						17 26	17 30				17 49	17 58				18 19	
Deansgate ⇌	d			17 00									17 33				17 51	18 00					
Rochdale 41	d										17 03												
Manchester Victoria ⇌	d		16 46		17 00			17 06	17 10	17 19	17 23			17 36	17 40	17 45			18 00	18 10			
Salford Central	d		16 49		17 03			17 09	17 12	17 22	17 27			17 39	17 43	17 48			18 03	18 13			
Salford Crescent	a		16 52	17 04	17 07			17 13	17 16	17 25	17 29	17 34	17 38	17 42	17 46	17 51	17 55	18 04	18 07	18 16			
	d		16 53	17 04	17 08			17 14	17 17	17 27	17 30	17 34	17 38	17 43	17 47	17 52	17 55	18 04	18 08	18 17			
Swinton	d		16 59						17 23							17 58				18 23			
Moorside	d		17 02						17 26							18 01				18 26			
Walkden	d		17 05						17 31							18 05				18 29			
Atherton	d		17 11					17 27	17 37						18 00	18 11				18 35			
Hag Fold	d		17 14						17 39							18 13				18 37			
Daisy Hill	d		17 17					17 31	17 43						18 04	18 17				18 40			
Kearsley	d													17 53									
Farnworth	d													17 55									
Moses Gate	d													17 57									
Bolton	a	17 05		17 14	17 19	17 31				17 37	17 42	17 45	17 48	18 01			18 06	18 14	18 19			18 32	
	d	17 06		17 15		17 32				17 37		17 45	17 49	18 01			18 07	18 15				18 33	
Westhoughton	d											17 53		18 09									
Hindley	d		17 21						17 48					18 13		18 22				18 45			
Ince	d		17 24						17 51							18 25				18 48			
Wigan North Western	a																			18 56			
Wigan Wallgate	a		17 31					17 39	17 54			18 01		18 22	18 12	18 28							
	d							17 40	17 55			18 02			18 15	18 29							
Pemberton	d								17 59							18 33							
Orrell	d								18 03							18 37							
Upholland	d								18 07							18 41							
Rainford	d								18 10							18 44							
Kirkby	a								18 22							18 55							
Gathurst	d							17 45							18 20								
Appley Bridge	d							17 48				18 09			18 24								
Parbold	d							17 53				18 13			18 28								
Hoscar	d														18 31								
Burscough Bridge	d							17 58				18 17			18 35								
New Lane	d														18 37								
Bescar Lane	d														18 41								
Meols Cop	d							18 05				18 26			18 46								
Southport	a							18 15				18 35			18 55								
Lostock	d			17 20						17 43			17 54				18 12	18 20					
Horwich Parkway	d			17 24						17 47			17 58				18 15	18 24					
Blackrod	d									17 51			18 01				18 19						
Adlington (Lancashire)	d									17 55			18 05										
Chorley	d	17 19		17 32		17 44				18 00			18 10				18 26	18 32				18 44	
Buckshaw Parkway	d			17 35						18 03			18 13					18 35					
Leyland	d			17 42						18 11								18 42					
Preston 8 65,97	a	17 30		17 51		17 55				18 16			18 25				18 38	18 48				18 55	
	d	17 32				17 58	18 08			18 18			18 26				18 40	18 49				19 00	19 04
Kirkham & Wesham 97	a	17 41								18 27							18 49						
Poulton-le-Fylde 97	a	17 51								18 35			18 43				18 59						
Layton 97	a	17 54								18 39							19 02						
Blackpool North 97	a	18 02								18 49			18 53				19 10	19 16					
Lancaster 6 65	a					18 13	18 23															19 15	19 20
	d					18 14	18 24														18 29	19 16	19 20
Oxenholme Lake District 65	a					18 28															18 45	19 30	
Windermere 83	a																				19 08		
Carnforth	d						18 34																19 29
Silverdale	d						18 40																19 35
Arnside	d						18 44																19 39
Grange-over-Sands	d						18 50																19 44
Kents Bank	d						18 53																19 48
Cark	d						18 58																19 52
Ulverston	d						19 06																20 00
Dalton	d						19 14																20 08
Roose	d						19 20																20 14
Barrow-in-Furness	a						19 29																20 24

A To Clitheroe
B To Glasgow Central
C From Stalybridge
D To Blackburn
E From Barrow-in-Furness
F To Edinburgh

Manchester - Bolton - Wigan, Kirkby, Southport, Preston, Blackpool North and Barrow-in-Furness

Network Diagram - see first Page of Table 82

		NT	NT A	NT	NT	NT	TP ◇**1** 🛒	NT	NT B	NT	NT C	TP ◇**1**	NT	NT	TP ◇**1**	NT B	TP ◇**1**	NT	NT	NT	NT D	TP ◇**1**
Manchester Airport 85 ✈	d			18 03			18 29					19 00	19 03		19 29		20 00			20 03	20 09	20 29
Heald Green 85	d						18 33								19 33						20 12	20 33
Buxton 86	d							17 59														
Hazel Grove 86	d							18 33														
Stockport 84	d							18 41														
Manchester Piccadilly 10 ⇌	d			18 22			18 46	18 54				19 16	19 20		19 46		20 16			20 20	20 32	20 46
Manchester Oxford Road	d			18 26			18 49	18 58				19 19	19 24		19 49		20 19			20 24	20a36	20 49
Deansgate ⇌	d			18 28			18 51	19 00					19 26		19 51					20 26		20 51
Rochdale 41	d		18 02																			
Manchester Victoria ⇌	d	18 20	18 23		18 33	18 45			19 00	19 10				19 28		20 00		20 10	20 22			
Salford Central	d	18 23	18 26		18 36	18 48			19 03	19 13				19 31		20 03		20 13	20 25			
Salford Crescent	a	18 26	18 30	18 34	18 39	18 51	18 56	19 04	19 07	19 16			19 29	19 34	19 56	20 07		20 16	20 29	20 33		20 56
	d	18 27	18 31	18 34	18 40	18 52	18 56	19 04	19 08	19 17			19 30	19 35	19 56	20 08		20 17	20 30	20 34		20 56
Swinton	d					18 58				19 23								20 23				
Moorside	d					19 01				19 26								20 26				
Walkden	d					19 04				19 29								20 29				
Atherton	d					19 10				19 35								20 35				
Hag Fold	d					19 12				19 37								20 37				
Daisy Hill	d					19 15				19 40								20 40				
Kearsley	d				18 47																	
Farnworth	d				18 49																	
Moses Gate	d				18 52																	
Bolton	a	18 37	18 42	18 45	18 55		19 06	19 19	19 20			19 32	19 40	19 45	20 06	20 19	20 32		20 40	20 45		21 06
	d	18 37		18 45	18 56		19 07					19 33	19 40	19 45	20 07		20 33		20 40	20 45		21 07
Westhoughton	d			18 53	19 03								19 48							20 53		
Hindley	d			18 57	19 09	19 20				19 45			19 52					20 45		20 57		
Ince	d					19 23				19 48								20 48				
Wigan North Western	a																					
Wigan Wallgate	a			19 02	19 18	19 30				19 55			19 57					20 55		21 02		
	d			19 03									19 59							21 03		
Pemberton	d																					
Orrell	d																					
Upholland	d																					
Rainford	d																					
Kirkby	a																					
Gathurst	d			19 08									20 03							21 08		
Appley Bridge	d			19 11									20 07							21 11		
Parbold	d			19 15									20 11							21 15		
Hoscar	d																			21 18		
Burscough Bridge	d			19 19									20 15							21 21		
New Lane	d																			21 24		
Bescar Lane	d																			21 27		
Meols Cop	d			19 27									20 23							21 32		
Southport	a			19 37									20 32							21 42		
Lostock	d	18 42					19 12							19 50					20 45			
Horwich Parkway	d	18 46					19 15							19 54	20 13		20 39		20 49			21 13
Blackrod	d	18 49												19 57					20 52			
Adlington (Lancashire)	d	18 53												20 01					20 56			
Chorley	d	18 58					19 23					19 44		20 06	20 21		20 46		21 01			21 21
Buckshaw Parkway	d	19 02					19 26							20 10	20 24				21 05			21 24
Leyland	d	19 10												20 18					21 12			
Preston 8 65,97	a	19 18					19 33					19 55		20 23	20 33		20 57		21 17			21 33
	d	19 19					19 38					19 58		20 25	20 38		20 59		21 19			21 38
Kirkham & Wesham 97	a	19 28												20 34					21 28			
Poulton-le-Fylde 97	a	19 36					19 56							20 42	20 56				21 36			21 56
Layton 97	a	19 43												20 46					21 40			
Blackpool North 97	a	19 52					20 06							20 54	21 06				21 48			22 06
Lancaster 6 65	a											20 13					21 14					
	d										19 24	20 14					21 15					
Oxenholme Lake District 65	a																					
Windermere 83	a																					
Carnforth	d										19a34	20 22					21 23					
Silverdale	d											20 28					21 29					
Arnside	d											20 32					21 33					
Grange-over-Sands	d											20 38					21 39					
Kents Bank	d											20 41					21 42					
Cark	d											20 46					21 47					
Ulverston	d											20 54					21 55					
Dalton	d											21 02					22 03					
Roose	d											21 08					22 09					
Barrow-in-Furness	a											21 17					22 18					

A To Blackburn
B To Clitheroe
C From Morecambe to Leeds
D From Wilmslow

Table 82

Mondays to Fridays
until 28 September

Manchester - Bolton - Wigan, Kirkby, Southport, Preston, Blackpool North and Barrow-in-Furness

Network Diagram - see first Page of Table 82

	NT A	NT	NT	NT	NT	NT B	NT C	TP ◇1	NT A	TP ◇1	NT B	NT	NT	NT	TP ◇1	NT	NT D	NT FO
Manchester Airport 85 ✈ d					21 03	21 09		21 29		22 00	22 08			22 19	22 29			
Heald Green 85 d						21 12		21 33			22 12				22 33			
Buxton 86 d																		
Hazel Grove 86 d																		
Stockport 84 d																22 34		
Manchester Piccadilly 10 ⇌ d					21 20	21 32	21 38	21 46		22 16	22 32			22 36	22 46	22 50		
Manchester Oxford Road d					21 24	21a36	21 44	21 49		22 19	22a36			22 39	22 49	22 53		
Deansgate ⇌ d					21 26		21a46	21 51						22 41	22 51	22 55		
Rochdale 41 d																		
Manchester Victoria ⇌ d	21 00	21 10		21 22					22 00			22 10	22 22				23 00	23 20
Salford Central d	21 03	21 13		21 25					22b04			22b13	22b25				23b03	23 23
Salford Crescent a	21 07	21 16		21 29	21 33			21 56	22 07			22 17	22 29	22 46	22 56	22 59	23 07	23 26
d	21 08	21 17		21 30	21 34			21 56	22 08			22 17	22 30	22 46	22 56	22 59	23 08	23 26
Swinton d		21 23										22 23						23 33
Moorside d		21 26										22 26						23 35
Walkden d		21 29										22 29						23 39
Atherton d		21 35										22 35						23 44
Hag Fold d		21 37										22 37						23 47
Daisy Hill d		21 40										22 40						23 50
Kearsley d																23 07		
Farnworth d																23 09		
Moses Gate d																23 11		
Bolton a	21 19			21 40	21 45			22 06	22 19	22 32			22 40	22 56	23 06	23 15	23 19	
d				21 40	21 45			22 07		22 33			22 40	22 57	23 07	23 15		
Westhoughton d					21 53									23 04		23 23		
Hindley d		21 45			21 57							22 45		23 08		23 27		23 54
Ince d		21 48										22 48						23 57
Wigan North Western a										22 48								
Wigan Wallgate a		21 55			22 02							22 55		23 13		23 38		00 04
d					22 03									23 15				
Pemberton d																		
Orrell d																		
Upholland d																		
Rainford d																		
Kirkby a																		
Gathurst d					22 08									23 19				
Appley Bridge d					22 11									23 23				
Parbold d					22 15									23 27				
Hoscar d																		
Burscough Bridge d					22 20									23 31				
New Lane d																		
Bescar Lane d																		
Meols Cop d					22 27									23 39				
Southport a					22 37									23 48				
Lostock d				21 45									22 45					
Horwich Parkway d				21 49				22 13					22 49		23 13			
Blackrod d				21 52									22 52					
Adlington (Lancashire) d				21 56									22 56					
Chorley d				22 01				22 21					23 01		23 21			
Buckshaw Parkway d				22 05				22 24					23 05		23 24			
Leyland d				22 12									23 12					
Preston 8 65,97 a				22 17				22 36		23 09			23 17		23 33			
d			21 51	22 19				22 38		23 13			23 19		23 35			
Kirkham & Wesham 97 a				22 28									23 28					
Poulton-le-Fylde 97 a				22 36				22 55					23 36		23 52			
Layton 97 a				22 43									23 40					
Blackpool North 97 a				22 53				23 04					23 48		00 02			
Lancaster 6 65 a			22 11							23 28								
d			22 11							23 29								
Oxenholme Lake District 65 a																		
Windermere 83 a																		
Carnforth d			22 21							23 37								
Silverdale d			22 27							23 43								
Arnside d			22 32							23 47								
Grange-over-Sands d			22 38							23 53								
Kents Bank d			22 41							23 56								
Cark d			22 46							00 01								
Ulverston d			22 54							00 09								
Dalton d			23 02							00 17								
Roose d			23 08							00 23								
Barrow-in-Furness a			23 16							00 31								

A To Clitheroe
B From Wilmslow
C To Warrington Central
D To Blackburn
b Fridays only

Table 82

Mondays to Fridays
until 28 September

Manchester - Bolton - Wigan, Kirkby, Southport, Preston, Blackpool North and Barrow-in-Furness

Network Diagram - see first Page of Table 82

	NT FX	NT	TP FX ◇1 A
Manchester Airport 85 ✈ d			23 18
Heald Green 85 d			
Buxton 86 d			
Hazel Grove 86 d			
Stockport 84 d			
Manchester Piccadilly 10 ⇌ d			23 38
Manchester Oxford Road d			
Deansgate ⇌ d			
Rochdale 41 d			
Manchester Victoria ⇌ d	23 20	23 23	
Salford Central d		23b26	
Salford Crescent a	23 25	23 29	23 43
d	23 26	23 30	
Swinton d	23 33		
Moorside d	23 35		
Walkden d	23 39		
Atherton d	23 44		
Hag Fold d	23 47		
Daisy Hill d	23 50		
Kearsley d			
Farnworth d			
Moses Gate d			
Bolton a		23 40	
d		23 40	
Westhoughton d			
Hindley d	23 54		
Ince d	23 57		
Wigan North Western a			
Wigan Wallgate a	00 04		
d			
Pemberton d			
Orrell d			
Upholland d			
Rainford d			
Kirkby a			
Gathurst d			
Appley Bridge d			
Parbold d			
Hoscar d			
Burscough Bridge d			
New Lane d			
Bescar Lane d			
Meols Cop d			
Southport a			
Lostock d		23 45	
Horwich Parkway d		23 49	
Blackrod d		23 52	
Adlington (Lancashire) d		23 56	
Chorley d		00 01	
Buckshaw Parkway d		00 05	
Leyland d		00 12	
Preston 8 65,97 a		00 17	
d		00 19	
Kirkham & Wesham 97 a		00 28	
Poulton-le-Fylde 97 a		00 36	
Layton 97 a		00 43	
Blackpool North 97 a		00 50	
Lancaster 6 65 a			
d			
Oxenholme Lake District 65 a			
Windermere 83 a			
Carnforth d			
Silverdale d			
Arnside d			
Grange-over-Sands d			
Kents Bank d			
Cark d			
Ulverston d			
Dalton d			
Roose d			
Barrow-in-Furness a			

A To York
b Fridays only

Manchester - Bolton - Wigan, Kirkby, Southport, Preston, Blackpool North and Barrow-in-Furness

Network Diagram - see first Page of Table 82

		TP MX ◇1	TP MO ◇1	TP MX ◇1	NT MX	NT MX	TP ◇1	TP MX ◇1 A	TP MO ◇1 A	TP ◇1	TP ◇1 B	NT C	NT D	TP 1	TP ◇1	TP ◇1 E 🍴	NT F	NT	NT	TP ◇1 G 🍴	NT	NT
Manchester Airport 85 ✈	d	22p00	22p30	22p29			00 01	00 38	00 48	04 00	04 12	04 38				05 45				06 18		
Heald Green 85	d			22p33												05 49						
Buxton 86	d																					
Hazel Grove 86	d																					
Stockport 84	d																					
Manchester Piccadilly 10 ⇌	d	22p16	22p46	22p46			00 16	00 53	01 03	04 15	04 30	04a51			05 46	06 03				06 33		
Manchester Oxford Road	d	22p19	22p49	22p49												06 06				06 36		
Deansgate ⇌	d		22p51	22p51																		
Rochdale 41	d																					
Manchester Victoria ⇌	d				23p20	23p23											05 55	06 00	06 17		06 38	
Salford Central	d																				06 40	
Salford Crescent	a		22p54	22p56	23p25	23p31		00 58	01 09		04 36				05 51		05 59	06 04	06 23		06 44	
	d		22p55	22p56	23p26	23p32									05 52		06 00	06 05	06 24		06 45	
Swinton	d				23p33																	
Moorside	d				23p35																	
Walkden	d				23p39																	
Atherton	d				23p44																	
Hag Fold	d				23p47																	
Daisy Hill	d				23p50																	
Kearsley	d																				06 52	
Farnworth	d																				06 54	
Moses Gate	d																				06 57	
Bolton	a	22p32	23p05	23p06		23p42	00s31			04s29						06 19	06 11	06 15	06 34	06 50	07 00	
	d	22p33	23p05	23p07		23p42										06 19		06 15	06 34	06 50	07 01	
Westhoughton	d																	06 23				
Hindley	d				23p54													06 27				
Ince	d				23p57																	
Wigan North Western	a	22p48								04 44					06 15						07 19	
Wigan Wallgate	a				00 06													06 32				
	d																	06 34				06 40
Pemberton	d																	06 38				
Orrell	d																	06 42				
Upholland	d																	06 45				
Rainford	d																	06 49				
Kirkby	a																	06 59				
Gathurst	d																					06 44
Appley Bridge	d																					06 48
Parbold	d																					06 52
Hoscar	d																					06 55
Burscough Bridge	d																					06 58
New Lane	d																					07 00
Bescar Lane	d																					07 04
Meols Cop	d																					07 09
Southport	a																					07 20
Lostock	d		23p10			23p47													06 39			
Horwich Parkway	d		23p14	23p13		23p51													06 43			
Blackrod	d		23p17			23p54													06 46			
Adlington (Lancashire)	d		23p20			23p58													06 50			
Chorley	d		23p25	23p21		00 03										06 31			06 55			
Buckshaw Parkway	d		23p28	23p24		00 07													06 59			
Leyland	d		23p36			00 14									06 27				07 06			
Preston 8 65,97	a	23p09	23p42	23p33		00 19	01s05			05s04					06 35	06 42			07 11	07 11		
	d	23p13	23p47	23p35		00 21							05 22		06 37	06 44			07 13	07 14		
Kirkham & Wesham 97	a		23p56			00 30									06 46				07 22			
Poulton-le-Fylde 97	a		00 05	23p52		00 38									06 56				07 30			
Layton 97	a					00 43									06 59				07 34			
Blackpool North 97	a		00 14	00 02		00 52	01 30			05 33					07 06				07 43			
Lancaster 8 65	a	23p28											05 42			06 59				07 30		
	d	23p29											05 42	05 46		07 00						
Oxenholme Lake District 65	a													06 21		07 15						
Windermere 83	a													06 41								
Carnforth	d	23p37											05 52									
Silverdale	d	23p43											05 58									
Arnside	d	23p47											06 03									
Grange-over-Sands	d	23p53											06 09									
Kents Bank	d	23p56											06 12									
Cark	d	00 01											06 17									
Ulverston	d	00 09											06 25									
Dalton	d	00 17											06 33									
Roose	d	00 23											06 39									
Barrow-in-Furness	a	00 31											06 47									

A To York
B To Scarborough
C To Liverpool Lime Street
D To Carlisle
E To Edinburgh
F To Clitheroe
G To Glasgow Central

Manchester - Bolton - Wigan, Kirkby, Southport, Preston, Blackpool North and Barrow-in-Furness

Network Diagram - see first Page of Table 82

		NT	NT A	TP ◇1 B	NT C	TP ◇1	NT D	NT	NT E	TP ◇1 🍴	NT	NT F	NT	NT	TP ◇1 G 🍴	NT H	NT I	NT	NT A	TP ◇1 J 🍴	NT	NT D	NT
Manchester Airport 85 ✈	d									07 00					07 25								
Heald Green 85	d														07 30								
Buxton 86	d		05 54											06 18				06 45					
Hazel Grove 86	d		06 31											06 58				07 25					
Stockport 84	d		06 41											07 10				07 37					
Manchester Piccadilly 10 ⇌	d		06 54	07 07						07 15				07 27	07 45			07 54		08 07			
Manchester Oxford Road	d		06 57	07a09						07 18				07 30				07 57		08a09			
Deansgate ⇌	d		06 59											07 32				07 59					
Rochdale 41	d																						
Manchester Victoria ⇌	d	06 45					07 01	07 06			07 17	07 23	07 27			07 47			08 00			08 03	08 11
Salford Central	d	06 48					07 04	07 09			07 19	07 26	07 30			07 50			08 03			08 08	08 13
Salford Crescent	a	06 51	07 03				07 07	07 12			07 24	07 29	07 33	07 37		07 53		08 04	08 07			08 12	08 17
	d	06 52	07 03				07 08	07 13			07 25	07 30	07 33	07 37		07 53		08 04	08 08			08 13	08 17
Swinton	d	06 58					07 14									08 00						08 19	
Moorside	d						07 17									08 02						08 22	
Walkden	d	07 03					07 20						07 42			08 06						08 25	
Atherton	d	07 08					07 26						07 48			08 11						08 31	
Hag Fold	d						07 28									08 14						08 33	
Daisy Hill	d	07 12					07 31						07 51			08 17						08 36	
Kearsley	d													07 45									
Farnworth	d													07 47									
Moses Gate	d													07 49									
Bolton	a		07 16					07 23		07 31	07 35	07 41		07 53	07 59			08 14	08 19				08 27
	d							07 23		07 31	07 35			07 53	07 59			08 15					08 28
Westhoughton	d							07 31	←					08 01									08 35
Hindley	d	07 16					07 39	07 35	07 39							08 21						08 43	08 39
Ince	d						→		07 42													→	08 42
Wigan North Western	a													08 16									
Wigan Wallgate	a	07 21						07 40	07 45				08 05			08 26							08 45
	d	07 23						07 41	07 46							08 28							08 47
Pemberton	d								07 50														
Orrell	d								07 54														
Upholland	d								07 58														
Rainford	d								08 01														
Kirkby	a								08 11														
Gathurst	d	07 27						07 46								08 32							08 51
Appley Bridge	d	07 31						07 49								08 36							08 55
Parbold	d	07 35						07 53															08 59
Hoscar	d							07 56															
Burscough Bridge	d	07 39						07 59								08 42							09 03
New Lane	d							08 02															
Bescar Lane	d							08 05															
Meols Cop	d	07 47						08 10															09 11
Southport	a	07 58						08 22								09 01							09 22
Lostock	d										07 42							08 20					
Horwich Parkway	d									07 38	07 46							08 24					
Blackrod	d										07 49												
Adlington (Lancashire)	d										07 53							08 29					
Chorley	d									07 46	07 58				08 11			08 34					
Buckshaw Parkway	d										08 01							08 37					
Leyland	d										08 08							08 43					
Preston 8 65,97	a									07 57	08 14				08 22			08 50					
	d					07 20				07 59	08 15				08 24		08 38	08 51					
Kirkham & Wesham 97	a									08 08	08 25												
Poulton-le-Fylde 97	a									08 18	08 33												
Layton 97	a									08 22	08 37												
Blackpool North 97	a									08 29	08 46							09 17					
Lancaster 8 65	a					07 36									08 39		08 58						
	d				07 10	07 36									08 40		08 58				09 39		
Oxenholme Lake District 65	a														08 54								
Windermere 83	a																						
Carnforth	d				07a19	07 45											09 08				09 49		
Silverdale	d					07 51											09 14				09 56		
Arnside	d					07 55											09 19				10 00		
Grange-over-Sands	d					08 00											09 25				10 06		
Kents Bank	d					08 04											09 28				10 10		
Cark	d					08 08											09 33				10 14		
Ulverston	d					08 16											09 42				10 23		
Dalton	d					08 24											09 50				10 31		
Roose	d					08 30											09 56				10 37		
Barrow-in-Furness	a					08 39											10 04				10 47		

A To Clitheroe
B To Liverpool Lime Street
C To Leeds
D To Kirkby
E From Manchester Victoria
F To Blackburn
G To Edinburgh
H From Huddersfield
I To Carlisle
J From Hull to Liverpool Lime Street

Manchester - Bolton - Wigan, Kirkby, Southport, Preston, Blackpool North and Barrow-in-Furness

Network Diagram - see first Page of Table 82

		NT	TP	NT	NT	EM	NT	NT	NT	TP	NT	NT	NT	TP		NT	NT	NT	NT	NT	NT
		A	◇1 🍴			◇ B	C	D		◇1 🍴		E		◇1 F 🍴							G
Manchester Airport 85 ✈	d		07 56		08 01					08 25				09 00				09 03			
Heald Green 85	d				08 05					08 29											
Buxton 86	d																				
Hazel Grove 86	d					08 17					08 30										
Stockport 84	d					08 24					08 41										
Manchester Piccadilly 10 ⇌	d		08 15		08 22	08 37				08 46	08 54			09 16				09 22			
Manchester Oxford Road	d		08 19		08 26	08a40				08 49	08 58			09 19				09 26			
Deansgate ⇌	d				08 28					08 51	09 00							09 28			
Rochdale 41	d							08 00											09 04		
Manchester Victoria ⇌	d			08 22			08 29	08 33	08 46			09 00	09 07			09 10	09 22		09 33	09 46	
Salford Central	d			08 25			08 32	08 36	08 49			09 03	09 10			09 13	09 25		09 36	09 49	
Salford Crescent	a			08 29	08 33		08 37	08 39	08 52	08 56	09 04	09 07	09 13			09 16	09 29	09 33	09 39	09 52	
	d			08 30	08 34		08 37	08 40	08 53	08 56	09 04	09 08	09 13			09 17	09 30	09 34	09 40	09 53	
Swinton	d								08 59							09 23				09 59	
Moorside	d															09 26					
Walkden	d								09 04							09 29				10 04	
Atherton	d								09 09							09 35				10 09	
Hag Fold	d															09 37					
Daisy Hill	d								09 13							09 40				10 13	
Kearsley	d							08 47											09 47		
Farnworth	d							08 49											09 49		
Moses Gate	d							08 52											09 52		
Bolton	a		08 32	08 40	08 44		08 49	08 55		09 06	09 14	09 19	09 23	09 32			09 40	09 45	09 55		
	d		08 32	08 40	08 45			08 56		09 07	09 15		09 24	09 33			09 40	09 45	09 56		
Westhoughton	d	←			08 53								09 31					09 53			
Hindley	d	08 43							09 17				09 35			09 45		09 57		10 17	
Ince	d	08 46														09 48					
Wigan North Western	a																				
Wigan Wallgate	a	08 49			09 00			09 16	09 22				09 46			09 51		10 02	10 15	10 22	
	d	08 51			09 05				09 24							09 52		10 03		10 24	
Pemberton	d	08 55														09 56					
Orrell	d	08 59														10 00					
Upholland	d	09 02														10 04					
Rainford	d	09 06														10 07					
Kirkby	a	09 16														10 17					
Gathurst	d								09 28											10 28	
Appley Bridge	d				09 11				09 32									10 10		10 32	
Parbold	d				09 15				09 36									10 14		10 36	
Hoscar	d								09 39												
Burscough Bridge	d				09 20				09 42									10 18		10 40	
New Lane	d								09 44												
Bescar Lane	d								09 48												
Meols Cop	d								09 53											10 48	
Southport	a				09 38				10 04									10 37		10 59	
Lostock	d			08 45							09 20						09 45				
Horwich Parkway	d		08 39	08 49						09 13	09 24						09 49				
Blackrod	d			08 52													09 52				
Adlington (Lancashire)	d			08 56													09 56				
Chorley	d		08 47	09 01						09 21	09 32			09 44			10 01				
Buckshaw Parkway	d			09 05						09 24	09 35						10 05				
Leyland	d			09 12							09 42						10 12				
Preston 8 65,97	a		08 58	09 17						09 33	09 50			09 55			10 17				
	d		08 59	09 19						09 38				09 58	10 07		10 19				
Kirkham & Wesham 97	a			09 28													10 28				
Poulton-le-Fylde 97	a		09 16	09 36						09 56							10 36				
Layton 97	a			09 43													10 43				
Blackpool North 97	a		09 25	09 52						10 05							10 53				
Lancaster 6 65	a													10 13	10 22						
	d														10 23						10 49
Oxenholme Lake District 65	a																				
Windermere 83	a																				
Carnforth	d														10 32						10a58
Silverdale	d																				
Arnside	d														10 41						
Grange-over-Sands	d														10 46						
Kents Bank	d																				
Cark	d																				
Ulverston	d														10 59						
Dalton	d																				
Roose	d																				
Barrow-in-Furness	a														11 17						

A From Manchester Victoria
B From Nottingham to Liverpool Lime Street
C To Blackburn
D From Todmorden
E To Clitheroe
F To Glasgow Central
G From Morecambe to Leeds

Manchester - Bolton - Wigan, Kirkby, Southport, Preston, Blackpool North and Barrow-in-Furness

Network Diagram - see first Page of Table 82

		TP		NT	NT	NT	TP	NT	NT	NT	NT	NT	TP	NT	NT	NT	NT	NT	TP	NT	NT	NT	NT
		◇1 🍴			A		◇1 B 🍴						◇1 🍴		A				◇1 C 🍴				
Manchester Airport 85 ✈	d	09 29					10 00			10 03			10 29						11 00		11 03		
Heald Green 85	d	09 33											10 33										
Buxton 86	d																						
Hazel Grove 86	d			09 30										10 31									
Stockport 84	d			09 41										10 41									
Manchester Piccadilly 10 ⇌	d	09 46		09 54			10 16			10 22			10 46	10 54					11 16		11 22		
Manchester Oxford Road	d	09 49		09 58			10 19			10 26			10 49	10 58					11 19		11 26		
Deansgate ⇌	d	09 51		10 00						10 28			10 51	11 00							11 28		
Rochdale 41	d										10 05											11 04	
Manchester Victoria ⇌	d				10 00	10 07		10 10	10 22		10 33	10 46			11 00	11 07	11 10			11 22		11 33	11 46
Salford Central	d				10 03	10 10		10 13	10 25		10 36	10 49			11 03	11 10	11 13			11 25		11 36	11 49
Salford Crescent	a	09 56		10 04	10 07	10 13		10 16	10 29	10 33	10 39	10 52	10 56	11 04	11 07	11 13	11 16			11 29	11 33	11 39	11 52
	d	09 56		10 04	10 08	10 13		10 17	10 30	10 34	10 40	10 53	10 56	11 04	11 08	11 13	11 17			11 30	11 34	11 40	11 53
Swinton	d							10 23				10 59					11 23						11 59
Moorside	d							10 26									11 26						
Walkden	d							10 29				11 04					11 29						12 04
Atherton	d							10 35				11 09					11 35						12 09
Hag Fold	d							10 37									11 37						
Daisy Hill	d							10 40				11 13					11 40						12 13
Kearsley	d										10 47											11 47	
Farnworth	d										10 49											11 49	
Moses Gate	d										10 52											11 52	
Bolton	a	10 06		10 14	10 19	10 23	10 32		10 40	10 45	10 55		11 06	11 14	11 19	11 23			11 32	11 40	11 45	11 55	
	d	10 07		10 15		10 24	10 33		10 40	10 45	10 56		11 07	11 15		11 24			11 33	11 40	11 45	11 56	
Westhoughton	d					10 31				10 53						11 31					11 53		
Hindley	d					10 35		10 45		10 57		11 17				11 35	11 45				11 57		12 17
Ince	d							10 48									11 48						
Wigan North Western	a																						
Wigan Wallgate	a					10 46		10 51		11 02	11 15	11 22				11 46	11 51				12 02	12 15	12 22
	d							10 52		11 03		11 24					11 52				12 03		12 24
Pemberton	d							10 56									11 56						
Orrell	d							11 00									12 00						
Upholland	d							11 04									12 04						
Rainford	d							11 07									12 07						
Kirkby	a							11 17									12 17						
Gathurst	d											11 28											12 28
Appley Bridge	d									11 10		11 32									12 10		12 32
Parbold	d									11 14		11 36									12 14		12 36
Hoscar	d											11 39											
Burscough Bridge	d									11 18		11 42									12 18		12 41
New Lane	d											11 44											
Bescar Lane	d											11 48											
Meols Cop	d											11 53											12 49
Southport	a									11 37		12 04									12 37		12 59
Lostock	d			10 20					10 45					11 20						11 45			
Horwich Parkway	d	10 13		10 24					10 49				11 13	11 24						11 49			
Blackrod	d								10 52											11 52			
Adlington (Lancashire)	d								10 56											11 56			
Chorley	d	10 21		10 32			10 44		11 01				11 21	11 32					11 44	12 01			
Buckshaw Parkway	d	10 24		10 35					11 05				11 24	11 35						12 05			
Leyland	d			10 42					11 12					11 42						12 12			
Preston 8 65,97	a	10 33		10 51			10 55		11 17				11 33	11 50					11 57	12 17			
	d	10 38	10 45				10 58		11 19				11 38						11 58	12 19			
Kirkham & Wesham 97	a								11 28											12 28			
Poulton-le-Fylde 97	a	10 56							11 36				11 56							12 36			
Layton 97	a								11 43											12 43			
Blackpool North 97	a	11 05							11 52				12 05							12 52			
Lancaster 6 65	a		11 00				11 13												12 13				
	d		11 01				11 14											11 32	12 14				
Oxenholme Lake District 65	a		11 17				11 28																
Windermere 83	a		11 39																				
Carnforth	d																	11 42	12 23				
Silverdale	d																	11 48					
Arnside	d																	11 53	12 32				
Grange-over-Sands	d																	11 59	12 38				
Kents Bank	d																	12 02					
Cark	d																	12 07					
Ulverston	d																	12 15	12 50				
Dalton	d																	12 23					
Roose	d																	12 29					
Barrow-in-Furness	a																	12 39	13 11				

A To Clitheroe
B To Edinburgh
C 🍴 to Preston

Table 82

Mondays to Fridays

from 1 October

Manchester - Bolton - Wigan, Kirkby, Southport, Preston, Blackpool North and Barrow-in-Furness

Network Diagram - see first Page of Table 82

	TP	NT	NT	NT	TP	NT	TP	NT	NT	NT	NT	TP	NT	NT	NT	TP	NT	NT	NT	TP FX	NT	NT
	◇1 🍴		A		◇1 B 🍴		◇1					◇1 🍴		A		◇1 C 🍴			D	◇1 E 🍴		
Manchester Airport 85 ✈ d	11 29				12 00				12 03			12 29				13 00				13 00		13 03
Heald Green 85 d	11 33											12 33										
Buxton 86 d																						
Hazel Grove 86 d		11 31											12 31									
Stockport 84 d		11 41											12 41									
Manchester Piccadilly 10 ⇌ d	11 46	11 54			12 16				12 22			12 46	12 54			13 16				13 16		13 22
Manchester Oxford Road d	11 49	11 58			12 19				12 26			12 49	12 58			13 19				13 19		13 26
Deansgate ⇌ d	11 51	12 00							12 28			12 51	13 00									13 28
Rochdale 41 d										12 04												
Manchester Victoria ⇌ d			12 00	12 07		12 10		12 22		12 33	12 46			13 00	13 07		13 10				13 22	
Salford Central d			12 03	12 10		12 13		12 25		12 36	12 49			13 03	13 10		13 13				13 25	
Salford Crescent a	11 56	12 04	12 07	12 13		12 16		12 29	12 33	12 39	12 52	12 56	13 04	13 07	13 13		13 16				13 29	13 33
d	11 56	12 04	12 08	12 13		12 17		12 30	12 34	12 40	12 53	12 56	13 04	13 08	13 13		13 17				13 30	13 34
Swinton d						12 23					12 59						13 23					
Moorside d						12 26											13 26					
Walkden d						12 29					13 04						13 29					
Atherton d						12 35					13 09						13 35					
Hag Fold d						12 37											13 37					
Daisy Hill d						12 40					13 13						13 40					
Kearsley d										12 47												
Farnworth d										12 49												
Moses Gate d										12 52												
Bolton a	12 06	12 14	12 19	12 23	12 32			12 40	12 45	12 55		13 06	13 14	13 19	13 23	13 32				13 32	13 40	13 45
d	12 07	12 15		12 24	12 33			12 40	12 45	12 56		13 07	13 15		13 24	13 33				13 33	13 40	13 45
Westhoughton d				12 31					12 53						13 31							13 53
Hindley d				12 35		12 45			12 57		13 17				13 35		13 45					13 57
Ince d						12 48											13 48					
Wigan North Western a																						
Wigan Wallgate a				12 46		12 51			13 02	13 15	13 22				13 46		13 51					14 02
d						12 52			13 03		13 24						13 52					14 03
Pemberton d						12 56											13 56					
Orrell d						13 00											14 00					
Upholland d						13 04											14 04					
Rainford d						13 07											14 07					
Kirkby a						13 17											14 17					
Gathurst d											13 28											
Appley Bridge d									13 10		13 32											14 10
Parbold d									13 14		13 36											14 14
Hoscar d											13 39											
Burscough Bridge d									13 18		13 42											14 18
New Lane d											13 44											
Bescar Lane d											13 48											
Meols Cop d											13 53											
Southport a									13 37		14 02											14 37
Lostock d		12 20						12 45					13 20								13 45	
Horwich Parkway d	12 13	12 24						12 49				13 13	13 24								13 49	
Blackrod d								12 52													13 52	
Adlington (Lancashire) d								12 56													13 56	
Chorley d	12 21	12 32			12 44			13 01				13 21	13 32			13 44				13 44	14 01	
Buckshaw Parkway d	12 24	12 35						13 05				13 24	13 35								14 05	
Leyland d		12 42						13 12					13 42								14 12	
Preston 8 65,97 a	12 33	12 50			12 55			13 17				13 33	13 50			13 55				13 55	14 17	
d	12 38				12 58		13 04	13 19				13 38				13 58				14 04	14 19	
Kirkham & Wesham 97 a								13 28													14 28	
Poulton-le-Fylde 97 a	12 56							13 36				13 56									14 36	
Layton 97 a								13 43													14 43	
Blackpool North 97 a	13 05							13 52				14 05									14 53	
Lancaster 6 65 a					13 13		13 19									14 13				14 19		
d					13 14		13 20											13 32	13 48	14 20		
Oxenholme Lake District 65 a					13 28		13 36															
Windermere 83 a							13 56															
Carnforth d																		13 42	13a58	14 28		
Silverdale d																		13 48				
Arnside d																		13 52		14 37		
Grange-over-Sands d																		13 58		14 42		
Kents Bank d																		14 02				
Cark d																		14 06				
Ulverston d																		14 15		14 55		
Dalton d																		14 23				
Roose d																		14 29				
Barrow-in-Furness a																		14 39		15 15		

A To Clitheroe
B To Edinburgh
C To Glasgow Central
D From Heysham Port to Leeds
E 🍴 to Preston

Table 82

Mondays to Fridays

from 1 October

Manchester - Bolton - Wigan, Kirkby, Southport, Preston, Blackpool North and Barrow-in-Furness

Network Diagram - see first Page of Table 82

	NT	NT	TP	NT	NT	NT	NT	TP FO	TP	NT	NT	NT	NT	TP	NT	NT	NT	NT	NT	TP	NT
			◇1 🍴		A			◇1	◇1 B 🍴					◇1 🍴		A			C	◇1 D 🍴	
Manchester Airport 85 ✈ d			13 29						14 00		14 03			14 29						15 00	
Heald Green 85 d			13 33											14 33							
Buxton 86 d																					
Hazel Grove 86 d				13 31											14 31						
Stockport 84 d				13 41											14 41						
Manchester Piccadilly 10 ⇌ d			13 46	13 54					14 16		14 22			14 46	14 54					15 16	
Manchester Oxford Road d			13 49	13 58					14 19		14 26			14 49	14 58					15 19	
Deansgate ⇌ d			13 51	14 00							14 28			14 51	15 00						
Rochdale 41 d	13 04											14 04									
Manchester Victoria ⇌ d	13 33	13 46			14 00	14 07	14 10			14 22		14 33	14 46			15 00	15 07	15 10			15 22
Salford Central d	13 36	13 49			14 03	14 10	14 13			14 25		14 36	14 49			15 03	15 10	15 13			15 25
Salford Crescent a	13 39	13 52	13 56	14 04	14 07	14 13	14 16			14 29	14 33	14 39	14 52	14 56	15 04	15 07	15 13	15 16			15 29
d	13 40	13 53	13 56	14 04	14 08	14 13	14 17			14 30	14 34	14 40	14 53	14 56	15 04	15 08	15 13	15 17			15 30
Swinton d		13 59					14 23						14 59					15 23			
Moorside d							14 26											15 26			
Walkden d		14 04					14 29						15 04					15 29			
Atherton d		14 09					14 35						15 09					15 35			
Hag Fold d							14 37											15 37			
Daisy Hill d		14 13					14 40						15 13					15 40			
Kearsley d	13 47											14 47									
Farnworth d	13 49											14 49									
Moses Gate d	13 52											14 52									
Bolton a	13 55		14 06	14 14	14 19	14 23			14 32	14 40	14 45	14 55		15 06	15 14	15 19	15 23			15 32	15 40
d	13 56		14 07	14 15		14 24			14 33	14 40	14 45	14 56		15 07	15 15		15 24			15 33	15 40
Westhoughton d						14 31					14 53						15 31				
Hindley d		14 17				14 35	14 45				14 57		15 17				15 35	15 45			
Ince d							14 48											15 48			
Wigan North Western a																					
Wigan Wallgate a	14 15	14 22				14 46	14 51				15 02	15 15	15 22				15 46	15 51			
d		14 24					14 52				15 03		15 24					15 58			
Pemberton d							14 56											16 02			
Orrell d							15 00											16 06			
Upholland d							15 04											16 09			
Rainford d							15 07											16 13			
Kirkby a							15 17											16 23			
Gathurst d		14 28											15 28								
Appley Bridge d		14 32									15 10		15 32								
Parbold d		14 36									15 14		15 36								
Hoscar d																					
Burscough Bridge d		14 41									15 18		15 40								
New Lane d																					
Bescar Lane d																					
Meols Cop d		14 49											15 48								
Southport a		15 01									15 37		15 59								
Lostock d				14 20						14 45					15 20						15 45
Horwich Parkway d			14 13	14 24						14 49				15 13	15 24						15 49
Blackrod d										14 52											15 52
Adlington (Lancashire) d										14 56											15 56
Chorley d			14 21	14 32					14 44	15 01				15 21	15 32					15 44	16 01
Buckshaw Parkway d			14 24	14 35						15 05				15 24	15 36						16 05
Leyland d				14 42						15 12					15 42						16 12
Preston 8 65,97 a			14 33	14 50					14 55	15 17				15 33	15 50					15 57	16 19
d			14 38						14 58	15 19				15 38						15 58	
Kirkham & Wesham 97 a										15 28											
Poulton-le-Fylde 97 a			14 56							15 36				15 56							
Layton 97 a										15 43											
Blackpool North 97 a			15 05							15 52				16 05							
Lancaster 6 65 a									15 13											16 14	
d								14 20	15 14										15 34	16 15	
Oxenholme Lake District 65 a									15 28												
Windermere 83 a																					
Carnforth d								14 28											15 44	16 23	
Silverdale d																			15 51	16 29	
Arnside d								14 37											15 55	16 33	
Grange-over-Sands d								14 42											16 01	16 39	
Kents Bank d																			16 05	16 42	
Cark d																			16 09	16 47	
Ulverston d								14 55											16 17	16 55	
Dalton d																			16 26	17 03	
Roose d																			16 32	17 09	
Barrow-in-Furness a								15 15											16 39	17 18	

A To Clitheroe
B To Edinburgh
C To Carlisle
D 🍴 to Preston

Table 82

Mondays to Fridays
from 1 October

Manchester - Bolton - Wigan, Kirkby, Southport, Preston, Blackpool North and Barrow-in-Furness

Network Diagram - see first Page of Table 82

Station		NT	NT	NT A	NT	TP ◇1	NT	NT	NT	NT B	TP ◇1 C	NT D	TP FX ◇1 E	TP ◇1	NT	NT A	NT	NT	NT	TP ◇1	NT	NT	NT A
Manchester Airport 85 ✈	d	15 03				15 29					16 00		16 00				16 03			16 29			
Heald Green 85	d					15 33														16 33			
Buxton 86	d																	15 22					
Hazel Grove 86	d						15 33											16 02				16 30	
Stockport 84	d						15 41											16 12				16 41	
Manchester Piccadilly 10	d	15 22				15 46	15 54				16 16		16 16				16 22	16 27		16 46		16 54	
Manchester Oxford Road	d	15 26				15 49	15 58				16 19		16 19				16 26	16 30		16 49		16 58	
Deansgate	d	15 28				15 51	16 00										16 28	16 33				17 00	
Rochdale 41	d		15 04																16 04				
Manchester Victoria	d		15 33	15 40	15 46			16 07	16 10						16 20	16 23			16 36		16 46		17 00
Salford Central	d		15 36	15 43	15 49			16 10	16 13						16 23	16 26			16 39		16 49		17 03
Salford Crescent	a	15 33	15 39	15 46	15 52	15 56	16 04	16 13	16 16						16 26	16 30	16 34	16 38	16 42		16 52	17 04	17 07
	d	15 34	15 40	15 47	15 53	15 56	16 04	16 13	16 17						16 27	16 31	16 34	16 38	16 43		16 53	17 04	17 08
Swinton	d				15 59				16 23												16 59		
Moorside	d								16 26												17 02		
Walkden	d				16 04				16 29												17 05		
Atherton	d				16 09				16 35												17 11		
Hag Fold	d								16 37												17 14		
Daisy Hill	d				16 13				16 40												17 17		
Kearsley	d		15 47																16 50				
Farnworth	d		15 49																16 52				
Moses Gate	d		15 52					16 21											16 55				
Bolton	a	15 45	15 55	15 59		16 06	16 19	16 25			16 32		16 32		16 37	16 42	16 45	16 48	16 58	17 05		17 14	17 19
	d	15 45	15 56			16 07		16 25			16 33		16 33		16 37		16 45	16 49	16 59	17 06		17 15	
Westhoughton	d	15 53						16 33									16 53		17 06				
Hindley	d	15 57			16 17			16 37	16 45								16 57		17 10		17 21		
Ince	d								16 48												17 24		
Wigan North Western	a																						
Wigan Wallgate	a	16 02	16 15		16 22			16 48	16 51								17 02		17 21		17 33		
	d	16 03			16 24				16 52								17 03						
Pemberton	d								16 56														
Orrell	d								17 00														
Upholland	d								17 04														
Rainford	d								17 07														
Kirkby	a								17 17														
Gathurst	d	16 08			16 28												17 08						
Appley Bridge	d	16 11			16 32												17 11						
Parbold	d	16 15			16 36												17 15						
Hoscar	d	16 18																					
Burscough Bridge	d	16 21			16 40												17 20						
New Lane	d	16 24																					
Bescar Lane	d	16 27																					
Meols Cop	d	16 32			16 48												17 27						
Southport	a	16 44			16 59												17 39						
Lostock	d					16 12									16 43			16 54				17 20	
Horwich Parkway	d					16 15									16 47			16 58				17 24	
Blackrod	d														16 51			17 01					
Adlington (Lancashire)	d														16 55			17 05					
Chorley	d					16 23					16 44		16 44		17 00			17 10		17 19		17 32	
Buckshaw Parkway	d					16 26									17 04			17 13				17 35	
Leyland	d														17 11			17 21				17 42	
Preston 8 65,97	a					16 35					16 55		16 55		17 19			17 26		17 30		17 51	
	d					16 38					17 00		17 04	17 04	17 21			17 28		17 32			
Kirkham & Wesham 97	a					16 47									17 30					17 41			
Poulton-le-Fylde 97	a					16 57									17 38					17 51			
Layton 97	a					17 00									17 43					17 54			
Blackpool North 97	a					17 07									17 52					18 02			
Lancaster 6 65	a										17 15		17 23	17 23				17 48					
	d									16 55	17 16	17 19	17 25	17 25				17 48					
Oxenholme Lake District 65	a										17 30		17 43	17 43									
Windermere 83	a												18 08	18 08									
Carnforth	d									17 05		17 28						18 00					
Silverdale	d									17 12		17 35						18 06					
Arnside	d									17 16		17 40						18 11					
Grange-over-Sands	d									17 22		17 46						18 19					
Kents Bank	d									17 26		17 49						18 23					
Cark	d									17 30		17 54						18 27					
Ulverston	d									17 39		18 02						18 36					
Dalton	d									17 48		18 10						18 44					
Roose	d									17 54		18 17						18 50					
Barrow-in-Furness	a									18 02		18 25						18 59					

A To Clitheroe
B To Millom
C To Edinburgh
D From Morecambe
E to Preston

Table 82

Mondays to Fridays
from 1 October

Manchester - Bolton - Wigan, Kirkby, Southport, Preston, Blackpool North and Barrow-in-Furness

Network Diagram - see first Page of Table 82

Station		TP ◇1 A		NT B	NT	NT	NT C	NT	NT	NT	NT D	NT	TP ◇1	NT	NT E	NT	TP ◇1 F	TP ◇1 G		NT	NT C	NT
Manchester Airport 85 ✈	d	17 00						17 03					17 29					18 00				18 03
Heald Green 85	d												17 33									
Buxton 86	d								16 30					16 59								
Hazel Grove 86	d								17 02					17 33								
Stockport 84	d								17 12					17 41								
Manchester Piccadilly 10	d	17 15						17 22	17 27				17 46	17 54				18 16				18 22
Manchester Oxford Road	d	17 18						17 26	17 30				17 49	17 58				18 19				18 26
Deansgate	d								17 33				17 51	18 00								18 28
Rochdale 41	d						17 03														18 02	
Manchester Victoria	d			17 06	17 10	17 19	17 23			17 36	17 40	17 45			18 00	18 10				18 20	18 23	
Salford Central	d			17 09	17 12	17 22	17 27			17 39	17 43	17 48			18 03	18 13				18 23	18 26	
Salford Crescent	a			17 13	17 16	17 25	17 29	17 34	17 38	17 42	17 46	17 51	17 55	18 04	18 07	18 16				18 26	18 30	18 34
	d			17 14	17 17	17 27	17 30	17 34	17 38	17 43	17 47	17 52	17 55	18 04	18 08	18 17				18 27	18 31	18 34
Swinton	d				17 23							17 58				18 23						
Moorside	d				17 26							18 01				18 26						
Walkden	d				17 31							18 05				18 29						
Atherton	d			17 27	17 37						18 00	18 11				18 35						
Hag Fold	d				17 39							18 13				18 37						
Daisy Hill	d			17 31	17 43						18 04	18 17				18 40						
Kearsley	d									17 53												
Farnworth	d									17 55												
Moses Gate	d									17 57												
Bolton	a	17 31				17 37	17 42	17 45	17 48	18 01			18 06	18 14	18 19			18 32		18 37	18 42	18 45
	d	17 32				17 37		17 45	17 49	18 01			18 07	18 15				18 33		18 37		18 45
Westhoughton	d							17 53		18 09												18 53
Hindley	d				17 48					18 13		18 22				18 45						18 57
Ince	d				17 51							18 25				18 48						
Wigan North Western	a															18 56						
Wigan Wallgate	a			17 39	17 54			18 01		18 24	18 12	18 28										19 02
	d			17 40	17 55			18 02			18 15	18 29										19 03
Pemberton	d				17 59							18 33										
Orrell	d				18 03							18 37										
Upholland	d				18 07							18 41										
Rainford	d				18 10							18 44										
Kirkby	a				18 20							18 54										
Gathurst	d			17 45							18 20											19 08
Appley Bridge	d			17 48				18 09			18 24											19 11
Parbold	d			17 53				18 13			18 28											19 15
Hoscar	d										18 31											
Burscough Bridge	d			17 58				18 17			18 35											19 19
New Lane	d										18 37											
Bescar Lane	d										18 41											
Meols Cop	d			18 05				18 26			18 46											19 27
Southport	a			18 17				18 37			18 57											19 39
Lostock	d					17 43			17 54				18 12	18 20						18 42		
Horwich Parkway	d					17 47			17 58				18 15	18 24						18 46		
Blackrod	d					17 51			18 01				18 19							18 49		
Adlington (Lancashire)	d					17 55			18 05											18 53		
Chorley	d	17 44				18 00			18 10				18 26	18 32				18 44		18 58		
Buckshaw Parkway	d					18 03			18 13					18 35						19 02		
Leyland	d					18 11								18 42						19 10		
Preston 8 65,97	a	17 55				18 16			18 25				18 38	18 48				18 55		19 18		
	d	17 58	18 08			18 18			18 26				18 40	18 49				19 00	19 04	19 19		
Kirkham & Wesham 97	a					18 27							18 49							19 28		
Poulton-le-Fylde 97	a					18 35			18 43				18 59							19 36		
Layton 97	a					18 39							19 02							19 43		
Blackpool North 97	a					18 51			18 55				19 10	19 16						19 52		
Lancaster 6 65	a	18 13	18 23															19 15	19 20			
	d	18 14	18 24														18 29	19 16	19 20			
Oxenholme Lake District 65	a	18 28															18 45	19 30				
Windermere 83	a																19 08					
Carnforth	d		18 34																19 29			
Silverdale	d		18 40																19 35			
Arnside	d		18 44																19 39			
Grange-over-Sands	d		18 50																19 44			
Kents Bank	d		18 53																19 48			
Cark	d		18 58																19 52			
Ulverston	d		19 06																20 00			
Dalton	d		19 14																20 08			
Roose	d		19 20																20 14			
Barrow-in-Furness	a		19 29																20 24			

A To Glasgow Central
B from 1 October until 19 October. From Stalybridge
C To Blackburn
D from 1 October until 19 October
E To Clitheroe
F From Barrow-in-Furness
G To Edinburgh

Table 82

Mondays to Fridays
from 1 October

Manchester - Bolton - Wigan, Kirkby, Southport, Preston, Blackpool North and Barrow-in-Furness

Network Diagram - see first Page of Table 82

	NT	NT	TP ◇1	NT	NT A	NT	NT B	TP ◇1	NT	NT	TP ◇1	NT A	TP ◇1	NT	NT	NT	NT C	TP ◇1	NT A	NT	NT	NT
Manchester Airport 85 ✈ d			18 29					19 00	19 03		19 29		20 00			20 03	20 09	20 29				
Heald Green 85 d			18 33								19 33						20 12	20 33				
Buxton 86 d				17 55																		
Hazel Grove 86 d				18 33																		
Stockport 84 d				18 41																		
Manchester Piccadilly 10 ⇌ d			18 46	18 54				19 16	19 20		19 46		20 16			20 20	20 32	20 46				
Manchester Oxford Road d			18 49	18 58				19 19	19 24		19 49		20 19			20 24	20a36	20 49				
Deansgate ⇌ d			18 51	19 00					19 26		19 51					20 26		20 51				
Rochdale 41 d																						
Manchester Victoria ⇌ d	18 33	18 45			19 00	19 10				19 28		20 00		20 10	20 22				21 00	21 10		21 22
Salford Central d	18 36	18 48			19 03	19 13				19 31		20 03		20 13	20 25				21 03	21 13		21 25
Salford Crescent a	18 39	18 51	18 56	19 04	19 07	19 16			19 29	19 34	19 56	20 07		20 16	20 29	20 33		20 56	21 07	21 16		21 29
d	18 40	18 52	18 56	19 04	19 08	19 17			19 30	19 35	19 56	20 08		20 17	20 30	20 34		20 56	21 08	21 17		21 30
Swinton d		18 58				19 23								20 23						21 23		
Moorside d		19 01				19 26								20 26						21 26		
Walkden d		19 04				19 29								20 29						21 29		
Atherton d		19 10				19 35								20 35						21 35		
Hag Fold d		19 12				19 37								20 37						21 37		
Daisy Hill d		19 15				19 40								20 40						21 40		
Kearsley d	18 47																					
Farnworth d	18 49																					
Moses Gate d	18 52																					
Bolton a	18 55		19 06	19 19	19 20			19 32	19 40	19 45	20 06	20 19	20 32		20 40	20 45		21 06	21 19			21 40
d	18 56		19 07					19 33	19 40	19 45	20 07		20 33		20 40	20 45		21 07				21 40
Westhoughton d	19 03								19 48							20 53						
Hindley d	19 09	19 20				19 45			19 52					20 45		20 57				21 45		
Ince d		19 23				19 48								20 48						21 48		
Wigan North Western a																						
Wigan Wallgate a	19 20	19 32				19 57			19 57					20 57		21 02				21 57		
d									19 59							21 03						
Pemberton d																						
Orrell d																						
Upholland d																						
Rainford d																						
Kirkby a																						
Gathurst d									20 03							21 08						
Appley Bridge d									20 07							21 11						
Parbold d									20 11							21 15						
Hoscar d																21 18						
Burscough Bridge d									20 15							21 21						
New Lane d																21 24						
Bescar Lane d																21 27						
Meols Cop d									20 23							21 32						
Southport a									20 34							21 42						
Lostock d			19 12							19 50					20 45							21 45
Horwich Parkway d			19 15							19 54	20 13		20 39		20 49			21 13				21 49
Blackrod d										19 57					20 52							21 52
Adlington (Lancashire) d										20 01					20 56							21 56
Chorley d			19 23					19 44		20 06	20 21		20 46		21 01			21 21				22 01
Buckshaw Parkway d			19 26							20 10	20 24				21 05			21 24				22 05
Leyland d										20 18					21 12							22 12
Preston 8 65,97 a			19 33					19 55		20 23	20 33		20 57		21 17			21 33				22 17
d			19 38					19 58		20 25	20 38		20 59		21 19			21 38			21 51	22 19
Kirkham & Wesham 97 a										20 34					21 28							22 28
Poulton-le-Fylde 97 a			19 56							20 42	20 56				21 36			21 56				22 36
Layton 97 a										20 46					21 40							22 43
Blackpool North 97 a			20 06							20 56	21 06				21 50			22 06				22 53
Lancaster 6 65 a								20 13					21 14								22 11	
d							19 24	20 14					21 15								22 11	
Oxenholme Lake District 65 a																						
Windermere 83 a																						
Carnforth d							19a34	20 22					21 23								22 21	
Silverdale d								20 28					21 29								22 27	
Arnside d								20 32					21 33								22 32	
Grange-over-Sands d								20 38					21 39								22 38	
Kents Bank d								20 41					21 42								22 41	
Cark d								20 46					21 47								22 46	
Ulverston d								20 54					21 55								22 54	
Dalton d								21 02					22 03								23 02	
Roose d								21 08					22 09								23 08	
Barrow-in-Furness a								21 17					22 18								23 16	

A To Clitheroe
B From Morecambe to Leeds
C From Wilmslow

Table 82

Mondays to Fridays
from 1 October

Manchester - Bolton - Wigan, Kirkby, Southport, Preston, Blackpool North and Barrow-in-Furness

Network Diagram - see first Page of Table 82

	NT	NT A	NT B	TP ◇1	NT C	TP ◇1	NT A	NT FO	NT FX	NT	NT	TP ◇1	NT	NT D	NT FO	NT FX	NT	TP FX ◇1 E
Manchester Airport 85 ✈ d	21 03	21 09		21 29		22 00	22 08				22 19	22 29						23 18
Heald Green 85 d		21 12		21 33			22 12					22 33						
Buxton 86 d																		
Hazel Grove 86 d																		
Stockport 84 d													22 34					
Manchester Piccadilly 10 ⇌ d	21 20	21 32	21 38	21 46		22 16	22 32				22 36	22 46	22 50					23 38
Manchester Oxford Road d	21 24	21a36	21 44	21 49		22 19	22a36				22 39	22 49	22 53					
Deansgate ⇌ d	21 26		21a46	21 51							22 41	22 51	22 55					
Rochdale 41 d																		
Manchester Victoria ⇌ d					22 00			22 10	22 10	22 22				23 00	23 20	23 20	23 23	
Salford Central d					22b04			22 13		22b25				23b03	23 23		23b26	
Salford Crescent a	21 33			21 56	22 07			22 17	22 17	22 29	22 46	22 56	22 59	23 07	23 26	23 25	23 29	23 43
d	21 34			21 56	22 08			22 17	22 17	22 30	22 46	22 56	22 59	23 08	23 26	23 26	23 30	
Swinton d								22 23	22 23						23 33	23 33		
Moorside d								22 26	22 26						23 35	23 35		
Walkden d								22 29	22 29						23 39	23 39		
Atherton d								22 35	22 35						23 44	23 44		
Hag Fold d								22 37	22 37						23 47	23 47		
Daisy Hill d								22 40	22 40						23 50	23 50		
Kearsley d													23 07					
Farnworth d													23 09					
Moses Gate d													23 11					
Bolton a	21 45			22 06	22 19	22 32				22 40	22 56	23 06	23 15	23 19			23 40	
d	21 45			22 07		22 33				22 40	22 57	23 07	23 15				23 40	
Westhoughton d	21 53										23 04		23 23					
Hindley d	21 57							22 45	22 45		23 08		23 27		23 54	23 54		
Ince d								22 48	22 48						23 57	23 57		
Wigan North Western a						22 48												
Wigan Wallgate a	22 02							22 57	22 57		23 13		23 40		00 06	00 06		
d	22 03										23 15							
Pemberton d																		
Orrell d																		
Upholland d																		
Rainford d																		
Kirkby a																		
Gathurst d	22 08										23 19							
Appley Bridge d	22 11										23 23							
Parbold d	22 15										23 27							
Hoscar d																		
Burscough Bridge d	22 20										23 31							
New Lane d																		
Bescar Lane d																		
Meols Cop d	22 27										23 39							
Southport a	22 39										23 50							
Lostock d										22 45							23 45	
Horwich Parkway d				22 13						22 49		23 13					23 49	
Blackrod d										22 52							23 52	
Adlington (Lancashire) d										22 56							23 56	
Chorley d				22 21						23 01		23 21					00 01	
Buckshaw Parkway d				22 24						23 05		23 24					00 05	
Leyland d										23 12							00 12	
Preston 8 65,97 a				22 36		23 09				23 17		23 33					00 17	
d				22 38		23 13				23 19		23 35					00 19	
Kirkham & Wesham 97 a										23 28							00 28	
Poulton-le-Fylde 97 a				22 55						23 36		23 52					00 36	
Layton 97 a										23 40							00 43	
Blackpool North 97 a				23 04						23 50		00 02					00 52	
Lancaster 6 65 a						23 28												
d						23 29												
Oxenholme Lake District 65 a																		
Windermere 83 a																		
Carnforth d						23 37												
Silverdale d						23 43												
Arnside d						23 47												
Grange-over-Sands d						23 53												
Kents Bank d						23 56												
Cark d						00 01												
Ulverston d						00 09												
Dalton d						00 17												
Roose d						00 23												
Barrow-in-Furness a						00 31												

A From Wilmslow
B To Warrington Central
C To Clitheroe
D To Blackburn
E To York
b Fridays only

Table 82

Saturdays until 29 September

Manchester - Bolton - Wigan, Kirkby, Southport, Preston, Blackpool North and Barrow-in-Furness

Network Diagram - see first Page of Table 82

Station		TP ◇1	TP ◇1	NT	NT	TP ◇1	TP ◇1	NT B	TP ◇1	TP 1	NT C	NT	TP ◇1 D	NT	TP ◇1 E	NT	NT	NT	NT C	TP ◇1 B	TP ◇1
Manchester Airport 85 ✈	d	22p00	22p29			00 01	04 00	04 34					05 45		06 18						
Heald Green 85	d		22p33										05 49								
Buxton 86	d																		05 59		
Hazel Grove 86	d																		06 33		
Stockport 84	d																		06 41		
Manchester Piccadilly 10 ⇌	d	22p16	22p46			00 16	04 15	04a47	05 43				06 03		06 33				06 54	07 07	
Manchester Oxford Road	d	22p19	22p49										06 06		06 36				06 57	07a09	
Deansgate ⇌	d		22p51																06 59		
Rochdale 41	d																				
Manchester Victoria ⇌	d			23p20	23p23						05 55	06 00		06 17		06 38		06 45			
Salford Central	d			23p23	23p26											06 40		06 48			
Salford Crescent	a		22p56	23p26	23p29				05 48		05 59	06 04		06 23		06 44		06 51	07 03		
	d		22p56	23p26	23p30				05 49		06 00	06 05		06 24		06 45		06 52	07 03		
Swinton	d			23p33														06 58			
Moorside	d			23p35																	
Walkden	d			23p39														07 03			
Atherton	d			23p44														07 08			
Hag Fold	d			23p47																	
Daisy Hill	d			23p50														07 12			
Kearsley	d															06 52					
Farnworth	d															06 54					
Moses Gate	d															06 57					
Bolton	a	22p32	23p06		23p40	00s31	04s29		05 59		06 11	06 15	06 19	06 34	06 50	07 00			07 16		
	d	22p33	23p07		23p40				05 59			06 15	06 19	06 34	06 50	07 01					
Westhoughton	d											06 23									
Hindley	d			23p54								06 27						07 16			
Ince	d			23p57																	
Wigan North Western	a	22p48														07 19					
Wigan Wallgate	a			00 04								06 32						07 21			
	d											06 34					06 40	07 23			
Pemberton	d											06 38									
Orrell	d											06 42									
Upholland	d											06 45									
Rainford	d											06 49									
Kirkby	a											07 01									
Gathurst	d																06 44	07 27			
Appley Bridge	d																06 48	07 31			
Parbold	d																06 52	07 35			
Hoscar	d																06 55				
Burscough Bridge	d																06 58	07 39			
New Lane	d																07 00				
Bescar Lane	d																07 04				
Meols Cop	d																07 09	07 47			
Southport	a																07 18	07 56			
Lostock	d				23p45									06 39							
Horwich Parkway	d		23p13		23p49				06 06					06 43							
Blackrod	d				23p52									06 46							
Adlington (Lancashire)	d				23p56									06 50							
Chorley	d		23p21		00 01				06 13				06 31	06 55							
Buckshaw Parkway	d		23p24		00 05									06 59							
Leyland	d				00 12				06 22					07 06							
Preston 8 65,97	a	23p09	23p33		00 17	01s05	05s04		06 26				06 42	07 11	07 11						
	d	23p13	23p35		00 19				06 37				06 44	07 13	07 14						07 20
Kirkham & Wesham 97	a				00 28				06 46					07 22							
Poulton-le-Fylde 97	a		23p52		00 36				06 56					07 30							
Layton 97	a				00 43				06 59					07 34							
Blackpool North 97	a		00 02		00 50	01 30	05 33		07 06					07 41							
Lancaster 6 65	a	23p28											06 59		07 30						07 36
	d	23p29								05 46			07 00								07 36
Oxenholme Lake District 65	a									06 21			07 15								
Windermere 83	a									06 41											
Carnforth	d	23p37																			07 45
Silverdale	d	23p43																			07 51
Arnside	d	23p47																			07 55
Grange-over-Sands	d	23p53																			08 00
Kents Bank	d	23p56																			08 04
Cark	d	00 01																			08 08
Ulverston	d	00 09																			08 16
Dalton	d	00 17																			08 24
Roose	d	00 23																			08 30
Barrow-in-Furness	a	00 31																			08 39

B To Liverpool Lime Street
C To Clitheroe
D To Edinburgh
E To Glasgow Central

Table 82

Saturdays until 29 September

Manchester - Bolton - Wigan, Kirkby, Southport, Preston, Blackpool North and Barrow-in-Furness

Network Diagram - see first Page of Table 82

Station		NT A	NT B	NT	NT C	TP ◇1	NT	NT D	TP ◇1 E	NT	NT	NT F	TP ◇1 G	NT	NT	NT H	TP ◇1	NT	NT	EM ◇ I	NT D	NT J	NT
Manchester Airport 85 ✈	d					07 00			07 25								07 56		08 01				
Heald Green 85	d								07 30										08 05				
Buxton 86	d																						
Hazel Grove 86	d										07 32									08 17			
Stockport 84	d										07 40									08 24			
Manchester Piccadilly 10 ⇌	d					07 15			07 45		07 54		08 07				08 15		08 22	08 37			
Manchester Oxford Road	d					07 18					07 58		08a09				08 19		08 26	08a40			
Deansgate ⇌	d										08 00								08 28				
Rochdale 41	d																					08 00	
Manchester Victoria ⇌	d		07 06	07 10			07 16	07 23		07 27		08 00		08 07	08 10			08 23			08 29	08 34	08 46
Salford Central	d		07 09	07 13			07 19	07 26		07 30		08 03		08 10	08 13			08 26			08 32	08 37	08 49
Salford Crescent	a		07 12	07 16			07 24	07 29		07 33	08 04	08 07		08 13	08 16			08 29	08 33		08 37	08 40	08 52
	d		07 13	07 16			07 25	07 30		07 33	08 04	08 08		08 13	08 17			08 30	08 34		08 37	08 41	08 53
Swinton	d		07 19												08 23								08 59
Moorside	d		07 22												08 26								
Walkden	d		07 25							07 43					08 29								09 04
Atherton	d		07 31							07 48					08 35								09 09
Hag Fold	d		07 33												08 37								
Daisy Hill	d		07 36							07 52					08 40								09 13
Kearsley	d																					08 48	
Farnworth	d																					08 50	
Moses Gate	d																					08 53	
Bolton	a			07 26		07 31	07 35	07 41	07 59		08 14	08 19		08 23			08 32	08 40	08 44		08 49	08 56	
	d			07 27		07 31	07 35		07 59		08 15			08 24			08 32	08 40	08 45			08 57	
Westhoughton	d			07 34	←									08 31					08 53				
Hindley	d		07 42	07 38	07 42									08 35	08 45								09 17
Ince	d		→		07 45										08 48								
Wigan North Western	a																						
Wigan Wallgate	a			07 43	07 48					08 03				08 44	08 51				09 00			09 14	09 22
	d			07 45	07 50										08 52				09 05				09 24
Pemberton	d				07 54										08 56								
Orrell	d				07 58										09 00								
Upholland	d				08 01										09 04								
Rainford	d				08 05										09 07								
Kirkby	a				08 17										09 19								
Gathurst	d			07 49																			09 28
Appley Bridge	d			07 53															09 11				09 32
Parbold	d			07 57															09 15				09 36
Hoscar	d			08 00																			09 39
Burscough Bridge	d			08 03															09 20				09 42
New Lane	d			08 05																			09 44
Bescar Lane	d			08 09																			09 48
Meols Cop	d			08 14																			09 53
Southport	a			08 23															09 36				10 02
Lostock	d						07 42				08 20							08 45					
Horwich Parkway	d					07 38	07 46				08 24						08 39	08 49					
Blackrod	d						07 49											08 52					
Adlington (Lancashire)	d						07 53				08 29							08 56					
Chorley	d					07 46	07 58		08 11		08 34						08 47	09 01					
Buckshaw Parkway	d						08 01				08 37							09 05					
Leyland	d						08 08				08 43							09 12					
Preston 8 65,97	a					07 57	08 14		08 22		08 50						08 58	09 17					
	d					07 59	08 15		08 24							08 42	08 59	09 19					
Kirkham & Wesham 97	a					08 08	08 25											09 28					
Poulton-le-Fylde 97	a					08 18	08 33										09 16	09 36					
Layton 97	a					08 22	08 37											09 43					
Blackpool North 97	a					08 29	08 44										09 25	09 50					
Lancaster 6 65	a								08 39							09 02							
	d	08 24														09 03							
Oxenholme Lake District 65	a																						
Windermere 83	a																						
Carnforth	d	08a33														09 13							
Silverdale	d															09 18							
Arnside	d															09 23							
Grange-over-Sands	d															09 29							
Kents Bank	d															09 32							
Cark	d															09 37							
Ulverston	d															09 45							
Dalton	d															09 53							
Roose	d															09 59							
Barrow-in-Furness	a															10 07							

A To Leeds
B To Kirkby
C From Manchester Victoria
D To Blackburn
E To Edinburgh
F To Clitheroe
G From Hull to Liverpool Lime Street
H To Carlisle
I From Nottingham to Liverpool Lime Street
J From Hebden Bridge

Table 82

Saturdays
until 29 September

Manchester - Bolton - Wigan, Kirkby, Southport, Preston, Blackpool North and Barrow-in-Furness

Network Diagram - see first Page of Table 82

		TP ◇1 A ⚒		NT	NT B	NT	NT	TP ◇1 C	TP ◇1 D ⚒		NT	NT		NT E	NT	NT	TP ◇1 ⚒	NT	NT B	NT	NT	NT F		TP ◇1	TP ◇1 G ⚒
Manchester Airport 85 ✈	d	08 25							09 00			09 03					09 29								10 00
Heald Green 85	d	08 29															09 33								
Buxton 86	d			07 56																					
Hazel Grove 86	d			08 33														09 32							
Stockport 84	d			08 41														09 42							
Manchester Piccadilly 10 ⇌	d	08 46		08 54					09 16			09 22					09 46	09 54							10 16
Manchester Oxford Road	d	08 49		08 58					09 19			09 26					09 49	09 58							10 19
Deansgate ⇌	d	08 51		09 00								09 28					09 51	10 00							
Rochdale 41	d														09 04										
Manchester Victoria ⇌	d				09 00	09 07	09 10				09 22			09 29	09 33	09 46			10 00	10 07	10 10				
Salford Central	d				09 03	09 10	09 13				09 25			09 32	09 37	09 49			10 03	10 10	10 13				
Salford Crescent	a	08 56		09 04	09 07	09 13	09 16				09 29	09 33		09 37	09 40	09 52	09 56	10 04	10 07	10 13	10 16				
	d	08 56		09 04	09 08	09 13	09 17				09 30	09 34		09 37	09 41	09 53	09 56	10 04	10 08	10 13	10 17				
Swinton	d						09 23									09 59					10 23				
Moorside	d						09 26														10 26				
Walkden	d						09 29									10 04					10 29				
Atherton	d						09 35									10 09					10 35				
Hag Fold	d						09 37														10 37				
Daisy Hill	d						09 40									10 13					10 40				
Kearsley	d														09 48										
Farnworth	d														09 50										
Moses Gate	d														09 53										
Bolton	a	09 06		09 14	09 19	09 23			09 32		09 40	09 44		09 49	09 56		10 06	10 14	10 19	10 23					10 32
	d	09 07		09 15		09 24			09 33		09 40	09 45			09 57		10 07	10 15		10 24					10 33
Westhoughton	d					09 31						09 53								10 31					
Hindley	d					09 35	09 45					09 57				10 17				10 35	10 45				
Ince	d						09 48														10 48				
Wigan North Western	a																								
Wigan Wallgate	a					09 44	09 51					10 02			10 13	10 22				10 44	10 51				
	d						09 52					10 03				10 24					10 52				
Pemberton	d						09 56														10 56				
Orrell	d						10 00														11 00				
Upholland	d						10 04														11 04				
Rainford	d						10 07														11 07				
Kirkby	a						10 19														11 19				
Gathurst	d															10 28									
Appley Bridge	d											10 10				10 32									
Parbold	d											10 14				10 36									
Hoscar	d																								
Burscough Bridge	d											10 18				10 40									
New Lane	d																								
Bescar Lane	d																								
Meols Cop	d															10 48									
Southport	a											10 35				10 57									
Lostock	d			09 20							09 45							10 20							
Horwich Parkway	d			09 24							09 49						10 13	10 24							
Blackrod	d										09 52														
Adlington (Lancashire)	d										09 56														
Chorley	d	09 19		09 32					09 44		10 01						10 21	10 32							10 44
Buckshaw Parkway	d			09 35							10 05						10 24	10 35							
Leyland	d			09 42							10 12							10 42							
Preston 8 65,97	a	09 30		09 50					09 55		10 17						10 33	10 50							10 55
	d	09 32						09 45	09 58	10 08	10 19						10 38							10 45	10 58
Kirkham & Wesham 97	a										10 28														
Poulton-le-Fylde 97	a									10 26	10 36						10 56								
Layton 97	a										10 43														
Blackpool North 97	a									10 35	10 51						11 05								
Lancaster 6 65	a	09 47						10 00	10 13															11 00	11 13
	d	09 48						10 01														10 49		11 01	11 14
Oxenholme Lake District 65	a	10 04																						11 17	11 28
Windermere 83	a	10 26																						11 39	
Carnforth	d							10 09														10a58			
Silverdale	d							10 15																	
Arnside	d							10 19																	
Grange-over-Sands	d							10 25																	
Kents Bank	d							10 28																	
Cark	d							10 33																	
Ulverston	d							10 41																	
Dalton	d							10 49																	
Roose	d							10 55																	
Barrow-in-Furness	a							11 04																	

A ⚒ to Preston
B To Clitheroe
C From Blackpool North
D To Glasgow Central
E To Blackburn
F From Morecambe to Leeds
G To Edinburgh

Table 82

Saturdays
until 29 September

Manchester - Bolton - Wigan, Kirkby, Southport, Preston, Blackpool North and Barrow-in-Furness

Network Diagram - see first Page of Table 82

		NT	NT	NT	NT	TP ◇1 ⚒	NT	NT A		NT	NT	NT B	TP ◇1 C ⚒	NT	NT	NT	NT	TP ◇1 ⚒		NT	NT A	NT	TP ◇1 D ⚒	NT	TP ◇1
Manchester Airport 85 ✈	d		10 03			10 29							11 00		11 03			11 29					12 00		
Heald Green 85	d					10 33												11 33							
Buxton 86	d																								
Hazel Grove 86	d						10 33													11 33					
Stockport 84	d						10 41													11 41					
Manchester Piccadilly 10 ⇌	d		10 22			10 46	10 54						11 16		11 22			11 46		11 54			12 16		
Manchester Oxford Road	d		10 26			10 49	10 58						11 19		11 26			11 49		11 58			12 19		
Deansgate ⇌	d		10 28			10 51	11 00								11 28			11 51		12 00					
Rochdale 41	d			10 05												11 04									
Manchester Victoria ⇌	d	10 22		10 33	10 46			11 00		11 07	11 10			11 22		11 33	11 46				12 00	12 07		12 10	
Salford Central	d	10 25		10 36	10 49			11 03		11 10	11 13			11 25		11 36	11 49				12 03	12 10		12 13	
Salford Crescent	a	10 29	10 33	10 39	10 52	10 56	11 04	11 07		11 13	11 16			11 29	11 33	11 39	11 52	11 56		12 04	12 07	12 13		12 16	
	d	10 30	10 35	10 40	10 53	10 56	11 04	11 08		11 13	11 17			11 30	11 35	11 40	11 53	11 56		12 04	12 08	12 13		12 17	
Swinton	d				10 59						11 23						11 59							12 23	
Moorside	d										11 26													12 26	
Walkden	d				11 04						11 29						12 04							12 29	
Atherton	d				11 09						11 35						12 09							12 35	
Hag Fold	d										11 37													12 37	
Daisy Hill	d				11 13						11 40						12 13							12 40	
Kearsley	d			10 47												11 47									
Farnworth	d			10 49												11 49									
Moses Gate	d			10 52												11 52									
Bolton	a	10 40	10 45	10 55		11 06	11 14	11 19		11 23			11 32	11 40	11 45	11 55		12 06		12 14	12 19	12 23	12 32		
	d	10 40	10 45	10 56		11 07	11 15			11 24			11 33	11 40	11 45	11 56		12 07		12 15		12 24	12 33		
Westhoughton	d		10 53							11 31					11 53							12 31			
Hindley	d		10 57		11 17					11 35	11 45				11 57		12 17					12 35		12 45	
Ince	d										11 48													12 48	
Wigan North Western	a																								
Wigan Wallgate	a		11 02	11 13	11 22					11 44	11 51				12 02	12 13	12 22					12 44		12 51	
	d		11 03		11 24						11 52				12 03		12 24							12 52	
Pemberton	d										11 56													12 56	
Orrell	d										12 00													13 00	
Upholland	d										12 04													13 04	
Rainford	d										12 07													13 07	
Kirkby	a										12 19													13 19	
Gathurst	d				11 28												12 28								
Appley Bridge	d		11 10		11 32										12 10		12 32								
Parbold	d		11 14		11 36										12 14		12 36								
Hoscar	d				11 39																				
Burscough Bridge	d		11 18		11 42										12 18		12 41								
New Lane	d				11 44																				
Bescar Lane	d				11 48																				
Meols Cop	d				11 53												12 49								
Southport	a		11 35		12 02										12 35		12 59								
Lostock	d	10 45					11 20							11 45						12 20					
Horwich Parkway	d	10 49				11 13	11 24							11 49				12 13		12 24					
Blackrod	d	10 52												11 52											
Adlington (Lancashire)	d	10 56												11 56											
Chorley	d	11 01				11 21	11 32						11 44	12 01				12 21		12 32			12 44		
Buckshaw Parkway	d	11 05				11 24	11 35							12 05				12 24		12 35					
Leyland	d	11 12					11 42							12 12						12 42					
Preston 8 65,97	a	11 17				11 33	11 50						11 55	12 17				12 33		12 50			12 55		
	d	11 19				11 38							11 58	12 19				12 38					12 58		13 04
Kirkham & Wesham 97	a	11 28												12 28											
Poulton-le-Fylde 97	a	11 36				11 56								12 36				12 56							
Layton 97	a	11 44												12 43											
Blackpool North 97	a	11 50				12 05								12 50				13 05							
Lancaster 6 65	a												12 13										13 13		13 19
	d											11 28	12 14										13 14		13 20
Oxenholme Lake District 65	a																						13 28		13 36
Windermere 83	a																								13 56
Carnforth	d											11 37	12 23												
Silverdale	d											11 43													
Arnside	d											11 48	12 32												
Grange-over-Sands	d											11 54	12 38												
Kents Bank	d											11 57													
Cark	d											12 02													
Ulverston	d											12 10	12 50												
Dalton	d											12 18													
Roose	d											12 24													
Barrow-in-Furness	a											12 32	13 11												

A To Clitheroe
B To Carlisle
C ⚒ to Preston
D To Edinburgh

Table 82

Saturdays
until 29 September

Manchester - Bolton - Wigan, Kirkby, Southport, Preston, Blackpool North and Barrow-in-Furness

Network Diagram - see first Page of Table 82

		NT	NT	NT	NT	TP ◇1 ✕	NT	NT A	NT	TP ◇1 B ✕	NT	NT C	NT D	TP ◇1 E ✕	TP ◇1 F ✕	NT	NT	NT	NT	TP ◇1 ✕	NT	NT A
Manchester Airport 85 ✈	d		12 03			12 29				13 00				13 00			13 03			13 29		
Heald Green 85	d					12 33														13 33		
Buxton 86	d																					
Hazel Grove 86	d						12 33														13 33	
Stockport 84	d						12 41														13 41	
Manchester Piccadilly	d		12 22			12 46	12 54			13 16				13 16			13 22			13 46	13 54	
Manchester Oxford Road	d		12 26			12 49	12 58			13 19				13 19			13 26			13 49	13 58	
Deansgate	d		12 28			12 51	13 00										13 28			13 51	14 00	
Rochdale 41	d			12 04														13 04				
Manchester Victoria	d	12 22		12 33	12 46			13 00	13 07		13 10					13 22		13 33	13 46			14 00
Salford Central	d	12 25		12 36	12 49			13 03	13 10		13 13					13 25		13 36	13 49			14 03
Salford Crescent	a	12 29	12 33	12 39	12 52	12 56	13 04	13 07	13 13		13 16					13 29	13 33	13 39	13 52	13 56	14 04	14 07
	d	12 30	12 35	12 40	12 53	12 56	13 04	13 08	13 13		13 17					13 30	13 34	13 40	13 53	13 56	14 04	14 08
Swinton	d				12 59						13 23								13 59			
Moorside	d										13 26											
Walkden	d				13 04						13 29								14 04			
Atherton	d				13 09						13 35								14 09			
Hag Fold	d										13 37											
Daisy Hill	d				13 13						13 40								14 13			
Kearsley	d			12 47														13 47				
Farnworth	d			12 49														13 49				
Moses Gate	d			12 52														13 52				
Bolton	a	12 40	12 45	12 55		13 06	13 14	13 19	13 23	13 32				13 32		13 40	13 45	13 55		14 06	14 14	14 19
	d	12 40	12 45	12 56		13 07	13 15		13 24	13 33				13 33		13 40	13 45	13 56		14 07	14 15	
Westhoughton	d		12 53						13 31								13 53					
Hindley	d		12 57		13 17				13 35		13 45						13 57		14 17			
Ince	d										13 48											
Wigan North Western	a																					
Wigan Wallgate	a		13 02	13 13	13 22				13 44		13 51						14 02	14 13	14 22			
	d		13 03		13 24						13 52						14 03		14 24			
Pemberton	d										13 56											
Orrell	d										14 00											
Upholland	d										14 04											
Rainford	d										14 07											
Kirkby	a										14 19											
Gathurst	d				13 28														14 28			
Appley Bridge	d		13 10		13 32												14 10		14 32			
Parbold	d		13 14		13 36												14 14		14 36			
Hoscar	d				13 39																	
Burscough Bridge	d		13 18		13 42												14 18		14 41			
New Lane	d				13 44																	
Bescar Lane	d				13 48																	
Meols Cop	d				13 53														14 49			
Southport	a		13 35		14 02												14 35		14 59			
Lostock	d	12 45					13 20									13 45					14 20	
Horwich Parkway	d	12 49				13 13	13 24									13 49				14 13	14 24	
Blackrod	d	12 52														13 52						
Adlington (Lancashire)	d	12 56														13 56						
Chorley	d	13 01				13 21	13 32			13 44				13 44		14 01				14 21	14 32	
Buckshaw Parkway	d	13 05				13 24	13 35									14 05				14 24	14 35	
Leyland	d	13 12					13 42									14 12					14 42	
Preston 65,97	a	13 17				13 33	13 50			13 55				13 55		14 17				14 33	14 50	
	d	13 19				13 38				13 58				13 58	13 58	14 19				14 38		
Kirkham & Wesham 97	a	13 28														14 28						
Poulton-le-Fylde 97	a	13 36				13 56										14 36				14 56		
Layton 97	a	13 43														14 43						
Blackpool North 97	a	13 50				14 05										14 50				15 05		
Lancaster 65	a									14 13				14 13	14 13							
	d											13 32	13 48	14 14								
Oxenholme Lake District 65	a													14 28								
Windermere 83	a																					
Carnforth	d											13 41	13a58									
Silverdale	d											13 47										
Arnside	d											13 52										
Grange-over-Sands	d											13 58										
Kents Bank	d											14 01										
Cark	d											14 06										
Ulverston	d											14 14										
Dalton	d											14 22										
Roose	d											14 28										
Barrow-in-Furness	a											14 36										

A To Clitheroe
B from 30 June until 8 September. To Glasgow Central
C To Carlisle
D From Heysham Port to Leeds
E until 23 June, 15 September, 22 September, 29 September. To Glasgow Central
F from 30 June until 4 August, 8 September. From Blackpool North to Glasgow Central

Table 82

Saturdays
until 29 September

Manchester - Bolton - Wigan, Kirkby, Southport, Preston, Blackpool North and Barrow-in-Furness

Network Diagram - see first Page of Table 82

		NT	NT	NT A	TP ◇1 B ✕		NT	NT	NT	NT	TP ◇1 ✕	NT	NT C	NT	TP ◇1 D ✕	NT	NT	NT	NT	NT C	NT	TP ◇1 ✕	NT
Manchester Airport 85 ✈	d				14 00			14 03			14 29				15 00			15 03				15 29	
Heald Green 85	d										14 33											15 33	
Buxton 86	d																						
Hazel Grove 86	d											14 33											15 33
Stockport 84	d											14 41											15 41
Manchester Piccadilly	d				14 16			14 22			14 46	14 54			15 16			15 22				15 46	15 54
Manchester Oxford Road	d				14 19			14 26			14 49	14 58			15 19			15 26				15 49	15 58
Deansgate	d							14 28			14 51	15 00						15 28				15 51	16 00
Rochdale 41	d								14 04										15 04				
Manchester Victoria	d	14 07	14 10				14 22		14 33	14 46			15 00	15 07		15 10	15 22		15 33	15 40	15 46		
Salford Central	d	14 10	14 13				14 25		14 36	14 49			15 03	15 10		15 13	15 25		15 36	15 43	15 49		
Salford Crescent	a	14 13	14 16				14 29	14 33	14 39	14 52	14 56	15 04	15 08	15 13		15 16	15 29	15 33	15 39	15 46	15 52	15 56	16 04
	d	14 13	14 17				14 30	14 35	14 40	14 53	14 56	15 04	15 08	15 13		15 17	15 30	15 35	15 40	15 47	15 53	15 56	16 04
Swinton	d		14 23							14 59						15 23					15 59		
Moorside	d		14 26													15 26							
Walkden	d		14 29							15 04						15 29					16 04		
Atherton	d		14 35							15 09						15 35					16 09		
Hag Fold	d		14 37													15 37							
Daisy Hill	d		14 40							15 13						15 40					16 13		
Kearsley	d								14 47										15 47				
Farnworth	d								14 49										15 49				
Moses Gate	d								14 52										15 52				
Bolton	a	14 23			14 32		14 40	14 45	14 55		15 06	15 14	15 19	15 23	15 32		15 40	15 45	15 55	15 59		16 06	16 14
	d	14 24			14 33		14 40	14 45	14 56		15 07	15 15		15 24	15 33		15 40	15 45	15 56			16 07	16 15
Westhoughton	d	14 31						14 53						15 31				15 53					
Hindley	d	14 35	14 45					14 57		15 17				15 35		15 45		15 57			16 17		
Ince	d		14 48													15 48							
Wigan North Western	a																						
Wigan Wallgate	a	14 44	14 51					15 02	15 13	15 22				15 44		15 51		16 02	16 13		16 22		
	d		14 52					15 03		15 24						15 52		16 03			16 24		
Pemberton	d		14 56													15 56							
Orrell	d		15 00													16 00							
Upholland	d		15 04													16 04							
Rainford	d		15 07													16 07							
Kirkby	a		15 19													16 19							
Gathurst	d									15 28								16 08			16 28		
Appley Bridge	d							15 10		15 32								16 11			16 32		
Parbold	d							15 14		15 36								16 15			16 36		
Hoscar	d																	16 18					
Burscough Bridge	d							15 18		15 40								16 21			16 40		
New Lane	d																	16 24					
Bescar Lane	d																	16 27					
Meols Cop	d									15 48								16 32			16 48		
Southport	a							15 35		15 57								16 42			16 57		
Lostock	d						14 45					15 20					15 45						16 20
Horwich Parkway	d						14 49				15 13	15 24					15 49					16 13	16 24
Blackrod	d						14 52										15 52						
Adlington (Lancashire)	d						14 56										15 56						
Chorley	d				14 44		15 01				15 21	15 32			15 44		16 01					16 21	16 32
Buckshaw Parkway	d						15 05				15 24	15 36					16 05					16 24	16 35
Leyland	d						15 12					15 42					16 12						16 42
Preston 65,97	a				14 55		15 17				15 33	15 51			15 57		16 19					16 33	16 50
	d				14 58	15 04	15 19				15 38				15 58							16 38	
Kirkham & Wesham 97	a						15 28															16 47	
Poulton-le-Fylde 97	a						15 36				15 56											16 57	
Layton 97	a						15 43															17 00	
Blackpool North 97	a						15 50				16 05											17 07	
Lancaster 65	a				15 13	15 20									16 14								
	d			14 22	15 14	15 20									16 15								
Oxenholme Lake District 65	a				15 28																		
Windermere 83	a																						
Carnforth	d			14 32		15 28									16 23								
Silverdale	d			14 38											16 29								
Arnside	d			14 42		15 37									16 33								
Grange-over-Sands	d			14 48		15 42									16 39								
Kents Bank	d			14 52											16 42								
Cark	d			14 56											16 47								
Ulverston	d			15 05		15 55									16 55								
Dalton	d			15 13											17 03								
Roose	d			15 19											17 09								
Barrow-in-Furness	a			15 26		16 15									17 18								

A To Carlisle
B To Edinburgh
C To Clitheroe
D ✕ to Preston

Table 82

Saturdays
until 29 September

Manchester - Bolton - Wigan, Kirkby, Southport, Preston, Blackpool North and Barrow-in-Furness

Network Diagram - see first Page of Table 82

		NT	NT	NT A	NT B	TP ◇1 C 🍴			NT	NT D	NT	NT	TP ◇1 🍴	NT	NT	NT D	NT		NT	NT	TP ◇1 E 🍴	TP ◇1	NT	NT F	NT
Manchester Airport 85 ✈	d					16 00					16 03		16 29								17 00				17 03
Heald Green 85	d												16 33												
Buxton 86	d																								
Hazel Grove 86	d														16 30										
Stockport 84	d														16 41										
Manchester Piccadilly 10 ⇌	d					16 16					16 22		16 46		16 54						17 15				17 23
Manchester Oxford Road	d					16 19					16 26		16 49		16 58						17 18				17 26
Deansgate ⇌	d										16 28				17 00										
Rochdale 41	d											16 04												17 03	
Manchester Victoria ⇌	d	16 07	16 10						16 20	16 23		16 36		16 46		17 00	17 07		17 10				17 19	17 23	
Salford Central	d	16 10	16 13						16 23	16 26		16 39		16 49		17 03	17 10		17 13				17 22	17 26	
Salford Crescent	a	16 13	16 16						16 26	16 30	16 34	16 42		16 52	17 04	17 07	17 13		17 17				17 25	17 30	17 34
	d	16 13	16 17						16 27	16 31	16 35	16 43		16 53	17 04	17 08	17 13		17 18				17 27	17 31	17 35
Swinton	d		16 23											16 59					17 24						
Moorside	d		16 26											17 02					17 27						
Walkden	d		16 29											17 05					17 30						
Atherton	d		16 35											17 11					17 36						
Hag Fold	d		16 37											17 14					17 38						
Daisy Hill	d		16 40											17 17					17 41						
Kearsley	d											16 50													
Farnworth	d											16 52													
Moses Gate	d											16 55													
Bolton	a	16 23				16 32			16 37	16 42	16 45	16 58	17 05		17 14	17 19	17 23				17 31		17 37	17 42	17 45
	d	16 24				16 33			16 37		16 46	16 59	17 06		17 15		17 24				17 32		17 37		17 46
Westhoughton	d	16 31									16 53	17 06					17 31								17 53
Hindley	d	16 35	16 45								16 57	17 10		17 21			17 35		17 46						
Ince	d		16 48											17 24					17 49						
Wigan North Western	a																								
Wigan Wallgate	a	16 44	16 51								17 02	17 19		17 27			17 44		17 52						18 01
	d		16 52								17 04			17 29					17 53						18 02
Pemberton	d		16 56																17 57						
Orrell	d		17 00																18 01						
Upholland	d		17 04																18 05						
Rainford	d		17 07																18 08						
Kirkby	a		17 19																18 19						
Gathurst	d										17 08			17 33											
Appley Bridge	d										17 12			17 37											18 09
Parbold	d										17 16			17 41											18 13
Hoscar	d																								
Burscough Bridge	d										17 20			17 45											18 17
New Lane	d																								
Bescar Lane	d																								
Meols Cop	d										17 28			17 53											
Southport	a										17 37			18 02											18 35
Lostock	d								16 43						17 20								17 43		
Horwich Parkway	d								16 47						17 24								17 47		
Blackrod	d								16 51														17 51		
Adlington (Lancashire)	d								16 55														17 55		
Chorley	d					16 44			17 00				17 19		17 32						17 44		18 00		
Buckshaw Parkway	d								17 04						17 35								18 04		
Leyland	d								17 12						17 42								18 11		
Preston 8 65,97	a					16 55			17 20				17 30		17 50						17 55		18 16		
	d					17 00	17 04		17 21				17 32								17 58	18 02	18 18		
Kirkham & Wesham 97	a								17 31				17 41										18 27		
Poulton-le-Fylde 97	a								17 39				17 51										18 35		
Layton 97	a								17 43				17 54										18 39		
Blackpool North 97	a								17 50				18 02										18 46		
Lancaster 6 65	a					17 16	17 20														18 13	18 18			
	d			16 40	17 00	17 16	17 21													17 32	18 14	18 18			
Oxenholme Lake District 65	a					17 30	17 37														18 28				
Windermere 83	a						18 00																		
Carnforth	d			16a49	17 10															17 43		18 31			
Silverdale	d				17 17															17 49		18 37			
Arnside	d				17 21															17 53		18 41			
Grange-over-Sands	d				17 27															17 59		18 46			
Kents Bank	d				17 31															18 03		18 50			
Cark	d				17 35															18 07		18 54			
Ulverston	d				17 44															18 16		19 02			
Dalton	d				17 53															18 24		19 10			
Roose	d				17 59															18 30		19 16			
Barrow-in-Furness	a				18 07															18 38		19 26			

A From Morecambe to Leeds
B To Millom
C To Edinburgh
D To Clitheroe
E To Glasgow Central
F To Blackburn

Table 82

Saturdays
until 29 September

Manchester - Bolton - Wigan, Kirkby, Southport, Preston, Blackpool North and Barrow-in-Furness

Network Diagram - see first Page of Table 82

		NT	NT		TP ◇1 🍴	NT	NT	NT A	TP ◇1 B 🍴	NT	NT	NT C	NT		NT	NT	TP ◇1 🍴	NT	NT A	NT	NT D	TP ◇1	NT		NT
Manchester Airport 85 ✈	d				17 29				18 00				18 03				18 29					19 00	19 03		
Heald Green 85	d				17 33												18 33								
Buxton 86	d																								
Hazel Grove 86	d						17 33											18 33							
Stockport 84	d						17 41											18 41							
Manchester Piccadilly 10 ⇌	d				17 46		17 54		18 16				18 22				18 46	18 54				19 16	19 20		
Manchester Oxford Road	d				17 49		17 58		18 19				18 26				18 49	18 58				19 19	19 24		
Deansgate ⇌	d				17 51		18 00						18 28				18 51	19 00					19 26		
Rochdale 41	d											18 02													
Manchester Victoria ⇌	d	17 36	17 40			17 50		18 00		18 08	18 20	18 23			18 33	18 45			19 00	19 10					19 28
Salford Central	d	17 39	17 43			17 53		18 03		18 12	18 23	18 26			18 36	18 48			19 03	19 13					19 31
Salford Crescent	a	17 42	17 46		17 55	17 58	18 04	18 07		18 16	18 26	18 30	18 34		18 39	18 51	18 56	19 04	19 08	19 16			19 29		19 34
	d	17 43	17 47		17 55	17 59	18 04	18 08		18 17	18 27	18 31	18 35		18 40	18 52	18 56	19 04	19 08	19 17			19 30		19 35
Swinton	d					18 05				18 23						18 58				19 23					
Moorside	d					18 08				18 26						19 01				19 26					
Walkden	d					18 11				18 29						19 04				19 29					
Atherton	d		18 00			18 17				18 35						19 10				19 35					
Hag Fold	d					18 19				18 37						19 12				19 37					
Daisy Hill	d		18 04			18 22				18 40						19 15				19 40					
Kearsley	d	17 53													18 47										
Farnworth	d	17 55													18 49										
Moses Gate	d	17 57													18 52										
Bolton	a	18 01			18 06		18 14	18 19	18 32		18 37	18 42	18 45		18 55		19 06	19 19	19 20			19 32	19 40		19 45
	d	18 01			18 07		18 15		18 33		18 37		18 46		18 56		19 07					19 33	19 40		19 45
Westhoughton	d	18 09											18 53		19 03								19 48		
Hindley	d	18 13				18 27				18 45			18 57		19 09	19 20				19 45			19 52		
Ince	d									18 48						19 23				19 48					
Wigan North Western	a									18 56															
Wigan Wallgate	a	18 22	18 12			18 32							19 02		19 18	19 30				19 55			19 57		
	d		18 15			18 33							19 04										19 59		
Pemberton	d					18 37																			
Orrell	d					18 41																			
Upholland	d					18 45																			
Rainford	d					18 48																			
Kirkby	a					19 00																			
Gathurst	d		18 20										19 08										20 03		
Appley Bridge	d		18 24										19 12										20 07		
Parbold	d		18 28										19 16										20 11		
Hoscar	d		18 31																						
Burscough Bridge	d		18 35										19 20										20 15		
New Lane	d		18 37																						
Bescar Lane	d		18 41																						
Meols Cop	d		18 46										19 28										20 23		
Southport	a		18 55										19 35										20 32		
Lostock	d				18 12		18 20				18 42						19 12								19 50
Horwich Parkway	d				18 15		18 24				18 46						19 15								19 54
Blackrod	d				18 19						18 49														19 57
Adlington (Lancashire)	d										18 53														20 01
Chorley	d				18 26		18 32		18 44		18 58						19 23					19 44			20 06
Buckshaw Parkway	d						18 35				19 02						19 26								20 10
Leyland	d						18 42				19 11														20 18
Preston 8 65,97	a				18 38		18 48		18 55		19 18						19 33					19 58			20 24
	d				18 40		18 49		18 58		19 20						19 38					20 01			20 25
Kirkham & Wesham 97	a				18 49						19 29														20 35
Poulton-le-Fylde 97	a				18 59						19 37						19 56								20 43
Layton 97	a				19 02						19 43														20 47
Blackpool North 97	a				19 10		19 16				19 50						20 06								20 54
Lancaster 6 65	a								19 13													20 17			
	d								19 15												19 24	20 17			
Oxenholme Lake District 65	a																								
Windermere 83	a																								
Carnforth	d								19 24												19a33	20 26			
Silverdale	d								19 30													20 32			
Arnside	d								19 34													20 36			
Grange-over-Sands	d								19 40													20 42			
Kents Bank	d								19 43													20 45			
Cark	d								19 48													20 50			
Ulverston	d								19 56													20 58			
Dalton	d								20 04													21 06			
Roose	d								20 10													21 12			
Barrow-in-Furness	a								20 19													21 20			

A To Clitheroe
B 🍴 to Preston
C To Blackburn
D From Morecambe to Leeds

Table 82

Saturdays
until 29 September

Manchester - Bolton - Wigan, Kirkby, Southport, Preston, Blackpool North and Barrow-in-Furness

Network Diagram - see first Page of Table 82

	TP ◇1	NT	TP ◇1	NT	NT	NT	NT	TP ◇1	NT	NT	NT	NT	NT	NT	NT	TP ◇1	NT	TP ◇1	NT	NT	NT	NT
		A					B		A					B	C		A		B			
Manchester Airport 85 ✈ d	19 29		20 00			20 03	20 09	20 29					21 03	21 09		21 29		22 00	22 08		22 19	
Heald Green 85 d	19 33						20 12	20 33						21 12		21 33			22 12			
Buxton 86 d																						
Hazel Grove 86 d																						
Stockport 84 d																						
Manchester Piccadilly 10 ⇌ d	19 46		20 16			20 20	20 32	20 46					21 22	21 32	21 38	21 46		22 16	22 32		22 36	
Manchester Oxford Road d	19 49		20 19			20 24	20a36	20 49					21 26	21a36	21 44	21 49		22 19	22a36		22 39	
Deansgate ⇌ d	19 51					20 26		20 51					21 28		21a46	21 51					22 41	
Rochdale 41 d																						
Manchester Victoria ⇌ d		20 00		20 10	20 22				21 00	21 10		21 22					22 01			22 22		22 45
Salford Central d		20 03		20 13	20 25				21 03	21 13		21 25					22 03			22 25		22 48
Salford Crescent a	19 56	20 07		20 16	20 29	20 33		20 56	21 07	21 16		21 30	21 34			21 56	22 07			22 29	22 46	22 51
d	19 56	20 08		20 17	20 30	20 35		20 56	21 08	21 17		21 31	21 35			21 56	22 08			22 30	22 46	22 52
Swinton d				20 23						21 23												22 58
Moorside d				20 26						21 26												23 01
Walkden d				20 29						21 29												23 04
Atherton d				20 35						21 35												23 10
Hag Fold d				20 37						21 37												23 12
Daisy Hill d				20 40						21 40												23 15
Kearsley d																						
Farnworth d																						
Moses Gate d																						
Bolton a	20 06	20 19	20 32		20 40	20 45		21 06	21 19			21 41	21 45			22 06	22 19	22 32		22 40	22 56	
d	20 07		20 33		20 40	20 45		21 07				21 41	21 45			22 07		22 33		22 40	22 57	
Westhoughton d						20 53							21 53								23 04	
Hindley d				20 45		20 57				21 45			21 57								23 08	23 20
Ince d				20 48						21 48												23 23
Wigan North Western a																						
Wigan Wallgate a				20 55		21 02				21 55			22 02								23 13	23 30
d						21 03							22 03								23 15	
Pemberton d																						
Orrell d																						
Upholland d																						
Rainford d																						
Kirkby a																						
Gathurst d						21 08							22 08								23 19	
Appley Bridge d						21 11							22 11								23 23	
Parbold d						21 15							22 15								23 27	
Hoscar d						21 18																
Burscough Bridge d						21 21							22 20								23 31	
New Lane d						21 24																
Bescar Lane d						21 27																
Meols Cop d						21 32							22 27								23 39	
Southport a						21 42							22 37								23 46	
Lostock d					20 45							21 46								22 45		
Horwich Parkway d	20 13		20 39		20 49			21 13				21 50				22 13				22 49		
Blackrod d					20 52							21 53								22 52		
Adlington (Lancashire) d					20 56							21 57								22 56		
Chorley d	20 21		20 46		21 01			21 21				22 02				22 21				23 01		
Buckshaw Parkway d	20 24				21 05			21 24				22 05				22 24				23 05		
Leyland d					21 12							22 12								23 12		
Preston 8 65,97 a	20 33		20 57		21 17			21 33				22 18				22 36		22 54		23 17		
d	20 38		21 02		21 19			21 38			21 59	22 19				22 38		22 55		23 19		
Kirkham & Wesham 97 a					21 28							22 29								23 28		
Poulton-le-Fylde 97 a	20 56				21 36			21 56				22 37				22 55				23 36		
Layton 97 a					21 40							22 43								23 42		
Blackpool North 97 a	21 06				21 48			22 06				22 50				23 04				23 48		
Lancaster 6 65 a			21 17								22 19							23 11				
d			21 18								22 19							23 11				
Oxenholme Lake District 65 a																						
Windermere 83 a																						
Carnforth d			21 26								22 29							23 20				
Silverdale d			21 32								22 35							23 26				
Arnside d			21 36								22 40							23 30				
Grange-over-Sands d			21 42								22 46							23 35				
Kents Bank d			21 45								22 49							23 39				
Cark d			21 50								22 54							23 43				
Ulverston d			21 58								23 02							23 51				
Dalton d			22 06								23 10							23 59				
Roose d			22 12								23 16							00 05				
Barrow-in-Furness a			22 21								23 24							00 15				

A To Clitheroe
B From Wilmslow
C To Warrington Central

Table 82

Saturdays
until 29 September

Manchester - Bolton - Wigan, Kirkby, Southport, Preston, Blackpool North and Barrow-in-Furness

Network Diagram - see first Page of Table 82

	TP ◇1	NT	NT	NT	NT
			A		
Manchester Airport 85 ✈ d	22 29				
Heald Green 85 d	22 33				
Buxton 86 d					
Hazel Grove 86 d					
Stockport 84 d		22 40			
Manchester Piccadilly 10 ⇌ d	22 46	22 54			
Manchester Oxford Road d	22 49	22 58			
Deansgate ⇌ d	22 51	23 00			
Rochdale 41 d					
Manchester Victoria ⇌ d			23 05	23 16	23 20
Salford Central d			23 08	23 19	23 23
Salford Crescent a	22 56	23 03	23 11	23 22	23 26
d	22 56	23 05	23 12	23 22	23 26
Swinton d					23 33
Moorside d					23 35
Walkden d					23 39
Atherton d					23 44
Hag Fold d					23 47
Daisy Hill d					23 50
Kearsley d		23 12			
Farnworth d		23 14			
Moses Gate d		23 17			
Bolton a	23 06	23 20	23 23	23 32	
d	23 07	23 21		23 33	
Westhoughton d		23 28			
Hindley d		23 32			23 54
Ince d					23 57
Wigan North Western a					
Wigan Wallgate a		23 41			00 04
d					
Pemberton d					
Orrell d					
Upholland d					
Rainford d					
Kirkby a					
Gathurst d					
Appley Bridge d					
Parbold d					
Hoscar d					
Burscough Bridge d					
New Lane d					
Bescar Lane d					
Meols Cop d					
Southport a					
Lostock d				23 38	
Horwich Parkway d	23 13			23 42	
Blackrod d				23 45	
Adlington (Lancashire) d				23 49	
Chorley d	23 21			23 54	
Buckshaw Parkway d	23 24			23 57	
Leyland d				00 04	
Preston 8 65,97 a	23 33			00 10	
d	23 35			00 11	
Kirkham & Wesham 97 a				00 21	
Poulton-le-Fylde 97 a	23 52			00 29	
Layton 97 a				00 34	
Blackpool North 97 a	00 02			00 40	
Lancaster 6 65 a					
d					
Oxenholme Lake District 65 a					
Windermere 83 a					
Carnforth d					
Silverdale d					
Arnside d					
Grange-over-Sands d					
Kents Bank d					
Cark d					
Ulverston d					
Dalton d					
Roose d					
Barrow-in-Furness a					

A To Blackburn

Table 82

Saturdays from 6 October

Manchester - Bolton - Wigan, Kirkby, Southport, Preston, Blackpool North and Barrow-in-Furness

Network Diagram - see first Page of Table 82

	TP ◇1	TP ◇1	NT	NT	TP ◇1	TP ◇1	TP ◇1	TP ◇1	NT	TP ◇1	TP 1	NT	NT	TP ◇1	NT	TP ◇1	NT	NT	NT	NT	TP ◇1	TP ◇1
						A		A	B			C		D		E				C	B	
Manchester Airport 85 ✈ d	22p00	22p29			00 01	00 38	04 00	04 15	04 34					05 45		06 18						
Heald Green 85 d		22p33												05 49								
Buxton 86 d																				05 54		
Hazel Grove 86 d																				06 31		
Stockport 84 d																				06 41		
Manchester Piccadilly 10 ⇌ d	22p16	22p46			00 16	00 53	04 15	04 30	04a47	05 43				06 03		06 33				06 54	07 07	
Manchester Oxford Road d	22p19	22p49												06 06		06 36				06 57	07a09	
Deansgate ⇌ d		22p51																		06 59		
Rochdale 41 d																						
Manchester Victoria ⇌ d			23p20	23p23								05 55	06 00		06 17		06 38		06 45			
Salford Central d			23p23	23p26													06 40		06 48			
Salford Crescent a		22p56	23p26	23p29		00 58		04 36		05 48		05 59	06 04		06 23		06 44		06 51	07 03		
d		22p56	23p26	23p30						05 49		06 00	06 05		06 24		06 45		06 52	07 03		
Swinton d			23p33																06 58			
Moorside d			23p35																			
Walkden d			23p39																07 03			
Atherton d			23p44																07 08			
Hag Fold d			23p47																			
Daisy Hill d			23p50																07 12			
Kearsley d																	06 52					
Farnworth d																	06 54					
Moses Gate d																	06 57					
Bolton a	22p32	23p06		23p40	00s31		04s29			05 59		06 11	06 15	06 19	06 34	06 50	07 00			07 16		
d	22p33	23p07		23p40						05 59			06 15	06 19	06 34	06 50	07 01					
Westhoughton d													06 23									
Hindley d			23p54										06 27						07 16			
Ince d			23p57																			
Wigan North Western a	22p48																07 19					
Wigan Wallgate a			00 06										06 32						07 21			
d													06 34					06 40	07 23			
Pemberton d													06 38									
Orrell d													06 42									
Upholland d													06 45									
Rainford d													06 49									
Kirkby a													07 03									
Gathurst d																		06 44	07 27			
Appley Bridge d																		06 48	07 31			
Parbold d																		06 52	07 35			
Hoscar d																		06 55				
Burscough Bridge d																		06 58	07 39			
New Lane d																		07 00				
Bescar Lane d																		07 04				
Meols Cop d																		07 09	07 47			
Southport a																		07 20	07 58			
Lostock d				23p45											06 39							
Horwich Parkway d		23p13		23p49						06 06					06 43							
Blackrod d				23p52											06 46							
Adlington (Lancashire) d				23p56											06 50							
Chorley d		23p21		00 01						06 13				06 31	06 55							
Buckshaw Parkway d		23p24		00 05											06 59							
Leyland d				00 12						06 22					07 06							
Preston 8 65,97 a	23p09	23p33		00 17	01s05		05s04			06 26				06 42	07 11	07 11						
d	23p13	23p35		00 19						06 37				06 44	07 13	07 14						07 20
Kirkham & Wesham 97 a				00 28						06 46					07 22							
Poulton-le-Fylde 97 a		23p52		00 36						06 56					07 30							
Layton 97 a				00 43						06 59					07 34							
Blackpool North 97 a		00 02		00 52	01 30		05 33			07 06					07 43							
Lancaster 6 65 a	23p28													06 59		07 30						07 36
d	23p29										05 46			07 00								07 36
Oxenholme Lake District 65 a											06 21			07 15								
Windermere 83 a											06 41											
Carnforth d	23p37																					07 45
Silverdale d	23p43																					07 51
Arnside d	23p47																					07 55
Grange-over-Sands d	23p53																					08 00
Kents Bank d	23p56																					08 04
Cark d	00 01																					08 08
Ulverston d	00 09																					08 16
Dalton d	00 17																					08 24
Roose d	00 23																					08 30
Barrow-in-Furness a	00 31																					08 39

A To York
B To Liverpool Lime Street
C To Clitheroe
D To Edinburgh
E To Glasgow Central

Table 82

Saturdays from 6 October

Manchester - Bolton - Wigan, Kirkby, Southport, Preston, Blackpool North and Barrow-in-Furness

Network Diagram - see first Page of Table 82

	NT	NT	NT	NT	TP ◇1	NT	NT	TP ◇1	NT	NT	NT	TP ◇1	NT	NT	NT	TP ◇1	NT	NT	EM ◇	NT	NT	NT
	A	B		C			D	E			F	G			H				I	D	J	
Manchester Airport 85 ✈ d					07 00			07 25								07 56		08 01				
Heald Green 85 d								07 30										08 05				
Buxton 86 d																						
Hazel Grove 86 d										07 32									08 17			
Stockport 84 d										07 40									08 24			
Manchester Piccadilly 10 ⇌ d					07 15			07 45		07 54		08 07				08 15		08 22	08 37			
Manchester Oxford Road d					07 18					07 58		08a09				08 19		08 26	08a40			
Deansgate ⇌ d										08 00								08 28				
Rochdale 41 d																					08 00	
Manchester Victoria ⇌ d		07 06	07 10			07 16	07 23		07 27		08 00		08 07	08 10			08 22			08 29	08 33	08 46
Salford Central d		07 09	07 13			07 19	07 26		07 30		08 03		08 10	08 13			08 25			08 32	08 36	08 49
Salford Crescent a		07 12	07 16			07 24	07 29		07 33	08 04	08 07		08 13	08 16			08 29	08 33		08 37	08 39	08 52
d		07 13	07 16			07 25	07 30		07 33	08 04	08 08		08 13	08 17			08 30	08 34		08 37	08 40	08 53
Swinton d		07 19												08 23								08 59
Moorside d		07 22												08 26								
Walkden d		07 25							07 42					08 29								09 04
Atherton d		07 31							07 48					08 35								09 09
Hag Fold d		07 33												08 37								
Daisy Hill d		07 36							07 51					08 40								09 13
Kearsley d																					08 47	
Farnworth d																					08 49	
Moses Gate d																					08 52	
Bolton a			07 26		07 31	07 35	07 41	07 59		08 14	08 19		08 23			08 32	08 40	08 44		08 49	08 55	
d			07 27		07 31	07 35		07 59		08 15			08 24			08 32	08 40	08 45			08 56	
Westhoughton d			07 34	←									08 31					08 53				
Hindley d		07 42	07 38	07 42									08 35	08 45								09 17
Ince d		→		07 45										08 48								
Wigan North Western a																						
Wigan Wallgate a			07 43	07 48					08 05				08 46	08 51				09 00			09 14	09 22
d			07 45	07 50										08 52				09 05				09 24
Pemberton d				07 54										08 56								
Orrell d				07 58										09 00								
Upholland d				08 01										09 04								
Rainford d				08 05										09 07								
Kirkby a				08 19										09 21								
Gathurst d			07 49																			09 28
Appley Bridge d			07 53															09 11				09 32
Parbold d			07 57															09 15				09 36
Hoscar d			08 00																			09 39
Burscough Bridge d			08 03															09 20				09 42
New Lane d			08 05																			09 44
Bescar Lane d			08 09																			09 48
Meols Cop d			08 14																			09 53
Southport a			08 25															09 38				10 04
Lostock d						07 42				08 20							08 45					
Horwich Parkway d					07 38	07 46				08 24						08 39	08 49					
Blackrod d						07 49											08 52					
Adlington (Lancashire) d						07 53				08 29							08 56					
Chorley d					07 46	07 58		08 11		08 34						08 47	09 01					
Buckshaw Parkway d						08 01				08 37							09 05					
Leyland d						08 08				08 43							09 12					
Preston 8 65,97 a					07 57	08 14		08 22		08 50						08 58	09 17					
d					07 59	08 15		08 24							08 42	08 59	09 19					
Kirkham & Wesham 97 a					08 08	08 25											09 28					
Poulton-le-Fylde 97 a					08 18	08 33										09 16	09 36					
Layton 97 a					08 22	08 37											09 43					
Blackpool North 97 a					08 29	08 46										09 25	09 52					
Lancaster 6 65 a								08 39							09 02							
d	08 24														09 03							
Oxenholme Lake District 65 a																						
Windermere 83 a																						
Carnforth d	08a33														09 13							
Silverdale d															09 18							
Arnside d															09 23							
Grange-over-Sands d															09 29							
Kents Bank d															09 32							
Cark d															09 37							
Ulverston d															09 45							
Dalton d															09 53							
Roose d															09 59							
Barrow-in-Furness a															10 07							

A To Leeds
B To Kirkby
C From Manchester Victoria
D To Blackburn
E To Edinburgh
F To Clitheroe
G From Hull to Liverpool Lime Street
H To Carlisle
I From Nottingham to Liverpool Lime Street
J From Hebden Bridge

Table 82

Saturdays from 6 October

Manchester - Bolton - Wigan, Kirkby, Southport, Preston, Blackpool North and Barrow-in-Furness

Network Diagram - see first Page of Table 82

	TP		NT	NT	NT	NT	TP	TP		NT	NT		NT	NT	NT	TP	NT	NT	NT	NT	NT		TP	TP
	◇1 A			B			◇1 C	◇1 D					E			◇1		B			F		◇1	◇1 G
Manchester Airport 85 d	08 25							09 00			09 03					09 29								10 00
Heald Green 85 d	08 29															09 33								
Buxton 86 d			07 51																					
Hazel Grove 86 d			08 31														09 31							
Stockport 84 d			08 41														09 41							
Manchester Piccadilly d	08 46		08 54					09 16			09 22					09 46	09 54							10 16
Manchester Oxford Road d	08 49		08 58					09 19			09 26					09 49	09 58							10 19
Deansgate d	08 51		09 00								09 28					09 51	10 00							
Rochdale 41 d														09 04										
Manchester Victoria d				09 00	09 07	09 10				09 22			09 29	09 32	09 46			10 00	10 07	10 10				
Salford Central d				09 03	09 10	09 13				09 25			09 32	09 36	09 49			10 03	10 10	10 13				
Salford Crescent a	08 56		09 04	09 07	09 13	09 16				09 29	09 33		09 37	09 39	09 52	09 56	10 04	10 07	10 13	10 16				
d	08 56		09 04	09 08	09 13	09 17				09 30	09 33		09 37	09 40	09 53	09 56	10 04	10 08	10 13	10 17				
Swinton d						09 23									09 59					10 23				
Moorside d						09 26														10 26				
Walkden d						09 29									10 04					10 29				
Atherton d						09 35									10 09					10 35				
Hag Fold d						09 37														10 37				
Daisy Hill d						09 40									10 13					10 40				
Kearsley d														09 47										
Farnworth d														09 49										
Moses Gate d														09 52										
Bolton a	09 06		09 14	09 19	09 23			09 32		09 40	09 44		09 49	09 55		10 06	10 14	10 19	10 23					10 32
d	09 07		09 15		09 24			09 33		09 40	09 45			09 56		10 07	10 15		10 24					10 33
Westhoughton d					09 31						09 53								10 31					
Hindley d					09 35	09 45					09 57				10 17				10 35	10 45				
Ince d						09 48														10 48				
Wigan North Western a																								
Wigan Wallgate a					09 46	09 51					10 02			10 15	10 22				10 46	10 51				
d						09 52					10 03				10 24					10 52				
Pemberton d						09 56														10 56				
Orrell d						10 00														11 00				
Upholland d						10 04														11 04				
Rainford d						10 07														11 07				
Kirkby a						10 21														11 21				
Gathurst d															10 28									
Appley Bridge d											10 10				10 32									
Parbold d											10 14				10 36									
Hoscar d																								
Burscough Bridge d											10 18				10 40									
New Lane d																								
Bescar Lane d																								
Meols Cop d															10 48									
Southport a											10 37				10 59									
Lostock d			09 20							09 45							10 20							
Horwich Parkway d			09 24							09 49						10 13	10 24							
Blackrod d										09 52														
Adlington (Lancashire) d										09 56														
Chorley d	09 19		09 32					09 44		10 01						10 21	10 32							10 44
Buckshaw Parkway d			09 35							10 05						10 24	10 35							
Leyland d			09 42							10 12							10 42							
Preston 8 65,97 a	09 30		09 50					09 55		10 17						10 33	10 50							10 55
d	09 32						09 45	09 58	10 08	10 19						10 38							10 45	10 58
Kirkham & Wesham 97 a										10 28														
Poulton-le-Fylde 97 a									10 26	10 36						10 56								
Layton 97 a										10 43														
Blackpool North 97 a									10 35	10 52						11 05								
Lancaster 6 65 a	09 47						10 00	10 13															11 00	11 13
d	09 48						10 01														10 49		11 01	11 14
Oxenholme Lake District 65 a	10 04																						11 17	11 28
Windermere 83 a	10 26																						11 39	
Carnforth d							10 09														10a58			
Silverdale d							10 15																	
Arnside d							10 19																	
Grange-over-Sands d							10 25																	
Kents Bank d							10 28																	
Cark d							10 33																	
Ulverston d							10 41																	
Dalton d							10 49																	
Roose d							10 55																	
Barrow-in-Furness a							11 04																	

A ⌶ to Preston
B To Clitheroe
C From Blackpool North
D To Glasgow Central
E To Blackburn
F From Morecambe to Leeds
G To Edinburgh

Table 82

Saturdays from 6 October

Manchester - Bolton - Wigan, Kirkby, Southport, Preston, Blackpool North and Barrow-in-Furness

Network Diagram - see first Page of Table 82

	NT	NT	NT	NT	TP	NT	NT		NT	NT	NT	TP	NT	NT	NT	NT	TP		NT	NT	NT	TP	NT	TP
					◇1		B				C	◇1 D					◇1			B		◇1 E		◇1
Manchester Airport 85 d		10 03			10 29							11 00		11 03			11 29					12 00		
Heald Green 85 d					10 33												11 33							
Buxton 86 d																								
Hazel Grove 86 d						10 31													11 31					
Stockport 84 d						10 41													11 41					
Manchester Piccadilly d		10 22			10 46	10 54						11 16		11 22			11 46		11 54			12 16		
Manchester Oxford Road d		10 26			10 49	10 58						11 19		11 26			11 49		11 58			12 19		
Deansgate d		10 28			10 51	11 00								11 28			11 51		12 00					
Rochdale 41 d			10 05												11 04									
Manchester Victoria d	10 22		10 33	10 46			11 00		11 07	11 10			11 22		11 33	11 46				12 00	12 07		12 10	
Salford Central d	10 25		10 36	10 49			11 03		11 10	11 13			11 25		11 36	11 49				12 03	12 10		12 13	
Salford Crescent a	10 29	10 33	10 39	10 52	10 56	11 04	11 07		11 13	11 16			11 29	11 33	11 39	11 52	11 56		12 04	12 07	12 13		12 16	
d	10 30	10 34	10 40	10 53	10 56	11 04	11 08		11 13	11 17			11 30	11 34	11 40	11 53	11 56		12 04	12 08	12 13		12 17	
Swinton d				10 59						11 23						11 59							12 23	
Moorside d										11 26													12 26	
Walkden d				11 04						11 29						12 04							12 29	
Atherton d				11 09						11 35						12 09							12 35	
Hag Fold d										11 37													12 37	
Daisy Hill d				11 13						11 40						12 13							12 40	
Kearsley d			10 47												11 47									
Farnworth d			10 49												11 49									
Moses Gate d			10 52												11 52									
Bolton a	10 40	10 45	10 55		11 06	11 14	11 19		11 23			11 32	11 40	11 45	11 55		12 06		12 14	12 19	12 23	12 32		
d	10 40	10 45	10 56		11 07	11 15			11 24			11 33	11 40	11 45	11 56		12 07		12 15		12 24	12 33		
Westhoughton d		10 53							11 31					11 53							12 31			
Hindley d		10 57		11 17					11 35	11 45				11 57		12 17					12 35		12 45	
Ince d										11 48													12 48	
Wigan North Western a																								
Wigan Wallgate a		11 02	11 15	11 22					11 46	11 51				12 02	12 15	12 22					12 46		12 51	
d		11 03		11 24						11 52				12 03		12 24							12 52	
Pemberton d										11 56													12 56	
Orrell d										12 00													13 00	
Upholland d										12 04													13 04	
Rainford d										12 07													13 07	
Kirkby a										12 21													13 21	
Gathurst d				11 28												12 28								
Appley Bridge d		11 10		11 32										12 10		12 32								
Parbold d		11 14		11 36										12 14		12 36								
Hoscar d				11 39																				
Burscough Bridge d		11 18		11 42										12 18		12 41								
New Lane d				11 44																				
Bescar Lane d				11 48																				
Meols Cop d				11 53												12 49								
Southport a		11 37		12 04										12 37		13 01								
Lostock d	10 45					11 20							11 45						12 20					
Horwich Parkway d	10 49				11 13	11 24							11 49				12 13		12 24					
Blackrod d	10 52												11 52											
Adlington (Lancashire) d	10 56												11 56											
Chorley d	11 01				11 21	11 32						11 44	12 01				12 21		12 32			12 44		
Buckshaw Parkway d	11 05				11 24	11 35							12 05				12 24		12 35					
Leyland d	11 12					11 42							12 12						12 42					
Preston 8 65,97 a	11 17				11 33	11 50						11 55	12 17				12 33		12 50			12 55		
d	11 19				11 38							11 58	12 19				12 38					12 58		13 04
Kirkham & Wesham 97 a	11 28												12 28											
Poulton-le-Fylde 97 a	11 36				11 56								12 36				12 56							
Layton 97 a	11 43												12 43											
Blackpool North 97 a	11 52				12 05								12 52				13 05							
Lancaster 6 65 a												12 13										13 13		13 19
d											11 28	12 14										13 14		13 20
Oxenholme Lake District 65 a																						13 28		13 36
Windermere 83 a																								13 56
Carnforth d											11 37	12 23												
Silverdale d											11 43													
Arnside d											11 48	12 32												
Grange-over-Sands d											11 54	12 38												
Kents Bank d											11 57													
Cark d											12 02													
Ulverston d											12 10	12 50												
Dalton d											12 18													
Roose d											12 24													
Barrow-in-Furness a											12 32	13 11												

B To Clitheroe
C To Carlisle
D ⌶ to Preston
E To Edinburgh

Table 82

Saturdays
from 6 October

Manchester - Bolton - Wigan, Kirkby, Southport, Preston, Blackpool North and Barrow-in-Furness

Network Diagram - see first Page of Table 82

	NT	NT	NT		NT	TP ◇■ 🍴	NT	NT B	NT	NT	NT	NT C	NT D	TP ◇■ E 🍴	NT	NT	NT	TP ◇■ 🍴	NT	NT B	NT	NT	NT C
Manchester Airport 85 ✈ d		12 03				12 29								13 00		13 03		13 29					
Heald Green 85 d						12 33												13 33					
Buxton 86 d																							
Hazel Grove 86 d							12 31												13 33				
Stockport 84 d							12 41												13 41				
Manchester Piccadilly ■ ⇌ d		12 22				12 46	12 54							13 16		13 22		13 46	13 54				
Manchester Oxford Road d		12 26				12 49	12 58							13 19		13 26		13 49	13 58				
Deansgate ⇌ d		12 28				12 51	13 00									13 28		13 51	14 00				
Rochdale 41 d			12 04						13 04														
Manchester Victoria ⇌ d	12 22		12 33		12 46			13 00	13 33	13 07	13 10				13 22		13 46			14 00	14 07	14 10	
Salford Central d	12 25		12 36		12 49			13 03	13 36	13 10	13 13				13 25		13 49			14 03	14 10	14 13	
Salford Crescent a	12 29	12 33	12 39		12 52	12 56	13 04	13 07	13 39	13 13	13 16				13 29	13 33	13 52	13 56	14 04	14 07	14 13	14 16	
d	12 30	12 34	12 40		12 53	12 56	13 04	13 08	13 40	13 13	13 17				13 30	13 34	13 53	13 56	14 04	14 08	14 13	14 17	
Swinton d					12 59						13 23						13 59					14 23	
Moorside d											13 26											14 26	
Walkden d					13 04						13 29						14 04					14 29	
Atherton d					13 09						13 35						14 09					14 35	
Hag Fold d											13 37											14 37	
Daisy Hill d					13 13						13 40						14 13					14 40	
Kearsley d			12 47						13 47														
Farnworth d			12 49						13 49														
Moses Gate d			12 52						13 52														
Bolton a	12 40	12 45	12 55			13 06	13 14	13 19	13 55	13 23				13 32	13 40	13 45		14 06	14 14	14 19	14 23		
d	12 40	12 45	12 56			13 07	13 15		13 56	13 24				13 33	13 40	13 45		14 07	14 15		14 24		
Westhoughton d		12 53								13 31						13 53					14 31		
Hindley d		12 57			13 17					13 35	13 45					13 57	14 17				14 35	14 45	
Ince d											13 48											14 48	
Wigan North Western a																							
Wigan Wallgate a		13 02	13 15		13 22				14 15	13 46	13 51					14 02	14 22				14 46	14 51	
d		13 03			13 24						13 52					14 03	14 24					14 52	
Pemberton d											13 56											14 56	
Orrell d											14 00											15 00	
Upholland d											14 04											15 04	
Rainford d											14 07											15 07	
Kirkby a											14 21											15 21	
Gathurst d					13 28												14 28						
Appley Bridge d		13 10			13 32											14 10	14 32						
Parbold d		13 14			13 36											14 14	14 36						
Hoscar d					13 39																		
Burscough Bridge d		13 18			13 42											14 18	14 41						
New Lane d					13 44																		
Bescar Lane d					13 48																		
Meols Cop d					13 53												14 49						
Southport a		13 37			14 04											14 37	15 01						
Lostock d	12 45						13 20								13 45				14 20				
Horwich Parkway d	12 49					13 13	13 24								13 49			14 13	14 24				
Blackrod d	12 52														13 52								
Adlington (Lancashire) d	12 56														13 56								
Chorley d	13 01					13 21	13 32							13 44	14 01			14 21	14 32				
Buckshaw Parkway d	13 05					13 24	13 35								14 05			14 24	14 35				
Leyland d	13 12						13 42								14 12				14 42				
Preston ■ 65,97 a	13 17					13 33	13 50							13 55	14 17			14 33	14 50				
d	13 19					13 38								13 58	14 19			14 38					
Kirkham & Wesham 97 a	13 28														14 28								
Poulton-le-Fylde 97 a	13 36					13 56									14 36			14 56					
Layton 97 a	13 45														14 43								
Blackpool North 97 a	13 55					14 05									14 50			15 05					
Lancaster ■ 65 a														14 13									
d												13 32	13 48	14 14									14 22
Oxenholme Lake District 65 a														14 28									
Windermere 83 a																							
Carnforth d												13 41	13a58										14 32
Silverdale d												13 47											14 38
Arnside d												13 52											14 42
Grange-over-Sands d												13 58											14 48
Kents Bank d												14 01											14 52
Cark d												14 06											14 56
Ulverston d												14 14											15 05
Dalton d												14 22											15 13
Roose d												14 28											15 19
Barrow-in-Furness a												14 36											15 26

B To Clitheroe
C To Carlisle
D From Heysham Port to Leeds
E To Glasgow Central

Table 82

Saturdays
from 6 October

Manchester - Bolton - Wigan, Kirkby, Southport, Preston, Blackpool North and Barrow-in-Furness

Network Diagram - see first Page of Table 82

	TP ◇■ A 🍴		NT	NT	NT	NT	TP ◇■ 🍴	NT	NT C		NT	TP ◇■ D 🍴	NT	NT	NT	NT	NT C	NT	TP ◇■ 🍴		NT	NT	NT	NT E
Manchester Airport 85 ✈ d	14 00			14 03			14 29					15 00			15 03				15 29					
Heald Green 85 d							14 33												15 33					
Buxton 86 d																								
Hazel Grove 86 d								14 31													15 33			
Stockport 84 d								14 41													15 41			
Manchester Piccadilly ■ ⇌ d	14 16			14 22			14 46	14 54				15 16			15 22				15 46		15 54			
Manchester Oxford Road d	14 19			14 26			14 49	14 58				15 19			15 26				15 49		15 58			
Deansgate ⇌ d				14 28			14 51	15 00							15 28				15 51		16 00			
Rochdale 41 d					14 04											15 04								
Manchester Victoria ⇌ d			14 22		14 33	14 46			15 00		15 07		15 10	15 22		15 33	15 40	15 46				16 07	16 10	
Salford Central d			14 25		14 36	14 49			15 03		15 10		15 13	15 25		15 36	15 43	15 49				16 10	16 13	
Salford Crescent a			14 29	14 33	14 39	14 52	14 56	15 04	15 07		15 13		15 16	15 29	15 33	15 39	15 46	15 52	15 56		16 04	16 13	16 16	
d			14 30	14 34	14 40	14 53	14 56	15 04	15 08		15 13		15 17	15 30	15 34	15 40	15 47	15 53	15 56		16 04	16 13	16 17	
Swinton d						14 59							15 23					15 59					16 23	
Moorside d													15 26										16 26	
Walkden d						15 04							15 29					16 04					16 29	
Atherton d						15 09							15 35					16 09					16 35	
Hag Fold d													15 37										16 37	
Daisy Hill d						15 13							15 40					16 13					16 40	
Kearsley d					14 47											15 47								
Farnworth d					14 49											15 49								
Moses Gate d					14 52											15 52								
Bolton a	14 32		14 40	14 45	14 55		15 06	15 14	15 19		15 23	15 32		15 40	15 45	15 55	15 59		16 06		16 14	16 23		
d	14 33		14 40	14 45	14 56		15 07	15 15			15 24	15 33		15 40	15 45	15 56			16 07		16 15	16 24		
Westhoughton d				14 53							15 31				15 53							16 31		
Hindley d				14 57		15 17					15 35		15 45		15 57			16 17				16 35	16 45	
Ince d													15 48										16 48	
Wigan North Western a																								
Wigan Wallgate a				15 02	15 15	15 22					15 46		15 51		16 02	16 15		16 22				16 46	16 51	
d				15 03		15 24							15 52		16 03			16 24					16 52	
Pemberton d													15 56										16 56	
Orrell d													16 00										17 00	
Upholland d													16 04										17 04	
Rainford d													16 07										17 07	
Kirkby a													16 21										17 21	
Gathurst d						15 28									16 08			16 28						
Appley Bridge d				15 10		15 32									16 11			16 32						
Parbold d				15 14		15 36									16 15			16 36						
Hoscar d															16 18									
Burscough Bridge d				15 18		15 40									16 21			16 40						
New Lane d															16 24									
Bescar Lane d															16 27									
Meols Cop d						15 48									16 32			16 48						
Southport a				15 37		15 59									16 44			16 59						
Lostock d			14 45					15 20						15 45							16 20			
Horwich Parkway d			14 49				15 13	15 24						15 49					16 13		16 24			
Blackrod d			14 52											15 52										
Adlington (Lancashire) d			14 56											15 56										
Chorley d	14 44		15 01				15 21	15 32				15 44		16 01					16 21		16 32			
Buckshaw Parkway d			15 05				15 24	15 36						16 05					16 24		16 35			
Leyland d			15 12					15 42						16 12							16 42			
Preston ■ 65,97 a	14 55		15 17				15 33	15 50				15 57		16 19					16 33		16 50			
d	14 58	15 04	15 19				15 38					15 58							16 38					
Kirkham & Wesham 97 a			15 28																16 47					
Poulton-le-Fylde 97 a			15 36				15 56												16 57					
Layton 97 a			15 43																17 00					
Blackpool North 97 a			15 52				16 05												17 07					
Lancaster ■ 65 a	15 13	15 20										16 14												
d	15 14	15 20										16 15												16 40
Oxenholme Lake District 65 a	15 28																							
Windermere 83 a																								
Carnforth d		15 28										16 23												16a49
Silverdale d												16 29												
Arnside d		15 37										16 33												
Grange-over-Sands d		15 42										16 39												
Kents Bank d												16 42												
Cark d												16 47												
Ulverston d		15 55										16 55												
Dalton d												17 03												
Roose d												17 09												
Barrow-in-Furness a		16 15										17 18												

A To Edinburgh
C To Clitheroe
D 🍴 to Preston
E From Morecambe to Leeds

Saturdays
from 6 October

Manchester - Bolton - Wigan, Kirkby, Southport, Preston, Blackpool North and Barrow-in-Furness

Network Diagram - see first Page of Table 82

Station		NT	TP		NT	NT	NT	NT	TP	NT	NT	NT	NT	NT	NT	TP	TP	NT	NT	NT	NT	NT	TP
			◇1						◇1							◇1	◇1						◇1
		A	B 🍴			C			🍴			C				D 🍴			E				🍴
Manchester Airport 85 ✈	d		16 00				16 03		16 29							17 00				17 03			17 29
Heald Green 85	d								16 33														17 33
Buxton 86	d																						
Hazel Grove 86	d										16 30												
Stockport 84	d										16 41												
Manchester Piccadilly 10 ⇌	d		16 16				16 22		16 46		16 54					17 15				17 22			17 46
Manchester Oxford Road	d		16 19				16 26		16 49		16 58					17 18				17 26			17 49
Deansgate ⇌	d						16 28				17 00												17 51
Rochdale 41	d							16 04											17 03				
Manchester Victoria ⇌	d				16 20	16 23		16 36		16 46		17 00	17 07	17 10				17 19	17 23		17 36	17 40	
Salford Central	d				16 23	16 26		16 39		16 49		17 03	17 10	17 13				17 22	17 26		17 39	17 43	
Salford Crescent	a				16 26	16 30	16 34	16 42		16 52	17 04	17 07	17 13	17 17				17 25	17 30	17 34	17 42	17 46	17 55
	d				16 27	16 31	16 34	16 43		16 53	17 04	17 08	17 13	17 17				17 27	17 31	17 34	17 43	17 47	17 55
Swinton	d									16 59				17 23									
Moorside	d									17 02				17 26									
Walkden	d									17 05				17 29									
Atherton	d									17 11				17 35								18 00	
Hag Fold	d									17 14				17 37									
Daisy Hill	d									17 17				17 40								18 04	
Kearsley	d							16 50													17 53		
Farnworth	d							16 52													17 55		
Moses Gate	d							16 55													17 57		
Bolton	a		16 32		16 37	16 42	16 45	16 58	17 05		17 14	17 19	17 23			17 31		17 37	17 42	17 45	18 01		18 06
	d		16 33		16 37		16 45	16 59	17 06		17 15		17 24			17 32		17 37		17 45	18 01		18 07
Westhoughton	d						16 53	17 06					17 31							17 53	18 09		
Hindley	d						16 57	17 10		17 21			17 35	17 45							18 13		
Ince	d									17 24				17 48									
Wigan North Western	a																						
Wigan Wallgate	a						17 02	17 19		17 27			17 46	17 51						18 01	18 24	18 12	
	d						17 03			17 29				17 52						18 02		18 15	
Pemberton	d													17 56									
Orrell	d													18 00									
Upholland	d													18 04									
Rainford	d													18 07									
Kirkby	a													18 21									
Gathurst	d						17 08			17 33												18 20	
Appley Bridge	d						17 11			17 37										18 09		18 24	
Parbold	d						17 15			17 41										18 13		18 28	
Hoscar	d																					18 31	
Burscough Bridge	d						17 20			17 45										18 17		18 35	
New Lane	d																					18 37	
Bescar Lane	d																					18 41	
Meols Cop	d						17 27			17 53												18 46	
Southport	a						17 39			18 04										18 37		18 58	
Lostock	d				16 43						17 20							17 43					18 12
Horwich Parkway	d				16 47						17 24							17 47					18 15
Blackrod	d				16 51													17 51					18 19
Adlington (Lancashire)	d				16 55													17 55					
Chorley	d		16 44		17 00				17 19		17 32					17 44		18 00					18 26
Buckshaw Parkway	d				17 04						17 35							18 04					
Leyland	d				17 11						17 42							18 11					
Preston 8 65,97	a		16 55		17 20				17 30		17 50					17 55		18 16					18 38
	d		17 00	17 04	17 21				17 32							17 58	18 02	18 18					18 40
Kirkham & Wesham 97	a				17 30				17 41									18 27					18 49
Poulton-le-Fylde 97	a				17 38				17 51									18 35					18 59
Layton 97	a				17 43				17 54									18 39					19 02
Blackpool North 97	a				17 52				18 02									18 48					19 10
Lancaster 8 65	a		17 16	17 20												18 13	18 18						
	d	17 00	17 16	17 21											17 32	18 14	18 18						
Oxenholme Lake District 65	a		17 30	17 37												18 28							
Windermere 83	a			18 00																			
Carnforth	d	17 10													17 43		18 31						
Silverdale	d	17 17													17 49		18 37						
Arnside	d	17 21													17 53		18 41						
Grange-over-Sands	d	17 27													17 59		18 46						
Kents Bank	d	17 31													18 03		18 50						
Cark	d	17 35													18 07		18 54						
Ulverston	d	17 44													18 16		19 02						
Dalton	d	17 53													18 24		19 10						
Roose	d	17 59													18 30		19 16						
Barrow-in-Furness	a	18 07													18 38		19 26						

A To Millom
B To Edinburgh
C To Clitheroe
D To Glasgow Central
E To Blackburn

Saturdays
from 6 October

Manchester - Bolton - Wigan, Kirkby, Southport, Preston, Blackpool North and Barrow-in-Furness

Network Diagram - see first Page of Table 82

Station		NT	NT	NT	TP	NT	NT	NT	NT	NT	NT	TP	NT	NT	NT	NT	TP	NT	NT	TP	NT	TP
					◇1							◇1					◇1			◇1		◇1
				A	B 🍴			C				🍴		A		D					A	
Manchester Airport 85 ✈	d				18 00				18 03			18 29					19 00	19 03		19 29		20 00
Heald Green 85	d											18 33								19 33		
Buxton 86	d																					
Hazel Grove 86	d		17 31										18 31									
Stockport 84	d		17 41										18 41									
Manchester Piccadilly 10 ⇌	d		17 54		18 16				18 22			18 46	18 54				19 16	19 20		19 46		20 16
Manchester Oxford Road	d		17 58		18 19				18 26			18 49	18 58				19 19	19 24		19 49		20 19
Deansgate ⇌	d		18 00						18 28			18 51	19 00					19 26		19 51		
Rochdale 41	d							18 02														
Manchester Victoria ⇌	d	17 50		18 00		18 08	18 20	18 23		18 33	18 45			19 00	19 10				19 28		20 00	
Salford Central	d	17 53		18 03		18 12	18 23	18 26		18 36	18 48			19 03	19 13				19 31		20 03	
Salford Crescent	a	17 58	18 04	18 07		18 16	18 26	18 30	18 34	18 39	18 51	18 56	19 04	19 07	19 16			19 29	19 34	19 56	20 07	
	d	17 59	18 04	18 08		18 17	18 27	18 31	18 34	18 40	18 52	18 56	19 04	19 08	19 17			19 30	19 35	19 56	20 08	
Swinton	d	18 05				18 23					18 58				19 23							
Moorside	d	18 08				18 26					19 01				19 26							
Walkden	d	18 11				18 29					19 04				19 29							
Atherton	d	18 17				18 35					19 10				19 35							
Hag Fold	d	18 19				18 37					19 12				19 37							
Daisy Hill	d	18 22				18 40					19 15				19 40							
Kearsley	d									18 47												
Farnworth	d									18 49												
Moses Gate	d									18 52												
Bolton	a		18 14	18 19	18 32		18 37	18 42	18 45	18 55		19 06	19 19	19 20			19 32	19 40	19 45	20 06	20 19	20 32
	d		18 15		18 33		18 37		18 45	18 56		19 07					19 33	19 40	19 45	20 07		20 33
Westhoughton	d								18 53	19 03								19 48				
Hindley	d	18 27				18 45			18 57	19 09	19 20				19 45			19 52				
Ince	d					18 48					19 23				19 48							
Wigan North Western	a					18 56																
Wigan Wallgate	a	18 32							19 02	19 20	19 32				19 57			19 57				
	d	18 33							19 03									19 59				
Pemberton	d	18 37																				
Orrell	d	18 41																				
Upholland	d	18 45																				
Rainford	d	18 48																				
Kirkby	a	19 02																				
Gathurst	d								19 07									20 03				
Appley Bridge	d								19 11									20 07				
Parbold	d								19 15									20 11				
Hoscar	d																					
Burscough Bridge	d								19 19									20 15				
New Lane	d																					
Bescar Lane	d																					
Meols Cop	d								19 27									20 23				
Southport	a								19 39									20 34				
Lostock	d		18 20				18 42					19 12							19 50			
Horwich Parkway	d		18 24				18 46					19 15							19 54	20 13		20 39
Blackrod	d						18 49												19 57			
Adlington (Lancashire)	d						18 53												20 01			
Chorley	d		18 32		18 44		18 58					19 23					19 44		20 06	20 21		20 46
Buckshaw Parkway	d		18 35				19 02					19 26							20 10	20 24		
Leyland	d		18 42				19 10												20 18			
Preston 8 65,97	a		18 48		18 55		19 18					19 33					19 58		20 24	20 33		20 57
	d		18 49		18 58		19 19					19 38					20 01		20 25	20 38		21 02
Kirkham & Wesham 97	a						19 28												20 34			
Poulton-le-Fylde 97	a						19 36					19 56							20 42	20 56		
Layton 97	a						19 43												20 47			
Blackpool North 97	a		19 16				19 52					20 06							20 56	21 06		
Lancaster 8 65	a				19 13												20 17					21 17
	d				19 15											19 24	20 17					21 18
Oxenholme Lake District 65	a																					
Windermere 83	a																					
Carnforth	d				19 24											19a33	20 26					21 26
Silverdale	d				19 30												20 32					21 32
Arnside	d				19 34												20 36					21 36
Grange-over-Sands	d				19 40												20 42					21 42
Kents Bank	d				19 43												20 45					21 45
Cark	d				19 48												20 50					21 50
Ulverston	d				19 56												20 58					21 58
Dalton	d				20 04												21 06					22 06
Roose	d				20 10												21 12					22 12
Barrow-in-Furness	a				20 19												21 20					22 21

A To Clitheroe
B 🍴 to Preston
C To Blackburn
D From Morecambe to Leeds

Saturdays from 6 October

Manchester - Bolton - Wigan, Kirkby, Southport, Preston, Blackpool North and Barrow-in-Furness

Network Diagram - see first Page of Table 82

	NT	NT	NT	NT	TP	NT	NT	NT	NT	NT	NT	NT	TP	NT	TP	NT	NT	NT	NT	TP	NT	NT
					◇1								◇1		◇1					◇1		
				A		B					A	C		B		A						D
Manchester Airport 85 ✈ d			20 03	20 09	20 29					21 03	21 09		21 29		22 00	22 08		22 19		22 29		
Heald Green 85 d				20 12	20 33						21 12		21 33			22 12				22 33		
Buxton 86 d																						
Hazel Grove 86 d																						
Stockport 84 d																					22 40	
Manchester Piccadilly 10 ⇌ d			20 20	20 32	20 46					21 20	21 32	21 38	21 46		22 16	22 32		22 36		22 46	22 54	
Manchester Oxford Road d			20 24	20a36	20 49					21 24	21a36	21 44	21 49		22 19	22a36		22 39		22 49	22 58	
Deansgate ⇌ d			20 26		20 51					21 26		21a46	21 51					22 41		22 51	23 00	
Rochdale 41 d																						
Manchester Victoria ⇌ d	20 10	20 22				21 00	21 10		21 22					22 00			22 22		22 45			23 05
Salford Central d	20 13	20 25				21 03	21 13		21 25					22 03			22 25		22 48			23 08
Salford Crescent a	20 16	20 29	20 33		20 56	21 07	21 16		21 29	21 33			21 56	22 07			22 29	22 46	22 51	22 56	23 02	23 11
d	20 17	20 30	20 34		20 56	21 08	21 17		21 30	21 34			21 56	22 08			22 30	22 46	22 52	22 56	23 04	23 12
Swinton d	20 23						21 23												22 58			
Moorside d	20 26						21 26												23 01			
Walkden d	20 29						21 29												23 04			
Atherton d	20 35						21 35												23 10			
Hag Fold d	20 37						21 37												23 12			
Daisy Hill d	20 40						21 40												23 15			
Kearsley d																					23 11	
Farnworth d																					23 13	
Moses Gate d																					23 16	
Bolton a		20 40	20 45		21 06	21 19			21 40	21 45			22 06	22 19	22 32		22 40	22 56		23 06	23 19	23 23
d		20 40	20 45		21 07				21 40	21 45			22 07		22 33		22 40	22 57		23 07	23 20	
Westhoughton d			20 53							21 53								23 04			23 27	
Hindley d	20 45		20 57				21 45			21 57								23 08	23 20		23 31	
Ince d	20 48						21 48												23 23			
Wigan North Western a																						
Wigan Wallgate a	20 57		21 02				21 57			22 02								23 13	23 32		23 41	
d			21 03							22 03								23 15				
Pemberton d																						
Orrell d																						
Upholland d																						
Rainford d																						
Kirkby a																						
Gathurst d			21 08							22 08								23 19				
Appley Bridge d			21 11							22 11								23 23				
Parbold d			21 15							22 15								23 27				
Hoscar d			21 18																			
Burscough Bridge d			21 21							22 20								23 31				
New Lane d			21 24																			
Bescar Lane d			21 27																			
Meols Cop d			21 32							22 27								23 39				
Southport a			21 44							22 39								23 50				
Lostock d		20 45							21 45								22 45					
Horwich Parkway d		20 49			21 13				21 49				22 13				22 49			23 13		
Blackrod d		20 52							21 52								22 52					
Adlington (Lancashire) d		20 56							21 56								22 56					
Chorley d		21 01			21 21				22 01				22 21				23 01			23 21		
Buckshaw Parkway d		21 05			21 24				22 05				22 24				23 05			23 24		
Leyland d		21 12							22 12								23 12					
Preston 8 65,97 a		21 17			21 33				22 18				22 36		22 54		23 17			23 33		
d		21 19			21 38			21 59	22 19				22 38		22 55		23 19			23 35		
Kirkham & Wesham 97 a		21 28							22 28								23 28					
Poulton-le-Fylde 97 a		21 36			21 56				22 36				22 55				23 36			23 52		
Layton 97 a		21 40							22 43								23 40					
Blackpool North 97 a		21 50			22 06				22 52				23 04				23 50			00 02		
Lancaster 6 65 a								22 19							23 11							
d								22 19							23 11							
Oxenholme Lake District 65 a																						
Windermere 83 a																						
Carnforth d								22 29							23 20							
Silverdale d								22 35							23 26							
Arnside d								22 40							23 30							
Grange-over-Sands d								22 46							23 35							
Kents Bank d								22 49							23 39							
Cark d								22 54							23 43							
Ulverston d								23 02							23 51							
Dalton d								23 10							23 59							
Roose d								23 16							00 05							
Barrow-in-Furness a								23 24							00 15							

A From Wilmslow
B To Clitheroe
C To Warrington Central
D To Blackburn

Saturdays from 6 October

Manchester - Bolton - Wigan, Kirkby, Southport, Preston, Blackpool North and Barrow-in-Furness

Network Diagram - see first Page of Table 82

	NT	NT
Manchester Airport 85 ✈ d		
Heald Green 85 d		
Buxton 86 d		
Hazel Grove 86 d		
Stockport 84 d		
Manchester Piccadilly 10 ⇌ d		
Manchester Oxford Road d		
Deansgate ⇌ d		
Rochdale 41 d		
Manchester Victoria ⇌ d	23 16	23 20
Salford Central d	23 19	23 23
Salford Crescent a	23 22	23 26
d	23 22	23 26
Swinton d		23 33
Moorside d		23 35
Walkden d		23 39
Atherton d		23 44
Hag Fold d		23 47
Daisy Hill d		23 50
Kearsley d		
Farnworth d		
Moses Gate d		
Bolton a	23 32	
d	23 33	
Westhoughton d		
Hindley d		23 54
Ince d		23 57
Wigan North Western a		
Wigan Wallgate a		00 06
d		
Pemberton d		
Orrell d		
Upholland d		
Rainford d		
Kirkby a		
Gathurst d		
Appley Bridge d		
Parbold d		
Hoscar d		
Burscough Bridge d		
New Lane d		
Bescar Lane d		
Meols Cop d		
Southport a		
Lostock d	23 38	
Horwich Parkway d	23 42	
Blackrod d	23 45	
Adlington (Lancashire) d	23 49	
Chorley d	23 54	
Buckshaw Parkway d	23 57	
Leyland d	00 04	
Preston 8 65,97 a	00 10	
d	00 11	
Kirkham & Wesham 97 a	00 21	
Poulton-le-Fylde 97 a	00 29	
Layton 97 a	00 33	
Blackpool North 97 a	00 42	
Lancaster 6 65 a		
d		
Oxenholme Lake District 65 a		
Windermere 83 a		
Carnforth d		
Silverdale d		
Arnside d		
Grange-over-Sands d		
Kents Bank d		
Cark d		
Ulverston d		
Dalton d		
Roose d		
Barrow-in-Furness a		

Table 82

Sundays until 24 June

Manchester - Bolton - Wigan, Kirkby, Southport, Preston, Blackpool North and Barrow-in-Furness

Network Diagram - see first Page of Table 82

	TP	TP	NT	NT	TP	TP	TP	TP	TP	NT	TP	NT	NT	NT	NT	TP	TP	TP	TP	NT	NT	TP
	◇1	◇1						◇1	◇1		◇1					◇1	◇1	◇1	◇1			◇1
						A		B	C	D				E	D			F	C			
					🚌	🚌	🚌											⌶				
Manchester Airport 85 ✈ d	22p00	22p29			00 05	01 20	05 30	06 11	07 50		07 55			08 34		08 47		09 00	09 03			09 30
Heald Green 85 d		22p33																				
Buxton 86 d																						
Hazel Grove 86 d																						
Stockport 84 d													08 24								09 22	
Manchester Piccadilly 10 ⇌ d	22p16	22p46			00 30	01a45	05 55	06 26	08 05		08 11		08 35	08 49		09 03		09 16	09 20		09 35	09 46
Manchester Oxford Road d	22p19	22p49									08 14		08 38	08 52		09 06		09 19			09 38	09 49
Deansgate ⇌ d		22p51									08 16		08 40	08a54		09 08					09 40	09 51
Rochdale 41 d																						
Manchester Victoria ⇌ d			23p16	23p20					08a20	08 01		08 25			09 00				09a35	09 25		
Salford Central d			23p19	23p23																		
Salford Crescent a		22p56	23p22	23p26				06 31		08 07	08 19	08 29	08 44		09 06	09 11				09 29	09 44	09 54
d		22p56	23p22	23p26						08 07	08 20	08 30	08 44		09 08	09 12				09 30	09 44	09 55
Swinton d				23p33																		
Moorside d				23p35																		
Walkden d				23p39																		
Atherton d				23p44																		
Hag Fold d				23p47																		
Daisy Hill d				23p50																		
Kearsley d																						
Farnworth d																						
Moses Gate d																						
Bolton a	22p32	23p06	23p32		00s55		06s20			08 19	08 30	08 40	08 54		09 19	09 22		09 32		09 40	09 54	10 05
d	22p33	23p07	23p33								08 30	08 40	08 55			09 23		09 33		09 40	09 55	10 05
Westhoughton d													09 02								10 02	
Hindley d				23p54									09 06								10 06	
Ince d				23p57																		
Wigan North Western a																						
Wigan Wallgate a				00 04									09 11								10 11	
d													09 13								10 13	
Pemberton d																						
Orrell d																						
Upholland d																						
Rainford d																						
Kirkby a																						
Gathurst d													09 17								10 17	
Appley Bridge d													09 21								10 21	
Parbold d													09 25								10 25	
Hoscar d																						
Burscough Bridge d													09 29								10 29	
New Lane d																						
Bescar Lane d																						
Meols Cop d													09 37								10 37	
Southport a													09 46								10 44	
Lostock d			23p38									08 45								09 45		
Horwich Parkway d		23p13	23p42								08 37	08 49				09 29				09 49		10 12
Blackrod d			23p45									08 52								09 52		
Adlington (Lancashire) d			23p49									08 56								09 56		
Chorley d		23p21	23p54								08 44	09 01				09 37		09 44		10 01		10 19
Buckshaw Parkway d		23p24	23p57								08 48	09 05				09 40				10 05		10 23
Leyland d			00 04									09 12								10 12		
Preston 8 65,97 a	22p54	23p33	00 10		01s30		06s55				08 57	09 18				09 50		09 57		10 18		10 33
d	22p55	23p35	00 11								08 58	09 20				09 52	10 07	10 00		10 20		10 35
Kirkham & Wesham 97 a			00 21									09 29								10 29		
Poulton-le-Fylde 97 a		23p52	00 29								09 15	09 37				10 09				10 37		10 52
Layton 97 a			00 34									09 42								10 42		
Blackpool North 97 a		00 02	00 40		02 10		07 35				09 23	09 49				10 18				10 49		11 01
Lancaster 6 65 a	23p11																10 22	10 15				
d	23p11																10 23	10 16				
Oxenholme Lake District 65 a																	10 39	10 30				
Windermere 83 a																	10 57					
Carnforth d	23p20																					
Silverdale d	23p26																					
Arnside d	23p30																					
Grange-over-Sands d	23p35																					
Kents Bank d	23p39																					
Cark d	23p43																					
Ulverston d	23p51																					
Dalton d	23p59																					
Roose d	00 05																					
Barrow-in-Furness a	00 15																					

A To Huddersfield
B To Middlesbrough
C To Newcastle
D To Clitheroe
E To Liverpool Lime Street
F To Edinburgh

The Sunday service between Manchester Victoria and Wigan Wallgate via Atherton is funded by TfGM and will operate whilst funding exists

Table 82

Sundays until 24 June

Manchester - Bolton - Wigan, Kirkby, Southport, Preston, Blackpool North and Barrow-in-Furness

Network Diagram - see first Page of Table 82

	NT	NT	TP	TP	TP	NT	NT	TP	NT	TP	TP	NT	NT	NT	NT	TP	NT	NT	NT	TP	TP	NT
			◇1	◇1	◇1			◇1		◇1	◇1					◇1				◇1	◇1	
	A			B	C		D		A		C	E					A		F	G	C	
				⌶																⌶		
Manchester Airport 85 ✈ d				10 00	10 03			10 30		11 00	11 03	11 05				11 30				12 00	12 03	12 08
Heald Green 85 d												11 08										12 11
Buxton 86 d																						
Hazel Grove 86 d																						
Stockport 84 d							10 12								11 15							
Manchester Piccadilly 10 ⇌ d				10 16	10 21		10 24	10 46		11 16	11 21	11 27			11 33	11 46				12 16	12 21	12 29
Manchester Oxford Road d				10 19			10 38	10 49		11 19		11a31			11 38	11 49				12 19		12a33
Deansgate ⇌ d							10 40	10 51							11 40	11 51						
Rochdale 41 d																						
Manchester Victoria ⇌ d	10 00	10 09			10a35	10 25			11 00		11a35		11 12	11 25			12 00	12 09			12a35	
Salford Central d																						
Salford Crescent a	10 06	10 16				10 29	10 44	10 54	11 06				11 16	11 29	11 44	11 54	12 06	12 13				
d	10 08	10 17				10 30	10 44	10 55	11 08				11 17	11 30	11 44	11 55	12 08	12 17				
Swinton d		10 23											11 23					12 23				
Moorside d		10 26											11 26					12 26				
Walkden d		10 29											11 29					12 29				
Atherton d		10 35											11 35					12 35				
Hag Fold d		10 37											11 37					12 37				
Daisy Hill d		10 40											11 40					12 40				
Kearsley d																						
Farnworth d																						
Moses Gate d																						
Bolton a	10 19			10 32		10 40	10 54	11 05	11 19	11 32				11 40	11 54	12 05	12 19			12 32		
d				10 33		10 40	10 55	11 05		11 33				11 40	11 55	12 05				12 33		
Westhoughton d							11 02								12 02							
Hindley d		10 45					11 06						11 45		12 06			12 45				
Ince d		10 48											11 48					12 48				
Wigan North Western a																						
Wigan Wallgate a		10 55					11 11						11 55		12 11			12 55				
d							11 13								12 13							
Pemberton d																						
Orrell d																						
Upholland d																						
Rainford d																						
Kirkby a																						
Gathurst d							11 17								12 17							
Appley Bridge d							11 21								12 21							
Parbold d							11 25								12 25							
Hoscar d																						
Burscough Bridge d							11 29								12 29							
New Lane d																						
Bescar Lane d																						
Meols Cop d							11 37								12 37							
Southport a							11 46								12 44							
Lostock d						10 45								11 45								
Horwich Parkway d						10 49		11 12						11 49		12 12						
Blackrod d						10 52								11 52								
Adlington (Lancashire) d						10 56								11 56								
Chorley d				10 44		11 01		11 19		11 44				12 01		12 19				12 44		
Buckshaw Parkway d						11 05		11 23						12 05		12 23						
Leyland d						11 12								12 12								
Preston 8 65,97 a				10 57		11 20		11 33		11 57				12 18		12 33				12 57		
d				10 58		11 21		11 35		11 58				12 20		12 35				12 58		
Kirkham & Wesham 97 a						11 31								12 29								
Poulton-le-Fylde 97 a						11 39		11 52						12 37		12 52						
Layton 97 a						11 44								12 42								
Blackpool North 97 a						11 49		12 01						12 49		13 01						
Lancaster 6 65 a				11 13						12 13										13 13		
d			10 28	11 14						12 14									12 48	13 14		
Oxenholme Lake District 65 a				11 28																13 28		
Windermere 83 a																						
Carnforth d			10 36							12 22									12a57			
Silverdale d			10 42							12 28												
Arnside d			10 46							12 32												
Grange-over-Sands d			10 52							12 38												
Kents Bank d			10 55							12 41												
Cark d			11 00							12 46												
Ulverston d			11 08							12 54												
Dalton d			11 16							13 02												
Roose d			11 22							13 08												
Barrow-in-Furness a			11 30							13 17												

A To Clitheroe
B To Glasgow Central
C To Newcastle
D From Chester
E From Alderley Edge
F From Morecambe to Leeds
G To Edinburgh

The Sunday service between Manchester Victoria and Wigan Wallgate via Atherton is funded by TfGM and will operate whilst funding exists

Table 82

Sundays until 24 June

Manchester - Bolton - Wigan, Kirkby, Southport, Preston, Blackpool North and Barrow-in-Furness

Network Diagram - see first Page of Table 82

	NT		NT A	TP ◇1	NT B	TP ◇1 C 🍴		TP ◇1 D	NT	NT	NT		TP ◇1	NT B	NT	NT E	TP ◇1 F 🍴	TP ◇1 D	NT	NT A	TP ◇1		NT B	TP ◇1
Manchester Airport 85 ✈ d				12 30		12 58		13 03					13 30				13 58	14 03			14 30			14 58
Heald Green 85 d																								
Buxton 86 d																								
Hazel Grove 86 d																								
Stockport 84 d			12 21								13 22									14 21				
Manchester Piccadilly 10 ⇌ d			12 35	12 46		13 16		13 21			13 35		13 46				14 16	14 21		14 35	14 46			15 16
Manchester Oxford Road d			12 38	12 49		13 19					13 38		13 49				14 19			14 38	14 49			15 19
Deansgate ⇌ d			12 40	12 51							13 40		13 51							14 40	14 51			
Rochdale 41 d																								
Manchester Victoria ⇌ d	12 25				13 00			13a35	13 12	13 25				14 00	14 12			14a35	14 25				15 00	
Salford Central d																								
Salford Crescent a	12 29		12 44	12 54	13 06				13 16	13 29	13 44		13 54	14 06	14 16				14 29	14 44	14 54		15 06	
d	12 30		12 44	12 55	13 08				13 17	13 30	13 44		13 55	14 08	14 17				14 30	14 44	14 55		15 08	
Swinton d									13 23						14 23									
Moorside d									13 26						14 26									
Walkden d									13 29						14 29									
Atherton d									13 35						14 35									
Hag Fold d									13 37						14 37									
Daisy Hill d									13 40						14 40									
Kearsley d																								
Farnworth d																								
Moses Gate d																								
Bolton a	12 40		12 54	13 05	13 19	13 32				13 41	13 54		14 05	14 19			14 32		14 40	14 54	15 05		15 19	15 32
d	12 40		12 55	13 05		13 33				13 41	13 55		14 05				14 33		14 40	14 55	15 05			15 33
Westhoughton d			13 02								14 02									15 02				
Hindley d			13 06						13 45		14 06				14 45					15 06				
Ince d									13 48						14 48									
Wigan North Western a																								
Wigan Wallgate a			13 11						13 55		14 11				14 55					15 11				
d			13 13								14 13									15 13				
Pemberton d																								
Orrell d																								
Upholland d																								
Rainford d																								
Kirkby a																								
Gathurst d			13 17								14 17									15 17				
Appley Bridge d			13 21								14 21									15 21				
Parbold d			13 25								14 25									15 25				
Hoscar d																								
Burscough Bridge d			13 29								14 29									15 29				
New Lane d																								
Bescar Lane d																								
Meols Cop d			13 37								14 37									15 37				
Southport a			13 46								14 44									15 46				
Lostock d	12 45									13 46									14 45					
Horwich Parkway d	12 49			13 12						13 50			14 12						14 49		15 12			
Blackrod d	12 52									13 53									14 52					
Adlington (Lancashire) d	12 56									13 57									14 56					
Chorley d	13 01			13 19		13 44				14 02			14 19				14 44		15 01		15 19			15 44
Buckshaw Parkway d	13 05			13 23						14 06			14 23						15 05		15 23			
Leyland d	13 12									14 13									15 13					
Preston 8 65,97 a	13 18			13 33		13 57				14 18			14 33				14 57		15 18		15 33			15 57
d	13 20			13 35		14 00	14 04			14 20			14 35				15 00		15 20		15 35			16 00
Kirkham & Wesham 97 a	13 29									14 29									15 29					
Poulton-le-Fylde 97 a	13 37			13 52						14 37			14 52						15 37		15 52			
Layton 97 a	13 42									14 42									15 43					
Blackpool North 97 a	13 49			14 01						14 49			15 01						15 49		16 01			
Lancaster 6 65 a						14 15	14 20										15 15							16 15
d						14 16	14 20									14 27	15 16							16 16
Oxenholme Lake District 65 a						14 30											15 30							
Windermere 83 a																								
Carnforth d							14 29									14a59								16 24
Silverdale d							14 35																	16 30
Arnside d							14 39																	16 34
Grange-over-Sands d							14 44																	16 40
Kents Bank d							14 48																	16 43
Cark d							14 52																	16 48
Ulverston d							15 00																	16 56
Dalton d							15 08																	17 04
Roose d							15 14																	17 10
Barrow-in-Furness a							15 24																	17 19

A From Chester
B To Clitheroe
C To Glasgow Central
D To Newcastle
E To Leeds
F To Edinburgh

The Sunday service between Manchester Victoria and Wigan Wallgate via Atherton is funded by TfGM and will operate whilst funding exists

Table 82

Sundays until 24 June

Manchester - Bolton - Wigan, Kirkby, Southport, Preston, Blackpool North and Barrow-in-Furness

Network Diagram - see first Page of Table 82

	TP ◇1 A	NT	NT	NT	TP ◇1	NT B	NT		NT	NT C	NT D	TP ◇1 E 🍴		TP ◇1 A	NT F	TP ◇1	NT B		TP ◇1 G 🍴	TP ◇1 A	NT	NT	NT	TP ◇1
Manchester Airport 85 ✈ d	15 03				15 30							15 58		16 03		16 30			16 58	17 03				17 30
Heald Green 85 d																								
Buxton 86 d																								
Hazel Grove 86 d																								
Stockport 84 d				15 22											16 21								17 22	
Manchester Piccadilly 10 ⇌ d	15 21			15 35	15 46							16 16		16 21	16 35	16 46			17 16	17 21			17 35	17 46
Manchester Oxford Road d				15 38	15 49							16 19			16 38	16 49			17 19				17 38	17 49
Deansgate ⇌ d				15 40	15 51										16 40	16 51							17 40	17 51
Rochdale 41 d																								
Manchester Victoria ⇌ d	15a35	15 12	15 25			16 00	16 12		16 25					16a35			17 00			17a35	17 12	17 25		
Salford Central d																								
Salford Crescent a		15 16	15 29	15 44	15 54	16 06	16 16		16 29						16 44	16 54	17 06				17 16	17 29	17 44	17 54
d		15 17	15 30	15 44	15 55	16 08	16 17		16 30						16 44	16 55	17 08				17 17	17 30	17 44	17 55
Swinton d		15 23					16 23														17 23			
Moorside d		15 26					16 26														17 26			
Walkden d		15 29					16 29														17 29			
Atherton d		15 35					16 35														17 35			
Hag Fold d		15 37					16 37														17 37			
Daisy Hill d		15 40					16 40														17 40			
Kearsley d																								
Farnworth d																								
Moses Gate d																								
Bolton a			15 40	15 54	16 05	16 19			16 40			16 32			16 54	17 05	17 19		17 32			17 40	17 54	18 05
d			15 40	15 55	16 05				16 40			16 33			16 55	17 05			17 33			17 40	17 55	18 05
Westhoughton d				16 02											17 02								18 02	
Hindley d		15 45		16 06			16 45								17 06						17 45		18 06	
Ince d		15 48					16 48														17 48			
Wigan North Western a																								
Wigan Wallgate a		15 55		16 11			16 55								17 11						17 55		18 11	
d				16 13											17 13								18 13	
Pemberton d																								
Orrell d																								
Upholland d																								
Rainford d																								
Kirkby a																								
Gathurst d				16 17											17 17								18 17	
Appley Bridge d				16 21											17 21								18 21	
Parbold d				16 25											17 25								18 25	
Hoscar d																								
Burscough Bridge d				16 29											17 29								18 29	
New Lane d																								
Bescar Lane d																								
Meols Cop d				16 37											17 37								18 37	
Southport a				16 44											17 46								18 46	
Lostock d			15 45						16 45													17 45		
Horwich Parkway d			15 49		16 12				16 49							17 12						17 49		18 12
Blackrod d			15 52						16 52													17 52		
Adlington (Lancashire) d			15 56						16 56													17 56		
Chorley d			16 01		16 19				17 01			16 44				17 19			17 44			18 01		18 19
Buckshaw Parkway d			16 05		16 23				17 05							17 23						18 05		18 23
Leyland d			16 12						17 12													18 12		
Preston 8 65,97 a			16 18		16 33				17 18			16 57				17 33			17 57			18 18		18 33
d			16 20		16 35				17 20			17 00	18 07			17 35			18 00			18 20		18 35
Kirkham & Wesham 97 a			16 29						17 29													18 29		
Poulton-le-Fylde 97 a			16 37		16 52				17 37							17 52						18 37		18 52
Layton 97 a			16 42						17 42													18 42		
Blackpool North 97 a			16 49		17 01				17 49							18 01						18 49		19 01
Lancaster 6 65 a												17 15	18 23						18 15					
d										17 30	18 04	17 16	18 23						18 16					
Oxenholme Lake District 65 a												17 30	18 40						18 30					
Windermere 83 a													19 01											
Carnforth d										17 40	18a13													
Silverdale d										17 46														
Arnside d										17 51														
Grange-over-Sands d										17 57														
Kents Bank d										18 00														
Cark d										18 04														
Ulverston d										18 12														
Dalton d										18 21														
Roose d										18 27														
Barrow-in-Furness a										18 34														

A To Newcastle
B To Clitheroe
C 20 May
D From Morecambe to Leeds
E To Edinburgh
F From Chester
G To Glasgow Central

The Sunday service between Manchester Victoria and Wigan Wallgate via Atherton is funded by TfGM and will operate whilst funding exists

Table 82

Manchester - Bolton - Wigan, Kirkby, Southport, Preston, Blackpool North and Barrow-in-Furness

Network Diagram - see first Page of Table 82

		NT A	TP ◇1 B 🍴	TP ◇1 B	TP ◇1 C	NT	NT	NT D	TP ◇1	NT A	NT E	TP ◇1	TP ◇1 F	NT	NT	TP ◇1	NT A	TP ◇1 G	NT	NT D	TP ◇1	NT A
Manchester Airport 85 ✈	d		17 58		18 03				18 30			18 58	19 03			19 30		20 03			20 30	
Heald Green 85	d																					
Buxton 86	d																					
Hazel Grove 86	d																					
Stockport 84	d							18 21							19 22					20 21		
Manchester Piccadilly 10 ⇌	d		18 16		18 21			18 35	18 46			19 16	19 21		19 35	19 46		20 21		20 35	20 46	
Manchester Oxford Road	d		18 19					18 38	18 49			19 19			19 38	19 49				20 38	20 49	
Deansgate ⇌	d							18 40	18 51						19 40	19 51				20 40	20 51	
Rochdale 41	d																					
Manchester Victoria ⇌	d	18 00			18a35	18 12	18 25			19 00			19a35	19 25			20 00	20a35	20 25			21 00
Salford Central	d																					
Salford Crescent	a	18 06				18 16	18 29	18 44	18 54	19 06				19 29	19 44	19 54	20 06		20 29	20 44	20 54	21 06
	d	18 08				18 17	18 30	18 44	18 55	19 08				19 30	19 44	19 55	20 08		20 30	20 44	20 55	21 08
Swinton	d					18 23																
Moorside	d					18 26																
Walkden	d					18 29																
Atherton	d					18 35																
Hag Fold	d					18 37																
Daisy Hill	d					18 40																
Kearsley	d																					
Farnworth	d																					
Moses Gate	d																					
Bolton	a	18 19	18 32				18 40	18 54	19 05	19 19		19 32		19 40	19 54	20 05	20 19		20 40	20 54	21 05	21 19
	d		18 33				18 40	18 55	19 05			19 33		19 40	19 55	20 05			20 40	20 55	21 05	
Westhoughton	d							19 02							20 02					21 02		
Hindley	d					18 45		19 06							20 06					21 06		
Ince	d					18 48																
Wigan North Western	a																					
Wigan Wallgate	a					18 55		19 11							20 11					21 11		
	d							19 13							20 13					21 13		
Pemberton	d																					
Orrell	d																					
Upholland	d																					
Rainford	d																					
Kirkby	a																					
Gathurst	d							19 17							20 17					21 17		
Appley Bridge	d							19 21							20 21					21 21		
Parbold	d							19 25							20 25					21 25		
Hoscar	d																					
Burscough Bridge	d							19 29							20 29					21 29		
New Lane	d																					
Bescar Lane	d																					
Meols Cop	d							19 37							20 37					21 37		
Southport	a							19 46							20 46					21 46		
Lostock	d						18 45							19 45					20 45			
Horwich Parkway	d						18 49		19 12					19 49		20 12			20 49		21 12	
Blackrod	d						18 52							19 52					20 52			
Adlington (Lancashire)	d						18 56							19 56					20 56			
Chorley	d		18 44				19 01		19 19			19 44		20 01		20 19			21 01		21 19	
Buckshaw Parkway	d						19 05		19 23					20 05		20 23			21 05		21 23	
Leyland	d						19 14							20 14					21 12			
Preston 8 65,97	a		18 55				19 19		19 33			19 57		20 19		20 33			21 18		21 33	
	d		19 00	19 06			19 21		19 35			20 06		20 21		20 35			21 20		21 35	
Kirkham & Wesham 97	a						19 30							20 30					21 29			
Poulton-le-Fylde 97	a						19 38		19 52					20 38		20 52			21 37		21 52	
Layton 97	a						19 42							20 43					21 42			
Blackpool North 97	a						19 49		20 01					20 49		21 01			21 49		22 01	
Lancaster 6 65	a		19 15	19 22								20 23										
	d		19 16	19 22							20 18	20 24										
Oxenholme Lake District 65	a		19 30																			
Windermere 83	a																					
Carnforth	d			19 31							20a27	20 32										
Silverdale	d			19 37																		
Arnside	d			19 41								20 41										
Grange-over-Sands	d			19 46								20 46										
Kents Bank	d			19 50																		
Cark	d			19 54																		
Ulverston	d			20 02								20 59										
Dalton	d			20 10																		
Roose	d			20 16																		
Barrow-in-Furness	a			20 26								21 19										

A To Clitheroe
B To Edinburgh
C To Middlesbrough
D From Chester
E From Morecambe to Leeds
F To Newcastle
G To Scarborough

The Sunday service between Manchester Victoria and Wigan Wallgate via Atherton is funded by TfGM and will operate whilst funding exists

Table 82

Manchester - Bolton - Wigan, Kirkby, Southport, Preston, Blackpool North and Barrow-in-Furness

Network Diagram - see first Page of Table 82

		TP ◇1 A	TP ◇1 B	NT	NT	TP ◇1	NT C	NT	NT D	NT E	TP ◇1	TP ◇1 A
Manchester Airport 85 ✈	d	21 03				21 30				22 27	22 30	23 22
Heald Green 85	d											
Buxton 86	d											
Hazel Grove 86	d											
Stockport 84	d				21 22				22 21			
Manchester Piccadilly 10 ⇌	d	21 21			21 35	21 46			22 35	22 41	22 46	23 39
Manchester Oxford Road	d				21 38	21 49			22 38	22 45	22 49	
Deansgate ⇌	d				21 40	21 51			22 40	22a47	22 51	
Rochdale 41	d											
Manchester Victoria ⇌	d	21a35		21 25			22 00					23a52
Salford Central	d											
Salford Crescent	a			21 29	21 44	21 54	22 06		22 44		22 54	
	d			21 30	21 44	21 55	22 08		22 44		22 55	
Swinton	d											
Moorside	d											
Walkden	d											
Atherton	d											
Hag Fold	d											
Daisy Hill	d											
Kearsley	d											
Farnworth	d											
Moses Gate	d											
Bolton	a			21 40	21 54	22 05	22 19		22 54		23 05	
	d			21 40	21 55	22 05			22 55		23 05	
Westhoughton	d				22 02				23 02			
Hindley	d				22 06				23 06			
Ince	d											
Wigan North Western	a											
Wigan Wallgate	a				22 15				23 15			
	d											
Pemberton	d											
Orrell	d											
Upholland	d											
Rainford	d											
Kirkby	a											
Gathurst	d											
Appley Bridge	d											
Parbold	d											
Hoscar	d											
Burscough Bridge	d											
New Lane	d											
Bescar Lane	d											
Meols Cop	d											
Southport	a											
Lostock	d			21 45							23 10	
Horwich Parkway	d			21 49							23 14	
Blackrod	d			21 52							23 17	
Adlington (Lancashire)	d			21 56							23 20	
Chorley	d			22 01		22 17					23 25	
Buckshaw Parkway	d			22 05							23 28	
Leyland	d			22 12							23 36	
Preston 8 65,97	a			22 18		22 28					23 42	
	d			22 20		22 29					23 47	
Kirkham & Wesham 97	a			22 29							23 56	
Poulton-le-Fylde 97	a			22 37		22 46					00 05	
Layton 97	a			22 42								
Blackpool North 97	a			22 49		22 55					00 14	
Lancaster 6 65	a											
	d		21 23				22 05					
Oxenholme Lake District 65	a											
Windermere 83	a											
Carnforth	d		21 31				22 15					
Silverdale	d		21 37				22 21					
Arnside	d		21 41				22 26					
Grange-over-Sands	d		21 47				22 32					
Kents Bank	d		21 50				22 35					
Cark	d		21 55				22 39					
Ulverston	d		22 02				22 47					
Dalton	d		22 10				22 56					
Roose	d		22 16				23 02					
Barrow-in-Furness	a		22 26				23 09					

A To York
B From Windermere
C To Blackburn
D From Chester
E To Liverpool Lime Street

The Sunday service between Manchester Victoria and Wigan Wallgate via Atherton is funded by TfGM and will operate whilst funding exists

1 July to 9 September

Manchester - Bolton - Wigan, Kirkby, Southport, Preston, Blackpool North and Barrow-in-Furness

Network Diagram - see first Page of Table 82

	TP	TP	NT	NT	TP	TP	NT	TP	NT		NT	NT	NT	TP	TP	TP	TP	NT	NT		TP	NT	NT	TP
	◇1	◇1			Bus	Bus	A	◇1				B	A	◇1	◇1	◇1 B	◇1 C ✠				◇1	A		◇1
Manchester Airport 85 ✈ d	22p00	22p29			00 05	05 30		07 55				08 34		08 47			09 00				09 30			
Heald Green 85 d		22p33																						
Buxton 86 d																								
Hazel Grove 86 d																								
Stockport 84 d											08 24								09 22					
Manchester Piccadilly 10 ⇌ d	22p16	22p46			00 30	05 55		08 11			08 35	08 49		09 03		09 07	09 16		09 35		09 46			
Manchester Oxford Road d	22p19	22p49						08 14			08 38	08 52		09 06		09a09	09 19		09 38		09 49			
Deansgate ⇌ d		22p51						08 16			08 40	08a54		09 08					09 40		09 51			
Rochdale 41 d																								
Manchester Victoria ⇌ d			23p16	23p20			08 01		08 25				09 00					09 25				10 00	10 09	
Salford Central d			23p19	23p23																				
Salford Crescent a		22p56	23p22	23p26			08 07	08 19	08 29		08 44		09 06	09 11				09 29	09 44		09 54	10 06	10 16	
d		22p56	23p22	23p26			08 07	08 20	08 30		08 44		09 08	09 12				09 30	09 44		09 55	10 08	10 17	
Swinton d				23p33																			10 23	
Moorside d				23p35																			10 26	
Walkden d				23p39																			10 29	
Atherton d				23p44																			10 35	
Hag Fold d				23p47																			10 37	
Daisy Hill d				23p50																			10 40	
Kearsley d																								
Farnworth d																								
Moses Gate d																								
Bolton a	22p32	23p06	23p32		00s55	06s20	08 19	08 30	08 40		08 54		09 19	09 22			09 32	09 40	09 54		10 05	10 19		
d	22p33	23p07	23p33					08 30	08 40		08 55			09 23			09 33	09 40	09 55		10 05			
Westhoughton d											09 02								10 02					
Hindley d				23p54							09 06								10 06				10 45	
Ince d				23p57																			10 48	
Wigan North Western a																								
Wigan Wallgate a				00 04							09 11								10 11				10 55	
d											09 13								10 13					
Pemberton d																								
Orrell d																								
Upholland d																								
Rainford d																								
Kirkby a																								
Gathurst d											09 17								10 17					
Appley Bridge d											09 21								10 21					
Parbold d											09 25								10 25					
Hoscar d																								
Burscough Bridge d											09 29								10 29					
New Lane d																								
Bescar Lane d																								
Meols Cop d											09 37								10 37					
Southport a											09 46								10 44					
Lostock d			23p38						08 45									09 45						
Horwich Parkway d		23p13	23p42					08 37	08 49					09 29				09 49			10 12			
Blackrod d			23p45						08 52									09 52						
Adlington (Lancashire) d			23p49						08 56									09 56						
Chorley d		23p21	23p54					08 44	09 01					09 37			09 44	10 01			10 19			
Buckshaw Parkway d		23p24	23p57					08 48	09 05					09 40				10 05			10 23			
Leyland d			00 04						09 12									10 12						
Preston 8 65,97 a	22p54	23p33	00 10		01s30	06s55		08 57	09 18					09 50			09 57	10 18			10 33			
d	22p55	23p35	00 11					08 58	09 20					09 52	10 07		10 00	10 20			10 35			
Kirkham & Wesham 97 a			00 21						09 29									10 29						
Poulton-le-Fylde 97 a		23p52	00 29					09 15	09 37					10 09				10 37			10 52			
Layton 97 a			00 34						09 42									10 42						
Blackpool North 97 a		00 02	00 40		02 10	07 35		09 23	09 49					10 18				10 49			11 01			
Lancaster 8 65 a	23p11														10 22		10 15							
d	23p11														10 23		10 16							10 28
Oxenholme Lake District 65 a															10 39		10 30							
Windermere 83 a															10 57									
Carnforth d	23p20																							10 36
Silverdale d	23p26																							10 42
Arnside d	23p30																							10 46
Grange-over-Sands d	23p35																							10 52
Kents Bank d	23p39																							10 55
Cark d	23p43																							11 00
Ulverston d	23p51																							11 08
Dalton d	23p59																							11 16
Roose d	00 05																							11 22
Barrow-in-Furness a	00 15																							11 30

A To Clitheroe
B To Liverpool Lime Street
C To Edinburgh

The Sunday service between Manchester Victoria and Wigan Wallgate via Atherton is funded by TfGM and will operate whilst funding exists

Table 82

Sundays

1 July to 9 September

Manchester - Bolton - Wigan, Kirkby, Southport, Preston, Blackpool North and Barrow-in-Furness

Network Diagram - see first Page of Table 82

	TP	NT	NT	TP	NT		TP	TP	NT	NT	NT	NT	TP	NT	NT		NT	TP	NT	NT	NT	TP	NT	
	◇1 A ✠		B	◇1	C		◇1 D	◇1	E				◇1	C			F	◇1 G ✠			B	◇1	C	
Manchester Airport 85 ✈ d	10 00			10 30				11 00	11 05				11 30					12 00	12 08			12 30		
Heald Green 85 d									11 08										12 11					
Buxton 86 d																								
Hazel Grove 86 d																								
Stockport 84 d			10 12									11 15									12 21			
Manchester Piccadilly 10 ⇌ d	10 16		10 24	10 46			11 07	11 16	11 27			11 33	11 46					12 16	12 29		12 35	12 46		
Manchester Oxford Road d	10 19		10 38	10 49			11a09	11 19	11a31			11 38	11 49					12 19	12a33		12 38	12 49		
Deansgate ⇌ d			10 40	10 51								11 40	11 51								12 40	12 51		
Rochdale 41 d																								
Manchester Victoria ⇌ d		10 25			11 00					11 12	11 25			12 00	12 09					12 25			13 00	
Salford Central d																								
Salford Crescent a		10 29	10 44	10 54	11 06					11 16	11 29	11 44	11 54	12 06	12 13					12 29	12 44	12 54	13 06	
d		10 30	10 44	10 55	11 08					11 17	11 30	11 44	11 55	12 08	12 17					12 30	12 44	12 55	13 08	
Swinton d										11 23					12 23									
Moorside d										11 26					12 26									
Walkden d										11 29					12 29									
Atherton d										11 35					12 35									
Hag Fold d										11 37					12 37									
Daisy Hill d										11 40					12 40									
Kearsley d																								
Farnworth d																								
Moses Gate d																								
Bolton a	10 32	10 40	10 54	11 05	11 19			11 32			11 40	11 54	12 05	12 19				12 32		12 40	12 54	13 05	13 19	
d	10 33	10 40	10 55	11 05				11 33			11 40	11 55	12 05					12 33		12 40	12 55	13 05		
Westhoughton d			11 02									12 02									13 02			
Hindley d			11 06							11 45		12 06			12 45						13 06			
Ince d										11 48					12 48									
Wigan North Western a																								
Wigan Wallgate a			11 11							11 55		12 11			12 55						13 11			
d			11 13									12 13									13 13			
Pemberton d																								
Orrell d																								
Upholland d																								
Rainford d																								
Kirkby a																								
Gathurst d			11 17									12 17									13 17			
Appley Bridge d			11 21									12 21									13 21			
Parbold d			11 25									12 25									13 25			
Hoscar d																								
Burscough Bridge d			11 29									12 29									13 29			
New Lane d																								
Bescar Lane d																								
Meols Cop d			11 37									12 37									13 37			
Southport a			11 46									12 44									13 46			
Lostock d		10 45									11 45									12 45				
Horwich Parkway d		10 49		11 12							11 49		12 12							12 49		13 12		
Blackrod d		10 52									11 52									12 52				
Adlington (Lancashire) d		10 56									11 56									12 56				
Chorley d	10 44	11 01		11 19				11 44			12 01		12 19					12 44		13 01		13 19		
Buckshaw Parkway d		11 05		11 23							12 05		12 23							13 05		13 23		
Leyland d		11 12									12 12									13 12				
Preston 8 65,97 a	10 57	11 20		11 33				11 57			12 18		12 33					12 57		13 18		13 33		
d	10 58	11 21		11 35				11 58			12 20		12 35					12 58		13 20		13 35		
Kirkham & Wesham 97 a		11 31									12 29									13 29				
Poulton-le-Fylde 97 a		11 39		11 52							12 37		12 52							13 37		13 52		
Layton 97 a		11 44									12 42									13 42				
Blackpool North 97 a		11 49		12 01							12 49		13 01							13 49		14 01		
Lancaster 8 65 a	11 13							12 13										13 13						
d	11 14							12 14									12 48	13 14						
Oxenholme Lake District 65 a	11 28																	13 28						
Windermere 83 a																								
Carnforth d								12 22									12a57							
Silverdale d								12 28																
Arnside d								12 32																
Grange-over-Sands d								12 38																
Kents Bank d								12 41																
Cark d								12 46																
Ulverston d								12 54																
Dalton d								13 02																
Roose d								13 08																
Barrow-in-Furness a								13 17																

A To Glasgow Central
B From Chester
C To Clitheroe
D To Liverpool Lime Street
E From Alderley Edge
F From Morecambe to Leeds
G To Edinburgh

The Sunday service between Manchester Victoria and Wigan Wallgate via Atherton is funded by TfGM and will operate whilst funding exists

Table 82

Sundays

1 July to 9 September

Manchester - Bolton - Wigan, Kirkby, Southport, Preston, Blackpool North and Barrow-in-Furness

Network Diagram - see first Page of Table 82

		TP ◇1 A 🍴		NT	NT	NT	TP ◇1	NT B	NT	NT C	TP ◇1 D 🍴	NT	NT E	TP ◇1	NT B	TP ◇1	NT	NT	NT	TP ◇1	NT B	NT
Manchester Airport 85 ✈	d	13 00					13 30				14 00			14 30		15 00				15 30		
Heald Green 85	d																					
Buxton 86	d																					
Hazel Grove 86	d																					
Stockport 84	d					13 22							14 21						15 22			
Manchester Piccadilly 10 ⇌	d	13 16				13 35	13 46				14 16		14 35	14 46		15 16			15 35	15 46		
Manchester Oxford Road	d	13 19				13 38	13 49				14 19		14 38	14 49		15 19			15 38	15 49		
Deansgate ⇌	d					13 40	13 51						14 40	14 51					15 40	15 51		
Rochdale 41	d																					
Manchester Victoria ⇌	d			13 12	13 25			14 00	14 12			14 25			15 00		15 12	15 25			16 00	16 12
Salford Central	d																					
Salford Crescent	a			13 16	13 29	13 44	13 54	14 06	14 16			14 29	14 44	14 54	15 06		15 16	15 29	15 44	15 54	16 06	16 16
	d			13 17	13 30	13 44	13 55	14 08	14 17			14 30	14 44	14 55	15 08		15 17	15 30	15 44	15 55	16 08	16 17
Swinton	d			13 23					14 23								15 23					16 23
Moorside	d			13 26					14 26								15 26					16 26
Walkden	d			13 29					14 29								15 29					16 29
Atherton	d			13 35					14 35								15 35					16 35
Hag Fold	d			13 37					14 37								15 37					16 37
Daisy Hill	d			13 40					14 40								15 40					16 40
Kearsley	d																					
Farnworth	d																					
Moses Gate	d																					
Bolton	a	13 32			13 41	13 54	14 05	14 19			14 32	14 40	14 54	15 05	15 19	15 32		15 40	15 54	16 05	16 19	
	d	13 33			13 41	13 55	14 05				14 33	14 40	14 55	15 05		15 33		15 40	15 55	16 05		
Westhoughton	d					14 02							15 02						16 02			
Hindley	d			13 45		14 06			14 45				15 06				15 45		16 06			16 45
Ince	d			13 48					14 48								15 48					16 48
Wigan North Western	a																					
Wigan Wallgate	a			13 55		14 11			14 55				15 11				15 55		16 11			16 55
	d					14 13							15 13						16 13			
Pemberton	d																					
Orrell	d																					
Upholland	d																					
Rainford	d																					
Kirkby	a																					
Gathurst	d					14 17							15 17						16 17			
Appley Bridge	d					14 21							15 21						16 21			
Parbold	d					14 25							15 25						16 25			
Hoscar	d																					
Burscough Bridge	d					14 29							15 29						16 29			
New Lane	d																					
Bescar Lane	d																					
Meols Cop	d					14 37							15 37						16 37			
Southport	a					14 44							15 46						16 44			
Lostock	d				13 46							14 45						15 45				
Horwich Parkway	d				13 50		14 12					14 49		15 12				15 49		16 12		
Blackrod	d				13 53							14 52						15 52				
Adlington (Lancashire)	d				13 57							14 56						15 56				
Chorley	d	13 44			14 02		14 19				14 44	15 01		15 19		15 44		16 01		16 19		
Buckshaw Parkway	d				14 06		14 23					15 05		15 23				16 05		16 23		
Leyland	d				14 13							15 13						16 12				
Preston 8 65,97	a	13 57			14 18		14 33				14 57	15 18		15 33		15 57		16 18		16 33		
	d	14 00	14 04		14 20		14 35				15 00	15 20		15 35		16 00		16 20		16 35		
Kirkham & Wesham 97	a				14 29							15 29						16 29				
Poulton-le-Fylde 97	a				14 37		14 52					15 37		15 52				16 37		16 52		
Layton 97	a				14 42							15 43						16 42				
Blackpool North 97	a				14 49		15 01					15 49		16 01				16 49		17 01		
Lancaster 6 65	a	14 15	14 20								15 15					16 15						
	d	14 16	14 20							14 27	15 16					16 16						
Oxenholme Lake District 65	a	14 30									15 30											
Windermere 83	a																					
Carnforth	d		14 29							14a59						16 24						
Silverdale	d		14 35													16 30						
Arnside	d		14 39													16 34						
Grange-over-Sands	d		14 44													16 40						
Kents Bank	d		14 48													16 43						
Cark	d		14 52													16 48						
Ulverston	d		15 00													16 55						
Dalton	d		15 08													17 03						
Roose	d		15 14													17 09						
Barrow-in-Furness	a		15 24													17 19						

A To Glasgow Central
B To Clitheroe
C To Leeds
D To Edinburgh
E From Chester

The Sunday service between Manchester Victoria and Wigan Wallgate via Atherton is funded by TfGM and will operate whilst funding exists

Table 82

Sundays

1 July to 9 September

Manchester - Bolton - Wigan, Kirkby, Southport, Preston, Blackpool North and Barrow-in-Furness

Network Diagram - see first Page of Table 82

		NT	NT A	TP ◇1 B 🍴		NT C	TP ◇1	NT D	TP ◇1 E 🍴	NT	TP ◇1 F 🍴	NT	NT	TP ◇1	NT D	TP ◇1 B 🍴		NT	NT	NT C	TP ◇1	NT D	TP ◇1
Manchester Airport 85 ✈	d			16 00			16 30		17 00					17 30		18 00					18 30		19 00
Heald Green 85	d																						
Buxton 86	d																						
Hazel Grove 86	d																						
Stockport 84	d					16 21							17 22							18 21			
Manchester Piccadilly 10 ⇌	d			16 16		16 35	16 46		17 16				17 35	17 46		18 16				18 35	18 46		19 16
Manchester Oxford Road	d			16 19		16 38	16 49		17 19				17 38	17 49		18 19				18 38	18 49		19 19
Deansgate ⇌	d					16 40	16 51						17 40	17 51						18 40	18 51		
Rochdale 41	d																						
Manchester Victoria ⇌	d	16 25						17 00		17 12		17 25			18 00			18 12	18 25			19 00	
Salford Central	d																						
Salford Crescent	a	16 29				16 44	16 54	17 06		17 16		17 29	17 44	17 54	18 06			18 16	18 29	18 44	18 54	19 06	
	d	16 30				16 44	16 55	17 08		17 17		17 30	17 44	17 55	18 08			18 17	18 30	18 44	18 55	19 08	
Swinton	d									17 23								18 23					
Moorside	d									17 26								18 26					
Walkden	d									17 29								18 29					
Atherton	d									17 35								18 35					
Hag Fold	d									17 37								18 37					
Daisy Hill	d									17 40								18 40					
Kearsley	d																						
Farnworth	d																						
Moses Gate	d																						
Bolton	a	16 40		16 32		16 54	17 05	17 19	17 32			17 40	17 54	18 05	18 19	18 32			18 40	18 54	19 05	19 19	19 32
	d	16 40		16 33		16 55	17 05		17 33			17 40	17 55	18 05		18 33			18 40	18 55	19 05		19 33
Westhoughton	d					17 02							18 02							19 02			
Hindley	d					17 06				17 45			18 06					18 45		19 06			
Ince	d									17 48								18 48					
Wigan North Western	a																						
Wigan Wallgate	a					17 11				17 55			18 11					18 55		19 11			
	d					17 13							18 13							19 13			
Pemberton	d																						
Orrell	d																						
Upholland	d																						
Rainford	d																						
Kirkby	a																						
Gathurst	d					17 17							18 17							19 17			
Appley Bridge	d					17 21							18 21							19 21			
Parbold	d					17 25							18 25							19 25			
Hoscar	d																						
Burscough Bridge	d					17 29							18 29							19 29			
New Lane	d																						
Bescar Lane	d																						
Meols Cop	d					17 37							18 37							19 37			
Southport	a					17 46							18 46							19 46			
Lostock	d	16 45										17 45							18 45				
Horwich Parkway	d	16 49					17 12					17 49		18 12					18 49		19 12		
Blackrod	d	16 52										17 52							18 52				
Adlington (Lancashire)	d	16 56										17 56							18 56				
Chorley	d	17 01		16 44			17 19		17 44			18 01		18 19		18 44			19 01		19 19		19 44
Buckshaw Parkway	d	17 05					17 23					18 05		18 23					19 05		19 23		
Leyland	d	17 12										18 12							19 14				
Preston 8 65,97	a	17 18		16 57			17 33		17 57			18 18		18 33		18 57			19 19		19 33		19 57
	d	17 20		17 00	18 07		17 35		18 03		18 03	18 20		18 35		19 00	19 06		19 21		19 35		20 00
Kirkham & Wesham 97	a	17 29										18 29							19 30				
Poulton-le-Fylde 97	a	17 37					17 52					18 37		18 52					19 38		19 52		
Layton 97	a	17 42										18 42							19 42				
Blackpool North 97	a	17 49					18 01					18 49		19 01					19 49		20 01		
Lancaster 6 65	a			17 15	18 23				18 18		18 18					19 15	19 22						20 15
	d		18 04	17 16	18 23				18 19		18 19					19 16	19 22						20 16
Oxenholme Lake District 65	a			17 30	18 40				18 33		18 33					19 30							
Windermere 83	a				19 01																		
Carnforth	d		18a13														19 31						20 24
Silverdale	d																19 37						
Arnside	d																19 41						20 33
Grange-over-Sands	d																19 46						20 38
Kents Bank	d																19 50						
Cark	d																19 54						
Ulverston	d																20 02						20 51
Dalton	d																20 10						
Roose	d																20 16						
Barrow-in-Furness	a																20 26						21 11

A From Morecambe to Leeds
B To Edinburgh
C From Chester
D To Clitheroe
E To Glasgow Central
F from 1 July until 29 July, 2 September, 9 September. From Blackpool North to Glasgow Central

The Sunday service between Manchester Victoria and Wigan Wallgate via Atherton is funded by TfGM and will operate whilst funding exists

Sundays

1 July to 9 September

Manchester - Bolton - Wigan, Kirkby, Southport, Preston, Blackpool North and Barrow-in-Furness

Network Diagram - see first Page of Table 82

		NT	NT	TP ◇■	NT A	NT B	NT	NT C	TP ◇■	NT A	TP ◇■ D	NT	NT	TP ◇■	NT E	NT	NT C	NT F	TP ◇■
Manchester Airport 85 ✈	d			19 30					20 30					21 30				22 27	22 30
Heald Green 85	d																		
Buxton 86	d																		
Hazel Grove 86	d																		
Stockport 84	d		19 22					20 21					21 22				22 21		
Manchester Piccadilly 10 ⇌	d		19 35	19 46				20 35	20 46				21 35	21 46			22 35	22 41	22 46
Manchester Oxford Road	d		19 38	19 49				20 38	20 49				21 38	21 49			22 38	22 45	22 49
Deansgate ⇌	d		19 40	19 51				20 40	20 51				21 40	21 51			22 40	22a47	22 51
Rochdale 41	d																		
Manchester Victoria ⇌	d	19 25			20 00		20 25			21 00		21 25			22 00				
Salford Central	d																		
Salford Crescent	a	19 29	19 44	19 54	20 06		20 29	20 44	20 54	21 06		21 29	21 44	21 54	22 06		22 44		22 54
	d	19 30	19 44	19 55	20 08		20 30	20 44	20 55	21 08		21 30	21 44	21 55	22 08		22 44		22 55
Swinton	d																		
Moorside	d																		
Walkden	d																		
Atherton	d																		
Hag Fold	d																		
Daisy Hill	d																		
Kearsley	d																		
Farnworth	d																		
Moses Gate	d																		
Bolton	a	19 40	19 54	20 05	20 19		20 40	20 54	21 05	21 19		21 40	21 54	22 05	22 19		22 54		23 05
	d	19 40	19 55	20 05			20 40	20 55	21 05			21 40	21 55	22 05			22 55		23 05
Westhoughton	d		20 02					21 02					22 02				23 02		
Hindley	d		20 06					21 06					22 06				23 06		
Ince	d																		
Wigan North Western	a																		
Wigan Wallgate	a		20 11					21 11					22 15				23 15		
	d		20 13					21 13											
Pemberton	d																		
Orrell	d																		
Upholland	d																		
Rainford	d																		
Kirkby	a																		
Gathurst	d		20 17					21 17											
Appley Bridge	d		20 21					21 21											
Parbold	d		20 25					21 25											
Hoscar	d																		
Burscough Bridge	d		20 29					21 29											
New Lane	d																		
Bescar Lane	d																		
Meols Cop	d		20 37					21 37											
Southport	a		20 46					21 46											
Lostock	d	19 45					20 45					21 45							23 10
Horwich Parkway	d	19 49		20 12			20 49		21 12			21 49							23 14
Blackrod	d	19 52					20 52					21 52							23 17
Adlington (Lancashire)	d	19 56					20 56					21 56							23 20
Chorley	d	20 01		20 19			21 01		21 19			22 01		22 17					23 25
Buckshaw Parkway	d	20 05		20 23			21 05		21 23			22 05							23 28
Leyland	d	20 14					21 12					22 12							23 36
Preston 8 65,97	a	20 19		20 33			21 18		21 33			22 18		22 28					23 42
	d	20 21		20 35			21 20		21 35			22 20		22 29					23 47
Kirkham & Wesham 97	a	20 30					21 29					22 29							23 56
Poulton-le-Fylde 97	a	20 38		20 52			21 37		21 52			22 37		22 46					00 05
Layton 97	a	20 43					21 42					22 42							
Blackpool North 97	a	20 49		21 01			21 49		22 01			22 49		22 55					00 14
Lancaster 6 65	a																		
	d					20 18					21 23					22 05			
Oxenholme Lake District 65	a																		
Windermere 83	a																		
Carnforth	d					20a27					21 31					22 15			
Silverdale	d										21 37					22 21			
Arnside	d										21 41					22 26			
Grange-over-Sands	d										21 47					22 32			
Kents Bank	d										21 50					22 35			
Cark	d										21 55					22 39			
Ulverston	d										22 02					22 47			
Dalton	d										22 10					22 56			
Roose	d										22 16					23 02			
Barrow-in-Furness	a										22 26					23 09			

A To Clitheroe
B From Morecambe to Leeds
C From Chester
D From Windermere
E To Blackburn
F To Liverpool Lime Street

The Sunday service between Manchester Victoria and Wigan Wallgate via Atherton is funded by TfGM and will operate whilst funding exists

Sundays

16 September to 30 September

Manchester - Bolton - Wigan, Kirkby, Southport, Preston, Blackpool North and Barrow-in-Furness

Network Diagram - see first Page of Table 82

		TP ◇■	TP ◇■	NT	NT	TP 🚌	TP A 🚌	TP 🚌	TP ◇■ B	NT C	TP ◇■	TP ◇■ D	NT	NT	NT E	NT C	TP ◇■	TP ◇■ F 🛒	TP ◇■ D	NT	NT	TP ◇■
Manchester Airport 85 ✈	d	22p00	22p29			00 05	01 20	05 30	06 11		07 47	07 50			08 34		08 47	09 00	09 03			
Heald Green 85	d		22p33																			
Buxton 86	d																					
Hazel Grove 86	d																					
Stockport 84	d													08 24							09 22	
Manchester Piccadilly 10 ⇌	d	22p16	22p46			00 30	01a45	05 55	06 26		08 02	08 08		08 35	08 49		09 03	09 16	09 20		09 35	
Manchester Oxford Road	d	22p19	22p49								08 05			08 38	08 52		09 06	09 19			09 38	
Deansgate ⇌	d		22p51								08 07			08 40	08a54		09 08				09 40	
Rochdale 41	d																					
Manchester Victoria ⇌	d			23p16	23p20					08 01		08a25	08 25			09 00			09a35	09 25		
Salford Central	d			23p19	23p23																	
Salford Crescent	a		22p56	23p22	23p26				06 31	08 07	08 10		08 29	08 44		09 05	09 11			09 29	09 44	
	d		22p56	23p22	23p26					08 07	08 11		08 30	08 44		09 07	09 12			09 30	09 44	
Swinton	d				23p33																	
Moorside	d				23p35																	
Walkden	d				23p39																	
Atherton	d				23p44																	
Hag Fold	d				23p47																	
Daisy Hill	d				23p50																	
Kearsley	d																					
Farnworth	d																					
Moses Gate	d																					
Bolton	a	22p32	23p06	23p32		00s55		06s20		08 19	08 21		08 40	08 54		09 17	09 22	09 32		09 40	09 54	
	d	22p33	23p07	23p33							08 21		08 40	08 55			09 23	09 33		09 40	09 55	
Westhoughton	d													09 02							10 02	
Hindley	d				23p54									09 06							10 06	
Ince	d				23p57																	
Wigan North Western	a																					
Wigan Wallgate	a				00 04									09 11							10 11	
	d													09 13							10 13	
Pemberton	d																					
Orrell	d																					
Upholland	d																					
Rainford	d																					
Kirkby	a																					
Gathurst	d													09 17							10 17	
Appley Bridge	d													09 21							10 21	
Parbold	d													09 25							10 25	
Hoscar	d																					
Burscough Bridge	d													09 29							10 29	
New Lane	d																					
Bescar Lane	d																					
Meols Cop	d													09 37							10 37	
Southport	a													09 46							10 44	
Lostock	d			23p38									08 45							09 45		
Horwich Parkway	d		23p13	23p42							08 28		08 49				09 29			09 49		
Blackrod	d			23p45									08 52							09 52		
Adlington (Lancashire)	d			23p49									08 56							09 56		
Chorley	d		23p21	23p54							08 35		09 01				09 37	09 44		10 01		
Buckshaw Parkway	d		23p24	23p57							08 39		09 05				09 40			10 05		
Leyland	d			00 04									09 12							10 12		
Preston 8 65,97	a	22p54	23p33	00 10		01s30		06s55			08 48		09 18				09 50	09 57		10 18		
	d	22p55	23p35	00 11							08 49		09 20				09 52	10 00		10 20		
Kirkham & Wesham 97	a			00 21									09 29							10 29		
Poulton-le-Fylde 97	a		23p52	00 29							09 06		09 37				10 09			10 37		
Layton 97	a			00 34									09 42							10 42		
Blackpool North 97	a		00 02	00 40		02 10		07 35			09 13		09 49				10 18			10 49		
Lancaster 6 65	a	23p11																10 15				
	d	23p11																10 16				10 23
Oxenholme Lake District 65	a																	10 30				10 39
Windermere 83	a																					10 57
Carnforth	d	23p20																				
Silverdale	d	23p26																				
Arnside	d	23p30																				
Grange-over-Sands	d	23p35																				
Kents Bank	d	23p39																				
Cark	d	23p43																				
Ulverston	d	23p51																				
Dalton	d	23p59																				
Roose	d	00 05																				
Barrow-in-Furness	a	00 15																				

A To Huddersfield
B To Middlesbrough
C To Clitheroe
D To Newcastle
E To Liverpool Lime Street
F To Edinburgh

The Sunday service between Manchester Victoria and Wigan Wallgate via Atherton is funded by TfGM and will operate whilst funding exists

Table 82

Sundays

16 September to 30 September

Manchester - Bolton - Wigan, Kirkby, Southport, Preston, Blackpool North and Barrow-in-Furness

Network Diagram - see first Page of Table 82

	TP ◇■		NT A	TP ◇■ B ✠	TP ◇■ C	NT		NT	NT D	TP ◇■	NT A	TP ◇■ C	NT E	NT	NT	NT		TP ◇■	NT A	NT	NT F	TP ◇■	TP ◇■ G ✠	TP ◇■ C
Manchester Airport 85 ✈ d	09 29			10 00	10 03					10 30		11 03	11 05					11 30					12 00	12 03
Heald Green 85 d													11 08											
Buxton 86 d																								
Hazel Grove 86 d																								
Stockport 84 d									10 12							11 15								
Manchester Piccadilly ⇌ d	09 46			10 14	10 20				10 24	10 46		11 21	11 27			11 33		11 46					12 16	12 21
Manchester Oxford Road d	09 49			10 17					10 38	10 49			11a31			11 38		11 49					12 19	
Deansgate ⇌ d	09 51								10 40	10 51						11 40		11 51						
Rochdale 41 d																								
Manchester Victoria ⇌ d			10 00		10a35	10 09		10 25			11 00	11a35		11 12	11 25				12 00	12 09				12a35
Salford Central d																								
Salford Crescent a	09 54		10 06			10 16		10 29	10 44	10 54	11 06			11 16	11 29	11 44		11 54	12 06	12 13				
d	09 55		10 08			10 17		10 30	10 44	10 55	11 08			11 17	11 30	11 44		11 55	12 08	12 17				
Swinton d						10 23								11 23						12 23				
Moorside d						10 26								11 26						12 26				
Walkden d						10 29								11 29						12 29				
Atherton d						10 35								11 35						12 35				
Hag Fold d						10 37								11 37						12 37				
Daisy Hill d						10 40								11 40						12 40				
Kearsley d																								
Farnworth d																								
Moses Gate d																								
Bolton a	10 05		10 19	10 30				10 40	10 54	11 05	11 19				11 40	11 54		12 05	12 19				12 32	
d	10 05			10 31				10 40	10 55	11 05					11 40	11 55		12 05					12 33	
Westhoughton d									11 02							12 02								
Hindley d						10 45			11 06					11 45		12 06				12 45				
Ince d						10 48								11 48						12 48				
Wigan North Western a																								
Wigan Wallgate a						10 55			11 11					11 55		12 11				12 55				
d									11 13							12 13								
Pemberton d																								
Orrell d																								
Upholland d																								
Rainford d																								
Kirkby a																								
Gathurst d									11 17							12 17								
Appley Bridge d									11 21							12 21								
Parbold d									11 25							12 25								
Hoscar d																								
Burscough Bridge d									11 29							12 29								
New Lane d																								
Bescar Lane d																								
Meols Cop d									11 37							12 37								
Southport a									11 46							12 44								
Lostock d								10 45							11 45									
Horwich Parkway d	10 12							10 49		11 12					11 49			12 12						
Blackrod d								10 52							11 52									
Adlington (Lancashire) d								10 56							11 56									
Chorley d	10 19			10 42				11 01		11 19					12 01			12 19					12 44	
Buckshaw Parkway d	10 23							11 05		11 23					12 05			12 23						
Leyland d								11 12							12 12									
Preston ■ 65,97 a	10 33			10 57				11 20		11 33					12 18			12 33					12 57	
d	10 35	10 41		10 58				11 21		11 35					12 20			12 35				12 48	12 58	
Kirkham & Wesham 97 a								11 31							12 29									
Poulton-le-Fylde 97 a	10 52							11 39		11 52					12 37			12 52						
Layton 97 a								11 44							12 42									
Blackpool North 97 a	11 02							11 49		12 01					12 49			13 01						
Lancaster ■ 65 a		10 56		11 13																		13 03	13 13	
d		10 57		11 14																	12 48	13 04	13 14	
Oxenholme Lake District 65 a				11 28																			13 28	
Windermere 83 a																								
Carnforth d		11 05																			12a57	13 12		
Silverdale d		11 11																				13 18		
Arnside d		11 15																				13 22		
Grange-over-Sands d		11 21																				13 28		
Kents Bank d		11 24																				13 31		
Cark d		11 29																				13 36		
Ulverston d		11 37																				13 44		
Dalton d		11 45																				13 52		
Roose d		11 51																				13 58		
Barrow-in-Furness a		12 00																				14 07		

A To Clitheroe
B To Glasgow Central
C To Newcastle
D From Chester
E From Alderley Edge
F From Morecambe to Leeds
G To Edinburgh

The Sunday service between Manchester Victoria and Wigan Wallgate via Atherton is funded by TfGM and will operate whilst funding exists

Table 82

Sundays

16 September to 30 September

Manchester - Bolton - Wigan, Kirkby, Southport, Preston, Blackpool North and Barrow-in-Furness

Network Diagram - see first Page of Table 82

	NT	NT		NT A	TP ◇■	NT B	TP ◇■ C ✠	TP ◇■ D	NT	NT	NT	TP ◇■		NT B	NT	NT E	TP ◇■ F ✠	TP ◇■ D	NT	NT A	TP ◇■	NT B		TP ◇■
Manchester Airport 85 ✈ d	12 08				12 30		12 58	13 03				13 30					13 58	14 03			14 30			14 58
Heald Green 85 d	12 11																							
Buxton 86 d																								
Hazel Grove 86 d																								
Stockport 84 d				12 21							13 22									14 21				
Manchester Piccadilly ⇌ d	12 29			12 35	12 46		13 16	13 21			13 35	13 46					14 16	14 21		14 35	14 46			15 16
Manchester Oxford Road d	12a33			12 38	12 49		13 19				13 38	13 49					14 19			14 38	14 49			15 19
Deansgate ⇌ d				12 40	12 51						13 40	13 51								14 40	14 51			
Rochdale 41 d																								
Manchester Victoria ⇌ d		12 25				13 00		13a35	13 12	13 25				14 00	14 12			14a35	14 25			15 00		
Salford Central d																								
Salford Crescent a		12 29		12 44	12 54	13 06			13 16	13 29	13 44	13 54		14 06	14 16				14 29	14 44	14 54	15 06		
d		12 30		12 44	12 55	13 08			13 17	13 30	13 44	13 55		14 08	14 17				14 30	14 44	14 55	15 08		
Swinton d									13 23						14 23									
Moorside d									13 26						14 26									
Walkden d									13 29						14 29									
Atherton d									13 35						14 35									
Hag Fold d									13 37						14 37									
Daisy Hill d									13 40						14 40									
Kearsley d																								
Farnworth d																								
Moses Gate d																								
Bolton a		12 40		12 54	13 05	13 19	13 32			13 41	13 54	14 05		14 19			14 32		14 40	14 54	15 05	15 19		15 32
d		12 40		12 55	13 05		13 33			13 41	13 55	14 05					14 33		14 40	14 55	15 05			15 33
Westhoughton d				13 02							14 02									15 02				
Hindley d				13 06					13 45		14 06				14 45					15 06				
Ince d									13 48						14 48									
Wigan North Western a																								
Wigan Wallgate a				13 11					13 55		14 11				14 55					15 11				
d				13 13							14 13									15 13				
Pemberton d																								
Orrell d																								
Upholland d																								
Rainford d																								
Kirkby a																								
Gathurst d				13 17							14 17									15 17				
Appley Bridge d				13 21							14 21									15 21				
Parbold d				13 25							14 25									15 25				
Hoscar d																								
Burscough Bridge d				13 29							14 29									15 29				
New Lane d																								
Bescar Lane d																								
Meols Cop d				13 37							14 37									15 37				
Southport a				13 46							14 44									15 46				
Lostock d		12 45								13 46									14 45					
Horwich Parkway d		12 49			13 12					13 50		14 12							14 49		15 12			
Blackrod d		12 52								13 53									14 52					
Adlington (Lancashire) d		12 56								13 57									14 56					
Chorley d		13 01			13 19		13 44			14 02		14 19					14 44		15 01		15 19			15 44
Buckshaw Parkway d		13 05			13 23					14 06		14 23							15 05		15 23			
Leyland d		13 12								14 13									15 13					
Preston ■ 65,97 a		13 18			13 33		13 57			14 18		14 33					14 57		15 18		15 33			15 57
d		13 20			13 35		14 00			14 20		14 35					15 00		15 20		15 35			16 00
Kirkham & Wesham 97 a		13 29								14 29									15 29					
Poulton-le-Fylde 97 a		13 37			13 52					14 37		14 52							15 37		15 52			
Layton 97 a		13 42								14 42									15 43					
Blackpool North 97 a		13 49			14 01					14 49		15 01							15 49		16 01			
Lancaster ■ 65 a							14 15										15 15							16 15
d							14 16									14 27	15 16							16 16
Oxenholme Lake District 65 a							14 30										15 30							
Windermere 83 a																								
Carnforth d																14a59								16 24
Silverdale d																								16 30
Arnside d																								16 34
Grange-over-Sands d																								16 40
Kents Bank d																								16 43
Cark d																								16 48
Ulverston d																								16 56
Dalton d																								17 04
Roose d																								17 10
Barrow-in-Furness a																								17 19

A From Chester
B To Clitheroe
C To Glasgow Central
D To Newcastle
E To Leeds
F To Edinburgh

The Sunday service between Manchester Victoria and Wigan Wallgate via Atherton is funded by TfGM and will operate whilst funding exists

Manchester - Bolton - Wigan, Kirkby, Southport, Preston, Blackpool North and Barrow-in-Furness

Network Diagram - see first Page of Table 82

Station			TP ◇1 A	NT	NT	NT	TP ◇1	NT B	TP ◇1 C 🍴	TP ◇1 A	NT	NT	NT D	TP ◇1	NT B	NT	NT	NT E	TP ◇1 F 🍴	TP ◇1 A	NT	NT	TP ◇1	NT B
Manchester Airport	85 ✈	d	15 03				15 30		15 58	16 03				16 30					16 58	17 03			17 30	
Heald Green	85	d																						
Buxton	86	d																						
Hazel Grove	86	d																						
Stockport	84	d				15 22							16 21									17 22		
Manchester Piccadilly 10	⇌	d	15 21			15 35	15 46		16 16	16 21			16 35	16 46					17 16	17 21		17 35	17 46	
Manchester Oxford Road		d				15 38	15 49		16 19				16 38	16 49					17 19			17 38	17 49	
Deansgate	⇌	d				15 40	15 51						16 40	16 51								17 40	17 51	
Rochdale	41	d																						
Manchester Victoria	⇌	d	15a35	15 12	15 25			16 00		16a35	16 12	16 25			17 00	17 12				17a35	17 25			18 00
Salford Central		d																						
Salford Crescent		a		15 16	15 29	15 44	15 54	16 06			16 16	16 29	16 44	16 54	17 06	17 16					17 29	17 44	17 54	18 06
		d		15 17	15 30	15 44	15 55	16 08			16 17	16 30	16 44	16 55	17 08	17 17					17 30	17 44	17 55	18 08
Swinton		d		15 23							16 23					17 23								
Moorside		d		15 26							16 26					17 26								
Walkden		d		15 29							16 29					17 29								
Atherton		d		15 35							16 35					17 35								
Hag Fold		d		15 37							16 37					17 37								
Daisy Hill		d		15 40							16 40					17 40								
Kearsley		d																						
Farnworth		d																						
Moses Gate		d																						
Bolton		a			15 40	15 54	16 05	16 19	16 32			16 40	16 54	17 05	17 19				17 32		17 40	17 54	18 05	18 19
		d			15 40	15 55	16 05		16 33			16 40	16 55	17 05					17 33		17 40	17 55	18 05	
Westhoughton		d				16 02							17 02									18 02		
Hindley		d		15 45		16 06					16 45		17 06			17 45						18 06		
Ince		d		15 48							16 48					17 48								
Wigan North Western		a																						
Wigan Wallgate		a		15 55		16 11					16 55		17 11			17 55						18 11		
		d				16 13							17 13									18 13		
Pemberton		d																						
Orrell		d																						
Upholland		d																						
Rainford		d																						
Kirkby		a																						
Gathurst		d				16 17							17 17									18 17		
Appley Bridge		d				16 21							17 21									18 21		
Parbold		d				16 25							17 25									18 25		
Hoscar		d																						
Burscough Bridge		d				16 29							17 29									18 29		
New Lane		d																						
Bescar Lane		d																						
Meols Cop		d				16 37							17 37									18 37		
Southport		a				16 44							17 46									18 46		
Lostock		d			15 45							16 45									17 45			
Horwich Parkway		d			15 49		16 12					16 49		17 12							17 49		18 12	
Blackrod		d			15 52							16 52									17 52			
Adlington (Lancashire)		d			15 56							16 56									17 56			
Chorley		d			16 01		16 19		16 44			17 01		17 19					17 44		18 01		18 19	
Buckshaw Parkway		d			16 05		16 23					17 05		17 23							18 05		18 23	
Leyland		d			16 12							17 12									18 12			
Preston 8	65,97	a			16 18		16 33		16 57			17 18		17 33					17 57		18 18		18 33	
		d			16 20		16 35		17 00			17 20		17 35					18 00		18 20		18 35	
Kirkham & Wesham	97	a			16 29							17 29									18 29			
Poulton-le-Fylde	97	a			16 37		16 52					17 37		17 52							18 37		18 52	
Layton	97	a			16 42							17 42									18 42			
Blackpool North	97	a			16 49		17 01					17 49		18 01							18 49		19 01	
Lancaster 6	65	a							17 15										18 15					
		d							17 16								17 30	18 04	18 16					
Oxenholme Lake District	65	a							17 30										18 30					
Windermere	83	a																						
Carnforth		d															17 40	18a13						
Silverdale		d															17 46							
Arnside		d															17 51							
Grange-over-Sands		d															17 57							
Kents Bank		d															18 00							
Cark		d															18 04							
Ulverston		d															18 12							
Dalton		d															18 21							
Roose		d															18 27							
Barrow-in-Furness		a															18 34							

A To Newcastle
B To Clitheroe
C To Edinburgh
D From Chester
E From Morecambe to Leeds
F To Glasgow Central

The Sunday service between Manchester Victoria and Wigan Wallgate via Atherton is funded by TfGM and will operate whilst funding exists

Manchester - Bolton - Wigan, Kirkby, Southport, Preston, Blackpool North and Barrow-in-Furness

Network Diagram - see first Page of Table 82

Station			TP ◇1 A 🍴		TP ◇1 B	NT	NT	NT C	TP ◇1	NT D	NT E	TP ◇1	TP ◇1 F	NT	NT	TP ◇1	NT D	TP ◇1 G	NT	NT C	TP ◇1	NT D	TP ◇1 H	TP ◇1 I
Manchester Airport	85 ✈	d	17 58		18 03				18 30			18 58	19 03			19 30		20 03			20 30		21 03	
Heald Green	85	d																						
Buxton	86	d																						
Hazel Grove	86	d																						
Stockport	84	d						18 21							19 22					20 21				
Manchester Piccadilly 10	⇌	d	18 16		18 21			18 35	18 46			19 16	19 21		19 35	19 46		20 21		20 35	20 46		21 21	
Manchester Oxford Road		d	18 19					18 38	18 49			19 19			19 38	19 49				20 38	20 49			
Deansgate	⇌	d						18 40	18 51						19 40	19 51				20 40	20 51			
Rochdale	41	d																						
Manchester Victoria	⇌	d			18a35	18 12	18 25			19 00			19a35	19 25			20 00	20a35	20 25			21 00	21a35	
Salford Central		d																						
Salford Crescent		a				18 16	18 29	18 44	18 54	19 06				19 29	19 44	19 54	20 06		20 29	20 44	20 54	21 06		
		d				18 17	18 30	18 44	18 55	19 08				19 30	19 44	19 55	20 08		20 30	20 44	20 55	21 08		
Swinton		d				18 23																		
Moorside		d				18 26																		
Walkden		d				18 29																		
Atherton		d				18 35																		
Hag Fold		d				18 37																		
Daisy Hill		d				18 40																		
Kearsley		d																						
Farnworth		d																						
Moses Gate		d																						
Bolton		a	18 32				18 40	18 54	19 05	19 19		19 32		19 40	19 54	20 05	20 19		20 40	20 54	21 05	21 19		
		d	18 33				18 40	18 55	19 05			19 33		19 40	19 55	20 05			20 40	20 55	21 05			
Westhoughton		d						19 02							20 02					21 02				
Hindley		d				18 45		19 06							20 06					21 06				
Ince		d				18 48																		
Wigan North Western		a																						
Wigan Wallgate		a				18 55		19 11							20 11					21 11				
		d						19 13							20 13					21 13				
Pemberton		d																						
Orrell		d																						
Upholland		d																						
Rainford		d																						
Kirkby		a																						
Gathurst		d						19 17							20 17					21 17				
Appley Bridge		d						19 21							20 21					21 21				
Parbold		d						19 25							20 25					21 25				
Hoscar		d																						
Burscough Bridge		d						19 29							20 29					21 29				
New Lane		d																						
Bescar Lane		d																						
Meols Cop		d						19 37							20 37					21 37				
Southport		a						19 46							20 46					21 46				
Lostock		d					18 45							19 45					20 45					
Horwich Parkway		d					18 49		19 12					19 49		20 12			20 49		21 12			
Blackrod		d					18 52							19 52					20 52					
Adlington (Lancashire)		d					18 56							19 56					20 56					
Chorley		d	18 44				19 01		19 19			19 44		20 01		20 19			21 01		21 19			
Buckshaw Parkway		d					19 05		19 23					20 05		20 23			21 05		21 23			
Leyland		d					19 14							20 14					21 12					
Preston 8	65,97	a	18 55				19 19		19 33			19 57		20 19		20 33			21 18		21 33			
		d	19 00	19 06			19 21		19 35			20 06		20 21		20 35			21 20		21 35			
Kirkham & Wesham	97	a					19 30							20 30					21 29					
Poulton-le-Fylde	97	a					19 38		19 52					20 38		20 52			21 37		21 52			
Layton	97	a					19 42							20 43					21 42					
Blackpool North	97	a					19 49		20 01					20 49		21 01			21 49		22 01			
Lancaster 6	65	a	19 15	19 22								20 23												
		d	19 16	19 22							20 18	20 24												21 23
Oxenholme Lake District	65	a	19 30																					
Windermere	83	a																						
Carnforth		d		19 31							20a27	20 32												21 31
Silverdale		d		19 37																				21 37
Arnside		d		19 41								20 41												21 41
Grange-over-Sands		d		19 46								20 46												21 47
Kents Bank		d		19 50																				21 50
Cark		d		19 54																				21 55
Ulverston		d		20 02								20 59												22 02
Dalton		d		20 10																				22 10
Roose		d		20 16																				22 16
Barrow-in-Furness		a		20 26								21 19												22 26

A To Edinburgh
B To Middlesbrough
C From Chester
D To Clitheroe
E From Morecambe to Leeds
F To Newcastle
G To Scarborough
H To York
I From Windermere

The Sunday service between Manchester Victoria and Wigan Wallgate via Atherton is funded by TfGM and will operate whilst funding exists

Manchester - Bolton - Wigan, Kirkby, Southport, Preston, Blackpool North and Barrow-in-Furness

Sundays
16 September to 30 September

Network Diagram - see first Page of Table 82

			NT	NT	TP	NT	NT	NT	NT	TP	TP
					◇1					◇1	◇1
						A		B	C		D
Manchester Airport	85 ✈	d			21 30				22 27	22 30	23 22
Heald Green	85	d									
Buxton	86	d									
Hazel Grove	86	d									
Stockport	84	d		21 22				22 21			
Manchester Piccadilly 10	⇌	d		21 35	21 46			22 35	22 41	22 46	23 40
Manchester Oxford Road		d		21 38	21 49			22 38	22 45	22 49	
Deansgate	⇌	d		21 40	21 51			22 40	22a47	22 51	
Rochdale	41	d									
Manchester Victoria	⇌	d	21 25			22 00					23a53
Salford Central		d									
Salford Crescent		a	21 29	21 44	21 54	22 06		22 44		22 54	
		d	21 30	21 44	21 55	22 08		22 44		22 55	
Swinton		d									
Moorside		d									
Walkden		d									
Atherton		d									
Hag Fold		d									
Daisy Hill		d									
Kearsley		d									
Farnworth		d									
Moses Gate		d									
Bolton		a	21 40	21 54	22 05	22 19		22 54		23 05	
		d	21 40	21 55	22 05			22 55		23 05	
Westhoughton		d		22 02				23 02			
Hindley		d		22 06				23 06			
Ince		d									
Wigan North Western		a									
Wigan Wallgate		a		22 15				23 15			
		d									
Pemberton		d									
Orrell		d									
Upholland		d									
Rainford		d									
Kirkby		a									
Gathurst		d									
Appley Bridge		d									
Parbold		d									
Hoscar		d									
Burscough Bridge		d									
New Lane		d									
Bescar Lane		d									
Meols Cop		d									
Southport		a									
Lostock		d	21 45							23 10	
Horwich Parkway		d	21 49							23 14	
Blackrod		d	21 52							23 17	
Adlington (Lancashire)		d	21 56							23 20	
Chorley		d	22 01		22 17					23 25	
Buckshaw Parkway		d	22 05							23 28	
Leyland		d	22 12							23 36	
Preston 8	65,97	a	22 18		22 28					23 42	
		d	22 20		22 29					23 47	
Kirkham & Wesham	97	a	22 29							23 56	
Poulton-le-Fylde	97	a	22 37		22 46					00 05	
Layton	97	a	22 42								
Blackpool North	97	a	22 49		22 55					00 14	
Lancaster 6	65	a									
		d					22 05				
Oxenholme Lake District	65	a									
Windermere	83	a									
Carnforth		d					22 15				
Silverdale		d					22 21				
Arnside		d					22 26				
Grange-over-Sands		d					22 32				
Kents Bank		d					22 35				
Cark		d					22 39				
Ulverston		d					22 47				
Dalton		d					22 56				
Roose		d					23 02				
Barrow-in-Furness		a					23 09				

A To Blackburn
B From Chester
C To Liverpool Lime Street
D To York

The Sunday service between Manchester Victoria and Wigan Wallgate via Atherton is funded by TfGM and will operate whilst funding exists

Table 82

Manchester - Bolton - Wigan, Kirkby, Southport, Preston, Blackpool North and Barrow-in-Furness

Sundays
from 7 October

Network Diagram - see first Page of Table 82

			TP	TP	NT	NT	TP	TP	TP	TP	TP	NT	TP	TP	TP	NT	NT	NT	NT	TP	TP	TP	TP	TP
			◇1	◇1							◇1		◇1	◇1	◇1					◇1	◇1	◇1	◇1	◇1
								A		B	C	D		E	F		G		D		H	I	J	K
							bus	bus	bus	bus												✕	✕	
Manchester Airport	85 ✈	d	22p00	22p29			00 05	01 20	05 30	06 05	06 11		07 47	07 50			08 34			08 47		09 00	09 00	09 03
Heald Green	85	d		22p33																				
Buxton	86	d																						
Hazel Grove	86	d																						
Stockport	84	d																						
Manchester Piccadilly 10	⇌	d	22p16	22p46			00 30	01a45	05 55	06a30	06 26		08 02	08 08	08 08		08 49			09 03	09 07	09 15	09 16	09 20
Manchester Oxford Road		d	22p19	22p49									08 05				08 52			09 06	09a09	09 18	09 19	
Deansgate	⇌	d		22p51									08 07				08a54			09 08				
Rochdale	41	d																						
Manchester Victoria	⇌	d			23p16	23p20						08 01		08a25	08a25	08 25		08 39	09 00					09a35
Salford Central		d			23p19	23p23																		
Salford Crescent		a		22p56	23p22	23p26					06 31	08 07	08 10			08 29		08 44	09 05	09 11				
		d		22p56	23p22	23p26						08 08	08 11			08 30		08 44	09 07	09 12				
Swinton		d				23p33																		
Moorside		d				23p35																		
Walkden		d				23p39																		
Atherton		d				23p44																		
Hag Fold		d				23p47																		
Daisy Hill		d				23p50																		
Kearsley		d																						
Farnworth		d																						
Moses Gate		d																						
Bolton		a	22p32	23p06	23p32		00s55		06s20			08 19	08 21			08 40		08 54	09 18	09 22		09 31	09 32	
		d	22p33	23p07	23p33								08 21			08 40		08 55		09 23		09 32	09 33	
Westhoughton		d																09 02						
Hindley		d				23p54												09 06						
Ince		d				23p57																		
Wigan North Western		a																						
Wigan Wallgate		a				00 06												09 11						
		d																09 13						
Pemberton		d																						
Orrell		d																						
Upholland		d																						
Rainford		d																						
Kirkby		a																						
Gathurst		d																09 17						
Appley Bridge		d																09 21						
Parbold		d																09 25						
Hoscar		d																						
Burscough Bridge		d																09 29						
New Lane		d																						
Bescar Lane		d																						
Meols Cop		d																09 37						
Southport		a																09 48						
Lostock		d			23p38											08 45								
Horwich Parkway		d		23p13	23p42								08 28			08 49				09 29				
Blackrod		d			23p45											08 52								
Adlington (Lancashire)		d			23p49											08 56								
Chorley		d		23p21	23p54								08 35			09 01				09 37		09 43	09 44	
Buckshaw Parkway		d		23p24	23p57								08 39			09 05				09 40				
Leyland		d			00 04											09 12								
Preston 8	65,97	a	22p54	23p33	00 10		01s30		06s55				08 48			09 18				09 50		09 57	09 57	
		d	22p55	23p35	00 11								08 49			09 20				09 52		10 00	10 00	
Kirkham & Wesham	97	a			00 21											09 29								
Poulton-le-Fylde	97	a		23p52	00 29								09 06			09 37				10 09				
Layton	97	a			00 33											09 42								
Blackpool North	97	a		00 02	00 42		02 10		07 35				09 13			09 51				10 18				
Lancaster 6	65	a	23p11																			10 15	10 15	
		d	23p11																			10 16	10 16	
Oxenholme Lake District	65	a																				10 30	10 30	
Windermere	83	a																						
Carnforth		d	23p20																					
Silverdale		d	23p26																					
Arnside		d	23p30																					
Grange-over-Sands		d	23p35																					
Kents Bank		d	23p39																					
Cark		d	23p43																					
Ulverston		d	23p51																					
Dalton		d	23p59																					
Roose		d	00 05																					
Barrow-in-Furness		a	00 15																					

A 7 October, 14 October, 21 October. To Huddersfield
B from 28 October. To Leeds
C 7 October, 14 October, 21 October. To Middlesbrough
D To Clitheroe
E 7 October, 14 October, 21 October. To Newcastle
F from 28 October. To Newcastle
G To Liverpool Lime Street
H from 28 October. To Liverpool Lime Street
I from 28 October. To Edinburgh
J 7 October, 14 October, 21 October. To Edinburgh
K To Newcastle

The Sunday service between Manchester Victoria and Wigan Wallgate via Atherton is funded by TfGM and will operate whilst funding exists

Table 82

Sundays
from 7 October

Manchester - Bolton - Wigan, Kirkby, Southport, Preston, Blackpool North and Barrow-in-Furness

Network Diagram - see first Page of Table 82

		NT	NT	TP	TP		NT	TP	TP	TP	TP	NT	NT	NT	TP	NT	TP	NT	NT	VT	NT	NT	TP
				◇■	◇■			◇■	◇■	◇■	◇■				◇■		◇■			◇■			◇■
							A	B ✕	C ✕	D	E			F		A	G	H		C ⊏			
Manchester Airport 85 ✈	d				09 29			10 00	10 00	10 03	10 03				10 30		11 03	11 05					11 30
Heald Green 85	d																	11 08					
Buxton 86	d																						
Hazel Grove 86	d																						
Stockport 84	d		09 22											10 12								11 15	
Manchester Piccadilly ■ ⇌	d		09 35		09 46			10 14	10 16	10 20	10 21			10 24	10 46		11 21	11 27				11 33	11 46
Manchester Oxford Road	d		09 38		09 49			10 17	10 19					10 38	10 49			11a31				11 38	11 49
Deansgate ⇌	d		09 40		09 51									10 40	10 51							11 40	11 51
Rochdale 41	d																						
Manchester Victoria ⇌	d	09 25					10 00			10a35	10a35	10 09	10 25			11 00	11a35		11 12		11 25		
Salford Central	d																						
Salford Crescent	a	09 29	09 44		09 54		10 06					10 15	10 29	10 44	10 54	11 06			11 16		11 29	11 44	11 54
	d	09 30	09 44		09 55		10 08					10 17	10 30	10 44	10 55	11 08			11 17		11 30	11 44	11 55
Swinton	d											10 23							11 23				
Moorside	d											10 26							11 26				
Walkden	d											10 29							11 29				
Atherton	d											10 35							11 35				
Hag Fold	d											10 37							11 37				
Daisy Hill	d											10 40							11 40				
Kearsley	d																						
Farnworth	d																						
Moses Gate	d																						
Bolton	a	09 40	09 54		10 05		10 19	10 30	10 32				10 40	10 54	11 05	11 19					11 40	11 54	12 05
	d	09 40	09 55		10 05			10 31	10 33				10 40	10 55	11 05						11 40	11 55	12 05
Westhoughton	d		10 02											11 02								12 02	
Hindley	d		10 06									10 45		11 06					11 45			12 06	
Ince	d											10 48							11 48				
Wigan North Western	a																						
Wigan Wallgate	a		10 11									10 57		11 11					11 57			12 11	
	d		10 13											11 13								12 13	
Pemberton	d																						
Orrell	d																						
Upholland	d																						
Rainford	d																						
Kirkby	a																						
Gathurst	d		10 17											11 17								12 17	
Appley Bridge	d		10 21											11 21								12 21	
Parbold	d		10 25											11 25								12 25	
Hoscar	d																						
Burscough Bridge	d		10 29											11 29								12 29	
New Lane	d																						
Bescar Lane	d																						
Meols Cop	d		10 37											11 37								12 37	
Southport	a		10 48											11 46								12 48	
Lostock	d	09 45											10 45								11 45		
Horwich Parkway	d	09 49			10 12								10 49		11 12						11 49		12 12
Blackrod	d	09 52											10 52								11 52		
Adlington (Lancashire)	d	09 56											10 56								11 56		
Chorley	d	10 01			10 19			10 42	10 44				11 01		11 19						12 01		12 19
Buckshaw Parkway	d	10 05			10 23								11 05		11 23						12 05		12 23
Leyland	d	10 12											11 12								12 12		
Preston ■ 65,97	a	10 18			10 33			10 57	10 57				11 18		11 33						12 18		12 33
	d	10 20			10 35	10 41		10 58	10 58				11 20		11 35					11 40	12 20		12 35
Kirkham & Wesham 97	a	10 29											11 29								12 29		
Poulton-le-Fylde 97	a	10 37			10 52								11 37		11 52						12 37		12 52
Layton 97	a	10 42											11 42								12 42		
Blackpool North 97	a	10 51			11 02								11 51		12 01						12 51		13 01
Lancaster ■ 65	a					10 56		11 13	11 13											11 54			
	d			10 23		10 57		11 14	11 14											11 55			
Oxenholme Lake District 65	a			10 39				11 28	11 28											12 08			
Windermere 83	a			10 57																			
Carnforth	d					11 05																	
Silverdale	d					11 11																	
Arnside	d					11 15																	
Grange-over-Sands	d					11 21																	
Kents Bank	d					11 24																	
Cark	d					11 29																	
Ulverston	d					11 37																	
Dalton	d					11 45																	
Roose	d					11 51																	
Barrow-in-Furness	a					12 00																	

A To Clitheroe
B 7 October, 14 October, 21 October. To Glasgow Central
C from 28 October. To Glasgow Central
D 7 October, 14 October, 21 October. To Newcastle
E from 28 October. To Newcastle
F From Chester
G To Newcastle
H From Alderley Edge

The Sunday service between Manchester Victoria and Wigan Wallgate via Atherton is funded by TfGM and will operate whilst funding exists

Table 82

Sundays
from 7 October

Manchester - Bolton - Wigan, Kirkby, Southport, Preston, Blackpool North and Barrow-in-Furness

Network Diagram - see first Page of Table 82

		NT	NT	NT	VT	TP	TP	TP	NT	NT	NT	TP	NT	NT	VT	TP	TP	TP	NT	NT	TP	NT
					◇■	◇■	◇■	◇■				◇■			◇■	◇■	◇■	◇■			◇■	
		A		B	C ⊏		D ✕	E			F		A		C ⊏	C ✕	G ✕	E				A
Manchester Airport 85 ✈	d						12 00	12 03	12 08			12 30				12 58	12 58	13 03			13 30	
Heald Green 85	d								12 11													
Buxton 86	d																					
Hazel Grove 86	d																					
Stockport 84	d										12 21									13 22		
Manchester Piccadilly ■ ⇌	d						12 16	12 21	12 29		12 35	12 46				13 16	13 16	13 21		13 35	13 46	
Manchester Oxford Road	d						12 19		12a33		12 38	12 49				13 19	13 19			13 38	13 49	
Deansgate ⇌	d										12 40	12 51								13 40	13 51	
Rochdale 41	d																					
Manchester Victoria ⇌	d	12 00	12 09					12a35		12 25			13 00	13 12				13a35	13 25			14 00
Salford Central	d																					
Salford Crescent	a	12 06	12 13							12 29	12 44	12 54	13 06	13 16					13 29	13 44	13 54	14 06
	d	12 08	12 17							12 30	12 44	12 55	13 08	13 17					13 30	13 44	13 55	14 08
Swinton	d		12 23											13 23								
Moorside	d		12 26											13 26								
Walkden	d		12 29											13 29								
Atherton	d		12 35											13 35								
Hag Fold	d		12 37											13 37								
Daisy Hill	d		12 40											13 40								
Kearsley	d																					
Farnworth	d																					
Moses Gate	d																					
Bolton	a	12 19					12 32			12 40	12 54	13 05	13 19			13 32	13 32		13 40	13 54	14 05	14 19
	d						12 33			12 40	12 55	13 05				13 33	13 33		13 40	13 55	14 05	
Westhoughton	d										13 02									14 02		
Hindley	d		12 45								13 06			13 45						14 06		
Ince	d		12 48											13 48								
Wigan North Western	a																					
Wigan Wallgate	a		12 57								13 11			13 57						14 11		
	d										13 13									14 13		
Pemberton	d																					
Orrell	d																					
Upholland	d																					
Rainford	d																					
Kirkby	a																					
Gathurst	d										13 17									14 17		
Appley Bridge	d										13 21									14 21		
Parbold	d										13 25									14 25		
Hoscar	d																					
Burscough Bridge	d										13 29									14 29		
New Lane	d																					
Bescar Lane	d																					
Meols Cop	d										13 37									14 37		
Southport	a										13 46									14 48		
Lostock	d									12 45									13 45			
Horwich Parkway	d									12 49		13 12							13 49		14 12	
Blackrod	d									12 52									13 52			
Adlington (Lancashire)	d									12 56									13 56			
Chorley	d						12 44			13 01		13 19				13 44	13 44		14 01		14 19	
Buckshaw Parkway	d									13 05		13 23							14 05		14 23	
Leyland	d									13 12									14 12			
Preston ■ 65,97	a						12 57			13 18		13 33				13 59	13 57		14 18		14 33	
	d				12 40	12 48	12 58			13 20		13 35			13 42	14 00	14 00		14 20		14 35	
Kirkham & Wesham 97	a									13 29									14 29			
Poulton-le-Fylde 97	a									13 37		13 52							14 37		14 52	
Layton 97	a									13 42									14 42			
Blackpool North 97	a									13 51		14 01							14 51		15 01	
Lancaster ■ 65	a				12 54	13 03	13 13								13 56	14 15	14 15					
	d			12 48	12 55	13 04	13 14								13 57	14 16	14 16					
Oxenholme Lake District 65	a				13 08		13 28								14 10	14 30	14 30					
Windermere 83	a																					
Carnforth	d			12a57		13 12																
Silverdale	d					13 18																
Arnside	d					13 22																
Grange-over-Sands	d					13 28																
Kents Bank	d					13 31																
Cark	d					13 36																
Ulverston	d					13 44																
Dalton	d					13 52																
Roose	d					13 58																
Barrow-in-Furness	a					14 07																

A To Clitheroe
B From Morecambe to Leeds
C from 28 October. To Glasgow Central
D To Edinburgh
E To Newcastle
F From Chester
G 7 October, 14 October, 21 October. To Glasgow Central

The Sunday service between Manchester Victoria and Wigan Wallgate via Atherton is funded by TfGM and will operate whilst funding exists

Table 82

Sundays
from 7 October

Manchester - Bolton - Wigan, Kirkby, Southport, Preston, Blackpool North and Barrow-in-Furness

Network Diagram - see first Page of Table 82

Station	NT	NT A	VT ◇1 B	TP ◇1 C	TP ◇1 D	NT	NT E	TP ◇1	NT F	TP ◇1	TP ◇1 D	NT	NT	NT	TP ◇1	NT F	TP ◇1 C	TP ◇1 D	NT	NT	NT E	TP ◇1
Manchester Airport 85 ✈ d				13 58	14 03			14 30		14 58	15 03				15 30		15 58	16 03				16 30
Heald Green 85 d																						
Buxton 86 d																						
Hazel Grove 86 d																						
Stockport 84 d							14 21							15 22							16 21	
Manchester Piccadilly 10 ⇌ d				14 16	14 21		14 35	14 46		15 16	15 21			15 35	15 46		16 16	16 21			16 35	16 46
Manchester Oxford Road d				14 19			14 38	14 49		15 19				15 38	15 49		16 19				16 38	16 49
Deansgate ⇌ d							14 40	14 51						15 40	15 51						16 40	16 51
Rochdale 41 d																						
Manchester Victoria ⇌ d	14 12				14a35	14 25			15 00		15a35	15 12	15 25			16 00		16a35	16 12	16 25		
Salford Central d																						
Salford Crescent a	14 16					14 29	14 44	14 54	15 06			15 16	15 29	15 44	15 54	16 06			16 16	16 29	16 44	16 54
d	14 17					14 30	14 44	14 55	15 08			15 17	15 30	15 44	15 55	16 08			16 17	16 30	16 44	16 55
Swinton d	14 23											15 23							16 23			
Moorside d	14 26											15 26							16 26			
Walkden d	14 29											15 29							16 29			
Atherton d	14 35											15 35							16 35			
Hag Fold d	14 37											15 37							16 37			
Daisy Hill d	14 40											15 40							16 40			
Kearsley d																						
Farnworth d																						
Moses Gate d																						
Bolton a				14 32		14 40	14 54	15 05	15 19	15 32			15 40	15 54	16 05	16 19	16 32			16 40	16 54	17 05
d				14 33		14 40	14 55	15 05		15 33			15 40	15 55	16 05		16 33			16 40	16 55	17 05
Westhoughton d							15 02							16 02							17 02	
Hindley d	14 45						15 06					15 45		16 06					16 45		17 06	
Ince d	14 48											15 48							16 48			
Wigan North Western a																						
Wigan Wallgate a	14 57						15 11					15 57		16 11					16 57		17 11	
d							15 13							16 13							17 13	
Pemberton d																						
Orrell d																						
Upholland d																						
Rainford d																						
Kirkby a																						
Gathurst d							15 17							16 17							17 17	
Appley Bridge d							15 21							16 21							17 21	
Parbold d							15 25							16 25							17 25	
Hoscar d																						
Burscough Bridge d							15 29							16 29							17 29	
New Lane d																						
Bescar Lane d																						
Meols Cop d							15 37							16 37							17 37	
Southport a							15 46							16 48							17 46	
Lostock d						14 45							15 45							16 45		
Horwich Parkway d						14 49		15 12					15 49		16 12					16 49		17 12
Blackrod d						14 52							15 52							16 52		
Adlington (Lancashire) d						14 56							15 56							16 56		
Chorley d				14 44		15 01		15 19		15 44			16 01		16 19		16 44			17 01		17 19
Buckshaw Parkway d						15 05		15 23					16 05		16 23					17 05		17 23
Leyland d						15 12							16 12							17 12		
Preston 8 65,97 a				14 57		15 18		15 33		15 57			16 18		16 33		16 57			17 18		17 33
d			14 42	15 00		15 20		15 35		16 00			16 20		16 35		17 00			17 20		17 35
Kirkham & Wesham 97 a						15 29							16 29							17 29		
Poulton-le-Fylde 97 a						15 37		15 52					16 37		16 52					17 37		17 52
Layton 97 a						15 42							16 42							17 42		
Blackpool North 97 a						15 51		16 01					16 51		17 01					17 51		18 01
Lancaster 6 65 a			14 56	15 15						16 15							17 15					
d		14 27		15 16						16 16							17 16					
Oxenholme Lake District 65 a				15 30													17 30					
Windermere 83 a																						
Carnforth d		14a59								16 24												
Silverdale d										16 30												
Arnside d										16 34												
Grange-over-Sands d										16 40												
Kents Bank d										16 43												
Cark d										16 48												
Ulverston d										16 56												
Dalton d										17 04												
Roose d										17 10												
Barrow-in-Furness a										17 19												

A To Leeds
B from 28 October. To Glasgow Central
C To Edinburgh
D To Newcastle
E From Chester
F To Clitheroe

The Sunday service between Manchester Victoria and Wigan Wallgate via Atherton is funded by TfGM and will operate whilst funding exists

Table 82

Sundays
from 7 October

Manchester - Bolton - Wigan, Kirkby, Southport, Preston, Blackpool North and Barrow-in-Furness

Network Diagram - see first Page of Table 82

Station	NT A	NT	NT	NT B	TP ◇1 C	TP ◇1 D	NT	NT	TP ◇1	NT A	TP ◇1 E		TP ◇1 F	NT	NT	NT G	TP ◇1	NT A	NT B	TP ◇1	TP ◇1 D
Manchester Airport 85 ✈ d					16 58	17 03			17 30		17 58		18 03				18 30			18 58	19 03
Heald Green 85 d																					
Buxton 86 d																					
Hazel Grove 86 d																					
Stockport 84 d								17 22								18 21					
Manchester Piccadilly 10 ⇌ d					17 16	17 21		17 35	17 46		18 16		18 21			18 35	18 46			19 16	19 21
Manchester Oxford Road d					17 19			17 38	17 49		18 19					18 38	18 49			19 19	
Deansgate ⇌ d								17 40	17 51							18 40	18 51				
Rochdale 41 d																					
Manchester Victoria ⇌ d	17 00	17 12				17a35	17 25			18 00			18a35	18 12	18 25			19 00			19a35
Salford Central d																					
Salford Crescent a	17 06	17 16					17 29	17 44	17 54	18 06				18 16	18 29	18 44	18 54	19 06			
d	17 08	17 17					17 30	17 44	17 55	18 08				18 17	18 30	18 44	18 55	19 08			
Swinton d		17 23												18 23							
Moorside d		17 26												18 26							
Walkden d		17 29												18 29							
Atherton d		17 35												18 35							
Hag Fold d		17 37												18 37							
Daisy Hill d		17 40												18 40							
Kearsley d																					
Farnworth d																					
Moses Gate d																					
Bolton a	17 19				17 32		17 40	17 54	18 05	18 19	18 32				18 40	18 54	19 05	19 19		19 32	
d					17 33		17 40	17 55	18 05		18 33				18 40	18 55	19 05			19 33	
Westhoughton d								18 02								19 02					
Hindley d		17 45						18 06						18 45		19 06					
Ince d		17 48												18 48							
Wigan North Western a																					
Wigan Wallgate a		17 57						18 11						18 57		19 11					
d								18 13								19 13					
Pemberton d																					
Orrell d																					
Upholland d																					
Rainford d																					
Kirkby a																					
Gathurst d								18 17								19 17					
Appley Bridge d								18 21								19 21					
Parbold d								18 25								19 25					
Hoscar d																					
Burscough Bridge d								18 29								19 29					
New Lane d																					
Bescar Lane d																					
Meols Cop d								18 37								19 37					
Southport a								18 48								19 46					
Lostock d							17 45								18 45						
Horwich Parkway d							17 49		18 12						18 49		19 12				
Blackrod d							17 52								18 52						
Adlington (Lancashire) d							17 56								18 56						
Chorley d					17 44		18 01		18 19		18 44				19 01		19 19			19 44	
Buckshaw Parkway d							18 05		18 23						19 05		19 23				
Leyland d							18 12								19 12						
Preston 8 65,97 a					17 57		18 18		18 33		18 55				19 18		19 33			19 57	
d					18 00		18 20		18 35		19 00	19 06			19 20		19 35			20 06	
Kirkham & Wesham 97 a							18 29								19 29						
Poulton-le-Fylde 97 a							18 37		18 52						19 37		19 52				
Layton 97 a							18 42								19 42						
Blackpool North 97 a							18 51		19 01						19 51		20 01				
Lancaster 6 65 a					18 15						19 15	19 22								20 23	
d			17 30	18 04	18 16						19 16	19 22							20 18	20 24	
Oxenholme Lake District 65 a					18 30						19 30										
Windermere 83 a																					
Carnforth d			17 40	18a13								19 31							20a27	20 32	
Silverdale d			17 46									19 37									
Arnside d			17 51									19 41								20 41	
Grange-over-Sands d			17 57									19 46								20 46	
Kents Bank d			18 00									19 50									
Cark d			18 04									19 54									
Ulverston d			18 12									20 02								20 59	
Dalton d			18 21									20 10									
Roose d			18 27									20 16									
Barrow-in-Furness a			18 34									20 26								21 19	

A To Clitheroe
B From Morecambe to Leeds
C To Glasgow Central
D To Newcastle
E To Edinburgh
F To Middlesbrough
G From Chester

The Sunday service between Manchester Victoria and Wigan Wallgate via Atherton is funded by TfGM and will operate whilst funding exists

Manchester - Bolton - Wigan, Kirkby, Southport, Preston, Blackpool North and Barrow-in-Furness

Sundays from 7 October

Network Diagram - see first Page of Table 82

		NT	NT	TP ◇1	NT A	TP ◇1 B	NT	NT C	TP ◇1	NT A	TP ◇1 D	TP ◇1 E	NT	NT	TP ◇1	NT F	NT	NT C	NT G	TP ◇1	TP ◇1 D
Manchester Airport 85 ✈	d			19 30		20 03			20 30		21 03				21 30				22 27	22 30	23 22
Heald Green 85	d																				
Buxton 86	d																				
Hazel Grove 86	d																				
Stockport 84	d		19 22					20 21						21 22				22 21			
Manchester Piccadilly 10 🚊	d		19 35	19 46		20 21		20 35	20 46		21 21			21 35	21 46			22 35	22 41	22 46	23 40
Manchester Oxford Road	d		19 38	19 49				20 38	20 49					21 38	21 49			22 38	22 45	22 49	
Deansgate 🚊	d		19 40	19 51				20 40	20 51					21 40	21 51			22 40	22a47	22 51	
Rochdale 41	d																				
Manchester Victoria 🚊	d	19 25			20 00	20a35	20 25			21 00	21a35		21 25			22 00					23a53
Salford Central	d																				
Salford Crescent	a	19 29	19 44	19 54	20 06		20 29	20 44	20 54	21 06			21 29	21 44	21 54	22 06		22 44		22 54	
	d	19 30	19 44	19 55	20 08		20 30	20 44	20 55	21 08			21 30	21 44	21 55	22 08		22 44		22 55	
Swinton	d																				
Moorside	d																				
Walkden	d																				
Atherton	d																				
Hag Fold	d																				
Daisy Hill	d																				
Kearsley	d																				
Farnworth	d																				
Moses Gate	d																				
Bolton	a	19 40	19 54	20 05	20 19		20 40	20 54	21 05	21 19			21 40	21 54	22 05	22 19		22 54		23 05	
	d	19 40	19 55	20 05			20 40	20 55	21 05				21 40	21 55	22 05			22 55		23 05	
Westhoughton	d		20 02					21 02						22 02				23 02			
Hindley	d		20 06					21 06						22 06				23 06			
Ince	d																				
Wigan North Western	a																				
Wigan Wallgate	a		20 11					21 11						22 15				23 15			
	d		20 13					21 13													
Pemberton	d																				
Orrell	d																				
Upholland	d																				
Rainford	d																				
Kirkby	a																				
Gathurst	d		20 17					21 17													
Appley Bridge	d		20 21					21 21													
Parbold	d		20 25					21 25													
Hoscar	d																				
Burscough Bridge	d		20 29					21 29													
New Lane	d																				
Bescar Lane	d																				
Meols Cop	d		20 37					21 37													
Southport	a		20 48					21 46													
Lostock	d	19 45					20 45						21 45							23 10	
Horwich Parkway	d	19 49		20 12			20 49		21 12				21 49							23 14	
Blackrod	d	19 52					20 52						21 52							23 17	
Adlington (Lancashire)	d	19 56					20 56						21 56							23 20	
Chorley	d	20 01		20 19			21 01		21 19				22 01		22 17					23 25	
Buckshaw Parkway	d	20 05		20 23			21 05		21 23				22 05							23 28	
Leyland	d	20 12					21 12						22 12							23 36	
Preston 8 65,97	a	20 18		20 33			21 18		21 33				22 18		22 28					23 42	
	d	20 20		20 35			21 20		21 35				22 20		22 29					23 47	
Kirkham & Wesham 97	a	20 29					21 29						22 29							23 56	
Poulton-le-Fylde 97	a	20 37		20 52			21 37		21 52				22 37		22 46					00 05	
Layton 97	a	20 42					21 42						22 42								
Blackpool North 97	a	20 51		21 01			21 51		22 01				22 51		22 55					00 14	
Lancaster 6 65	a																				
	d											21 23					22 05				
Oxenholme Lake District 65	a																				
Windermere 83	a																				
Carnforth	d											21 31					22 15				
Silverdale	d											21 37					22 21				
Arnside	d											21 41					22 26				
Grange-over-Sands	d											21 47					22 32				
Kents Bank	d											21 50					22 35				
Cark	d											21 55					22 39				
Ulverston	d											22 02					22 47				
Dalton	d											22 10					22 56				
Roose	d											22 16					23 02				
Barrow-in-Furness	a											22 26					23 09				

A To Clitheroe
B To Scarborough
C From Chester
D To York
E From Windermere
F To Blackburn
G To Liverpool Lime Street

The Sunday service between Manchester Victoria and Wigan Wallgate via Atherton is funded by TfGM and will operate whilst funding exists

Barrow-in-Furness, Blackpool North, Preston, Southport, Kirkby and Wigan - Bolton - Manchester

Mondays to Fridays until 28 September

Network Diagram - see first Page of Table 82

Miles	Miles	Miles	Miles	Miles			TP MX ◇1	TP MO ◇1 A	NT MX	TP MO ◇1 B	TP MX ◇1 C	TP ◇1 D	TP ◇1	TP ◇1	TP ◇1 D	NT E	TP ◇1	NT	TP ◇1 🛒	NT	NT	NT F	TP ◇1 G 🛒	NT
—	0	—	—	—	**Barrow-in-Furness**	d								04 35									05 31	
—	1¾	—	—	—	Roose	d																		
—	6	—	—	—	Dalton	d																		
—	9¼	—	—	—	Ulverston	d								04 51									05 47	
—	15¼	—	—	—	Cark	d																		
—	17¼	—	—	—	Kents Bank	d																		
—	19½	—	—	—	Grange-over-Sands	d								05 03									05 59	
—	22¾	—	—	—	Arnside	d								05 10									06 05	
—	25	—	—	—	Silverdale	d																		
—	28¾	—	—	—	Carnforth	d								05 19									06 15	
—	—	—	—	—	Windermere 83	d																		
—	—	—	—	—	Oxenholme Lake District 65	d																		
—	34¾	—	—	—	**Lancaster** 6 65	a								05 28									06 23	
—	—	—	—	—		d																	06 23	
0	—	—	—	—	**Blackpool North** 97	d	22p44	23p03	23p13				03 37			04 56			05 39					
1¾	—	—	—	—	Layton 97	d			23p16															
3¼	—	—	—	—	Poulton-le-Fylde 97	d	22p50	23p09	23p21							05 02			05 45					
9¾	—	—	—	—	Kirkham & Wesham 97	d		23p17	23p30															
—	55¾	—	—	—	**Preston** 8 65,97	a	23p08	23p28	23p40							05 20			06 03				06 42	
—	—	—	—	—		d	23p10	23p28	23p42				04u02				05 16		06 05				06 44	
21½	59¾	—	—	—	Leyland	d		23p34	23p48										06 10					
23¾	62	—	—	—	Buckshaw Parkway	d	23p17	23p38	23p52															
26	64¼	—	—	—	Chorley	d	23p21	23p42	23p57								05 26		06 16				06 53	
29	67¼	—	—	—	Adlington (Lancashire)	d		23p46	00 03															
31	69¼	—	—	—	Blackrod	d		23p50	00 06										06 22					
32½	70¾	—	—	—	Horwich Parkway	d	23p28	23p53	00 10								05 33		06 26				07 00	
34½	72¾	—	—	—	Lostock	d		23p57	00 14										06 30					
—	—	0	—	—	**Southport**	d																		06 23
—	—	1¼	—	—	Meols Cop	d																		06 28
—	—	4½	—	—	Bescar Lane	d																		
—	—	6½	—	—	New Lane	d																		
—	—	7¾	—	—	Burscough Bridge	d																		06 36
—	—	9¼	—	—	Hoscar	d																		
—	—	10¾	—	—	Parbold	d																		06 41
—	—	13	—	—	Appley Bridge	d																		06 45
—	—	14¾	—	—	Gathurst	d																		06 49
—	—	—	0	—	**Kirkby**	d																		
—	—	—	5¼	—	Rainford	d																		
—	—	—	7¼	—	Upholland	d																		
—	—	—	8½	—	Orrell	d																		
—	—	—	10½	—	Pemberton	d																		
—	—	17½	12¼	—	**Wigan Wallgate**	a																		06 54
—	—	—	—	—		d												06 03		06 31	06 36			06 55
—	—	—	—	0	Wigan North Western	d																		
—	—	18½	13¼	0¾	Ince	d												06 06			06 39			
—	—	20	14¾	—	Hindley	d												06 09		06 36	06 42			
—	—	22½	—	—	Westhoughton	d														06 41				07 03
37½	75¾	27	—	—	**Bolton**	a	23p34	00 02	00 19								05 42		06 34	06 52			07 08	07 11
—	—	—	—	—		d	23p35	00 02	00 20				04u31				05 43		06 35	06 53		06 56	07 08	07 12
38¼	76½	27¾	—	—	Moses Gate	d																06 59		
39¾	78	29¼	—	—	Farnworth	d																07 01		
40½	78¾	30	—	—	Kearsley	d																07 03		
—	—	—	17¼	—	Daisy Hill	d												06 13			06 46			
—	—	—	17½	—	Hag Fold	d												06 16			06 49			
—	—	—	18¾	—	Atherton	d												06 19			06 52			
—	—	—	22¼	—	Walkden	d												06 24			06 58			
—	—	—	24	—	Moorside	d												06 28			07 01			
—	—	—	24¾	—	Swinton	d												06 30			07 04			
46½	84¾	36	28¾	—	**Salford Crescent**	a	23p47										05 55	06 38	06 47	07 05	07 11	07 15		07 24
—	—	—	—	—		d	23p47			00 37	00 49	03 40			04 53		05 55	06 38	06 47	07 08	07 11	07 15		07 25
—	—	—	29¾	—	Salford Central	d												06 41			07 14	07 19		
—	—	—	30½	—	**Manchester Victoria** 🚊	a			00 37									06 46			07 20	07 26		
—	—	—	—	—	Rochdale 41	a																		
48	86¼	37½	—	—	Deansgate 🚊	a													06 51	07 11				07 28
48¼	86½	37¾	—	—	**Manchester Oxford Road**	a													06 52	07 13			07 23	07 30
48¾	87	38¼	—	—	**Manchester Piccadilly** 10 🚊	a	23p53	00 18		00 43	00 53	03 44	04 48		04 58		06 01		06 56	07 17			07 27	07 34
—	—	—	—	—	Stockport 84	a														07 34				
—	—	—	—	—	Hazel Grove 86	a														07 45				
—	—	—	—	—	Buxton 86	a																		
57	95¼	46½	—	—	Heald Green 85	a	00 16												07 10					
58½	96¾	48	—	—	**Manchester Airport** 85 ✈	a	00 24	00 32		00 57	01 10	04 00	05 07		05 19		06 18		07 17				07 47	07 53

A from 21 May until 24 September
B from 2 July until 10 September. From Middlesbrough
C From Newcastle
D From York
E To Colne
F From Blackburn
G 🛒 from Preston

Table 82

Mondays to Fridays
until 28 September

Barrow-in-Furness, Blackpool North, Preston, Southport, Kirkby and Wigan - Bolton - Manchester

Network Diagram - see first Page of Table 82

Station			NT	NT A	NT B	TP ◇1 ✠	NT C	NT	NT	NT	NT D	NT	NT B	TP ◇1 E ✠	TP ◇1 ✠	NT	NT	NT	NT B	TP ◇1 ✠	TP ◇1 F ✠	NT G	NT
Barrow-in-Furness		d												06 20								07 00	
Roose		d												06 24								07 04	
Dalton		d												06 31								07 10	
Ulverston		d												06 39								07 19	
Cark		d												06 47								07 26	
Kents Bank		d												06 51								07 32	
Grange-over-Sands		d												06 55								07 36	
Arnside		d												07 01								07 42	
Silverdale		d												07 05								07 47	
Carnforth		d		06 43										07 12								07 55	
Windermere	83	d																					
Oxenholme Lake District	65	d																					
Lancaster 6	65	a		06 52										07 21								08 04	
		d												07 22							07 47	08 05	
Blackpool North	97	d	06 19			06 40				06 53	07 02				07 10			07 18		07 36			
Layton	97	d	06 22			06 43									07 13			07 21		07 39			
Poulton-le-Fylde	97	d	06 27			06 47					07 08				07 17			07 26		07 43			
Kirkham & Wesham	97	d	06 36			06 56									07 26			07 35		07 52			
Preston 8	65,97	a	06 46			07 07				07 15	07 28			07 41	07 37			07 46		08 03	08 07	08 30	
		d	06 48			07 09				07 17	07 30			07 47				07 47		08 12			
Leyland		d	06 53							07 22	07 35							07 53					
Buckshaw Parkway		d	06 58							07 28								07 58					
Chorley		d	07 02			07 18				07 32				07 56				08 02		08 22			
Adlington (Lancashire)		d	07 07							07 37								08 07					
Blackrod		d	07 11							07 41								08 11					
Horwich Parkway		d	07 15			07 26				07 45								08 15					
Lostock		d	07 20			07 30				07 49								08 20					
Southport		d						06 53								07 21							
Meols Cop		d						06 58								07 26							
Bescar Lane		d						07 03															
New Lane		d						07 07															
Burscough Bridge		d						07 09								07 34							
Hoscar		d						07 13															
Parbold		d						07 16								07 39							
Appley Bridge		d						07 20								07 43							
Gathurst		d						07 23								07 47							
Kirkby		d										07 11											
Rainford		d										07 19											
Upholland		d										07 23											
Orrell		d										07 27											
Pemberton		d										07 30											
Wigan Wallgate		a						07 29				07 35				07 51							
		d					07 15	07 29				07 37				07 53	08 00						08 13
Wigan North Western		d							07 22		07a50												
Ince		d					07 18		07 25			07 40											08 16
Hindley		d					07 21		07 29			07 43				07 58							08 19
Westhoughton		d							07 33							08 03							
Bolton		a	07 25			07 34			07 42	07 54				08 08		08 11		08 25		08 34			
		d	07 25		07 30	07 35			07 43	07 55			07 59	08 08		08 12		08 25	08 31	08 35			
Moses Gate		d							07 46				08 02										
Farnworth		d							07 48				08 04										
Kearsley		d							07 50				08 06										
Daisy Hill		d					07 26	07 39				07 47					08 07						08 23
Hag Fold		d					07 29					07 50											08 26
Atherton		d					07 32	07 43				07 53					08 12						08 29
Walkden		d					07 38					07 59					08 18						08 35
Moorside		d					07 41					08 03											08 39
Swinton		d					07 44					08 06											08 42
Salford Crescent		a	07 38		07 43	07 47	07 51	07 59	08 02	08 07		08 13	08 17			08 24	08 29	08 38	08 43	08 47			08 50
		d	07 38		07 43	07 47	07 51	08 00	08 02	08 08		08 13	08 17			08 25	08 30	08 38	08 44	08 47			08 50
Salford Central		d	07 41		07 46		07 55	08 03	08 05			08 16	08 20				08 32	08 41	08 46				08 53
Manchester Victoria	⇌	a	07 47		07 53		08 00	08 08	08 12			08 20	08 25				08 38	08 48	08 52				08 59
Rochdale	41	a										08 51											
Deansgate	⇌	a				07 51				08 11						08 28							
Manchester Oxford Road		a				07 52				08 14				08 23		08 31				08 52			
Manchester Piccadilly 10	⇌	a				07 56				08 18				08 27		08 35				08 56			
Stockport	84	a								08 34													
Hazel Grove	86	a								08 48													
Buxton	86	a																					
Heald Green	85	a				08 10										08 47				09 10			
Manchester Airport	85 ✈	a				08 17								08 47		08 53				09 19			

A From Skipton
B From Clitheroe
C To Stalybridge
D To Liverpool Lime Street
E ✠ from Preston
F From Edinburgh
G From Millom

Table 82

Mondays to Fridays
until 28 September

Barrow-in-Furness, Blackpool North, Preston, Southport, Kirkby and Wigan - Bolton - Manchester

Network Diagram - see first Page of Table 82

Station			NT	NT	NT	NT A	TP ◇1 B ✠	NT C	NT	NT	NT	NT D	NT E	TP ◇1 ✠	NT	NT	NT	NT A	NT	TP ◇1 F ✠	NT	NT	NT	NT D
Barrow-in-Furness		d					07 29	08 00																
Roose		d						08 04																
Dalton		d					07 38	08 10																
Ulverston		d					07 46	08 19																
Cark		d					07 54	08 27																
Kents Bank		d						08 32																
Grange-over-Sands		d					08 01	08 36																
Arnside		d					08 07	08 42																
Silverdale		d					08 11	08 47																
Carnforth		d					08 18	08 54																
Windermere	83	d																						
Oxenholme Lake District	65	d																		09 11				
Lancaster 6	65	a					08 26	09 07												09 25				
		d					08 27													09 26				
Blackpool North	97	d									08 20			08 44									09 20	09 37
Layton	97	d									08 23												09 23	
Poulton-le-Fylde	97	d									08 28			08 50									09 28	
Kirkham & Wesham	97	d									08 37												09 37	09 52
Preston 8	65,97	a					08 45				08 47			09 08						09 45			09 47	10 02
		d			08 17		08 47				08 49	09 04		09 10			09 23			09 47			09 49	10 04
Leyland		d			08 23						08 54	09 09					09 29						09 54	10 09
Buckshaw Parkway		d			08 28						08 59			09 17			09 33						09 59	
Chorley		d			08 35		08 56				09 03			09 21			09 38			09 56			10 03	
Adlington (Lancashire)		d			08 39						09 08												10 08	
Blackrod		d			08 43						09 12												10 12	
Horwich Parkway		d			08 47						09 16			09 28			09 46						10 16	
Lostock		d			08 50						09 20						09 50						10 20	
Southport		d		07 58					08 25							09 02					09 24			
Meols Cop		d		08 03					08 30							09 07								
Bescar Lane		d																						
New Lane		d																						
Burscough Bridge		d		08 11					08 38							09 15					09 36			
Hoscar		d																						
Parbold		d		08 16					08 43							09 20					09 41			
Appley Bridge		d		08 20					08 47							09 24					09 45			
Gathurst		d		08 23					08 50							09 27								
Kirkby		d								08 21												09 32		
Rainford		d								08 29												09 40		
Upholland		d								08 33												09 44		
Orrell		d								08 36												09 47		
Pemberton		d								08 39												09 50		
Wigan Wallgate		a		08 28					08 55	08 45						09 32					09 51	09 56		
		d		08 29					08 56	08 50					09 20	09 32			09 46		09 53	09 58		
Wigan North Western		d	08 20									09a24												10a24
Ince		d								08 53												10 01		
Hindley		d	08 25	08 34						08 57					09 25	09 37					09 58	10 04		
Westhoughton		d	08 29						09 04						09 29				09 54		10 02			
Bolton		a	08 38		08 55		09 08		09 12		09 25			09 34	09 38		09 55		10 02	10 08	10 12		10 25	
		d	08 39		08 56	09 02	09 08		09 13		09 25		09 31	09 35	09 39		09 56	10 00	10 03	10 08	10 13		10 25	
Moses Gate		d	08 42												09 42									
Farnworth		d	08 44												09 44									
Kearsley		d	08 46												09 46									
Daisy Hill		d		08 39						09 01						09 41						10 09		
Hag Fold		d								09 04												10 12		
Atherton		d		08 43						09 06						09 45						10 15		
Walkden		d		08 49						09 12						09 50						10 20		
Moorside		d								09 15												10 24		
Swinton		d		08 54						09 18						09 55						10 26		
Salford Crescent		a	08 56	09 02	09 08	09 15			09 25	09 27	09 38		09 43	09 47	09 56	10 03	10 08	10 13	10 15		10 25	10 34	10 38	
		d	08 56	09 02	09 09	09 16			09 26	09 27	09 38		09 44	09 47	09 56	10 03	10 09	10 13	10 15		10 26	10 34	10 38	
Salford Central		d	08 59	09 04		09 18				09 31	09 41		09 46		09 59	10 05		10 16	10 17			10 36	10 41	
Manchester Victoria	⇌	a	09 06	09 11		09 26				09 38	09 47		09 52		10 06	10 12		10 21	10 25			10 43	10 47	
Rochdale	41	a																	10 51					
Deansgate	⇌	a			09 12				09 29					09 51			10 12				10 29			
Manchester Oxford Road		a			09 14		09 23		09 31					09 52			10 14			10 23	10 31			
Manchester Piccadilly 10	⇌	a			09 18		09 27		09 35					09 56			10 18			10 27	10 35			
Stockport	84	a			09 34												10 34							
Hazel Grove	86	a			09 45												10 45							
Buxton	86	a																						
Heald Green	85	a												10 10										
Manchester Airport	85 ✈	a					09 47		09 53					10 17						10 47	10 53			

A From Blackburn
B ✠ from Preston
C From Maryport
D To Liverpool South Parkway
E From Clitheroe
F From Glasgow Central

Barrow-in-Furness, Blackpool North, Preston, Southport, Kirkby and Wigan - Bolton - Manchester

Network Diagram - see first Page of Table 82

			NT A	NT B	TP ◇■ ⊼	NT	NT	NT	NT	TP ◇■ C ⊼	NT D	NT	NT	NT	NT E	NT B	TP ◇■ ⊼	NT	NT	NT	NT	TP ◇■ C ⊼	NT
Barrow-in-Furness		d								09 23	10 16												
Roose		d								09 27	10 20												
Dalton		d								09 34	10 26												
Ulverston		d								09 42	10 35												
Cark		d								09 50	10 42												
Kents Bank		d								09 54	10 47												
Grange-over-Sands		d								09 58	10 51												
Arnside		d								10 04	10 57												
Silverdale		d								10 08	11 01												
Carnforth		d	10 02							10 15	11 08												
Windermere	83	d																				10 49	
Oxenholme Lake District	65	d																				11 09	
Lancaster ■	65	a	10 12							10 25	11 20											11 26	
		d								10 26												11 26	
Blackpool North	97	d			09 43									10 20	10 37		10 44						
Layton	97	d												10 23									
Poulton-le-Fylde	97	d			09 49									10 28			10 50						
Kirkham & Wesham	97	d												10 37	10 52								
Preston ■	65,97	a			10 07					10 45				10 47	11 02		11 08					11 45	
		d			10 12			10 23		10 47				10 49	11 04		11 10			11 23		11 47	
Leyland		d						10 29						10 54	11 09					11 29			
Buckshaw Parkway		d						10 33						10 59			11 17			11 33			
Chorley		d			10 22			10 38		10 56				11 03			11 21			11 38		11 56	
Adlington (Lancashire)		d												11 08									
Blackrod		d												11 12									
Horwich Parkway		d						10 46						11 16			11 28			11 46			
Lostock		d						10 50						11 20						11 50			
Southport		d					09 55					10 24							10 55				11 24
Meols Cop		d					10 00												11 00				
Bescar Lane		d					10 05												11 05				
New Lane		d					10 09												11 09				
Burscough Bridge		d					10 11					10 36							11 11				11 36
Hoscar		d					10 15												11 15				
Parbold		d					10 18					10 41							11 18				11 41
Appley Bridge		d					10 22					10 45							11 22				11 45
Gathurst		d					10 25												11 25				
Kirkby		d											10 32										
Rainford		d											10 40										
Upholland		d											10 44										
Orrell		d											10 47										
Pemberton		d											10 50										
Wigan Wallgate		a					10 30					10 51	10 56						11 30				11 51
		d				10 20	10 32		10 48			10 53	10 58					11 20	11 32		11 48		11 53
Wigan North Western		d													11a24								
Ince		d											11 01										
Hindley		d				10 25	10 37					10 58	11 04					11 25	11 37				11 58
Westhoughton		d				10 29						11 02						11 29					12 02
Bolton		a			10 34	10 38		10 55	11 02	11 08		11 12		11 25			11 34	11 38		11 55	12 02	12 08	12 12
		d		10 31	10 35	10 39		10 56	11 03	11 08		11 13		11 25		11 31	11 35	11 39		11 56	12 03	12 08	12 13
Moses Gate		d				10 42												11 42					
Farnworth		d				10 44												11 44					
Kearsley		d				10 46												11 46					
Daisy Hill		d					10 41						11 09						11 41				
Hag Fold		d											11 12										
Atherton		d					10 45						11 15						11 45				
Walkden		d					10 50						11 20						11 50				
Moorside		d											11 24										
Swinton		d					10 55						11 26						11 55				
Salford Crescent		a		10 43	10 47	10 56	11 02	11 08	11 15			11 25	11 34	11 38		11 43	11 47	11 56	12 02	12 08	12 15		12 25
		d		10 44	10 47	10 56	11 03	11 09	11 15			11 26	11 34	11 38		11 44	11 47	11 56	12 03	12 09	12 15		12 26
Salford Central		d		10 46		10 59	11 05		11 17				11 36	11 41		11 46		11 59	12 05		12 17		
Manchester Victoria ⛴		a		10 52		11 06	11 11		11 25				11 43	11 47		11 52		12 06	12 11		12 25		
Rochdale	41	a							11 51												12 51		
Deansgate ⛴		a			10 51			11 12				11 29					11 51			12 12			12 29
Manchester Oxford Road		a			10 52			11 14		11 23		11 31					11 52			12 14		12 23	12 31
Manchester Piccadilly ■ ⛴		a			10 56			11 18		11 27		11 35					11 56			12 18		12 27	12 35
Stockport	84	a						11 34												12 34			
Hazel Grove	86	a						11 45												12 45			
Buxton	86	a																					
Heald Green	85	a			11 10												12 10						
Manchester Airport	85 ✈	a			11 17					11 50		11 53					12 17					12 47	12 53

A From Leeds to Morecambe
B From Clitheroe
C ⊼ from Preston
D From Sellafield
E To Liverpool South Parkway

Table 82 Mondays to Fridays
until 28 September

Barrow-in-Furness, Blackpool North, Preston, Southport, Kirkby and Wigan - Bolton - Manchester

Network Diagram - see first Page of Table 82

			NT	NT	NT A	NT B	TP ◇■	NT C	TP FO ◇■ ⊼	TP FX ◇■ ⊼	NT	NT	NT	NT	TP ◇■ D ⊼	NT E	NT	NT	NT	NT A	NT C	TP ◇■ ⊼	NT	NT
Barrow-in-Furness		d					11 25									12 11								
Roose		d														12 15								
Dalton		d														12 21								
Ulverston		d					11 41									12 29								
Cark		d														12 37								
Kents Bank		d														12 41								
Grange-over-Sands		d					11 53									12 45								
Arnside		d					11 59									12 51								
Silverdale		d														12 55								
Carnforth		d				12 02	12 09									13 03								
Windermere	83	d																						
Oxenholme Lake District	65	d													12 10									
Lancaster ■	65	a				12 11	12 18								12 26	13 16								
		d					12 18								12 26									
Blackpool North	97	d		11 20	11 37				11 44	11 44									12 20	12 37		12 44		
Layton	97	d		11 23															12 23					
Poulton-le-Fylde	97	d		11 28					11 50	11 50									12 28			12 50		
Kirkham & Wesham	97	d		11 37	11 52														12 37	12 52				
Preston ■	65,97	a		11 47	12 02		12 37		12 08	12 08					12 45				12 47	13 02		13 08		
		d		11 49	12 04				12 10	12 10			12 23		12 47				12 49	13 04		13 10		
Leyland		d		11 54	12 09								12 29						12 54	13 09				
Buckshaw Parkway		d		11 58					12 17	12 17			12 33						12 59			13 17		
Chorley		d		12 03					12 21	12 21			12 38		12 56				13 03			13 21		
Adlington (Lancashire)		d		12 08															13 08					
Blackrod		d		12 11															13 12					
Horwich Parkway		d		12 15					12 28	12 28			12 46						13 16			13 28		
Lostock		d		12 21									12 50						13 20					
Southport		d										12 00					12 24							12 54
Meols Cop		d										12 05												12 59
Bescar Lane		d																						13 04
New Lane		d																						13 08
Burscough Bridge		d										12 13					12 36							13 11
Hoscar		d																						13 15
Parbold		d										12 18					12 41							13 18
Appley Bridge		d										12 22					12 45							13 22
Gathurst		d										12 25												13 25
Kirkby		d	11 32															12 32						
Rainford		d	11 40															12 40						
Upholland		d	11 44															12 44						
Orrell		d	11 47															12 47						
Pemberton		d	11 50															12 50						
Wigan Wallgate		a	11 56									12 30					12 51	12 56						13 30
		d	11 58								12 20	12 32		12 48			12 53	12 58					13 20	13 32
Wigan North Western		d			12a24															13a24				
Ince		d	12 01															13 01						
Hindley		d	12 04								12 25	12 37					12 58	13 04					13 25	13 37
Westhoughton		d									12 29						13 02						13 29	
Bolton		a		12 25					12 34	12 34	12 38		12 55	13 02	13 08		13 12		13 25			13 34	13 38	
		d		12 25				12 31	12 35	12 35	12 39		12 56	13 03	13 08		13 13		13 25		13 31	13 35	13 39	
Moses Gate		d									12 42												13 42	
Farnworth		d									12 44												13 44	
Kearsley		d									12 46												13 46	
Daisy Hill		d	12 09									12 41						13 09						13 41
Hag Fold		d	12 12															13 12						
Atherton		d	12 15									12 45						13 15						13 45
Walkden		d	12 20									12 50						13 20						13 50
Moorside		d	12 24															13 24						
Swinton		d	12 26									12 55						13 26						13 55
Salford Crescent		a	12 34	12 38				12 43	12 47	12 47	12 56	13 02	13 08	13 15			13 25	13 34	13 38		13 43	13 47	13 56	14 02
		d	12 34	12 38				12 44	12 47	12 47	12 56	13 03	13 09	13 15			13 26	13 34	13 38		13 44	13 47	13 56	14 03
Salford Central		d	12 36	12 41				12 46			12 59	13 05		13 17				13 36	13 41		13 46		13 59	14 05
Manchester Victoria ⛴		a	12 43	12 47				12 52			13 06	13 11		13 25				13 43	13 47		13 52		14 06	14 11
Rochdale	41	a												13 51										
Deansgate ⛴		a							12 51	12 51			13 12				13 29					13 51		
Manchester Oxford Road		a							12 52	12 52			13 14		13 23		13 31					13 52		
Manchester Piccadilly ■ ⛴		a							12 56	12 56			13 18		13 27		13 35					13 56		
Stockport	84	a											13 34											
Hazel Grove	86	a											13 45											
Buxton	86	a																						
Heald Green	85	a							13 10	13 10												14 10		
Manchester Airport	85 ✈	a							13 16	13 17					13 47		13 53					14 17		

A To Liverpool South Parkway
B From Leeds to Heysham Port
C From Clitheroe
D From Edinburgh
E From Carlisle

Table 82 — Mondays to Fridays — until 28 September

Barrow-in-Furness, Blackpool North, Preston, Southport, Kirkby and Wigan - Bolton - Manchester

Network Diagram - see first Page of Table 82

		NT	NT	TP	NT	TP		TP	NT	NT	NT	NT	TP	NT	NT	NT		NT	TP	NT	NT	NT	NT	NT	NT
						FO		FX																	
				◇1		◇1		◇1					◇1						◇1						
				A							B	C							D					B	C
				⌶									⌶						⌶						
Barrow-in-Furness	d					13 25		13 25												14 16					
Roose	d																			14 20					
Dalton	d																			14 26					
Ulverston	d					13 41		13 41												14 35					
Cark	d																			14 42					
Kents Bank	d																			14 47					
Grange-over-Sands	d					13 53		13 53												14 51					
Arnside	d					13 59		13 59												14 57					
Silverdale	d																			15 01					
Carnforth	d					14 09		14 09												15 07					
Windermere 83	d			12 51																					
Oxenholme Lake District 65	d			13 09															14 10						
Lancaster 6 65	a			13 26		14 18		14 18											14 26	15 20					
	d			13 26				14 18											14 26						
Blackpool North 97	d									13 20	13 37		13 44										14 20	14 37	
Layton 97	d									13 23													14 23		
Poulton-le-Fylde 97	d									13 28			13 50										14 28		
Kirkham & Wesham 97	d									13 37	13 52												14 37	14 52	
Preston 8 65,97	a			13 45				14 37		13 47	14 02		14 08						14 45				14 47	15 02	
	d	13 23		13 47						13 49	14 04		14 10			14 23			14 47				14 49	15 04	
Leyland	d	13 29								13 54	14 09					14 29							14 54	15 09	
Buckshaw Parkway	d	13 33								13 59			14 17			14 33							14 59		
Chorley	d	13 38		13 56						14 03			14 21			14 38			14 56				15 03		
Adlington (Lancashire)	d									14 08													15 08		
Blackrod	d									14 11													15 12		
Horwich Parkway	d	13 46								14 15			14 28			14 46							15 16		
Lostock	d	13 50								14 21						14 50							15 20		
Southport	d				13 24										14 00						14 24				
Meols Cop	d														14 05										
Bescar Lane	d																								
New Lane	d																								
Burscough Bridge	d				13 36										14 13						14 36				
Hoscar	d																								
Parbold	d				13 41										14 18						14 41				
Appley Bridge	d				13 45										14 22						14 45				
Gathurst	d														14 25										
Kirkby	d								13 32													14 32			
Rainford	d								13 40													14 40			
Upholland	d								13 44													14 44			
Orrell	d								13 47													14 47			
Pemberton	d								13 50													14 50			
Wigan Wallgate	a				13 51				13 56						14 30						14 51	14 56			
	d		13 48		13 53				13 58					14 20	14 32			14 48			14 53	14 58			
Wigan North Western	d										14a24													15a24	
Ince	d								14 01													15 01			
Hindley	d				13 58				14 04					14 25	14 37						14 58	15 04			
Westhoughton	d				14 02									14 29							15 02				
Bolton	a	13 55	14 02	14 08	14 12					14 26			14 34	14 38		14 55		15 02	15 08		15 12		15 25		
	d	13 56	14 03	14 08	14 13					14 26		14 31	14 35	14 39		14 56		15 03	15 08		15 13		15 25		15 31
Moses Gate	d													14 42											
Farnworth	d													14 44											
Kearsley	d													14 46											
Daisy Hill	d								14 09						14 41							15 09			
Hag Fold	d								14 12													15 12			
Atherton	d								14 15						14 45							15 15			
Walkden	d								14 20						14 50							15 20			
Moorside	d								14 24													15 24			
Swinton	d								14 26						14 55							15 26			
Salford Crescent	a	14 08	14 15		14 25				14 34	14 38		14 43	14 47	14 56	15 02	15 08		15 15			15 25	15 33	15 38		15 43
	d	14 09	14 15		14 26				14 34	14 38		14 44	14 47	14 56	15 03	15 09		15 15			15 26	15 34	15 38		15 44
Salford Central	d		14 17						14 36	14 41		14 46		14 59	15 05			15 17				15 36	15 41		15 46
Manchester Victoria ⇌	a		14 25						14 43	14 47		14 52		15 06	15 11			15 25				15 43	15 47		15 54
Rochdale 41	a		14 51															15 51							
Deansgate ⇌	a	14 12			14 29								14 51			15 12					15 29				
Manchester Oxford Road	a	14 14		14 23	14 31								14 52			15 14			15 23		15 31				
Manchester Piccadilly 10 ⇌	a	14 18		14 27	14 35								14 56			15 18			15 27		15 35				
Stockport 84	a	14 34														15 34									
Hazel Grove 86	a	14 45														15 47									
Buxton 86	a																								
Heald Green 85	a												15 10												
Manchester Airport 85 ✈	a			14 47	14 53								15 17						15 47		15 53				

A ⌶ from Preston
B To Liverpool South Parkway
C From Clitheroe
D From Edinburgh

Table 82 — Mondays to Fridays — until 28 September

Barrow-in-Furness, Blackpool North, Preston, Southport, Kirkby and Wigan - Bolton - Manchester

Network Diagram - see first Page of Table 82

		TP		NT	NT	NT	NT	TP	NT	NT	TP	NT		NT	NT	NT	TP	NT	NT	NT	NT	TP		TP	NT
											FO											FX			
		◇1						◇1			◇1						◇1					◇1		◇1	
								A		B		C				D			E			F		G	
		⌶						⌶									⌶					⌶		⌶	
Barrow-in-Furness	d										15 24											15 24			16 20
Roose	d																								16 24
Dalton	d																								16 30
Ulverston	d										15 40											15 40			16 38
Cark	d										15 47											15 47			16 46
Kents Bank	d																								16 50
Grange-over-Sands	d										15 54											15 54			16 54
Arnside	d										16 00											16 00			17 00
Silverdale	d																								17 04
Carnforth	d									15 38	16 09											16 09			17 12
Windermere 83	d																								
Oxenholme Lake District 65	d																							16 07	
Lancaster 6 65	a									15 47	16 18											16 18		16 21	17 26
	d							15 22			16 18											16 18		16 22	
Blackpool North 97	d	14 44													15 20	15 37	15 44								
Layton 97	d														15 23										
Poulton-le-Fylde 97	d	14 50													15 28		15 50								
Kirkham & Wesham 97	d														15 37	15 52									
Preston 8 65,97	a	15 08						15 41			16 37				15 47	16 02	16 08					16 37		16 42	
	d	15 10				15 23		15 47							15 49	16 04	16 10			16 23		16 47		16 47	
Leyland	d					15 29									15 54	16 09				16 29					
Buckshaw Parkway	d	15 17				15 33									15 59		16 17			16 33					
Chorley	d	15 21				15 38		15 56							16 03		16 21			16 38		16 56		16 56	
Adlington (Lancashire)	d														16 08										
Blackrod	d														16 11										
Horwich Parkway	d	15 28				15 46									16 15		16 28			16 46					
Lostock	d					15 50									16 21					16 50					
Southport	d				14 54				15 24										15 58						
Meols Cop	d				14 59														16 03						
Bescar Lane	d				15 04																				
New Lane	d				15 08																				
Burscough Bridge	d				15 11				15 36										16 11						
Hoscar	d				15 15																				
Parbold	d				15 18				15 41										16 16						
Appley Bridge	d				15 22				15 45										16 20						
Gathurst	d				15 25														16 24						
Kirkby	d													15 32											
Rainford	d													15 40											
Upholland	d													15 44											
Orrell	d													15 47											
Pemberton	d													15 50											
Wigan Wallgate	a				15 30				15 51					15 56					16 29						
	d			15 20	15 32		15 48		15 53					15 58				16 20	16 30		16 48				
Wigan North Western	d															16a24									
Ince	d													16 01					16 33						
Hindley	d			15 25	15 37				15 58					16 04				16 25	16 37						
Westhoughton	d			15 29					16 02									16 29							
Bolton	a	15 34		15 38		15 55	16 02	16 08	16 12						16 25		16 34	16 38		16 55	17 02	17 08		17 08	
	d	15 35		15 39		15 56	16 03	16 08	16 13			16 17			16 25		16 35	16 39		16 56	17 03	17 08		17 08	
Moses Gate	d			15 42														16 42							
Farnworth	d			15 44														16 44							
Kearsley	d			15 46														16 46							
Daisy Hill	d				15 41									16 09					16 41						
Hag Fold	d													16 12											
Atherton	d				15 45									16 15					16 45						
Walkden	d				15 50									16 20					16 50						
Moorside	d													16 24											
Swinton	d				15 55									16 26					16 55						
Salford Crescent	a	15 47		15 56	16 02	16 08	16 15		16 25			16 30		16 34	16 38		16 47	16 56	17 02	17 08	17 15				
	d	15 47		15 56	16 03	16 09	16 15		16 26			16 30		16 34	16 38		16 47	16 56	17 03	17 09	17 15				
Salford Central	d			15 59	16 05		16 17					16 33		16 36	16 41			16 59	17 05		17 17				
Manchester Victoria ⇌	a			16 06	16 11		16 23					16 41		16 43	16 47			17 06	17 13		17 23				
Rochdale 41	a						16 51														17 51				
Deansgate ⇌	a	15 51				16 12											16 51			17 15					
Manchester Oxford Road	a	15 52				16 14		16 23	16 31								16 52			17 17		17 26		17 26	
Manchester Piccadilly 10 ⇌	a	15 56				16 18		16 27	16 35								16 56			17 21		17 29		17 29	
Stockport 84	a					16 34														17 32					
Hazel Grove 86	a					16 43														17 39					
Buxton 86	a					17 22														18 16					
Heald Green 85	a	16 10						16 40									17 10					17 41		17 41	
Manchester Airport 85 ✈	a	16 17						16 47	16 53								17 17					17 48		17 48	

A From Glasgow Central
B From Leeds to Morecambe
C From Clitheroe
D To Liverpool Lime Street
E To Huddersfield
F ⌶ from Preston
G From Edinburgh

Barrow-in-Furness, Blackpool North, Preston, Southport, Kirkby and Wigan - Bolton - Manchester

Network Diagram - see first Page of Table 82

			NT	NT	NT	NT	NT	TP	NT	NT	NT	NT	TP	NT	NT	NT	NT	TP	TP	NT	NT	NT	TP	NT
						A	B	◇1 ✠				B	◇1 ✠				A	◇1 C ✠	◇1 D			B	◇1 E ✠	
Barrow-in-Furness		d																	17 21					
Roose		d																						
Dalton		d																	17 30					
Ulverston		d																	17 38					
Cark		d																	17 46					
Kents Bank		d																						
Grange-over-Sands		d																	17 53					
Arnside		d																	17 59					
Silverdale		d																						
Carnforth		d																	18 09					
Windermere	83	d																17 06						
Oxenholme Lake District	65	d																17 30						
Lancaster 6	65	a																17 47	18 20					
		d																17 48					18 26	
Blackpool North	97	d			16 20	16 35		16 40					17 20				17 37							
Layton	97	d			16 23			16 44					17 23											
Poulton-le-Fylde	97	d			16 28			16 48					17 27											
Kirkham & Wesham	97	d			16 37	16 52		16 57									17 52							
Preston 8	65,97	a			16 47	17 02		17 08					17 45				18 02	18 06					18 45	
		d			16 49	17 04		17 10					17 47			17 56	18 04	18 08					18 47	
Leyland		d			16 54	17 09										18 01	18 09							
Buckshaw Parkway		d			16 59			17 17								18 05		18 15						
Chorley		d			17 03			17 21					17 56			18 10		18 19					18 56	
Adlington (Lancashire)		d			17 08											18 15								
Blackrod		d			17 12											18 18								
Horwich Parkway		d			17 16			17 28								18 21		18 26						
Lostock		d			17 20													18 30						
Southport		d	16 24							16 54				17 24										18 17
Meols Cop		d								16 59				17 29										18 22
Bescar Lane		d								17 04														18 27
New Lane		d								17 08														18 31
Burscough Bridge		d	16 36							17 11				17 37										18 33
Hoscar		d								17 15														18 37
Parbold		d	16 41							17 18				17 42										18 40
Appley Bridge		d	16 45							17 22				17 46										18 44
Gathurst		d								17 25														18 47
Kirkby		d		16 32											17 32									
Rainford		d		16 40											17 40									
Upholland		d		16 44											17 44									
Orrell		d		16 47											17 47									
Pemberton		d		16 50											17 50									
Wigan Wallgate		a	16 51	16 56						17 30				17 52	17 57									18 52
		d	16 53	16 58					17 20	17 32	17 39			17 54	17 59					18 20	18 32			18 53
Wigan North Western		d				17a24											18a24							
Ince		d		17 01											18 02									
Hindley		d	16 58	17 04					17 25	17 37					18 05					18 25	18 37			18 58
Westhoughton		d	17 02						17 29		17 47			18 02						18 29				19 02
Bolton		a	17 12		17 25			17 34	17 38		17 55		18 08	18 12		18 31		18 34		18 38			19 08	19 12
		d	17 13		17 25		17 31	17 35	17 39		17 56	18 02	18 08	18 13		18 31		18 35		18 39		19 02	19 08	19 13
Moses Gate		d							17 42											18 42				
Farnworth		d							17 44											18 44				
Kearsley		d							17 46											18 46				
Daisy Hill		d		17 08						17 41					18 09						18 41			
Hag Fold		d		17 11											18 12									
Atherton		d		17 14						17 45					18 15						18 45			
Walkden		d		17 19						17 50					18 20						18 50			
Moorside		d		17 23											18 24									
Swinton		d		17 25						17 55					18 26						18 55			
Salford Crescent		a	17 25	17 33	17 38		17 43	17 47	17 56	18 02	18 08	18 15		18 25	18 33	18 43		18 47		18 56	19 02	19 14		19 25
		d	17 26	17 33	17 38		17 44	17 47	17 56	18 03	18 09	18 15		18 26	18 33	18 43		18 47		18 56	19 03	19 15		19 26
Salford Central		d		17 36	17 41		17 46		17 59	18 05		18 17			18 36	18 46				18 59	19 05	19 17		
Manchester Victoria ⇌		a		17 43	17 47		17 53		18 06	18 09		18 24			18 43	18 52				19 06	19 11	19 23		
Rochdale	41	a										18 47												
Deansgate ⇌		a						17 51			18 12							18 51						19 29
Manchester Oxford Road		a	17 30					17 52			18 14		18 23	18 31				18 52					19 23	19 31
Manchester Piccadilly 10 ⇌		a	17 35					17 56			18 18		18 27	18 35				18 56					19 27	19 35
Stockport	84	a									18 34													
Hazel Grove	86	a									18 43													
Buxton	86	a									19 22													
Heald Green	85	a						18 10					18 40					19 10						
Manchester Airport	85 ✈	a	17 53					18 17					18 47	18 53				19 17					19 47	19 53

A To Liverpool Lime Street
B From Clitheroe
C ✠ from Preston
D To Windermere
E From Edinburgh

Barrow-in-Furness, Blackpool North, Preston, Southport, Kirkby and Wigan - Bolton - Manchester

Network Diagram - see first Page of Table 82

			NT	NT	NT	NT	NT	TP	TP	NT	NT	NT	TP	NT	NT	NT	NT	TP	TP ThX	TP ThO	NT	NT	NT
			A			B	C	◇1 ✠	◇1	D		E	◇1 F ✠			B	C	◇1	◇1 G ✠	◇1 G ✠			
Barrow-in-Furness		d								18 03													
Roose		d								18 07													
Dalton		d								18 13													
Ulverston		d								18 21													
Cark		d								18 29													
Kents Bank		d								18 33													
Grange-over-Sands		d								18 37													
Arnside		d								18 43													
Silverdale		d								18 47													
Carnforth		d	18 29							18 55													
Windermere	83	d							18 15														
Oxenholme Lake District	65	d							18 36				19 10						20 13	20 13			
Lancaster 6	65	a	18 42						18 52	19 05			19 26						20 26	20 26			
		d							18 52	19 06			19 26						20 26	20 26			
Blackpool North	97	d			18 20	18 37		18 44							19 20	19 37		19 44					20 20
Layton	97	d			18 23										19 23								20 23
Poulton-le-Fylde	97	d			18 28			18 50							19 28			19 50					20 28
Kirkham & Wesham	97	d			18 37	18 52									19 37								20 37
Preston 8	65,97	a			18 47	19 02		19 08	19 11	19 31			19 45		19 47	20 02		20 08	20 45	20 45			20 47
		d			18 49	19 04		19 10	19 16				19 47		19 49	20 04		20 10	20 47	20 47			20 49
Leyland		d			18 54	19 09									19 54	20 09							20 54
Buckshaw Parkway		d			18 59			19 17							19 59			20 17					20 59
Chorley		d			19 03			19 21	19 29				19 56		20 03			20 21	20 56	20 56			21 03
Adlington (Lancashire)		d			19 08										20 08								21 08
Blackrod		d			19 12										20 11								21 12
Horwich Parkway		d			19 16			19 28	19 36						20 15			20 28					21 16
Lostock		d			19 20										20 21								21 20
Southport		d									19 00			19 23								20 23	
Meols Cop		d									19 05			19 28								20 28	
Bescar Lane		d																					
New Lane		d																					
Burscough Bridge		d									19 13			19 36								20 36	
Hoscar		d																					
Parbold		d									19 18			19 41								20 41	
Appley Bridge		d									19 22			19 45								20 45	
Gathurst		d									19 25			19 48								20 48	
Kirkby		d		18 32																			
Rainford		d		18 40																			
Upholland		d		18 44																			
Orrell		d		18 47																			
Pemberton		d		18 50																			
Wigan Wallgate		a		18 56							19 30			19 53								20 53	
		d		18 58							19 32			19 55							20 27	20 55	
Wigan North Western		d				19a24										20a24							
Ince		d		19 01																	20 30		
Hindley		d		19 04							19 37			20 00							20 33	21 00	
Westhoughton		d												20 04								21 04	
Bolton		a			19 25			19 33	19 42				20 08	20 12	20 25			20 34	21 08	21 08		21 12	21 25
		d			19 25		19 31	19 34	19 43			20 02	20 08	20 13	20 25		20 31	20 35	21 08	21 08		21 13	21 25
Moses Gate		d																					
Farnworth		d																					
Kearsley		d																					
Daisy Hill		d		19 08							19 41										20 37		
Hag Fold		d		19 11																	20 40		
Atherton		d		19 14							19 45										20 43		
Walkden		d		19 19							19 50										20 49		
Moorside		d		19 23																	20 52		
Swinton		d		19 25							19 55										20 55		
Salford Crescent		a		19 33	19 38		19 44	19 47			20 02	20 15		20 25	20 38		20 43	20 47			21 02	21 25	21 38
		d		19 33	19 38		19 44	19 47			20 03	20 15		20 26	20 38		20 44	20 47			21 03	21 26	21 38
Salford Central		d		19 36	19 41		19 46				20 05	20 17			20 41		20 46				21 05		21 41
Manchester Victoria ⇌		a		19 43	19 47		19 53				20 11	20 24			20 47		20 52				21 11		21 47
Rochdale	41	a																					
Deansgate ⇌		a						19 51						20 29				20 51				21 29	
Manchester Oxford Road		a						19 52	19 57				20 23	20 31				20 52	21 23	21 23		21 31	
Manchester Piccadilly 10 ⇌		a						19 56	20 01				20 27	20 35				20 56	21 27	21 27		21 35	
Stockport	84	a																					
Hazel Grove	86	a																					
Buxton	86	a																					
Heald Green	85	a						20 10	20 15									21 10					
Manchester Airport	85 ✈	a						20 17	20 24				20 47	20 53				21 17	21 46	21 47		21 53	

A From Leeds to Morecambe
B To Liverpool Lime Street
C From Clitheroe
D From Carlisle
E From Blackburn
F From Glasgow Central
G From Edinburgh

Table 82

Mondays to Fridays
until 28 September

Barrow-in-Furness, Blackpool North, Preston, Southport, Kirkby and Wigan - Bolton - Manchester

Network Diagram - see first Page of Table 82

			NT	NT	TP	TP	NT	NT	NT	NT	NT		NT	NT	NT	TP	NT	TP	NT	NT	NT		NT	NT	NT	TP
							FO	FX	FO	FX	FX		FO	FX	FO			FO		FO	FX					
					◇1	◇1										◇1		◇1								◇1
			A	B										B	B			C							D	E
Barrow-in-Furness		d				20 08													21 43							
Roose		d				20 12													21 47							
Dalton		d				20 19													21 53							
Ulverston		d				20 27													22 01							
Cark		d				20 35													22 09							
Kents Bank		d				20 39													22 13							
Grange-over-Sands		d				20 43													22 17							
Arnside		d				20 49													22 23							
Silverdale		d				20 53													22 27							
Carnforth		d				21 01													22 35							
Windermere	83	d																								22 45
Oxenholme Lake District	65	d																22 10								23 06
Lancaster	65	a				21 10												22 26	22 45							23 23
		d				21 10												22 26	22 46						23 07	23 24
Blackpool North	97	d	20 37		20 44						21 20		21 20			21 44	22 14							22 20		
Layton	97	d									21 23		21 23											22 23		
Poulton-le-Fylde	97	d			20 50						21 28		21 28			21 50								22 28		
Kirkham & Wesham	97	d									21 37		21 37											22 37		
Preston	65,97	a	21 01		21 08	21 29					21 47		21 47			22 08	22 41	22 45	23 11					22 47	23 28	23 45
		d	21 04		21 10	21 31					21 49		21 49			22 10	22 43	22 47						22 49		
Leyland		d	21 09								21 54		21 54				22 48							22 54		
Buckshaw Parkway		d			21 17						21 59		21 59			22 17								22 59		
Chorley		d			21 21						22 03		22 03			22 21								23 03		
Adlington (Lancashire)		d									22 08		22 08											23 08		
Blackrod		d									22 12		22 12											23 12		
Horwich Parkway		d			21 28						22 16		22 16			22 28								23 16		
Lostock		d									22 20		22 20											23 20		
Southport		d							21 23	21 23													22 18			
Meols Cop		d							21 28	21 28													22 23			
Bescar Lane		d																					22 28			
New Lane		d																					22 32			
Burscough Bridge		d							21 36	21 36													22 34			
Hoscar		d																					22 38			
Parbold		d							21 41	21 41													22 41			
Appley Bridge		d							21 45	21 45													22 45			
Gathurst		d							21 48	21 48													22 48			
Kirkby		d																								
Rainford		d																								
Upholland		d																								
Orrell		d																								
Pemberton		d																								
Wigan Wallgate		a							21 53	21 53													22 53			
		d					21 27	21 27	21 55	21 55										22 27	22 27		22 55			
Wigan North Western		d	21a23			21 48											23a05									
Ince		d					21 30	21 30												22 30	22 30					
Hindley		d					21 33	21 33	22 00	22 00										22 33	22 33		23 00			
Westhoughton		d							22 04	22 04													23 04			
Bolton		a			21 34				22 12	22 12	22 25		22 25			22 34		23 06					23 12	23 25		
		d		21 31	21 35				22 13	22 13	22 25		22 25	22 31	22 31	22 35		23 06					23 13	23 25		
Moses Gate		d																								
Farnworth		d																								
Kearsley		d																								
Daisy Hill		d					21 37	21 37												22 37	22 37					
Hag Fold		d					21 40	21 40												22 40	22 40					
Atherton		d					21 43	21 43												22 43	22 43					
Walkden		d					21 49	21 49												22 49	22 49					
Moorside		d					21 52	21 52												22 52	22 52					
Swinton		d					21 55	21 55												22 55	22 55					
Salford Crescent		a		21 43	21 47		22 02	22 02	22 25	22 25	22 38		22 38	22 43	22 43	22 47				23 02	23 02		23 25	23 38		
		d		21 44	21 47		22 03	22 03	22 26	22 26	22 38		22 38	22 44	22 44	22 47				23 03	23 03		23 26	23 38		
Salford Central		d		21 46			22 05		22 28				22 41		22 46					23 05						
Manchester Victoria	⇌	a		21 52			22 11	22 11	22 34	22 34	22 47		22 47	22 52	22 52					23 13	23 13			23 47		
Rochdale	41	a																								
Deansgate	⇌	a			21 51											22 51							23 29			
Manchester Oxford Road		a			21 52	22 26										22 52		23s21					23 31			
Manchester Piccadilly	⇌	a			21 56	22 30										22 56		23 31					23 39			
Stockport	84	a																								
Hazel Grove	86	a																								
Buxton	86	a																								
Heald Green	85	a			22 09											23 09										
Manchester Airport	85 ✈	a			22 17	22 47										23 17										

A To Liverpool Lime Street
B From Clitheroe
C From Edinburgh
D From Morecambe
E To Blackpool North

Table 82

Mondays to Fridays
until 28 September

Barrow-in-Furness, Blackpool North, Preston, Southport, Kirkby and Wigan - Bolton - Manchester

Network Diagram - see first Page of Table 82

			NT	NT	TP	NT
					◇1	
				A		
Barrow-in-Furness		d				
Roose		d				
Dalton		d				
Ulverston		d				
Cark		d				
Kents Bank		d				
Grange-over-Sands		d				
Arnside		d				
Silverdale		d				
Carnforth		d				
Windermere	83	d				
Oxenholme Lake District	65	d				
Lancaster	65	a				
		d				
Blackpool North	97	d			22 44	23 13
Layton	97	d				23 16
Poulton-le-Fylde	97	d			22 50	23 21
Kirkham & Wesham	97	d				23 30
Preston	65,97	a			23 08	23 40
		d			23 10	23 42
Leyland		d				23 48
Buckshaw Parkway		d			23 17	23 52
Chorley		d			23 21	23 57
Adlington (Lancashire)		d				00 03
Blackrod		d				00 06
Horwich Parkway		d			23 28	00 10
Lostock		d				00 14
Southport		d	23 10			
Meols Cop		d	23 15			
Bescar Lane		d				
New Lane		d				
Burscough Bridge		d	23 23			
Hoscar		d				
Parbold		d	23 28			
Appley Bridge		d	23 32			
Gathurst		d	23 35			
Kirkby		d				
Rainford		d				
Upholland		d				
Orrell		d				
Pemberton		d				
Wigan Wallgate		a	23 44			
		d				
Wigan North Western		d				
Ince		d				
Hindley		d				
Westhoughton		d				
Bolton		a			23 34	00 19
		d		23 31	23 35	00 20
Moses Gate		d				
Farnworth		d				
Kearsley		d				
Daisy Hill		d				
Hag Fold		d				
Atherton		d				
Walkden		d				
Moorside		d				
Swinton		d				
Salford Crescent		a		23 43	23 47	
		d		23 44	23 47	
Salford Central		d				
Manchester Victoria	⇌	a		23 52		00 37
Rochdale	41	a				
Deansgate	⇌	a				
Manchester Oxford Road		a				
Manchester Piccadilly	⇌	a			23 53	
Stockport	84	a				
Hazel Grove	86	a				
Buxton	86	a				
Heald Green	85	a			00 16	
Manchester Airport	85 ✈	a			00 24	

A From Clitheroe

Barrow-in-Furness, Blackpool North, Preston, Southport, Kirkby and Wigan - Bolton - Manchester

Network Diagram - see first Page of Table 82

		TP MX ◇1	TP MO ◇1	NT MX	TP MX ◇1 A	TP ◇1 B	TP ◇1	TP ◇1	TP ◇1 B	NT C	TP ◇1	NT	TP ◇1 🚌	NT	NT	NT D	TP ◇1 E 🚌	NT	NT	NT F	NT G	TP ◇1 🚌	NT H
Barrow-in-Furness	d							04 35									05 31						
Roose	d																						
Dalton	d																						
Ulverston	d							04 51									05 47						
Cark	d																						
Kents Bank	d																						
Grange-over-Sands	d							05 03									05 59						
Arnside	d							05 10									06 05						
Silverdale	d																						
Carnforth	d							05 19									06 15			06 43			
Windermere 83	d																						
Oxenholme Lake District 65	d																						
Lancaster 6 65	a							05 28									06 23			06 52			
	d																06 23						
Blackpool North 97	d	22p44	23p03	23p13			03 37			04 56			05 39						06 19			06 40	
Layton 97	d			23p16															06 22			06 43	
Poulton-le-Fylde 97	d	22p50	23p09	23p21						05 02			05 45						06 27			06 47	
Kirkham & Wesham 97	d		23p17	23p30															06 36			06 56	
Preston 8 65,97	a	23p08	23p28	23p40						05 20			06 03				06 42		06 46			07 07	
	d	23p10	23p28	23p42			04u02				05 16		06 05				06 44		06 48			07 09	
Leyland	d		23p34	23p48									06 10						06 53				
Buckshaw Parkway	d	23p17	23p38	23p52															06 58				
Chorley	d	23p21	23p42	23p57							05 26		06 16				06 53		07 02			07 18	
Adlington (Lancashire)	d		23p46	00 03															07 07				
Blackrod	d		23p50	00 06									06 22						07 11				
Horwich Parkway	d	23p28	23p53	00 10							05 33		06 26				07 00		07 15			07 26	
Lostock	d		23p57	00 14									06 30						07 20			07 30	
Southport	d																	06 19					
Meols Cop	d																	06 24					
Bescar Lane	d																						
New Lane	d																						
Burscough Bridge	d																	06 32					
Hoscar	d																						
Parbold	d																	06 37					
Appley Bridge	d																	06 41					
Gathurst	d																	06 45					
Kirkby	d																						
Rainford	d																						
Upholland	d																						
Orrell	d																						
Pemberton	d																						
Wigan Wallgate	a																	06 52					
	d											06 01		06 31	06 34			06 53					07 15
Wigan North Western	d																						
Ince	d											06 04			06 37								07 18
Hindley	d											06 07		06 36	06 40								07 21
Westhoughton	d													06 41				07 01					
Bolton	a	23p34	00 02	00 19							05 42		06 34	06 52			07 08	07 11	07 25			07 34	
	d	23p35	00 02	00 20			04u31				05 43		06 35	06 53		06 56	07 08	07 12	07 25		07 30	07 35	
Moses Gate	d															06 59							
Farnworth	d															07 01							
Kearsley	d															07 03							
Daisy Hill	d											06 11			06 44								07 26
Hag Fold	d											06 14			06 47								07 29
Atherton	d											06 17			06 50								07 32
Walkden	d											06 22			06 56								07 38
Moorside	d											06 26			06 59								07 41
Swinton	d											06 28			07 02								07 44
Salford Crescent	a	23p47									05 55	06 38	06 47	07 05	07 11	07 16		07 24	07 38		07 43	07 47	07 51
	d	23p47			00 49	03 40			04 53		05 55	06 38	06 47	07 08	07 11	07 16		07 25	07 38		07 43	07 47	07 51
Salford Central	d											06 41			07 14	07 19			07 41		07 46		07 55
Manchester Victoria ⇌	a			00 37								06 46			07 20	07 26			07 47		07 54		08 00
Rochdale 41	a																						
Deansgate ⇌	a												06 51	07 11				07 28				07 51	
Manchester Oxford Road	a												06 52	07 13			07 23	07 30				07 52	
Manchester Piccadilly 10 ⇌	a	23p53	00 18		00 53	03 44	04 48		04 58		06 01		06 56	07 17			07 27	07 34				07 56	
Stockport 84	a													07 34									
Hazel Grove 86	a													07 47									
Buxton 86	a																						
Heald Green 85	a	00 16											07 10									08 10	
Manchester Airport 85 ✈	a	00 24	00 32		01 10	04 00	05 07		05 19		06 18		07 17				07 47	07 53				08 17	

A From Newcastle
B From York
C To Colne
D From Blackburn
E 🚌 from Preston
F From Skipton
G From Clitheroe
H from 1 October until 19 October. To Stalybridge

Barrow-in-Furness, Blackpool North, Preston, Southport, Kirkby and Wigan - Bolton - Manchester

Network Diagram - see first Page of Table 82

		NT	NT	NT	NT A	NT	NT B	TP ◇1 C 🚌	TP ◇1 🚌	NT	NT	NT	NT B	TP ◇1 🚌	TP ◇1 D 🚌	NT E	NT	NT	NT	NT	NT F	TP ◇1 C 🚌	NT G
Barrow-in-Furness	d							06 20								07 00						07 29	08 00
Roose	d							06 24								07 04							08 04
Dalton	d							06 31								07 10						07 38	08 10
Ulverston	d							06 39								07 19						07 46	08 19
Cark	d							06 47								07 26						07 54	08 27
Kents Bank	d							06 51								07 32							08 32
Grange-over-Sands	d							06 55								07 36						08 01	08 36
Arnside	d							07 01								07 42						08 07	08 42
Silverdale	d							07 05								07 47						08 11	08 47
Carnforth	d							07 12								07 55						08 18	08 54
Windermere 83	d																						
Oxenholme Lake District 65	d																						
Lancaster 6 65	a							07 21								08 04						08 26	09 07
	d							07 22							07 47	08 05						08 27	
Blackpool North 97	d			06 53	07 02				07 10			07 18		07 36									
Layton 97	d								07 13			07 21		07 39									
Poulton-le-Fylde 97	d				07 08				07 17			07 26		07 43									
Kirkham & Wesham 97	d								07 26			07 35		07 52									
Preston 8 65,97	a			07 15	07 28			07 41	07 37			07 46		08 03	08 07	08 30						08 45	
	d			07 17	07 30			07 47				07 47		08 12						08 17		08 47	
Leyland	d			07 22	07 35							07 53								08 23			
Buckshaw Parkway	d			07 28								07 58								08 28			
Chorley	d			07 32				07 56				08 02		08 22						08 35		08 56	
Adlington (Lancashire)	d			07 37								08 07								08 39			
Blackrod	d			07 41								08 11								08 43			
Horwich Parkway	d			07 45								08 15								08 47			
Lostock	d			07 49								08 20								08 50			
Southport	d	06 49								07 18									07 54				
Meols Cop	d	06 54								07 23									07 59				
Bescar Lane	d	06 59																					
New Lane	d	07 03																					
Burscough Bridge	d	07 05								07 31									08 07				
Hoscar	d	07 09																					
Parbold	d	07 12								07 36									08 12				
Appley Bridge	d	07 16								07 40									08 16				
Gathurst	d	07 19								07 44									08 19				
Kirkby	d					07 07																	
Rainford	d					07 15																	
Upholland	d					07 19																	
Orrell	d					07 23																	
Pemberton	d					07 26																	
Wigan Wallgate	a	07 27				07 33				07 49									08 26				
	d	07 27				07 35				07 51	07 58						08 11		08 27				
Wigan North Western	d		07 22		07a50													08 20					
Ince	d		07 25			07 38											08 14						
Hindley	d		07 29			07 41				07 56							08 17	08 25	08 32				
Westhoughton	d		07 33							08 01								08 29					
Bolton	a		07 42	07 54				08 08		08 11		08 25		08 34				08 38		08 55		09 08	
	d		07 43	07 55			07 59	08 08		08 12		08 25	08 31	08 35				08 39		08 56	09 02	09 08	
Moses Gate	d		07 46				08 02											08 42					
Farnworth	d		07 48				08 04											08 44					
Kearsley	d		07 50				08 06											08 46					
Daisy Hill	d	07 39				07 47					08 05						08 21		08 37				
Hag Fold	d					07 50											08 24						
Atherton	d	07 43				07 53					08 10						08 27		08 41				
Walkden	d					07 59					08 16						08 33		08 47				
Moorside	d					08 03											08 37						
Swinton	d					08 06											08 40		08 52				
Salford Crescent	a	07 59	08 02	08 07		08 13	08 17			08 24	08 29	08 38	08 43	08 47			08 50	08 56	09 02	09 08	09 15		
	d	08 00	08 02	08 08		08 13	08 17			08 25	08 30	08 38	08 44	08 47			08 50	08 56	09 02	09 09	09 16		
Salford Central	d	08 03	08 05			08 16	08 20				08 32	08 41	08 46				08 53	08 59	09 05		09 18		
Manchester Victoria ⇌	a	08 08	08 12			08 20	08 26				08 38	08 48	08 53				08 59	09 06	09 11		09 27		
Rochdale 41	a					08 51																	
Deansgate ⇌	a			08 11						08 28										09 12			
Manchester Oxford Road	a			08 14				08 23		08 31				08 52						09 14		09 23	
Manchester Piccadilly 10 ⇌	a			08 18				08 27		08 35				08 56						09 18		09 27	
Stockport 84	a			08 34																09 34			
Hazel Grove 86	a			08 50																09 47			
Buxton 86	a																						
Heald Green 85	a									08 47				09 10									
Manchester Airport 85 ✈	a							08 47		08 53				09 19								09 47	

A To Liverpool Lime Street
B From Clitheroe
C 🚌 from Preston
D From Edinburgh
E From Millom
F From Blackburn
G From Maryport

Table 82

Mondays to Fridays
from 1 October

Barrow-in-Furness, Blackpool North, Preston, Southport, Kirkby and Wigan - Bolton - Manchester

Network Diagram - see first Page of Table 82

		NT		NT	NT	NT A	NT B	TP ◇1 ⊼	NT	NT	NT	NT C		NT	TP ◇1 D ⊼	NT	NT	NT	NT A	NT E	NT B	TP ◇1 ⊼		NT	NT
Barrow-in-Furness	d																								
Roose	d																								
Dalton	d																								
Ulverston	d																								
Cark	d																								
Kents Bank	d																								
Grange-over-Sands	d																								
Arnside	d																								
Silverdale	d																								
Carnforth	d																			10 02					
Windermere 83	d																								
Oxenholme Lake District 65	d														09 11										
Lancaster ■ 65	a														09 25					10 12					
	d														09 26										
Blackpool North 97	d				08 20			08 44										09 20	09 37			09 43			
Layton 97	d				08 23													09 23							
Poulton-le-Fylde 97	d				08 28			08 50										09 28				09 49			
Kirkham & Wesham 97	d				08 37													09 37	09 52						
Preston ■ 65,97	a				08 47			09 08							09 45			09 47	10 02			10 07			
	d				08 49	09 04		09 10			09 23				09 47			09 49	10 04			10 12			
Leyland	d				08 54	09 09					09 29							09 54	10 09						
Buckshaw Parkway	d				08 59			09 17			09 33							09 59							
Chorley	d				09 03			09 21			09 38				09 56			10 03				10 22			
Adlington (Lancashire)	d				09 08													10 08							
Blackrod	d				09 12													10 12							
Horwich Parkway	d				09 16			09 28			09 46							10 16							
Lostock	d				09 20						09 50							10 20							
Southport	d	08 22								08 58						09 22									09 51
Meols Cop	d	08 27								09 03															09 56
Bescar Lane	d																								10 01
New Lane	d																								10 05
Burscough Bridge	d	08 35								09 11						09 34									10 07
Hoscar	d																								10 11
Parbold	d	08 40								09 16						09 39									10 14
Appley Bridge	d	08 44								09 20						09 43									10 18
Gathurst	d	08 47								09 23															10 21
Kirkby	d			08 19													09 28								
Rainford	d			08 27													09 36								
Upholland	d			08 31													09 40								
Orrell	d			08 34													09 43								
Pemberton	d			08 37													09 46								
Wigan Wallgate	a	08 54		08 45						09 30						09 49	09 54								10 28
	d	08 55		08 50					09 18	09 30				09 44		09 51	09 56							10 18	10 30
Wigan North Western	d					09a24													10a24						
Ince	d			08 53													09 59								
Hindley	d			08 57					09 23	09 35						09 56	10 02							10 23	10 35
Westhoughton	d	09 04							09 27					09 52		10 00								10 27	
Bolton	a	09 12			09 25			09 34	09 38		09 55			10 02	10 08	10 12		10 25				10 34		10 38	
	d	09 13			09 25		09 31	09 35	09 39		09 56	10 00		10 03	10 08	10 13		10 25			10 31	10 35		10 39	
Moses Gate	d								09 42															10 42	
Farnworth	d								09 44															10 44	
Kearsley	d								09 46															10 46	
Daisy Hill	d			09 01						09 39							10 07								10 39
Hag Fold	d			09 04													10 10								
Atherton	d			09 06						09 43							10 13								10 43
Walkden	d			09 12						09 48							10 18								10 48
Moorside	d			09 15													10 22								
Swinton	d			09 18						09 53							10 24								10 53
Salford Crescent	a	09 25		09 27	09 38		09 43	09 47	09 56	10 03	10 08	10 13		10 15		10 25	10 34	10 38			10 43	10 47		10 56	11 02
	d	09 26		09 27	09 38		09 44	09 47	09 56	10 03	10 09	10 13		10 15		10 26	10 34	10 38			10 44	10 47		10 56	11 03
Salford Central	d			09 31	09 41		09 46		09 59	10 05		10 16		10 17			10 36	10 41			10 46			10 59	11 05
Manchester Victoria ⇌	a			09 38	09 47		09 53		10 06	10 12		10 22		10 25			10 43	10 47			10 53			11 06	11 11
Rochdale 41	a													10 51											
Deansgate ⇌	a	09 29						09 51			10 12					10 29						10 51			
Manchester Oxford Road	a	09 31						09 52			10 14				10 23	10 31						10 52			
Manchester Piccadilly ■ ⇌	a	09 35						09 56			10 18				10 27	10 35						10 56			
Stockport 84	a										10 34														
Hazel Grove 86	a										10 47														
Buxton 86	a																								
Heald Green 85	a							10 10														11 10			
Manchester Airport 85 ✈	a	09 53						10 17							10 47	10 53						11 17			

A To Liverpool South Parkway
B From Clitheroe
C From Blackburn
D From Glasgow Central
E From Leeds to Morecambe

Table 82

Mondays to Fridays
from 1 October

Barrow-in-Furness, Blackpool North, Preston, Southport, Kirkby and Wigan - Bolton - Manchester

Network Diagram - see first Page of Table 82

		NT	NT	TP ◇1 A ⊼	NT B	NT	NT	NT		NT C	NT D	TP ◇1 ⊼	NT	NT	NT	NT	TP ◇1 A ⊼	NT		NT	NT	NT C	NT E	TP ◇1	NT D
Barrow-in-Furness	d			09 23	10 16																			11 25	
Roose	d			09 27	10 20																				
Dalton	d			09 34	10 26																				
Ulverston	d			09 42	10 35																			11 41	
Cark	d			09 50	10 42																				
Kents Bank	d			09 54	10 47																				
Grange-over-Sands	d			09 58	10 51																			11 53	
Arnside	d			10 04	10 57																			11 59	
Silverdale	d			10 08	11 01																				
Carnforth	d			10 15	11 08																		12 02	12 09	
Windermere 83	d																10 49								
Oxenholme Lake District 65	d																11 09								
Lancaster ■ 65	a			10 25	11 20												11 26						12 11	12 18	
	d			10 26													11 26							12 18	
Blackpool North 97	d							10 20		10 37		10 44									11 20	11 37			
Layton 97	d							10 23													11 23				
Poulton-le-Fylde 97	d							10 28				10 50									11 28				
Kirkham & Wesham 97	d							10 37		10 52											11 37	11 52			
Preston ■ 65,97	a			10 45				10 47		11 02		11 08					11 45				11 47	12 02		12 37	
	d	10 23		10 47				10 49		11 04		11 10			11 23		11 47				11 49	12 04			
Leyland	d	10 29						10 54		11 09					11 29						11 54	12 09			
Buckshaw Parkway	d	10 33						10 59				11 17			11 33						11 58				
Chorley	d	10 38		10 56				11 03				11 21			11 38		11 56				12 03				
Adlington (Lancashire)	d							11 08													12 08				
Blackrod	d							11 12													12 11				
Horwich Parkway	d	10 46						11 16				11 28			11 46						12 15				
Lostock	d	10 50						11 20							11 50						12 21				
Southport	d					10 20								10 51				11 20							
Meols Cop	d													10 56											
Bescar Lane	d													11 01											
New Lane	d													11 05											
Burscough Bridge	d					10 32								11 07				11 32							
Hoscar	d													11 11											
Parbold	d					10 37								11 14				11 37							
Appley Bridge	d					10 41								11 18				11 41							
Gathurst	d													11 21											
Kirkby	d						10 28													11 28					
Rainford	d						10 36													11 36					
Upholland	d						10 40													11 40					
Orrell	d						10 43													11 43					
Pemberton	d						10 46													11 46					
Wigan Wallgate	a					10 49	10 54							11 28				11 49		11 54					
	d		10 46			10 51	10 56						11 18	11 30		11 46		11 51		11 56					
Wigan North Western	d									11a24												12a24			
Ince	d						10 59													11 59					
Hindley	d					10 56	11 02						11 23	11 35				11 56		12 02					
Westhoughton	d					11 00							11 27					12 00							
Bolton	a	10 55	11 02	11 08		11 12		11 25				11 34	11 38		11 55	12 02	12 08	12 12			12 25				
	d	10 56	11 03	11 08		11 13		11 25			11 31	11 35	11 39		11 56	12 03	12 08	12 13			12 25				12 31
Moses Gate	d												11 42												
Farnworth	d												11 44												
Kearsley	d												11 46												
Daisy Hill	d						11 07							11 39						12 07					
Hag Fold	d						11 10													12 10					
Atherton	d						11 13							11 43						12 13					
Walkden	d						11 18							11 48						12 18					
Moorside	d						11 22													12 22					
Swinton	d						11 24							11 53						12 24					
Salford Crescent	a	11 08	11 15			11 25	11 34	11 38			11 43	11 47	11 56	12 02	12 08	12 15		12 25		12 34	12 38				12 43
	d	11 09	11 15			11 26	11 34	11 38			11 44	11 47	11 56	12 03	12 09	12 15		12 26		12 34	12 38				12 44
Salford Central	d		11 17				11 36	11 41			11 46		11 59	12 05		12 17				12 36	12 41				12 46
Manchester Victoria ⇌	a		11 25				11 43	11 47			11 53		12 06	12 11		12 25				12 43	12 47				12 53
Rochdale 41	a		11 51													12 51									
Deansgate ⇌	a	11 12				11 29						11 51			12 12			12 29							
Manchester Oxford Road	a	11 14		11 23		11 31						11 52			12 14		12 23	12 31							
Manchester Piccadilly ■ ⇌	a	11 18		11 27		11 35						11 56			12 18		12 27	12 35							
Stockport 84	a	11 34													12 34										
Hazel Grove 86	a	11 45													12 47										
Buxton 86	a																								
Heald Green 85	a											12 10													
Manchester Airport 85 ✈	a			11 50		11 53						12 17					12 47	12 53							

A ⊼ from Preston
B From Sellafield
C To Liverpool South Parkway
D From Clitheroe
E From Leeds to Heysham Port

Barrow-in-Furness, Blackpool North, Preston, Southport, Kirkby and Wigan - Bolton - Manchester

Network Diagram - see first Page of Table 82

		TP FO ◇1 ✠	TP FX ◇1 ✠	NT		NT	NT	NT	TP ◇1 A ✠	NT B	NT	NT	NT	NT C		NT D	TP ◇1 ✠	NT	NT	NT	NT	TP ◇1 E ✠	NT	TP FO ◇1
Barrow-in-Furness	d									12 11														13 25
Roose	d									12 15														
Dalton	d									12 21														
Ulverston	d									12 29														13 41
Cark	d									12 37														
Kents Bank	d									12 41														
Grange-over-Sands	d									12 45														13 53
Arnside	d									12 51														13 59
Silverdale	d									12 55														
Carnforth	d									13 03														14 09
Windermere 83	d																					12 51		
Oxenholme Lake District 65	d								12 10													13 09		
Lancaster 8 65	a								12 26	13 16												13 26		14 18
	d								12 26													13 26		
Blackpool North 97	d	11 44	11 44										12 20	12 37			12 44							
Layton 97	d												12 23											
Poulton-le-Fylde 97	d	11 50	11 50										12 28				12 50							
Kirkham & Wesham 97	d												12 37	12 52										
Preston 8 65,97	a	12 08	12 08						12 45				12 47	13 02			13 08					13 45		
	d	12 10	12 10				12 23		12 47				12 49	13 04			13 10			13 23		13 47		
Leyland	d						12 29						12 54	13 09						13 29				
Buckshaw Parkway	d	12 17	12 17				12 33						12 59				13 17			13 33				
Chorley	d	12 21	12 21				12 38		12 56				13 03				13 21			13 38		13 56		
Adlington (Lancashire)	d												13 08											
Blackrod	d												13 12											
Horwich Parkway	d	12 28	12 28				12 46						13 16				13 28			13 46				
Lostock	d						12 50						13 20							13 50				
Southport	d					11 56					12 20								12 50				13 20	
Meols Cop	d					12 01													12 55					
Bescar Lane	d																		13 00					
New Lane	d																		13 04					
Burscough Bridge	d					12 09					12 32								13 07				13 32	
Hoscar	d																		13 11					
Parbold	d					12 14					12 37								13 14				13 37	
Appley Bridge	d					12 18					12 41								13 18				13 41	
Gathurst	d					12 21													13 21					
Kirkby	d											12 28												
Rainford	d											12 36												
Upholland	d											12 40												
Orrell	d											12 43												
Pemberton	d											12 46												
Wigan Wallgate	a					12 28					12 49	12 54							13 28				13 49	
	d			12 18		12 30		12 46			12 51	12 56						13 18	13 30		13 46		13 51	
Wigan North Western	d													13a24										
Ince	d											12 59												
Hindley	d			12 23		12 35					12 56	13 02						13 23	13 35				13 56	
Westhoughton	d			12 27							13 00							13 27					14 00	
Bolton	a	12 34	12 34	12 38			12 55	13 02	13 08		13 12		13 25				13 34	13 38		13 55	14 02	14 08	14 12	
	d	12 35	12 35	12 39			12 56	13 03	13 08		13 13		13 25			13 31	13 35	13 39		13 56	14 03	14 08	14 13	
Moses Gate	d			12 42														13 42						
Farnworth	d			12 44														13 44						
Kearsley	d			12 46														13 46						
Daisy Hill	d					12 39						13 07							13 39					
Hag Fold	d											13 10												
Atherton	d					12 43						13 13							13 43					
Walkden	d					12 48						13 18							13 48					
Moorside	d											13 22												
Swinton	d					12 53						13 24							13 53					
Salford Crescent	a	12 47	12 47	12 56		13 02	13 08	13 15			13 25	13 34	13 38			13 43	13 47	13 56	14 02	14 08	14 15		14 25	
	d	12 47	12 47	12 56		13 03	13 09	13 15			13 26	13 34	13 38			13 44	13 47	13 56	14 03	14 09	14 15		14 26	
Salford Central	d			12 59		13 05		13 17				13 36	13 41			13 46		13 59	14 05		14 17			
Manchester Victoria ⇌	a			13 06		13 11		13 25				13 43	13 47			13 53		14 06	14 11		14 25			
Rochdale 41	a							13 51													14 51			
Deansgate ⇌	a	12 51	12 51				13 12				13 29						13 51			14 12			14 29	
Manchester Oxford Road	a	12 52	12 52				13 14		13 23		13 31						13 52			14 14		14 23	14 31	
Manchester Piccadilly 10 ⇌	a	12 56	12 56				13 18		13 27		13 35						13 56			14 18		14 27	14 35	
Stockport 84	a						13 34													14 34				
Hazel Grove 86	a						13 47													14 47				
Buxton 86	a																							
Heald Green 85	a	13 10	13 10														14 10							
Manchester Airport 85 ✈	a	13 16	13 17						13 47		13 53						14 17					14 47	14 53	

A From Edinburgh
B From Carlisle
C To Liverpool South Parkway
D From Clitheroe
E ✠ from Preston

Barrow-in-Furness, Blackpool North, Preston, Southport, Kirkby and Wigan - Bolton - Manchester

Network Diagram - see first Page of Table 82

		TP FX ◇1	NT	NT	NT A	NT B	TP ◇1 ✠	NT	NT	NT		NT	TP ◇1 C ✠	NT	NT	NT	NT	NT A	NT B	TP ◇1 ✠		NT	NT	NT	NT
Barrow-in-Furness	d	13 25												14 16											
Roose	d													14 20											
Dalton	d													14 26											
Ulverston	d	13 41												14 35											
Cark	d													14 42											
Kents Bank	d													14 47											
Grange-over-Sands	d	13 53												14 51											
Arnside	d	13 59												14 57											
Silverdale	d													15 01											
Carnforth	d	14 09												15 07											
Windermere 83	d																								
Oxenholme Lake District 65	d												14 10												
Lancaster 8 65	a	14 18											14 26	15 20											
	d	14 18											14 26												
Blackpool North 97	d			13 20	13 37		13 44										14 20	14 37		14 44					
Layton 97	d			13 23													14 23								
Poulton-le-Fylde 97	d			13 28			13 50										14 28			14 50					
Kirkham & Wesham 97	d			13 37	13 52												14 37	14 52							
Preston 8 65,97	a	14 37		13 47	14 02		14 08						14 45				14 47	15 02		15 08					
	d			13 49	14 04		14 10			14 23			14 47				14 49	15 04		15 10				15 23	
Leyland	d			13 54	14 09					14 29							14 54	15 09						15 29	
Buckshaw Parkway	d			13 59			14 17			14 33							14 59			15 17				15 33	
Chorley	d			14 03			14 21			14 38			14 56				15 03			15 21				15 38	
Adlington (Lancashire)	d			14 08													15 08								
Blackrod	d			14 11													15 12								
Horwich Parkway	d			14 15			14 28			14 46							15 16			15 28				15 46	
Lostock	d			14 21						14 50							15 20							15 50	
Southport	d								13 56						14 20								14 50		
Meols Cop	d								14 01														14 55		
Bescar Lane	d																						15 00		
New Lane	d																						15 04		
Burscough Bridge	d								14 09						14 32								15 07		
Hoscar	d																						15 11		
Parbold	d								14 14						14 37								15 14		
Appley Bridge	d								14 18						14 41								15 18		
Gathurst	d								14 21														15 21		
Kirkby	d		13 28													14 28									
Rainford	d		13 36													14 36									
Upholland	d		13 40													14 40									
Orrell	d		13 43													14 43									
Pemberton	d		13 46													14 46									
Wigan Wallgate	a		13 54						14 28						14 49	14 54							15 28		
	d		13 56					14 18	14 30			14 46			14 51	14 56						15 18	15 30		15 46
Wigan North Western	d				14a24													15a24							
Ince	d		13 59													14 59									
Hindley	d		14 02					14 23	14 35						14 56	15 02						15 23	15 35		
Westhoughton	d							14 27							15 00							15 27			
Bolton	a			14 26			14 34	14 38		14 55		15 02	15 08		15 12		15 25			15 34		15 38		15 55	16 02
	d			14 26		14 31	14 35	14 39		14 56		15 03	15 08		15 13		15 25		15 31	15 35		15 39		15 56	16 03
Moses Gate	d							14 42														15 42			
Farnworth	d							14 44														15 44			
Kearsley	d							14 46														15 46			
Daisy Hill	d		14 07						14 39							15 07							15 39		
Hag Fold	d		14 10													15 10									
Atherton	d		14 13						14 43							15 13							15 43		
Walkden	d		14 18						14 48							15 18							15 48		
Moorside	d		14 22													15 22									
Swinton	d		14 24						14 53							15 24							15 53		
Salford Crescent	a		14 34	14 38		14 43	14 47	14 56	15 02	15 08		15 15			15 25	15 33	15 38		15 43	15 47		15 56	16 02	16 08	16 15
	d		14 34	14 38		14 44	14 47	14 56	15 03	15 09		15 15			15 26	15 34	15 38		15 44	15 47		15 56	16 03	16 09	16 15
Salford Central	d		14 36	14 41		14 46		14 59	15 05			15 17				15 36	15 41		15 46			15 59	16 05		16 17
Manchester Victoria ⇌	a		14 43	14 47		14 53		15 06	15 11			15 25				15 43	15 47		15 55			16 06	16 11		16 23
Rochdale 41	a											15 51													16 51
Deansgate ⇌	a						14 51			15 12					15 29					15 51				16 12	
Manchester Oxford Road	a						14 52			15 14			15 23		15 31					15 52				16 14	
Manchester Piccadilly 10 ⇌	a						14 56			15 18			15 27		15 35					15 56				16 18	
Stockport 84	a									15 34														16 34	
Hazel Grove 86	a									15 50														16 43	
Buxton 86	a																							17 24	
Heald Green 85	a						15 10													16 10					
Manchester Airport 85 ✈	a						15 17						15 47		15 53					16 17					

A To Liverpool South Parkway
B From Clitheroe
C From Edinburgh

Table 82

Mondays to Fridays
from 1 October

Barrow-in-Furness, Blackpool North, Preston, Southport, Kirkby and Wigan - Bolton - Manchester

Network Diagram - see first Page of Table 82

		TP	NT	NT	TP	NT	NT	NT	NT	TP	NT	NT	NT	NT	TP	TP	NT	NT	NT	NT	NT	NT	TP
					FO										FX								
		◇1 A ✠		B	◇1	C			D	◇1 ✠		E			◇1 F ✠	◇1 G ✠					D	C	◇1 ✠
Barrow-in-Furness	d				15 24										15 24		16 20						
Roose	d																16 24						
Dalton	d																16 30						
Ulverston	d				15 40										15 40		16 38						
Cark	d				15 47										15 47		16 46						
Kents Bank	d																16 50						
Grange-over-Sands	d				15 54										15 54		16 54						
Arnside	d				16 00										16 00		17 00						
Silverdale	d																17 04						
Carnforth	d			15 38	16 09										16 09		17 12						
Windermere 83	d																						
Oxenholme Lake District 65	d															16 07							
Lancaster 6 65	a			15 47	16 18										16 18	16 21	17 26						
	d	15 22			16 18										16 18	16 22							
Blackpool North 97	d						15 20	15 37	15 44											16 20	16 35		16 40
Layton 97	d						15 23													16 23			16 44
Poulton-le-Fylde 97	d						15 28		15 50											16 28			16 48
Kirkham & Wesham 97	d						15 37	15 52												16 37	16 52		16 57
Preston 8 65,97	a	15 41			16 37			15 47	16 02	16 08					16 37	16 42				16 47	17 02		17 08
	d	15 47						15 49	16 04	16 10			16 23		16 47	16 47				16 49	17 04		17 10
Leyland	d							15 54	16 09				16 29							16 54	17 09		
Buckshaw Parkway	d							15 59		16 17			16 33							16 59			17 17
Chorley	d	15 56						16 03		16 21			16 38		16 56	16 56				17 03			17 21
Adlington (Lancashire)	d							16 08												17 08			
Blackrod	d							16 11												17 12			
Horwich Parkway	d							16 15		16 28			16 46							17 16			17 28
Lostock	d							16 21					16 50							17 20			
Southport	d		15 20									15 56						16 20					
Meols Cop	d											16 01											
Bescar Lane	d																						
New Lane	d																						
Burscough Bridge	d		15 32									16 09						16 32					
Hoscar	d																						
Parbold	d		15 37									16 14						16 37					
Appley Bridge	d		15 41									16 18						16 41					
Gathurst	d											16 22											
Kirkby	d						15 28												16 30				
Rainford	d						15 36												16 38				
Upholland	d						15 40												16 42				
Orrell	d						15 43												16 45				
Pemberton	d						15 46												16 48				
Wigan Wallgate	a		15 49				15 54					16 29						16 49	16 56				
	d		15 51				15 56				16 18	16 30		16 46				16 51	16 58				
Wigan North Western	d								16a24												17a24		
Ince	d						15 59					16 33							17 01				
Hindley	d		15 56				16 02				16 23	16 37						16 56	17 04				
Westhoughton	d		16 00								16 27							17 00					
Bolton	a	16 08	16 12					16 25		16 34	16 38		16 55	17 02	17 08	17 08		17 12		17 25			17 34
	d	16 08	16 13			16 17		16 25		16 35	16 39		16 56	17 03	17 08	17 08		17 13		17 25		17 31	17 35
Moses Gate	d										16 42												
Farnworth	d										16 44												
Kearsley	d										16 46												
Daisy Hill	d						16 07					16 41							17 08				
Hag Fold	d						16 10												17 11				
Atherton	d						16 13					16 45							17 14				
Walkden	d						16 18					16 50							17 19				
Moorside	d						16 22												17 23				
Swinton	d						16 24					16 55							17 25				
Salford Crescent	a		16 25			16 30	16 34	16 38		16 47	16 56	17 02	17 08	17 15				17 25	17 33	17 38		17 43	17 47
	d		16 26			16 30	16 34	16 38		16 47	16 56	17 03	17 09	17 15				17 26	17 33	17 38		17 44	17 47
Salford Central	d					16 33	16 36	16 41			16 59	17 05		17 17					17 36	17 41		17 46	
Manchester Victoria ⇌	a					16 42	16 43	16 47			17 06	17 13		17 23					17 43	17 47		17 54	
Rochdale 41	a													17 51									
Deansgate ⇌	a									16 51			17 15										17 51
Manchester Oxford Road	a	16 23	16 31							16 52			17 17		17 26	17 26		17 30					17 52
Manchester Piccadilly 10 ⇌	a	16 27	16 35							16 56			17 21		17 29	17 29		17 35					17 56
Stockport 84	a												17 32										
Hazel Grove 86	a												17 39										
Buxton 86	a												18 19										
Heald Green 85	a	16 40								17 10					17 41	17 41							18 10
Manchester Airport 85 ✈	a	16 47	16 53							17 17					17 48	17 48		17 53					18 17

A From Glasgow Central
B From Leeds to Morecambe
C From Clitheroe
D To Liverpool Lime Street
E To Huddersfield
F ✠ from Preston
G From Edinburgh

Table 82

Mondays to Fridays
from 1 October

Barrow-in-Furness, Blackpool North, Preston, Southport, Kirkby and Wigan - Bolton - Manchester

Network Diagram - see first Page of Table 82

		NT	NT	NT	NT	TP	NT	NT	NT	NT	TP	TP	NT	NT	NT	TP	NT	NT	NT	NT	NT	NT
					A	◇1 ✠				B	◇1 C ✠	◇1 D			A	◇1 E ✠		F			B	A
Barrow-in-Furness	d											17 21										
Roose	d																					
Dalton	d											17 30										
Ulverston	d											17 38										
Cark	d											17 46										
Kents Bank	d																					
Grange-over-Sands	d											17 53										
Arnside	d											17 59										
Silverdale	d																					
Carnforth	d											18 09						18 29				
Windermere 83	d										17 06											
Oxenholme Lake District 65	d										17 30											
Lancaster 6 65	a										17 47	18 20						18 42				
	d										17 48					18 26						
Blackpool North 97	d					17 20				17 37										18 20	18 37	
Layton 97	d					17 23														18 23		
Poulton-le-Fylde 97	d					17 27														18 28		
Kirkham & Wesham 97	d									17 52										18 37	18 52	
Preston 8 65,97	a					17 45				18 02	18 06					18 45				18 47	19 02	
	d					17 47			17 56	18 04	18 08					18 47				18 49	19 04	
Leyland	d								18 01	18 09										18 54	19 09	
Buckshaw Parkway	d								18 05		18 15									18 59		
Chorley	d					17 56			18 10		18 19					18 56				19 03		
Adlington (Lancashire)	d								18 15											19 08		
Blackrod	d								18 18											19 12		
Horwich Parkway	d								18 21		18 26									19 16		
Lostock	d										18 30									19 20		
Southport	d		16 50				17 20										18 14					
Meols Cop	d		16 55				17 25										18 19					
Bescar Lane	d		17 00														18 24					
New Lane	d		17 04														18 28					
Burscough Bridge	d		17 07				17 33										18 30					
Hoscar	d		17 11														18 34					
Parbold	d		17 14				17 38										18 37					
Appley Bridge	d		17 18				17 42										18 41					
Gathurst	d		17 21														18 44					
Kirkby	d							17 30											18 30			
Rainford	d							17 38											18 38			
Upholland	d							17 42											18 42			
Orrell	d							17 45											18 45			
Pemberton	d							17 48											18 48			
Wigan Wallgate	a		17 28				17 50	17 57									18 51		18 56			
	d	17 18	17 30	17 37			17 52	17 59					18 18	18 30			18 52		18 58			
Wigan North Western	d									18a24											19a24	
Ince	d							18 02											19 01			
Hindley	d	17 23	17 35					18 05					18 23	18 35			18 57		19 04			
Westhoughton	d	17 27		17 45			18 00						18 27				19 01					
Bolton	a	17 38		17 55		18 08	18 12		18 31		18 34		18 38			19 08	19 12			19 25		
	d	17 39		17 56	18 02	18 08	18 13		18 31		18 35		18 39		19 01	19 08	19 13			19 25		19 31
Moses Gate	d	17 42											18 42									
Farnworth	d	17 44											18 44									
Kearsley	d	17 46											18 46									
Daisy Hill	d		17 39					18 09						18 39					19 08			
Hag Fold	d							18 12											19 11			
Atherton	d		17 43					18 15						18 43					19 14			
Walkden	d		17 48					18 20						18 48					19 19			
Moorside	d							18 24											19 23			
Swinton	d		17 53					18 26						18 53					19 25			
Salford Crescent	a	17 56	18 02	18 08	18 15		18 25	18 33	18 43		18 47		18 56	19 02	19 13		19 25		19 33	19 38		19 44
	d	17 56	18 03	18 09	18 15		18 26	18 33	18 43		18 47		18 56	19 03	19 14		19 26		19 33	19 38		19 44
Salford Central	d	17 59	18 05		18 17			18 36	18 46				18 59	19 05	19 16				19 36	19 41		19 46
Manchester Victoria ⇌	a	18 06	18 11		18 24			18 43	18 52				19 06	19 11	19 23				19 43	19 47		19 54
Rochdale 41	a				18 47																	
Deansgate ⇌	a			18 12							18 51						19 29					
Manchester Oxford Road	a			18 14		18 23	18 31				18 52					19 23	19 31					
Manchester Piccadilly 10 ⇌	a			18 18		18 27	18 35				18 56					19 27	19 35					
Stockport 84	a			18 34																		
Hazel Grove 86	a			18 43																		
Buxton 86	a			19 24																		
Heald Green 85	a					18 40					19 10											
Manchester Airport 85 ✈	a					18 47	18 53				19 17					19 47	19 53					

A From Clitheroe
B To Liverpool Lime Street
C ✠ from Preston
D To Windermere
E From Edinburgh
F From Leeds to Morecambe

from 1 October

Barrow-in-Furness, Blackpool North, Preston, Southport, Kirkby and Wigan - Bolton - Manchester

Network Diagram - see first Page of Table 82

		TP	TP	NT	NT	NT	TP	NT	NT	NT	NT	TP	TP	TP	NT	NT	NT	NT	NT	TP	TP	NT	NT
													ThX	ThO								FO	FX
		◇1	◇1				◇1					◇1	◇1	◇1						◇1	◇1		
				A		B	C			D	E		F	F				D	E				
		⊼					⊼						⊼	⊼									
Barrow-in-Furness	d			18 03																	20 08		
Roose	d			18 07																	20 12		
Dalton	d			18 13																	20 19		
Ulverston	d			18 21																	20 27		
Cark	d			18 29																	20 35		
Kents Bank	d			18 33																	20 39		
Grange-over-Sands	d			18 37																	20 43		
Arnside	d			18 43																	20 49		
Silverdale	d			18 47																	20 53		
Carnforth	d			18 55																	21 01		
Windermere	83 d		18 15																				
Oxenholme Lake District	65 d		18 36				19 10						20 13	20 13									
Lancaster 6	65 a		18 52	19 05			19 26						20 26	20 26							21 10		
	d		18 52	19 06			19 26						20 26	20 26							21 10		
Blackpool North	97 d	18 44							19 20	19 37		19 44					20 20	20 37		20 44			
Layton	97 d								19 23								20 23						
Poulton-le-Fylde	97 d	18 50							19 28			19 50					20 28			20 50			
Kirkham & Wesham	97 d								19 37								20 37						
Preston 8	65,97 a	19 08	19 11	19 31			19 45		19 47	20 02		20 08	20 45	20 45			20 47	21 01		21 08	21 29		
	d	19 10	19 16				19 47		19 49	20 04		20 10	20 47	20 47			20 49	21 04		21 10	21 31		
Leyland	d								19 54	20 09							20 54	21 09					
Buckshaw Parkway	d	19 17							19 59			20 17					20 59			21 17			
Chorley	d	19 21	19 29				19 56		20 03			20 21	20 56	20 56			21 03			21 21			
Adlington (Lancashire)	d								20 08								21 08						
Blackrod	d								20 11								21 12						
Horwich Parkway	d	19 28	19 36						20 15			20 28					21 16			21 28			
Lostock	d								20 21								21 20						
Southport	d				18 56			19 19								20 20							
Meols Cop	d				19 01			19 24								20 25							
Bescar Lane	d																						
New Lane	d																						
Burscough Bridge	d				19 09			19 32								20 33							
Hoscar	d																						
Parbold	d				19 14			19 37								20 38							
Appley Bridge	d				19 18			19 41								20 42							
Gathurst	d				19 21			19 44								20 45							
Kirkby	d																						
Rainford	d																						
Upholland	d																						
Orrell	d																						
Pemberton	d																						
Wigan Wallgate	a				19 28			19 51								20 51							
	d				19 31			19 53							20 25	20 53						21 25	21 25
Wigan North Western	d									20a24								21a23			21 48		
Ince	d														20 28							21 28	21 28
Hindley	d				19 36			19 58							20 31	20 58						21 31	21 31
Westhoughton	d							20 02								21 02							
Bolton	a	19 33	19 42				20 08	20 12	20 25			20 34	21 08	21 08		21 12	21 25			21 34			
	d	19 34	19 43			20 02	20 08	20 13	20 25		20 31	20 35	21 08	21 08		21 13	21 25		21 31	21 35			
Moses Gate	d																						
Farnworth	d																						
Kearsley	d																						
Daisy Hill	d				19 40										20 35							21 35	21 35
Hag Fold	d														20 38							21 38	21 38
Atherton	d				19 44										20 41							21 41	21 41
Walkden	d				19 49										20 47							21 47	21 47
Moorside	d														20 50							21 50	21 50
Swinton	d				19 54										20 53							21 53	21 53
Salford Crescent	a	19 47			20 02	20 15		20 25	20 38		20 43	20 47			21 02	21 25	21 38		21 43	21 47		22 02	22 02
	d	19 47			20 03	20 15		20 26	20 38		20 44	20 47			21 03	21 26	21 38		21 44	21 47		22 03	22 03
Salford Central	d				20 05	20 17			20 41		20 46				21 05		21 41		21 46			22 05	
Manchester Victoria	⇌ a				20 11	20 25			20 47		20 53				21 11		21 47		21 53			22 11	22 11
Rochdale	41 a																						
Deansgate	⇌ a	19 51						20 29				20 51				21 29				21 51			
Manchester Oxford Road	a	19 52	19 57				20 23	20 31				20 52	21 23	21 23		21 31				21 52	22 26		
Manchester Piccadilly 10	⇌ a	19 56	20 01				20 27	20 35				20 56	21 27	21 27		21 35				21 56	22 30		
Stockport	84 a																						
Hazel Grove	86 a																						
Buxton	86 a																						
Heald Green	85 a	20 10	20 15									21 10								22 09			
Manchester Airport	85 ✈ a	20 17	20 24				20 47	20 53				21 17	21 46	21 47		21 53				22 17	22 47		

A From Carlisle
B From Blackburn
C From Glasgow Central
D To Liverpool Lime Street
E From Clitheroe
F From Edinburgh

Table 82 Mondays to Fridays

from 1 October

Barrow-in-Furness, Blackpool North, Preston, Southport, Kirkby and Wigan - Bolton - Manchester

Network Diagram - see first Page of Table 82

		NT	NT	NT	NT	NT	NT	TP	NT	TP	NT	NT	NT	NT	NT	NT	TP	NT	NT	TP	NT
		FO	FX	FX	FO	FX	FO			FO		FO	FX								
								◇1		◇1							◇1			◇1	
						A	A			B						C	D		A		
										⊼											
Barrow-in-Furness	d										21 43										
Roose	d										21 47										
Dalton	d										21 53										
Ulverston	d										22 01										
Cark	d										22 09										
Kents Bank	d										22 13										
Grange-over-Sands	d										22 17										
Arnside	d										22 23										
Silverdale	d										22 27										
Carnforth	d										22 35										
Windermere	83 d																22 45				
Oxenholme Lake District	65 d									22 10							23 06				
Lancaster 6	65 a									22 26	22 45						23 23				
	d									22 26	22 46					23 07	23 24				
Blackpool North	97 d			21 20	21 20			21 44	22 14						22 20					22 44	23 13
Layton	97 d			21 23	21 23										22 23						23 16
Poulton-le-Fylde	97 d			21 28	21 28			21 50							22 28					22 50	23 21
Kirkham & Wesham	97 d			21 37	21 37										22 37						23 30
Preston 8	65,97 a			21 47	21 47			22 08	22 41	22 45	23 11				22 47	23 28	23 45			23 08	23 40
	d			21 49	21 49			22 10	22 43	22 47					22 49					23 10	23 42
Leyland	d			21 54	21 54				22 48						22 54						23 48
Buckshaw Parkway	d			21 59	21 59			22 17							22 59					23 17	23 52
Chorley	d			22 03	22 03			22 21							23 03					23 21	23 57
Adlington (Lancashire)	d			22 08	22 08										23 08						00 03
Blackrod	d			22 12	22 12										23 12						00 06
Horwich Parkway	d			22 16	22 16			22 28							23 16					23 28	00 10
Lostock	d			22 20	22 20										23 20						00 14
Southport	d	21 19	21 19											22 14				23 10			
Meols Cop	d	21 24	21 24											22 19				23 15			
Bescar Lane	d													22 24							
New Lane	d													22 28							
Burscough Bridge	d	21 32	21 32											22 30				23 23			
Hoscar	d													22 34							
Parbold	d	21 37	21 37											22 37				23 28			
Appley Bridge	d	21 41	21 41											22 41				23 32			
Gathurst	d	21 44	21 44											22 44				23 35			
Kirkby	d																				
Rainford	d																				
Upholland	d																				
Orrell	d																				
Pemberton	d																				
Wigan Wallgate	a	21 51	21 51											22 51				23 46			
	d	21 53	21 53									22 25	22 25	22 53							
Wigan North Western	d								23a05												
Ince	d											22 28	22 28								
Hindley	d	21 58	21 58									22 31	22 31	22 58							
Westhoughton	d	22 02	22 02											23 02							
Bolton	a	22 12	22 12	22 25	22 25			22 34		23 06				23 12	23 25					23 34	00 19
	d	22 13	22 13	22 25	22 25	22 31	22 31	22 35		23 06				23 13	23 25				23 31	23 35	00 20
Moses Gate	d																				
Farnworth	d																				
Kearsley	d																				
Daisy Hill	d											22 35	22 35								
Hag Fold	d											22 38	22 38								
Atherton	d											22 41	22 41								
Walkden	d											22 47	22 47								
Moorside	d											22 50	22 50								
Swinton	d											22 53	22 53								
Salford Crescent	a	22 25	22 25	22 38	22 38	22 43	22 43	22 47				23 02	23 02	23 25	23 38				23 43	23 47	
	d	22 26	22 26	22 38	22 38	22 44	22 44	22 47				23 03	23 03	23 26	23 38				23 44	23 47	
Salford Central	d	22 28			22 41		22 46					23 05									
Manchester Victoria	⇌ a	22 34	22 34	22 47	22 47	22 53	22 53					23 13	23 13		23 47				23 53		00 37
Rochdale	41 a																				
Deansgate	⇌ a							22 51						23 29							
Manchester Oxford Road	a							22 52		23s21				23 31							
Manchester Piccadilly 10	⇌ a							22 56		23 31				23 39						23 53	
Stockport	84 a																				
Hazel Grove	86 a																				
Buxton	86 a																				
Heald Green	85 a							23 09												00 16	
Manchester Airport	85 ✈ a							23 17												00 24	

A From Clitheroe
B From Edinburgh
C From Morecambe
D To Blackpool North

Table 82

Saturdays until 29 September

Barrow-in-Furness, Blackpool North, Preston, Southport, Kirkby and Wigan - Bolton - Manchester

Network Diagram - see first Page of Table 82

		TP ◇1	NT	TP ◇1 A	TP ◇1 B	TP ◇1	TP ◇1	NT C	TP ◇1	TP ◇1	NT	NT	NT D	TP ◇1	NT	NT	TP ◇1 🚌	NT	NT	NT	NT E	NT	NT F
Barrow-in-Furness	d						04 35							05 31									
Roose	d																						
Dalton	d																						
Ulverston	d						04 51							05 47									
Cark	d																						
Kents Bank	d																						
Grange-over-Sands	d						05 03							05 59									
Arnside	d						05 10							06 05									
Silverdale	d																						
Carnforth	d						05 19							06 15									
Windermere 83	d																						
Oxenholme Lake District 65	d																						
Lancaster 6 65	a						05 28							06 23									
	d													06 23									
Blackpool North 97	d	22p44	23p13			03 37		04 56		05 39						06 19	06 40			06 53	07 02		
Layton 97	d		23p16													06 22	06 43						
Poulton-le-Fylde 97	d	22p50	23p21					05 02		05 45						06 27	06 47				07 08		
Kirkham & Wesham 97	d		23p30													06 36	06 56						
Preston 8 65,97	a	23p08	23p40					05 20		06 03				06 42		06 46	07 07			07 15	07 28		
	d	23p10	23p42			04u02			05 16	06 05				06 44		06 48	07 09			07 17	07 30		
Leyland	d		23p48							06 10						06 53				07 22	07 35		
Buckshaw Parkway	d	23p17	23p52													06 58				07 28			
Chorley	d	23p21	23p57						05 26	06 16				06 53		07 02	07 18			07 32			
Adlington (Lancashire)	d		00 03													07 07				07 37			
Blackrod	d		00 06							06 22						07 11				07 41			
Horwich Parkway	d	23p28	00 10						05 33	06 26				07 00		07 15	07 26			07 45			
Lostock	d		00 14							06 30						07 20	07 30			07 49			
Southport	d														06 23								
Meols Cop	d														06 28								
Bescar Lane	d																						
New Lane	d																						
Burscough Bridge	d														06 36								
Hoscar	d																						
Parbold	d														06 41								
Appley Bridge	d														06 45								
Gathurst	d														06 49								
Kirkby	d																					07 11	
Rainford	d																					07 19	
Upholland	d																					07 23	
Orrell	d																					07 27	
Pemberton	d																					07 30	
Wigan Wallgate	a														06 54							07 35	
	d										06 31	06 36			06 55			07 15				07 37	
Wigan North Western	d																		07 22		07a50		
Ince	d											06 39						07 18	07 25			07 40	
Hindley	d										06 36	06 42						07 21	07 29			07 43	
Westhoughton	d										06 41				07 03				07 33				
Bolton	a	23p34	00 19						05 42	06 34	06 52			07 08	07 11	07 25	07 34		07 42	07 54			
	d	23p35	00 20			04u31			05 43	06 35	06 53		06 56	07 08	07 12	07 25	07 35		07 43	07 55			07 59
Moses Gate	d												06 59						07 46				08 02
Farnworth	d												07 01						07 48				08 04
Kearsley	d												07 03						07 50				08 06
Daisy Hill	d											06 46						07 26				07 47	
Hag Fold	d											06 49						07 29				07 50	
Atherton	d											06 52						07 32				07 53	
Walkden	d											06 58						07 38				07 59	
Moorside	d											07 01						07 41				08 03	
Swinton	d											07 04						07 44				08 05	
Salford Crescent	a	23p47							05 55	06 47	07 05	07 11	07 15		07 24	07 38	07 47	07 53	08 02	08 07		08 13	08 17
	d	23p47		00 49	03 37				05 55	06 47	07 08	07 12	07 15		07 25	07 38	07 47	07 53	08 02	08 08		08 13	08 17
Salford Central	d											07 15	07 19			07 41		07 56	08 05			08 16	08 20
Manchester Victoria ⇌	a		00 37									07 18	07 25			07 47		07 59	08 12			08 20	08 25
Rochdale 41	a																					08 51	
Deansgate ⇌	a									06 51	07 11				07 28		07 51			08 11			
Manchester Oxford Road	a									06 52	07 13			07 23	07 30		07 52			08 14			
Manchester Piccadilly 10 ⇌	a	23p53		00 53	03 44	04 48			06 01	06 56	07 17			07 27	07 34		07 56			08 18			
Stockport 84	a										07 34									08 34			
Hazel Grove 86	a										07 45									08 45			
Buxton 86	a																						
Heald Green 85	a	00 16								07 10							08 10						
Manchester Airport 85 ✈	a	00 24		01 10	04 00	05 07			06 18	07 17				07 47	07 53		08 17						

A From Newcastle
B From York
C To Colne
D From Blackburn
E To Liverpool Lime Street
F From Clitheroe

Table 82

Saturdays until 29 September

Barrow-in-Furness, Blackpool North, Preston, Southport, Kirkby and Wigan - Bolton - Manchester

Network Diagram - see first Page of Table 82

		TP ◇1 A 🚌	NT	NT	NT B	NT C	TP ◇1 🚌	NT	NT	NT	NT	NT D	TP ◇1 A 🚌	NT	NT	NT	NT E	NT C	TP ◇1 🚌	TP ◇1 F	NT	NT	NT
Barrow-in-Furness	d	06 20											07 29										
Roose	d	06 24																					
Dalton	d	06 31											07 38										
Ulverston	d	06 39											07 46										
Cark	d	06 47											07 54										
Kents Bank	d	06 51																					
Grange-over-Sands	d	06 55											08 01										
Arnside	d	07 01											08 07										
Silverdale	d	07 05											08 11										
Carnforth	d	07 12			07 43								08 18										
Windermere 83	d																						
Oxenholme Lake District 65	d																						
Lancaster 6 65	a	07 21			07 52								08 26										
	d	07 22											08 27										
Blackpool North 97	d			07 18			07 44									08 20	08 38		08 44	09 14			
Layton 97	d			07 21			07 47									08 23							
Poulton-le-Fylde 97	d			07 26			07 51									08 28			08 50	09 20			
Kirkham & Wesham 97	d			07 35			08 00									08 37							
Preston 8 65,97	a	07 41		07 46			08 11						08 45			08 47	09 02		09 08	09 41			
	d	07 47		07 47			08 12				08 17		08 47			08 49	09 04		09 10				09 23
Leyland	d			07 53							08 23					08 54	09 09						09 29
Buckshaw Parkway	d			07 58							08 27					08 59			09 17				09 33
Chorley	d	07 56		08 02			08 22				08 34		08 56			09 03			09 21				09 38
Adlington (Lancashire)	d			08 07							08 39					09 08							
Blackrod	d			08 11							08 42					09 12							
Horwich Parkway	d			08 15							08 46					09 16			09 28				09 46
Lostock	d			08 20							08 50					09 20							09 50
Southport	d		07 21							07 53				08 25								09 02	
Meols Cop	d		07 26							07 58				08 30								09 07	
Bescar Lane	d									08 03													
New Lane	d									08 07													
Burscough Bridge	d		07 34							08 09				08 38								09 15	
Hoscar	d									08 13													
Parbold	d		07 39							08 16				08 43								09 20	
Appley Bridge	d		07 43							08 20				08 47								09 24	
Gathurst	d		07 47							08 23				08 50								09 27	
Kirkby	d														08 21								
Rainford	d														08 29								
Upholland	d														08 33								
Orrell	d														08 36								
Pemberton	d														08 39								
Wigan Wallgate	a		07 51							08 28				08 55	08 45							09 32	
	d		07 53					08 13		08 29				08 56	08 50						09 20	09 32	
Wigan North Western	d								08 20								09a24						
Ince	d							08 16							08 53								
Hindley	d		07 58					08 19	08 25	08 34					08 57						09 25	09 37	
Westhoughton	d		08 03						08 29					09 04							09 29		
Bolton	a	08 08	08 11	08 25			08 34		08 38		08 55		09 08	09 12		09 25			09 34		09 38		09 55
	d	08 08	08 12	08 25		08 31	08 35		08 39		08 56	09 02	09 08	09 13		09 25		09 31	09 35		09 39		09 56
Moses Gate	d								08 42												09 42		
Farnworth	d								08 44												09 44		
Kearsley	d								08 46												09 46		
Daisy Hill	d							08 23		08 39					09 01							09 41	
Hag Fold	d							08 26							09 04								
Atherton	d							08 29		08 43					09 06							09 45	
Walkden	d							08 35		08 49					09 12							09 50	
Moorside	d							08 39							09 15								
Swinton	d							08 42		08 54					09 18							09 55	
Salford Crescent	a		08 24	08 38		08 43	08 47	08 50	08 56	09 03	09 08	09 15		09 25	09 27	09 38		09 43	09 47		09 56	10 03	10 08
	d		08 25	08 38		08 44	08 47	08 51	08 56	09 03	09 09	09 16		09 26	09 27	09 38		09 44	09 47		09 56	10 03	10 09
Salford Central	d			08 41		08 46		08 54	08 59	09 06		09 18			09 31	09 41		09 46			09 59	10 05	
Manchester Victoria ⇌	a			08 47		08 52		08 57	09 06	09 11		09 26			09 38	09 47		09 52			10 06	10 12	
Rochdale 41	a											09 54											
Deansgate ⇌	a		08 28								09 12			09 29					09 51				10 12
Manchester Oxford Road	a	08 23	08 31				08 52				09 14		09 23	09 31					09 52				10 14
Manchester Piccadilly 10 ⇌	a	08 27	08 35				08 56				09 18		09 27	09 35					09 56				10 18
Stockport 84	a										09 34												10 34
Hazel Grove 86	a										09 45												10 45
Buxton 86	a																						
Heald Green 85	a		08 47				09 10												10 10				
Manchester Airport 85 ✈	a	08 47	08 52				09 19						09 47	09 51					10 17				

A 🚌 from Preston
B From Leeds
C From Clitheroe
D From Blackburn
E To Liverpool South Parkway
F To Barrow-in-Furness

Table 82

Saturdays until 29 September

Barrow-in-Furness, Blackpool North, Preston, Southport, Kirkby and Wigan - Bolton - Manchester

Network Diagram - see first Page of Table 82

		NT		NT	TP	NT	NT	NT	NT	NT	NT	TP		NT	TP	NT	NT	NT	NT	NT	TP	NT		NT	NT
					◇1							◇1			◇1						◇1				
		A			B	C				D	E			F					A		G	H			
					🍴										🍴						🍴				
Barrow-in-Furness	d					08 25															09 23	10 16			
Roose	d					08 29															09 27	10 20			
Dalton	d					08 36															09 34	10 26			
Ulverston	d					08 44															09 42	10 34			
Cark	d					08 52															09 50	10 42			
Kents Bank	d					08 57															09 54	10 46			
Grange-over-Sands	d					09 01															09 58	10 50			
Arnside	d					09 08															10 04	10 56			
Silverdale	d					09 13															10 08	11 01			
Carnforth	d					09 19					10 02										10 15	11 09			
Windermere 83	d											09 38													
Oxenholme Lake District 65	d				09 11							09 58													
Lancaster ■ 65	a				09 26	09 33					10 12	10 16									10 25	11 21			
	d				09 26							10 16									10 26				
Blackpool North 97	d								09 20	09 37					09 43										
Layton 97	d								09 23																
Poulton-le-Fylde 97	d								09 28						09 49										
Kirkham & Wesham 97	d								09 37																
Preston ■ 65,97	a				09 45				09 47	10 02		10 35			10 07						10 45				
	d				09 47				09 49	10 04					10 12			10 23			10 47				
Leyland	d								09 54	10 09								10 29							
Buckshaw Parkway	d								09 59									10 33							
Chorley	d				09 56				10 03						10 22			10 38			10 56				
Adlington (Lancashire)	d								10 08																
Blackrod	d								10 12																
Horwich Parkway	d								10 16									10 46							
Lostock	d								10 20									10 50							
Southport	d						09 24										09 55							10 24	
Meols Cop	d																10 00								
Bescar Lane	d																10 05								
New Lane	d																10 09								
Burscough Bridge	d						09 36										10 11							10 36	
Hoscar	d																10 15								
Parbold	d						09 41										10 18							10 41	
Appley Bridge	d						09 45										10 22							10 45	
Gathurst	d																10 25								
Kirkby	d							09 32																	10 32
Rainford	d							09 40																	10 40
Upholland	d							09 44																	10 44
Orrell	d							09 47																	10 47
Pemberton	d							09 50																	10 50
Wigan Wallgate	a						09 51	09 56									10 30							10 51	10 56
	d			09 46			09 53	09 58								10 20	10 32			10 48				10 53	10 58
Wigan North Western	d									10a24															
Ince	d							10 01																	11 01
Hindley	d						09 58	10 04								10 25	10 37							10 58	11 04
Westhoughton	d			09 54			10 02									10 29								11 02	
Bolton	a			10 02	10 08		10 12		10 25						10 34	10 38		10 55		11 02	11 08			11 12	
	d	10 00		10 03	10 08		10 13		10 25					10 31	10 35	10 39		10 56	11 00	11 04	11 08			11 13	
Moses Gate	d															10 42									
Farnworth	d															10 44									
Kearsley	d															10 46									
Daisy Hill	d							10 09									10 41								11 09
Hag Fold	d							10 12																	11 12
Atherton	d							10 15									10 45								11 15
Walkden	d							10 20									10 50								11 20
Moorside	d							10 24																	11 24
Swinton	d							10 26									10 55								11 26
Salford Crescent	a	10 13		10 15			10 25	10 34	10 38					10 44	10 47	10 56	11 02	11 08	11 12	11 16				11 25	11 34
	d	10 13		10 15			10 26	10 35	10 38					10 44	10 47	10 56	11 03	11 09	11 13	11 16				11 26	11 34
Salford Central	d	10 16		10 17				10 37	10 41					10 47		10 59	11 05		11 15	11 18					11 36
Manchester Victoria ⇌	a	10 22		10 25				10 41	10 47					10 52		11 06	11 11		11 23	11 25					11 43
Rochdale 41	a			10 51																11 51					
Deansgate ⇌	a						10 29								10 51			11 12						11 29	
Manchester Oxford Road	a				10 23		10 31								10 52			11 14			11 23			11 31	
Manchester Piccadilly 10 ⇌	a				10 27		10 35								10 56			11 18			11 27			11 35	
Stockport 84	a																	11 34							
Hazel Grove 86	a																	11 45							
Buxton 86	a																								
Heald Green 85	a														11 10										
Manchester Airport 85 ✈	a				10 47		10 53								11 17						11 47			11 53	

A From Blackburn
B From Glasgow Central
C From Maryport
D To Liverpool South Parkway
E From Leeds to Morecambe.
F From Clitheroe
G 🍴 from Preston
H From Sellafield

Table 82

Saturdays until 29 September

Barrow-in-Furness, Blackpool North, Preston, Southport, Kirkby and Wigan - Bolton - Manchester

Network Diagram - see first Page of Table 82

		NT	NT	NT	TP	NT	NT	NT		NT	TP	TP	NT	NT	NT	NT	NT	TP		TP	NT	TP	NT	NT	NT
					◇1						◇1	◇1						◇1		◇1		◇1			
			A	B							C	D				A	E	F		G	B				
					🍴						🍴							🍴		🍴		🍴			
Barrow-in-Furness	d											11 11													
Roose	d																								
Dalton	d																								
Ulverston	d											11 27													
Cark	d																								
Kents Bank	d																								
Grange-over-Sands	d											11 39													
Arnside	d											11 45													
Silverdale	d																								
Carnforth	d											11 55					12 02								
Windermere 83	d										10 49														
Oxenholme Lake District 65	d										11 09							12 07							
Lancaster ■ 65	a										11 26	12 04					12 12								
	d										11 26	12 04								12 15					
Blackpool North 97	d	10 20	10 37		10 44										11 15	11 37						11 44			
Layton 97	d	10 23													11 18										
Poulton-le-Fylde 97	d	10 28			10 50										11 23							11 50			
Kirkham & Wesham 97	d	10 37													11 32										
Preston ■ 65,97	a	10 47	11 02		11 08						11 45	12 23			11 42	12 02		12 37		12 33		12 08			
	d	10 49	11 04		11 10			11 23			11 47				11 49	12 04						12 10			12 23
Leyland	d	10 54	11 09					11 29							11 54	12 09									12 29
Buckshaw Parkway	d	10 59			11 17			11 33							11 59							12 17			12 33
Chorley	d	11 03			11 21			11 38			11 56				12 03							12 21			12 38
Adlington (Lancashire)	d	11 08													12 08										
Blackrod	d	11 12													12 12										
Horwich Parkway	d	11 16			11 28			11 46							12 16							12 28			12 46
Lostock	d	11 20						11 50							12 20										12 50
Southport	d						10 55						11 24											12 00	
Meols Cop	d						11 00																	12 05	
Bescar Lane	d						11 05																		
New Lane	d						11 09																		
Burscough Bridge	d						11 11						11 36											12 13	
Hoscar	d						11 15																		
Parbold	d						11 18						11 41											12 18	
Appley Bridge	d						11 22						11 45											12 22	
Gathurst	d						11 25																	12 25	
Kirkby	d													11 32											
Rainford	d													11 40											
Upholland	d													11 44											
Orrell	d													11 47											
Pemberton	d													11 50											
Wigan Wallgate	a						11 30						11 51	11 56										12 30	
	d					11 20	11 32			11 48			11 53	11 58									12 20	12 32	
Wigan North Western	d		11a24													12a24									
Ince	d													12 01											
Hindley	d					11 25	11 37						11 58	12 04									12 25	12 37	
Westhoughton	d					11 29							12 02										12 29		
Bolton	a	11 25			11 34	11 38		11 55		12 02	12 08		12 12		12 25							12 34	12 38		12 55
	d	11 25		11 31	11 35	11 39		11 56		12 03	12 08		12 13		12 25						12 31	12 35	12 39		12 56
Moses Gate	d					11 42																	12 42		
Farnworth	d					11 44																	12 44		
Kearsley	d					11 46																	12 46		
Daisy Hill	d						11 41							12 09										12 41	
Hag Fold	d													12 12											
Atherton	d						11 45							12 15										12 45	
Walkden	d						11 50							12 20										12 50	
Moorside	d													12 24											
Swinton	d						11 55							12 26										12 55	
Salford Crescent	a	11 38		11 43	11 47	11 56	12 02	12 08		12 15			12 25	12 34	12 38						12 43	12 47	12 56	13 02	13 08
	d	11 38		11 44	11 47	11 56	12 03	12 09		12 15			12 26	12 34	12 38						12 44	12 47	12 56	13 03	13 09
Salford Central	d	11 41		11 46		11 59	12 05			12 17				12 36	12 41						12 46		12 59	13 05	
Manchester Victoria ⇌	a	11 47		11 50		12 06	12 11			12 25				12 43	12 47						12 52		13 06	13 11	
Rochdale 41	a									12 51															
Deansgate ⇌	a				11 51			12 12					12 29									12 51			13 12
Manchester Oxford Road	a				11 52			12 14			12 23		12 31									12 52			13 14
Manchester Piccadilly 10 ⇌	a				11 56			12 18			12 27		12 35									12 56			13 18
Stockport 84	a							12 34																	13 34
Hazel Grove 86	a							12 45																	13 45
Buxton 86	a																								
Heald Green 85	a				12 10																	13 10			
Manchester Airport 85 ✈	a				12 17						12 47		12 53									13 17			

A To Liverpool South Parkway
B From Clitheroe
C 🍴 from Preston
D from 30 June until 8 September
E From Leeds to Heysham Port
F from 30 June until 8 September. From Glasgow Central to Blackpool North
G from 30 June until 8 September. From Edinburgh

Barrow-in-Furness, Blackpool North, Preston, Southport, Kirkby and Wigan - Bolton - Manchester

Network Diagram - see first Page of Table 82

			NT	TP	TP	TP	TP	NT	NT	NT	NT	NT	NT	TP	TP	NT	NT	NT	NT	TP	NT	NT	NT
				◇■ A 🍴	◇■ B 🍴	◇■ C	◇■ D 🍴	E				F	G	◇■ 🍴	◇■ H					◇■ I 🍴			
Barrow-in-Furness		d				11 25		12 11															
Roose		d						12 15															
Dalton		d						12 21															
Ulverston		d				11 41		12 29															
Cark		d						12 37															
Kents Bank		d						12 41															
Grange-over-Sands		d				11 53		12 45															
Arnside		d				11 59		12 51															
Silverdale		d						12 55															
Carnforth		d				12 09		13 03															
Windermere	83	d																		12 51			
Oxenholme Lake District	65	d		12 07			12 10													13 09			
Lancaster ■	65	a				12 18	12 26	13 16												13 26			
		d			12 15	12 18	12 26													13 26			
Blackpool North	97	d									12 20	12 37		12 44	13 15								13 20
Layton	97	d									12 23												13 23
Poulton-le-Fylde	97	d									12 28			12 50									13 28
Kirkham & Wesham	97	d									12 37												13 37
Preston ■	65,97	a		12 37	12 33	12 37	12 45				12 47	13 02		13 08	13 38					13 45			13 47
		d		12 47	12 47		12 47				12 49	13 04		13 10				13 23		13 47			13 49
Leyland		d									12 54	13 09						13 29					13 54
Buckshaw Parkway		d									12 59			13 17				13 33					13 59
Chorley		d		12 56	12 56		12 56				13 03			13 21				13 38		13 56			14 03
Adlington (Lancashire)		d									13 08												14 08
Blackrod		d									13 12												14 12
Horwich Parkway		d									13 16			13 28				13 46					14 16
Lostock		d									13 20							13 50					14 20
Southport		d							12 24								12 54				13 24		
Meols Cop		d															12 59						
Bescar Lane		d															13 04						
New Lane		d															13 08						
Burscough Bridge		d							12 36								13 11				13 36		
Hoscar		d															13 15						
Parbold		d							12 41								13 18				13 41		
Appley Bridge		d							12 45								13 22				13 45		
Gathurst		d															13 25						
Kirkby		d								12 32												13 32	
Rainford		d								12 40												13 40	
Upholland		d								12 44												13 44	
Orrell		d								12 47												13 47	
Pemberton		d								12 50												13 50	
Wigan Wallgate		a							12 51	12 56							13 30				13 51	13 56	
		d	12 48						12 53	12 58						13 20	13 32		13 48		13 53	13 58	
Wigan North Western		d										13a24											
Ince		d								13 01												14 01	
Hindley		d							12 58	13 04						13 25	13 37				13 58	14 04	
Westhoughton		d							13 02							13 29					14 02		
Bolton		a	13 02	13 08	13 08		13 08		13 12		13 25			13 34		13 38		13 55	14 02	14 08	14 12		14 25
		d	13 03	13 08	13 08		13 08		13 13		13 25		13 31	13 35		13 39		13 56	14 03	14 08	14 13		14 25
Moses Gate		d														13 42							
Farnworth		d														13 44							
Kearsley		d														13 46							
Daisy Hill		d								13 09							13 41					14 09	
Hag Fold		d								13 12												14 12	
Atherton		d								13 15							13 45					14 15	
Walkden		d								13 20							13 50					14 20	
Moorside		d								13 24												14 24	
Swinton		d								13 26							13 55					14 26	
Salford Crescent		a	13 15						13 25	13 34	13 38		13 43	13 47		13 56	14 02	14 08	14 15		14 25	14 34	14 38
		d	13 15						13 26	13 34	13 38		13 44	13 47		13 56	14 03	14 09	14 15		14 26	14 34	14 38
Salford Central		d	13 17							13 36	13 41		13 46			13 59	14 05		14 17			14 36	14 41
Manchester Victoria	⇌	a	13 25							13 43	13 47		13 52			14 06	14 11		14 25			14 43	14 47
Rochdale	41	a	13 51																14 51				
Deansgate	⇌	a							13 29					13 51				14 12			14 29		
Manchester Oxford Road		a		13 23	13 23		13 23		13 31					13 52				14 14		14 23	14 31		
Manchester Piccadilly ■	⇌	a		13 27	13 27		13 27		13 35					13 56				14 18		14 27	14 35		
Stockport	84	a																14 34					
Hazel Grove	86	a																14 45					
Buxton	86	a																					
Heald Green	85	a												14 10									
Manchester Airport	85 ✈	a		13 47	13 47		13 47		13 53					14 17						14 47	14 53		

A from 30 June until 8 September. From Glasgow Central
B 30 June, from 11 August until 8 September. From Edinburgh
C until 23 June, 15 September, 22 September, 29 September
D until 23 June, 15 September, 22 September, 29 September. From Edinburgh
E From Carlisle
F To Liverpool South Parkway
G From Clitheroe
H from 30 June until 4 August, 8 September. To Glasgow Central
I 🍴 from Preston

Barrow-in-Furness, Blackpool North, Preston, Southport, Kirkby and Wigan - Bolton - Manchester

Network Diagram - see first Page of Table 82

			NT	NT	TP	NT	NT	NT	NT	TP	TP	NT	NT	NT	NT	NT	NT	TP	NT	NT	NT	NT	TP	NT
			A	B	◇■ 🍴					◇■ C 🍴	◇■ D 🍴	E				A	B	◇■ 🍴					◇■ F 🍴	
Barrow-in-Furness		d								13 25		14 16												
Roose		d										14 20												
Dalton		d										14 26												
Ulverston		d								13 41		14 35												
Cark		d										14 42												
Kents Bank		d										14 47												
Grange-over-Sands		d								13 53		14 51												
Arnside		d								13 59		14 57												
Silverdale		d										15 01												
Carnforth		d								14 09		15 08												
Windermere	83	d																						
Oxenholme Lake District	65	d									14 07												15 10	
Lancaster ■	65	a								14 18	14 21	15 20											15 26	
		d								14 18	14 22												15 26	
Blackpool North	97	d	13 37		13 44										14 20	14 37		14 44						
Layton	97	d													14 23									
Poulton-le-Fylde	97	d			13 50										14 28			14 50						
Kirkham & Wesham	97	d													14 37									
Preston ■	65,97	a	14 02		14 08					14 37	14 41				14 47	15 02		15 08					15 45	
		d	14 04		14 10			14 23		14 47					14 49	15 04		15 10			15 23		15 47	
Leyland		d	14 09					14 29							14 54	15 09					15 29			
Buckshaw Parkway		d			14 17			14 33							14 59			15 17			15 33			
Chorley		d			14 21			14 38		14 56					15 03			15 21			15 38		15 56	
Adlington (Lancashire)		d													15 08									
Blackrod		d													15 12									
Horwich Parkway		d			14 28			14 46							15 16			15 28			15 46			
Lostock		d						14 50							15 20						15 50			
Southport		d					14 00						14 24							14 54				15 24
Meols Cop		d					14 05													14 59				
Bescar Lane		d																		15 04				
New Lane		d																		15 08				
Burscough Bridge		d					14 13						14 36							15 11				15 36
Hoscar		d																		15 15				
Parbold		d					14 18						14 41							15 18				15 41
Appley Bridge		d					14 22						14 45							15 22				15 45
Gathurst		d					14 25													15 25				
Kirkby		d												14 32										
Rainford		d												14 40										
Upholland		d												14 44										
Orrell		d												14 47										
Pemberton		d												14 50										
Wigan Wallgate		a					14 30						14 51	14 56						15 30				15 51
		d				14 20	14 32		14 48				14 53	14 58					15 20	15 32		15 48		15 53
Wigan North Western		d	14a24													15a24								
Ince		d												15 01										
Hindley		d				14 25	14 37						14 58	15 04					15 25	15 37				15 58
Westhoughton		d				14 29							15 02						15 29					16 02
Bolton		a			14 34	14 38		14 55	15 02	15 08			15 12		15 25			15 34	15 40		15 55	16 02	16 08	16 12
		d		14 31	14 35	14 39		14 56	15 03	15 08			15 13		15 25		15 31	15 35	15 41		15 56	16 03	16 08	16 13
Moses Gate		d				14 42													15 44					
Farnworth		d				14 44													15 46					
Kearsley		d				14 46													15 48					
Daisy Hill		d					14 41							15 09						15 41				
Hag Fold		d												15 12										
Atherton		d					14 45							15 15						15 45				
Walkden		d					14 50							15 20						15 50				
Moorside		d												15 24										
Swinton		d					14 55							15 26						15 55				
Salford Crescent		a		14 43	14 47	14 56	15 02	15 08	15 15				15 25	15 34	15 38		15 43	15 47	15 58	16 02	16 08	16 15		16 25
		d		14 44	14 47	14 56	15 03	15 09	15 15				15 26	15 34	15 38		15 44	15 47	15 58	16 03	16 09	16 15		16 26
Salford Central		d		14 46		14 59	15 05		15 17					15 36	15 41		15 48		16 01	16 05		16 17		
Manchester Victoria	⇌	a		14 52		15 06	15 11		15 25					15 43	15 47		15 54		16 08	16 11		16 23		
Rochdale	41	a							15 51													16 51		
Deansgate	⇌	a			14 51			15 12					15 29					15 51			16 12			
Manchester Oxford Road		a			14 52			15 14		15 23			15 31					15 52			16 14		16 23	16 31
Manchester Piccadilly ■	⇌	a			14 56			15 18		15 27			15 35					15 56			16 18		16 27	16 35
Stockport	84	a						15 34													16 34			
Hazel Grove	86	a						15 45													16 45			
Buxton	86	a																						
Heald Green	85	a			15 10													16 10					16 40	
Manchester Airport	85 ✈	a			15 17					15 47			15 53					16 17					16 47	16 53

A To Liverpool South Parkway
B From Clitheroe
C 🍴 from Preston
D From Edinburgh
E From Whitehaven
F From Glasgow Central

Barrow-in-Furness, Blackpool North, Preston, Southport, Kirkby and Wigan - Bolton - Manchester

Network Diagram - see first Page of Table 82

	NT A	NT B	NT C	NT	NT		NT D	TP ◇1 🛒	NT	NT	NT	NT	TP ◇1 E 🛒	TP ◇1	NT		NT	NT	NT D	NT C	TP ◇1 🛒	NT	NT	NT
Barrow-in-Furness d		15 18												16 22										
Roose d		15 22																						
Dalton d		15 28												16 31										
Ulverston d		15 36												16 39										
Cark d		15 44												16 47										
Kents Bank d		15 48																						
Grange-over-Sands d		15 52												16 54										
Arnside d		15 58												17 00										
Silverdale d		16 03												17 04										
Carnforth d	15 36	16 11												17 11										
Windermere 83 d																								
Oxenholme Lake District 65 d													16 07											
Lancaster 65 a	15 45	16 24											16 26	17 19										
d													16 26	17 20										
Blackpool North 97 d					15 20		15 37	15 44										16 20	16 35		16 40			
Layton 97 d					15 23													16 23			16 43			
Poulton-le-Fylde 97 d					15 28			15 50										16 28			16 48			
Kirkham & Wesham 97 d					15 37													16 37			16 57			
Preston 65,97 a					15 47		16 02	16 08					16 45	17 39				16 47	17 02		17 08			
d					15 49		16 04	16 10			16 23		16 47					16 49	17 04		17 10			17 23
Leyland d					15 54		16 09				16 29							16 54	17 09					17 29
Buckshaw Parkway d					15 59			16 17			16 33							16 59			17 17			17 33
Chorley d					16 03			16 21			16 38		16 56					17 03			17 21			17 38
Adlington (Lancashire) d					16 08													17 08						
Blackrod d					16 12													17 12						
Horwich Parkway d					16 16			16 28			16 46							17 16			17 28			17 46
Lostock d					16 20						16 50							17 20						17 50
Southport d										16 00					16 24								16 54	
Meols Cop d										16 05													16 59	
Bescar Lane d																							17 04	
New Lane d																							17 08	
Burscough Bridge d										16 13					16 36								17 11	
Hoscar d																							17 15	
Parbold d										16 18					16 41								17 18	
Appley Bridge d										16 22					16 45								17 22	
Gathurst d										16 25													17 25	
Kirkby d				15 32													16 32							
Rainford d				15 40													16 40							
Upholland d				15 44													16 44							
Orrell d				15 47													16 47							
Pemberton d				15 50													16 50							
Wigan Wallgate a				15 56						16 30					16 51		16 56						17 30	
d				15 58					16 20	16 32		16 48			16 53		16 58					17 20	17 32	
Wigan North Western d							16a24												17a24					
Ince d				16 01													17 01							
Hindley d				16 04					16 25	16 37					16 58		17 04					17 25	17 37	
Westhoughton d									16 29						17 02							17 29		
Bolton a					16 25			16 34	16 38		16 55	17 02	17 08		17 12			17 25			17 34	17 38		17 55
d			16 17		16 25			16 35	16 39		16 56	17 03	17 08		17 13			17 25		17 31	17 35	17 39		17 56
Moses Gate d									16 42													17 42		
Farnworth d									16 44													17 44		
Kearsley d									16 46													17 46		
Daisy Hill d				16 09						16 41							17 08						17 41	
Hag Fold d				16 12													17 11							
Atherton d				16 15						16 45							17 14						17 45	
Walkden d				16 20						16 50							17 19						17 50	
Moorside d				16 24													17 23							
Swinton d				16 26						16 55							17 25						17 55	
Salford Crescent a			16 30	16 33	16 38			16 47	16 56	17 02	17 08	17 15			17 25		17 33	17 38		17 43	17 47	17 56	18 02	18 08
d			16 30	16 34	16 38			16 47	16 56	17 03	17 09	17 15			17 26		17 33	17 38		17 44	17 47	17 56	18 03	18 09
Salford Central d			16 33	16 37	16 41				16 59	17 05		17 17					17 36	17 41		17 47		17 59	18 05	
Manchester Victoria 🚋 a			16 41	16 43	16 47				17 06	17 11		17 23					17 43	17 47		17 53		18 06	18 11	
Rochdale 41 a												17 51												
Deansgate 🚋 a								16 51			17 14				17 29						17 51			18 12
Manchester Oxford Road a								16 52			17 16		17 23		17 31						17 52			18 14
Manchester Piccadilly 🚋 a								16 56			17 20		17 27		17 35						17 56			18 18
Stockport 84 a											17 34													18 34
Hazel Grove 86 a											17 43													18 45
Buxton 86 a											18 25													
Heald Green 85 a								17 10					17 41								18 10			
Manchester Airport 85 ✈ a								17 17					17 48		17 53						18 17			

A From Leeds to Morecambe
B From Carlisle
C From Clitheroe
D To Liverpool Lime Street
E From Edinburgh

Barrow-in-Furness, Blackpool North, Preston, Southport, Kirkby and Wigan - Bolton - Manchester

Network Diagram - see first Page of Table 82

	NT A		TP ◇1 🛒	NT	NT	NT	NT B	TP ◇1 C 🛒	TP ◇1	NT	NT		NT A	TP ◇1 D 🛒	NT	NT E	NT F	NT	NT	NT B	NT A		TP ◇1	NT
Barrow-in-Furness d									17 21								18 03							
Roose d																	18 07							
Dalton d									17 30								18 13							
Ulverston d									17 38								18 21							
Cark d									17 46								18 29							
Kents Bank d																	18 33							
Grange-over-Sands d									17 53								18 37							
Arnside d									17 59								18 43							
Silverdale d																	18 47							
Carnforth d									18 09							18 26	18 55							
Windermere 83 d								17 06																
Oxenholme Lake District 65 d								17 30																
Lancaster 65 a								17 47	18 16							18 38	19 05							
d								17 48	18 17					18 26			19 06							
Blackpool North 97 d			17 20				17 37												18 20	18 37			18 44	
Layton 97 d			17 23																18 23					
Poulton-le-Fylde 97 d			17 27																18 28				18 50	
Kirkham & Wesham 97 d																			18 37					
Preston 65,97 a			17 45				18 02	18 06	18 36					18 45			19 31		18 47	19 00			19 08	
d			17 47			17 56	18 04	18 08						18 47					18 49	19 04			19 10	
Leyland d						18 01	18 09												18 54	19 09				
Buckshaw Parkway d						18 05		18 15											18 59				19 17	
Chorley d			17 56			18 09		18 19						18 56					19 03				19 21	
Adlington (Lancashire) d						18 15													19 08					
Blackrod d						18 19													19 12					
Horwich Parkway d						18 21		18 26											19 16				19 28	
Lostock d								18 30											19 20					
Southport d				17 24							17 54				18 17									19 00
Meols Cop d				17 29							17 59				18 22									19 05
Bescar Lane d											18 04				18 27									
New Lane d											18 08				18 31									
Burscough Bridge d				17 37							18 11				18 33									19 13
Hoscar d											18 15				18 37									
Parbold d				17 42							18 18				18 40									19 18
Appley Bridge d				17 46							18 22				18 44									19 22
Gathurst d											18 25				18 47									19 25
Kirkby d					17 32													18 32						
Rainford d					17 40													18 40						
Upholland d					17 44													18 44						
Orrell d					17 47													18 47						
Pemberton d					17 50													18 50						
Wigan Wallgate a				17 52	17 57						18 30				18 52			18 56						19 30
d				17 54	17 59					18 20	18 32				18 53			18 58						19 32
Wigan North Western d							18a24													19a24				
Ince d					18 02													19 01						
Hindley d					18 05					18 25	18 37				18 58			19 04						19 37
Westhoughton d				18 02						18 29					19 02									
Bolton a			18 08	18 12		18 30		18 34		18 38				19 08	19 12				19 25				19 34	
d	18 03		18 08	18 13		18 30		18 35		18 39			19 02	19 08	19 13				19 25		19 32		19 35	
Moses Gate d										18 42														
Farnworth d										18 44														
Kearsley d										18 46														
Daisy Hill d					18 09						18 41							19 08						19 41
Hag Fold d					18 12													19 11						
Atherton d					18 15						18 45							19 14						19 45
Walkden d					18 20						18 50							19 19						19 50
Moorside d					18 24													19 23						
Swinton d					18 26						18 55							19 25						19 55
Salford Crescent a	18 15			18 25	18 33	18 43		18 47		18 56	19 02		19 14		19 25			19 33	19 38		19 44		19 47	20 02
d	18 16			18 26	18 33	18 43		18 47		18 56	19 03		19 15		19 26			19 33	19 38		19 45		19 47	20 03
Salford Central d	18 18				18 36	18 46				18 59	19 05		19 17					19 36	19 41		19 47			20 05
Manchester Victoria 🚋 a	18 27				18 43	18 52				19 06	19 11		19 23					19 43	19 47		19 53			20 11
Rochdale 41 a	18 47																							
Deansgate 🚋 a								18 51							19 29								19 51	
Manchester Oxford Road a			18 23	18 31				18 52						19 23	19 31								19 52	
Manchester Piccadilly 🚋 a			18 27	18 35				18 56						19 27	19 35								19 56	
Stockport 84 a																								
Hazel Grove 86 a																								
Buxton 86 a																								
Heald Green 85 a			18 40					19 10															20 10	
Manchester Airport 85 ✈ a			18 47	18 53				19 17						19 50	19 53								20 17	

A From Clitheroe
B To Liverpool Lime Street
C 🛒 from Preston
D From Edinburgh
E From Leeds to Morecambe
F From Carlisle

Table 82

Saturdays
until 29 September

Barrow-in-Furness, Blackpool North, Preston, Southport, Kirkby and Wigan - Bolton - Manchester

Network Diagram - see first Page of Table 82

		NT	TP	NT	NT	NT	NT	TP		TP	NT	NT	NT	NT	NT	TP	TP	NT		NT	NT	TP	NT	NT	TP
			◇1					◇1		◇1						◇1	◇1					◇1			◇1
		A	B 🍴			C	D			E 🍴				C	D									D	
Barrow-in-Furness	d															19 33							21 43		
Roose	d															19 37							21 47		
Dalton	d															19 44							21 53		
Ulverston	d															19 52							22 01		
Cark	d															20 00							22 09		
Kents Bank	d															20 04							22 13		
Grange-over-Sands	d															20 08							22 17		
Arnside	d															20 14							22 23		
Silverdale	d															20 18							22 27		
Carnforth	d															20 25							22 35		
Windermere 83	d																					21 40			
Oxenholme Lake District 65	d		19 10							20 13												22 01			
Lancaster 6 65	a		19 26							20 26						20 34						22 17	22 45		
	d		19 26							20 26						20 35						22 17	22 46		
Blackpool North 97	d				19 20	19 37		19 44					20 20	20 37			20 42				21 20				21 44
Layton 97	d				19 23								20 23								21 23				
Poulton-le-Fylde 97	d				19 28			19 50					20 28				20 48				21 28				21 50
Kirkham & Wesham 97	d				19 37								20 37								21 37				
Preston 8 65,97	a		19 45		19 47	20 02		20 08		20 45			20 47	21 01		20 53	21 06				21 47	22 38	23 11		22 08
	d		19 47		19 49	20 04		20 10		20 47			20 49	21 04		21 10					21 49				22 10
Leyland	d				19 54	20 09							20 54	21 09							21 54				
Buckshaw Parkway	d				19 59			20 17					20 59								21 59				22 17
Chorley	d		19 56		20 03			20 21		20 56			21 03			21 21					22 03				22 21
Adlington (Lancashire)	d				20 08								21 08								22 08				
Blackrod	d				20 12								21 12								22 12				
Horwich Parkway	d				20 16			20 28					21 16			21 28					22 16				22 28
Lostock	d				20 20								21 20								22 20				
Southport	d			19 23								20 23								21 23					
Meols Cop	d			19 28								20 28								21 28					
Bescar Lane	d																								
New Lane	d																								
Burscough Bridge	d			19 36								20 36								21 36					
Hoscar	d																								
Parbold	d			19 41								20 41								21 41					
Appley Bridge	d			19 45								20 45								21 45					
Gathurst	d			19 48								20 48								21 48					
Kirkby	d																								
Rainford	d																								
Upholland	d																								
Orrell	d																								
Pemberton	d																								
Wigan Wallgate	a			19 53								20 53								21 53					
	d			19 55							20 27	20 55						21 27		21 55					
Wigan North Western	d					20a24								21a23											
Ince	d										20 30							21 30							
Hindley	d			20 00							20 33	21 00						21 33		22 00					
Westhoughton	d			20 04								21 04								22 04					
Bolton	a		20 08	20 12	20 25			20 34		21 08		21 12	21 25			21 34				22 12	22 25				22 34
	d	20 02	20 08	20 13	20 25		20 31	20 35		21 08		21 13	21 25		21 31	21 35				22 13	22 25			22 31	22 35
Moses Gate	d																								
Farnworth	d																								
Kearsley	d																								
Daisy Hill	d										20 37							21 37							
Hag Fold	d										20 40							21 40							
Atherton	d										20 43							21 43							
Walkden	d										20 49							21 49							
Moorside	d										20 52							21 52							
Swinton	d										20 55							21 55							
Salford Crescent	a	20 15		20 25	20 38		20 43	20 47			21 02	21 25	21 38		21 43	21 47		22 02		22 25	22 38			22 43	22 47
	d	20 15		20 26	20 38		20 44	20 47			21 03	21 26	21 38		21 44	21 47		22 03		22 26	22 38			22 44	22 47
Salford Central	d	20 17			20 41		20 46				21 05		21 41		21 46			22 05		22 28	22 41			22 46	
Manchester Victoria ⇌	a	20 24			20 47		20 52				21 11		21 47		21 52			22 11		22 34	22 47			22 52	
Rochdale 41	a																								
Deansgate ⇌	a			20 29				20 51				21 29				21 51									22 51
Manchester Oxford Road	a		20 23	20 31				20 52		21 23		21 31				21 52									22 52
Manchester Piccadilly 10 ⇌	a		20 27	20 35				20 56		21 27		21 35				21 56									22 56
Stockport 84	a																								
Hazel Grove 86	a																								
Buxton 86	a																								
Heald Green 85	a							21 10								22 09									23 09
Manchester Airport 85 ✈	a		20 47	20 53				21 17		21 47		21 53				22 17									23 17

A From Blackburn
B From Glasgow Central
C To Liverpool Lime Street
D From Clitheroe
E From Edinburgh

Table 82

Saturdays
until 29 September

Barrow-in-Furness, Blackpool North, Preston, Southport, Kirkby and Wigan - Bolton - Manchester

Network Diagram - see first Page of Table 82

		NT	NT	NT		NT	TP	NT	NT
							◇1		
		A							
Barrow-in-Furness	d								
Roose	d								
Dalton	d								
Ulverston	d								
Cark	d								
Kents Bank	d								
Grange-over-Sands	d								
Arnside	d								
Silverdale	d								
Carnforth	d								
Windermere 83	d								
Oxenholme Lake District 65	d								
Lancaster 6 65	a								
	d								
Blackpool North 97	d	22 14				22 20	22 44	23 02	
Layton 97	d					22 23		23 05	
Poulton-le-Fylde 97	d					22 28	22 50	23 10	
Kirkham & Wesham 97	d					22 37		23 19	
Preston 8 65,97	a	22 41				22 47	23 08	23 29	
	d	22 43				22 49	23 10	23 31	
Leyland	d	22 48				22 54		23 36	
Buckshaw Parkway	d					22 59	23 17	23 41	
Chorley	d					23 03	23 21	23 45	
Adlington (Lancashire)	d					23 08		23 50	
Blackrod	d					23 12		23 54	
Horwich Parkway	d					23 16	23 28	23 58	
Lostock	d					23 20		00 02	
Southport	d			22 18					23 10
Meols Cop	d			22 23					23 15
Bescar Lane	d			22 28					
New Lane	d			22 32					
Burscough Bridge	d			22 34					23 23
Hoscar	d			22 38					
Parbold	d			22 41					23 28
Appley Bridge	d			22 45					23 32
Gathurst	d			22 48					23 35
Kirkby	d								
Rainford	d								
Upholland	d								
Orrell	d								
Pemberton	d								
Wigan Wallgate	a			22 53					23 44
	d		22 27	22 55					
Wigan North Western	d	23a02							
Ince	d		22 30						
Hindley	d		22 33	23 00					
Westhoughton	d			23 04					
Bolton	a			23 12		23 25	23 34	00 07	
	d			23 13		23 25	23 35	00 07	
Moses Gate	d								
Farnworth	d								
Kearsley	d								
Daisy Hill	d		22 37						
Hag Fold	d		22 40						
Atherton	d		22 43						
Walkden	d		22 49						
Moorside	d		22 52						
Swinton	d		22 55						
Salford Crescent	a		23 02	23 25		23 38	23 47		
	d		23 03	23 26		23 38	23 47		
Salford Central	d		23 05						
Manchester Victoria ⇌	a		23 13			23 47		00 26	
Rochdale 41	a								
Deansgate ⇌	a			23 29					
Manchester Oxford Road	a			23 31					
Manchester Piccadilly 10 ⇌	a			23 39			23 53		
Stockport 84	a								
Hazel Grove 86	a								
Buxton 86	a								
Heald Green 85	a						00 16		
Manchester Airport 85 ✈	a						00 23		

A To Liverpool Lime Street

Barrow-in-Furness, Blackpool North, Preston, Southport, Kirkby and Wigan - Bolton - Manchester

Network Diagram - see first Page of Table 82

			TP ◇■	NT	TP ◇■ A	TP ◇■ B	TP ◇■	TP ◇■	NT C	TP ◇■	TP ◇■	NT	NT	NT D	TP ◇■	NT	NT	TP ◇■ 🛒	NT	NT	NT	NT E	NT	NT F
Barrow-in-Furness		d						04 35							05 31									
Roose		d																						
Dalton		d																						
Ulverston		d						04 51							05 47									
Cark		d																						
Kents Bank		d																						
Grange-over-Sands		d						05 03							05 59									
Arnside		d						05 10							06 05									
Silverdale		d																						
Carnforth		d						05 19							06 15									
Windermere	83	d																						
Oxenholme Lake District	65	d																						
Lancaster ■	65	a						05 28							06 23									
		d													06 23									
Blackpool North	97	d	22p44	23p13			03 37		04 56		05 39						06 19	06 40			06 53	07 02		
Layton	97	d		23p16													06 22	06 43						
Poulton-le-Fylde	97	d	22p50	23p21					05 02		05 45						06 27	06 47				07 08		
Kirkham & Wesham	97	d		23p30													06 36	06 56						
Preston ■	65,97	a	23p08	23p40					05 20		06 03				06 42		06 46	07 07			07 15	07 28		
		d	23p10	23p42			04u02			05 16	06 05				06 44		06 48	07 09			07 17	07 30		
Leyland		d		23p48							06 10						06 53				07 22	07 35		
Buckshaw Parkway		d	23p17	23p52													06 58				07 28			
Chorley		d	23p21	23p57						05 26	06 16				06 53		07 02	07 18			07 32			
Adlington (Lancashire)		d		00 03													07 07				07 37			
Blackrod		d		00 06							06 22						07 11				07 41			
Horwich Parkway		d	23p28	00 10						05 33	06 26				07 00		07 15	07 26			07 45			
Lostock		d		00 14							06 30						07 20	07 30			07 49			
Southport		d														06 19								
Meols Cop		d														06 24								
Bescar Lane		d																						
New Lane		d																						
Burscough Bridge		d														06 32								
Hoscar		d																						
Parbold		d														06 37								
Appley Bridge		d														06 41								
Gathurst		d														06 45								
Kirkby		d																					07 07	
Rainford		d																					07 15	
Upholland		d																					07 19	
Orrell		d																					07 23	
Pemberton		d																					07 26	
Wigan Wallgate		a														06 52							07 33	
		d										06 31	06 34			06 53			07 13				07 35	
Wigan North Western		d																		07 22		07a50		
Ince		d											06 37						07 16	07 25			07 38	
Hindley		d										06 36	06 40						07 19	07 29			07 41	
Westhoughton		d										06 41				07 01				07 33				
Bolton		a	23p34	00 19						05 42	06 34	06 52			07 08	07 11	07 25	07 34		07 42	07 54			
		d	23p35	00 20			04u31			05 43	06 35	06 53		06 56	07 08	07 12	07 25	07 35		07 43	07 55			07 59
Moses Gate		d												06 59						07 46				08 02
Farnworth		d												07 01						07 48				08 04
Kearsley		d												07 03						07 50				08 06
Daisy Hill		d											06 44						07 24				07 47	
Hag Fold		d											06 47						07 27				07 50	
Atherton		d											06 50						07 30				07 53	
Walkden		d											06 56						07 36				07 59	
Moorside		d											06 59						07 39				08 03	
Swinton		d											07 02						07 42				08 05	
Salford Crescent		a	23p47							05 55	06 47	07 05	07 11	07 15		07 24	07 38	07 47	07 51	08 02	08 07		08 13	08 17
		d	23p47		00 49	03 37				05 55	06 47	07 08	07 11	07 15		07 25	07 38	07 47	07 51	08 02	08 08		08 13	08 17
Salford Central		d											07 14	07 19			07 41		07 55	08 05			08 16	08 20
Manchester Victoria	⇌	a		00 37									07 20	07 25			07 47		08 01	08 12			08 20	08 26
Rochdale	41	a																					08 51	
Deansgate	⇌	a									06 51	07 11				07 28		07 51			08 11			
Manchester Oxford Road		a									06 52	07 13			07 23	07 30		07 52			08 14			
Manchester Piccadilly ■	⇌	a	23p53		00 53	03 44	04 48			06 01	06 56	07 17			07 27	07 34		07 56			08 18			
Stockport	84	a										07 34									08 34			
Hazel Grove	86	a										07 47									08 47			
Buxton	86	a																						
Heald Green	85	a	00 16								07 10							08 10						
Manchester Airport	85 ✈	a	00 24		01 10	04 00	05 07			06 18	07 17				07 47	07 53		08 17						

A From Newcastle
B From York
C To Colne
D From Blackburn
E To Liverpool Lime Street
F From Clitheroe

Barrow-in-Furness, Blackpool North, Preston, Southport, Kirkby and Wigan - Bolton - Manchester

Network Diagram - see first Page of Table 82

			TP ◇■ A 🛒	NT	NT	NT B	NT C	TP ◇■ 🛒	NT	NT	NT	NT	NT D	TP ◇■ A 🛒	NT	NT	NT	NT E	NT C	TP ◇■ 🛒	TP ◇■ F	NT	NT	NT
Barrow-in-Furness		d	06 20											07 29										
Roose		d	06 24																					
Dalton		d	06 31											07 38										
Ulverston		d	06 39											07 46										
Cark		d	06 47											07 54										
Kents Bank		d	06 51																					
Grange-over-Sands		d	06 55											08 01										
Arnside		d	07 01											08 07										
Silverdale		d	07 05											08 11										
Carnforth		d	07 12			07 43								08 18										
Windermere	83	d																						
Oxenholme Lake District	65	d																						
Lancaster ■	65	a	07 21			07 52								08 26										
		d	07 22											08 27										
Blackpool North	97	d			07 18			07 44									08 20	08 38		08 44	09 14			
Layton	97	d			07 21			07 47									08 23							
Poulton-le-Fylde	97	d			07 26			07 51									08 28			08 50	09 20			
Kirkham & Wesham	97	d			07 35			08 00									08 37							
Preston ■	65,97	a	07 41		07 46			08 11						08 45			08 47	09 02		09 08	09 41			
		d	07 47		07 47			08 12				08 17		08 47			08 49	09 04		09 10				09 23
Leyland		d			07 53							08 23					08 54	09 09						09 29
Buckshaw Parkway		d			07 58							08 27					08 59			09 17				09 33
Chorley		d	07 56		08 02			08 22				08 34		08 56			09 03			09 21				09 38
Adlington (Lancashire)		d			08 07							08 39					09 08							
Blackrod		d			08 11							08 42					09 12							
Horwich Parkway		d			08 15							08 46					09 16			09 28				09 46
Lostock		d			08 20							08 50					09 20							09 50
Southport		d		07 21							07 51					08 25							08 58	
Meols Cop		d		07 26							07 56					08 30							09 03	
Bescar Lane		d									08 01													
New Lane		d									08 05													
Burscough Bridge		d		07 34							08 07					08 38							09 11	
Hoscar		d									08 11													
Parbold		d		07 39							08 14					08 43							09 16	
Appley Bridge		d		07 43							08 18					08 47							09 20	
Gathurst		d		07 47							08 21					08 50							09 23	
Kirkby		d													08 17									
Rainford		d													08 25									
Upholland		d													08 29									
Orrell		d													08 32									
Pemberton		d													08 35									
Wigan Wallgate		a		07 51							08 28				08 43	08 55							09 30	
		d		07 53					08 11		08 29				08 48	08 56						09 18	09 30	
Wigan North Western		d								08 20								09a24						
Ince		d							08 14						08 51									
Hindley		d		07 58					08 17	08 25	08 34				08 55							09 23	09 35	
Westhoughton		d		08 03						08 29						09 04						09 27		
Bolton		a	08 08	08 11	08 25			08 34		08 38		08 55		09 08		09 13	09 25			09 34		09 38		09 55
		d	08 08	08 12	08 25		08 31	08 35		08 39		08 56	09 02	09 08		09 14	09 25		09 31	09 35		09 39		09 56
Moses Gate		d								08 42												09 42		
Farnworth		d								08 44												09 44		
Kearsley		d								08 46												09 46		
Daisy Hill		d							08 21		08 39				08 59								09 39	
Hag Fold		d							08 24						09 02									
Atherton		d							08 27		08 42				09 04								09 43	
Walkden		d							08 33		08 48				09 10								09 48	
Moorside		d							08 37						09 13									
Swinton		d							08 40		08 53				09 16								09 53	
Salford Crescent		a		08 24	08 38		08 43	08 47	08 50	08 56	09 03	09 08	09 15		09 27	09 26	09 38		09 43	09 47		09 56	10 03	10 08
		d		08 25	08 38		08 44	08 47	08 50	08 56	09 03	09 09	09 16		09 27	09 27	09 38		09 44	09 47		09 56	10 03	10 09
Salford Central		d			08 41		08 46		08 53	08 59	09 06		09 18		09 31		09 41		09 46			09 59	10 05	
Manchester Victoria	⇌	a			08 47		08 53		08 59	09 06	09 11		09 26		09 38		09 47		09 53			10 06	10 12	
Rochdale	41	a											09 54											
Deansgate	⇌	a		08 28								09 12				09 30				09 51				10 12
Manchester Oxford Road		a	08 23	08 31				08 52				09 14		09 23		09 32				09 52				10 14
Manchester Piccadilly ■	⇌	a	08 27	08 35				08 56				09 18		09 27		09 36				09 56				10 18
Stockport	84	a										09 34												10 34
Hazel Grove	86	a										09 47												10 47
Buxton	86	a																						
Heald Green	85	a		08 47				09 10												10 10				
Manchester Airport	85 ✈	a	08 47	08 53				09 19						09 47		09 54				10 17				

A 🛒 from Preston
B From Leeds
C From Clitheroe
D From Blackburn
E To Liverpool South Parkway
F To Barrow-in-Furness

Table 82

Saturdays from 6 October

Barrow-in-Furness, Blackpool North, Preston, Southport, Kirkby and Wigan - Bolton - Manchester

Network Diagram - see first Page of Table 82

			NT		NT	TP	NT	NT	NT	NT	NT	NT	TP		NT	TP	NT	NT	NT	NT	NT	TP	NT		NT	NT
						◇1							◇1			◇1						◇1				
			A			B	C				D	E			F					A		G	H			
						🛒										🛒						🛒				
Barrow-in-Furness		d					08 25															09 23	10 16			
Roose		d					08 29															09 27	10 20			
Dalton		d					08 36															09 34	10 26			
Ulverston		d					08 44															09 42	10 34			
Cark		d					08 52															09 50	10 42			
Kents Bank		d					08 57															09 54	10 46			
Grange-over-Sands		d					09 01															09 58	10 50			
Arnside		d					09 08															10 04	10 56			
Silverdale		d					09 13															10 08	11 01			
Carnforth		d					09 19					10 02										10 15	11 09			
Windermere	83	d											09 38													
Oxenholme Lake District	65	d				09 11							09 58													
Lancaster 8	65	a				09 26	09 33					10 12	10 16									10 25	11 21			
		d				09 26							10 16									10 26				
Blackpool North	97	d								09 20	09 37					09 43										
Layton	97	d								09 23																
Poulton-le-Fylde	97	d								09 28						09 49										
Kirkham & Wesham	97	d								09 37																
Preston 8	65,97	a				09 45				09 47	10 02		10 35			10 07						10 45				
		d				09 47				09 49	10 04					10 12			10 23			10 47				
Leyland		d								09 54	10 09								10 29							
Buckshaw Parkway		d								09 59									10 33							
Chorley		d				09 56				10 03						10 22			10 38			10 56				
Adlington (Lancashire)		d								10 08																
Blackrod		d								10 12																
Horwich Parkway		d								10 16									10 46							
Lostock		d								10 20									10 50							
Southport		d						09 22										09 51							10 20	
Meols Cop		d																09 56								
Bescar Lane		d																10 01								
New Lane		d																10 05								
Burscough Bridge		d						09 34										10 07							10 32	
Hoscar		d																10 11								
Parbold		d						09 39										10 14							10 37	
Appley Bridge		d						09 43										10 18							10 41	
Gathurst		d																10 21								
Kirkby		d							09 28																	10 28
Rainford		d							09 36																	10 36
Upholland		d							09 40																	10 40
Orrell		d							09 43																	10 43
Pemberton		d							09 46																	10 46
Wigan Wallgate		a						09 49	09 54									10 28							10 49	10 54
		d			09 44			09 51	09 56								10 18	10 30			10 46				10 51	10 56
Wigan North Western		d									10a24															
Ince		d							09 59																	10 59
Hindley		d						09 56	10 02								10 23	10 35							10 56	11 02
Westhoughton		d			09 52			10 00									10 27								11 00	
Bolton		a			10 02	10 08		10 12		10 25						10 34	10 38		10 55		11 02	11 08			11 12	
		d	10 00		10 03	10 08		10 13		10 25					10 31	10 35	10 39		10 56	11 00	11 04	11 08			11 13	
Moses Gate		d															10 42									
Farnworth		d															10 44									
Kearsley		d															10 46									
Daisy Hill		d							10 07									10 39								11 07
Hag Fold		d							10 10																	11 10
Atherton		d							10 13									10 43								11 13
Walkden		d							10 18									10 48								11 18
Moorside		d							10 22																	11 22
Swinton		d							10 24									10 53								11 24
Salford Crescent		a	10 13		10 15			10 25	10 34	10 38					10 44	10 47	10 56	11 02	11 08	11 12	11 16				11 25	11 34
		d	10 13		10 15			10 26	10 34	10 38					10 44	10 47	10 56	11 03	11 09	11 13	11 16				11 26	11 34
Salford Central		d	10 16		10 17				10 36	10 41					10 46		10 59	11 05		11 15	11 18					11 36
Manchester Victoria		a	10 22		10 25				10 43	10 47					10 52		11 06	11 11		11 23	11 25					11 43
Rochdale	41	a			10 51																11 51					
Deansgate		a						10 29								10 51			11 12						11 29	
Manchester Oxford Road		a				10 23		10 31								10 52			11 14			11 23			11 31	
Manchester Piccadilly 10		a				10 27		10 35								10 56			11 18			11 27			11 35	
Stockport	84	a																	11 34							
Hazel Grove	86	a																	11 47							
Buxton	86	a																								
Heald Green	85	a														11 10										
Manchester Airport	85 ✈	a				10 47		10 53								11 17						11 47			11 53	

A From Blackburn
B From Glasgow Central
C From Maryport
D To Liverpool South Parkway
E From Leeds to Morecambe.
F From Clitheroe
G 🛒 from Preston
H From Sellafield

Table 82

Saturdays from 6 October

Barrow-in-Furness, Blackpool North, Preston, Southport, Kirkby and Wigan - Bolton - Manchester

Network Diagram - see first Page of Table 82

			NT	NT	NT	TP	NT	NT	NT		NT	TP	NT	NT	NT	NT	NT	TP	NT		TP	NT	NT	NT	NT	TP
						◇1						◇1						◇1			◇1					◇1
				A	B							C				A	D		B							E
						🛒						🛒									🛒					🛒
Barrow-in-Furness		d																11 25								
Roose		d																								
Dalton		d																								
Ulverston		d																11 41								
Cark		d																								
Kents Bank		d																								
Grange-over-Sands		d																11 53								
Arnside		d																11 59								
Silverdale		d																								
Carnforth		d															12 02	12 09								
Windermere	83	d										10 49														
Oxenholme Lake District	65	d										11 09														12 10
Lancaster 8	65	a										11 26					12 12	12 18								12 26
		d										11 26						12 18								12 26
Blackpool North	97	d	10 20	10 37		10 44									11 15	11 37					11 44					
Layton	97	d	10 23												11 18											
Poulton-le-Fylde	97	d	10 28			10 50									11 23						11 50					
Kirkham & Wesham	97	d	10 37												11 32											
Preston 8	65,97	a	10 47	11 02		11 08						11 45			11 42	12 02		12 37			12 08					12 45
		d	10 49	11 04		11 10			11 23			11 47			11 49	12 04					12 10			12 23		12 47
Leyland		d	10 54	11 09					11 29						11 54	12 09								12 29		
Buckshaw Parkway		d	10 59			11 17			11 33						11 59						12 17			12 33		
Chorley		d	11 03			11 21			11 38			11 56			12 03						12 21			12 38		12 56
Adlington (Lancashire)		d	11 08												12 08											
Blackrod		d	11 12												12 12											
Horwich Parkway		d	11 16			11 28			11 46						12 16						12 28			12 46		
Lostock		d	11 20						11 50						12 20									12 50		
Southport		d						10 51					11 20										11 56			
Meols Cop		d						10 56															12 01			
Bescar Lane		d						11 01																		
New Lane		d						11 05																		
Burscough Bridge		d						11 07					11 32										12 09			
Hoscar		d						11 11																		
Parbold		d						11 14					11 37										12 14			
Appley Bridge		d						11 18					11 41										12 18			
Gathurst		d						11 21															12 21			
Kirkby		d												11 28												
Rainford		d												11 36												
Upholland		d												11 40												
Orrell		d												11 43												
Pemberton		d												11 46												
Wigan Wallgate		a						11 28					11 49	11 54									12 28			
		d					11 18	11 30			11 46		11 51	11 56								12 18	12 30		12 46	
Wigan North Western		d		11a24												12a24										
Ince		d												11 59												
Hindley		d					11 23	11 35					11 56	12 02								12 23	12 35			
Westhoughton		d					11 27						12 00									12 27				
Bolton		a	11 25			11 34	11 38		11 55		12 02	12 08	12 12		12 25						12 34	12 38		12 55	13 02	13 08
		d	11 25		11 31	11 35	11 39		11 56		12 03	12 08	12 13		12 25				12 31		12 35	12 39		12 56	13 03	13 08
Moses Gate		d					11 42															12 42				
Farnworth		d					11 44															12 44				
Kearsley		d					11 46															12 46				
Daisy Hill		d						11 39						12 07									12 39			
Hag Fold		d												12 10												
Atherton		d						11 43						12 13									12 43			
Walkden		d						11 48						12 18									12 48			
Moorside		d												12 22												
Swinton		d						11 53						12 24									12 53			
Salford Crescent		a	11 38		11 43	11 47	11 56	12 02	12 08		12 15		12 25	12 34	12 38				12 43		12 47	12 56	13 00	13 08	13 15	
		d	11 38		11 44	11 47	11 56	12 03	12 09		12 15		12 26	12 34	12 38				12 44		12 47	12 56	13 01	13 09	13 15	
Salford Central		d	11 41		11 46		11 59	12 05			12 17			12 36	12 41				12 46			12 59	13 05		13 17	
Manchester Victoria		a	11 47		11 53		12 06	12 11			12 25			12 43	12 47				12 53			13 06	13 11		13 25	
Rochdale	41	a									12 51														13 51	
Deansgate		a				11 51			12 12				12 29								12 51			13 12		
Manchester Oxford Road		a				11 52			12 14			12 23	12 31								12 52			13 14		13 23
Manchester Piccadilly 10		a				11 56			12 18			12 27	12 35								12 56			13 18		13 27
Stockport	84	a							12 34															13 34		
Hazel Grove	86	a							12 47															13 47		
Buxton	86	a																								
Heald Green	85	a				12 10															13 10					
Manchester Airport	85 ✈	a				12 17						12 47	12 53								13 17					13 47

A To Liverpool South Parkway
B From Clitheroe
C 🛒 from Preston
D From Leeds to Heysham Port
E From Edinburgh

Saturdays
from 6 October

Barrow-in-Furness, Blackpool North, Preston, Southport, Kirkby and Wigan - Bolton - Manchester

Network Diagram - see first Page of Table 82

		NT	NT	NT	NT	NT	NT	TP	NT	NT	NT	NT	TP	NT	NT	NT	NT	NT	TP	NT	NT	NT
		A				B	C	◇1 ✠					◇1 D ✠				B	C	◇1 ✠			
Barrow-in-Furness	d	12 11																				
Roose	d	12 15																				
Dalton	d	12 21																				
Ulverston	d	12 29																				
Cark	d	12 37																				
Kents Bank	d	12 41																				
Grange-over-Sands	d	12 45																				
Arnside	d	12 51																				
Silverdale	d	12 55																				
Carnforth	d	13 03																				
Windermere 83	d												12 51									
Oxenholme Lake District 65	d												13 09									
Lancaster 6 65	a	13 16											13 26									
	d												13 26									
Blackpool North 97	d				12 20	12 37		12 44								13 20	13 37		13 44			
Layton 97	d				12 23											13 23						
Poulton-le-Fylde 97	d				12 28			12 50								13 28			13 50			
Kirkham & Wesham 97	d				12 37											13 37						
Preston 8 65,97	a				12 47	13 02		13 08					13 45			13 47	14 02		14 08			
	d				12 49	13 04		13 10			13 23		13 47			13 49	14 04		14 10			14 23
Leyland	d				12 54	13 09					13 29					13 54	14 09					14 29
Buckshaw Parkway	d				12 59			13 17			13 33					13 59			14 17			14 33
Chorley	d				13 03			13 21			13 38		13 56			14 03			14 21			14 38
Adlington (Lancashire)	d				13 08											14 08						
Blackrod	d				13 12											14 12						
Horwich Parkway	d				13 16			13 28			13 46					14 16			14 28			14 46
Lostock	d				13 20						13 50					14 20						14 50
Southport	d		12 20							12 50				13 20							13 56	
Meols Cop	d									12 55											14 01	
Bescar Lane	d									13 00												
New Lane	d									13 04												
Burscough Bridge	d		12 32							13 07				13 32							14 09	
Hoscar	d									13 11												
Parbold	d		12 37							13 14				13 37							14 14	
Appley Bridge	d		12 41							13 18				13 41							14 18	
Gathurst	d									13 21											14 21	
Kirkby	d			12 28											13 28							
Rainford	d			12 36											13 36							
Upholland	d			12 40											13 40							
Orrell	d			12 43											13 43							
Pemberton	d			12 46											13 46							
Wigan Wallgate	a		12 49	12 54						13 28				13 49	13 54						14 28	
	d		12 51	12 56					13 18	13 30		13 46		13 51	13 56					14 18	14 30	
Wigan North Western	d					13a24											14a24					
Ince	d			12 59											13 59							
Hindley	d		12 56	13 02					13 23	13 35				13 56	14 02					14 23	14 35	
Westhoughton	d		13 00						13 27					14 00						14 27		
Bolton	a		13 12		13 25			13 34	13 38		13 55	14 02	14 08	14 12		14 25			14 34	14 38		14 55
	d		13 13		13 25		13 31	13 35	13 39		13 56	14 03	14 08	14 13		14 25		14 31	14 35	14 39		14 56
Moses Gate	d								13 42											14 42		
Farnworth	d								13 44											14 44		
Kearsley	d								13 46											14 46		
Daisy Hill	d			13 07						13 39					14 07						14 39	
Hag Fold	d			13 10											14 10							
Atherton	d			13 13						13 43					14 13						14 43	
Walkden	d			13 18						13 48					14 18						14 48	
Moorside	d			13 22											14 22							
Swinton	d			13 24						13 53					14 24						14 53	
Salford Crescent	a		13 25	13 34	13 38		13 43	13 47	13 56	14 02	14 08	14 15		14 25	14 34	14 38		14 43	14 47	14 56	15 02	15 08
	d		13 26	13 34	13 38		13 44	13 47	13 56	14 03	14 09	14 15		14 26	14 34	14 38		14 44	14 47	14 56	15 03	15 09
Salford Central	d			13 36	13 41		13 46		13 59	14 05		14 17			14 36	14 41		14 46		14 59	15 05	
Manchester Victoria ⇌	a			13 43	13 47		13 53		14 06	14 11		14 25			14 43	14 47		14 53		15 06	15 11	
Rochdale 41	a											14 51										
Deansgate ⇌	a		13 29					13 51			14 12			14 29					14 51			15 12
Manchester Oxford Road	a		13 31					13 52			14 14		14 23	14 31					14 52			15 14
Manchester Piccadilly 10 ⇌	a		13 35					13 56			14 18		14 27	14 35					14 56			15 18
Stockport 84	a										14 34											15 34
Hazel Grove 86	a										14 47											15 47
Buxton 86	a																					
Heald Green 85	a							14 10											15 10			
Manchester Airport 85 ✈	a		13 53					14 17					14 47	14 53					15 17			

A From Carlisle
B To Liverpool South Parkway
C From Clitheroe
D ✠ from Preston

Table 82

Saturdays
from 6 October

Barrow-in-Furness, Blackpool North, Preston, Southport, Kirkby and Wigan - Bolton - Manchester

Network Diagram - see first Page of Table 82

		NT	TP	TP	NT	NT	NT	NT	NT	NT	TP	NT	NT	NT	NT	TP	NT	NT	NT	NT	NT	NT	NT
			◇1 A ✠	◇1 B ✠	C				D	E	◇1 ✠					◇1 F ✠		G	H	E			I
Barrow-in-Furness	d		13 25		14 16														15 18				
Roose	d				14 20														15 22				
Dalton	d				14 26														15 28				
Ulverston	d		13 41		14 35														15 36				
Cark	d				14 42														15 44				
Kents Bank	d				14 47														15 48				
Grange-over-Sands	d		13 53		14 51														15 52				
Arnside	d		13 59		14 57														15 58				
Silverdale	d				15 01														16 03				
Carnforth	d		14 09		15 08													15 36	16 11				
Windermere 83	d																						
Oxenholme Lake District 65	d			14 07												15 10							
Lancaster 6 65	a		14 18	14 21	15 20											15 26		15 45	16 24				
	d		14 18	14 22												15 26							
Blackpool North 97	d							14 20	14 37		14 44											15 20	15 37
Layton 97	d							14 23														15 23	
Poulton-le-Fylde 97	d							14 28			14 50											15 28	
Kirkham & Wesham 97	d							14 37														15 37	
Preston 8 65,97	a		14 37	14 41				14 47	15 02		15 08					15 45						15 47	16 02
	d		14 47					14 49	15 04		15 10			15 23		15 47						15 49	16 04
Leyland	d							14 54	15 09					15 29								15 54	16 09
Buckshaw Parkway	d							14 59			15 17			15 33								15 59	
Chorley	d		14 56					15 03			15 21			15 38		15 56						16 03	
Adlington (Lancashire)	d							15 08														16 08	
Blackrod	d							15 12														16 12	
Horwich Parkway	d							15 16			15 28			15 46								16 16	
Lostock	d							15 20						15 50								16 20	
Southport	d					14 20							14 50				15 20						
Meols Cop	d												14 55										
Bescar Lane	d												15 00										
New Lane	d												15 04										
Burscough Bridge	d					14 32							15 07				15 32						
Hoscar	d												15 11										
Parbold	d					14 37							15 14				15 37						
Appley Bridge	d					14 41							15 18				15 41						
Gathurst	d												15 21										
Kirkby	d						14 28														15 28		
Rainford	d						14 36														15 36		
Upholland	d						14 40														15 40		
Orrell	d						14 43														15 43		
Pemberton	d						14 46														15 46		
Wigan Wallgate	a					14 49	14 54						15 28				15 49				15 54		
	d	14 46				14 51	14 56					15 18	15 30		15 46		15 51				15 56		
Wigan North Western	d								15a24														16a24
Ince	d						14 59														15 59		
Hindley	d					14 56	15 02					15 23	15 35				15 56				16 02		
Westhoughton	d					15 00						15 27					16 00						
Bolton	a	15 02	15 08			15 12		15 25			15 34	15 38		15 55	16 02	16 08	16 12					16 25	
	d	15 03	15 08			15 13		15 25		15 31	15 35	15 39		15 56	16 03	16 08	16 13			16 17		16 25	
Moses Gate	d											15 42											
Farnworth	d											15 44											
Kearsley	d											15 46											
Daisy Hill	d						15 07						15 39								16 07		
Hag Fold	d						15 10														16 10		
Atherton	d						15 13						15 43								16 13		
Walkden	d						15 18						15 48								16 18		
Moorside	d						15 22														16 22		
Swinton	d						15 24						15 53								16 24		
Salford Crescent	a	15 15				15 25	15 34	15 38		15 43	15 47	15 56	16 02	16 08	16 15		16 25			16 30	16 33	16 38	
	d	15 15				15 26	15 34	15 38		15 44	15 47	15 56	16 03	16 09	16 15		16 26			16 30	16 34	16 38	
Salford Central	d	15 17					15 36	15 41		15 46		15 59	16 05		16 17					16 33	16 37	16 41	
Manchester Victoria ⇌	a	15 25					15 43	15 47		15 55		16 06	16 11		16 23					16 42	16 43	16 47	
Rochdale 41	a	15 51													16 51								
Deansgate ⇌	a					15 29					15 51			16 12									
Manchester Oxford Road	a		15 23			15 31					15 52			16 14		16 23	16 31						
Manchester Piccadilly 10 ⇌	a		15 27			15 35					15 56			16 18		16 27	16 35						
Stockport 84	a													16 34									
Hazel Grove 86	a													16 47									
Buxton 86	a																						
Heald Green 85	a										16 10					16 40							
Manchester Airport 85 ✈	a		15 47			15 53					16 17					16 47	16 53						

A ✠ from Preston
B From Edinburgh
C From Whitehaven
D To Liverpool South Parkway
E From Clitheroe
F From Glasgow Central
G From Leeds to Morecambe
H From Carlisle
I To Liverpool Lime Street

Table 82

Saturdays from 6 October

Barrow-in-Furness, Blackpool North, Preston, Southport, Kirkby and Wigan - Bolton - Manchester

Network Diagram - see first Page of Table 82

		TP	NT	NT	NT	NT	TP	NT	TP	NT	NT	NT	NT	TP	NT	NT	NT	NT	TP	NT	NT	NT	NT
		◇1 ⊼					◇1 A ⊼		◇1			B	C	◇1 ⊼				C	◇1 ⊼				B
Barrow-in-Furness	d								16 22														
Roose	d																						
Dalton	d								16 31														
Ulverston	d								16 39														
Cark	d								16 47														
Kents Bank	d																						
Grange-over-Sands	d								16 54														
Arnside	d								17 00														
Silverdale	d								17 04														
Carnforth	d								17 11														
Windermere 83	d																						
Oxenholme Lake District 65	d						16 07																
Lancaster [6] 65	a						16 26		17 19														
	d						16 26		17 20														
Blackpool North 97	d	15 44									16 20	16 35		16 40					17 20				17 37
Layton 97	d										16 23			16 43					17 23				
Poulton-le-Fylde 97	d	15 50									16 28			16 48					17 27				
Kirkham & Wesham 97	d										16 37			16 57									
Preston [8] 65,97	a	16 08					16 45		17 39		16 47	17 02		17 08					17 45				18 02
	d	16 10			16 23		16 47				16 49	17 04		17 10			17 23		17 47			17 56	18 04
Leyland	d				16 29						16 54	17 09					17 29					18 01	18 09
Buckshaw Parkway	d	16 17			16 33						16 59			17 17			17 33					18 05	
Chorley	d	16 21			16 38		16 56				17 03			17 21			17 38		17 56			18 09	
Adlington (Lancashire)	d										17 08											18 15	
Blackrod	d										17 12											18 19	
Horwich Parkway	d	16 28			16 46						17 16			17 28			17 46					18 21	
Lostock	d				16 50						17 20						17 50						
Southport	d			15 56				16 20								16 50				17 20			
Meols Cop	d			16 01												16 55				17 25			
Bescar Lane	d															17 00							
New Lane	d															17 04							
Burscough Bridge	d			16 09				16 32								17 07				17 33			
Hoscar	d															17 11							
Parbold	d			16 14				16 37								17 14				17 38			
Appley Bridge	d			16 18				16 41								17 18				17 42			
Gathurst	d			16 21												17 21							
Kirkby	d									16 28											17 28		
Rainford	d									16 36											17 36		
Upholland	d									16 40											17 40		
Orrell	d									16 43											17 43		
Pemberton	d									16 46											17 46		
Wigan Wallgate	a			16 28				16 49		16 54						17 28				17 50	17 55		
	d		16 18	16 30		16 46		16 51		16 56					17 18	17 30				17 52	17 57		
Wigan North Western	d											17a24											18a24
Ince	d									16 59											18 00		
Hindley	d		16 23	16 35				16 56		17 02					17 23	17 35					18 03		
Westhoughton	d		16 27					17 00							17 27					18 00			
Bolton	a	16 34	16 38		16 55	17 02	17 08	17 12			17 25			17 34	17 38		17 55		18 08	18 12		18 30	
	d	16 35	16 39		16 56	17 03	17 08	17 13			17 25		17 31	17 35	17 39		17 56	18 02	18 08	18 13		18 30	
Moses Gate	d		16 42												17 42								
Farnworth	d		16 44												17 44								
Kearsley	d		16 46												17 46								
Daisy Hill	d			16 39						17 06						17 39					18 07		
Hag Fold	d									17 09											18 10		
Atherton	d			16 43						17 12						17 43					18 13		
Walkden	d			16 48						17 17						17 48					18 18		
Moorside	d									17 21											18 22		
Swinton	d			16 53						17 23						17 53					18 24		
Salford Crescent	a	16 47	16 56	17 02	17 08	17 15		17 25		17 33	17 38		17 43	17 47	17 56	18 02	18 08	18 14		18 25	18 33	18 43	
	d	16 47	16 56	17 03	17 09	17 15		17 26		17 33	17 38		17 44	17 47	17 56	18 03	18 09	18 15		18 26	18 33	18 43	
Salford Central	d		16 59	17 05		17 17				17 36	17 41		17 46		17 59	18 05		18 17			18 36	18 46	
Manchester Victoria ⇌	a		17 06	17 11		17 23				17 43	17 47		17 54		18 06	18 11		18 26			18 43	18 52	
Rochdale 41	a					17 51												18 49					
Deansgate ⇌	a	16 51			17 12			17 29						17 51			18 12						
Manchester Oxford Road	a	16 52			17 14		17 23	17 31						17 52			18 14		18 23	18 31			
Manchester Piccadilly [10] ⇌	a	16 56			17 18		17 27	17 35						17 56			18 18		18 27	18 35			
Stockport 84	a				17 34												18 34						
Hazel Grove 86	a				17 43												18 47						
Buxton 86	a				18 27																		
Heald Green 85	a	17 10					17 41							18 10					18 40				
Manchester Airport 85 ✈	a	17 17					17 48	17 53						18 17					18 47	18 53			

A From Edinburgh
B To Liverpool Lime Street
C From Clitheroe

Table 82

Saturdays from 6 October

Barrow-in-Furness, Blackpool North, Preston, Southport, Kirkby and Wigan - Bolton - Manchester

Network Diagram - see first Page of Table 82

		TP	TP	NT	NT	NT	TP	NT	NT	NT	NT	NT	NT	NT	TP	NT	NT	TP	NT	NT	NT	NT
		◇1 A ⊼	◇1			B	◇1 C ⊼		D	E			F	B	◇1		G	◇1 H ⊼			F	B
Barrow-in-Furness	d		17 21							18 03												
Roose	d									18 07												
Dalton	d		17 30							18 13												
Ulverston	d		17 38							18 21												
Cark	d		17 46							18 29												
Kents Bank	d									18 33												
Grange-over-Sands	d		17 53							18 37												
Arnside	d		17 59							18 43												
Silverdale	d									18 47												
Carnforth	d		18 09						18 26	18 55												
Windermere 83	d	17 06																				
Oxenholme Lake District 65	d	17 30																19 10				
Lancaster [6] 65	a	17 47	18 16						18 38	19 05								19 26				
	d	17 48	18 17				18 26			19 06								19 26				
Blackpool North 97	d											18 20	18 37		18 44					19 20	19 37	
Layton 97	d											18 23								19 23		
Poulton-le-Fylde 97	d											18 28			18 50					19 28		
Kirkham & Wesham 97	d											18 37								19 37		
Preston [8] 65,97	a	18 06	18 36				18 45			19 31		18 47	19 00		19 08			19 45		19 47	20 02	
	d	18 08					18 47					18 49	19 04		19 10			19 47		19 49	20 04	
Leyland	d											18 54	19 09							19 54	20 09	
Buckshaw Parkway	d	18 15										18 59			19 17					19 59		
Chorley	d	18 19					18 56					19 03			19 21			19 56		20 03		
Adlington (Lancashire)	d											19 08								20 08		
Blackrod	d											19 12								20 12		
Horwich Parkway	d	18 26										19 16			19 28					20 16		
Lostock	d	18 30										19 20								20 20		
Southport	d				17 50			18 14								18 56			19 19			
Meols Cop	d				17 55			18 19								19 01			19 24			
Bescar Lane	d				18 00			18 24														
New Lane	d				18 04			18 28														
Burscough Bridge	d				18 07			18 30								19 09			19 32			
Hoscar	d				18 11			18 34														
Parbold	d				18 14			18 37								19 14			19 37			
Appley Bridge	d				18 18			18 41								19 18			19 41			
Gathurst	d				18 21			18 44								19 21			19 44			
Kirkby	d										18 28											
Rainford	d										18 36											
Upholland	d										18 40											
Orrell	d										18 43											
Pemberton	d										18 46											
Wigan Wallgate	a				18 28			18 51			18 54					19 28			19 51			
	d			18 18	18 30			18 52			18 56					19 30			19 53			
Wigan North Western	d												19a24								20a24	
Ince	d										18 59											
Hindley	d			18 23	18 35			18 57			19 02					19 35			19 58			
Westhoughton	d			18 27				19 01											20 02			
Bolton	a	18 34		18 38			19 08	19 12				19 25			19 34			20 08	20 12	20 25		
	d	18 35		18 39		19 02	19 08	19 13				19 25		19 31	19 35		20 02	20 08	20 13	20 25		20 31
Moses Gate	d			18 42																		
Farnworth	d			18 44																		
Kearsley	d			18 46																		
Daisy Hill	d				18 39						19 06					19 39						
Hag Fold	d										19 09											
Atherton	d				18 43						19 12					19 43						
Walkden	d				18 48						19 17					19 48						
Moorside	d										19 21											
Swinton	d				18 53						19 23					19 53						
Salford Crescent	a	18 47		18 56	19 02	19 14		19 25			19 33	19 38		19 44	19 47	20 02	20 15		20 25	20 38		20 43
	d	18 47		18 56	19 03	19 15		19 26			19 33	19 38		19 44	19 47	20 03	20 15		20 26	20 38		20 44
Salford Central	d			18 59	19 05	19 17					19 36	19 41		19 46		20 05	20 17			20 41		20 46
Manchester Victoria ⇌	a			19 06	19 11	19 24					19 43	19 47		19 54		20 11	20 25			20 47		20 53
Rochdale 41	a																					
Deansgate ⇌	a	18 51						19 29							19 51				20 29			
Manchester Oxford Road	a	18 52					19 23	19 31							19 52			20 23	20 31			
Manchester Piccadilly [10] ⇌	a	18 56					19 27	19 35							19 56			20 27	20 35			
Stockport 84	a																					
Hazel Grove 86	a																					
Buxton 86	a																					
Heald Green 85	a	19 10													20 10							
Manchester Airport 85 ✈	a	19 17					19 50	19 53							20 17			20 47	20 53			

A ⊼ from Preston
B From Clitheroe
C From Edinburgh
D From Leeds to Morecambe
E From Carlisle
F To Liverpool Lime Street
G From Blackburn
H From Glasgow Central

Table 82

Saturdays
from 6 October

Barrow-in-Furness, Blackpool North, Preston, Southport, Kirkby and Wigan - Bolton - Manchester

Network Diagram - see first Page of Table 82

			TP ◇1	TP ◇1 A ✕	NT	NT	NT	NT B	NT C		TP ◇1	TP ◇1	NT	NT	NT	TP ◇1	NT	NT C	TP ◇1		NT B	NT	NT	NT	TP ◇1 D	TP ◇1 E
Barrow-in-Furness		d									19 33						21 43									
Roose		d									19 37						21 47									
Dalton		d									19 44						21 53									
Ulverston		d									19 52						22 01									
Cark		d									20 00						22 09									
Kents Bank		d									20 04						22 13									
Grange-over-Sands		d									20 08						22 17									
Arnside		d									20 14						22 23									
Silverdale		d									20 18						22 27									
Carnforth		d									20 25						22 35									
Windermere	83	d														21 40										
Oxenholme Lake District	65	d		20 13												22 01										
Lancaster 6	65	a		20 26							20 34					22 17	22 45									
		d		20 26							20 35					22 17	22 46									
Blackpool North	97	d	19 44				20 20	20 37				20 42			21 20				21 44		22 14			22 20	22 44	22 44
Layton	97	d					20 23								21 23									22 23		
Poulton-le-Fylde	97	d	19 50				20 28					20 48			21 28				21 50					22 28	22 50	22 50
Kirkham & Wesham	97	d					20 37								21 37									22 37		
Preston 8	65,97	a	20 08	20 45			20 47	21 01			20 53	21 06			21 47	22 38	23 11		22 08		22 41			22 47	23 07	23 08
		d	20 10	20 47			20 49	21 04			21 10				21 49				22 10		22 43			22 49	23 09	23 10
Leyland		d					20 54	21 09							21 54						22 48			22 54		
Buckshaw Parkway		d	20 17				20 59								21 59				22 17					22 59	23 17	23 17
Chorley		d	20 21	20 56			21 03				21 21				22 03				22 21					23 03	23 21	23 21
Adlington (Lancashire)		d					21 08								22 08									23 08		
Blackrod		d					21 12								22 12									23 12		
Horwich Parkway		d	20 28				21 16				21 28				22 16				22 28					23 16	23 28	23 28
Lostock		d					21 20								22 20									23 20		
Southport		d				20 19								21 19									22 18			
Meols Cop		d				20 24								21 24									22 23			
Bescar Lane		d																					22 28			
New Lane		d																					22 32			
Burscough Bridge		d				20 32								21 32									22 34			
Hoscar		d																					22 38			
Parbold		d				20 37								21 37									22 41			
Appley Bridge		d				20 41								21 41									22 45			
Gathurst		d				20 44								21 44									22 48			
Kirkby		d																								
Rainford		d																								
Upholland		d																								
Orrell		d																								
Pemberton		d																								
Wigan Wallgate		a				20 51								21 51									22 53			
		d			20 27	20 53							21 25	21 53								22 25	22 55			
Wigan North Western		d						21a23													23a02					
Ince		d			20 30								21 28									22 28				
Hindley		d			20 33	20 58							21 31	21 58								22 31	23 00			
Westhoughton		d				21 02								22 02									23 04			
Bolton		a	20 34	21 08		21 12	21 25				21 34			22 10	22 25				22 34				23 12	23 25	23 34	23 34
		d	20 35	21 08		21 13	21 25		21 31		21 35			22 11	22 25			22 31	22 35				23 13	23 25	23 35	23 35
Moses Gate		d																								
Farnworth		d																								
Kearsley		d																								
Daisy Hill		d			20 37								21 35									22 35				
Hag Fold		d			20 40								21 38									22 38				
Atherton		d			20 43								21 41									22 41				
Walkden		d			20 49								21 47									22 47				
Moorside		d			20 52								21 50									22 50				
Swinton		d			20 55								21 53									22 53				
Salford Crescent		a	20 47		21 02	21 25	21 38		21 43		21 47		22 02	22 25	22 38			22 43	22 47			23 02	23 25	23 38	23 47	23 47
		d	20 47		21 03	21 26	21 38		21 44		21 47		22 03	22 26	22 38			22 44	22 47			23 03	23 26	23 38	23 47	23 47
Salford Central		d			21 05		21 41		21 46				22 05	22 28	22 41			22 46				23 05				
Manchester Victoria	⇌	a			21 11		21 47		21 53				22 11	22 34	22 47			22 53				23 13		23 47		
Rochdale	41	a																								
Deansgate	⇌	a	20 51			21 29					21 51								22 51				23 29			
Manchester Oxford Road		a	20 52	21 23		21 31					21 52								22 52				23 31			
Manchester Piccadilly 10	⇌	a	20 56	21 27		21 35					21 56								22 56				23 39		23 53	23 53
Stockport	84	a																								
Hazel Grove	86	a																								
Buxton	86	a																								
Heald Green	85	a	21 10								22 09								23 09						00 16	00 16
Manchester Airport	85 ✈	a	21 17	21 47		21 53					22 17								23 17						00 23	00 23

A From Edinburgh
B To Liverpool Lime Street
C From Clitheroe
D from 27 October
E 6 October, 13 October, 20 October

Table 82

Saturdays
from 6 October

Barrow-in-Furness, Blackpool North, Preston, Southport, Kirkby and Wigan - Bolton - Manchester

Network Diagram - see first Page of Table 82

			NT	NT A	NT
Barrow-in-Furness		d			
Roose		d			
Dalton		d			
Ulverston		d			
Cark		d			
Kents Bank		d			
Grange-over-Sands		d			
Arnside		d			
Silverdale		d			
Carnforth		d			
Windermere	83	d			
Oxenholme Lake District	65	d			
Lancaster 6	65	a			
		d			
Blackpool North	97	d			23 02
Layton	97	d			23 05
Poulton-le-Fylde	97	d			23 10
Kirkham & Wesham	97	d			23 19
Preston 8	65,97	a			23 29
		d			23 31
Leyland		d			23 36
Buckshaw Parkway		d			23 41
Chorley		d			23 45
Adlington (Lancashire)		d			23 50
Blackrod		d			23 54
Horwich Parkway		d			23 58
Lostock		d			00 02
Southport		d	23 10		
Meols Cop		d	23 15		
Bescar Lane		d			
New Lane		d			
Burscough Bridge		d	23 23		
Hoscar		d			
Parbold		d	23 28		
Appley Bridge		d	23 32		
Gathurst		d	23 35		
Kirkby		d			
Rainford		d			
Upholland		d			
Orrell		d			
Pemberton		d			
Wigan Wallgate		a	23 44		
		d			
Wigan North Western		d			
Ince		d			
Hindley		d			
Westhoughton		d			
Bolton		a			00 07
		d		23 38	00 07
Moses Gate		d			
Farnworth		d			
Kearsley		d			
Daisy Hill		d			
Hag Fold		d			
Atherton		d			
Walkden		d			
Moorside		d			
Swinton		d			
Salford Crescent		a		23 48	
		d		23 51	
Salford Central		d			
Manchester Victoria	⇌	a		00 01	00 26
Rochdale	41	a			
Deansgate	⇌	a			
Manchester Oxford Road		a			
Manchester Piccadilly 10	⇌	a			
Stockport	84	a			
Hazel Grove	86	a			
Buxton	86	a			
Heald Green	85	a			
Manchester Airport	85 ✈	a			

A From Clitheroe

Table 82

Sundays until 24 June

Barrow-in-Furness, Blackpool North, Preston, Southport, Kirkby and Wigan - Bolton - Manchester

Network Diagram - see first Page of Table 82

		TP	NT	TP	TP	TP	TP	NT	NT	NT		NT	TP	NT	NT	NT	TP	NT	NT	TP		NT	NT	NT	TP
		◇■				◇■	◇■						◇■				◇■			◇■					◇■
						A		B		C		D		E			A		F			E		B	
				🚌	🚌					⌶															
Barrow-in-Furness	d																								09 17
Roose	d																								09 21
Dalton	d																								09 28
Ulverston	d																								09 36
Cark	d																								09 44
Kents Bank	d																								09 48
Grange-over-Sands	d																								09 52
Arnside	d																								09 58
Silverdale	d																								10 02
Carnforth	d																								10 09
Windermere 83	d																								
Oxenholme Lake District 65	d																								
Lancaster ■ 65	a																								10 17
	d																								10 21
Blackpool North 97	d	22p44	23p02	03 20	05 20		07 48		08 20	08 36			08 44	08 50				09 20		09 44		09 50			
Layton 97	d		23p05						08 23									09 23							
Poulton-le-Fylde 97	d	22p50	23p10				07 54		08 28	08 42			08 50	08 56				09 28		09 50		09 56			
Kirkham & Wesham 97	d		23p19						08 37	08 51								09 37							
Preston ■ 65,97	a	23p08	23p29				08 12		08 47	09 02			09 08	09 14				09 47		10 08		10 14			10 40
	d	23p10	23p31	04u00	06u00		08 14		08 49				09 10	09 15				09 49		10 10		10 15			10 47
Leyland	d		23p36						08 54					09 21				09 54				10 21			
Buckshaw Parkway	d	23p17	23p41						08 59				09 17					09 59		10 17					
Chorley	d	23p21	23p45				08 23		09 03				09 21					10 03		10 21					10 56
Adlington (Lancashire)	d		23p50						09 08									10 08							
Blackrod	d		23p54						09 12									10 12							
Horwich Parkway	d	23p28	23p58				08 30		09 16				09 28					10 16		10 28					
Lostock	d		00 02						09 20									10 20							
Southport	d															09 10								10 05	
Meols Cop	d															09 15								10 10	
Bescar Lane	d																								
New Lane	d																								
Burscough Bridge	d															09 23								10 18	
Hoscar	d																								
Parbold	d															09 28								10 23	
Appley Bridge	d															09 32								10 27	
Gathurst	d															09 35								10 30	
Kirkby	d																								
Rainford	d																								
Upholland	d																								
Orrell	d																								
Pemberton	d																								
Wigan Wallgate	a															09 40								10 35	
	d							08 40							09 15	09 41							10 15	10 36	
Wigan North Western	d													09a35								10a36			
Ince	d														09 18								10 18		
Hindley	d							08 45							09 22	09 46							10 22	10 41	
Westhoughton	d							08 49								09 51								10 46	
Bolton	a	23p34	00 07				08 37	08 57	09 25				09 34			09 59		10 25		10 34				10 54	11 08
	d	23p35	00 07	04u35	06u35		08 37	08 58	09 25			09 31	09 35			09 59		10 25	10 31	10 35				10 54	11 08
Moses Gate	d																								
Farnworth	d																								
Kearsley	d																								
Daisy Hill	d														09 26								10 26		
Hag Fold	d														09 29								10 29		
Atherton	d														09 31								10 31		
Walkden	d														09 37								10 37		
Moorside	d														09 40								10 40		
Swinton	d														09 43								10 43		
Salford Crescent	a	23p47					08 49	09 10	09 38			09 43	09 47		09 50	10 12		10 38	10 43	10 47			10 50	11 07	
	d	23p47				08 31	08 50	09 11	09 38			09 44	09 47		09 51	10 12	10 15	10 38	10 44	10 47			10 51	11 07	
Salford Central	d																								
Manchester Victoria ⇌	a		00 26						09 45			09 53			09 57			10 45	10 52				10 57		
Rochdale 41	a																								
Deansgate ⇌	a						08 53	09 14					09 51			10 16				10 51				11 11	
Manchester Oxford Road	a						08 55	09 17					09 52			10 18				10 52				11 13	11 23
Manchester Piccadilly ■ ⇌	a	23p53		05b00	07b00	08 36	08 59	09 21					09 56			10 22	10 25			10 56				11 19	11 27
Stockport 84	a							09 31								10 33								11 30	
Hazel Grove 86	a																								
Buxton 86	a																								
Heald Green 85	a	00 16																							
Manchester Airport 85 ✈	a	00 23		05 25	07 25	08 55	09 17						10 17				10 41			11 17					11 47

A From York
B To Chester
C To Carlisle
D From Blackburn
E To Liverpool Lime Street
F From Clitheroe
b Stops to pick up only

The Sunday service between Wigan Wallgate and Manchester Victoria via Atherton is funded by TfGM and will operate whilst funding exists

Table 82

Sundays until 24 June

Barrow-in-Furness, Blackpool North, Preston, Southport, Kirkby and Wigan - Bolton - Manchester

Network Diagram - see first Page of Table 82

		NT	NT	NT	TP	NT		NT	NT	TP	NT	NT	TP	NT	NT	NT		TP	NT	NT	NT	TP	NT	NT	NT
					◇■					◇■			◇■					◇■				◇■			
			A	B		C						B		C		D		E		A	B		C		
													⌶					⌶							
Barrow-in-Furness	d									10 30															
Roose	d																								
Dalton	d																								
Ulverston	d									10 46															
Cark	d																								
Kents Bank	d																								
Grange-over-Sands	d									10 58															
Arnside	d									11 04															
Silverdale	d																								
Carnforth	d		10 31							11 14										12 35					
Windermere 83	d																								
Oxenholme Lake District 65	d																	12 10							
Lancaster ■ 65	a		10 40							11 22								12 26		12 44					
	d									11 22								12 26							
Blackpool North 97	d	10 20			10 44	10 50					11 20		11 44	11 50					12 20			12 44	12 50		
Layton 97	d	10 23									11 23								12 23						
Poulton-le-Fylde 97	d	10 28			10 50	10 56					11 28		11 50	11 56					12 28			12 50	12 56		
Kirkham & Wesham 97	d	10 37									11 37								12 37						
Preston ■ 65,97	a	10 47			11 08	11 14				11 42	11 47		12 08	12 14				12 45	12 47			13 08	13 14		
	d	10 49			11 10	11 15				11 47	11 49		12 10	12 15				12 47	12 49			13 10	13 15		
Leyland	d	10 54				11 21					11 54			12 21					12 54				13 21		
Buckshaw Parkway	d	10 59			11 17						11 59		12 17						12 59			13 17			
Chorley	d	11 03			11 21					11 56	12 03		12 21					12 56	13 03			13 21			
Adlington (Lancashire)	d	11 08									12 08								13 08						
Blackrod	d	11 12									12 12								13 12						
Horwich Parkway	d	11 16			11 28						12 16		12 28						13 16			13 28			
Lostock	d	11 20									12 20								13 20						
Southport	d								11 05							12 05									13 05
Meols Cop	d								11 10							12 10									13 10
Bescar Lane	d																								
New Lane	d																								
Burscough Bridge	d								11 18							12 18									13 18
Hoscar	d																								
Parbold	d								11 23							12 23									13 23
Appley Bridge	d								11 27							12 27									13 27
Gathurst	d								11 30							12 30									13 30
Kirkby	d																								
Rainford	d																								
Upholland	d																								
Orrell	d																								
Pemberton	d																								
Wigan Wallgate	a								11 35							12 35									13 35
	d							11 15	11 36						12 15	12 36								13 15	13 36
Wigan North Western	d					11a35								12a35									13a35		
Ince	d							11 18							12 18									13 18	
Hindley	d							11 22	11 41						12 22	12 41								13 22	13 41
Westhoughton	d								11 46							12 46									13 46
Bolton	a	11 25			11 34				11 54	12 08	12 25		12 34			12 54		13 08	13 25			13 34			13 54
	d	11 25		11 31	11 35				11 54	12 08	12 25	12 31	12 35			12 54		13 08	13 25		13 31	13 35			13 54
Moses Gate	d																								
Farnworth	d																								
Kearsley	d																								
Daisy Hill	d							11 26							12 26									13 26	
Hag Fold	d							11 29							12 29									13 29	
Atherton	d							11 31							12 31									13 31	
Walkden	d							11 37							12 37									13 37	
Moorside	d							11 40							12 40									13 40	
Swinton	d							11 43							12 43									13 43	
Salford Crescent	a	11 38		11 43	11 47			11 50	12 07		12 38	12 43	12 47		12 50	13 07			13 38		13 43	13 47		13 50	14 07
	d	11 38		11 43	11 47			11 51	12 07		12 38	12 43	12 47		12 51	13 07			13 38		13 44	13 47		13 51	14 07
Salford Central	d																								
Manchester Victoria ⇌	a	11 45		11 52				11 57			12 45	12 52			12 57				13 45		13 52			13 57	
Rochdale 41	a																								
Deansgate ⇌	a				11 51				12 11				12 51			13 11						13 51			14 11
Manchester Oxford Road	a				11 52				12 13	12 23			12 52			13 13		13 23				13 52			14 13
Manchester Piccadilly ■ ⇌	a				11 56				12 19	12 27			12 59			13 19		13 27				13 56			14 19
Stockport 84	a								12 31							13 30									14 31
Hazel Grove 86	a																								
Buxton 86	a																								
Heald Green 85	a																								
Manchester Airport 85 ✈	a				12 17					12 48			13 17					13 47				14 17			

A From Leeds to Morecambe
B From Clitheroe
C To Liverpool Lime Street
D To Chester
E From Edinburgh

The Sunday service between Wigan Wallgate and Manchester Victoria via Atherton is funded by TfGM and will operate whilst funding exists

Sundays
until 24 June

Barrow-in-Furness, Blackpool North, Preston, Southport, Kirkby and Wigan - Bolton - Manchester

Network Diagram - see first Page of Table 82

		TP		NT	NT	TP	NT	NT	NT	TP	NT	NT		TP	NT	NT	NT	TP	NT	NT	TP	NT		NT	NT
		◇1				◇1				◇1				◇1				◇1			◇1				
					A		B		C	D ⚒		A			B					A		B			C
Barrow-in-Furness	d	12 25																14 25							
Roose	d	12 29																14 29							
Dalton	d	12 36																14 36							
Ulverston	d	12 44																14 44							
Cark	d	12 52																14 52							
Kents Bank	d	12 56																14 56							
Grange-over-Sands	d	13 00																15 00							
Arnside	d	13 06																15 06							
Silverdale	d	13 10																15 10							
Carnforth	d	13 17																15 17							
Windermere 83	d																								
Oxenholme Lake District 65	d									14 10															
Lancaster 6 65	a	13 26								14 26								15 26							
	d	13 26								14 26								15 26							
Blackpool North 97	d			13 20		13 44	13 50				14 20			14 44	14 50				15 20		15 44	15 50			
Layton 97	d			13 23							14 23								15 23						
Poulton-le-Fylde 97	d			13 28		13 50	13 56				14 28			14 50	14 56				15 28		15 50	15 56			
Kirkham & Wesham 97	d			13 37							14 37								15 37						
Preston 8 65,97	a	13 45		13 47		14 08	14 14			14 45	14 47			15 08	15 14			15 45	15 47		16 08	16 14			
	d	13 47		13 49		14 10	14 15			14 47	14 49			15 10	15 15			15 47	15 49		16 10	16 15			
Leyland	d			13 54			14 21				14 54				15 21				15 54			16 21			
Buckshaw Parkway	d			13 59		14 17					14 59			15 17					15 59		16 17				
Chorley	d	13 56		14 03		14 21				14 56	15 03			15 21				15 56	16 03		16 21				
Adlington (Lancashire)	d			14 08							15 08								16 08						
Blackrod	d			14 12							15 11								16 11						
Horwich Parkway	d			14 16		14 28					15 15			15 28					16 15		16 28				
Lostock	d			14 20							15 20								16 20						
Southport	d								14 05								15 05								16 05
Meols Cop	d								14 10								15 10								16 10
Bescar Lane	d																								
New Lane	d																								
Burscough Bridge	d								14 18								15 18								16 18
Hoscar	d																								
Parbold	d								14 23								15 23								16 23
Appley Bridge	d								14 27								15 27								16 27
Gathurst	d								14 30								15 30								16 30
Kirkby	d																								
Rainford	d																								
Upholland	d																								
Orrell	d																								
Pemberton	d																								
Wigan Wallgate	a								14 35								15 35								16 35
	d							14 15	14 36							15 15	15 36							16 15	16 36
Wigan North Western	d						14a35								15a35							16a35			
Ince	d							14 18								15 18								16 18	
Hindley	d							14 22	14 41							15 22	15 41							16 22	16 41
Westhoughton	d								14 46								15 46								16 46
Bolton	a	14 08		14 25		14 34			14 54	15 08	15 25			15 34			15 54	16 08	16 25		16 34				16 54
	d	14 08		14 25	14 31	14 35			14 54	15 08	15 25	15 30		15 35			15 54	16 08	16 25	16 31	16 35				16 54
Moses Gate	d																								
Farnworth	d																								
Kearsley	d																								
Daisy Hill	d							14 26								15 26								16 26	
Hag Fold	d							14 29								15 29								16 29	
Atherton	d							14 31								15 31								16 31	
Walkden	d							14 37								15 37								16 37	
Moorside	d							14 40								15 40								16 40	
Swinton	d							14 43								15 43								16 43	
Salford Crescent	a			14 38	14 43	14 47		14 50	15 07		15 38	15 42		15 47		15 50	16 07		16 38	16 43	16 47			16 50	17 07
	d			14 38	14 43	14 47		14 51	15 07		15 38	15 43		15 47		15 51	16 07		16 38	16 44	16 47			16 51	17 07
Salford Central	d																								
Manchester Victoria ⛴	a			14 45	14 52			14 57			15 45	15 52				15 57			16 45	16 52				16 57	
Rochdale 41	a																								
Deansgate ⛴	a					14 51			15 11					15 51			16 11				16 51				17 11
Manchester Oxford Road	a	14 23				14 52			15 13	15 23				15 52			16 13	16 23			16 52				17 13
Manchester Piccadilly 10 ⛴	a	14 27				14 56			15 19	15 27				15 56			16 19	16 27			16 56				17 19
Stockport 84	a								15 31								16 33								17 30
Hazel Grove 86	a																								
Buxton 86	a																								
Heald Green 85	a																								
Manchester Airport 85 ✈	a	14 47				15 17				15 47				16 17				16 46			17 17				

A From Clitheroe
B To Liverpool Lime Street
C To Chester
D From Edinburgh

The Sunday service between Wigan Wallgate and Manchester Victoria via Atherton is funded by TfGM and will operate whilst funding exists

Sundays
until 24 June

Barrow-in-Furness, Blackpool North, Preston, Southport, Kirkby and Wigan - Bolton - Manchester

Network Diagram - see first Page of Table 82

		TP	NT	NT	TP	NT	TP	NT		NT	NT	TP	NT	NT	TP	NT	NT	TP		NT	NT	TP	TP	NT	NT
		◇1			◇1		◇1					◇1			◇1			◇1				◇1	◇1		
		A ⚒		B		C		D				E ⚒		C		D	F	A ⚒			C			D	B
Barrow-in-Furness	d				16 17																				
Roose	d				16 21																				
Dalton	d				16 28																				
Ulverston	d				16 36																				
Cark	d				16 44																				
Kents Bank	d				16 48																				
Grange-over-Sands	d				16 52																				
Arnside	d				16 58																				
Silverdale	d				17 02																				
Carnforth	d			16 37	17 08																				19 04
Windermere 83	d																					18 01			
Oxenholme Lake District 65	d	16 10										17 07						18 10				18x22			
Lancaster 6 65	a	16 26		16 46	17 17							17 22						18 26				18 37			19 13
	d	16 26			17 17							17 22						18 26				18 38			
Blackpool North 97	d		16 20				16 44	16 50					17 20		17 44	17 50				18 20			18 40	18 50	
Layton 97	d		16 23										17 23							18 23					
Poulton-le-Fylde 97	d		16 28				16 50	16 56					17 28		17 50	17 56				18 28			18 46	18 56	
Kirkham & Wesham 97	d		16 37										17 37							18 37					
Preston 8 65,97	a	16 46	16 47		17 37		17 08	17 14				17 41	17 47		18 08	18 14		18 45		18 47		18 56	19 04	19 14	
	d	16 47	16 49				17 10	17 15				17 47	17 49		18 10	18 15		18 47		18 49		19 10		19 15	
Leyland	d		16 54					17 21					17 54			18 21				18 54				19 21	
Buckshaw Parkway	d		16 59				17 17						17 59		18 17					18 59		19 17			
Chorley	d	16 56	17 03				17 21					17 56	18 03		18 21			18 56		19 03		19 21			
Adlington (Lancashire)	d		17 08										18 08							19 08					
Blackrod	d		17 12										18 12							19 12					
Horwich Parkway	d		17 16				17 28						18 16		18 28					19 16		19 28			
Lostock	d		17 20										18 20							19 20					
Southport	d										17 05						18 05								
Meols Cop	d										17 10						18 10								
Bescar Lane	d																								
New Lane	d																								
Burscough Bridge	d										17 18						18 18								
Hoscar	d																								
Parbold	d										17 23						18 23								
Appley Bridge	d										17 27						18 27								
Gathurst	d										17 30						18 30								
Kirkby	d																								
Rainford	d																								
Upholland	d																								
Orrell	d																								
Pemberton	d																								
Wigan Wallgate	a										17 35						18 35								
	d									17 15	17 36						18 36								
Wigan North Western	d							17a35								18a35								19a35	
Ince	d									17 18															
Hindley	d									17 22	17 41						18 41								
Westhoughton	d										17 46						18 46								
Bolton	a	17 08	17 25				17 34				17 54	18 08	18 25		18 34		18 54	19 08		19 25		19 34			
	d	17 08	17 25			17 30	17 35				17 54	18 08	18 25	18 31	18 35		18 54	19 08		19 25	19 31	19 35			
Moses Gate	d																								
Farnworth	d																								
Kearsley	d																								
Daisy Hill	d									17 26															
Hag Fold	d									17 29															
Atherton	d									17 31															
Walkden	d									17 37															
Moorside	d									17 40															
Swinton	d									17 43															
Salford Crescent	a		17 38			17 42	17 47			17 50	18 07		18 38	18 43	18 47		19 08			19 38	19 44	19 47			
	d		17 38			17 43	17 47			17 51	18 07		18 38	18 44	18 47		19 09			19 38	19 44	19 47			
Salford Central	d																								
Manchester Victoria ⛴	a		17 45			17 52				17 57			18 45	18 52						19 45	19 52				
Rochdale 41	a																								
Deansgate ⛴	a						17 51				18 11				18 51		19 12					19 51			
Manchester Oxford Road	a	17 23					17 52				18 13	18 23			18 52		19 15	19 23				19 52			
Manchester Piccadilly 10 ⛴	a	17 27					17 56				18 19	18 27			18 56		19 19	19 27				19 56			
Stockport 84	a										18 33						19 30								
Hazel Grove 86	a																								
Buxton 86	a																								
Heald Green 85	a																								
Manchester Airport 85 ✈	a	17 47					18 17					18 45			19 17			19 47				20 17			

A From Edinburgh
B From Leeds to Morecambe
C From Clitheroe
D To Liverpool Lime Street
E From Glasgow Central
F To Chester

The Sunday service between Wigan Wallgate and Manchester Victoria via Atherton is funded by TfGM and will operate whilst funding exists

Sundays
until 24 June

Barrow-in-Furness, Blackpool North, Preston, Southport, Kirkby and Wigan - Bolton - Manchester

Network Diagram - see first Page of Table 82

		TP	NT	TP	NT	NT	TP	NT	NT	TP	NT	NT	NT	TP	NT	TP	NT	NT	NT	NT	NT	NT
		◇1		◇1 A 🍴		B	◇1	C	D	◇1 E 🍴		F		◇1 G	B	◇1	C		F			B
Barrow-in-Furness	d	18 17									20 02											
Roose	d	18 21									20 06											
Dalton	d	18 28									20 12											
Ulverston	d	18 36									20 21											
Cark	d	18 44									20 28											
Kents Bank	d	18 48									20 33											
Grange-over-Sands	d	18 52									20 37											
Arnside	d	18 58									20 43											
Silverdale	d	19 02									20 47											
Carnforth	d	19 08									20 54											
Windermere	83 d													20 40								
Oxenholme Lake District	65 d			19 07						20 10				21 01								
Lancaster 6	65 a	19 17		19 22						20 26	21 07			21 18								
	d	19 17		19 22						20 26												
Blackpool North	97 d				19 20		19 44	19 50				20 11	20 20			20 44	20 50		21 13	21 20	21 50	
Layton	97 d				19 23								20 23							21 23		
Poulton-le-Fylde	97 d				19 28		19 50	19 56				20 17	20 28			20 50	20 56		21 19	21 28	21 56	
Kirkham & Wesham	97 d				19 37								20 37							21 37		
Preston 8	65,97 a	19 37		19 41	19 47		20 08	20 14		20 45		20 34	20 47			21 08	21 14		21 36	21 47	22 14	
	d			19 47	19 49		20 10	20 15		20 47			20 49			21 10	21 15			21 49	22 15	
Leyland	d				19 54			20 21					20 54				21 21			21 54	22 21	
Buckshaw Parkway	d				19 59		20 17						20 59			21 17				21 59		
Chorley	d			19 56	20 03		20 21			20 56			21 03			21 21				22 03		
Adlington (Lancashire)	d				20 08								21 08							22 08		
Blackrod	d				20 12								21 12							22 12		
Horwich Parkway	d				20 16		20 28						21 16			21 28				22 16		
Lostock	d				20 20								21 20							22 20		
Southport	d		19 05						20 05									21 05				
Meols Cop	d		19 10						20 10									21 10				
Bescar Lane	d																					
New Lane	d																					
Burscough Bridge	d		19 18						20 18									21 18				
Hoscar	d																					
Parbold	d		19 23						20 23									21 23				
Appley Bridge	d		19 27						20 27									21 27				
Gathurst	d		19 30						20 30									21 30				
Kirkby	d																					
Rainford	d																					
Upholland	d																					
Orrell	d																					
Pemberton	d																					
Wigan Wallgate	a		19 35						20 35									21 35				
	d		19 36						20 36									21 36				
Wigan North Western	d							20a35									21a35				22a36	
Ince	d																					
Hindley	d		19 41						20 41									21 41				
Westhoughton	d		19 46						20 46									21 46				
Bolton	a		19 54	20 08	20 25		20 34		20 54	21 08			21 25			21 34		21 54		22 25		
	d		19 54	20 08	20 25	20 31	20 35		20 54	21 08			21 25		21 31	21 35		21 54		22 25		22 31
Moses Gate	d																					
Farnworth	d																					
Kearsley	d																					
Daisy Hill	d																					
Hag Fold	d																					
Atherton	d																					
Walkden	d																					
Moorside	d																					
Swinton	d																					
Salford Crescent	a		20 07		20 38	20 43	20 47		21 07				21 38		21 43	21 47		22 07		22 38		22 43
	d		20 07		20 38	20 43	20 47		21 07				21 38		21 43	21 47		22 07		22 38		22 44
Salford Central	d																					
Manchester Victoria	⇌ a				20 45	20 52							21 45		21 52					22 45		22 52
Rochdale	41 a																					
Deansgate	⇌ a		20 11				20 51		21 11							21 51		22 11				
Manchester Oxford Road	a		20 13	20 23			20 52		21 13	21 23						21 52		22 13				
Manchester Piccadilly 10	⇌ a		20 19	20 27			20 56		21 19	21 27						21 56		22 19				
Stockport	84 a		20 33						21 30									22 33				
Hazel Grove	86 a																					
Buxton	86 a																					
Heald Green	85 a																					
Manchester Airport	85 ✈ a			20 45			21 16			21 46						22 17						

A From Glasgow Central
B From Clitheroe
C To Liverpool Lime Street
D To Chester
E From Edinburgh
F To Leeds
G To Barrow-in-Furness

The Sunday service between Wigan Wallgate and Manchester Victoria via Atherton is funded by TfGM and will operate whilst funding exists

Sundays
until 24 June

Barrow-in-Furness, Blackpool North, Preston, Southport, Kirkby and Wigan - Bolton - Manchester

Network Diagram - see first Page of Table 82

		TP	NT	NT	NT	TP
		◇1 A 🍴			B	◇1
Barrow-in-Furness	d					
Roose	d					
Dalton	d					
Ulverston	d					
Cark	d					
Kents Bank	d					
Grange-over-Sands	d					
Arnside	d					
Silverdale	d					
Carnforth	d					
Windermere	83 d					
Oxenholme Lake District	65 d					
Lancaster 6	65 a					
	d	22 03				
Blackpool North	97 d			22 44		23 03
Layton	97 d					
Poulton-le-Fylde	97 d			22 50		23 09
Kirkham & Wesham	97 d					23 17
Preston 8	65,97 a	22 23		23 08		23 28
	d	22 29		23 09		23 28
Leyland	d			23 15		23 34
Buckshaw Parkway	d					23 38
Chorley	d	22 38				23 42
Adlington (Lancashire)	d					23 46
Blackrod	d					23 50
Horwich Parkway	d					23 53
Lostock	d					23 57
Southport	d		22 05			
Meols Cop	d		22 10			
Bescar Lane	d					
New Lane	d					
Burscough Bridge	d		22 18			
Hoscar	d					
Parbold	d		22 23			
Appley Bridge	d		22 27			
Gathurst	d		22 30			
Kirkby	d					
Rainford	d					
Upholland	d					
Orrell	d					
Pemberton	d					
Wigan Wallgate	a		22 35			
	d		22 36			
Wigan North Western	d			23a30		
Ince	d					
Hindley	d		22 41			
Westhoughton	d		22 46			
Bolton	a	22 50	22 54			00 02
	d	22 50	22 54		23 31	00 02
Moses Gate	d					
Farnworth	d					
Kearsley	d					
Daisy Hill	d					
Hag Fold	d					
Atherton	d					
Walkden	d					
Moorside	d					
Swinton	d					
Salford Crescent	a	23 02	23 07		23 43	
	d	23 05	23 07		23 43	
Salford Central	d					
Manchester Victoria	⇌ a				23 52	
Rochdale	41 a					
Deansgate	⇌ a	23 08	23 11			
Manchester Oxford Road	a	23 10	23 14			
Manchester Piccadilly 10	⇌ a	23 14	23 19			00 18
Stockport	84 a		23 33			
Hazel Grove	86 a					
Buxton	86 a					
Heald Green	85 a					
Manchester Airport	85 ✈ a	23 30				00 32

A From Edinburgh
B From Clitheroe

The Sunday service between Wigan Wallgate and Manchester Victoria via Atherton is funded by TfGM and will operate whilst funding exists

Table 82

Sundays
1 July to 9 September

Barrow-in-Furness, Blackpool North, Preston, Southport, Kirkby and Wigan - Bolton - Manchester

Network Diagram - see first Page of Table 82

		TP ◇1	NT	TP	TP	TP ◇1	NT	NT	NT	NT	TP ◇1	NT	NT	NT	NT	NT	TP ◇1	NT	NT	NT	TP ◇1	NT	NT
				🚌	🚌		A		B	C		D				E		D		A			F
Barrow-in-Furness	d																				09 17		
Roose	d																				09 21		
Dalton	d																				09 28		
Ulverston	d																				09 36		
Cark	d																				09 44		
Kents Bank	d																				09 48		
Grange-over-Sands	d																				09 52		
Arnside	d																				09 58		
Silverdale	d																				10 02		
Carnforth	d																				10 09		10 31
Windermere 83	d																						
Oxenholme Lake District 65	d																						
Lancaster 6 65	a																				10 17		10 40
	d																				10 21		
Blackpool North 97	d	22p44	23p02	03 20	05 20	07 48		08 20	08 36		08 44	08 50			09 20		09 44	09 50				10 20	
Layton 97	d		23p05					08 23							09 23							10 23	
Poulton-le-Fylde 97	d	22p50	23p10			07 54		08 28	08 42		08 50	08 56			09 28		09 50	09 56				10 28	
Kirkham & Wesham 97	d		23p19					08 37	08 51						09 37							10 37	
Preston 8 65,97	a	23p08	23p29			08 12		08 47	09 02		09 08	09 14			09 47		10 08	10 14			10 40	10 47	
	d	23p10	23p31	04u00	06u00	08 14		08 49			09 10	09 15			09 49		10 10	10 15			10 47	10 49	
Leyland	d		23p36					08 54				09 21			09 54			10 21				10 54	
Buckshaw Parkway	d	23p17	23p41					08 59			09 17				09 59		10 17					10 59	
Chorley	d	23p21	23p45			08 23		09 03			09 21				10 03		10 21				10 56	11 03	
Adlington (Lancashire)	d		23p50					09 08							10 08							11 08	
Blackrod	d		23p54					09 12							10 12							11 12	
Horwich Parkway	d	23p28	23p58			08 30		09 16			09 28				10 16		10 28					11 16	
Lostock	d		00 02					09 20							10 20							11 20	
Southport	d													09 10						10 05			
Meols Cop	d													09 15						10 10			
Bescar Lane	d																						
New Lane	d																						
Burscough Bridge	d													09 23						10 18			
Hoscar	d																						
Parbold	d													09 28						10 23			
Appley Bridge	d													09 32						10 27			
Gathurst	d													09 35						10 30			
Kirkby	d																						
Rainford	d																						
Upholland	d																						
Orrell	d																						
Pemberton	d																						
Wigan Wallgate	a													09 40						10 35			
	d						08 40						09 15	09 41					10 15	10 36			
Wigan North Western	d											09a35						10a36					
Ince	d												09 18						10 18				
Hindley	d						08 45						09 22	09 46					10 22	10 41			
Westhoughton	d						08 49							09 51						10 46			
Bolton	a	23p34	00 07			08 37	08 57	09 25			09 34			09 59	10 25		10 34			10 54	11 08	11 25	
	d	23p35	00 07	04u35	06u35	08 37	08 58	09 25		09 31	09 35			09 59	10 25	10 31	10 35			10 54	11 08	11 25	
Moses Gate	d																						
Farnworth	d																						
Kearsley	d																						
Daisy Hill	d												09 26						10 26				
Hag Fold	d												09 29						10 29				
Atherton	d												09 31						10 31				
Walkden	d												09 37						10 37				
Moorside	d												09 40						10 40				
Swinton	d												09 43						10 43				
Salford Crescent	a	23p47				08 49	09 10	09 38		09 43	09 47		09 50	10 12	10 38	10 43	10 47		10 50	11 07		11 38	
	d	23p47				08 50	09 11	09 38		09 44	09 47		09 51	10 12	10 38	10 44	10 47		10 51	11 07		11 38	
Salford Central	d																						
Manchester Victoria 🚊	a		00 26					09 45		09 53			09 57		10 45	10 52			10 57			11 45	
Rochdale 41	a																						
Deansgate 🚊	a					08 53	09 14				09 51			10 16			10 51			11 11			
Manchester Oxford Road	a					08 55	09 17				09 52			10 18			10 52			11 13	11 23		
Manchester Piccadilly 10 🚊	a	23p53		05b00	07b00	08 59	09 21				09 56			10 22			10 56			11 19	11 27		
Stockport 84	a						09 31							10 33						11 30			
Hazel Grove 86	a																						
Buxton 86	a																						
Heald Green 85	a	00 16																					
Manchester Airport 85 ✈	a	00 23		05 25	07 25	09 17					10 17						11 17				11 47		

A To Chester
B To Carlisle
C From Blackburn
D To Liverpool Lime Street
E From Clitheroe
F From Leeds to Morecambe
b Stops to pick up only

The Sunday service between Wigan Wallgate and Manchester Victoria via Atherton is funded by TfGM and will operate whilst funding exists

Table 82

Sundays
1 July to 9 September

Barrow-in-Furness, Blackpool North, Preston, Southport, Kirkby and Wigan - Bolton - Manchester

Network Diagram - see first Page of Table 82

		NT	TP ◇1	NT	NT	NT	TP ◇1	NT	NT	TP ◇1	NT	NT	NT	TP ◇1	NT	NT	NT	TP ◇1	NT	NT	NT	TP ◇1	NT
		A		B					A		B		C	D		E	A		B				
Barrow-in-Furness	d						10 30															12 25	
Roose	d																					12 29	
Dalton	d																					12 36	
Ulverston	d						10 46															12 44	
Cark	d																					12 52	
Kents Bank	d																					12 56	
Grange-over-Sands	d						10 58															13 00	
Arnside	d						11 04															13 06	
Silverdale	d																					13 10	
Carnforth	d						11 14									12 35						13 17	
Windermere 83	d																						
Oxenholme Lake District 65	d													12 10									
Lancaster 6 65	a						11 22							12 26		12 44						13 26	
	d						11 22							12 26								13 26	
Blackpool North 97	d		10 44	10 50				11 20		11 44	11 50				12 20			12 44	12 50				13 20
Layton 97	d							11 23							12 23								13 23
Poulton-le-Fylde 97	d		10 50	10 56				11 28		11 50	11 56				12 28			12 50	12 56				13 28
Kirkham & Wesham 97	d							11 37							12 37								13 37
Preston 8 65,97	a		11 08	11 14			11 42	11 47		12 08	12 14			12 45	12 47			13 08	13 14			13 45	13 47
	d		11 10	11 15			11 47	11 49		12 10	12 15			12 47	12 49			13 10	13 15			13 47	13 49
Leyland	d			11 21				11 54			12 21				12 54				13 21				13 54
Buckshaw Parkway	d		11 17					11 59		12 17					12 59			13 17					13 59
Chorley	d		11 21				11 56	12 03		12 21				12 56	13 03			13 21				13 56	14 03
Adlington (Lancashire)	d							12 08							13 08								14 08
Blackrod	d							12 12							13 12								14 12
Horwich Parkway	d		11 28					12 16		12 28					13 16			13 28					14 16
Lostock	d							12 20							13 20								14 20
Southport	d					11 05							12 05								13 05		
Meols Cop	d					11 10							12 10								13 10		
Bescar Lane	d																						
New Lane	d																						
Burscough Bridge	d					11 18							12 18								13 18		
Hoscar	d																						
Parbold	d					11 23							12 23								13 23		
Appley Bridge	d					11 27							12 27								13 27		
Gathurst	d					11 30							12 30								13 30		
Kirkby	d																						
Rainford	d																						
Upholland	d																						
Orrell	d																						
Pemberton	d																						
Wigan Wallgate	a					11 35							12 35								13 35		
	d				11 15	11 36						12 15	12 36							13 15	13 36		
Wigan North Western	d			11a35							12a35								13a35				
Ince	d				11 18							12 18								13 18			
Hindley	d				11 22	11 41						12 22	12 41							13 22	13 41		
Westhoughton	d					11 46							12 46								13 46		
Bolton	a		11 34			11 54	12 08	12 25		12 34			12 54	13 08	13 25			13 34			13 54	14 08	14 25
	d	11 31	11 35			11 54	12 08	12 25	12 31	12 35			12 54	13 08	13 25		13 31	13 35			13 54	14 08	14 25
Moses Gate	d																						
Farnworth	d																						
Kearsley	d																						
Daisy Hill	d				11 26							12 26								13 26			
Hag Fold	d				11 29							12 29								13 29			
Atherton	d				11 31							12 31								13 31			
Walkden	d				11 37							12 37								13 37			
Moorside	d				11 40							12 40								13 40			
Swinton	d				11 43							12 43								13 43			
Salford Crescent	a	11 43	11 47		11 50	12 07		12 38	12 43	12 47		12 50	13 07		13 38		13 43	13 47		13 50	14 07		14 38
	d	11 43	11 47		11 51	12 07		12 38	12 43	12 47		12 51	13 07		13 38		13 44	13 47		13 51	14 07		14 38
Salford Central	d																						
Manchester Victoria 🚊	a	11 52			11 57			12 45	12 52			12 57			13 45		13 52			13 57			14 45
Rochdale 41	a																						
Deansgate 🚊	a		11 51			12 11				12 51			13 11					13 51			14 11		
Manchester Oxford Road	a		11 52			12 13	12 23			12 52			13 13	13 23				13 52			14 13	14 23	
Manchester Piccadilly 10 🚊	a		11 56			12 19	12 27			12 59			13 19	13 27				13 56			14 19	14 27	
Stockport 84	a					12 31							13 30								14 31		
Hazel Grove 86	a																						
Buxton 86	a																						
Heald Green 85	a																						
Manchester Airport 85 ✈	a		12 17				12 48			13 17				13 47				14 17				14 47	

A From Clitheroe
B To Liverpool Lime Street
C To Chester
D From Edinburgh
E From Leeds to Morecambe

The Sunday service between Wigan Wallgate and Manchester Victoria via Atherton is funded by TfGM and will operate whilst funding exists

Table 82

Sundays
1 July to 9 September

Barrow-in-Furness, Blackpool North, Preston, Southport, Kirkby and Wigan - Bolton - Manchester

Network Diagram - see first Page of Table 82

		NT A		TP ◇1	NT B	NT	NT C	TP ◇1 D ⌶	NT	NT A	TP ◇1	NT B		NT	NT	TP ◇1	NT	NT A	TP ◇1	NT B	NT	NT C		TP ◇1 D ⌶	NT
Barrow-in-Furness	d															14 25									
Roose	d															14 29									
Dalton	d															14 36									
Ulverston	d															14 44									
Cark	d															14 52									
Kents Bank	d															14 56									
Grange-over-Sands	d															15 00									
Arnside	d															15 06									
Silverdale	d															15 10									
Carnforth	d															15 17									
Windermere 83	d																								
Oxenholme Lake District 65	d							14 10																16 10	
Lancaster 8 65	a							14 26								15 26								16 26	
	d							14 26								15 26								16 26	
Blackpool North 97	d			13 44	13 50				14 20		14 44	14 50					15 20		15 44	15 50					16 20
Layton 97	d								14 23								15 23								16 23
Poulton-le-Fylde 97	d			13 50	13 56				14 28		14 50	14 56					15 28		15 50	15 56					16 28
Kirkham & Wesham 97	d								14 37								15 37								16 37
Preston 8 65,97	a			14 08	14 14			14 45	14 47		15 08	15 14				15 45	15 47		16 08	16 14				16 46	16 47
	d			14 10	14 15			14 47	14 49		15 10	15 15				15 47	15 49		16 10	16 15				16 47	16 49
Leyland	d				14 21				14 54			15 21					15 54			16 21					16 54
Buckshaw Parkway	d			14 17					14 59		15 17						15 59		16 17						16 59
Chorley	d			14 21				14 56	15 03		15 21					15 56	16 03		16 21					16 56	17 03
Adlington (Lancashire)	d								15 08								16 08								17 08
Blackrod	d								15 11								16 11								17 12
Horwich Parkway	d			14 28					15 15		15 28						16 15		16 28						17 16
Lostock	d								15 20								16 20								17 20
Southport	d						14 05								15 05							16 05			
Meols Cop	d						14 10								15 10							16 10			
Bescar Lane	d																								
New Lane	d																								
Burscough Bridge	d						14 18								15 18							16 18			
Hoscar	d																								
Parbold	d						14 23								15 23							16 23			
Appley Bridge	d						14 27								15 27							16 27			
Gathurst	d						14 30								15 30							16 30			
Kirkby	d																								
Rainford	d																								
Upholland	d																								
Orrell	d																								
Pemberton	d																								
Wigan Wallgate	a						14 35								15 35							16 35			
	d					14 15	14 36							15 15	15 36						16 15	16 36			
Wigan North Western	d				14a35							15a35								16a35					
Ince	d					14 18								15 18							16 18				
Hindley	d					14 22	14 41							15 22	15 41						16 22	16 41			
Westhoughton	d						14 46								15 46							16 46			
Bolton	a			14 34			14 54	15 08	15 25		15 34				15 54	16 08	16 25		16 34			16 54		17 08	17 25
	d	14 31		14 35			14 54	15 08	15 25	15 30	15 35				15 54	16 08	16 25	16 31	16 35			16 54		17 08	17 25
Moses Gate	d																								
Farnworth	d																								
Kearsley	d																								
Daisy Hill	d					14 26								15 26							16 26				
Hag Fold	d					14 29								15 29							16 29				
Atherton	d					14 31								15 31							16 31				
Walkden	d					14 37								15 37							16 37				
Moorside	d					14 40								15 40							16 40				
Swinton	d					14 43								15 43							16 43				
Salford Crescent	a	14 43		14 47		14 50	15 07		15 38	15 42	15 47			15 50	16 07		16 38	16 43	16 47		16 50	17 07			17 38
	d	14 43		14 47		14 51	15 07		15 38	15 43	15 47			15 51	16 07		16 38	16 44	16 47		16 51	17 07			17 38
Salford Central	d																								
Manchester Victoria ⇌	a	14 52				14 57			15 45	15 52				15 57			16 45	16 52			16 57				17 45
Rochdale 41	a																								
Deansgate ⇌	a			14 51			15 11				15 51				16 11				16 51			17 11			
Manchester Oxford Road	a			14 52			15 13	15 23			15 52				16 13	16 23			16 52			17 13		17 23	
Manchester Piccadilly 10 ⇌	a			14 56			15 19	15 27			15 56				16 19	16 27			16 56			17 19		17 27	
Stockport 84	a						15 31								16 33							17 30			
Hazel Grove 86	a																								
Buxton 86	a																								
Heald Green 85	a																								
Manchester Airport 85 ✈	a			15 17				15 47			16 17					16 46			17 17					17 47	

A From Clitheroe
B To Liverpool Lime Street
C To Chester
D From Edinburgh

The Sunday service between Wigan Wallgate and Manchester Victoria via Atherton is funded by TfGM and will operate whilst funding exists

Table 82

Sundays
1 July to 9 September

Barrow-in-Furness, Blackpool North, Preston, Southport, Kirkby and Wigan - Bolton - Manchester

Network Diagram - see first Page of Table 82

		NT A	TP ◇1	NT B	TP ◇1	NT C	NT	NT		TP ◇1 D ⌶	NT	TP ◇1 E	NT B	TP ◇1	NT C	NT F	TP ◇1 G ⌶	NT		NT B	TP ◇1	TP ◇1	NT C	NT A	NT
Barrow-in-Furness	d		16 17																						
Roose	d		16 21																						
Dalton	d		16 28																						
Ulverston	d		16 36																						
Cark	d		16 44																						
Kents Bank	d		16 48																						
Grange-over-Sands	d		16 52																						
Arnside	d		16 58																						
Silverdale	d		17 02																						
Carnforth	d	16 37	17 08																					19 04	
Windermere 83	d																				18 01				
Oxenholme Lake District 65	d									17 07							18 10				18x22				
Lancaster 8 65	a	16 46	17 17							17 22							18 26				18 37			19 13	
	d		17 17							17 22							18 26				18 38				
Blackpool North 97	d				16 44	16 50					17 20	17 30		17 44	17 50			18 20				18 40	18 50		
Layton 97	d										17 23							18 23							
Poulton-le-Fylde 97	d				16 50	16 56					17 28			17 50	17 56			18 28				18 46	18 56		
Kirkham & Wesham 97	d										17 37							18 37							
Preston 8 65,97	a		17 37		17 08	17 14				17 41	17 47	17 53		18 08	18 14		18 45	18 47			18 56	19 04	19 14		
	d				17 10	17 15				17 47	17 49			18 10	18 15		18 47	18 49				19 10	19 15		
Leyland	d					17 21					17 54				18 21			18 54					19 21		
Buckshaw Parkway	d				17 17						17 59			18 17				18 59				19 17			
Chorley	d				17 21					17 56	18 03			18 21			18 56	19 03				19 21			
Adlington (Lancashire)	d										18 08							19 08							
Blackrod	d										18 12							19 12							
Horwich Parkway	d				17 28						18 16			18 28				19 16				19 28			
Lostock	d										18 20							19 20							
Southport	d							17 05								18 05									19 05
Meols Cop	d							17 10								18 10									19 10
Bescar Lane	d																								
New Lane	d																								
Burscough Bridge	d							17 18								18 18									19 18
Hoscar	d																								
Parbold	d							17 23								18 23									19 23
Appley Bridge	d							17 27								18 27									19 27
Gathurst	d							17 30								18 30									19 30
Kirkby	d																								
Rainford	d																								
Upholland	d																								
Orrell	d																								
Pemberton	d																								
Wigan Wallgate	a							17 35								18 35									19 35
	d						17 15	17 36								18 36									19 36
Wigan North Western	d					17a35									18a35								19a35		
Ince	d						17 18																		
Hindley	d						17 22	17 41								18 41									19 41
Westhoughton	d							17 46								18 46									19 46
Bolton	a				17 34			17 54		18 08	18 25			18 34		18 54	19 08	19 25				19 34			19 54
	d			17 30	17 35			17 54		18 08	18 25		18 31	18 35		18 54	19 08	19 25		19 31		19 35			19 54
Moses Gate	d																								
Farnworth	d																								
Kearsley	d																								
Daisy Hill	d						17 26																		
Hag Fold	d						17 29																		
Atherton	d						17 31																		
Walkden	d						17 37																		
Moorside	d						17 40																		
Swinton	d						17 43																		
Salford Crescent	a			17 42	17 47		17 50	18 07			18 38		18 43	18 47		19 07		19 38		19 44		19 47			20 07
	d			17 43	17 47		17 51	18 07			18 38		18 44	18 47		19 07		19 38		19 44		19 47			20 07
Salford Central	d																								
Manchester Victoria ⇌	a			17 52			17 57				18 45		18 52					19 45		19 52					
Rochdale 41	a																								
Deansgate ⇌	a				17 51			18 11						18 51		19 11						19 51			20 11
Manchester Oxford Road	a				17 52			18 13		18 23				18 52		19 13	19 23					19 52			20 13
Manchester Piccadilly 10 ⇌	a				17 56			18 19		18 27				18 56		19 19	19 27					19 56			20 19
Stockport 84	a							18 33								19 30									20 33
Hazel Grove 86	a																								
Buxton 86	a																								
Heald Green 85	a																								
Manchester Airport 85 ✈	a				18 17					18 45				19 17			19 47					20 17			

A From Leeds to Morecambe
B From Clitheroe
C To Liverpool Lime Street
D From Glasgow Central
E from 1 July until 29 July, 2 September, 9 September. To Glasgow Central
F To Chester
G From Edinburgh

The Sunday service between Wigan Wallgate and Manchester Victoria via Atherton is funded by TfGM and will operate whilst funding exists

Sundays

1 July to 9 September

Barrow-in-Furness, Blackpool North, Preston, Southport, Kirkby and Wigan - Bolton - Manchester

Network Diagram - see first Page of Table 82

		TP	TP	NT	NT	TP	NT	NT	TP	NT	NT	NT	TP	NT	TP	NT	NT	NT	NT	NT	NT	TP
		◇1	◇1			◇1			◇1				◇1		◇1							◇1
		A	B		C		D	E	F		G		H	C		D		G			C	F
		⌶	⌶						⌶													⌶
Barrow-in-Furness	d	18 17								20 02												
Roose	d	18 21								20 06												
Dalton	d	18 28								20 12												
Ulverston	d	18 36								20 21												
Cark	d	18 44								20 28												
Kents Bank	d	18 48								20 33												
Grange-over-Sands	d	18 52								20 37												
Arnside	d	18 58								20 43												
Silverdale	d	19 02								20 47												
Carnforth	d	19 08								20 54												
Windermere	83 d												20 40									
Oxenholme Lake District	65 d		19 07						20 10				21 01									
Lancaster 6	65 a	19 17	19 22						20 26	21 07			21 18									
	d	19 17	19 22						20 26													22 03
Blackpool North	97 d			19 20		19 44	19 50				20 11	20 20			20 44	20 50		21 13	21 20	21 50		
Layton	97 d			19 23								20 23							21 23			
Poulton-le-Fylde	97 d			19 28		19 50	19 56				20 17	20 28			20 50	20 56		21 19	21 28	21 56		
Kirkham & Wesham	97 d			19 37								20 37							21 37			
Preston 8	65,97 a	19 37	19 41	19 47		20 08	20 14		20 45		20 34	20 47			21 08	21 14		21 36	21 47	22 14		22 22
	d	19 47		19 49		20 10	20 15		20 47			20 49			21 10	21 15			21 49	22 15		22 29
Leyland	d			19 54			20 21					20 54				21 21			21 54	22 21		
Buckshaw Parkway	d			19 59		20 17						20 59			21 17				21 59			
Chorley	d	19 56		20 03		20 21			20 56			21 03			21 21				22 03			22 38
Adlington (Lancashire)	d			20 08								21 08							22 08			
Blackrod	d			20 12								21 12							22 12			
Horwich Parkway	d			20 16		20 28						21 16			21 28				22 16			
Lostock	d			20 20								21 20							22 20			
Southport	d							20 05									21 05					
Meols Cop	d							20 10									21 10					
Bescar Lane	d																					
New Lane	d																					
Burscough Bridge	d							20 18									21 18					
Hoscar	d																					
Parbold	d							20 23									21 23					
Appley Bridge	d							20 27									21 27					
Gathurst	d							20 30									21 30					
Kirkby	d																					
Rainford	d																					
Upholland	d																					
Orrell	d																					
Pemberton	d																					
Wigan Wallgate	a							20 35									21 35					
	d							20 36									21 36					
Wigan North Western	d						20a35									21a35				22a36		
Ince	d																					
Hindley	d							20 41									21 41					
Westhoughton	d							20 46									21 46					
Bolton	a	20 08		20 25		20 34		20 54	21 08			21 25			21 34		21 54		22 25			22 50
	d	20 08		20 25	20 31	20 35		20 54	21 08			21 25		21 31	21 35		21 54		22 25		22 31	22 50
Moses Gate	d																					
Farnworth	d																					
Kearsley	d																					
Daisy Hill	d																					
Hag Fold	d																					
Atherton	d																					
Walkden	d																					
Moorside	d																					
Swinton	d																					
Salford Crescent	a			20 38	20 43	20 47		21 07				21 38		21 43	21 47		22 07		22 38		22 43	23 02
	d			20 38	20 43	20 47		21 07				21 38		21 43	21 47		22 07		22 38		22 44	23 03
Salford Central	d																					
Manchester Victoria	⇌ a			20 45	20 52							21 45		21 52					22 45		22 52	
Rochdale	41 a																					
Deansgate	⇌ a					20 51		21 11							21 51		22 11					23 08
Manchester Oxford Road	a	20 23				20 52		21 13	21 23						21 52		22 13					23 10
Manchester Piccadilly 10	⇌ a	20 27				20 56		21 19	21 27						21 56		22 19					23 14
Stockport	84 a							21 30									22 33					
Hazel Grove	86 a																					
Buxton	86 a																					
Heald Green	85 a																					
Manchester Airport	85 ✈ a	20 47				21 16			21 46						22 17							23 29

A ⌶ from Preston
B From Glasgow Central
C From Clitheroe
D To Liverpool Lime Street
E To Chester
F From Edinburgh
G To Leeds
H To Barrow-in-Furness

The Sunday service between Wigan Wallgate and Manchester Victoria via Atherton is funded by TfGM and will operate whilst funding exists

Sundays

1 July to 9 September

Barrow-in-Furness, Blackpool North, Preston, Southport, Kirkby and Wigan - Bolton - Manchester

Network Diagram - see first Page of Table 82

		NT	NT	NT	TP
					◇1
				A	
Barrow-in-Furness	d				
Roose	d				
Dalton	d				
Ulverston	d				
Cark	d				
Kents Bank	d				
Grange-over-Sands	d				
Arnside	d				
Silverdale	d				
Carnforth	d				
Windermere	83 d				
Oxenholme Lake District	65 d				
Lancaster 6	65 a				
	d				
Blackpool North	97 d		22 44		23 03
Layton	97 d				
Poulton-le-Fylde	97 d		22 50		23 09
Kirkham & Wesham	97 d				23 17
Preston 8	65,97 a		23 08		23 28
	d		23 09		23 28
Leyland	d		23 15		23 34
Buckshaw Parkway	d				23 38
Chorley	d				23 42
Adlington (Lancashire)	d				23 46
Blackrod	d				23 50
Horwich Parkway	d				23 53
Lostock	d				23 57
Southport	d	22 05			
Meols Cop	d	22 10			
Bescar Lane	d				
New Lane	d				
Burscough Bridge	d	22 18			
Hoscar	d				
Parbold	d	22 23			
Appley Bridge	d	22 27			
Gathurst	d	22 30			
Kirkby	d				
Rainford	d				
Upholland	d				
Orrell	d				
Pemberton	d				
Wigan Wallgate	a	22 35			
	d	22 36			
Wigan North Western	d		23a30		
Ince	d				
Hindley	d	22 41			
Westhoughton	d	22 46			
Bolton	a	22 54			00 02
	d	22 54		23 31	00 02
Moses Gate	d				
Farnworth	d				
Kearsley	d				
Daisy Hill	d				
Hag Fold	d				
Atherton	d				
Walkden	d				
Moorside	d				
Swinton	d				
Salford Crescent	a	23 07		23 43	
	d	23 07		23 43	
Salford Central	d				
Manchester Victoria	⇌ a			23 52	
Rochdale	41 a				
Deansgate	⇌ a	23 11			
Manchester Oxford Road	a	23 14			
Manchester Piccadilly 10	⇌ a	23 19			00 18
Stockport	84 a	23 33			
Hazel Grove	86 a				
Buxton	86 a				
Heald Green	85 a				
Manchester Airport	85 ✈ a				00 32

A From Clitheroe

The Sunday service between Wigan Wallgate and Manchester Victoria via Atherton is funded by TfGM and will operate whilst funding exists

Table 82

Sundays
16 September to 30 September

Barrow-in-Furness, Blackpool North, Preston, Southport, Kirkby and Wigan - Bolton - Manchester

Network Diagram - see first Page of Table 82

		TP	NT	TP	TP	TP	TP	TP	NT	NT	NT	NT	TP	NT	NT	NT	NT	NT	TP	NT	NT	NT	TP
		◇1			◇1		◇1	◇1					◇1						◇1				◇1
					A		A		B		C	D		E				F		E		B	
				═		═					⊥												
Barrow-in-Furness	d																						09 17
Roose	d																						09 21
Dalton	d																						09 28
Ulverston	d																						09 36
Cark	d																						09 44
Kents Bank	d																						09 48
Grange-over-Sands	d																						09 52
Arnside	d																						09 58
Silverdale	d																						10 02
Carnforth	d																						10 09
Windermere 83	d																						
Oxenholme Lake District 65	d																						
Lancaster 6 65	a																						10 17
	d																						10 21
Blackpool North 97	d	22p44	23p02	03 20		05 20		07 48		08 20	08 36		08 44	08 50			09 20		09 44	09 50			
Layton 97	d		23p05							08 23							09 23						
Poulton-le-Fylde 97	d	22p50	23p10					07 54		08 28	08 42		08 50	08 56			09 28		09 50	09 56			
Kirkham & Wesham 97	d		23p19							08 37	08 51						09 37						
Preston 8 65,97	a	23p08	23p29					08 12		08 47	09 02		09 08	09 14			09 47		10 08	10 14			10 40
	d	23p10	23p31	04u00		06u00		08 14		08 49			09 10	09 15			09 49		10 10	10 15			10 47
Leyland	d		23p36							08 54				09 21			09 54			10 21			
Buckshaw Parkway	d	23p17	23p41							08 59			09 17				09 59		10 17				
Chorley	d	23p21	23p45					08 23		09 03			09 21				10 03		10 21				10 56
Adlington (Lancashire)	d		23p50							09 08							10 08						
Blackrod	d		23p54							09 12							10 12						
Horwich Parkway	d	23p28	23p58					08 30		09 16			09 28				10 16		10 28				
Lostock	d		00 02							09 20							10 20						
Southport	d															09 10						10 05	
Meols Cop	d															09 15						10 10	
Bescar Lane	d																						
New Lane	d																						
Burscough Bridge	d															09 23						10 18	
Hoscar	d																						
Parbold	d															09 28						10 23	
Appley Bridge	d															09 32						10 27	
Gathurst	d															09 35						10 30	
Kirkby	d																						
Rainford	d																						
Upholland	d																						
Orrell	d																						
Pemberton	d																						
Wigan Wallgate	a															09 40						10 35	
	d								08 40						09 15	09 41					10 15	10 36	
Wigan North Western	d													09a35						10a36			
Ince	d														09 18						10 18		
Hindley	d								08 45						09 22	09 46					10 22	10 41	
Westhoughton	d								08 49							09 51						10 46	
Bolton	a	23p34	00 07					08 37	08 57	09 25			09 34			09 59	10 25		10 34			10 54	11 08
	d	23p35	00 07	04u35		06u35		08 37	08 58	09 25		09 31	09 35			09 59	10 25	10 31	10 35			10 54	11 08
Moses Gate	d																						
Farnworth	d																						
Kearsley	d																						
Daisy Hill	d														09 26						10 26		
Hag Fold	d														09 29						10 29		
Atherton	d														09 31						10 31		
Walkden	d														09 37						10 37		
Moorside	d														09 40						10 40		
Swinton	d														09 43						10 43		
Salford Crescent	a	23p47						08 49	09 10	09 38		09 43	09 47		09 50	10 12	10 38	10 43	10 47		10 50	11 07	
	d	23p47			06 11		07 10	08 50	09 11	09 38		09 44	09 47		09 51	10 12	10 38	10 44	10 47		10 51	11 07	
Salford Central	d																						
Manchester Victoria ⇌	a		00 26							09 45		09 53			09 57		10 45	10 52			10 57		
Rochdale 41	a																						
Deansgate ⇌	a							08 53	09 14				09 51			10 16			10 51			11 11	
Manchester Oxford Road	a							08 55	09 17				09 52			10 18			10 52			11 13	11 23
Manchester Piccadilly 10 ⇌	a	23p53		05b00	06 17	07b00	07 15	08 59	09 21				09 56			10 22			10 56			11 19	11 27
Stockport 84	a								09 31							10 33						11 30	
Hazel Grove 86	a																						
Buxton 86	a																						
Heald Green 85	a	00 16																					
Manchester Airport 85 ✈	a	00 23		05 25	06 35	07 25	07 34	09 17					10 17						11 17				11 47

A From York
B To Chester
C To Carlisle
D From Blackburn
E To Liverpool Lime Street
F From Clitheroe
b Stops to pick up only

The Sunday service between Wigan Wallgate and Manchester Victoria via Atherton is funded by TfGM and will operate whilst funding exists

Table 82

Sundays
16 September to 30 September

Barrow-in-Furness, Blackpool North, Preston, Southport, Kirkby and Wigan - Bolton - Manchester

Network Diagram - see first Page of Table 82

		NT	NT	NT	TP	NT	NT	NT	TP	NT	NT	TP	NT	NT	NT	TP	NT	NT	NT	TP	NT	NT	NT
					◇1				◇1			◇1				◇1				◇1			
			A	B		C					B		C		D	E		A	B		C		
												⊥				⊥							
Barrow-in-Furness	d								10 30														
Roose	d																						
Dalton	d																						
Ulverston	d								10 46														
Cark	d																						
Kents Bank	d																						
Grange-over-Sands	d								10 58														
Arnside	d								11 04														
Silverdale	d																						
Carnforth	d		10 31						11 14									12 35					
Windermere 83	d																						
Oxenholme Lake District 65	d															12 10							
Lancaster 6 65	a		10 40						11 22							12 26		12 44					
	d								11 22							12 26							
Blackpool North 97	d	10 20			10 44	10 50				11 20		11 44	11 50				12 20			12 44	12 50		
Layton 97	d	10 23								11 23							12 23						
Poulton-le-Fylde 97	d	10 28			10 50	10 56				11 28		11 50	11 56				12 28			12 50	12 56		
Kirkham & Wesham 97	d	10 37								11 37							12 37						
Preston 8 65,97	a	10 47			11 08	11 14			11 42	11 47		12 08	12 14			12 45	12 47			13 08	13 14		
	d	10 49			11 10	11 15			11 47	11 49		12 10	12 15			12 47	12 49			13 10	13 15		
Leyland	d	10 54				11 21				11 54			12 21				12 54				13 21		
Buckshaw Parkway	d	10 59			11 17					11 59		12 17					12 59			13 17			
Chorley	d	11 03			11 21				11 56	12 03		12 21				12 56	13 03			13 21			
Adlington (Lancashire)	d	11 08								12 08							13 08						
Blackrod	d	11 12								12 12							13 12						
Horwich Parkway	d	11 16			11 28					12 16		12 28					13 16			13 28			
Lostock	d	11 20								12 20							13 20						
Southport	d							11 05							12 05								13 05
Meols Cop	d							11 10							12 10								13 10
Bescar Lane	d																						
New Lane	d																						
Burscough Bridge	d							11 18							12 18								13 18
Hoscar	d																						
Parbold	d							11 23							12 23								13 23
Appley Bridge	d							11 27							12 27								13 27
Gathurst	d							11 30							12 30								13 30
Kirkby	d																						
Rainford	d																						
Upholland	d																						
Orrell	d																						
Pemberton	d																						
Wigan Wallgate	a							11 35							12 35								13 35
	d						11 15	11 36						12 15	12 36							13 15	13 36
Wigan North Western	d					11a35							12a35								13a35		
Ince	d						11 18							12 18								13 18	
Hindley	d						11 22	11 41						12 22	12 41							13 22	13 41
Westhoughton	d							11 46							12 46								13 46
Bolton	a	11 25			11 34			11 54	12 08	12 25		12 34			12 54	13 08	13 25			13 34			13 54
	d	11 25		11 31	11 35			11 54	12 08	12 25	12 31	12 35			12 54	13 08	13 25		13 31	13 35			13 54
Moses Gate	d																						
Farnworth	d																						
Kearsley	d																						
Daisy Hill	d						11 26							12 26								13 26	
Hag Fold	d						11 29							12 29								13 29	
Atherton	d						11 31							12 31								13 31	
Walkden	d						11 37							12 37								13 37	
Moorside	d						11 40							12 40								13 40	
Swinton	d						11 43							12 43								13 43	
Salford Crescent	a	11 38		11 43	11 47		11 50	12 07		12 38	12 43	12 47		12 50	13 07		13 38		13 43	13 47		13 50	14 07
	d	11 38		11 43	11 47		11 51	12 07		12 38	12 43	12 47		12 51	13 07		13 38		13 44	13 47		13 51	14 07
Salford Central	d																						
Manchester Victoria ⇌	a	11 45		11 52			11 57			12 45	12 52			12 57			13 45		13 52			13 57	
Rochdale 41	a																						
Deansgate ⇌	a				11 51			12 11				12 51			13 11					13 51			14 11
Manchester Oxford Road	a				11 52			12 13	12 23			12 52			13 13	13 23				13 52			14 13
Manchester Piccadilly 10 ⇌	a				11 56			12 21	12 27			12 59			13 19	13 27				13 56			14 19
Stockport 84	a							12 31							13 30								14 31
Hazel Grove 86	a																						
Buxton 86	a																						
Heald Green 85	a																						
Manchester Airport 85 ✈	a				12 17				12 48			13 17				13 47				14 17			

A From Leeds to Morecambe
B From Clitheroe
C To Liverpool Lime Street
D To Chester
E From Edinburgh

The Sunday service between Wigan Wallgate and Manchester Victoria via Atherton is funded by TfGM and will operate whilst funding exists

Barrow-in-Furness, Blackpool North, Preston, Southport, Kirkby and Wigan - Bolton - Manchester

Network Diagram - see first Page of Table 82

Station	Table		TP ◇1	NT	NT	NT A	TP ◇1	NT B	NT	NT C	TP ◇1 D	NT	NT A	TP ◇1	NT B	NT	NT	TP ◇1	NT	NT A	TP ◇1	NT B	NT
Barrow-in-Furness		d	12 25	13 10														14 25					
Roose		d	12 29	13 14														14 29					
Dalton		d	12 36	13 20														14 36					
Ulverston		d	12 44	13 29														14 44					
Cark		d	12 52	13 36														14 52					
Kents Bank		d	12 56	13 41														14 56					
Grange-over-Sands		d	13 00	13 45														15 00					
Arnside		d	13 06	13 51														15 06					
Silverdale		d	13 10	13 55														15 10					
Carnforth		d	13 17	14 02														15 17					
Windermere	83	d																					
Oxenholme Lake District	65	d									14 10												
Lancaster 6	65	a	13 26	14 15							14 26							15 26					
		d	13 26								14 26							15 26					
Blackpool North	97	d			13 20		13 44	13 50				14 20		14 44	14 50				15 20		15 44	15 50	
Layton	97	d			13 23							14 23							15 23				
Poulton-le-Fylde	97	d			13 28		13 50	13 56				14 28		14 50	14 56				15 28		15 50	15 56	
Kirkham & Wesham	97	d			13 37							14 37							15 37				
Preston 8	65,97	a	13 45		13 47		14 08	14 14			14 45	14 47		15 08	15 14			15 45	15 47		16 08	16 14	
		d	13 47		13 49		14 10	14 15			14 47	14 49		15 10	15 15			15 47	15 49		16 10	16 15	
Leyland		d			13 54			14 21				14 54			15 21				15 54			16 21	
Buckshaw Parkway		d			13 59		14 17					14 59		15 17					15 59		16 17		
Chorley		d	13 56		14 03		14 21				14 56	15 03		15 21				15 56	16 03		16 21		
Adlington (Lancashire)		d			14 08							15 08							16 08				
Blackrod		d			14 12							15 11							16 11				
Horwich Parkway		d			14 16		14 28					15 15		15 28					16 15		16 28		
Lostock		d			14 20							15 20							16 20				
Southport		d								14 05							15 05						
Meols Cop		d								14 10							15 10						
Bescar Lane		d																					
New Lane		d																					
Burscough Bridge		d								14 18							15 18						
Hoscar		d																					
Parbold		d								14 23							15 23						
Appley Bridge		d								14 27							15 27						
Gathurst		d								14 30							15 30						
Kirkby		d																					
Rainford		d																					
Upholland		d																					
Orrell		d																					
Pemberton		d																					
Wigan Wallgate		a								14 35							15 35						
		d							14 15	14 36						15 15	15 36						16 15
Wigan North Western		d						14a35							15a35							16a35	
Ince		d							14 18							15 18							16 18
Hindley		d							14 22	14 41						15 22	15 41						16 22
Westhoughton		d								14 46							15 46						
Bolton		a	14 08		14 25		14 34			14 54	15 08	15 25		15 34			15 54	16 08	16 25		16 34		
		d	14 08		14 25	14 31	14 35			14 54	15 08	15 25	15 30	15 35			15 54	16 08	16 25	16 31	16 35		
Moses Gate		d																					
Farnworth		d																					
Kearsley		d																					
Daisy Hill		d							14 26							15 26							16 26
Hag Fold		d							14 29							15 29							16 29
Atherton		d							14 31							15 31							16 31
Walkden		d							14 37							15 37							16 37
Moorside		d							14 40							15 40							16 40
Swinton		d							14 43							15 43							16 43
Salford Crescent		a			14 38	14 43	14 47		14 50	15 07		15 38	15 42	15 47		15 50	16 07		16 38	16 43	16 47		16 50
		d			14 38	14 43	14 47		14 51	15 07		15 38	15 43	15 47		15 51	16 07		16 38	16 44	16 47		16 51
Salford Central		d																					
Manchester Victoria	⇌	a			14 45	14 52			14 57			15 45	15 52			15 57			16 45	16 52			16 57
Rochdale	41	a																					
Deansgate	⇌	a					14 51			15 11				15 51			16 11				16 51		
Manchester Oxford Road		a	14 23				14 52			15 13	15 23			15 52			16 13	16 23			16 52		
Manchester Piccadilly 10	⇌	a	14 27				14 56			15 19	15 27			15 56			16 19	16 27			16 56		
Stockport	84	a								15 31							16 33						
Hazel Grove	86	a																					
Buxton	86	a																					
Heald Green	85	a																					
Manchester Airport	85 ✈	a	14 47				15 17				15 47			16 17				16 46			17 17		

A From Clitheroe
B To Liverpool Lime Street
C To Chester
D From Edinburgh

The Sunday service between Wigan Wallgate and Manchester Victoria via Atherton is funded by TfGM and will operate whilst funding exists

Barrow-in-Furness, Blackpool North, Preston, Southport, Kirkby and Wigan - Bolton - Manchester

Network Diagram - see first Page of Table 82

Station	Table		NT A	TP ◇1 B	NT	NT C	NT D	TP ◇1	NT E	NT	NT	TP ◇1 F	NT	NT D	TP ◇1	NT E	NT A	TP ◇1 B	NT	NT C	TP ◇1	NT D	TP ◇1	NT E
Barrow-in-Furness		d																			18 17			
Roose		d																			18 21			
Dalton		d																			18 28			
Ulverston		d																			18 36			
Cark		d																			18 44			
Kents Bank		d																			18 48			
Grange-over-Sands		d																			18 52			
Arnside		d																			18 58			
Silverdale		d																			19 02			
Carnforth		d				16 37														19 04	19 08			
Windermere	83	d																						
Oxenholme Lake District	65	d		16 10								17 07						18 10						
Lancaster 6	65	a		16 26		16 46						17 22						18 26		19 13	19 17			
		d		16 26								17 22						18 26			19 17			
Blackpool North	97	d			16 20			16 44	16 50				17 20		17 44	17 50			18 20				18 44	18 50
Layton	97	d			16 23								17 23						18 23					
Poulton-le-Fylde	97	d			16 28			16 50	16 56				17 28		17 50	17 56			18 28				18 50	18 56
Kirkham & Wesham	97	d			16 37								17 37						18 37					
Preston 8	65,97	a		16 46	16 47			17 08	17 14			17 41	17 47		18 08	18 14		18 45	18 47		19 37		19 08	19 14
		d		16 47	16 49			17 10	17 15			17 47	17 49		18 10	18 15		18 47	18 49				19 10	19 15
Leyland		d			16 54				17 21				17 54			18 21			18 54					19 21
Buckshaw Parkway		d			16 59			17 17					17 59		18 17				18 59				19 17	
Chorley		d		16 56	17 03			17 21				17 56	18 03		18 21			18 56	19 03				19 21	
Adlington (Lancashire)		d			17 08								18 08						19 08					
Blackrod		d			17 12								18 12						19 12					
Horwich Parkway		d			17 16			17 28					18 16		18 28				19 16				19 28	
Lostock		d			17 20								18 20						19 20					
Southport		d	16 05								17 05						18 05							
Meols Cop		d	16 10								17 10						18 10							
Bescar Lane		d																						
New Lane		d																						
Burscough Bridge		d	16 18								17 18						18 18							
Hoscar		d																						
Parbold		d	16 23								17 23						18 23							
Appley Bridge		d	16 27								17 27						18 27							
Gathurst		d	16 30								17 30						18 30							
Kirkby		d																						
Rainford		d																						
Upholland		d																						
Orrell		d																						
Pemberton		d																						
Wigan Wallgate		a	16 35								17 35						18 35							
		d	16 36							17 15	17 36						18 36							
Wigan North Western		d							17a35							18a35								19a35
Ince		d								17 18														
Hindley		d	16 41							17 22	17 41						18 41							
Westhoughton		d	16 46								17 46						18 46							
Bolton		a	16 54	17 08	17 25			17 34			17 54	18 08	18 25		18 34		18 54	19 08	19 25				19 34	
		d	16 54	17 08	17 25		17 30	17 35			17 54	18 08	18 25	18 31	18 35		18 54	19 08	19 25			19 31	19 35	
Moses Gate		d																						
Farnworth		d																						
Kearsley		d																						
Daisy Hill		d								17 26														
Hag Fold		d								17 29														
Atherton		d								17 31														
Walkden		d								17 37														
Moorside		d								17 40														
Swinton		d								17 43														
Salford Crescent		a	17 07		17 38		17 42	17 47		17 50	18 07		18 38	18 43	18 47		19 08		19 38			19 44	19 47	
		d	17 07		17 38		17 43	17 47		17 51	18 07		18 38	18 44	18 47		19 09		19 38			19 44	19 47	
Salford Central		d																						
Manchester Victoria	⇌	a			17 45		17 52			17 57			18 45	18 52					19 45			19 52		
Rochdale	41	a																						
Deansgate	⇌	a	17 11					17 51			18 11				18 51		19 12						19 51	
Manchester Oxford Road		a	17 13	17 23				17 52			18 13	18 23			18 52		19 15	19 23					19 52	
Manchester Piccadilly 10	⇌	a	17 19	17 27				17 56			18 19	18 27			18 56		19 19	19 27					19 56	
Stockport	84	a	17 30								18 33						19 30							
Hazel Grove	86	a																						
Buxton	86	a																						
Heald Green	85	a																						
Manchester Airport	85 ✈	a		17 47				18 17				18 45			19 17			19 47					20 17	

A To Chester
B From Edinburgh
C From Leeds to Morecambe
D From Clitheroe
E To Liverpool Lime Street
F From Glasgow Central

The Sunday service between Wigan Wallgate and Manchester Victoria via Atherton is funded by TfGM and will operate whilst funding exists

16 September to 30 September

Barrow-in-Furness, Blackpool North, Preston, Southport, Kirkby and Wigan - Bolton - Manchester

Network Diagram - see first Page of Table 82

		NT	TP ◇1 A 🍴	NT		NT B	TP ◇1	NT C	NT D	TP ◇1 E 🍴	NT	NT F	NT	TP ◇1 G		NT B	TP ◇1	NT C	NT	NT F	NT	NT	NT B	TP ◇1 E 🍴
Barrow-in-Furness	d										20 02													
Roose	d										20 06													
Dalton	d										20 12													
Ulverston	d										20 21													
Cark	d										20 28													
Kents Bank	d										20 33													
Grange-over-Sands	d										20 37													
Arnside	d										20 43													
Silverdale	d										20 47													
Carnforth	d										20 54													
Windermere 83	d													20 40										
Oxenholme Lake District 65	d		19 07							20 10				21 01										
Lancaster 6 65	a		19 22							20 26	21 07			21 18										
	d		19 22							20 26														22 03
Blackpool North 97	d			19 20			19 44	19 50				20 11	20 20				20 44	20 50		21 13	21 20	21 50		
Layton 97	d			19 23									20 23								21 23			
Poulton-le-Fylde 97	d			19 28			19 50	19 56				20 17	20 28				20 50	20 56		21 19	21 28	21 56		
Kirkham & Wesham 97	d			19 37									20 37								21 37			
Preston 8 65,97	a		19 41	19 47			20 08	20 14		20 45		20 34	20 47				21 08	21 14		21 36	21 47	22 14		22 23
	d		19 47	19 49			20 10	20 15		20 47			20 49				21 10	21 15			21 49	22 15		22 29
Leyland	d			19 54				20 21					20 54					21 21			21 54	22 21		
Buckshaw Parkway	d			19 59			20 17						20 59				21 17				21 59			
Chorley	d		19 56	20 03			20 21			20 56			21 03				21 21				22 03			22 38
Adlington (Lancashire)	d			20 08									21 08								22 08			
Blackrod	d			20 12									21 12								22 12			
Horwich Parkway	d			20 16			20 28						21 16				21 28				22 16			
Lostock	d			20 20									21 20								22 20			
Southport	d	19 05							20 05										21 05					
Meols Cop	d	19 10							20 10										21 10					
Bescar Lane	d																							
New Lane	d																							
Burscough Bridge	d	19 18							20 18										21 18					
Hoscar	d																							
Parbold	d	19 23							20 23										21 23					
Appley Bridge	d	19 27							20 27										21 27					
Gathurst	d	19 30							20 30										21 30					
Kirkby	d																							
Rainford	d																							
Upholland	d																							
Orrell	d																							
Pemberton	d																							
Wigan Wallgate	a	19 35							20 35										21 35					
	d	19 36							20 36										21 36					
Wigan North Western	d							20a35										21a35				22a36		
Ince	d																							
Hindley	d	19 41							20 41										21 41					
Westhoughton	d	19 46							20 46										21 46					
Bolton	a	19 54	20 08	20 25			20 34		20 54	21 08			21 25				21 34		21 54		22 25			22 50
	d	19 54	20 08	20 25		20 31	20 35		20 54	21 08			21 25			21 31	21 35		21 54		22 25		22 31	22 50
Moses Gate	d																							
Farnworth	d																							
Kearsley	d																							
Daisy Hill	d																							
Hag Fold	d																							
Atherton	d																							
Walkden	d																							
Moorside	d																							
Swinton	d																							
Salford Crescent	a	20 07		20 38		20 43	20 47		21 07				21 38			21 43	21 47		22 07		22 38		22 43	23 02
	d	20 07		20 38		20 43	20 47		21 07				21 38			21 43	21 47		22 07		22 38		22 44	23 03
Salford Central	d																							
Manchester Victoria ⇌	a			20 45		20 52							21 45			21 52					22 45		22 52	
Rochdale 41	a																							
Deansgate ⇌	a	20 11					20 51		21 11								21 51		22 11					23 08
Manchester Oxford Road	a	20 13	20 23				20 52		21 13	21 23							21 52		22 13					23 10
Manchester Piccadilly 10 ⇌	a	20 19	20 27				20 56		21 19	21 27							21 56		22 19					23 14
Stockport 84	a	20 33							21 30										22 33					
Hazel Grove 86	a																							
Buxton 86	a																							
Heald Green 85	a																							
Manchester Airport 85 ✈	a		20 45				21 16			21 46							22 17							23 30

A From Glasgow Central
B From Clitheroe
C To Liverpool Lime Street
D To Chester
E From Edinburgh
F To Leeds
G To Barrow-in-Furness

The Sunday service between Wigan Wallgate and Manchester Victoria via Atherton is funded by TfGM and will operate whilst funding exists

16 September to 30 September

Barrow-in-Furness, Blackpool North, Preston, Southport, Kirkby and Wigan - Bolton - Manchester

Network Diagram - see first Page of Table 82

		NT	NT	NT A	TP ◇1
Barrow-in-Furness	d				
Roose	d				
Dalton	d				
Ulverston	d				
Cark	d				
Kents Bank	d				
Grange-over-Sands	d				
Arnside	d				
Silverdale	d				
Carnforth	d				
Windermere 83	d				
Oxenholme Lake District 65	d				
Lancaster 6 65	a				
	d				
Blackpool North 97	d		22 44		23 03
Layton 97	d				
Poulton-le-Fylde 97	d		22 50		23 09
Kirkham & Wesham 97	d				23 17
Preston 8 65,97	a		23 08		23 28
	d		23 09		23 28
Leyland	d		23 15		23 34
Buckshaw Parkway	d				23 38
Chorley	d				23 42
Adlington (Lancashire)	d				23 46
Blackrod	d				23 50
Horwich Parkway	d				23 53
Lostock	d				23 57
Southport	d	22 05			
Meols Cop	d	22 10			
Bescar Lane	d				
New Lane	d				
Burscough Bridge	d	22 18			
Hoscar	d				
Parbold	d	22 23			
Appley Bridge	d	22 27			
Gathurst	d	22 30			
Kirkby	d				
Rainford	d				
Upholland	d				
Orrell	d				
Pemberton	d				
Wigan Wallgate	a	22 35			
	d	22 36			
Wigan North Western	d		23a30		
Ince	d				
Hindley	d	22 41			
Westhoughton	d	22 46			
Bolton	a	22 54			00 02
	d	22 54		23 31	00 02
Moses Gate	d				
Farnworth	d				
Kearsley	d				
Daisy Hill	d				
Hag Fold	d				
Atherton	d				
Walkden	d				
Moorside	d				
Swinton	d				
Salford Crescent	a	23 07		23 43	
	d	23 07		23 43	
Salford Central	d				
Manchester Victoria ⇌	a			23 52	
Rochdale 41	a				
Deansgate ⇌	a	23 11			
Manchester Oxford Road	a	23 14			
Manchester Piccadilly 10 ⇌	a	23 19			00 18
Stockport 84	a	23 33			
Hazel Grove 86	a				
Buxton 86	a				
Heald Green 85	a				
Manchester Airport 85 ✈	a				00 32

A From Clitheroe

The Sunday service between Wigan Wallgate and Manchester Victoria via Atherton is funded by TfGM and will operate whilst funding exists

Sundays
from 7 October

Barrow-in-Furness, Blackpool North, Preston, Southport, Kirkby and Wigan - Bolton - Manchester

Network Diagram - see first Page of Table 82

		TP	TP	NT	NT	TP	TP	TP	TP	TP	NT	NT	NT	NT	NT	TP	TP	NT	NT	NT	NT	NT	NT
		◇1	◇1				◇1		◇1	◇1						◇1	◇1						
		A	B	C		bus	D	bus	D		A bus	E		F trolley	G	A	B	H			A bus		C
Barrow-in-Furness	d																						
Roose	d																						
Dalton	d																						
Ulverston	d																						
Cark	d																						
Kents Bank	d																						
Grange-over-Sands	d																						
Arnside	d																						
Silverdale	d																						
Carnforth	d																						
Windermere 83	d																						
Oxenholme Lake District 65	d																						
Lancaster 6 65	a																						
	d																						
Blackpool North 97	d	22p44	22p44		23p02	03 20		05 20		07 48			08 20	08 36		08 44	08 44	08 50				09 20	
Layton 97	d				23p05								08 23									09 23	
Poulton-le-Fylde 97	d	22p50	22p50		23p10					07 54			08 28	08 42		08 50	08 50	08 56				09 28	
Kirkham & Wesham 97	d				23p19								08 37	08 51								09 37	
Preston 8 65,97	a	23p07	23p08		23p29					08 12			08 47	09 02		09 08	09 08	09 14				09 47	
	d	23p09	23p10		23p31	04u00		06u00		08 14	08 28		08 49			09 09	09 10	09 15			09 28	09 49	
Leyland	d				23p36								08 54					09 21				09 54	
Buckshaw Parkway	d	23p17	23p17		23p41								08 59			09 17	09 17					09 59	
Chorley	d	23p21	23p21		23p45					08 23			09 03			09 21	09 21					10 03	
Adlington (Lancashire)	d				23p50								09 08									10 08	
Blackrod	d				23p54								09 12									10 12	
Horwich Parkway	d	23p28	23p28		23p58					08 30			09 16			09 28	09 28					10 16	
Lostock	d				00 02								09 20									10 20	
Southport	d																			09 06			
Meols Cop	d																			09 11			
Bescar Lane	d																						
New Lane	d																						
Burscough Bridge	d																			09 19			
Hoscar	d																						
Parbold	d																			09 24			
Appley Bridge	d																			09 28			
Gathurst	d																			09 31			
Kirkby	d																						
Rainford	d																						
Upholland	d																						
Orrell	d																						
Pemberton	d																						
Wigan Wallgate	a																			09 38			
	d											08 40							09 15	09 39			
Wigan North Western	d										09a25							09a35			10a25		
Ince	d																		09 18				
Hindley	d											08 45							09 22	09 44			
Westhoughton	d											08 49								09 49			
Bolton	a	23p34	23p34		00 07					08 37		08 57	09 25			09 34	09 34			09 59		10 25	
	d	23p35	23p35	23p38	00 07	04u35		06u35		08 37		08 58	09 25		09 31	09 35	09 35			09 59		10 25	10 31
Moses Gate	d																						
Farnworth	d																						
Kearsley	d																						
Daisy Hill	d																		09 26				
Hag Fold	d																		09 29				
Atherton	d																		09 31				
Walkden	d																		09 37				
Moorside	d																		09 40				
Swinton	d																		09 43				
Salford Crescent	a	23p47	23p47	23p48						08 49		09 10	09 38		09 43	09 47	09 47		09 50	10 12		10 38	10 44
	d	23p47	23p47	23p51			06 11		07 10	08 50		09 11	09 38		09 44	09 47	09 47		09 51	10 12		10 38	10 44
Salford Central	d																						
Manchester Victoria	a			00 01	00 26								09 45		09 53				09 57			10 45	10 52
Rochdale 41	a																						
Deansgate	a									08 53		09 14				09 51	09 51			10 16			
Manchester Oxford Road	a									08 55		09 17				09 52	09 52			10 18			
Manchester Piccadilly 10	a	23p53	23p53			05b00	06 17	07b00	07 15	08 59		09 21				09 56	09 56			10 22			
Stockport 84	a											09 31								10 33			
Hazel Grove 86	a																						
Buxton 86	a																						
Heald Green 85	a	00 16	00 16																				
Manchester Airport 85	a	00 23	00 23			05 25	06 35	07 25	07 34	09 17						10 17	10 17						

A from 28 October
B 7 October, 14 October, 21 October
C From Clitheroe
D 7 October, 14 October, 21 October. From York
E To Chester
F 7 October, 14 October, 21 October. To Carlisle
G From Blackburn
H 7 October, 14 October, 21 October. To Liverpool Lime Street
b Stops to pick up only

The Sunday service between Wigan Wallgate and Manchester Victoria via Atherton is funded by TfGM and will operate whilst funding exists

Sundays
from 7 October

Barrow-in-Furness, Blackpool North, Preston, Southport, Kirkby and Wigan - Bolton - Manchester

Network Diagram - see first Page of Table 82

		TP	TP	NT	NT	NT	NT	TP	TP	NT	NT	NT	TP	NT	NT	NT	NT	TP	TP	NT	VT	NT	TP
		◇1	◇1					◇1	◇1				◇1					◇1	◇1		◇1		◇1
		A	B	C		D	A bus	A	B		E	F		C			A bus	A	B		G buffet	F	A trolley
Barrow-in-Furness	d							09 17	09 17									10 30	10 30				
Roose	d							09 21	09 21														
Dalton	d							09 28	09 28														
Ulverston	d							09 36	09 36									10 46	10 46				
Cark	d							09 44	09 44														
Kents Bank	d							09 48	09 48														
Grange-over-Sands	d							09 52	09 52									10 58	10 58				
Arnside	d							09 58	09 58									11 04	11 04				
Silverdale	d							10 02	10 02														
Carnforth	d							10 09	10 09		10 31							11 14	11 14				
Windermere 83	d																						
Oxenholme Lake District 65	d																				11 23		
Lancaster 6 65	a							10 17	10 17		10 40							11 22	11 22		11 37		
	d							10 21	10 21									11 22	11 22		11 38		
Blackpool North 97	d	09 44	09 44	09 50						10 20			10 44	10 50						11 20			11 44
Layton 97	d									10 23										11 23			
Poulton-le-Fylde 97	d	09 50	09 50	09 56						10 28			10 50	10 56						11 28			11 50
Kirkham & Wesham 97	d									10 37										11 37			
Preston 8 65,97	a	10 08	10 08	10 14				10 40	10 40	10 47			11 08	11 14				11 42	11 42	11 47	11 56		12 08
	d	10 09	10 10	10 15			10 28	10 45	10 47	10 49			11 10	11 15			11 28	11 44	11 47	11 49			12 09
Leyland	d			10 21						10 54				11 21						11 54			
Buckshaw Parkway	d	10 17	10 17							10 59			11 17							11 59			12 17
Chorley	d	10 21	10 21					10 56	10 56	11 03			11 21					11 56	11 56	12 03			12 21
Adlington (Lancashire)	d									11 08										12 08			
Blackrod	d									11 12										12 12			
Horwich Parkway	d	10 28	10 28							11 16			11 28							12 16			12 28
Lostock	d									11 20										12 20			
Southport	d					10 05										11 01							
Meols Cop	d					10 10										11 06							
Bescar Lane	d																						
New Lane	d																						
Burscough Bridge	d					10 18										11 14							
Hoscar	d																						
Parbold	d					10 23										11 19							
Appley Bridge	d					10 27										11 23							
Gathurst	d					10 30										11 26							
Kirkby	d																						
Rainford	d																						
Upholland	d																						
Orrell	d																						
Pemberton	d																						
Wigan Wallgate	a					10 35										11 33							
	d				10 15	10 36									11 15	11 34							
Wigan North Western	d			10a36			11a25							11a35			13a25						
Ince	d				10 18										11 18								
Hindley	d				10 22	10 41									11 22	11 39							
Westhoughton	d					10 46										11 44							
Bolton	a	10 34	10 34			10 54		11 08	11 08	11 25			11 34			11 54		12 08	12 08	12 25			12 34
	d	10 35	10 35			10 54		11 08	11 08	11 25		11 31	11 35			11 54		12 08	12 08	12 25		12 31	12 35
Moses Gate	d																						
Farnworth	d																						
Kearsley	d																						
Daisy Hill	d				10 26										11 26								
Hag Fold	d				10 29										11 29								
Atherton	d				10 31										11 31								
Walkden	d				10 37										11 37								
Moorside	d				10 40										11 40								
Swinton	d				10 43										11 43								
Salford Crescent	a	10 47	10 47		10 50	11 06				11 38		11 43	11 47		11 50	12 07				12 38		12 43	12 47
	d	10 47	10 47		10 51	11 07				11 38		11 44	11 47		11 51	12 07				12 38		12 44	12 47
Salford Central	d																						
Manchester Victoria	a				10 57					11 45		11 53			11 57					12 45		12 53	
Rochdale 41	a																						
Deansgate	a	10 51	10 51			11 10							11 51			12 11							12 51
Manchester Oxford Road	a	10 52	10 52			11 13		11 23	11 23				11 52			12 13		12 23	12 23				12 52
Manchester Piccadilly 10	a	10 56	10 56			11 19		11 27	11 27				11 56			12 21		12 27	12 27				12 59
Stockport 84	a					11 30										12 31							
Hazel Grove 86	a																						
Buxton 86	a																						
Heald Green 85	a																						
Manchester Airport 85	a	11 17	11 17					11 47	11 47				12 17					12 48	12 48				13 17

A from 28 October
B 7 October, 14 October, 21 October
C 7 October, 14 October, 21 October. To Liverpool Lime Street
D To Chester
E From Leeds to Morecambe
F From Clitheroe
G from 28 October. From Glasgow Central

The Sunday service between Wigan Wallgate and Manchester Victoria via Atherton is funded by TfGM and will operate whilst funding exists

Table 82

Sundays from 7 October

Barrow-in-Furness, Blackpool North, Preston, Southport, Kirkby and Wigan - Bolton - Manchester

Network Diagram - see first Page of Table 82

Station			TP ◇1 A ⌶	NT B	NT	NT C	NT D 🚌	TP ◇1 E ⌶	TP ◇1 F ⌶	NT A	NT D	VT ◇1 G	NT H	NT I	TP ◇1 D	TP ◇1 A	NT B	NT	NT	NT D 🚌	TP ◇1 D	TP ◇1 A	NT A
Barrow-in-Furness		d																			12 25	12 25	
Roose		d																			12 29	12 29	
Dalton		d																			12 36	12 36	
Ulverston		d																			12 44	12 44	
Cark		d																			12 52	12 52	
Kents Bank		d																			12 56	12 56	
Grange-over-Sands		d																			13 00	13 00	
Arnside		d																			13 06	13 06	
Silverdale		d																			13 10	13 10	
Carnforth		d											12 35								13 17	13 17	
Windermere	83	d																					
Oxenholme Lake District	65	d						12 10	12 10			12 24											
Lancaster 6	65	a						12 26	12 26			12 37	12 44								13 26	13 26	
		d						12 26	12 26			12 38									13 26	13 26	
Blackpool North	97	d	11 44	11 50						12 20	12 20				12 42	12 44	12 50						13 20
Layton	97	d								12 23	12 23												13 23
Poulton-le-Fylde	97	d	11 50	11 56						12 28	12 28				12 48	12 50	12 56						13 28
Kirkham & Wesham	97	d								12 37	12 37												13 37
Preston 8	65,97	a	12 08	12 14				12 45	12 45	12 47	12 47	12 56			13 06	13 08	13 14				13 44	13 45	13 47
		d	12 10	12 15			12 28	12 46	12 47	12 49	12 50				13 08	13 10	13 15			13 28	13 46	13 47	13 49
Leyland		d		12 21						12 54	12 55						13 21						13 54
Buckshaw Parkway		d	12 17							12 59	13 00				13 17	13 17							13 59
Chorley		d	12 21					12 57	12 56	13 03	13 04				13 21	13 21					13 57	13 56	14 03
Adlington (Lancashire)		d								13 08	13 09												14 08
Blackrod		d								13 12	13 12												14 12
Horwich Parkway		d	12 28							13 16	13 16				13 28	13 28							14 16
Lostock		d								13 20	13 20												14 20
Southport		d				12 05													13 01				
Meols Cop		d				12 10													13 06				
Bescar Lane		d																					
New Lane		d																					
Burscough Bridge		d				12 18													13 14				
Hoscar		d																					
Parbold		d				12 23													13 19				
Appley Bridge		d				12 27													13 23				
Gathurst		d				12 30													13 26				
Kirkby		d																					
Rainford		d																					
Upholland		d																					
Orrell		d																					
Pemberton		d																					
Wigan Wallgate		a				12 35													13 33				
		d			12 15	12 36												13 15	13 34				
Wigan North Western		d		12a35			13a25										13a35			14a25			
Ince		d			12 18													13 18					
Hindley		d			12 22	12 41												13 22	13 39				
Westhoughton		d				12 46													13 44				
Bolton		a	12 34			12 54		13 09	13 08	13 25	13 25				13 34	13 34			13 54		14 09	14 08	14 25
		d	12 35			12 54		13 09	13 08	13 25	13 25			13 31	13 35	13 35			13 54		14 09	14 08	14 25
Moses Gate		d																					
Farnworth		d																					
Kearsley		d																					
Daisy Hill		d			12 26													13 26					
Hag Fold		d			12 29													13 29					
Atherton		d			12 31													13 31					
Walkden		d			12 37													13 37					
Moorside		d			12 40													13 40					
Swinton		d			12 43													13 43					
Salford Crescent		a	12 47		12 50	13 07				13 38	13 38			13 43	13 47	13 47		13 50	14 07				14 38
		d	12 47		12 51	13 07				13 38	13 38			13 44	13 47	13 47		13 51	14 07				14 38
Salford Central		d																					
Manchester Victoria	⇌	a			12 57					13 45	13 45			13 52				13 57					14 45
Rochdale	41	a																					
Deansgate	⇌	a	12 51			13 11									13 51	13 51			14 11				
Manchester Oxford Road		a	12 52			13 13		13 24	13 23						13 52	13 52			14 13		14 23	14 23	
Manchester Piccadilly 10	⇌	a	12 59			13 19		13 28	13 27						13 56	13 56			14 19		14 27	14 27	
Stockport	84	a				13 30													14 31				
Hazel Grove	86	a																					
Buxton	86	a																					
Heald Green	85	a																					
Manchester Airport	85 ✈	a	13 17					13 47	13 47						14 17	14 17					14 47	14 47	

A 7 October, 14 October, 21 October
B 7 October, 14 October, 21 October. To Liverpool Lime Street
C To Chester
D from 28 October
E from 28 October. From Edinburgh
F 7 October, 14 October, 21 October. From Edinburgh
G from 28 October. From Glasgow Central
H From Leeds to Morecambe
I From Clitheroe

The Sunday service between Wigan Wallgate and Manchester Victoria via Atherton is funded by TfGM and will operate whilst funding exists

Table 82

Sundays from 7 October

Barrow-in-Furness, Blackpool North, Preston, Southport, Kirkby and Wigan - Bolton - Manchester

Network Diagram - see first Page of Table 82

Station			NT A	VT ◇1 B	NT	NT C	TP ◇1 A	TP ◇1 D	NT E	NT	NT F	TP ◇1 G ⌶	TP ◇1 H ⌶	NT D	NT A	NT C	TP ◇1	NT I	NT	NT	TP ◇1	NT	NT C	TP ◇1
Barrow-in-Furness		d			13 10																14 25			
Roose		d			13 14																14 29			
Dalton		d			13 20																14 36			
Ulverston		d			13 29																14 44			
Cark		d			13 36																14 52			
Kents Bank		d			13 41																14 56			
Grange-over-Sands		d			13 45																15 00			
Arnside		d			13 51																15 06			
Silverdale		d			13 55																15 10			
Carnforth		d			14 02																15 17			
Windermere	83	d																						
Oxenholme Lake District	65	d		13 23								14 10	14 10											
Lancaster 6	65	a		13 37	14 15							14 26	14 26								15 26			
		d		13 38								14 26	14 26								15 26			
Blackpool North	97	d	13 20				13 44	13 44	13 50					14 20	14 20		14 44	14 50				15 20		15 44
Layton	97	d	13 23											14 23	14 23							15 23		
Poulton-le-Fylde	97	d	13 28				13 50	13 50	13 56					14 28	14 28		14 50	14 56				15 28		15 50
Kirkham & Wesham	97	d	13 37											14 37	14 37							15 37		
Preston 8	65,97	a	13 47	13 56			14 08	14 08	14 14			14 45	14 45	14 47	14 47		15 08	15 14			15 45	15 47		16 08
		d	13 50				14 09	14 10	14 15			14 46	14 47	14 49	14 50		15 10	15 15			15 47	15 49		16 10
Leyland		d	13 55						14 21					14 54	14 55			15 21				15 54		
Buckshaw Parkway		d	14 00				14 18	14 17						14 59	15 00		15 17					15 59		16 17
Chorley		d	14 04				14 22	14 21				14 57	14 56	15 03	15 04		15 21				15 56	16 03		16 21
Adlington (Lancashire)		d	14 09											15 08	15 09							16 08		
Blackrod		d	14 12											15 11	15 12							16 11		
Horwich Parkway		d	14 16				14 29	14 28						15 15	15 16		15 28					16 15		16 28
Lostock		d	14 20											15 20	15 20							16 20		
Southport		d									14 05									15 01				
Meols Cop		d									14 10									15 06				
Bescar Lane		d																						
New Lane		d																						
Burscough Bridge		d									14 18									15 14				
Hoscar		d																						
Parbold		d									14 23									15 19				
Appley Bridge		d									14 27									15 23				
Gathurst		d									14 30									15 26				
Kirkby		d																						
Rainford		d																						
Upholland		d																						
Orrell		d																						
Pemberton		d																						
Wigan Wallgate		a									14 35									15 33				
		d								14 15	14 36								15 15	15 34				
Wigan North Western		d							14a35									15a35						
Ince		d								14 18									15 18					
Hindley		d								14 22	14 41								15 22	15 39				
Westhoughton		d									14 46									15 44				
Bolton		a	14 25				14 35	14 34			14 54	15 09	15 08	15 25	15 25		15 34			15 54	16 08	16 25		16 34
		d	14 25			14 31	14 36	14 35			14 54	15 09	15 08	15 25	15 26	15 31	15 35			15 54	16 08	16 25	16 31	16 35
Moses Gate		d																						
Farnworth		d																						
Kearsley		d																						
Daisy Hill		d								14 26									15 26					
Hag Fold		d								14 29									15 29					
Atherton		d								14 31									15 31					
Walkden		d								14 37									15 37					
Moorside		d								14 40									15 40					
Swinton		d								14 43									15 43					
Salford Crescent		a	14 38			14 43	14 47	14 47		14 50	15 07			15 38	15 38	15 43	15 47		15 50	16 07		16 38	16 43	16 47
		d	14 38			14 44	14 47	14 47		14 51	15 07			15 38	15 38	15 44	15 47		15 51	16 07		16 38	16 44	16 47
Salford Central		d																						
Manchester Victoria	⇌	a	14 45			14 53				14 57				15 45	15 45	15 55			15 57			16 45	16 53	
Rochdale	41	a																						
Deansgate	⇌	a					14 51	14 51			15 11						15 51			16 11				16 51
Manchester Oxford Road		a					14 52	14 52			15 13	15 23	15 23				15 52			16 13	16 23			16 52
Manchester Piccadilly 10	⇌	a					14 56	14 56			15 19	15 27	15 27				15 56			16 19	16 27			16 56
Stockport	84	a									15 30									16 33				
Hazel Grove	86	a																						
Buxton	86	a																						
Heald Green	85	a																						
Manchester Airport	85 ✈	a					15 17	15 17				15 47	15 47				16 17				16 46			17 17

A from 28 October
B from 28 October. From Glasgow Central
C From Clitheroe
D 7 October, 14 October, 21 October
E 7 October, 14 October, 21 October. To Liverpool Lime Street
F To Chester
G from 28 October. From Edinburgh
H 7 October, 14 October, 21 October. From Edinburgh
I To Liverpool Lime Street

The Sunday service between Wigan Wallgate and Manchester Victoria via Atherton is funded by TfGM and will operate whilst funding exists

Table 82

Sundays
from 7 October

Barrow-in-Furness, Blackpool North, Preston, Southport, Kirkby and Wigan - Bolton - Manchester

Network Diagram - see first Page of Table 82

Station		NT A	NT	NT B	TP ◇1 C	NT	NT D	NT E	TP ◇1	NT A	NT	NT	TP ◇1 F	NT	NT E	TP ◇1	NT A	NT B	TP ◇1 C	NT	NT D	TP ◇1
Barrow-in-Furness	d																					18 17
Roose	d																					18 21
Dalton	d																					18 28
Ulverston	d																					18 36
Cark	d																					18 44
Kents Bank	d																					18 48
Grange-over-Sands	d																					18 52
Arnside	d																					18 58
Silverdale	d																					19 02
Carnforth	d						16 37														19 04	19 08
Windermere	83 d																					
Oxenholme Lake District	65 d				16 10								17 07						18 10			
Lancaster 8	65 a				16 26		16 46						17 22						18 26		19 13	19 17
	d				16 26								17 22						18 26			19 17
Blackpool North	97 d	15 50				16 20			16 44	16 50				17 20		17 44	17 50			18 20		
Layton	97 d					16 23								17 23						18 23		
Poulton-le-Fylde	97 d	15 56				16 28			16 50	16 56				17 28		17 50	17 56			18 28		
Kirkham & Wesham	97 d					16 37								17 37						18 37		
Preston 8	65,97 a	16 14			16 46	16 47			17 08	17 14			17 41	17 47		18 08	18 14		18 45	18 47		19 37
	d	16 15			16 47	16 49			17 10	17 15			17 47	17 49		18 10	18 15		18 47	18 49		
Leyland	d	16 21				16 54				17 21				17 54			18 21			18 54		
Buckshaw Parkway	d					16 59			17 17					17 59		18 17				18 59		
Chorley	d				16 56	17 03			17 21				17 56	18 03		18 21			18 56	19 03		
Adlington (Lancashire)	d					17 08								18 08						19 08		
Blackrod	d					17 12								18 12						19 12		
Horwich Parkway	d					17 16			17 28					18 16		18 28				19 16		
Lostock	d					17 20								18 20						19 20		
Southport	d			16 05								17 01						18 05				
Meols Cop	d			16 10								17 06						18 10				
Bescar Lane	d																					
New Lane	d																					
Burscough Bridge	d			16 18								17 14						18 18				
Hoscar	d																					
Parbold	d			16 23								17 19						18 23				
Appley Bridge	d			16 27								17 23						18 27				
Gathurst	d			16 30								17 26						18 30				
Kirkby	d																					
Rainford	d																					
Upholland	d																					
Orrell	d																					
Pemberton	d																					
Wigan Wallgate	a			16 35								17 33						18 35				
	d		16 15	16 36							17 15	17 34						18 36				
Wigan North Western	d	16a35								17a35							18a35					
Ince	d		16 18								17 18											
Hindley	d		16 22	16 41							17 22	17 39						18 41				
Westhoughton	d			16 46								17 44						18 46				
Bolton	a			16 54	17 08	17 25			17 34			17 54	18 08	18 25		18 34		18 54	19 08	19 25		
	d			16 54	17 08	17 25		17 31	17 35			17 54	18 08	18 25	18 31	18 35		18 54	19 08	19 25		
Moses Gate	d																					
Farnworth	d																					
Kearsley	d																					
Daisy Hill	d		16 26								17 26											
Hag Fold	d		16 29								17 29											
Atherton	d		16 31								17 31											
Walkden	d		16 37								17 37											
Moorside	d		16 40								17 40											
Swinton	d		16 43								17 43											
Salford Crescent	a		16 50	17 07		17 38		17 43	17 47		17 50	18 07		18 38	18 43	18 47		19 08		19 38		
	d		16 51	17 07		17 38		17 44	17 47		17 51	18 07		18 38	18 44	18 47		19 09		19 38		
Salford Central	d																					
Manchester Victoria	⇌ a		16 57			17 45		17 54			17 57			18 45	18 52					19 46		
Rochdale	41 a																					
Deansgate	⇌ a			17 11					17 51			18 11				18 51		19 12				
Manchester Oxford Road	a			17 13	17 23				17 52			18 13	18 23			18 52		19 15	19 23			
Manchester Piccadilly 10	⇌ a			17 19	17 27				17 56			18 19	18 27			18 56		19 19	19 27			
Stockport	84 a			17 30								18 33						19 30				
Hazel Grove	86 a																					
Buxton	86 a																					
Heald Green	85 a																					
Manchester Airport	85 ✈ a				17 47				18 17				18 45			19 17			19 47			

A To Liverpool Lime Street
B To Chester
C From Edinburgh
D From Leeds to Morecambe
E From Clitheroe
F From Glasgow Central

The Sunday service between Wigan Wallgate and Manchester Victoria via Atherton is funded by TfGM and will operate whilst funding exists

Table 82

Sundays
from 7 October

Barrow-in-Furness, Blackpool North, Preston, Southport, Kirkby and Wigan - Bolton - Manchester

Network Diagram - see first Page of Table 82

Station		NT A	TP ◇1	NT B	NT	TP ◇1 C	NT	NT A	TP ◇1	NT B	NT D	TP ◇1 E	NT	NT F	NT	TP ◇1 G	NT A	TP ◇1	NT B	NT	NT F	NT	NT
Barrow-in-Furness	d												20 02										
Roose	d												20 06										
Dalton	d												20 12										
Ulverston	d												20 21										
Cark	d												20 28										
Kents Bank	d												20 33										
Grange-over-Sands	d												20 37										
Arnside	d												20 43										
Silverdale	d												20 47										
Carnforth	d												20 54										
Windermere	83 d															20 40							
Oxenholme Lake District	65 d					19 07						20 10				21 01							
Lancaster 8	65 a					19 22						20 26	21 07			21 18							
	d					19 22						20 26											
Blackpool North	97 d		18 44	18 50			19 20		19 44	19 50				20 11	20 20			20 44	20 50		21 13	21 20	21 50
Layton	97 d						19 23								20 23							21 23	
Poulton-le-Fylde	97 d		18 50	18 56			19 28		19 50	19 56				20 17	20 28			20 50	20 56		21 19	21 28	21 56
Kirkham & Wesham	97 d						19 37								20 37							21 37	
Preston 8	65,97 a		19 08	19 14		19 41	19 47		20 08	20 14		20 45		20 34	20 47			21 08	21 14		21 36	21 47	22 14
	d		19 10	19 15		19 47	19 49		20 10	20 15		20 47			20 49			21 10	21 15			21 49	22 15
Leyland	d			19 21			19 54			20 21					20 54				21 21			21 54	22 21
Buckshaw Parkway	d		19 17				19 59		20 17						20 59			21 17				21 59	
Chorley	d		19 21			19 56	20 03		20 21			20 56			21 03			21 21				22 03	
Adlington (Lancashire)	d						20 08								21 08							22 08	
Blackrod	d						20 12								21 12							22 12	
Horwich Parkway	d		19 28				20 16		20 28						21 16			21 28				22 16	
Lostock	d						20 20								21 20							22 20	
Southport	d				19 01						20 05									21 01			
Meols Cop	d				19 06						20 10									21 06			
Bescar Lane	d																						
New Lane	d																						
Burscough Bridge	d				19 14						20 18									21 14			
Hoscar	d																						
Parbold	d				19 19						20 23									21 19			
Appley Bridge	d				19 23						20 27									21 23			
Gathurst	d				19 26						20 30									21 26			
Kirkby	d																						
Rainford	d																						
Upholland	d																						
Orrell	d																						
Pemberton	d																						
Wigan Wallgate	a				19 33						20 35									21 33			
	d				19 34						20 36									21 34			
Wigan North Western	d			19a35						20a35									21a35				22a36
Ince	d																						
Hindley	d				19 39						20 41									21 39			
Westhoughton	d				19 44						20 46									21 44			
Bolton	a		19 34		19 54	20 08	20 25		20 34		20 54	21 08			21 25			21 34		21 54		22 25	
	d	19 31	19 35		19 54	20 08	20 25	20 31	20 35		20 54	21 08			21 25		21 31	21 35		21 54		22 25	
Moses Gate	d																						
Farnworth	d																						
Kearsley	d																						
Daisy Hill	d																						
Hag Fold	d																						
Atherton	d																						
Walkden	d																						
Moorside	d																						
Swinton	d																						
Salford Crescent	a	19 44	19 47		20 07		20 38	20 43	20 47		21 07				21 38		21 43	21 47		22 07		22 38	
	d	19 44	19 47		20 07		20 38	20 44	20 47		21 07				21 38		21 44	21 47		22 07		22 38	
Salford Central	d																						
Manchester Victoria	⇌ a	19 54					20 45	20 53							21 45		21 53					22 45	
Rochdale	41 a																						
Deansgate	⇌ a		19 51		20 11				20 51		21 11							21 51		22 11			
Manchester Oxford Road	a		19 52		20 13	20 23			20 52		21 13	21 23						21 52		22 13			
Manchester Piccadilly 10	⇌ a		19 56		20 19	20 27			20 56		21 19	21 27						21 56		22 19			
Stockport	84 a				20 33						21 30									22 33			
Hazel Grove	86 a																						
Buxton	86 a																						
Heald Green	85 a																						
Manchester Airport	85 ✈ a		20 17			20 45			21 16			21 46						22 17					

A From Clitheroe
B To Liverpool Lime Street
C From Glasgow Central
D To Chester
E From Edinburgh
F To Leeds
G To Barrow-in-Furness

The Sunday service between Wigan Wallgate and Manchester Victoria via Atherton is funded by TfGM and will operate whilst funding exists

Table 82

Sundays from 7 October

Barrow-in-Furness, Blackpool North, Preston, Southport, Kirkby and Wigan - Bolton - Manchester

Network Diagram - see first Page of Table 82

		NT	TP	NT	NT	NT	TP
			◇■				◇■
		A	B			A	
			✠				
Barrow-in-Furness	d						
Roose	d						
Dalton	d						
Ulverston	d						
Cark	d						
Kents Bank	d						
Grange-over-Sands	d						
Arnside	d						
Silverdale	d						
Carnforth	d						
Windermere 83	d						
Oxenholme Lake District 65	d						
Lancaster ■ 65	a						
	d		22 03				
Blackpool North 97	d				22 44		23 03
Layton 97	d						
Poulton-le-Fylde 97	d				22 50		23 09
Kirkham & Wesham 97	d						23 17
Preston ■ 65,97	a		22 23		23 08		23 28
	d		22 29		23 09		23 28
Leyland	d				23 15		23 34
Buckshaw Parkway	d						23 38
Chorley	d		22 38				23 42
Adlington (Lancashire)	d						23 46
Blackrod	d						23 50
Horwich Parkway	d						23 53
Lostock	d						23 57
Southport	d			22 01			
Meols Cop	d			22 06			
Bescar Lane	d						
New Lane	d						
Burscough Bridge	d			22 14			
Hoscar	d						
Parbold	d			22 19			
Appley Bridge	d			22 23			
Gathurst	d			22 26			
Kirkby	d						
Rainford	d						
Upholland	d						
Orrell	d						
Pemberton	d						
Wigan Wallgate	a			22 33			
	d			22 34			
Wigan North Western	d				23a30		
Ince	d						
Hindley	d			22 39			
Westhoughton	d			22 44			
Bolton	a		22 50	22 54			00 02
	d	22 31	22 50	22 54		23 31	00 02
Moses Gate	d						
Farnworth	d						
Kearsley	d						
Daisy Hill	d						
Hag Fold	d						
Atherton	d						
Walkden	d						
Moorside	d						
Swinton	d						
Salford Crescent	a	22 43	23 02	23 07		23 43	
	d	22 44	23 03	23 07		23 44	
Salford Central	d						
Manchester Victoria ⇌	a	22 54				23 55	
Rochdale 41	a						
Deansgate ⇌	a		23 08	23 11			
Manchester Oxford Road	a		23 10	23 14			
Manchester Piccadilly ■ ⇌	a		23 14	23 19			00 18
Stockport 84	a			23 33			
Hazel Grove 86	a						
Buxton 86	a						
Heald Green 85	a						
Manchester Airport 85 ✈	a		23 30				00 32

A From Clitheroe
B From Edinburgh

The Sunday service between Wigan Wallgate and Manchester Victoria via Atherton is funded by TfGM and will operate whilst funding exists

Table 83

Mondays to Fridays

Oxenholme - Lake District - Windermere

Network Diagram - see first Page of Table 82

Miles			TP	TP	TP	TP	TP	TP	TP	TP	TP	TP	TP	TP	TP	TP	TP	TP	TP
			■	■	■	■	■	◇■	■	◇■	■	■	■	◇■	◇■	■	■	■	■
			A					B		C				B	D				
0	**Oxenholme Lake District**	d	06 21	07 21	08 27	09 14	10 27	11 18	12 28	13 37	14 27	15 38	16 28	17 49	18 46	19 37	20 27	21 15	22 20
2¼	Kendal	d	06 26	07 25	08 31	09 18	10 31	11 22	12 32	13 41	14 31	15 43	16 32	17 53	18 50	19 41	20 31	21 19	22 24
4	Burneside	d		07x29	08x35	09x22		11 26	12x36		14x35	15x46	16x36	17x57	18x54	19x45	20x35	21x23	22x28
6½	Staveley	d		07x34	08x40	09x27		11 31	12x41		14x40	15x51	16x41	18x02	18x59	19x50	20x40	21x28	22x33
10	**Windermere**	a	06 41	07 40	08 46	09 33	10 44	11 39	12 47	13 56	14 46	15 59	16 48	18 08	19 08	19 56	20 46	21 34	22 39

Saturdays

		TP	TP	TP	TP	TP	TP	TP	TP	TP	TP	TP	TP	TP	TP	TP	TP
		■	■	■	■	◇■	◇■	■	◇■	■	■	■	◇■	■	■	■	■
		A				B	C		C				B				
Oxenholme Lake District	d	06 21	07 21	08 27	09 11	10 05	11 18	12 28	13 37	14 33	15 38	16 28	17 38	18 37	19 37	20 23	21 15
Kendal	d	06 26	07 25	08 31	09 15	10 09	11 22	12 32	13 41	14 37	15 43	16 32	17 42	18 41	19 41	20 27	21 19
Burneside	d		07x29	08x35	09x19	10x13	11x26	12x36		14x41	15x46	16x36	17x46	18x45	19x45	20x31	21x23
Staveley	d		07x34	08x40	09x24	10x18	11x31	12x41		14x46	15x51	16x41	17x51	18x50	19x50	20x36	21x28
Windermere	a	06 41	07 40	08 46	09 30	10 26	11 39	12 47	13 56	14 52	15 59	16 48	18 00	18 56	19 56	20 42	21 34

Sundays until 9 September

		TP	TP	TP	TP	TP	TP	TP	TP	TP	TP	TP
		◇■	■	■	■	■	■	■	■	◇■	■	■
		B								B		
Oxenholme Lake District	d	10 40	11 35	12 29	13 35	14 37	15 35	16 29	17 37	18 40	19 29	20 16
Kendal	d	10 44	11 39	12 33	13 39	14 41	15 39	16 33	17 41	18 45	19 33	20 20
Burneside	d		11x43	12x37	13x43	14x45	15x43	16x37	17x45	18x48		20x24
Staveley	d		11x48	12x42	13x48	14x50	15x48	16x42	17x50	18x53		20x29
Windermere	a	10 57	11 54	12 48	13 54	14 56	15 54	16 48	17 56	19 01	19 45	20 35

Sundays from 16 September

		TP	TP	TP	TP	TP	TP	TP	TP	TP	TP	TP
		◇■	■	■	■	■	■	■	■	■	■	■
		A										
Oxenholme Lake District	d	10 40	11 35	12 29	13 35	14 37	15 35	16 29	17 37	18 37	19 29	20 16
Kendal	d	10 44	11 39	12 33	13 39	14 41	15 39	16 33	17 41	18 41	19 33	20 20
Burneside	d		11x43	12x37	13x43	14x45	15x43	16x37	17x45	18x45		20x24
Staveley	d		11x48	12x42	13x48	14x50	15x48	16x42	17x50	18x50		20x29
Windermere	a	10 57	11 54	12 48	13 54	14 56	15 54	16 48	17 56	18 56	19 45	20 35

A From Lancaster
B From Manchester Airport
C From Preston
D From Barrow-in-Furness

Windermere - Oxenholme - Lake District

Network Diagram - see first Page of Table 82

Miles			TP	TP	TP	TP	TP	TP	TP	TP	TP	TP	TP	TP	TP	TP	TP	TP	TP
			1	1	1	1	◇1	1	◇1	1	1	1	◇1	◇1	1	1	1	1	◇1
							A		A				A	A					B
0	Windermere	d	06 50	07 55	08 50	09 59	10 49	11 59	12 51	14 00	14 59	16 02	17 06	18 15	19 10	20 00	20 50	21 40	22 45
3½	Staveley	d	06x55	08x01		10x04	10x54	12x04		14x05	15x04		17x11	18x20		20x05	20x55	21x45	22x50
6	Burneside	d	07x00	08x06		10x09	10x59	12x09		14x10	15x09		17x16	18x25		20x10	21x00	21x50	22x55
7¾	Kendal	d	07 04	08 11	09 01	10 13	11 03	12 13	13 02	14 14	15 13	16 14	17 20	18 29	19 21	20 14	21 04	21 54	22 59
10	Oxenholme Lake District	a	07 09	08 16	09 06	10 18	11 08	12 18	13 07	14 19	15 18	16 19	17 25	18 34	19 27	20 19	21 09	21 59	23 04

Saturdays

		TP	TP	TP	TP	TP	TP	TP	TP	TP	TP	TP	TP	TP	TP	TP	TP
		1	1	1	◇1	◇1	1	◇1	1	1	1	◇1	1	1	1	1	◇1
					C	A		A				A					C
Windermere	d	06 50	07 55	08 50	09 38	10 49	11 59	12 51	14 00	14 59	16 02	17 06	18 02	19 00	20 00	20 47	21 40
Staveley	d	06x55	08x01		09x43	10x54	12x04		14x05	15x04		17x11	18x07	19x05	20x05		21x45
Burneside	d	07x00	08x06		09x48	10x59	12x09		14x10	15x09		17x16	18x12	19x10	20x10		21x50
Kendal	d	07 04	08 11	09 01	09 52	11 03	12 13	13 02	14 14	15 13	16 14	17 20	18 16	19 14	20 14	20 58	21 54
Oxenholme Lake District	a	07 09	08 16	09 06	09 57	11 08	12 18	13 07	14 19	15 18	16 19	17 25	18 21	19 19	20 19	21 04	21 59

Sundays
until 9 September

		TP	TP	TP	TP	TP	TP	TP	TP	TP	TP	TP
		1	1	1	1	1	1	1	◇1	1	1	◇1
									C			D
Windermere	d	11 01	11 59	12 58	13 58	15 00	15 58	16 58	18 01	19 06	19 49	20 40
Staveley	d		12x03	13x03	14x03		16x03	17x03	18 06			20x45
Burneside	d		12x08	13x08	14x08		16x08	17x08	18x11			20x50
Kendal	d	11 13	12 12	13 12	14 12	15 12	16 12	17 12	18 15	19 18	20 00	20 54
Oxenholme Lake District	a	11 18	12 18	13 17	14 17	15 17	16 17	17 17	18x21	19 23	20 05	20 59

Sundays
from 16 September

		TP	TP	TP	TP	TP	TP	TP	TP	TP	TP	TP
		1	1	1	1	1	1	1	1	1	1	◇1
												D
Windermere	d	11 01	11 59	12 58	13 58	15 00	15 58	16 58	18 04	19 00	19 49	20 40
Staveley	d		12x03	13x03	14x03		16x03	17x03	18x09	19x05		20x45
Burneside	d		12x08	13x08	14x08		16x08	17x08	18x14	19x10		20x50
Kendal	d	11 13	12 12	13 12	14 12	15 12	16 12	17 12	18 18	19 14	20 00	20 54
Oxenholme Lake District	a	11 18	12 18	13 17	14 17	15 17	16 17	17 17	18 23	19 19	20 05	20 59

A To Manchester Airport
B To Blackpool North
C To Preston
D To Barrow-in-Furness

until 29 June

Stoke-on-Trent and Crewe - Manchester Airport, Stockport and Manchester

Network Diagram - see first Page of Table 78

Miles	Miles	Miles			NT	NT	XC	VT	NT	VT	VT	NT	TP	NT	NT	VT	NT	NT	TP	AW	NT	NT	NT
					MX	MX	MX	MO	MX	MX	MO	MX											
							◇1	◇1		◇1	◇1		◇1			◇1			◇1				
					A			B	C		B		D				E		F		G	H	
								🛏		🛏	🛏												
—	—	—	London Euston 15 ⊖65	d				21p25		22p00	21p51												
—	—	—	Birmingham New Street 12 68	d			22p30																
—	—	—	Wolverhampton 7 68	d			22p48																
—	—	—	Stafford 65,68	d			23p01			23b38	23b53												
0	—	—	Stoke-on-Trent 50,68	d			23p21	23p29															
3	—	—	Longport 50	d																			
6¼	—	—	Kidsgrove 50	d																			
—	0	—	Crewe 10 65	d		23p12				00s03	00s21	00 44			05 48	06 11				06 27			
—	4¾	—	Sandbach	d		23p19									05 55								
—	8½	—	Holmes Chapel	d		23p24									06 00								
—	10½	—	Goostrey	d		23p27									06 03								
—	14¼	—	Chelford	d		23p31									06 07								
—	17¼	—	Alderley Edge	d		23p35									06 11								06 49
—	19	0	Wilmslow	d		23p39								05 46	06 15	06 27				06 45			06 52
—	—	2	Styal	d																			
—	—	4¼	Manchester Airport ✈	a								01 16		05 53									
—	20½	—	Handforth	d		23p42									06 18								06 55
11¾	—	—	Congleton	d																			
19¾	—	—	Macclesfield	a				23p45															
—	—	—		d				23p46										06 22					
22½	—	—	Prestbury	d														06 26					
24½	—	—	Adlington (Cheshire)	d														06 29					
26½	—	—	Poynton	d														06 33					
28	—	—	Bramhall	d														06 35					
29½	22¾	—	Cheadle Hulme	d		23p46									06 22			06 38					06 59
31¾	25	—	Stockport	a		23p51		23p59		00s26	00s50				06 27	06 36		06 43		06 55			07 04
—	—	—		d	23p48	23p51		00 01	00 05				05 53		06 27	06 37	06 41	06 43	06 53	06 55		06 58	07 04
31¾	26½	—	Heaton Chapel	d		23p55									06 31			06 46					07 08
34¾	28	—	Levenshulme	d		23p58									06 34			06 49					07 11
37¾	31	—	Manchester Piccadilly 10	a	00 02	00 07	00 12	00 12	00 18	00 35	01 00	01 36	06 05	06 25	06 42	06 49	06 52	06 58	07 02	07 07		07 10	07 21
—	—	—		d													06 54				06 58		
38¼	31½	—	Manchester Oxford Road	a													06 56				07 00		
38¾	32	—	Deansgate	a													06 59						

		NT	NT	NT	EM	XC	NT	NT	NT	NT	XC	NT	TP	NT	AW	NT	NT	TP	NT	NT	NT	VT	NT
					◇	◇1					◇1		◇1		◇			◇1				◇1	
		I		C	J				H				K	H	L		G	M	N	O			C
											⊼		⊼					⊼				⊠	
London Euston 15 ⊖65	d																					06 17	
Birmingham New Street 12 68	d					05 57					06 22												
Wolverhampton 7 68	d					06 16					06 40												
Stafford 65,68	d					06 30					06 55												
Stoke-on-Trent 50,68	d		06 30			06 51					07 14					07 17						07 45	
Longport 50	d		06 34													07 21							
Kidsgrove 50	d		06 38													07 25							
Crewe 10 65	d						06 33	06 49							07 27						07 22		
Sandbach	d						06 40	06 56													07 35		
Holmes Chapel	d						06 44	07 00													07 41		
Goostrey	d							07 03													07 45		
Chelford	d							07 08													07 51		
Alderley Edge	d						06 53	07 12				07 30									07 56		
Wilmslow	d						06 57	07 16				07 33			07 44						08 00		
Styal	d																						
Manchester Airport ✈	a						07 04																
Handforth	d							07 19				07 37									08 03		
Congleton	d		06 45			07 03										07 32							
Macclesfield	a		06 52			07 11					07 30					07 39						08 01	
	d		06 53			07 12				07 15	07 31					07 40						08 02	
Prestbury	d		06 57							07 21						07 44							
Adlington (Cheshire)	d		07 00							07 24						07 47							
Poynton	d		07 04							07 27						07 51							
Bramhall	d		07 07							07 31						07 54							
Cheadle Hulme	d		07 11					07 24		07 34		07 42				07 59					08 09		
Stockport	a		07 15			07 27		07 29		07 41	07 45	07 47			07 54	08 03					08 14	08 16	
	d	07 10	07 16	07 19	07 22	07 28		07 29	07 31	07 42	07 50	07 48	07 53	07 57	07 54	08 04			08 10		08 14	08 17	08 19
Heaton Chapel	d	07 15						07 33								08 07					08 18		
Levenshulme	d	07 18						07 36								08 10					08 21		
Manchester Piccadilly 10	a	07 26	07 27	07 31	07 34	07 37	07 42	07 44	07 45	07 56	07 59	07 59	08 02	08 09	08 10	08 21			08 25		08 27	08 28	08 32
	d	07 27			07 34												07 59	08 07		08 22	08 29		
Manchester Oxford Road	a	07 29			07 37												08 01	08 09		08 24	08 33		
Deansgate	a	07 32																		08 28			

A From Sheffield
B from 21 May until 25 June
C From Chester
D From Sheffield to Manchester Airport
E From Buxton to Clitheroe
F From Doncaster to Manchester Airport
G From Manchester Airport to Liverpool Lime Street
H From Hazel Grove
I From Buxton to Wigan North Western
J From Nottingham to Liverpool Lime Street
K From Cleethorpes to Manchester Airport
L From Cardiff Central
M From Hull to Liverpool Lime Street
N From Buxton
O From Manchester Airport to Southport
b Previous night, stops to set down only

Stoke-on-Trent and Crewe - Manchester Airport, Stockport and Manchester

Network Diagram - see first Page of Table 78

	XC	EM	NT	NT	NT	VT	NT	NT	XC	TP	VT	AW	NT	NT	TP	NT	VT	TP	NT	NT	EM	XC
	◇■	◇				◇■			◇■	◇■	◇■	◇			◇■		◇■	◇■			◇	◇■
		A					B			C		D		E	F	G		H	I	J	A	K
	🍴					⊠			🍴	🍴	⊠	🍴			🍴		⊠	🍴				🍴
London Euston ⊖65 d						06 36					06 55						07 20					
Birmingham New Street 68 d	06 57								07 31													07 57
Wolverhampton 68 d	07 15								07 49													08 15
Stafford 65,68 d	07 30								08 01													08 30
Stoke-on-Trent 50,68 d								07 57	08 20		08 25						08 48					08 55
Longport 50 d																						
Kidsgrove 50 d								08 04														
Crewe 65 d	07 52				07 55	08 11						08 28										
Sandbach d					08 02																	
Holmes Chapel d					08 06																	
Goostrey d																						
Chelford d																						
Alderley Edge d			07 53		08 15								08 49									
Wilmslow d	08 09		07 56		08 18	08 27						08 45	08 52									
Styal d			07 59																			
Manchester Airport ✈ a			08 04																			
Handforth d					08 21								08 55									
Congleton d								08 11														
Macclesfield a								08 18	08 36		08 41											09 11
d				08 06				08 19	08 37		08 41											09 12
Prestbury d				08 10				08 23														
Adlington (Cheshire) d								08 26														
Poynton d				08 15				08 30														
Bramhall d				08 17				08 33														
Cheadle Hulme d				08 20	08 26			08 37					08 59									
Stockport a	08 20			08 27	08 30	08 37		08 41	08 50		08 55	08 58	09 04				09 16					09 27
d	08 21	08 24		08 28	08 31	08 38	08 41	08 42	08 50	08 53	08 56	08 59	09 04			09 12	09 17		09 21		09 25	09 28
Heaton Chapel d					08 35			08 45					09 08			09 16						
Levenshulme d				08 32				08 48					09 11			09 19						
Manchester Piccadilly ⇌ a	08 34	08 36	08 42	08 42	08 45	08 49	08 52	08 56	08 59	09 02	09 07	09 15	09 20			09 28	09 28		09 36		09 36	09 39
d		08 37					08 54							09 01	09 07			09 16		09 22	09 37	
Manchester Oxford Road a		08 40					08 56							09 03	09 09			09 18		09 24	09 40	
Deansgate ⇌ a							09 00													09 28		

	NT	NT	VT	TP	NT	NT	XC	TP	VT	AW	NT	NT	TP	NT	VT	NT	NT	EM	XC	NT	NT
			◇■	◇■			◇■	◇■	◇■	◇			◇■		◇■			◇	◇■		
				L	B		M	C		N		E	O	G		I	J	P	K		
			⊠	🍴			🍴	🍴	⊠	🍴			🍴		⊠				🍴		
London Euston ⊖65 d			07 35						08 00						08 20						
Birmingham New Street 68 d							08 31												08 57		
Wolverhampton 68 d							08 49												09 15		
Stafford 65,68 d							09 01												09 30		
Stoke-on-Trent 50,68 d						08 58	09 20		09 25						09 48				09 55		
Longport 50 d																					
Kidsgrove 50 d						09 05															
Crewe 65 d	08 31	08 50	09 11							09 31										09 33	09 50
Sandbach d	08 38	08 57																		09 40	09 57
Holmes Chapel d	08 42	09 02																		09 44	10 02
Goostrey d	08 45	09 05																			10 05
Chelford d	08 50	09 09																			10 09
Alderley Edge d	08 54	09 13									09 48									09 53	10 13
Wilmslow d	08 57	09 17	09 27							09 48	09 51									09 57	10 17
Styal d																					
Manchester Airport ✈ a	09 04																			10 04	
Handforth d		09 20									09 54										10 20
Congleton d						09 12															
Macclesfield a						09 19			09 41										10 11		
d						09 20			09 41										10 12		
Prestbury d						09 24															
Adlington (Cheshire) d						09 27															
Poynton d						09 30															
Bramhall d						09 33															
Cheadle Hulme d		09 24				09 37					09 59										10 24
Stockport a		09 29	09 36			09 41	09 49		09 55	09 58	10 04				10 16				10 27		10 29
d		09 29	09 37		09 41	09 42	09 50	09 53	09 56	09 58	10 04			10 12	10 17	10 21		10 26	10 28		10 29
Heaton Chapel d		09 33				09 45					10 08			10 16							10 33
Levenshulme d		09 36				09 48					10 11			10 19							10 36
Manchester Piccadilly ⇌ a	09 42	09 44	09 49		09 52	09 56	09 59	10 02	10 07	10 15	10 20			10 28	10 28	10 36		10 36	10 39	10 42	10 44
d				09 46	09 54							10 01	10 07				10 22	10 37			
Manchester Oxford Road a				09 48	09 56							10 03	10 09				10 24	10 40			
Deansgate ⇌ a				09 51	10 00												10 28				

A From Nottingham to Liverpool Lime Street
B From Hazel Grove to Preston
C From Cleethorpes to Manchester Airport
D From Cardiff Central
E From Manchester Airport to Liverpool Lime Street
F From Newcastle to Liverpool Lime Street
G From Buxton
H From Manchester Airport to Barrow-in-Furness
I From Chester
J From Manchester Airport to Southport
K From Southampton Central
L From Manchester Airport to Windermere
M From Bristol Temple Meads
N From Carmarthen
O From Scarborough to Liverpool Lime Street
P From Norwich to Liverpool Lime Street

Stoke-on-Trent and Crewe - Manchester Airport, Stockport and Manchester

Network Diagram - see first Page of Table 78

	VT	NT	NT	XC	TP	VT	AW	NT	NT	TP	NT	VT	TP	NT	NT	EM	XC	NT	NT	VT	NT	NT
	◇■			◇■	◇■	◇■	◇			◇■		◇■	◇■			◇	◇■			◇■		
		A		B	C		D		E	F	G		H	I	J	K	L				A	
	⊠			🍴	🍴	⊠	🍴			🍴		⊠	🍴				🍴			⊠		
London Euston ⊖65 d	08 40					09 00						09 20								09 40		
Birmingham New Street 68 d				09 31													09 57					
Wolverhampton 68 d				09 49													10 15					
Stafford 65,68 d				10 01													10 30					
Stoke-on-Trent 50,68 d			09 58	10 20		10 25						10 48					10 55					10 58
Longport 50 d																						
Kidsgrove 50 d			10 05																			11 05
Crewe 65 d	10 11						10 31											10 34	10 50	11 11		
Sandbach d																		10 41	10 57			
Holmes Chapel d																		10 45	11 02			
Goostrey d																			11 05			
Chelford d																			11 09			
Alderley Edge d								10 49										10 54	11 13			
Wilmslow d	10 27						10 49	10 52										10 57	11 17	11 27		
Styal d																						
Manchester Airport ✈ a																		11 04				
Handforth d								10 55											11 20			
Congleton d			10 12																			11 12
Macclesfield a			10 19			10 41											11 11					11 19
d			10 20			10 41											11 12					11 20
Prestbury d			10 24																			11 24
Adlington (Cheshire) d			10 27																			11 27
Poynton d			10 30																			11 30
Bramhall d			10 33																			11 33
Cheadle Hulme d			10 37					10 59											11 24			11 37
Stockport a	10 36		10 41	10 49		10 55	10 58	11 04				11 16					11 27		11 29	11 36		11 41
d	10 37	10 41	10 42	10 50	10 53	10 56	10 58	11 04			11 12	11 17		11 21		11 26	11 28		11 29	11 37	11 41	11 42
Heaton Chapel d			10 45					11 08			11 16								11 33			11 45
Levenshulme d			10 48					11 11			11 19								11 36			11 48
Manchester Piccadilly ⇌ a	10 49	10 52	10 56	10 59	11 02	11 07	11 15	11 20			11 28	11 28		11 36		11 36	11 39	11 42	11 44	11 49	11 52	11 56
d		10 54							11 01	11 07			11 16		11 22	11 37					11 54	
Manchester Oxford Road a		10 56							11 03	11 09			11 18		11 24	11 40					11 56	
Deansgate ⇌ a		11 00													11 28						12 00	

	XC	TP	VT	AW	NT	NT	TP	NT	VT	NT	NT	EM	XC	NT	NT	VT	NT	NT	XC	TP	VT
	◇■	◇■	◇■	◇			◇■		◇■			◇	◇■			◇■			◇■	◇■	◇■
	M	C		N		E	F	G		I	J	K	L				A		O	C	
	🍴	🍴	⊠	🍴			🍴		⊠				🍴			⊠			🍴	🍴	🛒
London Euston ⊖65 d			10 00						10 20							10 40					11 00
Birmingham New Street 68 d	10 31												10 57						11 31		
Wolverhampton 68 d	10 49												11 15						11 49		
Stafford 65,68 d	11 01												11 30						12 01		
Stoke-on-Trent 50,68 d	11 20		11 25						11 48				11 55					11 58	12 20		12 25
Longport 50 d																					
Kidsgrove 50 d																		12 05			
Crewe 65 d				11 31										11 34	11 50	12 11					
Sandbach d														11 41	11 57						
Holmes Chapel d														11 45	12 02						
Goostrey d															12 05						
Chelford d															12 09						
Alderley Edge d					11 48									11 54	12 13						
Wilmslow d				11 48	11 51									11 57	12 17	12 27					
Styal d																					
Manchester Airport ✈ a														12 04							
Handforth d					11 54										12 20						
Congleton d																		12 12			
Macclesfield a			11 41										12 11					12 19			12 41
d			11 41										12 12					12 20			12 41
Prestbury d																		12 24			
Adlington (Cheshire) d																		12 27			
Poynton d																		12 30			
Bramhall d																		12 33			
Cheadle Hulme d					11 59										12 24			12 37			
Stockport a	11 49		11 55	11 58	12 04				12 16				12 27		12 29	12 36		12 41	12 49		12 55
d	11 50	11 53	11 56	11 58	12 04			12 12	12 17	12 21		12 26	12 28		12 29	12 37	12 41	12 42	12 50	12 53	12 56
Heaton Chapel d					12 08			12 16							12 33			12 45			
Levenshulme d					12 11			12 19							12 36			12 48			
Manchester Piccadilly ⇌ a	11 59	12 02	12 07	12 15	12 20			12 28	12 28	12 36		12 36	12 39	12 42	12 44	12 49	12 52	12 56	12 59	13 02	13 07
d						12 01	12 07				12 22	12 37					12 54				
Manchester Oxford Road a						12 03	12 09				12 24	12 40					12 56				
Deansgate ⇌ a											12 28						13 00				

A From Hazel Grove to Preston
B From Cardiff Central
C From Cleethorpes to Manchester Airport
D From Carmarthen
E From Manchester Airport to Liverpool Lime Street
F From Scarborough to Liverpool Lime Street
G From Buxton
H From Manchester Airport to Barrow-in-Furness
I From Chester
J From Manchester Airport to Southport
K From Norwich to Liverpool Lime Street
L From Bournemouth
M From Paignton
N From Milford Haven
O From Bristol Temple Meads

Table 84

Mondays to Fridays

until 29 June

Stoke-on-Trent and Crewe - Manchester Airport, Stockport and Manchester

Network Diagram - see first Page of Table 78

	AW	NT	NT	TP	NT	VT	TP FX	NT	NT	EM	XC	NT	NT	VT	NT	NT	XC	TP	VT	AW	NT	NT
	◇ A		B	◇1 C	D	◇1	◇1 E	F	G	◇ H	◇1 I			◇1	J		◇1 K	◇1 L	◇1	◇ M		B
London Euston ⊖65 d						11 20								11 40					12 00			
Birmingham New Street 68 d											11 57						12 31					
Wolverhampton 68 d											12 15						12 49					
Stafford 65,68 d											12 30						13 01					
Stoke-on-Trent 50,68 d						12 48					12 55					12 58	13 20		13 25			
Longport 50 d																						
Kidsgrove 50 d																13 05						
Crewe 65 d	12 31											12 34	12 50	13 11						13 31		
Sandbach d												12 41	12 57									
Holmes Chapel d												12 45	13 02									
Goostrey d													13 05									
Chelford d													13 09									
Alderley Edge d		12 49										12 54	13 13								13 48	
Wilmslow d	12 49	12 52										12 57	13 17	13 27						13 48	13 51	
Styal d																						
Manchester Airport a												13 04										
Handforth d		12 55											13 20								13 54	
Congleton d																13 12						
Macclesfield a											13 11					13 19			13 41			
Macclesfield d											13 12					13 20			13 41			
Prestbury d																13 24						
Adlington (Cheshire) d																13 27						
Poynton d																13 30						
Bramhall d																13 33						
Cheadle Hulme d		12 59											13 24			13 37					13 59	
Stockport a	12 58	13 04				13 16					13 27		13 29	13 36		13 41	13 49		13 55	13 58	14 04	
Stockport d	12 58	13 04			13 12	13 17		13 21		13 26	13 28		13 29	13 37	13 41	13 42	13 50	13 53	13 56	13 58	14 04	
Heaton Chapel d		13 08			13 16								13 33			13 45					14 08	
Levenshulme d		13 11			13 19								13 36			13 48					14 11	
Manchester Piccadilly a	13 15	13 20			13 28	13 28		13 36		13 36	13 39	13 42	13 44	13 49	13 52	13 56	13 59	14 02	14 07	14 15	14 20	
Manchester Piccadilly d			13 01	13 07			13 16		13 22	13 37					13 54							14 01
Manchester Oxford Road a			13 03	13 09			13 18		13 24	13 40					13 56							14 03
Deansgate a									13 28						14 00							

	TP	NT	VT	NT	NT	EM	XC	NT	NT	VT	NT	NT	XC	TP	VT	AW	NT	NT	TP	NT	VT	TP
	◇1 C	D	◇1	F	G	◇ H	◇1 I			◇1	J		◇1 N	◇1 L	◇1	◇ A		B	◇1 C	D	◇1	◇1 E
London Euston ⊖65 d			12 20							12 40					13 00						13 20	
Birmingham New Street 68 d							12 57						13 31									
Wolverhampton 68 d							13 15						13 49									
Stafford 65,68 d							13 30						14 01									
Stoke-on-Trent 50,68 d			13 48				13 55					13 58	14 20		14 25						14 48	
Longport 50 d																						
Kidsgrove 50 d												14 05										
Crewe 65 d								13 34	13 50	14 11						14 31						
Sandbach d								13 41	13 57													
Holmes Chapel d								13 45	14 02													
Goostrey d									14 05													
Chelford d									14 09													
Alderley Edge d								13 54	14 13								14 49					
Wilmslow d								13 57	14 17	14 27						14 49	14 52					
Styal d																						
Manchester Airport a								14 04														
Handforth d									14 20								14 55					
Congleton d												14 12										
Macclesfield a							14 11					14 19			14 41							
Macclesfield d							14 12					14 20			14 41							
Prestbury d												14 24										
Adlington (Cheshire) d												14 27										
Poynton d												14 30										
Bramhall d												14 33										
Cheadle Hulme d									14 24			14 37					14 59					
Stockport a			14 16				14 27		14 29	14 36		14 41	14 49		14 55	14 58	15 04				15 16	
Stockport d		14 12	14 17	14 21		14 26	14 28		14 29	14 37	14 41	14 42	14 50	14 53	14 56	14 58	15 04			15 12	15 17	
Heaton Chapel d		14 16							14 33			14 45					15 08			15 16		
Levenshulme d		14 19							14 36			14 48					15 11			15 19		
Manchester Piccadilly a		14 28	14 28	14 36		14 36	14 39	14 42	14 44	14 49	14 52	14 56	14 59	15 02	15 07	15 15	15 20			15 28	15 28	
Manchester Piccadilly d	14 07				14 22	14 37					14 54							15 01	15 07			15 16
Manchester Oxford Road a	14 09				14 24	14 40					14 56							15 03	15 09			15 18
Deansgate a					14 28						15 00											

A From Milford Haven
B From Manchester Airport to Liverpool Lime Street
C From Scarborough to Liverpool Lime Street
D From Buxton
E From Manchester Airport to Barrow-in-Furness
F From Chester
G From Manchester Airport to Southport
H From Norwich to Liverpool Lime Street
I From Bournemouth
J From Hazel Grove to Preston
K From Bristol Temple Meads
L From Cleethorpes to Manchester Airport
M From Fishguard Harbour
N From Paignton

Table 84

Mondays to Fridays

until 29 June

Stoke-on-Trent and Crewe - Manchester Airport, Stockport and Manchester

Network Diagram - see first Page of Table 78

	NT	NT	EM	XC	NT	NT	VT	NT	NT	XC	TP	VT	AW	NT	NT	TP	TP FX	NT	NT	VT	NT
	A	B	◇ C	◇1 D			◇1	E		◇1 F	◇1 G	◇1	◇ H		I	◇1 J	◇1 K	B	L	◇1	A
London Euston ⊖65 d							13 40					14 00								14 20	
Birmingham New Street 68 d				13 57						14 31											
Wolverhampton 68 d				14 15						14 49											
Stafford 65,68 d				14 30						15 01											
Stoke-on-Trent 50,68 d				14 55					14 58	15 20		15 25								15 48	
Longport 50 d																					
Kidsgrove 50 d									15 05												
Crewe 65 d					14 34	14 50	15 11						15 29								
Sandbach d					14 41	14 57															
Holmes Chapel d					14 45	15 02															
Goostrey d						15 05															
Chelford d						15 09															
Alderley Edge d					14 54	15 13								15 48							
Wilmslow d					14 57	15 17	15 27						15 47	15 51							
Styal d																					
Manchester Airport a					15 04																
Handforth d						15 20								15 54							
Congleton d									15 12												
Macclesfield a				15 11					15 19			15 41									
Macclesfield d				15 12					15 20			15 41									
Prestbury d									15 24												
Adlington (Cheshire) d									15 27												
Poynton d									15 30												
Bramhall d									15 33												
Cheadle Hulme d						15 24			15 37					15 59							
Stockport a				15 27		15 29	15 36		15 41	15 49		15 55	15 58	16 04						16 16	
Stockport d	15 21		15 26	15 28		15 29	15 37	15 41	15 42	15 50	15 53	15 56	15 58	16 04					16 12	16 17	16 21
Heaton Chapel d						15 33			15 45					16 08					16 16		
Levenshulme d						15 36			15 48					16 11					16 19		
Manchester Piccadilly a	15 36		15 36	15 39	15 41	15 44	15 49	15 52	15 56	15 59	16 02	16 07	16 15	16 20					16 25	16 28	16 36
Manchester Piccadilly d		15 22	15 37		15 42			15 54							16 01	16 07	16 16	16 22	16 27		
Manchester Oxford Road a		15 24	15 40		15 46			15 56							16 03	16 09	16 18	16 24	16 29		
Deansgate a		15 28						16 00										16 28	16 32		

	EM	XC	NT	NT	VT	NT	NT	XC	TP	VT	AW	NT	VT	NT	TP	TP	NT	NT	EM	XC	NT	NT
	◇ C	◇1 D			◇1	M		◇1 N	◇1 G	◇1	◇ O		◇1	I	◇1 J	◇1 P	A	B	◇ C	◇1 D		
London Euston ⊖65 d					14 40					15 00			15 20									
Birmingham New Street 68 d		14 57						15 31												15 57		
Wolverhampton 68 d		15 15						15 50												16 15		
Stafford 65,68 d		15 30						16 02												16 31		
Stoke-on-Trent 50,68 d		15 55					15 58	16 21		16 25			16 48							16 55		
Longport 50 d																						
Kidsgrove 50 d							16 05															
Crewe 65 d			15 33	15 50	16 12						16 31										16 34	16 50
Sandbach d			15 40	15 57																	16 41	16 57
Holmes Chapel d			15 44	16 02																	16 45	17 02
Goostrey d				16 05																		17 05
Chelford d				16 09																		17 09
Alderley Edge d			15 53	16 13								16 49									16 54	17 13
Wilmslow d			15 56	16 17	16 27						16 48	16 52									16 57	17 17
Styal d			15 59																			
Manchester Airport a			16 04																		17 04	
Handforth d				16 20								16 55										17 20
Congleton d							16 12															
Macclesfield a		16 11					16 19			16 41										17 11		
Macclesfield d		16 12					16 20			16 41										17 12		
Prestbury d							16 24															
Adlington (Cheshire) d							16 27															
Poynton d							16 30															
Bramhall d							16 33															
Cheadle Hulme d				16 24			16 37					16 59										17 24
Stockport a		16 27		16 29	16 36		16 41	16 49		16 54	16 58	17 04	17 16							17 27		17 29
Stockport d	16 26	16 28		16 29	16 37	16 41	16 42	16 50	16 53	16 55	16 58	17 04	17 17				17 21		17 26	17 28		17 29
Heaton Chapel d				16 33			16 45					17 08										17 33
Levenshulme d				16 36			16 48					17 11										17 36
Manchester Piccadilly a	16 36	16 39	16 42	16 44	16 49	16 52	16 56	16 59	17 02	17 07	17 14	17 20	17 28				17 36		17 37	17 39	17 42	17 44
Manchester Piccadilly d	16 37					16 54								17 01	17 07	17 15		17 22	17 37			
Manchester Oxford Road a	16 40					16 56								17 03	17 09	17 17		17 25	17 40			
Deansgate a						17 00																

A From Chester
B From Manchester Airport to Southport
C From Norwich to Liverpool Lime Street
D From Bournemouth
E From Hazel Grove to Bolton
F From Bristol Temple Meads
G From Cleethorpes to Manchester Airport
H From Carmarthen
I From Manchester Airport to Liverpool Lime Street
J From Scarborough to Liverpool Lime Street
K From Manchester Airport to Windermere
L From Buxton to Barrow-in-Furness
M From Hazel Grove to Preston
N From Penzance
O From Milford Haven
P From Manchester Airport to Barrow-in-Furness

Stoke-on-Trent and Crewe - Manchester Airport, Stockport and Manchester

Network Diagram - see first Page of Table 78

	VT	NT	XC	TP	VT	AW	NT	NT	TP	NT	VT	TP	NT	NT	EM	XC	NT	NT	VT	NT	NT
	◇■		◇■	◇■	◇■	◇			◇■		◇■	◇■			◇	◇■			◇■		
			A	B		C		D	E	F		G	H	I	J	K				L	
	☕		✕	✕	☕	✕			✕		☕	✕				✕			☕		
London Euston ■ ⊖65 d	15 40				16 00						16 20								16 40		
Birmingham New Street ■ 68 d			16 31													16 57					
Wolverhampton ■ 68 d			16 49													17 15					
Stafford 65,68 d			17 01													17 30					
Stoke-on-Trent 50,68 d		16 58	17 20		17 25						17 48					17 55					17 58
Longport 50 d																					
Kidsgrove 50 d		17 05																			18 05
Crewe ■ 65 d	17 11					17 30											17 33	17 50	18 11		
Sandbach d																	17 40	17 57			
Holmes Chapel d																	17 44	18 02			
Goostrey d																		18 05			
Chelford d																		18 09			
Alderley Edge d							17 48										17 53	18 13			
Wilmslow d	17 27					17 47	17 51										17 56	18 17	18 27		
Styal d																	17 59				
Manchester Airport ✈ a																	18 04				
Handforth d							17 54											18 20			
Congleton d		17 12																			18 12
Macclesfield a		17 19			17 41											18 11					18 19
d		17 20			17 41											18 12					18 20
Prestbury d		17 24																			18 24
Adlington (Cheshire) d		17 27																			18 27
Poynton d		17 30																			18 30
Bramhall d		17 33																			18 33
Cheadle Hulme d		17 36					17 59											18 24			18 37
Stockport a	17 36	17 41	17 49		17 55	17 57	18 04				18 16					18 27		18 29	18 37		18 41
d	17 37	17 42	17 50	17 53	17 56	17 58	18 04			18 12	18 17		18 21		18 26	18 28		18 29	18 38	18 41	18 42
Heaton Chapel d		17 45					18 08			18 16								18 33			18 45
Levenshulme d		17 48					18 11			18 19								18 36			18 48
Manchester Piccadilly ■ a	17 49	17 56	17 59	18 02	18 07	18 13	18 20			18 28	18 28		18 36		18 36	18 39	18 42	18 44	18 49	18 52	18 56
d								18 01	18 07			18 16		18 22	18 37					18 54	
Manchester Oxford Road a								18 03	18 09			18 18		18 24	18 40					18 56	
Deansgate a														18 28						19 00	

	XC	TP	VT	AW	NT	TP	NT	VT	TP	NT	NT	NT	EM	XC	NT	VT	NT	XC	TP	VT	AW	NT
				■																	■	
	◇■	◇■	◇■			◇■		◇■	◇■				◇	◇■		◇■		◇■	◇■	◇■		
	M	B		N	D	E	F		G	I		H	J	K				A	B		C	D
	✕	✕	☒	✕		✕		☒						✕		☒		✕	✕	☒	✕	
London Euston ■ ⊖65 d			17 00					17 20								17 40				18 00		
Birmingham New Street ■ 68 d	17 31													17 57				18 31				
Wolverhampton ■ 68 d	17 50													18 15				18 49				
Stafford 65,68 d	18 02													18 30				19 01				
Stoke-on-Trent 50,68 d	18 21		18 25					18 49						18 55			18 58	19 20		19 25		
Longport 50 d																						
Kidsgrove 50 d																	19 05					
Crewe ■ 65 d				18 31							18 34				18 50	19 11					19 31	
Sandbach d											18 41				18 57							
Holmes Chapel d											18 45				19 02							
Goostrey d															19 05							
Chelford d															19 09							
Alderley Edge d											18 54				19 13							
Wilmslow d				18 48							18 57				19 17	19 27					19 48	
Styal d																						
Manchester Airport ✈ a											19 05											
Handforth d															19 20							
Congleton d																	19 12					
Macclesfield a			18 41											19 11			19 19			19 41		
d			18 41											19 12			19 20			19 41		
Prestbury d																	19 24					
Adlington (Cheshire) d																	19 27					
Poynton d																	19 30					
Bramhall d																	19 33					
Cheadle Hulme d															19 24		19 37					
Stockport a	18 49		18 55	18 58				19 16						19 27	19 29	19 36	19 41	19 48		19 55	19 58	
d	18 50	18 53	18 56	18 58			19 12	19 17				19 21	19 26	19 28	19 29	19 37	19 42	19 50	19 53	19 56	19 58	
Heaton Chapel d							19 16										19 45					
Levenshulme d							19 19										19 48					
Manchester Piccadilly ■ a	18 59	19 02	19 07	19 15			19 28	19 28			19 31	19 35	19 36	19 39	19 43	19 49	19 56	19 59	20 02	20 07	20 15	
d					19 01	19 07			19 16	19 20	19 32		19 37									20 01
Manchester Oxford Road a					19 03	19 09			19 18	19 22	19 36		19 40									20 03
Deansgate a										19 26												

A From Bristol Temple Meads
B From Cleethorpes to Manchester Airport
C From Carmarthen
D From Manchester Airport to Liverpool Lime Street
E From Scarborough to Liverpool Lime Street
F From Buxton
G From Manchester Airport to Barrow-in-Furness
H From Chester
I From Manchester Airport to Southport
J From Norwich to Liverpool Lime Street
K From Bournemouth
L From Buxton to Bolton
M From Paignton
N From Milford Haven

Stoke-on-Trent and Crewe - Manchester Airport, Stockport and Manchester

Network Diagram - see first Page of Table 78

	TP	NT	VT	TP	NT	NT	NT	EM	XC	NT	VT	NT	XC	AW	TP	AW	VT	VT	VT	TP	NT	VT
																■	■		■			■
	◇■		◇■	◇■				◇	◇■		◇■		◇■		◇■		■	◇	■	◇■		■
	A	B		C	D		E	F	G				H	I	J	K	L	M	M	A	B	
			☒						✕		☒		✕			✕	☕	☕	☕			☕
London Euston ■ ⊖65 d			18 20								18 40						19 00	18 57	19 00			19 20
Birmingham New Street ■ 68 d									18 57				19 31									
Wolverhampton ■ 68 d									19 15				19 49									
Stafford 65,68 d									19 29				20 01									
Stoke-on-Trent 50,68 d			19 48						19 55			19 58	20 20				20 25		20 25			20 48
Longport 50 d																						
Kidsgrove 50 d												20 05										
Crewe ■ 65 d										19 50	20 12					20 23		20s33				
Sandbach d										19 57												
Holmes Chapel d										20 02												
Goostrey d										20 05												
Chelford d										20 09												
Alderley Edge d										20 13												
Wilmslow d						19 56				20 17	20 27					20 40						
Styal d																						
Manchester Airport ✈ a						20 04																
Handforth d										20 20												
Congleton d												20 12										
Macclesfield a									20 11			20 19					20 41		20 41			
d									20 12			20 20					20 41		20 41			
Prestbury d												20 24										
Adlington (Cheshire) d												20 27										
Poynton d												20 30										
Bramhall d												20 33										
Cheadle Hulme d										20 24		20 37										
Stockport a			20 16						20 27	20 29	20 36	20 41	20 48			20 50	20 55		20 55			21 16
d		20 12	20 17				20 21	20 26	20 28	20 29	20 37	20 42	20 50		20 54	20 51	20 56		20 56		21 12	21 17
Heaton Chapel d		20 16										20 45									21 16	
Levenshulme d		20 19										20 48									21 19	
Manchester Piccadilly ■ a		20 28	20 28			20 32	20 35	20 36	20 39	20 43	20 49	20 56	20 58		21 02	21 05	21 07	21 09	21 10		21 28	21 28
d	20 07			20 16	20 20	20 32		20 37						20 50						21 07		
Manchester Oxford Road a	20 09			20 18	20 22	20 36		20 40						20 52						21 09		
Deansgate a					20 26																	

	EM	NT	NT	NT	XC	NT	VT	NT	XC	VT	AW	AW	NT FO	TP	NT	TP	NT	NT	XC	NT	NT
	◇				◇■		◇■		◇■	◇■	◇			◇■		◇■			◇■		
	N	D		E	G				O		P	I	Q	A	B	C		E	G		D
							☕			☕	✕										
London Euston ■ ⊖65 d							19 40			20 00											
Birmingham New Street ■ 68 d					19 57				20 31										20 57		
Wolverhampton ■ 68 d					20 16				20 49										21 16		
Stafford 65,68 d					20 30		21 04												21 32		
Stoke-on-Trent 50,68 d					20 55			20 58	21 18	21 24									21 55		
Longport 50 d																					
Kidsgrove 50 d								21 05													
Crewe ■ 65 d						20 50	21 23				21 31									21 45	
Sandbach d						20 57														21 52	
Holmes Chapel d						21 02														21 58	
Goostrey d						21 05														22 01	
Chelford d						21 09														22 07	
Alderley Edge d						21 13														22 12	
Wilmslow d			20 56			21 17	21 38				21 48						21 55			22 15	
Styal d																					
Manchester Airport ✈ a			21 04														22 04				
Handforth d						21 20														22 19	
Congleton d								21 12													
Macclesfield a					21 11			21 19		21 40									22 11		
d					21 12			21 20		21 40									22 12		
Prestbury d								21 24													
Adlington (Cheshire) d								21 27													
Poynton d								21 30													
Bramhall d								21 33													
Cheadle Hulme d						21 24		21 37												22 24	
Stockport a					21 27	21 29		21 41	21 46	21 55	21 58								22 25	22 29	
d	21 20			21 21	21 28	21 29		21 42	21 49	21 56	21 59				22 12			22 21	22 26	22 29	
Heaton Chapel d								21 45							22 16						
Levenshulme d								21 48							22 19						
Manchester Piccadilly ■ a	21 32		21 32	21 35	21 39	21 43	21 57	21 57	21 59	22 07	22 13				22 28		22 31	22 35	22 35	22 43	
d		21 20	21 32									21 50	22 01	22 07		22 16	22 32				22 36
Manchester Oxford Road a		21 22	21 36									21 52	22 03	22 09		22 18	22 36				22 38
Deansgate a		21 26																			22 41

A From Scarborough to Liverpool Lime Street
B From Buxton
C From Manchester Airport to Barrow-in-Furness
D From Manchester Airport to Southport
E From Chester
F From Norwich to Liverpool Lime Street
G From Bournemouth
H From Exeter St Davids
I From Manchester Airport to Chester
J From Cleethorpes to Manchester Airport
K From Milford Haven
L MTWO
M ThFO
N From Norwich
O From Bristol Temple Meads
P From Carmarthen
Q From Manchester Airport to Liverpool Lime Street

until 29 June

Stoke-on-Trent and Crewe - Manchester Airport, Stockport and Manchester

Network Diagram - see first Page of Table 78

	NT	VT	TP	VT	NT	NT	XC	VT	AW	NT	NT	NT	XC	XC	AW	VT
													FX		FO	
		◇1	◇1	◇1			◇1	◇1	◇				◇1	◇1	◇	◇1
	A		B				C		D	E	F		G	H	I	
		☕		☕				☕								☕
London Euston [15] ⊖65 d		20 40		21 00				21 40								22 00
Birmingham New Street [12] 68 d							21 57						22 30	22 30	21 24	
Wolverhampton [7] 68 d							22 16						22 48	22 48	21 43	
Stafford 65,68 d							22 30						23 01	23 01		23s38
Stoke-on-Trent 50,68 d				22 28	22 18		22 55	23 07					23 21	23 22		
Longport 50 d																
Kidsgrove 50 d					22 25											
Crewe [10] 65 d		22 13							23 04			23 12				00s03
Sandbach d												23 19				
Holmes Chapel d												23 24				
Goostrey d												23 27				
Chelford d												23 31				
Alderley Edge d												23 35				
Wilmslow d		22 29				22 56			23 22			23 39				
Styal d																
Manchester Airport ✈ a						23 04										
Handforth d												23 42				
Congleton d					22 32											
Macclesfield a				22 44	22 40		23 11	23 23								
d				22 44	22 48		23 12	23 23								
Prestbury d					22 53											
Adlington (Cheshire) d					22 56											
Poynton d					22 59											
Bramhall d					23 02											
Cheadle Hulme d					23 05							23 46				
Stockport a		22 38		22 58	23 10		23 25	23 37	23 30			23 51				00s26
d	22 34	22 39	22 53	22 59	23 10		23 26	23 38	23 31	23 41	23 48	23 51				
Heaton Chapel d	22 38				23 14							23 55				
Levenshulme d	22 41				23 17							23 58				
Manchester Piccadilly [10] a	22 48	22 48	23 02	23 11	23 25	23 33	23 37	23 46	23 48	23 54	00 02	00 07	00 12	00 13	00 28	00 35
d	22 50															
Manchester Oxford Road a	22 52															
Deansgate a	22 55															

Mondays to Fridays

2 July to 28 September

	NT	NT	XC	VT	NT	VT	VT	NT	VT	VT	VT	VT	VT	TP	NT	NT	VT	NT	NT	TP	AW	NT
	MX	MX	MX	MO	MX	MX	MO	MX														
			◇1	◇1		◇1	◇1		◇1	◇1	◇1	◇1	◇1	◇1			◇1			◇1		
	F				J				K	L	K	L	M	N				O		P		Q
				☕		☕	☕		☕	☕	☕	☕	☕									
London Euston [15] ⊖65 d				21p25		22p00	21p51		23p30	23p30	00 30	00 30	01 30									
Birmingham New Street [12] 68 d			22p30																			
Wolverhampton [7] 68 d			22p48																			
Stafford 65,68 d			23p01			23b38	23b53															
Stoke-on-Trent 50,68 d			23p21	23p29					00s53	00s53	01s53	01s53	02s53									
Longport 50 d																						
Kidsgrove 50 d																						
Crewe [10] 65 d		23p12				00s03	00s21	00 44								05 48	06 11				06 27	
Sandbach d		23p19														05 55						
Holmes Chapel d		23p24														06 00						
Goostrey d		23p27														06 03						
Chelford d		23p31														06 07						
Alderley Edge d		23p35														06 11						
Wilmslow d		23p39													05 46	06 15	06 27				06 45	
Styal d																						
Manchester Airport ✈ a								01 16							05 53							
Handforth d		23p42														06 18						
Congleton d																						
Macclesfield a				23p45					01s10	01s10	02s10	02s10	03s12									
d				23p46															06 22			
Prestbury d																			06 26			
Adlington (Cheshire) d																			06 29			
Poynton d																			06 33			
Bramhall d																			06 35			
Cheadle Hulme d		23p46														06 22			06 38			
Stockport a		23p51		23p59		00s26	00s50		01s24	01s24	02s24	02s26	03s30			06 27	06 36		06 43		06 55	
d	23p48	23p51		00 01	00 05									05 53		06 27	06 37	06 41	06 43	06 53	06 55	
Heaton Chapel d		23p55														06 31			06 46			
Levenshulme d		23p58														06 34			06 49			
Manchester Piccadilly [10] a	00 02	00 07	00 12	00 12	00 18	00 35	01 00	01 36	01 37	01 43	02 37	02 39	03 43	06 05	06 25	06 42	06 49	06 52	06 58	07 02	07 07	
d																		06 54				06 58
Manchester Oxford Road a																		06 56				07 00
Deansgate a																		06 59				

A To Wigan Wallgate
B From Cleethorpes to Manchester Airport
C From Bournemouth
D From Cardiff Central
E From Buxton
F From Sheffield
G also 29 June
H FO until 22 June
I From Birmingham International
J From Chester
K 30 July, 6 August, 13 August, 3 September, 10 September
L MX from 31 July until 7 September, not from 14 August until 29 August
M from 30 July until 10 September, not from 14 August until 29 August
N From Sheffield to Manchester Airport
O From Buxton to Clitheroe
P From Doncaster to Manchester Airport
Q From Manchester Airport to Liverpool Lime Street
b Previous night, stops to set down only

2 July to 28 September

Stoke-on-Trent and Crewe - Manchester Airport, Stockport and Manchester

Network Diagram - see first Page of Table 78

	NT	NT	NT	NT	NT	EM	XC	NT	NT	NT	NT	XC	NT	TP	NT	AW	NT	NT	TP	NT	NT	NT
						◇	◇1					◇1		◇1		◇			◇1			
	A		B		C	D				A				E	A	F		G	H	I	J	
												🛒		🛒					🛒			
London Euston [15] ⊖65 d																						
Birmingham New Street [12] 68 d							05 57					06 22										
Wolverhampton [7] 68 d							06 16					06 40										
Stafford 65,68 d							06 30					06 55										
Stoke-on-Trent 50,68 d				06 30			06 51					07 14					07 17					
Longport 50 d				06 34													07 21					
Kidsgrove 50 d				06 38													07 25					
Crewe [10] 65 d								06 33	06 49							07 27						07 22
Sandbach d								06 40	06 56													07 35
Holmes Chapel d								06 44	07 00													07 41
Goostrey d									07 03													07 45
Chelford d									07 08													07 51
Alderley Edge d		06 49						06 53	07 12				07 30									07 56
Wilmslow d		06 52						06 57	07 16				07 33			07 44						08 00
Styal d																						
Manchester Airport ✈ a								07 04														
Handforth d		06 55							07 19				07 37									08 03
Congleton d				06 45			07 03										07 32					
Macclesfield a				06 52			07 11					07 30					07 39					
d				06 53			07 12				07 15	07 31					07 40					
Prestbury d				06 57							07 21						07 44					
Adlington (Cheshire) d				07 00							07 24						07 47					
Poynton d				07 04							07 27						07 51					
Bramhall d				07 07							07 31						07 54					
Cheadle Hulme d		06 59		07 11					07 24		07 34		07 42				07 59					08 09
Stockport a		07 04		07 15			07 27		07 29		07 41	07 45	07 47			07 54	08 03					08 14
d	06 58	07 04	07 10	07 16	07 19	07 22	07 28		07 29	07 31	07 42	07 50	07 48	07 53	07 57	07 54	08 04			08 10		08 14
Heaton Chapel d		07 08	07 15						07 33								08 07					08 18
Levenshulme d		07 11	07 18						07 36								08 10					08 21
Manchester Piccadilly [10] a	07 10	07 21	07 26	07 27	07 31	07 34	07 37	07 42	07 44	07 45	07 56	07 59	07 59	08 02	08 09	08 10	08 21			08 25		08 27
d			07 27			07 34												07 59	08 07		08 22	08 29
Manchester Oxford Road a			07 29			07 37												08 01	08 09		08 24	08 33
Deansgate a			07 32																		08 28	

	VT	NT	XC	EM	NT	NT	NT	VT	NT	NT	XC	TP	VT	AW	NT	NT	TP	NT	VT	TP	NT
	◇1		◇1	◇				◇1			◇1	◇1	◇1	◇			◇1		◇1	◇1	
		C		D					K			E		F		G	L	I		M	C
	⊠		🛒					⊠			🛒	🛒	⊠	🛒			🛒		⊠	🛒	
London Euston [15] ⊖65 d	06 17							06 36					06 55						07 20		
Birmingham New Street [12] 68 d			06 57								07 31										
Wolverhampton [7] 68 d			07 15								07 49										
Stafford 65,68 d			07 30								08 01										
Stoke-on-Trent 50,68 d	07 45									07 57	08 20		08 25						08 48		
Longport 50 d																					
Kidsgrove 50 d										08 04											
Crewe [10] 65 d			07 52				07 55	08 11						08 28							
Sandbach d							08 02														
Holmes Chapel d							08 06														
Goostrey d																					
Chelford d																					
Alderley Edge d					07 53		08 15								08 49						
Wilmslow d			08 09		07 56		08 18	08 27						08 45	08 52						
Styal d					07 59																
Manchester Airport ✈ a					08 04																
Handforth d							08 21								08 55						
Congleton d										08 11											
Macclesfield a	08 01									08 18	08 36		08 41								
d	08 02					08 06				08 19	08 37		08 41								
Prestbury d						08 10				08 23											
Adlington (Cheshire) d										08 26											
Poynton d						08 15				08 30											
Bramhall d						08 17				08 33											
Cheadle Hulme d						08 20	08 26			08 37					08 59						
Stockport a	08 16		08 20			08 27	08 30	08 37		08 41	08 50		08 55	08 58	09 04				09 16		
d	08 17	08 19	08 21	08 24		08 28	08 31	08 38	08 41	08 42	08 50	08 53	08 56	08 59	09 04			09 12	09 17		09 21
Heaton Chapel d							08 35			08 45					09 08			09 16			
Levenshulme d						08 32				08 48					09 11			09 19			
Manchester Piccadilly [10] a	08 28	08 32	08 34	08 36	08 42	08 42	08 45	08 49	08 52	08 56	08 59	09 02	09 07	09 15	09 20			09 28	09 28		09 36
d				08 37					08 54							09 01	09 07			09 16	
Manchester Oxford Road a				08 40					08 56							09 03	09 09			09 18	
Deansgate a									09 00												

A From Hazel Grove
B From Buxton to Wigan North Western
C From Chester
D From Nottingham to Liverpool Lime Street
E From Cleethorpes to Manchester Airport
F From Cardiff Central
G From Manchester Airport to Liverpool Lime Street
H From Hull to Liverpool Lime Street
I From Buxton
J From Manchester Airport to Southport
K From Hazel Grove to Preston
L From Newcastle to Liverpool Lime Street
M From Manchester Airport to Barrow-in-Furness

2 July to 28 September

Stoke-on-Trent and Crewe - Manchester Airport, Stockport and Manchester

Network Diagram - see first Page of Table 78

	NT A	EM ◇ B	XC ◇1 C ⊼	NT	NT	VT ◇1 ⊠	TP ◇1 D ⊼	NT E	NT	XC ◇1 F ⊼	TP ◇1 G ⊼	VT ◇1 ⊠	AW ◇ H ⊼	NT	NT I	TP ◇1 J ⊼	NT K	VT ◇1 ⊠	NT L	NT A	EM ◇ M	XC ◇1 C ⊼
London Euston ⊖65 d						07 35						08 00						08 20				
Birmingham New Street 68 d			07 57							08 31												08 57
Wolverhampton 68 d			08 15							08 49												09 15
Stafford 65,68 d			08 30							09 01												09 30
Stoke-on-Trent 50,68 d			08 55						08 58	09 20		09 25						09 48				09 55
Longport 50 d																						
Kidsgrove 50 d									09 05													
Crewe 65 d				08 31	08 50	09 11							09 31									
Sandbach d				08 38	08 57																	
Holmes Chapel d				08 42	09 02																	
Goostrey d				08 45	09 05																	
Chelford d				08 50	09 09																	
Alderley Edge d				08 54	09 13									09 48								
Wilmslow d				08 57	09 17	09 27							09 48	09 51								
Styal d																						
Manchester Airport a				09 04																		
Handforth d					09 20									09 54								
Congleton d									09 12													
Macclesfield a			09 11						09 19			09 41										10 11
d			09 12						09 20			09 41										10 12
Prestbury d									09 24													
Adlington (Cheshire) d									09 27													
Poynton d									09 30													
Bramhall d									09 33													
Cheadle Hulme d					09 24				09 37					09 59								
Stockport a			09 27		09 29	09 36			09 41	09 49		09 55	09 58	10 04				10 16				10 27
d		09 25	09 28		09 29	09 37		09 41	09 42	09 50	09 53	09 56	09 58	10 04			10 12	10 17	10 21		10 26	10 28
Heaton Chapel d					09 33				09 45					10 08			10 16					
Levenshulme d					09 36				09 48					10 11			10 19					
Manchester Piccadilly a		09 36	09 39	09 42	09 44	09 49		09 52	09 56	09 59	10 02	10 07	10 15	10 20			10 28	10 28	10 36		10 36	10 39
d	09 22	09 37					09 46	09 54							10 01	10 07				10 22	10 37	
Manchester Oxford Road a	09 24	09 40					09 48	09 56							10 03	10 09				10 24	10 40	
Deansgate a	09 28						09 51	10 00												10 28		

	NT	NT	VT ◇1 ⊠	NT E	NT	XC ◇1 N ⊼	TP ◇1 G ⊼	VT ◇1 ⊠	AW ◇ H ⊼	NT	NT I	TP ◇1 J ⊼	NT K	VT ◇1 ⊠	TP ◇1 O ⊼	NT L	NT A	EM ◇ M	XC ◇1 P ⊼	NT	NT
London Euston ⊖65 d			08 40					09 00						09 20							
Birmingham New Street 68 d						09 31													09 57		
Wolverhampton 68 d						09 49													10 15		
Stafford 65,68 d						10 01													10 30		
Stoke-on-Trent 50,68 d					09 58	10 20		10 25						10 48					10 55		
Longport 50 d																					
Kidsgrove 50 d					10 05																
Crewe 65 d	09 33	09 50	10 11						10 31											10 34	10 50
Sandbach d	09 40	09 57																		10 41	10 57
Holmes Chapel d	09 44	10 02																		10 45	11 02
Goostrey d		10 05																			11 05
Chelford d		10 09																			11 09
Alderley Edge d	09 53	10 13								10 49										10 54	11 13
Wilmslow d	09 57	10 17	10 27						10 49	10 52										10 57	11 17
Styal d																					
Manchester Airport a	10 04																			11 04	
Handforth d		10 20								10 55											11 20
Congleton d					10 12																
Macclesfield a					10 19			10 41											11 11		
d					10 20			10 41											11 12		
Prestbury d					10 24																
Adlington (Cheshire) d					10 27																
Poynton d					10 30																
Bramhall d					10 33																
Cheadle Hulme d		10 24			10 37					10 59											11 24
Stockport a		10 29	10 36		10 41	10 49		10 55	10 58	11 04				11 16					11 27		11 29
d		10 29	10 37	10 41	10 42	10 50	10 53	10 56	10 58	11 04			11 12	11 17		11 21		11 26	11 28		11 29
Heaton Chapel d		10 33			10 45					11 08			11 16								11 33
Levenshulme d		10 36			10 48					11 11			11 19								11 36
Manchester Piccadilly a	10 42	10 44	10 49	10 52	10 56	10 59	11 02	11 07	11 15	11 20			11 28	11 28		11 36		11 36	11 39	11 42	11 44
d				10 54							11 01	11 07			11 16		11 22	11 37			
Manchester Oxford Road a				10 56							11 03	11 09			11 18		11 24	11 40			
Deansgate a				11 00													11 28				

- **A** From Manchester Airport to Southport
- **B** From Nottingham to Liverpool Lime Street
- **C** From Southampton Central
- **D** From Manchester Airport to Windermere
- **E** From Hazel Grove to Preston
- **F** From Bristol Temple Meads
- **G** From Cleethorpes to Manchester Airport
- **H** From Carmarthen
- **I** From Manchester Airport to Liverpool Lime Street
- **J** From Scarborough to Liverpool Lime Street
- **K** From Buxton
- **L** From Chester
- **M** From Norwich to Liverpool Lime Street
- **N** From Cardiff Central
- **O** From Manchester Airport to Barrow-in-Furness
- **P** From Bournemouth

2 July to 28 September

Stoke-on-Trent and Crewe - Manchester Airport, Stockport and Manchester

Network Diagram - see first Page of Table 78

	VT ◇1 ⊠	NT A	NT	XC ◇1 B ⊼	TP ◇1 C ⊼	VT ◇1 ⊠	AW ◇ D ⊼	NT	NT E	TP ◇1 F ⊼	NT G	VT ◇1 ⊠	NT H	NT I	EM ◇ J	XC ◇1 K ⊼	NT	NT	VT ◇1 ⊠	NT A	NT	XC ◇1 L ⊼
London Euston ⊖65 d	09 40					10 00						10 20							10 40			
Birmingham New Street 68 d				10 31												10 57						11 31
Wolverhampton 68 d				10 49												11 15						11 49
Stafford 65,68 d				11 01												11 30						12 01
Stoke-on-Trent 50,68 d			10 58	11 20		11 25						11 48				11 55					11 58	12 20
Longport 50 d																						
Kidsgrove 50 d			11 05																		12 05	
Crewe 65 d	11 11						11 31										11 34	11 50	12 11			
Sandbach d																	11 41	11 57				
Holmes Chapel d																	11 45	12 02				
Goostrey d																		12 05				
Chelford d																		12 09				
Alderley Edge d								11 48									11 54	12 13				
Wilmslow d	11 27						11 48	11 51									11 57	12 17	12 27			
Styal d																						
Manchester Airport a																	12 04					
Handforth d								11 54										12 20				
Congleton d			11 12																		12 12	
Macclesfield a			11 19			11 41										12 11					12 19	
d			11 20			11 41										12 12					12 20	
Prestbury d			11 24																		12 24	
Adlington (Cheshire) d			11 27																		12 27	
Poynton d			11 30																		12 30	
Bramhall d			11 33																		12 33	
Cheadle Hulme d			11 37					11 59										12 24			12 37	
Stockport a	11 36		11 41	11 49		11 55	11 58	12 04				12 16				12 27		12 29	12 36		12 41	12 49
d	11 37	11 41	11 42	11 50	11 53	11 56	11 58	12 04			12 12	12 17	12 21		12 26	12 28		12 29	12 37	12 41	12 42	12 50
Heaton Chapel d			11 45					12 08			12 16							12 33			12 45	
Levenshulme d			11 48					12 11			12 19							12 36			12 48	
Manchester Piccadilly a	11 49	11 52	11 56	11 59	12 02	12 07	12 15	12 20			12 28	12 28	12 36		12 36	12 39	12 42	12 44	12 49	12 52	12 56	12 59
d		11 54							12 01	12 07				12 22	12 37					12 54		
Manchester Oxford Road a		11 56							12 03	12 09				12 24	12 40					12 56		
Deansgate a		12 00												12 28						13 00		

	TP ◇1 C ⊼	VT ◇1 ⊏	AW ◇ D ⊼	NT	NT E	TP ◇1 F ⊼	NT G	VT ◇1 ⊏	TP FX ◇1 M ⊼	NT H	NT I	EM ◇ J	XC ◇1 K ⊼	NT	NT	VT ◇1 ⊏	NT A	NT	XC ◇1 L ⊼	TP ◇1 C ⊼	VT ◇1 ⊏	AW ◇ N ⊼
London Euston ⊖65 d		11 00						11 20								11 40					12 00	
Birmingham New Street 68 d													11 57						12 31			
Wolverhampton 68 d													12 15						12 49			
Stafford 65,68 d													12 30						13 01			
Stoke-on-Trent 50,68 d		12 25						12 48					12 55					12 58	13 20		13 25	
Longport 50 d																						
Kidsgrove 50 d																		13 05				
Crewe 65 d			12 31											12 34	12 50	13 11						13 31
Sandbach d														12 41	12 57							
Holmes Chapel d														12 45	13 02							
Goostrey d															13 05							
Chelford d															13 09							
Alderley Edge d				12 49										12 54	13 13							
Wilmslow d			12 49	12 52										12 57	13 17	13 27						13 48
Styal d																						
Manchester Airport a														13 04								
Handforth d				12 55											13 20							
Congleton d																		13 12				
Macclesfield a		12 41											13 11					13 19			13 41	
d		12 41											13 12					13 20			13 41	
Prestbury d																		13 24				
Adlington (Cheshire) d																		13 27				
Poynton d																		13 30				
Bramhall d																		13 33				
Cheadle Hulme d				12 59											13 24			13 37				
Stockport a		12 55	12 58	13 04				13 16					13 27		13 29	13 36		13 41	13 49		13 55	13 58
d	12 53	12 56	12 58	13 04			13 12	13 17		13 21		13 26	13 28		13 29	13 37	13 41	13 42	13 50	13 53	13 56	13 58
Heaton Chapel d				13 08			13 16								13 33			13 45				
Levenshulme d				13 11			13 19								13 36			13 48				
Manchester Piccadilly a	13 02	13 07	13 15	13 20			13 28	13 28		13 36		13 36	13 39	13 42	13 44	13 49	13 52	13 56	13 59	14 02	14 07	14 15
d					13 01	13 07			13 16		13 22	13 37					13 54					
Manchester Oxford Road a					13 03	13 09			13 18		13 24	13 40					13 56					
Deansgate a											13 28						14 00					

- **A** From Hazel Grove to Preston
- **B** From Paignton
- **C** From Cleethorpes to Manchester Airport
- **D** From Milford Haven
- **E** From Manchester Airport to Liverpool Lime Street
- **F** From Scarborough to Liverpool Lime Street
- **G** From Buxton
- **H** From Chester
- **I** From Manchester Airport to Southport
- **J** From Norwich to Liverpool Lime Street
- **K** From Bournemouth
- **L** From Bristol Temple Meads
- **M** From Manchester Airport to Barrow-in-Furness
- **N** From Fishguard Harbour

Stoke-on-Trent and Crewe - Manchester Airport, Stockport and Manchester

Network Diagram - see first Page of Table 78

	NT		NT	TP	NT	VT	NT	NT	EM	XC	NT		NT	VT	NT	NT	XC	TP	VT	AW	NT		NT	TP
			A	B	C		D	E	F	G					H		I	J		K			A	B
London Euston ⊖65 d						12 20								12 40					13 00					
Birmingham New Street 68 d										12 57							13 31							
Wolverhampton 68 d										13 15							13 49							
Stafford 65,68 d										13 30							14 01							
Stoke-on-Trent 50,68 d						13 48				13 55						13 58	14 20		14 25					
Longport 50 d																								
Kidsgrove 50 d																14 05								
Crewe 65 d											13 34		13 50	14 11						14 31				
Sandbach d											13 41		13 57											
Holmes Chapel d											13 45		14 02											
Goostrey d													14 05											
Chelford d													14 09											
Alderley Edge d	13 48										13 54		14 13								14 49			
Wilmslow d	13 51										13 57		14 17	14 27						14 49	14 52			
Styal d																								
Manchester Airport a											14 04													
Handforth d	13 54												14 20								14 55			
Congleton d																14 12								
Macclesfield a										14 11						14 19			14 41					
d										14 12						14 20			14 41					
Prestbury d																14 24								
Adlington (Cheshire) d																14 27								
Poynton d																14 30								
Bramhall d																14 33								
Cheadle Hulme d	13 59												14 24			14 37					14 59			
Stockport a	14 04					14 16				14 27			14 29	14 36		14 41	14 49		14 55	14 58	15 04			
d	14 04				14 12	14 17	14 21		14 26	14 28			14 29	14 37	14 41	14 42	14 50	14 53	14 56	14 58	15 04			
Heaton Chapel d	14 08				14 16								14 33			14 45					15 08			
Levenshulme d	14 11				14 19								14 36			14 48					15 11			
Manchester Piccadilly a	14 20				14 28	14 28	14 36		14 36	14 39	14 42		14 44	14 49	14 52	14 56	14 59	15 02	15 07	15 15	15 20			
d			14 01	14 07				14 22	14 37						14 54								15 01	15 07
Manchester Oxford Road a			14 03	14 09				14 24	14 40						14 56								15 03	15 09
Deansgate a								14 28							15 00									

	NT	VT	TP	NT	NT	EM	XC		NT	NT	VT	NT	NT	XC	TP	VT	AW		NT	NT	TP	TP FX	NT	NT
	C		L	D	E	F	G					M		N	J		O			A	B	P	E	Q
London Euston ⊖65 d		13 20									13 40					14 00								
Birmingham New Street 68 d							13 57							14 31										
Wolverhampton 68 d							14 15							14 49										
Stafford 65,68 d							14 30							15 01										
Stoke-on-Trent 50,68 d		14 48					14 55						14 58	15 20		15 25								
Longport 50 d																								
Kidsgrove 50 d													15 05											
Crewe 65 d									14 34	14 50	15 11						15 29							
Sandbach d									14 41	14 57														
Holmes Chapel d									14 45	15 02														
Goostrey d										15 05														
Chelford d										15 09														
Alderley Edge d									14 54	15 13									15 48					
Wilmslow d									14 57	15 17	15 27						15 47		15 51					
Styal d																								
Manchester Airport a									15 04															
Handforth d										15 20									15 54					
Congleton d													15 12											
Macclesfield a							15 11						15 19			15 41								
d							15 12						15 20			15 41								
Prestbury d													15 24											
Adlington (Cheshire) d													15 27											
Poynton d													15 30											
Bramhall d													15 33											
Cheadle Hulme d										15 24			15 37						15 59					
Stockport a		15 16					15 27			15 29	15 36		15 41	15 49		15 55	15 58		16 04					
d	15 12	15 17		15 21		15 26	15 28			15 29	15 37	15 41	15 42	15 50	15 53	15 56	15 58		16 04					16 12
Heaton Chapel d	15 16									15 33			15 45						16 08					16 16
Levenshulme d	15 19									15 36			15 48						16 11					16 19
Manchester Piccadilly a	15 28	15 28		15 36		15 36	15 39		15 41	15 44	15 49	15 52	15 56	15 59	16 02	16 07	16 15		16 20					16 25
d			15 16		15 22	15 37			15 42			15 54								16 01	16 07	16 16	16 22	16 27
Manchester Oxford Road a			15 18		15 24	15 40			15 46			15 56								16 03	16 09	16 18	16 24	16 29
Deansgate a					15 28							16 00											16 28	16 32

A From Manchester Airport to Liverpool Lime Street
B From Scarborough to Liverpool Lime Street
C From Buxton
D From Chester
E From Manchester Airport to Southport
F From Norwich to Liverpool Lime Street
G From Bournemouth
H From Hazel Grove to Preston
I From Paignton
J From Cleethorpes to Manchester Airport
K From Milford Haven
L From Manchester Airport to Barrow-in-Furness
M From Hazel Grove to Bolton
N From Bristol Temple Meads
O From Carmarthen
P From Manchester Airport to Windermere
Q From Buxton to Barrow-in-Furness

Stoke-on-Trent and Crewe - Manchester Airport, Stockport and Manchester

Network Diagram - see first Page of Table 78

	VT	NT	EM		XC	NT	NT	VT	NT	NT	XC	TP	VT		AW	NT	VT	NT	TP	TP	NT	NT	EM	
		A	B		C				D		E	F			G			H	I	J	A	K	B	
London Euston ⊖65 d	14 20							14 40					15 00				15 20							
Birmingham New Street 68 d					14 57						15 31													
Wolverhampton 68 d					15 15						15 50													
Stafford 65,68 d					15 30						16 02													
Stoke-on-Trent 50,68 d	15 48				15 55					15 58	16 21		16 25				16 48							
Longport 50 d																								
Kidsgrove 50 d										16 05														
Crewe 65 d						15 33	15 50	16 12							16 31									
Sandbach d						15 40	15 57																	
Holmes Chapel d						15 44	16 02																	
Goostrey d							16 05																	
Chelford d							16 09																	
Alderley Edge d						15 53	16 13									16 49								
Wilmslow d						15 56	16 17	16 27							16 48	16 52								
Styal d						15 59																		
Manchester Airport a						16 04																		
Handforth d							16 20									16 55								
Congleton d										16 12														
Macclesfield a					16 11					16 19			16 41											
d					16 12					16 20			16 41											
Prestbury d										16 24														
Adlington (Cheshire) d										16 27														
Poynton d										16 30														
Bramhall d										16 33														
Cheadle Hulme d							16 24			16 37						16 59								
Stockport a	16 16				16 27		16 29	16 36		16 41	16 49		16 54		16 58	17 04	17 16							
d	16 17	16 21	16 26		16 28		16 29	16 37	16 41	16 42	16 50	16 53	16 55		16 58	17 04	17 17				17 21		17 26	
Heaton Chapel d							16 33			16 45						17 08								
Levenshulme d							16 36			16 48						17 11								
Manchester Piccadilly a	16 28	16 36	16 36		16 39	16 42	16 44	16 49	16 52	16 56	16 59	17 02	17 07		17 14	17 20	17 28				17 36		17 37	
d			16 37						16 54									17 01	17 07	17 15		17 22	17 37	
Manchester Oxford Road a			16 40						16 56									17 03	17 09	17 17		17 25	17 40	
Deansgate a									17 00															

	XC	NT	NT	VT	NT	XC	TP	VT	AW		NT	NT	TP	NT	VT	TP	NT	NT	EM		XC	NT	NT	VT
	C					L	F		M			H	I	N		J	A	K	B		C			
London Euston ⊖65 d				15 40				16 00							16 20									16 40
Birmingham New Street 68 d	15 57					16 31															16 57			
Wolverhampton 68 d	16 15					16 49															17 15			
Stafford 65,68 d	16 31					17 01															17 30			
Stoke-on-Trent 50,68 d	16 55				16 58	17 20		17 25							17 48						17 55			
Longport 50 d																								
Kidsgrove 50 d					17 05																			
Crewe 65 d		16 34	16 50	17 11					17 30													17 33	17 50	18 11
Sandbach d		16 41	16 57																			17 40	17 57	
Holmes Chapel d		16 45	17 02																			17 44	18 02	
Goostrey d			17 05																				18 05	
Chelford d			17 09																				18 09	
Alderley Edge d		16 54	17 13								17 48											17 53	18 13	
Wilmslow d		16 57	17 17	17 27					17 47		17 51											17 56	18 17	18 27
Styal d																						17 59		
Manchester Airport a		17 04																				18 04		
Handforth d			17 20								17 54												18 20	
Congleton d					17 12																			
Macclesfield a	17 11				17 19			17 41													18 11			
d	17 12				17 20			17 41													18 12			
Prestbury d					17 24																			
Adlington (Cheshire) d					17 27																			
Poynton d					17 30																			
Bramhall d					17 33																			
Cheadle Hulme d			17 24		17 36						17 59												18 24	
Stockport a	17 27		17 29	17 36	17 41	17 49		17 55	17 57		18 04				18 16						18 27		18 29	18 37
d	17 28		17 29	17 37	17 42	17 50	17 53	17 56	17 58		18 04			18 12	18 17		18 21		18 26		18 28		18 29	18 38
Heaton Chapel d			17 33		17 45						18 08			18 16									18 33	
Levenshulme d			17 36		17 48						18 11			18 19									18 36	
Manchester Piccadilly a	17 39	17 42	17 44	17 49	17 56	17 59	18 02	18 07	18 13		18 20			18 28	18 28		18 36		18 36		18 39	18 42	18 44	18 49
d												18 01	18 07			18 16		18 22	18 37					
Manchester Oxford Road a												18 03	18 09			18 18		18 24	18 40					
Deansgate a																		18 28						

A From Chester
B From Norwich to Liverpool Lime Street
C From Bournemouth
D From Hazel Grove to Preston
E From Penzance
F From Cleethorpes to Manchester Airport
G From Milford Haven
H From Manchester Airport to Liverpool Lime Street
I From Scarborough to Liverpool Lime Street
J From Manchester Airport to Barrow-in-Furness
K From Manchester Airport to Southport
L From Bristol Temple Meads
M From Carmarthen
N From Buxton

2 July to 28 September

Stoke-on-Trent and Crewe - Manchester Airport, Stockport and Manchester

Network Diagram - see first Page of Table 78

		NT	NT	XC	TP	VT	AW	NT	TP	NT	VT	TP	NT	NT	NT	EM	XC	NT	VT	NT	XC	TP	VT
		A		B	C		D	E	F	G		H	I		J	K	L				M	C	
London Euston ⊖65	d					17 00					17 20								17 40				18 00
Birmingham New Street 68	d			17 31													17 57				18 31		
Wolverhampton 68	d			17 50													18 15				18 49		
Stafford 65,68	d			18 02													18 30				19 01		
Stoke-on-Trent 50,68	d		17 58	18 21		18 25					18 49						18 55			18 58	19 20		19 25
Longport 50	d																						
Kidsgrove 50	d		18 05																	19 05			
Crewe 65	d						18 31							18 34				18 50	19 11				
Sandbach	d													18 41				18 57					
Holmes Chapel	d													18 45				19 02					
Goostrey	d																	19 05					
Chelford	d																	19 09					
Alderley Edge	d													18 54				19 13					
Wilmslow	d						18 48							18 57				19 17	19 27				
Styal	d																						
Manchester Airport	a													19 05									
Handforth	d																	19 20					
Congleton	d		18 12																	19 12			
Macclesfield	a		18 19			18 41											19 11			19 19			19 41
	d		18 20			18 41											19 12			19 20			19 41
Prestbury	d		18 24																	19 24			
Adlington (Cheshire)	d		18 27																	19 27			
Poynton	d		18 30																	19 30			
Bramhall	d		18 33																	19 33			
Cheadle Hulme	d		18 37															19 24		19 37			
Stockport	a		18 41	18 49		18 55	18 58				19 16						19 27	19 29	19 36	19 41	19 48		19 55
	d	18 41	18 42	18 50	18 53	18 56	18 58			19 12	19 17				19 21	19 26	19 28	19 29	19 37	19 42	19 50	19 53	19 56
Heaton Chapel	d		18 45							19 16										19 45			
Levenshulme	d		18 48							19 19										19 48			
Manchester Piccadilly	a	18 52	18 56	18 59	19 02	19 07	19 15			19 28	19 28			19 31	19 35	19 36	19 39	19 43	19 49	19 56	19 59	20 02	20 07
	d	18 54						19 01	19 07			19 16	19 20	19 32		19 37							
Manchester Oxford Road	a	18 56						19 03	19 09			19 18	19 22	19 36		19 40							
Deansgate	a	19 00											19 26										

		AW	NT	TP	NT	VT	TP	NT	NT	NT	EM	XC	NT	VT	NT	XC	AW	TP	AW	VT	VT	VT
		N	E	F	G		H	I		J	K	L				O	P	C	D	Q	R	R
London Euston ⊖65	d					18 20								18 40						19 00	18 57	19 00
Birmingham New Street 68	d											18 57				19 31						
Wolverhampton 68	d											19 15				19 49						
Stafford 65,68	d											19 29				20 01						
Stoke-on-Trent 50,68	d					19 48						19 55			19 58	20 20				20 25		20 25
Longport 50	d																					
Kidsgrove 50	d														20 05							
Crewe 65	d	19 31											19 50	20 12					20 23		20s33	
Sandbach	d												19 57									
Holmes Chapel	d												20 02									
Goostrey	d												20 05									
Chelford	d												20 09									
Alderley Edge	d												20 13									
Wilmslow	d	19 48							19 56				20 17	20 27					20 40			
Styal	d																					
Manchester Airport	a								20 04													
Handforth	d												20 20									
Congleton	d														20 12							
Macclesfield	a											20 11			20 19					20 41		20 41
	d											20 12			20 20					20 41		20 41
Prestbury	d														20 24							
Adlington (Cheshire)	d														20 27							
Poynton	d														20 30							
Bramhall	d														20 33							
Cheadle Hulme	d												20 24		20 37							
Stockport	a	19 58				20 16						20 27	20 29	20 36	20 41	20 48			20 50	20 55		20 55
	d	19 58			20 12	20 17				20 21	20 26	20 28	20 29	20 37	20 42	20 50		20 54	20 51	20 56		20 56
Heaton Chapel	d				20 16										20 45							
Levenshulme	d				20 19										20 48							
Manchester Piccadilly	a	20 15			20 28	20 28			20 32	20 35	20 36	20 39	20 43	20 49	20 56	20 58		21 02	21 05	21 07	21 09	21 10
	d		20 01	20 07			20 16	20 20	20 32		20 37						20 50					
Manchester Oxford Road	a		20 03	20 09			20 18	20 22	20 36		20 40						20 52					
Deansgate	a							20 26														

- **A** From Buxton to Bolton
- **B** From Paignton
- **C** From Cleethorpes to Manchester Airport
- **D** From Milford Haven
- **E** From Manchester Airport to Liverpool Lime Street
- **F** From Scarborough to Liverpool Lime Street
- **G** From Buxton
- **H** From Manchester Airport to Barrow-in-Furness
- **I** From Manchester Airport to Southport
- **J** From Chester
- **K** From Norwich to Liverpool Lime Street
- **L** From Bournemouth
- **M** From Bristol Temple Meads
- **N** From Carmarthen
- **O** From Exeter St Davids
- **P** From Manchester Airport to Chester
- **Q** MTWO
- **R** ThFO

2 July to 28 September

Stoke-on-Trent and Crewe - Manchester Airport, Stockport and Manchester

Network Diagram - see first Page of Table 78

		TP	NT	VT	EM	NT	NT	NT	XC	NT	VT	NT	XC	VT	AW	AW	NT FO	TP	NT	TP	NT	NT	XC
		A	B		C	D		E	F				G		H	I	J	A	B	K		E	F
London Euston ⊖65	d			19 20							19 40			20 00									
Birmingham New Street 68	d								19 57				20 31										20 57
Wolverhampton 68	d								20 16				20 49										21 16
Stafford 65,68	d								20 30		21 04												21 32
Stoke-on-Trent 50,68	d			20 48					20 55			20 58	21 18	21 24									21 55
Longport 50	d																						
Kidsgrove 50	d											21 05											
Crewe 65	d									20 50	21 23				21 31								
Sandbach	d									20 57													
Holmes Chapel	d									21 02													
Goostrey	d									21 05													
Chelford	d									21 09													
Alderley Edge	d									21 13													
Wilmslow	d						20 56			21 17	21 38				21 48						21 55		
Styal	d																						
Manchester Airport	a						21 04														22 04		
Handforth	d									21 20													
Congleton	d											21 12											
Macclesfield	a								21 11			21 19		21 40									22 11
	d								21 12			21 20		21 40									22 12
Prestbury	d											21 24											
Adlington (Cheshire)	d											21 27											
Poynton	d											21 30											
Bramhall	d											21 33											
Cheadle Hulme	d									21 24		21 37											
Stockport	a			21 16					21 27	21 29		21 41	21 46	21 55	21 58								22 25
	d		21 12	21 17	21 20			21 21	21 28	21 29		21 42	21 49	21 56	21 59				22 12			22 21	22 26
Heaton Chapel	d		21 16									21 45							22 16				
Levenshulme	d		21 19									21 48							22 19				
Manchester Piccadilly	a		21 28	21 28	21 32		21 32	21 35	21 39	21 43	21 57	21 57	21 59	22 07	22 13				22 28		22 31	22 35	22 35
	d	21 07				21 20	21 32									21 50	22 01	22 07		22 16	22 32		
Manchester Oxford Road	a	21 09				21 22	21 36									21 52	22 03	22 09		22 18	22 36		
Deansgate	a					21 26																	

		NT	NT	NT	VT	TP	VT	NT	NT	XC	VT	AW	NT	NT	NT	XC	AW FO	VT	VT
			D	L		M				F		N	B	O			P		Q
London Euston ⊖65	d				20 40		21 00				21 40							22 00	23 30
Birmingham New Street 68	d									21 57						22 30	21 24		
Wolverhampton 68	d									22 16						22 48	21 43		
Stafford 65,68	d									22 30						23 01		23s38	
Stoke-on-Trent 50,68	d						22 28	22 18		22 55	23 07					23 21			00s53
Longport 50	d																		
Kidsgrove 50	d							22 25											
Crewe 65	d	21 45			22 13							23 04			23 12			00s03	
Sandbach	d	21 52													23 19				
Holmes Chapel	d	21 58													23 24				
Goostrey	d	22 01													23 27				
Chelford	d	22 07													23 31				
Alderley Edge	d	22 12													23 35				
Wilmslow	d	22 15			22 29				22 56			23 22			23 39				
Styal	d																		
Manchester Airport	a								23 04										
Handforth	d	22 19													23 42				
Congleton	d							22 32											
Macclesfield	a						22 44	22 40		23 11	23 23								01s10
	d						22 44	22 48		23 12	23 23								
Prestbury	d							22 53											
Adlington (Cheshire)	d							22 56											
Poynton	d							22 59											
Bramhall	d							23 02											
Cheadle Hulme	d	22 24						23 05							23 46				
Stockport	a	22 29			22 38		22 58	23 10		23 25	23 37	23 30			23 51			00s26	01s24
	d	22 29		22 34	22 39	22 53	22 59	23 10		23 26	23 38	23 31	23 41	23 48	23 51				
Heaton Chapel	d			22 38				23 14							23 55				
Levenshulme	d			22 41				23 17							23 58				
Manchester Piccadilly	a	22 43		22 48	22 48	23 02	23 11	23 25	23 33	23 37	23 46	23 48	23 54	00 02	00 07	00 12	00 28	00 35	01 43
	d		22 36	22 50															
Manchester Oxford Road	a		22 38	22 52															
Deansgate	a		22 41	22 55															

- **A** From Scarborough to Liverpool Lime Street
- **B** From Buxton
- **C** From Norwich
- **D** From Manchester Airport to Southport
- **E** From Chester
- **F** From Bournemouth
- **G** From Bristol Temple Meads
- **H** From Carmarthen
- **I** From Manchester Airport to Chester
- **J** From Manchester Airport to Liverpool Lime Street
- **K** From Manchester Airport to Barrow-in-Furness
- **L** To Wigan Wallgate
- **M** From Cleethorpes to Manchester Airport
- **N** From Cardiff Central
- **O** From Sheffield
- **P** From Birmingham International
- **Q** from 27 July until 7 September, not from 13 August until 28 August

Stoke-on-Trent and Crewe - Manchester Airport, Stockport and Manchester

Network Diagram - see first Page of Table 78

	NT MX A	NT MX	XC MX ◇1	VT MO ◇1 ⊏	NT MX B	VT MX ◇1 ⊏	VT MO ◇1 ⊏	NT MX	TP ◇1 C	NT	NT	VT ◇1	NT D	NT	TP ◇1 E	AW	NT F	NT G	NT	NT H	NT	NT B
London Euston 15 ⊖65 d				21p25		22p00	21p51															
Birmingham New Street 12 68 d			22p30																			
Wolverhampton 7 68 d			22p48																			
Stafford 65,68 d			23p01			23b38	23b53															
Stoke-on-Trent 50,68 d			23p21	23p29																	06 30	
Longport 50 d																					06 34	
Kidsgrove 50 d																					06 38	
Crewe 10 65 d		23p12				00s03	00s21	00 44			05 48	06 11				06 27						
Sandbach d		23p19									05 55											
Holmes Chapel d		23p24									06 00											
Goostrey d		23p27									06 03											
Chelford d		23p31									06 07											
Alderley Edge d		23p35									06 11								06 49			
Wilmslow d		23p39								05 46	06 15	06 27				06 45			06 52			
Styal d																						
Manchester Airport ✈ a								01 16		05 53												
Handforth d		23p42									06 18								06 55			
Congleton d																					06 45	
Macclesfield a				23p45																	06 52	
d				23p46										06 22							06 53	
Prestbury d														06 26							06 57	
Adlington (Cheshire) d														06 29							07 00	
Poynton d														06 33							07 04	
Bramhall d														06 35							07 07	
Cheadle Hulme d		23p46									06 22			06 38					06 59		07 11	
Stockport a		23p51		23p59		00s26	00s50				06 27	06 36		06 43		06 55			07 04		07 15	
d	23p48	23p51		00 01	00 05				05 53		06 27	06 37	06 41	06 43	06 53	06 55		06 58	07 04	07 10	07 16	07 19
Heaton Chapel d		23p55									06 31			06 46					07 08	07 15		
Levenshulme d		23p58									06 34			06 49					07 11	07 18		
Manchester Piccadilly 10 a	00 02	00 07	00 12	00 12	00 18	00 35	01 00	01 36	06 05	06 25	06 42	06 49	06 52	06 58	07 02	07 07		07 10	07 21	07 26	07 27	07 31
d													06 54				06 58			07 27		
Manchester Oxford Road a													06 56				07 00			07 29		
Deansgate a													06 59							07 32		

	EM ◇ I	XC ◇1	NT	NT	NT G	NT	XC ◇1 ⌶	NT	TP ◇1 J ⌶	NT G	AW ◇ K	NT	NT F	TP ◇1 L ⌶	NT M	NT N	NT	VT ◇1 ⊠	NT B	XC ◇1 ⌶	EM ◇ I	NT
London Euston 15 ⊖65 d																		06 17				
Birmingham New Street 12 68 d		05 57					06 22													06 57		
Wolverhampton 7 68 d		06 16					06 40													07 15		
Stafford 65,68 d		06 30					06 55													07 30		
Stoke-on-Trent 50,68 d		06 51					07 14					07 17						07 45				
Longport 50 d												07 21										
Kidsgrove 50 d												07 25										
Crewe 10 65 d			06 33	06 49							07 27						07 22			07 52		
Sandbach d			06 40	06 56													07 35					
Holmes Chapel d			06 44	07 00													07 41					
Goostrey d				07 03													07 45					
Chelford d				07 08													07 51					
Alderley Edge d			06 53	07 12				07 30									07 56					07 53
Wilmslow d			06 57	07 16				07 33			07 44						08 00			08 09		07 56
Styal d																						07 59
Manchester Airport ✈ a			07 04																			08 04
Handforth d				07 19				07 37									08 03					
Congleton d		07 03										07 32										
Macclesfield a		07 11					07 30					07 39						08 01				
d		07 12				07 15	07 31					07 40						08 02				
Prestbury d						07 21						07 44										
Adlington (Cheshire) d						07 24						07 47										
Poynton d						07 27						07 51										
Bramhall d						07 31						07 54										
Cheadle Hulme d				07 24		07 34		07 42				07 59					08 09					
Stockport a		07 27		07 29		07 41	07 45	07 47			07 54	08 03					08 14	08 16		08 20		
d	07 22	07 28		07 29	07 31	07 42	07 50	07 48	07 53	07 57	07 54	08 04			08 10		08 14	08 17	08 19	08 21	08 24	
Heaton Chapel d				07 33								08 07					08 18					
Levenshulme d				07 36								08 10					08 21					
Manchester Piccadilly 10 a	07 34	07 37	07 42	07 44	07 45	07 56	07 59	07 59	08 02	08 09	08 10	08 21			08 25		08 27	08 28	08 32	08 34	08 36	08 42
d	07 34												07 59	08 07		08 22	08 29				08 37	
Manchester Oxford Road a	07 37												08 01	08 09		08 24	08 33				08 40	
Deansgate a																08 28						

- A From Sheffield
- B From Chester
- C From Sheffield to Manchester Airport
- D From Buxton to Clitheroe
- E From Doncaster to Manchester Airport
- F From Manchester Airport to Liverpool Lime Street
- G From Hazel Grove
- H From Buxton to Wigan North Western
- I From Nottingham to Liverpool Lime Street
- J From Cleethorpes to Manchester Airport
- K From Cardiff Central
- L From Hull to Liverpool Lime Street
- M From Buxton
- N From Manchester Airport to Southport
- b Previous night, stops to set down only

Stoke-on-Trent and Crewe - Manchester Airport, Stockport and Manchester

Network Diagram - see first Page of Table 78

	NT	NT	VT ◇1 ⊠	NT A	NT	XC ◇1 ⌶	TP ◇1 B ⌶	VT ◇1 ⊠	AW ◇ C ⌶	NT	NT D	TP ◇1 E ⌶	NT F	VT ◇1 ⊠	TP ◇1 G ⌶	NT H	NT I	EM ◇ J	XC ◇1 K ⌶	NT	NT
London Euston 15 ⊖65 d			06 36					06 55						07 20							
Birmingham New Street 12 68 d						07 31													07 57		
Wolverhampton 7 68 d						07 49													08 15		
Stafford 65,68 d						08 01													08 30		
Stoke-on-Trent 50,68 d					07 57	08 20		08 25						08 48					08 55		
Longport 50 d																					
Kidsgrove 50 d					08 04																
Crewe 10 65 d		07 55	08 11						08 28											08 31	08 50
Sandbach d		08 02																		08 38	08 57
Holmes Chapel d		08 06																		08 42	09 02
Goostrey d																				08 45	09 05
Chelford d																				08 50	09 09
Alderley Edge d		08 15								08 49										08 54	09 13
Wilmslow d		08 18	08 27						08 45	08 52										08 57	09 17
Styal d																					
Manchester Airport ✈ a																				09 04	
Handforth d		08 21								08 55											09 20
Congleton d					08 11																
Macclesfield a					08 18	08 36		08 41											09 11		
d	08 06				08 19	08 37		08 41											09 12		
Prestbury d	08 10				08 23																
Adlington (Cheshire) d					08 26																
Poynton d	08 15				08 30																
Bramhall d	08 17				08 33																
Cheadle Hulme d	08 20	08 26			08 37					08 59											09 24
Stockport a	08 27	08 30	08 37		08 41	08 50		08 55	08 58	09 04				09 16					09 27		09 29
d	08 28	08 31	08 38	08 41	08 42	08 50	08 53	08 56	08 59	09 04			09 12	09 17		09 21		09 25	09 28		09 29
Heaton Chapel d		08 35			08 45					09 08			09 16								09 33
Levenshulme d	08 32				08 48					09 11			09 19								09 36
Manchester Piccadilly 10 a	08 42	08 45	08 49	08 52	08 56	08 59	09 02	09 07	09 15	09 20			09 28	09 28		09 36		09 36	09 39	09 42	09 44
d				08 54							09 01	09 07			09 16		09 22	09 37			
Manchester Oxford Road a				08 56							09 03	09 09			09 18		09 24	09 40			
Deansgate a				09 00													09 28				

	VT ◇1 ⊠	TP ◇1 L ⌶	NT A	NT	XC ◇1 M ⌶	TP ◇1 B ⌶	VT ◇1 ⊠	AW ◇ N ⌶	NT	NT D	TP ◇1 O ⌶	NT F	VT ◇1 ⊠	NT H	NT I	EM ◇ P	XC ◇1 K ⌶	NT	NT	VT ◇1 ⊠	NT A	NT
London Euston 15 ⊖65 d	07 35						08 00						08 20							08 40		
Birmingham New Street 12 68 d					08 31												08 57					
Wolverhampton 7 68 d					08 49												09 15					
Stafford 65,68 d					09 01												09 30					
Stoke-on-Trent 50,68 d				08 58	09 20		09 25						09 48				09 55					09 58
Longport 50 d																						
Kidsgrove 50 d				09 05																		10 05
Crewe 10 65 d	09 11							09 31										09 33	09 50	10 11		
Sandbach d																		09 40	09 57			
Holmes Chapel d																		09 44	10 02			
Goostrey d																			10 05			
Chelford d																			10 09			
Alderley Edge d									09 48									09 53	10 13			
Wilmslow d	09 27							09 48	09 51									09 57	10 17	10 27		
Styal d																						
Manchester Airport ✈ a																		10 04				
Handforth d									09 54										10 20			
Congleton d				09 12																		10 12
Macclesfield a				09 19			09 41										10 11					10 19
d				09 20			09 41										10 12					10 20
Prestbury d				09 24																		10 24
Adlington (Cheshire) d				09 27																		10 27
Poynton d				09 30																		10 30
Bramhall d				09 33																		10 33
Cheadle Hulme d				09 37					09 59										10 24			10 37
Stockport a	09 36			09 41	09 49		09 55	09 58	10 04				10 16				10 27		10 29	10 36		10 41
d	09 37		09 41	09 42	09 50	09 53	09 56	09 58	10 04			10 12	10 17	10 21		10 26	10 28		10 29	10 37	10 41	10 42
Heaton Chapel d				09 45					10 08			10 16							10 33			10 45
Levenshulme d				09 48					10 11			10 19							10 36			10 48
Manchester Piccadilly 10 a	09 49		09 52	09 56	09 59	10 02	10 07	10 15	10 20			10 28	10 28	10 36		10 36	10 39	10 42	10 44	10 49	10 52	10 56
d		09 46	09 54							10 01	10 07				10 22	10 37					10 54	
Manchester Oxford Road a		09 48	09 56							10 03	10 09				10 24	10 40					10 56	
Deansgate a		09 51	10 00												10 28						11 00	

- A From Hazel Grove to Preston
- B From Cleethorpes to Manchester Airport
- C From Cardiff Central
- D From Manchester Airport to Liverpool Lime Street
- E From Newcastle to Liverpool Lime Street
- F From Buxton
- G From Manchester Airport to Barrow-in-Furness
- H From Chester
- I From Manchester Airport to Southport
- J From Nottingham to Liverpool Lime Street
- K From Southampton Central
- L From Manchester Airport to Windermere
- M From Bristol Temple Meads
- N From Carmarthen
- O From Scarborough to Liverpool Lime Street
- P From Norwich to Liverpool Lime Street

Stoke-on-Trent and Crewe - Manchester Airport, Stockport and Manchester

Network Diagram - see first Page of Table 78

	XC	TP	VT	AW	NT	NT	TP	NT	VT	TP	NT	NT	EM	XC	NT	NT	VT	NT	NT	XC	TP
	◇■ A	◇■ B	◇■ ⊠	◇ C		D	◇■ E	F	◇■ ⊠	◇■ G	H	I	◇ J	◇■ K			◇■ ⊠	L		◇■ M	◇■ B
London Euston ⊖65 d			09 00						09 20								09 40				
Birmingham New Street 68 d	09 31													09 57						10 31	
Wolverhampton 68 d	09 49													10 15						10 49	
Stafford 65,68 d	10 01													10 30						11 01	
Stoke-on-Trent 50,68 d	10 20		10 25						10 48					10 55					10 58	11 20	
Longport 50 d																					
Kidsgrove 50 d																			11 05		
Crewe 65 d				10 31											10 34	10 50	11 11				
Sandbach d															10 41	10 57					
Holmes Chapel d															10 45	11 02					
Goostrey d																11 05					
Chelford d																11 09					
Alderley Edge d					10 49										10 54	11 13					
Wilmslow d				10 49	10 52										10 57	11 17	11 27				
Styal d																					
Manchester Airport a															11 04						
Handforth d					10 55											11 20					
Congleton d																			11 12		
Macclesfield a			10 41											11 11					11 19		
Macclesfield d			10 41											11 12					11 20		
Prestbury d																			11 24		
Adlington (Cheshire) d																			11 27		
Poynton d																			11 30		
Bramhall d																			11 33		
Cheadle Hulme d					10 59											11 24			11 37		
Stockport a	10 49		10 55	10 58	11 04				11 16					11 27		11 29	11 36		11 41	11 49	
Stockport d	10 50	10 53	10 56	10 58	11 04			11 12	11 17		11 21		11 26	11 28		11 29	11 37	11 41	11 42	11 50	11 53
Heaton Chapel d					11 08			11 16								11 33			11 45		
Levenshulme d					11 11			11 19								11 36			11 48		
Manchester Piccadilly a	10 59	11 02	11 07	11 15	11 20			11 28	11 28		11 36		11 36	11 39	11 42	11 44	11 49	11 52	11 56	11 59	12 02
Manchester Piccadilly d						11 01	11 07			11 16		11 22	11 37					11 54			
Manchester Oxford Road a						11 03	11 09			11 18		11 24	11 40					11 56			
Deansgate a												11 28						12 00			

	VT	AW	NT	NT	TP	NT	VT	NT	NT	EM	XC	NT	NT	VT	NT	NT	XC	TP	VT	AW	NT	NT
	◇■ ⊠	◇ N		D	◇■ E	F	◇■ ⊠	H	I	◇ J	◇■ K			◇■ ⊠	L		◇■ O	◇■ B	◇■	◇ N		D
London Euston ⊖65 d	10 00						10 20							10 40					11 00			
Birmingham New Street 68 d											10 57						11 31					
Wolverhampton 68 d											11 15						11 49					
Stafford 65,68 d											11 30						12 01					
Stoke-on-Trent 50,68 d	11 25						11 48				11 55					11 58	12 20		12 25			
Longport 50 d																						
Kidsgrove 50 d																12 05						
Crewe 65 d		11 31										11 34	11 50	12 11						12 31		
Sandbach d												11 41	11 57									
Holmes Chapel d												11 45	12 02									
Goostrey d													12 05									
Chelford d													12 09									
Alderley Edge d			11 48									11 54	12 13								12 49	
Wilmslow d		11 48	11 51									11 57	12 17	12 27						12 49	12 52	
Styal d																						
Manchester Airport a												12 04										
Handforth d			11 54										12 20								12 55	
Congleton d																12 12						
Macclesfield a	11 41										12 11					12 19			12 41			
Macclesfield d	11 41										12 12					12 20			12 41			
Prestbury d																12 24						
Adlington (Cheshire) d																12 27						
Poynton d																12 30						
Bramhall d																12 33						
Cheadle Hulme d			11 59										12 24			12 37					12 59	
Stockport a	11 55	11 58	12 04				12 16				12 27		12 29	12 36		12 41	12 49		12 55	12 58	13 04	
Stockport d	11 56	11 58	12 04			12 12	12 17	12 21		12 26	12 28		12 29	12 37	12 41	12 42	12 50	12 53	12 56	12 58	13 04	
Heaton Chapel d			12 08			12 16							12 33			12 45					13 08	
Levenshulme d			12 11			12 19							12 36			12 48					13 11	
Manchester Piccadilly a	12 07	12 15	12 20			12 28	12 28	12 36		12 36	12 39	12 42	12 44	12 49	12 52	12 56	12 59	13 02	13 07	13 15	13 20	
Manchester Piccadilly d				12 01	12 07				12 22	12 37					12 54							13 01
Manchester Oxford Road a				12 03	12 09				12 24	12 40					12 56							13 03
Deansgate a									12 28						13 00							

A From Cardiff Central
B From Cleethorpes to Manchester Airport
C From Carmarthen
D From Manchester Airport to Liverpool Lime Street
E From Scarborough to Liverpool Lime Street
F From Buxton
G From Manchester Airport to Barrow-in-Furness
H From Chester
I From Manchester Airport to Southport
J From Norwich to Liverpool Lime Street
K From Bournemouth
L From Hazel Grove to Preston
M From Paignton
N From Milford Haven
O From Bristol Temple Meads

Stoke-on-Trent and Crewe - Manchester Airport, Stockport and Manchester

Network Diagram - see first Page of Table 78

	TP	NT	VT	TP FX	NT	NT	EM	XC	NT	NT	VT	NT	NT	XC	TP	VT	AW	NT	NT	TP	NT	VT
	◇■ A	B	◇■	◇■ C	D	E	◇ F	◇■ G			◇■	H		◇■ I	◇■ J	◇■	◇ K		L	◇■ A	B	◇■
London Euston ⊖65 d			11 20								11 40					12 00						12 20
Birmingham New Street 68 d								11 57						12 31								
Wolverhampton 68 d								12 15						12 49								
Stafford 65,68 d								12 30						13 01								
Stoke-on-Trent 50,68 d			12 48					12 55					12 58	13 20		13 25						13 48
Longport 50 d																						
Kidsgrove 50 d													13 05									
Crewe 65 d									12 34	12 50	13 11						13 31					
Sandbach d									12 41	12 57												
Holmes Chapel d									12 45	13 02												
Goostrey d										13 05												
Chelford d										13 09												
Alderley Edge d									12 54	13 13								13 48				
Wilmslow d									12 57	13 17	13 27						13 48	13 51				
Styal d																						
Manchester Airport a									13 04													
Handforth d										13 20								13 54				
Congleton d													13 12									
Macclesfield a								13 11					13 19			13 41						
Macclesfield d								13 12					13 20			13 41						
Prestbury d													13 24									
Adlington (Cheshire) d													13 27									
Poynton d													13 30									
Bramhall d													13 33									
Cheadle Hulme d										13 24			13 37					13 59				
Stockport a			13 16					13 27		13 29	13 36		13 41	13 49		13 55	13 58	14 04				14 16
Stockport d		13 12	13 17		13 21		13 26	13 28		13 29	13 37	13 41	13 42	13 50	13 53	13 56	13 58	14 04			14 12	14 17
Heaton Chapel d		13 16								13 33			13 45					14 08			14 16	
Levenshulme d		13 19								13 36			13 48					14 11			14 19	
Manchester Piccadilly a		13 28	13 28		13 36		13 36	13 39	13 42	13 44	13 49	13 52	13 56	13 59	14 02	14 07	14 15	14 20			14 28	14 28
Manchester Piccadilly d	13 07			13 16		13 22	13 37					13 54							14 01	14 07		
Manchester Oxford Road a	13 09			13 18		13 24	13 40					13 56							14 03	14 09		
Deansgate a						13 28						14 00										

	NT	NT	EM	XC	NT	NT	VT	NT	NT	XC	TP	VT	AW	NT	NT	TP	NT	VT	TP	NT	NT
	D	E	◇ F	◇■ G			◇■	H		◇■ M	◇■ J	◇■	◇ N		L	◇■ A	B	◇■	◇■ C	D	E
London Euston ⊖65 d							12 40					13 00						13 20			
Birmingham New Street 68 d				12 57						13 31											
Wolverhampton 68 d				13 15						13 49											
Stafford 65,68 d				13 30						14 01											
Stoke-on-Trent 50,68 d				13 55					13 58	14 20		14 25						14 48			
Longport 50 d																					
Kidsgrove 50 d									14 05												
Crewe 65 d					13 34	13 50	14 11						14 31								
Sandbach d					13 41	13 57															
Holmes Chapel d					13 45	14 02															
Goostrey d						14 05															
Chelford d						14 09															
Alderley Edge d					13 54	14 13								14 49							
Wilmslow d					13 57	14 17	14 27						14 49	14 52							
Styal d																					
Manchester Airport a					14 04																
Handforth d						14 20								14 55							
Congleton d									14 12												
Macclesfield a				14 11					14 19			14 41									
Macclesfield d				14 12					14 20			14 41									
Prestbury d									14 24												
Adlington (Cheshire) d									14 27												
Poynton d									14 30												
Bramhall d									14 33												
Cheadle Hulme d						14 24			14 37					14 59							
Stockport a				14 27		14 29	14 36		14 41	14 49		14 55	14 58	15 04				15 16			
Stockport d	14 21		14 26	14 28		14 29	14 37	14 41	14 42	14 50	14 53	14 56	14 58	15 04			15 12	15 17		15 21	
Heaton Chapel d						14 33			14 45					15 08			15 16				
Levenshulme d						14 36			14 48					15 11			15 19				
Manchester Piccadilly a	14 36		14 36	14 39	14 42	14 44	14 49	14 52	14 56	14 59	15 02	15 07	15 15	15 20			15 28	15 28		15 36	
Manchester Piccadilly d		14 22	14 37					14 54							15 01	15 07			15 16		15 22
Manchester Oxford Road a		14 24	14 40					14 56							15 03	15 09			15 18		15 24
Deansgate a		14 28						15 00													15 28

A From Scarborough to Liverpool Lime Street
B From Buxton
C From Manchester Airport to Barrow-in-Furness
D From Chester
E From Manchester Airport to Southport
F From Norwich to Liverpool Lime Street
G From Bournemouth
H From Hazel Grove to Preston
I From Bristol Temple Meads
J From Cleethorpes to Manchester Airport
K From Fishguard Harbour
L From Manchester Airport to Liverpool Lime Street
M From Paignton
N From Milford Haven

Stoke-on-Trent and Crewe - Manchester Airport, Stockport and Manchester

Network Diagram - see first Page of Table 78

	EM	XC	NT	NT	VT	NT	NT	XC	TP	VT	AW	NT	NT	TP	TP FX	NT	NT	VT	NT	EM	XC	NT
	◇ A	◇■ B			◇■	C		◇■ D	◇■ E	◇■	◇ F		G	◇■ H	◇■ I	J	K	◇■	L	◇ A	◇■ B	
London Euston ⊖65 d					13 40					14 00								14 20				
Birmingham New Street 68 d		13 57						14 31													14 57	
Wolverhampton 68 d		14 15						14 49													15 15	
Stafford 65,68 d		14 30						15 01													15 30	
Stoke-on-Trent 50,68 d		14 55					14 58	15 20		15 25								15 48			15 55	
Longport 50 d																						
Kidsgrove 50 d							15 05															
Crewe 65 d			14 34	14 50	15 11						15 29											15 33
Sandbach d			14 41	14 57																		15 40
Holmes Chapel d			14 45	15 02																		15 44
Goostrey d				15 05																		
Chelford d				15 09																		
Alderley Edge d			14 54	15 13								15 48										15 53
Wilmslow d			14 57	15 17	15 27						15 47	15 51										15 56
Styal d																						15 59
Manchester Airport a			15 04																			16 04
Handforth d				15 20								15 54										
Congleton d							15 12															
Macclesfield a		15 11					15 19			15 41											16 11	
d		15 12					15 20			15 41											16 12	
Prestbury d							15 24															
Adlington (Cheshire) d							15 27															
Poynton d							15 30															
Bramhall d							15 33															
Cheadle Hulme d				15 24			15 37					15 59										
Stockport a		15 27		15 29	15 36		15 41	15 49		15 55	15 58	16 04						16 16			16 27	
d	15 26	15 28		15 29	15 37	15 41	15 42	15 50	15 53	15 56	15 58	16 04					16 12	16 17	16 21	16 26	16 28	
Heaton Chapel d				15 33			15 45					16 08					16 16					
Levenshulme d				15 36			15 48					16 11					16 19					
Manchester Piccadilly a	15 36	15 39	15 41	15 44	15 49	15 52	15 56	15 59	16 02	16 07	16 15	16 20					16 25	16 28	16 36	16 36	16 39	16 42
d	15 37		15 42			15 54							16 01	16 07	16 16	16 22	16 27			16 37		
Manchester Oxford Road a	15 40		15 46			15 56							16 03	16 09	16 18	16 24	16 29			16 40		
Deansgate a						16 00										16 28	16 32					

	NT	VT	NT	NT	XC	TP	VT	AW	NT	VT	NT	TP	TP	NT	NT	EM	XC	NT	NT	VT	NT
		◇■	M		◇■ N	◇■ E	◇■	◇ O		◇■	G	◇■ H	◇■ P	L	J	◇ A	◇■ B			◇■	
London Euston ⊖65 d		14 40					15 00			15 20										15 40	
Birmingham New Street 68 d					15 31												15 57				
Wolverhampton 68 d					15 50												16 15				
Stafford 65,68 d					16 02												16 31				
Stoke-on-Trent 50,68 d				15 58	16 21		16 25			16 48							16 55				16 58
Longport 50 d																					
Kidsgrove 50 d				16 05																	17 05
Crewe 65 d	15 50	16 12						16 31										16 34	16 50	17 11	
Sandbach d	15 57																	16 41	16 57		
Holmes Chapel d	16 02																	16 45	17 02		
Goostrey d	16 05																		17 05		
Chelford d	16 09																		17 09		
Alderley Edge d	16 13								16 49									16 54	17 13		
Wilmslow d	16 17	16 27						16 48	16 52									16 57	17 17	17 27	
Styal d																					
Manchester Airport a																		17 04			
Handforth d	16 20								16 55										17 20		
Congleton d				16 12																	17 12
Macclesfield a				16 19			16 41										17 11				17 19
d				16 20			16 41										17 12				17 20
Prestbury d				16 24																	17 24
Adlington (Cheshire) d				16 27																	17 27
Poynton d				16 30																	17 30
Bramhall d				16 33																	17 33
Cheadle Hulme d	16 24			16 37					16 59										17 24		17 36
Stockport a	16 29	16 36		16 41	16 49		16 54	16 58	17 04	17 16							17 27		17 29	17 36	17 41
d	16 29	16 37	16 41	16 42	16 50	16 53	16 55	16 58	17 04	17 17				17 21		17 26	17 28		17 29	17 37	17 42
Heaton Chapel d	16 33			16 45					17 08										17 33		17 45
Levenshulme d	16 36			16 48					17 11										17 36		17 48
Manchester Piccadilly a	16 44	16 49	16 52	16 56	16 59	17 02	17 07	17 14	17 20	17 28				17 36		17 37	17 39	17 42	17 44	17 49	17 56
d			16 54								17 01	17 07	17 15		17 22	17 37					
Manchester Oxford Road a			16 56								17 03	17 09	17 17		17 25	17 40					
Deansgate a			17 00																		

A From Norwich to Liverpool Lime Street
B From Bournemouth
C From Hazel Grove to Bolton
D From Bristol Temple Meads
E From Cleethorpes to Manchester Airport
F From Carmarthen
G From Manchester Airport to Liverpool Lime Street
H From Scarborough to Liverpool Lime Street
I From Manchester Airport to Windermere
J From Manchester Airport to Southport
K From Buxton to Barrow-in-Furness
L From Chester
M From Hazel Grove to Preston
N From Penzance
O From Milford Haven
P From Manchester Airport to Barrow-in-Furness

Stoke-on-Trent and Crewe - Manchester Airport, Stockport and Manchester

Network Diagram - see first Page of Table 78

	XC	TP	VT	AW	NT	NT	TP	NT	VT	TP	NT	NT	EM	XC	NT	NT	VT	NT	NT	XC	TP	VT
	◇■ A	◇■ B	◇■	◇ C		D	◇■ E	F	◇■	◇■ G	H	I	◇ J	◇■ K			◇■	L		◇■ M	◇■ B	◇■ ⊠
London Euston ⊖65 d			16 00						16 20								16 40					17 00
Birmingham New Street 68 d	16 31													16 57						17 31		
Wolverhampton 68 d	16 49													17 15						17 50		
Stafford 65,68 d	17 01													17 30						18 02		
Stoke-on-Trent 50,68 d	17 20		17 25						17 48					17 55					17 58	18 21		18 25
Longport 50 d																						
Kidsgrove 50 d																			18 05			
Crewe 65 d				17 30											17 33	17 50	18 11					
Sandbach d															17 40	17 57						
Holmes Chapel d															17 44	18 02						
Goostrey d																18 05						
Chelford d																18 09						
Alderley Edge d					17 48										17 53	18 13						
Wilmslow d				17 47	17 51										17 56	18 17	18 27					
Styal d															17 59							
Manchester Airport a															18 04							
Handforth d					17 54											18 20						
Congleton d																			18 12			
Macclesfield a			17 41											18 11					18 19			18 41
d			17 41											18 12					18 20			18 41
Prestbury d																			18 24			
Adlington (Cheshire) d																			18 27			
Poynton d																			18 30			
Bramhall d																			18 33			
Cheadle Hulme d					17 59											18 24			18 37			
Stockport a	17 49		17 55	17 57	18 04				18 16					18 27		18 29	18 37		18 41	18 49		18 55
d	17 50	17 53	17 56	17 58	18 04			18 12	18 17		18 21		18 26	18 28		18 29	18 38	18 41	18 42	18 50	18 53	18 56
Heaton Chapel d					18 08			18 16								18 33			18 45			
Levenshulme d					18 11			18 19								18 36			18 48			
Manchester Piccadilly a	17 59	18 02	18 07	18 13	18 20			18 28	18 28		18 36		18 36	18 39	18 42	18 44	18 49	18 52	18 56	18 59	19 02	19 07
d						18 01	18 07			18 16		18 22	18 37					18 54				
Manchester Oxford Road a						18 03	18 09			18 18		18 24	18 40					18 56				
Deansgate a												18 28						19 00				

	AW	NT	TP	NT	VT	TP	NT	NT	NT	EM	XC	NT	VT	NT	XC	TP	VT	AW	NT	TP	NT	VT
	■ N	D	◇■ E	F	◇■ ⊠	◇■ G	I		H	◇ J	◇■ K		◇■ ⊠		◇■ A	◇■ B	◇■ ⊠	■ C	D	◇■ E	F	◇■ ⊠
London Euston ⊖65 d					17 20								17 40				18 00					18 20
Birmingham New Street 68 d											17 57				18 31							
Wolverhampton 68 d											18 15				18 49							
Stafford 65,68 d											18 30				19 01							
Stoke-on-Trent 50,68 d					18 49						18 55			18 58	19 20		19 25					19 48
Longport 50 d																						
Kidsgrove 50 d														19 05								
Crewe 65 d	18 31							18 34				18 50	19 11					19 31				
Sandbach d								18 41				18 57										
Holmes Chapel d								18 45				19 02										
Goostrey d												19 05										
Chelford d												19 09										
Alderley Edge d								18 54				19 13										
Wilmslow d	18 48							18 57				19 17	19 27					19 48				
Styal d																						
Manchester Airport a								19 05														
Handforth d												19 20										
Congleton d														19 12								
Macclesfield a											19 11			19 19			19 41					
d											19 12			19 20			19 41					
Prestbury d														19 24								
Adlington (Cheshire) d														19 27								
Poynton d														19 30								
Bramhall d														19 33								
Cheadle Hulme d												19 24		19 37								
Stockport a	18 58				19 16						19 27	19 29	19 36	19 41	19 48		19 55	19 58				20 16
d	18 58			19 12	19 17				19 21	19 26	19 28	19 29	19 37	19 42	19 50	19 53	19 56	19 58			20 12	20 17
Heaton Chapel d				19 16										19 45							20 16	
Levenshulme d				19 19										19 48							20 19	
Manchester Piccadilly a	19 15			19 28	19 28			19 31	19 35	19 36	19 39	19 43	19 49	19 56	19 59	20 02	20 07	20 15			20 28	20 28
d		19 01	19 07			19 16	19 20	19 32		19 37									20 01	20 07		
Manchester Oxford Road a		19 03	19 09			19 18	19 22	19 36		19 40									20 03	20 09		
Deansgate a							19 26															

A From Bristol Temple Meads
B From Cleethorpes to Manchester Airport
C From Carmarthen
D From Manchester Airport to Liverpool Lime Street
E From Scarborough to Liverpool Lime Street
F From Buxton
G From Manchester Airport to Barrow-in-Furness
H From Chester
I From Manchester Airport to Southport
J From Norwich to Liverpool Lime Street
K From Bournemouth
L From Buxton to Bolton
M From Paignton
N From Milford Haven

Table 84

Mondays to Fridays
from 1 October

Stoke-on-Trent and Crewe - Manchester Airport, Stockport and Manchester

Network Diagram - see first Page of Table 78

Station		TP	NT	NT	NT	EM	XC	NT	VT	NT	XC	AW	TP	AW	VT	VT	VT	TP	NT	VT	EM	NT
		◇1 A	B		C	◇ D	◇1 E ✠		◇1 ⊠		◇1 F ✠	G	◇1 H	■ I ✠	■ 1 J ⊡	◇ K ⊡	■ 1 K ⊡	◇1 L	M	■ 1 ⊡	◇ N	B
London Euston 15 ⊖65	d								18 40						19 00	18 57	19 00			19 20		
Birmingham New Street 12 68	d						18 57				19 31											
Wolverhampton 7 68	d						19 15				19 49											
Stafford 65,68	d						19 29				20 01											
Stoke-on-Trent 50,68	d						19 55			19 58	20 20				20 25		20 25			20 48		
Longport 50	d																					
Kidsgrove 50	d									20 05												
Crewe 10 65	d							19 50	20 12					20 23		20s33						
Sandbach	d							19 57														
Holmes Chapel	d							20 02														
Goostrey	d							20 05														
Chelford	d							20 09														
Alderley Edge	d							20 13														
Wilmslow	d			19 56				20 17	20 27					20 40								
Styal	d																					
Manchester Airport ✈	a			20 04																		
Handforth	d							20 20														
Congleton	d									20 12												
Macclesfield	a						20 11			20 19					20 41		20 41					
	d						20 12			20 20					20 41		20 41					
Prestbury	d									20 24												
Adlington (Cheshire)	d									20 27												
Poynton	d									20 30												
Bramhall	d									20 33												
Cheadle Hulme	d							20 24		20 37												
Stockport	a						20 27	20 29	20 36	20 41	20 48			20 50	20 55		20 55			21 16		
	d				20 21	20 26	20 28	20 29	20 37	20 42	20 50		20 54	20 51	20 56		20 56		21 12	21 17	21 20	
Heaton Chapel	d									20 45									21 16			
Levenshulme	d									20 48									21 19			
Manchester Piccadilly 10	a			20 32	20 35	20 36	20 39	20 43	20 49	20 56	20 58		21 02	21 05	21 07	21 09	21 10		21 28	21 28	21 32	
	d	20 16	20 20	20 32		20 37						20 50						21 07				21 20
Manchester Oxford Road	a	20 18	20 22	20 36		20 40						20 52						21 09				21 22
Deansgate	a		20 26																			21 26

Station		NT	NT	XC	NT	VT	NT	XC	VT	AW	AW	NT FO	TP	NT	TP	NT	NT	XC	NT	NT	NT	VT	TP
			C	◇1 E		◇1 ⊡		◇1 O	◇1 ⊡	◇ P ✠	G	Q	◇1 L	M	◇1 A		C	◇1 E		B	R	◇1 ⊡	◇1 H
London Euston 15 ⊖65	d					19 40			20 00													20 40	
Birmingham New Street 12 68	d			19 57				20 31										20 57					
Wolverhampton 7 68	d			20 16				20 49										21 16					
Stafford 65,68	d			20 30		21 04												21 32					
Stoke-on-Trent 50,68	d			20 55			20 58	21 18	21 24									21 55					
Longport 50	d																						
Kidsgrove 50	d						21 05																
Crewe 10 65	d				20 50	21 23				21 31									21 45			22 13	
Sandbach	d				20 57														21 52				
Holmes Chapel	d				21 02														21 58				
Goostrey	d				21 05														22 01				
Chelford	d				21 09														22 07				
Alderley Edge	d				21 13														22 12				
Wilmslow	d	20 56			21 17	21 38				21 48						21 55			22 15			22 29	
Styal	d																						
Manchester Airport ✈	a	21 04														22 04							
Handforth	d				21 20														22 19				
Congleton	d						21 12																
Macclesfield	a			21 11			21 19		21 40									22 11					
	d			21 12			21 20		21 40									22 12					
Prestbury	d						21 24																
Adlington (Cheshire)	d						21 27																
Poynton	d						21 30																
Bramhall	d						21 33																
Cheadle Hulme	d				21 24		21 37												22 24				
Stockport	a			21 27	21 29		21 41	21 46	21 55	21 58								22 25	22 29			22 38	
	d		21 21	21 28	21 29		21 42	21 49	21 56	21 59				22 12			22 21	22 26	22 29		22 34	22 39	22 53
Heaton Chapel	d						21 45							22 16							22 38		
Levenshulme	d						21 48							22 19							22 41		
Manchester Piccadilly 10	a	21 32	21 35	21 39	21 43	21 57	21 57	21 59	22 07	22 13				22 28		22 31	22 35	22 35	22 43		22 48	22 48	23 02
	d	21 32									21 50	22 01	22 07		22 16	22 32				22 36	22 50		
Manchester Oxford Road	a	21 36									21 52	22 03	22 09		22 18	22 36				22 38	22 52		
Deansgate	a																			22 41	22 55		

A From Manchester Airport to Barrow-in-Furness
B From Manchester Airport to Southport
C From Chester
D From Norwich to Liverpool Lime Street
E From Bournemouth
F From Exeter St Davids
G From Manchester Airport to Chester
H From Cleethorpes to Manchester Airport
I From Milford Haven
J MTWO
K ThFO
L From Scarborough to Liverpool Lime Street
M From Buxton
N From Norwich
O From Bristol Temple Meads
P From Carmarthen
Q From Manchester Airport to Liverpool Lime Street
R To Wigan Wallgate

Table 84

Mondays to Fridays
from 1 October

Stoke-on-Trent and Crewe - Manchester Airport, Stockport and Manchester

Network Diagram - see first Page of Table 78

Station		VT	NT	NT	XC	VT	AW	NT	NT	NT	XC	AW FO	VT
		◇1 ⊡			◇1 A	◇1 ⊡	◇ B	C	D		◇1	◇ E	◇1 ⊡
London Euston 15 ⊖65	d	21 00				21 40							22 00
Birmingham New Street 12 68	d				21 57						22 30	21 24	
Wolverhampton 7 68	d				22 16						22 48	21 43	
Stafford 65,68	d				22 30						23 01		23s38
Stoke-on-Trent 50,68	d	22 28	22 18		22 55	23 07					23 21		
Longport 50	d												
Kidsgrove 50	d		22 25										
Crewe 10 65	d						23 04			23 12			00s03
Sandbach	d									23 19			
Holmes Chapel	d									23 24			
Goostrey	d									23 27			
Chelford	d									23 31			
Alderley Edge	d									23 35			
Wilmslow	d			22 56			23 22			23 39			
Styal	d												
Manchester Airport ✈	a			23 04									
Handforth	d									23 42			
Congleton	d		22 32										
Macclesfield	a	22 44	22 40		23 11	23 23							
	d	22 44	22 48		23 12	23 23							
Prestbury	d		22 53										
Adlington (Cheshire)	d		22 56										
Poynton	d		22 59										
Bramhall	d		23 02										
Cheadle Hulme	d		23 05							23 46			
Stockport	a	22 58	23 10		23 25	23 37	23 30			23 51			00s26
	d	22 59	23 10		23 26	23 38	23 31	23 41	23 48	23 51			
Heaton Chapel	d		23 14							23 55			
Levenshulme	d		23 17							23 58			
Manchester Piccadilly 10	a	23 11	23 25	23 33	23 37	23 46	23 48	23 54	00 02	00 07	00 12	00 28	00 35
	d												
Manchester Oxford Road	a												
Deansgate	a												

Saturdays
until 30 June

Station		NT	NT	XC	XC	NT	AW	VT	NT	TP	NT	NT	TP	AW	NT	NT	NT	NT	EM	XC	NT	NT	NT
		D		◇1 F	◇1 G	H	◇ E	◇1 ⊡		◇1 I		J	◇1 K			L	C	H	◇ M	◇1			N
London Euston 15 ⊖65	d							22p00															
Birmingham New Street 12 68	d			22p30	22p30		21p24													05 57			
Wolverhampton 7 68	d			22p48	22p48		21p43													06 16			
Stafford 65,68	d			23p01	23p01			23b38												06 30			
Stoke-on-Trent 50,68	d			23p21	23p22															06 51			
Longport 50	d																						
Kidsgrove 50	d																						
Crewe 10 65	d		23p12					00s03	00 44					06 27							06 33	06 49	
Sandbach	d		23p19																		06 40	06 56	
Holmes Chapel	d		23p24																		06 44	07 00	
Goostrey	d		23p27																			07 03	
Chelford	d		23p31																			07 08	
Alderley Edge	d		23p35												06 49						06 53	07 12	
Wilmslow	d		23p39								05 46			06 45	06 52						06 57	07 16	
Styal	d																						
Manchester Airport ✈	a								01 16		05 53										07 04		
Handforth	d		23p42												06 55							07 19	
Congleton	d																			07 03			
Macclesfield	a																			07 11			
	d																			07 12			
Prestbury	d																						
Adlington (Cheshire)	d																						
Poynton	d																						
Bramhall	d																						
Cheadle Hulme	d		23p46												06 59							07 24	
Stockport	a		23p51					00s26						06 55	07 04					07 27		07 29	
	d	23p48	23p51			00 02				05 53		06 41	06 53	06 55	07 04		07 13	07 19	07 22	07 28		07 29	07 40
Heaton Chapel	d		23p55												07 08		07 16					07 33	
Levenshulme	d		23p58												07 11		07 19					07 36	
Manchester Piccadilly 10	a	00 02	00 07	00 12	00 13	00 18	00 28	00 35	01 36	06 05	06 25	06 52	07 02	07 07	07 21		07 26	07 31	07 34	07 38	07 42	07 44	07 52
	d											06 54				06 58			07 34				07 54
Manchester Oxford Road	a											06 56				07 00			07 37				07 56
Deansgate	a											06 59											08 00

A From Bournemouth
B From Cardiff Central
C From Buxton
D From Sheffield
E From Birmingham International
F 30 June
G not 30 June
H From Chester
I From Sheffield to Manchester Airport
J From Buxton to Clitheroe
K From Doncaster to Manchester Airport
L From Manchester Airport to Liverpool Lime Street
M From Nottingham to Liverpool Lime Street
N From Hazel Grove to Preston
b Previous night, stops to set down only

Stoke-on-Trent and Crewe - Manchester Airport, Stockport and Manchester

Saturdays until 30 June

Network Diagram - see first Page of Table 78

	NT	XC ◇■	TP ◇■ A	NT B	AW ◇ C	NT	NT D	TP ◇■ E	NT F	NT G	XC ◇■	NT H	EM ◇ I	NT	NT	VT ◇■	TP ◇■ J	NT K	NT	XC ◇■	TP ◇■ A	VT ◇■
London Euston ⊖65 d																06 36						06 55
Birmingham New Street 68 d		06 31									06 57									07 31		
Wolverhampton 68 d		06 49									07 15									07 49		
Stafford 65,68 d		07 01									07 30									08 01		
Stoke-on-Trent 50,68 d	06 57	07 19																	07 57	08 20		08 25
Longport 50 d																						
Kidsgrove 50 d	07 04																		08 04			
Crewe 65 d					07 27						07 53			07 30	07 55	08 11						
Sandbach d														07 37	08 02							
Holmes Chapel d														07 41	08 07							
Goostrey d														07 44								
Chelford d														07 49								
Alderley Edge d						07 49								07 53	08 15							
Wilmslow d					07 44	07 52					08 10			07 56	08 19	08 27						
Styal d														07 59								
Manchester Airport ✈ a														08 05								
Handforth d						07 55									08 22							
Congleton d	07 11																		08 11			
Macclesfield a	07 18	07 36																	08 18	08 36		08 41
d	07 19	07 37																	08 19	08 37		08 41
Prestbury d	07 23																		08 23			
Adlington (Cheshire) d	07 26																		08 26			
Poynton d	07 29																		08 30			
Bramhall d	07 32																		08 33			
Cheadle Hulme d	07 36					07 59									08 26				08 37			
Stockport a	07 40	07 49			08 01	08 04					08 20				08 31	08 36			08 41	08 49		08 55
d	07 41	07 50	07 53	07 57	08 01	08 04			08 13	08 19	08 20		08 24		08 31	08 37		08 41	08 42	08 50	08 53	08 56
Heaton Chapel d	07 44					08 08			08 16						08 35				08 45			
Levenshulme d	07 47					08 11			08 19										08 48			
Manchester Piccadilly a	07 56	07 59	08 02	08 09	08 20	08 20			08 26	08 32	08 35		08 36	08 42	08 45	08 49		08 52	08 56	08 59	09 02	09 07
d							07 59	08 07				08 22	08 37				08 46	08 54				
Manchester Oxford Road a							08 01	08 09				08 24	08 40				08 48	08 56				
Deansgate a												08 28					08 51	09 00				

	AW ◇ C	NT	NT D	TP ◇■ L	NT F	VT ◇■	NT G	NT H	EM ◇ I	XC ◇■ M	NT	NT	VT ◇■	NT N	NT	XC ◇■ O	TP ◇■ A	VT ◇■	AW ◇ P	NT	NT D
London Euston ⊖65 d						07 20							07 35					08 00			
Birmingham New Street 68 d										07 57						08 31					
Wolverhampton 68 d										08 15						08 49					
Stafford 65,68 d										08 30						09 01					
Stoke-on-Trent 50,68 d						08 48				08 55					08 58	09 20		09 25			
Longport 50 d																					
Kidsgrove 50 d															09 05						
Crewe 65 d	08 28										08 31	08 50	09 11						09 30		
Sandbach d											08 38	08 57									
Holmes Chapel d											08 42	09 02									
Goostrey d											08 45	09 05									
Chelford d											08 50	09 09									
Alderley Edge d		08 49									08 54	09 13								09 49	
Wilmslow d	08 45	08 52									08 57	09 17	09 27						09 47	09 52	
Styal d																					
Manchester Airport ✈ a											09 04										
Handforth d		08 55										09 20								09 55	
Congleton d															09 12						
Macclesfield a										09 11					09 19			09 41			
d										09 12					09 20			09 41			
Prestbury d															09 24						
Adlington (Cheshire) d															09 27						
Poynton d															09 30						
Bramhall d															09 33						
Cheadle Hulme d		08 59										09 24			09 37					09 59	
Stockport a	08 58	09 04				09 16				09 27		09 29	09 36		09 41	09 49		09 55	09 57	10 04	
d	08 59	09 04			09 13	09 17	09 21		09 25	09 28		09 29	09 37	09 42	09 42	09 50	09 53	09 56	09 58	10 04	
Heaton Chapel d		09 08			09 16							09 33			09 45					10 08	
Levenshulme d		09 11			09 19							09 36			09 48					10 11	
Manchester Piccadilly a	09 15	09 20			09 26	09 28	09 36		09 36	09 39	09 42	09 44	09 49	09 52	09 56	09 59	10 02	10 07	10 14	10 20	
d			09 01	09 07				09 22	09 37					09 54							10 01
Manchester Oxford Road a			09 03	09 09				09 24	09 40					09 56							10 03
Deansgate a								09 28						10 00							

A From Cleethorpes to Manchester Airport
B From Hazel Grove
C From Cardiff Central
D From Manchester Airport to Liverpool Lime Street
E From Hull to Liverpool Lime Street
F From Buxton
G From Chester
H From Manchester Airport to Southport
I From Nottingham to Liverpool Lime Street
J From Manchester Airport to Windermere
K From Buxton to Preston
L From Newcastle to Liverpool Lime Street
M From Southampton Central
N From Hazel Grove to Preston
O From Bristol Temple Meads
P From Carmarthen

Stoke-on-Trent and Crewe - Manchester Airport, Stockport and Manchester

Saturdays until 30 June

Network Diagram - see first Page of Table 78

	TP ◇■ A	NT B	VT ◇■	NT C	NT D	EM ◇ E	XC ◇■ F	NT	NT	VT ◇■	NT G	NT	XC ◇■ H	TP ◇■ I	VT ◇■	AW ◇ J	NT	NT K	TP ◇■ A	NT B	VT ◇■	TP ◇■ L
London Euston ⊖65 d			08 20							08 40					09 00						09 20	
Birmingham New Street 68 d							08 57						09 31									
Wolverhampton 68 d							09 15						09 49									
Stafford 65,68 d							09 30						10 01									
Stoke-on-Trent 50,68 d			09 48				09 55					09 58	10 20		10 25						10 48	
Longport 50 d																						
Kidsgrove 50 d												10 05										
Crewe 65 d								09 33	09 50	10 11						10 31						
Sandbach d								09 40	09 57													
Holmes Chapel d								09 44	10 02													
Goostrey d									10 05													
Chelford d									10 09													
Alderley Edge d								09 53	10 13								10 49					
Wilmslow d								09 57	10 17	10 27						10 49	10 52					
Styal d																						
Manchester Airport ✈ a								10 04														
Handforth d									10 20								10 55					
Congleton d												10 12										
Macclesfield a							10 11					10 19			10 41							
d							10 12					10 20			10 41							
Prestbury d												10 24										
Adlington (Cheshire) d												10 27										
Poynton d												10 30										
Bramhall d												10 33										
Cheadle Hulme d									10 24			10 37					10 59					
Stockport a			10 16				10 27		10 29	10 36		10 41	10 49		10 55	10 58	11 04				11 16	
d		10 13	10 17	10 21		10 26	10 28		10 29	10 37	10 41	10 42	10 50	10 53	10 56	10 58	11 04			11 13	11 17	
Heaton Chapel d		10 16							10 33			10 45					11 08			11 16		
Levenshulme d		10 19							10 36			10 48					11 11			11 19		
Manchester Piccadilly a		10 26	10 28	10 36		10 36	10 39	10 42	10 44	10 49	10 52	10 56	10 59	11 02	11 07	11 15	11 20			11 26	11 28	
d	10 07				10 22	10 37					10 54							11 01	11 07			11 16
Manchester Oxford Road a	10 09				10 24	10 40					10 56							11 03	11 09			11 18
Deansgate a					10 28						11 00											

	NT C	NT D	EM ◇ E	XC ◇■ M	NT	NT	VT ◇■	NT G	NT	XC ◇■ N	TP ◇■ I	VT ◇■	AW ◇ O	NT	NT K	TP ◇■ A	NT B	VT ◇■	NT C	NT D	EM ◇ E
London Euston ⊖65 d							09 40					10 00						10 20			
Birmingham New Street 68 d				09 57						10 31											
Wolverhampton 68 d				10 15						10 49											
Stafford 65,68 d				10 30						11 01											
Stoke-on-Trent 50,68 d				10 55					10 58	11 20		11 25						11 48			
Longport 50 d																					
Kidsgrove 50 d									11 05												
Crewe 65 d					10 34	10 50	11 11						11 31								
Sandbach d					10 41	10 57															
Holmes Chapel d					10 45	11 02															
Goostrey d						11 05															
Chelford d						11 09															
Alderley Edge d					10 54	11 13								11 49							
Wilmslow d					10 57	11 17	11 27						11 48	11 52							
Styal d																					
Manchester Airport ✈ a					11 04																
Handforth d						11 20								11 55							
Congleton d									11 12												
Macclesfield a				11 11					11 19			11 41									
d				11 12					11 20			11 41									
Prestbury d									11 24												
Adlington (Cheshire) d									11 27												
Poynton d									11 30												
Bramhall d									11 33												
Cheadle Hulme d						11 24			11 37					11 59							
Stockport a				11 27		11 29	11 36		11 41	11 49		11 55	11 58	12 04				12 16			
d	11 21		11 26	11 28		11 29	11 37	11 41	11 42	11 50	11 53	11 56	11 58	12 04			12 13	12 17	12 21		12 26
Heaton Chapel d						11 33			11 45					12 08			12 16				
Levenshulme d						11 36			11 48					12 11			12 19				
Manchester Piccadilly a	11 36		11 36	11 39	11 42	11 44	11 49	11 52	11 56	11 59	12 02	12 07	12 15	12 20			12 26	12 28	12 36		12 36
d		11 22	11 37					11 54							12 01	12 07				12 22	12 37
Manchester Oxford Road a		11 24	11 40					11 56							12 03	12 09				12 24	12 40
Deansgate a		11 28						12 00												12 28	

A From Scarborough to Liverpool Lime Street
B From Buxton
C From Chester
D From Manchester Airport to Southport
E From Norwich to Liverpool Lime Street
F From Southampton Central
G From Hazel Grove to Preston
H From Cardiff Central
I From Cleethorpes to Manchester Airport
J From Carmarthen
K From Manchester Airport to Liverpool Lime Street
L From Manchester Airport to Barrow-in-Furness
M From Bournemouth
N From Paignton
O From Milford Haven

Table 84

Saturdays until 30 June

Stoke-on-Trent and Crewe - Manchester Airport, Stockport and Manchester

Network Diagram - see first Page of Table 78

	XC	NT	NT	VT	NT	NT	XC	TP	VT	AW	NT	NT	TP	NT	VT	NT	NT	EM	XC	NT	NT	VT
	◇■ A			◇■	B		◇■ C	◇■ D	◇■	◇ E		F	◇■ G	H	◇■	I	J	◇ K	◇■ A			◇■
London Euston ⊖65 d				10 40					11 00						11 20							11 40
Birmingham New Street 68 d	10 57						11 31												11 57			
Wolverhampton 68 ⇌ d	11 15						11 49												12 15			
Stafford 65,68 d	11 30						12 01												12 30			
Stoke-on-Trent 50,68 d	11 55					11 58	12 20		12 25						12 48				12 55			
Longport 50 d																						
Kidsgrove 50 d						12 05																
Crewe 65 d		11 34	11 50	12 11						12 31										12 34	12 50	13 11
Sandbach d		11 41	11 57																	12 41	12 57	
Holmes Chapel d		11 45	12 02																	12 45	13 02	
Goostrey d			12 05																		13 05	
Chelford d			12 09																		13 09	
Alderley Edge d		11 54	12 13								12 49									12 54	13 13	
Wilmslow d		11 57	12 17	12 27						12 49	12 52									12 57	13 17	13 27
Styal d																						
Manchester Airport ✈ a		12 04																		13 04		
Handforth d			12 20								12 55										13 20	
Congleton d						12 12																
Macclesfield a	12 11					12 19			12 41										13 11			
d	12 12					12 20			12 41										13 12			
Prestbury d						12 24																
Adlington (Cheshire) d						12 27																
Poynton d						12 30																
Bramhall d						12 33																
Cheadle Hulme d			12 24			12 37					12 59										13 24	
Stockport a	12 27		12 29	12 36		12 41	12 49		12 55	12 58	13 04				13 16				13 27		13 29	13 36
d	12 28		12 29	12 37	12 41	12 42	12 50	12 53	12 56	12 58	13 04			13 13	13 17	13 21		13 26	13 28		13 29	13 37
Heaton Chapel d			12 33			12 45					13 08			13 16							13 33	
Levenshulme d			12 36			12 48					13 11			13 19							13 36	
Manchester Piccadilly ⇌ a	12 39	12 42	12 44	12 49	12 52	12 56	12 59	13 02	13 07	13 15	13 20			13 26	13 28	13 36		13 36	13 39	13 42	13 44	13 49
d					12 54							13 01	13 07				13 22	13 37				
Manchester Oxford Road a					12 56							13 03	13 09				13 24	13 40				
Deansgate ⇌ a					13 00												13 28					

	NT	NT	XC	TP	VT	AW	NT	NT	TP	NT	VT	TP	NT	NT	EM	XC	NT	NT	VT	NT	NT	XC
	B		◇■ L	◇■ D	◇■	◇ M		F	◇■ G	H	◇■	◇■ N	I	J	◇ K	◇■ A			◇■	B		◇■ O
London Euston ⊖65 d					12 00						12 20								12 40			
Birmingham New Street 68 d			12 31													12 57						13 31
Wolverhampton 68 ⇌ d			12 49													13 15						13 49
Stafford 65,68 d			13 01													13 30						14 01
Stoke-on-Trent 50,68 d		12 58	13 20		13 25						13 48					13 55					13 58	14 20
Longport 50 d																						
Kidsgrove 50 d		13 05																			14 05	
Crewe 65 d						13 31											13 34	13 50	14 11			
Sandbach d																	13 41	13 57				
Holmes Chapel d																	13 45	14 02				
Goostrey d																		14 05				
Chelford d																		14 09				
Alderley Edge d							13 49										13 54	14 13				
Wilmslow d						13 48	13 52										13 57	14 17	14 27			
Styal d																						
Manchester Airport ✈ a																	14 04					
Handforth d							13 55											14 20				
Congleton d		13 12																			14 12	
Macclesfield a		13 19			13 41											14 11					14 19	
d		13 20			13 41											14 12					14 20	
Prestbury d		13 24																			14 24	
Adlington (Cheshire) d		13 27																			14 27	
Poynton d		13 30																			14 30	
Bramhall d		13 33																			14 33	
Cheadle Hulme d		13 37					13 59											14 24			14 37	
Stockport a		13 41	13 49		13 55	13 58	14 04				14 16					14 27		14 29	14 36		14 41	14 49
d	13 41	13 42	13 50	13 53	13 56	13 58	14 04			14 15	14 17		14 21		14 26	14 28		14 29	14 37	14 41	14 42	14 50
Heaton Chapel d		13 45					14 08			14 18								14 33			14 45	
Levenshulme d		13 48					14 11			14 21								14 36			14 48	
Manchester Piccadilly ⇌ a	13 52	13 56	13 59	14 02	14 07	14 15	14 20			14 28	14 28		14 36		14 36	14 39	14 42	14 44	14 49	14 52	14 56	14 59
d	13 54							14 01	14 07			14 16		14 22	14 37					14 54		
Manchester Oxford Road a	13 56							14 03	14 09			14 18		14 24	14 40					14 56		
Deansgate ⇌ a	14 00													14 28						15 00		

A From Bournemouth
B From Hazel Grove to Preston
C From Bristol Temple Meads
D From Cleethorpes to Manchester Airport
E From Milford Haven
F From Manchester Airport to Liverpool Lime Street
G From Scarborough to Liverpool Lime Street
H From Buxton
I From Chester
J From Manchester Airport to Southport
K From Norwich to Liverpool Lime Street
L From Plymouth
M From Fishguard Harbour
N From Manchester Airport to Barrow-in-Furness
O From Paignton

Table 84

Saturdays until 30 June

Stoke-on-Trent and Crewe - Manchester Airport, Stockport and Manchester

Network Diagram - see first Page of Table 78

	TP	VT	AW	NT	NT	TP	NT	VT	TP	NT	NT	EM	XC	NT	NT	VT	NT	NT	XC	TP	VT
	◇■ A	◇■	◇ B		C	◇■ D	E	◇■	◇■ F	G	H	◇ I	◇■ J			◇■	K		◇■ L	◇■ A	◇■
London Euston ⊖65 d		13 00						13 20								13 40					14 00
Birmingham New Street 68 d													13 57						14 31		
Wolverhampton 68 ⇌ d													14 15						14 49		
Stafford 65,68 d													14 30						15 01		
Stoke-on-Trent 50,68 d		14 25						14 48					14 55					14 58	15 20		15 25
Longport 50 d																					
Kidsgrove 50 d																		15 05			
Crewe 65 d			14 31											14 34	14 50	15 11					
Sandbach d														14 41	14 57						
Holmes Chapel d														14 45	15 02						
Goostrey d															15 05						
Chelford d															15 09						
Alderley Edge d				14 49										14 54	15 13						
Wilmslow d			14 49	14 52										14 57	15 17	15 27					
Styal d																					
Manchester Airport ✈ a														15 04							
Handforth d				14 55											15 20						
Congleton d																		15 12			
Macclesfield a		14 41											15 11					15 19			15 41
d		14 41											15 12					15 20			15 41
Prestbury d																		15 24			
Adlington (Cheshire) d																		15 27			
Poynton d																		15 30			
Bramhall d																		15 33			
Cheadle Hulme d				14 59											15 24			15 37			
Stockport a		14 55	14 58	15 04				15 16					15 27		15 29	15 36		15 41	15 49		15 55
d	14 53	14 56	14 58	15 04			15 13	15 17		15 21		15 26	15 28		15 29	15 37	15 41	15 42	15 50	15 53	15 56
Heaton Chapel d				15 08			15 16								15 33			15 45			
Levenshulme d				15 11			15 19								15 36			15 48			
Manchester Piccadilly ⇌ a	15 02	15 07	15 15	15 20			15 26	15 28		15 36		15 36	15 39	15 42	15 44	15 49	15 52	15 56	15 59	16 02	16 07
d					15 01	15 07			15 16		15 22	15 37					15 54				
Manchester Oxford Road a					15 03	15 09			15 18		15 24	15 40					15 56				
Deansgate ⇌ a											15 28						16 00				

	AW	NT	NT	TP	NT	VT	TP	NT	NT	EM	XC	NT	NT	VT	NT	NT	XC	TP	VT	AW	NT	NT
	◇ M		C	◇■ D	E	◇■	◇■ N	G	H	◇ I	◇■ J			◇■	K		◇■ L	◇■ A	◇■	◇ B		C
London Euston ⊖65 d						14 20								14 40					15 00			
Birmingham New Street 68 d											14 57						15 31					
Wolverhampton 68 ⇌ d											15 15						15 49					
Stafford 65,68 d											15 30						16 01					
Stoke-on-Trent 50,68 d						15 48					15 55					15 58	16 19		16 25			
Longport 50 d																						
Kidsgrove 50 d																16 05						
Crewe 65 d	15 28											15 33	15 50	16 11						16 31		
Sandbach d												15 40	15 57									
Holmes Chapel d												15 44	16 02									
Goostrey d													16 05									
Chelford d													16 09									
Alderley Edge d		15 49										15 53	16 13								16 49	
Wilmslow d	15 45	15 52										15 56	16 17	16 27						16 48	16 52	
Styal d												15 59										
Manchester Airport ✈ a												16 04										
Handforth d		15 55											16 20								16 55	
Congleton d																16 12						
Macclesfield a											16 11					16 19			16 41			
d											16 12					16 20			16 41			
Prestbury d																16 24						
Adlington (Cheshire) d																16 27						
Poynton d																16 30						
Bramhall d																16 33						
Cheadle Hulme d		15 59											16 24			16 37					16 59	
Stockport a	15 58	16 04				16 16					16 27		16 29	16 36		16 41	16 48		16 54	16 58	17 04	
d	15 58	16 04			16 15	16 17		16 21		16 26	16 28		16 29	16 37	16 41	16 42	16 49	16 53	16 55	16 58	17 04	
Heaton Chapel d		16 08			16 18								16 33			16 45					17 08	
Levenshulme d		16 11			16 21								16 36			16 48					17 11	
Manchester Piccadilly ⇌ a	16 15	16 20			16 28	16 28		16 36		16 36	16 39	16 42	16 44	16 49	16 52	16 56	16 59	17 02	17 07	17 15	17 20	
d			16 01	16 07			16 16		16 22	16 37					16 54							17 01
Manchester Oxford Road a			16 03	16 09			16 18		16 24	16 40					16 56							17 03
Deansgate ⇌ a									16 28						17 00							

A From Cleethorpes to Manchester Airport
B From Milford Haven
C From Manchester Airport to Liverpool Lime Street
D From Scarborough to Liverpool Lime Street
E From Buxton
F From Manchester Airport to Barrow-in-Furness
G From Chester
H From Manchester Airport to Southport
I From Norwich to Liverpool Lime Street
J From Bournemouth
K From Hazel Grove to Preston
L From Bristol Temple Meads
M From Carmarthen
N From Manchester Airport to Windermere

Stoke-on-Trent and Crewe - Manchester Airport, Stockport and Manchester

Network Diagram - see first Page of Table 78

	TP ◇1 A	NT B	VT ◇1	NT C	NT D	EM ◇ E	XC ◇1 F	NT	NT	VT ◇1	NT	XC ◇1 G	TP ◇1 H	VT ◇1	AW ◇ I	NT	NT J	TP ◇1 A	NT B	VT ◇1	TP ◇1 K
London Euston ⊖65 d			15 20							15 40				16 00						16 20	
Birmingham New Street 68 d							15 57					16 31									
Wolverhampton 68 d							16 15					16 49									
Stafford 65,68 d							16 30					17 01									
Stoke-on-Trent 50,68 d			16 48				16 55				16 58	17 20		17 25						17 48	
Longport 50 d																					
Kidsgrove 50 d											17 05										
Crewe 65 d								16 34	16 50	17 11					17 28						
Sandbach d								16 41	16 57												
Holmes Chapel d								16 45	17 02												
Goostrey d									17 05												
Chelford d									17 09												
Alderley Edge d								16 54	17 13							17 49					
Wilmslow d								16 57	17 17	17 27					17 45	17 52					
Styal d																					
Manchester Airport ✈ a								17 04													
Handforth d									17 20							17 55					
Congleton d											17 12										
Macclesfield a							17 11				17 19			17 41							
d							17 12				17 20			17 41							
Prestbury d											17 24										
Adlington (Cheshire) d											17 27										
Poynton d											17 30										
Bramhall d											17 33										
Cheadle Hulme d									17 24		17 37					17 59					
Stockport a			17 16				17 27		17 29	17 36	17 41	17 49		17 55	17 58	18 04				18 16	
d		17 13	17 17	17 21		17 26	17 28		17 29	17 37	17 42	17 50	17 53	17 56	17 58	18 04			18 15	18 17	
Heaton Chapel d		17 16							17 33		17 45					18 08			18 18		
Levenshulme d		17 19							17 36		17 48					18 11			18 21		
Manchester Piccadilly a		17 26	17 28	17 36		17 37	17 39	17 42	17 44	17 49	17 56	17 59	18 02	18 07	18 15	18 20			18 28	18 28	
d	17 07				17 23	17 37											18 01	18 07			18 16
Manchester Oxford Road a	17 09				17 25	17 40											18 03	18 09			18 18
Deansgate a																					

	NT C	NT D	EM ◇ E	XC ◇1 F	NT	NT	VT ◇1	NT L	NT	XC ◇1 M	TP ◇1 H	VT ◇1	AW ■ N	NT J	TP ◇1 A	NT B	VT ◇1	TP ◇1 K	NT D	NT	NT C	EM ◇ E
London Euston ⊖65 d							16 40					17 00					17 20					
Birmingham New Street 68 d				16 57						17 31												
Wolverhampton 68 d				17 15						17 49												
Stafford 65,68 d				17 30						18 01												
Stoke-on-Trent 50,68 d				17 55					17 58	18 20		18 25					18 48					
Longport 50 d																						
Kidsgrove 50 d									18 05													
Crewe 65 d					17 33	17 50	18 11						18 31							18 34		
Sandbach d					17 40	17 57														18 41		
Holmes Chapel d					17 44	18 02														18 45		
Goostrey d						18 05																
Chelford d						18 09																
Alderley Edge d					17 53	18 13														18 54		
Wilmslow d					17 56	18 17	18 27						18 48							18 57		
Styal d					17 59																	
Manchester Airport ✈ a					18 04															19 05		
Handforth d						18 20																
Congleton d									18 12													
Macclesfield a				18 11					18 19			18 41										
d				18 12					18 20			18 41										
Prestbury d									18 24													
Adlington (Cheshire) d									18 27													
Poynton d									18 30													
Bramhall d									18 33													
Cheadle Hulme d						18 24			18 37													
Stockport a				18 27		18 29	18 36		18 41	18 49		18 55	18 58				19 16					
d	18 21		18 26	18 28		18 29	18 37	18 41	18 42	18 50	18 53	18 56	18 58			19 15	19 17				19 21	19 26
Heaton Chapel d						18 33			18 45							19 18						
Levenshulme d						18 36			18 48							19 21						
Manchester Piccadilly a	18 36		18 36	18 39	18 42	18 44	18 49	18 52	18 56	18 59	19 02	19 07	19 15			19 28	19 28			19 31	19 35	19 36
d		18 22	18 37					18 54						19 01	19 07			19 16	19 20	19 32		19 37
Manchester Oxford Road a		18 24	18 40					18 56						19 03	19 09			19 18	19 22	19 36		19 40
Deansgate a		18 28						19 00											19 26			

A From Scarborough to Liverpool Lime Street
B From Buxton
C From Chester
D From Manchester Airport to Southport
E From Norwich to Liverpool Lime Street
F From Bournemouth
G From Bristol Temple Meads
H From Cleethorpes to Manchester Airport
I From Carmarthen
J From Manchester Airport to Liverpool Lime Street
K From Manchester Airport to Barrow-in-Furness
L From Hazel Grove to Bolton
M From Paignton
N From Milford Haven

Stoke-on-Trent and Crewe - Manchester Airport, Stockport and Manchester

Network Diagram - see first Page of Table 78

	XC ◇1 A	NT	VT ◇1	NT	XC ◇1 B	TP ◇1 C	VT ◇1	AW ■ D	NT E	TP ◇1 F	NT G	VT ◇1	TP ◇1 H	NT I	NT	NT J	EM ◇ K	XC ◇1 A	NT	VT ◇1	NT	XC ◇1 B
London Euston ⊖65 d			17 40				18 00					18 20								18 40		
Birmingham New Street 68 d	17 57				18 31													18 57				19 31
Wolverhampton 68 d	18 15				18 49													19 15				19 49
Stafford 65,68 d	18 30				19 01													19 30				20 01
Stoke-on-Trent 50,68 d	18 55			18 58	19 20		19 25					19 48						19 55			19 58	20 20
Longport 50 d																						
Kidsgrove 50 d				19 05																	20 05	
Crewe 65 d		18 50	19 11					19 31											19 50	20 11		
Sandbach d		18 57																	19 57			
Holmes Chapel d		19 02																	20 02			
Goostrey d		19 05																	20 05			
Chelford d		19 09																	20 09			
Alderley Edge d		19 13																	20 13			
Wilmslow d		19 17	19 27					19 48							19 56				20 17	20 27		
Styal d																						
Manchester Airport ✈ a															20 04							
Handforth d		19 20																	20 20			
Congleton d				19 12																	20 12	
Macclesfield a	19 11			19 19			19 41											20 11			20 19	20 36
d	19 12			19 20			19 41											20 12			20 20	20 37
Prestbury d				19 24																	20 24	
Adlington (Cheshire) d				19 27																	20 27	
Poynton d				19 30																	20 30	
Bramhall d				19 33																	20 33	
Cheadle Hulme d		19 24		19 37															20 24		20 37	
Stockport a	19 27	19 29	19 36	19 41	19 49		19 55	19 58				20 16						20 27	20 29	20 36	20 41	20 49
d	19 28	19 29	19 37	19 42	19 50	19 53	19 56	19 58			20 15	20 17				20 21	20 26	20 28	20 29	20 37	20 42	20 50
Heaton Chapel d				19 45							20 18										20 45	
Levenshulme d				19 48							20 21										20 48	
Manchester Piccadilly a	19 39	19 43	19 49	19 56	19 59	20 02	20 07	20 15			20 28	20 28			20 31	20 35	20 36	20 39	20 43	20 49	20 56	20 59
d									20 01	20 07			20 16	20 20	20 32		20 37					
Manchester Oxford Road a									20 03	20 09			20 18	20 22	20 36		20 40					
Deansgate a														20 26								

	AW L	TP ◇1 C	VT ◇1	AW ■ M	TP ◇1 F	NT G	VT ◇1	NT I	NT	EM ◇ N	NT J	XC ◇1 A	NT	VT ◇1	NT	XC ◇1 B	AW ◇ D	NT E	TP ◇1 F	NT G	TP ◇1 H
London Euston ⊖65 d			19 00				19 20							19 40							
Birmingham New Street 68 d												19 57				20 31					
Wolverhampton 68 d												20 15				20 49					
Stafford 65,68 d												20 30				21 01					
Stoke-on-Trent 50,68 d			20 25				20 48					20 55			20 58	21 21					
Longport 50 d																					
Kidsgrove 50 d															21 05						
Crewe 65 d				20 28									20 50	21 19			21 33				
Sandbach d													20 57								
Holmes Chapel d													21 02								
Goostrey d													21 05								
Chelford d													21 09								
Alderley Edge d													21 13								
Wilmslow d				20 45					20 56				21 17	21 34			21 50				
Styal d																					
Manchester Airport ✈ a									21 05												
Handforth d													21 20								
Congleton d															21 12						
Macclesfield a			20 41									21 11			21 19	21 38					
d			20 41									21 12			21 20	21 39					
Prestbury d															21 24						
Adlington (Cheshire) d															21 27						
Poynton d															21 30						
Bramhall d															21 33						
Cheadle Hulme d													21 24		21 37						
Stockport a			20 55	20 58			21 16					21 27	21 29	21 44	21 41	21 53	22 00				
d		20 53	20 56	20 59		21 13	21 17			21 20	21 21	21 28	21 29	21 45	21 42	21 54	22 00			22 13	
Heaton Chapel d						21 16									21 45					22 16	
Levenshulme d						21 19									21 48					22 19	
Manchester Piccadilly a		21 02	21 07	21 15		21 26	21 28		21 31	21 32	21 35	21 39	21 43	21 53	21 57	22 04	22 15			22 26	
d	20 50				21 07			21 22	21 32									22 01	22 07		22 16
Manchester Oxford Road a	20 52				21 09			21 24	21 36									22 03	22 09		22 18
Deansgate a								21 28													

A From Bournemouth
B From Bristol Temple Meads
C From Cleethorpes to Manchester Airport
D From Carmarthen
E From Manchester Airport to Liverpool Lime Street
F From Scarborough to Liverpool Lime Street
G From Buxton
H From Manchester Airport to Barrow-in-Furness
I From Manchester Airport to Southport
J From Chester
K From Norwich to Liverpool Lime Street
L From Manchester Airport to Chester
M From Milford Haven
N From Norwich

Table 84

Saturdays until 30 June

Stoke-on-Trent and Crewe - Manchester Airport, Stockport and Manchester

Network Diagram - see first Page of Table 78

Station		NT	XC ◇■ A ✕	NT	VT ◇■ ⊡	NT B	NT C	NT D	NT	XC ◇■ E	VT ◇■ ⊡	NT F	AW ◇ G	NT	NT H	NT	XC ◇■
London Euston 15 ⊖65	d				20 20						21 00						
Birmingham New Street 12 68	d		20 57							21 57							22 31
Wolverhampton 7 68	d		21 15							22 16							22 49
Stafford 65,68	d		21 30							22 30	22 34						23 02
Stoke-on-Trent 50,68	d		21 53		22 05				22 18	22 51							23 21
Longport 50	d																
Kidsgrove 50	d								22 25								
Crewe 10 65	d			21 50							22 59		23 06			23 12	
Sandbach	d			21 57												23 19	
Holmes Chapel	d			22 02												23 24	
Goostrey	d			22 05												23 27	
Chelford	d			22 09												23 31	
Alderley Edge	d			22 13												23 35	
Wilmslow	d	21 55		22 17							23 15		23 24	23 15		23 39	
Styal	d																
Manchester Airport ✈	a	22 04												23 23			
Handforth	d			22 20												23 42	
Congleton	d								22 32								
Macclesfield	a		22 10		22 21				22 39	23 07							23 38
	d		22 11		22 21				22 40	23 08							23 39
Prestbury	d								22 44								
Adlington (Cheshire)	d								22 47								
Poynton	d								22 50								
Bramhall	d								22 53								
Cheadle Hulme	d			22 24					22 56							23 46	
Stockport	a		22 26	22 29	22 35				23 01	23 21	23 25		23 32			23 51	23 53
	d		22 27	22 29	22 36		22 40	22 48	23 01	23 22	23 26	23 22	23 33		23 42	23 51	23 54
Heaton Chapel	d						22 44		23 05							23 55	
Levenshulme	d						22 47		23 08							23 58	
Manchester Piccadilly 10	a	22 31	22 39	22 43	22 51		22 53	23 00	23 16	23 32	23 38	23 43	23 50	23 51	23 52	00 07	00 10
	d	22 32				22 36	22 54										
Manchester Oxford Road	a	22 36				22 38	22 56										
Deansgate	a					22 41	23 00										

Saturdays 7 July to 29 September

Station		NT F	NT	XC ◇■	NT D	AW ◇ I	VT ◇■ ⊡	NT	VT ◇■ J ⊡	VT ◇■ J ⊡	VT ◇■ J ⊡	TP ◇■ K	NT	NT L	TP ◇■ M	AW	NT	NT N	NT H	NT D	EM ◇ O	XC ◇■	NT
London Euston 15 ⊖65	d						22p00		23p30	00 30	01 30												
Birmingham New Street 12 68	d			22p30		21p24																05 57	
Wolverhampton 7 68	d			22p48		21p43																06 16	
Stafford 65,68	d			23p01			23b38															06 30	
Stoke-on-Trent 50,68	d			23p21					00s53	01s53	03s04											06 51	
Longport 50	d																						
Kidsgrove 50	d																						
Crewe 10 65	d		23p12				00s03	00 44								06 27							06 33
Sandbach	d		23p19																				06 40
Holmes Chapel	d		23p24																				06 44
Goostrey	d		23p27																				
Chelford	d		23p31																				
Alderley Edge	d		23p35														06 49						06 53
Wilmslow	d		23p39										05 46			06 45	06 52						06 57
Styal	d																						
Manchester Airport ✈	a							01 16					05 53										07 04
Handforth	d		23p42														06 55						
Congleton	d																					07 03	
Macclesfield	a								01s10	02s10	03s20											07 11	
	d																					07 12	
Prestbury	d																						
Adlington (Cheshire)	d																						
Poynton	d																						
Bramhall	d																						
Cheadle Hulme	d		23p46														06 59						
Stockport	a		23p51				00s26		01s24	02s24	03s34					06 55	07 04					07 27	
	d	23p48	23p51		00 02							05 53		06 41	06 53	06 55	07 04		07 13	07 19	07 22	07 28	
Heaton Chapel	d		23p55														07 08		07 16				
Levenshulme	d		23p58														07 11		07 19				
Manchester Piccadilly 10	a	00 02	00 07	00 12	00 18	00 28	00 35	01 36	01 43	02 37	03 45	06 05	06 25	06 52	07 02	07 07	07 21		07 26	07 31	07 34	07 38	07 42
	d													06 54				06 58			07 34		
Manchester Oxford Road	a													06 56				07 00			07 37		
Deansgate	a													06 59									

A From Newquay
B From Manchester Airport to Southport
C To Wigan Wallgate
D From Chester
E From Bournemouth
F From Sheffield
G From Maesteg
H From Buxton
I From Birmingham International
J from 28 July until 11 August, from 1 September until 8 September
K From Sheffield to Manchester Airport
L From Buxton to Clitheroe
M From Doncaster to Manchester Airport
N From Manchester Airport to Liverpool Lime Street
O From Nottingham to Liverpool Lime Street
b Previous night, stops to set down only

Table 84

Saturdays 7 July to 29 September

Stoke-on-Trent and Crewe - Manchester Airport, Stockport and Manchester

Network Diagram - see first Page of Table 78

Station		NT	NT A	NT	XC ◇■ ✕	TP ◇■ B ✕	NT C	AW ◇ D	NT	NT E	TP ◇■ F ✕	NT G	NT H	XC ◇■ ✕	NT I	EM ◇ J	NT	NT	VT ◇■ ⊡	TP ◇■ K ✕	NT L	NT	XC ◇■ ✕
London Euston 15 ⊖65	d																		06 36				
Birmingham New Street 12 68	d				06 31									06 57									07 31
Wolverhampton 7 68	d				06 49									07 15									07 49
Stafford 65,68	d				07 01									07 30									08 01
Stoke-on-Trent 50,68	d			06 57	07 19																	07 57	08 20
Longport 50	d																						
Kidsgrove 50	d			07 04																		08 04	
Crewe 10 65	d	06 49						07 27						07 53			07 30	07 55	08 11				
Sandbach	d	06 56															07 37	08 02					
Holmes Chapel	d	07 00															07 41	08 07					
Goostrey	d	07 03															07 44						
Chelford	d	07 08															07 49						
Alderley Edge	d	07 12							07 49								07 53	08 15					
Wilmslow	d	07 16						07 44	07 52					08 10			07 56	08 19	08 27				
Styal	d																07 59						
Manchester Airport ✈	a																08 05						
Handforth	d	07 19							07 55									08 22					
Congleton	d			07 11																		08 11	
Macclesfield	a			07 18	07 36																	08 18	08 36
	d			07 19	07 37																	08 19	08 37
Prestbury	d			07 23																		08 23	
Adlington (Cheshire)	d			07 26																		08 26	
Poynton	d			07 29																		08 30	
Bramhall	d			07 32																		08 33	
Cheadle Hulme	d	07 24		07 36					07 59									08 26				08 37	
Stockport	a	07 29		07 40	07 49			08 01	08 04					08 20				08 31	08 36			08 41	08 49
	d	07 29	07 40	07 41	07 50	07 53	07 57	08 01	08 04			08 13	08 19	08 20		08 24		08 31	08 37		08 41	08 42	08 50
Heaton Chapel	d	07 33		07 44					08 08			08 16						08 35				08 45	
Levenshulme	d	07 36		07 47					08 11			08 19										08 48	
Manchester Piccadilly 10	a	07 44	07 52	07 56	07 59	08 02	08 09	08 20	08 20			08 26	08 32	08 35		08 36	08 42	08 45	08 49		08 52	08 56	08 59
	d		07 54							07 59	08 07				08 22	08 37				08 46	08 54		
Manchester Oxford Road	a		07 56							08 01	08 09				08 24	08 40				08 48	08 56		
Deansgate	a		08 00												08 28					08 51	09 00		

Station		TP ◇■ B ✕	VT ◇■ ⊡	AW ◇ D ✕	NT	NT E	TP ◇■ M ✕	NT G	VT ◇■ ⊡	NT H	NT I	EM ◇ J	XC ◇■ N ✕	NT	NT	VT ◇■ ⊡	NT A	NT	XC ◇■ O ⊡	TP ◇■ B ✕	VT ◇■ ⊡	AW ◇ P ✕
London Euston 15 ⊖65	d		06 55						07 20							07 35					08 00	
Birmingham New Street 12 68	d												07 57						08 31			
Wolverhampton 7 68	d												08 15						08 49			
Stafford 65,68	d												08 30						09 01			
Stoke-on-Trent 50,68	d		08 25						08 48				08 55					08 58	09 20		09 25	
Longport 50	d																					
Kidsgrove 50	d																	09 05				
Crewe 10 65	d			08 28										08 31	08 50	09 11						09 30
Sandbach	d													08 38	08 57							
Holmes Chapel	d													08 42	09 02							
Goostrey	d													08 45	09 05							
Chelford	d													08 50	09 09							
Alderley Edge	d				08 49									08 54	09 13							
Wilmslow	d			08 45	08 52									08 57	09 17	09 27						09 47
Styal	d																					
Manchester Airport ✈	a													09 04								
Handforth	d				08 55										09 20							
Congleton	d																	09 12				
Macclesfield	a		08 41										09 11					09 19			09 41	
	d		08 41										09 12					09 20			09 41	
Prestbury	d																	09 24				
Adlington (Cheshire)	d																	09 27				
Poynton	d																	09 30				
Bramhall	d																	09 33				
Cheadle Hulme	d				08 59										09 24			09 37				
Stockport	a		08 55	08 58	09 04				09 16				09 27		09 29	09 36		09 41	09 49		09 55	09 57
	d	08 53	08 56	08 59	09 04			09 13	09 17	09 21		09 25	09 28		09 29	09 37	09 42	09 42	09 50	09 53	09 56	09 58
Heaton Chapel	d				09 08			09 16							09 33			09 45				
Levenshulme	d				09 11			09 19							09 36			09 48				
Manchester Piccadilly 10	a	09 02	09 07	09 15	09 20			09 26	09 28	09 36		09 36	09 39	09 42	09 44	09 49	09 52	09 56	09 59	10 02	10 07	10 14
	d					09 01	09 07				09 22	09 37					09 54					
Manchester Oxford Road	a					09 03	09 09				09 24	09 40					09 56					
Deansgate	a										09 28						10 00					

A From Hazel Grove to Preston
B From Cleethorpes to Manchester Airport
C From Hazel Grove
D From Cardiff Central
E From Manchester Airport to Liverpool Lime Street
F From Hull to Liverpool Lime Street
G From Buxton
H From Chester
I From Manchester Airport to Southport
J From Nottingham to Liverpool Lime Street
K From Manchester Airport to Windermere
L From Buxton to Preston
M From Newcastle to Liverpool Lime Street
N From Southampton Central
O From Bristol Temple Meads
P From Carmarthen

7 July to 29 September

Stoke-on-Trent and Crewe - Manchester Airport, Stockport and Manchester

Network Diagram - see first Page of Table 78

		NT	NT	TP	NT	VT	NT	NT	EM	XC	NT	NT	VT	NT	NT	XC	TP	VT	AW	NT	NT	TP	NT
				◇■		◇■			◇	◇■			◇■			◇■	◇■	◇■	◇			◇■	
			A	B	C		D	E	F	G				H		I	J		K		A	B	C
London Euston	⊖65 d					08 20							08 40					09 00					
Birmingham New Street	68 d									08 57						09 31							
Wolverhampton	68 d									09 15						09 49							
Stafford	65,68 d									09 30						10 01							
Stoke-on-Trent	50,68 d					09 48				09 55					09 58	10 20		10 25					
Longport	50 d																						
Kidsgrove	50 d														10 05								
Crewe	65 d										09 33	09 50	10 11						10 31				
Sandbach	d										09 40	09 57											
Holmes Chapel	d										09 44	10 02											
Goostrey	d											10 05											
Chelford	d											10 09											
Alderley Edge	d	09 49									09 53	10 13								10 49			
Wilmslow	d	09 52									09 57	10 17	10 27						10 49	10 52			
Styal	d																						
Manchester Airport	✈ a										10 04												
Handforth	d	09 55										10 20								10 55			
Congleton	d														10 12								
Macclesfield	a									10 11					10 19			10 41					
	d									10 12					10 20			10 41					
Prestbury	d														10 24								
Adlington (Cheshire)	d														10 27								
Poynton	d														10 30								
Bramhall	d														10 33								
Cheadle Hulme	d	09 59										10 24			10 37					10 59			
Stockport	a	10 04				10 16				10 27		10 29	10 36		10 41	10 49		10 55	10 58	11 04			
	d	10 04			10 13	10 17	10 21		10 26	10 28		10 29	10 37	10 41	10 42	10 50	10 53	10 56	10 58	11 04			11 13
Heaton Chapel	d	10 08			10 16							10 33			10 45					11 08			11 16
Levenshulme	d	10 11			10 19							10 36			10 48					11 11			11 19
Manchester Piccadilly	a	10 20			10 26	10 28	10 36		10 36	10 39	10 42	10 44	10 49	10 52	10 56	10 59	11 02	11 07	11 15	11 20			11 26
	d		10 01	10 07				10 22	10 37					10 54							11 01	11 07	
Manchester Oxford Road	a		10 03	10 09				10 24	10 40					10 56							11 03	11 09	
Deansgate	a							10 28						11 00									

		VT	TP	NT	NT	EM	XC	NT	NT	VT	NT	NT	XC	TP	VT	AW	NT	NT	TP	NT	VT	NT
		◇■	◇■			◇	◇■			◇■			◇■	◇■	◇■	◇			◇■		◇■	
			L	D	E	F	M				H		N	J		O		A	B	C		D
London Euston	⊖65 d	09 20								09 40					10 00						10 20	
Birmingham New Street	68 d						09 57						10 31									
Wolverhampton	68 d						10 15						10 49									
Stafford	65,68 d						10 30						11 01									
Stoke-on-Trent	50,68 d	10 48					10 55					10 58	11 20		11 25						11 48	
Longport	50 d																					
Kidsgrove	50 d											11 05										
Crewe	65 d							10 34	10 50	11 11						11 31						
Sandbach	d							10 41	10 57													
Holmes Chapel	d							10 45	11 02													
Goostrey	d								11 05													
Chelford	d								11 09													
Alderley Edge	d							10 54	11 13								11 49					
Wilmslow	d							10 57	11 17	11 27						11 48	11 52					
Styal	d																					
Manchester Airport	✈ a							11 04														
Handforth	d								11 20								11 55					
Congleton	d											11 12										
Macclesfield	a						11 11					11 19			11 41							
	d						11 12					11 20			11 41							
Prestbury	d											11 24										
Adlington (Cheshire)	d											11 27										
Poynton	d											11 30										
Bramhall	d											11 33										
Cheadle Hulme	d								11 24			11 37					11 59					
Stockport	a	11 16					11 27		11 29	11 36		11 41	11 49		11 55	11 58	12 04				12 16	
	d	11 17		11 21		11 26	11 28		11 29	11 37	11 41	11 42	11 50	11 53	11 56	11 58	12 04			12 13	12 17	12 21
Heaton Chapel	d								11 33			11 45					12 08			12 16		
Levenshulme	d								11 36			11 48					12 11			12 19		
Manchester Piccadilly	a	11 28		11 36		11 36	11 39	11 42	11 44	11 49	11 52	11 56	11 59	12 02	12 07	12 15	12 20			12 26	12 28	12 36
	d		11 16		11 22	11 37					11 54							12 01	12 07			
Manchester Oxford Road	a		11 18		11 24	11 40					11 56							12 03	12 09			
Deansgate	a				11 28						12 00											

A From Manchester Airport to Liverpool Lime Street
B From Scarborough to Liverpool Lime Street
C From Buxton
D From Chester
E From Manchester Airport to Southport
F From Norwich to Liverpool Lime Street
G From Southampton Central
H From Hazel Grove to Preston
I From Cardiff Central
J From Cleethorpes to Manchester Airport
K From Carmarthen
L From Manchester Airport to Barrow-in-Furness
M From Bournemouth
N From Paignton
O From Milford Haven

7 July to 29 September

Stoke-on-Trent and Crewe - Manchester Airport, Stockport and Manchester

Network Diagram - see first Page of Table 78

		NT	EM	XC	NT	NT	VT	NT	NT	XC	TP	VT	AW	NT	NT	TP	NT	VT	NT	NT	EM	XC	NT
			◇	◇■			◇■			◇■	◇■	◇■	◇			◇■		◇■			◇	◇■	
		A	B	C				D		E	F		G		H	I	J		K	A	B	C	
London Euston	⊖65 d						10 40					11 00						11 20					
Birmingham New Street	68 d			10 57						11 31												11 57	
Wolverhampton	68 d			11 15						11 49												12 15	
Stafford	65,68 d			11 30						12 01												12 30	
Stoke-on-Trent	50,68 d			11 55					11 58	12 20		12 25						12 48				12 55	
Longport	50 d																						
Kidsgrove	50 d								12 05														
Crewe	65 d				11 34	11 50	12 11						12 31										12 34
Sandbach	d				11 41	11 57																	12 41
Holmes Chapel	d				11 45	12 02																	12 45
Goostrey	d					12 05																	
Chelford	d					12 09																	
Alderley Edge	d				11 54	12 13								12 49									12 54
Wilmslow	d				11 57	12 17	12 27						12 49	12 52									12 57
Styal	d																						
Manchester Airport	✈ a				12 04																		13 04
Handforth	d					12 20								12 55									
Congleton	d								12 12														
Macclesfield	a			12 11					12 19			12 41										13 11	
	d			12 12					12 20			12 41										13 12	
Prestbury	d								12 24														
Adlington (Cheshire)	d								12 27														
Poynton	d								12 30														
Bramhall	d								12 33														
Cheadle Hulme	d					12 24			12 37					12 59									
Stockport	a			12 27		12 29	12 36		12 41	12 49		12 55	12 58	13 04				13 16				13 27	
	d		12 26	12 28		12 29	12 37	12 41	12 42	12 50	12 53	12 56	12 58	13 04			13 13	13 17	13 21		13 26	13 28	
Heaton Chapel	d					12 33			12 45					13 08			13 16						
Levenshulme	d					12 36			12 48					13 11			13 19						
Manchester Piccadilly	a		12 36	12 39	12 42	12 44	12 49	12 52	12 56	12 59	13 02	13 07	13 15	13 20			13 26	13 28	13 36		13 36	13 39	13 42
	d	12 22	12 37					12 54							13 01	13 07				13 22	13 37		
Manchester Oxford Road	a	12 24	12 40					12 56							13 03	13 09				13 24	13 40		
Deansgate	a	12 28						13 00												13 28			

		NT	VT	NT	NT	XC	TP	VT	AW	NT	NT	TP	NT	VT	TP	NT	NT	EM	XC	NT	NT	VT	NT
			◇■			◇■	◇■	◇■	◇			◇■		◇■	◇■			◇	◇■			◇■	
				D		L	F		M		H	I	J		N	K	A	B	C				D
London Euston	⊖65 d		11 40					12 00						12 20								12 40	
Birmingham New Street	68 d					12 31													12 57				
Wolverhampton	68 d					12 49													13 15				
Stafford	65,68 d					13 01													13 30				
Stoke-on-Trent	50,68 d				12 58	13 20		13 25						13 48					13 55				
Longport	50 d																						
Kidsgrove	50 d				13 05																		
Crewe	65 d	12 50	13 11						13 31											13 34	13 50	14 11	
Sandbach	d	12 57																		13 41	13 57		
Holmes Chapel	d	13 02																		13 45	14 02		
Goostrey	d	13 05																			14 05		
Chelford	d	13 09																			14 09		
Alderley Edge	d	13 13								13 49										13 54	14 13		
Wilmslow	d	13 17	13 27						13 48	13 52										13 57	14 17	14 27	
Styal	d																						
Manchester Airport	✈ a																			14 04			
Handforth	d	13 20								13 55											14 20		
Congleton	d				13 12																		
Macclesfield	a				13 19			13 41											14 11				
	d				13 20			13 41											14 12				
Prestbury	d				13 24																		
Adlington (Cheshire)	d				13 27																		
Poynton	d				13 30																		
Bramhall	d				13 33																		
Cheadle Hulme	d	13 24			13 37					13 59											14 24		
Stockport	a	13 29	13 36		13 41	13 49		13 55	13 58	14 04				14 16					14 27		14 29	14 36	
	d	13 29	13 37	13 41	13 42	13 50	13 53	13 56	13 58	14 04			14 15	14 17		14 21		14 26	14 28		14 29	14 37	14 41
Heaton Chapel	d	13 33			13 45					14 08			14 18								14 33		
Levenshulme	d	13 36			13 48					14 11			14 21								14 36		
Manchester Piccadilly	a	13 44	13 49	13 52	13 56	13 59	14 02	14 07	14 15	14 20			14 28	14 28		14 36		14 36	14 39	14 42	14 44	14 49	14 52
	d			13 54							14 01	14 07			14 16		14 22	14 37					14 54
Manchester Oxford Road	a			13 56							14 03	14 09			14 18		14 24	14 40					14 56
Deansgate	a			14 00													14 28						15 00

A From Manchester Airport to Southport
B From Norwich to Liverpool Lime Street
C From Bournemouth
D From Hazel Grove to Preston
E From Bristol Temple Meads
F From Cleethorpes to Manchester Airport
G From Milford Haven
H From Manchester Airport to Liverpool Lime Street
I From Scarborough to Liverpool Lime Street
J From Buxton
K From Chester
L From Plymouth
M From Fishguard Harbour
N From Manchester Airport to Barrow-in-Furness

Stoke-on-Trent and Crewe - Manchester Airport, Stockport and Manchester

Network Diagram - see first Page of Table 78

		NT		XC	TP	VT	AW	NT	NT	TP	NT	VT		TP	NT	NT	EM	XC	NT	NT	VT	NT		NT	XC
				◇1	◇1	◇1	◇			◇1		◇1		◇1			◇	◇1			◇1				◇1
				A	B		C		D	E	F			G	H	I	J	K				L			M
				☕	✕	☕	✕			✕		☕		✕				✕			☕				☕
London Euston [15] ⊖65	d					13 00						13 20									13 40				
Birmingham New Street [12] 68	d			13 31														13 57							14 31
Wolverhampton [7] 68 ⇌	d			13 49														14 15							14 49
Stafford 65,68	d			14 01														14 30							15 01
Stoke-on-Trent 50,68	d	13 58		14 20		14 25						14 48						14 55						14 58	15 20
Longport 50	d																							15 05	
Kidsgrove 50	d	14 05																							
Crewe [10] 65	d						14 31												14 34	14 50	15 11				
Sandbach	d																		14 41	14 57					
Holmes Chapel	d																		14 45	15 02					
Goostrey	d																			15 05					
Chelford	d																			15 09					
Alderley Edge	d							14 49											14 54	15 13					
Wilmslow	d						14 49	14 52											14 57	15 17	15 27				
Styal	d																								
Manchester Airport ✈	a																		15 04						
Handforth	d							14 55												15 20					
Congleton	d	14 12																						15 12	
Macclesfield	a	14 19				14 41												15 11						15 19	
	d	14 20				14 41												15 12						15 20	
Prestbury	d	14 24																						15 24	
Adlington (Cheshire)	d	14 27																						15 27	
Poynton	d	14 30																						15 30	
Bramhall	d	14 33																						15 33	
Cheadle Hulme	d	14 37						14 59												15 24				15 37	
Stockport	a	14 41		14 49		14 55	14 58	15 04				15 16						15 27		15 29	15 36			15 41	15 49
	d	14 42		14 50	14 53	14 56	14 58	15 04			15 13	15 17			15 21		15 26	15 28		15 29	15 37	15 41		15 42	15 50
Heaton Chapel	d	14 45						15 08			15 16									15 33				15 45	
Levenshulme	d	14 48						15 11			15 19									15 36				15 48	
Manchester Piccadilly [10] ⇌	a	14 56		14 59	15 02	15 07	15 15	15 20			15 26	15 28			15 36		15 36	15 39	15 42	15 44	15 49	15 52		15 56	15 59
	d								15 01	15 07				15 16		15 22	15 37					15 54			
Manchester Oxford Road	a								15 03	15 09				15 18		15 24	15 40					15 56			
Deansgate ⇌	a															15 28						16 00			

		TP	VT	AW	NT	NT	TP	NT		VT	TP	NT	NT	EM	XC	NT	NT	VT		NT	NT	XC	XC	TP	VT
		◇1	◇1	◇			◇1			◇1	◇1			◇	◇1			◇1				◇1	◇1	◇1	◇1
		B		N		D	E	F			O	H	I	J	K					L		P	Q	B	
		✕	☕	✕			✕			☕	✕				✕			☕				☕	☕	✕	☕
London Euston [15] ⊖65	d		14 00							14 20								14 40							15 00
Birmingham New Street [12] 68	d														14 57							15 31	15 31		
Wolverhampton [7] 68 ⇌	d														15 15							15 49	15 49		
Stafford 65,68	d														15 30							16 01	16 01		
Stoke-on-Trent 50,68	d		15 25							15 48					15 55						15 58	16 19	16 20		16 25
Longport 50	d																								
Kidsgrove 50	d																				16 05				
Crewe [10] 65	d			15 28												15 33	15 50	16 11							
Sandbach	d															15 40	15 57								
Holmes Chapel	d															15 44	16 02								
Goostrey	d																16 05								
Chelford	d																16 09								
Alderley Edge	d				15 49											15 53	16 13								
Wilmslow	d			15 45	15 52											15 56	16 17	16 27							
Styal	d															15 59									
Manchester Airport ✈	a															16 04									
Handforth	d				15 55												16 20								
Congleton	d																				16 12				
Macclesfield	a		15 41												16 11						16 19				16 41
	d		15 41												16 12						16 20				16 41
Prestbury	d																				16 24				
Adlington (Cheshire)	d																				16 27				
Poynton	d																				16 30				
Bramhall	d																				16 33				
Cheadle Hulme	d				15 59												16 24				16 37				
Stockport	a		15 55	15 58	16 04					16 16					16 27		16 29	16 36			16 41	16 48	16 49		16 54
	d	15 53	15 56	15 58	16 04			16 15		16 17		16 21		16 26	16 28		16 29	16 37		16 41	16 42	16 49	16 50	16 53	16 55
Heaton Chapel	d				16 08			16 18									16 33				16 45				
Levenshulme	d				16 11			16 21									16 36				16 48				
Manchester Piccadilly [10] ⇌	a	16 02	16 07	16 15	16 20			16 28		16 28		16 36		16 36	16 39	16 42	16 44	16 49		16 52	16 56	16 59	16 59	17 02	17 07
	d					16 01	16 07				16 16		16 22	16 37						16 54					
Manchester Oxford Road	a					16 03	16 09				16 18		16 24	16 40						16 56					
Deansgate ⇌	a												16 28							17 00					

A From Paignton
B From Cleethorpes to Manchester Airport
C From Milford Haven
D From Manchester Airport to Liverpool Lime Street
E From Scarborough to Liverpool Lime Street
F From Buxton
G From Manchester Airport to Barrow-in-Furness
H From Chester
I From Manchester Airport to Southport
J From Norwich to Liverpool Lime Street
K From Bournemouth
L From Hazel Grove to Preston
M From Bristol Temple Meads
N From Carmarthen
O From Manchester Airport to Windermere
P from 7 July until 8 September. From Bristol Temple Meads
Q from 15 September.From Penzance

Stoke-on-Trent and Crewe - Manchester Airport, Stockport and Manchester

Network Diagram - see first Page of Table 78

		AW	NT	NT		TP	NT	VT	NT	NT	EM	XC	NT	NT		VT	NT	XC	TP	VT	AW	NT	NT	TP
		◇				◇1		◇1			◇	◇1				◇1		◇1	◇1	◇1	◇			◇1
		A		B		C	D		E	F	G	H						I	J		K		B	C
		✕				✕		☕				✕				☕		☕	✕	☕	✕			✕
London Euston [15] ⊖65	d							15 20								15 40				16 00				
Birmingham New Street [12] 68	d											15 57						16 31						
Wolverhampton [7] 68 ⇌	d											16 15						16 49						
Stafford 65,68	d											16 30						17 01						
Stoke-on-Trent 50,68	d							16 48				16 55					16 58	17 20		17 25				
Longport 50	d																							
Kidsgrove 50	d																17 05							
Crewe [10] 65	d	16 31											16 34	16 50		17 11					17 28			
Sandbach	d												16 41	16 57										
Holmes Chapel	d												16 45	17 02										
Goostrey	d													17 05										
Chelford	d													17 09										
Alderley Edge	d		16 49										16 54	17 13								17 49		
Wilmslow	d	16 48	16 52										16 57	17 17		17 27					17 45	17 52		
Styal	d																							
Manchester Airport ✈	a												17 04											
Handforth	d		16 55											17 20								17 55		
Congleton	d																17 12							
Macclesfield	a											17 11					17 19			17 41				
	d											17 12					17 20			17 41				
Prestbury	d																17 24							
Adlington (Cheshire)	d																17 27							
Poynton	d																17 30							
Bramhall	d																17 33							
Cheadle Hulme	d		16 59											17 24			17 37					17 59		
Stockport	a	16 58	17 04					17 16				17 27		17 29		17 36	17 41	17 49		17 55	17 58	18 04		
	d	16 58	17 04				17 13	17 17	17 21		17 26	17 28		17 29		17 37	17 42	17 50	17 53	17 56	17 58	18 04		
Heaton Chapel	d		17 08				17 16							17 33			17 45					18 08		
Levenshulme	d		17 11				17 19							17 36			17 48					18 11		
Manchester Piccadilly [10] ⇌	a	17 15	17 20				17 26	17 28	17 36		17 37	17 39	17 42	17 44		17 49	17 56	17 59	18 02	18 07	18 15	18 20		
	d			17 01		17 07				17 23	17 37												18 01	18 07
Manchester Oxford Road	a			17 03		17 09				17 25	17 40												18 03	18 09
Deansgate ⇌	a																							

		NT	VT	TP	NT	NT	EM	XC	NT	NT		VT	NT	NT	XC	TP	VT	AW	NT	TP		NT	VT	TP	NT
			◇1	◇1			◇	◇1				◇1			◇1	◇1	◇1	■		◇1			◇1	◇1	
		D		L	E	F	G	H					M		N	J		A	B	C		D		L	F
			☕	✕				✕				☕			✕	✕	☕	✕					☕	✕	
London Euston [15] ⊖65	d		16 20									16 40					17 00						17 20		
Birmingham New Street [12] 68	d							16 57							17 31										
Wolverhampton [7] 68 ⇌	d							17 15							17 49										
Stafford 65,68	d							17 30							18 01										
Stoke-on-Trent 50,68	d		17 48					17 55						17 58	18 20		18 25						18 48		
Longport 50	d																								
Kidsgrove 50	d													18 05											
Crewe [10] 65	d								17 33	17 50		18 11						18 31							
Sandbach	d								17 40	17 57															
Holmes Chapel	d								17 44	18 02															
Goostrey	d									18 05															
Chelford	d									18 09															
Alderley Edge	d								17 53	18 13															
Wilmslow	d								17 56	18 17		18 27						18 48							
Styal	d								17 59																
Manchester Airport ✈	a								18 04																
Handforth	d									18 20															
Congleton	d													18 12											
Macclesfield	a							18 11						18 19			18 41								
	d							18 12						18 20			18 41								
Prestbury	d													18 24											
Adlington (Cheshire)	d													18 27											
Poynton	d													18 30											
Bramhall	d													18 33											
Cheadle Hulme	d									18 24				18 37											
Stockport	a		18 16					18 27		18 29		18 36		18 41	18 49		18 55	18 58					19 16		
	d	18 15	18 17		18 21		18 26	18 28		18 29		18 37	18 41	18 42	18 50	18 53	18 56	18 58				19 15	19 17		
Heaton Chapel	d	18 18								18 33				18 45								19 18			
Levenshulme	d	18 21								18 36				18 48								19 21			
Manchester Piccadilly [10] ⇌	a	18 28	18 28		18 36		18 36	18 39	18 42	18 44		18 49	18 52	18 56	18 59	19 02	19 07	19 15				19 28	19 28		
	d			18 16		18 22	18 37						18 54						19 01	19 07				19 16	19 20
Manchester Oxford Road	a			18 18		18 24	18 40						18 56						19 03	19 09				19 18	19 22
Deansgate ⇌	a					18 28							19 00												19 26

A From Milford Haven
B From Manchester Airport to Liverpool Lime Street
C From Scarborough to Liverpool Lime Street
D From Buxton
E From Chester
F From Manchester Airport to Southport
G From Norwich to Liverpool Lime Street
H From Bournemouth
I From Bristol Temple Meads
J From Cleethorpes to Manchester Airport
K From Carmarthen
L From Manchester Airport to Barrow-in-Furness
M From Hazel Grove to Bolton
N From Paignton

Table 84

Stoke-on-Trent and Crewe - Manchester Airport, Stockport and Manchester

Saturdays
7 July to 29 September

Network Diagram - see first Page of Table 78

	NT	NT	EM	XC	NT	VT	NT	XC	TP	VT	AW	NT	TP	NT	VT	TP	NT	NT	NT	EM	XC	NT
			◇	◇1		◇1		◇1	◇1	◇1	■		◇1		◇1	◇1				◇	◇1	
		A	B	C				D	E		F	G	H	I		J	K		A	B	C	
				🍴		☕		☕	🍴	☕	🍴				☕						🍴	
London Euston 15 ⊖65 d						17 40				18 00					18 20							
Birmingham New Street 12 68 d				17 57				18 31													18 57	
Wolverhampton 7 68 d				18 15				18 49													19 15	
Stafford 65,68 d				18 30				19 01													19 30	
Stoke-on-Trent 50,68 d				18 55			18 58	19 20		19 25					19 48						19 55	
Longport 50 d																						
Kidsgrove 50 d							19 05															
Crewe 10 65 d	18 34				18 50	19 11					19 31											19 50
Sandbach d	18 41				18 57																	19 57
Holmes Chapel d	18 45				19 02																	20 02
Goostrey d					19 05																	20 05
Chelford d					19 09																	20 09
Alderley Edge d	18 54				19 13																	20 13
Wilmslow d	18 57				19 17	19 27					19 48							19 56				20 17
Styal d																						
Manchester Airport ✈ a	19 05																	20 04				
Handforth d					19 20																	20 20
Congleton d							19 12															
Macclesfield a				19 11			19 19			19 41											20 11	
d				19 12			19 20			19 41											20 12	
Prestbury d							19 24															
Adlington (Cheshire) d							19 27															
Poynton d							19 30															
Bramhall d							19 33															
Cheadle Hulme d					19 24		19 37															20 24
Stockport a				19 27	19 29	19 36	19 41	19 49		19 55	19 58				20 16						20 27	20 29
d		19 21	19 26	19 28	19 29	19 37	19 42	19 50	19 53	19 56	19 58			20 15	20 17				20 21	20 26	20 28	20 29
Heaton Chapel d							19 45							20 18								
Levenshulme d							19 48							20 21								
Manchester Piccadilly 10 a	19 31	19 35	19 36	19 39	19 43	19 49	19 56	19 59	20 02	20 07	20 15			20 28	20 28			20 31	20 35	20 36	20 39	20 43
d	19 32		19 37									20 01	20 07			20 16	20 20	20 32		20 37		
Manchester Oxford Road a	19 36		19 40									20 03	20 09			20 18	20 22	20 36		20 40		
Deansgate a																	20 26					

	VT	NT	XC	AW	TP	VT	AW	TP	NT	VT	NT	NT	EM	NT	XC	NT	VT	NT	XC	AW	NT
	◇1		◇1		◇1	◇1	■	◇1		◇1			◇		◇1		◇1		◇1	◇	
			L	M	E		N	H	I		K		O	A	C				D	F	G
	☕		☕			☕	🍴			☕							☕		☕	🍴	
London Euston 15 ⊖65 d	18 40					19 00				19 20							19 40				
Birmingham New Street 12 68 d			19 31												19 57				20 31		
Wolverhampton 7 68 d			19 49												20 15				20 49		
Stafford 65,68 d			20 01												20 30				21 01		
Stoke-on-Trent 50,68 d		19 58	20 20			20 25				20 48					20 55			20 58	21 21		
Longport 50 d																					
Kidsgrove 50 d		20 05																21 05			
Crewe 10 65 d	20 11						20 28									20 50	21 19			21 33	
Sandbach d																20 57					
Holmes Chapel d																21 02					
Goostrey d																21 05					
Chelford d																21 09					
Alderley Edge d																21 13					
Wilmslow d	20 27						20 45					20 56				21 17	21 34			21 50	
Styal d																					
Manchester Airport ✈ a												21 05									
Handforth d																21 20					
Congleton d		20 12																21 12			
Macclesfield a		20 19	20 36			20 41									21 11			21 19	21 38		
d		20 20	20 37			20 41									21 12			21 20	21 39		
Prestbury d		20 24																21 24			
Adlington (Cheshire) d		20 27																21 27			
Poynton d		20 30																21 30			
Bramhall d		20 33																21 33			
Cheadle Hulme d		20 37														21 24		21 37			
Stockport a	20 36	20 41	20 49			20 55	20 58			21 16					21 27	21 29	21 44	21 41	21 53	22 00	
d	20 37	20 42	20 50		20 53	20 56	20 59		21 13	21 17			21 20	21 21	21 28	21 29	21 45	21 42	21 54	22 00	
Heaton Chapel d		20 45							21 16									21 45			
Levenshulme d		20 48							21 19									21 48			
Manchester Piccadilly 10 a	20 49	20 56	20 59		21 02	21 07	21 15		21 26	21 28		21 31	21 32	21 35	21 39	21 43	21 53	21 57	22 04	22 15	
d				20 50				21 07			21 22	21 32									22 01
Manchester Oxford Road a				20 52				21 09			21 24	21 36									22 03
Deansgate a											21 28										

A From Chester
B From Norwich to Liverpool Lime Street
C From Bournemouth
D From Bristol Temple Meads
E From Cleethorpes to Manchester Airport
F From Carmarthen
G From Manchester Airport to Liverpool Lime Street
H From Scarborough to Liverpool Lime Street
I From Buxton
J From Manchester Airport to Barrow-in-Furness
K From Manchester Airport to Southport
L From Exeter St Davids
M From Manchester Airport to Chester
N From Milford Haven
O From Norwich

Table 84

Stoke-on-Trent and Crewe - Manchester Airport, Stockport and Manchester

Saturdays
7 July to 29 September

Network Diagram - see first Page of Table 78

	TP	NT	TP	NT	XC	XC	NT	VT	NT	NT	NT	NT	XC	VT	NT	AW	NT	NT	NT	XC	VT	VT
	◇1		◇1		◇1	◇1		◇1					◇1	◇1		◇				◇1	◇1	◇1
	A	B	C		D	E			F	G	H		I		J	K		B			L	L
					🍴			☕						☕							☕	☕
London Euston 15 ⊖65 d								20 20						21 00							22 30	23 30
Birmingham New Street 12 68 d					20 57	20 57							21 57							22 31		
Wolverhampton 7 68 d					21 15	21 15							22 16							22 49		
Stafford 65,68 d					21 30	21 30							22 30	22 34						23 02		
Stoke-on-Trent 50,68 d					21 53	21 53		22 05				22 18	22 51							23 21	23s53	00s53
Longport 50 d																						
Kidsgrove 50 d												22 25										
Crewe 10 65 d							21 50							22 59		23 06			23 12			
Sandbach d							21 57												23 19			
Holmes Chapel d							22 02												23 24			
Goostrey d							22 05												23 27			
Chelford d							22 09												23 31			
Alderley Edge d							22 13												23 35			
Wilmslow d				21 55			22 17							23 15		23 24	23 15		23 39			
Styal d																						
Manchester Airport ✈ a				22 04													23 23					
Handforth d							22 20												23 42			
Congleton d												22 32										
Macclesfield a					22 10	22 11		22 21				22 39	23 07							23 38	00s10	01s10
d					22 11	22 12		22 21				22 40	23 08							23 39		
Prestbury d												22 44										
Adlington (Cheshire) d												22 47										
Poynton d												22 50										
Bramhall d												22 53										
Cheadle Hulme d							22 24					22 56							23 46			
Stockport a					22 26	22 27	22 29	22 35				23 01	23 21	23 25		23 32			23 51	23 53	00s24	01s24
d		22 13			22 27	22 28	22 29	22 36		22 40	22 48	23 01	23 22	23 26	23 22	23 33		23 42	23 51	23 54		
Heaton Chapel d		22 16								22 44		23 05							23 55			
Levenshulme d		22 19								22 47		23 08							23 58			
Manchester Piccadilly 10 a		22 26		22 31	22 39	22 39	22 43	22 51		22 53	23 00	23 16	23 32	23 38	23 43	23 50	23 51	23 52	00 07	00 10	00 37	01 37
d	22 07		22 16	22 32					22 36	22 54												
Manchester Oxford Road a	22 09		22 18	22 36					22 38	22 56												
Deansgate a									22 41	23 00												

Saturdays
from 6 October

	NT	NT	XC	NT	AW	VT	NT	TP	NT	NT	TP	AW	NT	NT	NT	NT	EM	XC	NT	NT	NT	NT
			◇1		◇	◇1		◇1			◇1						◇	◇1				
	J			H	M			N		O	P			Q	B	H	R				S	
						☕																
London Euston 15 ⊖65 d						22p00																
Birmingham New Street 12 68 d			22p30		21p24													05 57				
Wolverhampton 7 68 d			22p48		21p43													06 16				
Stafford 65,68 d			23p01			23b38												06 30				
Stoke-on-Trent 50,68 d			23p21															06 51				06 57
Longport 50 d																						
Kidsgrove 50 d																						07 04
Crewe 10 65 d		23p12				00s03	00 44					06 27							06 33	06 49		
Sandbach d		23p19																	06 40	06 56		
Holmes Chapel d		23p24																	06 44	07 00		
Goostrey d		23p27																		07 03		
Chelford d		23p31																		07 08		
Alderley Edge d		23p35											06 49						06 53	07 12		
Wilmslow d		23p39							05 46			06 45	06 52						06 57	07 16		
Styal d																						
Manchester Airport ✈ a							01 16		05 53										07 04			
Handforth d		23p42											06 55							07 19		
Congleton d																		07 03				07 11
Macclesfield a																		07 11				07 18
d																		07 12				07 19
Prestbury d																						07 23
Adlington (Cheshire) d																						07 26
Poynton d																						07 29
Bramhall d																						07 32
Cheadle Hulme d		23p46											06 59							07 24		07 36
Stockport a		23p51				00s26						06 55	07 04					07 27		07 29		07 40
d	23p48	23p51		00 02				05 53		06 41	06 53	06 55	07 04		07 12	07 19	07 22	07 28		07 29	07 40	07 41
Heaton Chapel d		23p55											07 08		07 16					07 33		07 44
Levenshulme d		23p58											07 11		07 19					07 36		07 47
Manchester Piccadilly 10 a	00 02	00 07	00 12	00 18	00 28	00 35	01 36	06 05	06 25	06 52	07 02	07 07	07 21		07 28	07 31	07 34	07 38	07 42	07 44	07 52	07 56
d										06 54				06 58			07 34				07 54	
Manchester Oxford Road a										06 56				07 00			07 37				07 56	
Deansgate a										06 59											08 00	

A From Scarborough to Liverpool Lime Street
B From Buxton
C From Manchester Airport to Barrow-in-Furness
D from 7 July until 8 September. From Newquay
E from 15 September.From Bournemouth
F From Manchester Airport to Southport
G To Wigan Wallgate
H From Chester
I From Bournemouth
J From Sheffield
K From Maesteg
L from 28 July until 11 August, from 1 September until 8 September
M From Birmingham International
N From Sheffield to Manchester Airport
O From Buxton to Clitheroe
P From Doncaster to Manchester Airport
Q From Manchester Airport to Liverpool Lime Street
R From Nottingham to Liverpool Lime Street
S From Hazel Grove to Preston
b Previous night, stops to set down only

Saturdays
from 6 October

Stoke-on-Trent and Crewe - Manchester Airport, Stockport and Manchester

Network Diagram - see first Page of Table 78

		XC	TP	NT	AW	NT	NT	TP	NT	NT	XC	NT	EM	NT	NT	VT	TP	NT	NT	XC	TP	VT	AW
		◇■	◇■		◇			◇■			◇■		◇			◇■	◇■			◇■	◇■	◇■	◇
			A	B	C		D	E	F	G		H	I				J	K			A		C
		✕	✕					✕			✕					⊡	✕			✕	✕	⊡	✕
London Euston ⊖65	d															06 36						06 55	
Birmingham New Street 68	d	06 31									06 57									07 31			
Wolverhampton 68 ⇌	d	06 49									07 15									07 49			
Stafford 65,68	d	07 01									07 30									08 01			
Stoke-on-Trent 50,68	d	07 19																	07 57	08 20		08 25	
Longport 50	d																						
Kidsgrove 50	d																		08 04				
Crewe 65	d				07 27						07 53			07 30	07 55	08 11							08 28
Sandbach	d													07 37	08 02								
Holmes Chapel	d													07 41	08 07								
Goostrey	d													07 44									
Chelford	d													07 49									
Alderley Edge	d					07 49								07 53	08 15								
Wilmslow	d				07 44	07 52					08 10			07 56	08 19	08 27							08 45
Styal	d													07 59									
Manchester Airport ✈	a													08 05									
Handforth	d					07 55									08 22								
Congleton	d																		08 11				
Macclesfield	a	07 36																	08 18	08 36		08 41	
	d	07 37																	08 19	08 37		08 41	
Prestbury	d																		08 23				
Adlington (Cheshire)	d																		08 26				
Poynton	d																		08 30				
Bramhall	d																		08 33				
Cheadle Hulme	d					07 59									08 26				08 37				
Stockport	a	07 49			08 01	08 04					08 20				08 31	08 36			08 41	08 49		08 55	08 58
	d	07 50	07 53	07 57	08 01	08 04			08 12	08 19	08 20		08 24		08 31	08 37		08 41	08 42	08 50	08 53	08 56	08 59
Heaton Chapel	d					08 08			08 16						08 35				08 45				
Levenshulme	d					08 11			08 19										08 48				
Manchester Piccadilly ⇌	a	07 59	08 02	08 09	08 20	08 20			08 28	08 32	08 35		08 36	08 42	08 45	08 49		08 52	08 56	08 59	09 02	09 07	09 15
	d						07 59	08 07				08 22	08 37				08 46	08 54					
Manchester Oxford Road	a						08 01	08 09				08 24	08 40				08 48	08 56					
Deansgate ⇌	a											08 28					08 51	09 00					

		NT	NT	TP	NT	VT	NT	NT	EM	XC	NT	NT	VT	NT	NT	XC	TP	VT	AW	NT	NT	TP
				◇■		◇■			◇	◇■			◇■			◇■	◇■	◇■	◇			◇■
			D	L	F		G	H	I	M				N		O	A		P		D	Q
				✕		⊡				✕			⊡			⊡	✕	⊡	✕			✕
London Euston ⊖65	d					07 20							07 35					08 00				
Birmingham New Street 68	d									07 57						08 31						
Wolverhampton 68 ⇌	d									08 15						08 49						
Stafford 65,68	d									08 30						09 01						
Stoke-on-Trent 50,68	d					08 48				08 55					08 58	09 20		09 25				
Longport 50	d																					
Kidsgrove 50	d														09 05							
Crewe 65	d										08 31	08 50	09 11						09 30			
Sandbach	d										08 38	08 57										
Holmes Chapel	d										08 42	09 02										
Goostrey	d										08 45	09 05										
Chelford	d										08 50	09 09										
Alderley Edge	d	08 49									08 54	09 13								09 49		
Wilmslow	d	08 52									08 57	09 17	09 27						09 47	09 52		
Styal	d																					
Manchester Airport ✈	a										09 04											
Handforth	d	08 55										09 20								09 55		
Congleton	d														09 12							
Macclesfield	a									09 11					09 19			09 41				
	d									09 12					09 20			09 41				
Prestbury	d														09 24							
Adlington (Cheshire)	d														09 27							
Poynton	d														09 30							
Bramhall	d														09 33							
Cheadle Hulme	d	08 59										09 24			09 37					09 59		
Stockport	a	09 04				09 16				09 27		09 29	09 36		09 41	09 49		09 55	09 57	10 04		
	d	09 04			09 12	09 17	09 21		09 25	09 28		09 29	09 37	09 41	09 42	09 50	09 53	09 56	09 58	10 04		
Heaton Chapel	d	09 08			09 16							09 33			09 45					10 08		
Levenshulme	d	09 11			09 19							09 36			09 48					10 11		
Manchester Piccadilly ⇌	a	09 20			09 28	09 28	09 36		09 36	09 39	09 42	09 44	09 49	09 52	09 56	09 59	10 02	10 07	10 14	10 20		
	d		09 01	09 07				09 22	09 37					09 54							10 01	10 07
Manchester Oxford Road	a		09 03	09 09				09 24	09 40					09 56							10 03	10 09
Deansgate ⇌	a							09 28						10 00								

A From Cleethorpes to Manchester Airport
B From Hazel Grove
C From Cardiff Central
D From Manchester Airport to Liverpool Lime Street
E From Hull to Liverpool Lime Street
F From Buxton
G From Chester
H From Manchester Airport to Southport
I From Nottingham to Liverpool Lime Street
J From Manchester Airport to Windermere
K From Buxton to Preston
L From Newcastle to Liverpool Lime Street
M From Southampton Central
N From Hazel Grove to Preston
O From Bristol Temple Meads
P From Carmarthen
Q From Scarborough to Liverpool Lime Street

Saturdays
from 6 October

Stoke-on-Trent and Crewe - Manchester Airport, Stockport and Manchester

Network Diagram - see first Page of Table 78

		NT	VT	NT	NT	EM	XC	NT	NT	VT	NT	NT	XC	TP	VT	AW	NT	NT	TP	NT	VT	TP	NT
			◇■			◇	◇■			◇■			◇■	◇■	◇■	◇			◇■		◇■	◇■	
		A		B	C	D	E				F		G	H		I		J	K	A		L	B
			⊡				✕			⊡			⊡	✕	⊡	✕					⊡	✕	
London Euston ⊖65	d		08 20							08 40					09 00						09 20		
Birmingham New Street 68	d						08 57						09 31										
Wolverhampton 68 ⇌	d						09 15						09 49										
Stafford 65,68	d						09 30						10 01										
Stoke-on-Trent 50,68	d		09 48				09 55					09 58	10 20		10 25						10 48		
Longport 50	d																						
Kidsgrove 50	d											10 05											
Crewe 65	d							09 33	09 50	10 11						10 31							
Sandbach	d							09 40	09 57														
Holmes Chapel	d							09 44	10 02														
Goostrey	d								10 05														
Chelford	d								10 09														
Alderley Edge	d							09 53	10 13								10 49						
Wilmslow	d							09 57	10 17	10 27						10 49	10 52						
Styal	d																						
Manchester Airport ✈	a							10 04															
Handforth	d								10 20								10 55						
Congleton	d											10 12											
Macclesfield	a						10 11					10 19			10 41								
	d						10 12					10 20			10 41								
Prestbury	d											10 24											
Adlington (Cheshire)	d											10 27											
Poynton	d											10 30											
Bramhall	d											10 33											
Cheadle Hulme	d								10 24			10 37					10 59						
Stockport	a		10 16				10 27		10 29	10 36		10 41	10 49		10 55	10 58	11 04				11 16		
	d	10 12	10 17	10 21		10 26	10 28		10 29	10 37	10 41	10 42	10 50	10 53	10 56	10 58	11 04			11 12	11 17		11 21
Heaton Chapel	d	10 16							10 33			10 45					11 08			11 16			
Levenshulme	d	10 19							10 36			10 48					11 11			11 19			
Manchester Piccadilly ⇌	a	10 28	10 28	10 36		10 36	10 39	10 42	10 44	10 49	10 52	10 56	10 59	11 02	11 07	11 15	11 20			11 28	11 28		11 36
	d				10 22	10 37					10 54							11 01	11 07			11 16	
Manchester Oxford Road	a				10 24	10 40					10 56							11 03	11 09			11 18	
Deansgate ⇌	a				10 28						11 00												

		NT	EM	XC	NT	NT	VT	NT	NT	XC	TP	VT	AW	NT	NT	TP	NT	VT	NT	NT	EM	XC
			◇	◇■			◇■			◇■	◇■	◇■	◇			◇■		◇■			◇	◇■
		C	D	M				F		N	H		O		J	K	A		B	C	D	M
				✕			⊡			⊡	✕	⊡	✕			✕		⊡				✕
London Euston ⊖65	d						09 40					10 00						10 20				
Birmingham New Street 68	d			09 57						10 31												10 57
Wolverhampton 68 ⇌	d			10 15						10 49												11 15
Stafford 65,68	d			10 30						11 01												11 30
Stoke-on-Trent 50,68	d			10 55					10 58	11 20		11 25						11 48				11 55
Longport 50	d																					
Kidsgrove 50	d								11 05													
Crewe 65	d				10 34	10 50	11 11						11 31									
Sandbach	d				10 41	10 57																
Holmes Chapel	d				10 45	11 02																
Goostrey	d					11 05																
Chelford	d					11 09																
Alderley Edge	d				10 54	11 13								11 49								
Wilmslow	d				10 57	11 17	11 27						11 48	11 52								
Styal	d																					
Manchester Airport ✈	a				11 04																	
Handforth	d					11 20								11 55								
Congleton	d								11 12													
Macclesfield	a			11 11					11 19			11 41										12 11
	d			11 12					11 20			11 41										12 12
Prestbury	d								11 24													
Adlington (Cheshire)	d								11 27													
Poynton	d								11 30													
Bramhall	d								11 33													
Cheadle Hulme	d					11 24			11 37					11 59								
Stockport	a			11 27		11 29	11 36		11 41	11 49		11 55	11 58	12 04				12 16				12 27
	d		11 26	11 28		11 29	11 37	11 41	11 42	11 50	11 53	11 56	11 58	12 04			12 12	12 17	12 21		12 26	12 28
Heaton Chapel	d					11 33			11 45					12 08			12 16					
Levenshulme	d					11 36			11 48					12 11			12 19					
Manchester Piccadilly ⇌	a		11 36	11 39	11 42	11 44	11 49	11 52	11 56	11 59	12 02	12 07	12 15	12 20			12 28	12 28	12 36		12 36	12 39
	d	11 22	11 37					11 54							12 01	12 07				12 22	12 37	
Manchester Oxford Road	a	11 24	11 40					11 56							12 03	12 09				12 24	12 40	
Deansgate ⇌	a	11 28						12 00												12 28		

A From Buxton
B From Chester
C From Manchester Airport to Southport
D From Norwich to Liverpool Lime Street
E From Southampton Central
F From Hazel Grove to Preston
G From Cardiff Central
H From Cleethorpes to Manchester Airport
I From Carmarthen
J From Manchester Airport to Liverpool Lime Street
K From Scarborough to Liverpool Lime Street
L From Manchester Airport to Barrow-in-Furness
M From Bournemouth
N From Paignton
O From Milford Haven

Saturdays
from 6 October

Stoke-on-Trent and Crewe - Manchester Airport, Stockport and Manchester

Network Diagram - see first Page of Table 78

Station		NT	NT	VT	NT	NT	XC	TP	VT	AW	NT	NT	TP	NT	VT	NT	NT	EM	XC	NT	NT	VT	NT
				◇1	A		◇1 B	◇1 C	◇1	◇ D		E	◇1 F	G	◇1	H	I	◇ J	◇1 K			◇1	A
London Euston 15 ⊖65	d			10 40					11 00						11 20							11 40	
Birmingham New Street 12 68	d						11 31												11 57				
Wolverhampton 7 68	d						11 49												12 15				
Stafford 65,68	d						12 01												12 30				
Stoke-on-Trent 50,68	d					11 58	12 20		12 25						12 48				12 55				
Longport 50	d																						
Kidsgrove 50	d					12 05																	
Crewe 10 65	d	11 34	11 50	12 11						12 31										12 34	12 50	13 11	
Sandbach	d	11 41	11 57																	12 41	12 57		
Holmes Chapel	d	11 45	12 02																	12 45	13 02		
Goostrey	d		12 05																		13 05		
Chelford	d		12 09																		13 09		
Alderley Edge	d	11 54	12 13								12 49									12 54	13 13		
Wilmslow	d	11 57	12 17	12 27						12 49	12 52									12 57	13 17	13 27	
Styal	d																						
Manchester Airport ✈	a	12 04																		13 04			
Handforth	d		12 20								12 55										13 20		
Congleton	d					12 12																	
Macclesfield	a					12 19			12 41										13 11				
	d					12 20			12 41										13 12				
Prestbury	d					12 24																	
Adlington (Cheshire)	d					12 27																	
Poynton	d					12 30																	
Bramhall	d					12 33																	
Cheadle Hulme	d		12 24			12 37					12 59										13 24		
Stockport	a		12 29	12 36		12 41	12 49		12 55	12 58	13 04				13 16				13 27		13 29	13 36	
	d		12 29	12 37	12 41	12 42	12 50	12 53	12 56	12 58	13 04			13 12	13 17	13 21		13 26	13 28		13 29	13 37	13 41
Heaton Chapel	d		12 33			12 45					13 08			13 16							13 33		
Levenshulme	d		12 36			12 48					13 11			13 19							13 36		
Manchester Piccadilly 10	a	12 42	12 44	12 49	12 52	12 56	12 59	13 02	13 07	13 15	13 20			13 28	13 28	13 36		13 36	13 39	13 42	13 44	13 49	13 52
	d				12 54							13 01	13 07				13 22	13 37					13 54
Manchester Oxford Road	a				12 56							13 03	13 09				13 24	13 40					13 56
Deansgate	a				13 00												13 28						14 00

Station		NT	XC	TP	VT	AW	NT	NT	TP	NT	VT	TP	NT	NT	EM	XC	NT	NT	VT	NT	NT	XC	TP
			◇1 B	◇1 C	◇1	◇ L		E	◇1 F	G	◇1	◇1 M	H	I	◇ J	◇1 K			◇1	A		◇1 N	◇1 C
London Euston 15 ⊖65	d				12 00						12 20								12 40				
Birmingham New Street 12 68	d		12 31													12 57						13 31	
Wolverhampton 7 68	d		12 49													13 15						13 49	
Stafford 65,68	d		13 01													13 30						14 01	
Stoke-on-Trent 50,68	d	12 58	13 20		13 25						13 48					13 55					13 58	14 20	
Longport 50	d																						
Kidsgrove 50	d	13 05																			14 05		
Crewe 10 65	d					13 31											13 34	13 50	14 11				
Sandbach	d																13 41	13 57					
Holmes Chapel	d																13 45	14 02					
Goostrey	d																	14 05					
Chelford	d																	14 09					
Alderley Edge	d						13 49										13 54	14 13					
Wilmslow	d					13 48	13 52										13 57	14 17	14 27				
Styal	d																						
Manchester Airport ✈	a																14 04						
Handforth	d						13 55											14 20					
Congleton	d	13 12																			14 12		
Macclesfield	a	13 19			13 41											14 11					14 19		
	d	13 20			13 41											14 12					14 20		
Prestbury	d	13 24																			14 24		
Adlington (Cheshire)	d	13 27																			14 27		
Poynton	d	13 30																			14 30		
Bramhall	d	13 33																			14 33		
Cheadle Hulme	d	13 37					13 59											14 24			14 37		
Stockport	a	13 41	13 49		13 55	13 58	14 04				14 16					14 27		14 29	14 36		14 41	14 49	
	d	13 42	13 50	13 53	13 56	13 58	14 04			14 12	14 17		14 21		14 26	14 28		14 29	14 37	14 41	14 42	14 50	14 53
Heaton Chapel	d	13 45					14 08			14 16								14 33			14 45		
Levenshulme	d	13 48					14 11			14 19								14 36			14 48		
Manchester Piccadilly 10	a	13 56	13 59	14 02	14 07	14 15	14 20			14 28	14 28		14 36		14 36	14 39	14 42	14 44	14 49	14 52	14 56	14 59	15 02
	d							14 01	14 07			14 16		14 22	14 37					14 54			
Manchester Oxford Road	a							14 03	14 09			14 18		14 24	14 40					14 56			
Deansgate	a													14 28						15 00			

A From Hazel Grove to Preston
B From Bristol Temple Meads
C From Cleethorpes to Manchester Airport
D From Milford Haven
E From Manchester Airport to Liverpool Lime Street
F From Scarborough to Liverpool Lime Street
G From Buxton
H From Chester
I From Manchester Airport to Southport
J From Norwich to Liverpool Lime Street
K From Bournemouth
L From Fishguard Harbour
M From Manchester Airport to Barrow-in-Furness
N From Paignton

Table 84

Saturdays
from 6 October

Stoke-on-Trent and Crewe - Manchester Airport, Stockport and Manchester

Network Diagram - see first Page of Table 78

Station		VT	AW	NT	NT	TP	NT	VT	TP	NT	NT	EM	XC	NT	NT	VT	NT	NT	XC	TP	VT	AW
		◇1	◇ A		B	◇1 C	D	◇1	◇1 E	F	G	◇ H	◇1 I			◇1	J		◇1 K	◇1 L	◇1	◇ M
London Euston 15 ⊖65	d	13 00						13 20								13 40					14 00	
Birmingham New Street 12 68	d												13 57						14 31			
Wolverhampton 7 68	d												14 15						14 49			
Stafford 65,68	d												14 30						15 01			
Stoke-on-Trent 50,68	d	14 25						14 48					14 55					14 58	15 20		15 25	
Longport 50	d																					
Kidsgrove 50	d																	15 05				
Crewe 10 65	d		14 31											14 34	14 50	15 11						15 28
Sandbach	d													14 41	14 57							
Holmes Chapel	d													14 45	15 02							
Goostrey	d														15 05							
Chelford	d														15 09							
Alderley Edge	d			14 49										14 54	15 13							
Wilmslow	d		14 49	14 52										14 57	15 17	15 27						15 45
Styal	d																					
Manchester Airport ✈	a													15 04								
Handforth	d			14 55											15 20							
Congleton	d																	15 12				
Macclesfield	a	14 41											15 11					15 19			15 41	
	d	14 41											15 12					15 20			15 41	
Prestbury	d																	15 24				
Adlington (Cheshire)	d																	15 27				
Poynton	d																	15 30				
Bramhall	d																	15 33				
Cheadle Hulme	d			14 59											15 24			15 37				
Stockport	a	14 55	14 58	15 04				15 16					15 27		15 29	15 36		15 41	15 49		15 55	15 58
	d	14 56	14 58	15 04			15 12	15 17		15 21		15 26	15 28		15 29	15 37	15 41	15 42	15 50	15 53	15 56	15 58
Heaton Chapel	d			15 08			15 16								15 33			15 45				
Levenshulme	d			15 11			15 19								15 36			15 48				
Manchester Piccadilly 10	a	15 07	15 15	15 20			15 28	15 28		15 36		15 36	15 39	15 42	15 44	15 49	15 52	15 56	15 59	16 02	16 07	16 15
	d				15 01	15 07			15 16		15 22	15 37					15 54					
Manchester Oxford Road	a				15 03	15 09			15 18		15 24	15 40					15 56					
Deansgate	a										15 28						16 00					

Station		NT	NT	TP	NT	VT	TP	NT	NT	EM	XC	NT	NT	VT	NT	NT	XC	TP	VT	AW	NT	NT	TP
			B	◇1 C	D	◇1	◇1 N	F	G	◇ H	◇1 I			◇1	J		◇1 O	◇1 L	◇1	◇ A		B	◇1 C
London Euston 15 ⊖65	d					14 20								14 40					15 00				
Birmingham New Street 12 68	d										14 57						15 31						
Wolverhampton 7 68	d										15 15						15 49						
Stafford 65,68	d										15 30						16 01						
Stoke-on-Trent 50,68	d					15 48					15 55					15 58	16 20		16 25				
Longport 50	d																						
Kidsgrove 50	d															16 05							
Crewe 10 65	d											15 33	15 50	16 11						16 31			
Sandbach	d											15 40	15 57										
Holmes Chapel	d											15 44	16 02										
Goostrey	d												16 05										
Chelford	d												16 09										
Alderley Edge	d	15 49										15 53	16 13								16 49		
Wilmslow	d	15 52										15 56	16 17	16 27						16 48	16 52		
Styal	d											15 59											
Manchester Airport ✈	a											16 04											
Handforth	d	15 55											16 20								16 55		
Congleton	d															16 12							
Macclesfield	a										16 11					16 19			16 41				
	d										16 12					16 20			16 41				
Prestbury	d															16 24							
Adlington (Cheshire)	d															16 27							
Poynton	d															16 30							
Bramhall	d															16 33							
Cheadle Hulme	d	15 59											16 24			16 37					16 59		
Stockport	a	16 04				16 16					16 27		16 29	16 36		16 41	16 49		16 54	16 58	17 04		
	d	16 04			16 12	16 17		16 21		16 26	16 28		16 29	16 37	16 41	16 42	16 50	16 53	16 55	16 58	17 04		
Heaton Chapel	d	16 08			16 16								16 33			16 45					17 08		
Levenshulme	d	16 11			16 19								16 36			16 48					17 11		
Manchester Piccadilly 10	a	16 20			16 28	16 28		16 36		16 36	16 39	16 42	16 44	16 49	16 52	16 56	16 59	17 02	17 07	17 15	17 20		
	d		16 01	16 07			16 16		16 22	16 37					16 54							17 01	17 07
Manchester Oxford Road	a		16 03	16 09			16 18		16 24	16 40					16 56							17 03	17 09
Deansgate	a								16 28						17 00								

A From Milford Haven
B From Manchester Airport to Liverpool Lime Street
C From Scarborough to Liverpool Lime Street
D From Buxton
E From Manchester Airport to Barrow-in-Furness
F From Chester
G From Manchester Airport to Southport
H From Norwich to Liverpool Lime Street
I From Bournemouth
J From Hazel Grove to Preston
K From Bristol Temple Meads
L From Cleethorpes to Manchester Airport
M From Carmarthen
N From Manchester Airport to Windermere
O From Penzance

Table 84

Saturdays from 6 October

Stoke-on-Trent and Crewe - Manchester Airport, Stockport and Manchester

Network Diagram - see first Page of Table 78

	NT A	VT	NT B	NT C	EM D	XC E	NT	NT	VT	NT	XC F	TP G	VT	AW H	NT	NT I	TP J	NT A	VT	TP K	NT B
London Euston ⊖65 d		15 20							15 40				16 00						16 20		
Birmingham New Street 68 d						15 57					16 31										
Wolverhampton 68 d						16 15					16 49										
Stafford 65,68 d						16 30					17 01										
Stoke-on-Trent 50,68 d		16 48				16 55				16 58	17 20		17 25						17 48		
Longport 50 d																					
Kidsgrove 50 d										17 05											
Crewe 65 d							16 34	16 50	17 11					17 28							
Sandbach d							16 41	16 57													
Holmes Chapel d							16 45	17 02													
Goostrey d								17 05													
Chelford d								17 09													
Alderley Edge d							16 54	17 13							17 49						
Wilmslow d							16 57	17 17	17 27					17 45	17 52						
Styal d																					
Manchester Airport a							17 04														
Handforth d								17 20							17 55						
Congleton d										17 12											
Macclesfield a						17 11				17 19			17 41								
d						17 12				17 20			17 41								
Prestbury d										17 24											
Adlington (Cheshire) d										17 27											
Poynton d										17 30											
Bramhall d										17 33											
Cheadle Hulme d								17 24		17 37					17 59						
Stockport a		17 16				17 27		17 29	17 36	17 41	17 49		17 55	17 58	18 04				18 16		
d	17 12	17 17	17 21		17 26	17 28		17 29	17 37	17 42	17 50	17 53	17 56	17 58	18 04			18 12	18 17		18 21
Heaton Chapel d	17 16							17 33		17 45					18 08			18 16			
Levenshulme d	17 19							17 36		17 48					18 11			18 19			
Manchester Piccadilly a	17 28	17 28	17 36		17 37	17 39	17 42	17 44	17 49	17 56	17 59	18 02	18 07	18 15	18 20			18 28	18 28		18 36
d				17 22	17 37											18 01	18 07			18 16	
Manchester Oxford Road a				17 25	17 40											18 03	18 09			18 18	
Deansgate a																					

	NT C	EM D	XC E	NT	NT	VT	NT L	NT	XC M	TP G	VT	AW N	NT I	TP J	NT A	VT	TP K	NT C	NT	NT B	EM D	XC E
London Euston ⊖65 d						16 40					17 00					17 20						
Birmingham New Street 68 d			16 57						17 31													17 57
Wolverhampton 68 d			17 15						17 49													18 15
Stafford 65,68 d			17 30						18 01													18 30
Stoke-on-Trent 50,68 d			17 55					17 58	18 20		18 25					18 48						18 55
Longport 50 d																						
Kidsgrove 50 d								18 05														
Crewe 65 d				17 33	17 50	18 11						18 31							18 34			
Sandbach d				17 40	17 57														18 41			
Holmes Chapel d				17 44	18 02														18 45			
Goostrey d					18 05																	
Chelford d					18 09																	
Alderley Edge d				17 53	18 13														18 54			
Wilmslow d				17 56	18 17	18 27						18 48							18 57			
Styal d				17 59																		
Manchester Airport a				18 04															19 05			
Handforth d					18 20																	
Congleton d								18 12														
Macclesfield a			18 11					18 19			18 41											19 11
d			18 12					18 20			18 41											19 12
Prestbury d								18 24														
Adlington (Cheshire) d								18 27														
Poynton d								18 30														
Bramhall d								18 33														
Cheadle Hulme d					18 24			18 37														
Stockport a			18 27		18 29	18 36		18 41	18 49		18 55	18 58				19 16						19 27
d		18 26	18 28		18 29	18 37	18 41	18 42	18 50	18 53	18 56	18 58			19 12	19 17				19 21	19 26	19 28
Heaton Chapel d					18 33			18 45							19 16							
Levenshulme d					18 36			18 48							19 19							
Manchester Piccadilly a		18 36	18 39	18 42	18 44	18 49	18 52	18 56	18 59	19 02	19 07	19 15			19 28	19 28			19 31	19 35	19 36	19 39
d	18 22	18 37					18 54						19 01	19 07			19 16	19 20	19 32		19 37	
Manchester Oxford Road a	18 24	18 40					18 56						19 03	19 09			19 18	19 22	19 36		19 40	
Deansgate a	18 28						19 00											19 26				

A From Buxton
B From Chester
C From Manchester Airport to Southport
D From Norwich to Liverpool Lime Street
E From Bournemouth
F From Bristol Temple Meads
G From Cleethorpes to Manchester Airport
H From Carmarthen
I From Manchester Airport to Liverpool Lime Street
J From Scarborough to Liverpool Lime Street
K From Manchester Airport to Barrow-in-Furness
L From Hazel Grove to Bolton
M From Paignton
N From Milford Haven

Table 84

Saturdays from 6 October

Stoke-on-Trent and Crewe - Manchester Airport, Stockport and Manchester

Network Diagram - see first Page of Table 78

	NT	VT	NT	XC A	TP B	VT	AW C	NT D	TP E	NT F	VT	TP G	NT H	NT	NT I	EM J	XC K	NT	VT	NT	XC L	AW M
London Euston ⊖65 d		17 40				18 00					18 20								18 40			
Birmingham New Street 68 d				18 31													18 57				19 31	
Wolverhampton 68 d				18 49													19 15				19 49	
Stafford 65,68 d				19 01													19 30				20 01	
Stoke-on-Trent 50,68 d			18 58	19 20		19 25					19 48						19 55			19 58	20 20	
Longport 50 d																						
Kidsgrove 50 d			19 05																	20 05		
Crewe 65 d	18 50	19 11					19 31											19 50	20 11			
Sandbach d	18 57																	19 57				
Holmes Chapel d	19 02																	20 02				
Goostrey d	19 05																	20 05				
Chelford d	19 09																	20 09				
Alderley Edge d	19 13																	20 13				
Wilmslow d	19 17	19 27					19 48							19 56				20 17	20 27			
Styal d																						
Manchester Airport a														20 04								
Handforth d	19 20																	20 20				
Congleton d			19 12																	20 12		
Macclesfield a			19 19			19 41											20 11			20 19	20 36	
d			19 20			19 41											20 12			20 20	20 37	
Prestbury d			19 24																	20 24		
Adlington (Cheshire) d			19 27																	20 27		
Poynton d			19 30																	20 30		
Bramhall d			19 33																	20 33		
Cheadle Hulme d	19 24		19 37															20 24		20 37		
Stockport a	19 29	19 36	19 41	19 49		19 55	19 58				20 16						20 27	20 29	20 36	20 41	20 49	
d	19 29	19 37	19 42	19 50	19 53	19 56	19 58			20 12	20 17				20 21	20 26	20 28	20 29	20 37	20 42	20 50	
Heaton Chapel d			19 45							20 16										20 45		
Levenshulme d			19 48							20 19										20 48		
Manchester Piccadilly a	19 43	19 49	19 56	19 59	20 02	20 07	20 15			20 28	20 28			20 31	20 35	20 36	20 39	20 43	20 49	20 56	20 59	
d								20 01	20 07			20 16	20 20	20 32		20 37						20 50
Manchester Oxford Road a								20 03	20 09			20 18	20 22	20 36		20 40						20 52
Deansgate a													20 26									

	TP B	VT	AW N	TP E	NT F	VT	NT H	NT	EM O	NT I	XC K	NT	VT	NT	XC A	AW C	NT D	TP E	NT F	TP G	NT
London Euston ⊖65 d		19 00				19 20							19 40								
Birmingham New Street 68 d											19 57				20 31						
Wolverhampton 68 d											20 15				20 49						
Stafford 65,68 d											20 30				21 01						
Stoke-on-Trent 50,68 d		20 25				20 48					20 55			20 58	21 21						
Longport 50 d																					
Kidsgrove 50 d														21 05							
Crewe 65 d			20 28									20 50	21 19			21 33					
Sandbach d												20 57									
Holmes Chapel d												21 02									
Goostrey d												21 05									
Chelford d												21 09									
Alderley Edge d												21 13									
Wilmslow d			20 45					20 56				21 17	21 34			21 50					21 55
Styal d																					
Manchester Airport a								21 05													22 04
Handforth d												21 20									
Congleton d														21 12							
Macclesfield a		20 41									21 11			21 19	21 38						
d		20 41									21 12			21 20	21 39						
Prestbury d														21 24							
Adlington (Cheshire) d														21 27							
Poynton d														21 30							
Bramhall d														21 33							
Cheadle Hulme d												21 24		21 37							
Stockport a		20 55	20 58			21 16					21 27	21 29	21 44	21 41	21 53	22 00					
d	20 53	20 56	20 59		21 12	21 17			21 20	21 21	21 28	21 29	21 45	21 42	21 54	22 00			22 12		
Heaton Chapel d					21 16									21 45					22 16		
Levenshulme d					21 19									21 48					22 19		
Manchester Piccadilly a	21 02	21 07	21 15		21 28	21 28		21 31	21 32	21 35	21 39	21 43	21 53	21 57	22 04	22 15			22 28		22 31
d				21 07			21 20	21 32									22 01	22 07		22 16	22 32
Manchester Oxford Road a				21 09			21 22	21 36									22 03	22 09		22 18	22 36
Deansgate a							21 26														

A From Bristol Temple Meads
B From Cleethorpes to Manchester Airport
C From Carmarthen
D From Manchester Airport to Liverpool Lime Street
E From Scarborough to Liverpool Lime Street
F From Buxton
G From Manchester Airport to Barrow-in-Furness
H From Manchester Airport to Southport
I From Chester
J From Norwich to Liverpool Lime Street
K From Bournemouth
L From Exeter St Davids
M From Manchester Airport to Chester
N From Milford Haven
O From Norwich

Table 84

Saturdays from 6 October

Stoke-on-Trent and Crewe - Manchester Airport, Stockport and Manchester

Network Diagram - see first Page of Table 78

		XC ◇■ A	NT	VT ◇■	NT B	NT C	NT D	VT ◇■ E	NT	XC ◇■ A	VT ◇■	NT F	AW ◇ G	NT	NT H	NT	XC ◇■
London Euston ⊖65	d			20 20				20 31			21 00						
Birmingham New Street 68	d	20 57								21 57							22 31
Wolverhampton 68	d	21 15								22 16							22 49
Stafford 65,68	d	21 30								22 30	22 34						23 02
Stoke-on-Trent 50,68	d	21 53		22 05					22 18	22 51							23 21
Longport 50	d																
Kidsgrove 50	d								22 25								
Crewe 65	d		21 50					22 36			22 59		23 06			23 12	
Sandbach	d		21 57													23 19	
Holmes Chapel	d		22 02													23 24	
Goostrey	d		22 05													23 27	
Chelford	d		22 09													23 31	
Alderley Edge	d		22 13													23 35	
Wilmslow	d		22 17								23 15		23 24	23 15		23 39	
Styal	d																
Manchester Airport	a													23 23			
Handforth	d		22 20													23 42	
Congleton	d								22 32								
Macclesfield	a	22 11		22 21					22 39	23 07							23 38
	d	22 12		22 21					22 40	23 08							23 39
Prestbury	d								22 44								
Adlington (Cheshire)	d								22 47								
Poynton	d								22 50								
Bramhall	d								22 53								
Cheadle Hulme	d		22 24						22 56							23 46	
Stockport	a	22 27	22 29	22 35					23 01	23 21	23 25		23 32			23 51	23 53
	d	22 28	22 29	22 36		22 40	22 48		23 01	23 22	23 26	23 22	23 33		23 41	23 51	23 54
Heaton Chapel	d					22 44			23 05							23 55	
Levenshulme	d					22 47			23 08							23 58	
Manchester Piccadilly	a	22 39	22 43	22 51		22 53	23 00	23 08	23 16	23 32	23 38	23 43	23 50	23 51	23 54	00 07	00 10
	d				22 36	22 54											
Manchester Oxford Road	a				22 38	22 56											
Deansgate	a				22 41	23 00											

Sundays until 24 June

		NT	XC ◇■	NT D	NT I	TP ◇■ J	AW	NT K	TP ◇■ L	NT H	NT I	NT	NT K	TP ◇■ M	AW	NT H	NT N	XC ◇■	VT ◇■	NT	VT ◇■	NT K	TP ◇■ F
London Euston ⊖65	d																		08 10		08 20		
Birmingham New Street 68	d		22p31															08 50					
Wolverhampton 68	d		22p49															09 19					
Stafford 65,68	d		23p02															09 33					
Stoke-on-Trent 50,68	d		23p21																		10 21		
Longport 50	d																						
Kidsgrove 50	d																						
Crewe 65	d	23p12					08 28								09 28			09 56	10 19				
Sandbach	d	23p19																					
Holmes Chapel	d	23p24																					
Goostrey	d	23p27																					
Chelford	d	23p31																					
Alderley Edge	d	23p35										09 19								10 19			
Wilmslow	d	23p39					08 48					09 23			09 47			10 13	10 34	10 23			
Styal	d																						
Manchester Airport	a																						
Handforth	d	23p42										09 26								10 26			
Congleton	d																						
Macclesfield	a		23p38																		10 36		
	d		23p39																		10 38		
Prestbury	d																						
Adlington (Cheshire)	d																						
Poynton	d																						
Bramhall	d																						
Cheadle Hulme	d	23p46										09 30								10 30			
Stockport	a	23p51	23p53									09 38						10 21	10 43	10 35	10 50		
	d	23p51	23p54	00 02	08 24	08 31				09 10	09 22	09 40		09 53		10 04	10 12	10 22	10 44	10 39	10 52		10 53
Heaton Chapel	d	23p55								09 13		09 44				10 08				10 43			
Levenshulme	d	23p58								09 16		09 47				10 11				10 46			
Manchester Piccadilly	a	00 07	00 10	00 15	08 33	08 42	09 10			09 23	09 33	09 54		10 04	10 17	10 20	10 22	10 37	10 55	10 56	11 03		11 06
	d				08 35			08 49	09 03		09 35		09 50				10 24					10 50	
Manchester Oxford Road	a				08 37			08 51	09 05		09 37		09 52				10 26					10 52	
Deansgate	a				08 40			08 54	09 08		09 40						10 40						

A From Bournemouth
B From Manchester Airport to Southport
C To Wigan Wallgate
D From Chester
E from 27 October
F From Sheffield
G From Maesteg
H From Buxton
I To Southport
J From Sheffield to Manchester Airport
K From Manchester Airport to Liverpool Lime Street
L From Manchester Airport to Windermere
M From Meadowhall
N From Chester to Southport

Table 84

Sundays until 24 June

Stoke-on-Trent and Crewe - Manchester Airport, Stockport and Manchester

Network Diagram - see first Page of Table 78

		AW ◇ A	NT	NT B	TP ◇■ C	NT	NT D	EM ◇ E	XC ◇■	NT	AW ◇ F	VT ◇■	NT G	TP ◇■ H	NT B	NT I	NT J	EM ◇ E	XC ◇■ K	NT	NT G	TP ◇■ H	VT ◇■
London Euston ⊖65	d											09 20											10 20
Birmingham New Street 68	d								10 01										11 01				
Wolverhampton 68	d								10 29										11 30				
Stafford 65,68	d								10 44										11 44				
Stoke-on-Trent 50,68	d								11 03			11 22							12 04				12 25
Longport 50	d																						
Kidsgrove 50	d																						
Crewe 65	d	10 28								10 56	11 23												
Sandbach	d									11 03													
Holmes Chapel	d									11 08													
Goostrey	d									11 11													
Chelford	d									11 15													
Alderley Edge	d					10 40				11 19										12 19			
Wilmslow	d	10 47				10 43				11 23	11 42									12 23			
Styal	d					10 47																	
Manchester Airport	a					10 55																	
Handforth	d									11 26										12 26			
Congleton	d																						
Macclesfield	a								11 19			11 37							12 21				12 40
	d		10 44						11 20			11 38							12 22				12 42
Prestbury	d		10 48																				
Adlington (Cheshire)	d		10 51																				
Poynton	d		10 54																				
Bramhall	d		10 57																				
Cheadle Hulme	d		11 00							11 30										12 30			
Stockport	a	10 58	11 05						11 37	11 37		11 51							12 35	12 37			12 55
	d	10 58	11 05	11 14			11 15	11 26	11 38	11 37		11 53		11 53	12 13		12 21	12 26	12 36	12 37		12 53	12 56
Heaton Chapel	d						11 19			11 41					12 16					12 41			
Levenshulme	d						11 22			11 44					12 19					12 44			
Manchester Piccadilly	a	11 12	11 19	11 25		11 25	11 28	11 37	11 47	11 53	12 02	12 04		12 06	12 26		12 31	12 35	12 44	12 57		13 06	13 08
	d				11 16	11 27	11 33	11 38					11 50			12 29	12 35	12 38			12 50		
Manchester Oxford Road	a				11 18	11 31	11 35	11 41					11 52			12 33	12 37	12 41			12 52		
Deansgate	a						11 40										12 40						

		AW ◇ F	NT B	NT	TP ◇■ C	NT D	EM ◇ E	XC ◇■ L	VT ◇■	NT	NT G	TP ◇■ H	AW ◇ M	NT	NT B	VT ◇■	NT J	EM ◇ N	XC ◇■ O	VT ◇■	NT	NT G
London Euston ⊖65	d								11 20							12 15				12 35		
Birmingham New Street 68	d							12 01											12 58			
Wolverhampton 68	d							12 28											13 26			
Stafford 65,68	d							12 43											13 40			
Stoke-on-Trent 50,68	d							13 04	13 11					13 25		13 50			14 00			
Longport 50	d																					
Kidsgrove 50	d													13 32								
Crewe 65	d	12 28								12 56			13 29							14 13		
Sandbach	d									13 03												
Holmes Chapel	d									13 08												
Goostrey	d									13 11												
Chelford	d									13 15												
Alderley Edge	d			12 51						13 19											14 19	
Wilmslow	d	12 47		12 54						13 23			13 49							14 29	14 23	
Styal	d			12 58																		
Manchester Airport	a			13 05																		
Handforth	d									13 26											14 26	
Congleton	d													13 39								
Macclesfield	a							13 20	13 26					13 46					14 16			
	d							13 21	13 28					13 47					14 17			
Prestbury	d													13 51								
Adlington (Cheshire)	d													13 54								
Poynton	d													13 57								
Bramhall	d													14 00								
Cheadle Hulme	d									13 30				14 03							14 30	
Stockport	a	12 58						13 38	13 41	13 37			14 00	14 08		14 18			14 29	14 38	14 37	
	d	12 58	13 15			13 22	13 26	13 38	13 42	13 37		13 53	14 00	14 08	14 15	14 19	14 21	14 26	14 30	14 39	14 37	
Heaton Chapel	d		13 18							13 41					14 18						14 41	
Levenshulme	d		13 21							13 44					14 21						14 44	
Manchester Piccadilly	a	13 15	13 29	13 31		13 33	13 37	13 46	13 53	13 55		14 06	14 19	14 21	14 29	14 29	14 33	14 37	14 40	14 50	14 53	
	d				13 16	13 35	13 38				13 50						14 35	14 38				14 50
Manchester Oxford Road	a				13 18	13 37	13 41				13 52						14 37	14 41				14 52
Deansgate	a					13 40											14 40					

A From Shrewsbury
B From Buxton
C From Manchester Airport to Barrow-in-Furness
D To Southport
E From Nottingham to Liverpool Lime Street
F From Cardiff Central
G From Manchester Airport to Liverpool Lime Street
H From Cleethorpes to Manchester Airport
I From Manchester Airport
J From Chester to Southport
K From Reading
L From Southampton Central
M From Carmarthen
N From Norwich to Liverpool Lime Street
O From Bournemouth

Sundays until 24 June

Stoke-on-Trent and Crewe - Manchester Airport, Stockport and Manchester

Network Diagram - see first Page of Table 78

		TP	VT	AW	XC	NT	VT	NT	TP	NT	EM	XC	VT	NT	NT	TP	VT	AW	XC	NT	VT	TP	NT
		◇1 A	◇1	◇ B	◇1	C	◇1		◇1 D	E	◇ F	◇1 G	◇1		H	◇1 I	◇1	◇ J	◇1 K	C	◇1	◇1 L	M
London Euston ⊖65	d		12 55				13 15						13 35				13 55				14 15		
Birmingham New Street 68	d				13 31							13 58							14 31				
Wolverhampton 68	d				14 01							14 25							15 01				
Stafford 65,68	d											14 39											
Stoke-on-Trent 50,68	d		14 26		14 32		14 50					14 57					15 26		15 36		15 50		
Longport 50	d																						
Kidsgrove 50	d																						
Crewe 65	d			14 28									15 13	14 56				15 28					
Sandbach	d													15 03									
Holmes Chapel	d													15 08									
Goostrey	d													15 11									
Chelford	d													15 15									
Alderley Edge	d							14 51						15 19									
Wilmslow	d			14 47				14 54					15 29	15 23				15 47					
Styal	d							14 58															
Manchester Airport ✈	a							15 04															
Handforth	d													15 26									
Congleton	d																						
Macclesfield	a		14 42		14 49							15 14					15 42		15 57				
	d		14 42		14 50							15 15					15 42		15 58				
Prestbury	d																						
Adlington (Cheshire)	d																						
Poynton	d																						
Bramhall	d																						
Cheadle Hulme	d													15 30									
Stockport	a		14 56	14 58	15 02		15 18					15 26	15 38	15 37			15 56	15 58	16 09		16 18		
	d	14 53	14 57	14 58	15 05	15 15	15 19			15 22	15 26	15 27	15 39	15 37		15 53	15 57	15 58	16 11	16 15	16 19		16 21
Heaton Chapel	d					15 18								15 41						16 18			
Levenshulme	d					15 21								15 44						16 21			
Manchester Piccadilly	a	15 06	15 09	15 15	15 17	15 29	15 29	15 32		15 33	15 37	15 38	15 50	15 53		16 06	16 09	16 15	16 22	16 29	16 29		16 33
	d								15 16	15 35	15 38				15 50							16 16	16 35
Manchester Oxford Road	a								15 18	15 37	15 41				15 52							16 18	16 37
Deansgate	a									15 40													16 40

		EM	XC	VT	NT	NT	NT	TP	VT	AW	XC	NT	VT	NT	NT	EM	XC	VT	NT	NT	TP	VT
		◇ N	◇1 G	◇1			H	◇1 I	◇1	■ B	◇1 O	C	◇1		E	◇ N	◇1 G	◇1		H	◇1 I	◇1
London Euston ⊖65	d			14 35					14 55				15 15					15 35				15 55
Birmingham New Street 68	d		14 58								15 31						15 58					
Wolverhampton 68	d		15 26								16 01						16 26					
Stafford 65,68	d		15 40														16 37					
Stoke-on-Trent 50,68	d		15 57			16 01			16 25		16 35		16 50				16 58					17 26
Longport 50	d																					
Kidsgrove 50	d					16 08																
Crewe 65	d			16 13						16 28								17 13	16 56			
Sandbach	d																		17 03			
Holmes Chapel	d																		17 08			
Goostrey	d																		17 11			
Chelford	d																		17 15			
Alderley Edge	d				16 19									16 51					17 19			
Wilmslow	d			16 29	16 23					16 47				16 54				17 29	17 23			
Styal	d													16 58								
Manchester Airport ✈	a													17 05								
Handforth	d				16 26														17 26			
Congleton	d					16 15																
Macclesfield	a		16 14			16 22			16 42		16 54						17 14					17 42
	d		16 15			16 23			16 42		16 55						17 15					17 42
Prestbury	d					16 27																
Adlington (Cheshire)	d					16 30																
Poynton	d					16 33																
Bramhall	d					16 36																
Cheadle Hulme	d				16 30	16 39													17 30			
Stockport	a		16 26	16 38	16 37	16 44			16 56	16 58	17 07		17 18				17 29	17 38	17 37			17 56
	d	16 26	16 27	16 39	16 37	16 44		16 53	16 57	16 58	17 08	17 15	17 19		17 22	17 29	17 30	17 39	17 37		17 53	17 57
Heaton Chapel	d				16 41							17 18							17 41			
Levenshulme	d				16 44							17 21							17 44			
Manchester Piccadilly	a	16 37	16 38	16 50	16 53	16 58		17 06	17 09	17 15	17 19	17 29	17 29	17 31	17 33	17 37	17 40	17 50	17 53		18 06	18 09
	d	16 38					16 50								17 35	17 38				17 50		
Manchester Oxford Road	a	16 41					16 52								17 37	17 41				17 52		
Deansgate	a														17 40							

A From Doncaster to Manchester Airport
B From Cardiff Central
C From Buxton
D From Manchester Airport to Barrow-in-Furness
E To Southport
F From Norwich to Liverpool Lime Street
G From Bournemouth
H From Manchester Airport to Liverpool Lime Street
I From Cleethorpes to Manchester Airport
J From Milford Haven
K From Paignton
L From Manchester Airport to Windermere
M From Chester to Southport
N From Nottingham to Liverpool Lime Street
O From Plymouth

Sundays until 24 June

Stoke-on-Trent and Crewe - Manchester Airport, Stockport and Manchester

Network Diagram - see first Page of Table 78

		AW	XC	NT	VT	TP	NT	EM	XC	VT	NT	NT	TP	VT	AW	XC	NT	VT	NT	TP	NT	EM	XC
		■ A	◇1 B	C	◇1	◇1 D	E	◇ F	◇1 G	◇1		H	◇1 I	◇1	■ J	◇1 K	C	◇1		◇1 D	L	◇ F	◇1 G
London Euston ⊖65	d				16 15					16 35				16 55				17 15					
Birmingham New Street 68	d		16 31						16 58							17 31							17 58
Wolverhampton 68	d		17 01						17 26							18 01							18 26
Stafford 65,68	d								17 39														18 36
Stoke-on-Trent 50,68	d		17 35		17 50				17 58					18 26		18 31		18 50					18 56
Longport 50	d																						
Kidsgrove 50	d																						
Crewe 65	d	17 28								18 13					18 28								
Sandbach	d																						
Holmes Chapel	d																						
Goostrey	d																						
Chelford	d																						
Alderley Edge	d										18 19								18 51				
Wilmslow	d	17 45								18 29	18 23				18 47				18 54				
Styal	d																		18 58				
Manchester Airport ✈	a																		19 05				
Handforth	d										18 26												
Congleton	d																						
Macclesfield	a		17 54						18 14					18 42		18 48							19 14
	d		17 55						18 15					18 42		18 50							19 14
Prestbury	d																						
Adlington (Cheshire)	d																						
Poynton	d																						
Bramhall	d																						
Cheadle Hulme	d										18 30												
Stockport	a	17 58	18 07		18 18				18 28	18 38	18 37			18 56	18 58	19 04		19 18					19 28
	d	17 58	18 08	18 15	18 19		18 21	18 26	18 29	18 39	18 37		18 53	18 57	18 58	19 05	19 15	19 19			19 22	19 26	19 29
Heaton Chapel	d			18 18							18 41						19 18						
Levenshulme	d			18 21							18 44						19 21						
Manchester Piccadilly	a	18 17	18 19	18 29	18 29		18 33	18 37	18 40	18 50	18 53		19 06	19 09	19 15	19 19	19 29	19 29	19 31		19 33	19 37	19 40
	d					18 16	18 35	18 38				18 50								19 16	19 35	19 38	
Manchester Oxford Road	a					18 18	18 37	18 41				18 52								19 18	19 37	19 41	
Deansgate	a						18 40														19 40		

		VT	NT	NT	TP	VT	AW	XC	NT	VT	NT	EM	XC	VT	NT	NT	NT	TP	VT	AW	XC	NT	VT
		◇1		H	◇1 I	◇1	■ A	◇1 M	C	◇1	E	◇ N	◇1 G	◇1			H	◇1 I	◇1	■ J	◇1 K	C	◇1
London Euston ⊖65	d	17 35				17 55				18 15				18 35					18 55				19 15
Birmingham New Street 68	d							18 31					18 58								19 31		
Wolverhampton 68	d							19 01					19 26								20 01		
Stafford 65,68	d												19 39										
Stoke-on-Trent 50,68	d					19 26		19 32		19 50			19 58			20 01			20 26		20 36		20 50
Longport 50	d																						
Kidsgrove 50	d															20 08							
Crewe 65	d	19 13	18 56				19 28							20 13						20 28			
Sandbach	d		19 03																				
Holmes Chapel	d		19 08																				
Goostrey	d		19 11																				
Chelford	d		19 15																				
Alderley Edge	d		19 19												20 19								
Wilmslow	d	19 29	19 23				19 47							20 29	20 23					20 46			
Styal	d																						
Manchester Airport ✈	a																						
Handforth	d		19 26												20 26								
Congleton	d															20 15							
Macclesfield	a					19 42		19 49					20 14			20 22			20 42		20 56		
	d					19 42		19 50					20 15			20 23			20 42		20 57		
Prestbury	d															20 27							
Adlington (Cheshire)	d															20 30							
Poynton	d															20 33							
Bramhall	d															20 36							
Cheadle Hulme	d		19 30												20 30	20 39							
Stockport	a	19 38	19 37			19 56	19 58	20 02		20 18			20 29	20 38	20 37	20 44			20 56	20 57	21 09		21 18
	d	19 39	19 37		19 53	19 57	19 58	20 05	20 15	20 19	20 21	20 26	20 30	20 39	20 37	20 44		20 53	20 57	20 57	21 10	21 13	21 19
Heaton Chapel	d		19 41						20 18						20 41							21 16	
Levenshulme	d		19 44						20 21						20 44							21 19	
Manchester Piccadilly	a	19 50	19 53		20 09	20 09	20 17	20 18	20 29	20 29	20 33	20 38	20 40	20 50	20 53	20 58		21 06	21 09	21 14	21 20	21 27	21 29
	d			19 50							20 35						20 50						
Manchester Oxford Road	a			19 52							20 37						20 52						
Deansgate	a										20 40												

A From Milford Haven
B From Plymouth
C From Buxton
D From Manchester Airport to Barrow-in-Furness
E From Chester to Southport
F From Norwich to Liverpool Lime Street
G From Bournemouth
H From Manchester Airport to Liverpool Lime Street
I From Cleethorpes to Manchester Airport
J From Cardiff Central
K From Bristol Temple Meads
L To Southport
M From Penzance
N From Norwich

Stoke-on-Trent and Crewe - Manchester Airport, Stockport and Manchester

Sundays until 24 June

Network Diagram - see first Page of Table 78

Station		NT		NT	EM	XC	VT	NT	NT	TP	VT	XC		AW	NT	VT	NT	XC	NT	VT	NT	NT		NT	NT
					◇	◇1	◇1			◇1	◇1	◇1		■		◇1		◇1		◇1					
				A	B	C			D	E		F		G	H		I	C			D	H			J
						🛒	🍴				🍴	🛒		🛒		🍴		🛒		🍴					
London Euston 15 ⊖65	d						19 35				19 55					20 15				20 35					
Birmingham New Street 12 68	d					19 58						20 31						20 58							
Wolverhampton 7 68	d					20 26						20 59						21 30							
Stafford 65,68	d					20 39												21 43		22 00					
Stoke-on-Trent 50,68	d					20 57					21 26	21 34				21 50		22 04							
Longport 50	d																								
Kidsgrove 50	d																								
Crewe 10 65	d						21 14	20 56						21 28						22 21					
Sandbach	d							21 03																	
Holmes Chapel	d							21 08																	
Goostrey	d							21 11																	
Chelford	d							21 15																	
Alderley Edge	d	20 51						21 19											22 19					22 51	
Wilmslow	d	20 54					21 30	21 23						21 45					22 23	22 36				22 54	
Styal	d	20 58																						22 58	
Manchester Airport ✈	a	21 05																						23 05	
Handforth	d							21 26											22 26						
Congleton	d																								
Macclesfield	a					21 15					21 42	21 51						22 20							
	d					21 15					21 42	21 52						22 21							
Prestbury	d																								
Adlington (Cheshire)	d																								
Poynton	d																								
Bramhall	d																								
Cheadle Hulme	d							21 30											22 30						
Stockport	a					21 28	21 39	21 37			21 56	22 05		21 58		22 18		22 32	22 37	22 45					
	d			21 22	21 24	21 29	21 40	21 37		21 53	21 57	22 07		21 58	22 13	22 19	22 21	22 33	22 37	22 46		23 13			23 16
Heaton Chapel	d							21 41							22 16				22 41			23 16			
Levenshulme	d							21 44							22 19				22 44			23 19			
Manchester Piccadilly 10	a	21 31		21 33	21 36	21 40	21 50	21 53		22 06	22 09	22 17		22 19	22 27	22 29	22 33	22 43	22 53	22 57		23 27		23 29	23 29
	d			21 35					21 50								22 35				22 41				
Manchester Oxford Road	a			21 37					21 52								22 37				22 43				
Deansgate	a			21 40													22 40				22 47				

Station		NT	XC	NT	VT	VT
			◇1		◇1	◇1
			C			
					🍴	🍴
London Euston 15 ⊖65	d				21 25	21 51
Birmingham New Street 12 68	d		21 59			
Wolverhampton 7 68	d		22 26			
Stafford 65,68	d		22 39			23s53
Stoke-on-Trent 50,68	d	22 39	22 59		23 29	
Longport 50	d					
Kidsgrove 50	d	22 46				
Crewe 10 65	d			22 56		00s21
Sandbach	d			23 03		
Holmes Chapel	d			23 08		
Goostrey	d			23 11		
Chelford	d			23 15		
Alderley Edge	d			23 19		
Wilmslow	d			23 23		
Styal	d					
Manchester Airport ✈	a					
Handforth	d			23 26		
Congleton	d	22 53				
Macclesfield	a	23 00	23 15		23 45	
	d	23 01	23 16		23 46	
Prestbury	d	23 05				
Adlington (Cheshire)	d	23 08				
Poynton	d	23 11				
Bramhall	d	23 14				
Cheadle Hulme	d	23 17		23 30		
Stockport	a	23 22	23 29	23 35	23 59	00s50
	d	23 23	23 30	23 37	00 01	
Heaton Chapel	d			23 41		
Levenshulme	d			23 44		
Manchester Piccadilly 10	a	23 37	23 41	23 53	00 12	01 00
	d					
Manchester Oxford Road	a					
Deansgate	a					

A To Wigan Wallgate
B From Norwich
C From Bournemouth
D From Manchester Airport to Liverpool Lime Street
E From Cleethorpes to Manchester Airport
F From Bristol Temple Meads
G From Milford Haven
H From Buxton
I From Chester to Wigan Wallgate
J From Sheffield

Stoke-on-Trent and Crewe - Manchester Airport, Stockport and Manchester

Sundays 1 July to 9 September

Network Diagram - see first Page of Table 78

Station		NT	XC	NT	VT	VT	VT	VT	NT	TP		AW	NT	TP	NT	NT	NT	NT	TP	AW		NT	TP	NT	XC
			◇1		◇1	◇1	◇1	◇1		◇1				◇1					◇1				◇1		◇1
				A	B	B	B	B	C	D			E	F	G	C		E	H			G	I	J	
					🍴	🍴	🍴	🍴																	🛒
London Euston 15 ⊖65	d				22p30	23p30	00 30	01 30																	
Birmingham New Street 12 68	d		22p31																						09 01
Wolverhampton 7 68	d		22p49																						09 19
Stafford 65,68	d		23p02																						09 33
Stoke-on-Trent 50,68	d		23p21		23b53	00s53	01s53	02s53																	
Longport 50	d																								
Kidsgrove 50	d																								
Crewe 10 65	d	23p12										08 28								09 28					09 56
Sandbach	d	23p19																							
Holmes Chapel	d	23p24																							
Goostrey	d	23p27																							
Chelford	d	23p31																							
Alderley Edge	d	23p35															09 19								
Wilmslow	d	23p39										08 48					09 23			09 47					10 13
Styal	d																								
Manchester Airport ✈	a																								
Handforth	d	23p42															09 26								
Congleton	d																								
Macclesfield	a		23p38		00s10	01s10	02s10	03s10																	
	d		23p39																						
Prestbury	d																								
Adlington (Cheshire)	d																								
Poynton	d																								
Bramhall	d																								
Cheadle Hulme	d	23p46															09 30								
Stockport	a	23p51	23p53		00s24	01s24	02s24	03s24									09 38								10 21
	d	23p51	23p54	00 02					08 24	08 31					09 10	09 22	09 40		09 53			10 04		10 12	10 22
Heaton Chapel	d	23p55													09 13		09 44					10 08			
Levenshulme	d	23p58													09 16		09 47					10 11			
Manchester Piccadilly 10	a	00 07	00 10	00 15	00 37	01 37	02 37	03 39	08 33	08 42		09 10			09 23	09 33	09 54		10 04	10 17		10 20		10 22	10 37
	d								08 35				08 49	09 03		09 35		09 50					10 07	10 24	
Manchester Oxford Road	a								08 37				08 51	09 05		09 37		09 52					10 09	10 26	
Deansgate	a								08 40				08 54	09 08		09 40								10 40	

Station		VT	NT	VT	NT	TP		AW	NT	NT	TP	NT	NT	XC	EM	NT		AW	VT	NT	TP	TP	NT	NT	NT
		◇1		◇1		◇1		◇			◇1			◇1	◇			◇	◇1		◇1	◇1			
					E	K		L		G	M		C		N			O		E	P	Q	G	R	J
		🍴		🍴										🛒				🛒	🍴						
London Euston 15 ⊖65	d	08 10		08 20															09 20						
Birmingham New Street 12 68	d													10 01											
Wolverhampton 7 68	d													10 19											
Stafford 65,68	d													10 33											
Stoke-on-Trent 50,68	d			10 21										10 52					11 22						
Longport 50	d																								
Kidsgrove 50	d																								
Crewe 10 65	d	10 19						10 28								10 56		11 23							
Sandbach	d															11 03									
Holmes Chapel	d															11 08									
Goostrey	d															11 11									
Chelford	d															11 15									
Alderley Edge	d		10 19									10 40				11 19									
Wilmslow	d	10 34	10 23					10 47				10 43				11 23		11 42							
Styal	d											10 47													
Manchester Airport ✈	a											10 55													
Handforth	d		10 26													11 26									
Congleton	d																								
Macclesfield	a			10 36										11 08					11 37						
	d			10 38					10 44					11 09					11 38						
Prestbury	d								10 48																
Adlington (Cheshire)	d								10 51																
Poynton	d								10 54																
Bramhall	d								10 57																
Cheadle Hulme	d		10 30						11 00							11 30									
Stockport	a	10 43	10 35	10 50				10 58	11 05					11 22		11 37			11 51						
	d	10 44	10 39	10 52		10 53		10 58	11 05	11 14			11 15	11 23	11 26	11 37			11 53		11 53		12 13		12 21
Heaton Chapel	d		10 43										11 19			11 41							12 16		
Levenshulme	d		10 46										11 22			11 44							12 19		
Manchester Piccadilly 10	a	10 55	10 56	11 03		11 06		11 12	11 19	11 25		11 25	11 28	11 31	11 37	11 53		12 02	12 04		12 06		12 26		12 31
	d				10 50						11 16	11 27	11 33		11 38					11 50		12 07		12 29	12 35
Manchester Oxford Road	a				10 52						11 18	11 31	11 35		11 41					11 52		12 09		12 33	12 37
Deansgate	a												11 40												12 40

A From Chester
B from 29 July until12 August, from 2 September
C To Southport
D From Sheffield to Manchester Airport
E From Manchester Airport to Liverpool Lime Street
F From Manchester Airport to Windermere
G From Buxton
H From Meadowhall
I From York to Liverpool Lime Street
J From Chester to Southport
K From Sheffield
L From Shrewsbury
M From Manchester Airport to Barrow-in-Furness
N From Nottingham to Liverpool Lime Street
O From Cardiff Central
P From Cleethorpes to Manchester Airport
Q From Newcastle to Liverpool Lime Street
R From Manchester Airport
b Previous night, stops to set down only

Table 84

Sundays

1 July to 9 September

Stoke-on-Trent and Crewe - Manchester Airport, Stockport and Manchester

Network Diagram - see first Page of Table 78

	EM A	XC B	NT	NT C	TP D	VT	AW E	TP F	NT G	NT	TP H	NT I	EM A	XC J	VT	NT	NT C	TP D	AW K	NT	TP F
London Euston ⊖65 d						10 20									11 20						
Birmingham New Street 68 d		11 01												12 01							
Wolverhampton 68 d		11 19												12 19							
Stafford 65,68 d		11 32												12 33							
Stoke-on-Trent 50,68 d		11 52				12 25								12 54	13 11					13 25	
Longport 50 d																					
Kidsgrove 50 d																				13 32	
Crewe 65 d							12 28									12 56			13 29		
Sandbach d																13 03					
Holmes Chapel d																13 08					
Goostrey d																13 11					
Chelford d																13 15					
Alderley Edge d			12 19							12 51						13 19					
Wilmslow d			12 23				12 47			12 54						13 23			13 49		
Styal d										12 58											
Manchester Airport a										13 05											
Handforth d			12 26													13 26					
Congleton d																				13 39	
Macclesfield a		12 09				12 40								13 10	13 26					13 46	
d		12 10				12 42								13 11	13 28					13 47	
Prestbury d																				13 51	
Adlington (Cheshire) d																				13 54	
Poynton d																				13 57	
Bramhall d																				14 00	
Cheadle Hulme d			12 30													13 30				14 03	
Stockport a		12 22	12 37			12 55	12 58							13 28	13 41	13 37			14 00	14 08	
d	12 26	12 27	12 37		12 53	12 56	12 58		13 15			13 22	13 26	13 29	13 42	13 37		13 53	14 00	14 08	
Heaton Chapel d			12 41						13 18							13 41					
Levenshulme d			12 44						13 21							13 44					
Manchester Piccadilly a	12 35	12 40	12 57		13 06	13 08	13 15		13 29	13 31		13 33	13 37	13 40	13 53	13 55		14 06	14 19	14 21	
d	12 38			12 50				13 07			13 16	13 35	13 38				13 50				14 07
Manchester Oxford Road a	12 41			12 52				13 09			13 18	13 37	13 41				13 52				14 09
Deansgate a												13 40									

	NT G	VT	NT L	EM M	XC N	VT	NT	XC	NT C	TP O	VT	AW E	TP P	NT G	VT	NT	TP H	NT I	EM M	XC N	VT	NT
London Euston ⊖65 d		12 15				12 35					12 55				13 15						13 35	
Birmingham New Street 68 d					13 01			13 31												14 01		
Wolverhampton 68 d					13 19			13 49												14 19		
Stafford 65,68 d					13 34															14 34		
Stoke-on-Trent 50,68 d		13 50			13 57			14 21			14 26				14 50					14 57		
Longport 50 d																						
Kidsgrove 50 d																						
Crewe 65 d						14 13						14 28									15 13	14 56
Sandbach d																						15 03
Holmes Chapel d																						15 08
Goostrey d																						15 11
Chelford d																						15 15
Alderley Edge d							14 19									14 51						15 19
Wilmslow d						14 29	14 23					14 47				14 54					15 29	15 23
Styal d																14 58						
Manchester Airport a																15 04						
Handforth d							14 26															15 26
Congleton d																						
Macclesfield a					14 14						14 42									15 14		
d					14 15						14 42									15 15		
Prestbury d																						
Adlington (Cheshire) d																						
Poynton d																						
Bramhall d																						
Cheadle Hulme d							14 30															15 30
Stockport a		14 18			14 28	14 38	14 37				14 56	14 58			15 18					15 28	15 38	15 37
d	14 15	14 19	14 21	14 26	14 29	14 39	14 37			14 53	14 57	14 58		15 15	15 19			15 22	15 26	15 29	15 39	15 37
Heaton Chapel d	14 18						14 41							15 18								15 41
Levenshulme d	14 21						14 44							15 21								15 44
Manchester Piccadilly a	14 29	14 29	14 33	14 37	14 40	14 50	14 53	14 57		15 06	15 09	15 15		15 29	15 29	15 32		15 33	15 37	15 40	15 50	15 53
d			14 35	14 38					14 50				15 07				15 16	15 35	15 38			
Manchester Oxford Road a			14 37	14 41					14 52				15 09				15 18	15 37	15 41			
Deansgate a			14 40															15 40				

A From Nottingham to Liverpool Lime Street
B From Reading
C From Manchester Airport to Liverpool Lime Street
D From Cleethorpes to Manchester Airport
E From Cardiff Central
F From Scarborough to Liverpool Lime Street
G From Buxton
H From Manchester Airport to Barrow-in-Furness
I To Southport
J From Southampton Central
K From Carmarthen
L From Chester to Southport
M From Norwich to Liverpool Lime Street
N From Bournemouth
O From Doncaster to Manchester Airport
P From Middlesbrough to Liverpool Lime Street

Table 84

Sundays

1 July to 9 September

Stoke-on-Trent and Crewe - Manchester Airport, Stockport and Manchester

Network Diagram - see first Page of Table 78

	XC A	NT B	TP C	VT	AW D	TP E	NT F	VT	TP G	NT H	EM I	XC J	VT	NT	NT	XC K	NT B	TP C	VT	AW L	TP M
London Euston ⊖65 d				13 55				14 15					14 35						14 55		
Birmingham New Street 68 d	14 31											15 01				15 31					
Wolverhampton 68 d	14 49											15 19				15 49					
Stafford 65,68 d												15 34									
Stoke-on-Trent 50,68 d	15 21			15 26				15 50				15 57			16 01	16 21			16 25		
Longport 50 d																					
Kidsgrove 50 d															16 08						
Crewe 65 d					15 28								16 13							16 28	
Sandbach d																					
Holmes Chapel d																					
Goostrey d																					
Chelford d																					
Alderley Edge d														16 19							
Wilmslow d					15 47								16 29	16 23						16 47	
Styal d																					
Manchester Airport a																					
Handforth d														16 26							
Congleton d															16 15						
Macclesfield a				15 42								16 14			16 22				16 42		
d				15 42								16 15			16 23				16 42		
Prestbury d															16 27						
Adlington (Cheshire) d															16 30						
Poynton d															16 33						
Bramhall d															16 36						
Cheadle Hulme d														16 30	16 39						
Stockport a				15 56	15 58			16 18				16 28	16 38	16 37	16 44				16 56	16 58	
d			15 53	15 57	15 58		16 15	16 19		16 21	16 26	16 29	16 39	16 37	16 44			16 53	16 57	16 58	
Heaton Chapel d							16 18							16 41							
Levenshulme d							16 21							16 44							
Manchester Piccadilly a	15 59		16 06	16 09	16 15		16 29	16 29		16 33	16 37	16 40	16 50	16 53	16 58	16 59		17 06	17 09	17 15	
d		15 50				16 07			16 16	16 35	16 38						16 50				17 07
Manchester Oxford Road a		15 52				16 09			16 18	16 37	16 41						16 52				17 09
Deansgate a										16 40											

	NT F	VT	NT	NT N	EM I	XC J	VT	NT	XC K	NT B	TP C	VT	AW D	TP E	NT F	VT	TP O	NT H	EM P	XC J	VT	NT
London Euston ⊖65 d		15 15					15 35					15 55				16 15					16 35	
Birmingham New Street 68 d						16 01			16 31											17 01		
Wolverhampton 68 d						16 19			16 49											17 19		
Stafford 65,68 d						16 34														17 36		
Stoke-on-Trent 50,68 d		16 50				16 57			17 21			17 26				17 50				17 57		
Longport 50 d																						
Kidsgrove 50 d																						
Crewe 65 d							17 13	16 56					17 28								18 13	
Sandbach d								17 03														
Holmes Chapel d								17 08														
Goostrey d								17 11														
Chelford d								17 15														
Alderley Edge d			16 51					17 19														18 19
Wilmslow d			16 54				17 29	17 23					17 45								18 29	18 23
Styal d			16 58																			
Manchester Airport a			17 05																			
Handforth d								17 26														18 26
Congleton d																						
Macclesfield a						17 14						17 42								18 14		
d						17 15						17 42								18 15		
Prestbury d																						
Adlington (Cheshire) d																						
Poynton d																						
Bramhall d																						
Cheadle Hulme d								17 30														18 30
Stockport a		17 18				17 28	17 38	17 37				17 56	17 58			18 18				18 28	18 38	18 37
d	17 15	17 19		17 22	17 29	17 29	17 39	17 37			17 53	17 57	17 58		18 15	18 19		18 21	18 26	18 29	18 39	18 37
Heaton Chapel d	17 18							17 41							18 18							18 41
Levenshulme d	17 21							17 44							18 21							18 44
Manchester Piccadilly a	17 29	17 29	17 31	17 33	17 37	17 40	17 50	17 53	17 56		18 06	18 09	18 17		18 29	18 29		18 33	18 37	18 40	18 50	18 53
d				17 35	17 38					17 50				18 07			18 16	18 35	18 38			
Manchester Oxford Road a				17 37	17 41					17 52				18 09			18 18	18 37	18 41			
Deansgate a				17 40														18 40				

A From Paignton
B From Manchester Airport to Liverpool Lime Street
C From Cleethorpes to Manchester Airport
D From Milford Haven
E From Scarborough to Liverpool Lime Street
F From Buxton
G From Manchester Airport to Windermere
H From Chester to Southport
I From Nottingham to Liverpool Lime Street
J From Bournemouth
K From Plymouth
L From Cardiff Central
M From Middlesbrough to Liverpool Lime Street
N To Southport
O From Manchester Airport to Barrow-in-Furness
P From Norwich to Liverpool Lime Street

Table 84

Sundays

1 July to 9 September

Stoke-on-Trent and Crewe - Manchester Airport, Stockport and Manchester

Network Diagram - see first Page of Table 78

		NT	TP	VT	AW	TP		NT	VT	NT	TP	NT	EM	XC	VT	NT		XC	NT	TP	VT	AW	TP	NT	VT
			◇■	◇■	■	◇■			◇■		◇■		◇	◇■	◇■			◇■		◇■	◇■	■	◇■		◇■
		A	B		C	D		E			F	G	H	I				J	A	B		K	L	E	
				⊡	✕				⊡					✕	⊡						⊡	✕			⊡
London Euston ⊖65	d			16 55					17 15						17 35						17 55				18 15
Birmingham New Street 68	d													18 01				18 31							
Wolverhampton 68	d													18 19				18 49							
Stafford 65,68	d													18 36											
Stoke-on-Trent 50,68	d			18 26					18 50					18 56				19 21			19 26				19 50
Longport 50	d																								
Kidsgrove 50	d																								
Crewe 65	d				18 28										19 13	18 56						19 28			
Sandbach	d															19 03									
Holmes Chapel	d															19 08									
Goostrey	d															19 11									
Chelford	d															19 15									
Alderley Edge	d									18 51						19 19									
Wilmslow	d				18 47					18 54					19 29	19 23						19 47			
Styal	d									18 58															
Manchester Airport ✈	a									19 05															
Handforth	d															19 26									
Congleton	d																								
Macclesfield	a			18 42										19 14							19 42				
	d			18 42										19 14							19 42				
Prestbury	d																								
Adlington (Cheshire)	d																								
Poynton	d																								
Bramhall	d																								
Cheadle Hulme	d															19 30									
Stockport	a			18 56	18 58				19 18					19 28	19 38	19 37					19 56	19 58			20 18
	d		18 53	18 57	18 58			19 15	19 19			19 22	19 26	19 29	19 39	19 37				19 53	19 57	19 58		20 15	20 19
Heaton Chapel	d							19 18								19 41								20 18	
Levenshulme	d							19 21								19 44								20 21	
Manchester Piccadilly	a		19 06	19 09	19 15			19 29	19 29	19 31		19 33	19 37	19 40	19 50	19 53		19 58		20 09	20 09	20 17		20 29	20 29
	d	18 50				19 07					19 16	19 35	19 38						19 50				20 07		
Manchester Oxford Road	a	18 52				19 09					19 18	19 37	19 41						19 52				20 09		
Deansgate	a											19 40													

		NT		EM	XC	VT	NT	NT	XC	NT	TP	VT		AW	TP	NT	VT	NT	NT	EM	XC	VT		NT	XC
				◇	◇■	◇■			◇■		◇■	◇■		■	◇■		◇■			◇	◇■	◇■			◇■
		M		N	I				O	A	B			C	D	E			P	N	I				O
					✕	⊡			✕			⊡					⊡					⊡			✕
London Euston ⊖65	d					18 35						18 55					19 15					19 35			
Birmingham New Street 68	d				19 01				19 31												20 01				20 31
Wolverhampton 68	d				19 19				19 49												20 19				20 52
Stafford 65,68	d				19 38																20 37				
Stoke-on-Trent 50,68	d				19 57			20 01	20 21			20 26					20 50				20 57				21 21
Longport 50	d																								
Kidsgrove 50	d							20 08																	
Crewe 65	d					20 13								20 28								21 14		20 56	
Sandbach	d																							21 03	
Holmes Chapel	d																							21 08	
Goostrey	d																							21 11	
Chelford	d																							21 15	
Alderley Edge	d						20 19											20 51						21 19	
Wilmslow	d					20 29	20 23							20 46				20 54				21 30		21 23	
Styal	d																	20 58							
Manchester Airport ✈	a																	21 05							
Handforth	d						20 26																	21 26	
Congleton	d							20 15																	
Macclesfield	a				20 14			20 22				20 42									21 15				
	d				20 15			20 23				20 42									21 15				
Prestbury	d							20 27																	
Adlington (Cheshire)	d							20 30																	
Poynton	d							20 33																	
Bramhall	d							20 36																	
Cheadle Hulme	d						20 30	20 39																21 30	
Stockport	a				20 28	20 38	20 37	20 44				20 56		20 57			21 18				21 28	21 39		21 37	
	d	20 21		20 26	20 29	20 39	20 37	20 44			20 53	20 57		20 57		21 13	21 19		21 22	21 24	21 29	21 40		21 37	
Heaton Chapel	d						20 41									21 16								21 41	
Levenshulme	d						20 44									21 19								21 44	
Manchester Piccadilly	a	20 33		20 38	20 40	20 50	20 53	20 58	21 00		21 06	21 09		21 14		21 27	21 29	21 31	21 33	21 36	21 40	21 50		21 53	21 56
	d	20 35								20 50					21 07				21 35						
Manchester Oxford Road	a	20 37								20 52					21 09				21 37						
Deansgate	a	20 40																	21 40						

A From Manchester Airport to Liverpool Lime Street
B From Cleethorpes to Manchester Airport
C From Cardiff Central
D From Middlesbrough to Liverpool Lime Street
E From Buxton
F From Manchester Airport to Barrow-in-Furness
G To Southport
H From Norwich to Liverpool Lime Street
I From Bournemouth
J From Penzance
K From Milford Haven
L From Scarborough to Liverpool Lime Street
M From Chester to Southport
N From Norwich
O From Bristol Temple Meads
P To Wigan Wallgate

Table 84

Sundays

1 July to 9 September

Stoke-on-Trent and Crewe - Manchester Airport, Stockport and Manchester

Network Diagram - see first Page of Table 78

		NT	TP	VT	AW	TP	NT	VT		NT	XC	NT	VT	NT	NT	NT	NT	NT		XC	NT	VT	VT	VT
			◇■	◇■	■	◇■		◇■			◇■		◇■							◇■		◇■	◇■	◇■
		A	B		C	D	E			F	G			A	E		H			G				I
				⊡	✕			⊡					⊡									⊡	⊡	⊡
London Euston ⊖65	d			19 55				20 15					20 35									21 25	21 51	23 30
Birmingham New Street 68	d										21 01									22 01				
Wolverhampton 68	d										21 19									22 19				
Stafford 65,68	d										21 37		22 00							22 37			23s53	
Stoke-on-Trent 50,68	d			21 26				21 50			21 57							22 39		22 57		23 29		00s53
Longport 50	d																							
Kidsgrove 50	d																	22 46						
Crewe 65	d				21 28								22 21								22 56		00s21	
Sandbach	d																				23 03			
Holmes Chapel	d																				23 08			
Goostrey	d																				23 11			
Chelford	d																				23 15			
Alderley Edge	d											22 19				22 51					23 19			
Wilmslow	d				21 45							22 23	22 36			22 54					23 23			
Styal	d															22 58								
Manchester Airport ✈	a															23 05								
Handforth	d											22 26									23 26			
Congleton	d																	22 53						
Macclesfield	a			21 42							22 14							23 00		23 12		23 45		01s10
	d			21 42							22 15							23 01		23 13		23 46		
Prestbury	d																	23 05						
Adlington (Cheshire)	d																	23 08						
Poynton	d																	23 11						
Bramhall	d																	23 14						
Cheadle Hulme	d											22 30						23 17			23 30			
Stockport	a			21 56	21 58			22 18			22 28	22 37	22 45					23 22		23 27	23 35	23 59	00s50	01s24
	d		21 53	21 57	21 58		22 13	22 19		22 21	22 29	22 37	22 46		23 13		23 16	23 23		23 28	23 37	00 01		
Heaton Chapel	d						22 16					22 41			23 16						23 41			
Levenshulme	d						22 19					22 44			23 19						23 44			
Manchester Piccadilly	a		22 06	22 09	22 19		22 27	22 29		22 33	22 40	22 53	22 57		23 27	23 29	23 29	23 37		23 41	23 53	00 12	01 00	01 37
	d	21 50				22 07				22 35				22 41										
Manchester Oxford Road	a	21 52				22 09				22 37				22 43										
Deansgate	a									22 40				22 47										

Sundays

16 September to 30 September

		NT	XC	NT	NT	TP	AW	NT	NT	NT		NT	TP	NT	TP	AW	NT	NT	XC	VT		NT	VT	AW	NT
			◇■			◇■							◇■		◇■				◇■	◇■			◇■	◇	
				J	K	L		A	E	K			M	A	N		E	O						P	
																			✕	⊡			⊡		
London Euston ⊖65	d																			08 10			08 20		
Birmingham New Street 68	d		22p31																09 01						
Wolverhampton 68	d		22p49																09 19						
Stafford 65,68	d		23p02																09 33						
Stoke-on-Trent 50,68	d		23p21																				10 21		
Longport 50	d																								
Kidsgrove 50	d																								
Crewe 65	d	23p12					08 28									09 28			09 56	10 19				10 28	
Sandbach	d	23p19																							
Holmes Chapel	d	23p24																							
Goostrey	d	23p27																							
Chelford	d	23p31																							
Alderley Edge	d	23p35										09 19										10 19			
Wilmslow	d	23p39					08 48					09 23				09 47			10 13	10 34		10 23		10 47	
Styal	d																								
Manchester Airport ✈	a																								
Handforth	d	23p42										09 26										10 26			
Congleton	d																								
Macclesfield	a		23p38																				10 36		
	d		23p39																				10 38		10 44
Prestbury	d																								10 48
Adlington (Cheshire)	d																								10 51
Poynton	d																								10 54
Bramhall	d																								10 57
Cheadle Hulme	d	23p46										09 30										10 30			11 00
Stockport	a	23p51	23p53									09 38							10 21	10 43		10 35	10 50	10 58	11 05
	d	23p51	23p54	00 02	08 24	08 31			09 10	09 22		09 40			09 53		10 04	10 12	10 22	10 44		10 39	10 52	10 58	11 05
Heaton Chapel	d	23p55							09 13			09 44					10 08					10 43			
Levenshulme	d	23p58							09 16			09 47					10 11					10 46			
Manchester Piccadilly	a	00 07	00 10	00 15	08 33	08 42	09 11		09 23	09 33		09 54			10 01	10 11	10 21	10 22	10 31	10 55		10 56	11 03	11 12	11 17
	d				08 35			08 49		09 35			09 46	09 50				10 24							
Manchester Oxford Road	a				08 37			08 51		09 37			09 48	09 52				10 26							
Deansgate	a				08 40			08 54		09 40			09 51					10 40							

A From Manchester Airport to Liverpool Lime Street
B From Cleethorpes to Manchester Airport
C From Milford Haven
D From Scarborough to Liverpool Lime Street
E From Buxton
F From Chester to Wigan Wallgate
G From Bournemouth
H From Sheffield
I 29 July, 5 August, 12 August, 2 September, 9 September
J From Chester
K To Southport
L From Sheffield to Manchester Airport
M From Manchester Airport to Barrow-in-Furness
N From Meadowhall
O From Chester to Southport
P From Shrewsbury

Stoke-on-Trent and Crewe - Manchester Airport, Stockport and Manchester

Network Diagram - see first Page of Table 78

		NT	NT	NT	NT	XC	EM	NT	AW	VT	NT	TP	NT	NT	NT	EM	XC	NT	TP	VT	AW	NT	NT
		A		B	C	◇■ ✕	◇ D		◇ E ✕	◇■ ⊡	A	◇■ F	B	G	H	◇ D	◇■ I ✕		◇■ F	◇■ ⊡	◇ E ✕	A	B
London Euston ⊖65	d									09 20										10 20			
Birmingham New Street 68	d					10 01											11 01						
Wolverhampton 68	d					10 19											11 19						
Stafford 65,68	d					10 33											11 32						
Stoke-on-Trent 50,68	d					10 52				11 22							11 52			12 25			
Longport 50	d																						
Kidsgrove 50	d																						
Crewe 65	d							10 56	11 23												12 29		
Sandbach	d							11 03															
Holmes Chapel	d							11 08															
Goostrey	d							11 11															
Chelford	d							11 15															
Alderley Edge	d		10 40					11 19										12 17					
Wilmslow	d		10 43					11 23	11 42									12 21			12 47		
Styal	d		10 47																				
Manchester Airport ✈	a		10 55																				
Handforth	d							11 26										12 24					
Congleton	d																						
Macclesfield	a					11 08				11 37							12 09			12 40			
	d					11 09				11 38							12 10			12 42			
Prestbury	d																						
Adlington (Cheshire)	d																						
Poynton	d																						
Bramhall	d																						
Cheadle Hulme	d							11 30										12 28					
Stockport	a					11 22		11 37		11 51							12 22	12 33		12 55	12 58		
	d			11 14	11 15	11 23	11 26	11 37		11 53		11 53	12 13		12 21	12 26	12 27	12 33	12 50	12 56	12 58		13 15
Heaton Chapel	d				11 19			11 41					12 17					12 37					13 18
Levenshulme	d				11 22			11 44					12 20					12 40					13 21
Manchester Piccadilly	a		11 25	11 25	11 28	11 31	11 37	11 53	12 02	12 04		12 06	12 27		12 31	12 37	12 40	12 48	13 03	13 08	13 12		13 29
	d	10 50	11 27		11 33		11 38				11 50			12 29	12 35	12 38						12 50	
Manchester Oxford Road	a	10 52	11 31		11 35		11 41				11 52			12 33	12 37	12 41						12 52	
Deansgate	a				11 40										12 40								

		NT	NT	EM	XC	VT	NT	NT	TP	AW	NT	NT	VT	NT	EM	XC	VT	NT	XC	NT	TP	VT
			C	◇ D	◇■ J ✕	◇■ ⊡		A	◇■ F	◇ E ✕		B	◇■ ⊡	H	◇ D	◇■ K ✕	◇■ ⊡		◇■ ✕	A	◇■ L	◇■ ⊡
London Euston ⊖65	d					11 20							12 17				12 37					12 57
Birmingham New Street 68	d				12 01											13 01			13 31			
Wolverhampton 68	d				12 19											13 19			13 49			
Stafford 65,68	d				12 33											13 34						
Stoke-on-Trent 50,68	d				12 54	13 11					13 25		13 50			13 57			14 21			14 26
Longport 50	d																					
Kidsgrove 50	d										13 32											
Crewe 65	d						12 56			13 29							14 13					
Sandbach	d						13 03															
Holmes Chapel	d						13 08															
Goostrey	d						13 11															
Chelford	d						13 15															
Alderley Edge	d	12 51					13 19											14 19				
Wilmslow	d	12 54					13 23			13 49							14 29	14 23				
Styal	d	12 58																				
Manchester Airport ✈	a	13 05																				
Handforth	d						13 26											14 26				
Congleton	d										13 39											
Macclesfield	a				13 10	13 26					13 46					14 14						14 42
	d				13 11	13 28					13 47					14 15						14 42
Prestbury	d										13 51											
Adlington (Cheshire)	d										13 54											
Poynton	d										13 57											
Bramhall	d										14 00											
Cheadle Hulme	d						13 30				14 03							14 30				
Stockport	a				13 28	13 41	13 37			14 00	14 08		14 18			14 28	14 38	14 37				14 56
	d		13 22	13 26	13 29	13 42	13 37		13 53	14 00	14 08	14 15	14 19	14 21	14 26	14 29	14 39	14 37			14 53	14 57
Heaton Chapel	d						13 41					14 18						14 41				
Levenshulme	d						13 44					14 21						14 44				
Manchester Piccadilly	a	13 31	13 33	13 37	13 40	13 53	13 55		14 06	14 19	14 21	14 29	14 29	14 33	14 37	14 40	14 50	14 53	14 57		15 06	15 09
	d		13 35	13 38				13 50						14 35	14 38					14 50		
Manchester Oxford Road	a		13 37	13 41				13 52						14 37	14 41					14 52		
Deansgate	a		13 40											14 40								

A From Manchester Airport to Liverpool Lime Street
B From Buxton
C To Southport
D From Nottingham to Liverpool Lime Street
E From Cardiff Central
F From Cleethorpes to Manchester Airport
G From Manchester Airport
H From Chester to Southport
I From Reading
J From Southampton Central
K From Bournemouth
L From Doncaster to Manchester Airport

Stoke-on-Trent and Crewe - Manchester Airport, Stockport and Manchester

Network Diagram - see first Page of Table 78

		AW	NT	VT	NT	TP	NT	EM	XC	VT	NT	XC	NT	TP	VT	AW	NT	VT	NT	EM	XC	VT	NT
		◇ A ✕	B	◇■ ⊡		◇■ C	D	◇ E	◇■ F ✕	◇■ ⊡		◇■ ✕	G	◇■ H	◇■ ⊡	◇ I ✕	B	◇■ ⊡	J	◇ K	◇■ F ✕	◇■ ⊡	
London Euston ⊖65	d			13 17						13 37					13 57			14 17				14 37	
Birmingham New Street 68	d								14 01			14 31									15 01		
Wolverhampton 68	d								14 19			14 49									15 19		
Stafford 65,68	d								14 34												15 34		
Stoke-on-Trent 50,68	d			14 50					14 56			15 21			15 26			15 50			15 57		
Longport 50	d																						
Kidsgrove 50	d																						
Crewe 65	d	14 28								15 13	14 56					15 28						16 13	
Sandbach	d										15 03												
Holmes Chapel	d										15 08												
Goostrey	d										15 11												
Chelford	d										15 15												
Alderley Edge	d				14 51						15 19												16 19
Wilmslow	d	14 47			14 54					15 29	15 23					15 47						16 29	16 23
Styal	d				14 58																		
Manchester Airport ✈	a				15 04																		
Handforth	d										15 26												16 26
Congleton	d																						
Macclesfield	a								15 13						15 42						16 14		
	d								15 14						15 42						16 15		
Prestbury	d																						
Adlington (Cheshire)	d																						
Poynton	d																						
Bramhall	d																						
Cheadle Hulme	d										15 30												16 30
Stockport	a	14 58		15 18					15 27	15 38	15 37				15 56	15 58		16 18			16 28	16 38	16 37
	d	14 58	15 15	15 19			15 22	15 26	15 28	15 39	15 37			15 53	15 57	15 58	16 15	16 19	16 21	16 26	16 29	16 39	16 37
Heaton Chapel	d		15 18								15 41						16 18						16 41
Levenshulme	d		15 21								15 44						16 21						16 44
Manchester Piccadilly	a	15 15	15 29	15 29	15 32		15 33	15 37	15 39	15 50	15 53	15 59		16 06	16 09	16 15	16 29	16 29	16 33	16 37	16 40	16 50	16 53
	d					15 16	15 35	15 38					15 50						16 35	16 38			
Manchester Oxford Road	a					15 18	15 37	15 41					15 52						16 37	16 41			
Deansgate	a						15 40												16 40				

		NT	XC	NT	TP	VT	AW	NT	VT	NT	NT	EM	XC	VT	NT	XC	NT	TP	VT	AW	NT	VT
			◇■ ✕	G	◇■ H	◇■ ⊡	■ A ✕	B	◇■ ⊡		D	◇ K	◇■ F ✕	◇■ ⊡		◇■ ✕	G	◇■ H	◇■ ⊡	■ L ✕	B	◇■ ⊡
London Euston ⊖65	d					14 57			15 17					15 37					15 57			16 17
Birmingham New Street 68	d		15 31										16 01			16 31						
Wolverhampton 68	d		15 49										16 19			16 49						
Stafford 65,68	d												16 34									
Stoke-on-Trent 50,68	d	16 01	16 21			16 25			16 50				16 57			17 21			17 26			17 50
Longport 50	d																					
Kidsgrove 50	d	16 08																				
Crewe 65	d						16 28							17 13	16 56					17 28		
Sandbach	d														17 03							
Holmes Chapel	d														17 08							
Goostrey	d														17 11							
Chelford	d														17 15							
Alderley Edge	d									16 51					17 19							
Wilmslow	d						16 47			16 54				17 29	17 23					17 45		
Styal	d									16 58												
Manchester Airport ✈	a									17 05												
Handforth	d														17 26							
Congleton	d	16 15																				
Macclesfield	a	16 22				16 42							17 14						17 42			
	d	16 23				16 42							17 15						17 42			
Prestbury	d	16 27																				
Adlington (Cheshire)	d	16 30																				
Poynton	d	16 33																				
Bramhall	d	16 36																				
Cheadle Hulme	d	16 39													17 30							
Stockport	a	16 44				16 56	16 58		17 18				17 28	17 38	17 37				17 56	17 58		18 18
	d	16 44			16 53	16 57	16 58	17 15	17 19		17 22	17 29	17 29	17 39	17 37			17 53	17 57	17 58	18 15	18 19
Heaton Chapel	d							17 18							17 41						18 18	
Levenshulme	d							17 21							17 44						18 21	
Manchester Piccadilly	a	16 58	16 59		17 06	17 09	17 15	17 29	17 29	17 31	17 33	17 37	17 40	17 50	17 53	17 56		18 06	18 09	18 17	18 29	18 29
	d			16 50							17 35	17 38					17 50					
Manchester Oxford Road	a			16 52							17 37	17 41					17 52					
Deansgate	a										17 40											

A From Cardiff Central
B From Buxton
C From Manchester Airport to Barrow-in-Furness
D To Southport
E From Norwich to Liverpool Lime Street
F From Bournemouth
G From Manchester Airport to Liverpool Lime Street
H From Cleethorpes to Manchester Airport
I From Carmarthen
J From Chester to Southport
K From Nottingham to Liverpool Lime Street
L From Milford Haven

Stoke-on-Trent and Crewe - Manchester Airport, Stockport and Manchester

Network Diagram - see first Page of Table 78

	TP	NT	EM	XC	VT	NT	XC	NT	TP	VT	AW	NT	VT	NT	TP	NT	EM	XC	VT	NT	XC	NT
	◇■ A ✠	B	◇ C	◇■ D ✠	◇■ ⊏		◇■ ✠	E	◇■ F	◇■ ⊏	■ G ✠	H	◇■ ⊏		◇■ A	I	◇ C	◇■ D ✠	◇■ ⊏		◇■ ✠	E
London Euston ⊖65 d					16 37					16 57			17 17						17 37			
Birmingham New Street 68 d				17 01			17 31											18 01			18 31	
Wolverhampton 68 ⇌ d				17 19			17 49											18 19			18 49	
Stafford 65,68 d				17 36														18 36				
Stoke-on-Trent 50,68 d				17 57			18 21			18 26			18 50					18 57			19 21	
Longport 50 d																						
Kidsgrove 50 d																						
Crewe 65 d					18 13						18 28								19 13	18 56		
Sandbach d																				19 03		
Holmes Chapel d																				19 08		
Goostrey d																				19 11		
Chelford d																				19 15		
Alderley Edge d						18 19								18 51						19 19		
Wilmslow d					18 29	18 23					18 47			18 54					19 29	19 23		
Styal d														18 58								
Manchester Airport ✈ a														19 05								
Handforth d						18 26														19 26		
Congleton d																						
Macclesfield a				18 14						18 42								19 15				
d				18 15						18 42								19 15				
Prestbury d																						
Adlington (Cheshire) d																						
Poynton d																						
Bramhall d																						
Cheadle Hulme d						18 30														19 30		
Stockport a				18 28	18 38	18 37				18 56	18 58		19 18					19 28	19 38	19 37		
d		18 21	18 26	18 29	18 39	18 37			18 53	18 57	18 58	19 15	19 19			19 22	19 26	19 29	19 39	19 37		
Heaton Chapel d						18 41						19 18								19 41		
Levenshulme d						18 44						19 21								19 44		
Manchester Piccadilly ⇌ a		18 33	18 37	18 40	18 50	18 53	18 56		19 06	19 09	19 15	19 29	19 29	19 31		19 33	19 37	19 40	19 50	19 53	19 58	
d	18 16	18 35	18 38					18 50							19 16	19 35	19 38					19 50
Manchester Oxford Road a	18 18	18 37	18 41					18 52							19 18	19 37	19 41					19 52
Deansgate ⇌ a		18 40														19 40						

	TP	VT	AW	NT	VT	NT	EM	XC	VT	NT	NT	XC	NT	TP	VT	AW	NT	VT	NT	NT	EM	XC
	◇■ F	◇■ ⊏	■ J ✠	H	◇■ ⊏	B	◇ K	◇■ D ✠	◇■ ⊏			◇■ ✠	E	◇■ F	◇■ ⊏	■ G	H	◇■ ⊏		L	◇ K	◇■ D
London Euston ⊖65 d		17 57			18 17				18 37						18 57			19 17				
Birmingham New Street 68 d								19 01				19 31										20 01
Wolverhampton 68 ⇌ d								19 19				19 49										20 19
Stafford 65,68 d								19 38														20 37
Stoke-on-Trent 50,68 d		19 26			19 50			19 57			20 01	20 21			20 26			20 50				20 57
Longport 50 d																						
Kidsgrove 50 d											20 08											
Crewe 65 d			19 28						20 13							20 28						
Sandbach d																						
Holmes Chapel d																						
Goostrey d																						
Chelford d																						
Alderley Edge d										20 19									20 51			
Wilmslow d			19 47						20 29	20 23						20 46			20 54			
Styal d																			20 58			
Manchester Airport ✈ a																			21 05			
Handforth d										20 26												
Congleton d											20 15											
Macclesfield a		19 42						20 14			20 22				20 42							21 15
d		19 42						20 15			20 23				20 42							21 15
Prestbury d											20 27											
Adlington (Cheshire) d											20 30											
Poynton d											20 33											
Bramhall d											20 36											
Cheadle Hulme d										20 30	20 39											
Stockport a		19 56	19 58		20 18			20 28	20 38	20 37	20 44				20 56	20 57		21 18				21 28
d	19 53	19 57	19 58	20 15	20 19	20 21	20 26	20 29	20 39	20 37	20 44			20 53	20 57	20 57	21 13	21 19		21 22	21 24	21 29
Heaton Chapel d				20 18						20 41							21 16					
Levenshulme d				20 21						20 44							21 19					
Manchester Piccadilly ⇌ a	20 09	20 09	20 17	20 29	20 29	20 33	20 38	20 40	20 50	20 53	20 58	21 00		21 06	21 09	21 14	21 27	21 29	21 31	21 33	21 36	21 40
d						20 35							20 50							21 35		
Manchester Oxford Road a						20 37							20 52							21 37		
Deansgate ⇌ a						20 40														21 40		

A From Manchester Airport to Barrow-in-Furness
B From Chester to Southport
C From Norwich to Liverpool Lime Street
D From Bournemouth
E From Manchester Airport to Liverpool Lime Street
F From Cleethorpes to Manchester Airport
G From Cardiff Central
H From Buxton
I To Southport
J From Milford Haven
K From Norwich
L To Wigan Wallgate

Stoke-on-Trent and Crewe - Manchester Airport, Stockport and Manchester

Network Diagram - see first Page of Table 78

	VT	NT	XC	NT	TP	VT	AW	NT	VT	NT	XC	NT	VT	NT	NT	NT	NT	NT	XC	NT	VT
	◇■ ⊏		◇■	A	◇■ B	◇■ ⊏	■ C ✠	D	◇■ ⊏	E	◇■ F		◇■ ⊏	A	D		G		◇■ F		◇■ ⊏
London Euston ⊖65 d	19 37					19 57			20 15				20 35								21 25
Birmingham New Street 68 d			20 31								21 01								22 01		
Wolverhampton 68 ⇌ d			20 52								21 19								22 19		
Stafford 65,68 d											21 37		22 00						22 37		
Stoke-on-Trent 50,68 d			21 21			21 26			21 50		21 57							22 39	22 57		23 29
Longport 50 d																					
Kidsgrove 50 d																		22 46			
Crewe 65 d	21 14	20 56					21 28						22 21							22 56	
Sandbach d		21 03																		23 03	
Holmes Chapel d		21 08																		23 08	
Goostrey d		21 11																		23 11	
Chelford d		21 15																		23 15	
Alderley Edge d		21 19										22 19				22 51				23 19	
Wilmslow d	21 30	21 23					21 45					22 23	22 36			22 54				23 23	
Styal d																22 58					
Manchester Airport ✈ a																23 05					
Handforth d		21 26										22 26								23 26	
Congleton d																		22 53			
Macclesfield a						21 42					22 14							23 00	23 12		23 45
d						21 42					22 15							23 01	23 13		23 46
Prestbury d																		23 05			
Adlington (Cheshire) d																		23 08			
Poynton d																		23 11			
Bramhall d																		23 14			
Cheadle Hulme d		21 30										22 30						23 17		23 30	
Stockport a	21 39	21 37				21 56	21 58		22 18		22 28	22 37	22 45					23 22	23 27	23 35	23 59
d	21 40	21 37			21 53	21 57	21 58	22 13	22 19	22 21	22 29	22 37	22 46		23 13		23 16	23 23	23 28	23 37	00 01
Heaton Chapel d		21 41						22 16				22 41			23 16					23 41	
Levenshulme d		21 44						22 19				22 44			23 19					23 44	
Manchester Piccadilly ⇌ a	21 50	21 53	21 56		22 06	22 09	22 19	22 27	22 29	22 33	22 40	22 53	22 57		23 27	23 29	23 29	23 37	23 41	23 53	00 12
d				21 50						22 35				22 41							
Manchester Oxford Road a				21 52						22 37				22 43							
Deansgate ⇌ a										22 40				22 47							

	VT
	◇■ ⊏
London Euston ⊖65 d	21 51
Birmingham New Street 68 d	
Wolverhampton 68 ⇌ d	
Stafford 65,68 d	23s53
Stoke-on-Trent 50,68 d	
Longport 50 d	
Kidsgrove 50 d	
Crewe 65 d	00s21
Sandbach d	
Holmes Chapel d	
Goostrey d	
Chelford d	
Alderley Edge d	
Wilmslow d	
Styal d	
Manchester Airport ✈ a	
Handforth d	
Congleton d	
Macclesfield a	
d	
Prestbury d	
Adlington (Cheshire) d	
Poynton d	
Bramhall d	
Cheadle Hulme d	
Stockport a	00s50
d	
Heaton Chapel d	
Levenshulme d	
Manchester Piccadilly ⇌ a	01 00
d	
Manchester Oxford Road a	
Deansgate ⇌ a	

A From Manchester Airport to Liverpool Lime Street
B From Cleethorpes to Manchester Airport
C From Milford Haven
D From Buxton
E From Chester to Wigan Wallgate
F From Bournemouth
G From Sheffield

Stoke-on-Trent and Crewe - Manchester Airport, Stockport and Manchester

Network Diagram - see first Page of Table 78

	NT	XC	NT	TP	AW	NT	NT	NT	NT		TP	NT	TP	AW	NT	NT	XC	VT	NT		VT	VT	AW	NT
		◇1	A	◇1 B		C	D	E			◇1 F	C	◇1 G		D	H	◇1	◇1			◇1 I	◇1 J	◇ K	
London Euston ⊖65 d																		08 10			08 20	08 20		
Birmingham New Street 68 d		22p31															09 01							
Wolverhampton 68 d		22p49															09 19							
Stafford 65,68 d		23p02															09 33							
Stoke-on-Trent 50,68 d		23p21																			10 21	10 23		
Longport 50 d																								
Kidsgrove 50 d																								
Crewe 65 d	23p12				08 28									09 28			09 56	10 19					10 28	
Sandbach d	23p19																							
Holmes Chapel d	23p24																							
Goostrey d	23p27																							
Chelford d	23p31																							
Alderley Edge d	23p35								09 19										10 19					
Wilmslow d	23p39				08 48				09 23					09 47			10 13	10 34	10 23				10 47	
Styal d																								
Manchester Airport a																								
Handforth d	23p42								09 26										10 26					
Congleton d																								
Macclesfield a		23p38																			10 36	10 39		
d		23p39																			10 38	10 40		10 44
Prestbury d																								10 48
Adlington (Cheshire) d																								10 51
Poynton d																								10 54
Bramhall d																								10 57
Cheadle Hulme d	23p46								09 30										10 30					11 00
Stockport a	23p51	23p53							09 38								10 21	10 43	10 35		10 50	10 52	10 58	11 05
d	23p51	23p54	00 02	08 31			09 08	09 22	09 40				09 53		10 04	10 12	10 22	10 44	10 39		10 52	10 53	10 58	11 05
Heaton Chapel d	23p55						09 12		09 44						10 08				10 43					
Levenshulme d	23p58						09 15		09 47						10 11				10 46					
Manchester Piccadilly a	00 07	00 10	00 15	08 42	09 11		09 23	09 33	09 54				10 01	10 11	10 21	10 22	10 31	10 55	10 56		11 03	11 05	11 12	11 17
d						08 49		09 35			09 46	09 50				10 24								
Manchester Oxford Road a						08 51		09 37			09 48	09 52				10 26								
Deansgate a						08 54		09 40			09 51					10 40								

	NT	NT	NT	NT	XC		EM	NT	AW	VT	NT	TP	NT	NT	NT		XC	EM	XC	NT	TP	VT	AW	NT
	C	D		E	◇1		◇ L		◇ M	◇1	C	◇1 N	D	O	H		◇1 P	◇ L	◇1 Q		◇1 N	◇1	◇ M	C
London Euston ⊖65 d										09 20												10 20		
Birmingham New Street 68 d					10 01												11 01		11 01					
Wolverhampton 68 d					10 19												11 19		11 19					
Stafford 65,68 d					10 33												11 32		11 32					
Stoke-on-Trent 50,68 d					10 52					11 22							11 52		11 52			12 25		
Longport 50 d																								
Kidsgrove 50 d																								
Crewe 65 d								10 56	11 23														12 29	
Sandbach d								11 03																
Holmes Chapel d								11 08																
Goostrey d								11 11																
Chelford d								11 15																
Alderley Edge d			10 40					11 19												12 17				
Wilmslow d			10 43					11 23	11 42											12 21			12 47	
Styal d			10 47																					
Manchester Airport a			10 55																					
Handforth d								11 26												12 24				
Congleton d																								
Macclesfield a					11 08					11 37							12 09		12 09			12 40		
d					11 09					11 38							12 10		12 10			12 42		
Prestbury d																								
Adlington (Cheshire) d																								
Poynton d																								
Bramhall d																								
Cheadle Hulme d								11 30												12 28				
Stockport a					11 22			11 37		11 51							12 22		12 22	12 33		12 55	12 58	
d		11 11		11 15	11 23		11 26	11 37		11 53		11 53	12 11		12 21		12 26	12 26	12 27	12 33	12 50	12 56	12 58	
Heaton Chapel d				11 19				11 41					12 15							12 37				
Levenshulme d				11 22				11 44					12 18							12 40				
Manchester Piccadilly a		11 23	11 25	11 28	11 31		11 37	11 53	12 02	12 04		12 06	12 25		12 31		12 34	12 37	12 40	12 48	13 03	13 08	13 12	
d	10 50		11 27	11 33			11 38				11 50			12 29	12 35			12 38						12 50
Manchester Oxford Road a	10 52		11 31	11 35			11 41				11 52			12 33	12 37			12 41						12 52
Deansgate a				11 40											12 40									

A From Chester
B From Sheffield to Manchester Airport
C From Manchester Airport to Liverpool Lime Street
D From Buxton
E To Southport
F From Manchester Airport to Barrow-in-Furness
G From Meadowhall
H From Chester to Southport
I from 7 October until 21 October
J from 28 October
K From Shrewsbury
L From Nottingham to Liverpool Lime Street
M From Cardiff Central
N From Cleethorpes to Manchester Airport
O From Manchester Airport
P from 28 October. From Reading
Q from 7 October until 21 October. From Reading

Stoke-on-Trent and Crewe - Manchester Airport, Stockport and Manchester

Network Diagram - see first Page of Table 78

	NT		NT	NT	EM	XC	VT	NT	NT	TP	AW		NT	NT	VT	NT	EM	XC	VT	NT	XC		NT	TP
	A			B	◇ C	◇1 D	◇1		E	◇1 F	◇ G			A	◇1	H	◇ C	◇1 I	◇1		◇1		E	◇1 J
London Euston ⊖65 d							11 20								12 17				12 37					
Birmingham New Street 68 d						12 01												13 01			13 31			
Wolverhampton 68 d						12 19												13 19			13 49			
Stafford 65,68 d						12 33												13 34						
Stoke-on-Trent 50,68 d						12 54	13 11						13 25		13 50			13 57			14 21			
Longport 50 d																								
Kidsgrove 50 d													13 32											
Crewe 65 d								12 56			13 29								14 13					
Sandbach d								13 03																
Holmes Chapel d								13 08																
Goostrey d								13 11																
Chelford d								13 15																
Alderley Edge d			12 51					13 19												14 19				
Wilmslow d			12 54					13 23			13 49								14 29	14 23				
Styal d			12 58																					
Manchester Airport a			13 05																					
Handforth d								13 26												14 26				
Congleton d													13 39											
Macclesfield a						13 10	13 26						13 46					14 14						
d						13 11	13 28						13 47					14 15						
Prestbury d													13 51											
Adlington (Cheshire) d													13 54											
Poynton d													13 57											
Bramhall d													14 00											
Cheadle Hulme d								13 30					14 03							14 30				
Stockport a						13 28	13 41	13 37			14 00		14 08		14 18			14 28	14 38	14 37				
d	13 12			13 22	13 26	13 29	13 42	13 37		13 53	14 00		14 08	14 12	14 19	14 21	14 26	14 29	14 39	14 37				14 53
Heaton Chapel d	13 16							13 41						14 16						14 41				
Levenshulme d	13 19							13 44						14 19						14 44				
Manchester Piccadilly a	13 27		13 31	13 33	13 37	13 40	13 53	13 55		14 06	14 19		14 21	14 27	14 29	14 33	14 37	14 40	14 50	14 53	14 57			15 06
d				13 35	13 38				13 50							14 35	14 38						14 50	
Manchester Oxford Road a				13 37	13 41				13 52							14 37	14 41						14 52	
Deansgate a				13 40												14 40								

	VT	AW	NT	VT	NT	TP	NT		EM	XC	VT	NT	XC	NT	TP	VT	AW		NT	VT	NT	EM	XC	VT
	◇1	◇ G	A	◇1		◇1 K	B		◇ L	◇1 I	◇1		◇1	E	◇1 F	◇1	◇ M		A	◇1	H	◇ C	◇1 I	◇1
London Euston ⊖65 d	12 57			13 17							13 37					13 57				14 17				14 37
Birmingham New Street 68 d										14 01			14 31										15 01	
Wolverhampton 68 d										14 19			14 49										15 19	
Stafford 65,68 d										14 34													15 34	
Stoke-on-Trent 50,68 d	14 26			14 50						14 56			15 21			15 26				15 50			15 57	
Longport 50 d																								
Kidsgrove 50 d																								
Crewe 65 d		14 28									15 13	14 56					15 28							16 13
Sandbach d												15 03												
Holmes Chapel d												15 08												
Goostrey d												15 11												
Chelford d												15 15												
Alderley Edge d					14 51							15 19												
Wilmslow d		14 47			14 54						15 29	15 23					15 47							16 29
Styal d					14 58																			
Manchester Airport a					15 04																			
Handforth d												15 26												
Congleton d																								
Macclesfield a	14 42									15 13						15 42							16 14	
d	14 42									15 14						15 42							16 15	
Prestbury d																								
Adlington (Cheshire) d																								
Poynton d																								
Bramhall d																								
Cheadle Hulme d												15 30												
Stockport a	14 56	14 58		15 18						15 27	15 38	15 37				15 56	15 58			16 18			16 28	16 38
d	14 57	14 58	15 12	15 19			15 22		15 26	15 28	15 39	15 37			15 53	15 57	15 58		16 12	16 19	16 21	16 26	16 29	16 39
Heaton Chapel d			15 16									15 41							16 16					
Levenshulme d			15 19									15 44							16 19					
Manchester Piccadilly a	15 09	15 15	15 27	15 29	15 32		15 33		15 37	15 39	15 50	15 53	15 59		16 06	16 09	16 15		16 27	16 29	16 33	16 37	16 40	16 50
d						15 16	15 35		15 38					15 50							16 35	16 38		
Manchester Oxford Road a						15 18	15 37		15 41					15 52							16 37	16 41		
Deansgate a							15 40														16 40			

A From Buxton
B To Southport
C From Nottingham to Liverpool Lime Street
D From Southampton Central
E From Manchester Airport to Liverpool Lime Street
F From Cleethorpes to Manchester Airport
G From Cardiff Central
H From Chester to Southport
I From Bournemouth
J From Doncaster to Manchester Airport
K From Manchester Airport to Barrow-in-Furness
L From Norwich to Liverpool Lime Street
M From Carmarthen

Stoke-on-Trent and Crewe - Manchester Airport, Stockport and Manchester

Sundays from 7 October

Network Diagram - see first Page of Table 78

	NT	NT	XC ◇1 A	NT B	TP ◇1 C	VT ◇1	AW D	NT E	VT ◇1	NT	NT F	EM ◇ G	XC ◇1 H	VT ◇1	NT	XC ◇1 I	NT B	TP ◇1 C	VT ◇1	AW J	NT E
London Euston 15 ⊖65 d						14 57			15 17					15 37					15 57		
Birmingham New Street 12 68 d			15 31										16 01			16 31					
Wolverhampton 7 68 d			15 49										16 19			16 49					
Stafford 65,68 d													16 34								
Stoke-on-Trent 50,68 d		16 01	16 21			16 25			16 50				16 57			17 21			17 26		
Longport 50 d																					
Kidsgrove 50 d		16 08																			
Crewe 10 65 d							16 28							17 13	16 56					17 28	
Sandbach d															17 03						
Holmes Chapel d															17 08						
Goostrey d															17 11						
Chelford d															17 15						
Alderley Edge d	16 19									16 51					17 19						
Wilmslow d	16 23						16 47			16 54				17 29	17 23					17 45	
Styal d										16 58											
Manchester Airport a										17 05											
Handforth d	16 26														17 26						
Congleton d		16 15																			
Macclesfield a		16 22				16 42							17 14						17 42		
d		16 23				16 42							17 15						17 42		
Prestbury d		16 27																			
Adlington (Cheshire) d		16 30																			
Poynton d		16 33																			
Bramhall d		16 36																			
Cheadle Hulme d	16 30	16 39													17 30						
Stockport a	16 37	16 44				16 56	16 58		17 18				17 28	17 38	17 37				17 56	17 58	
d	16 37	16 44			16 53	16 57	16 58	17 12	17 19		17 22	17 29	17 29	17 39	17 37			17 53	17 57	17 58	18 12
Heaton Chapel d	16 41							17 16							17 41						18 16
Levenshulme d	16 44							17 19							17 44						18 19
Manchester Piccadilly 10 a	16 53	16 58	16 59		17 06	17 09	17 15	17 27	17 29	17 31	17 33	17 37	17 40	17 50	17 53	17 56		18 06	18 09	18 17	18 27
d				16 50							17 35	17 38					17 50				
Manchester Oxford Road a				16 52							17 37	17 41					17 52				
Deansgate a											17 40										

	VT ◇1	TP ◇1 K	NT L	EM ◇ M	XC ◇1 H	VT ◇1	NT	XC ◇1 N	NT B	TP ◇1 C	VT ◇1	AW D	NT E	VT ◇1	NT	TP ◇1 K	NT F	EM ◇ M	XC ◇1 H	VT ◇1	NT	XC ◇1 O
London Euston 15 ⊖65 d	16 17					16 37					16 57			17 17						17 37		
Birmingham New Street 12 68 d					17 01			17 31											18 01			18 31
Wolverhampton 7 68 d					17 19			17 49											18 19			18 49
Stafford 65,68 d					17 36														18 36			
Stoke-on-Trent 50,68 d	17 50				17 57			18 21			18 26			18 50					18 57			19 21
Longport 50 d																						
Kidsgrove 50 d																						
Crewe 10 65 d						18 13						18 28								19 13	18 56	
Sandbach d																					19 03	
Holmes Chapel d																					19 08	
Goostrey d																					19 11	
Chelford d																					19 15	
Alderley Edge d							18 19								18 51						19 19	
Wilmslow d						18 29	18 23					18 47			18 54					19 29	19 23	
Styal d															18 58							
Manchester Airport a															19 05							
Handforth d							18 26														19 26	
Congleton d																						
Macclesfield a					18 14						18 42								19 15			
d					18 15						18 42								19 15			
Prestbury d																						
Adlington (Cheshire) d																						
Poynton d																						
Bramhall d																						
Cheadle Hulme d							18 30														19 30	
Stockport a	18 18				18 28	18 38	18 37				18 56	18 58		19 18					19 28	19 38	19 37	
d	18 19		18 21	18 26	18 29	18 39	18 37			18 53	18 57	18 58	19 12	19 19			19 22	19 26	19 29	19 39	19 37	
Heaton Chapel d							18 41						19 16								19 41	
Levenshulme d							18 44						19 19								19 44	
Manchester Piccadilly 10 a	18 29		18 33	18 37	18 40	18 50	18 53	18 56		19 06	19 09	19 15	19 27	19 29	19 31		19 33	19 37	19 40	19 50	19 53	19 58
d		18 16	18 35	18 38					18 50							19 16	19 35	19 38				
Manchester Oxford Road a		18 18	18 37	18 41					18 52							19 18	19 37	19 41				
Deansgate a			18 40														19 40					

A From Penzance
B From Manchester Airport to Liverpool Lime Street
C From Cleethorpes to Manchester Airport
D From Cardiff Central
E From Buxton
F To Southport
G From Nottingham to Liverpool Lime Street
H From Bournemouth
I From Plymouth
J From Milford Haven
K From Manchester Airport to Barrow-in-Furness
L From Chester to Southport
M From Norwich to Liverpool Lime Street
N From Bristol Temple Meads
O from 28 October. From Penzance

Stoke-on-Trent and Crewe - Manchester Airport, Stockport and Manchester

Sundays from 7 October

Network Diagram - see first Page of Table 78

	XC ◇1 A	NT B	TP ◇1 C	VT ◇1	AW D	NT E	VT ◇1	NT F	EM ◇ G	XC ◇1 H	XC ◇1 I	VT ◇1	NT	NT	XC ◇1 J	NT B	TP ◇1 C	VT ◇1	AW K	NT E	VT ◇1	NT
London Euston 15 ⊖65 d				17 57			18 17					18 37						18 57			19 17	
Birmingham New Street 12 68 d	18 31									19 01	19 01				19 31							
Wolverhampton 7 68 d	18 49									19 19	19 19				19 49							
Stafford 65,68 d										19 38	19 39											
Stoke-on-Trent 50,68 d	19 21			19 26			19 50			19 57	19 57			20 01	20 21			20 26			20 50	
Longport 50 d																						
Kidsgrove 50 d														20 08								
Crewe 10 65 d					19 28							20 13							20 28			
Sandbach d																						
Holmes Chapel d																						
Goostrey d																						
Chelford d																						
Alderley Edge d													20 19									20 51
Wilmslow d					19 47							20 29	20 23						20 46			20 54
Styal d																						20 58
Manchester Airport a																						21 05
Handforth d													20 26									
Congleton d														20 15								
Macclesfield a				19 42						20 14	20 14			20 22				20 42				
d				19 42						20 15	20 15			20 23				20 42				
Prestbury d														20 27								
Adlington (Cheshire) d														20 30								
Poynton d														20 33								
Bramhall d														20 36								
Cheadle Hulme d													20 30	20 39								
Stockport a				19 56	19 58		20 18			20 28	20 28	20 38	20 37	20 44				20 56	20 57		21 18	
d			19 53	19 57	19 58	20 12	20 19	20 21	20 26	20 29	20 29	20 39	20 37	20 44			20 53	20 57	20 57	21 12	21 19	
Heaton Chapel d						20 16							20 41							21 16		
Levenshulme d						20 19							20 44							21 19		
Manchester Piccadilly 10 a	19 58		20 09	20 09	20 17	20 27	20 29	20 33	20 38	20 40	20 40	20 50	20 53	20 58	21 00		21 06	21 09	21 14	21 27	21 29	21 31
d		19 50						20 35								20 50						
Manchester Oxford Road a		19 52						20 37								20 52						
Deansgate a								20 40														

	NT L	EM ◇ G	XC ◇1 M	VT ◇1	NT	XC ◇1 N	XC ◇1 A	NT B	TP ◇1 C	VT ◇1	AW D	NT E	VT ◇1	NT O	XC ◇1 M	NT	VT ◇1	NT B	NT E	NT	NT P
London Euston 15 ⊖65 d				19 37						19 57			20 15				20 35				
Birmingham New Street 12 68 d			20 01			20 31	20 31								21 01						
Wolverhampton 7 68 d			20 19			20 52	20 52								21 19						
Stafford 65,68 d			20 37												21 37		22 00				
Stoke-on-Trent 50,68 d			20 57			21 21	21 21			21 26			21 50		21 57						
Longport 50 d																					
Kidsgrove 50 d																					
Crewe 10 65 d				21 14	20 56						21 28						22 21				
Sandbach d					21 03																
Holmes Chapel d					21 08																
Goostrey d					21 11																
Chelford d					21 15																
Alderley Edge d					21 19											22 19				22 51	
Wilmslow d				21 30	21 23						21 45					22 23	22 36			22 54	
Styal d																				22 58	
Manchester Airport a																				23 05	
Handforth d					21 26											22 26					
Congleton d																					
Macclesfield a			21 15							21 42					22 14						
d			21 15							21 42					22 15						
Prestbury d																					
Adlington (Cheshire) d																					
Poynton d																					
Bramhall d																					
Cheadle Hulme d					21 30											22 30					
Stockport a			21 28	21 39	21 37					21 56	21 58		22 18		22 28	22 37	22 45				
d	21 22	21 24	21 29	21 40	21 37				21 53	21 57	21 58	22 12	22 19	22 21	22 29	22 37	22 46		23 12		23 16
Heaton Chapel d					21 41							22 16				22 41			23 16		
Levenshulme d					21 44							22 19				22 44			23 19		
Manchester Piccadilly 10 a	21 33	21 36	21 40	21 50	21 53	21 56	21 56		22 06	22 09	22 19	22 27	22 29	22 33	22 40	22 53	22 57		23 27	23 29	23 29
d	21 35							21 50						22 35				22 41			
Manchester Oxford Road a	21 37							21 52						22 37				22 43			
Deansgate a	21 40													22 40				22 47			

A from 7 October until 21 October
B From Manchester Airport to Liverpool Lime Street
C From Cleethorpes to Manchester Airport
D From Milford Haven
E From Buxton
F From Chester to Southport
G From Norwich
H from 7 October until 21 October. From Bournemouth
I from 28 October. From Bournemouth
J From Bristol Temple Meads
K From Cardiff Central
L To Wigan Wallgate
M From Bournemouth
N from 28 October. From Bristol Temple Meads
O From Chester to Wigan Wallgate
P From Sheffield

Table 84

Sundays from 7 October

Stoke-on-Trent and Crewe - Manchester Airport, Stockport and Manchester

Network Diagram - see first Page of Table 78

	NT	XC	NT	VT	VT
		◇1		◇1	◇1
		A			
				R	R
London Euston 15 ⊖65 d				21 25	21 51
Birmingham New Street 12 68 d		22 01			
Wolverhampton 7 68 d		22 19			
Stafford 65,68 d		22 37			23s53
Stoke-on-Trent 50,68 d	22 39	22 57		23 29	
Longport 50 d					
Kidsgrove 50 d	22 46				
Crewe 10 65 d			22 56		00s21
Sandbach d			23 03		
Holmes Chapel d			23 08		
Goostrey d			23 11		
Chelford d			23 15		
Alderley Edge d			23 19		
Wilmslow d			23 23		
Styal d					
Manchester Airport ✈ a					
Handforth d			23 26		
Congleton d	22 53				
Macclesfield a	23 00	23 12		23 45	
d	23 01	23 13		23 46	
Prestbury d	23 05				
Adlington (Cheshire) d	23 08				
Poynton d	23 11				
Bramhall d	23 14				
Cheadle Hulme d	23 17		23 30		
Stockport a	23 22	23 27	23 35	23 59	00s50
d	23 23	23 28	23 37	00 01	
Heaton Chapel d			23 41		
Levenshulme d			23 44		
Manchester Piccadilly 10 a	23 37	23 41	23 53	00 12	01 00
d					
Manchester Oxford Road a					
Deansgate a					

A From Bournemouth

Table 84

Mondays to Fridays until 29 June

Manchester, Stockport and Manchester Airport - Crewe and Stoke-on-Trent

Network Diagram - see first Page of Table 78

Miles	Miles	Miles		NT MX	VT	XC	NT	TP	NT	VT	XC	NT	NT	VT	NT	NT	VT	AW	NT	VT	VT
					◇1	◇1		◇1		◇1	◇1			◇1			◇1	◇		◇1	◇1
						A		B	C		D				E	F		G			
					⊠	🍴				⊠	🍴			⊠			⊠	🍴		⊠	⊠
0	0	—	Deansgate d																		
0½	0½	—	**Manchester Oxford Road** d																		
1	1	—	**Manchester Piccadilly** 10 a																		
—	—	—	d	23p38	05 05	05 11	05 35	05 44	05 50	05 55	06 00		06 06	06 10	06 18	06 21	06 27	06 30	06 32	06 35	06 43
4	4	—	Levenshulme d	23p43									06 11			06 28			06 37		
5½	5½	—	Heaton Chapel d	23p46									06 14			06 31			06 40		
7	7	—	**Stockport** a	23p50	05 12			05 52	05 59	06 02	06 07		06 18	06 17	06 27	06 34	06 34	06 38	06 44	06 43	06 50
—	—	—	d	23p50	05 13					06 03	06 08		06 19	06 18			06 35	06 39	06 45	06 43	06 51
9¼	9¼	—	Cheadle Hulme d	23p54									06 26						06 51		
9¾	—	—	Bramhall d																06 54		
12¼	—	—	Poynton d																06 57		
14¼	—	—	Adlington (Cheshire) d																07 01		
16¼	—	—	Prestbury d																07 04		
19	—	—	**Macclesfield** a											06 30			06 47		07 07	06 55	
—	—	—	d									06 03		06 31			06 48		07 08	06 56	
27	—	—	Congleton d									06 10							07 15		
—	11½	—	Handforth d	23p58									06 30								
—	—	0	**Manchester Airport** ✈ d				06 05														
—	—	2¼	Styal d																		
—	13	4	**Wilmslow** d	00 01			06 17			06 11			06 34					06 46			06 59
—	14¾	—	Alderley Edge d	00 04			06 20						06 37								
—	17¾	—	Chelford d	00 08			06 24														
—	21½	—	Goostrey d	00 12			06 29														
—	23½	—	Holmes Chapel d	00 15			06 32						06 47								
—	27¼	—	Sandbach d	00 20			06 36						06 53								
—	32	—	**Crewe** 10 65 a	00 30	05 34	05 44	06 46			06 27	06 32		07 04					07 05			07 15
32½	—	—	Kidsgrove 50 a									06 16									
35¾	—	—	Longport 50 a																		
38¾	—	—	**Stoke-on-Trent** 50,68 a			06 06						06 26		06 46			07 04		07 30	07 11	
—	—	—	Stafford 68 a		05 53	06 24					06 57						07 27				07 34
—	—	—	Wolverhampton 7 68 a			06 39					07 12						07 43				
—	—	—	Birmingham New Street 12 68 a			06 58					07 31						08 06				
—	—	—	London Euston 15 ⊖65 a		07 28					08 07				08 22			09 34			08 45	08 52

	NT	NT	VT	NT	XC	VT	NT	TP	NT	XC	AW	VT	NT	NT	NT	NT	VT	NT	XC	VT
			◇1		◇1	◇1		◇1		◇1	◇	◇1					◇1		◇1	◇1
		H			D		E	B	I	A	J					H			K	
			⊠		🍴	⊠		🍴		🍴	🍴	⊠					⊠		🍴	⊠
Deansgate d									07 11											
Manchester Oxford Road d									07 15											
Manchester Piccadilly 10 a									07 17											
d	06 46	06 49	07 00	07 03	07 07	07 15	07 17	07 20	07 21	07 26	07 30	07 35	07 38	07 46	07 48	07 52	07 55	08 04	08 07	08 15
Levenshulme d		06 55		07 09					07 28				07 43					08 09		
Heaton Chapel d		06 58		07 12					07 31				07 46					08 12		
Stockport a		07 01		07 16	07 15	07 22	07 26	07 28	07 34	07 34	07 38	07 43	07 50		07 57	08 01	08 03	08 16	08 15	08 22
d			07u07	07 18	07 16	07 23				07 35	07 39	07 43	07 51		07 58		08 04	08 17	08 16	08 23
Cheadle Hulme d				07 24									07 55		08 02			08 24		
Bramhall d															08 05					
Poynton d															08 08					
Adlington (Cheshire) d															08 11					
Prestbury d															08 14					
Macclesfield a										07 47		07 56			08 18					
d										07 49		07 56			08 18					
Congleton d															08 26					
Handforth d				07 28									07 59					08 28		
Manchester Airport ✈ d	07 11													08 11						
Styal d														08 18						
Wilmslow d	07 21			07 31							07 46		08 02	08 22			08 11	08 31		
Alderley Edge d	07 24			07 34									08a08	08 25				08 34		
Chelford d				07 38														08 38		
Goostrey d				07 43														08 43		
Holmes Chapel d	07 32			07 46										08 33				08 46		
Sandbach d	07 36			07 51										08 37				08 52		
Crewe 10 65 a	07 46			08 01							08 05			08 47			08 27	09 04		
Kidsgrove 50 a															08 32					
Longport 50 a																				
Stoke-on-Trent 50,68 a					07 43	07 48				08 06		08 12			08 42				08 43	08 48
Stafford 68 a					08 01					08 24									09 02	
Wolverhampton 7 68 a					08 15					08 39									09 15	
Birmingham New Street 12 68 a					08 32					08 58									09 32	
London Euston 15 ⊖65 a			08 58			09 23						09 52					10 04			10 23

A To Bournemouth
B From Manchester Airport to Cleethorpes
C To Sheffield
D To Bristol Temple Meads
E To Chester
F To Hazel Grove
G To Milford Haven
H To Buxton
I From Wigan Wallgate to Hazel Grove
J To Carmarthen
K To Paignton

Manchester, Stockport and Manchester Airport - Crewe and Stoke-on-Trent

Network Diagram - see first Page of Table 78

	NT A	TP ◇■ B	XC ◇■ C	AW ◇ D	VT ◇■ ⊠	NT	NT	NT	NT E	VT ◇■ ⊠	NT	XC ◇■ F	VT ◇■ ⊠	NT A	TP ◇■ B	XC ◇■ C	AW ◇ G	VT ◇■ ⊠	NT	NT	NT
Deansgate ⇌ d																					
Manchester Oxford Road d																					
Manchester Piccadilly 10 ⇌ a																					
d	08 17	08 20	08 27	08 30	08 35	08 38	08 46	08 48	08 52	08 55	09 04	09 07	09 15	09 17	09 20	09 27	09 30	09 35	09 38	09 46	09 48
Levenshulme d						08 43			08 58		09 09								09 43		
Heaton Chapel d						08 46			09 01		09 12								09 46		
Stockport a	08 27	08 28	08 34	08 38	08 42	08 50		08 57	09 04	09 03	09 16	09 15	09 22	09 27	09 28	09 34	09 38	09 42	09 50		09 57
d			08 35	08 39	08 43	08 51		08 58		09 04	09 17	09 16	09 23			09 35	09 39	09 43	09 51		09 58
Cheadle Hulme d						08 55		09 02			09 24								09 55		10 02
Bramhall d								09 05													10 05
Poynton d								09 08													10 08
Adlington (Cheshire) d								09 11													10 11
Prestbury d								09 14													10 14
Macclesfield a			08 47		08 55			09 18								09 47		09 55			10 18
d			08 49		08 56			09 18								09 49		09 56			10 18
Congleton d								09 26													10 26
Handforth d						08 59					09 28								09 59		
Manchester Airport ✈ d							09 11													10 11	
Styal d																					
Wilmslow d				08 46		09 02	09 21			09 11	09 31						09 46		10 02	10 21	
Alderley Edge d						09 05	09 24				09 34								10a08	10 24	
Chelford d											09 38										
Goostrey d											09 43										
Holmes Chapel d							09 32				09 46									10 32	
Sandbach d							09 36				09 51									10 36	
Crewe 10 65 a				09 07		09 23	09 46			09 27	10 01						10 05			10 46	
Kidsgrove 50 a								09 32													10 32
Longport 50 a																					
Stoke-on-Trent 50,68 a			09 06		09 11			09 42				09 43	09 48			10 06		10 11			10 42
Stafford 68 a			09 24									10 02				10 24					
Wolverhampton 7 68 ⇌ a			09 39									10 15				10 39					
Birmingham New Street 12 68 a			09 58									10 39				10 58					
London Euston 15 ⊖65 a					10 42					11 04			11 23					11 42			

	NT E	VT ◇■ ⊠	NT	XC ◇■ F	VT ◇■ ⊠	NT A	TP ◇■ B	XC ◇■ C	AW ◇ D	VT ◇■ ⊠	NT	NT	NT	NT E	VT ◇■ ⊠	NT	XC ◇■ F	VT ◇■	NT A
Deansgate ⇌ d																			
Manchester Oxford Road d																			
Manchester Piccadilly 10 ⇌ a																			
d	09 52	09 55	10 04	10 07	10 15	10 17	10 20	10 27	10 30	10 35	10 38	10 46	10 48	10 52	10 55	11 04	11 07	11 15	11 17
Levenshulme d	09 58		10 09								10 43			10 58		11 09			
Heaton Chapel d	10 01		10 12								10 46			11 01		11 12			
Stockport a	10 04	10 03	10 16	10 15	10 22	10 27	10 28	10 34	10 38	10 42	10 50		10 57	11 04	11 03	11 16	11 15	11 22	11 27
d		10 04	10 17	10 16	10 23			10 35	10 39	10 43	10 51		10 58		11 04	11 17	11 16	11 23	
Cheadle Hulme d			10 24								10 55		11 02			11 24			
Bramhall d													11 05						
Poynton d													11 08						
Adlington (Cheshire) d													11 11						
Prestbury d													11 14						
Macclesfield a								10 47		10 55			11 18						
d								10 49		10 56			11 18						
Congleton d													11 26						
Handforth d			10 28								10 59					11 28			
Manchester Airport ✈ d												11 11							
Styal d												11 18							
Wilmslow d		10 11	10 31						10 46		11 02	11 22			11 11	11 31			
Alderley Edge d			10 34								11a08	11 25				11 34			
Chelford d			10 38													11 38			
Goostrey d			10 43													11 43			
Holmes Chapel d			10 46									11 33				11 46			
Sandbach d			10 51									11 37				11 51			
Crewe 10 65 a		10 27	11 01						11 05			11 47			11 27	12 01			
Kidsgrove 50 a													11 32						
Longport 50 a																			
Stoke-on-Trent 50,68 a				10 43	10 48			11 06		11 11			11 42				11 43	11 48	
Stafford 68 a				11 01				11 24									12 02		
Wolverhampton 7 68 ⇌ a				11 15				11 39									12 15		
Birmingham New Street 12 68 a				11 32				11 58									12 39		
London Euston 15 ⊖65 a		12 04			12 23					12 42					13 03			13 23	

A To Chester
B From Manchester Airport to Cleethorpes
C To Bournemouth
D To Milford Haven
E To Buxton
F To Bristol Temple Meads
G To Carmarthen

Manchester, Stockport and Manchester Airport - Crewe and Stoke-on-Trent

Network Diagram - see first Page of Table 78

	TP ◇■ A	XC ◇■ B	AW ◇ C	VT ◇■	NT	NT	NT	NT D	VT ◇■	NT	XC ◇■ E	VT ◇■	NT F	TP ◇■ A	XC ◇■ B	AW ■ G	VT ◇■	NT	NT	NT	NT D
Deansgate ⇌ d																					
Manchester Oxford Road d																					
Manchester Piccadilly 10 ⇌ a																					
d	11 20	11 27	11 30	11 35	11 38	11 46	11 48	11 52	11 55	12 04	12 07	12 15	12 17	12 20	12 27	12 30	12 35	12 38	12 46	12 48	12 52
Levenshulme d					11 43			11 58		12 09								12 43			12 58
Heaton Chapel d					11 46			12 01		12 12								12 46			13 01
Stockport a	11 28	11 34	11 38	11 42	11 50		11 57	12 04	12 03	12 16	12 15	12 22	12 27	12 28	12 34	12 38	12 42	12 50		12 57	13 04
d		11 35	11 39	11 43	11 51		11 58		12 04	12 17	12 16	12 23			12 35	12 39	12 43	12 51		12 58	
Cheadle Hulme d					11 55		12 02			12 24								12 55		13 02	
Bramhall d							12 05													13 05	
Poynton d							12 08													13 08	
Adlington (Cheshire) d							12 11													13 11	
Prestbury d							12 14													13 14	
Macclesfield a		11 47		11 55			12 18								12 47		12 55			13 18	
d		11 49		11 56			12 18								12 49		12 56			13 18	
Congleton d							12 26													13 26	
Handforth d					11 59					12 28								12 59			
Manchester Airport ✈ d						12 11													13 11		
Styal d																			13 18		
Wilmslow d			11 46		12 02	12 21			12 11	12 31						12 46		13 02	13 22		
Alderley Edge d					12a08	12 24				12 34								13a08	13 25		
Chelford d										12 38											
Goostrey d										12 43											
Holmes Chapel d						12 32				12 46									13 33		
Sandbach d						12 36				12 51									13 37		
Crewe 10 65 a			12 05			12 46			12 27	13 01						13 05			13 47		
Kidsgrove 50 a							12 32													13 32	
Longport 50 a																					
Stoke-on-Trent 50,68 a		12 06		12 11			12 42				12 43	12 48			13 06		13 11			13 42	
Stafford 68 a		12 24									13 01				13 24						
Wolverhampton 7 68 ⇌ a		12 39									13 15				13 39						
Birmingham New Street 12 68 a		12 58									13 39				13 58						
London Euston 15 ⊖65 a				13 42					14 04			14 23					14 42				

	VT ◇■	NT	XC ◇■ H	VT ◇■	NT F	TP ◇■ A	XC ◇■ B	AW ■ I	VT ◇■	NT	NT	NT	NT D	VT ◇■	NT	XC ◇■ J	VT ◇■	NT F	TP ◇■ A
Deansgate ⇌ d																			
Manchester Oxford Road d																			
Manchester Piccadilly 10 ⇌ a																			
d	12 55	13 04	13 07	13 15	13 17	13 20	13 27	13 30	13 35	13 38	13 46	13 48	13 52	13 55	14 04	14 07	14 15	14 17	14 20
Levenshulme d		13 09								13 43			13 58		14 09				
Heaton Chapel d		13 12								13 46			14 01		14 12				
Stockport a	13 03	13 16	13 15	13 22	13 27	13 28	13 34	13 38	13 42	13 50		13 57	14 04	14 03	14 16	14 15	14 22	14 27	14 28
d	13 04	13 17	13 16	13 23			13 35	13 39	13 43	13 51		13 58		14 04	14 17	14 16	14 23		
Cheadle Hulme d		13 24								13 55		14 02			14 24				
Bramhall d												14 05							
Poynton d												14 08							
Adlington (Cheshire) d												14 11							
Prestbury d												14 14							
Macclesfield a							13 47		13 55			14 18							
d							13 49		13 56			14 18							
Congleton d												14 26							
Handforth d		13 28								13 59					14 28				
Manchester Airport ✈ d											14 11								
Styal d																			
Wilmslow d	13 11	13 31						13 46		14 02	14 21			14 11	14 31				
Alderley Edge d		13 34								14a08	14 24				14 34				
Chelford d		13 38													14 38				
Goostrey d		13 43													14 43				
Holmes Chapel d		13 46									14 32				14 46				
Sandbach d		13 51									14 36				14 51				
Crewe 10 65 a	13 27	14 01						14 05			14 46			14 27	15 01				
Kidsgrove 50 a												14 32							
Longport 50 a																			
Stoke-on-Trent 50,68 a			13 43	13 48			14 06		14 11			14 42				14 43	14 48		
Stafford 68 a			14 01				14 24									15 02			
Wolverhampton 7 68 ⇌ a			14 15				14 39									15 15			
Birmingham New Street 12 68 a			14 32				14 58									15 39			
London Euston 15 ⊖65 a	15 04			15 23					15 42					16 04			16 23		

A From Manchester Airport to Cleethorpes
B To Bournemouth
C To Carmarthen
D To Buxton
E To Exeter St Davids
F To Chester
G To Milford Haven
H To Bristol Temple Meads
I To Tenby
J To Paignton

Table 84

Mondays to Fridays
until 29 June

Manchester, Stockport and Manchester Airport - Crewe and Stoke-on-Trent

Network Diagram - see first Page of Table 78

		XC	AW	VT	NT	NT	NT	NT	VT	NT	XC	VT	NT	TP	XC	AW	VT	NT	NT	NT	NT	VT
		◇1 A	B	◇1				C	◇1		◇1 D	◇1	E	◇1 F	◇1 A	G	◇1				C	◇1
Deansgate	d																					
Manchester Oxford Road	d																					
Manchester Piccadilly	a																					
	d	14 27	14 30	14 35	14 38	14 46	14 48	14 52	14 55	15 04	15 07	15 15	15 17	15 20	15 27	15 30	15 35	15 38	15 46	15 48	15 52	15 55
Levenshulme	d				14 43			14 58		15 09								15 43			15 58	
Heaton Chapel	d				14 46			15 01		15 12								15 46			16 01	
Stockport	a	14 34	14 38	14 42	14 50		14 57	15 04	15 03	15 16	15 15	15 22	15 27	15 28	15 34	15 38	15 42	15 50		15 57	16 04	16 03
	d	14 35	14 39	14 43	14 51		14 58		15 04	15 17	15 16	15 23			15 35	15 39	15 43	15 51		15 58		16 04
Cheadle Hulme	d				14 55		15 02			15 24								15 55		16 02		
Bramhall	d						15 05													16 05		
Poynton	d						15 08													16 08		
Adlington (Cheshire)	d						15 11													16 11		
Prestbury	d						15 14													16 14		
Macclesfield	a	14 47		14 55			15 18								15 47		15 55			16 18		
	d	14 49		14 56			15 18								15 49		15 56			16 18		
Congleton	d						15 26													16 26		
Handforth	d				14 59					15 28								15 59				
Manchester Airport	d					15 11													16 11			
Styal	d																					
Wilmslow	d		14 46		15 02	15 21			15 11	15 31						15 46		16 02	16 21			16 11
Alderley Edge	d				15a08	15 24				15 34								16a08	16 24			
Chelford	d									15 38												
Goostrey	d									15 43												
Holmes Chapel	d					15 32				15 46									16 32			
Sandbach	d					15 36				15 51									16 36			
Crewe 65	a		15 05			15 46			15 27	16 01						16 05			16 46			16 27
Kidsgrove 50	a						15 32													16 32		
Longport 50	a																					
Stoke-on-Trent 50,68	a	15 06		15 11			15 42				15 43	15 48			16 06		16 11			16 42		
Stafford 68	a	15 24									16 02				16 24							
Wolverhampton 68	a	15 39									16 15				16 39							
Birmingham New Street 68	a	15 58									16 39				16 58							
London Euston ⊖65	a			16 42					17 04			17 23					17 42					18 03

		NT	XC	VT	NT	TP	XC	AW	VT	NT	NT	NT	NT	VT	NT	NT	XC	NT	VT	NT	TP
			◇1 D	◇1	E	◇1 F	◇1 A	B	◇1				C	◇1	H		◇1 I	E	◇1		◇1 F
Deansgate	d																			17 10	
Manchester Oxford Road	d																			17 13	
Manchester Piccadilly	a																			17 15	
	d	16 04	16 07	16 15	16 17	16 20	16 27	16 30	16 35	16 38	16 46	16 48	16 51	16 55	16 58	17 03	17 05	17 09	17 15	17 17	17 20
Levenshulme	d	16 09								16 43					17 03	17 08					
Heaton Chapel	d	16 12								16 46					17 06	17 11					
Stockport	a	16 16	16 15	16 22	16 27	16 28	16 34	16 38	16 42	16 50		16 58	17 02	17 03	17 10	17 15	17 12	17 17	17 22	17 27	17 28
	d	16 17	16 16	16 23			16 35	16 39	16 43	16 51		16 58		17 04		17 16	17 13		17 23	17 28	
Cheadle Hulme	d	16 24								16 55		17 02				17 24				17 32	
Bramhall	d											17 05								17 35	
Poynton	d											17 08								17 38	
Adlington (Cheshire)	d											17 11								17 41	
Prestbury	d											17 14								17 44	
Macclesfield	a						16 47		16 55			17 18					17 25			17 48	
	d						16 49		16 56			17 18					17 27			17 48	
Congleton	d											17 26								17 56	
Handforth	d	16 28								16 59						17 28					
Manchester Airport	d										17 11										
Styal	d										17 18										
Wilmslow	d	16 31						16 46		17 03	17 22			17 11		17 31					
Alderley Edge	d	16 34								17a09	17 25					17 34					
Chelford	d	16 38														17 38					
Goostrey	d	16 43														17 43					
Holmes Chapel	d	16 46									17 33					17 46					
Sandbach	d	16 51									17 37					17 51					
Crewe 65	a	17 01						17 05			17 47			17 27		18 01					
Kidsgrove 50	a											17 32									
Longport 50	a																				
Stoke-on-Trent 50,68	a		16 43	16 49			17 06		17 11			17 42					17 43		17 49	18 10	
Stafford 68	a		17 02				17 24										18 03				
Wolverhampton 68	a		17 15				17 39										18 15				
Birmingham New Street 68	a		17 32				17 58										18 38				
London Euston ⊖65	a			18 23					18 42					19 08					19 23		

A To Bournemouth
B To Milford Haven
C To Buxton
D To Bristol Temple Meads
E To Chester
F From Manchester Airport to Cleethorpes
G To Pembroke Dock
H To Hazel Grove
I To Cardiff Central

Table 84

Mondays to Fridays
until 29 June

Manchester, Stockport and Manchester Airport - Crewe and Stoke-on-Trent

Network Diagram - see first Page of Table 78

		NT	XC	AW	VT	NT	NT	NT	NT	VT	XC	NT	VT	NT	TP	NT	XC	AW	VT	NT	NT
		A	◇1 B	C	◇1				D	◇1	◇1 E		◇1	F	◇1 G	H	◇1 B	◇ I	◇1		
Deansgate	d															18 12					
Manchester Oxford Road	d															18 16					
Manchester Piccadilly	a															18 18					
	d	17 23	17 27	17 30	17 35	17 38	17 46	17 48	17 52	17 55	18 05	18 08	18 15	18 17	18 20	18 21	18 27	18 30	18 35	18 38	18 46
Levenshulme	d	17 28				17 43			17 58			18 13				18 28				18 43	
Heaton Chapel	d	17 31				17 46			18 01			18 16				18 31				18 46	
Stockport	a	17 35	17 35	17 38	17 42	17 50		17 57	18 04	18 03	18 12	18 20	18 22	18 27	18 28	18 34	18 34	18 38	18 42	18 50	
	d		17 35	17 39	17 43	17 51		17 58		18 04	18 13	18 21	18 23				18 35	18 39	18 43	18 51	
Cheadle Hulme	d					17 55		18 02				18 25								18 55	
Bramhall	d							18 05													
Poynton	d							18 08													
Adlington (Cheshire)	d							18 11													
Prestbury	d							18 14													
Macclesfield	a				17 55			18 18			18 25								18 55		
	d				17 56			18 18			18 26								18 56		
Congleton	d							18 26									18 54				
Handforth	d					17 59						18 29								18 59	
Manchester Airport	d						18 11														19 14
Styal	d						18 18														
Wilmslow	d		17 44	17 46		18 02	18 22			18 11		18 31						18 46		19 02	19 26
Alderley Edge	d					18 05	18 25					18 34								19a08	19a32
Chelford	d											18 38									
Goostrey	d											18 43									
Holmes Chapel	d						18 33					18 46									
Sandbach	d					18 16	18 37					18 50									
Crewe 65	a		18 04	18 07		18 26	18 47			18 27		19 00						19 05			
Kidsgrove 50	a							18 32													
Longport 50	a																				
Stoke-on-Trent 50,68	a				18 11			18 42			18 43		18 48				19 06		19 11		
Stafford 68	a		18 27								19 01						19 24				
Wolverhampton 68	a		18 39								19 15						19 39				
Birmingham New Street 68	a		18 58								19 32						19 58				
London Euston ⊖65	a				19 43					20 06			20 23						20 42		

		NT	NT	VT	NT	XC	VT	NT	TP	NT	XC	AW	NT	NT	NT	VT	NT	XC	VT	NT	TP	XC
			D	◇1		◇1 J	◇1	F	◇1 G	K	◇1 L	◇ C			D	◇1		◇1	◇1	F	◇1 M	◇1
Deansgate	d																					
Manchester Oxford Road	d												19 43									
Manchester Piccadilly	a												19 45									
	d	18 48	18 52	18 55	19 04	19 07	19 15	19 17	19 18	19 22	19 27	19 30	19 46	19 48	19 51	19 55	20 04	20 07	20 15	20 17	20 20	20 27
Levenshulme	d		18 58		19 09					19 28					19 58		20 09					
Heaton Chapel	d		19 01		19 12					19 31					20 01		20 12					
Stockport	a	18 57	19 04	19 03	19 16	19 15	19 22	19 27	19 26	19 34	19 34	19 38		19 57	20 04	20 03	20 15	20 15	20 22	20 27	20 28	20 34
	d	18 58		19 04	19 17	19 16	19 23				19 35	19 39		19 58		20 04	20 17	20 16	20 23			20 35
Cheadle Hulme	d	19 02			19 24									20 02			20 23					
Bramhall	d	19 05												20 05								
Poynton	d	19 08												20 08								
Adlington (Cheshire)	d	19 11												20 11								
Prestbury	d	19 14												20 14								
Macclesfield	a	19 18					19 35				19 47			20 18					20 35			20 47
	d	19 18					19 36				19 49			20 18					20 36			20 49
Congleton	d	19 26												20 26								
Handforth	d				19 28												20 27					
Manchester Airport	d												20 14									
Styal	d																					
Wilmslow	d			19 11	19 31							19 46	20a24			20 11	20 30					
Alderley Edge	d				19 34												20 33					
Chelford	d				19 38												20 37					
Goostrey	d				19 43												20 42					
Holmes Chapel	d				19 46												20 45					
Sandbach	d				19 51												20 51					
Crewe 65	a			19 27	20 01							20 05				20 27	21 03					
Kidsgrove 50	a	19 32												20 32								
Longport 50	a																					
Stoke-on-Trent 50,68	a	19 42				19 43	19 51				20 06			20 42				20 43	20 51			21 06
Stafford 68	a					20 03					20 25					20 47		21 02				21 24
Wolverhampton 68	a					20 16					20 40							21 15				21 39
Birmingham New Street 68	a					20 33					21 00							21 33				22 00
London Euston ⊖65	a			21 06			21 26									22 12			22 33			

A To Chinley
B To Bournemouth
C To Cardiff Central
D To Buxton
E To Plymouth
F To Chester
G From Manchester Airport to Cleethorpes
H From Wigan Wallgate to Buxton
I To Carmarthen
J To Bristol Temple Meads
K To Hazel Grove
L To Southampton Central
M From Manchester Airport to Sheffield

Table 84

Manchester, Stockport and Manchester Airport - Crewe and Stoke-on-Trent

Mondays to Fridays
until 29 June

Network Diagram - see first Page of Table 78

		AW ◇ A	NT	NT	NT B	NT	VT ◇1 ☕	NT C	TP ◇1 D	XC ◇1	AW E	NT	NT	NT B	NT	XC FO ◇1 F	XC FX ◇1 G	NT C	TP ◇1 H	AW ◇ E	NT
Deansgate	d																				
Manchester Oxford Road	d		20 43									21 43									22 43
Manchester Piccadilly 10	a		20 45									21 45									22 45
	d	20 30	20 46	20 48	20 51	21 04	21 15	21 17	21 20	21 27	21 35	21 46	21 48	21 52	22 04	22 07	22 07	22 17	22 20	22 35	22 46
Levenshulme	d				20 58	21 09								21 58	22 09						
Heaton Chapel	d				21 01	21 12								22 01	22 12						
Stockport	a	20 38		20 58	21 04	21 16	21 22	21 27	21 28	21 34	21 43		21 57	22 04	22 16	22 15	22 15	22 27	22 28	22 43	
	d	20 39		20 58		21 17	21 23			21 35	21 44		21 58		22 17	22 16	22 16			22 44	
Cheadle Hulme	d			21 02		21 24							22 02		22 24						
Bramhall	d			21 05									22 05								
Poynton	d			21 08									22 08								
Adlington (Cheshire)	d			21 11									22 11								
Prestbury	d			21 14									22 14								
Macclesfield	a			21 18			21 35			21 47			22 18			22 28	22 28				
	d			21 18			21 36			21 49			22 18			22 29	22 29				
Congleton	d			21 26									22 26								
Handforth	d					21 28									22 28						
Manchester Airport ✈	d		21 15									22 14									23 14
Styal	d																				
Wilmslow	d	20 46	21a25			21 31					21 51	22a22			22 31					22 52	23a22
Alderley Edge	d					21 34									22 34						
Chelford	d					21 38									22 38						
Goostrey	d					21 43									22 43						
Holmes Chapel	d					21 46									22 46						
Sandbach	d					21 51									22 51						
Crewe 10 65	a	21 04				22 01					22 11				23 01					23 10	
Kidsgrove 50	a			21 32									22 32								
Longport 50	a																				
Stoke-on-Trent 50,68	a			21 42			21 51			22 07			22 42			22 46	22 46				
Stafford 68	a									22 25						23 06	23 09				
Wolverhampton 7 68	a									22 39						23 19	23 22				
Birmingham New Street 12 68	a									22 58						23 39	23 39				
London Euston 15 ⊖65	a						23 48														

		NT	NT	NT B	NT	NT C	NT
Deansgate	d						
Manchester Oxford Road	d						
Manchester Piccadilly 10	a						
	d	22 48	23 04	23 10	23 14	23 17	23 38
Levenshulme	d		23 09				23 43
Heaton Chapel	d		23 12				23 46
Stockport	a	22 57	23 16	23 19	23 23	23 26	23 50
	d	22 58	23 16		23 23		23 50
Cheadle Hulme	d	23 02	23 23		23 27		23 54
Bramhall	d	23 05			23 30		
Poynton	d	23 08			23 33		
Adlington (Cheshire)	d	23 11			23 37		
Prestbury	d	23 14			23 40		
Macclesfield	a	23 20			23 46		
	d						
Congleton	d						
Handforth	d		23 27				23 58
Manchester Airport ✈	d						
Styal	d						
Wilmslow	d		23 31				00 01
Alderley Edge	d		23a37				00 04
Chelford	d						00 08
Goostrey	d						00 12
Holmes Chapel	d						00 15
Sandbach	d						00 20
Crewe 10 65	a						00 30
Kidsgrove 50	a						
Longport 50	a						
Stoke-on-Trent 50,68	a						
Stafford 68	a						
Wolverhampton 7 68	a						
Birmingham New Street 12 68	a						
London Euston 15 ⊖65	a						

A To Cardiff Central
B To Buxton
C To Chester
D From Manchester Airport to Cleethorpes
E To Shrewsbury
F also from 25 June until 28 June
G until 21 June
H From Manchester Airport to Sheffield

Table 84

Manchester, Stockport and Manchester Airport - Crewe and Stoke-on-Trent

Mondays to Fridays
2 July to 28 September

Network Diagram - see first Page of Table 78

		NT MX	VT ◇1 ⊠	XC ◇1 A 🍴	NT	TP ◇1 B	NT C	VT ◇1 ⊠	XC ◇1 D 🍴	NT	NT	VT ◇1 ⊠	NT E	NT F	VT ◇1 ⊠	AW ◇ G 🍴	NT	VT ◇1 ⊠	VT ◇1 ⊠	NT	NT H	VT ◇1 ⊠
Deansgate	d																					
Manchester Oxford Road	d																					
Manchester Piccadilly 10	a																					
	d	23p38	05 05	05 11	05 35	05 44	05 50	05 55	06 00		06 06	06 10	06 18	06 21	06 27	06 30	06 32	06 35	06 43	06 46	06 49	07 00
Levenshulme	d	23p43									06 11			06 28			06 37				06 55	
Heaton Chapel	d	23p46									06 14			06 31			06 40				06 58	
Stockport	a	23p50	05 12			05 52	05 59	06 02	06 07		06 18	06 17	06 27	06 34	06 34	06 38	06 44	06 43	06 50		07 01	
	d	23p50	05 13					06 03	06 08		06 19	06 18			06 35	06 39	06 45	06 43	06 51			07u07
Cheadle Hulme	d	23p54									06 26						06 51					
Bramhall	d																06 54					
Poynton	d																06 57					
Adlington (Cheshire)	d																07 01					
Prestbury	d																07 04					
Macclesfield	a											06 30			06 47		07 07	06 55				
	d									06 03		06 31			06 48		07 08	06 56				
Congleton	d									06 10							07 15					
Handforth	d	23p58									06 30											
Manchester Airport ✈	d				06 05															07 11		
Styal	d																					
Wilmslow	d	00 01			06 17			06 11			06 34					06 46			06 59	07 21		
Alderley Edge	d	00 04			06 20						06 37									07 24		
Chelford	d	00 08			06 24																	
Goostrey	d	00 12			06 29																	
Holmes Chapel	d	00 15			06 32						06 47									07 32		
Sandbach	d	00 20			06 36						06 53									07 36		
Crewe 10 65	a	00 30	05 34	05 44	06 46			06 27	06 32		07 04					07 05			07 15	07 46		
Kidsgrove 50	a									06 16												
Longport 50	a																					
Stoke-on-Trent 50,68	a			06 06						06 26		06 46			07 04		07 30	07 11				
Stafford 68	a		05 53	06 24					06 57						07 27				07 34			
Wolverhampton 7 68	a			06 39					07 12						07 43							
Birmingham New Street 12 68	a			06 58					07 31						08 06							
London Euston 15 ⊖65	a		07 28					08 07				08 22			09 34			08 45	08 52			08 58

		NT	XC ◇1 D 🍴	VT ◇1 ⊠	NT E	TP ◇1 B 🍴	NT I	XC ◇1 A 🍴	AW ◇ J 🍴	VT ◇1 ⊠	NT	NT	NT	NT H	VT ◇1 ⊠	NT	XC ◇1 K 🍴	VT ◇1 ⊠	NT E	TP ◇1 B 🍴	XC ◇1 A 🍴
Deansgate	d						07 11														
Manchester Oxford Road	d						07 15														
Manchester Piccadilly 10	a						07 17														
	d	07 03	07 07	07 15	07 17	07 20	07 21	07 26	07 30	07 35	07 38	07 46	07 48	07 52	07 55	08 04	08 07	08 15	08 17	08 20	08 27
Levenshulme	d	07 09					07 28				07 43					08 09					
Heaton Chapel	d	07 12					07 31				07 46					08 12					
Stockport	a	07 16	07 15	07 22	07 26	07 28	07 34	07 34	07 38	07 43	07 50		07 57	08 01	08 03	08 16	08 15	08 22	08 27	08 28	08 34
	d	07 18	07 16	07 23				07 35	07 39	07 43	07 51		07 58		08 04	08 17	08 16	08 23			08 35
Cheadle Hulme	d	07 24									07 55		08 02			08 24					
Bramhall	d												08 05								
Poynton	d												08 08								
Adlington (Cheshire)	d												08 11								
Prestbury	d												08 14								
Macclesfield	a							07 47		07 56			08 18								08 47
	d							07 49		07 56			08 18								08 49
Congleton	d												08 26								
Handforth	d	07 28									07 59					08 28					
Manchester Airport ✈	d											08 11									
Styal	d											08 18									
Wilmslow	d	07 31							07 46		08 02	08 22			08 11	08 31					
Alderley Edge	d	07 34									08a08	08 25				08 34					
Chelford	d	07 38														08 38					
Goostrey	d	07 43														08 43					
Holmes Chapel	d	07 46										08 33				08 46					
Sandbach	d	07 51										08 37				08 52					
Crewe 10 65	a	08 01							08 05			08 47			08 27	09 04					
Kidsgrove 50	a												08 32								
Longport 50	a																				
Stoke-on-Trent 50,68	a		07 43	07 48				08 06		08 12			08 42				08 43	08 48			09 06
Stafford 68	a		08 01					08 24									09 02				09 24
Wolverhampton 7 68	a		08 15					08 39									09 15				09 39
Birmingham New Street 12 68	a		08 32					08 58									09 32				09 58
London Euston 15 ⊖65	a			09 23						09 52					10 04			10 23			

A To Bournemouth
B From Manchester Airport to Cleethorpes
C To Sheffield
D To Bristol Temple Meads
E To Chester
F To Hazel Grove
G To Milford Haven
H To Buxton
I From Wigan Wallgate to Hazel Grove
J To Carmarthen
K To Paignton

Table 84

Mondays to Fridays
2 July to 28 September

Manchester, Stockport and Manchester Airport - Crewe and Stoke-on-Trent

Network Diagram - see first Page of Table 78

		AW	VT	NT	NT	NT	NT	VT	NT	XC	VT	NT	TP	XC	AW	VT	NT	NT	NT	NT	VT
		◇ A 🍴	◇1 ⊠				B	◇1 ⊠		◇1 C 🍴	◇1 ⊠	D	◇1 E 🍴	◇1 F 🍴	◇ G 🍴	◇1 ⊠				B	◇1 ⊠
Deansgate	d																				
Manchester Oxford Road	d																				
Manchester Piccadilly 10	a																				
	d	08 30	08 35	08 38	08 46	08 48	08 52	08 55	09 04	09 07	09 15	09 17	09 20	09 27	09 30	09 35	09 38	09 46	09 48	09 52	09 55
Levenshulme	d			08 43			08 58		09 09								09 43			09 58	
Heaton Chapel	d			08 46			09 01		09 12								09 46			10 01	
Stockport	a	08 38	08 42	08 50		08 57	09 04	09 03	09 16	09 15	09 22	09 27	09 28	09 34	09 38	09 42	09 50		09 57	10 04	10 03
	d	08 39	08 43	08 51		08 58		09 04	09 17	09 16	09 23			09 35	09 39	09 43	09 51		09 58		10 04
Cheadle Hulme	d			08 55		09 02			09 24								09 55		10 02		
Bramhall	d					09 05													10 05		
Poynton	d					09 08													10 08		
Adlington (Cheshire)	d					09 11													10 11		
Prestbury	d					09 14													10 14		
Macclesfield	a		08 55			09 18								09 47		09 55			10 18		
	d		08 56			09 18								09 49		09 56			10 18		
Congleton	d					09 26													10 26		
Handforth	d			08 59					09 28								09 59				
Manchester Airport ✈	d				09 11													10 11			
Styal	d																				
Wilmslow	d	08 46		09 02	09 21			09 11	09 31						09 46		10 02	10 21			10 11
Alderley Edge	d			09 05	09 24				09 34								10a08	10 24			
Chelford	d								09 38												
Goostrey	d								09 43												
Holmes Chapel	d				09 32				09 46									10 32			
Sandbach	d				09 36				09 51									10 36			
Crewe 10 65	a	09 07		09 23	09 46			09 27	10 01						10 05			10 46			10 27
Kidsgrove 50	a					09 32													10 32		
Longport 50	a																				
Stoke-on-Trent 50,68	a		09 11			09 42				09 43	09 48			10 06		10 11			10 42		
Stafford 68	a									10 02				10 24							
Wolverhampton 7 68	a									10 15				10 39							
Birmingham New Street 12 68	a									10 39				10 58							
London Euston 15 ⊖65	a		10 42					11 04			11 23					11 42					12 04

		NT	XC	VT	NT	TP	XC	AW	VT	NT	NT	NT	NT	VT	NT	XC	VT	NT	TP	XC	AW
			◇1 C 🍴	◇1 ⊠	D	◇1 E 🍴	◇1 F 🍴	◇ A 🍴	◇1 ⊠				B	◇1 ⊠		◇1 C 🍴	◇1 ☕	D	◇1 E 🍴	◇1 F 🍴	◇ G 🍴
Deansgate	d																				
Manchester Oxford Road	d																				
Manchester Piccadilly 10	a																				
	d	10 04	10 07	10 15	10 17	10 20	10 27	10 30	10 35	10 38	10 46	10 48	10 52	10 55	11 04	11 07	11 15	11 17	11 20	11 27	11 30
Levenshulme	d	10 09								10 43			10 58		11 09						
Heaton Chapel	d	10 12								10 46			11 01		11 12						
Stockport	a	10 16	10 15	10 22	10 27	10 28	10 34	10 38	10 42	10 50		10 57	11 04	11 03	11 16	11 15	11 22	11 27	11 28	11 34	11 38
	d	10 17	10 16	10 23			10 35	10 39	10 43	10 51		10 58		11 04	11 17	11 16	11 23			11 35	11 39
Cheadle Hulme	d	10 24								10 55		11 02			11 24						
Bramhall	d											11 05									
Poynton	d											11 08									
Adlington (Cheshire)	d											11 11									
Prestbury	d											11 14									
Macclesfield	a						10 47		10 55			11 18								11 47	
	d						10 49		10 56			11 18								11 49	
Congleton	d											11 26									
Handforth	d	10 28								10 59					11 28						
Manchester Airport ✈	d										11 11										
Styal	d										11 18										
Wilmslow	d	10 31						10 46		11 02	11 22			11 11	11 31						11 46
Alderley Edge	d	10 34								11a08	11 25				11 34						
Chelford	d	10 38													11 38						
Goostrey	d	10 43													11 43						
Holmes Chapel	d	10 46									11 33				11 46						
Sandbach	d	10 51									11 37				11 51						
Crewe 10 65	a	11 01						11 05			11 47			11 27	12 01						12 05
Kidsgrove 50	a											11 32									
Longport 50	a																				
Stoke-on-Trent 50,68	a		10 43	10 48			11 06		11 11			11 42				11 43	11 48			12 06	
Stafford 68	a		11 01				11 24									12 02				12 24	
Wolverhampton 7 68	a		11 15				11 39									12 15				12 39	
Birmingham New Street 12 68	a		11 32				11 58									12 39				12 58	
London Euston 15 ⊖65	a			12 23					12 42					13 03			13 23				

A To Milford Haven
B To Buxton
C To Bristol Temple Meads
D To Chester
E From Manchester Airport to Cleethorpes
F To Bournemouth
G To Carmarthen

Table 84

Mondays to Fridays
2 July to 28 September

Manchester, Stockport and Manchester Airport - Crewe and Stoke-on-Trent

Network Diagram - see first Page of Table 78

		VT	NT	NT	NT	NT	VT	NT	XC	VT	NT	TP	XC	AW	VT	NT	NT	NT	NT	VT	NT
		◇1 ☕				A	◇1 ☕		◇1 B 🍴	◇1 ☕	C	◇1 D 🍴	◇1 E 🍴	■ F 🍴	◇1 ☕				A	◇1 ☕	
Deansgate	d																				
Manchester Oxford Road	d																				
Manchester Piccadilly 10	a																				
	d	11 35	11 38	11 46	11 48	11 52	11 55	12 04	12 07	12 15	12 17	12 20	12 27	12 30	12 35	12 38	12 46	12 48	12 52	12 55	13 04
Levenshulme	d		11 43			11 58		12 09								12 43			12 58		13 09
Heaton Chapel	d		11 46			12 01		12 12								12 46			13 01		13 12
Stockport	a	11 42	11 50		11 57	12 04	12 03	12 16	12 15	12 22	12 27	12 28	12 34	12 38	12 42	12 50		12 57	13 04	13 03	13 16
	d	11 43	11 51		11 58		12 04	12 17	12 16	12 23			12 35	12 39	12 43	12 51		12 58		13 04	13 17
Cheadle Hulme	d		11 55		12 02			12 24								12 55		13 02			13 24
Bramhall	d				12 05													13 05			
Poynton	d				12 08													13 08			
Adlington (Cheshire)	d				12 11													13 11			
Prestbury	d				12 14													13 14			
Macclesfield	a	11 55			12 18								12 47		12 55			13 18			
	d	11 56			12 18								12 49		12 56			13 18			
Congleton	d				12 26													13 26			
Handforth	d		11 59					12 28								12 59					13 28
Manchester Airport ✈	d			12 11													13 11				
Styal	d																13 18				
Wilmslow	d		12 02	12 21			12 11	12 31						12 46		13 02	13 22			13 11	13 31
Alderley Edge	d		12a08	12 24				12 34								13a08	13 25				13 34
Chelford	d							12 38													13 38
Goostrey	d							12 43													13 43
Holmes Chapel	d			12 32				12 46									13 33				13 46
Sandbach	d			12 36				12 51									13 37				13 51
Crewe 10 65	a			12 46			12 27	13 01						13 05			13 47			13 27	14 01
Kidsgrove 50	a				12 32													13 32			
Longport 50	a																				
Stoke-on-Trent 50,68	a	12 11			12 42				12 43	12 48			13 06		13 11			13 42			
Stafford 68	a								13 01				13 24								
Wolverhampton 7 68	a								13 15				13 39								
Birmingham New Street 12 68	a								13 39				13 58								
London Euston 15 ⊖65	a	13 42					14 04			14 23					14 42					15 04	

		XC	VT	NT	TP	XC	AW	VT	NT	NT	NT	NT	VT	NT	XC	VT	NT	TP	XC	AW	VT
		◇1 G 🍴	◇1 ☕	C	◇1 D 🍴	◇1 E 🍴	■ H 🍴	◇1 ☕				A	◇1 ☕		◇1 I 🍴	◇1 ☕	C	◇1 D 🍴	◇1 E 🍴	■ F 🍴	◇1 ☕
Deansgate	d																				
Manchester Oxford Road	d																				
Manchester Piccadilly 10	a																				
	d	13 07	13 15	13 17	13 20	13 27	13 30	13 35	13 38	13 46	13 48	13 52	13 55	14 04	14 07	14 15	14 17	14 20	14 27	14 30	14 35
Levenshulme	d								13 43			13 58		14 09							
Heaton Chapel	d								13 46			14 01		14 12							
Stockport	a	13 15	13 22	13 27	13 28	13 34	13 38	13 42	13 50		13 57	14 04	14 03	14 16	14 15	14 22	14 27	14 28	14 34	14 38	14 42
	d	13 16	13 23			13 35	13 39	13 43	13 51		13 58		14 04	14 17	14 16	14 23			14 35	14 39	14 43
Cheadle Hulme	d								13 55		14 02			14 24							
Bramhall	d										14 05										
Poynton	d										14 08										
Adlington (Cheshire)	d										14 11										
Prestbury	d										14 14										
Macclesfield	a					13 47		13 55			14 18								14 47		14 55
	d					13 49		13 56			14 18								14 49		14 56
Congleton	d										14 26										
Handforth	d								13 59					14 28							
Manchester Airport ✈	d									14 11											
Styal	d																				
Wilmslow	d						13 46		14 02	14 21			14 11	14 31						14 46	
Alderley Edge	d								14a08	14 24				14 34							
Chelford	d													14 38							
Goostrey	d													14 43							
Holmes Chapel	d									14 32				14 46							
Sandbach	d									14 36				14 51							
Crewe 10 65	a						14 05			14 46			14 27	15 01						15 05	
Kidsgrove 50	a										14 32										
Longport 50	a																				
Stoke-on-Trent 50,68	a	13 43	13 48			14 06		14 11			14 42				14 43	14 48			15 06		15 11
Stafford 68	a	14 01				14 24									15 02				15 24		
Wolverhampton 7 68	a	14 15				14 39									15 15				15 39		
Birmingham New Street 12 68	a	14 32				14 58									15 39				15 58		
London Euston 15 ⊖65	a		15 23					15 42					16 04			16 23					16 42

A To Buxton
B To Exeter St Davids
C To Chester
D From Manchester Airport to Cleethorpes
E To Bournemouth
F To Milford Haven
G To Bristol Temple Meads
H To Tenby
I To Paignton

2 July to 28 September

Manchester, Stockport and Manchester Airport - Crewe and Stoke-on-Trent

Network Diagram - see first Page of Table 78

		NT	NT	NT	NT	VT	NT	XC	VT	NT	TP	XC	AW	VT	NT	NT	NT	NT	VT	NT	XC
					A	◇1 ⊏⊐		◇1 B ⊼	◇1 ⊏⊐	C	◇1 D ⊼	◇1 E ⊼	■ F ⊼	◇1 ⊏⊐				A	◇1 ⊏⊐		◇1 B ⊼
Deansgate	d																				
Manchester Oxford Road	d																				
Manchester Piccadilly	a																				
	d	14 38	14 46	14 48	14 52	14 55	15 04	15 07	15 15	15 17	15 20	15 27	15 30	15 35	15 38	15 46	15 48	15 52	15 55	16 04	16 07
Levenshulme	d	14 43			14 58		15 09								15 43			15 58		16 09	
Heaton Chapel	d	14 46			15 01		15 12								15 46			16 01		16 12	
Stockport	a	14 50		14 57	15 04	15 03	15 16	15 15	15 22	15 27	15 28	15 34	15 38	15 42	15 50		15 57	16 04	16 03	16 16	16 15
	d	14 51		14 58		15 04	15 17	15 16	15 23			15 35	15 39	15 43	15 51		15 58		16 04	16 17	16 16
Cheadle Hulme	d	14 55		15 02			15 24								15 55		16 02			16 24	
Bramhall	d			15 05													16 05				
Poynton	d			15 08													16 08				
Adlington (Cheshire)	d			15 11													16 11				
Prestbury	d			15 14													16 14				
Macclesfield	a			15 18								15 47		15 55			16 18				
	d			15 18								15 49		15 56			16 18				
Congleton	d			15 26													16 26				
Handforth	d	14 59					15 28								15 59					16 28	
Manchester Airport	d		15 11																		
Styal	d															16 11					
Wilmslow	d	15 02	15 21			15 11	15 31						15 46		16 02	16 21			16 11	16 31	
Alderley Edge	d	15a08	15 24				15 34								16a08	16 24				16 34	
Chelford	d						15 38													16 38	
Goostrey	d						15 43													16 43	
Holmes Chapel	d		15 32				15 46									16 32				16 46	
Sandbach	d		15 36				15 51									16 36				16 51	
Crewe 65	a		15 46			15 27	16 01						16 05			16 46			16 27	17 01	
Kidsgrove 50	a			15 32													16 32				
Longport 50	a																				
Stoke-on-Trent 50,68	a			15 42				15 43	15 48			16 06		16 11			16 42				16 43
Stafford 68	a							16 02				16 24									17 02
Wolverhampton 68	a							16 15				16 39									17 15
Birmingham New Street 68	a							16 39				16 58									17 32
London Euston ⊖65	a					17 04			17 23					17 42					18 03		

		VT	NT	TP	XC	AW	VT	NT	NT	NT	NT	VT	NT	NT	XC	NT	VT	NT	TP	NT	XC
		◇1 ⊏⊐	C	◇1 D ⊼	◇1 E ⊼	■ G ⊼	◇1 ⊏⊐				A	◇1 ⊏⊐	H		◇1 I ⊼	C	◇1 ⊠		◇1 D ⊼	J	◇1 E ⊼
Deansgate	d																	17 10			
Manchester Oxford Road	d																	17 13			
Manchester Piccadilly	a																	17 15			
	d	16 15	16 17	16 20	16 27	16 30	16 35	16 38	16 46	16 48	16 51	16 55	16 58	17 03	17 05	17 09	17 15	17 17	17 20	17 23	17 27
Levenshulme	d							16 43					17 03	17 08						17 28	
Heaton Chapel	d							16 46					17 06	17 11						17 31	
Stockport	a	16 22	16 27	16 28	16 34	16 38	16 42	16 50		16 58	17 02	17 03	17 10	17 15	17 12	17 17	17 22	17 27	17 28	17 35	17 35
	d	16 23			16 35	16 39	16 43	16 51		16 58		17 04		17 16	17 13		17 23	17 28			17 35
Cheadle Hulme	d							16 55		17 02				17 24				17 32			
Bramhall	d									17 05								17 35			
Poynton	d									17 08								17 38			
Adlington (Cheshire)	d									17 11								17 41			
Prestbury	d									17 14								17 44			
Macclesfield	a				16 47		16 55			17 18					17 25			17 48			
	d				16 49		16 56			17 18					17 27			17 48			
Congleton	d									17 26								17 56			
Handforth	d							16 59						17 28							
Manchester Airport	d								17 11												
Styal	d								17 18												
Wilmslow	d					16 46		17 03	17 22			17 11		17 31							17 44
Alderley Edge	d							17a09	17 25					17 34							
Chelford	d													17 38							
Goostrey	d													17 43							
Holmes Chapel	d								17 33					17 46							
Sandbach	d								17 37					17 51							
Crewe 65	a					17 05			17 47			17 27		18 01							18 04
Kidsgrove 50	a									17 32											
Longport 50	a																				
Stoke-on-Trent 50,68	a	16 49			17 06		17 11			17 42					17 43		17 49	18 10			
Stafford 68	a				17 24										18 03						18 27
Wolverhampton 68	a				17 39										18 15						18 39
Birmingham New Street 68	a				17 58										18 38						18 58
London Euston ⊖65	a	18 23					18 42					19 08					19 23				

A To Buxton
B To Bristol Temple Meads
C To Chester
D From Manchester Airport to Cleethorpes
E To Bournemouth
F To Pembroke Dock
G To Milford Haven
H To Hazel Grove
I To Cardiff Central
J To Chinley

2 July to 28 September

Manchester, Stockport and Manchester Airport - Crewe and Stoke-on-Trent

Network Diagram - see first Page of Table 78

		AW	VT	NT	NT	NT	NT	VT	XC	NT	VT	NT	TP	NT	XC	AW	VT	NT	NT	NT	NT	VT
		■ A ⊼	◇1 ⊠				B	◇1 ⊠	◇1 C ⊼		◇1 ⊠	D	◇1 E ⊼	F	◇1 G ⊼	◇ H ⊼	◇1 ⊠				B	◇1 ⊠
Deansgate	d													18 12								
Manchester Oxford Road	d													18 16								
Manchester Piccadilly	a													18 18								
	d	17 30	17 35	17 38	17 46	17 48	17 52	17 55	18 05	18 08	18 15	18 17	18 20	18 21	18 27	18 30	18 35	18 38	18 46	18 48	18 52	18 55
Levenshulme	d			17 43			17 58			18 13				18 28				18 43			18 58	
Heaton Chapel	d			17 46			18 01			18 16				18 31				18 46			19 01	
Stockport	a	17 38	17 42	17 50		17 57	18 04	18 03	18 12	18 20	18 22	18 27	18 28	18 34	18 34	18 38	18 42	18 50		18 57	19 04	19 03
	d	17 39	17 43	17 51		17 58		18 04	18 13	18 21	18 23				18 35	18 39	18 43	18 51		18 58		19 04
Cheadle Hulme	d			17 55		18 02				18 25								18 55		19 02		
Bramhall	d					18 05														19 05		
Poynton	d					18 08														19 08		
Adlington (Cheshire)	d					18 11														19 11		
Prestbury	d					18 14														19 14		
Macclesfield	a		17 55			18 18			18 25								18 55			19 18		
	d		17 56			18 18			18 26								18 56			19 18		
Congleton	d					18 26									18 54					19 26		
Handforth	d			17 59						18 29								18 59				
Manchester Airport	d				18 11														19 14			
Styal	d				18 18																	
Wilmslow	d	17 46		18 02	18 22			18 11		18 31						18 46		19 02	19 26			19 11
Alderley Edge	d			18 05	18 25					18 34								19a08	19a32			
Chelford	d									18 38												
Goostrey	d									18 43												
Holmes Chapel	d				18 33					18 46												
Sandbach	d			18 16	18 37					18 50												
Crewe 65	a	18 07		18 26	18 47			18 27		19 00						19 05						19 27
Kidsgrove 50	a					18 32														19 32		
Longport 50	a																					
Stoke-on-Trent 50,68	a		18 11			18 42			18 43		18 48				19 06		19 11			19 42		
Stafford 68	a								19 01						19 24							
Wolverhampton 68	a								19 15						19 39							
Birmingham New Street 68	a								19 32						19 58							
London Euston ⊖65	a		19 42					20 06			20 23						20 42					21 06

		NT	XC	VT	NT	TP	NT	XC	AW	NT	NT	NT	VT	NT	XC	VT	NT	TP	XC	AW	NT
			◇1 I ⊼	◇1 ⊏⊐	D	◇1 E	J	◇1 K ⊼	◇ A			B	◇1 ⊏⊐		◇1	◇1 ⊏⊐	D	◇1 L	◇1	◇ A	
Deansgate	d																				
Manchester Oxford Road	d									19 43											20 43
Manchester Piccadilly	a									19 45											20 45
	d	19 04	19 07	19 15	19 17	19 18	19 22	19 27	19 30	19 46	19 48	19 51	19 55	20 04	20 07	20 15	20 17	20 20	20 27	20 30	20 46
Levenshulme	d	19 09					19 28					19 58		20 09							
Heaton Chapel	d	19 12					19 31					20 01		20 12							
Stockport	a	19 16	19 15	19 22	19 27	19 26	19 34	19 34	19 38		19 57	20 04	20 03	20 15	20 15	20 22	20 27	20 28	20 34	20 38	
	d	19 17	19 16	19 23				19 35	19 39		19 58		20 04	20 17	20 16	20 23			20 35	20 39	
Cheadle Hulme	d	19 24									20 02			20 23							
Bramhall	d										20 05										
Poynton	d										20 08										
Adlington (Cheshire)	d										20 11										
Prestbury	d										20 14										
Macclesfield	a			19 35				19 47			20 18					20 35			20 47		
	d			19 36				19 49			20 18					20 36			20 49		
Congleton	d										20 26										
Handforth	d	19 28												20 27							
Manchester Airport	d									20 14											21 15
Styal	d																				
Wilmslow	d	19 31							19 46	20a24			20 11	20 30						20 46	21a25
Alderley Edge	d	19 34												20 33							
Chelford	d	19 38												20 37							
Goostrey	d	19 43												20 42							
Holmes Chapel	d	19 46												20 45							
Sandbach	d	19 51												20 51							
Crewe 65	a	20 01							20 05				20 27	21 03						21 04	
Kidsgrove 50	a										20 32										
Longport 50	a																				
Stoke-on-Trent 50,68	a		19 43	19 51				20 06			20 42				20 43	20 51			21 06		
Stafford 68	a		20 03					20 25					20 47		21 02				21 24		
Wolverhampton 68	a		20 16					20 40							21 15				21 39		
Birmingham New Street 68	a		20 33					21 00							21 33				22 00		
London Euston ⊖65	a			21 26									22 12			22 33					

A To Cardiff Central
B To Buxton
C To Plymouth
D To Chester
E From Manchester Airport to Cleethorpes
F From Wigan Wallgate to Buxton
G To Bournemouth
H To Carmarthen
I To Bristol Temple Meads
J To Hazel Grove
K To Southampton Central
L From Manchester Airport to Sheffield

Table 84

Mondays to Fridays

2 July to 28 September

Manchester, Stockport and Manchester Airport - Crewe and Stoke-on-Trent

Network Diagram - see first Page of Table 78

		NT	NT	NT	VT	NT	TP	XC	AW	NT	NT	NT	NT	XC	NT	TP	AW	NT	NT	NT	NT	NT
					◇■		◇■	◇■						◇■		◇■	◇					
			A		🍴	B	C		D			A			B	E	D				A	
Deansgate ⇌	d																					
Manchester Oxford Road	d									21 43								22 43				
Manchester Piccadilly ■10 ⇌	a									21 45								22 45				
	d	20 48	20 51	21 04	21 15	21 17	21 20	21 27	21 35	21 46	21 48	21 52	22 04	22 07	22 17	22 20	22 35	22 46	22 48	23 04	23 10	23 14
Levenshulme	d		20 58	21 09								21 58	22 09							23 09		
Heaton Chapel	d		21 01	21 12								22 01	22 12							23 12		
Stockport	a	20 58	21 04	21 16	21 22	21 27	21 28	21 34	21 43		21 57	22 04	22 16	22 15	22 27	22 28	22 43		22 57	23 16	23 19	23 23
	d	20 58		21 17	21 23			21 35	21 44		21 58		22 17	22 16			22 44		22 58	23 16		23 23
Cheadle Hulme	d	21 02		21 24							22 02		22 24						23 02	23 23		23 27
Bramhall	d	21 05									22 05								23 05			23 30
Poynton	d	21 08									22 08								23 08			23 33
Adlington (Cheshire)	d	21 11									22 11								23 11			23 37
Prestbury	d	21 14									22 14								23 14			23 40
Macclesfield	a	21 18			21 35			21 47			22 18			22 28					23 20			23 46
	d	21 18			21 36			21 49			22 18			22 29								
Congleton	d	21 26									22 26											
Handforth	d			21 28									22 28							23 27		
Manchester Airport ✈	d									22 14								23 14				
Styal	d																					
Wilmslow	d			21 31					21 51	22a22			22 31				22 52	23a22		23 31		
Alderley Edge	d			21 34									22 34							23a37		
Chelford	d			21 38									22 38									
Goostrey	d			21 43									22 43									
Holmes Chapel	d			21 46									22 46									
Sandbach	d			21 51									22 51									
Crewe ■10 65	a			22 01					22 11				23 01				23 10					
Kidsgrove 50	a	21 32									22 32											
Longport 50	a																					
Stoke-on-Trent 50,68	a	21 42			21 51			22 07			22 42			22 46								
Stafford 68	a							22 25						23 06								
Wolverhampton ■7 68 ⇌	a							22 39						23 19								
Birmingham New Street ■12 68	a							22 58						23 39								
London Euston ■15 ⊖65	a				23 48																	

		NT	NT
		B	
Deansgate ⇌	d		
Manchester Oxford Road	d		
Manchester Piccadilly ■10 ⇌	a		
	d	23 17	23 38
Levenshulme	d		23 43
Heaton Chapel	d		23 46
Stockport	a	23 26	23 50
	d		23 50
Cheadle Hulme	d		23 54
Bramhall	d		
Poynton	d		
Adlington (Cheshire)	d		
Prestbury	d		
Macclesfield	a		
	d		
Congleton	d		
Handforth	d		23 58
Manchester Airport ✈	d		
Styal	d		
Wilmslow	d		00 01
Alderley Edge	d		00 04
Chelford	d		00 08
Goostrey	d		00 12
Holmes Chapel	d		00 15
Sandbach	d		00 20
Crewe ■10 65	a		00 30
Kidsgrove 50	a		
Longport 50	a		
Stoke-on-Trent 50,68	a		
Stafford 68	a		
Wolverhampton ■7 68 ⇌	a		
Birmingham New Street ■12 68	a		
London Euston ■15 ⊖65	a		

A To Buxton
B To Chester
C From Manchester Airport to Cleethorpes
D To Shrewsbury
E From Manchester Airport to Sheffield

Table 84

Mondays to Fridays

from 1 October

Manchester, Stockport and Manchester Airport - Crewe and Stoke-on-Trent

Network Diagram - see first Page of Table 78

		NT	VT	XC	NT	TP	NT	VT	XC	NT	NT	VT	NT	NT	VT	AW	NT	VT	VT	NT	NT	VT
		MX	◇■	◇■		◇■		◇■	◇■			◇■			◇■	◇		◇■	◇■			◇■
				A		B	C		D				E	F		G					H	
			⊠	⊥				⊠	⊥			⊠			⊠	⊥		⊠	⊠			⊠
Deansgate ⇌	d																					
Manchester Oxford Road	d																					
Manchester Piccadilly ■10 ⇌	a																					
	d	23p38	05 05	05 11	05 35	05 44	05 50	05 55	06 00		06 06	06 10	06 18	06 21	06 27	06 30	06 32	06 35	06 43	06 46	06 49	07 00
Levenshulme	d	23p43									06 11			06 28			06 37				06 55	
Heaton Chapel	d	23p46									06 14			06 31			06 40				06 58	
Stockport	a	23p50	05 12			05 52	05 59	06 02	06 07		06 18	06 17	06 27	06 34	06 34	06 38	06 44	06 43	06 50		07 01	
	d	23p50	05 13					06 03	06 08		06 19	06 18			06 35	06 39	06 45	06 43	06 51			07u07
Cheadle Hulme	d	23p54									06 26						06 51					
Bramhall	d																06 54					
Poynton	d																06 57					
Adlington (Cheshire)	d																07 01					
Prestbury	d																07 04					
Macclesfield	a											06 30			06 47		07 07	06 55				
	d									06 03		06 31			06 48		07 08	06 56				
Congleton	d									06 10							07 15					
Handforth	d	23p58									06 30											
Manchester Airport ✈	d				06 05															07 11		
Styal	d																					
Wilmslow	d	00 01			06 17			06 11			06 34					06 46			06 59	07 21		
Alderley Edge	d	00 04			06 20						06 37									07 24		
Chelford	d	00 08			06 24																	
Goostrey	d	00 12			06 29																	
Holmes Chapel	d	00 15			06 32						06 47									07 32		
Sandbach	d	00 20			06 36						06 53									07 36		
Crewe ■10 65	a	00 30	05 34	05 44	06 46			06 27	06 32		07 04					07 05			07 15	07 46		
Kidsgrove 50	a									06 16												
Longport 50	a																					
Stoke-on-Trent 50,68	a			06 06						06 26		06 46			07 04		07 30	07 11				
Stafford 68	a		05 53	06 24					06 57						07 27				07 34			
Wolverhampton ■7 68 ⇌	a			06 39					07 12						07 43							
Birmingham New Street ■12 68	a			06 58					07 31						08 06							
London Euston ■15 ⊖65	a		07 28					08 07				08 22			09 34			08 45	08 52			08 58

		NT	XC	VT	NT	TP	NT	XC	AW	VT	NT	NT	NT	NT	VT	NT	XC	VT	NT	TP	XC
			◇■	◇■		◇■		◇■	◇	◇■					◇■		◇■	◇■		◇■	◇■
			D		E	B	I	A	J					H			K		E	B	A
			⊥	⊠		⊥		⊥	⊥	⊠					⊠		⊥	⊠		⊥	⊥
Deansgate ⇌	d						07 11														
Manchester Oxford Road	d						07 15														
Manchester Piccadilly ■10 ⇌	a						07 17														
	d	07 03	07 07	07 15	07 17	07 20	07 21	07 26	07 30	07 35	07 38	07 46	07 48	07 52	07 55	08 04	08 07	08 15	08 17	08 20	08 27
Levenshulme	d	07 09					07 28				07 43					08 09					
Heaton Chapel	d	07 12					07 31				07 46					08 12					
Stockport	a	07 16	07 15	07 22	07 26	07 28	07 34	07 34	07 38	07 43	07 50		07 57	08 01	08 03	08 16	08 15	08 22	08 27	08 28	08 34
	d	07 18	07 16	07 23				07 35	07 39	07 43	07 51		07 58		08 04	08 17	08 16	08 23			08 35
Cheadle Hulme	d	07 24									07 55		08 02			08 24					
Bramhall	d												08 05								
Poynton	d												08 08								
Adlington (Cheshire)	d												08 11								
Prestbury	d												08 14								
Macclesfield	a							07 47		07 56			08 18								08 47
	d							07 49		07 56			08 18								08 49
Congleton	d												08 26								
Handforth	d	07 28									07 59					08 28					
Manchester Airport ✈	d											08 11									
Styal	d											08 18									
Wilmslow	d	07 31							07 46		08 02	08 22			08 11	08 31					
Alderley Edge	d	07 34									08a08	08 25				08 34					
Chelford	d	07 38														08 38					
Goostrey	d	07 43														08 43					
Holmes Chapel	d	07 46										08 33				08 46					
Sandbach	d	07 51										08 37				08 52					
Crewe ■10 65	a	08 01							08 05			08 47			08 27	09 04					
Kidsgrove 50	a												08 32								
Longport 50	a																				
Stoke-on-Trent 50,68	a		07 43	07 48				08 06		08 12			08 42				08 43	08 48			09 06
Stafford 68	a		08 01					08 24									09 02				09 24
Wolverhampton ■7 68 ⇌	a		08 15					08 39									09 15				09 39
Birmingham New Street ■12 68	a		08 32					08 58									09 32				09 58
London Euston ■15 ⊖65	a			09 23						09 52					10 04			10 23			

A To Bournemouth
B From Manchester Airport to Cleethorpes
C To Sheffield
D To Bristol Temple Meads
E To Chester
F To Hazel Grove
G To Milford Haven
H To Buxton
I From Wigan Wallgate to Hazel Grove
J To Carmarthen
K To Paignton

Manchester, Stockport and Manchester Airport - Crewe and Stoke-on-Trent

Network Diagram - see first Page of Table 78

		AW	VT	NT	NT	NT	NT	VT	NT	XC	VT	NT	TP	XC	AW	VT	NT	NT	NT	NT	VT
		A					B			C		D	E	F	G					B	
Deansgate	d																				
Manchester Oxford Road	d																				
Manchester Piccadilly	a																				
	d	08 30	08 35	08 38	08 46	08 48	08 52	08 55	09 04	09 07	09 15	09 17	09 20	09 27	09 30	09 35	09 38	09 46	09 48	09 52	09 55
Levenshulme	d			08 43			08 58		09 09								09 43			09 58	
Heaton Chapel	d			08 46			09 01		09 12								09 46			10 01	
Stockport	a	08 38	08 42	08 50		08 57	09 04	09 03	09 16	09 15	09 22	09 27	09 28	09 34	09 38	09 42	09 50		09 57	10 04	10 03
	d	08 39	08 43	08 51		08 58		09 04	09 17	09 16	09 23			09 35	09 39	09 43	09 51		09 58		10 04
Cheadle Hulme	d			08 55		09 02			09 24								09 55		10 02		
Bramhall	d					09 05													10 05		
Poynton	d					09 08													10 08		
Adlington (Cheshire)	d					09 11													10 11		
Prestbury	d					09 14													10 14		
Macclesfield	a		08 55			09 18								09 47		09 55			10 18		
	d		08 56			09 18								09 49		09 56			10 18		
Congleton	d					09 26													10 26		
Handforth	d			08 59					09 28								09 59				
Manchester Airport	d				09 11													10 11			
Styal	d																				
Wilmslow	d	08 46		09 02	09 21			09 11	09 31						09 46		10 02	10 21			10 11
Alderley Edge	d			09 05	09 24				09 34								10a08	10 24			
Chelford	d								09 38												
Goostrey	d								09 43												
Holmes Chapel	d				09 32				09 46									10 32			
Sandbach	d				09 36				09 51									10 36			
Crewe 65	a	09 07		09 23	09 46			09 27	10 01						10 05			10 46			10 27
Kidsgrove 50	a					09 32													10 32		
Longport 50	a																				
Stoke-on-Trent 50,68	a		09 11			09 42				09 43	09 48			10 06		10 11			10 42		
Stafford 68	a									10 02				10 24							
Wolverhampton 68	a									10 15				10 39							
Birmingham New Street 68	a									10 39				10 58							
London Euston ⊖65	a		10 42					11 04			11 23					11 42					12 04

		NT	XC	VT	NT	TP	XC	AW	VT	NT	NT	NT	NT	VT	NT	XC	VT	NT	TP	XC	AW
			C		D	E	F	A					B			C		D	E	F	G
Deansgate	d																				
Manchester Oxford Road	d																				
Manchester Piccadilly	a																				
	d	10 04	10 07	10 15	10 17	10 20	10 27	10 30	10 35	10 38	10 46	10 48	10 52	10 55	11 04	11 07	11 15	11 17	11 20	11 27	11 30
Levenshulme	d	10 09								10 43			10 58		11 09						
Heaton Chapel	d	10 12								10 46			11 01		11 12						
Stockport	a	10 16	10 15	10 22	10 27	10 28	10 34	10 38	10 42	10 50		10 57	11 04	11 03	11 16	11 15	11 22	11 27	11 28	11 34	11 38
	d	10 17	10 16	10 23			10 35	10 39	10 43	10 51		10 58		11 04	11 17	11 16	11 23			11 35	11 39
Cheadle Hulme	d	10 24								10 55		11 02			11 24						
Bramhall	d											11 05									
Poynton	d											11 08									
Adlington (Cheshire)	d											11 11									
Prestbury	d											11 14									
Macclesfield	a						10 47		10 55			11 18								11 47	
	d						10 49		10 56			11 18								11 49	
Congleton	d											11 26									
Handforth	d	10 28								10 59					11 28						
Manchester Airport	d										11 11										
Styal	d										11 18										
Wilmslow	d	10 31						10 46		11 02	11 22			11 11	11 31						11 46
Alderley Edge	d	10 34								11a08	11 25				11 34						
Chelford	d	10 38													11 38						
Goostrey	d	10 43													11 43						
Holmes Chapel	d	10 46									11 33				11 46						
Sandbach	d	10 51									11 37				11 51						
Crewe 65	a	11 01						11 05			11 47			11 27	12 01						12 05
Kidsgrove 50	a											11 32									
Longport 50	a																				
Stoke-on-Trent 50,68	a		10 43	10 48			11 06		11 11			11 42				11 43	11 48			12 06	
Stafford 68	a		11 01				11 24									12 02				12 24	
Wolverhampton 68	a		11 15				11 39									12 15				12 39	
Birmingham New Street 68	a		11 32				11 58									12 39				12 58	
London Euston ⊖65	a			12 23					12 42					13 03			13 23				

A To Milford Haven
B To Buxton
C To Bristol Temple Meads
D To Chester
E From Manchester Airport to Cleethorpes
F To Bournemouth
G To Carmarthen

Manchester, Stockport and Manchester Airport - Crewe and Stoke-on-Trent

Network Diagram - see first Page of Table 78

		VT	NT	NT	NT	NT	VT	NT	XC	VT	NT	TP	XC	AW	VT	NT	NT	NT	NT	VT	NT
						A			B		C	D	E	F					A		
Deansgate	d																				
Manchester Oxford Road	d																				
Manchester Piccadilly	a																				
	d	11 35	11 38	11 46	11 48	11 52	11 55	12 04	12 07	12 15	12 17	12 20	12 27	12 30	12 35	12 38	12 46	12 48	12 52	12 55	13 04
Levenshulme	d		11 43			11 58		12 09								12 43			12 58		13 09
Heaton Chapel	d		11 46			12 01		12 12								12 46			13 01		13 12
Stockport	a	11 42	11 50		11 57	12 04	12 03	12 16	12 15	12 22	12 27	12 28	12 34	12 38	12 42	12 50		12 57	13 04	13 03	13 16
	d	11 43	11 51		11 58		12 04	12 17	12 16	12 23			12 35	12 39	12 43	12 51		12 58		13 04	13 17
Cheadle Hulme	d		11 55		12 02			12 24								12 55		13 02			13 24
Bramhall	d				12 05													13 05			
Poynton	d				12 08													13 08			
Adlington (Cheshire)	d				12 11													13 11			
Prestbury	d				12 14													13 14			
Macclesfield	a	11 55			12 18								12 47		12 55			13 18			
	d	11 56			12 18								12 49		12 56			13 18			
Congleton	d				12 26													13 26			
Handforth	d		11 59					12 28								12 59					13 28
Manchester Airport	d			12 11													13 11				
Styal	d																13 18				
Wilmslow	d		12 02	12 21			12 11	12 31						12 46		13 02	13 22			13 11	13 31
Alderley Edge	d		12a08	12 24				12 34								13a08	13 25				13 34
Chelford	d							12 38													13 38
Goostrey	d							12 43													13 43
Holmes Chapel	d			12 32				12 46									13 33				13 46
Sandbach	d			12 36				12 51									13 37				13 51
Crewe 65	a			12 46			12 27	13 01						13 05			13 47			13 27	14 01
Kidsgrove 50	a				12 32													13 32			
Longport 50	a																				
Stoke-on-Trent 50,68	a	12 11			12 42				12 43	12 48			13 06		13 11			13 42			
Stafford 68	a								13 01				13 24								
Wolverhampton 68	a								13 15				13 39								
Birmingham New Street 68	a								13 39				13 58								
London Euston ⊖65	a	13 42					14 04			14 23					14 42					15 04	

		XC	VT	NT	TP	XC	AW	VT	NT	NT	NT	NT	VT	NT	XC	VT	NT	TP	XC	AW	VT
		G		C	D	E	H					A			I		C	D	E	F	
Deansgate	d																				
Manchester Oxford Road	d																				
Manchester Piccadilly	a																				
	d	13 07	13 15	13 17	13 20	13 27	13 30	13 35	13 38	13 46	13 48	13 52	13 55	14 04	14 07	14 15	14 17	14 20	14 27	14 30	14 35
Levenshulme	d								13 43			13 58		14 09							
Heaton Chapel	d								13 46			14 01		14 12							
Stockport	a	13 15	13 22	13 27	13 28	13 34	13 38	13 42	13 50		13 57	14 04	14 03	14 16	14 15	14 22	14 27	14 28	14 34	14 38	14 42
	d	13 16	13 23			13 35	13 39	13 43	13 51		13 58		14 04	14 17	14 16	14 23			14 35	14 39	14 43
Cheadle Hulme	d								13 55		14 02			14 24							
Bramhall	d										14 05										
Poynton	d										14 08										
Adlington (Cheshire)	d										14 11										
Prestbury	d										14 14										
Macclesfield	a					13 47		13 55			14 18								14 47		14 55
	d					13 49		13 56			14 18								14 49		14 56
Congleton	d										14 26										
Handforth	d								13 59					14 28							
Manchester Airport	d									14 11											
Styal	d																				
Wilmslow	d						13 46		14 02	14 21			14 11	14 31						14 46	
Alderley Edge	d								14a08	14 24				14 34							
Chelford	d													14 38							
Goostrey	d													14 43							
Holmes Chapel	d									14 32				14 46							
Sandbach	d									14 36				14 51							
Crewe 65	a						14 05			14 46			14 27	15 01						15 05	
Kidsgrove 50	a										14 32										
Longport 50	a																				
Stoke-on-Trent 50,68	a	13 43	13 48			14 06		14 11			14 42				14 43	14 48			15 06		15 11
Stafford 68	a	14 01				14 24									15 02				15 24		
Wolverhampton 68	a	14 15				14 39									15 15				15 39		
Birmingham New Street 68	a	14 32				14 58									15 39				15 58		
London Euston ⊖65	a		15 23					15 42					16 04			16 23					16 42

A To Buxton
B To Exeter St Davids
C To Chester
D From Manchester Airport to Cleethorpes
E To Bournemouth
F To Milford Haven
G To Bristol Temple Meads
H To Tenby
I To Paignton

Manchester, Stockport and Manchester Airport - Crewe and Stoke-on-Trent

Network Diagram - see first Page of Table 78

Station			NT	NT	NT	NT	VT	NT	XC	VT	NT	TP	XC	AW	VT	NT	NT	NT	NT	VT	NT	XC
						A	◇1 ▭		◇1 B ⌶	◇1 ▭	C	◇1 D ⌶	◇1 E ⌶	■ F ⌶	◇1 ▭				A	◇1 ▭		◇1 B ⌶
Deansgate		d																				
Manchester Oxford Road		d																				
Manchester Piccadilly 10		a																				
		d	14 38	14 46	14 48	14 52	14 55	15 04	15 07	15 15	15 17	15 20	15 27	15 30	15 35	15 38	15 46	15 48	15 52	15 55	16 04	16 07
Levenshulme		d	14 43			14 58		15 09								15 43			15 58		16 09	
Heaton Chapel		d	14 46			15 01		15 12								15 46			16 01		16 12	
Stockport		a	14 50		14 57	15 04	15 03	15 16	15 15	15 22	15 27	15 28	15 34	15 38	15 42	15 50		15 57	16 04	16 03	16 16	16 15
		d	14 51		14 58		15 04	15 17	15 16	15 23			15 35	15 39	15 43	15 51		15 58		16 04	16 17	16 16
Cheadle Hulme		d	14 55		15 02			15 24								15 55		16 02			16 24	
Bramhall		d			15 05													16 05				
Poynton		d			15 08													16 08				
Adlington (Cheshire)		d			15 11													16 11				
Prestbury		d			15 14													16 14				
Macclesfield		a			15 18								15 47		15 55			16 18				
		d			15 18								15 49		15 56			16 18				
Congleton		d			15 26													16 26				
Handforth		d	14 59					15 28								15 59					16 28	
Manchester Airport ✈		d		15 11													16 11					
Styal		d																				
Wilmslow		d	15 02	15 21			15 11	15 31						15 46		16 02	16 21			16 11	16 31	
Alderley Edge		d	15a08	15 24				15 34								16a08	16 24				16 34	
Chelford		d						15 38													16 38	
Goostrey		d						15 43													16 43	
Holmes Chapel		d		15 32				15 46									16 32				16 46	
Sandbach		d		15 36				15 51									16 36				16 51	
Crewe 10	65	a		15 46			15 27	16 01						16 05			16 46			16 27	17 01	
Kidsgrove	50	a			15 32													16 32				
Longport	50	a																				
Stoke-on-Trent	50,68	a			15 42				15 43	15 48			16 06		16 11			16 42				16 43
Stafford	68	a							16 02				16 24									17 02
Wolverhampton 7	68	a							16 15				16 39									17 15
Birmingham New Street 12	68	a							16 39				16 58									17 32
London Euston 15	⊖65	a					17 04			17 23					17 42					18 03		

Station			VT	NT	TP	XC	AW	VT	NT	NT	NT	NT	VT	NT	NT	XC	NT	VT	NT	TP	NT	XC
			◇1 ▭	C	◇1 D ⌶	◇1 E ⌶	■ G ⌶	◇1 ▭				A	◇1 ▭	H		◇1 I ⌶	C	◇1 ⊠		◇1 D ⌶	J	◇1 E ⌶
Deansgate		d																	17 10			
Manchester Oxford Road		d																	17 13			
Manchester Piccadilly 10		a																	17 15			
		d	16 15	16 17	16 20	16 27	16 30	16 35	16 38	16 46	16 48	16 51	16 55	16 58	17 03	17 05	17 09	17 15	17 17	17 20	17 23	17 27
Levenshulme		d							16 43					17 03	17 08						17 28	
Heaton Chapel		d							16 46					17 06	17 11						17 31	
Stockport		a	16 22	16 27	16 28	16 34	16 38	16 42	16 50		16 58	17 02	17 03	17 10	17 15	17 12	17 17	17 22	17 27	17 28	17 35	17 35
		d	16 23			16 35	16 39	16 43	16 51		16 58		17 04		17 16	17 13		17 23	17 28			17 35
Cheadle Hulme		d							16 55		17 02				17 24				17 32			
Bramhall		d									17 05								17 35			
Poynton		d									17 08								17 38			
Adlington (Cheshire)		d									17 11								17 41			
Prestbury		d									17 14								17 44			
Macclesfield		a				16 47		16 55			17 18					17 25			17 48			
		d				16 49		16 56			17 18					17 27			17 48			
Congleton		d									17 26								17 56			
Handforth		d							16 59						17 28							
Manchester Airport ✈		d								17 11												
Styal		d								17 18												
Wilmslow		d					16 46		17 03	17 22			17 11		17 31							17 44
Alderley Edge		d							17a09	17 25					17 34							
Chelford		d													17 38							
Goostrey		d													17 43							
Holmes Chapel		d								17 33					17 46							
Sandbach		d								17 37					17 51							
Crewe 10	65	a					17 05			17 47			17 27		18 01							18 04
Kidsgrove	50	a									17 32											
Longport	50	a																				
Stoke-on-Trent	50,68	a	16 49			17 06		17 11			17 42					17 43		17 49	18 10			
Stafford	68	a				17 24										18 03						18 27
Wolverhampton 7	68	a				17 39										18 15						18 39
Birmingham New Street 12	68	a				17 58										18 38						18 58
London Euston 15	⊖65	a	18 23					18 42					19 08					19 23				

A To Buxton
B To Bristol Temple Meads
C To Chester
D From Manchester Airport to Cleethorpes
E To Bournemouth
F To Pembroke Dock
G To Milford Haven
H To Hazel Grove
I To Cardiff Central
J To Chinley

Manchester, Stockport and Manchester Airport - Crewe and Stoke-on-Trent

Network Diagram - see first Page of Table 78

Station			AW	VT	NT	NT	NT	NT	VT	XC	NT	VT	NT	TP	NT	XC	AW	VT	NT	NT	NT	NT	VT
			■ A ⌶	◇1 ⊠				B	◇1 ⊠	◇1 C ⌶		◇1 ⊠	D	◇1 E ⌶	F	◇1 G ⌶	◇ H ⌶	◇1 ⊠				B	◇1 ⊠
Deansgate		d													18 12								
Manchester Oxford Road		d													18 16								
Manchester Piccadilly 10		a													18 18								
		d	17 30	17 35	17 38	17 46	17 48	17 52	17 55	18 05	18 08	18 15	18 17	18 20	18 21	18 27	18 30	18 35	18 38	18 46	18 48	18 52	18 55
Levenshulme		d			17 43			17 58			18 13				18 28				18 43			18 58	
Heaton Chapel		d			17 46			18 01			18 16				18 31				18 46			19 01	
Stockport		a	17 38	17 42	17 50		17 57	18 04	18 03	18 12	18 20	18 22	18 27	18 28	18 34	18 34	18 38	18 42	18 50		18 57	19 04	19 03
		d	17 39	17 43	17 51		17 58		18 04	18 13	18 21	18 23				18 35	18 39	18 43	18 51		18 58		19 04
Cheadle Hulme		d			17 55		18 02				18 25								18 55		19 02		
Bramhall		d					18 05														19 05		
Poynton		d					18 08														19 08		
Adlington (Cheshire)		d					18 11														19 11		
Prestbury		d					18 14														19 14		
Macclesfield		a		17 55			18 18			18 25								18 55			19 18		
		d		17 56			18 18			18 26								18 56			19 18		
Congleton		d					18 26									18 54					19 26		
Handforth		d			17 59						18 29								18 59				
Manchester Airport ✈		d				18 11														19 14			
Styal		d				18 18																	
Wilmslow		d	17 46		18 02	18 22			18 11		18 31						18 46		19 02	19 26			19 11
Alderley Edge		d			18 05	18 25					18 34								19a08	19a32			
Chelford		d									18 38												
Goostrey		d									18 43												
Holmes Chapel		d				18 33					18 46												
Sandbach		d			18 16	18 37					18 50												
Crewe 10	65	a	18 07		18 26	18 47			18 27		19 00						19 05						19 27
Kidsgrove	50	a					18 32														19 32		
Longport	50	a																					
Stoke-on-Trent	50,68	a		18 11			18 42			18 43		18 48				19 06		19 11			19 42		
Stafford	68	a								19 01						19 24							
Wolverhampton 7	68	a								19 15						19 39							
Birmingham New Street 12	68	a								19 32						19 58							
London Euston 15	⊖65	a		19 42					20 06			20 23						20 42					21 06

Station			NT	XC	VT	NT	TP	NT	XC	AW	NT	NT	NT	VT	NT	XC	VT	NT	TP	XC	AW	NT
				◇1 I ⌶	◇1 ▭	D	◇1 E	J	◇1 K ⌶	◇ A			B	◇1 ▭		◇1	◇1 ▭	D	◇1 L	◇1	◇ A	
Deansgate		d																				
Manchester Oxford Road		d									19 43											20 43
Manchester Piccadilly 10		a									19 45											20 45
		d	19 04	19 07	19 15	19 17	19 18	19 22	19 27	19 30	19 46	19 48	19 51	19 55	20 04	20 07	20 15	20 17	20 20	20 27	20 30	20 46
Levenshulme		d	19 09					19 28					19 58		20 09							
Heaton Chapel		d	19 12					19 31					20 01		20 12							
Stockport		a	19 16	19 15	19 22	19 27	19 26	19 34	19 34	19 38		19 57	20 04	20 03	20 15	20 15	20 22	20 27	20 28	20 34	20 38	
		d	19 17	19 16	19 23				19 35	19 39		19 58		20 04	20 17	20 16	20 23			20 35	20 39	
Cheadle Hulme		d	19 24									20 02			20 23							
Bramhall		d										20 05										
Poynton		d										20 08										
Adlington (Cheshire)		d										20 11										
Prestbury		d										20 14										
Macclesfield		a			19 35				19 47			20 18					20 35			20 47		
		d			19 36				19 49			20 18					20 36			20 49		
Congleton		d										20 26										
Handforth		d	19 28												20 27							
Manchester Airport ✈		d									20 14											21 15
Styal		d																				
Wilmslow		d	19 31							19 46	20a24			20 11	20 30						20 46	21a25
Alderley Edge		d	19 34												20 33							
Chelford		d	19 38												20 37							
Goostrey		d	19 43												20 42							
Holmes Chapel		d	19 46												20 45							
Sandbach		d	19 51												20 51							
Crewe 10	65	a	20 01							20 05				20 27	21 03						21 04	
Kidsgrove	50	a										20 32										
Longport	50	a																				
Stoke-on-Trent	50,68	a		19 43	19 51				20 06			20 42				20 43	20 51			21 06		
Stafford	68	a		20 03					20 25					20 47		21 02				21 24		
Wolverhampton 7	68	a		20 16					20 40							21 15				21 39		
Birmingham New Street 12	68	a		20 33					21 00							21 33				22 00		
London Euston 15	⊖65	a			21 26									22 12			22 33					

A To Cardiff Central
B To Buxton
C To Plymouth
D To Chester
E From Manchester Airport to Cleethorpes
F From Wigan Wallgate to Buxton
G To Bournemouth
H To Carmarthen
I To Bristol Temple Meads
J To Hazel Grove
K To Southampton Central
L From Manchester Airport to Sheffield

Manchester, Stockport and Manchester Airport - Crewe and Stoke-on-Trent

Network Diagram - see first Page of Table 78

	NT	NT	NT	VT	NT	TP	XC	AW	NT	NT	NT	NT	XC	NT	TP	AW	NT	NT	NT	NT	NT
				◇■		◇■	◇■						◇■		◇■	◇					
		A			B	C		D			A			B	E	D				A	
Deansgate d																					
Manchester Oxford Road d									21 43								22 43				
Manchester Piccadilly a									21 45								22 45				
Manchester Piccadilly d	20 48	20 51	21 04	21 15	21 17	21 20	21 27	21 35	21 46	21 48	21 52	22 04	22 07	22 17	22 20	22 35	22 46	22 48	23 04	23 10	23 14
Levenshulme d		20 58	21 09								21 58	22 09							23 09		
Heaton Chapel d		21 01	21 12								22 01	22 12							23 12		
Stockport a	20 58	21 04	21 16	21 22	21 27	21 28	21 34	21 43		21 57	22 04	22 16	22 15	22 27	22 28	22 43		22 57	23 16	23 19	23 23
Stockport d	20 58		21 17	21 23			21 35	21 44		21 58		22 17	22 16			22 44		22 58	23 16		23 23
Cheadle Hulme d	21 02		21 24							22 02		22 24						23 02	23 23		23 27
Bramhall d	21 05									22 05								23 05			23 30
Poynton d	21 08									22 08								23 08			23 33
Adlington (Cheshire) d	21 11									22 11								23 11			23 37
Prestbury d	21 14									22 14								23 14			23 40
Macclesfield a	21 18			21 35			21 47			22 18			22 28					23 20			23 46
Macclesfield d	21 18			21 36			21 49			22 18			22 29								
Congleton d	21 26									22 26											
Handforth d			21 28									22 28							23 27		
Manchester Airport d									22 14								23 14				
Styal d																					
Wilmslow d			21 31					21 51	22a22			22 31				22 52	23a22		23 31		
Alderley Edge d			21 34									22 34							23a37		
Chelford d			21 38									22 38									
Goostrey d			21 43									22 43									
Holmes Chapel d			21 46									22 46									
Sandbach d			21 51									22 51									
Crewe 65 a			22 01					22 11				23 01				23 10					
Kidsgrove 50 a	21 32									22 32											
Longport 50 a																					
Stoke-on-Trent 50,68 a	21 42			21 51			22 07			22 42			22 46								
Stafford 68 a							22 25						23 06								
Wolverhampton 68 a							22 39						23 19								
Birmingham New Street 68 a							22 58						23 39								
London Euston ⊖65 a				23 48																	

	NT	NT
	B	
Deansgate d		
Manchester Oxford Road d		
Manchester Piccadilly a		
Manchester Piccadilly d	23 17	23 38
Levenshulme d		23 43
Heaton Chapel d		23 46
Stockport a	23 26	23 50
Stockport d		23 50
Cheadle Hulme d		23 54
Bramhall d		
Poynton d		
Adlington (Cheshire) d		
Prestbury d		
Macclesfield a		
Macclesfield d		
Congleton d		
Handforth d		23 58
Manchester Airport d		
Styal d		
Wilmslow d		00 01
Alderley Edge d		00 04
Chelford d		00 08
Goostrey d		00 12
Holmes Chapel d		00 15
Sandbach d		00 20
Crewe 65 a		00 30
Kidsgrove 50 a		
Longport 50 a		
Stoke-on-Trent 50,68 a		
Stafford 68 a		
Wolverhampton 68 a		
Birmingham New Street 68 a		
London Euston ⊖65 a		

A To Buxton
B To Chester
C From Manchester Airport to Cleethorpes
D To Shrewsbury
E From Manchester Airport to Sheffield

Manchester, Stockport and Manchester Airport - Crewe and Stoke-on-Trent

Network Diagram - see first Page of Table 78

	NT	XC	VT	NT	TP	NT	VT	NT	XC	NT	VT	NT	AW	VT	NT	NT	NT	VT	NT	XC
		◇■	◇■		◇■		◇■		◇■		◇■		◇	◇■				◇■		◇■
		A			B	C			D			E	F				G			H
Deansgate d																				
Manchester Oxford Road d																				
Manchester Piccadilly a																				
Manchester Piccadilly d	23p38	05 11	05 25	05 35	05 44	05 50	05 55		06 00	06 06	06 10	06 17	06 30	06 35	06 44	06 46	06 49	06 55	07 03	07 07
Levenshulme d	23p43									06 11							06 55		07 09	
Heaton Chapel d	23p46									06 14							06 58		07 12	
Stockport a	23p50		05 33		05 52	05 59	06 02		06 07	06 18	06 17	06 27	06 38	06 43	06 52		07 01	07 03	07 16	07 14
Stockport d	23p50		05 34				06 03		06 08	06 19	06 18		06 39	06 43	06 53			07 04	07 18	07 16
Cheadle Hulme d	23p54									06 26					06 57				07 24	
Bramhall d															07 00					
Poynton d															07 03					
Adlington (Cheshire) d															07 06					
Prestbury d															07 09					
Macclesfield a									06 20		06 30			06 55	07 13					
Macclesfield d								06 03	06 21		06 31			06 56	07 13					
Congleton d								06 10							07 21					
Handforth d	23p58									06 30									07 28	
Manchester Airport d				06 05												07 11				
Styal d																				
Wilmslow d	00 01		05 41	06 14			06 11			06 33			06 46			07 21		07 11	07 31	
Alderley Edge d	00 04			06 17						06 36						07 24			07 34	
Chelford d	00 08			06 21															07 38	
Goostrey d	00 12			06 25															07 43	
Holmes Chapel d	00 15			06 28						06 44						07 32			07 46	
Sandbach d	00 20			06 33						06 49						07 36			07 51	
Crewe 65 a	00 30	05 41	05 57	06 43			06 27			06 59			07 05			07 46		07 27	08 01	
Kidsgrove 50 a								06 16							07 28					
Longport 50 a																				
Stoke-on-Trent 50,68 a		06 07						06 26	06 38		06 46			07 11	07 40					07 43
Stafford 68 a		06 25	06 17						06 57											08 02
Wolverhampton 68 a		06 39							07 12											08 17
Birmingham New Street 68 a		06 57							07 31											08 39
London Euston ⊖65 a			07 52				08 09				08 27			08 46				09 04		

	VT	NT	TP	NT	XC	AW	VT	NT	NT	NT	NT	VT	NT	XC	VT	NT	TP	XC	AW	VT	NT
	◇■		◇■		◇■	◇	◇■					◇■		◇■	◇■		◇■	◇■	◇	◇■	
		E	B	I	A	J					G			K		E	B	A	F		
Deansgate d				07 11																	
Manchester Oxford Road d				07 15																	
Manchester Piccadilly a				07 17																	
Manchester Piccadilly d	07 15	07 17	07 20	07 21	07 27	07 30	07 35	07 38	07 46	07 48	07 52	07 55	08 04	08 07	08 15	08 17	08 20	08 27	08 30	08 35	08 38
Levenshulme d				07 28				07 43			07 58		08 09								08 43
Heaton Chapel d				07 31				07 46					08 12								08 46
Stockport a	07 22	07 27	07 28	07 34	07 34	07 38	07 43	07 50		07 57	08 02	08 03	08 16	08 15	08 22	08 27	08 28	08 34	08 38	08 43	08 50
Stockport d	07 23				07 35	07 39	07 43	07 51		07 58		08 04	08 17	08 16	08 23			08 35	08 39	08 43	08 51
Cheadle Hulme d								07 55		08 02			08 24								08 55
Bramhall d										08 05											
Poynton d										08 08											
Adlington (Cheshire) d										08 11											
Prestbury d										08 14											
Macclesfield a					07 47		07 55			08 18								08 47		08 55	
Macclesfield d					07 49		07 56			08 18								08 49		08 56	
Congleton d										08 26											
Handforth d								07 59					08 28								08 59
Manchester Airport d									08 11												
Styal d									08 18												
Wilmslow d						07 46		08 01	08 22			08 11	08 31						08 46		09 02
Alderley Edge d								08a07	08 25				08 34								09a08
Chelford d													08 38								
Goostrey d													08 43								
Holmes Chapel d									08 33				08 46								
Sandbach d									08 37				08 51								
Crewe 65 a						08 05			08 47			08 27	09 01						09 05		
Kidsgrove 50 a										08 32											
Longport 50 a																					
Stoke-on-Trent 50,68 a	07 48				08 06		08 11			08 42				08 43	08 48			09 06		09 11	
Stafford 68 a					08 25									09 02				09 25			
Wolverhampton 68 a					08 39									09 15				09 39			
Birmingham New Street 68 a					08 58									09 39				09 58			
London Euston ⊖65 a	09 23						09 42					10 04			10 23					10 42	

A To Bournemouth
B From Manchester Airport to Cleethorpes
C To Sheffield
D To Bristol Temple Meads
E To Chester
F To Milford Haven
G To Buxton
H To Newquay
I From Wigan Wallgate to Hazel Grove
J To Carmarthen
K To Paignton

Table 84

Saturdays until 30 June

Manchester, Stockport and Manchester Airport - Crewe and Stoke-on-Trent

Network Diagram - see first Page of Table 78

Station		NT	NT	NT A	VT ◇■	NT	XC ◇■ B	VT ◇■	NT C	TP ◇■ D	XC ◇■ E	AW ◇ F	VT ◇■	NT	NT	NT	NT A	VT ◇■	NT	XC ◇■ B
Deansgate	d																			
Manchester Oxford Road	d																			
Manchester Piccadilly	a																			
	d	08 46	08 48	08 52	08 55	09 04	09 07	09 15	09 17	09 20	09 27	09 30	09 35	09 38	09 46	09 48	09 52	09 55	10 04	10 07
Levenshulme	d			08 58		09 09								09 43			09 58		10 09	
Heaton Chapel	d			09 01		09 12								09 46			10 01		10 12	
Stockport	a		08 57	09 04	09 03	09 16	09 15	09 22	09 27	09 28	09 34	09 38	09 42	09 50		09 57	10 04	10 03	10 16	10 15
	d		08 58		09 04	09 17	09 16	09 23			09 35	09 39	09 43	09 51		09 58		10 04	10 17	10 16
Cheadle Hulme	d		09 02			09 24								09 55		10 02			10 24	
Bramhall	d		09 05													10 05				
Poynton	d		09 08													10 08				
Adlington (Cheshire)	d		09 11													10 11				
Prestbury	d		09 14													10 14				
Macclesfield	a		09 18								09 47		09 55			10 18				
	d		09 18								09 49		09 56			10 18				
Congleton	d		09 26													10 26				
Handforth	d					09 28								09 59					10 28	
Manchester Airport	d	09 11													10 11					
Styal	d																			
Wilmslow	d	09 21			09 11	09 31						09 46		10 02	10 21			10 11	10 31	
Alderley Edge	d	09 24				09 34								10a08	10 24				10 34	
Chelford	d					09 38													10 38	
Goostrey	d					09 43													10 43	
Holmes Chapel	d	09 32				09 46									10 32				10 46	
Sandbach	d	09 36				09 51									10 36				10 51	
Crewe 65	a	09 46			09 27	10 01						10 05			10 46			10 27	11 01	
Kidsgrove 50	a		09 32													10 32				
Longport 50	a																			
Stoke-on-Trent 50,68	a		09 42				09 43	09 48			10 06		10 11			10 42				10 43
Stafford 68	a						10 02				10 25									11 02
Wolverhampton 68	a						10 15				10 39									11 16
Birmingham New Street 68	a						10 39				10 58									11 39
London Euston ⊖65	a				11 04			11 23					11 42					12 04		

Station		VT ◇■	NT C	TP ◇■ D	XC ◇■ E	AW ◇ G	VT ◇■	NT	NT	NT	NT A	VT ◇■	NT	XC ◇■ B	VT ◇■	NT C	TP ◇■ D	XC ◇■ E	AW ◇ F	VT ◇■	NT	NT
Deansgate	d																					
Manchester Oxford Road	d																					
Manchester Piccadilly	a																					
	d	10 15	10 17	10 20	10 27	10 30	10 35	10 38	10 46	10 48	10 52	10 55	11 04	11 07	11 15	11 17	11 20	11 27	11 30	11 35	11 38	11 46
Levenshulme	d							10 43			10 58		11 09								11 43	
Heaton Chapel	d							10 46			11 01		11 12								11 46	
Stockport	a	10 22	10 27	10 28	10 34	10 38	10 42	10 50		10 57	11 04	11 03	11 16	11 15	11 22	11 27	11 28	11 34	11 38	11 42	11 50	
	d	10 23			10 35	10 39	10 43	10 51		10 58		11 04	11 17	11 16	11 23			11 35	11 39	11 43	11 51	
Cheadle Hulme	d							10 55		11 02			11 24								11 55	
Bramhall	d									11 05												
Poynton	d									11 08												
Adlington (Cheshire)	d									11 11												
Prestbury	d									11 14												
Macclesfield	a				10 47		10 55			11 18								11 47		11 55		
	d				10 49		10 56			11 18								11 49		11 56		
Congleton	d									11 26												
Handforth	d							10 59					11 28								11 59	
Manchester Airport	d								11 11													12 11
Styal	d								11 18													
Wilmslow	d					10 46		11 02	11 22			11 11	11 31						11 46		12 02	12 21
Alderley Edge	d							11a08	11 25				11 34								12a08	12 24
Chelford	d												11 38									
Goostrey	d												11 43									
Holmes Chapel	d								11 33				11 46									12 32
Sandbach	d								11 37				11 51									12 36
Crewe 65	a					11 05			11 47			11 27	12 01						12 05			12 46
Kidsgrove 50	a									11 32												
Longport 50	a																					
Stoke-on-Trent 50,68	a	10 48			11 06		11 11			11 42				11 43	11 48			12 06		12 11		
Stafford 68	a				11 25									12 02				12 24				
Wolverhampton 68	a				11 39									12 16				12 39				
Birmingham New Street 68	a				11 58									12 39				12 58				
London Euston ⊖65	a	12 23					12 42					13 04			13 23					13 42		

A To Buxton
B To Bristol Temple Meads
C To Chester
D From Manchester Airport to Cleethorpes
E To Bournemouth
F To Carmarthen
G To Milford Haven

Table 84

Saturdays until 30 June

Manchester, Stockport and Manchester Airport - Crewe and Stoke-on-Trent

Network Diagram - see first Page of Table 78

Station		NT	NT A	VT ◇■	NT	XC ◇■ B	VT ◇■	NT C	TP ◇■ D	XC ◇■ E	AW ■ F	VT ◇■	NT	NT	NT	NT A	VT ◇■	NT	XC ◇■ G	VT ◇■
Deansgate	d																			
Manchester Oxford Road	d																			
Manchester Piccadilly	a																			
	d	11 48	11 52	11 55	12 04	12 07	12 15	12 17	12 20	12 27	12 30	12 35	12 38	12 46	12 48	12 52	12 55	13 04	13 07	13 15
Levenshulme	d		11 58		12 09								12 43			12 58		13 09		
Heaton Chapel	d		12 01		12 12								12 46			13 01		13 12		
Stockport	a	11 57	12 04	12 03	12 16	12 15	12 22	12 27	12 28	12 34	12 38	12 42	12 50		12 57	13 04	13 03	13 16	13 15	13 22
	d	11 58		12 04	12 17	12 16	12 23			12 35	12 39	12 43	12 51		12 58		13 04	13 17	13 16	13 23
Cheadle Hulme	d	12 02			12 24								12 55		13 02			13 24		
Bramhall	d	12 05													13 05					
Poynton	d	12 08													13 08					
Adlington (Cheshire)	d	12 11													13 11					
Prestbury	d	12 14													13 14					
Macclesfield	a	12 18								12 47		12 55			13 18					
	d	12 18								12 49		12 56			13 18					
Congleton	d	12 26													13 26					
Handforth	d				12 28								12 59					13 28		
Manchester Airport	d													13 11						
Styal	d													13 18						
Wilmslow	d			12 11	12 31						12 46		13 02	13 22			13 11	13 31		
Alderley Edge	d				12 34								13a08	13 25				13 34		
Chelford	d				12 38													13 38		
Goostrey	d				12 43													13 43		
Holmes Chapel	d				12 46									13 33				13 46		
Sandbach	d				12 51									13 37				13 51		
Crewe 65	a			12 27	13 01						13 05			13 47			13 27	14 01		
Kidsgrove 50	a	12 32													13 32					
Longport 50	a																			
Stoke-on-Trent 50,68	a	12 42				12 43	12 48			13 06		13 11			13 42				13 43	13 48
Stafford 68	a					13 02				13 25									14 02	
Wolverhampton 68	a					13 15				13 39									14 16	
Birmingham New Street 68	a					13 39				13 58									14 39	
London Euston ⊖65	a			14 04			14 23					14 42					15 04			15 23

Station		NT C	TP ◇■ D	XC ◇■ E	AW ■ H	VT ◇■	NT	NT	NT	NT A	VT ◇■	NT	XC ◇■ G	VT ◇■	NT C	TP ◇■ D	XC ◇■ E	AW ■ F	VT ◇■	NT	NT	NT
Deansgate	d																					
Manchester Oxford Road	d																					
Manchester Piccadilly	a																					
	d	13 17	13 20	13 27	13 30	13 35	13 38	13 46	13 48	13 52	13 55	14 04	14 07	14 15	14 17	14 20	14 27	14 30	14 35	14 38	14 46	14 48
Levenshulme	d						13 43			13 58		14 09								14 43		
Heaton Chapel	d						13 46			14 01		14 12								14 46		
Stockport	a	13 27	13 28	13 34	13 38	13 42	13 50		13 57	14 04	14 03	14 16	14 15	14 22	14 27	14 28	14 34	14 38	14 42	14 50		14 57
	d			13 35	13 39	13 43	13 51		13 58		14 04	14 17	14 16	14 23			14 35	14 39	14 43	14 51		14 58
Cheadle Hulme	d						13 55		14 02			14 24								14 55		15 02
Bramhall	d								14 05													15 05
Poynton	d								14 08													15 08
Adlington (Cheshire)	d								14 11													15 11
Prestbury	d								14 14													15 14
Macclesfield	a			13 47		13 55			14 18								14 47		14 55			15 18
	d			13 49		13 56			14 18								14 49		14 56			15 18
Congleton	d								14 26													15 26
Handforth	d						13 59					14 28								14 59		
Manchester Airport	d							14 11													15 11	
Styal	d																					
Wilmslow	d				13 46		14 02	14 21			14 11	14 31						14 46		15 02	15 21	
Alderley Edge	d						14a08	14 24				14 34								15a08	15 24	
Chelford	d											14 38										
Goostrey	d											14 43										
Holmes Chapel	d							14 32				14 46									15 32	
Sandbach	d							14 36				14 51									15 36	
Crewe 65	a				14 05			14 46			14 27	15 01						15 05			15 46	
Kidsgrove 50	a								14 32													15 32
Longport 50	a																					
Stoke-on-Trent 50,68	a			14 06		14 11			14 42				14 43	14 48			15 06		15 11			15 42
Stafford 68	a			14 25									15 02				15 25					
Wolverhampton 68	a			14 39									15 16				15 39					
Birmingham New Street 68	a			14 58									15 39				15 58					
London Euston ⊖65	a					15 42					16 04			16 23					16 42			

A To Buxton
B To Paignton
C To Chester
D From Manchester Airport to Cleethorpes
E To Bournemouth
F To Milford Haven
G To Bristol Temple Meads
H To Pembroke Dock

Manchester, Stockport and Manchester Airport - Crewe and Stoke-on-Trent

Network Diagram - see first Page of Table 78

Station		NT A	VT ◇1	NT	XC ◇1 B	VT ◇1	NT C	TP ◇1 D	XC ◇1 E	AW F	VT ◇1	NT	NT	NT	NT A	VT ◇1	NT	XC ◇1 B	VT ◇1	NT C	TP ◇1 D
Deansgate	d																				
Manchester Oxford Road	d																				
Manchester Piccadilly 10	a																				
	d	14 52	14 55	15 04	15 07	15 15	15 17	15 20	15 27	15 30	15 35	15 38	15 46	15 48	15 52	15 55	16 04	16 07	16 15	16 17	16 20
Levenshulme	d	14 58		15 09								15 43			15 58		16 09				
Heaton Chapel	d	15 01		15 12								15 46			16 01		16 12				
Stockport	a	15 04	15 03	15 16	15 15	15 22	15 27	15 28	15 34	15 38	15 42	15 50		15 57	16 04	16 03	16 16	16 15	16 22	16 27	16 28
	d		15 04	15 17	15 16	15 23			15 35	15 39	15 43	15 51		15 58		16 04	16 17	16 16	16 23		
Cheadle Hulme	d			15 24								15 55		16 02			16 24				
Bramhall	d													16 05							
Poynton	d													16 08							
Adlington (Cheshire)	d													16 11							
Prestbury	d													16 14							
Macclesfield	a								15 47		15 55			16 18							
	d								15 49		15 56			16 18							
Congleton	d													16 26							
Handforth	d			15 28								15 59					16 28				
Manchester Airport	d												16 11								
Styal	d																				
Wilmslow	d		15 11	15 31						15 46		16 02	16 21			16 11	16 31				
Alderley Edge	d			15 34								16a08	16 24				16 34				
Chelford	d			15 38													16 38				
Goostrey	d			15 43													16 43				
Holmes Chapel	d			15 46									16 32				16 46				
Sandbach	d			15 51									16 36				16 51				
Crewe 10 65	a		15 27	16 01						16 05			16 46			16 27	17 01				
Kidsgrove 50	a													16 32							
Longport 50	a																				
Stoke-on-Trent 50,68	a				15 43	15 48			16 06		16 11			16 42				16 43	16 48		
Stafford 68	a				16 02				16 24									17 02			
Wolverhampton 7 68	a				16 16				16 39									17 16			
Birmingham New Street 12 68	a				16 39				16 58									17 39			
London Euston 15 ⊖65	a		17 04			17 23					17 42					18 04			18 23		

Station		XC ◇1 E	AW G	VT ◇1	NT	NT	NT	NT A	VT ◇1	NT	XC ◇1 H	NT I	VT ◇1	NT C	TP ◇1 D	XC ◇1 E	AW H	VT ◇1	NT	NT	NT
Deansgate	d																				
Manchester Oxford Road	d																				
Manchester Piccadilly 10	a																				
	d	16 27	16 30	16 35	16 38	16 46	16 48	16 51	16 55	17 03	17 06	17 09	17 15	17 17	17 20	17 27	17 30	17 35	17 38	17 46	17 48
Levenshulme	d				16 43			16 58		17 08		17 14							17 43		
Heaton Chapel	d				16 46			17 01		17 11		17 17							17 46		
Stockport	a	16 34	16 38	16 42	16 50		16 58	17 04	17 03	17 15		17 21	17 22	17 27	17 28	17 35	17 38	17 42	17 50		17 57
	d	16 35	16 39	16 43	16 51		16 58		17 04	17 16			17 23			17 36	17 39	17 43	17 51		17 58
Cheadle Hulme	d				16 55		17 02			17 24									17 55		18 02
Bramhall	d						17 05														18 05
Poynton	d						17 08														18 08
Adlington (Cheshire)	d						17 11														18 11
Prestbury	d						17 14														18 14
Macclesfield	a	16 47		16 55			17 18				17 25							17 55			18 18
	d	16 49		16 56			17 18				17 26							17 56			18 18
Congleton	d						17 26									17 54					18 26
Handforth	d				16 59					17 28									17 59		
Manchester Airport	d					17 11														18 11	
Styal	d					17 18														18 18	
Wilmslow	d		16 46		17 02	17 22			17 11	17 31							17 46		18 02	18 22	
Alderley Edge	d				17a08	17 25				17 34									18a08	18 25	
Chelford	d									17 38											
Goostrey	d									17 43											
Holmes Chapel	d					17 33				17 46										18 33	
Sandbach	d					17 37				17 51										18 37	
Crewe 10 65	a		17 05			17 47			17 27	18 01							18 05			18 47	
Kidsgrove 50	a						17 32														18 32
Longport 50	a																				
Stoke-on-Trent 50,68	a	17 06		17 11			17 42				17 43		17 49			18 07		18 11			18 42
Stafford 68	a	17 25									18 03					18 26					
Wolverhampton 7 68	a	17 39									18 16					18 40					
Birmingham New Street 12 68	a	17 58									18 38					18 58					
London Euston 15 ⊖65	a			18 42					19 04				19 23					19 42			

A To Buxton
B To Bristol Temple Meads
C To Chester
D From Manchester Airport to Cleethorpes
E To Bournemouth
F To Pembroke Dock
G To Milford Haven
H To Cardiff Central
I To Hazel Grove

Manchester, Stockport and Manchester Airport - Crewe and Stoke-on-Trent

Network Diagram - see first Page of Table 78

Station		NT A	VT ◇1	XC ◇1 B	NT	VT ◇1	NT C	TP ◇1 D	XC ◇1 E	AW ◇ F	VT ◇1	NT	NT	NT	NT A	VT ◇1	NT	XC ◇1 B	NT C	TP ◇1 D	NT G
Deansgate	d																				
Manchester Oxford Road	d																				
Manchester Piccadilly 10	a																				
	d	17 52	17 55	18 05	18 08	18 15	18 17	18 20	18 27	18 30	18 35	18 38	18 46	18 48	18 52	18 55	19 04	19 07	19 17	19 18	19 22
Levenshulme	d	17 58			18 13							18 43			18 58		19 09				19 28
Heaton Chapel	d	18 01			18 16							18 46			19 01		19 12				19 31
Stockport	a	18 04	18 03	18 12	18 20	18 22	18 27	18 28	18 34	18 38	18 42	18 50		18 57	19 04	19 03	19 16	19 15	19 27	19 26	19 34
	d		18 04	18 13	18 22	18 23			18 35	18 39	18 43	18 51		18 58		19 04	19 17	19 16			
Cheadle Hulme	d				18 30							18 55		19 02			19 24				
Bramhall	d													19 05							
Poynton	d													19 08							
Adlington (Cheshire)	d													19 11							
Prestbury	d													19 14							
Macclesfield	a			18 25							18 55			19 18							
	d			18 26							18 56			19 18							
Congleton	d								18 54					19 26							
Handforth	d				18 34							18 59					19 28				
Manchester Airport	d												19 14								
Styal	d																				
Wilmslow	d		18 11		18 37					18 46		19 02	19 26			19 11	19 31				
Alderley Edge	d				18 40							19a08	19a32				19 34				
Chelford	d				18 44												19 38				
Goostrey	d				18 48												19 43				
Holmes Chapel	d				18 51												19 46				
Sandbach	d				18 56												19 51				
Crewe 10 65	a		18 27		19 06					19 08						19 27	20 01				
Kidsgrove 50	a													19 32							
Longport 50	a																				
Stoke-on-Trent 50,68	a			18 43		18 48			19 06		19 11			19 42				19 43			
Stafford 68	a			19 02					19 25									20 02			
Wolverhampton 7 68	a			19 16					19 39									20 16			
Birmingham New Street 12 68	a			19 33					19 58									20 33			
London Euston 15 ⊖65	a		20 04			20 24					20 59					21 18					

Station		XC ◇1 H	AW I	VT ◇1	NT	NT	NT A	NT	XC ◇1	NT C	TP ◇1 J	XC ◇1	AW I	VT ◇1	NT	NT	NT A	NT	XC ◇1	NT C	TP ◇1 D	XC ◇1
Deansgate	d																					
Manchester Oxford Road	d				19 43										20 43							
Manchester Piccadilly 10	a				19 45										20 45							
	d	19 27	19 30	19 35	19 46	19 48	19 51	20 04	20 07	20 17	20 20	20 27	20 30	20 35	20 46	20 48	20 52	21 04	21 07	21 17	21 20	21 27
Levenshulme	d						19 58	20 09									20 58	21 09				
Heaton Chapel	d						20 01	20 12									21 01	21 12				
Stockport	a	19 34	19 38	19 42		19 57	20 04	20 16	20 15	20 27	20 28	20 34	20 38	20 42		20 57	21 04	21 16		21 27	21 28	21 35
	d	19 35	19 39	19 43		19 58		20 17	20 16			20 35	20 39	20 43		20 58		21 17				21 36
Cheadle Hulme	d					20 02		20 24								21 02		21 24				
Bramhall	d					20 05										21 05						
Poynton	d					20 08										21 08						
Adlington (Cheshire)	d					20 11										21 11						
Prestbury	d					20 14										21 14						
Macclesfield	a	19 47		19 55		20 18						20 47		20 55		21 18						21 48
	d	19 49		19 56		20 18						20 49		20 56		21 18						21 50
Congleton	d					20 26										21 26						
Handforth	d							20 28										21 28				
Manchester Airport	d				20 14										21 14							
Styal	d																					
Wilmslow	d		19 46		20a24			20 31					20 46		21a24			21 31				
Alderley Edge	d							20 34										21 34				
Chelford	d							20 38										21 38				
Goostrey	d							20 43										21 43				
Holmes Chapel	d							20 46										21 46				
Sandbach	d							20 51										21 51				
Crewe 10 65	a		20 05					21 01					21 05					22 01				
Kidsgrove 50	a					20 32										21 32						
Longport 50	a																					
Stoke-on-Trent 50,68	a	20 06		20 11		20 42			20 43			21 06		21 11		21 42			21 43			22 07
Stafford 68	a	20 25							21 02			21 26							22 02			22 32
Wolverhampton 7 68	a	20 39							21 15			21 39							22 14			22 45
Birmingham New Street 12 68	a	20 58							21 32			21 58							22 32			23 02
London Euston 15 ⊖65	a			22 00										23 02								

A To Buxton
B To Bristol Temple Meads
C To Chester
D From Manchester Airport to Cleethorpes
E To Bournemouth
F To Carmarthen
G To Hazel Grove
H To Southampton Central
I To Cardiff Central
J From Manchester Airport to Sheffield

Saturdays
until 30 June

Manchester, Stockport and Manchester Airport - Crewe and Stoke-on-Trent

Network Diagram - see first Page of Table 78

		AW	NT	NT	NT	NT	NT	TP	AW	NT	NT	NT	NT	NT	NT	NT
								◇1								
		A			B		C	D	A				B		C	
Deansgate	d															
Manchester Oxford Road	d		21 43							22 43						
Manchester Piccadilly	a		21 45							22 45						
	d	21 35	21 46	21 48	21 54	22 04	22 17	22 20	22 35	22 46	22 48	23 04	23 10	23 14	23 17	23 37
Levenshulme	d				22 00	22 09						23 09				23 42
Heaton Chapel	d				22 03	22 12						23 12				23 45
Stockport	a	21 43		21 58	22 06	22 16	22 27	22 28	22 43		22 57	23 16	23 19	23 23	23 26	23 49
	d	21 44		21 58		22 17			22 44		22 58	23 16		23 23		23 50
Cheadle Hulme	d			22 02		22 24					23 02	23 21		23 27		23 54
Bramhall	d			22 05							23 05			23 30		
Poynton	d			22 08							23 08			23 33		
Adlington (Cheshire)	d			22 11							23 11			23 37		
Prestbury	d			22 14							23 14			23 40		
Macclesfield	a			22 18							23 20			23 46		
	d			22 18												
Congleton	d			22 26												
Handforth	d					22 28						23 25				23 58
Manchester Airport ✈	d		22 14							23 14						
Styal	d															
Wilmslow	d	21 51	22a22			22 31			22 52	23a22		23 28				00 01
Alderley Edge	d					22 34						23 31				00a07
Chelford	d					22 38						23 35				
Goostrey	d					22 43						23 40				
Holmes Chapel	d					22 46						23 43				
Sandbach	d					22 51						23 48				
Crewe 10 65	a	22 11				23 01			23 10			23 58				
Kidsgrove 50	a			22 32												
Longport 50	a															
Stoke-on-Trent 50,68	a			22 42												
Stafford 68	a															
Wolverhampton 7 68	a															
Birmingham New Street 12 68	a															
London Euston 15 ⊖65	a															

Saturdays
7 July to 29 September

		NT	XC	VT	NT	TP	NT	VT	NT	XC	NT	VT	NT	AW	VT	NT	NT	NT	VT	NT	XC	XC
			◇1	◇1		◇1		◇1		◇1		◇1		◇	◇1				◇1		◇1	◇1
			E			F	G			H			C	I				B			J	K
Deansgate	d																					
Manchester Oxford Road	d																					
Manchester Piccadilly 10	a																					
	d	23p38	05 11	05 25	05 35	05 44	05 50	05 55		06 00	06 06	06 10	06 17	06 30	06 35	06 44	06 46	06 49	06 55	07 03	07 07	07 07
Levenshulme	d	23p43									06 11							06 55		07 09		
Heaton Chapel	d	23p46									06 14							06 58		07 12		
Stockport	a	23p50		05 33		05 52	05 59	06 02		06 07	06 18	06 17	06 27	06 38	06 43	06 52		07 01	07 03	07 16	07 15	07 14
	d	23p50		05 34				06 03		06 08	06 19	06 18		06 39	06 43	06 53			07 04	07 18	07 16	07 16
Cheadle Hulme	d	23p54									06 26					06 57				07 24		
Bramhall	d															07 00						
Poynton	d															07 03						
Adlington (Cheshire)	d															07 06						
Prestbury	d															07 09						
Macclesfield	a									06 20		06 30			06 55	07 13						
	d								06 03	06 21		06 31			06 56	07 13						
Congleton	d								06 10							07 21						
Handforth	d	23p58									06 30									07 28		
Manchester Airport ✈	d				06 05												07 11					
Styal	d																					
Wilmslow	d	00 01		05 41	06 14			06 11			06 33			06 46			07 21		07 11	07 31		
Alderley Edge	d	00 04			06 17						06 36						07 24			07 34		
Chelford	d	00 08			06 21															07 38		
Goostrey	d	00 12			06 25															07 43		
Holmes Chapel	d	00 15			06 28						06 44						07 32			07 46		
Sandbach	d	00 20			06 33						06 49						07 36			07 51		
Crewe 10 65	a	00 30	05 41	05 57	06 43			06 27			06 59			07 05			07 46		07 27	08 01		
Kidsgrove 50	a								06 16							07 28						
Longport 50	a																					
Stoke-on-Trent 50,68	a		06 07						06 26	06 38		06 46			07 11	07 40					07 43	07 43
Stafford 68	a		06 25	06 17						06 57											08 02	08 02
Wolverhampton 7 68	a		06 39							07 12											08 16	08 17
Birmingham New Street 12 68	a		06 57							07 31											08 38	08 39
London Euston 15 ⊖65	a			07 52				08 09				08 27			08 46				09 04			

A To Shrewsbury
B To Buxton
C To Chester
D From Manchester Airport to Sheffield
E To Bournemouth
F From Manchester Airport to Cleethorpes
G To Sheffield
H To Bristol Temple Meads
I To Milford Haven
J from 15 September. To Bristol Temple Meads
K from 7 July until 8 September. To Newquay

Saturdays
7 July to 29 September

Manchester, Stockport and Manchester Airport - Crewe and Stoke-on-Trent

Network Diagram - see first Page of Table 78

		VT	NT	TP	NT	XC	AW	VT	NT	NT	NT	NT	VT	NT	XC	VT	NT	TP	XC	AW	VT
		◇1		◇1		◇1	◇	◇1					◇1		◇1	◇1		◇1	◇1	◇	◇1
			A	B	C	D	E					F			G		A	B	D	H	
Deansgate	d				07 11																
Manchester Oxford Road	d				07 15																
Manchester Piccadilly 10	a				07 17																
	d	07 15	07 17	07 20	07 21	07 27	07 30	07 35	07 38	07 46	07 48	07 52	07 55	08 04	08 07	08 15	08 17	08 20	08 27	08 30	08 35
Levenshulme	d				07 28				07 43			07 58		08 09							
Heaton Chapel	d				07 31				07 46					08 12							
Stockport	a	07 22	07 27	07 28	07 34	07 34	07 38	07 43	07 50		07 57	08 02	08 03	08 16	08 15	08 22	08 27	08 28	08 34	08 38	08 43
	d	07 23				07 35	07 39	07 43	07 51		07 58		08 04	08 17	08 16	08 23			08 35	08 39	08 43
Cheadle Hulme	d								07 55		08 02			08 24							
Bramhall	d										08 05										
Poynton	d										08 08										
Adlington (Cheshire)	d										08 11										
Prestbury	d										08 14										
Macclesfield	a					07 47		07 55			08 18								08 47		08 55
	d					07 49		07 56			08 18								08 49		08 56
Congleton	d										08 26										
Handforth	d								07 59					08 28							
Manchester Airport ✈	d									08 11											
Styal	d									08 18											
Wilmslow	d						07 46		08 01	08 22			08 11	08 31						08 46	
Alderley Edge	d								08a07	08 25				08 34							
Chelford	d													08 38							
Goostrey	d													08 43							
Holmes Chapel	d									08 33				08 46							
Sandbach	d									08 37				08 51							
Crewe 10 65	a						08 05			08 47			08 27	09 01						09 05	
Kidsgrove 50	a										08 32										
Longport 50	a																				
Stoke-on-Trent 50,68	a	07 48				08 06		08 11			08 42				08 43	08 48			09 06		09 11
Stafford 68	a					08 25									09 02				09 25		
Wolverhampton 7 68	a					08 39									09 15				09 39		
Birmingham New Street 12 68	a					08 58									09 39				09 58		
London Euston 15 ⊖65	a	09 23						09 42					10 04			10 23					10 42

		NT	NT	NT	NT	VT	NT	XC	VT	NT	TP	XC	AW	VT	NT	NT	NT	NT	VT	NT	XC
						◇1		◇1	◇1		◇1	◇1	◇	◇1					◇1		◇1
					F			I		A	B	D	E					F			I
Deansgate	d																				
Manchester Oxford Road	d																				
Manchester Piccadilly 10	a																				
	d	08 38	08 46	08 48	08 52	08 55	09 04	09 07	09 15	09 17	09 20	09 27	09 30	09 35	09 38	09 46	09 48	09 52	09 55	10 04	10 07
Levenshulme	d	08 43			08 58		09 09								09 43			09 58		10 09	
Heaton Chapel	d	08 46			09 01		09 12								09 46			10 01		10 12	
Stockport	a	08 50		08 57	09 04	09 03	09 16	09 15	09 22	09 27	09 28	09 34	09 38	09 42	09 50		09 57	10 04	10 03	10 16	10 15
	d	08 51		08 58		09 04	09 17	09 16	09 23			09 35	09 39	09 43	09 51		09 58		10 04	10 17	10 16
Cheadle Hulme	d	08 55		09 02			09 24								09 55		10 02			10 24	
Bramhall	d			09 05													10 05				
Poynton	d			09 08													10 08				
Adlington (Cheshire)	d			09 11													10 11				
Prestbury	d			09 14													10 14				
Macclesfield	a			09 18								09 47		09 55			10 18				
	d			09 18								09 49		09 56			10 18				
Congleton	d			09 26													10 26				
Handforth	d	08 59					09 28								09 59					10 28	
Manchester Airport ✈	d		09 11													10 11					
Styal	d																				
Wilmslow	d	09 02	09 21			09 11	09 31						09 46		10 02	10 21			10 11	10 31	
Alderley Edge	d	09a08	09 24				09 34								10a08	10 24				10 34	
Chelford	d						09 38													10 38	
Goostrey	d						09 43													10 43	
Holmes Chapel	d		09 32				09 46									10 32				10 46	
Sandbach	d		09 36				09 51									10 36				10 51	
Crewe 10 65	a		09 46			09 27	10 01						10 05			10 46			10 27	11 01	
Kidsgrove 50	a			09 32													10 32				
Longport 50	a																				
Stoke-on-Trent 50,68	a			09 42				09 43	09 48			10 06		10 11			10 42				10 43
Stafford 68	a							10 02				10 25									11 02
Wolverhampton 7 68	a							10 15				10 39									11 16
Birmingham New Street 12 68	a							10 39				10 58									11 39
London Euston 15 ⊖65	a					11 04			11 23					11 42					12 04		

A To Chester
B From Manchester Airport to Cleethorpes
C From Wigan Wallgate to Hazel Grove
D To Bournemouth
E To Carmarthen
F To Buxton
G To Paignton
H To Milford Haven
I To Bristol Temple Meads

Table 84

Saturdays

7 July to 29 September

Manchester, Stockport and Manchester Airport - Crewe and Stoke-on-Trent

Network Diagram - see first Page of Table 78

Station		VT	NT	TP	XC	AW	VT	NT	NT	NT	NT	VT	NT	XC	VT	NT	TP	XC	AW	VT	NT
		◇1	A	◇1 B	◇1 C	◇ D	◇1				E	◇1		◇1 F	◇1	A	◇1 B	◇1 C	◇ G	◇1	
Deansgate	d																				
Manchester Oxford Road	d																				
Manchester Piccadilly	a																				
	d	10 15	10 17	10 20	10 27	10 30	10 35	10 38	10 46	10 48	10 52	10 55	11 04	11 07	11 15	11 17	11 20	11 27	11 30	11 35	11 38
Levenshulme	d							10 43			10 58		11 09								11 43
Heaton Chapel	d							10 46			11 01		11 12								11 46
Stockport	a	10 22	10 27	10 28	10 34	10 38	10 42	10 50		10 57	11 04	11 03	11 16	11 15	11 22	11 27	11 28	11 34	11 38	11 42	11 50
	d	10 23			10 35	10 39	10 43	10 51		10 58		11 04	11 17	11 16	11 23			11 35	11 39	11 43	11 51
Cheadle Hulme	d							10 55		11 02			11 24								11 55
Bramhall	d									11 05											
Poynton	d									11 08											
Adlington (Cheshire)	d									11 11											
Prestbury	d									11 14											
Macclesfield	a				10 47		10 55			11 18								11 47		11 55	
	d				10 49		10 56			11 18								11 49		11 56	
Congleton	d									11 26											
Handforth	d							10 59					11 28								11 59
Manchester Airport	d								11 11												
Styal	d								11 18												
Wilmslow	d					10 46		11 02	11 22			11 11	11 31						11 46		12 02
Alderley Edge	d							11a08	11 25				11 34								12a08
Chelford	d												11 38								
Goostrey	d												11 43								
Holmes Chapel	d								11 33				11 46								
Sandbach	d								11 37				11 51								
Crewe	65 a					11 05			11 47			11 27	12 01						12 05		
Kidsgrove	50 a									11 32											
Longport	50 a																				
Stoke-on-Trent	50,68 a	10 48			11 06		11 11			11 42				11 43	11 48			12 06		12 11	
Stafford	68 a				11 25									12 02				12 24			
Wolverhampton	68 a				11 39									12 16				12 39			
Birmingham New Street	68 a				11 58									12 39				12 58			
London Euston	⊖65 a	12 23					12 42					13 04			13 23					13 42	

Station		NT	NT	NT	VT	NT	XC	VT	NT	TP	XC	AW	VT	NT	NT	NT	NT	VT	NT	XC
				E	◇1		◇1 H	◇1	A	◇1 B	◇1 C	D	◇1				E	◇1		◇1 F
Deansgate	d																			
Manchester Oxford Road	d																			
Manchester Piccadilly	a																			
	d	11 46	11 48	11 52	11 55	12 04	12 07	12 15	12 17	12 20	12 27	12 30	12 35	12 38	12 46	12 48	12 52	12 55	13 04	13 07
Levenshulme	d			11 58		12 09								12 43			12 58		13 09	
Heaton Chapel	d			12 01		12 12								12 46			13 01		13 12	
Stockport	a		11 57	12 04	12 03	12 16	12 15	12 22	12 27	12 28	12 34	12 38	12 42	12 50		12 57	13 04	13 03	13 16	13 15
	d		11 58		12 04	12 17	12 16	12 23			12 35	12 39	12 43	12 51		12 58		13 04	13 17	13 16
Cheadle Hulme	d		12 02			12 24								12 55		13 02			13 24	
Bramhall	d		12 05													13 05				
Poynton	d		12 08													13 08				
Adlington (Cheshire)	d		12 11													13 11				
Prestbury	d		12 14													13 14				
Macclesfield	a		12 18								12 47		12 55			13 18				
	d		12 18								12 49		12 56			13 18				
Congleton	d		12 26													13 26				
Handforth	d					12 28								12 59					13 28	
Manchester Airport	d	12 11													13 11					
Styal	d														13 18					
Wilmslow	d	12 21			12 11	12 31						12 46		13 02	13 22			13 11	13 31	
Alderley Edge	d	12 24				12 34								13a08	13 25				13 34	
Chelford	d					12 38													13 38	
Goostrey	d					12 43													13 43	
Holmes Chapel	d	12 32				12 46									13 33				13 46	
Sandbach	d	12 36				12 51									13 37				13 51	
Crewe	65 a	12 46			12 27	13 01						13 05			13 47			13 27	14 01	
Kidsgrove	50 a		12 32													13 32				
Longport	50 a																			
Stoke-on-Trent	50,68 a		12 42				12 43	12 48			13 06		13 11			13 42				13 43
Stafford	68 a						13 02				13 25									14 02
Wolverhampton	68 a						13 15				13 39									14 16
Birmingham New Street	68 a						13 39				13 58									14 39
London Euston	⊖65 a				14 04			14 23					14 42					15 04		

A To Chester
B From Manchester Airport to Cleethorpes
C To Bournemouth
D To Milford Haven
E To Buxton
F To Bristol Temple Meads
G To Carmarthen
H To Exeter St Davids

Table 84

Saturdays

7 July to 29 September

Manchester, Stockport and Manchester Airport - Crewe and Stoke-on-Trent

Network Diagram - see first Page of Table 78

Station		VT	NT	TP	XC	AW	VT	NT	NT	NT	NT	VT	NT	XC	VT	NT	TP	XC	AW	VT	NT	NT
		◇1	A	◇1 B	◇1 C	D	◇1				E	◇1		◇1 F	◇1	A	◇1 B	◇1 C	G	◇1		
Deansgate	d																					
Manchester Oxford Road	d																					
Manchester Piccadilly	a																					
	d	13 15	13 17	13 20	13 27	13 30	13 35	13 38	13 46	13 48	13 52	13 55	14 04	14 07	14 15	14 17	14 20	14 27	14 30	14 35	14 38	14 46
Levenshulme	d							13 43			13 58		14 09								14 43	
Heaton Chapel	d							13 46			14 01		14 12								14 46	
Stockport	a	13 22	13 27	13 28	13 34	13 38	13 42	13 50		13 57	14 04	14 03	14 16	14 15	14 22	14 27	14 28	14 34	14 38	14 42	14 50	
	d	13 23			13 35	13 39	13 43	13 51		13 58		14 04	14 17	14 16	14 23			14 35	14 39	14 43	14 51	
Cheadle Hulme	d							13 55		14 02			14 24								14 55	
Bramhall	d									14 05												
Poynton	d									14 08												
Adlington (Cheshire)	d									14 11												
Prestbury	d									14 14												
Macclesfield	a				13 47		13 55			14 18								14 47		14 55		
	d				13 49		13 56			14 18								14 49		14 56		
Congleton	d									14 26												
Handforth	d							13 59					14 28								14 59	
Manchester Airport	d								14 11													15 11
Styal	d																					
Wilmslow	d					13 46		14 02	14 21			14 11	14 31						14 46		15 02	15 21
Alderley Edge	d							14a08	14 24				14 34								15a08	15 24
Chelford	d												14 38									
Goostrey	d												14 43									
Holmes Chapel	d								14 32				14 46									15 32
Sandbach	d								14 36				14 51									15 36
Crewe	65 a					14 05			14 46			14 27	15 01						15 05			15 46
Kidsgrove	50 a									14 32												
Longport	50 a																					
Stoke-on-Trent	50,68 a	13 48			14 06		14 11			14 42				14 43	14 48			15 06		15 11		
Stafford	68 a				14 25									15 02				15 25				
Wolverhampton	68 a				14 39									15 16				15 39				
Birmingham New Street	68 a				14 58									15 39				15 58				
London Euston	⊖65 a	15 23					15 42					16 04			16 23					16 42		

Station		NT	NT	VT	NT	XC	VT	NT	TP	XC	AW	VT	NT	NT	NT	NT	VT	NT	XC	VT	NT
			E	◇1		◇1 F	◇1	A	◇1 B	◇1 C	D	◇1				E	◇1		◇1 F	◇1	A
Deansgate	d																				
Manchester Oxford Road	d																				
Manchester Piccadilly	a																				
	d	14 48	14 52	14 55	15 04	15 07	15 15	15 17	15 20	15 27	15 30	15 35	15 38	15 46	15 48	15 52	15 55	16 04	16 07	16 15	16 17
Levenshulme	d		14 58		15 09								15 43			15 58		16 09			
Heaton Chapel	d		15 01		15 12								15 46			16 01		16 12			
Stockport	a	14 57	15 04	15 03	15 16	15 15	15 22	15 27	15 28	15 34	15 38	15 42	15 50		15 57	16 04	16 03	16 16	16 15	16 22	16 27
	d	14 58		15 04	15 17	15 16	15 23			15 35	15 39	15 43	15 51		15 58		16 04	16 17	16 16	16 23	
Cheadle Hulme	d	15 02			15 24								15 55		16 02			16 24			
Bramhall	d	15 05													16 05						
Poynton	d	15 08													16 08						
Adlington (Cheshire)	d	15 11													16 11						
Prestbury	d	15 14													16 14						
Macclesfield	a	15 18								15 47		15 55			16 18						
	d	15 18								15 49		15 56			16 18						
Congleton	d	15 26													16 26						
Handforth	d				15 28								15 59					16 28			
Manchester Airport	d													16 11							
Styal	d																				
Wilmslow	d			15 11	15 31						15 46		16 02	16 21			16 11	16 31			
Alderley Edge	d				15 34								16a08	16 24				16 34			
Chelford	d				15 38													16 38			
Goostrey	d				15 43													16 43			
Holmes Chapel	d				15 46									16 32				16 46			
Sandbach	d				15 51									16 36				16 51			
Crewe	65 a			15 27	16 01						16 05			16 46			16 27	17 01			
Kidsgrove	50 a	15 32													16 32						
Longport	50 a																				
Stoke-on-Trent	50,68 a	15 42				15 43	15 48			16 06		16 11			16 42				16 43	16 48	
Stafford	68 a					16 02				16 24									17 02		
Wolverhampton	68 a					16 16				16 39									17 16		
Birmingham New Street	68 a					16 39				16 58									17 39		
London Euston	⊖65 a			17 04			17 23					17 42					18 04			18 23	

A To Chester
B From Manchester Airport to Cleethorpes
C To Bournemouth
D To Pembroke Dock
E To Buxton
F To Bristol Temple Meads
G To Milford Haven

Manchester, Stockport and Manchester Airport - Crewe and Stoke-on-Trent

Network Diagram - see first Page of Table 78

		TP	XC	AW	VT	NT	NT	NT	NT	VT	NT	XC	NT	VT	NT	TP	XC	AW	VT	NT	NT
		◇■ A	◇■ B	■ C	◇■				D	◇■		◇■ E	F	◇■	G	◇■ A	◇■ B	■ E	◇■		
Deansgate	d																				
Manchester Oxford Road	d																				
Manchester Piccadilly 10	a																				
	d	16 20	16 27	16 30	16 35	16 38	16 46	16 48	16 51	16 55	17 03	17 06	17 09	17 15	17 17	17 20	17 27	17 30	17 35	17 38	17 46
Levenshulme	d					16 43			16 58		17 08		17 14							17 43	
Heaton Chapel	d					16 46			17 01		17 11		17 17							17 46	
Stockport	a	16 28	16 34	16 38	16 42	16 50		16 58	17 04	17 03	17 15		17 21	17 22	17 27	17 28	17 35	17 38	17 42	17 50	
	d		16 35	16 39	16 43	16 51		16 58		17 04	17 16			17 23			17 36	17 39	17 43	17 51	
Cheadle Hulme	d					16 55		17 02			17 24									17 55	
Bramhall	d							17 05													
Poynton	d							17 08													
Adlington (Cheshire)	d							17 11													
Prestbury	d							17 14													
Macclesfield	a		16 47		16 55			17 18				17 25							17 55		
	d		16 49		16 56			17 18				17 26							17 56		
Congleton	d							17 26									17 54				
Handforth	d					16 59					17 28									17 59	
Manchester Airport ✈	d						17 11														18 11
Styal	d						17 18														18 18
Wilmslow	d			16 46		17 02	17 22			17 11	17 31							17 46		18 02	18 22
Alderley Edge	d					17a08	17 25				17 34									18a08	18 25
Chelford	d										17 38										
Goostrey	d										17 43										
Holmes Chapel	d						17 33				17 46										18 33
Sandbach	d						17 37				17 51										18 37
Crewe 10 65	a			17 05			17 47			17 27	18 01							18 05			18 47
Kidsgrove 50	a							17 32													
Longport 50	a																				
Stoke-on-Trent 50,68	a		17 06		17 11			17 42				17 43		17 49			18 07		18 11		
Stafford 68	a		17 25									18 03					18 26				
Wolverhampton 7 68	a		17 39									18 16					18 40				
Birmingham New Street 12 68	a		17 58									18 38					18 58				
London Euston 15 ⊖65	a				18 42					19 04				19 23					19 42		

		NT	NT	VT	XC	NT	VT	NT	TP	XC	AW	VT	NT	NT	NT	NT	VT	NT	XC	NT	TP
			D	◇■	◇■ H		◇■	G	◇■ A	◇■ B	◇ I	◇■				D	◇■		◇■ H	G	◇■ A
Deansgate	d																				
Manchester Oxford Road	d																				
Manchester Piccadilly 10	a																				
	d	17 48	17 52	17 55	18 05	18 08	18 15	18 17	18 20	18 27	18 30	18 35	18 38	18 46	18 48	18 52	18 55	19 04	19 07	19 17	19 18
Levenshulme	d		17 58			18 13							18 43			18 58		19 09			
Heaton Chapel	d		18 01			18 16							18 46			19 01		19 12			
Stockport	a	17 57	18 04	18 03	18 12	18 20	18 22	18 27	18 28	18 34	18 38	18 42	18 50		18 57	19 04	19 03	19 16	19 15	19 27	19 26
	d	17 58		18 04	18 13	18 22	18 23			18 35	18 39	18 43	18 51		18 58		19 04	19 17	19 16		
Cheadle Hulme	d	18 02				18 30							18 55		19 02			19 24			
Bramhall	d	18 05													19 05						
Poynton	d	18 08													19 08						
Adlington (Cheshire)	d	18 11													19 11						
Prestbury	d	18 14													19 14						
Macclesfield	a	18 18			18 25							18 55			19 18						
	d	18 18			18 26							18 56			19 18						
Congleton	d	18 26								18 54					19 26						
Handforth	d					18 34							18 59					19 28			
Manchester Airport ✈	d													19 14							
Styal	d																				
Wilmslow	d			18 11		18 37					18 46		19 02	19 26			19 11	19 31			
Alderley Edge	d					18 40							19a08	19a32				19 34			
Chelford	d					18 44												19 38			
Goostrey	d					18 48												19 43			
Holmes Chapel	d					18 51												19 46			
Sandbach	d					18 56												19 51			
Crewe 10 65	a			18 27		19 06					19 08						19 27	20 01			
Kidsgrove 50	a	18 32													19 32						
Longport 50	a																				
Stoke-on-Trent 50,68	a	18 42			18 43		18 48			19 06		19 11			19 42				19 43		
Stafford 68	a				19 02					19 25									20 02		
Wolverhampton 7 68	a				19 16					19 39									20 16		
Birmingham New Street 12 68	a				19 33					19 58									20 33		
London Euston 15 ⊖65	a			20 04			20 24					20 59					21 18				

A From Manchester Airport to Cleethorpes
B To Bournemouth
C To Milford Haven
D To Buxton
E To Cardiff Central
F To Hazel Grove
G To Chester
H To Bristol Temple Meads
I To Carmarthen

Manchester, Stockport and Manchester Airport - Crewe and Stoke-on-Trent

Network Diagram - see first Page of Table 78

		NT	XC	AW	VT	NT	NT	NT	NT	XC	NT	TP	XC	AW	VT	NT	NT	NT	NT	XC	NT	TP
		A	◇■ B	C	◇■			D		◇■	E	◇■ F	◇■	C	◇■			D		◇■	E	◇■ G
Deansgate	d																					
Manchester Oxford Road	d					19 43										20 43						
Manchester Piccadilly 10	a					19 45										20 45						
	d	19 22	19 27	19 30	19 35	19 46	19 48	19 51	20 04	20 07	20 17	20 20	20 27	20 30	20 35	20 46	20 48	20 52	21 04	21 07	21 17	21 20
Levenshulme	d	19 28						19 58	20 09									20 58	21 09			
Heaton Chapel	d	19 31						20 01	20 12									21 01	21 12			
Stockport	a	19 34	19 34	19 38	19 42		19 57	20 04	20 16	20 15	20 27	20 28	20 34	20 38	20 42		20 57	21 04	21 16		21 27	21 28
	d		19 35	19 39	19 43		19 58		20 17	20 16			20 35	20 39	20 43		20 58		21 17			
Cheadle Hulme	d						20 02		20 24								21 02		21 24			
Bramhall	d						20 05										21 05					
Poynton	d						20 08										21 08					
Adlington (Cheshire)	d						20 11										21 11					
Prestbury	d						20 14										21 14					
Macclesfield	a		19 47		19 55		20 18						20 47		20 55		21 18					
	d		19 49		19 56		20 18						20 49		20 56		21 18					
Congleton	d						20 26										21 26					
Handforth	d								20 28										21 28			
Manchester Airport ✈	d					20 14										21 14						
Styal	d																					
Wilmslow	d			19 46		20a24			20 31					20 46		21a24			21 31			
Alderley Edge	d								20 34										21 34			
Chelford	d								20 38										21 38			
Goostrey	d								20 43										21 43			
Holmes Chapel	d								20 46										21 46			
Sandbach	d								20 51										21 51			
Crewe 10 65	a			20 05					21 01					21 05					22 01			
Kidsgrove 50	a						20 32										21 32					
Longport 50	a																					
Stoke-on-Trent 50,68	a		20 06		20 11		20 42			20 43			21 06		21 11		21 42			21 43		
Stafford 68	a		20 25							21 02			21 26							22 02		
Wolverhampton 7 68	a		20 39							21 15			21 39							22 14		
Birmingham New Street 12 68	a		20 58							21 32			21 58							22 32		
London Euston 15 ⊖65	a				22 00										23 02							

		XC	AW	NT	NT	NT	NT	NT	TP	AW	NT	NT	NT	NT	NT	NT	NT
		◇■	H			D		E	◇■ F	H				D		E	
Deansgate	d																
Manchester Oxford Road	d			21 43							22 43						
Manchester Piccadilly 10	a			21 45							22 45						
	d	21 27	21 35	21 46	21 48	21 54	22 04	22 17	22 20	22 35	22 46	22 48	23 04	23 10	23 14	23 17	23 37
Levenshulme	d					22 00	22 09						23 09				23 42
Heaton Chapel	d					22 03	22 12						23 12				23 45
Stockport	a	21 35	21 43		21 58	22 06	22 16	22 27	22 28	22 43		22 57	23 16	23 19	23 23	23 26	23 49
	d	21 36	21 44		21 58		22 17			22 44		22 58	23 16		23 23		23 50
Cheadle Hulme	d				22 02		22 24					23 02	23 21		23 27		23 54
Bramhall	d				22 05							23 05			23 30		
Poynton	d				22 08							23 08			23 33		
Adlington (Cheshire)	d				22 11							23 11			23 37		
Prestbury	d				22 14							23 14			23 40		
Macclesfield	a	21 48			22 18							23 20			23 46		
	d	21 50			22 18												
Congleton	d				22 26												
Handforth	d						22 28						23 25				23 58
Manchester Airport ✈	d			22 14							23 14						
Styal	d																
Wilmslow	d		21 51	22a22			22 31			22 52	23a22		23 28				00 01
Alderley Edge	d						22 34						23 31				00a07
Chelford	d						22 38						23 35				
Goostrey	d						22 43						23 40				
Holmes Chapel	d						22 46						23 43				
Sandbach	d						22 51						23 48				
Crewe 10 65	a		22 11				23 01			23 10			23 58				
Kidsgrove 50	a				22 32												
Longport 50	a																
Stoke-on-Trent 50,68	a	22 07			22 42												
Stafford 68	a	22 32															
Wolverhampton 7 68	a	22 45															
Birmingham New Street 12 68	a	23 02															
London Euston 15 ⊖65	a																

A To Hazel Grove
B To Southampton Central
C To Cardiff Central
D To Buxton
E To Chester
F From Manchester Airport to Sheffield
G From Manchester Airport to Cleethorpes
H To Shrewsbury

Manchester, Stockport and Manchester Airport - Crewe and Stoke-on-Trent

Network Diagram - see first Page of Table 78

Station			NT	XC A	VT	NT	TP B	NT C	VT	NT	XC D	NT	VT	NT E	AW F	VT	NT	NT	NT G	VT	NT	XC D
Deansgate		d																				
Manchester Oxford Road		d																				
Manchester Piccadilly		a																				
		d	23p38	05 11	05 25	05 35	05 44	05 50	05 55		06 00	06 06	06 10	06 17	06 30	06 35	06 44	06 46	06 49	06 55	07 03	07 07
Levenshulme		d	23p43									06 11							06 55		07 09	
Heaton Chapel		d	23p46									06 14							06 58		07 12	
Stockport		a	23p50		05 33		05 52	05 59	06 02		06 07	06 18	06 17	06 27	06 38	06 43	06 52		07 01	07 03	07 16	07 15
		d	23p50		05 34				06 03		06 08	06 19	06 18		06 39	06 43	06 53			07 04	07 18	07 16
Cheadle Hulme		d	23p54									06 26					06 57				07 24	
Bramhall		d															07 00					
Poynton		d															07 03					
Adlington (Cheshire)		d															07 06					
Prestbury		d															07 09					
Macclesfield		a									06 20		06 30			06 55	07 13					
		d								06 03	06 21		06 31			06 56	07 13					
Congleton		d								06 10							07 21					
Handforth		d	23p58									06 30									07 28	
Manchester Airport		d				06 05												07 11				
Styal		d																				
Wilmslow		d	00 01		05 41	06 14			06 11			06 33			06 46			07 21		07 11	07 31	
Alderley Edge		d	00 04			06 17						06 36						07 24			07 34	
Chelford		d	00 08			06 21															07 38	
Goostrey		d	00 12			06 25															07 43	
Holmes Chapel		d	00 15			06 28						06 44						07 32			07 46	
Sandbach		d	00 20			06 33						06 49						07 36			07 51	
Crewe	65	a	00 30	05 41	05 57	06 43			06 27			06 59			07 05			07 46		07 27	08 01	
Kidsgrove	50	a								06 16							07 28					
Longport	50	a																				
Stoke-on-Trent	50,68	a		06 07						06 26	06 38		06 46			07 11	07 40					07 43
Stafford	68	a		06 25	06 17						06 57											08 02
Wolverhampton	68	a		06 39							07 12											08 16
Birmingham New Street	68	a		06 57							07 31											08 38
London Euston	⊖65	a			07 52				08 09				08 27			08 46				09 04		

Station			VT	NT E	TP B	NT H	XC A	AW I	VT	NT	NT	NT	NT G	VT	NT	XC J	VT	NT E	TP B	XC A	AW F	VT	NT
Deansgate		d				07 11																	
Manchester Oxford Road		d				07 15																	
Manchester Piccadilly		a				07 17																	
		d	07 15	07 17	07 20	07 21	07 27	07 30	07 35	07 38	07 46	07 48	07 52	07 55	08 04	08 07	08 15	08 17	08 20	08 27	08 30	08 35	08 38
Levenshulme		d				07 28				07 43			07 57		08 09								08 43
Heaton Chapel		d				07 31				07 46					08 12								08 46
Stockport		a	07 22	07 27	07 28	07 34	07 34	07 38	07 43	07 50		07 57	08 02	08 03	08 16	08 15	08 22	08 27	08 28	08 34	08 38	08 43	08 50
		d	07 23				07 35	07 39	07 43	07 51		07 58		08 04	08 17	08 16	08 23			08 35	08 39	08 43	08 51
Cheadle Hulme		d								07 55		08 02			08 24								08 55
Bramhall		d										08 05											
Poynton		d										08 08											
Adlington (Cheshire)		d										08 11											
Prestbury		d										08 14											
Macclesfield		a					07 47		07 55			08 18								08 47		08 55	
		d					07 49		07 56			08 18								08 49		08 56	
Congleton		d										08 26											
Handforth		d								07 59					08 28								08 59
Manchester Airport		d									08 11												
Styal		d									08 18												
Wilmslow		d						07 46		08 01	08 22			08 11	08 31						08 46		09 02
Alderley Edge		d								08a07	08 25				08 34								09a08
Chelford		d													08 38								
Goostrey		d													08 43								
Holmes Chapel		d									08 33				08 46								
Sandbach		d									08 37				08 51								
Crewe	65	a						08 05			08 47			08 27	09 01						09 05		
Kidsgrove	50	a										08 32											
Longport	50	a																					
Stoke-on-Trent	50,68	a	07 48				08 06		08 11			08 42				08 43	08 48			09 06		09 11	
Stafford	68	a					08 25									09 02				09 25			
Wolverhampton	68	a					08 39									09 15				09 39			
Birmingham New Street	68	a					08 58									09 39				09 58			
London Euston	⊖65	a	09 23						09 42					10 04			10 23					10 42	

A To Bournemouth
B From Manchester Airport to Cleethorpes
C To Sheffield
D To Bristol Temple Meads
E To Chester
F To Milford Haven
G To Buxton
H From Wigan Wallgate to Hazel Grove
I To Carmarthen
J To Paignton

Table 84

Saturdays
from 6 October

Manchester, Stockport and Manchester Airport - Crewe and Stoke-on-Trent

Network Diagram - see first Page of Table 78

Station			NT	NT	NT A	VT	NT	XC B	VT	NT C	TP D	XC E	AW F	VT	NT	NT	NT	NT A	VT	NT	XC B
Deansgate		d																			
Manchester Oxford Road		d																			
Manchester Piccadilly		a																			
		d	08 46	08 48	08 52	08 55	09 04	09 07	09 15	09 17	09 20	09 27	09 30	09 35	09 38	09 46	09 48	09 52	09 55	10 04	10 07
Levenshulme		d			08 58		09 09								09 43			09 58		10 09	
Heaton Chapel		d			09 01		09 12								09 46			10 01		10 12	
Stockport		a		08 57	09 04	09 03	09 16	09 15	09 22	09 27	09 28	09 34	09 38	09 42	09 50		09 57	10 04	10 03	10 16	10 15
		d		08 58		09 04	09 17	09 16	09 23			09 35	09 39	09 43	09 51		09 58		10 04	10 17	10 16
Cheadle Hulme		d		09 02			09 24								09 55		10 02			10 24	
Bramhall		d		09 05													10 05				
Poynton		d		09 08													10 08				
Adlington (Cheshire)		d		09 11													10 11				
Prestbury		d		09 14													10 14				
Macclesfield		a		09 18								09 47		09 55			10 18				
		d		09 18								09 49		09 56			10 18				
Congleton		d		09 26													10 26				
Handforth		d					09 28								09 59					10 28	
Manchester Airport		d	09 11													10 11					
Styal		d																			
Wilmslow		d	09 21			09 11	09 31						09 46		10 02	10 21			10 11	10 31	
Alderley Edge		d	09 24				09 34								10a08	10 24				10 34	
Chelford		d					09 38													10 38	
Goostrey		d					09 43													10 43	
Holmes Chapel		d	09 32				09 46									10 32				10 46	
Sandbach		d	09 36				09 51									10 36				10 51	
Crewe	65	a	09 46			09 27	10 01						10 05			10 46			10 27	11 01	
Kidsgrove	50	a		09 32													10 32				
Longport	50	a																			
Stoke-on-Trent	50,68	a		09 42				09 43	09 48			10 06		10 11			10 42				10 43
Stafford	68	a						10 02				10 25									11 02
Wolverhampton	68	a						10 15				10 39									11 16
Birmingham New Street	68	a						10 39				10 58									11 39
London Euston	⊖65	a				11 04			11 23					11 42					12 04		

Station			VT	NT C	TP D	XC E	AW G	VT	NT	NT	NT	NT A	VT	NT	XC B	VT	NT C	TP D	XC E	AW F	VT	NT	NT
Deansgate		d																					
Manchester Oxford Road		d																					
Manchester Piccadilly		a																					
		d	10 15	10 17	10 20	10 27	10 30	10 35	10 38	10 46	10 48	10 52	10 55	11 04	11 07	11 15	11 17	11 20	11 27	11 30	11 35	11 38	11 46
Levenshulme		d							10 43			10 58		11 09								11 43	
Heaton Chapel		d							10 46			11 01		11 12								11 46	
Stockport		a	10 22	10 27	10 28	10 34	10 38	10 42	10 50		10 57	11 04	11 03	11 16	11 15	11 22	11 27	11 28	11 34	11 38	11 42	11 50	
		d	10 23			10 35	10 39	10 43	10 51		10 58		11 04	11 17	11 16	11 23			11 35	11 39	11 43	11 51	
Cheadle Hulme		d							10 55		11 02			11 24								11 55	
Bramhall		d									11 05												
Poynton		d									11 08												
Adlington (Cheshire)		d									11 11												
Prestbury		d									11 14												
Macclesfield		a				10 47		10 55			11 18								11 47		11 55		
		d				10 49		10 56			11 18								11 49		11 56		
Congleton		d									11 26												
Handforth		d							10 59					11 28								11 59	
Manchester Airport		d								11 11													12 11
Styal		d								11 18													
Wilmslow		d					10 46		11 02	11 22			11 11	11 31						11 46		12 02	12 21
Alderley Edge		d							11a08	11 25				11 34								12a08	12 24
Chelford		d												11 38									
Goostrey		d												11 43									
Holmes Chapel		d								11 33				11 46									12 32
Sandbach		d								11 37				11 51									12 36
Crewe	65	a					11 05			11 47			11 27	12 01						12 05			12 46
Kidsgrove	50	a									11 32												
Longport	50	a																					
Stoke-on-Trent	50,68	a	10 48			11 06		11 11			11 42				11 43	11 48			12 06		12 11		
Stafford	68	a				11 25									12 02				12 24				
Wolverhampton	68	a				11 39									12 16				12 39				
Birmingham New Street	68	a				11 58									12 39				12 58				
London Euston	⊖65	a	12 23					12 42					13 04			13 23					13 42		

A To Buxton
B To Bristol Temple Meads
C To Chester
D From Manchester Airport to Cleethorpes
E To Bournemouth
F To Carmarthen
G To Milford Haven

Manchester, Stockport and Manchester Airport - Crewe and Stoke-on-Trent

Network Diagram - see first Page of Table 78

		NT	NT	VT	NT	XC	VT	NT	TP	XC	AW	VT	NT	NT	NT	NT	VT	NT	XC	VT
				◇1		◇1	◇1		◇1	◇1	■	◇1					◇1		◇1	◇1
			A			B		C	D	E	F					A			G	
Deansgate	d																			
Manchester Oxford Road	d																			
Manchester Piccadilly 10	a																			
	d	11 48	11 52	11 55	12 04	12 07	12 15	12 17	12 20	12 27	12 30	12 35	12 38	12 46	12 48	12 52	12 55	13 04	13 07	13 15
Levenshulme	d		11 58		12 09								12 43			12 58		13 09		
Heaton Chapel	d		12 01		12 12								12 46			13 01		13 12		
Stockport	a	11 57	12 04	12 03	12 16	12 15	12 22	12 27	12 28	12 34	12 38	12 42	12 50		12 57	13 04	13 03	13 16	13 15	13 22
	d	11 58		12 04	12 17	12 16	12 23			12 35	12 39	12 43	12 51		12 58		13 04	13 17	13 16	13 23
Cheadle Hulme	d	12 02			12 24								12 55		13 02			13 24		
Bramhall	d	12 05													13 05					
Poynton	d	12 08													13 08					
Adlington (Cheshire)	d	12 11													13 11					
Prestbury	d	12 14													13 14					
Macclesfield	a	12 18								12 47		12 55			13 18					
	d	12 18								12 49		12 56			13 18					
Congleton	d	12 26													13 26					
Handforth	d				12 28								12 59					13 28		
Manchester Airport	d													13 11						
Styal	d													13 18						
Wilmslow	d			12 11	12 31						12 46		13 02	13 22			13 11	13 31		
Alderley Edge	d				12 34								13a08	13 25				13 34		
Chelford	d				12 38													13 38		
Goostrey	d				12 43													13 43		
Holmes Chapel	d				12 46									13 33				13 46		
Sandbach	d				12 51									13 37				13 51		
Crewe 10 65	a			12 27	13 01						13 05			13 47			13 27	14 01		
Kidsgrove 50	a	12 32													13 32					
Longport 50	a																			
Stoke-on-Trent 50,68	a	12 42				12 43	12 48			13 06		13 11			13 42				13 43	13 48
Stafford 68	a					13 02				13 25									14 02	
Wolverhampton 7 68	a					13 15				13 39									14 16	
Birmingham New Street 12 68	a					13 39				13 58									14 39	
London Euston 15 ⊖65	a			14 04			14 23					14 42					15 04			15 23

		NT	TP	XC	AW	VT	NT	NT	NT	NT	VT	NT	XC	VT	NT	TP	XC	AW	VT	NT	NT	NT
			◇1	◇1	■	◇1					◇1		◇1	◇1		◇1	◇1	■	◇1			
		C	D	E	H					A			I		C	D	E	F				
Deansgate	d																					
Manchester Oxford Road	d																					
Manchester Piccadilly 10	a																					
	d	13 17	13 20	13 27	13 30	13 35	13 38	13 46	13 48	13 52	13 55	14 04	14 07	14 15	14 17	14 20	14 27	14 30	14 35	14 38	14 46	14 48
Levenshulme	d						13 43			13 58		14 09								14 43		
Heaton Chapel	d						13 46			14 01		14 12								14 46		
Stockport	a	13 27	13 28	13 34	13 38	13 42	13 50		13 57	14 04	14 03	14 16	14 15	14 22	14 27	14 28	14 34	14 38	14 42	14 50		14 57
	d			13 35	13 39	13 43	13 51		13 58		14 04	14 17	14 16	14 23			14 35	14 39	14 43	14 51		14 58
Cheadle Hulme	d						13 55		14 02			14 24								14 55		15 02
Bramhall	d								14 05													15 05
Poynton	d								14 08													15 08
Adlington (Cheshire)	d								14 11													15 11
Prestbury	d								14 14													15 14
Macclesfield	a			13 47		13 55			14 18								14 47		14 55			15 18
	d			13 49		13 56			14 18								14 49		14 56			15 18
Congleton	d								14 26													15 26
Handforth	d						13 59					14 28								14 59		
Manchester Airport	d							14 11													15 11	
Styal	d																					
Wilmslow	d				13 46		14 02	14 21			14 11	14 31						14 46		15 02	15 21	
Alderley Edge	d						14a08	14 24				14 34								15a08	15 24	
Chelford	d											14 38										
Goostrey	d											14 43										
Holmes Chapel	d							14 32				14 46									15 32	
Sandbach	d							14 36				14 51									15 36	
Crewe 10 65	a				14 05			14 46			14 27	15 01						15 05			15 46	
Kidsgrove 50	a								14 32													15 32
Longport 50	a																					
Stoke-on-Trent 50,68	a			14 06		14 11			14 42				14 43	14 48			15 06		15 11			15 42
Stafford 68	a			14 25									15 02				15 25					
Wolverhampton 7 68	a			14 39									15 16				15 39					
Birmingham New Street 12 68	a			14 58									15 39				15 58					
London Euston 15 ⊖65	a					15 42					16 04			16 23					16 42			

A To Buxton
B To Exeter St Davids
C To Chester
D From Manchester Airport to Cleethorpes
E To Bournemouth
F To Milford Haven
G To Bristol Temple Meads
H To Pembroke Dock
I To Paignton

Table 84

Saturdays
from 6 October

Manchester, Stockport and Manchester Airport - Crewe and Stoke-on-Trent

Network Diagram - see first Page of Table 78

		NT	VT	NT	XC	VT	NT	TP	XC	AW	VT	NT	NT	NT	NT	VT	NT	XC	VT	NT	TP
			◇1		◇1	◇1		◇1	◇1	■	◇1					◇1		◇1	◇1		◇1
		A			B		C	D	E	F					A			B		C	D
Deansgate	d																				
Manchester Oxford Road	d																				
Manchester Piccadilly 10	a																				
	d	14 52	14 55	15 04	15 07	15 15	15 17	15 20	15 27	15 30	15 35	15 38	15 46	15 48	15 52	15 55	16 04	16 07	16 15	16 17	16 20
Levenshulme	d	14 58		15 09								15 43			15 58		16 09				
Heaton Chapel	d	15 01		15 12								15 46			16 01		16 12				
Stockport	a	15 04	15 03	15 16	15 15	15 22	15 27	15 28	15 34	15 38	15 42	15 50		15 57	16 04	16 03	16 16	16 15	16 22	16 27	16 28
	d		15 04	15 17	15 16	15 23			15 35	15 39	15 43	15 51		15 58		16 04	16 17	16 16	16 23		
Cheadle Hulme	d			15 24								15 55		16 02			16 24				
Bramhall	d													16 05							
Poynton	d													16 08							
Adlington (Cheshire)	d													16 11							
Prestbury	d													16 14							
Macclesfield	a								15 47		15 55			16 18							
	d								15 49		15 56			16 18							
Congleton	d													16 26							
Handforth	d			15 28								15 59					16 28				
Manchester Airport	d												16 11								
Styal	d																				
Wilmslow	d		15 11	15 31						15 46		16 02	16 21			16 11	16 31				
Alderley Edge	d			15 34								16a08	16 24				16 34				
Chelford	d			15 38													16 38				
Goostrey	d			15 43													16 43				
Holmes Chapel	d			15 46									16 32				16 46				
Sandbach	d			15 51									16 36				16 51				
Crewe 10 65	a		15 27	16 01						16 05			16 46			16 27	17 01				
Kidsgrove 50	a													16 32							
Longport 50	a																				
Stoke-on-Trent 50,68	a				15 43	15 48			16 06		16 11			16 42				16 43	16 48		
Stafford 68	a				16 02				16 24									17 02			
Wolverhampton 7 68	a				16 16				16 39									17 16			
Birmingham New Street 12 68	a				16 39				16 58									17 39			
London Euston 15 ⊖65	a		17 04			17 23					17 42					18 04			18 23		

		XC	AW	VT	NT	NT	NT	NT	VT	NT	XC	NT	VT	NT	TP	XC	AW	VT	NT	NT	NT
		◇1	■	◇1					◇1		◇1		◇1		◇1	◇1	■	◇1			
		E	G					A			H	I		C	D	E	H				
Deansgate	d																				
Manchester Oxford Road	d																				
Manchester Piccadilly 10	a																				
	d	16 27	16 30	16 35	16 38	16 46	16 48	16 51	16 55	17 03	17 06	17 09	17 15	17 17	17 20	17 27	17 30	17 35	17 38	17 46	17 48
Levenshulme	d				16 43			16 58		17 08		17 14							17 43		
Heaton Chapel	d				16 46			17 01		17 11		17 17							17 46		
Stockport	a	16 34	16 38	16 42	16 50		16 58	17 04	17 03	17 15		17 21	17 22	17 27	17 28	17 35	17 38	17 42	17 50		17 57
	d	16 35	16 39	16 43	16 51		16 58		17 04	17 16			17 23			17 36	17 39	17 43	17 51		17 58
Cheadle Hulme	d				16 55		17 02			17 24									17 55		18 02
Bramhall	d						17 05														18 05
Poynton	d						17 08														18 08
Adlington (Cheshire)	d						17 11														18 11
Prestbury	d						17 14														18 14
Macclesfield	a	16 47		16 55			17 18				17 25							17 55			18 18
	d	16 49		16 56			17 18				17 26							17 56			18 18
Congleton	d						17 26									17 54					18 26
Handforth	d				16 59					17 28									17 59		
Manchester Airport	d					17 11														18 11	
Styal	d					17 18														18 18	
Wilmslow	d		16 46		17 02	17 22			17 11	17 31							17 46		18 02	18 22	
Alderley Edge	d				17a08	17 25				17 34									18a08	18 25	
Chelford	d									17 38											
Goostrey	d									17 43											
Holmes Chapel	d					17 33				17 46										18 33	
Sandbach	d					17 37				17 51										18 37	
Crewe 10 65	a		17 05			17 47			17 27	18 01							18 05			18 47	
Kidsgrove 50	a						17 32														18 32
Longport 50	a																				
Stoke-on-Trent 50,68	a	17 06		17 11			17 42				17 43		17 49			18 07		18 11			18 42
Stafford 68	a	17 25									18 03					18 26					
Wolverhampton 7 68	a	17 39									18 16					18 40					
Birmingham New Street 12 68	a	17 58									18 38					18 58					
London Euston 15 ⊖65	a			18 42					19 04				19 23					19 42			

A To Buxton
B To Bristol Temple Meads
C To Chester
D From Manchester Airport to Cleethorpes
E To Bournemouth
F To Pembroke Dock
G To Milford Haven
H To Cardiff Central
I To Hazel Grove

Saturdays from 6 October

Manchester, Stockport and Manchester Airport - Crewe and Stoke-on-Trent

Network Diagram - see first Page of Table 78

		NT	VT	XC	NT	VT	NT	TP	XC	AW	VT	NT	NT	NT	NT	VT	NT	XC	NT	TP	NT
			◇1	◇1		◇1		◇1	◇1	◇	◇1					◇1		◇1		◇1	
		A		B			C	D	E	F					A			B	C	D	G
Deansgate	d																				
Manchester Oxford Road	d																				
Manchester Piccadilly	a																				
	d	17 52	17 55	18 05	18 08	18 15	18 17	18 20	18 27	18 30	18 35	18 38	18 46	18 48	18 52	18 55	19 04	19 07	19 17	19 18	19 22
Levenshulme	d	17 58			18 13							18 43			18 58		19 09				19 28
Heaton Chapel	d	18 01			18 16							18 46			19 01		19 12				19 31
Stockport	a	18 04	18 03	18 12	18 20	18 22	18 27	18 28	18 34	18 38	18 42	18 50		18 57	19 04	19 03	19 16	19 15	19 27	19 26	19 34
	d		18 04	18 13	18 22	18 23			18 35	18 39	18 43	18 51		18 58		19 04	19 17	19 16			
Cheadle Hulme	d				18 30							18 55		19 02			19 24				
Bramhall	d													19 05							
Poynton	d													19 08							
Adlington (Cheshire)	d													19 11							
Prestbury	d													19 14							
Macclesfield	a			18 25							18 55			19 18							
	d			18 26							18 56			19 18							
Congleton	d								18 54					19 26							
Handforth	d				18 34							18 59					19 28				
Manchester Airport	d												19 14								
Styal	d																				
Wilmslow	d		18 11		18 37					18 46		19 02	19 26			19 11	19 31				
Alderley Edge	d				18 40							19a08	19a32				19 34				
Chelford	d				18 44												19 38				
Goostrey	d				18 48												19 43				
Holmes Chapel	d				18 51												19 46				
Sandbach	d				18 56												19 51				
Crewe 65	a		18 27		19 06					19 08						19 27	20 01				
Kidsgrove 50	a													19 32							
Longport 50	a																				
Stoke-on-Trent 50,68	a			18 43		18 48			19 06		19 11			19 42				19 43			
Stafford 68	a			19 02					19 25									20 02			
Wolverhampton 68	a			19 16					19 39									20 16			
Birmingham New Street 68	a			19 33					19 58									20 33			
London Euston ⊖65	a		20 04			20 24					20 59					21 18					

		XC	AW	VT	NT	NT	NT	NT	XC	NT	TP	XC	AW	VT	NT	NT	NT	NT	XC	NT	TP	XC
		◇1		◇1					◇1		◇1	◇1		◇1					◇1		◇1	◇1
		H	I				A			C	J		I				A			C	D	
Deansgate	d																					
Manchester Oxford Road	d				19 43										20 43							
Manchester Piccadilly	a				19 45										20 45							
	d	19 27	19 30	19 35	19 46	19 48	19 51	20 04	20 07	20 17	20 20	20 27	20 30	20 35	20 46	20 48	20 52	21 04	21 07	21 17	21 20	21 27
Levenshulme	d						19 58	20 09									20 58	21 09				
Heaton Chapel	d						20 01	20 12									21 01	21 12				
Stockport	a	19 34	19 38	19 42		19 57	20 04	20 16	20 15	20 27	20 28	20 34	20 38	20 42		20 57	21 04	21 16		21 27	21 28	21 35
	d	19 35	19 39	19 43		19 58		20 17	20 16			20 35	20 39	20 43		20 58		21 17				21 36
Cheadle Hulme	d					20 02		20 24								21 02		21 24				
Bramhall	d					20 05										21 05						
Poynton	d					20 08										21 08						
Adlington (Cheshire)	d					20 11										21 11						
Prestbury	d					20 14										21 14						
Macclesfield	a	19 47		19 55		20 18						20 47		20 55		21 18						21 48
	d	19 49		19 56		20 18						20 49		20 56		21 18						21 50
Congleton	d					20 26										21 26						
Handforth	d							20 28										21 28				
Manchester Airport	d				20 14										21 14							
Styal	d																					
Wilmslow	d		19 46		20a24			20 31					20 46		21a24			21 31				
Alderley Edge	d							20 34										21 34				
Chelford	d							20 38										21 38				
Goostrey	d							20 43										21 43				
Holmes Chapel	d							20 46										21 46				
Sandbach	d							20 51										21 51				
Crewe 65	a		20 05					21 01					21 05					22 01				
Kidsgrove 50	a					20 32										21 32						
Longport 50	a																					
Stoke-on-Trent 50,68	a	20 06		20 11		20 42			20 43			21 06		21 11		21 42			21 43			22 07
Stafford 68	a	20 25							21 02			21 26							22 02			22 32
Wolverhampton 68	a	20 39							21 15			21 39							22 14			22 45
Birmingham New Street 68	a	20 58							21 32			21 58							22 32			23 02
London Euston ⊖65	a			22 00										23 02								

A To Buxton
B To Bristol Temple Meads
C To Chester
D From Manchester Airport to Cleethorpes
E To Bournemouth
F To Carmarthen
G To Hazel Grove
H To Southampton Central
I To Cardiff Central
J From Manchester Airport to Sheffield

Saturdays from 6 October

Manchester, Stockport and Manchester Airport - Crewe and Stoke-on-Trent

Network Diagram - see first Page of Table 78

		AW	NT	NT	NT	NT	NT	TP	AW	NT	NT	NT	NT	NT	NT	NT
								◇1								
		A			B		C	D	A				B		C	
Deansgate	d															
Manchester Oxford Road	d		21 43							22 43						
Manchester Piccadilly	a		21 45							22 45						
	d	21 35	21 46	21 48	21 52	22 04	22 17	22 20	22 35	22 46	22 48	23 04	23 10	23 14	23 17	23 37
Levenshulme	d				21 58	22 09						23 09				23 42
Heaton Chapel	d				22 01	22 12						23 12				23 45
Stockport	a	21 43		21 58	22 04	22 16	22 27	22 28	22 43		22 57	23 16	23 19	23 23	23 26	23 49
	d	21 44		21 58		22 17			22 44		22 58	23 16		23 23		23 50
Cheadle Hulme	d			22 02		22 24					23 02	23 21		23 27		23 54
Bramhall	d			22 05							23 05			23 30		
Poynton	d			22 08							23 08			23 33		
Adlington (Cheshire)	d			22 11							23 11			23 37		
Prestbury	d			22 14							23 14			23 40		
Macclesfield	a			22 18							23 20			23 46		
	d			22 18												
Congleton	d			22 26												
Handforth	d					22 28						23 25				23 58
Manchester Airport	d		22 14							23 14						
Styal	d															
Wilmslow	d	21 51	22a22			22 31			22 52	23a22		23 28				00 01
Alderley Edge	d					22 34						23 31				00a07
Chelford	d					22 38						23 35				
Goostrey	d					22 43						23 40				
Holmes Chapel	d					22 46						23 43				
Sandbach	d					22 51						23 48				
Crewe 65	a	22 11				23 01			23 10			23 58				
Kidsgrove 50	a			22 32												
Longport 50	a															
Stoke-on-Trent 50,68	a			22 42												
Stafford 68	a															
Wolverhampton 68	a															
Birmingham New Street 68	a															
London Euston ⊖65	a															

Sundays until 24 June

		NT	VT	XC	VT	NT	NT	NT	TP	NT	XC	VT	NT	AW	NT	NT
			◇1	◇1	◇1				◇1		◇1	◇1		◇		
				F				B	D		F		G	H	B	
Deansgate	d												09 15			
Manchester Oxford Road	d												09 18			
Manchester Piccadilly	a												09 21			
	d	23p37	08 05	08 10	08 20	08 41	08 50	08 55	08 58	09 04	09 07	09 20	09 22	09 30	09 51	10 03
Levenshulme	d	23p42						09 00		09 09					09 58	10 08
Heaton Chapel	d	23p45						09 03		09 12					10 01	10 11
Stockport	a	23p49	08 13	08 17	08 28		08 59	09 07	09 06	09 17	09 15	09 27	09 31	09 39	10 04	10 15
	d	23p50	08 14	08 19	08 28		09 01			09 17	09 16	09 27		09 39		10 17
Cheadle Hulme	d	23p54					09 06			09 21						10 23
Bramhall	d						09 09									
Poynton	d						09 12									
Adlington (Cheshire)	d						09 15									
Prestbury	d						09 18									
Macclesfield	a				08 41		09 22				09 28	09 40				
	d				08 42						09 29	09 40				
Congleton	d															
Handforth	d	23p58								09 25						10 27
Manchester Airport	d					09 06										
Styal	d					09 10										
Wilmslow	d	00 01	08 22	08 26		09 15				09 28				09 47		10 30
Alderley Edge	d	00a07				09a22				09 31						10a36
Chelford	d									09 35						
Goostrey	d									09 40						
Holmes Chapel	d									09 43						
Sandbach	d									09 48						
Crewe 65	a		08 39	08 44						09 58				10 06		
Kidsgrove 50	a															
Longport 50	a															
Stoke-on-Trent 50,68	a				08 59						09 45	09 57				
Stafford 68	a		09 01	09 06							10 09					
Wolverhampton 68	a			09 26							10 25					
Birmingham New Street 68	a			09 58							10 56					
London Euston ⊖65	a		10 57		11 02							12 08				

A To Shrewsbury
B To Buxton
C To Chester
D From Manchester Airport to Sheffield
F To Bournemouth
G From Wigan Wallgate to Chester
H To Cardiff Central

Manchester, Stockport and Manchester Airport - Crewe and Stoke-on-Trent

Network Diagram - see first Page of Table 78

	XC	VT	AW	VT	NT	NT	NT	XC	VT	TP	AW	VT	NT	NT	VT	NT	XC	VT	TP	AW
	◇1 A ✕	◇1 ⊐	■ B ✕	◇1 ⊐		C		◇1 A ✕	◇1 ⊐	◇1 D	■ E ✕	◇1 ⊐		C	◇1 ⊐		◇1 A ✕	◇1 ⊐	◇1 F	■ B ✕
Deansgate ⇌ d																				
Manchester Oxford Road d																				
Manchester Piccadilly 10 ⇌ a																				
d	10 06	10 20	10 30	10 35	10 41	10 53	11 04	11 05	11 15	11 18	11 24	11 35	11 41	11 52	11 55	12 04	12 06	12 15	12 20	12 30
Levenshulme d						10 59	11 10							11 58		12 09				
Heaton Chapel d						11 02	11 13							12 01		12 12				
Stockport a	10 14	10 28	10 39	10 42		11 05	11 17	11 12	11 23	11 27	11 34	11 43	11 49	12 04	12 04	12 16	12 15	12 23	12 28	12 39
d	10 16	10 29	10 39	10 42			11 17	11 14	11 23		11 40	11 43	11 51		12 05	12 16	12 15	12 23		12 40
Cheadle Hulme d							11 22						11 56			12 22				
Bramhall d													11 59							
Poynton d													12 02							
Adlington (Cheshire) d													12 04							
Prestbury d													12 07							
Macclesfield a	10 28			10 55				11 27				11 56	12 11				12 28			
d	10 29			10 55				11 27				11 56	12 11				12 29			
Congleton d													12 19							
Handforth d							11 26									12 26				
Manchester Airport ✈ d					11 08															
Styal d					11 12															
Wilmslow d		10 36	10 48		11 16		11 29				11 47				12 12	12 29				12 48
Alderley Edge d					11a21		11 32									12a35				
Chelford d							11 36													
Goostrey d							11 41													
Holmes Chapel d							11 44													
Sandbach d							11 49													
Crewe 10 65 a		10 53	11 07				11 59				12 07				12 28					13 07
Kidsgrove 50 a													12 25							
Longport 50 a																				
Stoke-on-Trent 50,68 a	10 46			11 12				11 44	11 50			12 13	12 37				12 46	12 50		
Stafford 68 a	11 04							12 02									13 06			
Wolverhampton 7 68 ⇌ a	11 24							12 23									13 21			
Birmingham New Street 12 68 a	11 56							12 52									13 56			
London Euston 15 ⊖65 a		12 56		12 59					13 28			13 47			14 09			14 27		

	VT	XC	EM	NT	NT	VT	XC	NT	VT	TP	AW	VT	XC	NT	VT	NT	XC	VT	TP	AW
	◇1 ⊐	◇1 G ✕	◇ H		C	◇1 ⊐	◇1 A ✕		◇1 ⊐	◇1 D	■ E ✕	◇1 ⊐	◇1 I ✕	C	◇1 ⊐		◇1 A ✕	◇1 ⊐	◇1 D	■ B ✕
Deansgate ⇌ d																				
Manchester Oxford Road d				12 43																
Manchester Piccadilly 10 ⇌ a				12 45																
d	12 35	12 41	12 44	12 47	12 52	12 55	13 03	13 04	13 15	13 20	13 30	13 35	13 42	13 52	13 55	14 04	14 05	14 15	14 20	14 30
Levenshulme d					12 58			13 09						13 58		14 09				
Heaton Chapel d					13 01			13 12						14 01		14 12				
Stockport a	12 44	12 49	12 53		13 04	13 04	13 11	13 16	13 22	13 29	13 39	13 42	13 50	14 04	14 03	14 16	14 12	14 22	14 28	14 38
d	12 44	12 50				13 05	13 13	13 17	13 22		13 40	13 42	13 51		14 04	14 17	14 14	14 22		14 39
Cheadle Hulme d								13 21								14 22				
Bramhall d																				
Poynton d																				
Adlington (Cheshire) d																				
Prestbury d																				
Macclesfield a	12 57	13 03					13 25					13 55	14 03				14 26			
d	12 57	13 04					13 26					13 55	14 04				14 27			
Congleton d																				
Handforth d								13 25								14 26				
Manchester Airport ✈ d				13 12																
Styal d				13 16																
Wilmslow d				13 23		13 12		13 28			13 47				14 11	14 29				14 47
Alderley Edge d				13a29				13 31								14a35				
Chelford d								13 35												
Goostrey d								13 40												
Holmes Chapel d								13 43												
Sandbach d								13 48												
Crewe 10 65 a						13 28		13 58			14 07				14 27					15 07
Kidsgrove 50 a																				
Longport 50 a																				
Stoke-on-Trent 50,68 a	13 14	13 21					13 43		13 49			14 12	14 21				14 44	14 49		
Stafford 68 a							14 01										15 05			
Wolverhampton 7 68 ⇌ a		13 52					14 20						14 53				15 19			
Birmingham New Street 12 68 a		14 27					14 56						15 27				15 56			
London Euston 15 ⊖65 a	14 47					15 09			15 27			15 47			16 09			16 27		

A To Bournemouth
B To Milford Haven
C To Buxton
D From Manchester Airport to Cleethorpes
E To Cardiff Central
F To Doncaster
G To Paignton
H To Norwich
I To Bristol Temple Meads

Manchester, Stockport and Manchester Airport - Crewe and Stoke-on-Trent

Network Diagram - see first Page of Table 78

	VT	NT	NT	XC	NT	VT	XC	NT	VT	TP	AW	VT	XC	NT	VT	XC	NT	VT	TP	AW	VT
	◇1 ⊐			◇1 A ✕	B	◇1 ⊐	◇1 C ✕		◇1 ⊐	◇1 D	■ E ✕	◇1 ⊐	◇1 A ✕	B	◇1 ⊐	◇1 C ✕		◇1 ⊐	◇1 D	■ E ✕	◇1 ⊐
Deansgate ⇌ d																					
Manchester Oxford Road d																					
Manchester Piccadilly 10 ⇌ a																					
d	14 35	14 41	14 41	14 42	14 52	14 55	15 02	15 04	15 15	15 20	15 30	15 35	15 42	15 52	15 55	16 02	16 04	16 15	16 20	16 30	16 35
Levenshulme d					14 58			15 09						15 58			16 09				
Heaton Chapel d					15 01			15 12						16 01			16 12				
Stockport a	14 42		14 49	14 50	15 04	15 03	15 10	15 16	15 22	15 28	15 39	15 42	15 50	16 04	16 03	16 09	16 16	16 22	16 28	16 39	16 42
d	14 42		14 51	14 51		15 04	15 11	15 17	15 22		15 39	15 42	15 51		16 04	16 11	16 17	16 23		16 39	16 42
Cheadle Hulme d			14 56					15 22									16 22				
Bramhall d			14 59																		
Poynton d			15 02																		
Adlington (Cheshire) d			15 04																		
Prestbury d			15 07																		
Macclesfield a	14 55		15 11	15 03			15 23					15 55	16 03			16 23					16 55
d	14 55		15 11	15 04			15 24					15 55	16 04			16 24					16 55
Congleton d			15 19																		
Handforth d								15 26									16 26				
Manchester Airport ✈ d		15 06																			
Styal d		15 10																			
Wilmslow d		15 14				15 11		15 29			15 47				16 11		16 29			16 47	
Alderley Edge d		15a20						15 32									16a35				
Chelford d								15 36													
Goostrey d								15 40													
Holmes Chapel d								15 43													
Sandbach d								15 48													
Crewe 10 65 a						15 27		15 58			16 06				16 27					17 06	
Kidsgrove 50 a			15 25																		
Longport 50 a																					
Stoke-on-Trent 50,68 a	15 12		15 37	15 21			15 43		15 49			16 12	16 22			16 43		16 48			17 12
Stafford 68 a							16 05									17 05					
Wolverhampton 7 68 ⇌ a				15 53			16 21						16 53			17 20					
Birmingham New Street 12 68 a				16 27			16 52						17 28			17 56					
London Euston 15 ⊖65 a	16 47					17 09			17 27			17 47			18 09			18 27			18 47

	NT	XC	NT	VT	XC	NT	VT	TP	AW	VT	XC	NT	VT	XC	NT	VT	TP	AW	VT	NT
		◇1 F ✕	B	◇1 ⊐	◇1 C ✕		◇1 ⊐	◇1 D	■ E ✕	◇1 ⊐	◇1 A ✕	B	◇1 ⊐	◇1 G ✕		◇1 ⊐	◇1 D	■ E ✕	◇1 ⊐	
Deansgate ⇌ d																				
Manchester Oxford Road d																				
Manchester Piccadilly 10 ⇌ a																				
d	16 41	16 42	16 52	16 55	17 02	17 04	17 15	17 20	17 30	17 35	17 42	17 52	17 55	18 02	18 04	18 15	18 20	18 30	18 35	18 41
Levenshulme d			16 58			17 09						17 58			18 09					
Heaton Chapel d			17 01			17 12						18 01			18 12					
Stockport a		16 50	17 04	17 03	17 09	17 16	17 22	17 28	17 39	17 42	17 50	18 04	18 03	18 09	18 16	18 22	18 28	18 39	18 42	
d		16 51		17 04	17 11	17 17	17 22		17 39	17 42	17 51		18 04	18 11	18 17	18 22		18 39	18 42	
Cheadle Hulme d						17 22									18 22					
Bramhall d																				
Poynton d																				
Adlington (Cheshire) d																				
Prestbury d																				
Macclesfield a		17 03			17 23					17 55	18 03			18 23					18 55	
d		17 04			17 24					17 55	18 04			18 24					18 55	
Congleton d																				
Handforth d						17 26									18 26					
Manchester Airport ✈ d	17 06																			19 06
Styal d	17 10																			19 10
Wilmslow d	17 15			17 11		17 29			17 47				18 11		18 29			18 47		19 15
Alderley Edge d	17a21					17 32									18a35					19a21
Chelford d						17 36														
Goostrey d						17 40														
Holmes Chapel d						17 43														
Sandbach d						17 48														
Crewe 10 65 a				17 27		17 58			18 07				18 27					19 06		
Kidsgrove 50 a																				
Longport 50 a																				
Stoke-on-Trent 50,68 a		17 21			17 44		17 49			18 12	18 21			18 43		18 49			19 12	
Stafford 68 a					18 05									19 02						
Wolverhampton 7 68 ⇌ a		17 53			18 20						18 53			19 20						
Birmingham New Street 12 68 a		18 27			18 56						19 27			19 50						
London Euston 15 ⊖65 a				19 09			19 27			19 47			20 09			20 27			20 47	

A To Bristol Temple Meads
B To Buxton
C To Bournemouth
D From Manchester Airport to Cleethorpes
E To Cardiff Central
F To Paignton
G To Southampton Central

Manchester, Stockport and Manchester Airport - Crewe and Stoke-on-Trent

Network Diagram - see first Page of Table 78

		XC	NT	NT	VT	XC	NT	VT	TP	AW	VT	XC	NT	NT	XC	TP	VT	AW	NT	NT	VT	NT
		◇1			◇1	◇1		◇1	◇1	◇	◇1	◇1			◇1	◇1	◇1	◇			◇1	
		A		B		C			D	E		A	B			D		E		B		
Deansgate ⇌	d																					
Manchester Oxford Road	d																					
Manchester Piccadilly 10 ⇌	a																					
	d	18 42	18 42	18 52	18 55	19 02	19 04	19 15	19 20	19 30	19 35	19 42	19 52	20 04	20 07	20 18	20 20	20 30	20 41	20 52	20 55	21 04
Levenshulme	d			18 58			19 09						19 58	20 09						20 58		21 09
Heaton Chapel	d			19 01			19 12						20 01	20 12						21 01		21 12
Stockport	a	18 50	18 50	19 04	19 03	19 09	19 16	19 22	19 28	19 39	19 41	19 50	20 04	20 16	20 15	20 26	20 27	20 38		21 04	21 03	21 16
	d	18 51	18 52		19 04	19 11	19 17	19 22		19 39	19 41	19 51		20 17	20 16		20 27	20 39			21 03	21 17
Cheadle Hulme	d		18 57				19 22							20 22								21 22
Bramhall	d		19 00																			
Poynton	d		19 03																			
Adlington (Cheshire)	d		19 06																			
Prestbury	d		19 09																			
Macclesfield	a	19 03	19 13			19 23					19 54	20 04			20 28		20 40				21 15	
	d	19 04	19 13			19 24					19 54	20 05			20 29		20 40				21 15	
Congleton	d		19 21																			
Handforth	d						19 26							20 26								21 26
Manchester Airport ✈	d																		21 06			
Styal	d																		21 10			
Wilmslow	d				19 11		19 29			19 47				20 29				20 47	21 14			21 29
Alderley Edge	d						19 32							20a37					21a20			21 32
Chelford	d						19 36															21 36
Goostrey	d						19 40															21 40
Holmes Chapel	d						19 43															21 43
Sandbach	d						19 48															21 48
Crewe 10 65	a				19 27		19 58			20 07								21 07				21 58
Kidsgrove 50	a		19 28																			
Longport 50	a																					
Stoke-on-Trent 50,68	a	19 21	19 40			19 43		19 49			20 11	20 22			20 46		20 57				21 32	
Stafford 68	a					20 04						20 44			21 08							
Wolverhampton 7 68 ⇌	a	19 53				20 20						20 57			21 21							
Birmingham New Street 12 68	a	20 27				20 50						21 27			21 50							
London Euston 15 ⊖65	a				21 09			21 31			21 58						22 56				23 49	

		XC	TP	AW	NT	NT	NT	XC	TP	AW	NT	NT	TP
		◇1	◇1					◇1	◇1				◇1
			F			B			F		B		F
Deansgate ⇌	d												
Manchester Oxford Road	d												
Manchester Piccadilly 10 ⇌	a												
	d	21 07	21 20	21 34	21 41	21 52	22 04	22 07	22 15	22 35	22 52	23 04	23 20
Levenshulme	d					21 58	22 09				22 58	23 09	
Heaton Chapel	d					22 01	22 12				23 01	23 12	
Stockport	a	21 15	21 28		21 49	22 04	22 16	22 15	22 23		23 04	23 16	23 28
	d	21 16			21 52		22 17	22 16				23 17	
Cheadle Hulme	d				21 56		22 22					23 21	
Bramhall	d				21 59								
Poynton	d				22 02								
Adlington (Cheshire)	d				22 05								
Prestbury	d				22 08								
Macclesfield	a	21 28			22 12			22 28					
	d	21 29			22 13			22 29					
Congleton	d				22 20								
Handforth	d						22 26					23 25	
Manchester Airport ✈	d												
Styal	d												
Wilmslow	d			21 50			22 29			22 50		23 28	
Alderley Edge	d						22a35					23a35	
Chelford	d												
Goostrey	d												
Holmes Chapel	d												
Sandbach	d												
Crewe 10 65	a			22 13						23 10			
Kidsgrove 50	a				22 26								
Longport 50	a												
Stoke-on-Trent 50,68	a	21 46			22 36			22 46					
Stafford 68	a	22 06						23 04					
Wolverhampton 7 68 ⇌	a	22 20						23 18					
Birmingham New Street 12 68	a	22 52						23 49					
London Euston 15 ⊖65	a												

A To Bristol Temple Meads
B To Buxton
C To Reading
D From Manchester Airport to Cleethorpes
E To Cardiff Central
F From Manchester Airport to Sheffield

Manchester, Stockport and Manchester Airport - Crewe and Stoke-on-Trent

Network Diagram - see first Page of Table 78

		NT	VT	VT	VT	XC	NT	NT	NT	TP	NT	VT	NT	XC	AW	NT
			◇1	◇1	◇1	◇1				◇1		◇1		◇1	◇	
			B			C			D	E			F	C	G	D
Deansgate ⇌	d												09 15			
Manchester Oxford Road	d												09 18			
Manchester Piccadilly 10 ⇌	a												09 21			
	d	23p37	06 50	08 05	08 20	08 27	08 41	08 50	08 55	08 58	09 04	09 20	09 22	09 27	09 30	09 51
Levenshulme	d	23p42							09 00		09 09					09 58
Heaton Chapel	d	23p45							09 03		09 12					10 01
Stockport	a	23p49	06 58	08 13	08 28	08 34		08 59	09 07	09 06	09 17	09 27	09 31	09 35	09 39	10 04
	d	23p50	06 58	08 14	08 28	08 36		09 01			09 17	09 27		09 36	09 39	
Cheadle Hulme	d	23p54						09 06			09 21					
Bramhall	d							09 09								
Poynton	d							09 12								
Adlington (Cheshire)	d							09 15								
Prestbury	d							09 18								
Macclesfield	a		07 11		08 41			09 22				09 40		09 48		
	d		07 12		08 42							09 40		09 49		
Congleton	d															
Handforth	d	23p58									09 25					
Manchester Airport ✈	d						09 06									
Styal	d						09 10									
Wilmslow	d	00 01		08 22		08 43	09 15				09 28				09 47	
Alderley Edge	d	00a07					09a22				09 31					
Chelford	d										09 35					
Goostrey	d										09 40					
Holmes Chapel	d										09 43					
Sandbach	d										09 48					
Crewe 10 65	a			08 39		09 01					09 58				10 06	
Kidsgrove 50	a															
Longport 50	a															
Stoke-on-Trent 50,68	a		07 29		08 59							09 57		10 05		
Stafford 68	a			09 01		09 25								10 26		
Wolverhampton 7 68 ⇌	a					09 40								10 42		
Birmingham New Street 12 68	a					09 58								10 59		
London Euston 15 ⊖65	a		09 23	10 57	11 02							12 08				

		NT	VT	XC	AW	VT	NT	NT	NT	VT	TP	AW	XC	VT	NT	NT	VT	NT	VT	TP	XC
			◇1	◇1	2	◇1				◇1	◇1	2	◇1	◇1			◇1		◇1	◇1	◇1
				C	H			D			I	G	C			D				J	C
Deansgate ⇌	d																				
Manchester Oxford Road	d																				
Manchester Piccadilly 10 ⇌	a																				
	d	10 03	10 20	10 27	10 30	10 35	10 41	10 53	11 04	11 15	11 18	11 24	11 27	11 35	11 41	11 52	11 55	12 04	12 15	12 20	12 26
Levenshulme	d	10 08						10 59	11 10							11 58		12 09			
Heaton Chapel	d	10 11						11 02	11 13							12 01		12 12			
Stockport	a	10 15	10 28	10 34	10 39	10 42		11 05	11 17	11 23	11 27	11 34	11 34	11 43	11 49	12 04	12 04	12 16	12 23	12 28	12 35
	d	10 17	10 29	10 36	10 39	10 42			11 17	11 23		11 40	11 36	11 43	11 51		12 05	12 16	12 23		12 35
Cheadle Hulme	d	10 23							11 22						11 56			12 22			
Bramhall	d														11 59						
Poynton	d														12 02						
Adlington (Cheshire)	d														12 04						
Prestbury	d														12 07						
Macclesfield	a			10 48		10 55							11 49	11 56	12 11						12 48
	d			10 49		10 55							11 49	11 56	12 11						12 49
Congleton	d														12 19						
Handforth	d	10 27							11 26									12 26			
Manchester Airport ✈	d						11 08														
Styal	d						11 12														
Wilmslow	d	10 30	10 36		10 48		11 16		11 29			11 47					12 12	12 29			
Alderley Edge	d	10a36					11a21		11 32									12a35			
Chelford	d								11 36												
Goostrey	d								11 41												
Holmes Chapel	d								11 44												
Sandbach	d								11 49												
Crewe 10 65	a		10 53		11 07				11 59			12 07					12 28				
Kidsgrove 50	a														12 25						
Longport 50	a																				
Stoke-on-Trent 50,68	a			11 06		11 12				11 50			12 06	12 13	12 37				12 50		13 06
Stafford 68	a			11 27									12 24								13 24
Wolverhampton 7 68 ⇌	a			11 41									12 40								13 40
Birmingham New Street 12 68	a			12 00									12 58								13 58
London Euston 15 ⊖65	a		12 56			12 59				13 28				13 47			14 09		14 27		

B From 29 July until 12 August, from 2 September
C To Bournemouth
D To Buxton
E From Manchester Airport to Sheffield
F From Wigan Wallgate to Chester
G To Cardiff Central
H To Milford Haven
I From Manchester Airport to Cleethorpes
J To Doncaster

Manchester, Stockport and Manchester Airport - Crewe and Stoke-on-Trent

Network Diagram - see first Page of Table 78

		AW	VT	EM	NT	NT	VT	NT	XC	VT	TP	XC	AW	VT	NT	VT	NT	XC	VT	TP	XC
		■	◇■	◇			◇■		◇■	◇■	◇■	◇■	■	◇■		◇■		◇■	◇■	◇■	◇■
		A		B		C			D		E	F	G		C			H		E	F
		⊼	⊡				⊡		⊼	⊡		⊼	⊼	⊡		⊡		⊼	⊡		⊼
Deansgate ⇌	d																				
Manchester Oxford Road	d				12 43																
Manchester Piccadilly 10 ⇌	a				12 45																
	d	12 30	12 35	12 44	12 47	12 52	12 55	13 04	13 07	13 15	13 20	13 27	13 30	13 35	13 52	13 55	14 04	14 07	14 15	14 20	14 27
Levenshulme	d					12 58		13 09							13 58		14 09				
Heaton Chapel	d					13 01		13 12							14 01		14 12				
Stockport	a	12 39	12 44	12 53		13 04	13 04	13 16		13 22	13 28	13 35	13 39	13 42	14 04	14 03	14 16		14 22	14 28	14 34
	d	12 40	12 44				13 05	13 17		13 22		13 36	13 40	13 42		14 04	14 17		14 22		14 36
Cheadle Hulme	d							13 21									14 22				
Bramhall	d																				
Poynton	d																				
Adlington (Cheshire)	d																				
Prestbury	d																				
Macclesfield	a		12 57									13 48		13 55							14 48
	d		12 57									13 49		13 55							14 49
Congleton	d																				
Handforth	d							13 25									14 26				
Manchester Airport ✈	d				13 12																
Styal	d				13 16																
Wilmslow	d	12 48			13 23		13 12	13 28					13 47			14 11	14 29				
Alderley Edge	d				13a29			13 31									14a35				
Chelford	d							13 35													
Goostrey	d							13 40													
Holmes Chapel	d							13 43													
Sandbach	d							13 48													
Crewe 10 65	a	13 07					13 28	13 58					14 07			14 27					
Kidsgrove 50	a																				
Longport 50	a																				
Stoke-on-Trent 50,68	a		13 14						13 42	13 49		14 06		14 12				14 42	14 49		15 06
Stafford 68	a											14 24									15 24
Wolverhampton 7 68 ⇌	a								14 13			14 40						15 13			15 40
Birmingham New Street 12 68	a								14 31			14 58						15 31			15 58
London Euston 15 ⊖65	a		14 47				15 09			15 27				15 47		16 09			16 27		

		AW	VT	NT	NT	NT	VT	NT	XC	VT	TP	XC	AW	VT	NT	VT	NT	XC	VT	TP	XC	AW
		■	◇■				◇■		◇■	◇■	◇■	◇■	■	◇■		◇■		◇■	◇■	◇■	◇■	■
		A				C			H		E	F	G		C			H		E	F	G
		⊼	⊡				⊡		⊼	⊡		⊼	⊼	⊡		⊡		⊼	⊡		⊼	⊼
Deansgate ⇌	d																					
Manchester Oxford Road	d																					
Manchester Piccadilly 10 ⇌	a																					
	d	14 30	14 35	14 41	14 41	14 52	14 55	15 04	15 07	15 15	15 20	15 27	15 30	15 35	15 52	15 55	16 04	16 07	16 15	16 20	16 27	16 30
Levenshulme	d					14 58		15 09							15 58		16 09					
Heaton Chapel	d					15 01		15 12							16 01		16 12					
Stockport	a	14 38	14 42		14 49	15 04	15 03	15 16		15 22	15 28	15 35	15 39	15 42	16 04	16 03	16 16		16 22	16 28	16 34	16 39
	d	14 39	14 42		14 51		15 04	15 17		15 22		15 36	15 39	15 42		16 04	16 17		16 23		16 36	16 39
Cheadle Hulme	d				14 56			15 22									16 22					
Bramhall	d				14 59																	
Poynton	d				15 02																	
Adlington (Cheshire)	d				15 04																	
Prestbury	d				15 07																	
Macclesfield	a		14 55		15 11							15 48		15 55							16 48	
	d		14 55		15 11							15 49		15 55							16 49	
Congleton	d				15 19																	
Handforth	d							15 26									16 26					
Manchester Airport ✈	d			15 06																		
Styal	d			15 10																		
Wilmslow	d	14 47		15 14			15 11	15 29					15 47			16 11	16 29					16 47
Alderley Edge	d			15a20				15 32									16a35					
Chelford	d							15 36														
Goostrey	d							15 40														
Holmes Chapel	d							15 43														
Sandbach	d							15 48														
Crewe 10 65	a	15 07					15 27	15 58					16 06			16 27						17 06
Kidsgrove 50	a				15 25																	
Longport 50	a																					
Stoke-on-Trent 50,68	a		15 12		15 37				15 42	15 49		16 06		16 12				16 42	16 48		17 06	
Stafford 68	a											16 24									17 25	
Wolverhampton 7 68 ⇌	a								16 13			16 40						17 13			17 40	
Birmingham New Street 12 68	a								16 31			16 58						17 31			17 58	
London Euston 15 ⊖65	a		16 47				17 09			17 27				17 47		18 09			18 27			

A To Milford Haven
B To Norwich
C To Buxton
D To Paignton
E From Manchester Airport to Cleethorpes
F To Bournemouth
G To Cardiff Central
H To Bristol Temple Meads

Manchester, Stockport and Manchester Airport - Crewe and Stoke-on-Trent

Network Diagram - see first Page of Table 78

		VT	NT	NT	VT	NT	XC	VT	TP	XC	AW	VT	NT	VT	NT	XC	VT	TP	XC	AW	VT
		◇■			◇■		◇■	◇■	◇■	◇■	■	◇■		◇■		◇■	◇■	◇■	◇■	■	◇■
				A			B		C	D	E		A			F		C	G	E	
		⊡			⊡		⊼	⊡		⊼	⊼	⊡		⊡		⊼	⊡		⊼	⊼	⊡
Deansgate ⇌	d																				
Manchester Oxford Road	d																				
Manchester Piccadilly 10 ⇌	a																				
	d	16 35	16 41	16 52	16 55	17 04	17 07	17 15	17 20	17 27	17 30	17 35	17 52	17 55	18 04	18 07	18 15	18 20	18 27	18 30	18 35
Levenshulme	d			16 58		17 09							17 58		18 09						
Heaton Chapel	d			17 01		17 12							18 01		18 12						
Stockport	a	16 42		17 04	17 03	17 16		17 22	17 28	17 34	17 39	17 42	18 04	18 03	18 16		18 22	18 28	18 34	18 39	18 42
	d	16 42			17 04	17 17		17 22		17 36	17 39	17 42		18 04	18 17		18 22		18 36	18 39	18 42
Cheadle Hulme	d					17 22									18 22						
Bramhall	d																				
Poynton	d																				
Adlington (Cheshire)	d																				
Prestbury	d																				
Macclesfield	a	16 55								17 48		17 55							18 48		18 55
	d	16 55								17 49		17 55							18 49		18 55
Congleton	d																				
Handforth	d					17 26									18 26						
Manchester Airport ✈	d		17 06																		
Styal	d		17 10																		
Wilmslow	d		17 15		17 11	17 29					17 47			18 11	18 29					18 47	
Alderley Edge	d		17a21			17 32									18a35						
Chelford	d					17 36															
Goostrey	d					17 40															
Holmes Chapel	d					17 43															
Sandbach	d					17 48															
Crewe 10 65	a				17 27	17 58					18 07			18 27						19 06	
Kidsgrove 50	a																				
Longport 50	a																				
Stoke-on-Trent 50,68	a	17 12					17 42	17 49		18 06		18 12				18 42	18 49		19 06		19 12
Stafford 68	a									18 25									19 24		
Wolverhampton 7 68 ⇌	a						18 13			18 40						19 13			19 40		
Birmingham New Street 12 68	a						18 31			18 58						19 31			19 58		
London Euston 15 ⊖65	a	18 47			19 09			19 27				19 47		20 09			20 27				20 47

		NT	NT	NT	VT	NT	XC	VT	TP	XC	AW	VT	NT	NT	XC	TP	VT	AW	NT	NT	VT	NT
					◇■		◇■	◇■	◇■	◇■	◇	◇■			◇■	◇■	◇■	◇			◇■	
				A			F		C	H	E		A		F	C		E		A		
					⊡		⊼	⊡		⊼		⊡					⊡				⊡	
Deansgate ⇌	d																					
Manchester Oxford Road	d																					
Manchester Piccadilly 10 ⇌	a																					
	d	18 41	18 42	18 52	18 55	19 04	19 07	19 15	19 20	19 27	19 30	19 35	19 52	20 04	20 07	20 18	20 20	20 30	20 41	20 52	20 55	21 04
Levenshulme	d			18 58		19 09							19 58	20 09						20 58		21 09
Heaton Chapel	d			19 01		19 12							20 01	20 12						21 01		21 12
Stockport	a		18 50	19 04	19 03	19 16		19 22	19 28	19 34	19 39	19 41	20 04	20 16	20 15	20 26	20 27	20 38		21 04	21 03	21 16
	d		18 52		19 04	19 17		19 22		19 36	19 39	19 41		20 17	20 16		20 27	20 39			21 03	21 17
Cheadle Hulme	d		18 57			19 22								20 22								21 22
Bramhall	d		19 00																			
Poynton	d		19 03																			
Adlington (Cheshire)	d		19 06																			
Prestbury	d		19 09																			
Macclesfield	a		19 13							19 48		19 54			20 28		20 40				21 15	
	d		19 13							19 49		19 54			20 29		20 40				21 15	
Congleton	d		19 21																			
Handforth	d					19 26								20 26								21 26
Manchester Airport ✈	d	19 06																	21 06			
Styal	d	19 10																	21 10			
Wilmslow	d	19 15			19 11	19 29					19 47			20 29				20 47	21 14			21 29
Alderley Edge	d	19a21				19 32								20a37					21a20			21 32
Chelford	d					19 36																21 36
Goostrey	d					19 40																21 40
Holmes Chapel	d					19 43																21 43
Sandbach	d					19 48																21 48
Crewe 10 65	a				19 27	19 58					20 07							21 07				21 58
Kidsgrove 50	a		19 28																			
Longport 50	a																					
Stoke-on-Trent 50,68	a		19 40				19 42	19 49		20 06		20 11			20 46		20 57				21 32	
Stafford 68	a									20 26					21 08							
Wolverhampton 7 68 ⇌	a						20 13			20 39					21 21							
Birmingham New Street 12 68	a						20 31			20 58					21 39							
London Euston 15 ⊖65	a				21 09			21 31				21 58					22 56				23 49	

A To Buxton
B To Paignton
C From Manchester Airport to Cleethorpes
D To Bournemouth
E To Cardiff Central
F To Bristol Temple Meads
G To Southampton Central
H To Reading

Manchester, Stockport and Manchester Airport - Crewe and Stoke-on-Trent

Sundays
1 July to 9 September

Network Diagram - see first Page of Table 78

		XC	TP	AW	NT	NT	NT	XC	TP	AW	NT	NT	TP
		◇1	◇1					◇1	◇1				◇1
			A			B			A		B		A
Deansgate	d												
Manchester Oxford Road	d												
Manchester Piccadilly	a												
	d	21 07	21 20	21 34	21 41	21 52	22 04	22 07	22 15	22 35	22 52	23 04	23 20
Levenshulme	d					21 58	22 09				22 58	23 09	
Heaton Chapel	d					22 01	22 12				23 01	23 12	
Stockport	a	21 15	21 28		21 49	22 04	22 16	22 15	22 23		23 04	23 16	23 28
	d	21 16			21 52		22 17	22 16				23 17	
Cheadle Hulme	d				21 56		22 22					23 21	
Bramhall	d				21 59								
Poynton	d				22 02								
Adlington (Cheshire)	d				22 05								
Prestbury	d				22 08								
Macclesfield	a	21 28			22 12			22 28					
	d	21 29			22 13			22 29					
Congleton	d				22 20								
Handforth	d						22 26					23 25	
Manchester Airport	d												
Styal	d												
Wilmslow	d			21 50			22 29			22 50		23 28	
Alderley Edge	d						22a35					23a35	
Chelford	d												
Goostrey	d												
Holmes Chapel	d												
Sandbach	d												
Crewe 65	a			22 13						23 10			
Kidsgrove 50	a				22 26								
Longport 50	a												
Stoke-on-Trent 50,68	a	21 46			22 36			22 46					
Stafford 68	a	22 06						23 04					
Wolverhampton 68	a	22 20						23 18					
Birmingham New Street 68	a	22 39						23 36					
London Euston 65	a												

Sundays
16 September to 30 September

		NT	VT	VT	XC	NT	NT	NT	TP	NT	VT	NT	XC	AW	NT	NT
			◇1	◇1	◇1				◇1		◇1		◇1	◇		
					D			B	A			E	D	F	B	
Deansgate	d											09 15				
Manchester Oxford Road	d											09 18				
Manchester Piccadilly	a											09 21				
	d	23p37	08 05	08 20	08 27	08 41	08 50	08 55	08 58	09 04	09 20	09 22	09 27	09 30	09 51	10 03
Levenshulme	d	23p42						09 00		09 09					09 58	10 08
Heaton Chapel	d	23p45						09 03		09 12					10 01	10 11
Stockport	a	23p49	08 13	08 28	08 34		08 59	09 07	09 06	09 17	09 27	09 31	09 35	09 39	10 04	10 15
	d	23p50	08 14	08 28	08 36		09 01			09 17	09 27		09 36	09 39		10 17
Cheadle Hulme	d	23p54					09 06			09 21						10 23
Bramhall	d						09 09									
Poynton	d						09 12									
Adlington (Cheshire)	d						09 15									
Prestbury	d						09 18									
Macclesfield	a			08 41			09 22				09 40		09 48			
	d			08 42							09 40		09 49			
Congleton	d															
Handforth	d	23p58								09 25						10 27
Manchester Airport	d					09 06										
Styal	d					09 10										
Wilmslow	d	00 01	08 22		08 43	09 15				09 28				09 47		10 30
Alderley Edge	d	00a07				09a22				09 31						10a36
Chelford	d									09 35						
Goostrey	d									09 40						
Holmes Chapel	d									09 43						
Sandbach	d									09 48						
Crewe 65	a		08 39		09 01					09 58				10 06		
Kidsgrove 50	a															
Longport 50	a															
Stoke-on-Trent 50,68	a			08 59							09 57		10 05			
Stafford 68	a		09 01		09 25								10 26			
Wolverhampton 68	a				09 40								10 42			
Birmingham New Street 68	a				09 58								10 59			
London Euston 65	a		10 57	11 02							12 08					

A From Manchester Airport to Sheffield
B To Buxton
D To Bournemouth
E From Wigan Wallgate to Chester
F To Cardiff Central

Manchester, Stockport and Manchester Airport - Crewe and Stoke-on-Trent

Sundays
16 September to 30 September

Network Diagram - see first Page of Table 78

		VT	XC	AW	VT	NT	NT	NT	VT	TP	AW	XC	VT	NT	NT	VT	NT	VT	TP	XC	AW
		◇1	◇1		◇1				◇1	◇1		◇1	◇1			◇1		◇1	◇1	◇1	
			A	B			C			D	E	A			C				F	A	B
Deansgate	d																				
Manchester Oxford Road	d																				
Manchester Piccadilly	a																				
	d	10 20	10 27	10 31	10 35	10 41	10 53	11 04	11 15	11 18	11 24	11 27	11 35	11 41	11 52	11 55	12 04	12 15	12 18	12 26	12 30
Levenshulme	d						10 59	11 10							11 58		12 09				
Heaton Chapel	d						11 02	11 13							12 01		12 12				
Stockport	a	10 28	10 34	10 40	10 42		11 05	11 17	11 23	11 27	11 34	11 34	11 43	11 50	12 04	12 04	12 16	12 23	12 28	12 35	12 39
	d	10 29	10 36	10 40	10 42			11 17	11 23		11 40	11 36	11 43	11 51		12 05	12 16	12 23		12 35	12 40
Cheadle Hulme	d							11 22						11 56			12 22				
Bramhall	d													11 59							
Poynton	d													12 02							
Adlington (Cheshire)	d													12 05							
Prestbury	d													12 08							
Macclesfield	a		10 48		10 55							11 49	11 56	12 11						12 48	
	d		10 49		10 55							11 49	11 56	12 12						12 49	
Congleton	d													12 20							
Handforth	d							11 26									12 26				
Manchester Airport	d					11 08															
Styal	d					11 12															
Wilmslow	d	10 36		10 48		11 16		11 29			11 47					12 12	12 29				12 48
Alderley Edge	d					11a21		11 32									12a35				
Chelford	d							11 36													
Goostrey	d							11 41													
Holmes Chapel	d							11 44													
Sandbach	d							11 49													
Crewe 65	a	10 53		11 07				11 59			12 07					12 28					13 07
Kidsgrove 50	a													12 26							
Longport 50	a																				
Stoke-on-Trent 50,68	a		11 06		11 12				11 50			12 06	12 13	12 37				12 50		13 06	
Stafford 68	a		11 27									12 24								13 24	
Wolverhampton 68	a		11 41									12 40								13 40	
Birmingham New Street 68	a		12 00									12 58								13 58	
London Euston 65	a	12 56			12 59				13 28				13 47			14 09		14 27			

		VT	EM	NT	NT	VT	NT	XC	VT	TP	XC	AW	VT	NT	VT	NT	XC	VT	TP	XC	AW
		◇1	◇			◇1		◇1	◇1	◇1	◇1		◇1		◇1		◇1	◇1	◇1	◇1	
			G		C					D	A	E		C					D	A	B
Deansgate	d																				
Manchester Oxford Road	d			12 43																	
Manchester Piccadilly	a			12 45																	
	d	12 35	12 44	12 47	12 52	12 55	13 04	13 07	13 15	13 20	13 27	13 30	13 35	13 52	13 55	14 04	14 07	14 15	14 20	14 27	14 30
Levenshulme	d				12 58		13 09							13 58		14 09					
Heaton Chapel	d				13 01		13 12							14 01		14 12					
Stockport	a	12 44	12 53		13 04	13 04	13 16		13 22	13 28	13 35	13 39	13 42	14 04	14 03	14 16		14 22	14 28	14 34	14 38
	d	12 44				13 05	13 17		13 22		13 36	13 40	13 42		14 04	14 17		14 22		14 36	14 39
Cheadle Hulme	d						13 21									14 22					
Bramhall	d																				
Poynton	d																				
Adlington (Cheshire)	d																				
Prestbury	d																				
Macclesfield	a	12 57									13 48		13 55							14 48	
	d	12 57									13 49		13 55							14 49	
Congleton	d																				
Handforth	d						13 25									14 26					
Manchester Airport	d			13 12																	
Styal	d			13 16																	
Wilmslow	d			13 23		13 12	13 28					13 47			14 11	14 29					14 47
Alderley Edge	d			13a29			13 31									14a35					
Chelford	d						13 35														
Goostrey	d						13 40														
Holmes Chapel	d						13 43														
Sandbach	d						13 48														
Crewe 65	a					13 28	13 58					14 07			14 27						15 07
Kidsgrove 50	a																				
Longport 50	a																				
Stoke-on-Trent 50,68	a	13 14						13 42	13 49		14 06		14 12				14 42	14 49		15 06	
Stafford 68	a										14 24									15 24	
Wolverhampton 68	a							14 13			14 40						15 13			15 40	
Birmingham New Street 68	a							14 31			14 58						15 31			15 58	
London Euston 65	a	14 47				15 05			15 26				15 47		16 05			16 26			

A To Bournemouth
B To Milford Haven
C To Buxton
D From Manchester Airport to Cleethorpes
E To Cardiff Central
F To Doncaster
G To Norwich

16 September to 30 September

Manchester, Stockport and Manchester Airport - Crewe and Stoke-on-Trent

Network Diagram - see first Page of Table 78

	VT	NT	NT	NT	VT	NT	XC	VT	TP	XC	AW	VT	NT	VT	NT	XC	VT	TP	XC	AW	VT
				A					B	C	D		A					B	C	D	
Deansgate d																					
Manchester Oxford Road d																					
Manchester Piccadilly a																					
Manchester Piccadilly d	14 35	14 41	14 41	14 52	14 55	15 04	15 07	15 15	15 20	15 27	15 30	15 35	15 52	15 55	16 04	16 07	16 15	16 20	16 27	16 30	16 35
Levenshulme d				14 58		15 09							15 58		16 09						
Heaton Chapel d				15 01		15 12							16 01		16 12						
Stockport a	14 42		14 49	15 04	15 03	15 16		15 22	15 28	15 35	15 39	15 42	16 04	16 03	16 16		16 22	16 28	16 34	16 39	16 42
Stockport d	14 42		14 51		15 04	15 17		15 22		15 36	15 39	15 42		16 04	16 17		16 23		16 36	16 39	16 42
Cheadle Hulme d			14 56			15 22									16 22						
Bramhall d			14 59																		
Poynton d			15 02																		
Adlington (Cheshire) d			15 04																		
Prestbury d			15 07																		
Macclesfield a	14 55		15 11							15 48		15 55							16 48		16 55
Macclesfield d	14 55		15 11							15 49		15 55							16 49		16 55
Congleton d			15 19																		
Handforth d						15 26									16 26						
Manchester Airport d		15 06																			
Styal d		15 10																			
Wilmslow d		15 14			15 11	15 29					15 47			16 11	16 29					16 47	
Alderley Edge d		15a20				15 32									16a35						
Chelford d						15 36															
Goostrey d						15 40															
Holmes Chapel d						15 43															
Sandbach d						15 48															
Crewe 65 a					15 27	15 58					16 06			16 27						17 06	
Kidsgrove 50 a			15 25																		
Longport 50 a																					
Stoke-on-Trent 50,68 a	15 12		15 37				15 42	15 49		16 06		16 12				16 42	16 48		17 06		17 12
Stafford 68 a										16 24									17 25		
Wolverhampton 68 a							16 13			16 40						17 13			17 40		
Birmingham New Street 68 a							16 31			16 58						17 31			17 58		
London Euston 65 a	16 47				17 07			17 27				17 46		18 07			18 26				18 47

	NT	NT	VT	NT	XC	VT	TP	XC	AW	VT	NT	VT	NT	XC	VT	TP	XC	AW	VT	NT
		A					B	C	D		A					B	E	D		
Deansgate d																				
Manchester Oxford Road d																				
Manchester Piccadilly a																				
Manchester Piccadilly d	16 41	16 52	16 55	17 04	17 07	17 15	17 20	17 27	17 30	17 35	17 52	17 55	18 04	18 07	18 15	18 20	18 27	18 30	18 35	18 41
Levenshulme d		16 58		17 09							17 58		18 09							
Heaton Chapel d		17 01		17 12							18 01		18 12							
Stockport a		17 04	17 03	17 16		17 22	17 28	17 34	17 39	17 42	18 04	18 03	18 16		18 22	18 28	18 34	18 39	18 42	
Stockport d			17 04	17 17		17 22		17 36	17 39	17 42		18 04	18 17		18 22		18 36	18 39	18 42	
Cheadle Hulme d				17 22									18 22							
Bramhall d																				
Poynton d																				
Adlington (Cheshire) d																				
Prestbury d																				
Macclesfield a								17 48		17 55							18 48		18 55	
Macclesfield d								17 49		17 55							18 49		18 55	
Congleton d																				
Handforth d				17 26									18 26							
Manchester Airport d	17 06																			19 06
Styal d	17 10																			19 10
Wilmslow d	17 15		17 11	17 29					17 47			18 11	18 29					18 47		19 15
Alderley Edge d	17a21			17 32									18a35							19a21
Chelford d				17 36																
Goostrey d				17 40																
Holmes Chapel d				17 43																
Sandbach d				17 48																
Crewe 65 a			17 27	17 58					18 07			18 27						19 06		
Kidsgrove 50 a																				
Longport 50 a																				
Stoke-on-Trent 50,68 a					17 42	17 49		18 06		18 12				18 42	18 49		19 06		19 12	
Stafford 68 a								18 25									19 24			
Wolverhampton 68 a					18 13			18 40						19 13			19 40			
Birmingham New Street 68 a					18 31			18 58						19 31			19 58			
London Euston 65 a			19 05			19 26				19 47		20 05			20 26				20 47	

A To Buxton
B From Manchester Airport to Cleethorpes
C To Bournemouth
D To Cardiff Central
E To Southampton Central

16 September to 30 September

Manchester, Stockport and Manchester Airport - Crewe and Stoke-on-Trent

Network Diagram - see first Page of Table 78

	NT	NT	VT	NT	XC	VT	TP	XC	AW	VT	NT	NT	XC	TP	VT	AW	NT	NT	VT	NT	XC
		A					B	C	D		A			B		D		A			
Deansgate d																					
Manchester Oxford Road d																					
Manchester Piccadilly a																					
Manchester Piccadilly d	18 42	18 52	18 55	19 04	19 07	19 15	19 20	19 27	19 30	19 35	19 52	20 04	20 07	20 18	20 20	20 30	20 41	20 52	20 55	21 04	21 07
Levenshulme d		18 58		19 09							19 58	20 09						20 58		21 09	
Heaton Chapel d		19 01		19 12							20 01	20 12						21 01		21 12	
Stockport a	18 50	19 04	19 03	19 16		19 22	19 28	19 34	19 39	19 41	20 04	20 16	20 15	20 26	20 27	20 38		21 04	21 03	21 16	21 15
Stockport d	18 52		19 04	19 17		19 22		19 36	19 39	19 41		20 17	20 16		20 27	20 39			21 03	21 17	21 16
Cheadle Hulme d	18 57			19 22								20 22								21 22	
Bramhall d	19 00																				
Poynton d	19 03																				
Adlington (Cheshire) d	19 06																				
Prestbury d	19 09																				
Macclesfield a	19 13							19 48		19 54			20 28		20 40				21 15		21 28
Macclesfield d	19 13							19 49		19 54			20 29		20 40				21 15		21 29
Congleton d	19 21																				
Handforth d				19 26								20 26								21 26	
Manchester Airport d																	21 06				
Styal d																	21 10				
Wilmslow d			19 11	19 29					19 47			20 29				20 47	21 14			21 29	
Alderley Edge d				19 32								20a37					21a20			21 32	
Chelford d				19 36																21 36	
Goostrey d				19 40																21 40	
Holmes Chapel d				19 43																21 43	
Sandbach d				19 48																21 48	
Crewe 65 a			19 27	19 58					20 07							21 07				21 58	
Kidsgrove 50 a	19 28																				
Longport 50 a																					
Stoke-on-Trent 50,68 a	19 40				19 42	19 49		20 06		20 11			20 46		20 57				21 32		21 46
Stafford 68 a								20 26					21 08								22 06
Wolverhampton 68 a					20 13			20 39					21 21								22 20
Birmingham New Street 68 a					20 31			20 58					21 39								22 39
London Euston 65 a			21 08			21 31				21 58					22 56				23 49		

	TP	AW	NT	NT	NT	XC	TP	AW	NT	NT	TP
	E			A			E		A		E
Deansgate d											
Manchester Oxford Road d											
Manchester Piccadilly a											
Manchester Piccadilly d	21 20	21 34	21 41	21 52	22 04	22 07	22 15	22 35	22 52	23 04	23 20
Levenshulme d				21 58	22 09				22 58	23 09	
Heaton Chapel d				22 01	22 12				23 01	23 12	
Stockport a	21 28		21 49	22 04	22 16	22 15	22 23		23 04	23 16	23 28
Stockport d			21 52		22 17	22 16				23 17	
Cheadle Hulme d			21 56		22 22					23 21	
Bramhall d			21 59								
Poynton d			22 02								
Adlington (Cheshire) d			22 05								
Prestbury d			22 08								
Macclesfield a			22 12			22 28					
Macclesfield d			22 13			22 29					
Congleton d			22 20								
Handforth d					22 26					23 25	
Manchester Airport d											
Styal d											
Wilmslow d		21 50			22 29			22 50		23 28	
Alderley Edge d					22a35					23a35	
Chelford d											
Goostrey d											
Holmes Chapel d											
Sandbach d											
Crewe 65 a		22 13						23 10			
Kidsgrove 50 a			22 26								
Longport 50 a											
Stoke-on-Trent 50,68 a			22 36			22 46					
Stafford 68 a						23 04					
Wolverhampton 68 a						23 18					
Birmingham New Street 68 a						23 36					
London Euston 65 a											

A To Buxton
B From Manchester Airport to Cleethorpes
C To Reading
D To Cardiff Central
E From Manchester Airport to Sheffield

Table 84

Sundays
from 7 October

Manchester, Stockport and Manchester Airport - Crewe and Stoke-on-Trent

Network Diagram - see first Page of Table 78

Station		NT	VT	VT	XC	NT	NT	NT	TP	NT	VT	NT
			◇1 ☕	◇1 ☕	◇1 D 🛒			E	◇1 F		◇1 ☕	G
Deansgate ⇌	d											09 15
Manchester Oxford Road	d											09 18
Manchester Piccadilly 10 ⇌	a											09 21
	d	23p37	08 05	08 20	08 27	08 41	08 50	08 55	08 58	09 04	09 20	09 22
Levenshulme	d	23p42						09 00		09 09		
Heaton Chapel	d	23p45						09 03		09 12		
Stockport	a	23p49	08 13	08 28	08 34		08 59	09 07	09 06	09 17	09 27	09 31
	d	23p50	08 14	08 28	08 36		09 01			09 17	09 27	
Cheadle Hulme	d	23p54					09 06			09 21		
Bramhall	d						09 09					
Poynton	d						09 12					
Adlington (Cheshire)	d						09 15					
Prestbury	d						09 18					
Macclesfield	a			08 41			09 22				09 40	
	d			08 42							09 40	
Congleton	d											
Handforth	d	23p58								09 25		
Manchester Airport ✈	d					09 06						
Styal	d					09 10						
Wilmslow	d	00 01	08 22		08 43	09 15				09 28		
Alderley Edge	d	00a07				09a22				09 31		
Chelford	d									09 35		
Goostrey	d									09 40		
Holmes Chapel	d									09 43		
Sandbach	d									09 48		
Crewe 10 65	a		08 39		09 01					09 58		
Kidsgrove 50	a											
Longport 50	a											
Stoke-on-Trent 50,68	a			08 59							09 57	
Stafford 68	a		09 01		09 25							
Wolverhampton 7 68 ⇌	a				09 40							
Birmingham New Street 12 68	a				09 58							
London Euston 15 ⊖65	a		10 57	11 02							12 08	

Station		XC	AW	NT	NT	VT	XC	AW	VT	NT	NT	NT	VT	TP	AW	XC	VT	NT	NT	VT
		◇1 D 🛒	◇ H 🛒	E		◇1 ☕	◇1 D 🛒	■ I 🛒	◇1 ☕		E		◇1 ☕	◇1 J	■ H 🛒	◇1 D 🛒	◇1 ☕		E	◇1 ☕
Deansgate ⇌	d																			
Manchester Oxford Road	d																			
Manchester Piccadilly 10 ⇌	a																			
	d	09 27	09 30	09 51	10 03	10 20	10 27	10 31	10 35	10 41	10 52	11 04	11 15	11 18	11 24	11 27	11 35	11 41	11 52	11 55
Levenshulme	d			09 58	10 08						10 58	11 10							11 58	
Heaton Chapel	d			10 01	10 11						11 01	11 13							12 01	
Stockport	a	09 35	09 39	10 04	10 15	10 28	10 34	10 40	10 42		11 04	11 17	11 23	11 27	11 34	11 34	11 43	11 50	12 04	12 04
	d	09 36	09 39		10 17	10 29	10 36	10 40	10 42			11 17	11 23		11 40	11 36	11 43	11 51		12 05
Cheadle Hulme	d				10 23							11 22						11 56		
Bramhall	d																	11 59		
Poynton	d																	12 02		
Adlington (Cheshire)	d																	12 05		
Prestbury	d																	12 08		
Macclesfield	a	09 48					10 48		10 55							11 49	11 56	12 11		
	d	09 49					10 49		10 55							11 49	11 56	12 12		
Congleton	d																	12 20		
Handforth	d				10 27							11 26								
Manchester Airport ✈	d									11 08										
Styal	d									11 12										
Wilmslow	d		09 47		10 30	10 36		10 48		11 16		11 29			11 47					12 12
Alderley Edge	d				10a36					11a21		11 32								
Chelford	d											11 36								
Goostrey	d											11 41								
Holmes Chapel	d											11 44								
Sandbach	d											11 49								
Crewe 10 65	a		10 06			10 53		11 07				11 59			12 07					12 28
Kidsgrove 50	a																	12 26		
Longport 50	a																			
Stoke-on-Trent 50,68	a	10 05					11 06		11 12				11 50			12 06	12 13	12 37		
Stafford 68	a	10 26					11 27									12 24				
Wolverhampton 7 68 ⇌	a	10 42					11 41									12 40				
Birmingham New Street 12 68	a	10 59					12 00									12 58				
London Euston 15 ⊖65	a					12 56			12 59				13 28				13 47			14 09

D To Bournemouth
E To Buxton
F From Manchester Airport to Sheffield
G From Wigan Wallgate to Chester
H To Cardiff Central
I To Milford Haven
J From Manchester Airport to Cleethorpes

Table 84

Sundays
from 7 October

Manchester, Stockport and Manchester Airport - Crewe and Stoke-on-Trent

Network Diagram - see first Page of Table 78

Station		NT	VT	TP	XC	AW	VT	EM	NT	NT	VT	NT	XC	VT	TP	XC	AW	VT	NT	VT	NT
			◇1 ☕	◇1 A	◇1 B 🛒	■ C 🛒	◇1 ☕	◇ D		E	◇1 ☕		◇1 🛒	◇1 ☕	◇1 F	◇1 B 🛒	■ G 🛒	◇1 ☕	E	◇1 ☕	
Deansgate ⇌	d																				
Manchester Oxford Road	d								12 43												
Manchester Piccadilly 10 ⇌	a								12 45												
	d	12 04	12 15	12 18	12 26	12 30	12 35	12 44	12 47	12 52	12 55	13 04	13 07	13 15	13 20	13 27	13 30	13 35	13 52	13 55	14 04
Levenshulme	d	12 09								12 58		13 09							13 58		14 09
Heaton Chapel	d	12 12								13 01		13 12							14 01		14 12
Stockport	a	12 16	12 23	12 28	12 35	12 39	12 44	12 53		13 04	13 04	13 16		13 22	13 28	13 35	13 39	13 42	14 04	14 03	14 16
	d	12 16	12 23		12 35	12 40	12 44				13 05	13 17		13 22		13 36	13 40	13 42		14 04	14 17
Cheadle Hulme	d	12 22										13 21									14 22
Bramhall	d																				
Poynton	d																				
Adlington (Cheshire)	d																				
Prestbury	d																				
Macclesfield	a				12 48		12 57									13 48		13 55			
	d				12 49		12 57									13 49		13 55			
Congleton	d																				
Handforth	d	12 26										13 25									14 26
Manchester Airport ✈	d								13 12												
Styal	d								13 16												
Wilmslow	d	12 29				12 48			13 23		13 12	13 28					13 47			14 11	14 29
Alderley Edge	d	12a35							13a29			13 31									14a35
Chelford	d											13 35									
Goostrey	d											13 40									
Holmes Chapel	d											13 43									
Sandbach	d											13 48									
Crewe 10 65	a					13 07					13 28	13 58					14 07			14 27	
Kidsgrove 50	a																				
Longport 50	a																				
Stoke-on-Trent 50,68	a		12 50		13 06		13 14						13 42	13 49		14 06		14 12			
Stafford 68	a				13 24											14 24					
Wolverhampton 7 68 ⇌	a				13 40								14 13			14 40					
Birmingham New Street 12 68	a				13 58								14 31			14 58					
London Euston 15 ⊖65	a		14 27				14 47				15 05			15 26				15 47		16 05	

Station		XC	VT	TP	XC	AW	VT	NT	NT	NT	VT	NT	XC	VT	TP	XC	AW	VT	NT	VT	NT	XC
		◇1 🛒	◇1 ☕	◇1 F	◇1 B 🛒	■ C 🛒	◇1 ☕			E	◇1 ☕		◇1 🛒	◇1 ☕	◇1 F	◇1 B 🛒	■ G 🛒	◇1 ☕	E	◇1 ☕		◇1 🛒
Deansgate ⇌	d																					
Manchester Oxford Road	d																					
Manchester Piccadilly 10 ⇌	a																					
	d	14 07	14 15	14 20	14 27	14 30	14 35	14 41	14 41	14 52	14 55	15 04	15 07	15 15	15 20	15 27	15 30	15 35	15 52	15 55	16 04	16 07
Levenshulme	d									14 58		15 09							15 58		16 09	
Heaton Chapel	d									15 01		15 12							16 01		16 12	
Stockport	a		14 22	14 28	14 34	14 38	14 42		14 49	15 04	15 03	15 16		15 22	15 28	15 35	15 39	15 42	16 04	16 03	16 16	
	d		14 22		14 36	14 39	14 42		14 51		15 04	15 17		15 22		15 36	15 39	15 42		16 04	16 17	
Cheadle Hulme	d								14 56			15 22									16 22	
Bramhall	d								14 59													
Poynton	d								15 02													
Adlington (Cheshire)	d								15 04													
Prestbury	d								15 07													
Macclesfield	a				14 48		14 55		15 11							15 48		15 55				
	d				14 49		14 55		15 11							15 49		15 55				
Congleton	d								15 19													
Handforth	d											15 26									16 26	
Manchester Airport ✈	d							15 06														
Styal	d							15 10														
Wilmslow	d					14 47		15 14			15 11	15 29					15 47			16 11	16 29	
Alderley Edge	d							15a20				15 32									16a35	
Chelford	d											15 36										
Goostrey	d											15 40										
Holmes Chapel	d											15 43										
Sandbach	d											15 48										
Crewe 10 65	a					15 07					15 27	15 58					16 06			16 27		
Kidsgrove 50	a								15 25													
Longport 50	a																					
Stoke-on-Trent 50,68	a	14 42	14 49		15 06		15 12		15 37				15 42	15 49		16 06		16 12				16 42
Stafford 68	a				15 24											16 24						
Wolverhampton 7 68 ⇌	a	15 13			15 40								16 13			16 40						17 13
Birmingham New Street 12 68	a	15 31			15 58								16 31			16 58						17 31
London Euston 15 ⊖65	a		16 26				16 47				17 07			17 27				17 46		18 07		

A To Doncaster
B To Bournemouth
C To Milford Haven
D To Norwich
E To Buxton
F From Manchester Airport to Cleethorpes
G To Cardiff Central

Table 84 **Sundays** from 7 October

Manchester, Stockport and Manchester Airport - Crewe and Stoke-on-Trent

Network Diagram - see first Page of Table 78

Station			VT	TP	XC	AW	VT	NT	NT	VT	NT	XC	VT	TP	XC	AW	VT	NT	VT	NT	XC	VT
				A	B	C			D					A	B	C		D				
Deansgate		d																				
Manchester Oxford Road		d																				
Manchester Piccadilly		a																				
		d	16 15	16 20	16 27	16 30	16 35	16 41	16 52	16 55	17 04	17 07	17 15	17 20	17 27	17 30	17 35	17 52	17 55	18 04	18 07	18 15
Levenshulme		d							16 58		17 09							17 58		18 09		
Heaton Chapel		d							17 01		17 12							18 01		18 12		
Stockport		a	16 22	16 28	16 34	16 39	16 42		17 04	17 03	17 16		17 22	17 28	17 34	17 39	17 42	18 04	18 03	18 16		18 22
		d	16 23		16 36	16 39	16 42			17 04	17 17		17 22		17 36	17 39	17 42		18 04	18 17		18 22
Cheadle Hulme		d									17 22									18 22		
Bramhall		d																				
Poynton		d																				
Adlington (Cheshire)		d																				
Prestbury		d																				
Macclesfield		a			16 48		16 55								17 48		17 55					
		d			16 49		16 55								17 49		17 55					
Congleton		d																				
Handforth		d									17 26									18 26		
Manchester Airport		d						17 06														
Styal		d						17 10														
Wilmslow		d				16 47		17 15		17 11	17 29					17 47			18 11	18 29		
Alderley Edge		d						17a21			17 32									18a35		
Chelford		d									17 36											
Goostrey		d									17 40											
Holmes Chapel		d									17 43											
Sandbach		d									17 48											
Crewe	65	a				17 06				17 27	17 58					18 07			18 27			
Kidsgrove	50	a																				
Longport	50	a																				
Stoke-on-Trent	50,68	a	16 48		17 06		17 12					17 42	17 49		18 06		18 12				18 42	18 49
Stafford	68	a			17 25										18 25							
Wolverhampton	68	a			17 40							18 13			18 40						19 13	
Birmingham New Street	68	a			17 58							18 31			18 58						19 31	
London Euston	⊖65	a	18 26				18 47			19 05			19 26				19 47		20 05			20 26

Station			TP	XC	AW	VT	NT	NT	NT	VT	NT	XC	VT	TP	XC	AW	VT	NT	NT	XC	TP	VT	AW
			A	E	C				D					A	F	C		D			A		C
Deansgate		d																					
Manchester Oxford Road		d																					
Manchester Piccadilly		a																					
		d	18 20	18 27	18 30	18 35	18 41	18 42	18 52	18 55	19 04	19 07	19 15	19 20	19 27	19 30	19 35	19 52	20 04	20 07	20 18	20 20	20 30
Levenshulme		d							18 58		19 09							19 58	20 09				
Heaton Chapel		d							19 01		19 12							20 01	20 12				
Stockport		a	18 28	18 34	18 39	18 42		18 50	19 04	19 03	19 16		19 22	19 28	19 34	19 39	19 41	20 04	20 16	20 15	20 26	20 27	20 38
		d		18 36	18 39	18 42		18 52		19 04	19 17		19 22		19 36	19 39	19 41		20 17	20 16		20 27	20 39
Cheadle Hulme		d						18 57			19 22								20 22				
Bramhall		d						19 00															
Poynton		d						19 03															
Adlington (Cheshire)		d						19 06															
Prestbury		d						19 09															
Macclesfield		a		18 48		18 55		19 13							19 48		19 54			20 28		20 40	
		d		18 49		18 55		19 13							19 49		19 54			20 29		20 40	
Congleton		d						19 21															
Handforth		d									19 26								20 26				
Manchester Airport		d					19 06																
Styal		d					19 10																
Wilmslow		d			18 47		19 15			19 11	19 29					19 47			20 29				20 47
Alderley Edge		d					19a21				19 32								20a37				
Chelford		d									19 36												
Goostrey		d									19 40												
Holmes Chapel		d									19 43												
Sandbach		d									19 48												
Crewe	65	a			19 06					19 27	19 58					20 07							21 07
Kidsgrove	50	a						19 28															
Longport	50	a																					
Stoke-on-Trent	50,68	a		19 06		19 12		19 40				19 42	19 49		20 06		20 11			20 46		20 57	
Stafford	68	a		19 24											20 26					21 08			
Wolverhampton	68	a		19 40								20 13			20 39					21 21			
Birmingham New Street	68	a		19 58								20 31			20 58					21 39			
London Euston	⊖65	a				20 47				21 08			21 31				21 58					22 56	

A From Manchester Airport to Cleethorpes
B To Bournemouth
C To Cardiff Central
D To Buxton
E To Southampton Central
F To Reading

Table 84 **Sundays** from 7 October

Manchester, Stockport and Manchester Airport - Crewe and Stoke-on-Trent

Network Diagram - see first Page of Table 78

Station			NT	NT	VT	NT	XC	TP	AW	NT	NT	NT	XC	TP	AW	NT	NT	TP
				A				B			A			B		A		B
Deansgate		d																
Manchester Oxford Road		d																
Manchester Piccadilly		a																
		d	20 41	20 52	20 55	21 04	21 07	21 20	21 34	21 41	21 52	22 04	22 07	22 15	22 35	22 52	23 04	23 20
Levenshulme		d		20 58		21 09					21 58	22 09				22 58	23 09	
Heaton Chapel		d		21 01		21 12					22 01	22 12				23 01	23 12	
Stockport		a		21 04	21 03	21 16	21 15	21 28		21 49	22 04	22 16	22 15	22 23		23 04	23 16	23 28
		d			21 03	21 17	21 16			21 52		22 17	22 16				23 17	
Cheadle Hulme		d				21 22				21 56		22 22					23 21	
Bramhall		d								21 59								
Poynton		d								22 02								
Adlington (Cheshire)		d								22 05								
Prestbury		d								22 08								
Macclesfield		a			21 15		21 28			22 12			22 28					
		d			21 15		21 29			22 13			22 29					
Congleton		d								22 20								
Handforth		d				21 26						22 26					23 25	
Manchester Airport		d	21 06															
Styal		d	21 10															
Wilmslow		d	21 14			21 29			21 50			22 29			22 50		23 28	
Alderley Edge		d	21a20			21 32						22a35					23a35	
Chelford		d				21 36												
Goostrey		d				21 40												
Holmes Chapel		d				21 43												
Sandbach		d				21 48												
Crewe	65	a				21 58			22 13						23 10			
Kidsgrove	50	a								22 26								
Longport	50	a																
Stoke-on-Trent	50,68	a			21 32		21 46			22 36			22 46					
Stafford	68	a					22 06						23 04					
Wolverhampton	68	a					22 20						23 18					
Birmingham New Street	68	a					22 39						23 36					
London Euston	⊖65	a			23 49													

A To Buxton
B From Manchester Airport to Sheffield

Manchester - Manchester Airport

Network Diagram - see first Page of Table 78

Miles			NT	TP	TP	TP	TP	TP	NT	NT	TP	AW	TP	TP	NT	NT	TP	TP	TP	NT	NT	TP	NT
			MO	MX	MO	MX	MO		MO	MX													
				◇1	◇1	◇1	◇1	◇1			◇1		◇1	◇1			◇1	◇1	◇1			◇1	
			A		B		C																
—	Deansgate	d																					
—	Manchester Oxford Road	d	23p47																				06 58
0	Manchester Piccadilly [10]	a	23p50																				07 01
—		d	23p52	23p55	00 44	00 54	01 10	03 44	04 21	04 21	04 44	04 49	04 50	05 00	05 35	05 58	06 03	06 08	06 12	06 15	06 46	06 54	07 03
3½	Mauldeth Road	d	≀	00 04	≀		≀								05 42					06 22	06 53		
4½	Burnage	d	≀	00 07	≀		≀								05 44					06 24	06 55		
5½	East Didsbury	d	≀	00 10	≀		≀								05 46					06 26	06 57		
6¾	Gatley	d	≀	00 13	≀		≀								05 49					06 29	06 59		
8¼	Heald Green	d	≀	00 17	≀		≀								05 52					06 32	07 02		
9¾	Manchester Airport ✈	a	00 07	00 24	00 57	01 10	01 24	04 00	04 33	04 34	05 00	05 09	05 07	05 19	05 57	06 14	06 18	06 24	06 29	06 39	07 07	07 12	07 22
—	Wilmslow	84 a													06 11						07 20		
—	Crewe [10]	84 a													06 46						07 46		

		TP	NT	NT	TP	TP	NT	NT	TP	NT	TP	NT	TP	TP	NT	NT	TP	TP	NT	TP	NT	TP	TP
		◇1			◇1	◇1 ≍			◇1 ≍		◇1 ≍		◇1 ≍	◇1 ≍			◇1 ≍	◇1 ≍		◇1 ≍		◇1 ≍	◇1 ≍
Deansgate	d		07 11				07 28								08 29								
Manchester Oxford Road	d		07 15			07 24	07 32			07 58				08 24	08 33			08 54	08 58				09 24
Manchester Piccadilly [10]	a		07 17			07 27	07 34			08 01				08 27	08 35			08 56	09 01				09 27
	d	07 06		07 14	07 23	07 29	07 36	07 46	07 54	08 03	08 06	08 14	08 24	08 29	08 37	08 46	08 54	08 58	09 03	09 06	09 14	09 24	09 29
Mauldeth Road	d			07 21				07 53				08 21				08 53					09 21		
Burnage	d			07 23				07 55				08 23				08 55					09 23		
East Didsbury	d			07 25				07 57				08 25				08 57				09 16	09 25		
Gatley	d			07 27				07 59				08 27				08 59					09 27		
Heald Green	d			07 30				08 02				08 30			08 47	09 02		09 10			09 30		
Manchester Airport ✈	a	07 29		07 38	07 42	07 47	07 53	08 07	08 12	08 22	08 26	08 38	08 42	08 47	08 53	09 07	09 12	09 19	09 22	09 33	09 38	09 42	09 47
Wilmslow	84 a							08 21								09 20							
Crewe [10]	84 a							08 47								09 46							

		NT	NT	TP	TP	NT	TP	NT	TP	TP	NT	NT	TP	TP	NT	TP	NT	TP	TP	NT	NT	TP
				◇1 ≍	◇1 ≍		◇1 ≍		◇1 ≍	◇1 ≍			◇1 ≍	◇1 ≍		◇1 ≍		◇1 ≍	◇1 ≍			◇1 ≍
Deansgate	d	09 29			09 51						10 29			10 51						11 29		
Manchester Oxford Road	d	09 33			09 54	09 58				10 24	10 33			10 54	10 58				11 24	11 33		
Manchester Piccadilly [10]	a	09 35			09 56	10 01				10 27	10 35			10 56	11 01				11 27	11 35		
	d	09 37	09 46	09 54	09 58	10 03	10 06	10 14	10 24	10 29	10 37	10 46	10 54	10 58	11 03	11 06	11 14	11 24	11 29	11 37	11 46	11 54
Mauldeth Road	d		09 53					10 21				10 53					11 21				11 53	
Burnage	d		09 55					10 23				10 55					11 23				11 55	
East Didsbury	d		09 57					10 25				10 57					11 25				11 57	
Gatley	d		09 59					10 27				10 59					11 27				11 59	
Heald Green	d		10 02		10 10			10 30				11 02		11 10			11 30				12 02	
Manchester Airport ✈	a	09 53	10 07	10 12	10 17	10 22	10 26	10 38	10 42	10 47	10 53	11 08	11 12	11 17	11 22	11 26	11 38	11 45	11 50	11 53	12 07	12 12
Wilmslow	84 a		10 20									11 21									12 20	
Crewe [10]	84 a		10 46									11 47									12 46	

		TP	NT	TP	NT	TP	TP	NT	NT	TP	TP	TP	TP	NT	TP	NT	TP	TP	NT	NT	TP	TP	NT
										FO	FX	FO	FX										
		◇1 ≍		◇1 ≍		◇1 ≍	◇1 ≍			◇1 ≍	◇1 ≍	◇1 ≍	◇1 ≍		◇1 ≍		◇1 ≍	◇1 ≍			◇1 ≍	◇1 ≍	
Deansgate	d	11 51						12 29				12 51	12 51						13 29			13 51	
Manchester Oxford Road	d	11 54	11 58				12 24	12 33				12 54	12 54	12 58				13 24	13 33			13 54	13 58
Manchester Piccadilly [10]	a	11 56	12 01				12 27	12 35				12 56	12 56	13 01				13 27	13 35			13 56	14 01
	d	11 58	12 03	12 06	12 14	12 24	12 29	12 37	12 46	12 54	12 54	12 58	12 58	13 03	13 06	13 14	13 24	13 29	13 37	13 46	13 54	13 58	14 03
Mauldeth Road	d				12 21				12 53							13 21				13 53			
Burnage	d				12 23				12 55							13 23				13 55			
East Didsbury	d				12 25				12 57							13 25				13 57			
Gatley	d				12 27				12 59							13 27				13 59			
Heald Green	d	12 10			12 30				13 02			13 10	13 10			13 30				14 02		14 10	
Manchester Airport ✈	a	12 17	12 22	12 26	12 38	12 42	12 47	12 53	13 07	13 11	13 12	13 16	13 17	13 22	13 26	13 38	13 42	13 47	13 53	14 07	14 12	14 17	14 22
Wilmslow	84 a								13 21											14 20			
Crewe [10]	84 a								13 47											14 46			

		TP	NT	TP	TP	NT	NT	TP	TP	NT	TP	NT	TP	TP	NT	NT	TP	TP	NT	TP	NT	TP	TP
		◇1 ≍		◇1 ≍	◇1 ≍			◇1 ≍	◇1 ≍		◇1 ≍		◇1 ≍	◇1 ≍			◇1 ≍	◇1 ≍		◇1 ≍		◇1 ≍	◇1 ≍
Deansgate	d					14 29			14 51						15 29			15 51					
Manchester Oxford Road	d				14 24	14 33			14 54	14 58				15 24	15 33			15 54	15 58				16 24
Manchester Piccadilly [10]	a				14 27	14 35			14 56	15 01				15 27	15 35			15 56	16 01				16 27
	d	14 06	14 14	14 24	14 29	14 37	14 46	14 54	14 58	15 03	15 06	15 14	15 24	15 29	15 37	15 46	15 54	15 58	16 03	16 06	16 14	16 24	16 29
Mauldeth Road	d		14 21				14 53					15 21				15 53					16 21		
Burnage	d		14 23				14 55					15 23				15 55					16 23		
East Didsbury	d		14 25				14 57					15 25				15 57					16 25		
Gatley	d		14 27				14 59					15 27				15 59					16 27		
Heald Green	d		14 30				15 02		15 10			15 30				16 02		16 10			16 30		16 40
Manchester Airport ✈	a	14 26	14 38	14 42	14 47	14 53	15 07	15 12	15 17	15 22	15 26	15 38	15 42	15 47	15 53	16 07	16 12	16 17	16 22	16 26	16 38	16 42	16 47
Wilmslow	84 a						15 20									16 20							
Crewe [10]	84 a						15 46									16 46							

A from 21 May
B from 2 July until 10 September
C from 21 May until 25 June, from 17 September

Manchester - Manchester Airport

Network Diagram - see first Page of Table 78

		NT	NT	TP	TP	NT	TP	NT	TP	NT	NT	TP	TP	NT	TP	NT	NT	TP	TP	NT	NT	TP
																		FX				
				◇1 ≍	◇1 ≍		◇1 ≍		◇1 ≍			◇1 ≍	◇1 ≍		◇1 ≍			◇1 ≍	◇1 ≍			◇1 ≍
Deansgate	d				16 51								17 51			18 12						
Manchester Oxford Road	d	16 33			16 54	16 58			17 27	17 33			17 54	17 58		18 16			18 24	18 33		
Manchester Piccadilly [10]	a	16 35			16 56	17 01			17 29	17 35			17 56	18 01		18 18			18 27	18 35		
	d	16 37	16 46	16 54	16 58	17 03	17 06	17 14	17 31	17 37	17 46	17 54	17 58	18 03	18 06		18 14	18 24	18 29	18 37	18 46	18 54
Mauldeth Road	d		16 53					17 21			17 53						18 21				18 53	
Burnage	d		16 55					17 23			17 55						18 23				18 55	
East Didsbury	d		16 57				17 17	17 25			17 57						18 25				18 57	
Gatley	d		16 59				17 20	17 27			17 59						18 27				18 59	
Heald Green	d		17 02		17 10		17 23	17 30	17 41		18 02		18 10				18 30		18 40		19 02	
Manchester Airport ✈	a	16 53	17 07	17 12	17 17	17 22	17 32	17 39	17 48	17 53	18 07	18 12	18 17	18 22	18 26		18 38	18 42	18 47	18 53	19 08	19 13
Wilmslow	84 a		17 21								18 21										19 23	
Crewe [10]	84 a		17 47								18 47											

		NT	TP	NT	TP	NT	TP	NT	AW	TP	TP	TP	TP	NT	TP	NT	AW	TP	NT	TP	TP	TP	TP
																				ThFO	MWFO	ThX	ThO
			◇1 ≍		◇1 ≍		◇1 ≍			◇1 ≍	◇1	◇1 ≍	◇1 ≍		◇1		◇ ≍	◇1		◇1	◇1	◇1 ≍	◇1 ≍
Deansgate	d					19 29				19 51				20 29				20 51					
Manchester Oxford Road	d	18 58			19 24	19 33		19 43	19 49	19 54	19 59		20 24	20 33		20 43	20 49	20 54	20 58			21 24	21 24
Manchester Piccadilly [10]	a	19 01			19 27	19 35		19 45	19 52	19 56	20 01		20 27	20 35		20 45	20 52	20 56	21 01			21 27	21 27
	d	19 03	19 06	19 14	19 29	19 37	19 40	19 46	19 54	19 58	20 03	20 13	20 29	20 37	20 40	20 46	20 54	20 58	21 03	21 06	21 06	21 29	21 29
Mauldeth Road	d			19 21				19 53				20 21				20 53				21 15	21 15		
Burnage	d			19 23				19 55				20 23				20 55				21 17	21 17		
East Didsbury	d			19 25				19 57				20 26				20 57				21 20	21 20		
Gatley	d			19 27				19 59				20 29				20 59				21 23	21 23		
Heald Green	d			19 30				20 02		20 10	20 15	20 32				21 02		21 10		21 26	21 26		
Manchester Airport ✈	a	19 24	19 28	19 38	19 47	19 53	19 59	20 07	20 18	20 17	20 24	20 39	20 47	20 53	20 57	21 07	21 18	21 17	21 20	21 36	21 38	21 46	21 47
Wilmslow	84 a							20 24								21 25							
Crewe [10]	84 a																						

		NT	TP	NT	TP	TP	TP	NT	TP	TP	TP
			◇1		◇1	◇1	◇1		◇1	◇1	◇1
Deansgate	d	21 29			21 51				22 51		
Manchester Oxford Road	d	21 33		21 43	21 54	22 27		22 43	22 54		
Manchester Piccadilly [10]	a	21 35		21 45	21 56	22 30		22 45	22 56		
	d	21 37	21 40	21 46	21 58	22 32	22 40	22 46	22 58	23 06	23 55
Mauldeth Road	d			21 53				22 53			00 04
Burnage	d			21 55				22 55			00 07
East Didsbury	d			21 57				22 57			00 10
Gatley	d			21 59				22 59			00 13
Heald Green	d			22 02	22 09			23 02	23 09		00 17
Manchester Airport ✈	a	21 53	21 57	22 10	22 17	22 47	22 57	23 08	23 17	23 26	00 24
Wilmslow	84 a			22 22				23 22			
Crewe [10]	84 a										

Saturdays

		TP	TP	TP	NT	TP	TP	TP	AW	NT	NT	TP	TP	TP	NT	NT	TP	NT	TP	NT	NT	TP	TP
		◇1	◇1	◇1		◇1	◇1	◇1				◇1	◇1	◇1			◇1		◇1			◇1	◇1
Deansgate	d																			07 11			
Manchester Oxford Road	d																	06 58		07 15			07 24
Manchester Piccadilly [10]	a																	07 01		07 17			07 27
	d	23p55	00 54	03 44	04 15	04 44	04 50	04 54	05 00	05 35	05 58	06 03	06 08	06 12	06 15	06 46	06 54	07 03	07 06		07 14	07 23	07 29
Mauldeth Road	d	00 04								05 42					06 22	06 53					07 21		
Burnage	d	00 07								05 44					06 24	06 55					07 23		
East Didsbury	d	00 10								05 46					06 26	06 57					07 25		
Gatley	d	00 13								05 49					06 29	06 59					07 27		
Heald Green	d	00 17								05 52					06 32	07 02					07 30		
Manchester Airport ✈	a	00 24	01 10	04 00	04 30	05 00	05 07	05 10	05 19	05 57	06 14	06 18	06 24	06 29	06 39	07 07	07 12	07 22	07 29		07 38	07 42	07 47
Wilmslow	84 a									06 11						07 20							
Crewe [10]	84 a									06 43						07 46							

		NT	NT	TP	NT	TP	NT	TP	TP	NT	NT	NT	TP	TP	NT	TP	NT	TP	TP	NT	NT	NT	TP
				◇1		◇1 ≍		◇1	◇1 ≍				◇1	◇1 ≍		◇1 ≍		◇1 ≍	◇1 ≍				◇1 ≍
										C	D									C	D		
Deansgate	d	07 28								08 29	08 29									09 29	09 30		
Manchester Oxford Road	d	07 32			07 58				08 24	08 33	08 33			08 54	08 58				09 24	09 33	09 34		
Manchester Piccadilly [10]	a	07 34			08 01				08 27	08 35	08 35			08 56	09 01				09 27	09 35	09 36		
	d	07 36	07 46	07 54	08 03	08 06	08 14	08 24	08 29	08 37	08 37	08 46	08 54	08 58	09 03	09 06	09 14	09 24	09 29	09 37	09 38	09 46	09 54
Mauldeth Road	d		07 53				08 21			≀	≀	08 53					09 21			≀	≀	09 53	
Burnage	d		07 55				08 23			≀	≀	08 55					09 23			≀	≀	09 55	
East Didsbury	d		07 57				08 25			≀	≀	08 57				09 16	09 25			≀	≀	09 57	
Gatley	d		07 59				08 27			≀	≀	08 59					09 27			≀	≀	09 59	
Heald Green	d		08 02				08 30			08 47	08 47	09 02		09 10			09 30			≀	≀	10 02	
Manchester Airport ✈	a	07 53	08 07	08 12	08 22	08 26	08 38	08 42	08 47	08 52	08 53	09 08	09 12	09 19	09 22	09 26	09 38	09 42	09 47	09 51	09 54	10 07	10 12
Wilmslow	84 a		08 21									09 21										10 20	
Crewe [10]	84 a		08 47									09 46										10 46	

C until 29 September

D from 6 October

Table 85

Saturdays

Manchester - Manchester Airport

Network Diagram - see first Page of Table 78

	TP ◇1 ⊼	NT	TP ◇1 ⊼	NT	TP ◇1 ⊼	TP ◇1 ⊼	NT	NT	TP ◇1 ⊼	TP ◇1 ⊼	NT	TP ◇1 ⊼	NT	TP ◇1 ⊼	TP ◇1 ⊼	NT	NT	TP ◇1 ⊼	TP ◇1 ⊼	NT	TP ◇1 ⊼
Deansgate d	09 51						10 29			10 51						11 29			11 51		
Manchester Oxford Road d	09 54	09 58				10 24	10 33			10 54	10 58				11 24	11 33			11 54	11 58	
Manchester Piccadilly 10 a	09 56	10 01				10 27	10 35			10 56	11 01				11 27	11 35			11 56	12 01	
d	09 58	10 03	10 06	10 14	10 24	10 29	10 37	10 46	10 54	10 58	11 03	11 06	11 14	11 24	11 29	11 37	11 46	11 54	11 58	12 03	12 06
Mauldeth Road d				10 21				10 53					11 21				11 53				
Burnage d				10 23				10 55					11 23				11 55				
East Didsbury d				10 25				10 57					11 25				11 57				
Gatley d				10 27				10 59					11 27				11 59				
Heald Green d	10 10			10 30				11 02		11 10			11 30				12 02		12 10		
Manchester Airport ✈ a	10 17	10 22	10 26	10 38	10 42	10 47	10 53	11 07	11 12	11 17	11 22	11 26	11 38	11 42	11 47	11 53	12 07	12 12	12 17	12 22	12 26
Wilmslow 84 a								11 21									12 20				
Crewe 10 84 a								11 47									12 46				

	NT	TP ◇1 ⊼	TP ◇1 ⊼	NT	NT	TP ◇1 ⊼	TP ◇1 ⊼	NT	TP ◇1 ⊼	NT	TP ◇1 ⊼	TP ◇1 ⊼	NT	NT	TP ◇1 ⊼	TP ◇1 ⊼	NT	TP ◇1 ⊼	NT	TP ◇1 ⊼	TP ◇1 ⊼	NT
Deansgate d				12 29			12 51						13 29			13 51						14 29
Manchester Oxford Road d			12 24	12 33			12 54	12 58				13 24	13 33			13 54	13 58				14 24	14 33
Manchester Piccadilly 10 a			12 27	12 35			12 56	13 01				13 27	13 35			13 56	14 01				14 27	14 35
d	12 14	12 24	12 29	12 37	12 46	12 54	12 58	13 03	13 06	13 14	13 24	13 29	13 37	13 46	13 54	13 58	14 03	14 06	14 14	14 24	14 29	14 37
Mauldeth Road d	12 21				12 53					13 21				13 53					14 21			
Burnage d	12 23				12 55					13 23				13 55					14 23			
East Didsbury d	12 25				12 57					13 25				13 57					14 25			
Gatley d	12 27				12 59					13 27				13 59					14 27			
Heald Green d	12 30				13 02		13 10			13 30				14 02		14 10			14 30			
Manchester Airport ✈ a	12 38	12 42	12 47	12 53	13 07	13 12	13 17	13 22	13 26	13 38	13 42	13 47	13 53	14 07	14 12	14 17	14 22	14 26	14 38	14 42	14 47	14 53
Wilmslow 84 a					13 21									14 20								
Crewe 10 84 a					13 47									14 46								

	NT	TP ◇1 ⊼	TP ◇1 ⊼	NT	TP ◇1 ⊼	NT	TP ◇1 ⊼	TP ◇1 ⊼	NT	NT	TP ◇1 ⊼	TP ◇1 ⊼	NT	TP ◇1 ⊼	NT	TP ◇1 ⊼	TP ◇1 ⊼	NT	NT	TP ◇1 ⊼	TP ◇1 ⊼
Deansgate d			14 51						15 29			15 51									16 51
Manchester Oxford Road d			14 54	14 58				15 24	15 33			15 54	15 58				16 24	16 33			16 54
Manchester Piccadilly 10 a			14 56	15 01				15 27	15 35			15 56	16 01				16 27	16 35			16 56
d	14 46	14 54	14 58	15 03	15 06	15 14	15 24	15 29	15 37	15 46	15 54	15 58	16 03	16 06	16 14	16 24	16 29	16 37	16 46	16 54	16 58
Mauldeth Road d	14 53					15 21				15 53					16 21				16 53		
Burnage d	14 55					15 23				15 55					16 23				16 55		
East Didsbury d	14 57					15 25				15 57					16 25				16 57		
Gatley d	14 59					15 27				15 59					16 27				16 59		
Heald Green d	15 02		15 10			15 30				16 02		16 10			16 30		16 40		17 02		17 10
Manchester Airport ✈ a	15 07	15 12	15 17	15 22	15 26	15 38	15 42	15 47	15 53	16 07	16 12	16 17	16 22	16 26	16 38	16 42	16 47	16 53	17 07	17 12	17 17
Wilmslow 84 a	15 20									16 20									17 21		
Crewe 10 84 a	15 46									16 46									17 47		

	NT	TP ◇1 ⊼	NT	TP ◇1 ⊼	NT	NT	TP ◇1 ⊼	TP ◇1 ⊼	NT	TP ◇1 ⊼	NT	TP ◇1 ⊼	TP ◇1 ⊼	NT	NT	TP ◇1 ⊼	NT	TP ◇1 ⊼	NT	TP ◇1 ⊼	NT	TP ◇1
Deansgate d					17 29			17 51													19 29	
Manchester Oxford Road d	16 58			17 24	17 33			17 54	17 58				18 24	18 33			18 58			19 24	19 33	
Manchester Piccadilly 10 a	17 01			17 27	17 35			17 56	18 01				18 27	18 35			19 01			19 27	19 35	
d	17 03	17 06	17 14	17 29	17 37	17 46	17 54	17 58	18 03	18 06	18 14	18 24	18 29	18 37	18 46	18 54	19 03	19 06	19 14	19 32	19 37	19 40
Mauldeth Road d			17 21			17 53					18 21				18 53				19 21			
Burnage d			17 23			17 55					18 23				18 55				19 23			
East Didsbury d		17 17	17 25			17 57					18 25				18 57				19 25			
Gatley d		17 20	17 27			17 59					18 27				18 59				19 27			
Heald Green d		17 23	17 30	17 41		18 02		18 10			18 30		18 40		19 02				19 30			
Manchester Airport ✈ a	17 22	17 32	17 38	17 48	17 53	18 07	18 12	18 17	18 22	18 26	18 38	18 42	18 47	18 53	19 08	19 13	19 24	19 28	19 38	19 50	19 53	19 59
Wilmslow 84 a						18 21									19 23							
Crewe 10 84 a						18 47																

	NT	AW ◇ ⊼	TP ◇1	TP ◇1 ⊼	TP ◇1 ⊼	NT	TP ◇1	NT	TP ◇1	NT	TP ◇1	TP ◇1 ⊼	NT	TP ◇1	NT	TP ◇1	TP ◇1	NT	TP ◇1	TP ◇1
Deansgate d			19 51			20 29			20 51				21 29			21 51			22 51	
Manchester Oxford Road d	19 43	19 49	19 54		20 24	20 33		20 43	20 54	20 58		21 24	21 33		21 43	21 54		22 43	22 54	
Manchester Piccadilly 10 a	19 45	19 52	19 56		20 27	20 35		20 45	20 56	21 01		21 27	21 35		21 45	21 56		22 45	22 56	
d	19 46	19 54	19 58	20 06	20 32	20 37	20 40	20 46	20 58	21 03	21 06	21 29	21 37	21 40	21 46	21 58	22 40	22 46	22 58	23 55
Mauldeth Road d	19 53			20 15				20 53			21 15				21 53			22 53		00 04
Burnage d	19 55			20 17				20 55			21 17				21 55			22 55		00 07
East Didsbury d	19 57			20 20				20 57			21 20				21 57			22 57		00 10
Gatley d	19 59			20 23				20 59			21 23				21 59			22 59		00 13
Heald Green d	20 02		20 10	20 26				21 02	21 10		21 26				22 02	22 09		23 02	23 09	00 17
Manchester Airport ✈ a	20 07	20 13	20 17	20 36	20 47	20 53	20 57	21 07	21 17	21 24	21 36	21 47	21 53	21 57	22 08	22 17	22 57	23 08	23 17	00 23
Wilmslow 84 a	20 24							21 24							22 22			23 22		
Crewe 10 84 a																				

Table 85

Sundays
until 24 June

Manchester - Manchester Airport

Network Diagram - see first Page of Table 78

	TP ◇1	TP ◇1	TP 🚌	TP 🚌	NT	TP ◇1	NT	TP 🚌	TP ◇1	TP ◇1	NT	TP ◇1	TP ◇1	NT	TP ◇1	TP ◇1	NT	NT	NT	TP ◇1	NT	NT
Deansgate d																08 53		09 15		09 51		10 16
Manchester Oxford Road d																08 56	09 01	09 18		09 54	10 00	10 19
Manchester Piccadilly 10 a																08 59	09 03	09 21		09 56	10 03	10 22
d	23p55	00 31	03 55	05u00	05 41	06 18	06 41	07u00	07 27	07 30	07 41	08 13	08 38	08 41	08 47	09 00	09 05		09 41	09 58	10 07	
Mauldeth Road d	00 04				05 48		06 50				07 48			08 48					09 48			
Burnage d	00 07				05 50		06 52				07 50			08 50					09 50			
East Didsbury d	00 10				05 52		06 54				07 52			08 52					09 52			
Gatley d	00 13				05 54		06 56				07 54			08 54					09 54			
Heald Green d	00 17				05 57		06 59				07 57			08 57					09 57			
Manchester Airport ✈ a	00 23	00 46	04 20	05 25	06 03	06 35	07 05	07 25	07 40	07 46	08 02	08 26	08 55	09 04	09 07	09 17	09 21		10 03	10 17	10 24	
Wilmslow 84 a														09 15								
Crewe 10 84 a																						

	TP ◇1	TP ◇1	NT	TP ◇1	NT	TP ◇1	NT	TP ◇1	NT	TP ◇1	NT	TP ◇1	NT	TP ◇1	TP ◇1	NT	TP ◇1 ⊼	NT	TP ◇1	NT	TP ◇1	TP ◇1 ⊼
Deansgate d				10 51			11 11			11 51			12 11				12 51			13 11		
Manchester Oxford Road d				10 54	11 03		11 17	11 24	11 38	11 54	12 00		12 17		12 24	12 43	12 54	13 00		13 17		13 24
Manchester Piccadilly 10 a				10 56	11 06		11 19	11 27	11 40	11 56	12 03		12 19		12 27	12 45	12 59	13 03		13 19		13 27
d	10 16	10 27	10 41	10 58	11 08	11 10		11 29	11 41	11 58	12 07	12 10		12 13	12 29	12 47	13 01	13 04	13 10		13 13	13 30
Mauldeth Road d			10 48						11 48							12 54						
Burnage d			10 50						11 50							12 56						
East Didsbury d			10 52						11 52							12 58						
Gatley d			10 54						11 54							13 00						
Heald Green d			10 57						11 57							13 03						
Manchester Airport ✈ a	10 29	10 41	11 01	11 17	11 24	11 24		11 47	12 04	12 17	12 21	12 24		12 27	12 48	13 08	13 17	13 19	13 24		13 27	13 47
Wilmslow 84 a			11 16													13 19						
Crewe 10 84 a																						

	NT	TP ◇1	NT	TP ◇1	NT	TP ◇1	TP ◇1	NT	TP ◇1	NT	TP ◇1	NT	TP ◇1	TP ◇1 ⊼	NT	TP ◇1	NT	TP ◇1	NT	TP ◇1	TP ◇1
Deansgate d		13 51			14 11				14 51			15 11				15 51			16 11		
Manchester Oxford Road d		13 54	14 01		14 17		14 24		14 54	15 00		15 17		15 24		15 54	16 00		16 17		16 24
Manchester Piccadilly 10 a		13 56	14 03		14 19		14 27		14 56	15 02		15 19		15 27		15 56	16 02		16 19		16 27
d	13 41	13 58	14 04	14 10		14 13	14 29	14 41	14 58	15 04	15 10		15 13	15 29	15 41	15 58	16 04	16 10		16 13	16 29
Mauldeth Road d	13 48							14 48							15 48						
Burnage d	13 50							14 50							15 50						
East Didsbury d	13 52							14 52							15 52						
Gatley d	13 54							14 54							15 54						
Heald Green d	13 57							14 57							15 57						
Manchester Airport ✈ a	14 03	14 17	14 21	14 24		14 27	14 47	15 01	15 17	15 20	15 24		15 28	15 47	16 03	16 17	16 21	16 25		16 34	16 46
Wilmslow 84 a								15 13													
Crewe 10 84 a																					

	NT	TP ◇1	NT	TP ◇1	NT	TP ◇1	TP ◇1 ⊼	NT	TP ◇1	NT	TP ◇1	NT	TP ◇1	TP ◇1 ⊼	NT	TP ◇1	NT	TP ◇1	TP ◇1	NT	TP ◇1 ⊼	NT
Deansgate d		16 51			17 11				17 51			18 11				18 51				19 13		
Manchester Oxford Road d		16 54	17 00		17 17		17 24		17 54	18 00		18 17		18 24		18 54	19 00			19 17	19 24	
Manchester Piccadilly 10 a		16 56	17 02		17 19		17 27		17 56	18 02		18 19		18 27		18 56	19 02			19 19	19 27	
d	16 41	16 58	17 04	17 10		17 13	17 29	17 41	17 58	18 04	18 10		18 13	18 29	18 41	18 58	19 04	19 10	19 13		19 29	19 41
Mauldeth Road d	16 48							17 48							18 48							19 48
Burnage d	16 50							17 50							18 50							19 50
East Didsbury d	16 52							17 52							18 52							19 52
Gatley d	16 54							17 54							18 54							19 54
Heald Green d	16 57							17 57							18 57							19 57
Manchester Airport ✈ a	17 02	17 17	17 21	17 24		17 27	17 47	18 03	18 17	18 21	18 24		18 27	18 45	19 02	19 17	19 21	19 26	19 27		19 47	20 02
Wilmslow 84 a	17 13														19 13							
Crewe 10 84 a																						

	TP ◇1	NT	TP ◇1	NT	TP ◇1	TP ◇1 ⊼	NT	TP ◇1	NT	TP ◇1	NT	TP ◇1	TP ◇1 ⊼	AW	NT	TP ◇1	NT	NT	TP ◇1	AW	NT
Deansgate d	19 51			20 11				20 51			21 11					21 51		22 11			
Manchester Oxford Road d	19 54	20 00		20 17		20 24		20 54	21 00		21 17		21 24			21 54	22 00	22 17			
Manchester Piccadilly 10 a	19 56	20 02		20 19		20 27		20 56	21 02		21 19		21 27			21 56	22 02	22 19			
d	19 58	20 04	20 10		20 13	20 29	20 41	20 58	21 04	21 09		21 13	21 29	21 34	21 41	21 58	22 04		22 13	22 35	22 46
Mauldeth Road d							20 48								21 48						22 53
Burnage d							20 50								21 50						22 55
East Didsbury d							20 52								21 52						22 57
Gatley d							20 54								21 54						22 59
Heald Green d							20 57								21 57						23 02
Manchester Airport ✈ a	20 17	20 26	20 24		20 30	20 45	21 01	21 16	21 20	21 24		21 27	21 46		22 03	22 17	22 21		22 27		23 09
Wilmslow 84 a							21 12							21 50						22 50	
Crewe 10 84 a														22 13						23 10	

Sundays until 24 June

Manchester - Manchester Airport

Network Diagram - see first Page of Table 78

	NT	TP ◇1	TP ◇1 🛒	NT	NT
Deansgate d			23 08	23 11	
Manchester Oxford Road d	22 47		23 11	23 17	23 47
Manchester Piccadilly 10 a	22 50		23 14	23 19	23 50
d	22 52	23 09	23 15		23 52
Mauldeth Road d					
Burnage d					
East Didsbury d					
Gatley d					
Heald Green d					
Manchester Airport a	23 15	23 24	23 30		00 07
Wilmslow 84 a					
Crewe 10 84 a					

Sundays 1 July to 9 September

	TP ◇1	TP ◇1	TP 🚌	TP ◇1	TP 🚌	TP ◇1	NT	TP ◇1	NT		TP 🚌	TP ◇1	TP ◇1	NT	TP ◇1	TP ◇1	NT	TP ◇1	TP ◇1		NT	NT	TP ◇1	NT
Deansgate d																			08 53			09 15		
Manchester Oxford Road d																			08 56		09 01	09 18		
Manchester Piccadilly 10 a																			08 59		09 03	09 21		
d	23p55	00 31	03 55	04 06	05u00	05 21	05 41	06 38	06 41		07u00	07 27	07 38	07 41	08 13	08 38	08 41	08 47	09 00		09 05		09 38	09 41
Mauldeth Road d	00 04						05 48		06 50					07 48			08 48							09 48
Burnage d	00 07						05 50		06 52					07 50			08 50							09 50
East Didsbury d	00 10						05 52		06 54					07 52			08 52							09 52
Gatley d	00 13						05 54		06 56					07 54			08 54							09 54
Heald Green d	00 17						05 57		06 59					07 57			08 57							09 57
Manchester Airport a	00 23	00 46	04 20	04 23	05 25	05 38	06 03	06 55	07 05		07 25	07 40	07 55	08 02	08 26	08 55	09 04	09 07	09 17		09 21		09 55	10 03
Wilmslow 84 a																	09 15							
Crewe 10 84 a																								

	TP ◇1	NT	NT	TP ◇1	TP ◇1		NT	TP ◇1	NT	NT	TP ◇1	TP ◇1	NT	TP ◇1	NT		NT	TP ◇1	TP ◇1	TP ◇1	NT	TP ◇1 🛒	NT	NT
Deansgate d	09 51		10 16					10 51		11 11				11 51			12 11					12 51		13 11
Manchester Oxford Road d	09 54	10 00	10 19					10 54	11 03	11 17	11 24		11 38	11 54	12 00		12 17		12 24		12 43	12 54	13 00	13 17
Manchester Piccadilly 10 a	09 56	10 03	10 22					10 56	11 06	11 19	11 27		11 40	11 56	12 03		12 19		12 27		12 45	12 59	13 03	13 19
d	09 58	10 07		10 16	10 38		10 41	10 58	11 08		11 29	11 38	11 41	11 58	12 07			12 13	12 29	12 38	12 47	13 01	13 04	
Mauldeth Road d							10 48						11 48								12 54			
Burnage d							10 50						11 50								12 56			
East Didsbury d							10 52						11 52								12 58			
Gatley d							10 54						11 54								13 00			
Heald Green d							10 57						11 57								13 03			
Manchester Airport a	10 17	10 24		10 29	10 55		11 01	11 17	11 24		11 47	11 55	12 04	12 17	12 21			12 27	12 48	12 55	13 08	13 17	13 19	
Wilmslow 84 a							11 16														13 19			
Crewe 10 84 a																								

	TP ◇1		TP ◇1 🛒	TP ◇1	NT	TP ◇1	NT	NT	TP ◇1	TP ◇1	TP ◇1		NT	TP ◇1	NT	NT	TP ◇1	TP ◇1 🛒	TP ◇1	NT	TP ◇1		NT	NT
Deansgate d						13 51		14 11						14 51		15 11					15 51			16 11
Manchester Oxford Road d			13 24			13 54	14 01	14 17		14 24				14 54	15 00	15 17		15 24			15 54		16 00	16 17
Manchester Piccadilly 10 a			13 27			13 56	14 03	14 19		14 27				14 56	15 02	15 19		15 27			15 56		16 02	16 19
d	13 13		13 30	13 38	13 41	13 58	14 04		14 13	14 29	14 38		14 41	14 58	15 04		15 13	15 29	15 38	15 41	15 58		16 04	
Mauldeth Road d					13 48								14 48							15 48				
Burnage d					13 50								14 50							15 50				
East Didsbury d					13 52								14 52							15 52				
Gatley d					13 54								14 54							15 54				
Heald Green d					13 57								14 57							15 57				
Manchester Airport a	13 27		13 47	13 55	14 03	14 17	14 21		14 27	14 47	14 55		15 01	15 17	15 20		15 28	15 47	15 55	16 03	16 17		16 21	
Wilmslow 84 a													15 13											
Crewe 10 84 a																								

	TP ◇1	TP ◇1	TP ◇1	NT	TP ◇1	NT	NT		TP ◇1	TP ◇1 🛒	TP ◇1	NT	TP ◇1	NT	NT	TP ◇1	TP ◇1 🛒		TP ◇1	NT	TP ◇1	NT	NT	TP ◇1
Deansgate d					16 51		17 11						17 51		18 11						18 51		19 11	
Manchester Oxford Road d		16 24			16 54	17 00	17 17			17 24			17 54	18 00	18 17		18 24				18 54	19 00	19 17	
Manchester Piccadilly 10 a		16 27			16 56	17 02	17 19			17 27			17 56	18 02	18 19		18 27				18 56	19 02	19 19	
d	16 13	16 29	16 38	16 41	16 58	17 04			17 13	17 29	17 38	17 41	17 58	18 04		18 13	18 29		18 38	18 41	18 58	19 04		19 13
Mauldeth Road d				16 48								17 48								18 48				
Burnage d				16 50								17 50								18 50				
East Didsbury d				16 52								17 52								18 52				
Gatley d				16 54								17 54								18 54				
Heald Green d				16 57								17 57								18 57				
Manchester Airport a	16 34	16 46	16 55	17 02	17 17	17 21			17 27	17 47	17 55	18 03	18 17	18 21		18 27	18 45		18 55	19 02	19 17	19 21		19 27
Wilmslow 84 a				17 13																19 13				
Crewe 10 84 a																								

Sundays 1 July to 9 September

Manchester - Manchester Airport

Network Diagram - see first Page of Table 78

	TP ◇1 🛒	TP ◇1	NT		TP ◇1	NT	NT	TP ◇1	TP ◇1 🛒	TP ◇1	NT	TP ◇1	NT		NT	TP ◇1	TP ◇1 🛒	AW	NT	TP ◇1	NT	NT	TP ◇1	
Deansgate d					19 51		20 11					20 51			21 11					21 51		22 11		
Manchester Oxford Road d	19 24				19 54	20 00	20 17		20 24			20 54	21 00		21 17		21 24			21 54	22 00	22 17		
Manchester Piccadilly 10 a	19 27				19 56	20 02	20 19		20 27			20 56	21 02		21 19		21 27			21 56	22 02	22 19		
d	19 29	19 38	19 41		19 58	20 04		20 13	20 29	20 38	20 41	20 58	21 04			21 13	21 29	21 34	21 41	21 58	22 04		22 13	
Mauldeth Road d			19 48								20 48								21 48					
Burnage d			19 50								20 50								21 50					
East Didsbury d			19 52								20 52								21 52					
Gatley d			19 54								20 54								21 54					
Heald Green d			19 57								20 57								21 57					
Manchester Airport a	19 47	19 55	20 02		20 17	20 26		20 30	20 47	20 55	21 01	21 16	21 20			21 27	21 46		22 03	22 17	22 21		22 27	
Wilmslow 84 a											21 12							21 50						
Crewe 10 84 a																		22 13						

	AW	TP ◇1	NT	NT	TP ◇1 🛒	NT	NT
Deansgate d					23 08	23 11	
Manchester Oxford Road d				22 47	23 11	23 17	23 47
Manchester Piccadilly 10 a				22 50	23 14	23 19	23 50
d	22 35	22 38	22 46	22 52	23 15		23 52
Mauldeth Road d			22 53				
Burnage d			22 55				
East Didsbury d			22 57				
Gatley d			22 59				
Heald Green d			23 02				
Manchester Airport a		22 55	23 09	23 15	23 29		00 07
Wilmslow 84 a	22 50						
Crewe 10 84 a	23 10						

Sundays 16 September to 21 October

	TP ◇1	TP ◇1	TP 🚌	TP 🚌	NT	TP ◇1	NT	TP 🚌	TP ◇1		TP ◇1	NT	TP ◇1	TP ◇1	NT	TP ◇1	TP ◇1	NT	NT		TP ◇1	NT	NT	TP ◇1
Deansgate d																	08 53	09 15			09 51		10 16	
Manchester Oxford Road d																	08 56	09 18			09 54	10 00	10 19	
Manchester Piccadilly 10 a																	08 59	09 21			09 56	10 03	10 22	
d	23p55	00 31	03 55	05u00	05 41	06 18	06 41	07u00	07 08		07 17	07 41	07 50	08 39	08 41	08 47	09 00		09 41		09 58	10 07		10 16
Mauldeth Road d	00 04				05 48		06 50					07 48			08 48				09 48					
Burnage d	00 07				05 50		06 52					07 50			08 50				09 50					
East Didsbury d	00 10				05 52		06 54					07 52			08 52				09 52					
Gatley d	00 13				05 54		06 56					07 54			08 54				09 54					
Heald Green d	00 17				05 57		06 59					07 57			08 57				09 57					
Manchester Airport a	00 23	00 46	04 20	05 25	06 03	06 35	07 05	07 25	07 22		07 34	08 02	08 05	08 55	09 04	09 07	09 17		10 03		10 17	10 24		10 29
Wilmslow 84 a															09 15									
Crewe 10 84 a																								

	TP ◇1	NT	TP ◇1	TP ◇1	NT A		NT B	TP ◇1	NT	TP ◇1	NT	TP ◇1	NT	TP ◇1	TP ◇1		NT	TP ◇1 🛒	NT	TP ◇1	NT	TP ◇1	TP ◇1 🛒	NT
Deansgate d			10 51		11 11		11 11			11 51			12 11					12 51			13 11			
Manchester Oxford Road d			10 54		11 16		11 17	11 24	11 38	11 54	12 00		12 18		12 24		12 43	12 54	13 00		13 17		13 24	
Manchester Piccadilly 10 a			10 56		11 19		11 19	11 27	11 40	11 56	12 02		12 21		12 27		12 45	12 59	13 03		13 19		13 27	
d	10 28	10 41	10 58	11 10				11 29	11 41	11 58	12 06	12 10		12 13	12 29		12 47	13 01	13 04	13 10		13 13	13 30	13 41
Mauldeth Road d		10 48							11 48								12 54							13 48
Burnage d		10 50							11 50								12 56							13 50
East Didsbury d		10 52							11 52								12 58							13 52
Gatley d		10 54							11 54								13 00							13 54
Heald Green d		10 57							11 57								13 03							13 57
Manchester Airport a	10 42	11 01	11 17	11 24				11 47	12 04	12 17	12 20	12 24		12 34	12 48		13 08	13 17	13 19	13 24		13 27	13 47	14 03
Wilmslow 84 a		11 16															13 19							
Crewe 10 84 a																								

	TP ◇1		NT	TP ◇1	NT	TP ◇1	TP ◇1	NT	TP ◇1	NT	TP ◇1		NT	TP ◇1	TP ◇1 🛒	NT	TP ◇1	NT	TP ◇1	NT	TP ◇1		TP ◇1	NT
Deansgate d	13 51				14 11				14 51				15 11				15 51			16 11				
Manchester Oxford Road d	13 54		14 01		14 17		14 24		14 54	15 00			15 17		15 24		15 54	16 00		16 17			16 24	
Manchester Piccadilly 10 a	13 56		14 03		14 19		14 27		14 56	15 02			15 19		15 27		15 56	16 02		16 19			16 27	
d	13 58		14 04	14 10		14 13	14 29	14 41	14 58	15 04	15 10			15 13	15 29	15 41	15 58	16 04	16 10		16 13		16 29	16 41
Mauldeth Road d								14 48								15 48								16 48
Burnage d								14 50								15 50								16 50
East Didsbury d								14 52								15 52								16 52
Gatley d								14 54								15 54								16 54
Heald Green d								14 57								15 57								16 57
Manchester Airport a	14 17		14 21	14 24		14 34	14 47	15 01	15 17	15 20	15 24			15 34	15 47	16 03	16 17	16 21	16 24		16 34		16 46	17 02
Wilmslow 84 a								15 13																17 13
Crewe 10 84 a																								

A from 7 October until 21 October

B from 16 September until 30 September

Sundays

16 September to 21 October

Manchester - Manchester Airport

Network Diagram - see first Page of Table 78

		TP	NT	TP	NT	TP	TP	NT		TP	NT	TP	NT	TP	TP	NT	TP	NT		TP	TP	NT	TP	NT	TP
		◇1		◇1		◇1	◇1			◇1		◇1		◇1	◇1		◇1			◇1	◇1		◇1		◇1
							🛒								🛒								🛒		
Deansgate 🚊	d	16 51			17 11					17 51			18 11				18 51					19 13			19 51
Manchester Oxford Road	d	16 54	17 00		17 17		17 24			17 54	18 00		18 17		18 24		18 54	19 00				19 17	19 24		19 54
Manchester Piccadilly 10 🚊	a	16 56	17 02		17 19		17 27			17 56	18 02		18 19		18 27		18 56	19 02				19 19	19 27		19 56
	d	16 58	17 04	17 10		17 13	17 29	17 41		17 58	18 04	18 10		18 13	18 29	18 41	18 58	19 04		19 10	19 13		19 29	19 41	19 58
Mauldeth Road	d							17 48								18 48								19 48	
Burnage	d							17 50								18 50								19 50	
East Didsbury	d							17 52								18 52								19 52	
Gatley	d							17 54								18 54								19 54	
Heald Green	d							17 57								18 57								19 57	
Manchester Airport ✈	a	17 17	17 21	17 24		17 27	17 47	18 03		18 17	18 21	18 24		18 27	18 45	19 02	19 17	19 21		19 26	19 27		19 47	20 02	20 17
Wilmslow 84	a															19 13									
Crewe 10 84	a																								

		NT	TP	NT		TP	TP	NT	TP	NT	TP	NT	TP	TP		AW	NT	TP	NT	NT	TP	AW	NT	NT	
			◇1			◇1	◇1		◇1		◇1		◇1	◇1				◇1			◇1				
							🛒							🛒											
Deansgate 🚊	d			20 11					20 51			21 11						21 51		22 11					
Manchester Oxford Road	d	20 00		20 17			20 24		20 54	21 00		21 17		21 24				21 54	22 00	22 17				22 47	
Manchester Piccadilly 10 🚊	a	20 02		20 19			20 27		20 56	21 02		21 19		21 27				21 56	22 02	22 19				22 50	
	d	20 04	20 10			20 13	20 29	20 41	20 58	21 04	21 09		21 13	21 29		21 34	21 41	21 58	22 04		22 13	22 35	22 46	22 52	
Mauldeth Road	d							20 48									21 48						22 53		
Burnage	d							20 50									21 50						22 55		
East Didsbury	d							20 52									21 52						22 57		
Gatley	d							20 54									21 54						22 59		
Heald Green	d							20 57									21 57						23 02		
Manchester Airport ✈	a	20 21	20 24			20 30	20 45	21 01	21 16	21 20	21 24		21 27	21 46			22 03	22 17	22 21		22 27		23 09	23 15	
Wilmslow 84	a							21 12								21 50						22 50			
Crewe 10 84	a															22 13						23 10			

		TP	TP	NT	NT
		◇1	◇1		
			🛒		
Deansgate 🚊	d		23 08	23 11	
Manchester Oxford Road	d		23 11	23 17	23 47
Manchester Piccadilly 10 🚊	a		23 14	23 19	23 50
	d	23 10	23 15		23 52
Mauldeth Road	d				
Burnage	d				
East Didsbury	d				
Gatley	d				
Heald Green	d				
Manchester Airport ✈	a	23 24	23 30		00 07
Wilmslow 84	a				
Crewe 10 84	a				

Sundays

from 28 October

		TP	TP	NT	TP	NT	TP	TP	TP	TP		NT	TP	TP	NT	TP	TP	NT	NT	TP		NT	NT	TP	TP
		◇1						◇1	◇1				◇1			◇1	◇1			◇1				◇1	◇1
			🚌	🚌	🚌	🚌	🚌			🚌				🚌											
Deansgate 🚊	d																08 53	09 15		09 51			10 16		
Manchester Oxford Road	d																08 56	09 18		09 54		10 00	10 19		
Manchester Piccadilly 10 🚊	a																08 59	09 21		09 56		10 03	10 22		
	d	23p55	05u00	05 25	05 55	06 25	07u00	07 22	07 38	07 40		07 41	08 39	08 40	08 41	08 47	09 00		09 41	09 58		10 07		10 16	10 37
Mauldeth Road	d	00 04		05 36		06 36						07 48			08 48				09 48						
Burnage	d	00 07		05 41		06 41						07 50			08 50				09 50						
East Didsbury	d	00 10		05 47		06 47						07 52			08 52				09 52						
Gatley	d	00 13		05 52		06 52						07 54			08 54				09 54						
Heald Green	d	00 17		06 00		07 00						07 57			08 57				09 57						
Manchester Airport ✈	a	00 23	05 25	06 05	06 20	07 05	07 25	07 40	07 55	08 05		08 02	08 52	09 05	09 04	09 07	09 17		10 03	10 17		10 24		10 29	10 54
Wilmslow 84	a														09 15										
Crewe 10 84	a																								

		NT	TP	TP	NT	TP		NT	TP	NT	TP	NT	TP	TP	NT	TP		NT	TP	NT	TP	TP	NT	TP	NT
			◇1	◇1		◇1			◇1		◇1		◇1	◇1		◇1			◇1		◇1	◇1		◇1	
																🛒						🛒			
Deansgate 🚊	d		10 51		11 11				11 51			12 11				12 51				13 11				13 51	
Manchester Oxford Road	d		10 54		11 16	11 24		11 38	11 54	12 00		12 18		12 24	12 43	12 54		13 00		13 17		13 26		13 54	14 01
Manchester Piccadilly 10 🚊	a		10 56		11 19	11 27		11 40	11 56	12 02		12 21		12 27	12 45	12 59		13 03		13 19		13 28		13 56	14 03
	d	10 41	10 58	11 10		11 29		11 41	11 58	12 06	12 10		12 13	12 29	12 47	13 01		13 04	13 10		13 13	13 30	13 41	13 58	14 04
Mauldeth Road	d	10 48						11 48							12 54								13 48		
Burnage	d	10 50						11 50							12 56								13 50		
East Didsbury	d	10 52						11 52							12 58								13 52		
Gatley	d	10 54						11 54							13 00								13 54		
Heald Green	d	10 57						11 57							13 03								13 57		
Manchester Airport ✈	a	11 01	11 17	11 24		11 47		12 04	12 17	12 20	12 24		12 34	12 48	13 08	13 17		13 19	13 24		13 27	13 47	14 03	14 17	14 21
Wilmslow 84	a	11 16													13 19										
Crewe 10 84	a																								

Sundays

from 28 October

Manchester - Manchester Airport

Network Diagram - see first Page of Table 78

		TP		NT	TP	TP	NT	TP	NT	TP	NT	TP		TP	NT	TP	NT	TP	NT	TP	TP	NT		TP	NT
		◇1			◇1	◇1		◇1		◇1		◇1		◇1		◇1		◇1		◇1	◇1			◇1	
														🛒											
Deansgate 🚊	d			14 11				14 51			15 11					15 51			16 11					16 51	
Manchester Oxford Road	d			14 17		14 24		14 54	15 00		15 17			15 24		15 54	16 00		16 17		16 24			16 54	17 00
Manchester Piccadilly 10 🚊	a			14 19		14 27		14 56	15 02		15 19			15 27		15 56	16 02		16 19		16 27			16 56	17 02
	d	14 10			14 13	14 29	14 41	14 58	15 04	15 10		15 13		15 29	15 41	15 58	16 04	16 10		16 13	16 29	16 41		16 58	17 04
Mauldeth Road	d						14 48								15 48							16 48			
Burnage	d						14 50								15 50							16 50			
East Didsbury	d						14 52								15 52							16 52			
Gatley	d						14 54								15 54							16 54			
Heald Green	d						14 57								15 57							16 57			
Manchester Airport ✈	a	14 24			14 34	14 47	15 01	15 17	15 20	15 24		15 34		15 47	16 03	16 17	16 21	16 24		16 34	16 46	17 02		17 17	17 21
Wilmslow 84	a						15 13															17 13			
Crewe 10 84	a																								

		TP	NT	TP	TP	NT	TP	NT		TP	NT	TP	TP	NT	TP	NT	TP	TP		NT	TP	NT	TP	NT	TP
		◇1		◇1	◇1		◇1			◇1		◇1	◇1		◇1		◇1	◇1			◇1		◇1		◇1
					🛒								🛒								🛒				
Deansgate 🚊	d		17 11				17 51				18 11				18 51					19 13			19 51		
Manchester Oxford Road	d		17 17		17 24		17 54	18 00			18 17		18 24		18 54	19 00				19 17	19 24		19 54	20 00	
Manchester Piccadilly 10 🚊	a		17 19		17 27		17 56	18 02			18 19		18 27		18 56	19 02				19 19	19 27		19 56	20 02	
	d	17 10		17 13	17 29	17 41	17 58	18 04		18 10		18 13	18 29	18 41	18 58	19 04	19 10	19 13			19 29	19 41	19 58	20 04	20 10
Mauldeth Road	d					17 48								18 48								19 48			
Burnage	d					17 50								18 50								19 50			
East Didsbury	d					17 52								18 52								19 52			
Gatley	d					17 54								18 54								19 54			
Heald Green	d					17 57								18 57								19 57			
Manchester Airport ✈	a	17 24		17 27	17 47	18 03	18 17	18 21		18 24		18 27	18 45	19 02	19 17	19 21	19 26	19 27			19 47	20 02	20 17	20 21	20 24
Wilmslow 84	a													19 13											
Crewe 10 84	a																								

		NT	TP	TP		NT	TP	NT	TP	NT	TP	TP	AW	NT		TP	NT	NT	TP	AW	NT	NT	TP	TP	
			◇1	◇1			◇1		◇1		◇1	◇1				◇1			◇1				◇1	◇1	
				🛒								🛒												🛒	
Deansgate 🚊	d	20 11					20 51			21 11						21 51		22 11						23 08	
Manchester Oxford Road	d	20 17		20 24			20 54	21 00		21 17		21 24				21 54	22 00	22 17				22 47		23 11	
Manchester Piccadilly 10 🚊	a	20 19		20 27			20 56	21 02		21 19		21 27				21 56	22 02	22 19				22 50		23 14	
	d		20 13	20 29		20 41	20 58	21 04	21 09		21 13	21 29	21 34	21 41		21 58	22 04		22 13	22 35	22 46	22 52	23 10	23 15	
Mauldeth Road	d					20 48								21 48							22 53				
Burnage	d					20 50								21 50							22 55				
East Didsbury	d					20 52								21 52							22 57				
Gatley	d					20 54								21 54							22 59				
Heald Green	d					20 57								21 57							23 02				
Manchester Airport ✈	a		20 30	20 45		21 01	21 16	21 20	21 24		21 27	21 46		22 03		22 17	22 21		22 27		23 09	23 15	23 24	23 30	
Wilmslow 84	a					21 12							21 50							22 50					
Crewe 10 84	a												22 13							23 10					

		NT	NT
Deansgate 🚊	d	23 11	
Manchester Oxford Road	d	23 17	23 47
Manchester Piccadilly 10 🚊	a	23 19	23 50
	d		23 52
Mauldeth Road	d		
Burnage	d		
East Didsbury	d		
Gatley	d		
Heald Green	d		
Manchester Airport ✈	a		00 07
Wilmslow 84	a		
Crewe 10 84	a		

Manchester Airport - Manchester

Network Diagram - see first Page of Table 78

Miles			TP MX	TP	TP MX	TP MO	NT MX	TP	TP	NT	TP	AW	TP	TP	NT	TP	TP	NT	NT	TP	TP	TP	NT
			◇■	◇■	◇■	◇■		◇■	◇■		◇■	◇ ⊼	◇■	◇■ ⊼		◇■ ⊼	◇■ ⊼			◇■ ⊼	◇■ ⊼	◇■ ⊼	
—	Crewe 10	84 d					00 44																06 33
—	Wilmslow	84 d													05 46								06 57
0	Manchester Airport	✈ d	23p52	00 01	00 38	00 48	01 20	04 00	04 12	04 38	05 15	05 33	05 37	05 45	06 01	06 18	06 23	06 41	06 46	06 55	07 00	07 05	07 17
1½	Heald Green	d												05 49	06 04				06 49				07 20
4	Gatley	d													06 07				06 52				07 23
5¼	East Didsbury	d													06 10				06 55				07 26
6¼	Burnage	d													06 12				06 57				07 28
7¼	Mauldeth Road	d													06 14				06 59				07 30
—	Manchester Piccadilly 10	a	00 09	00 15	00 51	01 01	01 36	04 14	04 27	04 51	05 33	05 48	05 51	06 00	06 25	06 31	06 39	06 56	07 11	07 13	07 14	07 22	07 42
—		d										05 50		06 03		06 33		06 58			07 15		
—	Manchester Oxford Road	a										05 52		06 05		06 35		07 00			07 17		
—	Deansgate	a																					

		TP	TP	NT	NT	TP	TP	NT	TP	NT	TP	TP	NT	NT	TP	TP	NT	TP	NT	TP	TP	NT	NT
		◇■ ⊼	◇■ ⊼			◇■ ⊼	◇■ ⊼		◇■ ⊼		◇■ ⊼	◇■ ⊼			◇■ ⊼	◇■ ⊼		◇■ ⊼		◇■ ⊼	◇■ ⊼		
Crewe 10	84 d																		08 31				
Wilmslow	84 d									07 56									08 57				
Manchester Airport	✈ d	07 25	07 35	07 38	07 46	07 53	07 56	08 01	08 05	08 17	08 25	08 35	08 41	08 46	08 55	09 00	09 03	09 05	09 17	09 29	09 35	09 41	09 46
Heald Green	d	07 30		07 42	07 49			08 05		08 20	08 29			08 49					09 20	09 33			09 49
Gatley	d			07 45	07 52		08 02			08 23	08 32			08 52					09 23				09 52
East Didsbury	d			07 48	07 55		08 05			08 26	08 35			08 55					09 26				09 55
Burnage	d				07 57					08 28				08 57					09 28				09 57
Mauldeth Road	d				07 59					08 30				08 59					09 30				09 59
Manchester Piccadilly 10	a	07 43	07 49	07 57	08 11	08 12	08 14	08 21	08 22	08 42	08 44	08 49	08 58	09 11	09 13	09 14	09 18	09 22	09 42	09 44	09 52	09 59	10 11
	d			07 59			08 15	08 22			08 46		09 01			09 16	09 22			09 46		10 01	
Manchester Oxford Road	a			08 01			08 17	08 24			08 48		09 03			09 18	09 24			09 48		10 03	
Deansgate	a							08 28			08 51						09 28			09 51			

		TP	TP	NT	TP	NT	TP	TP	NT	NT	TP	TP	NT	TP	NT	TP	TP	NT	NT	TP	TP	NT
		◇■ ⊼	◇■ ⊼		◇■ ⊼		◇■ ⊼	◇■ ⊼			◇■ ⊼	◇■ ⊼		◇■ ⊼		◇■ ⊼	◇■ ⊼			◇■ ⊼	◇■ ⊼	
Crewe 10	84 d					09 33									10 34							
Wilmslow	84 d					09 57									10 57							
Manchester Airport	✈ d	09 55	10 00	10 03	10 05	10 17	10 29	10 35	10 41	10 46	10 55	11 00	11 03	11 05	11 17	11 29	11 35	11 41	11 46	11 55	12 00	12 03
Heald Green	d					10 20	10 33			10 49					11 20	11 33			11 49			
Gatley	d					10 23				10 52					11 23				11 52			
East Didsbury	d					10 26				10 55					11 26				11 55			
Burnage	d					10 28				10 57					11 28				11 57			
Mauldeth Road	d					10 30				10 59					11 30				11 59			
Manchester Piccadilly 10	a	10 13	10 14	10 18	10 22	10 42	10 44	10 52	10 59	11 11	11 13	11 14	11 18	11 22	11 42	11 44	11 52	11 59	12 11	12 13	12 14	12 18
	d		10 16	10 22			10 46		11 01			11 16	11 22			11 46		12 01			12 16	12 22
Manchester Oxford Road	a		10 18	10 24			10 48		11 03			11 18	11 24			11 48		12 03			12 18	12 24
Deansgate	a			10 28			10 51						11 28			11 51						12 28

		TP	NT	TP	TP	NT	NT	TP	TP	NT	TP	NT	TP	TP	NT	NT	TP	TP	NT	TP	NT	TP	TP
		◇■ ⊼		◇■ ⊼	◇■ ⊼			◇■ ⊼	◇■ ⊼		◇■ ⊼		◇■ ⊼	◇■ ⊼			◇■ ⊼	◇■ ⊼		◇■ ⊼		◇■ ⊼	◇■ ⊼
Crewe 10	84 d		11 34									12 34									13 34		
Wilmslow	84 d		11 57									12 57									13 57		
Manchester Airport	✈ d	12 05	12 17	12 29	12 35	12 41	12 46	12 55	13 00	13 03	13 05	13 17	13 29	13 35	13 41	13 46	13 55	14 00	14 03	14 05	14 17	14 29	14 35
Heald Green	d		12 20	12 33			12 49					13 20	13 33			13 49					14 20	14 33	
Gatley	d		12 23				12 52					13 23				13 52					14 23		
East Didsbury	d		12 26				12 55					13 26				13 55					14 26		
Burnage	d		12 28				12 57					13 28				13 57					14 28		
Mauldeth Road	d		12 30				12 59					13 30				13 59					14 30		
Manchester Piccadilly 10	a	12 22	12 42	12 44	12 52	12 59	13 11	13 13	13 14	13 18	13 22	13 42	13 44	13 52	13 59	14 11	14 13	14 14	14 18	14 22	14 42	14 44	14 52
	d			12 46		13 01			13 16	13 22			13 46		14 01			14 16	14 22			14 46	
Manchester Oxford Road	a			12 48		13 03			13 18	13 24			13 48		14 03			14 18	14 24			14 48	
Deansgate	a			12 51						13 28			13 51						14 28			14 51	

		NT	NT	TP	TP	NT	TP	NT	TP	NT	NT	TP	TP	NT	TP	NT	TP	TP	NT	NT	TP	TP	NT
				◇■ ⊼	◇■ ⊼		◇■ ⊼		◇■ ⊼			◇■ ⊼	◇■ ⊼		◇■ ⊼		◇■ ⊼	◇■ ⊼			◇■ ⊼	◇■ ⊼	
Crewe 10	84 d							14 34								15 33							
Wilmslow	84 d							14 57								15 56							
Manchester Airport	✈ d	14 41	14 46	14 55	15 00	15 03	15 05	15 17	15 35	15 41	15 46	15 55	16 00	16 03	16 05	16 17	16 29	16 35	16 41	16 46	16 55	17 00	17 03
Heald Green	d		14 49					15 20			15 49					16 20	16 33			16 49			
Gatley	d		14 52					15 23			15 52					16 23				16 52			
East Didsbury	d		14 55					15 26			15 55					16 26				16 55			
Burnage	d		14 57					15 28			15 57					16 28				16 57			
Mauldeth Road	d		14 59					15 30			15 59					16 30				16 59			
Manchester Piccadilly 10	a	14 59	15 11	15 13	15 14	15 18	15 22	15 41	15 52	15 59	16 11	16 13	16 14	16 18	16 22	16 42	16 44	16 52	16 59	17 11	17 13	17 14	17 21
	d	15 01			15 16	15 22		15 42		16 01			16 16	16 22			16 46		17 01			17 15	17 22
Manchester Oxford Road	a	15 03			15 18	15 24		15 46		16 03			16 18	16 24			16 48		17 03			17 17	17 25
Deansgate	a					15 28								16 28									

Manchester Airport - Manchester

Network Diagram - see first Page of Table 78

		TP FX	NT	TP	NT	NT	TP	TP	NT	NT	TP	NT	NT	TP	TP	NT	NT	TP	TP	NT	NT	TP
		◇■ ⊼		◇■ ⊼			◇■ ⊼	◇■ ⊼			◇■			◇■	◇■			◇■	◇■			◇■
Crewe 10	84 d		16 34							17 33							18 34					
Wilmslow	84 d		16 57							17 56							18 57					
Manchester Airport	✈ d	17 05	17 17	17 35	17 41	17 46	17 55	18 00	18 03	18 17	18 35	18 41	18 46	18 55	19 00	19 03	19 09	19 20	19 29	19 41	19 46	19 55
Heald Green	d		17 20			17 49				18 20			18 49				19 12		19 33		19 49	
Gatley	d		17 23			17 52				18 23			18 52				19 15				19 52	
East Didsbury	d		17 26			17 55				18 26			18 55				19 18				19 55	
Burnage	d		17 28			17 57				18 28			18 57				19 20				19 57	
Mauldeth Road	d		17 30			17 59				18 30			18 59				19 22				19 59	
Manchester Piccadilly 10	a	17 22	17 42	17 52	17 59	18 11	18 13	18 14	18 18	18 42	18 52	18 59	19 11	19 13	19 14	19 18	19 31	19 36	19 44	19 59	20 11	20 13
	d				18 01			18 16	18 22			19 01			19 16	19 20	19 32		19 46	20 01		
Manchester Oxford Road	a				18 03			18 18	18 24			19 03			19 18	19 22	19 36		19 48	20 03		
Deansgate	a								18 28							19 26			19 51			

		TP	NT	NT	TP	TP	AW	TP	NT FO A	NT FX B	NT	TP	NT FX	TP	AW	NT FO	TP	TP	NT	NT	TP	TP	NT
		◇■			◇■	◇■		◇■				◇■		◇■			◇■	◇■			◇■	◇■	
Crewe 10	84 d																						
Wilmslow	84 d			19 56							20 56								21 55				22 56
Manchester Airport	✈ d	20 00	20 03	20 09	20 20	20 29	20 32	20 47	21 03	21 03	21 09	21 20	21 24	21 29	21 32	21 42	21 47	22 00	22 08	22 19	22 22	22 29	23 09
Heald Green	d			20 12		20 33		20 51			21 12			21 33			21 51		22 12			22 33	23 12
Gatley	d			20 15				20 54			21 15						21 54		22 15				23 15
East Didsbury	d			20 18				20 57			21 18						21 57		22 17				23 18
Burnage	d			20 20				20 59			21 20						21 59		22 19				23 20
Mauldeth Road	d			20 22				21 02			21 22						22 02		22 21				23 22
Manchester Piccadilly 10	a	20 14	20 18	20 32	20 36	20 44	20 48	21 13	21 19	21 18	21 32	21 36	21 38	21 44	21 48	21 59	22 13	22 14	22 31	22 34	22 36	22 44	23 33
	d	20 16	20 20	20 32		20 46	20 50		21 20	21 20	21 32			21 46	21 50	22 01		22 16	22 32	22 36		22 46	
Manchester Oxford Road	a	20 18	20 22	20 36		20 48	20 52		21 22	21 22	21 36			21 48	21 52	22 03		22 18	22 36	22 38		22 48	
Deansgate	a		20 26			20 51			21 26	21 26				21 51						22 41		22 51	

		TP	TP
		◇■	◇■
Crewe 10	84 d		
Wilmslow	84 d		
Manchester Airport	✈ d	23 18	23 52
Heald Green	d		
Gatley	d		
East Didsbury	d		
Burnage	d		
Mauldeth Road	d		
Manchester Piccadilly 10	a	23 34	00 09
	d		
Manchester Oxford Road	a		
Deansgate	a		

Saturdays

		TP	TP	TP	NT	TP	TP	NT	TP	AW	TP	TP	NT	TP	TP	NT	NT	TP	TP	TP	NT	TP	TP
		◇■	◇■	◇■		◇■	◇■		◇■	◇ ⊼	◇■	◇■ ⊼		◇■ ⊼	◇■ ⊼			◇■ ⊼	◇■ ⊼	◇■ ⊼		◇■ ⊼	◇■ ⊼
Crewe 10	84 d				00 44																06 33		
Wilmslow	84 d												05 46								06 57		
Manchester Airport	✈ d	23p52	00 01	00 38	01 20	04 00	04 15	04 34	05 20	05 33	05 37	05 45	06 01	06 18	06 23	06 41	06 46	06 55	07 00	07 05	07 17	07 25	07 33
Heald Green	d											05 49	06 04				06 49				07 20	07 30	
Gatley	d												06 07				06 52				07 23		
East Didsbury	d												06 10				06 55				07 26		
Burnage	d												06 12				06 57				07 28		
Mauldeth Road	d												06 14				06 59				07 30		
Manchester Piccadilly 10	a	00 09	00 15	00 51	01 36	04 14	04 29	04 47	05 35	05 48	05 51	06 00	06 25	06 31	06 39	06 56	07 11	07 13	07 14	07 22	07 42	07 43	07 48
	d									05 50		06 03		06 33		06 58			07 15				
Manchester Oxford Road	a									05 52		06 05		06 35		07 00			07 17				
Deansgate	a																						

		NT	NT	TP	TP	NT	TP	NT	TP	TP	NT	NT	TP	TP	NT	TP	NT	TP	TP	NT	NT	TP	TP
				◇■ ⊼	◇■ ⊼		◇■ ⊼		◇■ ⊼	◇■ ⊼			◇■ ⊼	◇■ ⊼		◇■ ⊼		◇■ ⊼	◇■ ⊼			◇■ ⊼	◇■ ⊼
Crewe 10	84 d							07 30									08 31						
Wilmslow	84 d							07 56									08 57						
Manchester Airport	✈ d	07 38	07 46	07 53	07 56	08 01	08 05	08 17	08 25	08 35	08 41	08 46	08 55	09 00	09 03	09 05	09 17	09 29	09 35	09 41	09 46	09 55	10 00
Heald Green	d	07 42	07 49			08 05		08 20	08 29			08 49					09 20	09 33			09 49		
Gatley	d	07 45	07 52		08 02			08 23	08 32			08 52					09 23				09 52		
East Didsbury	d	07 48	07 55		08 05			08 26	08 35			08 55					09 26				09 55		
Burnage	d		07 57					08 28				08 57					09 28				09 57		
Mauldeth Road	d		07 59					08 30				08 59					09 30				09 59		
Manchester Piccadilly 10	a	07 57	08 11	08 12	08 14	08 21	08 22	08 42	08 44	08 49	08 59	09 11	09 13	09 14	09 18	09 22	09 42	09 44	09 52	09 59	10 11	10 13	10 14
	d	07 59			08 15	08 22			08 46		09 01			09 16	09 22			09 46		10 01			10 16
Manchester Oxford Road	a	08 01			08 17	08 24			08 48		09 03			09 18	09 24			09 48		10 03			10 18
Deansgate	a					08 28			08 51						09 28			09 51					

A until 28 September

B until 27 September, from 1 October

Manchester Airport - Manchester

Network Diagram - see first Page of Table 78

Saturdays

		NT		TP	NT	TP	TP	NT	NT	TP	TP	NT		TP	NT	TP	TP	NT	NT	TP	TP	NT		TP	NT
				◇1		◇1 ⌶	◇1 ⌶			◇1 ⌶	◇1 ⌶			◇1 ⌶		◇1 ⌶	◇1 ⌶			◇1 ⌶	◇1 ⌶			◇1 ⌶	
Crewe 10	84 d				09 33										10 34										11 34
Wilmslow	84 d				09 57										10 57										11 57
Manchester Airport ✈	d	10 03		10 05	10 17	10 29	10 35	10 41	10 46	10 55	11 00	11 03		11 05	11 17	11 29	11 35	11 41	11 46	11 55	12 00	12 03		12 05	12 17
Heald Green	d				10 20	10 33			10 49						11 20	11 33			11 49						12 20
Gatley	d				10 23				10 52						11 23				11 52						12 23
East Didsbury	d				10 26				10 55						11 26				11 55						12 26
Burnage	d				10 28				10 57						11 28				11 57						12 28
Mauldeth Road	d				10 30				10 59						11 30				11 59						12 30
Manchester Piccadilly 10	a	10 18		10 22	10 42	10 44	10 52	10 59	11 11	11 13	11 14	11 18		11 22	11 42	11 44	11 52	11 59	12 11	12 13	12 14	12 18		12 22	12 42
	d	10 22				10 46		11 01			11 16	11 22				11 46		12 01			12 16	12 22			
Manchester Oxford Road	a	10 24				10 48		11 03			11 18	11 24				11 48		12 03			12 18	12 24			
Deansgate	a	10 28				10 51						11 28				11 51						12 28			

		TP	TP	NT	NT	TP	TP	NT		TP	NT	TP	TP	NT	NT	TP	TP	NT		TP	NT	TP	TP	NT	NT
		◇1 ⌶	◇1 ⌶			◇1 ⌶	◇1 ⌶			◇1 ⌶		◇1 ⌶	◇1 ⌶			◇1 ⌶	◇1 ⌶			◇1 ⌶		◇1 ⌶	◇1		
Crewe 10	84 d										12 34										13 34				
Wilmslow	84 d										12 57										13 57				
Manchester Airport ✈	d	12 29	12 35	12 41	12 46	12 55	13 00	13 03		13 05	13 17	13 29	13 35	13 41	13 46	13 55	14 00	14 03		14 05	14 17	14 29	14 35	14 41	14 46
Heald Green	d	12 33			12 49						13 20	13 33			13 49						14 20	14 33			14 49
Gatley	d				12 52						13 23				13 52						14 23				14 52
East Didsbury	d				12 55						13 26				13 55						14 26				14 55
Burnage	d				12 57						13 28				13 57						14 28				14 57
Mauldeth Road	d				12 59						13 30				13 59						14 30				14 59
Manchester Piccadilly 10	a	12 44	12 52	12 59	13 11	13 13	13 14	13 18		13 22	13 42	13 44	13 52	13 59	14 11	14 13	14 14	14 18		14 22	14 42	14 44	14 52	14 59	15 11
	d	12 46		13 01			13 16	13 22				13 46		14 01			14 16	14 22				14 46		15 01	
Manchester Oxford Road	a	12 48		13 03			13 18	13 24				13 48		14 03			14 18	14 24				14 48		15 03	
Deansgate	a	12 51						13 28				13 51						14 28				14 51			

		TP	TP	NT		TP	NT	TP	TP	NT	NT	TP	TP	NT		TP	NT	TP	TP	NT	NT	TP	TP	NT	
		◇1 ⌶	◇1 ⌶			◇1 ⌶		◇1 ⌶	◇1 ⌶			◇1 ⌶	◇1 ⌶			◇1		◇1 ⌶	◇1			◇1 ⌶	◇1 ⌶	A	
Crewe 10	84 d						14 34										15 33								
Wilmslow	84 d						14 57										15 56								
Manchester Airport ✈	d	14 55	15 00	15 03		15 05	15 17	15 29	15 35	15 41	15 46	15 55	16 00	16 03		16 05	16 17	16 29	16 35	16 41	16 46	16 55	17 00	17 03	
Heald Green	d						15 20	15 33			15 49						16 20	16 33			16 49				
Gatley	d						15 23				15 52						16 23				16 52				
East Didsbury	d						15 26				15 55						16 26				16 55				
Burnage	d						15 28				15 57						16 28				16 57				
Mauldeth Road	d						15 30				15 59						16 30				16 59				
Manchester Piccadilly 10	a	15 13	15 14	15 18		15 22	15 42	15 44	15 52	15 59	16 11	16 13	16 14	16 18		16 22	16 42	16 44	16 52	16 59	17 11	17 13	17 14	17 21	
	d		15 16	15 22				15 46		16 01			16 16	16 22				16 46		17 01			17 15	17 22	
Manchester Oxford Road	a		15 18	15 24				15 48		16 03			16 18	16 24				16 48		17 03			17 17	17 25	
Deansgate	a			15 28				15 51						16 28											

		NT	TP	NT	TP	NT	NT	TP	TP	NT		NT	TP	NT	NT	TP	TP	NT	NT	TP		TP	NT	NT	TP
		B	◇1		◇1			◇1 ⌶	◇1 ⌶				◇1			◇1	◇1			◇1		◇1			◇1
Crewe 10	84 d			16 34								17 33							18 34						
Wilmslow	84 d			16 57								17 56							18 57						
Manchester Airport ✈	d	17 03	17 05	17 17	17 35	17 41	17 46	17 55	18 00	18 03		18 17	18 35	18 41	18 46	18 55	19 00	19 03	19 09	19 20		19 29	19 41	19 46	19 55
Heald Green	d			17 20			17 49					18 20			18 49				19 12			19 33		19 49	
Gatley	d			17 23			17 52					18 23			18 52				19 15					19 52	
East Didsbury	d			17 26			17 55					18 26			18 55				19 18					19 55	
Burnage	d			17 28			17 57					18 28			18 57				19 20					19 57	
Mauldeth Road	d			17 30			17 59					18 30			18 59				19 22					19 59	
Manchester Piccadilly 10	a	17 21	17 22	17 42	17 52	17 59	18 11	18 13	18 14	18 18		18 42	18 52	18 59	19 11	19 13	19 14	19 18	19 31	19 36		19 44	19 59	20 11	20 13
	d	17 23				18 01			18 16	18 22				19 01			19 16	19 20	19 32			19 46	20 01		
Manchester Oxford Road	a	17 25				18 03			18 18	18 24				19 03			19 18	19 22	19 36			19 48	20 03		
Deansgate	a									18 28								19 26				19 51			

		TP	NT	NT	TP	TP		AW	TP	NT	NT	NT	TP	TP	NT	TP		TP	NT	NT	TP	TP	TP	TP	TP
		◇1			◇1	◇1			◇1	A	B		◇1	◇1		◇1		◇1			◇1	◇1	◇1 C	◇1 D	C 🚌
Crewe 10	84 d																								
Wilmslow	84 d			19 56								20 56							21 55						
Manchester Airport ✈	d	20 00	20 03	20 09	20 20	20 29		20 32	20 47	21 03	21 03	21 09	21 20	21 29	21 41	21 47		22 00	22 08	22 19	22 22	22 29	22 55	23 24	23 25
Heald Green	d			20 12		20 33			20 51			21 12		21 33		21 51			22 12			22 33			
Gatley	d			20 15					20 54			21 15				21 54			22 15						
East Didsbury	d			20 18					20 57			21 18				21 57			22 17						
Burnage	d			20 20					20 59			21 20				21 59			22 19						
Mauldeth Road	d			20 22					21 02			21 22				22 02			22 21						
Manchester Piccadilly 10	a	20 14	20 18	20 31	20 36	20 44		20 48	21 13	21 18	21 18	21 31	21 36	21 44	22 00	22 13		22 14	22 31	22 34	22 36	22 44	23 09	23 39	23 50
	d	20 16	20 20	20 32		20 46		20 50		21 20	21 22	21 32		21 46	22 01			22 16	22 32	22 36		22 46			
Manchester Oxford Road	a	20 18	20 22	20 36		20 48		20 52		21 22	21 24	21 36		21 48	22 03			22 18	22 36	22 38		22 48			
Deansgate	a		20 26			20 51				21 26	21 28			21 51						22 41		22 51			

A from 6 October
B until 29 September
C from 27 October
D until 20 October

Manchester Airport - Manchester

Network Diagram - see first Page of Table 78

Saturdays

		NT
Crewe 10	84 d	
Wilmslow	84 d	23 15
Manchester Airport ✈	d	23 27
Heald Green	d	23 30
Gatley	d	23 33
East Didsbury	d	23 36
Burnage	d	23 38
Mauldeth Road	d	23 40
Manchester Piccadilly 10	a	23 51
	d	
Manchester Oxford Road	a	
Deansgate	a	

Sundays

until 24 June

		TP	TP	TP	TP	NT	NT	TP	TP	NT		NT	TP	TP	TP	TP	NT	TP	NT	TP		TP	NT	TP	NT
		🚌	🚌	🚌	◇1			◇1	◇1				◇1	◇1	◇1 ⌶	◇1		◇1		◇1 ⌶		◇1		◇1	
Crewe 10	84 d																								
Wilmslow	84 d																								
Manchester Airport ✈	d	00 05	01 20	05 30	06 11	06 14	07 30	07 50	07 55	08 24		08 34	08 40	08 47	09 00	09 03	09 06	09 30	09 35	10 00		10 03	10 06	10 30	10 35
Heald Green	d					06 17	07 33			08 27							09 09						10 09		
Gatley	d					06 20	07 36			08 30							09 12						10 12		
East Didsbury	d					06 23	07 39			08 33							09 15						10 15		
Burnage	d					06 25	07 41			08 35							09 17						10 17		
Mauldeth Road	d					06 27	07 43			08 37							09 19						10 19		
Manchester Piccadilly 10	a	00 30	01 45	05 55	06 24	06 36	07 54	08 03	08 08	08 47		08 47	08 54	09 01	09 14	09 19	09 29	09 44	09 48	10 14		10 18	10 26	10 44	10 48
	d								08 11			08 49		09 03	09 16			09 46	09 50	10 16				10 46	10 50
Manchester Oxford Road	a								08 13			08 51		09 05	09 18			09 48	09 52	10 18				10 48	10 52
Deansgate	a								08 16			08 54		09 08				09 51						10 51	

		TP	TP	TP	NT	TP		NT	TP	TP	NT	TP	NT	TP	TP	TP		NT	TP	NT	TP	TP	TP	NT	TP
		◇1	◇1	◇1		◇1			◇1 ⌶	◇1		◇1		◇1	◇1 ⌶	◇1			◇1		◇1	◇1 ⌶	◇1		◇1
Crewe 10	84 d																								
Wilmslow	84 d				10 43													12 54							
Manchester Airport ✈	d	10 44	11 00	11 03	11 05	11 30		11 33	12 00	12 03	12 08	12 30	12 35	12 55	12 58	13 03		13 09	13 30	13 35	13 55	13 58	14 03	14 09	14 30
Heald Green	d				11 08						12 11							13 12						14 12	
Gatley	d				11 11						12 14							13 15						14 15	
East Didsbury	d				11 14						12 17							13 18						14 18	
Burnage	d				11 16						12 19							13 20						14 20	
Mauldeth Road	d				11 18						12 21							13 22						14 22	
Manchester Piccadilly 10	a	10 58	11 14	11 18	11 25	11 44		11 48	12 14	12 18	12 29	12 44	12 49	13 09	13 14	13 18		13 31	13 44	13 48	14 09	14 14	14 18	14 31	14 44
	d		11 16		11 27	11 46		11 50	12 16		12 29	12 46	12 50		13 16				13 46	13 50		14 16			14 46
Manchester Oxford Road	a		11 18		11 31	11 48		11 52	12 18		12 33	12 48	12 52		13 18				13 48	13 52		14 18			14 48
Deansgate	a					11 51						12 51							13 51						14 51

		NT		TP	TP	TP	NT	TP	NT	TP	TP	TP		NT	TP	NT	TP	TP	TP	NT	TP	NT		TP	TP
				◇1	◇1	◇1		◇1		◇1	◇1 ⌶	◇1			◇1		◇1	◇1 ⌶	◇1		◇1			◇1	◇1 ⌶
Crewe 10	84 d																								
Wilmslow	84 d						14 54													16 54					
Manchester Airport ✈	d	14 35		14 55	14 58	15 03	15 09	15 30	15 35	15 55	15 58	16 03		16 09	16 30	16 35	16 55	16 58	17 03	17 09	17 30	17 35		17 55	17 58
Heald Green	d						15 11							16 12						17 12					
Gatley	d						15 14							16 15						17 15					
East Didsbury	d						15 18							16 18						17 18					
Burnage	d						15 20							16 20						17 20					
Mauldeth Road	d						15 22							16 22						17 22					
Manchester Piccadilly 10	a	14 48		15 09	15 14	15 18	15 32	15 44	15 48	16 09	16 14	16 18		16 31	16 44	16 48	17 09	17 14	17 18	17 31	17 44	17 48		18 09	18 14
	d	14 50			15 16			15 46	15 50		16 16				16 46	16 50		17 16			17 46	17 50			18 16
Manchester Oxford Road	a	14 52			15 18			15 48	15 52		16 18				16 48	16 52		17 18			17 48	17 52			18 18
Deansgate	a							15 51							16 51						17 51				

		TP	NT	TP	NT	TP	TP	TP		NT	TP	NT	TP	TP	NT	TP	NT	TP		TP	NT	TP	NT	TP	NT
		◇1		◇1		◇1	◇1	◇1			◇1		◇1	◇1		◇1		◇1		◇1		◇1		◇1	
Crewe 10	84 d																								
Wilmslow	84 d									18 54											20 54				
Manchester Airport ✈	d	18 03	18 09	18 30	18 35	18 55	18 58	19 03		19 09	19 30	19 35	19 55	20 03	20 09	20 30	20 35	20 55		21 03	21 09	21 30	21 35	21 55	22 09
Heald Green	d		18 12							19 12					20 12						21 12				22 12
Gatley	d		18 15							19 15					20 15						21 15				22 15
East Didsbury	d		18 18							19 18					20 18						21 18				22 18
Burnage	d		18 20							19 20					20 20						21 20				22 20
Mauldeth Road	d		18 22							19 22					20 22						21 22				22 22
Manchester Piccadilly 10	a	18 18	18 31	18 44	18 48	19 09	19 14	19 18		19 31	19 44	19 48	20 09	20 18	20 31	20 44	20 48	21 09		21 18	21 31	21 44	21 48	22 09	22 31
	d			18 46	18 50		19 16				19 46	19 50				20 46	20 50					21 46	21 50		
Manchester Oxford Road	a			18 48	18 52		19 18				19 48	19 52				20 48	20 52					21 48	21 52		
Deansgate	a			18 51							19 51					20 51						21 51			

Table 85

Manchester Airport - Manchester

Sundays
until 24 June

Network Diagram - see first Page of Table 78

	TP	NT	TP
	◇1		◇1
Crewe 10 84 d			
Wilmslow 84 d		22 54	
Manchester Airport ✈ d	22 55	23 09	23 22
Heald Green d		23 12	
Gatley d		23 15	
East Didsbury d		23 18	
Burnage d		23 20	
Mauldeth Road d		23 22	
Manchester Piccadilly 10 a	23 09	23 29	23 35
d			
Manchester Oxford Road a			
Deansgate a			

Sundays
1 July to 9 September

	TP	TP	TP	TP	NT	TP	TP	NT	TP	TP	NT	NT	TP	TP	TP	NT	TP	TP	NT	TP	NT	TP
	[bus]	◇1	◇1	[bus]		◇1	◇1		◇1	◇1			◇1	◇1	◇1 [trolley]		◇1	◇1		◇1 [trolley]		◇1
Crewe 10 84 d																						
Wilmslow 84 d																						
Manchester Airport ✈ d	00 05	01 22	04 43	05 30	06 14	06 24	07 24	07 30	07 55	08 06	08 24	08 34	08 40	08 47	09 00	09 06	09 22	09 30	09 35	10 00	10 06	10 20
Heald Green d					06 17			07 33			08 27					09 09					10 09	
Gatley d					06 20			07 36			08 30					09 12					10 12	
East Didsbury d					06 23			07 39			08 33					09 15					10 15	
Burnage d					06 25			07 41			08 35					09 17					10 17	
Mauldeth Road d					06 27			07 43			08 37					09 19					10 19	
Manchester Piccadilly 10 a	00 30	01 36	04 57	05 55	06 36	06 38	07 37	07 54	08 08	08 24	08 47	08 47	08 54	09 01	09 14	09 29	09 37	09 44	09 48	10 14	10 26	10 37
d									08 11			08 49		09 03	09 16			09 46	09 50	10 16		
Manchester Oxford Road a									08 13			08 51		09 05	09 18			09 48	09 52	10 18		
Deansgate a									08 16			08 54		09 08				09 51				

	TP	NT	TP	TP	NT	TP	TP	NT	TP	NT	TP	TP	NT	TP	TP	NT	TP	TP	NT	TP	TP	NT
	◇1		◇1	◇1		◇1	◇1		◇1 [trolley]		◇1	◇1		◇1	◇1 [trolley]		◇1	◇1		◇1	◇1 [trolley]	
Crewe 10 84 d																						
Wilmslow 84 d					10 43											12 54						
Manchester Airport ✈ d	10 30	10 35	10 44	11 00	11 05	11 20	11 30	11 33	12 00	12 08	12 20	12 30	12 35	12 55	13 00	13 09	13 20	13 30	13 35	13 55	14 00	14 09
Heald Green d					11 08					12 11						13 12						14 12
Gatley d					11 11					12 14						13 15						14 15
East Didsbury d					11 14					12 17						13 18						14 18
Burnage d					11 16					12 19						13 20						14 20
Mauldeth Road d					11 18					12 21						13 22						14 22
Manchester Piccadilly 10 a	10 44	10 48	10 58	11 14	11 25	11 35	11 44	11 48	12 14	12 29	12 37	12 44	12 49	13 09	13 14	13 31	13 37	13 44	13 48	14 09	14 14	14 31
d	10 46	10 50		11 16	11 27		11 46	11 50	12 16	12 29		12 46	12 50		13 16			13 46	13 50		14 16	
Manchester Oxford Road a	10 48	10 52		11 18	11 31		11 48	11 52	12 18	12 33		12 48	12 52		13 18			13 48	13 52		14 18	
Deansgate a	10 51						11 51					12 51						13 51				

	TP	TP	NT	TP	TP	NT	TP	TP	NT	TP	TP	NT	TP	TP	NT	TP	TP	NT	TP	TP	NT
	◇1	◇1		◇1	◇1		◇1	◇1		◇1	◇1 [trolley]		◇1	◇1		◇1	◇1 [trolley]		◇1	◇1	
Crewe 10 84 d																					
Wilmslow 84 d						14 54												16 54			
Manchester Airport ✈ d	14 20	14 30	14 35	14 55	15 00	15 09	15 20	15 30	15 35	15 55	16 00	16 09	16 20	16 30	16 35	16 55	17 00	17 09	17 20	17 30	17 35
Heald Green d						15 11						16 12						17 12			
Gatley d						15 14						16 15						17 15			
East Didsbury d						15 18						16 18						17 18			
Burnage d						15 20						16 20						17 20			
Mauldeth Road d						15 22						16 22						17 22			
Manchester Piccadilly 10 a	14 37	14 44	14 48	15 09	15 14	15 32	15 37	15 44	15 48	16 09	16 14	16 31	16 37	16 44	16 48	17 09	17 14	17 31	17 37	17 44	17 48
d		14 46	14 50		15 16			15 46	15 50		16 16			16 46	16 50		17 16			17 46	17 50
Manchester Oxford Road a		14 48	14 52		15 18			15 48	15 52		16 18			16 48	16 52		17 18			17 48	17 52
Deansgate a		14 51						15 51						16 51						17 51	

	TP	TP	NT	TP	TP	NT	TP	TP	NT	TP	TP	NT	TP	NT	TP	TP	NT	TP	NT	TP	TP	NT
	◇1	◇1 [trolley]		◇1	◇1		◇1	◇1		◇1	◇1		◇1		◇1	◇1		◇1		◇1	◇1	
Crewe 10 84 d																						
Wilmslow 84 d									18 54										20 54			
Manchester Airport ✈ d	17 55	18 00	18 09	18 20	18 30	18 35	18 55	19 00	19 09	19 20	19 30	19 35	19 55	20 09	20 20	20 30	20 35	20 55	21 09	21 20	21 30	21 35
Heald Green d			18 12						19 12					20 12					21 12			
Gatley d			18 15						19 15					20 15					21 15			
East Didsbury d			18 18						19 18					20 18					21 18			
Burnage d			18 20						19 20					20 20					21 20			
Mauldeth Road d			18 22						19 22					20 22					21 22			
Manchester Piccadilly 10 a	18 09	18 14	18 31	18 37	18 44	18 48	19 09	19 14	19 31	19 37	19 44	19 48	20 09	20 31	20 37	20 44	20 48	21 09	21 31	21 37	21 44	21 48
d		18 16			18 46	18 50		19 16			19 46	19 50				20 46	20 50				21 46	21 50
Manchester Oxford Road a		18 18			18 48	18 52		19 18			19 48	19 52				20 48	20 52				21 48	21 52
Deansgate a					18 51						19 51					20 51					21 51	

Table 85

Manchester Airport - Manchester

Sundays
1 July to 9 September

Network Diagram - see first Page of Table 78

	TP	NT	TP	NT	TP
	◇1		◇1		◇1
Crewe 10 84 d					
Wilmslow 84 d				22 54	
Manchester Airport ✈ d	21 55	22 09	22 55	23 09	23 20
Heald Green d		22 12		23 12	
Gatley d		22 15		23 15	
East Didsbury d		22 18		23 18	
Burnage d		22 20		23 20	
Mauldeth Road d		22 22		23 22	
Manchester Piccadilly 10 a	22 09	22 31	23 09	23 29	23 37
d					
Manchester Oxford Road a					
Deansgate a					

Sundays
16 September to 21 October

	TP	TP	TP	TP	NT	NT	TP	TP	NT	TP	TP	TP	TP	NT	TP	NT	TP	TP	NT	TP	NT	TP
	[bus]	[bus]	[bus]	◇1			◇1	◇1		◇1	◇1	◇1 [trolley]	◇1		◇1		◇1 [trolley]	◇1		◇1		◇1
Crewe 10 84 d																						
Wilmslow 84 d																						
Manchester Airport ✈ d	00 05	01 20	05 30	06 11	06 14	07 09	07 47	07 50	08 34	08 40	08 47	09 00	09 03	09 06	09 29	09 35	10 00	10 03	10 06	10 30	10 35	10 44
Heald Green d					06 17	07 12								09 09					10 09			
Gatley d					06 20	07 15								09 12					10 12			
East Didsbury d					06 23	07 18								09 15					10 15			
Burnage d					06 25	07 20								09 17					10 17			
Mauldeth Road d					06 27	07 22								09 19					10 19			
Manchester Piccadilly 10 a	00 30	01 45	05 55	06 24	06 36	07 31	08 00	08 04	08 47	08 54	09 01	09 14	09 19	09 29	09 42	09 48	10 12	10 17	10 26	10 44	10 48	10 58
d							08 02		08 49		09 03	09 16			09 46	09 50	10 14			10 46	10 50	
Manchester Oxford Road a							08 04		08 51		09 05	09 18			09 48	09 52	10 16			10 48	10 52	
Deansgate a							08 07		08 54		09 08				09 51					10 51		

	TP	NT	TP	NT	TP	TP	NT	TP	NT	TP	TP	TP	NT	TP	NT	TP	TP	TP	NT	TP	NT	TP
	◇1		◇1		◇1 [trolley]	◇1		◇1		◇1	◇1 [trolley]	◇1		◇1		◇1	◇1 [trolley]	◇1		◇1		◇1
Crewe 10 84 d																						
Wilmslow 84 d		10 43											12 54									
Manchester Airport ✈ d	11 03	11 05	11 30	11 33	12 00	12 03	12 08	12 30	12 35	12 55	12 58	13 03	13 09	13 30	13 35	13 55	13 58	14 03	14 09	14 30	14 35	14 55
Heald Green d		11 08					12 11						13 12						14 12			
Gatley d		11 11					12 14						13 15						14 15			
East Didsbury d		11 14					12 17						13 18						14 18			
Burnage d		11 16					12 19						13 20						14 20			
Mauldeth Road d		11 18					12 21						13 22						14 22			
Manchester Piccadilly 10 a	11 18	11 25	11 44	11 48	12 14	12 18	12 29	12 44	12 49	13 09	13 14	13 18	13 31	13 44	13 48	14 09	14 14	14 18	14 31	14 44	14 48	15 09
d		11 27	11 46	11 50	12 16		12 29	12 46	12 50		13 16			13 46	13 50		14 16			14 46	14 50	
Manchester Oxford Road a		11 31	11 48	11 52	12 18		12 33	12 48	12 52		13 18			13 48	13 52		14 18			14 48	14 52	
Deansgate a			11 51					12 51						13 51						14 51		

	TP	TP	NT	TP	NT	TP	TP	TP	NT	TP	NT	TP	TP	TP	NT	TP	NT	TP	TP	TP	NT
	◇1	◇1		◇1		◇1	◇1 [trolley]	◇1		◇1		◇1	◇1 [trolley]	◇1		◇1		◇1	◇1 [trolley]	◇1	
Crewe 10 84 d																					
Wilmslow 84 d			14 54												16 54						
Manchester Airport ✈ d	14 58	15 03	15 09	15 30	15 35	15 55	15 58	16 03	16 09	16 30	16 35	16 55	16 58	17 03	17 09	17 30	17 35	17 55	17 58	18 03	18 09
Heald Green d			15 11						16 12						17 12						18 12
Gatley d			15 14						16 15						17 15						18 15
East Didsbury d			15 18						16 18						17 18						18 18
Burnage d			15 20						16 20						17 20						18 20
Mauldeth Road d			15 22						16 22						17 22						18 22
Manchester Piccadilly 10 a	15 14	15 18	15 32	15 44	15 48	16 09	16 14	16 18	16 31	16 44	16 48	17 09	17 14	17 18	17 31	17 44	17 48	18 09	18 14	18 18	18 31
d	15 16			15 46	15 50		16 16			16 46	16 50		17 16			17 46	17 50		18 16		
Manchester Oxford Road a	15 18			15 48	15 52		16 18			16 48	16 52		17 18			17 48	17 52		18 18		
Deansgate a				15 51						16 51						17 51					

	TP	NT	TP	TP	TP	NT	TP	NT	TP	TP	NT	TP	NT	TP	TP	NT	TP	NT	TP	NT	TP	NT
	◇1		◇1	◇1	◇1		◇1		◇1	◇1		◇1		◇1	◇1		◇1		◇1		◇1	
Crewe 10 84 d																						
Wilmslow 84 d						18 54										20 54						22 54
Manchester Airport ✈ d	18 30	18 35	18 55	18 58	19 03	19 09	19 30	19 35	19 55	20 03	20 09	20 30	20 35	20 55	21 03	21 09	21 30	21 35	21 55	22 09	22 55	23 09
Heald Green d						19 12					20 12					21 12				22 12		23 12
Gatley d						19 15					20 15					21 15				22 15		23 15
East Didsbury d						19 18					20 18					21 18				22 18		23 18
Burnage d						19 20					20 20					21 20				22 20		23 20
Mauldeth Road d						19 22					20 22					21 22				22 22		23 22
Manchester Piccadilly 10 a	18 44	18 48	19 09	19 14	19 18	19 31	19 44	19 48	20 09	20 18	20 31	20 44	20 48	21 09	21 18	21 31	21 44	21 48	22 09	22 31	23 09	23 29
d	18 46	18 50		19 16			19 46	19 50				20 46	20 50				21 46	21 50				
Manchester Oxford Road a	18 48	18 52		19 18			19 48	19 52				20 48	20 52				21 48	21 52				
Deansgate a	18 51						19 51					20 51					21 51					

Table 85

Manchester Airport - Manchester

Sundays

16 September to 21 October

Network Diagram - see first Page of Table 78

			TP
			◇1
Crewe [10]	84	d	
Wilmslow	84	d	
Manchester Airport	✈	d	23 22
Heald Green		d	
Gatley		d	
East Didsbury		d	
Burnage		d	
Mauldeth Road		d	
Manchester Piccadilly [10]	🚇	a	23 35
		d	
Manchester Oxford Road		a	
Deansgate	🚇	a	

Sundays

from 28 October

			TP	TP	TP	TP	TP	NT	NT	TP	NT		TP	TP	TP	TP	NT	TP	NT	TP	TP		NT	TP	NT	TP
										◇1			◇1	◇1	◇1	◇1		◇1		◇1	◇1			◇1		◇1
			🚌	🚌	🚌	🚌	🚌	🚌	🚌						⊼					⊼						
Crewe [10]	84	d																								
Wilmslow	84	d																								
Manchester Airport	✈	d	00 05	01 20	05 05	05 30	06 05	06 10	07 10	07 47	08 34		08 40	08 47	09 00	09 03	09 06	09 29	09 35	10 00	10 03		10 06	10 30	10 35	10 44
Heald Green		d						06 15	07 15								09 09						10 09			
Gatley		d						06 23	07 23								09 12						10 12			
East Didsbury		d						06 31	07 31								09 15						10 15			
Burnage		d						06 36	07 36								09 17						10 17			
Mauldeth Road		d						06 41	07 41								09 19						10 19			
Manchester Piccadilly [10]	🚇	a	00 30	01 45	05 30	05 55	06 30	06 52	07 52	08 00	08 47		08 54	09 01	09 14	09 19	09 29	09 42	09 48	10 14	10 18		10 26	10 44	10 48	10 58
		d								08 02	08 49			09 03	09 15			09 46	09 50	10 16				10 46	10 50	
Manchester Oxford Road		a								08 04	08 51			09 05	09 17			09 48	09 52	10 18				10 48	10 52	
Deansgate	🚇	a								08 07	08 54			09 08				09 51						10 51		

			TP	NT	TP	NT	TP		TP	NT	TP	NT	TP	TP	TP	NT	TP		NT	TP	TP	TP	NT	TP	NT	TP
			◇1		◇1		◇1		◇1		◇1		◇1	◇1	◇1		◇1			◇1	◇1	◇1		◇1		◇1
							⊼							⊼							⊼					
Crewe [10]	84	d																								
Wilmslow	84	d		10 43												12 54										
Manchester Airport	✈	d	11 03	11 05	11 30	11 33	12 00		12 03	12 08	12 30	12 35	12 55	12 58	13 03	13 09	13 30		13 35	13 55	13 58	14 03	14 09	14 30	14 35	14 55
Heald Green		d		11 08						12 11						13 12							14 12			
Gatley		d		11 11						12 14						13 15							14 15			
East Didsbury		d		11 14						12 17						13 18							14 18			
Burnage		d		11 16						12 19						13 20							14 20			
Mauldeth Road		d		11 18						12 21						13 22							14 22			
Manchester Piccadilly [10]	🚇	a	11 18	11 25	11 44	11 48	12 14		12 18	12 29	12 44	12 49	13 09	13 14	13 18	13 31	13 44		13 48	14 09	14 14	14 18	14 31	14 44	14 48	15 09
		d		11 27	11 46	11 50	12 16			12 29	12 46	12 50		13 16			13 46		13 50		14 16			14 46	14 50	
Manchester Oxford Road		a		11 31	11 48	11 52	12 18			12 33	12 48	12 52		13 18			13 48		13 52		14 18			14 48	14 52	
Deansgate	🚇	a			11 51						12 51						13 51							14 51		

			TP		TP	NT	TP	NT	TP	TP	TP	NT	TP		NT	TP	TP	TP	NT	TP	NT	TP	TP		TP	NT
			◇1		◇1		◇1		◇1	◇1	◇1		◇1			◇1	◇1	◇1		◇1		◇1	◇1		◇1	
										⊼							⊼						⊼			
Crewe [10]	84	d																								
Wilmslow	84	d				14 54													16 54							
Manchester Airport	✈	d	14 58		15 03	15 09	15 30	15 35	15 55	15 58	16 03	16 09	16 30		16 35	16 55	16 58	17 03	17 09	17 30	17 35	17 55	17 58		18 03	18 09
Heald Green		d				15 11						16 12							17 12							18 12
Gatley		d				15 14						16 15							17 15							18 15
East Didsbury		d				15 18						16 18							17 18							18 18
Burnage		d				15 20						16 20							17 20							18 20
Mauldeth Road		d				15 22						16 22							17 22							18 22
Manchester Piccadilly [10]	🚇	a	15 14		15 18	15 32	15 44	15 48	16 09	16 14	16 18	16 31	16 44		16 48	17 09	17 14	17 18	17 31	17 44	17 48	18 09	18 14		18 18	18 31
		d	15 16				15 46	15 50		16 16			16 46		16 50		17 16			17 46	17 50		18 16			
Manchester Oxford Road		a	15 18				15 48	15 52		16 18			16 48		16 52		17 18			17 48	17 52		18 18			
Deansgate	🚇	a					15 51						16 51							17 51						

			TP	NT	TP	TP	TP	NT	TP		NT	TP	TP	NT	TP	NT	TP	TP	NT		TP	NT	TP	NT	TP	NT
			◇1		◇1	◇1	◇1		◇1			◇1	◇1		◇1		◇1	◇1			◇1		◇1		◇1	
Crewe [10]	84	d																								
Wilmslow	84	d						18 54											20 54							22 54
Manchester Airport	✈	d	18 30	18 35	18 55	18 58	19 03	19 09	19 30		19 35	19 55	20 03	20 09	20 30	20 35	20 55	21 03	21 09		21 30	21 35	21 55	22 09	22 55	23 09
Heald Green		d						19 12						20 12					21 12					22 12		23 12
Gatley		d						19 15						20 15					21 15					22 15		23 15
East Didsbury		d						19 18						20 18					21 18					22 18		23 18
Burnage		d						19 20						20 20					21 20					22 20		23 20
Mauldeth Road		d						19 22						20 22					21 22					22 22		23 22
Manchester Piccadilly [10]	🚇	a	18 44	18 48	19 09	19 14	19 18	19 31	19 44		19 48	20 09	20 18	20 31	20 44	20 48	21 09	21 18	21 31		21 44	21 48	22 09	22 31	23 09	23 29
		d	18 46	18 50		19 16			19 46		19 50				20 46	20 50					21 46	21 50				
Manchester Oxford Road		a	18 48	18 52		19 18			19 48		19 52				20 48	20 52					21 48	21 52				
Deansgate	🚇	a	18 51						19 51						20 51						21 51					

			TP
			◇1
Crewe [10]	84	d	
Wilmslow	84	d	
Manchester Airport	✈	d	23 22
Heald Green		d	
Gatley		d	
East Didsbury		d	
Burnage		d	
Mauldeth Road		d	
Manchester Piccadilly [10]	🚇	a	23 35
		d	
Manchester Oxford Road		a	
Deansgate	🚇	a	

Table 86

Manchester - Hazel Grove and Buxton

Mondays to Fridays

until 28 September

Network Diagram - see first Page of Table 78

Miles				NT MX	NT A	NT	NT	NT B	NT	NT C	NT	NT D		NT	NT D	NT	NT D	NT	NT D	NT	NT D	NT		NT D	NT	NT D
—	Deansgate	🚇	d					07 11		08 12		09 12			10 12		11 12		12 12		13 12			14 12		15 12
—	Manchester Oxford Road		d					07 15		08 15		09 16			10 16		11 16		12 16		13 16			14 16		15 16
0	**Manchester Picc. [10]**	84 🚇	d	23p10	05 50	06 21	06 49	07 21	07 52	08 20	08 52	09 21		09 52	10 21	10 52	11 21	11 52	12 21	12 52	13 21	13 52		14 21	14 52	15 21
3	Levenshulme	84	d			06 28	06 55	07 28		08 28	08 58	09 28		09 58	10 28	10 58	11 28	11 58	12 28	12 58	13 28	13 58		14 28	14 58	15 28
4½	Heaton Chapel	84	d			06 31	06 58	07 31		08 31	09 01	09 31		10 01	10 31	11 01	11 31	12 01	12 31	13 01	13 31	14 01		14 31	15 01	15 31
6	**Stockport**	84	d	23p20	06 00	06 35	07 02	07 35	08 01	08 35	09 05	09 35		10 05	10 35	11 05	11 35	12 05	12 35	13 05	13 35	14 05		14 35	15 05	15 35
7	Davenport		d	23p23		06 39	07 06	07 39	08 05	08 39	09 09	09 39		10 09	10 39	11 09	11 39	12 09	12 39	13 09	13 39	14 09		14 39	15 09	15 39
7¾	Woodsmoor		d	23p25		06 41	07 08	07 41	08 07	08 41	09 11	09 41		10 11	10 41	11 11	11 41	12 11	12 41	13 11	13 41	14 11		14 41	15 11	15 41
8¾	**Hazel Grove**		a	23p27	06 06	06 45	07 10	07 45	08 09	08 48	09 13	09 45		10 13	10 45	11 13	11 45	12 13	12 45	13 13	13 45	14 13		14 45	15 13	15 47
—			d	23p28			07 10		08 10		09 13			10 13		11 13		12 13		13 13		14 13			15 13	
11	Middlewood		d	23p32			07 15				09 18			10 18				12 18				14 18				
12½	Disley		d	23p36			07 19		08 17		09 22			10 22		11 20		12 22		13 20		14 22			15 20	
14¼	New Mills Newtown		d	23p40			07 22		08 20		09 25			10 25		11 24		12 25		13 24		14 25			15 24	
15¼	Furness Vale		d	23p42			07 25		08 23		09 28			10 28		11 26		12 28		13 26		14 28			15 26	
16¼	Whaley Bridge		d	23p45			07 28		08 26		09 31			10 31		11 29		12 31		13 29		14 31			15 29	
20½	Chapel-en-le-Frith		d	23p52			07 35		08 33		09 38			10 38		11 36		12 38		13 36		14 38			15 36	
22¾	Dove Holes		d	23p57			07 40				09 43			10 43				12 43				14 43				
25¾	**Buxton**		a	00 07			07 50		08 44		09 53			10 53		11 50		12 53		13 50		14 53			15 50	

			NT	NT D	NT	NT	NT D	NT E		NT	NT B	NT	NT	NT	NT	NT	NT
Deansgate	🚇	d		16 12			17 15				18 12						
Manchester Oxford Road		d		16 16			17 19				18 16						
Manchester Picc. [10]	84 🚇	d	15 52	16 21	16 51	16 58	17 23	17 23		17 52	18 21	18 52	19 22	19 51	20 51	21 52	23 10
Levenshulme	84	d	15 58	16 28		17 03		17 28		17 58	18 28	18 58	19 28	19 58	20 58	21 58	
Heaton Chapel	84	d	16 01	16 31		17 06		17 31		18 01	18 31	19 01	19 31	20 01	21 01	22 01	
Stockport	84	d	16 05	16 35	17 03	17 10	17 32	17 35		18 05	18 35	19 05	19 35	20 05	21 05	22 05	23 20
Davenport		d	16 09	16 39	17 06	17 14		17 39		18 09	18 39	19 09	19 39	20 09	21 09	22 09	23 23
Woodsmoor		d	16 11	16 41	17 08	17 16		17 41		18 11	18 41	19 11	19 41	20 11	21 11	22 11	23 25
Hazel Grove		a	16 13	16 43	17 10	17 20	17 39	17 43		18 13	18 43	19 13	19 45	20 13	21 13	22 13	23 27
		d	16 13	16 46	17 11		17 39			18 13	18 46	19 13		20 13	21 13	22 13	23 28
Middlewood		d	16 18		17 15					18 18		19 18		20 18	21 18	22 18	23 32
Disley		d	16 22	16 53	17 19		17 46			18 22	18 53	19 22		20 22	21 22	22 22	23 36
New Mills Newtown		d	16 25	16 56	17 23		17 50			18 25	18 56	19 25		20 25	21 25	22 25	23 40
Furness Vale		d	16 28	16 59	17 26		17 52			18 28	18 59	19 28		20 28	21 28	22 28	23 42
Whaley Bridge		d	16 31	17 02	17 29		17 55			18 31	19 02	19 31		20 31	21 31	22 31	23 45
Chapel-en-le-Frith		d	16 38	17 09	17 36		18 03			18 38	19 09	19 38		20 38	21 38	22 38	23 52
Dove Holes		d	16 43		17 41					18 43		19 43		20 43	21 43	22 43	23 57
Buxton		a	16 53	17 22	17 51		18 16			18 54	19 22	19 53		20 53	21 53	22 53	00 07

Mondays to Fridays

from 1 October

			NT MX	NT A	NT	NT	NT B	NT	NT C	NT	NT D		NT	NT D	NT	NT D	NT	NT D	NT	NT D	NT		NT D	NT	NT D	NT
Deansgate	🚇	d					07 11		08 12		09 12			10 12		11 12		12 12		13 12			14 12		15 12	
Manchester Oxford Road		d					07 15		08 15		09 16			10 16		11 16		12 16		13 16			14 16		15 16	
Manchester Picc. [10]	84 🚇	d	23p10	05 50	06 21	06 49	07 21	07 52	08 20	08 52	09 21		09 52	10 21	10 52	11 21	11 52	12 21	12 52	13 21	13 52		14 21	14 52	15 21	15 52
Levenshulme	84	d			06 28	06 55	07 28		08 28	08 58	09 28		09 58	10 28	10 58	11 28	11 58	12 28	12 58	13 28	13 58		14 28	14 58	15 28	15 58
Heaton Chapel	84	d			06 31	06 58	07 31		08 31	09 01	09 31		10 01	10 31	11 01	11 31	12 01	12 31	13 01	13 31	14 01		14 31	15 01	15 31	16 01
Stockport	84	d	23p20	06 00	06 35	07 02	07 35	08 01	08 35	09 05	09 35		10 05	10 35	11 05	11 35	12 05	12 35	13 05	13 35	14 05		14 35	15 05	15 35	16 05
Davenport		d	23p23		06 39	07 06	07 39	08 05	08 39	09 09	09 39		10 09	10 39	11 09	11 39	12 09	12 39	13 09	13 39	14 09		14 39	15 09	15 39	16 09
Woodsmoor		d	23p25		06 41	07 08	07 41	08 07	08 41	09 11	09 41		10 11	10 41	11 11	11 41	12 11	12 41	13 11	13 41	14 11		14 41	15 11	15 41	16 11
Hazel Grove		a	23p27	06 06	06 47	07 10	07 47	08 09	08 50	09 13	09 47		10 13	10 47	11 13	11 45	12 13	12 47	13 13	13 47	14 13		14 47	15 13	15 50	16 13
		d	23p28			07 10		08 10		09 13			10 13		11 13		12 13		13 13		14 13			15 13		16 13
Middlewood		d	23p32			07 15				09 18			10 18				12 18				14 18					16 18
Disley		d	23p36			07 19		08 17		09 22			10 22		11 20		12 22		13 20		14 22			15 20		16 22
New Mills Newtown		d	23p40			07 22		08 20		09 25			10 25		11 24		12 25		13 24		14 25			15 24		16 25
Furness Vale		d	23p42			07 25		08 23		09 28			10 28		11 26		12 28		13 26		14 28			15 26		16 28
Whaley Bridge		d	23p45			07 28		08 26		09 31			10 31		11 29		12 31		13 29		14 31			15 29		16 31
Chapel-en-le-Frith		d	23p52			07 35		08 33		09 38			10 38		11 36		12 38		13 36		14 38			15 36		16 38
Dove Holes		d	23p57			07 40				09 43			10 43				12 43				14 43					16 43
Buxton		a	00 09			07 52		08 44		09 55			10 55		11 52		12 55		13 52		14 55			15 52		16 55

			NT D	NT	NT	NT D	NT E		NT	NT B	NT	NT	NT	NT	NT	NT
Deansgate	🚇	d	16 12			17 15				18 12						
Manchester Oxford Road		d	16 16			17 19				18 16						
Manchester Picc. [10]	84 🚇	d	16 21	16 51	16 58	17 23	17 23		17 52	18 21	18 52	19 22	19 51	20 51	21 52	23 10
Levenshulme	84	d	16 28		17 03		17 28		17 58	18 28	18 58	19 28	19 58	20 58	21 58	
Heaton Chapel	84	d	16 31		17 06		17 31		18 01	18 31	19 01	19 31	20 01	21 01	22 01	
Stockport	84	d	16 35	17 03	17 10	17 32	17 35		18 05	18 35	19 05	19 35	20 05	21 05	22 05	23 20
Davenport		d	16 39	17 06	17 14		17 39		18 09	18 39	19 09	19 39	20 09	21 09	22 09	23 23
Woodsmoor		d	16 41	17 08	17 16		17 41		18 11	18 41	19 11	19 41	20 11	21 11	22 11	23 25
Hazel Grove		a	16 43	17 10	17 22	17 39	17 43		18 13	18 43	19 13	19 47	20 13	21 13	22 13	23 27
		d	16 46	17 11		17 39			18 13	18 46	19 13		20 13	21 13	22 13	23 28
Middlewood		d		17 15					18 18		19 18		20 18	21 18	22 18	23 32
Disley		d	16 53	17 19		17 46			18 22	18 53	19 22		20 22	21 22	22 22	23 36
New Mills Newtown		d	16 56	17 23		17 50			18 25	18 56	19 25		20 25	21 25	22 25	23 40
Furness Vale		d	16 59	17 26		17 52			18 28	18 59	19 28		20 28	21 28	22 28	23 42
Whaley Bridge		d	17 02	17 29		17 55			18 31	19 02	19 31		20 31	21 31	22 31	23 45
Chapel-en-le-Frith		d	17 09	17 36		18 03			18 38	19 09	19 38		20 38	21 38	22 38	23 52
Dove Holes		d		17 41					18 43		19 43		20 43	21 43	22 43	23 57
Buxton		a	17 24	17 53		18 19			18 56	19 24	19 55		20 55	21 55	22 55	00 09

A To Sheffield
B From Wigan Wallgate
C From Blackpool North
D From Preston
E To Chinley

Table 86

Manchester - Hazel Grove and Buxton

Saturdays until 29 September

Network Diagram - see first Page of Table 78

		NT	NT A	NT	NT B	NT	NT C	NT	NT D	NT	NT D	NT	NT D	NT	NT D	NT	NT D	NT	NT D	NT	NT D	NT	NT D
Deansgate	d				07 11		08 12		09 12		10 12		11 12		12 12		13 12		14 12		15 12		16 12
Manchester Oxford Road	d				07 15		08 15		09 16		10 16		11 16		12 16		13 16		14 16		15 16		16 16
Manchester Picc. 84	d	23p10	05 50	06 49	07 21	07 52	08 20	08 52	09 21	09 52	10 21	10 52	11 21	11 52	12 21	12 52	13 21	13 52	14 21	14 52	15 21	15 52	16 21
Levenshulme 84	d			06 55	07 28	07 58	08 28	08 58	09 28	09 58	10 28	10 58	11 28	11 58	12 28	12 58	13 28	13 58	14 28	14 58	15 28	15 58	16 28
Heaton Chapel 84	d			06 58	07 31		08 31	09 01	09 31	10 01	10 31	11 01	11 31	12 01	12 31	13 01	13 31	14 01	14 31	15 01	15 31	16 01	16 31
Stockport 84	d	23p20	06 00	07 02	07 35	08 03	08 35	09 05	09 35	10 05	10 35	11 05	11 35	12 05	12 35	13 05	13 35	14 05	14 35	15 05	15 35	16 05	16 35
Davenport	d	23p23		07 06	07 39	08 07	08 39	09 09	09 39	10 09	10 39	11 09	11 39	12 09	12 39	13 09	13 39	14 09	14 39	15 09	15 39	16 09	16 39
Woodsmoor	d	23p25		07 08	07 41	08 09	08 41	09 11	09 41	10 11	10 41	11 11	11 41	12 11	12 41	13 11	13 41	14 11	14 41	15 11	15 41	16 11	16 41
Hazel Grove	a	23p27	06 06	07 10	07 45	08 11	08 45	09 13	09 45	10 13	10 45	11 13	11 45	12 13	12 45	13 13	13 45	14 13	14 45	15 13	15 45	16 13	16 45
	d	23p28		07 10		08 11		09 13		10 13		11 13		12 13		13 13		14 13		15 13		16 13	
Middlewood	d	23p32		07 15				09 18		10 18				12 18				14 18				16 18	
Disley	d	23p36		07 19		08 18		09 22		10 22		11 20		12 22		13 20		14 22		15 20		16 22	
New Mills Newtown	d	23p40		07 22		08 22		09 25		10 25		11 24		12 25		13 24		14 25		15 24		16 28	
Furness Vale	d	23p42		07 25		08 24		09 28		10 28		11 26		12 28		13 26		14 28		15 26		16 30	
Whaley Bridge	d	23p45		07 28		08 27		09 31		10 31		11 29		12 31		13 29		14 31		15 29		16 33	
Chapel-en-le-Frith	d	23p52		07 35		08 34		09 38		10 38		11 36		12 38		13 36		14 38		15 36		16 40	
Dove Holes	d	23p57		07 40				09 43		10 43				12 43				14 43				16 45	
Buxton	a	00 07		07 50		08 48		09 53		10 53		11 48		12 53		13 50		14 53		15 50		16 55	

		NT	NT	NT D	NT	NT D	NT	NT	NT	NT	NT	NT
Deansgate	d			17 14		18 12						
Manchester Oxford Road	d			17 18		18 16						
Manchester Picc. 84	d	16 51	17 09	17 22	17 52	18 21	18 52	19 22	19 51	20 52	21 54	23 10
Levenshulme 84	d	16 58	17 14	17 28	17 58	18 28	18 58	19 28	19 58	20 58	22 00	
Heaton Chapel 84	d	17 01	17 17	17 31	18 01	18 31	19 01	19 31	20 01	21 01	22 03	
Stockport 84	d	17 05	17 32	17 35	18 05	18 35	19 05	19 35	20 05	21 05	22 07	23 20
Davenport	d	17 09		17 39	18 09	18 39	19 09	19 39	20 09	21 09	22 11	23 23
Woodsmoor	d	17 11		17 41	18 11	18 41	19 11	19 41	20 11	21 11	22 13	23 25
Hazel Grove	a	17 13	17 39	17 43	18 13	18 45	19 13	19 45	20 13	21 13	22 15	23 27
	d	17 13		17 46	18 13		19 13		20 13	21 13	22 15	23 28
Middlewood	d			17 50			19 18		20 18	21 18	22 20	23 32
Disley	d	17 20		17 54	18 20		19 22		20 22	21 22	22 24	23 36
New Mills Newtown	d	17 26		17 58	18 24		19 25		20 25	21 25	22 27	23 42
Furness Vale	d	17 29		18 00	18 26		19 28		20 28	21 28	22 30	23 45
Whaley Bridge	d	17 32		18 03	18 29		19 31		20 31	21 31	22 33	23 48
Chapel-en-le-Frith	d	17 39		18 10	18 36		19 38		20 38	21 38	22 40	23 55
Dove Holes	d			18 15			19 43		20 43	21 43	22 45	00 01
Buxton	a	17 52		18 25	18 50		19 53		20 53	21 53	22 53	00 10

Saturdays from 6 October

		NT	NT A	NT	NT B	NT	NT C	NT	NT D	NT	NT D	NT	NT D	NT	NT D	NT	NT D	NT	NT D	NT	NT D	NT	NT D
Deansgate	d				07 11		08 12		09 12		10 12		11 12		12 12		13 12		14 12		15 12		16 12
Manchester Oxford Road	d				07 15		08 15		09 16		10 16		11 16		12 16		13 16		14 16		15 16		16 16
Manchester Picc. 84	d	23p10	05 50	06 49	07 21	07 52	08 20	08 52	09 21	09 52	10 21	10 52	11 21	11 52	12 21	12 52	13 21	13 52	14 21	14 52	15 21	15 52	16 21
Levenshulme 84	d			06 55	07 28	07 57	08 28	08 58	09 28	09 58	10 28	10 58	11 28	11 58	12 28	12 58	13 28	13 58	14 28	14 58	15 28	15 58	16 28
Heaton Chapel 84	d			06 58	07 31		08 31	09 01	09 31	10 01	10 31	11 01	11 31	12 01	12 31	13 01	13 31	14 01	14 31	15 01	15 31	16 01	16 31
Stockport 84	d	23p20	06 00	07 02	07 35	08 02	08 35	09 05	09 35	10 05	10 35	11 05	11 35	12 05	12 35	13 05	13 35	14 05	14 35	15 05	15 35	16 05	16 35
Davenport	d	23p23		07 06	07 39	08 06	08 39	09 09	09 39	10 09	10 39	11 09	11 39	12 09	12 39	13 09	13 39	14 09	14 39	15 09	15 39	16 09	16 39
Woodsmoor	d	23p25		07 08	07 41	08 08	08 41	09 11	09 41	10 11	10 41	11 11	11 41	12 11	12 41	13 11	13 41	14 11	14 41	15 11	15 41	16 11	16 41
Hazel Grove	a	23p27	06 06	07 10	07 47	08 11	08 47	09 13	09 47	10 13	10 47	11 13	11 47	12 13	12 47	13 13	13 47	14 13	14 47	15 13	15 47	16 13	16 47
	d	23p28		07 10		08 11		09 13		10 13		11 13		12 13		13 13		14 13		15 13		16 13	
Middlewood	d	23p32		07 15				09 18		10 18				12 18				14 18				16 18	
Disley	d	23p36		07 19		08 18		09 22		10 22		11 20		12 22		13 20		14 22		15 20		16 22	
New Mills Newtown	d	23p40		07 22		08 21		09 25		10 25		11 24		12 25		13 24		14 25		15 24		16 25	
Furness Vale	d	23p42		07 25		08 24		09 28		10 28		11 26		12 28		13 26		14 28		15 26		16 28	
Whaley Bridge	d	23p45		07 28		08 27		09 31		10 31		11 29		12 31		13 29		14 31		15 29		16 31	
Chapel-en-le-Frith	d	23p52		07 35		08 34		09 38		10 38		11 36		12 38		13 36		14 38		15 36		16 38	
Dove Holes	d	23p57		07 40				09 43		10 43				12 43				14 43				16 43	
Buxton	a	00 09		07 52		08 50		09 55		10 55		11 52		12 55		13 52		14 55		15 52		16 55	

		NT	NT	NT D	NT	NT D	NT	NT	NT	NT	NT	NT
Deansgate	d			17 12		18 12						
Manchester Oxford Road	d			17 16		18 16						
Manchester Picc. 84	d	16 51	17 09	17 21	17 52	18 21	18 52	19 22	19 51	20 52	21 52	23 10
Levenshulme 84	d	16 58	17 14	17 28	17 58	18 28	18 58	19 28	19 58	20 58	21 58	
Heaton Chapel 84	d	17 01	17 17	17 31	18 01	18 31	19 01	19 31	20 01	21 01	22 01	
Stockport 84	d	17 05	17 32	17 35	18 05	18 35	19 05	19 35	20 05	21 05	22 05	23 20
Davenport	d	17 09		17 39	18 09	18 39	19 09	19 39	20 09	21 09	22 09	23 23
Woodsmoor	d	17 11		17 41	18 11	18 41	19 11	19 41	20 11	21 11	22 11	23 25
Hazel Grove	a	17 13	17 41	17 43	18 13	18 47	19 13	19 47	20 13	21 13	22 13	23 27
	d	17 13		17 46	18 13		19 13		20 13	21 13	22 13	23 28
Middlewood	d			17 50			19 18		20 18	21 18	22 18	23 32
Disley	d	17 20		17 54	18 20		19 22		20 22	21 22	22 22	23 36
New Mills Newtown	d	17 24		17 58	18 24		19 25		20 25	21 25	22 25	23 40
Furness Vale	d	17 26		18 00	18 26		19 28		20 28	21 28	22 28	23 42
Whaley Bridge	d	17 29		18 03	18 29		19 31		20 31	21 31	22 31	23 45
Chapel-en-le-Frith	d	17 36		18 10	18 36		19 38		20 38	21 38	22 38	23 52
Dove Holes	d			18 15			19 43		20 43	21 43	22 43	23 57
Buxton	a	17 52		18 27	18 52		19 55		20 55	21 55	22 55	00 09

A To Sheffield
B From Wigan Wallgate
C From Blackpool North
D From Preston

Table 86

Manchester - Hazel Grove and Buxton

Sundays until 30 September

Network Diagram - see first Page of Table 78

		NT	NT	NT	NT	NT	NT	NT	NT	NT	NT	NT	NT	NT	NT	NT	NT
Deansgate	d																
Manchester Oxford Road	d																
Manchester Picc. 84	d	23p10	08 55	09 51	10 53	11 52	12 52	13 52	14 52	15 52	16 52	17 52	18 52	19 52	20 52	21 52	22 52
Levenshulme 84	d		09 00	09 58	10 59	11 58	12 58	13 58	14 58	15 58	16 58	17 58	18 58	19 58	20 58	21 58	22 58
Heaton Chapel 84	d		09 03	10 01	11 02	12 01	13 01	14 01	15 01	16 01	17 01	18 01	19 01	20 01	21 01	22 01	23 01
Stockport 84	d	23p20	09 10	10 06	11 06	12 05	13 05	14 05	15 05	16 05	17 05	18 05	19 05	20 05	21 05	22 05	23 05
Davenport	d	23p23	09 13	10 10	11 10	12 09	13 09	14 09	15 09	16 09	17 09	18 09	19 09	20 09	21 09	22 09	23 09
Woodsmoor	d	23p25	09 15	10 12	11 12	12 11	13 11	14 11	15 11	16 11	17 11	18 11	19 11	20 11	21 11	22 11	23 11
Hazel Grove	a	23p27	09 17	10 14	11 14	12 13	13 13	14 13	15 13	16 13	17 13	18 13	19 13	20 13	21 13	22 13	23 13
	d	23p28	09 18	10 15	11 14	12 13	13 13	14 13	15 13	16 13	17 13	18 13	19 13	20 13	21 13	22 13	23 13
Middlewood	d	23p32	09 22	10 19	11 19	12 18	13 18	14 18	15 18	16 18	17 18	18 18	19 18	20 18	21 18	22 18	23 18
Disley	d	23p36	09 26	10 23	11 23	12 22	13 22	14 22	15 22	16 22	17 22	18 22	19 22	20 22	21 22	22 22	23 22
New Mills Newtown	d	23p42	09 30	10 27	11 26	12 25	13 25	14 25	15 25	16 25	17 25	18 25	19 25	20 25	21 25	22 25	23 25
Furness Vale	d	23p45	09 32	10 29	11 29	12 28	13 28	14 28	15 28	16 28	17 28	18 28	19 28	20 28	21 28	22 28	23 28
Whaley Bridge	d	23p48	09 35	10 32	11 32	12 31	13 31	14 31	15 31	16 31	17 31	18 31	19 31	20 31	21 31	22 31	23 31
Chapel-en-le-Frith	d	23p55	09 42	10 39	11 39	12 38	13 38	14 38	15 38	16 38	17 38	18 38	19 38	20 38	21 38	22 38	23 38
Dove Holes	d	00 01	09 47	10 44	11 44	12 43	13 43	14 43	15 43	16 43	17 43	18 43	19 43	20 43	21 43	22 43	23 43
Buxton	a	00 10	09 57	10 53	11 53	12 53	13 53	14 53	15 53	16 53	17 53	18 53	19 53	20 53	21 53	22 53	23 53

Sundays from 7 October

		NT	NT	NT	NT	NT	NT	NT	NT	NT	NT	NT	NT	NT	NT	NT	NT
Deansgate	d																
Manchester Oxford Road	d																
Manchester Picc. 84	d	23p10	08 55	09 51	10 52	11 52	12 52	13 52	14 52	15 52	16 52	17 52	18 52	19 52	20 52	21 52	22 52
Levenshulme 84	d		09 00	09 58	10 58	11 58	12 58	13 58	14 58	15 58	16 58	17 58	18 58	19 58	20 58	21 58	22 58
Heaton Chapel 84	d		09 03	10 01	11 01	12 01	13 01	14 01	15 01	16 01	17 01	18 01	19 01	20 01	21 01	22 01	23 01
Stockport 84	d	23p20	09 10	10 05	11 05	12 05	13 05	14 05	15 05	16 05	17 05	18 05	19 05	20 05	21 05	22 05	23 05
Davenport	d	23p23	09 13	10 09	11 09	12 09	13 09	14 09	15 09	16 09	17 09	18 09	19 09	20 09	21 09	22 09	23 09
Woodsmoor	d	23p25	09 15	10 11	11 11	12 11	13 11	14 11	15 11	16 11	17 11	18 11	19 11	20 11	21 11	22 11	23 11
Hazel Grove	a	23p27	09 17	10 13	11 13	12 13	13 13	14 13	15 13	16 13	17 13	18 13	19 13	20 13	21 13	22 13	23 13
	d	23p28	09 18	10 13	11 13	12 13	13 13	14 13	15 13	16 13	17 13	18 13	19 13	20 13	21 13	22 13	23 13
Middlewood	d	23p32	09 22	10 18	11 18	12 18	13 18	14 18	15 18	16 18	17 18	18 18	19 18	20 18	21 18	22 18	23 18
Disley	d	23p36	09 26	10 22	11 22	12 22	13 22	14 22	15 22	16 22	17 22	18 22	19 22	20 22	21 22	22 22	23 22
New Mills Newtown	d	23p40	09 30	10 25	11 25	12 25	13 25	14 25	15 25	16 25	17 25	18 25	19 25	20 25	21 25	22 25	23 25
Furness Vale	d	23p42	09 32	10 28	11 28	12 28	13 28	14 28	15 28	16 28	17 28	18 28	19 28	20 28	21 28	22 28	23 28
Whaley Bridge	d	23p45	09 35	10 31	11 31	12 31	13 31	14 31	15 31	16 31	17 31	18 31	19 31	20 31	21 31	22 31	23 31
Chapel-en-le-Frith	d	23p52	09 42	10 38	11 38	12 38	13 38	14 38	15 38	16 38	17 38	18 38	19 38	20 38	21 38	22 38	23 38
Dove Holes	d	23p57	09 47	10 43	11 43	12 43	13 43	14 43	15 43	16 43	17 43	18 43	19 43	20 43	21 43	22 43	23 43
Buxton	a	00 09	09 59	10 55	11 55	12 55	13 55	14 55	15 55	16 55	17 55	18 55	19 55	20 55	21 55	22 55	23 55

Table 86

Buxton and Hazel Grove - Manchester

Mondays to Fridays

until 28 September

Network Diagram - see first Page of Table 78

Miles				NT	NT	NT	NT	NT	NT	NT	EM	NT		NT	NT	NT	NT	NT	NT	NT	NT	NT		NT	NT	NT
				A		B		C			◇ D			E		E		E		E		E			E	
0	**Buxton**		d	05 59		06 23		06 50		07 24		07 48			08 27		09 27		10 30		11 27			12 30		13 25
3	Dove Holes		d			06 29		06 56		07 30					08 33		09 33				11 33					13 31
5¼	Chapel-en-le-Frith		d	06 08		06 34		07 01		07 35		07 57			08 38		09 38		10 39		11 38			12 39		13 36
9½	Whaley Bridge		d	06 14		06 40		07 07		07 41		08 03			08 44		09 44		10 45		11 44			12 45		13 42
10½	Furness Vale		d	06 17		06 43		07 10		07 44		08 06			08 47		09 47		10 48		11 47			12 48		13 45
11½	New Mills Newtown		d	06 20		06 46		07 13		07 47		08 10			08 50		09 50		10 51		11 50			12 51		13 48
13¼	Disley		d	06 24		06 49		07 17		07 51		08 14			08 53		09 53		10 55		11 53			12 55		13 51
14¾	Middlewood		d			06 53		07 21		07 55					08 57		09 57				11 57					13 55
17	**Hazel Grove**		a	06 32		06 59		07 27		08 00		08 22			09 03		10 03		11 03		12 03			13 03		14 01
—			d	06 33	06 50	07 00	07 22	07 27	07 48	08 01	08 17	08 22		08 32	09 04	09 32	10 04	10 33	11 04	11 33	12 04	12 33		13 04	13 33	14 01
18	Woodsmoor		d	06 35	06 52	07 02	07 24	07 30	07 50	08 03				08 34	09 06	09 34	10 06	10 35	11 06	11 35	12 06	12 35		13 06	13 35	14 03
18¾	Davenport		d	06 37	06 54	07 04	07 27	07 32	07 53	08 06				08 37	09 08	09 37	10 08	10 37	11 08	11 37	12 08	12 37		13 08	13 37	14 05
19¾	**Stockport**	84	a	06 41	06 58	07 08	07 31	07 37	07 57	08 10	08 24			08 41	09 12	09 41	10 12	10 41	11 12	11 41	12 12	12 41		13 12	13 41	14 09
21¼	Heaton Chapel	84	a			07 15		07 41							09 16		10 16		11 16		12 16			13 16		14 16
22¾	Levenshulme	84	a			07 18		07 44							09 19		10 19		11 19		12 19			13 19		14 19
25¾	**Manchester Picc.** 10	84	a	06 52	07 10	07 26	07 45	07 52	08 09	08 25	08 36	08 39		08 52	09 28	09 52	10 28	10 52	11 28	11 52	12 28	12 52		13 28	13 52	14 28
—	Manchester Oxford Road		a	06 56		07 29		07 56			08 40			08 56		09 56		10 56		11 56		12 56			13 56	
—	Deansgate		a	06 59		07 32		07 59						09 00		10 00		11 00		12 00		13 00			14 00	

			NT	NT	NT	NT	NT	NT		NT	NT	NT	NT	NT	NT	NT	NT
			E		F	G	E	C		C		F					
Buxton		d		14 30		15 27		16 30		16 59	17 27	17 59	18 27	19 27	20 27	21 27	22 56
Dove Holes		d				15 33					17 33		18 33	19 33	20 33	21 33	23 02
Chapel-en-le-Frith		d		14 39		15 38		16 39		17 08	17 38	18 08	18 38	19 38	20 38	21 38	23 07
Whaley Bridge		d		14 45		15 44		16 45		17 14	17 44	18 14	18 44	19 44	20 44	21 44	23 13
Furness Vale		d		14 48		15 47		16 48		17 17	17 47	18 17	18 47	19 47	20 47	21 47	23 16
New Mills Newtown		d		14 51		15 50		16 51		17 20	17 50	18 20	18 50	19 50	20 50	21 50	23 19
Disley		d		14 55		15 53		16 55		17 24	17 53	18 24	18 53	19 53	20 53	21 53	23 22
Middlewood		d				15 57					17 57		18 57	19 57	20 57	21 57	23 26
Hazel Grove		a		15 03		16 03		17 03		17 32	18 03	18 32	19 03	20 03	21 03	22 03	23 31
		d	14 33	15 04	15 33	16 04	16 30	17 04		17 33	18 04	18 33	19 04	20 04	21 04	22 04	23 32
Woodsmoor		d	14 35	15 06	15 35	16 06	16 32	17 06		17 35	18 06	18 35	19 06	20 06	21 06	22 06	23 34
Davenport		d	14 37	15 08	15 37	16 08	16 35	17 08		17 37	18 08	18 37	19 08	20 08	21 08	22 08	23 36
Stockport	84	a	14 41	15 12	15 41	16 12	16 40	17 12		17 41	18 12	18 41	19 12	20 12	21 12	22 12	23 40
Heaton Chapel	84	a		15 16		16 16		17 16			18 16		19 16	20 16	21 16	22 16	
Levenshulme	84	a		15 19		16 19		17 19			18 19		19 19	20 19	21 19	22 19	
Manchester Picc. 10	84	a	14 52	15 28	15 52	16 25	16 52	17 25		17 52	18 28	18 52	19 28	20 28	21 28	22 28	23 54
Manchester Oxford Road		a	14 56		15 56	16 29	16 56	17 29		17 56		18 56					
Deansgate		a	15 00		16 00	16 32	17 00	17 32		18 00		19 00					

Mondays to Fridays

from 1 October

			NT	NT	NT	NT	NT	NT	NT	EM	NT		NT	NT	NT	NT	NT	NT	NT	NT	NT		NT	NT	NT	NT
			A		B		C			◇ D			E		E		E		E		E			E		E
Buxton		d	05 54		06 18		06 45		07 19		07 43			08 22		09 22		10 25		11 22			12 25		13 20	
Dove Holes		d			06 24		06 51		07 25					08 28		09 28				11 28					13 26	
Chapel-en-le-Frith		d	06 03		06 29		06 56		07 30		07 52			08 33		09 33		10 34		11 33			12 34		13 31	
Whaley Bridge		d	06 09		06 35		07 02		07 36		07 58			08 39		09 39		10 40		11 39			12 40		13 37	
Furness Vale		d	06 12		06 38		07 05		07 39		08 01			08 42		09 42		10 43		11 42			12 43		13 40	
New Mills Newtown		d	06 15		06 41		07 08		07 42		08 05			08 45		09 45		10 46		11 45			12 46		13 43	
Disley		d	06 19		06 44		07 12		07 46		08 09			08 48		09 48		10 50		11 48			12 50		13 46	
Middlewood		d			06 48		07 16		07 50					08 52		09 52				11 52					13 50	
Hazel Grove		a	06 30		06 57		07 25		07 58		08 21			09 01		10 01		11 01		12 01			13 01		14 01	
		d	06 31	06 48	06 58	07 20	07 25	07 46	07 59	08 17	08 21		08 30	09 02	09 30	10 02	10 31	11 02	11 31	12 02	12 31		13 02	13 31	14 01	14 31
Woodsmoor		d	06 33	06 50	07 00	07 22	07 28	07 48	08 01				08 32	09 04	09 32	10 04	10 33	11 04	11 33	12 04	12 33		13 04	13 33	14 03	14 33
Davenport		d	06 35	06 52	07 02	07 25	07 30	07 51	08 04				08 35	09 06	09 35	10 06	10 35	11 06	11 35	12 06	12 35		13 06	13 35	14 05	14 35
Stockport	84	a	06 41	06 58	07 08	07 31	07 37	07 57	08 10	08 24			08 41	09 12	09 41	10 12	10 41	11 12	11 41	12 12	12 41		13 12	13 41	14 09	14 41
Heaton Chapel	84	a			07 15		07 41							09 16		10 16		11 16		12 16			13 16		14 16	
Levenshulme	84	a			07 18		07 44							09 19		10 19		11 19		12 19			13 19		14 19	
Manchester Picc. 10	84	a	06 52	07 10	07 26	07 45	07 52	08 09	08 25	08 36	08 39		08 52	09 28	09 52	10 28	10 52	11 28	11 52	12 28	12 52		13 28	13 52	14 28	14 52
Manchester Oxford Road		a	06 56		07 29		07 56			08 40			08 56		09 56		10 56		11 56		12 56			13 56		14 56
Deansgate		a	06 59		07 32		07 59						09 00		10 00		11 00		12 00		13 00			14 00		15 00

			NT	NT	NT	NT	NT		NT	NT	NT	NT	NT	NT	NT	NT
				F	G	E	C		C		F					
Buxton		d	14 25		15 22		16 30		16 59	17 25	17 55	18 22	19 22	20 22	21 22	22 51
Dove Holes		d			15 28					17 31		18 28	19 28	20 28	21 28	22 57
Chapel-en-le-Frith		d	14 34		15 33		16 34		17 05	17 36	18 04	18 33	19 33	20 33	21 33	23 02
Whaley Bridge		d	14 40		15 39		16 40		17 11	17 42	18 10	18 39	19 39	20 39	21 39	23 08
Furness Vale		d	14 43		15 42		16 43		17 14	17 45	18 13	18 42	19 42	20 42	21 42	23 11
New Mills Newtown		d	14 46		15 45		16 46		17 17	17 48	18 16	18 45	19 45	20 45	21 45	23 14
Disley		d	14 50		15 48		16 50		17 21	17 51	18 20	18 48	19 48	20 48	21 48	23 17
Middlewood		d			15 52					17 55		18 52	19 52	20 52	21 52	23 21
Hazel Grove		a	15 01		16 01		17 01		17 32	18 03	18 32	19 01	20 01	21 01	22 01	23 29
		d	15 02	15 33	16 02	16 30	17 02		17 33	18 04	18 33	19 02	20 02	21 02	22 02	23 30
Woodsmoor		d	15 04	15 35	16 04	16 32	17 04		17 35	18 06	18 35	19 04	20 04	21 04	22 04	23 32
Davenport		d	15 06	15 37	16 06	16 35	17 06		17 37	18 08	18 37	19 06	20 06	21 06	22 06	23 34
Stockport	84	a	15 12	15 41	16 12	16 40	17 12		17 41	18 12	18 41	19 12	20 12	21 12	22 12	23 40
Heaton Chapel	84	a	15 16		16 16		17 16			18 16		19 16	20 16	21 16	22 16	
Levenshulme	84	a	15 19		16 19		17 19			18 19		19 19	20 19	21 19	22 19	
Manchester Picc. 10	84	a	15 28	15 52	16 25	16 52	17 25		17 52	18 28	18 52	19 28	20 28	21 28	22 28	23 54
Manchester Oxford Road		a		15 56	16 29	16 56	17 29		17 56		18 56					
Deansgate		a		16 00	16 32	17 00	17 32		18 00		19 00					

A To Clitheroe
B To Wigan North Western
C To Blackpool North
D From Nottingham to Liverpool Lime Street
E To Preston
F To Bolton
G To Barrow-in-Furness

Table 86

Buxton and Hazel Grove - Manchester

Saturdays

until 29 September

Network Diagram - see first Page of Table 78

			NT	NT	NT	NT	NT	EM	NT	NT	NT		NT	NT	NT	NT	NT	NT	NT	NT	NT		NT	NT	NT	NT
			A		B			◇ C	B		B			B		B		B		B			B		B	
Buxton		d	05 59	06 27			07 27		07 56	08 27			09 27		10 30		11 27		12 30		13 27			14 30		15 27
Dove Holes		d		06 33			07 33		08 02	08 33			09 33				11 33				13 33					15 33
Chapel-en-le-Frith		d	06 08	06 38			07 38		08 07	08 38			09 38		10 39		11 38		12 39		13 38			14 39		15 38
Whaley Bridge		d	06 14	06 44			07 44		08 13	08 44			09 44		10 45		11 44		12 45		13 44			14 45		15 44
Furness Vale		d	06 17	06 47			07 47		08 16	08 47			09 47		10 48		11 47		12 48		13 47			14 48		15 47
New Mills Newtown		d	06 20	06 50			07 50		08 19	08 50			09 50		10 51		11 50		12 51		13 50			14 51		15 50
Disley		d	06 24	06 53			07 53		08 22	08 53			09 53		10 55		11 53		12 55		13 53			14 55		15 53
Middlewood		d		06 57			07 57		08 26	08 57			09 57				11 57				13 57					15 57
Hazel Grove		a	06 32	07 03			08 03		08 32	09 03			10 03		11 03		12 03		13 03		14 03			15 03		16 03
		d	06 33	07 03	07 32	07 48	08 03	08 17	08 33	09 04	09 32		10 04	10 33	11 04	11 33	12 04	12 33	13 04	13 33	14 04		14 33	15 04	15 33	16 04
Woodsmoor		d	06 35	07 05	07 34	07 50	08 05		08 35	09 06	09 34		10 06	10 35	11 06	11 35	12 06	12 35	13 06	13 35	14 06		14 35	15 06	15 35	16 06
Davenport		d	06 37	07 07	07 36	07 53	08 07		08 37	09 08	09 37		10 08	10 37	11 08	11 37	12 08	12 37	13 08	13 37	14 08		14 37	15 08	15 37	16 08
Stockport	84	a	06 41	07 12	07 40	07 57	08 12	08 24	08 41	09 12	09 41		10 12	10 41	11 12	11 41	12 12	12 41	13 12	13 41	14 14		14 41	15 12	15 41	16 14
Heaton Chapel	84	a		07 16			08 16			09 16			10 16		11 16		12 16		13 16		14 18			15 16		16 18
Levenshulme	84	a		07 19			08 19			09 19			10 19		11 19		12 19		13 19		14 21			15 19		16 21
Manchester Picc. 10	84	a	06 52	07 26	07 52	08 09	08 26	08 36	08 52	09 26	09 52		10 26	10 52	11 26	11 52	12 26	12 52	13 26	13 52	14 28		14 52	15 26	15 52	16 28
Manchester Oxford Road		a	06 56		07 56			08 40	08 56		09 56			10 56		11 56		12 56		13 56			14 56		15 56	
Deansgate		a	06 59		08 00				09 00		10 00			11 00		12 00		13 00		14 00			15 00		16 00	

			NT	NT	NT	NT	NT		NT	NT	NT	NT	NT
			B		D		E						
Buxton		d		16 30		17 27			18 27	19 27	20 27	21 27	22 56
Dove Holes		d				17 33			18 33	19 33	20 33	21 33	23 02
Chapel-en-le-Frith		d		16 39		17 38			18 38	19 38	20 38	21 38	23 07
Whaley Bridge		d		16 45		17 44			18 44	19 44	20 44	21 44	23 13
Furness Vale		d		16 48		17 47			18 47	19 47	20 47	21 47	23 16
New Mills Newtown		d		16 51		17 50			18 50	19 50	20 50	21 50	23 19
Disley		d		16 55		17 53			18 53	19 53	20 53	21 53	23 22
Middlewood		d				17 57			18 57	19 57	20 57	21 57	23 26
Hazel Grove		a		17 03		18 03			19 03	20 03	21 03	22 03	23 32
		d	16 30	17 04	17 33	18 04	18 33		19 04	20 04	21 04	22 04	23 33
Woodsmoor		d	16 32	17 06	17 35	18 06	18 35		19 06	20 06	21 06	22 06	23 35
Davenport		d	16 34	17 08	17 37	18 08	18 37		19 08	20 08	21 08	22 08	23 37
Stockport	84	a	16 40	17 12	17 41	18 14	18 41		19 14	20 14	21 12	22 12	23 41
Heaton Chapel	84	a		17 16		18 18			19 18	20 18	21 16	22 16	
Levenshulme	84	a		17 19		18 21			19 21	20 21	21 19	22 19	
Manchester Picc. 10	84	a	16 52	17 26	17 52	18 28	18 52		19 28	20 28	21 26	22 26	23 52
Manchester Oxford Road		a	16 56		17 56		18 56						
Deansgate		a	17 00		18 00		19 00						

Saturdays

from 6 October

			NT	NT	NT	NT	NT	EM	NT	NT	NT		NT	NT	NT	NT	NT	NT	NT	NT	NT		NT	NT	NT	NT
			A		B			◇ C	B		B			B		B		B		B			B		B	
Buxton		d	05 54	06 22			07 22		07 51	08 22			09 27		10 25		11 22		12 25		13 22			14 25		15 22
Dove Holes		d		06 28			07 28		07 57	08 28			09 33				11 28				13 28					15 28
Chapel-en-le-Frith		d	06 03	06 33			07 33		08 02	08 33			09 38		10 34		11 33		12 34		13 33			14 34		15 33
Whaley Bridge		d	06 09	06 39			07 39		08 08	08 39			09 44		10 40		11 39		12 40		13 39			14 40		15 39
Furness Vale		d	06 12	06 42			07 42		08 11	08 42			09 47		10 43		11 42		12 43		13 42			14 43		15 42
New Mills Newtown		d	06 15	06 45			07 45		08 14	08 45			09 50		10 46		11 45		12 46		13 45			14 46		15 45
Disley		d	06 19	06 48			07 48		08 17	08 48			09 53		10 50		11 48		12 50		13 48			14 50		15 48
Middlewood		d		06 52			07 52		08 21	08 52			09 57				11 52				13 52					15 52
Hazel Grove		a	06 30	07 01			08 01		08 30	09 01			10 03		11 01		12 01		13 01		14 01			15 01		16 01
		d	06 31	07 01	07 32	07 48	08 01	08 17	08 31	09 02	09 31		10 04	10 31	11 02	11 31	12 02	12 31	13 02	13 33	14 02		14 31	15 02	15 33	16 02
Woodsmoor		d	06 33	07 03	07 34	07 50	08 03		08 33	09 04	09 33		10 06	10 33	11 04	11 33	12 04	12 33	13 04	13 35	14 04		14 33	15 04	15 35	16 04
Davenport		d	06 35	07 05	07 36	07 53	08 05		08 35	09 06	09 35		10 08	10 35	11 06	11 35	12 06	12 35	13 06	13 37	14 06		14 35	15 06	15 37	16 06
Stockport	84	a	06 41	07 12	07 40	07 57	08 12	08 24	08 41	09 12	09 41		10 12	10 41	11 12	11 41	12 12	12 41	13 12	13 41	14 12		14 41	15 12	15 41	16 12
Heaton Chapel	84	a		07 16			08 16			09 16			10 16		11 16		12 16		13 16		14 16			15 16		16 16
Levenshulme	84	a		07 19			08 19			09 19			10 19		11 19		12 19		13 19		14 19			15 19		16 19
Manchester Picc. 10	84	a	06 52	07 28	07 52	08 09	08 28	08 36	08 52	09 28	09 52		10 28	10 52	11 28	11 52	12 28	12 52	13 28	13 52	14 28		14 52	15 28	15 52	16 28
Manchester Oxford Road		a	06 56		07 56			08 40	08 56		09 56			10 56		11 56		12 56		13 56			14 56		15 56	
Deansgate		a	06 59		08 00				09 00		10 00			11 00		12 00		13 00		14 00			15 00		16 00	

			NT	NT	NT	NT	NT		NT	NT	NT	NT	NT
			B		D		E						
Buxton		d		16 25		17 22			18 22	19 22	20 22	21 22	22 51
Dove Holes		d				17 28			18 28	19 28	20 28	21 28	22 57
Chapel-en-le-Frith		d		16 34		17 33			18 33	19 33	20 33	21 33	23 02
Whaley Bridge		d		16 40		17 39			18 39	19 39	20 39	21 39	23 08
Furness Vale		d		16 43		17 42			18 42	19 42	20 42	21 42	23 11
New Mills Newtown		d		16 46		17 45			18 45	19 45	20 45	21 45	23 14
Disley		d		16 50		17 48			18 48	19 48	20 48	21 48	23 17
Middlewood		d				17 52			18 52	19 52	20 52	21 52	23 21
Hazel Grove		a		17 01		18 01			19 01	20 01	21 01	22 01	23 29
		d	16 30	17 02	17 31	18 02	18 31		19 02	20 02	21 02	22 02	23 30
Woodsmoor		d	16 32	17 04	17 33	18 04	18 33		19 04	20 04	21 04	22 04	23 32
Davenport		d	16 34	17 06	17 35	18 06	18 35		19 06	20 06	21 06	22 06	23 34
Stockport	84	a	16 40	17 12	17 41	18 12	18 41		19 12	20 12	21 12	22 12	23 40
Heaton Chapel	84	a		17 16		18 16			19 16	20 16	21 16	22 16	
Levenshulme	84	a		17 19		18 19			19 19	20 19	21 19	22 19	
Manchester Picc. 10	84	a	16 52	17 28	17 52	18 28	18 52		19 28	20 28	21 28	22 28	23 54
Manchester Oxford Road		a	16 56		17 56		18 56						
Deansgate		a	17 00		18 00		19 00						

A To Clitheroe
B To Preston
C From Nottingham to Liverpool Lime Street
D To Blackpool North
E To Bolton

Table 86

Buxton and Hazel Grove - Manchester

Sundays
until 30 September

Network Diagram - see first Page of Table 78

			NT	NT	NT	NT	NT	NT	NT	NT	NT	NT	NT	NT	NT	NT	NT
Buxton		d	08 23	09 19	10 27	11 26	12 27	13 27	14 27	15 27	16 27	17 27	18 27	19 27	20 27	21 27	22 27
Dove Holes		d	08 29	09 25	10 33	11 32	12 33	13 33	14 33	15 33	16 33	17 33	18 33	19 33	20 33	21 33	22 33
Chapel-en-le-Frith		d	08 34	09 30	10 38	11 37	12 38	13 38	14 38	15 38	16 38	17 38	18 38	19 38	20 38	21 38	22 38
Whaley Bridge		d	08 40	09 36	10 44	11 43	12 44	13 44	14 44	15 44	16 44	17 44	18 44	19 44	20 44	21 44	22 44
Furness Vale		d	08 43	09 39	10 47	11 46	12 47	13 47	14 47	15 47	16 47	17 47	18 47	19 47	20 47	21 47	22 47
New Mills Newtown		d	08 46	09 42	10 50	11 49	12 50	13 50	14 50	15 50	16 50	17 50	18 50	19 50	20 50	21 50	22 50
Disley		d	08 49	09 45	10 53	11 52	12 53	13 53	14 53	15 53	16 53	17 53	18 53	19 53	20 53	21 53	22 53
Middlewood		d	08 53	09 49	10 57	11 56	12 57	13 57	14 57	15 57	16 57	17 57	18 57	19 57	20 57	21 57	22 57
Hazel Grove		a	08 59	09 55	11 02	12 02	13 03	14 03	15 03	16 03	17 03	18 03	19 03	20 03	21 03	22 03	23 03
		d	08 59	09 55	11 03	12 02	13 04	14 04	15 04	16 04	17 04	18 04	19 04	20 04	21 04	22 04	23 04
Woodsmoor		d	09 01	09 57	11 05	12 04	13 06	14 06	15 06	16 06	17 06	18 06	19 06	20 06	21 06	22 06	23 06
Davenport		d	09 03	09 59	11 07	12 06	13 08	14 08	15 08	16 08	17 08	18 08	19 08	20 08	21 08	22 08	23 08
Stockport	84	a	09 09	10 04	11 13	12 13	13 14	14 14	15 14	16 14	17 14	18 14	19 14	20 14	21 12	22 12	23 12
Heaton Chapel	84	a	09 13	10 08		12 17	13 18	14 18	15 18	16 18	17 18	18 18	19 18	20 18	21 16	22 16	23 16
Levenshulme	84	a	09 16	10 11		12 20	13 21	14 21	15 21	16 21	17 21	18 21	19 21	20 21	21 19	22 19	23 19
Manchester Picc. 10	84 ⇌	a	09 23	10 21	11 25	12 27	13 29	14 29	15 29	16 29	17 29	18 29	19 29	20 29	21 27	22 27	23 27
Manchester Oxford Road		a															
Deansgate	⇌	a															

Sundays
from 7 October

			NT	NT	NT	NT	NT	NT	NT	NT	NT	NT	NT	NT	NT	NT	NT
Buxton		d	08 21	09 14	10 22	11 21	12 22	13 22	14 22	15 22	16 22	17 22	18 22	19 22	20 22	21 22	22 22
Dove Holes		d	08 27	09 20	10 28	11 27	12 28	13 28	14 28	15 28	16 28	17 28	18 28	19 28	20 28	21 28	22 28
Chapel-en-le-Frith		d	08 32	09 25	10 33	11 32	12 33	13 33	14 33	15 33	16 33	17 33	18 33	19 33	20 33	21 33	22 33
Whaley Bridge		d	08 38	09 31	10 39	11 38	12 39	13 39	14 39	15 39	16 39	17 39	18 39	19 39	20 39	21 39	22 39
Furness Vale		d	08 41	09 34	10 42	11 41	12 42	13 42	14 42	15 42	16 42	17 42	18 42	19 42	20 42	21 42	22 42
New Mills Newtown		d	08 44	09 37	10 45	11 44	12 45	13 45	14 45	15 45	16 45	17 45	18 45	19 45	20 45	21 45	22 45
Disley		d	08 47	09 40	10 48	11 47	12 48	13 48	14 48	15 48	16 48	17 48	18 48	19 48	20 48	21 48	22 48
Middlewood		d	08 51	09 44	10 52	11 51	12 52	13 52	14 52	15 52	16 52	17 52	18 52	19 52	20 52	21 52	22 52
Hazel Grove		a	08 57	09 53	11 00	12 00	13 01	14 01	15 01	16 01	17 01	18 01	19 01	20 01	21 01	22 01	23 01
		d	08 58	09 53	11 01	12 00	13 02	14 02	15 02	16 02	17 02	18 02	19 02	20 02	21 02	22 02	23 02
Woodsmoor		d	09 00	09 55	11 03	12 02	13 04	14 04	15 04	16 04	17 04	18 04	19 04	20 04	21 04	22 04	23 04
Davenport		d	09 02	09 57	11 05	12 04	13 06	14 06	15 06	16 06	17 06	18 06	19 06	20 06	21 06	22 06	23 06
Stockport	84	a	09 08	10 04	11 11	12 11	13 12	14 12	15 12	16 12	17 12	18 12	19 12	20 12	21 12	22 12	23 12
Heaton Chapel	84	a	09 12	10 08		12 15	13 16	14 16	15 16	16 16	17 16	18 16	19 16	20 16	21 16	22 16	23 16
Levenshulme	84	a	09 15	10 11		12 18	13 19	14 19	15 19	16 19	17 19	18 19	19 19	20 19	21 19	22 19	23 19
Manchester Picc. 10	84 ⇌	a	09 23	10 21	11 23	12 25	13 27	14 27	15 27	16 27	17 27	18 27	19 27	20 27	21 27	22 27	23 27
Manchester Oxford Road		a															
Deansgate	⇌	a															

Network Diagram for Tables 88, 89, 90, 91

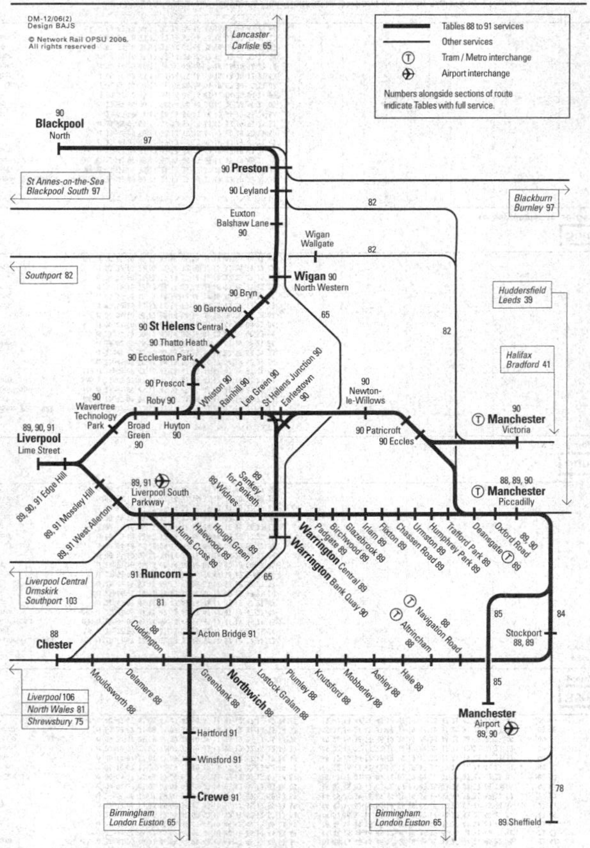

Manchester - Northwich and Chester

Mondays to Fridays
until 28 September

Network Diagram - see first Page of Table 88

Miles			NT MX	NT	NT	NT	NT	NT	NT	NT	NT	NT	NT	NT	NT	NT	NT	NT	NT	NT	NT	NT	NT A	NT FO B
0	**Manchester Picc.** 10 84 ⇌	d	23p17	06 18	07 17	08 17	09 17	10 17	11 17	12 17	13 17	14 17	15 17	16 17	....	17 09	....	18 17	19 17	20 17	21 17	22 17	23 17	23 17
6½	**Stockport** 84	d	23p27	06 30	07 30	08 30	09 30	10 30	11 30	12 30	13 30	14 30	15 30	16 30	16 58	17 19	17 58	18 30	19 30	20 30	21 30	22 30	23 27	23 27
14¾	Navigation Road ⇌	d	23p41	06 44	07 44	08 44	09 44	10 44	11 44	12 44	13 44	14 44	15 44	16 44	17 12	17 33	18 12	18 44	19 44	20 44	21 44	22 44	23 41	23 41
15¼	**Altrincham** ⇌	a	23p43	06 46	07 46	08 46	09 46	10 46	11 46	12 46	13 46	14 46	15 46	16 46	17 14	17 35	18 14	18 46	19 46	20 46	21 46	22 46	23 43	23 43
—		d	23p43	06 46	07 46	08 46	09 46	10 46	11 46	12 46	13 46	14 46	15 46	16 46	17 14	17 35	18 14	18 46	19 46	20 46	21 46	22 46	23 43	23 43
16	Hale	d	23p46	06 49	07 49	08 49	09 49	10 49	11 49	12 49	13 49	14 49	15 49	16 49	17 17	17 38	18 17	18 49	19 49	20 49	21 49	22 49	23 46	23 46
17¾	Ashley	d	23p49	06 52	07 52	08 52	09 52	10 52	11 52	12 52	13 52	14 52	15 52	16 52	17 20	17 41	18 20	18 52	19 52	20 52	21 52	22 52	23 49	23 49
18½	Mobberley	d	23p52	06 55	07 55	08 55	09 55	10 55	11 55	12 55	13 55	14 55	15 55	16 55	17 23	17 44	18 23	18 55	19 55	20 55	21 55	22 55	23 52	23 52
22¼	Knutsford	d	23p57	06 59	07 59	08 59	09 59	10 59	11 59	12 59	13 59	14 59	15 59	16 59	17 27	17 49	18 27	18 59	19 59	20 59	21 59	22 59	23 57	23 57
24¾	Plumley	d	00 01	07 03	08 03	09 03	10 03	11 03	12 03	13 03	14 03	15 03	16 03	17 03	17 31	17 53	18 31	19 03	20 03	21 03	22 03	23 03	00 01	00 01
26¾	Lostock Gralam	d	00 04	07 07	08 07	09 07	10 07	11 07	12 07	13 07	14 07	15 07	16 07	17 07	17 35	17 56	18 35	19 07	20 07	21 07	22 07	23 07	00 04	00 04
28¼	**Northwich**	d	00 10	07 12	08 12	09 12	10 12	11 12	12 12	13 12	14 12	15 12	16 12	17 12	17 40	18 02	18 40	19 12	20 12	21 12	22 12	23 12	00 10	00 10
30	Greenbank	d	00 14	07 17	08 17	09 17	10 17	11 17	12 17	13 17	14 17	15 17	16 17	17 17	17 45	18 06	18 45	19 17	20 17	21 17	22 17	23 17	00 14	00 14
32¾	Cuddington	d	00 19	07 22	08 22	09 22	10 22	11 22	12 22	13 22	14 22	15 22	16 22	17 22	17 50	18 11	18 50	19 22	20 22	21 22	22 22	23 22	00 19	00 19
35¾	Delamere	d	00 24	07 26	08 26	09 26	10 26	11 26	12 26	13 26	14 26	15 26	16 26	17 26	17 54	18 16	18 54	19 26	20 26	21 26	22 26	23 26	00 24	00 24
38¾	Mouldsworth	d	00 28	07 31	08 31	09 31	10 31	11 31	12 31	13 31	14 31	15 31	16 31	17 31	17 59	18 21	18 59	19 31	20 31	21 31	22 31	23 31	00 28	00 28
45¼	**Chester** 81	a	00 40	07 45	08 45	09 45	10 45	11 43	12 45	13 45	14 45	15 45	16 45	17 45	18 13	18 32	19 13	19 45	20 45	21 45	22 45	23 45	00 40	00 43

Mondays to Fridays
from 1 October

		NT MX	NT	NT	NT	NT	NT	NT	NT	NT	NT	NT	NT	NT	NT	NT	NT	NT	NT	NT	NT FO	NT FX	NT
Manchester Picc. 10 84 ⇌	d	23p17	06 18	07 17	08 17	09 17	10 17	11 17	12 17	13 17	14 17	15 17	16 17	....	17 09	....	18 17	19 17	20 17	21 17	22 17	22 17	23 17
Stockport 84	d	23p27	06 30	07 30	08 30	09 30	10 30	11 30	12 30	13 30	14 30	15 30	16 30	16 58	17 19	17 58	18 30	19 30	20 30	21 30	22 30	22 30	23 27
Navigation Road ⇌	d	23p41	06 44	07 44	08 44	09 44	10 44	11 44	12 44	13 44	14 44	15 44	16 44	17 12	17 33	18 12	18 44	19 44	20 44	21 44	22 44	22 44	23 41
Altrincham ⇌	a	23p43	06 46	07 46	08 46	09 46	10 46	11 46	12 46	13 46	14 46	15 46	16 46	17 14	17 35	18 14	18 46	19 46	20 46	21 46	22 46	22 46	23 43
	d	23p43	06 46	07 46	08 46	09 46	10 46	11 46	12 46	13 46	14 46	15 46	16 46	17 14	17 35	18 14	18 46	19 46	20 46	21 46	22 46	22 46	23 43
Hale	d	23p46	06 49	07 49	08 49	09 49	10 49	11 49	12 49	13 49	14 49	15 49	16 49	17 17	17 38	18 17	18 49	19 49	20 49	21 49	22 49	22 49	23 46
Ashley	d	23p49	06 52	07 52	08 52	09 52	10 52	11 52	12 52	13 52	14 52	15 52	16 52	17 20	17 41	18 20	18 52	19 52	20 52	21 52	22 52	22 52	23 49
Mobberley	d	23p52	06 55	07 55	08 55	09 55	10 55	11 55	12 55	13 55	14 55	15 55	16 55	17 23	17 44	18 23	18 55	19 55	20 55	21 55	22 55	22 55	23 52
Knutsford	d	23p57	06 59	07 59	08 59	09 59	10 59	11 59	12 59	13 59	14 59	15 59	16 59	17 27	17 49	18 27	18 59	19 59	20 59	21 59	22 59	22 59	23 57
Plumley	d	00 01	07 03	08 03	09 03	10 03	11 03	12 03	13 03	14 03	15 03	16 03	17 03	17 31	17 53	18 31	19 03	20 03	21 03	22 03	23 03	23 03	00 01
Lostock Gralam	d	00 04	07 07	08 07	09 07	10 07	11 07	12 07	13 07	14 07	15 07	16 07	17 07	17 35	17 56	18 35	19 07	20 07	21 07	22 07	23 07	23 07	00 04
Northwich	d	00 10	07 12	08 12	09 12	10 12	11 12	12 12	13 12	14 12	15 12	16 12	17 12	17 40	18 02	18 40	19 12	20 12	21 12	22 12	23 12	23 12	00 10
Greenbank	d	00 14	07 17	08 17	09 17	10 17	11 17	12 17	13 17	14 17	15 17	16 17	17 17	17 45	18 06	18 45	19 17	20 17	21 17	22 17	23 17	23 17	00 14
Cuddington	d	00 19	07 22	08 22	09 22	10 22	11 22	12 22	13 22	14 22	15 22	16 22	17 22	17 50	18 11	18 50	19 22	20 22	21 22	22 22	23 22	23 22	00 19
Delamere	d	00 24	07 26	08 26	09 26	10 26	11 26	12 26	13 26	14 26	15 26	16 26	17 26	17 54	18 16	18 54	19 26	20 26	21 26	22 26	23 26	23 26	00 24
Mouldsworth	d	00 28	07 31	08 31	09 31	10 31	11 31	12 31	13 31	14 31	15 31	16 31	17 31	17 59	18 21	18 59	19 31	20 31	21 31	22 31	23 31	23 31	00 28
Chester 81	a	00 42	07 46	08 46	09 45	10 44	11 44	12 44	13 44	14 44	15 44	16 44	17 44	18 12	18 34	19 15	19 44	20 44	21 44	22 44	23 44	23 46	00 42

Saturdays
until 29 September

		NT C	NT D	NT	NT	NT	NT	NT	NT	NT	NT	NT	NT	NT	NT	NT	NT	NT	NT	NT	NT
Manchester Picc. 10 84 ⇌	d	23p17	23p17	06 17	07 17	08 17	09 17	10 17	11 17	12 17	13 17	14 17	15 17	16 17	17 17	18 17	19 17	20 17	21 17	22 17	23 17
Stockport 84	d	23p27	23p27	06 30	07 30	08 30	09 30	10 30	11 30	12 30	13 30	14 30	15 30	16 30	17 30	18 30	19 30	20 30	21 30	22 30	23 27
Navigation Road ⇌	d	23p41	23p41	06 44	07 44	08 44	09 44	10 44	11 44	12 44	13 44	14 44	15 44	16 44	17 44	18 44	19 44	20 44	21 44	22 44	23 41
Altrincham ⇌	a	23p43	23p43	06 46	07 46	08 46	09 46	10 46	11 46	12 46	13 46	14 46	15 46	16 46	17 46	18 46	19 46	20 46	21 46	22 46	23 43
	d	23p43	23p43	06 46	07 46	08 46	09 46	10 46	11 46	12 46	13 46	14 46	15 46	16 46	17 46	18 46	19 46	20 46	21 46	22 46	23 43
Hale	d	23p46	23p46	06 49	07 49	08 49	09 49	10 49	11 49	12 49	13 49	14 49	15 49	16 49	17 49	18 49	19 49	20 49	21 49	22 49	23 46
Ashley	d	23p49	23p49	06 52	07 52	08 52	09 52	10 52	11 52	12 52	13 52	14 52	15 52	16 52	17 52	18 52	19 52	20 52	21 52	22 52	23 49
Mobberley	d	23p52	23p52	06 55	07 55	08 55	09 55	10 55	11 55	12 55	13 55	14 55	15 55	16 55	17 55	18 55	19 55	20 55	21 55	22 55	23 52
Knutsford	d	23p57	23p57	06 59	07 59	08 59	09 59	10 59	11 59	12 59	13 59	14 59	15 59	16 59	17 59	18 59	19 59	20 59	21 59	22 59	23 57
Plumley	d	00 01	00 01	07 03	08 03	09 03	10 03	11 03	12 03	13 03	14 03	15 03	16 03	17 03	18 03	19 03	20 03	21 03	22 03	23 03	00 01
Lostock Gralam	d	00 04	00 04	07 07	08 07	09 07	10 07	11 07	12 07	13 07	14 07	15 07	16 07	17 07	18 07	19 07	20 07	21 07	22 07	23 07	00 04
Northwich	d	00 10	00 10	07 12	08 12	09 12	10 12	11 12	12 12	13 12	14 12	15 12	16 12	17 12	18 12	19 12	20 12	21 12	22 12	23 12	00 10
Greenbank	d	00 14	00 14	07 17	08 17	09 17	10 17	11 17	12 17	13 17	14 17	15 17	16 17	17 17	18 17	19 17	20 17	21 17	22 17	23 17	00 14
Cuddington	d	00 19	00 19	07 22	08 22	09 22	10 22	11 22	12 22	13 22	14 22	15 22	16 22	17 22	18 22	19 22	20 22	21 22	22 22	23 22	00 19
Delamere	d	00 24	00 24	07 26	08 26	09 26	10 26	11 26	12 26	13 26	14 26	15 26	16 26	17 26	18 26	19 26	20 26	21 26	22 26	23 26	00 24
Mouldsworth	d	00 28	00 28	07 31	08 31	09 31	10 31	11 31	12 31	13 31	14 31	15 31	16 31	17 31	18 31	19 31	20 31	21 31	22 31	23 31	00 28
Chester 81	a	00 40	00 43	07 45	08 45	09 45	10 45	11 45	12 45	13 45	14 45	15 45	16 45	17 45	18 45	19 45	20 45	21 45	22 45	23 45	00 43

A until 9 August, FX from 13 August until 27 September
B from 10 August until 28 September
C until 4 August
D from 11 August until 29 September

On Sundays only, National Rail Tickets to stations between Hale and Mouldsworth inclusive are valid for travel on Metrolink services between Manchester City Centre and Altrincham

Table 88

Manchester - Northwich and Chester

Saturdays
from 6 October

Network Diagram - see first Page of Table 88

		NT	NT	NT	NT	NT	NT	NT	NT	NT	NT	NT	NT	NT	NT	NT	NT	NT	NT	NT
Manchester Picc. 10 84 ⇌	d	23p17	06 17	07 17	08 17	09 17	10 17	11 17	12 17	13 17	14 17	15 17	16 17	17 17	18 17	19 17	20 17	21 17	22 17	23 17
Stockport 84	d	23p27	06 30	07 30	08 30	09 30	10 30	11 30	12 30	13 30	14 30	15 30	16 30	17 30	18 30	19 30	20 30	21 30	22 30	23 27
Navigation Road ⇌	d	23p41	06 44	07 44	08 44	09 44	10 44	11 44	12 44	13 44	14 44	15 44	16 44	17 44	18 44	19 44	20 44	21 44	22 44	23 41
Altrincham ⇌	a	23p43	06 46	07 46	08 46	09 46	10 46	11 46	12 46	13 46	14 46	15 46	16 46	17 46	18 46	19 46	20 46	21 46	22 46	23 43
	d	23p43	06 46	07 46	08 46	09 46	10 46	11 46	12 46	13 46	14 46	15 46	16 46	17 46	18 46	19 46	20 46	21 46	22 46	23 43
Hale	d	23p46	06 49	07 49	08 49	09 49	10 49	11 49	12 49	13 49	14 49	15 49	16 49	17 49	18 49	19 49	20 49	21 49	22 49	23 46
Ashley	d	23p49	06 52	07 52	08 52	09 52	10 52	11 52	12 52	13 52	14 52	15 52	16 52	17 52	18 52	19 52	20 52	21 52	22 52	23 49
Mobberley	d	23p52	06 55	07 55	08 55	09 55	10 55	11 55	12 55	13 55	14 55	15 55	16 55	17 55	18 55	19 55	20 55	21 55	22 55	23 52
Knutsford	d	23p57	06 59	07 59	08 59	09 59	10 59	11 59	12 59	13 59	14 59	15 59	16 59	17 59	18 59	19 59	20 59	21 59	22 59	23 57
Plumley	d	00 01	07 03	08 03	09 03	10 03	11 03	12 03	13 03	14 03	15 03	16 03	17 03	18 03	19 03	20 03	21 03	22 03	23 03	00 01
Lostock Gralam	d	00 04	07 07	08 07	09 07	10 07	11 07	12 07	13 07	14 07	15 07	16 07	17 07	18 07	19 07	20 07	21 07	22 07	23 07	00 04
Northwich	d	00 10	07 12	08 12	09 12	10 12	11 12	12 12	13 12	14 12	15 12	16 12	17 12	18 12	19 12	20 12	21 12	22 12	23 12	00 10
Greenbank	d	00 14	07 17	08 17	09 17	10 17	11 17	12 17	13 17	14 17	15 17	16 17	17 17	18 17	19 17	20 17	21 17	22 17	23 17	00 14
Cuddington	d	00 19	07 22	08 22	09 22	10 22	11 22	12 22	13 22	14 22	15 22	16 22	17 22	18 22	19 22	20 22	21 22	22 22	23 22	00 19
Delamere	d	00 24	07 26	08 26	09 26	10 26	11 26	12 26	13 26	14 26	15 26	16 26	17 26	18 26	19 26	20 26	21 26	22 26	23 26	00 24
Mouldsworth	d	00 28	07 31	08 31	09 31	10 31	11 31	12 31	13 31	14 31	15 31	16 31	17 31	18 31	19 31	20 31	21 31	22 31	23 31	00 28
Chester 81	a	00 42	07 47	08 47	09 47	10 47	11 47	12 47	13 47	14 47	15 47	16 47	17 47	18 47	19 47	20 47	21 47	22 47	23 47	00 45

Sundays
until 24 June

		NT	NT	NT	NT	NT	NT	NT	NT
Manchester Picc. 10 84 ⇌	d	23p17	09 22	11 22	13 22	15 22	17 22	19 22	21 22
Stockport 84	d	23p27	09 31	11 31	13 31	15 32	17 31	19 31	21 31
Navigation Road ⇌	d	23p41	09 45	11 45	13 45	15 45	17 45	19 45	21 45
Altrincham ⇌	a	23p43	09 47	11 47	13 47	15 47	17 47	19 47	21 47
	d	23p43	09 47	11 47	13 47	15 48	17 47	19 47	21 47
Hale	d	23p46	09 50	11 50	13 50	15 50	17 50	19 50	21 50
Ashley	d	23p49	09 53	11 53	13 53	15 53	17 53	19 53	21 53
Mobberley	d	23p52	09 56	11 56	13 56	15 56	17 56	19 56	21 56
Knutsford	d	23p57	10 00	12 00	14 00	16 01	18 00	20 00	22 00
Plumley	d	00 01	10 05	12 04	14 04	16 05	18 04	20 04	22 04
Lostock Gralam	d	00 04	10 08	12 08	14 08	16 08	18 08	20 08	22 08
Northwich	d	00 10	10 13	12 13	14 13	16 14	18 13	20 13	22 13
Greenbank	d	00 14	10 18	12 18	14 18	16 18	18 18	20 18	22 18
Cuddington	d	00 19	10 23	12 23	14 23	16 23	18 23	20 23	22 23
Delamere	d	00 24	10 27	12 27	14 27	16 28	18 27	20 27	22 27
Mouldsworth	d	00 28	10 32	12 32	14 32	16 32	18 32	20 32	22 32
Chester 81	a	00 43	10 46	12 43	14 46	16 46	18 46	20 46	22 46

Sundays
1 July to 9 September

		NT	NT	NT	NT	NT	NT	NT	NT
Manchester Picc. 10 84 ⇌	d	23p17	09 22	11 22	13 22	15 22	17 22	19 22	21 22
Stockport 84	d	23p27	09 31	11 31	13 31	15 32	17 31	19 31	21 31
Navigation Road ⇌	d	23p41	09 45	11 45	13 45	15 45	17 45	19 45	21 45
Altrincham ⇌	a	23p43	09 47	11 47	13 47	15 47	17 47	19 47	21 47
	d	23p43	09 47	11 47	13 47	15 48	17 47	19 47	21 47
Hale	d	23p46	09 50	11 50	13 50	15 50	17 50	19 50	21 50
Ashley	d	23p49	09 53	11 53	13 53	15 53	17 53	19 53	21 53
Mobberley	d	23p52	09 56	11 56	13 56	15 56	17 56	19 56	21 56
Knutsford	d	23p57	10 00	12 00	14 00	16 01	18 00	20 00	22 00
Plumley	d	00 01	10 05	12 04	14 04	16 05	18 04	20 04	22 04
Lostock Gralam	d	00 04	10 08	12 08	14 08	16 08	18 08	20 08	22 08
Northwich	d	00 10	10 13	12 13	14 13	16 14	18 13	20 13	22 13
Greenbank	d	00 14	10 18	12 18	14 18	16 18	18 18	20 18	22 18
Cuddington	d	00 19	10 23	12 23	14 23	16 23	18 23	20 23	22 23
Delamere	d	00 24	10 27	12 27	14 27	16 28	18 27	20 27	22 27
Mouldsworth	d	00 28	10 32	12 32	14 32	16 32	18 32	20 32	22 32
Chester 81	a	00 43	10 46	12 43	14 46	16 46	18 46	20 48	22 46

Sundays
16 September to 30 September

		NT	NT	NT	NT	NT	NT	NT	NT
Manchester Picc. 10 84 ⇌	d	23p17	09 22	11 22	13 22	15 22	17 22	19 22	21 22
Stockport 84	d	23p27	09 31	11 31	13 31	15 32	17 31	19 31	21 31
Navigation Road ⇌	d	23p41	09 45	11 45	13 45	15 45	17 45	19 45	21 45
Altrincham ⇌	a	23p43	09 47	11 47	13 47	15 47	17 47	19 47	21 47
	d	23p43	09 47	11 47	13 47	15 48	17 47	19 47	21 47
Hale	d	23p46	09 50	11 50	13 50	15 50	17 50	19 50	21 50
Ashley	d	23p49	09 53	11 53	13 53	15 53	17 53	19 53	21 53
Mobberley	d	23p52	09 56	11 56	13 56	15 56	17 56	19 56	21 56
Knutsford	d	23p57	10 00	12 00	14 00	16 01	18 00	20 00	22 00
Plumley	d	00 01	10 05	12 04	14 04	16 05	18 04	20 04	22 04
Lostock Gralam	d	00 04	10 08	12 08	14 08	16 08	18 08	20 08	22 08
Northwich	d	00 10	10 13	12 13	14 13	16 14	18 13	20 13	22 13
Greenbank	d	00 14	10 18	12 18	14 18	16 18	18 18	20 18	22 18
Cuddington	d	00 19	10 23	12 23	14 23	16 23	18 23	20 23	22 23
Delamere	d	00 24	10 27	12 27	14 27	16 28	18 27	20 27	22 27
Mouldsworth	d	00 28	10 32	12 32	14 32	16 32	18 32	20 32	22 32
Chester 81	a	00 43	10 46	12 43	14 46	16 46	18 46	20 43	22 46

On Sundays only, National Rail Tickets to stations between Hale and Mouldsworth inclusive are valid for travel on Metrolink services between Manchester City Centre and Altrincham

Manchester - Northwich and Chester

Sundays
from 7 October

Network Diagram - see first Page of Table 88

			NT	NT	NT	NT	NT	NT	NT	NT
Manchester Picc. 10	84	d	23p17	09 22	11 21	13 22	15 22	17 22	19 22	21 22
Stockport	84	d	23p27	09 31	11 30	13 31	15 31	17 31	19 31	21 31
Navigation Road		d	23p41	09 45	11 44	13 45	15 45	17 45	19 45	21 45
Altrincham		a	23p43	09 47	11 46	13 47	15 47	17 47	19 47	21 47
		d	23p43	09 47	11 47	13 47	15 47	17 47	19 47	21 47
Hale		d	23p46	09 50	11 49	13 50	15 50	17 50	19 50	21 50
Ashley		d	23p49	09 53	11 52	13 53	15 53	17 53	19 53	21 53
Mobberley		d	23p52	09 56	11 55	13 56	15 56	17 56	19 56	21 56
Knutsford		d	23p57	10 00	12 00	14 00	16 00	18 00	20 00	22 00
Plumley		d	00 01	10 05	12 04	14 04	16 04	18 04	20 04	22 04
Lostock Gralam		d	00 04	10 08	12 07	14 08	16 08	18 08	20 08	22 08
Northwich		d	00 10	10 13	12 13	14 13	16 13	18 13	20 13	22 13
Greenbank		d	00 14	10 18	12 17	14 18	16 18	18 18	20 18	22 18
Cuddington		d	00 19	10 23	12 22	14 23	16 23	18 23	20 23	22 23
Delamere		d	00 24	10 27	12 27	14 27	16 27	18 27	20 27	22 27
Mouldsworth		d	00 28	10 32	12 31	14 32	16 32	18 32	20 32	22 32
Chester	81	a	00 45	10 46	12 46	14 46	16 46	18 46	20 48	22 48

On Sundays only, National Rail Tickets to stations between Hale and Mouldsworth inclusive are valid for travel on Metrolink services between Manchester City Centre and Altrincham

Chester and Northwich - Manchester

Mondays to Fridays
until 28 September

Network Diagram - see first Page of Table 88

Miles				NT MX	NT	NT	NT	NT	NT	NT	NT	NT	NT	NT	NT	NT	NT	NT	NT	NT	NT	NT	NT
0	**Chester**	81	d	22p48	06 05	06 35	06 59	07 35	08 07	09 07	10 07	11 07	12 07	13 07	14 07	15 07	16 07	17 07	18 07	19 07	20 07	21 07	22 48
6½	Mouldsworth		d	22p59	06 16	06 46	07 10	07 46	08 18	09 18	10 18	11 18	12 18	13 18	14 18	15 18	16 18	17 18	18 18	19 18	20 18	21 18	22 59
9½	Delamere		d	23p04	06 21	06 51	07 15	07 51	08 23	09 23	10 23	11 23	12 23	13 23	14 23	15 23	16 23	17 23	18 23	19 23	20 23	21 23	23 04
12½	Cuddington		d	23p08	06 25	06 55	07 19	07 55	08 27	09 27	10 27	11 27	12 27	13 27	14 27	15 27	16 27	17 27	18 27	19 27	20 27	21 27	23 08
15¼	Greenbank		d	23p13	06 30	07 00	07 24	08 00	08 32	09 32	10 32	11 32	12 32	13 32	14 32	15 32	16 32	17 32	18 32	19 32	20 32	21 32	23 13
17	**Northwich**		d	23p17	06 35	07 05	07 29	08 05	08 37	09 37	10 37	11 37	12 37	13 37	14 37	15 37	16 37	17 37	18 37	19 37	20 37	21 37	23 17
18½	Lostock Gralam		d	23p20	06 38	07 08	07 32	08 08	08 40	09 40	10 40	11 40	12 40	13 40	14 40	15 40	16 40	17 40	18 40	19 40	20 40	21 40	23 20
20½	Plumley		d	23p24	06 41	07 11	07 36	08 11	08 43	09 43	10 43	11 43	12 43	13 43	14 43	15 43	16 43	17 43	18 43	19 43	20 43	21 43	23 24
23	Knutsford		d	23p29	06 46	07 17	07 41	08 17	08 49	09 49	10 49	11 49	12 49	13 49	14 49	15 49	16 49	17 49	18 49	19 49	20 49	21 49	23 29
26¼	Mobberley		d	23p33	06 50	07 21	07 45	08 21	08 53	09 53	10 53	11 53	12 53	13 53	14 53	15 53	16 53	17 53	18 53	19 53	20 53	21 53	23 33
27½	Ashley		d	23p36	06 54	07 24	07 49	08 24	08 56	09 56	10 56	11 56	12 56	13 56	14 56	15 56	16 56	17 56	18 56	19 56	20 56	21 56	23 36
29¼	Hale		d	23p39	06 57	07 28	07 53	08 28	08 59	09 59	10 59	11 59	12 59	13 59	14 59	15 59	16 59	17 59	18 59	19 59	20 59	21 59	23 39
30	**Altrincham**		a	23p44	07 01	07 32	07 57	08 32	09 04	10 04	11 04	12 04	13 04	14 04	15 04	16 04	17 04	18 04	19 04	20 04	21 04	22 04	23 44
—			d	23p44	07 02	07 33	07 58	08 33	09 04	10 04	11 04	12 04	13 04	14 04	15 04	16 04	17 04	18 04	19 04	20 04	21 04	22 04	23 44
30½	Navigation Road		d	23p46	07 04	07 35	08 00	08 35	09 06	10 06	11 06	12 06	13 06	14 06	15 06	16 06	17 06	18 06	19 06	20 06	21 06	22 06	23 46
38¾	**Stockport**	84	a	00 02	07 18	07 56	08 19	08 56	09 21	10 21	11 21	12 21	13 21	14 21	15 21	16 21	17 21	18 21	19 21	20 21	21 21	22 21	00 02
44¾	**Manchester Picc.** 10	81	a	00 18	07 31		08 32		09 36	10 36	11 36	12 36	13 36	14 36	15 36	16 36	17 36	18 36	19 35	20 35	21 35	22 35	00 18

Mondays to Fridays
from 1 October

			NT MX	NT	NT	NT	NT	NT	NT	NT	NT	NT	NT	NT	NT	NT	NT	NT	NT	NT	NT	NT
Chester	81	d	22p44	06 01	06 35	06 59	07 35	08 03	09 03	10 03	11 03	12 03	13 03	14 03	15 03	16 03	17 03	18 03	19 03	20 03	21 03	22 44
Mouldsworth		d	22p55	06 12	06 46	07 10	07 46	08 14	09 14	10 14	11 14	12 14	13 14	14 14	15 14	16 14	17 14	18 14	19 14	20 14	21 14	22 55
Delamere		d	23p00	06 17	06 51	07 15	07 51	08 19	09 19	10 19	11 19	12 19	13 19	14 19	15 19	16 19	17 19	18 19	19 19	20 19	21 19	23 00
Cuddington		d	23p04	06 21	06 55	07 19	07 55	08 23	09 23	10 23	11 23	12 23	13 23	14 23	15 23	16 23	17 23	18 23	19 23	20 23	21 23	23 04
Greenbank		d	23p09	06 26	07 00	07 24	08 00	08 28	09 28	10 28	11 28	12 28	13 28	14 28	15 28	16 28	17 28	18 28	19 28	20 28	21 28	23 09
Northwich		d	23p13	06 31	07 05	07 29	08 05	08 33	09 33	10 33	11 33	12 33	13 33	14 33	15 33	16 33	17 33	18 33	19 33	20 33	21 33	23 13
Lostock Gralam		d	23p16	06 34	07 08	07 32	08 08	08 36	09 36	10 36	11 36	12 36	13 36	14 36	15 36	16 36	17 36	18 36	19 36	20 36	21 36	23 16
Plumley		d	23p20	06 37	07 11	07 36	08 11	08 39	09 39	10 39	11 39	12 39	13 39	14 39	15 39	16 39	17 39	18 39	19 39	20 39	21 39	23 20
Knutsford		d	23p25	06 42	07 17	07 41	08 17	08 45	09 45	10 45	11 45	12 45	13 45	14 45	15 45	16 45	17 45	18 45	19 45	20 45	21 45	23 25
Mobberley		d	23p29	06 46	07 21	07 45	08 21	08 49	09 49	10 49	11 49	12 49	13 49	14 49	15 49	16 49	17 49	18 49	19 49	20 49	21 49	23 29
Ashley		d	23p32	06 50	07 24	07 49	08 24	08 52	09 52	10 52	11 52	12 52	13 52	14 52	15 52	16 52	17 52	18 52	19 52	20 52	21 52	23 32
Hale		d	23p35	06 53	07 28	07 53	08 28	08 55	09 55	10 55	11 55	12 55	13 55	14 55	15 55	16 55	17 55	18 55	19 55	20 55	21 55	23 35
Altrincham		a	23p40	06 57	07 32	07 57	08 32	09 00	10 00	11 00	12 00	13 00	14 00	15 00	16 00	17 00	18 00	19 00	20 00	21 00	22 00	23 40
		d	23p40	06 58	07 33	07 58	08 33	09 00	10 00	11 00	12 00	13 00	14 00	15 00	16 00	17 00	18 00	19 00	20 00	21 00	22 00	23 40
Navigation Road		d	23p42	07 00	07 35	08 00	08 35	09 02	10 02	11 02	12 02	13 02	14 02	15 02	16 02	17 02	18 02	19 02	20 02	21 02	22 02	23 42
Stockport	84	a	00 02	07 18	07 56	08 19	08 56	09 21	10 21	11 21	12 21	13 21	14 21	15 21	16 21	17 21	18 21	19 21	20 21	21 21	22 21	00 02
Manchester Picc. 10	81	a	00 18	07 31		08 32		09 36	10 36	11 36	12 36	13 36	14 36	15 36	16 36	17 36	18 36	19 35	20 35	21 35	22 35	00 18

Saturdays
until 29 September

			NT	NT	NT	NT	NT	NT	NT	NT	NT	NT	NT	NT	NT	NT	NT	NT	NT	NT
Chester	81	d	22p48	06 05	07 03	08 07	09 07	10 07	11 07	12 07	13 07	14 07	15 07	16 07	17 07	18 07	19 07	20 07	21 33	22 49
Mouldsworth		d	22p59	06 16	07 14	08 18	09 18	10 18	11 18	12 18	13 18	14 18	15 18	16 18	17 18	18 18	19 18	20 18	21 45	23 00
Delamere		d	23p04	06 21	07 19	08 23	09 23	10 23	11 23	12 23	13 23	14 23	15 23	16 23	17 23	18 23	19 23	20 23	21 49	23 05
Cuddington		d	23p08	06 25	07 23	08 27	09 27	10 27	11 27	12 27	13 27	14 27	15 27	16 27	17 27	18 27	19 27	20 27	21 54	23 09
Greenbank		d	23p13	06 30	07 28	08 32	09 32	10 32	11 32	12 32	13 32	14 32	15 32	16 32	17 32	18 32	19 32	20 32	21 58	23 14
Northwich		d	23p17	06 35	07 33	08 37	09 37	10 37	11 37	12 37	13 37	14 37	15 37	16 37	17 37	18 37	19 37	20 37	22 03	23 18
Lostock Gralam		d	23p20	06 38	07 36	08 40	09 40	10 40	11 40	12 40	13 40	14 40	15 40	16 40	17 40	18 40	19 40	20 40	22 06	23 21
Plumley		d	23p24	06 41	07 40	08 43	09 43	10 43	11 43	12 43	13 43	14 43	15 43	16 43	17 43	18 43	19 43	20 43	22 10	23 25
Knutsford		d	23p29	06 46	07 45	08 49	09 49	10 49	11 49	12 49	13 49	14 49	15 49	16 49	17 49	18 49	19 49	20 49	22 15	23 30
Mobberley		d	23p33	06 50	07 49	08 53	09 53	10 53	11 53	12 53	13 53	14 53	15 53	16 53	17 53	18 53	19 53	20 53	22 19	23 34
Ashley		d	23p36	06 54	07 53	08 56	09 56	10 56	11 56	12 56	13 56	14 56	15 56	16 56	17 56	18 56	19 56	20 56	22 23	23 37
Hale		d	23p39	06 57	07 57	08 59	09 59	10 59	11 59	12 59	13 59	14 59	15 59	16 59	17 59	18 59	19 59	20 59	22 26	23 40
Altrincham		a	23p44	07 01	08 01	09 04	10 04	11 04	12 04	13 04	14 04	15 04	16 04	17 04	18 04	19 04	20 04	21 04	22 30	23 45
		d	23p44	07 02	08 02	09 04	10 04	11 04	12 04	13 04	14 04	15 04	16 04	17 04	18 04	19 04	20 04	21 04	22 31	23 45
Navigation Road		d	23p46	07 04	08 04	09 06	10 06	11 06	12 06	13 06	14 06	15 06	16 06	17 06	18 06	19 06	20 06	21 06	22 33	23 47
Stockport	84	a	00 02	07 18	08 19	09 21	10 21	11 21	12 21	13 21	14 21	15 21	16 21	17 21	18 21	19 21	20 21	21 21	22 47	00 02
Manchester Picc. 10	81	a	00 18	07 31	08 32	09 36	10 36	11 36	12 36	13 36	14 36	15 36	16 36	17 36	18 36	19 35	20 35	21 35	23 00	00 15

Saturdays
from 6 October

			NT	NT	NT	NT	NT	NT	NT	NT	NT	NT	NT	NT	NT	NT	NT	NT	NT	NT
Chester	81	d	22p44	06 01	06 59	08 03	09 03	10 03	11 03	12 03	13 03	14 03	15 03	16 03	17 03	18 03	19 03	20 03	21 33	22 45
Mouldsworth		d	22p55	06 12	07 10	08 14	09 14	10 14	11 14	12 14	13 14	14 14	15 14	16 14	17 14	18 14	19 14	20 14	21 45	22 56
Delamere		d	23p00	06 17	07 15	08 19	09 19	10 19	11 19	12 19	13 19	14 19	15 19	16 19	17 19	18 19	19 19	20 19	21 49	23 01
Cuddington		d	23p04	06 21	07 19	08 23	09 23	10 23	11 23	12 23	13 23	14 23	15 23	16 23	17 23	18 23	19 23	20 23	21 54	23 05
Greenbank		d	23p09	06 26	07 24	08 28	09 28	10 28	11 28	12 28	13 28	14 28	15 28	16 28	17 28	18 28	19 28	20 28	21 58	23 10
Northwich		d	23p13	06 31	07 29	08 33	09 33	10 33	11 33	12 33	13 33	14 33	15 33	16 33	17 33	18 33	19 33	20 33	22 03	23 14
Lostock Gralam		d	23p16	06 34	07 32	08 36	09 36	10 36	11 36	12 36	13 36	14 36	15 36	16 36	17 36	18 36	19 36	20 36	22 06	23 17
Plumley		d	23p20	06 37	07 36	08 39	09 39	10 39	11 39	12 39	13 39	14 39	15 39	16 39	17 39	18 39	19 39	20 39	22 10	23 21
Knutsford		d	23p25	06 42	07 41	08 45	09 45	10 45	11 45	12 45	13 45	14 45	15 45	16 45	17 45	18 45	19 45	20 45	22 15	23 26
Mobberley		d	23p29	06 46	07 45	08 49	09 49	10 49	11 49	12 49	13 49	14 49	15 49	16 49	17 49	18 49	19 49	20 49	22 19	23 30
Ashley		d	23p32	06 50	07 49	08 52	09 52	10 52	11 52	12 52	13 52	14 52	15 52	16 52	17 52	18 52	19 52	20 52	22 23	23 33
Hale		d	23p35	06 53	07 53	08 55	09 55	10 55	11 55	12 55	13 55	14 55	15 55	16 55	17 55	18 55	19 55	20 55	22 26	23 36
Altrincham		a	23p40	06 57	07 57	09 00	10 00	11 00	12 00	13 00	14 00	15 00	16 00	17 00	18 00	19 00	20 00	21 00	22 30	23 41
		d	23p40	06 58	07 58	09 00	10 00	11 00	12 00	13 00	14 00	15 00	16 00	17 00	18 00	19 00	20 00	21 00	22 31	23 41
Navigation Road		d	23p42	07 00	08 00	09 02	10 02	11 02	12 02	13 02	14 02	15 02	16 02	17 02	18 02	19 02	20 02	21 02	22 33	23 43
Stockport	84	a	00 02	07 18	08 19	09 21	10 21	11 21	12 21	13 21	14 21	15 21	16 21	17 21	18 21	19 21	20 21	21 21	22 47	00 02
Manchester Picc. 10	81	a	00 18	07 31	08 32	09 36	10 36	11 36	12 36	13 36	14 36	15 36	16 36	17 36	18 36	19 35	20 35	21 35	23 00	00 15

On Sundays only, National Rail Tickets from stations between Mouldsworth and Hale inclusive are valid for travel on Metrolink services between Altrincham and Manchester City Centre

Chester and Northwich - Manchester

Sundays until 24 June

Network Diagram - see first Page of Table 88

			NT	NT	NT	NT	NT	NT	NT	NT
Chester	81	d	22p49	08 58	11 07	13 07	15 07	17 07	19 07	21 07
Mouldsworth		d	23p00	09 09	11 18	13 18	15 18	17 18	19 18	21 18
Delamere		d	23p05	09 14	11 23	13 23	15 23	17 23	19 23	21 23
Cuddington		d	23p09	09 18	11 27	13 27	15 27	17 27	19 27	21 27
Greenbank		d	23p14	09 23	11 32	13 32	15 32	17 32	19 32	21 32
Northwich		d	23p18	09 28	11 37	13 37	15 37	17 37	19 37	21 37
Lostock Gralam		d	23p21	09 31	11 40	13 40	15 40	17 40	19 40	21 40
Plumley		d	23p25	09 34	11 43	13 43	15 43	17 43	19 43	21 43
Knutsford		d	23p30	09 40	11 49	13 49	15 49	17 49	19 49	21 49
Mobberley		d	23p34	09 44	11 53	13 53	15 53	17 53	19 53	21 53
Ashley		d	23p37	09 47	11 56	13 56	15 56	17 56	19 56	21 56
Hale		d	23p40	09 50	11 59	13 59	15 59	17 59	19 59	21 59
Altrincham		a	23p45	09 55	12 04	14 04	16 04	18 04	20 04	22 04
		d	23p45	09 55	12 04	14 04	16 04	18 04	20 04	22 04
Navigation Road		d	23p47	09 57	12 06	14 06	16 06	18 06	20 06	22 06
Stockport	84	a	00 02	10 12	12 21	14 21	16 21	18 21	20 21	22 21
Manchester Picc. [10]	81	a	00 15	10 22	12 31	14 33	16 33	18 33	20 33	22 33

Sundays 1 July to 9 September

			NT	NT	NT	NT	NT	NT	NT	NT
Chester	81	d	22p49	08 58	11 07	13 07	15 07	17 07	19 07	21 07
Mouldsworth		d	23p00	09 09	11 18	13 18	15 18	17 18	19 18	21 18
Delamere		d	23p05	09 14	11 23	13 23	15 23	17 23	19 23	21 23
Cuddington		d	23p09	09 18	11 27	13 27	15 27	17 27	19 27	21 27
Greenbank		d	23p14	09 23	11 32	13 32	15 32	17 32	19 32	21 32
Northwich		d	23p18	09 28	11 37	13 37	15 37	17 37	19 37	21 37
Lostock Gralam		d	23p21	09 31	11 40	13 40	15 40	17 40	19 40	21 40
Plumley		d	23p25	09 34	11 43	13 43	15 43	17 43	19 43	21 43
Knutsford		d	23p30	09 40	11 49	13 49	15 49	17 49	19 49	21 49
Mobberley		d	23p34	09 44	11 53	13 53	15 53	17 53	19 53	21 53
Ashley		d	23p37	09 47	11 56	13 56	15 56	17 56	19 56	21 56
Hale		d	23p40	09 50	11 59	13 59	15 59	17 59	19 59	21 59
Altrincham		a	23p45	09 55	12 04	14 04	16 04	18 04	20 04	22 04
		d	23p45	09 55	12 04	14 04	16 04	18 04	20 04	22 04
Navigation Road		d	23p47	09 57	12 06	14 06	16 06	18 06	20 06	22 06
Stockport	84	a	00 02	10 12	12 21	14 21	16 21	18 21	20 21	22 21
Manchester Picc. [10]	81	a	00 15	10 22	12 31	14 33	16 33	18 33	20 33	22 33

Sundays 16 September to 30 September

			NT	NT	NT	NT	NT	NT	NT	NT
Chester	81	d	22p49	08 58	11 07	13 07	15 07	17 07	19 07	21 07
Mouldsworth		d	23p00	09 09	11 18	13 18	15 18	17 18	19 18	21 18
Delamere		d	23p05	09 14	11 23	13 23	15 23	17 23	19 23	21 23
Cuddington		d	23p09	09 18	11 27	13 27	15 27	17 27	19 27	21 27
Greenbank		d	23p14	09 23	11 32	13 32	15 32	17 32	19 32	21 32
Northwich		d	23p18	09 28	11 37	13 37	15 37	17 37	19 37	21 37
Lostock Gralam		d	23p21	09 31	11 40	13 40	15 40	17 40	19 40	21 40
Plumley		d	23p25	09 34	11 43	13 43	15 43	17 43	19 43	21 43
Knutsford		d	23p30	09 40	11 49	13 49	15 49	17 49	19 49	21 49
Mobberley		d	23p34	09 44	11 53	13 53	15 53	17 53	19 53	21 53
Ashley		d	23p37	09 47	11 56	13 56	15 56	17 56	19 56	21 56
Hale		d	23p40	09 50	11 59	13 59	15 59	17 59	19 59	21 59
Altrincham		a	23p45	09 55	12 04	14 04	16 04	18 04	20 04	22 04
		d	23p45	09 55	12 04	14 04	16 04	18 04	20 04	22 04
Navigation Road		d	23p47	09 57	12 06	14 06	16 06	18 06	20 06	22 06
Stockport	84	a	00 02	10 12	12 21	14 21	16 21	18 21	20 21	22 21
Manchester Picc. [10]	81	a	00 15	10 22	12 31	14 33	16 33	18 33	20 33	22 33

Sundays from 7 October

			NT	NT	NT	NT	NT	NT	NT	NT
Chester	81	d	22p45	08 54	11 03	13 03	15 03	17 03	19 03	21 03
Mouldsworth		d	22p56	09 05	11 14	13 14	15 14	17 14	19 14	21 14
Delamere		d	23p01	09 10	11 19	13 19	15 19	17 19	19 19	21 19
Cuddington		d	23p05	09 14	11 23	13 23	15 23	17 23	19 23	21 23
Greenbank		d	23p10	09 19	11 28	13 28	15 28	17 28	19 28	21 28
Northwich		d	23p14	09 24	11 33	13 33	15 33	17 33	19 33	21 33
Lostock Gralam		d	23p17	09 27	11 36	13 36	15 36	17 36	19 36	21 36
Plumley		d	23p21	09 30	11 39	13 39	15 39	17 39	19 39	21 39
Knutsford		d	23p26	09 36	11 45	13 45	15 45	17 45	19 45	21 45
Mobberley		d	23p30	09 40	11 49	13 49	15 49	17 49	19 49	21 49
Ashley		d	23p33	09 43	11 52	13 52	15 52	17 52	19 52	21 52
Hale		d	23p36	09 46	11 55	13 55	15 55	17 55	19 55	21 55
Altrincham		a	23p41	09 51	12 00	14 00	16 00	18 00	20 00	22 00
		d	23p41	09 51	12 00	14 00	16 00	18 00	20 00	22 00
Navigation Road		d	23p43	09 53	12 02	14 02	16 02	18 02	20 02	22 02
Stockport	84	a	00 02	10 12	12 21	14 21	16 21	18 21	20 21	22 21
Manchester Picc. [10]	81	a	00 15	10 22	12 31	14 33	16 33	18 33	20 33	22 33

On Sundays only, National Rail Tickets from stations between Mouldsworth and Hale inclusive are valid for travel on Metrolink services between Altrincham and Manchester City Centre

Liverpool - Warrington Central - Manchester and Manchester Airport

Network Diagram - see first Page of Table 88

Miles			NT MO	NT MO	NT MO	NT MX	NT MO	NT MX	NT	NT	NT	NT	TP	NT	EM	NT	NT	NT	TP	NT	EM	NT	NT
			A	A	A								◇[1] B ✠		◇ C				◇[1] B ✠		◇ C		
0	**Liverpool Lime Street** [10] 90,91	d	22p01	23p01	23p01	23p38	03 38	03 38	05 13	05 49		06 13	06 15	06 21	06 47	06 50	07 13		07 15	07 26	07 42	07 45	08 13
1¾	Edge Hill 90,91	d				23p42				05 53						06 54				07 30			
3¾	Mossley Hill 91	d				23p47				05 58				06 29		06 59				07 35		07 53	
4½	West Allerton 91	d				23p50				06 00				06 31		07 01				07 37		07 56	
—	Liverpool Central [10] 103	d																					
5½	L'pool Sth Parkway [7] 91,103	d				23p53				06 03			06 25	06 34	06 57	07 04			07 25	07 40	07 53	07 59	
7¼	Hunts Cross 103	d				23p56				06 07						07 08					07 59	08 04	
8¼	Halewood	d				23p59				06 09						07 10						08 07	
10½	Hough Green	d				00 03				06 13				06 41		07 14				07 47		08 11	
12¾	Widnes	d				00 06				06 17				06 44	07 07	07 18			07 33		08 05	08 15	
16	Sankey for Penketh	d				00 11				06 22						07 23						08 20	
18½	**Warrington Central**	a				00 16				06 28			06 37	06 52	07 15	07 29			07 39	07 56	08 13	08 25	
—		d				00 17					06 02		06 38	06 53	07 15			07 22	07 40	07 57	08 13	08 25	
20¼	Padgate	d									06 05			06 56				07 25		08 00			
21¾	Birchwood	d									06 08		06 43	06 59	07 20			07 28	07 45	08 03	08 18	08 30	
24½	Glazebrook	d									06 13			07 04				07 33		08 08			
25¾	Irlam	d									06 16			07 07				07 36	07 50	08 11		08 37	
28	Flixton	d									06 20			07 11				07 40		08 15		08 41	
28½	Chassen Road	d									06 22			07 13				07 42		08 17		08 43	
29	Urmston	d									06 24			07 15				07 44		08 19		08 46	
30¼	Humphrey Park	d									06 26			07 17				07 46		08 21		08 49	
31	Trafford Park	d									06 29			07 20				07 49		08 24		08 52	
34	Deansgate 84,85	a									06 36			07 29				07 58		08 32		09 00	
34½	**Manchester Oxford Road** 84,85	a	00 12	23p47	01 12						06 41	06 57	07 00	07 36	07 38		07 57	08 03	08 04	08 36	08 38	09 04	08 57
35	**ManchesterPicc** [10] 78,84,85	a		23p50		00 40	04 20	04 20	05 57			07 01	07 09		07 41		08 01		08 08		08 41		09 01
—	Stockport 84	a													07 53						08 53		
—	Sheffield [7] 78	a													08 34						09 35		
44¾	**Manchester Airport** 85	a		00 07			04 33	04 34	06 14			07 22					08 22						09 22

		TP	NT	EM	NT	NT	TP	NT	EM	NT	NT	NT	TP	NT	EM	NT	NT	TP	NT	EM	NT	NT	TP
		◇[1] B ✠		◇ C			◇[1] B ✠		◇ C			D	◇[1] B ✠		◇ C			◇[1] B ✠		◇ C			◇[1] B ✠
Liverpool Lime Street [10] 90,91	d	08 22	08 26	08 52	08 55	09 13	09 22	09 27	09 52	09 55	10 13	10 16	10 22	10 27	10 52	10 55	11 13	11 22	11 27	11 52	11 55	12 13	12 22
Edge Hill 90,91	d		08 30		08 59					09 59						10 59					11 59		
Mossley Hill 91	d		08 35		09 04			09 35		10 04				10 35		11 04			11 35		12 04		
West Allerton 91	d		08 37		09 06			09 37		10 06				10 37		11 06			11 37		12 06		
Liverpool Central [10] 103	d																						
L'pool Sth Parkway [7] 91,103	d	08 32	08 40	09 03	09 09		09 32	09 40	10 03	10 09		10a27	10 32	10 40	11 03	11 09		11 32	11 40	12 03	12 09		12 32
Hunts Cross 103	d				09 13					10 13						11 13					12 13		
Halewood	d				09 16					10 16						11 16					12 16		
Hough Green	d		08 47		09 20			09 47		10 20				10 47		11 20			11 47		12 20		
Widnes	d		08 50	09 11	09 23			09 50	10 11	10 23				10 50	11 11	11 23			11 50	12 11	12 23		
Sankey for Penketh	d				09 28					10 28						11 28					12 28		
Warrington Central	a	08 44	08 58	09 18	09 33		09 44	09 58	10 18	10 33			10 44	10 58	11 18	11 33		11 44	11 58	12 18	12 33		12 44
	d	08 45	08 59	09 19	09 34		09 45	09 59	10 19	10 34			10 45	10 59	11 19	11 34		11 45	11 59	12 19	12 34		12 45
Padgate	d		09 02					10 02						11 02					12 02				
Birchwood	d	08 50	09 05		09 38		09 50	10 05		10 38			10 50	11 05		11 38		11 50	12 05		12 38		12 50
Glazebrook	d							10 10											12 10				
Irlam	d		09 11		09 44			10 13		10 44				11 11		11 44			12 13		12 44		
Flixton	d		09 15					10 17						11 15					12 17				
Chassen Road	d							10 19											12 19				
Urmston	d		09 18		09 49			10 21		10 49				11 18		11 49			12 21		12 49		
Humphrey Park	d		09 20											11 20									
Trafford Park	d		09 23											11 23									
Deansgate 84,85	a		09 31		09 59			10 31		10 59				11 31		11 59			12 31		12 59		
Manchester Oxford Road 84,85	a	09 05	09 36	09 39	10 04	09 57	10 05	10 36	10 39	11 04	10 57		11 05	11 36	11 39	12 04	11 57	12 05	12 36	12 39	13 04	12 57	13 05
ManchesterPicc [10] 78,84,85	a	09 09		09 41		10 01	10 09		10 41		11 01		11 09		11 41		12 01	12 09		12 41		13 01	13 09
Stockport 84	a			09 53					10 53						11 53					12 53			
Sheffield [7] 78	a			10 35					11 34						12 35					13 35			
Manchester Airport 85	a					10 22					11 22						12 22					13 22	

A from 21 May
B To Scarborough
C To Norwich
D From Preston

Liverpool - Warrington Central - Manchester and Manchester Airport

Network Diagram - see first Page of Table 88

	NT	EM	NT	NT	TP	NT	EM	NT	NT	TP	NT	EM	NT	NT	TP	NT	EM	NT	NT	TP	NT
		◇ A			◇■ B		◇ A			◇■ B		◇ A			◇■ C		◇ A			◇■ B	
Liverpool Lime Street ■ 90,91 d	12 27	12 52	12 55	13 13	13 22	13 27	13 52	13 55	14 13	14 22	14 27	14 52	14 55	15 13	15 22	15 27	15 52	15 55	16 13	16 22	16 27
Edge Hill 90,91 d			12 59					13 59					14 59					15 59			
Mossley Hill 91 d	12 35		13 04			13 35		14 04			14 35		15 04			15 35		16 04			16 35
West Allerton 91 d	12 37		13 06			13 37		14 06			14 37		15 06			15 37		16 06			16 37
Liverpool Central ■ 103 d																					
L'pool Sth Parkway ■ 91,103 ✈ d	12 40	13 03	13 09		13 32	13 40	14 03	14 09		14 32	14 40	15 03	15 09		15 32	15 40	16 03	16 09		16 32	16 40
Hunts Cross 103 d			13 13					14 13					15 13					16 13			
Halewood d			13 16					14 16					15 16					16 16			
Hough Green d	12 47		13 20			13 47		14 20			14 47		15 20			15 47		16 20			16 47
Widnes d	12 50	13 11	13 23			13 50	14 11	14 23			14 50	15 11	15 23			15 50	16 11	16 23			16 50
Sankey for Penketh d			13 28					14 28					15 28					16 28			
Warrington Central a	12 58	13 18	13 33		13 44	13 58	14 18	14 33		14 44	14 58	15 18	15 33		15 44	15 58	16 18	16 33		16 44	16 58
d	12 59	13 19	13 34		13 45	13 59	14 19	14 34		14 45	14 59	15 19	15 34		15 45	15 59	16 19	16 34		16 45	16 59
Padgate d	13 02					14 02					15 02					16 02					17 02
Birchwood d	13 05		13 38		13 50	14 05		14 38		14 50	15 05		15 38		15 50	16 05		16 38		16 50	17 05
Glazebrook d						14 10										16 10					
Irlam d	13 11		13 44			14 13		14 44			15 11		15 44			16 13		16 44			17 11
Flixton d	13 15					14 17					15 15					16 17					17 15
Chassen Road d						14 19										16 19					
Urmston d	13 18		13 49			14 21		14 49			15 18		15 49			16 21		16 49			17 18
Humphrey Park d	13 20										15 20										17 20
Trafford Park d	13 23										15 23										17 23
Deansgate 84,85 a	13 31		13 59			14 31		14 59			15 31		15 59			16 30		16 59			17 31
Manchester Oxford Road 84,85 a	13 36	13 39	14 04	13 57	14 05	14 36	14 39	15 04	14 57	15 05	15 36	15 39	16 04	15 57	16 05	16 36	16 38	17 04	16 57	17 05	17 36
ManchesterPicc ■ 78,84,85 a		13 41		14 01	14 09		14 41		15 01	15 09		15 41		16 01	16 09		16 41		17 01	17 09	
Stockport 84 a		13 53					14 53					15 53					16 53				
Sheffield ■ 78 a		14 35					15 35					16 34					17 40				
Manchester Airport 85 ✈ a				14 22					15 22					16 22					17 22		

	EM	NT	NT	TP	NT	EM	NT	NT	TP	NT	EM	NT	TP	NT	EM	NT	NT	TP	NT	EM	NT	TP
	◇ D			◇■ B		◇ A			◇■ B		◇ D		◇■ E		◇ D			◇■ F		◇ D		◇■ F
Liverpool Lime Street ■ 90,91 d	16 52	16 55	17 06	17 22	17 25	17 52	17 55	18 13	18 22	18 25	18 52	18 55	19 22		19 52	19 55	20 09	20 22	20 55	21 37	21 55	22 30
Edge Hill 90,91 d		16 59			17 29		17 59			18 29		18 59				19 59			20 59		21 59	
Mossley Hill 91 d		17 04			17 34		18 04			18 34		19 04				20 04			21 04		22 04	
West Allerton 91 d		17 06			17 36		18 06			18 36		19 06				20 06			21 06		22 06	
Liverpool Central ■ 103 d																						
L'pool Sth Parkway ■ 91,103 ✈ d	17 03	17 09		17 32	17 39	18 03	18 09		18 32	18 39	19 03	19 09	19 32		20 03	20 09		20 32	21 09	21 47	22 09	22 40
Hunts Cross 103 d		17 13			17 43		18 13			18 43		19 13				20 13			21 13		22 13	
Halewood d		17 16			17 46		18 16			18 46		19 16				20 16			21 16		22 16	
Hough Green d		17 20			17 50		18 20			18 50		19 20				20 20			21 20		22 20	
Widnes d	17 11	17 23			17 53	18 11	18 23			18 53	19 11	19 23			20 11	20 23			21 23	21 55	22 23	
Sankey for Penketh d		17 28			17 58		18 28			18 58		19 28				20 28			21 28		22 28	
Warrington Central a	17 18	17 33		17 44	18 03	18 18	18 33		18 44	19 03	19 18	19 34	19 44		20 18	20 34		20 44	21 33	22 03	22 33	22 52
d	17 19	17 34		17 45	18 04	18 19	18 34		18 45	19 04	19 19		19 45	19 56	20 19			20 45	21 34	22 03	22 34	22 53
Padgate d					18 07					19 07				19 59					21 37		22 37	
Birchwood d		17 38		17 50	18 10		18 38		18 50	19 10			19 50	20 02				20 50	21 40		22 40	22 58
Glazebrook d										19 15				20 07					21 45		22 45	
Irlam d		17 44			18 16		18 44			19 18				20 10					21 48		22 48	
Flixton d					18 20									20 14					21 52		22 52	
Chassen Road d														20 16					21 54		22 54	
Urmston d		17 49			18 23		18 49			19 23				20 18					21 56		22 56	
Humphrey Park d														20 20					21 58		22 58	
Trafford Park d														20 23					22 01		23 01	
Deansgate 84,85 a		17 59			18 31		18 59			19 31				20 31					22 08		23 08	
Manchester Oxford Road 84,85 a	17 38	18 04	17 57	18 05	18 36	18 39	19 04	18 57	19 05	19 36	19 39		20 05	20 36	20 39		20 57	21 06	22 13	22 23	23 13	23 14
ManchesterPicc ■ 78,84,85 a	17 41		18 01	18 09		18 41		19 01	19 09		19 41		20 09		20 41		21 01	21 09		22 26		23 19
Stockport 84 a	17 53					18 53					19 53				20 53					22 37		
Sheffield ■ 78 a	18 41					19 33					20 36				21 35					23 35		
Manchester Airport 85 ✈ a			18 22					19 24									21 20					

A To Norwich
B To Scarborough
C To Middlesbrough
D To Nottingham
E To Hull
F To York

Liverpool - Warrington Central - Manchester and Manchester Airport

Network Diagram - see first Page of Table 88

	NT
Liverpool Lime Street ■ 90,91 d	23 38
Edge Hill 90,91 d	23 42
Mossley Hill 91 d	23 47
West Allerton 91 d	23 50
Liverpool Central ■ 103 d	
L'pool Sth Parkway ■ 91,103 ✈ d	23 53
Hunts Cross 103 d	23 56
Halewood d	23 59
Hough Green d	00 03
Widnes d	00 06
Sankey for Penketh d	00 11
Warrington Central a	00 16
d	00 17
Padgate d	
Birchwood d	
Glazebrook d	
Irlam d	
Flixton d	
Chassen Road d	
Urmston d	
Humphrey Park d	
Trafford Park d	
Deansgate 84,85 a	
Manchester Oxford Road 84,85 a	
ManchesterPicc ■ 78,84,85 a	00 40
Stockport 84 a	
Sheffield ■ 78 a	
Manchester Airport 85 ✈ a	

Saturdays

	NT	NT	NT	NT	NT	TP	NT	EM	NT	NT	TP	NT	EM	NT	NT	TP	NT	EM	NT	NT	TP	NT
						◇■ A		◇ B			◇■ A		◇ B			◇■ A		◇ B			◇■ A	
Liverpool Lime Street ■ 90,91 d	23p38	03 38	05 13	05 49	06 13	06 15	06 25	06 49	06 55	07 13	07 15	07 26	07 42	07 45	08 13	08 22	08 26	08 52	08 55	09 13	09 22	09 27
Edge Hill 90,91 d	23p42			05 53					06 59			07 30					08 30		08 59			
Mossley Hill 91 d	23p47			05 58			06 33		07 04			07 35		07 53			08 35		09 04			09 35
West Allerton 91 d	23p50			06 00			06 35		07 06			07 37		07 56			08 37		09 06			09 37
Liverpool Central ■ 103 d																						
L'pool Sth Parkway ■ 91,103 ✈ d	23p53			06 03		06 25	06 38	06 59	07 09		07 25	07 40	07 52	07 59		08 32	08 40	09 03	09 09		09 32	09 40
Hunts Cross 103 d	23p56			06 07					07 13				07 59	08 04					09 13			
Halewood d	23p59			06 09					07 16					08 07					09 16			
Hough Green d	00 03			06 13			06 46		07 20			07 47		08 11			08 47		09 20			09 47
Widnes d	00 06			06 17			06 49	07 07	07 23		07 33		08 05	08 15			08 50	09 11	09 23			09 50
Sankey for Penketh d	00 11			06 22					07 28					08 20					09 28			
Warrington Central a	00 16			06 28		06 37	06 57	07 15	07 34		07 39	07 56	08 13	08 25		08 44	08 58	09 18	09 33		09 44	09 58
d	00 17					06 38	06 58	07 15			07 40	07 57	08 13	08 25		08 45	08 59	09 19	09 34		09 45	09 59
Padgate d							07 01					08 00					09 02					10 02
Birchwood d						06 43	07 04	07 20			07 45	08 03	08 18	08 30		08 50	09 05		09 38		09 50	10 05
Glazebrook d							07 09					08 08										10 10
Irlam d							07 12				07 50	08 11		08 37			09 11		09 44			10 13
Flixton d							07 16					08 15		08 41			09 15					10 17
Chassen Road d							07 18					08 17		08 43								10 19
Urmston d							07 20					08 19		08 46			09 18		09 49			10 21
Humphrey Park d							07 22					08 21		08 49			09 20					
Trafford Park d							07 25					08 24		08 52			09 23					
Deansgate 84,85 a							07 32					08 32		09 00			09 31		09 59			10 31
Manchester Oxford Road 84,85 a					06 57	07 00	07 37	07 38		07 57	08 04	08 36	08 38	09 04	08 57	09 05	09 36	09 39	10 04	09 57	10 05	10 36
ManchesterPicc ■ 78,84,85 a	00 40	04 14	05 57		07 01	07 09		07 41		08 01	08 08		08 41		09 01	09 09		09 41		10 01	10 09	
Stockport 84 a								07 53					08 53					09 53				
Sheffield ■ 78 a								08 34					09 35					10 35				
Manchester Airport 85 ✈ a		04 30	06 14		07 22					08 22					09 22					10 22		

A To Scarborough
B To Norwich

Liverpool - Warrington Central - Manchester and Manchester Airport

Network Diagram - see first Page of Table 88

	EM	NT	NT	TP	NT	EM	NT	NT	TP	NT	EM	NT	NT	TP	NT	EM	NT	NT	TP	NT	EM	NT
	◇			◇1		◇			◇1		◇			◇1		◇			◇1		◇	
	A			B		A			B		A			B		A			B		A	
				⌶					⌶					⌶					⌶			
Liverpool Lime Street 10 90,91 d	09 52	09 55	10 13	10 22	10 27	10 52	10 55	11 13	11 22	11 27	11 52	11 55	12 13	12 22	12 27	12 52	12 55	13 13	13 22	13 27	13 52	13 55
Edge Hill 90,91 d		09 59					10 59					11 59					12 59					13 59
Mossley Hill 91 d		10 04			10 35		11 04			11 35		12 04			12 35		13 04			13 35		14 04
West Allerton 91 d		10 06			10 37		11 06			11 37		12 06			12 37		13 06			13 37		14 06
Liverpool Central 10 103 d																						
L'pool Sth Parkway 7 91,103 ✈ d	10 03	10 09		10 32	10 40	11 03	11 09		11 32	11 40	12 03	12 09		12 32	12 40	13 03	13 09		13 32	13 40	14 03	14 09
Hunts Cross 103 d		10 13					11 13					12 13					13 13					14 13
Halewood d		10 16					11 16					12 16					13 16					14 16
Hough Green d		10 20			10 47		11 20			11 47		12 20			12 47		13 20			13 47		14 20
Widnes d	10 11	10 23			10 50	11 11	11 23			11 50	12 11	12 23			12 50	13 11	13 23			13 50	14 11	14 23
Sankey for Penketh d		10 28					11 28					12 28					13 28					14 28
Warrington Central a	10 18	10 33		10 44	10 58	11 18	11 33		11 44	11 58	12 18	12 33		12 44	12 58	13 18	13 33		13 44	13 58	14 18	14 33
d	10 19	10 34		10 45	10 59	11 19	11 34		11 45	11 59	12 19	12 34		12 45	12 59	13 19	13 34		13 45	13 59	14 19	14 34
Padgate d					11 02					12 02					13 02					14 02		
Birchwood d		10 38		10 50	11 05		11 38		11 50	12 05		12 38		12 50	13 05		13 38		13 50	14 05		14 38
Glazebrook d										12 10										14 10		
Irlam d		10 44			11 11		11 44			12 13		12 44			13 11		13 44			14 13		14 44
Flixton d					11 15					12 17					13 15					14 17		
Chassen Road d										12 19										14 19		
Urmston d		10 49			11 18		11 49			12 21		12 49			13 18		13 49			14 21		14 49
Humphrey Park d					11 20										13 20							
Trafford Park d					11 23										13 23							
Deansgate 84,85 ⇌ a		10 59			11 31		11 59			12 31		12 59			13 31		13 59			14 31		14 59
Manchester Oxford Road 84,85 a	10 39	11 04	10 57	11 05	11 36	11 39	12 04	11 57	12 05	12 36	12 39	13 04	12 57	13 05	13 36	13 39	14 04	13 57	14 05	14 36	14 39	15 04
ManchesterPicc 10 78,84,85 ⇌ a	10 41		11 01	11 09		11 41		12 01	12 09		12 41		13 01	13 09		13 41		14 01	14 09		14 41	
Stockport 84 a	10 53					11 53					12 53					13 53					14 53	
Sheffield 7 78 ⇌ a	11 35					12 35					13 35					14 35					15 36	
Manchester Airport 85 ✈ a			11 22					12 22					13 22					14 22				

	NT	TP	NT	EM	NT	NT	TP	NT	EM	NT	NT	TP	NT	EM	NT	NT	TP	NT	EM	NT	NT
		◇1		◇			◇1		◇			◇1		◇			◇1		◇		
		B		A			B		A			B		C			B		A		
		⌶																			
Liverpool Lime Street 10 90,91 d	14 13	14 22	14 27	14 52	14 55	15 13	15 22	15 27	15 52	15 55	16 13	16 22	16 27	16 52	16 55	17 06	17 22	17 25	17 52	17 55	18 13
Edge Hill 90,91 d					14 59					15 59					16 59			17 29		17 59	
Mossley Hill 91 d			14 35		15 04			15 35		16 04			16 35		17 04			17 34		18 04	
West Allerton 91 d			14 37		15 06			15 37		16 06			16 37		17 06			17 36		18 06	
Liverpool Central 10 103 d																					
L'pool Sth Parkway 7 91,103 ✈ d		14 32	14 40	15 03	15 09		15 32	15 40	16 03	16 09		16 32	16 40	17 03	17 09		17 32	17 39	18 03	18 09	
Hunts Cross 103 d					15 13					16 13					17 13			17 43		18 13	
Halewood d					15 16					16 16					17 16			17 46		18 16	
Hough Green d			14 47		15 20			15 47		16 20			16 47		17 20			17 50		18 20	
Widnes d			14 50	15 11	15 23			15 50	16 11	16 23			16 50	17 11	17 23			17 54	18 11	18 23	
Sankey for Penketh d					15 28					16 28					17 28			17 58		18 28	
Warrington Central a		14 44	14 58	15 18	15 33		15 44	15 58	16 18	16 33		16 44	16 58	17 18	17 33		17 44	18 03	18 18	18 33	
d		14 45	14 59	15 19	15 34		15 45	15 59	16 19	16 34		16 45	16 59	17 19	17 34		17 45	18 04	18 19	18 34	
Padgate d			15 02					16 02					17 02					18 07			
Birchwood d		14 50	15 05		15 38		15 50	16 05		16 38		16 50	17 05		17 38		17 50	18 10		18 38	
Glazebrook d								16 10													
Irlam d			15 11		15 44			16 13		16 44			17 11		17 44			18 16		18 44	
Flixton d			15 15					16 17					17 15					18 20			
Chassen Road d								16 19													
Urmston d			15 18		15 49			16 21		16 49			17 18		17 49			18 23		18 49	
Humphrey Park d			15 20										17 20								
Trafford Park d			15 23										17 23								
Deansgate 84,85 ⇌ a			15 31		15 59			16 30		16 59			17 31		17 59			18 31		18 59	
Manchester Oxford Road 84,85 a	14 57	15 05	15 36	15 39	16 04	15 57	16 05	16 36	16 38	17 04	16 57	17 05	17 36	17 38	18 04	17 57	18 05	18 36	18 39	19 04	18 57
ManchesterPicc 10 78,84,85 ⇌ a	15 01	15 09		15 41		16 01	16 09		16 41		17 01	17 09		17 41		18 01	18 09		18 41		19 01
Stockport 84 a				15 53					16 53					17 53					18 53		
Sheffield 7 78 ⇌ a				16 35					17 37					18 35					19 35		
Manchester Airport 85 ✈ a	15 22					16 22					17 22					18 22					19 24

A To Norwich

B To Scarborough

C To Nottingham

Table 89

Saturdays

Liverpool - Warrington Central - Manchester and Manchester Airport

Network Diagram - see first Page of Table 88

	TP	NT	EM	NT	TP	NT	EM	NT	NT	TP	EM	NT	EM	NT	TP	TP	NT
	◇1		◇		◇1		◇			◇1	◇		◇		◇1	◇1	
	A		B		C		B			C	B		B		D	E	
Liverpool Lime Street 10 90,91 d	18 22	18 25	18 52	18 55	19 22		19 52	19 55	20 09	20 22	20 52	20 55	21 37	21 55	22 30	22 30	23 38
Edge Hill 90,91 d		18 29		18 59				19 59				20 59		21 59			23 42
Mossley Hill 91 d		18 34		19 04				20 04				21 04		22 04			23 47
West Allerton 91 d		18 36		19 06				20 06				21 06		22 06			23 49
Liverpool Central 10 103 d																	
L'pool Sth Parkway 7 91,103 ✈ d	18 32	18 39	19 03	19 09	19 32		20 03	20 09		20 32	21 03	21 09	21 47	22 09	22 40	22 40	23 52
Hunts Cross 103 d		18 43		19 13				20 13				21 13		22 13			23 56
Halewood d		18 46		19 16				20 16				21 16		22 16			23 59
Hough Green d		18 50		19 20				20 20				21 20		22 20			00 03
Widnes d		18 53	19 11	19 23			20 11	20 23			21 11	21 23	21 55	22 23			00 06
Sankey for Penketh d		18 58		19 28				20 28				21 28		22 28			00 11
Warrington Central a	18 44	19 03	19 18	19 34	19 44		20 18	20 34		20 44	21 18	21 33	22 03	22 33	22 52	22 52	00 16
d	18 45	19 04	19 19		19 45	19 56	20 19			20 45	21 19	21 34	22 03	22 34	22 53	22 53	00 17
Padgate d		19 07				19 59						21 37		22 37			
Birchwood d	18 50	19 10			19 50	20 02				20 50		21 40		22 40	22 58	22 58	
Glazebrook d		19 15				20 07						21 45		22 45			
Irlam d		19 18				20 10						21 48		22 48			
Flixton d						20 14						21 52		22 52			
Chassen Road d						20 16						21 54		22 54			
Urmston d		19 23				20 18						21 56		22 56			
Humphrey Park d						20 20						21 58		22 58			
Trafford Park d						20 23						22 01		23 01			
Deansgate 84,85 ⇌ a		19 31				20 31						22 08		23 08			
Manchester Oxford Road 84,85 a	19 05	19 36	19 39		20 05	20 36	20 39		20 57	21 06	21 38	22 13	22 26	23 13	23 13	23 14	
ManchesterPicc 10 78,84,85 ⇌ a	19 09		19 41		20 09		20 41		21 01	21 09	21 41		22 29		23 17	23 19	00 39
Stockport 84 a			19 53				20 53				21 52		22 41				
Sheffield 7 78 ⇌ a			20 35				21 34				22 31		23 39				
Manchester Airport 85 ✈ a									21 24								

Sundays

until 24 June

	NT	NT	NT	NT	NT	NT	NT	NT	NT	NT	NT	EM	NT	NT	EM	NT	NT	EM	NT	NT	EM	NT
												◇			◇			◇			◇	
												F			F			F			F	
Liverpool Lime Street 10 90,91 d	23p38	08 01	08 26	09 01	09 26	10 01	10 26	11 01	11 26	12 01	12 26	12 52	13 01	13 26	13 52	14 01	14 26	14 52	15 01	15 26	15 52	16 01
Edge Hill 90,91 d	23p42																					
Mossley Hill 91 d	23p47		08 34		09 34		10 34		11 34		12 34			13 34			14 34			15 34		
West Allerton 91 d	23p49		08 36		09 36		10 36		11 36		12 36			13 36			14 36			15 36		
Liverpool Central 10 103 d																						
L'pool Sth Parkway 7 91,103 ✈ d	23p52		08 39		09 39		10 39		11 39		12 39	13 03		13 39	14 03		14 39	15 03		15 39	16 03	
Hunts Cross 103 d	23p56		08 43		09 43		10 43		11 43		12 43			13 43			14 43			15 43		
Halewood d	23p59		08 46		09 46		10 46		11 46		12 46			13 46			14 46			15 46		
Hough Green d	00 03		08 50		09 50		10 50		11 50		12 50			13 50			14 50			15 50		
Widnes d	00 06		08 53		09 53		10 53		11 53		12 53	13 11		13 53	14 11		14 53	15 11		15 53	16 11	
Sankey for Penketh d	00 11																					
Warrington Central a	00 16		09 01		10 01		11 01		12 01		13 01	13 18		14 01	14 18		15 01	15 18		16 01	16 18	
d	00 17		09 02		10 02		11 02		12 02		13 02	13 19		14 02	14 19		15 02	15 19		16 02	16 19	
Padgate d																						
Birchwood d			09 06		10 06		11 06		12 06		13 06			14 06			15 06			16 06		
Glazebrook d																						
Irlam d			09 12		10 12		11 12		12 12		13 12			14 12			15 12			16 12		
Flixton d																						
Chassen Road d																						
Urmston d			09 17		10 17		11 17		12 17		13 17			14 17			15 17			16 17		
Humphrey Park d																						
Trafford Park d																						
Deansgate 84,85 ⇌ a			09 29		10 27		11 27		12 27		13 27			14 27			15 27			16 27		
Manchester Oxford Road 84,85 a		09 00	09 33	09 59	10 31	10 59	11 31	11 59	12 30	12 59	13 31	13 39	13 57	14 31	14 39	14 59	15 31	15 39	15 59	16 31	16 38	16 59
ManchesterPicc 10 78,84,85 ⇌ a	00 39	09 03		10 03		11 06		12 03		13 03		13 41	14 03		14 41	15 02		15 41	16 02		16 41	17 02
Stockport 84 a												13 53			14 53			15 53			16 53	
Sheffield 7 78 ⇌ a												14 39			15 37			16 36			17 36	
Manchester Airport 85 ✈ a		09 21		10 24		11 24		12 21		13 19			14 21			15 20			16 21			17 21

A To Scarborough

B To Nottingham

C To York

D until 23 June, from 15 September until 20 October. To York

E from 30 June until 8 September, from 27 October. To York

F To Norwich

Table 89

Sundays until 24 June

Liverpool - Warrington Central - Manchester and Manchester Airport

Network Diagram - see first Page of Table 88

		NT	EM ◇ A	NT	NT	EM ◇ B	NT	NT	EM ◇ A	NT	NT	EM ◇ A	NT	NT	NT	EM ◇ A	NT	NT	NT Bus	NT	NT	NT Bus
Liverpool Lime Street 10 90,91	d	16 26	16 52	17 01	17 26	17 52	18 01	18 26	18 52	19 01	19 26	19 52	20 01	20 26	21 01	21 21	21 26	22 01	22 01	22 26	23 01	23 01
Edge Hill 90,91	d																					
Mossley Hill 91	d	16 34			17 34			18 34			19 34			20 34			21 34			22 34		
West Allerton 91	d	16 36			17 36			18 36			19 36			20 36			21 36			22 36		
Liverpool Central 10 103	d																					
L'pool Sth Parkway 7 91,103 ✈	d	16 39	17 03		17 39	18 03		18 39	19 03		19 39	20 03		20 39		21 31	21 39			22 39		
Hunts Cross 103	d	16 43			17 43			18 43			19 43			20 43			21 43			22 43		
Halewood	d	16 46			17 46			18 46			19 46			20 46			21 46			22 46		
Hough Green	d	16 50			17 50			18 50			19 50			20 50			21 50			22 50		
Widnes	d	16 53	17 11		17 53	18 11		18 53	19 11		19 53	20 11		20 53		21 39	21 53			22 53		
Sankey for Penketh	d																					
Warrington Central	a	17 01	17 18		18 01	18 18		19 01	19 18		20 01	20 18		21 01		21 47	22 01			23 01		
	d	17 02	17 19		18 02	18 19		19 02	19 19		20 02	20 19		21 02		21 47	22 02			23 02		
Padgate	d																					
Birchwood	d	17 06			18 06			19 06			20 06			21 06			22 06			23 06		
Glazebrook	d																					
Irlam	d	17 12			18 12			19 12			20 12			21 12			22 12			23 12		
Flixton	d																					
Chassen Road	d																					
Urmston	d	17 17			18 17			19 17			20 17			21 17			22 17			23 17		
Humphrey Park	d																					
Trafford Park	d																					
Deansgate 84,85	a	17 27			18 27			19 27			20 27			21 27			22 27			23 27		
Manchester Oxford Road 84,85	a	17 31	17 38	17 59	18 31	18 39	18 59	19 31	19 39	19 59	20 31	20 39	20 59	21 31	21 59	22 06	22 31	22 47	00 12	23 32	23 47	01 12
ManchesterPicc 10 78,84,85	a		17 41	18 02		18 41	19 02		19 41	20 02		20 41	21 02		22 02	22 09		22 50			23 50	
Stockport 84	a		17 53			18 53			19 53			20 53				22 20						
Sheffield 7 78	a		18 37			19 34			20 34			21 36				23 25						
Manchester Airport 85 ✈	a			18 21			19 21			20 26			21 20		22 21			23 15			00 07	

Sundays 1 July to 9 September

		NT	NT	TP ◇1 C	NT	NT	TP ◇1 D	NT	NT	TP ◇1 E	NT	NT	TP ◇1 D	NT	NT	TP ◇1 E	NT	EM ◇ B	NT	TP ◇1 D	NT	EM ◇ B	NT
Liverpool Lime Street 10 90,91	d	23p38	08 01	08 22	08 26	09 01	09 22	09 26	10 01	10 22	10 26	11 01	11 22	11 26	12 01	12 22	12 26	12 52	13 01	13 22	13 26	13 52	14 01
Edge Hill 90,91	d	23p42																					
Mossley Hill 91	d	23p47			08 34			09 34			10 34			11 34			12 34				13 34		
West Allerton 91	d	23p49			08 36			09 36			10 36			11 36			12 36				13 36		
Liverpool Central 10 103	d																						
L'pool Sth Parkway 7 91,103 ✈	d	23p52		08 32	08 39		09 32	09 39		10 32	10 39		11 32	11 39		12 32	12 39	13 03		13 32	13 39	14 03	
Hunts Cross 103	d	23p56			08 43			09 43			10 43			11 43			12 43				13 43		
Halewood	d	23p59			08 46			09 46			10 46			11 46			12 46				13 46		
Hough Green	d	00 03			08 50			09 50			10 50			11 50			12 50				13 50		
Widnes	d	00 06			08 53			09 53			10 53			11 53			12 53	13 11			13 53	14 11	
Sankey for Penketh	d	00 11																					
Warrington Central	a	00 16		08 44	09 01		09 44	10 01		10 44	11 01		11 44	12 01		12 44	13 01	13 18		13 44	14 01	14 18	
	d	00 17		08 45	09 02		09 45	10 02		10 45	11 02		11 45	12 02		12 45	13 02	13 19		13 45	14 02	14 19	
Padgate	d																						
Birchwood	d			08 50	09 06		09 50	10 06		10 50	11 06		11 50	12 06		12 50	13 06			13 50	14 06		
Glazebrook	d																						
Irlam	d				09 12			10 12			11 12			12 12			13 12				14 12		
Flixton	d																						
Chassen Road	d																						
Urmston	d				09 17			10 17			11 17			12 17			13 17				14 17		
Humphrey Park	d																						
Trafford Park	d																						
Deansgate 84,85	a				09 29			10 27			11 27			12 27			13 27				14 27		
Manchester Oxford Road 84,85	a		09 00	09 05	09 33	09 59	10 05	10 31	10 59	11 05	11 31	11 59	12 05	12 30	12 59	13 05	13 31	13 39	13 57	14 05	14 31	14 39	14 59
ManchesterPicc 10 78,84,85	a	00 39	09 03	09 09		10 03	10 09		11 06	11 09		12 03	12 09		13 03	13 09		13 41	14 03	14 09		14 41	15 02
Stockport 84	a																	13 53				14 53	
Sheffield 7 78	a																	14 39				15 37	
Manchester Airport 85 ✈	a		09 21			10 24			11 24			12 21			13 19				14 21				15 20

A To Nottingham
B To Norwich
C To Hull
D To Scarborough
E To Middlesbrough

Table 89

Sundays 1 July to 9 September

Liverpool - Warrington Central - Manchester and Manchester Airport

Network Diagram - see first Page of Table 88

		TP ◇1 A	NT	EM ◇ B	NT	TP ◇1 C	NT	EM ◇ B	NT	TP ◇1 A	NT	EM ◇ D	NT	TP ◇1 C	NT	EM ◇ B	NT	TP ◇1 C	NT	EM ◇ D	NT	TP ◇1 E	NT
Liverpool Lime Street 10 90,91	d	14 22	14 26	14 52	15 01	15 22	15 26	15 52	16 01	16 22	16 26	16 52	17 01	17 22	17 26	17 52	18 01	18 22	18 26	18 52	19 01	19 22	19 26
Edge Hill 90,91	d																						
Mossley Hill 91	d		14 34				15 34				16 34				17 34				18 34				19 34
West Allerton 91	d		14 36				15 36				16 36				17 36				18 36				19 36
Liverpool Central 10 103	d																						
L'pool Sth Parkway 7 91,103 ✈	d	14 32	14 39	15 03		15 32	15 39	16 03		16 32	16 39	17 03		17 32	17 39	18 03		18 32	18 39	19 03		19 32	19 39
Hunts Cross 103	d		14 43				15 43				16 43				17 43				18 43				19 43
Halewood	d		14 46				15 46				16 46				17 46				18 46				19 46
Hough Green	d		14 50				15 50				16 50				17 50				18 50				19 50
Widnes	d		14 53	15 11			15 53	16 11			16 53	17 11			17 53	18 11			18 53	19 11			19 53
Sankey for Penketh	d																						
Warrington Central	a	14 44	15 01	15 18		15 44	16 01	16 18		16 44	17 01	17 18		17 44	18 01	18 18		18 44	19 01	19 18		19 44	20 01
	d	14 45	15 02	15 19		15 45	16 02	16 19		16 45	17 02	17 19		17 45	18 02	18 19		18 45	19 02	19 19		19 45	20 02
Padgate	d																						
Birchwood	d	14 50	15 06			15 50	16 06			16 50	17 06			17 50	18 06			18 50	19 06			19 50	20 06
Glazebrook	d																						
Irlam	d		15 12				16 12				17 12				18 12				19 12				20 12
Flixton	d																						
Chassen Road	d																						
Urmston	d		15 17				16 17				17 17				18 17				19 17				20 17
Humphrey Park	d																						
Trafford Park	d																						
Deansgate 84,85	a		15 27				16 27				17 27				18 27				19 27				20 27
Manchester Oxford Road 84,85	a	15 05	15 31	15 39	15 59	16 05	16 31	16 38	16 59	17 05	17 31	17 38	17 59	18 05	18 31	18 39	18 59	19 05	19 31	19 39	19 59	20 05	20 31
ManchesterPicc 10 78,84,85	a	15 09		15 41	16 02	16 09		16 41	17 02	17 09		17 41	18 02	18 09		18 41	19 02	19 09		19 41	20 02	20 09	
Stockport 84	a			15 53				16 53				17 53				18 53				19 53			
Sheffield 7 78	a			16 36				17 36				18 37				19 34				20 34			
Manchester Airport 85 ✈	a				16 21				17 21				18 21				19 21				20 26		

		EM ◇ D	NT	TP ◇1 F	NT	NT	EM ◇ D	NT	TP ◇1 E	NT	NT Bus	NT	NT	NT Bus
Liverpool Lime Street 10 90,91	d	19 52	20 01	20 22	20 26	21 01	21 21	21 26	21 52	22 01	22 01	22 26	23 01	23 01
Edge Hill 90,91	d													
Mossley Hill 91	d				20 34			21 34				22 34		
West Allerton 91	d				20 36			21 36				22 36		
Liverpool Central 10 103	d													
L'pool Sth Parkway 7 91,103 ✈	d	20 03		20 32	20 39		21 31	21 39	22 02			22 39		
Hunts Cross 103	d				20 43			21 43				22 43		
Halewood	d				20 46			21 46				22 46		
Hough Green	d				20 50			21 50				22 50		
Widnes	d	20 11			20 53		21 39	21 53				22 53		
Sankey for Penketh	d													
Warrington Central	a	20 18		20 44	21 01		21 47	22 01	22 14			23 01		
	d	20 19		20 45	21 02		21 47	22 02	22 15			23 02		
Padgate	d													
Birchwood	d			20 50	21 06			22 06	22 20			23 06		
Glazebrook	d													
Irlam	d				21 12			22 12				23 12		
Flixton	d													
Chassen Road	d													
Urmston	d				21 17			22 17				23 17		
Humphrey Park	d													
Trafford Park	d													
Deansgate 84,85	a				21 27			22 27				23 27		
Manchester Oxford Road 84,85	a	20 39	20 59	21 05	21 31	21 59	22 06	22 31	22 35	22 47	00 12	23 32	23 47	01 12
ManchesterPicc 10 78,84,85	a	20 41	21 02	21 09		22 02	22 09		22 39	22 50			23 50	
Stockport 84	a	20 53					22 20							
Sheffield 7 78	a	21 36					23 25							
Manchester Airport 85 ✈	a		21 20			22 21				23 15			00 07	

A To Middlesbrough
B To Norwich
C To Scarborough
D To Nottingham
E To York
F To Newcastle

Sundays
from 16 September

Liverpool - Warrington Central - Manchester and Manchester Airport

Network Diagram - see first Page of Table 88

	NT	NT	NT	NT	NT	NT	NT	NT	NT	EM	NT	NT	EM	NT	NT	EM	NT	NT	EM	NT	NT	EM
										◇ A			◇ A			◇ A			◇ A			◇ B
Liverpool Lime Street 90,91 d	23p38	08 26	09 01	09 26	10 26	11 01	11 26	12 01	12 26	12 52	13 01	13 26	13 52	14 01	14 26	14 52	15 01	15 26	15 52	16 01	16 26	16 52
Edge Hill 90,91 d	23p42																					
Mossley Hill 91 d	23p47	08 34		09 34	10 34		11 34		12 34			13 34			14 34			15 34			16 34	
West Allerton 91 d	23p49	08 36		09 36	10 36		11 36		12 36			13 36			14 36			15 36			16 36	
Liverpool Central 103 d																						
L'pool Sth Parkway 91,103 d	23p52	08 39		09 39	10 39		11 39		12 39	13 03		13 39	14 03		14 39	15 03		15 39	16 03		16 39	17 03
Hunts Cross 103 d	23p56	08 43		09 43	10 43		11 43		12 43			13 43			14 43			15 43			16 43	
Halewood d	23p59	08 46		09 46	10 46		11 46		12 46			13 46			14 46			15 46			16 46	
Hough Green d	00 03	08 50		09 50	10 50		11 50		12 50			13 50			14 50			15 50			16 50	
Widnes d	00 06	08 53		09 53	10 53		11 53		12 53	13 11		13 53	14 11		14 53	15 11		15 53	16 11		16 53	17 11
Sankey for Penketh d	00 11																					
Warrington Central a	00 16	09 01		10 01	11 01		12 01		13 01	13 18		14 01	14 18		15 01	15 18		16 01	16 18		17 01	17 18
d	00 17	09 02		10 02	11 02		12 02		13 02	13 19		14 02	14 19		15 02	15 19		16 02	16 19		17 02	17 19
Padgate d																						
Birchwood d		09 06		10 06	11 06		12 06		13 06			14 06			15 06			16 06			17 06	
Glazebrook d																						
Irlam d		09 12		10 12	11 12		12 12		13 12			14 12			15 12			16 12			17 12	
Flixton d																						
Chassen Road d																						
Urmston d		09 17		10 17	11 17		12 17		13 17			14 17			15 17			16 17			17 17	
Humphrey Park d																						
Trafford Park d																						
Deansgate 84,85 a		09 29		10 27	11 27		12 27		13 27			14 27			15 27			16 27			17 27	
Manchester Oxford Road 84,85 a		09 33	09 59	10 31	11 31	11 59	12 30	12 59	13 31	13 39	13 57	14 31	14 39	14 59	15 31	15 39	15 59	16 31	16 38	16 59	17 31	17 38
ManchesterPicc 78,84,85 a	00 39		10 03			12 02		13 03		13 41	14 03		14 41	15 02		15 41	16 02		16 41	17 02		17 41
Stockport 84 a										13 53			14 53			15 53			16 53			17 53
Sheffield 78 a										14 39			15 37			16 36			17 36			18 37
Manchester Airport 85 a			10 24			12 20		13 19			14 21			15 20			16 21			17 21		

	NT	NT	EM	NT	NT	EM	NT	NT	EM	NT	NT	NT	EM	NT	NT	NT	NT	NT	NT
			◇ A			◇ B			◇ B				◇ B			bus			bus
Liverpool Lime Street 90,91 d	17 01	17 26	17 52	18 01	18 26	18 52	19 01	19 26	19 52	20 01	20 26	21 01	21 21	21 26	22 01	22 01	22 26	23 01	23 01
Edge Hill 90,91 d																			
Mossley Hill 91 d		17 34			18 34			19 34			20 34			21 34			22 34		
West Allerton 91 d		17 36			18 36			19 36			20 36			21 36			22 36		
Liverpool Central 103 d																			
L'pool Sth Parkway 91,103 d		17 39	18 03		18 39	19 03		19 39	20 03		20 39		21 31	21 39			22 39		
Hunts Cross 103 d		17 43			18 43			19 43			20 43			21 43			22 43		
Halewood d		17 46			18 46			19 46			20 46			21 46			22 46		
Hough Green d		17 50			18 50			19 50			20 50			21 50			22 50		
Widnes d		17 53	18 11		18 53	19 11		19 53	20 11		20 53		21 39	21 53			22 53		
Sankey for Penketh d																			
Warrington Central a		18 01	18 18		19 01	19 18		20 01	20 18		21 01		21 47	22 01			23 01		
d		18 02	18 19		19 02	19 19		20 02	20 19		21 02		21 47	22 02			23 02		
Padgate d																			
Birchwood d		18 06			19 06			20 06			21 06			22 06			23 06		
Glazebrook d																			
Irlam d		18 12			19 12			20 12			21 12			22 12			23 12		
Flixton d																			
Chassen Road d																			
Urmston d		18 17			19 17			20 17			21 17			22 17			23 17		
Humphrey Park d																			
Trafford Park d																			
Deansgate 84,85 a		18 27			19 27			20 27			21 27			22 27			23 27		
Manchester Oxford Road 84,85 a	17 59	18 31	18 39	18 59	19 31	19 39	19 59	20 31	20 39	20 59	21 31	21 59	22 06	22 31	22 47	00 12	23 32	23 47	01 12
ManchesterPicc 78,84,85 a	18 02		18 41	19 02		19 41	20 02		20 41	21 02		22 02	22 09		22 50			23 50	
Stockport 84 a			18 53			19 53			20 53				22 20						
Sheffield 78 a			19 34			20 34			21 36				23 25						
Manchester Airport 85 a	18 21			19 21			20 21			21 20		22 21			23 15			00 07	

A To Norwich
B To Nottingham

Table 89

Mondays to Fridays

Manchester Airport and Manchester - Warrington Central - Liverpool

Network Diagram - see first Page of Table 88

Miles		NT MO	NT MX	NT	NT	NT	NT	NT	NT	TP	NT	EM	NT	NT	TP	NT	EM	NT	NT	TP	NT	EM
		A bus								◇1		◇ B			◇1 C		◇ B			◇1 D		◇ B
0	**Manchester Airport** 85 d			04 38					06 41					07 38					08 41			
—	Sheffield 78 d											06 20					07 35					08 42
—	Stockport 84 d											07 22					08 24					09 25
9¾	**ManchesterPicc** 78,84,85 d			04 53					06 58	07 07		07 34		07 59	08 07		08 37		09 01	09 07		09 37
10¼	**Manchester Oxford Road** 84,85 d	23p00	23p27				06 22	06 46	07 01	07 10		07 37	07 39	08 03	08 12	08 15	08 41	08 44	09 04	09 12	09 15	09 41
10½	Deansgate 84,85 d		23p29				06 24						07 41			08 17		08 46			09 17	
13¾	Trafford Park d		23p34				06 29						07 46								09 22	
14½	Humphrey Park d		23p36				06 31														09 24	
15¾	Urmston d		23p38				06 33	06 53					07 49			08 24		08 52			09 27	
16¼	Chassen Road d		23p40				06 35									08 26						
16¾	Flixton d		23p43				06 38						07 52			08 28					09 30	
19	Irlam d		23p47				06 42	06 58					07 56			08 32		08 57			09 34	
20¼	Glazebrook d		23p50				06 45						07 59			08 35						
23	Birchwood d		23p54				06 49	07 04		07 23			08 04		08 25	08 40		09 03		09 25	09 40	
24½	Padgate d		23p57				06 52						08 07					09 06				
26¼	**Warrington Central** a		00 01				06 56	07 12		07 27		07 53	08 10		08 30	08 45	08 57	09 09		09 30	09 45	09 57
—	d		00 02		06 03	06 37	06 56			07 28	07 35	07 53	08 11		08 30	08 45	08 57	09 10		09 30	09 45	09 57
28¾	Sankey for Penketh d		00 05		06 07	06 41	07 00				07 39		08 15					09 14				
32½	Widnes d		00 11		06 12	06 46	07 06				07 44	08 01	08 20			08 53	09 05	09 19			09 53	10 05
34¼	Hough Green d		00 13		06 15	06 49	07 09				07 47	08 05	08 24			08 56		09 23			09 56	
36½	Halewood d		00 18		06 20	06 54	07 13				07 52		08 28					09 27				
37½	Hunts Cross 89 d		00 21		06 23	06 57	07 17				07 55	08s10	08 32					09 30				
39¾	L'pool Sth Parkway 91,103 d		00 27		06 27	07 01	07 22				07 59	08 18	08 37		08 47	09 06	09 15	09 36		09 47	10 06	10 15
—	Liverpool Central 103 a																					
40¾	West Allerton 91 a				06 31	07 05	07 25				08 03		08 40			09 09		09 39			10 10	
41	Mossley Hill 91 a				06 33	07 07	07 28				08 06		08 43			09 12		09 41			10 12	
43	Edge Hill 90,91 a				06 39	07 13	07 32				08 11		08 48					09 47				
44¾	**Liverpool Lime Street** 90,91 a	01 11	00 41	05 36	06 45	07 19	07 40		07 49	07 53	08 18	08 31	08 55	08 59	08 58	09 24	09 31	09 53	09 48	09 58	10 24	10 31

	NT	NT	TP	NT	EM	NT	NT	TP	NT	EM	NT	NT	TP	NT	EM	NT	NT	TP	NT	EM	NT	NT
			◇1 E		◇ F			◇1 E		◇ F			◇1 E		◇ F			◇1 E		◇ F		
Manchester Airport 85 d		09 41					10 41					11 41					12 41					13 41
Sheffield 78 d					09 42					10 42					11 42					12 42		
Stockport 84 d					10 26					11 26					12 26					13 26		
ManchesterPicc 78,84,85 d		10 01	10 07		10 37		11 01	11 07		11 37		12 01	12 07		12 37		13 01	13 07		13 37		14 01
Manchester Oxford Road 84,85 d	09 44	10 04	10 12	10 16	10 41	10 44	11 04	11 12	11 16	11 41	11 44	12 04	12 12	12 16	12 41	12 44	13 04	13 12	13 16	13 41	13 44	14 04
Deansgate 84,85 d	09 46			10 18		10 46			11 18		11 46			12 18		12 46			13 18		13 46	
Trafford Park d									11 23										13 23			
Humphrey Park d									11 25										13 25			
Urmston d	09 52			10 24		10 52			11 27		11 52			12 24		12 52			13 27		13 52	
Chassen Road d				10 26										12 26								
Flixton d				10 29					11 30					12 29					13 30			
Irlam d	09 57			10 33		10 57			11 34		11 57			12 33		12 57			13 34		13 57	
Glazebrook d				10 36										12 36								
Birchwood d	10 03		10 25	10 40		11 03		11 25	11 40		12 03		12 25	12 40		13 03		13 25	13 40		14 03	
Padgate d	10 06					11 06					12 06					13 06					14 06	
Warrington Central a	10 09		10 30	10 45	10 57	11 09		11 30	11 45	11 57	12 09		12 30	12 45	12 57	13 09		13 30	13 45	13 57	14 09	
d	10 10		10 30	10 46	10 57	11 10		11 30	11 46	11 57	12 10		12 30	12 46	12 57	13 10		13 30	13 46	13 57	14 10	
Sankey for Penketh d	10 14					11 14					12 14					13 14					14 14	
Widnes d	10 19			10 54	11 05	11 19			11 54	12 05	12 19			12 54	13 05	13 19			13 54	14 05	14 19	
Hough Green d	10 23			10 57		11 23			11 57		12 23			12 57		13 23			13 57		14 23	
Halewood d	10 27					11 27					12 27					13 27					14 27	
Hunts Cross 89 d	10 30					11 30					12 30					13 30					14 30	
L'pool Sth Parkway 91,103 d	10 36		10 47	11 06	11 15	11 36		11 47	12 06	12 15	12 36		12 47	13 06	13 15	13 36		13 47	14 06	14 15	14 36	
Liverpool Central 103 a																						
West Allerton 91 a	10 39			11 10		11 39			12 10		12 39			13 10		13 39			14 10		14 39	
Mossley Hill 91 a	10 41			11 13		11 41			12 13		12 41			13 13		13 41			14 13		14 41	
Edge Hill 90,91 a	10 47					11 47					12 47					13 47					14 47	
Liverpool Lime Street 90,91 a	10 53	10 48	10 58	11 24	11 31	11 53	11 48	11 58	12 24	12 31	12 53	12 48	12 58	13 24	13 31	13 53	13 48	13 58	14 24	14 31	14 53	14 48

A from 21 May
B From Nottingham
C From Hull
D From Newcastle
E From Scarborough
F From Norwich

Manchester Airport and Manchester - Warrington Central - Liverpool

Network Diagram - see first Page of Table 88

	TP	NT	EM	NT	NT	TP	NT	EM	NT	NT	TP	NT	EM	NT	NT	TP	NT	EM	NT	NT	TP
	◇1 A ⊥		◇ B			◇1 A ⊥		◇ B			◇1 A ⊥		◇ B			◇1 A ⊥		◇ B			◇1 A ⊥
Manchester Airport 85 ✈ d					14 41					15 41					16 41					17 41	
Sheffield 7 78 d			13 42					14 42					15 42					16 42			
Stockport 84 d			14 26					15 26					16 26					17 26			
ManchesterPicc 10 78,84,85 d	14 07		14 37		15 01	15 07		15 37		16 01	16 07		16 37		17 01	17 07		17 37		18 01	18 07
Manchester Oxford Road 84,85 d	14 12	14 16	14 41	14 44	15 04	15 12	15 16	15 41	15 44	16 04	16 12	16 16	16 41	16 43	17 04	17 11	17 13	17 42	17 44	18 04	18 12
Deansgate 84,85 d		14 18		14 46			15 18		15 46			16 18		16 45			17 15		17 46		
Trafford Park d							15 23							16 51			17 20		17 51		
Humphrey Park d							15 25										17 22		17 53		
Urmston d		14 24		14 52			15 27		15 52			16 24		16 54			17 25		17 55		
Chassen Road d		14 26										16 26					17 27		17 57		
Flixton d		14 29					15 30					16 29		16 57			17 29		18 00		
Irlam d		14 33		14 57			15 34		15 57			16 33		17 01			17 33	17 52	18 04		
Glazebrook d		14 36										16 36					17 36		18 07		
Birchwood d	14 25	14 40		15 03		15 25	15 40		16 03		16 25	16 40		17 07		17 25	17 41	17 58	18 11		18 25
Padgate d				15 06					16 06			16 43		17 10			17 44		18 14		
Warrington Central a	14 30	14 45	14 57	15 09		15 30	15 45	15 57	16 09		16 30	16 47	16 57	17 13		17 30	17 48	18 03	18 18		18 30
d	14 30	14 46	14 57	15 10		15 30	15 45	15 57	16 10		16 30	16 47	16 57	17 14		17 30	17 48	18 03	18 18		18 30
Sankey for Penketh d				15 14					16 14					17 18			17 52				
Widnes d		14 54	15 05	15 19			15 53	16 05	16 19			16 55	17 05	17 23			17 58	18 11			
Hough Green d		14 57		15 23			15 56		16 23			16 58		17 27			18 01		18 28		
Halewood d				15 27			16 01		16 27					17 31			18 06				
Hunts Cross 89 d				15 30					16 30					17 34			18 09		18 33		
L'pool Sth Parkway 7 91,103 ✈ d	14 47	15 06	15 15	15 36		15 47	16 07	16 15	16 36		16 47	17 07	17 15	17 39		17 47	18 14	18 22	18 38		18 47
Liverpool Central 10 103 a																					
West Allerton 91 a		15 10		15 39			16 11		16 39			17 11		17 42			18 18		18 41		
Mossley Hill 91 a		15 13		15 41			16 13		16 42			17 13		17 45			18 20		18 44		
Edge Hill 90,91 a				15 47					16 47					17 50			18 30		18 49		
Liverpool Lime Street 10 90,91 a	14 58	15 24	15 31	15 53	15 48	15 58	16 25	16 31	16 54	16 48	16 58	17 25	17 31	17 58	17 48	18 01	18 38	18 35	18 57	19 00	19 01

	NT	EM	NT	NT	TP	NT	EM	NT	NT	TP	NT	EM	NT	TP	NT	NT	NT FO	TP	NT	NT
		◇ B			◇1 A ⊥		◇ B			◇1 A		◇ B		◇1 A				◇1 A		
Manchester Airport 85 ✈ d				18 41					19 41								21 42			
Sheffield 7 78 d		17 40					18 43					19 42								
Stockport 84 d		18 26					19 26					20 26								
ManchesterPicc 10 78,84,85 d		18 37		19 01	19 07		19 37		20 01	20 07		20 37		21 07	21 38		22 01	22 07		
Manchester Oxford Road 84,85 d	18 16	18 41	18 44	19 04	19 12		19 41	19 44	20 04	20 12		20 41	20 44	21 12	21 44		22 04	22 12		23 27
Deansgate 84,85 d	18 18		18 46					19 46					20 46		21 46					23 29
Trafford Park d	18 23		18 51					19 51					20 51		21 51					23 34
Humphrey Park d	18 25		18 53					19 53					20 53		21 53					23 36
Urmston d	18 27		18 55					19 55					20 55		21 55					23 38
Chassen Road d	18 29		18 57					19 57					20 57		21 57					23 40
Flixton d	18 32		19 00					20 00					21 00		22 00					23 43
Irlam d	18 36		19 04					20 04					21 04		22 04					23 47
Glazebrook d			19 07					20 07					21 07		22 07					23 50
Birchwood d	18 41		19 11		19 25			20 11		20 25			21 11	21 25	22 11			22 25		23 54
Padgate d			19 14					20 14					21 14		22 14					23 57
Warrington Central a	18 46	18 57	19 20		19 30		19 57	20 18		20 30		20 57	21 20	21 30	22 20			22 30		00 01
d	18 47	18 57			19 30	19 49	19 57	20 18		20 30	20 49	20 57		21 30		21 49		22 30	22 58	00 02
Sankey for Penketh d	18 51					19 53					20 53					21 53			23 02	00 05
Widnes d	18 56	19 05				19 58	20 05				20 58	21 05				21 58			23 07	00 11
Hough Green d	18 59					20 02		20 28			21 01					22 01			23 10	00 13
Halewood d	19 04					20 06					21 06					22 06			23 15	00 18
Hunts Cross 89 d	19 07	19 12				20 09		20 33			21 09					22 09			23 18	00 21
L'pool Sth Parkway 7 91,103 ✈ d	19 13	19 18			19 47	20 13	20 16	20 38		20 47	21 12	21 20		21 47		22 12		22 47	23 22	00 27
Liverpool Central 10 103 a																				
West Allerton 91 a	19 16					20 16		20 41			21 15					22 15			23 25	
Mossley Hill 91 a	19 18					20 18		20 44			21 18					22 18			23 27	
Edge Hill 90,91 a	19 26					20 24					21 23					22 23			23 32	
Liverpool Lime Street 10 90,91 a	19 35	19 35		19 48	20 01	20 30	20 35	20 56	20 48	21 01	21 30	21 35		22 01		22 30	22 48	23 01	23 39	00 41

A From Scarborough
B From Norwich

Manchester Airport and Manchester - Warrington Central - Liverpool

Network Diagram - see first Page of Table 88

	NT	NT	NT	NT	NT	NT	TP	NT	EM	NT	NT	TP	NT	EM	NT	NT	TP	NT	EM	NT	NT	TP
							◇1		◇ A			◇1 B ⊥		◇ A			◇1 C ⊥		◇ A			◇1 D ⊥
Manchester Airport 85 ✈ d		04 34				06 41					07 38					08 41					09 41	
Sheffield 7 78 d									06 20					07 35					08 42			
Stockport 84 d									07 22					08 24					09 25			
ManchesterPicc 10 78,84,85 d		04 49				06 58	07 07		07 34		07 59	08 07		08 37		09 01	09 07		09 37		10 01	10 07
Manchester Oxford Road 84,85 d	23p27				06 22	07 01	07 10		07 37	07 39	08 03	08 12	08 15	08 41	08 44	09 04	09 12	09 16	09 41	09 44	10 04	10 12
Deansgate 84,85 d	23p29				06 24					07 41			08 17		08 46			09 18		09 46		
Trafford Park d	23p34				06 29					07 46								09 23				
Humphrey Park d	23p36				06 31													09 25				
Urmston d	23p38				06 33					07 49			08 24		08 52			09 27		09 52		
Chassen Road d	23p40				06 35								08 26									
Flixton d	23p43				06 38					07 52			08 28					09 30				
Irlam d	23p47				06 42					07 56			08 32		08 57			09 34		09 57		
Glazebrook d	23p50				06 45					07 59			08 35									
Birchwood d	23p54				06 49		07 23			08 04		08 25	08 40		09 03		09 25	09 40		10 03		10 25
Padgate d	23p57				06 52					08 07					09 06					10 06		
Warrington Central a	00 01				06 56		07 27		07 53	08 10		08 30	08 45	08 57	09 09		09 30	09 45	09 57	10 09		10 30
d	00 02		06 03	06 37	06 56		07 28	07 40	07 53	08 11		08 30	08 45	08 57	09 10		09 30	09 46	09 57	10 10		10 30
Sankey for Penketh d	00 05		06 07	06 41	07 00			07 44		08 15					09 14					10 14		
Widnes d	00 11		06 12	06 46	07 06			07 49	08 01	08 20			08 53	09 05	09 19			09 54	10 05	10 19		
Hough Green d	00 13		06 15	06 49	07 09			07 52	08 05	08 24			08 56		09 23			09 57		10 23		
Halewood d	00 18		06 20	06 54	07 13			07 57		08 28					09 27					10 27		
Hunts Cross 89 d	00 21		06 23	06 57	07 17			08 00	08s10	08 32					09 30					10 30		
L'pool Sth Parkway 7 91,103 ✈ d	00 27		06 27	07 01	07 22			08 03	08 18	08 37		08 47	09 06	09 15	09 36		09 47	10 06	10 15	10 36		10 47
Liverpool Central 10 103 a																						
West Allerton 91 a			06 31	07 05	07 25			08 06		08 40			09 09		09 39			10 10		10 39		
Mossley Hill 91 a			06 33	07 07	07 28			08 09		08 43			09 12		09 41			10 12		10 41		
Edge Hill 90,91 a			06 39	07 13	07 34			08 14		08 48					09 47					10 47		
Liverpool Lime Street 10 90,91 a	00 41	05 32	06 45	07 20	07 40	07 49	07 53	08 21	08 31	08 55	08 59	08 58	09 24	09 31	09 53	09 48	09 58	10 23	10 31	10 53	10 48	10 58

	NT	EM	NT	NT	TP	NT	EM	NT	NT	TP	NT	EM	NT	NT	TP	NT	EM	NT	NT	TP	NT	EM
		◇ E			◇1 D		◇ E			◇1 D ⊥		◇ E			◇1 D ⊥		◇ E			◇1 D		◇ E
Manchester Airport 85 ✈ d				10 41					11 41					12 41					13 41			
Sheffield 7 78 d		09 42					10 42					11 42					12 42					13 42
Stockport 84 d		10 26					11 26					12 26					13 26					14 26
ManchesterPicc 10 78,84,85 d		10 37		11 01	11 07		11 37		12 01	12 07		12 37		13 01	13 07		13 37		14 01	14 07		14 37
Manchester Oxford Road 84,85 d	10 16	10 41	10 44	11 04	11 12	11 16	11 41	11 44	12 04	12 12	12 16	12 41	12 44	13 04	13 12	13 16	13 41	13 44	14 04	14 12	14 16	14 41
Deansgate 84,85 d	10 18		10 46			11 18		11 46			12 18		12 46			13 18		13 46			14 18	
Trafford Park d						11 23										13 23						
Humphrey Park d						11 25										13 25						
Urmston d	10 24		10 52			11 27		11 52			12 24		12 52			13 27		13 52			14 24	
Chassen Road d	10 26										12 26										14 26	
Flixton d	10 29					11 30					12 29					13 30					14 29	
Irlam d	10 33		10 57			11 34		11 57			12 33		12 57			13 34		13 57			14 33	
Glazebrook d	10 36										12 36										14 36	
Birchwood d	10 40		11 03		11 25	11 40		12 03		12 25	12 40		13 03		13 25	13 40		14 03		14 25	14 40	
Padgate d			11 06					12 06					13 06					14 06				
Warrington Central a	10 45	10 57	11 09		11 30	11 45	11 57	12 09		12 30	12 45	12 57	13 09		13 30	13 45	13 57	14 09		14 30	14 45	14 57
d	10 46	10 57	11 10		11 30	11 46	11 57	12 10		12 30	12 46	12 57	13 10		13 30	13 46	13 57	14 10		14 30	14 46	14 57
Sankey for Penketh d			11 14					12 14					13 14					14 14				
Widnes d	10 54	11 05	11 19			11 54	12 05	12 19			12 54	13 05	13 19			13 54	14 05	14 19			14 54	15 05
Hough Green d	10 57		11 23			11 57		12 23			12 57		13 23			13 57		14 23			14 57	
Halewood d			11 27					12 27					13 27					14 27				
Hunts Cross 89 d			11 30					12 30					13 30					14 30				
L'pool Sth Parkway 7 91,103 ✈ d	11 06	11 15	11 36		11 47	12 06	12 15	12 36		12 47	13 06	13 15	13 36		13 47	14 06	14 15	14 36		14 47	15 06	15 15
Liverpool Central 10 103 a																						
West Allerton 91 a	11 10		11 39			12 10		12 39			13 10		13 39			14 10		14 39			15 10	
Mossley Hill 91 a	11 13		11 41			12 13		12 41			13 13		13 41			14 13		14 41			15 13	
Edge Hill 90,91 a			11 47					12 47					13 47					14 47				
Liverpool Lime Street 10 90,91 a	11 24	11 31	11 53	11 48	11 58	12 24	12 31	12 53	12 48	12 58	13 24	13 31	13 53	13 48	13 58	14 24	14 31	14 53	14 48	14 58	15 24	15 31

A From Nottingham
B From Hull
C From Newcastle
D From Scarborough
E From Norwich

Table 89

Saturdays

Manchester Airport and Manchester - Warrington Central - Liverpool

Network Diagram - see first Page of Table 88

		NT	NT	TP	NT	EM	NT	NT	TP	NT	EM	NT	NT	TP	NT	EM	NT	NT	TP	NT	EM	NT
				◇1 A		◇ B			◇1 A		◇ B			◇1 A		◇ B			◇1 A		◇ B	
Manchester Airport 85 ✈	d		14 41					15 41					16 41					17 41				
Sheffield 7 78	d					14 42					15 42					16 42					17 40	
Stockport 84	d					15 26					16 26					17 26					18 26	
ManchesterPicc 10 78,84,85	d		15 01	15 07		15 37		16 01	16 07		16 37		17 01	17 07		17 37		18 01	18 07		18 37	
Manchester Oxford Road 84,85	d	14 44	15 04	15 12	15 16	15 41	15 44	16 04	16 12	16 16	16 41	16 43	17 04	17 11	17 13	17 42	17 44	18 04	18 12	18 16	18 41	18 44
Deansgate 84,85	d	14 46			15 18		15 46			16 18		16 45			17 15		17 46			18 18		18 46
Trafford Park	d				15 23							16 51			17 20		17 51			18 23		18 51
Humphrey Park	d				15 25										17 22		17 53			18 25		18 53
Urmston	d	14 52			15 27		15 52			16 24		16 54			17 25		17 55			18 27		18 55
Chassen Road	d									16 26					17 27		17 57			18 29		18 57
Flixton	d				15 30					16 29		16 57			17 29		18 00			18 32		19 00
Irlam	d	14 57			15 34		15 57			16 33		17 01			17 33	17 52	18 04			18 36		19 04
Glazebrook	d									16 36					17 36		18 07					19 07
Birchwood	d	15 03		15 25	15 40		16 03		16 25	16 40		17 07		17 25	17 41	17 58	18 11		18 25	18 41		19 11
Padgate	d	15 06					16 06			16 43		17 10			17 44		18 14					19 14
Warrington Central	a	15 09		15 30	15 45	15 57	16 09		16 30	16 47	16 57	17 13		17 30	17 48	18 03	18 18		18 30	18 46	18 57	19 20
	d	15 10		15 30	15 45	15 57	16 10		16 30	16 47	16 57	17 14		17 30	17 48	18 03	18 18		18 30	18 47	18 57	
Sankey for Penketh	d	15 14					16 14					17 18			17 52					18 51		
Widnes	d	15 19			15 53	16 05	16 19			16 55	17 05	17 23			17 58	18 11				18 56	19 05	
Hough Green	d	15 23			15 56		16 23			16 58		17 27			18 01		18 28			18 59		
Halewood	d	15 27			16 01		16 27					17 31			18 06					19 04		
Hunts Cross 89	d	15 30					16 30					17 34			18 09		18 33			19 07	19 12	
L'pool Sth Parkway 7 91,103 ✈	d	15 36		15 47	16 07	16 15	16 36		16 47	17 07	17 15	17 39		17 47	18 14	18 22	18 38		18 47	19 11	19 18	
Liverpool Central 10 103	a																					
West Allerton 91	a	15 39			16 11		16 39			17 11		17 42			18 18		18 41			19 15		
Mossley Hill 91	a	15 41			16 13		16 41			17 13		17 45			18 20		18 44			19 18		
Edge Hill 90,91	a	15 47					16 47					17 50			18 30		18 50			19 26		
Liverpool Lime Street 10 90,91	a	15 53	15 48	15 58	16 25	16 31	16 54	16 48	16 58	17 25	17 31	17 58	17 48	18 01	18 38	18 35	18 57	19 00	19 01	19 35	19 35	

		NT	TP	NT	EM	NT	NT	TP	NT	EM	NT	TP	NT	NT	NT	TP	NT	NT
			◇1 A		◇ B			◇1 A		◇ B		◇1 A				◇1 A		
Manchester Airport 85 ✈	d	18 41					19 41								21 41			
Sheffield 7 78	d				18 42					19 42								
Stockport 84	d				19 26					20 26								
ManchesterPicc 10 78,84,85	d	19 01	19 07		19 37		20 01	20 07		20 37		21 07	21 38		22 01	22 07		
Manchester Oxford Road 84,85	d	19 04	19 12		19 41	19 44	20 04	20 12		20 41	20 44	21 12	21 44		22 04	22 12		23 20
Deansgate 84,85	d					19 46					20 46		21 46					23 22
Trafford Park	d					19 51					20 51		21 51					23 27
Humphrey Park	d					19 53					20 53		21 53					23 29
Urmston	d					19 55					20 55		21 55					23 31
Chassen Road	d					19 57					20 57		21 57					23 33
Flixton	d					20 00					21 00		22 00					23 36
Irlam	d					20 04					21 04		22 04					23 40
Glazebrook	d					20 07					21 07		22 07					23 43
Birchwood	d		19 25			20 11		20 25			21 11	21 25	22 11			22 25		23 47
Padgate	d					20 14					21 14		22 14					23 50
Warrington Central	a		19 30		19 57	20 18		20 30		20 57	21 20	21 30	22 20			22 30		23 54
	d		19 30	19 34	19 57	20 18		20 30	20 49	20 57		21 30		21 49		22 30	22 49	23 54
Sankey for Penketh	d			19 38					20 53					21 53			22 53	23 58
Widnes	d			19 43	20 05				20 58	21 05				21 58			22 58	00 04
Hough Green	d			19 46		20 28			21 01					22 01			23 01	00 06
Halewood	d			19 51					21 06					22 06			23 06	00 11
Hunts Cross 89	d			19 54		20 33			21 09					22 09			23 09	00 14
L'pool Sth Parkway 7 91,103 ✈	d		19 47	19 59	20 15	20 38		20 47	21 15	21 20		21 47		22 12		22 47	23 12	00 20
Liverpool Central 10 103	a																	
West Allerton 91	a			20 03		20 41			21 19					22 15			23 15	
Mossley Hill 91	a			20 05		20 44			21 21					22 18			23 18	
Edge Hill 90,91	a			20 11					21 27					22 23			23 23	
Liverpool Lime Street 10 90,91	a	19 48	20 01	20 18	20 30	20 55	20 48	21 01	21 34	21 35		22 01		22 30	22 48	23 01	23 30	00 34

A From Scarborough

B From Norwich

Table 89

Sundays
until 24 June

Manchester Airport and Manchester - Warrington Central - Liverpool

Network Diagram - see first Page of Table 88

		NT	NT	NT	NT	NT	NT	NT	NT	EM	NT	NT	EM	NT	NT	EM	NT	NT	EM	NT	NT	EM	NT
										◇ A			◇ A			◇ A			◇ B			◇ B	
Manchester Airport 85 ✈	d				08 34		09 35		10 35			11 33			12 35			13 35			14 35		
Sheffield 7 78	d									10 41			11 38			12 41			13 38			14 39	
Stockport 84	d									11 26			12 26			13 26			14 26			15 26	
ManchesterPicc 10 78,84,85	d				08 49		09 50		10 50	11 38		11 50	12 38		12 50	13 38		13 50	14 38		14 50	15 38	
Manchester Oxford Road 84,85	d	23p20	08 08	08 45	08 52	09 45	09 53	10 45	10 53	11 42	11 45	11 53	12 42	12 45	12 53	13 42	13 45	13 53	14 42	14 45	14 53	15 42	15 45
Deansgate 84,85	d	23p22	08 10	08 47	08 54	09 47		10 47			11 47			12 47			13 47			14 47			15 47
Trafford Park	d	23p27																					
Humphrey Park	d	23p29																					
Urmston	d	23p31	08 16	08 53		09 53		10 53			11 53			12 53			13 53			14 53			15 53
Chassen Road	d	23p33																					
Flixton	d	23p36																					
Irlam	d	23p40	08 21	08 58		09 58		10 58			11 58			12 58			13 58			14 58			15 58
Glazebrook	d	23p43																					
Birchwood	d	23p47	08 27	09 04		10 04		11 04			12 04			13 04			14 04			15 04			16 04
Padgate	d	23p50																					
Warrington Central	a	23p54	08 31	09 09		10 09		11 09		11 58	12 09		12 58	13 09		13 58	14 09		14 58	15 09		15 58	16 09
	d	23p54	08 31	09 09		10 09		11 09		11 59	12 09		12 58	13 09		13 58	14 09		14 58	15 09		15 58	16 09
Sankey for Penketh	d	23p58																					
Widnes	d	00 04	08 39	09 17		10 17		11 17		12 06	12 17		13 06	13 17		14 06	14 17		15 06	15 17		16 06	16 17
Hough Green	d	00 06	08 44	09 21		10 21		11 21			12 21			13 21			14 21			15 21			16 21
Halewood	d	00 11	08 48	09 25		10 25		11 25			12 25			13 25			14 25			15 25			16 25
Hunts Cross 89	d	00 14	08 51	09 28		10 28		11 28			12 28			13 28			14 28			15 28			16 28
L'pool Sth Parkway 7 91,103 ✈	d	00 20	08 55	09 33		10 33		11 33		12 17	12 33		13 17	13 33		14 16	14 33		15 16	15 33		16 16	16 33
Liverpool Central 10 103	a																						
West Allerton 91	a		08 58	09 36		10 36		11 36			12 36			13 36			14 36			15 36			16 36
Mossley Hill 91	a		09 02	09 39		10 39		11 39			12 39			13 39			14 39			15 39			16 39
Edge Hill 90,91	a																						
Liverpool Lime Street 10 90,91	a	00 34	09 13	09 50	09 52	10 50	10 54	11 50	11 54	12 30	12 50	12 54	13 30	13 50	13 54	14 30	14 50	14 54	15 30	15 50	15 54	16 30	16 50

		NT	EM	NT	NT	EM	NT	NT	EM	NT	NT	EM	NT	NT	NT	NT	NT	NT	NT	NT
			◇ A			◇ A			◇ B			◇ B								Bus
Manchester Airport 85 ✈	d	15 35			16 35			17 35			18 35			19 35		20 35		21 35	22 27	
Sheffield 7 78	d		15 38			16 44			17 44			18 37								
Stockport 84	d		16 26			17 29			18 26			19 26								
ManchesterPicc 10 78,84,85	d	15 50	16 38		16 50	17 38		17 50	18 38		18 50	19 38		19 50		20 50		21 50	22 41	
Manchester Oxford Road 84,85	d	15 53	16 42	16 45	16 53	17 42	17 45	17 53	18 42	18 45	18 53	19 42	19 45	19 53	20 45	20 53	21 45	21 53	22 45	23 00
Deansgate 84,85	d			16 47			17 47			18 47			19 47		20 47		21 47		22 47	
Trafford Park	d																			
Humphrey Park	d																			
Urmston	d			16 53			17 53			18 53			19 53		20 53		21 53		22 53	
Chassen Road	d																			
Flixton	d																			
Irlam	d			16 58			17 58			18 58			19 58		20 58		21 58		22 58	
Glazebrook	d																			
Birchwood	d			17 04			18 04			19 04			20 04		21 04		22 04		23 04	
Padgate	d																			
Warrington Central	a		16 58	17 09		17 58	18 09		18 58	19 09		19 58	20 09		21 09		22 09		23 09	
	d		16 58	17 09		17 58	18 09		18 58	19 09		19 58	20 09		21 09		22 09		23 09	
Sankey for Penketh	d																			
Widnes	d		17 06	17 17		18 06	18 17		19 06	19 17		20 06	20 17		21 17		22 17		23 17	
Hough Green	d			17 21			18 21			19 21			20 21		21 21		22 21		23 21	
Halewood	d			17 25			18 25			19 25			20 25		21 25		22 25		23 25	
Hunts Cross 89	d			17 28			18 28			19 28			20 28		21 28		22 28		23 28	
L'pool Sth Parkway 7 91,103 ✈	d		17 16	17 33		18 16	18 33		19 17	19 33		20 16	20 33		21 33		22 33		23 33	
Liverpool Central 10 103	a																			
West Allerton 91	a			17 36			18 36			19 36			20 36		21 36		22 36		23 36	
Mossley Hill 91	a			17 39			18 39			19 39			20 39		21 39		22 39		23 39	
Edge Hill 90,91	a																			
Liverpool Lime Street 10 90,91	a	16 54	17 30	17 50	17 54	18 30	18 50	18 54	19 30	19 50	19 54	20 30	20 50	20 54	21 50	21 54	22 50	22 54	23 50	01 11

A From Nottingham

B From Norwich

1 July to 9 September

Manchester Airport and Manchester - Warrington Central - Liverpool

Network Diagram - see first Page of Table 88

	NT	NT	NT	NT	TP	NT	NT	TP	NT	NT	TP	EM	NT	NT	TP	EM	NT	NT	TP	EM	NT	NT
					◇1			◇1 A			◇1	◇ B			◇1 C	◇ B			◇1 D	◇ B		
Manchester Airport 85 ✈ d				08 34			09 35			10 35				11 33				12 35				13 35
Sheffield 7 78 ⇌ d												10 41				11 38				12 41		
Stockport 84 d												11 26				12 26				13 26		
ManchesterPicc 10 78,84,85 ⇌ d				08 49	09 07		09 50	10 07		10 50	11 07	11 38		11 50	12 07	12 38		12 50	13 07	13 38		13 50
Manchester Oxford Road 84,85 d	23p20	08 08	08 45	08 52	09 12	09 45	09 53	10 11	10 45	10 53	11 12	11 42	11 45	11 53	12 12	12 42	12 45	12 53	13 12	13 42	13 45	13 53
Deansgate 84,85 ⇌ d	23p22	08 10	08 47	08 54		09 47			10 47				11 47				12 47				13 47	
Trafford Park d	23p27																					
Humphrey Park d	23p29																					
Urmston d	23p31	08 16	08 53			09 53			10 53				11 53				12 53				13 53	
Chassen Road d	23p33																					
Flixton d	23p36																					
Irlam d	23p40	08 21	08 58			09 58			10 58				11 58				12 58				13 58	
Glazebrook d	23p43																					
Birchwood d	23p47	08 27	09 04		09 25	10 04		10 25	11 04		11 25		12 04		12 25		13 04		13 25		14 04	
Padgate d	23p50																					
Warrington Central a	23p54	08 31	09 09		09 30	10 09		10 29	11 09		11 30	11 58	12 09		12 30	12 58	13 09		13 30	13 58	14 09	
d	23p54	08 31	09 09		09 30	10 09		10 30	11 09		11 30	11 59	12 09		12 30	12 58	13 09		13 30	13 58	14 09	
Sankey for Penketh d	23p58																					
Widnes d	00 04	08 39	09 17			10 17			11 17			12 06	12 17			13 06	13 17			14 06	14 17	
Hough Green d	00 06	08 44	09 21			10 21			11 21				12 21				13 21				14 21	
Halewood d	00 11	08 48	09 25			10 25			11 25				12 25				13 25				14 25	
Hunts Cross 89 d	00 14	08 51	09 28			10 28			11 28				12 28				13 28				14 28	
L'pool Sth Parkway 7 91,103 ✈ d	00 20	08 55	09 33		09 47	10 33		10 45	11 33		11 47	12 17	12 33		12 47	13 17	13 33		13 47	14 16	14 33	
Liverpool Central 10 103 a																						
West Allerton 91 a		08 58	09 36			10 36			11 36				12 36				13 36				14 36	
Mossley Hill 91 a		09 02	09 39			10 39			11 39				12 39				13 39				14 39	
Edge Hill 90,91 a																						
Liverpool Lime Street 10 90,91 a	00 34	09 13	09 50	09 52	10 00	10 50	10 54	10 57	11 50	11 54	11 59	12 30	12 50	12 54	12 58	13 30	13 50	13 54	13 58	14 30	14 50	14 54

	TP	EM	NT	NT	TP	EM	NT	NT	TP	EM	NT	NT	TP	EM	NT	NT	TP	EM	NT	NT	TP	EM
	◇1 D	◇ E			◇1 F	◇ E			◇1 D	◇ B			◇1 F	◇ B			◇1 D	◇ E			◇1 F	◇ E
Manchester Airport 85 ✈ d				14 35				15 35				16 35				17 35				18 35		
Sheffield 7 78 ⇌ d		13 38				14 39				15 38				16 44				17 44				18 37
Stockport 84 d		14 26				15 26				16 26				17 29				18 26				19 26
ManchesterPicc 10 78,84,85 ⇌ d	14 07	14 38		14 50	15 07	15 38		15 50	16 07	16 38		16 50	17 07	17 38		17 50	18 07	18 38		18 50	19 07	19 38
Manchester Oxford Road 84,85 d	14 12	14 42	14 45	14 53	15 12	15 42	15 45	15 53	16 12	16 42	16 45	16 53	17 12	17 42	17 45	17 53	18 12	18 42	18 45	18 53	19 12	19 42
Deansgate 84,85 ⇌ d			14 47				15 47				16 47				17 47				18 47			
Trafford Park d																						
Humphrey Park d																						
Urmston d			14 53				15 53				16 53				17 53				18 53			
Chassen Road d																						
Flixton d																						
Irlam d			14 58				15 58				16 58				17 58				18 58			
Glazebrook d																						
Birchwood d	14 25		15 04		15 25		16 04		16 25		17 04		17 25		18 04		18 25		19 04		19 25	
Padgate d																						
Warrington Central a	14 30	14 58	15 09		15 30	15 58	16 09		16 30	16 58	17 09		17 30	17 58	18 09		18 30	18 58	19 09		19 30	19 58
d	14 30	14 58	15 09		15 30	15 58	16 09		16 30	16 58	17 09		17 30	17 58	18 09		18 30	18 58	19 09		19 30	19 58
Sankey for Penketh d																						
Widnes d		15 06	15 17			16 06	16 17			17 06	17 17			18 06	18 17			19 06	19 17			20 06
Hough Green d			15 21				16 21				17 21				18 21				19 21			
Halewood d			15 25				16 25				17 25				18 25				19 25			
Hunts Cross 89 d			15 28				16 28				17 28				18 28				19 28			
L'pool Sth Parkway 7 91,103 ✈ d	14 47	15 16	15 33		15 47	16 16	16 33		16 47	17 16	17 33		17 47	18 16	18 33		18 47	19 17	19 33		19 47	20 16
Liverpool Central 10 103 a																						
West Allerton 91 a			15 36				16 36				17 36				18 36				19 36			
Mossley Hill 91 a			15 39				16 39				17 39				18 39				19 39			
Edge Hill 90,91 a																						
Liverpool Lime Street 10 90,91 a	14 58	15 30	15 50	15 54	15 58	16 30	16 50	16 54	16 58	17 30	17 50	17 54	17 58	18 30	18 50	18 54	18 58	19 30	19 50	19 54	19 58	20 30

A From York
B From Nottingham
C From Newcastle
D From Scarborough
E From Norwich
F From Middlesbrough

1 July to 9 September

Manchester Airport and Manchester - Warrington Central - Liverpool

Network Diagram - see first Page of Table 88

	NT	NT	TP	NT	NT	TP	NT	NT	TP	NT	NT
			◇1 A			◇1 B			◇1 A		Bus
Manchester Airport 85 ✈ d		19 35			20 35			21 35		22 27	
Sheffield 7 78 ⇌ d											
Stockport 84 d											
ManchesterPicc 10 78,84,85 ⇌ d		19 50	20 07		20 50	21 07		21 50	22 07	22 41	
Manchester Oxford Road 84,85 d	19 45	19 53	20 12	20 45	20 53	21 12	21 45	21 53	22 12	22 45	23 00
Deansgate 84,85 ⇌ d	19 47			20 47			21 47			22 47	
Trafford Park d											
Humphrey Park d											
Urmston d	19 53			20 53			21 53			22 53	
Chassen Road d											
Flixton d											
Irlam d	19 58			20 58			21 58			22 58	
Glazebrook d											
Birchwood d	20 04		20 25	21 04		21 25	22 04		22 25	23 04	
Padgate d											
Warrington Central a	20 09		20 30	21 09		21 30	22 09		22 30	23 09	
d	20 09		20 30	21 09		21 30	22 09		22 30	23 09	
Sankey for Penketh d											
Widnes d	20 17			21 17			22 17			23 17	
Hough Green d	20 21			21 21			22 21			23 21	
Halewood d	20 25			21 25			22 25			23 25	
Hunts Cross 89 d	20 28			21 28			22 28			23 28	
L'pool Sth Parkway 7 91,103 ✈ d	20 33		20 47	21 33		21 47	22 33		22 47	23 33	
Liverpool Central 10 103 a											
West Allerton 91 a	20 36			21 36			22 36			23 36	
Mossley Hill 91 a	20 39			21 39			22 39			23 39	
Edge Hill 90,91 a											
Liverpool Lime Street 10 90,91 a	20 50	20 54	20 58	21 50	21 54	21 58	22 50	22 54	22 58	23 50	01 11

Sundays

from 16 September

	NT	NT	NT	NT	TP	NT	NT	NT	NT	EM	NT	NT	EM	NT	NT	EM	NT	NT	EM	NT	NT	EM
					◇1 C					◇ D			◇ D			◇ D			◇ D			◇ E
Manchester Airport 85 ✈ d				08 34			09 35		10 35			11 33			12 35			13 35			14 35	
Sheffield 7 78 ⇌ d										10 41			11 38			12 41			13 38			14 39
Stockport 84 d										11 26			12 26			13 26			14 26			15 26
ManchesterPicc 10 78,84,85 ⇌ d				08 49	09 07		09 50		10 50	11 38		11 50	12 38		12 50	13 38		13 50	14 38		14 50	15 38
Manchester Oxford Road 84,85 d	23p20	08 08	08 45	08 52	09 11	09 45	09 53	10 45	10 53	11 42	11 45	11 53	12 42	12 45	12 53	13 42	13 45	13 53	14 42	14 45	14 53	15 42
Deansgate 84,85 ⇌ d	23p22	08 10	08 47	08 54		09 47		10 47			11 47			12 47			13 47			14 47		
Trafford Park d	23p27																					
Humphrey Park d	23p29																					
Urmston d	23p31	08 16	08 53			09 53		10 53			11 53			12 53			13 53			14 53		
Chassen Road d	23p33																					
Flixton d	23p36																					
Irlam d	23p40	08 21	08 58			09 58		10 58			11 58			12 58			13 58			14 58		
Glazebrook d	23p43																					
Birchwood d	23p47	08 27	09 04		09 24	10 04		11 04			12 04			13 04			14 04			15 04		
Padgate d	23p50																					
Warrington Central a	23p54	08 31	09 09		09 29	10 09		11 09		11 58	12 09		12 58	13 09		13 58	14 09		14 58	15 09		15 58
d	23p54	08 31	09 09		09 29	10 09		11 09		11 59	12 09		12 58	13 09		13 58	14 09		14 58	15 09		15 58
Sankey for Penketh d	23p58																					
Widnes d	00 04	08 39	09 17			10 17		11 17		12 06	12 17		13 06	13 17		14 06	14 17		15 06	15 17		16 06
Hough Green d	00 06	08 44	09 21			10 21		11 21			12 21			13 21			14 21			15 21		
Halewood d	00 11	08 48	09 25			10 25		11 25			12 25			13 25			14 25			15 25		
Hunts Cross 89 d	00 14	08 51	09 28			10 28		11 28			12 28			13 28			14 28			15 28		
L'pool Sth Parkway 7 91,103 ✈ d	00 20	08 55	09 33		09 46	10 33		11 33		12 17	12 33		13 17	13 33		14 16	14 33		15 16	15 33		16 16
Liverpool Central 10 103 a																						
West Allerton 91 a		08 58	09 36			10 36		11 36			12 36			13 36			14 36			15 36		
Mossley Hill 91 a		09 02	09 39			10 39		11 39			12 39			13 39			14 39			15 39		
Edge Hill 90,91 a																						
Liverpool Lime Street 10 90,91 a	00 34	09 13	09 50	09 52	09 59	10 50	10 54	11 50	11 54	12 30	12 50	12 54	13 30	13 50	13 54	14 30	14 50	14 54	15 30	15 50	15 54	16 30

A From Scarborough
B From Middlesbrough
C from 28 October
D From Nottingham
E From Norwich

Table 89

Sundays
from 16 September

Manchester Airport and Manchester - Warrington Central - Liverpool

Network Diagram - see first Page of Table 88

	NT	NT	EM ◇ A	NT	NT	EM ◇ A	NT	NT	EM ◇ B	NT	NT	EM ◇ B	NT	NT	NT	NT	NT	NT	NT	NT 🚌
Manchester Airport 85 ✈ d		15 35			16 35			17 35			18 35			19 35		20 35		21 35	22 27	
Sheffield 7 78 ⇌ d			15 38			16 44			17 44			18 37								
Stockport 84 d			16 26			17 29			18 26			19 26								
Manchester Picc. 10 78,84,85 ⇌ d		15 50	16 38		16 50	17 38		17 50	18 38		18 50	19 38		19 50		20 50		21 50	22 41	
Manchester Oxford Road 84,85 d	15 45	15 53	16 42	16 45	16 53	17 42	17 45	17 53	18 42	18 45	18 53	19 42	19 45	19 53	20 45	20 53	21 45	21 53	22 45	23 00
Deansgate 84,85 ⇌ d	15 47			16 47			17 47			18 47			19 47		20 47		21 47		22 47	
Trafford Park d																				
Humphrey Park d																				
Urmston d	15 53			16 53			17 53			18 53			19 53		20 53		21 53		22 53	
Chassen Road d																				
Flixton d																				
Irlam d	15 58			16 58			17 58			18 58			19 58		20 58		21 58		22 58	
Glazebrook d																				
Birchwood d	16 04			17 04			18 04			19 04			20 04		21 04		22 04		23 04	
Padgate d																				
Warrington Central a	16 09		16 58	17 09		17 58	18 09		18 58	19 09		19 58	20 09		21 09		22 09		23 09	
d	16 09		16 58	17 09		17 58	18 09		18 58	19 09		19 58	20 09		21 09		22 09		23 09	
Sankey for Penketh d																				
Widnes d	16 17		17 06	17 17		18 06	18 17		19 06	19 17		20 06	20 17		21 17		22 17		23 17	
Hough Green d	16 21			17 21			18 21			19 21			20 21		21 21		22 21		23 21	
Halewood d	16 25			17 25			18 25			19 25			20 25		21 25		22 25		23 25	
Hunts Cross 89 d	16 28			17 28			18 28			19 28			20 28		21 28		22 28		23 28	
L'pool Sth Parkway 7 91,103 ✈ d	16 33		17 16	17 33		18 16	18 33		19 17	19 33		20 16	20 33		21 33		22 33		23 33	
Liverpool Central 10 103 a																				
West Allerton 91 a	16 36			17 36			18 36			19 36			20 36		21 36		22 36		23 36	
Mossley Hill 91 a	16 39			17 39			18 39			19 39			20 39		21 39		22 39		23 39	
Edge Hill 90,91 a																				
Liverpool Lime Street 10 90,91 a	16 50	16 54	17 30	17 50	17 54	18 30	18 50	18 54	19 30	19 50	19 54	20 30	20 50	20 54	21 50	21 54	22 50	22 54	23 50	01 11

A From Nottingham
B From Norwich

Table 90

Mondays to Fridays
until 28 September

Liverpool and St Helens - Newton-le-Willows, Wigan, Preston and Manchester

Network Diagram - see first Page of Table 88

Miles	Miles	Miles	Miles		NT A 🚌	AW B 🚌	NT MX 🚌	NT A	NT A 🚌	NT MX 🚌	AW MX 🚌	NT MX 🚌	NT MO	NT MX	TP ◇1 C	NT	NT	AW D	NT	NT	NT	TP ◇1 E
0	0	0	—	**Liverpool Lime Street** 10 89,91 d	22p01		22p12	23p01	23p01	23p02		23p16	03 38	03 38		05 13	05 31		05 46	06 01	06 13	
1¾	1¾	1¾	—	Edge Hill 89,91 d			22p19			23p09		23p23					05 35		05 50	06 05		
2½	2½	2½	—	Wavertree Technology Park d	22p16		22p29		23p16	23p19		23p33				05 19	05 37		05 52	06 07	06 19	
3½	3½	3½	—	Broad Green d	22p26		22p39		23p26	23p29		23p43					05 40		05 55	06 10		
5	5	5	—	Roby d	22p33		22p46		23p33	23p36		23p50					05 44		05 59	06 14		
5½	5½	5½	—	Huyton d	22p37		22p50		23p37	23p40		23p54					05 46		06 01	06 16		
—	7¾	—	—	Prescot d						23p50							05 51			06 21		
—	8¾	—	—	Eccleston Park d						23p56							05 53			06 23		
—	9¾	—	—	Thatto Heath d						00 06							05 56			06 26		
—	11¼	—	—	**St Helens Central** a						00 16							05 59			06 29		
—	—	—	—	d						00 16							06 00			06 30		
—	15	—	—	Garswood d						00 36							06 07			06 37		
—	16¼	—	—	Bryn d						00 43							06 10			06 40		
7½	—	7½	—	Whiston d	22p47		23p00		23p47			00 04							06 05			
9	—	9	—	Rainhill d	22p57		23p10		23p57			00 14							06 08			
10¾	—	10¾	—	Lea Green d	23p05		23p18		00 05			00 22							06 11			
12	—	12	—	**St Helens Junction** d	23p12		23p25		00 12			00 29				05 29			06 14		06 29	
—	—	—	—	Warrington Bank Quay d		23p09					23p59							06 06				
14¾	—	14¾	—	Earlestown 8 d	23p24	23p34	23b37		00 24		00 24	00s41						06 12	06 19			
—	—	—	—	Warrington Bank Quay a																		
16¾	—	16¾	0	**Newton-le-Willows** d	23p33	23p44	23b45		00 33		00 34	00s49				05 35		06 15	06 22		06 35	
—	20	23¼	—	**Wigan North Western** 65 a						00s56							06 21			06 51		
—	—	—	—	d											04 44							06 15
—	28¾	31½	—	Euxton Balshaw Lane d						01s21												
—	31	34¾	—	Leyland 82 a						01s33												06 27
—	35	38¾	—	**Preston** 8 65,82 a						01 48					05s04							06 35
—	52½	—	—	Blackpool North 97 a											05 33							07 06
26¾	—	—	10½	Patricroft d			00s15					01s19							06 34			
27¾	—	—	11½	Eccles d	23p57		00s25		00 57			01s29							06 36			
31¾	—	—	—	**Manchester Victoria** ⇌ a			00 44					01 48							06 47			
—	—	—	15¾	**Manchester Oxford Road** a	00 12	00 14		23p47	01 12									06 35			06 57	
—	—	—	16¼	**Manchester Piccadilly** 10 ⇌ a		00 19		23p50			01 09		04 20	04 20		05 57		06 45			07 01	
—	—	—	26	**Manchester Airport** 85 ✈ a				00 07					04 33	04 34		06 14					07 22	

	NT	NT	NT MO	NT MX	AW ◇ F	NT	NT	NT	NT	AW D 🍴	NT G	NT	NT	AW ◇ H 🍴	NT	NT	NT	NT	NT	NT	NT	NT I
Liverpool Lime Street 10 89,91 d	06 16	06 21	06 31	06 31		06 46	06 57	07 01	07 13		07 16	07 26	07 31		07 46	07 57	08 01	08 13	08 16	08 26	08 31	08 44
Edge Hill 89,91 d	06 20		06 35	06 35		06 50		07 05			07 20	07 30	07 35		07 50		08 05		08 20	08 30	08 35	08 50
Wavertree Technology Park d	06 22		06 37	06 37		06 52		07 07	07 19		07 22		07 37		07 52		08 07	08 19	08 22		08 37	08 52
Broad Green d	06 25		06 40	06 40		06 55		07 10			07 25		07 40		07 55		08 10		08 25		08 40	08 55
Roby d	06 29		06 44	06 44		06 59		07 14			07 29		07 44		07 59		08 14		08 29		08 44	08 59
Huyton d	06 31		06 46	06 46		07 01	07 06	07 16			07 31		07 46		08 01	08 06	08 16		08 31		08 46	09 01
Prescot d			06 51	06 51				07 21					07 51				08 21				08 51	
Eccleston Park d			06 53	06 53				07 23					07 53				08 23				08 53	
Thatto Heath d			06 56	06 56				07 26					07 56				08 26				08 56	
St Helens Central a			06 59	06 59			07 15	07 29					07 59			08 15	08 29				08 59	
d			07 00	07 00			07 15	07 30					08 00			08 15	08 30				09 00	
Garswood d			07 07	07 07				07 37					08 07				08 37				09 07	
Bryn d			07 10	07 10				07 40					08 10				08 40				09 10	
Whiston d	06 35					07 05					07 35				08 05				08 35			09 05
Rainhill d	06 38					07 08					07 38				08 08				08 38			09 08
Lea Green d	06 41					07 11			07 28		07 41				08 11				08 41			09 11
St Helens Junction d	06 44					07 14			07 31		07 44				08 14			08 29	08 44			09 14
Warrington Bank Quay d					07 07					07 39				08 08								
Earlestown 8 d	06 50				07 14	07 19				07 46	07 49			08 16	08 19				08 50			09 19
Warrington Bank Quay a	07 01																		09 01			
Newton-le-Willows d					07 17	07 22			07 37	07 49	07 52			08 19	08 22			08 35				09 22
Wigan North Western 65 a			07 19	07 21			07 30	07 49					08 19			08 30	08 49				09 19	
d							07 31									08 31						
Euxton Balshaw Lane d							07 41									08 41						
Leyland 82 a							07 46									08 46						
Preston 8 65,82 a							07 56									08 56						
Blackpool North 97 a																						
Patricroft d						07 34					08 04				08 34							09 34
Eccles d						07 36					08 06				08 36							09 36
Manchester Victoria ⇌ a						07 49					08 19				08 50							09 47
Manchester Oxford Road a		07 36			07 41				07 57	08 09		08 36		08 41				08 57		09 36		
Manchester Piccadilly 10 ⇌ a					07 50				08 01	08 18				08 50				09 01				
Manchester Airport 85 ✈ a									08 22									09 22				

A MO from 21 May until 24 September
B MO from 21 May until 24 September. From Chester
C From Manchester Airport
D From Chester
E From Manchester Piccadilly
F From Llandudno Junction
G To Huddersfield
H From Llandudno
I To Stalybridge
b Previous night, stops to set down only

until 28 September

Liverpool and St Helens - Newton-le-Willows, Wigan, Preston and Manchester

Network Diagram - see first Page of Table 88

	NT	NT	AW	NT	NT	NT	NT	NT	NT	NT	NT	AW	NT	NT	NT	NT	NT	NT	NT	NT	AW	NT
			◇ A ✕		B							◇ A ✕		B				C	D		◇ A ✕	
Liverpool Lime Street 10 89,91 d	08 57	09 01		09 13		09 16	09 27	09 31	09 46	09 57	10 01		10 13		10 16	10 27	10 31	10 46	10 57	11 01		11 13
Edge Hill 89,91 d		09 05				09 20		09 35	09 50		10 05				10 20		10 35	10 50		11 05		
Wavertree Technology Park d		09 07		09 19		09 22		09 37	09 52		10 07		10 19		10 22		10 37	10 52		11 07		11 19
Broad Green d		09 10				09 25		09 40	09 55		10 10				10 25		10 40	10 55		11 10		
Roby d		09 14				09 29		09 44	09 59		10 14				10 29		10 44	10 59		11 14		
Huyton d	09 06	09 16				09 31		09 46	10 01	10 06	10 16				10 31		10 46	11 01	11 06	11 16		
Prescot d		09 21						09 51			10 21						10 51			11 21		
Eccleston Park d		09 23						09 53			10 23						10 53			11 23		
Thatto Heath d		09 26						09 56			10 26						10 56			11 26		
St Helens Central a	09 15	09 29						09 59		10 15	10 29						10 59		11 15	11 29		
d	09 15	09 30						10 00		10 15	10 30						11 00		11 15	11 30		
Garswood d		09 37						10 07			10 37						11 07			11 37		
Bryn d		09 40						10 10			10 40						11 10			11 40		
Whiston d						09 35			10 05						10 35			11 05				
Rainhill d						09 38			10 08						10 38			11 08				
Lea Green d						09 41			10 11						10 41			11 11				
St Helens Junction d				09 29		09 44			10 14				10 29		10 44			11 14				11 29
Warrington Bank Quay d			09 19		09 22							10 19		10 22							11 19	
Earlestown 8 d			09 26		09a33	09 50			10 19			10 26		10a33	10 50			11 19			11 26	
Warrington Bank Quay a						10 01									11 02							
Newton-le-Willows d			09 29	09 35					10 22			10 29	10 35					11 22			11 29	11 35
Wigan North Western 65 a	09 30	09 51						10 21		10 30	10 51						11 19		11 30	11 51		
d	09 31									10 31									11 31			
Euxton Balshaw Lane d	09 41									10 41									11 41			
Leyland 82 a	09 46									10 46									11 46			
Preston 8 65,82 a	09 54									10 54									11 54			
Blackpool North 97 a	10 19									11 20									12 19			
Patricroft d									10 34									11 34				
Eccles d									10 36									11 36				
Manchester Victoria a									10 47									11 49				
Manchester Oxford Road a			09 48	09 57			10 36					10 48	10 57			11 36					11 48	11 57
Manchester Piccadilly 10 a			09 57	10 01								10 57	11 01								11 57	12 01
Manchester Airport 85 ✈ a				10 22									11 22									12 22

	NT	NT	NT	NT	NT	NT	NT	AW	NT	NT	NT	NT	NT	NT	NT	NT	AW	NT	NT	NT	NT
	B				C	D		◇ A ✕		B				C	D		◇ A ✕		B		
Liverpool Lime Street 10 89,91 d		11 16	11 27	11 31	11 46	11 57	12 01		12 13		12 16	12 27	12 31	12 46	12 57	13 01		13 13		13 16	13 27
Edge Hill 89,91 d		11 20		11 35	11 50		12 05				12 20		12 35	12 50		13 05				13 20	
Wavertree Technology Park d		11 22		11 37	11 52		12 07		12 19		12 22		12 37	12 52		13 07		13 19		13 22	
Broad Green d		11 25		11 40	11 55		12 10				12 25		12 40	12 55		13 10				13 25	
Roby d		11 29		11 44	11 59		12 14				12 29		12 44	12 59		13 14				13 29	
Huyton d		11 31		11 46	12 01	12 06	12 16				12 31		12 46	13 01	13 06	13 16				13 31	
Prescot d				11 51			12 21						12 51			13 21					
Eccleston Park d				11 53			12 23						12 53			13 23					
Thatto Heath d				11 56			12 26						12 56			13 26					
St Helens Central a				11 59		12 15	12 29						12 59		13 15	13 29					
d				12 00		12 15	12 30						13 00		13 15	13 30					
Garswood d				12 07			12 37						13 07			13 37					
Bryn d				12 10			12 40						13 10			13 40					
Whiston d		11 35			12 05						12 35			13 05						13 35	
Rainhill d		11 38			12 08						12 38			13 08						13 38	
Lea Green d		11 41			12 11						12 41			13 11						13 41	
St Helens Junction d		11 44			12 14				12 29		12 44			13 14				13 29		13 44	
Warrington Bank Quay d	11 22							12 19		12 22							13 19		13 22		
Earlestown 8 d	11a33	11 50			12 19			12 26		12a33	12 50			13 19			13 26		13a33	13 50	
Warrington Bank Quay a		12 01									13 01									14 01	
Newton-le-Willows d					12 22			12 29	12 35					13 22			13 29	13 35			
Wigan North Western 65 a				12 19		12 30	12 51						13 21		13 30	13 51					
d						12 31									13 31						
Euxton Balshaw Lane d						12 41									13 41						
Leyland 82 a						12 46									13 46						
Preston 8 65,82 a						12 54									13 54						
Blackpool North 97 a						13 19									14 19						
Patricroft d					12 34									13 34							
Eccles d					12 36									13 36							
Manchester Victoria a					12 50									13 47							
Manchester Oxford Road a			12 36					12 48	12 57			13 36					13 48	13 57			14 36
Manchester Piccadilly 10 a								12 57	13 01								13 57	14 01			
Manchester Airport 85 ✈ a									13 22									14 22			

A From Llandudno
B To Liverpool Lime Street
C To Stalybridge
D From Liverpool South Parkway

until 28 September

Liverpool and St Helens - Newton-le-Willows, Wigan, Preston and Manchester

Network Diagram - see first Page of Table 88

	NT	NT	NT	NT	AW	NT	NT	NT	NT	NT	NT	NT	NT	AW	NT	NT	NT	NT	NT	NT	NT	NT
		A	B		◇ C ✕		D				A	B		◇ C ✕		D				E	B	
Liverpool Lime Street 10 89,91 d	13 31	13 46	13 57	14 01		14 13		14 16	14 27	14 31	14 46	14 57	15 02		15 13		15 16	15 27	15 31	15 46	15 57	16 01
Edge Hill 89,91 d	13 35	13 50		14 05				14 20		14 35	14 50		15 05				15 20		15 35	15 50		16 05
Wavertree Technology Park d	13 37	13 52		14 07		14 19		14 22		14 37	14 52		15 07		15 19		15 22		15 37	15 52		16 07
Broad Green d	13 40	13 55		14 10				14 25		14 40	14 55		15 10				15 25		15 40	15 55		16 10
Roby d	13 44	13 59		14 14				14 29		14 44	14 59		15 14				15 29		15 44	15 59		16 14
Huyton d	13 46	14 01	14 06	14 16				14 31		14 46	15 01	15 06	15 16				15 31		15 46	16 01	16 06	16 16
Prescot d	13 51			14 21						14 51			15 21						15 51			16 21
Eccleston Park d	13 53			14 23						14 53			15 23						15 53			16 23
Thatto Heath d	13 56			14 26						14 56			15 26						15 56			16 26
St Helens Central a	13 59		14 15	14 29						14 59		15 15	15 29						15 59		16 15	16 29
d	14 00		14 15	14 30						15 00		15 15	15 30						16 00		16 15	16 30
Garswood d	14 07			14 37						15 07			15 37						16 07			16 37
Bryn d	14 10			14 40						15 10			15 40						16 10			16 40
Whiston d		14 05						14 35			15 05						15 35			16 05		
Rainhill d		14 08						14 38			15 08						15 38			16 08		
Lea Green d		14 11						14 41			15 11						15 41			16 11		
St Helens Junction d		14 14				14 29		14 44			15 14				15 29		15 44			16 14		
Warrington Bank Quay d					14 19		14 22							15 19		15 22						
Earlestown 8 d		14 19			14 26		14a33	14 50			15 19			15 26		15a33	15 50			16 19		
Warrington Bank Quay a								15 01									16 01					
Newton-le-Willows d		14 22			14 29	14 35					15 22			15 29	15 35					16 22		
Wigan North Western 65 a	14 19		14 30	14 51						15 21		15 30	15 51						16 19		16 30	16 51
d			14 31									15 31									16 30	
Euxton Balshaw Lane d			14 41									15 41									16 40	
Leyland 82 a			14 46									15 46									16 45	
Preston 8 65,82 a			14 54									15 54									16 54	
Blackpool North 97 a			15 21									16 20									17 20	
Patricroft d		14 34									15 34									16 34		
Eccles d		14 36									15 36									16 36		
Manchester Victoria a		14 50									15 49									16 49		
Manchester Oxford Road a					14 48	14 57			15 36					15 48	15 57			16 36				
Manchester Piccadilly 10 a					14 57	15 01								15 57	16 01							
Manchester Airport 85 ✈ a						15 22									16 22							

	AW	NT	NT	NT	AW	NT	NT	NT	NT	NT	NT	NT	NT	NT	AW	NT	NT	NT	NT	NT	NT
	◇ C ✕		D		◇ C ✕			E	B						◇ C ✕						
Liverpool Lime Street 10 89,91 d		16 13		16 16		16 27	16 31	16 46	16 57	17 01	17 06	17 10	17 19	17 27		17 35	17 44	17 48	18 01	18 13	18 16
Edge Hill 89,91 d				16 20			16 35	16 50		17 05		17 14		17 31		17 39		17 52	18 05		18 20
Wavertree Technology Park d		16 19		16 22			16 37	16 52		17 07	17 12	17 16		17 33		17 41	17 49	17 54	18 07	18 19	18 22
Broad Green d				16 25			16 40	16 55		17 10		17 19		17 36		17 44	17 52	17 57	18 10		18 25
Roby d				16 29			16 44	16 59		17 14		17 23		17 40		17 48		18 01	18 14		18 29
Huyton d				16 31			16 46	17 01	17 06	17 16	17 19	17 25	17 29	17 42		17 50	17 57	18 03	18 16		18 31
Prescot d							16 51			17 21			17 33				18 02		18 21		
Eccleston Park d							16 53			17 23			17 36				18 05		18 23		
Thatto Heath d							16 56			17 26			17 38				18 07		18 26		
St Helens Central a							16 59		17 15	17 29			17 42	17 51			18 11		18 29		
d							17 00		17 15	17 30			17 42	17 51			18 11		18 30		
Garswood d							17 07			17 37			17 49				18 19		18 37		
Bryn d							17 10			17 40			17 52				18 22		18 40		
Whiston d				16 35				17 05				17 28				17 54		18 07			18 35
Rainhill d				16 38				17 08				17 32				17 57		18 10			18 38
Lea Green d				16 41				17 11			17 26	17 35				18 00		18 13			18 41
St Helens Junction d		16 29		16 44				17 14			17 29	17 39				18 03		18 16		18 29	18 44
Warrington Bank Quay d	16 19		16 22		16 51										17 49						
Earlestown 8 d	16 26		16a33	16 49	16 59			17 19				17 44			17 57	18 08		18 21			18 50
Warrington Bank Quay a																					19 01
Newton-le-Willows d	16 29	16 35		16 52	17 02			17 22			17 35	17 47			18 00	18 11		18 24		18 35	
Wigan North Western 65 a							17 19		17 30	17 52			18 02	18 04			18 30		18 49		
d									17 31					18 05			18 31		18 49		
Euxton Balshaw Lane d									17 41					18 16			18 41		19 01		
Leyland 82 a									17 46					18 21			18 46		19 06		
Preston 8 65,82 a									17 54					18 31			18 54		19 15		
Blackpool North 97 a									18 23								19 22				
Patricroft d				17 04				17 34				17 59				18 23					
Eccles d				17 06				17 36				18 01				18 25		18 36			
Manchester Victoria a				17 20				17 47				18 14				18 41		18 49			
Manchester Oxford Road a	16 48	16 57			17 21	17 36					17 57				18 19					18 57	
Manchester Piccadilly 10 a	16 57	17 01			17 30						18 01				18 28					19 01	
Manchester Airport 85 ✈ a		17 22									18 22									19 24	

A To Stalybridge
B From Liverpool South Parkway
C From Llandudno
D To Liverpool Lime Street
E To Huddersfield

until 28 September

Liverpool and St Helens - Newton-le-Willows, Wigan, Preston and Manchester

Network Diagram - see first Page of Table 88

		NT	AW	NT	NT	AW	NT	NT	NT	NT	AW	NT	NT	NT	NT	AW	NT	NT	TP	AW FO	NT FO	AW FX	NT FX
			◇ A			B	C				◇ A					◇ A			◇■ D	B			
Liverpool Lime Street ■ 89,91	d	18 31		18 46	19 01			19 12	19 23	19 42		20 09	20 12	20 25	20 42		21 12	21 42			22 12		22 12
Edge Hill 89,91	d	18 35		18 50	19 05			19 16		19 46			20 16		20 46		21 16	21 46			22 16		22 19
Wavertree Technology Park	d	18 37		18 52	19 07			19 18		19 48		20 15	20 18		20 48		21 18	21 48			22 18		22 29
Broad Green	d	18 40		18 55	19 10			19 21		19 51			20 21		20 51		21 21	21 51			22 21		22 39
Roby	d	18 44		18 59	19 14			19 25		19 55			20 25		20 55		21 25	21 55			22 25		22 46
Huyton	d	18 46		19 01	19 16			19 27	19 32	19 57			20 27	20 34	20 57		21 27	21 57			22 27		22 50
Prescot	d	18 51			19 21					20 02					21 02			22 02					
Eccleston Park	d	18 53			19 23					20 04					21 04			22 04					
Thatto Heath	d	18 56			19 26					20 07					21 07			22 07					
St Helens Central	a	18 59			19 29				19 40	20 10				20 42	21 10			22 10					
	d	19 00			19 30				19 41	20 11				20 43	21 11			22 11					
Garswood	d	19 07			19 37					20 18					21 18			22 18					
Bryn	d	19 10			19 40					20 21					21 21			22 21					
Whiston	d			19 05				19 31					20 31				21 31				22 31		23 00
Rainhill	d			19 08				19 34					20 34				21 34				22 34		23 10
Lea Green	d			19 11				19 37					20 37				21 37				22 37		23 18
St Helens Junction	d			19 14				19 40				20 25	20 40				21 40				22 40		23 25
Warrington Bank Quay	d		18 46			19 19	19 22				20 19					21 19				22 19		22 28	
Earlestown ■	d		18 57	19 19		19 26	19a33	19 45			20 26		20 45			21 26	21 45			22 26	22 45	22 53	23s37
Warrington Bank Quay	a																						
Newton-le-Willows	d		19 00	19 22		19 29		19 48			20 29	20 35	20 48			21 29	21 48			22 29	22 48	23 03	23s45
Wigan North Western 65	a	19 19			19 51				19 54	20 32				20 57	21 32			22 28					
	d								19 55					20 57				22 28	21 48				
Euxton Balshaw Lane	d								20 05					21 08				22 39					
Leyland 82	a								20 10					21 16				22 44					
Preston ■ 65,82	a								20 18					21 22				22 55					
Blackpool North 97	a								20 42					21 52				23 21					
Patricroft	d			19 34				20 00					21 00				22 00				23 00		00s15
Eccles	d			19 36				20 02					21 02				22 02				23 02		00s25
Manchester Victoria	a			19 49				20 16					21 15				22 15				23 15		00 44
Manchester Oxford Road	a		19 21			19 48					20 48	20 57				21 48			22 26	22 50		23 33	
Manchester Piccadilly ■	a		19 29			19 52					20 52	21 01				21 57			22 30	22 58		23 38	
Manchester Airport 85	a					20 18					21 18	21 20							22 47				

		TP	NT FO	NT FX	NT FO	AW FX	NT FX
		◇■ E					
Liverpool Lime Street ■ 89,91	d		23 02	23 02	23 16		23 16
Edge Hill 89,91	d		23 06	23 09	23 20		23 23
Wavertree Technology Park	d		23 08	23 19	23 22		23 33
Broad Green	d		23 11	23 29	23 26		23 43
Roby	d		23 15	23 36	23 30		23 50
Huyton	d		23 17	23 40	23 32		23 54
Prescot	d		23 22	23 50			
Eccleston Park	d		23 24	23 56			
Thatto Heath	d		23 27	00 06			
St Helens Central	a		23 30	00 16			
	d		23 31	00 16			
Garswood	d		23 38	00 36			
Bryn	d		23 41	00 43			
Whiston	d				23 36		00 04
Rainhill	d				23 39		00 14
Lea Green	d				23 42		00 22
St Helens Junction	d				23 45		00 29
Warrington Bank Quay	d					23 59	
Earlestown ■	d				23 50	00 24	00 41
Warrington Bank Quay	a						
Newton-le-Willows	d				23 53	00 34	00 49
Wigan North Western 65	a		23 48	00s56			
	d	22 51	23 48				
Euxton Balshaw Lane	d		23 59	01s21			
Leyland 82	a		00 04	01s33			
Preston ■ 65,82	a	23 09	00 13	01 48			
Blackpool North 97	a						
Patricroft	d				00 05		01 19
Eccles	d				00 08		01 29
Manchester Victoria	a				00 21		01 48
Manchester Oxford Road	a						
Manchester Piccadilly ■	a					01 09	
Manchester Airport 85	a						

A From Llandudno
B From Chester
C To Liverpool Lime Street
D From Barrow-in-Furness
E From Manchester Airport to Barrow-in-Furness

from 1 October

Liverpool and St Helens - Newton-le-Willows, Wigan, Preston and Manchester

Network Diagram - see first Page of Table 88

		NT MO	AW MO	NT MX	NT MO	NT MO	NT MX	AW MX	NT MX	NT MO	NT MX	TP	NT	NT	AW	NT	NT	NT	TP	NT	NT	NT	AW
			A									◇■ B			A				◇■ C				◇ D
Liverpool Lime Street ■ 89,91	d	22p01		22p12	23p01	23p01	23p02		23p16	03 38	03 38		05 13	05 31		05 46	06 01	06 13		06 16	06 21	06 31	
Edge Hill 89,91	d			22p19			23p09		23p23					05 35		05 50	06 05			06 20		06 35	
Wavertree Technology Park	d	22p16		22p29		23p16	23p19		23p33				05 19	05 37		05 52	06 07	06 19		06 22		06 37	
Broad Green	d	22p26		22p39		23p26	23p29		23p43					05 40		05 55	06 10			06 25		06 40	
Roby	d	22p33		22p46		23p33	23p36		23p50					05 44		05 59	06 14			06 29		06 44	
Huyton	d	22p37		22p50		23p37	23p40		23p54					05 46		06 01	06 16			06 31		06 46	
Prescot	d						23p50							05 51			06 21					06 51	
Eccleston Park	d						23p56							05 53			06 23					06 53	
Thatto Heath	d						00 06							05 56			06 26					06 56	
St Helens Central	a						00 16							05 59			06 29					06 59	
	d						00 16							06 00			06 30					07 00	
Garswood	d						00 36							06 07			06 37					07 07	
Bryn	d						00 43							06 10			06 40					07 10	
Whiston	d	22p47		23p00		23p47			00 04							06 05				06 35			
Rainhill	d	22p57		23p10		23p57			00 14							06 08				06 38			
Lea Green	d	23p05		23p18		00 05			00 22							06 11				06 41			
St Helens Junction	d	23p12		23p25		00 12			00 29				05 29			06 14		06 29		06 44			
Warrington Bank Quay	d		23p09					23p59							06 06								07 07
Earlestown ■	d	23p24	23p34	23b37		00 24		00 24	00s41						06 12	06 19				06 50			07 14
Warrington Bank Quay	a																			07 01			
Newton-le-Willows	d	23p33	23p44	23b45		00 33		00 34	00s49				05 35		06 15	06 22		06 35					07 17
Wigan North Western 65	a						00s56							06 23			06 53					07 23	
	d											04 44							06 15				
Euxton Balshaw Lane	d						01s21																
Leyland 82	a						01s33												06 27				
Preston ■ 65,82	a						01 48					05s04							06 35				
Blackpool North 97	a											05 33							07 06				
Patricroft	d			00s15					01s19							06 34							
Eccles	d	23p57		00s25		00 57			01s29							06 36							
Manchester Victoria	a			00 44					01 48							06 47							
Manchester Oxford Road	a	00 12	00 14		23p47	01 12									06 35			06 57			07 36		07 41
Manchester Piccadilly ■	a		00 19		23p50			01 09		04 20	04 20		05 57		06 45			07 01					07 50
Manchester Airport 85	a				00 07					04 33	04 34		06 14					07 22					

		NT	NT	NT	NT	AW	NT	NT	NT	AW	NT	NT	NT	NT	NT	NT	NT	NT	NT	NT	AW	NT	NT
						A	E			◇ F								G			◇ F		H
Liverpool Lime Street ■ 89,91	d	06 46	06 57	07 01	07 13		07 16	07 26	07 31		07 46	07 57	08 01	08 13	08 16	08 26	08 31	08 44	08 57	09 01		09 13	
Edge Hill 89,91	d	06 50		07 05			07 20	07 30	07 35		07 50		08 05		08 20	08 30	08 35	08 50		09 05			
Wavertree Technology Park	d	06 52		07 07	07 19		07 22		07 37		07 52		08 07	08 19	08 22		08 37	08 52		09 07		09 19	
Broad Green	d	06 55		07 10			07 25		07 40		07 55		08 10		08 25		08 40	08 55		09 10			
Roby	d	06 59		07 14			07 29		07 44		07 59		08 14		08 29		08 44	08 59		09 14			
Huyton	d	07 01	07 06	07 16			07 31		07 46		08 01	08 06	08 16		08 31		08 46	09 01	09 06	09 16			
Prescot	d			07 21					07 51				08 21				08 51			09 21			
Eccleston Park	d			07 23					07 53				08 23				08 53			09 23			
Thatto Heath	d			07 26					07 56				08 26				08 56			09 26			
St Helens Central	a		07 15	07 29					07 59			08 15	08 29				08 59		09 15	09 29			
	d		07 15	07 30					08 00			08 15	08 30				09 00		09 15	09 30			
Garswood	d			07 37					08 07				08 37				09 07			09 37			
Bryn	d			07 40					08 10				08 40				09 10			09 40			
Whiston	d	07 05					07 35				08 05				08 35			09 05					
Rainhill	d	07 08					07 38				08 08				08 38			09 08					
Lea Green	d	07 11			07 28		07 41				08 11				08 41			09 11					
St Helens Junction	d	07 14			07 31		07 44				08 14			08 29	08 44			09 14				09 29	
Warrington Bank Quay	d					07 39				08 08											09 19		09 22
Earlestown ■	d	07 19				07 46	07 49			08 16	08 19				08 50			09 19			09 26		09a33
Warrington Bank Quay	a														09 01								
Newton-le-Willows	d	07 22			07 37	07 49	07 52			08 19	08 22			08 35				09 22			09 29	09 35	
Wigan North Western 65	a		07 30	07 53					08 23			08 30	08 53				09 23		09 30	09 53			
	d		07 31									08 31							09 31				
Euxton Balshaw Lane	d		07 41									08 41							09 41				
Leyland 82	a		07 46									08 46							09 46				
Preston ■ 65,82	a		07 56									08 56							09 54				
Blackpool North 97	a																		10 19				
Patricroft	d	07 34					08 04				08 34							09 34					
Eccles	d	07 36					08 06				08 36							09 36					
Manchester Victoria	a	07 49					08 19				08 50							09 47					
Manchester Oxford Road	a				07 57	08 09		08 36		08 41				08 57		09 36					09 48	09 57	
Manchester Piccadilly ■	a				08 01	08 18				08 50				09 01							09 57	10 01	
Manchester Airport 85	a				08 22									09 22								10 22	

A From Chester
B From Manchester Airport
C From Manchester Piccadilly
D From Llandudno Junction
E To Huddersfield
F From Llandudno
G To Stalybridge
H To Liverpool Lime Street
b Previous night, stops to set down only

from 1 October

Liverpool and St Helens - Newton-le-Willows, Wigan, Preston and Manchester

Network Diagram - see first Page of Table 88

		NT		NT	NT	NT	NT	NT	AW	NT	NT	NT		NT	NT	NT	NT	NT	AW	NT	NT	NT		NT	NT
									◇ A		B					C	D		◇ A		B				
Liverpool Lime Street 10 89,91	d	09 16		09 27	09 31	09 46	09 57	10 01		10 13		10 16		10 27	10 31	10 46	10 57	11 02		11 13		11 16		11 27	11 31
Edge Hill 89,91	d	09 20			09 35	09 50		10 05				10 20			10 35	10 50		11 05				11 20			11 35
Wavertree Technology Park	d	09 22			09 37	09 52		10 07		10 19		10 22			10 37	10 52		11 07		11 19		11 22			11 37
Broad Green	d	09 25			09 40	09 55		10 10				10 25			10 40	10 55		11 10				11 25			11 40
Roby	d	09 29			09 44	09 59		10 14				10 29			10 44	10 59		11 14				11 29			11 44
Huyton	d	09 31			09 46	10 01	10 06	10 16				10 31			10 46	11 01	11 06	11 16				11 31			11 46
Prescot	d				09 51			10 21							10 51			11 21							11 51
Eccleston Park	d				09 53			10 23							10 53			11 23							11 53
Thatto Heath	d				09 56			10 26							10 56			11 26							11 56
St Helens Central	a				09 59		10 15	10 29							10 59		11 15	11 29							11 59
	d				10 00		10 15	10 30							11 00		11 15	11 30							12 00
Garswood	d				10 07			10 37							11 07			11 37							12 07
Bryn	d				10 10			10 40							11 10			11 40							12 10
Whiston	d	09 35				10 05						10 35				11 05						11 35			
Rainhill	d	09 38				10 08						10 38				11 08						11 38			
Lea Green	d	09 41				10 11						10 41				11 11						11 41			
St Helens Junction	d	09 44				10 14				10 29		10 44				11 14				11 29		11 44			
Warrington Bank Quay	d								10 19		10 22								11 19		11 22				
Earlestown 8	d	09 50				10 19			10 26		10a33	10 50				11 19			11 26		11a33	11 50			
Warrington Bank Quay	a	10 01										11 02										12 01			
Newton-le-Willows	d					10 22			10 29	10 35						11 22			11 29	11 35					
Wigan North Western 65	a				10 23		10 30	10 53							11 19		11 30	11 53							12 23
	d						10 31										11 31								
Euxton Balshaw Lane	d						10 41										11 41								
Leyland 82	a						10 46										11 46								
Preston 8 65,82	a						10 54										11 54								
Blackpool North 97	a						11 20										12 19								
Patricroft	d					10 34										11 34									
Eccles	d					10 36										11 36									
Manchester Victoria	a					10 47										11 49									
Manchester Oxford Road	a			10 36					10 48	10 57				11 36					11 48	11 57				12 36	
Manchester Piccadilly 10	a								10 57	11 01									11 57	12 01					
Manchester Airport 85 ✈	a									11 22										12 22					

		NT	NT	NT	AW	NT	NT	NT		NT	NT	NT	NT	NT	AW	NT	NT	NT		NT	NT	NT	NT	NT	AW
		C	D		◇ A		B					C	D		◇ A		B					C	D		◇ A
Liverpool Lime Street 10 89,91	d	11 46	11 57	12 02		12 13		12 16		12 27	12 31	12 46	12 57	13 02		13 13		13 16		13 27	13 31	13 46	13 57	14 01	
Edge Hill 89,91	d	11 50		12 05				12 20			12 35	12 50		13 05				13 20			13 35	13 50		14 05	
Wavertree Technology Park	d	11 52		12 07		12 19		12 22			12 37	12 52		13 07		13 19		13 22			13 37	13 52		14 07	
Broad Green	d	11 55		12 10				12 25			12 40	12 55		13 10				13 25			13 40	13 55		14 10	
Roby	d	11 59		12 14				12 29			12 44	12 59		13 14				13 29			13 44	13 59		14 14	
Huyton	d	12 01	12 06	12 16				12 31			12 46	13 01	13 06	13 16				13 31			13 46	14 01	14 06	14 16	
Prescot	d			12 21							12 51			13 21							13 51			14 21	
Eccleston Park	d			12 23							12 53			13 23							13 53			14 23	
Thatto Heath	d			12 26							12 56			13 26							13 56			14 26	
St Helens Central	a		12 15	12 29							12 59		13 15	13 29							13 59		14 15	14 29	
	d		12 15	12 30							13 00		13 15	13 30							14 00		14 15	14 30	
Garswood	d			12 37							13 07			13 37							14 07			14 37	
Bryn	d			12 40							13 10			13 40							14 10			14 40	
Whiston	d	12 05						12 35				13 05						13 35				14 05			
Rainhill	d	12 08						12 38				13 08						13 38				14 08			
Lea Green	d	12 11						12 41				13 11						13 41				14 11			
St Helens Junction	d	12 14				12 29		12 44				13 14				13 29		13 44				14 14			
Warrington Bank Quay	d				12 19		12 22								13 19		13 22								14 19
Earlestown 8	d	12 19			12 26		12a33	12 50				13 19			13 26		13a33	13 50				14 19			14 26
Warrington Bank Quay	a							13 01										14 01							
Newton-le-Willows	d	12 22			12 29	12 35						13 22			13 29	13 35						14 22			14 29
Wigan North Western 65	a		12 30	12 53							13 23		13 30	13 53							14 23		14 30	14 53	
	d		12 31										13 31										14 31		
Euxton Balshaw Lane	d		12 41										13 41										14 41		
Leyland 82	a		12 46										13 46										14 46		
Preston 8 65,82	a		12 54										13 54										14 54		
Blackpool North 97	a		13 19										14 19										15 21		
Patricroft	d	12 34										13 34										14 34			
Eccles	d	12 36										13 36										14 36			
Manchester Victoria	a	12 50										13 47										14 50			
Manchester Oxford Road	a				12 48	12 57				13 36					13 48	13 57				14 36					14 48
Manchester Piccadilly 10	a				12 57	13 01									13 57	14 01									14 57
Manchester Airport 85 ✈	a					13 22										14 22									

A From Llandudno
B To Liverpool Lime Street
C To Stalybridge
D From Liverpool South Parkway

from 1 October

Liverpool and St Helens - Newton-le-Willows, Wigan, Preston and Manchester

Network Diagram - see first Page of Table 88

		NT	NT	NT		NT	NT	NT	NT	NT	AW	NT	NT	NT		NT	NT	NT	NT	NT	AW	NT	NT	NT	
			A					B	C		◇ D		A					E	C		◇ D		A		
Liverpool Lime Street 10 89,91	d	14 13		14 16		14 27	14 31	14 46	14 57	15 02		15 13		15 16		15 27	15 31	15 46	15 57	16 02		16 13		16 16	
Edge Hill 89,91	d			14 20			14 35	14 50		15 05				15 20			15 35	15 50		16 05				16 20	
Wavertree Technology Park	d	14 19		14 22			14 37	14 52		15 07		15 19		15 22			15 37	15 52		16 07		16 19		16 22	
Broad Green	d			14 25			14 40	14 55		15 10				15 25			15 40	15 55		16 10				16 25	
Roby	d			14 29			14 44	14 59		15 14				15 29			15 44	15 59		16 14				16 29	
Huyton	d			14 31			14 46	15 01	15 06	15 16				15 31			15 46	16 01	16 06	16 16				16 31	
Prescot	d						14 51			15 21							15 51			16 21					
Eccleston Park	d						14 53			15 23							15 53			16 23					
Thatto Heath	d						14 56			15 26							15 56			16 26					
St Helens Central	a						14 59		15 15	15 29							15 59		16 15	16 29					
	d						15 00		15 15	15 30							16 00		16 15	16 30					
Garswood	d						15 07			15 37							16 07			16 37					
Bryn	d						15 10			15 40							16 10			16 40					
Whiston	d			14 35				15 05						15 35				16 05						16 35	
Rainhill	d			14 38				15 08						15 38				16 08						16 38	
Lea Green	d			14 41				15 11						15 41				16 11						16 41	
St Helens Junction	d	14 29		14 44				15 14				15 29		15 44				16 14				16 29		16 44	
Warrington Bank Quay	d		14 22								15 19		15 22								16 19		16 22		
Earlestown 8	d		14a33	14 50				15 19			15 26		15a33	15 50				16 19			16 26		16a33	16 49	
Warrington Bank Quay	a			15 01										16 01											
Newton-le-Willows	d	14 35						15 22			15 29	15 35						16 22			16 29	16 35		16 52	
Wigan North Western 65	a						15 23		15 30	15 53							16 19		16 30	16 53					
	d								15 31										16 30						
Euxton Balshaw Lane	d								15 41										16 40						
Leyland 82	a								15 46										16 45						
Preston 8 65,82	a								15 54										16 54						
Blackpool North 97	a								16 20										17 20						
Patricroft	d							15 34										16 34						17 04	
Eccles	d							15 36										16 36						17 06	
Manchester Victoria	a							15 49										16 49						17 20	
Manchester Oxford Road	a	14 57				15 36					15 48	15 57				16 36					16 48	16 57			
Manchester Piccadilly 10	a	15 01									15 57	16 01									16 57	17 01			
Manchester Airport 85 ✈	a	15 22										16 22										17 22			

		AW	NT	NT	NT	NT	NT	NT	NT	NT		NT	AW	NT	NT	NT	NT	NT	NT	NT		AW	NT	NT	AW
		◇ D			E	C							◇ D									◇ D			F
Liverpool Lime Street 10 89,91	d		16 27	16 31	16 46	16 57	17 01	17 06	17 10	17 19		17 27		17 35	17 44	17 48	18 01	18 13	18 16	18 31			18 46	19 01	
Edge Hill 89,91	d			16 35	16 50		17 05		17 14			17 31		17 39		17 52	18 05		18 20	18 35			18 50	19 05	
Wavertree Technology Park	d			16 37	16 52		17 07	17 12	17 16			17 33		17 41	17 49	17 54	18 07	18 19	18 22	18 37			18 52	19 07	
Broad Green	d			16 40	16 55		17 10		17 19			17 36		17 44	17 52	17 57	18 10		18 25	18 40			18 55	19 10	
Roby	d			16 44	16 59		17 14		17 23			17 40		17 48		18 01	18 14		18 29	18 44			18 59	19 14	
Huyton	d			16 46	17 01	17 06	17 16	17 19	17 25	17 29		17 42		17 50	17 57	18 03	18 16		18 31	18 46			19 01	19 16	
Prescot	d			16 51			17 21			17 33					18 02		18 21			18 51				19 21	
Eccleston Park	d			16 53			17 23			17 36					18 05		18 23			18 53				19 23	
Thatto Heath	d			16 56			17 26			17 38					18 07		18 26			18 56				19 26	
St Helens Central	a			16 59		17 15	17 29			17 42		17 51			18 11		18 29			18 59				19 29	
	d			17 00		17 15	17 30			17 42		17 51			18 11		18 30			19 00				19 30	
Garswood	d			17 07			17 37			17 49					18 19		18 37			19 07				19 37	
Bryn	d			17 10			17 40			17 52					18 22		18 40			19 10				19 40	
Whiston	d				17 05				17 28					17 54		18 07			18 35				19 05		
Rainhill	d				17 08				17 32					17 57		18 10			18 38				19 08		
Lea Green	d				17 11			17 26	17 35					18 00		18 13			18 41				19 11		
St Helens Junction	d				17 14			17 29	17 39					18 03		18 16		18 29	18 44				19 14		
Warrington Bank Quay	d	16 51											17 49									18 46			19 19
Earlestown 8	d	16 59			17 19				17 44				17 57	18 08		18 21			18 50			18 57	19 19		19 26
Warrington Bank Quay	a																		19 01						
Newton-le-Willows	d	17 02			17 22			17 35	17 47				18 00	18 11		18 24		18 35				19 00	19 22		19 29
Wigan North Western 65	a			17 23		17 30	17 54			18 06		18 04			18 30		18 49			19 23				19 53	
	d					17 31						18 05			18 31		18 49								
Euxton Balshaw Lane	d					17 41						18 16			18 41		19 01								
Leyland 82	a					17 46						18 21			18 46		19 06								
Preston 8 65,82	a					17 54						18 31			18 54		19 15								
Blackpool North 97	a					18 23									19 22										
Patricroft	d				17 34				17 59					18 23									19 34		
Eccles	d				17 36				18 01					18 25		18 36							19 36		
Manchester Victoria	a				17 47				18 14					18 41		18 49							19 49		
Manchester Oxford Road	a	17 21	17 36					17 57					18 19					18 57				19 21			19 48
Manchester Piccadilly 10	a	17 30						18 01					18 28					19 01				19 29			19 52
Manchester Airport 85 ✈	a							18 22										19 24							20 18

A To Liverpool Lime Street
B To Stalybridge
C From Liverpool South Parkway
D From Llandudno
E To Huddersfield
F From Chester

Table 90

Mondays to Fridays

from 1 October

Liverpool and St Helens - Newton-le-Willows, Wigan, Preston and Manchester

Network Diagram - see first Page of Table 88

		NT A	NT	NT	NT	AW ◇ B	NT	NT	NT	NT	AW ◇ B	NT	NT	TP ◇ C	AW FO D	NT FO	AW FX	NT FX	TP ◇ E	NT FO	NT FX	NT FO	AW FX
Liverpool Lime Street 89,91	d		19 12	19 23	19 42		20 09	20 12	20 25	20 42		21 12	21 42			22 12		22 12		23 02	23 02	23 16	
Edge Hill 89,91	d		19 16		19 46			20 16		20 46		21 16	21 46			22 16		22 19		23 06	23 09	23 20	
Wavertree Technology Park	d		19 18		19 48		20 15	20 18		20 48		21 18	21 48			22 18		22 29		23 08	23 19	23 22	
Broad Green	d		19 21		19 51			20 21		20 51		21 21	21 51			22 21		22 39		23 11	23 29	23 26	
Roby	d		19 25		19 55			20 25		20 55		21 25	21 55			22 25		22 46		23 15	23 36	23 30	
Huyton	d		19 27	19 32	19 57			20 27	20 34	20 57		21 27	21 57			22 27		22 50		23 17	23 40	23 32	
Prescot	d				20 02					21 02			22 02							23 22	23 50		
Eccleston Park	d				20 04					21 04			22 04							23 24	23 56		
Thatto Heath	d				20 07					21 07			22 07							23 27	00 06		
St Helens Central	a			19 40	20 10				20 42	21 10			22 10							23 30	00 16		
	d			19 41	20 11				20 43	21 11			22 11							23 31	00 16		
Garswood	d				20 18					21 18			22 18							23 38	00 36		
Bryn	d				20 21					21 21			22 21							23 41	00 43		
Whiston	d		19 31					20 31				21 31				22 31		23 00				23 36	
Rainhill	d		19 34					20 34				21 34				22 34		23 10				23 39	
Lea Green	d		19 37					20 37				21 37				22 37		23 18				23 42	
St Helens Junction	d		19 40				20 25	20 40				21 40				22 40		23 25				23 45	
Warrington Bank Quay	d	19 22				20 19					21 19				22 19		22 28						23 59
Earlestown	d	19a33	19 45			20 26		20 45			21 26	21 45			22 26	22 45	22 53	23 37				23 50	00 24
Warrington Bank Quay	a																						
Newton-le-Willows	d		19 48			20 29	20 35	20 48			21 29	21 48			22 29	22 48	23 03	23 45				23 53	00 34
Wigan North Western 65	a			19 54	20 34				20 57	21 34			22 28							23 48	00s56		
	d			19 55					20 57				22 28	21 48					22 51	23 48			
Euxton Balshaw Lane	d			20 05					21 08				22 39							23 59	01s21		
Leyland 82	a			20 10					21 16				22 44							00 04	01s33		
Preston 65,82	a			20 18					21 22				22 55						23 09	00 13	01 48		
Blackpool North 97	a			20 42					21 52				23 21										
Patricroft	d		20 00					21 00				22 00				23 00		00 15				00 05	
Eccles	d		20 02					21 02				22 02				23 02		00 25				00 08	
Manchester Victoria	a		20 16					21 15				22 15				23 15		00 44				00 21	
Manchester Oxford Road	a					20 48	20 57				21 48			22 26	22 50		23 33						
Manchester Piccadilly	a					20 52	21 01				21 57			22 30	22 58		23 38						01 09
Manchester Airport 85	a					21 18	21 20							22 47									

		NT FX
Liverpool Lime Street 89,91	d	23 16
Edge Hill 89,91	d	23 23
Wavertree Technology Park	d	23 33
Broad Green	d	23 43
Roby	d	23 50
Huyton	d	23 54
Prescot	d	
Eccleston Park	d	
Thatto Heath	d	
St Helens Central	a	
	d	
Garswood	d	
Bryn	d	
Whiston	d	00 04
Rainhill	d	00 14
Lea Green	d	00 22
St Helens Junction	d	00 29
Warrington Bank Quay	d	
Earlestown	d	00 41
Warrington Bank Quay	a	
Newton-le-Willows	d	00 49
Wigan North Western 65	a	
	d	
Euxton Balshaw Lane	d	
Leyland 82	a	
Preston 65,82	a	
Blackpool North 97	a	
Patricroft	d	01 19
Eccles	d	01 29
Manchester Victoria	a	01 48
Manchester Oxford Road	a	
Manchester Piccadilly	a	
Manchester Airport 85	a	

A To Liverpool Lime Street
B From Llandudno
C From Barrow-in-Furness
D From Chester
E From Manchester Airport to Barrow-in-Furness

Table 90

Saturdays

Liverpool and St Helens - Newton-le-Willows, Wigan, Preston and Manchester

Network Diagram - see first Page of Table 88

		NT	NT	NT	NT	NT	AW A	NT	NT	NT	AW ◇ B	NT	NT	NT	NT C	NT	NT	NT	AW D	NT E	NT	NT	AW F
Liverpool Lime Street 89,91	d	23p02	23p16	03 38	05 13	05 31		05 46	06 01	06 13		06 16	06 25	06 31	06 46	06 57	07 01	07 13		07 16	07 26	07 31	
Edge Hill 89,91	d	23p06	23p20			05 35		05 50	06 05			06 20		06 35	06 50		07 05			07 20	07 30	07 35	
Wavertree Technology Park	d	23p08	23p22		05 19	05 37		05 52	06 07	06 19		06 22		06 37	06 52		07 07	07 19		07 22		07 37	
Broad Green	d	23p11	23p26			05 40		05 55	06 10			06 25		06 40	06 55		07 10			07 25		07 40	
Roby	d	23p15	23p30			05 44		05 59	06 14			06 29		06 44	06 59		07 14			07 29		07 44	
Huyton	d	23p17	23p32			05 46		06 01	06 16			06 31		06 46	07 01	07 06	07 16			07 31		07 46	
Prescot	d	23p22				05 51			06 21					06 51			07 21					07 51	
Eccleston Park	d	23p24				05 53			06 23					06 53			07 23					07 53	
Thatto Heath	d	23p27				05 56			06 26					06 56			07 26					07 56	
St Helens Central	a	23p30				05 59			06 29					06 59		07 15	07 29					07 59	
	d	23p31				06 00			06 30					07 00		07 15	07 30					08 00	
Garswood	d	23p38				06 07			06 37					07 07			07 37					08 07	
Bryn	d	23p41				06 10			06 40					07 10			07 40					08 10	
Whiston	d		23p36					06 05				06 35			07 05					07 35			
Rainhill	d		23p39					06 08				06 38			07 08					07 38			
Lea Green	d		23p42					06 11				06 41			07 11			07 28		07 41			
St Helens Junction	d		23p45		05 29			06 14		06 29		06 44			07 14			07 31		07 44			
Warrington Bank Quay	d						06 06				06 40								07 39				08 08
Earlestown	d		23p50				06 12	06 19			06 47	06 50			07 19				07 46	07 49			08 16
Warrington Bank Quay	a											07 01											
Newton-le-Willows	d		23p53		05 35		06 15	06 22		06 35	06 50				07 22			07 37	07 49	07 52			08 19
Wigan North Western 65	a	23p48				06 21			06 51					07 21		07 30	07 51					08 21	
	d	23p48														07 31							
Euxton Balshaw Lane	d	23p59														07 41							
Leyland 82	a	00 04														07 46							
Preston 65,82	a	00 13														07 54							
Blackpool North 97	a															08 21							
Patricroft	d		00 05					06 34							07 34					08 04			
Eccles	d		00 08					06 36							07 36					08 06			
Manchester Victoria	a		00 21					06 47							07 49					08 19			
Manchester Oxford Road	a						06 35			06 57	07 09		07 37					07 57	08 09		08 36		08 41
Manchester Piccadilly	a			04 14	05 57		06 45			07 01	07 18							08 01	08 18				08 45
Manchester Airport 85	a			04 30	06 14					07 22								08 22					

		NT	NT	NT	NT	NT	NT	NT C	NT	NT	AW F	NT	NT G	NT	NT	NT	NT C	NT	NT	AW F	NT	NT G	NT
Liverpool Lime Street 89,91	d	07 46	08 01	08 13	08 16	08 26	08 31	08 44	08 57	09 01		09 13		09 16	09 27	09 31	09 46	09 57	10 01		10 13		10 16
Edge Hill 89,91	d	07 50	08 05		08 20	08 30	08 35	08 50		09 05				09 20		09 35	09 50		10 05				10 20
Wavertree Technology Park	d	07 52	08 07	08 19	08 22		08 37	08 52		09 07		09 19		09 22		09 37	09 52		10 07		10 19		10 22
Broad Green	d	07 55	08 10		08 25		08 40	08 55		09 10				09 25		09 40	09 55		10 10				10 25
Roby	d	07 59	08 14		08 29		08 44	08 59		09 14				09 29		09 44	09 59		10 14				10 29
Huyton	d	08 01	08 16		08 31		08 46	09 01	09 06	09 16				09 31		09 46	10 01	10 06	10 16				10 31
Prescot	d		08 21				08 51			09 21						09 51			10 21				
Eccleston Park	d		08 23				08 53			09 23						09 53			10 23				
Thatto Heath	d		08 26				08 56			09 26						09 56			10 26				
St Helens Central	a		08 29				08 59		09 15	09 29						09 59		10 15	10 29				
	d		08 30				09 00		09 15	09 30						10 00		10 15	10 30				
Garswood	d		08 37				09 07			09 37						10 07			10 37				
Bryn	d		08 40				09 10			09 40						10 10			10 40				
Whiston	d	08 05			08 35			09 05						09 35			10 05						10 35
Rainhill	d	08 08			08 38			09 08						09 38			10 08						10 38
Lea Green	d	08 11			08 41			09 11						09 41			10 11						10 41
St Helens Junction	d	08 14		08 29	08 44			09 14				09 29		09 44			10 14				10 29		10 44
Warrington Bank Quay	d										09 19		09 22							10 19		10 22	
Earlestown	d	08 19			08 50			09 19			09 26		09a33	09 50			10 19			10 26		10a33	10 50
Warrington Bank Quay	a				09 01									10 01									11 01
Newton-le-Willows	d	08 22		08 35				09 22			09 29	09 35					10 22			10 29	10 35		
Wigan North Western 65	a		08 51				09 21		09 30	09 51						10 21		10 30	10 51				
	d								09 31									10 31					
Euxton Balshaw Lane	d								09 41									10 41					
Leyland 82	a								09 46									10 46					
Preston 65,82	a								09 54									10 54					
Blackpool North 97	a								10 21									11 21					
Patricroft	d	08 34						09 34									10 34						
Eccles	d	08 36						09 36									10 36						
Manchester Victoria	a	08 50						09 47									10 49						
Manchester Oxford Road	a			08 57		09 36					09 48	09 57			10 36					10 48	10 57		
Manchester Piccadilly	a			09 01							09 52	10 01								10 52	11 01		
Manchester Airport 85	a			09 22								10 22									11 22		

A From Chester
B From Holyhead
C To Stalybridge
D From Shrewsbury
E To Huddersfield
F From Llandudno
G To Liverpool Lime Street

Table 90

Saturdays

Liverpool and St Helens - Newton-le-Willows, Wigan, Preston and Manchester

Network Diagram - see first Page of Table 88

		NT	NT	NT A	NT B	NT	AW ◇ C	NT	NT D	NT	NT	NT	NT A	NT B	NT	AW ◇ C	NT	NT D	NT	NT	NT	NT A
Liverpool Lime Street 10 89,91	d	10 27	10 31	10 46	10 57	11 01		11 13		11 16	11 27	11 31	11 46	11 57	12 01		12 13		12 16	12 27	12 31	12 46
Edge Hill 89,91	d		10 35	10 50		11 05				11 20		11 35	11 50		12 05				12 20		12 35	12 50
Wavertree Technology Park	d		10 37	10 52		11 07		11 19		11 22		11 37	11 52		12 07		12 19		12 22		12 37	12 52
Broad Green	d		10 40	10 55		11 10				11 25		11 40	11 55		12 10				12 25		12 40	12 55
Roby	d		10 44	10 59		11 14				11 29		11 44	11 59		12 14				12 29		12 44	12 59
Huyton	d		10 46	11 01	11 06	11 16				11 31		11 46	12 01	12 06	12 16				12 31		12 46	13 01
Prescot	d		10 51			11 21						11 51			12 21						12 51	
Eccleston Park	d		10 53			11 23						11 53			12 23						12 53	
Thatto Heath	d		10 56			11 26						11 56			12 26						12 56	
St Helens Central	a		10 59		11 15	11 29						11 59		12 15	12 29						12 59	
	d		11 00		11 15	11 30						12 00		12 15	12 30						13 00	
Garswood	d		11 07			11 37						12 07			12 37						13 07	
Bryn	d		11 10			11 40						12 10			12 40						13 10	
Whiston	d			11 05						11 35			12 05						12 35			13 05
Rainhill	d			11 08						11 38			12 08						12 38			13 08
Lea Green	d			11 11						11 41			12 11						12 41			13 11
St Helens Junction	d			11 14				11 29		11 44			12 14				12 29		12 44			13 14
Warrington Bank Quay	d						11 19		11 22							12 19		12 22				
Earlestown 8	d			11 19			11 26		11a33	11 50			12 19			12 26		12a33	12 50			13 19
Warrington Bank Quay	a									12 01									13 01			
Newton-le-Willows	d			11 22			11 29	11 35					12 22			12 29	12 35					13 22
Wigan North Western 65	a		11 21		11 30	11 51						12 21		12 30	12 51						13 21	
	d				11 31									12 31								
Euxton Balshaw Lane	d				11 41									12 41								
Leyland 82	a				11 46									12 46								
Preston 8 65,82	a				11 54									12 54								
Blackpool North 97	a				12 21									13 21								
Patricroft	d			11 34									12 34									13 34
Eccles	d			11 36									12 36									13 36
Manchester Victoria	a			11 49									12 49									13 49
Manchester Oxford Road	a	11 36					11 48	11 57			12 36					12 48	12 57			13 36		
Manchester Piccadilly 10	a						11 52	12 01								12 52	13 01					
Manchester Airport 85	a							12 22									13 22					

		NT B	NT	AW ◇ C	NT	NT D	NT	NT	NT	NT A	NT B	NT	AW ◇ C	NT	NT D	NT	NT	NT	NT A	NT B	NT	AW ◇ C	NT
Liverpool Lime Street 10 89,91	d	12 57	13 01		13 13		13 16	13 27	13 31	13 46	13 57	14 01		14 13		14 16	14 27	14 31	14 46	14 57	15 01		15 13
Edge Hill 89,91	d		13 05				13 20		13 35	13 50		14 05				14 20		14 35	14 50		15 05		
Wavertree Technology Park	d		13 07		13 19		13 22		13 37	13 52		14 07		14 19		14 22		14 37	14 52		15 07		15 19
Broad Green	d		13 10				13 25		13 40	13 55		14 10				14 25		14 40	14 55		15 10		
Roby	d		13 14				13 29		13 44	13 59		14 14				14 29		14 44	14 59		15 14		
Huyton	d	13 06	13 16				13 31		13 46	14 01	14 06	14 16				14 31		14 46	15 01	15 06	15 16		
Prescot	d		13 21						13 51			14 21						14 51			15 21		
Eccleston Park	d		13 23						13 53			14 23						14 53			15 23		
Thatto Heath	d		13 26						13 56			14 26						14 56			15 26		
St Helens Central	a	13 15	13 29						13 59		14 15	14 29						14 59		15 15	15 29		
	d	13 15	13 30						14 00		14 15	14 30						15 00		15 15	15 30		
Garswood	d		13 37						14 07			14 37						15 07			15 37		
Bryn	d		13 40						14 10			14 40						15 10			15 40		
Whiston	d						13 35			14 05						14 35			15 05				
Rainhill	d						13 38			14 08						14 38			15 08				
Lea Green	d						13 41			14 11						14 41			15 11				
St Helens Junction	d				13 29		13 44			14 14				14 29		14 44			15 14				15 29
Warrington Bank Quay	d			13 19		13 22							14 19		14 22							15 19	
Earlestown 8	d			13 26		13a33	13 50			14 19			14 26		14a33	14 50			15 19			15 26	
Warrington Bank Quay	a						14 01									15 01							
Newton-le-Willows	d			13 29	13 35					14 22			14 29	14 35					15 22			15 29	15 35
Wigan North Western 65	a	13 30	13 51						14 21		14 30	14 51						15 21		15 30	15 51		
	d	13 31									14 31									15 31			
Euxton Balshaw Lane	d	13 41									14 41									15 41			
Leyland 82	a	13 46									14 46									15 46			
Preston 8 65,82	a	13 54									14 54									15 54			
Blackpool North 97	a	14 21									15 21									16 21			
Patricroft	d									14 34									15 34				
Eccles	d									14 36									15 36				
Manchester Victoria	a									14 50									15 49				
Manchester Oxford Road	a			13 48	13 57			14 36					14 48	14 57			15 36					15 48	15 57
Manchester Piccadilly 10	a			13 52	14 01								14 57	15 01								15 52	16 01
Manchester Airport 85	a				14 22									15 22									16 22

A To Stalybridge
B From Liverpool South Parkway
C From Llandudno
D To Liverpool Lime Street

Table 90

Saturdays

Liverpool and St Helens - Newton-le-Willows, Wigan, Preston and Manchester

Network Diagram - see first Page of Table 88

		NT A	NT	NT	NT	NT B	NT C	NT	AW ◇ D	NT	NT A	NT	NT	NT	NT	NT C	NT	AW ◇ D	NT	NT	NT	NT
Liverpool Lime Street 10 89,91	d		15 16	15 27	15 31	15 46	15 57	16 01		16 13		16 16	16 27	16 31	16 46	16 57	17 01		17 06	17 10	17 19	17 27
Edge Hill 89,91	d		15 20		15 35	15 50		16 05				16 20		16 35	16 50		17 05			17 14		17 31
Wavertree Technology Park	d		15 22		15 37	15 52		16 07		16 19		16 22		16 37	16 52		17 07		17 12	17 16		17 33
Broad Green	d		15 25		15 40	15 55		16 10				16 25		16 40	16 55		17 10			17 19		17 36
Roby	d		15 29		15 44	15 59		16 14				16 29		16 44	16 59		17 14			17 23		17 40
Huyton	d		15 31		15 46	16 01	16 06	16 16				16 31		16 46	17 01	17 06	17 16		17 19	17 25	17 29	17 42
Prescot	d				15 51			16 21						16 51			17 21				17 33	
Eccleston Park	d				15 53			16 23						16 53			17 23				17 36	
Thatto Heath	d				15 56			16 26						16 56			17 26				17 38	
St Helens Central	a				15 59		16 15	16 29						16 59		17 15	17 29				17 42	17 51
	d				16 00		16 15	16 30						17 00		17 15	17 30				17 42	17 51
Garswood	d				16 07			16 37						17 07			17 37				17 49	
Bryn	d				16 10			16 40						17 10			17 40				17 52	
Whiston	d		15 35			16 05						16 35			17 05					17 28		
Rainhill	d		15 38			16 08						16 38			17 08					17 32		
Lea Green	d		15 41			16 11						16 41			17 11				17 26	17 35		
St Helens Junction	d		15 44			16 14				16 29		16 44			17 14				17 29	17 39		
Warrington Bank Quay	d	15 22							16 19		16 22							17 19				
Earlestown 8	d	15a33	15 50			16 19			16 26		16a33	16 49			17 19			17 26		17 44		
Warrington Bank Quay	a		16 01																			
Newton-le-Willows	d					16 22			16 29	16 35		16 52			17 22			17 29	17 35	17 47		
Wigan North Western 65	a				16 21		16 30	16 51						17 21		17 30	17 52				18 04	18 05
	d						16 31									17 31						18 05
Euxton Balshaw Lane	d						16 41									17 41						18 16
Leyland 82	a						16 46									17 46						18 21
Preston 8 65,82	a						16 54									17 54						18 31
Blackpool North 97	a						17 21									18 24						
Patricroft	d					16 34						17 04			17 34					17 59		
Eccles	d					16 36						17 06			17 36					18 01		
Manchester Victoria	a					16 49						17 20			17 47					18 15		
Manchester Oxford Road	a			16 36					16 48	16 57			17 36					17 48	17 57			
Manchester Piccadilly 10	a								16 57	17 01								17 57	18 01			
Manchester Airport 85	a									17 22									18 22			

		NT	NT	NT	NT	AW ◇ D	NT	NT	NT	NT	NT	AW ◇ D	NT A	NT	NT	NT	AW ◇ D	NT	NT	NT	NT	AW ◇ D	NT
Liverpool Lime Street 10 89,91	d	17 35	17 44	17 48	18 01		18 13	18 16	18 31	18 46	19 01			19 12	19 23	19 42		20 09	20 12	20 25	20 42		21 12
Edge Hill 89,91	d	17 39		17 52	18 05			18 20	18 35	18 50	19 05			19 16		19 46			20 16		20 46		21 16
Wavertree Technology Park	d	17 41	17 49	17 54	18 07		18 19	18 22	18 37	18 52	19 07			19 18		19 48		20 15	20 18		20 48		21 18
Broad Green	d	17 44	17 52	17 57	18 10			18 25	18 40	18 55	19 10			19 21		19 51			20 21		20 51		21 21
Roby	d	17 48		18 01	18 14			18 29	18 44	18 59	19 14			19 25		19 55			20 25		20 55		21 25
Huyton	d	17 50	17 57	18 03	18 16			18 31	18 46	19 01	19 16			19 27	19 32	19 57			20 27	20 34	20 57		21 27
Prescot	d		18 02		18 21				18 51		19 21					20 02					21 02		
Eccleston Park	d		18 05		18 23				18 53		19 23					20 04					21 04		
Thatto Heath	d		18 07		18 26				18 56		19 26					20 07					21 07		
St Helens Central	a		18 11		18 29				18 59		19 29				19 40	20 10				20 42	21 10		
	d		18 11		18 30				19 00		19 30				19 41	20 11				20 43	21 11		
Garswood	d		18 19		18 37				19 07		19 37					20 18					21 18		
Bryn	d		18 22		18 40				19 10		19 40					20 21					21 21		
Whiston	d	17 54		18 07				18 35		19 05				19 31					20 31				21 31
Rainhill	d	17 57		18 10				18 38		19 08				19 34					20 34				21 34
Lea Green	d	18 00		18 13				18 41		19 11				19 37					20 37				21 37
St Helens Junction	d	18 03		18 16			18 29	18 44		19 14				19 40				20 25	20 40				21 40
Warrington Bank Quay	d					18 19						19 19	19 22				20 19					21 19	
Earlestown 8	d	18 08		18 21		18 26		18 50		19 19		19 26	19a33	19 45			20 26		20 45			21 26	21 45
Warrington Bank Quay	a							19 01															
Newton-le-Willows	d	18 11		18 24		18 29	18 35			19 22		19 29		19 48			20 29	20 35	20 48			21 29	21 48
Wigan North Western 65	a		18 30		18 49				19 21		19 51				19 54	20 32				20 57	21 32		
	d		18 31		18 49										19 55					20 57			
Euxton Balshaw Lane	d		18 41		19 01										20 05					21 08			
Leyland 82	a		18 46		19 06										20 10					21 16			
Preston 8 65,82	a		18 54		19 15										20 18					21 22			
Blackpool North 97	a		19 21												20 44					21 53			
Patricroft	d	18 23								19 34				20 00					21 00				22 00
Eccles	d	18 25		18 36						19 36				20 02					21 02				22 02
Manchester Victoria	a	18 41		18 49						19 49				20 15					21 15				22 15
Manchester Oxford Road	a					18 48	18 57					19 48					20 48	20 57				21 48	
Manchester Piccadilly 10	a					18 57	19 01					19 52					20 57	21 01				21 57	
Manchester Airport 85	a						19 24					20 13						21 24					

A To Liverpool Lime Street
B To Stalybridge
C From Liverpool South Parkway
D From Llandudno

Table 90

Saturdays

Liverpool and St Helens - Newton-le-Willows, Wigan, Preston and Manchester

Network Diagram - see first Page of Table 88

		NT	AW	NT	TP	NT	NT	NT	AW
					◇■				
			A		B	C	D		E
Liverpool Lime Street ■ 89,91	d	21 42		22 12	22 30	23 02	23 02	23 16	
Edge Hill 89,91	d	21 46		22 16		23 06	23 06	23 20	
Wavertree Technology Park	d	21 48		22 18		23 08	23 08	23 22	
Broad Green	d	21 51		22 21		23 11	23 11	23 26	
Roby	d	21 55		22 25		23 15	23 15	23 30	
Huyton	d	21 57		22 27		23 17	23 17	23 32	
Prescot	d	22 02				23 22	23 22		
Eccleston Park	d	22 04				23 24	23 24		
Thatto Heath	d	22 07				23 27	23 27		
St Helens Central	a	22 10				23 30	23 30		
	d	22 11				23 31	23 31		
Garswood	d	22 18				23 38	23 38		
Bryn	d	22 21				23 41	23 41		
Whiston	d			22 31				23 36	
Rainhill	d			22 34				23 39	
Lea Green	d			22 37				23 42	
St Helens Junction	d			22 40				23 45	
Warrington Bank Quay	d		22 19						23 50
Earlestown ■	d		22 27	22 45				23 50	23 58
Warrington Bank Quay	a								
Newton-le-Willows	d		22 30	22 48				23 53	00 02
Wigan North Western 65	a	22 28				23 48	23 50		
	d	22 28				23 48			
Euxton Balshaw Lane	d	22 39				23 59			
Leyland 82	a	22 44				00 04			
Preston ■ 65,82	a	22 55				00 13			
Blackpool North 97	a	23 22							
Patricroft	d			23 00				00 05	
Eccles	d			23 02				00 08	
Manchester Victoria ⇌	a			23 15				00 21	
Manchester Oxford Road	a		22 50		23 14				
Manchester Piccadilly ■ ⇌	a		22 58		23 19				00 26
Manchester Airport 85 ✈	a								

Sundays until 9 September

		NT	NT	AW	NT	NT	AW	NT	NT	AW	NT	NT	AW	NT	NT	AW	NT	NT	AW	NT	NT
										◇											
				A			A			F			A			A			A		
Liverpool Lime Street ■ 89,91	d	23p02	23p16		08 01	08 31		09 01	09 31		10 01	10 31		11 01	11 31		12 01	12 31		13 01	13 31
Edge Hill 89,91	d	23p06	23p20																		
Wavertree Technology Park	d	23p08	23p22		08 07	08 37		09 07	09 37		10 07	10 37		11 07	11 37		12 07	12 37		13 07	13 37
Broad Green	d	23p11	23p26		08 10	08 40		09 10	09 40		10 10	10 40		11 10	11 40		12 10	12 40		13 10	13 40
Roby	d	23p15	23p30		08 13	08 43		09 13	09 43		10 13	10 43		11 13	11 43		12 13	12 43		13 13	13 43
Huyton	d	23p17	23p32		08 16	08 46		09 16	09 46		10 16	10 46		11 16	11 46		12 16	12 46		13 16	13 46
Prescot	d	23p22				08 50			09 50			10 50			11 50			12 50			13 50
Eccleston Park	d	23p24																			
Thatto Heath	d	23p27				08 54			09 54			10 54			11 54			12 54			13 54
St Helens Central	a	23p30				08 57			09 57			10 57			11 57			12 57			13 57
	d	23p31				08 58			09 58			10 58			11 58			12 58			13 58
Garswood	d	23p38				09 05			10 05			11 05			12 05			13 05			14 05
Bryn	d	23p41																			
Whiston	d		23p36		08 19			09 19			10 19			11 19			12 19			13 19	
Rainhill	d		23p39		08 22			09 22			10 22			11 22			12 22			13 22	
Lea Green	d		23p42		08 26			09 26			10 26			11 26			12 26			13 26	
St Helens Junction	d		23p45		08 29			09 29			10 29			11 29			12 29			13 29	
Warrington Bank Quay	d			23p50			09 10			10 12			11 03			12 03			13 03		
Earlestown ■	d		23p50	23p58	08 33		09 16	09 33		10 19	10 33		11 10	11 33		12 10	12 33		13 10	13 33	
Warrington Bank Quay	a																				
Newton-le-Willows	d		23p53	00 02	08 36		09 19	09 36		10 22	10 36		11 13	11 36		12 13	12 36		13 13	13 36	
Wigan North Western 65	a	23p48				09 13			10 13			11 13			12 13			13 13			14 13
	d	23p48				09 14			10 14			11 14			12 14			13 14			14 14
Euxton Balshaw Lane	d	23p59				09 24			10 26			11 24			12 24			13 24			14 24
Leyland 82	a	00 04				09 29			10 31			11 29			12 29			13 29			14 29
Preston ■ 65,82	a	00 13				09 37			10 39			11 37			12 37			13 37			14 37
Blackpool North 97	a					10 07			11 09			12 07			13 07			14 07			15 07
Patricroft	d		00 05																		
Eccles	d		00 08		08 49			09 49			10 49			11 49			12 49			13 49	
Manchester Victoria ⇌	a		00 21																		
Manchester Oxford Road	a				09 00		09 39	09 59		10 41	10 59		11 32	11 59		12 32	12 59		13 32	13 57	
Manchester Piccadilly ■ ⇌	a			00 26	09 03		09 48	10 03		10 50	11 06		11 41	12 03		12 41	13 03		13 41	14 03	
Manchester Airport 85 ✈	a				09 21			10 24			11 24			12 21			13 19			14 21	

A From Chester
B from 27 October. To Huddersfield
C until 20 October
D from 27 October
E until 20 October. From Chester
F From Holyhead

Table 90

Sundays until 9 September

Liverpool and St Helens - Newton-le-Willows, Wigan, Preston and Manchester

Network Diagram - see first Page of Table 88

		AW	NT	NT	AW	NT	NT	AW	NT	NT	AW	NT	NT	AW	NT	NT	AW	NT	NT	AW	NT	NT	AW
											◇			◇									
		A			A			A			B			B			A			A			A
Liverpool Lime Street ■ 89,91	d		14 01	14 31		15 01	15 31		16 01	16 31		17 01	17 31		18 01	18 31		19 01	19 31		20 01	20 31	
Edge Hill 89,91	d																						
Wavertree Technology Park	d		14 07	14 37		15 07	15 37		16 07	16 37		17 07	17 37		18 07	18 37		19 07	19 37		20 07	20 37	
Broad Green	d		14 10	14 40		15 10	15 40		16 10	16 40		17 10	17 40		18 10	18 40		19 10	19 40		20 10	20 40	
Roby	d		14 13	14 43		15 13	15 43		16 13	16 43		17 13	17 43		18 13	18 43		19 13	19 43		20 13	20 43	
Huyton	d		14 16	14 46		15 16	15 46		16 16	16 46		17 16	17 46		18 16	18 46		19 16	19 46		20 16	20 46	
Prescot	d			14 50			15 50			16 50			17 50			18 50			19 50			20 50	
Eccleston Park	d																						
Thatto Heath	d			14 54			15 54			16 54			17 54			18 54			19 54			20 54	
St Helens Central	a			14 57			15 57			16 57			17 57			18 57			19 57			20 57	
	d			14 58			15 58			16 58			17 58			18 58			19 58			20 58	
Garswood	d			15 05			16 05			17 05			18 05			19 05			20 05			21 05	
Bryn	d																						
Whiston	d		14 19			15 19			16 19			17 19			18 19			19 19			20 19		
Rainhill	d		14 22			15 22			16 22			17 22			18 22			19 22			20 22		
Lea Green	d		14 26			15 26			16 26			17 26			18 26			19 26			20 26		
St Helens Junction	d		14 29			15 29			16 29			17 29			18 29			19 29			20 29		
Warrington Bank Quay	d	14 03			15 03			16 03			17 03			18 03			19 03			20 03			21 03
Earlestown ■	d	14 10	14 33		15 10	15 33		16 10	16 33		17 10	17 33		18 10	18 33		19 10	19 33		20 10	20 33		21 10
Warrington Bank Quay	a																						
Newton-le-Willows	d	14 13	14 36		15 13	15 36		16 13	16 36		17 13	17 36		18 13	18 36		19 13	19 36		20 13	20 36		21 13
Wigan North Western 65	a			15 13			16 13			17 13			18 13			19 13			20 13			21 13	
	d			15 14			16 14			17 14			18 14			19 14			20 14			21 14	
Euxton Balshaw Lane	d			15 24			16 24			17 24			18 24			19 24			20 24			21 24	
Leyland 82	a			15 29			16 29			17 29			18 29			19 29			20 29			21 29	
Preston ■ 65,82	a			15 37			16 37			17 37			18 37			19 37			20 37			21 37	
Blackpool North 97	a			16 07			17 07			18 07			19 07			20 07			21 07			22 07	
Patricroft	d																						
Eccles	d		14 49			15 49			16 49			17 49			18 49			19 49			20 49		
Manchester Victoria ⇌	a																						
Manchester Oxford Road	a	14 32	14 59		15 32	15 59		16 32	16 59		17 32	17 59		18 32	18 59		19 32	19 59		20 32	20 59		21 32
Manchester Piccadilly ■ ⇌	a	14 41	15 02		15 41	16 02		16 41	17 02		17 41	18 02		18 41	19 02		19 41	20 02		20 41	21 02		21 41
Manchester Airport 85 ✈	a		15 20			16 21			17 21			18 21			19 21			20 26			21 20		

		NT	NT	NT	NT	NT	AW	NT
							A	
					🚌		🚌	🚌
Liverpool Lime Street ■ 89,91	d	21 01	21 31	22 01	22 01	23 01		23 01
Edge Hill 89,91	d							
Wavertree Technology Park	d	21 07	21 37		22 16			23 16
Broad Green	d	21 10	21 40		22 26			23 26
Roby	d	21 13	21 43		22 33			23 33
Huyton	d	21 16	21 46		22 37			23 37
Prescot	d		21 50					
Eccleston Park	d							
Thatto Heath	d		21 54					
St Helens Central	a		21 57					
	d		21 58					
Garswood	d		22 05					
Bryn	d							
Whiston	d	21 19			22 47			23 47
Rainhill	d	21 22			22 57			23 57
Lea Green	d	21 26			23 05			00 05
St Helens Junction	d	21 29			23 12			00 12
Warrington Bank Quay	d						23 09	
Earlestown ■	d	21 33			23 24		23 34	00 24
Warrington Bank Quay	a							
Newton-le-Willows	d	21 36			23 33		23 44	00 33
Wigan North Western 65	a		22 13					
	d		22 14					
Euxton Balshaw Lane	d		22 24					
Leyland 82	a		22 29					
Preston ■ 65,82	a		22 37					
Blackpool North 97	a		23 07					
Patricroft	d							
Eccles	d	21 49			23 57			00 57
Manchester Victoria ⇌	a							
Manchester Oxford Road	a	21 59		22 47	00 12	23 47	00 14	01 12
Manchester Piccadilly ■ ⇌	a	22 02		22 50		23 50	00 19	
Manchester Airport 85 ✈	a	22 21		23 15		00 07		

A From Chester
B From Holyhead

Table 90

Sundays

16 September to 21 October

Liverpool and St Helens - Newton-le-Willows, Wigan, Preston and Manchester

Network Diagram - see first Page of Table 88

		NT	NT	AW	NT	NT	AW	NT	NT	AW		VT	NT	AW	NT	NT	AW	NT	NT	AW		NT	NT	AW	NT
				A			A			◇ A		◇1 B		A ✕			A ✕			A ✕				A ✕	
Liverpool Lime Street 10 89,91	d	23p02	23p16		08 01	08 31		09 01	09 31				10 31		11 01	11 31		12 01	12 31			13 01	13 31		14 01
Edge Hill 89,91	d	23p06	23p20																						
Wavertree Technology Park	d	23p08	23p22		08 07	08 37		09 07	09 37				10 37		11 07	11 37		12 07	12 37			13 07	13 37		14 07
Broad Green	d	23p11	23p26		08 10	08 40		09 10	09 40				10 40		11 10	11 40		12 10	12 40			13 10	13 40		14 10
Roby	d	23p15	23p30		08 13	08 43		09 13	09 43				10 43		11 13	11 43		12 13	12 43			13 13	13 43		14 13
Huyton	d	23p17	23p32		08 16	08 46		09 16	09 46				10 46		11 16	11 46		12 16	12 46			13 16	13 46		14 16
Prescot	d	23p22				08 50			09 50				10 50			11 50			12 50				13 50		
Eccleston Park	d	23p24																							
Thatto Heath	d	23p27				08 54			09 54				10 54			11 54			12 54				13 54		
St Helens Central	a	23p30				08 57			09 57				10 57			11 57			12 57				13 57		
	d	23p31				08 58			09 58				10 58			11 58			12 58				13 58		
Garswood	d	23p38				09 05			10 05				11 05			12 05			13 05				14 05		
Bryn	d	23p41																							
Whiston	d		23p36		08 19			09 19							11 19			12 19				13 19			14 19
Rainhill	d		23p39		08 22			09 22							11 22			12 22				13 22			14 22
Lea Green	d		23p42		08 26			09 26							11 26			12 26				13 26			14 26
St Helens Junction	d		23p45		08 29			09 29							11 29			12 29				13 29			14 29
Warrington Bank Quay	d			23p50			09 10			10 12				11 03			12 03			13 03				14 03	
Earlestown 8	d		23p50	23p58	08 33		09 16	09 33		10 19				11 10	11 33		12 10	12 33		13 10		13 33		14 10	14 33
Warrington Bank Quay	a											10d37													
Newton-le-Willows	d		23p53	00 02	08 36		09 19	09 36		10 22				11 13	11 36		12 13	12 36		13 13		13 36		14 13	14 36
Wigan North Western 65	a	23p48				09 13			10 13			10 48	11 13			12 13			13 13				14 13		
	d	23p48				09 14			10 14			10 48	11 14			12 14			13 14				14 14		
Euxton Balshaw Lane	d	23p59				09 24			10 26				11 24			12 24			13 24				14 24		
Leyland 82	a	00 04				09 29			10 31				11 29			12 29			13 29				14 29		
Preston 8 65,82	a	00 13				09 37			10 39			11 02	11 37			12 37			13 37				14 37		
Blackpool North 97	a					10 07			11 09				12 07			13 07			14 07				15 07		
Patricroft	d		00 05																						
Eccles	d		00 08		08 49			09 49							11 49			12 49				13 49			14 49
Manchester Victoria	a		00 21		08 59																				
Manchester Oxford Road	a						09 39	09 59		10 41				11 32	11 59		12 32	12 59		13 32		13 57		14 32	14 59
Manchester Piccadilly 10	a			00 26			09 48	10 03		10 50				11 41	12 02		12 41	13 03		13 41		14 03		14 41	15 02
Manchester Airport 85 ✈	a							10 24							12 20			13 19				14 21			15 20

		NT	AW	NT	NT	AW		NT	NT	AW	NT	NT	AW	NT	NT	AW		NT	NT	AW	NT	NT	AW	NT	NT
			A ✕			A				◇ C ✕			◇ A			A				A			A		
Liverpool Lime Street 10 89,91	d	14 31		15 01	15 31			16 01	16 31		17 01	17 31		18 01	18 31			19 01	19 31		20 01	20 31		21 01	21 31
Edge Hill 89,91	d																								
Wavertree Technology Park	d	14 37		15 07	15 37			16 07	16 37		17 07	17 37		18 07	18 37			19 07	19 37		20 07	20 37		21 07	21 37
Broad Green	d	14 40		15 10	15 40			16 10	16 40		17 10	17 40		18 10	18 40			19 10	19 40		20 10	20 40		21 10	21 40
Roby	d	14 43		15 13	15 43			16 13	16 43		17 13	17 43		18 13	18 43			19 13	19 43		20 13	20 43		21 13	21 43
Huyton	d	14 46		15 16	15 46			16 16	16 46		17 16	17 46		18 16	18 46			19 16	19 46		20 16	20 46		21 16	21 46
Prescot	d	14 50			15 50				16 50			17 50			18 50				19 50			20 50			21 50
Eccleston Park	d																								
Thatto Heath	d	14 54			15 54				16 54			17 54			18 54				19 54			20 54			21 54
St Helens Central	a	14 57			15 57				16 57			17 57			18 57				19 57			20 57			21 57
	d	14 58			15 58				16 58			17 58			18 58				19 58			20 58			21 58
Garswood	d	15 05			16 05				17 05			18 05			19 05				20 05			21 05			22 05
Bryn	d																								
Whiston	d			15 19				16 19			17 19			18 19				19 19			20 19			21 19	
Rainhill	d			15 22				16 22			17 22			18 22				19 22			20 22			21 22	
Lea Green	d			15 26				16 26			17 26			18 26				19 26			20 26			21 26	
St Helens Junction	d			15 29				16 29			17 29			18 29				19 29			20 29			21 29	
Warrington Bank Quay	d		15 03			16 03				17 03			18 03			19 03				20 03			21 03		
Earlestown 8	d		15 10	15 33		16 10		16 33		17 10	17 33		18 10	18 33		19 10		19 33		20 10	20 33		21 10	21 33	
Warrington Bank Quay	a																								
Newton-le-Willows	d		15 13	15 36		16 13		16 36		17 13	17 36		18 13	18 36		19 13		19 36		20 13	20 36		21 13	21 36	
Wigan North Western 65	a	15 13			16 13				17 13			18 13			19 13				20 13			21 13			22 13
	d	15 14			16 14				17 14			18 14			19 14				20 14			21 14			22 14
Euxton Balshaw Lane	d	15 24			16 24				17 24			18 24			19 24				20 24			21 24			22 24
Leyland 82	a	15 29			16 29				17 29			18 29			19 29				20 29			21 29			22 29
Preston 8 65,82	a	15 37			16 37				17 37			18 37			19 37				20 37			21 37			22 37
Blackpool North 97	a	16 07			17 07				18 07			19 07			20 07				21 07			22 07			23 07
Patricroft	d																								
Eccles	d			15 49				16 49			17 49			18 49				19 49			20 49			21 49	
Manchester Victoria	a																								
Manchester Oxford Road	a		15 32	15 59		16 32		16 59		17 32	17 59		18 32	18 59		19 32		19 59		20 32	20 59		21 32	21 59	
Manchester Piccadilly 10	a		15 41	16 02		16 41		17 02		17 41	18 02		18 41	19 02		19 41		20 02		20 41	21 02		21 41	22 02	
Manchester Airport 85 ✈	a			16 21				17 21			18 21			19 21				20 21			21 20			22 21	

A From Chester

B From Crewe to Lancaster

C From Holyhead

Table 90

Sundays

16 September to 21 October

Liverpool and St Helens - Newton-le-Willows, Wigan, Preston and Manchester

Network Diagram - see first Page of Table 88

		NT		NT	NT	AW	NT
				🚌		A 🚌	🚌
Liverpool Lime Street 10 89,91	d	22 01		22 01	23 01		23 01
Edge Hill 89,91	d						
Wavertree Technology Park	d			22 16			23 16
Broad Green	d			22 26			23 26
Roby	d			22 33			23 33
Huyton	d			22 37			23 37
Prescot	d						
Eccleston Park	d						
Thatto Heath	d						
St Helens Central	a						
	d						
Garswood	d						
Bryn	d						
Whiston	d			22 47			23 47
Rainhill	d			22 57			23 57
Lea Green	d			23 05			00 05
St Helens Junction	d			23 12			00 12
Warrington Bank Quay	d					23 09	
Earlestown 8	d			23 24		23 34	00 24
Warrington Bank Quay	a						
Newton-le-Willows	d			23 33		23 44	00 33
Wigan North Western 65	a						
	d						
Euxton Balshaw Lane	d						
Leyland 82	a						
Preston 8 65,82	a						
Blackpool North 97	a						
Patricroft	d						
Eccles	d			23 57			00 57
Manchester Victoria	a						
Manchester Oxford Road	a	22 47		00 12	23 47	00 14	01 12
Manchester Piccadilly 10	a	22 50			23 50	00 19	
Manchester Airport 85 ✈	a	23 15			00 07		

Sundays

from 28 October

		NT	AW	NT	NT	NT	NT	AW	NT	AW		NT	NT	AW	NT	NT	AW	NT	NT	AW		NT	NT	AW	NT
			A 🚌					A 🚌		A 🚌				A 🚌			A 🚌			A 🚌				A ✕	
Liverpool Lime Street 10 89,91	d	23p16		08 01	08 31	09 01	09 31		10 31			11 01	11 31		12 01	12 31		13 01	13 31			14 01	14 31		15 01
Edge Hill 89,91	d	23p20																							
Wavertree Technology Park	d	23p22		08 07	08 37	09 07	09 37		10 37			11 07	11 37		12 07	12 37		13 07	13 37			14 07	14 37		15 07
Broad Green	d	23p26		08 10	08 40	09 10	09 40		10 40			11 10	11 40		12 10	12 40		13 10	13 40			14 10	14 40		15 10
Roby	d	23p30		08 13	08 43	09 13	09 43		10 43			11 13	11 43		12 13	12 43		13 13	13 43			14 13	14 43		15 13
Huyton	d	23p32		08 16	08 46	09 16	09 46		10 46			11 16	11 46		12 16	12 46		13 16	13 46			14 16	14 46		15 16
Prescot	d				08 50		09 50		10 50				11 50			12 50			13 50				14 50		
Eccleston Park	d																								
Thatto Heath	d				08 54		09 54		10 54				11 54			12 54			13 54				14 54		
St Helens Central	a				08 57		09 57		10 57				11 57			12 57			13 57				14 57		
	d				08 58		09 58		10 58				11 58			12 58			13 58				14 58		
Garswood	d				09 05		10 05		11 05				12 05			13 05			14 05				15 05		
Bryn	d																								
Whiston	d	23p36		08 19		09 19						11 19			12 19			13 19				14 19			15 19
Rainhill	d	23p39		08 22		09 22						11 22			12 22			13 22				14 22			15 22
Lea Green	d	23p42		08 26		09 26						11 26			12 26			13 26				14 26			15 26
St Helens Junction	d	23p45		08 29		09 29						11 29			12 29			13 29				14 29			15 29
Warrington Bank Quay	d		00 22					09 41		10 49				11 40			12 36			13 36				15 03	
Earlestown 8	d	23p50	00 47	08 33		09 33		10 06		11 14		11 33		12 05	12 33		13 01	13 33		14 01		14 33		15 10	15 33
Warrington Bank Quay	a																								
Newton-le-Willows	d	23p53	00 57	08 36		09 36		10 16		11 24		11 36		12 15	12 36		13 11	13 36		14 11		14 36		15 13	15 36
Wigan North Western 65	a				09 15		10 15		11 15				12 15			13 15			14 15				15 13		
	d																						15 14		
Euxton Balshaw Lane	d																						15 24		
Leyland 82	a																						15 29		
Preston 8 65,82	a																						15 37		
Blackpool North 97	a																						16 07		
Patricroft	d	00 05																							
Eccles	d	00 08		08 49		09 49						11 49			12 49			13 49				14 49			15 49
Manchester Victoria	a	00 21		08 59																					
Manchester Oxford Road	a					09 59		10 46		11 54		11 59		12 45	12 59		13 41	13 57		14 41		14 59		15 32	15 59
Manchester Piccadilly 10	a		01 32			10 03		10 51		11 59		12 02		12 50	13 03		13 46	14 03		14 46		15 02		15 41	16 02
Manchester Airport 85 ✈	a					10 24						12 20			13 19			14 21				15 20			16 21

A From Chester

Table 90

Sundays from 28 October

Liverpool and St Helens - Newton-le-Willows, Wigan, Preston and Manchester

Network Diagram - see first Page of Table 88

		NT	AW	NT	NT	AW	NT	NT	AW	NT	NT	AW	NT	NT	AW	NT	NT	AW	NT	NT	NT	NT	NT
			A			◇ B 🛒			◇ A			A			A			A				🚌	
Liverpool Lime Street 10 89,91	d	15 31		16 01	16 31		17 01	17 31		18 01	18 31		19 01	19 31		20 01	20 31		21 01	21 31	22 01	22 01	23 01
Edge Hill 89,91	d																						
Wavertree Technology Park	d	15 37		16 07	16 37		17 07	17 37		18 07	18 37		19 07	19 37		20 07	20 37		21 07	21 37		22 16	
Broad Green	d	15 40		16 10	16 40		17 10	17 40		18 10	18 40		19 10	19 40		20 10	20 40		21 10	21 40		22 26	
Roby	d	15 43		16 13	16 43		17 13	17 43		18 13	18 43		19 13	19 43		20 13	20 43		21 13	21 43		22 33	
Huyton	d	15 46		16 16	16 46		17 16	17 46		18 16	18 46		19 16	19 46		20 16	20 46		21 16	21 46		22 37	
Prescot	d	15 50			16 50			17 50			18 50			19 50			20 50			21 50			
Eccleston Park	d																						
Thatto Heath	d	15 54			16 54			17 54			18 54			19 54			20 54			21 54			
St Helens Central	a	15 57			16 57			17 57			18 57			19 57			20 57			21 57			
	d	15 58			16 58			17 58			18 58			19 58			20 58			21 58			
Garswood	d	16 05			17 05			18 05			19 05			20 05			21 05			22 05			
Bryn	d																						
Whiston	d			16 19			17 19			18 19			19 19			20 19			21 19			22 47	
Rainhill	d			16 22			17 22			18 22			19 22			20 22			21 22			22 57	
Lea Green	d			16 26			17 26			18 26			19 26			20 26			21 26			23 05	
St Helens Junction	d			16 29			17 29			18 29			19 29			20 29			21 29			23 12	
Warrington Bank Quay	d		16 03			17 03			18 03			19 03			20 03			21 03					
Earlestown 8	d		16 10	16 33		17 10	17 33		18 10	18 33		19 10	19 33		20 10	20 33		21 10	21 33			23 24	
Warrington Bank Quay	a																						
Newton-le-Willows	d		16 13	16 36		17 13	17 36		18 13	18 36		19 13	19 36		20 13	20 36		21 13	21 36			23 33	
Wigan North Western 65	a	16 13			17 13			18 13			19 13			20 13			21 13			22 13			
	d	16 14			17 14			18 14			19 14			20 14			21 14			22 14			
Euxton Balshaw Lane	d	16 24			17 24			18 24			19 24			20 24			21 24			22 24			
Leyland 82	a	16 29			17 29			18 29			19 29			20 29			21 29			22 29			
Preston 8 65,82	a	16 37			17 37			18 37			19 37			20 37			21 37			22 37			
Blackpool North 97	a	17 07			18 07			19 07			20 07			21 07			22 07			23 07			
Patricroft	d																						
Eccles	d			16 49			17 49			18 49			19 49			20 49			21 49			23 57	
Manchester Victoria	a																						
Manchester Oxford Road	a		16 32	16 59		17 32	17 59		18 32	18 59		19 32	19 59		20 32	20 59		21 32	21 59		22 47	00 12	23 47
Manchester Piccadilly 10	a		16 41	17 02		17 41	18 02		18 41	19 02		19 41	20 02		20 41	21 02		21 41	22 02		22 50		23 50
Manchester Airport 85 ✈	a			17 21			18 21			19 21			20 21			21 20			22 21		23 15		00 07

		AW	NT
		A 🚌	🚌
Liverpool Lime Street 10 89,91	d		23 01
Edge Hill 89,91	d		
Wavertree Technology Park	d		23 16
Broad Green	d		23 26
Roby	d		23 33
Huyton	d		23 37
Prescot	d		
Eccleston Park	d		
Thatto Heath	d		
St Helens Central	a		
	d		
Garswood	d		
Bryn	d		
Whiston	d		23 47
Rainhill	d		23 57
Lea Green	d		00 05
St Helens Junction	d		00 12
Warrington Bank Quay	d	23 09	
Earlestown 8	d	23 34	00 24
Warrington Bank Quay	a		
Newton-le-Willows	d	23 44	00 33
Wigan North Western 65	a		
	d		
Euxton Balshaw Lane	d		
Leyland 82	a		
Preston 8 65,82	a		
Blackpool North 97	a		
Patricroft	d		
Eccles	d		00 57
Manchester Victoria	a		
Manchester Oxford Road	a	00 14	01 12
Manchester Piccadilly 10	a	00 19	
Manchester Airport 85 ✈	a		

A From Chester
B From Holyhead

Table 90

Mondays to Fridays until 28 September

Manchester, Preston, Wigan and Newton-le-Willows - St Helens and Liverpool

Network Diagram - see first Page of Table 88

Miles	Miles	Miles	Miles			NT MX	NT	NT MX	NT MX	NT	NT	NT MX	AW MX	NT	NT	NT	AW	AW	NT	NT	VT	NT	NT
						🚌	A 🚌	🚌	🚌	A 🚌	A 🚌	🚌	🚌				B	◇ C 🛒			◇ 1 D ⊠		E
—	—	—	0	**Manchester Airport** 85 ✈	d									04 38				05 33					
—	—	—	9¾	**Manchester Piccadilly** 10	d								23p50	04 53				05 50					
—	—	—	10¼	**Manchester Oxford Road**	d					23p00			23p55					05 53					
0	—	—	—	**Manchester Victoria**	d				22p39			23p09				05 39				06 09			
4	—	—	14½	Eccles	d				22p58	23p15		23p28				05 46				06 16			
5	—	—	15½	Patricroft	d				23p08			23p38				05 49				06 19			
—	—	—	—	Blackpool North 97	d																		
—	0	0	—	**Preston** 8 65,82	d																06 16		
—	4	4	—	Leyland 82	d																		
—	6¾	6¾	—	Euxton Balshaw Lane	d																		
—	15	15	—	**Wigan North Western** 65	a																06 27		
—	—	—	—		d	22p25	22p50	23p15			23p42								06 08		06 27	06 38	
15½	—	22	26	**Newton-le-Willows**	d				23p38	23p40		00 08	00 25			06 01		06 12		06 31			
—	—	—	—	Warrington Bank Quay	d												06 06				06a38		
17	—	23½	27½	Earlestown 8	d				23p46	23p48		00 16	00 35			06 04	06a12	06 15		06 34			06 50
—	—	—	—	Warrington Bank Quay	a								01 00					06 25					07 01
19¾	—	26¼	30¼	**St Helens Junction**	d				23p58	00 01		00 28				06 09				06 39			
21	—	27½	31½	Lea Green	d				00 05	00 07		00 35				06 12				06 42			
22¾	—	29¼	33¼	Rainhill	d				00 13	00 15		00 43				06 16				06 46			
24¼	—	30¼	34¼	Whiston	d				00 23	00 25		00 53				06 19				06 49			
—	18¾	—	—	Bryn	d	22p38													06 15			06 45	
—	20	—	—	Garswood	d	22p45	23p10	23p35			00 02								06 19			06 49	
—	23¼	—	—	**St Helens Central**	a	23p05	23p30	23p55			00 22								06 25			06 55	
—	—	—	—		d	23p05	23p30	23p55			00 22				05 56				06 26			06 56	
—	25¼	—	—	Thatto Heath	d	23p15	23p40	00 05			00 32				05 59				06 29			06 59	
—	26¼	—	—	Eccleston Park	d	23p25									06 02				06 32			07 02	
—	27¼	—	—	Prescot	d	23p31	23p50	00 21			00 42				06 04				06 34			07 04	
26¼	29½	32¾	36¾	Huyton	d	23p41	00 01	00 31	00 33	00 35	00 52	01 03			06 08	06 23			06 38	06 53		07 08	
26¾	30	33¼	37¼	Roby	d	23p45	00 04	00 35	00 37	00 39	00 56	01 07			06 10	06 25			06 40	06 55		07 10	
28¼	31½	34¾	38¾	Broad Green	d	23p52	00 11	00 42	00 44	00 46	01 03	01 14			06 13	06 28			06 43	06 58		07 13	
29¾	32½	35¾	39¾	Wavertree Technology Park	d	00 02	00 21	00 52	00 54	00 56	01 13	01 24			06 16	06 31			06 46	07 01		07 16	
30	33¼	36½	40½	Edge Hill 89,91	d	00 12			01 04			01 34			06 19	06 34			06 49	07 04		07 19	
31¾	35	38¼	42¼	**Liverpool Lime Street** 10 89,91	a	00 19	00 36	01 09	01 11	01 11	01 28	01 41		05 36	06 26	06 43			06 58	07 13		07 26	

		NT	AW	AW	NT	NT	NT	NT	NT	AW	NT	NT	AW	NT	AW	NT	NT	NT	NT	NT	AW	NT	NT	NT
			◇ F	◇ C 🛒						B 🛒			◇ C 🛒		◇ G 🛒			E			◇ C 🛒			H
Manchester Airport 85 ✈	d				06 41							07 38										08 41		
Manchester Piccadilly 10	d			06 50	06 58							07 53	07 50								08 50	09 01		
Manchester Oxford Road	d			06 53	07 01							08 03	07 53								08 53	09 04		
Manchester Victoria	d						07 09				07 39					08 09				08 39				
Eccles	d						07 16				07 46					08 16				08 46				
Patricroft	d						07 19				07 49					08 19				08 49				
Blackpool North 97	d								07 02															
Preston 8 65,82	d								07 30															09 04
Leyland 82	d								07 35															09 09
Euxton Balshaw Lane	d								07 40															09 14
Wigan North Western 65	a								07 50															09 24
	d	06 47				07 08		07 38	07 50					07 58			08 28						09 08	09 24
Newton-le-Willows	d	07 00		07 12	07 19		07 31				08 01	08 21	08 12			08 31				09 01	09 12	09 22		
Warrington Bank Quay	d		07 07							07 39					08 08									
Earlestown 8	d	07 03	07a14	07 15			07 34			07a46	08 04		08 15		08a15	08 34		08 50		09 04	09 15			
Warrington Bank Quay	a			07 22									08 23					09 01			09 25			
St Helens Junction	d	07 09			07 24		07 39				08 09	08 26				08 39				09 09		09 27		
Lea Green	d	07 12					07 42				08 12	08 29				08 42				09 12				
Rainhill	d	07 16			07 29		07 46				08 16	08 34				08 46				09 16				
Whiston	d	07 19					07 49				08 19	08 37				08 49				09 19				
Bryn	d					07 15		07 45						08 05			08 35						09 15	
Garswood	d					07 19		07 49	07 59					08 09			08 39						09 19	
St Helens Central	a					07 25		07 55	08 06					08 15			08 45						09 25	09 39
	d					07 26		07 56	08 06					08 16			08 46		08 56				09 26	09 39
Thatto Heath	d					07 29		07 59						08 19			08 49		08 59				09 29	
Eccleston Park	d					07 32		08 02						08 22			08 52		09 02				09 32	
Prescot	d					07 34		08 04	08 12					08 24			08 54		09 04				09 34	
Huyton	d	07 23			07 34	07 38	07 53	08 08	08 16		08 23	08 41		08 28		08 53	08 58		09 08	09 23			09 38	09 48
Roby	d	07 25				07 40	07 55	08 10			08 25			08 30		08 55	09 00		09 10	09 25			09 40	
Broad Green	d	07 28				07 43	07 58	08 13	08 20		08 28	08 45		08 33		08 58	09 03		09 13	09 28			09 43	
Wavertree Technology Park	d	07 31			07 39	07 46	08 01	08 16	08 24		08 31	08 48		08 36		09 01	09 06		09 16	09 31		09 38	09 46	
Edge Hill 89,91	d	07 34				07 49	08 04	08 19			08 34			08 39		09 04	09 09		09 19	09 34			09 49	
Liverpool Lime Street 10 89,91	a	07 43			07 49	07 56	08 13	08 28	08 35		08 43	08 59		08 48		09 13	09 18		09 28	09 43		09 48	09 58	10 02

A MO from 21 May until 24 September
B From Chester to Manchester Piccadilly
C To Llandudno
D To Birmingham New Street
E From Liverpool Lime Street
F From Llandudno Junction to Manchester Piccadilly
G From Llandudno to Manchester Piccadilly
H To Liverpool South Parkway

Table 90

Mondays to Fridays
until 28 September

Manchester, Preston, Wigan and Newton-le-Willows - St Helens and Liverpool

Network Diagram - see first Page of Table 88

		AW ◇ A	NT	NT	NT B	NT	AW ◇ C	NT	NT	NT D	AW ◇ A	NT	NT	NT B	NT	AW ◇ C	NT	NT	NT D	AW ◇ A	NT	NT	NT B
Manchester Airport 85 ✈	d							09 41									10 41						
Manchester Piccadilly	d						09 50	10 01								10 50	11 01						
Manchester Oxford Road	d						09 53	10 04								10 53	11 04						
Manchester Victoria	d					09 39									10 39								
Eccles	d					09 46									10 46								
Patricroft	d					09 49									10 49								
Blackpool North 97	d									09 37									10 37				
Preston 65,82	d									10 04									11 04				
Leyland 82	d									10 09									11 09				
Euxton Balshaw Lane	d									10 14									11 14				
Wigan North Western 65	a									10 24									11 24				
	d			09 38					10 08	10 24			10 38					11 08	11 24			11 38	
Newton-le-Willows	d					10 01	10 12	10 22							11 01	11 12	11 22						
Warrington Bank Quay	d	09 19	09 22								10 19	10 22								11 19	11 22		
Earlestown	d	09a26	09 34		09 50	10 04	10 15				10a26	10 34		10 50	11 04	11 15				11a26	11 34		11 50
Warrington Bank Quay	a				10 01		10 25							11 02		11 25							12 01
St Helens Junction	d		09 39			10 09		10 27				10 39			11 09		11 27				11 39		
Lea Green	d		09 42			10 12						10 42			11 12						11 42		
Rainhill	d		09 46			10 16						10 46			11 16						11 46		
Whiston	d		09 49			10 19						10 49			11 19						11 49		
Bryn	d			09 45					10 15				10 45					11 15				11 45	
Garswood	d			09 49					10 19				10 49					11 19				11 49	
St Helens Central	a			09 55					10 25	10 39			10 55					11 25	11 39			11 55	
	d			09 56					10 26	10 39			10 56					11 26	11 39			11 56	
Thatto Heath	d			09 59					10 29				10 59					11 29				11 59	
Eccleston Park	d			10 02					10 32				11 02					11 32				12 02	
Prescot	d			10 04					10 34				11 04					11 34				12 04	
Huyton	d		09 53	10 08		10 23			10 38	10 48		10 53	11 08		11 23			11 38	11 48		11 53	12 08	
Roby	d		09 55	10 10		10 25			10 40			10 55	11 10		11 25			11 40			11 55	12 10	
Broad Green	d		09 58	10 13		10 28			10 43			10 58	11 13		11 28			11 43			11 58	12 13	
Wavertree Technology Park	d		10 01	10 16		10 31		10 38	10 46			11 01	11 16		11 31		11 38	11 46			12 01	12 16	
Edge Hill 89,91	d		10 04	10 19		10 34			10 49			11 04	11 19		11 34			11 49			12 04	12 19	
Liverpool Lime Street 89,91	a		10 13	10 26		10 43		10 48	10 56	11 02		11 13	11 28		11 43		11 48	11 56	12 02		12 13	12 28	

		NT	AW ◇ C	NT	NT	NT D	AW ◇ A	NT	NT	NT B	NT	AW ◇ C	NT	NT	NT D	AW ◇ A	NT	NT	NT B	NT	AW ◇ C	NT
Manchester Airport 85 ✈	d			11 41									12 41									13 41
Manchester Piccadilly	d		11 50	12 01								12 50	13 01								13 50	14 01
Manchester Oxford Road	d		11 53	12 04								12 53	13 04								13 53	14 04
Manchester Victoria	d	11 39									12 39									13 39		
Eccles	d	11 46									12 46									13 46		
Patricroft	d	11 49									12 49									13 49		
Blackpool North 97	d					11 37									12 37							
Preston 65,82	d					12 04									13 04							
Leyland 82	d					12 09									13 09							
Euxton Balshaw Lane	d					12 14									13 14							
Wigan North Western 65	a					12 24									13 24							
	d				12 08	12 24			12 38					13 08	13 24			13 38				
Newton-le-Willows	d	12 01	12 12	12 22							13 01	13 12	13 22							14 01	14 12	14 22
Warrington Bank Quay	d						12 19	12 22								13 19	13 22					
Earlestown	d	12 04	12 15				12a26	12 34		12 50	13 04	13 15				13a26	13 34		13 50	14 04	14 15	
Warrington Bank Quay	a		12 25							13 01		13 25							14 01		14 25	
St Helens Junction	d	12 09		12 27				12 39			13 09		13 27				13 39			14 09		14 27
Lea Green	d	12 12						12 42			13 12						13 42			14 12		
Rainhill	d	12 16						12 46			13 16						13 46			14 16		
Whiston	d	12 19						12 49			13 19						13 49			14 19		
Bryn	d				12 15				12 45					13 15				13 45				
Garswood	d				12 19				12 49					13 19				13 49				
St Helens Central	a				12 25	12 39			12 55					13 25	13 39			13 55				
	d				12 26	12 39			12 56					13 26	13 39			13 56				
Thatto Heath	d				12 29				12 59					13 29				13 59				
Eccleston Park	d				12 32				13 02					13 32				14 02				
Prescot	d				12 34				13 04					13 34				14 04				
Huyton	d	12 23			12 38	12 48		12 53	13 08		13 23			13 38	13 48		13 53	14 08		14 23		
Roby	d	12 25			12 40			12 55	13 10		13 25			13 40			13 55	14 10		14 25		
Broad Green	d	12 28			12 43			12 58	13 13		13 28			13 43			13 58	14 13		14 28		
Wavertree Technology Park	d	12 31		12 38	12 46			13 01	13 16		13 31		13 38	13 46			14 01	14 16		14 31		14 38
Edge Hill 89,91	d	12 34			12 49			13 04	13 19		13 34			13 49			14 04	14 19		14 34		
Liverpool Lime Street 89,91	a	12 43		12 48	12 58	13 02		13 13	13 26		13 43		13 48	13 56	14 02		14 13	14 26		14 43		14 48

A From Llandudno to Manchester Piccadilly
B From Liverpool Lime Street
C To Llandudno
D To Liverpool South Parkway

Table 90

Mondays to Fridays
until 28 September

Manchester, Preston, Wigan and Newton-le-Willows - St Helens and Liverpool

Network Diagram - see first Page of Table 88

		NT	NT A	AW ◇ B	NT	NT	NT C	NT	AW ◇ D	NT	NT	NT A	AW ◇ B	NT	NT	NT C	NT	AW ◇ D	NT	NT	NT	AW ◇ B	NT
Manchester Airport 85 ✈	d									14 41									15 41				
Manchester Piccadilly	d								14 50	15 01								15 50	16 01				
Manchester Oxford Road	d								14 53	15 04								15 53	16 04				
Manchester Victoria	d							14 39									15 39						
Eccles	d							14 46									15 46						
Patricroft	d							14 49									15 49						
Blackpool North 97	d		13 37									14 37									15 37		
Preston 65,82	d		14 04									15 04									16 04		
Leyland 82	d		14 09									15 09									16 09		
Euxton Balshaw Lane	d		14 14									15 14									16 14		
Wigan North Western 65	a		14 24									15 24									16 24		
	d	14 08	14 24			14 38					15 08	15 24			15 38					16 08	16 24		
Newton-le-Willows	d							15 01	15 12	15 22							16 01	16 12	16 22				
Warrington Bank Quay	d			14 19	14 22								15 19	15 22								16 19	16 22
Earlestown	d			14a26	14 34		14 50	15 04	15 15				15a26	15 34		15 50	16 04	16 15				16a26	16 34
Warrington Bank Quay	a						15 01		15 25							16 01		16 26					
St Helens Junction	d				14 39			15 09		15 27				15 39			16 09		16 27				16 39
Lea Green	d				14 42			15 12						15 42			16 12						16 42
Rainhill	d				14 46			15 16						15 46			16 16						16 46
Whiston	d				14 49			15 19						15 49			16 19						16 49
Bryn	d	14 15				14 45					15 15				15 45					16 15			
Garswood	d	14 19				14 49					15 19				15 49					16 19			
St Helens Central	a	14 25	14 39			14 55					15 25	15 39			15 55					16 25	16 39		
	d	14 26	14 39			14 56					15 26	15 39			15 56					16 26	16 39		
Thatto Heath	d	14 29				14 59					15 29				15 59					16 29			
Eccleston Park	d	14 32				15 02					15 32				16 02					16 32			
Prescot	d	14 34				15 04					15 34				16 04					16 34			
Huyton	d	14 38	14 48		14 53	15 08		15 23			15 38	15 48		15 53	16 08		16 23			16 38	16 48		16 53
Roby	d	14 40			14 55	15 10		15 25			15 40			15 55	16 10		16 25			16 40			16 55
Broad Green	d	14 43			14 58	15 13		15 28			15 43			15 58	16 13		16 28			16 43			16 58
Wavertree Technology Park	d	14 46			15 01	15 16		15 31		15 38	15 46			16 01	16 16		16 31		16 38	16 46			17 01
Edge Hill 89,91	d	14 49			15 04	15 19		15 34			15 49			16 04	16 19		16 34			16 49			17 04
Liverpool Lime Street 89,91	a	14 58	15 02		15 13	15 26		15 43		15 48	15 58	16 02		16 13	16 28		16 43		16 48	16 56	17 05		17 13

		NT	AW ◇ B	NT	AW ◇ D	NT	NT	NT	NT	AW E	NT	AW ◇ B	NT	AW ◇ D	NT	NT	NT	NT	NT	NT C	AW ◇ B	NT
Manchester Airport 85 ✈	d					16 41										17 41						
Manchester Piccadilly	d				16 50	17 01				17 19				17 50		18 01						
Manchester Oxford Road	d				16 53	17 04				17 22				17 53		18 04						
Manchester Victoria	d			16 39					17 09				17 37									18 39
Eccles	d			16 46					17 16				17 46			18 11						18 46
Patricroft	d			16 49					17 19				17 49									18 49
Blackpool North 97	d							16 35										17 37				
Preston 65,82	d							17 04										18 04				
Leyland 82	d							17 09										18 09				
Euxton Balshaw Lane	d							17 14										18 14				
Wigan North Western 65	a							17 24										18 24				
	d	16 38					17 08	17 24			17 38				18 08		18 21	18 24	18 35			
Newton-le-Willows	d			17 01	17 12	17 22			17 31	17 40			18 01	18 12		18 24	18 33					19 01
Warrington Bank Quay	d		16 51									17 49									18 46	
Earlestown	d		16a59	17 04	17 15				17 34	17 44		17a57	18 04	18 15			18 36			18 50	18a57	19 04
Warrington Bank Quay	a				17 25					17 52				18 23						19 01		
St Helens Junction	d			17 09		17 27			17 39				18 09			18 29	18 41					19 09
Lea Green	d			17 12					17 42				18 12			18 32	18 44					19 12
Rainhill	d			17 16					17 46				18 16			18 36	18 48					19 16
Whiston	d			17 19					17 49				18 19				18 51					19 19
Bryn	d	16 45					17 15				17 45				18 15				18 45			
Garswood	d	16 49					17 19				17 49				18 19				18 49			
St Helens Central	a	16 55					17 25	17 39			17 55				18 25			18 39	18 55			
	d	16 56					17 26	17 39			17 56				18 26			18 39	18 56			
Thatto Heath	d	16 59					17 29				17 59				18 29				18 59			
Eccleston Park	d	17 02					17 32				18 02				18 32				19 02			
Prescot	d	17 04					17 34				18 04				18 34				19 04			
Huyton	d	17 08		17 23			17 38	17 48	17 53		18 08		18 23		18 38	18 41	18 55	18 48	19 08			19 23
Roby	d	17 10		17 25			17 40		17 55		18 10		18 25			18 43	18 57		19 10			19 25
Broad Green	d	17 13		17 28			17 43		17 58		18 13		18 28			18 47	19 00		19 13			19 28
Wavertree Technology Park	d	17 16		17 31		17 38	17 46		18 01		18 16		18 31		18 43	18 50	19 03		19 16			19 31
Edge Hill 89,91	d	17 19		17 34			17 49		18 04		18 19		18 34		18 46		19 06		19 19			19 35
Liverpool Lime Street 89,91	a	17 26		17 43		17 48	17 56	18 02	18 13		18 26		18 43		18 52	19 00	19 15	19 03	19 28			19 43

A To Liverpool South Parkway
B From Llandudno to Manchester Piccadilly
C From Liverpool Lime Street
D To Llandudno
E To Chester

until 28 September

Manchester, Preston, Wigan and Newton-le-Willows - St Helens and Liverpool

Network Diagram - see first Page of Table 88

Station		AW A	NT	NT	NT	AW B	NT	NT	AW A	NT	NT	NT	AW ◇ C	NT	NT	AW A	NT	AW ◇ D	NT FX	NT	AW A	NT FO	AW FO E
Manchester Airport 85 ✈	d		18 41							19 41						20 32			21 24		21 32	21 42	
Manchester Piccadilly 10	d	18 50	19 01						19 50	20 01						20 50			21a38		21 50	22 01	
Manchester Oxford Road	d	18 53	19 04						19 53	20 04						20 53					21 53	22 04	
Manchester Victoria	d							19 39							20 39					21 39			
Eccles	d							19 46							20 46					21 46			
Patricroft	d							19 49							20 49					21 49			
Blackpool North 97	d				18 37							19 37					20 37						
Preston 8 65,82	d				19 04							20 04					21 04						
Leyland 82	d				19 09							20 09					21 09						
Euxton Balshaw Lane	d				19 14							20 14					21 14						
Wigan North Western 65	a				19 24							20 24					21 23						
	d			19 08	19 24						20 08	20 24		20 38			21 23						
Newton-le-Willows	d	19 12	19 22					20 01	20 12	20 22					21 01	21 12				22 01	22 12	22 22	
Warrington Bank Quay	d					19 19	19 22						20 19					21 19					22 19
Earlestown 8	d	19 16				19a26	19 34	20 04	20 15				20a26		21 04	21 15		21a26		22 04	22 15		22a26
Warrington Bank Quay	a	19 24							20 25							21 24					22 23		
St Helens Junction	d		19 27				19 39	20 09		20 27					21 09					22 09		22 27	
Lea Green	d						19 42	20 12							21 12					22 12			
Rainhill	d						19 46	20 16							21 16					22 16			
Whiston	d						19 49	20 19							21 19					22 19			
Bryn	d			19 15							20 15			20 45			21 30						
Garswood	d			19 19							20 19			20 49			21 34						
St Helens Central	a			19 25	19 39						20 25	20 39		20 55			21 40						
	d			19 26	19 39						20 26	20 39		20 56			21 41						
Thatto Heath	d			19 29							20 29			20 59			21 44						
Eccleston Park	d			19 32							20 32			21 02			21 47						
Prescot	d			19 34							20 34			21 04			21 49						
Huyton	d			19 38	19 48		19 53	20 23			20 38	20 48		21 08	21 23		21 53			22 23			
Roby	d			19 40			19 55	20 25			20 40			21 10	21 25		21 55			22 25			
Broad Green	d			19 43			19 58	20 28			20 43			21 13	21 28		21 58			22 28			
Wavertree Technology Park	d		19 38	19 46			20 01	20 31		20 38	20 46			21 16	21 31		22 03			22 31		22 38	
Edge Hill 89,91	d			19 49			20 04	20 34			20 49			21 19	21 34		22 06			22 34			
Liverpool Lime Street 10 89,91	a		19 48	19 58	20 00		20 13	20 43		20 48	20 56	21 00		21 28	21 43		22 16			22 43		22 48	

Station		AW FO A	NT FO	AW FX F 🚌	NT FO	NT FX 🚌	NT FO	AW FX 🚌	NT FO	AW FO A	NT FX 🚌	NT FX 🚌	NT FX 🚌	AW FX F 🚌	AW FX 🚌
Manchester Airport 85 ✈	d														
Manchester Piccadilly 10	d	22 12						22 35		23 14					23 50
Manchester Oxford Road	d	22 29						22 40		23 17					23 55
Manchester Victoria	d				22 39				23 09			22 39	23 09		
Eccles	d				22 46				23 16			22 58	23 28		
Patricroft	d				22 49				23 19			23 08	23 38		
Blackpool North 97	d						22 14								
Preston 8 65,82	d						22 43								
Leyland 82	d						22 48								
Euxton Balshaw Lane	d						22 53								
Wigan North Western 65	a						23 02								
	d		22 25			22 25	23 03				23 15				
Newton-le-Willows	d	22 47			23 01			23 10	23 31	23 36		23 38	00 08		00 25
Warrington Bank Quay	d			22 28										23 59	
Earlestown 8	d	22 50		22a53	23 04			23 20	23 34	23 39		23 46	00 16	00a24	00 35
Warrington Bank Quay	a	22 58						23 45		23 47					01 00
St Helens Junction	d				23 09				23 39			23 58	00 28		
Lea Green	d				23 12				23 42			00 05	00 35		
Rainhill	d				23 16				23 46			00 13	00 43		
Whiston	d				23 19				23 49			00 23	00 53		
Bryn	d		22 32			22 38	23 10								
Garswood	d		22 36			22 45	23 14				23 35				
St Helens Central	a		22 42			23 05	23 20				23 55				
	d		22 43			23 05	23 21				23 55				
Thatto Heath	d		22 46			23 15	23 24				00 05				
Eccleston Park	d		22 49			23 25	23 27								
Prescot	d		22 51			23 31	23 29				00 21				
Huyton	d		22 55		23 23	23 41	23 33		23 53		00 31	00 33	01 03		
Roby	d		22 57		23 25	23 45	23 35		23 55		00 35	00 37	01 07		
Broad Green	d		23 00		23 28	23 52	23 38		23 58		00 42	00 44	01 14		
Wavertree Technology Park	d		23 03		23 31	00 02	23 41		00 01		00 52	00 54	01 24		
Edge Hill 89,91	d		23 06		23 34	00 12	23 46		00 04			01 04	01 34		
Liverpool Lime Street 10 89,91	a		23 13		23 43	00 19	23 54		00 13		01 09	01 11	01 41		

A To Chester
B From Chester to Manchester Airport
C From Llandudno to Manchester Airport
D From Llandudno to Manchester Piccadilly
E From Chester to Manchester Piccadilly
F To Manchester Piccadilly

from 1 October

Manchester, Preston, Wigan and Newton-le-Willows - St Helens and Liverpool

Network Diagram - see first Page of Table 88

Station		NT MX 🚌	NT MO 🚌	NT MX 🚌	NT MX 🚌	NT MO 🚌	NT MO 🚌	NT MX 🚌	AW MX 🚌	NT	NT	NT	AW A	AW ◇ B	NT	NT	VT ◇1 C	NT	NT D	NT	AW ◇ E	AW ◇ B	NT
Manchester Airport 85 ✈	d									04 38				05 33									06 41
Manchester Piccadilly 10	d								23p50	04 53				05 50								06 50	06 58
Manchester Oxford Road	d					23p00			23p55					05 53								06 53	07 01
Manchester Victoria	d				22p39			23p09				05 39				06 09							
Eccles	d				22p58	23p15		23p28				05 46				06 16							
Patricroft	d				23p08			23p38				05 49				06 19							
Blackpool North 97	d																						
Preston 8 65,82	d																06 16						
Leyland 82	d																						
Euxton Balshaw Lane	d																						
Wigan North Western 65	a																06 27						
	d	22p25	22p50	23p15			23p42								06 08		06 27	06 38		06 47			
Newton-le-Willows	d				23p38	23p40		00 08	00 25			06 01		06 12		06 31				07 00		07 12	07 19
Warrington Bank Quay	d												06 06				06a38				07 07		
Earlestown 8	d				23p46	23p48		00 16	00 35			06 04	06a12	06 15		06 34			06 50	07 03	07a14	07 15	
Warrington Bank Quay	a								01 00					06 25					07 01			07 22	
St Helens Junction	d				23p58	00 01		00 28				06 09				06 39				07 09			07 24
Lea Green	d				00 05	00 07		00 35				06 12				06 42				07 12			
Rainhill	d				00 13	00 15		00 43				06 16				06 46				07 16			07 29
Whiston	d				00 23	00 25		00 53				06 19				06 49				07 19			
Bryn	d	22p38													06 15			06 45					
Garswood	d	22p45	23p10	23p35			00 02								06 19			06 49					
St Helens Central	a	23p05	23p30	23p55			00 22								06 25			06 55					
	d	23p05	23p30	23p55			00 22				05 56				06 26			06 56					
Thatto Heath	d	23p15	23p40	00 05			00 32				05 59				06 29			06 59					
Eccleston Park	d	23p25									06 02				06 32			07 02					
Prescot	d	23p31	23p50	00 21			00 42				06 04				06 34			07 04					
Huyton	d	23p41	00 01	00 31	00 33	00 35	00 52	01 03			06 08	06 23			06 38	06 53		07 08		07 23			07 34
Roby	d	23p45	00 04	00 35	00 37	00 39	00 56	01 07			06 10	06 25			06 40	06 55		07 10		07 25			
Broad Green	d	23p52	00 11	00 42	00 44	00 46	01 03	01 14			06 13	06 28			06 43	06 58		07 13		07 28			
Wavertree Technology Park	d	00 02	00 21	00 52	00 54	00 56	01 13	01 24			06 16	06 31			06 46	07 01		07 16		07 31			07 39
Edge Hill 89,91	d	00 12			01 04			01 34			06 19	06 34			06 49	07 04		07 19		07 34			
Liverpool Lime Street 10 89,91	a	00 19	00 36	01 09	01 11	01 11	01 28	01 41		05 36	06 30	06 43			07 00	07 13		07 30		07 43			07 49

Station		NT	NT	NT	NT	AW A	NT	NT	AW ◇ B	NT	AW ◇ F	NT	NT	NT D	NT	NT	AW ◇ B	NT	NT	NT G	AW ◇ F	NT	NT	NT D
Manchester Airport 85 ✈	d						07 38											08 41						
Manchester Piccadilly 10	d						07 53		07 50								08 50	09 01						
Manchester Oxford Road	d						08 03		07 53								08 53	09 04						
Manchester Victoria	d		07 09					07 39				08 09				08 39								
Eccles	d		07 16					07 46				08 16				08 46								
Patricroft	d		07 19					07 49				08 19				08 49								
Blackpool North 97	d				07 02																			
Preston 8 65,82	d				07 30															09 04				
Leyland 82	d				07 35															09 09				
Euxton Balshaw Lane	d				07 40															09 14				
Wigan North Western 65	a				07 50															09 24				
	d	07 08		07 38	07 50					07 58			08 28						09 08	09 24			09 38	
Newton-le-Willows	d		07 31				08 21	08 01	08 12			08 31				09 01	09 12	09 22						
Warrington Bank Quay	d					07 39					08 08										09 19	09 22		
Earlestown 8	d		07 34			07a46		08 04	08 15		08a15	08 34		08 50		09 04	09 15				09a26	09 34		09 50
Warrington Bank Quay	a								08 23					09 01			09 25							10 01
St Helens Junction	d		07 39				08 26	08 09				08 39				09 09		09 27				09 39		
Lea Green	d		07 42				08 29	08 12				08 42				09 12						09 42		
Rainhill	d		07 46				08 34	08 16				08 46				09 16						09 46		
Whiston	d		07 49				08 37	08 19				08 49				09 19						09 49		
Bryn	d	07 15		07 45						08 05			08 35						09 15				09 45	
Garswood	d	07 19		07 49	07 59					08 09			08 39						09 19				09 49	
St Helens Central	a	07 25		07 55	08 06					08 15			08 45						09 25	09 39			09 55	
	d	07 26		07 56	08 06					08 16			08 46		08 56				09 26	09 39			09 56	
Thatto Heath	d	07 29		07 59						08 19			08 49		08 59				09 29				09 59	
Eccleston Park	d	07 32		08 02						08 22			08 52		09 02				09 32				10 02	
Prescot	d	07 34		08 04	08 12					08 24			08 54		09 04				09 34				10 04	
Huyton	d	07 38	07 53	08 08	08 16		08 41	08 23		08 28		08 53	08 58		09 08	09 23			09 38	09 48		09 53	10 08	
Roby	d	07 40	07 55	08 10				08 25		08 30		08 55	09 00		09 10	09 25			09 40			09 55	10 10	
Broad Green	d	07 43	07 58	08 13	08 20		08 45	08 28		08 33		08 58	09 03		09 13	09 28			09 43			09 58	10 13	
Wavertree Technology Park	d	07 46	08 01	08 16	08 24		08 48	08 31		08 36		09 01	09 06		09 16	09 31		09 38	09 46			10 01	10 16	
Edge Hill 89,91	d	07 49	08 04	08 19				08 34		08 39		09 04	09 09		09 19	09 34			09 49			10 04	10 19	
Liverpool Lime Street 10 89,91	a	08 00	08 13	08 30	08 35		08 59	08 43		08 52		09 13	09 20		09 30	09 43		09 48	10 00	10 02		10 13	10 30	

A From Chester to Manchester Piccadilly
B To Llandudno
C To Birmingham New Street
D From Liverpool Lime Street
E From Llandudno Junction to Manchester Piccadilly
F From Llandudno to Manchester Piccadilly
G To Liverpool South Parkway

Manchester, Preston, Wigan and Newton-le-Willows - St Helens and Liverpool

Network Diagram - see first Page of Table 88

	NT	AW ◇A	NT	NT	NT B	AW ◇C	NT	NT	NT D	NT E	AW ◇A	NT	NT	NT B	AW ◇C	NT	NT	NT D	NT	AW ◇A	NT
Manchester Airport 85 ✈ d			09 41									10 41									11 41
Manchester Piccadilly 10 d		09 50	10 01								10 50	11 01								11 50	12 01
Manchester Oxford Road d		09 53	10 04								10 53	11 04								11 53	12 04
Manchester Victoria d	09 39									10 39									11 39		
Eccles d	09 46									10 46									11 46		
Patricroft d	09 49									10 49									11 49		
Blackpool North 97 d					09 37									10 37							
Preston 8 65,82 d					10 04									11 04							
Leyland 82 d					10 09									11 09							
Euxton Balshaw Lane d					10 14									11 14							
Wigan North Western 65 a					10 24									11 24							
d				10 08	10 24			10 38					11 08	11 24			11 38				
Newton-le-Willows d	10 01	10 12	10 22							11 01	11 12	11 22							12 01	12 12	12 22
Warrington Bank Quay d						10 19	10 22								11 19	11 22					
Earlestown 8 d	10 04	10 15				10a26	10 34		10 50	11 04	11 15				11a26	11 34		11 50	12 04	12 15	
Warrington Bank Quay a		10 25							11 02		11 25							12 01		12 25	
St Helens Junction d	10 09		10 27				10 39			11 09		11 27				11 39			12 09		12 27
Lea Green d	10 12						10 42			11 12						11 42			12 12		
Rainhill d	10 16						10 46			11 16						11 46			12 16		
Whiston d	10 19						10 49			11 19						11 49			12 19		
Bryn d				10 15				10 45					11 15				11 45				
Garswood d				10 19				10 49					11 19				11 49				
St Helens Central a				10 25	10 39			10 55					11 25	11 39			11 55				
d				10 26	10 39			10 56					11 26	11 39			11 56				
Thatto Heath d				10 29				10 59					11 29				11 59				
Eccleston Park d				10 32				11 02					11 32				12 02				
Prescot d				10 34				11 04					11 34				12 04				
Huyton d	10 23			10 38	10 48		10 53	11 08		11 23			11 38	11 48		11 53	12 08		12 23		
Roby d	10 25			10 40			10 55	11 10		11 25			11 40			11 55	12 10		12 25		
Broad Green d	10 28			10 43			10 58	11 13		11 28			11 43			11 58	12 13		12 28		
Wavertree Technology Park d	10 31		10 38	10 46			11 01	11 16		11 31		11 38	11 46			12 01	12 16		12 31		12 38
Edge Hill 89,91 d	10 34			10 49			11 04	11 19		11 34			11 49			12 04	12 19		12 34		
Liverpool Lime Street 10 89,91 a	10 43		10 48	11 00	11 02		11 13	11 30		11 43		11 48	12 00	12 02		12 13	12 30		12 43		12 48

	NT	NT B	AW ◇C	NT	NT	NT D	NT	AW ◇A	NT	NT	NT B	AW ◇C	NT	NT	NT D	NT	AW ◇A	NT	NT	NT B	AW ◇C	NT
Manchester Airport 85 ✈ d									12 41									13 41				
Manchester Piccadilly 10 d								12 50	13 01								13 50	14 01				
Manchester Oxford Road d								12 53	13 04								13 53	14 04				
Manchester Victoria d							12 39									13 39						
Eccles d							12 46									13 46						
Patricroft d							12 49									13 49						
Blackpool North 97 d		11 37									12 37									13 37		
Preston 8 65,82 d		12 04									13 04									14 04		
Leyland 82 d		12 09									13 09									14 09		
Euxton Balshaw Lane d		12 14									13 14									14 14		
Wigan North Western 65 a		12 24									13 24									14 24		
d	12 08	12 24			12 38					13 08	13 24			13 38					14 08	14 24		
Newton-le-Willows d							13 01	13 12	13 22							14 01	14 12	14 22				
Warrington Bank Quay d			12 19	12 22								13 19	13 22								14 19	14 22
Earlestown 8 d			12a26	12 34		12 50	13 04	13 15				13a26	13 34		13 50	14 04	14 15				14a26	14 34
Warrington Bank Quay a						13 01		13 25							14 01		14 25					
St Helens Junction d				12 39			13 09		13 27				13 39			14 09		14 27				14 39
Lea Green d				12 42			13 12						13 42			14 12						14 42
Rainhill d				12 46			13 16						13 46			14 16						14 46
Whiston d				12 49			13 19						13 49			14 19						14 49
Bryn d	12 15				12 45					13 15				13 45					14 15			
Garswood d	12 19				12 49					13 19				13 49					14 19			
St Helens Central a	12 25	12 39			12 55					13 25	13 39			13 55					14 25	14 39		
d	12 26	12 39			12 56					13 26	13 39			13 56					14 26	14 39		
Thatto Heath d	12 29				12 59					13 29				13 59					14 29			
Eccleston Park d	12 32				13 02					13 32				14 02					14 32			
Prescot d	12 34				13 04					13 34				14 04					14 34			
Huyton d	12 38	12 48		12 53	13 08		13 23			13 38	13 48		13 53	14 08		14 23			14 38	14 48		14 53
Roby d	12 40			12 55	13 10		13 25			13 40			13 55	14 10		14 25			14 40			14 55
Broad Green d	12 43			12 58	13 13		13 28			13 43			13 58	14 13		14 28			14 43			14 58
Wavertree Technology Park d	12 46			13 01	13 16		13 31		13 38	13 46			14 01	14 16		14 31		14 38	14 46			15 01
Edge Hill 89,91 d	12 49			13 04	13 19		13 34			13 49			14 04	14 19		14 34			14 49			15 04
Liverpool Lime Street 10 89,91 a	13 00	13 02		13 13	13 30		13 43		13 48	14 00	14 02		14 13	14 30		14 43		14 48	15 00	15 02		15 13

A To Llandudno
B To Liverpool South Parkway
C From Llandudno to Manchester Piccadilly
D From Liverpool Lime Street
E from 1 October until 19 October

Manchester, Preston, Wigan and Newton-le-Willows - St Helens and Liverpool

Network Diagram - see first Page of Table 88

	NT	NT A	NT	AW ◇B	NT	NT	NT C	AW ◇D	NT	NT	NT A	NT	AW ◇B	NT	NT	NT	AW ◇D	NT	NT	AW ◇D	NT
Manchester Airport 85 ✈ d					14 41									15 41							
Manchester Piccadilly 10 d				14 50	15 01								15 50	16 01							
Manchester Oxford Road d				14 53	15 04								15 53	16 04							
Manchester Victoria d			14 39									15 39									16 39
Eccles d			14 46									15 46									16 46
Patricroft d			14 49									15 49									16 49
Blackpool North 97 d							14 37									15 37					
Preston 8 65,82 d							15 04									16 04					
Leyland 82 d							15 09									16 09					
Euxton Balshaw Lane d							15 14									16 14					
Wigan North Western 65 a							15 24									16 24					
d	14 38					15 08	15 24			15 38					16 08	16 24			16 38		
Newton-le-Willows d			15 01	15 12	15 22							16 01	16 12	16 22							17 01
Warrington Bank Quay d								15 19	15 22								16 19	16 22		16 51	
Earlestown 8 d		14 50	15 04	15 15				15a26	15 34		15 50	16 04	16 15				16a26	16 34		16a59	17 04
Warrington Bank Quay a		15 01		15 25							16 01		16 26								
St Helens Junction d			15 09		15 27				15 39			16 09		16 27				16 39			17 09
Lea Green d			15 12						15 42			16 12						16 42			17 12
Rainhill d			15 16						15 46			16 16						16 46			17 16
Whiston d			15 19						15 49			16 19						16 49			17 19
Bryn d	14 45					15 15				15 45					16 15				16 45		
Garswood d	14 49					15 19				15 49					16 19				16 49		
St Helens Central a	14 55					15 25	15 39			15 55					16 25	16 39			16 55		
d	14 56					15 26	15 39			15 56					16 26	16 39			16 56		
Thatto Heath d	14 59					15 29				15 59					16 29				16 59		
Eccleston Park d	15 02					15 32				16 02					16 32				17 02		
Prescot d	15 04					15 34				16 04					16 34				17 04		
Huyton d	15 08		15 23			15 38	15 48		15 53	16 08		16 23			16 38	16 48		16 53	17 08		17 23
Roby d	15 10		15 25			15 40			15 55	16 10		16 25			16 40			16 55	17 10		17 25
Broad Green d	15 13		15 28			15 43			15 58	16 13		16 28			16 43			16 58	17 13		17 28
Wavertree Technology Park d	15 16		15 31		15 38	15 46			16 01	16 16		16 31		16 38	16 46			17 01	17 16		17 31
Edge Hill 89,91 d	15 19		15 34			15 49			16 04	16 19		16 34			16 49			17 04	17 19		17 34
Liverpool Lime Street 10 89,91 a	15 30		15 43		15 48	16 00	16 02		16 13	16 30		16 43		16 48	17 00	17 05		17 13	17 30		17 43

	AW ◇B	NT	NT	NT	NT	AW E	NT	AW ◇D	NT	AW ◇B	NT	NT	NT	NT	NT	NT A	AW ◇D	NT	AW E	NT	NT	NT
Manchester Airport 85 ✈ d		16 41										17 41								18 41		
Manchester Piccadilly 10 d	16 50	17 01				17 19				17 50		18 01							18 50	19 01		
Manchester Oxford Road d	16 53	17 04				17 22				17 53		18 04							18 53	19 04		
Manchester Victoria d					17 09				17 37									18 39				
Eccles d					17 16				17 46			18 11						18 46				
Patricroft d					17 19				17 49									18 49				
Blackpool North 97 d				16 35										17 37								18 37
Preston 8 65,82 d				17 04										18 04								19 04
Leyland 82 d				17 09										18 09								19 09
Euxton Balshaw Lane d				17 14										18 14								19 14
Wigan North Western 65 a				17 24										18 24								19 24
d			17 08	17 24			17 38				18 08		18 21	18 24	18 35						19 08	19 24
Newton-le-Willows d	17 12	17 22			17 31	17 40			18 01	18 12		18 24	18 33					19 01	19 12	19 22		
Warrington Bank Quay d								17 49									18 46					
Earlestown 8 d	17 15				17 34	17 44		17a57	18 04	18 15			18 36			18 50	18a57	19 04	19 16			
Warrington Bank Quay a	17 25					17 52				18 23						19 01			19 24			
St Helens Junction d		17 27			17 39				18 09			18 29	18 41					19 09		19 27		
Lea Green d					17 42				18 12			18 32	18 44					19 12				
Rainhill d					17 46				18 16			18 36	18 48					19 16				
Whiston d					17 49				18 19				18 51					19 19				
Bryn d			17 15				17 45				18 15				18 45						19 15	
Garswood d			17 19				17 49				18 19				18 49						19 19	
St Helens Central a			17 25	17 39			17 55				18 25			18 39	18 55						19 25	19 39
d			17 26	17 39			17 56				18 26			18 39	18 56						19 26	19 39
Thatto Heath d			17 29				17 59				18 29				18 59						19 29	
Eccleston Park d			17 32				18 02				18 32				19 02						19 32	
Prescot d			17 34				18 04				18 34				19 04						19 34	
Huyton d			17 38	17 48	17 53		18 08		18 23		18 38	18 41	18 55	18 48	19 08			19 23			19 38	19 48
Roby d			17 40		17 55		18 10		18 25			18 43	18 57		19 10			19 25			19 40	
Broad Green d			17 43		17 58		18 13		18 28			18 47	19 00		19 13			19 28			19 43	
Wavertree Technology Park d		17 38	17 46		18 01		18 16		18 31		18 43	18 50	19 03		19 16			19 31		19 38	19 46	
Edge Hill 89,91 d			17 49		18 04		18 19		18 34		18 46		19 06		19 19			19 35			19 49	
Liverpool Lime Street 10 89,91 a		17 48	18 00	18 04	18 13		18 30		18 43		18 56	19 00	19 15	19 04	19 30			19 43		19 48	20 00	20 04

A From Liverpool Lime Street
B To Llandudno
C To Liverpool South Parkway
D From Llandudno to Manchester Piccadilly
E To Chester

Mondays to Fridays

from 1 October

Manchester, Preston, Wigan and Newton-le-Willows - St Helens and Liverpool

Network Diagram - see first Page of Table 88

	AW	NT	NT	AW	NT		NT	NT	AW	NT	NT	AW
	A			B					◇ C ✠			B
Manchester Airport 85 ✈ d					19 41							20 32
Manchester Piccadilly ⇌ d				19 50	20 01							20 50
Manchester Oxford Road d				19 53	20 04							20 53
Manchester Victoria ⇌ d			19 39								20 39	
Eccles d			19 46								20 46	
Patricroft d			19 49								20 49	
Blackpool North 97 d								19 37				
Preston 65,82 d								20 04				
Leyland 82 d								20 09				
Euxton Balshaw Lane d								20 14				
Wigan North Western 65 a								20 24				
d							20 08	20 24		20 38		
Newton-le-Willows d			20 01	20 12	20 22						21 01	21 12
Warrington Bank Quay d	19 19	19 22							20 19			
Earlestown d	19a26	19 34	20 04	20 15					20a26		21 04	21 15
Warrington Bank Quay a				20 25								21 24
St Helens Junction d		19 39	20 09		20 27						21 09	
Lea Green d		19 42	20 12								21 12	
Rainhill d		19 46	20 16								21 16	
Whiston d		19 49	20 19								21 19	
Bryn d							20 15			20 45		
Garswood d							20 19			20 49		
St Helens Central a							20 25	20 39		20 55		
d							20 26	20 39		20 56		
Thatto Heath d							20 29			20 59		
Eccleston Park d							20 32			21 02		
Prescot d							20 34			21 04		
Huyton d		19 53	20 23				20 38	20 48		21 08	21 23	
Roby d		19 55	20 25				20 40			21 10	21 25	
Broad Green d		19 58	20 28				20 43			21 13	21 28	
Wavertree Technology Park d		20 01	20 31		20 38		20 46			21 16	21 31	
Edge Hill 89,91 d		20 04	20 34				20 49			21 19	21 34	
Liverpool Lime Street 89,91 a		20 13	20 43		20 48		21 00	21 04		21 30	21 43	

	NT	AW	NT FX		NT	AW	NT FO	AW FO	AW FO	NT FO	AW FX	NT FO
		◇ D				B		E	B		F 🚌	
Manchester Airport 85 ✈ d			21 24			21 32	21 42					
Manchester Piccadilly ⇌ d			21a38			21 50	22 01		22 12			
Manchester Oxford Road d						21 53	22 04		22 29			
Manchester Victoria ⇌ d					21 39							22 39
Eccles d					21 46							22 46
Patricroft d					21 49							22 49
Blackpool North 97 d	20 37											
Preston 65,82 d	21 04											
Leyland 82 d	21 09											
Euxton Balshaw Lane d	21 14											
Wigan North Western 65 a	21 23											
d	21 23									22 25		
Newton-le-Willows d					22 01	22 12	22 22		22 47			23 01
Warrington Bank Quay d		21 19						22 19			22 28	
Earlestown d		21a26			22 04	22 15		22a26	22 50		22a53	23 04
Warrington Bank Quay a						22 23			22 58			
St Helens Junction d					22 09		22 27					23 09
Lea Green d					22 12							23 12
Rainhill d					22 16							23 16
Whiston d					22 19							23 19
Bryn d	21 30									22 32		
Garswood d	21 34									22 36		
St Helens Central a	21 40									22 42		
d	21 41									22 43		
Thatto Heath d	21 44									22 46		
Eccleston Park d	21 47									22 49		
Prescot d	21 49									22 51		
Huyton d	21 53				22 23					22 55		23 23
Roby d	21 55				22 25					22 57		23 25
Broad Green d	21 58				22 28					23 00		23 28
Wavertree Technology Park d	22 03				22 31		22 38			23 03		23 31
Edge Hill 89,91 d	22 06				22 34					23 06		23 34
Liverpool Lime Street 89,91 a	22 16				22 43		22 48			23 17		23 43

	NT FX		NT FO	AW FX	NT FO	AW FO	NT FX	NT FX	NT FX	AW FX	AW FX
	🚌			🚌		B	🚌	🚌	🚌	F 🚌	🚌
Manchester Airport 85 ✈ d											
Manchester Piccadilly ⇌ d				22 35		23 14					23 50
Manchester Oxford Road d				22 40		23 17					23 55
Manchester Victoria ⇌ d					23 09			22 39	23 09		
Eccles d					23 16			22 58	23 28		
Patricroft d					23 19			23 08	23 38		
Blackpool North 97 d			22 14								
Preston 65,82 d			22 43								
Leyland 82 d			22 48								
Euxton Balshaw Lane d			22 53								
Wigan North Western 65 a			23 02								
d	22 25		23 03				23 15				
Newton-le-Willows d				23 10	23 31	23 36		23 38	00 08		00 25
Warrington Bank Quay d										23 59	
Earlestown d				23 20	23 34	23 39		23 46	00 16	00a24	00 35
Warrington Bank Quay a				23 45		23 47					01 00
St Helens Junction d					23 39			23 58	00 28		
Lea Green d					23 42			00 05	00 35		
Rainhill d					23 46			00 13	00 43		
Whiston d					23 49			00 23	00 53		
Bryn d	22 38		23 10								
Garswood d	22 45		23 14				23 35				
St Helens Central a	23 05		23 20				23 55				
d	23 05		23 21				23 55				
Thatto Heath d	23 15		23 24				00 05				
Eccleston Park d	23 25		23 27								
Prescot d	23 31		23 29				00 21				
Huyton d	23 41		23 33		23 53		00 31	00 33	01 03		
Roby d	23 45		23 35		23 55		00 35	00 37	01 07		
Broad Green d	23 52		23 38		23 58		00 42	00 44	01 14		
Wavertree Technology Park d	00 02		23 41		00 01		00 52	00 54	01 24		
Edge Hill 89,91 d	00 12		23 46		00 04			01 04	01 34		
Liverpool Lime Street 89,91 a	00 19		23 56		00 13		01 09	01 11	01 41		

A From Chester to Manchester Airport
B To Chester
C From Llandudno to Manchester Airport
D From Llandudno to Manchester Piccadilly
E From Chester to Manchester Piccadilly
F To Manchester Piccadilly

Saturdays

Manchester, Preston, Wigan and Newton-le-Willows - St Helens and Liverpool

Network Diagram - see first Page of Table 88

	NT	NT	NT	NT	AW	AW	NT	NT	VT		NT	AW
					A	◇ B ✠			◇ C			◇ D
Manchester Airport 85 ✈ d		04 34				05 33						
Manchester Piccadilly ⇌ d		04 49				05 50						
Manchester Oxford Road d						05 53						
Manchester Victoria ⇌ d	23p09			05 39				06 09				
Eccles d	23p16			05 46				06 16				
Patricroft d	23p19			05 49				06 19				
Blackpool North 97 d												
Preston 65,82 d									06 17			
Leyland 82 d												
Euxton Balshaw Lane d												
Wigan North Western 65 a									06 28			
d							06 08		06 28		06 38	
Newton-le-Willows d	23p31			06 01		06 12		06 31				
Warrington Bank Quay d					06 06				06a39			06 40
Earlestown d	23p34			06 04	06a12	06 15		06 34				06a47
Warrington Bank Quay a						06 25						
St Helens Junction d	23p39			06 09				06 39				
Lea Green d	23p42			06 12				06 42				
Rainhill d	23p46			06 16				06 46				
Whiston d	23p49			06 19				06 49				
Bryn d							06 15				06 45	
Garswood d							06 19				06 49	
St Helens Central a							06 25				06 55	
d			05 56				06 26				06 56	
Thatto Heath d			05 59				06 29				06 59	
Eccleston Park d			06 02				06 32				07 02	
Prescot d			06 04				06 34				07 04	
Huyton d	23p53		06 08	06 23			06 38	06 53			07 08	
Roby d	23p55		06 10	06 25			06 40	06 55			07 10	
Broad Green d	23p58		06 13	06 28			06 43	06 58			07 13	
Wavertree Technology Park d	00 01		06 16	06 31			06 46	07 01			07 16	
Edge Hill 89,91 d	00 04		06 19	06 34			06 49	07 04			07 19	
Liverpool Lime Street 89,91 a	00 13	05 32	06 28	06 43			06 58	07 13			07 28	

	NT	NT	AW	NT	NT	NT	NT		NT	AW	NT	AW
	E		◇ B ✠							F ✠		◇ B ✠
Manchester Airport 85 ✈ d				06 41								
Manchester Piccadilly ⇌ d			06 50	06 58								07 50
Manchester Oxford Road d			06 53	07 01								07 53
Manchester Victoria ⇌ d						07 09					07 39	
Eccles d						07 16					07 46	
Patricroft d						07 19					07 49	
Blackpool North 97 d									07 02			
Preston 65,82 d									07 30			
Leyland 82 d									07 35			
Euxton Balshaw Lane d									07 40			
Wigan North Western 65 a									07 50			
d		06 47			07 08		07 38		07 50			
Newton-le-Willows d		07 00	07 12	07 19		07 31					08 01	08 12
Warrington Bank Quay d										07 39		
Earlestown d	06 50	07 03	07 15			07 34				07a46	08 04	08 15
Warrington Bank Quay a	07 01		07 22									08 23
St Helens Junction d		07 09		07 24		07 39					08 09	
Lea Green d		07 12				07 42					08 12	
Rainhill d		07 16		07 29		07 46					08 16	
Whiston d		07 19				07 49					08 19	
Bryn d					07 15		07 45					
Garswood d					07 19		07 49		07 59			
St Helens Central a					07 25		07 55		08 06			
d					07 26		07 56		08 06			
Thatto Heath d					07 29		07 59					
Eccleston Park d					07 32		08 02					
Prescot d					07 34		08 04		08 12			
Huyton d		07 23		07 34	07 38	07 53	08 08		08 16		08 23	
Roby d		07 25			07 40	07 55	08 10				08 25	
Broad Green d		07 28			07 43	07 58	08 13		08 20		08 28	
Wavertree Technology Park d		07 31		07 39	07 46	08 01	08 16		08 24		08 31	
Edge Hill 89,91 d		07 34			07 49	08 04	08 19				08 34	
Liverpool Lime Street 89,91 a		07 43		07 49	07 58	08 13	08 28		08 34		08 43	

	NT	AW	NT	NT	NT		NT	NT	AW	NT	NT	NT
		G ✠			E				◇ B ✠			H
Manchester Airport 85 ✈ d										08 41		
Manchester Piccadilly ⇌ d									08 50	09 01		
Manchester Oxford Road d									08 53	09 04		
Manchester Victoria ⇌ d			08 09					08 39				
Eccles d			08 16					08 46				
Patricroft d			08 19					08 49				
Blackpool North 97 d												08 38
Preston 65,82 d												09 04
Leyland 82 d												09 09
Euxton Balshaw Lane d												09 14
Wigan North Western 65 a												09 24
d	07 58			08 28							09 08	09 24
Newton-le-Willows d			08 31					09 01	09 12	09 22		
Warrington Bank Quay d		08 08										
Earlestown d		08a15	08 34		08 50			09 04	09 15			
Warrington Bank Quay a					09 01				09 25			
St Helens Junction d			08 39					09 09		09 27		
Lea Green d			08 42					09 12				
Rainhill d			08 46					09 16				
Whiston d			08 49					09 19				
Bryn d	08 05			08 35							09 15	
Garswood d	08 09			08 39							09 19	
St Helens Central a	08 15			08 45							09 25	09 39
d	08 16			08 46			08 56				09 26	09 39
Thatto Heath d	08 19			08 49			08 59				09 29	
Eccleston Park d	08 22			08 52			09 02				09 32	
Prescot d	08 24			08 54			09 04				09 34	
Huyton d	08 28		08 53	08 58			09 08	09 23			09 38	09 48
Roby d	08 30		08 55	09 00			09 10	09 25			09 40	
Broad Green d	08 33		08 58	09 03			09 13	09 28			09 43	
Wavertree Technology Park d	08 36		09 01	09 06			09 16	09 31		09 38	09 46	
Edge Hill 89,91 d	08 39		09 04	09 09			09 19	09 34			09 49	
Liverpool Lime Street 89,91 a	08 48		09 13	09 18			09 28	09 43		09 48	09 58	10 02

	AW	NT	NT		NT	NT	AW	NT	NT	NT	AW	NT
	G ✠				E		◇ B ✠			H	G ✠	
Manchester Airport 85 ✈ d								09 41				
Manchester Piccadilly ⇌ d							09 50	10 01				
Manchester Oxford Road d							09 53	10 04				
Manchester Victoria ⇌ d						09 39						
Eccles d						09 46						
Patricroft d						09 49						
Blackpool North 97 d										09 37		
Preston 65,82 d										10 04		
Leyland 82 d										10 09		
Euxton Balshaw Lane d										10 14		
Wigan North Western 65 a										10 24		
d			09 38						10 08	10 24		
Newton-le-Willows d						10 01	10 12	10 22				
Warrington Bank Quay d	09 19	09 22									10 19	10 22
Earlestown d	09a26	09 34			09 50	10 04	10 15				10a26	10 34
Warrington Bank Quay a					10 01		10 25					
St Helens Junction d		09 39				10 09		10 27				10 39
Lea Green d		09 42				10 12						10 42
Rainhill d		09 46				10 16						10 46
Whiston d		09 49				10 19						10 49
Bryn d			09 45						10 15			
Garswood d			09 49						10 19			
St Helens Central a			09 55						10 25	10 39		
d			09 56						10 26	10 39		
Thatto Heath d			09 59						10 29			
Eccleston Park d			10 02						10 32			
Prescot d			10 04						10 34			
Huyton d		09 53	10 08			10 23			10 38	10 48		10 53
Roby d		09 55	10 10			10 25			10 40			10 55
Broad Green d		09 58	10 13			10 28			10 43			10 58
Wavertree Technology Park d		10 01	10 16			10 31		10 38	10 46			11 01
Edge Hill 89,91 d		10 04	10 21			10 34			10 49			11 04
Liverpool Lime Street 89,91 a		10 13	10 29			10 41		10 48	10 58	11 02		11 13

A From Chester to Manchester Piccadilly
B To Llandudno
C To Birmingham New Street
D From Holyhead to Manchester Piccadilly
E From Liverpool Lime Street
F From Shrewsbury to Manchester Piccadilly
G From Llandudno to Manchester Piccadilly
H To Liverpool South Parkway

Manchester, Preston, Wigan and Newton-le-Willows - St Helens and Liverpool

Network Diagram - see first Page of Table 88

	NT	NT A	NT	AW ◇ B	NT	NT	NT C	AW ◇ D	NT	NT	NT A	NT	AW ◇ B	NT	NT	NT C	AW ◇ D	NT	NT	NT A	NT
Manchester Airport 85 ✈ d					10 41									11 41							
Manchester Piccadilly 10 d				10 50	11 01								11 50	12 01							
Manchester Oxford Road d				10 53	11 04								11 53	12 04							
Manchester Victoria d			10 39									11 39									12 39
Eccles d			10 46									11 46									12 46
Patricroft d			10 49									11 49									12 49
Blackpool North 97 d							10 37									11 37					
Preston 8 65,82 d							11 04									12 04					
Leyland 82 d							11 09									12 09					
Euxton Balshaw Lane d							11 14									12 14					
Wigan North Western 65 a							11 24									12 24					
d	10 38					11 08	11 24			11 38					12 08	12 24			12 38		
Newton-le-Willows d			11 01	11 12	11 22							12 01	12 12	12 22							13 01
Warrington Bank Quay d								11 19	11 22								12 19	12 22			
Earlestown 8 d		10 50	11 04	11 15				11a26	11 34		11 50	12 04	12 15				12a26	12 34		12 50	13 04
Warrington Bank Quay a		11 01		11 25							12 01		12 25							13 01	
St Helens Junction d			11 09		11 27				11 39			12 09		12 27				12 39			13 09
Lea Green d			11 12						11 42			12 12						12 42			13 12
Rainhill d			11 16						11 46			12 16						12 46			13 16
Whiston d			11 19						11 49			12 19						12 49			13 19
Bryn d	10 45					11 15				11 45					12 15				12 45		
Garswood d	10 49					11 19				11 49					12 19				12 49		
St Helens Central a	10 55					11 25	11 39			11 55					12 25	12 39			12 55		
d	10 56					11 26	11 39			11 56					12 26	12 39			12 56		
Thatto Heath d	10 59					11 29				11 59					12 29				12 59		
Eccleston Park d	11 02					11 32				12 02					12 32				13 02		
Prescot d	11 04					11 34				12 04					12 34				13 04		
Huyton d	11 08		11 23			11 38	11 48		11 53	12 08		12 23			12 38	12 48		12 53	13 08		13 23
Roby d	11 10		11 25			11 40			11 55	12 10		12 25			12 40			12 55	13 10		13 25
Broad Green d	11 13		11 28			11 43			11 58	12 13		12 28			12 43			12 58	13 13		13 28
Wavertree Technology Park d	11 16		11 31		11 38	11 46			12 01	12 16		12 31		12 38	12 46			13 01	13 16		13 31
Edge Hill 89,91 d	11 19		11 34			11 49			12 04	12 19		12 34			12 49			13 04	13 19		13 34
Liverpool Lime Street 10 89,91 a	11 28		11 41		11 48	11 58	12 02		12 13	12 28		12 41		12 48	12 58	13 02		13 13	13 28		13 43

	AW ◇ B	NT	NT	NT C	AW ◇ D	NT	NT	NT A	NT	AW ◇ B	NT	NT	NT C	AW ◇ D	NT	NT	NT A	NT	AW ◇ B	NT	NT	NT C
Manchester Airport 85 ✈ d		12 41									13 41									14 41		
Manchester Piccadilly 10 d	12 50	13 01								13 50	14 01								14 50	15 01		
Manchester Oxford Road d	12 53	13 04								13 53	14 04								14 53	15 04		
Manchester Victoria d									13 39									14 39				
Eccles d									13 46									14 46				
Patricroft d									13 49									14 49				
Blackpool North 97 d				12 37									13 37									14 37
Preston 8 65,82 d				13 04									14 04									15 04
Leyland 82 d				13 09									14 09									15 09
Euxton Balshaw Lane d				13 14									14 14									15 14
Wigan North Western 65 a				13 24									14 24									15 24
d			13 08	13 24			13 38					14 08	14 24			14 38					15 08	15 24
Newton-le-Willows d	13 12	13 22							14 01	14 12	14 22							15 01	15 12	15 22		
Warrington Bank Quay d					13 19	13 22								14 19	14 22							
Earlestown 8 d	13 15				13a26	13 34		13 50	14 04	14 15				14a26	14 34		14 50	15 04	15 15			
Warrington Bank Quay a	13 25							14 01		14 25							15 01		15 25			
St Helens Junction d		13 27				13 39			14 09		14 27				14 39			15 09		15 27		
Lea Green d						13 42			14 12						14 42			15 12				
Rainhill d						13 46			14 16						14 46			15 16				
Whiston d						13 49			14 19						14 49			15 19				
Bryn d			13 15				13 45					14 15				14 45					15 15	
Garswood d			13 19				13 49					14 19				14 49					15 19	
St Helens Central a			13 25	13 39			13 55					14 25	14 39			14 55					15 25	15 39
d			13 26	13 39			13 56					14 26	14 39			14 56					15 26	15 39
Thatto Heath d			13 29				13 59					14 29				14 59					15 29	
Eccleston Park d			13 32				14 02					14 32				15 02					15 32	
Prescot d			13 34				14 04					14 34				15 04					15 34	
Huyton d			13 38	13 48		13 53	14 08		14 23			14 38	14 48		14 53	15 08		15 23			15 38	15 48
Roby d			13 40			13 55	14 10		14 25			14 40			14 55	15 10		15 25			15 40	
Broad Green d			13 43			13 58	14 13		14 28			14 43			14 58	15 13		15 28			15 43	
Wavertree Technology Park d		13 38	13 46			14 01	14 16		14 31		14 38	14 46			15 01	15 16		15 31		15 38	15 46	
Edge Hill 89,91 d			13 49			14 04	14 19		14 34			14 49			15 04	15 19		15 34			15 49	
Liverpool Lime Street 10 89,91 a		13 48	13 58	14 02		14 13	14 28		14 41		14 48	14 58	15 02		15 13	15 28		15 41		15 48	15 58	16 02

A From Liverpool Lime Street
B To Llandudno
C To Liverpool South Parkway
D From Llandudno to Manchester Piccadilly

Manchester, Preston, Wigan and Newton-le-Willows - St Helens and Liverpool

Network Diagram - see first Page of Table 88

	AW ◇ A	NT	NT	NT B	NT	AW ◇ C	NT	NT	NT	AW ◇ A	NT	NT	NT	AW ◇ C	NT	NT	NT	AW ◇ A	NT	NT	NT
Manchester Airport 85 ✈ d							15 41								16 41						
Manchester Piccadilly 10 d						15 50	16 01							16 50	17 01						
Manchester Oxford Road d						15 53	16 04							16 53	17 04						
Manchester Victoria d					15 39								16 39						17 09		17 39
Eccles d					15 46								16 46						17 16		17 46
Patricroft d					15 49								16 49						17 19		17 49
Blackpool North 97 d									15 37								16 35				
Preston 8 65,82 d									16 04								17 04				
Leyland 82 d									16 09								17 09				
Euxton Balshaw Lane d									16 14								17 14				
Wigan North Western 65 a									16 24								17 24				
d			15 38					16 08	16 24			16 38				17 08	17 24			17 38	
Newton-le-Willows d					16 01	16 12	16 22						17 01	17 12	17 22				17 31		18 01
Warrington Bank Quay d	15 19	15 22								16 19	16 22							17 19			
Earlestown 8 d	15a26	15 34		15 50	16 04	16 15				16a26	16 34		17 04	17 15				17a26	17 34		18 04
Warrington Bank Quay a				16 01		16 25								17 25							
St Helens Junction d		15 39			16 09		16 27				16 39		17 09		17 27				17 39		18 09
Lea Green d		15 42			16 12						16 42		17 12						17 42		18 12
Rainhill d		15 46			16 16						16 46		17 16						17 46		18 16
Whiston d		15 49			16 19						16 49		17 19						17 49		18 19
Bryn d			15 45					16 15				16 45				17 15				17 45	
Garswood d			15 49					16 19				16 49				17 19				17 49	
St Helens Central a			15 55					16 25	16 39			16 55				17 25	17 39			17 55	
d			15 56					16 26	16 39			16 56				17 26	17 39			17 56	
Thatto Heath d			15 59					16 29				16 59				17 29				17 59	
Eccleston Park d			16 02					16 32				17 02				17 32				18 02	
Prescot d			16 04					16 34				17 04				17 34				18 04	
Huyton d		15 53	16 08		16 23			16 38	16 48		16 53	17 08	17 23			17 38	17 48		17 53	18 08	18 23
Roby d		15 55	16 10		16 25			16 40			16 55	17 10	17 25			17 40			17 55	18 10	18 25
Broad Green d		15 58	16 13		16 28			16 43			16 58	17 13	17 28			17 43			17 58	18 13	18 28
Wavertree Technology Park d		16 01	16 16		16 31		16 38	16 46			17 01	17 16	17 31		17 38	17 46			18 01	18 16	18 31
Edge Hill 89,91 d		16 04	16 19		16 34			16 49			17 04	17 19	17 34			17 49			18 04	18 19	18 34
Liverpool Lime Street 10 89,91 a		16 13	16 28		16 41		16 48	16 58	17 05		17 13	17 28	17 41		17 48	17 58	18 02		18 13	18 28	18 41

	AW ◇ C	NT	NT	AW ◇ A	NT	NT	NT	NT B	NT	AW D	NT	NT	NT	AW ◇ E	NT	NT	AW D	NT	NT	NT	AW ◇ A	NT
Manchester Airport 85 ✈ d			17 41								18 41							19 41				
Manchester Piccadilly 10 d	17 50		18 01							18 50	19 01						19 50	20 01				
Manchester Oxford Road d	17 53		18 04							18 53	19 04						19 53	20 04				
Manchester Victoria d									18 39							19 39						
Eccles d			18 11						18 46							19 46						
Patricroft d									18 49							19 49						
Blackpool North 97 d						17 37							18 37							19 37		
Preston 8 65,82 d						18 04							19 04							20 04		
Leyland 82 d						18 09							19 09							20 09		
Euxton Balshaw Lane d						18 14							19 14							20 14		
Wigan North Western 65 a						18 24							19 24							20 24		
d		18 08			18 21	18 24	18 35					19 08	19 24						20 08	20 24		20 38
Newton-le-Willows d	18 12		18 24		18 33				19 01	19 12	19 22					20 01	20 12	20 22				
Warrington Bank Quay d				18 19										19 19	19 22						20 19	
Earlestown 8 d	18 15			18a26	18 36			18 50	19 04	19 16				19a26	19 34	20 04	20 15				20a26	
Warrington Bank Quay a	18 24							19 01		19 26							20 29					
St Helens Junction d			18 29		18 41				19 09		19 27				19 39	20 09		20 27				
Lea Green d			18 32		18 44				19 12						19 42	20 12						
Rainhill d			18 36		18 48				19 16						19 46	20 16						
Whiston d					18 51				19 19						19 49	20 19						
Bryn d		18 15					18 45					19 15							20 15			20 45
Garswood d		18 19					18 49					19 19							20 19			20 49
St Helens Central a		18 25				18 39	18 55					19 25	19 39						20 25	20 39		20 55
d		18 26				18 39	18 56					19 26	19 39						20 26	20 39		20 56
Thatto Heath d		18 29					18 59					19 29							20 29			20 59
Eccleston Park d		18 32					19 02					19 32							20 32			21 02
Prescot d		18 34					19 04					19 34							20 34			21 04
Huyton d		18 38	18 41		18 55	18 48	19 08		19 23			19 38	19 48		19 53	20 23			20 38	20 48		21 08
Roby d			18 43		18 57		19 10		19 25			19 40			19 55	20 25			20 40			21 10
Broad Green d			18 47		19 00		19 13		19 28			19 43			19 58	20 28			20 43			21 13
Wavertree Technology Park d		18 43	18 50		19 03		19 16		19 31		19 38	19 46			20 01	20 31		20 38	20 46			21 16
Edge Hill 89,91 d		18 46			19 06		19 19		19 34			19 49			20 04	20 34			20 49			21 19
Liverpool Lime Street 10 89,91 a		18 54	19 00		19 15	19 02	19 28		19 41		19 48	19 58	20 02		20 13	20 43		20 48	20 58	21 02		21 28

A From Llandudno to Manchester Piccadilly
B From Liverpool Lime Street
C To Llandudno
D To Chester
E From Llandudno to Manchester Airport

Table 90

Saturdays

Manchester, Preston, Wigan and Newton-le-Willows - St Helens and Liverpool

Network Diagram - see first Page of Table 88

	NT	AW	NT	AW	NT	AW	NT	AW	NT	AW	NT	NT	AW	TP	NT	AW	AW	AW
		A		◇ B		A		C		D			E 🚌	◇1 F		D	G	E 🚌
Manchester Airport 85 ✈ d		20 32					21 41							22 55				
Manchester Piccadilly 10 ⇌ d		20 50				21 50	22 01			22 26			22 26	23a09		23 14		23 14
Manchester Oxford Road d		20 53				21 53	22 04			22 29			22 31			23 17		23 19
Manchester Victoria ⇌ d	20 39				21 39						22 39				23 09			
Eccles d	20 46				21 46						22 46				23 16			
Patricroft d	20 49				21 49						22 49				23 19			
Blackpool North 97 d			20 37									22 14						
Preston 8 65,82 d			21 04									22 43						
Leyland 82 d			21 09									22 48						
Euxton Balshaw Lane d			21 14									22 53						
Wigan North Western 65 a			21 23									23 02						
d			21 23						22 25			23 03						
Newton-le-Willows d	20 59	21 12			22 01	22 12	22 22			22 47	23 01		23 01		23 31	23 36		23 49
Warrington Bank Quay d				21 19				22 19									23 50	
Earlestown 8 d	21 04	21 15		21a26	22 04	22 15		22a26		22 50	23 04		23 11		23 34	23 39	23a58	23 59
Warrington Bank Quay a		21 26				22 23				22 58			23 36			23 47		00 24
St Helens Junction d	21 09				22 09		22 27				23 09				23 39			
Lea Green d	21 12				22 12						23 12				23 42			
Rainhill d	21 16				22 16						23 16				23 46			
Whiston d	21 19				22 19						23 19				23 49			
Bryn d			21 30						22 32			23 10						
Garswood d			21 34						22 36			23 14						
St Helens Central a			21 40						22 42			23 20						
d			21 41						22 43			23 21						
Thatto Heath d			21 44						22 46			23 24						
Eccleston Park d			21 47						22 49			23 27						
Prescot d			21 49						22 51			23 29						
Huyton d	21 23		21 53		22 23				22 55		23 23	23 33			23 53			
Roby d	21 25		21 55		22 25				22 57		23 25	23 35			23 55			
Broad Green d	21 28		21 58		22 28				23 00		23 28	23 38			23 57			
Wavertree Technology Park d	21 31		22 03		22 31		22 38		23 03		23 31	23 41			00 01			
Edge Hill 89,91 d	21 34		22 06		22 34				23 06		23 34	23 46			00 04			
Liverpool Lime Street 10 89,91 a	21 43		22 14		22 43		22 48		23 15		23 43	23 54			00 13			

Sundays

until 9 September

	NT	AW	NT	NT	AW	NT	NT	AW	AW	VT	NT	AW	NT	AW	VT	NT	AW	NT	NT	AW
		A 🚌			C			◇ J	A	◇1 K ☕		C 🛒		A	◇1 K ☕		C 🛒			A 🛒
Manchester Airport 85 ✈ d				08 34			09 35						10 35					11 33		
Manchester Piccadilly 10 ⇌ d		07 28		08 49			09 50		09 56				10 50	10 55				11 50		11 56
Manchester Oxford Road d		07 33		08 52			09 53		09 59				10 53	10 59				11 53		11 59
Manchester Victoria ⇌ d	23p09																			
Eccles d	23p16			09 00			10 00						11 00					12 00		
Patricroft d	23p19																			
Blackpool North 97 d						08 50					09 50					10 50			11 50	
Preston 8 65,82 d						09 15				10 17	10 15				11 17	11 15			12 15	
Leyland 82 d						09 21					10 21					11 21			12 21	
Euxton Balshaw Lane d						09 25					10 25					11 25			12 25	
Wigan North Western 65 a						09 35				10 28	10 36				11 28	11 35			12 35	
d			08 36			09 36				10 28	10 36				11 28	11 36			12 36	
Newton-le-Willows d	23p31	08 03		09 13			10 13		10 18				11 13	11 20				12 13		12 18
Warrington Bank Quay d					09 10			10 12		10a39		11 03			11a39		12 03			
Earlestown 8 d	23p34	08 13		09 16	09a16		10 16	10a19	10 21			11a10	11 16	11 23			12a10	12 16		12 21
Warrington Bank Quay a		08 38							10 27					11 29						12 27
St Helens Junction d	23p39			09 21			10 21						11 21					12 21		
Lea Green d	23p42			09 24			10 24						11 24					12 24		
Rainhill d	23p46			09 28			10 28						11 28					12 28		
Whiston d	23p49			09 31			10 31						11 31					12 31		
Bryn d																				
Garswood d			08 46			09 46					10 46					11 46			12 46	
St Helens Central a			08 52			09 52					10 52					11 52			12 52	
d			08 53			09 53					10 53					11 53			12 53	
Thatto Heath d			08 56			09 56					10 56					11 56			12 56	
Eccleston Park d																				
Prescot d			09 00			10 00					11 00					12 00			13 00	
Huyton d	23p53		09 05	09 35		10 05	10 35				11 05		11 35			12 05		12 35	13 05	
Roby d	23p55		09 07	09 37		10 07	10 37				11 07		11 37			12 07		12 37	13 07	
Broad Green d	23p57		09 10	09 40		10 10	10 40				11 10		11 40			12 10		12 40	13 10	
Wavertree Technology Park d	00 01		09 13	09 43		10 13	10 43				11 13		11 43			12 13		12 43	13 13	
Edge Hill 89,91 d	00 04																			
Liverpool Lime Street 10 89,91 a	00 13		09 26	09 52		10 24	10 54				11 24		11 54			12 24		12 54	13 24	

A To Chester
B From Llandudno to Manchester Piccadilly
C From Chester to Manchester Piccadilly
D until 20 October. To Chester
E from 27 October. To Chester
F from 27 October
G until 20 October. From Chester to Manchester Piccadilly
J From Holyhead to Manchester Piccadilly
K To Birmingham New Street

Table 90

Sundays

until 9 September

Manchester, Preston, Wigan and Newton-le-Willows - St Helens and Liverpool

Network Diagram - see first Page of Table 88

	AW	NT	NT	AW	AW	NT	NT	AW	AW	NT	NT	AW	AW	NT	NT	AW	AW	NT	NT	AW	AW	NT
	A 🛒			B 🛒	A 🛒			B 🛒	A 🛒			B 🛒	A			B 🛒	◇ C 🛒			B	◇ C 🛒	
Manchester Airport 85 ✈ d		12 35				13 35				14 35				15 35				16 35				17 35
Manchester Piccadilly 10 ⇌ d		12 50		12 56		13 50		13 56		14 50		14 56		15 50		15 56		16 50		16 56		17 50
Manchester Oxford Road d		12 53		12 59		13 53		13 59		14 53		14 59		15 53		15 59		16 53		16 59		17 53
Manchester Victoria ⇌ d																						
Eccles d		13 00				14 00				15 00				16 00				17 00				18 00
Patricroft d																						
Blackpool North 97 d			12 50				13 50				14 50				15 50				16 50			
Preston 8 65,82 d			13 15				14 15				15 15				16 15				17 15			
Leyland 82 d			13 21				14 21				15 21				16 21				17 21			
Euxton Balshaw Lane d			13 25				14 25				15 25				16 25				17 25			
Wigan North Western 65 a			13 35				14 35				15 35				16 35				17 35			
d			13 36				14 36				15 36				16 36				17 36			
Newton-le-Willows d		13 13		13 18		14 13		14 18		15 13		15 18		16 13		16 18		17 13		17 18		18 13
Warrington Bank Quay d	13 03				14 03				15 03				16 03				17 03				18 03	
Earlestown 8 d	13a10	13 16		13 21	14a10	14 16		14 21	15a10	15 16		15 21	16a10	16 16		16 21	17a10	17 16		17 21	18a10	18 16
Warrington Bank Quay a				13 28				14 27				15 28				16 27				17 27		
St Helens Junction d		13 21				14 21				15 21				16 21				17 21				18 21
Lea Green d		13 24				14 24				15 24				16 24				17 24				18 24
Rainhill d		13 28				14 28				15 28				16 28				17 28				18 28
Whiston d		13 31				14 31				15 31				16 31				17 31				18 31
Bryn d																						
Garswood d			13 46				14 46				15 46				16 46				17 46			
St Helens Central a			13 52				14 52				15 52				16 52				17 52			
d			13 53				14 53				15 53				16 53				17 53			
Thatto Heath d			13 56				14 56				15 56				16 56				17 56			
Eccleston Park d																						
Prescot d			14 00				15 00				16 00				17 00				18 00			
Huyton d		13 35	14 05			14 35	15 05			15 35	16 05			16 35	17 05			17 35	18 05			18 35
Roby d		13 37	14 07			14 37	15 07			15 37	16 07			16 37	17 07			17 37	18 07			18 37
Broad Green d		13 40	14 10			14 40	15 10			15 40	16 10			16 40	17 10			17 40	18 10			18 40
Wavertree Technology Park d		13 43	14 13			14 43	15 13			15 43	16 13			16 43	17 13			17 43	18 13			18 43
Edge Hill 89,91 d																						
Liverpool Lime Street 10 89,91 a		13 54	14 24			14 54	15 24			15 54	16 24			16 54	17 24			17 54	18 24			18 54

	NT	AW	AW	NT	NT	AW	AW	NT	NT	AW	AW	NT	NT	AW	NT	AW	NT	AW	NT	NT
		B 🛒	A			B	A			B	A			B		B 🚌	🚌	A 🚌	🚌	🚌
Manchester Airport 85 ✈ d				18 35				19 35				20 35			21 35					
Manchester Piccadilly 10 ⇌ d		17 56		18 50		18 56		19 50		19 56		20 50		20 56	21 50	22 14				
Manchester Oxford Road d		17 59		18 53		18 59		19 53		19 59		20 53		20 59	21 53	22 19			23 00	
Manchester Victoria ⇌ d																				
Eccles d				19 00				20 00				21 00			22 00				23 15	
Patricroft d																				
Blackpool North 97 d	17 50				18 50				19 50				20 50							
Preston 8 65,82 d	18 15				19 15				20 15				21 15							
Leyland 82 d	18 21				19 21				20 21				21 21							
Euxton Balshaw Lane d	18 25				19 25				20 25				21 25							
Wigan North Western 65 a	18 35				19 35				20 35				21 35							
d	18 36				19 36				20 36				21 36				22 50			23 42
Newton-le-Willows d		18 18		19 13		19 18		20 13		20 18		21 13		21 18	22 13	22 49			23 40	
Warrington Bank Quay d			19 03				20 03				21 03							23 09		
Earlestown 8 d		18 21	19a10	19 16		19 21	20a10	20 16		20 21	21a10	21 16		21 21	22 16	22 59		23a34	23 48	
Warrington Bank Quay a		18 27				19 28				20 29				21 27		23 24				
St Helens Junction d				19 21				20 21				21 21			22 21				00 01	
Lea Green d				19 24				20 24				21 24			22 24				00 07	
Rainhill d				19 28				20 28				21 28			22 28				00 15	
Whiston d				19 31				20 31				21 31			22 31				00 25	
Bryn d																				
Garswood d	18 46				19 46				20 46				21 46				23 10			00 02
St Helens Central a	18 52				19 52				20 52				21 52				23 30			00 22
d	18 53				19 53				20 53				21 53				23 30			00 22
Thatto Heath d	18 56				19 56				20 56				21 56				23 40			00 32
Eccleston Park d																				
Prescot d	19 00				20 00				21 00				22 00				23 50			00 42
Huyton d	19 05			19 35	20 05			20 35	21 05			21 35	22 05		22 35		00 01		00 35	00 52
Roby d	19 07			19 37	20 07			20 37	21 07			21 37	22 07		22 37		00 04		00 39	00 56
Broad Green d	19 10			19 40	20 10			20 40	21 10			21 40	22 10		22 40		00 11		00 46	01 03
Wavertree Technology Park d	19 13			19 43	20 13			20 43	21 13			21 43	22 13		22 43		00 21		00 56	01 13
Edge Hill 89,91 d																				
Liverpool Lime Street 10 89,91 a	19 24			19 54	20 24			20 54	21 24			21 54	22 24		22 54		00 36		01 11	01 28

A From Chester to Manchester Piccadilly
B To Chester
C From Holyhead to Manchester Piccadilly

Sundays
16 September to 21 October

Manchester, Preston, Wigan and Newton-le-Willows - St Helens and Liverpool

Network Diagram - see first Page of Table 88

		NT	TP	AW	NT	NT	AW	TP	NT	NT		AW	AW	VT	NT	AW	NT	AW	VT	NT		AW	NT	NT	AW
			A	B			C	◇1				◇ C	B	◇1 D		C		B	◇1 D			C			B
Manchester Airport 85	d		01 20			08 34				09 35							10 35						11 33		
Manchester Piccadilly 10	d		01a45	07 28		08 49				09 50			09 56				10 50	10 55					11 50		11 56
Manchester Oxford Road	d			07 33		08 52				09 53			09 59				10 53	10 59					11 53		11 59
Manchester Victoria	d	23p09						09 15																	
Eccles	d	23p16				09 00				10 00							11 00						12 00		
Patricroft	d	23p19																							
Blackpool North 97	d								08 50						09 50					10 50				11 50	
Preston 8 65,82	d								09 15					10 17	10 15				11 17	11 15				12 15	
Leyland 82	d								09 21						10 21					11 21				12 21	
Euxton Balshaw Lane	d								09 25						10 25					11 25				12 25	
Wigan North Western 65	a								09 35					10 28	10 36				11 28	11 35				12 35	
	d				08 36				09 36					10 28	10 36				11 28	11 36				12 36	
Newton-le-Willows	d	23p31		08 03		09 13		09 33		10 13			10 18				11 13	11 20					12 13		12 18
Warrington Bank Quay	d						09 10					10 12		10a39		11 03			11a39			12 03			
Earlestown 8	d	23p34		08 13		09 16	09a16			10 16		10a19	10 21			11a10	11 16	11 23				12a10	12 16		12 21
Warrington Bank Quay	a			08 38									10 27					11 29							12 27
St Helens Junction	d	23p39				09 21				10 21							11 21						12 21		
Lea Green	d	23p42				09 24				10 24							11 24						12 24		
Rainhill	d	23p46				09 28				10 28							11 28						12 28		
Whiston	d	23p49				09 31				10 31							11 31						12 31		
Bryn	d																								
Garswood	d				08 46				09 46						10 46					11 46				12 46	
St Helens Central	a				08 52				09 52						10 52					11 52				12 52	
	d				08 53				09 53						10 53					11 53				12 53	
Thatto Heath	d				08 56				09 56						10 56					11 56				12 56	
Eccleston Park	d																								
Prescot	d				09 00				10 00						11 00					12 00				13 00	
Huyton	d	23p53			09 05	09 35			10 05	10 35					11 05		11 35			12 05			12 35	13 05	
Roby	d	23p55			09 07	09 37			10 07	10 37					11 07		11 37			12 07			12 37	13 07	
Broad Green	d	23p57			09 10	09 40			10 10	10 40					11 10		11 40			12 10			12 40	13 10	
Wavertree Technology Park	d	00 01			09 13	09 43			10 13	10 43					11 13		11 43			12 13			12 43	13 13	
Edge Hill 89,91	d	00 04																							
Liverpool Lime Street 10 89,91	a	00 13			09 26	09 52		09 56	10 24	10 54					11 24		11 54			12 24			12 54	13 24	

		AW	NT	NT	AW	AW		NT	NT	AW	AW	NT	NT	AW	AW	NT		NT	AW	AW	NT	NT	AW	AW	NT
		C			B	C				B	C			B	C				B	◇ E			B	◇ C	
Manchester Airport 85	d		12 35					13 35				14 35				15 35					16 35				17 35
Manchester Piccadilly 10	d		12 50		12 56			13 50		13 56		14 50		14 56		15 50			15 56		16 50		16 56		17 50
Manchester Oxford Road	d		12 53		12 59			13 53		13 59		14 53		14 59		15 53			15 59		16 53		16 59		17 53
Manchester Victoria	d																								
Eccles	d		13 00					14 00				15 00				16 00					17 00				18 00
Patricroft	d																								
Blackpool North 97	d			12 50					13 50				14 50					15 50				16 50			
Preston 8 65,82	d			13 15					14 15				15 15					16 15				17 15			
Leyland 82	d			13 21					14 21				15 21					16 21				17 21			
Euxton Balshaw Lane	d			13 25					14 25				15 25					16 25				17 25			
Wigan North Western 65	a			13 35					14 35				15 35					16 35				17 35			
	d			13 36					14 36				15 36					16 36				17 36			
Newton-le-Willows	d		13 13		13 18			14 13		14 18		15 13		15 18		16 13			16 18		17 13		17 18		18 13
Warrington Bank Quay	d	13 03				14 03					15 03				16 03					17 03				18 03	
Earlestown 8	d	13a10	13 16		13 21	14a10		14 16		14 21	15a10	15 16		15 21	16a10	16 16			16 21	17a10	17 16		17 21	18a10	18 16
Warrington Bank Quay	a				13 28					14 27				15 28					16 27				17 27		
St Helens Junction	d		13 21					14 21				15 21				16 21					17 21				18 21
Lea Green	d		13 24					14 24				15 24				16 24					17 24				18 24
Rainhill	d		13 28					14 28				15 28				16 28					17 28				18 28
Whiston	d		13 31					14 31				15 31				16 31					17 31				18 31
Bryn	d																								
Garswood	d			13 46					14 46				15 46					16 46				17 46			
St Helens Central	a			13 52					14 52				15 52					16 52				17 52			
	d			13 53					14 53				15 53					16 53				17 53			
Thatto Heath	d			13 56					14 56				15 56					16 56				17 56			
Eccleston Park	d																								
Prescot	d			14 00					15 00				16 00					17 00				18 00			
Huyton	d		13 35	14 05				14 35	15 05			15 35	16 05			16 35		17 05			17 35	18 05			18 35
Roby	d		13 37	14 07				14 37	15 07			15 37	16 07			16 37		17 07			17 37	18 07			18 37
Broad Green	d		13 40	14 10				14 40	15 10			15 40	16 10			16 40		17 10			17 40	18 10			18 40
Wavertree Technology Park	d		13 43	14 13				14 43	15 13			15 43	16 13			16 43		17 13			17 43	18 13			18 43
Edge Hill 89,91	d																								
Liverpool Lime Street 10 89,91	a		13 54	14 24				14 54	15 24			15 54	16 24			16 54		17 24			17 54	18 24			18 54

A To Huddersfield
B To Chester
C From Chester to Manchester Piccadilly
D To Birmingham New Street
E From Holyhead to Manchester Piccadilly

Sundays
16 September to 21 October

Manchester, Preston, Wigan and Newton-le-Willows - St Helens and Liverpool

Network Diagram - see first Page of Table 88

		NT		AW	AW	NT	NT	AW	AW	NT	NT	AW		AW	NT	NT	AW	NT	AW	NT	AW	NT		NT
				A	B			A	B			A		B			A		A		B			
Manchester Airport 85	d					18 35				19 35					20 35			21 35						
Manchester Piccadilly 10	d			17 56		18 50		18 56		19 50		19 56			20 50		20 56	21 50	22 14					
Manchester Oxford Road	d			17 59		18 53		18 59		19 53		19 59			20 53		20 59	21 53	22 19			23 00		
Manchester Victoria	d																							
Eccles	d					19 00				20 00					21 00			22 00				23 15		
Patricroft	d																							
Blackpool North 97	d	17 50					18 50				19 50					20 50								
Preston 8 65,82	d	18 15					19 15				20 15					21 15								
Leyland 82	d	18 21					19 21				20 21					21 21								
Euxton Balshaw Lane	d	18 25					19 25				20 25					21 25								
Wigan North Western 65	a	18 35					19 35				20 35					21 35								
	d	18 36					19 36				20 36					21 36				22 50				23 42
Newton-le-Willows	d			18 18		19 13		19 18		20 13		20 18			21 13		21 18	22 13	22 49			23 40		
Warrington Bank Quay	d				19 03				20 03					21 03							23 09			
Earlestown 8	d			18 21	19a10	19 16		19 21	20a10	20 16		20 21		21a10	21 16		21 21	22 16	22 59		23a34	23 48		
Warrington Bank Quay	a			18 27				19 28				20 29					21 27		23 24					
St Helens Junction	d					19 21				20 21					21 21			22 21				00 01		
Lea Green	d					19 24				20 24					21 24			22 24				00 07		
Rainhill	d					19 28				20 28					21 28			22 28				00 15		
Whiston	d					19 31				20 31					21 31			22 31				00 25		
Bryn	d																							
Garswood	d	18 46					19 46				20 46					21 46				23 10				00 02
St Helens Central	a	18 52					19 52				20 52					21 52				23 30				00 22
	d	18 53					19 53				20 53					21 53				23 30				00 22
Thatto Heath	d	18 56					19 56				20 56					21 56				23 40				00 32
Eccleston Park	d																							
Prescot	d	19 00					20 00				21 00					22 00				23 50				00 42
Huyton	d	19 05				19 35	20 05			20 35	21 05				21 35	22 05		22 35		00 01		00 35		00 52
Roby	d	19 07				19 37	20 07			20 37	21 07				21 37	22 07		22 37		00 04		00 39		00 56
Broad Green	d	19 10				19 40	20 10			20 40	21 10				21 40	22 10		22 40		00 11		00 46		01 03
Wavertree Technology Park	d	19 13				19 43	20 13			20 43	21 13				21 43	22 13		22 43		00 21		00 56		01 13
Edge Hill 89,91	d																							
Liverpool Lime Street 10 89,91	a	19 24				19 54	20 24			20 54	21 24				21 54	22 24		22 54		00 36		01 11		01 28

Sundays
from 28 October

		NT	AW	AW		AW	NT	NT	AW	NT		AW	NT	AW	NT	AW	NT	AW	NT	AW		NT	AW	AW	NT
			A	B		A			A			B		A		B		A		B			A	B	
Manchester Airport 85	d							08 34					09 35				10 35					11 33			
Manchester Piccadilly 10	d		23p14			07 28		08 49	08 49				09 50	09 47			10 50	10 45				11 50	11 45		
Manchester Oxford Road	d		23p19			07 33		08 52	08 54				09 53	09 52			10 53	10 50				11 53	11 50		
Manchester Victoria	d	23p09																							
Eccles	d	23p16						09 00					10 00				11 00					12 00			
Patricroft	d	23p19																							
Blackpool North 97	d																								
Preston 8 65,82	d																								
Leyland 82	d																								
Euxton Balshaw Lane	d																								
Wigan North Western 65	a																								
	d						08 36			09 36					10 36				11 36						12 36
Newton-le-Willows	d	23p31	23p49			08 03		09 13	09 24				10 13	10 22			11 13	11 20				12 13	12 20		
Warrington Bank Quay	d			00 22								09 41				10 49				11 40				12 36	
Earlestown 8	d	23p34	23p59	00a47		08 13		09 16	09 34			10a06	10 16	10 32		11a14	11 16	11 30		12a05		12 16	12 30	13a01	
Warrington Bank Quay	a		00 24			08 38			09 59					10 57				11 55					12 55		
St Helens Junction	d	23p39						09 21					10 21				11 21					12 21			
Lea Green	d	23p42						09 24					10 24				11 24					12 24			
Rainhill	d	23p46						09 28					10 28				11 28					12 28			
Whiston	d	23p49						09 31					10 31				11 31					12 31			
Bryn	d																								
Garswood	d						08 46			09 46					10 46				11 46						12 46
St Helens Central	a						08 52			09 52					10 52				11 52						12 52
	d						08 53			09 53					10 53				11 53						12 53
Thatto Heath	d						08 56			09 56					10 56				11 56						12 56
Eccleston Park	d																								
Prescot	d						09 00			10 00					11 00				12 00						13 00
Huyton	d	23p53					09 05	09 35		10 05			10 35		11 05		11 35		12 05			12 35			13 05
Roby	d	23p55					09 07	09 37		10 07			10 37		11 07		11 37		12 07			12 37			13 07
Broad Green	d	23p57					09 10	09 40		10 10			10 40		11 10		11 40		12 10			12 40			13 10
Wavertree Technology Park	d	00 01					09 13	09 43		10 13			10 43		11 13		11 43		12 13			12 43			13 13
Edge Hill 89,91	d	00 04																							
Liverpool Lime Street 10 89,91	a	00 13					09 26	09 52		10 24			10 54		11 24		11 54		12 24			12 54			13 24

A To Chester
B From Chester to Manchester Piccadilly

Sundays
from 28 October

Manchester, Preston, Wigan and Newton-le-Willows - St Helens and Liverpool

Network Diagram - see first Page of Table 88

Station		NT	AW	AW	NT	NT		NT	AW	NT	NT	AW	AW	NT	NT	AW		AW	NT	NT	AW	AW	NT	NT	AW
			A ═	B ═					B ⌶			A ⌶	B			A ⌶		◇ C ⌶			A	◇ B			A ⌶
Manchester Airport 85 ✈	d	12 35				13 35				14 35				15 35					16 35				17 35		
Manchester Piccadilly 10 ⇌	d	12 50	12 45			13 50				14 50		14 56		15 50		15 56			16 50		16 56		17 50		17 56
Manchester Oxford Road	d	12 53	12 50			13 53				14 53		14 59		15 53		15 59			16 53		16 59		17 53		17 59
Manchester Victoria ⇌	d																								
Eccles	d	13 00				14 00				15 00				16 00					17 00				18 00		
Patricroft	d																								
Blackpool North 97	d										14 50				15 50					16 50				17 50	
Preston 8 65,82	d										15 15				16 15					17 15				18 15	
Leyland 82	d										15 21				16 21					17 21				18 21	
Euxton Balshaw Lane	d										15 25				16 25					17 25				18 25	
Wigan North Western 65	a										15 35				16 35					17 35				18 35	
	d				13 36			14 36			15 36				16 36					17 36				18 36	
Newton-le-Willows	d	13 13	13 20			14 13				15 13		15 18		16 13		16 18			17 13		17 18		18 13		18 18
Warrington Bank Quay	d			13 36					15 03				16 03					17 03				18 03			
Earlestown 8	d	13 16	13 30	14a01		14 16			15a10	15 16		15 21	16a10	16 16		16 21		17a10	17 16		17 21	18a10	18 16		18 21
Warrington Bank Quay	a		13 55									15 28				16 27					17 27				18 27
St Helens Junction	d	13 21				14 21				15 21				16 21					17 21				18 21		
Lea Green	d	13 24				14 24				15 24				16 24					17 24				18 24		
Rainhill	d	13 28				14 28				15 28				16 28					17 28				18 28		
Whiston	d	13 31				14 31				15 31				16 31					17 31				18 31		
Bryn	d																								
Garswood	d				13 46			14 46			15 46				16 46					17 46				18 46	
St Helens Central	a				13 52			14 52			15 52				16 52					17 52				18 52	
	d				13 53			14 53			15 53				16 53					17 53				18 53	
Thatto Heath	d				13 56			14 56			15 56				16 56					17 56				18 56	
Eccleston Park	d																								
Prescot	d				14 00			15 00			16 00				17 00					18 00				19 00	
Huyton	d	13 35			14 05	14 35		15 05		15 35	16 05			16 35	17 05				17 35	18 05			18 35	19 05	
Roby	d	13 37			14 07	14 37		15 07		15 37	16 07			16 37	17 07				17 37	18 07			18 37	19 07	
Broad Green	d	13 40			14 10	14 40		15 10		15 40	16 10			16 40	17 10				17 40	18 10			18 40	19 10	
Wavertree Technology Park	d	13 43			14 13	14 43		15 13		15 43	16 13			16 43	17 13				17 43	18 13			18 43	19 13	
Edge Hill 89,91	d																								
Liverpool Lime Street 10 89,91	a	13 54			14 24	14 54		15 24		15 54	16 24			16 54	17 24				17 54	18 24			18 54	19 24	

Station		AW		NT	NT	AW	AW	NT	NT	AW	AW	NT		NT	AW	NT	AW	NT	AW	NT	NT
		B				A	B			A	B				A		A ═	═	B ═	═	═
Manchester Airport 85 ✈	d			18 35				19 35				20 35				21 35					
Manchester Piccadilly 10 ⇌	d			18 50		18 56		19 50		19 56		20 50			20 56	21 50	22 14				
Manchester Oxford Road	d			18 53		18 59		19 53		19 59		20 53			20 59	21 53	22 19			23 00	
Manchester Victoria ⇌	d																				
Eccles	d			19 00				20 00				21 00				22 00				23 15	
Patricroft	d																				
Blackpool North 97	d				18 50				19 50					20 50							
Preston 8 65,82	d				19 15				20 15					21 15							
Leyland 82	d				19 21				20 21					21 21							
Euxton Balshaw Lane	d				19 25				20 25					21 25							
Wigan North Western 65	a				19 35				20 35					21 35							
	d				19 36				20 36					21 36				22 50			23 42
Newton-le-Willows	d			19 13		19 18		20 13		20 18		21 13			21 18	22 13	22 49			23 40	
Warrington Bank Quay	d	19 03					20 03				21 03								23 09		
Earlestown 8	d	19a10		19 16		19 21	20a10	20 16		20 21	21a10	21 16			21 21	22 16	22 59		23a34	23 48	
Warrington Bank Quay	a					19 28				20 29					21 27		23 24				
St Helens Junction	d			19 21				20 21				21 21				22 21				00 01	
Lea Green	d			19 24				20 24				21 24				22 24				00 07	
Rainhill	d			19 28				20 28				21 28				22 28				00 15	
Whiston	d			19 31				20 31				21 31				22 31				00 25	
Bryn	d																				
Garswood	d				19 46				20 46					21 46				23 10			00 02
St Helens Central	a				19 52				20 52					21 52				23 30			00 22
	d				19 53				20 53					21 53				23 30			00 22
Thatto Heath	d				19 56				20 56					21 56				23 40			00 32
Eccleston Park	d																				
Prescot	d				20 00				21 00					22 00				23 50			00 42
Huyton	d			19 35	20 05			20 35	21 05			21 35		22 05		22 35		00 01		00 35	00 52
Roby	d			19 37	20 07			20 37	21 07			21 37		22 07		22 37		00 04		00 39	00 56
Broad Green	d			19 40	20 10			20 40	21 10			21 40		22 10		22 40		00 11		00 46	01 03
Wavertree Technology Park	d			19 43	20 13			20 43	21 13			21 43		22 13		22 43		00 21		00 56	01 13
Edge Hill 89,91	d																				
Liverpool Lime Street 10 89,91	a			19 54	20 24			20 54	21 24			21 54		22 24		22 54		00 36		01 11	01 28

A To Chester
B From Chester to Manchester Piccadilly
C From Holyhead to Manchester Piccadilly

Liverpool - Runcorn and Crewe

Network Diagram - see first Page of Table 88

Miles	Station		LM	VT	NT	VT	TP	NT	LM	EM	NT		VT	LM	TP	NT	LM	EM	NT	VT	LM		TP	NT	LM
			MX ◇1	◇1 ⊠	A	◇1 ⊠	◇1 B ⌶	C	◇1	◇ D	A		◇1 ⊠	◇1	◇1 B ⌶	C	◇1	◇ D	C	◇1 ⊠	◇1		◇1 B ⌶	C	◇1
0	Liverpool Lime Street 10 90	d	23p34	05 27	05 49	06 05	06 15	06 21	06 30	06 47	06 50		07 00	07 04	07 15	07 26	07 34	07 42	07 45	07 48	08 04		08 22	08 26	08 34
1¾	Edge Hill 90	d			05 53						06 54					07 30								08 30	
3¾	Mossley Hill	d			05 58			06 29			06 59					07 35			07 53					08 35	
4½	West Allerton	d			06 00			06 31			07 01					07 37			07 56					08 37	
5½	Liverpool South Parkway 7 ✈	a	23p44		06 03		06 25	06 34	06 39	06 57	07 04			07 13	07 25	07 40	07 43	07 52	07 59		08 15		08 32	08 40	08 43
—		d	23p45						06 40					07 14			07 44				08 15				08 44
13	Runcorn	a	23p53	05 42		06 20			06 47					07 21			07 51			08 03	08 24				08 51
—		d	23p53	05 43		06 21			06 48				07u15	07 22			07 52			08 04	08 24				08 52
21	Acton Bridge	d	00 02						06 57					07 32							08 34				09 02
23¾	Hartford	d	00 07						07 02					07 36			08 04								09 06
28	Winsford	d	00 11						07 06								08 08								
35½	Crewe 10 65	a	00 22	06 00					07 14					07 48			08 19				08 47				09 20
—	Birmingham New Street 12 65	a							08 17					08 47			09 18				09 47				10 17
—	London Euston ⊖65	a		07 50		08 22							09 01							09 56					

Station		VT	EM	NT	LM	TP	NT		LM	VT	EM	NT	LM	NT	TP	NT	LM		VT	EM	NT	LM	NT	TP	NT
		◇1 ⊠	◇ D	C	◇1	◇1 B ⌶	C		◇1	◇1 ⊠	◇ D	C	◇1	E	◇1 B ⌶	C	◇1		◇1 ⊠	◇ D	C	◇1	F	◇1 B ⌶	C
Liverpool Lime Street 10 90	d	08 48	08 52	08 55	09 04	09 22	09 27		09 34	09 48	09 52	09 55	10 04	10 16	10 22	10 27	10 34		10 48	10 52	10 55	11 04	11 16	11 22	11 27
Edge Hill 90	d			08 59								09 59									10 59				
Mossley Hill	d			09 04			09 35					10 04				10 35					11 04				11 35
West Allerton	d			09 06			09 37					10 06				10 37					11 06				11 37
Liverpool South Parkway 7 ✈	a		09 02	09 09	09 15	09 32	09 40		09 43		10 02	10 09	10 15	10 27	10 32	10 40	10 43			11 02	11 09	11 15	11 27	11 32	11 40
	d				09 15				09 44				10 15				10 44					11 15			
Runcorn	a	09 03			09 24				09 51	10 03			10 24				10 51		11 03			11 24			
	d	09 04			09 25				09 52	10 04			10 25				10 52		11 04			11 25			
Acton Bridge	d																								
Hartford	d								10 04								11 04								
Winsford	d								10 08								11 08								
Crewe 10 65	a				09 44				10 19				10 45				11 19					11 45			
Birmingham New Street 12 65	a				10 47				11 18				11 47				12 17					12 47			
London Euston ⊖65	a	10 56								11 56									12 56						

Station		LM	VT		EM	NT	LM	NT	TP	NT	LM	VT	EM		NT	LM	NT	TP	NT	LM	VT	EM	NT		LM
		◇1	◇1 ⊓		◇ D	C	◇1	F	◇1 B ⌶	C	◇1	◇1 ⊓	◇ D		C	◇1	F	◇1 B ⌶	C	◇1	◇1 ⊓	◇ D	C		1
Liverpool Lime Street 10 90	d	11 34	11 48		11 52	11 55	12 04	12 16	12 22	12 27	12 34	12 48	12 52		12 55	13 04	13 16	13 22	13 27	13 34	13 48	13 52	13 55		14 04
Edge Hill 90	d					11 59									12 59								13 59		
Mossley Hill	d					12 04				12 35					13 04				13 35				14 04		
West Allerton	d					12 06				12 37					13 06				13 37				14 06		
Liverpool South Parkway 7 ✈	a	11 43			12 02	12 09	12 15	12 27	12 32	12 40	12 43		13 02		13 09	13 15	13 27	13 32	13 40	13 43		14 02	14 09		14 15
	d	11 44					12 15				12 44					13 15				13 44					14 15
Runcorn	a	11 51	12 03				12 24				12 51	13 03				13 24				13 51	14 03				14 24
	d	11 52	12 04				12 25				12 52	13 04				13 25				13 52	14 04				14 25
Acton Bridge	d										13 02														
Hartford	d	12 04									13 06									14 04					
Winsford	d	12 08																		14 08					
Crewe 10 65	a	12 19					12 45				13 20					13 45				14 19					14 45
Birmingham New Street 12 65	a	13 17					13 47				14 17					14 47				15 20					15 47
London Euston ⊖65	a		13 56									14 56									15 56				

Station		NT	TP	NT	LM	VT	EM	NT	LM		NT	TP	NT	LM	VT	EM	NT	LM	NT		TP	NT	LM	VT	EM
		F	◇1 B ⌶	C	◇1	◇1 ⊓	◇ D	C	◇1		F	◇1 G ⌶	C	◇1	◇1 ⊓	◇ D	C	◇1	F		◇1 B ⌶	C	◇1	◇1 ⊓	◇ H
Liverpool Lime Street 10 90	d	14 16	14 22	14 27	14 34	14 48	14 52	14 55	15 04		15 16	15 22	15 27	15 34	15 48	15 52	15 55	16 04	16 16		16 22	16 27	16 34	16 48	16 52
Edge Hill 90	d							14 59									15 59								
Mossley Hill	d			14 35				15 04					15 35				16 04					16 35			
West Allerton	d			14 37				15 06					15 37				16 06					16 37			
Liverpool South Parkway 7 ✈	a	14 27	14 32	14 40	14 43		15 02	15 09	15 15		15 27	15 32	15 40	15 43		16 02	16 09	16 15	16 27		16 32	16 40	16 43		17 02
	d				14 44				15 15					15 44				16 15					16 44		
Runcorn	a				14 51	15 03			15 24					15 51	16 03			16 24					16 52	17 03	
	d				14 52	15 04			15 25					15 52	16 04			16 25					16 52	17 04	
Acton Bridge	d																						17 01		
Hartford	d				15 04									16 04									17 06		
Winsford	d				15 08									16 08											
Crewe 10 65	a				15 19				15 45					16 19				16 45					17 19		
Birmingham New Street 12 65	a				16 17				16 47					17 20				17 47					18 17		
London Euston ⊖65	a					16 59									17 56									18 59	

A To Warrington Central
B To Scarborough
C To Manchester Oxford Road
D To Norwich
E From Preston
F From Blackpool North
G To Middlesbrough
H To Nottingham

Table 91

Mondays to Fridays

Liverpool - Runcorn and Crewe

Network Diagram - see first Page of Table 88

	NT	LM	TP	NT	LM	VT	EM	NT	LM	TP	NT	LM	VT	EM	NT	LM	TP	LM	VT	EM	NT	LM
		◇1	◇1		◇1	◇1	◇		◇1	◇1		◇1	◇1	◇		◇1	◇1	◇1	◇1	◇		◇1
	A		B	A			C	A		B	A			D	E		F			D	E	
			⌶			⊠							⊠						⊡			
Liverpool Lime Street 10 90 d	16 55	17 04	17 22	17 25	17 34	17 48	17 52	17 55	18 04	18 22	18 25	18 34	18 48	18 52	18 55	19 11	19 22	19 34	19 48	19 52	19 55	20 04
Edge Hill 90 d	16 59			17 29				17 59			18 29				18 59						19 59	
Mossley Hill d	17 04			17 34				18 04			18 34				19 04						20 04	
West Allerton d	17 06			17 36				18 06			18 36				19 06						20 06	
Liverpool South Parkway 7 ✈ a	17 09	17 15	17 32	17 39	17 43		18 02	18 09	18 14	18 32	18 39	18 43		19 02	19 09	19 20	19 32	19 43		20 02	20 09	20 15
d		17 15			17 44				18 15			18 44				19 21		19 44				20 15
Runcorn a		17 24			17 51	18 03			18 24			18 51	19 03			19 28		19 51	20 03			20 24
d		17 25			17 52	18 04			18 24			18 52	19 04			19 29		19 52	20 04			20 24
Acton Bridge d					18 01											19 40						
Hartford d					18 06							19 04						20 04				
Winsford d		17 39							18 38			19 08						20 08				
Crewe 10 65 a		17 47			18 20				18 47			19 16	19 21			19 53		20 16	20 21			20 45
Birmingham New Street 12 65 a		18 48			19 17				19 48			20 18				20 47		21 18				21 47
London Euston ⊖65 a						20 02							21 05						22 09			

	TP	LM	VT	NT	LM	EM	NT	TP	LM	LM	NT
	◇1	◇1	◇1		◇1	◇		◇1	◇1	◇1	
	G			A		D	A	G			H
			⊡								
Liverpool Lime Street 10 90 d	20 22	20 34	20 48	20 55	21 34	21 37	21 55	22 30	22 34	23 34	23 38
Edge Hill 90 d				20 59			21 59				23 42
Mossley Hill d				21 04			22 04				23 47
West Allerton d				21 06			22 06				23 50
Liverpool South Parkway 7 ✈ a	20 32	20 43		21 09	21 43	21 47	22 09	22 40	22 44	23 44	23 53
d		20 44			21 44				22 45	23 45	
Runcorn a		20 51	21 03		21 51				22 54	23 53	
d		20 52	21 04		21 52				22 54	23 53	
Acton Bridge d									23 03	00 02	
Hartford d		21 04			22 04				23 08	00 07	
Winsford d		21 08			22 08				23 12	00 11	
Crewe 10 65 a		21 16	21 21		22 18				23 21	00 22	
Birmingham New Street 12 65 a		22 17			23 18						
London Euston ⊖65 a			23 56								

Saturdays

	LM	VT	NT	TP	NT	LM	VT	EM	NT	LM	TP	VT	NT	LM	EM	NT	VT	LM	TP	NT	LM	VT
	◇1	◇1		◇1		◇1	◇1	◇		◇1	◇1	◇1		◇1	◇		◇1	◇1	◇1		◇1	◇1
			E	B	A			C	E		B		A		C	A			B	A		
		⊡		⌶			⊡				⌶	⊡					⊡		⌶			⊡
Liverpool Lime Street 10 90 d	23p34	05 47	05 49	06 15	06 25	06 32	06 45	06 49	06 55	07 04	07 15	07 19	07 26	07 34	07 42	07 45	07 48	08 04	08 22	08 26	08 34	08 48
Edge Hill 90 d			05 53						06 59				07 30							08 30		
Mossley Hill d			05 58		06 33				07 04				07 35			07 53				08 35		
West Allerton d			06 00		06 35				07 06				07 37			07 56				08 37		
Liverpool South Parkway 7 ✈ a	23p44		06 03	06 25	06 38	06 41		06 59	07 09	07 14	07 25		07 40	07 43	07 52	07 59		08 14	08 32	08 40	08 43	
d	23p45					06 42				07 14				07 44				08 15			08 44	
Runcorn a	23p53	06 02				06 49	07 00			07 22		07 35		07 51			08 03	08 24			08 51	09 03
d	23p53	06 03				06 50	07 01			07 22		07 36		07 52			08 04	08 24			08 52	09 04
Acton Bridge d	00 02									07 32								08 34			09 02	
Hartford d	00 07					07 02				07 36				08 04							09 06	
Winsford d	00 11					07 06								08 08								
Crewe 10 65 a	00 22					07 14	07 18			07 47		07 52		08 19				08 47			09 20	
Birmingham New Street 12 65 a						08 17				08 47				09 18				09 47			10 17	
London Euston ⊖65 a		08 05					08 59					09 46					10 00					11 01

	EM	NT	LM	TP	NT	LM	VT	EM	NT	LM	NT	TP	NT	LM	VT	EM	NT	LM	NT	TP	NT	LM
	◇		◇1	◇1		◇1	◇1	◇		◇1		◇1		◇1	◇1	◇		◇1		◇1		◇1
	C	A		B	A			C	A		I	B	A			C	A		I	B	A	
				⌶			⊡					⌶			⊡					⌶		
Liverpool Lime Street 10 90 d	08 52	08 55	09 04	09 22	09 27	09 34	09 48	09 52	09 55	10 04	10 16	10 22	10 27	10 34	10 48	10 52	10 55	11 04	11 16	11 22	11 27	11 34
Edge Hill 90 d		08 59							09 59								10 59					
Mossley Hill d		09 04			09 35				10 04				10 35				11 04				11 35	
West Allerton d		09 06			09 37				10 06				10 37				11 06				11 37	
Liverpool South Parkway 7 ✈ a	09 02	09 09	09 15	09 32	09 40	09 43		10 02	10 09	10 15	10 27	10 32	10 40	10 43		11 02	11 09	11 15	11 27	11 32	11 40	11 43
d			09 15			09 44				10 15				10 44				11 15				11 44
Runcorn a			09 24			09 51	10 03			10 24				10 51	11 03			11 24				11 51
d			09 24			09 52	10 04			10 25				10 52	11 04			11 25				11 52
Acton Bridge d																						
Hartford d						10 04								11 04								12 04
Winsford d						10 08								11 08								12 08
Crewe 10 65 a			09 44			10 19				10 45				11 19				11 45				12 19
Birmingham New Street 12 65 a			10 47			11 17				11 47				12 17				12 47				13 17
London Euston ⊖65 a							11 56								12 56							

A To Manchester Oxford Road
B To Scarborough
C To Norwich
D To Nottingham
E To Warrington Central
F To Hull
G To York
H To Manchester Piccadilly
I From Blackpool North

Table 91

Saturdays

Liverpool - Runcorn and Crewe

Network Diagram - see first Page of Table 88

	VT	EM	NT	LM	NT	TP	NT	LM	VT	EM	NT	LM	NT	TP	NT	LM	VT	EM	NT	LM	NT
	◇1	◇		◇1		◇1		◇1	◇1	◇		◇1		◇1		◇1	◇1	◇		◇1	
		A	B		C	D	B			A	B		C	D	B			A	B		C
	⊡					⌶			⊡					⌶			⊡				
Liverpool Lime Street 10 90 d	11 48	11 52	11 55	12 04	12 16	12 22	12 27	12 34	12 48	12 52	12 55	13 04	13 16	13 22	13 27	13 34	13 48	13 52	13 55	14 04	14 16
Edge Hill 90 d			11 59								12 59								13 59		
Mossley Hill d			12 04				12 35				13 04				13 35				14 04		
West Allerton d			12 06				12 37				13 06				13 37				14 06		
Liverpool South Parkway 7 ✈ a		12 02	12 09	12 15	12 27	12 32	12 40	12 43		13 02	13 09	13 15	13 27	13 32	13 40	13 43		14 02	14 09	14 15	14 27
d				12 15				12 44				13 15				13 44				14 15	
Runcorn a	12 03			12 24				12 51	13 03			13 24				13 51	14 03			14 24	
d	12 04			12 25				12 52	13 04			13 25				13 52	14 04			14 25	
Acton Bridge d								13 02													
Hartford d								13 06								14 04					
Winsford d																14 08					
Crewe 10 65 a				12 45				13 20				13 45				14 19				14 45	
Birmingham New Street 12 65 a				13 47				14 17				14 47				15 18				15 47	
London Euston ⊖65 a	13 56								14 56								15 56				

	TP	NT	LM	VT	EM	NT	LM	NT	TP	NT	LM	VT	EM	NT	LM	NT	TP	NT	LM	VT	EM	NT
	◇1		◇1	◇1	◇		◇1		◇1		◇1	◇1	◇		◇1		◇1		◇1	◇1	◇	
	D	B			A	B		C	D	B			A	B		C	D	B			E	B
	⌶			⊡								⊡								⊡		
Liverpool Lime Street 10 90 d	14 22	14 27	14 34	14 48	14 52	14 55	15 04	15 16	15 22	15 27	15 34	15 48	15 52	15 55	16 04	16 16	16 22	16 27	16 34	16 48	16 52	16 55
Edge Hill 90 d						14 59								15 59								16 59
Mossley Hill d		14 35				15 04				15 35				16 04				16 35				17 04
West Allerton d		14 37				15 06				15 37				16 06				16 37				17 06
Liverpool South Parkway 7 ✈ a	14 32	14 40	14 43		15 02	15 09	15 15	15 27	15 32	15 40	15 43		16 02	16 09	16 15	16 27	16 32	16 40	16 43		17 02	17 09
d			14 44				15 15				15 44				16 15				16 44			
Runcorn a			14 51	15 03			15 24				15 51	16 03			16 24				16 51	17 03		
d			14 52	15 04			15 25				15 52	16 04			16 25				16 52	17 04		
Acton Bridge d																			17 02			
Hartford d			15 04								16 04								17 06			
Winsford d			15 08								16 08											
Crewe 10 65 a			15 19				15 45				16 19				16 45				17 20			
Birmingham New Street 12 65 a			16 17				16 47				17 18				17 47				18 17			
London Euston ⊖65 a				16 56								17 56								18 56		

	LM	TP	NT	LM	VT	EM	NT	LM	TP	NT	LM	VT	EM	NT	LM	TP	LM	VT	VT	EM	NT
	◇1	◇1		◇1	◇1	◇		◇1	◇1		◇1	◇1	◇		◇1	◇1	◇1	◇1	◇1	◇	
		D	B			A	B		D	B			E	F		G		H	I	E	F
					⊡							⊡						⊡	⊡		
Liverpool Lime Street 10 90 d	17 04	17 22	17 25	17 34	17 48	17 52	17 55	18 04	18 22	18 25	18 34	18 48	18 52	18 55	19 04	19 22	19 34	19 48	19 48	19 52	19 55
Edge Hill 90 d			17 29				17 59			18 29				18 59							19 59
Mossley Hill d			17 34				18 04			18 34				19 04							20 04
West Allerton d			17 36				18 06			18 36				19 06							20 06
Liverpool South Parkway 7 ✈ a	17 15	17 32	17 39	17 43		18 02	18 09	18 14	18 32	18 39	18 43		19 02	19 09	19 14	19 32	19 43			20 02	20 09
d	17 15			17 44				18 15			18 44				19 14		19 44				
Runcorn a	17 24			17 51	18 03			18 24			18 51	19 03			19 23		19 51	20 03	20 03		
d	17 25			17 52	18 04			18 24			18 52	19 04			19 23		19 52	20 04	20 04		
Acton Bridge d				18 02											19 36						
Hartford d				18 06							19 04						20 04				
Winsford d	17 39							18 38			19 08						20 08				
Crewe 10 65 a	17 47			18 20				18 46			19 19				19 49		20 16		20b23		
Birmingham New Street 12 65 a	18 47			19 17				19 47			20 17				20 47		21 19				
London Euston ⊖65 a					19 56							21 15						22 14	22 14		

	TP	LM	EM	NT	LM	EM	NT	LM	TP	NT
	◇1	◇1	◇		◇1	◇		1	◇1	
	G		E	B		E	B		G	J
Liverpool Lime Street 10 90 d	20 22	20 34	20 52	20 55	21 34	21 37	21 55	22 04	22 30	23 38
Edge Hill 90 d				20 59			21 59			23 42
Mossley Hill d				21 04			22 04			23 47
West Allerton d				21 06			22 06			23 49
Liverpool South Parkway 7 ✈ a	20 32	20 43	21 02	21 09	21 43	21 47	22 09	22 14	22 40	23 52
d		20 44			21 44			22 14		
Runcorn a		20 51			21 51			22 22		
d		20 52			21 52			22 23		
Acton Bridge d										
Hartford d		21 03			22 04			22 34		
Winsford d		21 08			22 08			22 39		
Crewe 10 65 a		21 16			22 21			22 48		
Birmingham New Street 12 65 a		22 20			23 21					
London Euston ⊖65 a										

A To Norwich
B To Manchester Oxford Road
C From Blackpool North
D To Scarborough
E To Nottingham
F To Warrington Central
G To York
H until 30 June, from 15 September
I from 7 July until 8 September
J To Manchester Piccadilly
b Stops to pick up only

Table 91

Liverpool - Runcorn and Crewe

Sundays until 24 June

Network Diagram - see first Page of Table 88

	VT ◇1 ☕	NT A	VT ◇1 ☕	NT A	VT ◇1 ☕	NT A	VT ◇1 ☕	NT A	LM ◇1	VT ◇1 ☕	NT A	LM ◇1	VT ◇1 ☕	EM ◇ B	NT A	LM ◇1	VT ◇1 ☕	EM ◇ B	NT A	LM ◇1	VT ◇1 ☕	EM ◇ B
Liverpool Lime Street 10 90 d	08 15	08 26	08 38	09 26	09 38	10 26	10 38	11 26	11 34	11 48	12 26	12 34	12 48	12 52	13 26	13 34	13 48	13 52	14 26	14 34	14 48	14 52
Edge Hill 90 d																						
Mossley Hill d		08 34		09 34		10 34		11 34			12 34				13 34				14 34			
West Allerton d		08 36		09 36		10 36		11 36			12 36				13 36				14 36			
Liverpool South Parkway 7 ✈ a		08 39		09 39		10 39		11 39	11 43		12 39	12 43		13 02	13 39	13 43		14 02	14 39	14 43		15 02
d									11 44			12 44				13 44				14 44		
Runcorn a	08 34		08 53		09 53		10 53		11 51	12 03		12 51	13 03			13 51	14 03			14 51	15 03	
d	08 35		08 54		09 54		10 54		11 52	12 04		12 52	13 04			13 52	14 04			14 52	15 04	
Acton Bridge d																						
Hartford d									12 04			13 03				14 03				15 03		
Winsford d									12 08			13 08				14 08				15 08		
Crewe 10 65 a	08 52		09 11		10 12		11 12		12 20			13 19				14 18				15 20		
Birmingham New Street 12 65 a									13 27			14 31				15 31				16 35		
London Euston ⊖65 a	11 06		11 37		12 32		13 11			14 01			15 01				16 01				17 01	

	NT A	LM ◇1	VT ◇1 ☕	EM ◇ B	VT ◇1 ☕	NT A	LM ◇1	VT ◇1 ☕	EM ◇ C	NT A	LM ◇1	VT ◇1 ☕	EM ◇ B	NT A	LM ◇1	VT ◇1 ☕	EM ◇ C	NT A	LM ◇1	VT ◇1 ☕	EM ◇ C	NT A
Liverpool Lime Street 10 90 d	15 26	15 34	15 48	15 52	16 18	16 26	16 34	16 48	16 52	17 26	17 34	17 48	17 52	18 26	18 34	18 48	18 52	19 26	19 34	19 48	19 52	20 26
Edge Hill 90 d																						
Mossley Hill d	15 34					16 34				17 34				18 34				19 34				20 34
West Allerton d	15 36					16 36				17 36				18 36				19 36				20 36
Liverpool South Parkway 7 ✈ a	15 39	15 43		16 02		16 39	16 43		17 02	17 39	17 43		18 02	18 39	18 43		19 02	19 39	19 43		20 02	20 39
d		15 44					16 44				17 44				18 44				19 44			
Runcorn a		15 51	16 03		16 33		16 51	17 03			17 51	18 03			18 51	19 03			19 51	20 03		
d		15 52	16 04		16 34		16 52	17 04			17 52	18 04			18 52	19 04			19 52	20 04		
Acton Bridge d																						
Hartford d		16 03					17 03				18 03				19 03				20 03			
Winsford d		16 08					17 08				18 08				19 08				20 08			
Crewe 10 65 a		16 18			16 51		17 18				18 20				19 20				20 16	20 22		
Birmingham New Street 12 65 a		17 32					18 32				19 32				20 32				21 32			
London Euston ⊖65 a			18 01		18 44			19 01				20 01				21 01				22 27		

	LM ◇1	VT ◇1 ☕	EM ◇ C	NT A	LM ◇1	NT A
Liverpool Lime Street 10 90 d	20 34	20 48	21 21	21 26	21 34	22 26
Edge Hill 90 d						
Mossley Hill d				21 34		22 34
West Allerton d				21 36		22 36
Liverpool South Parkway 7 ✈ a	20 43		21 31	21 39	21 43	22 39
d	20 44				21 44	
Runcorn a	20 51	21 03			21 51	
d	20 52	21 04			21 52	
Acton Bridge d						
Hartford d	21 03				22 03	
Winsford d	21 08				22 08	
Crewe 10 65 a	21 16	21 21			22 18	
Birmingham New Street 12 65 a	22 26				23 26	
London Euston ⊖65 a		23 54				

Sundays 1 July to 9 September

	VT ◇1 D ☕	VT ◇1 ☕	TP ◇1 E	NT A	VT ◇1 ☕	TP ◇1 F	NT A	VT ◇1 ☕	TP ◇1 G	NT A	VT ◇1 ☕	TP ◇1 F	NT A	LM ◇1	VT ◇1 ☕	TP ◇1 G	NT A	LM ◇1	VT ◇1 ☕	EM ◇ B	TP ◇1 F	NT A
Liverpool Lime Street 10 90 d	06 55	08 15	08 22	08 26	08 38	09 22	09 26	09 38	10 22	10 26	10 38	11 22	11 26	11 34	11 48	12 22	12 26	12 34	12 48	12 52	13 22	13 26
Edge Hill 90 d																						
Mossley Hill d				08 34			09 34			10 34			11 34				12 34					13 34
West Allerton d				08 36			09 36			10 36			11 36				12 36					13 36
Liverpool South Parkway 7 ✈ a			08 32	08 39		09 32	09 39		10 32	10 39		11 32	11 39	11 43		12 32	12 39	12 43		13 02	13 32	13 39
d														11 44				12 44				
Runcorn a	07 10	08 34			08 53			09 53			10 53			11 51	12 03			12 51	13 03			
d	07 11	08 35			08 54			09 54			10 54			11 52	12 04			12 52	13 04			
Acton Bridge d																						
Hartford d														12 03				13 03				
Winsford d														12 08				13 08				
Crewe 10 65 a	07 29	08 52			09 11			10 12			11 12			12 20				13 19				
Birmingham New Street 12 65 a														13 16				14 15				
London Euston ⊖65 a	09 37	11 06			11 37			12 32			13 11				14 01				15 01			

A To Manchester Oxford Road
B To Norwich
C To Nottingham
D from 29 July until 12 August, from 2 September
E To Hull
F To Scarborough
G To Middlesbrough

Table 91

Liverpool - Runcorn and Crewe

Sundays 1 July to 9 September

Network Diagram - see first Page of Table 88

	LM ◇1	VT ◇1 ☕	EM ◇ A	TP ◇1 B	NT C	LM ◇1	VT ◇1 ☕	EM ◇ A	TP ◇1 D	NT C	LM ◇1	VT ◇1 ☕	EM ◇ A	VT ◇1 ☕	TP ◇1 B	NT C	LM ◇1	VT ◇1 ☕	EM ◇ E	TP ◇1 D	NT C	LM ◇1
Liverpool Lime Street 10 90 d	13 34	13 48	13 52	14 22	14 26	14 34	14 48	14 52	15 22	15 26	15 34	15 48	15 52	16 18	16 22	16 26	16 34	16 48	16 52	17 22	17 26	17 34
Edge Hill 90 d																						
Mossley Hill d					14 34					15 34						16 34					17 34	
West Allerton d					14 36					15 36						16 36					17 36	
Liverpool South Parkway 7 ✈ a	13 43		14 02	14 32	14 39	14 43		15 02	15 32	15 39	15 43		16 02		16 32	16 39	16 43		17 02	17 32	17 39	17 43
d	13 44					14 44					15 44						16 44					17 44
Runcorn a	13 51	14 03				14 51	15 03				15 51	16 03		16 33			16 51	17 03				17 51
d	13 52	14 04				14 52	15 04				15 52	16 04		16 34			16 52	17 04				17 52
Acton Bridge d																						
Hartford d	14 03					15 03					16 03						17 03					18 03
Winsford d	14 08					15 08					16 08						17 08					18 08
Crewe 10 65 a	14 18					15 20					16 18			16 51			17 18					18 20
Birmingham New Street 12 65 a	15 15					16 15					17 15						18 15					19 15
London Euston ⊖65 a		16 01					17 01					18 01		18 44				19 01				

	VT ◇1 ☕	EM ◇ A	TP ◇1 D	NT C	LM ◇1	VT ◇1 ☕	EM ◇ E	TP ◇1 F	NT C	LM ◇1	VT ◇1 ☕	EM ◇ E	TP ◇1 G	NT C	LM ◇1	VT ◇1 ☕	EM ◇ E	NT C	LM ◇1	TP ◇1 F	NT C
Liverpool Lime Street 10 90 d	17 48	17 52	18 22	18 26	18 34	18 48	18 52	19 22	19 26	19 34	19 48	19 52	20 22	20 26	20 34	20 48	21 21	21 26	21 34	21 52	22 26
Edge Hill 90 d																					
Mossley Hill d				18 34					19 34					20 34				21 34			22 34
West Allerton d				18 36					19 36					20 36				21 36			22 36
Liverpool South Parkway 7 ✈ a		18 02	18 32	18 39	18 43		19 02	19 32	19 39	19 43		20 02	20 32	20 39	20 43		21 31	21 39	21 43	22 02	22 39
d					18 44					19 44					20 44				21 44		
Runcorn a	18 03				18 51	19 03				19 51	20 03				20 51	21 03			21 51		
d	18 04				18 52	19 04				19 52	20 04				20 52	21 04			21 52		
Acton Bridge d																					
Hartford d					19 03					20 03					21 03				22 03		
Winsford d					19 08					20 08					21 08				22 08		
Crewe 10 65 a					19 20					20 16	20 22				21 16	21 21			22 18		
Birmingham New Street 12 65 a					20 15					21 15					22 16				23 17		
London Euston ⊖65 a	20 01					21 01					22 27					23 54					

Sundays 16 September to 21 October

	VT ◇1 ☕	NT C	VT ◇1 ☕	NT C	VT ◇1 ☕	NT C	VT ◇1 ☕	NT C	LM ◇1	VT ◇1 ☕	NT C	LM ◇1	VT ◇1 ☕	EM ◇ A	NT C	LM ◇1	VT ◇1 ☕	EM ◇ A	NT C	LM ◇1	VT ◇1 ☕	EM ◇ A
Liverpool Lime Street 10 90 d	08 15	08 26	08 38	09 26	09 38	10 26	10 38	11 26	11 34	11 48	12 26	12 34	12 48	12 52	13 26	13 34	13 48	13 52	14 26	14 34	14 48	14 52
Edge Hill 90 d																						
Mossley Hill d		08 34		09 34		10 34		11 34			12 34				13 34				14 34			
West Allerton d		08 36		09 36		10 36		11 36			12 36				13 36				14 36			
Liverpool South Parkway 7 ✈ a		08 39		09 39		10 39		11 39	11 43		12 39	12 43		13 02	13 39	13 43		14 02	14 39	14 43		15 02
d									11 44			12 44				13 44				14 44		
Runcorn a	08 34		08 53		09 53		10 53		11 51	12 03		12 51	13 03			13 51	14 03			14 51	15 03	
d	08 35		08 54		09 54		10 54		11 52	12 04		12 52	13 04			13 52	14 04			14 52	15 04	
Acton Bridge d																						
Hartford d									12 03			13 03				14 03				15 03		
Winsford d									12 08			13 08				14 08				15 08		
Crewe 10 65 a	08 52		09 11		10 12		11 12		12 20			13 19				14 18				15 20		
Birmingham New Street 12 65 a									13 16			14 15				15 15				16 15		
London Euston ⊖65 a	11 06		11 37		12 32		13 11			14 01			15 01				16 01				17 01	

	NT C	LM ◇1	VT ◇1 ☕	EM ◇ A	VT ◇1 ☕	NT C	LM ◇1	VT ◇1 ☕	EM ◇ E	NT C	LM ◇1	VT ◇1 ☕	EM ◇ A	NT C	LM ◇1	VT ◇1 ☕	EM ◇ E	NT C	LM ◇1	VT ◇1 ☕	EM ◇ E	NT C
Liverpool Lime Street 10 90 d	15 26	15 34	15 48	15 52	16 18	16 26	16 34	16 48	16 52	17 26	17 34	17 48	17 52	18 26	18 34	18 48	18 52	19 26	19 34	19 48	19 52	20 26
Edge Hill 90 d																						
Mossley Hill d	15 34					16 34				17 34				18 34				19 34				20 34
West Allerton d	15 36					16 36				17 36				18 36				19 36				20 36
Liverpool South Parkway 7 ✈ a	15 39	15 43		16 02		16 39	16 43		17 02	17 39	17 43		18 02	18 39	18 43		19 02	19 39	19 43		20 02	20 39
d		15 44					16 44				17 44				18 44				19 44			
Runcorn a		15 51	16 03		16 33		16 51	17 03			17 51	18 03			18 51	19 03			19 51	20 03		
d		15 52	16 04		16 34		16 52	17 04			17 52	18 04			18 52	19 04			19 52	20 04		
Acton Bridge d																						
Hartford d		16 03					17 03				18 03				19 03				20 03			
Winsford d		16 08					17 08				18 08				19 08				20 08			
Crewe 10 65 a		16 18			16 51		17 18				18 20				19 20				20 16	20 22		
Birmingham New Street 12 65 a		17 15					18 15				19 15				20 15				21 15			
London Euston ⊖65 a			18 01		18 44			19 01				20 01				21 01				22 27		

A To Norwich
B To Middlesbrough
C To Manchester Oxford Road
D To Scarborough
E To Nottingham
F To York
G To Newcastle

Liverpool - Runcorn and Crewe

Sundays
16 September to 21 October

Network Diagram - see first Page of Table 88

			LM		VT	EM	NT	LM	NT
			◇1		◇1 🍴	◇ A	B	◇1	B
Liverpool Lime Street 10	90	d	20 34		20 48	21 21	21 26	21 34	22 26
Edge Hill	90	d							
Mossley Hill		d					21 34		22 34
West Allerton		d					21 36		22 36
Liverpool South Parkway 7 ✈		a	20 43			21 31	21 39	21 43	22 39
		d	20 44					21 44	
Runcorn		a	20 51		21 03			21 51	
		d	20 52		21 04			21 52	
Acton Bridge		d							
Hartford		d	21 03					22 03	
Winsford		d	21 08					22 08	
Crewe 10	65	a	21 16		21 21			22 18	
Birmingham New Street 12	65	a	22 16					23 17	
London Euston	⊖65	a			23 54				

Sundays
from 28 October

			VT	NT	VT	NT	VT	NT	VT	NT	LM		VT	NT	LM	VT	EM	NT	LM	VT	EM		NT	LM	VT	EM
			◇1 🍴	B	◇1 🍴	B	◇1 🍴	B	◇1 🍴	B	◇1		◇1 🍴	B	◇1	◇1 🍴	◇ C	B	◇1	◇1 🍴	◇ C		B	◇1	◇1 🍴	◇ C
Liverpool Lime Street 10	90	d	08 15	08 26	08 38	09 26	09 38	10 26	10 38	11 26	11 34		11 48	12 26	12 34	12 48	12 52	13 26	13 34	13 48	13 52		14 26	14 34	14 48	14 52
Edge Hill	90	d																								
Mossley Hill		d		08 34		09 34		10 34		11 34				12 34				13 34					14 34			
West Allerton		d		08 36		09 36		10 36		11 36				12 36				13 36					14 36			
Liverpool South Parkway 7 ✈		a		08 39		09 39		10 39		11 39	11 43			12 39	12 43		13 02	13 39	13 43		14 02		14 39	14 43		15 02
		d									11 44				12 44				13 44					14 44		
Runcorn		a	08 34		08 53		09 53		10 53		11 51		12 03		12 51	13 03			13 51	14 03				14 51	15 03	
		d	08 35		08 54		09 54		10 54		11 52		12 04		12 52	13 04			13 52	14 04				14 52	15 04	
Acton Bridge		d																								
Hartford		d									12 03				13 03				14 03					15 03		
Winsford		d									12 08				13 08				14 08					15 08		
Crewe 10	65	a	08 52		09 11		10 12		11 12		12 20				13 19				14 18					15 20		
Birmingham New Street 12	65	a									13 16				14 15				15 15					16 15		
London Euston	⊖65	a	11 06		11 37		12 32		13 11				14 01			15 01				16 01					17 01	

			NT	LM	VT	EM	VT		NT	LM	VT	EM	NT	LM	VT	EM	NT		LM	VT	EM	NT	LM	VT	EM	NT
			B	◇1	◇1 🍴	◇ C	◇1 🍴		B	◇1	◇1 🍴	◇ A	B	◇1	◇1 🍴	◇ C	B		◇1	◇1 🍴	◇ A	B	◇1	◇1 🍴	◇ A	B
Liverpool Lime Street 10	90	d	15 26	15 34	15 48	15 52	16 18		16 26	16 34	16 48	16 52	17 26	17 34	17 48	17 52	18 26		18 34	18 48	18 52	19 26	19 34	19 48	19 52	20 26
Edge Hill	90	d																								
Mossley Hill		d	15 34						16 34				17 34				18 34					19 34				20 34
West Allerton		d	15 36						16 36				17 36				18 36					19 36				20 36
Liverpool South Parkway 7 ✈		a	15 39	15 43		16 02			16 39	16 43		17 02	17 39	17 43		18 02	18 39		18 43		19 02	19 39	19 43		20 02	20 39
		d		15 44						16 44				17 44					18 44				19 44			
Runcorn		a		15 51	16 03		16 33			16 51	17 03			17 51	18 03				18 51	19 03			19 51	20 03		
		d		15 52	16 04		16 34			16 52	17 04			17 52	18 04				18 52	19 04			19 52	20 04		
Acton Bridge		d																								
Hartford		d		16 03						17 03				18 03					19 03				20 03			
Winsford		d		16 08						17 08				18 08					19 08				20 08			
Crewe 10	65	a		16 18			16 51			17 18				18 20					19 20				20 16	20 22		
Birmingham New Street 12	65	a		17 15						18 15				19 15					20 15				21 15			
London Euston	⊖65	a			18 01		18 44				19 01				20 01					21 01				22 27		

			LM		VT	EM	NT	LM	NT
			◇1		◇1 🍴	◇ A	B	◇1	B
Liverpool Lime Street 10	90	d	20 34		20 48	21 21	21 26	21 34	22 26
Edge Hill	90	d							
Mossley Hill		d					21 34		22 34
West Allerton		d					21 36		22 36
Liverpool South Parkway 7 ✈		a	20 43			21 31	21 39	21 43	22 39
		d	20 44					21 44	
Runcorn		a	20 51		21 03			21 51	
		d	20 52		21 04			21 52	
Acton Bridge		d							
Hartford		d	21 03					22 03	
Winsford		d	21 08					22 08	
Crewe 10	65	a	21 16		21 21			22 18	
Birmingham New Street 12	65	a	22 16					23 17	
London Euston	⊖65	a			23 54				

A To Nottingham
B To Manchester Oxford Road
C To Norwich

Mondays to Fridays

Crewe and Runcorn - Liverpool

Network Diagram - see first Page of Table 88

Miles				VT MO	NT MX	VT	VT MX	VT	VT	LM	NT	LM		NT	LM	NT	LM	VT	NT	LM	EM	LM		NT	TP	LM
				◇1 A 🍴	B	◇1 C 🍴	◇1 D 🍴	◇1 C 🍴	◇1 D 🍴	◇1	E	◇1		E	◇1	B	1	◇1 ⊠	E	◇1	◇ F	◇1		B	◇1 G 🛒	◇1 H
—	London Euston	⊖65	d	21p21		23p45	23p45	01 00	01 00									05 27								
—	Birmingham New Street 12	65	d														06 01			06 36		07 01				07 36
0	**Crewe** 10	65	d	23p45		01s27	01s41	02s42	02s50	05 40		06 02			06 32		06 57	07 24		07 34		07 57				08 31
7½	Winsford		d									06 10			06 41		07 05			07 43		08 05				
11¾	Hartford		d									06 15			06 46		07 10			07 48		08 10				
14½	Acton Bridge		d									06 19			06 51		07 14			07 52		08 14				
22½	**Runcorn**		a	00 07		01s46	02s02	03s01	03s09	05 58		06 27			06 59		07 22	07 41		08 00		08 22				08 50
—			d	00 07						06 01		06 28			06 59		07 22	07 41		08 01		08 22				08 50
30	**Liverpool South Parkway** 7 ✈		a							06 10		06 36			07 08		07 31			08 09		08 31				08 59
—			d		00 27					06 10	06 27	06 37		07 01	07 08	07 22	07 31		07 59	08 10	08 18	08 31		08 37	08 47	08 59
31	West Allerton		d								06 31			07 05		07 25			08 03					08 40		
31¾	Mossley Hill		d								06 33			07 07		07 28			08 06					08 43		
33¾	Edge Hill	90	d								06 39			07 13		07 32			08 11					08 48		
35½	**Liverpool Lime Street** 10	90	a	00 30	00 41	02 07	02 21	03 19	03 27	06 22	06 45	06 49		07 19	07 22	07 40	07 43	08 01	08 18	08 21	08 31	08 44		08 55	08 58	09 10

			VT	NT	EM	LM	NT	TP		LM	VT	NT	EM	LM	NT	NT	TP	LM		VT	NT	EM	LM	NT	NT	TP
			◇1 ⊠	B	◇ F	◇1 I	B	◇1 J 🛒		◇1	◇1 ⊠	B	◇ F	◇1	K	B	◇1 L 🛒	◇1		◇1 ⊠	B	◇ M	◇1	K	B	◇1 L 🛒
London Euston	⊖65	d	07 07								08 07									09 07						
Birmingham New Street 12	65	d				08 01				08 36				09 01				09 36					10 01			
Crewe 10	65	d				08 57				09 31				09 57				10 31					10 57			
Winsford		d				09 06																	11 06			
Hartford		d				09 12								10 10									11 12			
Acton Bridge		d												10 14												
Runcorn		a	08 55			09 22				09 50	09 55			10 22				10 50		10 55			11 21			
		d	08 55			09 22				09 50	09 55			10 22				10 50		10 55			11 22			
Liverpool South Parkway 7 ✈		a				09 31				09 59				10 31				10 59					11 30			
		d		09 06	09 15	09 31	09 36	09 47		09 59		10 06	10 15	10 31	10 36	10 36	10 47	10 59			11 06	11 15	11 31	11 36	11 36	11 47
West Allerton		d		09 09			09 39					10 10				10 39					11 10				11 39	
Mossley Hill		d		09 12			09 41					10 12				10 41					11 13				11 41	
Edge Hill	90	d					09 47									10 47									11 47	
Liverpool Lime Street 10	90	a	09 15	09 24	09 31	09 43	09 53	09 58		10 10	10 15	10 24	10 31	10 43	10 49	10 53	10 58	11 10		11 15	11 24	11 31	11 43	11 49	11 53	11 58

			LM	VT		NT	EM	LM	NT	NT	TP	LM	VT	NT		EM	LM	NT	NT	TP	LM	VT	NT	EM		LM
			◇1	◇1 ⊠		B	◇ M	◇1	K	B	◇1 L 🛒	◇1	◇1 🍴	B		◇ M	◇1	K	B	◇1 L 🛒	◇1	◇1 🍴	B	◇ M		◇1
London Euston	⊖65	d		10 07									11 07									12 07				
Birmingham New Street 12	65	d	10 36					11 01				11 36					12 01				12 36					13 01
Crewe 10	65	d	11 31					11 57				12 31					12 57				13 31					13 57
Winsford		d															13 06									14 06
Hartford		d						12 10									13 12									14 12
Acton Bridge		d						12 14																		
Runcorn		a	11 50	11 55				12 22				12 50	12 55				13 21				13 50	13 55				14 21
		d	11 50	11 55				12 22				12 50	12 55				13 22				13 50	13 55				14 22
Liverpool South Parkway 7 ✈		a	11 59					12 31				12 59					13 30				13 59					14 30
		d	11 59			12 06	12 15	12 31	12 36	12 36	12 47	12 59		13 06		13 15	13 31	13 36	13 36	13 47	13 59		14 06	14 15		14 31
West Allerton		d				12 10				12 39				13 10					13 39				14 10			
Mossley Hill		d				12 13				12 41				13 13					13 41				14 13			
Edge Hill	90	d								12 47									13 47							
Liverpool Lime Street 10	90	a	12 10	12 15		12 24	12 31	12 43	12 49	12 53	12 58	13 10	13 15	13 24		13 31	13 43	13 49	13 53	13 58	14 10	14 15	14 24	14 31		14 43

			NT	NT	TP	LM	VT	NT	EM	LM		NT	NT	TP	LM	VT	NT	EM	LM	NT		NT	TP	LM	VT	NT
			K	B	◇1 L 🛒	◇1	◇1 🍴	B	◇ M	◇1		K	B	◇1 L 🛒	◇1	◇1 🍴	B	◇ M	◇1	K		B	◇1 L 🛒	◇1	◇1 🍴	B
London Euston	⊖65	d					13 07									14 07									15 07	
Birmingham New Street 12	65	d				13 36				14 01					14 36				15 01					15 36		
Crewe 10	65	d				14 31				14 57					15 31				15 57					16 31		
Winsford		d								15 06																
Hartford		d								15 12									16 10							
Acton Bridge		d																	16 14							
Runcorn		a				14 50	14 55			15 21					15 50	15 55			16 22					16 50	16 55	
		d				14 50	14 55			15 22					15 50	15 55			16 22					16 50	16 55	
Liverpool South Parkway 7 ✈		a				14 59				15 30					15 59				16 31					16 59		
		d	14 36	14 36	14 47	14 59		15 06	15 15	15 31		15 36	15 36	15 47	15 59		16 07	16 15	16 31	16 36		16 36	16 47	16 59		17 07
West Allerton		d		14 39				15 10					15 39				16 11					16 39				17 11
Mossley Hill		d		14 41				15 13					15 41				16 13					16 42				17 13
Edge Hill	90	d		14 47									15 47									16 47				
Liverpool Lime Street 10	90	a	14 49	14 53	14 58	15 10	15 15	15 24	15 31	15 43		15 49	15 53	15 58	16 10	16 15	16 25	16 31	16 44	16 49		16 54	16 58	17 10	17 15	17 25

A from 21 May
B From Manchester Oxford Road
C 30 July, 6 August, 13 August, 3 September, 10 September
D from 31 July until 7 September, not from 14 August until 29 August
E From Warrington Central
F From Nottingham
G From Hull
H From Birmingham International
I From Walsall
J From Newcastle
K To Blackpool North
L From Scarborough
M From Norwich

Table 91

Mondays to Fridays

Crewe and Runcorn - Liverpool

Network Diagram - see first Page of Table 88

	EM	LM	NT	TP	LM	VT	NT	EM	LM	NT	TP	LM	VT	NT	EM	LM	VT	TP	LM	VT	NT	EM
	◇ A	◇■	B	◇■ C ⌶	◇■	◇■ ⊏	B	◇ A	◇■	B	◇■ C ⌶	◇■	◇■ ⊠	B	◇ A	◇■	◇■ ⊠	◇■ C ⌶	◇■	◇■ ⊠	D	◇ A
London Euston ⊖65 d						16 07							17 07				17 33			18 07		
Birmingham New Street 65 d		16 01			16 36				17 01			17 36				18 01			18 36			
Crewe 65 d		16 57			17 31				17 57			18 31	18 44			19 02	19 16		19 31	19 44		
Winsford d		17 06							18 06							19 10			19 42			
Hartford d		17 12							18 12			18 44							19 47			
Acton Bridge d												18 48										
Runcorn a		17 21			17 50	17 55			18 21			18 56	19 02			19 22	19 33		19 57	20 01		
d		17 22			17 50	17 55			18 22			18 57	19 02			19 23	19 33		19 57	20 01		
Liverpool South Parkway ✈ a		17 30			17 59				18 30			19 05				19 31			20 06			
d	17 15	17 31	17 39	17 47	17 59		18 14	18 22	18 31	18 38	18 47	19 06		19 13	19 18	19 32		19 47	20 06		20 13	20 16
West Allerton d			17 42				18 18			18 41				19 16							20 16	
Mossley Hill d			17 45				18 20			18 44				19 18							20 18	
Edge Hill 90 d			17 50				18 30			18 49				19 26							20 24	
Liverpool Lime Street 90 a	17 31	17 43	17 58	18 01	18 10	18 15	18 38	18 35	18 43	18 57	19 01	19 16	19 22	19 35	19 35	19 44	19 51	20 01	20 18	20 19	20 30	20 35

	VT	NT	TP	LM	VT	NT	EM	TP	LM	VT	NT	TP	LM	VT	VT	NT	VT	VT
														FO	FX		FX	
	◇■ ⊠	B	◇■ C	◇■	■ ⊏	D	◇ A	◇■ C	◇■	◇■ ⊏	D	◇■ C	◇■	◇■ E ⊏	◇■ F ⊏	D	◇■ G ⊏	◇■ H ⊏
London Euston ⊖65 d	18 33				19 07					20 07				21 07	21 07		23 45	23 45
Birmingham New Street 65 d				19 36					20 36				21 36					
Crewe 65 d	20 17			20 31					21 31				22 31	22 48	22 51		01s41	01s55
Winsford d				20 40					21 39				22 39					
Hartford d				20 45					21 44				22 44					
Acton Bridge d													22 48					
Runcorn a	20 34			20 56	21 01				21 54	21 59			22 56	23 05	23 08		02s02	02s16
d	20 34			20 56	21 01				21 54	21 59			22 57	23 05	23 08			
Liverpool South Parkway ✈ a				21 05					22 05				23 07					
d		20 38	20 47	21 05		21 12	21 20	21 47	22 05		22 12	22 47	23 08			23 22		
West Allerton d		20 41				21 15					22 15					23 25		
Mossley Hill d		20 44				21 18					22 18					23 27		
Edge Hill 90 d						21 23					22 23					23 32		
Liverpool Lime Street 90 a	20 53	20 56	21 01	21 16	21 21	21 30	21 35	22 01	22 15	22 20	22 30	23 01	23 23	23 24	23 27	23 39	02 21	02 34

Saturdays

	NT	VT	VT	LM	NT	LM	NT	LM	NT	LM	NT	LM	EM	LM	NT	TP	LM	VT	NT	EM	LM	NT
	B	◇■ I ⊏	◇■ I ⊏	■	D	■	D	◇■	B	◇■	D	◇■	◇ J	◇■	B	◇■ K ⌶	◇■	◇■ ⊏	B	◇ J	◇■	B
London Euston ⊖65 d		23p45	01 00															07 07				
Birmingham New Street 65 d										06 01		06 36		07 01			07 36				08 01	
Crewe 65 d		01s55	03s00	05 48		06 12		06 32		06 57		07 35		08 00			08 31	08 43			08 57	
Winsford d								06 41		07 05		07 44		08 07							09 07	
Hartford d								06 46		07 10		07 49		08 12							09 12	
Acton Bridge d								06 51				07 53		08 16								
Runcorn a		02s16	03s19	06 07		06 31		06 59		07 20		08 02		08 24			08 50	09 00			09 21	
d				06 08		06 31		06 59		07 21		08 03		08 25			08 50	09 00			09 22	
Liverpool South Parkway ✈ a				06 15		06 39		07 08		07 30		08 11		08 33			08 59				09 30	
d	00 27			06 15	06 27	06 39	07 01	07 08	07 22	07 30	08 03	08 12	08 18	08 34	08 37	08 47	08 59		09 06	09 15	09 31	09 36
West Allerton d					06 31		07 05		07 25		08 06				08 40				09 09			09 39
Mossley Hill d					06 33		07 07		07 28		08 09				08 43				09 12			09 41
Edge Hill 90 d					06 39		07 13		07 34		08 14				08 48							09 47
Liverpool Lime Street 90 a	00 41	02 34	03 38	06 26	06 45	06 53	07 20	07 22	07 40	07 42	08 21	08 24	08 31	08 46	08 55	08 58	09 12	09 21	09 24	09 31	09 43	09 53

	TP	LM	VT	NT	EM	LM	NT	NT	TP	LM	VT	NT	EM	LM	NT	NT	TP	LM	VT	NT	EM	LM
	◇■ L ⌶	◇■	◇■ ⊏	B	◇ J	◇■	M	B	◇■ C ⌶	◇■	◇■ ⊏	B	◇ A	◇■	M	B	◇■ C	◇■	◇■ ⊏	B	◇ A	◇■
London Euston ⊖65 d			08 07								09 07								10 07			
Birmingham New Street 65 d		08 36				09 01				09 36				10 01				10 36				11 01
Crewe 65 d		09 31				09 57				10 31				10 57				11 31				11 57
Winsford d														11 07								
Hartford d						10 10								11 12								12 10
Acton Bridge d						10 14																12 14
Runcorn a		09 50	09 55			10 22				10 50	10 55			11 21				11 50	11 55			12 22
d		09 50	09 55			10 23				10 50	10 55			11 22				11 50	11 55			12 23
Liverpool South Parkway ✈ a		09 59				10 31				10 59				11 30				11 59				12 31
d	09 47	09 59		10 06	10 15	10 32	10 36	10 36	10 47	10 59		11 06	11 15	11 31	11 36	11 36	11 47	11 59		12 06	12 15	12 32
West Allerton d				10 10				10 39				11 10				11 39				12 10		
Mossley Hill d				10 12				10 41				11 13				11 41				12 13		
Edge Hill 90 d								10 47								11 47						
Liverpool Lime Street 90 a	09 58	10 10	10 15	10 23	10 31	10 44	10 49	10 53	10 58	11 10	11 15	11 24	11 31	11 43	11 49	11 53	11 58	12 10	12 15	12 24	12 31	12 44

A From Norwich
B From Manchester Oxford Road
C From Scarborough
D From Warrington Central
E until 15 June, from 22 June
F until 21 June
G from 30 July until 6 September, not from 13 August until 28 August
H 27 July, 3 August, 10 August, 31 August, 7 September
I from 28 July until 11 August, from 1 September until 8 September
J From Nottingham
K From Hull
L From Newcastle
M To Blackpool North

Table 91

Saturdays

Crewe and Runcorn - Liverpool

Network Diagram - see first Page of Table 88

	NT	NT	TP	LM	VT	NT	EM	LM	NT	NT	TP	LM	VT	NT	EM	LM	NT	NT	TP	LM	VT
	A	B	◇■ C ⌶	◇■	◇■ ⊏	B	◇ D	◇■	A	B	◇■ C ⌶	◇■	◇■ ⊏	B	◇ D	◇■	A	B	◇■ C	◇■	◇■ ⊏
London Euston ⊖65 d					11 07								12 07								13 07
Birmingham New Street 65 d				11 36				12 01				12 36				13 01				13 36	
Crewe 65 d				12 31				12 57				13 31				13 57				14 31	
Winsford d								13 07								14 07					
Hartford d								13 12								14 12					
Acton Bridge d																					
Runcorn a				12 50	12 55			13 21				13 50	13 55			14 21				14 50	14 55
d				12 50	12 55			13 22				13 50	13 55			14 22				14 50	14 55
Liverpool South Parkway ✈ a				12 59				13 30				13 59				14 30				14 59	
d	12 36	12 36	12 47	12 59		13 06	13 15	13 31	13 36	13 36	13 47	13 59		14 06	14 15	14 31	14 36	14 36	14 47	14 59	
West Allerton d		12 39				13 10				13 39				14 10				14 39			
Mossley Hill d		12 41				13 13				13 41				14 13				14 41			
Edge Hill 90 d		12 47								13 47								14 47			
Liverpool Lime Street 90 a	12 49	12 53	12 58	13 10	13 15	13 24	13 31	13 43	13 49	13 53	13 58	14 10	14 15	14 24	14 31	14 43	14 49	14 53	14 58	15 10	15 15

	NT	EM	LM	NT	NT	TP	LM	VT	NT	EM	LM	NT	NT	TP	LM	VT	NT	EM	LM	NT	TP	LM
	B	◇ D	◇■	A	B	◇■ C ⌶	◇■	◇■ ⊏	B	◇ D	◇■	A	B	◇■ C ⌶	◇■	◇■ ⊏	B	◇ D	◇■	B	◇■ C ⌶	◇■
London Euston ⊖65 d								14 07								15 07						
Birmingham New Street 65 d			14 01				14 36				15 01				15 36				16 01			16 36
Crewe 65 d			14 57				15 31				15 57				16 31				16 57			17 31
Winsford d			15 07																17 07			
Hartford d			15 12								16 10								17 12			
Acton Bridge d											16 14											
Runcorn a			15 21				15 50	15 55			16 22				16 50	16 55			17 21			17 50
d			15 22				15 50	15 55			16 23				16 50	16 55			17 22			17 50
Liverpool South Parkway ✈ a			15 30				15 59				16 31				16 59				17 30			17 59
d	15 06	15 15	15 31	15 36	15 36	15 47	15 59		16 07	16 15	16 32	16 36	16 36	16 47	16 59		17 07	17 15	17 31	17 39	17 47	17 59
West Allerton d	15 10				15 39				16 11				16 39				17 11			17 42		
Mossley Hill d	15 13				15 41				16 13				16 41				17 13			17 45		
Edge Hill 90 d					15 47								16 47							17 50		
Liverpool Lime Street 90 a	15 24	15 31	15 43	15 49	15 53	15 58	16 10	16 15	16 25	16 31	16 44	16 49	16 54	16 58	17 10	17 15	17 25	17 31	17 43	17 58	18 01	18 10

	VT	NT	EM	LM	VT	NT	TP	LM	VT	NT	EM	LM	TP	VT	NT	EM	LM	VT	NT	TP	VT
	◇■ ⊏	B	◇ D	◇■	◇■ ⊏	B	◇■ C ⌶	◇■	◇■ ⊏	B	◇ D	◇■	◇■ C	◇■ ⊏	E	◇ D	◇■	◇■ ⊏	B	◇■ C	◇■ ⊏
London Euston ⊖65 d	16 07				16 33				17 07					18 07				18 33			19 07
Birmingham New Street 65 d				17 01				17 36				18 01					19 01				
Crewe 65 d				17 57				18 33				18 59					19 58				20 47
Winsford d				18 07								19 08					20 07				
Hartford d				18 12				18 44				19 13					20 12				
Acton Bridge d																	20 16				
Runcorn a	17 55			18 21	18 31			18 52	18 59			19 22		19 55			20 24	20 31			21 05
d	17 55			18 22	18 31			18 53	18 59			19 23		19 55			20 25	20 32			21 05
Liverpool South Parkway ✈ a				18 30				19 02				19 31					20 33				
d		18 14	18 22	18 31		18 38	18 47	19 02		19 11	19 18	19 32	19 47		19 59	20 15	20 34		20 38	20 47	
West Allerton d		18 18				18 41				19 15					20 03				20 41		
Mossley Hill d		18 20				18 44				19 18					20 05				20 44		
Edge Hill 90 d		18 30				18 50				19 26					20 11						
Liverpool Lime Street 90 a	18 15	18 38	18 35	18 43	18 52	18 57	19 01	19 14	19 17	19 35	19 35	19 44	20 01	20 15	20 18	20 30	20 46	20 52	20 55	21 01	21 25

	NT	EM	LM	TP	NT	VT	TP	NT	VT
	E	◇ D	◇■	◇■ C	E	◇■ ⊏	◇■ C	E	◇■ F ⊏
London Euston ⊖65 d						20 11			23 45
Birmingham New Street 65 d			20 01						
Crewe 65 d			21 06			22 06			01s35
Winsford d			21 14						
Hartford d			21 19						
Acton Bridge d									
Runcorn a			21 29			22 24			01s54
d			21 29			22 24			
Liverpool South Parkway ✈ a			21 38						
d	21 15	21 20	21 38	21 47	22 12		22 47	23 12	
West Allerton d	21 19				22 15			23 15	
Mossley Hill d	21 21				22 18			23 18	
Edge Hill 90 d	21 27				22 23			23 23	
Liverpool Lime Street 90 a	21 34	21 35	21 50	22 01	22 30	22 46	23 01	23 30	02 16

A To Blackpool North
B From Manchester Oxford Road
C From Scarborough
D From Norwich
E From Warrington Central
F from 28 July until 11 August, from 1 September until 8 September

Table 91

Crewe and Runcorn - Liverpool

Sundays
until 24 June

Network Diagram - see first Page of Table 88

	NT	NT	NT	NT	VT	LM	NT	VT	LM	EM	NT	VT	LM	EM	NT	VT	LM	VT	EM	NT	LM	VT
					◇1	◇1		◇1	◇1	◇		◇1	◇1	◇		◇1	◇1	◇1	◇		◇1	◇1
	A	A	A	A			A			B	A			B	A				B	A		
					⊡			⊡				⊡				⊡		⊡				⊡
London Euston ⊖65 d					08 15			09 15				10 15				11 15		12 02				13 02
Birmingham New Street 12 65 d						09 34			10 35				11 33				12 28				13 28	
Crewe 10 65 d					10 30	10 38		11 32	11 38			12 34	12 38			13 15	13 31	13 45			14 30	14 45
Winsford d						10 45			11 45				12 45				13 38				14 37	
Hartford d						10 50			11 50				12 50				13 43				14 42	
Acton Bridge d																						
Runcorn a					10 47	11 00		11 49	12 01			12 51	13 01			13 32	13 54	14 02			14 53	15 02
d					10 47	11 00		11 49	12 01			12 51	13 01			13 32	13 54	14 02			14 53	15 02
Liverpool South Parkway 7 ✈ a						11 09			12 10				13 10				14 03				15 02	
d	00 20	08 55	09 33	10 33		11 09	11 33		12 10	12 17	12 33		13 10	13 17	13 33		14 03		14 16	14 33	15 02	
West Allerton d		08 58	09 36	10 36			11 36				12 36				13 36					14 36		
Mossley Hill d		09 02	09 39	10 39			11 39				12 39				13 39					14 39		
Edge Hill 90 d																						
Liverpool Lime Street 10 90 a	00 34	09 13	09 50	10 50	11 09	11 20	11 50	12 10	12 21	12 30	12 50	13 12	13 21	13 30	13 50	13 54	14 14	14 24	14 30	14 50	15 13	15 24

	EM	NT	LM	VT	EM	NT	LM	VT	EM	NT	LM	VT	EM	NT	LM	VT	EM	NT	LM	VT	EM	NT
	◇		◇1	◇1	◇		◇1	◇1	◇		◇1	◇1	◇		◇1	◇1	◇		◇1	◇1	◇	
	C	A			C	A			B	A			B	A			C	A			C	A
				⊡				⊡				⊡				⊡				⊡		
London Euston ⊖65 d				14 02				15 02				16 02				17 02				18 02		
Birmingham New Street 12 65 d			14 28				15 28				16 28				17 28				18 28			
Crewe 10 65 d			15 30	15 45			16 31				17 31				18 31				19 31			
Winsford d			15 37				16 38				17 38				18 38				19 38			
Hartford d			15 42				16 43				17 43				18 43				19 43			
Acton Bridge d																						
Runcorn a			15 53	16 02			16 54	16 57			17 53	17 57			18 54	18 57			19 54	19 58		
d			15 53	16 02			16 54	16 57			17 54	17 57			18 54	18 57			19 54	19 58		
Liverpool South Parkway 7 ✈ a			16 02				17 03				18 02				19 03				20 03			
d	15 16	15 33	16 02		16 16	16 33	17 03		17 16	17 33	18 03		18 16	18 33	19 03		19 17	19 33	20 03		20 16	20 33
West Allerton d		15 36				16 36				17 36				18 36				19 36				20 36
Mossley Hill d		15 39				16 39				17 39				18 39				19 39				20 39
Edge Hill 90 d																						
Liverpool Lime Street 10 90 a	15 30	15 50	16 13	16 24	16 30	16 50	17 14	17 16	17 30	17 50	18 14	18 16	18 30	18 50	19 14	19 19	19 30	19 50	20 14	20 16	20 30	20 50

	LM	VT	NT	VT	VT	NT	NT	VT
	◇1	◇1		◇1	◇1			◇1
			A			A	D	
		⊡		⊡	⊡			⊡
London Euston ⊖65 d		19 02		20 02	20 05			21 21
Birmingham New Street 12 65 d	19 16							
Crewe 10 65 d	20 23	20 50		21 46	21 55			23 45
Winsford d	20 30							
Hartford d	20 35							
Acton Bridge d								
Runcorn a	20 45	21 07		22 03	22 12			00 07
d	20 46	21 07		22 03	22 12			00 07
Liverpool South Parkway 7 ✈ a	20 54							
d	20 55		21 33			22 33	23 33	
West Allerton d			21 36			22 36	23 36	
Mossley Hill d			21 39			22 39	23 39	
Edge Hill 90 d								
Liverpool Lime Street 10 90 a	21 06	21 28	21 50	22 23	22 33	22 50	23 50	00 30

Sundays
1 July to 9 September

	NT	VT	VT	NT	NT	TP	NT	TP	VT	LM	NT	TP	VT	LM	EM	NT	TP	VT	LM	EM	NT	VT
		◇1	◇1			◇1		◇1	◇1	◇1		◇1	◇1	◇1	◇		◇1	◇1	◇1	◇		◇1
	A	E	E	A	A	F	A	G			A	F			B	A	H			B	A	
		⊡	⊡						⊡				⊡					⊡				⊡
London Euston ⊖65 d		23p45	01 00						08 15				09 15					10 15				11 15
Birmingham New Street 12 65 d										09 42				10 42					11 42			
Crewe 10 65 d		01s35	02s42						10 30	10 38			11 32	11 38				12 34	12 38			13 15
Winsford d										10 45				11 45					12 45			
Hartford d										10 50				11 50					12 50			
Acton Bridge d																						
Runcorn a		01s54	03s01						10 47	11 00			11 49	12 01				12 51	13 01			13 32
d									10 47	11 01			11 49	12 01				12 51	13 01			13 32
Liverpool South Parkway 7 ✈ a										11 09				12 10					13 10			
d	00 20			08 55	09 33	09 47	10 33	10 45		11 10	11 33	11 47		12 10	12 17	12 33	12 47		13 10	13 17	13 33	
West Allerton d				08 58	09 36		10 36				11 36					12 36					13 36	
Mossley Hill d				09 02	09 39		10 39				11 39					12 39					13 39	
Edge Hill 90 d																						
Liverpool Lime Street 10 90 a	00 34	02 16	03 19	09 13	09 50	10 00	10 50	10 57	11 09	11 21	11 50	11 59	12 10	12 21	12 30	12 50	12 58	13 12	13 21	13 30	13 50	13 54

A From Manchester Oxford Road
B From Nottingham
C From Norwich
D From Manchester Airport
E from 29 July until 12 August, from 2 September
F From Manchester Piccadilly
G From York
H From Newcastle

Table 91

Crewe and Runcorn - Liverpool

Sundays
1 July to 9 September

Network Diagram - see first Page of Table 88

	TP	LM	VT	EM	NT	TP	LM	VT	EM	NT	TP	LM	VT	EM	NT	TP	LM	VT	EM	NT	TP	LM
	◇1	◇1	◇1	◇		◇1	◇1	◇1	◇		◇1	◇1	◇1	◇		◇1	◇1	◇1	◇		◇1	◇1
	A			B	C	A			D	C	E			D	C	A			B	C	E	
			⊡					⊡					⊡					⊡				
London Euston ⊖65 d			12 02					13 02					14 02					15 02				
Birmingham New Street 12 65 d		12 35					13 35					14 35					15 35					16 35
Crewe 10 65 d		13 31	13 45				14 31	14 45				15 31	15 45				16 31					17 31
Winsford d		13 38					14 38					15 38					16 38					17 38
Hartford d		13 43					14 43					15 43					16 43					17 43
Acton Bridge d																						
Runcorn a		13 54	14 02				14 53	15 02				15 53	16 02				16 54	16 57				17 54
d		13 54	14 02				14 54	15 02				15 54	16 02				16 54	16 57				17 54
Liverpool South Parkway 7 ✈ a		14 03					15 02					16 02					17 03					18 03
d	13 47	14 03		14 16	14 33	14 47	15 03		15 16	15 33	15 47	16 03		16 16	16 33	16 47	17 03		17 16	17 33	17 47	18 03
West Allerton d					14 36					15 36					16 36					17 36		
Mossley Hill d					14 39					15 39					16 39					17 39		
Edge Hill 90 d																						
Liverpool Lime Street 10 90 a	13 58	14 14	14 24	14 30	14 50	14 58	15 14	15 24	15 30	15 50	15 58	16 14	16 24	16 30	16 50	16 58	17 14	17 16	17 30	17 50	17 58	18 14

	VT	EM	NT	TP	LM	VT	EM	NT	TP	LM	VT	EM	NT	TP	LM	VT	NT	TP	VT	VT	NT
	◇1	◇		◇1	◇1	◇1	◇		◇1	◇1	◇1	◇		◇1	◇1	◇1		◇1	◇1	◇1	
		B	C	A			D	C	E			D	C	A			C	E			C
	⊡					⊡					⊡					⊡			⊡	⊡	
London Euston ⊖65 d	16 02					17 02					18 02					19 02			20 02	20 05	
Birmingham New Street 12 65 d					17 35					18 35					19 35						
Crewe 10 65 d					18 31					19 31					20 31	20 50			21 46	21 55	
Winsford d					18 38					19 38					20 38						
Hartford d					18 43					19 43					20 43						
Acton Bridge d																					
Runcorn a	17 57				18 54	18 57				19 53	19 58				20 54	21 07			22 03	22 12	
d	17 57				18 54	18 57				19 54	19 58				20 54	21 07			22 03	22 12	
Liverpool South Parkway 7 ✈ a					19 03					20 02					21 03						
d		18 16	18 33	18 47	19 03		19 17	19 33	19 47	20 03		20 16	20 33	20 47	21 03		21 33	21 47			22 33
West Allerton d			18 36					19 36					20 36				21 36				22 36
Mossley Hill d			18 39					19 39					20 39				21 39				22 39
Edge Hill 90 d																					
Liverpool Lime Street 10 90 a	18 16	18 30	18 50	18 58	19 14	19 19	19 30	19 50	19 58	20 14	20 16	20 30	20 50	20 58	21 14	21 28	21 50	21 58	22 23	22 33	22 50

	TP	NT	VT	VT
	◇1		◇1	◇1
	A	F		G
			⊡	⊡
London Euston ⊖65 d			21 21	23 45
Birmingham New Street 12 65 d				
Crewe 10 65 d			23 45	01s27
Winsford d				
Hartford d				
Acton Bridge d				
Runcorn a			00 07	01s46
d			00 07	
Liverpool South Parkway 7 ✈ a				
d	22 47	23 33		
West Allerton d		23 36		
Mossley Hill d		23 39		
Edge Hill 90 d				
Liverpool Lime Street 10 90 a	22 58	23 50	00 30	02 07

Sundays
16 September to 21 October

	NT	NT	NT	NT	VT	LM	NT	VT	LM	EM	NT	VT	LM	EM	NT	VT	LM	VT	EM	NT	LM	VT
					◇1	◇1		◇1	◇1	◇		◇1	◇1	◇		◇1	◇1	◇1	◇		◇1	◇1
	C	C	C	C			C			B	C			B	C				B	C		
					⊡			⊡				⊡				⊡		⊡				⊡
London Euston ⊖65 d					08 15			09 15				10 15				11 15		12 05				13 05
Birmingham New Street 12 65 d						09 42			10 42				11 42				12 35				13 35	
Crewe 10 65 d					10 30	10 38		11 32	11 38			12 34	12 38			13 15	13 31	13 45			14 31	14 45
Winsford d						10 45			11 45				12 45				13 38				14 38	
Hartford d						10 50			11 50				12 50				13 43				14 43	
Acton Bridge d																						
Runcorn a					10 47	11 00		11 49	12 01			12 51	13 01			13 32	13 54	14 02			14 53	15 02
d					10 47	11 01		11 49	12 01			12 51	13 01			13 32	13 54	14 02			14 54	15 02
Liverpool South Parkway 7 ✈ a						11 09			12 10				13 10				14 03				15 02	
d	00 20	08 55	09 33	10 33		11 10	11 33		12 10	12 17	12 33		13 10	13 17	13 33		14 03		14 16	14 33	15 03	
West Allerton d		08 58	09 36	10 36			11 36				12 36				13 36					14 36		
Mossley Hill d		09 02	09 39	10 39			11 39				12 39				13 39					14 39		
Edge Hill 90 d																						
Liverpool Lime Street 10 90 a	00 34	09 13	09 50	10 50	11 09	11 21	11 50	12 10	12 21	12 30	12 50	13 12	13 21	13 30	13 50	13 54	14 14	14 24	14 30	14 50	15 14	15 24

A From Scarborough
B From Nottingham
C From Manchester Oxford Road
D From Norwich
E From Middlesbrough
F From Manchester Airport
G from 29 July until 12 August, from 2 September

Table 91

Crewe and Runcorn - Liverpool

Sundays

16 September to 21 October

Network Diagram - see first Page of Table 88

		EM	NT	LM	VT	EM	NT	LM	VT	EM	NT	LM	VT	EM	NT	LM	VT	EM	NT	LM	VT	EM	NT
		◇		◇1	◇1	◇		◇1	◇1	◇		◇1	◇1	◇		◇1	◇1	◇		◇1	◇1	◇	
		A	B			C	B			A	B			A	B			C	B			C	B
					☕				☕				☕				☕				☕		
London Euston ⊖65	d				14 05				15 05				16 05				17 05				18 05		
Birmingham New Street 12 65	d			14 35				15 35				16 35				17 35				18 35			
Crewe 10 65	d			15 31	15 45			16 31				17 31				18 31				19 31			
Winsford	d			15 38				16 38				17 38				18 38				19 38			
Hartford	d			15 43				16 43				17 43				18 43				19 43			
Acton Bridge	d																						
Runcorn	a			15 53	16 02			16 54	16 57			17 54	17 57			18 54	18 57			19 53	19 58		
	d			15 54	16 02			16 54	16 57			17 54	17 57			18 54	18 57			19 54	19 58		
Liverpool South Parkway 7 ✈	a			16 02				17 03				18 03				19 03				20 02			
	d	15 16	15 33	16 03		16 16	16 33	17 03		17 16	17 33	18 03		18 16	18 33	19 03		19 17	19 33	20 03		20 16	20 33
West Allerton	d		15 36				16 36				17 36				18 36				19 36				20 36
Mossley Hill	d		15 39				16 39				17 39				18 39				19 39				20 39
Edge Hill 90	d																						
Liverpool Lime Street 10 90	a	15 30	15 50	16 14	16 24	16 30	16 50	17 14	17 16	17 30	17 50	18 14	18 16	18 30	18 50	19 14	19 19	19 30	19 50	20 14	20 16	20 30	20 50

		LM	VT	NT	VT	VT	NT	NT	VT
		◇1	◇1		◇1	◇1			◇1
				B			B	D	
			☕		☕	☕			☕
London Euston ⊖65	d		19 05		20 05	20 08			21 21
Birmingham New Street 12 65	d	19 35							
Crewe 10 65	d	20 31	20 49		21 46	21 55			23 45
Winsford	d	20 38							
Hartford	d	20 43							
Acton Bridge	d								
Runcorn	a	20 54	21 06		22 03	22 12			00 07
	d	20 54	21 06		22 03	22 12			00 07
Liverpool South Parkway 7 ✈	a	21 03							
	d	21 03		21 33			22 33	23 33	
West Allerton	d			21 36			22 36	23 36	
Mossley Hill	d			21 39			22 39	23 39	
Edge Hill 90	d								
Liverpool Lime Street 10 90	a	21 14	21 27	21 50	22 23	22 33	22 50	23 50	00 30

Sundays

from 28 October

		NT	NT	NT	TP	NT	VT	LM	NT	VT	LM	EM	NT	VT	LM	EM	NT	VT	LM	VT	EM	NT	LM
					◇1		◇1	◇1		◇1	◇1	◇		◇1	◇1	◇		◇1	◇1	◇1	◇		◇1
		B	B	B	E	B			B			A	B			A	B				A	B	
							☕			☕				☕				☕		☕			
London Euston ⊖65	d						08 15			09 15				10 15				11 15		12 05			
Birmingham New Street 12 65	d							09 42			10 42				11 42				12 35				13 35
Crewe 10 65	d						10 32	10 38		11 32	11 38			12 34	12 38			13 15	13 31	13 45			14 31
Winsford	d							10 45			11 45				12 45				13 38				14 38
Hartford	d							10 50			11 50				12 50				13 43				14 43
Acton Bridge	d																						
Runcorn	a						10 49	11 00		11 49	12 01			12 51	13 01			13 32	13 54	14 02			14 53
	d						10 49	11 01		11 49	12 01			12 51	13 01			13 32	13 54	14 02			14 54
Liverpool South Parkway 7 ✈	a							11 09			12 10				13 10				14 03				15 02
	d	00 20	08 55	09 33	09 46	10 33		11 10	11 33		12 10	12 17	12 33		13 10	13 17	13 33		14 03		14 16	14 33	15 03
West Allerton	d		08 58	09 36		10 36			11 36				12 36				13 36					14 36	
Mossley Hill	d		09 02	09 39		10 39			11 39				12 39				13 39					14 39	
Edge Hill 90	d																						
Liverpool Lime Street 10 90	a	00 34	09 13	09 50	09 59	10 50	11 09	11 21	11 50	12 10	12 21	12 30	12 50	13 12	13 21	13 30	13 50	13 54	14 14	14 24	14 30	14 50	15 14

		VT	EM	NT	LM	VT	EM	NT	LM	VT	EM	NT	LM	VT	EM	NT	LM	VT	EM	NT	LM	VT	EM
		◇1	◇		◇1	◇1	◇		◇1	◇1	◇		◇1	◇1	◇		◇1	◇1	◇		◇1	◇1	◇
			A	B			C	B			A	B			A	B			C	B			C
		☕				☕				☕				☕				☕				☕	
London Euston ⊖65	d	13 05				14 05				15 05				16 05				17 05				18 05	
Birmingham New Street 12 65	d				14 35				15 35				16 35				17 35				18 35		
Crewe 10 65	d	14 45			15 31	15 45			16 31				17 31				18 31				19 31		
Winsford	d				15 38				16 38				17 38				18 38				19 38		
Hartford	d				15 43				16 43				17 43				18 43				19 43		
Acton Bridge	d																						
Runcorn	a	15 02			15 53	16 02			16 54	16 57			17 54	17 57			18 54	18 57			19 53	19 58	
	d	15 02			15 54	16 02			16 54	16 57			17 54	17 57			18 54	18 57			19 54	19 58	
Liverpool South Parkway 7 ✈	a				16 02				17 03				18 03				19 03				20 02		
	d		15 16	15 33	16 03		16 16	16 33	17 03		17 16	17 33	18 03		18 16	18 33	19 03		19 17	19 33	20 03		20 16
West Allerton	d			15 36				16 36				17 36				18 36				19 36			
Mossley Hill	d			15 39				16 39				17 39				18 39				19 39			
Edge Hill 90	d																						
Liverpool Lime Street 10 90	a	15 24	15 30	15 50	16 14	16 24	16 30	16 50	17 14	17 16	17 30	17 50	18 14	18 16	18 30	18 50	19 14	19 19	19 30	19 50	20 14	20 16	20 30

A From Nottingham
B From Manchester Oxford Road
C From Norwich
D From Manchester Airport
E From Manchester Piccadilly

Table 91

Crewe and Runcorn - Liverpool

Sundays

from 28 October

Network Diagram - see first Page of Table 88

		NT	LM	VT	NT	VT	VT	NT	NT	VT
			◇1	◇1		◇1	◇1			◇1
		A			A			A	B	
				☕		☕	☕			☕
London Euston ⊖65	d			19 05		20 05	20 08			21 21
Birmingham New Street 12 65	d		19 35							
Crewe 10 65	d		20 31	20 49		21 46	21 55			23 45
Winsford	d		20 38							
Hartford	d		20 43							
Acton Bridge	d									
Runcorn	a		20 54	21 06		22 03	22 12			00 07
	d		20 54	21 06		22 03	22 12			00 07
Liverpool South Parkway 7 ✈	a		21 03							
	d	20 33	21 03		21 33			22 33	23 33	
West Allerton	d	20 36			21 36			22 36	23 36	
Mossley Hill	d	20 39			21 39			22 39	23 39	
Edge Hill 90	d									
Liverpool Lime Street 10 90	a	20 50	21 14	21 27	21 50	22 23	22 33	22 50	23 50	00 30

A From Manchester Oxford Road
B From Manchester Airport

Manchester and Bolton - Blackburn - Clitheroe

Mondays to Fridays

until 28 September

Network Diagram - see first page of Table 94

Miles			NT	NT	NT	NT	NT	NT	NT	NT	NT	NT	NT	NT	NT	NT	NT	NT	NT	NT	NT	NT
0	**Manchester Victoria** 82 ⇌	d		05 55		07 23	08 00	08 29	09 00	10 00	11 00	12 00	13 00	14 00	15 00	15 40	16 23	17 00	17 23	18 00	18 23	19 00
0¾	Salford Central 82	d				07 26	08 03	08 32	09 03	10 03	11 03	12 03	13 03	14 03	15 03	15 43	16 26	17 03	17 27	18 03	18 26	19 03
—	Manchester Piccadilly 10 82 ⇌	d			06 54																	
1¾	Salford Crescent 82	d		06 00	07 03	07 30	08 08	08 37	09 08	10 08	11 08	12 08	13 08	14 08	15 08	15 47	16 31	17 08	17 30	18 08	18 31	19 08
10¾	**Bolton** 82	d		06 12	07 19	07 42	08 20	08 49	09 20	10 20	11 20	12 20	13 20	14 20	15 20	16 00	16 43	17 20	17 43	18 20	18 43	19 20
12½	Hall I' Th' Wood	d		06 17	07 24	07 47	08 25	08 54	09 25	10 25	11 25	12 25	13 25	14 25	15 25	16 05	16 48	17 25	17 48	18 25	18 48	19 25
13½	Bromley Cross	d		06 20	07 27	07 53	08 28	08 57	09 28	10 28	11 28	12 28	13 28	14 28	15 28	16 10	16 51	17 28	17 55	18 28	18 54	19 28
16½	Entwistle	d				07x59	08x34		09x34	10x34	11x34	12x34	13x34	14x34	15x34	16x16	16x57	17x34		18x34		19x34
20¼	Darwen	a		06 31	07 39	08 06	08 41	09 09	09 41	10 41	11 41	12 41	13 41	14 41	15 41	16 23	17 04	17 41	18 07	18 41	19 06	19 41
—		d		06 42	07 39	08 11	08 41	09 11	09 41	10 41	11 41	12 41	13 41	14 41	15 41	16 23	17 11	17 41	18 07	18 41	19 11	19 41
—	Blackpool North 97	d																				
—	Preston 8 97	d																				
24½	**Blackburn**	a		06 49	07 46	08 20	08 51	09 20	09 50	10 50	11 50	12 50	13 50	14 50	15 50	16 30	17 20	17 51	18 16	18 48	19 21	19 51
—		d	06 25	06 52	07 47		08 52		09 52	10 52	11 52	12 52	13 52	14 52	15 52	16 31	17 20	17 53		18 49		19 52
27¼	Ramsgreave & Wilpshire	d	06 31	06 58	07 53		08 58		09 58	10 58	11 58	12 58	13 58	14 58	15 58	16 37	17 26	17 59		18 55		19 58
29¾	Langho	d	06 35	07 02	07 57		09 02		10 02	11 02	12 02	13 02	14 02	15 02	16 02	16 41	17 31	18 03		18 59		20 02
31¾	Whalley	d	06 39	07 06	08 01		09 06		10 06	11 06	12 06	13 06	14 06	15 06	16 06	16 45	17 35	18 07		19 03		20 06
34¼	**Clitheroe**	a	06 50	07 17	08 12		09 17		10 17	11 17	12 17	13 17	14 17	15 17	16 17	16 56	17 45	18 18		19 14		20 17

		NT	NT	NT FO	NT FX	NT FX	NT FO
Manchester Victoria 82 ⇌	d	20 00	21 00	22 00	22 00	23 00	23 00
Salford Central 82	d	20 03	21 03	22 04			23 03
Manchester Piccadilly 10 82 ⇌	d						
Salford Crescent 82	d	20 08	21 08	22 08	22 08	23 08	23 08
Bolton 82	d	20 20	21 20	22 20	22 20	23 20	23 20
Hall I' Th' Wood	d	20 25	21 25	22 25	22 25	23 25	23 25
Bromley Cross	d	20 28	21 28	22 28	22 28	23 28	23 28
Entwistle	d	20x34	21x34	22x34	22x34	23x34	23x34
Darwen	a	20 41	21 41	22 41	22 41	23 41	23 41
	d	20 41	21 41	22 41	22 41	23 41	23 41
Blackpool North 97	d						
Preston 8 97	d						
Blackburn	a	20 50	21 50	22 50	22 50	23 51	23 51
	d	20 52	21 52	22 51	22 51		
Ramsgreave & Wilpshire	d	20 58	21 58	22 57	22 57		
Langho	d	21 02	22 02	23 01	23 01		
Whalley	d	21 06	22 06	23 05	23 05		
Clitheroe	a	21 17	22 17	23 16	23 16		

Mondays to Fridays

from 1 October

		NT	NT	NT	NT	NT	NT	NT	NT	NT	NT	NT	NT	NT	NT	NT	NT	NT	NT	NT	NT	NT
Manchester Victoria 82 ⇌	d		05 55		07 23	08 00	08 29	09 00	10 00	11 00	12 00	13 00	14 00	15 00	15 40	16 23	17 00	17 23	18 00	18 23	19 00	20 00
Salford Central 82	d				07 26	08 03	08 32	09 03	10 03	11 03	12 03	13 03	14 03	15 03	15 43	16 26	17 03	17 27	18 03	18 26	19 03	20 03
Manchester Piccadilly 10 82 ⇌	d			06 54																		
Salford Crescent 82	d		06 00	07 03	07 30	08 08	08 37	09 08	10 08	11 08	12 08	13 08	14 08	15 08	15 47	16 31	17 08	17 30	18 08	18 31	19 08	20 08
Bolton 82	d		06 12	07 19	07 42	08 20	08 49	09 20	10 20	11 20	12 20	13 20	14 20	15 20	16 00	16 43	17 20	17 43	18 20	18 43	19 20	20 20
Hall I' Th' Wood	d		06 17	07 24	07 47	08 25	08 54	09 25	10 25	11 25	12 25	13 25	14 25	15 25	16 05	16 48	17 25	17 48	18 25	18 48	19 25	20 25
Bromley Cross	d		06 20	07 27	07 53	08 28	08 57	09 28	10 28	11 28	12 28	13 28	14 28	15 28	16 10	16 51	17 28	17 55	18 28	18 54	19 28	20 28
Entwistle	d				07x59	08x34		09x34	10x34	11x34	12x34	13x34	14x34	15x34	16x16	16x57	17x34		18x34		19x34	20x34
Darwen	a		06 31	07 39	08 06	08 41	09 09	09 41	10 41	11 41	12 41	13 41	14 41	15 41	16 23	17 04	17 41	18 07	18 41	19 06	19 41	20 41
	d		06 42	07 39	08 11	08 41	09 11	09 41	10 41	11 41	12 41	13 41	14 41	15 41	16 23	17 11	17 41	18 07	18 41	19 11	19 41	20 41
Blackpool North 97	d																					
Preston 8 97	d																					
Blackburn	a		06 49	07 46	08 20	08 51	09 20	09 50	10 50	11 50	12 50	13 50	14 50	15 50	16 30	17 20	17 51	18 16	18 48	19 21	19 51	20 50
	d	06 25	06 52	07 47		08 52		09 52	10 52	11 52	12 52	13 52	14 52	15 52	16 31	17 20	17 53		18 49		19 52	20 52
Ramsgreave & Wilpshire	d	06 31	06 58	07 53		08 58		09 58	10 58	11 58	12 58	13 58	14 58	15 58	16 37	17 26	17 59		18 55		19 58	20 58
Langho	d	06 35	07 02	07 57		09 02		10 02	11 02	12 02	13 02	14 02	15 02	16 02	16 41	17 31	18 03		18 59		20 02	21 02
Whalley	d	06 39	07 06	08 01		09 06		10 06	11 06	12 06	13 06	14 06	15 06	16 06	16 45	17 35	18 07		19 03		20 06	21 06
Clitheroe	a	06 52	07 19	08 14		09 19		10 19	11 19	12 19	13 19	14 19	15 19	16 19	16 58	17 47	18 20		19 16		20 19	21 19

		NT	NT FO	NT FX	NT FX	NT FO
Manchester Victoria 82 ⇌	d	21 00	22 00	22 00	23 00	23 00
Salford Central 82	d	21 03	22 04			23 03
Manchester Piccadilly 10 82 ⇌	d					
Salford Crescent 82	d	21 08	22 08	22 08	23 08	23 08
Bolton 82	d	21 20	22 20	22 20	23 20	23 20
Hall I' Th' Wood	d	21 25	22 25	22 25	23 25	23 25
Bromley Cross	d	21 28	22 28	22 28	23 28	23 28
Entwistle	d	21x34	22x34	22x34	23x34	23x34
Darwen	a	21 41	22 41	22 41	23 41	23 41
	d	21 41	22 41	22 41	23 41	23 41
Blackpool North 97	d					
Preston 8 97	d					
Blackburn	a	21 50	22 50	22 50	23 51	23 51
	d	21 52	22 51	22 51		
Ramsgreave & Wilpshire	d	21 58	22 57	22 57		
Langho	d	22 02	23 01	23 01		
Whalley	d	22 06	23 05	23 05		
Clitheroe	a	22 19	23 18	23 18		

Manchester and Bolton - Blackburn - Clitheroe

Saturdays

until 29 September

Network Diagram - see first page of Table 94

		NT	NT	NT	NT	NT	NT	NT	NT	NT	NT	NT	NT	NT	NT	NT	NT	NT	NT	NT	NT	NT	NT
Manchester Victoria 82 ⇌	d		05 55		07 23	08 00	08 29	09 00	09 29	10 00	11 00	12 00	13 00	14 00	15 00	15 40	16 23	17 00	17 23	18 00	18 23	19 00	20 00
Salford Central 82	d				07 26	08 03	08 32	09 03	09 32	10 03	11 03	12 03	13 03	14 03	15 03	15 43	16 26	17 03	17 26	18 03	18 26	19 03	20 03
Manchester Piccadilly 10 82 ⇌	d			06 54																			
Salford Crescent 82	d		06 00	07 03	07 30	08 08	08 37	09 08	09 37	10 08	11 08	12 08	13 08	14 08	15 08	15 47	16 31	17 08	17 31	18 08	18 31	19 08	20 08
Bolton 82	d		06 12	07 19	07 42	08 20	08 49	09 20	09 49	10 20	11 20	12 20	13 20	14 20	15 20	16 00	16 43	17 20	17 43	18 20	18 43	19 20	20 20
Hall I' Th' Wood	d		06 17	07 24	07 47	08 25	08 54	09 25	09 54	10 25	11 25	12 25	13 25	14 25	15 25	16 05	16 48	17 25	17 48	18 25	18 48	19 25	20 25
Bromley Cross	d		06 20	07 27	07 53	08 28	08 57	09 28	09 57	10 28	11 28	12 28	13 28	14 28	15 28	16 10	16 51	17 28	17 55	18 28	18 54	19 28	20 28
Entwistle	d				07x59	08x34		09x34		10x34	11x34	12x34	13x34	14x34	15x34	16x16	16x57	17x34		18x34		19x34	20x34
Darwen	a		06 31	07 39	08 06	08 41	09 09	09 41	10 09	10 41	11 41	12 41	13 41	14 41	15 41	16 23	17 04	17 41	18 07	18 41	19 06	19 41	20 41
	d		06 42	07 39	08 11	08 41	09 11	09 41	10 11	10 41	11 41	12 41	13 41	14 41	15 41	16 23	17 11	17 41	18 07	18 41	19 11	19 41	20 41
Blackpool North 97	d																						
Preston 8 97	d																						
Blackburn	a		06 49	07 46	08 20	08 51	09 20	09 50	10 20	10 50	11 50	12 50	13 50	14 50	15 49	16 30	17 19	17 51	18 21	18 48	19 21	19 51	20 50
	d	06 25	06 52	07 47		08 52		09 52		10 52	11 52	12 52	13 52	14 52	15 52	16 31	17 19	17 53		18 49		19 52	20 52
Ramsgreave & Wilpshire	d	06 31	06 58	07 53		08 58		09 58		10 58	11 58	12 58	13 58	14 58	15 58	16 37	17 25	17 59		18 55		19 58	20 58
Langho	d	06 35	07 02	07 57		09 03		10 02		11 02	12 02	13 02	14 02	15 02	16 02	16 41	17 30	18 03		18 59		20 02	21 02
Whalley	d	06 39	07 06	08 01		09 07		10 06		11 06	12 06	13 06	14 06	15 06	16 06	16 45	17 34	18 07		19 03		20 06	21 06
Clitheroe	a	06 50	07 17	08 12		09 17		10 17		11 17	12 17	13 17	14 17	15 17	16 17	16 56	17 44	18 18		19 14		20 17	21 17

		NT	NT	NT
Manchester Victoria 82 ⇌	d	21 00	22 01	23 05
Salford Central 82	d	21 03	22 03	23 08
Manchester Piccadilly 10 82 ⇌	d			
Salford Crescent 82	d	21 08	22 08	23 12
Bolton 82	d	21 20	22 20	23 24
Hall I' Th' Wood	d	21 25	22 25	23 29
Bromley Cross	d	21 28	22 28	23 32
Entwistle	d	21x34	22x34	23x38
Darwen	a	21 41	22 41	23 45
	d	21 41	22 41	23 45
Blackpool North 97	d			
Preston 8 97	d			
Blackburn	a	21 50	22 50	23 54
	d	21 52	22 52	
Ramsgreave & Wilpshire	d	21 58	22 58	
Langho	d	22 02	23 02	
Whalley	d	22 06	23 06	
Clitheroe	a	22 17	23 17	

Saturdays

from 6 October

		NT	NT	NT	NT	NT	NT	NT	NT	NT	NT	NT	NT	NT	NT	NT	NT	NT	NT	NT	NT	NT	NT
Manchester Victoria 82 ⇌	d		05 55		07 23	08 00	08 29	09 00	09 29	10 00	11 00	12 00	13 00	14 00	15 00	15 40	16 23	17 00	17 23	18 00	18 23	19 00	20 00
Salford Central 82	d				07 26	08 03	08 32	09 03	09 32	10 03	11 03	12 03	13 03	14 03	15 03	15 43	16 26	17 03	17 26	18 03	18 26	19 03	20 03
Manchester Piccadilly 10 82 ⇌	d			06 54																			
Salford Crescent 82	d		06 00	07 03	07 30	08 08	08 37	09 08	09 37	10 08	11 08	12 08	13 08	14 08	15 08	15 47	16 31	17 08	17 31	18 08	18 31	19 08	20 08
Bolton 82	d		06 12	07 19	07 42	08 20	08 49	09 20	09 49	10 20	11 20	12 20	13 20	14 20	15 20	16 00	16 43	17 20	17 43	18 20	18 43	19 20	20 20
Hall I' Th' Wood	d		06 17	07 24	07 47	08 25	08 54	09 25	09 54	10 25	11 25	12 25	13 25	14 25	15 25	16 05	16 48	17 25	17 48	18 25	18 48	19 25	20 25
Bromley Cross	d		06 20	07 27	07 53	08 28	08 57	09 28	09 57	10 28	11 28	12 28	13 28	14 28	15 28	16 10	16 51	17 28	17 55	18 28	18 54	19 28	20 28
Entwistle	d				07x59	08x34		09x34		10x34	11x34	12x34	13x34	14x34	15x34	16x16	16x57	17x34		18x34		19x34	20x34
Darwen	a		06 31	07 39	08 06	08 41	09 09	09 41	10 09	10 41	11 41	12 41	13 41	14 41	15 41	16 23	17 04	17 41	18 07	18 41	19 06	19 41	20 41
	d		06 42	07 39	08 11	08 41	09 11	09 41	10 11	10 41	11 41	12 41	13 41	14 41	15 41	16 23	17 11	17 41	18 07	18 41	19 11	19 41	20 41
Blackpool North 97	d																						
Preston 8 97	d																						
Blackburn	a		06 49	07 46	08 20	08 51	09 20	09 50	10 20	10 50	11 50	12 50	13 50	14 50	15 49	16 30	17 19	17 51	18 21	18 48	19 21	19 51	20 50
	d	06 25	06 52	07 47		08 52		09 52		10 52	11 52	12 52	13 52	14 52	15 52	16 31	17 19	17 53		18 49		19 52	20 52
Ramsgreave & Wilpshire	d	06 31	06 58	07 53		08 58		09 58		10 58	11 58	12 58	13 58	14 58	15 58	16 37	17 25	17 59		18 55		19 58	20 58
Langho	d	06 35	07 02	07 57		09 02		10 02		11 02	12 02	13 02	14 02	15 02	16 02	16 41	17 30	18 03		18 59		20 02	21 02
Whalley	d	06 39	07 06	08 01		09 06		10 06		11 06	12 06	13 06	14 06	15 06	16 06	16 45	17 34	18 07		19 03		20 06	21 06
Clitheroe	a	06 52	07 19	08 14		09 19		10 19		11 19	12 19	13 19	14 19	15 19	16 19	16 58	17 46	18 20		19 16		20 19	21 19

		NT	NT	NT
Manchester Victoria 82 ⇌	d	21 00	22 00	23 05
Salford Central 82	d	21 03	22 03	23 08
Manchester Piccadilly 10 82 ⇌	d			
Salford Crescent 82	d	21 08	22 08	23 12
Bolton 82	d	21 20	22 20	23 24
Hall I' Th' Wood	d	21 25	22 25	23 29
Bromley Cross	d	21 28	22 28	23 32
Entwistle	d	21x34	22x34	23x38
Darwen	a	21 41	22 41	23 45
	d	21 41	22 41	23 45
Blackpool North 97	d			
Preston 8 97	d			
Blackburn	a	21 50	22 50	23 54
	d	21 52	22 51	
Ramsgreave & Wilpshire	d	21 58	22 57	
Langho	d	22 02	23 01	
Whalley	d	22 06	23 05	
Clitheroe	a	22 19	23 18	

Table 94

Manchester and Bolton - Blackburn - Clitheroe

Sundays
until 30 September

Network Diagram - see first page of Table 94

	NT	NT 🚌	NT A	NT B	NT B	NT	NT	NT	NT	NT	NT	NT	NT	NT	NT	NT	NT	NT
Manchester Victoria 82 ⇌ d	08 01		09 00	09 00		10 00	11 00	12 00	13 00	14 00	15 00	16 00	17 00	18 00	19 00	20 00	21 00	22 00
Salford Central 82 d																		
Manchester Piccadilly 10 82 ⇌ d																		
Salford Crescent 82 d	08 07		09 07	09 08		10 08	11 08	12 08	13 08	14 08	15 08	16 08	17 08	18 08	19 08	20 08	21 08	22 08
Bolton 82 d	08 20		09 17	09 20		10 20	11 20	12 20	13 20	14 20	15 20	16 20	17 20	18 20	19 20	20 20	21 20	22 20
Hall I' Th' Wood d	08 25		09 22	09 25		10 25	11 25	12 25	13 25	14 25	15 25	16 25	17 25	18 25	19 25	20 25	21 25	22 25
Bromley Cross d	08 28		09 25	09 28		10 28	11 28	12 28	13 28	14 28	15 28	16 28	17 28	18 28	19 28	20 28	21 28	22 28
Entwistle d	08x34		09x32	09x34		10x34	11x34	12x34	13x34	14x34	15x34	16x34	17x34	18x34	19x34	20x34	21x34	22x34
Darwen a	08 41		09 38	09 41		10 41	11 41	12 41	13 41	14 41	15 41	16 41	17 41	18 41	19 41	20 41	21 41	22 41
d	08 41		09 38	09 41		10 41	11 41	12 41	13 41	14 41	15 41	16 41	17 41	18 41	19 41	20 41	21 41	22 41
Blackpool North 97 d		08 36																
Preston 8 97 d		09 05			10 00													
Blackburn a	08 48	09 25	09 46	09 48	10 18	10 48	11 48	12 48	13 48	14 48	15 48	16 48	17 48	18 48	19 48	20 48	21 48	22 50
d	08 54	09 27	09 49	09 50	10 21	10 50	11 50	12 50	13 50	14 50	15 50	16 50	17 50	18 50	19 50	20 50	21 50	
Ramsgreave & Wilpshire d	09 00	09 34	09 55	09 56	10 27	10 56	11 56	12 56	13 56	14 56	15 56	16 56	17 56	18 56	19 56	20 56	21 56	
Langho d	09 04	09 39	09 58	10 00	10 32	11 00	12 00	13 00	14 00	15 00	16 00	17 00	18 00	19 00	20 00	21 00	22 00	
Whalley d	09 08	09 43	10 02	10 04	10 37	11 04	12 04	13 04	14 04	15 04	16 04	17 04	18 04	19 04	20 04	21 04	22 04	
Clitheroe a	09 19	09 50	10 14	10 15	10 43	11 15	12 15	13 15	14 15	15 15	16 15	17 15	18 15	19 15	20 15	21 15	22 15	

Sundays
from 7 October

	NT	NT C 🚌	NT	NT	NT	NT	NT	NT	NT	NT	NT	NT	NT	NT	NT	NT
Manchester Victoria 82 ⇌ d	08 01		09 00	10 00	11 00	12 00	13 00	14 00	15 00	16 00	17 00	18 00	19 00	20 00	21 00	22 00
Salford Central 82 d																
Manchester Piccadilly 10 82 ⇌ d																
Salford Crescent 82 d	08 08		09 07	10 08	11 08	12 08	13 08	14 08	15 08	16 08	17 08	18 08	19 08	20 08	21 08	22 08
Bolton 82 d	08 20		09 19	10 20	11 20	12 20	13 20	14 20	15 20	16 20	17 20	18 20	19 20	20 20	21 20	22 20
Hall I' Th' Wood d	08 25		09 24	10 25	11 25	12 25	13 25	14 25	15 25	16 25	17 25	18 25	19 25	20 25	21 25	22 25
Bromley Cross d	08 28		09 27	10 28	11 28	12 28	13 28	14 28	15 28	16 28	17 28	18 28	19 28	20 28	21 28	22 28
Entwistle d	08x34		09x33	10x34	11x34	12x34	13x34	14x34	15x34	16x34	17x34	18x34	19x34	20x34	21x34	22x34
Darwen a	08 41		09 40	10 41	11 41	12 41	13 41	14 41	15 41	16 41	17 41	18 41	19 41	20 41	21 41	22 41
d	08 41		09 40	10 41	11 41	12 41	13 41	14 41	15 41	16 41	17 41	18 41	19 41	20 41	21 41	22 41
Blackpool North 97 d		08 36														
Preston 8 97 d		09 05														
Blackburn a	08 48	09 25	09 48	10 48	11 48	12 48	13 48	14 48	15 48	16 48	17 48	18 48	19 48	20 48	21 48	22 50
d	08 54	09 27	09 50	10 50	11 50	12 50	13 50	14 50	15 50	16 50	17 50	18 50	19 50	20 50	21 50	
Ramsgreave & Wilpshire d	09 00	09 34	09 56	10 56	11 56	12 56	13 56	14 56	15 56	16 56	17 56	18 56	19 56	20 56	21 56	
Langho d	09 04	09 39	10 00	11 00	12 00	13 00	14 00	15 00	16 00	17 00	18 00	19 00	20 00	21 00	22 00	
Whalley d	09 08	09 43	10 04	11 04	12 04	13 04	14 04	15 04	16 04	17 04	18 04	19 04	20 04	21 04	22 04	
Clitheroe a	09 21	09 50	10 17	11 17	12 17	13 17	14 17	15 17	16 17	17 17	18 17	19 17	20 17	21 17	22 17	

A 16 September, 23 September, 30 September
B until 9 September
C 7 October, 14 October, 21 October

Table 94

Clitheroe - Blackburn - Bolton and Manchester

Mondays to Fridays
until 28 September

Network Diagram - see first page of Table 94

Miles		NT	NT	NT	NT	NT	NT	NT	NT	NT	NT	NT	NT	NT	NT	NT	NT	NT	NT	NT	NT
0	**Clitheroe** d		06 40	07 07	07 40		08 26		09 40	10 40	11 40	12 40	13 40	14 40	15 26	16 40	17 09	18 09	18 40		19 40
2½	Whalley d		06 46	07 13	07 46		08 32		09 46	10 46	11 46	12 46	13 46	14 46	15 32	16 46	17 15	18 15	18 46		19 46
4½	Langho d		06 50	07 17	07 50		08 36		09 50	10 50	11 50	12 50	13 50	14 50	15 36	16 49	17 19	18 19	18 50		19 50
7	Ramsgreave & Wilpshire d		06 55	07 22	07 55		08 41		09 55	10 55	11 55	12 55	13 55	14 55	15 41	16 55	17 24	18 24	18 55		19 55
9¾	**Blackburn** a		07 01	07 29	08 01		08 47		10 01	11 01	12 01	13 01	14 01	15 01	15 47	17 01	17 30	18 30	19 01		20 01
—	d	06 28	07 02	07 30	08 03	08 32	09 03	09 31	10 03	11 03	12 03	13 03	14 03	15 03	15 51	17 03	17 31	18 31	19 03	19 31	20 03
—	Preston 8 97 a																				
—	Blackpool North 97 a																				
14	Darwen a	06 35	07 09	07 37	08 10	08 39	09 11	09 38	10 10	11 10	12 10	13 10	14 10	15 10	15 58	17 10	17 38	18 38	19 10	19 38	20 10
—	d	06 35	07 09	07 40	08 10	08 42	09 11	09 41	10 10	11 10	12 10	13 10	14 10	15 10	15 58	17 10	17 41	18 41	19 10	19 42	20 10
17¾	Entwistle d	06x42	07x16		08x17				10x17	11x17	12x17	13x17	14x17	15x17		17x17	17x48	18x48	19x17	19x49	20x17
20¾	Bromley Cross d	06 48	07 22	07 51	08 23	08 52	09 22	09 52	10 23	11 23	12 23	13 23	14 23	15 23	16 09	17 23	17 54	18 54	19 23	19 54	20 23
21¾	Hall I' Th' Wood d	06 50	07 24	07 53	08 25	08 55	09 25	09 55	10 25	11 25	12 25	13 25	14 25	15 25	16 12	17 25	17 56	18 56	19 25	19 57	20 25
23½	**Bolton** 82 a	06 55	07 30	07 58	08 30	09 02	09 30	10 00	10 30	11 30	12 30	13 30	14 30	15 30	16 17	17 30	18 01	19 01	19 31	20 02	20 30
32½	Salford Crescent 82 a	07 15	07 43	08 17	08 43	09 15	09 43	10 13	10 43	11 43	12 43	13 43	14 43	15 43	16 30	17 43	18 15	19 14	19 44	20 15	20 43
—	Manchester Piccadilly 10 82 ⇌ a																				
33½	Salford Central 82 a	07 18	07 46	08 20	08 46	09 18	09 46	10 16	10 46	11 46	12 46	13 46	14 46	15 46	16 33	17 46	18 17	19 17	19 46	20 17	20 46
34¼	**Manchester Victoria** 82 ⇌ a	07 26	07 53	08 25	08 52	09 26	09 52	10 21	10 52	11 52	12 52	13 52	14 52	15 54	16 41	17 53	18 24	19 23	19 53	20 24	20 52

	NT	NT FX	NT FO	NT	NT
Clitheroe d	20 40	21 40	21 40	22 40	23 24
Whalley d	20 46	21 46	21 46	22 46	23 30
Langho d	20 50	21 50	21 50	22 50	23 34
Ramsgreave & Wilpshire d	20 55	21 55	21 55	22 55	23 39
Blackburn a	21 01	22 01	22 01	23 01	23 45
d	21 03	22 03	22 03	23 03	
Preston 8 97 a					
Blackpool North 97 a					
Darwen a	21 10	22 10	22 10	23 10	
d	21 10	22 10	22 10	23 10	
Entwistle d	21x17	22x17	22x17	23x17	
Bromley Cross d	21 23	22 23	22 23	23 23	
Hall I' Th' Wood d	21 25	22 25	22 25	23 25	
Bolton 82 a	21 30	22 30	22 30	23 30	
Salford Crescent 82 a	21 43	22 43	22 43	23 43	
Manchester Piccadilly 10 82 ⇌ a					
Salford Central 82 a	21 46		22 46		
Manchester Victoria 82 ⇌ a	21 52	22 52	22 52	23 52	

Mondays to Fridays
from 1 October

	NT	NT	NT	NT	NT	NT	NT	NT	NT	NT	NT	NT	NT	NT	NT	NT	NT	NT	NT	NT	NT
Clitheroe d		06 40	07 06	07 39		08 26		09 40	10 40	11 40	12 40	13 40	14 40	15 26	16 40	17 09	18 08	18 40		19 40	20 40
Whalley d		06 46	07 12	07 45		08 32		09 46	10 46	11 46	12 46	13 46	14 46	15 32	16 46	17 15	18 14	18 46		19 46	20 46
Langho d		06 50	07 16	07 49		08 36		09 50	10 50	11 50	12 50	13 50	14 50	15 36	16 49	17 19	18 18	18 50		19 50	20 50
Ramsgreave & Wilpshire d		06 55	07 21	07 54		08 41		09 55	10 55	11 55	12 55	13 55	14 55	15 41	16 55	17 24	18 23	18 55		19 55	20 55
Blackburn a		07 01	07 28	08 01		08 48		10 01	11 01	12 01	13 01	14 01	15 01	15 47	17 01	17 30	18 29	19 01		20 01	21 01
d	06 28	07 02	07 29	08 03	08 32	09 03	09 31	10 03	11 03	12 03	13 03	14 03	15 03	15 51	17 03	17 31	18 30	19 03	19 31	20 03	21 03
Preston 8 97 a																					
Blackpool North 97 a																					
Darwen a	06 35	07 09	07 37	08 10	08 39	09 11	09 38	10 10	11 10	12 10	13 10	14 10	15 10	15 58	17 10	17 38	18 37	19 10	19 38	20 10	21 10
d	06 35	07 09	07 40	08 10	08 42	09 11	09 41	10 10	11 10	12 10	13 10	14 10	15 10	15 58	17 10	17 41	18 40	19 10	19 42	20 10	21 10
Entwistle d	06x42	07x16		08x17				10x17	11x17	12x17	13x17	14x17	15x17		17x17	17x48	18x47	19x17	19x49	20x17	21x17
Bromley Cross d	06 48	07 22	07 51	08 23	08 52	09 22	09 52	10 23	11 23	12 23	13 23	14 23	15 23	16 09	17 23	17 54	18 53	19 23	19 54	20 23	21 23
Hall I' Th' Wood d	06 50	07 24	07 53	08 25	08 55	09 25	09 55	10 25	11 25	12 25	13 25	14 25	15 25	16 12	17 25	17 56	18 55	19 25	19 57	20 25	21 25
Bolton 82 a	06 55	07 30	07 58	08 30	09 02	09 30	10 00	10 30	11 30	12 30	13 30	14 30	15 30	16 17	17 30	18 01	19 00	19 31	20 02	20 30	21 30
Salford Crescent 82 a	07 16	07 43	08 17	08 43	09 15	09 43	10 13	10 43	11 43	12 43	13 43	14 43	15 43	16 30	17 43	18 15	19 13	19 44	20 15	20 43	21 43
Manchester Piccadilly 10 82 ⇌ a																					
Salford Central 82 a	07 19	07 46	08 20	08 46	09 18	09 46	10 16	10 46	11 46	12 46	13 46	14 46	15 46	16 33	17 46	18 17	19 16	19 46	20 17	20 46	21 46
Manchester Victoria 82 ⇌ a	07 26	07 54	08 26	08 53	09 27	09 53	10 22	10 53	11 53	12 53	13 53	14 53	15 55	16 42	17 54	18 24	19 23	19 54	20 25	20 53	21 53

	NT FX	NT FO	NT	NT
Clitheroe d	21 40	21 40	22 40	23 24
Whalley d	21 46	21 46	22 46	23 30
Langho d	21 50	21 50	22 50	23 34
Ramsgreave & Wilpshire d	21 55	21 55	22 55	23 39
Blackburn a	22 01	22 01	23 01	23 45
d	22 03	22 03	23 03	
Preston 8 97 a				
Blackpool North 97 a				
Darwen a	22 10	22 10	23 10	
d	22 10	22 10	23 10	
Entwistle d	22x17	22x17	23x17	
Bromley Cross d	22 23	22 23	23 23	
Hall I' Th' Wood d	22 25	22 25	23 25	
Bolton 82 a	22 30	22 30	23 30	
Salford Crescent 82 a	22 43	22 43	23 43	
Manchester Piccadilly 10 82 ⇌ a				
Salford Central 82 a		22 46		
Manchester Victoria 82 ⇌ a	22 53	22 53	23 53	

Clitheroe - Blackburn - Bolton and Manchester

Network Diagram - see first page of Table 94

Saturdays until 29 September

		NT	NT	NT	NT	NT	NT	NT	NT	NT	NT	NT	NT	NT	NT	NT	NT	NT	NT	NT	NT	NT	NT
Clitheroe	d		07 07	07 41		08 26		09 40		10 40	11 40	12 40	13 40	14 40	15 26	16 40	17 09	18 09	18 40		19 40	20 40	21 40
Whalley	d		07 13	07 47		08 32		09 46		10 46	11 46	12 46	13 46	14 46	15 32	16 46	17 15	18 15	18 46		19 46	20 46	21 46
Langho	d		07 17	07 51		08 36		09 50		10 50	11 50	12 50	13 50	14 50	15 36	16 50	17 19	18 19	18 50		19 50	20 50	21 50
Ramsgreave & Wilpshire	d		07 22	07 56		08 41		09 55		10 55	11 55	12 55	13 55	14 55	15 41	16 55	17 24	18 24	18 55		19 55	20 55	21 55
Blackburn	a		07 28	08 02		08 47		10 01		11 01	12 01	13 01	14 01	15 01	15 47	17 01	17 30	18 30	19 01		20 01	21 01	22 01
	d	06 28	07 29	08 03	08 32	09 03	09 31	10 03	10 31	11 03	12 03	13 03	14 03	15 03	15 51	17 03	17 31	18 31	19 03	19 31	20 03	21 03	22 03
Preston 8 97	a																						
Blackpool North 97	a																						
Darwen	a	06 35	07 37	08 10	08 39	09 11	09 38	10 11	10 38	11 10	12 10	13 10	14 10	15 10	15 58	17 10	17 38	18 38	19 10	19 38	20 10	21 10	22 10
	d	06 35	07 40	08 10	08 42	09 11	09 41	10 11	10 39	11 10	12 10	13 10	14 10	15 10	15 58	17 10	17 41	18 41	19 10	19 42	20 10	21 10	22 10
Entwistle	d	06x42		08x17				10x18	10x46	11x17	12x17	13x17	14x17	15x17		17x17	17x48	18x48	19x17	19x49	20x17	21x17	22x17
Bromley Cross	d	06 48	07 51	08 23	08 52	09 22	09 52	10 23	10 51	11 23	12 23	13 23	14 23	15 23	16 09	17 23	17 54	18 54	19 23	19 54	20 23	21 23	22 23
Hall I' Th' Wood	d	06 50	07 53	08 25	08 55	09 25	09 55	10 26	10 54	11 25	12 25	13 25	14 25	15 25	16 12	17 25	17 56	18 56	19 26	19 57	20 25	21 25	22 25
Bolton 82	a	06 55	07 58	08 30	09 02	09 30	10 00	10 31	10 59	11 30	12 30	13 30	14 30	15 30	16 17	17 30	18 01	19 01	19 31	20 02	20 30	21 30	22 30
Salford Crescent 82	a	07 15	08 17	08 43	09 15	09 43	10 13	10 44	11 12	11 43	12 43	13 43	14 43	15 43	16 30	17 43	18 15	19 14	19 44	20 15	20 43	21 43	22 43
Manchester Piccadilly 10 82 ⇌	a																						
Salford Central 82	a	07 19	08 20	08 46	09 18	09 46	10 16	10 47	11 15	11 46	12 46	13 46	14 46	15 46	16 33	17 46	18 18	19 17	19 47	20 17	20 46	21 46	22 46
Manchester Victoria 82 ⇌	a	07 25	08 25	08 52	09 26	09 52	10 22	10 52	11 23	11 50	12 52	13 52	14 52	15 54	16 41	17 53	18 27	19 23	19 53	20 24	20 52	21 52	22 52

		NT	NT
Clitheroe	d	22 46	23 24
Whalley	d	22 52	23 30
Langho	d	22 56	23 34
Ramsgreave & Wilpshire	d	23 01	23 39
Blackburn	a	23 07	23 45
	d	23 09	
Preston 8 97	a		
Blackpool North 97	a		
Darwen	a	23 16	
	d	23 16	
Entwistle	d	23x23	
Bromley Cross	d	23 29	
Hall I' Th' Wood	d	23 31	
Bolton 82	a	23 37	
Salford Crescent 82	a		
Manchester Piccadilly 10 82 ⇌	a		
Salford Central 82	a		
Manchester Victoria 82 ⇌	a		

Saturdays from 6 October

		NT	NT	NT	NT	NT	NT	NT	NT	NT	NT	NT	NT	NT	NT	NT	NT	NT	NT	NT	NT	NT	NT
Clitheroe	d		07 07	07 40		08 26		09 40		10 40	11 40	12 40	13 40	14 40	15 26	16 40	17 09	18 09	18 40		19 40	20 40	21 40
Whalley	d		07 13	07 46		08 32		09 46		10 46	11 46	12 46	13 46	14 46	15 32	16 46	17 15	18 15	18 46		19 46	20 46	21 46
Langho	d		07 17	07 50		08 36		09 50		10 50	11 50	12 50	13 50	14 50	15 36	16 50	17 19	18 19	18 50		19 50	20 50	21 50
Ramsgreave & Wilpshire	d		07 22	07 55		08 41		09 55		10 55	11 55	12 55	13 55	14 55	15 41	16 55	17 24	18 24	18 55		19 55	20 55	21 55
Blackburn	a		07 28	08 02		08 47		10 01		11 01	12 01	13 01	14 01	15 01	15 47	17 01	17 30	18 30	19 01		20 01	21 01	22 01
	d	06 28	07 29	08 03	08 32	09 03	09 31	10 03	10 31	11 03	12 03	13 03	14 03	15 03	15 51	17 03	17 31	18 31	19 03	19 31	20 03	21 03	22 03
Preston 8 97	a																						
Blackpool North 97	a																						
Darwen	a	06 35	07 37	08 10	08 39	09 11	09 38	10 10	10 38	11 10	12 10	13 10	14 10	15 10	15 58	17 10	17 38	18 38	19 10	19 38	20 10	21 10	22 10
	d	06 35	07 40	08 10	08 42	09 11	09 41	10 10	10 39	11 10	12 10	13 10	14 10	15 10	15 58	17 10	17 41	18 41	19 10	19 42	20 10	21 10	22 10
Entwistle	d	06x42		08x17				10x17	10x46	11x17	12x17	13x17	14x17	15x17		17x17	17x48	18x48	19x17	19x49	20x17	21x17	22x17
Bromley Cross	d	06 48	07 51	08 23	08 52	09 22	09 52	10 23	10 51	11 23	12 23	13 23	14 23	15 23	16 09	17 23	17 54	18 54	19 23	19 54	20 23	21 23	22 23
Hall I' Th' Wood	d	06 50	07 53	08 25	08 55	09 25	09 55	10 25	10 54	11 25	12 25	13 25	14 25	15 25	16 12	17 25	17 56	18 56	19 25	19 57	20 25	21 25	22 25
Bolton 82	a	06 55	07 58	08 30	09 02	09 30	10 00	10 31	10 59	11 30	12 30	13 30	14 30	15 30	16 17	17 30	18 01	19 01	19 31	20 02	20 30	21 30	22 30
Salford Crescent 82	a	07 15	08 17	08 43	09 15	09 43	10 13	10 44	11 12	11 43	12 43	13 43	14 43	15 43	16 30	17 43	18 14	19 14	19 44	20 15	20 43	21 43	22 43
Manchester Piccadilly 10 82 ⇌	a																						
Salford Central 82	a	07 19	08 20	08 46	09 18	09 46	10 16	10 46	11 15	11 46	12 46	13 46	14 46	15 46	16 33	17 46	18 17	19 17	19 46	20 17	20 46	21 46	22 46
Manchester Victoria 82 ⇌	a	07 25	08 26	08 53	09 26	09 53	10 22	10 52	11 23	11 53	12 53	13 53	14 53	15 55	16 42	17 54	18 26	19 24	19 54	20 25	20 53	21 53	22 53

		NT	NT
Clitheroe	d	22 46	23 24
Whalley	d	22 52	23 30
Langho	d	22 56	23 34
Ramsgreave & Wilpshire	d	23 01	23 39
Blackburn	a	23 07	23 45
	d	23 09	
Preston 8 97	a		
Blackpool North 97	a		
Darwen	a	23 16	
	d	23 16	
Entwistle	d	23x23	
Bromley Cross	d	23 29	
Hall I' Th' Wood	d	23 31	
Bolton 82	a	23 36	
Salford Crescent 82	a	23 48	
Manchester Piccadilly 10 82 ⇌	a		
Salford Central 82	a		
Manchester Victoria 82 ⇌	a	00 01	

Table 94

Clitheroe - Blackburn - Bolton and Manchester

Network Diagram - see first page of Table 94

Sundays until 30 September

		NT	NT	NT	NT	NT	NT	NT	NT	NT	NT	NT A	NT	NT	NT 🚲	NT	NT	NT
Clitheroe	d		09 40	10 40	11 40	12 40	13 40	14 40	15 40	16 40	17 40	17 51	18 40	19 40	19 57	20 40	21 40	22 40
Whalley	d		09 46	10 46	11 46	12 46	13 46	14 46	15 46	16 46	17 46	17 57	18 46	19 46	20 04	20 46	21 46	22 46
Langho	d		09 50	10 50	11 50	12 50	13 50	14 50	15 50	16 50	17 50	18 02	18 50	19 50	20 09	20 50	21 50	22 50
Ramsgreave & Wilpshire	d		09 55	10 55	11 55	12 55	13 55	14 55	15 55	16 55	17 55	18 07	18 55	19 55	20 14	20 55	21 55	22 55
Blackburn	a		10 01	11 01	12 01	13 01	14 01	15 01	16 01	17 01	18 01	18 21	19 01	20 01	20 22	21 01	22 01	23 01
	d	09 03	10 03	11 03	12 03	13 03	14 03	15 02	16 05	17 02	18 03	18 27	19 03	20 03	20 25	21 03	22 03	23 03
Preston 8 97	a											18 48			20 47			
Blackpool North 97	a														21 16			
Darwen	a	09 10	10 10	11 10	12 10	13 10	14 10	15 10	16 12	17 10	18 10		19 10	20 10		21 10	22 10	23 10
	d	09 10	10 10	11 10	12 10	13 10	14 10	15 10	16 12	17 10	18 10		19 10	20 10		21 10	22 10	23 10
Entwistle	d	09x17	10x17	11x17	12x17	13x17	14x17	15x17		17x17	18x17		19x17	20x17		21x17	22x17	23x17
Bromley Cross	d	09 23	10 23	11 23	12 23	13 23	14 23	15 22	16 23	17 22	18 23		19 23	20 23		21 23	22 23	23 23
Hall I' Th' Wood	d	09 25	10 25	11 25	12 25	13 25	14 25	15 25	16 26	17 25	18 25		19 25	20 25		21 25	22 25	23 25
Bolton 82	a	09 30	10 31	11 30	12 30	13 30	14 30	15 30	16 31	17 30	18 30		19 31	20 30		21 30	22 30	23 30
Salford Crescent 82	a	09 43	10 43	11 43	12 43	13 43	14 43	15 42	16 43	17 42	18 43		19 44	20 43		21 43	22 43	23 43
Manchester Piccadilly 10 82 ⇌	a																	
Salford Central 82	a																	
Manchester Victoria 82 ⇌	a	09 53	10 52	11 52	12 52	13 52	14 52	15 52	16 52	17 52	18 52		19 52	20 52		21 52	22 52	23 52

Sundays from 7 October

		NT	NT	NT	NT	NT	NT	NT	NT	NT	NT	NT	NT	NT	NT B 🚲	NT	NT	NT
Clitheroe	d	22p46		09 40	10 40	11 40	12 40	13 40	14 40	15 40	16 40	17 40	18 40	19 40	19 57	20 40	21 40	22 40
Whalley	d	22p52		09 46	10 46	11 46	12 46	13 46	14 46	15 46	16 46	17 46	18 46	19 46	20 04	20 46	21 46	22 46
Langho	d	22p56		09 50	10 50	11 50	12 50	13 50	14 50	15 50	16 50	17 50	18 50	19 50	20 09	20 50	21 50	22 50
Ramsgreave & Wilpshire	d	23p01		09 55	10 55	11 55	12 55	13 55	14 55	15 55	16 55	17 55	18 55	19 55	20 14	20 55	21 55	22 55
Blackburn	a	23p07		10 01	11 01	12 01	13 01	14 01	15 01	16 01	17 01	18 01	19 01	20 01	20 22	21 01	22 01	23 01
	d	23p09	09 03	10 03	11 03	12 03	13 03	14 03	15 03	16 03	17 03	18 03	19 03	20 03	20 25	21 03	22 03	23 03
Preston 8 97	a														20 47			
Blackpool North 97	a														21 16			
Darwen	a	23p16	09 10	10 10	11 10	12 10	13 10	14 10	15 10	16 10	17 10	18 10	19 10	20 10		21 10	22 10	23 10
	d	23p16	09 10	10 10	11 10	12 10	13 10	14 10	15 10	16 10	17 10	18 10	19 10	20 10		21 10	22 10	23 10
Entwistle	d	23b23	09x17	10x17	11x17	12x17	13x17	14x17	15x17	16x17	17x17	18x17	19x17	20x17		21x17	22x17	23x17
Bromley Cross	d	23p29	09 23	10 23	11 23	12 23	13 23	14 23	15 23	16 23	17 23	18 23	19 23	20 23		21 23	22 23	23 23
Hall I' Th' Wood	d	23p31	09 25	10 25	11 25	12 25	13 25	14 25	15 25	16 25	17 25	18 25	19 25	20 25		21 25	22 25	23 25
Bolton 82	a	23p36	09 30	10 31	11 30	12 30	13 30	14 30	15 30	16 30	17 30	18 30	19 31	20 30		21 30	22 30	23 30
Salford Crescent 82	a	23p48	09 43	10 44	11 43	12 43	13 43	14 43	15 43	16 43	17 43	18 43	19 44	20 43		21 43	22 43	23 43
Manchester Piccadilly 10 82 ⇌	a																	
Salford Central 82	a																	
Manchester Victoria 82 ⇌	a	00 01	09 53	10 52	11 53	12 53	13 52	14 53	15 55	16 53	17 54	18 52	19 54	20 53		21 53	22 54	23 55

A until 9 September

B 7 October, 14 October, 21 October

b Previous night, stops on request

Network Diagram for Tables 97, 98, 99, 100

DM-15/08
Design BAJS

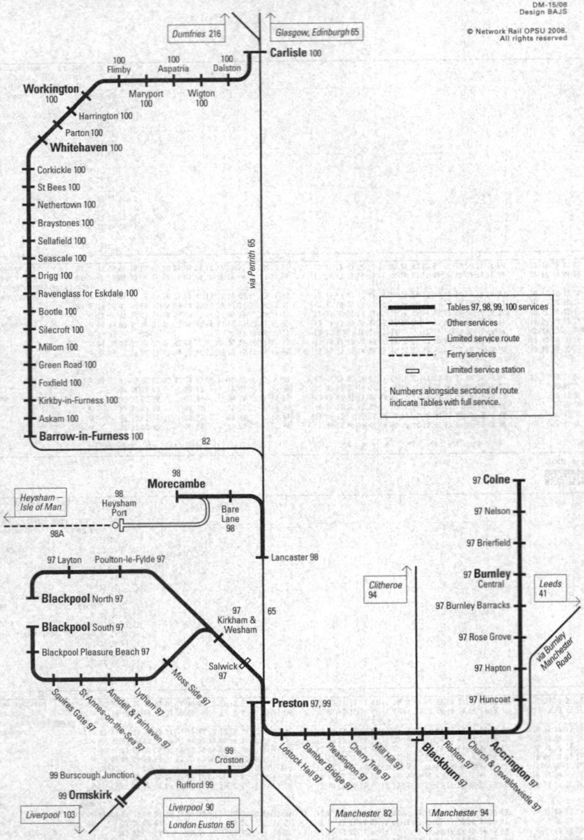

Table 97

Mondays to Fridays
until 28 September

Blackpool - Preston - Blackburn, Accrington, Burnley and Colne

Network Diagram - see first Page of Table 97

Miles	Miles			NT	TP	NT	NT	NT	TP	NT	NT	NT	TP	NT	NT	NT	TP	NT	NT	TP	NT	NT	NT
				MX	◇1				◇1				◇1				◇1			◇1			
					A			G	A ✠		C	G	A ✠	D		E	✠	C	G	✠		C	G
—	0	**Blackpool North**	d		03 37		04 56	05 29	05 39		06 19	06 28	06 40	06 53		07 02	07 10	07 18	07 29	07 36		08 20	08 29
—	1¼	Layton	d								06 22		06 43				07 13	07 21		07 39		08 23	
—	3¼	Poulton-le-Fylde	d				05 02	05 35	05 45		06 27	06 34	06 47			07 08	07 17	07 26	07 35	07 43		08 28	08 35
0	—	**Blackpool South**	d	23p30						05 42					06 42						07 42		
0½	—	Blackpool Pleasure Beach	d	23p32						05 44					06 44						07 44		
1¾	—	Squires Gate	d	23p34						05 46					06 46						07 46		
3¼	—	St Annes-on-the-Sea	d	23p38						05 50					06 50						07 50		
5¼	—	Ansdell & Fairhaven	d	23p41						05 53					06 53						07 53		
6½	—	Lytham	d	23p44						05 56					06 56						07 56		
9	—	Moss Side	d	23p49						06 01					07 01						08 01		
12¼	9¾	Kirkham & Wesham	d	23p56						06 08	06 36		06 56		07 09		07 26	07 35		07 52	08 09	08 37	
14¾	12¼	Salwick	d												07 13						08 13		
20	17½	**Preston** 8	a	00 08			05 20	05 52	06 03	06 19	06 46	06 52	07 07	07 15	07 20	07 28	07 37	07 46	07 52	08 03	08 20	08 47	08 52
—	—		d			04 47	05 22	05 54		06 21		06 54			07 22				07 54		08 22		08 54
22¾	—	Lostock Hall	d							06 26					07 27						08 27		
24	—	Bamber Bridge	d							06 29					07 30						08 30		
29	—	Pleasington	d							06x37					07x38						08x38		
30	—	Cherry Tree	d							06 40					07 41						08 41		
30¾	—	Mill Hill (Lancashire)	d							06 42					07 43						08 43		
32	—	**Blackburn**	a			05 03	05 38	06 09		06 45		07 09			07 50				08 09		08 47		09 09
—	—	Clitheroe 94	a																				
—	—	**Blackburn**	d			05 04	05 39	06 10		06 48		07 10			07 51				08 10		08 48		09 10
35¾	—	Rishton	d				05 44			06 53					07 56						08 53		
37½	—	Church & Oswaldtwistle	d				05 47			06 56					07 59						08 56		
38¾	—	**Accrington**	d			05 11	05 50	06 17		06 59		07 17			08 02				08 17		08 59		09 17
40	—	Huncoat	d				05x54			07x03					08x06						09x03		
41½	—	Hapton	d				05x57			07x06					08x09						09x06		
43	—	Rose Grove	d				06 00			07 09					08 12						09 09		
—	—	Burnley Manchester Road 41	a					06 26				07 26							08 26				09 26
—	—	Leeds 10 41	a					07 39				08 39							09 39				10 38
44	—	Burnley Barracks	d							07x12					08x15						09x12		
44½	—	**Burnley Central**	d			05 21	06 05			07 15					08 18						09 15		
46¾	—	Brierfield	d				06 09			07 19					08 22						09 19		
48	—	Nelson	d				06 12			07 22					08 25						09 22		
50	—	**Colne**	a			05 35	06 22			07 30					08 35						09 32		

		TP	NT	NT	NT	NT	TP	NT	NT	NT	NT	TP	NT	NT	NT	NT	TP	NT	NT	NT	NT	TP	NT
		◇1					◇1					◇1					◇1					◇1	
		A ✠		C	G	F	A ✠		C	G	F	A ✠		C	G	F	A ✠		C	G	F	A ✠	
Blackpool North	d	08 44		09 20	09 29	09 37	09 43		10 20	10 29	10 37	10 44		11 20	11 29	11 37	11 44		12 20	12 29	12 37	12 44	
Layton	d			09 23					10 23					11 23					12 23				
Poulton-le-Fylde	d	08 50		09 28	09 35		09 49		10 28	10 35		10 50		11 28	11 35		11 50		12 28	12 35		12 50	
Blackpool South	d		08 44					09 44					10 44					11 44					12 44
Blackpool Pleasure Beach	d		08 46					09 46					10 46					11 46					12 46
Squires Gate	d		08 48					09 48					10 48					11 48					12 48
St Annes-on-the-Sea	d		08 52					09 52					10 52					11 52					12 52
Ansdell & Fairhaven	d		08 55					09 55					10 55					11 55					12 55
Lytham	d		08 58					09 58					10 58					11 58					12 58
Moss Side	d		09 03					10 03					11 03					12 03					13 03
Kirkham & Wesham	d		09 10	09 37		09 52		10 10	10 37		10 52		11 10	11 37		11 52		12 10	12 37		12 52		13 10
Salwick	d																						
Preston 8	a	09 08	09 20	09 47	09 52	10 02	10 07	10 20	10 47	10 52	11 02	11 08	11 20	11 47	11 52	12 02	12 08	12 20	12 47	12 52	13 02	13 08	13 20
	d		09 22		09 54			10 22		10 54			11 22		11 54			12 22		12 54			13 22
Lostock Hall	d		09 27					10 27					11 27					12 27					13 27
Bamber Bridge	d		09 30					10 30					11 30					12 30					13 30
Pleasington	d		09x38					10x38					11x38					12x38					13x38
Cherry Tree	d		09 41					10 41					11 41					12 41					13 41
Mill Hill (Lancashire)	d		09 43					10 43					11 43					12 43					13 43
Blackburn	a		09 46		10 09			10 46		11 09			11 46		12 09			12 46		13 09			13 46
Clitheroe 94	a																						
Blackburn	d		09 48		10 10			10 48		11 10			11 48		12 10			12 48		13 10			13 48
Rishton	d		09 53					10 53					11 53					12 53					13 53
Church & Oswaldtwistle	d		09 56					10 56					11 56					12 56					13 56
Accrington	d		09 59		10 17			10 59		11 17			11 59		12 17			12 59		13 17			13 59
Huncoat	d		10x03					11x03					12x03					13x03					14x03
Hapton	d		10x06					11x06					12x06					13x06					14x06
Rose Grove	d		10 09					11 09					12 09					13 09					14 09
Burnley Manchester Road 41	a				10 26					11 27					12 26					13 26			
Leeds 10 41	a				11 39					12 39					13 40					14 39			
Burnley Barracks	d		10x12					11x12					12x12					13x12					14x12
Burnley Central	d		10 15					11 15					12 15					13 15					14 15
Brierfield	d		10 19					11 19					12 19					13 19					14 19
Nelson	d		10 22					11 22					12 22					13 22					14 22
Colne	a		10 32					11 32					12 32					13 32					14 32

A To Manchester Airport
C To Manchester Victoria
D To Hazel Grove
E To Liverpool Lime Street
F To Liverpool South Parkway
G To York

until 28 September

Blackpool - Preston - Blackburn, Accrington, Burnley and Colne

Network Diagram - see first Page of Table 97

		NT	NT	NT	TP	NT	NT	NT	NT	TP	NT	NT	NT	NT	TP	NT	NT	NT	NT	TP	NT	NT
					◇1					◇1					◇1					◇1		
		A	G	C	D		A	G	C	D		A	G	E	D		A	F	E	D		G
Blackpool North	d	13 20	13 29	13 37	13 44		14 20	14 29	14 37	14 44		15 20	15 29	15 37	15 44		16 20	16 29	16 35	16 40		17 14
Layton	d	13 23					14 23					15 23					16 23			16 44		
Poulton-le-Fylde	d	13 28	13 35		13 50		14 28	14 35		14 50		15 28	15 35		15 50		16 28	16 35		16 48		17 20
Blackpool South	d					13 44					14 44					15 44					16 44	
Blackpool Pleasure Beach	d					13 46					14 46					15 46					16 46	
Squires Gate	d					13 48					14 48					15 48					16 48	
St Annes-on-the-Sea	d					13 52					14 52					15 52					16 52	
Ansdell & Fairhaven	d					13 55					14 55					15 55					16 55	
Lytham	d					13 58					14 58					15 58					16 58	
Moss Side	d					14 03					15 03					16 02					17 03	
Kirkham & Wesham	d	13 37		13 52		14 10	14 37		14 52		15 10	15 37		15 52		16 10	16 37		16 52	16 57	17 10	17 29
Salwick	d															16 15						
Preston [8]	a	13 47	13 52	14 02	14 08	14 20	14 47	14 52	15 02	15 08	15 20	15 47	15 52	16 02	16 08	16 22	16 47	16 52	17 02	17 08	17 20	17 44
	d		13 54			14 22		14 54			15 22		15 54			16 22		16 54			17 22	17 44
Lostock Hall	d					14 27					15 27					16 27					17 27	17 51
Bamber Bridge	d					14 30					15 30					16 30					17 30	17 54
Pleasington	d					14x38					15x38					16x38					17x38	18x01
Cherry Tree	d					14 41					15 41					16 41					17 41	18 05
Mill Hill (Lancashire)	d					14 43					15 43					16 43					17 44	18 08
Blackburn	a		14 10			14 46		15 09			15 47		16 09			16 48		17 09			17 48	18 11
Clitheroe 94	a																					
Blackburn	d		14 10			14 48		15 10			15 48		16 10			16 50		17 10			17 58	18 11
Rishton	d					14 53					15 53					16 55					18 03	
Church & Oswaldtwistle	d					14 56					15 56					16 58					18 06	
Accrington	d		14 17			14 59		15 17			15 59		16 17			17 01		17 17			18 09	18 19
Huncoat	d					15x03					16x03					17x05					18x13	
Hapton	d					15x06					16x06					17x08					18x16	
Rose Grove	d					15 09					16 09					17 11					18 19	
Burnley Manchester Road 41	a		14 26					15 26					16 26					17 26				18 27
Leeds [10] 41	a		15 39					16 39					17 39					18 39				19 39
Burnley Barracks	d					15x12					16x12					17x14					18x22	
Burnley Central	d					15 15					16 15					17 18					18 25	
Brierfield	d					15 19					16 19					17 21					18 29	
Nelson	d					15 22					16 22					17 24					18 32	
Colne	a					15 32					16 32					17 34					18 42	

		TP	NT	NT	NT	NT	NT	TP	NT	NT	NT	TP	NT	NT	NT	NT	TP	NT	NT	TP	NT	NT	NT
		◇1						◇1				◇1					◇1			◇1			
		D	E		A	G	E	D		A	E	D		A	G	E	D		A	D		H	A
Blackpool North	d	17 20	17 37		18 20	18 29	18 37	18 44		19 20	19 37	19 44		20 20	20 29	20 37	20 44		21 20	21 44		22 14	22 20
Layton	d	17 23			18 23					19 23				20 23					21 23				22 23
Poulton-le-Fylde	d	17 27			18 28	18 35		18 50		19 28		19 50		20 28	20 35		20 50		21 28	21 50			22 28
Blackpool South	d			17 44					18 44				19 44					20 44			22 00		
Blackpool Pleasure Beach	d			17 46					18 46				19 46					20 46			22 02		
Squires Gate	d			17 48					18 48				19 48					20 48			22 04		
St Annes-on-the-Sea	d			17 52					18 52				19 52					20 52			22 08		
Ansdell & Fairhaven	d			17 55					18 55				19 55					20 55			22 11		
Lytham	d			17 58					18 58				19 58					20 58			22 14		
Moss Side	d			18 03					19 03				20 03					21 03			22 19		
Kirkham & Wesham	d		17 52	18 10	18 37		18 52		19 10	19 37			20 10	20 37				21 10	21 37		22 26		22 37
Salwick	d																						
Preston [8]	a	17 45	18 02	18 20	18 47	18 52	19 02	19 08	19 20	19 47	20 02	20 08	20 20	20 47	20 53	21 01	21 08	21 20	21 47	22 08	22 36	22 41	22 47
	d			18 24		18 54			19 22				20 22		20 54			21 22			22 38		
Lostock Hall	d			18 30					19 27				20 27					21 27			22 43		
Bamber Bridge	d			18 33					19 30				20 30					21 30			22 46		
Pleasington	d			18x41					19x38				20x38					21x38			22x54		
Cherry Tree	d			18 44					19 41				20 41					21 41			22 57		
Mill Hill (Lancashire)	d			18 46					19 43				20 43					21 43			22 59		
Blackburn	a			18 52		19 09			19 46				20 46		21 10			21 46			23 04		
Clitheroe 94	a																						
Blackburn	d			18 53		19 10			19 48				20 48		21 10			21 48			23 05		
Rishton	d			18 58					19 53				20 53					21 53			23 10		
Church & Oswaldtwistle	d			19 01					19 56				20 56					21 56			23 13		
Accrington	d			19 04		19 17			19 59				20 59		21 18			21 59			23 16		
Huncoat	d			19x08					20x03				21x03					22x03			23x20		
Hapton	d			19x11					20x06				21x06					22x06			23x23		
Rose Grove	d			19 14					20 09				21 09					22 09			23 26		
Burnley Manchester Road 41	a					19 26									21 27								
Leeds [10] 41	a					20 38									22 38								
Burnley Barracks	d			19x17					20x12				21x12					22x12			23x29		
Burnley Central	d			19 20					20 15				21 15					22 15			23 32		
Brierfield	d			19 24					20 19				21 19					22 19			23 36		
Nelson	d			19 27					20 22				21 22					22 22			23 39		
Colne	a			19 37					20 32				21 32					22 32			23 49		

A To Manchester Victoria
C To Liverpool South Parkway
D To Manchester Airport
E To Liverpool Lime Street
F To Selby
G To York
H To Wigan North Western

until 28 September

Blackpool - Preston - Blackburn, Accrington, Burnley and Colne

Network Diagram - see first Page of Table 97

		TP	NT	NT
		◇1		
		A	B	
Blackpool North	d	22 44	23 13	
Layton	d		23 16	
Poulton-le-Fylde	d	22 50	23 21	
Blackpool South	d			23 30
Blackpool Pleasure Beach	d			23 32
Squires Gate	d			23 34
St Annes-on-the-Sea	d			23 38
Ansdell & Fairhaven	d			23 41
Lytham	d			23 44
Moss Side	d			23 49
Kirkham & Wesham	d		23 30	23 56
Salwick	d			
Preston [8]	a	23 08	23 40	00 08
	d			
Lostock Hall	d			
Bamber Bridge	d			
Pleasington	d			
Cherry Tree	d			
Mill Hill (Lancashire)	d			
Blackburn	a			
Clitheroe 94	a			
Blackburn	d			
Rishton	d			
Church & Oswaldtwistle	d			
Accrington	d			
Huncoat	d			
Hapton	d			
Rose Grove	d			
Burnley Manchester Road 41	a			
Leeds [10] 41	a			
Burnley Barracks	d			
Burnley Central	d			
Brierfield	d			
Nelson	d			
Colne	a			

Mondays to Fridays

from 1 October

		NT MX	TP	NT	NT	NT	TP	NT	NT	NT	TP	NT	NT	NT	TP	NT	NT	TP	NT	NT	NT	TP	NT
			◇1				◇1				◇1				◇1			◇1				◇1	
			A			C	A		B	C	A	D		E		B	C			B	C	A	
Blackpool North	d		03 37		04 56	05 29	05 39		06 19	06 28	06 40	06 53		07 02	07 10	07 18	07 29	07 36		08 20	08 29	08 44	
Layton	d								06 22		06 43				07 13	07 21		07 39		08 23			
Poulton-le-Fylde	d				05 02	05 35	05 45		06 27	06 34	06 47			07 08	07 17	07 26	07 35	07 43		08 28	08 35	08 50	
Blackpool South	d	23p30						05 42					06 42						07 42				08 44
Blackpool Pleasure Beach	d	23p32						05 44					06 44						07 44				08 46
Squires Gate	d	23p34						05 46					06 46						07 46				08 48
St Annes-on-the-Sea	d	23p38						05 50					06 50						07 50				08 52
Ansdell & Fairhaven	d	23p41						05 53					06 53						07 53				08 55
Lytham	d	23p44						05 56					06 56						07 56				08 58
Moss Side	d	23p49						06 01					07 01						08 01				09 03
Kirkham & Wesham	d	23p56						06 08	06 36		06 56		07 09		07 26	07 35		07 52	08 09	08 37			09 10
Salwick	d												07 13						08 13				
Preston [8]	a	00 10			05 20	05 52	06 03	06 19	06 46	06 52	07 07	07 15	07 20	07 28	07 37	07 46	07 52	08 03	08 20	08 47	08 52	09 08	09 20
	d			04 47	05 22	05 54		06 21		06 54			07 22				07 54		08 22		08 54		09 22
Lostock Hall	d							06 26					07 27						08 27				09 27
Bamber Bridge	d							06 29					07 30						08 30				09 30
Pleasington	d							06x37					07x38						08x38				09x38
Cherry Tree	d							06 40					07 41						08 41				09 41
Mill Hill (Lancashire)	d							06 42					07 43						08 43				09 43
Blackburn	a			05 03	05 38	06 09		06 45		07 09			07 50				08 09		08 47		09 09		09 46
Clitheroe 94	a																						
Blackburn	d			05 04	05 39	06 10		06 48		07 10			07 51				08 10		08 48		09 10		09 48
Rishton	d				05 44			06 53					07 56						08 53				09 53
Church & Oswaldtwistle	d				05 47			06 56					07 59						08 56				09 56
Accrington	d			05 11	05 50	06 17		06 59		07 17			08 02				08 17		08 59		09 17		09 59
Huncoat	d				05x54			07x03					08x06						09x03				10x03
Hapton	d				05x57			07x06					08x09						09x06				10x06
Rose Grove	d				06 00			07 09					08 12						09 09				10 09
Burnley Manchester Road 41	a					06 26				07 26							08 26				09 26		
Leeds [10] 41	a					07 39				08 39							09 39				10 38		
Burnley Barracks	d							07x12					08x15						09x12				10x12
Burnley Central	d			05 21	06 05			07 15					08 18						09 15				10 15
Brierfield	d				06 09			07 19					08 22						09 19				10 19
Nelson	d				06 12			07 22					08 25						09 22				10 22
Colne	a			05 37	06 24			07 34					08 37						09 34				10 34

A To Manchester Airport
B To Manchester Victoria
C To York
D To Hazel Grove
E To Liverpool Lime Street

Table 97

Mondays to Fridays
from 1 October

Blackpool - Preston - Blackburn, Accrington, Burnley and Colne

Network Diagram - see first Page of Table 97

Station		NT	NT	NT	TP	NT	NT	NT	NT	TP	NT	NT	NT	NT	TP	NT	NT	NT	NT	TP	NT	NT	NT
		A	E	C	◇1 D ✠		A	E	C	◇1 D ✠		A	E	C	◇1 D ✠		A	E	C	◇1 D ✠		A	E
Blackpool North	d	09 20	09 29	09 37	09 43		10 20	10 29	10 37	10 44		11 20	11 29	11 37	11 44		12 20	12 29	12 37	12 44		13 20	13 29
Layton	d	09 23					10 23					11 23					12 23					13 23	
Poulton-le-Fylde	d	09 28	09 35		09 49		10 28	10 35		10 50		11 28	11 35		11 50		12 28	12 35		12 50		13 28	13 35
Blackpool South	d					09 44					10 44					11 44					12 44		
Blackpool Pleasure Beach	d					09 46					10 46					11 46					12 46		
Squires Gate	d					09 48					10 48					11 48					12 48		
St Annes-on-the-Sea	d					09 52					10 52					11 52					12 52		
Ansdell & Fairhaven	d					09 55					10 55					11 55					12 55		
Lytham	d					09 58					10 58					11 58					12 58		
Moss Side	d					10 03					11 03					12 03					13 03		
Kirkham & Wesham	d	09 37		09 52		10 10	10 37		10 52		11 10	11 37		11 52		12 10	12 37		12 52		13 10	13 37	
Salwick	d																						
Preston 8	a	09 47	09 52	10 02	10 07	10 20	10 47	10 52	11 02	11 08	11 20	11 47	11 52	12 02	12 08	12 20	12 47	12 52	13 02	13 08	13 20	13 47	13 52
	d		09 54			10 22		10 54			11 22		11 54			12 22		12 54			13 22		13 54
Lostock Hall	d					10 27					11 27					12 27					13 27		
Bamber Bridge	d					10 30					11 30					12 30					13 30		
Pleasington	d					10x38					11x38					12x38					13x38		
Cherry Tree	d					10 41					11 41					12 41					13 41		
Mill Hill (Lancashire)	d					10 43					11 43					12 43					13 43		
Blackburn	a		10 09			10 46		11 09			11 46		12 09			12 46		13 09			13 46		14 10
Clitheroe 94	a																						
Blackburn	d		10 10			10 48		11 10			11 48		12 10			12 48		13 10			13 48		14 10
Rishton	d					10 53					11 53					12 53					13 53		
Church & Oswaldtwistle	d					10 56					11 56					12 56					13 56		
Accrington	d		10 17			10 59		11 17			11 59		12 17			12 59		13 17			13 59		14 17
Huncoat	d					11x03					12x03					13x03					14x03		
Hapton	d					11x06					12x06					13x06					14x06		
Rose Grove	d					11 09					12 09					13 09					14 09		
Burnley Manchester Road 41	a		10 26					11 27					12 26					13 26					14 26
Leeds 10 41	a		11 39					12 39					13 40					14 39					15 39
Burnley Barracks	d					11x12					12x12					13x12					14x12		
Burnley Central	d					11 15					12 15					13 15					14 15		
Brierfield	d					11 19					12 19					13 19					14 19		
Nelson	d					11 22					12 22					13 22					14 22		
Colne	a					11 34					12 34					13 34					14 34		

Station		NT	TP	NT	NT	NT	NT	TP	NT	NT	NT	NT	TP	NT	NT	NT	NT	TP	NT	NT	TP	NT
		C	◇1 D ✠		A	E	C	◇1 D ✠		A	E	F	◇1 D ✠		A	G	F	◇1 D ✠		E	◇1 D ✠	F
Blackpool North	d	13 37	13 44		14 20	14 29	14 37	14 44		15 20	15 29	15 37	15 44		16 20	16 29	16 35	16 40		17 14	17 20	17 37
Layton	d				14 23					15 23					16 23			16 44			17 23	
Poulton-le-Fylde	d		13 50		14 28	14 35		14 50		15 28	15 35		15 50		16 28	16 35		16 48		17 20	17 27	
Blackpool South	d			13 44					14 44					15 44					16 44			
Blackpool Pleasure Beach	d			13 46					14 46					15 46					16 46			
Squires Gate	d			13 48					14 48					15 48					16 48			
St Annes-on-the-Sea	d			13 52					14 52					15 52					16 52			
Ansdell & Fairhaven	d			13 55					14 55					15 55					16 55			
Lytham	d			13 58					14 58					15 58					16 58			
Moss Side	d			14 03					15 03					16 02					17 03			
Kirkham & Wesham	d	13 52		14 10	14 37		14 52		15 10	15 37		15 52		16 10	16 37		16 52	16 57	17 10	17 29		17 52
Salwick	d													16 15								
Preston 8	a	14 02	14 08	14 20	14 47	14 52	15 02	15 08	15 20	15 47	15 52	16 02	16 08	16 22	16 47	16 52	17 02	17 08	17 20	17 44	17 45	18 02
	d			14 22		14 54			15 22		15 54			16 22		16 54			17 22	17 44		
Lostock Hall	d			14 27					15 27					16 27					17 27	17 51		
Bamber Bridge	d			14 30					15 30					16 30					17 30	17 54		
Pleasington	d			14x38					15x38					16x38					17x38	18x01		
Cherry Tree	d			14 41					15 41					16 41					17 41	18 05		
Mill Hill (Lancashire)	d			14 43					15 43					16 43					17 43	18 08		
Blackburn	a			14 46		15 09			15 47		16 09			16 48		17 09			17 48	18 11		
Clitheroe 94	a																					
Blackburn	d			14 48		15 10			15 48		16 10			16 50		17 10			17 58	18 11		
Rishton	d			14 53					15 53					16 55					18 03			
Church & Oswaldtwistle	d			14 56					15 56					16 58					18 06			
Accrington	d			14 59		15 17			15 59		16 17			17 01		17 17			18 09	18 19		
Huncoat	d			15x03					16x03					17x05					18x13			
Hapton	d			15x06					16x06					17x08					18x16			
Rose Grove	d			15 09					16 09					17 11					18 19			
Burnley Manchester Road 41	a					15 26					16 26					17 26				18 27		
Leeds 10 41	a					16 39					17 39					18 39				19 39		
Burnley Barracks	d			15x12					16x12					17x14					18x22			
Burnley Central	d			15 15					16 15					17 18					18 25			
Brierfield	d			15 19					16 19					17 21					18 29			
Nelson	d			15 22					16 22					17 24					18 32			
Colne	a			15 34					16 34					17 37					18 42			

A To Manchester Victoria
C To Liverpool South Parkway
D To Manchester Airport
E To York
F To Liverpool Lime Street
G To Selby

Table 97

Mondays to Fridays
from 1 October

Blackpool - Preston - Blackburn, Accrington, Burnley and Colne

Network Diagram - see first Page of Table 97

Station		NT	NT	NT	NT	TP	NT	NT	NT	TP	NT	NT	NT	NT	TP	NT	NT	TP	NT	NT	NT	TP	NT
			A	B	C	◇1 D ✠		A	C	◇1 D		A	B	C	◇1 D		A	◇1 D		E	A	◇1 D	A
Blackpool North	d		18 20	18 29	18 37	18 44		19 20	19 37	19 44		20 20	20 29	20 37	20 44		21 20	21 44		22 14	22 20	22 44	23 13
Layton	d		18 23					19 23				20 23					21 23				22 23		23 16
Poulton-le-Fylde	d		18 28	18 35		18 50		19 28		19 50		20 28	20 35		20 50		21 28	21 50			22 28	22 50	23 21
Blackpool South	d	17 44					18 44				19 44					20 44			22 00				
Blackpool Pleasure Beach	d	17 46					18 46				19 46					20 46			22 02				
Squires Gate	d	17 48					18 48				19 48					20 48			22 04				
St Annes-on-the-Sea	d	17 52					18 52				19 52					20 52			22 08				
Ansdell & Fairhaven	d	17 55					18 55				19 55					20 55			22 11				
Lytham	d	17 58					18 58				19 58					20 58			22 14				
Moss Side	d	18 03					19 03				20 03					21 03			22 19				
Kirkham & Wesham	d	18 10	18 37		18 52		19 10	19 37			20 10	20 37				21 10	21 37		22 26		22 37		23 30
Salwick	d																						
Preston 8	a	18 20	18 47	18 52	19 02	19 08	19 20	19 47	20 02	20 08	20 20	20 47	20 53	21 01	21 08	21 20	21 47	22 08	22 36	22 41	22 47	23 08	23 40
	d	18 24		18 54			19 22				20 22		20 54			21 22			22 38				
Lostock Hall	d	18 30					19 27				20 27					21 27			22 43				
Bamber Bridge	d	18 33					19 30				20 30					21 30			22 46				
Pleasington	d	18x41					19x38				20x38					21x38			22x54				
Cherry Tree	d	18 44					19 41				20 41					21 41			22 57				
Mill Hill (Lancashire)	d	18 46					19 43				20 43					21 43			22 59				
Blackburn	a	18 52		19 09			19 46				20 46		21 10			21 46			23 04				
Clitheroe 94	a																						
Blackburn	d	18 53		19 10			19 48				20 48		21 10			21 48			23 05				
Rishton	d	18 58					19 53				20 53					21 53			23 10				
Church & Oswaldtwistle	d	19 01					19 56				20 56					21 56			23 13				
Accrington	d	19 04		19 17			19 59				20 59		21 18			21 59			23 16				
Huncoat	d	19x08					20x03				21x03					22x03			23x20				
Hapton	d	19x11					20x06				21x06					22x06			23x23				
Rose Grove	d	19 14					20 09				21 09					22 09			23 26				
Burnley Manchester Road 41	a			19 26									21 27										
Leeds 10 41	a			20 38									22 38										
Burnley Barracks	d	19x17					20x12				21x12					22x12			23x29				
Burnley Central	d	19 20					20 15				21 15					22 15			23 32				
Brierfield	d	19 24					20 19				21 19					22 19			23 36				
Nelson	d	19 27					20 22				21 22					22 22			23 39				
Colne	a	19 39					20 34				21 34					22 34			23 51				

Station		NT
Blackpool North	d	
Layton	d	
Poulton-le-Fylde	d	
Blackpool South	d	23 30
Blackpool Pleasure Beach	d	23 32
Squires Gate	d	23 34
St Annes-on-the-Sea	d	23 38
Ansdell & Fairhaven	d	23 41
Lytham	d	23 44
Moss Side	d	23 49
Kirkham & Wesham	d	23 56
Salwick	d	
Preston 8	a	00 10
	d	
Lostock Hall	d	
Bamber Bridge	d	
Pleasington	d	
Cherry Tree	d	
Mill Hill (Lancashire)	d	
Blackburn	a	
Clitheroe 94	a	
Blackburn	d	
Rishton	d	
Church & Oswaldtwistle	d	
Accrington	d	
Huncoat	d	
Hapton	d	
Rose Grove	d	
Burnley Manchester Road 41	a	
Leeds 10 41	a	
Burnley Barracks	d	
Burnley Central	d	
Brierfield	d	
Nelson	d	
Colne	a	

A To Manchester Victoria
B To York
C To Liverpool Lime Street
D To Manchester Airport
E To Wigan North Western

Blackpool - Preston - Blackburn, Accrington, Burnley and Colne

Network Diagram - see first Page of Table 97

	NT	TP ◇1 A	NT	NT	NT H	TP ◇1 A	NT	NT C	NT H	TP ◇1 A	NT D	NT	NT E	NT C	NT H	TP ◇1 A	NT	NT C	NT H	NT F	TP ◇1 A	NT
Blackpool North d		03 37		04 56	05 29	05 39		06 19	06 28	06 40	06 53		07 02	07 18	07 29	07 44		08 20	08 29	08 38	08 44	
Layton d								06 22		06 43				07 21		07 47		08 23				
Poulton-le-Fylde d				05 02	05 35	05 45		06 27	06 34	06 47			07 08	07 26	07 35	07 51		08 28	08 35		08 50	
Blackpool South d	23p30						05 42					06 42					07 42					08 44
Blackpool Pleasure Beach d	23p32						05 44					06 44					07 44					08 46
Squires Gate d	23p34						05 46					06 46					07 46					08 48
St Annes-on-the-Sea d	23p38						05 50					06 50					07 50					08 52
Ansdell & Fairhaven d	23p41						05 53					06 53					07 53					08 55
Lytham d	23p44						05 56					06 56					07 56					08 58
Moss Side d	23p49						06 01					07 01					08 01					09 03
Kirkham & Wesham d	23p56						06 08	06 36		06 56		07 09		07 35		08 00	08 09	08 37				09 10
Salwick d												07 13					08 13					
Preston 8 a	00 08			05 20	05 52	06 03	06 19	06 46	06 52	07 07	07 15	07 20	07 28	07 46	07 52	08 11	08 20	08 47	08 52	09 02	09 08	09 20
d			04 47	05 22	05 54		06 21		06 54			07 22			07 54		08 22		08 54			09 22
Lostock Hall d							06 26					07 27					08 27					09 27
Bamber Bridge d							06 29					07 30					08 30					09 30
Pleasington d							06x37					07x38					08x38					09x38
Cherry Tree d							06 40					07 41					08 41					09 41
Mill Hill (Lancashire) d							06 42					07 43					08 43					09 43
Blackburn a			05 03	05 38	06 09		06 45		07 09			07 50			08 09		08 46		09 09			09 46
Clitheroe 94 a																						
Blackburn d			05 04	05 39	06 10		06 48		07 10			07 51			08 10		08 48		09 10			09 48
Rishton d				05 44			06 53					07 56					08 53					09 53
Church & Oswaldtwistle d				05 47			06 56					07 59					08 56					09 56
Accrington d			05 11	05 50	06 17		06 59		07 17			08 02			08 17		08 59		09 17			09 59
Huncoat d				05x54			07x03					08x06					09x03					10x03
Hapton d				05x57			07x06					08x09					09x06					10x06
Rose Grove d				06 00			07 09					08 12					09 09					10 09
Burnley Manchester Road 41 a					06 26				07 26						08 26				09 26			
Leeds 10 41 a					07 39				08 39						09 39				10 38			
Burnley Barracks d							07x12					08x15					09x12					10x12
Burnley Central d			05 21	06 05			07 15					08 18					09 15					10 15
Brierfield d				06 09			07 19					08 22					09 19					10 19
Nelson d				06 12			07 22					08 25					09 22					10 22
Colne a			05 35	06 22			07 32					08 35					09 32					10 32

	TP ◇1 G	NT C	NT H	NT F	TP ◇1 A	NT	NT C	NT H	NT F	TP ◇1 A	NT	NT C	NT H	NT F	TP ◇1 A	NT	NT C	NT H	NT F	TP ◇1 A	NT	TP ◇1 I
Blackpool North d	09 14	09 20	09 29	09 37	09 43		10 20	10 29	10 37	10 44		11 15	11 29	11 37	11 44		12 20	12 29	12 37	12 44		13 15
Layton d		09 23					10 23					11 18					12 23					
Poulton-le-Fylde d	09 20	09 28	09 35		09 49		10 28	10 35		10 50		11 23	11 35		11 50		12 28	12 35		12 50		
Blackpool South d						09 44					10 44					11 44					12 44	
Blackpool Pleasure Beach d						09 46					10 46					11 46					12 46	
Squires Gate d						09 48					10 48					11 48					12 48	
St Annes-on-the-Sea d						09 52					10 52					11 52					12 52	
Ansdell & Fairhaven d						09 55					10 55					11 55					12 55	
Lytham d						09 58					10 58					11 58					12 58	
Moss Side d						10 03					11 03					12 03					13 03	
Kirkham & Wesham d		09 37				10 10	10 37				11 10	11 32				12 10	12 37				13 10	
Salwick d																						
Preston 8 a	09 41	09 47	09 52	10 02	10 07	10 20	10 47	10 52	11 02	11 08	11 20	11 42	11 52	12 02	12 08	12 20	12 47	12 51	13 02	13 08	13 20	13 38
d			09 54			10 22		10 54			11 22		11 54			12 22		12 53			13 22	
Lostock Hall d						10 27					11 27					12 27					13 27	
Bamber Bridge d						10 30					11 30					12 30					13 30	
Pleasington d						10x38					11x38					12x38					13x38	
Cherry Tree d						10 41					11 41					12 41					13 41	
Mill Hill (Lancashire) d						10 43					11 43					12 43					13 43	
Blackburn a			10 09			10 46		11 09			11 46		12 09			12 46		13 08			13 46	
Clitheroe 94 a																						
Blackburn d			10 10			10 48		11 10			11 48		12 10			12 48		13 09			13 48	
Rishton d						10 53					11 53					12 53					13 53	
Church & Oswaldtwistle d						10 56					11 56					12 56					13 56	
Accrington d			10 18			10 59		11 17			11 59		12 17			12 59		13 16			13 59	
Huncoat d						11x03					12x03					13x03					14x03	
Hapton d						11x06					12x06					13x06					14x06	
Rose Grove d						11 09					12 09					13 09					14 09	
Burnley Manchester Road 41 a			10 26					11 27					12 26					13 25				
Leeds 10 41 a			11 39					12 39					13 39					14 39				
Burnley Barracks d						11x12					12x12					13x12					14x12	
Burnley Central d						11 15					12 15					13 15					14 15	
Brierfield d						11 19					12 19					13 19					14 19	
Nelson d						11 22					12 22					13 22					14 22	
Colne a						11 32					12 32					13 32					14 32	

A To Manchester Airport
C To Manchester Victoria
D To Hazel Grove
E To Liverpool Lime Street
F To Liverpool South Parkway
G To Barrow-in-Furness
H To York
I from 30 June until 8 September

Blackpool - Preston - Blackburn, Accrington, Burnley and Colne

Network Diagram - see first Page of Table 97

	NT A	NT G	NT C	TP ◇1 D	NT	NT A	NT G	NT C	TP ◇1 D	NT	NT A	NT G	NT E	TP ◇1 D	NT	NT A	NT F	NT E	TP ◇1 D	NT	NT G
Blackpool North d	13 20	13 29	13 37	13 44		14 20	14 29	14 37	14 44		15 20	15 29	15 37	15 44		16 20	16 29	16 35	16 40		17 14
Layton d	13 23					14 23					15 23					16 23			16 43		
Poulton-le-Fylde d	13 28	13 35		13 50		14 28	14 35		14 50		15 28	15 35		15 50		16 28	16 35		16 48		17 20
Blackpool South d					13 44					14 44					15 44					16 44	
Blackpool Pleasure Beach d					13 46					14 46					15 46					16 46	
Squires Gate d					13 48					14 48					15 48					16 48	
St Annes-on-the-Sea d					13 52					14 52					15 52					16 52	
Ansdell & Fairhaven d					13 55					14 55					15 55					16 55	
Lytham d					13 58					14 58					15 58					16 58	
Moss Side d					14 03					15 03					16 03					17 03	
Kirkham & Wesham d	13 37				14 10	14 37				15 10	15 37				16 10	16 37			16 57	17 10	17 29
Salwick d															16 15						
Preston 8 a	13 47	13 52	14 02	14 08	14 20	14 47	14 52	15 02	15 08	15 20	15 47	15 52	16 02	16 08	16 22	16 47	16 52	17 02	17 08	17 20	17 42
d		13 54			14 22		14 54			15 22		15 54			16 22		16 54			17 22	17 44
Lostock Hall d					14 27					15 27					16 27					17 27	17 51
Bamber Bridge d					14 30					15 30					16 30					17 30	17 54
Pleasington d					14x38					15x38					16x38					17x38	18x01
Cherry Tree d					14 41					15 41					16 41					17 41	18 05
Mill Hill (Lancashire) d					14 43					15 43					16 43					17 43	18 08
Blackburn a		14 09			14 46		15 09			15 46		16 09			16 48		17 09			17 47	18 11
Clitheroe 94 a																					
Blackburn d		14 10			14 48		15 10			15 48		16 10			16 50		17 10			17 48	18 11
Rishton d					14 53					15 53					16 55					17 53	
Church & Oswaldtwistle d					14 56					15 56					16 58					17 56	
Accrington d		14 17			14 59		15 17			15 59		16 17			17 01		17 17			17 59	18 19
Huncoat d					15x03					16x03					17x05					18x03	
Hapton d					15x06					16x06					17x08					18x06	
Rose Grove d					15 09					16 09					17 11					18 09	
Burnley Manchester Road 41 a		14 26					15 26					16 26					17 26				18 27
Leeds 10 41 a		15 39					16 39					17 39					18 39				19 39
Burnley Barracks d					15x12					16x12					17x14					18x12	
Burnley Central d					15 15					16 15					17 16					18 15	
Brierfield d					15 19					16 19					17 21					18 19	
Nelson d					15 22					16 22					17 24					18 22	
Colne a					15 32					16 32					17 34					18 32	

	TP ◇1 D	NT E	NT	NT A	NT G	NT E	TP ◇1 D	NT	NT A	NT E	TP ◇1 D	NT	NT A	NT G	NT E	TP ◇1 D	NT	NT A	TP ◇1 D	NT	NT E	NT A
Blackpool North d	17 20	17 37		18 20	18 29	18 37	18 44		19 20	19 37	19 44		20 20	20 29	20 37	20 42		21 20	21 44		22 14	22 20
Layton d	17 23			18 23					19 23				20 23					21 23				22 23
Poulton-le-Fylde d	17 27			18 28	18 35		18 50		19 28		19 50		20 28	20 35		20 48		21 28	21 50			22 28
Blackpool South d			17 44					18 44				19 44					20 44			22 00		
Blackpool Pleasure Beach d			17 46					18 46				19 46					20 46			22 02		
Squires Gate d			17 48					18 48				19 48					20 48			22 04		
St Annes-on-the-Sea d			17 52					18 52				19 52					20 52			22 08		
Ansdell & Fairhaven d			17 55					18 55				19 55					20 55			22 11		
Lytham d			17 58					18 58				19 58					20 58			22 14		
Moss Side d			18 03					19 03				20 03					21 03			22 19		
Kirkham & Wesham d			18 10	18 37				19 10	19 37			20 10	20 37				21 10	21 37		22 26		22 37
Salwick d																						
Preston 8 a	17 45	18 02	18 22	18 47	18 52	19 00	19 08	19 20	19 47	20 02	20 08	20 20	20 47	20 53	21 01	21 06	21 20	21 47	22 08	22 36	22 41	22 47
d			18 24		18 54			19 22				20 22		20 54			21 22			22 38		
Lostock Hall d			18 30					19 27				20 27					21 27			22 43		
Bamber Bridge d			18 33					19 30				20 30					21 30			22 46		
Pleasington d			18x41					19x38				20x38					21x38			22x54		
Cherry Tree d			18 44					19 41				20 41					21 41			22 57		
Mill Hill (Lancashire) d			18 46					19 43				20 43					21 43			22 59		
Blackburn a			18 52		19 09			19 46				20 46		21 10			21 46			23 06		
Clitheroe 94 a																						
Blackburn d			18 53		19 10			19 48				20 48		21 10			21 48					
Rishton d			18 58					19 53				20 53					21 53					
Church & Oswaldtwistle d			19 01					19 56				20 56					21 56					
Accrington d			19 04		19 17			19 59				20 59		21 18			21 59					
Huncoat d			19x08					20x03				21x03					22x03					
Hapton d			19x11					20x06				21x06					22x06					
Rose Grove d			19 14					20 09				21 09					22 09					
Burnley Manchester Road 41 a					19 26									21 27								
Leeds 10 41 a					20 38									22 35								
Burnley Barracks d			19x17					20x12				21x12					22x12					
Burnley Central d			19 20					20 15				21 15					22 15					
Brierfield d			19 24					20 19				21 19					22 19					
Nelson d			19 27					20 22				21 22					22 22					
Colne a			19 37					20 32				21 32					22 32					

A To Manchester Victoria
C To Liverpool South Parkway
D To Manchester Airport
E To Liverpool Lime Street
F To Hull
G To York

Blackpool - Preston - Blackburn, Accrington, Burnley and Colne

Network Diagram - see first Page of Table 97

		TP	NT	NT	NT
		◇1			
		A	B	(bus)	
Blackpool North	d	22 44	23 02		
Layton	d		23 05		
Poulton-le-Fylde	d	22 50	23 10		
Blackpool South	d				23 30
Blackpool Pleasure Beach	d				23 32
Squires Gate	d				23 34
St Annes-on-the-Sea	d				23 38
Ansdell & Fairhaven	d				23 41
Lytham	d				23 44
Moss Side	d				23 49
Kirkham & Wesham	d		23 19		23 56
Salwick	d				
Preston 8	a	23 08	23 29		00 08
	d				
Lostock Hall	d				
Bamber Bridge	d				
Pleasington	d				
Cherry Tree	d				
Mill Hill (Lancashire)	d				
Blackburn	a				
Clitheroe 94	a				
Blackburn	d			23 14	
Rishton	d			23 24	
Church & Oswaldtwistle	d			23 36	
Accrington	d			23 40	
Huncoat	d			23 46	
Hapton	d			23 52	
Rose Grove	d			23 58	
Burnley Manchester Road 41	a				
Leeds 10 41	a				
Burnley Barracks	d			00 02	
Burnley Central	d			00 07	
Brierfield	d			00 15	
Nelson	d			00 20	
Colne	a			00 28	

Saturdays
from 6 October

		NT	TP	NT	NT	NT	TP	NT	NT	NT	TP	NT	NT	NT	NT	NT	TP	NT	NT	NT	NT	TP	NT
			◇1				◇1				◇1						◇1					◇1	
			A			C	A		B	C	A 🚲	D		E	B	C	A 🚲		B	C	F	A 🚲	
Blackpool North	d		03 37		04 56	05 29	05 39		06 19	06 28	06 40	06 53		07 02	07 18	07 29	07 44		08 20	08 29	08 38	08 44	
Layton	d								06 22		06 43				07 21		07 47		08 23				
Poulton-le-Fylde	d				05 02	05 35	05 45		06 27	06 34	06 47			07 08	07 26	07 35	07 51		08 28	08 35		08 50	
Blackpool South	d	23p30						05 42					06 42					07 42					08 44
Blackpool Pleasure Beach	d	23p32						05 44					06 44					07 44					08 46
Squires Gate	d	23p34						05 46					06 46					07 46					08 48
St Annes-on-the-Sea	d	23p38						05 50					06 50					07 50					08 52
Ansdell & Fairhaven	d	23p41						05 53					06 53					07 53					08 55
Lytham	d	23p44						05 56					06 56					07 56					08 58
Moss Side	d	23p49						06 01					07 01					08 01					09 03
Kirkham & Wesham	d	23p56						06 08	06 36		06 56		07 09		07 35		08 00	08 09	08 37				09 10
Salwick	d												07 13					08 13					
Preston 8	a	00 10			05 20	05 52	06 03	06 19	06 46	06 52	07 07	07 15	07 20	07 28	07 46	07 52	08 11	08 20	08 47	08 52	09 02	09 08	09 20
	d			04 47	05 22	05 54		06 21		06 54			07 22			07 54		08 22		08 54			09 22
Lostock Hall	d							06 26					07 27					08 27					09 27
Bamber Bridge	d							06 29					07 30					08 30					09 30
Pleasington	d							06x37					07x38					08x38					09x38
Cherry Tree	d							06 40					07 41					08 41					09 41
Mill Hill (Lancashire)	d							06 42					07 43					08 43					09 43
Blackburn	a			05 03	05 38	06 09		06 45		07 09			07 50			08 09		08 46		09 09			09 46
Clitheroe 94	a																						
Blackburn	d			05 04	05 39	06 10		06 48		07 10			07 51			08 10		08 48		09 10			09 48
Rishton	d				05 44			06 53					07 56					08 53					09 53
Church & Oswaldtwistle	d				05 47			06 56					07 59					08 56					09 56
Accrington	d			05 11	05 50	06 17		06 59		07 17			08 02			08 17		08 59		09 17			09 59
Huncoat	d				05x54			07x03					08x06					09x03					10x03
Hapton	d				05x57			07x06					08x09					09x06					10x06
Rose Grove	d				06 00			07 09					08 12					09 09					10 09
Burnley Manchester Road 41	a					06 26				07 26						08 26				09 26			
Leeds 10 41	a					07 39				08 39						09 39				10 38			
Burnley Barracks	d							07x12					08x15					09x12					10x12
Burnley Central	d			05 21	06 05			07 15					08 18					09 15					10 15
Brierfield	d				06 09			07 19					08 22					09 19					10 19
Nelson	d				06 12			07 22					08 25					09 22					10 22
Colne	a			05 37	06 24			07 34					08 37					09 34					10 34

A To Manchester Airport
B To Manchester Victoria
C To York
D To Hazel Grove
E To Liverpool Lime Street
F To Liverpool South Parkway

Table 97

Blackpool - Preston - Blackburn, Accrington, Burnley and Colne

Network Diagram - see first Page of Table 97

		TP	NT	NT	NT	TP	NT	NT	NT	NT	TP	NT	NT	NT	NT	TP	NT	NT	NT	NT	TP	NT	NT
		◇1				◇1					◇1					◇1					◇1		
		A	B	F	D	E 🚲		B	F	D	E 🚲		B	F	D	E 🚲		B	F	D	E 🚲		B
Blackpool North	d	09 14	09 20	09 29	09 37	09 43		10 20	10 29	10 37	10 44		11 15	11 29	11 37	11 44		12 20	12 29	12 37	12 44		13 20
Layton	d		09 23					10 23					11 18					12 23					13 23
Poulton-le-Fylde	d	09 20	09 28	09 35		09 49		10 28	10 35		10 50		11 23	11 35		11 50		12 28	12 35		12 50		13 28
Blackpool South	d						09 44					10 44					11 44					12 44	
Blackpool Pleasure Beach	d						09 46					10 46					11 46					12 46	
Squires Gate	d						09 48					10 48					11 48					12 48	
St Annes-on-the-Sea	d						09 52					10 52					11 52					12 52	
Ansdell & Fairhaven	d						09 55					10 55					11 55					12 55	
Lytham	d						09 58					10 58					11 58					12 58	
Moss Side	d						10 03					11 03					12 03					13 03	
Kirkham & Wesham	d		09 37				10 10	10 37				11 10	11 32				12 10	12 37				13 10	13 37
Salwick	d																						
Preston 8	a	09 41	09 47	09 52	10 02	10 07	10 20	10 47	10 52	11 02	11 08	11 20	11 42	11 52	12 02	12 08	12 20	12 47	12 51	13 02	13 08	13 20	13 47
	d			09 54			10 22		10 54			11 22		11 54			12 22		12 53			13 22	
Lostock Hall	d						10 27					11 27					12 27					13 27	
Bamber Bridge	d						10 30					11 30					12 30					13 30	
Pleasington	d						10x38					11x38					12x38					13x38	
Cherry Tree	d						10 41					11 41					12 41					13 41	
Mill Hill (Lancashire)	d						10 43					11 43					12 43					13 43	
Blackburn	a			10 09			10 46		11 09			11 46		12 09			12 46		13 08			13 46	
Clitheroe 94	a																						
Blackburn	d			10 10			10 48		11 10			11 48		12 10			12 48		13 09			13 48	
Rishton	d						10 53					11 53					12 53					13 53	
Church & Oswaldtwistle	d						10 56					11 56					12 56					13 56	
Accrington	d			10 18			10 59		11 17			11 59		12 17			12 59		13 16			13 59	
Huncoat	d						11x03					12x03					13x03					14x03	
Hapton	d						11x06					12x06					13x06					14x06	
Rose Grove	d						11 09					12 09					13 09					14 09	
Burnley Manchester Road 41	a			10 26					11 27					12 26					13 25				
Leeds 10 41	a			11 39					12 39					13 39					14 39				
Burnley Barracks	d						11x12					12x12					13x12					14x12	
Burnley Central	d						11 15					12 15					13 15					14 15	
Brierfield	d						11 19					12 19					13 19					14 19	
Nelson	d						11 22					12 22					13 22					14 22	
Colne	a						11 34					12 34					13 34					14 34	

		NT	NT	TP	NT	NT	NT	NT	TP	NT	NT	NT	NT	TP	NT	NT	NT	NT	TP	NT	NT	TP
				◇1					◇1					◇1					◇1			◇1
		F	D	E 🚲		B	F	D	E 🚲		B	F	G	E 🚲		B	H	G	E 🚲		F	E 🚲
Blackpool North	d	13 29	13 37	13 44		14 20	14 29	14 37	14 44		15 20	15 29	15 37	15 44		16 20	16 29	16 35	16 40		17 14	17 20
Layton	d					14 23					15 23					16 23			16 43			17 23
Poulton-le-Fylde	d	13 35		13 50		14 28	14 35		14 50		15 28	15 35		15 50		16 28	16 35		16 48		17 20	17 27
Blackpool South	d				13 44					14 44					15 44					16 44		
Blackpool Pleasure Beach	d				13 46					14 46					15 46					16 46		
Squires Gate	d				13 48					14 48					15 48					16 48		
St Annes-on-the-Sea	d				13 52					14 52					15 52					16 52		
Ansdell & Fairhaven	d				13 55					14 55					15 55					16 55		
Lytham	d				13 58					14 58					15 58					16 58		
Moss Side	d				14 03					15 03					16 03					17 03		
Kirkham & Wesham	d				14 10	14 37				15 10	15 37				16 10	16 37			16 57	17 10	17 29	
Salwick	d														16 15							
Preston 8	a	13 52	14 02	14 08	14 20	14 47	14 52	15 02	15 08	15 20	15 47	15 52	16 02	16 08	16 22	16 47	16 52	17 02	17 08	17 20	17 42	17 45
	d	13 54			14 22		14 54			15 22		15 54			16 22		16 54			17 22	17 44	
Lostock Hall	d				14 27					15 27					16 27					17 27	17 51	
Bamber Bridge	d				14 30					15 30					16 30					17 30	17 54	
Pleasington	d				14x38					15x38					16x38					17x38	18x01	
Cherry Tree	d				14 41					15 41					16 41					17 41	18 05	
Mill Hill (Lancashire)	d				14 43					15 43					16 43					17 43	18 08	
Blackburn	a	14 09			14 46		15 09			15 46		16 09			16 48		17 09			17 47	18 11	
Clitheroe 94	a																					
Blackburn	d	14 10			14 48		15 10			15 48		16 10			16 50		17 10			17 48	18 11	
Rishton	d				14 53					15 53					16 55					17 53		
Church & Oswaldtwistle	d				14 56					15 56					16 58					17 56		
Accrington	d	14 17			14 59		15 17			15 59		16 17			17 01		17 17			17 59	18 19	
Huncoat	d				15x03					16x03					17x05					18x03		
Hapton	d				15x06					16x06					17x08					18x06		
Rose Grove	d				15 09					16 09					17 11					18 09		
Burnley Manchester Road 41	a	14 26					15 26					16 26					17 26				18 27	
Leeds 10 41	a	15 39					16 39					17 39					18 39				19 39	
Burnley Barracks	d				15x12					16x12					17x14					18x12		
Burnley Central	d				15 15					16 15					17 16					18 15		
Brierfield	d				15 19					16 19					17 21					18 19		
Nelson	d				15 22					16 22					17 24					18 22		
Colne	a				15 34					16 34					17 36					18 34		

A To Barrow-in-Furness
B To Manchester Victoria
D To Liverpool South Parkway
E To Manchester Airport
F To York
G To Liverpool Lime Street
H To Hull

Table 97

Saturdays from 6 October

Blackpool - Preston - Blackburn, Accrington, Burnley and Colne

Network Diagram - see first Page of Table 97

		NT	NT	NT	NT	NT	TP	NT	NT	NT	TP	NT	NT	NT	NT	TP	NT	NT	TP	NT	NT	NT	TP
							◇1				◇1					◇1			◇1				◇1
		A		B	C	A	D		B	A	D		B	C	A	D		B	D		A	B	E
Blackpool North	d	17 37		18 20	18 29	18 37	18 44		19 20	19 37	19 44		20 20	20 29	20 37	20 42		21 20	21 44		22 14	22 20	22 44
Layton	d			18 23					19 23				20 23					21 23				22 23	
Poulton-le-Fylde	d			18 28	18 35		18 50		19 28		19 50		20 28	20 35		20 48		21 28	21 50			22 28	22 50
Blackpool South	d		17 44					18 44				19 44					20 44			22 00			
Blackpool Pleasure Beach	d		17 46					18 46				19 46					20 46			22 02			
Squires Gate	d		17 48					18 48				19 48					20 48			22 04			
St Annes-on-the-Sea	d		17 52					18 52				19 52					20 52			22 08			
Ansdell & Fairhaven	d		17 55					18 55				19 55					20 55			22 11			
Lytham	d		17 58					18 58				19 58					20 58			22 14			
Moss Side	d		18 03					19 03				20 03					21 03			22 19			
Kirkham & Wesham	d		18 10	18 37				19 10	19 37			20 10	20 37				21 10	21 37		22 26		22 37	
Salwick	d																						
Preston 8	a	18 02	18 22	18 47	18 52	19 00	19 08	19 20	19 47	20 02	20 08	20 20	20 47	20 53	21 01	21 06	21 20	21 47	22 08	22 36	22 41	22 47	23 07
	d		18 24		18 54			19 22				20 22		20 54			21 22			22 38			
Lostock Hall	d		18 30					19 27				20 27					21 27			22 43			
Bamber Bridge	d		18 33					19 30				20 30					21 30			22 46			
Pleasington	d		18x41					19x38				20x38					21x38			22x54			
Cherry Tree	d		18 44					19 41				20 41					21 41			22 57			
Mill Hill (Lancashire)	d		18 46					19 43				20 43					21 43			22 59			
Blackburn	a		18 52		19 09			19 46				20 46		21 10			21 46			23 08			
Clitheroe 94	a																						
Blackburn	d		18 53		19 10			19 48				20 48		21 10			21 48						
Rishton	d		18 58					19 53				20 53					21 53						
Church & Oswaldtwistle	d		19 01					19 56				20 56					21 56						
Accrington	d		19 04		19 17			19 59				20 59		21 18			21 59						
Huncoat	d		19x08					20x03				21x03					22x03						
Hapton	d		19x11					20x06				21x06					22x06						
Rose Grove	d		19 14					20 09				21 09					22 09						
Burnley Manchester Road 41	a				19 26									21 27									
Leeds 10 41	a				20 38									22 35									
Burnley Barracks	d		19x17					20x12				21x12					22x12						
Burnley Central	d		19 20					20 15				21 15					22 15						
Brierfield	d		19 24					20 19				21 19					22 19						
Nelson	d		19 27					20 22				21 22					22 22						
Colne	a		19 39					20 34				21 34					22 34						

		TP	NT	NT	NT
		◇1			
		F	B		
				bus	
Blackpool North	d	22 44	23 02		
Layton	d		23 05		
Poulton-le-Fylde	d	22 50	23 10		
Blackpool South	d				23 30
Blackpool Pleasure Beach	d				23 32
Squires Gate	d				23 34
St Annes-on-the-Sea	d				23 38
Ansdell & Fairhaven	d				23 41
Lytham	d				23 44
Moss Side	d				23 49
Kirkham & Wesham	d		23 19		23 56
Salwick	d				
Preston 8	a	23 08	23 29		00 08
	d				
Lostock Hall	d				
Bamber Bridge	d				
Pleasington	d				
Cherry Tree	d				
Mill Hill (Lancashire)	d				
Blackburn	a				
Clitheroe 94	a				
Blackburn	d			23 14	
Rishton	d			23 24	
Church & Oswaldtwistle	d			23 36	
Accrington	d			23 40	
Huncoat	d			23 46	
Hapton	d			23 52	
Rose Grove	d			23 58	
Burnley Manchester Road 41	a				
Leeds 10 41	a				
Burnley Barracks	d			00 02	
Burnley Central	d			00 07	
Brierfield	d			00 15	
Nelson	d			00 20	
Colne	a			00 28	

A To Liverpool Lime Street
B To Manchester Victoria
C To York
D To Manchester Airport
E from 27 October. To Manchester Airport
F 6 October, 13 October, 20 October. To Manchester Airport

Table 97

Sundays until 9 September

Blackpool - Preston - Blackburn, Accrington, Burnley and Colne

Network Diagram - see first Page of Table 97

		NT	NT	TP	TP	TP	NT	NT	NT	TP	NT	NT	NT	NT	NT	TP	NT	NT	NT	TP	NT	NT	NT
						◇1				◇1						◇1				◇1			
				A	A	A		B	C	A	D	E	B	C		A	D	E	B	A	D	E	B
		bus		bus	bus				trolley														
Blackpool North	d			03 20	05 20	07 48		08 20	08 36	08 44	08 50	09 01	09 20			09 44	09 50	10 11	10 20	10 44	10 50	11 13	11 20
Layton	d							08 23					09 23						10 23				11 23
Poulton-le-Fylde	d					07 54		08 28	08 42	08 50	08 56	09 07	09 28			09 50	09 56	10 17	10 28	10 50	10 56	11 19	11 28
Blackpool South	d		23p30												09 28								
Blackpool Pleasure Beach	d		23p32												09 30								
Squires Gate	d		23p34												09 32								
St Annes-on-the-Sea	d		23p38												09 36								
Ansdell & Fairhaven	d		23p41												09 39								
Lytham	d		23p44												09 42								
Moss Side	d		23p49												09 47								
Kirkham & Wesham	d		23p56					08 37	08 51				09 37		09 54				10 37				11 37
Salwick	d																						
Preston 8	a		00 08			08 12		08 47	09 02	09 08	09 14	09 24	09 47		10 04	10 08	10 14	10 34	10 47	11 08	11 14	11 36	11 47
	d						08 16		09 05			09 27		10 00	10 05			10 37				11 37	
Lostock Hall	d						08 21		09 11					10 05	10 11								
Bamber Bridge	d						08 24		09 14					10 08	10 14								
Pleasington	d														10x21								
Cherry Tree	d														10 24								
Mill Hill (Lancashire)	d														10 27								
Blackburn	a						08 35		09 25			09 42		10 18	10 30			10 53				11 53	
Clitheroe 94	a								09 50					10 43									
Blackburn	d	23p14					08 37					09 44			10 31			10 54				11 54	
Rishton	d	23p24													10 36								
Church & Oswaldtwistle	d	23p36													10 39								
Accrington	d	23p40					08 44					09 51			10 42			11 01				12 01	
Huncoat	d	23p46													10x47								
Hapton	d	23p52													10x50								
Rose Grove	d	23p58					08 51								10 53								
Burnley Manchester Road 41	a											10 00						11 10				12 10	
Leeds 10 41	a											11 21						12 22				13 22	
Burnley Barracks	d	00 02													10x56								
Burnley Central	d	00 07					08 56								10 58								
Brierfield	d	00 15					09 00								11 03								
Nelson	d	00 20					09 03								11 06								
Colne	a	00 28					09 13								11 15								

		NT	TP	NT	NT	NT	NT	TP	NT	NT	NT	NT	TP	NT	NT	NT	NT	TP	NT	NT	NT	NT	TP
			◇1					◇1					◇1					◇1					◇1
			A	D	E	B		A	D	E	B		A	D	E	B		A	D	E	B		A
			trolley																				
Blackpool North	d		11 44	11 50	12 11	12 20		12 44	12 50	13 13	13 20		13 44	13 50	14 11	14 20		14 44	14 50	15 13	15 20		15 44
Layton	d					12 23					13 23					14 23					15 23		
Poulton-le-Fylde	d		11 50	11 56	12 17	12 28		12 50	12 56	13 19	13 28		13 50	13 56	14 17	14 28		14 50	14 56	15 19	15 28		15 50
Blackpool South	d	11 27					12 24					13 27					14 27					15 27	
Blackpool Pleasure Beach	d	11 29					12 26					13 29					14 29					15 29	
Squires Gate	d	11 31					12 28					13 31					14 31					15 31	
St Annes-on-the-Sea	d	11 35					12 32					13 35					14 35					15 35	
Ansdell & Fairhaven	d	11 38					12 35					13 38					14 38					15 38	
Lytham	d	11 41					12 38					13 41					14 41					15 41	
Moss Side	d	11 46					12 43					13 46					14 46					15 46	
Kirkham & Wesham	d	11 53				12 37	12 50				13 37	13 53				14 37	14 53				15 37	15 53	
Salwick	d																						
Preston 8	a	12 03	12 08	12 14	12 34	12 47	13 01	13 08	13 14	13 36	13 47	14 03	14 08	14 14	14 34	14 47	15 04	15 08	15 14	15 36	15 47	16 03	16 08
	d	12 05			12 37					13 37		14 05			14 37					15 37		16 05	
Lostock Hall	d	12 11										14 11										16 11	
Bamber Bridge	d	12 14										14 14										16 14	
Pleasington	d	12x21										14x21										16x21	
Cherry Tree	d	12 24										14 24										16 24	
Mill Hill (Lancashire)	d	12 27										14 27										16 27	
Blackburn	a	12 30			12 52					13 53		14 30			14 52					15 53		16 30	
Clitheroe 94	a																						
Blackburn	d	12 31			12 54					13 54		14 31			14 54					15 54		16 31	
Rishton	d	12 36										14 36										16 36	
Church & Oswaldtwistle	d	12 39										14 39										16 39	
Accrington	d	12 42			13 01					14 01		14 42			15 01					16 01		16 42	
Huncoat	d	12x47										14x47										16x47	
Hapton	d	12x50										14x50										16x50	
Rose Grove	d	12 53										14 53										16 53	
Burnley Manchester Road 41	a				13 10					14 10					15 10					16 10			
Leeds 10 41	a				14 22					15 22					16 22					17 21			
Burnley Barracks	d	12x56										14x56										16x56	
Burnley Central	d	12 58										14 58										16 58	
Brierfield	d	13 03										15 03										17 03	
Nelson	d	13 06										15 06										17 06	
Colne	a	13 15										15 15										17 15	

A To Manchester Airport
B To Manchester Victoria
C To Carlisle
D To Liverpool Lime Street
E To York

Table 97

Sundays

until 9 September

Blackpool - Preston - Blackburn, Accrington, Burnley and Colne

Network Diagram - see first Page of Table 97

		NT A	NT B	NT C	NT	TP ◇1 D	NT A	NT B	NT C	TP ◇1 E	NT	TP ◇1 D	NT A	NT B	NT C	NT	TP ◇1 D	NT A	NT B	NT C	NT	TP ◇1 D
Blackpool North	d	15 50	16 11	16 20		16 44	16 50	17 11	17 20	17 30		17 44	17 50	18 11	18 20		18 40	18 50	19 13	19 20		19 44
Layton	d			16 23					17 23						18 23					19 23		
Poulton-le-Fylde	d	15 56	16 17	16 28		16 50	16 56	17 17	17 28			17 50	17 56	18 17	18 28		18 46	18 56	19 19	19 28		19 50
Blackpool South	d				16 27						17 24					18 27					19 27	
Blackpool Pleasure Beach	d				16 29						17 26					18 29					19 29	
Squires Gate	d				16 31						17 28					18 31					19 31	
St Annes-on-the-Sea	d				16 35						17 32					18 35					19 35	
Ansdell & Fairhaven	d				16 38						17 35					18 38					19 38	
Lytham	d				16 41						17 38					18 41					19 41	
Moss Side	d				16 46						17 43					18 46					19 46	
Kirkham & Wesham	d			16 37	16 53				17 37		17 50				18 37	18 53				19 37	19 53	
Salwick	d																					
Preston 8	a	16 14	16 34	16 47	17 04	17 08	17 14	17 34	17 47	17 53	18 00	18 08	18 14	18 34	18 47	19 04	19 04	19 14	19 36	19 47	20 03	20 08
	d		16 37					17 37			18 05			18 37					19 37		20 05	
Lostock Hall	d										18 11										20 11	
Bamber Bridge	d										18 14										20 14	
Pleasington	d										18x21										20x21	
Cherry Tree	d										18 24										20 24	
Mill Hill (Lancashire)	d										18 27										20 27	
Blackburn	a		16 52					17 52			18 30			18 52					19 53		20 30	
Clitheroe 94	a																					
Blackburn	d		16 54					17 54			18 31			18 54					19 54		20 31	
Rishton	d										18 36										20 36	
Church & Oswaldtwistle	d										18 39										20 39	
Accrington	d		17 01					18 01			18 42			19 01					20 01		20 42	
Huncoat	d										18x47										20x47	
Hapton	d										18x50										20x50	
Rose Grove	d										18 53										20 53	
Burnley Manchester Road 41	a		17 10					18 10						19 10					20 10			
Leeds 10 41	a		18 21					19 22						20 22					21 22			
Burnley Barracks	d										18x56										20x56	
Burnley Central	d										18 58										20 58	
Brierfield	d										19 03										21 03	
Nelson	d										19 06										21 06	
Colne	a										19 15										21 15	

		NT A	NT	NT C	NT	TP ◇1 D	NT A	NT	NT C	NT	NT F	TP ◇1	NT F	TP ◇1 D
Blackpool North	d	19 50	20 11	20 20		20 44	20 50	21 13	21 20		21 50	21 56	22 44	23 03
Layton	d			20 23					21 23					
Poulton-le-Fylde	d	19 56	20 17	20 28		20 50	20 56	21 19	21 28		21 56	22 02	22 50	23 09
Blackpool South	d				20 27					21 27				
Blackpool Pleasure Beach	d				20 29					21 29				
Squires Gate	d				20 31					21 31				
St Annes-on-the-Sea	d				20 35					21 35				
Ansdell & Fairhaven	d				20 38					21 38				
Lytham	d				20 41					21 41				
Moss Side	d				20 46					21 46				
Kirkham & Wesham	d			20 37	20 53				21 37	21 53				23 17
Salwick	d													
Preston 8	a	20 14	20 34	20 47	21 03	21 08	21 14	21 36	21 47	22 03	22 14	22 20	23 08	23 28
	d		20 37		21 05			21 39		22 05				
Lostock Hall	d				21 10					22 11				
Bamber Bridge	d				21 13					22 14				
Pleasington	d				21x20					22x21				
Cherry Tree	d				21 23					22 24				
Mill Hill (Lancashire)	d				21 26					22 27				
Blackburn	a		20 52		21 29			21 54		22 30				
Clitheroe 94	a													
Blackburn	d		20 54		21 29			21 55		22 31				
Rishton	d				21 34					22 36				
Church & Oswaldtwistle	d				21 37					22 39				
Accrington	d		21 01		21 40			22 02		22 42				
Huncoat	d				21x45					22x47				
Hapton	d				21x48					22x50				
Rose Grove	d				21 51					22 53				
Burnley Manchester Road 41	a		21 10					22 12						
Leeds 10 41	a		22 21					23 23						
Burnley Barracks	d				21x54					22x56				
Burnley Central	d				22a00					22 58				
Brierfield	d									23 03				
Nelson	d									23 06				
Colne	a									23 15				

A To Liverpool Lime Street
B To York
C To Manchester Victoria
D To Manchester Airport
E from 1 July
F To Wigan North Western

Table 97

Sundays

16 September to 21 October

Blackpool - Preston - Blackburn, Accrington, Burnley and Colne

Network Diagram - see first Page of Table 97

		NT 🚌	NT	TP A 🚌	TP A 🚌	TP ◇1 A	NT B	NT D	NT E ⚲	TP ◇1 A	NT F	NT G	NT D	NT	TP ◇1 A	NT F	NT G	NT D	TP ◇1 A	NT F	NT G
Blackpool North	d			03 20	05 20	07 48		08 20	08 36	08 44	08 50	09 01	09 20		09 44	09 50	10 11	10 20	10 44	10 50	11 13
Layton	d							08 23					09 23					10 23			
Poulton-le-Fylde	d					07 54		08 28	08 42	08 50	08 56	09 07	09 28		09 50	09 56	10 17	10 28	10 50	10 56	11 19
Blackpool South	d		23p30											09 28							
Blackpool Pleasure Beach	d		23p32											09 30							
Squires Gate	d		23p34											09 32							
St Annes-on-the-Sea	d		23p38											09 36							
Ansdell & Fairhaven	d		23p41											09 39							
Lytham	d		23p44											09 42							
Moss Side	d		23p49											09 47							
Kirkham & Wesham	d		23p56					08 37	08 51				09 37	09 54				10 37			
Salwick	d																				
Preston 8	a		00 08			08 12		08 47	09 02	09 08	09 14	09 24	09 47	10 04	10 08	10 14	10 34	10 47	11 08	11 14	11 36
	d						08 16		09 05			09 27		10 05			10 37				11 37
Lostock Hall	d						08 21		09 11					10 11							
Bamber Bridge	d						08 24		09 14					10 14							
Pleasington	d													10x21							
Cherry Tree	d													10 24							
Mill Hill (Lancashire)	d													10 27							
Blackburn	a						08 35		09 25			09 42		10 30			10 52				11 53
Clitheroe 94	a								09 50												
Blackburn	d	23p14					08 37					09 44		10 31			10 54				11 54
Rishton	d	23p24												10 36							
Church & Oswaldtwistle	d	23p36												10 39							
Accrington	d	23p40					08 44					09 51		10 42			11 01				12 01
Huncoat	d	23p46												10x47							
Hapton	d	23p52												10x50							
Rose Grove	d	23p58					08 51							10 53							
Burnley Manchester Road 41	a											10 00					11 10				12 10
Leeds 10 41	a											11 20					12 17				13 16
Burnley Barracks	d	00 02												10x56							
Burnley Central	d	00 07					08 56							10 58							
Brierfield	d	00 15					09 00							11 03							
Nelson	d	00 20					09 03							11 06							
Colne	a	00 28					09 13							11 15							

		NT D	NT	TP ◇1 A ⚲	NT F	NT G	NT D	NT	TP ◇1 A	NT F	NT G	NT D	NT	TP ◇1 A	NT F	NT G	NT D	NT	TP ◇1 A	NT F	NT G
Blackpool North	d	11 20		11 44	11 50	12 11	12 20		12 44	12 50	13 13	13 20		13 44	13 50	14 11	14 20		14 44	14 50	15 13
Layton	d	11 23					12 23					13 23					14 23				
Poulton-le-Fylde	d	11 28		11 50	11 56	12 17	12 28		12 50	12 56	13 19	13 28		13 50	13 56	14 17	14 28		14 50	14 56	15 19
Blackpool South	d		11 27					12 24					13 27					14 27			
Blackpool Pleasure Beach	d		11 29					12 26					13 29					14 29			
Squires Gate	d		11 31					12 28					13 31					14 31			
St Annes-on-the-Sea	d		11 35					12 32					13 35					14 35			
Ansdell & Fairhaven	d		11 38					12 35					13 38					14 38			
Lytham	d		11 41					12 38					13 41					14 41			
Moss Side	d		11 46					12 43					13 46					14 46			
Kirkham & Wesham	d	11 37	11 53				12 37	12 50				13 37	13 53				14 37	14 53			
Salwick	d																				
Preston 8	a	11 47	12 03	12 08	12 14	12 34	12 47	13 01	13 08	13 14	13 36	13 47	14 03	14 08	14 14	14 34	14 47	15 04	15 08	15 14	15 36
	d		12 05			12 37					13 37		14 05			14 37					15 37
Lostock Hall	d		12 11										14 11								
Bamber Bridge	d		12 14										14 14								
Pleasington	d		12x21										14x21								
Cherry Tree	d		12 24										14 24								
Mill Hill (Lancashire)	d		12 27										14 27								
Blackburn	a		12 30			12 52					13 53		14 30			14 52					15 53
Clitheroe 94	a																				
Blackburn	d		12 31			12 54					13 54		14 31			14 54					15 54
Rishton	d		12 36										14 36								
Church & Oswaldtwistle	d		12 39										14 39								
Accrington	d		12 42			13 01					14 01		14 42			15 01					16 01
Huncoat	d		12x47										14x47								
Hapton	d		12x50										14x50								
Rose Grove	d		12 53										14 53								
Burnley Manchester Road 41	a					13 10					14 10					15 10					16 10
Leeds 10 41	a					14 16					15 16					16 16					17 16
Burnley Barracks	d		12x56										14x56								
Burnley Central	d		12 58										14 58								
Brierfield	d		13 03										15 03								
Nelson	d		13 06										15 06								
Colne	a		13 15										15 15								

A To Manchester Airport
D To Manchester Victoria
E To Carlisle
F To Liverpool Lime Street
G To York

Table 97

Sundays
16 September to 21 October

Blackpool - Preston - Blackburn, Accrington, Burnley and Colne

Network Diagram - see first Page of Table 97

		NT A	NT	TP ◇1 D	NT E	NT G	NT A	NT	TP ◇1 D	NT E	NT A	NT A	NT	TP ◇1 D	NT E	NT G	NT A	NT	TP ◇1 D	NT E
Blackpool North	d	15 20		15 44	15 50	16 11	16 20		16 44	16 50	17 11	17 20		17 44	17 50	18 11	18 20		18 44	18 50
Layton	d	15 23					16 23					17 23					18 23			
Poulton-le-Fylde	d	15 28		15 50	15 56	16 17	16 28		16 50	16 56	17 17	17 28		17 50	17 56	18 17	18 28		18 50	18 56
Blackpool South	d		15 27					16 27					17 24					18 27		
Blackpool Pleasure Beach	d		15 29					16 29					17 26					18 29		
Squires Gate	d		15 31					16 31					17 28					18 31		
St Annes-on-the-Sea	d		15 35					16 35					17 32					18 35		
Ansdell & Fairhaven	d		15 38					16 38					17 35					18 38		
Lytham	d		15 41					16 41					17 38					18 41		
Moss Side	d		15 46					16 46					17 43					18 46		
Kirkham & Wesham	d	15 37	15 53				16 37	16 53				17 37	17 50				18 37	18 53		
Salwick	d																			
Preston 8	a	15 47	16 03	16 08	16 14	16 34	16 47	17 04	17 08	17 14	17 34	17 47	18 00	18 08	18 14	18 34	18 47	19 04	19 08	19 14
	d		16 05			16 37					17 37		18 05			18 37				
Lostock Hall	d		16 11										18 11							
Bamber Bridge	d		16 14										18 14							
Pleasington	d		16 21										18 21							
Cherry Tree	d		16 24										18 24							
Mill Hill (Lancashire)	d		16 27										18 27							
Blackburn	a		16 30			16 52					17 52		18 30			18 52				
Clitheroe 94	a																			
Blackburn	d		16 31			16 54					17 54		18 31			18 54				
Rishton	d		16 36										18 36							
Church & Oswaldtwistle	d		16 39										18 39							
Accrington	d		16 42			17 01					18 01		18 42			19 01				
Huncoat	d		16 47										18 47							
Hapton	d		16 50										18 50							
Rose Grove	d		16 53										18 53							
Burnley Manchester Road 41	a					17 10					18 10					19 10				
Leeds 10 41	a					18 16					19 16					20 19				
Burnley Barracks	d		16 56										18 56							
Burnley Central	d		16 58										18 58							
Brierfield	d		17 03										19 03							
Nelson	d		17 06										19 06							
Colne	a		17 15										19 15							

		NT G	NT A	NT	TP ◇1 D	NT E	NT	NT A	NT	TP ◇1 D	NT E	NT	NT A	NT	NT H	TP ◇1	NT H	TP ◇1 D
Blackpool North	d	19 13	19 20		19 44	19 50	20 11	20 20		20 44	20 50	21 13	21 20		21 50	21 56	22 44	23 03
Layton	d		19 23					20 23					21 23					
Poulton-le-Fylde	d	19 19	19 28		19 50	19 56	20 17	20 28		20 50	20 56	21 19	21 28		21 56	22 02	22 50	23 09
Blackpool South	d			19 27					20 27					21 27				
Blackpool Pleasure Beach	d			19 29					20 29					21 29				
Squires Gate	d			19 31					20 31					21 31				
St Annes-on-the-Sea	d			19 35					20 35					21 35				
Ansdell & Fairhaven	d			19 38					20 38					21 38				
Lytham	d			19 41					20 41					21 41				
Moss Side	d			19 46					20 46					21 46				
Kirkham & Wesham	d		19 37	19 53				20 37	20 53				21 37	21 53				23 17
Salwick	d																	
Preston 8	a	19 36	19 47	20 03	20 08	20 14	20 34	20 47	21 03	21 08	21 14	21 36	21 47	22 03	22 14	22 20	23 08	23 28
	d	19 37		20 05			20 37		21 05			21 39		22 05				
Lostock Hall	d			20 11					21 10					22 11				
Bamber Bridge	d			20 14					21 13					22 14				
Pleasington	d			20 21					21x20					22 21				
Cherry Tree	d			20 24					21 23					22 24				
Mill Hill (Lancashire)	d			20 27					21 26					22 27				
Blackburn	a	19 53		20 30			20 52		21 29			21 54		22 30				
Clitheroe 94	a																	
Blackburn	d	19 54		20 31			20 54		21 29			21 55		22 31				
Rishton	d			20 36					21 34					22 36				
Church & Oswaldtwistle	d			20 39					21 37					22 39				
Accrington	d	20 01		20 42			21 01		21 40			22 02		22 42				
Huncoat	d			20 47					21x45					22 47				
Hapton	d			20 50					21x48					22 50				
Rose Grove	d			20 53					21 51					22 53				
Burnley Manchester Road 41	a	20 10					21 10					22 12						
Leeds 10 41	a	21 16					22 20					23 18						
Burnley Barracks	d			20 56					21x54					22 56				
Burnley Central	d			20 58					22a00					22 58				
Brierfield	d			21 03										23 03				
Nelson	d			21 06										23 06				
Colne	a			21 15										23 15				

A To Manchester Victoria
D To Manchester Airport
E To Liverpool Lime Street
G To York
H To Wigan North Western

Table 97

Sundays
from 28 October

Blackpool - Preston - Blackburn, Accrington, Burnley and Colne

Network Diagram - see first Page of Table 97

		NT 🚌	NT	TP A 🚌	TP A 🚌	TP ◇1 A	NT	NT B	TP ◇1 A	NT G	NT B	NT D	NT E	TP ◇1 A	NT G	NT B	TP ◇1 A	NT G	NT B	NT D	NT E	TP ◇1 A 🛒	NT G
Blackpool North	d			03 20	05 20	07 48		08 20	08 44	09 01	09 20			09 44	10 11	10 20	10 44	11 13	11 20			11 44	12 11
Layton	d							08 23			09 23					10 23			11 23				
Poulton-le-Fylde	d					07 54		08 28	08 50	09 07	09 28			09 50	10 17	10 28	10 50	11 19	11 28			11 50	12 17
Blackpool South	d		23p30									09 28								11 27			
Blackpool Pleasure Beach	d		23p32									09 30								11 29			
Squires Gate	d		23p34									09 32								11 31			
St Annes-on-the-Sea	d		23p38									09 36								11 35			
Ansdell & Fairhaven	d		23p41									09 39								11 38			
Lytham	d		23p44									09 42								11 41			
Moss Side	d		23p49									09 47								11 46			
Kirkham & Wesham	d		23p56					08 37			09 37	09 54				10 37			11 37	11 53			
Salwick	d																						
Preston 8	a		00 08			08 12		08 47	09 08	09 24	09 47	10 04		10 08	10 34	10 47	11 08	11 36	11 47	12 03		12 08	12 34
	d						08 16			09 27		10 05	10 05		10 37			11 37		12 05	12 05		12 37
Lostock Hall	d						08 21					10 11	10 11							12 11	12 11		
Bamber Bridge	d						08 24					10 14	10 14							12 14	12 14		
Pleasington	d											10x21	10x21							12x21	12x21		
Cherry Tree	d											10 24	10 24							12 24	12 24		
Mill Hill (Lancashire)	d											10 27	10 27							12 27	12 27		
Blackburn	a						08 35			09 42		10 30	10 30		10 52			11 53		12 30	12 30		12 52
Clitheroe 94	a																						
Blackburn	d	23p14					08 37			09 44		10 31	10 31		10 54			11 54		12 31	12 31		12 54
Rishton	d	23p24										10 36	10 36							12 36	12 36		
Church & Oswaldtwistle	d	23p36										10 39	10 39							12 39	12 39		
Accrington	d	23p40					08 44			09 51		10 42	10 42		11 01			12 01		12 42	12 42		13 01
Huncoat	d	23p46										10x47	10x47							12x47	12x47		
Hapton	d	23p52										10x50	10x50							12x50	12x50		
Rose Grove	d	23p58					08 51					10 53	10 53							12 53	12 53		
Burnley Manchester Road 41	a									10 00					11 10			12 10					13 10
Leeds 10 41	a									11 21					12 22			13 22					14 22
Burnley Barracks	d	00 02										10x56	10x56							12x56	12x56		
Burnley Central	d	00 07					08 56					10 58	10 58							12 58	12 58		
Brierfield	d	00 15					09 00					11 03	11 03							13 03	13 03		
Nelson	d	00 20					09 03					11 06	11 06							13 06	13 06		
Colne	a	00 28					09 15					11 17	11 17							13 17	13 17		

		NT B	NT D	TP ◇1 A	NT G	NT B	NT D	NT E	TP ◇1 A	NT G	NT B	NT D	TP ◇1 A	NT F	NT G	NT B	NT D	NT E	TP ◇1 A	NT F	NT G	NT B	NT D
Blackpool North	d	12 20		12 42	13 13	13 20			13 44	14 11	14 20		14 44	14 50	15 13	15 20			15 44	15 50	16 11	16 20	
Layton	d	12 23				13 23					14 23					15 23						16 23	
Poulton-le-Fylde	d	12 28		12 48	13 19	13 28			13 50	14 17	14 28		14 50	14 56	15 19	15 28			15 50	15 56	16 17	16 28	
Blackpool South	d		12 24				13 27					14 27					15 27						16 27
Blackpool Pleasure Beach	d		12 26				13 29					14 29					15 29						16 29
Squires Gate	d		12 28				13 31					14 31					15 31						16 31
St Annes-on-the-Sea	d		12 32				13 35					14 35					15 35						16 35
Ansdell & Fairhaven	d		12 35				13 38					14 38					15 38						16 38
Lytham	d		12 38				13 41					14 41					15 41						16 41
Moss Side	d		12 43				13 46					14 46					15 46						16 46
Kirkham & Wesham	d	12 37	12 50			13 37	13 53				14 37	14 53				15 37	15 53					16 37	16 53
Salwick	d																						
Preston 8	a	12 47	13 01	13 06	13 36	13 47	14 03		14 08	14 34	14 47	15 04	15 08	15 14	15 36	15 47	16 03		16 08	16 14	16 34	16 47	17 04
	d				13 37		14 05	14 05		14 37					15 37		16 05	16 05			16 37		
Lostock Hall	d						14 11	14 11									16 11	16 11					
Bamber Bridge	d						14 14	14 14									16 14	16 14					
Pleasington	d						14x21	14x21									16x21	16x21					
Cherry Tree	d						14 24	14 24									16 24	16 24					
Mill Hill (Lancashire)	d						14 27	14 27									16 27	16 27					
Blackburn	a				13 53		14 30	14 30		14 52					15 53		16 30	16 30			16 52		
Clitheroe 94	a																						
Blackburn	d				13 54		14 31	14 31		14 54					15 54		16 31	16 31			16 54		
Rishton	d						14 36	14 36									16 36	16 36					
Church & Oswaldtwistle	d						14 39	14 39									16 39	16 39					
Accrington	d				14 01		14 42	14 42		15 01					16 01		16 42	16 42			17 01		
Huncoat	d						14x47	14x47									16x47	16x47					
Hapton	d						14x50	14x50									16x50	16x50					
Rose Grove	d						14 53	14 53									16 53	16 53					
Burnley Manchester Road 41	a				14 10					15 10					16 10						17 10		
Leeds 10 41	a				15 22					16 22					17 21						18 21		
Burnley Barracks	d						14x56	14x56									16x56	16x56					
Burnley Central	d						14 58	14 58									16 58	16 58					
Brierfield	d						15 03	15 03									17 03	17 03					
Nelson	d						15 06	15 06									17 06	17 06					
Colne	a						15 17	15 17									17 17	17 17					

A To Manchester Airport
B To Manchester Victoria
D 28 October, 4 November
E from 11 November
F To Liverpool Lime Street
G To York

Sundays
from 28 October

Blackpool - Preston - Blackburn, Accrington, Burnley and Colne

Network Diagram - see first Page of Table 97

		TP ◇1	NT	NT	NT	NT	NT	TP ◇1	NT	NT	NT	NT	TP ◇1	NT	NT	NT	NT	NT	TP ◇1	NT	NT	NT
		A	B	F	C	D	E	A	B	F	C	D	A	B	F	C	D	E	A	B		C
Blackpool North	d	16 44	16 50	17 11	17 20			17 44	17 50	18 11	18 20		18 44	18 50	19 13	19 20			19 44	19 50	20 11	20 20
Layton	d				17 23						18 23					19 23						20 23
Poulton-le-Fylde	d	16 50	16 56	17 17	17 28			17 50	17 56	18 17	18 28		18 50	18 56	19 19	19 28			19 50	19 56	20 17	20 28
Blackpool South	d					17 24						18 27					19 27					
Blackpool Pleasure Beach	d					17 26						18 29					19 29					
Squires Gate	d					17 28						18 31					19 31					
St Annes-on-the-Sea	d					17 32						18 35					19 35					
Ansdell & Fairhaven	d					17 35						18 38					19 38					
Lytham	d					17 38						18 41					19 41					
Moss Side	d					17 43						18 46					19 46					
Kirkham & Wesham	d				17 37	17 50					18 37	18 53				19 37	19 53					20 37
Salwick	d																					
Preston 8	a	17 08	17 14	17 34	17 47	18 00		18 08	18 14	18 34	18 47	19 04	19 08	19 14	19 36	19 47	20 03		20 08	20 14	20 34	20 47
	d			17 37		18 05	18 05			18 37					19 37		20 05	20 05			20 37	
Lostock Hall	d					18 11	18 11										20 11	20 11				
Bamber Bridge	d					18 14	18 14										20 14	20 14				
Pleasington	d					18x21	18x21										20x21	20x21				
Cherry Tree	d					18 24	18 24										20 24	20 24				
Mill Hill (Lancashire)	d					18 27	18 27										20 27	20 27				
Blackburn	a			17 52		18 30	18 30			18 52					19 53		20 30	20 30			20 52	
Clitheroe 94	a																					
Blackburn	d			17 54		18 31	18 31			18 54					19 54		20 31	20 31			20 54	
Rishton	d					18 36	18 36										20 36	20 36				
Church & Oswaldtwistle	d					18 39	18 39										20 39	20 39				
Accrington	d			18 01		18 42	18 42			19 01					20 01		20 42	20 42			21 01	
Huncoat	d					18x47	18x47										20x47	20x47				
Hapton	d					18x50	18x50										20x50	20x50				
Rose Grove	d					18 53	18 53										20 53	20 53				
Burnley Manchester Road 41	a			18 10						19 10					20 10						21 10	
Leeds 10 41	a			19 22						20 22					21 22						22 21	
Burnley Barracks	d					18x56	18x56										20x56	20x56				
Burnley Central	d					18 58	18 58										20 58	20 58				
Brierfield	d					19 03	19 03										21 03	21 03				
Nelson	d					19 06	19 06										21 06	21 06				
Colne	a					19 17	19 17										21 17	21 17				

		NT	TP ◇1	NT	NT	NT	NT	NT	NT	TP ◇1	NT	TP ◇1
		D	A	B		C	D	E	G		G	A
Blackpool North	d		20 44	20 50	21 13	21 20			21 50	21 56	22 44	23 03
Layton	d					21 23						
Poulton-le-Fylde	d		20 50	20 56	21 19	21 28			21 56	22 02	22 50	23 09
Blackpool South	d	20 27					21 27					
Blackpool Pleasure Beach	d	20 29					21 29					
Squires Gate	d	20 31					21 31					
St Annes-on-the-Sea	d	20 35					21 35					
Ansdell & Fairhaven	d	20 38					21 38					
Lytham	d	20 41					21 41					
Moss Side	d	20 46					21 46					
Kirkham & Wesham	d	20 53				21 37	21 53					23 17
Salwick	d											
Preston 8	a	21 03	21 08	21 14	21 36	21 47	22 03		22 14	22 20	23 08	23 28
	d	21 05			21 39		22 05	22 05				
Lostock Hall	d	21 10					22 11	22 11				
Bamber Bridge	d	21 13					22 14	22 14				
Pleasington	d	21x20					22x21	22x21				
Cherry Tree	d	21 23					22 24	22 24				
Mill Hill (Lancashire)	d	21 26					22 27	22 27				
Blackburn	a	21 29			21 54		22 30	22 30				
Clitheroe 94	a											
Blackburn	d	21 29			21 55		22 31	22 31				
Rishton	d	21 34					22 36	22 36				
Church & Oswaldtwistle	d	21 37					22 39	22 39				
Accrington	d	21 40			22 02		22 42	22 42				
Huncoat	d	21x45					22x47	22x47				
Hapton	d	21x48					22x50	22x50				
Rose Grove	d	21 51					22 53	22 53				
Burnley Manchester Road 41	a				22 12							
Leeds 10 41	a				23 23							
Burnley Barracks	d	21x54					22x56	22x56				
Burnley Central	d	22a02					22 58	22 58				
Brierfield	d						23 03	23 03				
Nelson	d						23 06	23 06				
Colne	a						23 17	23 17				

A To Manchester Airport
B To Liverpool Lime Street
C To Manchester Victoria
D 28 October, 4 November
E from 11 November
F To York
G To Wigan North Western

Mondays to Fridays
until 28 September

Colne, Burnley, Accrington and Blackburn - Preston - Blackpool

Network Diagram - see first Page of Table 97

Miles	Miles			TP MX ◇1	NT	TP ◇1	TP MX ◇1	NT MX	TP ◇1	TP ◇1	TP ◇1	NT	NT	NT	TP ◇1	NT	NT	NT	NT	NT	TP ◇1	NT	NT
				A	B	C	D	E	A	A	F		E		A		E	G		H	A	E	G
0	—	**Colne**	d									05 40				06 46			07 47				
2	—	Nelson	d									05 45				06 51			07 52				
3¼	—	Brierfield	d									05 48				06 54			07 55				
5½	—	**Burnley Central**	d									05 53				06 59			08 00				
—	—	Burnley Barracks	d									05x55				07x01			08x02				
—	—	Leeds 10 41	d											05 51				06 51					07 51
—	—	Burnley Manchester Road 41	d											06 57				07 57					08 57
7	—	Rose Grove	d									05 58				07 05			08 05				
8½	—	Hapton	d									06x01							08x08				
10	—	Huncoat	d									06x04				07x09			08x11				
11¾	—	Accrington	d									06 09		07 06		07 14		08 06	08 16				09 06
12½	—	Church & Oswaldtwistle	d									06 11				07 16			08 18				
14¼	—	Rishton	d									06 14				07 19			08 21				
18	—	**Blackburn**	a									06 23		07 16		07 24		08 14	08 27				09 14
—	—	Clitheroe 94	d																				
—	—	**Blackburn**	d									06 25		07 16		07 35		08 15	08 35				09 15
19¼	—	Mill Hill (Lancashire)	d									06 28				07 38		08 18	08 38				
20	—	Cherry Tree	d									06 30				07 40			08 40				
21	—	Pleasington	d									06x32				07x42			08x42				
26	—	Bamber Bridge	d									06 39		07 26		07 49		08 27	08 49				
27¼	—	Lostock Hall	d									06 42		07 28		07 52		08 30	08 52				
30	—	**Preston** 8	a									06 50		07 36		08 00		08 38	09 00				09 32
—	—		d	23p35	23p39	23p47	23p51	00 21			06 37	07 00	07 13	07 38	07 59	08 02	08 15	08 40	09 02	08 51	08 59	09 19	09 34
35¼	5¼	Salwick	d									07 07				08 09							
37¾	7¾	Kirkham & Wesham	d			23p56		00 30			06 46	07 11	07 22		08 09	08 13	08 25		09 11			09 28	
41	—	Moss Side	d									07 17				08 19			09 17				
43½	—	Lytham	d									07 21				08 23			09 21				
44¾	—	Ansdell & Fairhaven	d									07 24				08 26			09 24				
46¾	—	St Annes-on-the-Sea	d									07 28				08 30			09 28				
48¼	—	Squires Gate	d									07 32				08 34			09 32				
49½	—	Blackpool Pleasure Beach	d									07 34				08 36			09 34				
50	—	**Blackpool South**	a									07 37				08 41			09 39				
—	14¼	Poulton-le-Fylde	d	23p52	23p56	00 05	00 08	00 38			06 56		07 30	07 54	08 18		08 33	08 56			09 16	09 36	09 51
—	16¼	Layton	d					00 43			06 59		07 34		08 22		08 37					09 43	
—	17½	**Blackpool North**	a	00 02	00 05	00 14	00 16	00 50	01 30	05 33	07 06		07 41	08 05	08 29		08 44	09 05		09 17	09 25	09 50	10 01

		TP ◇1	NT	NT	NT	NT	TP ◇1	NT	NT	NT	NT	TP ◇1	NT	NT	NT	NT	TP ◇1	NT	NT	NT	NT	TP ◇1	NT
		A	I		E	G	A	I		E	G	A	K		E	G	A	K		E	G	A	K
Colne	d			08 40					09 50					10 50					11 50				
Nelson	d			08 45					09 55					10 55					11 55				
Brierfield	d			08 48					09 58					10 58					11 58				
Burnley Central	d			09 03					10 03					11 03					12 03				
Burnley Barracks	d			09x05					10x05					11x05					12x05				
Leeds 10 41	d					08 51					09 53					10 53					11 53		
Burnley Manchester Road 41	d					09 57					10 57					11 57					12 57		
Rose Grove	d			09 08					10 08					11 08					12 08				
Hapton	d			09x11					10x11					11x11					12x11				
Huncoat	d			09x14					10x14					11x14					12x14				
Accrington	d			09 19		10 06			10 19		11 06			11 19		12 06			12 19		13 06		
Church & Oswaldtwistle	d			09 21					10 21					11 21					12 21				
Rishton	d			09 24					10 24					11 24					12 24				
Blackburn	a			09 33		10 14			10 34		11 14			11 33		12 14			12 33		13 14		
Clitheroe 94	d																						
Blackburn	d			09 35		10 15			10 35		11 15			11 35		12 15			12 35		13 15		
Mill Hill (Lancashire)	d			09 38					10 38					11 38					12 38				
Cherry Tree	d			09 40					10 40					11 40					12 40				
Pleasington	d			09x42					10x42					11x42					12x42				
Bamber Bridge	d			09 49					10 49					11 49					12 49				
Lostock Hall	d			09 52					10 52					11 52					12 52				
Preston 8	a			10 00		10 32			11 00		11 32			12 00		12 32			13 00		13 32		
	d	09 38	09 55	10 02	10 19	10 34	10 38	10 55	11 02	11 19	11 34	11 38	11 55	12 02	12 19	12 34	12 38	12 55	13 02	13 19	13 34	13 38	13 55
Salwick	d													12 09									
Kirkham & Wesham	d		10 05	10 11	10 28			11 05	11 11	11 28			12 05	12 13	12 28			13 05	13 11	13 28			14 05
Moss Side	d			10 17					11 17					12 19					13 17				
Lytham	d			10 21					11 21					12 23					13 21				
Ansdell & Fairhaven	d			10 24					11 24					12 26					13 24				
St Annes-on-the-Sea	d			10 28					11 28					12 30					13 28				
Squires Gate	d			10 32					11 32					12 34					13 32				
Blackpool Pleasure Beach	d			10 34					11 34					12 36					13 34				
Blackpool South	a			10 39					11 39					12 41					13 39				
Poulton-le-Fylde	d	09 56			10 36	10 51	10 56			11 36	11 50	11 56			12 36	12 50	12 56			13 36	13 50	13 56	
Layton	d				10 43					11 43					12 43					13 43			
Blackpool North	a	10 05	10 19		10 51	11 01	11 05	11 20		11 50	12 00	12 05	12 19		12 50	13 00	13 05	13 19		13 50	14 00	14 05	14 19

A From Manchester Airport
B MO from 21 May until 24 September. From Wigan North Western
C MO from 21 May until 24 September. From Manchester Airport
D From Windermere
E From Manchester Victoria
F From Manchester Piccadilly
G From York
H From Buxton
I From Liverpool Lime Street
K From Liverpool South Parkway

Colne, Burnley, Accrington and Blackburn - Preston - Blackpool

Network Diagram - see first Page of Table 97

		NT	NT A	NT F	TP ◇1 C 🍴	NT D	NT	NT A	NT F	TP ◇1 C 🍴	NT D	NT	NT F	TP ◇1 C 🍴	NT D	NT	NT A	TP ◇1 C 🍴	NT F	NT D	NT	NT A
Colne	d	12 50					13 50					14 50				15 50					16 50	
Nelson	d	12 55					13 55					14 55				15 55					16 55	
Brierfield	d	12 58					13 58					14 58				15 58					16 58	
Burnley Central	d	13 03					14 03					15 03				16 03					17 03	
Burnley Barracks	d	13x05					14x05					15x05				16x05					17x05	
Leeds 10 41	d			12 53					13 53				14 53						15 52			
Burnley Manchester Road 41	d			13 57					14 57				15 57						16 58			
Rose Grove	d	13 08					14 08					15 08				16 08					17 08	
Hapton	d	13x11					14x11					15x11				16x11					17x11	
Huncoat	d	13x14					14x14					15x14				16x14					17x14	
Accrington	d	13 19		14 06			14 19		15 06			15 19	16 06			16 19			17 06		17 19	
Church & Oswaldtwistle	d	13 21					14 21					15 21				16 21					17 21	
Rishton	d	13 24					14 24					15 24				16 24					17 24	
Blackburn	a	13 33		14 14			14 33		15 14			15 33	16 14			16 33			17 14		17 33	
Clitheroe 94	d																					
Blackburn	d	13 35		14 15			14 35		15 15			15 35	16 15			16 35			17 15		17 35	
Mill Hill (Lancashire)	d	13 38					14 38					15 38				16 38					17 38	
Cherry Tree	d	13 40					14 40					15 40				16 40					17 40	
Pleasington	d	13x42					14x42					15x42				16x42					17x42	
Bamber Bridge	d	13 49					14 49					15 49				16 49					17 49	
Lostock Hall	d	13 52					14 52					15 52				16 52					17 52	
Preston 8	a	14 00		14 32			15 00		15 32			16 00	16 32			17 00			17 32		18 00	
	d	14 02	14 19	14 34	14 38	14 55	15 02	15 19	15 34	15 38	15 55	16 02	16 34	16 38	16 56	17 02	17 21	17 32	17 35	17 55	18 02	18 18
Salwick	d											16 09										
Kirkham & Wesham	d	14 11	14 28			15 05	15 11	15 28			16 05	16 13		16 47	17 05	17 11	17 30	17 41		18 05	18 11	18 27
Moss Side	d	14 17					15 17					16 19				17 17					18 17	
Lytham	d	14 21					15 21					16 23				17 21					18 21	
Ansdell & Fairhaven	d	14 24					15 24					16 26				17 24					18 24	
St Annes-on-the-Sea	d	14 28					15 28					16 30				17 28					18 28	
Squires Gate	d	14 32					15 32					16 34				17 32					18 32	
Blackpool Pleasure Beach	d	14 34					15 34					16 36				17 34					18 34	
Blackpool South	a	14 39					15 39					16 41				17 39					18 39	
Poulton-le-Fylde	d		14 36	14 50	14 56			15 36	15 50	15 56			16 50	16 57	17 13		17 38	17 51	17 56	18 13		18 35
Layton	d		14 43					15 43						17 00			17 43	17 54				18 39
Blackpool North	a		14 51	15 00	15 05	15 21		15 50	16 00	16 05	16 20		17 00	17 07	17 20		17 50	18 02	18 06	18 23		18 49

		NT E	NT F	TP ◇1 C 🍴	NT E	NT G	NT	NT	NT A	NT F	NT	TP ◇1 C 🍴	NT G	NT A	NT F	NT	TP ◇1 C	NT	NT A	NT G	TP ◇1 C	NT A	NT F
Colne	d						17 50				18 54					19 50		20 50					
Nelson	d						17 55				18 59					19 55		20 55					
Brierfield	d						17 58				19 02					19 58		20 58					
Burnley Central	d						18 03				19 07					20 03		21 03					
Burnley Barracks	d						18x05				19x09					20x05		21x05					
Leeds 10 41	d		16 51							17 51					18 51								20 51
Burnley Manchester Road 41	d		17 57							18 57					19 57								21 56
Rose Grove	d						18 08				19 12					20 08		21 08					
Hapton	d						18x11				19x15					20x11		21x11					
Huncoat	d						18x14				19x18					20x14		21x14					
Accrington	d		18 06				18 19			19 06	19 23				20 06	20 19		21 19					22 05
Church & Oswaldtwistle	d						18 21				19 25					20 21		21 21					
Rishton	d						18 24				19 28					20 24		21 24					
Blackburn	a		18 14				18 33			19 14	19 33				20 14	20 33		21 33					22 13
Clitheroe 94	d																						
Blackburn	d		18 15				18 35	18 44		19 15	19 35				20 15	20 35		21 35					22 14
Mill Hill (Lancashire)	d						18 38				19 38					20 38		21 38					
Cherry Tree	d						18 40				19 40					20 40		21 40					
Pleasington	d						18x42				19x42					20x42		21x42					
Bamber Bridge	d						18 49				19 49					20 49		21 49					
Lostock Hall	d						18 52				19 52					20 52		21 52					
Preston 8	a		18 33				19 00	19 05		19 32	20 00				20 32	21 00		22 02					22 31
	d	18 26	18 34	18 40	18 49	18 55	19 02	19 08	19 19	19 34	20 02	19 38	20 19	20 25	20 34	21 02	20 38		21 19	21 24	21 38	22 19	22 32
Salwick	d																						
Kirkham & Wesham	d			18 49		19 05	19 11		19 28		20 11			20 34		21 11			21 28			22 28	
Moss Side	d						19 17				20 17					21 17							
Lytham	d						19 21				20 21					21 21							
Ansdell & Fairhaven	d						19 24				20 24					21 24							
St Annes-on-the-Sea	d						19 28				20 28					21 28							
Squires Gate	d						19 32				20 32					21 32							
Blackpool Pleasure Beach	d						19 34				20 34					21 34							
Blackpool South	a						19 39				20 39					21 39							
Poulton-le-Fylde	d	18 43	18 50	18 59					19 36	19 50		19 56		20 42	20 50		20 56		21 36		21 56	22 36	22 49
Layton	d			19 02					19 43					20 47					21 40			22 43	
Blackpool North	a	18 53	18 58	19 10	19 16	19 22		19 33	19 52	20 00		20 06	20 42	20 54	21 00		21 06		21 48	21 52	22 06	22 53	22 59

A From Manchester Victoria
C From Manchester Airport
D From Liverpool South Parkway
E From Buxton
F From York
G From Liverpool Lime Street

Colne, Burnley, Accrington and Blackburn - Preston - Blackpool

Network Diagram - see first Page of Table 97

		NT	TP ◇1 A	NT	NT B	NT C	NT FO	TP ◇1 A	TP ◇1 D
Colne	d	21 45		22 55			23 50		
Nelson	d	21 50		23 00			23 55		
Brierfield	d	21 53		23 03					
Burnley Central	d	21 58		23 08			00 01		
Burnley Barracks	d	22x00		23x10					
Leeds 10 41	d								
Burnley Manchester Road 41	d								
Rose Grove	d	22 03		23 13					
Hapton	d	22x06							
Huncoat	d	22x09							
Accrington	d	22 14		23 20			00 11		
Church & Oswaldtwistle	d	22 16							
Rishton	d	22 19							
Blackburn	a	22 24		23 28			00 19		
Clitheroe 94	d								
Blackburn	d	22 25		23 30			00 19		
Mill Hill (Lancashire)	d	22 28		23 33					
Cherry Tree	d	22 30							
Pleasington	d	22x32							
Bamber Bridge	d	22 39		23 41					
Lostock Hall	d	22 42		23 43					
Preston 8	a	22 50		23 54			00 36		
	d	22 51	22 38		22 57	23 19		23 35	23 51
Salwick	d								
Kirkham & Wesham	d	23 01				23 28			
Moss Side	d	23 07							
Lytham	d	23 11							
Ansdell & Fairhaven	d	23 14							
St Annes-on-the-Sea	d	23 18							
Squires Gate	d	23 21							
Blackpool Pleasure Beach	d	23 24							
Blackpool South	a	23 28							
Poulton-le-Fylde	d		22 55			23 36		23 52	00 08
Layton	d					23 40			
Blackpool North	a		23 04		23 21	23 48		00 02	00 16

Mondays to Fridays
from 1 October

		TP MX ◇1 A	NT MO E	TP MO ◇1 A	TP MX ◇1 D	NT MX C	TP ◇1 A	TP ◇1 A	TP ◇1 F	NT	NT C	NT	TP ◇1 A 🍴	NT	NT C	NT G	NT	NT H	TP ◇1 A 🍴	NT C	NT G	TP ◇1 A 🍴	NT B
Colne	d									05 40				06 46			07 47						
Nelson	d									05 45				06 51			07 52						
Brierfield	d									05 48				06 54			07 55						
Burnley Central	d									05 53				06 59			08 00						
Burnley Barracks	d									05x55				07x01			08x02						
Leeds 10 41	d											05 51				06 51					07 51		
Burnley Manchester Road 41	d											06 57				07 57					08 57		
Rose Grove	d									05 58				07 05			08 05						
Hapton	d									06x01							08x08						
Huncoat	d									06x04				07x09			08x11						
Accrington	d									06 09		07 06		07 14		08 06	08 16				09 06		
Church & Oswaldtwistle	d									06 11				07 16			08 18						
Rishton	d									06 14				07 19			08 21						
Blackburn	a									06 23		07 16		07 24		08 14	08 27				09 14		
Clitheroe 94	d																						
Blackburn	d									06 25		07 16		07 35		08 15	08 35				09 15		
Mill Hill (Lancashire)	d									06 28				07 38		08 18	08 38						
Cherry Tree	d									06 30				07 40			08 40						
Pleasington	d									06x32				07x42			08x42						
Bamber Bridge	d									06 39		07 26		07 49		08 27	08 49						
Lostock Hall	d									06 42		07 28		07 52		08 30	08 52						
Preston 8	a									06 50		07 36		08 00		08 38	09 00				09 32		
	d	23p35	23p39	23p47	23p51	00 21			06 37	07 00	07 13	07 38	07 59	08 02	08 15	08 40	09 02	08 51	08 59	09 19	09 34	09 38	09 55
Salwick	d									07 07				08 09									
Kirkham & Wesham	d			23p56		00 30			06 46	07 11	07 22		08 09	08 13	08 25		09 11			09 28			10 05
Moss Side	d									07 17				08 19			09 17						
Lytham	d									07 21				08 23			09 21						
Ansdell & Fairhaven	d									07 24				08 26			09 24						
St Annes-on-the-Sea	d									07 28				08 30			09 28						
Squires Gate	d									07 32				08 34			09 32						
Blackpool Pleasure Beach	d									07 34				08 36			09 34						
Blackpool South	a									07 40				08 43			09 41						
Poulton-le-Fylde	d	23p52	23p56	00 05	00 08	00 38			06 56		07 30	07 54	08 18		08 33	08 56			09 16	09 36	09 51	09 56	
Layton	d					00 43			06 59		07 34		08 22		08 37					09 43			
Blackpool North	a	00 02	00 05	00 14	00 16	00 52	01 30	05 33	07 06		07 43	08 05	08 29		08 46	09 05		09 17	09 25	09 52	10 01	10 05	10 19

A From Manchester Airport
B From Liverpool Lime Street
C From Manchester Victoria
D From Windermere
E From Wigan North Western
F From Manchester Piccadilly
G From York
H From Buxton

Table 97

Mondays to Fridays

from 1 October

Colne, Burnley, Accrington and Blackburn - Preston - Blackpool

Network Diagram - see first Page of Table 97

		NT	NT	NT	TP	NT	NT	NT	NT	TP	NT	NT	NT	NT	TP	NT	NT	NT	NT	TP	NT	NT	NT
			A	G	◇1 B	C		A	G	◇1 B	E		A	G	◇1 B	E		A	G	◇1 B	E		A
Colne	d	08 40					09 50					10 50					11 50					12 50	
Nelson	d	08 45					09 55					10 55					11 55					12 55	
Brierfield	d	08 48					09 58					10 58					11 58					12 58	
Burnley Central	d	09 03					10 03					11 03					12 03					13 03	
Burnley Barracks	d	09x05					10x05					11x05					12x05					13x05	
Leeds 10	41 d			08 51					09 53					10 53					11 53				
Burnley Manchester Road	41 d			09 57					10 57					11 57					12 57				
Rose Grove	d	09 08					10 08					11 08					12 08					13 08	
Hapton	d	09x11					10x11					11x11					12x11					13x11	
Huncoat	d	09x14					10x14					11x14					12x14					13x14	
Accrington	d	09 19		10 06			10 19		11 06			11 19		12 06			12 19		13 06			13 19	
Church & Oswaldtwistle	d	09 21					10 21					11 21					12 21					13 21	
Rishton	d	09 24					10 24					11 24					12 24					13 24	
Blackburn	a	09 33		10 14			10 34		11 14			11 33		12 14			12 33		13 14			13 33	
Clitheroe	94 d																						
Blackburn	d	09 35		10 15			10 35		11 15			11 35		12 15			12 35		13 15			13 35	
Mill Hill (Lancashire)	d	09 38					10 38					11 38					12 38					13 38	
Cherry Tree	d	09 40					10 40					11 40					12 40					13 40	
Pleasington	d	09x42					10x42					11x42					12x42					13x42	
Bamber Bridge	d	09 49					10 49					11 49					12 49					13 49	
Lostock Hall	d	09 52					10 52					11 52					12 52					13 52	
Preston 8	a	10 00		10 32			11 00		11 32			12 00		12 32			13 00		13 32			14 00	
	d	10 02	10 19	10 34	10 38	10 55	11 02	11 19	11 34	11 38	11 55	12 02	12 19	12 34	12 38	12 55	13 02	13 19	13 34	13 38	13 55	14 02	14 19
Salwick	d											12 09											
Kirkham & Wesham	d	10 11	10 28			11 05	11 11	11 28			12 05	12 13	12 28			13 05	13 11	13 28			14 05	14 11	14 28
Moss Side	d	10 17					11 17					12 19					13 17					14 17	
Lytham	d	10 21					11 21					12 23					13 21					14 21	
Ansdell & Fairhaven	d	10 24					11 24					12 26					13 24					14 24	
St Annes-on-the-Sea	d	10 28					11 28					12 30					13 28					14 28	
Squires Gate	d	10 32					11 32					12 34					13 32					14 32	
Blackpool Pleasure Beach	d	10 34					11 34					12 36					13 34					14 34	
Blackpool South	a	10 41					11 41					12 43					13 41					14 41	
Poulton-le-Fylde	d		10 36	10 51	10 56			11 36	11 50	11 56			12 36	12 50	12 56			13 36	13 50	13 56			14 36
Layton	d		10 43					11 43					12 43					13 43					14 43
Blackpool North	a		10 53	11 01	11 05	11 20		11 52	12 00	12 05	12 19		12 52	13 00	13 05	13 19		13 52	14 00	14 05	14 19		14 53

		NT	TP	NT	NT	NT	NT	TP	NT	NT	NT	TP	NT	NT	NT	TP	NT	NT	NT	NT	NT	NT
		G	◇1 B	E		A	G	◇1 B	E		G	◇1 B	E		A	◇1 B	G	E		A	F	G
Colne	d				13 50					14 50				15 50					16 50			
Nelson	d				13 55					14 55				15 55					16 55			
Brierfield	d				13 58					14 58				15 58					16 58			
Burnley Central	d				14 03					15 03				16 03					17 03			
Burnley Barracks	d				14x05					15x05				16x05					17x05			
Leeds 10	41 d	12 53					13 53				14 53						15 52					16 51
Burnley Manchester Road	41 d	13 57					14 57				15 57						16 58					17 57
Rose Grove	d				14 08					15 08				16 08					17 08			
Hapton	d				14x11					15x11				16x11					17x11			
Huncoat	d				14x14					15x14				16x14					17x14			
Accrington	d	14 06			14 19		15 06			15 19	16 06			16 19			17 06		17 19			18 06
Church & Oswaldtwistle	d				14 21					15 21				16 21					17 21			
Rishton	d				14 24					15 24				16 24					17 24			
Blackburn	a	14 14			14 33		15 14			15 33	16 14			16 33			17 14		17 33			18 14
Clitheroe	94 d																					
Blackburn	d	14 15			14 35		15 15			15 35	16 15			16 35			17 15		17 35			18 15
Mill Hill (Lancashire)	d				14 38					15 38				16 38					17 38			
Cherry Tree	d				14 40					15 40				16 40					17 40			
Pleasington	d				14x42					15x42				16x42					17x42			
Bamber Bridge	d				14 49					15 49				16 49					17 49			
Lostock Hall	d				14 52					15 52				16 52					17 52			
Preston 8	a	14 32			15 00		15 32			16 00	16 32			17 00			17 32		18 00			18 33
	d	14 34	14 38	14 55	15 02	15 19	15 34	15 38	15 55	16 02	16 34	16 38	16 56	17 02	17 21	17 32	17 35	17 55	18 02	18 18	18 26	18 34
Salwick	d									16 09												
Kirkham & Wesham	d			15 05	15 11	15 28			16 05	16 13		16 47	17 05	17 11	17 30	17 41		18 05	18 11	18 27		
Moss Side	d				15 17					16 19				17 17					18 17			
Lytham	d				15 21					16 23				17 21					18 21			
Ansdell & Fairhaven	d				15 24					16 26				17 24					18 24			
St Annes-on-the-Sea	d				15 28					16 30				17 28					18 28			
Squires Gate	d				15 32					16 34				17 32					18 32			
Blackpool Pleasure Beach	d				15 34					16 36				17 34					18 34			
Blackpool South	a				15 41					16 43				17 41					18 41			
Poulton-le-Fylde	d	14 50	14 56			15 36	15 50	15 56			16 50	16 57	17 13		17 38	17 51	17 56	18 13		18 35	18 43	18 50
Layton	d					15 43						17 00			17 43	17 54				18 39		
Blackpool North	a	15 00	15 05	15 21		15 52	16 00	16 05	16 20		17 00	17 07	17 20		17 52	18 02	18 06	18 23		18 51	18 55	18 58

A From Manchester Victoria
B From Manchester Airport
C From Liverpool Lime Street
E From Liverpool South Parkway
F From Buxton
G From York

Table 97

Mondays to Fridays

from 1 October

Colne, Burnley, Accrington and Blackburn - Preston - Blackpool

Network Diagram - see first Page of Table 97

		TP	NT	NT	NT	NT	NT	NT	NT	TP	NT	NT	NT	NT	TP	NT	NT	NT	TP	NT	NT	NT	TP
		◇1 A	B	C			D	E		◇1 A	C	D	E		◇1 A		D	C	◇1 A	D	E		◇1 A
Colne	d				17 50				18 54					19 50		20 50						21 45	
Nelson	d				17 55				18 59					19 55		20 55						21 50	
Brierfield	d				17 58				19 02					19 58		20 58						21 53	
Burnley Central	d				18 03				19 07					20 03		21 03						21 58	
Burnley Barracks	d				18x05				19x09					20x05		21x05						22x00	
Leeds 10	41 d							17 51					18 51								20 51		
Burnley Manchester Road	41 d							18 57					19 57								21 56		
Rose Grove	d				18 08				19 12					20 08		21 08						22 03	
Hapton	d				18x11				19x15					20x11		21x11						22x06	
Huncoat	d				18x14				19x18					20x14		21x14						22x09	
Accrington	d				18 19			19 06	19 23				20 06	20 19		21 19					22 05	22 14	
Church & Oswaldtwistle	d				18 21				19 25					20 21		21 21						22 16	
Rishton	d				18 24				19 28					20 24		21 24						22 19	
Blackburn	a				18 33			19 14	19 33				20 14	20 33		21 33					22 13	22 24	
Clitheroe	94 d																						
Blackburn	d				18 35	18 44		19 15	19 35				20 15	20 35		21 35					22 14	22 25	
Mill Hill (Lancashire)	d				18 38				19 38					20 38		21 38						22 28	
Cherry Tree	d				18 40				19 40					20 40		21 40						22 30	
Pleasington	d				18x42				19x42					20x42		21x42						22x32	
Bamber Bridge	d				18 49				19 49					20 49		21 49						22 39	
Lostock Hall	d				18 52				19 52					20 52		21 52						22 42	
Preston 8	a				19 00	19 05		19 32	20 00				20 32	21 00		22 04					22 31	22 50	
	d	18 40	18 49	18 55	19 02	19 08	19 19	19 34	20 02	19 38	20 19	20 25	20 34	21 02	20 38		21 19	21 24	21 38	22 19	22 32	22 51	22 38
Salwick	d																						
Kirkham & Wesham	d	18 49		19 05	19 11		19 28		20 11			20 34		21 11			21 28			22 28		23 01	
Moss Side	d				19 17				20 17					21 17								23 07	
Lytham	d				19 21				20 21					21 21								23 11	
Ansdell & Fairhaven	d				19 24				20 24					21 24								23 14	
St Annes-on-the-Sea	d				19 28				20 28					21 28								23 18	
Squires Gate	d				19 32				20 32					21 32								23 21	
Blackpool Pleasure Beach	d				19 34				20 34					21 34								23 24	
Blackpool South	a				19 41				20 41					21 41								23 30	
Poulton-le-Fylde	d	18 59					19 36	19 50		19 56		20 42	20 50		20 56		21 36		21 56	22 36	22 49		22 55
Layton	d	19 02					19 43					20 47					21 40			22 43			
Blackpool North	a	19 10	19 16	19 22		19 33	19 52	20 00		20 06	20 42	20 56	21 00		21 06		21 50	21 52	22 06	22 53	22 59		23 04

		NT	NT	NT	NT	TP	TP
			C	D	FO	◇1 A	◇1 F
Colne	d	22 55			23 50		
Nelson	d	23 00			23 55		
Brierfield	d	23 03					
Burnley Central	d	23 08			00 01		
Burnley Barracks	d	23 10					
Leeds 10	41 d						
Burnley Manchester Road	41 d						
Rose Grove	d	23 13					
Hapton	d						
Huncoat	d						
Accrington	d	23 20			00 11		
Church & Oswaldtwistle	d						
Rishton	d						
Blackburn	a	23 28			00 19		
Clitheroe	94 d						
Blackburn	d	23 30			00 19		
Mill Hill (Lancashire)	d	23 33					
Cherry Tree	d						
Pleasington	d						
Bamber Bridge	d	23 41					
Lostock Hall	d	23 43					
Preston 8	a	23 56			00 36		
	d		22 57	23 19		23 35	23 51
Salwick	d						
Kirkham & Wesham	d			23 28			
Moss Side	d						
Lytham	d						
Ansdell & Fairhaven	d						
St Annes-on-the-Sea	d						
Squires Gate	d						
Blackpool Pleasure Beach	d						
Blackpool South	a						
Poulton-le-Fylde	d			23 36		23 52	00 08
Layton	d			23 40			
Blackpool North	a		23 21	23 50		00 02	00 16

A From Manchester Airport
B From Buxton
C From Liverpool Lime Street
D From Manchester Victoria
E From York
F From Windermere

Colne, Burnley, Accrington and Blackburn - Preston - Blackpool

Network Diagram - see first Page of Table 97

		TP	TP	NT	TP	TP	TP	NT	NT	NT	NT	TP	NT	NT	NT	NT	NT	TP	NT	NT	NT	NT	TP
		◇1	◇1		◇1	◇1	◇1					◇1						◇1					◇1
		A	B	C	A	A	D		C		E	A		C	F		G	A	C	F		E	A
Colne	d							05 40					06 50			07 50					08 50		
Nelson	d							05 45					06 55			07 55					08 55		
Brierfield	d							05 48					06 58			07 58					08 58		
Burnley Central	d							05 53					07 03			08 03					09 03		
Burnley Barracks	d							05x55					07x05			08x05					09x05		
Leeds 10	41 d									05 51					06 51					07 51			
Burnley Manchester Road	41 d									06 57					07 57					08 57			
Rose Grove	d							05 58					07 08			08 08					09 08		
Hapton	d							06x01					07x11			08x11					09x11		
Huncoat	d							06x04					07x14			08x14					09x14		
Accrington	d							06 09		07 06			07 19		08 06	08 19				09 06	09 19		
Church & Oswaldtwistle	d							06 11					07 21			08 21					09 21		
Rishton	d							06 14					07 24			08 24					09 24		
Blackburn	a							06 23		07 16			07 33		08 14	08 33				09 14	09 33		
Clitheroe	94 d																						
Blackburn	d							06 25		07 16			07 35		08 15	08 35				09 15	09 35		
Mill Hill (Lancashire)	d							06 28					07 38		08 18	08 38					09 38		
Cherry Tree	d							06 30					07 40			08 40					09 40		
Pleasington	d							06x32					07x42			08x42					09x42		
Bamber Bridge	d							06 39		07 26			07 49		08 27	08 49					09 49		
Lostock Hall	d							06 42		07 28			07 52		08 30	08 52					09 52		
Preston 8	a							06 50		07 36			08 00		08 38	09 00				09 32	10 00		
	d	23p35	23p51	00 19			06 37	07 00	07 13	07 38	07 55	07 59	08 02	08 15	08 40	09 02	08 55	08 59	09 19	09 34	10 02	09 55	10 08
Salwick	d							07 07					08 09										
Kirkham & Wesham	d			00 28			06 46	07 11	07 22			08 09	08 13	08 25		09 11			09 28		10 11		
Moss Side	d							07 17					08 19			09 17					10 17		
Lytham	d							07 21					08 23			09 21					10 21		
Ansdell & Fairhaven	d							07 24					08 26			09 24					10 24		
St Annes-on-the-Sea	d							07 28					08 30			09 28					10 28		
Squires Gate	d							07 32					08 34			09 32					10 32		
Blackpool Pleasure Beach	d							07 34					08 36			09 34					10 34		
Blackpool South	a							07 38					08 41			09 39					10 39		
Poulton-le-Fylde	d	23p52	00 08	00 36			06 56		07 30	07 54		08 18		08 33	08 56			09 16	09 36	09 51			10 26
Layton	d			00 43			06 59		07 34			08 22		08 37					09 43				
Blackpool North	a	00 02	00 16	00 50	01 30	05 33	07 06		07 41	08 05	08 21	08 29		08 44	09 05		09 21	09 25	09 50	10 01		10 21	10 35

		NT	NT	NT	TP	NT	NT	NT	NT	TP	NT	NT	NT	NT	TP	TP	NT	NT	NT	NT	TP	NT	NT
					◇1					◇1					◇1	◇1					◇1		
		C			A	E	C	F		A	I	C	F		A	J	I	C	F		A	I	C
Colne	d			09 50					10 50					11 50						12 50			
Nelson	d			09 55					10 55					11 55						12 55			
Brierfield	d			09 58					10 58					11 58						12 58			
Burnley Central	d			10 03					11 03					12 03						13 03			
Burnley Barracks	d			10x05					11x05					12x05						13x05			
Leeds 10	41 d		08 51					09 53					10 53						11 53				
Burnley Manchester Road	41 d		09 57					10 57					11 57						12 57				
Rose Grove	d			10 08					11 08					12 08						13 08			
Hapton	d			10x11					11x11					12x11						13x11			
Huncoat	d			10x14					11x14					12x14						13x14			
Accrington	d		10 06	10 19				11 06	11 19				12 06	12 19					13 06	13 19			
Church & Oswaldtwistle	d			10 21					11 21					12 21						13 21			
Rishton	d			10 24					11 24					12 24						13 24			
Blackburn	a		10 14	10 33				11 14	11 33				12 14	12 33					13 14	13 33			
Clitheroe	94 d																						
Blackburn	d		10 15	10 35				11 15	11 35				12 15	12 35					13 15	13 35			
Mill Hill (Lancashire)	d			10 38					11 38					12 38						13 38			
Cherry Tree	d			10 40					11 40					12 40						13 40			
Pleasington	d			10x42					11x42					12x42						13x42			
Bamber Bridge	d			10 49					11 49					12 49						13 49			
Lostock Hall	d			10 52					11 52					12 52						13 52			
Preston 8	a		10 32	11 00				11 32	12 00				12 32	13 00					13 32	14 00			
	d	10 19	10 34	11 02	10 38	10 55	11 19	11 34	12 02	11 38	11 55	12 19	12 34	13 02	12 38	12 48	12 55	13 19	13 34	14 02	13 38	13 55	14 19
Salwick	d								12 09														
Kirkham & Wesham	d	10 28		11 11			11 28		12 13			12 28		13 11				13 28		14 11			14 28
Moss Side	d			11 17					12 19					13 17						14 17			
Lytham	d			11 21					12 23					13 21						14 21			
Ansdell & Fairhaven	d			11 24					12 26					13 24						14 24			
St Annes-on-the-Sea	d			11 28					12 30					13 28						14 28			
Squires Gate	d			11 32					12 34					13 32						14 32			
Blackpool Pleasure Beach	d			11 34					12 36					13 34						14 34			
Blackpool South	a			11 39					12 41					13 39						14 39			
Poulton-le-Fylde	d	10 36	10 51		10 56		11 36	11 50		11 56		12 36	12 50		12 56			13 36	13 50		13 56		14 36
Layton	d	10 43					11 44					12 43						13 45					14 43
Blackpool North	a	10 51	11 01		11 05	11 21	11 50	12 00		12 05	12 21	12 50	13 00		13 05	13 12	13 21	13 50	14 00		14 05	14 21	14 50

A From Manchester Airport
B From Windermere
C From Manchester Victoria
D From Manchester Piccadilly
E From Liverpool Lime Street
F From York
G From Wigan North Western
I From Liverpool South Parkway
J from 30 June until 8 September. From Glasgow Central

Colne, Burnley, Accrington and Blackburn - Preston - Blackpool

Network Diagram - see first Page of Table 97

		NT	NT	TP	NT	NT	NT	NT	TP	NT	NT	TP	NT	NT	NT	TP	NT	NT	NT	NT	NT	TP
				◇1					◇1			◇1				◇1						◇1
		A		B	C	D	A		B	C	A	B		C	D	B	A		C	D	A	B
Colne	d		13 50					14 50					15 50					16 50				
Nelson	d		13 55					14 55					15 55					16 55				
Brierfield	d		13 58					14 58					15 58					16 58				
Burnley Central	d		14 03					15 03					16 03					17 03				
Burnley Barracks	d		14x05					15x05					16x05					17x05				
Leeds 10	41 d	12 53					13 53				14 53						15 52				16 51	
Burnley Manchester Road	41 d	13 57					14 57				15 57						16 58				17 57	
Rose Grove	d		14 08					15 08					16 08					17 08				
Hapton	d		14x11					15x11					16x11					17x11				
Huncoat	d		14x14					15x14					16x14					17x14				
Accrington	d	14 06	14 19				15 06	15 19			16 06		16 19				17 06	17 19			18 06	
Church & Oswaldtwistle	d		14 21					15 21					16 21					17 21				
Rishton	d		14 24					15 24					16 24					17 24				
Blackburn	a	14 14	14 33				15 14	15 33			16 14		16 33				17 14	17 34			18 14	
Clitheroe	94 d																					
Blackburn	d	14 15	14 35				15 15	15 35			16 15		16 35				17 15	17 35			18 15	
Mill Hill (Lancashire)	d		14 38					15 38					16 38					17 38				
Cherry Tree	d		14 40					15 40					16 40					17 40				
Pleasington	d		14x42					15x42					16x42					17x42				
Bamber Bridge	d		14 49					15 49					16 49					17 49				
Lostock Hall	d		14 52					15 52					16 52					17 52				
Preston 8	a	14 32	15 00				15 32	16 00			16 32		17 00				17 32	18 00			18 33	
	d	14 34	15 02	14 38	14 55	15 19	15 34	16 02	15 38	15 55	16 34	16 38	17 02	16 55	17 21	17 32	17 35	18 02	17 55	18 18	18 34	18 40
Salwick	d							16 09														
Kirkham & Wesham	d		15 11			15 28		16 13				16 47	17 11		17 31	17 41		18 11		18 27		18 49
Moss Side	d		15 17					16 19					17 17					18 17				
Lytham	d		15 21					16 23					17 21					18 21				
Ansdell & Fairhaven	d		15 24					16 26					17 24					18 24				
St Annes-on-the-Sea	d		15 28					16 30					17 28					18 28				
Squires Gate	d		15 32					16 34					17 32					18 32				
Blackpool Pleasure Beach	d		15 34					16 36					17 34					18 34				
Blackpool South	a		15 39					16 41					17 39					18 39				
Poulton-le-Fylde	d	14 50		14 56		15 36	15 50		15 56		16 50	16 57		17 12	17 39	17 51	17 56			18 35	18 50	18 59
Layton	d					15 43						17 00			17 43	17 54				18 39		19 02
Blackpool North	a	15 00		15 05	15 21	15 50	16 00		16 05	16 21	17 00	17 07		17 21	17 50	18 02	18 06		18 24	18 46	19 00	19 10

		NT	NT	NT	NT	NT	NT	TP	NT	NT	NT	NT	TP	NT	NT	NT	TP	NT	NT	NT	TP	NT	NT
								◇1					◇1				◇1				◇1		
			E	F	D	A		B	F	D	A		B		D	F	B	D	A		B		F
Colne	d	17 50					18 50					19 50		20 50						21 45		22 55	
Nelson	d	17 55					18 55					19 55		20 55						21 50		23 00	
Brierfield	d	17 58					18 58					19 58		20 58						21 53		23 03	
Burnley Central	d	18 03					19 03					20 03		21 03						21 58		23 08	
Burnley Barracks	d	18x05					19x05					20x05		21x05						22x00		23x10	
Leeds 10	41 d					17 51					18 51								20 51				
Burnley Manchester Road	41 d					18 57					19 57								21 56				
Rose Grove	d	18 08					19 08					20 08		21 08						22 03		23 13	
Hapton	d	18x11					19x11					20x11		21x11						22x06			
Huncoat	d	18x14					19x14					20x14		21x14						22x09			
Accrington	d	18 19				19 06	19 19				20 06	20 19		21 19					22 05	22 14		23 20	
Church & Oswaldtwistle	d	18 21					19 21					20 21		21 21						22 16			
Rishton	d	18 24					19 24					20 24		21 24						22 19			
Blackburn	a	18 34				19 14	19 33				20 14	20 33		21 33					22 13	22 24		23 28	
Clitheroe	94 d																						
Blackburn	d	18 35				19 15	19 35				20 15	20 35		21 35					22 14	22 25		23 30	
Mill Hill (Lancashire)	d	18 38					19 38					20 38		21 38						22 28		23 33	
Cherry Tree	d	18 40					19 40					20 40		21 40						22 30			
Pleasington	d	18x42					19x42					20x42		21x42						22x32			
Bamber Bridge	d	18 49					19 49					20 49		21 49						22 39		23 41	
Lostock Hall	d	18 52					19 52					20 52		21 52						22 42		23 43	
Preston 8	a	19 00				19 32	20 00				20 32	21 00		22 02					22 31	22 50		23 54	
	d	19 02	18 49	18 55	19 20	19 34	20 02	19 38	20 19	20 25	20 34	21 02	20 38		21 19	21 24	21 38	22 19	22 32	22 51	22 38		22 57
Salwick	d																						
Kirkham & Wesham	d	19 11			19 29		20 11			20 35		21 11			21 28			22 29		23 01			
Moss Side	d	19 17					20 17					21 17								23 07			
Lytham	d	19 21					20 21					21 21								23 11			
Ansdell & Fairhaven	d	19 24					20 24					21 24								23 14			
St Annes-on-the-Sea	d	19 28					20 28					21 28								23 18			
Squires Gate	d	19 32					20 32					21 32								23 21			
Blackpool Pleasure Beach	d	19 34					20 34					21 34								23 24			
Blackpool South	a	19 39					20 39					21 39								23 28			
Poulton-le-Fylde	d				19 37	19 50		19 56		20 43	20 50		20 56		21 36		21 56	22 37	22 49		22 55		
Layton	d				19 43					20 47					21 40			22 43					
Blackpool North	a		19 16	19 21	19 50	20 00		20 06	20 44	20 54	21 00		21 06		21 48	21 53	22 06	22 50	22 59		23 04		23 22

A From York
B From Manchester Airport
C From Liverpool South Parkway
D From Manchester Victoria
E From Hazel Grove
F From Liverpool Lime Street

Table 97

Saturdays
until 29 September

Colne, Burnley, Accrington and Blackburn - Preston - Blackpool

Network Diagram - see first Page of Table 97

		NT A	TP ◇1 B
Colne	d		
Nelson	d		
Brierfield	d		
Burnley Central	d		
Burnley Barracks	d		
Leeds 10 41	d		
Burnley Manchester Road 41	d		
Rose Grove	d		
Hapton	d		
Huncoat	d		
Accrington	d		
Church & Oswaldtwistle	d		
Rishton	d		
Blackburn	a		
Clitheroe 94	d		
Blackburn	d		
Mill Hill (Lancashire)	d		
Cherry Tree	d		
Pleasington	d		
Bamber Bridge	d		
Lostock Hall	d		
Preston 8	a		
	d	23 19	23 35
Salwick	d		
Kirkham & Wesham	d	23 28	
Moss Side	d		
Lytham	d		
Ansdell & Fairhaven	d		
St Annes-on-the-Sea	d		
Squires Gate	d		
Blackpool Pleasure Beach	d		
Blackpool South	a		
Poulton-le-Fylde	d	23 36	23 52
Layton	d	23 42	
Blackpool North	a	23 48	00 02

Saturdays
from 6 October

		TP ◇1 B	TP ◇1 C	NT A	TP ◇1 B	TP ◇1 B	TP ◇1 D	NT	NT A	NT		NT E	TP ◇1 B ⌶	NT	NT A	NT F	NT	NT G	TP ◇1 B ⌶	NT A		NT F	NT	NT E	TP ◇1 B
Colne	d							05 40						06 50			07 50						08 50		
Nelson	d							05 45						06 55			07 55						08 55		
Brierfield	d							05 48						06 58			07 58						08 58		
Burnley Central	d							05 53						07 03			08 03						09 03		
Burnley Barracks	d							05x55						07x05			08x05						09x05		
Leeds 10 41	d									05 51						06 51						07 51			
Burnley Manchester Road 41	d									06 57						07 57						08 57			
Rose Grove	d							05 58						07 08			08 08						09 08		
Hapton	d							06x01						07x11			08x11						09x11		
Huncoat	d							06x04						07x14			08x14						09x14		
Accrington	d							06 09		07 06				07 19		08 06	08 19					09 06	09 19		
Church & Oswaldtwistle	d							06 11						07 21			08 21						09 21		
Rishton	d							06 14						07 24			08 24						09 24		
Blackburn	a							06 23		07 16				07 33		08 14	08 33					09 14	09 33		
Clitheroe 94	d																								
Blackburn	d							06 25		07 16				07 35		08 15	08 35					09 15	09 35		
Mill Hill (Lancashire)	d							06 28						07 38		08 18	08 38						09 38		
Cherry Tree	d							06 30						07 40			08 40						09 40		
Pleasington	d							06x32						07x42			08x42						09x42		
Bamber Bridge	d							06 39		07 26				07 49		08 27	08 49						09 49		
Lostock Hall	d							06 42		07 28				07 52		08 30	08 52						09 52		
Preston 8	a							06 50		07 36				08 00		08 38	09 00					09 32	10 00		
	d	23p35	23p51	00 19			06 37	07 00	07 13	07 38		07 55	07 59	08 02	08 15	08 40	09 02	08 55	08 59	09 19		09 34	10 02	09 55	10 08
Salwick	d							07 07						08 09											
Kirkham & Wesham	d			00 28			06 46	07 11	07 22				08 09	08 13	08 25		09 11			09 28			10 11		
Moss Side	d							07 17						08 19			09 17						10 17		
Lytham	d							07 21						08 23			09 21						10 21		
Ansdell & Fairhaven	d							07 24						08 26			09 24						10 24		
St Annes-on-the-Sea	d							07 28						08 30			09 28						10 28		
Squires Gate	d							07 32						08 34			09 32						10 32		
Blackpool Pleasure Beach	d							07 34						08 36			09 34						10 34		
Blackpool South	a							07 40						08 43			09 41						10 41		
Poulton-le-Fylde	d	23p52	00 08	00 36			06 56		07 30	07 54			08 18		08 33	08 56			09 16	09 36		09 51			10 26
Layton	d			00 43			06 59		07 34				08 22		08 37					09 43					
Blackpool North	a	00 02	00 16	00 52	01 30	05 33	07 06		07 43	08 05		08 21	08 29		08 46	09 05		09 21	09 25	09 52		10 01		10 21	10 35

A From Manchester Victoria
B From Manchester Airport
C From Windermere
D From Manchester Piccadilly
E From Liverpool Lime Street
F From York
G From Wigan North Western

Table 97

Saturdays
from 6 October

Colne, Burnley, Accrington and Blackburn - Preston - Blackpool

Network Diagram - see first Page of Table 97

		NT A	NT	NT	TP ◇1 B ⌶	NT C		NT A	NT D	NT	TP ◇1 B ⌶	NT E	NT A	NT D	NT	TP ◇1 B ⌶		NT E	NT A	NT D	NT	TP ◇1 B ⌶	NT E	NT A	NT D
Colne	d			09 50						10 50					11 50						12 50				
Nelson	d			09 55						10 55					11 55						12 55				
Brierfield	d			09 58						10 58					11 58						12 58				
Burnley Central	d			10 03						11 03					12 03						13 03				
Burnley Barracks	d			10x05						11x05					12x05						13x05				
Leeds 10 41	d		08 51						09 53					10 53						11 53					12 53
Burnley Manchester Road 41	d		09 57						10 57					11 57						12 57					13 57
Rose Grove	d			10 08						11 08					12 08						13 08				
Hapton	d			10x11						11x11					12x11						13x11				
Huncoat	d			10x14						11x14					12x14						13x14				
Accrington	d		10 06	10 19					11 06	11 19				12 06	12 19					13 06	13 19				14 06
Church & Oswaldtwistle	d			10 21						11 21					12 21						13 21				
Rishton	d			10 24						11 24					12 24						13 24				
Blackburn	a		10 14	10 33					11 14	11 33				12 14	12 33					13 14	13 33				14 14
Clitheroe 94	d																								
Blackburn	d		10 15	10 35					11 15	11 35				12 15	12 35					13 15	13 35				14 15
Mill Hill (Lancashire)	d			10 38						11 38					12 38						13 38				
Cherry Tree	d			10 40						11 40					12 40						13 40				
Pleasington	d			10x42						11x42					12x42						13x42				
Bamber Bridge	d			10 49						11 49					12 49						13 49				
Lostock Hall	d			10 52						11 52					12 52						13 52				
Preston 8	a		10 32	11 00					11 32	12 00				12 32	13 00					13 32	14 00				14 32
	d	10 19	10 34	11 02	10 38	10 55		11 19	11 34	12 02	11 38	11 55	12 19	12 34	13 02	12 38		12 55	13 19	13 34	14 02	13 38	13 55	14 19	14 34
Salwick	d									12 09															
Kirkham & Wesham	d	10 28		11 11				11 28		12 13			12 28		13 11				13 28		14 11			14 28	
Moss Side	d			11 17						12 19					13 17						14 17				
Lytham	d			11 21						12 23					13 21						14 21				
Ansdell & Fairhaven	d			11 24						12 26					13 24						14 24				
St Annes-on-the-Sea	d			11 28						12 30					13 28						14 28				
Squires Gate	d			11 32						12 34					13 32						14 32				
Blackpool Pleasure Beach	d			11 34						12 36					13 34						14 34				
Blackpool South	a			11 41						12 43					13 41						14 41				
Poulton-le-Fylde	d	10 36	10 51		10 56			11 36	11 50		11 56		12 36	12 50		12 56			13 36	13 50		13 56		14 36	14 50
Layton	d	10 43						11 43					12 43						13 45					14 43	
Blackpool North	a	10 52	11 01		11 05	11 21		11 52	12 00		12 05	12 21	12 52	13 00		13 05		13 21	13 55	14 00		14 05	14 21	14 50	15 00

		NT		TP ◇1 B ⌶	NT E	NT A	NT D	NT	TP ◇1 B ⌶	NT E	NT D	TP ◇1 B ⌶		NT	NT E	NT A	TP ◇1 B ⌶	NT D	NT	NT E	NT A	NT D		TP ◇1 B ⌶	NT
Colne	d	13 50						14 50						15 50					16 50						17 50
Nelson	d	13 55						14 55						15 55					16 55						17 55
Brierfield	d	13 58						14 58						15 58					16 58						17 58
Burnley Central	d	14 03						15 03						16 03					17 03						18 03
Burnley Barracks	d	14x05						15x05						16x05					17x05						18x05
Leeds 10 41	d						13 53				14 53							15 52				16 51			
Burnley Manchester Road 41	d						14 57				15 57							16 58				17 57			
Rose Grove	d	14 08						15 08						16 08					17 08						18 08
Hapton	d	14x11						15x11						16x11					17x11						18x11
Huncoat	d	14x14						15x14						16x14					17x14						18x14
Accrington	d	14 19					15 06	15 19			16 06			16 19				17 06	17 19			18 06			18 19
Church & Oswaldtwistle	d	14 21						15 21						16 21					17 21						18 21
Rishton	d	14 24						15 24						16 24					17 24						18 24
Blackburn	a	14 33					15 14	15 33			16 14			16 33				17 14	17 34			18 14			18 34
Clitheroe 94	d																								
Blackburn	d	14 35					15 15	15 35			16 15			16 35				17 15	17 35			18 15			18 35
Mill Hill (Lancashire)	d	14 38						15 38						16 38					17 38						18 38
Cherry Tree	d	14 40						15 40						16 40					17 40						18 40
Pleasington	d	14x42						15x42						16x42					17x42						18x42
Bamber Bridge	d	14 49						15 49						16 49					17 49						18 49
Lostock Hall	d	14 52						15 52						16 52					17 52						18 52
Preston 8	a	15 00					15 32	16 00			16 32			17 00				17 32	18 00			18 33			19 00
	d	15 02		14 38	14 55	15 19	15 34	16 02	15 38	15 55	16 34	16 38		17 02	16 55	17 21	17 32	17 35	18 02	17 55	18 18	18 34		18 40	19 02
Salwick	d							16 09																	
Kirkham & Wesham	d	15 11				15 28		16 13				16 47		17 11		17 30	17 41		18 11		18 27			18 49	19 11
Moss Side	d	15 17						16 19						17 17					18 17						19 17
Lytham	d	15 21						16 23						17 21					18 21						19 21
Ansdell & Fairhaven	d	15 24						16 26						17 24					18 24						19 24
St Annes-on-the-Sea	d	15 28						16 30						17 28					18 28						19 28
Squires Gate	d	15 32						16 34						17 32					18 32						19 32
Blackpool Pleasure Beach	d	15 34						16 36						17 34					18 34						19 34
Blackpool South	a	15 41						16 43						17 41					18 41						19 41
Poulton-le-Fylde	d			14 56		15 36	15 50		15 56		16 50	16 57			17 12	17 38	17 51	17 56			18 35	18 50		18 59	
Layton	d					15 43						17 00				17 43	17 54				18 39			19 02	
Blackpool North	a			15 05	15 21	15 52	16 00		16 05	16 21	17 00	17 07			17 21	17 52	18 02	18 06		18 24	18 48	19 00		19 10	

A From Manchester Victoria
B From Manchester Airport
C From Liverpool Lime Street
D From York
E From Liverpool South Parkway

Colne, Burnley, Accrington and Blackburn - Preston - Blackpool

Saturdays
from 6 October

Network Diagram - see first Page of Table 97

		NT A	NT B	NT C	NT D	NT	TP ◇1 E ⚲	NT B	NT C	NT D	NT	TP ◇1 E	NT	NT C	NT B	TP ◇1 E	NT C	NT D	NT	TP ◇1 E	NT	NT B	NT C
Colne	d					18 50					19 50		20 50						21 45		22 55		
Nelson	d					18 55					19 55		20 55						21 50		23 00		
Brierfield	d					18 58					19 58		20 58						21 53		23 03		
Burnley Central	d					19 03					20 03		21 03						21 58		23 08		
Burnley Barracks	d					19x05					20x05		21x05						22x00		23x10		
Leeds 10 41	d				17 51					18 51								20 51					
Burnley Manchester Road 41	d				18 57					19 57								21 56					
Rose Grove	d					19 08					20 08		21 08						22 03		23 13		
Hapton	d					19x11					20x11		21x11						22x06				
Huncoat	d					19x14					20x14		21x14						22x09				
Accrington	d				19 06	19 19				20 06	20 19		21 19					22 05	22 14		23 20		
Church & Oswaldtwistle	d					19 21					20 21		21 21						22 16				
Rishton	d					19 24					20 24		21 24						22 19				
Blackburn	a				19 14	19 33				20 14	20 33		21 33					22 13	22 24		23 28		
Clitheroe 94	d																						
Blackburn	d				19 15	19 35				20 15	20 35		21 35					22 14	22 25		23 30		
Mill Hill (Lancashire)	d					19 38					20 38		21 38						22 28		23 33		
Cherry Tree	d					19 40					20 40		21 40						22 30				
Pleasington	d					19x42					20x42		21x42						22x32				
Bamber Bridge	d					19 49					20 49		21 49						22 39		23 41		
Lostock Hall	d					19 52					20 52		21 52						22 42		23 43		
Preston 8	a				19 32	20 00				20 32	21 00		22 04					22 31	22 50		23 56		
	d	18 49	18 55	19 19	19 34	20 02	19 38	20 19	20 25	20 34	21 02	20 38		21 19	21 24	21 38	22 19	22 32	22 51	22 38		22 57	23 19
Salwick	d																						
Kirkham & Wesham	d			19 28		20 11			20 34		21 11			21 28			22 28		23 01				23 28
Moss Side	d					20 17					21 17								23 07				
Lytham	d					20 21					21 21								23 11				
Ansdell & Fairhaven	d					20 24					21 24								23 14				
St Annes-on-the-Sea	d					20 28					21 28								23 18				
Squires Gate	d					20 32					21 32								23 21				
Blackpool Pleasure Beach	d					20 34					21 34								23 24				
Blackpool South	a					20 41					21 41								23 30				
Poulton-le-Fylde	d			19 36	19 50		19 56		20 42	20 50		20 56		21 36		21 56	22 36	22 49		22 55			23 36
Layton	d			19 43					20 47					21 40			22 43						23 40
Blackpool North	a	19 16	19 21	19 52	20 00		20 06	20 44	20 56	21 00		21 06		21 50	21 53	22 06	22 52	22 59		23 04		23 22	23 50

		TP ◇1 E
Colne	d	
Nelson	d	
Brierfield	d	
Burnley Central	d	
Burnley Barracks	d	
Leeds 10 41	d	
Burnley Manchester Road 41	d	
Rose Grove	d	
Hapton	d	
Huncoat	d	
Accrington	d	
Church & Oswaldtwistle	d	
Rishton	d	
Blackburn	a	
Clitheroe 94	d	
Blackburn	d	
Mill Hill (Lancashire)	d	
Cherry Tree	d	
Pleasington	d	
Bamber Bridge	d	
Lostock Hall	d	
Preston 8	a	
	d	23 35
Salwick	d	
Kirkham & Wesham	d	
Moss Side	d	
Lytham	d	
Ansdell & Fairhaven	d	
St Annes-on-the-Sea	d	
Squires Gate	d	
Blackpool Pleasure Beach	d	
Blackpool South	a	
Poulton-le-Fylde	d	23 52
Layton	d	
Blackpool North	a	00 02

A From Hazel Grove
B From Liverpool Lime Street
C From Manchester Victoria
D From York
E From Manchester Airport

Colne, Burnley, Accrington and Blackburn - Preston - Blackpool

Sundays
until 9 September

Network Diagram - see first Page of Table 97

		TP ◇1 A	NT B	TP A 🚌	TP A 🚌	NT	TP ◇1 A	NT B	NT C	TP ◇1 A	NT B	NT	NT	TP ◇1 A	NT C	NT D	NT B	TP ◇1 A	NT C	NT D	NT	NT B	NT
Colne	d											09 16											11 35
Nelson	d											09 21											11 40
Brierfield	d											09 24											11 43
Burnley Central	d											09 29											11 48
Burnley Barracks	d											09x31											11x50
Leeds 10 41	d												08 45			09 35				10 35			
Burnley Manchester Road 41	d												09 50			10 39				11 39			
Rose Grove	d											09 34											11 53
Hapton	d											09x37											11x56
Huncoat	d											09x40											11x59
Accrington	d											09 45	09 59			10 48				11 47			12 04
Church & Oswaldtwistle	d											09 47											12 06
Rishton	d											09 50											12 09
Blackburn	a											09 55	10 07			10 56				11 55			12 14
Clitheroe 94	d																						
Blackburn	d											09 57	10 07			10 56				11 56			12 16
Mill Hill (Lancashire)	d											10 00											12 19
Cherry Tree	d											10 02											12 21
Pleasington	d											10x04											12x23
Bamber Bridge	d											10 11											12 30
Lostock Hall	d											10 14											12 33
Preston 8	a											10 22	10 27			11 13				12 13			12 41
	d	23p35	00 11			08 49	08 58	09 20	09 39	09 52	10 20	10 23	10 29	10 35	10 40	11 15	11 21	11 35	11 39	12 14	11 44	12 20	12 42
Salwick	d																						
Kirkham & Wesham	d		00 21			08 58		09 29			10 29	10 33					11 31				11 53	12 29	12 52
Moss Side	d					09 06						10 39									12 01		12 58
Lytham	d					09 10						10 43									12 05		13 02
Ansdell & Fairhaven	d					09 13						10 46									12 08		13 05
St Annes-on-the-Sea	d					09 17						10 50									12 12		13 09
Squires Gate	d					09 20						10 54									12 15		13 13
Blackpool Pleasure Beach	d					09 23						10 56									12 18		13 15
Blackpool South	a					09 26						11 01									12 21		13 20
Poulton-le-Fylde	d	23p52	00 29				09 15	09 37	09 57	10 09	10 37		10 46	10 52	10 57	11 32	11 39	11 52	11 57	12 31		12 37	
Layton	d		00 34					09 42			10 42						11 44					12 42	
Blackpool North	a	00 02	00 40	02 10	07 35		09 23	09 49	10 07	10 18	10 49		10 53	11 01	11 09	11 39	11 49	12 01	12 07	12 38		12 49	

		TP ◇1 A	NT C	NT D	NT B	TP ◇1 A	NT C	NT D	NT	NT B	NT	TP ◇1 A	NT C	NT D	NT B	TP ◇1 A	NT C	NT D	NT	NT B	NT	TP ◇1 A	NT C
Colne	d										13 35										15 35		
Nelson	d										13 40										15 40		
Brierfield	d										13 43										15 43		
Burnley Central	d										13 48										15 48		
Burnley Barracks	d										13x50										15x50		
Leeds 10 41	d			11 35				12 35						13 35				14 35					
Burnley Manchester Road 41	d			12 39				13 39						14 39				15 39					
Rose Grove	d										13 53										15 53		
Hapton	d										13x56										15x56		
Huncoat	d										13x59										15x59		
Accrington	d			12 47				13 47			14 04			14 47				15 47			16 04		
Church & Oswaldtwistle	d										14 06										16 06		
Rishton	d										14 09										16 09		
Blackburn	a			12 55				13 55			14 14			14 55				15 55			16 14		
Clitheroe 94	d																						
Blackburn	d			12 56				13 56			14 16			14 56				15 56			16 16		
Mill Hill (Lancashire)	d										14 19										16 19		
Cherry Tree	d										14 21										16 21		
Pleasington	d										14x23										16x23		
Bamber Bridge	d										14 30										16 30		
Lostock Hall	d										14 33										16 33		
Preston 8	a			13 13				14 13			14 41			15 13				16 13			16 41		
	d	12 35	12 39	13 14	13 20	13 35	13 39	14 14	13 44	14 20	14 42	14 35	14 39	15 14	15 20	15 35	15 39	16 14	15 44	16 20	16 41	16 35	16 39
Salwick	d																						
Kirkham & Wesham	d				13 29				13 53	14 29	14 52				15 29				15 53	16 29	16 52		
Moss Side	d								14 01		14 59								16 01		16 58		
Lytham	d								14 05		15 03								16 05		17 02		
Ansdell & Fairhaven	d								14 08		15 06								16 08		17 05		
St Annes-on-the-Sea	d								14 12		15 10								16 12		17 09		
Squires Gate	d								14 15		15 13								16 15		17 13		
Blackpool Pleasure Beach	d								14 18		15 16								16 18		17 15		
Blackpool South	a								14 21		15 20								16 21		17 20		
Poulton-le-Fylde	d	12 52	12 57	13 31	13 37	13 52	13 57	14 30		14 37		14 52	14 57	15 32	15 37	15 52	15 57	16 31		16 37		16 52	16 57
Layton	d				13 42					14 42					15 43					16 42			
Blackpool North	a	13 01	13 07	13 38	13 49	14 01	14 07	14 38		14 49		15 01	15 07	15 39	15 49	16 01	16 07	16 38		16 49		17 01	17 07

A From Manchester Airport
B From Manchester Victoria
C From Liverpool Lime Street
D From York

Table 97

Sundays until 9 September

Colne, Burnley, Accrington and Blackburn - Preston - Blackpool

Network Diagram - see first Page of Table 97

		NT	NT	TP	NT	NT	NT	NT	NT	TP	NT	NT	NT	TP	NT	NT	NT	NT	NT	TP	NT	NT
				◇■						◇■				◇■						◇■		
		A	B	C	D	A		B		C	D	A	B	C	D	A		B		C	D	E
Colne	d								17 35										19 35			
Nelson	d								17 40										19 40			
Brierfield	d								17 43										19 43			
Burnley Central	d								17 48										19 48			
Burnley Barracks	d								17x50										19x50			
Leeds ■ 41	d	15 35				16 35						17 35				18 35						
Burnley Manchester Road 41	d	16 39				17 39						18 39				19 39						
Rose Grove	d								17 53										19 53			
Hapton	d								17x56										19x56			
Huncoat	d								17x59										19x59			
Accrington	d	16 47				17 47			18 04			18 47				19 47			20 04			
Church & Oswaldtwistle	d								18 06										20 06			
Rishton	d								18 09										20 09			
Blackburn	a	16 55				17 55			18 14			18 55				19 56			20 14			
Clitheroe 94	d																					19 57
Blackburn	d	16 56				17 56			18 16			18 56				19 57			20 16			20 25
Mill Hill (Lancashire)	d								18 19										20 19			
Cherry Tree	d								18 21										20 21			
Pleasington	d								18x23										20x23			
Bamber Bridge	d								18 30										20 30			20 34
Lostock Hall	d								18 33										20 33			20 38
Preston ■	a	17 13				18 13			18 41			19 13				20 14			20 41			20 47
	d	17 14	17 20	17 35	17 39	18 14	17 44	18 20	18 41	18 35	18 39	19 14	19 21	19 35	19 39	20 15	19 44	20 21	20 41	20 35	20 39	20 49
Salwick	d																					
Kirkham & Wesham	d		17 29				17 53	18 29	18 52				19 30				19 53	20 30	20 52			20 59
Moss Side	d						18 01		18 58								20 01		20 58			
Lytham	d						18 05		19 02								20 05		21 02			
Ansdell & Fairhaven	d						18 08		19 05								20 08		21 05			
St Annes-on-the-Sea	d						18 12		19 09								20 12		21 09			
Squires Gate	d						18 15		19 13								20 15		21 13			
Blackpool Pleasure Beach	d						18 18		19 15								20 18		21 15			
Blackpool South	a						18 21		19 20								20 21		21 20			
Poulton-le-Fylde	d	17 31	17 37	17 52	17 57	18 31		18 37		18 52	18 57	19 31	19 38	19 52	19 57	20 32		20 38		20 52	20 57	21 07
Layton	d		17 42					18 42					19 42					20 43				
Blackpool North	a	17 38	17 49	18 01	18 07	18 38		18 49		19 01	19 07	19 38	19 49	20 01	20 07	20 39		20 49		21 01	21 07	21 16

		NT	NT	TP	NT	NT	NT	NT	TP	NT	NT	TP
				◇■					◇■			◇■
		A	B	C	D	A		B	C	D	F	C
Colne	d						21 35					
Nelson	d						21 40					
Brierfield	d						21 43					
Burnley Central	d						21 48					
Burnley Barracks	d						21x50					
Leeds ■ 41	d	19 35				20 35						
Burnley Manchester Road 41	d	20 39				21 39						
Rose Grove	d						21 53					
Hapton	d						21x56					
Huncoat	d						21x59					
Accrington	d	20 47				21 47	22 04					
Church & Oswaldtwistle	d						22 06					
Rishton	d						22 09					
Blackburn	a	20 55				21 55	22 14					
Clitheroe 94	d											
Blackburn	d	20 56				21 56	22 16					
Mill Hill (Lancashire)	d						22 19					
Cherry Tree	d						22 21					
Pleasington	d						22x23					
Bamber Bridge	d						22 30					
Lostock Hall	d						22 33					
Preston ■	a	21 13				22 13	22 44					
	d	21 14	21 20	21 35	21 39	22 14		22 20	22 29	22 39	23 39	23 47
Salwick	d											
Kirkham & Wesham	d		21 29					22 29				23 56
Moss Side	d											
Lytham	d											
Ansdell & Fairhaven	d											
St Annes-on-the-Sea	d											
Squires Gate	d											
Blackpool Pleasure Beach	d											
Blackpool South	a											
Poulton-le-Fylde	d	21 31	21 37	21 52	21 57	22 31		22 37	22 46	22 57	23 56	00 05
Layton	d		21 42					22 42				
Blackpool North	a	21 38	21 49	22 01	22 07	22 38		22 49	22 55	23 07	00 05	00 14

A From York
B From Manchester Victoria
C From Manchester Airport
D From Liverpool Lime Street
E From Carlisle
F From Wigan North Western

Table 97

Sundays 16 September to 21 October

Colne, Burnley, Accrington and Blackburn - Preston - Blackpool

Network Diagram - see first Page of Table 97

		TP	NT	TP	TP	TP	NT	NT	NT	TP	NT	NT	NT	TP	NT	NT	NT
		◇■				◇■				◇■				◇■			
		A	C	A (bus)	A (bus)	A		C	F	A	C			A	F	G	C
Colne	d											09 16					
Nelson	d											09 21					
Brierfield	d											09 24					
Burnley Central	d											09 29					
Burnley Barracks	d											09x31					
Leeds ■ 41	d												08 36			09 35	
Burnley Manchester Road 41	d												09 50			10 39	
Rose Grove	d											09 34					
Hapton	d											09x37					
Huncoat	d											09x40					
Accrington	d											09 45	09 59			10 48	
Church & Oswaldtwistle	d											09 47					
Rishton	d											09 50					
Blackburn	a											09 55	10 07			10 56	
Clitheroe 94	d																
Blackburn	d											09 57	10 07			10 56	
Mill Hill (Lancashire)	d											10 00					
Cherry Tree	d											10 02					
Pleasington	d											10x04					
Bamber Bridge	d											10 11					
Lostock Hall	d											10 14					
Preston ■	a											10 22	10 27			11 13	
	d	23p35	00 11			08 49	08 49	09 20	09 39	09 52	10 20	10 23	10 29	10 35	10 40	11 15	11 21
Salwick	d																
Kirkham & Wesham	d		00 21				08 58	09 29			10 29	10 33					11 31
Moss Side	d						09 06					10 39					
Lytham	d						09 10					10 43					
Ansdell & Fairhaven	d						09 13					10 46					
St Annes-on-the-Sea	d						09 17					10 50					
Squires Gate	d						09 20					10 54					
Blackpool Pleasure Beach	d						09 23					10 56					
Blackpool South	a						0926					11 01					
Poulton-le-Fylde	d	23p52	00 29			09 06		09 37	09 57	10 09	10 37		10 46	10 52	10 57	11 32	11 39
Layton	d		00 34					09 42			10 42						11 44
Blackpool North	a	00 02	00 42	02 10	07 35	09 13		09 51	10 07	10 18	10 49		10 53	11 02	11 09	11 39	11 49

		TP	NT	NT	NT	NT	NT	TP	NT	NT	NT	TP	NT	NT	NT	NT	NT
		◇■						◇■				◇■					
		A	F	H		C		A	F	H	C	A	F	G		C	
Colne	d						11 35										13 35
Nelson	d						11 40										13 40
Brierfield	d						11 43										13 43
Burnley Central	d						11 48										13 48
Burnley Barracks	d						11x50										13x50
Leeds ■ 41	d			10 35						11 35				12 35			
Burnley Manchester Road 41	d			11 39						12 39				13 39			
Rose Grove	d						11 53										13 53
Hapton	d						11x56										13x56
Huncoat	d						11x59										13x59
Accrington	d			11 47			12 04			12 47				13 47			14 04
Church & Oswaldtwistle	d						12 06										14 06
Rishton	d						12 09										14 09
Blackburn	a			11 55			12 14			12 55				13 55			14 14
Clitheroe 94	d																
Blackburn	d			11 56			12 16			12 56				13 56			14 16
Mill Hill (Lancashire)	d						12 19										14 19
Cherry Tree	d						12 21										14 21
Pleasington	d						12x23										14x23
Bamber Bridge	d						12 30										14 30
Lostock Hall	d						12 33										14 33
Preston ■	a			12 13			12 41			13 13				14 13			14 41
	d	11 35	11 39	12 14	11 44	12 20	12 42	12 35	12 39	13 14	13 20	13 35	13 39	14 14	13 44	14 20	14 42
Salwick	d																
Kirkham & Wesham	d				11 53	12 29	12 52				13 29				13 53	14 29	14 52
Moss Side	d				12 01		12 58								14 01		14 59
Lytham	d				12 05		13 02								14 05		15 03
Ansdell & Fairhaven	d				12 08		13 05								14 08		15 06
St Annes-on-the-Sea	d				12 12		13 09								14 12		15 10
Squires Gate	d				12 15		13 13								14 15		15 13
Blackpool Pleasure Beach	d				12 18		13 15								14 18		15 16
Blackpool South	a				12 21		13 20								14 21		15 20
Poulton-le-Fylde	d	11 52	11 57	12 31		12 37		12 52	12 57	13 31	13 37	13 52	13 57	14 30		14 37	
Layton	d					12 42					13 42					14 42	
Blackpool North	a	12 01	12 07	12 38		12 49		13 01	13 07	13 38	13 49	14 01	14 07	14 38		14 49	

A From Manchester Airport
C From Manchester Victoria
F From Liverpool Lime Street
G From York
H From Bradford Interchange

Colne, Burnley, Accrington and Blackburn - Preston - Blackpool

Sundays

16 September to 21 October

Network Diagram - see first Page of Table 97

		TP ◇1 B	NT C	NT D	NT E	TP ◇1 B	NT C	NT D	NT	NT E	NT	TP ◇1 B	NT C	NT D	NT E	TP ◇1 B
Colne	d										15 35					
Nelson	d										15 40					
Brierfield	d										15 43					
Burnley Central	d										15 48					
Burnley Barracks	d										15x50					
Leeds 41	d			13 35				14 35						15 35		
Burnley Manchester Road 41	d			14 39				15 39						16 39		
Rose Grove	d										15 53					
Hapton	d										15x56					
Huncoat	d										15x59					
Accrington	d			14 47				15 47			16 04			16 47		
Church & Oswaldtwistle	d										16 06					
Rishton	d										16 09					
Blackburn	a			14 55				15 55			16 14			16 55		
Clitheroe 94	d															
Blackburn	d			14 56				15 56			16 16			16 56		
Mill Hill (Lancashire)	d										16 19					
Cherry Tree	d										16 21					
Pleasington	d										16x23					
Bamber Bridge	d										16 30					
Lostock Hall	d										16 33					
Preston	a			15 13				16 13			16 41			17 13		
	d	14 35	14 39	15 14	15 20	15 35	15 39	16 14	15 44	16 20	16 41	16 35	16 39	17 14	17 20	17 35
Salwick	d															
Kirkham & Wesham	d				15 29				15 53	16 29	16 52				17 29	
Moss Side	d								16 01		16 58					
Lytham	d								16 05		17 02					
Ansdell & Fairhaven	d								16 08		17 05					
St Annes-on-the-Sea	d								16 12		17 09					
Squires Gate	d								16 15		17 13					
Blackpool Pleasure Beach	d								16 18		17 15					
Blackpool South	a								16 21		17 20					
Poulton-le-Fylde	d	14 52	14 57	15 32	15 37	15 52	15 57	16 31		16 37		16 52	16 57	17 31	17 37	17 52
Layton	d				15 42					16 42					17 42	
Blackpool North	a	15 01	15 07	15 39	15 51	16 01	16 07	16 38		16 49		17 01	17 07	17 38	17 49	18 01

		NT C	NT D	NT	NT E	NT	TP ◇1 B	NT C	NT D	NT E	TP ◇1 B	NT C	NT D	NT	NT E	NT
Colne	d					17 35										19 35
Nelson	d					17 40										19 40
Brierfield	d					17 43										19 43
Burnley Central	d					17 48										19 48
Burnley Barracks	d					17x50										19x50
Leeds 41	d		16 35						17 35				18 35			
Burnley Manchester Road 41	d		17 39						18 39				19 39			
Rose Grove	d					17 53										19 53
Hapton	d					17x56										19x56
Huncoat	d					17x59										19x59
Accrington	d		17 47			18 04			18 47				19 47			20 04
Church & Oswaldtwistle	d					18 06										20 06
Rishton	d					18 09										20 09
Blackburn	a		17 55			18 14			18 55				19 56			20 14
Clitheroe 94	d															
Blackburn	d		17 56			18 16			18 56				19 57			20 16
Mill Hill (Lancashire)	d					18 19										20 19
Cherry Tree	d					18 21										20 21
Pleasington	d					18x23										20x23
Bamber Bridge	d					18 30										20 30
Lostock Hall	d					18 33										20 33
Preston	a		18 13			18 41			19 13				20 14			20 41
	d	17 39	18 14	17 44	18 20	18 41	18 35	18 39	19 14	19 21	19 35	19 39	20 15	19 44	20 21	20 41
Salwick	d															
Kirkham & Wesham	d			17 53	18 29	18 52				19 30				19 53	20 30	20 52
Moss Side	d			18 01		18 58								20 01		20 58
Lytham	d			18 05		19 02								20 05		21 02
Ansdell & Fairhaven	d			18 08		19 05								20 08		21 05
St Annes-on-the-Sea	d			18 12		19 09								20 12		21 09
Squires Gate	d			18 15		19 13								20 15		21 13
Blackpool Pleasure Beach	d			18 18		19 15								20 18		21 15
Blackpool South	a			18 21		19 20								20 21		21 20
Poulton-le-Fylde	d	17 57	18 31		18 37		18 52	18 57	19 31	19 38	19 52	19 57	20 32		20 38	
Layton	d				18 42					19 42					20 43	
Blackpool North	a	18 07	18 38		18 49		19 01	19 07	19 38	19 49	20 01	20 07	20 39		20 49	

B From Manchester Airport
C From Liverpool Lime Street
D From York
E From Manchester Victoria

Table 97

Colne, Burnley, Accrington and Blackburn - Preston - Blackpool

Sundays

16 September to 21 October

Network Diagram - see first Page of Table 97

		TP ◇1 A	NT B	NT C	NT D	NT E	TP ◇1 A	NT B	NT D	NT	NT E	TP ◇1 A	NT B	NT G	TP ◇1 A
Colne	d									21 35					
Nelson	d									21 40					
Brierfield	d									21 43					
Burnley Central	d									21 48					
Burnley Barracks	d									21x50					
Leeds 41	d				19 35				20 35						
Burnley Manchester Road 41	d				20 39				21 39						
Rose Grove	d									21 53					
Hapton	d									21x56					
Huncoat	d									21x59					
Accrington	d				20 47				21 47	22 04					
Church & Oswaldtwistle	d									22 06					
Rishton	d									22 09					
Blackburn	a				20 55				21 55	22 14					
Clitheroe 94	d			19 57											
Blackburn	d			20 25	20 56				21 56	22 16					
Mill Hill (Lancashire)	d									22 19					
Cherry Tree	d									22 21					
Pleasington	d									22x23					
Bamber Bridge	d			20 34						22 30					
Lostock Hall	d			20 38						22 33					
Preston	a			20 47	21 13				22 13	22 44					
	d	20 35	20 39	20 49	21 14	21 20	21 35	21 39	22 14		22 20	22 29	22 39	23 39	23 47
Salwick	d														
Kirkham & Wesham	d			20 59		21 29					22 29				23 56
Moss Side	d														
Lytham	d														
Ansdell & Fairhaven	d														
St Annes-on-the-Sea	d														
Squires Gate	d														
Blackpool Pleasure Beach	d														
Blackpool South	a														
Poulton-le-Fylde	d	20 52	20 57	21 07	21 31	21 37	21 52	21 57	22 31		22 37	22 46	22 57	23 56	00 05
Layton	d					21 42					22 42				
Blackpool North	a	21 01	21 07	21 16	21 38	21 49	22 01	22 07	22 38		22 49	22 55	23 07	00 05	00 14

Sundays

from 28 October

		TP ◇1 A	NT H	TP A (bus)	TP A (bus)	TP ◇1 A	NT I	NT J	NT H	TP ◇1 A	NT H	NT I	NT	TP ◇1 A	NT K	NT H	TP ◇1 A	NT I	NT L	NT H	TP ◇1 A	NT I	NT J
Colne	d							09 16				09 16										11 35	11 35
Nelson	d							09 21				09 21										11 40	11 40
Brierfield	d							09 24				09 24										11 43	11 43
Burnley Central	d							09 29				09 29										11 48	11 48
Burnley Barracks	d							09x31				09x31										11x50	11x50
Leeds 41	d												08 45		09 35				10 35				
Burnley Manchester Road 41	d												09 50		10 39				11 39				
Rose Grove	d							09 34				09 34										11 53	11 53
Hapton	d							09x37				09x37										11x56	11x56
Huncoat	d							09x40				09x40										11x59	11x59
Accrington	d							09 45				09 45	09 59		10 48				11 47			12 04	12 04
Church & Oswaldtwistle	d							09 47				09 47										12 06	12 06
Rishton	d							09 50				09 50										12 09	12 09
Blackburn	a							09 55				09 55	10 07		10 56				11 55			12 14	12 14
Clitheroe 94	d																						
Blackburn	d							09 57				09 57	10 07		10 56				11 56			12 16	12 16
Mill Hill (Lancashire)	d							10 00				10 00										12 19	12 19
Cherry Tree	d							10 02				10 02										12 21	12 21
Pleasington	d							10x04				10x04										12x23	12x23
Bamber Bridge	d							10 11				10 11										12 30	12 30
Lostock Hall	d							10 14				10 14										12 33	12 33
Preston	a							10 22				10 22	10 27		11 13				12 13			12 41	12 42
	d	23p35	00 11			08 49	08 49		09 20	09 52	10 20	10 23	10 29	10 35	11 15	11 20	11 35	11 44	12 14	12 20	12 35	12 42	
Salwick	d																						
Kirkham & Wesham	d		00 21				08 58		09 29		10 29	10 33				11 29		11 53		12 29		12 52	
Moss Side	d						09 06					10 39						12 01				12 58	
Lytham	d						09 10					10 43						12 05				13 02	
Ansdell & Fairhaven	d						09 13					10 46						12 08				13 05	
St Annes-on-the-Sea	d						09 17					10 50						12 12				13 09	
Squires Gate	d						09 20					10 54						12 15				13 13	
Blackpool Pleasure Beach	d						09 23					10 56						12 18				13 15	
Blackpool South	a						09 28					11 03						12 23				13 22	
Poulton-le-Fylde	d	23p52	00 29			09 06			09 37	10 09	10 37		10 46	10 52	11 32	11 37	11 52		12 31	12 37	12 52		
Layton	d		00 33						09 42		10 42					11 42				12 42			
Blackpool North	a	00 02	00 42	02 10	07 35	09 13			09 51	10 18	10 51		10 53	11 02	11 39	11 51	12 01		12 38	12 51	13 01		

A From Manchester Airport
B From Liverpool Lime Street
C From Carlisle
D From York
E From Manchester Victoria
G From Wigan North Western
H From Manchester Victoria
I 28 October, 4 November
J not from 28 October until 4 November
K From York
L From Bradford Interchange

Table 97

Sundays from 28 October

Colne, Burnley, Accrington and Blackburn - Preston - Blackpool

Network Diagram - see first Page of Table 97

		NT	NT	TP	NT	NT	NT	NT	NT	TP	NT	NT	TP	NT	NT	NT	NT	NT	NT	TP	NT	NT	NT
				◇1						◇1			◇1							◇1			
		A	B	C	D	E	B	E	F	C	D	B	C	H	D	E	B	E	F	C	H	D	B
Colne	d							13 35	13 35									15 35	15 35				
Nelson	d							13 40	13 40									15 40	15 40				
Brierfield	d							13 43	13 43									15 43	15 43				
Burnley Central	d							13 48	13 48									15 48	15 48				
Burnley Barracks	d							13x50	13x50									15x50	15x50				
Leeds 10	41 d	11 35			12 35						13 35				14 35							15 35	
Burnley Manchester Road	41 d	12 39			13 39						14 39				15 39							16 39	
Rose Grove	d							13 53	13 53									15 53	15 53				
Hapton	d							13x56	13x56									15x56	15x56				
Huncoat	d							13x59	13x59									15x59	15x59				
Accrington	d	12 47			13 47			14 04	14 04		14 47				15 47			16 04	16 04			16 47	
Church & Oswaldtwistle	d							14 06	14 06									16 06	16 06				
Rishton	d							14 09	14 09									16 09	16 09				
Blackburn	a	12 55			13 55			14 14	14 14		14 55				15 55			16 14	16 14			16 55	
Clitheroe	94 d																						
Blackburn	d	12 56			13 56			14 16	14 16		14 56				15 56			16 16	16 16			16 56	
Mill Hill (Lancashire)	d							14 19	14 19									16 19	16 19				
Cherry Tree	d							14 21	14 21									16 21	16 21				
Pleasington	d							14x23	14x23									16x23	16x23				
Bamber Bridge	d							14 30	14 30									16 30	16 30				
Lostock Hall	d							14 33	14 33									16 33	16 33				
Preston 8	a	13 13			14 13			14 41	14 42		15 13				16 13			16 41	16 42			17 13	
	d	13 14	13 20	13 35	14 14	13 44	14 20	14 42		14 35	15 14	15 20	15 35	15 39	16 14	15 44	16 20	16 41		16 35	16 39	17 14	17 20
Salwick	d																						
Kirkham & Wesham	d		13 29			13 53	14 29	14 52				15 29				15 53	16 29	16 52					17 29
Moss Side	d					14 01		14 59								16 01		16 58					
Lytham	d					14 05		15 03								16 05		17 02					
Ansdell & Fairhaven	d					14 08		15 06								16 08		17 05					
St Annes-on-the-Sea	d					14 12		15 10								16 12		17 09					
Squires Gate	d					14 15		15 13								16 15		17 13					
Blackpool Pleasure Beach	d					14 18		15 16								16 18		17 15					
Blackpool South	a					14 23		15 22								16 23		17 22					
Poulton-le-Fylde	d	13 31	13 37	13 52	14 30		14 37			14 52	15 32	15 37	15 52	15 57	16 31		16 37			16 52	16 57	17 31	17 37
Layton	d		13 42				14 42					15 42					16 42						17 42
Blackpool North	a	13 38	13 51	14 01	14 38		14 51			15 01	15 39	15 51	16 01	16 07	16 38		16 51			17 01	17 07	17 38	17 51

		TP	NT	NT	NT	NT	NT	NT	TP	NT	NT	NT	TP	NT	NT	NT	NT	NT	NT	TP	NT	NT
		◇1							◇1				◇1							◇1		
		C	H	D	E	B	E	F	C	H	D	B	C	H	E	D	B	E	F	C	H	D
Colne	d						17 35	17 35										19 35	19 35			
Nelson	d						17 40	17 40										19 40	19 40			
Brierfield	d						17 43	17 43										19 43	19 43			
Burnley Central	d						17 48	17 48										19 48	19 48			
Burnley Barracks	d						17x50	17x50										19x50	19x50			
Leeds 10	41 d			16 35							17 35					18 35						19 35
Burnley Manchester Road	41 d			17 39							18 39					19 39						20 39
Rose Grove	d						17 53	17 53										19 53	19 53			
Hapton	d						17x56	17x56										19x56	19x56			
Huncoat	d						17x59	17x59										19x59	19x59			
Accrington	d			17 47			18 04	18 04			18 47					19 47		20 04	20 04			20 47
Church & Oswaldtwistle	d						18 06	18 06										20 06	20 06			
Rishton	d						18 09	18 09										20 09	20 09			
Blackburn	a			17 55			18 14	18 14			18 55					19 56		20 14	20 14			20 55
Clitheroe	94 d																					
Blackburn	d			17 56			18 16	18 16			18 56					19 57		20 16	20 16			20 56
Mill Hill (Lancashire)	d						18 19	18 19										20 19	20 19			
Cherry Tree	d						18 21	18 21										20 21	20 21			
Pleasington	d						18x23	18x23										20x23	20x23			
Bamber Bridge	d						18 30	18 30										20 30	20 30			
Lostock Hall	d						18 33	18 33										20 33	20 33			
Preston 8	a			18 13			18 41	18 42			19 13					20 14		20 41	20 42			21 13
	d	17 35	17 39	18 14	17 44	18 20	18 41		18 35	18 39	19 14	19 20	19 35	19 39	19 44	20 15	20 20	20 41		20 35	20 39	21 14
Salwick	d																					
Kirkham & Wesham	d				17 53	18 29	18 52					19 29			19 53		20 29	20 52				
Moss Side	d				18 01		18 58								20 01			20 58				
Lytham	d				18 05		19 02								20 05			21 02				
Ansdell & Fairhaven	d				18 08		19 05								20 08			21 05				
St Annes-on-the-Sea	d				18 12		19 09								20 12			21 09				
Squires Gate	d				18 15		19 13								20 15			21 13				
Blackpool Pleasure Beach	d				18 18		19 15								20 18			21 15				
Blackpool South	a				18 23		19 22								20 23			21 22				
Poulton-le-Fylde	d	17 52	17 57	18 31		18 37			18 52	18 57	19 31	19 37	19 52	19 57		20 32	20 37			20 52	20 57	21 31
Layton	d					18 42						19 42					20 42					
Blackpool North	a	18 01	18 07	18 38		18 51			19 01	19 07	19 38	19 51	20 01	20 07		20 39	20 51			21 01	21 07	21 38

A From Halifax
B From Manchester Victoria
C From Manchester Airport
D From York
E 28 October, 4 November
F not from 28 October until 4 November
H From Liverpool Lime Street

Table 97

Sundays from 28 October

Colne, Burnley, Accrington and Blackburn - Preston - Blackpool

Network Diagram - see first Page of Table 97

		NT	TP	NT	NT	NT	NT	TP	NT	NT	TP
			◇1					◇1			◇1
		A	B	C	D		A	B	C	E	B
Colne	d					21 35					
Nelson	d					21 40					
Brierfield	d					21 43					
Burnley Central	d					21 48					
Burnley Barracks	d					21x50					
Leeds 10	41 d				20 35						
Burnley Manchester Road	41 d				21 39						
Rose Grove	d					21 53					
Hapton	d					21x56					
Huncoat	d					21x59					
Accrington	d				21 47	22 04					
Church & Oswaldtwistle	d					22 06					
Rishton	d					22 09					
Blackburn	a				21 55	22 14					
Clitheroe	94 d										
Blackburn	d				21 56	22 16					
Mill Hill (Lancashire)	d					22 19					
Cherry Tree	d					22 21					
Pleasington	d					22x23					
Bamber Bridge	d					22 30					
Lostock Hall	d					22 33					
Preston 8	a				22 13	22 44					
	d	21 20	21 35	21 39	22 14		22 20	22 29	22 39	23 39	23 47
Salwick	d										
Kirkham & Wesham	d	21 29					22 29				23 56
Moss Side	d										
Lytham	d										
Ansdell & Fairhaven	d										
St Annes-on-the-Sea	d										
Squires Gate	d										
Blackpool Pleasure Beach	d										
Blackpool South	a										
Poulton-le-Fylde	d	21 37	21 52	21 57	22 31		22 37	22 46	22 57	23 56	00 05
Layton	d	21 42					22 42				
Blackpool North	a	21 51	22 01	22 07	22 38		22 51	22 55	23 07	00 05	00 14

A From Manchester Victoria
B From Manchester Airport
C From Liverpool Lime Street
D From York
E From Wigan North Western

Table 98

Mondays to Fridays

Lancaster - Morecambe and Heysham

Network Diagram - see first Page of Table 97

Miles			TP 1	NT	NT	NT	NT	NT	NT	NT	NT	NT	NT	NT	NT	NT	NT	NT	NT	NT	NT	NT	NT
0	Lancaster 6 82	d	05 46	06 38	07 25	07 58	08 35	09 15	10 04	10 19	11 22	12 02	12 28	13 44	14 27	15 25	16 03	16 19	16 49	17 38	18 33	18 49	19 40
2½	Bare Lane	d	05 52	06 44	07 31	08 04	08 41	09 21	10 10	10 27	11 28	12 08	12 34	13 50	14 33	15 31	16 09	16 26	16 55	17 44	18 39	18 55	19 46
4¼	Morecambe	a	05 56	06 49	07 36	08 09	08 46	09 26	10 15	10 31	11 33	12 13	12 39	13 55	14 38	15 36	16 13	16 30	17 00	17 49	18 44	19 01	19 50
—		d											12 42										
8½	Heysham Port	a											12 57										

		NT	NT	NT	NT
Lancaster 6 82	d	20 22	21 03	22 06	22 35
Bare Lane	d	20 28	21 09	22 12	22 41
Morecambe	a	20 32	21 13	22 16	22 45
	d				
Heysham Port	a				

Saturdays

		TP 1	NT	NT	NT	NT	NT	NT	NT	NT	NT	NT	NT	NT	NT	NT	NT	NT	NT	NT	NT	NT	NT
Lancaster 6 82	d	05 46	06 38	07 25	07 57	08 35	09 15	10 05	10 19	11 23	12 02	12 25	13 24	14 27	15 25	15 49	16 03	17 04	17 37	18 21	18 47	19 40	20 22
Bare Lane	d	05 52	06 44	07 31	08 03	08 41	09 21	10 11	10 26	11 29	12 08	12 31	13 30	14 33	15 31	15 56	16 09	17 10	17 43	18 27	18 53	19 46	20 28
Morecambe	a	05 56	06 49	07 36	08 08	08 46	09 26	10 16	10 32	11 34	12 13	12 36	13 35	14 38	15 36	16 02	16 14	17 15	17 48	18 32	18 59	19 50	20 32
	d											12 39											
Heysham Port	a											12 54											

		NT	NT	NT
Lancaster 6 82	d	21 03	22 06	22 35
Bare Lane	d	21 09	22 12	22 41
Morecambe	a	21 13	22 16	22 46
	d			
Heysham Port	a			

Sundays

		NT	NT A	NT A	NT	NT	NT A	NT	NT	NT A	NT A	NT	NT	NT
Lancaster 6 82	d	10 45	11 05	12 00	12 05	13 01	13 20	14 27	15 05	15 45	16 26	16 51	19 25	21 18
Bare Lane	d	10 51	11 11	12 06	12 11	13 07	13 26	14 34	15 11	15 51	16 32	16 56	19 31	21 24
Morecambe	a	10 57	11 16	12 11	12 16	13 13	13 32	14 38	15 16	15 56	16 37	17 03	19 37	21 29
	d			12 14			13 34							
Heysham Port	a			12 27			13 47							

Table 98

Mondays to Fridays

Heysham and Morecambe - Lancaster

Network Diagram - see first Page of Table 97

Miles			NT	NT	NT	NT	NT	NT	NT	NT	NT	NT	NT	NT	NT	NT	NT	NT	NT	NT	NT	NT	NT
0	Heysham Port	d											13 15										
4¼	Morecambe	a											13 25										
—		d	06 19	07 03	07 42	08 11	08 51	09 32	10 34	10 55	11 39	12 32	13 29	13 58	14 42	15 45	16 19	16 34	17 03	17 56	19 00	19 08	19 55
6	Bare Lane	d	06 23	07 07	07 46	08 15	08 55	09 36	10 38	10 59	11 43	12 36	13 36	14 02	14 46	15 49	16a23	16 38	17 07	18 00	19 04	19 12	19 59
8½	Lancaster 6 82	a	06 30	07 14	07 53	08 21	09 03	09 43	10 45	11 06	11 50	12 43	13 42	14 09	14 53	15 56		16 45	17 14	18 07	19 11	19 19	20 06

		NT	NT	NT	NT
Heysham Port	d				
Morecambe	a				
	d	20 40	21 36	22 20	22 55
Bare Lane	d	20 44	21 40	22 24	22 59
Lancaster 6 82	a	20 51	21 47	22 31	23 05

Saturdays

		NT	NT	NT	NT	NT	NT	NT	NT	NT	NT	NT	NT	NT	NT	NT	NT	NT	NT	NT	NT	NT	NT
Heysham Port	d											13 15											
Morecambe	a											13 25											
	d	06 19	07 03	07 38	08 11	08 51	09 41	10 34	10 54	11 40	12 32	13 29	13 58	14 42	15 44	16 19	16 40	17 20	17 56	18 58	19 09	19 55	20 40
Bare Lane	d	06 23	07 07	07 42	08 15	08 55	09 45	10 38	10 58	11 44	12 36	13 36	14 02	14 46	15 48	16 24	16 44	17 24	18 00	19 02	19 13	19 59	20 44
Lancaster 6 82	a	06 30	07 14	07 49	08 22	09 03	09 52	10 45	11 05	11 51	12 43	13 42	14 09	14 53	15 55	16 30	16 50	17 31	18 07	19 09	19 20	20 06	20 51

		NT	NT
Heysham Port	d		
Morecambe	a		
	d	21 36	22 20
Bare Lane	d	21 40	22 24
Lancaster 6 82	a	21 47	22 31

Sundays

		NT	NT A	NT	NT A	NT	NT A	NT	NT	NT A	NT A	NT	NT	NT
Heysham Port	d				12 46		14 00							
Morecambe	a				12 56		14 10							
	d	11 20	11 35	12 20	13 00	13 23	14 17	14 46	15 21	16 02	16 42	17 45	20 00	21 41
Bare Lane	d	11 24	11 39	12 24	13 07	13 27	14 24	14a50	15 25	16 06	16 46	17 49	20 04	21 45
Lancaster 6 82	a	11 31	11 46	12 30	13 13	13 34	14 30		15 32	16 13	16 53	17 55	20 11	21 51

A until 9 September

Table 98A

Mondays to Fridays

To and from The Isle of Man via Heysham and Liverpool

One Class only on ship

		VT ◇ A	VT ◇ B	VT ◇ C	VT ◇	VT ◇ D	VT ◇ E	VT ◇ F	VT ◇ G	VT ◇ H	VT ◇ I
Liverpool Landing Stage	d	21p30		11 15		18 15	18 45	19 00	19 15	20 00	20 30
Heysham Port	d		02 15		14 15						
Douglas (Isle of Man)	a	00 15	05 45	14 00	17 45	21 00	21 30	21 45	22 00	22 45	23 15

Saturdays

		VT ◇	VT ◇ J	VT ◇ K	VT ◇ L	VT ◇ M	VT ◇ N	VT ◇ O	VT ◇ P
Liverpool Landing Stage	d		11 15		18 45	19 00	19 15	20 30	21 00
Heysham Port	d	02 15		14 15					
Douglas (Isle of Man)	a	05 45	14 00	17 45	21 30	21 45	22 00	23 15	23 45

Sundays

		VT ◇ Q	VT ◇ R	VT ◇ S	VT ◇ T	VT ◇ U	VT ◇ V
Liverpool Landing Stage	d			19 00	19 15	20 30	21 30
Heysham Port	d	02 15	14 15				
Douglas (Isle of Man)	a	05 45	17 45	21 45	22 00	23 15	00 15

Mondays to Fridays

		VT ◇ W	VT ◇ X	VT ◇ Y	VT ◇ Z	VT ◇ [	VT ◇ D	VT ◇ AA	VT ◇ BB	VT ◇ CC	VT ◇ DD	VT ◇ EE	VT ◇ FF	VT ◇ GG
Douglas (Isle of Man)	d	06 00	07 30	08 00	08 15	08 45	13 45	14 30	15 00	15 30	16 00	16 30	19 15	19 45
Heysham Port	a			11 45	11 45	12 15							22 45	23 15
Liverpool Landing Stage	a	08 45	10 15				16 30	17 15	17 45	18 15	18 45	19 15		

Saturdays

		VT ◇ HH	VT ◇ II	VT ◇ L	VT ◇ L	VT ◇ P	VT ◇ HH	VT ◇ JJ	VT ◇ KK	VT ◇ LL	VT ◇ MM	VT ◇ NN	VT ◇ OO
Douglas (Isle of Man)	d	06 00	07 30	07 30	08 00	08 00	08 15	08 45	10 00	15 00	15 30	16 30	20 00
Heysham Port	a			11 00		11 30	11 45	12 15					23 30
Liverpool Landing Stage	a	08 45	10 15		10 45				12 45	17 45	18 15	19 15	

Sundays

		VT ◇ V	VT ◇ PP	VT ◇ QQ	VT ◇ RR	VT ◇ SS	VT ◇ V	VT ◇
Douglas (Isle of Man)	d	08 00	08 45	15 00	15 30	16 30	17 30	19 45
Heysham Port	a	11 30	12 15					23 15
Liverpool Landing Stage	a			17 45	18 15	19 15	20 15	

A 4 June
B not 1 June
C MFO until 28 May, MThFO from 11 June until 10 September, not 21 June, 13 July, 19 July, also MFO from 14 September until 1 October
D 29 May, 30 May
E 4 June, from 6 June until 8 June
F until 28 May
G from 13 June until 2 November, not from 23 August until 3 September, 30 October, 31 October
H 1 June, 11 June, 12 June
I from 23 August until 3 September
J until 29 September, not 2 June, 9 June
K until 3 November
L 9 June
M 19 May, 26 May
N from 16 June until 3 November, not 25 August, 1 September
O 25 August, 1 September
P 2 June
Q 8 July, 22 July, 5 August, 12 August, 9 September, 23 September, 30 September, 7 October, 4 November, 2 December
R from 27 May until 4 November, not 17 June, 15 July, 19 August, 16 September, 7 October, 21 October
S 20 May, 27 May, 10 June
T from 17 June until 4 November, not 26 August, 2 September
U 26 August, 2 September
V 3 June
W 24 August
X MFO until 28 May, MThFO from 11 June until 10 September, not 21 June, 13 July, 19 July, 2 August, 24 August, also MFO from 14 September until 1 October
Y 30 May, 31 May
Z 1 June, 23 August, 24 August
[not from 30 May until 1 June, 23 August, 24 August
AA 31 May
BB until 2 November, not from 29 May until 31 May, 5 June, 11 June, 12 June, 30 July, 31 July, from 23 August until 3 September, 30 October, 31 October
CC 23 August, 24 August
DD 11 June, 12 June
EE from 27 August until 3 September
FF from 30 May until 1 June
GG not from 30 May until 1 June
HH 25 August
II until 29 September, not 2 June, 9 June, 25 August
JJ until 3 November, not 25 August
KK from 6 October until 3 November
LL until 29 September, not 2 June, 25 August, 1 September
MM 2 June, 25 August
NN 1 September
OO 19 May, 26 May, 2 June, 9 June, 23 June, 30 June, 14 July, 28 July, 18 August, 25 August, 1 September, 15 September, from 13 October, not 3 November, 1 December
PP until 4 November, not 3 June, 7 October
QQ until 4 November, not 3 June, 26 August, 2 September
RR 26 August
SS 2 September

Table 99

Mondays to Saturdays

Ormskirk - Preston

Network Diagram - see first Page of Table 97

Miles			NT	NT	NT	NT	NT	NT	NT	NT	NT	NT	NT	NT
0	Ormskirk	d	06 58	08 06	09 17	10 36	12 17	13 36	15 17	16 36	17 52	19 06	20 47	22 47
2½	Burscough Junction	d	07 02	08 10	09 21	10 40	12 21	13 40	15 21	16 40	17 56	19 10	20 51	22 51
5½	Rufford	d	07 07	08 15	09 25	10 45	12 25	13 45	15 25	16 45	18 01	19 15	20 55	22 55
8	Croston	d	07 11	08 19	09 30	10 49	12 30	13 50	15 30	16 49	18 06	19 19	21 00	23 00
15	Preston ■	a	07 29	08 36	09 47	11 08	12 47	14 08	15 47	17 08	18 23	19 38	21 17	23 14

Table 99

Mondays to Saturdays

Preston - Ormskirk

Network Diagram - see first Page of Table 97

Miles			NT	NT	NT	NT	NT	NT	NT	NT	NT	NT	NT	NT
0	Preston ■	d	06 25	07 33	08 41	09 59	11 29	12 59	14 29	15 59	17 10	18 34	20 08	22 08
7	Croston	d	06 36	07 45	08 52	10 11	11 41	13 11	14 41	16 11	17 22	18 47	20 19	22 20
9½	Rufford	d	06 41	07 50	08 57	10 16	11 46	13 16	14 46	16 16	17 27	18 51	20 24	22 24
12½	Burscough Junction	d	06 46	07 55	09 02	10 21	11 51	13 21	14 51	16 21	17 32	18 56	20 29	22 29
15	Ormskirk	a	06 55	08 04	09 11	10 30	12 00	13 30	15 00	16 30	17 41	19 05	20 38	22 38

For connections to Liverpool Central please refer to Table 103

No Sunday Service

Table 100

Mondays to Fridays

Barrow-in-Furness - Whitehaven and Carlisle

Network Diagram - see first Page of Table 97

Miles			NT	NT	NT	NT	NT	NT	NT	NT	NT	NT	NT	NT	NT	NT	NT	NT	NT	NT	NT
—	Lancaster ■ 82	d			05 42				08 58					15 34		16 55					
0	Barrow-in-Furness	d		06 00	06 50	08 01		09 10	10 11	11 22	12 31	13 31	14 54	16 41	17 28	18 05		19 35		21 25	
6	Askam	d		06 10	07 00	08 11		09 20	10 21	11 32	12 41	13 41	15 04	16 51	17 40	18 15		19 45		21 35	
9¼	Kirkby-in-Furness	d		06 14	07x04	08x15		09x24	10x25	11x36	12x45	13x45	15x08	16x55	17x44	18x19		19x49		21x39	
11¼	Foxfield	d		06x18	07x08	08x18		09x27	10x29	11x39	12x48	13x48	15x11	16x58	17x48	18x22		19x52		21x42	
13½	Green Road	d		06x22	07x12	08x22		09x31	10x32	11x43	12x52	13x52	15x15	17x02	17x51	18x26		19x56		21x46	
16	Millom	a		06 29	07 19	08 28		09 37	10 39	11 49	12 58	13 58	15 21	17 08	17 58	18 35		20 05		21 55	
—		d		06 29	07 19	08 29		09 38	10 39	11 49	12 59	13 58	15 22	17 09	17 58						
19	Silecroft	d		06x34	07x24			09x42	10x44	11x54	13x03	14x03	15x26	17x13	18x03						
24½	Bootle	d		06x41	07x31			09x49	10x50	12x00	13x10	14x09	15x33	17x20	18x09						
29¼	Ravenglass for Eskdale	d		06 47	07 37	08 44		09 55	10 56	12 06	13 15	14 15	15 39	17 26	18 15						
31	Drigg	d		06x51	07x41			09x58	10x59	12x09	13x18	14x18	15x42	17x29	18x18						
33¼	Seascale	d		06x54	07x44	08x49		10x01	11x02	12x12	13x21	14x21	15x45	17x32	18x21						
35	Sellafield	d		07 02	07 51	08a58		10 10	11 07	12 18	13 28	14 27	15 51	17 39	18 27						
37	Braystones	d		07x05	07x54							14x31			18x31						
38¼	Nethertown	d		07x08	07x57							14x33			18x33						
41¼	St Bees	d		07 12	08 01			10 20	11 20	12 27	13 38	14 38	16 00	17 49	18 45						
44¾	Corkickle	d		07x17	08x06			10x25	11x25	12x32	13x43	14x43	16x05	17x54	18x50						
45¾	Whitehaven	a		07 20	08 10			10 27	11 27	12 36	13 45	14 46	16 09	17 57	18 53						
—		d	06 30	07 25	08 11		09 02	10 28	11 29	12 37	13 47	14 48	16 11	17 58	18 55		19 31		20 30		21 50
47	Parton	d	06x33	07x29	08x15		09x05	10x31	11x32	12x41	13x50	14x51	16x15	18x02	18x58		19x34		20x33		21x53
50½	Harrington	d	06x41	07x37	08x23		09x13	10x40	11x40	12x49	13x58	14x59	16x23	18x10	19x06		19x42		20x41		22x01
52¼	Workington	d	06 48	07 43	08 29		09 20	10 46	11 47	12 55	14 05	15 06	16 29	18 16	19 12		19 49		20 48		22a10
56	Flimby	d	06x52	07x48	08x34		09x24	10x50	11x51	13x00	14x09	15x10	16x34	18x21	19x17		19x53		20x52		
58	Maryport	d	06 56	07 51	08 37		09 28	10 54	11 55	13 03	14 13	15 14	16 37	18 26	19 20		19 57		20 56		
65½	Aspatria	d	07x05	08x01	08x47		09x37	11x03	12x04	13x13	14x22	15x23	16x47	18x36	19x30		20x06		21x05		
71¾	Wigton	d	07 15	08 11	08 57		09 47	11 13	12 14	13 23	14 32	15 33	16 57	18 46	19 40		20 16		21 15		
81¼	Dalston	d	07x24	08x19	09x05		09x56	11x22	12x23	13x31	14x41	15x42	17x05	18x54	19x48		20x25		21x24		
85¼	Carlisle ■	a	07 38	08 35	09 22		10 13	11 37	12 39	13 47	14 57	15 58	17 21	19 08	20 04		20 41		21 39		

Saturdays

		NT	NT	NT	NT	NT	NT	NT	NT	NT	NT	NT	NT	NT	NT	NT	NT	NT	NT	NT
Lancaster ■ 82	d							09 03			11 28		13 32	14 22		17 00				
Barrow-in-Furness	d		06 00	07 05	08 01		09 07	10 11	11 22		12 34	13 50	14 50	15 33	17 25	18 10		19 35		21 25
Askam	d		06 10	07 15	08 11		09 17	10 21	11 32		12 44	14 00	15 00	15 43	17 35	18 20		19 45		21 35
Kirkby-in-Furness	d		06x14	07x19	08x15		09x21	10x25	11x36		12x48	14x04	15x04	15x47	17x39	18x24		19x49		21x39
Foxfield	d		06x17	07x23	08x18		09x24	10x28	11x39		12x51	14x07	15x07	15x50	17x42	18x27		19x52		21x42
Green Road	d		06x21	07x27	08x22		09x28	10x32	11x43		12x55	14x11	15x11	15x54	17x46	18x31		19x56		21x46
Millom	a		06 25	07 34	08 28		09 34	10 38	11 49		13 01	14 17	15 17	16 00	17 52	18 40		20 05		21 55
	d		06 26	07 34	08 29		09 35	10 39	11 50		13 02	14 18	15 18	16 01	17 53					
Silecroft	d		06x30	07x39			09x39	10x43	11x54		13x06	14x22	15x22	16x05	17x57					
Bootle	d		06x37	07x46			09x46	10x50	12x01		13x13	14x29	15x29	16x12	18x04					
Ravenglass for Eskdale	d		06 42	07 52	08 44		09 52	10 56	12 07		13 19	14 35	15 35	16 18	18 10					
Drigg	d		06x45	07x56			09x55	10x59	12x10		13x22	14x38	15x38	16x21	18x13					
Seascale	d		06x50	07x59	08x49		09x58	11x04	12x13		13x25	14x41	15x41	16x24	18x16					
Sellafield	d		06 55	08 06	08a58		10 04	11 10	12 19		13 31	14 47	15 51	16 30	18 22					
Braystones	d		06x59	08x09										16x34	18x26					
Nethertown	d		07x01	08x12										16x36	18x28					
St Bees	d		07 06	08 16			10 14	11 19	12 29		13 40	14 56	16 01	16 46	18 33					
Corkickle	d		07x11	08x21			10x19	11x24	12x34		13x45	15x01	16x06	16x51	18x38					
Whitehaven	a		07 15	08 25			10 22	11 27	12 41		13 49	15 05	16 09	16 54	18 41					
	d	06 30	07 19	08 26		09 15	10 24	11 29		12 54	13 50	15 06	16 11	16 56	18 43		19 31		20 30	
Parton	d	06x33	07x23	08x30		09x18	10x27	11x32		12x57	13x54	15x10	16x15	17x00	18x46		19x34		20x33	
Harrington	d	06x41	07x31	08x38		09x26	10x35	11x40		13x05	14x02	15x18	16x23	17x08	18x54		19x42		20x41	
Workington	d	06 48	07 37	08 44		09 33	10 42	11 47		13 12	14 09	15 24	16 29	17 14	19 01		19 49		20 48	
Flimby	d	06x52	07x42	08x49		09x37	10x46	11x51		13x16	14x13	15x29	16x34	17x19	19x05		19x53		20x52	
Maryport	d	06 56	07 45	08 52		09 41	10 50	11 55		13 20	14 17	15 32	16 37	17 22	19 09		19 57		20 56	
Aspatria	d	07x05	07x55	09x02		09x50	10x59	12x04		13x29	14x26	15x42	16x47	17x32	19x18		20x06		21x05	
Wigton	d	07 15	08 05	09 12		10 00	11 09	12 14		13 39	14 36	15 52	16 57	17 42	19 28		20 16		21 15	
Dalston	d	07x24	08x13	09x20		10x08	11x18	12x23		13x48	14x45	16x00	17x05	17x50	19x37		20x25		21x24	
Carlisle ■	a	07 38	08 27	09 36		10 24	11 34	12 39		14 04	15 01	16 16	17 21	18 06	19 53		20 41		21 39	

Sundays

		NT	NT	NT
Lancaster ■ 82	d			
Barrow-in-Furness	d			
Askam	d			
Kirkby-in-Furness	d			
Foxfield	d			
Green Road	d			
Millom	a			
	d			
Silecroft	d			
Bootle	d			
Ravenglass for Eskdale	d			
Drigg	d			
Seascale	d			
Sellafield	d			
Braystones	d			
Nethertown	d			
St Bees	d			
Corkickle	d			
Whitehaven	a			
	d	12 57	16 28	20 28
Parton	d	13x00	16x31	20x31
Harrington	d	13x08	16x39	20x39
Workington	d	13 15	16 46	20 46
Flimby	d	13x19	16x50	20x50
Maryport	d	13 23	16 54	20 54
Aspatria	d	13x32	17x03	21x03
Wigton	d	13 42	17 13	21 13
Dalston	d	13x50	17x21	21x21
Carlisle ■	a	14 07	17 37	21 38

No Sunday Service Barrow-in-Furness to Whitehaven

Carlisle and Whitehaven - Barrow-in-Furness

Network Diagram - see first Page of Table 97

Mondays to Fridays

Miles			NT	NT	NT	NT	NT	NT	NT	NT	NT		NT	NT	NT	NT	NT	NT	NT	NT	NT		NT	NT
0	**Carlisle**	d				07 44		08 44	09 40	10 43	11 50		12 47	14 20	15 12	16 31	17 27	18 13	19 15		20 33		21 50	
4	Dalston	d				07x52		08x52	09x48	10x51	11x58		12x55	14x28	15x20	16x39	17x35	18x21	19x23		20x41		21x58	
11½	Wigton	d				08 01		09 01	09 57	11 00	12 07		13 04	14 37	15 29	16 48	17 44	18 30	19 32		20 50		22 07	
19¾	Aspatria	d				08x11		09x11	10x07	11x10	12x17		13x14	14x47	15x39	16x58	17x54	18x40	19x42		21x00		22x17	
27¼	Maryport	d		06 00		08 21		09 21	10 17	11 20	12 27		13 24	14 57	15 49	17 08	18 04	18 50	19 52		21 10		22 27	
29¼	Flimby	d		06x03		08x24		09x24	10x20	11x23	12x30		13x27	15x02	15x52	17x11	18x07	18x53	19x55		21x13		22x30	
33	**Workington**	d		06 09		08 33		09 33	10 29	11 32	12 39		13 36	15 09	16 01	17 20	18 16	19 02	20 04		21 22		22 39	
34¾	Harrington	d		06x13		08x36		09x36	10x32	11x35	12x42		13x39	15x12	16x04	17x23	18x19	19x05	20x07		21x25		22x42	
38¼	Parton	d		06x21		08x45		09x45	10x42	11x44	12x52		13x48	15x21	16x13	17x32	18x28	19x14	20x16		21x34		22x51	
39½	**Whitehaven**	a		06 26		08 54		09 49	10 47	11 50	13 00		13 54	15 27	16 19	17 38	18 34	19 23	20 25		21 43		23 00	
—		d		06 28	07 28			09 51	10 48	11 51			13 56	15 28	16 20	17 39	18 35							
40½	Corkickle	d		06x30	07x30			09x53	10x50	11x53			13x58	15x30	16x22	17x41	18x37							
44	St Bees	d		06 35	07 35			09 58	10 56	11 59			14 03	15 36	16 28	17 50	18 43							
47	Nethertown	d		06x39						12x03				15x40		17x54								
48¼	Braystones	d		06x42						12x05				15x42		17x57								
50¼	Sellafield	d		06 48	07 48		09 07	10 09	11 08	12 11			14 14	15 54	16 42	18 03	18 54							
52	Seascale	d		06x51	07x51		09x10	10x14	11x11	12x14			14x17	15x57	16x45	18x07	18x57							
54¼	Drigg	d		06x54	07x54		09x13	10x17	11x14	12x17			14x20	16x01	16x49	18x11	19x00							
56	Ravenglass for Eskdale	d		06 57	07 57		09 16	10 20	11 18	12 21			14 23	16 04	16 52	18 14	19 03							
60¾	Bootle	d		07x03	08x03		09x22	10x26	11x23	12x26			14x29	16x10	16x58	18x20	19x09							
66¼	Silecroft	d		07x09	08x09		09x28	10x32	11x30	12x33			14x35	16x17	17x05	18x27	19x15							
69¼	Millom	a		07 16	08 14		09 35	10 39	11 37	12 40			14 42	16 24	17 12	18 34	19 22							
—		d	06 10	07 17	08 15		09 36	10 40	11 37	12 40			14 43	16 25	17 13	18 34	19 23			20 12				22 02
71¾	Green Road	d	06x14	07x21	08x19		09x40	10x44	11x41	12x44			14x47	16x29	17x17	18x39	19x27			20x16				22x06
73¾	Foxfield	d	06x17	07x24	08x22		09x43	10x47	11x44	12x47			14x50	16x33	17x21	18x43	19x30			20x19				22x09
76	Kirkby-in-Furness	d	06x21	07x28	08x26		09x47	10x51	11x48	12x51			14x54	16x38	17x26	18x47	19x34			20x23				22x13
79¼	Askam	d	06 26	07 33	08 31		09 52	10 56	11 53	12 56			14 59	16 43	17 31	18 52	19 39			20 28				22 18
85¼	**Barrow-in-Furness**	a	06 42	07 49	08 49		10 07	11 14	12 09	13 12			15 17	17 01	17 47	19 10	19 57			20 45				22 35
—	Lancaster 82	a	08 04	09 07			11 20		13 16						19 05									

Saturdays

		NT	NT	NT	NT	NT	NT	NT	NT	NT		NT	NT	NT	NT	NT	NT	NT	NT	NT		NT	NT
Carlisle	d			07 44		08 37	09 40	10 43	11 39			12 48	14 21	15 25	16 30	17 40	18 15	19 00	20 05			21 45	
Dalston	d			07x52		08x45	09x48	10x51	11x47			12x56	14x29	15x33	16x38	17x48	18 24	19x08	20x13			21x53	
Wigton	d			08 01		08 54	09 57	11 00	11 56			13 05	14 38	15 42	16 47	17 57	18 33	19 17	20 22			22 02	
Aspatria	d			08x11		09x04	10x07	11x10	12x06			13x15	14x48	15x52	16x57	18x07	18 43	19x27	20x32			22x12	
Maryport	d		06 26	08 21		09 14	10 17	11 20	12 16			13 25	14 58	16 02	17 07	18 17	18 54	19 37	20 42			22 22	
Flimby	d		06x29	08x24		09x17	10x20	11x23	12x19			13x28	15x01	16x05	17x10	18x20	18 57	19x40	20x45			22x25	
Workington	d		06 37	08 33		09 26	10 29	11 32	12 28			13 37	15 10	16 14	17 19	18 29	19 06	19 49	20 54			22 34	
Harrington	d		06x41	08x36		09x29	10x32	11x35	12x31			13x40	15x14	16x18	17x23	18x32	19 10	19x52	20x57			22x37	
Parton	d		06x49	08x45		09x38	10x40	11x44	12x40			13x49	15x22	16x26	17x31	18x41	19x19	20x01	21x06			22x46	
Whitehaven	a		06 55	08 54		09 44	10 47	11 50	12 49			13 55	15 28	16 32	17 37	18 47	19 28	20 10	21 15			22 55	
	d		06 57			09 45	10 48	11 51		12 54		13 57	15 30	16 34	17 39	18 48							
Corkickle	d		06x59			09x47	10x50	11x53		12x56		13x59	15x32	16x36	17x41	18x50							
St Bees	d		07 10			09 53	10 56	11 59		13 01		14 04	15 37	16 43	17 46	18 56							
Nethertown	d		07x14				11x00						15x41		17x50								
Braystones	d		07x16				11x02						15x44		17x53								
Sellafield	d		07 22		09 07	10 03	11 08	12 10		13 12		14 15	15 50	16 53	17 59	19 06							
Seascale	d		07x25		09x10	10x06	11x11	12x13		13x15		14x18	15x53	16x56	18x02	19x09							
Drigg	d		07x28		09x13	10x09	11x14	12x16		13x18		14x21	15x56	16x59	18x05	19x12							
Ravenglass for Eskdale	d		07 32		09 16	10 13	11 18	12 20		13 21		14 24	15 59	17 03	18 08	19 16							
Bootle	d		07x37		09x22	10x18	11x23	12x25		13x27		14x30	16x05	17x08	18x14	19x21							
Silecroft	d		07x44		09x28	10x25	11x30	12x32		13x33		14x36	16x11	17x15	18x20	19x28							
Millom	a		07 51		09 35	10 32	11 37	12 39		13 40		14 43	16 18	17 22	18 27	19 35							
	d	06 10	07 51		09 36	10 32	11 37	12 39		13 41		14 44	16 19	17 22	18 28	19 36				20 12			22 02
Green Road	d	06x14	07x55		09x40	10x36	11x41	12x43		13x45		14x48	16x23	17x26	18x32	19x40				20x16			22x06
Foxfield	d	06x17	07x59		09x43	10x40	11x44	12x47		13x48		14x51	16x26	17x30	18x35	19x43				20x19			22x09
Kirkby-in-Furness	d	06x21	08x03		09x47	10x44	11x48	12x51		13x52		14x55	16x30	17x34	18x39	19x47				20x23			22x13
Askam	d	06 26	08 08		09 52	10 49	11 53	12 56		13 57		15 00	16 35	17 39	18 44	19 52				20 28			22 18
Barrow-in-Furness	a	06 42	08 24		10 07	11 07	12 09	13 14		14 13		15 16	16 53	17 55	19 02	20 10				20 45			22 35
Lancaster 82	a		09 33		11 21		13 16			15 20		16 24		19 05									

Sundays

		NT	NT	NT
Carlisle	d	15 00	19 00	21 50
Dalston	d	15x08	19x08	21x58
Wigton	d	15 17	19 17	22 07
Aspatria	d	15x27	19x27	22x17
Maryport	d	15 37	19 37	22 27
Flimby	d	15x40	19x40	22x30
Workington	d	15 49	19 49	22 39
Harrington	d	15x52	19x52	22x42
Parton	d	16x01	20x01	22x51
Whitehaven	a	16 10	20 10	23 00
	d			
Corkickle	d			
St Bees	d			
Nethertown	d			
Braystones	d			
Sellafield	d			
Seascale	d			
Drigg	d			
Ravenglass for Eskdale	d			
Bootle	d			
Silecroft	d			
Millom	a			
	d			
Green Road	d			
Foxfield	d			
Kirkby-in-Furness	d			
Askam	d			
Barrow-in-Furness	a			
Lancaster 82	a			

No Sunday Service Whitehaven to Barrow-in-Furness

Network Diagram for Tables 101, 103, 106, 109

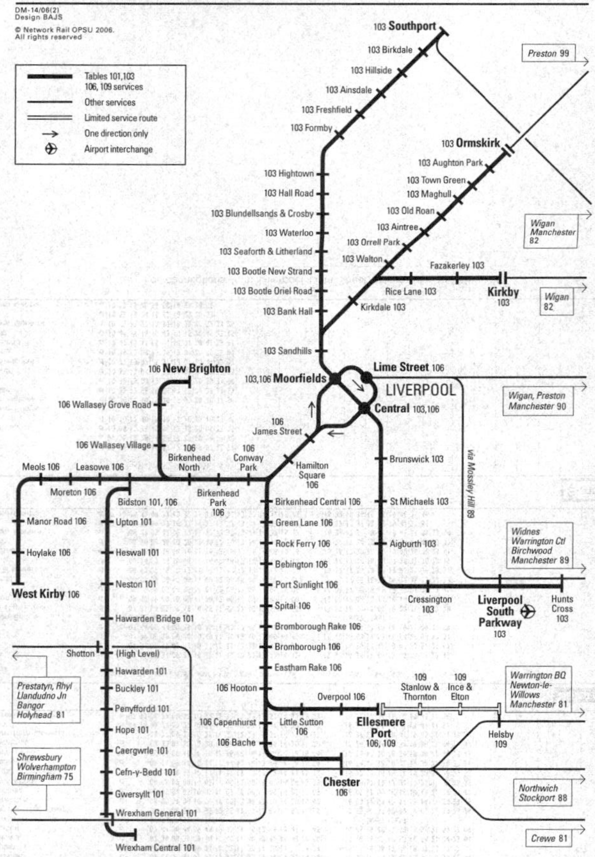

Table 101

Mondays to Fridays

Wrexham - Bidston

Network Diagram - see first Page of Table 101

Miles			AW	AW	AW	AW	AW	AW	AW	AW	AW	AW	AW	AW	AW	AW
0	**Wrexham Central**	d		07 28	08 30	09 30	10 30	11 30	12 30	13 30	14 30	15 30	16 30	17 43	19 44	21 55
0½	**Wrexham General**	a		07 30	08 32	09 32	10 32	11 32	12 32	13 32	14 32	15 32	16 32	17 45	19 46	21 57
—		d	06 31	07 30	08 32	09 32	10 32	11 32	12 32	13 32	14 32	15 32	16 32	17 45	19 46	21 57
2¼	Gwersyllt	d	06 35	07 34	08 36	09 36	10 36	11 36	12 36	13 36	14 36	15 36	16 36	17 49	19 50	22 01
4	Cefn-y-Bedd	d	06 40	07 39	08 41	09 41	10 41	11 41	12 41	13 41	14 41	15 41	16 41	17 54	19 55	22 06
4¾	Caergwrle	d	06 42	07 41	08 43	09 43	10 43	11 43	12 43	13 43	14 43	15 43	16 43	17 56	19 57	22 08
5¼	Hope (Flintshire)	d	06 44	07 43	08 45	09 45	10 45	11 45	12 45	13 45	14 45	15 45	16 45	17 58	19 59	22 10
7¼	Penyffordd	d	06 48	07 47	08 49	09 49	10 49	11 49	12 49	13 49	14 49	15 49	16 49	18 02	20 03	22 14
8½	Buckley	d	06 51	07 50	08 52	09 52	10 52	11 52	12 52	13 52	14 52	15 52	16 52	18 05	20 06	22 17
10½	Hawarden	d	06 55	07 54	08 56	09 56	10 56	11 56	12 56	13 56	14 56	15 56	16 56	18 09	20 10	22 21
12¾	Shotton High Level	d	06 59	07 59	09 00	10 00	11 00	12 00	13 00	14 00	15 00	16 00	17 00	18 13	20 14	22 25
13¼	Hawarden Bridge	d	07x01	08x01									17x02			
18¾	Neston	d	07 10	08 10	09 10	10 10	11 10	12 10	13 10	14 10	15 10	16 10	17 11	18 23	20 24	22 35
21¼	Heswall	d	07 15	08 15	09 15	10 15	11 15	12 15	13 15	14 15	15 15	16 15	17 16	18 28	20 29	22 40
25½	Upton	d	07 21	08 21	09 21	10 21	11 21	12 21	13 21	14 21	15 21	16 21	17 22	18 34	20 35	22 46
27½	**Bidston**	a	07 30	08 30	09 31	10 30	11 30	12 30	13 30	14 30	15 30	16 30	17 31	18 45	20 44	22 55

Saturdays

		AW	AW	AW	AW	AW	AW	AW	AW	AW	AW	AW	AW	AW	AW
Wrexham Central	d		07 28	08 30	09 30	10 30	11 30	12 30	13 30	14 30	15 30	16 30	17 43	19 44	21 55
Wrexham General	a		07 30	08 32	09 32	10 32	11 32	12 32	13 32	14 32	15 32	16 32	17 45	19 46	21 57
	d	06 31	07 30	08 32	09 32	10 32	11 32	12 32	13 32	14 32	15 32	16 32	17 45	19 46	21 57
Gwersyllt	d	06 35	07 34	08 36	09 36	10 36	11 36	12 36	13 36	14 36	15 36	16 36	17 49	19 50	22 01
Cefn-y-Bedd	d	06 40	07 39	08 41	09 41	10 41	11 41	12 41	13 41	14 41	15 41	16 41	17 54	19 55	22 06
Caergwrle	d	06 42	07 41	08 43	09 43	10 43	11 43	12 43	13 43	14 43	15 43	16 43	17 56	19 57	22 08
Hope (Flintshire)	d	06 44	07 43	08 45	09 45	10 45	11 45	12 45	13 45	14 45	15 45	16 45	17 58	19 59	22 10
Penyffordd	d	06 48	07 47	08 49	09 49	10 49	11 49	12 49	13 49	14 49	15 49	16 49	18 02	20 03	22 14
Buckley	d	06 51	07 50	08 52	09 52	10 52	11 52	12 52	13 52	14 52	15 52	16 52	18 05	20 06	22 17
Hawarden	d	06 55	07 54	08 56	09 56	10 56	11 56	12 56	13 56	14 56	15 56	16 56	18 09	20 10	22 21
Shotton High Level	d	06 59	07 59	09 00	10 00	11 00	12 00	13 00	14 00	15 00	16 00	17 00	18 13	20 14	22 25
Hawarden Bridge	d	07x01	08x01									17x02			
Neston	d	07 10	08 10	09 10	10 10	11 10	12 10	13 10	14 10	15 10	16 10	17 11	18 23	20 24	22 35
Heswall	d	07 15	08 15	09 15	10 15	11 15	12 15	13 15	14 15	15 15	16 15	17 16	18 28	20 29	22 40
Upton	d	07 21	08 21	09 21	10 21	11 21	12 21	13 21	14 21	15 21	16 21	17 22	18 34	20 35	22 46
Bidston	a	07 30	08 30	09 31	10 30	11 30	12 30	13 30	14 30	15 30	16 30	17 31	18 45	20 44	22 55

Sundays

		AW	AW	AW	AW	AW	AW
Wrexham Central	d		11 11	13 41	16 11	18 41	21 11
Wrexham General	a		11 13	13 43	16 13	18 43	21 13
	d	08 44	11 14	13 44	16 14	18 44	21 14
Gwersyllt	d	08 48	11 18	13 48	16 18	18 48	21 18
Cefn-y-Bedd	d	08 53	11 23	13 53	16 23	18 53	21 23
Caergwrle	d	08 55	11 25	13 55	16 25	18 55	21 25
Hope (Flintshire)	d	08 57	11 27	13 57	16 27	18 57	21 27
Penyffordd	d	09 01	11 31	14 01	16 31	19 01	21 31
Buckley	d	09 04	11 34	14 04	16 34	19 04	21 34
Hawarden	d	09 08	11 38	14 08	16 38	19 08	21 38
Shotton High Level	d	09 12	11 42	14 12	16 42	19 12	21 42
Hawarden Bridge	d						
Neston	d	09 22	11 52	14 22	16 52	19 22	21 52
Heswall	d	09 27	11 57	14 27	16 57	19 27	21 57
Upton	d	09 33	12 03	14 33	17 03	19 33	22 03
Bidston	a	09 42	12 12	14 42	17 12	19 42	22 12

For connections to Liverpool Lime Street please refer to Table 106

Table 101

Mondays to Fridays

Bidston - Wrexham

Network Diagram - see first Page of Table 101

Miles			AW	AW	AW	AW	AW	AW	AW	AW	AW	AW	AW	AW	AW	AW	AW
0	**Bidston**	d		07 31	08 31	09 32	10 32	11 32	12 32	13 32	14 32	15 32	16 34	17 45	18 46	20 56	22 56
2	Upton	d		07 32	08 32	09 33	10 33	11 33	12 33	13 33	14 33	15 33	16 36	17 46	18 47	20 57	22 57
6¼	Heswall	d		07 39	08 39	09 40	10 40	11 40	12 40	13 40	14 40	15 40	16 43	17 53	18 54	21 04	23 04
8¾	Neston	d		07 44	08 44	09 45	10 45	11 45	12 45	13 45	14 45	15 45	16 48	17 58	18 59	21 09	23 09
14¼	Hawarden Bridge	d		07x53	08x53								16x57	18x07			
14¾	Shotton High Level	d		07 55	08 55	09 55	10 55	11 55	12 55	13 55	14 55	15 55	16 59	18 09	19 09	21 19	23 20
17½	Hawarden	d		08 00	09 00	10 00	11 00	12 00	13 00	14 00	15 00	16 00	17 04	18 14	19 14	21 24	23 25
19	Buckley	d		08 05	09 05	10 05	11 05	12 05	13 05	14 05	15 05	16 05	17 09	18 19	19 19	21 29	23 30
20¼	Penyffordd	d		08 08	09 08	10 08	11 08	12 08	13 08	14 08	15 08	16 08	17 12	18 22	19 22	21 32	23 33
22¼	Hope (Flintshire)	d		08 12	09 12	10 12	11 12	12 12	13 12	14 12	15 12	16 12	17 16	18 26	19 26	21 36	23 37
22¾	Caergwrle	d		08 14	09 14	10 14	11 14	12 14	13 14	14 14	15 14	16 14	17 18	18 28	19 28	21 38	23 39
23½	Cefn-y-Bedd	d		08 16	09 16	10 16	11 16	12 16	13 16	14 16	15 16	16 16	17 20	18 30	19 30	21 40	23 41
25¼	Gwersyllt	d		08 20	09 20	10 20	11 20	12 20	13 20	14 20	15 20	16 20	17 24	18 34	19 34	21 44	23 47
27	**Wrexham General**	a		08 27	09 27	10 27	11 27	12 27	13 27	14 27	15 27	16 27	17 31	18 41	19 41	21 51	23 54
—		d	07 10	08 27	09 27	10 27	11 27	12 27	13 27	14 27	15 27	16 27	17 31	18 41	19 41	21 51	
27½	**Wrexham Central**	a	07 13	08 32	09 32	10 32	11 32	12 32	13 32	14 32	15 32	16 32	17 36	18 46	19 46	21 56	

Saturdays

		AW	AW	AW	AW	AW	AW	AW	AW	AW	AW	AW	AW	AW	AW	AW
Bidston	d		07 31	08 31	09 32	10 32	11 32	12 32	13 32	14 32	15 32	16 34	17 45	18 46	20 56	22 56
Upton	d		07 32	08 32	09 33	10 33	11 33	12 33	13 33	14 33	15 33	16 36	17 46	18 47	20 57	22 57
Heswall	d		07 39	08 39	09 40	10 40	11 40	12 40	13 40	14 40	15 40	16 43	17 53	18 54	21 04	23 04
Neston	d		07 44	08 44	09 45	10 45	11 45	12 45	13 45	14 45	15 45	16 48	17 58	18 59	21 09	23 09
Hawarden Bridge	d		07x53	08x53								16x57	18x07			
Shotton High Level	d		07 55	08 55	09 55	10 55	11 55	12 55	13 55	14 55	15 55	16 59	18 09	19 09	21 19	23 20
Hawarden	d		08 00	09 00	10 00	11 00	12 00	13 00	14 00	15 00	16 00	17 04	18 14	19 14	21 24	23 25
Buckley	d		08 05	09 05	10 05	11 05	12 05	13 05	14 05	15 05	16 05	17 09	18 19	19 19	21 29	23 30
Penyffordd	d		08 08	09 08	10 08	11 08	12 08	13 08	14 08	15 08	16 08	17 12	18 22	19 22	21 32	23 33
Hope (Flintshire)	d		08 12	09 12	10 12	11 12	12 12	13 12	14 12	15 12	16 12	17 16	18 26	19 26	21 36	23 37
Caergwrle	d		08 14	09 14	10 14	11 14	12 14	13 14	14 14	15 14	16 14	17 18	18 28	19 28	21 38	23 39
Cefn-y-Bedd	d		08 16	09 16	10 16	11 16	12 16	13 16	14 16	15 16	16 16	17 20	18 30	19 30	21 40	23 41
Gwersyllt	d		08 20	09 20	10 20	11 20	12 20	13 20	14 20	15 20	16 20	17 24	18 34	19 34	21 44	23 47
Wrexham General	a		08 27	09 27	10 27	11 27	12 27	13 27	14 27	15 27	16 27	17 31	18 41	19 41	21 51	23 54
	d	07 10	08 27	09 27	10 27	11 27	12 27	13 27	14 27	15 27	16 27	17 31	18 41	19 41	21 51	
Wrexham Central	a	07 13	08 32	09 32	10 32	11 32	12 32	13 32	14 32	15 32	16 32	17 36	18 46	19 46	21 56	

Sundays

		AW	AW	AW	AW	AW	AW
Bidston	d	09 57	12 27	14 57	17 27	19 57	22 27
Upton	d	09 58	12 28	14 58	17 28	19 58	22 28
Heswall	d	10 05	12 35	15 05	17 35	20 05	22 35
Neston	d	10 10	12 40	15 10	17 40	20 10	22 40
Hawarden Bridge	d						
Shotton High Level	d	10 20	12 50	15 20	17 50	20 20	22 50
Hawarden	d	10 25	12 55	15 25	17 55	20 25	22 55
Buckley	d	10 30	13 00	15 30	18 00	20 30	23 00
Penyffordd	d	10 33	13 03	15 33	18 03	20 33	23 03
Hope (Flintshire)	d	10 37	13 07	15 37	18 07	20 37	23 07
Caergwrle	d	10 39	13 09	15 39	18 09	20 39	23 09
Cefn-y-Bedd	d	10 41	13 11	15 41	18 11	20 41	23 11
Gwersyllt	d	10 45	13 15	15 45	18 15	20 45	23 15
Wrexham General	a	10 52	13 22	15 52	18 22	20 52	23 25
	d	10 53	13 23	15 53	18 23	20 53	
Wrexham Central	a	10 58	13 28	15 58	18 28	20 58	

For connections from Liverpool Lime Street please refer to Table 106

Llandudno - Blaenau Ffestiniog

Network Diagram - see first Page of Table 81

Miles				AW	AW	AW	AW	AW	AW
				◇	◇	◇	◇	◇	◇
0	**Llandudno**	81	d			10 22	13 22	16 20	19 03
1¾	Deganwy	81	d			10x26	13x26	16x24	19x07
3	**Llandudno Junction**	81	d	05 35	07 39	10 34	13 34	16 33	19 20
5	Glan Conwy		d		07x42	10x37	13x37	16x36	19x23
8½	Tal-y-Cafn		d		07 48	10 43	13 43	16 42	19 29
11½	Dolgarrog		d		07x53	10x48	13x48	16x47	19x34
14½	North Llanrwst		d		08x00	10x54	13x54	16x53	19x40
15	Llanrwst		d	05 53	08 02	10 56	13 56	16 55	19 42
18½	Betws-y-Coed		d	05 59	08 08	11 02	14 02	17 01	19 48
22¾	Pont-y-Pant		d		08x16	11x10	14x10	17x09	19x56
24¼	Dolwyddelan		d		08x19	11x13	14x13	17x12	19x59
26	Roman Bridge		d		08x23	11x17	14x17	17x16	20x03
31	**Blaenau Ffestiniog**		a	06 29	08 42	11 36	14 36	17 35	20 20

Saturdays

			AW	AW	AW	AW	AW	AW
			◇	◇	◇	◇	◇	◇
Llandudno	81	d			10 22	13 22	16 20	19 03
Deganwy	81	d			10x26	13x26	16x24	19x07
Llandudno Junction	81	d	05 35	07 39	10 34	13 34	16 33	19 20
Glan Conwy		d		07x42	10x37	13x37	16x36	19x23
Tal-y-Cafn		d		07 48	10 43	13 43	16 42	19 29
Dolgarrog		d		07x53	10x48	13x48	16x47	19x34
North Llanrwst		d		08x00	10x54	13x54	16x53	19x40
Llanrwst		d	05 53	08 02	10 56	13 56	16 55	19 42
Betws-y-Coed		d	05 59	08 08	11 02	14 02	17 01	19 48
Pont-y-Pant		d		08x16	11x10	14x10	17x09	19x56
Dolwyddelan		d		08x19	11x13	14x13	17x12	19x59
Roman Bridge		d		08x23	11x17	14x17	17x16	20x03
Blaenau Ffestiniog		a	06 29	08 42	11 36	14 36	17 35	20 20

Sundays
until 9 September

			AW	AW	AW
			◇	◇	◇
Llandudno	81	d	10 22	13 30	
Deganwy	81	d	10x26	13x34	
Llandudno Junction	81	d	10 32	13 40	16 15
Glan Conwy		d	10x35	13x43	16x18
Tal-y-Cafn		d	10 41	13 49	16 24
Dolgarrog		d	10x46	13x54	16x29
North Llanrwst		d	10x52	14x00	16x35
Llanrwst		d	10 54	14 02	16 37
Betws-y-Coed		d	11 00	14 08	16 43
Pont-y-Pant		d	11x08	14x16	16x51
Dolwyddelan		d	11x11	14x19	16x54
Roman Bridge		d	11x15	14x23	16x58
Blaenau Ffestiniog		a	11 32	14 40	17 15

For connections from Crewe, Chester, Rhyl and Bangor (Gwynedd) please refer to Table 81

On Sundays from 16th September 2012 until 8th December 2012
A bus service is available at Llandudno Junction Station to various destinations between Blaenau Ffestiniog & Llandudno, please contact Traveline 0871 200 22 33 for further information on these services or contact a staff member at Llandudno Junction upon arrival

Blaenau Ffestiniog - Llandudno

Network Diagram - see first Page of Table 81

Miles				AW	AW	AW	AW	AW	AW
				◇	◇	◇	◇	◇	◇
—	**Blaenau Ffestiniog**		d	06 30	08 46	11 46	14 57	17 37	20 23
—	Roman Bridge		d	06x40	08x56	11x56	15x07	17x47	20x33
6¾	Dolwyddelan		d	06x43	09x00	12x00	15x11	17x51	20x37
8¼	Pont-y-Pant		d	06x46	09x03	12x03	15x14	17x54	20x40
12½	Betws-y-Coed		d	06 56	09 13	12 13	15 24	18 04	20 50
16	Llanrwst		d	07 02	09 19	12 19	15 30	18 10	20 56
16½	North Llanrwst		d	07x03	09x20	12x20	15x31	18x11	20x57
19½	Dolgarrog		d	07x09	09x27	12x27	15x38	18x18	21x04
22½	Tal-y-Cafn		d	07x15	09x33	12x33	15x44	18x24	21x10
26	Glan Conwy		d	07x21	09x39	12x39	15x50	18x30	21x16
28	**Llandudno Junction**	81	a	07 31	09 44	12 44	15 56	18 35	21 21
29¼	Deganwy	81	a		10x06	13x06	16x07	18x44	21x35
31	**Llandudno**	81	a		10 13	13 13	16 17	18 54	21 46

Saturdays

			AW	AW	AW	AW	AW	AW
			◇	◇	◇	◇	◇	◇
Blaenau Ffestiniog		d	06 30	08 46	11 46	14 57	17 37	20 23
Roman Bridge		d	06x40	08x56	11x56	15x07	17x47	20x33
Dolwyddelan		d	06x43	09x00	12x00	15x11	17x51	20x37
Pont-y-Pant		d	06x46	09x03	12x03	15x14	17x54	20x40
Betws-y-Coed		d	06 56	09 13	12 13	15 24	18 04	20 50
Llanrwst		d	07 02	09 19	12 19	15 30	18 10	20 56
North Llanrwst		d	07x03	09x20	12x20	15x31	18x11	20x57
Dolgarrog		d	07x09	09x27	12x27	15x38	18x18	21x04
Tal-y-Cafn		d	07x15	09x33	12x33	15x44	18x24	21x10
Glan Conwy		d	07x21	09x39	12x39	15x50	18x30	21x16
Llandudno Junction	81	a	07 31	09 45	12 45	15 56	18 35	21 21
Deganwy	81	a		10x03	13x03	16x03	18x44	21x35
Llandudno	81	a		10 13	13 13	16 13	18 54	21 46

Sundays
until 9 September

			AW	AW	AW
			◇	◇	◇
Blaenau Ffestiniog		d	11 45	15 03	17 30
Roman Bridge		d	11x55	15x13	17x40
Dolwyddelan		d	11x58	15x16	17x44
Pont-y-Pant		d	12x01	15x19	17x48
Betws-y-Coed		d	12 11	15 29	17 57
Llanrwst		d	12 17	15 35	18 03
North Llanrwst		d	12x18	15x36	18x05
Dolgarrog		d	12x24	15x42	18x11
Tal-y-Cafn		d	12x29	15x48	18x17
Glan Conwy		d	12x35	15x54	18x23
Llandudno Junction	81	a	12 40	15 59	18 29
Deganwy	81	a	12x45		18x34
Llandudno	81	a	12 55		18 44

For connections to Bangor (Gwynedd), Rhyl, Chester and Crewe please refer to Table 81

On Sundays from 16th September 2012 until 8th December 2012
A bus service is available at Llandudno Junction Station to various destinations between Blaenau Ffestiniog & Llandudno, please contact Traveline 0871 200 22 33 for further information on these services or contact a staff member at Llandudno Junction upon arrival

Hunts Cross and Liverpool - Kirkby, Ormskirk and Southport

Network Diagram - see first Page of Table 101

Miles	Miles	Miles			ME MX A	ME MX	ME MO B	ME C	ME C	ME SX	ME SO	ME	ME SX	ME SO	ME	ME SX	ME SO	ME	ME SX	ME SO	ME SX	ME SO	ME
0	—	—	**Hunts Cross** 89	d	23p06	23p21										06 06	06 06		06 21	06 21			
1½	—	—	**Liverpool Sth Parkway** 89	d	23p09	23p24										06 09	06 09		06 24	06 24			
2½	—	—	Cressington	d	23p12	23p27										06 12	06 12		06 27	06 27			
3¼	—	—	Aigburth	d	23p14	23p29										06 14	06 14		06 29	06 29			
4½	—	—	St Michaels	d	23p16	23p31										06 16	06 16		06 31	06 31			
5¾	—	—	Brunswick	d	23p19	23p34										06 19	06 19		06 34	06 34			
7¼	0	0	**Liverpool Central** 10	a	23p23	23p38										06 23	06 23		06 38	06 38			
—	—	—		d	23p23	23p38	23p38	23p40	23p55			05 55	06 08	06 08	06 10	06 23	06 23	06 25	06 38	06 38	06 40	06 40	06 50
7¾	0½	0½	**Moorfields** 10	d	23p25	23p40	23p40	23p42	23p57			05 57	06 10	06 10	06 12	06 25	06 25	06 27	06 40	06 40	06 42	06 42	06 52
9¼	2	2	Sandhills	d	23p29	23p44	23p44	23p46	00 01	05 59	05 59	06 01	06 14	06 14	06 16	06 29	06 29	06 31	06 44	06 44	06 46	06 46	06 56
—	3	3	Kirkdale	d				23p49	00 04			06 04			06 19			06 34			06 49	06 49	06 59
—	—	4¼	Rice Lane	d					00 07			06 07						06 37					07 02
—	—	5¾	Fazakerley	d					00 10			06 10						06 40					07 03
—	—	7½	**Kirkby**	a					00 13			06 13						06 43					07 08
—	4¼	—	Walton (Merseyside)	d				23p52							06 22						06 52	06 52	
—	4½	—	Orrell Park	d				23p53							06 23						06 53	06 53	
—	5½	—	Aintree	d				23p56							06 26						06 56	06 56	
—	6¼	—	Old Roan	d				23p58							06 28						06 58	06 58	
—	8	—	Maghull	d				00 01							06 31						07 01	07 01	
—	10½	—	Town Green	d				00 05							06 35						07 05	07 05	
—	11½	—	Aughton Park	d				00 07							06 37						07 07	07 07	
—	12¾	—	**Ormskirk**	a				00 12							06 43						07 11	07 12	
10	—	—	Bank Hall	d	23p31	23p46	23p46			06 01	06 01		06 16	06 16		06 31	06 31		06 46	06 46			
10¾	—	—	Bootle Oriel Road	d	23p33	23p48	23p48			06 03	06 03		06 18	06 18		06 33	06 33		06 48	06 48			
11	—	—	Bootle New Strand	d	23p35	23p50	23p50			06 05	06 05		06 20	06 20		06 35	06 35		06 50	06 50			
12	—	—	Seaforth & Litherland	d	23p37	23p52	23p52			06 07	06 07		06 22	06 22		06 37	06 37		06 52	06 52			
13¼	—	—	Waterloo (Merseyside)	d	23p39	23p54	23p54			06 09	06 09		06 24	06 24		06 39	06 39		06 54	06 54			
14¼	—	—	Blundellsands & Crosby	d	23p42	23p57	23p57			06 12	06 12		06 27	06 27		06 42	06 42		06 57	06 57			
15	—	—	Hall Road	d	23p44	23p59	23p59			06 14	06 14		06 29	06 29		06 44	06 44		06 59	06 59			
17	—	—	Hightown	d	23p47	00 02	00 02			06 17	06 17		06 32	06 32		06 47	06 47		07 02	07 02			
19	—	—	Formby	d	23p51	00 06	00 06			06 21	06 21		06 36	06 36		06 51	06 51		07 06	07 06			
20	—	—	Freshfield	d	23p53	00 08	00 08			06 23	06 23		06 38	06 38		06 53	06 53		07 08	07 08			
22¾	—	—	Ainsdale	d	23p57	00 12	00 12			06 27	06 27		06 42	06 42		06 57	06 57		07 12	07 12			
24½	—	—	Hillside	d	23p59	00 15	00 15			06 30	06 30		06 45	06 45		07 00	07 00		07 15	07 15			
25¼	—	—	Birkdale	d	00 02	00 17	00 17			06 32	06 32		06 47	06 47		07 02	07 02		07 17	07 17			
26¼	—	—	**Southport**	a	00 09	00 24	00 24			06 37	06 39		06 52	06 54		07 07	07 09		07 22	07 24			

		ME	ME	ME SX	ME SO	ME	ME	ME SX	ME SO	ME	ME	ME SX	ME SO	ME	ME	ME SX	ME SO	ME	ME	ME SX	ME SO	ME	ME
Hunts Cross 89	d	06 36		06 51	06 51			07 06	07 06			07 21	07 21			07 36	07 36			07 51	07 51		
Liverpool Sth Parkway 89	d	06 39		06 54	06 54			07 09	07 09			07 24	07 24			07 39	07 39			07 54	07 54		
Cressington	d	06 42		06 57	06 57			07 12	07 12			07 27	07 27			07 42	07 42			07 57	07 57		
Aigburth	d	06 44		06 59	06 59			07 14	07 14			07 29	07 29			07 44	07 44			07 59	07 59		
St Michaels	d	06 46		07 01	07 01			07 16	07 16			07 31	07 31			07 46	07 46			08 01	08 01		
Brunswick	d	06 49		07 04	07 04			07 19	07 19			07 34	07 34			07 49	07 49			08 04	08 04		
Liverpool Central 10	a	06 53		07 08	07 08			07 23	07 23			07 38	07 38			07 53	07 53			08 08	08 08		
	d	06 53	06 55	07 08	07 08	07 10	07 20	07 23	07 23	07 25	07 35	07 38	07 38	07 40	07 50	07 53	07 53	07 55	08 05	08 08	08 08	08 10	08 20
Moorfields 10	d	06 55	06 57	07 10	07 10	07 12	07 22	07 25	07 25	07 27	07 37	07 40	07 40	07 42	07 52	07 55	07 55	07 57	08 07	08 10	08 10	08 12	08 22
Sandhills	d	06 59	07 01	07 14	07 14	07 16	07 26	07 29	07 29	07 31	07 41	07 44	07 44	07 46	07 56	07 59	07 59	08 01	08 11	08 14	08 14	08 16	08 26
Kirkdale	d		07 04			07 19	07 29			07 34	07 44			07 49	07 59			08 04	08 14			08 19	08 29
Rice Lane	d						07 32				07 47				08 02				08 17				08 32
Fazakerley	d						07 34				07 49				08 04				08 19				08 34
Kirkby	a						07 38				07 53				08 08				08 23				08 38
Walton (Merseyside)	d		07 07			07 22				07 37				07 52				08 07				08 22	
Orrell Park	d		07 08			07 23				07 38				07 53				08 08				08 23	
Aintree	d		07 11			07 26				07 41				07 56				08 11				08 26	
Old Roan	d		07 13			07 28				07 43				07 58				08 13				08 28	
Maghull	d		07 16			07 31				07 46				08 01				08 16				08 31	
Town Green	d		07 20			07 35				07 50				08 05				08 20				08 35	
Aughton Park	d		07 22			07 37				07 52				08 07				08 22				08 37	
Ormskirk	a		07 28			07 43				07 58				08 13				08 28				08 43	
Bank Hall	d	07 01		07 16	07 16			07 31	07 31			07 46	07 46			08 01	08 01			08 16	08 16		
Bootle Oriel Road	d	07 03		07 18	07 18			07 33	07 33			07 48	07 48			08 03	08 03			08 18	08 18		
Bootle New Strand	d	07 05		07 20	07 20			07 35	07 35			07 50	07 50			08 05	08 05			08 20	08 20		
Seaforth & Litherland	d	07 07		07 22	07 22			07 37	07 37			07 52	07 52			08 07	08 07			08 22	08 22		
Waterloo (Merseyside)	d	07 09		07 24	07 24			07 39	07 39			07 54	07 54			08 09	08 09			08 24	08 24		
Blundellsands & Crosby	d	07 12		07 27	07 27			07 42	07 42			07 57	07 57			08 12	08 12			08 27	08 27		
Hall Road	d	07 14		07 29	07 29			07 44	07 44			07 59	07 59			08 14	08 14			08 29	08 29		
Hightown	d	07 17		07 32	07 32			07 47	07 47			08 02	08 02			08 17	08 17			08 32	08 32		
Formby	d	07 21		07 36	07 36			07 51	07 51			08 06	08 06			08 21	08 21			08 36	08 36		
Freshfield	d	07 23		07 38	07 38			07 53	07 53			08 08	08 08			08 23	08 23			08 38	08 38		
Ainsdale	d	07 27		07 42	07 42			07 57	07 57			08 12	08 12			08 27	08 27			08 42	08 42		
Hillside	d	07 30		07 45	07 45			08 00	08 00			08 15	08 15			08 30	08 30			08 45	08 45		
Birkdale	d	07 32		07 47	07 47			08 02	08 02			08 17	08 17			08 32	08 32			08 47	08 47		
Southport	a	07 39		07 52	07 54			08 07	08 09			08 22	08 24			08 37	08 39			08 52	08 54		

A until 22 September, from 25 September B from 21 May C not 14 May

Table 103 Mondays to Saturdays

Hunts Cross and Liverpool - Kirkby, Ormskirk and Southport

Network Diagram - see first Page of Table 101

		ME SX	ME SO	ME	ME	ME SX	ME SO	ME	ME	ME SX	ME SO	ME SO	ME SX	ME	ME	ME	ME	ME	ME	ME	ME	ME	ME
Hunts Cross 89	d	08 06	08 06			08 21	08 21			08 36	08 36				08 51			09 06			09 21		
Liverpool Sth Parkway 89	d	08 09	08 09			08 24	08 24			08 39	08 39				08 54			09 09			09 24		
Cressington	d	08 12	08 12			08 27	08 27			08 42	08 42				08 57			09 12			09 27		
Aigburth	d	08 14	08 14			08 29	08 29			08 44	08 44				08 59			09 14			09 29		
St Michaels	d	08 16	08 16			08 31	08 31			08 46	08 46				09 01			09 16			09 31		
Brunswick	d	08 19	08 19			08 34	08 34			08 49	08 49				09 04			09 19			09 34		
Liverpool Central 10	a	08 23	08 23			08 38	08 38			08 53	08 53				09 08			09 23			09 38		
	d	08 23	08 23	08 25	08 35	08 38	08 38	08 40	08 50	08 53	08 53	08 55	08 57	09 05	09 08	09 10	09 20	09 23	09 25	09 35	09 38	09 40	09 50
Moorfields 10	d	08 25	08 25	08 27	08 37	08 40	08 40	08 42	08 52	08 55	08 55	08 57	08 58	09 07	09 10	09 12	09 22	09 25	09 27	09 37	09 40	09 42	09 52
Sandhills	d	08 29	08 29	08 31	08 41	08 44	08 44	08 46	08 56	08 59	08 59	09 01	09 01	09 11	09 14	09 16	09 26	09 29	09 31	09 41	09 44	09 46	09 56
Kirkdale	d			08 34	08 44			08 49	08 59			09 04	09 04	09 14		09 19	09 29		09 34	09 44		09 49	09 59
Rice Lane	d				08 47				09 02					09 17			09 32			09 47			10 02
Fazakerley	d				08 49				09 05					09 19			09 34			09 49			10 04
Kirkby	a				08 53				09 08					09 23			09 38			09 53			10 08
Walton (Merseyside)	d			08 37				08 52				09 07	09 07			09 22			09 37			09 52	
Orrell Park	d			08 38				08 53				09 08	09 08			09 23			09 38			09 53	
Aintree	d			08 41				08 56				09 11	09 11			09 26			09 41			09 56	
Old Roan	d			08 43				08 58				09 13	09 13			09 28			09 43			09 58	
Maghull	d			08 46				09 01				09 16	09 16			09 31			09 46			10 01	
Town Green	d			08 50				09 05				09 20	09 20			09 35			09 50			10 05	
Aughton Park	d			08 52				09 07				09 22	09 22			09 37			09 52			10 07	
Ormskirk	a			08 58				09 13				09 28	09 28			09 43			09 58			10 13	
Bank Hall	d	08 31	08 31			08 46	08 46			09 01	09 01				09 16			09 31			09 46		
Bootle Oriel Road	d	08 33	08 33			08 48	08 48			09 03	09 03				09 18			09 33			09 48		
Bootle New Strand	d	08 35	08 35			08 50	08 50			09 05	09 05				09 20			09 35			09 50		
Seaforth & Litherland	d	08 37	08 37			08 52	08 52			09 07	09 07				09 22			09 37			09 52		
Waterloo (Merseyside)	d	08 39	08 39			08 54	08 54			09 09	09 09				09 24			09 39			09 54		
Blundellsands & Crosby	d	08 42	08 42			08 57	08 57			09 12	09 12				09 27			09 42			09 57		
Hall Road	d	08 44	08 44			08 59	08 59			09 14	09 14				09 29			09 44			09 59		
Hightown	d	08 47	08 47			09 02	09 02			09 17	09 17				09 32			09 47			10 02		
Formby	d	08 51	08 51			09 06	09 06			09 21	09 21				09 36			09 51			10 06		
Freshfield	d	08 53	08 53			09 08	09 08			09 23	09 23				09 38			09 53			10 08		
Ainsdale	d	08 57	08 57			09 12	09 12			09 27	09 27				09 42			09 57			10 12		
Hillside	d	09 00	09 00			09 15	09 15			09 30	09 30				09 45			10 00			10 15		
Birkdale	d	09 02	09 02			09 17	09 17			09 32	09 32				09 47			10 02			10 17		
Southport	a	09 07	09 09			09 22	09 24			09 37	09 39				09 54			10 09			10 24		

		ME	ME	ME	ME	ME	ME	ME	ME	ME	ME	ME	ME	ME	ME	ME	ME	ME	ME	ME	ME	ME
Hunts Cross 89	d	09 36			09 51			10 06			10 21			10 36			10 51			11 06		
Liverpool Sth Parkway 89	d	09 39			09 54			10 09			10 24			10 39			10 54			11 09		
Cressington	d	09 42			09 57			10 12			10 27			10 42			10 57			11 12		
Aigburth	d	09 44			09 59			10 14			10 29			10 44			10 59			11 14		
St Michaels	d	09 46			10 01			10 16			10 31			10 46			11 01			11 16		
Brunswick	d	09 49			10 04			10 19			10 34			10 49			11 04			11 19		
Liverpool Central 10	a	09 53			10 08			10 23			10 38			10 53			11 08			11 23		
	d	09 53	09 55	10 05	10 08	10 10	10 20	10 23	10 25	10 35	10 38	10 40	10 50	10 53	10 55	11 05	11 08	11 10	11 20	11 23	11 25	11 35
Moorfields 10	d	09 55	09 57	10 07	10 10	10 12	10 22	10 25	10 27	10 37	10 40	10 42	10 52	10 55	10 57	11 07	11 10	11 12	11 22	11 25	11 27	11 37
Sandhills	d	09 59	10 01	10 11	10 14	10 16	10 26	10 29	10 31	10 41	10 44	10 46	10 56	10 59	11 01	11 11	11 14	11 16	11 26	11 29	11 31	11 41
Kirkdale	d		10 04	10 14		10 19	10 29		10 34	10 44		10 49	10 59		11 04	11 14		11 19	11 29		11 34	11 44
Rice Lane	d			10 17			10 32			10 47			11 02			11 17			11 32			11 47
Fazakerley	d			10 19			10 34			10 49			11 04			11 19			11 34			11 49
Kirkby	a			10 23			10 38			10 53			11 08			11 23			11 38			11 53
Walton (Merseyside)	d		10 07			10 22			10 37			10 52			11 07			11 22			11 37	
Orrell Park	d		10 08			10 23			10 38			10 53			11 08			11 23			11 38	
Aintree	d		10 11			10 26			10 41			10 56			11 11			11 26			11 41	
Old Roan	d		10 13			10 28			10 43			10 58			11 13			11 28			11 43	
Maghull	d		10 16			10 31			10 46			11 01			11 16			11 31			11 46	
Town Green	d		10 20			10 35			10 50			11 05			11 20			11 35			11 50	
Aughton Park	d		10 22			10 37			10 52			11 07			11 22			11 37			11 52	
Ormskirk	a		10 28			10 43			10 58			11 13			11 28			11 43			11 58	
Bank Hall	d	10 01			10 16			10 31			10 46			11 01			11 16			11 31		
Bootle Oriel Road	d	10 03			10 18			10 33			10 48			11 03			11 18			11 33		
Bootle New Strand	d	10 05			10 20			10 35			10 50			11 05			11 20			11 35		
Seaforth & Litherland	d	10 07			10 22			10 37			10 52			11 07			11 22			11 37		
Waterloo (Merseyside)	d	10 09			10 24			10 39			10 54			11 09			11 24			11 39		
Blundellsands & Crosby	d	10 12			10 27			10 42			10 57			11 12			11 27			11 42		
Hall Road	d	10 14			10 29			10 44			10 59			11 14			11 29			11 44		
Hightown	d	10 17			10 32			10 47			11 02			11 17			11 32			11 47		
Formby	d	10 21			10 36			10 51			11 06			11 21			11 36			11 51		
Freshfield	d	10 23			10 38			10 53			11 08			11 23			11 38			11 53		
Ainsdale	d	10 27			10 42			10 57			11 12			11 27			11 42			11 57		
Hillside	d	10 30			10 45			11 00			11 15			11 30			11 45			12 00		
Birkdale	d	10 32			10 47			11 02			11 17			11 32			11 47			12 02		
Southport	a	10 39			10 54			11 09			11 24			11 39			11 54			12 09		

Hunts Cross and Liverpool - Kirkby, Ormskirk and Southport

Network Diagram - see first Page of Table 101

		ME	ME	ME	ME	ME	ME	ME	ME	ME	ME	ME	ME	ME	ME	ME	ME	ME	ME	ME	ME	ME	ME
Hunts Cross	89 d	11 21			11 36			11 51			12 06			12 21			12 36			12 51			13 06
Liverpool Sth Parkway 7 89 ✈	d	11 24			11 39			11 54			12 09			12 24			12 39			12 54			13 09
Cressington	d	11 27			11 42			11 57			12 12			12 27			12 42			12 57			13 12
Aigburth	d	11 29			11 44			11 59			12 14			12 29			12 44			12 59			13 14
St Michaels	d	11 31			11 46			12 01			12 16			12 31			12 46			13 01			13 16
Brunswick	d	11 34			11 49			12 04			12 19			12 34			12 49			13 04			13 19
Liverpool Central 10	a	11 38			11 53			12 08			12 23			12 38			12 53			13 08			13 23
	d	11 38	11 40	11 50	11 53	11 55	12 05	12 08	12 10	12 20	12 23	12 25	12 35	12 38	12 40	12 50	12 53	12 55	13 05	13 08	13 10	13 20	13 23
Moorfields 10	d	11 40	11 42	11 52	11 55	11 57	12 07	12 10	12 12	12 22	12 25	12 27	12 37	12 40	12 42	12 52	12 55	12 57	13 07	13 10	13 12	13 22	13 25
Sandhills	d	11 44	11 46	11 56	11 59	12 01	12 11	12 14	12 16	12 26	12 29	12 31	12 41	12 44	12 46	12 56	12 59	13 01	13 11	13 14	13 16	13 26	13 29
Kirkdale	d		11 49	11 59		12 04	12 14		12 19	12 29		12 34	12 44		12 49	12 59		13 04	13 14		13 19	13 29	
Rice Lane	d			12 02			12 17			12 32			12 47			13 02			13 17			13 32	
Fazakerley	d			12 04			12 19			12 34			12 49			13 04			13 19			13 34	
Kirkby	a			12 08			12 23			12 38			12 53			13 08			13 23			13 38	
Walton (Merseyside)	d		11 52			12 07			12 22			12 37			12 52			13 07			13 22		
Orrell Park	d		11 53			12 08			12 23			12 38			12 53			13 08			13 23		
Aintree	d		11 56			12 11			12 26			12 41			12 56			13 11			13 26		
Old Roan	d		11 58			12 13			12 28			12 43			12 58			13 13			13 28		
Maghull	d		12 01			12 16			12 31			12 46			13 01			13 16			13 31		
Town Green	d		12 05			12 20			12 35			12 50			13 05			13 20			13 35		
Aughton Park	d		12 07			12 22			12 37			12 52			13 07			13 22			13 37		
Ormskirk	a		12 13			12 28			12 43			12 58			13 13			13 28			13 43		
Bank Hall	d	11 46			12 01			12 16			12 31			12 46			13 01			13 16			13 31
Bootle Oriel Road	d	11 48			12 03			12 18			12 33			12 48			13 03			13 18			13 33
Bootle New Strand	d	11 50			12 05			12 20			12 35			12 50			13 05			13 20			13 35
Seaforth & Litherland	d	11 52			12 07			12 22			12 37			12 52			13 07			13 22			13 37
Waterloo (Merseyside)	d	11 54			12 09			12 24			12 39			12 54			13 09			13 24			13 39
Blundellsands & Crosby	d	11 57			12 12			12 27			12 42			12 57			13 12			13 27			13 42
Hall Road	d	11 59			12 14			12 29			12 44			12 59			13 14			13 29			13 44
Hightown	d	12 02			12 17			12 32			12 47			13 02			13 17			13 32			13 47
Formby	d	12 06			12 21			12 36			12 51			13 06			13 21			13 36			13 51
Freshfield	d	12 08			12 23			12 38			12 53			13 08			13 23			13 38			13 53
Ainsdale	d	12 12			12 27			12 42			12 57			13 12			13 27			13 42			13 57
Hillside	d	12 15			12 30			12 45			13 00			13 15			13 30			13 45			14 00
Birkdale	d	12 17			12 32			12 47			13 02			13 17			13 32			13 47			14 02
Southport	a	12 24			12 39			12 54			13 09			13 24			13 39			13 54			14 09

		ME	ME	ME	ME	ME	ME	ME	ME	ME	ME	ME	ME SX	ME SO	ME	ME	ME SX	ME SO	ME	ME	ME	ME SX
Hunts Cross	89 d			13 21			13 36			13 51			14 06	14 06			14 21	14 21			14 36	
Liverpool Sth Parkway 7 89 ✈	d			13 24			13 39			13 54			14 09	14 09			14 24	14 24			14 39	
Cressington	d			13 27			13 42			13 57			14 12	14 12			14 27	14 27			14 42	
Aigburth	d			13 29			13 44			13 59			14 14	14 14			14 29	14 29			14 44	
St Michaels	d			13 31			13 46			14 01			14 16	14 16			14 31	14 31			14 46	
Brunswick	d			13 34			13 49			14 04			14 19	14 19			14 34	14 34			14 49	
Liverpool Central 10	a			13 38			13 53			14 08			14 23	14 23			14 38	14 38			14 53	
	d	13 25	13 35	13 38	13 40	13 50	13 53	13 55	14 05	14 08	14 10	14 20	14 23	14 23	14 25	14 35	14 38	14 38	14 40	14 50	14 53	14 55
Moorfields 10	d	13 27	13 37	13 40	13 42	13 52	13 55	13 57	14 07	14 10	14 12	14 22	14 25	14 25	14 27	14 37	14 40	14 40	14 42	14 52	14 55	14 57
Sandhills	d	13 31	13 41	13 44	13 46	13 56	13 59	14 01	14 11	14 14	14 16	14 26	14 29	14 29	14 31	14 41	14 44	14 44	14 46	14 56	14 59	15 01
Kirkdale	d	13 34	13 44		13 49	13 59		14 04	14 14		14 19	14 29			14 34	14 44			14 49	14 59		15 04
Rice Lane	d		13 47			14 02			14 17			14 32				14 47				15 02		
Fazakerley	d		13 49			14 04			14 19			14 34				14 49				15 04		
Kirkby	a		13 53			14 08			14 23			14 38				14 53				15 08		
Walton (Merseyside)	d	13 37			13 52			14 07			14 22				14 37				14 52			15 07
Orrell Park	d	13 38			13 53			14 08			14 23				14 38				14 53			15 08
Aintree	d	13 41			13 56			14 11			14 26				14 41				14 56			15 11
Old Roan	d	13 43			13 58			14 13			14 28				14 43				14 58			15 13
Maghull	d	13 46			14 01			14 16			14 31				14 46				15 01			15 16
Town Green	d	13 50			14 05			14 20			14 35				14 50				15 05			15 20
Aughton Park	d	13 52			14 07			14 22			14 37				14 52				15 07			15 22
Ormskirk	a	13 58			14 13			14 28			14 43				14 58				15 13			15 27
Bank Hall	d			13 46			14 01			14 16			14 31	14 31			14 46	14 46			15 01	
Bootle Oriel Road	d			13 48			14 03			14 18			14 33	14 33			14 48	14 48			15 03	
Bootle New Strand	d			13 50			14 05			14 20			14 35	14 35			14 50	14 50			15 05	
Seaforth & Litherland	d			13 52			14 07			14 22			14 37	14 37			14 52	14 52			15 07	
Waterloo (Merseyside)	d			13 54			14 09			14 24			14 39	14 39			14 54	14 54			15 09	
Blundellsands & Crosby	d			13 57			14 12			14 27			14 42	14 42			14 57	14 57			15 12	
Hall Road	d			13 59			14 14			14 29			14 44	14 44			14 59	14 59			15 14	
Hightown	d			14 02			14 17			14 32			14 47	14 47			15 02	15 02			15 17	
Formby	d			14 06			14 21			14 36			14 51	14 51			15 06	15 06			15 21	
Freshfield	d			14 08			14 23			14 38			14 53	14 53			15 08	15 08			15 23	
Ainsdale	d			14 12			14 27			14 42			14 57	14 57			15 12	15 12			15 27	
Hillside	d			14 15			14 30			14 45			15 00	15 00			15 15	15 15			15 30	
Birkdale	d			14 17			14 32			14 47			15 02	15 02			15 17	15 17			15 32	
Southport	a			14 24			14 39			14 54			15 07	15 09			15 22	15 24			15 39	

Hunts Cross and Liverpool - Kirkby, Ormskirk and Southport

Network Diagram - see first Page of Table 101

		ME SO	ME	ME	ME	ME	ME SX	ME SO	ME	ME	ME SX	ME SO	ME	ME	ME SX	ME SO	ME	ME	ME SX	ME SO	ME	ME	ME SX
Hunts Cross	89 d			14 51			15 06	15 06			15 21	15 21			15 36	15 36			15 51	15 51			16 06
Liverpool Sth Parkway 7 89 ✈	d			14 54			15 09	15 09			15 24	15 24			15 39	15 39			15 54	15 54			16 09
Cressington	d			14 57			15 12	15 12			15 27	15 27			15 42	15 42			15 57	15 57			16 12
Aigburth	d			14 59			15 14	15 14			15 29	15 29			15 44	15 44			15 59	15 59			16 14
St Michaels	d			15 01			15 16	15 16			15 31	15 31			15 46	15 46			16 01	16 01			16 16
Brunswick	d			15 04			15 19	15 19			15 34	15 34			15 49	15 49			16 04	16 04			16 19
Liverpool Central 10	a			15 08			15 23	15 23			15 38	15 38			15 53	15 53			16 08	16 08			16 23
	d	14 55	15 05	15 08	15 10	15 20	15 23	15 23	15 25	15 35	15 38	15 38	15 40	15 50	15 53	15 53	15 55	16 05	16 08	16 08	16 10	16 20	16 23
Moorfields 10	d	14 57	15 07	15 10	15 12	15 22	15 25	15 25	15 27	15 37	15 40	15 40	15 42	15 52	15 55	15 55	15 57	16 07	16 10	16 10	16 12	16 22	16 25
Sandhills	d	15 01	15 11	15 14	15 16	15 26	15 29	15 29	15 31	15 41	15 44	15 44	15 46	15 56	15 59	15 59	16 01	16 11	16 14	16 14	16 16	16 26	16 29
Kirkdale	d	15 04	15 14		15 19	15 29			15 34	15 44			15 49	15 59			16 04	16 14			16 19	16 29	
Rice Lane	d		15 17			15 32				15 47				16 02				16 17				16 32	
Fazakerley	d		15 19			15 34				15 49				16 04				16 19				16 34	
Kirkby	a		15 23			15 38				15 53				16 08				16 23				16 38	
Walton (Merseyside)	d	15 07			15 22				15 37				15 52				16 07				16 22		
Orrell Park	d	15 08			15 23				15 38				15 53				16 08				16 23		
Aintree	d	15 11			15 26				15 41				15 56				16 11				16 26		
Old Roan	d	15 13			15 28				15 43				15 58				16 13				16 28		
Maghull	d	15 16			15 31				15 46				16 01				16 16				16 31		
Town Green	d	15 20			15 35				15 50				16 05				16 20				16 35		
Aughton Park	d	15 22			15 37				15 52				16 07				16 22				16 37		
Ormskirk	a	15 28			15 43				15 58				16 13				16 28				16 43		
Bank Hall	d			15 16			15 31	15 31			15 46	15 46			16 01	16 01			16 16	16 16			16 31
Bootle Oriel Road	d			15 18			15 33	15 33			15 48	15 48			16 03	16 03			16 18	16 18			16 33
Bootle New Strand	d			15 20			15 35	15 35			15 50	15 50			16 05	16 05			16 20	16 20			16 35
Seaforth & Litherland	d			15 22			15 37	15 37			15 52	15 52			16 07	16 07			16 22	16 22			16 37
Waterloo (Merseyside)	d			15 24			15 39	15 39			15 54	15 54			16 09	16 09			16 24	16 24			16 39
Blundellsands & Crosby	d			15 27			15 42	15 42			15 57	15 57			16 12	16 12			16 27	16 27			16 42
Hall Road	d			15 29			15 44	15 44			15 59	15 59			16 14	16 14			16 29	16 29			16 44
Hightown	d			15 32			15 47	15 47			16 02	16 02			16 17	16 17			16 32	16 32			16 47
Formby	d			15 36			15 51	15 51			16 06	16 06			16 21	16 21			16 36	16 36			16 51
Freshfield	d			15 38			15 53	15 53			16 08	16 08			16 23	16 23			16 38	16 38			16 53
Ainsdale	d			15 42			15 57	15 57			16 12	16 12			16 27	16 27			16 42	16 42			16 57
Hillside	d			15 45			16 00	16 00			16 15	16 15			16 30	16 30			16 45	16 45			17 00
Birkdale	d			15 47			16 02	16 02			16 17	16 17			16 32	16 32			16 47	16 47			17 02
Southport	a			15 54			16 07	16 09			16 22	16 24			16 37	16 39			16 52	16 54			17 07

		ME SO	ME	ME	ME SX	ME SO	ME	ME	ME SX	ME SO	ME	ME	ME SX	ME SO	ME	ME SX	ME	ME	ME	ME	ME	ME	ME
Hunts Cross	89 d	16 06			16 21	16 21			16 36	16 36			16 51	16 51				17 06			17 21		
Liverpool Sth Parkway 7 89 ✈	d	16 09			16 24	16 24			16 39	16 39			16 54	16 54				17 09			17 24		
Cressington	d	16 12			16 27	16 27			16 42	16 42			16 57	16 57				17 12			17 27		
Aigburth	d	16 14			16 29	16 29			16 44	16 44			16 59	16 59				17 14			17 29		
St Michaels	d	16 16			16 31	16 31			16 46	16 46			17 01	17 01				17 16			17 31		
Brunswick	d	16 19			16 34	16 34			16 49	16 49			17 04	17 04				17 19			17 34		
Liverpool Central 10	a	16 23			16 38	16 38			16 53	16 53			17 08	17 08				17 23			17 38		
	d	16 23	16 25	16 35	16 38	16 38	16 40	16 50	16 53	16 53	16 55	17 05	17 08	17 08	17 10	17 13	17 20	17 23	17 25	17 35	17 38	17 40	17 50
Moorfields 10	d	16 25	16 27	16 37	16 40	16 40	16 42	16 52	16 55	16 55	16 57	17 07	17 10	17 10	17 12	17 15	17 22	17 25	17 27	17 37	17 40	17 42	17 52
Sandhills	d	16 29	16 31	16 41	16 44	16 44	16 46	16 56	16 59	16 59	17 01	17 11	17 14	17 14	17 16	17 19	17 26	17 29	17 31	17 41	17 44	17 46	17 56
Kirkdale	d		16 34	16 44			16 49	16 59			17 04	17 14			17 19		17 29		17 34	17 44		17 49	17 59
Rice Lane	d			16 47				17 02				17 17					17 32			17 47			18 02
Fazakerley	d			16 49				17 04				17 19					17 34			17 49			18 04
Kirkby	a			16 53				17 08				17 23					17 38			17 53			18 08
Walton (Merseyside)	d		16 37				16 52				17 07				17 22				17 37			17 52	
Orrell Park	d		16 38				16 53				17 08				17 23				17 38			17 53	
Aintree	d		16 41				16 56				17 11				17 26				17 41			17 56	
Old Roan	d		16 43				16 58				17 13				17 28				17 43			17 58	
Maghull	d		16 46				17 01				17 16				17 31				17 46			18 01	
Town Green	d		16 50				17 05				17 20				17 35				17 50			18 05	
Aughton Park	d		16 52				17 07				17 22				17 37				17 52			18 07	
Ormskirk	a		16 58				17 13				17 28				17 43				17 58			18 13	
Bank Hall	d	16 31			16 46	16 46			17 01	17 01			17 16	17 16		17 21		17 31			17 46		
Bootle Oriel Road	d	16 33			16 48	16 48			17 03	17 03			17 18	17 18		17 23		17 33			17 48		
Bootle New Strand	d	16 35			16 50	16 50			17 05	17 05			17 20	17 20		17 25		17 35			17 50		
Seaforth & Litherland	d	16 37			16 52	16 52			17 07	17 07			17 22	17 22		17 27		17 37			17 52		
Waterloo (Merseyside)	d	16 39			16 54	16 54			17 09	17 09			17 24	17 24		17 29		17 39			17 54		
Blundellsands & Crosby	d	16 42			16 57	16 57			17 12	17 12			17 27	17 27		17 32		17 42			17 57		
Hall Road	d	16 44			16 59	16 59			17 14	17 14			17 29	17 29		17 34		17 44			17 59		
Hightown	d	16 47			17 02	17 02			17 17	17 17			17 32	17 32		17 37		17 47			18 02		
Formby	d	16 51			17 06	17 06			17 21	17 21			17 36	17 36		17 41		17 51			18 06		
Freshfield	d	16 53			17 08	17 08			17 23	17 23			17 38	17 38		17 43		17 53			18 08		
Ainsdale	d	16 57			17 12	17 12			17 27	17 27			17 42	17 42		17 47		17 57			18 12		
Hillside	d	17 00			17 15	17 15			17 30	17 30			17 45	17 45		17 50		18 00			18 15		
Birkdale	d	17 02			17 17	17 17			17 32	17 32			17 47	17 47		17 52		18 02			18 17		
Southport	a	17 09			17 22	17 24			17 37	17 39			17 52	17 54		17 59		18 09			18 24		

Hunts Cross and Liverpool - Kirkby, Ormskirk and Southport

Network Diagram - see first Page of Table 101

		ME	ME	ME	ME	ME	ME	ME	ME	ME	ME	ME	ME	ME	ME	ME	ME	ME	ME	ME SO	ME SX	ME
Hunts Cross	89 d	17 36			17 51			18 06			18 21			18 36			18 51		19 06			19 21
Liverpool Sth Parkway 89	d	17 39			17 54			18 09			18 24			18 39			18 54		19 09			19 24
Cressington	d	17 42			17 57			18 12			18 27			18 42			18 57		19 12			19 27
Aigburth	d	17 44			17 59			18 14			18 29			18 44			18 59		19 14			19 29
St Michaels	d	17 46			18 01			18 16			18 31			18 46			19 01		19 16			19 31
Brunswick	d	17 49			18 04			18 19			18 34			18 49			19 04		19 19			19 34
Liverpool Central 10	a	17 53			18 08			18 23			18 38			18 53			19 08		19 23			19 38
	d	17 53	17 55	18 05	18 08	18 10	18 20	18 23	18 25	18 35	18 38	18 40	18 50	18 53	18 55	19 05	19 08	19 10	19 23	19 25	19 25	19 38
Moorfields 10	d	17 55	17 57	18 07	18 10	18 12	18 22	18 25	18 27	18 37	18 40	18 42	18 52	18 55	18 57	19 07	19 10	19 12	19 25	19 27	19 27	19 40
Sandhills	d	17 59	18 01	18 11	18 14	18 16	18 26	18 29	18 31	18 41	18 44	18 46	18 56	18 59	19 01	19 11	19 14	19 16	19 29	19 31	19 31	19 44
Kirkdale	d		18 04	18 14		18 19	18 29		18 34	18 44		18 49	18 59		19 04	19 14		19 19		19 34	19 34	
Rice Lane	d			18 17			18 32			18 47			19 02			19 17				19 37	19 37	
Fazakerley	d			18 19			18 34			18 49			19 04			19 19				19 40	19 40	
Kirkby	a			18 23			18 38			18 53			19 08			19 23				19 43	19 45	
Walton (Merseyside)	d		18 07			18 22			18 37			18 52			19 07			19 22				
Orrell Park	d		18 08			18 23			18 38			18 53			19 08			19 23				
Aintree	d		18 11			18 26			18 41			18 56			19 11			19 26				
Old Roan	d		18 13			18 28			18 43			18 58			19 13			19 28				
Maghull	d		18 16			18 31			18 46			19 01			19 16			19 31				
Town Green	d		18 20			18 35			18 50			19 05			19 20			19 35				
Aughton Park	d		18 22			18 37			18 52			19 07			19 22			19 37				
Ormskirk	a		18 28			18 43			18 58			19 13			19 28			19 43				
Bank Hall	d	18 01			18 16			18 31			18 46			19 01			19 16		19 31			19 46
Bootle Oriel Road	d	18 03			18 18			18 33			18 48			19 03			19 18		19 33			19 48
Bootle New Strand	d	18 05			18 20			18 35			18 50			19 05			19 20		19 35			19 50
Seaforth & Litherland	d	18 07			18 22			18 37			18 52			19 07			19 22		19 37			19 52
Waterloo (Merseyside)	d	18 09			18 24			18 39			18 54			19 09			19 24		19 39			19 54
Blundellsands & Crosby	d	18 12			18 27			18 42			18 57			19 12			19 27		19 42			19 57
Hall Road	d	18 14			18 29			18 44			18 59			19 14			19 29		19 44			19 59
Hightown	d	18 17			18 32			18 47			19 02			19 17			19 32		19 47			20 02
Formby	d	18 21			18 36			18 51			19 06			19 21			19 36		19 51			20 06
Freshfield	d	18 23			18 38			18 53			19 08			19 23			19 38		19 53			20 08
Ainsdale	d	18 27			18 42			18 57			19 12			19 27			19 42		19 57			20 12
Hillside	d	18 30			18 45			19 00			19 15			19 30			19 45		20 00			20 15
Birkdale	d	18 32			18 47			19 02			19 17			19 32			19 47		20 02			20 17
Southport	a	18 39			18 54			19 09			19 24			19 39			19 54		20 09			20 24

		ME	ME	ME SO	ME SX	ME	ME	ME	ME	ME	ME	ME	ME	ME	ME	ME	ME	ME	ME	ME	ME	ME	ME
Hunts Cross	89 d		19 36			19 51		20 06		20 21		20 36		20 51		21 06		21 21		21 36		21 51	
Liverpool Sth Parkway 89	d		19 39			19 54		20 09		20 24		20 39		20 54		21 09		21 24		21 39		21 54	
Cressington	d		19 42			19 57		20 12		20 27		20 42		20 57		21 12		21 27		21 42		21 57	
Aigburth	d		19 44			19 59		20 14		20 29		20 44		20 59		21 14		21 29		21 44		21 59	
St Michaels	d		19 46			20 01		20 16		20 31		20 46		21 01		21 16		21 31		21 46		22 01	
Brunswick	d		19 49			20 04		20 19		20 34		20 49		21 04		21 19		21 34		21 49		22 04	
Liverpool Central 10	a		19 53			20 08		20 23		20 38		20 53		21 08		21 23		21 38		21 53		22 08	
	d	19 40	19 53	19 55	19 55	20 08	20 10	20 23	20 25	20 38	20 40	20 53	20 55	21 08	21 10	21 23	21 25	21 38	21 40	21 53	21 55	22 08	22 10
Moorfields 10	d	19 42	19 55	19 57	19 57	20 10	20 12	20 25	20 27	20 40	20 42	20 55	20 57	21 10	21 12	21 25	21 27	21 40	21 42	21 55	21 57	22 10	22 12
Sandhills	d	19 46	19 59	20 01	20 01	20 14	20 16	20 29	20 31	20 44	20 46	20 59	21 01	21 14	21 16	21 29	21 31	21 44	21 46	21 59	22 01	22 14	22 16
Kirkdale	d	19 49		20 04	20 04		20 19		20 34		20 49		21 04		21 19		21 34		21 49		22 04		22 19
Rice Lane	d			20 07	20 07				20 37				21 07				21 37				22 07		
Fazakerley	d			20 10	20 10				20 40				21 10				21 40				22 10		
Kirkby	a			20 13	20 15				20 43				21 13				21 43				22 13		
Walton (Merseyside)	d	19 52					20 22				20 52				21 22				21 52				22 22
Orrell Park	d	19 53					20 23				20 53				21 23				21 53				22 23
Aintree	d	19 56					20 26				20 56				21 26				21 56				22 26
Old Roan	d	19 58					20 28				20 58				21 28				21 58				22 28
Maghull	d	20 01					20 31				21 01				21 31				22 01				22 31
Town Green	d	20 05					20 35				21 05				21 35				22 05				22 35
Aughton Park	d	20 07					20 37				21 07				21 37				22 07				22 37
Ormskirk	a	20 13					20 43				21 13				21 43				22 13				22 43
Bank Hall	d		20 01			20 16		20 31		20 46		21 01		21 16		21 31		21 46		22 01		22 16	
Bootle Oriel Road	d		20 03			20 18		20 33		20 48		21 03		21 18		21 33		21 48		22 03		22 18	
Bootle New Strand	d		20 05			20 20		20 35		20 50		21 05		21 20		21 35		21 50		22 05		22 20	
Seaforth & Litherland	d		20 07			20 22		20 37		20 52		21 07		21 22		21 37		21 52		22 07		22 22	
Waterloo (Merseyside)	d		20 09			20 24		20 39		20 54		21 09		21 24		21 39		21 54		22 09		22 24	
Blundellsands & Crosby	d		20 12			20 27		20 42		20 57		21 12		21 27		21 42		21 57		22 12		22 27	
Hall Road	d		20 14			20 29		20 44		20 59		21 14		21 29		21 44		21 59		22 14		22 29	
Hightown	d		20 17			20 32		20 47		21 02		21 17		21 32		21 47		22 02		22 17		22 32	
Formby	d		20 21			20 36		20 51		21 06		21 21		21 36		21 51		22 06		22 21		22 36	
Freshfield	d		20 23			20 38		20 53		21 08		21 23		21 38		21 53		22 08		22 23		22 38	
Ainsdale	d		20 27			20 42		20 57		21 12		21 27		21 42		21 57		22 12		22 27		22 42	
Hillside	d		20 30			20 45		21 00		21 15		21 30		21 45		22 00		22 15		22 30		22 45	
Birkdale	d		20 32			20 47		21 02		21 17		21 32		21 47		22 02		22 17		22 32		22 47	
Southport	a		20 39			20 54		21 09		21 24		21 39		21 54		22 09		22 24		22 39		22 54	

Hunts Cross and Liverpool - Kirkby, Ormskirk and Southport

Network Diagram - see first Page of Table 101

		ME	ME	ME	ME	ME	ME	ME	ME	ME	ME	ME	ME	ME
Hunts Cross	89 d	22 06		22 21		22 36		22 51		23 06		23 21		
Liverpool Sth Parkway 89	d	22 09		22 24		22 39		22 54		23 09		23 24		
Cressington	d	22 12		22 27		22 42		22 57		23 12		23 27		
Aigburth	d	22 14		22 29		22 44		22 59		23 14		23 29		
St Michaels	d	22 16		22 31		22 46		23 01		23 16		23 31		
Brunswick	d	22 19		22 34		22 49		23 04		23 19		23 34		
Liverpool Central 10	a	22 23		22 38		22 53		23 08		23 23		23 38		
	d	22 23	22 25	22 38	22 40	22 53	22 55	23 08	23 10	23 23	23 25	23 38	23 40	23 55
Moorfields 10	d	22 25	22 27	22 40	22 42	22 55	22 57	23 10	23 12	23 25	23 27	23 40	23 42	23 57
Sandhills	d	22 29	22 31	22 44	22 46	22 59	23 01	23 14	23 16	23 29	23 31	23 44	23 46	00 01
Kirkdale	d		22 34		22 49		23 04		23 19		23 34		23 49	00 04
Rice Lane	d		22 37				23 07				23 37			00 07
Fazakerley	d		22 40				23 10				23 40			00 10
Kirkby	a		22 43				23 13				23 43			00 13
Walton (Merseyside)	d				22 52				23 22				23 52	
Orrell Park	d				22 53				23 23				23 53	
Aintree	d				22 56				23 26				23 56	
Old Roan	d				22 58				23 28				23 58	
Maghull	d				23 01				23 31				00 01	
Town Green	d				23 05				23 35				00 05	
Aughton Park	d				23 07				23 37				00 07	
Ormskirk	a				23 13				23 42				00 12	
Bank Hall	d	22 31		22 46		23 01		23 16		23 31		23 46		
Bootle Oriel Road	d	22 33		22 48		23 03		23 18		23 33		23 48		
Bootle New Strand	d	22 35		22 50		23 05		23 20		23 35		23 50		
Seaforth & Litherland	d	22 37		22 52		23 07		23 22		23 37		23 52		
Waterloo (Merseyside)	d	22 39		22 54		23 09		23 24		23 39		23 54		
Blundellsands & Crosby	d	22 42		22 57		23 12		23 27		23 42		23 57		
Hall Road	d	22 44		22 59		23 14		23 29		23 44		23 59		
Hightown	d	22 47		23 02		23 17		23 32		23 47		00 02		
Formby	d	22 51		23 06		23 21		23 36		23 51		00 06		
Freshfield	d	22 53		23 08		23 23		23 38		23 53		00 08		
Ainsdale	d	22 57		23 12		23 27		23 42		23 57		00 12		
Hillside	d	23 00		23 15		23 30		23 45		23 59		00 15		
Birkdale	d	23 02		23 17		23 32		23 47		00 02		00 17		
Southport	a	23 09		23 24		23 39		23 54		00 09		00 24		

Sundays

		ME	ME	ME	ME	ME	ME	ME	ME	ME	ME	ME	ME	ME	ME	ME	ME	ME	ME A	ME	ME	ME
Hunts Cross	89 d	23p06	23p21					08 06			08 36			09 06			09 36				10 06	
Liverpool Sth Parkway 89	d	23p09	23p24					08 09			08 39			09 09			09 39				10 09	
Cressington	d	23p12	23p27					08 12			08 42			09 12			09 42				10 12	
Aigburth	d	23p14	23p29					08 14			08 44			09 14			09 44				10 14	
St Michaels	d	23p16	23p31					08 16			08 46			09 16			09 46				10 16	
Brunswick	d	23p19	23p34					08 19			08 49			09 19			09 49				10 19	
Liverpool Central 10	a	23p23	23p38					08 23			08 53			09 23			09 53				10 23	
	d	23p23	23p38	23p40	23p55	08 08	08 10	08 23	08 25	08 40	08 53	08 55	09 10	09 23	09 25	09 40	09 53	09 55	10 08	10 10	10 23	10 25
Moorfields 10	d	23p25	23p40	23p42	23p57	08 10	08 12	08 25	08 27	08 42	08 55	08 57	09 12	09 25	09 27	09 42	09 55	09 57	10 10	10 12	10 25	10 27
Sandhills	d	23p29	23p44	23p46	00 01	08 14	08 16	08 29	08 31	08 46	08 59	09 01	09 16	09 29	09 31	09 46	09 59	10 01	10 14	10 16	10 29	10 31
Kirkdale	d			23p49	00 04		08 19		08 34	08 49		09 04	09 19		09 34	09 49		10 04		10 19		10 34
Rice Lane	d				00 07				08 37			09 07			09 37			10 07				10 37
Fazakerley	d				00 10				08 40			09 10			09 40			10 10				10 40
Kirkby	a				00 13				08 43			09 13			09 43			10 13				10 43
Walton (Merseyside)	d			23p52			08 22			08 52			09 22			09 52				10 22		
Orrell Park	d			23p53			08 23			08 53			09 23			09 53				10 23		
Aintree	d			23p56			08 26			08 56			09 26			09 56				10 26		
Old Roan	d			23p58			08 28			08 58			09 28			09 58				10 28		
Maghull	d			00 01			08 31			09 01			09 31			10 01				10 31		
Town Green	d			00 05			08 35			09 05			09 35			10 05				10 35		
Aughton Park	d			00 07			08 37			09 07			09 37			10 07				10 37		
Ormskirk	a			00 12			08 43			09 13			09 43			10 13				10 43		
Bank Hall	d	23p31	23p46			08 16		08 31			09 01			09 31			10 01		10 16		10 31	
Bootle Oriel Road	d	23p33	23p48			08 18		08 33			09 03			09 33			10 03		10 18		10 33	
Bootle New Strand	d	23p35	23p50			08 20		08 35			09 05			09 35			10 05		10 20		10 35	
Seaforth & Litherland	d	23p37	23p52			08 22		08 37			09 07			09 37			10 07		10 22		10 37	
Waterloo (Merseyside)	d	23p39	23p54			08 24		08 39			09 09			09 39			10 09		10 24		10 39	
Blundellsands & Crosby	d	23p42	23p57			08 27		08 42			09 12			09 42			10 12		10 27		10 42	
Hall Road	d	23p44	23p59			08 29		08 44			09 14			09 44			10 14		10 29		10 44	
Hightown	d	23p47	00 02			08 32		08 47			09 17			09 47			10 17		10 32		10 47	
Formby	d	23p51	00 06			08 36		08 51			09 21			09 51			10 21		10 36		10 51	
Freshfield	d	23p53	00 08			08 38		08 53			09 23			09 53			10 23		10 38		10 53	
Ainsdale	d	23p57	00 12			08 42		08 57			09 27			09 57			10 27		10 42		10 57	
Hillside	d	23p59	00 15			08 45		09 00			09 30			10 00			10 30		10 45		11 00	
Birkdale	d	00 02	00 17			08 47		09 02			09 32			10 02			10 32		10 47		11 02	
Southport	a	00 09	00 24			08 52		09 09			09 39			10 09			10 39		10 54		11 09	

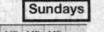

A until 23 September

Hunts Cross and Liverpool - Kirkby, Ormskirk and Southport

Network Diagram - see first Page of Table 101

		ME		ME	ME	ME	ME	ME	ME	ME	ME	ME	ME	ME	ME
		A		A				A		B	A				
Hunts Cross 89	d					22 36				23 06	23 06				
Liverpool Sth Parkway 7 89 ✈	d					22 39				23 09	23 09				
Cressington	d					22 42				23 12	23 12				
Aigburth	d					22 44				23 14	23 14				
St Michaels	d					22 46				23 16	23 16				
Brunswick	d					22 49				23 19	23 19				
Liverpool Central 10	a					22 53				23 23	23 23				
	d	10 38		22 38	22 40	22 53	22 55	23 08	23 10	23 23	23 23	23 25	23 38	23 40	23 55
Moorfields 10	d	10 40		22 40	22 42	22 55	22 57	23 10	23 12	23 25	23 25	23 27	23 40	23 42	23 57
Sandhills	d	10 44		22 44	22 46	22 59	23 01	23 14	23 16	23 29	23a29	23 31	23 44	23 46	00 01
Kirkdale	d				22 49		23 04		23 19			23 34		23 49	00 04
Rice Lane	d						23 07					23 37			00 07
Fazakerley	d						23 10					23 40			00 10
Kirkby	a						23 13					23 43			00 13
Walton (Merseyside)	d		and at the same minutes past each hour until		22 52				23 22					23 52	
Orrell Park	d				22 53				23 23					23 53	
Aintree	d				22 56				23 26					23 56	
Old Roan	d				22 58				23 28					23 58	
Maghull	d				23 01				23 31					00 01	
Town Green	d				23 05				23 35					00 05	
Aughton Park	d				23 07				23 37					00 07	
Ormskirk	a				23 13				23 42					00 12	
Bank Hall	d	10 46		22 46		23 01		23 16		23 31			23 46		
Bootle Oriel Road	d	10 48		22 48		23 03		23 18		23 33			23 48		
Bootle New Strand	d	10 50		22 50		23 05		23 20		23 35			23 50		
Seaforth & Litherland	d	10 52		22 52		23 07		23 22		23 37			23 52		
Waterloo (Merseyside)	d	10 54		22 54		23 09		23 24		23 39			23 54		
Blundellsands & Crosby	d	10 57		22 57		23 12		23 27		23 42			23 57		
Hall Road	d	10 59		22 59		23 14		23 29		23 44			23 59		
Hightown	d	11 02		23 02		23 17		23 32		23 47			00 02		
Formby	d	11 06		23 06		23 21		23 36		23 51			00 06		
Freshfield	d	11 08		23 08		23 23		23 38		23 53			00 08		
Ainsdale	d	11 12		23 12		23 27		23 42		23 57			00 12		
Hillside	d	11 15		23 15		23 30		23 45		23 59			00 15		
Birkdale	d	11 17		23 17		23 32		23 47		00 02			00 17		
Southport	a	11 24		23 24		23 39		23 54		00 09			00 24		

A until 23 September

B from 30 September

Southport, Ormskirk and Kirby - Liverpool and Hunts Cross

Network Diagram - see first Page of Table 101

Miles	Miles	Miles			ME	ME	ME	ME	ME	ME	ME	ME	ME	ME	ME	ME	ME	ME	ME	ME	ME	ME	ME
					A	A															SX	SO	
0	—	—	**Southport**	d	22p58	23p16				05 38		05 53		06 08		06 23		06 43			06 58	06 58	
1	—	—	Birkdale	d	23p02	23p20				05 42		05 57		06 12		06 27		06 47			07 02	07 02	
2	—	—	Hillside	d	23p04	23p22				05 44		05 59		06 14		06 29		06 49			07 04	07 04	
3½	—	—	Ainsdale	d	23p07	23p25				05 47		06 02		06 17		06 32		06 52			07 07	07 07	
6¼	—	—	Freshfield	d	23p11	23p29				05 51		06 06		06 21		06 36		06 56			07 11	07 11	
7¼	—	—	Formby	d	23p13	23p31				05 53		06 08		06 23		06 38		06 58			07 13	07 13	
9¼	—	—	Hightown	d	23p17	23p35				05 57		06 12		06 27		06 42		07 02			07 17	07 17	
11¼	—	—	Hall Road	d	23p20	23p38				06 00		06 15		06 30		06 45		07 05			07 20	07 20	
12	—	—	Blundellsands & Crosby	d	23p22	23p40				06 02		06 17		06 32		06 47		07 07			07 22	07 22	
13	—	—	Waterloo (Merseyside)	d	23p25	23p43				06 05		06 20		06 35		06 50		07 10			07 25	07 25	
14¼	—	—	Seaforth & Litherland	d	23p27	23p45				06 07		06 22		06 37		06 52		07 12			07 27	07 27	
15¼	—	—	Bootle New Strand	d	23p30	23p48				06 10		06 25		06 40		06 55		07 15			07 30	07 30	
15½	—	—	Bootle Oriel Road	d	23p31	23p49				06 11		06 26		06 41		06 56		07 16			07 31	07 31	
16¼	—	—	Bank Hall	d	23p33	23p51				06 18		06 33		06 48		07 03		07 18			07 33	07 33	
—	0	—	**Ormskirk**	d					05 50				06 20				06 50			07 05			
—	1¼	—	Aughton Park	d					05 53				06 23				06 53			07 08			
—	2¼	—	Town Green	d					05 55				06 25				06 55			07 10			
—	4¾	—	Maghull	d					06 00				06 30				07 00			07 15			
—	6½	—	Old Roan	d					06 03				06 33				07 03			07 18			
—	7¼	—	Aintree	d					06 05				06 35				07 05			07 20			
—	8¼	—	Orrell Park	d					06 07				06 37				07 07			07 22			
—	8½	—	Walton (Merseyside)	d					06 09				06 39				07 09			07 24			
—	—	0	**Kirkby**	d			05 48				06 18				06 48				07 13				07 28
—	—	1¾	Fazakerley	d			05 51				06 21				06 51				07 16				07 31
—	—	3¼	Rice Lane	d			05 54				06 24				06 54				07 19				07 34
—	9¼	4½	Kirkdale	d			05 57		06 12		06 27		06 42		06 57		07 12		07 22	07 27			07 37
17	10¾	5½	Sandhills	d	23p36	23p55	06 00	06 06	06 14	06 21	06 30	06 36	06 44	06 51	07 00	07 06	07 14	07 21	07 25	07 29	07 36	07 36	07 40
18½	12¼	7	**Moorfields** 10	d	23p40	23p58	06 03	06 10	06 18	06 25	06 33	06 40	06 48	06 55	07 03	07 10	07 18	07 25	07 28	07 33	07 40	07 40	07 43
19	12¾	7½	**Liverpool Central** 10	a	23p43	00 01	06 06	06 13	06 20	06 28	06 36	06 43	06 50	06 58	07 06	07 13	07 20	07 28	07 31	07 35	07 43	07 43	07 46
—	—	—		d	23p44			06 14		06 29		06 43		06 59		07 14		07 29			07 44	07 44	
20½	—	—	Brunswick	d	23p47			06 17		06 32		06 47		07 02		07 17		07 32			07 47	07 47	
21¾	—	—	St Michaels	d	23p50			06 20		06 35		06 49		07 05		07 20		07 35			07 50	07 50	
23	—	—	Aigburth	d	23p52			06 22		06 37		06 52		07 07		07 22		07 37			07 52	07 52	
23¾	—	—	Cressington	d	23p54			06 24		06 39		06 54		07 09		07 24		07 39			07 54	07 54	
24¾	—	—	**Liverpool Sth Parkway** 7 89 ✈	d	23p57			06 27		06 42		06 56		07 12		07 27		07 42			07 57	07 57	
26¼	—	—	**Hunts Cross** 89	a	00 02			06 32		06 47		07 02		07 17		07 32		07 47			08 01	08 02	

		ME	ME	ME	ME	ME	ME	ME	ME	ME	ME	ME	ME	ME	ME	ME	ME	ME	ME	ME	ME	ME	ME
									SX	SO		SX				SX							
Southport	d		07 13			07 28			07 38	07 43		07 48		07 58		08 03		08 13			08 28		
Birkdale	d		07 17			07 32			07 42	07 47		07 52		08 02		08 07		08 17			08 32		
Hillside	d		07 19			07 34			07 44	07 49		07 54		08 04		08 09		08 19			08 34		
Ainsdale	d		07 22			07 37			07 47	07 52		07 57		08 07		08 12		08 22			08 37		
Freshfield	d		07 26			07 41			07 51	07 56		08 01		08 11		08 16		08 26			08 41		
Formby	d		07 28			07 43			07 53	07 58		08 03		08 13		08 18		08 28			08 43		
Hightown	d		07 32			07 47			07 57	08 02		08 07		08 17		08 22		08 32			08 47		
Hall Road	d		07 35			07 50			08 00	08 05		08 10		08 20		08 25		08 35			08 50		
Blundellsands & Crosby	d		07 37			07 52			08 02	08 07		08 12		08 22		08 27		08 37			08 52		
Waterloo (Merseyside)	d		07 40			07 55			08 05	08 10		08 15		08 25		08 30		08 40			08 55		
Seaforth & Litherland	d		07 42			07 57			08 07	08 12		08 17		08 27		08 32		08 42			08 57		
Bootle New Strand	d		07 45			08 00			08 10	08 15		08 20		08 30		08 35		08 45			09 00		
Bootle Oriel Road	d		07 46			08 01			08 11	08 16		08 21		08 31		08 36		08 46			09 01		
Bank Hall	d		07 48			08 03			08 18	08 18		08 23		08 33		08 38		08 48			09 03		
Ormskirk	d	07 20			07 35			07 50					08 05				08 20			08 35			08 50
Aughton Park	d	07 23			07 38			07 53					08 08				08 23			08 38			08 53
Town Green	d	07 25			07 40			07 55					08 10				08 25			08 40			08 55
Maghull	d	07 30			07 45			08 00					08 15				08 30			08 45			09 00
Old Roan	d	07 33			07 48			08 03					08 18				08 33			08 48			09 03
Aintree	d	07 35			07 50			08 05					08 20				08 35			08 50			09 05
Orrell Park	d	07 37			07 52			08 07					08 22				08 37			08 52			09 07
Walton (Merseyside)	d	07 39			07 54			08 09					08 24				08 39			08 54			09 09
Kirkby	d			07 43			07 58				08 13				08 28				08 43			08 58	
Fazakerley	d			07 46			08 01				08 16				08 31				08 46			09 01	
Rice Lane	d			07 49			08 04				08 19				08 34				08 49			09 04	
Kirkdale	d	07 42		07 52	07 57		08 07	08 12			08 22		08 27		08 37		08 42		08 52	08 57		09 07	09 12
Sandhills	d	07 44	07 51	07 55	07 59	08 06	08 10	08 14	08 21	08 21	08 25	08 27	08 29	08 36	08 40	08 42	08 44	08 51	08 55	08 59	09 06	09 10	09 14
Moorfields 10	d	07 48	07 55	07 58	08 03	08 10	08 13	08 18	08 25	08 25	08 28	08 31	08 33	08 40	08 43	08 46	08 48	08 55	08 58	09 03	09 10	09 13	09 18
Liverpool Central 10	a	07 50	07 58	08 01	08 05	08 13	08 16	08 20	08 28	08 28	08 31	08 33	08 35	08 43	08 46	08 48	08 50	08 58	09 01	09 05	09 13	09 16	09 20
	d		07 59			08 14			08 29	08 29				08 44				08 59			09 14		
Brunswick	d		08 02			08 17			08 32	08 32				08 47				09 02			09 17		
St Michaels	d		08 05			08 20			08 35	08 35				08 50				09 05			09 20		
Aigburth	d		08 07			08 22			08 37	08 37				08 52				09 07			09 22		
Cressington	d		08 09			08 24			08 39	08 39				08 54				09 09			09 24		
Liverpool Sth Parkway 7 89 ✈	d		08 12			08 27			08 42	08 42				08 57				09 12			09 27		
Hunts Cross 89	a		08 17			08 32			08 47	08 47				09 02				09 17			09 32		

A not 14 May

Southport, Ormskirk and Kirby - Liverpool and Hunts Cross

Network Diagram - see first Page of Table 101

		ME	ME	ME	ME		ME	ME	ME	ME	ME	ME	ME	ME	ME		ME	ME	ME	ME	ME	ME	ME	ME	ME
Southport	d	08 43			08 58				09 13			09 28			09 43				09 58			10 13			10 28
Birkdale	d	08 47			09 02				09 17			09 32			09 47				10 02			10 17			10 32
Hillside	d	08 49			09 04				09 19			09 34			09 49				10 04			10 19			10 34
Ainsdale	d	08 52			09 07				09 22			09 37			09 52				10 07			10 22			10 37
Freshfield	d	08 56			09 11				09 26			09 41			09 56				10 11			10 26			10 41
Formby	d	08 58			09 13				09 28			09 43			09 58				10 13			10 28			10 43
Hightown	d	09 02			09 17				09 32			09 47			10 02				10 17			10 32			10 47
Hall Road	d	09 05			09 20				09 35			09 50			10 05				10 20			10 35			10 50
Blundellsands & Crosby	d	09 07			09 22				09 37			09 52			10 07				10 22			10 37			10 52
Waterloo (Merseyside)	d	09 10			09 25				09 40			09 55			10 10				10 25			10 40			10 55
Seaforth & Litherland	d	09 12			09 27				09 42			09 57			10 12				10 27			10 42			10 57
Bootle New Strand	d	09 15			09 30				09 45			10 00			10 15				10 30			10 45			11 00
Bootle Oriel Road	d	09 16			09 31				09 46			10 01			10 16				10 31			10 46			11 01
Bank Hall	d	09 18			09 33				09 48			10 03			10 18				10 33			10 48			11 03
Ormskirk	d			09 05				09 20			09 35			09 50				10 05			10 20			10 35	
Aughton Park	d			09 08				09 23			09 38			09 53				10 08			10 23			10 38	
Town Green	d			09 10				09 25			09 40			09 55				10 10			10 25			10 40	
Maghull	d			09 15				09 30			09 45			10 00				10 15			10 30			10 45	
Old Roan	d			09 18				09 33			09 48			10 03				10 18			10 33			10 48	
Aintree	d			09 20				09 35			09 50			10 05				10 20			10 35			10 50	
Orrell Park	d			09 22				09 37			09 52			10 07				10 22			10 37			10 52	
Walton (Merseyside)	d			09 24				09 39			09 54			10 09				10 24			10 39			10 54	
Kirby	d		09 13				09 28			09 43			09 58				10 13			10 28			10 43		
Fazakerley	d		09 16				09 31			09 46			10 01				10 16			10 31			10 46		
Rice Lane	d		09 19				09 34			09 49			10 04				10 19			10 34			10 49		
Kirkdale	d		09 22	09 27			09 37	09 42		09 52	09 57		10 07	10 12			10 22	10 27		10 37	10 42		10 52	10 57	
Sandhills	d	09 21	09 25	09 29	09 36		09 40	09 44	09 51	09 55	09 59	10 06	10 10	10 14	10 21		10 25	10 29	10 36	10 40	10 44	10 51	10 55	10 59	11 06
Moorfields [10]	d	09 25	09 28	09 33	09 40		09 43	09 48	09 55	09 58	10 03	10 10	10 13	10 18	10 25		10 28	10 33	10 40	10 43	10 48	10 55	10 58	11 03	11 10
Liverpool Central [10]	a	09 28	09 31	09 35	09 43		09 46	09 50	09 58	10 01	10 05	10 13	10 16	10 20	10 28		10 31	10 35	10 43	10 46	10 50	10 58	11 01	11 05	11 13
	d	09 29			09 44				09 59			10 14			10 29				10 44			10 59			11 14
Brunswick	d	09 32			09 47				10 02			10 17			10 32				10 47			11 02			11 17
St Michaels	d	09 35			09 50				10 05			10 20			10 35				10 50			11 05			11 20
Aigburth	d	09 37			09 52				10 07			10 22			10 37				10 52			11 07			11 22
Cressington	d	09 39			09 54				10 09			10 24			10 39				10 54			11 09			11 24
Liverpool Sth Parkway [7] 89 ✈	d	09 42			09 57				10 12			10 27			10 42				10 57			11 12			11 27
Hunts Cross 89	a	09 47			10 02				10 17			10 32			10 47				11 02			11 17			11 32

			ME	ME	ME	ME	ME	ME	ME	ME	ME		ME	ME	ME	ME	ME	ME	ME	ME	ME		ME	ME	ME
Southport	d				10 43			10 58			11 13				11 28			11 43			11 58				12 13
Birkdale	d				10 47			11 02			11 17				11 32			11 47			12 02				12 17
Hillside	d				10 49			11 04			11 19				11 34			11 49			12 04				12 19
Ainsdale	d				10 52			11 07			11 22				11 37			11 52			12 07				12 22
Freshfield	d				10 56			11 11			11 26				11 41			11 56			12 11				12 26
Formby	d				10 58			11 13			11 28				11 43			11 58			12 13				12 28
Hightown	d				11 02			11 17			11 32				11 47			12 02			12 17				12 32
Hall Road	d				11 05			11 20			11 35				11 50			12 05			12 20				12 35
Blundellsands & Crosby	d				11 07			11 22			11 37				11 52			12 07			12 22				12 37
Waterloo (Merseyside)	d				11 10			11 25			11 40				11 55			12 10			12 25				12 40
Seaforth & Litherland	d				11 12			11 27			11 42				11 57			12 12			12 27				12 42
Bootle New Strand	d				11 15			11 30			11 45				12 00			12 15			12 30				12 45
Bootle Oriel Road	d				11 16			11 31			11 46				12 01			12 16			12 31				12 46
Bank Hall	d				11 18			11 33			11 48				12 03			12 18			12 33				12 48
Ormskirk	d			10 50			11 05			11 20				11 35			11 50			12 05				12 20	
Aughton Park	d			10 53			11 08			11 23				11 38			11 53			12 08				12 23	
Town Green	d			10 55			11 10			11 25				11 40			11 55			12 10				12 25	
Maghull	d			11 00			11 15			11 30				11 45			12 00			12 15				12 30	
Old Roan	d			11 03			11 18			11 33				11 48			12 03			12 18				12 33	
Aintree	d			11 05			11 20			11 35				11 50			12 05			12 20				12 35	
Orrell Park	d			11 07			11 22			11 37				11 52			12 07			12 22				12 37	
Walton (Merseyside)	d			11 09			11 24			11 39				11 54			12 09			12 24				12 39	
Kirby	d		10 58			11 13			11 28				11 43			11 58			12 13				12 28		
Fazakerley	d		11 01			11 16			11 31				11 46			12 01			12 16				12 31		
Rice Lane	d		11 04			11 19			11 34				11 49			12 04			12 19				12 34		
Kirkdale	d		11 07	11 12		11 22	11 27		11 37	11 42			11 52	11 57		12 07	12 12		12 22	12 27			12 37	12 42	
Sandhills	d		11 10	11 14	11 21	11 25	11 29	11 36	11 40	11 44	11 51		11 55	11 59	12 06	12 10	12 14	12 21	12 25	12 29	12 36		12 40	12 44	12 51
Moorfields [10]	d		11 13	11 18	11 25	11 28	11 33	11 40	11 43	11 48	11 55		11 58	12 03	12 10	12 13	12 18	12 25	12 28	12 33	12 40		12 43	12 48	12 55
Liverpool Central [10]	a		11 16	11 20	11 28	11 31	11 35	11 43	11 46	11 50	11 58		12 01	12 05	12 13	12 16	12 20	12 28	12 31	12 35	12 43		12 46	12 50	12 58
	d				11 29			11 44			11 59				12 14			12 29			12 44				12 59
Brunswick	d				11 32			11 47			12 02				12 17			12 32			12 47				13 02
St Michaels	d				11 35			11 50			12 05				12 20			12 35			12 50				13 05
Aigburth	d				11 37			11 52			12 07				12 22			12 37			12 52				13 07
Cressington	d				11 39			11 54			12 09				12 24			12 39			12 54				13 09
Liverpool Sth Parkway [7] 89 ✈	d				11 42			11 57			12 12				12 27			12 42			12 57				13 12
Hunts Cross 89	a				11 47			12 02			12 17				12 32			12 47			13 02				13 17

Southport, Ormskirk and Kirby - Liverpool and Hunts Cross

Network Diagram - see first Page of Table 101

		ME	ME	ME	ME	ME	ME		ME	ME	ME	ME	ME	ME	ME	ME	ME		ME	ME	ME	ME	ME	ME	ME
Southport	d			12 28			12 43				12 58			13 13			13 28				13 43			13 58	
Birkdale	d			12 32			12 47				13 02			13 17			13 32				13 47			14 02	
Hillside	d			12 34			12 49				13 04			13 19			13 34				13 49			14 04	
Ainsdale	d			12 37			12 52				13 07			13 22			13 37				13 52			14 07	
Freshfield	d			12 41			12 56				13 11			13 26			13 41				13 56			14 11	
Formby	d			12 43			12 58				13 13			13 28			13 43				13 58			14 13	
Hightown	d			12 47			13 02				13 17			13 32			13 47				14 02			14 17	
Hall Road	d			12 50			13 05				13 20			13 35			13 50				14 05			14 20	
Blundellsands & Crosby	d			12 52			13 07				13 22			13 37			13 52				14 07			14 22	
Waterloo (Merseyside)	d			12 55			13 10				13 25			13 40			13 55				14 10			14 25	
Seaforth & Litherland	d			12 57			13 12				13 27			13 42			13 57				14 12			14 27	
Bootle New Strand	d			13 00			13 15				13 30			13 45			14 00				14 15			14 30	
Bootle Oriel Road	d			13 01			13 16				13 31			13 46			14 01				14 16			14 31	
Bank Hall	d			13 03			13 18				13 33			13 48			14 03				14 18			14 33	
Ormskirk	d		12 35			12 50				13 05			13 20			13 35				13 50			14 05		
Aughton Park	d		12 38			12 53				13 08			13 23			13 38				13 53			14 08		
Town Green	d		12 40			12 55				13 10			13 25			13 40				13 55			14 10		
Maghull	d		12 45			13 00				13 15			13 30			13 45				14 00			14 15		
Old Roan	d		12 48			13 03				13 18			13 33			13 48				14 03			14 18		
Aintree	d		12 50			13 05				13 20			13 35			13 50				14 05			14 20		
Orrell Park	d		12 52			13 07				13 22			13 37			13 52				14 07			14 22		
Walton (Merseyside)	d		12 54			13 09				13 24			13 39			13 54				14 09			14 24		
Kirby	d	12 43			12 58				13 13			13 28			13 43				13 58			14 13			14 28
Fazakerley	d	12 46			13 01				13 16			13 31			13 46				14 01			14 16			14 31
Rice Lane	d	12 49			13 04				13 19			13 34			13 49				14 04			14 19			14 34
Kirkdale	d	12 52	12 57		13 07	13 12			13 22	13 27		13 37	13 42		13 52	13 57			14 07	14 12		14 22	14 27		14 37
Sandhills	d	12 55	12 59	13 06	13 10	13 14	13 21		13 25	13 29	13 36	13 40	13 44	13 51	13 55	13 59	14 06		14 10	14 14	14 21	14 25	14 29	14 36	14 40
Moorfields [10]	d	12 58	13 03	13 10	13 13	13 18	13 25		13 28	13 33	13 40	13 43	13 48	13 55	13 58	14 03	14 10		14 13	14 18	14 25	14 28	14 33	14 40	14 43
Liverpool Central [10]	a	13 01	13 05	13 13	13 16	13 20	13 28		13 31	13 35	13 43	13 46	13 50	13 58	14 01	14 05	14 13		14 16	14 20	14 28	14 31	14 35	14 43	14 46
	d			13 14			13 29				13 44			13 59			14 14				14 29			14 44	
Brunswick	d			13 17			13 32				13 47			14 02			14 17				14 32			14 47	
St Michaels	d			13 20			13 35				13 50			14 05			14 20				14 35			14 50	
Aigburth	d			13 22			13 37				13 52			14 07			14 22				14 37			14 52	
Cressington	d			13 24			13 39				13 54			14 09			14 24				14 39			14 54	
Liverpool Sth Parkway [7] 89 ✈	d			13 27			13 42				13 57			14 12			14 27				14 42			14 57	
Hunts Cross 89	a			13 32			13 47				14 02			14 17			14 32				14 47			15 02	

		ME	ME		ME	ME	ME	ME	ME	ME	ME	ME	ME		ME	ME	ME	ME	ME	ME	ME	ME	ME		ME
Southport	d		14 13				14 28			14 43			14 58				15 13			15 28			15 43		
Birkdale	d		14 17				14 32			14 47			15 02				15 17			15 32			15 47		
Hillside	d		14 19				14 34			14 49			15 04				15 19			15 34			15 49		
Ainsdale	d		14 22				14 37			14 52			15 07				15 22			15 37			15 52		
Freshfield	d		14 26				14 41			14 56			15 11				15 26			15 41			15 56		
Formby	d		14 28				14 43			14 58			15 13				15 28			15 43			15 58		
Hightown	d		14 32				14 47			15 02			15 17				15 32			15 47			16 02		
Hall Road	d		14 35				14 50			15 05			15 20				15 35			15 50			16 05		
Blundellsands & Crosby	d		14 37				14 52			15 07			15 22				15 37			15 52			16 07		
Waterloo (Merseyside)	d		14 40				14 55			15 10			15 25				15 40			15 55			16 10		
Seaforth & Litherland	d		14 42				14 57			15 12			15 27				15 42			15 57			16 12		
Bootle New Strand	d		14 45				15 00			15 15			15 30				15 45			16 00			16 15		
Bootle Oriel Road	d		14 46				15 01			15 16			15 31				15 46			16 01			16 16		
Bank Hall	d		14 48				15 03			15 18			15 33				15 48			16 03			16 18		
Ormskirk	d	14 20				14 35			14 50			15 05				15 20			15 35			15 50			
Aughton Park	d	14 23				14 38			14 53			15 08				15 23			15 38			15 53			
Town Green	d	14 25				14 40			14 55			15 10				15 25			15 40			15 55			
Maghull	d	14 30				14 45			15 00			15 15				15 30			15 45			16 00			
Old Roan	d	14 33				14 48			15 03			15 18				15 33			15 48			16 03			
Aintree	d	14 35				14 50			15 05			15 20				15 35			15 50			16 05			
Orrell Park	d	14 37				14 52			15 07			15 22				15 37			15 52			16 07			
Walton (Merseyside)	d	14 39				14 54			15 09			15 24				15 39			15 54			16 09			
Kirby	d				14 43			14 58			15 13				15 28			15 43			15 58				16 13
Fazakerley	d				14 46			15 01			15 16				15 31			15 46			16 01				16 16
Rice Lane	d				14 49			15 04			15 19				15 34			15 49			16 04				16 19
Kirkdale	d	14 42			14 52	14 57		15 07	15 12		15 22	15 27			15 37	15 42		15 52	15 57		16 07	16 12			16 22
Sandhills	d	14 44	14 51		14 55	14 59	15 06	15 10	15 14	15 21	15 25	15 29	15 36		15 40	15 44	15 51	15 55	15 59	16 06	16 10	16 14	16 21		16 25
Moorfields [10]	d	14 48	14 55		14 58	15 03	15 10	15 13	15 18	15 25	15 28	15 33	15 40		15 43	15 48	15 55	15 58	16 03	16 10	16 13	16 18	16 25		16 28
Liverpool Central [10]	a	14 50	14 58		15 01	15 05	15 13	15 16	15 20	15 28	15 31	15 35	15 43		15 46	15 50	15 58	16 01	16 05	16 13	16 16	16 20	16 28		16 31
	d		14 59				15 14			15 29			15 44				15 59			16 14			16 29		
Brunswick	d		15 02				15 17			15 32			15 47				16 02			16 17			16 32		
St Michaels	d		15 05				15 20			15 35			15 50				16 05			16 20			16 35		
Aigburth	d		15 07				15 22			15 37			15 52				16 07			16 22			16 37		
Cressington	d		15 09				15 24			15 39			15 54				16 09			16 24			16 39		
Liverpool Sth Parkway [7] 89 ✈	d		15 12				15 27			15 42			15 57				16 12			16 27			16 42		
Hunts Cross 89	a		15 17				15 32			15 47			16 02				16 17			16 32			16 47		

Southport, Ormskirk and Kirby - Liverpool and Hunts Cross

Network Diagram - see first Page of Table 101

		ME	ME	ME	ME	ME	ME	ME	ME	ME	ME	ME	ME	ME	ME	ME	ME	ME	ME	ME	ME	ME	ME
Southport	d		15 58			16 13			16 28			16 43			16 58			17 13			17 28		
Birkdale	d		16 02			16 17			16 32			16 47			17 02			17 17			17 32		
Hillside	d		16 04			16 19			16 34			16 49			17 04			17 19			17 34		
Ainsdale	d		16 07			16 22			16 37			16 52			17 07			17 22			17 37		
Freshfield	d		16 11			16 26			16 41			16 56			17 11			17 26			17 41		
Formby	d		16 13			16 28			16 43			16 58			17 13			17 28			17 43		
Hightown	d		16 17			16 32			16 47			17 02			17 17			17 32			17 47		
Hall Road	d		16 20			16 35			16 50			17 05			17 20			17 35			17 50		
Blundellsands & Crosby	d		16 22			16 37			16 52			17 07			17 22			17 37			17 52		
Waterloo (Merseyside)	d		16 25			16 40			16 55			17 10			17 25			17 40			17 55		
Seaforth & Litherland	d		16 27			16 42			16 57			17 12			17 27			17 42			17 57		
Bootle New Strand	d		16 30			16 45			17 00			17 15			17 30			17 45			18 00		
Bootle Oriel Road	d		16 31			16 46			17 01			17 16			17 31			17 46			18 01		
Bank Hall	d		16 33			16 48			17 03			17 18			17 33			17 48			18 03		
Ormskirk	d	16 05			16 20			16 35			16 50			17 05			17 20			17 35			17 50
Aughton Park	d	16 08			16 23			16 38			16 53			17 08			17 23			17 38			17 53
Town Green	d	16 10			16 25			16 40			16 55			17 10			17 25			17 40			17 55
Maghull	d	16 15			16 30			16 45			17 00			17 15			17 30			17 45			18 00
Old Roan	d	16 18			16 33			16 48			17 03			17 18			17 33			17 48			18 03
Aintree	d	16 20			16 35			16 50			17 05			17 20			17 35			17 50			18 05
Orrell Park	d	16 22			16 37			16 52			17 07			17 22			17 37			17 52			18 07
Walton (Merseyside)	d	16 24			16 39			16 54			17 09			17 24			17 39			17 54			18 09
Kirkby	d			16 28			16 43			16 58			17 13			17 28			17 43			17 58	
Fazakerley	d			16 31			16 46			17 01			17 16			17 31			17 46			18 01	
Rice Lane	d			16 34			16 49			17 04			17 19			17 34			17 49			18 04	
Kirkdale	d	16 27		16 37	16 42		16 52	16 57		17 07	17 12		17 22	17 27		17 37	17 42		17 52	17 57		18 07	18 12
Sandhills	d	16 29	16 36	16 40	16 44	16 51	16 55	16 59	17 06	17 10	17 14	17 21	17 25	17 29	17 36	17 40	17 44	17 51	17 55	17 59	18 06	18 10	18 14
Moorfields 10	d	16 33	16 40	16 43	16 48	16 55	16 58	17 03	17 10	17 13	17 18	17 25	17 28	17 33	17 40	17 43	17 48	17 55	17 58	18 03	18 10	18 13	18 18
Liverpool Central 10	a	16 35	16 43	16 46	16 50	16 58	17 01	17 05	17 13	17 16	17 20	17 28	17 31	17 35	17 43	17 46	17 50	17 58	18 01	18 05	18 13	18 16	18 20
	d		16 44			16 59			17 14			17 29			17 44			17 59			18 14		
Brunswick	d		16 47			17 02			17 17			17 32			17 47			18 02			18 17		
St Michaels	d		16 50			17 05			17 20			17 35			17 50			18 05			18 20		
Aigburth	d		16 52			17 07			17 22			17 37			17 52			18 07			18 22		
Cressington	d		16 54			17 09			17 24			17 39			17 54			18 09			18 24		
Liverpool Sth Parkway 7 89 ✈	d		16 57			17 12			17 27			17 42			17 57			18 12			18 27		
Hunts Cross 89	a		17 02			17 17			17 32			17 47			18 02			18 17			18 32		

		ME	ME	ME	ME	ME	ME	ME	ME	ME	ME	ME	ME	ME	ME	ME	ME	ME	ME	ME	ME	ME	ME
Southport	d	17 43			17 58			18 13			18 28			18 43			18 58			19 13		19 28	
Birkdale	d	17 47			18 02			18 17			18 32			18 47			19 02			19 17		19 32	
Hillside	d	17 49			18 04			18 19			18 34			18 49			19 04			19 19		19 34	
Ainsdale	d	17 52			18 07			18 22			18 37			18 52			19 07			19 22		19 37	
Freshfield	d	17 56			18 11			18 26			18 41			18 56			19 11			19 26		19 41	
Formby	d	17 58			18 13			18 28			18 43			18 58			19 13			19 28		19 43	
Hightown	d	18 02			18 17			18 32			18 47			19 02			19 17			19 32		19 47	
Hall Road	d	18 05			18 20			18 35			18 50			19 05			19 20			19 35		19 50	
Blundellsands & Crosby	d	18 07			18 22			18 37			18 52			19 07			19 22			19 37		19 52	
Waterloo (Merseyside)	d	18 10			18 25			18 40			18 55			19 10			19 25			19 40		19 55	
Seaforth & Litherland	d	18 12			18 27			18 42			18 57			19 12			19 27			19 42		19 57	
Bootle New Strand	d	18 15			18 30			18 45			19 00			19 15			19 30			19 45		20 00	
Bootle Oriel Road	d	18 16			18 31			18 46			19 01			19 16			19 31			19 46		20 01	
Bank Hall	d	18 18			18 33			18 48			19 03			19 18			19 33			19 48		20 03	
Ormskirk	d			18 05			18 20			18 35			18 50			19 05			19 20				19 50
Aughton Park	d			18 08			18 23			18 38			18 53			19 08			19 23				19 53
Town Green	d			18 10			18 25			18 40			18 55			19 10			19 25				19 55
Maghull	d			18 15			18 30			18 45			19 00			19 15			19 30				20 00
Old Roan	d			18 18			18 33			18 48			19 03			19 18			19 33				20 03
Aintree	d			18 20			18 35			18 50			19 05			19 20			19 35				20 05
Orrell Park	d			18 22			18 37			18 52			19 07			19 22			19 37				20 07
Walton (Merseyside)	d			18 24			18 39			18 54			19 09			19 24			19 39				20 09
Kirkby	d		18 13			18 28			18 43			18 58			19 13			19 28			19 48		
Fazakerley	d		18 16			18 31			18 46			19 01			19 16			19 31			19 51		
Rice Lane	d		18 19			18 34			18 49			19 04			19 19			19 34			19 54		
Kirkdale	d		18 22	18 27		18 37	18 42		18 52	18 57		19 07	19 12		19 22	19 27		19 37	19 42		19 57		20 12
Sandhills	d	18 21	18 25	18 29	18 36	18 40	18 44	18 51	18 55	18 59	19 06	19 10	19 14	19 21	19 25	19 29	19 36	19 40	19 44	19 51	20 00	20 06	20 14
Moorfields 10	d	18 25	18 28	18 33	18 40	18 43	18 48	18 55	18 58	19 03	19 10	19 13	19 18	19 25	19 28	19 33	19 40	19 43	19 48	19 55	20 03	20 10	20 18
Liverpool Central 10	a	18 28	18 31	18 35	18 43	18 46	18 50	18 58	19 01	19 05	19 13	19 16	19 20	19 28	19 31	19 35	19 43	19 46	19 50	19 58	20 06	20 13	20 20
	d	18 29			18 44			18 59			19 14			19 29			19 44			19 59		20 14	
Brunswick	d	18 32			18 47			19 02			19 17			19 32			19 47			20 02		20 17	
St Michaels	d	18 35			18 50			19 05			19 20			19 35			19 50			20 05		20 20	
Aigburth	d	18 37			18 52			19 07			19 22			19 37			19 52			20 07		20 22	
Cressington	d	18 39			18 54			19 09			19 24			19 39			19 54			20 09		20 24	
Liverpool Sth Parkway 7 89 ✈	d	18 42			18 57			19 12			19 27			19 42			19 57			20 12		20 27	
Hunts Cross 89	a	18 47			19 02			19 16			19 32			19 47			20 02			20 16		20 32	

Southport, Ormskirk and Kirby - Liverpool and Hunts Cross

Network Diagram - see first Page of Table 101

		ME	ME	ME	ME	ME	ME	ME	ME	ME	ME	ME	ME	ME	ME	ME	ME	ME	ME	ME	ME	ME
Southport	d	19 43		19 58		20 13		20 28		20 43		20 58		21 13		21 28		21 43		21 58		22 13
Birkdale	d	19 47		20 02		20 17		20 32		20 47		21 02		21 17		21 32		21 47		22 02		22 17
Hillside	d	19 49		20 04		20 19		20 34		20 49		21 04		21 19		21 34		21 49		22 04		22 19
Ainsdale	d	19 52		20 07		20 22		20 37		20 52		21 07		21 22		21 37		21 52		22 07		22 22
Freshfield	d	19 56		20 11		20 26		20 41		20 56		21 11		21 26		21 41		21 56		22 11		22 26
Formby	d	19 58		20 13		20 28		20 43		20 58		21 13		21 28		21 43		21 58		22 13		22 28
Hightown	d	20 02		20 17		20 32		20 47		21 02		21 17		21 32		21 47		22 02		22 17		22 32
Hall Road	d	20 05		20 20		20 35		20 50		21 05		21 20		21 35		21 50		22 05		22 20		22 35
Blundellsands & Crosby	d	20 07		20 22		20 37		20 52		21 07		21 22		21 37		21 52		22 07		22 22		22 37
Waterloo (Merseyside)	d	20 10		20 25		20 40		20 55		21 10		21 25		21 40		21 55		22 10		22 25		22 40
Seaforth & Litherland	d	20 12		20 27		20 42		20 57		21 12		21 27		21 42		21 57		22 12		22 27		22 42
Bootle New Strand	d	20 15		20 30		20 45		21 00		21 15		21 30		21 45		22 00		22 15		22 30		22 45
Bootle Oriel Road	d	20 16		20 31		20 46		21 01		21 16		21 31		21 46		22 01		22 16		22 31		22 46
Bank Hall	d	20 18		20 33		20 48		21 03		21 18		21 33		21 48		22 03		22 18		22 33		22 48
Ormskirk	d				20 20				20 50				21 20				21 50				22 20	
Aughton Park	d				20 23				20 53				21 23				21 53				22 23	
Town Green	d				20 25				20 55				21 25				21 55				22 25	
Maghull	d				20 30				21 00				21 30				22 00				22 30	
Old Roan	d				20 33				21 03				21 33				22 03				22 33	
Aintree	d				20 35				21 05				21 35				22 05				22 35	
Orrell Park	d				20 37				21 07				21 37				22 07				22 37	
Walton (Merseyside)	d				20 39				21 09				21 39				22 09				22 39	
Kirkby	d		20 18				20 48				21 18				21 48				22 18			
Fazakerley	d		20 21				20 51				21 21				21 51				22 21			
Rice Lane	d		20 24				20 54				21 24				21 54				22 24			
Kirkdale	d		20 27		20 42		20 57		21 12		21 27		21 42		21 57		22 12		22 27		22 42	
Sandhills	d	20 21	20 30	20 36	20 44	20 51	21 00	21 06	21 14	21 21	21 30	21 36	21 44	21 51	22 00	22 06	22 14	22 21	22 30	22 36	22 44	22 51
Moorfields 10	d	20 25	20 33	20 40	20 48	20 55	21 03	21 10	21 18	21 25	21 33	21 40	21 48	21 55	22 03	22 10	22 18	22 25	22 33	22 40	22 48	22 55
Liverpool Central 10	a	20 28	20 36	20 43	20 50	20 58	21 06	21 13	21 20	21 28	21 36	21 43	21 50	21 58	22 06	22 13	22 20	22 28	22 36	22 43	22 50	22 58
	d	20 29		20 44		20 59		21 14		21 29		21 44		21 59		22 14		22 29		22 44		22 59
Brunswick	d	20 32		20 47		21 02		21 17		21 32		21 47		22 02		22 17		22 32		22 47		23 02
St Michaels	d	20 35		20 50		21 05		21 20		21 35		21 50		22 05		22 20		22 35		22 50		23 05
Aigburth	d	20 37		20 52		21 07		21 22		21 37		21 52		22 07		22 22		22 37		22 52		23 07
Cressington	d	20 39		20 54		21 09		21 24		21 39		21 54		22 09		22 24		22 39		22 54		23 09
Liverpool Sth Parkway 7 89 ✈	d	20 42		20 57		21 12		21 27		21 42		21 57		22 12		22 27		22 42		22 57		23 12
Hunts Cross 89	a	20 47		21 02		21 17		21 32		21 47		22 01		22 17		22 32		22 47		23 02		23 18

		ME	ME	ME	ME	ME	ME	ME	ME
Southport	d		22 28		22 43		22 58		23 16
Birkdale	d		22 32		22 47		23 02		23 20
Hillside	d		22 34		22 49		23 04		23 22
Ainsdale	d		22 37		22 52		23 07		23 25
Freshfield	d		22 41		22 56		23 11		23 29
Formby	d		22 43		22 58		23 13		23 31
Hightown	d		22 47		23 02		23 17		23 35
Hall Road	d		22 50		23 05		23 20		23 38
Blundellsands & Crosby	d		22 52		23 07		23 22		23 40
Waterloo (Merseyside)	d		22 55		23 10		23 25		23 43
Seaforth & Litherland	d		22 57		23 12		23 27		23 45
Bootle New Strand	d		23 00		23 15		23 30		23 48
Bootle Oriel Road	d		23 01		23 16		23 31		23 49
Bank Hall	d		23 03		23 18		23 33		23 51
Ormskirk	d			22 50				23 20	
Aughton Park	d			22 53				23 23	
Town Green	d			22 55				23 25	
Maghull	d			23 00				23 30	
Old Roan	d			23 03				23 33	
Aintree	d			23 05				23 35	
Orrell Park	d			23 07				23 37	
Walton (Merseyside)	d			23 09				23 39	
Kirkby	d	22 48				23 18			
Fazakerley	d	22 51				23 21			
Rice Lane	d	22 54				23 24			
Kirkdale	d	22 57		23 12		23 27		23 42	
Sandhills	d	23 00	23 06	23 14	23 21	23 30	23 36	23 44	23 55
Moorfields 10	d	23 03	23 10	23 18	23 25	23 33	23 40	23 48	23 58
Liverpool Central 10	a	23 06	23 13	23 20	23 28	23 36	23 43	23 50	00 01
	d		23 14		23 29		23 44		
Brunswick	d		23 17		23 32		23 47		
St Michaels	d		23 20		23 35		23 50		
Aigburth	d		23 22		23 37		23 52		
Cressington	d		23 24		23 39		23 54		
Liverpool Sth Parkway 7 89 ✈	d		23 27		23 42		23 57		
Hunts Cross 89	a		23 32		23 47		00 02		

Table 103

Sundays

Southport, Ormskirk and Kirby - Liverpool and Hunts Cross

Network Diagram - see first Page of Table 101

		ME	ME	ME	ME	ME	ME	ME	ME	ME	ME	ME	ME	ME	ME	ME	ME	ME	ME	ME A	ME	ME	ME
Southport	d	22p58	23p16			07 58			08 28			08 58			09 28			09 58		10 13		10 28	
Birkdale	d	23p02	23p20			08 02			08 32			09 02			09 32			10 02		10 17		10 32	
Hillside	d	23p04	23p22			08 04			08 34			09 04			09 34			10 04		10 19		10 34	
Ainsdale	d	23p07	23p25			08 07			08 37			09 07			09 37			10 07		10 22		10 37	
Freshfield	d	23p11	23p29			08 11			08 41			09 11			09 41			10 11		10 26		10 41	
Formby	d	23p13	23p31			08 13			08 43			09 13			09 43			10 13		10 28		10 43	
Hightown	d	23p17	23p35			08 17			08 47			09 17			09 47			10 17		10 32		10 47	
Hall Road	d	23p20	23p38			08 20			08 50			09 20			09 50			10 20		10 35		10 50	
Blundellsands & Crosby	d	23p22	23p40			08 22			08 52			09 22			09 52			10 22		10 37		10 52	
Waterloo (Merseyside)	d	23p25	23p43			08 25			08 55			09 25			09 55			10 25		10 40		10 55	
Seaforth & Litherland	d	23p27	23p45			08 27			08 57			09 27			09 57			10 27		10 42		10 57	
Bootle New Strand	d	23p30	23p48			08 30			09 00			09 30			10 00			10 30		10 45		11 00	
Bootle Oriel Road	d	23p31	23p49			08 31			09 01			09 31			10 01			10 31		10 46		11 01	
Bank Hall	d	23p33	23p51			08 33			09 03			09 33			10 03			10 33		10 48		11 03	
Ormskirk	d						08 20			08 50			09 20			09 50			10 20				10 50
Aughton Park	d						08 23			08 53			09 23			09 53			10 23				10 53
Town Green	d						08 25			08 55			09 25			09 55			10 25				10 55
Maghull	d						08 30			09 00			09 30			10 00			10 30				11 00
Old Roan	d						08 33			09 03			09 33			10 03			10 33				11 03
Aintree	d						08 35			09 05			09 35			10 05			10 35				11 05
Orrell Park	d						08 37			09 07			09 37			10 07			10 37				11 07
Walton (Merseyside)	d						08 39			09 09			09 39			10 09			10 39				11 09
Kirkby	d				08 18			08 48			09 18			09 48			10 18				10 48		
Fazakerley	d				08 21			08 51			09 21			09 51			10 21				10 51		
Rice Lane	d				08 24			08 54			09 24			09 54			10 24				10 54		
Kirkdale	d				08 27		08 42	08 57		09 12	09 27		09 42	09 57		10 12	10 27		10 42		10 57		11 12
Sandhills	d	23p36	23p55		08 30	08 36	08 44	09 00	09 06	09 14	09 30	09 36	09 44	10 00	10 06	10 14	10 30	10 36	10 44	10 51	11 00	11 06	11 14
Moorfields 10	d	23p40	23p58		08 33	08 40	08 48	09 03	09 10	09 18	09 33	09 40	09 48	10 03	10 10	10 18	10 33	10 40	10 48	10 55	11 03	11 10	11 18
Liverpool Central 10	a	23p43	00 01		08 36	08 43	08 50	09 06	09 13	09 20	09 36	09 43	09 50	10 06	10 13	10 20	10 36	10 43	10 50	10 58	11 06	11 13	11 20
	d	23p44		08 14		08 44			09 14			09 44			10 14			10 44				11 14	
Brunswick	d	23p47		08 17		08 47			09 17			09 47			10 17			10 47				11 17	
St Michaels	d	23p50		08 20		08 50			09 20			09 50			10 20			10 50				11 20	
Aigburth	d	23p52		08 22		08 52			09 22			09 52			10 22			10 52				11 22	
Cressington	d	23p54		08 24		08 54			09 24			09 54			10 24			10 54				11 24	
Liverpool Sth Parkway 7 89 ✈	d	23p57		08 27		08 57			09 27			09 57			10 27			10 57				11 27	
Hunts Cross 89	a	00 02		08 32		09 02			09 32			10 02			10 32			11 02				11 32	

		ME A		ME A	ME	ME	ME	ME
Southport	d	10 43		22 43		22 58		23 16
Birkdale	d	10 47		22 47		23 02		23 20
Hillside	d	10 49		22 49		23 04		23 22
Ainsdale	d	10 52		22 52		23 07		23 25
Freshfield	d	10 56		22 56		23 11		23 29
Formby	d	10 58		22 58		23 13		23 31
Hightown	d	11 02		23 02		23 17		23 35
Hall Road	d	11 05		23 05		23 20		23 38
Blundellsands & Crosby	d	11 07		23 07		23 22		23 40
Waterloo (Merseyside)	d	11 10		23 10		23 25		23 43
Seaforth & Litherland	d	11 12		23 12		23 27		23 45
Bootle New Strand	d	11 15		23 15		23 30		23 48
Bootle Oriel Road	d	11 16		23 16		23 31		23 49
Bank Hall	d	11 18	and at	23 18		23 33		23 51
Ormskirk	d		the same				23 20	
Aughton Park	d		minutes				23 23	
Town Green	d		past				23 25	
Maghull	d		each				23 30	
Old Roan	d		hour until				23 33	
Aintree	d						23 35	
Orrell Park	d						23 37	
Walton (Merseyside)	d						23 39	
Kirkby	d				23 18			
Fazakerley	d				23 21			
Rice Lane	d				23 24			
Kirkdale	d				23 27		23 42	
Sandhills	d	11 21		23 21	23 30	23 36	23 44	23 55
Moorfields 10	d	11 25		23 25	23 33	23 40	23 48	23 58
Liverpool Central 10	a	11 28		23 28	23 36	23 43	23 50	00 01
	d					23 44		
Brunswick	d					23 47		
St Michaels	d					23 50		
Aigburth	d					23 52		
Cressington	d					23 54		
Liverpool Sth Parkway 7 89 ✈	d					23 57		
Hunts Cross 89	a					00 02		

A until 23 September

Table 106

Mondays to Saturdays

Liverpool and Birkenhead - New Brighton, West Kirby, Ellesmere Port and Chester

Network Diagram - see first Page of Table 101

Miles	Miles	Miles	Miles			ME A	ME A	ME A	ME A	ME A	ME	ME	ME	ME	ME	ME	ME	ME	ME	ME	ME	ME	ME
0	—	0	0	Moorfields 10	d	23p26	23p31	23p41	23p46	23p56	05 36	05 56	06 06	06 16	06 21	06 26	06 41	06 46	06 51	06 56	07 11	07 16	07 21
0½	—	0½	0½	Liverpool Lime Street 10	d	23p28	23p33	23p43	23p48	23p58	05 38	05 58	06 08	06 18	06 23	06 28	06 43	06 48	06 53	06 58	07 13	07 18	07 23
1	—	1	1	Liverpool Central 10	d	23p30	23p35	23p45	23p50	23p59	05 40	06 00	06 10	06 20	06 25	06 30	06 45	06 50	06 55	07 00	07 15	07 20	07 25
1½	—	1½	1½	James Street	d	23p32	23p37	23p47	23p52	00 02	05 42	06 02	06 12	06 22	06 27	06 32	06 47	06 52	06 57	07 02	07 17	07 22	07 27
2¾	—	2¾	2¾	Hamilton Square	d	23p35	23p40	23p50	23p55	00a05	05 45	06 05	06 15	06 25	06 30	06 35	06 50	06 55	07 00	07 05	07 20	07 25	07 30
—	—	3¼	3¼	Conway Park	d		23p42		23p57					06 27	06 32			06 57	07 02			07 27	07 32
—	—	4	4	Birkenhead Park	d		23p44		23p59					06 29	06 34			06 59	07 04			07 29	07 34
—	—	4¾	4¾	Birkenhead North	d		23p47		00 02					06 32	06 37			07 02	07 07			07 32	07 37
—	—	—	6¼	Wallasey Village	d				00 07					06 37				07 07				07 37	
—	—	—	6½	Wallasey Grove Road	d				00 08					06 38				07 08				07 38	
—	—	—	7¾	**New Brighton**	a				00 13					06 43				07 13				07 43	
—	—	5¼	—	Bidston	d		23p50								06 40				07 10				07 40
—	—	6½	—	Leasowe	d		23p52								06 42				07 12				07 42
—	—	7	—	Moreton (Merseyside)	d		23p54								06 44				07 14				07 44
—	—	8¼	—	Meols	d		23p58								06 48				07 18				07 48
—	—	9½	—	Manor Road	d		23p59								06 50				07 20				07 50
—	—	10	—	Hoylake	d		00 02								06 52				07 22				07 52
—	—	11¼	—	**West Kirby**	a		00 07								06 57				07 27				07 57
3	—	—	—	Birkenhead Central	d	23p37		23p52			05 47	06 07	06 17			06 37	06 52			07 07	07 22		
3¾	—	—	—	Green Lane	d	23p39		23p54			05 49	06 09	06 19			06 39	06 54			07 09	07 24		
4½	—	—	—	Rock Ferry	d	23p42		23p57			05 52	06 12	06 22			06 42	06 57			07 12	07 27		
5½	—	—	—	Bebington	d	23p44		23p59			05 54	06 14	06 24			06 44	06 59			07 14	07 29		
6½	—	—	—	Port Sunlight	d	23p46		00 01			05 56	06 16	06 26			06 46	07 01			07 16	07 31		
7	—	—	—	Spital	d	23p48		00 03			05 58	06 18	06 28			06 48	07 03			07 18	07 33		
7¾	—	—	—	Bromborough Rake	d	23p50		00 05			06 00	06 20	06 30			06 50	07 05			07 20	07 35		
8½	—	—	—	Bromborough	d	23p52		00 07			06 02	06 22	06 32			06 52	07 07			07 22	07 37		
9	—	—	—	Eastham Rake	d	23p55		00 10			06 05	06 25	06 35			06 55	07 10			07 25	07 40		
10	0	—	—	Hooton	d	23p57		00 12			06 07	06 27	06 37			06 57	07 12			07 27	07 42		
—	1½	—	—	Little Sutton	d	00 01						06 31				07 01				07 31			
—	2½	—	—	Overpool	d	00 03						06 33				07 03				07 33			
—	4	—	—	**Ellesmere Port**	a	00 07						06 38				07 08				07 38			
13	—	—	—	Capenhurst	d			00 17			06 12		06 42				07 17				07 47		
16¾	—	—	—	Bache	d			00 22			06 17		06 47				07 22				07 52		
18¼	—	—	—	**Chester**	a			00 26			06 26		06 56				07 26				07 56		

		ME	ME	ME	ME	ME	ME	ME SX	ME SO	ME	ME SX	ME	ME SX	ME	ME	ME SX	ME	ME	ME	ME SX	ME	ME SO	ME SX
Moorfields 10	d	07 26	07 31	07 36	07 41	07 46	07 51	07 53	07 56	08 01	08 03	08 06		08 11	08 16	08 18	08 21	08 26	08 31	08 33	08 36	08 41	08 41
Liverpool Lime Street 10	d	07 28	07 33	07 38	07 43	07 48	07 53	07 55	07 58	08 03	08 05	08 08		08 13	08 18	08 20	08 23	08 28	08 33	08 35	08 38	08 43	08 43
Liverpool Central 10	d	07 30	07 35	07 40	07 45	07 50	07 55	07 57	08 00	08 05	08a07	08 10		08 15	08 20	08 22	08 25	08 30	08 35	08 37	08 40	08 45	08 45
James Street	d	07 32	07 37	07 42	07 47	07 52	07 57	07 59	08 02	08 07		08 12		08 17	08 22	08 24	08 27	08 32	08 37	08 39	08 42	08 47	08 47
Hamilton Square	d	07 35	07 40	07 45	07 50	07 55	08 00	08 02	08 05	08 10		08 15		08 20	08 25	08 27	08 30	08 35	08 40	08 42	08 45	08 50	08 50
Conway Park	d		07 42	07 47		07 57	08 02			08 12		08 17			08 27		08 32		08 42		08 47		
Birkenhead Park	d		07 44	07 49		07 59	08 04			08 14		08 19			08 29		08 34		08 44		08 49		
Birkenhead North	d		07 47	07 52		08 02	08 07			08 17		08 22			08 32		08 37		08 47		08 52		
Wallasey Village	d		07 52			08 07				08 22					08 37				08 52				
Wallasey Grove Road	d		07 53			08 08				08 23					08 38				08 53				
New Brighton	a		07 58			08 13				08 28					08 43				08 58				
Bidston	d			07 55			08 10					08 25					08 40				08 55		
Leasowe	d			07 57			08 12					08 27					08 42				08 57		
Moreton (Merseyside)	d			07 59			08 14					08 29					08 44				08 59		
Meols	d			08 03			08 18					08 33					08 48				09 03		
Manor Road	d			08 05			08 20					08 35					08 50				09 05		
Hoylake	d			08 07			08 22					08 37					08 52				09 07		
West Kirby	a			08 12			08 27					08 42					08 57				09 12		
Birkenhead Central	d	07 37			07 52			08 05	08 07					08 22		08 30		08 37		08a44		08 52	08 53
Green Lane	d	07 39			07 54			08 07	08 09					08 24		08 32		08 39				08 54	08 55
Rock Ferry	d	07 42			07 57			08 09	08 12					08 27		08 34		08 42				08 57	08 57
Bebington	d	07 44			07 59			08 12	08 14					08 29		08 37		08 44				08 59	09 00
Port Sunlight	d	07 46			08 01			08 14	08 16					08 31		08 39		08 46				09 01	09 02
Spital	d	07 48			08 03			08 16	08 18					08 33		08 41		08 48				09 03	09 04
Bromborough Rake	d	07 50			08 05			08 18	08 20					08 35		08 43		08 50				09 05	09 06
Bromborough	d	07 52			08 07			08 20	08 22					08 37		08 45		08 52				09 07	09 08
Eastham Rake	d	07 55			08 10			08 22	08 25					08 40		08 47		08 55				09 10	09 10
Hooton	d	07 57			08 12			08 24	08 27				08 29	08 42		08 49		08 57				09 12	09 12
Little Sutton	d	08 01							08 31				08 34					09 01					
Overpool	d	08 03							08 33				08 36					09 03					
Ellesmere Port	a	08 08							08 38				08 39					09 08					
Capenhurst	d				08 17			08 29						08 47		08 54						09 17	09 17
Bache	d				08 22			08 35						08 52		09 00						09 22	09 23
Chester	a				08 27			08 38						08 57		09 06						09 27	09 27

A not 14 May

Liverpool and Birkenhead - New Brighton, West Kirby, Ellesmere Port and Chester

Network Diagram - see first Page of Table 101

		ME	ME SX	ME SO	ME	ME SO	ME SX	ME	ME	ME	ME	ME SO	ME SX	ME	ME	ME	ME	ME	ME	ME	ME	ME	ME
Moorfields	d	08 46	08 48	08 48	08 51	08 56	08 56	09 01	09 06	09 11	09 16	09 18	09 19	09 21	09 26	09 31	09 36	09 41	09 46	09 48	09 51	09 56	10 01
Liverpool Lime Street	d	08 48	08 50	08 50	08 53	08 58	08 58	09 03	09 08	09 13	09 18	09 20	09 21	09 23	09 28	09 33	09 38	09 43	09 48	09 50	09 53	09 58	10 03
Liverpool Central	d	08 50	08 52	08 52	08 55	09 00	09 00	09 05	09 10	09 15	09 20	09 22	09 23	09 25	09 30	09 35	09 40	09 45	09 50	09 52	09 55	10 00	10 05
James Street	d	08 52	08 54	08 54	08 57	09 02	09 02	09 07	09 12	09 17	09 22	09 24	09 25	09 27	09 32	09 37	09 42	09 47	09 52	09 54	09 57	10 02	10 07
Hamilton Square	d	08 55	08 57	08 57	09 00	09 05	09 05	09 10	09 15	09 20	09 25	09 27	09 28	09 30	09 35	09 40	09 45	09 50	09 55	09 57	10 00	10 05	10 10
Conway Park	d	08 57	09 00		09 02			09 12	09 17		09 27			09 32		09 42	09 47		09 57		10 02		10 12
Birkenhead Park	d	08 59	09 02		09 04			09 14	09 19		09 29			09 34		09 44	09 49		09 59		10 04		10 14
Birkenhead North	d	09 02	09a05		09 07			09 17	09 22		09 32			09 37		09 47	09 52		10 02		10 07		10 17
Wallasey Village	d	09 07						09 22			09 37					09 52			10 07				10 22
Wallasey Grove Road	d	09 08						09 23			09 38					09 53			10 08				10 23
New Brighton	a	09 13						09 28			09 43					09 58			10 13				10 28
Bidston	d				09 10				09 25					09 40			09 55				10 10		
Leasowe	d				09 12				09 27					09 42			09 57				10 12		
Moreton (Merseyside)	d				09 14				09 29					09 44			09 59				10 14		
Meols	d				09 18				09 33					09 48			10 03				10 18		
Manor Road	d				09 20				09 35					09 50			10 05				10 20		
Hoylake	d				09 22				09 37					09 52			10 07				10 22		
West Kirby	a				09 27				09 42					09 57			10 12				10 27		
Birkenhead Central	d			09 00		09 07	09 07			09 22		09 30	09 30		09 37			09 52		10 00		10 07	
Green Lane	d			09 02		09 09	09 09			09 24		09 32	09 32		09 39			09 54		10 02		10 09	
Rock Ferry	d			09 04		09 12	09 12			09 27		09 34	09 35		09 42			09 57		10 04		10 12	
Bebington	d			09 07		09 14	09 14			09 29		09 37	09 37		09 44			09 59		10 07		10 14	
Port Sunlight	d			09 09		09 16	09 16			09 31		09 39	09 39		09 46			10 01		10 09		10 16	
Spital	d			09 11		09 18	09 18			09 33		09 41	09 41		09 48			10 03		10 11		10 18	
Bromborough Rake	d			09 13		09 20	09 20			09 35		09 43	09 43		09 50			10 05		10 13		10 20	
Bromborough	d			09 15		09 22	09 22			09 37		09 45	09 45		09 52			10 07		10 15		10 22	
Eastham Rake	d			09 17		09 25	09 25			09 40		09 47	09 48		09 55			10 10		10 17		10 25	
Hooton	d			09 19		09 27	09 27			09 42		09 49	09 50		09 57			10 12		10 19		10 27	
Little Sutton	d			09 24			09 31					09 54	09 54							10 24			
Overpool	d			09 26			09 33					09 56	09 56							10 26			
Ellesmere Port	a			09 32			09 38					10 00	10 00							10 30			
Capenhurst	d									09 47								10 17					
Bache	d					09 36				09 52					10 06			10 22				10 36	
Chester	a					09 41				09 57					10 11			10 27				10 41	

		ME	ME	ME	ME	ME	ME	ME	ME	ME	ME	ME	ME	ME	ME	ME	ME	ME	ME	ME	ME	ME
Moorfields	d	10 06	10 11	10 16	10 18	10 21	10 26	10 31	10 36	10 41	10 46	10 48	10 51	10 56	11 01	11 06	11 11	11 16	11 18	11 21	11 26	11 31
Liverpool Lime Street	d	10 08	10 13	10 18	10 20	10 23	10 28	10 33	10 38	10 43	10 48	10 50	10 53	10 58	11 03	11 08	11 13	11 18	11 20	11 23	11 28	11 33
Liverpool Central	d	10 10	10 15	10 20	10 22	10 25	10 30	10 35	10 40	10 45	10 50	10 52	10 55	11 00	11 05	11 10	11 15	11 20	11 22	11 25	11 30	11 35
James Street	d	10 12	10 17	10 22	10 24	10 27	10 32	10 37	10 42	10 47	10 52	10 54	10 57	11 02	11 07	11 12	11 17	11 22	11 24	11 27	11 32	11 37
Hamilton Square	d	10 15	10 20	10 25	10 27	10 30	10 35	10 40	10 45	10 50	10 55	10 57	11 00	11 05	11 10	11 15	11 20	11 25	11 27	11 30	11 35	11 40
Conway Park	d	10 17		10 27		10 32		10 42	10 47		10 57		11 02		11 12	11 17		11 27		11 32		11 42
Birkenhead Park	d	10 19		10 29		10 34		10 44	10 49		10 59		11 04		11 14	11 19		11 29		11 34		11 44
Birkenhead North	d	10 22		10 32		10 37		10 47	10 52		11 02		11 07		11 17	11 22		11 32		11 37		11 47
Wallasey Village	d			10 37				10 52			11 07				11 22			11 37				11 52
Wallasey Grove Road	d			10 38				10 53			11 08				11 23			11 38				11 53
New Brighton	a			10 43				10 58			11 13				11 28			11 43				11 58
Bidston	d	10 25				10 40			10 55				11 10			11 25				11 40		
Leasowe	d	10 27				10 42			10 57				11 12			11 27				11 42		
Moreton (Merseyside)	d	10 29				10 44			10 59				11 14			11 29				11 44		
Meols	d	10 33				10 48			11 03				11 18			11 33				11 48		
Manor Road	d	10 35				10 50			11 05				11 20			11 35				11 50		
Hoylake	d	10 37				10 52			11 07				11 22			11 37				11 52		
West Kirby	a	10 42				10 57			11 12				11 27			11 42				11 57		
Birkenhead Central	d		10 22		10 30		10 37			10 52		11 00		11 07			11 22		11 30		11 37	
Green Lane	d		10 24		10 32		10 39			10 54		11 02		11 09			11 24		11 32		11 39	
Rock Ferry	d		10 27		10 34		10 42			10 57		11 04		11 12			11 27		11 34		11 42	
Bebington	d		10 29		10 37		10 44			10 59		11 07		11 14			11 29		11 37		11 44	
Port Sunlight	d		10 31		10 39		10 46			11 01		11 09		11 16			11 31		11 39		11 46	
Spital	d		10 33		10 41		10 48			11 03		11 11		11 18			11 33		11 41		11 48	
Bromborough Rake	d		10 35		10 43		10 50			11 05		11 13		11 20			11 35		11 43		11 50	
Bromborough	d		10 37		10 45		10 52			11 07		11 15		11 22			11 37		11 45		11 52	
Eastham Rake	d		10 40		10 47		10 55			11 10		11 17		11 25			11 40		11 47		11 55	
Hooton	d		10 42		10 49		10 57			11 12		11 19		11 27			11 42		11 49		11 57	
Little Sutton	d				10 54							11 24							11 54			
Overpool	d				10 56							11 26							11 56			
Ellesmere Port	a				11 00							11 30							12 00			
Capenhurst	d		10 47							11 17							11 47					
Bache	d		10 52				11 06			11 22				11 36			11 52				12 06	
Chester	a		10 57				11 11			11 27				11 41			11 57				12 11	

Liverpool and Birkenhead - New Brighton, West Kirby, Ellesmere Port and Chester

Network Diagram - see first Page of Table 101

		ME	ME	ME	ME	ME	ME	ME	ME	ME	ME	ME	ME	ME	ME	ME	ME	ME	ME	ME	ME	ME	ME
Moorfields	d	11 36	11 41	11 46	11 48	11 51	11 56	12 01	12 06	12 11	12 16	12 18	12 21	12 26	12 31	12 36	12 41	12 46	12 48	12 51	12 56	13 01	13 06
Liverpool Lime Street	d	11 38	11 43	11 48	11 50	11 53	11 58	12 03	12 08	12 13	12 18	12 20	12 23	12 28	12 33	12 38	12 43	12 48	12 50	12 53	12 58	13 03	13 08
Liverpool Central	d	11 40	11 45	11 50	11 52	11 55	12 00	12 05	12 10	12 15	12 20	12 22	12 25	12 30	12 35	12 40	12 45	12 50	12 52	12 55	13 00	13 05	13 10
James Street	d	11 42	11 47	11 52	11 54	11 57	12 02	12 07	12 12	12 17	12 22	12 24	12 27	12 32	12 37	12 42	12 47	12 52	12 54	12 57	13 02	13 07	13 12
Hamilton Square	d	11 45	11 50	11 55	11 57	12 00	12 05	12 10	12 15	12 20	12 25	12 27	12 30	12 35	12 40	12 45	12 50	12 55	12 57	13 00	13 05	13 10	13 15
Conway Park	d	11 47		11 57		12 02		12 12	12 17		12 27		12 32		12 42	12 47		12 57		13 02		13 12	13 17
Birkenhead Park	d	11 49		11 59		12 04		12 14	12 19		12 29		12 34		12 44	12 49		12 59		13 04		13 14	13 19
Birkenhead North	d	11 52		12 02		12 07		12 17	12 22		12 32		12 37		12 47	12 52		13 02		13 07		13 17	13 22
Wallasey Village	d			12 07				12 22			12 37				12 52			13 07				13 22	
Wallasey Grove Road	d			12 08				12 23			12 38				12 53			13 08				13 23	
New Brighton	a			12 13				12 28			12 43				12 58			13 13				13 28	
Bidston	d	11 55				12 10			12 25				12 40			12 55				13 10			13 25
Leasowe	d	11 57				12 12			12 27				12 42			12 57				13 12			13 27
Moreton (Merseyside)	d	11 59				12 14			12 29				12 44			12 59				13 14			13 29
Meols	d	12 03				12 18			12 33				12 48			13 03				13 18			13 33
Manor Road	d	12 05				12 20			12 35				12 50			13 05				13 20			13 35
Hoylake	d	12 07				12 22			12 37				12 52			13 07				13 22			13 37
West Kirby	a	12 12				12 27			12 42				12 57			13 12				13 27			13 42
Birkenhead Central	d		11 52		12 00		12 07			12 22		12 30		12 37			12 52		13 00		13 07		
Green Lane	d		11 54		12 02		12 09			12 24		12 32		12 39			12 54		13 02		13 09		
Rock Ferry	d		11 57		12 04		12 12			12 27		12 34		12 42			12 57		13 04		13 12		
Bebington	d		11 59		12 07		12 14			12 29		12 37		12 44			12 59		13 07		13 14		
Port Sunlight	d		12 01		12 09		12 16			12 31		12 39		12 46			13 01		13 09		13 16		
Spital	d		12 03		12 11		12 18			12 33		12 41		12 48			13 03		13 11		13 18		
Bromborough Rake	d		12 05		12 13		12 20			12 35		12 43		12 50			13 05		13 13		13 20		
Bromborough	d		12 07		12 15		12 22			12 37		12 45		12 52			13 07		13 15		13 22		
Eastham Rake	d		12 10		12 17		12 25			12 40		12 47		12 55			13 10		13 17		13 25		
Hooton	d		12 12		12 19		12 27			12 42		12 49		12 57			13 12		13 19		13 27		
Little Sutton	d				12 24							12 54							13 24				
Overpool	d				12 26							12 56							13 26				
Ellesmere Port	a				12 31							13 00							13 30				
Capenhurst	d		12 17							12 47							13 17						
Bache	d		12 22				12 36			12 52				13 06			13 22				13 36		
Chester	a		12 27				12 41			12 57				13 11			13 27				13 41		

		ME	ME	ME	ME	ME	ME	ME	ME	ME	ME	ME	ME	ME	ME	ME	ME	ME	ME	ME	ME	ME
Moorfields	d	13 11	13 16	13 18	13 21	13 26	13 31	13 36	13 41	13 46	13 48	13 51	13 56	14 01	14 06	14 11	14 16	14 18	14 21	14 26	14 31	14 36
Liverpool Lime Street	d	13 13	13 18	13 20	13 23	13 28	13 33	13 38	13 43	13 48	13 50	13 53	13 58	14 03	14 08	14 13	14 18	14 20	14 23	14 28	14 33	14 38
Liverpool Central	d	13 15	13 20	13 22	13 25	13 30	13 35	13 40	13 45	13 50	13 52	13 55	14 00	14 05	14 10	14 15	14 20	14 22	14 25	14 30	14 35	14 40
James Street	d	13 17	13 22	13 24	13 27	13 32	13 37	13 42	13 47	13 52	13 54	13 57	14 02	14 07	14 12	14 17	14 22	14 24	14 27	14 32	14 37	14 42
Hamilton Square	d	13 20	13 25	13 27	13 30	13 35	13 40	13 45	13 50	13 55	13 57	14 00	14 05	14 10	14 15	14 20	14 25	14 27	14 30	14 35	14 40	14 45
Conway Park	d		13 27		13 32		13 42	13 47		13 57		14 02		14 12	14 17		14 27		14 32		14 42	14 47
Birkenhead Park	d		13 29		13 34		13 44	13 49		13 59		14 04		14 14	14 19		14 29		14 34		14 44	14 49
Birkenhead North	d		13 32		13 37		13 47	13 52		14 02		14 07		14 17	14 22		14 32		14 37		14 47	14 52
Wallasey Village	d		13 37				13 52			14 07				14 22			14 37				14 52	
Wallasey Grove Road	d		13 38				13 53			14 08				14 23			14 38				14 53	
New Brighton	a		13 43				13 58			14 13				14 28			14 43				14 58	
Bidston	d				13 40			13 55				14 10			14 25				14 40			14 55
Leasowe	d				13 42			13 57				14 12			14 27				14 42			14 57
Moreton (Merseyside)	d				13 44			13 59				14 14			14 29				14 44			14 59
Meols	d				13 48			14 03				14 18			14 33				14 48			15 03
Manor Road	d				13 50			14 05				14 20			14 35				14 50			15 05
Hoylake	d				13 52			14 07				14 22			14 37				14 52			15 07
West Kirby	a				13 57			14 12				14 27			14 42				14 57			15 12
Birkenhead Central	d	13 22		13 30		13 37			13 52		14 00		14 07			14 22		14 30		14 37		
Green Lane	d	13 24		13 32		13 39			13 54		14 02		14 09			14 24		14 32		14 39		
Rock Ferry	d	13 27		13 34		13 42			13 57		14 04		14 12			14 27		14 34		14 42		
Bebington	d	13 29		13 37		13 44			13 59		14 07		14 14			14 29		14 37		14 44		
Port Sunlight	d	13 31		13 39		13 46			14 01		14 09		14 16			14 31		14 39		14 46		
Spital	d	13 33		13 41		13 48			14 03		14 11		14 18			14 33		14 41		14 48		
Bromborough Rake	d	13 35		13 43		13 50			14 05		14 13		14 20			14 35		14 43		14 50		
Bromborough	d	13 37		13 45		13 52			14 07		14 15		14 22			14 37		14 45		14 52		
Eastham Rake	d	13 40		13 47		13 55			14 10		14 17		14 25			14 40		14 47		14 55		
Hooton	d	13 42		13 49		13 57			14 12		14 19		14 27			14 42		14 49		14 57		
Little Sutton	d			13 54							14 24							14 54				
Overpool	d			13 56							14 26							14 56				
Ellesmere Port	a			14 00							14 30							15 00				
Capenhurst	d	13 47							14 17							14 47						
Bache	d	13 52				14 06			14 22				14 36			14 52				15 06		
Chester	a	13 57				14 11			14 27				14 41			14 57				15 11		

Liverpool and Birkenhead - New Brighton, West Kirby, Ellesmere Port and Chester

Network Diagram - see first Page of Table 101

		ME	ME	ME	ME	ME	ME	ME	ME	ME	ME	ME	ME	ME	ME	ME	ME	ME	ME	ME	ME	ME SX	ME
Moorfields 10	d	14 41	14 46	14 48	14 51	14 56	15 01	15 06	15 11	15 16	15 18	15 21	15 26	15 31	15 36	15 41	15 46	15 48	15 51	15 56	16 01	16 03	16 06
Liverpool Lime Street 10	d	14 43	14 48	14 50	14 53	14 58	15 03	15 08	15 13	15 18	15 20	15 23	15 28	15 33	15 38	15 43	15 48	15 50	15 53	15 58	16 03	16 05	16 08
Liverpool Central 10	d	14 45	14 50	14 52	14 55	15 00	15 05	15 10	15 15	15 20	15 22	15 25	15 30	15 35	15 40	15 45	15 50	15 52	15 55	16 00	16 05	16 07	16 10
James Street	d	14 47	14 52	14 54	14 57	15 02	15 07	15 12	15 17	15 22	15 24	15 27	15 32	15 37	15 42	15 47	15 52	15 54	15 57	16 02	16 07	16 09	16 12
Hamilton Square	d	14 50	14 55	14 57	15 00	15 05	15 10	15 15	15 20	15 25	15 27	15 30	15 35	15 40	15 45	15 50	15 55	15 57	16 00	16 05	16 10	16 12	16 15
Conway Park	d		14 57		15 02		15 12	15 17		15 27		15 32		15 42	15 47		15 57		16 02		16 12		16 17
Birkenhead Park	d		14 59		15 04		15 14	15 19		15 29		15 34		15 44	15 49		15 59		16 04		16 14		16 19
Birkenhead North	d		15 02		15 07		15 17	15 22		15 32		15 37		15 47	15 52		16 02		16 07		16 17		16 22
Wallasey Village	d		15 07				15 22			15 37				15 52			16 07				16 22		
Wallasey Grove Road	d		15 08				15 23			15 38				15 53			16 08				16 23		
New Brighton	a		15 13				15 28			15 43				15 58			16 13				16 28		
Bidston	d				15 10			15 25				15 40			15 55				16 10				16 25
Leasowe	d				15 12			15 27				15 42			15 57				16 12				16 27
Moreton (Merseyside)	d				15 14			15 29				15 44			15 59				16 14				16 29
Meols	d				15 18			15 33				15 48			16 03				16 18				16 33
Manor Road	d				15 20			15 35				15 50			16 05				16 20				16 35
Hoylake	d				15 22			15 37				15 52			16 07				16 22				16 37
West Kirby	a				15 27			15 42				15 57			16 12				16 27				16 42
Birkenhead Central	d	14 52		15 00		15 07			15 22		15 30		15 37			15 52		16 00		16 07		16 15	
Green Lane	d	14 54		15 02		15 09			15 24		15 32		15 39			15 54		16 02		16 09		16 17	
Rock Ferry	d	14 57		15 04		15 12			15 27		15 34		15 42			15 57		16 04		16 12		16 19	
Bebington	d	14 59		15 07		15 14			15 29		15 37		15 44			15 59		16 07		16 14		16 22	
Port Sunlight	d	15 01		15 09		15 16			15 31		15 39		15 46			16 01		16 09		16 16		16 24	
Spital	d	15 03		15 11		15 18			15 33		15 41		15 48			16 03		16 11		16 18		16 26	
Bromborough Rake	d	15 05		15 13		15 20			15 35		15 43		15 50			16 05		16 13		16 20		16 28	
Bromborough	d	15 07		15 15		15 22			15 37		15 45		15 52			16 07		16 15		16 22		16 30	
Eastham Rake	d	15 10		15 17		15 25			15 40		15 47		15 55			16 10		16 17		16 25		16 32	
Hooton	d	15 12		15 19		15 27			15 42		15 49		15 57			16 12		16 19		16 27		16a34	
Little Sutton	d			15 24							15 54							16 24					
Overpool	d			15 26							15 56							16 26					
Ellesmere Port	a			15 30							16 00							16 30					
Capenhurst	d	15 17							15 47							16 17							
Bache	d	15 22				15 36			15 52				16 06			16 22				16 36			
Chester	a	15 27				15 41			15 57				16 11			16 27				16 41			

		ME	ME	ME	ME	ME	ME	ME SX	ME	ME	ME	ME	ME	ME SO	ME SX	ME	ME SX	ME	ME	ME	ME	ME	ME SO
Moorfields 10	d	16 11	16 16	16 18	16 21	16 26	16 31	16 33	16 36	16 41	16 46	16 48	16 51	16 56	16 56	17 01	17 03	17 06	17 11	17 16	17 18	17 21	17 26
Liverpool Lime Street 10	d	16 13	16 18	16 20	16 23	16 28	16 33	16 35	16 38	16 43	16 48	16 50	16 53	16 58	16 58	17 03	17 05	17 08	17 13	17 18	17 20	17 23	17 28
Liverpool Central 10	d	16 15	16 20	16 22	16 25	16 30	16 35	16 37	16 40	16 45	16 50	16 52	16 55	17 00	17 00	17 05	17 07	17 10	17 15	17 20	17 22	17 25	17 30
James Street	d	16 17	16 22	16 24	16 27	16 32	16 37	16 39	16 42	16 47	16 52	16 54	16 57	17 02	17 02	17 07	17 09	17 12	17 17	17 22	17 24	17 27	17 32
Hamilton Square	d	16 20	16 25	16 27	16 30	16 35	16 40	16 42	16 45	16 50	16 55	16 57	17 00	17 05	17 05	17 10	17 12	17 15	17 20	17 25	17 27	17 30	17 35
Conway Park	d		16 27		16 32		16 42		16 47		16 57		17 02			17 12		17 17		17 27		17 32	
Birkenhead Park	d		16 29		16 34		16 44		16 49		16 59		17 04			17 14		17 19		17 29		17 34	
Birkenhead North	d		16 32		16 37		16 47		16 52		17 02		17 07			17 17		17 22		17 32		17 37	
Wallasey Village	d		16 37				16 52				17 07					17 22				17 37			
Wallasey Grove Road	d		16 38				16 53				17 08					17 23				17 38			
New Brighton	a		16 43				16 58				17 13					17 28				17 43			
Bidston	d				16 40				16 55				17 10					17 25				17 40	
Leasowe	d				16 42				16 57				17 12					17 27				17 42	
Moreton (Merseyside)	d				16 44				16 59				17 14					17 29				17 44	
Meols	d				16 48				17 03				17 18					17 33				17 48	
Manor Road	d				16 50				17 05				17 20					17 35				17 50	
Hoylake	d				16 52				17 07				17 22					17 37				17 52	
West Kirby	a				16 57				17 12				17 27					17 42				17 57	
Birkenhead Central	d	16 22		16 30		16 37		16 45		16 52		17 00		17 07	17 07		17 15		17 22		17 30		17 37
Green Lane	d	16 24		16 32		16 39		16 47		16 54		17 02		17 09	17 09		17 17		17 24		17 32		17 39
Rock Ferry	d	16 27		16 34		16 42		16 49		16 57		17 04		17 12	17 12		17 19		17 27		17 34		17 42
Bebington	d	16 29		16 37		16 44		16 52		16 59		17 07		17 14	17 14		17 22		17 29		17 37		17 44
Port Sunlight	d	16 31		16 39		16 46		16 54		17 01		17 09		17 16	17 16		17 24		17 31		17 39		17 46
Spital	d	16 33		16 41		16 48		16 56		17 03		17 11		17 18	17 18		17 26		17 33		17 41		17 48
Bromborough Rake	d	16 35		16 43		16 50		16 58		17 05		17 13		17 20	17 20		17 28		17 35		17 43		17 50
Bromborough	d	16 37		16 45		16 52		17 00		17 07		17 15		17 22	17 22		17 30		17 37		17 45		17 52
Eastham Rake	d	16 40		16 47		16 55		17 02		17 10		17 17		17 25	17 25		17 32		17 40		17 47		17 55
Hooton	d	16 42		16 49		16 57		17 04		17 12		17 19		17 27	17 27		17 34		17 42		17 49		17 57
Little Sutton	d			16 54				17 09				17 24					17 39				17 54		
Overpool	d			16 56				17 11				17 26					17 41				17 56		
Ellesmere Port	a			17 00				17 16				17 30					17 46				18 00		
Capenhurst	d	16 47								17 17					17 32				17 47				
Bache	d	16 52				17 06				17 22				17 36	17 37				17 52				18 06
Chester	a	16 57				17 11				17 27				17 41	17 41				17 57				18 11

Liverpool and Birkenhead - New Brighton, West Kirby, Ellesmere Port and Chester

Network Diagram - see first Page of Table 101

		ME SX	ME	ME SX	ME	ME	ME	ME	ME	ME	ME	ME	ME	ME	ME	ME	ME	ME	ME	ME	ME	ME
Moorfields 10	d	17 26	17 31	17 33	17 36	17 41	17 46	17 48	17 51	17 56	18 01	18 06	18 11	18 16	18 18	18 21	18 26	18 31	18 36	18 41	18 46	18 48
Liverpool Lime Street 10	d	17 28	17 33	17 35	17 38	17 43	17 48	17 50	17 53	17 58	18 03	18 08	18 13	18 18	18 20	18 23	18 28	18 33	18 38	18 43	18 48	18 50
Liverpool Central 10	d	17 30	17 35	17 37	17 40	17 45	17 50	17 52	17 55	18 00	18 05	18 10	18 15	18 20	18 22	18 25	18 30	18 35	18 40	18 45	18 50	18 52
James Street	d	17 32	17 37	17 39	17 42	17 47	17 52	17 54	17 57	18 02	18 07	18 12	18 17	18 22	18 24	18 27	18 32	18 37	18 42	18 47	18 52	18 54
Hamilton Square	d	17 35	17 40	17 42	17 45	17 50	17 55	17 57	18 00	18 05	18 10	18 15	18 20	18 25	18 27	18 30	18 35	18 40	18 45	18 50	18 55	18 57
Conway Park	d		17 42		17 47		17 57		18 02		18 12	18 17		18 27		18 32		18 42	18 47		18 57	
Birkenhead Park	d		17 44		17 49		17 59		18 04		18 14	18 19		18 29		18 34		18 44	18 49		18 59	
Birkenhead North	d		17 47		17 52		18 02		18 07		18 17	18 22		18 32		18 37		18 47	18 52		19 02	
Wallasey Village	d		17 52				18 07				18 22			18 37				18 52			19 07	
Wallasey Grove Road	d		17 53				18 08				18 23			18 38				18 53			19 08	
New Brighton	a		17 58				18 13				18 28			18 43				18 58			19 13	
Bidston	d				17 55				18 10			18 25				18 40			18 55			
Leasowe	d				17 57				18 12			18 27				18 42			18 57			
Moreton (Merseyside)	d				17 59				18 14			18 29				18 44			18 59			
Meols	d				18 03				18 18			18 33				18 48			19 03			
Manor Road	d				18 05				18 20			18 35				18 50			19 05			
Hoylake	d				18 07				18 22			18 37				18 52			19 07			
West Kirby	a				18 12				18 27			18 42				18 57			19 12			
Birkenhead Central	d	17 37		17 45		17 52		18 00		18 07			18 22		18 30		18 37			18 52		19 00
Green Lane	d	17 39		17 47		17 54		18 02		18 09			18 24		18 32		18 39			18 54		19 02
Rock Ferry	d	17 42		17 49		17 57		18 04		18 12			18 27		18 34		18 42			18 57		19 04
Bebington	d	17 44		17 52		17 59		18 07		18 14			18 29		18 37		18 44			18 59		19 07
Port Sunlight	d	17 46		17 54		18 01		18 09		18 16			18 31		18 39		18 46			19 01		19 09
Spital	d	17 48		17 56		18 03		18 11		18 18			18 33		18 41		18 48			19 03		19 11
Bromborough Rake	d	17 50		17 58		18 05		18 13		18 20			18 35		18 43		18 50			19 05		19 13
Bromborough	d	17 52		18 00		18 07		18 15		18 22			18 37		18 45		18 52			19 07		19 15
Eastham Rake	d	17 55		18 02		18 10		18 17		18 25			18 40		18 47		18 55			19 10		19 17
Hooton	d	17 57		18 04		18 12		18 19		18 27			18 42		18 49		18 57			19 12		19 19
Little Sutton	d			18 09				18 24							18 54							19 24
Overpool	d			18 11				18 26							18 56							19 26
Ellesmere Port	a			18 16				18 30							19 00							19 30
Capenhurst	d	18 02				18 17							18 47							19 17		
Bache	d	18 07				18 22				18 36			18 52				19 06			19 22		
Chester	a	18 11				18 26				18 39			18 56				19 10			19 26		

		ME	ME	ME	ME	ME	ME	ME	ME	ME	ME	ME	ME	ME	ME	ME	ME	ME	ME	ME	ME	ME	ME
Moorfields 10	d	18 51	18 56	19 01	19 06	19 11	19 16	19 26	19 31	19 41	19 46	19 56	20 01	20 11	20 16	20 26	20 31	20 41	20 46	20 56	21 01	21 11	21 16
Liverpool Lime Street 10	d	18 53	18 58	19 03	19 08	19 13	19 18	19 28	19 33	19 43	19 48	19 58	20 03	20 13	20 18	20 28	20 33	20 43	20 48	20 58	21 03	21 13	21 18
Liverpool Central 10	d	18 55	19 00	19 05	19 10	19 15	19 20	19 30	19 35	19 45	19 50	20 00	20 05	20 15	20 20	20 30	20 35	20 45	20 50	21 00	21 05	21 15	21 20
James Street	d	18 57	19 02	19 07	19 12	19 17	19 22	19 32	19 37	19 47	19 52	20 02	20 07	20 17	20 22	20 32	20 37	20 47	20 52	21 02	21 07	21 17	21 22
Hamilton Square	d	19 00	19 05	19 10	19 15	19 20	19 25	19 35	19 40	19 50	19 55	20 05	20 10	20 20	20 25	20 35	20 40	20 50	20 55	21 05	21 10	21 20	21 25
Conway Park	d	19 02		19 12	19 17		19 27		19 42		19 57		20 12		20 27		20 42		20 57		21 12		21 27
Birkenhead Park	d	19 04		19 14	19 19		19 29		19 44		19 59		20 14		20 29		20 44		20 59		21 14		21 29
Birkenhead North	d	19 07		19 17	19 22		19 32		19 47		20 02		20 17		20 32		20 47		21 02		21 17		21 32
Wallasey Village	d			19 22			19 37				20 07				20 37				21 07				21 37
Wallasey Grove Road	d			19 23			19 38				20 08				20 38				21 08				21 38
New Brighton	a			19 28			19 43				20 13				20 43				21 13				21 43
Bidston	d	19 10			19 25				19 50				20 20				20 50				21 20		
Leasowe	d	19 12			19 27				19 52				20 22				20 52				21 22		
Moreton (Merseyside)	d	19 14			19 29				19 54				20 24				20 54				21 24		
Meols	d	19 18			19 33				19 58				20 28				20 58				21 28		
Manor Road	d	19 20			19 35				20 00				20 30				21 00				21 30		
Hoylake	d	19 22			19 37				20 02				20 32				21 02				21 32		
West Kirby	a	19 27			19 42				20 07				20 37				21 07				21 37		
Birkenhead Central	d		19 07			19 22		19 37		19 52		20 07		20 22		20 37		20 52		21 07		21 22	
Green Lane	d		19 09			19 24		19 39		19 54		20 09		20 24		20 39		20 54		21 09		21 24	
Rock Ferry	d		19 12			19 27		19 42		19 57		20 12		20 27		20 42		20 57		21 12		21 27	
Bebington	d		19 14			19 29		19 44		19 59		20 14		20 29		20 44		20 59		21 14		21 29	
Port Sunlight	d		19 16			19 31		19 46		20 01		20 16		20 31		20 46		21 01		21 16		21 31	
Spital	d		19 18			19 33		19 48		20 03		20 18		20 33		20 48		21 03		21 18		21 33	
Bromborough Rake	d		19 20			19 35		19 50		20 05		20 20		20 35		20 50		21 05		21 20		21 35	
Bromborough	d		19 22			19 37		19 52		20 07		20 22		20 37		20 52		21 07		21 22		21 37	
Eastham Rake	d		19 25			19 40		19 55		20 10		20 25		20 40		20 55		21 10		21 25		21 40	
Hooton	d		19 27			19 42		19 57		20 12		20 27		20 42		20 57		21 12		21 27		21 42	
Little Sutton	d							20 01				20 31				21 01				21 31			
Overpool	d							20 03				20 33				21 03				21 33			
Ellesmere Port	a							20 08				20 38				21 08				21 38			
Capenhurst	d					19 47				20 17				20 47				21 17				21 47	
Bache	d		19 36			19 52				20 22				20 52				21 22				21 52	
Chester	a		19 41			19 56				20 26				20 56				21 26				21 56	

Liverpool and Birkenhead - New Brighton, West Kirby, Ellesmere Port and Chester

Network Diagram - see first Page of Table 101

		ME	ME	ME	ME	ME	ME	ME	ME	ME	ME	ME	ME	ME	ME	ME	ME	ME	ME	ME	ME	ME
Moorfields 10	d	21 26	21 31	21 41	21 46	21 56	22 01	22 11	22 16	22 26	22 31	22 41	22 46	22 56	23 01	23 11	23 16	23 26	23 31	23 41	23 46	23 56
Liverpool Lime Street 10	d	21 28	21 33	21 43	21 48	21 58	22 03	22 13	22 18	22 28	22 33	22 43	22 48	22 58	23 03	23 13	23 18	23 28	23 33	23 43	23 48	23 58
Liverpool Central 10	d	21 30	21 35	21 45	21 50	22 00	22 05	22 15	22 20	22 30	22 35	22 45	22 50	23 00	23 05	23 15	23 20	23 30	23 35	23 45	23 50	23 59
James Street	d	21 32	21 37	21 47	21 52	22 02	22 07	22 17	22 22	22 32	22 37	22 47	22 52	23 02	23 07	23 17	23 22	23 32	23 37	23 47	23 52	00 02
Hamilton Square	d	21 35	21 40	21 50	21 55	22 05	22 10	22 20	22 25	22 35	22 40	22 50	22 55	23 05	23 10	23 20	23 25	23 35	23 40	23 50	23 55	00a05
Conway Park	d		21 42		21 57		22 12		22 27		22 42		22 57		23 12		23 27		23 42		23 57	
Birkenhead Park	d		21 44		21 59		22 14		22 29		22 44		22 59		23 14		23 29		23 44		23 59	
Birkenhead North	d		21 47		22 02		22 17		22 32		22 47		23 02		23 17		23 32		23 47		00 02	
Wallasey Village	d				22 07				22 37				23 07				23 37				00 07	
Wallasey Grove Road	d				22 08				22 38				23 08				23 38				00 08	
New Brighton	a				22 13				22 43				23 13				23 43				00 13	
Bidston	d		21 50				22 20				22 50				23 20				23 50			
Leasowe	d		21 52				22 22				22 52				23 22				23 52			
Moreton (Merseyside)	d		21 54				22 24				22 54				23 24				23 54			
Meols	d		21 58				22 28				22 58				23 28				23 58			
Manor Road	d		22 00				22 30				23 00				23 30				23 59			
Hoylake	d		22 02				22 32				23 02				23 32				00 02			
West Kirby	a		22 07				22 37				23 07				23 37				00 07			
Birkenhead Central	d	21 37		21 52		22 07		22 22		22 37		22 52		23 07		23 22		23 37		23 52		
Green Lane	d	21 39		21 54		22 09		22 24		22 39		22 54		23 09		23 24		23 39		23 54		
Rock Ferry	d	21 42		21 57		22 12		22 27		22 42		22 57		23 12		23 27		23 42		23 57		
Bebington	d	21 44		21 59		22 14		22 29		22 44		22 59		23 14		23 29		23 44		23 59		
Port Sunlight	d	21 46		22 01		22 16		22 31		22 46		23 01		23 16		23 31		23 46		00 01		
Spital	d	21 48		22 03		22 18		22 33		22 48		23 03		23 18		23 33		23 48		00 03		
Bromborough Rake	d	21 50		22 05		22 20		22 35		22 50		23 05		23 20		23 35		23 50		00 05		
Bromborough	d	21 52		22 07		22 22		22 37		22 52		23 07		23 22		23 37		23 52		00 07		
Eastham Rake	d	21 55		22 10		22 25		22 40		22 55		23 10		23 25		23 40		23 55		00 10		
Hooton	d	21 57		22 12		22 27		22 42		22 57		23 12		23 27		23 42		23 57		00 12		
Little Sutton	d	22 01				22 31				23 01				23 31				00 01				
Overpool	d	22 03				22 33				23 03				23 33				00 03				
Ellesmere Port	a	22 08				22 38				23 08				23 37				00 07				
Capenhurst	d			22 17				22 47				23 17				23 47				00 17		
Bache	d			22 22				22 52				23 22				23 52				00 22		
Chester	a			22 26				22 56				23 26				23 56				00 26		

Sundays

		ME	ME	ME	ME	ME	ME	ME	ME	ME	ME	ME	ME	ME	ME	ME	ME	ME	ME		ME	ME
Moorfields 10	d	23p26	23p31	23p41	23p46	23p56	07 56	08 01	08 11	08 16	08 25	08 31	08 41	08 46	08 56	09 01	09 11	09 16	09 26	and at the same minutes past each hour until	22 26	22 31
Liverpool Lime Street 10	d	23p28	23p33	23p43	23p48	23p58	07 58	08 03	08 13	08 18	08 27	08 33	08 43	08 48	08 58	09 03	09 13	09 18	09 28		22 28	22 33
Liverpool Central 10	d	23p30	23p35	23p45	23p50	23p59	08 00	08 05	08 15	08 20	08 29	08 35	08 45	08 50	09 00	09 05	09 15	09 20	09 30		22 30	22 35
James Street	d	23p32	23p37	23p47	23p52	00 02	08 02	08 07	08 17	08 22	08 31	08 37	08 47	08 52	09 02	09 07	09 17	09 22	09 32		22 32	22 37
Hamilton Square	d	23p35	23p40	23p50	23p55	00a05	08 05	08 10	08 20	08 25	08 34	08 40	08 50	08 55	09 05	09 10	09 20	09 25	09 35		22 35	22 40
Conway Park	d		23p42		23p57			08 12		08 27		08 42		08 57		09 12		09 27				22 42
Birkenhead Park	d		23p44		23p59			08 14		08 29		08 44		08 59		09 14		09 29				22 44
Birkenhead North	d		23p47		00 02			08 17		08 32		08 47		09 02		09 17		09 32				22 47
Wallasey Village	d				00 07					08 37				09 07				09 37				
Wallasey Grove Road	d				00 08					08 38				09 08				09 38				
New Brighton	a				00 13					08 43				09 13				09 43				
Bidston	d		23p50					08 20				08 50				09 20						22 50
Leasowe	d		23p52					08 22				08 52				09 22						22 52
Moreton (Merseyside)	d		23p54					08 24				08 54				09 24						22 54
Meols	d		23p58					08 28				08 58				09 28						22 58
Manor Road	d		23p59					08 30				09 00				09 30						23 00
Hoylake	d		00 02					08 32				09 02				09 32						23 02
West Kirby	a		00 07					08 37				09 07				09 37						23 07
Birkenhead Central	d	23p37		23p52			08 07		08 22		08 37		08 52		09 07		09 22		09 37		22 37	
Green Lane	d	23p39		23p54			08 09		08 24		08 39		08 54		09 09		09 24		09 39		22 39	
Rock Ferry	d	23p42		23p57			08 12		08 27		08 41		08 57		09 12		09 27		09 42		22 42	
Bebington	d	23p44		23p59			08 14		08 29		08 44		08 59		09 14		09 29		09 44		22 44	
Port Sunlight	d	23p46		00 01			08 16		08 31		08 46		09 01		09 16		09 31		09 46		22 46	
Spital	d	23p48		00 03			08 18		08 33		08 48		09 03		09 18		09 33		09 48		22 48	
Bromborough Rake	d	23p50		00 05			08 20		08 35		08 50		09 05		09 20		09 35		09 50		22 50	
Bromborough	d	23p52		00 07			08 22		08 37		08 52		09 07		09 22		09 37		09 52		22 52	
Eastham Rake	d	23p55		00 10			08 25		08 40		08 54		09 10		09 25		09 40		09 55		22 55	
Hooton	d	23p57		00 12			08 27		08 42		08 56		09 12		09 27		09 42		09 57		22 57	
Little Sutton	d	00 01					08 31				09 01				09 31				10 01		23 01	
Overpool	d	00 03					08 33				09 03				09 33				10 03		23 03	
Ellesmere Port	a	00 07					08 38				09 08				09 38				10 08		23 08	
Capenhurst	d			00 17					08 47				09 17				09 47					
Bache	d			00 22					08 52				09 22				09 52					
Chester	a			00 26					08 56				09 26				09 56					

Liverpool and Birkenhead - New Brighton, West Kirby, Ellesmere Port and Chester

Network Diagram - see first Page of Table 101

		ME	ME	ME	ME	ME	ME	ME	ME	ME	ME	ME
Moorfields 10	d	22 41	22 46	22 56	23 01	23 11	23 16	23 26	23 31	23 41	23 46	23 56
Liverpool Lime Street 10	d	22 43	22 48	22 58	23 03	23 13	23 18	23 28	23 33	23 43	23 48	23 58
Liverpool Central 10	d	22 45	22 50	23 00	23 05	23 15	23 20	23 30	23 35	23 45	23 50	23 59
James Street	d	22 47	22 52	23 02	23 07	23 17	23 22	23 32	23 37	23 47	23 52	00 02
Hamilton Square	d	22 50	22 55	23 05	23 10	23 20	23 25	23 35	23 40	23 50	23 55	00a05
Conway Park	d		22 57		23 12		23 27		23 42		23 57	
Birkenhead Park	d		22 59		23 14		23 29		23 44		23 59	
Birkenhead North	d		23 02		23 17		23 32		23 47		00 02	
Wallasey Village	d		23 07				23 37				00 07	
Wallasey Grove Road	d		23 08				23 38				00 08	
New Brighton	a		23 13				23 43				00 13	
Bidston	d				23 20				23 50			
Leasowe	d				23 22				23 52			
Moreton (Merseyside)	d				23 24				23 54			
Meols	d				23 28				23 58			
Manor Road	d				23 30				23 59			
Hoylake	d				23 32				00 02			
West Kirby	a				23 37				00 07			
Birkenhead Central	d	22 52		23 07		23 22		23 37		23 52		
Green Lane	d	22 54		23 09		23 24		23 39		23 54		
Rock Ferry	d	22 57		23 12		23 27		23 42		23 57		
Bebington	d	22 59		23 14		23 29		23 44		23 59		
Port Sunlight	d	23 01		23 16		23 31		23 46		00 01		
Spital	d	23 03		23 18		23 33		23 48		00 03		
Bromborough Rake	d	23 05		23 20		23 35		23 50		00 05		
Bromborough	d	23 07		23 22		23 37		23 52		00 07		
Eastham Rake	d	23 10		23 25		23 40		23 55		00 10		
Hooton	d	23 12		23 27		23 42		23 57		00 12		
Little Sutton	d			23 31				00 01				
Overpool	d			23 33				00 03				
Ellesmere Port	a			23 37				00 07				
Capenhurst	d	23 17				23 47				00 17		
Bache	d	23 22				23 52				00 22		
Chester	a	23 26				23 56				00 26		

Chester, Ellesmere Port, West Kirby and New Brighton - Birkenhead and Liverpool

Network Diagram - see first Page of Table 101

Miles	Miles	Miles	Miles			ME	ME	ME	ME	ME	ME	ME	ME	ME		ME	ME	ME	ME	ME	ME	ME	ME	ME
0	—	—	—	**Chester**	d						05 55					06 30						07 00		
1½	—	—	—	Bache	d						05 58					06 33						07 03		
5¼	—	—	—	Capenhurst	d						06 04					06 39						07 09		
—	0	—	—	**Ellesmere Port**	d									06 17					06 47					
—	1½	—	—	Overpool	d									06 20					06 50					
—	2½	—	—	Little Sutton	d									06 22					06 52					
8¼	4	—	—	Hooton	d		05 39			05 59	06 09			06 26		06 44			06 56			07 14		
9¼	—	—	—	Eastham Rake	d		05 41			06 01	06 11			06 28		06 46			06 58			07 16		
9¾	—	—	—	Bromborough	d		05 43			06 03	06 13			06 31		06 48			07 01			07 18		
10½	—	—	—	Bromborough Rake	d		05 45			06 05	06 15			06 33		06 50			07 03			07 20		
11¼	—	—	—	Spital	d		05 47			06 07	06 17			06 35		06 52			07 05			07 22		
11¾	—	—	—	Port Sunlight	d		05 49			06 09	06 19			06 37		06 54			07 07			07 24		
12¾	—	—	—	Bebington	d		05 51			06 11	06 21			06 39		06 56			07 09			07 26		
13¾	—	—	—	Rock Ferry	d	05 44	05 54			06 14	06 24			06 42		06 59			07 12			07 29		
14½	—	—	—	Green Lane	d	05 47	05 57			06 17	06 27			06 44		07 02			07 14			07 32		
15	—	—	—	Birkenhead Central	d	05 49	05 59			06 19	06 34			06 49		07 04			07 19			07 34		
—	—	0	—	**West Kirby**	d				05 51				06 21					06 51			07 06			07 21
—	—	1	—	Hoylake	d				05 54				06 24					06 54			07 09			07 24
—	—	1¾	—	Manor Road	d				05 56				06 26					06 56			07 11			07 26
—	—	3	—	Meols	d				05 58				06 28					06 58			07 13			07 28
—	—	4¼	—	Moreton (Merseyside)	d				06 01				06 31					07 01			07 16			07 31
—	—	4¾	—	Leasowe	d				06 03				06 33					07 03			07 18			07 33
—	—	5¾	—	Bidston	d				06 06				06 36					07 06			07 21			07 36
—	—	—	0	**New Brighton**	d			05 53				06 23					06 53			07 08			07 23	
—	—	—	1¼	Wallasey Grove Road	d			05 57				06 27					06 57			07 12			07 27	
—	—	—	1½	Wallasey Village	d			05 59				06 29					06 59			07 14			07 29	
—	—	6½	3	Birkenhead North	d			06 04	06 09			06 34	06 39				07 04	07 09		07 19	07 24		07 34	07 39
—	—	7½	3¾	Birkenhead Park	d			06 06	06 11			06 36	06 41				07 06	07 11		07 21	07 26		07 36	07 41
—	—	8¼	4½	Conway Park	d			06 09	06 14			06 39	06 44				07 09	07 14		07 24	07 29		07 39	07 44
15½	—	8¾	5	Hamilton Square	d	05 51	06 01	06 11	06 16	06 21	06 36	06 41	06 46	06 51		07 06	07 11	07 16	07 21	07 26	07 31	07 36	07 41	07 46
16¾	—	8¾	6¼	James Street	d	05 54	06 04	06 14	06 19	06 24	06 39	06 44	06 49	06 54		07 09	07 14	07 19	07 24	07 29	07 34	07 39	07 44	07 49
17¼	—	10¼	7¾	Moorfields [10]	a	05 56	06 06	06 16	06 21	06 26	06 41	06 46	06 51	06 56		07 11	07 16	07 21	07 26	07 31	07 36	07 41	07 46	07 51
17¾	—	10¾	8¼	Liverpool Lime Street [10]	a	05 58	06 08	06 18	06 23	06 28	06 43	06 48	06 53	06 58		07 13	07 18	07 23	07 28	07 33	07 38	07 43	07 48	07 53
18½	—	11¼	8¾	**Liverpool Central** [10]	a	06 00	06 10	06 20	06 25	06 30	06 45	06 50	06 55	07 00		07 15	07 20	07 25	07 30	07 35	07 40	07 45	07 50	07 55

		ME SX	ME SO	ME	ME SX	ME	ME SO	ME SX	ME	ME SX		ME	ME	ME	ME SX	ME	ME SO	ME SX	ME	ME SX		ME SO	ME	ME SO	ME SX
Chester	d				07 22		07 30			07 37					07 52		08 00			08 07				08 15	
Bache	d				07 26		07 33			07 41					07 56		08 03			08 11				08 18	
Capenhurst	d				07 32		07 39			07 47					08 02		08 09			08 17				08 24	
Ellesmere Port	d	07 17	07 19					07 31					07 49					08 01				08 12			08 17
Overpool	d	07 20	07 22					07 34					07 52					08 04				08 15			08 20
Little Sutton	d	07 22	07 24					07 36					07 54					08 06				08 17			08 22
Hooton	d	07 26	07 29		07 36		07 44	07 44		07 51			07 59		08 06		08 14	08 14		08 21		08 21		08 29	08 29
Eastham Rake	d	07 28	07 31		07 38		07 46	07 46		07 53			08 01		08 08		08 16	08 16		08 23		08 23		08 31	08 31
Bromborough	d	07 31	07 33		07 41		07 48	07 48		07 56			08 03		08 11		08 18	08 18		08 26		08 26		08 33	08 33
Bromborough Rake	d	07 33	07 35		07 43		07 50	07 50		07 58			08 05		08 13		08 20	08 20		08 28		08 28		08 35	08 35
Spital	d	07 35	07 37		07 45		07 52	07 52		08 00			08 07		08 15		08 22	08 22		08 30		08 30		08 37	08 37
Port Sunlight	d	07 37	07 39		07 47		07 54	07 54		08 02			08 09		08 17		08 24	08 24		08 32		08 32		08 39	08 39
Bebington	d	07 39	07 41		07 49		07 56	07 56		08 04			08 11		08 19		08 26	08 26		08 34		08 34		08 41	08 41
Rock Ferry	d	07 42	07 44		07 52		07 59	07 59		08 07			08 14		08 22		08 29	08 29		08 37		08 37		08 44	08 44
Green Lane	d	07 44	07 47		07 54		08 02	08 02		08 09			08 17		08 24		08 32	08 32		08 39		08 39		08 47	08 47
Birkenhead Central	d	07 47	07 49		07 57		08 04	08 04		08 12			08 19		08 27		08 34	08 34		08 42		08 42		08 49	08 49
West Kirby	d					07 36						07 51				08 06							08 21		
Hoylake	d					07 39						07 54				08 09							08 24		
Manor Road	d					07 41						07 56				08 11							08 26		
Meols	d					07 43						07 58				08 13							08 28		
Moreton (Merseyside)	d					07 46						08 01				08 16							08 31		
Leasowe	d					07 48						08 03				08 18							08 33		
Bidston	d					07 51						08 06				08 21							08 36		
New Brighton	d			07 38					07 53					08 08					08 23						
Wallasey Grove Road	d			07 42					07 57					08 12					08 27						
Wallasey Village	d			07 44					07 59					08 14					08 29						
Birkenhead North	d			07 49		07 54			08 04			08 09		08 19		08 24			08 34				08 39		
Birkenhead Park	d			07 51		07 56			08 06			08 11		08 21		08 26			08 36				08 41		
Conway Park	d			07 54		07 59			08 09			08 14		08 24		08 29			08 39				08 44		
Hamilton Square	d	07 49	07 51	07 56	07 59	08 01	08 06	08 06	08 11	08 14		08 16	08 21	08 26	08 29	08 31	08 36	08 36	08 41	08 44		08 44	08 46	08 51	08 51
James Street	d	07 52	07 54	07 59	08 02	08 04	08 09	08 09	08 14	08 17		08 19	08 24	08 29	08 32	08 34	08 39	08 39	08 44	08 47		08 47	08 49	08 54	08 54
Moorfields [10]	a	07 53	07 56	08 01	08 03	08 06	08 11	08 11	08 16	08 18		08 21	08 26	08 31	08 33	08 36	08 41	08 41	08 46	08 48		08 48	08 51	08 56	08 56
Liverpool Lime Street [10]	a	07 55	07 58	08 03	08 05	08 08	08 13	08 13	08 18	08 20		08 23	08 28	08 33	08 35	08 38	08 43	08 43	08 48	08 50		08 50	08 53	08 58	08 58
Liverpool Central [10]	a	07 57	08 00	08 05	08 07	08 10	08 15	08 15	08 20	08 22		08 25	08 30	08 35	08 37	08 40	08 45	08 45	08 50	08 52		08 52	08 55	09 00	09 00

Chester, Ellesmere Port, West Kirby and New Brighton - Birkenhead and Liverpool

Network Diagram - see first Page of Table 101

		ME	ME	ME	ME	ME SO		ME SX	ME	ME	ME	ME	ME	ME	ME	ME		ME	ME	ME	ME	ME	ME	ME	ME
Chester	d			08 31						08 45			09 01					09 15			09 31				09 45
Bache	d			08 35						08 48			09 05					09 18			09 35				09 48
Capenhurst	d									08 54								09 24							09 54
Ellesmere Port	d					08 42		08 42							09 12								09 42		
Overpool	d					08 45		08 45							09 15								09 45		
Little Sutton	d					08 47		08 47							09 17								09 47		
Hooton	d			08 44		08 51		08 52		08 59			09 14		09 21			09 29			09 44		09 51		09 59
Eastham Rake	d			08 46		08 53		08 54		09 01			09 16		09 23			09 31			09 46		09 53		10 01
Bromborough	d			08 48		08 56		08 56		09 03			09 18		09 26			09 33			09 48		09 56		10 03
Bromborough Rake	d			08 50		08 58		08 58		09 05			09 20		09 28			09 35			09 50		09 58		10 05
Spital	d			08 52		09 00		09 00		09 07			09 22		09 30			09 37			09 52		10 00		10 07
Port Sunlight	d			08 54		09 02		09 02		09 09			09 24		09 32			09 39			09 54		10 02		10 09
Bebington	d			08 56		09 04		09 04		09 11			09 26		09 34			09 41			09 56		10 04		10 11
Rock Ferry	d			08 59		09 07		09 07		09 14			09 29		09 37			09 44			09 59		10 07		10 14
Green Lane	d			09 02		09 09		09 10		09 17			09 32		09 39			09 47			10 02		10 09		10 17
Birkenhead Central	d			09 04		09 12		09 12		09 19			09 34		09 42			09 49			10 04		10 12		10 19
West Kirby	d		08 36						08 51			09 06				09 21				09 36				09 51	
Hoylake	d		08 39						08 54			09 09				09 24				09 39				09 54	
Manor Road	d		08 41						08 56			09 11				09 26				09 41				09 56	
Meols	d		08 43						08 58			09 13				09 28				09 43				09 58	
Moreton (Merseyside)	d		08 46						09 01			09 16				09 31				09 46				10 01	
Leasowe	d		08 48						09 03			09 18				09 33				09 48				10 03	
Bidston	d		08 51						09 06			09 21				09 36				09 51				10 06	
New Brighton	d	08 38			08 53						09 08			09 23					09 38			09 53			
Wallasey Grove Road	d	08 42			08 57						09 12			09 27					09 42			09 57			
Wallasey Village	d	08 44			08 59						09 14			09 29					09 44			09 59			
Birkenhead North	d	08 49	08 54		09 04				09 09		09 19	09 24		09 34		09 39			09 49	09 54		10 04		10 09	
Birkenhead Park	d	08 51	08 56		09 06				09 11		09 21	09 26		09 36		09 41			09 51	09 56		10 06		10 11	
Conway Park	d	08 54	08 59		09 09				09 14		09 24	09 29		09 39		09 44			09 54	09 59		10 09		10 14	
Hamilton Square	d	08 56	09 01	09 06	09 11	09 14		09 14	09 16	09 21	09 26	09 31	09 36	09 41	09 44	09 46		09 51	09 56	10 01	10 06	10 11	10 14	10 16	10 21
James Street	d	08 59	09 04	09 09	09 14	09 17		09 17	09 19	09 24	09 29	09 34	09 39	09 44	09 47	09 49		09 54	09 59	10 04	10 09	10 14	10 17	10 19	10 24
Moorfields [10]	a	09 01	09 06	09 11	09 16	09 18		09 19	09 21	09 26	09 31	09 36	09 41	09 46	09 48	09 51		09 56	10 01	10 06	10 11	10 16	10 18	10 21	10 26
Liverpool Lime Street [10]	a	09 03	09 08	09 13	09 18	09 20		09 21	09 23	09 28	09 33	09 38	09 43	09 48	09 50	09 53		09 58	10 03	10 08	10 13	10 18	10 20	10 23	10 28
Liverpool Central [10]	a	09 05	09 10	09 15	09 20	09 22		09 23	09 25	09 30	09 35	09 40	09 45	09 50	09 52	09 55		10 00	10 05	10 10	10 15	10 20	10 22	10 25	10 30

		ME		ME	ME	ME	ME	ME	ME	ME	ME	ME		ME	ME	ME	ME	ME	ME	ME	ME	ME		ME	ME
Chester	d				10 01				10 15			10 31					10 45			11 01					11 15
Bache	d				10 05				10 18			10 35					10 48			11 05					11 18
Capenhurst	d								10 24								10 54								11 24
Ellesmere Port	d						10 12								10 42							11 12			
Overpool	d						10 15								10 45							11 15			
Little Sutton	d						10 17								10 47							11 17			
Hooton	d				10 14		10 21		10 29			10 44			10 51		10 59			11 14		11 21			11 29
Eastham Rake	d				10 16		10 23		10 31			10 46			10 53		11 01			11 16		11 23			11 31
Bromborough	d				10 18		10 26		10 33			10 48			10 56		11 03			11 18		11 26			11 33
Bromborough Rake	d				10 20		10 28		10 35			10 50			10 58		11 05			11 20		11 28			11 35
Spital	d				10 22		10 30		10 37			10 52			11 00		11 07			11 22		11 30			11 37
Port Sunlight	d				10 24		10 32		10 39			10 54			11 02		11 09			11 24		11 32			11 39
Bebington	d				10 26		10 34		10 41			10 56			11 04		11 11			11 26		11 34			11 41
Rock Ferry	d				10 29		10 37		10 44			10 59			11 07		11 14			11 29		11 37			11 44
Green Lane	d				10 32		10 39		10 47			11 02			11 09		11 17			11 32		11 39			11 47
Birkenhead Central	d				10 34		10 42		10 49			11 04			11 12		11 19			11 34		11 42			11 49
West Kirby	d			10 06				10 21			10 36					10 51			11 06					11 21	
Hoylake	d			10 09				10 24			10 39					10 54			11 09					11 24	
Manor Road	d			10 11				10 26			10 41					10 56			11 11					11 26	
Meols	d			10 13				10 28			10 43					10 58			11 13					11 28	
Moreton (Merseyside)	d			10 16				10 31			10 46					11 01			11 16					11 31	
Leasowe	d			10 18				10 33			10 48					11 03			11 18					11 33	
Bidston	d			10 21				10 36			10 51					11 06			11 21					11 36	
New Brighton	d	10 08				10 23				10 38				10 53				11 08			11 23				
Wallasey Grove Road	d	10 12				10 27				10 42				10 57				11 12			11 27				
Wallasey Village	d	10 14				10 29				10 44				10 59				11 14			11 29				
Birkenhead North	d	10 19		10 24		10 34		10 39		10 49	10 54			11 04		11 09		11 19	11 24		11 34			11 39	
Birkenhead Park	d	10 21		10 26		10 36		10 41		10 51	10 56			11 06		11 11		11 21	11 26		11 36			11 41	
Conway Park	d	10 24		10 29		10 39		10 44		10 54	10 59			11 09		11 14		11 24	11 29		11 39			11 44	
Hamilton Square	d	10 26		10 31	10 36	10 41	10 44	10 46	10 51	10 56	11 01	11 06		11 11	11 14	11 16	11 21	11 26	11 31	11 36	11 41	11 44		11 46	11 51
James Street	d	10 29		10 34	10 39	10 44	10 47	10 49	10 54	10 59	11 04	11 09		11 14	11 17	11 19	11 24	11 29	11 34	11 39	11 44	11 47		11 49	11 54
Moorfields [10]	a	10 31		10 36	10 41	10 46	10 48	10 51	10 56	11 01	11 06	11 11		11 16	11 18	11 21	11 26	11 31	11 36	11 41	11 46	11 48		11 51	11 56
Liverpool Lime Street [10]	a	10 33		10 38	10 43	10 48	10 50	10 53	10 58	11 03	11 08	11 13		11 18	11 20	11 23	11 28	11 33	11 38	11 43	11 48	11 50		11 53	11 58
Liverpool Central [10]	a	10 35		10 40	10 45	10 50	10 52	10 55	11 00	11 05	11 10	11 15		11 20	11 22	11 25	11 30	11 35	11 40	11 45	11 50	11 52		11 55	12 00

Chester, Ellesmere Port, West Kirby and New Brighton - Birkenhead and Liverpool

Network Diagram - see first Page of Table 101

		ME	ME	ME	ME	ME	ME	ME		ME	ME	ME	ME	ME	ME	ME	ME	ME		ME	ME	ME	ME	ME	ME
Chester	d			11 31				11 45				12 01				12 15				12 31				12 45	
Bache	d			11 35				11 48				12 05				12 18				12 35				12 48	
Capenhurst	d							11 54								12 24								12 54	
Ellesmere Port	d					11 42								12 12								12 42			
Overpool	d					11 45								12 15								12 45			
Little Sutton	d					11 47								12 17								12 47			
Hooton	d			11 44		11 51		11 59				12 14		12 21		12 29				12 44		12 51		12 59	
Eastham Rake	d			11 46		11 53		12 01				12 16		12 23		12 31				12 46		12 53		13 01	
Bromborough	d			11 48		11 56		12 03				12 18		12 26		12 33				12 48		12 56		13 03	
Bromborough Rake	d			11 50		11 58		12 05				12 20		12 28		12 35				12 50		12 58		13 05	
Spital	d			11 52		12 00		12 07				12 22		12 30		12 37				12 52		13 00		13 07	
Port Sunlight	d			11 54		12 02		12 09				12 24		12 32		12 39				12 54		13 02		13 09	
Bebington	d			11 56		12 04		12 11				12 26		12 34		12 41				12 56		13 04		13 11	
Rock Ferry	d			11 59		12 07		12 14				12 29		12 37		12 44				12 59		13 07		13 14	
Green Lane	d			12 02		12 09		12 17				12 32		12 39		12 47				13 02		13 09		13 17	
Birkenhead Central	d			12 04		12 12		12 19				12 34		12 42		12 49				13 04		13 12		13 19	
West Kirby	d		11 36				11 51				12 06				12 21			12 36					12 51		
Hoylake	d		11 39				11 54				12 09				12 24			12 39					12 54		
Manor Road	d		11 41				11 56				12 11				12 26			12 41					12 56		
Meols	d		11 43				11 58				12 13				12 28			12 43					12 58		
Moreton (Merseyside)	d		11 46				12 01				12 16				12 31			12 46					13 01		
Leasowe	d		11 48				12 03				12 18				12 33			12 48					13 03		
Bidston	d		11 51				12 06				12 21				12 36			12 51					13 06		
New Brighton	d	11 38			11 53					12 08			12 23				12 38				12 53				13 08
Wallasey Grove Road	d	11 42			11 57					12 12			12 27				12 42				12 57				13 12
Wallasey Village	d	11 44			11 59					12 14			12 29				12 44				12 59				13 14
Birkenhead North	d	11 49	11 54		12 04		12 09			12 19	12 24		12 34		12 39		12 49	12 54			13 04		13 09		13 19
Birkenhead Park	d	11 51	11 56		12 06		12 11			12 21	12 26		12 36		12 41		12 51	12 56			13 06		13 11		13 21
Conway Park	d	11 54	11 59		12 09		12 14			12 24	12 29		12 39		12 44		12 54	12 59			13 09		13 14		13 24
Hamilton Square	d	11 56	12 01	12 06	12 11	12 14	12 16	12 21		12 26	12 31	12 36	12 41	12 44	12 46	12 51	12 56	13 01		13 06	13 11	13 14	13 16	13 21	13 26
James Street	d	11 59	12 04	12 09	12 14	12 17	12 19	12 24		12 29	12 34	12 39	12 44	12 47	12 49	12 54	12 59	13 04		13 09	13 14	13 17	13 19	13 24	13 29
Moorfields 10	a	12 01	12 06	12 11	12 16	12 18	12 21	12 26		12 31	12 36	12 41	12 46	12 48	12 51	12 56	13 01	13 06		13 11	13 16	13 18	13 21	13 26	13 31
Liverpool Lime Street 10	a	12 03	12 08	12 13	12 18	12 20	12 23	12 28		12 33	12 38	12 43	12 48	12 50	12 53	12 58	13 03	13 08		13 13	13 18	13 20	13 23	13 28	13 33
Liverpool Central 10	a	12 05	12 10	12 15	12 20	12 22	12 25	12 30		12 35	12 40	12 45	12 50	12 52	12 55	13 00	13 05	13 10		13 15	13 20	13 22	13 25	13 30	13 35

		ME	ME	ME		ME	ME	ME	ME	ME	ME	ME	ME	ME		ME	ME	ME	ME	ME	ME	ME	ME	ME	
Chester	d		13 01					13 15			13 31					13 45			14 01				14 15		
Bache	d		13 05					13 18			13 35					13 48			14 05				14 18		
Capenhurst	d							13 24								13 54							14 24		
Ellesmere Port	d					13 12							13 42								14 12				
Overpool	d					13 15							13 45								14 15				
Little Sutton	d					13 17							13 47								14 17				
Hooton	d		13 14			13 21		13 29			13 44		13 51			13 59			14 14		14 21		14 29		
Eastham Rake	d		13 16			13 23		13 31			13 46		13 53			14 01			14 16		14 23		14 31		
Bromborough	d		13 18			13 26		13 33			13 48		13 56			14 03			14 18		14 26		14 33		
Bromborough Rake	d		13 20			13 28		13 35			13 50		13 58			14 05			14 20		14 28		14 35		
Spital	d		13 22			13 30		13 37			13 52		14 00			14 07			14 22		14 30		14 37		
Port Sunlight	d		13 24			13 32		13 39			13 54		14 02			14 09			14 24		14 32		14 39		
Bebington	d		13 26			13 34		13 41			13 56		14 04			14 11			14 26		14 34		14 41		
Rock Ferry	d		13 29			13 37		13 44			13 59		14 07			14 14			14 29		14 37		14 44		
Green Lane	d		13 32			13 39		13 47			14 02		14 09			14 17			14 32		14 39		14 47		
Birkenhead Central	d		13 34			13 42		13 49			14 04		14 12			14 19			14 34		14 42		14 49		
West Kirby	d	13 06					13 21			13 36				13 51				14 06				14 21			
Hoylake	d	13 09					13 24			13 39				13 54				14 09				14 24			
Manor Road	d	13 11					13 26			13 41				13 56				14 11				14 26			
Meols	d	13 13					13 28			13 43				13 58				14 13				14 28			
Moreton (Merseyside)	d	13 16					13 31			13 46				14 01				14 16				14 31			
Leasowe	d	13 18					13 33			13 48				14 03				14 18				14 33			
Bidston	d	13 21					13 36			13 51				14 06				14 21				14 36			
New Brighton	d			13 23					13 38			13 53					14 08			14 23				14 38	
Wallasey Grove Road	d			13 27					13 42			13 57					14 12			14 27				14 42	
Wallasey Village	d			13 29					13 44			13 59					14 14			14 29				14 44	
Birkenhead North	d	13 24		13 34			13 39		13 49	13 54		14 04		14 09			14 19	14 24		14 34		14 39		14 49	
Birkenhead Park	d	13 26		13 36			13 41		13 51	13 56		14 06		14 11			14 21	14 26		14 36		14 41		14 51	
Conway Park	d	13 29		13 39			13 44		13 54	13 59		14 09		14 14			14 24	14 29		14 39		14 44		14 54	
Hamilton Square	d	13 31	13 36	13 41		13 44	13 46	13 51	13 56	14 01	14 06	14 11	14 14	14 16		14 21	14 26	14 31	14 36	14 41	14 44	14 46	14 51	14 56	
James Street	d	13 34	13 39	13 44		13 47	13 49	13 54	13 59	14 04	14 09	14 14	14 17	14 19		14 24	14 29	14 34	14 39	14 44	14 47	14 49	14 54	14 59	
Moorfields 10	a	13 36	13 41	13 46		13 48	13 51	13 56	14 01	14 06	14 11	14 16	14 18	14 21		14 26	14 31	14 36	14 41	14 46	14 48	14 51	14 56	15 01	
Liverpool Lime Street 10	a	13 38	13 43	13 48		13 50	13 53	13 58	14 03	14 08	14 13	14 18	14 20	14 23		14 28	14 33	14 38	14 43	14 48	14 50	14 53	14 58	15 03	
Liverpool Central 10	a	13 40	13 45	13 50		13 52	13 55	14 00	14 05	14 10	14 15	14 20	14 22	14 25		14 30	14 35	14 40	14 45	14 50	14 52	14 55	15 00	15 05	

Chester, Ellesmere Port, West Kirby and New Brighton - Birkenhead and Liverpool

Network Diagram - see first Page of Table 101

		ME	ME	ME	ME	ME	ME	ME	ME	ME		ME	ME	ME	ME	ME	ME	ME	ME	ME		ME	ME	ME	ME
Chester	d		14 31				14 45			15 01					15 15			15 31					15 45		
Bache	d		14 35				14 48			15 05					15 18			15 35					15 48		
Capenhurst	d						14 54								15 24								15 54		
Ellesmere Port	d				14 42								15 12							15 42					
Overpool	d				14 45								15 15							15 45					
Little Sutton	d				14 47								15 17							15 47					
Hooton	d		14 44		14 51		14 59			15 14			15 21		15 29			15 44		15 51			15 59		
Eastham Rake	d		14 46		14 53		15 01			15 16			15 23		15 31			15 46		15 53			16 01		
Bromborough	d		14 48		14 56		15 03			15 18			15 26		15 33			15 48		15 56			16 03		
Bromborough Rake	d		14 50		14 58		15 05			15 20			15 28		15 35			15 50		15 58			16 05		
Spital	d		14 52		15 00		15 07			15 22			15 30		15 37			15 52		16 00			16 07		
Port Sunlight	d		14 54		15 02		15 09			15 24			15 32		15 39			15 54		16 02			16 09		
Bebington	d		14 56		15 04		15 11			15 26			15 34		15 41			15 56		16 04			16 11		
Rock Ferry	d		14 59		15 07		15 14			15 29			15 37		15 44			15 59		16 07			16 14		
Green Lane	d		15 02		15 09		15 17			15 32			15 39		15 47			16 02		16 09			16 17		
Birkenhead Central	d		15 04		15 12		15 19			15 34			15 42		15 49			16 04		16 12			16 19		
West Kirby	d	14 36				14 51			15 06					15 21			15 36					15 51			16 06
Hoylake	d	14 39				14 54			15 09					15 24			15 39					15 54			16 09
Manor Road	d	14 41				14 56			15 11					15 26			15 41					15 56			16 11
Meols	d	14 43				14 58			15 13					15 28			15 43					15 58			16 13
Moreton (Merseyside)	d	14 46				15 01			15 16					15 31			15 46					16 01			16 16
Leasowe	d	14 48				15 03			15 18					15 33			15 48					16 03			16 18
Bidston	d	14 51				15 06			15 21					15 36			15 51					16 06			16 21
New Brighton	d			14 53				15 08				15 23				15 38			15 53					16 08	
Wallasey Grove Road	d			14 57				15 12				15 27				15 42			15 57					16 12	
Wallasey Village	d			14 59				15 14				15 29				15 44			15 59					16 14	
Birkenhead North	d	14 54		15 04		15 09		15 19	15 24			15 34		15 39		15 49	15 54		16 04			16 09		16 19	16 24
Birkenhead Park	d	14 56		15 06		15 11		15 21	15 26			15 36		15 41		15 51	15 56		16 06			16 11		16 21	16 26
Conway Park	d	14 59		15 09		15 14		15 24	15 29			15 39		15 44		15 54	15 59		16 09			16 14		16 24	16 29
Hamilton Square	d	15 01	15 06	15 11	15 14	15 16	15 21	15 26	15 31	15 36		15 41	15 44	15 46	15 51	15 56	16 01	16 06	16 11	16 14		16 16	16 21	16 26	16 31
James Street	d	15 04	15 09	15 14	15 17	15 19	15 24	15 29	15 34	15 39		15 44	15 47	15 49	15 54	15 59	16 04	16 09	16 14	16 17		16 19	16 24	16 29	16 34
Moorfields 10	a	15 06	15 11	15 16	15 18	15 21	15 26	15 31	15 36	15 41		15 46	15 48	15 51	15 56	16 01	16 06	16 11	16 16	16 18		16 21	16 26	16 31	16 36
Liverpool Lime Street 10	a	15 08	15 13	15 18	15 20	15 23	15 28	15 33	15 38	15 43		15 48	15 50	15 53	15 58	16 03	16 08	16 13	16 18	16 20		16 23	16 28	16 33	16 38
Liverpool Central 10	a	15 10	15 15	15 20	15 22	15 25	15 30	15 35	15 40	15 45		15 50	15 52	15 55	16 00	16 05	16 10	16 15	16 20	16 22		16 25	16 30	16 35	16 40

		ME	ME	ME	ME	ME		ME	ME	ME	ME	ME	ME	ME	ME	ME		ME	ME	ME	ME	ME	ME	ME	ME
Chester	d	16 01				16 15				16 31				16 45				17 01				17 15			17 31
Bache	d	16 05				16 18				16 35				16 48				17 05				17 18			17 35
Capenhurst	d					16 24								16 54								17 24			
Ellesmere Port	d			16 12								16 42								17 12					
Overpool	d			16 15								16 45								17 15					
Little Sutton	d			16 17								16 47								17 17					
Hooton	d	16 14		16 21		16 29				16 44		16 51		16 59				17 14		17 21		17 29			17 44
Eastham Rake	d	16 16		16 23		16 31				16 46		16 53		17 01				17 16		17 23		17 31			17 46
Bromborough	d	16 18		16 26		16 33				16 48		16 56		17 03				17 18		17 26		17 33			17 48
Bromborough Rake	d	16 20		16 28		16 35				16 50		16 58		17 05				17 20		17 28		17 35			17 50
Spital	d	16 22		16 30		16 37				16 52		17 00		17 07				17 22		17 30		17 37			17 52
Port Sunlight	d	16 24		16 32		16 39				16 54		17 02		17 09				17 24		17 32		17 39			17 54
Bebington	d	16 26		16 34		16 41				16 56		17 04		17 11				17 26		17 34		17 41			17 56
Rock Ferry	d	16 29		16 37		16 44				16 59		17 07		17 14				17 29		17 37		17 44			17 59
Green Lane	d	16 32		16 39		16 47				17 02		17 09		17 17				17 32		17 39		17 47			18 02
Birkenhead Central	d	16 34		16 42		16 49				17 04		17 12		17 19				17 34		17 42		17 49			18 04
West Kirby	d				16 21				16 36				16 51			17 06					17 21			17 36	
Hoylake	d				16 24				16 39				16 54			17 09					17 24			17 39	
Manor Road	d				16 26				16 41				16 56			17 11					17 26			17 41	
Meols	d				16 28				16 43				16 58			17 13					17 28			17 43	
Moreton (Merseyside)	d				16 31				16 46				17 01			17 16					17 31			17 46	
Leasowe	d				16 33				16 48				17 03			17 18					17 33			17 48	
Bidston	d				16 36				16 51				17 06			17 21					17 36			17 51	
New Brighton	d		16 23					16 38			16 53				17 08				17 23				17 38		
Wallasey Grove Road	d		16 27					16 42			16 57				17 12				17 27				17 42		
Wallasey Village	d		16 29					16 44			16 59				17 14				17 29				17 44		
Birkenhead North	d		16 34		16 39			16 49	16 54		17 04		17 09		17 19	17 24			17 34		17 39		17 49	17 54	
Birkenhead Park	d		16 36		16 41			16 51	16 56		17 06		17 11		17 21	17 26			17 36		17 41		17 51	17 56	
Conway Park	d		16 39		16 44			16 54	16 59		17 09		17 14		17 24	17 29			17 39		17 44		17 54	17 59	
Hamilton Square	d	16 36	16 41	16 44	16 46	16 51		16 56	17 01	17 06	17 11	17 14	17 16	17 21	17 26	17 31		17 36	17 41	17 44	17 46	17 51	17 56	18 01	18 06
James Street	d	16 39	16 44	16 47	16 49	16 54		16 59	17 04	17 09	17 14	17 17	17 19	17 24	17 29	17 34		17 39	17 44	17 47	17 49	17 54	17 59	18 04	18 09
Moorfields 10	a	16 41	16 46	16 48	16 51	16 56		17 01	17 06	17 11	17 16	17 18	17 21	17 26	17 31	17 36		17 41	17 46	17 48	17 51	17 56	18 01	18 06	18 11
Liverpool Lime Street 10	a	16 43	16 48	16 50	16 53	16 58		17 03	17 08	17 13	17 18	17 20	17 23	17 28	17 33	17 38		17 43	17 48	17 50	17 53	17 58	18 03	18 08	18 13
Liverpool Central 10	a	16 45	16 50	16 52	16 55	17 00		17 05	17 10	17 15	17 20	17 22	17 25	17 30	17 35	17 40		17 45	17 50	17 52	17 55	18 00	18 05	18 10	18 15

Table 106

Mondays to Saturdays

Chester, Ellesmere Port, West Kirby and New Brighton - Birkenhead and Liverpool

Network Diagram - see first Page of Table 101

		ME		ME	ME	ME	ME	ME	ME	ME	ME	ME		ME	ME	ME	ME	ME	ME	ME	ME	ME		ME	ME
Chester	d					17 45			18 01					18 15			18 30				19 00				
Bache	d					17 48			18 05					18 18			18 33				19 03				
Capenhurst	d					17 54								18 24			18 39				19 09				
Ellesmere Port	d			17 42							18 12								18 46					19 16	
Overpool	d			17 45							18 15								18 49					19 19	
Little Sutton	d			17 47							18 17								18 51					19 21	
Hooton	d			17 51		17 59			18 14		18 21			18 29			18 44		18 59		19 14			19 29	
Eastham Rake	d			17 53		18 01			18 16		18 23			18 31			18 46		19 01		19 16			19 31	
Bromborough	d			17 56		18 03			18 18		18 26			18 33			18 48		19 03		19 18			19 33	
Bromborough Rake	d			17 58		18 05			18 20		18 28			18 35			18 50		19 05		19 20			19 35	
Spital	d			18 00		18 07			18 22		18 30			18 37			18 52		19 07		19 22			19 37	
Port Sunlight	d			18 02		18 09			18 24		18 32			18 39			18 54		19 09		19 24			19 39	
Bebington	d			18 04		18 11			18 26		18 34			18 41			18 56		19 11		19 26			19 41	
Rock Ferry	d			18 07		18 14			18 29		18 37			18 44			18 59		19 14		19 29			19 44	
Green Lane	d			18 09		18 17			18 32		18 39			18 47			19 02		19 17		19 32			19 47	
Birkenhead Central	d			18 12		18 19			18 34		18 42			18 49			19 04		19 19		19 34			19 49	
West Kirby	d				17 51			18 06				18 21				18 36				19 01					19 31
Hoylake	d				17 54			18 09				18 24				18 39				19 04					19 34
Manor Road	d				17 56			18 11				18 26				18 41				19 06					19 36
Meols	d				17 58			18 13				18 28				18 43				19 08					19 38
Moreton (Merseyside)	d				18 01			18 16				18 31				18 46				19 11					19 41
Leasowe	d				18 03			18 18				18 33				18 48				19 13					19 43
Bidston	d				18 06			18 21				18 36				18 51				19 16					19 46
New Brighton	d	17 53					18 08			18 23					18 38			18 53				19 23			
Wallasey Grove Road	d	17 57					18 12			18 27					18 42			18 57				19 27			
Wallasey Village	d	17 59					18 14			18 29					18 44			18 59				19 29			
Birkenhead North	d	18 04			18 09		18 19	18 24		18 34		18 39			18 49	18 54		19 04		19 19		19 34			19 49
Birkenhead Park	d	18 06			18 11		18 21	18 26		18 36		18 41			18 51	18 56		19 06		19 21		19 36			19 51
Conway Park	d	18 09			18 14		18 24	18 29		18 39		18 44			18 54	18 59		19 09		19 24		19 39			19 54
Hamilton Square	d	18 11		18 14	18 16	18 21	18 26	18 31	18 36	18 41	18 44	18 46		18 51	18 56	19 01	19 06	19 11	19 21	19 26	19 36	19 41		19 51	19 56
James Street	d	18 14		18 17	18 19	18 24	18 29	18 34	18 39	18 44	18 47	18 49		18 54	18 59	19 04	19 09	19 14	19 24	19 29	19 39	19 44		19 54	19 59
Moorfields	a	18 16		18 18	18 21	18 26	18 31	18 36	18 41	18 46	18 48	18 51		18 56	19 01	19 06	19 11	19 16	19 26	19 31	19 41	19 46		19 56	20 01
Liverpool Lime Street	a	18 18		18 20	18 23	18 28	18 33	18 38	18 43	18 48	18 50	18 53		18 58	19 03	19 08	19 13	19 18	19 28	19 33	19 43	19 48		19 58	20 03
Liverpool Central	a	18 20		18 22	18 25	18 30	18 35	18 40	18 45	18 50	18 52	18 55		19 00	19 05	19 10	19 15	19 20	19 30	19 35	19 45	19 50		20 00	20 05

		ME	ME	ME	ME	ME	ME	ME		ME	ME	ME	ME	ME	ME	ME	ME	ME		ME	ME	ME	ME	ME	ME
Chester	d	19 30				20 00					20 30				21 00					21 30				22 00	
Bache	d	19 33				20 03					20 33				21 03					21 33				22 03	
Capenhurst	d	19 39				20 09					20 39				21 09					21 39				22 09	
Ellesmere Port	d			19 49				20 19					20 49				21 19					21 49			
Overpool	d			19 52				20 22					20 52				21 22					21 52			
Little Sutton	d			19 54				20 24					20 54				21 24					21 54			
Hooton	d	19 44		19 59		20 14		20 29			20 44		20 59		21 14		21 29			21 44		21 59		22 14	
Eastham Rake	d	19 46		20 01		20 16		20 31			20 46		21 01		21 16		21 31			21 46		22 01		22 16	
Bromborough	d	19 48		20 03		20 18		20 33			20 48		21 03		21 18		21 33			21 48		22 03		22 18	
Bromborough Rake	d	19 50		20 05		20 20		20 35			20 50		21 05		21 20		21 35			21 50		22 05		22 20	
Spital	d	19 52		20 07		20 22		20 37			20 52		21 07		21 22		21 37			21 52		22 07		22 22	
Port Sunlight	d	19 54		20 09		20 24		20 39			20 54		21 09		21 24		21 39			21 54		22 09		22 24	
Bebington	d	19 56		20 11		20 26		20 41			20 56		21 11		21 26		21 41			21 56		22 11		22 26	
Rock Ferry	d	19 59		20 14		20 29		20 44			20 59		21 14		21 29		21 44			21 59		22 14		22 29	
Green Lane	d	20 02		20 17		20 32		20 47			21 02		21 17		21 32		21 47			22 02		22 17		22 32	
Birkenhead Central	d	20 04		20 19		20 34		20 49			21 04		21 19		21 34		21 49			22 04		22 19		22 34	
West Kirby	d				20 01					20 31				21 01				21 31					22 01		
Hoylake	d				20 04					20 34				21 04				21 34					22 04		
Manor Road	d				20 06					20 36				21 06				21 36					22 06		
Meols	d				20 08					20 38				21 08				21 38					22 08		
Moreton (Merseyside)	d				20 11					20 41				21 11				21 41					22 11		
Leasowe	d				20 13					20 43				21 13				21 43					22 13		
Bidston	d				20 16					20 46				21 16				21 46					22 16		
New Brighton	d		19 53				20 23					20 53				21 23					21 53				22 23
Wallasey Grove Road	d		19 57				20 27					20 57				21 27					21 57				22 27
Wallasey Village	d		19 59				20 29					20 59				21 29					21 59				22 29
Birkenhead North	d		20 04		20 19		20 34			20 49		21 04		21 19		21 34		21 49			22 04		22 19		22 34
Birkenhead Park	d		20 06		20 21		20 36			20 51		21 06		21 21		21 36		21 51			22 06		22 21		22 36
Conway Park	d		20 09		20 24		20 39			20 54		21 09		21 24		21 39		21 54			22 09		22 24		22 39
Hamilton Square	d	20 06	20 11	20 21	20 26	20 36	20 41	20 51		20 56	21 06	21 11	21 21	21 26	21 36	21 41	21 51	21 56		22 06	22 11	22 21	22 26	22 36	22 41
James Street	d	20 09	20 14	20 24	20 29	20 39	20 44	20 54		20 59	21 09	21 14	21 24	21 29	21 39	21 44	21 54	21 59		22 09	22 14	22 24	22 29	22 39	22 44
Moorfields	a	20 11	20 16	20 26	20 31	20 41	20 46	20 56		21 01	21 11	21 16	21 26	21 31	21 41	21 46	21 56	22 01		22 11	22 16	22 26	22 31	22 41	22 46
Liverpool Lime Street	a	20 13	20 18	20 28	20 33	20 43	20 48	20 58		21 03	21 13	21 18	21 28	21 33	21 43	21 48	21 58	22 03		22 13	22 18	22 28	22 33	22 43	22 48
Liverpool Central	a	20 15	20 20	20 30	20 35	20 45	20 50	21 00		21 05	21 15	21 20	21 30	21 35	21 45	21 50	22 00	22 05		22 15	22 20	22 30	22 35	22 45	22 50

Table 106

Mondays to Saturdays

Chester, Ellesmere Port, West Kirby and New Brighton - Birkenhead and Liverpool

Network Diagram - see first Page of Table 101

		ME	ME	ME		ME	ME	ME	ME	ME	ME
Chester	d			22 30					23 00		
Bache	d			22 33					23 03		
Capenhurst	d			22 39					23 09		
Ellesmere Port	d	22 19					22 49				23 19
Overpool	d	22 22					22 52				23 22
Little Sutton	d	22 24					22 54				23 24
Hooton	d	22 29		22 44			22 59		23 14		23 29
Eastham Rake	d	22 31		22 46			23 01		23 16		23 31
Bromborough	d	22 33		22 48			23 03		23 18		23 33
Bromborough Rake	d	22 35		22 50			23 05		23 20		23 35
Spital	d	22 37		22 52			23 07		23 22		23 37
Port Sunlight	d	22 39		22 54			23 09		23 24		23 39
Bebington	d	22 41		22 56			23 11		23 26		23 41
Rock Ferry	d	22 44		22 59			23 14		23 29		23 44
Green Lane	d	22 47		23 02			23 17		23 32		23 47
Birkenhead Central	d	22 49		23 04			23 19		23 34		23 49
West Kirby	d		22 31					23 01			
Hoylake	d		22 34					23 04			
Manor Road	d		22 36					23 06			
Meols	d		22 38					23 08			
Moreton (Merseyside)	d		22 41					23 11			
Leasowe	d		22 43					23 13			
Bidston	d		22 46					23 16			
New Brighton	d					22 53				23 23	
Wallasey Grove Road	d					22 57				23 27	
Wallasey Village	d					22 59				23 29	
Birkenhead North	d		22 49			23 04		23 19		23 34	
Birkenhead Park	d		22 51			23 06		23 21		23 36	
Conway Park	d		22 54			23 09		23 24		23 39	
Hamilton Square	d	22 51	22 56	23 06		23 11	23 21	23 26	23 36	23 41	23 51
James Street	d	22 54	22 59	23 09		23 14	23 24	23 29	23 39	23 44	23 54
Moorfields	a	22 56	23 01	23 11		23 16	23 26	23 31	23 41	23 46	23 56
Liverpool Lime Street	a	22 58	23 03	23 13		23 18	23 28	23 33	23 43	23 48	23 58
Liverpool Central	a	23 00	23 05	23 15		23 20	23 30	23 35	23 45	23 50	23 59

Sundays

		ME	ME	ME	ME	ME	ME	ME	ME	ME		ME	ME	ME	ME		ME	ME	ME		ME	ME
Chester	d							08 00					08 30						23 00			
Bache	d							08 03					08 33						23 03			
Capenhurst	d							08 09					08 39						23 09			
Ellesmere Port	d					07 49				08 19					08 49		22 49					23 19
Overpool	d					07 52				08 22					08 52		22 52					23 22
Little Sutton	d					07 54				08 24					08 54		22 54					23 24
Hooton	d			07 44		07 58		08 14		08 29			08 44		08 59		22 59		23 14			23 29
Eastham Rake	d			07 46		08 00		08 16		08 31			08 46		09 01		23 01		23 16			23 31
Bromborough	d			07 48		08 03		08 18		08 33			08 48		09 03		23 03		23 18			23 33
Bromborough Rake	d			07 50		08 05		08 20		08 35			08 50		09 05		23 05		23 20			23 35
Spital	d			07 52		08 07		08 22		08 37			08 52		09 07		23 07		23 22			23 37
Port Sunlight	d			07 54		08 09		08 24		08 39			08 54		09 09		23 09		23 24			23 39
Bebington	d			07 56		08 11		08 26		08 41			08 56		09 11		23 11		23 26			23 41
Rock Ferry	d	07 44	07 49	07 59		08 14		08 29		08 44			08 59		09 14	and at	23 14		23 29			23 44
Green Lane	d	07 47	07 52	08 02		08 16		08 32		08 47			09 02		09 17	the same	23 17		23 32			23 47
Birkenhead Central	d	07 49	07 54	08 04		08 19		08 34		08 49			09 04		09 19	minutes	23 19		23 34			23 49
West Kirby	d						08 01					08 31				past		23 01				
Hoylake	d						08 04					08 34				each		23 04				
Manor Road	d						08 06					08 36				hour until		23 06				
Meols	d						08 08					08 38						23 08				
Moreton (Merseyside)	d						08 11					08 41						23 11				
Leasowe	d						08 13					08 43						23 13				
Bidston	d						08 16					08 46						23 16				
New Brighton	d				07 53				08 23					08 53							23 23	
Wallasey Grove Road	d				07 57				08 27					08 57							23 27	
Wallasey Village	d				07 59				08 29					08 59							23 29	
Birkenhead North	d				08 04		08 19		08 34			08 49		09 04				23 19			23 34	
Birkenhead Park	d				08 06		08 21		08 36			08 51		09 06				23 21			23 36	
Conway Park	d				08 09		08 24		08 39			08 54		09 09				23 24			23 39	
Hamilton Square	d	07 51	07 56	08 06	08 11	08 21	08 26	08 36	08 41	08 51		08 56	09 06	09 11	09 21		23 21	23 26	23 36		23 41	23 51
James Street	d	07 54	07 59	08 09	08 14	08 24	08 29	08 39	08 44	08 54		08 59	09 09	09 14	09 24		23 24	23 29	23 39		23 44	23 54
Moorfields	a	07 56	08 01	08 11	08 16	08 25	08 31	08 41	08 46	08 56		09 01	09 11	09 16	09 26		23 26	23 31	23 41		23 46	23 56
Liverpool Lime Street	a	07 58	08 03	08 13	08 18	08 27	08 33	08 43	08 48	08 58		09 03	09 13	09 18	09 28		23 28	23 33	23 43		23 48	23 58
Liverpool Central	a	08 00	08 05	08 15	08 20	08 29	08 35	08 45	08 50	09 00		09 05	09 15	09 20	09 30		23 30	23 35	23 45		23 50	23 59

Table 109

Mondays to Fridays

Helsby - Ellesmere Port

Network Diagram - see first Page of Table 101

Miles				NT	NT	NT	NT
—	Warrington Bank Quay	81	d	05 49			
0	**Helsby**		d	06 03	06 33	15 17	15 48
2	Ince & Elton		d	06 06	06 36	15 20	15 51
2¾	Stanlow & Thornton		d	06 08	06 38	15 22	15 53
5¼	**Ellesmere Port**		a	06 15	06 45	15 28	15 59

Saturdays

			NT	NT	NT	NT
Warrington Bank Quay	81	d	05 49			
Helsby		d	06 03	06 33	15 17	15 48
Ince & Elton		d	06 06	06 36	15 20	15 51
Stanlow & Thornton		d	06 08	06 38	15 22	15 53
Ellesmere Port		a	06 15	06 45	15 28	15 59

Table 109

Mondays to Fridays

Ellesmere Port - Helsby

Network Diagram - see first Page of Table 101

Miles				NT	NT	NT	NT
0	**Ellesmere Port**		d	06 19	06 53	15 34	16 04
2½	Stanlow & Thornton		d	06 23	06 57	15 38	16 08
3¼	Ince & Elton		d	06 26	07 00	15 41	16 11
5¼	**Helsby**		a	06 30	07 03	15 45	16 14
—	Warrington Bank Quay	81	a		07 23		16 34

Saturdays

			NT	NT	NT	NT
Ellesmere Port		d	06 19	06 56	15 34	16 04
Stanlow & Thornton		d	06 23	07 00	15 38	16 08
Ince & Elton		d	06 26	07 03	15 41	16 11
Helsby		a	06 30	07 07	15 45	16 14
Warrington Bank Quay	81	a				16 34

No Sunday Service

Network Diagram for Tables 114, 115

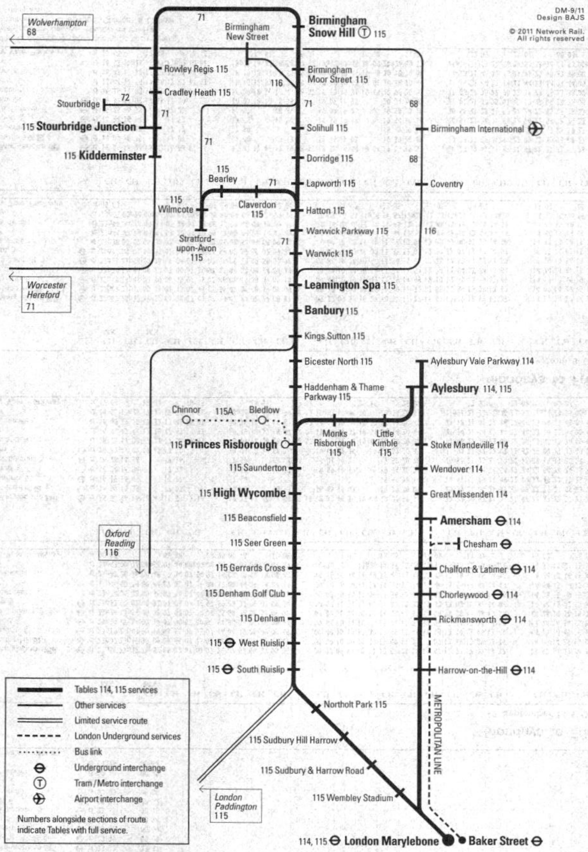

Table 114

Mondays to Fridays

until 27 July

London - Amersham and Aylesbury

Network Diagram - see first Page of Table 114

Miles			CH MX	CH ◇ A	CH MX	CH	CH ◇	CH	CH	CH	CH ◇	CH ◇	CH ◇	CH	CH ◇	CH	CH	CH	CH	CH ◇	CH	CH	CH ◇
0	**London Marylebone** 10	⊖ d	22p57	23p27	23p57	06 32	07 03	07 24	07 57	08 27	08 57	09 27	09 57	10 27	10 57	11 27	11 57	12 27	12 57	13 27	13 57	14 27	14 57
9	Harrow-on-the-Hill 3 §	⊖ d	23p09	23p39	00 09	06 45	07 15	07 36	08 09	08 39	09 09	09 39	10 09	10 39	11 09	11 39	12 09	12 39	13 09	13 39	14 09	14 39	15 09
17	Rickmansworth §	⊖ d	23p19	23p49	00 19	06 55	07 25	07 46	08 19	08 49	09 19	09 49	10 19	10 49	11 19	11 49	12 19	12 49	13 19	13 49	14 19	14 49	15 19
19¾	Chorleywood §	⊖ d	23p24	23p54	00 24	07 00	07 30	07 51	08 24	08 54	09 24	09 54	10 24	10 54	11 24	11 54	12 24	12 54	13 24	13 54	14 24	14 54	15 24
21½	Chalfont & Latimer §	⊖ d	23p28	23p58	00 28	07 04	07 34	07 55	08 28	08 58	09 28	09 58	10 28	10 58	11 28	11 58	12 28	12 58	13 28	13 58	14 28	14 58	15 28
23½	**Amersham** §	⊖ d	23p32	00 02	00 32	07 08	07 38	07 59	08 32	09 02	09 32	10 02	10 32	11 02	11 32	12 02	12 32	13 02	13 32	14 02	14 32	15 02	15 32
28¾	Great Missenden	d	23p38	00 08	00 38	07 14	07 44	08 05	08 38	09 08	09 38	10 08	10 38	11 08	11 38	12 08	12 38	13 08	13 38	14 08	14 38	15 08	15 38
33¼	Wendover	d	23p44	00 14	00 44	07 20	07 50	08 11	08 44	09 14	09 44	10 14	10 44	11 14	11 44	12 14	12 44	13 14	13 44	14 14	14 44	15 14	15 44
35¼	Stoke Mandeville	d	23p48	00 18	00 48	07 24	07 54	08 15	08 48	09 18	09 48	10 18	10 48	11 18	11 48	12 18	12 48	13 18	13 48	14 18	14 48	15 18	15 48
37¾	**Aylesbury**	d	23p53	00a26	00a56	07 44	08a02	08 20	09 05	09a26	09 59	10a26	10 53	11a26	11 53	12a26	12 53	13a26	13 53	14a26	14 53	15a26	15 53
40½	**Aylesbury Vale Parkway**	a	00 03			07 54		08 29	09 16		10 08		11 02		12 05		13 05		14 02		15 02		16 02

		CH	CH	CH	CH	CH	CH	CH	CH	CH	CH	CH	CH	CH	CH	CH	CH	CH ◇	CH	CH	CH	CH	CH ◇
London Marylebone 10	⊖ d	15 27	15 56	16 26	16 43	16 53	17 16	17 27	17 46	17 59	18 19	18 33	18 50	19 04	19 27	19 57	20 27	20 57	21 27	21 57	22 27	22 57	23 27
Harrow-on-the-Hill 3 §	⊖ d	15 39	16 09	16 39		17 07		17 40		18 13		18 45	19 03		19 39	20 09	20 39	21 09	21 39	22 09	22 39	23 09	23 39
Rickmansworth §	⊖ d	15 49	16 19	16 49		17 17		17 50							19 49	20 19	20 49	21 19	21 49	22 19	22 49	23 19	23 49
Chorleywood §	⊖ d	15 54	16 24	16 54		17 22		17 55		18 27		18 59	19 17		19 54	20 24	20 54	21 24	21 54	22 24	22 54	23 24	23 54
Chalfont & Latimer §	⊖ d	15 58	16 28	16 58		17 26		17 59		18 31		19 03	19 21		19 58	20 28	20 58	21 28	21 58	22 28	22 58	23 28	23 58
Amersham §	⊖ d	16 02	16 32	17 02	17 15	17 30		18 03	18 18	18 35		19 07	19 25		20 02	20 32	21 02	21 32	22 02	22 32	23 02	23 32	00 02
Great Missenden	d	16 08	16 38	17 08	17 22	17 36	17 51	18 09	18 26	18 41	18 57	19 13	19 31	19 44	20 08	20 38	21 08	21 38	22 08	22 38	23 08	23 38	00 08
Wendover	d	16 14	16 44	17 14	17 28	17 42	17 57	18 15	18 32	18 47	19 03	19 19	19 37	19 51	20 14	20 44	21 14	21 44	22 14	22 44	23 14	23 44	00 14
Stoke Mandeville	d	16 18	16 48	17 18	17 32	17 46	18 01	18 19	18 37	18 51	19 07	19 23	19 41	19 55	20 18	20 48	21 18	21 48	22 18	22 48	23 18	23 48	00 18
Aylesbury	d	16a26	16 53	17a25	17 37	17a52	18 06	18a26	18 42	18a58	19 12	19a32	19a49	20 09	20a26	20 53	21a26	21 53	22a26	22 53	23a26	23 53	00a26
Aylesbury Vale Parkway	a		17 04		17 46		18 15		18 51		19 21			20 18		21 02		22 02		23 02		00 03	

		CH
London Marylebone 10	⊖ d	23 57
Harrow-on-the-Hill 3 §	⊖ d	00 09
Rickmansworth §	⊖ d	00 19
Chorleywood §	⊖ d	00 24
Chalfont & Latimer §	⊖ d	00 28
Amersham §	⊖ d	00 32
Great Missenden	d	00 38
Wendover	d	00 44
Stoke Mandeville	d	00 48
Aylesbury	d	00a56
Aylesbury Vale Parkway	a	

Mondays to Fridays

30 July to 7 September

		CH MX	CH ◇	CH MX	CH B	CH B	CH	CH ◇	CH	CH	CH	CH ◇	CH ◇	CH ◇	CH	CH ◇	CH	CH	CH	CH	CH ◇	CH	CH
London Marylebone 10	⊖ d	22p57	23p27	23p57	00 57	01 57	06 32	07 03	07 24	07 57	08 27	08 57	09 27	09 57	10 27	10 57	11 27	11 57	12 27	12 57	13 27	13 57	14 27
Harrow-on-the-Hill 3 §	⊖ d	23p09	23p39	00 09			06 45	07 15	07 36	08 09	08 39	09 09	09 39	10 09	10 39	11 09	11 39	12 09	12 39	13 09	13 39	14 09	14 39
Rickmansworth §	⊖ d	23p19	23p49	00 19			06 55	07 25	07 46	08 19	08 49	09 19	09 49	10 19	10 49	11 19	11 49	12 19	12 49	13 19	13 49	14 19	14 49
Chorleywood §	⊖ d	23p24	23p54	00 24			07 00	07 30	07 51	08 24	08 54	09 24	09 54	10 24	10 54	11 24	11 54	12 24	12 54	13 24	13 54	14 24	14 54
Chalfont & Latimer §	⊖ d	23p28	23p58	00 28			07 04	07 34	07 55	08 28	08 58	09 28	09 58	10 28	10 58	11 28	11 58	12 28	12 58	13 28	13 58	14 28	14 58
Amersham §	⊖ d	23p32	00 02	00 32	01 28	02 28	07 08	07 38	07 59	08 32	09 02	09 32	10 02	10 32	11 02	11 32	12 02	12 32	13 02	13 32	14 02	14 32	15 02
Great Missenden	d	23p38	00 08	00 38	01 34	02 34	07 14	07 44	08 05	08 38	09 08	09 38	10 08	10 38	11 08	11 38	12 08	12 38	13 08	13 38	14 08	14 38	15 08
Wendover	d	23p44	00 14	00 44	01 40	02 40	07 20	07 50	08 11	08 44	09 14	09 44	10 14	10 44	11 14	11 44	12 14	12 44	13 14	13 44	14 14	14 44	15 14
Stoke Mandeville	d	23p48	00 18	00 48	01 44	02 44	07 24	07 54	08 15	08 48	09 18	09 48	10 18	10 48	11 18	11 48	12 18	12 48	13 18	13 48	14 18	14 48	15 18
Aylesbury	d	23p53	00a26	00a56	01a52	02a52	07 44	08a02	08 20	09 05	09a26	09 59	10a26	10 53	11a26	11 53	12a26	12 53	13a26	13 53	14a26	14 53	15a26
Aylesbury Vale Parkway	a	00 03					07 54		08 29	09 16		10 08		11 02		12 05		13 05		14 02		15 02	

		CH ◇	CH	CH	CH	CH	CH	CH	CH	CH	CH	CH	CH	CH	CH	CH	CH	CH	CH ◇	CH	CH	CH	CH
London Marylebone 10	⊖ d	14 57	15 27	15 56	16 26	16 43	16 53	17 16	17 27	17 46	17 59	18 19	18 33	18 50	19 04	19 27	19 57	20 27	20 57	21 27	21 57	22 27	22 57
Harrow-on-the-Hill 3 §	⊖ d	15 09	15 39	16 09	16 39		17 07		17 40		18 13		18 45	19 03		19 39	20 09	20 39	21 09	21 39	22 09	22 39	23 09
Rickmansworth §	⊖ d	15 19	15 49	16 19	16 49		17 17		17 50							19 49	20 19	20 49	21 19	21 49	22 19	22 49	23 19
Chorleywood §	⊖ d	15 24	15 54	16 24	16 54		17 22		17 55		18 27		18 59	19 17		19 54	20 24	20 54	21 24	21 54	22 24	22 54	23 24
Chalfont & Latimer §	⊖ d	15 28	15 58	16 28	16 58		17 26		17 59		18 31		19 03	19 21		19 58	20 28	20 58	21 28	21 58	22 28	22 58	23 28
Amersham §	⊖ d	15 32	16 02	16 32	17 02	17 15	17 30		18 03	18 18	18 35		19 07	19 25		20 02	20 32	21 02	21 32	22 02	22 32	23 02	23 32
Great Missenden	d	15 38	16 08	16 38	17 08	17 22	17 36	17 51	18 09	18 26	18 41	18 57	19 13	19 31	19 44	20 08	20 38	21 08	21 38	22 08	22 38	23 08	23 38
Wendover	d	15 44	16 14	16 44	17 14	17 28	17 42	17 57	18 15	18 32	18 47	19 03	19 19	19 37	19 51	20 14	20 44	21 14	21 44	22 14	22 44	23 14	23 44
Stoke Mandeville	d	15 48	16 18	16 48	17 18	17 32	17 46	18 01	18 19	18 37	18 51	19 07	19 23	19 41	19 55	20 18	20 48	21 18	21 48	22 18	22 48	23 18	23 48
Aylesbury	d	15 53	16a26	16 53	17a25	17 37	17a52	18 06	18a26	18 42	18a58	19 12	19a32	19a49	20 09	20a26	20 53	21a26	21 53	22a26	22 53	23a26	23 53
Aylesbury Vale Parkway	a	16 02		17 04		17 46		18 15		18 51		19 21			20 18		21 02		22 02		23 02		00 03

§ London Underground Limited (Metropolitan Line) services operate between Harrow-on-the-Hill, Rickmansworth, Chorleywood, Chalfont & Latimer and Amersham

A not 14 May

B not from 14 August

Table 114

Mondays to Fridays

30 July to 7 September

London - Amersham and Aylesbury

Network Diagram - see first Page of Table 114

		CH ◇	CH
London Marylebone 10	⊖ d	23 27	23 57
Harrow-on-the-Hill 3 §	⊖ d	23 39	00 09
Rickmansworth §	⊖ d	23 49	00 19
Chorleywood §	⊖ d	23 54	00 24
Chalfont & Latimer §	⊖ d	23 58	00 28
Amersham §	⊖ d	00 02	00 32
Great Missenden	d	00 08	00 38
Wendover	d	00 14	00 44
Stoke Mandeville	d	00 18	00 48
Aylesbury	d	00a26	00a56
Aylesbury Vale Parkway	a		

Mondays to Fridays

10 September to 5 October

		CH MX	CH ◇	CH MX	CH	CH ◇	CH	CH	CH	CH ◇	CH ◇	CH ◇	CH	CH ◇	CH	CH	CH	CH	CH ◇	CH	CH	CH ◇	CH
London Marylebone 10	⊖ d	22p57	23p27	23p57	06 32	07 03	07 24	07 57	08 27	08 57	09 27	09 57	10 27	10 57	11 27	11 57	12 27	12 57	13 27	13 57	14 27	14 57	15 27
Harrow-on-the-Hill 3 §	⊖ d	23p09	23p39	00 09	06 45	07 15	07 36	08 09	08 39	09 09	09 39	10 09	10 39	11 09	11 39	12 09	12 39	13 09	13 39	14 09	14 39	15 09	15 39
Rickmansworth §	⊖ d	23p19	23p49	00 19	06 55	07 25	07 46	08 19	08 49	09 19	09 49	10 19	10 49	11 19	11 49	12 19	12 49	13 19	13 49	14 19	14 49	15 19	15 49
Chorleywood §	⊖ d	23p24	23p54	00 24	07 00	07 30	07 51	08 24	08 54	09 24	09 54	10 24	10 54	11 24	11 54	12 24	12 54	13 24	13 54	14 24	14 54	15 24	15 54
Chalfont & Latimer §	⊖ d	23p28	23p58	00 28	07 04	07 34	07 55	08 28	08 58	09 28	09 58	10 28	10 58	11 28	11 58	12 28	12 58	13 28	13 58	14 28	14 58	15 28	15 58
Amersham §	⊖ d	23p32	00 02	00 32	07 08	07 38	07 59	08 32	09 02	09 32	10 02	10 32	11 02	11 32	12 02	12 32	13 02	13 32	14 02	14 32	15 02	15 32	16 02
Great Missenden	d	23p38	00 08	00 38	07 14	07 44	08 05	08 38	09 08	09 38	10 08	10 38	11 08	11 38	12 08	12 38	13 08	13 38	14 08	14 38	15 08	15 38	16 08
Wendover	d	23p44	00 14	00 44	07 20	07 50	08 11	08 44	09 14	09 44	10 14	10 44	11 14	11 44	12 14	12 44	13 14	13 44	14 14	14 44	15 14	15 44	16 14
Stoke Mandeville	d	23p48	00 18	00 48	07 24	07 54	08 15	08 48	09 18	09 48	10 18	10 48	11 18	11 48	12 18	12 48	13 18	13 48	14 18	14 48	15 18	15 48	16 18
Aylesbury	d	23p53	00a26	00a56	07 44	08a02	08 20	09 05	09a26	09 59	10a26	10 53	11a26	11 53	12a26	12 53	13a26	13 53	14a26	14 53	15a26	15 53	16a26
Aylesbury Vale Parkway	a	00 03			07 54		08 29	09 16		10 08		11 02		12 05		13 05		14 02		15 02		16 02	

		CH	CH	CH	CH	CH	CH	CH	CH	CH	CH	CH	CH	CH	CH	CH	CH ◇	CH	CH	CH	CH	CH ◇	CH
London Marylebone 10	⊖ d	15 56	16 26	16 43	16 53	17 16	17 27	17 46	17 59	18 19	18 33	18 50	19 04	19 27	19 57	20 27	20 57	21 27	21 57	22 27	22 57	23 27	23 57
Harrow-on-the-Hill 3 §	⊖ d	16 09	16 39		17 07		17 40		18 13		18 45	19 03		19 39	20 09	20 39	21 09	21 39	22 09	22 39	23 09	23 39	00 09
Rickmansworth §	⊖ d	16 19	16 49		17 17		17 50							19 49	20 19	20 49	21 19	21 49	22 19	22 49	23 19	23 49	00 19
Chorleywood §	⊖ d	16 24	16 54		17 22		17 55		18 27		18 59	19 17		19 54	20 24	20 54	21 24	21 54	22 24	22 54	23 24	23 54	00 24
Chalfont & Latimer §	⊖ d	16 28	16 58		17 26		17 59		18 31		19 03	19 21		19 58	20 28	20 58	21 28	21 58	22 28	22 58	23 28	23 58	00 28
Amersham §	⊖ d	16 32	17 02	17 15	17 30		18 03	18 18	18 35		19 07	19 25		20 02	20 32	21 02	21 32	22 02	22 32	23 02	23 32	00 02	00 32
Great Missenden	d	16 38	17 08	17 22	17 36	17 51	18 09	18 26	18 41	18 57	19 13	19 31	19 44	20 08	20 38	21 08	21 38	22 08	22 38	23 08	23 38	00 08	00 38
Wendover	d	16 44	17 14	17 28	17 42	17 57	18 15	18 32	18 47	19 03	19 19	19 37	19 51	20 14	20 44	21 14	21 44	22 14	22 44	23 14	23 44	00 14	00 44
Stoke Mandeville	d	16 48	17 18	17 32	17 46	18 01	18 19	18 37	18 51	19 07	19 23	19 41	19 55	20 18	20 48	21 18	21 48	22 18	22 48	23 18	23 48	00 18	00 48
Aylesbury	d	16 53	17a25	17 37	17a52	18 06	18a26	18 42	18a58	19 12	19a32	19a49	20 09	20a26	20 53	21a26	21 53	22a26	22 53	23a26	23 53	00a26	00a56
Aylesbury Vale Parkway	a	17 04		17 46		18 15		18 51		19 21			20 18		21 02		22 02		23 02		00 03		

Mondays to Fridays

from 8 October

		CH MX	CH ◇	CH MX	CH	CH ◇	CH	CH	CH	CH ◇	CH ◇	CH ◇	CH	CH ◇	CH	CH	CH	CH	CH ◇	CH	CH	CH ◇	CH
London Marylebone 10	⊖ d	22p57	23p27	23p57	06 32	07 03	07 24	07 57	08 27	08 57	09 27	09 57	10 27	10 57	11 27	11 57	12 27	12 57	13 27	13 57	14 27	14 57	15 27
Harrow-on-the-Hill 3 §	⊖ d	23p09	23p39	00 09	06 45	07 15	07 36	08 09	08 39	09 09	09 39	10 09	10 39	11 09	11 39	12 09	12 39	13 09	13 39	14 09	14 39	15 09	15 39
Rickmansworth §	⊖ d	23p19	23p49	00 19	06 55	07 25	07 46	08 19	08 49	09 19	09 49	10 19	10 49	11 19	11 49	12 19	12 49	13 19	13 49	14 19	14 49	15 19	15 49
Chorleywood §	⊖ d	23p24	23p54	00 24	07 00	07 30	07 51	08 24	08 54	09 24	09 54	10 24	10 54	11 24	11 54	12 24	12 54	13 24	13 54	14 24	14 54	15 24	15 54
Chalfont & Latimer §	⊖ d	23p28	23p58	00 28	07 04	07 34	07 55	08 28	08 58	09 28	09 58	10 28	10 58	11 28	11 58	12 28	12 58	13 28	13 58	14 28	14 58	15 28	15 58
Amersham §	⊖ d	23p32	00 02	00 32	07 08	07 38	07 59	08 32	09 02	09 32	10 02	10 32	11 02	11 32	12 02	12 32	13 02	13 32	14 02	14 32	15 02	15 32	16 02
Great Missenden	d	23p38	00 08	00 38	07 14	07 44	08 05	08 38	09 08	09 38	10 08	10 38	11 08	11 38	12 08	12 38	13 08	13 38	14 08	14 38	15 08	15 38	16 08
Wendover	d	23p44	00 14	00 44	07 20	07 50	08 11	08 44	09 14	09 44	10 14	10 44	11 14	11 44	12 14	12 44	13 14	13 44	14 14	14 44	15 14	15 44	16 14
Stoke Mandeville	d	23p48	00 18	00 48	07 24	07 54	08 15	08 48	09 18	09 48	10 18	10 48	11 18	11 48	12 18	12 48	13 18	13 48	14 18	14 48	15 18	15 48	16 18
Aylesbury	d	23p53	00a26	00a56	07 44	08a02	08 20	09 05	09a26	09 59	10a26	10 53	11a26	11 53	12a26	12 53	13a26	13 53	14a26	14 53	15a26	15 53	16a26
Aylesbury Vale Parkway	a	00 03			07 54		08 29	09 16		10 08		11 02		12 05		13 05		14 02		15 02		16 02	

		CH	CH	CH	CH	CH	CH	CH	CH	CH	CH	CH	CH	CH	CH	CH	CH ◇	CH	CH	CH	CH	CH ◇	CH
London Marylebone 10	⊖ d	15 56	16 26	16 43	16 53	17 16	17 27	17 46	17 59	18 19	18 33	18 50	19 04	19 27	19 57	20 27	20 57	21 27	21 57	22 27	22 57	23 27	23 57
Harrow-on-the-Hill 3 §	⊖ d	16 09	16 39		17 07		17 40		18 13		18 45	19 03		19 39	20 09	20 39	21 09	21 39	22 09	22 39	23 09	23 39	00 09
Rickmansworth §	⊖ d	16 19	16 49		17 17		17 50							19 49	20 19	20 49	21 19	21 49	22 19	22 49	23 19	23 49	00 19
Chorleywood §	⊖ d	16 24	16 54		17 22		17 55		18 27		18 59	19 17		19 54	20 24	20 54	21 24	21 54	22 24	22 54	23 24	23 54	00 24
Chalfont & Latimer §	⊖ d	16 28	16 58		17 26		17 59		18 31		19 03	19 21		19 58	20 28	20 58	21 28	21 58	22 28	22 58	23 28	23 58	00 28
Amersham §	⊖ d	16 32	17 02	17 15	17 30		18 03	18 18	18 35		19 07	19 25		20 02	20 32	21 02	21 32	22 02	22 32	23 02	23 32	00 02	00 32
Great Missenden	d	16 38	17 08	17 22	17 36	17 51	18 09	18 26	18 41	18 57	19 13	19 31	19 44	20 08	20 38	21 08	21 38	22 08	22 38	23 08	23 38	00 08	00 38
Wendover	d	16 44	17 14	17 28	17 42	17 57	18 15	18 32	18 47	19 03	19 19	19 37	19 51	20 14	20 44	21 14	21 44	22 14	22 44	23 14	23 44	00 14	00 44
Stoke Mandeville	d	16 48	17 18	17 32	17 46	18 01	18 19	18 37	18 51	19 07	19 23	19 41	19 55	20 18	20 48	21 18	21 48	22 18	22 48	23 18	23 48	00 18	00 48
Aylesbury	d	16 53	17a25	17 37	17a52	18 06	18a26	18 42	18a58	19 12	19a32	19a49	20 09	20a26	20 53	21a26	21 53	22a26	22 53	23a26	23 53	00a26	00a56
Aylesbury Vale Parkway	a	17 04		17 46		18 15		18 51		19 21			20 18		21 02		22 02		23 02		00 03		

§ London Underground Limited (Metropolitan Line) services operate between Harrow-on-the-Hill, Rickmansworth, Chorleywood, Chalfont & Latimer and Amersham

London - Amersham and Aylesbury

Saturdays until 21 July

Network Diagram - see first Page of Table 114

		CH	CH	CH	CH	CH	CH	CH	CH	CH	CH	CH	CH	CH	CH	CH	CH	CH	CH	CH	CH	CH	CH
			◇			◇			◇					◇				◇			◇		
London Marylebone 10	⊖ d	22p57	23p27	23p57		07 27	07 57	08 27	08 57	09 27	09 57	10 27	10 57	11 27	11 57	12 27	12 57	13 27	13 57	14 27	14 57	15 27	15 57
Harrow-on-the-Hill 3 §	⊖ d	23p09	23p39	00 09		07 39	08 09	08 39	09 09	09 39	10 09	10 39	11 09	11 39	12 09	12 39	13 09	13 39	14 09	14 39	15 09	15 39	16 09
Rickmansworth §	⊖ d	23p19	23p49	00 19		07 49	08 19	08 49	09 19	09 49	10 19	10 49	11 19	11 49	12 19	12 49	13 19	13 49	14 19	14 49	15 19	15 49	16 19
Chorleywood §	⊖ d	23p24	23p54	00 24		07 54	08 24	08 54	09 24	09 54	10 24	10 54	11 24	11 54	12 24	12 54	13 24	13 54	14 24	14 54	15 24	15 54	16 24
Chalfont & Latimer §	⊖ d	23p28	23p58	00 28		07 58	08 28	08 58	09 28	09 58	10 28	10 58	11 28	11 58	12 28	12 58	13 28	13 58	14 28	14 58	15 28	15 58	16 28
Amersham §	⊖ d	23p32	00 02	00 32	07 05	08 02	08 32	09 02	09 32	10 02	10 32	11 02	11 32	12 02	12 32	13 02	13 32	14 02	14 32	15 02	15 32	16 02	16 32
Great Missenden	d	23p38	00 08	00 38	07 11	08 08	08 38	09 08	09 38	10 08	10 38	11 08	11 38	12 08	12 38	13 08	13 38	14 08	14 38	15 08	15 38	16 08	16 38
Wendover	d	23p44	00 14	00 44	07 17	08 14	08 44	09 14	09 44	10 14	10 44	11 14	11 44	12 14	12 44	13 14	13 44	14 14	14 44	15 14	15 44	16 14	16 44
Stoke Mandeville	d	23p48	00 18	00 48	07 21	08 18	08 48	09 18	09 48	10 18	10 48	11 18	11 48	12 18	12 48	13 18	13 48	14 18	14 48	15 18	15 48	16 18	16 48
Aylesbury	d	23p53	00a26	00a56	07a29	08a26	08 53	09a26	09 53	10a26	10 53	11a26	11 53	12a26	12 53	13a26	13 53	14a26	14 53	15a26	15 53	16a26	16 53
Aylesbury Vale Parkway	a	00 03					09 02		10 02		11 02		12 02		13 02		14 02		15 02		16 02		17 02

		CH	CH	CH	CH	CH	CH	CH	CH	CH	CH	CH	CH
										◇			
London Marylebone 10	⊖ d	16 27	16 57	17 27	17 57	18 27	18 57	19 27	19 57	20 57	21 57	22 57	23 57
Harrow-on-the-Hill 3 §	⊖ d	16 39	17 09	17 39	18 09	18 39	19 09	19 39	20 09	21 09	22 09	23 09	00 09
Rickmansworth §	⊖ d	16 49	17 19	17 49	18 19	18 49	19 19	19 49	20 19	21 19	22 19	23 19	00 19
Chorleywood §	⊖ d	16 54	17 24	17 54	18 24	18 54	19 24	19 54	20 24	21 24	22 24	23 24	00 24
Chalfont & Latimer §	⊖ d	16 58	17 28	17 58	18 28	18 58	19 28	19 58	20 28	21 28	22 28	23 28	00 28
Amersham §	⊖ d	17 02	17 32	18 02	18 32	19 02	19 32	20 02	20 32	21 32	22 32	23 32	00 32
Great Missenden	d	17 08	17 38	18 08	18 38	19 08	19 38	20 08	20 38	21 38	22 38	23 38	00 38
Wendover	d	17 14	17 44	18 14	18 44	19 14	19 44	20 14	20 44	21 44	22 44	23 44	00 44
Stoke Mandeville	d	17 18	17 48	18 18	18 48	19 18	19 48	20 18	20 48	21 48	22 48	23 48	00 48
Aylesbury	d	17a26	17 53	18a26	18 53	19a26	19 53	20a26	20 53	21 53	22 53	23 53	00a56
Aylesbury Vale Parkway	a		18 02		19 02		20 02		21 02	22 02	23 02	00 03	

Saturdays 28 July to 8 September

		CH	CH	CH	CH	CH	CH	CH	CH	CH	CH	CH	CH	CH	CH	CH	CH	CH	CH	CH	CH	CH	CH
			◇					◇			◇					◇				◇			◇
					A	A																	
London Marylebone 10	⊖ d	22p57	23p27	23p57	00 57	01 57		07 27	07 57	08 27	08 57	09 27	09 57	10 27	10 57	11 27	11 57	12 27	12 57	13 27	13 57	14 27	14 57
Harrow-on-the-Hill 3 §	⊖ d	23p09	23p39	00 09				07 39	08 09	08 39	09 09	09 39	10 09	10 39	11 09	11 39	12 09	12 39	13 09	13 39	14 09	14 39	15 09
Rickmansworth §	⊖ d	23p19	23p49	00 19				07 49	08 19	08 49	09 19	09 49	10 19	10 49	11 19	11 49	12 19	12 49	13 19	13 49	14 19	14 49	15 19
Chorleywood §	⊖ d	23p24	23p54	00 24				07 54	08 24	08 54	09 24	09 54	10 24	10 54	11 24	11 54	12 24	12 54	13 24	13 54	14 24	14 54	15 24
Chalfont & Latimer §	⊖ d	23p28	23p58	00 28				07 58	08 28	08 58	09 28	09 58	10 28	10 58	11 28	11 58	12 28	12 58	13 28	13 58	14 28	14 58	15 28
Amersham §	⊖ d	23p32	00 02	00 32	01 28	02 28	07 05	08 02	08 32	09 02	09 32	10 02	10 32	11 02	11 32	12 02	12 32	13 02	13 32	14 02	14 32	15 02	15 32
Great Missenden	d	23p38	00 08	00 38	01 34	02 34	07 11	08 08	08 38	09 08	09 38	10 08	10 38	11 08	11 38	12 08	12 38	13 08	13 38	14 08	14 38	15 08	15 38
Wendover	d	23p44	00 14	00 44	01 40	02 40	07 17	08 14	08 44	09 14	09 44	10 14	10 44	11 14	11 44	12 14	12 44	13 14	13 44	14 14	14 44	15 14	15 44
Stoke Mandeville	d	23p48	00 18	00 48	01 44	02 44	07 21	08 18	08 48	09 18	09 48	10 18	10 48	11 18	11 48	12 18	12 48	13 18	13 48	14 18	14 48	15 18	15 48
Aylesbury	d	23p53	00a26	00a56	01a52	02a52	07a29	08a26	08 53	09a26	09 53	10a26	10 53	11a26	11 53	12a26	12 53	13a26	13 53	14a26	14 53	15a26	15 53
Aylesbury Vale Parkway	a	00 03							09 02		10 02		11 02		12 02		13 02		14 02		15 02		16 02

		CH	CH	CH	CH	CH	CH	CH	CH	CH	CH	CH	CH	CH	CH
												◇			
London Marylebone 10	⊖ d	15 27	15 57	16 27	16 57	17 27	17 57	18 27	18 57	19 27	19 57	20 57	21 57	22 57	23 57
Harrow-on-the-Hill 3 §	⊖ d	15 39	16 09	16 39	17 09	17 39	18 09	18 39	19 09	19 39	20 09	21 09	22 09	23 09	00 09
Rickmansworth §	⊖ d	15 49	16 19	16 49	17 19	17 49	18 19	18 49	19 19	19 49	20 19	21 19	22 19	23 19	00 19
Chorleywood §	⊖ d	15 54	16 24	16 54	17 24	17 54	18 24	18 54	19 24	19 54	20 24	21 24	22 24	23 24	00 24
Chalfont & Latimer §	⊖ d	15 58	16 28	16 58	17 28	17 58	18 28	18 58	19 28	19 58	20 28	21 28	22 28	23 28	00 28
Amersham §	⊖ d	16 02	16 32	17 02	17 32	18 02	18 32	19 02	19 32	20 02	20 32	21 32	22 32	23 32	00 32
Great Missenden	d	16 08	16 38	17 08	17 38	18 08	18 38	19 08	19 38	20 08	20 38	21 38	22 38	23 38	00 38
Wendover	d	16 14	16 44	17 14	17 44	18 14	18 44	19 14	19 44	20 14	20 44	21 44	22 44	23 44	00 44
Stoke Mandeville	d	16 18	16 48	17 18	17 48	18 18	18 48	19 18	19 48	20 18	20 48	21 48	22 48	23 48	00 48
Aylesbury	d	16a26	16 53	17a26	17 53	18a26	18 53	19a26	19 53	20a26	20 53	21 53	22 53	23 53	00a56
Aylesbury Vale Parkway	a		17 02		18 02		19 02		20 02		21 02	22 02	23 02	00 03	

Saturdays 15 September to 6 October

		CH	CH	CH	CH	CH	CH	CH	CH	CH	CH	CH	CH	CH	CH	CH	CH	CH	CH	CH	CH	CH	CH
			◇			◇			◇					◇				◇			◇		
London Marylebone 10	⊖ d	22p57	23p27	23p57		07 27	07 57	08 27	08 57	09 27	09 57	10 27	10 57	11 27	11 57	12 27	12 57	13 27	13 57	14 27	14 57	15 27	15 57
Harrow-on-the-Hill 3 §	⊖ d	23p09	23p39	00 09		07 39	08 09	08 39	09 09	09 39	10 09	10 39	11 09	11 39	12 09	12 39	13 09	13 39	14 09	14 39	15 09	15 39	16 09
Rickmansworth §	⊖ d	23p19	23p49	00 19		07 49	08 19	08 49	09 19	09 49	10 19	10 49	11 19	11 49	12 19	12 49	13 19	13 49	14 19	14 49	15 19	15 49	16 19
Chorleywood §	⊖ d	23p24	23p54	00 24		07 54	08 24	08 54	09 24	09 54	10 24	10 54	11 24	11 54	12 24	12 54	13 24	13 54	14 24	14 54	15 24	15 54	16 24
Chalfont & Latimer §	⊖ d	23p28	23p58	00 28		07 58	08 28	08 58	09 28	09 58	10 28	10 58	11 28	11 58	12 28	12 58	13 28	13 58	14 28	14 58	15 28	15 58	16 28
Amersham §	⊖ d	23p32	00 02	00 32	07 05	08 02	08 32	09 02	09 32	10 02	10 32	11 02	11 32	12 02	12 32	13 02	13 32	14 02	14 32	15 02	15 32	16 02	16 32
Great Missenden	d	23p38	00 08	00 38	07 11	08 08	08 38	09 08	09 38	10 08	10 38	11 08	11 38	12 08	12 38	13 08	13 38	14 08	14 38	15 08	15 38	16 08	16 38
Wendover	d	23p44	00 14	00 44	07 17	08 14	08 44	09 14	09 44	10 14	10 44	11 14	11 44	12 14	12 44	13 14	13 44	14 14	14 44	15 14	15 44	16 14	16 44
Stoke Mandeville	d	23p48	00 18	00 48	07 21	08 18	08 48	09 18	09 48	10 18	10 48	11 18	11 48	12 18	12 48	13 18	13 48	14 18	14 48	15 18	15 48	16 18	16 48
Aylesbury	d	23p53	00a26	00a56	07a29	08a26	08 53	09a26	09 53	10a26	10 53	11a26	11 53	12a26	12 53	13a26	13 53	14a26	14 53	15a26	15 53	16a26	16 53
Aylesbury Vale Parkway	a	00 03					09 02		10 02		11 02		12 02		13 02		14 02		15 02		16 02		17 02

§ London Underground Limited (Metropolitan Line) services operate between Harrow-on-the-Hill, Rickmansworth, Chorleywood, Chalfont & Latimer and Amersham

A not from 18 August

London - Amersham and Aylesbury

Saturdays 15 September to 6 October

Network Diagram - see first Page of Table 114

		CH	CH	CH	CH	CH	CH	CH	CH	CH	CH	CH	CH
										◇			
London Marylebone 10	⊖ d	16 27	16 57	17 27	17 57	18 27	18 57	19 27	19 57	20 57	21 57	22 57	23 57
Harrow-on-the-Hill 3 §	⊖ d	16 39	17 09	17 39	18 09	18 39	19 09	19 39	20 09	21 09	22 09	23 09	00 09
Rickmansworth §	⊖ d	16 49	17 19	17 49	18 19	18 49	19 19	19 49	20 19	21 19	22 19	23 19	00 19
Chorleywood §	⊖ d	16 54	17 24	17 54	18 24	18 54	19 24	19 54	20 24	21 24	22 24	23 24	00 24
Chalfont & Latimer §	⊖ d	16 58	17 28	17 58	18 28	18 58	19 28	19 58	20 28	21 28	22 28	23 28	00 28
Amersham §	⊖ d	17 02	17 32	18 02	18 32	19 02	19 32	20 02	20 32	21 32	22 32	23 32	00 32
Great Missenden	d	17 08	17 38	18 08	18 38	19 08	19 38	20 08	20 38	21 38	22 38	23 38	00 38
Wendover	d	17 14	17 44	18 14	18 44	19 14	19 44	20 14	20 44	21 44	22 44	23 44	00 44
Stoke Mandeville	d	17 18	17 48	18 18	18 48	19 18	19 48	20 18	20 48	21 48	22 48	23 48	00 48
Aylesbury	d	17a26	17 53	18a26	18 53	19a26	19 53	20a26	20 53	21 53	22 53	23 53	00a56
Aylesbury Vale Parkway	a		18 02		19 02		20 02		21 02	22 02	23 02	00 03	

Saturdays from 13 October

		CH	CH	CH	CH	CH	CH	CH	CH	CH	CH	CH	CH	CH	CH	CH	CH	CH	CH	CH	CH	CH	CH
			◇			◇			◇					◇				◇			◇		
London Marylebone 10	⊖ d	22p57	23p27	23p57		07 27	07 57	08 27	08 57	09 27	09 57	10 27	10 57	11 27	11 57	12 27	12 57	13 27	13 57	14 27	14 57	15 27	15 57
Harrow-on-the-Hill 3 §	⊖ d	23p09	23p39	00 09		07 39	08 09	08 39	09 09	09 39	10 09	10 39	11 09	11 39	12 09	12 39	13 09	13 39	14 09	14 39	15 09	15 39	16 09
Rickmansworth §	⊖ d	23p19	23p49	00 19		07 49	08 19	08 49	09 19	09 49	10 19	10 49	11 19	11 49	12 19	12 49	13 19	13 49	14 19	14 49	15 19	15 49	16 19
Chorleywood §	⊖ d	23p24	23p54	00 24		07 54	08 24	08 54	09 24	09 54	10 24	10 54	11 24	11 54	12 24	12 54	13 24	13 54	14 24	14 54	15 24	15 54	16 24
Chalfont & Latimer §	⊖ d	23p28	23p58	00 28		07 58	08 28	08 58	09 28	09 58	10 28	10 58	11 28	11 58	12 28	12 58	13 28	13 58	14 28	14 58	15 28	15 58	16 28
Amersham §	⊖ d	23p32	00 02	00 32	07 05	08 02	08 32	09 02	09 32	10 02	10 32	11 02	11 32	12 02	12 32	13 02	13 32	14 02	14 32	15 02	15 32	16 02	16 32
Great Missenden	d	23p38	00 08	00 38	07 11	08 08	08 38	09 08	09 38	10 08	10 38	11 08	11 38	12 08	12 38	13 08	13 38	14 08	14 38	15 08	15 38	16 08	16 38
Wendover	d	23p44	00 14	00 44	07 17	08 14	08 44	09 14	09 44	10 14	10 44	11 14	11 44	12 14	12 44	13 14	13 44	14 14	14 44	15 14	15 44	16 14	16 44
Stoke Mandeville	d	23p48	00 18	00 48	07 21	08 18	08 48	09 18	09 48	10 18	10 48	11 18	11 48	12 18	12 48	13 18	13 48	14 18	14 48	15 18	15 48	16 18	16 48
Aylesbury	d	23p53	00a26	00a56	07a29	08a26	08 53	09a26	09 53	10a26	10 53	11a26	11 53	12a26	12 53	13a26	13 53	14a26	14 53	15a26	15 53	16a26	16 53
Aylesbury Vale Parkway	a	00 03					09 02		10 02		11 02		12 02		13 02		14 02		15 02		16 02		17 02

		CH	CH	CH	CH	CH	CH	CH	CH	CH	CH	CH	CH
										◇			
London Marylebone 10	⊖ d	16 27	16 57	17 27	17 57	18 27	18 57	19 27	19 57	20 57	21 57	22 57	23 57
Harrow-on-the-Hill 3 §	⊖ d	16 39	17 09	17 39	18 09	18 39	19 09	19 39	20 09	21 09	22 09	23 09	00 09
Rickmansworth §	⊖ d	16 49	17 19	17 49	18 19	18 49	19 19	19 49	20 19	21 19	22 19	23 19	00 19
Chorleywood §	⊖ d	16 54	17 24	17 54	18 24	18 54	19 24	19 54	20 24	21 24	22 24	23 24	00 24
Chalfont & Latimer §	⊖ d	16 58	17 28	17 58	18 28	18 58	19 28	19 58	20 28	21 28	22 28	23 28	00 28
Amersham §	⊖ d	17 02	17 32	18 02	18 32	19 02	19 32	20 02	20 32	21 32	22 32	23 32	00 32
Great Missenden	d	17 08	17 38	18 08	18 38	19 08	19 38	20 08	20 38	21 38	22 38	23 38	00 38
Wendover	d	17 14	17 44	18 14	18 44	19 14	19 44	20 14	20 44	21 44	22 44	23 44	00 44
Stoke Mandeville	d	17 18	17 48	18 18	18 48	19 18	19 48	20 18	20 48	21 48	22 48	23 48	00 48
Aylesbury	d	17a26	17 53	18a26	18 53	19a26	19 53	20a26	20 53	21 53	22 53	23 53	00a56
Aylesbury Vale Parkway	a		18 02		19 02		20 02		21 02	22 02	23 02	00 03	

Sundays until 22 July

		CH	CH	CH	CH	CH	CH	CH	CH	CH	CH	CH	CH	CH	CH	CH	CH	CH	CH	CH	CH	CH	CH
						◇				◇				◇									
London Marylebone 10	⊖ d	22p57		23p57		08 27	09 27	10 27	11 27	12 27	13 27	14 27		15 27		16 27		17 27		18 27		19 27	
Harrow-on-the-Hill 3 §	⊖ d	23p09		00 09		08 39	09 39	10 39	11 39	12 39	13 39	14 39		15 39		16 39		17 39		18 39		19 39	
Rickmansworth §	⊖ d	23p19		00 19		08 49	09 49	10 49	11 49	12 49	13 49	14 49		15 49		16 49		17 49		18 49		19 49	
Chorleywood §	⊖ d	23p24		00 24		08 54	09 54	10 54	11 54	12 54	13 54	14 54		15 54		16 54		17 54		18 54		19 54	
Chalfont & Latimer §	⊖ d	23p28		00 28		08 58	09 58	10 58	11 58	12 58	13 58	14 58		15 58		16 58		17 58		18 58		19 58	
Amersham §	⊖ d	23p32	00 02	00 32	08 32	09 02	10 02	11 02	12 02	13 02	14 02	15 02	15 32	16 02	16 32	17 02	17 32	18 02	18 32	19 02	19 32	20 02	20 32
Great Missenden	d	23p38	00 08	00 38	08 38	09 08	10 08	11 08	12 08	13 08	14 08	15 08	15 38	16 08	16 38	17 08	17 38	18 08	18 38	19 08	19 38	20 08	20 38
Wendover	d	23p44	00 14	00 44	08 44	09 14	10 14	11 14	12 14	13 14	14 14	15 14	15 44	16 14	16 44	17 14	17 44	18 14	18 44	19 14	19 44	20 14	20 44
Stoke Mandeville	d	23p48	00 18	00 48	08 48	09 18	10 18	11 18	12 18	13 18	14 18	15 18	15 48	16 18	16 48	17 18	17 48	18 18	18 48	19 18	19 48	20 18	20 48
Aylesbury	d	23p53	00a26	00a56	08a56	09 23	10 23	11 23	12 23	13 23	14 23	15 23	15a56	16 23	16a56	17 23	17a56	18 23	18a56	19 23	19a56	20 23	20a56
Aylesbury Vale Parkway	a	00 03				09 32	10 32	11 32	12 32	13 32	14 32	15 32		16 32		17 32		18 32		19 32		20 32	

		CH	CH	CH	CH	CH
						◇
London Marylebone 10	⊖ d	20 27		21 27	22 27	23 27
Harrow-on-the-Hill 3 §	⊖ d	20 39		21 39	22 39	23 39
Rickmansworth §	⊖ d	20 49		21 49	22 49	23 49
Chorleywood §	⊖ d	20 54		21 54	22 54	23 54
Chalfont & Latimer §	⊖ d	20 58		21 58	22 58	23 58
Amersham §	⊖ d	21 02	21 32	22 02	23 02	00 02
Great Missenden	d	21 08	21 38	22 08	23 08	00 08
Wendover	d	21 14	21 44	22 14	23 14	00 14
Stoke Mandeville	d	21 18	21 48	22 18	23 18	00 18
Aylesbury	d	21 23	21a56	22 23	23 23	00a26
Aylesbury Vale Parkway	a	21 32		22 32	23 32	

§ London Underground Limited (Metropolitan Line) services operate between Harrow-on-the-Hill, Rickmansworth, Chorleywood, Chalfont & Latimer and Amersham

Table 114

29 July to 9 September

London - Amersham and Aylesbury

Network Diagram - see first Page of Table 114

		CH	CH	CH	CH	CH	CH	CH	CH	CH
								◇		
					A	A				
London Marylebone [10]	⊖ d	22p57		23p57	00 57	01 57		08 27	09 27	10 27
Harrow-on-the-Hill [3] §	⊖ d	23p09		00 09				08 39	09 39	10 39
Rickmansworth §	⊖ d	23p19		00 19				08 49	09 49	10 49
Chorleywood §	⊖ d	23p24		00 24				08 54	09 54	10 54
Chalfont & Latimer §	⊖ d	23p28		00 28				08 58	09 58	10 58
Amersham §	⊖ d	23p32	00 02	00 32	01 28	02 28	08 32	09 02	10 02	11 02
Great Missenden	d	23p38	00 08	00 38	01 34	02 34	08 38	09 08	10 08	11 08
Wendover	d	23p44	00 14	00 44	01 40	02 40	08 44	09 14	10 14	11 14
Stoke Mandeville	d	23p48	00 18	00 48	01 44	02 44	08 48	09 18	10 18	11 18
Aylesbury	d	23p53	00a26	00a56	01a52	02a52	08a56	09 23	10 23	11 23
Aylesbury Vale Parkway	a	00 03						09 32	10 32	11 32

		CH	CH	CH	CH	CH	CH	CH	CH	CH	CH	CH	CH	CH
			◇				◇							
London Marylebone [10]	⊖ d	11 27	12 27	13 27	14 27		15 27		16 27		17 27		18 27	
Harrow-on-the-Hill [3] §	⊖ d	11 39	12 39	13 39	14 39		15 39		16 39		17 39		18 39	
Rickmansworth §	⊖ d	11 49	12 49	13 49	14 49		15 49		16 49		17 49		18 49	
Chorleywood §	⊖ d	11 54	12 54	13 54	14 54		15 54		16 54		17 54		18 54	
Chalfont & Latimer §	⊖ d	11 58	12 58	13 58	14 58		15 58		16 58		17 58		18 58	
Amersham §	⊖ d	12 02	13 02	14 02	15 02	15 32	16 02	16 32	17 02	17 32	18 02	18 32	19 02	19 32
Great Missenden	d	12 08	13 08	14 08	15 08	15 38	16 08	16 38	17 08	17 38	18 08	18 38	19 08	19 38
Wendover	d	12 14	13 14	14 14	15 14	15 44	16 14	16 44	17 14	17 44	18 14	18 44	19 14	19 44
Stoke Mandeville	d	12 18	13 18	14 18	15 18	15 48	16 18	16 48	17 18	17 48	18 18	18 48	19 18	19 48
Aylesbury	d	12 23	13 23	14 23	15 23	15a56	16 23	16a56	17 23	17a56	18 23	18a56	19 23	19a56
Aylesbury Vale Parkway	a	12 32	13 32	14 32	15 32		16 32		17 32		18 32		19 32	

		CH	CH	CH	CH	CH	CH	CH
								◇
London Marylebone [10]	⊖ d	19 27		20 27		21 27	22 27	23 27
Harrow-on-the-Hill [3] §	⊖ d	19 39		20 39		21 39	22 39	23 39
Rickmansworth §	⊖ d	19 49		20 49		21 49	22 49	23 49
Chorleywood §	⊖ d	19 54		20 54		21 54	22 54	23 54
Chalfont & Latimer §	⊖ d	19 58		20 58		21 58	22 58	23 58
Amersham §	⊖ d	20 02	20 32	21 02	21 32	22 02	23 02	00 02
Great Missenden	d	20 08	20 38	21 08	21 38	22 08	23 08	00 08
Wendover	d	20 14	20 44	21 14	21 44	22 14	23 14	00 14
Stoke Mandeville	d	20 18	20 48	21 18	21 48	22 18	23 18	00 18
Aylesbury	d	20 23	20a56	21 23	21a56	22 23	23 23	00a26
Aylesbury Vale Parkway	a	20 32		21 32		22 32	23 32	

16 September to 30 September

		CH	CH	CH	CH	CH	CH	CH	CH	CH
						◇				◇
London Marylebone [10]	⊖ d	22p57		23p57		08 27	09 27	10 27	11 27	12 27
Harrow-on-the-Hill [3] §	⊖ d	23p09		00 09		08 39	09 39	10 39	11 39	12 39
Rickmansworth §	⊖ d	23p19		00 19		08 49	09 49	10 49	11 49	12 49
Chorleywood §	⊖ d	23p24		00 24		08 54	09 54	10 54	11 54	12 54
Chalfont & Latimer §	⊖ d	23p28		00 28		08 58	09 58	10 58	11 58	12 58
Amersham §	⊖ d	23p32	00 02	00 32	08 32	09 02	10 02	11 02	12 02	13 02
Great Missenden	d	23p38	00 08	00 38	08 38	09 08	10 08	11 08	12 08	13 08
Wendover	d	23p44	00 14	00 44	08 44	09 14	10 14	11 14	12 14	13 14
Stoke Mandeville	d	23p48	00 18	00 48	08 48	09 18	10 18	11 18	12 18	13 18
Aylesbury	d	23p53	00a26	00a56	08a56	09 23	10 23	11 23	12 23	13 23
Aylesbury Vale Parkway	a	00 03				09 32	10 32	11 32	12 32	13 32

		CH	CH	CH	CH	CH	CH	CH	CH	CH	CH	CH	CH	CH
					◇									
London Marylebone [10]	⊖ d	13 27	14 27		15 27		16 27		17 27		18 27		19 27	
Harrow-on-the-Hill [3] §	⊖ d	13 39	14 39		15 39		16 39		17 39		18 39		19 39	
Rickmansworth §	⊖ d	13 49	14 49		15 49		16 49		17 49		18 49		19 49	
Chorleywood §	⊖ d	13 54	14 54		15 54		16 54		17 54		18 54		19 54	
Chalfont & Latimer §	⊖ d	13 58	14 58		15 58		16 58		17 58		18 58		19 58	
Amersham §	⊖ d	14 02	15 02	15 32	16 02	16 32	17 02	17 32	18 02	18 32	19 02	19 32	20 02	20 32
Great Missenden	d	14 08	15 08	15 38	16 08	16 38	17 08	17 38	18 08	18 38	19 08	19 38	20 08	20 38
Wendover	d	14 14	15 14	15 44	16 14	16 44	17 14	17 44	18 14	18 44	19 14	19 44	20 14	20 44
Stoke Mandeville	d	14 18	15 18	15 48	16 18	16 48	17 18	17 48	18 18	18 48	19 18	19 48	20 18	20 48
Aylesbury	d	14 23	15 23	15a56	16 23	16a56	17 23	17a56	18 23	18a56	19 23	19a56	20 23	20a56
Aylesbury Vale Parkway	a	14 32	15 32		16 32		17 32		18 32		19 32		20 32	

		CH	CH	CH	CH	CH
						◇
London Marylebone [10]	⊖ d	20 27		21 27	22 27	23 27
Harrow-on-the-Hill [3] §	⊖ d	20 39		21 39	22 39	23 39
Rickmansworth §	⊖ d	20 49		21 49	22 49	23 49
Chorleywood §	⊖ d	20 54		21 54	22 54	23 54
Chalfont & Latimer §	⊖ d	20 58		21 58	22 58	23 58
Amersham §	⊖ d	21 02	21 32	22 02	23 02	00 02
Great Missenden	d	21 08	21 38	22 08	23 08	00 08
Wendover	d	21 14	21 44	22 14	23 14	00 14
Stoke Mandeville	d	21 18	21 48	22 18	23 18	00 18
Aylesbury	d	21 23	21a56	22 23	23 23	00a26
Aylesbury Vale Parkway	a	21 32		22 32	23 32	

from 7 October

		CH	CH	CH	CH	CH	CH	CH	CH	CH
						◇				◇
London Marylebone [10]	⊖ d	22p57		23p57		08 27	09 27	10 27	11 27	12 27
Harrow-on-the-Hill [3] §	⊖ d	23p09		00 09		08 39	09 39	10 39	11 39	12 39
Rickmansworth §	⊖ d	23p19		00 19		08 49	09 49	10 49	11 49	12 49
Chorleywood §	⊖ d	23p24		00 24		08 54	09 54	10 54	11 54	12 54
Chalfont & Latimer §	⊖ d	23p28		00 28		08 58	09 58	10 58	11 58	12 58
Amersham §	⊖ d	23p32	00 02	00 32	08 32	09 02	10 02	11 02	12 02	13 02
Great Missenden	d	23p38	00 08	00 38	08 38	09 08	10 08	11 08	12 08	13 08
Wendover	d	23p44	00 14	00 44	08 44	09 14	10 14	11 14	12 14	13 14
Stoke Mandeville	d	23p48	00 18	00 48	08 48	09 18	10 18	11 18	12 18	13 18
Aylesbury	d	23p53	00a26	00a56	08a56	09 23	10 23	11 23	12 23	13 23
Aylesbury Vale Parkway	a	00 03				09 32	10 32	11 32	12 32	13 32

		CH	CH	CH	CH	CH	CH	CH	CH	CH	CH	CH	CH	CH
					◇									
London Marylebone [10]	⊖ d	13 27	14 27		15 27		16 27		17 27		18 27		19 27	
Harrow-on-the-Hill [3] §	⊖ d	13 39	14 39		15 39		16 39		17 39		18 39		19 39	
Rickmansworth §	⊖ d	13 49	14 49		15 49		16 49		17 49		18 49		19 49	
Chorleywood §	⊖ d	13 54	14 54		15 54		16 54		17 54		18 54		19 54	
Chalfont & Latimer §	⊖ d	13 58	14 58		15 58		16 58		17 58		18 58		19 58	
Amersham §	⊖ d	14 02	15 02	15 32	16 02	16 32	17 02	17 32	18 02	18 32	19 02	19 32	20 02	20 32
Great Missenden	d	14 08	15 08	15 38	16 08	16 38	17 08	17 38	18 08	18 38	19 08	19 38	20 08	20 38
Wendover	d	14 14	15 14	15 44	16 14	16 44	17 14	17 44	18 14	18 44	19 14	19 44	20 14	20 44
Stoke Mandeville	d	14 18	15 18	15 48	16 18	16 48	17 18	17 48	18 18	18 48	19 18	19 48	20 18	20 48
Aylesbury	d	14 23	15 23	15a56	16 23	16a56	17 23	17a56	18 23	18a56	19 23	19a56	20 23	20a56
Aylesbury Vale Parkway	a	14 32	15 32		16 32		17 32		18 32		19 32		20 32	

§ London Underground Limited (Metropolitan Line) services operate between Harrow-on-the-Hill, Rickmansworth, Chorleywood, Chalfont & Latimer and Amersham

A not from 19 August

Table 114

from 7 October

London - Amersham and Aylesbury

Network Diagram - see first Page of Table 114

		CH	CH	CH	CH	CH
						◇
London Marylebone [10]	⊖ d	20 27		21 27	22 27	23 27
Harrow-on-the-Hill [3] §	⊖ d	20 39		21 39	22 39	23 39
Rickmansworth §	⊖ d	20 49		21 49	22 49	23 49
Chorleywood §	⊖ d	20 54		21 54	22 54	23 54
Chalfont & Latimer §	⊖ d	20 58		21 58	22 58	23 58
Amersham §	⊖ d	21 02	21 32	22 02	23 02	00 02
Great Missenden	d	21 08	21 38	22 08	23 08	00 08
Wendover	d	21 14	21 44	22 14	23 14	00 14
Stoke Mandeville	d	21 18	21 48	22 18	23 18	00 18
Aylesbury	d	21 23	21a56	22 23	23 23	00a26
Aylesbury Vale Parkway	a	21 32		22 32	23 32	

§ London Underground Limited (Metropolitan Line) services operate between Harrow-on-the-Hill, Rickmansworth, Chorleywood, Chalfont & Latimer and Amersham

Table 114

Aylesbury and Amersham - London

Mondays to Fridays
until 27 July

Network Diagram - see first Page of Table 114

Miles			CH	CH	CH	CH	CH	CH	CH	CH	CH	CH	CH	CH	CH	CH	CH	CH	CH	CH	CH	CH	CH
														◇						◇	◇		◇
0	**Aylesbury Vale Parkway**	d	05 30	06 00		06 34		07 06		07 39		08 09		09 00	09 30		10 30		11 30		12 30		13 30
2¾	**Aylesbury**	d	05 35	06 05	06 23	06 39	06 55	07 11	07 27	07 44	07 58	08 14	08 30	09 05	09 35	10 05	10 35	11 05	11 35	12 05	12 35	13 05	13 35
5¼	Stoke Mandeville	d	05 39	06 09	06 27	06 43	06 59	07 15	07 31	07 48	08 02	08 18	08 34	09 09	09 39	10 09	10 39	11 09	11 39	12 09	12 39	13 09	13 39
7¼	Wendover	d	05 43	06 13	06 31	06 47	07 03	07 20	07 35	07 52	08 06	08 22	08 38	09 13	09 43	10 13	10 43	11 13	11 43	12 13	12 43	13 13	13 43
11¾	Great Missenden	d	05 49	06 19	06 37	06 53	07 09	07 26	07 41	07 58	08 12	08 28	08 44	09 19	09 49	10 19	10 49	11 19	11 49	12 19	12 49	13 19	13 49
17	**Amersham** §	⊖ d	05 56	06 26	06 44	07 00	07 16	07 32	07 48	08 05	08 19	08 35	08 51	09 26	09 56	10 26	10 56	11 26	11 56	12 26	12 56	13 26	13 56
19	Chalfont & Latimer §	⊖ d		06 30	06 48		07 20		07 52		08 23		08 55	09 30	10 00	10 30	11 00	11 30	12 00	12 30	13 00	13 30	14 00
21¼	Chorleywood §	⊖ d		06 33	06 51		07 23		07 55		08 27		08 58	09 33	10 03	10 33	11 03	11 33	12 03	12 33	13 03	13 33	14 03
23½	Rickmansworth §	⊖ d			06 56				08 00		08 31		09 03	09 38	10 08	10 38	11 08	11 38	12 08	12 38	13 08	13 38	14 08
31½	Harrow-on-the-Hill 3 §	⊖ d	06 18	06 48	07 07		07 39		08 11		08 42		09 14	09 49	10 19	10 49	11 19	11 49	12 19	12 49	13 19	13 49	14 19
40½	**London Marylebone** 10	⊖ a	06 33	07 05	07 23	07 39	07 55	08 11	08 30	08 44	08 58	09 14	09 30	10 05	10 35	11 05	11 35	12 05	12 35	13 05	13 35	14 05	14 35

		CH	CH	CH	CH	CH	CH	CH	CH	CH	CH	CH	CH	CH	CH	CH	CH	CH	CH
				◇			◇						◇	◇		◇			
Aylesbury Vale Parkway	d		14 30		15 30		16 30		17 27			18 35		19 30		20 30		21 30	22 30
Aylesbury	d	14 05	14 35	15 05	15 35	16 05	16 35	17 03	17 32	17 52	18 23	18 52	19 11	19 35	20 05	20 35	21 05	21 35	22 35
Stoke Mandeville	d	14 09	14 39	15 09	15 39	16 09	16 39	17 07	17 36	17 56	18 27	18 56	19 15	19 39	20 09	20 39	21 09	21 39	22 39
Wendover	d	14 13	14 43	15 13	15 43	16 13	16 43	17 11	17 40	18 00	18 31	19 00	19 19	19 43	20 13	20 43	21 13	21 43	22 43
Great Missenden	d	14 19	14 49	15 19	15 49	16 19	16 49	17 17	17 46	18 06	18 37	19 06	19 25	19 49	20 19	20 49	21 19	21 49	22 49
Amersham §	⊖ d	14 26	14 56	15 26	15 56	16 26	16 56	17 24	17 53	18 13	18 44	19 13	19 32	19 56	20 26	20 56	21 26	21 56	22 56
Chalfont & Latimer §	⊖ d	14 30	15 00	15 30	16 00	16 30	17 00	17 28	17 57	18 17	18 48	19 17	19 36	20 00	20 30	21 00	21 30	22 00	23 00
Chorleywood §	⊖ d	14 33	15 03	15 33	16 03	16 33	17 03	17 31	18 00	18 20	18 52	19 20	19 40	20 03	20 33	21 03	21 33	22 03	23 03
Rickmansworth §	⊖ d	14 38	15 08	15 38	16 08	16 38	17 08	17 36	18 05	18 25	18 56	19 25	19 44	20 08	20 38	21 08	21 38	22 08	23 08
Harrow-on-the-Hill 3 §	⊖ d	14 49	15 19	15 49	16 19	16 49	17 19	17 49	18 17	18 36	19 08	19 36	19 56	20 19	20 49	21 19	21 49	22 19	23 19
London Marylebone 10	⊖ a	15 05	15 35	16 05	16 35	17 05	17 35	18 05	18 39	18 53	19 23	19 52	20 11	20 35	21 05	21 35	22 05	22 35	23 35

Mondays to Fridays
30 July to 7 September

		CH	CH	CH	CH	CH	CH	CH	CH	CH	CH	CH	CH	CH	CH	CH	CH	CH	CH	CH	CH	CH	CH
													◇						◇	◇		◇	
Aylesbury Vale Parkway	d	05 30	06 00		06 34		07 06		07 39		08 09		09 00	09 30		10 30		11 30		12 30		13 30	
Aylesbury	d	05 35	06 05	06 23	06 39	06 55	07 11	07 27	07 44	07 58	08 14	08 30	09 05	09 35	10 05	10 35	11 05	11 35	12 05	12 35	13 05	13 35	14 05
Stoke Mandeville	d	05 39	06 09	06 27	06 43	06 59	07 15	07 31	07 48	08 02	08 18	08 34	09 09	09 39	10 09	10 39	11 09	11 39	12 09	12 39	13 09	13 39	14 09
Wendover	d	05 43	06 13	06 31	06 47	07 03	07 20	07 35	07 52	08 06	08 22	08 38	09 13	09 43	10 13	10 43	11 13	11 43	12 13	12 43	13 13	13 43	14 13
Great Missenden	d	05 49	06 19	06 37	06 53	07 09	07 26	07 41	07 58	08 12	08 28	08 44	09 19	09 49	10 19	10 49	11 19	11 49	12 19	12 49	13 19	13 49	14 19
Amersham §	⊖ d	05 56	06 26	06 44	07 00	07 16	07 32	07 48	08 05	08 19	08 35	08 51	09 26	09 56	10 26	10 56	11 26	11 56	12 26	12 56	13 26	13 56	14 26
Chalfont & Latimer §	⊖ d		06 30	06 48		07 20		07 52		08 23		08 55	09 30	10 00	10 30	11 00	11 30	12 00	12 30	13 00	13 30	14 00	14 30
Chorleywood §	⊖ d		06 33	06 51		07 23		07 55		08 27		08 58	09 33	10 03	10 33	11 03	11 33	12 03	12 33	13 03	13 33	14 03	14 33
Rickmansworth §	⊖ d			06 56				08 00		08 31		09 03	09 38	10 08	10 38	11 08	11 38	12 08	12 38	13 08	13 38	14 08	14 38
Harrow-on-the-Hill 3 §	⊖ d	06 18	06 48	07 07		07 39		08 11		08 42		09 14	09 49	10 19	10 49	11 19	11 49	12 19	12 49	13 19	13 49	14 19	14 49
London Marylebone 10	⊖ a	06 33	07 05	07 23	07 39	07 55	08 11	08 30	08 44	08 58	09 14	09 30	10 05	10 35	11 05	11 35	12 05	12 35	13 05	13 35	14 05	14 35	15 05

		CH	CH	CH	CH	CH	CH	CH	CH	CH	CH	CH	CH	CH	CH	CH	CH	CH
			◇			◇						◇	◇		◇			
Aylesbury Vale Parkway	d	14 30		15 30		16 30		17 27			18 35		19 30		20 30		21 30	22 30
Aylesbury	d	14 35	15 05	15 35	16 05	16 35	17 03	17 32	17 52	18 23	18 52	19 11	19 35	20 05	20 35	21 05	21 35	22 35
Stoke Mandeville	d	14 39	15 09	15 39	16 09	16 39	17 07	17 36	17 56	18 27	18 56	19 15	19 39	20 09	20 39	21 09	21 39	22 39
Wendover	d	14 43	15 13	15 43	16 13	16 43	17 11	17 40	18 00	18 31	19 00	19 19	19 43	20 13	20 43	21 13	21 43	22 43
Great Missenden	d	14 49	15 19	15 49	16 19	16 49	17 17	17 46	18 06	18 37	19 06	19 25	19 49	20 19	20 49	21 19	21 49	22 49
Amersham §	⊖ d	14 56	15 26	15 56	16 26	16 56	17 24	17 53	18 13	18 44	19 13	19 32	19 56	20 26	20 56	21 26	21 56	22 56
Chalfont & Latimer §	⊖ d	15 00	15 30	16 00	16 30	17 00	17 28	17 57	18 17	18 48	19 17	19 36	20 00	20 30	21 00	21 30	22 00	23 00
Chorleywood §	⊖ d	15 03	15 33	16 03	16 33	17 03	17 31	18 00	18 20	18 52	19 20	19 40	20 03	20 33	21 03	21 33	22 03	23 03
Rickmansworth §	⊖ d	15 08	15 38	16 08	16 38	17 08	17 36	18 05	18 25	18 56	19 25	19 44	20 08	20 38	21 08	21 38	22 08	23 08
Harrow-on-the-Hill 3 §	⊖ d	15 19	15 49	16 19	16 49	17 19	17 49	18 17	18 36	19 08	19 36	19 56	20 19	20 49	21 19	21 49	22 19	23 19
London Marylebone 10	⊖ a	15 35	16 05	16 35	17 05	17 35	18 05	18 39	18 53	19 23	19 52	20 11	20 35	21 05	21 35	22 05	22 35	23 35

Mondays to Fridays
10 September to 5 October

		CH	CH	CH	CH	CH	CH	CH	CH	CH	CH	CH	CH	CH	CH	CH	CH	CH	CH	CH	CH	CH	CH
													◇						◇	◇		◇	
Aylesbury Vale Parkway	d	05 30	06 00		06 34		07 06		07 39		08 09		09 00	09 30		10 30		11 30		12 30		13 30	
Aylesbury	d	05 35	06 05	06 23	06 39	06 55	07 11	07 27	07 44	07 58	08 14	08 30	09 05	09 35	10 05	10 35	11 05	11 35	12 05	12 35	13 05	13 35	14 05
Stoke Mandeville	d	05 39	06 09	06 27	06 43	06 59	07 15	07 31	07 48	08 02	08 18	08 34	09 09	09 39	10 09	10 39	11 09	11 39	12 09	12 39	13 09	13 39	14 09
Wendover	d	05 43	06 13	06 31	06 47	07 03	07 20	07 35	07 52	08 06	08 22	08 38	09 13	09 43	10 13	10 43	11 13	11 43	12 13	12 43	13 13	13 43	14 13
Great Missenden	d	05 49	06 19	06 37	06 53	07 09	07 26	07 41	07 58	08 12	08 28	08 44	09 19	09 49	10 19	10 49	11 19	11 49	12 19	12 49	13 19	13 49	14 19
Amersham §	⊖ d	05 56	06 26	06 44	07 00	07 16	07 32	07 48	08 05	08 19	08 35	08 51	09 26	09 56	10 26	10 56	11 26	11 56	12 26	12 56	13 26	13 56	14 26
Chalfont & Latimer §	⊖ d		06 30	06 48		07 20		07 52		08 23		08 55	09 30	10 00	10 30	11 00	11 30	12 00	12 30	13 00	13 30	14 00	14 30
Chorleywood §	⊖ d		06 33	06 51		07 23		07 55		08 27		08 58	09 33	10 03	10 33	11 03	11 33	12 03	12 33	13 03	13 33	14 03	14 33
Rickmansworth §	⊖ d			06 56				08 00		08 31		09 03	09 38	10 08	10 38	11 08	11 38	12 08	12 38	13 08	13 38	14 08	14 38
Harrow-on-the-Hill 3 §	⊖ d	06 18	06 48	07 07		07 39		08 11		08 42		09 14	09 49	10 19	10 49	11 19	11 49	12 19	12 49	13 19	13 49	14 19	14 49
London Marylebone 10	⊖ a	06 33	07 05	07 23	07 39	07 55	08 11	08 30	08 44	08 58	09 14	09 30	10 05	10 35	11 05	11 35	12 05	12 35	13 05	13 35	14 05	14 35	15 05

§ London Underground Limited (Metropolitan Line) services operate between Harrow-on-the-Hill, Rickmansworth, Chorleywood, Chalfont & Latimer and Amersham

Table 114

Aylesbury and Amersham - London

Mondays to Fridays
10 September to 5 October

Network Diagram - see first Page of Table 114

		CH	CH	CH	CH	CH	CH	CH	CH	CH	CH	CH	CH	CH	CH	CH	CH	CH
			◇			◇						◇	◇		◇			
Aylesbury Vale Parkway	d	14 30		15 30		16 30		17 27			18 35		19 30		20 30		21 30	22 30
Aylesbury	d	14 35	15 05	15 35	16 05	16 35	17 03	17 32	17 52	18 23	18 52	19 11	19 35	20 05	20 35	21 05	21 35	22 35
Stoke Mandeville	d	14 39	15 09	15 39	16 09	16 39	17 07	17 36	17 56	18 27	18 56	19 15	19 39	20 09	20 39	21 09	21 39	22 39
Wendover	d	14 43	15 13	15 43	16 13	16 43	17 11	17 40	18 00	18 31	19 00	19 19	19 43	20 13	20 43	21 13	21 43	22 43
Great Missenden	d	14 49	15 19	15 49	16 19	16 49	17 17	17 46	18 06	18 37	19 06	19 25	19 49	20 19	20 49	21 19	21 49	22 49
Amersham §	⊖ d	14 56	15 26	15 56	16 26	16 56	17 24	17 53	18 13	18 44	19 13	19 32	19 56	20 26	20 56	21 26	21 56	22 56
Chalfont & Latimer §	⊖ d	15 00	15 30	16 00	16 30	17 00	17 28	17 57	18 17	18 48	19 17	19 36	20 00	20 30	21 00	21 30	22 00	23 00
Chorleywood §	⊖ d	15 03	15 33	16 03	16 33	17 03	17 31	18 00	18 20	18 52	19 20	19 40	20 03	20 33	21 03	21 33	22 03	23 03
Rickmansworth §	⊖ d	15 08	15 38	16 08	16 38	17 08	17 36	18 05	18 25	18 56	19 25	19 44	20 08	20 38	21 08	21 38	22 08	23 08
Harrow-on-the-Hill 3 §	⊖ d	15 19	15 49	16 19	16 49	17 19	17 49	18 17	18 36	19 08	19 36	19 56	20 19	20 49	21 19	21 49	22 19	23 19
London Marylebone 10	⊖ a	15 35	16 05	16 35	17 05	17 35	18 05	18 39	18 53	19 23	19 52	20 11	20 35	21 05	21 35	22 05	22 35	23 35

Mondays to Fridays
from 8 October

		CH	CH	CH	CH	CH	CH	CH	CH	CH	CH	CH	CH	CH	CH	CH	CH	CH	CH	CH	CH	CH	CH
													◇						◇	◇		◇	
Aylesbury Vale Parkway	d	05 27	05 57		06 31		07 03		07 36		08 06		08 57	09 27		10 27		11 27		12 27		13 27	
Aylesbury	d	05 32	06 02	06 20	06 36	06 52	07 08	07 24	07 41	07 55	08 11	08 27	09 02	09 32	10 02	10 32	11 02	11 32	12 02	12 32	13 02	13 32	14 02
Stoke Mandeville	d	05 36	06 06	06 24	06 40	06 56	07 12	07 28	07 45	07 59	08 15	08 31	09 06	09 36	10 06	10 36	11 06	11 36	12 06	12 36	13 06	13 36	14 06
Wendover	d	05 40	06 10	06 28	06 44	07 00	07 17	07 32	07 49	08 03	08 19	08 35	09 10	09 40	10 10	10 40	11 10	11 40	12 10	12 40	13 10	13 40	14 10
Great Missenden	d	05 46	06 16	06 34	06 50	07 06	07 23	07 38	07 55	08 09	08 25	08 41	09 16	09 46	10 16	10 46	11 16	11 46	12 16	12 46	13 16	13 46	14 16
Amersham §	⊖ d	05 53	06 23	06 41	06 57	07 13	07 29	07 45	08 02	08 16	08 32	08 48	09 23	09 53	10 23	10 53	11 23	11 53	12 23	12 53	13 23	13 53	14 23
Chalfont & Latimer §	⊖ d		06 27	06 45		07 17		07 49		08 21		08 52	09 27	09 57	10 27	10 57	11 27	11 57	12 27	12 57	13 27	13 57	14 27
Chorleywood §	⊖ d		06 32	06 50		07 22		07 54		08 25		08 57	09 32	10 02	10 32	11 02	11 32	12 02	12 32	13 02	13 32	14 02	14 32
Rickmansworth §	⊖ d			06 56				08 00		08 31		09 03	09 38	10 08	10 38	11 08	11 38	12 08	12 38	13 08	13 38	14 08	14 38
Harrow-on-the-Hill 3 §	⊖ d	06 18	06 48	07 07		07 39		08 11		08 42		09 14	09 49	10 19	10 49	11 19	11 49	12 19	12 49	13 19	13 49	14 19	14 49
London Marylebone 10	⊖ a	06 33	07 05	07 23	07 39	07 55	08 11	08 30	08 44	08 58	09 14	09 30	10 05	10 35	11 05	11 35	12 05	12 35	13 05	13 35	14 05	14 35	15 05

		CH	CH	CH	CH	CH	CH	CH	CH	CH	CH	CH	CH	CH	CH	CH	CH	CH
			◇			◇						◇	◇		◇			
Aylesbury Vale Parkway	d	14 27		15 27		16 27		17 24			18 35		19 27		20 27		21 27	22 27
Aylesbury	d	14 32	15 02	15 32	16 02	16 32	17 00	17 29	17 49	18 20	18 49	19 08	19 32	20 02	20 32	21 02	21 32	22 32
Stoke Mandeville	d	14 36	15 06	15 36	16 06	16 36	17 04	17 33	17 53	18 24	18 53	19 12	19 36	20 06	20 36	21 06	21 36	22 36
Wendover	d	14 40	15 10	15 40	16 10	16 40	17 08	17 37	17 57	18 28	18 57	19 16	19 40	20 10	20 40	21 10	21 40	22 40
Great Missenden	d	14 46	15 16	15 46	16 16	16 46	17 14	17 43	18 03	18 34	19 03	19 22	19 46	20 16	20 46	21 16	21 46	22 46
Amersham §	⊖ d	14 53	15 23	15 53	16 23	16 53	17 21	17 50	18 10	18 41	19 10	19 29	19 53	20 23	20 53	21 23	21 53	22 53
Chalfont & Latimer §	⊖ d	14 57	15 27	15 57	16 27	16 57	17 25	17 54	18 14	18 45	19 14	19 33	19 57	20 27	20 57	21 27	21 57	22 57
Chorleywood §	⊖ d	15 02	15 32	16 02	16 32	17 02	17 30	17 59	18 19	18 50	19 19	19 38	20 02	20 32	21 02	21 32	22 02	23 02
Rickmansworth §	⊖ d	15 08	15 38	16 08	16 38	17 08	17 36	18 05	18 25	18 56	19 25	19 44	20 08	20 38	21 08	21 38	22 08	23 08
Harrow-on-the-Hill 3 §	⊖ d	15 19	15 49	16 19	16 49	17 19	17 49	18 17	18 36	19 08	19 36	19 56	20 19	20 49	21 19	21 49	22 19	23 19
London Marylebone 10	⊖ a	15 35	16 05	16 35	17 05	17 35	18 05	18 39	18 53	19 23	19 52	20 11	20 35	21 05	21 35	22 05	22 35	23 35

Saturdays
until 21 July

		CH	CH	CH	CH	CH	CH	CH	CH	CH	CH	CH	CH	CH	CH	CH	CH	CH	CH	CH	CH	CH	CH
		◇															◇		◇			◇	
Aylesbury Vale Parkway	d			07 00	07 30		08 30		09 30		10 30		11 30		12 30		13 30		14 30		15 30		16 30
Aylesbury	d	06 05	06 35	07 05	07 35	08 05	08 35	09 05	09 35	10 05	10 35	11 05	11 35	12 05	12 35	13 05	13 35	14 05	14 35	15 05	15 35	16 05	16 35
Stoke Mandeville	d	06 09	06 39	07 09	07 39	08 09	08 39	09 09	09 39	10 09	10 39	11 09	11 39	12 09	12 39	13 09	13 39	14 09	14 39	15 09	15 39	16 09	16 39
Wendover	d	06 13	06 43	07 13	07 43	08 13	08 43	09 13	09 43	10 13	10 43	11 13	11 43	12 13	12 43	13 13	13 43	14 13	14 43	15 13	15 43	16 13	16 43
Great Missenden	d	06 19	06 49	07 19	07 49	08 19	08 49	09 19	09 49	10 19	10 49	11 19	11 49	12 19	12 49	13 19	13 49	14 19	14 49	15 19	15 49	16 19	16 49
Amersham §	⊖ d	06 26	06a58	07 26	07 56	08 26	08 56	09 26	09 56	10 26	10 56	11 26	11 56	12 26	12 56	13 26	13 56	14 26	14 56	15 26	15 56	16 26	16 56
Chalfont & Latimer §	⊖ d	06 30		07 30	08 00	08 30	09 00	09 30	10 00	10 30	11 00	11 30	12 00	12 30	13 00	13 30	14 00	14 30	15 00	15 30	16 00	16 30	17 00
Chorleywood §	⊖ d	06 33		07 33	08 03	08 33	09 03	09 33	10 03	10 33	11 03	11 33	12 03	12 33	13 03	13 33	14 03	14 33	15 03	15 33	16 03	16 33	17 03
Rickmansworth §	⊖ d	06 38		07 38	08 08	08 38	09 08	09 38	10 08	10 38	11 08	11 38	12 08	12 38	13 08	13 38	14 08	14 38	15 08	15 38	16 08	16 38	17 08
Harrow-on-the-Hill 3 §	⊖ d	06 49		07 49	08 19	08 49	09 19	09 49	10 19	10 49	11 19	11 49	12 19	12 49	13 19	13 49	14 19	14 49	15 19	15 49	16 19	16 49	17 19
London Marylebone 10	⊖ a	07 05		08 05	08 35	09 05	09 35	10 05	10 35	11 05	11 35	12 05	12 35	13 05	13 35	14 05	14 35	15 05	15 35	16 05	16 35	17 05	17 35

		CH	CH	CH	CH	CH	CH	CH	CH	CH
				◇				◇		
Aylesbury Vale Parkway	d		17 30		18 30		19 46	20 46	21 46	
Aylesbury	d	17 05	17 35	18 05	18 35	19 05	20 05	21 05	22 05	23 20
Stoke Mandeville	d	17 09	17 39	18 09	18 39	19 09	20 09	21 09	22 09	23 24
Wendover	d	17 13	17 43	18 13	18 43	19 13	20 13	21 13	22 13	23 28
Great Missenden	d	17 19	17 49	18 19	18 49	19 19	20 19	21 19	22 19	23 34
Amersham §	⊖ d	17 26	17 56	18 26	18 56	19 26	20 26	21 26	22 26	23a43
Chalfont & Latimer §	⊖ d	17 30	18 00	18 30	19 00	19 30	20 30	21 30	22 30	
Chorleywood §	⊖ d	17 33	18 03	18 33	19 03	19 33	20 33	21 33	22 33	
Rickmansworth §	⊖ d	17 38	18 08	18 38	19 08	19 38	20 38	21 38	22 38	
Harrow-on-the-Hill 3 §	⊖ d	17 49	18 19	18 49	19 19	19 49	20 49	21 49	22 49	
London Marylebone 10	⊖ a	18 05	18 35	19 05	19 35	20 05	21 05	22 05	23 05	

§ London Underground Limited (Metropolitan Line) services operate between Harrow-on-the-Hill, Rickmansworth, Chorleywood, Chalfont & Latimer and Amersham

Aylesbury and Amersham - London

Saturdays
28 July to 8 September

Network Diagram - see first Page of Table 114

		CH	CH	CH	CH	CH	CH	CH	CH	CH	CH	CH	CH	CH	CH	CH	CH	CH	CH	CH	CH	CH	CH
		◇															◇		◇			◇	
Aylesbury Vale Parkway	d			07 00	07 30		08 30		09 30		10 30		11 30		12 30		13 30		14 30		15 30		16 30
Aylesbury	d	06 05	06 35	07 05	07 35	08 05	08 35	09 05	09 35	10 05	10 35	11 05	11 35	12 05	12 35	13 05	13 35	14 05	14 35	15 05	15 35	16 05	16 35
Stoke Mandeville	d	06 09	06 39	07 09	07 39	08 09	08 39	09 09	09 39	10 09	10 39	11 09	11 39	12 09	12 39	13 09	13 39	14 09	14 39	15 09	15 39	16 09	16 39
Wendover	d	06 13	06 43	07 13	07 43	08 13	08 43	09 13	09 43	10 13	10 43	11 13	11 43	12 13	12 43	13 13	13 43	14 13	14 43	15 13	15 43	16 13	16 43
Great Missenden	d	06 19	06 49	07 19	07 49	08 19	08 49	09 19	09 49	10 19	10 49	11 19	11 49	12 19	12 49	13 19	13 49	14 19	14 49	15 19	15 49	16 19	16 49
Amersham §	⊖ d	06 26	06a58	07 26	07 56	08 26	08 56	09 26	09 56	10 26	10 56	11 26	11 56	12 26	12 56	13 26	13 56	14 26	14 56	15 26	15 56	16 26	16 56
Chalfont & Latimer §	⊖ d	06 30		07 30	08 00	08 30	09 00	09 30	10 00	10 30	11 00	11 30	12 00	12 30	13 00	13 30	14 00	14 30	15 00	15 30	16 00	16 30	17 00
Chorleywood §	⊖ d	06 33		07 33	08 03	08 33	09 03	09 33	10 03	10 33	11 03	11 33	12 03	12 33	13 03	13 33	14 03	14 33	15 03	15 33	16 03	16 33	17 03
Rickmansworth §	⊖ d	06 38		07 38	08 08	08 38	09 08	09 38	10 08	10 38	11 08	11 38	12 08	12 38	13 08	13 38	14 08	14 38	15 08	15 38	16 08	16 38	17 08
Harrow-on-the-Hill [3] §	⊖ d	06 49		07 49	08 19	08 49	09 19	09 49	10 19	10 49	11 19	11 49	12 19	12 49	13 19	13 49	14 19	14 49	15 19	15 49	16 19	16 49	17 19
London Marylebone [10]	⊖ a	07 05		08 05	08 35	09 05	09 35	10 05	10 35	11 05	11 35	12 05	12 35	13 05	13 35	14 05	14 35	15 05	15 35	16 05	16 35	17 05	17 35

		CH	CH	CH	CH	CH	CH	CH	CH	CH
				◇				◇		
Aylesbury Vale Parkway	d		17 30		18 30		19 46	20 46	21 46	
Aylesbury	d	17 05	17 35	18 05	18 35	19 05	20 05	21 05	22 05	23 20
Stoke Mandeville	d	17 09	17 39	18 09	18 39	19 09	20 09	21 09	22 09	23 24
Wendover	d	17 13	17 43	18 13	18 43	19 13	20 13	21 13	22 13	23 28
Great Missenden	d	17 19	17 49	18 19	18 49	19 19	20 19	21 19	22 19	23 34
Amersham §	⊖ d	17 26	17 56	18 26	18 56	19 26	20 26	21 26	22 26	23a43
Chalfont & Latimer §	⊖ d	17 30	18 00	18 30	19 00	19 30	20 30	21 30	22 30	
Chorleywood §	⊖ d	17 33	18 03	18 33	19 03	19 33	20 33	21 33	22 33	
Rickmansworth §	⊖ d	17 38	18 08	18 38	19 08	19 38	20 38	21 38	22 38	
Harrow-on-the-Hill [3] §	⊖ d	17 49	18 19	18 49	19 19	19 49	20 49	21 49	22 49	
London Marylebone [10]	⊖ a	18 05	18 35	19 05	19 35	20 05	21 05	22 05	23 05	

Saturdays
15 September to 6 October

		CH	CH	CH	CH	CH	CH	CH	CH	CH	CH	CH	CH	CH	CH	CH	CH	CH	CH	CH	CH	CH	CH
		◇															◇		◇			◇	
Aylesbury Vale Parkway	d			07 00	07 30		08 30		09 30		10 30		11 30		12 30		13 30		14 30		15 30		16 30
Aylesbury	d	06 05	06 35	07 05	07 35	08 05	08 35	09 05	09 35	10 05	10 35	11 05	11 35	12 05	12 35	13 05	13 35	14 05	14 35	15 05	15 35	16 05	16 35
Stoke Mandeville	d	06 09	06 39	07 09	07 39	08 09	08 39	09 09	09 39	10 09	10 39	11 09	11 39	12 09	12 39	13 09	13 39	14 09	14 39	15 09	15 39	16 09	16 39
Wendover	d	06 13	06 43	07 13	07 43	08 13	08 43	09 13	09 43	10 13	10 43	11 13	11 43	12 13	12 43	13 13	13 43	14 13	14 43	15 13	15 43	16 13	16 43
Great Missenden	d	06 19	06 49	07 19	07 49	08 19	08 49	09 19	09 49	10 19	10 49	11 19	11 49	12 19	12 49	13 19	13 49	14 19	14 49	15 19	15 49	16 19	16 49
Amersham §	⊖ d	06 26	06a58	07 26	07 56	08 26	08 56	09 26	09 56	10 26	10 56	11 26	11 56	12 26	12 56	13 26	13 56	14 26	14 56	15 26	15 56	16 26	16 56
Chalfont & Latimer §	⊖ d	06 30		07 30	08 00	08 30	09 00	09 30	10 00	10 30	11 00	11 30	12 00	12 30	13 00	13 30	14 00	14 30	15 00	15 30	16 00	16 30	17 00
Chorleywood §	⊖ d	06 33		07 33	08 03	08 33	09 03	09 33	10 03	10 33	11 03	11 33	12 03	12 33	13 03	13 33	14 03	14 33	15 03	15 33	16 03	16 33	17 03
Rickmansworth §	⊖ d	06 38		07 38	08 08	08 38	09 08	09 38	10 08	10 38	11 08	11 38	12 08	12 38	13 08	13 38	14 08	14 38	15 08	15 38	16 08	16 38	17 08
Harrow-on-the-Hill [3] §	⊖ d	06 49		07 49	08 19	08 49	09 19	09 49	10 19	10 49	11 19	11 49	12 19	12 49	13 19	13 49	14 19	14 49	15 19	15 49	16 19	16 49	17 19
London Marylebone [10]	⊖ a	07 05		08 05	08 35	09 05	09 35	10 05	10 35	11 05	11 35	12 05	12 35	13 05	13 35	14 05	14 35	15 05	15 35	16 05	16 35	17 05	17 35

		CH	CH	CH	CH	CH	CH	CH	CH	CH
				◇				◇		
Aylesbury Vale Parkway	d		17 30		18 30		19 46	20 46	21 46	
Aylesbury	d	17 05	17 35	18 05	18 35	19 05	20 05	21 05	22 05	23 20
Stoke Mandeville	d	17 09	17 39	18 09	18 39	19 09	20 09	21 09	22 09	23 24
Wendover	d	17 13	17 43	18 13	18 43	19 13	20 13	21 13	22 13	23 28
Great Missenden	d	17 19	17 49	18 19	18 49	19 19	20 19	21 19	22 19	23 34
Amersham §	⊖ d	17 26	17 56	18 26	18 56	19 26	20 26	21 26	22 26	23a43
Chalfont & Latimer §	⊖ d	17 30	18 00	18 30	19 00	19 30	20 30	21 30	22 30	
Chorleywood §	⊖ d	17 33	18 03	18 33	19 03	19 33	20 33	21 33	22 33	
Rickmansworth §	⊖ d	17 38	18 08	18 38	19 08	19 38	20 38	21 38	22 38	
Harrow-on-the-Hill [3] §	⊖ d	17 49	18 19	18 49	19 19	19 49	20 49	21 49	22 49	
London Marylebone [10]	⊖ a	18 05	18 35	19 05	19 35	20 05	21 05	22 05	23 05	

Saturdays
from 13 October

		CH	CH	CH	CH	CH	CH	CH	CH	CH	CH	CH	CH	CH	CH	CH	CH	CH	CH	CH	CH	CH	CH
		◇															◇		◇			◇	
Aylesbury Vale Parkway	d			06 57	07 27		08 27		09 27		10 27		11 27		12 27		13 27		14 27		15 27		16 27
Aylesbury	d	06 02	06 32	07 02	07 32	08 02	08 32	09 02	09 32	10 02	10 32	11 02	11 32	12 02	12 32	13 02	13 32	14 02	14 32	15 02	15 32	16 02	16 32
Stoke Mandeville	d	06 06	06 36	07 06	07 36	08 06	08 36	09 06	09 36	10 06	10 36	11 06	11 36	12 06	12 36	13 06	13 36	14 06	14 36	15 06	15 36	16 06	16 36
Wendover	d	06 10	06 40	07 10	07 40	08 10	08 40	09 10	09 40	10 10	10 40	11 10	11 40	12 10	12 40	13 10	13 40	14 10	14 40	15 10	15 40	16 10	16 40
Great Missenden	d	06 16	06 46	07 16	07 46	08 16	08 46	09 16	09 46	10 16	10 46	11 16	11 46	12 16	12 46	13 16	13 46	14 16	14 46	15 16	15 46	16 16	16 46
Amersham §	⊖ d	06 23	06a55	07 23	07 53	08 23	08 53	09 23	09 53	10 23	10 53	11 23	11 53	12 23	12 53	13 23	13 53	14 23	14 53	15 23	15 53	16 23	16 53
Chalfont & Latimer §	⊖ d	06 27		07 27	07 57	08 27	08 57	09 27	09 57	10 27	10 57	11 27	11 57	12 27	12 57	13 27	13 57	14 27	14 57	15 27	15 57	16 27	16 57
Chorleywood §	⊖ d	06 32		07 32	08 02	08 32	09 02	09 32	10 02	10 32	11 02	11 32	12 02	12 32	13 02	13 32	14 02	14 32	15 02	15 32	16 02	16 32	17 02
Rickmansworth §	⊖ d	06 38		07 38	08 08	08 38	09 08	09 38	10 08	10 38	11 08	11 38	12 08	12 38	13 08	13 38	14 08	14 38	15 08	15 38	16 08	16 38	17 08
Harrow-on-the-Hill [3] §	⊖ d	06 49		07 49	08 19	08 49	09 19	09 49	10 19	10 49	11 19	11 49	12 19	12 49	13 19	13 49	14 19	14 49	15 19	15 49	16 19	16 49	17 19
London Marylebone [10]	⊖ a	07 05		08 05	08 35	09 05	09 35	10 05	10 35	11 05	11 35	12 05	12 35	13 05	13 35	14 05	14 35	15 05	15 35	16 05	16 35	17 05	17 35

§ London Underground Limited (Metropolitan Line) services operate between Harrow-on-the-Hill, Rickmansworth, Chorleywood, Chalfont & Latimer and Amersham

Aylesbury and Amersham - London

Saturdays
from 13 October

Network Diagram - see first Page of Table 114

		CH	CH	CH	CH	CH	CH	CH	CH	CH
				◇				◇		
Aylesbury Vale Parkway	d		17 27		18 27		19 43	20 43	21 43	
Aylesbury	d	17 02	17 32	18 02	18 32	19 02	20 02	21 02	22 02	23 17
Stoke Mandeville	d	17 06	17 36	18 06	18 36	19 06	20 06	21 06	22 06	23 21
Wendover	d	17 10	17 40	18 10	18 40	19 10	20 10	21 10	22 10	23 25
Great Missenden	d	17 16	17 46	18 16	18 46	19 16	20 16	21 16	22 16	23 31
Amersham §	⊖ d	17 23	17 53	18 23	18 53	19 23	20 23	21 23	22 23	23a40
Chalfont & Latimer §	⊖ d	17 27	17 57	18 27	18 57	19 27	20 27	21 27	22 27	
Chorleywood §	⊖ d	17 32	18 02	18 32	19 02	19 32	20 32	21 32	22 32	
Rickmansworth §	⊖ d	17 38	18 08	18 38	19 08	19 38	20 38	21 38	22 38	
Harrow-on-the-Hill [3] §	⊖ d	17 49	18 19	18 49	19 19	19 49	20 49	21 49	22 49	
London Marylebone [10]	⊖ a	18 05	18 35	19 05	19 35	20 05	21 05	22 05	23 05	

Sundays
until 22 July

		CH	CH	CH	CH	CH	CH	CH	CH	CH	CH	CH	CH	CH	CH	CH	CH	CH	CH	CH	CH	CH	CH
		◇							◇									◇					
Aylesbury Vale Parkway	d	07 30	08 30	09 00	10 00	11 00	12 00	13 00	14 00	15 00		16 00		17 00		18 00		19 00		20 00		21 00	
Aylesbury	d	07 35	08 35	09 05	10 05	11 05	12 05	13 05	14 05	15 05	15 35	16 05	16 35	17 05	17 35	18 05	18 35	19 05	19 35	20 05	20 35	21 05	21 35
Stoke Mandeville	d	07 39	08 39	09 09	10 09	11 09	12 09	13 09	14 09	15 09	15 39	16 09	16 39	17 09	17 39	18 09	18 39	19 09	19 39	20 09	20 39	21 09	21 39
Wendover	d	07 43	08 43	09 13	10 13	11 13	12 13	13 13	14 13	15 13	15 43	16 13	16 43	17 13	17 43	18 13	18 43	19 13	19 43	20 13	20 43	21 13	21 43
Great Missenden	d	07 49	08 49	09 19	10 19	11 19	12 19	13 19	14 19	15 19	15 49	16 19	16 49	17 19	17 49	18 19	18 49	19 19	19 49	20 19	20 49	21 19	21 49
Amersham §	⊖ d	07 56	08 56	09 26	10 26	11 26	12 26	13 26	14 26	15 26	15a58	16 26	16a58	17 26	17a58	18 26	18a58	19 26	19a58	20 26	20a58	21 26	21a58
Chalfont & Latimer §	⊖ d	08 00	09 00	09 30	10 30	11 30	12 30	13 30	14 30	15 30		16 30		17 30		18 30		19 30		20 30		21 30	
Chorleywood §	⊖ d	08 03	09 03	09 33	10 33	11 33	12 33	13 33	14 33	15 33		16 33		17 33		18 33		19 33		20 33		21 33	
Rickmansworth §	⊖ d	08 08	09 08	09 38	10 38	11 38	12 38	13 38	14 38	15 38		16 38		17 38		18 38		19 38		20 38		21 38	
Harrow-on-the-Hill [3] §	⊖ d	08 19	09 19	09 49	10 49	11 49	12 49	13 49	14 49	15 49		16 49		17 49		18 49		19 49		20 49		21 49	
London Marylebone [10]	⊖ a	08 35	09 35	10 05	11 05	12 05	13 05	14 05	15 05	16 05		17 05		18 05		19 05		20 05		21 05		22 05	

		CH	CH
			◇
Aylesbury Vale Parkway	d	22 00	
Aylesbury	d	22 05	22 35
Stoke Mandeville	d	22 09	22 39
Wendover	d	22 13	22 43
Great Missenden	d	22 19	22 49
Amersham §	⊖ d	22a28	22 56
Chalfont & Latimer §	⊖ d		23 00
Chorleywood §	⊖ d		23 03
Rickmansworth §	⊖ d		23 08
Harrow-on-the-Hill [3] §	⊖ d		23 19
London Marylebone [10]	⊖ a		23 35

Sundays
29 July to 9 September

		CH	CH	CH	CH	CH	CH	CH	CH	CH	CH	CH	CH	CH	CH	CH	CH	CH	CH	CH	CH	CH	CH
		◇ A	◇							◇									◇				
Aylesbury Vale Parkway	d	06 30	07 30	08 30	09 00	10 00	11 00	12 00	13 00	14 00	15 00		16 00		17 00		18 00		19 00		20 00		21 00
Aylesbury	d	06 35	07 35	08 35	09 05	10 05	11 05	12 05	13 05	14 05	15 05	15 35	16 05	16 35	17 05	17 35	18 05	18 35	19 05	19 35	20 05	20 35	21 05
Stoke Mandeville	d	06 39	07 39	08 39	09 09	10 09	11 09	12 09	13 09	14 09	15 09	15 39	16 09	16 39	17 09	17 39	18 09	18 39	19 09	19 39	20 09	20 39	21 09
Wendover	d	06 43	07 43	08 43	09 13	10 13	11 13	12 13	13 13	14 13	15 13	15 43	16 13	16 43	17 13	17 43	18 13	18 43	19 13	19 43	20 13	20 43	21 13
Great Missenden	d	06 49	07 49	08 49	09 19	10 19	11 19	12 19	13 19	14 19	15 19	15 49	16 19	16 49	17 19	17 49	18 19	18 49	19 19	19 49	20 19	20 49	21 19
Amersham §	⊖ d	06 56	07 56	08 56	09 26	10 26	11 26	12 26	13 26	14 26	15 26	15a58	16 26	16a58	17 26	17a58	18 26	18a58	19 26	19a58	20 26	20a58	21 26
Chalfont & Latimer §	⊖ d	07 00	08 00	09 00	09 30	10 30	11 30	12 30	13 30	14 30	15 30		16 30		17 30		18 30		19 30		20 30		21 30
Chorleywood §	⊖ d	07 03	08 03	09 03	09 33	10 33	11 33	12 33	13 33	14 33	15 33		16 33		17 33		18 33		19 33		20 33		21 33
Rickmansworth §	⊖ d	07 08	08 08	09 08	09 38	10 38	11 38	12 38	13 38	14 38	15 38		16 38		17 38		18 38		19 38		20 38		21 38
Harrow-on-the-Hill [3] §	⊖ d	07 19	08 19	09 19	09 49	10 49	11 49	12 49	13 49	14 49	15 49		16 49		17 49		18 49		19 49		20 49		21 49
London Marylebone [10]	⊖ a	07 35	08 35	09 35	10 05	11 05	12 05	13 05	14 05	15 05	16 05		17 05		18 05		19 05		20 05		21 05		22 05

		CH	CH	CH
				◇
Aylesbury Vale Parkway	d		22 00	
Aylesbury	d	21 35	22 05	22 35
Stoke Mandeville	d	21 39	22 09	22 39
Wendover	d	21 43	22 13	22 43
Great Missenden	d	21 49	22 19	22 49
Amersham §	⊖ d	21a58	22a28	22 56
Chalfont & Latimer §	⊖ d			23 00
Chorleywood §	⊖ d			23 03
Rickmansworth §	⊖ d			23 08
Harrow-on-the-Hill [3] §	⊖ d			23 19
London Marylebone [10]	⊖ a			23 35

§ London Underground Limited (Metropolitan Line) services operate between Harrow-on-the-Hill, Rickmansworth, Chorleywood, Chalfont & Latimer and Amersham

A not from 19 August

Sundays

16 September to 30 September

Aylesbury and Amersham - London

Network Diagram - see first Page of Table 114

			CH	CH	CH	CH	CH	CH	CH	CH	CH	CH	CH	CH	CH	CH	CH	CH	CH	CH	CH	CH	CH	CH
			◇							◇									◇					
Aylesbury Vale Parkway		d	07 30	08 30	09 00	10 00	11 00	12 00	13 00	14 00	15 00		16 00		17 00		18 00		19 00		20 00		21 00	
Aylesbury		d	07 35	08 35	09 05	10 05	11 05	12 05	13 05	14 05	15 05	15 35	16 05	16 35	17 05	17 35	18 05	18 35	19 05	19 35	20 05	20 35	21 05	21 35
Stoke Mandeville		d	07 39	08 39	09 09	10 09	11 09	12 09	13 09	14 09	15 09	15 39	16 09	16 39	17 09	17 39	18 09	18 39	19 09	19 39	20 09	20 39	21 09	21 39
Wendover		d	07 43	08 43	09 13	10 13	11 13	12 13	13 13	14 13	15 13	15 43	16 13	16 43	17 13	17 43	18 13	18 43	19 13	19 43	20 13	20 43	21 13	21 43
Great Missenden		d	07 49	08 49	09 19	10 19	11 19	12 19	13 19	14 19	15 19	15 49	16 19	16 49	17 19	17 49	18 19	18 49	19 19	19 49	20 19	20 49	21 19	21 49
Amersham §	⊖	d	07 56	08 56	09 26	10 26	11 26	12 26	13 26	14 26	15 26	15a58	16 26	16a58	17 26	17a58	18 26	18a58	19 26	19a58	20 26	20a58	21 26	21a58
Chalfont & Latimer §	⊖	d	08 00	09 00	09 30	10 30	11 30	12 30	13 30	14 30	15 30		16 30		17 30		18 30		19 30		20 30		21 30	
Chorleywood §	⊖	d	08 03	09 03	09 33	10 33	11 33	12 33	13 33	14 33	15 33		16 33		17 33		18 33		19 33		20 33		21 33	
Rickmansworth §	⊖	d	08 08	09 08	09 38	10 38	11 38	12 38	13 38	14 38	15 38		16 38		17 38		18 38		19 38		20 38		21 38	
Harrow-on-the-Hill 3 §	⊖	d	08 19	09 19	09 49	10 49	11 49	12 49	13 49	14 49	15 49		16 49		17 49		18 49		19 49		20 49		21 49	
London Marylebone 10	⊖	a	08 35	09 35	10 05	11 05	12 05	13 05	14 05	15 05	16 05		17 05		18 05		19 05		20 05		21 05		22 05	

			CH	CH
				◇
Aylesbury Vale Parkway		d	22 00	
Aylesbury		d	22 05	22 35
Stoke Mandeville		d	22 09	22 39
Wendover		d	22 13	22 43
Great Missenden		d	22 19	22 49
Amersham §	⊖	d	22a28	22 56
Chalfont & Latimer §	⊖	d		23 00
Chorleywood §	⊖	d		23 03
Rickmansworth §	⊖	d		23 08
Harrow-on-the-Hill 3 §	⊖	d		23 19
London Marylebone 10	⊖	a		23 35

Sundays

from 7 October

			CH	CH	CH	CH	CH	CH	CH	CH	CH	CH	CH	CH	CH	CH	CH	CH	CH	CH	CH	CH	CH	CH
			◇							◇									◇					
Aylesbury Vale Parkway		d	07 27	08 27	08 57	09 57	10 57	11 57	12 57	13 57	14 57		15 57		16 57		17 57		18 57		19 57		20 57	
Aylesbury		d	07 32	08 32	09 02	10 02	11 02	12 02	13 02	14 02	15 02	15 32	16 02	16 32	17 02	17 32	18 02	18 32	19 02	19 32	20 02	20 32	21 02	21 32
Stoke Mandeville		d	07 36	08 36	09 06	10 06	11 06	12 06	13 06	14 06	15 06	15 36	16 06	16 36	17 06	17 36	18 06	18 36	19 06	19 36	20 06	20 36	21 06	21 36
Wendover		d	07 40	08 40	09 10	10 10	11 10	12 10	13 10	14 10	15 10	15 40	16 10	16 40	17 10	17 40	18 10	18 40	19 10	19 40	20 10	20 40	21 10	21 40
Great Missenden		d	07 46	08 46	09 16	10 16	11 16	12 16	13 16	14 16	15 16	15 46	16 16	16 46	17 16	17 46	18 16	18 46	19 16	19 46	20 16	20 46	21 16	21 46
Amersham §	⊖	d	07 53	08 53	09 23	10 23	11 23	12 23	13 23	14 23	15 23	15a55	16 23	16a55	17 23	17a55	18 23	18a55	19 23	19a55	20 23	20a55	21 23	21a55
Chalfont & Latimer §	⊖	d	07 57	08 57	09 27	10 27	11 27	12 27	13 27	14 27	15 27		16 27		17 27		18 27		19 27		20 27		21 27	
Chorleywood §	⊖	d	08 02	09 02	09 32	10 32	11 32	12 32	13 32	14 32	15 32		16 32		17 32		18 32		19 32		20 32		21 32	
Rickmansworth §	⊖	d	08 08	09 08	09 38	10 38	11 38	12 38	13 38	14 38	15 38		16 38		17 38		18 38		19 38		20 38		21 38	
Harrow-on-the-Hill 3 §	⊖	d	08 19	09 19	09 49	10 49	11 49	12 49	13 49	14 49	15 49		16 49		17 49		18 49		19 49		20 49		21 49	
London Marylebone 10	⊖	a	08 35	09 35	10 05	11 05	12 05	13 05	14 05	15 05	16 05		17 05		18 05		19 05		20 05		21 05		22 05	

			CH	CH
				◇
Aylesbury Vale Parkway		d	21 57	
Aylesbury		d	22 02	22 32
Stoke Mandeville		d	22 06	22 36
Wendover		d	22 10	22 40
Great Missenden		d	22 16	22 46
Amersham §	⊖	d	22a25	22 53
Chalfont & Latimer §	⊖	d		22 57
Chorleywood §	⊖	d		23 02
Rickmansworth §	⊖	d		23 08
Harrow-on-the-Hill 3 §	⊖	d		23 19
London Marylebone 10	⊖	a		23 35

§ London Underground Limited (Metropolitan Line) services operate between Harrow-on-the-Hill, Rickmansworth, Chorleywood, Chalfont & Latimer and Amersham

Mondays to Fridays

until 27 July

London - High Wycombe, Aylesbury, Banbury, Stratford-upon-Avon, Birmingham Snow Hill and Kidderminster

Network Diagram - see first Page of Table 114

Miles	Miles	Miles				CH	CH	CH	CH	CH	CH	CH	CH	CH	CH	LM	CH	CH	CH	CH	CH	CH	CH
						MX	MX	MO	MO	MX	MX	MO	MX	MO	MX								
						◇	◇						◇										◇ 🍴
								A	A			A											
—	—	—	**London Marylebone** 10	⊖	d	22p37	23p07	22p45		23p20	23p30	23p45	00 05		00 10				06 00	06 12	06 20	06 40	07 00
—	—	0	**London Paddington** 15	⊖	d																		
6½	—	—	Wembley Stadium		d			22p54		23p29	23p39	23p54			00 19				06 09		06 29	06 49	
8	—	—	Sudbury & Harrow Road		d																		
8¾	—	—	Sudbury Hill Harrow		d																		
9¾	—	—	Northolt Park		d			22p59			23p44	23p59			00 24				06 14		06 34		
11½	—	—	South Ruislip §	⊖	d			23p02			23p47	00 02			00 27				06 17		06 37		
13¼	—	—	West Ruislip 3 §	⊖	d			23p06			23p51	00 06			00 31					06 26		06 57	
16	—	—	Denham		d			23p10			23p55	00 10			00 35				06 23	06 31	06 43	07 01	
17	—	—	Denham Golf Club		d			23p13			23p58	00 13			00 38							07 04	
18¾	—	—	Gerrards Cross 1		d			23p17		23p42	00 02	00 17	00 24		00 42				06 27	06 36	06 47	07 07	
21¼	—	—	Seer Green		d			23p21			00 06	00 21			00 46				06 32			07 12	
23	—	—	Beaconsfield		d			23p25		23p48	00 10	00 25	00 30		00 50				06 35	06 42	06 53	07 15	
27¼	—	—	**High Wycombe** 1		d			23p31		23p54	00 16	00 31	00 36		00 56			06 10	06 41	06 48	07a06	07a24	07 25
32¾	—	—	Saunderton		d			23p37			00 22	00 37			01 02			06 17	06 47				
36	—	—	**Princes Risborough** 2		d			23p42	23p48	00 03	00 29	00 42	00 45	00 48	01 09			06 22	06 54	06 58			07 34
—	1½	—	Monks Risborough		d				23p51		00 32			00 51	01 12				06 57				
—	3	—	Little Kimble		d				23p55		00 36			00 55	01 16				07 01				
—	7½	—	**Aylesbury**		a				00 06		00 51			01 06	01 29				07 14				
4¾	—	—	Haddenham & Thame Parkway		d			23p49		00 10		00 49	00 51					06 30		07 04			07 41
54¾	—	—	**Bicester North** 3		d	23p20	23p50	00 02		00 23		01 02	01 04					06 45		07 17			07 53
65¼	—	—	Kings Sutton		d			00 13		00 33								06 56		07 28			
68¾	—	—	**Banbury**		d	23p39	00 03	00a22		00a45		01a20	01a24					07 02		07a41			08 07
88¾	—	—	**Leamington Spa** 6		d	23p56	00 21										06 52	07 22					08 25
90¾	—	—	Warwick		d	23p59	00 25										06 56	07 26					08 30
92	—	—	Warwick Parkway		d	00 04	00 29										06 59	07 30					08 33
94¾	—	—	Hatton		d												07 06	07 35					
—	—	7¾	Claverdon		d											06x34	07 12						
—	—	10	Bearley		d											06x38	07 17						
—	—	11½	Wilmcote		d											06 42	07 21						
—	—	15¼	**Stratford-upon-Avon**		a											06 48	07 27						
99	—	—	Lapworth		a																		
101½	—	—	Dorridge		a	00 13												07 42					08 43
104¾	—	—	Solihull		a	00 18	00 40											07 50					08 48
111¼	—	—	**Birmingham Moor Street**		a	00 33	00 55											08 02					08 59
112	—	—	**Birmingham Snow Hill**	🚌	a													08 10					09 07
—	—	—	Rowley Regis		a																		
—	—	—	Cradley Heath		a																		
—	—	—	**Stourbridge Junction** 2		a																		
—	—	—	**Kidderminster**		a																		

			CH	CH	CH	CH	CH	CH	CH	CH	CH	CH	CH	CH	CH	CH	CH	CH	CH	CH	CH	CH	CH	CH
														BZ										
			◇		◇					◇	◇			◇ 🍴	◇		◇ 🍴		◇	◇		◇ 🍴		
London Marylebone 10	⊖	d	07 08	07 12	07 33		07 43	07 46	08 00	08 03	08 06	08 10	08 30	08 37	08 41	08 45	09 07		09 10	09 14	09 17	09 37	09 40	09 43
London Paddington 15	⊖	d																						
Wembley Stadium		d		07 21				07 55				08 19	08 39			08 54					09 26			09 52
Sudbury & Harrow Road		d																						
Sudbury Hill Harrow		d		07 25					08 10				08 43								09 30			
Northolt Park		d		07 27			07 54					08 24				08 59				09 25				
South Ruislip §	⊖	d		07 31				08 01	08a19				08 55								09 35			
West Ruislip 3 §	⊖	d					07 59					08 29				09 04								10 00
Denham		d		07 36				08 07				08 34	09 01			09 08					09 40			10 04
Denham Golf Club		d						08 09								09 11								10 07
Gerrards Cross 1		d	07 27	07 41			08 06	08 13			08 27	08 39	09a12			09 15				09 35	09 45		09 59	10 11
Seer Green		d	07 32					08 17				08 43								09 40				10 15
Beaconsfield		d	07 35				08 12	08 20			08 33	08 47				09 21				09 43	09 51		10 05	10 19
High Wycombe 1		d	07 41	07 51	07 57		08 18	08a28		08 29	08 39	09a00			09 08	09a30	09 31		09 35	09 49	10a03		10 11	10a30
Saunderton		d	07 47								08 45				09 14					09 56				
Princes Risborough 2		d	07 53	08a05	08 06	08 16	08 27			08 38	08 50				09 20			09 24	09 44	10a08			10 20	
Monks Risborough		d				08 19												09 27						
Little Kimble		d				08 23												09 31						
Aylesbury		a				08 34												09 42						
Haddenham & Thame Parkway		d	08 00		08 12		08 33				08 57				09 27				09 50				10 27	
Bicester North 3		d	08 13		08 23		08 46			08 52	09a16				09 41		09 52		10 01				10a47	
Kings Sutton		d	08 26												09 52									
Banbury		d	08 32		08 38		09a04			09 05				09 30	10a04		10 05		10 15			10 30		
Leamington Spa 6		d	08 51		08 56					09 22				09 47			10 23		10 33			10 48		
Warwick		d	08 56		09 01					09 27							10 27		10 37					
Warwick Parkway		d			09 04					09 30				09 53			10 31					10 54		
Hatton		d	09 04		09 09																			
Claverdon		d	09 09																					
Bearley		d	09 14																					
Wilmcote		d	09 18																					
Stratford-upon-Avon		a	09 31																11 09					
Lapworth		a			09 15																			
Dorridge		a			09 19					09 40							10 40							
Solihull		a			09 25					09 46				10 05			10 46					11 05		
Birmingham Moor Street		a			09 39					09 54				10 17			10 54					11 19		
Birmingham Snow Hill	🚌	a								10 05							11 04							
Rowley Regis		a																						
Cradley Heath		a																						
Stourbridge Junction 2		a																						
Kidderminster		a																						

§ London Underground Limited (Central Line) also operate services between South Ruislip and West Ruislip at frequent intervals

A from 21 May until 23 July

BZ Business Zone available offering greater comfort and an enhanced working environment. Supplement payable

London - High Wycombe, Aylesbury, Banbury, Stratford-upon-Avon, Birmingham Snow Hill and Kidderminster

Network Diagram - see first Page of Table 114

		CH	CH	CH	CH		CH	CH	CH	CH	CH	CH	CH	CH	CH		CH	CH	CH	CH	CH	CH	CH	CH	CH
		◇ H		◇	◇			◇ H	◇		◇ H		◇	◇			◇ H				◇ H	◇			◇ H
London Marylebone ⊖	d	10 07		10 10	10 13		10 17	10 37	10 40	10 43	11 07		11 10	11 13	11 16		11 37		11 40	11 43	12 07	12 10	12 13	12 16	12 37
London Paddington ⊖	d																								
Wembley Stadium	d						10 26			10 52					11 25					11 52				12 25	
Sudbury & Harrow Road	d																								
Sudbury Hill Harrow	d						10 30																	12 29	
Northolt Park	d						10 32								11 30									12 31	
South Ruislip § ⊖	d						10 36								11 33									12 35	
West Ruislip § ⊖	d									11 00										12 00					
Denham	d						10 41			11 04					11 39					12 04				12 40	
Denham Golf Club	d														11 41									12 43	
Gerrards Cross	d				10 32		10a52		10 59	11 10				11 32	11a52				11 59	12 10			12 32	12a53	
Seer Green	d									11 14										12 14					
Beaconsfield	d				10 38				11 05	11 18				11 38					12 05	12 18			12 38		
High Wycombe	d	10 31		10 37	10 44				11 11	11a30	11 31		11 35	11 44					12 11	12a30	12 31	12 35	12 44		
Saunderton	d				10 50									11 50									12 50		
Princes Risborough	d		10 24	10a53	10 55				11 20			11 24	11 44	12a07				12 17	12 20			12 44	13a02		
Monks Risborough	d		10 27									11 27						12 20							
Little Kimble	d		10 31									11 31						12 24							
Aylesbury	a		10 42									11 43						12 38							
Haddenham & Thame Parkway	d				11 02				11 26				11 50						12 27			12 50			
Bicester North	d	10 52			11 14				11 40		11 52		12 01						12a47		12 52	13 01			
Kings Sutton	d								11 54													13 12			
Banbury	d	11 05			11a32			11 33	12 00		12 05		12a21				12 29				13 05	13a24			13 29
Leamington Spa	d	11 23						11 50	12 19		12 23						12 47				13 23				13 47
Warwick	d	11 27							12 23		12 27										13 27				
Warwick Parkway	d	11 31						11 56			12 31						12 52				13 31				13 52
Hatton	d								12 31																
Claverdon	d								12 36																
Bearley	d								12 41																
Wilmcote	d																								
Stratford-upon-Avon	a								12 54																
Lapworth	a																								
Dorridge	a	11 40									12 40										13 40				
Solihull	a	11 46						12 07			12 46						13 05				13 46				14 04
Birmingham Moor Street	a	11 54						12 25			12 54						13 19				13 54				14 19
Birmingham Snow Hill	a	12 04									13 04										14 04				
Rowley Regis	a																								
Cradley Heath	a																								
Stourbridge Junction	a																								
Kidderminster	a																								

			CH	CH	CH	CH	CH	CH	CH	CH	CH BZ		CH	CH	CH	CH	CH	CH	CH	CH	CH		CH	CH	CH
					◇ H		◇			◇	◇				◇ H		◇			◇ H				◇	
London Marylebone ⊖	d		12 40	12 43	13 07		13 10	13 13	13 16		13 37		13 40	13 43	14 07		14 10	14 13	14 16	14 37	14 40		14 43	15 07	
London Paddington ⊖	d																								
Wembley Stadium	d			12 52					13 25					13 52					14 25				14 52		
Sudbury & Harrow Road	d																								
Sudbury Hill Harrow	d								13 29										14 29						
Northolt Park	d								13 31										14 31						
South Ruislip § ⊖	d								13 35										14 35						
West Ruislip § ⊖	d			13 00										14 00									15 00		
Denham	d			13 04					13 40					14 04					14 40				15 04		
Denham Golf Club	d								13 43										14 43						
Gerrards Cross	d		12 59	13 10				13 32	13a53				13 59	14 10				14 32	14a53		14 59		15 10		
Seer Green	d			13 14										14 14									15 14		
Beaconsfield	d		13 05	13 18				13 38					14 05	14 18				14 38			15 05		15 18		
High Wycombe	d		13 11	13a30	13 31		13 37	13 44					14 11	14a30	14 31		14 37	14 44			15 11		15a30	15 31	
Saunderton	d							13 50										14 50							
Princes Risborough	d		13 20			13 24	13 46	14a02					14 20			14 24	14 46	15a02			15 20				15 24
Monks Risborough	d					13 27										14 27									15 27
Little Kimble	d					13 31										14 31									15 31
Aylesbury	a					13 42										14 42									15 42
Haddenham & Thame Parkway	d		13 27				13 52						14 27				14 52				15 27				
Bicester North	d		13a47		13 52		14 05						14a47		14 52		15 05				15a47			15 52	
Kings Sutton	d																								
Banbury	d				14 05		14a25				14 30				15 05		15a24			15 29				16 06	
Leamington Spa	d				14 23					14 32	14 47				15 23					15 47				16 23	
Warwick	d				14 27					14 37					15 27									16 28	
Warwick Parkway	d				14 31						14 53				15 31					15 52				16 31	
Hatton	d									14 45															
Claverdon	d									14 51															
Bearley	d									14 56															
Wilmcote	d									15 00															
Stratford-upon-Avon	a									15 07															
Lapworth	a																								
Dorridge	a				14 40										15 40									16 41	
Solihull	a				14 46						15 05				15 46					16 04				16 46	
Birmingham Moor Street	a				14 54						15 19				15 54					16 13				17 01	
Birmingham Snow Hill	a				15 04										16 04					16 21					
Rowley Regis	a																								
Cradley Heath	a																								
Stourbridge Junction	a																								
Kidderminster	a																								

§ London Underground Limited (Central Line) also operate services between South Ruislip and West Ruislip at frequent intervals

BZ Business Zone available offering greater comfort and an enhanced working environment. Supplement payable

London - High Wycombe, Aylesbury, Banbury, Stratford-upon-Avon, Birmingham Snow Hill and Kidderminster

Network Diagram - see first Page of Table 114

		CH	CH	CH	CH MX	CH MX	CH MO	MO	CH MX	CH MX	CH MO	CH MX	CH MO	CH	CH MO	CH MX	CH		CH	CH	CH	CH	CH BZ	CH	CH
		◇			◇				◇					◇					◇				◇	◇	◇
London Marylebone ⊖	d	15 10	15 13	15 16	15 37	15 40	15 43		16 07		16 10	16 13	16 00	16 30	16 33	16 36			16 49	16 56	16 40	16 43	16 46	17 07	17 10
London Paddington ⊖	d																								
Wembley Stadium	d			15 25			15 52						16 09						16 59		16 49				
Sudbury & Harrow Road	d																				16 52				
Sudbury Hill Harrow	d			15 29																	16 54				
Northolt Park	d			15 31									16 14								16 57				
South Ruislip § ⊖	d			15 35									16 27								17 10				
West Ruislip § ⊖	d						16 00						16 31								17 13				
Denham	d			15 40			16 04					16 29	16 36							17 12					
Denham Golf Club	d			15 43								16 32													
Gerrards Cross	d		15 32	15a53		15 59	16 10					16 35	16a46			16 55				17 17	17a26				
Seer Green	d						16 14					16 40				17 00									
Beaconsfield	d		15 38			16 05	16 18				16 30	16 43				17 03				17 23					
High Wycombe	d	15 35	15 44			16 11	16a32				16 36	16a55			16 57	17a15			17 16	17a35					17 36
Saunderton	d		15 50								16 42								17 23						
Princes Risborough	d	15 44	16a02			16 20				16 24	16 48				17 06		17 16		17 28						17 45
Monks Risborough	d									16 27							17 19								
Little Kimble	d									16 31							17 23								
Aylesbury	a									16 42							17 37					17 36			
Haddenham & Thame Parkway	d	15 50				16 27					16 54				17 12				17 34						17 51
Bicester North	d	16 01				16a46			16 49		17a12				17a34				17 45						18 03
Kings Sutton	d	16 12																							18 13
Banbury	d	16 17			16 33				17 02										18a03				17 43	18 04	18 19
Leamington Spa	d	16 35			16 50				17 20														18 01	18 21	18 36
Warwick	d	16 39							17 25																18 41
Warwick Parkway	d				16 55				17 29					17 39									18 07	18 27	
Hatton	d	16 47																							18 48
Claverdon	d	16 54																							18 54
Bearley	d	16 59																							
Wilmcote	d	17 03																							19 01
Stratford-upon-Avon	a	17 14																							19 12
Lapworth	a																								
Dorridge	a								17 38														18 18	18 39	
Solihull	a				17 07				17 44					17 51									18 24	18 44	
Birmingham Moor Street	a				17 17				17 55					18 00									18 36	19 01	
Birmingham Snow Hill	a				17 27				18 03					18 12										19 04	
Rowley Regis	a																							19 24	
Cradley Heath	a																							19 29	
Stourbridge Junction	a																							19 35	
Kidderminster	a																							19 49	

		CH	CH		CH	CH	CH	CH	CH	CH	CH	CH	CH BZ		CH	CH	CH	CH	CH	CH	CH	CH	CH		CH
							◇						◇ H		◇	◇							◇		
London Marylebone ⊖	d	17 13	17 16		17 19	17 23	17 37	17 40	17 43	17 46	17 50	17 56	18 07		18 10	18 13		18 16	18 19	18 22	18 25	18 29	18 37		18 40
London Paddington ⊖	d																								
Wembley Stadium	d	17 22				17 32			17 52									18 25				18 38			
Sudbury & Harrow Road	d					17 36																18 41			
Sudbury Hill Harrow	d					17 39																18 43			
Northolt Park	d				17 30	17 42						18 07										18 46			
South Ruislip § ⊖	d					17 52						18 11										19 02			
West Ruislip § ⊖	d				17 36	18a02					18 05										18 40	19a08			
Denham	d				17 40						18 09										18 45				
Denham Golf Club	d				17 43						18 12														
Gerrards Cross	d	17 35							18 07		18 16	18a26								18 41	18 49				
Seer Green	d	17 39							18 11											18 46					
Beaconsfield	d	17 43			17 50				18 15		18 22							18 42			18 55				
High Wycombe	d	17 49			18a02			18 04	18 21		18a34							18 49		18 54	19a07				19 09
Saunderton	d	17 55							18 27											19 00					
Princes Risborough	d	18 02						18 13	18a39							18 48	18 52	19 02		19a13					19 18
Monks Risborough	d	18 05															18 55								
Little Kimble	d	18 09															18 59								
Aylesbury	a	18 23	18 05							18 41							19 10	19 23	19 11						
Haddenham & Thame Parkway	d						18 11	18 20								18 56									19 24
Bicester North	d						18 23	18a39								19 10							19 23		19a42
Kings Sutton	d																								
Banbury	d						18 37								19 05	19a30							19 36		
Leamington Spa	d						18 54								19 23								19 53		
Warwick	d						18 59								19 28								19 58		
Warwick Parkway	d						19 02						19 20		19 32								20 01		
Hatton	d																								
Claverdon	d																								
Bearley	d																								
Wilmcote	d																								
Stratford-upon-Avon	a																								
Lapworth	a																								
Dorridge	a						19 12								19 42								20 12		
Solihull	a						19 17						19 31		19 48								20 17		
Birmingham Moor Street	a						19 26						19 40		19 58								20 26		
Birmingham Snow Hill	a						19 36						19 43		20 11								20 37		
Rowley Regis	a												20 01												
Cradley Heath	a																								
Stourbridge Junction	a												20 12												
Kidderminster	a												20 30												

§ London Underground Limited (Central Line) also operate services between South Ruislip and West Ruislip at frequent intervals

BZ Business Zone available offering greater comfort and an enhanced working environment. Supplement payable

Mondays to Fridays
until 27 July

London - High Wycombe, Aylesbury, Banbury, Stratford-upon-Avon, Birmingham Snow Hill and Kidderminster

Network Diagram - see first Page of Table 114

	CH	CH	CH	CH	CH	CH ◇	CH	CH	CH ◇	CH ◇	CH
London Marylebone ⊖ d	18 44	18 47	18 54	18 58	19 04	19 15	19 18	19 21	19 37	19 40	19 43
London Paddington ⊖ d											
Wembley Stadium d				19 07				19 30			
Sudbury & Harrow Road d											
Sudbury Hill Harrow d											
Northolt Park d			19 06					19 35			
South Ruislip § ⊖ d				19 13				19 38			
West Ruislip § ⊖ d			19 11								19 58
Denham d				19 20				19 44			20 03
Denham Golf Club d				19 23							20 05
Gerrards Cross d		19 08	19 18	19 27			19 37	19 49			20 09
Seer Green d		19 12					19 41				
Beaconsfield d	19 09	19 15	19 24				19 45			20 03	20 16
High Wycombe d	19 15	19a27	19 30	19a43			19 51	20a05		20 09	20 22
Saunderton d			19 37								20 28
Princes Risborough d	19 24		19 43				20 00			20 19	20 36
Monks Risborough d			19 47								20 40
Little Kimble d			19 50								20 43
Aylesbury a			20 04		20 08						20 58
Haddenham & Thame Parkway d	19 30						20 06		20 13	20 26	
Bicester North d	19 43					20 00	20 19		20 25	20a46	
Kings Sutton d	19 54										
Banbury d	20 01					20 13	20a38		20 39		
Leamington Spa d	20 22					20 31			20 57		
Warwick d	20 27								21 01		
Warwick Parkway d						20 36			21 05		
Hatton d	20 36										
Claverdon d	20 42										
Bearley d	20 48										
Wilmcote d	20 53										
Stratford-upon-Avon a	21 04										
Lapworth a											
Dorridge a						20 46			21 14		
Solihull a						20 51			21 20		
Birmingham Moor Street a						21 00			21 28		
Birmingham Snow Hill a						21 04			21 37		
Rowley Regis a						21 19					
Cradley Heath a						21 25					
Stourbridge Junction a						21 32					
Kidderminster a						21 49					

	CH	CH ◇	CH ◇	CH	CH ◇	CH	CH ◇	CH	CH	CH ◇	CH
London Marylebone ⊖ d	19 46	20 10	20 14	20 17	20 37	20 40	21 07	21 10		21 37	21 40
London Paddington ⊖ d											
Wembley Stadium d	19 55			20 26		20 50		21 20			21 50
Sudbury & Harrow Road d	19 58					20 53					
Sudbury Hill Harrow d	20 00					20 55					
Northolt Park d	20 03			20 31				21 25			
South Ruislip § ⊖ d	20 06			20 34				21 28			
West Ruislip § ⊖ d						21 01					21 58
Denham d				20 40		21 06		21 34			22 03
Denham Golf Club d						21 09		21 37			
Gerrards Cross d	20 15		20 33	20 45		21 13		21 41			22 08
Seer Green d	20 19					21 17		21 45			
Beaconsfield d	20 23		20 40	20 51		21 21		21 49			22 14
High Wycombe d	20a36		20 46	20 57	21 02	21 27	21 32	21 55		22 02	22 20
Saunderton d			20 52					22 01			22 27
Princes Risborough d			20 58	21 07	21 12	21a40	21 42	22 09		22 12	22 33
Monks Risborough d				21 11				22 12			22 37
Little Kimble d				21 14				22 16			22 40
Aylesbury a				21 28				22 31			22 54
Haddenham & Thame Parkway d			21 05		21 18		21 48			22 18	
Bicester North d		20 53	21 19		21 29		21 59			22 29	
Kings Sutton d			21 29								
Banbury d		21 06	21a42		21 45		22 13			22 43	
Leamington Spa d		21 24			22 04		22 30		22 40	23 00	
Warwick d					22 09		22 34		22 45	23 05	
Warwick Parkway d		21 30			22 12		22 37			23 09	
Hatton d							22 42				
Claverdon d											
Bearley d											
Wilmcote d											
Stratford-upon-Avon a									23 12		
Lapworth a							22 48				
Dorridge a		21 39			22 22		22 52			23 18	
Solihull a		21 45			22 27		22 59			23 24	
Birmingham Moor Street a		21 57			22 42		23 08			23 39	
Birmingham Snow Hill a		22 00					23 12				
Rowley Regis a		22 24					23 38				
Cradley Heath a		22 29					23 44				
Stourbridge Junction a		22 35					23 52				
Kidderminster a		22 50									

	CH ◇	CH	CH	CH ◇	CH ◇	CH	CH	CH ◇	CH	CH
London Marylebone ⊖ d	22 07	22 10	22 13	22 37	22 40	22 43	23 00	23 07	23 20	23 30
London Paddington ⊖ d										
Wembley Stadium d			22 22			22 52	23 09		23 29	23 39
Sudbury & Harrow Road d										
Sudbury Hill Harrow d										
Northolt Park d			22 27				23 14			23 44
South Ruislip § ⊖ d			22 31				23 20			23 47
West Ruislip § ⊖ d						23 00				23 51
Denham d			22 36			23 04	23 26			23 55
Denham Golf Club d			22 39				23 29			23 58
Gerrards Cross d		22 29	22 43		22 59	23 09	23 33		23 42	00 02
Seer Green d			22 47				23 37			00 06
Beaconsfield d		22 36	22 51		23 06	23 15	23 41		23 48	00 10
High Wycombe d		22 42	23a03		23 12	23 21	23 47		23 54	00 16
Saunderton d						23 27				00 22
Princes Risborough d		22 51			23 21	23 34	00a01		00 03	00 29
Monks Risborough d						23 37				00 32
Little Kimble d						23 41				00 36
Aylesbury a						23 55				00 51
Haddenham & Thame Parkway d		22 58			23 28				00 10	
Bicester North d	22 50	23a17		23 20	23a47			23 50	00 23	
Kings Sutton d									00 33	
Banbury d	23 04			23 39				00 03	00a45	
Leamington Spa d	23 23			23 56				00 21		
Warwick d	23 27			23 59				00 25		
Warwick Parkway d	23 31			00 04				00 29		
Hatton d										
Claverdon d										
Bearley d										
Wilmcote d										
Stratford-upon-Avon a										
Lapworth a										
Dorridge a	23 40			00 13						
Solihull a	23 46			00 18				00 40		
Birmingham Moor Street a	23 59			00 33				00 55		
Birmingham Snow Hill a										
Rowley Regis a										
Cradley Heath a										
Stourbridge Junction a										
Kidderminster a										

§ London Underground Limited (Central Line) also operate services between South Ruislip and West Ruislip at frequent intervals

Mondays to Fridays
30 July to 7 September

London - High Wycombe, Aylesbury, Banbury, Stratford-upon-Avon, Birmingham Snow Hill and Kidderminster

Network Diagram - see first Page of Table 114

	CH MX ◇	CH MX ◇	CH MO	CH MO	CH MX	CH MX	CH MO	CH MX ◇	CH MO	CH MX
London Marylebone ⊖ d	22p37	23p07	22p45		23p20	23p30	23p45	00 05		00 10
London Paddington ⊖ d										
Wembley Stadium d			22p54		23p29	23p39	23p54			00 19
Sudbury & Harrow Road d										
Sudbury Hill Harrow d										
Northolt Park d			22p59			23p44	23p59			00 24
South Ruislip § ⊖ d			23p02			23p47	00 02			00 27
West Ruislip § ⊖ d			23p06			23p51	00 06			00 31
Denham d			23p10			23p55	00 10			00 35
Denham Golf Club d			23p13			23p58	00 13			00 38
Gerrards Cross d			23p17		23p42	00 02	00 17	00 24		00 42
Seer Green d			23p21			00 06	00 21			00 46
Beaconsfield d			23p25		23p48	00 10	00 25	00 30		00 50
High Wycombe d			23p31		23p54	00 16	00 31	00 36		00 56
Saunderton d			23p37			00 22	00 37			01 02
Princes Risborough d			23p42	23p48	00 03	00 29	00 42	00 45	00 48	01 09
Monks Risborough d				23p51		00 32			00 51	01 12
Little Kimble d				23p55		00 36			00 55	01 16
Aylesbury a				00 06		00 51			01 06	01 29
Haddenham & Thame Parkway d			23p49		00 10		00 49	00 51		
Bicester North d	23p20	23p50	00 02		00 23		01 02	01 04		
Kings Sutton d			00 13		00 33					
Banbury d	23p39	00 03	00a22		00a45		01a20	01a24		
Leamington Spa d	23p56	00 21								
Warwick d	23p59	00 25								
Warwick Parkway d	00 04	00 29								
Hatton d										
Claverdon d										
Bearley d										
Wilmcote d										
Stratford-upon-Avon a										
Lapworth a										
Dorridge a	00 13									
Solihull a	00 18	00 40								
Birmingham Moor Street a	00 33	00 55								
Birmingham Snow Hill a										
Rowley Regis a										
Cradley Heath a										
Stourbridge Junction a										
Kidderminster a										

	CH A	CH A	CH A	CH ◇ A	CH A	LM	CH	CH	CH	CH	CH
London Marylebone ⊖ d	00 40	00 57	01 10	01 30	01 57				06 00	06 12	06 20
London Paddington ⊖ d											
Wembley Stadium d									06 09		06 29
Sudbury & Harrow Road d											
Sudbury Hill Harrow d											
Northolt Park d									06 14		06 34
South Ruislip § ⊖ d									06 17		06 37
West Ruislip § ⊖ d										06 26	
Denham d	00 57		01 27						06 23	06 31	06 43
Denham Golf Club d	00 59		01 29								
Gerrards Cross d	01 04		01 34						06 27	06 36	06 47
Seer Green d	01 08		01 38						06 32		
Beaconsfield d	01 12		01 42						06 35	06 42	06 53
High Wycombe d	01a24		01 48					06 10	06 41	06 48	07a06
Saunderton d			01 54					06 17	06 47		
Princes Risborough d			02 01	02 05				06 22	06 54	06 58	
Monks Risborough d									06 57		
Little Kimble d									07 01		
Aylesbury a		01 52	02 20		02 52				07 14		
Haddenham & Thame Parkway d				02 11				06 30		07 04	
Bicester North d				02 23				06 45		07 17	
Kings Sutton d								06 56		07 28	
Banbury d				02 36				07 02		07a41	
Leamington Spa d				02 54			06 52	07 22			
Warwick d				02 59			06 56	07 26			
Warwick Parkway d				03 02			06 59	07 30			
Hatton d							07 06	07 35			
Claverdon d						06x34	07 12				
Bearley d						06x38	07 17				
Wilmcote d						06 42	07 21				
Stratford-upon-Avon a						06 48	07 27				
Lapworth a											
Dorridge a				03 12				07 42			
Solihull a								07 50			
Birmingham Moor Street a				03 23				08 02			
Birmingham Snow Hill a				03 32				08 10			
Rowley Regis a											
Cradley Heath a											
Stourbridge Junction a											
Kidderminster a											

§ London Underground Limited (Central Line) also operate services between South Ruislip and West Ruislip at frequent intervals

A not from 14 August

Table 115

Mondays to Fridays
30 July to 7 September

London - High Wycombe, Aylesbury, Banbury, Stratford-upon-Avon, Birmingham Snow Hill and Kidderminster

Network Diagram - see first Page of Table 114

		CH	CH	CH	CH	CH	CH	CH	CH	CH	CH	CH	CH	CH	CH BZ	CH	CH	CH	CH	CH	CH	CH	CH
			◇ H	◇		◇					◇	◇			◇ H	◇		◇ H		◇	◇		◇ H
London Marylebone 10 ⊖	d	06 40	07 00	07 08	07 12	07 33		07 43	07 46	08 00	08 03	08 06	08 10	08 30	08 37	08 41	08 45	09 07		09 10	09 14	09 17	09 37
London Paddington 15 ⊖	d																						
Wembley Stadium	d	06 49			07 21				07 55				08 19	08 39			08 54					09 26	
Sudbury & Harrow Road	d																						
Sudbury Hill Harrow	d				07 25					08 10				08 43								09 30	
Northolt Park	d				07 27			07 54					08 24				08 59				09 25		
South Ruislip § ⊖	d				07 31				08 01	08a19				08 55								09 35	
West Ruislip 3 § ⊖	d	06 57						07 59					08 29				09 04						
Denham	d	07 01			07 36				08 07				08 34	09 01			09 08					09 40	
Denham Golf Club	d	07 04							08 09								09 11						
Gerrards Cross 1	d	07 07		07 27	07 41			08 06	08 13			08 27	08 39	09a12			09 15				09 35	09 45	
Seer Green	d	07 12		07 32					08 17				08 43								09 40		
Beaconsfield	d	07 15		07 35				08 12	08 20			08 33	08 47				09 21				09 43	09 51	
High Wycombe 1	d	07a24	07 25	07 41	07 51	07 57		08 18	08a28		08 29	08 39	09a00			09 08	09a30	09 31		09 35	09 49	10a03	
Saunderton	d			07 47								08 45				09 14					09 56		
Princes Risborough 2	d		07 34	07 53	08a05	08 06	08 16	08 27			08 38	08 50				09 20			09 24	09 44	10a08		
Monks Risborough	d						08 19												09 27				
Little Kimble	d						08 23												09 31				
Aylesbury	a						08 34												09 42				
Haddenham & Thame Parkway	d		07 41	08 00		08 12		08 33				08 57				09 27				09 50			
Bicester North 3	d		07 53	08 13		08 23		08 46			08 52	09a16				09 41		09 52		10 01			
Kings Sutton	d			08 26												09 52							
Banbury	d		08 07	08 32		08 38		09a04			09 05				09 30	10a04		10 05		10 15			10 30
Leamington Spa 8	d		08 25	08 51		08 56					09 22				09 47			10 23		10 33			10 48
Warwick	d		08 30	08 56		09 01					09 27							10 27		10 37			
Warwick Parkway	d		08 33			09 04					09 30				09 53			10 31					10 54
Hatton	d			09 04		09 09																	
Claverdon	d			09 09																			
Bearley	d			09 14																			
Wilmcote	d			09 18																			
Stratford-upon-Avon	a			09 31																11 09			
Lapworth	a					09 15																	
Dorridge	a		08 43			09 19					09 40							10 40					
Solihull	a		08 48			09 25					09 46				10 05			10 46					11 05
Birmingham Moor Street	a		08 59			09 39					09 54				10 17			10 54					11 19
Birmingham Snow Hill	a		09 07								10 05							11 04					
Rowley Regis	a																						
Cradley Heath	a																						
Stourbridge Junction 2	a																						
Kidderminster	a																						

		CH	CH	CH	CH	CH	CH	CH	CH	CH	CH	CH	CH	CH	CH	CH	CH	CH	CH	CH	CH	CH
				◇ H		◇	◇		◇ H	◇		◇ H		◇	◇		◇ H				◇ H	◇
London Marylebone 10 ⊖	d	09 40	09 43	10 07		10 10	10 13	10 17	10 37	10 40	10 43	11 07		11 10	11 13	11 16	11 37		11 40	11 43	12 07	12 10
London Paddington 15 ⊖	d																					
Wembley Stadium	d		09 52					10 26			10 52					11 25				11 52		
Sudbury & Harrow Road	d																					
Sudbury Hill Harrow	d							10 30														
Northolt Park	d							10 32								11 30						
South Ruislip § ⊖	d							10 36								11 33						
West Ruislip 3 § ⊖	d		10 00								11 01									12 00		
Denham	d		10 04					10 41			11 05					11 39				12 04		
Denham Golf Club	d		10 07													11 41						
Gerrards Cross 1	d	09 59	10 11				10 32	10a52		10 59	11 10				11 32	11a52			11 59	12 10		
Seer Green	d		10 15								11 14									12 14		
Beaconsfield	d	10 05	10 19				10 38			11 05	11 18				11 38				12 05	12 18		
High Wycombe 1	d	10 11	10a30	10 31		10 37	10 44			11 11	11a30	11 31		11 35	11 44				12 11	12a30	12 31	12 35
Saunderton	d						10 50								11 50							
Princes Risborough 2	d	10 20			10 24	10a53	10 55			11 20			11 24	11 44	12a07			12 17	12 20			12 44
Monks Risborough	d				10 27								11 27					12 20				
Little Kimble	d				10 31								11 31					12 24				
Aylesbury	a				10 42								11 43					12 38				
Haddenham & Thame Parkway	d	10 27					11 02			11 26				11 50					12 27			12 50
Bicester North 3	d	10a47		10 52			11 14			11 40		11 52		12 01					12a47		12 52	13 01
Kings Sutton	d									11 54												13 12
Banbury	d			11 05			11a32		11 33	12 00		12 05		12a21			12 29				13 05	13a24
Leamington Spa 8	d			11 23					11 50	12 19		12 23					12 47				13 23	
Warwick	d			11 27						12 23		12 27									13 27	
Warwick Parkway	d			11 31					11 56			12 31					12 52				13 31	
Hatton	d									12 31												
Claverdon	d									12 36												
Bearley	d									12 41												
Wilmcote	d																					
Stratford-upon-Avon	a									12 54												
Lapworth	a																					
Dorridge	a			11 40								12 40									13 40	
Solihull	a			11 46					12 07			12 46					13 05				13 46	
Birmingham Moor Street	a			11 54					12 25			12 54					13 19				13 54	
Birmingham Snow Hill	a			12 04								13 04									14 04	
Rowley Regis	a																					
Cradley Heath	a																					
Stourbridge Junction 2	a																					
Kidderminster	a																					

§ London Underground Limited (Central Line) also operate services between South Ruislip and West Ruislip at frequent intervals

BZ Business Zone available offering greater comfort and an enhanced working environment. Supplement payable

Table 115

Mondays to Fridays
30 July to 7 September

London - High Wycombe, Aylesbury, Banbury, Stratford-upon-Avon, Birmingham Snow Hill and Kidderminster

Network Diagram - see first Page of Table 114

		CH	CH	CH	CH	CH	CH	CH	CH	CH	CH	CH	CH BZ	CH	CH	CH	CH	CH	CH	CH	CH	CH	CH
				◇ H			◇ H		◇			◇	◇			◇ H		◇			◇ H		
London Marylebone 10 ⊖	d	12 13	12 16	12 37	12 40	12 43	13 07		13 10	13 13	13 16		13 37	13 40	13 43	14 07		14 10	14 13	14 16	14 37	14 40	14 43
London Paddington 15 ⊖	d																						
Wembley Stadium	d		12 25			12 52					13 25				13 52					14 25			14 52
Sudbury & Harrow Road	d																						
Sudbury Hill Harrow	d		12 29								13 29									14 29			
Northolt Park	d		12 31								13 31									14 31			
South Ruislip § ⊖	d		12 35								13 35									14 35			
West Ruislip 3 § ⊖	d					13 00									14 00								15 00
Denham	d		12 40			13 04					13 40				14 04					14 40			15 04
Denham Golf Club	d		12 43								13 43									14 43			
Gerrards Cross 1	d	12 32	12a53		12 59	13 10				13 32	13a53			13 59	14 10				14 32	14a53		14 59	15 10
Seer Green	d					13 14									14 14								15 14
Beaconsfield	d	12 38			13 05	13 18				13 38				14 05	14 18				14 38			15 05	15 18
High Wycombe 1	d	12 44			13 11	13a30	13 31		13 37	13 44				14 11	14a30	14 31		14 37	14 44			15 11	15a30
Saunderton	d	12 50								13 50									14 50				
Princes Risborough 2	d	13a02			13 20			13 24	13 46	14a02				14 20			14 24	14 46	15a02			15 20	
Monks Risborough	d							13 27									14 27						
Little Kimble	d							13 31									14 31						
Aylesbury	a							13 42									14 42						
Haddenham & Thame Parkway	d				13 27				13 52					14 27				14 52				15 27	
Bicester North 3	d				13a47		13 52		14 05					14a47		14 52		15 05				15a47	
Kings Sutton	d																						
Banbury	d			13 29			14 05		14a25				14 30			15 05		15a24			15 29		
Leamington Spa 8	d			13 47			14 23					14 32	14 47			15 23					15 47		
Warwick	d						14 27					14 37				15 27							
Warwick Parkway	d			13 52			14 31						14 53			15 31					15 52		
Hatton	d											14 45											
Claverdon	d											14 51											
Bearley	d											14 56											
Wilmcote	d											15 00											
Stratford-upon-Avon	a											15 07											
Lapworth	a																						
Dorridge	a						14 40									15 40							
Solihull	a			14 04			14 46						15 05			15 46					16 04		
Birmingham Moor Street	a			14 19			14 54						15 19			15 54					16 13		
Birmingham Snow Hill	a						15 04									16 04					16 21		
Rowley Regis	a																						
Cradley Heath	a																						
Stourbridge Junction 2	a																						
Kidderminster	a																						

		CH	CH	CH	CH	CH	CH	CH	CH	CH	CH	CH	CH	CH	CH	CH	CH	CH	CH	CH	CH	CH
		◇		◇			◇			◇					◇				◇			
London Marylebone 10 ⊖	d	15 07		15 10	15 13	15 16	15 37	15 40	15 43	16 07		16 10	16 13	16 00	16 30	16 33	16 36		16 49	16 56	16 40	16 43
London Paddington 15 ⊖	d																					
Wembley Stadium	d					15 25			15 52					16 09					16 59		16 49	
Sudbury & Harrow Road	d																				16 52	
Sudbury Hill Harrow	d					15 29															16 54	
Northolt Park	d					15 31								16 14							16 57	
South Ruislip § ⊖	d					15 35								16 27							17 10	
West Ruislip 3 § ⊖	d								16 00					16 31							17 13	
Denham	d					15 40			16 04				16 29	16 36						17 12		
Denham Golf Club	d					15 43							16 32									
Gerrards Cross 1	d				15 32	15a53		15 59	16 10				16 35	16a46			16 55			17 17	17a26	
Seer Green	d								16 14				16 40				17 00					
Beaconsfield	d				15 38			16 05	16 18			16 30	16 43				17 03			17 23		
High Wycombe 1	d	15 31		15 35	15 44			16 11	16a32			16 36	16a55			16 57	17a15		17 16	17a35		
Saunderton	d				15 50							16 42							17 23			
Princes Risborough 2	d		15 24	15 44	16a02			16 20			16 24	16 48				17 06		17 16	17 28			
Monks Risborough	d		15 27								16 27							17 19				
Little Kimble	d		15 31								16 31							17 23				
Aylesbury	a		15 42								16 42							17 37				17 36
Haddenham & Thame Parkway	d			15 50				16 27				16 54				17 12			17 34			
Bicester North 3	d	15 52		16 01				16a46		16 49		17a12				17a34			17 45			
Kings Sutton	d			16 12																		
Banbury	d	16 06		16 17			16 33			17 02									18a03			
Leamington Spa 8	d	16 23		16 35			16 50			17 20												
Warwick	d	16 28		16 39						17 25												
Warwick Parkway	d	16 31					16 55			17 29					17 39							
Hatton	d			16 47																		
Claverdon	d			16 54																		
Bearley	d			16 59																		
Wilmcote	d			17 03																		
Stratford-upon-Avon	a			17 14																		
Lapworth	a																					
Dorridge	a	16 41								17 38												
Solihull	a	16 46					17 07			17 44					17 51							
Birmingham Moor Street	a	17 01					17 17			17 55					18 00							
Birmingham Snow Hill	a						17 27			18 03					18 12							
Rowley Regis	a																					
Cradley Heath	a																					
Stourbridge Junction 2	a																					
Kidderminster	a																					

§ London Underground Limited (Central Line) also operate services between South Ruislip and West Ruislip at frequent intervals

BZ Business Zone available offering greater comfort and an enhanced working environment. Supplement payable

Table 115

Mondays to Fridays

30 July to 7 September

London - High Wycombe, Aylesbury, Banbury, Stratford-upon-Avon, Birmingham Snow Hill and Kidderminster

Network Diagram - see first Page of Table 114

Station		CH BZ ◇	CH ◇	CH ◇	CH	CH	CH	CH	CH ◇	CH		CH	CH	CH	CH	CH BZ ◇ ✠	CH ◇	CH ◇	CH	CH		CH	CH	CH	CH
London Marylebone 10 ⊖	d	16 46	17 07	17 10	17 13	17 16	17 19	17 23	17 37	17 40		17 43	17 46	17 50	17 56	18 07	18 10	18 13		18 16		18 19	18 22	18 25	18 29
London Paddington 15 ⊖	d																								
Wembley Stadium	d				17 22			17 32				17 52								18 25					18 38
Sudbury & Harrow Road	d							17 36																	18 41
Sudbury Hill Harrow	d							17 39																	18 43
Northolt Park	d						17 30	17 42							18 07										18 46
South Ruislip § ⊖	d							17 52							18 11										19 02
West Ruislip 3 § ⊖	d						17 36	18a02						18 05										18 40	19a08
Denham	d						17 40							18 09										18 45	
Denham Golf Club	d						17 43							18 12											
Gerrards Cross 1	d				17 35							18 07		18 16	18a26								18 41	18 49	
Seer Green	d				17 39							18 11											18 46		
Beaconsfield	d				17 43		17 50					18 15		18 22						18 42				18 55	
High Wycombe 1	d			17 36	17 49		18a02			18 04		18 21		18a34						18 49			18 54	19a07	
Saunderton	d				17 55							18 27											19 00		
Princes Risborough 2	d			17 45	18 02					18 13		18a39						18 48	18 52	19 02			19a13		
Monks Risborough	d				18 05														18 55						
Little Kimble	d				18 09														18 59						
Aylesbury	a				18 23	18 05							18 41						19 10	19 23		19 11			
Haddenham & Thame Parkway	d			17 51					18 11	18 20								18 56							
Bicester North 3	d			18 03					18 23	18a39								19 10							
Kings Sutton	d			18 13																					
Banbury	d	17 43	18 04	18 19					18 37								19 05	19a30							
Leamington Spa 8	d	18 01	18 21	18 36					18 54								19 23								
Warwick	d			18 41					18 59								19 28								
Warwick Parkway	d	18 07	18 27						19 02							19 20	19 32								
Hatton	d			18 48																					
Claverdon	d			18 54																					
Bearley	d																								
Wilmcote	d			19 01																					
Stratford-upon-Avon	a			19 12																					
Lapworth	a																								
Dorridge	a	18 18	18 39						19 12								19 42								
Solihull	a	18 24	18 44						19 17							19 31	19 48								
Birmingham Moor Street	a	18 36	19 01						19 26							19 40	19 58								
Birmingham Snow Hill	a		19 04						19 36							19 43	20 11								
Rowley Regis	a		19 24													20 01									
Cradley Heath	a		19 29																						
Stourbridge Junction 2	a		19 35													20 12									
Kidderminster	a		19 49													20 30									

Station		CH ◇	CH	CH	CH	CH		CH	CH	CH ◇	CH	CH	CH ◇	CH ◇	CH	CH		CH ◇	CH ◇	CH	CH ◇	CH	CH ◇	CH	CH
London Marylebone 10 ⊖	d	18 37	18 40	18 44	18 47	18 54		18 58	19 04	19 15	19 18	19 21	19 37	19 40	19 43	19 46		20 10	20 14	20 17	20 37	20 40	21 07	21 10	
London Paddington 15 ⊖	d																								
Wembley Stadium	d							19 07				19 30				19 55				20 26		20 50		21 20	
Sudbury & Harrow Road	d															19 58						20 53			
Sudbury Hill Harrow	d															20 00						20 55			
Northolt Park	d					19 06						19 35				20 03				20 31				21 25	
South Ruislip § ⊖	d							19 13				19 38				20 06				20 34				21 28	
West Ruislip 3 § ⊖	d					19 11									19 58							21 01			
Denham	d							19 20				19 44			20 03					20 40		21 06		21 34	
Denham Golf Club	d							19 23							20 05							21 09		21 37	
Gerrards Cross 1	d				19 08	19 18		19 27			19 37	19 49			20 09	20 15			20 33	20 45		21 13		21 41	
Seer Green	d				19 12						19 41					20 19						21 17		21 45	
Beaconsfield	d			19 09	19 15	19 24					19 45			20 03	20 16	20 23			20 40	20 51		21 21		21 49	
High Wycombe 1	d		19 09	19 15	19a27	19 30		19a43			19 51	20a05		20 09	20 22	20a36			20 46	20 57	21 02	21 27	21 32	21 55	
Saunderton	d					19 37									20 28				20 52					22 01	
Princes Risborough 2	d		19 18	19 24		19 43					20 00			20 19	20 36				20 58	21 07	21 12	21a40	21 42	22 09	
Monks Risborough	d					19 47									20 40					21 11				22 12	
Little Kimble	d					19 50									20 43					21 14				22 16	
Aylesbury	a					20 04			20 08						20 58					21 28				22 31	
Haddenham & Thame Parkway	d		19 24	19 30							20 06		20 13	20 26					21 05		21 18		21 48		
Bicester North 3	d	19 23	19a42	19 43						20 00	20 19		20 25	20a46				20 53	21 19		21 29		21 59		
Kings Sutton	d			19 54															21 29						
Banbury	d	19 36		20 01						20 13	20a38		20 39					21 06	21a42		21 45		22 13		
Leamington Spa 8	d	19 53		20 22						20 31			20 57					21 24			22 04		22 30		22 40
Warwick	d	19 58		20 27									21 01								22 09		22 34		22 45
Warwick Parkway	d	20 01								20 36			21 05					21 30			22 12		22 37		
Hatton	d			20 36																			22 42		
Claverdon	d			20 42																					
Bearley	d			20 48																					
Wilmcote	d			20 53																					
Stratford-upon-Avon	a			21 04																					23 12
Lapworth	a																						22 48		
Dorridge	a	20 12								20 46			21 14					21 39			22 22		22 52		
Solihull	a	20 17								20 51			21 20					21 45			22 27		22 59		
Birmingham Moor Street	a	20 26								21 00			21 28					21 57			22 42		23 08		
Birmingham Snow Hill	a	20 37								21 04			21 37					22 00					23 12		
Rowley Regis	a									21 19								22 24					23 38		
Cradley Heath	a									21 25								22 29					23 44		
Stourbridge Junction 2	a									21 32								22 35					23 52		
Kidderminster	a									21 49								22 50							

§ London Underground Limited (Central Line) also operate services between South Ruislip and West Ruislip at frequent intervals

BZ Business Zone available offering greater comfort and an enhanced working environment. Supplement payable

Table 115

Mondays to Fridays

30 July to 7 September

London - High Wycombe, Aylesbury, Banbury, Stratford-upon-Avon, Birmingham Snow Hill and Kidderminster

Network Diagram - see first Page of Table 114

Station		CH ◇		CH	CH ◇	CH	CH	CH ◇	CH ◇	CH	CH	CH ◇		CH	CH
London Marylebone 10 ⊖	d	21 37		21 40	22 07	22 10	22 13	22 37	22 40	22 43	23 00	23 07		23 20	23 30
London Paddington 15 ⊖	d														
Wembley Stadium	d			21 50			22 22			22 52	23 09			23 29	23 39
Sudbury & Harrow Road	d														
Sudbury Hill Harrow	d														
Northolt Park	d						22 27				23 14				23 44
South Ruislip § ⊖	d						22 31				23 20				23 47
West Ruislip 3 § ⊖	d			21 58						23 00					23 51
Denham	d			22 03			22 36			23 04	23 26				23 55
Denham Golf Club	d						22 39				23 29				23 58
Gerrards Cross 1	d			22 08		22 29	22 43		22 59	23 09	23 33			23 42	00 02
Seer Green	d						22 47				23 37				00 06
Beaconsfield	d			22 14		22 36	22 51		23 06	23 15	23 41			23 48	00 10
High Wycombe 1	d	22 02		22 20		22 42	23a03		23 12	23 21	23 47			23 54	00 16
Saunderton	d			22 27						23 27					00 22
Princes Risborough 2	d	22 12		22 33		22 51			23 21	23 34	00a01			00 03	00 29
Monks Risborough	d			22 37						23 37					00 32
Little Kimble	d			22 40						23 41					00 36
Aylesbury	a			22 54						23 55					00 51
Haddenham & Thame Parkway	d	22 18				22 58			23 28					00 10	
Bicester North 3	d	22 29			22 50	23a17		23 20	23a47			23 50		00 23	
Kings Sutton	d													00 33	
Banbury	d	22 43			23 04			23 39				00 03		00a45	
Leamington Spa 8	d	23 00			23 23			23 56				00 21			
Warwick	d	23 05			23 27			23 59				00 25			
Warwick Parkway	d	23 09			23 31			00 04				00 29			
Hatton	d														
Claverdon	d														
Bearley	d														
Wilmcote	d														
Stratford-upon-Avon	a														
Lapworth	a														
Dorridge	a	23 18			23 40			00 13							
Solihull	a	23 24			23 46			00 18				00 40			
Birmingham Moor Street	a	23 39			23 59			00 33				00 55			
Birmingham Snow Hill	a														
Rowley Regis	a														
Cradley Heath	a														
Stourbridge Junction 2	a														
Kidderminster	a														

§ London Underground Limited (Central Line) also operate services between South Ruislip and West Ruislip at frequent intervals

London - High Wycombe, Aylesbury, Banbury, Stratford-upon-Avon, Birmingham Snow Hill and Kidderminster

Network Diagram - see first Page of Table 114

		CH MX ◇	CH MX ◇	CH MO	CH MO	CH MX	CH MX	CH MO	CH MX ◇	CH MO			CH MX	LM	CH	CH	CH	CH	CH	CH		CH ◇ H	CH ◇	CH	CH ◇
London Marylebone [10] ⊖	d	22p37	23p07	22p45		23p20	23p30	23p45	00 05				00 10				06 00	06 12	06 20	06 40		07 00	07 08	07 12	07 33
London Paddington [15] ⊖	d																								
Wembley Stadium	d			22p54		23p29	23p39	23p54					00 19				06 09		06 29	06 49				07 21	
Sudbury & Harrow Road	d																								
Sudbury Hill Harrow	d																							07 25	
Northolt Park	d			22p59			23p44	23p59					00 24				06 14		06 34					07 27	
South Ruislip § ⊖	d			23p02			23p47	00 02					00 27				06 17		06 37					07 31	
West Ruislip [3] § ⊖	d			23p06			23p51	00 06					00 31					06 26		06 57					
Denham	d			23p10			23p55	00 10					00 35				06 23	06 31	06 43	07 01				07 36	
Denham Golf Club	d			23p13			23p58	00 13					00 38							07 04					
Gerrards Cross [1]	d			23p17		23p42	00 02	00 17	00 24				00 42				06 27	06 36	06 47	07 07			07 27	07 41	
Seer Green	d			23p21			00 06	00 21					00 46				06 32			07 12			07 32		
Beaconsfield	d			23p25		23p48	00 10	00 25	00 30				00 50				06 35	06 42	06 53	07 15			07 35		
High Wycombe [1]	d			23p31		23p54	00 16	00 31	00 36				00 56			06 10	06 41	06 48	07a06	07a24		07 25	07 41	07 51	07 57
Saunderton	d			23p37			00 22	00 37					01 02			06 17	06 47						07 47		
Princes Risborough [2]	d			23p42	23p48	00 03	00 29	00 42	00 45	00 48			01 09			06 22	06 54	06 58				07 34	07 53	08a05	08 06
Monks Risborough	d				23p51		00 32			00 51			01 12				06 57								
Little Kimble	d				23p55		00 36			00 55			01 16				07 01								
Aylesbury	a				00 06		00 51			01 06			01 29				07 14								
Haddenham & Thame Parkway	d			23p49		00 10		00 49	00 51							06 30		07 04				07 41	08 00		08 12
Bicester North [3]	d	23p20	23p50	00 02		00 23		01 02	01 04							06 45		07 17				07 53	08 13		08 23
Kings Sutton	d			00 13		00 33										06 56		07 28					08 26		
Banbury	d	23p39	00 03	00a22		00a45		01a20	01a24							07 02		07a41				08 07	08 32		08 38
Leamington Spa [8]	d	23p56	00 21												06 52	07 22						08 25	08 51		08 56
Warwick	d	23p59	00 25												06 56	07 26						08 30	08 56		09 01
Warwick Parkway	d	00 04	00 29												06 59	07 30						08 33			09 04
Hatton	d														07 06	07 35							09 04		09 09
Claverdon	d													06x34	07 12								09 09		
Bearley	d													06x38	07 17								09 14		
Wilmcote	d													06 42	07 21								09 18		
Stratford-upon-Avon	a													06 48	07 27								09 31		
Lapworth	a																								09 15
Dorridge	a	00 13														07 42						08 43			09 19
Solihull	a	00 18	00 40													07 50						08 48			09 25
Birmingham Moor Street	a	00 33	00 55													08 02						08 59			09 39
Birmingham Snow Hill ⇌	a															08 10						09 07			
Rowley Regis	a																								
Cradley Heath	a																								
Stourbridge Junction [2]	a																								
Kidderminster	a																								

		CH	CH	CH	CH	CH ◇		CH ◇	CH	CH	CH BZ ◇ H	CH ◇	CH	CH ◇ H	CH	CH ◇		CH ◇	CH	CH ◇ H	CH	CH	CH ◇ H	CH	CH ◇
London Marylebone [10] ⊖	d		07 43	07 46	08 00	08 03		08 06	08 10	08 30	08 37	08 41	08 45	09 07		09 10		09 14	09 17	09 37	09 40	09 43	10 07		10 10
London Paddington [15] ⊖	d																								
Wembley Stadium	d			07 55					08 19	08 39			08 54						09 26			09 52			
Sudbury & Harrow Road	d																								
Sudbury Hill Harrow	d				08 10					08 43									09 30						
Northolt Park	d		07 54						08 24				08 59					09 25							
South Ruislip § ⊖	d			08 01	08a19					08 55									09 35						
West Ruislip [3] § ⊖	d		07 59						08 29				09 04									10 00			
Denham	d			08 07					08 34	09 01			09 08						09 40			10 04			
Denham Golf Club	d			08 09									09 11									10 07			
Gerrards Cross [1]	d		08 06	08 13				08 27	08 39	09a12			09 15					09 35	09 45		09 59	10 11			
Seer Green	d			08 17					08 43									09 40				10 15			
Beaconsfield	d		08 12	08 20				08 33	08 47				09 21					09 43	09 51		10 05	10 19			
High Wycombe [1]	d		08 18	08a28		08 29		08 39	09a00			09 08	09a30	09 31		09 35		09 49	10a03		10 11	10a30	10 31		10 37
Saunderton	d							08 45				09 14						09 56							
Princes Risborough [2]	d	08 16	08 27			08 38		08 50				09 20			09 24	09 44		10a08			10 20			10 24	10a53
Monks Risborough	d	08 19													09 27									10 27	
Little Kimble	d	08 23													09 31									10 31	
Aylesbury	a	08 34													09 42									10 42	
Haddenham & Thame Parkway	d		08 33					08 57				09 27				09 50					10 27				
Bicester North [3]	d		08 46			08 52		09a16				09 41		09 52		10 01					10a47		10 52		
Kings Sutton	d											09 52													
Banbury	d		09a04			09 05					09 30	10a04		10 05		10 15				10 30			11 05		
Leamington Spa [8]	d					09 22					09 47			10 23		10 33				10 48			11 23		
Warwick	d					09 27								10 27		10 37							11 27		
Warwick Parkway	d					09 30					09 53			10 31						10 54			11 31		
Hatton	d																								
Claverdon	d																								
Bearley	d																								
Wilmcote	d																								
Stratford-upon-Avon	a															11 09									
Lapworth	a																								
Dorridge	a					09 40								10 40									11 40		
Solihull	a					09 46					10 05			10 46						11 05			11 46		
Birmingham Moor Street	a					09 54					10 17			10 54						11 19			11 54		
Birmingham Snow Hill ⇌	a					10 05								11 04									12 04		
Rowley Regis	a																								
Cradley Heath	a																								
Stourbridge Junction [2]	a																								
Kidderminster	a																								

§ London Underground Limited (Central Line) also operate services between South Ruislip and West Ruislip at frequent intervals

BZ Business Zone available offering greater comfort and an enhanced working environment. Supplement payable

London - High Wycombe, Aylesbury, Banbury, Stratford-upon-Avon, Birmingham Snow Hill and Kidderminster

Network Diagram - see first Page of Table 114

		CH ◇		CH	CH ◇ H	CH ◇	CH	CH ◇ H	CH	CH ◇	CH ◇	CH		CH ◇ H	CH	CH	CH	CH ◇ H	CH ◇	CH	CH	CH ◇ H		CH	CH
London Marylebone [10] ⊖	d	10 13		10 17	10 37	10 40	10 43	11 07		11 10	11 13	11 16		11 37		11 40	11 43	12 07	12 10	12 13	12 16	12 37		12 40	12 43
London Paddington [15] ⊖	d																								
Wembley Stadium	d			10 26			10 52					11 25					11 52				12 25				12 52
Sudbury & Harrow Road	d																								
Sudbury Hill Harrow	d			10 30																	12 29				
Northolt Park	d			10 32								11 30									12 31				
South Ruislip § ⊖	d			10 36								11 33									12 35				
West Ruislip [3] § ⊖	d						11 01										12 00								13 00
Denham	d			10 41			11 05					11 39					12 04				12 40				13 04
Denham Golf Club	d											11 41									12 43				
Gerrards Cross [1]	d	10 32		10a52		10 59	11 10				11 32	11a52				11 59	12 10			12 32	12a53			12 59	13 10
Seer Green	d						11 14										12 14								13 14
Beaconsfield	d	10 38				11 05	11 18				11 38					12 05	12 18			12 38				13 05	13 18
High Wycombe [1]	d	10 44				11 11	11a30	11 31		11 35	11 44					12 11	12a30	12 31	12 35	12 44				13 11	13a30
Saunderton	d	10 50									11 50									12 50					
Princes Risborough [2]	d	10 55				11 20			11 24	11 44	12a07				12 17	12 20			12 44	13a02				13 20	
Monks Risborough	d								11 27						12 20										
Little Kimble	d								11 31						12 24										
Aylesbury	a								11 43						12 38										
Haddenham & Thame Parkway	d	11 02				11 26				11 50						12 27			12 50					13 27	
Bicester North [3]	d	11 14				11 40		11 52		12 01						12a47		12 52	13 01					13a47	
Kings Sutton	d					11 54													13 12						
Banbury	d	11a32			11 33	12 00		12 05		12a21				12 29				13 05	13a24			13 29			
Leamington Spa [8]	d				11 50	12 19		12 23						12 47				13 23				13 47			
Warwick	d					12 23		12 27										13 27							
Warwick Parkway	d				11 56			12 31						12 52				13 31				13 52			
Hatton	d					12 31																			
Claverdon	d					12 36																			
Bearley	d					12 41																			
Wilmcote	d																								
Stratford-upon-Avon	a					12 54																			
Lapworth	a																								
Dorridge	a							12 40										13 40							
Solihull	a				12 07			12 46						13 05				13 46				14 04			
Birmingham Moor Street	a				12 25			12 54						13 19				13 54				14 19			
Birmingham Snow Hill ⇌	a							13 04										14 04							
Rowley Regis	a																								
Cradley Heath	a																								
Stourbridge Junction [2]	a																								
Kidderminster	a																								

		CH ◇ H	CH	CH ◇	CH	CH	CH ◇	CH BZ ◇		CH	CH	CH ◇ H	CH	CH ◇	CH	CH	CH ◇ H	CH		CH	CH ◇	CH	CH ◇	CH	CH
London Marylebone [10] ⊖	d	13 07		13 10	13 13	13 16		13 37		13 40	13 43	14 07		14 10	14 13	14 16	14 37	14 40		14 43	15 07		15 10	15 13	15 16
London Paddington [15] ⊖	d																								
Wembley Stadium	d					13 25					13 52					14 25				14 52					15 25
Sudbury & Harrow Road	d																								
Sudbury Hill Harrow	d					13 29										14 29									15 29
Northolt Park	d					13 31										14 31									15 31
South Ruislip § ⊖	d					13 35										14 35									15 35
West Ruislip [3] § ⊖	d										14 00									15 00					
Denham	d					13 40					14 04					14 40				15 04					15 40
Denham Golf Club	d					13 43										14 43									15 43
Gerrards Cross [1]	d				13 32	13a53				13 59	14 10				14 32	14a53		14 59		15 10				15 32	15a53
Seer Green	d										14 14									15 14					
Beaconsfield	d				13 38					14 05	14 18				14 38			15 05		15 18				15 38	
High Wycombe [1]	d	13 31		13 37	13 44					14 11	14a30	14 31		14 37	14 44			15 11		15a30	15 31		15 35	15 44	
Saunderton	d				13 50										14 50									15 50	
Princes Risborough [2]	d		13 24	13 46	14a02					14 20			14 24	14 46	15a02			15 20				15 24	15 44	16a02	
Monks Risborough	d		13 27										14 27									15 27			
Little Kimble	d		13 31										14 31									15 31			
Aylesbury	a		13 42										14 42									15 42			
Haddenham & Thame Parkway	d			13 52						14 27				14 52				15 27					15 50		
Bicester North [3]	d	13 52		14 05						14a47		14 52		15 05				15a47			15 52		16 01		
Kings Sutton	d																						16 12		
Banbury	d	14 05		14a25				14 30				15 05		15a24			15 29				16 06		16 17		
Leamington Spa [8]	d	14 23					14 32	14 47				15 23					15 47				16 23		16 35		
Warwick	d	14 27					14 37					15 27									16 28		16 39		
Warwick Parkway	d	14 31						14 53				15 31					15 52				16 31				
Hatton	d						14 45																16 47		
Claverdon	d						14 51																16 54		
Bearley	d						14 56																16 59		
Wilmcote	d						15 00																17 03		
Stratford-upon-Avon	a						15 07																17 14		
Lapworth	a																								
Dorridge	a	14 40										15 40									16 41				
Solihull	a	14 46						15 05				15 46					16 04				16 46				
Birmingham Moor Street	a	14 54						15 19				15 54					16 13				17 01				
Birmingham Snow Hill ⇌	a	15 04										16 04					16 21								
Rowley Regis	a																								
Cradley Heath	a																								
Stourbridge Junction [2]	a																								
Kidderminster	a																								

§ London Underground Limited (Central Line) also operate services between South Ruislip and West Ruislip at frequent intervals

BZ Business Zone available offering greater comfort and an enhanced working environment. Supplement payable

London - High Wycombe, Aylesbury, Banbury, Stratford-upon-Avon, Birmingham Snow Hill and Kidderminster

Network Diagram - see first Page of Table 114

	CH	CH	CH		CH	CH	CH	CH	CH	CH	CH	CH	CH		CH	CH	CH	CH	CH BZ	CH	CH	CH	CH	
	◇				◇					◇					◇				◇	◇	◇			
London Marylebone 10 ⊖ d	15 37	15 40	15 43		16 07		16 10	16 13	16 00	16 30	16 33	16 36			16 49	16 56	16 40	16 43	16 46	17 07	17 10	17 13	17 16	
London Paddington 15 ⊖ d																								
Wembley Stadium d			15 52						16 09						16 59		16 49					17 22		
Sudbury & Harrow Road d																	16 52							
Sudbury Hill Harrow d																	16 54							
Northolt Park d									16 14								16 57							
South Ruislip § ⊖ d									16 27								17 10							
West Ruislip 3 § ⊖ d			16 00						16 31								17 13							
Denham d			16 04					16 29	16 36							17 12								
Denham Golf Club d								16 32																
Gerrards Cross 1 d		15 59	16 10					16 35	16a46			16 55				17 17	17a26					17 35		
Seer Green d			16 14					16 40				17 00										17 39		
Beaconsfield d		16 05	16 18				16 30	16 43				17 03				17 23						17 43		
High Wycombe 1 d		16 11	16a32				16 36	16a55			16 57	17a15			17 16	17a35					17 36	17 49		
Saunderton d							16 42								17 23							17 55		
Princes Risborough 2 d		16 20				16 24	16 48				17 06		17 16		17 28						17 45	18 02		
Monks Risborough d						16 27							17 19									18 05		
Little Kimble d						16 31							17 23									18 09		
Aylesbury a						16 42							17 37					17 36				18 23	18 05	
Haddenham & Thame Parkway d		16 27					16 54				17 12				17 34						17 51			
Bicester North 3 d		16a46			16 49		17a12				17a34				17 45						18 03			
Kings Sutton d																					18 13			
Banbury d	16 33				17 02										18a03				17 43	18 04	18 19			
Leamington Spa 8 d	16 50				17 20														18 01	18 21	18 36			
Warwick d					17 25																18 41			
Warwick Parkway d	16 55				17 29					17 39									18 07	18 27				
Hatton d																					18 48			
Claverdon d																					18 54			
Bearley d																								
Wilmcote d																					19 01			
Stratford-upon-Avon a																					19 12			
Lapworth a																								
Dorridge a					17 38														18 18	18 39				
Solihull a	17 07				17 44					17 51									18 24	18 44				
Birmingham Moor Street a	17 17				17 55					18 00									18 36	19 01				
Birmingham Snow Hill a	17 27				18 03					18 12										19 04				
Rowley Regis a																				19 24				
Cradley Heath a																				19 29				
Stourbridge Junction 2 a																				19 35				
Kidderminster a																				19 49				

	CH	CH	CH	CH	CH	CH	CH	CH	CH BZ		CH	CH	CH	CH	CH	CH	CH	CH	CH		CH	CH	CH	CH
			◇						◇		◇	◇							◇					
London Marylebone 10 ⊖ d	17 19	17 23	17 37	17 40	17 43	17 46	17 50	17 56	18 07		18 10	18 13		18 16	18 19	18 22	18 25	18 29	18 37		18 40	18 44	18 47	18 54
London Paddington 15 ⊖ d																								
Wembley Stadium d		17 32			17 52									18 25				18 38						
Sudbury & Harrow Road d		17 36																18 41						
Sudbury Hill Harrow d		17 39																18 43						
Northolt Park d	17 30	17 42						18 07										18 46						19 06
South Ruislip § ⊖ d		17 52						18 11										19 02						
West Ruislip 3 § ⊖ d	17 36	18a02					18 05										18 40	19a08						19 11
Denham d	17 40						18 09										18 45							
Denham Golf Club d	17 43						18 12																	
Gerrards Cross 1 d					18 07		18 16	18a26								18 41	18 49						19 08	19 18
Seer Green d					18 11											18 46							19 12	
Beaconsfield d	17 50				18 15		18 22							18 42			18 55					19 09	19 15	19 24
High Wycombe 1 d	18a02			18 04	18 21		18a34							18 49		18 54	19a07				19 09	19 15	19a27	19 30
Saunderton d					18 27											19 00								19 37
Princes Risborough 2 d				18 13	18a39							18 48	18 52	19 02		19a13					19 18	19 24		19 43
Monks Risborough d													18 55											19 47
Little Kimble d													18 59											19 50
Aylesbury a						18 41							19 10	19 23	19 11									20 04
Haddenham & Thame Parkway d			18 11	18 20								18 56									19 24	19 30		
Bicester North 3 d			18 23	18a39								19 10							19 23		19a42	19 43		
Kings Sutton d																						19 54		
Banbury d			18 37								19 05	19a30							19 36			20 01		
Leamington Spa 8 d			18 54								19 23								19 53			20 22		
Warwick d			18 59								19 28								19 58			20 27		
Warwick Parkway d			19 02						19 20		19 32								20 01					
Hatton d																						20 36		
Claverdon d																						20 42		
Bearley d																						20 48		
Wilmcote d																						20 53		
Stratford-upon-Avon a																						21 04		
Lapworth a																								
Dorridge a			19 12								19 42								20 12					
Solihull a			19 17						19 31		19 48								20 17					
Birmingham Moor Street a			19 26						19 40		19 58								20 26					
Birmingham Snow Hill a			19 36						19 43		20 11								20 37					
Rowley Regis a									20 01															
Cradley Heath a																								
Stourbridge Junction 2 a									20 12															
Kidderminster a									20 30															

§ London Underground Limited (Central Line) also operate services between South Ruislip and West Ruislip at frequent intervals

BZ Business Zone available offering greater comfort and an enhanced working environment. Supplement payable

Table 115

Mondays to Fridays

from 10 September

London - High Wycombe, Aylesbury, Banbury, Stratford-upon-Avon, Birmingham Snow Hill and Kidderminster

Network Diagram - see first Page of Table 114

	CH	CH	CH	CH	CH		CH	CH	CH	CH	CH	CH	CH	CH	CH		CH	CH	CH	CH	CH	CH	CH	CH
			◇				◇	◇			◇	◇		◇			◇			◇		◇		
London Marylebone 10 ⊖ d	18 58	19 04	19 15	19 18	19 21		19 37	19 40	19 43	19 46	20 10	20 14	20 17	20 37	20 40		21 07	21 10		21 37	21 40	22 07	22 10	22 13
London Paddington 15 ⊖ d																								
Wembley Stadium d	19 07				19 30					19 55			20 26		20 50			21 20			21 50			22 22
Sudbury & Harrow Road d										19 58					20 53									
Sudbury Hill Harrow d										20 00					20 55									
Northolt Park d					19 35					20 03			20 31					21 25						22 27
South Ruislip § ⊖ d	19 13				19 38					20 06			20 34					21 28						22 31
West Ruislip 3 § ⊖ d									19 58						21 01						21 58			
Denham d	19 20				19 44				20 03				20 40		21 06			21 34			22 03			22 36
Denham Golf Club d	19 23								20 05						21 09			21 37						22 39
Gerrards Cross 1 d	19 27			19 37	19 49				20 09	20 15		20 33	20 45		21 13			21 41			22 08		22 29	22 43
Seer Green d				19 41						20 19					21 17			21 45						22 47
Beaconsfield d				19 45				20 03	20 16	20 23		20 40	20 51		21 21			21 49			22 14		22 36	22 51
High Wycombe 1 d	19a43			19 51	20a05			20 09	20 22	20a36		20 46	20 57	21 02	21 27		21 32	21 55		22 02	22 20		22 42	23a03
Saunderton d									20 28			20 52						22 01			22 27			
Princes Risborough 2 d				20 00				20 19	20 36			20 58	21 07	21 12	21a40		21 42	22 09		22 12	22 33		22 51	
Monks Risborough d									20 40				21 11					22 12			22 37			
Little Kimble d									20 43				21 14					22 16			22 40			
Aylesbury a		20 08							20 58				21 28					22 31			22 54			
Haddenham & Thame Parkway d				20 06			20 13	20 26				21 05		21 18			21 48			22 18			22 58	
Bicester North 3 d			20 00	20 19			20 25	20a46			20 53	21 19		21 29			21 59			22 29		22 50	23a17	
Kings Sutton d												21 29												
Banbury d			20 13	20a38			20 39				21 06	21a42		21 45			22 13			22 43		23 04		
Leamington Spa 8 d			20 31				20 57				21 24			22 04			22 30		22 40	23 00		23 23		
Warwick d							21 01							22 09			22 34		22 45	23 05		23 27		
Warwick Parkway d			20 36				21 05				21 30			22 12			22 37			23 09		23 31		
Hatton d																	22 42							
Claverdon d																								
Bearley d																								
Wilmcote d																								
Stratford-upon-Avon a																			23 12					
Lapworth a																	22 48							
Dorridge a			20 46				21 14				21 39			22 22			22 52			23 18		23 40		
Solihull a			20 51				21 20				21 45			22 27			22 59			23 24		23 46		
Birmingham Moor Street a			21 00				21 28				21 57			22 42			23 08			23 39		23 59		
Birmingham Snow Hill a			21 04				21 37				22 00						23 12							
Rowley Regis a			21 19								22 24						23 38							
Cradley Heath a			21 25								22 29						23 44							
Stourbridge Junction 2 a			21 32								22 35						23 52							
Kidderminster a			21 49								22 50													

	CH		CH	CH	CH	CH	CH	CH
	◇		◇			◇		
London Marylebone 10 ⊖ d	22 37		22 40	22 43	23 00	23 07	23 20	23 30
London Paddington 15 ⊖ d								
Wembley Stadium d				22 52	23 09		23 29	23 39
Sudbury & Harrow Road d								
Sudbury Hill Harrow d								
Northolt Park d					23 14			23 44
South Ruislip § ⊖ d					23 20			23 47
West Ruislip 3 § ⊖ d				23 00				23 51
Denham d				23 04	23 26			23 55
Denham Golf Club d					23 29			23 58
Gerrards Cross 1 d			22 59	23 09	23 33		23 42	00 02
Seer Green d					23 37			00 06
Beaconsfield d			23 06	23 15	23 41		23 48	00 10
High Wycombe 1 d			23 12	23 21	23 47		23 54	00 16
Saunderton d				23 27				00 22
Princes Risborough 2 d			23 21	23 34	00a01		00 03	00 29
Monks Risborough d				23 37				00 32
Little Kimble d				23 41				00 36
Aylesbury a				23 55				00 51
Haddenham & Thame Parkway d			23 28				00 10	
Bicester North 3 d	23 20		23a47			23 50	00 23	
Kings Sutton d							00 33	
Banbury d	23 39					00 03	00a45	
Leamington Spa 8 d	23 56					00 21		
Warwick d	23 59					00 25		
Warwick Parkway d	00 04					00 29		
Hatton d								
Claverdon d								
Bearley d								
Wilmcote d								
Stratford-upon-Avon a								
Lapworth a								
Dorridge a	00 13							
Solihull a	00 18					00 40		
Birmingham Moor Street a	00 33					00 55		
Birmingham Snow Hill a								
Rowley Regis a								
Cradley Heath a								
Stourbridge Junction 2 a								
Kidderminster a								

§ London Underground Limited (Central Line) also operate services between South Ruislip and West Ruislip at frequent intervals

London - High Wycombe, Aylesbury, Banbury, Stratford-upon-Avon, Birmingham Snow Hill and Kidderminster

Network Diagram - see first Page of Table 114

		CH ◇	CH ◇	CH	CH	CH ◇	CH	CH	CH	CH ◇	CH	CH	CH ◇	CH ◇	CH	CH ◇	CH ◇	CH	CH ◇	CH	CH ◇	CH	CH ◇
London Marylebone ⊖	d	22p37	23p07	23p20	23p30	00 05	00 10		06 30	07 00	07 30		08 00	08 23	08 30	08 54	09 00	09 03	09 30		09 33	09 37	10 00
London Paddington ⊖	d																						
Wembley Stadium	d			23p29	23p39		00 19		06 39		07 39				08 39			09 12				09 46	
Sudbury & Harrow Road	d																						
Sudbury Hill Harrow	d																						
Northolt Park	d				23p44		00 24		06 44		07 44				08 44							09 51	
South Ruislip § ⊖	d				23p47		00 27		06 47		07 47				08 47							09 54	
West Ruislip § ⊖	d				23p51		00 31		06 51		07 51				08 51			09 20					
Denham	d				23p55		00 35		06 55		07 55				08 55			09 24				10 00	
Denham Golf Club	d				23p58		00 38		06 58		07 58				08 58							10 02	
Gerrards Cross	d			23p42	00 02	00 24	00 42		07 01		08 01			08 40	09 01			09 29			09 53	10a10	
Seer Green	d				00 06		00 46		07 06		08 06				09 06			09 33					
Beaconsfield	d			23p48	00 10	00 30	00 50		07 09		08 09			08 45	09 09			09 36			10 00		
High Wycombe	d			23p54	00 16	00 36	00 56	06 10	07 15	07 23	08 15		08 23	08 51	09a18		09 23	09a46			10 06		10 23
Saunderton	d				00 22		01 02	06 17	07 21		08 21			08 58							10 12		
Princes Risborough	d			00 03	00 29	00 45	01 09	06 23	07 28	07 33	08 28		08 33	09 04			09 33			09 38	10 19		10 33
Monks Risborough	d				00 32		01 12		07 31		08 31									09 41			
Little Kimble	d				00 36		01 16		07 35		08 35									09 45			
Aylesbury	a				00 51		01 29		07 49		08 49									09 55			
Haddenham & Thame Parkway	d			00 10		00 51		06 30		07 39			08 39	09 10			09 39				10 26		10 39
Bicester North	d	23p20	23p50	00 23		01 04		06 45		07 50			08 50	09 21		09 38	09 50		10 12		10 40		10 50
Kings Sutton	d			00 33				06 55					09 01								10 51		
Banbury	d	23p39	00 03	00a45		01 19		07 02		08 03		08 08	09 06	09 35		09 51	10 04		10 28		11a03		11 04
Leamington Spa	d	23p56	00 21			01a50		07 21		08 21		08 28	09 25	09 54		10 08	10 23		10 46				11 22
Warwick	d	23p59	00 25					07 25		08 26		08 32	09 29	09 58		10 14	10 27						11 26
Warwick Parkway	d	00 04	00 29					07 29		08 29		08 36	09 33	10 02			10 31		10 51				11 30
Hatton	d							07 34				08 43		10 07									
Claverdon	d											08 49											
Bearley	d											08 54											
Wilmcote	d											08 58											
Stratford-upon-Avon	a											09 09				10 40							
Lapworth	a									08 37				10 12									
Dorridge	a	00 13						07 42		08 42			09 42	10 17			10 40						11 39
Solihull	a	00 18	00 40					07 47		08 47			09 48	10 22			10 46		11 04				11 45
Birmingham Moor Street	a	00 33	00 55					08 03		08 59			10 01	10 35			10 54		11 17				11 54
Birmingham Snow Hill	a									09 07			10 09				11 02						12 02
Rowley Regis	a																						
Cradley Heath	a																						
Stourbridge Junction	a																						
Kidderminster	a																						

		CH	CH ◇	CH	CH ◇	CH	CH ◇	CH	CH ◇	CH	CH ◇	CH ◇	CH	CH ◇	CH	CH ◇	CH ◇	CH	CH ◇	CH	CH	CH ◇	CH
London Marylebone ⊖	d	10 03	10 30		10 33	10 37	11 00	11 03	11 30		11 37	12 00	12 03	12 30		12 37	13 00	13 03	13 30		13 37	14 00	14 03
London Paddington ⊖	d																						
Wembley Stadium	d	10 12				10 46		11 12			11 46		12 12			12 46		13 12			13 46		14 12
Sudbury & Harrow Road	d																						
Sudbury Hill Harrow	d																						
Northolt Park	d					10 51		11 17					12 17					13 17					14 17
South Ruislip § ⊖	d					10 54		11 20					12 20					13 20					14 20
West Ruislip § ⊖	d	10 20						11 24					12 24					13 24					14 24
Denham	d	10 24				11 00		11 28					12 28					13 28					14 28
Denham Golf Club	d					11 02		11 31					12 31					13 31					14 31
Gerrards Cross	d	10 29			10 53	11a10		11 34			11 58		12 34			12 58		13 34			13 58		14 34
Seer Green	d	10 33						11 39					12 39					13 39					14 39
Beaconsfield	d	10 36			11 00			11 42			12 04		12 42			13 04		13 42			14 04		14 42
High Wycombe	d	10a46			11 06		11 23	11a51			12 10	12 23	12a51			13 10	13 23	13a51			14 10	14 23	14a49
Saunderton	d				11 12						12 17					13 17					14 17		
Princes Risborough	d			10 38	11 19		11 33			11 38	12 23	12 33			12 38	13 23	13 33			13 38	14 23	14 33	
Monks Risborough	d			10 41						11 41					12 41					13 41			
Little Kimble	d			10 45						11 45					12 45					13 45			
Aylesbury	a			11 00						11 59					12 55					13 55			
Haddenham & Thame Parkway	d				11 26		11 39				12 29	12 39				13 29	13 39				14 29	14 39	
Bicester North	d		11 12		11 40		11 50		12 13		12 42	12 50		13 12		13 42	13 50		14 12		14 42	14 50	
Kings Sutton	d										12 54										14 54		
Banbury	d		11 28		11 58		12 04		12 28		13a03	13 04		13 28		13 58	14 04		14 28		15a03	15 04	
Leamington Spa	d		11 46		12 17		12 22		12 46			13 22		13 46		14 17	14 22		14 46			15 22	
Warwick	d				12 21		12 26					13 26				14 22	14 26					15 26	
Warwick Parkway	d		11 51				12 30		12 51			13 30		13 51			14 30		14 51			15 30	
Hatton	d				12 29											14 29							
Claverdon	d				12 35											14 34							
Bearley	d				12 40																		
Wilmcote	d				12 43																		
Stratford-upon-Avon	a				12 53											14 50							
Lapworth	a																						
Dorridge	a						12 39					13 39					14 39					15 39	
Solihull	a		12 04				12 45		13 04			13 45		14 04			14 45		15 04			15 45	
Birmingham Moor Street	a		12 17				12 54		13 17			13 54		14 17			14 54		15 17			15 54	
Birmingham Snow Hill	a						13 02					14 02					15 02					16 02	
Rowley Regis	a																						
Cradley Heath	a																						
Stourbridge Junction	a																						
Kidderminster	a																						

§ London Underground Limited (Central Line) also operate services between South Ruislip and West Ruislip at frequent intervals

London - High Wycombe, Aylesbury, Banbury, Stratford-upon-Avon, Birmingham Snow Hill and Kidderminster

Network Diagram - see first Page of Table 114

		CH ◇	CH	CH ◇	CH ◇	CH	CH	CH ◇	CH	CH	CH ◇	CH	CH	CH ◇	CH ◇	CH	CH ◇	CH	CH	CH ◇	CH	CH
London Marylebone ⊖	d	14 30		14 33	15 00		15 03	15 30	15 33	15 37	16 00		16 03	16 30	16 33	16 37	17 00		17 03	17 30	17 33	17 37
London Paddington ⊖	d																					
Wembley Stadium	d			14 43			15 12			15 46			16 12			16 46			17 12			17 46
Sudbury & Harrow Road	d																					
Sudbury Hill Harrow	d																					
Northolt Park	d						15 17						16 17						17 17			
South Ruislip § ⊖	d						15 20						16 20						17 20			
West Ruislip § ⊖	d						15 24			15 54						16 54						17 54
Denham	d			14 53			15 28			15 58			16 26			16 58			17 26			17 58
Denham Golf Club	d						15 31						16 28						17 28			
Gerrards Cross	d			14 58			15 34		15 53	16 03			16 32		16 53	17 03			17 32		17 50	18 03
Seer Green	d						15 39			16 08						17 08						18 08
Beaconsfield	d			15 04			15 42		16 00	16 11			16 39		17 00	17 11			17 39		17 55	18 11
High Wycombe	d			15 10	15 23		15 48		16 06	16a21	16 23		16 45		17 06	17a21	17 23		17 45		18 01	18a21
Saunderton	d			15 17					16 12						17 12						18 08	
Princes Risborough	d		14 38	15 23	15 33	15 38	16a01		16 19		16 33	16 38	16a58		17 19		17 33	17 38	17a58		18 13	
Monks Risborough	d		14 41			15 41						16 41						17 41				
Little Kimble	d		14 45			15 45						16 45						17 45				
Aylesbury	a		14 55			15 55						16 55						17 55				
Haddenham & Thame Parkway	d			15 29	15 39				16 26		16 39				17 26		17 39				18 19	
Bicester North	d	15 13		15 42	15 50			16 15	16 40		16 50			17 14	17 40		17 50			18 14	18a33	
Kings Sutton	d								16 51						17 51							
Banbury	d	15 28		15 58	16 04			16 28	17a03		17 04			17 28	18 00		18 04			18 28		
Leamington Spa	d	15 46		16 17	16 23			16 46			17 22			17 46	18 19		18 24			18 46		
Warwick	d			16 22	16 27						17 26				18 23		18 28					
Warwick Parkway	d	15 51			16 31			16 51			17 30			17 51			18 32			18 51		
Hatton	d			16 29											18 31							
Claverdon	d			16 35											18 38							
Bearley	d			16 40											18 43							
Wilmcote	d			16 45											18 47							
Stratford-upon-Avon	a			16 55											18 59							
Lapworth	a																					
Dorridge	a				16 40						17 39						18 43					
Solihull	a	16 04			16 46			17 04			17 45			18 04			18 48			19 04		
Birmingham Moor Street	a	16 17			16 54			17 17			17 54			18 17			18 57			19 17		
Birmingham Snow Hill	a				17 02						18 02						19 05					
Rowley Regis	a																					
Cradley Heath	a																					
Stourbridge Junction	a																					
Kidderminster	a																					

		CH ◇	CH	CH ◇	CH	CH ◇	CH	CH ◇	CH	CH ◇	CH	CH	CH ◇	CH	CH	CH ◇	CH	CH	CH ◇	CH	CH	CH	CH
London Marylebone ⊖	d	18 00	18 03	18 30		18 33	18 37	19 00	19 04	19 30	19 33	19 37	20 00	20 04	20 35	21 00	21 04	21 35	22 10	22 14	22 40	23 10	23 14
London Paddington ⊖	d																						
Wembley Stadium	d		18 12				18 46		19 13			19 46		20 13			21 13			22 23	22 49	23 19	23 23
Sudbury & Harrow Road	d																						
Sudbury Hill Harrow	d																						
Northolt Park	d		18 17						19 18					20 18			21 18			22 28			23 28
South Ruislip § ⊖	d		18 20						19 21					20 21			21 21			22 31			23 31
West Ruislip § ⊖	d						18 54					19 54		20 25			21 25			22 35			23 35
Denham	d		18 26				18 58		19 27			19 58		20 29			21 29			22 39			23 39
Denham Golf Club	d		18 28						19 29					20 32			21 32			22 42			23 42
Gerrards Cross	d		18 32			18 53	19 03		19 33		19 52	20 03		20 36	20 54		21 36	21 54		22 46	23 02	23 32	23 46
Seer Green	d						19 08					20 08		20 40			21 40			22 50			23 50
Beaconsfield	d		18 39			19 00	19 11		19 40		19 59	20 11		20 44	21 01		21 44	22 01		22 54	23 09	23 39	23 54
High Wycombe	d	18 23	18a49			19 06	19 17	19 23	19 46		20 05	20a21	20 23	20 50	21 07	21 23	21 50	22 07		23 01	23 15	23 45	00 01
Saunderton	d					19 12					20 11				21 13		21 56			23 07			00 07
Princes Risborough	d	18 33			18 38	19 19	19 28	19 33	19 56		20 18		20 33	21 00	21 20	21 33	22 03	22 17		23 14	23 25	23 55	00 14
Monks Risborough	d				18 41		19 32		20 00					21 04			22 06			23 17			00 17
Little Kimble	d				18 45				20 03					21 07			22 10			23 21			00 21
Aylesbury	a				18 55		19 48		20 18					21 22			22 23			23 34			00 35
Haddenham & Thame Parkway	d	18 39				19 26		19 39			20 25		20 39		21 27	21 40		22 24			23 32	00 02	
Bicester North	d	18 50		19 12		19 40		19 50		20 14	20a40		20 51		21 41	21 51		22a42	22 52		23 45	00 15	
Kings Sutton	d					19 51									21 51						23 55		
Banbury	d	19 04		19 28		20 09		20 04		20 33			21 04		22a03	22 08			23 05		00a06	00a33	
Leamington Spa	d	19 23		19 46		20 28		20 22		20 52			21 22			22 26			23 24				
Warwick	d	19 27				20 33		20 26					21 26			22 31			23 28				
Warwick Parkway	d	19 31		19 51				20 30		20 57			21 30			22 34			23 32				
Hatton	d					20 40		20 35															
Claverdon	d					20 46																	
Bearley	d					20 51																	
Wilmcote	d					20 56																	
Stratford-upon-Avon	a					21 06																	
Lapworth	a							20 40															
Dorridge	a	19 41						20 45					21 40			22 44			23 41				
Solihull	a	19 47		20 04				20 50		21 09			21 44			22 49			23 49				
Birmingham Moor Street	a	19 56		20 17				21 00		21 22			21 55			23 01			00 01				
Birmingham Snow Hill	a	20 04						21 08					22 03			23 09							
Rowley Regis	a																						
Cradley Heath	a																						
Stourbridge Junction	a																						
Kidderminster	a																						

§ London Underground Limited (Central Line) also operate services between South Ruislip and West Ruislip at frequent intervals

Saturdays until 21 July

London - High Wycombe, Aylesbury, Banbury, Stratford-upon-Avon, Birmingham Snow Hill and Kidderminster

Network Diagram - see first Page of Table 114

		CH
London Marylebone ⊖	d	23 45
London Paddington ⊖	d	
Wembley Stadium	d	23 54
Sudbury & Harrow Road	d	
Sudbury Hill Harrow	d	
Northolt Park	d	
South Ruislip § ⊖	d	
West Ruislip § ⊖	d	
Denham	d	
Denham Golf Club	d	
Gerrards Cross	d	00 07
Seer Green	d	
Beaconsfield	d	00 14
High Wycombe	d	00 20
Saunderton	d	
Princes Risborough	d	00 30
Monks Risborough	d	
Little Kimble	d	
Aylesbury	a	
Haddenham & Thame Parkway	d	00 37
Bicester North	d	00 50
Kings Sutton	d	01 00
Banbury	d	01a11
Leamington Spa	d	
Warwick	d	
Warwick Parkway	d	
Hatton	d	
Claverdon	d	
Bearley	d	
Wilmcote	d	
Stratford-upon-Avon	a	
Lapworth	a	
Dorridge	a	
Solihull	a	
Birmingham Moor Street	a	
Birmingham Snow Hill	a	
Rowley Regis	a	
Cradley Heath	a	
Stourbridge Junction	a	
Kidderminster	a	

Saturdays 28 July to 8 September

		CH	CH	CH	CH	CH	CH	CH	CH	CH	CH	CH	CH	CH	CH	CH	CH	CH	CH	CH	CH	CH	CH
		◇	◇			◇		A	A	A	◇ A	A			◇			◇	◇		◇	◇	
London Marylebone ⊖	d	22p37	23p07	23p20	23p30	00 05	00 10	00 40	00 57	01 10	01 30	01 57		06 30	07 00	07 30		08 00	08 23	08 30	08 54	09 00	09 03
London Paddington ⊖	d																						
Wembley Stadium	d			23p29	23p39		00 19							06 39		07 39				08 39			09 12
Sudbury & Harrow Road	d																						
Sudbury Hill Harrow	d																						
Northolt Park	d				23p44		00 24							06 44		07 44				08 44			
South Ruislip § ⊖	d				23p47		00 27							06 47		07 47				08 47			
West Ruislip § ⊖	d				23p51		00 31							06 51		07 51				08 51			09 20
Denham	d				23p55		00 35	01 02		01 27				06 55		07 55				08 55			09 24
Denham Golf Club	d				23p58		00 38	01 04		01 29				06 58		07 58				08 58			
Gerrards Cross	d			23p42	00 02	00 24	00 42	01 09		01 34				07 01		08 01			08 40	09 01			09 29
Seer Green	d				00 06		00 46	01 13		01 38				07 06		08 06				09 06			09 33
Beaconsfield	d			23p48	00 10	00 30	00 50	01 17		01 42				07 09		08 09			08 45	09 09			09 36
High Wycombe	d			23p54	00 16	00 36	00 56	01a28		01 48			06 10	07 15	07 23	08 15		08 23	08 51	09a18		09 23	09a46
Saunderton	d				00 22		01 02			01 54			06 17	07 21		08 21			08 58				
Princes Risborough	d			00 03	00 29	00 45	01 09			02 01	02 05		06 23	07 28	07 33	08 28		08 33	09 04			09 33	
Monks Risborough	d				00 32		01 12							07 31		08 31							
Little Kimble	d				00 36		01 16							07 35		08 35							
Aylesbury	a				00 51		01 29		01 52	02 20		02 52		07 49		08 49							
Haddenham & Thame Parkway	d			00 10		00 51					02 11		06 30		07 39			08 39	09 10			09 39	
Bicester North	d	23p20	23p50	00 23		01 04					02 23		06 45		07 50			08 50	09 21		09 38	09 50	
Kings Sutton	d			00 33									06 55					09 01					
Banbury	d	23p39	00 03	00a45		01 19					02 36		07 02		08 03		08 08	09 06	09 35		09 51	10 04	
Leamington Spa	d	23p56	00 21			01a50					02 54		07 21		08 21		08 28	09 25	09 54		10 08	10 23	
Warwick	d	23p59	00 25								02 59		07 25		08 26		08 32	09 29	09 58		10 14	10 27	
Warwick Parkway	d	00 04	00 29								03 02		07 29		08 29		08 36	09 33	10 02			10 31	
Hatton	d												07 34				08 43		10 07				
Claverdon	d																08 49						
Bearley	d																08 54						
Wilmcote	d																08 58						
Stratford-upon-Avon	a																09 09				10 40		
Lapworth	a														08 37				10 12				
Dorridge	a	00 13									03 12		07 42		08 42			09 42	10 17			10 40	
Solihull	a	00 18	00 40										07 47		08 47			09 48	10 22			10 46	
Birmingham Moor Street	a	00 33	00 55								03 23		08 03		08 59			10 01	10 35			10 54	
Birmingham Snow Hill	a										03 32				09 07			10 09				11 02	
Rowley Regis	a																						
Cradley Heath	a																						
Stourbridge Junction	a																						
Kidderminster	a																						

§ London Underground Limited (Central Line) also operate services between South Ruislip and West Ruislip at frequent intervals

A not from 18 August

Saturdays 28 July to 8 September

London - High Wycombe, Aylesbury, Banbury, Stratford-upon-Avon, Birmingham Snow Hill and Kidderminster

Network Diagram - see first Page of Table 114

		CH	CH	CH	CH	CH	CH	CH	CH	CH	CH	CH	CH	CH	CH	CH	CH	CH	CH	CH	CH	CH	CH
		◇		◇		◇		◇		◇		◇		◇		◇	◇		◇		◇	◇	
London Marylebone ⊖	d	09 30		09 33	09 37	10 00	10 03	10 30		10 33	10 37	11 00	11 03	11 30		11 37	12 00	12 03	12 30		12 37	13 00	13 03
London Paddington ⊖	d																						
Wembley Stadium	d				09 46		10 12				10 46		11 12			11 46		12 12			12 46		13 12
Sudbury & Harrow Road	d																						
Sudbury Hill Harrow	d																						
Northolt Park	d				09 51						10 51		11 17					12 17					13 17
South Ruislip § ⊖	d				09 54						10 54		11 20					12 20					13 20
West Ruislip § ⊖	d						10 20						11 24					12 24					13 24
Denham	d				10 00		10 24				11 00		11 28					12 28					13 28
Denham Golf Club	d				10 02						11 02		11 31					12 31					13 31
Gerrards Cross	d			09 53	10a10		10 29			10 53	11a10		11 34			11 58		12 34			12 58		13 34
Seer Green	d						10 33						11 39					12 39					13 39
Beaconsfield	d			10 00			10 36			11 00			11 42			12 04		12 42			13 04		13 42
High Wycombe	d			10 06		10 23	10a46			11 06		11 23	11a51			12 10	12 23	12a51			13 10	13 23	13a51
Saunderton	d			10 12						11 12						12 17					13 17		
Princes Risborough	d		09 38	10 19		10 33			10 38	11 19		11 33			11 38	12 23	12 33			12 38	13 23	13 33	
Monks Risborough	d		09 41						10 41						11 41					12 41			
Little Kimble	d		09 45						10 45						11 45					12 45			
Aylesbury	a		09 55						11 00						11 59					12 55			
Haddenham & Thame Parkway	d			10 26		10 39				11 26		11 39				12 29	12 39				13 29	13 39	
Bicester North	d	10 12		10 40		10 50		11 12		11 40		11 50		12 13		12 42	12 50		13 12		13 42	13 50	
Kings Sutton	d			10 51												12 54							
Banbury	d	10 28		11a03		11 04		11 28		11 58		12 04		12 28		13a03	13 04		13 28		13 58	14 04	
Leamington Spa	d	10 46				11 22		11 46		12 17		12 22		12 46			13 22		13 46		14 17	14 22	
Warwick	d					11 26				12 21		12 26					13 26				14 22	14 26	
Warwick Parkway	d	10 51				11 30		11 51				12 30		12 51			13 30		13 51			14 30	
Hatton	d									12 29											14 29		
Claverdon	d									12 35											14 34		
Bearley	d									12 40													
Wilmcote	d									12 43													
Stratford-upon-Avon	a									12 53											14 50		
Lapworth	a																						
Dorridge	a					11 39						12 39					13 39					14 39	
Solihull	a	11 04				11 45		12 04				12 45		13 04			13 45		14 04			14 45	
Birmingham Moor Street	a	11 17				11 54		12 17				12 54		13 17			13 54		14 17			14 54	
Birmingham Snow Hill	a					12 02						13 02					14 02					15 02	
Rowley Regis	a																						
Cradley Heath	a																						
Stourbridge Junction	a																						
Kidderminster	a																						

		CH	CH	CH	CH	CH	CH	CH	CH	CH	CH	CH	CH	CH	CH	CH	CH	CH	CH	CH	CH	CH
		◇			◇		◇		◇	◇			◇			◇			◇	◇		◇
London Marylebone ⊖	d	13 30		13 37	14 00	14 03	14 30		14 33	15 00		15 03	15 30	15 33	15 37	16 00		16 03	16 30	16 33	16 37	17 00
London Paddington ⊖	d																					
Wembley Stadium	d			13 46		14 12			14 43			15 12			15 46			16 12			16 46	
Sudbury & Harrow Road	d																					
Sudbury Hill Harrow	d																					
Northolt Park	d					14 17						15 17						16 17				
South Ruislip § ⊖	d					14 20						15 20						16 20				
West Ruislip § ⊖	d					14 24						15 24			15 54						16 54	
Denham	d					14 28			14 53			15 28			15 58			16 26			16 58	
Denham Golf Club	d					14 31						15 31						16 28				
Gerrards Cross	d			13 58		14 34			14 58			15 34		15 53	16 03			16 32		16 53	17 03	
Seer Green	d					14 39						15 39			16 08						17 08	
Beaconsfield	d			14 04		14 42			15 04			15 42		16 00	16 11			16 39		17 00	17 11	
High Wycombe	d			14 10	14 23	14a49			15 10	15 23		15 48		16 06	16a21	16 23		16 45		17 06	17a21	17 23
Saunderton	d			14 17					15 17					16 12						17 12		
Princes Risborough	d		13 38	14 23	14 33			14 38	15 23	15 33	15 38	16a01		16 19		16 33	16 38	16a58		17 19		17 33
Monks Risborough	d		13 41					14 41			15 41						16 41					
Little Kimble	d		13 45					14 45			15 45						16 45					
Aylesbury	a		13 55					14 55			15 55						16 55					
Haddenham & Thame Parkway	d			14 29	14 39				15 29	15 39				16 26		16 39				17 26		17 39
Bicester North	d	14 12		14 42	14 50		15 13		15 42	15 50			16 15	16 40		16 50			17 14	17 40		17 50
Kings Sutton	d			14 54										16 51						17 51		
Banbury	d	14 28		15a03	15 04		15 28		15 58	16 04			16 28	17a03		17 04			17 28	18 00		18 04
Leamington Spa	d	14 46			15 22		15 46		16 17	16 23			16 46			17 22			17 46	18 19		18 24
Warwick	d				15 26				16 22	16 27						17 26				18 23		18 28
Warwick Parkway	d	14 51			15 30		15 51			16 31			16 51			17 30			17 51			18 32
Hatton	d								16 29											18 31		
Claverdon	d								16 35											18 38		
Bearley	d								16 40											18 43		
Wilmcote	d								16 45											18 47		
Stratford-upon-Avon	a								16 55											18 59		
Lapworth	a																					
Dorridge	a				15 39					16 40						17 39						18 43
Solihull	a	15 04			15 45		16 04			16 46			17 04			17 45			18 04			18 48
Birmingham Moor Street	a	15 17			15 54		16 17			16 54			17 17			17 54			18 17			18 57
Birmingham Snow Hill	a				16 02					17 02						18 02						19 05
Rowley Regis	a																					
Cradley Heath	a																					
Stourbridge Junction	a																					
Kidderminster	a																					

§ London Underground Limited (Central Line) also operate services between South Ruislip and West Ruislip at frequent intervals

Table 115

Saturdays
28 July to 8 September

London - High Wycombe, Aylesbury, Banbury, Stratford-upon-Avon, Birmingham Snow Hill and Kidderminster

Network Diagram - see first Page of Table 114

		CH	CH	CH ◇	CH	CH	CH ◇	CH	CH ◇	CH	CH ◇	CH	CH ◇	CH	CH ◇	CH	CH	CH ◇	CH	CH	CH ◇	CH	CH
London Marylebone ⊖	d		17 03	17 30	17 33	17 37	18 00	18 03	18 30		18 33	18 37	19 00	19 04	19 30	19 33	19 37	20 00	20 04	20 35	21 00	21 04	21 35
London Paddington ⊖	d																						
Wembley Stadium	d		17 12			17 46		18 12				18 46		19 13			19 46		20 13			21 13	
Sudbury & Harrow Road	d																						
Sudbury Hill Harrow	d																						
Northolt Park	d		17 17					18 17						19 18					20 18			21 18	
South Ruislip § ⊖	d		17 20					18 20						19 21					20 21			21 21	
West Ruislip § ⊖	d					17 54						18 54					19 54		20 25			21 25	
Denham	d		17 26			17 58		18 26				18 58		19 27			19 58		20 29			21 29	
Denham Golf Club	d		17 28					18 28						19 29					20 32			21 32	
Gerrards Cross	d		17 32		17 50	18 03		18 32			18 53	19 03		19 33		19 52	20 03		20 36	20 54		21 36	21 54
Seer Green	d					18 08						19 08					20 08		20 40			21 40	
Beaconsfield	d		17 39		17 55	18 11		18 39			19 00	19 11		19 40		19 59	20 11		20 44	21 01		21 44	22 01
High Wycombe	d		17 45		18 01	18a21	18 23	18a49			19 06	19 17	19 23	19 46		20 05	20a21	20 23	20 50	21 07	21 23	21 50	22 07
Saunderton	d				18 08						19 12					20 11				21 13		21 56	
Princes Risborough	d	17 38	17a58		18 13		18 33			18 38	19 19	19 28	19 33	19 56		20 18		20 33	21 00	21 20	21 33	22 03	22 17
Monks Risborough	d	17 41								18 41		19 32		20 00					21 04			22 06	
Little Kimble	d	17 45								18 45				20 03					21 07			22 10	
Aylesbury	a	17 55								18 55		19 48		20 18					21 22			22 23	
Haddenham & Thame Parkway	d				18 19		18 39				19 26		19 39			20 25		20 39		21 27	21 40		22 24
Bicester North	d			18 14	18a33		18 50		19 12		19 40		19 50		20 14	20a40		20 51		21 41	21 51		22a42
Kings Sutton	d										19 51									21 51			
Banbury	d			18 28			19 04		19 28		20 09		20 04		20 33			21 04		22a03	22 08		
Leamington Spa	d			18 46			19 23		19 46		20 28		20 22		20 52			21 22			22 26		
Warwick	d						19 27				20 33		20 26					21 26			22 31		
Warwick Parkway	d			18 51			19 31		19 51				20 30		20 57			21 30			22 34		
Hatton	d										20 40		20 35										
Claverdon	d										20 46												
Bearley	d										20 51												
Wilmcote	d										20 56												
Stratford-upon-Avon	a										21 06												
Lapworth	a												20 40										
Dorridge	a						19 41						20 45					21 40			22 44		
Solihull	a			19 04			19 47		20 04				20 50		21 09			21 44			22 49		
Birmingham Moor Street	a			19 17			19 56		20 17				21 00		21 22			21 55			23 01		
Birmingham Snow Hill	a						20 04						21 08					22 03			23 09		
Rowley Regis	a																						
Cradley Heath	a																						
Stourbridge Junction	a																						
Kidderminster	a																						

		CH ◇	CH	CH	CH	CH	CH
London Marylebone ⊖	d	22 10	22 14	22 40	23 10	23 14	23 45
London Paddington ⊖	d						
Wembley Stadium	d		22 23	22 49	23 19	23 23	23 54
Sudbury & Harrow Road	d						
Sudbury Hill Harrow	d						
Northolt Park	d		22 28			23 28	
South Ruislip § ⊖	d		22 31			23 31	
West Ruislip § ⊖	d		22 35			23 35	
Denham	d		22 39			23 39	
Denham Golf Club	d		22 42			23 42	
Gerrards Cross	d		22 46	23 02	23 32	23 46	00 07
Seer Green	d		22 50			23 50	
Beaconsfield	d		22 54	23 09	23 39	23 54	00 14
High Wycombe	d		23 01	23 15	23 45	00 01	00 20
Saunderton	d		23 07			00 07	
Princes Risborough	d		23 14	23 25	23 55	00 14	00 30
Monks Risborough	d		23 17			00 17	
Little Kimble	d		23 21			00 21	
Aylesbury	a		23 34			00 35	
Haddenham & Thame Parkway	d			23 32	00 02		00 37
Bicester North	d	22 52		23 45	00 15		00 50
Kings Sutton	d			23 55			01 00
Banbury	d	23 05		00a06	00a33		01a11
Leamington Spa	d	23 24					
Warwick	d	23 28					
Warwick Parkway	d	23 32					
Hatton	d						
Claverdon	d						
Bearley	d						
Wilmcote	d						
Stratford-upon-Avon	a						
Lapworth	a						
Dorridge	a	23 41					
Solihull	a	23 49					
Birmingham Moor Street	a	00 01					
Birmingham Snow Hill	a						
Rowley Regis	a						
Cradley Heath	a						
Stourbridge Junction	a						
Kidderminster	a						

§ London Underground Limited (Central Line) also operate services between South Ruislip and West Ruislip at frequent intervals

Table 115

Saturdays
from 15 September

London - High Wycombe, Aylesbury, Banbury, Stratford-upon-Avon, Birmingham Snow Hill and Kidderminster

Network Diagram - see first Page of Table 114

		CH ◇	CH ◇	CH	CH	CH ◇	CH	CH	CH	CH ◇	CH	CH	CH ◇	CH ◇	CH	CH ◇	CH ◇	CH	CH ◇	CH	CH ◇	CH	CH ◇
London Marylebone ⊖	d	22p37	23p07	23p20	23p30	00 05	00 10		06 30	07 00	07 30		08 00	08 23	08 30	08 54	09 00	09 03	09 30		09 33	09 37	10 00
London Paddington ⊖	d																						
Wembley Stadium	d			23p29	23p39		00 19		06 39		07 39				08 39			09 12				09 46	
Sudbury & Harrow Road	d																						
Sudbury Hill Harrow	d																						
Northolt Park	d				23p44		00 24		06 44		07 44				08 44							09 51	
South Ruislip § ⊖	d				23p47		00 27		06 47		07 47				08 47							09 54	
West Ruislip § ⊖	d				23p51		00 31		06 51		07 51				08 51			09 20					
Denham	d				23p55		00 35		06 55		07 55				08 55			09 24				10 00	
Denham Golf Club	d				23p58		00 38		06 58		07 58				08 58							10 02	
Gerrards Cross	d			23p42	00 02	00 24	00 42		07 01		08 01			08 40	09 01			09 29			09 53	10a10	
Seer Green	d				00 06		00 46		07 06		08 06				09 06			09 33					
Beaconsfield	d			23p48	00 10	00 30	00 50		07 09		08 09			08 45	09 09			09 36			10 00		
High Wycombe	d			23p54	00 16	00 36	00 56	06 10	07 15	07 23	08 15		08 23	08 51	09a18		09 23	09a46			10 06		10 23
Saunderton	d				00 22		01 02	06 17	07 21		08 21			08 58							10 12		
Princes Risborough	d			00 03	00 29	00 45	01 09	06 23	07 28	07 33	08 28		08 33	09 04			09 33			09 38	10 19		10 33
Monks Risborough	d				00 32		01 12		07 31		08 31									09 41			
Little Kimble	d				00 36		01 16		07 35		08 35									09 45			
Aylesbury	a				00 51		01 29		07 49		08 49									09 55			
Haddenham & Thame Parkway	d			00 10		00 51		06 30		07 39			08 39	09 10			09 39				10 26		10 39
Bicester North	d	23p20	23p50	00 23		01 04		06 45		07 50			08 50	09 21		09 38	09 50		10 12		10 40		10 50
Kings Sutton	d			00 33				06 55					09 01								10 51		
Banbury	d	23p39	00 03	00a45		01 19		07 02		08 03		08 08	09 06	09 35		09 51	10 04		10 28		11a03		11 04
Leamington Spa	d	23p56	00 21			01a50		07 21		08 21		08 28	09 25	09 54		10 08	10 23		10 46				11 22
Warwick	d	23p59	00 25					07 25		08 26		08 32	09 29	09 58		10 14	10 27						11 26
Warwick Parkway	d	00 04	00 29					07 29		08 29		08 36	09 33	10 02			10 31		10 51				11 30
Hatton	d							07 34				08 43		10 07									
Claverdon	d											08 49											
Bearley	d											08 54											
Wilmcote	d											08 58											
Stratford-upon-Avon	a											09 09				10 40							
Lapworth	a									08 37				10 12									
Dorridge	a	00 13						07 42		08 42			09 42	10 17			10 40						11 39
Solihull	a	00 18	00 40					07 47		08 47			09 48	10 22			10 46		11 04				11 45
Birmingham Moor Street	a	00 33	00 55					08 03		08 59			10 01	10 35			10 54		11 17				11 54
Birmingham Snow Hill	a									09 07			10 09				11 02						12 02
Rowley Regis	a																						
Cradley Heath	a																						
Stourbridge Junction	a																						
Kidderminster	a																						

		CH	CH ◇	CH	CH ◇	CH	CH ◇	CH	CH ◇	CH	CH ◇	CH ◇	CH	CH ◇	CH	CH ◇	CH ◇	CH	CH ◇	CH	CH	CH ◇	CH
London Marylebone ⊖	d	10 03	10 30		10 33	10 37	11 00	11 03	11 30		11 37	12 00	12 03	12 30		12 37	13 00	13 03	13 30		13 37	14 00	14 03
London Paddington ⊖	d																						
Wembley Stadium	d	10 12				10 46		11 12			11 46		12 12			12 46		13 12			13 46		14 12
Sudbury & Harrow Road	d																						
Sudbury Hill Harrow	d																						
Northolt Park	d					10 51		11 17					12 17					13 17					14 17
South Ruislip § ⊖	d					10 54		11 20					12 20					13 20					14 20
West Ruislip § ⊖	d	10 20						11 24					12 24					13 24					14 24
Denham	d	10 24				11 00		11 28					12 28					13 28					14 28
Denham Golf Club	d					11 02		11 31					12 31					13 31					14 31
Gerrards Cross	d	10 29			10 53	11a10		11 34			11 58		12 34			12 58		13 34			13 58		14 34
Seer Green	d	10 33						11 39					12 39					13 39					14 39
Beaconsfield	d	10 36			11 00			11 42			12 04		12 42			13 04		13 42			14 04		14 42
High Wycombe	d	10a46			11 06		11 23	11a51			12 10	12 23	12a51			13 10	13 23	13a51			14 10	14 23	14a49
Saunderton	d				11 12						12 17					13 17					14 17		
Princes Risborough	d			10 38	11 19		11 33			11 38	12 23	12 33			12 38	13 23	13 33			13 38	14 23	14 33	
Monks Risborough	d			10 41						11 41					12 41					13 41			
Little Kimble	d			10 45						11 45					12 45					13 45			
Aylesbury	a			11 00						11 59					12 55					13 55			
Haddenham & Thame Parkway	d				11 26		11 39				12 29	12 39				13 29	13 39				14 29	14 39	
Bicester North	d		11 12		11 40		11 50		12 13		12 42	12 50		13 12		13 42	13 50		14 12		14 42	14 50	
Kings Sutton	d										12 54										14 54		
Banbury	d		11 28		11 58		12 04		12 28		13a03	13 04		13 28		13 58	14 04		14 28		15a03	15 04	
Leamington Spa	d		11 46		12 17		12 22		12 46			13 22		13 46		14 17	14 22		14 46			15 22	
Warwick	d				12 21		12 26					13 26				14 22	14 26					15 26	
Warwick Parkway	d		11 51				12 30		12 51			13 30		13 51			14 30		14 51			15 30	
Hatton	d				12 29											14 29							
Claverdon	d				12 35											14 34							
Bearley	d				12 40																		
Wilmcote	d				12 43																		
Stratford-upon-Avon	a				12 53											14 50							
Lapworth	a																						
Dorridge	a						12 39					13 39					14 39					15 39	
Solihull	a		12 04				12 45		13 04			13 45		14 04			14 45		15 04			15 45	
Birmingham Moor Street	a		12 17				12 54		13 17			13 54		14 17			14 54		15 17			15 54	
Birmingham Snow Hill	a						13 02					14 02					15 02					16 02	
Rowley Regis	a																						
Cradley Heath	a																						
Stourbridge Junction	a																						
Kidderminster	a																						

§ London Underground Limited (Central Line) also operate services between South Ruislip and West Ruislip at frequent intervals

Saturdays
from 15 September

London - High Wycombe, Aylesbury, Banbury, Stratford-upon-Avon, Birmingham Snow Hill and Kidderminster

Network Diagram - see first Page of Table 114

Station		CH ◇		CH	CH ◇	CH ◇	CH	CH	CH ◇	CH	CH	CH ◇		CH	CH	CH ◇	CH ◇	CH	CH ◇	CH	CH	CH ◇		CH	CH
London Marylebone 10 ⊖	d	14 30			14 33	15 00		15 03	15 30	15 33	15 37	16 00			16 03	16 30	16 33	16 37	17 00		17 03	17 30		17 33	17 37
London Paddington 15 ⊖	d																								
Wembley Stadium	d				14 43			15 12			15 46				16 12			16 46			17 12				17 46
Sudbury & Harrow Road	d																								
Sudbury Hill Harrow	d																								
Northolt Park	d							15 17							16 17						17 17				
South Ruislip § ⊖	d							15 20							16 20						17 20				
West Ruislip 3 § ⊖	d							15 24			15 54							16 54							17 54
Denham	d				14 53			15 28			15 58				16 26			16 58			17 26				17 58
Denham Golf Club	d							15 31							16 28						17 28				
Gerrards Cross 1	d				14 58			15 34		15 53	16 03				16 32		16 53	17 03			17 32			17 50	18 03
Seer Green	d							15 39			16 08							17 08							18 08
Beaconsfield	d				15 04			15 42		16 00	16 11				16 39		17 00	17 11			17 39			17 55	18 11
High Wycombe 1	d				15 10	15 23		15 48		16 06	16a21	16 23			16 45		17 06	17a21	17 23		17 45			18 01	18a21
Saunderton	d				15 17					16 12							17 12							18 08	
Princes Risborough 2	d			14 38	15 23	15 33	15 38	16a01		16 19		16 33		16 38	16a58		17 19		17 33	17 38	17a58			18 13	
Monks Risborough	d			14 41			15 41							16 41						17 41					
Little Kimble	d			14 45			15 45							16 45						17 45					
Aylesbury	a			14 55			15 55							16 55						17 55					
Haddenham & Thame Parkway	d				15 29	15 39				16 26		16 39					17 26		17 39					18 19	
Bicester North 3	d	15 13			15 42	15 50			16 15	16 40		16 50				17 14	17 40		17 50			18 14		18a33	
Kings Sutton	d									16 51							17 51								
Banbury	d	15 28			15 58	16 04			16 28	17a03		17 04				17 28	18 00		18 04			18 28			
Leamington Spa 8	d	15 46			16 17	16 23			16 46			17 22				17 46	18 19		18 24			18 46			
Warwick	d				16 22	16 27						17 26					18 23		18 28						
Warwick Parkway	d	15 51				16 31			16 51			17 30				17 51			18 32			18 51			
Hatton	d				16 29												18 31								
Claverdon	d				16 35												18 38								
Bearley	d				16 40												18 43								
Wilmcote	d				16 45												18 47								
Stratford-upon-Avon	a				16 55												18 59								
Lapworth	a																								
Dorridge	a					16 40						17 39							18 43						
Solihull	a	16 04				16 46			17 04			17 45				18 04			18 48			19 04			
Birmingham Moor Street	a	16 17				16 54			17 17			17 54				18 17			18 57			19 17			
Birmingham Snow Hill	a					17 02						18 02							19 05						
Rowley Regis	a																								
Cradley Heath	a																								
Stourbridge Junction 2	a																								
Kidderminster	a																								

Station		CH ◇	CH	CH ◇	CH	CH ◇	CH	CH ◇		CH	CH ◇	CH	CH	CH ◇	CH	CH	CH ◇	CH		CH	CH ◇	CH	CH	CH	CH
London Marylebone 10 ⊖	d	18 00	18 03	18 30		18 33	18 37	19 00		19 04	19 30	19 33	19 37	20 00	20 04	20 35	21 00	21 04		21 35	22 10	22 14	22 40	23 10	23 14
London Paddington 15 ⊖	d																								
Wembley Stadium	d		18 12				18 46			19 13			19 46		20 13			21 13				22 23	22 49	23 19	23 23
Sudbury & Harrow Road	d																								
Sudbury Hill Harrow	d																								
Northolt Park	d		18 17							19 18					20 18			21 18				22 28			23 28
South Ruislip § ⊖	d		18 20							19 21					20 21			21 21				22 31			23 31
West Ruislip 3 § ⊖	d						18 54						19 54		20 25			21 25				22 35			23 35
Denham	d		18 26				18 58			19 27			19 58		20 29			21 29				22 39			23 39
Denham Golf Club	d		18 28							19 29					20 32			21 32				22 42			23 42
Gerrards Cross 1	d		18 32			18 53	19 03			19 33		19 52	20 03		20 36	20 54		21 36		21 54		22 46	23 02	23 32	23 46
Seer Green	d						19 08						20 08		20 40			21 40				22 50			23 50
Beaconsfield	d		18 39			19 00	19 11			19 40		19 59	20 11		20 44	21 01		21 44		22 01		22 54	23 09	23 39	23 54
High Wycombe 1	d	18 23	18a49			19 06	19 17	19 23		19 46		20 05	20a21	20 23	20 50	21 07	21 23	21 50		22 07		23 01	23 15	23 45	00 01
Saunderton	d					19 12						20 11				21 13		21 56				23 07			00 07
Princes Risborough 2	d	18 33			18 38	19 19	19 28	19 33		19 56		20 18		20 33	21 00	21 20	21 33	22 03		22 17		23 14	23 25	23 55	00 14
Monks Risborough	d				18 41		19 32			20 00					21 04			22 06				23 17			00 17
Little Kimble	d				18 45					20 03					21 07			22 10				23 21			00 21
Aylesbury	a				18 55		19 48			20 18					21 22			22 23				23 34			00 35
Haddenham & Thame Parkway	d	18 39				19 26		19 39				20 25		20 39		21 27	21 40			22 24			23 32	00 02	
Bicester North 3	d	18 50		19 12		19 40		19 50			20 14	20a40		20 51		21 41	21 51			22a42	22 52		23 45	00 15	
Kings Sutton	d					19 51										21 51							23 55		
Banbury	d	19 04		19 28		20 09		20 04			20 33			21 04		22a03	22 08				23 05		00a06	00a33	
Leamington Spa 8	d	19 23		19 46		20 28		20 22			20 52			21 22			22 26				23 24				
Warwick	d	19 27				20 33		20 26						21 26			22 31				23 28				
Warwick Parkway	d	19 31		19 51				20 30			20 57			21 30			22 34				23 32				
Hatton	d					20 40		20 35																	
Claverdon	d					20 46																			
Bearley	d					20 51																			
Wilmcote	d					20 56																			
Stratford-upon-Avon	a					21 06																			
Lapworth	a							20 40																	
Dorridge	a	19 41						20 45						21 40			22 44				23 41				
Solihull	a	19 47		20 04				20 50			21 09			21 44			22 49				23 49				
Birmingham Moor Street	a	19 56		20 17				21 00			21 22			21 55			23 01				00 01				
Birmingham Snow Hill	a	20 04						21 08						22 03			23 09								
Rowley Regis	a																								
Cradley Heath	a																								
Stourbridge Junction 2	a																								
Kidderminster	a																								

§ London Underground Limited (Central Line) also operate services between South Ruislip and West Ruislip at frequent intervals

Saturdays
from 15 September

London - High Wycombe, Aylesbury, Banbury, Stratford-upon-Avon, Birmingham Snow Hill and Kidderminster

Network Diagram - see first Page of Table 114

Station		CH
London Marylebone 10 ⊖	d	23 45
London Paddington 15 ⊖	d	
Wembley Stadium	d	23 54
Sudbury & Harrow Road	d	
Sudbury Hill Harrow	d	
Northolt Park	d	
South Ruislip § ⊖	d	
West Ruislip 3 § ⊖	d	
Denham	d	
Denham Golf Club	d	
Gerrards Cross 1	d	00 07
Seer Green	d	
Beaconsfield	d	00 14
High Wycombe 1	d	00 20
Saunderton	d	
Princes Risborough 2	d	00 30
Monks Risborough	d	
Little Kimble	d	
Aylesbury	a	
Haddenham & Thame Parkway	d	00 37
Bicester North 3	d	00 50
Kings Sutton	d	01 00
Banbury	d	01a11
Leamington Spa 8	d	
Warwick	d	
Warwick Parkway	d	
Hatton	d	
Claverdon	d	
Bearley	d	
Wilmcote	d	
Stratford-upon-Avon	a	
Lapworth	a	
Dorridge	a	
Solihull	a	
Birmingham Moor Street	a	
Birmingham Snow Hill	a	
Rowley Regis	a	
Cradley Heath	a	
Stourbridge Junction 2	a	
Kidderminster	a	

Sundays
until 22 July

Station		CH ◇	CH	CH	CH	CH	CH ◇	CH	CH ◇	CH ◇		CH	CH	CH ◇	CH	CH ◇	CH	CH	CH ◇	CH ◇		CH ◇	CH	CH	CH
London Marylebone 10 ⊖	d	22p10	23p10	23p14	23p45	00 10	07 35	07 50	08 15	09 00		08 52	09 36	10 00	09 52	10 33	11 00	10 52	11 33	11 36		12 00	11 52	12 33	13 00
London Paddington 15 ⊖	d																								
Wembley Stadium	d		23p19	23p23	23p54	00 19	07 44	07 59				09 01	09 45		10 01			11 01		11 45			12 01		
Sudbury & Harrow Road	d																								
Sudbury Hill Harrow	d																								
Northolt Park	d			23p28		00 24		08 04				09 06			10 06			11 06					12 06		
South Ruislip § ⊖	d			23p31		00 27	07 51	08 07				09 13			10 13			11 13					12 13		
West Ruislip 3 § ⊖	d			23p35		00 31		08 11				09 17			10 17			11 17					12 17		
Denham	d			23p39		00 35	07 56	08 15				09 21			10 21			11 21					12 21		
Denham Golf Club	d			23p42		00 38		08 18				09 24						11 24							
Gerrards Cross 1	d		23p32	23p46	00 07	00 42	08 01	08 22	08 33	09 17		09 28	09 58	10 17	10 26		11 17	11 28		11 58		12 17	12 26		13 17
Seer Green	d			23p50		00 46		08 26				09 32			10 31			11 32					12 31		
Beaconsfield	d		23p39	23p54	00 14	00 50	08 08	08 30	08 39	09 23		09 36	10 04	10 23	10 34		11 23	11 36		12 04		12 23	12 34		13 23
High Wycombe 1	d		23p45	00 01	00 20	00 56	08 14	08 36	08 45	09 29		09 42	10 10	10 29	10 40		11 29	11 42		12 10		12 29	12 40		13 29
Saunderton	d			00 07		01 02		08 42				09 48			10 47			11 48					12 47		
Princes Risborough 2	d		23p55	00 14	00 30	01 09	08 23	08 50	08 54	09 39		09 55	10 19	10 39	10 53		11 39	11 55		12 19		12 39	12 53		13 39
Monks Risborough	d			00 17		01 12		08 53				09 58			10 57			11 58					12 57		
Little Kimble	d			00 21		01 16		08 57				10 02			11 00			12 02					13 00		
Aylesbury	a			00 35		01 29		09 10				10 15			11 14			12 15					13 14		
Haddenham & Thame Parkway	d		00 02		00 37		08 29		09 00	09 45			10 26	10 45			11 45			12 26		12 45			13 45
Bicester North 3	d	22p52	00 15		00 50		08a46		09 12	09 57			10 42	10 57		11 16	11 57		12 16	12 42		12 57		13 16	13 57
Kings Sutton	d				01 00				09 22				10 54							12 54					
Banbury	d	23p05	00a33		01a11				09 28	10 11			11 01	11 11		11 29	12 11		12 29	13 01		13 11		13 40	14 11
Leamington Spa 8	d	23p24							09 45	10 28			11 20	11 28		11 47	12 28		12 47	13 20		13 28		14 00	14 28
Warwick	d	23p28							09 50	10 33			11 25	11 33			12 33			13 25		13 33			14 33
Warwick Parkway	d	23p32							09 53	10 36				11 36		11 53	12 36		12 53			13 36		14 06	14 36
Hatton	d								09 59				11 32	11 42						13 32		13 42			
Claverdon	d																								
Bearley	d																								
Wilmcote	d												11 43							13 43					
Stratford-upon-Avon	a												11 54							13 54					
Lapworth	a								10 05					11 48								13 48			
Dorridge	a	23p41							10 09	10 46				11 52		12 02	12 46		13 02			13 52		14 16	14 46
Solihull	a	23p49							10 15	10 52				11 58		12 08	12 52		13 08			13 58		14 21	14 52
Birmingham Moor Street	a	00 01							10 23	11 02				12 06		12 25	13 01		13 25			14 06		14 37	15 01
Birmingham Snow Hill	a								10 31	11 10				12 14			13 09					14 14			15 09
Rowley Regis	a																								
Cradley Heath	a																								
Stourbridge Junction 2	a																								
Kidderminster	a																								

§ London Underground Limited (Central Line) also operate services between South Ruislip and West Ruislip at frequent intervals

Table 115

Sundays
until 22 July

London - High Wycombe, Aylesbury, Banbury, Stratford-upon-Avon, Birmingham Snow Hill and Kidderminster

Network Diagram - see first Page of Table 114

		CH	CH	CH	CH	CH	CH	CH	CH	CH	CH	CH	CH	CH	CH	CH	CH	CH	CH	CH	CH	CH	CH
			◇	◇	◇		◇		◇		◇	◇	■		◇		◇		◇	◇	◇		◇
London Marylebone ⊖	d	12 52	13 33	13 36	14 00	13 52	14 33	14 36	15 00	14 52	15 33	15 36	16 00	15 52	16 33	16 36	17 00	16 52	17 33	17 36	18 00	17 52	18 33
London Paddington ⊖	d																						
Wembley Stadium	d	13 01		13 45		14 01		14 45		15 01		15 45		16 01		16 45		17 01		17 45		18 01	
Sudbury & Harrow Road	d																						
Sudbury Hill Harrow	d																						
Northolt Park	d	13 06				14 06				15 06				16 06				17 06				18 06	
South Ruislip § ⊖	d	13 13				14 13				15 13				16 13				17 13				18 13	
West Ruislip § ⊖	d	13 17				14 17				15 17				16 17				17 17				18 17	
Denham	d	13 21				14 21				15 21				16 21				17 21				18 21	
Denham Golf Club	d	13 24								15 24								17 24					
Gerrards Cross	d	13 28		13 58	14 17	14 26		14 58	15 17	15 28		15 58	16 17	16 26		16 58	17 17	17 28		17 58	18 17	18 26	
Seer Green	d	13 32				14 31				15 32				16 31				17 32				18 31	
Beaconsfield	d	13 36		14 04	14 23	14 34		15 04	15 23	15 36		16 04	16 23	16 34		17 04	17 23	17 36		18 04	18 23	18 34	
High Wycombe	d	13 42		14 10	14 29	14 40		15 10	15 29	15 42		16 10	16 29	16 40		17 10	17 29	17 42		18 10	18 29	18 40	
Saunderton	d	13 48				14 47				15 48				16 47				17 48				18 47	
Princes Risborough	d	13 55		14 19	14 39	14 53		15 19	15 38	15 55		16 19	16 39	16 53		17 19	17 39	17 55		18 19	18 39	18 53	
Monks Risborough	d	13 58				14 57				15 58				16 57				17 58				18 57	
Little Kimble	d	14 02				15 00				16 02				17 00				18 02				19 00	
Aylesbury	a	14 15				15 14				16 15				17 14				18 15				19 14	
Haddenham & Thame Parkway	d			14 26	14 45			15 26	15 44			16 26	16 45			17 26	17 45			18 26	18 45		
Bicester North	d		14 16	14 42	14 57		15 16	15a42	15 56		16 16	16 42	16 57		17 16	17a42	17 57		18 16	18 42	18 57		19 16
Kings Sutton	d			14 54								16 54								18 54			
Banbury	d		14 31	15 01	15 11		15 31		16 09		16 31	17 01	17 11		17 31		18 11		18 31	19 01	19 11		19 31
Leamington Spa	d		14 49	15 20	15 28		15 49		16 26		16 49	17 20	17 28		17 49		18 28		18 49	19 20	19 28		19 49
Warwick	d			15 25	15 33				16 31			17 25	17 33				18 33			19 25	19 33		
Warwick Parkway	d		14 55		15 36		15 55		16 34		16 55		17 36		17 55		18 36		18 55		19 36		19 55
Hatton	d			15 32			16 00					17 32			18 00					19 32			20 00
Claverdon	d																						
Bearley	d																						
Wilmcote	d			15 43								17 43								19 43			
Stratford-upon-Avon	a			15 54								17 54								19 54			
Lapworth	a						16 05								18 05								20 05
Dorridge	a		15 04		15 46		16 10		16 44		17 04		17 46		18 10		18 46		19 04		19 46		20 10
Solihull	a		15 10		15 52		16 16		16 50		17 10		17 52		18 16		18 55		19 10		19 55		20 16
Birmingham Moor Street	a		15 26		16 01		16 31		17 04		17 26		18 01		18 31		19 04		19 25		20 04		20 31
Birmingham Snow Hill	a				16 09				17 13				18 09				19 12				20 12		
Rowley Regis	a																						
Cradley Heath	a																						
Stourbridge Junction	a																						
Kidderminster	a																						

		CH	CH	CH	CH	CH	CH	CH	CH	CH	CH	CH	CH	CH	CH	CH	CH
			◇		◇		◇		◇	◇			◇				
London Marylebone ⊖	d	18 36	19 00	18 52	19 33	19 36	20 00	20 04	20 33	21 00	21 03	21 33	22 00	22 03	22 45		23 45
London Paddington ⊖	d																
Wembley Stadium	d	18 45		19 01		19 45		20 12			21 12			22 12	22 54		23 54
Sudbury & Harrow Road	d																
Sudbury Hill Harrow	d																
Northolt Park	d			19 06				20 17			21 17			22 17	22 59		23 59
South Ruislip § ⊖	d			19 13				20 20			21 20			22 20	23 02		00 02
West Ruislip § ⊖	d			19 17				20 24			21 24			22 24	23 06		00 06
Denham	d			19 21				20 28			21 28			22 28	23 10		00 10
Denham Golf Club	d			19 24							21 31				23 13		00 13
Gerrards Cross	d	18 58	19 17	19 28		19 58	20 17	20 33	20 50	21 17	21 35	21 52		22 33	23 17		00 17
Seer Green	d			19 32				20 38			21 39			22 38	23 21		00 21
Beaconsfield	d	19 04	19 23	19 36		20 04	20 23	20 41	20 56	21 23	21 43	21 59		22 41	23 25		00 25
High Wycombe	d	19 10	19 29	19 42		20 10	20 29	20 47	21 02	21 29	21 49	22 05		22 47	23 31		00 31
Saunderton	d			19 48				20 54			21 55			22 54	23 37		00 37
Princes Risborough	d	19 19	19 39	19 55		20 19	20 39	21 00	21 12	21 39	22 02	22 14		23 00	23 42	23 48	00 42
Monks Risborough	d			19 58				21 04			22 05			23 04		23 51	
Little Kimble	d			20 02				21 07			22 09			23 07		23 55	
Aylesbury	a			20 15				21 22			22 22			23 21		00 06	
Haddenham & Thame Parkway	d	19 26	19 45			20 26	20 45		21 18	21 45		22 21			23 49		00 49
Bicester North	d	19 42	19 57		20 16	20 42	20 57		21 30	21 57		22a37	22 42		00 02		01 02
Kings Sutton	d					20 54									00 13		
Banbury	d	20a02	20 11		20 31	21a04	21 11		21 44	22 11			22 55		00a22		01a20
Leamington Spa	d		20 28		20 49		21 28		22 01	22 28			23 13				
Warwick	d		20 33				21 33			22 33			23 17				
Warwick Parkway	d		20 36		20 55		21 36		22 07	22 36			23 21				
Hatton	d									22 42							
Claverdon	d																
Bearley	d																
Wilmcote	d																
Stratford-upon-Avon	a																
Lapworth	a									22 47							
Dorridge	a		20 46		21 04		21 46		22 16	22 52			23 30				
Solihull	a		20 55		21 10		21 55		22 22	23 00			23 36				
Birmingham Moor Street	a		21 04		21 25		22 04		22 37	23 09			23 46				
Birmingham Snow Hill	a		21 12				22 12			23 17			23 54				
Rowley Regis	a																
Cradley Heath	a																
Stourbridge Junction	a																
Kidderminster	a																

§ London Underground Limited (Central Line) also operate services between South Ruislip and West Ruislip at frequent intervals

Table 115

Sundays
29 July to 9 September

London - High Wycombe, Aylesbury, Banbury, Stratford-upon-Avon, Birmingham Snow Hill and Kidderminster

Network Diagram - see first Page of Table 114

		CH	CH	CH	CH	CH	CH	CH	CH	CH	CH	CH	CH	CH	CH	CH	CH	CH	CH	CH	CH	CH	CH
		◇								◇		◇		◇	◇			◇		◇			◇
							A	A	A	A	A												
London Marylebone ⊖	d	22p10	23p10	23p14	23p45	00 10	00 40	00 57	01 10	01 30	01 57	07 35	07 50	08 15	09 00	08 52	09 36	10 00	09 52	10 33	11 00	10 52	11 33
London Paddington ⊖	d																						
Wembley Stadium	d		23p19	23p23	23p54	00 19						07 44	07 59			09 01	09 45		10 01			11 01	
Sudbury & Harrow Road	d																						
Sudbury Hill Harrow	d																						
Northolt Park	d			23p28		00 24							08 04			09 06			10 06			11 06	
South Ruislip § ⊖	d			23p31		00 27						07 51	08 07			09 13			10 13			11 13	
West Ruislip § ⊖	d			23p35		00 31							08 11			09 17			10 17			11 17	
Denham	d			23p39		00 35	00 57		01 27			07 56	08 15			09 21			10 21			11 21	
Denham Golf Club	d			23p42		00 38	00 59		01 29				08 18			09 24						11 24	
Gerrards Cross	d		23p32	23p46	00 07	00 42	01 04		01 34			08 01	08 22	08 33	09 17	09 28	09 58	10 17	10 26		11 17	11 28	
Seer Green	d			23p50		00 46	01 08		01 38				08 26			09 32			10 31			11 32	
Beaconsfield	d		23p39	23p54	00 14	00 50	01 12		01 42			08 08	08 30	08 39	09 23	09 36	10 04	10 23	10 34		11 23	11 36	
High Wycombe	d		23p45	00 01	00 20	00 56	01a24		01 48			08 14	08 36	08 45	09 29	09 42	10 10	10 29	10 40		11 29	11 42	
Saunderton	d			00 07		01 02			01 54				08 42			09 48			10 47			11 48	
Princes Risborough	d		23p55	00 14	00 30	01 09			02 01	02 05		08 23	08 50	08 54	09 39	09 55	10 19	10 39	10 53		11 39	11 55	
Monks Risborough	d			00 17		01 12							08 53			09 58			10 57			11 58	
Little Kimble	d			00 21		01 16							08 57			10 02			11 00			12 02	
Aylesbury	a			00 35		01 26		01 52	02 20		02 52		09 10			10 15			11 14			12 15	
Haddenham & Thame Parkway	d		00 02		00 37					02 11		08 29		09 00	09 45		10 26	10 45			11 45		
Bicester North	d	22p52	00 15		00 50					02 23		08a46		09 12	09 57		10 42	10 57		11 16	11 57		12 16
Kings Sutton	d				01 00									09 22			10 54						
Banbury	d	23p05	00a33		01a11					02 36				09 28	10 11		11 01	11 11		11 29	12 11		12 29
Leamington Spa	d	23p24								02 54				09 45	10 28		11 20	11 28		11 47	12 28		12 47
Warwick	d	23p28								02 59				09 50	10 33		11 25	11 33			12 33		
Warwick Parkway	d	23p32								03 02				09 53	10 36			11 36		11 53	12 36		12 53
Hatton	d													09 59			11 32	11 42					
Claverdon	d																						
Bearley	d																						
Wilmcote	d																11 43						
Stratford-upon-Avon	a																11 54						
Lapworth	a													10 05				11 48					
Dorridge	a	23p41								03 12				10 09	10 46			11 52		12 02	12 46		13 02
Solihull	a	23p49												10 15	10 52			11 58		12 08	12 52		13 08
Birmingham Moor Street	a	00 01								03 23				10 23	11 02			12 06		12 25	13 01		13 25
Birmingham Snow Hill	a									03 32				10 31	11 10			12 14			13 09		
Rowley Regis	a																						
Cradley Heath	a																						
Stourbridge Junction	a																						
Kidderminster	a																						

		CH	CH	CH	CH	CH	CH	CH	CH	CH	CH	CH	CH	CH	CH	CH	CH	CH	CH	CH	CH	CH	CH
		◇	◇					◇	◇	◇		◇		◇		◇	◇	■		◇		◇	
London Marylebone ⊖	d	11 36	12 00	11 52	12 33	13 00	12 52	13 33	13 36	14 00	13 52	14 33	14 36	15 00	14 52	15 33	15 36	16 00	15 52	16 33	16 36	17 00	16 52
London Paddington ⊖	d																						
Wembley Stadium	d	11 45		12 01			13 01		13 45		14 01		14 45		15 01		15 45		16 01		16 45		17 01
Sudbury & Harrow Road	d																						
Sudbury Hill Harrow	d																						
Northolt Park	d			12 06			13 06				14 06				15 06				16 06				17 06
South Ruislip § ⊖	d			12 13			13 13				14 13				15 13				16 13				17 13
West Ruislip § ⊖	d			12 17			13 17				14 17				15 17				16 17				17 17
Denham	d			12 21			13 21				14 21				15 21				16 21				17 21
Denham Golf Club	d						13 24								15 24								17 24
Gerrards Cross	d	11 58	12 17	12 26		13 17	13 28		13 58	14 17	14 26		14 58	15 17	15 28		15 58	16 17	16 26		16 58	17 17	17 28
Seer Green	d			12 31			13 32				14 31				15 32				16 31				17 32
Beaconsfield	d	12 04	12 23	12 34		13 23	13 36		14 04	14 23	14 34		15 04	15 23	15 36		16 04	16 23	16 34		17 04	17 23	17 36
High Wycombe	d	12 10	12 29	12 40		13 29	13 42		14 10	14 29	14 40		15 10	15 29	15 42		16 10	16 29	16 40		17 10	17 29	17 42
Saunderton	d			12 47			13 48				14 47				15 48				16 47				17 48
Princes Risborough	d	12 19	12 39	12 53		13 39	13 55		14 19	14 39	14 53		15 19	15 38	15 55		16 19	16 39	16 53		17 19	17 39	17 55
Monks Risborough	d			12 57			13 58				14 57				15 58				16 57				17 58
Little Kimble	d			13 00			14 02				15 00				16 02				17 00				18 02
Aylesbury	a			13 14			14 15				15 14				16 15				17 14				18 15
Haddenham & Thame Parkway	d	12 26	12 45			13 45			14 26	14 45			15 26	15 44			16 26	16 45			17 26	17 45	
Bicester North	d	12 42	12 57		13 16	13 57		14 16	14 42	14 57		15 16	15a42	15 56		16 16	16 42	16 57		17 16	17a42	17 57	
Kings Sutton	d	12 54							14 54								16 54						
Banbury	d	13 01	13 11		13 40	14 11		14 31	15 01	15 11		15 31		16 09		16 31	17 01	17 11		17 31		18 11	
Leamington Spa	d	13 20	13 28		14 00	14 28		14 49	15 20	15 28		15 49		16 26		16 49	17 20	17 28		17 49		18 28	
Warwick	d	13 25	13 33			14 33			15 25	15 33				16 31			17 25	17 33				18 33	
Warwick Parkway	d		13 36		14 06	14 36		14 55		15 36		15 55		16 34		16 55		17 36		17 55		18 36	
Hatton	d	13 32	13 42						15 32			16 00					17 32			18 00			
Claverdon	d																						
Bearley	d																						
Wilmcote	d	13 43							15 43								17 43						
Stratford-upon-Avon	a	13 54							15 54								17 54						
Lapworth	a		13 48									16 05								18 05			
Dorridge	a		13 52		14 16	14 46		15 04		15 46		16 10		16 44		17 04		17 46		18 10		18 46	
Solihull	a		13 58		14 21	14 52		15 10		15 52		16 16		16 50		17 10		17 52		18 16		18 55	
Birmingham Moor Street	a		14 06		14 37	15 01		15 26		16 01		16 31		17 04		17 26		18 01		18 31		19 04	
Birmingham Snow Hill	a		14 14			15 09				16 09				17 13				18 09				19 12	
Rowley Regis	a																						
Cradley Heath	a																						
Stourbridge Junction	a																						
Kidderminster	a																						

§ London Underground Limited (Central Line) also operate services between South Ruislip and West Ruislip at frequent intervals

A not from 19 August

London - High Wycombe, Aylesbury, Banbury, Stratford-upon-Avon, Birmingham Snow Hill and Kidderminster

Sundays
29 July to 9 September

Network Diagram - see first Page of Table 114

		CH ◇	CH ◇	CH ◇	CH	CH ◇	CH	CH ◇	CH	CH ◇	CH	CH ◇	CH	CH ◇	CH ◇	CH	CH	CH ◇	CH	CH	CH	CH
London Marylebone 10 ⊖	d	17 33	17 36	18 00	17 52	18 33	18 36	19 00	18 52	19 33	19 36	20 00	20 04	20 33	21 00	21 03	21 33	22 00	22 03	22 45		23 45
London Paddington 15 ⊖	d																					
Wembley Stadium	d		17 45		18 01		18 45		19 01		19 45		20 12			21 12			22 12	22 54		23 54
Sudbury & Harrow Road	d																					
Sudbury Hill Harrow	d																					
Northolt Park	d				18 06				19 06				20 17			21 17			22 17	22 59		23 59
South Ruislip § ⊖	d				18 13				19 13				20 20			21 20			22 20	23 02		00 02
West Ruislip 3 § ⊖	d				18 17				19 17				20 24			21 24			22 24	23 06		00 06
Denham	d				18 21				19 21				20 28			21 28			22 28	23 10		00 10
Denham Golf Club	d								19 24							21 31				23 13		00 13
Gerrards Cross 1	d		17 58	18 17	18 26		18 58	19 17	19 28		19 58	20 17	20 33	20 50	21 17	21 35	21 52		22 33	23 17		00 17
Seer Green	d				18 31				19 32				20 38			21 39			22 38	23 21		00 21
Beaconsfield	d		18 04	18 23	18 34		19 04	19 23	19 36		20 04	20 23	20 41	20 56	21 23	21 43	21 59		22 41	23 25		00 25
High Wycombe 1	d		18 10	18 29	18 40		19 10	19 29	19 42		20 10	20 29	20 47	21 02	21 29	21 49	22 05		22 47	23 31		00 31
Saunderton	d				18 47				19 48				20 54			21 55			22 54	23 37		00 37
Princes Risborough 2	d		18 19	18 39	18 53		19 19	19 39	19 55		20 19	20 39	21 00	21 12	21 39	22 02	22 14		23 00	23 42	23 48	00 42
Monks Risborough	d				18 57				19 58				21 04			22 05			23 04		23 51	
Little Kimble	d				19 00				20 02				21 07			22 09			23 07		23 55	
Aylesbury	a				19 14				20 15				21 22			22 22			23 21		00 06	
Haddenham & Thame Parkway	d		18 26	18 45			19 26	19 45			20 26	20 45		21 18	21 45		22 21			23 49		00 49
Bicester North 3	d	18 16	18 42	18 57		19 16	19 42	19 57		20 16	20 42	20 57		21 30	21 57		22a37	22 42		00 02		01 02
Kings Sutton	d		18 54								20 54									00 13		
Banbury	d	18 31	19 01	19 11		19 31	20a02	20 11		20 31	21a04	21 11		21 44	22 11			22 55		00a22		01a20
Leamington Spa 8	d	18 49	19 20	19 28		19 49		20 28		20 49		21 28		22 01	22 28			23 13				
Warwick	d		19 25	19 33				20 33				21 33			22 33			23 17				
Warwick Parkway	d	18 55		19 36		19 55		20 36		20 55		21 36		22 07	22 36			23 21				
Hatton	d		19 32			20 00									22 42							
Claverdon	d																					
Bearley	d																					
Wilmcote	d		19 43																			
Stratford-upon-Avon	a		19 54																			
Lapworth	a					20 05									22 47							
Dorridge	a	19 04		19 46		20 10		20 46		21 04		21 46		22 16	22 52			23 30				
Solihull	a	19 10		19 55		20 16		20 55		21 10		21 55		22 22	23 00			23 36				
Birmingham Moor Street	a	19 25		20 04		20 31		21 04		21 25		22 04		22 37	23 09			23 46				
Birmingham Snow Hill	a			20 12				21 12				22 12			23 17			23 54				
Rowley Regis	a																					
Cradley Heath	a																					
Stourbridge Junction 2	a																					
Kidderminster	a																					

Sundays
from 16 September

		CH ◇	CH	CH	CH	CH	CH ◇	CH	CH ◇	CH ◇	CH	CH	CH ◇	CH	CH ◇	CH	CH	CH ◇	CH ◇	CH ◇	CH	CH	CH
London Marylebone 10 ⊖	d	22p10	23p10	23p14	23p45	00 10	07 35	07 50	08 15	09 00	08 52	09 36	10 00	09 52	10 33	11 00	10 52	11 33	11 36	12 00	11 52	12 33	13 00
London Paddington 15 ⊖	d																						
Wembley Stadium	d		23p19	23p23	23p54	00 19	07 44	07 59			09 01	09 45		10 01			11 01		11 45		12 01		
Sudbury & Harrow Road	d																						
Sudbury Hill Harrow	d																						
Northolt Park	d			23p28		00 24		08 04			09 06			10 06			11 06				12 06		
South Ruislip § ⊖	d			23p31		00 27	07 51	08 07			09 13			10 13			11 13				12 13		
West Ruislip 3 § ⊖	d			23p35		00 31		08 11			09 17			10 17			11 17				12 17		
Denham	d			23p39		00 35	07 56	08 15			09 21			10 21			11 21				12 21		
Denham Golf Club	d			23p42		00 38		08 18			09 24						11 24						
Gerrards Cross 1	d		23p32	23p46	00 07	00 42	08 01	08 22	08 33	09 17	09 28	09 58	10 17	10 26		11 17	11 28		11 58	12 17	12 26		13 17
Seer Green	d			23p50		00 46		08 26			09 32			10 31			11 32				12 31		
Beaconsfield	d		23p39	23p54	00 14	00 50	08 08	08 30	08 39	09 23	09 36	10 04	10 23	10 34		11 23	11 36		12 04	12 23	12 34		13 23
High Wycombe 1	d		23p45	00 01	00 20	00 56	08 14	08 36	08 45	09 29	09 42	10 10	10 29	10 40		11 29	11 42		12 10	12 29	12 40		13 29
Saunderton	d			00 07		01 02		08 42			09 48			10 47			11 48				12 47		
Princes Risborough 2	d		23p55	00 14	00 30	01 09	08 23	08 50	08 54	09 39	09 55	10 19	10 39	10 53		11 39	11 55		12 19	12 39	12 53		13 39
Monks Risborough	d			00 17		01 12		08 53			09 58			10 57			11 58				12 57		
Little Kimble	d			00 21		01 16		08 57			10 02			11 00			12 02				13 00		
Aylesbury	a			00 35		01 29		09 10			10 15			11 14			12 15				13 14		
Haddenham & Thame Parkway	d		00 02		00 37		08 29		09 00	09 45		10 26	10 45			11 45			12 26	12 45			13 45
Bicester North 3	d	22p52	00 15		00 50		08a46		09 12	09 57		10 42	10 57		11 16	11 57		12 16	12 42	12 57		13 16	13 57
Kings Sutton	d				01 00				09 22			10 54							12 54				
Banbury	d	23p05	00a33		01a11				09 28	10 11		11 01	11 11		11 29	12 11		12 29	13 01	13 11		13 40	14 11
Leamington Spa 8	d	23p24							09 45	10 28		11 20	11 28		11 47	12 28		12 47	13 20	13 28		14 00	14 28
Warwick	d	23p28							09 50	10 33		11 25	11 33			12 33			13 25	13 33			14 33
Warwick Parkway	d	23p32							09 53	10 36			11 36		11 53	12 36		12 53		13 36		14 06	14 36
Hatton	d								09 59			11 32	11 42						13 32	13 42			
Claverdon	d																						
Bearley	d																						
Wilmcote	d											11 43							13 43				
Stratford-upon-Avon	a											11 54							13 54				
Lapworth	a								10 05				11 48							13 48			
Dorridge	a	23p41							10 09	10 46			11 52		12 02	12 46		13 02		13 52		14 16	14 46
Solihull	a	23p49							10 15	10 52			11 58		12 08	12 52		13 08		13 58		14 21	14 52
Birmingham Moor Street	a	00 01							10 23	11 02			12 06		12 25	13 01		13 25		14 06		14 37	15 01
Birmingham Snow Hill	a								10 31	11 10			12 14			13 09				14 14			15 09
Rowley Regis	a																						
Cradley Heath	a																						
Stourbridge Junction 2	a																						
Kidderminster	a																						

§ London Underground Limited (Central Line) also operate services between South Ruislip and West Ruislip at frequent intervals

Table 115

London - High Wycombe, Aylesbury, Banbury, Stratford-upon-Avon, Birmingham Snow Hill and Kidderminster

Sundays
from 16 September

Network Diagram - see first Page of Table 114

		CH	CH ◇	CH ◇	CH ◇	CH	CH ◇	CH	CH ◇	CH	CH ◇	CH ◇	CH ■	CH	CH ◇	CH	CH ◇	CH	CH ◇	CH ◇	CH ◇	CH	CH ◇
London Marylebone 10 ⊖	d	12 52	13 33	13 36	14 00	13 52	14 33	14 36	15 00	14 52	15 33	15 36	16 00	15 52	16 33	16 36	17 00	16 52	17 33	17 36	18 00	17 52	18 33
London Paddington 15 ⊖	d																						
Wembley Stadium	d	13 01		13 45		14 01		14 45		15 01		15 45		16 01		16 45		17 01		17 45		18 01	
Sudbury & Harrow Road	d																						
Sudbury Hill Harrow	d																						
Northolt Park	d	13 06				14 06				15 06				16 06				17 06				18 06	
South Ruislip § ⊖	d	13 13				14 13				15 13				16 13				17 13				18 13	
West Ruislip 3 § ⊖	d	13 17				14 17				15 17				16 17				17 17				18 17	
Denham	d	13 21				14 21				15 21				16 21				17 21				18 21	
Denham Golf Club	d	13 24								15 24								17 24					
Gerrards Cross 1	d	13 28		13 58	14 17	14 26		14 58	15 17	15 28		15 58	16 17	16 26		16 58	17 17	17 28		17 58	18 17	18 26	
Seer Green	d	13 32				14 31				15 32				16 31				17 32				18 31	
Beaconsfield	d	13 36		14 04	14 23	14 34		15 04	15 23	15 36		16 04	16 23	16 34		17 04	17 23	17 36		18 04	18 23	18 34	
High Wycombe 1	d	13 42		14 10	14 29	14 40		15 10	15 29	15 42		16 10	16 29	16 40		17 10	17 29	17 42		18 10	18 29	18 40	
Saunderton	d	13 48				14 47				15 48				16 47				17 48				18 47	
Princes Risborough 2	d	13 55		14 19	14 39	14 53		15 19	15 38	15 55		16 19	16 39	16 53		17 19	17 39	17 55		18 19	18 39	18 53	
Monks Risborough	d	13 58				14 57				15 58				16 57				17 58				18 57	
Little Kimble	d	14 02				15 00				16 02				17 00				18 02				19 00	
Aylesbury	a	14 15				15 14				16 15				17 14				18 15				19 14	
Haddenham & Thame Parkway	d			14 26	14 45			15 26	15 44			16 26	16 45			17 26	17 45			18 26	18 45		
Bicester North 3	d		14 16	14 42	14 57		15 16	15a42	15 56		16 16	16 42	16 57		17 16	17a42	17 57		18 16	18 42	18 57		19 16
Kings Sutton	d			14 54								16 54								18 54			
Banbury	d		14 31	15 01	15 11		15 31		16 09		16 31	17 01	17 11		17 31		18 11		18 31	19 01	19 11		19 31
Leamington Spa 8	d		14 49	15 20	15 28		15 49		16 26		16 49	17 20	17 28		17 49		18 28		18 49	19 20	19 28		19 49
Warwick	d			15 25	15 33				16 31			17 25	17 33				18 33			19 25	19 33		
Warwick Parkway	d		14 55		15 36		15 55		16 34		16 55		17 36		17 55		18 36		18 55		19 36		19 55
Hatton	d			15 32			16 00					17 32			18 00					19 32			20 00
Claverdon	d																						
Bearley	d																						
Wilmcote	d			15 43								17 42								19 43			
Stratford-upon-Avon	a			15 54								17 54								19 54			
Lapworth	a						16 05								18 05								20 05
Dorridge	a		15 04		15 46		16 10		16 44		17 04		17 46		18 10		18 46		19 04		19 46		20 10
Solihull	a		15 10		15 52		16 16		16 50		17 10		17 52		18 16		18 55		19 10		19 55		20 16
Birmingham Moor Street	a		15 26		16 01		16 31		17 04		17 26		18 01		18 31		19 04		19 25		20 04		20 31
Birmingham Snow Hill	a				16 09				17 13				18 09				19 12				20 12		
Rowley Regis	a																						
Cradley Heath	a																						
Stourbridge Junction 2	a																						
Kidderminster	a																						

		CH	CH ◇	CH	CH ◇	CH	CH ◇	CH	CH ◇	CH ◇	CH	CH	CH ◇	CH	CH	CH	CH
London Marylebone 10 ⊖	d	18 36	19 00	18 52	19 33	19 36	20 00	20 04	20 33	21 00	21 03	21 33	22 00	22 03	22 45		23 45
London Paddington 15 ⊖	d																
Wembley Stadium	d	18 45		19 01		19 45		20 12			21 12			22 12	22 54		23 54
Sudbury & Harrow Road	d																
Sudbury Hill Harrow	d																
Northolt Park	d			19 06				20 17			21 17			22 17	22 59		23 59
South Ruislip § ⊖	d			19 13				20 20			21 20			22 20	23 02		00 02
West Ruislip 3 § ⊖	d			19 17				20 24			21 24			22 24	23 06		00 06
Denham	d			19 21				20 28			21 28			22 28	23 10		00 10
Denham Golf Club	d			19 24							21 31				23 13		00 13
Gerrards Cross 1	d	18 58	19 17	19 28		19 58	20 17	20 33	20 50	21 17	21 35	21 52		22 33	23 17		00 17
Seer Green	d			19 32				20 38			21 39			22 38	23 21		00 21
Beaconsfield	d	19 04	19 23	19 36		20 04	20 23	20 41	20 56	21 23	21 43	21 59		22 41	23 25		00 25
High Wycombe 1	d	19 10	19 29	19 42		20 10	20 29	20 47	21 02	21 29	21 49	22 05		22 47	23 31		00 31
Saunderton	d			19 48				20 54			21 55			22 54	23 37		00 37
Princes Risborough 2	d	19 19	19 39	19 55		20 19	20 39	21 00	21 12	21 39	22 02	22 14		23 00	23 42	23 48	00 42
Monks Risborough	d			19 58				21 04			22 05			23 04		23 51	
Little Kimble	d			20 02				21 07			22 09			23 07		23 55	
Aylesbury	a			20 15				21 22			22 22			23 21		00 06	
Haddenham & Thame Parkway	d	19 26	19 45			20 26	20 45		21 18	21 45		22 21			23 49		00 49
Bicester North 3	d	19 42	19 57		20 16	20 42	20 57		21 30	21 57		22a37	22 42		00 02		01 02
Kings Sutton	d					20 54									00 13		
Banbury	d	20a02	20 11		20 31	21a04	21 11		21 44	22 11			22 55		00a22		01a20
Leamington Spa 8	d		20 28		20 49		21 28		22 01	22 28			23 13				
Warwick	d		20 33				21 33			22 33			23 17				
Warwick Parkway	d		20 36		20 55		21 36		22 07	22 36			23 21				
Hatton	d									22 42							
Claverdon	d																
Bearley	d																
Wilmcote	d																
Stratford-upon-Avon	a																
Lapworth	a									22 47							
Dorridge	a		20 46		21 04		21 46		22 16	22 52			23 30				
Solihull	a		20 55		21 10		21 55		22 22	23 00			23 36				
Birmingham Moor Street	a		21 04		21 25		22 04		22 37	23 09			23 46				
Birmingham Snow Hill	a		21 12				22 12			23 17			23 54				
Rowley Regis	a																
Cradley Heath	a																
Stourbridge Junction 2	a																
Kidderminster	a																

§ London Underground Limited (Central Line) also operate services between South Ruislip and West Ruislip at frequent intervals

Kidderminster, Birmingham Snow Hill, Stratford-upon-Avon, Banbury, Aylesbury and High Wycombe - London

Network Diagram - see first Page of Table 114

Miles	Miles	Miles			CH	CH	CH	CH	CH	CH	CH	CH	CH	CH	CH	CH	CH	CH	CH	CH	CH	CH	CH
					MX	MX																	
																	◇ ⚲						
—	—	—	Kidderminster	d																			
—	—	—	Stourbridge Junction ■	d																			
—	—	—	Cradley Heath	d																			
—	—	—	Rowley Regis	d																			
0	—	—	Birmingham Snow Hill	d																			
0¾	—	—	Birmingham Moor Street	d													05 46						
7¼	—	—	Solihull	d													05 54						
10½	—	—	Dorridge	d													05 59						
13	—	—	Lapworth	d																			
—	—	0	Stratford-upon-Avon	d														06 10					
—	—	2¾	Wilmcote	d														06 16					
—	—	4¼	Bearley	d														06 19					
—	—	7¼	Claverdon	d														06 25					
17¼	—	9¼	Hatton	d														06 31					
20	—	12	Warwick Parkway	d									05 40				06 09						
21¼	—	13¼	Warwick	d													06 12	06 38					
23¼	—	15¼	Leamington Spa ■	d									05 45				06 17	06a45					
43¼	—	—	Banbury	d						05 24		05 42	06 03			06 12	06 36						06 52
46¾	—	—	Kings Sutton	d						05 29						06 18							
57¼	—	—	Bicester North ■	d						05 41		05 57	06 15			06 29	06 48					06 54	07 06
70¼	—	—	Haddenham & Thame Parkway	d						05 53		06 09	06 26			06 42						07 07	07 19
—	0	—	Aylesbury	d		23p00	05 05	05 15	05 25		05 48				06 20				06 39				
—	4½	—	Little Kimble	d		23p08	05 13				05 56				06 28								
—	6	—	Monks Risborough	d		23p12	05 17				06 00				06 32								
76	7½	—	Princes Risborough ■	d		23p16	05 21	05 29	05 39	06 00	06 04	06 16	06 33		06 37	06 49						07 14	07 28
79¼	—	—	Saunderton	d		23p21	05 26				06 09				06 42								
84¼	—	—	High Wycombe ■	d	23p22	23p27	05 32	05 39	05 55	06 10	06 16	06 26			06 48	06 59					07 10	07 25	
89	—	—	Beaconsfield	d	23p29	23p33	05 38	05 45	06 02	06 16	06 22	06 33			06 55	07 05					07 17	07 32	
90¾	—	—	Seer Green	d		23p36	05 41		06 05			06 36			06 58						07 20		
93¼	—	—	Gerrards Cross ■	d	23p35	23p41	05 46	05 51	06 10	06 22	06 28	06 41		06 52	07 03	07 11				07 19	07 25	07 38	
95	—	—	Denham Golf Club	d		23p44	05 49							06 55							07 29		
96	—	—	Denham	d		23p47	05 52	05 56	06 14		06 32				07 07						07 31		
98¾	—	—	West Ruislip ■ § ⊖	d		23p51	06 01				06 37				07 12						07 36		
100½	—	—	South Ruislip § ⊖	d		23p55	06 05		06 20					07 02						07 27			
102¼	—	—	Northolt Park	d		23p59	06 08				06 42			07 06						07 31			
103¼	—	—	Sudbury Hill Harrow	d										07 09						07 34			
104	—	—	Sudbury & Harrow Road	d										07 12						07 37			
105½	—	—	Wembley Stadium	d	23p48	00 04	06 13		06 27		06 47			07 15							07 45		
—	—	12	London Paddington ■ ⊖	a																			
112	—	—	London Marylebone ■ ⊖	a	00 06	00 20	06 30	06 19	06 44	06 48	07 00	07 04	07 10	07 29	07 32	07 35	07 38		07 39	07 51	07 58	08 02	08 04

		CH	CH	CH	CH	CH	CH	CH	CH	CH	CH	CH	CH	CH	CH	CH	CH	CH	CH	CH	CH	CH	CH
		BZ						BZ															
		◇ ⚲						◇ ⚲				◇					◇	◇ ⚲					◇
Kidderminster	d																06 10						
Stourbridge Junction ■	d																06 18						
Cradley Heath	d																06 24						
Rowley Regis	d																06 30						
Birmingham Snow Hill	d																06 46						
Birmingham Moor Street	d	06 19						06 55									06 59	07 33					
Solihull	d	06 29						07 03									07 08	07 41					
Dorridge	d	06 35															07 13						
Lapworth	d																						
Stratford-upon-Avon	d											06 47											07 35
Wilmcote	d																						07 41
Bearley	d																						07 45
Claverdon	d																						07 51
Hatton	d																07 20						08 02
Warwick Parkway	d	06 45						07 16				07 08					07 25	07 53					08 09
Warwick	d											07 11					07 29						
Leamington Spa ■	d	06 52										07 23					07 33	07 58					08 15
Banbury	d	07 11					07 17					07 40					07 51	08 16				08 00	08 34
Kings Sutton	d																					08 06	
Bicester North ■	d						07 29					07 52					08 05					08 17	08 46
Haddenham & Thame Parkway	d						07 40					08 03					08 17						08 57
Aylesbury	d		07 11			07 20				07 40	07 44		07 50						08 14				
Little Kimble	d					07 28							07 58										
Monks Risborough	d					07 32							08 02										
Princes Risborough ■	d					07 37				07 58			08a08			08 12	08 24					08 42	
Saunderton	d					07 42										08 17						08 47	
High Wycombe ■	d				07 42	07 48	07 54			08 08					08 18	08 23	08 34				08 48	08 53	
Beaconsfield	d				07 49	07 54	08 01			08 15						08 30	08 41				08 55	09 00	
Seer Green	d				07 52										08 26							09 03	
Gerrards Cross ■	d			07 50	07 56	08 00			08 13						08 31	08 35	08 47				09 01	09 08	
Denham Golf Club	d															08 39					09 04		
Denham	d			07 54					08 18							08 41					09 07		
West Ruislip ■ § ⊖	d					08a08								08 29						08 58		09 14	
South Ruislip § ⊖	d				08 04											08 47				09 02			
Northolt Park	d			08 01										08 34	08 41							09 20	
Sudbury Hill Harrow	d													08 38						09 06			
Sudbury & Harrow Road	d													08 41						09 09			
Wembley Stadium	d			08 06											08 48					09 12		09 25	
London Paddington ■ ⊖	a																						
London Marylebone ■ ⊖	a	08 06	08 11	08 18	08 21		08 24	08 25	08 38	08 42	08 44	08 48		08 55	09 02	09 05	09 08	09 09	09 14	09 25	09 28	09 38	09 42

§ London Underground Limited (Central Line) also operate services between South Ruislip and West Ruislip at frequent intervals

BZ Business Zone available offering greater comfort and an enhanced working environment. Supplement payable

Table 115 — Mondays to Fridays until 27 July

Kidderminster, Birmingham Snow Hill, Stratford-upon-Avon, Banbury, Aylesbury and High Wycombe - London

Network Diagram - see first Page of Table 114

		CH	CH	CH	CH	CH	CH	CH	CH	CH	CH	CH	CH	CH	CH	CH	CH	CH	CH	CH	CH	CH	CH
				◇	◇ ⚲				◇ ⚲	◇ ⚲				◇	◇ ⚲			◇	◇ ⚲				◇
Kidderminster	d			06 59	07 30					08 09													
Stourbridge Junction ■	d			07 07	07 40					08 22													
Cradley Heath	d			07 14	07 46					08 28													
Rowley Regis	d			07 22	07 53					08 34													
Birmingham Snow Hill	d			07 44	08 12				08 22	08 52					09 12								
Birmingham Moor Street	d			07 47	08 15				08 25	08 55					09 15				09 55				
Solihull	d			07 55	08 24				08 37	09 03					09 23				10 03				
Dorridge	d			08 00	08 29				08 50						09 28								
Lapworth	d			08 04					08 54						09 32								
Stratford-upon-Avon	d																						09 55
Wilmcote	d																						10 00
Bearley	d																						10 04
Claverdon	d																						10 09
Hatton	d			08 10					09 00														10 15
Warwick Parkway	d			08 16	08 39					09 15					09 40				10 15				
Warwick	d			08 19	08 43				09 05						09 44								10 23
Leamington Spa ■	d			08 25	08 48				09 10						09 49				10 21				10 27
Banbury	d			08 43	09 08				09 29					09 45	10 07				10 38				10 48
Kings Sutton	d													09 51									
Bicester North ■	d			08 56				09 24	09 41					10 02	10 20			10 27					11 02
Haddenham & Thame Parkway	d			09 07				09 37						10 15				10 39					11 14
Aylesbury	d	08 50									09 50											10 59	
Little Kimble	d	08 58									09 58											11 07	
Monks Risborough	d	09 02									10 02											11 11	
Princes Risborough ■	d	09a08		09 14				09 44			10a08		10 10	10 22				10 46			11 10	11a17	11 21
Saunderton	d			09 19									10 15								11 15		
High Wycombe ■	d		09 12	09 25			09 41	09 54				10 11	10 21	10 32	10 40		10 45	10 56			11 21		11 31
Beaconsfield	d		09 18	09 32			09 48					10 18	10 27				10 51	11 02			11 28		
Seer Green	d						09 51										10 54						
Gerrards Cross ■	d		09 24	09 38		09 47	09 56					10 24	10 33			10 44	10 59	11 08		11 19	11 34		
Denham Golf Club	d					09 50														11 22			
Denham	d		09 28			09 53						10 28				10 48				11 25			
West Ruislip ■ § ⊖	d		09 32				10 02									11 01	11 06						
South Ruislip § ⊖	d		09 36									10 33								11 30			
Northolt Park	d					10 00							10 42							11 34			
Sudbury Hill Harrow	d											10 38								11 37			
Sudbury & Harrow Road	d																						
Wembley Stadium	d		09 43			10 06						10 42					11 15			11 41			
London Paddington ■ ⊖	a															11 32							
London Marylebone ■ ⊖	a		09 55	09 58	09 59	10 21	10 25	10 27	10 28	10 29		10 58	10 59	11 00	11 15		11 30	11 31	11 32	11 58	11 59		12 00

		CH	CH	CH	CH	CH	CH	CH	CH	CH	CH	CH	CH	CH	CH	CH	CH	CH	CH	CH	CH	CH
					BZ																	
		◇ ⚲			◇ ⚲		◇			◇ ⚲		◇	◇ ⚲					◇			◇	
Kidderminster	d																					
Stourbridge Junction ■	d																					
Cradley Heath	d																					
Rowley Regis	d																					
Birmingham Snow Hill	d	10 12								11 12								12 12				
Birmingham Moor Street	d	10 15			10 55					11 15			11 55					12 15			12 55	
Solihull	d	10 23			11 04					11 23			12 03					12 23			13 03	
Dorridge	d	10 28								11 28								12 28				
Lapworth	d																					
Stratford-upon-Avon	d											11 20										13 06
Wilmcote	d											11 25										13 11
Bearley	d																					13 15
Claverdon	d											11 32										13 20
Hatton	d											11 38										13 27
Warwick Parkway	d	10 39			11 15					11 39			12 15					12 39			13 15	
Warwick	d	10 42								11 42		11 46						12 42				13 35
Leamington Spa ■	d	10 47			11 21					11 47		11 51	12 20					12 47			13 20	13a41
Banbury	d	11 05			11 39				11 44	12 04		12 11	12 38				12 47	13 04			13 39	
Kings Sutton	d								11 50													
Bicester North ■	d	11 17		11 25					12 01	12 16		12 25					13 02	13 16		13 25		
Haddenham & Thame Parkway	d			11 38					12 14			12 38					13 14			13 38		
Aylesbury	d							11 54						12 50								
Little Kimble	d							12 02						12 58								
Monks Risborough	d							12 06						13 02								
Princes Risborough ■	d			11 45			12 10	12a12	12 21			12 45		13a08		13 10	13 21			13 45		
Saunderton	d						12 15									13 15						
High Wycombe ■	d	11 38	11 44	11 55			12 21		12 31	12 37	12 44	12 55				13 21	13 31	13 37	13 44	13 55		
Beaconsfield	d		11 50	12 01			12 28				12 50	13 01				13 28			13 50	14 01		
Seer Green	d		11 53								12 53								13 53			
Gerrards Cross ■	d		11 58	12 07		12 19	12 34				12 58	13 07			13 19	13 34			13 58	14 07		
Denham Golf Club	d					12 22									13 22							
Denham	d		12 02			12 25					13 02				13 25				14 02			
West Ruislip ■ § ⊖	d		12 06								13 06								14 06			
South Ruislip § ⊖	d					12 30									13 30							
Northolt Park	d					12 34									13 34							
Sudbury Hill Harrow	d					12 37									13 37							
Sudbury & Harrow Road	d																					
Wembley Stadium	d		12 15			12 41					13 15				13 41				14 15			
London Paddington ■ ⊖	a																					
London Marylebone ■ ⊖	a	12 09	12 29	12 30	12 31	12 58	12 59		13 00	13 07	13 29	13 30	13 31		13 58	13 59	14 00	14 09	14 29	14 30	14 31	

§ London Underground Limited (Central Line) also operate services between South Ruislip and West Ruislip at frequent intervals

BZ Business Zone available offering greater comfort and an enhanced working environment. Supplement payable

Kidderminster, Birmingham Snow Hill, Stratford-upon-Avon, Banbury, Aylesbury and High Wycombe - London

Network Diagram - see first Page of Table 114

		CH	CH	CH	CH	CH	CH		CH	CH	CH	CH	CH	CH	CH	CH	CH		CH	CH	CH	CH	CH	CH	CH
					◇	◇				◇				◇	◇				◇				◇	◇	◇
Kidderminster	d																								
Stourbridge Junction [2]	d																								
Cradley Heath	d																								
Rowley Regis	d																								
Birmingham Snow Hill	d					13 12									14 12									15 12	
Birmingham Moor Street	d					13 15				13 55					14 15				14 55					15 15	
Solihull	d					13 23				14 03					14 23				15 03					15 23	
Dorridge	d					13 28									14 28									15 28	
Lapworth	d																								
Stratford-upon-Avon	d																								15 20
Wilmcote	d																								15 25
Bearley	d																								15 30
Claverdon	d																								15 36
Hatton	d																								15 42
Warwick Parkway	d					13 39				14 15					14 39				15 15					15 39	
Warwick	d					13 42									14 42									15 42	15 49
Leamington Spa [8]	d					13 47				14 21					14 47				15 20					15 47	15a55
Banbury	d				13 44	14 04				14 39				14 45	15 04				15 39				15 44	16 04	
Kings Sutton	d				13 50																		15 50		
Bicester North [3]	d				14 01	14 16			14 25					15 01	15 16		15 25						16 01	16 16	
Haddenham & Thame Parkway	d				14 14				14 38					15 14			15 38						16 14		
Aylesbury	d	13 50									14 50									15 50					
Little Kimble	d	13 58									14 58									15 58					
Monks Risborough	d	14 02									15 02									16 02					
Princes Risborough [2]	d	14a08		14 10	14 21				14 45		15a08		15 10	15 21			15 45			16a08		16 10	16 21		
Saunderton	d			14 15									15 15									16 15			
High Wycombe [1]	d			14 21	14 31	14 37	14 44		14 55				15 21	15 31	15 37	15 44	15 55					16 21	16 31	16 37	
Beaconsfield	d			14 28			14 50		15 01				15 28			15 50	16 01					16 28			
Seer Green	d						14 53									15 53									
Gerrards Cross [1]	d		14 19	14 34			14 58		15 07			15 19	15 34			15 58	16 07				16 19	16 34			
Denham Golf Club	d		14 22									15 22									16 22				
Denham	d		14 25				15 02					15 25				16 02					16 25				
West Ruislip [3] § ⊖	d						15 06									16 06									
South Ruislip § ⊖	d		14 30									15 30									16 30				
Northolt Park	d		14 34									15 34									16 34				
Sudbury Hill Harrow	d		14 37									15 37									16 37				
Sudbury & Harrow Road	d																								
Wembley Stadium	d		14 41				15 15					15 41				16 15					16 41				
London Paddington [15] ⊖	a																								
London Marylebone [10] ⊖	a		14 58	14 59	15 00	15 07	15 29		15 30	15 31		15 57	15 59	16 00	16 11	16 30	16 31		16 32		16 57	16 59	17 00	17 11	

		CH	CH		CH	CH	CH	CH	CH	CH BZ	CH	CH	CH		CH	CH	CH	CH	CH	CH	CH	CH	CH		CH
										◇	◇	◇						◇	◇			◇			
Kidderminster	d																								
Stourbridge Junction [2]	d																								
Cradley Heath	d																								
Rowley Regis	d																								
Birmingham Snow Hill	d											16 12							16 52						
Birmingham Moor Street	d									15 55		16 15							16 55			17 10			
Solihull	d									16 04		16 23							17 03			17 19			
Dorridge	d											16 28										17 25			
Lapworth	d																								
Stratford-upon-Avon	d																								
Wilmcote	d																								
Bearley	d																								
Claverdon	d																								
Hatton	d																								
Warwick Parkway	d									16 17		16 39							17 15			17 35			
Warwick	d											16 42							17 18			17 38			
Leamington Spa [8]	d									16 24		16 47							17 23			17 43			
Banbury	d									16 42		17 06							17 42			18 02			
Kings Sutton	d																								
Bicester North [3]	d		16 23						16 48	16 55	17 02	17 18					17 23		17 54		18 00	18 14			
Haddenham & Thame Parkway	d		16 36							17 07	17 15						17 36				18 11	18 25			
Aylesbury	d				16 53													17 34					18 22		
Little Kimble	d				17 01													17 42					18 30		
Monks Risborough	d				17 05													17 46					18 34		
Princes Risborough [2]	d		16 43		17a11				17 15		17 23						17 43	17 50			18 18		18a41		
Saunderton	d								17 20									17 55							
High Wycombe [1]	d	16 43	16 53				17 03	17 23	17 28		17 33	17 39			17 45		17 54	18 02		18 16	18 28	18 38			18 43
Beaconsfield	d	16 49	16 59				17 09				17 39				17 52		18 00			18 23	18 34				18 50
Seer Green	d	16 52							17 35						17 55						18 37				
Gerrards Cross [1]	d	16 57	17 05			17 10	17 15	17 33	17 40				17 52		18 00		18 06			18 29	18 42				18 56
Denham Golf Club	d						17 18						17 56							18 32					
Denham	d	17 01					17 21						17 59							18 35					19 00
West Ruislip [3] § ⊖	d	17 05					17 31									18 08				18 40					
South Ruislip § ⊖	d					17 18		17 41										18 18							
Northolt Park	d		17 15					17 45									18 17								19 07
Sudbury Hill Harrow	d					17 23										18 14									19 10
Sudbury & Harrow Road	d																								
Wembley Stadium	d	17 15					17 40				17 57		18 09					18 26		18 49					19 14
London Paddington [15] ⊖	a																								
London Marylebone [10] ⊖	a	17 30	17 33			17 41	17 58	18 02	18 10	17 46	18 13	18 19	18 27		18 30	18 34	18 38	18 45	18 46	19 05	19 08	19 09			19 30

§ London Underground Limited (Central Line) also operate services between South Ruislip and West Ruislip at frequent intervals

BZ Business Zone available offering greater comfort and an enhanced working environment. Supplement payable

Table 115

Mondays to Fridays
until 27 July

Kidderminster, Birmingham Snow Hill, Stratford-upon-Avon, Banbury, Aylesbury and High Wycombe - London

Network Diagram - see first Page of Table 114

		CH	CH	CH	CH	CH	CH	CH	CH		CH	CH	CH	CH	CH	CH	CH	CH	CH		CH	CH	CH	CH	CH
			◇	◇		◇					◇	◇		◇		◇		◇					◇	◇	◇
Kidderminster	d																								
Stourbridge Junction [2]	d																								
Cradley Heath	d																								
Rowley Regis	d																								
Birmingham Snow Hill	d					17 52					18 12	18 40						19 48					20 37		21 42
Birmingham Moor Street	d					17 55					18 15	18 43						19 51					20 40		21 45
Solihull	d					18 04					18 24	18 52						19 59					20 48		21 53
Dorridge	d					18 11					18 29	18 57						20 04					20 53		21 58
Lapworth	d										18 33												20 57		
Stratford-upon-Avon	d			17 40												19 20									
Wilmcote	d			17 46												19 25									
Bearley	d			17 50																					
Claverdon	d			17 56												19 32									
Hatton	d			18 01							18 39					19 37							21 03		
Warwick Parkway	d					18 21					18 44	19 06						20 14					21 08		22 08
Warwick	d			18 08							18 47					19 44		20 17					21 11		22 11
Leamington Spa [8]	d			18 12		18 28					18 53	19 12				19 49		20 22					21 16		22 17
Banbury	d		18 13	18 31		18 46					19 13	19 34				20 08		20 42					21 34	22 05	22 34
Kings Sutton	d		18 18								19 18					20 13									22 39
Bicester North [3]	d		18 30	18 45		19 00		19 07			19 29	19 49		20 00		20 24		20 54	21 02				21 46	22 19	22 49
Haddenham & Thame Parkway	d		18 44					19 19			19 41			20 13		20 35		21 06	21 15				21 56	22 32	23 00
Aylesbury	d								19 22						20 16						21 26				
Little Kimble	d								19 30						20 24						21 34				
Monks Risborough	d								19 34						20 28						21 38				
Princes Risborough [2]	d	18 44	18 52					19 26	19 38		19 49	20 04			20 32	20 42			21 22		21a45	21 51	22 03	22 39	23 08
Saunderton	d		18 57					19 31								20 47						21 56		22 44	
High Wycombe [1]	d	18 54	19 04		19 11	19 22	19 31	19 38	19 48		19 59	20 13	20 19	20 29	20 43	20 53	21 02	21 20	21 32			22 02	22 12	22 51	23 17
Beaconsfield	d	19 00			19 19		19 38	19 44					20 26		20 49		21 09		21 38			22 09	22 18	22 57	
Seer Green	d							19 47					20 29				21 12					22 12		23 00	
Gerrards Cross [1]	d	19 06			19 25		19 44	19 52	19 58				20 34		20 55		21 17		21 44			22 17	22 24	23 05	
Denham Golf Club	d				19 28								20 37				21 20					22 20		23 08	
Denham	d				19 31			19 56					20 40				21 23					22 23		23 11	
West Ruislip [3] § ⊖	d				19 40				20 12						21 07		21 31					22 31		23 16	
South Ruislip § ⊖	d	19 14						20 01					20 46						21 52			22 35		23 20	
Northolt Park	d								20 18				20 49				21 36					22 38		23 23	
Sudbury Hill Harrow	d								20 21																
Sudbury & Harrow Road	d																								
Wembley Stadium	d	19 21			19 49			20 08	20 25				20 55		21 16		21 41	21 37	21 59			22 44	22 37	23 29	23 34
London Paddington [15] ⊖	a																								
London Marylebone [10] ⊖	a	19 37	19 38	19 39	20 05	19 56	20 12	20 24	20 41		20 28	20 44	21 11	21 15	21 32	21 22	21 58	21 53	22 15			23 01	22 53	23 45	23 50

		CH	CH	CH	CH
Kidderminster	d				
Stourbridge Junction [2]	d				
Cradley Heath	d				
Rowley Regis	d				
Birmingham Snow Hill	d				
Birmingham Moor Street	d				
Solihull	d				
Dorridge	d				
Lapworth	d				
Stratford-upon-Avon	d	22 00	23 15		
Wilmcote	d	22 05			
Bearley	d				
Claverdon	d				
Hatton	d	22 17			
Warwick Parkway	d				
Warwick	d	22 24	23 34		
Leamington Spa [8]	d	22a30	23 38		
Banbury	d		23a57		
Kings Sutton	d				
Bicester North [3]	d				
Haddenham & Thame Parkway	d				
Aylesbury	d				23 00
Little Kimble	d				23 08
Monks Risborough	d				23 12
Princes Risborough [2]	d				23 16
Saunderton	d				23 21
High Wycombe [1]	d			23 22	23 27
Beaconsfield	d			23 29	23 33
Seer Green	d				23 36
Gerrards Cross [1]	d			23 35	23 41
Denham Golf Club	d				23 44
Denham	d				23 47
West Ruislip [3] § ⊖	d				23 51
South Ruislip § ⊖	d				23 55
Northolt Park	d				23 59
Sudbury Hill Harrow	d				
Sudbury & Harrow Road	d				
Wembley Stadium	d			23 48	00 04
London Paddington [15] ⊖	a				
London Marylebone [10] ⊖	a			00 06	00 20

§ London Underground Limited (Central Line) also operate services between South Ruislip and West Ruislip at frequent intervals

Table 115

Mondays to Fridays

30 July to 7 September

Kidderminster, Birmingham Snow Hill, Stratford-upon-Avon, Banbury, Aylesbury and High Wycombe - London

Network Diagram - see first Page of Table 114

		CH MX	CH MX	CH	CH	CH	CH	CH	CH	CH	CH	CH	CH	CH ◇ ⌶	CH	CH	CH	CH	CH	CH	CH BZ ◇ ⌶	CH	CH
Kidderminster	d																						
Stourbridge Junction 2	d																						
Cradley Heath	d																						
Rowley Regis	d																						
Birmingham Snow Hill ⇌	d																						
Birmingham Moor Street	d													05 46							06 19		
Solihull	d													05 54							06 29		
Dorridge	d													05 59							06 35		
Lapworth	d																						
Stratford-upon-Avon	d														06 10								
Wilmcote	d														06 16								
Bearley	d														06 19								
Claverdon	d														06 25								
Hatton	d														06 31								
Warwick Parkway	d									05 40				06 09							06 45		
Warwick	d													06 12	06 38								
Leamington Spa 8	d									05 45				06 17	06a45						06 52		
Banbury	d						05 24		05 42	06 03			06 12	06 36						06 52	07 11		
Kings Sutton	d						05 29						06 18										
Bicester North 3	d						05 41		05 57	06 15			06 29	06 48					06 54	07 06			
Haddenham & Thame Parkway	d						05 53		06 09	06 26			06 42						07 07	07 19			
Aylesbury	d		23p00	05 05	05 15	05 25		05 48				06 20				06 39						07 11	
Little Kimble	d		23p08	05 13				05 56				06 28											
Monks Risborough	d		23p12	05 17				06 00				06 32											
Princes Risborough 2	d		23p16	05 21	05 29	05 39	06 00	06 04	06 16	06 33		06 37	06 49						07 14	07 28			
Saunderton	d		23p21	05 26				06 09				06 42											
High Wycombe 1	d	23p22	23p27	05 32	05 39	05 55	06 10	06 16	06 26			06 48	06 59					07 10	07 25				
Beaconsfield	d	23p29	23p33	05 38	05 45	06 02	06 16	06 22	06 33			06 55	07 05					07 17	07 32				
Seer Green	d		23p36	05 41		06 05			06 36			06 58						07 20					
Gerrards Cross 1	d	23p35	23p41	05 46	05 51	06 10	06 22	06 28	06 41		06 52	07 03	07 11				07 19	07 25	07 38				07 50
Denham Golf Club	d		23p44	05 49							06 55							07 29					
Denham	d		23p47	05 52	05 56	06 14		06 32				07 07						07 31					07 54
West Ruislip 3 § ⊖	d		23p51	06 01				06 37				07 12						07 36					
South Ruislip § ⊖	d		23p55	06 05		06 20					07 02						07 27						
Northolt Park	d		23p59	06 08				06 42			07 06						07 31						08 01
Sudbury Hill Harrow	d										07 09						07 34						
Sudbury & Harrow Road	d										07 12						07 37						
Wembley Stadium	d	23p48	00 04	06 13		06 27		06 47			07 15							07 45					08 06
London Paddington 15 ⊖	a																						
London Marylebone 10 ⊖	a	00 06	00 20	06 30	06 19	06 44	06 48	07 00	07 04	07 10	07 29	07 32	07 35	07 38		07 39	07 51	07 58	08 02	08 04	08 06	08 11	08 18

		CH	CH	CH	CH BZ ◇ ⌶	CH	CH	CH	CH ◇	CH	CH	CH	CH	CH ◇	CH ◇ ⌶	CH	CH	CH	CH	CH ◇	CH	CH	CH ◇
Kidderminster	d													06 10									06 59
Stourbridge Junction 2	d													06 18									07 07
Cradley Heath	d													06 24									07 14
Rowley Regis	d													06 30									07 22
Birmingham Snow Hill ⇌	d													06 46									07 44
Birmingham Moor Street	d				06 55									06 59	07 33								07 47
Solihull	d				07 03									07 08	07 41								07 55
Dorridge	d													07 13									08 00
Lapworth	d																						08 04
Stratford-upon-Avon	d								06 47											07 35			
Wilmcote	d																			07 41			
Bearley	d																			07 45			
Claverdon	d																			07 51			
Hatton	d													07 20						08 02			08 10
Warwick Parkway	d				07 16				07 08					07 25	07 53					08 09			08 16
Warwick	d								07 11					07 29									08 19
Leamington Spa 8	d								07 23					07 33	07 58					08 15			08 25
Banbury	d			07 17					07 40					07 51	08 16				08 00	08 34			08 43
Kings Sutton	d																		08 06				
Bicester North 3	d			07 29					07 52					08 05					08 17	08 46			08 56
Haddenham & Thame Parkway	d			07 40					08 03					08 17						08 57			09 07
Aylesbury	d		07 20				07 40	07 44		07 50						08 14					08 50		
Little Kimble	d		07 28							07 58											08 58		
Monks Risborough	d		07 32							08 02											09 02		
Princes Risborough 2	d		07 37				07 58			08a08			08 12	08 24					08 42		09a08		09 14
Saunderton	d		07 42										08 17						08 47				09 19
High Wycombe 1	d	07 42	07 48	07 54			08 08					08 18	08 23	08 34				08 48	08 53			09 12	09 25
Beaconsfield	d	07 49	07 54	08 01			08 15						08 30	08 41				08 55	09 00			09 18	09 32
Seer Green	d	07 52										08 26							09 03				
Gerrards Cross 1	d	07 56	08 00			08 13						08 31	08 35	08 47				09 01	09 08			09 24	09 38
Denham Golf Club	d												08 39					09 04					
Denham	d					08 18							08 41					09 07				09 28	
West Ruislip 3 § ⊖	d		08a08								08 29						08 58		09 14			09 32	
South Ruislip § ⊖	d	08 04											08 47				09 02					09 36	
Northolt Park	d										08 34	08 41							09 20				
Sudbury Hill Harrow	d										08 38						09 06						
Sudbury & Harrow Road	d										08 41						09 09						
Wembley Stadium	d											08 48					09 12		09 25			09 43	
London Paddington 15 ⊖	a																						
London Marylebone 10 ⊖	a	08 21		08 24	08 25	08 38	08 42	08 44	08 48		08 55	09 02	09 05	09 08	09 09	09 14	09 25	09 28	09 38	09 42		09 55	09 58

§ London Underground Limited (Central Line) also operate services between South Ruislip and West Ruislip at frequent intervals

BZ Business Zone available offering greater comfort and an enhanced working environment. Supplement payable

Table 115

Mondays to Fridays

30 July to 7 September

Kidderminster, Birmingham Snow Hill, Stratford-upon-Avon, Banbury, Aylesbury and High Wycombe - London

Network Diagram - see first Page of Table 114

		CH ◇ ⌶	CH	CH	CH	CH ◇ ⌶	CH ◇ ⌶	CH	CH	CH	CH ◇	CH ◇ ⌶	CH	CH	CH ◇	CH ◇ ⌶	CH	CH	CH	CH ◇	CH ◇ ⌶	CH
Kidderminster	d	07 30					08 09															
Stourbridge Junction 2	d	07 40					08 22															
Cradley Heath	d	07 46					08 28															
Rowley Regis	d	07 53					08 34															
Birmingham Snow Hill ⇌	d	08 12				08 22	08 52					09 12									10 12	
Birmingham Moor Street	d	08 15				08 25	08 55					09 15				09 55					10 15	
Solihull	d	08 24				08 37	09 03					09 23				10 03					10 23	
Dorridge	d	08 29				08 50						09 28									10 28	
Lapworth	d					08 54						09 32										
Stratford-upon-Avon	d																			09 55		
Wilmcote	d																			10 00		
Bearley	d																			10 04		
Claverdon	d																			10 09		
Hatton	d					09 00														10 15		
Warwick Parkway	d	08 39					09 15					09 40				10 15					10 39	
Warwick	d	08 43				09 05						09 44								10 23	10 42	
Leamington Spa 8	d	08 48				09 10						09 49				10 21				10 27	10 47	
Banbury	d	09 08				09 29					09 45	10 07				10 38				10 48	11 05	
Kings Sutton	d										09 51											
Bicester North 3	d				09 24	09 41					10 02	10 20			10 27					11 02	11 17	
Haddenham & Thame Parkway	d				09 37						10 15				10 39					11 14		
Aylesbury	d							09 50											10 59			
Little Kimble	d							09 58											11 07			
Monks Risborough	d							10 02											11 11			
Princes Risborough 2	d				09 44			10a08		10 10	10 22				10 46			11 10	11a17	11 21		
Saunderton	d									10 15								11 15				
High Wycombe 1	d			09 41	09 54				10 11	10 21	10 32	10 40		10 45	10 56			11 21		11 31	11 38	11 44
Beaconsfield	d			09 48					10 18	10 27				10 51	11 02			11 28				11 50
Seer Green	d			09 51										10 54								11 53
Gerrards Cross 1	d		09 47	09 56					10 24	10 33			10 44	10 59	11 08		11 19	11 34				11 58
Denham Golf Club	d		09 50														11 22					
Denham	d		09 53						10 28				10 48				11 25					12 02
West Ruislip 3 § ⊖	d			10 02									11 01	11 06								12 06
South Ruislip § ⊖	d								10 33								11 30					
Northolt Park	d		10 00							10 42							11 34					
Sudbury Hill Harrow	d								10 38								11 37					
Sudbury & Harrow Road	d																					
Wembley Stadium	d		10 06						10 42					11 15			11 41					12 15
London Paddington 15 ⊖	a												11 32									
London Marylebone 10 ⊖	a	09 59	10 21	10 25	10 27	10 28	10 29		10 58	10 59	11 00	11 15		11 30	11 31	11 32	11 58	11 59		12 00	12 09	12 29

		CH	CH BZ ◇ ⌶	CH	CH ◇	CH	CH	CH ◇ ⌶	CH	CH ◇	CH ◇ ⌶	CH	CH	CH	CH	CH ◇	CH	CH	CH ◇	CH	CH	CH	CH
Kidderminster	d																						
Stourbridge Junction 2	d																						
Cradley Heath	d																						
Rowley Regis	d																						
Birmingham Snow Hill ⇌	d							11 12								12 12							
Birmingham Moor Street	d		10 55					11 15			11 55					12 15			12 55				
Solihull	d		11 04					11 23			12 03					12 23			13 03				
Dorridge	d							11 28								12 28							
Lapworth	d																						
Stratford-upon-Avon	d									11 20										13 06			
Wilmcote	d									11 25										13 11			
Bearley	d																			13 15			
Claverdon	d									11 32										13 20			
Hatton	d									11 38										13 27			
Warwick Parkway	d		11 15					11 39			12 15					12 39			13 15				
Warwick	d							11 42		11 46						12 42				13 35			
Leamington Spa 8	d		11 21					11 47		11 51	12 20					12 47			13 20	13a41			
Banbury	d		11 39				11 44	12 04		12 11	12 38				12 47	13 04			13 39				
Kings Sutton	d						11 50																
Bicester North 3	d	11 25					12 01	12 16		12 25					13 02	13 16		13 25					
Haddenham & Thame Parkway	d	11 38					12 14			12 38					13 14			13 38					
Aylesbury	d					11 54						12 50									13 50		
Little Kimble	d					12 02						12 58									13 58		
Monks Risborough	d					12 06						13 02									14 02		
Princes Risborough 2	d	11 45			12 10	12a12	12 21			12 45		13a08		13 10	13 21			13 45			14a08		14 10
Saunderton	d				12 15									13 15									14 15
High Wycombe 1	d	11 55			12 21		12 31	12 37	12 44	12 55				13 21	13 31	13 37	13 44	13 55					14 21
Beaconsfield	d	12 01			12 28				12 50	13 01				13 28			13 50	14 01					14 28
Seer Green	d								12 53								13 53						
Gerrards Cross 1	d	12 07		12 19	12 34				12 58	13 07			13 19	13 34			13 58	14 07				14 19	14 34
Denham Golf Club	d			12 22									13 22									14 22	
Denham	d			12 25					13 02				13 25				14 02					14 25	
West Ruislip 3 § ⊖	d								13 06								14 06						
South Ruislip § ⊖	d			12 30									13 30									14 30	
Northolt Park	d			12 34									13 34									14 34	
Sudbury Hill Harrow	d			12 37									13 37									14 37	
Sudbury & Harrow Road	d																						
Wembley Stadium	d			12 41					13 15				13 41				14 15					14 41	
London Paddington 15 ⊖	a																						
London Marylebone 10 ⊖	a	12 30	12 31	12 58	12 59		13 00	13 07	13 29	13 30	13 31		13 58	13 59	14 00	14 09	14 29	14 30	14 31			14 58	14 59

§ London Underground Limited (Central Line) also operate services between South Ruislip and West Ruislip at frequent intervals

BZ Business Zone available offering greater comfort and an enhanced working environment. Supplement payable

Kidderminster, Birmingham Snow Hill, Stratford-upon-Avon, Banbury, Aylesbury and High Wycombe - London

30 July to 7 September

Network Diagram - see first Page of Table 114

		CH ◇	CH ◇	CH	CH	CH ◇	CH	CH	CH	CH ◇	CH ◇	CH	CH	CH ◇	CH	CH	CH	CH ◇	CH ◇	CH ◇	CH	CH
Kidderminster	d																					
Stourbridge Junction	d																					
Cradley Heath	d																					
Rowley Regis	d																					
Birmingham Snow Hill	d		13 12								14 12								15 12			
Birmingham Moor Street	d		13 15			13 55					14 15			14 55					15 15			
Solihull	d		13 23			14 03					14 23			15 03					15 23			
Dorridge	d		13 28								14 28								15 28			
Lapworth	d																					
Stratford-upon-Avon	d																			15 20		
Wilmcote	d																			15 25		
Bearley	d																			15 30		
Claverdon	d																			15 36		
Hatton	d																			15 42		
Warwick Parkway	d		13 39			14 15					14 39			15 15					15 39			
Warwick	d		13 42								14 42								15 42	15 49		
Leamington Spa	d		13 47			14 21					14 47			15 20					15 47	15a55		
Banbury	d	13 44	14 04			14 39				14 45	15 04			15 39				15 44	16 04			
Kings Sutton	d	13 50																15 50				
Bicester North	d	14 01	14 16		14 25					15 01	15 16		15 25					16 01	16 16			16 23
Haddenham & Thame Parkway	d	14 14			14 38					15 14			15 38					16 14				16 36
Aylesbury	d						14 50								15 50							
Little Kimble	d						14 58								15 58							
Monks Risborough	d						15 02								16 02							
Princes Risborough	d	14 21			14 45		15a08		15 10	15 21			15 45		16a08		16 10	16 21				16 43
Saunderton	d								15 15								16 15					
High Wycombe	d	14 31	14 37	14 44	14 55				15 21	15 31	15 37	15 44	15 55				16 21	16 31	16 37		16 43	16 53
Beaconsfield	d			14 50	15 01				15 28			15 50	16 01				16 28				16 49	16 59
Seer Green	d			14 53								15 53									16 52	
Gerrards Cross	d			14 58	15 07			15 19	15 34			15 58	16 07			16 19	16 34				16 57	17 05
Denham Golf Club	d							15 22								16 22						
Denham	d			15 02				15 25				16 02				16 25					17 01	
West Ruislip §	⊖ d			15 06								16 06									17 05	
South Ruislip §	⊖ d							15 30								16 30						
Northolt Park	d							15 34								16 34						17 15
Sudbury Hill Harrow	d							15 37								16 37						
Sudbury & Harrow Road	d																					
Wembley Stadium	d			15 15				15 41				16 15				16 41					17 15	
London Paddington	⊖ a																					
London Marylebone	⊖ a	15 00	15 07	15 29	15 30	15 31		15 57	15 59	16 00	16 11	16 30	16 31	16 32		16 57	16 59	17 00	17 11		17 30	17 33

		CH	CH	CH	CH	CH	CH BZ ◇ ✠	CH ◇	CH ◇	CH	CH	CH	CH	CH ◇	CH ◇	CH	CH	CH ◇	CH	CH	CH	CH ◇	CH ◇
Kidderminster	d																						
Stourbridge Junction	d																						
Cradley Heath	d																						
Rowley Regis	d																						
Birmingham Snow Hill	d								16 12						16 52								
Birmingham Moor Street	d						15 55		16 15						16 55			17 10					
Solihull	d						16 04		16 23						17 03			17 19					
Dorridge	d								16 28									17 25					
Lapworth	d																						
Stratford-upon-Avon	d																						17 40
Wilmcote	d																						17 46
Bearley	d																						17 50
Claverdon	d																						17 56
Hatton	d																						18 01
Warwick Parkway	d						16 17		16 39						17 15			17 35					
Warwick	d								16 42						17 18			17 38					18 08
Leamington Spa	d						16 24		16 47						17 23			17 43					18 12
Banbury	d						16 42		17 06						17 42			18 02				18 13	18 31
Kings Sutton	d																					18 18	
Bicester North	d					16 48	16 55	17 02	17 18				17 23		17 54		18 00	18 14				18 30	18 45
Haddenham & Thame Parkway	d						17 07	17 15					17 36				18 11	18 25				18 44	
Aylesbury	d	16 53												17 34					18 22				
Little Kimble	d	17 01												17 42					18 30				
Monks Risborough	d	17 05												17 46					18 34				
Princes Risborough	d	17a11				17 15		17 23					17 43	17 50			18 18		18a41		18 44	18 52	
Saunderton	d					17 20								17 55								18 57	
High Wycombe	d			17 03	17 23	17 28		17 33	17 39		17 45		17 54	18 02		18 16	18 28	18 38		18 43	18 54	19 04	
Beaconsfield	d			17 09				17 39			17 52		18 00			18 23	18 34			18 50	19 00		
Seer Green	d					17 35					17 55						18 37						
Gerrards Cross	d		17 10	17 15	17 33	17 40				17 52	18 00		18 06			18 29	18 42			18 56	19 06		
Denham Golf Club	d			17 18						17 56						18 32							
Denham	d			17 21						17 59						18 35				19 00			
West Ruislip §	⊖ d			17 31								18 08				18 40							
South Ruislip §	⊖ d		17 18		17 41									18 18							19 14		
Northolt Park	d				17 45								18 17							19 07			
Sudbury Hill Harrow	d		17 23									18 14								19 10			
Sudbury & Harrow Road	d																						
Wembley Stadium	d			17 40				17 57		18 09				18 26		18 49				19 14	19 21		
London Paddington	⊖ a																						
London Marylebone	⊖ a		17 41	17 58	18 02	18 10	17 46	18 13	18 19	18 27	18 30	18 34	18 38	18 45	18 46	19 05	19 08	19 09		19 30	19 37	19 38	19 39

§ London Underground Limited (Central Line) also operate services between South Ruislip and West Ruislip at frequent intervals

BZ Business Zone available offering greater comfort and an enhanced working environment. Supplement payable

Kidderminster, Birmingham Snow Hill, Stratford-upon-Avon, Banbury, Aylesbury and High Wycombe - London

30 July to 7 September

Network Diagram - see first Page of Table 114

		CH	CH ◇	CH	CH	CH	CH ◇	CH ◇	CH	CH ◇	CH	CH ◇	CH	CH ◇	CH	CH	CH	CH ◇	CH ◇	CH ◇	CH	CH	CH
Kidderminster	d																						
Stourbridge Junction	d																						
Cradley Heath	d																						
Rowley Regis	d																						
Birmingham Snow Hill	d		17 52				18 12	18 40						19 48				20 37		21 42			
Birmingham Moor Street	d		17 55				18 15	18 43						19 51				20 40		21 45			
Solihull	d		18 04				18 24	18 52						19 59				20 48		21 53			
Dorridge	d		18 11				18 29	18 57						20 04				20 53		21 58			
Lapworth	d						18 33											20 57					
Stratford-upon-Avon	d											19 20									22 00	23 15	
Wilmcote	d											19 25									22 05		
Bearley	d																						
Claverdon	d											19 32											
Hatton	d						18 39					19 37						21 03			22 17		
Warwick Parkway	d		18 21				18 44	19 06						20 14				21 08		22 08			
Warwick	d						18 47					19 44		20 17				21 11		22 11	22 24	23 34	
Leamington Spa	d		18 28				18 53	19 12				19 49		20 22				21 16		22 17	22a30	23 38	
Banbury	d		18 46				19 13	19 34				20 08		20 42				21 34	22 05	22 34		23a57	
Kings Sutton	d						19 18					20 13								22 39			
Bicester North	d		19 00		19 07		19 29	19 49		20 00		20 24		20 54	21 02			21 46	22 19	22 49			
Haddenham & Thame Parkway	d				19 19		19 41			20 13		20 35		21 06	21 15			21 56	22 32	23 00			
Aylesbury	d					19 22					20 16					21 26							
Little Kimble	d					19 30					20 24					21 34							
Monks Risborough	d					19 34					20 28					21 38							
Princes Risborough	d				19 26	19 38	19 49	20 04			20 32	20 42			21 22	21a45	21 51	22 03	22 39	23 08			
Saunderton	d				19 31							20 47					21 56		22 44				
High Wycombe	d	19 11	19 22	19 31	19 38	19 48	19 59	20 13	20 19	20 29	20 43	20 53	21 02	21 20	21 32		22 02	22 12	22 51	23 17			23 22
Beaconsfield	d	19 19		19 38	19 44				20 26		20 49		21 09		21 38		22 09	22 18	22 57				23 29
Seer Green	d				19 47				20 29				21 12				22 12		23 00				
Gerrards Cross	d	19 25		19 44	19 52	19 58			20 34		20 55		21 17		21 44		22 17	22 24	23 05				23 35
Denham Golf Club	d	19 28							20 37				21 20				22 20		23 08				
Denham	d	19 31			19 56				20 40				21 23				22 23		23 11				
West Ruislip §	⊖ d	19 40				20 12					21 07		21 31				22 31		23 16				
South Ruislip §	⊖ d				20 01				20 46						21 52		22 35		23 20				
Northolt Park	d					20 18			20 49				21 36				22 38		23 23				
Sudbury Hill Harrow	d					20 21																	
Sudbury & Harrow Road	d																						
Wembley Stadium	d	19 49			20 08	20 25			20 55		21 16		21 41	21 37	21 59		22 44	22 37	23 29	23 34			23 48
London Paddington	⊖ a																						
London Marylebone	⊖ a	20 05	19 56	20 12	20 24	20 41	20 28	20 44	21 11	21 15	21 32	21 22	21 58	21 53	22 15		23 01	22 53	23 45	23 50			00 06

		CH
Kidderminster	d	
Stourbridge Junction	d	
Cradley Heath	d	
Rowley Regis	d	
Birmingham Snow Hill	d	
Birmingham Moor Street	d	
Solihull	d	
Dorridge	d	
Lapworth	d	
Stratford-upon-Avon	d	
Wilmcote	d	
Bearley	d	
Claverdon	d	
Hatton	d	
Warwick Parkway	d	
Warwick	d	
Leamington Spa	d	
Banbury	d	
Kings Sutton	d	
Bicester North	d	
Haddenham & Thame Parkway	d	
Aylesbury	d	23 00
Little Kimble	d	23 08
Monks Risborough	d	23 12
Princes Risborough	d	23 16
Saunderton	d	23 21
High Wycombe	d	23 27
Beaconsfield	d	23 33
Seer Green	d	23 36
Gerrards Cross	d	23 41
Denham Golf Club	d	23 44
Denham	d	23 47
West Ruislip §	⊖ d	23 51
South Ruislip §	⊖ d	23 55
Northolt Park	d	23 59
Sudbury Hill Harrow	d	
Sudbury & Harrow Road	d	
Wembley Stadium	d	00 04
London Paddington	⊖ a	
London Marylebone	⊖ a	00 20

§ London Underground Limited (Central Line) also operate services between South Ruislip and West Ruislip at frequent intervals

Table 115

Mondays to Fridays
from 10 September

Kidderminster, Birmingham Snow Hill, Stratford-upon-Avon, Banbury, Aylesbury and High Wycombe - London

Network Diagram - see first Page of Table 114

		CH MX	CH MX	CH	CH	CH	CH	CH	CH	CH	CH	CH	CH	CH ◇ H	CH	CH A	CH B	CH	CH	CH	CH	CH BZ ◇ H	CH A
Kidderminster	d																						
Stourbridge Junction 2	d																						
Cradley Heath	d																						
Rowley Regis	d																						
Birmingham Snow Hill	d																						
Birmingham Moor Street	d													05 46								06 19	
Solihull	d													05 54								06 29	
Dorridge	d													05 59								06 35	
Lapworth	d																						
Stratford-upon-Avon	d														06 10								
Wilmcote	d														06 16								
Bearley	d														06 19								
Claverdon	d														06 25								
Hatton	d														06 31								
Warwick Parkway	d									05 40				06 09								06 45	
Warwick	d													06 12	06 38								
Leamington Spa 8	d									05 45				06 17	06a45							06 52	
Banbury	d						05 24		05 42	06 03			06 12	06 36							06 52	07 11	
Kings Sutton	d						05 29						06 18										
Bicester North 3	d						05 41		05 57	06 15			06 29	06 48						06 54	07 06		
Haddenham & Thame Parkway	d						05 53		06 09	06 26			06 42							07 07	07 19		
Aylesbury	d		23p00	05 05	05 15	05 25		05 48				06 20				06 36	06 39						07 08
Little Kimble	d		23p08	05 13				05 56				06 28											
Monks Risborough	d		23p12	05 17				06 00				06 32											
Princes Risborough 2	d		23p16	05 21	05 29	05 39	06 00	06 04	06 16	06 33		06 37	06 49							07 14	07 28		
Saunderton	d		23p21	05 26				06 09				06 42											
High Wycombe 1	d	23p22	23p27	05 32	05 39	05 55	06 10	06 16	06 26			06 48	06 59						07 10	07 25			
Beaconsfield	d	23p29	23p33	05 38	05 45	06 02	06 16	06 22	06 33			06 55	07 05						07 17	07 32			
Seer Green	d		23p36	05 41		06 05			06 36			06 58							07 20				
Gerrards Cross 1	d	23p35	23p41	05 46	05 51	06 10	06 22	06 28	06 41		06 52	07 03	07 11					07 19	07 25	07 38			
Denham Golf Club	d		23p44	05 49							06 55								07 29				
Denham	d		23p47	05 52	05 56	06 14		06 32				07 07							07 31				
West Ruislip 3 § ⊖	d		23p51	06 01				06 37				07 12							07 36				
South Ruislip § ⊖	d		23p55	06 05		06 20					07 02							07 27					
Northolt Park	d		23p59	06 08				06 42			07 06							07 31					
Sudbury Hill Harrow	d										07 09							07 34					
Sudbury & Harrow Road	d										07 12							07 37					
Wembley Stadium	d	23p48	00 04	06 13		06 27		06 47			07 15								07 45				
London Paddington 15 ⊖	a																						
London Marylebone 10 ⊖	a	00 06	00 20	06 30	06 19	06 44	06 48	07 00	07 04	07 10	07 29	07 32	07 35	07 38		07 39	07 39	07 51	07 58	08 02	08 04	08 06	08 11

§ London Underground Limited (Central Line) also operate services between South Ruislip and West Ruislip at frequent intervals

A from 8 October

B from 10 September until 5 October

BZ Business Zone available offering greater comfort and an enhanced working environment. Supplement payable

Table 115

Mondays to Fridays
from 10 September

Kidderminster, Birmingham Snow Hill, Stratford-upon-Avon, Banbury, Aylesbury and High Wycombe - London

Network Diagram - see first Page of Table 114

		CH A	CH	CH	CH	CH	CH BZ ◇ H	CH	CH	CH B	CH A	CH ◇	CH	CH	CH	CH	CH ◇	CH ◇ H	CH B	CH A	CH	CH	CH
Kidderminster	d																06 10						
Stourbridge Junction 2	d																06 18						
Cradley Heath	d																06 24						
Rowley Regis	d																06 30						
Birmingham Snow Hill	d																06 46						
Birmingham Moor Street	d						06 55										06 59	07 33					
Solihull	d						07 03										07 08	07 41					
Dorridge	d																07 13						
Lapworth	d																						
Stratford-upon-Avon	d											06 47											
Wilmcote	d																						
Bearley	d																						
Claverdon	d																						
Hatton	d																07 20						
Warwick Parkway	d						07 16					07 08					07 25	07 53					
Warwick	d											07 11					07 29						
Leamington Spa 8	d											07 23					07 33	07 58					
Banbury	d					07 17						07 40					07 51	08 16					08 00
Kings Sutton	d																						08 06
Bicester North 3	d					07 29						07 52					08 05						08 17
Haddenham & Thame Parkway	d					07 40						08 03					08 17						
Aylesbury	d	07 11			07 20				07 40	07 41	07 44		07 50						08 11	08 14			
Little Kimble	d				07 28								07 58										
Monks Risborough	d				07 32								08 02										
Princes Risborough 2	d				07 37				07 58				08a08			08 12	08 24						08 42
Saunderton	d				07 42											08 17							08 47
High Wycombe 1	d			07 42	07 48	07 54			08 08						08 18	08 23	08 34					08 48	08 53
Beaconsfield	d			07 49	07 54	08 01			08 15							08 30	08 41					08 55	09 00
Seer Green	d			07 52											08 26								09 03
Gerrards Cross 1	d		07 50	07 56	08 00			08 13							08 31	08 35	08 47					09 01	09 08
Denham Golf Club	d															08 39						09 04	
Denham	d		07 54					08 18								08 41						09 07	
West Ruislip 3 § ⊖	d				08a08									08 29							08 58		09 14
South Ruislip § ⊖	d			08 04												08 47					09 02		
Northolt Park	d		08 01											08 34	08 41								09 20
Sudbury Hill Harrow	d													08 38							09 06		
Sudbury & Harrow Road	d													08 41							09 09		
Wembley Stadium	d		08 06												08 48						09 12		09 25
London Paddington 15 ⊖	a																						
London Marylebone 10 ⊖	a	08 11	08 18	08 21		08 24	08 25	08 38	08 42	08 44	08 44	08 48		08 55	09 02	09 05	09 08	09 09	09 14	09 14	09 25	09 28	09 38

		CH ◇	CH	CH	CH ◇	CH ◇ H	CH	CH	CH	CH ◇ H	CH ◇ H	CH	CH	CH	CH ◇	CH ◇ H	CH	CH	CH ◇	CH ◇ H	CH	CH
Kidderminster	d				06 59	07 30					08 09											
Stourbridge Junction 2	d				07 07	07 40					08 22											
Cradley Heath	d				07 14	07 46					08 28											
Rowley Regis	d				07 22	07 53					08 34											
Birmingham Snow Hill	d				07 44	08 12				08 22	08 52					09 12						
Birmingham Moor Street	d				07 47	08 15				08 25	08 55					09 15				09 55		
Solihull	d				07 55	08 24				08 37	09 03					09 23				10 03		
Dorridge	d				08 00	08 29				08 50						09 28						
Lapworth	d				08 04					08 54						09 32						
Stratford-upon-Avon	d	07 35																				
Wilmcote	d	07 41																				
Bearley	d	07 45																				
Claverdon	d	07 51																				
Hatton	d	08 02			08 10					09 00												
Warwick Parkway	d	08 09			08 16	08 39					09 15					09 40				10 15		
Warwick	d				08 19	08 43				09 05						09 44						
Leamington Spa 8	d	08 15			08 25	08 48				09 10						09 49				10 21		
Banbury	d	08 34			08 43	09 08				09 29					09 45	10 07				10 38		
Kings Sutton	d														09 51							
Bicester North 3	d	08 46			08 56				09 24	09 41					10 02	10 20			10 27			
Haddenham & Thame Parkway	d	08 57			09 07				09 37						10 15				10 39			
Aylesbury	d		08 50									09 50										
Little Kimble	d		08 58									09 58										
Monks Risborough	d		09 02									10 02										
Princes Risborough 2	d		09a08		09 14				09 44			10a08		10 10	10 22				10 46			11 10
Saunderton	d				09 19									10 15								11 15
High Wycombe 1	d			09 12	09 25			09 41	09 54				10 11	10 21	10 32	10 40		10 45	10 56			11 21
Beaconsfield	d			09 18	09 32			09 48					10 18	10 27				10 51	11 02			11 28
Seer Green	d							09 51										10 54				
Gerrards Cross 1	d			09 24	09 38		09 47	09 56					10 24	10 33			10 44	10 59	11 08		11 19	11 34
Denham Golf Club	d						09 50														11 22	
Denham	d			09 28			09 53						10 28				10 48				11 25	
West Ruislip 3 § ⊖	d			09 32				10 02									11 01	11 06				
South Ruislip § ⊖	d			09 36									10 33								11 30	
Northolt Park	d						10 00							10 42							11 34	
Sudbury Hill Harrow	d												10 38								11 37	
Sudbury & Harrow Road	d																					
Wembley Stadium	d			09 43			10 06						10 42					11 15			11 41	
London Paddington 15 ⊖	a																11 32					
London Marylebone 10 ⊖	a	09 42		09 55	09 58	09 59	10 21	10 25	10 27	10 28	10 29		10 58	10 59	11 00	11 15		11 30	11 31	11 32	11 58	11 59

§ London Underground Limited (Central Line) also operate services between South Ruislip and West Ruislip at frequent intervals

A from 10 September until 5 October

B from 8 October

BZ Business Zone available offering greater comfort and an enhanced working environment. Supplement payable

Table 115

Mondays to Fridays

from 10 September

Kidderminster, Birmingham Snow Hill, Stratford-upon-Avon, Banbury, Aylesbury and High Wycombe - London

Network Diagram - see first Page of Table 114

	CH	CH ◇	CH ◇ H	CH	CH	CH BZ ◇ H	CH	CH ◇	CH	CH	CH ◇ H	CH	CH ◇	CH ◇ H	CH	CH	CH	CH	CH ◇	CH	CH	CH ◇
Kidderminster d																						
Stourbridge Junction 2 d																						
Cradley Heath d																						
Rowley Regis d																						
Birmingham Snow Hill d			10 12								11 12								12 12			
Birmingham Moor Street d			10 15			10 55					11 15			11 55					12 15			12 55
Solihull d			10 23			11 04					11 23			12 03					12 23			13 03
Dorridge d			10 28								11 28								12 28			
Lapworth d																						
Stratford-upon-Avon d		09 55											11 20									
Wilmcote d		10 00											11 25									
Bearley d		10 04																				
Claverdon d		10 09											11 32									
Hatton d		10 15											11 38									
Warwick Parkway d			10 39			11 15					11 39			12 15					12 39			13 15
Warwick d		10 23	10 42								11 42		11 46						12 42			
Leamington Spa 8 d		10 27	10 47			11 21					11 47		11 51	12 20					12 47			13 20
Banbury d		10 48	11 05			11 39				11 44	12 04		12 11	12 38				12 47	13 04			13 39
Kings Sutton d										11 50												
Bicester North 3 d		11 02	11 17		11 25					12 01	12 16		12 25					13 02	13 16		13 25	
Haddenham & Thame Parkway d		11 14			11 38					12 14			12 38					13 14			13 38	
Aylesbury d	10 59								11 54						12 50							
Little Kimble d	11 07								12 02						12 58							
Monks Risborough d	11 11								12 06						13 02							
Princes Risborough 2 d	11a17	11 21			11 45			12 10	12a12	12 21			12 45		13a08		13 10	13 21			13 45	
Saunderton d								12 15									13 15					
High Wycombe 1 d		11 31	11 38	11 44	11 55			12 21		12 31	12 37	12 44	12 55				13 21	13 31	13 37	13 44	13 55	
Beaconsfield d				11 50	12 01			12 28				12 50	13 01				13 28			13 50	14 01	
Seer Green d				11 53								12 53								13 53		
Gerrards Cross 1 d				11 58	12 07		12 19	12 34				12 58	13 07			13 19	13 34			13 58	14 07	
Denham Golf Club d							12 22									13 22						
Denham d				12 02			12 25					13 02				13 25				14 02		
West Ruislip 3 § ⊖ d				12 06								13 06								14 06		
South Ruislip § ⊖ d							12 30									13 30						
Northolt Park d							12 34									13 34						
Sudbury Hill Harrow d							12 37									13 37						
Sudbury & Harrow Road d																						
Wembley Stadium d				12 15			12 41					13 15				13 41				14 15		
London Paddington 15 ⊖ a																						
London Marylebone 10 ⊖ a		12 00	12 09	12 29	12 30	12 31	12 58	12 59		13 00	13 07	13 29	13 30	13 31		13 58	13 59	14 00	14 09	14 29	14 30	14 31

	CH	CH	CH	CH	CH ◇	CH ◇	CH	CH	CH ◇	CH	CH	CH	CH ◇	CH ◇	CH	CH	CH ◇	CH	CH	CH	CH ◇
Kidderminster d																					
Stourbridge Junction 2 d																					
Cradley Heath d																					
Rowley Regis d																					
Birmingham Snow Hill d						13 12								14 12							
Birmingham Moor Street d						13 15			13 55					14 15			14 55				
Solihull d						13 23			14 03					14 23			15 03				
Dorridge d						13 28								14 28							
Lapworth d																					
Stratford-upon-Avon d	13 06																				
Wilmcote d	13 11																				
Bearley d	13 15																				
Claverdon d	13 20																				
Hatton d	13 27																				
Warwick Parkway d						13 39			14 15					14 39			15 15				
Warwick d	13 35					13 42								14 42							
Leamington Spa 8 d	13a41					13 47			14 21					14 47			15 20				
Banbury d					13 44	14 04			14 39				14 45	15 04			15 39				15 44
Kings Sutton d					13 50																15 50
Bicester North 3 d					14 01	14 16		14 25					15 01	15 16		15 25					16 01
Haddenham & Thame Parkway d					14 14			14 38					15 14			15 38					16 14
Aylesbury d		13 50								14 50								15 50			
Little Kimble d		13 58								14 58								15 58			
Monks Risborough d		14 02								15 02								16 02			
Princes Risborough 2 d		14a08		14 10	14 21			14 45		15a08		15 10	15 21			15 45		16a08		16 10	16 21
Saunderton d				14 15								15 15								16 15	
High Wycombe 1 d				14 21	14 31	14 37	14 44	14 55				15 21	15 31	15 37	15 44	15 55				16 21	16 31
Beaconsfield d				14 28			14 50	15 01				15 28			15 50	16 01				16 28	
Seer Green d							14 53								15 53						
Gerrards Cross 1 d			14 19	14 34			14 58	15 07			15 19	15 34			15 58	16 07			16 19	16 34	
Denham Golf Club d			14 22								15 22								16 22		
Denham d			14 25				15 02				15 25				16 02				16 25		
West Ruislip 3 § ⊖ d							15 06								16 06						
South Ruislip § ⊖ d			14 30								15 30								16 30		
Northolt Park d			14 34								15 34								16 34		
Sudbury Hill Harrow d			14 37								15 37								16 37		
Sudbury & Harrow Road d																					
Wembley Stadium d			14 41				15 15				15 41				16 15				16 41		
London Paddington 15 ⊖ a																					
London Marylebone 10 ⊖ a			14 58	14 59	15 00	15 07	15 29	15 30	15 31		15 57	15 59	16 00	16 11	16 30	16 31	16 32		16 57	16 59	17 00

§ London Underground Limited (Central Line) also operate services between South Ruislip and West Ruislip at frequent intervals

BZ Business Zone available offering greater comfort and an enhanced working environment. Supplement payable

Table 115

Mondays to Fridays

from 10 September

Kidderminster, Birmingham Snow Hill, Stratford-upon-Avon, Banbury, Aylesbury and High Wycombe - London

Network Diagram - see first Page of Table 114

	CH ◇	CH ◇	CH	CH	CH	CH	CH	CH	CH	CH BZ ◇ H	CH ◇	CH ◇	CH	CH	CH	CH	CH ◇	CH ◇	CH	CH	CH ◇	CH
Kidderminster d																						
Stourbridge Junction 2 d																						
Cradley Heath d																						
Rowley Regis d																						
Birmingham Snow Hill d	15 12										16 12						16 52					
Birmingham Moor Street d	15 15								15 55		16 15						16 55			17 10		
Solihull d	15 23								16 04		16 23						17 03			17 19		
Dorridge d	15 28										16 28									17 25		
Lapworth d																						
Stratford-upon-Avon d		15 20																				
Wilmcote d		15 25																				
Bearley d		15 30																				
Claverdon d		15 36																				
Hatton d		15 42																				
Warwick Parkway d	15 39								16 17		16 39						17 15			17 35		
Warwick d	15 42	15 49									16 42						17 18			17 38		
Leamington Spa 8 d	15 47	15a55							16 24		16 47						17 23			17 43		
Banbury d	16 04								16 42		17 06						17 42			18 02		
Kings Sutton d																						
Bicester North 3 d	16 16			16 23					16 48	16 55	17 02	17 18				17 23		17 54		18 00	18 14	
Haddenham & Thame Parkway d				16 36						17 07	17 15					17 36				18 11	18 25	
Aylesbury d					16 53												17 34					18 22
Little Kimble d					17 01												17 42					18 30
Monks Risborough d					17 05												17 46					18 34
Princes Risborough 2 d				16 43	17a11				17 15		17 23					17 43	17 50			18 18		18a41
Saunderton d									17 20								17 55					
High Wycombe 1 d	16 37		16 43	16 53			17 03	17 23	17 28		17 33	17 39		17 45		17 54	18 02		18 16	18 28	18 38	
Beaconsfield d			16 49	16 59			17 09				17 39			17 52		18 00			18 23	18 34		
Seer Green d			16 52						17 35					17 55						18 37		
Gerrards Cross 1 d			16 57	17 05		17 10	17 15	17 33	17 40				17 52	18 00		18 06			18 29	18 42		
Denham Golf Club d							17 18						17 56						18 32			
Denham d			17 01				17 21						17 59						18 35			
West Ruislip 3 § ⊖ d			17 05				17 31								18 08				18 40			
South Ruislip § ⊖ d						17 18		17 41									18 18					
Northolt Park d				17 15				17 45								18 17						
Sudbury Hill Harrow d						17 23									18 14							
Sudbury & Harrow Road d																						
Wembley Stadium d			17 15				17 40				17 57		18 09				18 26		18 49			
London Paddington 15 ⊖ a																						
London Marylebone 10 ⊖ a	17 11		17 30	17 33		17 41	17 58	18 02	18 10	17 46	18 13	18 19	18 27	18 30	18 34	18 38	18 45	18 46	19 05	19 08	19 09	

	CH	CH	CH ◇	CH ◇	CH	CH ◇	CH	CH	CH	CH ◇	CH ◇	CH	CH ◇	CH	CH ◇	CH	CH ◇	CH	CH	CH	CH ◇	CH ◇
Kidderminster d																						
Stourbridge Junction 2 d																						
Cradley Heath d																						
Rowley Regis d																						
Birmingham Snow Hill d						17 52				18 12	18 40						19 48				20 37	
Birmingham Moor Street d						17 55				18 15	18 43						19 51				20 40	
Solihull d						18 04				18 24	18 52						19 59				20 48	
Dorridge d						18 11				18 29	18 57						20 04				20 53	
Lapworth d										18 33											20 57	
Stratford-upon-Avon d				17 40											19 20							
Wilmcote d				17 46											19 25							
Bearley d				17 50																		
Claverdon d				17 56											19 32							
Hatton d				18 01						18 39					19 37						21 03	
Warwick Parkway d						18 21				18 44	19 06						20 14				21 08	
Warwick d				18 08						18 47					19 44		20 17				21 11	
Leamington Spa 8 d				18 12		18 28				18 53	19 12				19 49		20 22				21 16	
Banbury d			18 13	18 31		18 46				19 13	19 34				20 08		20 42				21 34	22 05
Kings Sutton d			18 18							19 18					20 13							
Bicester North 3 d			18 30	18 45		19 00		19 07		19 29	19 49		20 00		20 24		20 54	21 02			21 46	22 19
Haddenham & Thame Parkway d			18 44					19 19		19 41			20 13		20 35		21 06	21 15			21 56	22 32
Aylesbury d									19 22					20 16					21 26			
Little Kimble d									19 30					20 24					21 34			
Monks Risborough d									19 34					20 28					21 38			
Princes Risborough 2 d		18 44	18 52					19 26	19 38	19 49	20 04			20 32	20 42			21 22	21a45	21 51	22 03	22 39
Saunderton d			18 57					19 31							20 47					21 56		22 44
High Wycombe 1 d	18 43	18 54	19 04		19 11	19 22	19 31	19 38	19 48	19 59	20 13	20 19	20 29	20 43	20 53	21 02	21 20	21 32		22 02	22 12	22 51
Beaconsfield d	18 50	19 00			19 19		19 38	19 44				20 26		20 49		21 09		21 38		22 09	22 18	22 57
Seer Green d								19 47				20 29				21 12				22 12		23 00
Gerrards Cross 1 d	18 56	19 06			19 25		19 44	19 52	19 58			20 34		20 55		21 17		21 44		22 17	22 24	23 05
Denham Golf Club d					19 28							20 37				21 20				22 20		23 08
Denham d	19 00				19 31			19 56				20 40				21 23				22 23		23 11
West Ruislip 3 § ⊖ d					19 40				20 12					21 07		21 31				22 31		23 16
South Ruislip § ⊖ d		19 14						20 01				20 46						21 52		22 35		23 20
Northolt Park d	19 07								20 18			20 49				21 36				22 38		23 23
Sudbury Hill Harrow d	19 10								20 21													
Sudbury & Harrow Road d																						
Wembley Stadium d	19 14	19 21			19 49			20 08	20 25			20 55		21 16		21 41	21 37	21 59		22 44	22 37	23 29
London Paddington 15 ⊖ a																						
London Marylebone 10 ⊖ a	19 30	19 37	19 38	19 39	20 05	19 56	20 12	20 24	20 41	20 28	20 44	21 11	21 15	21 32	21 22	21 58	21 53	22 15		23 01	22 53	23 45

§ London Underground Limited (Central Line) also operate services between South Ruislip and West Ruislip at frequent intervals

BZ Business Zone available offering greater comfort and an enhanced working environment. Supplement payable

Table 115

Mondays to Fridays
from 10 September

Kidderminster, Birmingham Snow Hill, Stratford-upon-Avon, Banbury, Aylesbury and High Wycombe - London

Network Diagram - see first Page of Table 114

		CH	CH	CH	CH	CH
		◇				
Kidderminster	d					
Stourbridge Junction 2	d					
Cradley Heath	d					
Rowley Regis	d					
Birmingham Snow Hill ⇌	d	21 42				
Birmingham Moor Street	d	21 45				
Solihull	d	21 53				
Dorridge	d	21 58				
Lapworth	d					
Stratford-upon-Avon	d		22 00	23 15		
Wilmcote	d		22 05			
Bearley	d					
Claverdon	d					
Hatton	d		22 17			
Warwick Parkway	d	22 08				
Warwick	d	22 11	22 24	23 34		
Leamington Spa 8	d	22 17	22a30	23 38		
Banbury	d	22 34		23a57		
Kings Sutton	d	22 39				
Bicester North 3	d	22 49				
Haddenham & Thame Parkway	d	23 00				
Aylesbury	d					23 00
Little Kimble	d					23 08
Monks Risborough	d					23 12
Princes Risborough 2	d	23 08				23 16
Saunderton	d					23 21
High Wycombe 1	d	23 17			23 22	23 27
Beaconsfield	d				23 29	23 33
Seer Green	d					23 36
Gerrards Cross 1	d				23 35	23 41
Denham Golf Club	d					23 44
Denham	d					23 47
West Ruislip 3 § ⊖	d					23 51
South Ruislip § ⊖	d					23 55
Northolt Park	d					23 59
Sudbury Hill Harrow	d					
Sudbury & Harrow Road	d					
Wembley Stadium	d	23 34			23 48	00 04
London Paddington 15 ⊖	a					
London Marylebone 10 ⊖	a	23 50			00 06	00 20

Saturdays
until 21 July

		CH	CH	CH	CH	CH	CH	CH	CH	CH	CH	CH	CH	CH	CH	CH	CH	CH	CH	CH	CH	CH	CH
									◇	◇			◇	◇		◇		◇		◇			◇
Kidderminster	d												06 37	07 14						08 13			
Stourbridge Junction 2	d												06 45	07 22						08 26			
Cradley Heath	d												06 51	07 28						08 32			
Rowley Regis	d												06 57	07 34						08 37			
Birmingham Snow Hill ⇌	d												07 12	07 52						08 52			09 12
Birmingham Moor Street	d								06 15	06 44			07 15	07 55				08 15		08 55			09 15
Solihull	d								06 24	06 53			07 24	08 04				08 25		09 05			09 23
Dorridge	d								06 29	06 58			07 29					08 30					09 28
Lapworth	d								06 33														
Stratford-upon-Avon	d															08 00							
Wilmcote	d																						
Bearley	d																						
Claverdon	d															08 10							
Hatton	d								06 39							08 17							
Warwick Parkway	d								06 44	07 07			07 39	08 18				08 39		09 19			09 38
Warwick	d								06 47				07 42			08 24		08 43					09 41
Leamington Spa 8	d								06 52	07 14			07 47	08 24		08 29		08 48		09 24			09 47
Banbury	d					06 05	06 29		07 10	07 31			08 05	08 44		08 49		09 10		09 45	09 25		10 05
Kings Sutton	d						06 34									08 54					09 31		
Bicester North 3	d					06 19	06 45		07 23	07 44			08 17			09 05		09 22			09 42		10 18
Haddenham & Thame Parkway	d					06 31	06 57		07 33	07 55			08 28			09 18		09 33			09 55		10 28
Aylesbury	d		23p00	05 15	05 55			06 55			07 50	08 10			08 55		09 10					10 10	
Little Kimble	d		23p08	05 23	06 03			07 03			07 58						09 18					10 18	
Monks Risborough	d		23p12	05 27	06 07			07 07			08 02				09 06		09 22					10 22	
Princes Risborough 2	d		23p16	05 31	06 11	06 38		07 11	07 41		08 06	08 24	08 35		09 10	09 25	09a31	09 41			10 09	10a28	10 36
Saunderton	d		23p21	05 36	06 16			07 16			08 11	08 29				09 30					10 15		
High Wycombe 1	d	23p22	23p27	05 42	06 22	06 48	07 11	07 22	07 50		08 17	08 50	08 45		09 20	09 37		09 50	09 54		10 21		10 45
Beaconsfield	d	23p29	23p33	05 49	06 29	06 54		07 29	07 56		08 24	08 56			09 26	09 43			10 01		10 28		
Seer Green	d		23p36	05 52	06 32			07 32			08 27				09 29						10 31		
Gerrards Cross 1	d	23p35	23p41	05 57	06 37	07 00		07 37	08 02		08 32	09 02			09 35	09 49			10 07		10 36		
Denham Golf Club	d		23p44	06 00	06 40			07 40			08 35				09 39								
Denham	d		23p47	06 03	06 43			07 43			08 38	09 06			09 41				10 11				
West Ruislip 3 § ⊖	d		23p51	06 07	06 47			07 47			08 42				09 46								
South Ruislip § ⊖	d		23p55	06 11	06 51			07 51			08 46	09 12							10 16				
Northolt Park	d		23p59	06 15	06 55			07 55			08 50	09 15							10 20				
Sudbury Hill Harrow	d																						
Sudbury & Harrow Road	d																						
Wembley Stadium	d	23p48	00 04	06 20	07 00	07 12		08 00			08 55	09 20			09 54				10 25				
London Paddington 15 ⊖	a																						
London Marylebone 10 ⊖	a	00 06	00 20	06 33	07 13	07 25	07 42	08 13	08 22	08 32	09 08	09 33	09 12	09 39	10 08	10 12		10 16	10 38	10 42	10 59		11 12

§ London Underground Limited (Central Line) also operate services between South Ruislip and West Ruislip at frequent intervals

Table 115

Saturdays
until 21 July

Kidderminster, Birmingham Snow Hill, Stratford-upon-Avon, Banbury, Aylesbury and High Wycombe - London

Network Diagram - see first Page of Table 114

		CH	CH	CH	CH	CH	CH	CH	CH	CH	CH	CH	CH	CH	CH	CH	CH	CH	CH	CH	CH	CH	CH
				◇	◇			◇			◇			◇	◇	◇			◇		◇		
Kidderminster	d				09 03																		
Stourbridge Junction 2	d				09 16																		
Cradley Heath	d				09 22																		
Rowley Regis	d				09 28																		
Birmingham Snow Hill ⇌	d				09 52			10 12						11 12					12 12				
Birmingham Moor Street	d				09 55			10 15			10 55			11 15		11 55			12 15		12 55		
Solihull	d				10 05			10 24			11 03			11 23		12 04			12 23		13 05		
Dorridge	d							10 30						11 28					12 28				
Lapworth	d																						
Stratford-upon-Avon	d			09 19											11 34								
Wilmcote	d			09 25											11 41								
Bearley	d			09 28											11 44								
Claverdon	d			09 34											11 50								
Hatton	d			09 41											11 57								
Warwick Parkway	d				10 19			10 39			11 15			11 38		12 20			12 38		13 18		
Warwick	d			09 48				10 43						11 41	12 04				12 41				
Leamington Spa 8	d			09 54	10 25			10 48			11 20			11 47	12 08	12 26			12 47		13 24		
Banbury	d			10 14	10 46			11 08		11 12	11 40			12 04	12 26	12 46			13 08	13 12	13 44		
Kings Sutton	d									11 18										13 18			
Bicester North 3	d			10 33	10 58			11 22		11 33	11 54			12 20	12 38	12 58			13 22	13 29	13 56		
Haddenham & Thame Parkway	d			10 46				11 33		11 46				12 31	12 48				13 33	13 42			
Aylesbury	d					11 10						12 10					13 10					14 10	
Little Kimble	d					11 18						12 18					13 18					14 18	
Monks Risborough	d					11 22						12 22					13 22					14 22	
Princes Risborough 2	d			10 54		11a30		11 41		11 54		12a28		12 38	12 55		13a30		13 40	13 50		14a28	
Saunderton	d			10 59						11 59					13 00					13 55			
High Wycombe 1	d		10 54	11 06			11 24	11 50		12 06			12 19	12 48	13 07			13 19	13 50	14 01			14 19
Beaconsfield	d		11 01	11 12			11 31			12 12			12 26		13 13			13 26		14 08			14 26
Seer Green	d						11 34						12 29					13 29					14 29
Gerrards Cross 1	d	10 42	11 07	11 18			11 39		12 06	12 18			12 34		13 19			13 34		14 14			14 34
Denham Golf Club	d	10 46					11 42						12 37					13 37					14 37
Denham	d	10 49	11 11				11 45		12 10				12 40					13 40					14 40
West Ruislip 3 § ⊖	d	10 56					11 49						12 45					13 45					14 45
South Ruislip § ⊖	d		11 16						12 16				12 49					13 49					14 49
Northolt Park	d		11 20						12 19				12 53					13 53					14 53
Sudbury Hill Harrow	d																						
Sudbury & Harrow Road	d																						
Wembley Stadium	d	11 04	11 25				11 58		12 25				12 58		13 29			13 58		14 26			14 58
London Paddington 15 ⊖	a																						
London Marylebone 10 ⊖	a	11 21	11 38	11 42	11 46		12 12	12 16	12 38	12 42	12 46		13 11	13 16	13 43	13 46		14 12	14 16	14 39	14 42		15 11

		CH	CH	CH	CH	CH	CH	CH	CH	CH	CH	CH	CH	CH	CH	CH	CH	CH	CH	CH	CH	CH
		◇	◇	◇			◇		◇			◇		◇	◇			◇			◇	
Kidderminster	d																					
Stourbridge Junction 2	d																					
Cradley Heath	d																					
Rowley Regis	d																					
Birmingham Snow Hill ⇌	d	13 12					14 12					15 12						16 12				
Birmingham Moor Street	d	13 15		13 55			14 15		14 55			15 15			15 55			16 15			16 55	
Solihull	d	13 23		14 03			14 23		15 03			15 23			16 03			16 23			17 03	
Dorridge	d	13 28					14 28					15 28						16 28				
Lapworth	d																					
Stratford-upon-Avon	d		13 19											15 19								
Wilmcote	d		13 25											15 25								
Bearley	d		13 28																			
Claverdon	d		13 33											15 32								
Hatton	d		13 41											15 42								
Warwick Parkway	d	13 38		14 15			14 38		15 15			15 38			16 15			16 38			17 15	
Warwick	d	13 41	13 48				14 41					15 41		15 49				16 41				
Leamington Spa 8	d	13 47	13 54	14 21			14 47		15 21			15 47		15 55	16 21			16 47			17 21	
Banbury	d	14 08	14 13	14 42			15 08	15 12	15 41			16 07		16 15	16 44			17 07		17 12	17 43	
Kings Sutton	d							15 18												17 18		
Bicester North 3	d	14 21	14 28	14 55			15 22	15 30	15 54			16 21		16 31	16 58			17 21		17 31	17 57	
Haddenham & Thame Parkway	d	14 31	14 41				15 33	15 42				16 32		16 44				17 32		17 44		
Aylesbury	d				15 10						16 10						17 10					
Little Kimble	d				15 18						16 18						17 18					
Monks Risborough	d				15 22						16 22						17 22					
Princes Risborough 2	d	14 38	14 49		15a30		15 40	15 50		16 09	16a30	16 40		16 51		17 14	17a30	17 40		17 51		18 14
Saunderton	d		14 54					15 55						16 57						17 57		
High Wycombe 1	d	14 49	15 01			15 19	15 49	16 02		16 19		16 49	16 54	17 05		17 24		17 49	17 54	18 06		18 24
Beaconsfield	d		15 07			15 26		16 08		16 26			17 01	17 12		17 31			18 01	18 12		18 31
Seer Green	d					15 29				16 29						17 34						18 34
Gerrards Cross 1	d		15 13			15 34		16 14		16 34			17 07	17 18		17 39			18 07	18 18		18 39
Denham Golf Club	d					15 37				16 37						17 42						18 42
Denham	d					15 40		16 18		16 40			17 11			17 45			18 11			18 45
West Ruislip 3 § ⊖	d					15 45				16 45						17 49						18 49
South Ruislip § ⊖	d					15 49				16 49			17 16						18 16			
Northolt Park	d					15 53				16 53			17 20						18 20			
Sudbury Hill Harrow	d																					
Sudbury & Harrow Road	d																					
Wembley Stadium	d		15 25			15 58		16 28		16 58			17 25			17 58			18 25			18 58
London Paddington 15 ⊖	a																					
London Marylebone 10 ⊖	a	15 16	15 38	15 42		16 11	16 16	16 42	16 46	17 11		17 16	17 38	17 41	17 46	18 11		18 16	18 38	18 42	18 46	19 11

§ London Underground Limited (Central Line) also operate services between South Ruislip and West Ruislip at frequent intervals

Saturdays until 21 July

Kidderminster, Birmingham Snow Hill, Stratford-upon-Avon, Banbury, Aylesbury and High Wycombe - London

Network Diagram - see first Page of Table 114

	CH	CH ◇	CH ◇	CH	CH	CH ◇	CH	CH	CH ◇	CH	CH ◇	CH ◇	CH	CH ◇	CH	CH	CH ◇	CH
Kidderminster d																		
Stourbridge Junction d																		
Cradley Heath d																		
Rowley Regis d																		
Birmingham Snow Hill d		17 12				17 52			18 42			19 42		20 42			21 20	
Birmingham Moor Street d		17 15				17 55			18 45			19 45		20 45			21 23	
Solihull d		17 23				18 03			18 53			19 53		20 53			21 31	
Dorridge d		17 28							18 58			19 58		20 58			21 38	
Lapworth d												20 03		21 03			21 43	
Stratford-upon-Avon d			17 40								19 16				21 16			
Wilmcote d											19 22							
Bearley d											19 25							
Claverdon d											19 31							
Hatton d											19 36	20 09		21 09			21 49	
Warwick Parkway d		17 38				18 15			19 08		19 43	20 14		21 14			21 54	
Warwick d		17 41	18 02			18 18			19 11		19 46	20 17		21 17	21 37		21 57	
Leamington Spa d		17 47	18 06			18 24			19 17		19 52	20 23		21 21	21a48		22 03	
Banbury d		18 06	18 24			18 46			19 34		20 11	20 46		21 39			22 20	
Kings Sutton d											20 16						22 25	
Bicester North d		18 19	18 36		18 43	19 01			19 47		20 27	20 58		21 52			22 35	
Haddenham & Thame Parkway d		18 30			18 54				19 58		20 39	21 09		22 02			22 47	
Aylesbury d	18 10							19 08					21 20			22 20		22 45
Little Kimble d	18 18							19 16					21 28					22 53
Monks Risborough d	18 22							19 20					21 32					22 57
Princes Risborough d	18a28	18 38			19 01			19 24	20 06		20 46	21 16	21 36	22 10		22 34	22 55	23 01
Saunderton d					19 06			19 29			20 51		21 41					23 06
High Wycombe d		18 47		18 58	19 13		19 28	19 48	20 15	20 28	20 58	21 25	21 47	22 19		22 44	23 05	23 12
Beaconsfield d				19 05	19 19		19 35	19 54		20 35	21 04	21 31	21 54	22 25		22 50		23 19
Seer Green d							19 38			20 38	21 07		21 57			22 53		23 22
Gerrards Cross d				19 11	19 25		19 43	20 00		20 43	21 12	21 37	22 02	22 30		22 58		23 27
Denham Golf Club d							19 46			20 46	21 16		22 05			23 02		23 30
Denham d				19 15			19 49	20 04		20 49	21 18		22 08			23 04		23 33
West Ruislip § d							19 53			20 53	21 23		22 12			23 09		23 37
South Ruislip § d				19 20				20 10			21 27		22 16			23 13		23 41
Northolt Park d				19 24				20 13		20 59	21 30		22 20			23 16		23 45
Sudbury Hill Harrow d																		
Sudbury & Harrow Road d																		
Wembley Stadium d				19 29			20 02	20 18		21 04	21 35		22 25			23 21	23 25	23 50
London Paddington a																		
London Marylebone a		19 16	19 22	19 42	19 46	19 49	20 16	20 31	20 42	21 17	21 46	21 57	22 38	22 58		23 34	23 37	00 03

Saturdays 28 July to 8 September

	CH	CH	CH	CH	CH	CH	CH	CH ◇	CH ◇	CH	CH	CH ◇	CH ◇	CH	CH ◇	CH	CH ◇	CH	CH ◇	CH	CH	CH ◇
Kidderminster d												06 37	07 14						08 13			
Stourbridge Junction d												06 45	07 22						08 26			
Cradley Heath d												06 51	07 28						08 32			
Rowley Regis d												06 57	07 34						08 37			
Birmingham Snow Hill d												07 12	07 52						08 52			09 12
Birmingham Moor Street d								06 15	06 44			07 15	07 55				08 15		08 55			09 15
Solihull d								06 24	06 53			07 24	08 04				08 25		09 05			09 23
Dorridge d								06 29	06 58			07 29					08 30					09 28
Lapworth d								06 33														
Stratford-upon-Avon d															08 00							
Wilmcote d																						
Bearley d																						
Claverdon d															08 10							
Hatton d								06 39							08 17							
Warwick Parkway d								06 44	07 07			07 39	08 18				08 39		09 19			09 38
Warwick d								06 47				07 42			08 24		08 43					09 41
Leamington Spa d								06 52	07 14			07 47	08 24		08 29		08 48		09 24			09 47
Banbury d					06 05	06 29		07 10	07 31			08 05	08 44		08 49		09 10		09 45	09 25		10 05
Kings Sutton d						06 34									08 54					09 31		
Bicester North d					06 19	06 45		07 23	07 44			08 17			09 05		09 22			09 42		10 18
Haddenham & Thame Parkway d					06 31	06 57		07 33	07 55			08 28			09 18		09 33			09 55		10 28
Aylesbury d		23p00	05 15	05 55			06 55			07 50	08 10			08 55		09 10					10 10	
Little Kimble d		23p08	05 23	06 03			07 03			07 58						09 18					10 18	
Monks Risborough d		23p12	05 27	06 07			07 07			08 02				09 06		09 22					10 22	
Princes Risborough d		23p16	05 31	06 11	06 38		07 11	07 41		08 06	08 24	08 35		09 10	09 25	09a31	09 41			10 09	10a28	10 36
Saunderton d		23p21	05 36	06 16			07 16			08 11	08 29				09 30					10 15		
High Wycombe d	23p22	23p27	05 42	06 22	06 48	07 11	07 22	07 50		08 17	08 50	08 45		09 20	09 37		09 50	09 54		10 21		10 45
Beaconsfield d	23p29	23p33	05 49	06 29	06 54		07 29	07 56		08 24	08 56			09 26	09 43			10 01		10 28		
Seer Green d		23p36	05 52	06 32			07 32			08 27				09 29						10 31		
Gerrards Cross d	23p35	23p41	05 57	06 37	07 00		07 37	08 02		08 32	09 02			09 35	09 49			10 07		10 36		
Denham Golf Club d		23p44	06 00	06 40			07 40			08 35				09 39								
Denham d		23p47	06 03	06 43			07 43			08 38	09 06			09 41				10 11				
West Ruislip § d		23p51	06 07	06 47			07 47			08 42				09 46								
South Ruislip § d		23p55	06 11	06 51			07 51			08 46	09 12							10 16				
Northolt Park d		23p59	06 15	06 55			07 55			08 50	09 15							10 20				
Sudbury Hill Harrow d																						
Sudbury & Harrow Road d																						
Wembley Stadium d	23p48	00 04	06 20	07 00	07 12		08 00			08 55	09 20			09 54				10 25				
London Paddington a																						
London Marylebone a	00 06	00 20	06 33	07 13	07 25	07 42	08 13	08 22	08 32	09 08	09 33	09 12	09 39	10 08	10 12		10 16	10 38	10 42	10 59		11 12

§ London Underground Limited (Central Line) also operate services between South Ruislip and West Ruislip at frequent intervals

Saturdays 28 July to 8 September

Kidderminster, Birmingham Snow Hill, Stratford-upon-Avon, Banbury, Aylesbury and High Wycombe - London

Network Diagram - see first Page of Table 114

	CH	CH	CH ◇	CH ◇	CH	CH	CH ◇	CH	CH	CH ◇	CH	CH	CH ◇	CH ◇	CH ◇	CH	CH	CH ◇	CH	CH ◇	CH	CH
Kidderminster d				09 03																		
Stourbridge Junction d				09 16																		
Cradley Heath d				09 22																		
Rowley Regis d				09 28																		
Birmingham Snow Hill d				09 52			10 12						11 12					12 12				
Birmingham Moor Street d				09 55			10 15			10 55			11 15		11 55			12 15		12 55		
Solihull d				10 05			10 24			11 03			11 23		12 04			12 23		13 05		
Dorridge d							10 30						11 28					12 28				
Lapworth d																						
Stratford-upon-Avon d			09 19											11 34								
Wilmcote d			09 25											11 41								
Bearley d			09 28											11 44								
Claverdon d			09 34											11 50								
Hatton d			09 41											11 57								
Warwick Parkway d				10 19			10 39			11 15			11 38		12 20			12 38		13 18		
Warwick d			09 48				10 43						11 41	12 04				12 41				
Leamington Spa d			09 54	10 25			10 48			11 20			11 47	12 08	12 26			12 47		13 24		
Banbury d			10 14	10 46			11 08		11 12	11 40			12 04	12 26	12 46			13 08	13 12	13 44		
Kings Sutton d									11 18										13 18			
Bicester North d			10 33	10 58			11 22		11 33	11 54			12 20	12 38	12 58			13 22	13 29	13 56		
Haddenham & Thame Parkway d			10 46				11 33		11 46				12 31	12 48				13 33	13 42			
Aylesbury d					11 10						12 10					13 10					14 10	
Little Kimble d					11 18						12 18					13 18					14 18	
Monks Risborough d					11 22						12 22					13 22					14 22	
Princes Risborough d			10 54		11a30		11 41		11 54		12a28		12 38	12 55		13a30		13 40	13 50		14a28	
Saunderton d			10 59						11 59					13 00					13 55			
High Wycombe d		10 54	11 06			11 24	11 50		12 06			12 19	12 48	13 07			13 19	13 50	14 01			14 19
Beaconsfield d		11 01	11 12			11 31			12 12			12 26		13 13			13 26		14 08			14 26
Seer Green d						11 34						12 29					13 29					14 29
Gerrards Cross d	10 42	11 07	11 18			11 39		12 06	12 18			12 34		13 19			13 34		14 14			14 34
Denham Golf Club d	10 46					11 42						12 37					13 37					14 37
Denham d	10 49	11 11				11 45		12 10				12 40					13 40					14 40
West Ruislip § d	10 56					11 49						12 45					13 45					14 45
South Ruislip § d		11 16						12 16				12 49					13 49					14 49
Northolt Park d		11 20						12 19				12 53					13 53					14 53
Sudbury Hill Harrow d																						
Sudbury & Harrow Road d																						
Wembley Stadium d	11 04	11 25				11 58		12 25				12 58		13 29			13 58		14 26			14 58
London Paddington a																						
London Marylebone a	11 21	11 38	11 42	11 46		12 12	12 16	12 38	12 42	12 46		13 11	13 16	13 43	13 46		14 12	14 16	14 39	14 42		15 11

	CH ◇	CH ◇	CH ◇	CH	CH	CH ◇	CH	CH ◇	CH	CH	CH ◇	CH	CH ◇	CH ◇	CH	CH	CH ◇	CH	CH	CH ◇	CH
Kidderminster d																					
Stourbridge Junction d																					
Cradley Heath d																					
Rowley Regis d																					
Birmingham Snow Hill d	13 12					14 12					15 12						16 12				
Birmingham Moor Street d	13 15		13 55			14 15		14 55			15 15			15 55			16 15			16 55	
Solihull d	13 23		14 03			14 23		15 03			15 23			16 03			16 23			17 03	
Dorridge d	13 28					14 28					15 28						16 28				
Lapworth d																					
Stratford-upon-Avon d		13 19											15 19								
Wilmcote d		13 25											15 25								
Bearley d		13 28																			
Claverdon d		13 33											15 32								
Hatton d		13 41											15 42								
Warwick Parkway d	13 38		14 15			14 38		15 15			15 38			16 15			16 38			17 15	
Warwick d	13 41	13 48				14 41					15 41		15 49				16 41				
Leamington Spa d	13 47	13 54	14 21			14 47		15 21			15 47		15 55	16 21			16 47			17 21	
Banbury d	14 08	14 13	14 42			15 08	15 12	15 41			16 07		16 15	16 44			17 07		17 12	17 43	
Kings Sutton d							15 18												17 18		
Bicester North d	14 21	14 28	14 55			15 22	15 30	15 54			16 21		16 31	16 58			17 21		17 31	17 57	
Haddenham & Thame Parkway d	14 31	14 41				15 33	15 42				16 32		16 44				17 32		17 44		
Aylesbury d				15 10						16 10						17 10					
Little Kimble d				15 18						16 18						17 18					
Monks Risborough d				15 22						16 22						17 22					
Princes Risborough d	14 38	14 49		15a30		15 40	15 50		16 09	16a30	16 40		16 51		17 14	17a30	17 40		17 51		18 14
Saunderton d		14 54					15 55						16 57						17 57		
High Wycombe d	14 49	15 01			15 19	15 49	16 02		16 19		16 49	16 54	17 05		17 24		17 49	17 54	18 06		18 24
Beaconsfield d		15 07			15 26		16 08		16 26			17 01	17 12		17 31			18 01	18 12		18 31
Seer Green d					15 29				16 29						17 34						18 34
Gerrards Cross d		15 13			15 34		16 14		16 34			17 07	17 18		17 39			18 07	18 18		18 39
Denham Golf Club d					15 37				16 37						17 42						18 42
Denham d					15 40		16 18		16 40			17 11			17 45			18 11			18 45
West Ruislip § d					15 45				16 45						17 49						18 49
South Ruislip § d					15 49				16 49			17 16						18 16			
Northolt Park d					15 53				16 53			17 20						18 20			
Sudbury Hill Harrow d																					
Sudbury & Harrow Road d																					
Wembley Stadium d		15 25			15 58		16 28		16 58			17 25			17 58			18 25			18 58
London Paddington a																					
London Marylebone a	15 16	15 38	15 42		16 11	16 16	16 42	16 46	17 11		17 16	17 38	17 41	17 46	18 11		18 16	18 38	18 42	18 46	19 11

§ London Underground Limited (Central Line) also operate services between South Ruislip and West Ruislip at frequent intervals

Table 115

Saturdays
28 July to 8 September

Kidderminster, Birmingham Snow Hill, Stratford-upon-Avon, Banbury, Aylesbury and High Wycombe - London

Network Diagram - see first Page of Table 114

		CH	CH	CH	CH	CH	CH	CH	CH	CH	CH	CH	CH	CH	CH	CH	CH	CH	CH
			◇	◇			◇			◇		◇	◇		◇			◇	
Kidderminster	d																		
Stourbridge Junction	d																		
Cradley Heath	d																		
Rowley Regis	d																		
Birmingham Snow Hill	d		17 12				17 52			18 42			19 42		20 42			21 20	
Birmingham Moor Street	d		17 15				17 55			18 45			19 45		20 45			21 23	
Solihull	d		17 23				18 03			18 53			19 53		20 53			21 31	
Dorridge	d		17 28							18 58			19 58		20 58			21 38	
Lapworth	d												20 03		21 03			21 43	
Stratford-upon-Avon	d			17 40								19 16				21 16			
Wilmcote	d											19 22							
Bearley	d											19 25							
Claverdon	d											19 31							
Hatton	d											19 36	20 09		21 09			21 49	
Warwick Parkway	d		17 38				18 15			19 08		19 43	20 14		21 14			21 54	
Warwick	d		17 41	18 02			18 18			19 11		19 46	20 17		21 17	21 37		21 57	
Leamington Spa	d		17 47	18 06			18 24			19 17		19 52	20 23		21 21	21a48		22 03	
Banbury	d		18 06	18 24			18 46			19 34		20 11	20 46		21 39			22 20	
Kings Sutton	d											20 16						22 25	
Bicester North	d		18 19	18 36		18 43	19 01			19 47		20 27	20 58		21 52			22 35	
Haddenham & Thame Parkway	d		18 30			18 54				19 58		20 39	21 09		22 02			22 47	
Aylesbury	d	18 10							19 08					21 20			22 20		22 45
Little Kimble	d	18 18							19 16					21 28					22 53
Monks Risborough	d	18 22							19 20					21 32					22 57
Princes Risborough	d	18a28	18 38			19 01			19 24	20 06		20 46	21 16	21 36	22 10		22 34	22 55	23 01
Saunderton	d					19 06			19 29			20 51		21 41					23 06
High Wycombe	d		18 47		18 58	19 13		19 28	19 48	20 15	20 28	20 58	21 25	21 47	22 19		22 44	23 05	23 12
Beaconsfield	d				19 05	19 19		19 35	19 54		20 35	21 04	21 31	21 54	22 25		22 50		23 19
Seer Green	d							19 38			20 38	21 07		21 57			22 53		23 22
Gerrards Cross	d				19 11	19 25		19 43	20 00		20 43	21 12	21 37	22 02	22 30		22 58		23 27
Denham Golf Club	d							19 46			20 46	21 16		22 05			23 02		23 30
Denham	d				19 15			19 49	20 04		20 49	21 18		22 08			23 04		23 33
West Ruislip §	⊖ d							19 53			20 53	21 23		22 12			23 09		23 37
South Ruislip §	⊖ d				19 20				20 10			21 27		22 16			23 13		23 41
Northolt Park	d				19 24				20 13		20 59	21 30		22 20			23 16		23 45
Sudbury Hill Harrow	d																		
Sudbury & Harrow Road	d																		
Wembley Stadium	d				19 29			20 02	20 18		21 04	21 35		22 25			23 21	23 25	23 50
London Paddington	⊖ a																		
London Marylebone	⊖ a		19 16	19 22	19 42	19 46	19 49	20 16	20 31	20 42	21 17	21 46	21 57	22 38	22 58		23 34	23 37	00 03

Saturdays
from 15 September

		CH	CH	CH	CH	CH	CH	CH	CH	CH	CH	CH	CH	CH	CH	CH	CH	CH	CH	CH	CH	CH	CH
									◇	◇			◇	◇		◇		◇		◇			◇
Kidderminster	d												06 37	07 14						08 13			
Stourbridge Junction	d												06 45	07 22						08 26			
Cradley Heath	d												06 51	07 28						08 32			
Rowley Regis	d												06 57	07 34						08 37			
Birmingham Snow Hill	d												07 12	07 52						08 52			09 12
Birmingham Moor Street	d								06 15	06 44			07 15	07 55				08 15		08 55			09 15
Solihull	d								06 24	06 53			07 24	08 04				08 25		09 05			09 23
Dorridge	d								06 29	06 58			07 29					08 30					09 28
Lapworth	d								06 33														
Stratford-upon-Avon	d															08 00							
Wilmcote	d																						
Bearley	d																						
Claverdon	d															08 10							
Hatton	d								06 39							08 17							
Warwick Parkway	d								06 44	07 07			07 39	08 18				08 39		09 19			09 38
Warwick	d								06 47				07 42			08 24		08 43					09 41
Leamington Spa	d								06 52	07 14			07 47	08 24		08 29		08 48		09 24			09 47
Banbury	d					06 05	06 29		07 10	07 31			08 05	08 44		08 49		09 10		09 45	09 25		10 05
Kings Sutton	d						06 34									08 54					09 31		
Bicester North	d					06 19	06 45		07 23	07 44			08 17			09 05		09 22			09 42		10 18
Haddenham & Thame Parkway	d					06 31	06 57		07 33	07 55			08 28			09 18		09 33			09 55		10 28
Aylesbury	d		23p00	05 15	05 55			06 55			07 50	08 10			08 55		09 10					10 10	
Little Kimble	d		23p08	05 23	06 03			07 03			07 58						09 18					10 18	
Monks Risborough	d		23p12	05 27	06 07			07 07			08 02				09 06		09 22					10 22	
Princes Risborough	d		23p16	05 31	06 11	06 38		07 11	07 41		08 06	08 24	08 35		09 10	09 25	09a31	09 41			10 09	10a28	10 36
Saunderton	d		23p21	05 36	06 16			07 16			08 11	08 29				09 30					10 15		
High Wycombe	d	23p22	23p27	05 42	06 22	06 48	07 11	07 22	07 50		08 17	08 50	08 45		09 20	09 37		09 50	09 54		10 21		10 45
Beaconsfield	d	23p29	23p33	05 49	06 29	06 54		07 29	07 56		08 24	08 56			09 26	09 43			10 01		10 28		
Seer Green	d		23p36	05 52	06 32			07 32			08 27				09 29						10 31		
Gerrards Cross	d	23p35	23p41	05 57	06 37	07 00		07 37	08 02		08 32	09 02			09 35	09 49			10 07		10 36		
Denham Golf Club	d		23p44	06 00	06 40			07 40			08 35				09 39								
Denham	d		23p47	06 03	06 43			07 43			08 38	09 06			09 41				10 11				
West Ruislip §	⊖ d		23p51	06 07	06 47			07 47			08 42				09 46								
South Ruislip §	⊖ d		23p55	06 11	06 51			07 51			08 46	09 12							10 16				
Northolt Park	d		23p59	06 15	06 55			07 55			08 50	09 15							10 20				
Sudbury Hill Harrow	d																						
Sudbury & Harrow Road	d																						
Wembley Stadium	d	23p48	00 04	06 20	07 00	07 12		08 00			08 55	09 20			09 54				10 25				
London Paddington	⊖ a																						
London Marylebone	⊖ a	00 06	00 20	06 33	07 13	07 25	07 42	08 13	08 22	08 32	09 08	09 33	09 12	09 39	10 08	10 12		10 16	10 38	10 42	10 59		11 12

§ London Underground Limited (Central Line) also operate services between South Ruislip and West Ruislip at frequent intervals

Table 115

Saturdays
from 15 September

Kidderminster, Birmingham Snow Hill, Stratford-upon-Avon, Banbury, Aylesbury and High Wycombe - London

Network Diagram - see first Page of Table 114

		CH	CH	CH	CH	CH	CH	CH	CH	CH	CH	CH	CH	CH	CH	CH	CH	CH	CH	CH	CH	CH	CH
				◇	◇			◇			◇			◇	◇	◇			◇		◇		
Kidderminster	d				09 03																		
Stourbridge Junction	d				09 16																		
Cradley Heath	d				09 22																		
Rowley Regis	d				09 28																		
Birmingham Snow Hill	d				09 52			10 12						11 12					12 12				
Birmingham Moor Street	d				09 55			10 15			10 55			11 15		11 55			12 15		12 55		
Solihull	d				10 05			10 24			11 03			11 23		12 04			12 23		13 05		
Dorridge	d							10 30						11 28					12 28				
Lapworth	d																						
Stratford-upon-Avon	d			09 19											11 34								
Wilmcote	d			09 25											11 41								
Bearley	d			09 28											11 44								
Claverdon	d			09 34											11 50								
Hatton	d			09 41											11 57								
Warwick Parkway	d				10 19			10 39			11 15			11 38		12 20			12 38		13 18		
Warwick	d			09 48				10 43						11 41	12 04				12 41				
Leamington Spa	d			09 54	10 25			10 48			11 20			11 47	12 08	12 26			12 47		13 24		
Banbury	d			10 14	10 46			11 08		11 12	11 40			12 04	12 26	12 46			13 08	13 12	13 44		
Kings Sutton	d									11 18										13 18			
Bicester North	d			10 33	10 58			11 22		11 33	11 54			12 20	12 38	12 58			13 22	13 29	13 56		
Haddenham & Thame Parkway	d			10 46				11 33		11 46				12 31	12 48				13 33	13 42			
Aylesbury	d					11 10						12 10					13 10					14 10	
Little Kimble	d					11 18						12 18					13 18					14 18	
Monks Risborough	d					11 22						12 22					13 22					14 22	
Princes Risborough	d			10 54		11a30		11 41		11 54		12a28		12 38	12 55		13a30		13 40	13 50		14a28	
Saunderton	d			10 59						11 59					13 00					13 55			
High Wycombe	d		10 54	11 06			11 24	11 50		12 06			12 19	12 48	13 07			13 19	13 50	14 01			14 19
Beaconsfield	d		11 01	11 12			11 31			12 12			12 26		13 13			13 26		14 08			14 26
Seer Green	d						11 34						12 29					13 29					14 29
Gerrards Cross	d	10 42	11 07	11 18			11 39		12 06	12 18			12 34		13 19			13 34		14 14			14 34
Denham Golf Club	d	10 46					11 42						12 37					13 37					14 37
Denham	d	10 49	11 11				11 45		12 10				12 40					13 40					14 40
West Ruislip §	⊖ d	10 56					11 49						12 45					13 45					14 45
South Ruislip §	⊖ d		11 16						12 16				12 49					13 49					14 49
Northolt Park	d		11 20						12 19				12 53					13 53					14 53
Sudbury Hill Harrow	d																						
Sudbury & Harrow Road	d																						
Wembley Stadium	d	11 04	11 25				11 58		12 25				12 58		13 29			13 58		14 26			14 58
London Paddington	⊖ a																						
London Marylebone	⊖ a	11 21	11 38	11 42	11 46		12 12	12 16	12 38	12 42	12 46		13 11	13 16	13 43	13 46		14 12	14 16	14 39	14 42		15 11

		CH	CH	CH	CH	CH	CH	CH	CH	CH	CH	CH	CH	CH	CH	CH	CH	CH	CH	CH	CH	CH
		◇	◇	◇			◇		◇			◇		◇	◇			◇			◇	
Kidderminster	d																					
Stourbridge Junction	d																					
Cradley Heath	d																					
Rowley Regis	d																					
Birmingham Snow Hill	d	13 12					14 12					15 12						16 12				
Birmingham Moor Street	d	13 15		13 55			14 15		14 55			15 15			15 55			16 15			16 55	
Solihull	d	13 23		14 03			14 23		15 03			15 23			16 03			16 23			17 03	
Dorridge	d	13 28					14 28					15 28						16 28				
Lapworth	d																					
Stratford-upon-Avon	d		13 19											15 19								
Wilmcote	d		13 25											15 25								
Bearley	d		13 28																			
Claverdon	d		13 33											15 32								
Hatton	d		13 41											15 42								
Warwick Parkway	d	13 38		14 15			14 38		15 15			15 38			16 15			16 38			17 15	
Warwick	d	13 41	13 48				14 41					15 41		15 49				16 41				
Leamington Spa	d	13 47	13 54	14 21			14 47		15 21			15 47		15 55	16 21			16 47			17 21	
Banbury	d	14 08	14 13	14 42			15 08	15 12	15 41			16 07		16 15	16 44			17 07		17 12	17 43	
Kings Sutton	d							15 18												17 18		
Bicester North	d	14 21	14 28	14 55			15 22	15 30	15 54			16 21		16 31	16 58			17 21		17 31	17 57	
Haddenham & Thame Parkway	d	14 31	14 41				15 33	15 42				16 32		16 44				17 32		17 44		
Aylesbury	d				15 10						16 10						17 10					
Little Kimble	d				15 18						16 18						17 18					
Monks Risborough	d				15 22						16 22						17 22					
Princes Risborough	d	14 38	14 49		15a30		15 40	15 50		16 09	16a30	16 40		16 51		17 14	17a30	17 40		17 51		18 14
Saunderton	d		14 54					15 55						16 57						17 57		
High Wycombe	d	14 49	15 01			15 19	15 49	16 02		16 19		16 49	16 54	17 05		17 24		17 49	17 54	18 06		18 24
Beaconsfield	d		15 07			15 26		16 08		16 26			17 01	17 12		17 31			18 01	18 12		18 31
Seer Green	d					15 29				16 29						17 34						18 34
Gerrards Cross	d		15 13			15 34		16 14		16 34			17 07	17 18		17 39			18 07	18 18		18 39
Denham Golf Club	d					15 37				16 37						17 42						18 42
Denham	d					15 40		16 18		16 40			17 11			17 45			18 11			18 45
West Ruislip §	⊖ d					15 45				16 45						17 49						18 49
South Ruislip §	⊖ d					15 49				16 49			17 16						18 16			
Northolt Park	d					15 53				16 53			17 20						18 20			
Sudbury Hill Harrow	d																					
Sudbury & Harrow Road	d																					
Wembley Stadium	d		15 25			15 58		16 28		16 58			17 25			17 58			18 25			18 58
London Paddington	⊖ a																					
London Marylebone	⊖ a	15 16	15 38	15 42		16 11	16 16	16 42	16 46	17 11		17 16	17 38	17 41	17 46	18 11		18 16	18 38	18 42	18 46	19 11

§ London Underground Limited (Central Line) also operate services between South Ruislip and West Ruislip at frequent intervals

Saturdays
from 15 September

Kidderminster, Birmingham Snow Hill, Stratford-upon-Avon, Banbury, Aylesbury and High Wycombe - London

Network Diagram - see first Page of Table 114

	CH	CH ◇	CH ◇	CH	CH	CH ◇	CH		CH	CH ◇	CH	CH ◇	CH ◇	CH	CH ◇	CH	CH		CH ◇	CH
Kidderminster d																				
Stourbridge Junction 2 d																				
Cradley Heath d																				
Rowley Regis d																				
Birmingham Snow Hill d		17 12				17 52				18 42			19 42		20 42				21 20	
Birmingham Moor Street d		17 15				17 55				18 45			19 45		20 45				21 23	
Solihull d		17 23				18 03				18 53			19 53		20 53				21 31	
Dorridge d		17 28								18 58			19 58		20 58				21 38	
Lapworth d													20 03		21 03				21 43	
Stratford-upon-Avon d			17 40									19 16				21 16				
Wilmcote d												19 22								
Bearley d												19 25								
Claverdon d												19 31								
Hatton d												19 36	20 09		21 09				21 49	
Warwick Parkway d		17 38				18 15				19 08		19 43	20 14		21 14				21 54	
Warwick d		17 41	18 02			18 18				19 11		19 46	20 17		21 17	21 37			21 57	
Leamington Spa 8 d		17 47	18 06			18 24				19 17		19 52	20 23		21 21	21a48			22 03	
Banbury d		18 06	18 24			18 46				19 34		20 11	20 46		21 39				22 20	
Kings Sutton d												20 16							22 25	
Bicester North 3 d		18 19	18 36		18 43	19 01				19 47		20 27	20 58		21 52				22 35	
Haddenham & Thame Parkway d		18 30			18 54					19 58		20 39	21 09		22 02				22 47	
Aylesbury d	18 10								19 08					21 20			22 20			22 45
Little Kimble d	18 18								19 16					21 28						22 53
Monks Risborough d	18 22								19 20					21 32						22 57
Princes Risborough 2 d	18a28	18 38			19 01				19 24	20 06		20 46	21 16	21 36	22 10		22 34		22 55	23 01
Saunderton d					19 06				19 29			20 51		21 41						23 06
High Wycombe 1 d		18 47		18 58	19 13		19 28		19 48	20 15	20 28	20 58	21 25	21 47	22 19		22 44		23 05	23 12
Beaconsfield d				19 05	19 19		19 35		19 54		20 35	21 04	21 31	21 54	22 25		22 50			23 19
Seer Green d							19 38				20 38	21 07		21 57			22 53			23 22
Gerrards Cross 1 d				19 11	19 25		19 43		20 00		20 43	21 12	21 37	22 02	22 30		22 58			23 27
Denham Golf Club d							19 46				20 46	21 16		22 05			23 02			23 30
Denham d				19 15			19 49		20 04		20 49	21 18		22 08			23 04			23 33
West Ruislip 3 § ⊖ d							19 53				20 53	21 23		22 12			23 09			23 37
South Ruislip § ⊖ d				19 20					20 10			21 27		22 16			23 13			23 41
Northolt Park d				19 24					20 13		20 59	21 30		22 20			23 16			23 45
Sudbury Hill Harrow d																				
Sudbury & Harrow Road d																				
Wembley Stadium d				19 29			20 02		20 18		21 04	21 35		22 25			23 21		23 25	23 50
London Paddington 15 ⊖ a																				
London Marylebone 10 ⊖ a		19 16	19 22	19 42	19 46	19 49	20 16		20 31	20 42	21 17	21 46	21 57	22 38	22 58		23 34		23 37	00 03

Sundays
until 22 July

	CH	CH	CH	CH	CH ◇	CH	CH	CH ◇	CH ◇		CH ◇	CH	CH	CH ◇	CH ◇	CH	CH ◇	CH ◇	CH ◇		CH	CH ◇	CH ◇	CH
Kidderminster d																								
Stourbridge Junction 2 d																								
Cradley Heath d																								
Rowley Regis d																								
Birmingham Snow Hill d													09 40				10 40					11 40		
Birmingham Moor Street d								08 55			09 13		09 43		10 13		10 43		11 13			11 43		12 13
Solihull d								09 04			09 22		09 52		10 22		10 52		11 22			11 52		12 22
Dorridge d								09 09			09 27		09 57		10 27		10 57		11 27			11 57		12 27
Lapworth d																	11 02							
Stratford-upon-Avon d														10 00									12 00	
Wilmcote d														10 05									12 05	
Bearley d																								
Claverdon d																								
Hatton d														10 15			11 08						12 15	
Warwick Parkway d								09 18			09 37		10 08		10 37		11 13		11 37			12 08		12 37
Warwick d								09 22			09 41			10 23	10 41				11 41				12 23	12 41
Leamington Spa 8 d								09 27			09 46		10 16	10 27	10 46		11 18		11 46			12 16	12 27	12 46
Banbury d						08 57		09 45	09 50		10 06		10 34	10 47	11 06		11 36		12 06			12 34	12 47	13 06
Kings Sutton d						09 03								10 52									12 52	
Bicester North 3 d				08 25	08 55	09 14		09 58	10 04		10 20		10 46	11 04	11 20		11 48	12 04	12 20			12 46	13 04	13 20
Haddenham & Thame Parkway d				08 37	09 08	09 27			10 17				10 57	11 17			11 59	12 17				12 57	13 17	
Aylesbury d	22p45	07 23	08 23				09 23					10 23				11 23					12 23			
Little Kimble d	22p53	07 31	08 31				09 31					10 31				11 31					12 31			
Monks Risborough d	22p57	07 35	08 35				09 35					10 35				11 35					12 35			
Princes Risborough 2 d	23p01	07 39	08 39	08 44	09 15	09 34	09 39		10 24			10 39	11 05	11 24		11 39	12 06	12 24			12 39	13 05	13 24	
Saunderton d	23p06	07 44		08 49			09 44					10 44				11 44					12 44			
High Wycombe 1 d	23p12	07 50	08 49	08 56	09 25	09 44	09 50		10 34			10 50	11 14	11 34		11 50	12 15	12 34			12 50	13 14	13 34	
Beaconsfield d	23p19	07 57	08 55	09 02	09 32		09 57		10 40			10 57	11 21	11 40		11 57	12 21	12 40			12 57	13 21	13 40	
Seer Green d	23p22	08 00		09 05			10 00					11 00				12 00					13 00			
Gerrards Cross 1 d	23p27	08 05	09 01	09 10	09 38		10 05		10 46			11 05	11 27	11 46		12 05	12 27	12 46			13 05	13 27	13 46	
Denham Golf Club d	23p30	08 08					10 08									12 08								
Denham d	23p33	08 11		09 14			10 11					11 09				12 11					13 09			
West Ruislip 3 § ⊖ d	23p37	08 15	09 08				10 15					11 13				12 15					13 13			
South Ruislip § ⊖ d	23p41	08 19		09 19			10 19					11 17				12 19					13 17			
Northolt Park d	23p45	08 23		09 23			10 23					11 21				12 23					13 21			
Sudbury Hill Harrow d																								
Sudbury & Harrow Road d																								
Wembley Stadium d	23p50	08 28		09 28			10 28		10 58			11 26		11 58		12 28		12 58			13 26		13 58	
London Paddington 15 ⊖ a																								
London Marylebone 10 ⊖ a	00 03	08 41	09 28	09 41	10 01	10 15	10 41	10 46	11 11		11 14	11 39	11 47	12 11	12 14	12 41	12 47	13 11	13 14		13 39	13 47	14 11	14 14

§ London Underground Limited (Central Line) also operate services between South Ruislip and West Ruislip at frequent intervals

Sundays
until 22 July

Kidderminster, Birmingham Snow Hill, Stratford-upon-Avon, Banbury, Aylesbury and High Wycombe - London

Network Diagram - see first Page of Table 114

	CH	CH ◇	CH ◇	CH ◇	CH		CH ◇	CH ◇	CH ◇	CH	CH ◇	CH	CH ◇	CH	CH ◇		CH ◇	CH ◇	CH	CH ◇	CH	CH ◇	CH	CH
Kidderminster d																								
Stourbridge Junction 2 d																								
Cradley Heath d																								
Rowley Regis d																								
Birmingham Snow Hill d		12 40					13 40				14 40				15 40					16 40				17 40
Birmingham Moor Street d		12 43		13 13			13 43		14 13		14 43		15 13		15 43			16 13		16 43		17 13		17 43
Solihull d		12 52		13 22			13 52		14 22		14 52		15 22		15 52			16 22		16 52		17 22		17 52
Dorridge d		12 57		13 27			13 57		14 27		14 57		15 27		15 57			16 27		16 57		17 27		17 57
Lapworth d							14 02								16 02									18 02
Stratford-upon-Avon d								14 00									16 00							
Wilmcote d								14 05									16 05							
Bearley d																								
Claverdon d																								
Hatton d							14 08	14 15							16 08		16 15							18 08
Warwick Parkway d		13 08		13 37			14 13		14 37		15 08		15 37		16 13			16 37		17 08		17 37		18 13
Warwick d				13 41				14 23	14 41				15 41				16 23	16 41				17 41		
Leamington Spa 8 d		13 16		13 46			14 18	14 27	14 46		15 16		15 46		16 18		16 27	16 46		17 16		17 46		18 18
Banbury d		13 34		14 06			14 36	14 47	15 06		15 34		16 06		16 36		16 47	17 06		17 34		18 06		18 36
Kings Sutton d								14 52									16 52							
Bicester North 3 d		13 46	14 04	14 20			14 48	15 04	15 20		15 46	16 04	16 20		16 48		17 04	17 20		17 46	18 04	18 20		18 48
Haddenham & Thame Parkway d		13 57	14 17				14 59	15 17			15 57	16 17			16 59		17 17			17 57	18 17			18 59
Aylesbury d	13 23				14 23					15 23				16 23					17 23				18 23	
Little Kimble d	13 31				14 31					15 31				16 31					17 31				18 31	
Monks Risborough d	13 35				14 35					15 35				16 35					17 35				18 35	
Princes Risborough 2 d	13 39	14 05	14 24		14 39		15 06	15 24		15 39	16 05	16 24		16 39	17 06		17 24		17 39	18 05	18 24		18 39	19 06
Saunderton d	13 44				14 44					15 44				16 44					17 44				18 44	
High Wycombe 1 d	13 50	14 14	14 34		14 50		15 15	15 34		15 50	16 14	16 34		16 50	17 15		17 34		17 50	18 14	18 34		18 50	19 15
Beaconsfield d	13 57	14 21	14 40		14 57		15 21	15 40		15 57	16 21	16 40		16 57	17 21		17 40		17 57	18 21	18 40		18 57	19 21
Seer Green d	14 00				15 00					16 00				17 00					18 00				19 00	
Gerrards Cross 1 d	14 05	14 27	14 46		15 05		15 27	15 46		16 05	16 27	16 46		17 05	17 27		17 46		18 05	18 27	18 46		19 05	19 27
Denham Golf Club d	14 08									16 08									18 08					
Denham d	14 11				15 09					16 11				17 09					18 11				19 09	
West Ruislip 3 § ⊖ d	14 15				15 13					16 15				17 13					18 15				19 13	
South Ruislip § ⊖ d	14 19				15 17					16 19				17 17					18 19				19 17	
Northolt Park d	14 23				15 21					16 23				17 21					18 23				19 21	
Sudbury Hill Harrow d																								
Sudbury & Harrow Road d																								
Wembley Stadium d	14 28		14 58		15 26			15 58		16 28		16 58		17 26			17 58		18 28		18 58		19 26	
London Paddington 15 ⊖ a																								
London Marylebone 10 ⊖ a	14 41	14 47	15 11	15 14	15 39		15 48	16 11	16 14	16 41	16 47	17 11	17 14	17 39	17 48		18 11	18 14	18 41	18 47	19 11	19 14	19 39	19 48

	CH ◇		CH ◇	CH	CH ◇	CH ◇	CH ◇	CH ◇	CH	CH ◇
Kidderminster d										
Stourbridge Junction 2 d										
Cradley Heath d										
Rowley Regis d										
Birmingham Snow Hill d					18 40	19 15		20 15		21 15
Birmingham Moor Street d			18 13		18 43	19 18		20 18		21 18
Solihull d			18 22		18 52	19 26		20 26		21 26
Dorridge d			18 27		18 57	19 34		20 34		21 34
Lapworth d						19 38				
Stratford-upon-Avon d	18 00						20 00			
Wilmcote d	18 05						20 05			
Bearley d										
Claverdon d										
Hatton d	18 15					19 44	20 15			
Warwick Parkway d			18 37		19 08	19 49		20 46		21 46
Warwick d	18 23		18 41			19 52	20 23	20 49		21 49
Leamington Spa 8 d	18 27		18 46		19 16	19 57	20 27	20 54		21 54
Banbury d	18 47		19 06		19 34	20 15	20 47	21 13		22 15
Kings Sutton d	18 52					20 20				22 20
Bicester North 3 d	19 04		19 20		19 46	20 31	21 04	21 28		22 31
Haddenham & Thame Parkway d	19 17				19 57	20 42		21 42		22 44
Aylesbury d				19 23					22 28	
Little Kimble d				19 31					22 36	
Monks Risborough d				19 35					22 40	
Princes Risborough 2 d	19 24			19 39	20 05	20 49		21 49	22a47	22 51
Saunderton d				19 44		20 54		21 54		22 56
High Wycombe 1 d	19 34			19 50	20 14	21 00		22 00		23 02
Beaconsfield d	19 40			19 57	20 21	21 07		22 07		23 09
Seer Green d				20 00		21 10		22 10		23 12
Gerrards Cross 1 d	19 46			20 05	20 27	21 15		22 15		23 17
Denham Golf Club d				20 08				22 18		
Denham d				20 11		21 19		22 21		23 21
West Ruislip 3 § ⊖ d				20 15		21 24		22 26		23 26
South Ruislip § ⊖ d				20 19		21 28		22 30		23 30
Northolt Park d				20 23		21 31		22 33		23 33
Sudbury Hill Harrow d										
Sudbury & Harrow Road d										
Wembley Stadium d	19 58			20 28		21 37		22 39		23 39
London Paddington 15 ⊖ a										
London Marylebone 10 ⊖ a	20 11		20 14	20 41	20 47	21 50	21 58	22 52		23 52

§ London Underground Limited (Central Line) also operate services between South Ruislip and West Ruislip at frequent intervals

Table 115

Sundays
29 July to 9 September

Kidderminster, Birmingham Snow Hill, Stratford-upon-Avon, Banbury, Aylesbury and High Wycombe - London

Network Diagram - see first Page of Table 114

		CH	CH	CH	CH	CH	CH	CH	CH	CH		CH	CH	CH	CH	CH	CH	CH	CH	CH		CH	CH	CH	CH
								◇	◇				◇	◇	◇			◇	◇			◇	◇	◇	
			A		A			A																	
Kidderminster	d																								
Stourbridge Junction 2	d																								
Cradley Heath	d																								
Rowley Regis	d																								
Birmingham Snow Hill	d							07 40									09 40					10 40			
Birmingham Moor Street	d							07 43					08 55		09 13		09 43		10 13			10 43		11 13	
Solihull	d							07 51					09 04		09 22		09 52		10 22			10 52		11 22	
Dorridge	d							07 56					09 09		09 27		09 57		10 27			10 57		11 27	
Lapworth	d																					11 02			
Stratford-upon-Avon	d																	10 00							
Wilmcote	d																	10 05							
Bearley	d																								
Claverdon	d																								
Hatton	d																	10 15				11 08			
Warwick Parkway	d							08 06					09 18		09 37		10 08		10 37			11 13		11 37	
Warwick	d							08 09					09 22		09 41			10 23	10 41					11 41	
Leamington Spa 8	d							08 15					09 27		09 46		10 16	10 27	10 46			11 18		11 46	
Banbury	d							08 33		08 57			09 45	09 50	10 06		10 34	10 47	11 06			11 36		12 06	
Kings Sutton	d									09 03								10 52							
Bicester North 3	d				07 26		08 25	08 50	08 55	09 14			09 58	10 04	10 20		10 46	11 04	11 20			11 48	12 04	12 20	
Haddenham & Thame Parkway	d				07 39		08 37		09 08	09 27				10 17			10 57	11 17				11 59	12 17		
Aylesbury	d	22p45	06 27	07 23		08 23						09 23				10 23				11 23					12 23
Little Kimble	d	22p53	06 35	07 31		08 31						09 31				10 31				11 31					12 31
Monks Risborough	d	22p57	06 39	07 35		08 35						09 35				10 35				11 35					12 35
Princes Risborough 2	d	23p01	06 43	07 39	07 46	08 39	08 44		09 15	09 34		09 39		10 24		10 39	11 05	11 24		11 39		12 06	12 24		12 39
Saunderton	d	23p06	06 48	07 44	07 51		08 49					09 44				10 44				11 44					12 44
High Wycombe 1	d	23p12	06 55	07 50	07 57	08 49	08 56		09 25	09 44		09 50		10 34		10 50	11 14	11 34		11 50		12 15	12 34		12 50
Beaconsfield	d	23p19	07 02	07 57	08 04	08 55	09 02		09 32			09 57		10 40		10 57	11 21	11 40		11 57		12 21	12 40		12 57
Seer Green	d	23p22	07 05	08 00	08 07		09 05					10 00				11 00				12 00					13 00
Gerrards Cross 1	d	23p27	07 10	08 05	08 12	09 01	09 10		09 38			10 05		10 46		11 05	11 27	11 46		12 05		12 27	12 46		13 05
Denham Golf Club	d	23p30	07 13	08 08								10 08								12 08					
Denham	d	23p33	07 16	08 11	08 16		09 14					10 11				11 09				12 11					13 09
West Ruislip 3 § ⊖	d	23p37	07 21	08 15	08 21	09 08						10 15				11 13				12 15					13 13
South Ruislip § ⊖	d	23p41	07 25	08 19	08 25		09 19					10 19				11 17				12 19					13 17
Northolt Park	d	23p45	07 28	08 23	08 28		09 23					10 23				11 21				12 23					13 21
Sudbury Hill Harrow	d																								
Sudbury & Harrow Road	d																								
Wembley Stadium	d	23p50	07 34	08 28	08 34		09 28					10 28		10 58		11 26		11 58		12 28			12 58		13 26
London Paddington 15 ⊖	a																								
London Marylebone 10 ⊖	a	00 03	07 47	08 41	08 47	09 28	09 41	09 47	10 01	10 15		10 41	10 46	11 11	11 14	11 39	11 47	12 11	12 14	12 41		12 47	13 11	13 14	13 39

		CH	CH	CH	CH	CH		CH	CH	CH	CH	CH	CH	CH	CH	CH		CH	CH	CH	CH	CH	CH	CH	CH
		◇	◇			◇		◇	◇		◇	◇	◇		◇			◇		◇	◇	◇		◇	
Kidderminster	d																								
Stourbridge Junction 2	d																								
Cradley Heath	d																								
Rowley Regis	d																								
Birmingham Snow Hill	d	11 40				12 40					13 40				14 40					15 40				16 40	
Birmingham Moor Street	d	11 43		12 13		12 43			13 13		13 43		14 13		14 43			15 13		15 43		16 13		16 43	
Solihull	d	11 52		12 22		12 52			13 22		13 52		14 22		14 52			15 22		15 52		16 22		16 52	
Dorridge	d	11 57		12 27		12 57			13 27		13 57		14 27		14 57			15 27		15 57		16 27		16 57	
Lapworth	d										14 02									16 02					
Stratford-upon-Avon	d		12 00									14 00									16 00				
Wilmcote	d		12 05									14 05									16 05				
Bearley	d																								
Claverdon	d																								
Hatton	d		12 15								14 08	14 15								16 08	16 15				
Warwick Parkway	d	12 08		12 37		13 08			13 37		14 13		14 37		15 08			15 37		16 13		16 37		17 08	
Warwick	d		12 23	12 41					13 41			14 23	14 41					15 41			16 23	16 41			
Leamington Spa 8	d	12 16	12 27	12 46		13 16			13 46		14 18	14 27	14 46		15 16			15 46		16 18	16 27	16 46		17 16	
Banbury	d	12 34	12 47	13 06		13 34			14 06		14 36	14 47	15 06		15 34			16 06		16 36	16 47	17 06		17 34	
Kings Sutton	d		12 52									14 52									16 52				
Bicester North 3	d	12 46	13 04	13 20		13 46		14 04	14 20		14 48	15 04	15 20		15 46	16 04		16 20		16 48	17 04	17 20		17 46	18 04
Haddenham & Thame Parkway	d	12 57	13 17			13 57		14 17			14 59	15 17			15 57	16 17				16 59	17 17			17 57	18 17
Aylesbury	d				13 23					14 23				15 23					16 23				17 23		
Little Kimble	d				13 31					14 31				15 31					16 31				17 31		
Monks Risborough	d				13 35					14 35				15 35					16 35				17 35		
Princes Risborough 2	d	13 05	13 24		13 39	14 05		14 24		14 39	15 06	15 24		15 39	16 05	16 24			16 39	17 06	17 24		17 39	18 05	18 24
Saunderton	d				13 44					14 44				15 44					16 44				17 44		
High Wycombe 1	d	13 14	13 34		13 50	14 14		14 34		14 50	15 15	15 34		15 50	16 14	16 34			16 50	17 15	17 34		17 50	18 14	18 34
Beaconsfield	d	13 21	13 40		13 57	14 21		14 40		14 57	15 21	15 40		15 57	16 21	16 40			16 57	17 21	17 40		17 57	18 21	18 40
Seer Green	d				14 00					15 00				16 00					17 00				18 00		
Gerrards Cross 1	d	13 27	13 46		14 05	14 27		14 46		15 05	15 27	15 46		16 05	16 27	16 46			17 05	17 27	17 46		18 05	18 27	18 46
Denham Golf Club	d				14 08									16 08									18 08		
Denham	d				14 11					15 09				16 11					17 09				18 11		
West Ruislip 3 § ⊖	d				14 15					15 13				16 15					17 13				18 15		
South Ruislip § ⊖	d				14 19					15 17				16 19					17 17				18 19		
Northolt Park	d				14 23					15 21				16 23					17 21				18 23		
Sudbury Hill Harrow	d																								
Sudbury & Harrow Road	d																								
Wembley Stadium	d		13 58		14 28			14 58		15 26		15 58		16 28		16 58			17 26		17 58		18 28		18 58
London Paddington 15 ⊖	a																								
London Marylebone 10 ⊖	a	13 47	14 11	14 14	14 41	14 47		15 11	15 14	15 39	15 48	16 11	16 14	16 41	16 47	17 11		17 14	17 39	17 48	18 11	18 14	18 41	18 47	19 11

§ London Underground Limited (Central Line) also operate services between South Ruislip and West Ruislip at frequent intervals

A not from 19 August

Table 115

Sundays
29 July to 9 September

Kidderminster, Birmingham Snow Hill, Stratford-upon-Avon, Banbury, Aylesbury and High Wycombe - London

Network Diagram - see first Page of Table 114

		CH		CH	CH	CH	CH	CH	CH	CH	CH	CH		CH	CH
		◇				◇	◇		◇	◇	◇	◇			◇
Kidderminster	d														
Stourbridge Junction 2	d														
Cradley Heath	d														
Rowley Regis	d														
Birmingham Snow Hill	d				17 40				18 40	19 15		20 15			21 15
Birmingham Moor Street	d	17 13			17 43		18 13		18 43	19 18		20 18			21 18
Solihull	d	17 22			17 52		18 22		18 52	19 26		20 26			21 26
Dorridge	d	17 27			17 57		18 27		18 57	19 34		20 34			21 34
Lapworth	d				18 02					19 38					
Stratford-upon-Avon	d					18 00					20 00				
Wilmcote	d					18 05					20 05				
Bearley	d														
Claverdon	d														
Hatton	d				18 08	18 15				19 44	20 15				
Warwick Parkway	d	17 37			18 13		18 37		19 08	19 49		20 46			21 46
Warwick	d	17 41				18 23	18 41			19 52	20 23	20 49			21 49
Leamington Spa 8	d	17 46			18 18	18 27	18 46		19 16	19 57	20 27	20 54			21 54
Banbury	d	18 06			18 36	18 47	19 06		19 34	20 15	20 47	21 13			22 15
Kings Sutton	d					18 52				20 20					22 20
Bicester North 3	d	18 20			18 48	19 04	19 20		19 46	20 31	21 04	21 28			22 31
Haddenham & Thame Parkway	d				18 59	19 17			19 57	20 42		21 42			22 44
Aylesbury	d			18 23				19 23						22 28	
Little Kimble	d			18 31				19 31						22 36	
Monks Risborough	d			18 35				19 35						22 40	
Princes Risborough 2	d			18 39	19 06	19 24		19 39	20 05	20 49		21 49		22a47	22 51
Saunderton	d			18 44				19 44		20 54		21 54			22 56
High Wycombe 1	d			18 50	19 15	19 34		19 50	20 14	21 00		22 00			23 02
Beaconsfield	d			18 57	19 21	19 40		19 57	20 21	21 07		22 07			23 09
Seer Green	d			19 00				20 00		21 10		22 10			23 12
Gerrards Cross 1	d			19 05	19 27	19 46		20 05	20 27	21 15		22 15			23 17
Denham Golf Club	d							20 08				22 18			
Denham	d			19 09				20 11		21 19		22 21			23 21
West Ruislip 3 § ⊖	d			19 13				20 15		21 24		22 26			23 26
South Ruislip § ⊖	d			19 17				20 19		21 28		22 30			23 30
Northolt Park	d			19 21				20 23		21 31		22 33			23 33
Sudbury Hill Harrow	d														
Sudbury & Harrow Road	d														
Wembley Stadium	d			19 26		19 58		20 28		21 37		22 39			23 39
London Paddington 15 ⊖	a														
London Marylebone 10 ⊖	a	19 14		19 39	19 48	20 11	20 14	20 41	20 47	21 50	21 58	22 52			23 52

Sundays
from 16 September

		CH	CH	CH	CH	CH	CH	CH	CH	CH		CH	CH	CH	CH	CH	CH	CH	CH	CH		CH	CH	CH	CH
						◇			◇	◇		◇			◇	◇		◇	◇	◇			◇	◇	
Kidderminster	d																								
Stourbridge Junction 2	d																								
Cradley Heath	d																								
Rowley Regis	d																								
Birmingham Snow Hill	d													09 40				10 40					11 40		
Birmingham Moor Street	d								08 55			09 13		09 43		10 13		10 43		11 13			11 43		12 13
Solihull	d								09 04			09 22		09 52		10 22		10 52		11 22			11 52		12 22
Dorridge	d								09 09			09 27		09 57		10 27		10 57		11 27			11 57		12 27
Lapworth	d																	11 02							
Stratford-upon-Avon	d														10 00									12 00	
Wilmcote	d														10 05									12 05	
Bearley	d																								
Claverdon	d																								
Hatton	d														10 15			11 08						12 15	
Warwick Parkway	d								09 18			09 37		10 08		10 37		11 13		11 37			12 08		12 37
Warwick	d								09 22			09 41			10 23	10 41				11 41				12 23	12 41
Leamington Spa 8	d								09 27			09 46		10 16	10 27	10 46		11 18		11 46			12 16	12 27	12 46
Banbury	d						08 57		09 45	09 50		10 06		10 34	10 47	11 06		11 36		12 06			12 34	12 47	13 06
Kings Sutton	d						09 03								10 52									12 52	
Bicester North 3	d				08 25	08 55	09 14		09 58	10 04		10 20		10 46	11 04	11 20		11 48	12 04	12 20			12 46	13 04	13 20
Haddenham & Thame Parkway	d				08 37	09 08	09 27			10 17				10 57	11 17			11 59	12 17				12 57	13 17	
Aylesbury	d	22p45	07 23	08 23				09 23					10 23				11 23					12 23			
Little Kimble	d	22p53	07 31	08 31				09 31					10 31				11 31					12 31			
Monks Risborough	d	22p57	07 35	08 35				09 35					10 35				11 35					12 35			
Princes Risborough 2	d	23p01	07 39	08 39	08 44	09 15	09 34	09 39		10 24			10 39	11 05	11 24		11 39	12 06	12 24			12 39	13 05	13 24	
Saunderton	d	23p06	07 44		08 49			09 44					10 44				11 44					12 44			
High Wycombe 1	d	23p12	07 50	08 49	08 56	09 25	09 44	09 50		10 34			10 50	11 14	11 34		11 50	12 15	12 34			12 50	13 14	13 34	
Beaconsfield	d	23p19	07 57	08 55	09 02	09 32		09 57		10 40			10 57	11 21	11 40		11 57	12 21	12 40			12 57	13 21	13 40	
Seer Green	d	23p22	08 00		09 05			10 00					11 00				12 00					13 00			
Gerrards Cross 1	d	23p27	08 05	09 01	09 10	09 38		10 05		10 46			11 05	11 27	11 46		12 05	12 27	12 46			13 05	13 27	13 46	
Denham Golf Club	d	23p30	08 08					10 08									12 08								
Denham	d	23p33	08 11		09 14			10 11					11 09				12 11					13 09			
West Ruislip 3 § ⊖	d	23p37	08 15	09 08				10 15					11 13				12 15					13 13			
South Ruislip § ⊖	d	23p41	08 19		09 19			10 19					11 17				12 19					13 17			
Northolt Park	d	23p45	08 23		09 23			10 23					11 21				12 23					13 21			
Sudbury Hill Harrow	d																								
Sudbury & Harrow Road	d																								
Wembley Stadium	d	23p50	08 28		09 28			10 28		10 58			11 26		11 58		12 28		12 58			13 26		13 58	
London Paddington 15 ⊖	a																								
London Marylebone 10 ⊖	a	00 03	08 41	09 28	09 41	10 01	10 15	10 41	10 46	11 11		11 14	11 39	11 47	12 11	12 14	12 41	12 47	13 11	13 14		13 39	13 47	14 11	14 14

§ London Underground Limited (Central Line) also operate services between South Ruislip and West Ruislip at frequent intervals

Table 115

Sundays
from 16 September

Kidderminster, Birmingham Snow Hill, Stratford-upon-Avon, Banbury, Aylesbury and High Wycombe - London

Network Diagram - see first Page of Table 114

		CH	CH	CH	CH	CH		CH	CH	CH	CH	CH	CH	CH	CH	CH		CH	CH	CH	CH	CH	CH	CH	CH
			◇	◇	◇			◇	◇	◇		◇		◇		◇		◇	◇		◇		◇		
Kidderminster	d																								
Stourbridge Junction 2	d																								
Cradley Heath	d																								
Rowley Regis	d																								
Birmingham Snow Hill	d		12 40					13 40				14 40				15 40					16 40				17 40
Birmingham Moor Street	d		12 43		13 13			13 43		14 13		14 43		15 13		15 43			16 13		16 43		17 13		17 43
Solihull	d		12 52		13 22			13 52		14 22		14 52		15 22		15 52			16 22		16 52		17 22		17 52
Dorridge	d		12 57		13 27			13 57		14 27		14 57		15 27		15 57			16 27		16 57		17 27		17 57
Lapworth	d							14 02								16 02									18 02
Stratford-upon-Avon	d								14 00									16 00							
Wilmcote	d								14 05									16 05							
Bearley	d																								
Claverdon	d																								
Hatton	d							14 08	14 15							16 08		16 15							18 08
Warwick Parkway	d		13 08		13 37			14 13		14 37		15 08		15 37		16 13			16 37		17 08		17 37		18 13
Warwick	d				13 41				14 23	14 41				15 41				16 23	16 41				17 41		
Leamington Spa 8	d		13 16		13 46			14 18	14 27	14 46		15 16		15 46		16 18		16 27	16 46		17 16		17 46		18 18
Banbury	d		13 34		14 06			14 36	14 47	15 06		15 34		16 06		16 36		16 47	17 06		17 34		18 06		18 36
Kings Sutton	d								14 52									16 52							
Bicester North 3	d		13 46	14 04	14 20			14 48	15 04	15 20		15 46	16 04	16 20		16 48		17 04	17 20		17 46	18 04	18 20		18 48
Haddenham & Thame Parkway	d		13 57	14 17				14 59	15 17			15 57	16 17			16 59		17 17			17 57	18 17			18 59
Aylesbury	d	13 23				14 23					15 23				16 23					17 23				18 23	
Little Kimble	d	13 31				14 31					15 31				16 31					17 31				18 31	
Monks Risborough	d	13 35				14 35					15 35				16 35					17 35				18 35	
Princes Risborough 2	d	13 39	14 05	14 24		14 39		15 06	15 24		15 39	16 05	16 24		16 39	17 06		17 24		17 39	18 05	18 24		18 39	19 06
Saunderton	d	13 44				14 44					15 44				16 44					17 44				18 44	
High Wycombe 1	d	13 50	14 14	14 34		14 50		15 15	15 34		15 50	16 14	16 34		16 50	17 15		17 34		17 50	18 14	18 34		18 50	19 15
Beaconsfield	d	13 57	14 21	14 40		14 57		15 21	15 40		15 57	16 21	16 40		16 57	17 21		17 40		17 57	18 21	18 40		18 57	19 21
Seer Green	d	14 00				15 00					16 00				17 00					18 00				19 00	
Gerrards Cross 1	d	14 05	14 27	14 46		15 05		15 27	15 46		16 05	16 27	16 46		17 05	17 27		17 46		18 05	18 27	18 46		19 05	19 27
Denham Golf Club	d	14 08									16 08									18 08					
Denham	d	14 11				15 09					16 11				17 09					18 11				19 09	
West Ruislip 3 § ⊖	d	14 15				15 13					16 15				17 13					18 15				19 13	
South Ruislip § ⊖	d	14 19				15 17					16 19				17 17					18 19				19 17	
Northolt Park	d	14 23				15 21					16 23				17 21					18 23				19 21	
Sudbury Hill Harrow	d																								
Sudbury & Harrow Road	d																								
Wembley Stadium	d	14 28		14 58		15 26			15 58		16 28		16 58		17 26			17 58		18 28		18 58		19 26	
London Paddington 15 ⊖	a																								
London Marylebone 10 ⊖	a	14 41	14 47	15 11	15 14	15 39		15 48	16 11	16 14	16 41	16 47	17 11	17 14	17 39	17 48		18 11	18 14	18 41	18 47	19 11	19 14	19 39	19 48

		CH		CH	CH	CH	CH	CH	CH	CH	CH
		◇		◇		◇	◇	◇	◇		◇
Kidderminster	d										
Stourbridge Junction 2	d										
Cradley Heath	d										
Rowley Regis	d										
Birmingham Snow Hill	d					18 40	19 15		20 15		21 15
Birmingham Moor Street	d			18 13		18 43	19 18		20 18		21 18
Solihull	d			18 22		18 52	19 26		20 26		21 26
Dorridge	d			18 27		18 57	19 34		20 34		21 34
Lapworth	d						19 38				
Stratford-upon-Avon	d	18 00						20 00			
Wilmcote	d	18 05						20 05			
Bearley	d										
Claverdon	d										
Hatton	d	18 15					19 44	20 15			
Warwick Parkway	d			18 37		19 08	19 49		20 46		21 46
Warwick	d	18 23		18 41			19 52	20 23	20 49		21 49
Leamington Spa 8	d	18 27		18 46		19 16	19 57	20 27	20 54		21 54
Banbury	d	18 47		19 06		19 34	20 15	20 47	21 13		22 15
Kings Sutton	d	18 52					20 20				22 20
Bicester North 3	d	19 04		19 20		19 46	20 31	21 04	21 28		22 31
Haddenham & Thame Parkway	d	19 17				19 57	20 42		21 42		22 44
Aylesbury	d				19 23					22 28	
Little Kimble	d				19 31					22 36	
Monks Risborough	d				19 35					22 40	
Princes Risborough 2	d	19 24			19 39	20 05	20 49		21 49	22a47	22 51
Saunderton	d				19 44		20 54		21 54		22 56
High Wycombe 1	d	19 34			19 50	20 14	21 00		22 00		23 02
Beaconsfield	d	19 40			19 57	20 21	21 07		22 07		23 09
Seer Green	d				20 00		21 10		22 10		23 12
Gerrards Cross 1	d	19 46			20 05	20 27	21 15		22 15		23 17
Denham Golf Club	d				20 08				22 18		
Denham	d				20 11		21 19		22 21		23 21
West Ruislip 3 § ⊖	d				20 15		21 24		22 26		23 26
South Ruislip § ⊖	d				20 19		21 28		22 30		23 30
Northolt Park	d				20 23		21 31		22 33		23 33
Sudbury Hill Harrow	d										
Sudbury & Harrow Road	d										
Wembley Stadium	d	19 58			20 28		21 37		22 39		23 39
London Paddington 15 ⊖	a										
London Marylebone 10 ⊖	a	20 11		20 14	20 41	20 47	21 50	21 58	22 52		23 52

§ London Underground Limited (Central Line) also operate services between South Ruislip and West Ruislip at frequent intervals

Table 115A

Mondays to Fridays

Chinnor - Princes Risborough

Bus Service

		CH	CH	CH	CH	CH	CH	CH	CH	CH	CH	CH	CH	CH	CH
Chinnor, Lower Road	d	06 08	06 48	07 14	07 56	08 30	09 16	09 42	17 01	17 28	18 28	19 04	19 39	20 15	21 12
Chinnor, Estover Way	d	06 10	06 50	07 16	07 58	08 32	09 18	09 44	17 03	17 30	18 30	19 06	19 41	20 17	21 14
Chinnor, The Wheatsheaf	d	06 11	06 51	07 17	07 59	08 33	09 19	09 45	17 04	17 31	18 31	19 07	19 42	20 18	21 15
Chinnor, The Red Lion	d	06 14	06 54	07 20	08 02	08a36	09 22	09 48	17a07	17 34	18a34	19a10	19a45	20a21	21a17
Bledlow, Village Hall	d	06 17	06 57	07 23	08 05		09 25	09 51		17 37					
Princes Risborough	a	06 24	07 04	07 30	08 12		09 32	09 58		17 50					

No Saturday or Sunday service

Table 115A

Mondays to Fridays

Princes Risborough - Chinnor

Bus Service

		CH	CH	CH	CH	CH	CH	CH	CH	CH	CH	CH	CH	CH	CH
Princes Risborough	d				07 38	08 12			16 51	17 18	18 18	18 54	19 29	20 05	21 02
Bledlow, Village Hall	d				07 52	08 27			16 58	17 25	18 25	19 01	19 36	20 12	21 09
Chinnor, Lower Road	d	06 08	06 48	07 14	07 56	08 30	09 16	09 42	17 01	17 28	18 28	19 04	19 39	20 15	21 12
Chinnor, Estover Way	d	06 10	06 50	07 16	07 58	08 32	09 18	09 44	17 03	17 30	18 30	19 06	19 41	20 17	21 14
Chinnor, The Wheatsheaf	d	06 11	06 51	07 17	07 59	08 33	09 19	09 45	17 04	17 31	18 31	19 07	19 42	20 18	21 15
Chinnor, The Red Lion	a	06 14	06 54	07 20	08 02	08 36	09 22	09 48	17 07	17 34	18 34	19 10	19 45	20 21	21 17

No Saturday or Sunday service

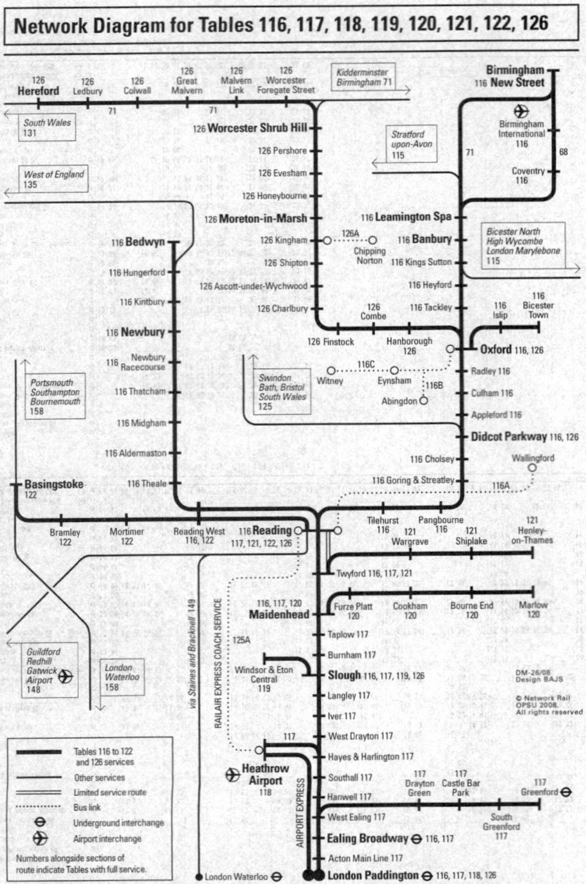

London and Reading - Bedwyn, Oxford, Bicester, Banbury and Birmingham

Network Diagram - see first Page of Table 116

Miles	Miles			GW MO A	GW MO A	GW ■ A	GW MX ■	GW MO ◇■ A	GW MO ■ A	GW MX ◇■	CH MX	GW B		GW MX ■	GW MX ◇■	GW MO ◇■ A	GW MX ■	GW B	GW MO A	GW MX ■	GW MX ◇■	GW ■		GW ■	CH
0	—	London Paddington ⊖	d			22p43	22p45	23p03		23p18				23p29	23p30	23p37					00 22				
5¾	—	Ealing Broadway ⊖	d			22p50	22p54							23p37											
18½	—	Slough	d			23p16	23p12			23p36				23p54		00 03					00 39				
24¼	—	Maidenhead	d			23p24	23p24			23p44				00 01											
31	—	Twyford	d			23p32	23p32		←					00 09						←					
36	0	Reading	d	23p13		23p53	23p41	23p47	23p53	23p58				00 24	00 08	00 14	00 20			00 24	01 00	05 18			
—	1	Reading West	d	23p29		→								→			00s23					05 20			
—	5¼	Theale	d	23p44													00s29					05 26			
—	8¾	Aldermaston	d	23p50													00s34					05 31			
—	10¾	Midgham	d	23p58													00s37					05 35			
—	13½	Thatcham	d	00 05													00s42					05 40			
—	16½	Newbury Racecourse	d	00 15													00s47					05 44			
—	17	Newbury	a	00 25													00 52					05 47			
—	—		d																			05 47			
—	22½	Kintbury	d																			05 54			
—	25½	Hungerford	d																			05 58			
—	30½	Bedwyn	a																			06 08			
38¾	—	Tilehurst	d				23p45		23p57											00 29					
41½	—	Pangbourne	d				23p49		00 02											00 33					
44¾	—	Goring & Streatley	d				23p53		00 07											00 37					
48½	—	Cholsey	d				23p57		00 12											00 42					
53¼	—	Didcot Parkway	a				00 07	00s01	00 20						00 25	00s30				00 51	01 19				
—	—		d		23p45		00 07					00 25						00 40	00 40	00 51	01 19				
55¼	—	Appleford	d																	00 56					
56¼	—	Culham	d																	00 58					
58½	—	Radley	d				00 15					00 40							00 55	01 02					
63½	0	Oxford	a		00 10		00 26			00 28		00 55						01 05	01 10	01 15	01 34				
—	—		d								00 38													05 40	05 45
—	5¾	Islip	d																						05 58
—	11¾	Bicester Town	a																						06 10
72½	—	Tackley	d								00 48													05 49	
75¼	—	Heyford	d								00 53													05 52	
82¾	—	Kings Sutton	d								01 01													06 02	
86¼	—	Banbury	a								01 11													06 11	
106¼	—	Leamington Spa	a																						
115¾	—	Coventry	a																						
126½	—	Birmingham International	a																						
135	—	Birmingham New Street	a																						

		GW ■	GW ■	GW ■	GW ◇■	XC ◇■	GW ■	GW ■		GW ◇■	GW ■	XC ◇■	GW ■	GW ■	GW ■	CH	GW ■	GW ◇■		XC ◇■	GW ■	GW ■	GW ■	GW ◇■	GW ◇■ C
London Paddington ⊖	d		05 18	05 22	05 36					05 48			05 57	06 20				06 30				06 48	06 57	07 00	07 06
Ealing Broadway ⊖	d			05 30									06 05										07 05		
Slough	d		05 34	05 54	05 52					06 05			06 29	06 35								07 04	07 29		
Maidenhead	d			06 02									06 37										07 37		
Twyford	d			06 10							←		06 45				←						07 45		
Reading	d	05 49	05 52	06 21	06 07	06 11		06 15		06 22	06 21	06 41	06 53	06 51	06 52		06 53	06 56		07 09	07 12	07 22	07 53	07 26	07 33
Reading West	d			→				06 17					→		06 54						07 14		→		
Theale	d							06 23							07 00						07 20				
Aldermaston	d							06 28							07 05						07 25				
Midgham	d							06 32							07 09						07 29				
Thatcham	d							06 37							07 14						07 34				
Newbury Racecourse	d							06 41							07 18						07 38				
Newbury	a							06 47							07 21						07 44				07 47
	d														07 21										
Kintbury	d														07 28										
Hungerford	d														07 32										
Bedwyn	a														07 42										
Tilehurst	d	05 54									06 25						06 57					07 27			
Pangbourne	d	05 58									06 29						07 01					07 31			
Goring & Streatley	d	06 03									06 34						07 06					07 36			
Cholsey	d	06 08					←				06 39						07 11					07 41			
Didcot Parkway	a	06 18	06 08		06 20		06 18			06 39	06 47			07 06			07 19	07 10				07 49		07 40	
	d	06 25	06 09				06 25			06 39	06 47			07 08			07 25					07 49			
Appleford	d	→															07 30								
Culham	d						06 31										07 32								
Radley	d									06 48							07 36								
Oxford	a		06 22			06 34	06 41			06 56	07 02	07 05		07 22			07 46			07 35		08 02			
	d					06 36	06 45					07 07				07 32				07 36					
Islip	d															07 45									
Bicester Town	a															07 58									
Tackley	d						06 53																		
Heyford	d						06 58																		
Kings Sutton	d						07 06																		
Banbury	a					06 52	07 14					07 24								07 53					
Leamington Spa	a					07 10						07 42								08 11					
Coventry	a					07 22														08 23					
Birmingham International	a					07 37														08 37					
Birmingham New Street	a					07 48						08 15								08 48					

A from 21 May until 18 June
B 14 May
C The Devon Express

London and Reading - Bedwyn, Oxford, Bicester, Banbury and Birmingham

Network Diagram - see first Page of Table 116

		GW	GW	XC	GW	GW	CH	GW	XC	GW	GW	GW	GW	GW	GW	GW	GW	GW	XC	GW	GW	GW
		1	◇1 🍴	◇1 🛒	1	1		1	◇1 🛒	1	1	◇1 🍴	1	1	1	◇1 🍴	1	◇1 🍴	◇1 🛒	1	◇1 🍴	1
London Paddington 15 ⊖	d		07 15		07 18	07 21					07 27	07 48	07 50		07 57	08 00		08 15		08 18	08 22	
Ealing Broadway ⊖	d										07 35				08 05							
Slough 3	d					07 36					07 59		08 06		08 29						08 36	
Maidenhead 3	d										08 07				08 38							
Twyford 3	d							←			08 15			←	08 46							←
Reading 7	d	07 34	07 42	07 40	07 48	07 52		07 53	08 11	08 12	08 23	08 16	08 22	08 23	08 55	08 27	08 34	08 42	08 41	08 48	08 52	08 55
Reading West	d									08 14	→				→							
Theale	d				07 56					08 20							08 41			08 56		
Aldermaston	d				08 01					08 25							08 46					
Midgham	d									08 29												
Thatcham	d				08 08					08 34							08 53			09 04		
Newbury Racecourse	d									08 38												
Newbury	a				08 13					08 44							08 59			09 13		
	d				08 13												08 59					
Kintbury	d				08 20												09 05					
Hungerford	d				08 24												09 09					
Bedwyn	a				08 34												09 20					
Tilehurst	d							07 57						08 27								09 00
Pangbourne	d							08 01						08 31								09 04
Goring & Streatley	d							08 06						08 36								09 09
Cholsey	d							08 11						08 41								09 14
Didcot Parkway	a	07 57	07 56					08 20				08 32		08 50		08 40		08 56				09 22
	d	08 08						08 25						08 55								09 25
Appleford	d	08 13												09 00								
Culham	d	08 15												09 01								
Radley	d	08 19						08 33						09 06								09 33
Oxford	a	08 31		08 05		08 19		08 43	08 34				08 49	09 15					09 04		09 20	09 43
	d			08 07			08 35		08 36				08 53						09 07			
Islip	d						08 48															
Bicester Town	a						09 01															
Tackley	d												09 01									
Heyford	d												09 06									
Kings Sutton	d												09 15									
Banbury	a			08 26					08 52				09 22						09 25			
Leamington Spa 8	a			08 43					09 10										09 42			
Coventry	a								09 22													
Birmingham International	a								09 37													
Birmingham New Street 12	a			09 18					09 48										10 18			

		GW	GW	XC	GW	GW	CH	GW	XC	GW	GW	GW	GW	GW	GW	GW	XC	GW	GW	GW	CH	GW	XC
		1	◇1 🍴	◇1 🛒	1	1		1	◇1 🛒	1	◇1 🍴	1	◇1 🛒	1	1	◇1 ⊘	◇1 🛒	1	◇1 🍴	◇1		1	◇1 🛒
London Paddington 15 ⊖	d	08 27	08 30			08 51				08 55	09 15	09 18	09 21		09 27	09 30			09 48	09 50			
Ealing Broadway ⊖	d	08 35								09 03					09 35								
Slough 3	d	08 59				09 06				09 27			09 36		09 57					10 06			
Maidenhead 3	d	09 06								09 35					10 04								
Twyford 3	d	09 16						←		09 43				←	10 12							←	
Reading 7	d	09 23	08 57	09 11	09 14	09 22		09 23	09 40	09 53	09 42	09 48	09 52	09 53	10 23	09 57	10 11	10 12	10 16	10 22		10 23	10 41
Reading West	d	→			09 16					→					→			10 14					
Theale	d				09 22							09 56						10 20					
Aldermaston	d				09 27													10 25					
Midgham	d				09 31													10 29					
Thatcham	d				09 36							10 04						10 34					
Newbury Racecourse	d				09 40													10 38					
Newbury	a				09 46							10 10						10 44					
	d											10 10											
Kintbury	d											10 17											
Hungerford	d											10 21											
Bedwyn	a											10 31											
Tilehurst	d							09 27						09 57								10 27	
Pangbourne	d							09 31						10 01								10 31	
Goring & Streatley	d							09 36						10 06								10 36	
Cholsey	d							09 41						10 11								10 41	
Didcot Parkway	a		09 11			09 37		09 50			09 56			10 18		10 11			10 32			10 49	
	d					09 38		09 55						10 25								10 55	
Appleford	d																					11 00	
Culham	d							10 01															
Radley	d							10 03														11 03	
Oxford	a			09 34		09 53		10 14	10 01				10 18	10 41			10 34			10 47		11 14	11 04
	d			09 36			10 00		10 07								10 36				11 00		11 07
Islip	d						10 13														11 13		
Bicester Town	a						10 25														11 25		
Tackley	d																						
Heyford	d																						
Kings Sutton	d																						
Banbury	a			09 53					10 24								10 52						11 24
Leamington Spa 8	a			10 11					10 41								11 10						11 41
Coventry	a			10 23													11 22						
Birmingham International	a			10 37													11 37						
Birmingham New Street 12	a			10 48					11 18								11 48						12 18

London and Reading - Bedwyn, Oxford, Bicester, Banbury and Birmingham

Network Diagram - see first Page of Table 116

		GW	GW	GW	GW	GW	GW	GW	GW	XC	GW	GW	GW	XC	GW	GW	GW	GW	GW	GW	GW	XC	GW
		1	◇1 🍴	1	◇1 🍴	1	1	1	◇1 ⊘	◇1 🛒	1	◇1	1	◇1 🛒	1	◇1 🍴	1	◇1 🛒	1	1	◇1 🍴	◇1 🛒	1
London Paddington 15 ⊖	d	09 57	10 15	10 18	10 22			10 27	10 30			10 50			10 57	11 15	11 18	11 20		11 27	11 30		
Ealing Broadway ⊖	d	10 05						10 35							11 05					11 35			
Slough 3	d	10 27			10 36			10 57				11 06			11 27			11 36		11 57			
Maidenhead 3	d	10 34						11 04							11 34					12 04			
Twyford 3	d	10 42					←	11 12					←		11 42				←	12 12			
Reading 7	d	10 53	10 42	10 48	10 52		10 53	11 23	10 57	11 11	11 12	11 21	11 23	11 40	11 53	11 42	11 48	11 52	11 53	12 23	11 57	12 11	12 12
Reading West	d	→						→			11 14				→					→			12 14
Theale	d			10 56							11 20						11 56						12 20
Aldermaston	d										11 25												12 25
Midgham	d										11 29												12 29
Thatcham	d			11 04							11 34						12 04						12 34
Newbury Racecourse	d										11 38												12 38
Newbury	a			11 10							11 44						12 10						12 44
	d			11 10													12 10						
Kintbury	d			11 17													12 17						
Hungerford	d			11 21													12 21						
Bedwyn	a			11 31													12 31						
Tilehurst	d						10 57						11 27						11 57				
Pangbourne	d						11 01						11 31						12 01				
Goring & Streatley	d						11 06						11 36						12 06				
Cholsey	d						11 11						11 41						12 11				
Didcot Parkway	a		10 56				11 19		11 11			11 37	11 50			11 56			12 20		12 11		
	d						11 25					11 38	11 55						12 25				
Appleford	d																						
Culham	d																						
Radley	d												12 03										
Oxford	a				11 18		11 41			11 34		11 50	12 14	12 01				12 18	12 41			12 34	
	d					11 23				11 36				12 07								12 36	
Islip	d																						
Bicester Town	a																						
Tackley	d					11 32																	
Heyford	d					11 36																	
Kings Sutton	d					11 45																	
Banbury	a					11 51				11 52				12 24								12 52	
Leamington Spa 8	a									12 11				12 42								13 10	
Coventry	a									12 24												13 22	
Birmingham International	a									12 37												13 37	
Birmingham New Street 12	a									12 48				13 18								13 48	

		GW	GW	GW	XC	GW	GW	GW	GW	CH	GW	GW	GW	XC	GW	GW	GW	XC	GW	GW	GW	GW
		◇1 A 🍴	◇1 🛒	1	◇1 🛒	1	◇1 🍴	◇1 🍴	◇1 🛒		1	1	◇1 🍴	◇1 🛒	1	◇1 🛒	1	◇1 🛒	1	◇1 🍴	1	◇1 🛒
London Paddington 15 ⊖	d	11 48	11 50			11 57	12 15	12 18	12 21			12 27	12 30			12 50			12 57	13 15	13 18	13 21
Ealing Broadway ⊖	d					12 05						12 35							13 05			
Slough 3	d		12 06			12 27			12 36			12 57				13 06			13 27			13 36
Maidenhead 3	d					12 34						13 04							13 34			
Twyford 3	d			←		12 42					←	13 12					←		13 42			
Reading 7	d	12 16	12 22	12 23	12 41	12 53	12 42	12 48	12 52		12 53	13 23	12 57	13 11	13 12	13 22	13 23	13 40	13 53	13 42	13 48	13 52
Reading West	d					→						→			13 14				→			
Theale	d							12 56							13 20						13 56	
Aldermaston	d														13 25							
Midgham	d														13 29							
Thatcham	d							13 04							13 34						14 04	
Newbury Racecourse	d														13 38							
Newbury	a							13 12							13 44						14 10	
	d							13 12													14 10	
Kintbury	d																				14 17	
Hungerford	d							13 21													14 21	
Bedwyn	a							13 30													14 31	
Tilehurst	d			12 27							12 57						13 27					
Pangbourne	d			12 31							13 01						13 31					
Goring & Streatley	d			12 36							13 06						13 36					
Cholsey	d			12 41							13 11						13 41					
Didcot Parkway	a	12 32		12 49			12 56				13 19		13 11			13 37	13 49			13 56		
	d			12 55							13 25					13 38	13 55					
Appleford	d			13 00																		
Culham	d																14 01					
Radley	d			13 03													14 03					
Oxford	a		12 48	13 14	13 02				13 18		13 41			13 34		13 50	14 14	14 02				14 18
	d				13 07					13 30				13 36				14 07				
Islip	d									13 43												
Bicester Town	a									13 55												
Tackley	d																					
Heyford	d																					
Kings Sutton	d																					
Banbury	a				13 24									13 52				14 25				
Leamington Spa 8	a				13 42									14 10				14 41				
Coventry	a													14 22								
Birmingham International	a													14 37								
Birmingham New Street 12	a				14 18									14 48				15 18				

A The Cheltenham Spa Express

London and Reading - Bedwyn, Oxford, Bicester, Banbury and Birmingham

Network Diagram - see first Page of Table 116

		GW	GW	GW	GW	XC	GW	GW	GW	CH	GW	XC	GW	GW	GW	GW	GW	GW	GW	XC	GW	GW	GW
		■	■	■	◇■	◇■	■	◇■	◇■		■	◇■	■	◇■	■	◇■	■	■	◇■	◇■	■	◇■	■
					☕	🛒		☕	🛒			🛒		☕		🛒			☕	🛒		🛒	
London Paddington ■15 ⊖	d			13 27	13 30			13 48	13 50				13 57	14 15	14 18	14 21		14 27	14 30			14 50	
Ealing Broadway ⊖	d			13 35									14 05					14 35					
Slough ■3	d			13 57					14 06				14 27			14 36		14 57				15 06	
Maidenhead ■3	d			14 04									14 34					15 04					
Twyford ■3	d		←	14 12							←		14 42				←	15 12					←
Reading ■7	d		13 53	14 23	13 57	14 11	14 12	14 16	14 22		14 23	14 41	14 53	14 42	14 48	14 52	14 53	15 23	14 57	15 11	15 12	15 22	15 23
Reading West	d			→			14 14						→					→			15 14		
Theale	d						14 20								14 56						15 20		
Aldermaston	d						14 25														15 25		
Midgham	d						14 29														15 29		
Thatcham	d						14 34								15 04						15 34		
Newbury Racecourse	d						14 38														15 38		
Newbury	a						14 44								15 10						15 44		
	d														15 10								
Kintbury	d														15 17								
Hungerford	d														15 21								
Bedwyn	a														15 31								
Tilehurst	d		13 57								14 27						14 57						15 27
Pangbourne	d		14 01								14 31						15 01						15 31
Goring & Streatley	d		14 06								14 36						15 06						15 36
Cholsey	d		14 11								14 41						15 11						15 41
Didcot Parkway	a		14 20		14 11			14 32			14 49			14 56			15 21		15 11			15 37	15 49
	d		14 25								14 55						15 25					15 38	15 55
Appleford	d										15 00												
Culham	d																						16 01
Radley	d										15 03												16 03
Oxford	a		14 42			14 34			14 48		15 14	15 02				15 18	15 41			15 34		15 50	16 14
	d	14 24				14 36				15 00		15 07								15 36			
Islip	d									15 13													
Bicester Town	a									15 25													
Tackley	d	14 33																					
Heyford	d	14 37																					
Kings Sutton	d	14 46																					
Banbury	a	14 52				14 53						15 24								15 52			
Leamington Spa ■8	a					15 11						15 42								16 10			
Coventry	a					15 24														16 22			
Birmingham International	a					15 37														16 37			
Birmingham New Street ■12	a					15 48						16 18								16 48			

		XC	GW	GW	GW	GW	GW	CH	GW	GW	GW	XC	GW	GW	GW	GW	XC	GW	GW	GW	GW	GW
		◇■	■	◇■	■	◇■	■		■	■	◇■	◇■	■	◇■	◇■	■	◇■	■	■	◇■	■	◇■
		🛒		☕		🛒					☕	🛒		☕	☕		🛒			☕		🛒
London Paddington ■15 ⊖	d		14 57	15 15	15 18	15 22				15 27	15 30			15 48	15 51				15 57	16 15	16 18	16 22
Ealing Broadway ⊖	d		15 05							15 35									16 05			
Slough ■3	d		15 27			15 36				15 59					16 06				16 27			16 38
Maidenhead ■3	d		15 34							16 07									16 34			
Twyford ■3	d		15 42						←	16 15						←			16 42			
Reading ■7	d	15 40	15 53	15 42	15 48	15 52			15 53	16 25	15 57	16 11	16 12	16 16	16 22	16 25	16 40		16 53	16 41	16 48	16 52
Reading West	d		→							→			16 14						→			
Theale	d				15 56								16 20								16 56	
Aldermaston	d												16 25								17 01	
Midgham	d												16 29									
Thatcham	d				16 04								16 34								17 08	
Newbury Racecourse	d												16 38									
Newbury	a				16 10								16 44								17 14	
	d				16 10													17 08			17 24	
Kintbury	d				16 17													17 14			→	
Hungerford	d				16 21													17 19				
Bedwyn	a				16 31													17 28				
Tilehurst	d								15 57							16 29						
Pangbourne	d								16 01							16 34						
Goring & Streatley	d								16 06							16 39						
Cholsey	d								16 11							16 43						
Didcot Parkway	a			15 56					16 19		16 11			16 32		16 50				16 54		17 08
	d								16 25							16 55						17 09
Appleford	d															17 00						
Culham	d															17 02						
Radley	d								16 33							17 06						
Oxford	a	16 05				16 18			16 43			16 34			16 47	17 15	17 03					17 24
	d	16 07					16 23	16 26				16 36					17 07					
Islip	d							16 39														
Bicester Town	a							16 51														
Tackley	d						16 32															
Heyford	d						16 36															
Kings Sutton	d						16 45															
Banbury	a	16 25					16 51					16 52					17 27					
Leamington Spa ■8	a	16 43										17 11					17 47					
Coventry	a											17 23										
Birmingham International	a											17 37										
Birmingham New Street ■12	a	17 18										17 48					18 18					

London and Reading - Bedwyn, Oxford, Bicester, Banbury and Birmingham

Network Diagram - see first Page of Table 116

		GW	GW	GW	GW	GW	XC	GW	CH	GW	GW	GW	GW	GW	GW	XC	GW	GW	GW	GW	GW	GW	XC
		■	■	◇■	◇■	■	◇■	■		◇■	■	◇■	◇■	◇■	◇■	◇■	■	◇■	■	◇■	■	◇■	◇■
															A								
				☕	☕		🛒					☕	☕	☕	⊘	🛒		☕		☕		☕	🛒
London Paddington ■15 ⊖	d		16 27	16 30	16 36					16 49		17 00	17 03	17 06	17 15		17 18	17 22	17 25	17 30		17 33	
Ealing Broadway ⊖	d		16 35																17 33				
Slough ■3	d		16 57							17 04									17 58				
Maidenhead ■3	d		17 04														17 40		18 10				
Twyford ■3	d	←	17 12								←			17 28			17 48		18 17		←		
Reading ■7	d	16 53	17 23	16 57	17 04		17 11	17 12		17 20	17 23	17 26	17 32	17 36	17 43	17 41	17 57	17 50	18 28	17 56	17 57	18 04	18 11
Reading West	d		→					17 14									→		→				
Theale	d							17 20						17 45									
Aldermaston	d							17 25															
Midgham	d							17 29															
Thatcham	d							17 34						17 55									
Newbury Racecourse	d					←		17 38															
Newbury	a				17 18	17 14		17 44					17 47	18 02								18 18	
	d				17 19	17 24								18 02									
Kintbury	d					17 31								18 10									
Hungerford	d				17a28	17 35								18 16									
Bedwyn	a					17 45								18 24									
Tilehurst	d	16 57									17 27										18 01		
Pangbourne	d	17 01									17 31										18 06		
Goring & Streatley	d	17 06									17 36										18 11		
Cholsey	d	17 11									17 41										18 16		
Didcot Parkway	a	17 20		17 11						17 35	17 49	17 40			17 56					18 09	18 22		
	d	17 25								17 37	17 55										18 25		
Appleford	d	17 30																					
Culham	d	17 32																			18 31		
Radley	d	17 36									18 03										18 35		
Oxford	a	17 44					17 34			17 50	18 12					18 05		18 15			18 45		18 34
	d	17 45					17 36		17 45							18 07							18 36
Islip	d								17 58														
Bicester Town	a								18 10														
Tackley	d	17 54																					
Heyford	d	17 58																					
Kings Sutton	d	18 07																					
Banbury	a	18 15					17 53									18 25							18 53
Leamington Spa ■8	a						18 11									18 45							19 10
Coventry	a						18 22																19 22
Birmingham International	a						18 37																19 37
Birmingham New Street ■12	a						18 48									19 18							19 48

		GW	GW	GW	GW	GW	GW	GW	GW	GW	GW	XC	GW	GW	GW	CH	GW	GW	GW	GW	GW	XC	GW
																	FO	FX					
		■	■	■	◇■	■	◇■	◇■	■	◇■	◇■	◇■	■	■	◇■		■	■	◇■	■	◇■	◇■	■
								B							C								
					☕		☕	☕		☕	☕	🛒			☕				☕		☕	🛒	
London Paddington ■15 ⊖	d			17 36	17 48		17 50	18 00		18 06	18 15		18 15	18 18	18 22		18 25	18 25	18 30		18 33		
Ealing Broadway ⊖	d												18 23				18 33	18 33					
Slough ■3	d												18 47				18 59	18 59					
Maidenhead ■3	d			17 58			18 09						18 57	18 40			19 10	19 10					
Twyford ■3	d			18 07		←			←	18 28			19 05	18 48			19 18	19 18		←			
Reading ■7	d		18 12	18 18	18 16	18 18	18 22	18 27	18 28	18 37	18 43	18 41	19 18	18 57	18 50		19 27	19 27	18 56	18 57	19 02	19 11	
Reading West	d		18 14	→									→	→			→	→					
Theale	d		18 20							18 45													
Aldermaston	d		18 25																				
Midgham	d		18 29																				
Thatcham	d		18 34							18 55													
Newbury Racecourse	d		18 38																				
Newbury	a		18 44							19 02											19 16		
	d	18 26								19 02											19 17		19 27
Kintbury	d	18 32								19 10													19 33
Hungerford	d	18 37								19 16											19 27		19 38
Bedwyn	a	18 46								19 24											19 35		19 47
Tilehurst	d					18 24			18 33											19 01			
Pangbourne	d					18 29			18 38											19 06			
Goring & Streatley	d					18 34			18 43											19 11			
Cholsey	d					18 40			18 49											19 16			
Didcot Parkway	a				18 32	18 46		18 40	18 57		18 56								19 10	19 22			
	d					18 46			18 58											19 25			
Appleford	d								19 03														
Culham	d																						
Radley	d					18 54														19 33			
Oxford	a					19 04	18 47		19 16			19 11			19 19					19 43		19 34	
	d								19 17			19 12				19 30						19 36	
Islip	d															19 43							
Bicester Town	a															19 55							
Tackley	d								19 27														
Heyford	d								19 31														
Kings Sutton	d								19 40														
Banbury	a								19 48			19 30										19 52	
Leamington Spa ■8	a											19 49										20 10	
Coventry	a																					20 22	
Birmingham International	a																					20 37	
Birmingham New Street ■12	a											20 18										20 48	

A The Red Dragon

B The Bristolian

C The Cathedrals Express

London and Reading - Bedwyn, Oxford, Bicester, Banbury and Birmingham

Network Diagram - see first Page of Table 116

		GW		GW	GW	GW	GW	GW	GW	GW	GW	XC		GW	GW	GW	GW	GW	GW	GW	GW	GW		GW	GW
									FO	FX				FO	FX	FO			FX	FO					
		1		◇1 ⊏	1	1	◇1 ⌶	◇1 ⊏	1	1	1 A ✕	◇1		1	◇1 ⊏	1	1	1	◇1 ⊏	◇1 ⊏	1	◇1 ⊏		1	◇1 ⊏
London Paddington 15 ⊖	d			18 47			18 51	19 00			19 03			19 12	19 15			19 18	19 22	19 22	19 27	19 30			19 45
Ealing Broadway ⊖	d																				19 35				
Slough 3	d						19 06												19 36	19 36	19 59				
Maidenhead 3	d																	19 40			20 09				
Twyford 3	d			19 09	←				←	←						←		19 48			20 17			←	
Reading 7	d	19 12		19 18	19 18	19 21	19 22	19 27	19 27	19 27	19u33	19 40		19 43	19 41	19 43	19 42	19 57	19 52	19 52	20 23	19 57		19 57	20 12
Reading West	d	19 15												→			19 44	→			→				
Theale	d	19 20				19 28											19 50								
Aldermaston	d	19 25															19 55								
Midgham	d	19 29															19 59								
Thatcham	d	19 34				19 39											20 04								
Newbury Racecourse	d	19 39				19 52											20 08								
Newbury	a	19 44				19 56					19 50						20 11								20 28
	d					19 56											20 33								
Kintbury	d					20 03											20 39								
Hungerford	d					20 08											20 43								
Bedwyn	a					20 17											20 53								
Tilehurst	d				19 24				19 31	19 31														20 01	
Pangbourne	d				19 28				19 35	19 35														20 06	
Goring & Streatley	d				19 33				19 40	19 40														20 11	
Cholsey	d				19 38				19 46	19 46														20 16	
Didcot Parkway	a			19 32	19 47			19 41	19 53	19 53					19 56	20 00						20 11		20 22	
	d				19 55				20 01	20 08						20 08								20 25	
Appleford	d									20 13						20 13									
Culham	d				20 03																			20 31	
Radley	d									20 18						20 18								20 35	
Oxford	a				20 13		19 48		20 18	20 27		20 05				20 28			20 18	20 21				20 45	
	d											20 07													
Islip	d																								
Bicester Town	a																								
Tackley	d																								
Heyford	d																								
Kings Sutton	d																								
Banbury	a											20 27													
Leamington Spa 8	a											20 45													
Coventry	a																								
Birmingham International	a																								
Birmingham New Street 12	a											21 22													

		XC	GW	GW	CH	GW	GW	GW		GW	XC	GW	GW	GW	GW	GW	GW	XC		GW	GW	GW	GW	GW	XC
		◇1	◇1 ⊏	◇1 ⌶		1	1	◇1 ⊏		◇1 ⊘	◇1	1	◇1 ⌶	1	1	◇1 ⊏	◇1 ⊏	◇1		1	◇1	1	1	◇1 ⊏	◇1
London Paddington 15 ⊖	d		19 48	19 50			19 57	20 00		20 15			20 20		20 27	20 35	20 45				20 48		20 57	21 15	
Ealing Broadway ⊖	d						20 05								20 35								21 05		
Slough 3	d			20 06			20 27						20 36		20 57						21 05		21 27		
Maidenhead 3	d		20 06				20 34								21 04								21 34		
Twyford 3	d					←	20 42							←	21 12							←	21 42		
Reading 7	d	20 11	20 18	20 22		20 23	20 53	20 27		20 41	20 40	20 41	20 52	20 53	21 23	21 02	21 11	21 11			21 20	21 23	21 58	21 41	21 46
Reading West	d						→					20 44			→								→		
Theale	d											20 50													
Aldermaston	d											20 55													
Midgham	d											20 58													
Thatcham	d											21 03													
Newbury Racecourse	d											21 08													
Newbury	a											21 11				21 17									
	d											21 22													
Kintbury	d											21 29													
Hungerford	d											21 33													
Bedwyn	a											21 43													
Tilehurst	d					20 27								20 57								21 27			
Pangbourne	d					20 31								21 01								21 31			
Goring & Streatley	d					20 36								21 06								21 36			
Cholsey	d					20 41								21 11								21 41			
Didcot Parkway	a		20 32			20 50		20 41		20 56				21 19			21 25					21 52		22 00	
	d					20 56								21 25								21 52			
Appleford	d					21 00																21 56			
Culham	d																					21 59			
Radley	d					21 05								21 33								22 03			
Oxford	a	20 34		20 47		21 14					21 05		21 19	21 43				21 34			21 51	22 14			22 28
	d	20 36		20 55	21 00						21 08							21 36		21 41					22 30
Islip	d				21 13																				
Bicester Town	a				21 25																				
Tackley	d			21 04																21 50					
Heyford	d			21 08																21 54					
Kings Sutton	d			21 17																22 03					
Banbury	a	20 52		21 23							21 31							21 52		22 09					22 53
Leamington Spa 8	a	21 10									21 51							22 10							23 12
Coventry	a	21 22																22 22							23 25
Birmingham International	a	21 37																22 33							23 36
Birmingham New Street 12	a	21 48									22 17							22 45							23 57

London and Reading - Bedwyn, Oxford, Bicester, Banbury and Birmingham

Network Diagram - see first Page of Table 116

		GW	GW	GW		GW	GW	GW	GW	GW	CH	GW	GW	GW		GW	GW	GW	GW	GW	GW	GW	GW	GW
								FX	FO		FO			FO		FX				FO	FX			
		◇1	1	1		1	◇1 ⊏	◇1 ⊏	◇1 ⌶	1		1	1	◇1 ⊏		◇1 ⊏	◇1	1	1	◇1 ⊏	◇1 ⊏	1	◇1	1
London Paddington 15 ⊖	d	21 18				21 27	21 45	21 48	21 48				21 58	22 15		22 15	22 18			22 45	22 45	22 45	22 48	
Ealing Broadway ⊖	d					21 35							22 06									22 54		
Slough 3	d	21 35				22 07		22 03	22 03				22 39				22 36					23 12	23 06	
Maidenhead 3	d					22 14							22 47				22 44					23 24	23 14	
Twyford 3	d		←			22 22						←	22 55						←			23 32		←
Reading 7	d	21 50	21 58	22 01		22 32	22 11	22 22	22 22			22 32	23 04	22 41		22 49	22 58	23 00	23 04	23 11	23 19	23 41	23 28	23 41
Reading West	d			22 03		→							→					23 02				→		
Theale	d			22 10														23 08						
Aldermaston	d			22 15														23 13						
Midgham	d			22 18														23 17						
Thatcham	d			22 23														23 22						
Newbury Racecourse	d			22 28														23 26						
Newbury	a			22 31														23 29						
	d			22 31														23 29						
Kintbury	d			22 37														23 36						
Hungerford	d			22 42														23 40						
Bedwyn	a			22 52														23 50						
Tilehurst	d		22 02									22 35							23 08					23 45
Pangbourne	d		22 06									22 40							23 12					23 49
Goring & Streatley	d		22 10									22 43							23 16					23 53
Cholsey	d		22 15									22 48							23 21					23 57
Didcot Parkway	a		22 25				22 31					22 58		23 01		23 08			23 31	23 29	23 38			00 07
	d		22 25									22 58							23 31					00 07
Appleford	d											23 03												
Culham	d											23 05												
Radley	d											23 09												00 15
Oxford	a	22 18	22 41					22 47	22 47			23 21					23 28		23 48				23 56	00 26
	d									23 06	23 12													
Islip	d										23 25													
Bicester Town	a										23 37													
Tackley	d									23 15														
Heyford	d									23 19														
Kings Sutton	d									23 28														
Banbury	a									23 34														
Leamington Spa 8	a																							
Coventry	a																							
Birmingham International	a																							
Birmingham New Street 12	a																							

		GW	GW	GW	GW	GW	GW	GW
			FX	FO		FO	FX	FO
		◇1	1	1	◇1 ⊏	1	1	1
London Paddington 15 ⊖	d	23 18	23 29	23 29	23 30	23 42		
Ealing Broadway ⊖	d		23 37	23 37				
Slough 3	d	23 36	23 54	23 54		23 58		
Maidenhead 3	d	23 44	00 01	00 01		00 08		
Twyford 3	d		00 09	00 09			←	←
Reading 7	d	23 58	00 24	00 24	00 08	00 21	00 24	00 24
Reading West	d		→	→				
Theale	d							
Aldermaston	d							
Midgham	d							
Thatcham	d							
Newbury Racecourse	d							
Newbury	a							
	d							
Kintbury	d							
Hungerford	d							
Bedwyn	a							
Tilehurst	d						00 29	00 29
Pangbourne	d						00 33	00 33
Goring & Streatley	d						00 37	00 37
Cholsey	d						00 42	00 42
Didcot Parkway	a				00 25	00 43	00 51	00 51
	d					00 44	00 51	00 51
Appleford	d						00 56	00 56
Culham	d						00 58	00 58
Radley	d						01 02	01 02
Oxford	a	00 28				01 02	01 15	01 16
	d							
Islip	d							
Bicester Town	a							
Tackley	d							
Heyford	d							
Kings Sutton	d							
Banbury	a							
Leamington Spa 8	a							
Coventry	a							
Birmingham International	a							
Birmingham New Street 12	a							

London and Reading - Bedwyn, Oxford, Bicester, Banbury and Birmingham

Network Diagram - see first Page of Table 116

		GW A 🚌	GW A 🚌	GW ■ A	GW MO ■ B	GW MX ■	GW ◇■ A ⊡	GW MO ◇■ B ⊡	GW MO ■ B	GW ■ A	GW MX ◇■	CH MX	GW MX ■	GW MX ◇■ ⊡	GW ◇■ A ⊡	GW MO ◇■ B ⊡	GW MX ■	GW MX ■	GW B 🚌	GW A 🚌	GW MO ◇■ B	GW MX ■	GW MX ◇■
London Paddington ⊖	d			22p43	22p43	22p45	23p03	23p03			23p18		23p29	23p30	23p37	23p37					23p47		00 22
Ealing Broadway ⊖	d			22p50	22p50	22p54							23p37								23p55		
Slough	d			23p16	23p16	23p12					23p36		23p54		00 03	23p55					00 08		00 39
Maidenhead	d			23p24	23p25	23p24					23p44		00 01								00 16		
Twyford	d			23p32	23p32	23p32							00 09										
Reading	d	23p13		23p53	23p53	23p41	23p47	23p47	23p53	23p53	23p58		00 24	00 08	00 14	00 14	00 24	00 20			00 28		01 00
Reading West	d	23p29																00s23					
Theale	d	23p44																00s29					
Aldermaston	d	23p50																00s34					
Midgham	d	23p58																00s37					
Thatcham	d	00 05																00s42					
Newbury Racecourse	d	00 15																00s47					
Newbury	a	00 25																00 52					
	d																						
Kintbury	d																						
Hungerford	d																						
Bedwyn	a																						
Tilehurst	d					23p45			23p57	23p57							00 29						
Pangbourne	d					23p49			00 01	00 02							00 33						
Goring & Streatley	d					23p53			00 07	00 07							00 37						
Cholsey	d					23p57			00 12	00 12							00 42						
Didcot Parkway	a					00 07	00s01	00s02	00 18	00 20				00 25	00s30	00s32	00 51				00 43	00 51	01 19
	d		23p45			00 07			00 19								00 51		00 40	00 40	00 45	00 51	01 19
Appleford	d																					00 56	
Culham	d																					00 58	
Radley	d					00 15			00 26											00 55		01 02	
Oxford	a		00 10			00 26			00 35		00 28								01 05	01 10	00 57	01 15	01 34
	d											00 38											
Islip	d																						
Bicester Town	a																						
Tackley	d											00 48											
Heyford	d											00 53											
Kings Sutton	d											01 01											
Banbury	a											01 11											
Leamington Spa	a																						
Coventry	a																						
Birmingham International	a																						
Birmingham New Street	a																						

		GW ■	GW ■	CH	GW ■	GW ■	GW ■	GW ◇■ ⊡	XC ◇■ 🛒	GW ■	GW ■	GW ◇■	GW ■	XC ◇■ 🛒	GW ■	GW ■	GW ■	CH	GW ■	GW ◇■ ⊡	XC ◇■ 🛒	GW ■	GW ■
London Paddington ⊖	d					05 18	05 22	05 36				05 48			05 57	06 20				06 30			06 48
Ealing Broadway ⊖	d						05 30								06 05								
Slough	d					05 34	05 54	05 52				06 05			06 29	06 35							07 04
Maidenhead	d						06 02								06 37								
Twyford	d						06 10								06 45								
Reading	d	05 18			05 49	05 52	06 21	06 07	06 11		06 15	06 22	06 21	06 41	06 53	06 51	06 52		06 53	06 56	07 09	07 12	07 22
Reading West	d	05 20									06 17						06 54					07 14	
Theale	d	05 26									06 23						07 00					07 20	
Aldermaston	d	05 31									06 28						07 05					07 25	
Midgham	d	05 35									06 32						07 09					07 29	
Thatcham	d	05 40									06 37						07 14					07 34	
Newbury Racecourse	d	05 44									06 41						07 18					07 38	
Newbury	a	05 47									06 47						07 21					07 44	
	d	05 47															07 21						
Kintbury	d	05 54															07 28						
Hungerford	d	05 58															07 32						
Bedwyn	a	06 08															07 42						
Tilehurst	d				05 54								06 25						06 57				07 27
Pangbourne	d				05 58								06 29						07 01				07 31
Goring & Streatley	d				06 03								06 34						07 06				07 36
Cholsey	d				06 08								06 39						07 11				07 41
Didcot Parkway	a				06 18	06 08		06 20		06 18		06 39	06 47			07 06			07 19	07 10			07 49
	d				06 25	06 09				06 25		06 39	06 47			07 08			07 25				07 49
Appleford	d																		07 30				
Culham	d									06 31									07 32				
Radley	d											06 48							07 36				
Oxford	a					06 22			06 34	06 41		06 56	07 02	07 05		07 22			07 46		07 35		08 02
	d		05 40	05 45					06 36	06 45				07 07				07 32			07 36		
Islip	d			05 58														07 45					
Bicester Town	a			06 10														07 58					
Tackley	d		05 49							06 53													
Heyford	d		05 52							06 58													
Kings Sutton	d		06 02							07 06													
Banbury	a		06 11						06 52	07 14				07 24							07 53		
Leamington Spa	a								07 10					07 42							08 11		
Coventry	a								07 22												08 23		
Birmingham International	a								07 37												08 37		
Birmingham New Street	a								07 48					08 15							08 48		

A 25 June

B from 2 July until 10 September

London and Reading - Bedwyn, Oxford, Bicester, Banbury and Birmingham

Network Diagram - see first Page of Table 116

		GW ■	GW ◇■ ⊡	GW ◇■ A ⊡	GW ■	GW ◇■ ⊡	XC ◇■ 🛒	GW ■	GW ■	CH	GW ■	XC ◇■ 🛒	GW ■	GW ■	GW ◇■ ⊡	GW ■	GW ■	GW ■	GW ◇■ ⊡	GW ■	GW ◇■ ⊡	XC ◇■ 🛒
London Paddington ⊖	d	06 57	07 00	07 06		07 15		07 18	07 21					07 27	07 48	07 50		07 57	08 00		08 15	
Ealing Broadway ⊖	d	07 05												07 35				08 05				
Slough	d	07 29							07 36					07 59		08 06		08 29				
Maidenhead	d	07 37												08 07				08 38				
Twyford	d	07 45												08 15				08 46				
Reading	d	07 53	07 26	07 33	07 34	07 42	07 40	07 48	07 52		07 53	08 11	08 12	08 23	08 16	08 22	08 23	08 55	08 27	08 34	08 42	08 41
Reading West	d												08 14									
Theale	d							07 56					08 20							08 41		
Aldermaston	d							08 01					08 25							08 46		
Midgham	d												08 29									
Thatcham	d							08 08					08 34							08 53		
Newbury Racecourse	d												08 38									
Newbury	a			07 47				08 13					08 44							08 59		
	d							08 13												08 59		
Kintbury	d							08 20												09 05		
Hungerford	d							08 24												09 09		
Bedwyn	a							08 34												09 20		
Tilehurst	d										07 57						08 27					
Pangbourne	d										08 01						08 31					
Goring & Streatley	d										08 06						08 36					
Cholsey	d										08 11						08 41					
Didcot Parkway	a		07 40		07 57	07 56					08 20				08 32		08 50		08 40		08 56	
	d				08 08						08 25						08 55					
Appleford	d				08 13												09 00					
Culham	d				08 15												09 01					
Radley	d				08 19						08 33						09 06					
Oxford	a				08 31		08 05		08 19		08 43	08 34				08 49	09 15					09 04
	d						08 07			08 35		08 36				08 53						09 07
Islip	d									08 48												
Bicester Town	a									09 01												
Tackley	d															09 01						
Heyford	d															09 06						
Kings Sutton	d															09 15						
Banbury	a						08 26					08 52				09 22						09 25
Leamington Spa	a						08 43					09 10										09 42
Coventry	a											09 22										
Birmingham International	a											09 37										
Birmingham New Street	a						09 18					09 48										10 18

		GW ■	GW ◇■ ⊡	GW ■	GW ■	GW ◇■ ⊡	XC ◇■ 🛒	GW ■	GW ■	CH	GW ■	XC ◇■ 🛒	GW ■	GW ◇■ ⊡	GW ■	GW ◇■ 🛒	GW ■	GW ■	GW ◇■ Ø	XC ◇■ 🛒	GW ■	GW ◇■ ⊡	GW ◇■
London Paddington ⊖	d	08 18	08 22		08 27	08 30			08 51				08 55	09 15	09 18	09 21		09 27	09 30			09 48	09 50
Ealing Broadway ⊖	d				08 35								09 03					09 35					
Slough	d		08 36		08 59				09 06				09 27			09 36		09 57					10 06
Maidenhead	d				09 06								09 35					10 04					
Twyford	d				09 16								09 43					10 12					
Reading	d	08 48	08 52	08 55	09 23	08 57	09 11	09 14	09 22		09 23	09 40	09 53	09 42	09 48	09 52	09 53	10 23	09 57	10 11	10 12	10 16	10 22
Reading West	d							09 16													10 14		
Theale	d	08 56						09 22							09 56						10 20		
Aldermaston	d							09 27													10 25		
Midgham	d							09 31													10 29		
Thatcham	d	09 04						09 36							10 04						10 34		
Newbury Racecourse	d							09 40													10 38		
Newbury	a	09 13						09 46							10 10						10 44		
	d														10 10								
Kintbury	d														10 17								
Hungerford	d														10 21								
Bedwyn	a														10 31								
Tilehurst	d			09 00							09 27						09 57						
Pangbourne	d			09 04							09 31						10 01						
Goring & Streatley	d			09 09							09 36						10 06						
Cholsey	d			09 14							09 41						10 11						
Didcot Parkway	a			09 22		09 11			09 37		09 50			09 56			10 18		10 11			10 32	
	d			09 25					09 38		09 55						10 25						
Appleford	d																						
Culham	d										10 01												
Radley	d			09 33							10 03												
Oxford	a		09 20	09 43			09 34		09 53		10 14	10 01				10 18	10 41			10 34			10 47
	d						09 36			10 00		10 07								10 36			
Islip	d									10 13													
Bicester Town	a									10 25													
Tackley	d																						
Heyford	d																						
Kings Sutton	d																						
Banbury	a						09 53					10 24								10 52			
Leamington Spa	a						10 11					10 41								11 10			
Coventry	a						10 23													11 22			
Birmingham International	a						10 37													11 37			
Birmingham New Street	a						10 48					11 18								11 48			

A The Devon Express

London and Reading - Bedwyn, Oxford, Bicester, Banbury and Birmingham

Network Diagram - see first Page of Table 116

		CH	GW	XC	GW	GW	GW	GW	GW	GW	GW	GW	XC	GW	GW	GW	XC	GW	GW	GW	GW	GW
			1	◇1	1	◇1	1	◇1	1	1	1	◇1	◇1	1	◇1	1	◇1	1	◇1	1	◇1	1
				⊼		⊐		⊐				⌀	⊼				⊼		⊐		⊼	
London Paddington 15 ⊖	d				09 57	10 15	10 18	10 22			10 27	10 30			10 50			10 57	11 15	11 18	11 20	
Ealing Broadway ⊖	d				10 05						10 35							11 05				
Slough 3	d				10 27			10 36			10 57				11 06			11 27			11 36	
Maidenhead 3	d				10 34						11 04							11 34				
Twyford 3	d		←		10 42					←	11 12					←		11 42				←
Reading 7	d		10 23	10 41	10 53	10 42	10 48	10 52		10 53	11 23	10 57	11 11	11 12	11 21	11 23	11 40	11 53	11 42	11 48	11 52	11 53
Reading West	d				→						→			11 14				→				
Theale	d						10 56							11 20						11 56		
Aldermaston	d													11 25								
Midgham	d													11 29								
Thatcham	d						11 04							11 34						12 04		
Newbury Racecourse	d													11 38								
Newbury	a						11 10							11 44						12 10		
	d						11 10													12 10		
Kintbury	d						11 17													12 17		
Hungerford	d						11 21													12 21		
Bedwyn	a						11 31													12 31		
Tilehurst	d		10 27							10 57						11 27						11 57
Pangbourne	d		10 31							11 01						11 31						12 01
Goring & Streatley	d		10 36							11 06						11 36						12 06
Cholsey	d		10 41							11 11						11 41						12 11
Didcot Parkway	a		10 49			10 56				11 19		11 11			11 37	11 50			11 56			12 20
	d		10 55							11 25					11 38	11 55						12 25
Appleford	d		11 00																			
Culham	d																					
Radley	d		11 03													12 03						
Oxford	a		11 14	11 04				11 18		11 41			11 34		11 50	12 14	12 01				12 18	12 41
	d	11 00		11 07					11 23				11 36				12 07					
Islip	d	11 13																				
Bicester Town	a	11 25																				
Tackley	d								11 32													
Heyford	d								11 36													
Kings Sutton	d								11 45													
Banbury	a			11 24					11 51				11 52				12 24					
Leamington Spa 8	a			11 41									12 11				12 42					
Coventry	a												12 24									
Birmingham International	a												12 37									
Birmingham New Street 12	a			12 18									12 48				13 18					

		GW	GW	XC	GW	GW	GW	GW	XC	GW	GW	GW	GW	CH	GW	GW	GW	XC	GW	GW	GW	XC	GW
		1	◇1	◇1	1	◇1 A	◇1	1	◇1	1	◇1	◇1	◇1		1	1	◇1	◇1	1	◇1	1	◇1	1
			⊐	⊼		⊐	⊼		⊼		⊐	⊐	⊼				⊐	⊼		⊼		⊼	
London Paddington 15 ⊖	d	11 27	11 30			11 48	11 50			11 57	12 15	12 18	12 21			12 27	12 30			12 50			12 57
Ealing Broadway ⊖	d	11 35								12 05						12 35							13 05
Slough 3	d	11 57					12 06			12 27			12 36			12 57				13 06			13 27
Maidenhead 3	d	12 04								12 34						13 04							13 34
Twyford 3	d	12 12						←		12 42					←	13 12					←		13 42
Reading 7	d	12 23	11 57	12 11	12 12	12 16	12 22	12 23	12 41	12 53	12 42	12 48	12 52		12 53	13 23	12 57	13 11	13 12	13 22	13 23	13 40	13 53
Reading West	d	→			12 14					→						→			13 14				→
Theale	d				12 20							12 56							13 20				
Aldermaston	d				12 25														13 25				
Midgham	d				12 29														13 29				
Thatcham	d				12 34							13 04							13 34				
Newbury Racecourse	d				12 38														13 38				
Newbury	a				12 44							13 12							13 44				
	d											13 12											
Kintbury	d																						
Hungerford	d											13 21											
Bedwyn	a											13 30											
Tilehurst	d							12 27							12 57						13 27		
Pangbourne	d							12 31							13 01						13 31		
Goring & Streatley	d							12 36							13 06						13 36		
Cholsey	d							12 41							13 11						13 41		
Didcot Parkway	a		12 11			12 32		12 49			12 56				13 19		13 11			13 37	13 49		
	d							12 55							13 25					13 38	13 55		
Appleford	d							13 00															
Culham	d																				14 01		
Radley	d							13 03													14 03		
Oxford	a			12 34			12 48	13 14	13 02				13 18		13 41			13 34		13 50	14 14	14 02	
	d			12 36					13 07					13 30				13 36				14 07	
Islip	d													13 43									
Bicester Town	a													13 55									
Tackley	d																						
Heyford	d																						
Kings Sutton	d																						
Banbury	a			12 52					13 24									13 52				14 25	
Leamington Spa 8	a			13 10					13 42									14 10				14 41	
Coventry	a			13 22														14 22					
Birmingham International	a			13 37														14 37					
Birmingham New Street 12	a			13 48					14 18									14 48				15 18	

A The Cheltenham Spa Express

London and Reading - Bedwyn, Oxford, Bicester, Banbury and Birmingham

Network Diagram - see first Page of Table 116

		GW	GW	GW	GW	GW	GW	GW	XC	GW	GW	GW	CH	GW	XC	GW	GW	GW	GW	GW	GW	GW	XC
		◇1	1	◇1	1	1	1	◇1	◇1	1	◇1	◇1		1	◇1	1	◇1	1	◇1	1	1	◇1	◇1
		⊐		⊼				⊐	⊼		⊐	⊼			⊼		⊐		⊼			⊐	⊼
London Paddington 15 ⊖	d	13 15	13 18	13 21			13 27	13 30			13 48	13 50				13 57	14 15	14 18	14 21		14 27	14 30	
Ealing Broadway ⊖	d						13 35									14 05					14 35		
Slough 3	d			13 36			13 57					14 06				14 27			14 36		14 57		
Maidenhead 3	d						14 04									14 34					15 04		
Twyford 3	d					←	14 12							←		14 42				←	15 12		
Reading 7	d	13 42	13 48	13 52		13 53	14 23	13 57	14 11	14 12	14 16	14 22		14 23	14 41	14 53	14 42	14 48	14 52	14 53	15 23	14 57	15 11
Reading West	d						→			14 14						→					→		
Theale	d		13 56							14 20								14 56					
Aldermaston	d									14 25													
Midgham	d									14 29													
Thatcham	d		14 04							14 34								15 04					
Newbury Racecourse	d									14 38													
Newbury	a		14 10							14 44								15 10					
	d		14 10															15 10					
Kintbury	d		14 17															15 17					
Hungerford	d		14 21															15 21					
Bedwyn	a		14 31															15 31					
Tilehurst	d					13 57								14 27						14 57			
Pangbourne	d					14 01								14 31						15 01			
Goring & Streatley	d					14 06								14 36						15 06			
Cholsey	d					14 11								14 41						15 11			
Didcot Parkway	a	13 56				14 20		14 11			14 32			14 49			14 56			15 21		15 11	
	d					14 25								14 55						15 25			
Appleford	d													15 00									
Culham	d																						
Radley	d													15 03									
Oxford	a			14 18		14 42			14 34			14 48		15 14	15 02				15 18	15 41			15 34
	d				14 24				14 36				15 00		15 07								15 36
Islip	d												15 13										
Bicester Town	a												15 25										
Tackley	d				14 33																		
Heyford	d				14 37																		
Kings Sutton	d				14 46																		
Banbury	a				14 52				14 53						15 24								15 52
Leamington Spa 8	a								15 11						15 42								16 10
Coventry	a								15 24														16 22
Birmingham International	a								15 37														16 37
Birmingham New Street 12	a								15 48						16 18								16 48

		GW	GW	GW	XC	GW	GW	GW	GW	GW	CH	GW	GW	GW	XC	GW	GW	GW	GW	XC	GW	GW
		1	◇1	1	◇1	1	◇1	1	◇1	1		1	1	◇1	◇1	1	◇1	◇1	1	◇1	1	1
			⊼		⊼		⊐		⊼					⊐	⊼		⊐	⊐		⊼		
London Paddington 15 ⊖	d		14 50			14 57	15 15	15 18	15 22				15 27	15 30			15 48	15 51				15 57
Ealing Broadway ⊖	d					15 05							15 35									16 05
Slough 3	d		15 06			15 27			15 36				15 59					16 06				16 27
Maidenhead 3	d					15 34							16 07									16 34
Twyford 3	d			←		15 42						←	16 15						←			16 42
Reading 7	d	15 12	15 22	15 23	15 40	15 53	15 42	15 48	15 52			15 53	16 25	15 57	16 11	16 12	16 16	16 22	16 25	16 40		16 53
Reading West	d	15 14				→							→			16 14						→
Theale	d	15 20						15 56								16 20						
Aldermaston	d	15 25														16 25						
Midgham	d	15 29														16 29						
Thatcham	d	15 34						16 04								16 34						
Newbury Racecourse	d	15 38														16 38						
Newbury	a	15 44						16 10								16 44						
	d							16 10													17 08	
Kintbury	d							16 17													17 14	
Hungerford	d							16 21													17 19	
Bedwyn	a							16 31													17 28	
Tilehurst	d			15 27								15 57							16 29			
Pangbourne	d			15 31								16 01							16 34			
Goring & Streatley	d			15 36								16 06							16 39			
Cholsey	d			15 41								16 11							16 43			
Didcot Parkway	a		15 37	15 49			15 56					16 19		16 11			16 32		16 50			
	d		15 38	15 55								16 25							16 55			
Appleford	d																		17 00			
Culham	d			16 01															17 02			
Radley	d			16 03								16 33							17 06			
Oxford	a		15 50	16 14	16 05				16 18			16 43			16 34			16 47	17 15	17 03		
	d				16 07					16 23	16 26				16 36					17 07		
Islip	d										16 39											
Bicester Town	a										16 51											
Tackley	d									16 32												
Heyford	d									16 36												
Kings Sutton	d									16 45												
Banbury	a				16 25					16 51					16 52					17 27		
Leamington Spa 8	a				16 43										17 11					17 47		
Coventry	a														17 23							
Birmingham International	a														17 37							
Birmingham New Street 12	a				17 18										17 48					18 18		

Table 116

Mondays to Fridays

25 June to 14 September

London and Reading - Bedwyn, Oxford, Bicester, Banbury and Birmingham

Network Diagram - see first Page of Table 116

		GW	GW	GW	GW	GW	GW	GW	GW	XC	GW	CH	GW	GW	GW	GW	GW	GW	XC	GW	GW	GW	GW
		◇1 ☕	1	◇1 🛒	1	1	◇1 ☕	◇1 ☕	1	◇1 🛒	1		◇1	1	◇1 ☕	◇1 ☕	◇1 ☕	◇1 A ⌀	◇1 🛒	1	◇1 ☕	1	◇1 ☕
London Paddington 15 ⊖	d	16 15	16 18	16 22		16 27	16 30	16 36					16 49		17 00	17 03	17 06	17 15		17 18	17 22	17 25	17 30
Ealing Broadway ⊖	d					16 35																17 33	
Slough 3	d			16 38		16 57							17 04									17 58	
Maidenhead 3	d					17 04														17 40		18 10	
Twyford 3	d				←	17 12								←			17 28			17 48		18 17	
Reading 7	d	16 41	16 48	16 52	16 53	17 23	16 57	17 04		17 11	17 12		17 20	17 23	17 26	17 32	17 36	17 43	17 41	17 57	17 50	18 28	17 56
Reading West	d					→					17 14									→		→	
Theale	d		16 56								17 20						17 45						
Aldermaston	d		17 01								17 25												
Midgham	d										17 29												
Thatcham	d		17 08								17 34						17 55						
Newbury Racecourse	d								←		17 38												
Newbury	a		17 14					17 18	17 14		17 44					17 47	18 02						
	d		17 24					17 19	17 24								18 02						
Kintbury	d		→						17 31								18 10						
Hungerford	d							17a28	17 35								18 16						
Bedwyn	a								17 45								18 24						
Tilehurst	d				16 57									17 27									
Pangbourne	d				17 01									17 31									
Goring & Streatley	d				17 06									17 36									
Cholsey	d				17 11									17 41									
Didcot Parkway	a	16 54		17 08	17 20		17 11						17 35	17 49	17 40			17 56					18 09
	d			17 09	17 25								17 37	17 55									
Appleford	d				17 30																		
Culham	d				17 32																		
Radley	d				17 36									18 03									
Oxford	a			17 24	17 44					17 34			17 50	18 12					18 05		18 15		
	d				17 45					17 36		17 45							18 07				
Islip	d											17 58											
Bicester Town	a											18 10											
Tackley	d				17 54																		
Heyford	d				17 58																		
Kings Sutton	d				18 07																		
Banbury	a				18 15					17 53									18 25				
Leamington Spa 8	a									18 11									18 45				
Coventry	a									18 22													
Birmingham International	a									18 37													
Birmingham New Street 12	a									18 48									19 18				

		GW	GW	XC	GW	GW	GW	GW	GW	GW	GW	GW	GW	GW	XC	GW	GW	GW	CH	GW	GW	GW
		1	◇1 ☕	◇1 🛒	1	1	1	◇1 ☕	1	◇1 ☕	◇1 B ☕	1	◇1 ☕	◇1 ☕	◇1 🛒	1	1	◇1 C ☕		FO 1	FX 1	◇1 ☕
London Paddington 15 ⊖	d		17 33				17 36	17 48		17 50	18 00		18 06	18 15		18 15	18 18	18 22		18 25	18 25	18 30
Ealing Broadway ⊖	d															18 23				18 33	18 33	
Slough 3	d															18 47				18 59	18 59	
Maidenhead 3	d						17 58			18 09						18 57	18 40			19 10	19 10	
Twyford 3	d	←					18 07		←			←	18 28			19 05	18 48			19 18	19 18	
Reading 7	d	17 57	18 04	18 11		18 12	18 18	18 16	18 18	18 22	18 27	18 28	18 37	18 43	18 41	19 18	18 57	18 50		19 27	19 27	18 56
Reading West	d					18 14	→									→	→			→	→	
Theale	d					18 20							18 45									
Aldermaston	d					18 25																
Midgham	d					18 29																
Thatcham	d					18 34							18 55									
Newbury Racecourse	d					18 38																
Newbury	a		18 18			18 44							19 02									
	d				18 26								19 02									
Kintbury	d				18 32								19 10									
Hungerford	d				18 37								19 16									
Bedwyn	a				18 46								19 24									
Tilehurst	d	18 01							18 24			18 33										
Pangbourne	d	18 06							18 29			18 38										
Goring & Streatley	d	18 11							18 34			18 43										
Cholsey	d	18 16							18 40			18 49										
Didcot Parkway	a	18 22						18 32	18 46		18 40	18 57		18 56								19 10
	d	18 25							18 46			18 58										
Appleford	d											19 03										
Culham	d	18 31																				
Radley	d	18 35							18 54													
Oxford	a	18 45		18 34					19 04	18 47		19 16			19 11			19 19				
	d			18 36								19 17			19 12				19 30			
Islip	d																		19 43			
Bicester Town	a																		19 55			
Tackley	d											19 27										
Heyford	d											19 31										
Kings Sutton	d											19 40										
Banbury	a			18 53								19 48			19 30							
Leamington Spa 8	a			19 10											19 49							
Coventry	a			19 22																		
Birmingham International	a			19 37																		
Birmingham New Street 12	a			19 48											20 18							

A The Red Dragon

B The Bristolian

C The Cathedrals Express

Table 116

Mondays to Fridays

25 June to 14 September

London and Reading - Bedwyn, Oxford, Bicester, Banbury and Birmingham

Network Diagram - see first Page of Table 116

		GW	GW	XC	GW	GW	GW	GW	GW	GW	GW	GW	GW	GW	XC	GW	GW	GW	GW	GW	GW	GW	GW
		1	◇1 ☕	◇1 🛒	1	1	◇1 ☕	1	1	◇1 🛒	◇1 ☕	FO 1	FX 1	B 1 A ✕	◇1	FO 1	FX ◇1 ☕	FO 1	1	1	FX ◇1 ☕	FO ◇1 ☕	1
London Paddington 15 ⊖	d		18 33				18 47			18 51	19 00			19 03		19 12	19 15			19 18	19 22	19 22	19 27
Ealing Broadway ⊖	d																						19 35
Slough 3	d									19 06											19 36	19 36	19 59
Maidenhead 3	d																			19 40			20 09
Twyford 3	d	←					19 09	←				←	←					←		19 48			20 17
Reading 7	d	18 57	19 02	19 11		19 12	19 18	19 18	19 21	19 22	19 27	19 27	19 27	19u33	19 40	19 43	19 41	19 43	19 42	19 57	19 52	19 52	20 23
Reading West	d					19 15										→			19 44	→			→
Theale	d					19 20			19 28										19 50				
Aldermaston	d					19 25													19 55				
Midgham	d					19 29													19 59				
Thatcham	d					19 34			19 39										20 04				
Newbury Racecourse	d					19 39			19 52										20 08				
Newbury	a		19 16			19 44			19 56					19 50					20 11				
	d		19 17		19 27				19 56										20 33				
Kintbury	d				19 33				20 03										20 39				
Hungerford	d		19 27		19 38				20 08										20 43				
Bedwyn	a		19 35		19 47				20 17										20 53				
Tilehurst	d	19 01						19 24				19 31	19 31										
Pangbourne	d	19 06						19 28				19 35	19 35										
Goring & Streatley	d	19 11						19 33				19 40	19 40										
Cholsey	d	19 16						19 38				19 46	19 46										
Didcot Parkway	a	19 22					19 32	19 47			19 41	19 53	19 53				19 56	20 00					
	d	19 25						19 55				20 01	20 08					20 08					
Appleford	d												20 13					20 13					
Culham	d							20 03															
Radley	d	19 33											20 18					20 18					
Oxford	a	19 43		19 34				20 13		19 48		20 18	20 27		20 05			20 28			20 18	20 21	
	d			19 36											20 07								
Islip	d																						
Bicester Town	a																						
Tackley	d																						
Heyford	d																						
Kings Sutton	d																						
Banbury	a			19 52											20 27								
Leamington Spa 8	a			20 10											20 45								
Coventry	a			20 22																			
Birmingham International	a			20 37																			
Birmingham New Street 12	a			20 48											21 22								

		GW	GW	GW	XC	GW	GW	CH	GW	GW	GW	GW	XC	GW	GW	GW	GW	GW	GW	XC	GW	GW	GW
		◇1 ☕	1	◇1 ☕	◇1	◇1 ☕	◇1 🛒		1	1	◇1 ☕	◇1 ⌀	◇1	1	◇1 🛒	1	1	◇1 ☕	◇1 ☕	◇1	1	◇1	1
London Paddington 15 ⊖	d	19 30		19 45		19 48	19 50			19 57	20 00	20 15			20 20		20 27	20 35	20 45			20 48	
Ealing Broadway ⊖	d									20 05							20 35						
Slough 3	d						20 06			20 27					20 36		20 57					21 05	
Maidenhead 3	d					20 06				20 34							21 04						
Twyford 3	d		←						←	20 42						←	21 12						←
Reading 7	d	19 57	19 57	20 12	20 11	20 18	20 22		20 23	20 53	20 27	20 41	20 40	20 41	20 52	20 53	21 23	21 02	21 11	21 11		21 20	21 23
Reading West	d									→				20 44			→						
Theale	d													20 50									
Aldermaston	d													20 55									
Midgham	d													20 58									
Thatcham	d													21 03									
Newbury Racecourse	d													21 08									
Newbury	a			20 28										21 11				21 17					
	d													21 22									
Kintbury	d													21 29									
Hungerford	d													21 33									
Bedwyn	a													21 43									
Tilehurst	d		20 01						20 27							20 57							21 27
Pangbourne	d		20 06						20 31							21 01							21 31
Goring & Streatley	d		20 11						20 36							21 06							21 36
Cholsey	d		20 16						20 41							21 11							21 41
Didcot Parkway	a	20 11	20 22			20 32			20 50		20 41	20 56				21 19			21 25				21 52
	d		20 25						20 56							21 25							21 52
Appleford	d								21 00														21 56
Culham	d		20 31																				21 59
Radley	d		20 35						21 05							21 33							22 03
Oxford	a		20 45		20 34		20 47		21 14				21 05		21 19	21 43				21 34		21 51	22 14
	d				20 36		20 55	21 00					21 08							21 36	21 41		
Islip	d							21 13															
Bicester Town	a							21 25															
Tackley	d						21 04														21 50		
Heyford	d						21 08														21 54		
Kings Sutton	d						21 17														22 03		
Banbury	a				20 52		21 23						21 31							21 52	22 09		
Leamington Spa 8	a				21 10								21 51							22 10			
Coventry	a				21 22																		
Birmingham International	a				21 37																		
Birmingham New Street 12	a				21 48								22 17							22 45			

A Restaurant for customers joining at Pad, Reading + Newbury. The Armada

London and Reading - Bedwyn, Oxford, Bicester, Banbury and Birmingham

Mondays to Fridays

25 June to 14 September

Network Diagram - see first Page of Table 116

Station		GW	GW	XC	GW	GW	GW	GW	GW	GW FO	GW FX	GW	CH FO	GW	GW	GW FO	GW FX	GW	GW	GW	GW FO	GW FX
		1	◇1 ⊡	◇1	◇1	1	1	1	◇1 ⊡	◇1 ✕	◇1 ⊡	1		1	1	◇1 ⊡	◇1 ⊡	◇1	1	1	◇1 ⊡	◇1 ⊡
London Paddington 15 ⊖	d	20 57	21 15		21 18			21 27	21 45	21 48	21 48				21 58	22 15	22 15	22 18			22 45	22 45
Ealing Broadway ⊖	d	21 05						21 35							22 06							
Slough 3	d	21 27			21 35			22 07		22 03	22 03				22 39			22 36				
Maidenhead 3	d	21 34						22 14							22 47			22 44				
Twyford 3	d	21 42				←		22 22						←	22 55					←		
Reading 7	d	21 58	21 41	21 46	21 50	21 58	22 01	22 32	22 11	22 22	22 22			22 32	23 04	22 41	22 49	22 58	23 00	23 04	23 11	23 19
Reading West	d	→					22 03	→							→				23 02			
Theale	d						22 10												23 08			
Aldermaston	d						22 15												23 13			
Midgham	d						22 18												23 17			
Thatcham	d						22 23												23 22			
Newbury Racecourse	d						22 28												23 26			
Newbury	a						22 31												23 29			
	d						22 31												23 29			
Kintbury	d						22 37												23 36			
Hungerford	d						22 42												23 40			
Bedwyn	a						22 52												23 50			
Tilehurst	d					22 02								22 35						23 08		
Pangbourne	d					22 06								22 40						23 12		
Goring & Streatley	d					22 10								22 43						23 16		
Cholsey	d					22 15								22 48						23 21		
Didcot Parkway	a		22 00			22 25			22 31					22 58		23 01	23 08			23 31	23 29	23 38
	d					22 25								22 58						23 31		
Appleford	d													23 03								
Culham	d													23 05								
Radley	d													23 09								
Oxford	a			22 28	22 18	22 41				22 47	22 47			23 21				23 28		23 48		
	d			22 30								23 06	23 12									
Islip	d												23 25									
Bicester Town	a												23 37									
Tackley	d											23 15										
Heyford	d											23 19										
Kings Sutton	d											23 28										
Banbury	a			22 53								23 34										
Leamington Spa 8	a			23 12																		
Coventry	a																					
Birmingham International	a																					
Birmingham New Street 12	a			23 49																		

Station		GW	GW	GW	GW	GW FX	GW FO	GW	GW FO	GW FX	GW FO
		1	◇1	1	◇1	1	1	◇1 ⊡	1	1	1
London Paddington 15 ⊖	d	22 45	22 48		23 18	23 29	23 29	23 30	23 42		
Ealing Broadway ⊖	d	22 54				23 37	23 37				
Slough 3	d	23 12	23 06		23 36	23 54	23 54		23 58		
Maidenhead 3	d	23 24	23 14		23 44	00 01	00 01		00 08		
Twyford 3	d	23 32		←		00 09	00 09			←	←
Reading 7	d	23 41	23 28	23 41	23 58	00 24	00 24	00 08	00 21	00 24	00 24
Reading West	d	→				→	→				
Theale	d										
Aldermaston	d										
Midgham	d										
Thatcham	d										
Newbury Racecourse	d										
Newbury	a										
	d										
Kintbury	d										
Hungerford	d										
Bedwyn	a										
Tilehurst	d			23 45						00 29	00 29
Pangbourne	d			23 49						00 33	00 33
Goring & Streatley	d			23 53						00 37	00 37
Cholsey	d			23 57						00 42	00 42
Didcot Parkway	a			00 07				00 25	00 43	00 51	00 51
	d			00 07					00 44	00 51	00 51
Appleford	d									00 56	00 56
Culham	d									00 58	00 58
Radley	d			00 15						01 02	01 02
Oxford	a		23 56	00 26	00 28				01 02	01 15	01 16
	d										
Islip	d										
Bicester Town	a										
Tackley	d										
Heyford	d										
Kings Sutton	d										
Banbury	a										
Leamington Spa 8	a										
Coventry	a										
Birmingham International	a										
Birmingham New Street 12	a										

London and Reading - Bedwyn, Oxford, Bicester, Banbury and Birmingham

Mondays to Fridays

from 17 September

Network Diagram - see first Page of Table 116

Station		GW MO	GW MO	GW MX	GW MO	GW MO	GW MX	CH MX	GW MX	GW MX	GW	GW	GW MX	GW MO	GW MX	GW MX	GW	CH	GW	GW	GW	GW	GW
		🚌	1	1	◇1 ⊡	1	◇1		1	◇1 ⊡	◇1 A ⊡	◇1 B ⊡	1	🚌	1	◇1	1		1	1	1	1	◇1 ⊡
London Paddington 15 ⊖	d		22p43	22p45	23p03		23p18		23p29	23p30	23p37	23p37				00 22					05 18	05 22	05 36
Ealing Broadway ⊖	d		22p50	22p54					23p37													05 30	
Slough 3	d		23p16	23p12			23p36		23p54		00 02	00 02				00 39					05 34	05 54	05 52
Maidenhead 3	d		23p24	23p24			23p44		00 01													06 02	
Twyford 3	d		23p32	23p32		←			00 09						←							06 10	
Reading 7	d		23p53	23p41	23p46	23p53	23p58		00 24	00 08	00 14	00 14	00 20		00 24	01 00	05 18			05 49	05 52	06 21	06 07
Reading West	d		→						→				00s23				05 20					→	
Theale	d												00s29				05 26						
Aldermaston	d												00s34				05 31						
Midgham	d												00s37				05 35						
Thatcham	d												00s42				05 40						
Newbury Racecourse	d												00s47				05 44						
Newbury	a												00 52				05 47						
	d																05 47						
Kintbury	d																05 54						
Hungerford	d																05 58						
Bedwyn	a																06 08						
Tilehurst	d			23p45		23p59									00 29					05 54			
Pangbourne	d			23p49		00 03									00 33					05 58			
Goring & Streatley	d			23p53		00 09									00 37					06 03			
Cholsey	d			23p57		00 14									00 42					06 08			
Didcot Parkway	a			00 07	00s04	00 21				00 25	00s31	00s33			00 51	01 19				06 18	06 08		06 20
	d	23p45		00 07										00 40	00 51	01 19				06 25	06 09		
Appleford	d														00 56					→			
Culham	d														00 58								
Radley	d			00 15										00 55	01 02								
Oxford	a	00 10		00 26			00 28							01 10	01 15	01 34					06 22		
	d							00 38										05 45	05 45				
Islip	d																	05 58					
Bicester Town	a																	06 10					
Tackley	d							00 48											05 54				
Heyford	d							00 53											05 58				
Kings Sutton	d							01 01											06 07				
Banbury	a							01 11											06 14				
Leamington Spa 8	a																						
Coventry	a																						
Birmingham International	a																						
Birmingham New Street 12	a																						

Station		XC	GW	GW	GW	GW	XC	GW	GW	GW	CH	GW	GW	XC	GW	GW	GW	GW	GW	GW	GW	XC	GW
		◇1 ✕	1	1	◇1	1	◇1 ✕	1	1	1		1	◇1 ⊡	◇1 ✕	1	1	1	◇1 ⊡	◇1 C ⊡	1	◇1 ⊡	◇1 ✕	1
London Paddington 15 ⊖	d				05 48			05 57	06 20				06 30			06 48	06 57	07 00	07 06		07 15		07 18
Ealing Broadway ⊖	d							06 05									07 05						
Slough 3	d				06 05			06 29	06 35							07 04	07 29						
Maidenhead 3	d							06 37									07 37						
Twyford 3	d					←		06 45				←					07 45						
Reading 7	d	06 11		06 15	06 22	06 21	06 41	06 53	06 51	06 52		06 53	06 56	07 09	07 12	07 22	07 53	07 26	07 33	07 34	07 42	07 40	07 48
Reading West	d			06 17				→		06 54					07 14		→						
Theale	d			06 23						07 00					07 20								07 56
Aldermaston	d			06 28						07 05					07 25								08 01
Midgham	d			06 32						07 09					07 29								
Thatcham	d			06 37						07 14					07 34								08 08
Newbury Racecourse	d			06 41						07 18					07 38								
Newbury	a			06 47						07 21					07 44				07 47				08 13
	d									07 21													08 13
Kintbury	d									07 28													08 20
Hungerford	d									07 32													08 24
Bedwyn	a									07 42													08 34
Tilehurst	d					06 25						06 57				07 27							
Pangbourne	d					06 29						07 01				07 31							
Goring & Streatley	d					06 34						07 06				07 36							
Cholsey	d		←			06 39						07 11				07 41							
Didcot Parkway	a		06 18		06 39	06 47			07 06			07 19	07 10			07 49		07 40		07 57	07 56		
	d		06 25		06 39	06 47			07 08			07 25				07 49				08 08			
Appleford	d											07 30								08 13			
Culham	d		06 31									07 32								08 15			
Radley	d				06 48							07 36								08 19			
Oxford	a	06 34	06 41		06 56	07 02	07 05		07 22			07 46		07 35		08 02				08 31		08 05	
	d	06 36	06 45				07 07				07 32			07 36								08 07	
Islip	d										07 45												
Bicester Town	a										07 58												
Tackley	d		06 53																				
Heyford	d		06 58																				
Kings Sutton	d		07 06																				
Banbury	a	06 52	07 14				07 24							07 53								08 26	
Leamington Spa 8	a	07 10					07 42							08 11								08 43	
Coventry	a	07 22												08 23									
Birmingham International	a	07 37												08 37									
Birmingham New Street 12	a	07 48					08 15							08 48								09 18	

A MO from 17 September until 22 October

B MO from 29 October

C The Devon Express

London and Reading - Bedwyn, Oxford, Bicester, Banbury and Birmingham

Network Diagram - see first Page of Table 116

		GW ■		CH	GW ■	XC ◇■ ✠	GW ■	GW ■	GW ◇■ ⊡	GW ■	GW ■	GW ■		GW ◇■ ⊡	GW ■	GW ◇■ ⊡	XC ◇■ ✠	GW ■	GW ◇■ ⊡	GW ■	GW ◇■ ⊡	GW ■		XC ◇■ ✠	GW ■
London Paddington 15 ⊖	d	07 21						07 27	07 48	07 50		07 57		08 00		08 15		08 18	08 22	08 27	08 30				
Ealing Broadway ⊖	d							07 35				08 05								08 35					
Slough 3	d	07 36						07 59		08 06		08 29							08 36	08 59					
Maidenhead 3	d							08 07				08 39								09 06					
Twyford 3	d				←			08 15			←	08 48								09 16		←			
Reading 7	d	07 52			07 53	08 11	08 12	08 23	08 16	08 22	08 23	08 56		08 27	08 34	08 42	08 41	08 48	08 52	09 25	08 57	08 56		09 11	09 14
Reading West	d						08 14	→				→								→					09 16
Theale	d						08 20								08 41			08 56							09 22
Aldermaston	d						08 25								08 46										09 27
Midgham	d						08 29																		09 31
Thatcham	d						08 34								08 53			09 04							09 36
Newbury Racecourse	d						08 38																		09 40
Newbury	a						08 44								08 59			09 13							09 46
	d														08 59										
Kintbury	d														09 05										
Hungerford	d														09 09										
Bedwyn	a														09 20										
Tilehurst	d				07 57						08 27											09 00			
Pangbourne	d				08 01						08 31											09 05			
Goring & Streatley	d				08 06						08 36											09 10			
Cholsey	d				08 11						08 41											09 15			
Didcot Parkway	a				08 20				08 32		08 50			08 40		08 56					09 11	09 22			
	d				08 25						08 55											09 25			
Appleford	d										09 00														
Culham	d										09 01														
Radley	d				08 33						09 06											09 33			
Oxford	a	08 19			08 43	08 34				08 49	09 15						09 04		09 20			09 43		09 34	
	d			08 35		08 36				08 53							09 07							09 36	
Islip	d			08 48																					
Bicester Town	a			09 01																					
Tackley	d									09 01															
Heyford	d									09 06															
Kings Sutton	d									09 15															
Banbury	a					08 52				09 22							09 25							09 53	
Leamington Spa 8	a					09 10											09 42							10 11	
Coventry	a					09 22																		10 23	
Birmingham International	a					09 37																		10 37	
Birmingham New Street 12	a					09 48											10 18							10 48	

		GW ■	CH	GW ■	XC ◇■ ✠	GW ■	GW ◇■ ⊡	GW ■		GW ◇■ ✠	GW ■	GW ■	GW ◇■ Ø	XC ◇■ ✠	GW ■	GW ◇■ ⊡	GW ◇■	CH		GW ■	XC ◇■ ✠	GW ■	GW ◇■ ⊡	GW ■	GW ◇■ ⊡
London Paddington 15 ⊖	d	08 51				08 55	09 15	09 18		09 21		09 27	09 30			09 48	09 50					09 57	10 15	10 18	10 22
Ealing Broadway ⊖	d					09 03						09 35										10 05			
Slough 3	d	09 06				09 27				09 36		09 57					10 06					10 27			10 36
Maidenhead 3	d					09 35						10 04										10 34			
Twyford 3	d			←		09 43					←	10 12								←		10 42			
Reading 7	d	09 22		09 25	09 40	09 53	09 42	09 48		09 52	09 53	10 23	09 57	10 11	10 12	10 16	10 22			10 23	10 41	10 53	10 42	10 48	10 52
Reading West	d					→						→			10 14							→			
Theale	d							09 56							10 20									10 56	
Aldermaston	d														10 25										
Midgham	d														10 29										
Thatcham	d							10 04							10 34									11 04	
Newbury Racecourse	d														10 38										
Newbury	a							10 10							10 44									11 10	
	d							10 10																11 10	
Kintbury	d							10 17																11 17	
Hungerford	d							10 21																11 21	
Bedwyn	a							10 31																11 31	
Tilehurst	d			09 28							09 57									10 27					
Pangbourne	d			09 34							10 01									10 31					
Goring & Streatley	d			09 39							10 06									10 36					
Cholsey	d			09 44							10 11									10 41					
Didcot Parkway	a	09 37		09 51			09 56				10 18		10 11			10 32				10 49			10 56		
	d	09 38		09 55							10 25									10 55					
Appleford	d																			11 00					
Culham	d			10 01																					
Radley	d			10 03																11 03					
Oxford	a	09 53		10 14	10 01					10 18	10 41			10 34			10 47			11 14	11 04				11 18
	d		10 00		10 07									10 36				11 00			11 07				
Islip	d		10 13															11 13							
Bicester Town	a		10 25															11 25							
Tackley	d																								
Heyford	d																								
Kings Sutton	d																								
Banbury	a				10 24									10 52							11 24				
Leamington Spa 8	a				10 41									11 10							11 41				
Coventry	a													11 22											
Birmingham International	a													11 37											
Birmingham New Street 12	a				11 18									11 48							12 18				

London and Reading - Bedwyn, Oxford, Bicester, Banbury and Birmingham

Network Diagram - see first Page of Table 116

		GW ■	GW ■	GW ■		GW ◇■ Ø	XC ◇■ ✠	GW ■	GW ◇■	GW ■	XC ◇■ ✠	GW ■	GW ◇■ ⊡	GW ■		GW ◇■ ✠	GW ■	GW ■	GW ◇■ ⊡	XC ◇■ ✠	GW ■	GW ◇■ A ⊡	GW ◇■ ✠	GW ■
London Paddington 15 ⊖	d			10 27		10 30			10 50			10 57	11 15	11 18		11 20		11 27	11 30			11 48	11 50	
Ealing Broadway ⊖	d			10 35								11 05						11 35						
Slough 3	d			10 57					11 06			11 27				11 36		11 57					12 06	
Maidenhead 3	d			11 04								11 34						12 04						
Twyford 3	d		←	11 12						←		11 42					←	12 12						←
Reading 7	d		10 53	11 23		10 57	11 11	11 12	11 21	11 23	11 40	11 53	11 42	11 48		11 52	11 53	12 23	11 57	12 11	12 12	12 16	12 22	12 23
Reading West	d			→				11 14				→						→			12 14			
Theale	d							11 20						11 56							12 20			
Aldermaston	d							11 25													12 25			
Midgham	d							11 29													12 29			
Thatcham	d							11 34						12 04							12 34			
Newbury Racecourse	d							11 38													12 38			
Newbury	a							11 44						12 10							12 44			
	d													12 10										
Kintbury	d													12 17										
Hungerford	d													12 21										
Bedwyn	a													12 31										
Tilehurst	d		10 57							11 27							11 57							12 27
Pangbourne	d		11 01							11 31							12 01							12 31
Goring & Streatley	d		11 06							11 36							12 06							12 36
Cholsey	d		11 11							11 41							12 11							12 41
Didcot Parkway	a		11 19			11 11			11 37	11 50			11 56				12 20		12 11			12 32		12 49
	d		11 25						11 38	11 55							12 25							12 55
Appleford	d																							13 00
Culham	d																							
Radley	d									12 03														13 03
Oxford	a		11 41				11 34		11 50	12 14	12 01					12 18	12 41			12 34			12 48	13 14
	d	11 23					11 36				12 07									12 36				
Islip	d																							
Bicester Town	a																							
Tackley	d	11 32																						
Heyford	d	11 36																						
Kings Sutton	d	11 45																						
Banbury	a	11 51					11 52				12 24									12 52				
Leamington Spa 8	a						12 11				12 42									13 10				
Coventry	a						12 24													13 22				
Birmingham International	a						12 37													13 37				
Birmingham New Street 12	a						12 48				13 18									13 48				

		XC ◇■ ✠	GW ■	GW ◇■ ⊡	GW ◇■ ⊡	GW ◇■ ✠	CH	GW ■	GW ■	GW ◇■ ⊡		XC ◇■ ✠	GW ■	GW ◇■ ✠	GW ■	XC ◇■ ✠	GW ■	GW ◇■ ⊡	GW ■	GW ◇■ ✠		GW ■	GW ■	GW ■	GW ◇■ ⊡
London Paddington 15 ⊖	d		11 57	12 15	12 18	12 21			12 27	12 30				12 50			12 57	13 15	13 18	13 21				13 27	13 30
Ealing Broadway ⊖	d		12 05						12 35								13 05							13 35	
Slough 3	d		12 27			12 36			12 57					13 06			13 27			13 36				13 57	
Maidenhead 3	d		12 34						13 04								13 34							14 04	
Twyford 3	d		12 42					←	13 12						←		13 42						←	14 12	
Reading 7	d	12 41	12 53	12 42	12 48	12 52		12 53	13 23	12 57		13 11	13 12	13 22	13 23	13 40	13 53	13 42	13 48	13 52			13 53	14 23	13 57
Reading West	d		→						→				13 14				→							→	
Theale	d				12 56								13 20						13 56						
Aldermaston	d												13 25												
Midgham	d												13 29												
Thatcham	d				13 04								13 34						14 04						
Newbury Racecourse	d												13 38												
Newbury	a				13 12								13 44						14 10						
	d				13 12														14 10						
Kintbury	d																		14 17						
Hungerford	d				13 21														14 21						
Bedwyn	a				13 30														14 31						
Tilehurst	d							12 57							13 27								13 57		
Pangbourne	d							13 01							13 31								14 01		
Goring & Streatley	d							13 06							13 36								14 06		
Cholsey	d							13 11							13 41								14 11		
Didcot Parkway	a			12 56				13 19		13 11				13 37	13 49			13 56					14 20		14 11
	d							13 25						13 38	13 55								14 25		
Appleford	d																								
Culham	d														14 01										
Radley	d														14 03										
Oxford	a	13 02				13 18		13 41				13 34		13 50	14 14	14 02				14 18			14 42		
	d	13 07					13 30					13 36				14 07						14 24			
Islip	d						13 43																		
Bicester Town	a						13 55																		
Tackley	d																					14 33			
Heyford	d																					14 37			
Kings Sutton	d																					14 46			
Banbury	a	13 24										13 52				14 25						14 52			
Leamington Spa 8	a	13 42										14 10				14 41									
Coventry	a											14 22													
Birmingham International	a											14 37													
Birmingham New Street 12	a	14 18										14 48				15 18									

A The Cheltenham Spa Express

London and Reading - Bedwyn, Oxford, Bicester, Banbury and Birmingham

Network Diagram - see first Page of Table 116

		XC	GW	GW	GW	CH		GW	XC	GW	GW	GW	GW	GW	GW	GW		XC	GW	GW	GW	XC	GW	GW	GW
		◇1	1	◇1	◇1			1	◇1	1	◇1	1	◇1	1	1	◇1		◇1	1	◇1	1	◇1	1	◇1	1
		⊥		⊏	⊥				⊥		⊏		⊥			⊏		⊥		⊥		⊥		⊏	
London Paddington 15 ⊖	d			13 48	13 50					13 57	14 15	14 18	14 21		14 27	14 30				14 50			14 57	15 15	15 18
Ealing Broadway ⊖	d									14 05					14 35								15 05		
Slough 3	d				14 06					14 27			14 36		14 57					15 06			15 27		
Maidenhead 3	d									14 34					15 04								15 34		
Twyford 3	d							←		14 42				←	15 12						←		15 42		
Reading 7	d	14 11	14 12	14 16	14 22			14 23	14 41	14 53	14 42	14 48	14 52	14 53	15 23	14 57		15 11	15 12	15 22	15 23	15 40	15 53	15 42	15 48
Reading West	d		14 14							→					→				15 14				→		
Theale	d		14 20									14 56							15 20						15 56
Aldermaston	d		14 25																15 25						
Midgham	d		14 29																15 29						
Thatcham	d		14 34									15 04							15 34						16 04
Newbury Racecourse	d		14 38																15 38						
Newbury	a		14 44									15 10							15 44						16 10
	d											15 10													16 10
Kintbury	d											15 17													16 17
Hungerford	d											15 21													16 21
Bedwyn	a											15 31													16 31
Tilehurst	d							14 27						14 57							15 27				
Pangbourne	d							14 31						15 01							15 31				
Goring & Streatley	d							14 36						15 06							15 36				
Cholsey	d							14 41						15 11							15 41				
Didcot Parkway	a			14 32				14 49			14 56			15 21		15 11				15 37	15 49			15 56	
	d							14 55						15 25						15 38	15 55				
Appleford	d							15 00																	
Culham	d																				16 01				
Radley	d							15 03													16 03				
Oxford	a	14 34			14 48			15 14	15 02				15 18	15 41				15 34		15 50	16 14	16 05			
	d	14 36				15 00			15 07									15 36				16 07			
Islip	d					15 13																			
Bicester Town	a					15 25																			
Tackley	d																								
Heyford	d																								
Kings Sutton	d																								
Banbury	a	14 53							15 24									15 52				16 25			
Leamington Spa 8	a	15 11							15 42									16 10				16 43			
Coventry	a	15 24																16 22							
Birmingham International	a	15 37																16 37							
Birmingham New Street 12	a	15 48							16 18									16 48				17 18			

		GW		GW	CH	GW	GW	GW	XC	GW	GW	GW		GW	XC	GW	GW	GW	GW	GW	GW	GW		GW	GW
		◇1		1		1	1	◇1	◇1	1	◇1	◇1		1	◇1	1	1	◇1	1	◇1	1	1		◇1	◇1
		⊥						⊏	⊥		⊏	⊏			⊥			⊏		⊥				⊏	⊏
London Paddington 15 ⊖	d	15 22					15 27	15 30			15 48	15 51					15 57	16 15	16 18	16 22		16 27		16 30	16 33
Ealing Broadway ⊖	d						15 35										16 05					16 35			
Slough 3	d	15 36					15 59					16 06					16 27			16 38		16 57			
Maidenhead 3	d						16 07										16 34					17 04			
Twyford 3	d					←	16 15							←			16 42				←	17 12			
Reading 7	d	15 52				15 53	16 25	15 57	16 11	16 12	16 16	16 22		16 25	16 40		16 53	16 41	16 48	16 52	16 53	17 23		16 57	17 04
Reading West	d						→			16 14							→					→			
Theale	d									16 20									16 56						
Aldermaston	d									16 25									17 01						
Midgham	d									16 29															
Thatcham	d									16 34									17 08						
Newbury Racecourse	d									16 38															
Newbury	a									16 44									17 14						17 18
	d															17 08			17 24						17 19
Kintbury	d															17 14			→						
Hungerford	d															17 19									
Bedwyn	a															17 28									17a28
Tilehurst	d					15 57								16 29							16 57				
Pangbourne	d					16 01								16 34							17 01				
Goring & Streatley	d					16 06								16 39							17 06				
Cholsey	d					16 11								16 43							17 11				
Didcot Parkway	a					16 19		16 11			16 32			16 50				16 54		17 08	17 20			17 11	
	d					16 25								16 55						17 09	17 25				
Appleford	d													17 00							17 30				
Culham	d													17 02							17 32				
Radley	d					16 33								17 06							17 36				
Oxford	a	16 18				16 47			16 34			16 47		17 15	17 03					17 24	17 44				
	d			16 23	16 26				16 36						17 07						17 45				
Islip	d				16 39																				
Bicester Town	a				16 51																				
Tackley	d			16 32																	17 54				
Heyford	d			16 36																	17 58				
Kings Sutton	d			16 45																	18 07				
Banbury	a			16 51					16 52						17 27						18 15				
Leamington Spa 8	a								17 11						17 47										
Coventry	a								17 23																
Birmingham International	a								17 37																
Birmingham New Street 12	a								17 48						18 18										

London and Reading - Bedwyn, Oxford, Bicester, Banbury and Birmingham

Network Diagram - see first Page of Table 116

		GW	XC	GW	CH	GW	GW	GW		GW	GW	GW	XC	GW	GW	GW	GW	GW		GW	XC	GW	GW	GW	GW
		1	◇1	1		◇1	1	◇1		◇1	◇1	◇1	◇1	1	◇1	1	◇1	1		◇1	◇1	1	1	1	◇1
												A													
			⊥					⊏		⊏	⊏	⊘	⊥		⊏		⊏			⊏	⊥				⊏
London Paddington 15 ⊖	d					16 49		17 00		17 03	17 06	17 15		17 18	17 22	17 25	17 30			17 33				17 36	17 48
Ealing Broadway ⊖	d															17 33									
Slough 3	d					17 04										17 58									
Maidenhead 3	d													17 40		18 10								17 58	
Twyford 3	d						←				17 28			17 48		18 17		←						18 07	
Reading 7	d		17 11	17 12		17 20	17 23	17 26		17 32	17 36	17 43	17 41	17 57	17 50	18 28	17 56	17 57		18 04	18 11		18 12	18 18	18 16
Reading West	d			17 14										→		→							18 14	→	
Theale	d			17 20							17 45												18 20		
Aldermaston	d			17 25																			18 25		
Midgham	d			17 29																			18 29		
Thatcham	d			17 34							17 55												18 34		
Newbury Racecourse	d	←		17 38																			18 38		
Newbury	a	17 14		17 44						17 47	18 02									18 18			18 44		
	d	17 24									18 02											18 26			
Kintbury	d	17 31									18 10											18 32			
Hungerford	d	17 35									18 16											18 37			
Bedwyn	a	17 45									18 24											18 46			
Tilehurst	d						17 27											18 01							
Pangbourne	d						17 31											18 06							
Goring & Streatley	d						17 36											18 11							
Cholsey	d						17 41											18 16							
Didcot Parkway	a					17 35	17 49	17 40				17 56					18 09	18 22							18 32
	d					17 37	17 55											18 25							
Appleford	d																								
Culham	d																	18 31							
Radley	d						18 03											18 35							
Oxford	a		17 34			17 50	18 12						18 05		18 15			18 45			18 34				
	d		17 36		17 45								18 07								18 36				
Islip	d				17 58																				
Bicester Town	a				18 10																				
Tackley	d																								
Heyford	d																								
Kings Sutton	d																								
Banbury	a		17 53										18 25								18 53				
Leamington Spa 8	a		18 11										18 45								19 10				
Coventry	a		18 22																		19 22				
Birmingham International	a		18 37																		19 37				
Birmingham New Street 12	a		18 48										19 18								19 48				

		GW	GW	GW		GW	GW	GW	XC	GW	GW	GW	CH	GW FO		GW FX	GW	GW	GW	XC	GW	GW	GW	GW
		1	◇1	◇1		1	◇1	◇1	◇1	1	1	◇1		1		1	◇1	1	◇1	◇1	1	1	◇1	1
				B								C												
			⊏	⊏			⊏	⊏	⊥			⊏					⊏		⊏	⊥			⊏	
London Paddington 15 ⊖	d		17 50	18 00			18 06	18 15		18 15	18 18	18 22		18 25		18 25	18 30		18 33				18 47	
Ealing Broadway ⊖	d									18 23				18 33		18 33								
Slough 3	d									18 47				18 59		18 59								
Maidenhead 3	d		18 09							18 57	18 40			19 10		19 10								
Twyford 3	d	←				←	18 28			19 05	18 48			19 18		19 18		←					19 09	←
Reading 7	d	18 18	18 22	18 27		18 28	18 37	18 43	18 41	19 18	18 57	18 50		19 27		19 27	18 56	18 57	19 02	19 11		19 12	19 18	19 18
Reading West	d									→	→			→		→						19 15		
Theale	d						18 45															19 20		
Aldermaston	d																					19 25		
Midgham	d																					19 29		
Thatcham	d						18 55															19 34		
Newbury Racecourse	d																					19 39		
Newbury	a						19 02												19 16			19 44		
	d						19 02												19 17		19 27			
Kintbury	d						19 10														19 33			
Hungerford	d						19 16												19 27		19 38			
Bedwyn	a						19 24												19 35		19 47			
Tilehurst	d	18 24				18 33												19 01						19 24
Pangbourne	d	18 29				18 38												19 06						19 28
Goring & Streatley	d	18 34				18 43												19 11						19 33
Cholsey	d	18 40				18 49												19 16						19 38
Didcot Parkway	a	18 46		18 40		18 57		18 56									19 10	19 22					19 32	19 47
	d	18 46				19 02												19 25						19 55
Appleford	d					19 07																		
Culham	d																							20 03
Radley	d	18 54																19 33						
Oxford	a	19 04	18 47			19 17			19 11			19 20						19 43		19 34				20 13
	d					19 18			19 12				19 30							19 36				
Islip	d												19 43											
Bicester Town	a												19 55											
Tackley	d					19 27																		
Heyford	d					19 31																		
Kings Sutton	d					19 40																		
Banbury	a					19 48			19 30											19 52				
Leamington Spa 8	a								19 49											20 10				
Coventry	a																			20 22				
Birmingham International	a																			20 37				
Birmingham New Street 12	a								20 18											20 48				

A The Red Dragon

B The Bristolian

C The Cathedrals Express

London and Reading - Bedwyn, Oxford, Bicester, Banbury and Birmingham

Network Diagram - see first Page of Table 116

		GW	GW	GW	GW	GW	GW	XC	GW	GW	GW	GW	GW	GW	GW	GW	GW	GW	GW	XC	GW	GW	CH
					FO	FX			FO	FX	FO			FX	FO								
		1	◇1	◇1	1	1	1 A	◇1	1	◇1	1	1	1	◇1	◇1	1	◇1	1	◇1	◇1	◇1	◇1	
			🛒	☕			✕			☕				☕	☕		☕		☕		☕	🛒	
London Paddington 15 ⊖	d		18 51	19 00			19 03		19 12	19 15			19 18	19 22	19 22	19 27	19 30		19 45		19 48	19 50	
Ealing Broadway ⊖	d															19 35							
Slough 3	d		19 06											19 36	19 36	19 59						20 06	
Maidenhead 3	d												19 40			20 09					20 06		
Twyford 3	d				←	←					←		19 48			20 17		←					
Reading 7	d	19 21	19 22	19 27	19 27	19 27	19u33	19 40	19 43	19 41	19 43	19 42	19 57	19 52	19 52	20 23	19 57	19 57	20 12	20 11	20 18	20 22	
Reading West	d								→			19 44	→			→							
Theale	d	19 28										19 50											
Aldermaston	d											19 55											
Midgham	d											19 59											
Thatcham	d	19 39										20 04											
Newbury Racecourse	d	19 52										20 08											
Newbury	a	19 56					19 50					20 11							20 28				
	d	19 56										20 33											
Kintbury	d	20 03										20 39											
Hungerford	d	20 08										20 43											
Bedwyn	a	20 17										20 53											
Tilehurst	d				19 31	19 31												20 01					
Pangbourne	d				19 35	19 35												20 06					
Goring & Streatley	d				19 40	19 40												20 11					
Cholsey	d				19 46	19 46												20 16					
Didcot Parkway	a			19 41	19 53	19 53				19 56	20 00						20 11	20 22			20 32		
	d				20 01	20 08					20 08							20 25					
Appleford	d					20 13					20 13												
Culham	d																	20 31					
Radley	d					20 18					20 18							20 35					
Oxford	a		19 48		20 18	20 27		20 05			20 28			20 18	20 21			20 45		20 34		20 47	
	d							20 07												20 36		20 55	21 00
Islip	d																						21 13
Bicester Town	a																						21 25
Tackley	d																					21 04	
Heyford	d																					21 08	
Kings Sutton	d																					21 17	
Banbury	a							20 27												20 52		21 23	
Leamington Spa 8	a							20 45												21 10			
Coventry	a																			21 22			
Birmingham International	a																			21 37			
Birmingham New Street 12	a							21 22												21 48			

		GW	GW	GW	GW	XC	GW	GW	GW	GW	GW	GW	XC	GW	GW	GW	GW	GW	XC	GW	GW	GW	GW
		1	1	◇1	◇1	◇1	1	◇1	1	1	◇1	◇1	◇1	1	◇1	1	1	◇1	◇1	◇1	1	1	1
				☕	⊘			🛒			☕	☕						☕					
London Paddington 15 ⊖	d		19 57	20 00	20 15			20 20		20 27	20 35	20 45			20 48		20 57	21 15		21 18			21 27
Ealing Broadway ⊖	d		20 05							20 35							21 05						21 35
Slough 3	d		20 27					20 36		20 57					21 05		21 27			21 35			22 07
Maidenhead 3	d		20 34							21 04							21 34						22 14
Twyford 3	d	←	20 42						←	21 12						←	21 42				←		22 22
Reading 7	d	20 23	20 53	20 27	20 41	20 40	20 41	20 52	20 53	21 23	21 02	21 11	21 11		21 20	21 23	21 58	21 41	21 46	21 50	21 58	22 01	22 32
Reading West	d		→				20 44			→							→					22 03	→
Theale	d						20 50															22 10	
Aldermaston	d						20 55															22 15	
Midgham	d						20 58															22 18	
Thatcham	d						21 03															22 23	
Newbury Racecourse	d						21 08															22 28	
Newbury	a						21 11				21 17											22 31	
	d						21 22															22 31	
Kintbury	d						21 29															22 37	
Hungerford	d						21 33															22 42	
Bedwyn	a						21 43															22 52	
Tilehurst	d	20 27							20 57							21 27					22 02		
Pangbourne	d	20 31							21 01							21 31					22 06		
Goring & Streatley	d	20 36							21 06							21 36					22 10		
Cholsey	d	20 41							21 11							21 41					22 15		
Didcot Parkway	a	20 50		20 41	20 56				21 19			21 25				21 52		22 00			22 25		
	d	20 56							21 25							21 52					22 25		
Appleford	d	21 00														21 56							
Culham	d															21 59							
Radley	d	21 05							21 33							22 03							
Oxford	a	21 14				21 05		21 19	21 43				21 34		21 51	22 14			22 28	22 18	22 41		
	d					21 08							21 36	21 41					22 30				
Islip	d																						
Bicester Town	a																						
Tackley	d													21 50									
Heyford	d													21 54									
Kings Sutton	d													22 03									
Banbury	a					21 31							21 52	22 09					22 53				
Leamington Spa 8	a					21 51							22 10						23 12				
Coventry	a												22 22						23 25				
Birmingham International	a												22 33						23 36				
Birmingham New Street 12	a					22 17							22 45						23 57				

A. Restaurant for customers joining at Pad, Reading + Newbury. The Armada

London and Reading - Bedwyn, Oxford, Bicester, Banbury and Birmingham

Network Diagram - see first Page of Table 116

		GW	GW	GW	GW	CH	GW	GW	GW	GW	GW	GW	GW	GW	GW	GW	GW	GW	GW	GW	GW	GW
			FO	FX		FO			FO	FX	FO	FX			FO	FX					FX	FO
		◇1	◇1	◇1	1		1	1	◇1	◇1	◇1	◇1	1	1	◇1	◇1	1	◇1	1	◇1	1	1
		☕	🛒	☕					☕	☕					☕	☕						
London Paddington 15 ⊖	d	21 45	21 48	21 48				21 58	22 15	22 15	22 18	22 18			22 45	22 45	22 45	22 48		23 18	23 29	23 29
Ealing Broadway ⊖	d							22 06									22 54				23 37	23 37
Slough 3	d		22 03	22 03				22 39			22 36	22 37					23 12	23 06		23 36	23 54	23 54
Maidenhead 3	d							22 47			22 44	22 45					23 24	23 14		23 44	00 01	00 01
Twyford 3	d						←	22 55						←			23 32		←		00 09	00 09
Reading 7	d	22 11	22 22	22 22			22 32	23 04	22 41	22 49	22 58	22 58	23 00	23 04	23 11	23 19	23 41	23 28	23 41	23 58	00 24	00 24
Reading West	d							→					23 02				→				→	→
Theale	d												23 08									
Aldermaston	d												23 13									
Midgham	d												23 17									
Thatcham	d												23 22									
Newbury Racecourse	d												23 26									
Newbury	a												23 29									
	d												23 29									
Kintbury	d												23 36									
Hungerford	d												23 40									
Bedwyn	a												23 50									
Tilehurst	d						22 35							23 08					23 45			
Pangbourne	d						22 40							23 12					23 49			
Goring & Streatley	d						22 43							23 16					23 53			
Cholsey	d						22 48							23 21					23 57			
Didcot Parkway	a	22 31					22 58		23 01	23 08				23 31	23 29	23 38			00 07			
	d						22 58							23 31					00 07			
Appleford	d						23 03															
Culham	d						23 05															
Radley	d						23 09												00 15			
Oxford	a		22 47	22 47			23 21				23 28	23 28		23 48				23 56	00 26	00 28		
	d				23 06	23 12																
Islip	d					23 25																
Bicester Town	a					23 37																
Tackley	d				23 15																	
Heyford	d				23 19																	
Kings Sutton	d				23 28																	
Banbury	a				23 34																	
Leamington Spa 8	a																					
Coventry	a																					
Birmingham International	a																					
Birmingham New Street 12	a																					

		GW	GW	GW	GW
			FO	FX	FO
		◇1	1	1	1
		☕			
London Paddington 15 ⊖	d	23 30	23 42		
Ealing Broadway ⊖	d				
Slough 3	d		23 58		
Maidenhead 3	d		00 08		
Twyford 3	d			←	←
Reading 7	d	00 08	00 21	00 24	00 24
Reading West	d				
Theale	d				
Aldermaston	d				
Midgham	d				
Thatcham	d				
Newbury Racecourse	d				
Newbury	a				
	d				
Kintbury	d				
Hungerford	d				
Bedwyn	a				
Tilehurst	d			00 29	00 29
Pangbourne	d			00 33	00 33
Goring & Streatley	d			00 37	00 37
Cholsey	d			00 42	00 42
Didcot Parkway	a	00 25	00 43	00 51	00 51
	d		00 44	00 51	00 51
Appleford	d			00 56	00 56
Culham	d			00 58	00 58
Radley	d			01 02	01 02
Oxford	a		01 02	01 15	01 16
	d				
Islip	d				
Bicester Town	a				
Tackley	d				
Heyford	d				
Kings Sutton	d				
Banbury	a				
Leamington Spa 8	a				
Coventry	a				
Birmingham International	a				
Birmingham New Street 12	a				

London and Reading - Bedwyn, Oxford, Bicester, Banbury and Birmingham

Network Diagram - see first Page of Table 116

		GW	GW	CH	GW	GW	GW	GW	GW	GW	GW	GW	GW	GW	GW	GW	XC	GW	GW	GW	CH	GW	XC
		1	◇1		1	◇1 🍴	1	1	1	◇1	1	1	1	1	◇1	1	◇1 🛒	1	1	◇1		1	◇1 🛒
London Paddington 15 ⊖	d	22p45	23p18		23p29	23p30		23p42		00 22					05 21				05 25	05 50			
Ealing Broadway ⊖	d	22p54			23p37														05 33				
Slough 3	d	23p12	23p36		23p54			23p58		00 39					05 38				05 51	06 06			
Maidenhead 3	d	23p24	23p44		00 01			00 08											06 02				
Twyford 3	d	23p32			00 09				←										06 10				
Reading 7	d	23p41	23p58		00 24	00 08	00 20	00 21	00 24	00 56	05 08	05 41		05 46	05 54		06 11	06 12	06 21	06 22			06 46
Reading West	d				→		00s23				05 11	05 44						06 14					
Theale	d						00s29				05 17	05 50						06 20					
Aldermaston	d						00s34				05 22	05 55						06 25					
Midgham	d						00s37				05 25	05 58						06 29					
Thatcham	d						00s42				05 30	06 03						06 34					
Newbury Racecourse	d						00s47				05 35	06 08						06 38					
Newbury	a						00 52				05 37	06 10						06 44					
	d										05 37	06 10											
Kintbury	d										05 44	06 17											
Hungerford	d										05 48	06 21											
Bedwyn	a										05 57	06 30											
Tilehurst	d	23p45							00 29					05 50					06 25				
Pangbourne	d	23p49							00 33					05 54					06 29				
Goring & Streatley	d	23p53							00 37					05 59					06 34				
Cholsey	d	23p57							00 42					06 04		←			06 39			←	
Didcot Parkway	a	00 07				00 25		00 43	00 51	01 13				06 12	06 07	06 12			06 46	06 37		06 46	
	d	00 07						00 44	00 51	01 14				06 13	06 08	06 13			06 47	06 38		06 47	
Appleford	d								00 56					→		06 17			→				
Culham	d								00 58							06 20							
Radley	d	00 15							01 02							06 24						06 54	
Oxford	a	00 26	00 28					01 02	01 16	01 28					06 22	06 32	06 36			06 52		07 03	07 10
	d			00 38									06 16				06 38				07 00		07 12
Islip	d																				07 13		
Bicester Town	a																				07 25		
Tackley	d			00 48									06 25										
Heyford	d			00 53									06 29										
Kings Sutton	d			01 01									06 38										
Banbury	a			01 11									06 46				06 54						07 32
Leamington Spa 8	a																07 12						07 50
Coventry	a																07 24						
Birmingham International	a																07 37						
Birmingham New Street 12	a																07 48						08 17

		GW	GW	GW	GW	GW	GW	XC	GW	GW	GW	CH	GW	GW	XC	GW	GW	GW	GW	XC	GW	GW	GW
		1	1	◇1	1	1	◇1 🍴	◇1 🛒	1	◇1	1		1	1	◇1 🛒	1	◇1	1	1 🍴	◇1 🛒	1	◇1	1
London Paddington 15 ⊖	d		05 57	06 21		06 27	06 30			06 50						06 57	07 21	07 27	07 30			07 50	
Ealing Broadway ⊖	d		06 05			06 35										07 05		07 35					
Slough 3	d		06 31	06 38		06 57				07 06						07 27	07 38	07 57				08 06	
Maidenhead 3	d		06 42			07 04										07 34		08 04					
Twyford 3	d		06 50		←	07 12							←			07 42		08 12					←
Reading 7	d	06 48	06 56	06 54	06 56	07 23	06 59	07 11	07 11	07 22			07 23	07 35	07 47	07 53	07 53	08 23	07 57	08 11	08 18	08 22	08 23
Reading West	d		→			→			07 14									→			08 20		
Theale	d	06 55							07 20					07 44							08 27		
Aldermaston	d								07 25												08 32		
Midgham	d								07 29												08 36		
Thatcham	d	07 04							07 34					07 52							08 41		
Newbury Racecourse	d								07 38												08 45		
Newbury	a	07 09							07 43					07 58							08 50		
	d	07 09												07 58									
Kintbury	d	07 16												08 04									
Hungerford	d	07 20												08 09									
Bedwyn	a	07 29												08 18									
Tilehurst	d				07 00								07 27			07 57							08 27
Pangbourne	d				07 04								07 31			08 01							08 31
Goring & Streatley	d				07 09								07 36			08 06							08 36
Cholsey	d				07 14								07 41			08 11							08 41
Didcot Parkway	a				07 30		07 12						07 49			08 19			08 12				08 48
	d				07 30								07 51			08 25							08 55
Appleford	d																						09 00
Culham	d												07 56										
Radley	d												08 00										09 03
Oxford	a			07 18	07 43			07 34		07 48			08 09		08 13	08 40	08 19			08 34		08 48	09 14
	d							07 36			07 53	08 07			08 15					08 36			
Islip	d											08 20											
Bicester Town	a											08 32											
Tackley	d										08 02												
Heyford	d										08 06												
Kings Sutton	d										08 15												
Banbury	a							07 52			08 23				08 32					08 52			
Leamington Spa 8	a							08 10							08 49					09 10			
Coventry	a							08 22												09 22			
Birmingham International	a							08 37												09 37			
Birmingham New Street 12	a							08 48							09 18					09 48			

London and Reading - Bedwyn, Oxford, Bicester, Banbury and Birmingham

Network Diagram - see first Page of Table 116

		XC	GW	GW	GW	GW	GW	GW	CH	GW	GW	GW	XC	GW	GW	GW	XC	GW	GW	GW	GW	GW
		◇1 🛒	1	1	◇1 🍴	1	1	◇1 🍴		1	◇1 🍴	1 A 🍴	◇1 🛒	1	◇1	1	◇1 🛒	1	1	1	1	◇1
London Paddington 15 ⊖	d			07 57	08 15	08 18		08 21		08 27	08 30	08 35			08 50				08 57	09 18		09 21
Ealing Broadway ⊖	d			08 05						08 35									09 05			
Slough 3	d			08 27				08 39		08 57					09 06				09 27			09 39
Maidenhead 3	d			08 34						09 04									09 34			
Twyford 3	d			08 42			←			09 12						←			09 42		←	
Reading 7	d	08 40		08 53	08 42	08 48	08 53	08 54		09 23	08 57	09u04	09 11	09 12	09 22	09 23	09 40		09 53	09 48	09 53	09 54
Reading West	d			→						→				09 14					→			
Theale	d					08 55								09 20						09 56		
Aldermaston	d													09 25								
Midgham	d													09 29								
Thatcham	d					09 05								09 34						10 04		
Newbury Racecourse	d													09 38								
Newbury	a					09 11						09 20		09 44						10 10		
	d		08 58			09 24														10 10		
Kintbury	d		09 04			09 31														10 17		
Hungerford	d		09 09			09 35														10 21		
Bedwyn	a		09 17			09 44														10 31		
Tilehurst	d						08 57									09 27					09 57	
Pangbourne	d						09 01									09 31					10 01	
Goring & Streatley	d						09 06									09 36					10 06	
Cholsey	d						09 11									09 41					10 11	
Didcot Parkway	a				08 55		09 19				09 12					09 48					10 18	
	d						09 25									09 55					10 25	
Appleford	d																					
Culham	d															10 01						
Radley	d															10 03						
Oxford	a	09 04					09 40	09 18					09 34		09 48	10 14	10 04				10 40	10 19
	d	09 07							09 28				09 36				10 07	10 16				
Islip	d								09 41													
Bicester Town	a								09 53													
Tackley	d																	10 25				
Heyford	d																	10 29				
Kings Sutton	d																	10 38				
Banbury	a	09 23											09 52				10 23	10 46				
Leamington Spa 8	a	09 41											10 12				10 41					
Coventry	a												10 22									
Birmingham International	a												10 37									
Birmingham New Street 12	a	10 18											10 48				11 18					

		GW	GW	XC	GW	GW	CH	GW	XC	GW	GW	GW	GW	GW	GW	GW	XC	GW	GW	GW	XC	GW	GW
		1	◇1 🍴	◇1 🛒	1	◇1		1	◇1 🛒	1	◇1 🍴	1	1	◇1 🍴	1	◇1 🍴	◇1 🛒	1	◇1 🛒	1	◇1 🛒	1	1
London Paddington 15 ⊖	d	09 27	09 30			09 50				09 57	10 15	10 18		10 21	10 27	10 30			10 50				10 57
Ealing Broadway ⊖	d	09 35								10 05					10 35								11 05
Slough 3	d	09 57				10 06				10 27				10 39	10 57				11 06				11 27
Maidenhead 3	d	10 04								10 34					11 04								11 34
Twyford 3	d	10 12						←		10 42			←		11 12					←			11 42
Reading 7	d	10 23	09 57	10 11	10 12	10 22		10 23	10 40	10 53	10 42	10 48	10 53	10 54	11 23	10 57	11 11	11 12	11 22	11 23	11 40		11 53
Reading West	d	→			10 14					→					→			11 14					→
Theale	d				10 20							10 56						11 20					
Aldermaston	d				10 25													11 25					
Midgham	d				10 29													11 29					
Thatcham	d				10 34							11 04						11 34					
Newbury Racecourse	d				10 38													11 38					
Newbury	a				10 44							11 10						11 44					
	d											11 23											
Kintbury	d											11 30											
Hungerford	d											11 34											
Bedwyn	a											11 44											
Tilehurst	d							10 27					10 57							11 27			
Pangbourne	d							10 31					11 01							11 31			
Goring & Streatley	d							10 36					11 06							11 36			
Cholsey	d							10 41					11 11							11 41			
Didcot Parkway	a		10 12					10 48			10 55		11 19			11 12				11 49			
	d							10 55					11 25							11 55			
Appleford	d							11 00															
Culham	d																						
Radley	d							11 03												12 03			
Oxford	a			10 34		10 48		11 14	11 04				11 40	11 19			11 34		11 48	12 14	12 04		
	d			10 36			11 00		11 07								11 36				12 07	12 16	
Islip	d						11 13																
Bicester Town	a						11 25																
Tackley	d																					12 25	
Heyford	d																					12 29	
Kings Sutton	d																					12 38	
Banbury	a			10 52					11 23								11 52				12 23	12 46	
Leamington Spa 8	a			11 10					11 41								12 10				12 41		
Coventry	a			11 22													12 22						
Birmingham International	a			11 37													12 37						
Birmingham New Street 12	a			11 48					12 18								12 48				13 18		

A The Torbay Express

Table 116

Saturdays
until 23 June

London and Reading - Bedwyn, Oxford, Bicester, Banbury and Birmingham

Network Diagram - see first Page of Table 116

		GW	GW	GW	CH	GW	GW	XC	GW	GW	GW	XC	GW	GW	GW	GW	GW	GW	GW	GW	XC	GW
		1	1	◇1 ⊼		1	◇1 Ø	◇1 ⊼	1	◇1	1	◇1 ⊼	1	◇1 ⊏	1	1	◇1	1	◇1 ⊏	1 ⊏	◇1 ⊼	1
London Paddington 15 ⊖	d	11 18		11 21		11 27	11 30			11 50			11 57	12 15	12 18		12 21	12 27	12 30	12 35		
Ealing Broadway ⊖	d					11 35							12 05					12 35				
Slough 3	d			11 39		11 57				12 06			12 27				12 39	12 57				
Maidenhead 3	d					12 04							12 34					13 04				
Twyford 3	d		←			12 12					←		12 42			←		13 12				
Reading 7	d	11 48	11 53	11 54		12 23	11 58	12 11	12 12	12 22	12 23	12 40	12 53	12 42	12 48	12 53	12 54	13 23	12 57	13u06	13 11	
Reading West	d					→			12 14				→					→				
Theale	d	11 56							12 20						12 56							
Aldermaston	d								12 25													
Midgham	d								12 29													
Thatcham	d	12 04							12 34						13 04							
Newbury Racecourse	d								12 38													
Newbury	a	12 10							12 44						13 16					13 21		
	d	12 25																				13 26
Kintbury	d	12 31																				13 32
Hungerford	d	12 36																				13 37
Bedwyn	a	12 45																				13 45
Tilehurst	d		11 57								12 27					12 57						
Pangbourne	d		12 01								12 31					13 01						
Goring & Streatley	d		12 06								12 36					13 06						
Cholsey	d		12 11								12 41					13 11						
Didcot Parkway	a		12 19				12 12				12 48			12 55		13 19			13 12			
	d		12 25								12 55					13 25						
Appleford	d										13 00											
Culham	d																					
Radley	d										13 03											
Oxford	a		12 40	12 20				12 34		12 48	13 14	13 04				13 40	13 19				13 34	
	d				12 30			12 36				13 07									13 36	
Islip	d				12 43																	
Bicester Town	a				12 55																	
Tackley	d																					
Heyford	d																					
Kings Sutton	d																					
Banbury	a							12 52				13 23									13 52	
Leamington Spa 8	a							13 10				13 41									14 10	
Coventry	a							13 22													14 22	
Birmingham International	a							13 37													14 37	
Birmingham New Street 12	a							13 48				14 18									14 48	

		GW	CH	GW	GW	XC	GW	GW	GW	GW	GW	GW	GW	XC	GW	GW	CH	GW	XC	GW	GW	GW	GW
		1		◇1 ⊼	1	◇1 ⊼	1	1	1	1	◇1 ⊼	1	◇1 ⊏	◇1 ⊼	1	◇1 ⊼		1	◇1 ⊼	1	◇1 ⊏	1	1
London Paddington 15 ⊖	d			12 50				12 57	13 18		13 21	13 27	13 30			13 50				13 57	14 15	14 18	
Ealing Broadway ⊖	d							13 05				13 35								14 05			
Slough 3	d			13 06				13 27			13 39	13 57				14 06				14 27			
Maidenhead 3	d							13 34				14 04								14 34			
Twyford 3	d				←			13 42		←		14 12						←		14 42			←
Reading 7	d	13 12		13 22	13 23	13 40		13 53	13 48	13 53	13 54	14 23	13 59	14 11	14 12	14 22		14 23	14 40	14 53	14 42	14 48	14 53
Reading West	d	13 14						→				→			14 14					→			
Theale	d	13 20							13 56						14 20							14 56	
Aldermaston	d	13 25													14 25								
Midgham	d	13 29													14 29								
Thatcham	d	13 34							14 04						14 34							15 04	
Newbury Racecourse	d	13 38													14 38								
Newbury	a	13 44							14 10						14 44							15 10	
	d								14 10													15 10	
Kintbury	d								14 17													15 17	
Hungerford	d								14 21													15 21	
Bedwyn	a								14 31													15 31	
Tilehurst	d				13 27					13 57								14 27					14 57
Pangbourne	d				13 31					14 01								14 31					15 01
Goring & Streatley	d				13 36					14 06								14 36					15 06
Cholsey	d				13 41					14 11								14 41					15 11
Didcot Parkway	a				13 48					14 19			14 12					14 48			14 55		15 19
	d				13 55					14 25								14 55					15 25
Appleford	d																	15 00					
Culham	d				14 01																		
Radley	d				14 03													15 03					
Oxford	a			13 48	14 14	14 04				14 40	14 19			14 34		14 48		15 14	15 04				15 40
	d		13 41			14 07	14 16							14 36			14 57		15 07				
Islip	d		13 54														15 10						
Bicester Town	a		14 06														15 22						
Tackley	d						14 25																
Heyford	d						14 29																
Kings Sutton	d						14 38																
Banbury	a					14 23	14 46							14 52					15 23				
Leamington Spa 8	a					14 41								15 10					15 41				
Coventry	a													15 22									
Birmingham International	a													15 37									
Birmingham New Street 12	a					15 18								15 48					16 18				

Table 116

Saturdays
until 23 June

London and Reading - Bedwyn, Oxford, Bicester, Banbury and Birmingham

Network Diagram - see first Page of Table 116

		GW	GW	GW	XC	GW	GW	CH	GW	XC	GW	GW	GW	GW	GW	GW	GW	XC	GW	GW	GW	XC	CH
		◇1 ⊼	1	◇1 ⊏	◇1 ⊼	1	◇1		1	◇1 ⊼	1	1	1	1	◇1 ⊼	1	◇1 ⊏	◇1 ⊼	1	◇1	1	◇1 ⊼	
London Paddington 15 ⊖	d	14 21	14 27	14 30			14 50					14 57	15 18		15 21	15 27	15 30			15 50			
Ealing Broadway ⊖	d		14 35									15 05				15 35							
Slough 3	d	14 39	14 57				15 06					15 27			15 39	15 57				16 06			
Maidenhead 3	d		15 04									15 34				16 04							
Twyford 3	d		15 12						←			15 42		←		16 12					←		
Reading 7	d	14 54	15 23	14 57	15 11	15 12	15 22		15 23	15 40		15 53	15 48	15 53	15 54	16 23	15 59	16 11	16 12	16 22	16 23	16 40	
Reading West	d		→			15 14						→				→			16 14				
Theale	d					15 20							15 56						16 20				
Aldermaston	d					15 25													16 25				
Midgham	d					15 29													16 29				
Thatcham	d					15 34							16 04						16 34				
Newbury Racecourse	d					15 38													16 38				
Newbury	a					15 44							16 10						16 44				
	d												16 10										
Kintbury	d												16 17										
Hungerford	d												16 21										
Bedwyn	a												16 31										
Tilehurst	d								15 27					15 57							16 27		
Pangbourne	d								15 31					16 01							16 31		
Goring & Streatley	d								15 36					16 06							16 36		
Cholsey	d								15 41					16 11							16 41		
Didcot Parkway	a			15 12					15 48					16 19			16 12				16 48		
	d								15 55					16 25							16 55		
Appleford	d																				17 00		
Culham	d								16 01														
Radley	d								16 03												17 03		
Oxford	a	15 18			15 34		15 48		16 14	16 04				16 40	16 19			16 34		16 48	17 14	17 04	
	d				15 36			16 00		16 07	16 16							16 36				17 07	17 10
Islip	d							16 13															17 23
Bicester Town	a							16 25															17 35
Tackley	d										16 25												
Heyford	d										16 29												
Kings Sutton	d										16 38												
Banbury	a				15 52					16 23	16 46							16 52				17 23	
Leamington Spa 8	a				16 10					16 41								17 10				17 41	
Coventry	a				16 22													17 22					
Birmingham International	a				16 37													17 37					
Birmingham New Street 12	a				16 48					17 18								17 48				18 18	

		GW	GW	GW	GW	GW	GW	GW	XC	GW	GW	GW	XC	GW	GW	GW	GW	GW	GW	GW	XC	GW
		1	◇1 ⊏	1	1	◇1 ⊏	1	◇1 ⊏	◇1 ⊼	1	◇1 ⊼	1	◇1 ⊼	1	1	1	1	◇1 ⊏	1	◇1 ⊏	◇1 ⊼	1
London Paddington 15 ⊖	d	15 57	16 15	16 18		16 21	16 27	16 30			16 50				16 57	17 18		17 21	17 27	17 30		
Ealing Broadway ⊖	d	16 05					16 35								17 05				17 35			
Slough 3	d	16 27				16 39	16 57				17 06				17 27			17 39	17 57			
Maidenhead 3	d	16 34					17 04								17 34				18 04			
Twyford 3	d	16 42			←		17 12					←			17 42		←		18 12			
Reading 7	d	16 53	16 42	16 48	16 53	16 54	17 23	16 57	17 11	17 12	17 22	17 23	17 40		17 53	17 48	17 53	17 54	18 23	17 57	18 11	18 12
Reading West	d	→					→			17 14					→				→			18 14
Theale	d			16 56						17 20						17 56						18 20
Aldermaston	d									17 25												18 25
Midgham	d									17 29												18 29
Thatcham	d			17 04						17 34						18 04						18 34
Newbury Racecourse	d									17 38												18 38
Newbury	a			17 10						17 44						18 10						18 44
	d			17 10												18 10						
Kintbury	d			17 17												18 17						
Hungerford	d			17 21												18 21						
Bedwyn	a			17 31												18 31						
Tilehurst	d				16 57							17 27					17 57					
Pangbourne	d				17 01							17 31					18 01					
Goring & Streatley	d				17 06							17 36					18 06					
Cholsey	d				17 11							17 41					18 11					
Didcot Parkway	a		16 55		17 19			17 12				17 48					18 19			18 12		
	d				17 25							17 55					18 25					
Appleford	d																					
Culham	d											18 01										
Radley	d											18 03										
Oxford	a				17 40	17 18			17 34		17 48	18 14	18 04				18 40	18 18			18 34	
	d								17 36				18 07	18 16							18 36	
Islip	d																					
Bicester Town	a																					
Tackley	d													18 25								
Heyford	d													18 29								
Kings Sutton	d													18 38								
Banbury	a								17 52				18 23	18 46							18 52	
Leamington Spa 8	a								18 10				18 41								19 10	
Coventry	a								18 22												19 22	
Birmingham International	a								18 37												19 37	
Birmingham New Street 12	a								18 48				19 18								19 48	

Table 116

Saturdays until 23 June

London and Reading - Bedwyn, Oxford, Bicester, Banbury and Birmingham

Network Diagram - see first Page of Table 116

		CH	GW ◇1	GW 1	XC ◇1	GW 1	GW ◇1	GW 1	GW 1	GW ◇1	GW 1	GW ◇1	XC ◇1	GW ◇1	CH	GW 1	GW 1	GW 1	GW ◇1	XC ◇1	GW 1	GW ◇1	GW 1
London Paddington 15 ⊖	d		17 50			17 57	18 15	18 18		18 21	18 27	18 30		18 50				18 57	19 06			19 21	
Ealing Broadway ⊖	d					18 05					18 35							19 05					
Slough 3	d		18 06			18 27				18 39	18 57			19 06				19 27				19 38	
Maidenhead 3	d					18 34					19 04							19 34					
Twyford 3	d			←		18 42			←		19 12						←	19 42					←
Reading 7	d		18 22	18 23	18 40	18 53	18 42	18 48	18 53	18 54	19 23	18 57	19 11	19 23			19 23	19 53	19 32	19 40	19 49	19 52	19 53
Reading West	d					→					→							→			19 52		
Theale	d							18 56													19 58		
Aldermaston	d																				20 03		
Midgham	d																				20 06		
Thatcham	d							19 04													20 11		
Newbury Racecourse	d																				20 16		
Newbury	a							19 10											19 48		20 18		
	d							19 10													20 18		
Kintbury	d							19 17													20 25		
Hungerford	d							19 21													20 29		
Bedwyn	a							19 31													20 38		
Tilehurst	d			18 27					18 57								19 27						19 57
Pangbourne	d			18 31					19 01								19 31						20 01
Goring & Streatley	d			18 36					19 06								19 37						20 06
Cholsey	d			18 41					19 11								19 41						20 11
Didcot Parkway	a			18 48			18 55		19 19			19 12					19 49						20 19
	d			18 55					19 25								19 55						20 25
Appleford	d			19 00																			
Culham	d																20 01						
Radley	d			19 03													20 03						
Oxford	a		18 48	19 14	19 04				19 40	19 18			19 34	19 48			20 14			20 04		20 20	20 40
	d	18 41			19 07								19 36		19 48	19 56				20 07			
Islip	d	18 54													20 01								
Bicester Town	a	19 06													20 13								
Tackley	d															20 05							
Heyford	d															20 09							
Kings Sutton	d															20 18							
Banbury	a				19 23								19 52			20 25				20 28			
Leamington Spa 8	a				19 41								20 10							20 45			
Coventry	a												20 22										
Birmingham International	a												20 37										
Birmingham New Street 12	a				20 18								20 48							21 18			

		GW 1	GW ◇1	XC ◇1	GW ◇1	CH	GW 1	GW 1	GW ◇1	GW ◇1	GW ◇1	XC ◇1	GW 1	GW ◇1	GW 1	GW 1	GW 1	GW ◇1	XC ◇1	GW ◇1	GW 1	XC ◇1
London Paddington 15 ⊖	d	19 27	19 30		19 50			19 57	20 00	20 06	20 15			20 20			20 27	20 30		20 50		
Ealing Broadway ⊖	d	19 35						20 05									20 35					
Slough 3	d	19 57			20 06			20 27						20 35			20 57			21 06		
Maidenhead 3	d	20 04						20 34									21 04					
Twyford 3	d	20 12					←	20 42								←	21 12				←	
Reading 7	d	20 23	19 57	20 11	20 22		20 23	20 53	20 27	20 33	20 42	20 40	20 49	20 51		20 53	21 23	20 57	21 11	21 22	21 23	21 40
Reading West	d	→						→					20 52				→					
Theale	d												20 58									
Aldermaston	d												21 03									
Midgham	d												21 06									
Thatcham	d												21 11									
Newbury Racecourse	d												21 16									
Newbury	a									20 47			21 18									
	d												21 32									
Kintbury	d												21 39									
Hungerford	d												21 43									
Bedwyn	a												21 52									
Tilehurst	d						20 27									20 57					21 27	
Pangbourne	d						20 31									21 01					21 31	
Goring & Streatley	d						20 37									21 06					21 36	
Cholsey	d						20 41									21 11					21 41	
Didcot Parkway	a		20 11				20 49		20 41		20 55					21 19		21 12		21 39	21 48	
	d						20 55									21 25				21 40	21 55	
Appleford	d						21 00															
Culham	d																				22 01	
Radley	d						21 03														22 03	
Oxford	a			20 34	20 47		21 14					21 04		21 19		21 40			21 34	21 53	22 14	22 03
	d			20 36		21 00						21 07			21 20				21 36			22 07
Islip	d					21 13																
Bicester Town	a					21 25																
Tackley	d														21 29							
Heyford	d														21 33							
Kings Sutton	d														21 42							
Banbury	a			20 52								21 23			21 49				21 52			22 28
Leamington Spa 8	a			21 10								21 44							22 10			22 45
Coventry	a			21 22								21 55							22 22			
Birmingham International	a			21 37								22 10							22 36			
Birmingham New Street 12	a			21 48								22 21							22 48			23 16

Table 116

Saturdays until 23 June

London and Reading - Bedwyn, Oxford, Bicester, Banbury and Birmingham

Network Diagram - see first Page of Table 116

		GW 1	GW ◇1	CH	GW 1	GW ◇1	GW 1	GW ◇1	GW 1	GW ◇1	GW ◇1	GW 1	GW ◇1	GW 1	GW	GW 1	GW ◇1	GW 1	GW 1	GW ◇1	GW ◇1	GW 1
London Paddington 15 ⊖	d	20 57	21 17			21 30		21 50	21 57	22 00	22 15		22 35			22 45	23 00		23 20	23 30	23 33	
Ealing Broadway ⊖	d	21 05							22 05							22 55			23 28			
Slough 3	d	21 27	21 35					22 06	22 27		22 32					23 21	23 17		23 54		23 50	
Maidenhead 3	d	21 34							22 34							23 32			00 05			
Twyford 3	d	21 42			←				22 42			←				23 39		←	00 13			←
Reading 7	d	21 53	21 52		21 53	21 57	22 03	22 23	22 55	22 27	22 51	22 55	23 02	23 12		23 49	23 34	23 49	00 20	23 59	00 08	00 20
Reading West	d	→					22 06		→					23 14		→			→			
Theale	d						22 12							23 20								
Aldermaston	d						22 17							23 25								
Midgham	d						22 20							23 29								
Thatcham	d						22 25							23 34								
Newbury Racecourse	d						22 30							23 38								
Newbury	a						22 32							23 41								
	d						22 32							23 41								
Kintbury	d						22 39							23 48								
Hungerford	d						22 43							23 52								
Bedwyn	a						22 51							00 01								
Tilehurst	d				21 57							22 59						23 53				00 24
Pangbourne	d				22 01																	
Goring & Streatley	d				22 06							23 06						00 03				00 31
Cholsey	d				22 11							23 11						00 08				00 36
Didcot Parkway	a		22 07		22 19	22 12		22 37		22 41	23 06	23 18	23 22				23 51	00 14		00 18	00 22	00 44
	d		22 08		22 25			22 38			23 07	23 20					23 51	00 15			00 24	00 45
Appleford	d																					00s49
Culham	d																					00s51
Radley	d				22 34							23 27						00s22				00s55
Oxford	a		22 20		22 43			22 50			23 20	23 38					00 04	00 32			00 38	01 05
	d			22 25											23 47							
Islip	d			22 38																		
Bicester Town	a			22 50																		
Tackley	d														00s06							
Heyford	d														00s20							
Kings Sutton	d																					
Banbury	a														00 45							
Leamington Spa 8	a																					
Coventry	a																					
Birmingham International	a																					
Birmingham New Street 12	a																					

Saturdays 30 June to 8 September

		GW 1	GW ◇1	CH	GW 1	GW ◇1	GW 1	GW 1	GW 1	GW ◇1	GW 1	GW 1	GW 1	GW 1	GW ◇1	GW 1	XC ◇1	GW 1	GW 1	GW ◇1	CH	GW 1	XC ◇1
London Paddington 15 ⊖	d	22p45	23p18		23p29	23p30		23p42		00 22					05 21				05 25	05 50			
Ealing Broadway ⊖	d	22p54			23p37														05 33				
Slough 3	d	23p12	23p36		23p54			23p58		00 39					05 38				05 51	06 06			
Maidenhead 3	d	23p24	23p44		00 01			00 08											06 02				
Twyford 3	d	23p32			00 09				←										06 10				
Reading 7	d	23p41	23p58		00 24	00 08	00 20	00 21	00 24	00 56	05 08	05 41		05 46	05 54		06 11	06 12	06 21	06 22			06 46
Reading West	d				→		00s23				05 11	05 44						06 14					
Theale	d						00s29				05 17	05 50						06 20					
Aldermaston	d						00s34				05 22	05 55						06 25					
Midgham	d						00s37				05 25	05 58						06 29					
Thatcham	d						00s42				05 30	06 03						06 34					
Newbury Racecourse	d						00s47				05 35	06 08						06 38					
Newbury	a						00 52				05 37	06 10						06 44					
	d										05 37	06 10											
Kintbury	d										05 44	06 17											
Hungerford	d										05 48	06 21											
Bedwyn	a										05 57	06 30											
Tilehurst	d	23p45							00 29					05 50					06 25				
Pangbourne	d	23p49							00 33					05 54					06 29				
Goring & Streatley	d	23p53							00 37					05 59					06 34				
Cholsey	d	23p57							00 42					06 04		←			06 39			←	
Didcot Parkway	a	00 07				00 25		00 43	00 51	01 13				06 12	06 07	06 12			06 46	06 37		06 46	
	d	00 07						00 44	00 51	01 14				06 13	06 08	06 13			06 47	06 38		06 47	
Appleford	d								00 56					→		06 17			→				
Culham	d								00 58							06 20							
Radley	d	00 15							01 02							06 24						06 54	
Oxford	a	00 26	00 28					01 02	01 16	01 28					06 22	06 32	06 36			06 52		07 03	07 10
	d			00 38									06 16				06 38				07 00		07 12
Islip	d																				07 13		
Bicester Town	a																				07 25		
Tackley	d			00 48									06 25										
Heyford	d			00 53									06 29										
Kings Sutton	d			01 01									06 38										
Banbury	a			01 11									06 46				06 54						07 32
Leamington Spa 8	a																07 12						07 50
Coventry	a																07 24						
Birmingham International	a																07 37						
Birmingham New Street 12	a																07 48						08 17

30 June to 8 September

London and Reading - Bedwyn, Oxford, Bicester, Banbury and Birmingham

Network Diagram - see first Page of Table 116

Station		GW	GW	GW	GW	GW	GW	XC	GW	GW	GW	CH	GW	GW	XC	GW	GW	GW	GW	XC	GW	GW	GW
		1	1	◇1	1	1	◇1 ⊞	◇1 ✠	1	◇1	1		1	1	◇1 ✠	1	◇1	1	■ 1 ⊞	◇1 ✠	1	◇1	1
London Paddington 15 ⊖	d		05 57	06 21		06 27	06 30			06 50						06 57	07 21	07 27	07 30			07 50	
Ealing Broadway ⊖	d		06 05			06 35										07 05		07 35					
Slough 3	d		06 31	06 38		06 57				07 06						07 27	07 38	07 57				08 06	
Maidenhead 3	d		06 42			07 04										07 34		08 04					
Twyford 3	d		06 50		←	07 12							←			07 42		08 12					←
Reading 7	d	06 48	06 56	06 54	06 56	07 23	06 59	07 11	07 11	07 22			07 23	07 35	07 47	07 53	07 53	08 23	07 57	08 11	08 18	08 22	08 23
Reading West	d		→			→			07 14									→			08 20		
Theale	d	06 55							07 20					07 44							08 27		
Aldermaston	d								07 25												08 32		
Midgham	d								07 29												08 36		
Thatcham	d	07 04							07 34					07 52							08 41		
Newbury Racecourse	d								07 38												08 45		
Newbury	a	07 09							07 43					07 58							08 50		
	d	07 09												07 58									
Kintbury	d	07 16												08 04									
Hungerford	d	07 20												08 09									
Bedwyn	a	07 29												08 18									
Tilehurst	d				07 00								07 27			07 57							08 27
Pangbourne	d				07 04								07 31			08 01							08 31
Goring & Streatley	d				07 09								07 36			08 06							08 36
Cholsey	d				07 14								07 41			08 11							08 41
Didcot Parkway	a				07 30		07 12						07 49			08 19			08 12				08 48
	d				07 30								07 51			08 25							08 55
Appleford	d																						09 00
Culham	d												07 56										
Radley	d												08 00										09 03
Oxford	a			07 18	07 43			07 34		07 48			08 09		08 13	08 40	08 19			08 34		08 48	09 14
	d							07 36			07 53	08 07			08 15					08 36			
Islip	d											08 20											
Bicester Town	a											08 32											
Tackley	d										08 02												
Heyford	d										08 06												
Kings Sutton	d										08 15												
Banbury	a							07 52			08 23				08 32					08 52			
Leamington Spa 8	a							08 10							08 49					09 10			
Coventry	a							08 22												09 22			
Birmingham International	a							08 37												09 37			
Birmingham New Street 12	a							08 48							09 18					09 48			

Station		XC	GW	GW	GW	GW	GW	GW	GH	GW	GW	GW	XC	GW	GW	GW	XC	GW	GW	GW	GW	GW
		◇1 ✠	1	1	◇1 ⊞	1	1	◇1 ⊞		1	◇1 ⊞	■ 1 A ⊞	◇1 ✠	1	◇1	1	◇1 ✠	1	1	1	1	◇1
London Paddington 15 ⊖	d			07 57	08 15	08 18		08 21		08 27	08 30	08 35			08 50				08 57	09 18		09 21
Ealing Broadway ⊖	d			08 05						08 35									09 05			
Slough 3	d			08 27				08 39		08 57					09 06				09 27			09 39
Maidenhead 3	d			08 34						09 04									09 34			
Twyford 3	d			08 42			←			09 12						←			09 42		←	
Reading 7	d	08 40		08 53	08 42	08 48	08 53	08 54		09 23	08 57	09u04	09 11	09 12	09 22	09 23	09 40		09 53	09 48	09 53	09 54
Reading West	d			→						→				09 14					→			
Theale	d					08 55								09 20						09 56		
Aldermaston	d													09 25								
Midgham	d													09 29								
Thatcham	d					09 05								09 34						10 04		
Newbury Racecourse	d													09 38								
Newbury	a					09 11						09 20		09 44						10 10		
	d		08 58			09 24														10 10		
Kintbury	d		09 04			09 31														10 17		
Hungerford	d		09 09			09 35														10 21		
Bedwyn	a		09 17			09 44														10 31		
Tilehurst	d						08 57									09 27					09 57	
Pangbourne	d						09 01									09 31					10 01	
Goring & Streatley	d						09 06									09 36					10 06	
Cholsey	d						09 11									09 41					10 11	
Didcot Parkway	a				08 55		09 19				09 12					09 48					10 18	
	d						09 25									09 55					10 25	
Appleford	d																					
Culham	d															10 01						
Radley	d															10 03						
Oxford	a	09 04					09 40	09 18					09 34		09 48	10 14	10 04				10 40	10 19
	d	09 07							09 28				09 36				10 07	10 16				
Islip	d								09 41													
Bicester Town	a								09 53													
Tackley	d																	10 25				
Heyford	d																	10 29				
Kings Sutton	d																	10 38				
Banbury	a	09 23											09 52				10 23	10 46				
Leamington Spa 8	a	09 41											10 12				10 41					
Coventry	a												10 22									
Birmingham International	a												10 37									
Birmingham New Street 12	a	10 18											10 48				11 18					

A The Torbay Express

30 June to 8 September

London and Reading - Bedwyn, Oxford, Bicester, Banbury and Birmingham

Network Diagram - see first Page of Table 116

Station		GW	GW	XC	GW	GW	CH	GW	XC	GW	GW	GW	GW	GW	GW	GW	XC	GW	GW	GW	XC	GW	GW
		1	◇1 ⊞	◇1 ✠	1	◇1		1	◇1 ✠	1	◇1 ⊞	1	1	◇1 ⊞	1	◇1 ⊞	◇1 ✠	1	◇1 ✠	1	◇1 ✠	1	1
London Paddington 15 ⊖	d	09 27	09 30			09 50				09 57	10 15	10 18		10 21	10 27	10 30			10 50				10 57
Ealing Broadway ⊖	d	09 35								10 05					10 35								11 05
Slough 3	d	09 57				10 06				10 27				10 39	10 57				11 06				11 27
Maidenhead 3	d	10 04								10 34					11 04								11 34
Twyford 3	d	10 12						←		10 42			←		11 12					←			11 42
Reading 7	d	10 23	09 57	10 11	10 12	10 22		10 23	10 40	10 53	10 42	10 48	10 53	10 54	11 23	10 57	11 11	11 12	11 22	11 23	11 40		11 53
Reading West	d	→			10 14					→					→			11 14					→
Theale	d				10 20							10 56						11 20					
Aldermaston	d				10 25													11 25					
Midgham	d				10 29													11 29					
Thatcham	d				10 34							11 04						11 34					
Newbury Racecourse	d				10 38													11 38					
Newbury	a				10 44							11 10						11 44					
	d											11 23											
Kintbury	d											11 30											
Hungerford	d											11 34											
Bedwyn	a											11 44											
Tilehurst	d							10 27					10 57							11 27			
Pangbourne	d							10 31					11 01							11 31			
Goring & Streatley	d							10 36					11 06							11 36			
Cholsey	d							10 41					11 11							11 41			
Didcot Parkway	a		10 12					10 48			10 55		11 19			11 12				11 49			
	d							10 55					11 25							11 55			
Appleford	d							11 00															
Culham	d																						
Radley	d							11 03												12 03			
Oxford	a			10 34		10 48		11 14	11 04				11 40	11 19			11 34		11 48	12 14	12 04		
	d			10 36			11 00		11 07								11 36				12 07	12 16	
Islip	d						11 13																
Bicester Town	a						11 25																
Tackley	d																					12 25	
Heyford	d																					12 29	
Kings Sutton	d																					12 38	
Banbury	a			10 52					11 23								11 52				12 23	12 46	
Leamington Spa 8	a			11 10					11 41								12 10				12 41		
Coventry	a			11 22													12 22						
Birmingham International	a			11 37													12 37						
Birmingham New Street 12	a			11 48					12 18								12 48				13 18		

Station		GW	GW	GW	CH	GW	GW	XC	GW	GW	GW	XC	GW	GW	GW	GW	GW	GW	GW	GW	XC	GW
		1	1	◇1 ✠		1	◇1 ⊘	◇1 ✠	1	◇1	1	◇1 ✠	1	◇1 ⊞	1	1	◇1	1	◇1 ⊞	■ 1 ⊞	◇1 ✠	1
London Paddington 15 ⊖	d	11 18		11 21		11 27	11 30			11 50			11 57	12 15	12 18		12 21	12 27	12 30	12 35		
Ealing Broadway ⊖	d					11 35							12 05					12 35				
Slough 3	d			11 39		11 57				12 06			12 27				12 39	12 57				
Maidenhead 3	d					12 04							12 34					13 04				
Twyford 3	d		←			12 12					←		12 42			←		13 12				
Reading 7	d	11 48	11 53	11 54		12 23	11 58	12 11	12 12	12 22	12 23	12 40	12 53	12 42	12 48	12 53	12 54	13 23	12 57	13u06	13 11	
Reading West	d					→			12 14				→					→				
Theale	d	11 56							12 20						12 56							
Aldermaston	d								12 25													
Midgham	d								12 29													
Thatcham	d	12 04							12 34						13 04							
Newbury Racecourse	d								12 38													
Newbury	a	12 10							12 44						13 16					13 21		
	d	12 25																				13 26
Kintbury	d	12 31																				13 32
Hungerford	d	12 36																				13 37
Bedwyn	a	12 45																				13 45
Tilehurst	d		11 57								12 27					12 57						
Pangbourne	d		12 01								12 31					13 01						
Goring & Streatley	d		12 06								12 36					13 06						
Cholsey	d		12 11								12 41					13 11						
Didcot Parkway	a		12 19				12 12				12 48			12 55		13 19			13 12			
	d		12 25								12 55					13 25						
Appleford	d										13 00											
Culham	d																					
Radley	d										13 03											
Oxford	a		12 40	12 20				12 34		12 48	13 14	13 04				13 40	13 19				13 34	
	d				12 30			12 36				13 07									13 36	
Islip	d				12 43																	
Bicester Town	a				12 55																	
Tackley	d																					
Heyford	d																					
Kings Sutton	d																					
Banbury	a							12 52				13 23									13 52	
Leamington Spa 8	a							13 10				13 41									14 10	
Coventry	a							13 22													14 22	
Birmingham International	a							13 37													14 37	
Birmingham New Street 12	a							13 48				14 18									14 48	

London and Reading - Bedwyn, Oxford, Bicester, Banbury and Birmingham

Saturdays
30 June to 8 September

Network Diagram - see first Page of Table 116

		GW ■	CH	GW ◇■ 🛒	GW ■	XC ◇■ 🛒	GW ■	GW ■	GW ■	GW ■	GW ◇■ 🛒	GW ■	GW ◇■ ☕	XC ◇■ 🛒	GW ■	GW ◇■ 🛒	CH	GW ■	XC ◇■ 🛒	GW ■	GW ◇■ ☕	GW ■	GW ■
London Paddington 15 ⊖	d			12 50				12 57	13 18		13 21	13 27	13 30			13 50				13 57	14 15	14 18	
Ealing Broadway ⊖	d							13 05				13 35								14 05			
Slough 3	d			13 06				13 27			13 39	13 57				14 06				14 27			
Maidenhead 3	d							13 34				14 04								14 34			
Twyford 3	d				←			13 42		←		14 12						←		14 42			←
Reading 7	d	13 12		13 22	13 23	13 40		13 53	13 48	13 53	13 54	14 23	13 59	14 11	14 12	14 22		14 23	14 40	14 53	14 42	14 48	14 53
Reading West	d	13 14						→				→			14 14					→			
Theale	d	13 20							13 56						14 20							14 56	
Aldermaston	d	13 25													14 25								
Midgham	d	13 29													14 29								
Thatcham	d	13 34							14 04						14 34							15 04	
Newbury Racecourse	d	13 38													14 38								
Newbury	a	13 44							14 10						14 44							15 10	
	d								14 10													15 10	
Kintbury	d								14 17													15 17	
Hungerford	d								14 21													15 21	
Bedwyn	a								14 31													15 31	
Tilehurst	d				13 27					13 57								14 27					14 57
Pangbourne	d				13 31					14 01								14 31					15 01
Goring & Streatley	d				13 36					14 06								14 36					15 06
Cholsey	d				13 41					14 11								14 41					15 11
Didcot Parkway	a				13 48					14 19			14 12					14 48			14 55		15 19
	d				13 55					14 25								14 55					15 25
Appleford	d																	15 00					
Culham	d				14 01																		
Radley	d				14 03													15 03					
Oxford	a			13 48	14 14	14 04				14 40	14 19			14 34		14 48		15 14	15 04				15 40
	d		13 41			14 07	14 16							14 36			14 57		15 07				
Islip	d		13 54														15 10						
Bicester Town	a		14 06														15 22						
Tackley	d						14 25																
Heyford	d						14 29																
Kings Sutton	d						14 38																
Banbury	a					14 23	14 46							14 52					15 23				
Leamington Spa 8	a					14 41								15 10					15 41				
Coventry	a													15 22									
Birmingham International	a													15 37									
Birmingham New Street 12	a					15 18								15 48					16 18				

		GW ◇■ 🛒	GW ■	GW ◇■ ☕	XC ◇■ 🛒	GW ■	GW ◇■	CH	GW ■	XC ◇■ 🛒	GW ■	GW ■	GW ■	GW ■	GW ◇■ 🛒	GW ■	GW ◇■ ☕	XC ◇■ 🛒	GW ■	GW ◇■	GW ■	XC ◇■ 🛒	CH
London Paddington 15 ⊖	d	14 21	14 27	14 30			14 50					14 57	15 18		15 21	15 27	15 30			15 50			
Ealing Broadway ⊖	d		14 35									15 05				15 35							
Slough 3	d	14 39	14 57				15 06					15 27			15 39	15 57				16 06			
Maidenhead 3	d		15 04									15 34				16 04							
Twyford 3	d		15 12						←			15 42		←		16 12					←		
Reading 7	d	14 54	15 23	14 57	15 11	15 12	15 22		15 23	15 40		15 53	15 48	15 53	15 54	16 23	15 59	16 11	16 12	16 22	16 23	16 40	
Reading West	d		→			15 14						→				→			16 14				
Theale	d					15 20							15 56						16 20				
Aldermaston	d					15 25													16 25				
Midgham	d					15 29													16 29				
Thatcham	d					15 34							16 04						16 34				
Newbury Racecourse	d					15 38													16 38				
Newbury	a					15 44							16 10						16 44				
	d												16 10										
Kintbury	d												16 17										
Hungerford	d												16 21										
Bedwyn	a												16 31										
Tilehurst	d								15 27					15 57							16 27		
Pangbourne	d								15 31					16 01							16 31		
Goring & Streatley	d								15 36					16 06							16 36		
Cholsey	d								15 41					16 11							16 41		
Didcot Parkway	a			15 12					15 48					16 19			16 12				16 48		
	d								15 55					16 25							16 55		
Appleford	d																				17 00		
Culham	d								16 01														
Radley	d								16 03												17 03		
Oxford	a	15 18			15 34		15 48		16 14	16 04				16 40	16 19			16 34		16 48	17 14	17 04	
	d				15 36			16 00		16 07	16 16							16 36				17 07	17 10
Islip	d							16 13															17 23
Bicester Town	a							16 25															17 35
Tackley	d										16 25												
Heyford	d										16 29												
Kings Sutton	d										16 38												
Banbury	a				15 52					16 23	16 46							16 52				17 23	
Leamington Spa 8	a				16 10					16 41								17 10				17 41	
Coventry	a				16 22													17 22					
Birmingham International	a				16 37													17 37					
Birmingham New Street 12	a				16 48					17 18								17 48				18 18	

London and Reading - Bedwyn, Oxford, Bicester, Banbury and Birmingham

Saturdays
30 June to 8 September

Network Diagram - see first Page of Table 116

		GW ■	GW ◇■ ☕	GW ■	GW ■	GW ◇■ ☕	GW ■	GW ◇■ ☕	XC ◇■ 🛒	GW ■	GW ◇■ 🛒	GW ■	XC ◇■ 🛒	GW ■	GW ■	GW ■	GW ■	GW ◇■ ☕	GW ■	GW ◇■ ☕	XC ◇■ 🛒	GW ■
London Paddington 15 ⊖	d	15 57	16 15	16 18		16 21	16 27	16 30			16 50				16 57	17 18		17 21	17 27	17 30		
Ealing Broadway ⊖	d	16 05					16 35								17 05				17 35			
Slough 3	d	16 27				16 39	16 57				17 06				17 27			17 39	17 57			
Maidenhead 3	d	16 34					17 04								17 34				18 04			
Twyford 3	d	16 42			←		17 12					←			17 42		←		18 12			
Reading 7	d	16 53	16 42	16 48	16 53	16 54	17 23	16 57	17 11	17 12	17 22	17 23	17 40		17 53	17 48	17 53	17 54	18 23	17 57	18 11	18 12
Reading West	d	→					→			17 14					→				→			18 14
Theale	d			16 56						17 20						17 56						18 20
Aldermaston	d									17 25												18 25
Midgham	d									17 29												18 29
Thatcham	d			17 04						17 34						18 04						18 34
Newbury Racecourse	d									17 38												18 38
Newbury	a			17 10						17 44						18 10						18 44
	d			17 10												18 10						
Kintbury	d			17 17												18 17						
Hungerford	d			17 21												18 21						
Bedwyn	a			17 31												18 31						
Tilehurst	d				16 57							17 27					17 57					
Pangbourne	d				17 01							17 31					18 01					
Goring & Streatley	d				17 06							17 36					18 06					
Cholsey	d				17 11							17 41					18 11					
Didcot Parkway	a		16 55		17 19			17 12				17 48					18 19			18 12		
	d				17 25							17 55					18 25					
Appleford	d																					
Culham	d											18 01										
Radley	d											18 03										
Oxford	a				17 40	17 18			17 34		17 48	18 14	18 04				18 40	18 18			18 34	
	d								17 36				18 07	18 16							18 36	
Islip	d																					
Bicester Town	a																					
Tackley	d													18 25								
Heyford	d													18 29								
Kings Sutton	d													18 38								
Banbury	a								17 52				18 23	18 46							18 52	
Leamington Spa 8	a								18 10				18 41								19 10	
Coventry	a								18 22												19 22	
Birmingham International	a								18 37												19 37	
Birmingham New Street 12	a								18 48				19 18								19 48	

		CH	GW ◇■ 🛒	GW ■	XC ◇■ 🛒	GW ■	GW ◇■ ☕	GW ■	GW ■	GW ◇■ ☕	GW ■	GW ◇■ ☕	XC ◇■ 🛒	GW ◇■	CH	GW ■	GW ■	GW ■	GW ◇■ ☕	XC ◇■	GW ■	GW ◇■	GW ■
London Paddington 15 ⊖	d		17 50			17 57	18 15	18 18		18 21	18 27	18 30		18 50				18 57	19 06			19 21	
Ealing Broadway ⊖	d					18 05					18 35							19 05					
Slough 3	d		18 06			18 27				18 39	18 57			19 06				19 27				19 38	
Maidenhead 3	d					18 34					19 04							19 34					
Twyford 3	d			←		18 42			←		19 12						←	19 42					←
Reading 7	d		18 22	18 23	18 40	18 53	18 42	18 48	18 53	18 54	19 23	18 57	19 11	19 23			19 23	19 53	19 32	19 40	19 49	19 52	19 53
Reading West	d					→					→							→			19 52		
Theale	d							18 56													19 58		
Aldermaston	d																				20 03		
Midgham	d																				20 06		
Thatcham	d							19 04													20 11		
Newbury Racecourse	d																				20 16		
Newbury	a							19 10											19 48		20 18		
	d							19 10													20 18		
Kintbury	d							19 17													20 25		
Hungerford	d							19 21													20 29		
Bedwyn	a							19 31													20 38		
Tilehurst	d			18 27					18 57								19 27						19 57
Pangbourne	d			18 31					19 01								19 31						20 01
Goring & Streatley	d			18 36					19 06								19 37						20 06
Cholsey	d			18 41					19 11								19 41						20 11
Didcot Parkway	a			18 48			18 55		19 19			19 12					19 49						20 19
	d			18 55					19 25								19 55						20 25
Appleford	d			19 00																			
Culham	d																20 01						
Radley	d			19 03													20 03						
Oxford	a		18 48	19 14	19 04				19 40	19 18			19 34	19 48			20 14			20 04		20 20	20 40
	d	18 41			19 07								19 36		19 48	19 56				20 07			
Islip	d	18 54													20 01								
Bicester Town	a	19 06													20 13								
Tackley	d															20 05							
Heyford	d															20 09							
Kings Sutton	d															20 18							
Banbury	a				19 23								19 52			20 25				20 28			
Leamington Spa 8	a				19 41								20 10							20 45			
Coventry	a												20 22										
Birmingham International	a												20 37										
Birmingham New Street 12	a				20 18								20 48							21 18			

Saturdays

30 June to 8 September

London and Reading - Bedwyn, Oxford, Bicester, Banbury and Birmingham

Network Diagram - see first Page of Table 116

		GW	GW	XC	GW	CH	GW	GW	GW	GW	GW	XC	GW	GW	GW	GW	GW	GW	XC	GW	GW	XC
		1	◇1 ☕	◇1	◇1 🍴		1	1	◇1 ☕	◇1 ☕	◇1 ☕	◇1	1	◇1	1	1	1	◇1 ☕	◇1	◇1 🍴	1	◇1 🍴
London Paddington 15 ⊖	d	19 27	19 30		19 50			19 57	20 00	20 06	20 15			20 20			20 27	20 30		20 50		
Ealing Broadway ⊖	d	19 35						20 05									20 35					
Slough 3	d	19 57			20 06			20 27						20 35			20 57			21 06		
Maidenhead 3	d	20 04						20 34									21 04					
Twyford 3	d	20 12					←	20 42								←	21 12				←	
Reading 7	d	20 23	19 57	20 11	20 22		20 23	20 53	20 27	20 33	20 42	20 40	20 49	20 51		20 53	21 23	20 57	21 11	21 22	21 23	21 40
Reading West	d	→						→					20 52				→					
Theale	d												20 58									
Aldermaston	d												21 03									
Midgham	d												21 06									
Thatcham	d												21 11									
Newbury Racecourse	d												21 16									
Newbury	a									20 47			21 18									
	d												21 32									
Kintbury	d												21 39									
Hungerford	d												21 43									
Bedwyn	a												21 52									
Tilehurst	d						20 27									20 57					21 27	
Pangbourne	d						20 31									21 01					21 31	
Goring & Streatley	d						20 37									21 06					21 36	
Cholsey	d						20 41									21 11					21 41	
Didcot Parkway	a		20 11				20 49		20 41		20 55					21 19		21 12		21 39	21 48	
	d						20 55									21 25				21 40	21 55	
Appleford	d						21 00															
Culham	d																				22 01	
Radley	d						21 03														22 03	
Oxford	a			20 34	20 47		21 14					21 04		21 19		21 40			21 34	21 53	22 14	22 03
	d			20 36		21 00						21 07			21 20				21 36			22 07
Islip	d					21 13																
Bicester Town	a					21 25																
Tackley	d														21 29							
Heyford	d														21 33							
Kings Sutton	d														21 42							
Banbury	a			20 52								21 23			21 49				21 52			22 28
Leamington Spa 8	a			21 10								21 44							22 10			22 45
Coventry	a			21 22								21 55							22 22			
Birmingham International	a			21 37								22 10							22 36			
Birmingham New Street 12	a			21 48								22 21							22 48			23 16

		GW	GW	CH	GW	GW	GW	GW	GW	GW	GW	GW	GW	GW	GW	GW	GW	GW	GW	GW	GW	GW
		1	◇1		1	◇1 ☕	1	◇1	1	◇1 ☕	◇1	1	◇1 ☕	1	🚌	1	◇1	1	1	◇1 ☕	◇1	1
London Paddington 15 ⊖	d	20 57	21 17			21 30		21 50	21 57	22 00	22 15		22 35			22 45	23 00		23 20	23 30	23 33	
Ealing Broadway ⊖	d	21 05							22 05							22 55			23 28			
Slough 3	d	21 27	21 35					22 06	22 27		22 32					23 21	23 17		23 54		23 50	
Maidenhead 3	d	21 34							22 34							23 32			00 05			
Twyford 3	d	21 42			←				22 42			←				23 39		←	00 13			←
Reading 7	d	21 53	21 52		21 53	21 57	22 03	22 23	22 53	22 27	22 51	22 53	23 02	23 12		23 49	23 34	23 49	00 20	23 59	00 08	00 20
Reading West	d	→					22 06		→					23 14		→			→			
Theale	d						22 12							23 20								
Aldermaston	d						22 17							23 25								
Midgham	d						22 20							23 29								
Thatcham	d						22 25							23 34								
Newbury Racecourse	d						22 30							23 38								
Newbury	a						22 32							23 41								
	d						22 32							23 41								
Kintbury	d						22 39							23 48								
Hungerford	d						22 43							23 52								
Bedwyn	a						22 51							00 01								
Tilehurst	d				21 57							22 57						23 53				00 24
Pangbourne	d				22 01							23 01						23 58				
Goring & Streatley	d				22 06							23 06						00 03				00 31
Cholsey	d				22 11							23 11						00 08				00 36
Didcot Parkway	a		22 07		22 19	22 12		22 37		22 41	23 06	23 19	23 21				23 51	00 14		00 18	00 22	00 44
	d		22 08		22 25			22 38			23 07	23 20					23 51	00 15			00 24	00 45
Appleford	d																					00s49
Culham	d																					00s51
Radley	d				22 34							23 27						00s22				00s55
Oxford	a		22 20		22 43			22 50			23 20	23 38					00 04	00 32			00 38	01 05
	d			22 25											23 47							
Islip	d			22 38																		
Bicester Town	a			22 50																		
Tackley	d														00s06							
Heyford	d														00s20							
Kings Sutton	d																					
Banbury	a														00 45							
Leamington Spa 8	a																					
Coventry	a																					
Birmingham International	a																					
Birmingham New Street 12	a																					

Saturdays

15 September to 20 October

London and Reading - Bedwyn, Oxford, Bicester, Banbury and Birmingham

Network Diagram - see first Page of Table 116

		GW	GW	CH	GW	GW	GW	GW	GW	GW	GW	GW	GW	GW	GW	GW	XC	GW	GW	GW	CH	GW	XC
		1	◇1		1	◇1 ☕	1	1	1	◇1	1	1	1	1	◇1	1	◇1 🍴	1	1	◇1		1	◇1 🍴
London Paddington 15 ⊖	d	22p45	23p18		23p29	23p30		23p42		00 22					05 21				05 25	05 50			
Ealing Broadway ⊖	d	22p54			23p37														05 33				
Slough 3	d	23p12	23p36		23p54			23p58		00 39					05 38				05 51	06 06			
Maidenhead 3	d	23p24	23p44		00 01			00 08											06 02				
Twyford 3	d	23p32			00 09				←										06 10				
Reading 7	d	23p41	23p58		00 24	00 08	00 20	00 21	00 24	00 56	05 08	05 41		05 46	05 54		06 11	06 12	06 21	06 22			06 46
Reading West	d				→		00s23				05 11	05 44						06 14					
Theale	d						00s29				05 17	05 50						06 20					
Aldermaston	d						00s34				05 22	05 55						06 25					
Midgham	d						00s37				05 25	05 58						06 29					
Thatcham	d						00s42				05 30	06 03						06 34					
Newbury Racecourse	d						00s47				05 35	06 08						06 38					
Newbury	a						00 52				05 37	06 10						06 44					
	d										05 37	06 10											
Kintbury	d										05 44	06 17											
Hungerford	d										05 48	06 21											
Bedwyn	a										05 57	06 30											
Tilehurst	d	23p45							00 29					05 50					06 25				
Pangbourne	d	23p49							00 33					05 54					06 29				
Goring & Streatley	d	23p53							00 37					05 59					06 34				
Cholsey	d	23p57							00 42					06 04		←			06 39			←	
Didcot Parkway	a	00 07				00 25		00 43	00 51	01 13				06 12	06 07	06 12			06 46	06 37		06 46	
	d	00 07						00 44	00 51	01 14				06 13	06 08	06 13			06 47	06 38		06 47	
Appleford	d								00 56					→		06 17			→				
Culham	d								00 58							06 20							
Radley	d	00 15							01 02							06 24						06 54	
Oxford	a	00 26	00 28					01 02	01 16	01 28					06 22	06 32	06 36			06 52		07 03	07 10
	d			00 38									06 16				06 38				07 00		07 12
Islip	d																				07 13		
Bicester Town	a																				07 25		
Tackley	d			00 48									06 25										
Heyford	d			00 53									06 29										
Kings Sutton	d			01 01									06 38										
Banbury	a			01 11									06 46				06 54						07 32
Leamington Spa 8	a																07 12						07 50
Coventry	a																07 24						
Birmingham International	a																07 37						
Birmingham New Street 12	a																07 48						08 17

		GW	GW	GW	GW	GW	GW	XC	GW	GW	GW	CH	GW	XC	GW	GW	GW	GW	GW	XC	GW	GW	GW
		1	1	◇1	1	1	◇1 ☕	◇1 🍴	1	◇1	1		1	◇1 🍴	1	1	◇1	1	1 ☕	◇1 🍴	1	◇1	1
London Paddington 15 ⊖	d		05 57	06 21		06 27	06 30			06 50						06 57	07 21	07 27	07 30			07 50	
Ealing Broadway ⊖	d		06 05			06 35										07 05		07 35					
Slough 3	d		06 31	06 38		06 57				07 06						07 27	07 38	07 57				08 06	
Maidenhead 3	d		06 42			07 04										07 34		08 04					
Twyford 3	d		06 50		←	07 12							←			07 42		08 12					←
Reading 7	d	06 48	06 56	06 54	06 56	07 23	06 59	07 11	07 11	07 22			07 23	07 47	07 48	07 53	07 53	08 23	07 57	08 11	08 18	08 22	08 23
Reading West	d		→			→			07 14									→			08 20		
Theale	d	06 55							07 20						07 57						08 27		
Aldermaston	d								07 25												08 32		
Midgham	d								07 29												08 36		
Thatcham	d	07 04							07 34						08 05						08 41		
Newbury Racecourse	d								07 38												08 45		
Newbury	a	07 09							07 43						08 11						08 50		
	d	07 09													08 11								
Kintbury	d	07 16													08 17								
Hungerford	d	07 20													08 22								
Bedwyn	a	07 29													08 31								
Tilehurst	d				07 00								07 27			07 57							08 27
Pangbourne	d				07 04								07 31			08 01							08 31
Goring & Streatley	d				07 09								07 36			08 06							08 36
Cholsey	d				07 14								07 41			08 11							08 41
Didcot Parkway	a				07 30		07 12						07 49			08 19			08 12				08 48
	d				07 30								07 51			08 25							08 55
Appleford	d																						09 00
Culham	d												07 56										
Radley	d												08 00										09 03
Oxford	a			07 18	07 43			07 34		07 48			08 09	08 13		08 40	08 19			08 34		08 48	09 14
	d							07 36			07 53	08 07		08 15						08 36			
Islip	d											08 20											
Bicester Town	a											08 32											
Tackley	d										08 02												
Heyford	d										08 06												
Kings Sutton	d										08 15												
Banbury	a							07 52			08 23			08 32						08 52			
Leamington Spa 8	a							08 10						08 49						09 10			
Coventry	a							08 22												09 22			
Birmingham International	a							08 37												09 37			
Birmingham New Street 12	a							08 48						09 18						09 48			

Table 116

Saturdays

15 September to 20 October

London and Reading - Bedwyn, Oxford, Bicester, Banbury and Birmingham

Network Diagram - see first Page of Table 116

		XC		GW	GW	GW	GW	GW	GW	CH	GW	GW		XC	GW	GW	GW	XC	GW	GW	GW	GW		GW	GW
		◇■ H		■	■	◇■ ⊏	◇■ ⊏	■	◇■ ⊏		■	◇■ ⊏		◇■ H	■	◇■	■	◇■ H	■	■	■	■		◇■	■
London Paddington [15] ⊖	d				07 57	08 15	08 18		08 21		08 27	08 30				08 50				08 57	09 18			09 21	09 27
Ealing Broadway ⊖	d				08 05						08 35									09 05					09 35
Slough [3]	d				08 27				08 39		08 57					09 06				09 27				09 39	09 57
Maidenhead [3]	d				08 34						09 04									09 34					10 04
Twyford [3]	d				08 42			←			09 12						←			09 42		←			10 12
Reading [7]	d	08 40			08 53	08 42	08 48	08 53	08 54		09 23	08 57		09 11	09 12	09 22	09 23	09 40		09 53	09 48	09 53		09 54	10 23
Reading West	d				→						→				09 14					→					→
Theale	d						08 58								09 20						09 56				
Aldermaston	d														09 25										
Midgham	d														09 29										
Thatcham	d						09 07								09 34						10 04				
Newbury Racecourse	d														09 38										
Newbury	a						09 13								09 44						10 10				
	d			08 58			09 14														10 10				
Kintbury	d			09 04																	10 17				
Hungerford	d			09 09			09 23														10 21				
Bedwyn	a			09 17			09 30														10 31				
Tilehurst	d							08 57									09 27					09 57			
Pangbourne	d							09 01									09 31					10 01			
Goring & Streatley	d							09 06									09 36					10 06			
Cholsey	d							09 11									09 41					10 11			
Didcot Parkway	a					08 55		09 19				09 12					09 48					10 18			
	d							09 25									09 55					10 25			
Appleford	d																								
Culham	d																10 01								
Radley	d																10 03								
Oxford	a	09 04						09 40	09 18					09 34		09 48	10 14	10 04				10 40		10 19	
	d	09 07								09 28				09 36				10 07	10 16						
Islip	d									09 41															
Bicester Town	a									09 53															
Tackley	d																		10 25						
Heyford	d																		10 29						
Kings Sutton	d																		10 38						
Banbury	a	09 23												09 52				10 23	10 46						
Leamington Spa [8]	a	09 41												10 12				10 41							
Coventry	a													10 22											
Birmingham International	a													10 37											
Birmingham New Street [12]	a	10 18												10 48				11 18							

		GW	XC	GW	GW	CH	GW	XC		GW	GW	GW	GW	GW	GW	GW	XC	GW		GW	GW	XC	GW	GW	GW
		◇■ ⊏	◇■ H	■	◇■		■	◇■ H		■	◇■ ⊏	■	■	◇■ ⊏	■	◇■ ⊏	◇■ H	■		◇■ H	■	◇■ H	■	■	■
London Paddington [15] ⊖	d	09 30			09 50					09 57	10 15	10 18		10 21	10 27	10 30				10 50				10 57	11 18
Ealing Broadway ⊖	d									10 05					10 35									11 05	
Slough [3]	d				10 06					10 27				10 39	10 57					11 06				11 27	
Maidenhead [3]	d									10 34					11 04									11 34	
Twyford [3]	d						←			10 42			←		11 12						←			11 42	
Reading [7]	d	09 57	10 11	10 12	10 22		10 23	10 40		10 53	10 42	10 48	10 53	10 54	11 23	10 57	11 11	11 12		11 22	11 23	11 40		11 53	11 48
Reading West	d			10 14						→					→			11 14						→	
Theale	d			10 20								10 56						11 20							11 56
Aldermaston	d			10 25														11 25							
Midgham	d			10 29														11 29							
Thatcham	d			10 34								11 04						11 34							12 04
Newbury Racecourse	d			10 38														11 38							
Newbury	a			10 44								11 10						11 44							12 10
	d											11 10													12 10
Kintbury	d											11 17													12 17
Hungerford	d											11 21													12 21
Bedwyn	a											11 31													12 31
Tilehurst	d						10 27						10 57								11 27				
Pangbourne	d						10 31						11 01								11 31				
Goring & Streatley	d						10 36						11 06								11 36				
Cholsey	d						10 41						11 11								11 41				
Didcot Parkway	a	10 12					10 48				10 55		11 19			11 12					11 49				
	d						10 55						11 25								11 55				
Appleford	d						11 00																		
Culham	d																								
Radley	d						11 03														12 03				
Oxford	a		10 34		10 48		11 14	11 04					11 40	11 19			11 34			11 48	12 14	12 04			
	d		10 36			11 00		11 07									11 36					12 07	12 16		
Islip	d					11 13																			
Bicester Town	a					11 25																			
Tackley	d																						12 25		
Heyford	d																						12 29		
Kings Sutton	d																						12 38		
Banbury	a		10 52					11 23									11 52					12 23	12 46		
Leamington Spa [8]	a		11 10					11 41									12 10					12 41			
Coventry	a		11 22														12 22								
Birmingham International	a		11 37														12 37								
Birmingham New Street [12]	a		11 48					12 18									12 48					13 18			

Table 116

Saturdays

15 September to 20 October

London and Reading - Bedwyn, Oxford, Bicester, Banbury and Birmingham

Network Diagram - see first Page of Table 116

		GW	GW	CH		GW	GW	XC	GW	GW	GW	XC	GW	GW		GW	GW	GW	GW	GW	XC	GW	CH	GW	
		■	◇■ H			■	◇■ ⊘	◇■ H	■	◇■	■	◇■ H	■	◇■ ⊏		◇■ ⊏	■	◇■	■	◇■ ⊏	◇■ H	■		◇■ H	
London Paddington [15] ⊖	d		11 21			11 27	11 30			11 50			11 57	12 15		12 18		12 21	12 27	12 30				12 50	
Ealing Broadway ⊖	d					11 35							12 05						12 35						
Slough [3]	d		11 39			11 57				12 06			12 27					12 39	12 57					13 06	
Maidenhead [3]	d					12 04							12 34						13 04						
Twyford [3]	d	←				12 12					←		12 42				←		13 12						
Reading [7]	d	11 53	11 54			12 23	11 58	12 11	12 12	12 22	12 23	12 40	12 53	12 42		12 48	12 53	12 54	13 23	12 57	13 11	13 12		13 22	
Reading West	d					→			12 14				→						→			13 14			
Theale	d								12 20							12 57						13 20			
Aldermaston	d								12 25													13 25			
Midgham	d								12 29													13 29			
Thatcham	d								12 34							13 05						13 34			
Newbury Racecourse	d								12 38													13 38			
Newbury	a								12 44							13 12						13 44			
	d															13 13									
Kintbury	d																								
Hungerford	d															13 21									
Bedwyn	a															13 29									
Tilehurst	d	11 57									12 27						12 57								
Pangbourne	d	12 01									12 31						13 01								
Goring & Streatley	d	12 06									12 36						13 06								
Cholsey	d	12 11									12 41						13 11								
Didcot Parkway	a	12 19					12 12				12 48			12 55			13 19			13 12					
	d	12 25									12 55						13 25								
Appleford	d										13 00														
Culham	d																								
Radley	d										13 03														
Oxford	a	12 40	12 20					12 34		12 48	13 14	13 04					13 40	13 19			13 34			13 48	
	d			12 30				12 36				13 07									13 36		13 41		
Islip	d			12 43																			13 54		
Bicester Town	a			12 55																			14 06		
Tackley	d																								
Heyford	d																								
Kings Sutton	d																								
Banbury	a							12 52				13 23									13 52				
Leamington Spa [8]	a							13 10				13 41									14 10				
Coventry	a							13 22													14 22				
Birmingham International	a							13 37													14 37				
Birmingham New Street [12]	a							13 48				14 18									14 48				

		GW	XC	GW	GW	GW	GW	GW	GW	GW		XC	GW	GW	CH	GW	XC	GW	GW	GW		GW	GW	GW	GW
		■	◇■ H	■	■	■	■	◇■ H	■	◇■ ⊏		◇■ H	■	◇■ H		■	◇■ H	■	◇■ ⊏	■		■	◇■ H	■	◇■ ⊏
London Paddington [15] ⊖	d				12 57	13 18		13 21	13 27	13 30				13 50				13 57	14 15	14 18			14 21	14 27	14 30
Ealing Broadway ⊖	d				13 05				13 35									14 05						14 35	
Slough [3]	d				13 27			13 39	13 57					14 06				14 27					14 39	14 57	
Maidenhead [3]	d				13 34				14 04									14 34						15 04	
Twyford [3]	d	←			13 42		←		14 12							←		14 42				←		15 12	
Reading [7]	d	13 23	13 40		13 53	13 48	13 53	13 54	14 23	13 59		14 11	14 12	14 22		14 23	14 40	14 53	14 42	14 48		14 53	14 54	15 23	14 57
Reading West	d				→				→				14 14					→						→	
Theale	d					13 56							14 20							14 56					
Aldermaston	d												14 25												
Midgham	d												14 29												
Thatcham	d					14 04							14 34							15 04					
Newbury Racecourse	d												14 38												
Newbury	a					14 10							14 44							15 10					
	d					14 10														15 10					
Kintbury	d					14 17														15 17					
Hungerford	d					14 21														15 21					
Bedwyn	a					14 31														15 31					
Tilehurst	d	13 27					13 57									14 27						14 57			
Pangbourne	d	13 31					14 01									14 31						15 01			
Goring & Streatley	d	13 36					14 06									14 36						15 06			
Cholsey	d	13 41					14 11									14 41						15 11			
Didcot Parkway	a	13 48					14 19			14 12						14 48			14 55			15 19			15 12
	d	13 55					14 25									14 55						15 25			
Appleford	d															15 00									
Culham	d	14 01																							
Radley	d	14 03														15 03									
Oxford	a	14 14	14 04				14 40	14 19				14 34		14 48		15 14	15 04					15 40	15 18		
	d		14 07	14 16								14 36			14 57		15 07								
Islip	d														15 10										
Bicester Town	a														15 22										
Tackley	d			14 25																					
Heyford	d			14 29																					
Kings Sutton	d			14 38																					
Banbury	a		14 23	14 46								14 52					15 23								
Leamington Spa [8]	a		14 41									15 10					15 41								
Coventry	a											15 22													
Birmingham International	a											15 37													
Birmingham New Street [12]	a		15 18									15 48					16 18								

London and Reading - Bedwyn, Oxford, Bicester, Banbury and Birmingham

Network Diagram - see first Page of Table 116

		XC	GW	GW	CH	GW	XC	GW	GW	GW	GW	GW	GW	GW	XC	GW	GW	GW	XC	CH	GW	GW	GW
		◇1 ⌶	1	◇1		1	◇1 ⌶	1	1	1	1	◇1 ⌶	1	◇1 ⊐	◇1 ⌶	1	◇1	1	◇1 ⌶		1	◇1 ⊐	1
London Paddington ⊖	d			14 50					14 57	15 18		15 21	15 27	15 30			15 50				15 57	16 15	16 18
Ealing Broadway ⊖	d								15 05				15 35								16 05		
Slough	d			15 06					15 27			15 39	15 57				16 06				16 27		
Maidenhead	d								15 34				16 04								16 34		
Twyford	d					←			15 42		←		16 12					←			16 42		
Reading	d	15 11	15 12	15 22		15 23	15 40		15 53	15 48	15 53	15 54	16 23	15 59	16 11	16 12	16 22	16 23	16 40		16 53	16 42	16 48
Reading West	d		15 14						→				→			16 14					→		
Theale	d		15 20							15 56						16 20							16 56
Aldermaston	d		15 25													16 25							
Midgham	d		15 29													16 29							
Thatcham	d		15 34							16 04						16 34							17 04
Newbury Racecourse	d		15 38													16 38							
Newbury	a		15 44							16 10						16 44							17 10
	d									16 10													17 10
Kintbury	d									16 17													17 17
Hungerford	d									16 21													17 21
Bedwyn	a									16 31													17 31
Tilehurst	d					15 27					15 57							16 27					
Pangbourne	d					15 31					16 01							16 31					
Goring & Streatley	d					15 36					16 06							16 36					
Cholsey	d					15 41					16 11							16 41					
Didcot Parkway	a					15 48					16 19			16 12				16 48				16 55	
	d					15 55					16 25							16 55					
Appleford	d																	17 00					
Culham	d					16 01																	
Radley	d					16 03												17 03					
Oxford	a	15 34		15 48		16 14	16 04				16 40	16 19			16 34		16 48	17 14	17 04				
	d	15 36			16 00		16 07	16 16							16 36				17 07	17 10			
Islip	d				16 13															17 23			
Bicester Town	a				16 25															17 35			
Tackley	d							16 25															
Heyford	d							16 29															
Kings Sutton	d							16 38															
Banbury	a	15 52					16 23	16 46							16 52				17 23				
Leamington Spa	a	16 10					16 41								17 10				17 41				
Coventry	a	16 22													17 22								
Birmingham International	a	16 37													17 37								
Birmingham New Street	a	16 48					17 18								17 48				18 18				

		GW	GW	GW	GW	XC	GW	GW	GW	XC	GW	GW	GW	GW	GW	GW	GW	XC	GW	CH	GW	GW
		1	◇1 ⊐	1	◇1 ⊐	◇1 ⌶	1	◇1 ⌶	1	◇1 ⌶	1	1	1	1	◇1 ⊐	1	◇1 ⊐	◇1 ⌶	1		◇1 ⌶	1
London Paddington ⊖	d		16 21	16 27	16 30			16 50				16 57	17 18		17 21	17 27	17 30				17 50	
Ealing Broadway ⊖	d			16 35								17 05				17 35						
Slough	d		16 39	16 57				17 06				17 27			17 39	17 57					18 06	
Maidenhead	d			17 04								17 34				18 04						
Twyford	d	←		17 12					←			17 42		←		18 12						←
Reading	d	16 53	16 54	17 23	16 57	17 11	17 12	17 22	17 23	17 40		17 53	17 48	17 53	17 54	18 23	17 57	18 11	18 12		18 22	18 23
Reading West	d			→			17 14					→				→			18 14			
Theale	d						17 20						17 56						18 20			
Aldermaston	d						17 25												18 25			
Midgham	d						17 29												18 29			
Thatcham	d						17 34						18 04						18 34			
Newbury Racecourse	d						17 38												18 38			
Newbury	a						17 44						18 10						18 44			
	d												18 10									
Kintbury	d												18 17									
Hungerford	d												18 21									
Bedwyn	a												18 31									
Tilehurst	d	16 57							17 27					17 57								18 27
Pangbourne	d	17 01							17 31					18 01								18 31
Goring & Streatley	d	17 06							17 36					18 06								18 36
Cholsey	d	17 11							17 41					18 11								18 41
Didcot Parkway	a	17 19			17 12				17 48					18 19			18 12					18 48
	d	17 25							17 55					18 25								18 55
Appleford	d																					19 00
Culham	d								18 01													
Radley	d								18 03													19 03
Oxford	a	17 40	17 18			17 34		17 48	18 14	18 04				18 40	18 18			18 34			18 48	19 14
	d					17 36				18 07	18 16							18 36		18 41		
Islip	d																			18 54		
Bicester Town	a																			19 06		
Tackley	d										18 25											
Heyford	d										18 29											
Kings Sutton	d										18 38											
Banbury	a					17 52				18 23	18 46							18 52				
Leamington Spa	a					18 10				18 41								19 10				
Coventry	a					18 22												19 22				
Birmingham International	a					18 37												19 37				
Birmingham New Street	a					18 48				19 18								19 48				

London and Reading - Bedwyn, Oxford, Bicester, Banbury and Birmingham

Network Diagram - see first Page of Table 116

		XC	GW	GW	GW	GW	GW	GW	GW	XC	GW	CH	GW	GW	GW	GW	GW	XC	GW	GW	GW	GW	GW
		◇1 ⌶	1	◇1 ⊐	1	1	◇1 ⊐	1	◇1 ⊐	◇1 ⌶	◇1		1	1	1	◇1 ⊐	◇1 ⊐	◇1	1	◇1	1	1	◇1 ⊐
London Paddington ⊖	d		17 57	18 15	18 18		18 21	18 27	18 30		18 50				18 57	19 06	19 15			19 21		19 27	19 30
Ealing Broadway ⊖	d		18 05					18 35							19 05							19 35	
Slough	d		18 27				18 39	18 57			19 06				19 27					19 38		19 57	
Maidenhead	d		18 34					19 04							19 34							20 04	
Twyford	d		18 42			←		19 12						←	19 42						←	20 12	
Reading	d	18 40	18 53	18 42	18 48	18 53	18 54	19 23	18 57	19 11	19 23			19 23	19 53	19 32	19 42	19 40	19 49	19 52	19 53	20 23	19 57
Reading West	d		→					→							→				19 52			→	
Theale	d				18 56														19 58				
Aldermaston	d																		20 03				
Midgham	d																		20 06				
Thatcham	d				19 04														20 11				
Newbury Racecourse	d																		20 16				
Newbury	a				19 10											19 48			20 18				
	d				19 10														20 18				
Kintbury	d				19 17														20 25				
Hungerford	d				19 21														20 29				
Bedwyn	a				19 31														20 38				
Tilehurst	d					18 57								19 27							19 57		
Pangbourne	d					19 01								19 31							20 01		
Goring & Streatley	d					19 06								19 36							20 06		
Cholsey	d					19 11								19 41							20 11		
Didcot Parkway	a			18 55		19 19			19 12					19 48			19 55				20 19		20 11
	d					19 25								19 55							20 25		
Appleford	d																						
Culham	d													20 01									
Radley	d													20 03									
Oxford	a	19 04				19 40	19 18			19 34	19 48			20 14				20 04		20 20	20 40		
	d	19 07								19 36		19 48	19 56					20 07					
Islip	d											20 01											
Bicester Town	a											20 13											
Tackley	d												20 05										
Heyford	d												20 09										
Kings Sutton	d												20 18										
Banbury	a	19 23								19 52			20 25					20 28					
Leamington Spa	a	19 41								20 10								20 45					
Coventry	a									20 22													
Birmingham International	a									20 37													
Birmingham New Street	a	20 18								20 48								21 18					

		XC	GW	CH	GW	GW	GW	GW	GW	XC	GW	GW	GW	GW	GW	GW	XC	XC	GW	GW	XC	GW
		◇1	◇1 ⌶		1	1	◇1 ⊐	◇1 ⊐	◇1 ⊐	◇1	1	◇1	1	1	1	◇1 ⊐	◇1 A	◇1 B	1	◇1 ⌶	◇1 ⌶	1
London Paddington ⊖	d		19 50			19 57	20 00	20 06	20 15			20 20			20 27	20 30				20 50		
Ealing Broadway ⊖	d					20 05									20 35							
Slough	d		20 06			20 27						20 35			20 57					21 06		
Maidenhead	d					20 34									21 04							
Twyford	d				←	20 42								←	21 12				←			
Reading	d	20 11	20 22		20 23	20 53	20 27	20 33	20 42	20 40	20 49	20 51		20 53	21 23	20 57	21 11	21 11	21 23	21 25	21 40	
Reading West	d					→					20 52				→							
Theale	d										20 58											
Aldermaston	d										21 03											
Midgham	d										21 06											
Thatcham	d										21 11											
Newbury Racecourse	d										21 16											
Newbury	a							20 47			21 18											
	d										21 32											
Kintbury	d										21 39											
Hungerford	d										21 43											
Bedwyn	a										21 52											
Tilehurst	d				20 27									20 57					21 27			
Pangbourne	d				20 31									21 01					21 31			
Goring & Streatley	d				20 37									21 06					21 36			
Cholsey	d				20 41									21 11					21 41			←
Didcot Parkway	a				20 49		20 41		20 55					21 19		21 12			21 48	21 41		21 48
	d				20 55									21 25					21 55	21 42		21 55
Appleford	d				21 00														→			
Culham	d																					22 01
Radley	d				21 03																	22 03
Oxford	a	20 34	20 47		21 14					21 04		21 19		21 40			21 33	21 34		21 55	22 03	22 14
	d	20 36		21 00						21 07			21 20				21 36	21 36			22 07	
Islip	d			21 13																		
Bicester Town	a			21 25																		
Tackley	d												21 29									
Heyford	d												21 33									
Kings Sutton	d												21 42									
Banbury	a	20 52								21 23			21 49				21 52	21 52			22 28	
Leamington Spa	a	21 10								21 44							22 10	22 10			22 45	
Coventry	a	21 22								21 55							22 22	22 22				
Birmingham International	a	21 37								22 10							22 36	22 36				
Birmingham New Street	a	21 48								22 21							22 48	22 48			23 16	

A not 15 September

B 15 September

Table 116

Saturdays
15 September to 20 October

London and Reading - Bedwyn, Oxford, Bicester, Banbury and Birmingham

Network Diagram - see first Page of Table 116

		GW	GW	CH	GW	GW	GW	GW	GW	GW	GW	GW	GW	GW	GW	GW	GW	GW	GW	GW	GW	GW
		1	◇1		1	◇1 ☕	1	◇1	1	◇1 ☕	◇1	1	◇1 ☕	1	🚌	1	◇1	1	1	◇1 ☕	◇1	1
London Paddington [15] ⊖	d	20 57	21 17			21 30		21 50	21 57	22 00	22 15		22 35			22 45	23 00		23 20	23 30	23 33	
Ealing Broadway ⊖	d	21 05							22 05							22 55			23 28			
Slough [3]	d	21 27	21 35					22 06	22 27		22 32					23 21	23 17		23 54		23 50	
Maidenhead [3]	d	21 34							22 34							23 32			00 05			
Twyford [3]	d	21 46			←				22 45			←				23 39		←	00 13			←
Reading [7]	d	21 55	21 51		21 55	21 58	22 03	22 23	22 56	22 27	22 51	22 56	23 02	23 12		23 49	23 34	23 49	00 20	23 59	00 08	00 20
Reading West	d	→					22 06		→					23 14		→			→			
Theale	d						22 12							23 20								
Aldermaston	d						22 17							23 25								
Midgham	d						22 20							23 29								
Thatcham	d						22 25							23 34								
Newbury Racecourse	d						22 30							23 38								
Newbury	a						22 32							23 41								
	d						22 32							23 41								
Kintbury	d						22 39							23 48								
Hungerford	d						22 43							23 52								
Bedwyn	a						22 51							00 01								
Tilehurst	d				22 01							23 00						23 53				00 24
Pangbourne	d				22 05																	
Goring & Streatley	d				22 10							23 06						00 03				00 31
Cholsey	d				22 15							23 11						00 08				00 36
Didcot Parkway	a		22 07		22 23	22 13		22 37		22 41	23 07	23 19	23 22				23 51	00 14		00 18	00 22	00 44
	d		22 08		22 25			22 38			23 07	23 20					23 51	00 15			00 24	00 45
Appleford	d																					00s49
Culham	d																					00s51
Radley	d				22 34							23 27						00s22				00s55
Oxford	a		22 20		22 43			22 50			23 20	23 38					00 04	00 32			00 39	01 07
	d			22 25											23 48							
Islip	d			22 38																		
Bicester Town	a			22 50																		
Tackley	d														00s08							
Heyford	d														00s22							
Kings Sutton	d																					
Banbury	a														00 47							
Leamington Spa [8]	a																					
Coventry	a																					
Birmingham International	a																					
Birmingham New Street [12]	a																					

Saturdays
from 27 October

		GW	GW	CH	GW	GW	GW	GW	GW	GW	GW	GW	GW	GW	GW	GW	XC	GW	GW	GW	CH	GW	XC
		1	◇1		1	◇1 ☕	1	1	1	◇1	1	1	1	1	◇1	1	◇1 trolley	1	1	◇1		1	◇1 trolley
London Paddington [15] ⊖	d	22p45	23p18		23p29	23p30		23p42		00 22					05 21				05 25	05 50			
Ealing Broadway ⊖	d	22p54			23p37														05 33				
Slough [3]	d	23p12	23p36		23p54			23p58		00 39					05 38				05 51	06 06			
Maidenhead [3]	d	23p24	23p44		00 01			00 08											06 02				
Twyford [3]	d	23p32			00 09				←										06 10				
Reading [7]	d	23p41	23p58		00 24	00 08	00 20	00 21	00 24	00 56	05 08	05 41		05 46	05 54		06 11	06 12	06 21	06 22			06 46
Reading West	d				→		00s23				05 11	05 44						06 14					
Theale	d						00s29				05 17	05 50						06 20					
Aldermaston	d						00s34				05 22	05 55						06 25					
Midgham	d						00s37				05 25	05 58						06 29					
Thatcham	d						00s42				05 30	06 03						06 34					
Newbury Racecourse	d						00s47				05 35	06 08						06 38					
Newbury	a						00 52				05 37	06 10						06 44					
	d										05 37	06 10											
Kintbury	d										05 44	06 17											
Hungerford	d										05 48	06 21											
Bedwyn	a										05 57	06 30											
Tilehurst	d	23p45							00 29					05 50					06 25				
Pangbourne	d	23p49							00 33					05 54					06 29				
Goring & Streatley	d	23p53							00 37					05 59					06 34				
Cholsey	d	23p57							00 42					06 04		←			06 39			←	
Didcot Parkway	a	00 07				00 25		00 43	00 51	01 13				06 12	06 07	06 12			06 46	06 37		06 46	
	d	00 07						00 44	00 51	01 14				06 13	06 08	06 13			06 47	06 38		06 47	
Appleford	d								00 56					→		06 17			→				
Culham	d								00 58							06 20							
Radley	d	00 15							01 02							06 24						06 54	
Oxford	a	00 26	00 28					01 02	01 16	01 28					06 22	06 32	06 36			06 52		07 03	07 10
	d			00 38									06 16				06 38				07 00		07 12
Islip	d																				07 13		
Bicester Town	a																				07 25		
Tackley	d			00 48									06 25										
Heyford	d			00 53									06 29										
Kings Sutton	d			01 01									06 38										
Banbury	a			01 11									06 46				06 54						07 32
Leamington Spa [8]	a																07 12						07 50
Coventry	a																07 24						
Birmingham International	a																07 37						
Birmingham New Street [12]	a																07 48						08 17

Table 116

Saturdays
from 27 October

London and Reading - Bedwyn, Oxford, Bicester, Banbury and Birmingham

Network Diagram - see first Page of Table 116

		GW	GW	GW	GW	GW	GW	XC	GW	GW	GW	CH	GW	XC	GW	GW	GW	GW	GW	XC	GW	GW	GW
		1	1	◇1	1	1	◇1 ☕	◇1 trolley	1	◇1	1		1	◇1 trolley	1	1	◇1	1	1 ☕	◇1 trolley	1	◇1	1
London Paddington [15] ⊖	d		05 57	06 21		06 27	06 30			06 50						06 57	07 21	07 27	07 30			07 50	
Ealing Broadway ⊖	d		06 05			06 35										07 05		07 35					
Slough [3]	d		06 31	06 38		06 57				07 06						07 27	07 38	07 57				08 06	
Maidenhead [3]	d		06 42			07 04										07 34		08 04					
Twyford [3]	d		06 50		←	07 12							←			07 42		08 12					←
Reading [7]	d	06 48	06 56	06 54	06 56	07 23	06 59	07 11	07 11	07 22			07 23	07 47	07 48	07 53	07 53	08 23	07 57	08 11	08 18	08 22	08 23
Reading West	d		→			→			07 14									→			08 20		
Theale	d	06 55							07 20						07 57						08 27		
Aldermaston	d								07 25												08 32		
Midgham	d								07 29												08 36		
Thatcham	d	07 04							07 34						08 05						08 41		
Newbury Racecourse	d								07 38												08 45		
Newbury	a	07 09							07 43						08 11						08 50		
	d	07 09													08 11								
Kintbury	d	07 16													08 17								
Hungerford	d	07 20													08 22								
Bedwyn	a	07 29													08 31								
Tilehurst	d				07 00								07 27			07 57							08 27
Pangbourne	d				07 04								07 31			08 01							08 31
Goring & Streatley	d				07 09								07 36			08 06							08 36
Cholsey	d				07 14								07 41			08 11							08 41
Didcot Parkway	a				07 30		07 12						07 49			08 19			08 12				08 48
	d				07 30								07 51			08 25							08 55
Appleford	d																						09 00
Culham	d												07 56										
Radley	d												08 00										09 03
Oxford	a			07 18	07 43			07 34		07 48			08 09	08 13		08 40	08 19			08 34		08 48	09 14
	d							07 36			07 53	08 07		08 15						08 36			
Islip	d											08 20											
Bicester Town	a											08 32											
Tackley	d										08 02												
Heyford	d										08 06												
Kings Sutton	d										08 15												
Banbury	a							07 52			08 23			08 32						08 52			
Leamington Spa [8]	a							08 10						08 49						09 10			
Coventry	a							08 22												09 22			
Birmingham International	a							08 37												09 37			
Birmingham New Street [12]	a							08 48						09 18						09 48			

		XC	GW	GW	GW	GW	GW	GW	CH	GW	GW	XC	GW	GW	GW	XC	GW	GW	GW	GW	GW	GW
		◇1 trolley	1	1	◇1 ☕	◇1 ☕	1	◇1 ☕		1	◇1 ☕	◇1 trolley	1	◇1	1	◇1 trolley	1	1	1	1	◇1	1
London Paddington [15] ⊖	d			07 57	08 15	08 18		08 21		08 27	08 30			08 50				08 57	09 18		09 21	09 27
Ealing Broadway ⊖	d			08 05						08 35								09 05				09 35
Slough [3]	d			08 27				08 39		08 57				09 06				09 27			09 39	09 57
Maidenhead [3]	d			08 34						09 04								09 34				10 04
Twyford [3]	d			08 42			←			09 12					←			09 42		←		10 12
Reading [7]	d	08 40		08 53	08 42	08 48	08 53	08 54		09 23	08 57	09 11	09 12	09 22	09 23	09 40		09 53	09 48	09 53	09 54	10 23
Reading West	d			→						→			09 14					→				→
Theale	d					08 58							09 20						09 56			
Aldermaston	d												09 25									
Midgham	d												09 29									
Thatcham	d					09 07							09 34						10 04			
Newbury Racecourse	d												09 38									
Newbury	a					09 13							09 44						10 10			
	d		08 58			09 14													10 10			
Kintbury	d		09 04																10 17			
Hungerford	d		09 09			09 23													10 21			
Bedwyn	a		09 17			09 30													10 31			
Tilehurst	d						08 57								09 27					09 57		
Pangbourne	d						09 01								09 31					10 01		
Goring & Streatley	d						09 06								09 36					10 06		
Cholsey	d						09 11								09 41					10 11		
Didcot Parkway	a				08 55		09 19				09 12				09 48					10 18		
	d						09 25								09 55					10 25		
Appleford	d																					
Culham	d														10 01							
Radley	d														10 03							
Oxford	a	09 04					09 40	09 18				09 34		09 48	10 14	10 04				10 40	10 19	
	d	09 07							09 28			09 36				10 07	10 16					
Islip	d								09 41													
Bicester Town	a								09 53													
Tackley	d																10 25					
Heyford	d																10 29					
Kings Sutton	d																10 38					
Banbury	a	09 23										09 52				10 23	10 46					
Leamington Spa [8]	a	09 41										10 12				10 41						
Coventry	a											10 22										
Birmingham International	a											10 37										
Birmingham New Street [12]	a	10 18										10 48				11 18						

London and Reading - Bedwyn, Oxford, Bicester, Banbury and Birmingham

Network Diagram - see first Page of Table 116

		GW	XC	GW	GW	CH	GW	XC	GW	GW	GW	GW	GW	GW	GW	XC	GW	GW	GW	XC	GW	GW	GW
		◇1 ⊡	◇1 ✕	1	◇1		1	◇1 ✕	1	◇1 ⊡	1	1	◇1 ⊡	1	◇1 ⊡	◇1 ✕	1	◇1 ✕	1	◇1 ✕	1	1	1
London Paddington 15 ⊖	d	09 30			09 50				09 57	10 15	10 18		10 21	10 27	10 30			10 50				10 57	11 18
Ealing Broadway ⊖	d								10 05					10 35								11 05	
Slough 3	d				10 06				10 27				10 39	10 57				11 06				11 27	
Maidenhead 3	d								10 34					11 04								11 34	
Twyford 3	d						←		10 42			←		11 12					←			11 42	
Reading 7	d	09 57	10 11	10 12	10 22		10 23	10 40	10 53	10 42	10 48	10 53	10 54	11 23	10 57	11 11	11 12	11 22	11 23	11 40		11 53	11 48
Reading West	d			10 14					→					→			11 14					→	
Theale	d			10 20							10 56						11 20						11 56
Aldermaston	d			10 25													11 25						
Midgham	d			10 29													11 29						
Thatcham	d			10 34							11 04						11 34						12 04
Newbury Racecourse	d			10 38													11 38						
Newbury	a			10 44							11 10						11 44						12 10
	d										11 10												12 10
Kintbury	d										11 17												12 17
Hungerford	d										11 21												12 21
Bedwyn	a										11 31												12 31
Tilehurst	d						10 27					10 57							11 27				
Pangbourne	d						10 31					11 01							11 31				
Goring & Streatley	d						10 36					11 06							11 36				
Cholsey	d						10 41					11 11							11 41				
Didcot Parkway	a	10 12					10 48			10 55		11 19			11 12				11 49				
	d						10 55					11 25							11 55				
Appleford	d						11 00																
Culham	d																						
Radley	d						11 03												12 03				
Oxford	a		10 34		10 48		11 14	11 04				11 40	11 19			11 34		11 48	12 14	12 04			
	d		10 36			11 00		11 07								11 36				12 07	12 16		
Islip	d					11 13																	
Bicester Town	a					11 25																	
Tackley	d																				12 25		
Heyford	d																				12 29		
Kings Sutton	d																				12 38		
Banbury	a		10 52					11 23								11 52				12 23	12 46		
Leamington Spa 8	a		11 10					11 41								12 10				12 41			
Coventry	a		11 22													12 22							
Birmingham International	a		11 37													12 37							
Birmingham New Street 12	a		11 48					12 18								12 48				13 18			

		GW	GW	CH	GW	GW	XC	GW	GW	GW	XC	GW	GW	GW	GW	GW	GW	GW	XC	GW	CH	GW
		1	◇1 ✕		1	◇1 ⊘	◇1 ✕	1	◇1	1	◇1 ✕	1	◇1 ⊡	◇1 ⊡	1	◇1	1	◇1 ⊡	◇1 ✕	1		◇1 ✕
London Paddington 15 ⊖	d		11 21		11 27	11 30			11 50			11 57	12 15	12 18		12 21	12 27	12 30				12 50
Ealing Broadway ⊖	d				11 35							12 05					12 35					
Slough 3	d		11 39		11 57				12 06			12 27				12 39	12 57					13 06
Maidenhead 3	d				12 04							12 34					13 04					
Twyford 3	d	←			12 12					←		12 42			←		13 12					
Reading 7	d	11 53	11 54		12 23	11 58	12 11	12 12	12 22	12 23	12 40	12 53	12 42	12 48	12 53	12 54	13 23	12 57	13 11	13 12		13 22
Reading West	d				→			12 14				→					→			13 14		
Theale	d							12 20						12 57						13 20		
Aldermaston	d							12 25												13 25		
Midgham	d							12 29												13 29		
Thatcham	d							12 34						13 05						13 34		
Newbury Racecourse	d							12 38												13 38		
Newbury	a							12 44						13 12						13 44		
	d													13 13								
Kintbury	d																					
Hungerford	d													13 21								
Bedwyn	a													13 29								
Tilehurst	d	11 57								12 27					12 57							
Pangbourne	d	12 01								12 31					13 01							
Goring & Streatley	d	12 06								12 36					13 06							
Cholsey	d	12 11								12 41					13 11							
Didcot Parkway	a	12 19				12 12				12 48			12 55		13 19			13 12				
	d	12 25								12 55					13 25							
Appleford	d									13 00												
Culham	d																					
Radley	d									13 03												
Oxford	a	12 40	12 20				12 34		12 48	13 14	13 04				13 40	13 19			13 34			13 48
	d			12 30			12 36				13 07								13 36		13 41	
Islip	d			12 43																	13 54	
Bicester Town	a			12 55																	14 06	
Tackley	d																					
Heyford	d																					
Kings Sutton	d																					
Banbury	a						12 52				13 23								13 52			
Leamington Spa 8	a						13 10				13 41								14 10			
Coventry	a						13 22												14 22			
Birmingham International	a						13 37												14 37			
Birmingham New Street 12	a						13 48				14 18								14 48			

London and Reading - Bedwyn, Oxford, Bicester, Banbury and Birmingham

Network Diagram - see first Page of Table 116

		GW	XC	GW	GW	GW	GW	GW	GW	GW	XC	GW	GW	CH	GW	XC	GW	GW	GW	GW	GW	GW	GW
		1	◇1 ✕	1	1	1	1	◇1 ✕	1	◇1 ⊡	◇1 ✕	1	◇1 ✕		1	◇1 ✕	1	◇1 ⊡	1	1	◇1 ✕	1	◇1 ⊡
London Paddington 15 ⊖	d				12 57	13 18		13 21	13 27	13 30			13 50				13 57	14 15	14 18		14 21	14 27	14 30
Ealing Broadway ⊖	d				13 05				13 35								14 05					14 35	
Slough 3	d				13 27			13 39	13 57				14 06				14 27				14 39	14 57	
Maidenhead 3	d				13 34				14 04								14 34					15 04	
Twyford 3	d	←			13 42		←		14 12						←		14 42			←		15 12	
Reading 7	d	13 23	13 40		13 53	13 48	13 53	13 54	14 23	13 59	14 11	14 12	14 22		14 23	14 40	14 53	14 42	14 48	14 53	14 54	15 23	14 57
Reading West	d				→				→			14 14					→					→	
Theale	d					13 56						14 20							14 56				
Aldermaston	d											14 25											
Midgham	d											14 29											
Thatcham	d					14 04						14 34							15 04				
Newbury Racecourse	d											14 38											
Newbury	a					14 10						14 44							15 10				
	d					14 10													15 10				
Kintbury	d					14 17													15 17				
Hungerford	d					14 21													15 21				
Bedwyn	a					14 31													15 31				
Tilehurst	d	13 27					13 57								14 27					14 57			
Pangbourne	d	13 31					14 01								14 31					15 01			
Goring & Streatley	d	13 36					14 06								14 36					15 06			
Cholsey	d	13 41					14 11								14 41					15 11			
Didcot Parkway	a	13 48					14 19			14 12					14 48			14 55		15 19			15 12
	d	13 55					14 25								14 55					15 25			
Appleford	d														15 00								
Culham	d	14 01																					
Radley	d	14 03													15 03								
Oxford	a	14 14	14 04				14 40	14 19			14 34		14 48		15 14	15 04				15 40	15 18		
	d		14 07	14 16							14 36			14 57		15 07							
Islip	d													15 10									
Bicester Town	a													15 22									
Tackley	d			14 25																			
Heyford	d			14 29																			
Kings Sutton	d			14 38																			
Banbury	a		14 23	14 46							14 52					15 23							
Leamington Spa 8	a		14 41								15 10					15 41							
Coventry	a										15 22												
Birmingham International	a										15 37												
Birmingham New Street 12	a		15 18								15 48					16 18							

		XC	GW	GW	CH	GW	XC	GW	GW	GW	GW	GW	GW	GW	XC	GW	GW	GW	XC	CH	GW	GW	GW
		◇1 ✕	1	◇1		1	◇1 ✕	1	1	1	1	◇1 ✕	1	◇1 ⊡	◇1 ✕	1	◇1	1	◇1 ✕		1	◇1 ⊡	1
London Paddington 15 ⊖	d			14 50					14 57	15 18		15 21	15 27	15 30			15 50				15 57	16 15	16 18
Ealing Broadway ⊖	d								15 05				15 35								16 05		
Slough 3	d			15 06					15 27			15 39	15 57				16 06				16 27		
Maidenhead 3	d								15 34				16 04								16 34		
Twyford 3	d					←			15 42		←		16 12					←			16 42		
Reading 7	d	15 11	15 12	15 22		15 23	15 40		15 53	15 48	15 53	15 54	16 23	15 59	16 11	16 12	16 22	16 23	16 40		16 53	16 42	16 48
Reading West	d		15 14						→				→			16 14					→		
Theale	d		15 20							15 56						16 20							16 56
Aldermaston	d		15 25													16 25							
Midgham	d		15 29													16 29							
Thatcham	d		15 34							16 04						16 34							17 04
Newbury Racecourse	d		15 38													16 38							
Newbury	a		15 44							16 10						16 44							17 10
	d									16 10													17 10
Kintbury	d									16 17													17 17
Hungerford	d									16 21													17 21
Bedwyn	a									16 31													17 31
Tilehurst	d					15 27					15 57							16 27					
Pangbourne	d					15 31					16 01							16 31					
Goring & Streatley	d					15 36					16 06							16 36					
Cholsey	d					15 41					16 11							16 41					
Didcot Parkway	a					15 48					16 19			16 12				16 48				16 55	
	d					15 55					16 25							16 55					
Appleford	d																	17 00					
Culham	d					16 01																	
Radley	d					16 03												17 03					
Oxford	a	15 34		15 48		16 14	16 04				16 40	16 19			16 34		16 48	17 14	17 04				
	d	15 36			16 00		16 07	16 16							16 36				17 07	17 10			
Islip	d				16 13															17 23			
Bicester Town	a				16 25															17 35			
Tackley	d							16 25															
Heyford	d							16 29															
Kings Sutton	d							16 38															
Banbury	a	15 52					16 23	16 46							16 52				17 23				
Leamington Spa 8	a	16 10					16 41								17 10				17 41				
Coventry	a	16 22													17 22								
Birmingham International	a	16 37													17 37								
Birmingham New Street 12	a	16 48					17 18								17 48				18 18				

Saturdays
from 27 October

London and Reading - Bedwyn, Oxford, Bicester, Banbury and Birmingham

Network Diagram - see first Page of Table 116

		GW 1		GW ◇1	GW 1	GW ◇1	XC ◇1	GW 1	GW ◇1	GW 1	XC ◇1	GW 1		GW 1	GW 1	GW 1	GW ◇1	GW 1	GW ◇1	XC ◇1	GW 1	CH		GW ◇1	GW 1
London Paddington 15 ⊖	d			16 21	16 27	16 30			16 50					16 57	17 18		17 21	17 27	17 30					17 50	
Ealing Broadway ⊖	d				16 35									17 05				17 35							
Slough 3	d			16 39	16 57				17 06					17 27			17 39	17 57						18 06	
Maidenhead 3	d				17 04									17 34				18 04							
Twyford 3	d	←			17 12					←				17 42		←		18 12							←
Reading 7	d	16 53		16 54	17 23	16 57	17 11	17 12	17 22	17 23	17 40			17 53	17 48	17 53	17 54	18 23	17 57	18 11	18 12			18 22	18 23
Reading West	d				→			17 14						→				→			18 14				
Theale	d							17 20							17 56						18 20				
Aldermaston	d							17 25													18 25				
Midgham	d							17 29													18 29				
Thatcham	d							17 34							18 04						18 34				
Newbury Racecourse	d							17 38													18 38				
Newbury	a							17 44							18 10						18 44				
	d														18 10										
Kintbury	d														18 17										
Hungerford	d														18 21										
Bedwyn	a														18 31										
Tilehurst	d	16 57								17 27						17 57									18 27
Pangbourne	d	17 01								17 31						18 01									18 31
Goring & Streatley	d	17 06								17 36						18 06									18 36
Cholsey	d	17 11								17 41						18 11									18 41
Didcot Parkway	a	17 19				17 12				17 48						18 19			18 12						18 48
	d	17 25								17 55						18 25									18 55
Appleford	d																								19 00
Culham	d									18 01															
Radley	d									18 03															19 03
Oxford	a	17 40		17 18			17 34		17 48	18 14	18 04					18 40	18 18			18 34				18 48	19 14
	d						17 36				18 07	18 16								18 36		18 41			
Islip	d																					18 54			
Bicester Town	a																					19 06			
Tackley	d											18 25													
Heyford	d											18 29													
Kings Sutton	d											18 38													
Banbury	a						17 52				18 23	18 46								18 52					
Leamington Spa 8	a						18 10				18 41									19 10					
Coventry	a						18 22													19 22					
Birmingham International	a						18 37													19 37					
Birmingham New Street 12	a						18 48				19 18									19 48					

		XC ◇1	GW 1	GW ◇1	GW 1	GW 1	GW ◇1	GW 1		GW ◇1	XC ◇1	GW ◇1	CH	GW 1	GW 1	GW 1	GW ◇1	GW ◇1		XC ◇1	GW 1	GW ◇1	GW 1	GW 1	GW ◇1
London Paddington 15 ⊖	d		17 57	18 15	18 18		18 21	18 27		18 30		18 50				18 57	19 06	19 15				19 21		19 27	19 30
Ealing Broadway ⊖	d		18 05					18 35								19 05								19 35	
Slough 3	d		18 27				18 39	18 57				19 06				19 27						19 38		19 57	
Maidenhead 3	d		18 34					19 04								19 34								20 04	
Twyford 3	d		18 42			←		19 12							←	19 42							←	20 12	
Reading 7	d	18 40	18 53	18 42	18 48	18 53	18 54	19 23		18 57	19 11	19 23			19 23	19 53	19 32	19 42		19 40	19 49	19 52	19 53	20 23	19 57
Reading West	d		→					→								→					19 52			→	
Theale	d				18 56																19 58				
Aldermaston	d																				20 03				
Midgham	d																				20 06				
Thatcham	d				19 04																20 11				
Newbury Racecourse	d																				20 16				
Newbury	a				19 10												19 48				20 18				
	d				19 10																20 18				
Kintbury	d				19 17																20 25				
Hungerford	d				19 21																20 29				
Bedwyn	a				19 31																20 38				
Tilehurst	d					18 57									19 27								19 57		
Pangbourne	d					19 01									19 31								20 01		
Goring & Streatley	d					19 06									19 36								20 06		
Cholsey	d					19 11									19 41								20 11		
Didcot Parkway	a			18 55		19 19				19 12					19 48			19 55					20 19		20 11
	d					19 25									19 55								20 25		
Appleford	d																								
Culham	d														20 01										
Radley	d														20 03										
Oxford	a	19 04				19 40	19 18				19 34	19 48			20 14					20 04		20 20	20 40		
	d	19 07									19 36		19 48	19 56						20 07					
Islip	d												20 01												
Bicester Town	a												20 13												
Tackley	d													20 05											
Heyford	d													20 09											
Kings Sutton	d													20 18											
Banbury	a	19 23									19 52			20 25						20 28					
Leamington Spa 8	a	19 41									20 10									20 45					
Coventry	a										20 22														
Birmingham International	a										20 37														
Birmingham New Street 12	a	20 18									20 48									21 18					

Saturdays
from 27 October

London and Reading - Bedwyn, Oxford, Bicester, Banbury and Birmingham

Network Diagram - see first Page of Table 116

		XC ◇1	GW ◇1	CH		GW 1	GW 1	GW ◇1	GW ◇1	GW ◇1	XC ◇1	GW 1	GW ◇1	GW 1		GW 1	GW 1	GW ◇1	XC ◇1	GW 1	GW ◇1	XC ◇1	GW 1	GW 1
London Paddington 15 ⊖	d		19 50				19 57	20 00	20 06	20 15			20 20				20 27	20 30			20 50			20 57
Ealing Broadway ⊖	d						20 05										20 35							21 05
Slough 3	d		20 06				20 27						20 35				20 57				21 06			21 27
Maidenhead 3	d						20 34										21 04							21 34
Twyford 3	d					←	20 42									←	21 12			←				21 46
Reading 7	d	20 11	20 22			20 23	20 53	20 27	20 33	20 42	20 40	20 49	20 51			20 53	21 23	20 57	21 11	21 23	21 25	21 40		21 55
Reading West	d						→					20 52					→							→
Theale	d											20 58												
Aldermaston	d											21 03												
Midgham	d											21 06												
Thatcham	d											21 11												
Newbury Racecourse	d											21 16												
Newbury	a								20 47			21 18												
	d											21 32												
Kintbury	d											21 39												
Hungerford	d											21 43												
Bedwyn	a											21 52												
Tilehurst	d					20 27										20 57				21 27				
Pangbourne	d					20 31										21 01				21 31				
Goring & Streatley	d					20 37										21 06				21 36				
Cholsey	d					20 41										21 11				21 41			←	
Didcot Parkway	a					20 49		20 41		20 55						21 19		21 12		21 48	21 41		21 48	
	d					20 55										21 25				21 55	21 42		21 55	
Appleford	d					21 00														→				
Culham	d																						22 01	
Radley	d					21 03																	22 03	
Oxford	a	20 34	20 47			21 14					21 04		21 19			21 40			21 33		21 55	22 03	22 14	
	d	20 36		21 00							21 07			21 20					21 36			22 07		
Islip	d			21 13																				
Bicester Town	a			21 25																				
Tackley	d													21 29										
Heyford	d													21 33										
Kings Sutton	d													21 42										
Banbury	a	20 52									21 23			21 49					21 52			22 28		
Leamington Spa 8	a	21 10									21 44								22 10			22 45		
Coventry	a	21 22									21 55								22 22					
Birmingham International	a	21 37									22 10								22 36					
Birmingham New Street 12	a	21 48									22 21								22 48			23 16		

		GW ◇1	CH	GW 1	GW ◇1	GW 1	GW ◇1	GW 1	GW ◇1	GW ◇1		GW 1	GW ◇1	GW 1	GW	GW 1	GW ◇1	GW 1	GW 1	GW ◇1		GW ◇1	GW 1
London Paddington 15 ⊖	d	21 17			21 30		21 50	21 57	22 00	22 15			22 35			22 45	23 00		23 20	23 30		23 33	
Ealing Broadway ⊖	d							22 05								22 55			23 28				
Slough 3	d	21 35					22 06	22 27		22 32						23 21	23 17		23 54			23 50	
Maidenhead 3	d							22 34								23 32			00 05				
Twyford 3	d			←				22 45				←				23 39		←	00 13				←
Reading 7	d	21 51		21 55	21 58	22 03	22 22	22 56	22 27	22 51		22 56	23 02	23 12		23 49	23 34	23 49	00 20	23 59		00 08	00 20
Reading West	d					22 06		→						23 14		→			→				
Theale	d					22 12								23 20									
Aldermaston	d					22 17								23 25									
Midgham	d					22 20								23 29									
Thatcham	d					22 25								23 34									
Newbury Racecourse	d					22 30								23 38									
Newbury	a					22 32								23 41									
	d					22 32								23 41									
Kintbury	d					22 39								23 48									
Hungerford	d					22 43								23 52									
Bedwyn	a					22 51								00 01									
Tilehurst	d			22 01								23 02						23 56					00 24
Pangbourne	d			22 05								23 06						00 01					
Goring & Streatley	d			22 10								23 11						00 06					00 31
Cholsey	d			22 15								23 15						00 11					00 36
Didcot Parkway	a	22 07		22 23	22 13		22 37		22 41	23 07		23 23	23 26				23 51	00 17		00 18		00 22	00 44
	d	22 08		22 25			22 37			23 07		23 23					23 51	00 18				00 24	00 45
Appleford	d																						00s49
Culham	d																						00s51
Radley	d			22 34								23 31						00s25					00s55
Oxford	a	22 20		22 43			22 50			23 20		23 41					00 04	00 35				00 39	01 07
	d		22 25												23 51								
Islip	d		22 38																				
Bicester Town	a		22 50																				
Tackley	d														00s11								
Heyford	d														00s25								
Kings Sutton	d																						
Banbury	a														00 50								
Leamington Spa 8	a																						
Coventry	a																						
Birmingham International	a																						
Birmingham New Street 12	a																						

Sundays until 24 June

London and Reading - Bedwyn, Oxford, Bicester, Banbury and Birmingham

Network Diagram - see first Page of Table 116

	GW	GW	GW	GW	GW	GW	GW	GW	GW	GW	GW	GW	GW	GW	GW	GW	GW	GW	XC	CH	GW	GW
	1		1	◇1	1	1	◇1	◇1	1	1		1	1	◇1		◇1	1	◇1	◇1		◇1	1
		🚌					⌶				🚌			⌶	🚌			⌶	🍴			
London Paddington 15 ⊖ d			22p45	23p00		23p20	23p30	23p33					07 29	08 00		08 03		08 30			08 42	
Ealing Broadway ⊖ d			22p55			23p28							07 36									
Slough 3 d			23p21	23p17		23p54		23p50					07 58			08 25					09 04	
Maidenhead 3 d			23p32			00 05							08 08			08 33						
Twyford 3 d			23p39		←	00 13				←			08 17				←					
Reading 7 d	23p12		23p49	23p34	23p49	00 20	23p59	00 08	00 15	00 20	08 00		08 48	08 35	08 36	08 44	08 48	09 06	09 11		09 21	
Reading West d	23p14		→			→			00s18		08 16		→									
Theale d	23p20								00s24		08 31				09 02							
Aldermaston d	23p25								00s29		08 37											
Midgham d	23p29								00s32		08 45											
Thatcham d	23p34								00s37		08 52				09 17							
Newbury Racecourse d	23p38								00s42													
Newbury a	23p41								00 45		09 05				09 30							
d	23p41											09 20										
Kintbury d	23p48											09 26										
Hungerford d	23p52											09 31										
Bedwyn a	00 01											09 38										
Tilehurst d					23p53					00 24							08 52					
Pangbourne d																	08 56					
Goring & Streatley d					00 03					00 31							09 01					
Cholsey d					00 08					00 36							09 06					
Didcot Parkway a				23p51	00 14		00 18	00 22		00 44				08 48		08 58	09 11	09 20			09 36	
d				23p51	00 15			00 24		00 45						09 00	09 14				09 37	
Appleford d										00s49												
Culham d										00s51												
Radley d					00s22					00s55							09 21					
Oxford a				00 04	00 32			00 38		01 05						09 12	09 30		09 34		09 51	
d		23p47																	09 37	09 36		10 00
Islip d																				09 49		
Bicester Town a																				10 01		
Tackley d		00s06																				10 09
Heyford d		00s20																				10 13
Kings Sutton d																						10 22
Banbury a		00 45																	09 53			10 30
Leamington Spa 8 a																			10 11			
Coventry a																			10 22			
Birmingham International a																			10 38			
Birmingham New Street 12 a																			10 50			

	GW	GW	GW	GW	GW	GW	GW	XC	GW	GW	CH	GW	GW	GW	GW	GW	XC	GW	GW	GW	GW	GW
	1	◇1	1		1		1	◇1	◇1	◇1		1	◇1	1		◇1	◇1	◇1	1	1	◇1	1
		⌶		🚌		🚌		🍴	⌶	⌶			⌶		🚌	⌶	🍴	⌶			⌶	
London Paddington 15 ⊖ d	08 43	09 03							09 35	09 42		09 43	10 03			10 37		10 42		10 43	11 03	
Ealing Broadway ⊖ d	08 50											09 50								10 50		
Slough 3 d	09 16								09 59			10 16						11 06		11 16		
Maidenhead 3 d	09 27											10 27								11 27		
Twyford 3 d	09 35		←									10 35		←						11 35		←
Reading 7 d	09 43	09 38	09 43	09 42		09 52	09 59	10 11	10 12	10 18		10 43	10 38	10 43	10 52	11 12	11 11	11 21		11 43	11 38	11 43
Reading West d	→					10 08						→			11 08					→		
Theale d				10 08		10 23									11 23							
Aldermaston d						10 29									11 29							
Midgham d						10 37									11 37							
Thatcham d				10 23		10 44									11 44							
Newbury Racecourse d															11 54							
Newbury a				10 36		10 57									12 04							
d					10 45														12 15			
Kintbury d					10 51														12 21			
Hungerford d					10 56														12 26			
Bedwyn a					11 03														12 33			
Tilehurst d			09 47											10 47								11 47
Pangbourne d			09 51											10 52								11 52
Goring & Streatley d			09 56											10 57								11 57
Cholsey d			10 01											11 02								12 02
Didcot Parkway a		09 51	10 08						10 28	10 32			10 52	11 09		11 25		11 36			11 51	12 09
d			10 09						10 28					11 10				11 37				12 10
Appleford d			10 14																			
Culham d																						
Radley d			10 19											11 17								12 17
Oxford a			10 28				10 30	10 35	10 43					11 27			11 35	11 50				12 27
d								10 37			10 56						11 37					
Islip d											11 09											
Bicester Town a											11 21											
Tackley d																						
Heyford d																						
Kings Sutton d																						
Banbury a								10 53									11 53					
Leamington Spa 8 a								11 11									12 11					
Coventry a								11 22									12 22					
Birmingham International a								11 38									12 38					
Birmingham New Street 12 a								11 50									12 50					

Sundays until 24 June

London and Reading - Bedwyn, Oxford, Bicester, Banbury and Birmingham

Network Diagram - see first Page of Table 116

	GW	CH	XC	GW	GW	GW	GW	GW	GW	XC	GW	XC	GW	CH	GW	GW	GW	XC	GW	GW	GW
			◇1	◇1	◇1	1	◇1	1		◇1	◇1	◇1	◇1		1	1	◇1	◇1	1	1	
	🚌		🍴	⌶			⌶		🚌	🍴	⌶	🍴	⌶				⌶	🍴			🚌
London Paddington 15 ⊖ d				11 37	11 42	11 43	12 03				12 37		12 42			12 43	13 03				
Ealing Broadway ⊖ d						11 50										12 50					
Slough 3 d					12 03	12 16							13 07			13 16					
Maidenhead 3 d						12 27										13 27					
Twyford 3 d						12 35		←								13 35				←	
Reading 7 d	11 52		12 11	12 12	12 20	12 43	12 38	12 43	12 52	12 54	13 13	13 11	13 21			13 43	13 38	13 40		13 43	13 52
Reading West d						→			13 08							→					
Theale d	12 18								13 23												14 18
Aldermaston d									13 29												
Midgham d									13 37												
Thatcham d	12 33								13 44												14 33
Newbury Racecourse d									13 54												
Newbury a	12 46								14 04												14 46
d															14 15						
Kintbury d															14 21						
Hungerford d															14 26						
Bedwyn a															14 33						
Tilehurst d								12 47												13 47	
Pangbourne d								12 52												13 52	
Goring & Streatley d								12 57												13 57	
Cholsey d								13 02												14 02	
Didcot Parkway a				12 26	12 35		12 51	13 08			13 25		13 37				13 51			14 09	
d					12 36			13 10					13 38							14 10	
Appleford d								13 15													
Culham d																					
Radley d								13 19												14 18	
Oxford a			12 34		12 48			13 28		13 15		13 35	13 50					14 03		14 28	
d		12 33	12 37							13 17		13 37		13 56				14 05	14 20		
Islip d		12 46												14 09							
Bicester Town a		12 58												14 21							
Tackley d																			14 29		
Heyford d																			14 33		
Kings Sutton d																			14 42		
Banbury a			12 53							13 33		13 53						14 22	14 50		
Leamington Spa 8 a			13 11							13 50		14 11						14 40			
Coventry a			13 22									14 22									
Birmingham International a			13 37									14 35									
Birmingham New Street 12 a			13 48							14 19		14 48						15 09			

	XC	GW	GW	GW	GW	XC	GW	GW	GW	CH	XC	GW	GW	GW	XC	GW	GW	XC	GW	GW	GW	GW
	◇1	◇1	◇1	1	◇1	◇1	1		◇1		◇1	◇1	1	◇1	◇1	1		◇1	1	◇1	◇1	◇1
	🍴	⌶	⌶		⌶	🍴		🚌	⌶		🍴			⌶	🍴		🚌	🍴			⌶	
London Paddington 15 ⊖ d		13 37	13 42	13 43	14 03				14 37			14 42	14 43	15 03						15 27	15 37	
Ealing Broadway ⊖ d				13 50									14 50									
Slough 3 d			14 06	14 16								15 03	15 16							15 50		
Maidenhead 3 d				14 27									15 27							16 01		
Twyford 3 d				14 35			←						15 35			←				16 10		←
Reading 7 d	14 09	14 13	14 21	14 42	14 38	14 40	14 42	14 52	15 13		15 11	15 21	15 43	15 38	15 40	15 43	15 52	16 11		16 16	16 12	16 16
Reading West d				→				15 08					→							→		
Theale d								15 23									16 18					
Aldermaston d								15 29														
Midgham d								15 37														
Thatcham d								15 44									16 33					
Newbury Racecourse d								15 54														
Newbury a								16 04									16 46					
d																			16 54			
Kintbury d																			17 00			
Hungerford d																			17 05			
Bedwyn a																			17 13			
Tilehurst d							14 47									15 47						
Pangbourne d							14 52									15 52						
Goring & Streatley d							14 57									15 57						
Cholsey d							15 02									16 02						
Didcot Parkway a		14 26	14 36		14 51		15 09		15 26			15 35		15 51		16 09					16 25	
d			14 37				15 10					15 36				16 10						
Appleford d							15 14															
Culham d																						
Radley d							15 19									16 17						
Oxford a	14 35		14 50			15 03	15 27				15 35	15 50			16 03	16 25		16 35				16 41
d	14 37					15 06				15 33	15 37				16 06			16 37				
Islip d										15 46												
Bicester Town a										15 58												
Tackley d																						
Heyford d																						
Kings Sutton d																						
Banbury a	14 53					15 23					15 53				16 23			16 53				
Leamington Spa 8 a	15 11					15 41					16 11				16 41			17 11				
Coventry a	15 22										16 22							17 22				
Birmingham International a	15 35										16 35							17 35				
Birmingham New Street 12 a	15 48					16 12					16 48				17 12			17 48				

Table 116

Sundays until 24 June

London and Reading - Bedwyn, Oxford, Bicester, Banbury and Birmingham

Network Diagram - see first Page of Table 116

		GW	CH	GW	GW	XC	GW	GW	GW	GW	XC	GW	GW	GW	GW	XC	GW	GW	GW	XC	CH	GW
		◇1		1	◇1	◇1	1	1		◇1	◇1	◇1	1	◇1	◇1	◇1	1		◇1	◇1		◇1
					☕	🍴			🚌	☕	🍴			☕	☕	🍴		🚌	☕	🍴		☕
London Paddington 15 ⊖	d	15 42		15 43	16 03					16 37		16 42	16 43	16 57	17 03				17 37			17 42
Ealing Broadway ⊖	d			15 50									16 50									
Slough 3	d	16 05		16 16								17 04	17 16									18 04
Maidenhead 3	d			16 27								17 11	17 27									18 14
Twyford 3	d			16 35				←					17 35				←					
Reading 7	d	16 21		16 43	16 38	16 41		16 43	16 52	17 13	17 09	17 25	17 43	17 32	17 37	17 40	17 43	17 52	18 13	18 11		18 24
Reading West	d			→					17 08				→									
Theale	d								17 23									18 18				
Aldermaston	d								17 29													
Midgham	d								17 37													
Thatcham	d								17 44									18 33				
Newbury Racecourse	d								17 54													
Newbury	a								18 04									18 46				
	d																					
Kintbury	d																					
Hungerford	d																					
Bedwyn	a																					
Tilehurst	d							16 47									17 47					
Pangbourne	d							16 52									17 52					
Goring & Streatley	d							16 57									17 57					
Cholsey	d							17 02									18 02					
Didcot Parkway	a	16 38			16 51			17 09		17 26		17 39		17 46	17 51		18 09		18 26			18 39
	d	16 39						17 10				17 39					18 10					18 39
Appleford	d																18 14					
Culham	d																					
Radley	d							17 17									18 19					
Oxford	a	16 50				17 04		17 25			17 35	17 50				18 03	18 27			18 35		18 50
	d		16 56			17 06	17 19				17 37					18 06				18 37	18 37	
Islip	d		17 09																		18 50	
Bicester Town	a		17 21																		19 02	
Tackley	d						17 28															
Heyford	d						17 32															
Kings Sutton	d						17 41															
Banbury	a					17 23	17 50				17 53					18 23				18 53		
Leamington Spa 8	a					17 41					18 11					18 41				19 11		
Coventry	a										18 22									19 22		
Birmingham International	a										18 35									19 35		
Birmingham New Street 12	a					18 09					18 48					19 11				19 48		

		GW	GW	GW	XC	GW	GW	GW	XC	GW	CH	GW	GW	XC	GW	GW	GW	XC	GW	GW	GW	GW	XC
		1	1	◇1	◇1	1		◇1	◇1	◇1		1	◇1	◇1	1		◇1	◇1	◇1	1	1	◇1	◇1
				☕	🍴		🚌	☕	🍴				☕	🍴		🚌	☕		☕			☕	
London Paddington 15 ⊖	d		17 43	18 03				18 37		18 42		18 43	19 03				19 37		19 42		19 43	20 03	
Ealing Broadway ⊖	d		17 51									18 50									19 50		
Slough 3	d		18 16							19 07		19 16							20 06		20 16		
Maidenhead 3	d		18 27							19 14		19 27									20 27		
Twyford 3	d		18 35			←						19 35			←						20 35		
Reading 7	d		18 43	18 38	18 41	18 43	18 58	19 12	19 11	19 28		19 43	19 38	19 40	19 43	19 52	20 13	20 11	20 21		20 43	20 38	20 41
Reading West	d		→				19 14					→									→		
Theale	d						19 29									20 18							
Aldermaston	d						19 35																
Midgham	d						19 43																
Thatcham	d						19 50									20 33							
Newbury Racecourse	d						20 00																
Newbury	a						20 10									20 46							
	d	18 55																		20 55			
Kintbury	d	19 01																		21 01			
Hungerford	d	19 06																		21 06			
Bedwyn	a	19 14																		21 14			
Tilehurst	d					18 47									19 47								
Pangbourne	d					18 52									19 52								
Goring & Streatley	d					18 57									19 57								
Cholsey	d					19 02									20 02								
Didcot Parkway	a			18 51		19 09		19 25		19 43			19 51		20 09		20 26		20 36			20 51	
	d					19 10				19 44					20 10				20 37				
Appleford	d																						
Culham	d																						
Radley	d					19 17									20 17								
Oxford	a				19 03	19 25			19 35	19 55				20 03	20 25			20 35	20 50				21 03
	d				19 06				19 37		19 56			20 06				20 37					21 06
Islip	d										20 09												
Bicester Town	a										20 21												
Tackley	d																						
Heyford	d																						
Kings Sutton	d																						
Banbury	a				19 23				19 53					20 24				20 53					21 23
Leamington Spa 8	a				19 41				20 11					20 41				21 11					21 41
Coventry	a				19 53				20 22					20 53				21 22					21 52
Birmingham International	a				20 03				20 35					21 03				21 35					22 02
Birmingham New Street 12	a				20 15				20 48					21 15				21 48					22 14

Table 116

Sundays until 24 June

London and Reading - Bedwyn, Oxford, Bicester, Banbury and Birmingham

Network Diagram - see first Page of Table 116

		GW	GW	GW	CH	XC	GW	GW	GW	GW	GW	XC	GW	GW	GW	GW	GW	GW	GW	GW	GW	GW	GW
		1		◇1		◇1	◇1		1	1	◇1	◇1	1	◇1	◇1		1	◇1	1			◇1	◇1
			🚌	☕				🚌			☕			☕		🚌		☕		🚌	🚌	☕	
London Paddington 15 ⊖	d			20 37			20 42			20 43	21 03			21 37	21 42		21 43	22 03				22 37	22 42
Ealing Broadway ⊖	d									20 50							21 50						
Slough 3	d						21 01			21 16					22 06		22 16						23 02
Maidenhead 3	d									21 27							22 31						
Twyford 3	d	←								21 35			←				22 41		←				
Reading 7	d	20 43	20 44	21 13		21 11	21 24	21 36		21 47	21 38	21 40	21 47	22 12	22 22	22 36	22 50	22 45	22 50	23 13		23 17	23 22
Reading West	d		20 52							→						22 52	→			23 29			
Theale	d		21 07					22 02								23 07				23 44			
Aldermaston	d		21 13													23 13				23 50			
Midgham	d		21 21													23 21				23 58			
Thatcham	d		21 28					22 17								23 28				00 05			
Newbury Racecourse	d		21 38													23 38				00 15			
Newbury	a		21 48					22 30								23 48				00 25			
	d								22 38														
Kintbury	d								22 44														
Hungerford	d								22 49														
Bedwyn	a								22 57														
Tilehurst	d	20 47											21 51						22 53				
Pangbourne	d	20 52											21 56						22 58				
Goring & Streatley	d	20 57											22 00						23 02				
Cholsey	d	21 02											22 05						23 07				
Didcot Parkway	a	21 09		21 26			21 40				21 51		22 12	22 27	22 38			22 59	23 16			23s32	23 39
	d	21 14					21 40						22 14		22 40						23 27		
Appleford	d																						
Culham	d																						
Radley	d	21 22											22 21								23 42		
Oxford	a	21 30				21 35	21 53					22 04	22 30		22 51						23 57		
	d				21 33	21 37						22 06											
Islip	d				21 46																		
Bicester Town	a				21 58																		
Tackley	d																						
Heyford	d																						
Kings Sutton	d																						
Banbury	a					21 53						22 22											
Leamington Spa 8	a					22 11						22 40											
Coventry	a					22 22						22 52											
Birmingham International	a					22 32						23 02											
Birmingham New Street 12	a					22 42						23 13											

		GW	GW	GW	GW	GW
			1	◇1	1	◇1
		🚌		☕		☕
London Paddington 15 ⊖	d		22 43	23 03		23 37
Ealing Broadway ⊖	d		22 50			
Slough 3	d		23 16			00 03
Maidenhead 3	d		23 24			
Twyford 3	d		23 32		←	
Reading 7	d		23 53	23 47	23 53	00 14
Reading West	d		→			
Theale	d					
Aldermaston	d					
Midgham	d					
Thatcham	d					
Newbury Racecourse	d					
Newbury	a					
	d					
Kintbury	d					
Hungerford	d					
Bedwyn	a					
Tilehurst	d				23 57	
Pangbourne	d				00 02	
Goring & Streatley	d				00 07	
Cholsey	d				00 12	
Didcot Parkway	a			00s01	00 20	00s30
	d	23 45				
Appleford	d					
Culham	d					
Radley	d					
Oxford	a	00 10				
	d					
Islip	d					
Bicester Town	a					
Tackley	d					
Heyford	d					
Kings Sutton	d					
Banbury	a					
Leamington Spa 8	a					
Coventry	a					
Birmingham International	a					
Birmingham New Street 12	a					

Sundays

1 July to 9 September

London and Reading - Bedwyn, Oxford, Bicester, Banbury and Birmingham

Network Diagram - see first Page of Table 116

		GW 1	GW (bus)	GW 1	GW ◇1	GW 1	GW 1	GW ◇1 ⊏	GW ◇1	GW 1	GW 1	GW	GW 1	GW ◇1 ⊏	GW ◇1	GW 1	GW	GW ◇1 ⊏	XC ◇1 ⌶	CH	GW ◇1	GW 1	GW 1
London Paddington 15 ⊖	d			22p45	23p00		23p20	23p30	23p33				07 29	08 00	08 03			08 30			08 42		08 43
Ealing Broadway ⊖	d			22p55			23p28						07 36										08 51
Slough 3	d			23p21	23p17		23p54		23p50				07 58		08 21						08 59		09 16
Maidenhead 3	d			23p32			00 05						08 08		08 28								09 27
Twyford 3	d			23p39		←	00 13				←		08 16			←							09 35
Reading 7	d	23p12		23p49	23p34	23p49	00 20	23p59	00 08	00 15	00 20	08 14	08 48	08 34	08 44	08 48	08 44	09 06	09 11		09 16		09 43
Reading West	d	23p14		→			→			00s18		08 17	→										→
Theale	d	23p20								00s24		08 23					08 51						
Aldermaston	d	23p25								00s29		08 28											
Midgham	d	23p29								00s32		08 31											
Thatcham	d	23p34								00s37		08 36					09 00						
Newbury Racecourse	d	23p38								00s42													
Newbury	a	23p41								00 45		08 43					09 05						
	d	23p41															09 06						
Kintbury	d	23p48															09 12						
Hungerford	d	23p52															09 17						
Bedwyn	a	00 01															09 24						
Tilehurst	d					23p53					00 24					08 52							
Pangbourne	d					23p58										08 56							
Goring & Streatley	d					00 03					00 31					09 01							
Cholsey	d					00 08					00 36					09 06							
Didcot Parkway	a				23p51	00 14		00 18	00 22		00 44			08 49	08 59	09 11		09 22			09 33		
	d				23p51	00 15			00 24		00 45				09 02	09 14					09 34		
Appleford	d										00s49												
Culham	d										00s51												
Radley	d					00s22					00s55					09 21							
Oxford	a				00 04	00 32			00 38		01 05				09 13	09 30			09 34		09 48		
	d		23p47																09 37	09 36		10 00	
Islip	d																			09 49			
Bicester Town	a																			10 01			
Tackley	d		00s06																			10 09	
Heyford	d		00s20																			10 13	
Kings Sutton	d																					10 22	
Banbury	a		00 45																09 53			10 30	
Leamington Spa 8	a																		10 11				
Coventry	a																						
Birmingham International	a																						
Birmingham New Street 12	a																		10 55				

		GW ◇1 ⊏	GW ◇1 ⊏	GW 1	GW 1 A	GW 1	GW ◇1 ⊏	XC ◇1 ⌶	GW ◇1 ⊏	CH	GW 1	GW ◇1 ⊏	GW 1	GW 1 A	GW ◇1 ⊏	XC ◇1 ⌶	GW ◇1 ⊏	GW 1	GW ◇1 ⊏	GW 1	GW 1 A	GW ◇1 ⊏	CH
London Paddington 15 ⊖	d	08 57	09 03		09 03		09 37		09 42		09 43	10 03		10 03	10 37		10 42	10 43	11 03		11 03	11 37	
Ealing Broadway ⊖	d										09 50							10 50					
Slough 3	d				09 23				09 59		10 16			10 23			11 00	11 16			11 23		
Maidenhead 3	d				09 30						10 27			10 30				11 27			11 30		
Twyford 3	d			←							10 35		←					11 35		←			
Reading 7	d	09 33	09 38	09 43	09 43	09 59	10 06	10 11	10 11		10 43	10 38	10 43	10 43	11 12	11 11	11 21	11 43	11 38	11 43	11 43	12 12	
Reading West	d				09 47						→			10 47				→					
Theale	d				09 53									10 53							11 51		
Aldermaston	d				09 58									10 58									
Midgham	d				10 01									11 01									
Thatcham	d				10 06									11 06							11 59		
Newbury Racecourse	d													11 11									
Newbury	a	09 48			10 12									11 16							12 05		
	d				10 12																12 05		
Kintbury	d				10 19																12 12		
Hungerford	d				10 23																12 16		
Bedwyn	a				10 32																12 25		
Tilehurst	d			09 47									10 47							11 47			
Pangbourne	d			09 52									10 52							11 52			
Goring & Streatley	d			09 57									10 57							11 57			
Cholsey	d			10 02									11 02							12 02			
Didcot Parkway	a		09 51	10 09			10 19		10 28			10 51	11 09		11 25		11 36		11 51	12 09		12 26	
	d			10 10					10 28				11 10				11 37			12 10			
Appleford	d			10 14																			
Culham	d																						
Radley	d			10 19									11 17							12 17			
Oxford	a			10 28		10 31		10 35	10 43				11 27			11 35	11 50			12 27			
	d							10 37		10 56						11 37							12 33
Islip	d									11 09													12 46
Bicester Town	a									11 21													12 58
Tackley	d																						
Heyford	d																						
Kings Sutton	d																						
Banbury	a							10 53								11 53							
Leamington Spa 8	a							11 11								12 11							
Coventry	a																						
Birmingham International	a																						
Birmingham New Street 12	a							11 54								12 54							

A 1 to Reading

Table 116

Sundays

1 July to 9 September

London and Reading - Bedwyn, Oxford, Bicester, Banbury and Birmingham

Network Diagram - see first Page of Table 116

		XC ◇1 ⌶	GW ◇1	GW 1	GW ◇1 ⊏	GW ◇1 ⊏	GW 1	GW 1 A	XC ◇1 ⌶	GW ◇1 ⊏	XC ◇1 ⌶	GW ◇1 ⊏	CH	GW 1	GW ◇1 ⊏	XC ◇1 ⌶	GW 1 A	GW 1	GW 1	GW ◇1 ⊏	XC ◇1 ⌶	GW ◇1 ⊏
London Paddington 15 ⊖	d		11 42	11 43	11 57	12 03		12 03		12 37		12 42		12 43	13 03		13 03			13 37		13 42
Ealing Broadway ⊖	d			11 50										12 50								
Slough 3	d		12 00	12 16				12 23				13 01		13 16			13 23					14 00
Maidenhead 3	d			12 27				12 30						13 27			13 30					
Twyford 3	d			12 35			←							13 35					←			
Reading 7	d	12 11	12 21	12 43	12 33	12 38	12 43	12 43	12 54	13 12	13 11	13 21		13 43	13 38	13 40	13 43		13 43	14 12	14 11	14 21
Reading West	d			→				12 47						→								
Theale	d							12 53									13 51					
Aldermaston	d							12 58														
Midgham	d							13 01														
Thatcham	d							13 06									13 59					
Newbury Racecourse	d							13 11														
Newbury	a				12 48			13 16									14 05					
	d																14 05					
Kintbury	d																14 12					
Hungerford	d																14 16					
Bedwyn	a																14 25					
Tilehurst	d						12 47												13 47			
Pangbourne	d						12 53												13 52			
Goring & Streatley	d						12 58												13 57			
Cholsey	d						13 03												14 02			
Didcot Parkway	a		12 36			12 51	13 09			13 25		13 36			13 50				14 09	14 25		14 36
	d		12 37				13 10					13 37							14 10			14 37
Appleford	d						13 15															
Culham	d																					
Radley	d						13 19												14 17			
Oxford	a	12 35	12 49				13 28		13 15		13 35	13 50				14 03			14 27		14 35	14 50
	d	12 37							13 17		13 37		13 56			14 05		14 20			14 37	
Islip	d												14 09									
Bicester Town	a												14 21									
Tackley	d																	14 29				
Heyford	d																	14 33				
Kings Sutton	d																	14 42				
Banbury	a	12 53							13 33		13 53					14 22		14 50			14 53	
Leamington Spa 8	a	13 11							13 50		14 11					14 40					15 11	
Coventry	a																				15 22	
Birmingham International	a																				15 35	
Birmingham New Street 12	a	13 54							14 19		14 54					15 09					15 48	

		GW 1	GW ◇1 ⊏	GW ◇1 ⊏	XC ◇1 ⌶	GW 1	GW 1 A	GW ◇1 ⊏	CH	XC ◇1 ⌶	GW ◇1	GW 1	GW ◇1 ⊏	XC ◇1 ⌶	GW 1	GW 1 A	XC ◇1 ⌶	GW ◇1	GW ◇1 ⊏	GW ◇1	GW ◇1	CH	GW 1
London Paddington 15 ⊖	d	13 43	13 57	14 03			14 03	14 37			14 42	14 43	15 03			15 03		15 27	15 37		15 42		15 43
Ealing Broadway ⊖	d	13 50										14 50											15 50
Slough 3	d	14 16					14 23				15 00	15 16				15 23		15 50			16 00		16 16
Maidenhead 3	d	14 27					14 30					15 27				15 30		16 01					16 27
Twyford 3	d	14 35				←						15 35			←			16 10		←			16 35
Reading 7	d	14 43	14 33	14 38	14 40	14 43	14 43	15 12		15 11	15 21	15 43	15 38	15 40	15 43	15 43	16 11	16 16	16 12	16 16	16 21		16 43
Reading West	d	→					14 46					→						→					→
Theale	d						14 52									15 51							
Aldermaston	d						14 57																
Midgham	d						15 01																
Thatcham	d						15 06									15 59							
Newbury Racecourse	d						15 10																
Newbury	a		14 48				15 15									16 05							
	d															16 05							
Kintbury	d															16 12							
Hungerford	d															16 16							
Bedwyn	a															16 25							
Tilehurst	d					14 47									15 47								
Pangbourne	d					14 52									15 52								
Goring & Streatley	d					14 57									15 57								
Cholsey	d					15 02									16 02								
Didcot Parkway	a			14 51		15 09		15 25			15 35		15 51		16 09				16 25		16 36		
	d					15 10					15 36				16 10						16 37		
Appleford	d					15 14																	
Culham	d																						
Radley	d					15 19									16 17								
Oxford	a				15 04	15 27				15 35	15 50			16 04	16 25		16 35			16 41	16 50		
	d				15 06				15 33	15 37				16 06			16 37					16 56	
Islip	d								15 46													17 09	
Bicester Town	a								15 58													17 21	
Tackley	d																						
Heyford	d																						
Kings Sutton	d																						
Banbury	a				15 23					15 53				16 23			16 53						
Leamington Spa 8	a				15 41					16 11				16 41			17 11						
Coventry	a									16 22							17 22						
Birmingham International	a									16 35							17 35						
Birmingham New Street 12	a				16 12					16 48				17 12			17 48						

A 1 to Reading

Sundays
1 July to 9 September

London and Reading - Bedwyn, Oxford, Bicester, Banbury and Birmingham

Network Diagram - see first Page of Table 116

		GW	GW	XC	GW	GW	GW	GW	XC	GW	GW	GW	XC	GW	GW	GW	XC	CH	GW	GW	GW	GW
		◇1 ⊐	◇1 ⊐	◇1 ⚒	1 A	1	1	◇1 ⊐	◇1 ⚒	◇1	1	◇1 ⊐	◇1 ⚒	1	1 A	◇1 ⊐	◇1 ⚒		◇1 ⊐	1	◇1 ⊐	◇1 ⊐
London Paddington [15] ⊖	d	15 57	16 03		16 03			16 37		16 42	16 43	17 03			17 03	17 37			17 42	17 43	17 57	18 03
Ealing Broadway ⊖	d										16 50									17 50		
Slough [3]	d				16 23					17 00	17 16				17 23				17 58	18 16		
Maidenhead [3]	d				16 30					17 07	17 27				17 30				18 07	18 27		
Twyford [3]	d						←				17 35			←						18 35		
Reading [7]	d	16 33	16 38	16 40	16 43		16 43	17 12	17 11	17 22	17 43	17 38	17 40	17 43	17 43	18 12	18 11		18 21	18 43	18 32	18 38
Reading West	d				16 46						→									→		
Theale	d				16 52										17 51							
Aldermaston	d				16 57																	
Midgham	d				17 01																	
Thatcham	d				17 06										17 59							
Newbury Racecourse	d				17 10																	
Newbury	a	16 48			17 15										18 05						18 48	
	d														18 05							
Kintbury	d														18 12							
Hungerford	d														18 16							
Bedwyn	a														18 25							
Tilehurst	d						16 47							17 47								
Pangbourne	d						16 52							17 52								
Goring & Streatley	d						16 57							17 57								
Cholsey	d						17 02							18 02								
Didcot Parkway	a		16 51				17 09	17 25		17 36		17 51		18 09		18 25			18 36			18 51
	d						17 10			17 37				18 10					18 36			
Appleford	d													18 14								
Culham	d																					
Radley	d						17 17							18 19								
Oxford	a			17 03			17 25		17 35	17 50			18 04	18 27			18 35		18 50			
	d			17 06		17 19			17 37				18 06				18 37	18 37				
Islip	d																	18 50				
Bicester Town	a																	19 02				
Tackley	d					17 28																
Heyford	d					17 32																
Kings Sutton	d					17 41																
Banbury	a			17 23		17 50			17 53				18 23				18 53					
Leamington Spa [8]	a			17 41					18 11				18 41				19 11					
Coventry	a								18 22								19 22					
Birmingham International	a								18 35								19 35					
Birmingham New Street [12]	a			18 09					18 48				19 11				19 48					

		XC	GW	GW	GW	XC	GW	CH	GW	GW	XC	GW	GW	GW	XC	GW	GW	GW	GW	XC	GW	GW	GW
		◇1 ⚒	1	1 A	◇1 ⊐	◇1 ⚒	◇1		1	◇1 ⊐	◇1 ⚒	1	1 A	◇1 ⊐	◇1	◇1 ⊐	1	◇1 ⊐	◇1 ⊐	◇1	1	1	◇1 ⊐
London Paddington [15] ⊖	d			18 11	18 37		18 42		18 43	19 03			19 03	19 37		19 42	19 43	19 57	20 03				20 37
Ealing Broadway ⊖	d								18 50								19 50						
Slough [3]	d			18 29			19 02		19 16				19 23			20 00	20 16						
Maidenhead [3]	d			18 36			19 09		19 27				19 30				20 27						
Twyford [3]	d		←						19 35			←					20 35				←		
Reading [7]	d	18 41	18 43	18 49	19 12	19 11	19 22		19 43	19 38	19 40	19 43	19 43	20 12	20 11	20 21	20 43	20 33	20 38	20 41	20 43	20 44	21 06
Reading West	d			18 52					→								→					20 47	
Theale	d			18 58									19 51									20 53	
Aldermaston	d			19 03																		20 58	
Midgham	d			19 06																		21 01	
Thatcham	d			19 11									19 59									21 06	
Newbury Racecourse	d			19 16																		21 11	
Newbury	a			19 20									20 05					20 49				21 16	
	d												20 05										
Kintbury	d												20 12										
Hungerford	d												20 16										
Bedwyn	a												20 25										
Tilehurst	d		18 47									19 47									20 47		
Pangbourne	d		18 52									19 52									20 52		
Goring & Streatley	d		18 57									19 57									20 57		
Cholsey	d		19 02									20 02									21 02		
Didcot Parkway	a		19 09		19 25		19 37			19 51		20 09		20 25		20 36			20 51		21 12		21 19
	d		19 10				19 38					20 10				20 37					21 13		
Appleford	d																						
Culham	d																						
Radley	d		19 17									20 17									21 21		
Oxford	a	19 03	19 25			19 35	19 50				20 03	20 25			20 35	20 50				21 04	21 31		
	d	19 06				19 37		19 56			20 06				20 37					21 06			
Islip	d							20 09															
Bicester Town	a							20 21															
Tackley	d																						
Heyford	d																						
Kings Sutton	d																						
Banbury	a	19 23				19 53					20 24				20 53					21 23			
Leamington Spa [8]	a	19 41				20 11					20 41				21 11					21 41			
Coventry	a	19 53				20 22					20 53				21 22					21 52			
Birmingham International	a	20 03				20 35					21 03				21 35					22 02			
Birmingham New Street [12]	a	20 15				20 48					21 15				21 48					22 14			

A 1 to Reading

Sundays
1 July to 9 September

London and Reading - Bedwyn, Oxford, Bicester, Banbury and Birmingham

Network Diagram - see first Page of Table 116

		CH	XC	GW	GW	GW	XC	GW	GW	GW	GW	GW	GW	GW	GW	GW	GW	GW	GW	GW	GW	GW
			◇1	◇1	1	◇1 ⊐	◇1	1	1	◇1 ⊐	◇1	1	1	◇1 ⊐	1	1 A	◇1	1	◇1 ⊐	1	◇1 ⊐	◇1
London Paddington [15] ⊖	d			20 42	20 43	21 03				21 37	21 42		21 43	22 03		22 15	22 42	22 43	23 03		23 37	23 47
Ealing Broadway ⊖	d				20 50								21 50			22 24		22 50				23 55
Slough [3]	d			20 58	21 16						21 59		22 16			22 46	22 58	23 16			23 55	00 08
Maidenhead [3]	d				21 27								22 31			22 56		23 25				00 16
Twyford [3]	d				21 35			←					22 39		←	23 04		23 32		←		
Reading [7]	d		21 11	21 21	21 47	21 38	21 40	21 47	21 44	22 12	22 22	22 44	22 54	22 50	22 54	23 12	23 21	23 53	23 47	23 53	00 14	00 28
Reading West	d				→							22 47	→			23 15		→				
Theale	d								21 51			22 53				23 21						
Aldermaston	d											22 58										
Midgham	d											23 01										
Thatcham	d								22 00			23 06				23 30						
Newbury Racecourse	d											23 11										
Newbury	a								22 05			23 15				23 37						
	d								22 06													
Kintbury	d								22 12													
Hungerford	d								22 17													
Bedwyn	a								22 25													
Tilehurst	d							21 52							22 58					23 57		
Pangbourne	d							21 56							23 03					00 01		
Goring & Streatley	d							22 01							23 07					00 07		
Cholsey	d							22 06							23 12					00 12		
Didcot Parkway	a			21 36		21 51		22 13		22 29	22 38			23 05	23 19		23 35		00s02	00 18	00s32	00 43
	d			21 37				22 14			22 38				23 20		23 38			00 19		00 45
Appleford	d																					
Culham	d																					
Radley	d							22 21							23 27					00 26		
Oxford	a		21 35	21 49			22 04	22 29			22 50				23 36		23 51			00 35		00 57
	d	21 33	21 37				22 06															
Islip	d	21 46																				
Bicester Town	a	21 58																				
Tackley	d																					
Heyford	d																					
Kings Sutton	d																					
Banbury	a		21 53				22 22															
Leamington Spa [8]	a		22 11				22 40															
Coventry	a		22 22				22 52															
Birmingham International	a		22 32				23 02															
Birmingham New Street [12]	a		22 42				23 13															

Sundays
16 September to 21 October

		GW	GW	GW	GW	GW	GW	GW	GW	GW	GW	GW	GW	GW	GW	GW	GW	GW	XC	CH	GW	GW	GW
		1	🚌	1	◇1	1	1	◇1 ⊐	◇1	1	1		1	◇1 ⊐	◇1	1		◇1 ⊐	◇1 ⚒		◇1	1	◇1 ⊐
London Paddington [15] ⊖	d			22p45	23p00		23p20	23p30	23p33				07 29	07 57	08 03			08 30			08 42	08 43	08 57
Ealing Broadway ⊖	d			22p55			23p28						07 36									08 50	
Slough [3]	d			23p21	23p17		23p54		23p50				07 58		08 25						09 05	09 16	
Maidenhead [3]	d			23p32			00 05						08 08		08 32							09 27	
Twyford [3]	d			23p39		←	00 13				←		08 16			←						09 35	
Reading [7]	d	23p12		23p49	23p34	23p49	00 20	23p59	00 08	00 15	00 20	08 14	08 47	08 32	08 44	08 47	08 44	09 06	09 11		09 21	09 43	09 32
Reading West	d	23p14		→			→			00s18		08 17	→									→	
Theale	d	23p20								00s24		08 23					08 51						
Aldermaston	d	23p25								00s29		08 28											
Midgham	d	23p29								00s32		08 31											
Thatcham	d	23p34								00s37		08 36					09 00						
Newbury Racecourse	d	23p38								00s42													
Newbury	a	23p41								00 45		08 43					09 05						09 48
	d	23p41															09 06						
Kintbury	d	23p48															09 12						
Hungerford	d	23p52															09 17						
Bedwyn	a	00 01															09 24						
Tilehurst	d					23p53					00 24					08 52							
Pangbourne	d															08 57							
Goring & Streatley	d					00 03					00 31					09 02							
Cholsey	d					00 08					00 36					09 07							
Didcot Parkway	a				23p51	00 14		00 18	00 22		00 44			08 46	08 58	09 12		09 20			09 36		
	d				23p51	00 15			00 24		00 45				09 00	09 14					09 37		
Appleford	d										00s49												
Culham	d										00s51												
Radley	d					00s22					00s55					09 21							
Oxford	a				00 04	00 32			00 39		01 07				09 12	09 30			09 34		09 51		
	d		23p48																09 37	09 36			
Islip	d																			09 49			
Bicester Town	a																			10 01			
Tackley	d		00s08																				
Heyford	d		00s22																				
Kings Sutton	d																						
Banbury	a		00 47																09 53				
Leamington Spa [8]	a																		10 11				
Coventry	a																		10 22				
Birmingham International	a																		10 38				
Birmingham New Street [12]	a																		10 50				

A 1 to Reading

London and Reading - Bedwyn, Oxford, Bicester, Banbury and Birmingham

Network Diagram - see first Page of Table 116

		GW ◇1 🍴	GW 1	GW 1	GW 1	GW ◇1 🍴	XC ◇1 🛒	GW ◇1 🍴	CH	GW 1	GW ◇1 🍴	GW 1	GW 1	XC ◇1 🛒	GW ◇1 🍴	GW ◇1 🍴	GW 1	GW ◇1 🍴	GW 1	GW 1	CH	XC ◇1 🛒	GW ◇1 🍴
London Paddington 15 ⊖	d	09 03				09 30		09 35		09 43	10 03				10 37	10 42	10 43	11 03					11 37
Ealing Broadway ⊖	d									09 50							10 50						
Slough 3	d							09 59		10 16						11 06	11 16						
Maidenhead 3	d									10 27							11 27						
Twyford 3	d		←							10 35		←					11 35		←				
Reading 7	d	09 38	09 43	09 44	10 00	10 06	10 11	10 12		10 43	10 38	10 43	10 44	11 11	11 13	11 21	11 43	11 38	11 43	11 44		12 11	12 13
Reading West	d			09 47						→			10 47				→						
Theale	d			09 53									10 53							11 51			
Aldermaston	d			09 58									10 58										
Midgham	d			10 01									11 01										
Thatcham	d			10 06									11 06							12 00			
Newbury Racecourse	d												11 11										
Newbury	a			10 12									11 15							12 05			
	d			10 12																12 06			
Kintbury	d			10 18																12 12			
Hungerford	d			10 23																12 17			
Bedwyn	a			10 31																12 25			
Tilehurst	d		09 49									10 49							11 49				
Pangbourne	d		09 53									10 53							11 53				
Goring & Streatley	d		09 58									10 58							11 58				
Cholsey	d		10 03									11 03							12 03				
Didcot Parkway	a	09 51	10 10			10 19		10 28			10 51	11 10			11 26	11 36		11 51	12 10				12 26
	d		10 11					10 28				11 11				11 37			12 11				
Appleford	d		10 15																				
Culham	d																						
Radley	d		10 20									11 18							12 18				
Oxford	a		10 29		10 30		10 35	10 43				11 28		11 35		11 50			12 27			12 34	
	d						10 37		10 56					11 37							12 33	12 36	
Islip	d								11 09												12 46		
Bicester Town	a								11 21												12 58		
Tackley	d																						
Heyford	d																						
Kings Sutton	d																						
Banbury	a						10 53							11 53								12 52	
Leamington Spa 8	a						11 11							12 11								13 11	
Coventry	a						11 22							12 22								13 22	
Birmingham International	a						11 38							12 38								13 36	
Birmingham New Street 12	a						11 51							12 50								13 48	

		GW ◇1	GW 1	GW ◇1 🍴	GW ◇1 🍴	GW 1	GW 1	XC ◇1 🛒	XC ◇1 🛒	GW ◇1 🍴	GW ◇1 🍴	CH	GW 1	GW ◇1 🍴	XC ◇1 🛒	GW 1	GW 1	XC ◇1 🛒	GW ◇1 🍴	GW ◇1 🍴	GW 1	GW ◇1 🍴
London Paddington 15 ⊖	d	11 42	11 43	11 57	12 03					12 37	12 42		12 43	13 03					13 37	13 42	13 43	13 57
Ealing Broadway ⊖	d		11 50										12 50								13 50	
Slough 3	d	12 03	12 16								13 07		13 16							14 06	14 16	
Maidenhead 3	d		12 27										13 27								14 27	
Twyford 3	d		12 35			←							13 35			←					14 35	
Reading 7	d	12 20	12 43	12 32	12 38	12 43	12 44	12 54	13 11	13 13	13 21		13 43	13 38	13 41	13 43	13 44	14 09	14 13	14 21	14 43	14 32
Reading West	d		→				12 47						→								→	
Theale	d						12 53										13 51					
Aldermaston	d						12 58															
Midgham	d						13 01															
Thatcham	d						13 06										14 00					
Newbury Racecourse	d						13 11															
Newbury	a			12 48			13 15										14 05					14 48
	d																14 06					
Kintbury	d																14 12					
Hungerford	d																14 17					
Bedwyn	a																14 25					
Tilehurst	d					12 49										13 50						
Pangbourne	d					12 53										13 54						
Goring & Streatley	d					12 58										14 00						
Cholsey	d					13 03										14 05						
Didcot Parkway	a	12 37			12 51	13 10				13 26	13 37			13 51		14 12			14 26	14 36		
	d	12 38				13 11					13 38					14 13				14 37		
Appleford	d					13 16																
Culham	d																					
Radley	d					13 20										14 20						
Oxford	a	12 50				13 29		13 15	13 35		13 50				14 03	14 30		14 35		14 50		
	d							13 17	13 37			13 56			14 04			14 37				
Islip	d											14 09										
Bicester Town	a											14 21										
Tackley	d																					
Heyford	d																					
Kings Sutton	d																					
Banbury	a							13 33	13 53						14 22			14 53				
Leamington Spa 8	a							13 50	14 11						14 40			15 11				
Coventry	a								14 22									15 22				
Birmingham International	a								14 35									15 35				
Birmingham New Street 12	a							14 19	14 48						15 09			15 48				

Table 116

Sundays

16 September to 21 October

London and Reading - Bedwyn, Oxford, Bicester, Banbury and Birmingham

Network Diagram - see first Page of Table 116

		GW ◇1 🍴	XC ◇1 🛒	GW 1	GW 1	CH	XC ◇1 🛒	GW ◇1 🍴	GW ◇1	GW 1	GW ◇1 🍴	XC ◇1 🛒	GW 1	GW 1	XC ◇1 🛒	GW ◇1	GW ◇1 🍴	GW ◇1	GW ◇1	CH	GW 1	GW ◇1 🍴	GW ◇1 🍴
London Paddington 15 ⊖	d	14 03						14 37	14 42	14 43	15 03					15 27	15 37		15 42		15 43	15 57	16 03
Ealing Broadway ⊖	d									14 50											15 50		
Slough 3	d								15 05	15 16						15 50			16 05		16 16		
Maidenhead 3	d									15 27						16 01					16 27		
Twyford 3	d			←						15 35			←			16 10		←			16 35		
Reading 7	d	14 38	14 40	14 43	14 44		15 09	15 13	15 21	15 43	15 38	15 40	15 43	15 44	16 09	16 19	16 13	16 19	16 21		16 43	16 32	16 38
Reading West	d				14 47					→						→					→		
Theale	d				14 53									15 51									
Aldermaston	d				14 58																		
Midgham	d				15 01																		
Thatcham	d				15 06									16 00									
Newbury Racecourse	d				15 11																		
Newbury	a				15 15									16 05								16 47	
	d													16 06									
Kintbury	d													16 12									
Hungerford	d													16 17									
Bedwyn	a													16 25									
Tilehurst	d			14 50									15 50										
Pangbourne	d			14 54									15 54										
Goring & Streatley	d			15 00									16 00										
Cholsey	d			15 05									16 05										
Didcot Parkway	a	14 51		15 12				15 26	15 35		15 51		16 12				16 26		16 38				16 51
	d			15 13					15 36				16 13						16 39				
Appleford	d			15 17																			
Culham	d																						
Radley	d			15 22									16 21										
Oxford	a		15 04	15 30			15 35		15 50			16 04	16 31		16 35			16 45	16 50				
	d		15 06			15 33	15 37					16 06			16 37					16 56			
Islip	d					15 46														17 09			
Bicester Town	a					15 58														17 21			
Tackley	d																						
Heyford	d																						
Kings Sutton	d																						
Banbury	a		15 23				15 53					16 23			16 53								
Leamington Spa 8	a		15 41				16 11					16 41			17 11								
Coventry	a						16 22								17 22								
Birmingham International	a						16 35								17 35								
Birmingham New Street 12	a		16 12				16 48					17 12			17 48								

		XC ◇1 🛒	GW 1	GW 1	XC ◇1 🛒	GW ◇1 🍴	GW ◇1	GW 1	GW ◇1 🍴	XC ◇1 🛒	GW 1	GW 1	XC ◇1 🛒	GW ◇1 🍴	CH	GW ◇1 🍴	GW 1	GW ◇1 🍴	GW ◇1 🍴	XC ◇1 🛒	GW 1	GW 1
London Paddington 15 ⊖	d					16 37	16 42	16 43	17 03					17 37		17 42	17 43	17 57	18 03			
Ealing Broadway ⊖	d							16 50									17 50					
Slough 3	d						17 04	17 16								18 04	18 16					
Maidenhead 3	d						17 11	17 27								18 13	18 27					
Twyford 3	d		←					17 35			←						18 35				←	
Reading 7	d	16 41	16 43	16 44	17 09	17 13	17 25	17 43	17 38	17 40	17 43	17 44	18 11	18 15		18 24	18 43	18 32	18 38	18 41	18 43	18 44
Reading West	d			16 47				→									→					18 47
Theale	d			16 53								17 51										18 53
Aldermaston	d			16 58																		18 58
Midgham	d			17 01																		19 01
Thatcham	d			17 06								18 00										19 06
Newbury Racecourse	d			17 11																		19 11
Newbury	a			17 15								18 05						18 49				19 15
	d											18 06										
Kintbury	d											18 12										
Hungerford	d											18 17										
Bedwyn	a											18 25										
Tilehurst	d		16 50								17 50										18 50	
Pangbourne	d		16 54								17 54										18 54	
Goring & Streatley	d		17 00								18 00										19 00	
Cholsey	d		17 05								18 05										19 05	
Didcot Parkway	a		17 12			17 26	17 39		17 51		18 12			18 28		18 39			18 51		19 12	
	d		17 13				17 39				18 13					18 39					19 13	
Appleford	d										18 18											
Culham	d																					
Radley	d		17 20								18 23										19 20	
Oxford	a	17 04	17 30		17 35		17 50			18 04	18 31		18 35			18 50				19 03	19 31	
	d	17 06			17 37					18 06			18 37		18 37					19 06		
Islip	d														18 50							
Bicester Town	a														19 02							
Tackley	d																					
Heyford	d																					
Kings Sutton	d																					
Banbury	a	17 23			17 53					18 23			18 53							19 23		
Leamington Spa 8	a	17 41			18 11					18 41			19 11							19 41		
Coventry	a				18 22								19 22							19 53		
Birmingham International	a				18 35								19 35							20 03		
Birmingham New Street 12	a	18 09			18 48					19 11			19 48							20 15		

London and Reading - Bedwyn, Oxford, Bicester, Banbury and Birmingham

Sundays
16 September to 21 October

Network Diagram - see first Page of Table 116

		XC	GW	GW	CH	GW	GW	XC	GW	GW	XC	GW	GW	GW	GW	GW	XC	GW	GW	CH	XC	GW	GW
		◇1 🛒	◇1 ☕	◇1		1	◇1 ☕	◇1 🛒	1	1	◇1	◇1 ☕	◇1 ☕	1	◇1 ☕	◇1 ☕	◇1	1	1		◇1	◇1 ☕	◇1
London Paddington 15 ⊖	d		18 37	18 42		18 43	19 03					19 37	19 42	19 43	19 57	20 03						20 37	20 42
Ealing Broadway ⊖	d					18 50								19 50									
Slough 3	d			19 07		19 16							20 04	20 16									21 04
Maidenhead 3	d			19 14		19 27								20 27									
Twyford 3	d					19 35			←					20 35				←					
Reading 7	d	19 11	19 15	19 28		19 43	19 38	19 40	19 43	19 44	20 11	20 15	20 21	20 43	20 32	20 38	20 41	20 43	20 44		21 11	21 15	21 26
Reading West	d					→								→					20 47				
Theale	d									19 51									20 53				
Aldermaston	d																		20 58				
Midgham	d																		21 01				
Thatcham	d									20 00									21 06				
Newbury Racecourse	d																		21 11				
Newbury	a									20 05					20 49				21 16				
	d									20 06													
Kintbury	d									20 12													
Hungerford	d									20 17													
Bedwyn	a									20 25													
Tilehurst	d								19 50									20 50					
Pangbourne	d								19 54									20 54					
Goring & Streatley	d								20 00									21 00					
Cholsey	d								20 05									21 05					
Didcot Parkway	a		19 28	19 43			19 51		20 12			20 28	20 36			20 51		21 12				21 28	21 44
	d			19 44					20 13				20 37					21 13					21 44
Appleford	d																						
Culham	d																						
Radley	d								20 21									21 21					
Oxford	a	19 35		19 55				20 03	20 31		20 35		20 50				21 04	21 30			21 35		21 56
	d	19 37			19 56			20 06			20 37						21 06			21 33	21 37		
Islip	d				20 09															21 46			
Bicester Town	a				20 21															21 58			
Tackley	d																						
Heyford	d																						
Kings Sutton	d																						
Banbury	a	19 53						20 24			20 53						21 23				21 53		
Leamington Spa 8	a	20 11						20 41			21 11						21 41				22 11		
Coventry	a	20 22						20 53			21 22						21 52				22 22		
Birmingham International	a	20 35						21 03			21 35						22 02				22 32		
Birmingham New Street 12	a	20 48						21 15			21 48						22 14				22 42		

		GW	GW	XC	GW	GW	GW	GW	GW	GW	GW	GW	GW	GW	GW	GW	GW	GW	GW	GW	GW
		1	◇1 ☕	◇1	1	1	◇1 ☕	◇1	1	1	◇1 ☕	1	1 A	🚌	◇1 ☕	◇1	🚌	1	◇1 ☕	1	◇1 ☕
London Paddington 15 ⊖	d	20 43	21 03				21 37	21 42		21 43	22 03		22 15		22 37	22 42		22 43	23 03		23 37
Ealing Broadway ⊖	d	20 50								21 50			22 24					22 50			
Slough 3	d	21 16						22 06		22 16			22 46			23 02		23 16			00 02
Maidenhead 3	d	21 27								22 31			22 56					23 24			
Twyford 3	d	21 35			←					22 39		←	23 04					23 32		←	
Reading 7	d	21 43	21 38	21 40	21 43	21 44	22 14	22 22	22 44	22 54	22 50	22 54	23 12		23 17	23 21		23 53	23 46	23 53	00 14
Reading West	d	→							22 47	→			23 15					→			
Theale	d					21 51			22 53				23 21								
Aldermaston	d								22 58												
Midgham	d								23 01												
Thatcham	d					22 00			23 06				23 30								
Newbury Racecourse	d								23 11												
Newbury	a					22 05			23 15				23 37								
	d					22 06															
Kintbury	d					22 12															
Hungerford	d					22 17															
Bedwyn	a					22 25															
Tilehurst	d				21 50							23 00								23 59	
Pangbourne	d				21 54							23 05								00 03	
Goring & Streatley	d				22 00							23 09								00 09	
Cholsey	d				22 05							23 14								00 14	
Didcot Parkway	a		21 53		22 12		22 28	22 38			23 07	23 23			23s32	23 37			00s04	00 21	00s31
	d				22 13			22 40						23 30			23 45				
Appleford	d																				
Culham	d																				
Radley	d				22 21																
Oxford	a			22 06	22 29			22 51						23 55			00 10				
	d			22 06																	
Islip	d																				
Bicester Town	a																				
Tackley	d																				
Heyford	d																				
Kings Sutton	d																				
Banbury	a			22 25																	
Leamington Spa 8	a			22 42																	
Coventry	a			22 53																	
Birmingham International	a			23 03																	
Birmingham New Street 12	a			23 14																	

A 1 to Reading

London and Reading - Bedwyn, Oxford, Bicester, Banbury and Birmingham

Sundays
from 28 October

Network Diagram - see first Page of Table 116

		GW	GW	GW	GW	GW	GW	GW	GW	GW	GW	GW	GW	GW	GW	GW	GW	GW	XC	CH	GW	GW	GW
		1	🚌	1	◇1	1	1	◇1 ☕	◇1	1	1		1	◇1 ☕	◇1	1		◇1 ☕	◇1 🛒		◇1	1	◇1 ☕
London Paddington 15 ⊖	d			22p45	23p00		23p20	23p30	23p33				07 29	08 00	08 03			08 30			08 42	08 43	08 57
Ealing Broadway ⊖	d			22p55			23p28						07 36									08 50	
Slough 3	d			23p21	23p17		23p54		23p50				07 58		08 25						09 05	09 16	
Maidenhead 3	d			23p32			00 05						08 08		08 32							09 27	
Twyford 3	d			23p39		←	00 13				←		08 16			←						09 35	
Reading 7	d	23p12		23p49	23p34	23p49	00 20	23p59	00 08	00 15	00 20	08 14	08 47	08 34	08 44	08 47	08 44	09 06	09 11		09 21	09 43	09 32
Reading West	d	23p14		→			→			00s18		08 17	→									→	
Theale	d	23p20								00s24		08 23					08 51						
Aldermaston	d	23p25								00s29		08 28											
Midgham	d	23p29								00s32		08 31											
Thatcham	d	23p34								00s37		08 36					09 00						
Newbury Racecourse	d	23p38								00s42													
Newbury	a	23p41								00 45		08 43					09 05						09 48
	d	23p41															09 06						
Kintbury	d	23p48															09 12						
Hungerford	d	23p52															09 17						
Bedwyn	a	00 01															09 24						
Tilehurst	d					23p56					00 24					08 52							
Pangbourne	d					00 01										08 57							
Goring & Streatley	d					00 06					00 31					09 02							
Cholsey	d					00 11					00 36					09 07							
Didcot Parkway	a				23p51	00 17		00 18	00 22		00 44			08 51	08 58	09 12		09 24			09 36		
	d				23p51	00 18			00 24		00 45				09 00	09 14					09 37		
Appleford	d										00s49												
Culham	d										00s51												
Radley	d					00s25					00s55					09 21							
Oxford	a				00 04	00 35			00 39		01 07				09 12	09 30			09 34		09 51		
	d		23p51																09 37	09 36			
Islip	d																			09 49			
Bicester Town	a																			10 01			
Tackley	d		00s11																				
Heyford	d		00s25																				
Kings Sutton	d																						
Banbury	a		00 50																09 53				
Leamington Spa 8	a																		10 11				
Coventry	a																		10 22				
Birmingham International	a																		10 38				
Birmingham New Street 12	a																		10 50				

		GW	GW	GW	GW	GW	XC	GW	CH	GW	GW	GW	GW	XC	GW	GW	GW	GW	GW	GW	CH	XC	GW
		◇1 ☕	1	1	1	◇1 ☕	◇1 🛒	◇1 ☕		1	◇1 ☕	1	1	◇1 🛒	◇1 ☕	◇1 ☕	1	◇1 ☕	1	1		◇1 🛒	◇1 ☕
London Paddington 15 ⊖	d	09 03				09 30		09 35		09 43	10 03				10 37	10 42	10 43	11 03					11 37
Ealing Broadway ⊖	d									09 50							10 50						
Slough 3	d							09 59		10 16						11 06	11 16						
Maidenhead 3	d									10 27							11 27						
Twyford 3	d		←							10 35		←					11 35		←				
Reading 7	d	09 38	09 43	09 44	10 00	10 06	10 11	10 12		10 43	10 38	10 43	10 44	11 11	11 13	11 21	11 43	11 38	11 43	11 44		12 11	12 13
Reading West	d			09 47						→			10 47				→						
Theale	d			09 53									10 53							11 51			
Aldermaston	d			09 58									10 58										
Midgham	d			10 01									11 01										
Thatcham	d			10 06									11 06							12 00			
Newbury Racecourse	d												11 11										
Newbury	a			10 12									11 15							12 05			
	d			10 12																12 06			
Kintbury	d			10 18																12 12			
Hungerford	d			10 23																12 17			
Bedwyn	a			10 31																12 25			
Tilehurst	d		09 49									10 49							11 49				
Pangbourne	d		09 53									10 53							11 53				
Goring & Streatley	d		09 58									10 58							11 58				
Cholsey	d		10 03									11 03							12 03				
Didcot Parkway	a	09 51	10 10			10 19		10 28			10 51	11 10			11 26	11 36		11 51	12 10				12 26
	d		10 11					10 28				11 11				11 37			12 11				
Appleford	d		10 15																				
Culham	d																						
Radley	d		10 20									11 18							12 18				
Oxford	a		10 29		10 30		10 35	10 43				11 29		11 35		11 50			12 27			12 34	
	d						10 37		10 56					11 37							12 33	12 36	
Islip	d								11 09												12 46		
Bicester Town	a								11 21												12 58		
Tackley	d																						
Heyford	d																						
Kings Sutton	d																						
Banbury	a						10 53							11 53								12 52	
Leamington Spa 8	a						11 11							12 11								13 11	
Coventry	a						11 22							12 22								13 22	
Birmingham International	a						11 38							12 38								13 36	
Birmingham New Street 12	a						11 51							12 50								13 48	

Sundays from 28 October

London and Reading - Bedwyn, Oxford, Bicester, Banbury and Birmingham

Network Diagram - see first Page of Table 116

Station		GW	GW	GW	GW	GW	GW	XC	XC	GW	GW	CH	GW	GW	XC	GW	GW	XC	GW	GW	GW	GW
		◇1	1	◇1	◇1	1	1	◇1	◇1	◇1	◇1		1	◇1	◇1	1	1	◇1	◇1	◇1	1	◇1
London Paddington 15 ⊖	d	11 42	11 43	11 57	12 03					12 37	12 42		12 43	13 03					13 37	13 42	13 43	13 57
Ealing Broadway ⊖	d		11 50										12 50								13 50	
Slough 3	d	12 03	12 16								13 07		13 16							14 06	14 16	
Maidenhead 3	d		12 27										13 27								14 27	
Twyford 3	d		12 35			←							13 35			←					14 35	
Reading 7	d	12 20	12 43	12 32	12 38	12 43	12 44	12 54	13 11	13 13	13 21		13 43	13 38	13 41	13 43	13 44	14 09	14 13	14 21	14 43	14 32
Reading West	d		→				12 47						→								→	
Theale	d						12 53										13 51					
Aldermaston	d						12 58															
Midgham	d						13 01															
Thatcham	d						13 06										14 00					
Newbury Racecourse	d						13 11															
Newbury	a			12 48			13 15										14 05					14 48
	d																14 06					
Kintbury	d																14 12					
Hungerford	d																14 17					
Bedwyn	a																14 25					
Tilehurst	d					12 49										13 50						
Pangbourne	d					12 53										13 54						
Goring & Streatley	d					12 58										14 00						
Cholsey	d					13 03										14 05						
Didcot Parkway	a	12 37			12 51	13 10				13 26	13 37			13 51		14 12			14 26	14 36		
	d	12 38				13 11					13 38					14 13				14 37		
Appleford	d					13 16																
Culham	d																					
Radley	d					13 20										14 20						
Oxford	a	12 50				13 29		13 15	13 35		13 50				14 04	14 30		14 35		14 50		
	d							13 17	13 37			13 56			14 06			14 37				
Islip	d											14 09										
Bicester Town	a											14 21										
Tackley	d																					
Heyford	d																					
Kings Sutton	d																					
Banbury	a							13 33	13 53						14 22			14 53				
Leamington Spa 8	a							13 50	14 11						14 40			15 11				
Coventry	a								14 22									15 22				
Birmingham International	a								14 35									15 35				
Birmingham New Street 12	a							14 19	14 48						15 09			15 48				

Station		GW	XC	GW	GW	CH	XC	GW	GW	GW	GW	XC	GW	GW	XC	GW	GW	GW	GW	CH	GW	GW	GW
		◇1	◇1	1	1		◇1	◇1	◇1	1	◇1	◇1	1	1	◇1	◇1	◇1	◇1	◇1		1	◇1	◇1
London Paddington 15 ⊖	d	14 03						14 37	14 42	14 43	15 03					15 27	15 37		15 42		15 43	15 57	16 03
Ealing Broadway ⊖	d									14 50											15 50		
Slough 3	d								15 05	15 16						15 50			16 05		16 16		
Maidenhead 3	d									15 27						16 01					16 27		
Twyford 3	d			←						15 35			←			16 10		←			16 35		
Reading 7	d	14 38	14 40	14 43	14 44		15 09	15 13	15 21	15 43	15 38	15 40	15 43	15 44	16 09	16 19	16 13	16 19	16 21		16 43	16 32	16 38
Reading West	d				14 47					→						→					→		
Theale	d				14 53									15 51									
Aldermaston	d				14 58																		
Midgham	d				15 01																		
Thatcham	d				15 06									16 00									
Newbury Racecourse	d				15 11																		
Newbury	a				15 15									16 05								16 47	
	d													16 06									
Kintbury	d													16 12									
Hungerford	d													16 17									
Bedwyn	a													16 25									
Tilehurst	d			14 50									15 50										
Pangbourne	d			14 54									15 54										
Goring & Streatley	d			15 00									16 00										
Cholsey	d			15 05									16 05										
Didcot Parkway	a	14 51		15 12				15 26	15 35		15 51		16 12				16 26		16 38				16 51
	d			15 13					15 36				16 13						16 39				
Appleford	d			15 17																			
Culham	d																						
Radley	d			15 22									16 21										
Oxford	a		15 04	15 30			15 35		15 50			16 04	16 31		16 35			16 45	16 50				
	d		15 06			15 33	15 37					16 06			16 37					16 56			
Islip	d					15 46														17 09			
Bicester Town	a					15 58														17 21			
Tackley	d																						
Heyford	d																						
Kings Sutton	d																						
Banbury	a		15 23				15 53					16 23			16 53								
Leamington Spa 8	a		15 41				16 11					16 41			17 11								
Coventry	a						16 22								17 22								
Birmingham International	a						16 35								17 35								
Birmingham New Street 12	a		16 12				16 48					17 12			17 48								

Table 116

Sundays from 28 October

London and Reading - Bedwyn, Oxford, Bicester, Banbury and Birmingham

Network Diagram - see first Page of Table 116

Station		XC	GW	GW	XC	GW	GW	GW	GW	XC	GW	GW	XC	GW	CH	GW	GW	GW	GW	XC	GW	GW
		◇1	1	1	◇1	◇1	◇1	1	◇1	◇1	1	1	◇1	◇1		◇1	1	◇1	◇1	◇1	1	1
London Paddington 15 ⊖	d					16 37	16 42	16 43	17 03					17 37		17 42	17 43	17 57	18 03			
Ealing Broadway ⊖	d							16 50									17 50					
Slough 3	d						17 04	17 16								18 04	18 16					
Maidenhead 3	d						17 11	17 27								18 13	18 27					
Twyford 3	d		←					17 35			←						18 35				←	
Reading 7	d	16 41	16 43	16 44	17 09	17 13	17 25	17 43	17 38	17 40	17 43	17 44	18 11	18 15		18 24	18 43	18 32	18 38	18 41	18 43	18 44
Reading West	d			16 47				→									→					18 47
Theale	d			16 53								17 51										18 53
Aldermaston	d			16 58																		18 58
Midgham	d			17 01																		19 01
Thatcham	d			17 06								18 00										19 06
Newbury Racecourse	d			17 11																		19 11
Newbury	a			17 15								18 05						18 49				19 15
	d											18 06										
Kintbury	d											18 12										
Hungerford	d											18 17										
Bedwyn	a											18 25										
Tilehurst	d		16 50								17 50										18 50	
Pangbourne	d		16 54								17 54										18 54	
Goring & Streatley	d		17 00								18 00										19 00	
Cholsey	d		17 05								18 05										19 05	
Didcot Parkway	a		17 12			17 26	17 39		17 51		18 12			18 28		18 39			18 51		19 12	
	d		17 13				17 39				18 13					18 39					19 13	
Appleford	d										18 18											
Culham	d																					
Radley	d		17 20								18 23										19 20	
Oxford	a	17 05	17 30		17 35		17 50			18 04	18 31		18 35			18 50				19 03	19 31	
	d	17 07			17 37					18 06			18 37		18 37					19 06		
Islip	d														18 50							
Bicester Town	a														19 02							
Tackley	d																					
Heyford	d																					
Kings Sutton	d																					
Banbury	a	17 23			17 53					18 23			18 53							19 23		
Leamington Spa 8	a	17 41			18 11					18 41			19 11							19 41		
Coventry	a				18 22								19 22							19 53		
Birmingham International	a				18 35								19 35							20 03		
Birmingham New Street 12	a	18 09			18 48					19 11			19 48							20 15		

Station		XC	GW	GW	CH	GW	GW	XC	GW	GW	XC	GW	GW	GW	GW	GW	XC	GW	GW	CH	XC	GW	GW
		◇1	◇1	◇1		1	◇1	◇1	1	1	◇1	◇1	◇1	1	◇1	◇1	◇1	1	1		◇1	◇1	◇1
London Paddington 15 ⊖	d		18 37	18 42		18 43	19 03					19 37	19 42	19 43	19 57	20 03						20 37	20 42
Ealing Broadway ⊖	d					18 50								19 50									
Slough 3	d			19 07		19 16							20 04	20 16									21 04
Maidenhead 3	d			19 15		19 27								20 27									
Twyford 3	d					19 35			←					20 35				←					
Reading 7	d	19 09	19 15	19 28		19 43	19 38	19 40	19 43	19 44	20 11	20 15	20 21	20 43	20 32	20 38	20 41	20 43	20 44		21 09	21 15	21 26
Reading West	d					→								→					20 47				
Theale	d									19 51									20 53				
Aldermaston	d																		20 58				
Midgham	d																		21 01				
Thatcham	d									20 00									21 06				
Newbury Racecourse	d																		21 11				
Newbury	a									20 05					20 49				21 16				
	d									20 06													
Kintbury	d									20 12													
Hungerford	d									20 17													
Bedwyn	a									20 25													
Tilehurst	d								19 50									20 50					
Pangbourne	d								19 55									20 54					
Goring & Streatley	d								20 00									21 00					
Cholsey	d								20 05									21 05					
Didcot Parkway	a		19 28	19 43			19 51		20 12			20 28	20 36			20 51		21 12				21 28	21 41
	d			19 44					20 13				20 37					21 13					21 42
Appleford	d																						
Culham	d																						
Radley	d								20 21									21 21					
Oxford	a	19 35		19 55				20 03	20 31		20 35		20 50				21 04	21 30			21 35		21 54
	d	19 37			19 56			20 06			20 37						21 06			21 33	21 37		
Islip	d				20 09															21 46			
Bicester Town	a				20 21															21 58			
Tackley	d																						
Heyford	d																						
Kings Sutton	d																						
Banbury	a	19 53						20 24			20 53						21 23				21 53		
Leamington Spa 8	a	20 11						20 41			21 11						21 41				22 11		
Coventry	a	20 22						20 53			21 22						21 52				22 22		
Birmingham International	a	20 35						21 03			21 35						22 02				22 32		
Birmingham New Street 12	a	20 48						21 15			21 48						22 14				22 42		

Table 116

Sundays from 28 October

London and Reading - Bedwyn, Oxford, Bicester, Banbury and Birmingham

Network Diagram - see first Page of Table 116

		GW	GW	XC	GW	GW	GW	GW	GW	GW	GW	GW	GW	GW	GW	GW	GW	GW	GW	GW	GW
		[1]	◇[1]	◇[1]	[1]	[1]	◇[1]	◇[1]	[1]	[1]	◇[1]	[1]	[1]		◇[1]	◇[1]		[1]	◇[1]	[1]	◇[1]
													A	🚌			🚌				
			☕				☕				☕				☕				☕		☕
London Paddington [15] ⊖	d	20 43	21 03				21 37	21 42		21 43	22 03		22 15		22 37	22 42		22 43	23 03		23 37
Ealing Broadway ⊖	d	20 50								21 50			22 24					22 50			
Slough [3]	d	21 16						22 06		22 16			22 46			23 02		23 16			00 02
Maidenhead [3]	d	21 27								22 31			22 56					23 24			
Twyford [3]	d	21 35			←					22 39		←	23 04					23 32		←	
Reading [7]	d	21 43	21 38	21 40	21 43	21 44	22 14	22 22	22 44	22 54	22 50	22 54	23 12		23 17	23 21		23 53	23 46	23 53	00 14
Reading West	d	→							22 47	→			23 15					→			
Theale	d					21 51			22 53				23 21								
Aldermaston	d								22 58												
Midgham	d								23 01												
Thatcham	d					22 00			23 06				23 30								
Newbury Racecourse	d								23 11												
Newbury	a					22 05			23 15				23 37								
	d					22 06															
Kintbury	d					22 12															
Hungerford	d					22 17															
Bedwyn	a					22 25															
Tilehurst	d				21 50							23 00								23 59	
Pangbourne	d				21 54							23 05								00 03	
Goring & Streatley	d				22 00							23 09								00 09	
Cholsey	d				22 05							23 14								00 14	
Didcot Parkway	a		21 53		22 12		22 28	22 38			23 07	23 23			23s32	23 37			00s04	00 21	00s33
	d				22 13			22 40						23 30			23 45				
Appleford	d																				
Culham	d																				
Radley	d				22 21																
Oxford	a			22 06	22 29			22 51						23 55			00 10				
	d			22 06																	
Islip	d																				
Bicester Town	a																				
Tackley	d																				
Heyford	d																				
Kings Sutton	d																				
Banbury	a			22 25																	
Leamington Spa [8]	a			22 42																	
Coventry	a			22 53																	
Birmingham International	a			23 03																	
Birmingham New Street [12]	a			23 14																	

A [1] to Reading

Table 116

Mondays to Fridays until 22 June

Birmingham, Banbury, Bicester, Oxford and Bedwyn - Reading and London

Network Diagram - see first Page of Table 116

Miles	Miles			GW	GW	GW	GW	GW	GW	GW	GW	GW	GW	GW	CH	GW	GW	GW	GW	GW	GW	GW	GW
				MO	MO	MX	MX	MO	MO	MO	MX	MO	MO	MX	MX	MO	MX	MO					
				◇[1]	◇[1]	◇[1]	◇[1]	[1]			◇[1]	◇[1]		[1]			[1]	[1]	[1]	◇[1]	[1]	[1]	[1]
				A	A			A	A				A										
									🚌	🚌			🚌			🚌							
					☕		☕													☕			
0	—	Birmingham New Street [12]	d																				
8½	—	Birmingham International	d																				
19¼	—	Coventry	d																				
28¾	—	Leamington Spa [8]	d												23p38								
48¾	—	Banbury	d											23p45	23p57								
52¼	—	Kings Sutton	d											23p50									
59¾	—	Heyford	d											23p58									
62½	—	Tackley	d											00 03									
—	0	Bicester Town	d																				
—	6	Islip	d																				
71½	11¾	Oxford	a											00 13	00 21								
—	—		d	22p46		23p09				00 05	00 07			00 27		03 38	04 00		05 03		05 24		05 43
76½	—	Radley	d											00 33					05 09				05 49
78¾	—	Culham	d											00 37									
79¾	—	Appleford	d											00 39									
81½	—	Didcot Parkway	a	22p58		23p23				00 30	00 20			00 46		04 03	04 12		05 17		05 36		05 58
—	—		d	22p59	23p12	23p23	23p35	23p50			00 21	00 35		00 46			04 12	04 12	05 18	05 41	05 46		06 00
86¾	—	Cholsey	d					23p56						00 52			04 18	04 18	05 23		05 52		
90¼	—	Goring & Streatley	d					00 01						00 57			04 23	04 23	05 28		05 57		
93½	—	Pangbourne	d					00 06						01 01			04 28	04 28	05 33		06 02		
96¼	—	Tilehurst	d					00 10						01 06			04 32	04 32	05 37		06 06		
—	0	Bedwyn	d																				
—	5	Hungerford	d																				
—	8	Kintbury	d																				
—	13½	Newbury	a																				
—	—		d						23p30				23p50									05 40	
—	14	Newbury Racecourse	d										23p55									05 42	
—	17	Thatcham	d						23p41				00 05									05 47	
—	19¾	Midgham	d										00 15									05 51	
—	21¾	Aldermaston	d										00 22									05 55	
—	25¾	Theale	d						23p59				00 34									06 00	
—	29½	Reading West	d										00 49									06 07	
99	30½	Reading [7]	a	23p17	23p28	23p40	23p53	00 16	00 25		00 38	00 51	01 05	01 12			04 38	04 38	05 43	05 56	06 12	06 12	06 16
—	—		d	23p22	23p30	23p41	23p55	00 16			00 39	00 53		01 15			04 39	04 39	05 44	05 57	06 15		06 16
104	—	Twyford [3]	a					00 22				00 59		01 21			04 45	04 45	05 50		06 21		06 23
110¾	—	Maidenhead [3]	a			23p54		00 30				01 06		01 29			04 53	04 53	05 58		06 28		06 31
116½	—	Slough [3]	a	23p43		00 01		00 38			00 55	01 14		01 37			05 00	05 00	06 10		06 40		
129¼	—	Ealing Broadway ⊖	a					01 01				01 30		01 53			05 25	05 25	06 35		07 05		
135	—	London Paddington [15] ⊖	a	00 05	00 13	00 28	00 33	01 10			01 17	01 39		02 05			05 41	05 41	06 46	06 24	07 17		06 54

		GW	GW	GW	GW	GW	GW	GW	GW	GW	GW	GW	GW	GW	GW	GW	GW	CH	GW	GW	GW	GW	GW
		[1]	◇[1]	[1]	[1]	◇[1]	[1]	[1]	[1]	◇[1]	◇[1]	[1]	[1]	[1]	◇[1]	◇[1]	[1]		◇[1]	[1]	◇[1]	[1]	◇[1]
						☕				☕	☕				☕	☕			☕				☕
Birmingham New Street [12]	d																						
Birmingham International	d																						
Coventry	d																						
Leamington Spa [8]	d																						
Banbury	d																06 07						
Kings Sutton	d																06 11						
Heyford	d																06 21						
Tackley	d																06 25						
Bicester Town	d																	06 17					
Islip	d																	06 28					
Oxford	a																06 35	06 43					
	d		05 59					06 07		06 27							06 36		06 56				
Radley	d							06 13									06 42						
Culham	d							06 17									06 46						
Appleford	d							06 19									06 48						
Didcot Parkway	a		06 12					06 25		06 39							06 56		07 07				
	d		06 13		06 20	06 30		06 31	06 37	06 39	06 47				06 59		07 01		07 09		07 14		07 20
Cholsey	d				06 25			06 37	06 43								07 07				07 20		
Goring & Streatley	d				06 30			06 42	06 48								07 12				07 26		
Pangbourne	d				06 35			06 47	06 53								07 17				07 33		
Tilehurst	d				06 40			06 51	06 58								07 21				07 40		
Bedwyn	d			05 55								06 13											
Hungerford	d			06 01								06 18				06 40							
Kintbury	d			06 05								06 23											
Newbury	a			06 12								06 30				06 49							
	d	05 58		06 12								06 30				06 50				06 56			
Newbury Racecourse	d											06 32								06 58			
Thatcham	d	06 02		06 17								06 37				06 57				07 03			
Midgham	d											06 42								07 07			
Aldermaston	d											06 45								07 11			
Theale	d	06 10		06 25								06 50				07 07				07 16			
Reading West	d	06 17		06 32			←					06 57	←	←						07 23		←	
Reading [7]	a	06 21	06 30	06 36	06 46	06 43	06 46	06 58	07 05	06 54	07 00	07 02	07 05	06 58	07 14	07 19	07 28		07 25	07 29		07 28	07 34
	d	06 22	06 31	06 36	06 46	06 44	06 46	07 10	07 07	06 56	07 01		07 07	07 10	07 16	07 21	07 30		07 27			07 30	07 36
Twyford [3]	a			06 43	→		06 53	→	→					07 16			→					07 37	
Maidenhead [3]	a		06 42				07 02			07 07			07 18	07 24							07 59	07 45	
Slough [3]	a	06 40	06 50			06 58								07 36								07 55	
Ealing Broadway ⊖	a													08 03								08 18	
London Paddington [15] ⊖	a	07 01	07 08	07 14		07 16	07 29			07 30	07 32		07 43	08 16	07 44	07 53			07 59		08 26	08 32	08 07

A from 21 May until 18 June

Birmingham, Banbury, Bicester, Oxford and Bedwyn - Reading and London

Network Diagram - see first Page of Table 116

		GW ◇■ ☕	GW ■	XC ◇■ 🍴	GW ◇■ ☕	GW ■	GW ■	GW ■	GW ◇■ 🍴	GW ◇■ ☕	GW ◇■ A ☕⊘	XC ◇■	GW ◇■ ☕	GW ◇■ ☕	GW ■	GW ◇■ A ☕⊘	GW ■	GW ■	GW ■	GW ■	XC ◇■ 🍴	GW ◇■ B ☕
Birmingham New Street ■	d			06 04								06 33									07 04	
Birmingham International	d			06 14																	07 14	
Coventry	d			06 25																	07 25	
Leamington Spa ■	d			06 38								07 00									07 38	
Banbury	d		06 27	06 57								07 22							07 26		07 55	
Kings Sutton	d		06 33																07 31			
Heyford	d		06 41																07 40			
Tackley	d		06 46																07 44			
Bicester Town	d																					
Islip	d																					
Oxford	a		06 58	07 14								07 41							07 55		08 14	
	d		07 00	07 16				07 21	07 33			07 43				07 52			07 56	08 06	08 16	
Radley	d		07 06					07 27											08 02			
Culham	d		07 10					07 31											08 06			
Appleford	d		07 12					07 33											08 09			
Didcot Parkway	a		07 19					07 40											08 15	08 18		
	d		07 28		07 29			07 49		07 47			07 55	08 01					08 15	08 20		08 29
Cholsey	d		07 34					07 55											08 22			
Goring & Streatley	d		07 39					08 00											08 27			
Pangbourne	d		07 44					08 04											08 32			
Tilehurst	d		07 48					08 09											08 37			
Bedwyn	d	06 47					07 07											07 56				
Hungerford	d	06 54					07 12				07 34							08 01				
Kintbury	d	07 00					07 17											08 06				
Newbury	a	07 08					07 24				07 46							08 14				
	d	07 09					07 24				07 49						07 55					
Newbury Racecourse	d						07 26										07 57					
Thatcham	d	07 16					07 32										08 02					
Midgham	d						07 36										08 07					
Aldermaston	d						07 40										08 10					
Theale	d	07 25					07 45										08 16					
Reading West	d	07 34				←	07 52								←		08 23					
Reading ■	a	07 37	07 53	07 39	07 43	07 53	07 56	08 17	07 57	08 00	08 06	08 10	08 12	08 16	08 17	08 21	08 27		08 46	08 35	08 39	08 44
	d	07 39	07 55		07 45	07 55		08 19	07 58	08 02	08 08		08 14	08 17	08 19	08 23			08 48	08 35		08 45
Twyford ■	a		→			08 02		→							08 25				→			
Maidenhead ■	a					08 10									08 33							
Slough ■	a					08 20																
Ealing Broadway ⊖	a																					
London Paddington ■ ⊖	a	08 09			08 14	08 48			08 31	08 33	08 38		08 40	08 44	08 58	08 51				09 06		09 14

		GW ■	GW ◇■ ☕	GW ■	CH	GW ◇■ A ☕⊘	GW ■	GW ◇■ ☕	GW ■	GW ■	XC ◇■	GW ◇■ ☕	GW ◇■ C ☕⊘	GW ■	GW ■	GW ◇■	GW ■	XC ◇■ 🍴	GW ◇■ ☕	GW ■	GW ◇■	GW ■	CH
Birmingham New Street ■	d										07 33							08 04					
Birmingham International	d																	08 14					
Coventry	d																	08 25					
Leamington Spa ■	d										08 04							08 38					
Banbury	d										08 21							08 55					
Kings Sutton	d																						
Heyford	d																						
Tackley	d																						
Bicester Town	d				08 02																		09 07
Islip	d				08 13																		09 18
Oxford	a				08 28						08 41							09 14					09 32
	d			08 21						08 36	08 44		08 51			09 01	09 07	09 16			09 31		
Radley	d			08 27													09 13						
Culham	d																09 17						
Appleford	d									08 45													
Didcot Parkway	a			08 36						08 51						09 14	09 24						
	d			08 37		08 47		08 53		09 01		08 59				09 15	09 31		09 29				
Cholsey	d			08 43						09 07							09 37						
Goring & Streatley	d			08 48						09 12							09 42						
Pangbourne	d			08 53						09 17							09 47						
Tilehurst	d			08 57						09 21							09 51						
Bedwyn	d													08 41									
Hungerford	d													08 46									
Kintbury	d													08 51									
Newbury	a													08 58									
	d		08 29						08 38					08 58						09 22			
Newbury Racecourse	d								08 40											09 25			
Thatcham	d								08 45					09 03						09 30			
Midgham	d								08 49											09 34			
Aldermaston	d								08 53											09 38			
Theale	d								08 58					09 11						09 43			
Reading West	d	←					←		09 05						←					09 50		←	
Reading ■	a	08 46	08 50	09 03		09 01	09 03	09 07	09 10	09 27	09 11	09 14	09 14	09 20	09 27	09 32	09 57	09 39	09 44	09 54	09 54	09 57	
	d	08 48	08 52	09 03		09 02	09 03	09 08		09 33		09 16	09 18	09 21	09 33	09 37	10 03		09 46		09 55	10 03	
Twyford ■	a	08 54		→			09 09			→					09 39		→					10 09	
Maidenhead ■	a	09 02					09 17								09 47							10 17	
Slough ■	a						09 29								09 54	09 52					10 10	10 24	
Ealing Broadway ⊖	a						09 54								10 19							10 49	
London Paddington ■ ⊖	a	09 27	09 21			09 29	10 03	09 39				09 44	09 47	09 56	10 31	10 12			10 15		10 30	11 01	

A ☕ from Reading ⊘ to Reading
B The Bristolian
C The Cathedrals Express. ☕ from Reading ⊘ to Reading

Birmingham, Banbury, Bicester, Oxford and Bedwyn - Reading and London

Network Diagram - see first Page of Table 116

		GW ◇■ ☕	GW ■	XC ◇■ 🍴	GW ■	GW ◇■ 🍴	GW ◇■ ☕	GW ■	GW ■	XC ◇■ 🍴	GW ■	GW ◇■ ☕	GW ◇■	GW ◇■ A ☕	GW ■	GW ■	XC ◇■ 🍴	CH	GW ■	GW ◇■ 🍴	GW ◇■ ☕	GW ■	GW ■
Birmingham New Street ■	d			08 33						09 04							09 33						
Birmingham International	d									09 14													
Coventry	d									09 25													
Leamington Spa ■	d			09 00						09 38							10 00						
Banbury	d			09 19					09 39	09 55							10 19						
Kings Sutton	d								09 45														
Heyford	d								09 53														
Tackley	d								09 58														
Bicester Town	d																	10 30					
Islip	d																	10 41					
Oxford	a			09 41					10 08	10 14							10 41	10 56					
	d		09 36	09 43		10 01			10 08	10 16			10 31			10 36	10 43			11 01			11 07
Radley	d								10 14														11 13
Culham	d																						
Appleford	d		09 44													10 44							
Didcot Parkway	a		09 50						10 23							10 51							11 22
	d	09 53	10 01				10 16		10 31			10 29		10 47		11 01					11 17		11 31
Cholsey	d		10 07						10 37							11 07							11 37
Goring & Streatley	d		10 12						10 42							11 12							11 42
Pangbourne	d		10 17						10 47							11 17							11 47
Tilehurst	d		10 21						10 51							11 21							11 51
Bedwyn	d				09 36														10 38				
Hungerford	d				09 41														10 43				
Kintbury	d				09 46														10 48				
Newbury	a				09 53														10 55				
	d				09 53						10 13								10 55				
Newbury Racecourse	d										10 15												
Thatcham	d				09 58						10 20								11 00				
Midgham	d										10 24												
Aldermaston	d										10 28												
Theale	d				10 06						10 33								11 08				
Reading West	d							←			10 40				←							←	
Reading ■	a	10 06	10 28	10 10	10 16	10 25	10 31	10 28	10 58	10 39	10 45	10 44	10 54	11 00	10 58	11 28	11 07		11 20	11 24	11 30	11 28	11 58
	d	10 08	10 33		10 18	10 26	10 32	10 33	11 03			10 45	10 55	11 02	11 03	11 33			11 20	11 26	11 32	11 33	12 03
Twyford ■	a		→					10 39	→						11 09	→						11 39	→
Maidenhead ■	a							10 47							11 17							11 47	
Slough ■	a					10 39		10 54					11 09		11 24					11 39		11 54	
Ealing Broadway ⊖	a							11 18							11 49							12 19	
London Paddington ■ ⊖	a	10 37			10 56	11 00	11 07	11 32				11 14	11 29	11 32	12 01				11 55	11 59	12 00	12 31	

		XC ◇■ 🍴	GW ◇■ ☕	GW ■	GW ◇■ 🍴	GW ■	GW ◇■ ☕	GW ■	XC ◇■ 🍴	CH	GW ■	GW ◇■ 🍴	GW ◇■ ☕	GW ■	GW ■	XC ◇■ 🍴	GW ■	GW ◇■ ☕	GW ◇■ 🍴	GW ◇■ ☕	GW ■	GW ■
Birmingham New Street ■	d	10 04							10 33							11 04						
Birmingham International	d	10 14														11 14						
Coventry	d	10 25														11 25						
Leamington Spa ■	d	10 38							11 00							11 38						
Banbury	d	10 55							11 19							11 55						
Kings Sutton	d																					
Heyford	d																					
Tackley	d																					
Bicester Town	d									11 30												
Islip	d									11 41												
Oxford	a	11 14							11 40	11 56						12 14						
	d	11 16			11 31			11 37	11 43			12 01			12 07	12 16			12 31			12 37
Radley	d														12 13							
Culham	d																					
Appleford	d														12 17							
Didcot Parkway	a							11 51							12 24							12 49
	d		11 29				11 53	12 01					12 16		12 31			12 29		12 47		13 01
Cholsey	d							12 07							12 37							13 07
Goring & Streatley	d							12 12							12 42							13 12
Pangbourne	d							12 17							12 47							13 17
Tilehurst	d							12 21							12 51							13 21
Bedwyn	d										11 38											
Hungerford	d										11 43											
Kintbury	d										11 48											
Newbury	a										11 55											
	d			11 13							11 55						12 13					
Newbury Racecourse	d			11 15													12 15					
Thatcham	d			11 20							12 00						12 20					
Midgham	d			11 24													12 24					
Aldermaston	d			11 28													12 28					
Theale	d			11 33							12 08						12 33					
Reading West	d			11 40		←								←			12 40				←	
Reading ■	a	11 39	11 43	11 45	11 54	11 58	12 06	12 27	12 10		12 17	12 24	12 30	12 27	12 57	12 39	12 45	12 44	12 54	13 00	12 57	13 29
	d		11 44		11 55	12 03	12 08	12 33			12 18	12 26	12 32	12 33	13 03			12 45	12 55	13 02	13 03	13 33
Twyford ■	a					12 09		→						12 39	→						13 09	→
Maidenhead ■	a					12 17								12 47							13 17	
Slough ■	a				12 09	12 24						12 39		12 54					13 09		13 24	
Ealing Broadway ⊖	a					12 49								13 19							13 49	
London Paddington ■ ⊖	a		12 14		12 29	13 02	12 37				12 52	13 06	13 00	13 31				13 14	13 29	13 32	14 01	

A The Red Dragon

Table 116

Mondays to Fridays

until 22 June

Birmingham, Banbury, Bicester, Oxford and Bedwyn - Reading and London

Network Diagram - see first Page of Table 116

	XC ◇1 ✕	GW ◇1 ✕	GW 1	GW ◇1 ⊡	GW 1	GW 1	GW 1	XC ◇1 ✕	GW ◇1 ⊡	GW 1	GW ◇1 ✕	GW 1	GW ◇1 ⊡	GW 1	XC ◇1 ✕	GW ◇1 ⊡	GW ◇1 ✕	GW ◇1 ⊡	GW 1	GW 1	XC ◇1 ✕	CH
Birmingham New Street 12 d	11 33							12 04							12 33						13 04	
Birmingham International d								12 14													13 14	
Coventry d								12 25													13 25	
Leamington Spa d	12 00							12 38							13 00						13 38	
Banbury d	12 19						12 42	12 55							13 21						13 55	
Kings Sutton d							12 48															
Heyford d							12 56															
Tackley d							13 01															
Bicester Town d																						14 00
Islip d																						14 11
Oxford a	12 40						13 11	13 14							13 40						14 14	14 28
Oxford d	12 43	13 01				13 07		13 16			13 31			13 37	13 43		14 01			14 07	14 16	
Radley d						13 13														14 13		
Culham d						13 17																
Appleford d																				14 17		
Didcot Parkway a						13 24								13 49						14 24		
Didcot Parkway d				13 16		13 31			13 29				13 53	14 01				14 16		14 31		
Cholsey d						13 37								14 07						14 37		
Goring & Streatley d						13 42								14 12						14 42		
Pangbourne d						13 47								14 17						14 47		
Tilehurst d						13 51								14 21						14 51		
Bedwyn d			12 38													13 32						
Hungerford d			12 43													13 39						
Kintbury d			12 48																			
Newbury a			12 55													13 48						
Newbury d			13 03							13 13						13 48						
Newbury Racecourse d										13 15												
Thatcham d			13 08							13 20						13 55						
Midgham d										13 24												
Aldermaston d										13 28												
Theale d			13 16							13 33						14 04						
Reading West d					←					13 40		←							←			
Reading 7 a	13 07	13 24	13 27	13 31	13 29	13 58		13 39	13 43	13 45	13 54	13 58	14 06	14 27	14 10	14 15	14 24	14 31	14 27	14 58	14 39	
Reading d		13 26	13 29	13 32	13 33	14 03			13 44		13 55	14 03	14 08	14 33		14 17	14 26	14 32	14 33	15 03		
Twyford 3 a					13 39	→						14 09		→					14 39	→		
Maidenhead 3 a					13 47							14 17							14 47			
Slough 3 a		13 39			13 54						14 09	14 24					14 39		14 54			
Ealing Broadway ⊖ a					14 19							14 49							15 19			
London Paddington 15 ⊖ a		14 01	14 09	14 06	14 31				14 14		14 29	15 01	14 37			14 44	15 00	15 08	15 32			

	GW ◇1 ⊡	GW 1	GW ◇1	GW ◇1 A ⊡⊘	GW 1	GW 1	XC ◇1 ✕	GW 1	GW ◇1 ✕	GW ◇1 ⊡	GW 1	GW 1	XC ◇1 ✕	GW ◇1 ⊡	GW 1	GW ◇1 ⊡	GW 1	GW ◇1 B ⊡	GW 1	GW 1	XC ◇1 ✕
Birmingham New Street 12 d							13 33						14 04								14 33
Birmingham International d													14 14								
Coventry d													14 25								
Leamington Spa d							14 00						14 38								15 00
Banbury d							14 19						14 55							15 08	15 19
Kings Sutton d																				15 14	
Heyford d																				15 22	
Tackley d																				15 27	
Bicester Town d																					
Islip d																					
Oxford a							14 40						15 14							15 39	15 41
Oxford d			14 31			14 37	14 43		15 01			15 07	15 16			15 31			15 37		15 43
Radley d												15 13							15 43		
Culham d												15 17									
Appleford d																					
Didcot Parkway a						14 51						15 24							15 51		
Didcot Parkway d	14 29			14 47		15 01				15 16		15 31		15 29				15 53	16 01		
Cholsey d						15 07						15 37							16 07		
Goring & Streatley d						15 12						15 42							16 12		
Pangbourne d						15 17						15 47							16 17		
Tilehurst d						15 21						15 51							16 21		
Bedwyn d								14 38													
Hungerford d								14 43													
Kintbury d								14 48													
Newbury a								14 55													
Newbury d		14 13						14 55							15 13						
Newbury Racecourse d		14 15													15 15						
Thatcham d		14 20						15 00							15 20						
Midgham d		14 24													15 24						
Aldermaston d		14 28													15 28						
Theale d		14 33						15 08							15 33						
Reading West d		14 40			←						←				15 40		←				
Reading 7 a	14 43	14 45	14 54	15 00	14 58	15 27	15 07	15 20	15 24	15 31	15 27	15 58	15 39	15 43	15 45	15 54	15 58	16 06	16 27		16 10
Reading d	14 44		14 55	15 02	15 03	15 33		15 20	15 26	15 32	15 33	16 03		15 44		15 55	16 03	16 08	16 33		
Twyford 3 a					15 09	→					15 39	→					16 09		→		
Maidenhead 3 a					15 17						15 47						16 17				
Slough 3 a			15 09		15 24				15 39		15 54					16 09	16 24				
Ealing Broadway ⊖ a					15 49						16 19						16 49				
London Paddington 15 ⊖ a	15 14		15 29	15 32	16 02			15 54	16 01	16 09	16 31			16 14		16 27	17 02	16 39			

A ⊡ from Reading ⊘ to Reading

B The Cheltenham Spa Express

Table 116

Mondays to Fridays

until 22 June

Birmingham, Banbury, Bicester, Oxford and Bedwyn - Reading and London

Network Diagram - see first Page of Table 116

	CH	GW 1	GW ◇1 ✕	GW 1	GW ◇1 ⊡	GW 1	XC ◇1 ✕	GW ◇1 ⊡	GW 1	GW ◇1	GW ◇1 ⊡	GW 1	GW 1	XC ◇1 ✕	GW ◇1 ⊡	GW 1	GW 1	GW 1 ✕	GW ◇1 ⊡	GW 1	GW 1	XC ◇1 ✕
Birmingham New Street 12 d							15 04							15 33								16 04
Birmingham International d							15 14															16 14
Coventry d							15 25															16 25
Leamington Spa d							15 38							16 00								16 38
Banbury d							15 55							16 19								16 55
Kings Sutton d																						
Heyford d																						
Tackley d																						
Bicester Town d	15 30																					
Islip d	15 41																					
Oxford a	15 56						16 14							16 40								17 14
Oxford d			16 01			16 07	16 16			16 31			16 37	16 43			16 47	17 01			17 07	17 16
Radley d						16 13							16 43								17 13	
Culham d																					17 17	
Appleford d						16 17																
Didcot Parkway a						16 24							16 51				17 04				17 24	
Didcot Parkway d					16 16	16 31		16 29			16 47		17 05						17 16		17 31	
Cholsey d						16 37							17 11								17 37	
Goring & Streatley d						16 42							17 16								17 42	
Pangbourne d						16 47							17 20								17 47	
Tilehurst d						16 51							17 25								17 51	
Bedwyn d		15 36														16 44						
Hungerford d		15 41													16 39	16 49						
Kintbury d		15 46														16 54						
Newbury a		15 53													16 48	17 03						
Newbury d		15 53							16 13						16 48							
Newbury Racecourse d									16 15													
Thatcham d		15 58							16 20						16 55							
Midgham d									16 24													
Aldermaston d									16 28													
Theale d		16 06							16 33						17 04							
Reading West d				←					16 40			←								←		
Reading 7 a		16 16	16 24	16 27	16 31	16 59	16 39	16 43	16 45	16 54	17 00	16 59	17 31	17 07	17 15			17 24	17 31	17 31	17 57	17 39
Reading d		16 19	16 26	16 33	16 34	17 03		16 44		16 55	17 02	17 03	17 33		17 17			17 26	17 32	17 33	18 00	
Twyford 3 a				16 39		→						17 09	→							17 39	→	
Maidenhead 3 a				16 47								17 17			17 28					17 47		
Slough 3 a			16 39	16 54						17 09		17 24						17 39		17 54		
Ealing Broadway ⊖ a				17 21								17 49								18 19		
London Paddington 15 ⊖ a		16 57	17 00	17 31	17 09			17 14		17 34	17 30	18 01			17 54			17 59	18 02	18 31		

	CH	GW 1	GW ◇1 ⊡	GW ◇1 ⊡	GW 1	GW ◇1 ⊡	GW 1	XC ◇1 ✕	GW 1	GW 1	GW 1 ✕	GW ◇1 ⊡	GW 1	GW 1	XC ◇1 ✕	GW 1	GW ◇1 ⊡	GW 1	GW ◇1 A ⊡⊘	GW 1	GW 1	XC ◇1 ✕
Birmingham New Street 12 d								16 33							17 04							17 33
Birmingham International d															17 14							
Coventry d															17 25							
Leamington Spa d								17 00							17 38							18 00
Banbury d								17 19	17 23						17 55							18 19
Kings Sutton d									17 27													
Heyford d									17 36													
Tackley d									17 40													
Bicester Town d	16 57																					
Islip d	17 08																					
Oxford a	17 23							17 39	17 52						18 14							18 40
Oxford d				17 31			17 37	17 43			18 01			18 07	18 16			18 31			18 37	18 43
Radley d							17 43							18 13							18 43	
Culham d														18 17								
Appleford d							17 47														18 47	
Didcot Parkway a							17 54							18 24							18 56	
Didcot Parkway d			17 29			17 53	18 01					18 16		18 31			18 29		18 47		19 01	
Cholsey d							18 07							18 37							19 07	
Goring & Streatley d							18 12							18 42							19 12	
Pangbourne d							18 17							18 47							19 17	
Tilehurst d							18 21							18 51							19 21	
Bedwyn d										17 36						17 55						
Hungerford d										17 41						18 00						
Kintbury d										17 46						18 05						
Newbury a										17 53						18 12						
Newbury d		17 13								17 53						18 13						
Newbury Racecourse d		17 15														18 15						
Thatcham d		17 20								17 58						18 20						
Midgham d		17 24														18 24						
Aldermaston d		17 28								18 04						18 28						
Theale d		17 33								18 09						18 33						
Reading West d		17 40			←								←			18 40				←		
Reading 7 a		17 45	17 44	17 54	17 57	18 06	18 27	18 09		18 21	18 24	18 31	18 27	19 00	18 39	18 45	18 46	18 55	19 01	19 00	19 27	19 07
Reading d			17 46	17 56	18 00	18 08	18 33			18 22	18 26	18 32	18 33	19 03			18 47	18 57	19 02	19 03	19 33	
Twyford 3 a					18 06		→						18 39	→						19 09	→	
Maidenhead 3 a					18 17								18 47							19 21		
Slough 3 a				18 10	18 24						18 39		18 54					19 09		19 29		
Ealing Broadway ⊖ a					18 49								19 19							19 53		
London Paddington 15 ⊖ a			18 14	18 28	19 00	18 39				18 54	18 59	19 02	19 31				19 14	19 31	19 32	20 02		

A ⊡ from Reading ⊘ to Reading

Table 116

Mondays to Fridays
until 22 June

Birmingham, Banbury, Bicester, Oxford and Bedwyn - Reading and London

Network Diagram - see first Page of Table 116

		CH	GW	GW	GW	GW	GW	GW	XC	GW	GW FO	GW FX	GW	GW	GW	GW	XC	GW	GW	GW	GW	GW
			1	1	1	◇1 ⌶	1	1	◇1 ⌶	◇1 ⊡	◇1	◇1	1	◇1 ⊡	◇1 ⊡	1	◇1 ⌶	◇1 ⊡	◇1	1	1	1
Birmingham New Street 12	d								18 04								18 33					
Birmingham International	d								18 14													
Coventry	d								18 25													
Leamington Spa 8	d								18 38								19 00					
Banbury	d							18 37	18 55								19 19					
Kings Sutton	d							18 43														
Heyford	d							18 51														
Tackley	d							18 56														
Bicester Town	d	18 18																				
Islip	d	18 29																				
Oxford	a	18 44						19 08	19 14								19 39					
	d				19 01	19 06			19 16		19 31	19 31				19 37	19 42		20 01			
Radley	d				19 07																	
Culham	d																					
Appleford	d																					
Didcot Parkway	a				19 16											19 49						
	d				19 32					19 29				19 47		20 01		20 00				
Cholsey	d				19 37											20 07						
Goring & Streatley	d				19 42											20 12						
Pangbourne	d				19 47											20 17						
Tilehurst	d				19 51											20 21						
Bedwyn	d			19 03																		19 55
Hungerford	d			19 08																		20 00
Kintbury	d			19 13																		20 05
Newbury	a			19 22																		20 12
	d		18 53												19 49						19 55	20 12
Newbury Racecourse	d																				19 57	
Thatcham	d		18 58																		20 02	20 17
Midgham	d																				20 06	
Aldermaston	d																				20 10	
Theale	d		19 06																		20 15	20 25
Reading West	d						←						←							←	20 21	
Reading 7	a		19 16		19 57	19 32	19 27		19 39	19 44	19 54	19 54	19 57	20 00	20 06	20 27	20 10	20 14	20 24	20 27	20 27	20 34
	d		19 18		19 58	19 32	19 33			19 45	19 55	19 55	19 58	20 02	20 08	20 33		20 15	20 26	20 33		20 34
Twyford 3	a				→		19 42						20 04			→				20 39		
Maidenhead 3	a						19 50						20 12							20 47		
Slough 3	a					19 47	19 57				20 09	20 09	20 19						20 39	20 54		
Ealing Broadway ⊖	a						20 22						20 49							21 19		
London Paddington 15 ⊖	a		19 54			20 06	20 31			20 14	20 30	20 31	20 59	20 32	20 39			20 46	21 01	21 31		21 08

		GW	XC	CH	GW	GW	GW	GW	GW	GW	XC	GW	GW	GW	XC	GW	GW	GW	GW	GW	GW FX	GW FO	XC
		1	◇1 ⌶		◇1 ⊡	◇1 ⊡	1	◇1 ⊡	1	1	◇1 ⌶	1	◇1	1	◇1	◇1 ⊡	1	1	◇1	◇1 ⊡	◇1 ⊡	◇1 ⊡	◇1
Birmingham New Street 12	d		19 04								19 33				20 04								20 33
Birmingham International	d		19 14												20 14								
Coventry	d		19 25												20 25								
Leamington Spa 8	d		19 38								20 05				20 38								21 00
Banbury	d		19 55				20 01				20 23				20 55								21 19
Kings Sutton	d						20 07																
Heyford	d						20 15																
Tackley	d						20 20																
Bicester Town	d			20 00																			
Islip	d			20 11																			
Oxford	a		20 14	20 26			20 32				20 40				21 14								21 40
	d	20 07	20 16			20 31				20 37	20 42		21 01		21 16			21 21	21 32				21 43
Radley	d	20 13																21 27					
Culham	d	20 17																21 31					
Appleford	d									20 45													
Didcot Parkway	a	20 24								20 51								21 38					
	d	20 31			20 29			20 47		21 01						21 29		21 44			21 53	21 53	
Cholsey	d	20 37								21 08								21 50					
Goring & Streatley	d	20 42								21 13								21 55					
Pangbourne	d	20 47								21 19								21 59					
Tilehurst	d	20 51								21 22								22 02					
Bedwyn	d											20 33					21 06						
Hungerford	d											20 38					21 11						
Kintbury	d											20 43					21 16						
Newbury	a											20 50					21 23						
	d											20 50					21 23			21 42			
Newbury Racecourse	d											20 52					21 25						
Thatcham	d											20 57					21 30						
Midgham	d											21 02					21 35						
Aldermaston	d											21 05					21 38						
Theale	d											21 10					21 43						
Reading West	d								←			21 17		←			21 50						
Reading 7	a	20 58	20 39		20 44	20 54		21 00	20 58	21 29	21 07	21 22	21 24	21 29	21 40	21 43	21 55	22 12	21 55	21 59	22 11	22 11	22 17
	d	21 14			20 45	20 55		21 02	21 14	21 33			21 26	21 33		21 44			21 56	22 01	22 12	22 12	
Twyford 3	a	→							21 20	→				21 39									
Maidenhead 3	a								21 28					21 47									
Slough 3	a					21 09			21 40				21 39	21 58					22 13				
Ealing Broadway ⊖	a								22 04					22 21									
London Paddington 15 ⊖	a				21 14	21 29		21 32	22 16				22 00	22 33		22 14			22 39	22 30	22 44	22 45	

Table 116

Mondays to Fridays
until 22 June

Birmingham, Banbury, Bicester, Oxford and Bedwyn - Reading and London

Network Diagram - see first Page of Table 116

		GW	CH	GW	XC	GW	GW FO	GW FX	GW	GW	GW FX	GW FO	GW	GW	XC	GW	CH FO	GW	CH
		1		◇	◇1	1	◇1	◇1	◇1 ⊡	1	1	1	◇1	1	◇1	◇1 ⊡		1	
Birmingham New Street 12	d				21 04										22 04				
Birmingham International	d				21 14										22 14				
Coventry	d				21 25										22 25				
Leamington Spa 8	d				21 38										22 38				23 38
Banbury	d			21 38	21 55						22 25	22 25			22 55			23 45	23 57
Kings Sutton	d			21 42							22 31	22 31						23 50	
Heyford	d			21 51							22 38	22 39						23 58	
Tackley	d			21 55							22 44	22 44						00 03	
Bicester Town	d		21 30														23 42		
Islip	d		21 41														23 53		
Oxford	a		21 56	22 05	22 14						22 56	22 56			23 14		00 08	00 13	00 21
	d	21 51		22 11	22 16		22 34	22 34		22 52			23 09		23 15			00 27	
Radley	d	21 57								22 58								00 33	
Culham	d									23 02								00 37	
Appleford	d									23 04								00 39	
Didcot Parkway	a	22 06		22 24						23 11			23 23					00 46	
	d	22 08		22 27					22 52	23 11			23 23			23 35		00 46	
Cholsey	d	22 14								23 18								00 52	
Goring & Streatley	d	22 19								23 23								00 57	
Pangbourne	d	22 24								23 26								01 01	
Tilehurst	d	22 27								23 30								01 06	
Bedwyn	d					21 55								23 00					
Hungerford	d					22 00								23 05					
Kintbury	d					22 05								23 10					
Newbury	a					22 12								23 17					
	d					22 13								23 17					
Newbury Racecourse	d					22 15								23 19					
Thatcham	d					22 20								23 24					
Midgham	d					22 24								23 29					
Aldermaston	d					22 28								23 32					
Theale	d					22 33								23 37					
Reading West	d					22 40								23 44					
Reading 7	a	22 37		22 44	22 41	22 45	22 58	22 58	23 06	23 40			23 40	23 49	23 52	23 53		01 12	
	d			22 44			22 59	22 59	23 08				23 41			23 55		01 15	
Twyford 3	a																	01 21	
Maidenhead 3	a												23 54					01 29	
Slough 3	a			23 01			23 12	23 15					00 01					01 37	
Ealing Broadway ⊖	a																	01 53	
London Paddington 15 ⊖	a			23 25			23 36	23 36	23 41				00 28			00 33		02 05	

Mondays to Fridays
25 June to 14 September

		GW MO	GW	GW MO	GW	GW MX	GW MO	GW MX	GW MO	XC MX	GW	GW	GW MO	GW MO	GW	GW MX	GW	GW	GW MX	CH MX	GW	GW	GW
		◇1 A	◇1 B	◇1 A ⊡	◇1 B ⊡	◇1	1 A	◇1 ⊡	1 A	◇1	1 B	B 🚌	1 A	◇1 A	B 🚌	◇1	◇1 B	B 🚌	1		B 🚌	1 C	1 B
Birmingham New Street 12	d									22p04													
Birmingham International	d																						
Coventry	d																						
Leamington Spa 8	d									22p53										23p38			
Banbury	d									23p16									23p45	23p57			
Kings Sutton	d																		23p50				
Heyford	d																		23p58				
Tackley	d																		00 03				
Bicester Town	d																						
Islip	d																						
Oxford	a									23p35									00 13	00 21			
	d	22p46	22p46			23p09	23p15			23p36				00⌇01	00⌇05	00 07			00 27		03⌇38	04⌇00	
Radley	d						23p22												00 33				
Culham	d																		00 37				
Appleford	d																		00 39				
Didcot Parkway	a	22p58	22p58			23p23	23p30							00⌇13	00⌇30	00 20			00 46		04⌇03	04⌇12	
	d	22p59	22p59	23p12	23p12	23p23	23p30	23p35			23p50			00⌇14		00 21	00⌇35		00 46			04⌇12	04⌇12
Cholsey	d						23p36				23p56								00 52			04⌇18	04⌇18
Goring & Streatley	d						23p42				00⌇01								00 57			04⌇23	04⌇23
Pangbourne	d						23p46				00⌇06								01 01			04⌇28	04⌇28
Tilehurst	d						23p50				00⌇10								01 06			04⌇32	04⌇32
Bedwyn	d																						
Hungerford	d																						
Kintbury	d																						
Newbury	a																						
	d											23p30	23p45					23p50					
Newbury Racecourse	d												23p47					23p55					
Thatcham	d											23p41	23p52					00⌇05					
Midgham	d												23p57					00⌇15					
Aldermaston	d												00⌇01					00⌇22					
Theale	d											23p59	00⌇06					00⌇34					
Reading West	d								←				00s13					00⌇49					
Reading 7	a	23p15	23p17	23p28	23p28	23p40	23p56	23p53	23p56	00 07	00⌇16	00⌇25	00⌇17	00⌇30		00 38	00⌇51	01⌇05	01 12			04⌇38	04⌇38
	d	23p22	23p22	23p30	23p30	23p41	23p56	23p55	23p56		00⌇16			00⌇32		00 39	00⌇53		01 15			04⌇39	04⌇39
Twyford 3	a						→		00⌇02		00⌇22			00⌇38			00⌇59		01 21			04⌇45	04⌇45
Maidenhead 3	a					23p54			00⌇10		00⌇30			00⌇45			01⌇06		01 29			04⌇53	04⌇53
Slough 3	a	23p42	23p43			00 01			00⌇20		00⌇38			00⌇53		00 55	01⌇14		01 37			05⌇00	05⌇00
Ealing Broadway ⊖	a								00⌇43		01⌇01			01⌇09			01⌇30		01 53			05⌇25	05⌇25
London Paddington 15 ⊖	a	00⌇02	00⌇05	00⌇05	00⌇13	00 28		00 33	00⌇52		01⌇10			01⌇18		01 17	01⌇39		02 05			05⌇41	05⌇41

A from 2 July until 10 September
B 25 June
C not 25 June

25 June to 14 September

Birmingham, Banbury, Bicester, Oxford and Bedwyn - Reading and London

Network Diagram - see first Page of Table 116

Station		GW ■	GW ◇■ ☕	GW ■	GW ■	GW ■		GW ■	GW ◇■	GW ■	GW ■	GW ◇■ ☕	GW ■	GW ■	GW ■	GW ◇■ ☕		GW ◇■ ☕	GW ■	GW ■	GW ■	GW ◇■ ☕	GW ◇■ ☕	GW ■	CH
Birmingham New Street ■	d																								
Birmingham International	d																								
Coventry	d																								
Leamington Spa ■	d																								
Banbury	d																							06 07	
Kings Sutton	d																							06 11	
Heyford	d																							06 21	
Tackley	d																							06 25	
Bicester Town	d																								06 17
Islip	d																								06 28
Oxford	a																							06 35	06 43
	d	05 03		05 24		05 43			05 59					06 07		06 27								06 36	
Radley	d	05 09				05 49								06 13										06 42	
Culham	d													06 17										06 46	
Appleford	d													06 19										06 48	
Didcot Parkway	a	05 17		05 36		05 58			06 12					06 25		06 39								06 56	
	d	05 18	05 41	05 46		06 00			06 13		06 20	06 30		06 31	06 37	06 39		06 47				06 59		07 01	
Cholsey	d	05 23		05 52							06 25			06 37	06 43									07 07	
Goring & Streatley	d	05 28		05 57							06 30			06 42	06 48									07 12	
Pangbourne	d	05 33		06 02							06 35			06 47	06 53									07 17	
Tilehurst	d	05 37		06 06							06 40			06 51	06 58									07 21	
Bedwyn	d									05 55									06 13						
Hungerford	d									06 01									06 18				06 40		
Kintbury	d									06 05									06 23						
Newbury	a									06 12									06 30				06 49		
	d				05 40			05 58		06 12									06 30				06 50		
Newbury Racecourse	d				05 42														06 32						
Thatcham	d				05 47			06 02		06 17									06 37				06 57		
Midgham	d				05 51														06 42						
Aldermaston	d				05 55														06 45						
Theale	d				06 00			06 10		06 25									06 50				07 07		
Reading West	d				06 07			06 17		06 32			←						06 57	←	←				
Reading ■	a	05 43	05 56	06 12	06 12	06 16		06 21	06 30	06 36	06 46	06 43	06 46	06 58	07 05	06 54		07 00	07 02	07 05	06 58	07 14	07 19	07 28	
	d	05 44	05 57	06 15		06 16		06 22	06 31	06 36	06 46	06 44	06 46	07 10	07 07	06 56		07 01		07 07	07 10	07 16	07 21	07 30	
Twyford ■	a	05 50		06 21		06 23				06 43	→		06 53	→	→						07 16			→	
Maidenhead ■	a	05 58		06 28		06 31			06 42				07 02			07 07				07 18	07 24				
Slough ■	a	06 10		06 40				06 40	06 50			06 58									07 36				
Ealing Broadway ⊖	a	06 35		07 05																	08 03				
London Paddington ■ ⊖	a	06 46	06 24	07 17		06 54		07 01	07 08	07 14		07 16	07 29			07 30		07 32		07 43	08 16	07 44	07 53		

Station		GW ◇■ ☕		GW ■	GW ◇■	GW ■	GW ◇■ ☕	GW ◇■ ☕	GW ■	XC ◇■ 🛒	GW ◇■ ☕	GW ■		GW ■	GW ■	GW ◇■ 🛒	GW ◇■ ☕	GW ◇■ A ☕Ø	XC ◇■	GW ◇■ ☕	GW ◇■ ☕	GW ■		GW ◇■ A ☕Ø	GW ■
Birmingham New Street ■	d									06 04									06 33						
Birmingham International	d									06 14															
Coventry	d									06 25															
Leamington Spa ■	d									06 38									07 00						
Banbury	d								06 27	06 57									07 22						
Kings Sutton	d								06 33																
Heyford	d								06 41																
Tackley	d								06 46																
Bicester Town	d																								
Islip	d																								
Oxford	a								06 58	07 14									07 41						
	d	06 56							07 00	07 16					07 21	07 33			07 43					07 52	
Radley	d								07 06						07 27										
Culham	d								07 10						07 31										
Appleford	d								07 12						07 33										
Didcot Parkway	a	07 07							07 19						07 40										
	d	07 09			07 14		07 20		07 28		07 29				07 49		07 47			07 55	08 01				
Cholsey	d				07 20				07 34						07 55										
Goring & Streatley	d				07 26				07 39						08 00										
Pangbourne	d				07 33				07 44						08 04										
Tilehurst	d				07 40				07 48						08 09										
Bedwyn	d							06 47						07 07											
Hungerford	d							06 54						07 12				07 34							
Kintbury	d							07 00						07 17											
Newbury	a							07 08						07 24				07 46							
	d			06 56				07 09						07 24				07 49							07 55
Newbury Racecourse	d			06 58										07 26											07 57
Thatcham	d			07 03				07 16						07 32											08 02
Midgham	d			07 07										07 36											08 07
Aldermaston	d			07 11										07 40											08 10
Theale	d			07 16				07 25						07 45											08 16
Reading West	d			07 23		←		07 34				←		07 52								←			08 23
Reading ■	a	07 25		07 29		07 28	07 34	07 37	07 53	07 39	07 43	07 53		07 56	08 17	07 57	08 00	08 06	08 10	08 12	08 16	08 17		08 21	08 27
	d	07 27				07 30	07 36	07 39	07 55		07 45	07 55			08 19	07 58	08 02	08 08		08 14	08 17	08 19		08 23	
Twyford ■	a					07 37			→			08 02			→							08 25			
Maidenhead ■	a				07 59	07 45						08 10										08 33			
Slough ■	a					07 55						08 20													
Ealing Broadway ⊖	a					08 18																			
London Paddington ■ ⊖	a	07 59			08 26	08 32	08 07	08 09			08 14	08 48				08 31	08 33	08 38		08 40	08 44	08 58		08 51	

A ☕ from Reading Ø to Reading

25 June to 14 September

Birmingham, Banbury, Bicester, Oxford and Bedwyn - Reading and London

Network Diagram - see first Page of Table 116

Station		GW ■	GW ■	GW ■	XC ◇■ 🛒	GW ◇■ A ☕	GW ■	GW ◇■ ☕		GW ■	CH	GW ◇■ B ☕Ø	GW ■	GW ◇■ ☕	GW ■	GW ■	XC ◇■	GW ◇■ ☕		GW ◇■ C ☕Ø	GW ■	GW ■	GW ◇■	GW ■	XC ◇■ 🛒
Birmingham New Street ■	d				07 04												07 33								08 04
Birmingham International	d				07 14																				08 14
Coventry	d				07 25																				08 25
Leamington Spa ■	d				07 38												08 04								08 38
Banbury	d		07 26		07 55												08 21								08 55
Kings Sutton	d		07 31																						
Heyford	d		07 40																						
Tackley	d		07 44																						
Bicester Town	d										08 02														
Islip	d										08 13														
Oxford	a		07 55		08 14						08 28						08 41								09 14
	d		07 56	08 06	08 16					08 21						08 36	08 44			08 51			09 01	09 07	09 16
Radley	d		08 02							08 27														09 13	
Culham	d		08 06																					09 17	
Appleford	d		08 09													08 45									
Didcot Parkway	a		08 15	08 18						08 36						08 51							09 14	09 24	
	d		08 15	08 20		08 29				08 37		08 47		08 53		09 01		08 59					09 15	09 31	
Cholsey	d		08 22							08 43						09 07								09 37	
Goring & Streatley	d		08 27							08 48						09 12								09 42	
Pangbourne	d		08 32							08 53						09 17								09 47	
Tilehurst	d		08 37							08 57						09 21								09 51	
Bedwyn	d	07 56																			08 41				
Hungerford	d	08 01																			08 46				
Kintbury	d	08 06																			08 51				
Newbury	a	08 14																			08 58				
	d							08 29							08 38						08 58				
Newbury Racecourse	d														08 40										
Thatcham	d														08 45						09 03				
Midgham	d														08 49										
Aldermaston	d														08 53										
Theale	d														08 58						09 11				
Reading West	d						←						←		09 05							←			
Reading ■	a		08 46	08 35	08 39	08 44	08 46	08 50		09 03		09 01	09 03	09 07	09 10	09 27	09 11	09 14		09 14	09 20	09 27	09 32	09 57	09 39
	d		08 48	08 35		08 45	08 48	08 52		09 03		09 02	09 03	09 08		09 33		09 16		09 18	09 21	09 33	09 37	10 03	
Twyford ■	a		→				08 54			→			09 09			→						09 39		→	
Maidenhead ■	a						09 02						09 17									09 47			
Slough ■	a												09 29									09 54	09 52		
Ealing Broadway ⊖	a												09 54									10 19			
London Paddington ■ ⊖	a			09 06		09 14	09 27	09 21				09 29	10 03	09 39				09 44		09 47	09 56	10 31	10 12		

Station		GW ◇■ ☕	GW ■	GW ◇■		GW ■	CH	GW ◇■ ☕	GW ■	XC ◇■ 🛒	GW ■	GW ◇■ 🛒	GW ◇■ ☕	GW ■		GW ■	XC ◇■ 🛒	GW ■	GW ◇■ ☕	GW ◇■	GW ◇■ D ☕	GW ■	GW ■	XC ◇■ 🛒
Birmingham New Street ■	d									08 33							09 04							09 33
Birmingham International	d																09 14							
Coventry	d																09 25							
Leamington Spa ■	d									09 00							09 38							10 00
Banbury	d									09 19						09 39	09 55							10 19
Kings Sutton	d															09 45								
Heyford	d															09 53								
Tackley	d															09 58								
Bicester Town	d						09 07																	
Islip	d						09 18																	
Oxford	a						09 32			09 41						10 08	10 14							10 41
	d			09 31					09 36	09 43		10 01				10 08	10 16			10 31			10 36	10 43
Radley	d															10 14								
Culham	d																							
Appleford	d								09 44														10 44	
Didcot Parkway	a								09 50							10 23							10 51	
	d	09 29						09 53	10 01				10 16			10 31			10 29		10 47		11 01	
Cholsey	d								10 07							10 37							11 07	
Goring & Streatley	d								10 12							10 42							11 12	
Pangbourne	d								10 17							10 47							11 17	
Tilehurst	d								10 21							10 51							11 21	
Bedwyn	d										09 36													
Hungerford	d										09 41													
Kintbury	d										09 46													
Newbury	a										09 53													
	d		09 22								09 53							10 13						
Newbury Racecourse	d		09 25															10 15						
Thatcham	d		09 30								09 58							10 20						
Midgham	d		09 34															10 24						
Aldermaston	d		09 38															10 28						
Theale	d		09 43								10 06							10 33						
Reading West	d		09 50			←								←				10 40				←		
Reading ■	a	09 44	09 54	09 54		09 57		10 06	10 28	10 10	10 16	10 25	10 31	10 28		10 58	10 39	10 45	10 44	10 54	11 00	10 58	11 28	11 07
	d	09 46		09 55		10 03		10 08	10 33		10 18	10 26	10 32	10 33		11 03			10 45	10 55	11 02	11 03	11 33	
Twyford ■	a					10 09			→					10 39		→						11 09	→	
Maidenhead ■	a					10 17								10 47								11 17		
Slough ■	a			10 10		10 24						10 39		10 54						11 09		11 24		
Ealing Broadway ⊖	a					10 49								11 18								11 49		
London Paddington ■ ⊖	a	10 15		10 30		11 01		10 37			10 56	11 00	11 07	11 32					11 14	11 29	11 32	12 01		

A The Bristolian
B ☕ from Reading Ø to Reading
C The Cathedrals Express. ☕ from Reading Ø to Reading
D The Red Dragon

Birmingham, Banbury, Bicester, Oxford and Bedwyn - Reading and London

Network Diagram - see first Page of Table 116

Station		CH	GW 1	GW ◇1 🍴	GW ◇1 🛒	GW 1	GW 1	XC ◇1 🍴	GW ◇1 🛒	GW 1	GW ◇1 🍴	GW 1	GW ◇1 🛒	GW 1	XC ◇1 🍴	CH	GW 1	GW ◇1 🍴	GW ◇1 🛒	GW 1	GW 1	XC ◇1 🍴	GW 1
Birmingham New Street 12	d							10 04							10 33							11 04	
Birmingham International	d							10 14														11 14	
Coventry	d							10 25														11 25	
Leamington Spa 8	d							10 38							11 00							11 38	
Banbury	d							10 55							11 19							11 55	
Kings Sutton	d																						
Heyford	d																						
Tackley	d																						
Bicester Town	d	10 30														11 30							
Islip	d	10 41														11 41							
Oxford	a	10 56						11 14							11 40	11 56						12 14	
	d			11 01			11 07	11 16			11 31			11 37	11 43			12 01			12 07	12 16	
Radley	d						11 13														12 13		
Culham	d																						
Appleford	d																				12 17		
Didcot Parkway	a						11 22							11 51							12 24		
	d				11 17		11 31		11 29				11 53	12 01					12 16		12 31		
Cholsey	d						11 37							12 07							12 37		
Goring & Streatley	d						11 42							12 12							12 42		
Pangbourne	d						11 47							12 17							12 47		
Tilehurst	d						11 51							12 21							12 51		
Bedwyn	d		10 38														11 38						
Hungerford	d		10 43														11 43						
Kintbury	d		10 48														11 48						
Newbury	a		10 55														11 55						
	d		10 55							11 13							11 55						12 13
Newbury Racecourse	d									11 15													12 15
Thatcham	d		11 00							11 20							12 00						12 20
Midgham	d									11 24													12 24
Aldermaston	d									11 28													12 28
Theale	d		11 08							11 33							12 08						12 33
Reading West	d					←				11 40		←								←			12 40
Reading 7	a		11 20	11 24	11 30	11 28	11 58	11 39	11 43	11 45	11 54	11 58	12 06	12 27	12 10		12 17	12 24	12 30	12 27	12 57	12 39	12 45
	d		11 20	11 26	11 32	11 33	12 03		11 44		11 55	12 03	12 08	12 33			12 18	12 26	12 32	12 33	13 03		
Twyford 3	a					11 39	→					12 09		→						12 39	→		
Maidenhead 3	a					11 47						12 17								12 47			
Slough 3	a			11 39		11 54					12 09	12 24						12 39		12 54			
Ealing Broadway ⊖	a					12 19						12 49								13 19			
London Paddington 15 ⊖	a		11 55	11 59	12 00	12 31			12 14		12 29	13 02	12 37				12 52	13 06	13 00	13 31			

Station		GW ◇1 🛒	GW ◇1 🍴	GW ◇1 🛒	GW 1	GW 1	XC ◇1 🍴	GW ◇1 🍴	GW 1	GW ◇1 🛒	GW 1	GW 1	GW 1	XC ◇1 🍴	GW ◇1 🛒	GW 1	GW ◇1 🍴	GW 1	GW ◇1 🛒	GW 1	XC ◇1 🍴	GW ◇1 🛒	GW ◇1 🍴
Birmingham New Street 12	d						11 33							12 04							12 33		
Birmingham International	d													12 14									
Coventry	d													12 25									
Leamington Spa 8	d						12 00							12 38							13 00		
Banbury	d						12 19						12 42	12 55							13 21		
Kings Sutton	d												12 48										
Heyford	d												12 56										
Tackley	d												13 01										
Bicester Town	d																						
Islip	d																						
Oxford	a						12 40						13 11	13 14							13 40		
	d		12 31			12 37	12 43	13 01				13 07		13 16			13 31			13 37	13 43		14 01
Radley	d											13 13											
Culham	d																						
Appleford	d											13 17											
Didcot Parkway	a					12 49						13 24								13 49			
	d	12 29		12 47		13 01				13 16		13 31			13 29				13 53	14 01			
Cholsey	d					13 07						13 37								14 07			
Goring & Streatley	d					13 12						13 42								14 12			
Pangbourne	d					13 17						13 47								14 17			
Tilehurst	d					13 21						13 51								14 21			
Bedwyn	d								12 38													13 32	
Hungerford	d								12 43													13 39	
Kintbury	d								12 48														
Newbury	a								12 55													13 48	
	d								13 03							13 13						13 48	
Newbury Racecourse	d															13 15							
Thatcham	d								13 08							13 20						13 55	
Midgham	d															13 24							
Aldermaston	d															13 28							
Theale	d								13 16							13 33						14 04	
Reading West	d				←						←					13 40		←					
Reading 7	a	12 44	12 54	13 00	12 57	13 29	13 07	13 24	13 27	13 31	13 29	13 58		13 39	13 43	13 45	13 54	13 58	14 06	14 27	14 10	14 15	14 24
	d	12 45	12 55	13 02	13 03	13 33		13 26	13 29	13 32	13 33	14 03			13 44		13 55	14 03	14 08	14 33		14 17	14 26
Twyford 3	a				13 09	→					13 39	→						14 09		→			
Maidenhead 3	a				13 17						13 47							14 17					
Slough 3	a		13 09		13 24			13 39			13 54						14 09	14 24					14 39
Ealing Broadway ⊖	a				13 49						14 19							14 49					
London Paddington 15 ⊖	a	13 14	13 29	13 32	14 01			14 01	14 09	14 06	14 31				14 14		14 29	15 01	14 37			14 44	15 00

Birmingham, Banbury, Bicester, Oxford and Bedwyn - Reading and London

Network Diagram - see first Page of Table 116

Station		GW ◇1 🛒	GW 1	GW 1	XC ◇1 🍴	CH	GW ◇1 🛒	GW 1	GW ◇1	GW ◇1 A 🛒⊘	GW 1	GW 1	XC ◇1 🍴	GW 1 B	GW FX 1 C	GW ◇1 🍴	GW ◇1 🛒	GW 1	GW 1	XC ◇1 🍴	GW ◇1 🛒	GW 1
Birmingham New Street 12	d				13 04								13 33							14 04		
Birmingham International	d				13 14															14 14		
Coventry	d				13 25															14 25		
Leamington Spa 8	d				13 38								14 00							14 38		
Banbury	d				13 55								14 19							14 55		
Kings Sutton	d																					
Heyford	d																					
Tackley	d																					
Bicester Town	d					14 00																
Islip	d					14 11																
Oxford	a				14 14	14 28							14 40							15 14		
	d			14 07	14 16				14 31			14 37	14 43			15 01			15 07	15 16		
Radley	d			14 13															15 13			
Culham	d																					
Appleford	d			14 17															15 17			
Didcot Parkway	a			14 24								14 51							15 24			
	d	14 16		14 31			14 29			14 47		15 01					15 16		15 31		15 29	
Cholsey	d			14 37								15 07							15 37			
Goring & Streatley	d			14 42								15 12							15 42			
Pangbourne	d			14 47								15 17							15 47			
Tilehurst	d			14 51								15 21							15 51			
Bedwyn	d													14 38	14 38							
Hungerford	d													14 43	14 43							
Kintbury	d													14 48	14 48							
Newbury	a													14 55	14 55							
	d							14 13						14 55	14 55							15 13
Newbury Racecourse	d							14 15														15 15
Thatcham	d							14 20						15 00	15 00							15 20
Midgham	d							14 24														15 24
Aldermaston	d							14 28														15 28
Theale	d							14 33						15 08	15 08							15 33
Reading West	d		←					14 40			←							←				15 40
Reading 7	a	14 31	14 27	14 58	14 39		14 43	14 45	14 54	15 00	14 58	15 27	15 07	15 19	15 20	15 24	15 31	15 27	15 58	15 39	15 43	15 45
	d	14 32	14 33	15 03			14 44		14 55	15 02	15 03	15 33		15 20	15 20	15 26	15 32	15 33	16 03		15 44	
Twyford 3	a		14 39	→							15 09	→						15 39	→			
Maidenhead 3	a		14 47								15 17							15 47				
Slough 3	a		14 54						15 09		15 24					15 39		15 54				
Ealing Broadway ⊖	a		15 19								15 49							16 19				
London Paddington 15 ⊖	a	15 08	15 32				15 14		15 29	15 32	16 02			15 54	15 54	16 01	16 09	16 31			16 14	

Station		GW ◇1 🛒	GW 1	GW ◇1 D 🛒	GW 1	GW 1	XC ◇1 🍴	CH	GW 1	GW ◇1 🍴	GW 1	GW ◇1 🛒	GW 1	XC ◇1 🍴	GW ◇1 🛒	GW 1	GW ◇1	GW ◇1 🛒	GW 1	GW 1	XC ◇1 🍴	GW ◇1 🛒	GW 1
Birmingham New Street 12	d						14 33							15 04							15 33		
Birmingham International	d													15 14									
Coventry	d													15 25									
Leamington Spa 8	d						15 00							15 38							16 00		
Banbury	d					15 08	15 19							15 55							16 19		
Kings Sutton	d					15 14																	
Heyford	d					15 22																	
Tackley	d					15 27																	
Bicester Town	d							15 30															
Islip	d							15 41															
Oxford	a					15 39	15 41	15 56						16 14							16 40		
	d	15 31			15 37		15 43			16 01			16 07	16 16			16 31			16 37	16 43		
Radley	d				15 43								16 13							16 43			
Culham	d																						
Appleford	d												16 17										
Didcot Parkway	a				15 51								16 24							16 51			
	d			15 53	16 01							16 16	16 31		16 29			16 47		17 05			
Cholsey	d				16 07								16 37							17 11			
Goring & Streatley	d				16 12								16 42							17 16			
Pangbourne	d				16 17								16 47							17 20			
Tilehurst	d				16 21								16 51							17 25			
Bedwyn	d								15 36														16 44
Hungerford	d								15 41													16 39	16 49
Kintbury	d								15 46														16 54
Newbury	a								15 53													16 48	17 03
	d								15 53							16 13						16 48	
Newbury Racecourse	d															16 15							
Thatcham	d								15 58							16 20						16 55	
Midgham	d															16 24							
Aldermaston	d															16 28							
Theale	d								16 06							16 33						17 04	
Reading West	d		←								←					16 40			←				
Reading 7	a	15 54	15 58	16 06	16 27		16 10		16 16	16 24	16 27	16 31	16 59	16 39	16 43	16 45	16 54	17 00	16 59	17 31	17 07	17 15	
	d	15 55	16 03	16 08	16 33				16 19	16 26	16 33	16 34	17 03		16 44		16 55	17 02	17 03	17 33		17 17	
Twyford 3	a		16 09		→						16 39		→						17 09	→			
Maidenhead 3	a		16 17								16 47								17 17			17 28	
Slough 3	a	16 09	16 24							16 39	16 54						17 09		17 24				
Ealing Broadway ⊖	a		16 49								17 21								17 49				
London Paddington 15 ⊖	a	16 27	17 02	16 39					16 57	17 00	17 31	17 09			17 14		17 34	17 30	18 01			17 54	

A 🛒 from Reading ⊘ to Reading
B FO from 6 July until 31 August
C also 29 June, from 7 September until 14 September
D The Cheltenham Spa Express

25 June to 14 September

Birmingham, Banbury, Bicester, Oxford and Bedwyn - Reading and London

Network Diagram - see first Page of Table 116

		GW ■	GW ■ 🛒	GW ◇■ ☕		GW ■	GW ■	XC ◇■ 🛒	CH	GW ■	GW ◇■ ☕	GW ◇■ ☕	GW ■	GW ◇■ ☕		GW ■	XC ◇■ 🛒	GW ■	GW ■	GW ■ 🛒	GW ◇■ ☕	GW ■	GW ■	XC ◇■ 🛒
Birmingham New Street	d							16 04									16 33							17 04
Birmingham International	d							16 14																17 14
Coventry	d							16 25																17 25
Leamington Spa	d							16 38									17 00							17 38
Banbury	d							16 55									17 19	17 23						17 55
Kings Sutton	d																	17 27						
Heyford	d																	17 36						
Tackley	d																	17 40						
Bicester Town	d								16 57															
Islip	d								17 08															
Oxford	a							17 14	17 23								17 39	17 52						18 14
	d	16 47	17 01				17 07	17 16				17 31				17 37	17 43			18 01			18 07	18 16
Radley	d						17 13									17 43							18 13	
Culham	d						17 17																18 17	
Appleford	d															17 47								
Didcot Parkway	a	17 04					17 24									17 54							18 24	
	d			17 16			17 31				17 29			17 53		18 01					18 16		18 31	
Cholsey	d						17 37									18 07							18 37	
Goring & Streatley	d						17 42									18 12							18 42	
Pangbourne	d						17 47									18 17							18 47	
Tilehurst	d						17 51									18 21							18 51	
Bedwyn	d																		17 36					
Hungerford	d																		17 41					
Kintbury	d																		17 46					
Newbury	a																		17 53					
	d									17 13									17 53					
Newbury Racecourse	d									17 15														
Thatcham	d									17 20									17 58					
Midgham	d									17 24														
Aldermaston	d									17 28									18 04					
Theale	d									17 33									18 09					
Reading West	d					←				17 40			←									←		
Reading	a		17 24	17 31		17 31	17 57	17 39		17 45	17 44	17 54	17 57	18 06		18 27	18 09		18 21	18 24	18 31	18 27	19 00	18 39
	d		17 26	17 32		17 33	18 00				17 46	17 56	18 00	18 08		18 33			18 22	18 26	18 32	18 33	19 03	
Twyford	a					17 39	→						18 06			→						18 39	→	
Maidenhead	a					17 47							18 17									18 47		
Slough	a		17 39			17 54						18 10	18 24							18 39		18 54		
Ealing Broadway	⊖ a					18 19							18 49									19 19		
London Paddington	⊖ a		17 59	18 02		18 31					18 14	18 28	19 00	18 39					18 54	18 59	19 02	19 31		

		GW ■	GW ◇■ ☕	GW ■	GW ◇■ A ☕⊘	GW ■	GW ■	XC ◇■ 🛒	CH	GW ■		GW ■	GW ■	GW ◇■ 🛒	GW ■	GW ■	XC ◇■ 🛒	GW ◇■ ☕	GW FO ◇■	GW FX ◇■		GW ■	GW ◇■ ☕	GW ◇■ B ☕	GW ◇■ C ☕
Birmingham New Street	d							17 33									18 04								
Birmingham International	d																18 14								
Coventry	d																18 25								
Leamington Spa	d							18 00									18 38								
Banbury	d							18 19								18 37	18 55								
Kings Sutton	d															18 43									
Heyford	d															18 51									
Tackley	d															18 56									
Bicester Town	d								18 18																
Islip	d								18 29																
Oxford	a							18 40	18 44							19 08	19 14								
	d			18 31			18 37	18 43					19 01	19 06			19 16		19 31	19 31					
Radley	d						18 43						19 07												
Culham	d																								
Appleford	d						18 47																		
Didcot Parkway	a						18 56						19 16												
	d		18 29		18 47		19 01						19 32					19 29					19 47		
Cholsey	d						19 07						19 37												
Goring & Streatley	d						19 12						19 42												
Pangbourne	d						19 17						19 47												
Tilehurst	d						19 21						19 51												
Bedwyn	d	17 55										19 03													
Hungerford	d	18 00										19 08													
Kintbury	d	18 05										19 13													
Newbury	a	18 12										19 22													
	d	18 13								18 53														19 49	19 49
Newbury Racecourse	d	18 15																							
Thatcham	d	18 20								18 58															
Midgham	d	18 24																							
Aldermaston	d	18 28																							
Theale	d	18 33								19 06															
Reading West	d	18 40				←									←							←			
Reading	a	18 45	18 46	18 55	19 01	19 00	19 27	19 07		19 16			19 57	19 32	19 27		19 39	19 44	19 54	19 54		19 57	20 00	20 06	20 06
	d		18 47	18 57	19 02	19 03	19 33			19 18			19 58	19 32	19 33			19 45	19 55	19 55		19 58	20 02	20 08	20 08
Twyford	a					19 09	→						→		19 42							20 04			
Maidenhead	a					19 21									19 50							20 12			
Slough	a			19 09		19 29								19 47	19 57				20 09	20 09		20 19			
Ealing Broadway	⊖ a					19 53									20 22							20 49			
London Paddington	⊖ a		19 14	19 31	19 32	20 02				19 54				20 06	20 31			20 14	20 30	20 31		20 59	20 32	20 39	20 39

A ☕ from Reading ⊘ to Reading

B from 2 July until 31 August. The Atlantic Coast Express

C from 25 June until 29 June, from 3 September until 14 September

25 June to 14 September

Birmingham, Banbury, Bicester, Oxford and Bedwyn - Reading and London

Network Diagram - see first Page of Table 116

		GW ■	XC ◇■ 🛒	GW ◇■ ☕	GW ◇■	GW ■		GW ■	GW ■	GW ■	XC ◇■ 🛒	CH	GW ◇■ ☕	GW ◇■ ☕	GW ■	GW ◇■ ☕		GW ■	GW ■	XC ◇■ 🛒	GW ■	GW ◇■	GW ■	XC ◇■	GW ◇■ ☕
Birmingham New Street	d		18 33								19 04									19 33				20 04	
Birmingham International	d										19 14													20 14	
Coventry	d										19 25													20 25	
Leamington Spa	d		19 00								19 38									20 05				20 38	
Banbury	d		19 19								19 55				20 01					20 23				20 55	
Kings Sutton	d														20 07										
Heyford	d														20 15										
Tackley	d														20 20										
Bicester Town	d											20 00													
Islip	d											20 11													
Oxford	a		19 39								20 14	20 26			20 32					20 40				21 14	
	d	19 37	19 42		20 01					20 07	20 16			20 31					20 37	20 42		21 01		21 16	
Radley	d									20 13															
Culham	d									20 17															
Appleford	d																		20 45						
Didcot Parkway	a	19 49								20 24									20 51						
	d	20 01		20 00						20 31			20 29			20 47			21 01						21 29
Cholsey	d	20 07								20 37									21 08						
Goring & Streatley	d	20 12								20 42									21 13						
Pangbourne	d	20 17								20 47									21 19						
Tilehurst	d	20 21								20 51									21 22						
Bedwyn	d								19 55												20 33				
Hungerford	d								20 00												20 38				
Kintbury	d								20 05												20 43				
Newbury	a								20 12												20 50				
	d							19 55	20 12												20 50				
Newbury Racecourse	d							19 57													20 52				
Thatcham	d							20 02	20 17												20 57				
Midgham	d							20 06													21 02				
Aldermaston	d							20 10													21 05				
Theale	d							20 15	20 25												21 10				
Reading West	d					←		20 21										←			21 17		←		
Reading	a	20 27	20 10	20 14	20 24	20 27		20 27	20 34	20 58	20 39		20 44	20 54		21 00		20 58	21 29	21 07	21 22	21 24	21 29	21 40	21 43
	d	20 33		20 15	20 26	20 33			20 34	21 14			20 45	20 55		21 02		21 14	21 33			21 26	21 33		21 44
Twyford	a	→				20 39				→								21 20	→				21 39		
Maidenhead	a					20 47												21 28					21 47		
Slough	a				20 39	20 54								21 09				21 40				21 39	21 58		
Ealing Broadway	⊖ a					21 19												22 04					22 21		
London Paddington	⊖ a			20 46	21 01	21 31			21 08				21 14	21 29		21 32		22 16				22 00	22 33		22 14

		GW ■		GW ■	GW ◇■	GW ◇■ ☕	GW FX ◇■ ☕	GW FO ◇■ ☕	XC ◇■	GW ■	CH	GW ◇		XC ◇■	GW ■	GW FO ◇■	GW FX ◇■	GW ◇■ ☕	GW ■	GW FX ■	GW FO ■	GW ◇■		GW ■	GW ◇■ ☕
Birmingham New Street	d								20 33					21 04											
Birmingham International	d													21 14											
Coventry	d													21 25											
Leamington Spa	d								21 00					21 38											
Banbury	d								21 19			21 38		21 55						22 25	22 25				
Kings Sutton	d											21 42								22 31	22 31				
Heyford	d											21 51								22 38	22 39				
Tackley	d											21 55								22 44	22 44				
Bicester Town	d										21 30														
Islip	d										21 41														
Oxford	a								21 40		21 56	22 05		22 14						22 56	22 56				
	d			21 21	21 32				21 43	21 51		22 11		22 16		22 34	22 34		22 52			23 09			
Radley	d			21 27						21 57									22 58						
Culham	d			21 31															23 02						
Appleford	d																		23 04						
Didcot Parkway	a			21 38						22 06		22 24							23 11			23 23			
	d			21 44			21 53	21 53		22 08		22 27						22 52	23 11			23 23			23 35
Cholsey	d			21 50						22 14									23 18						
Goring & Streatley	d			21 55						22 19									23 23						
Pangbourne	d			21 59						22 24									23 26						
Tilehurst	d			22 02						22 27									23 30						
Bedwyn	d	21 06													21 55									23 00	
Hungerford	d	21 11													22 00									23 05	
Kintbury	d	21 16													22 05									23 10	
Newbury	a	21 23													22 12									23 17	
	d	21 23				21 42									22 13									23 17	
Newbury Racecourse	d	21 25													22 15									23 19	
Thatcham	d	21 30													22 20									23 24	
Midgham	d	21 35													22 24									23 29	
Aldermaston	d	21 38													22 28									23 32	
Theale	d	21 43													22 33									23 37	
Reading West	d	21 50													22 40									23 44	
Reading	a	21 55		22 12	21 55	21 59	22 11	22 11	22 17	22 37		22 44		22 41	22 45	22 58	22 58	23 06	23 40			23 40		23 49	23 53
	d				21 56	22 01	22 12	22 12				22 44				22 59	22 59	23 08				23 41			23 55
Twyford	a																								
Maidenhead	a																					23 54			
Slough	a				22 13							23 01				23 12	23 15					00 01			
Ealing Broadway	⊖ a																								
London Paddington	⊖ a				22 39	22 30	22 44	22 45				23 25				23 36	23 36	23 41				00 28			00 33

Birmingham, Banbury, Bicester, Oxford and Bedwyn - Reading and London

Mondays to Fridays
25 June to 14 September

Network Diagram - see first Page of Table 116

		XC	CH	GW	CH
			FO		
		◇1		1	
Birmingham New Street 12	d	22 04			
Birmingham International	d				
Coventry	d				
Leamington Spa 8	d	22 53			23 38
Banbury	d	23 16		23 45	23 57
Kings Sutton	d			23 50	
Heyford	d			23 58	
Tackley	d			00 03	
Bicester Town	d		23 42		
Islip	d		23 53		
Oxford	a	23 35	00 08	00 13	00 22
	d	23 36		00 27	
Radley	d			00 33	
Culham	d			00 37	
Appleford	d			00 39	
Didcot Parkway	a			00 46	
	d			00 46	
Cholsey	d			00 52	
Goring & Streatley	d			00 57	
Pangbourne	d			01 01	
Tilehurst	d			01 06	
Bedwyn	d				
Hungerford	d				
Kintbury	d				
Newbury	a				
	d				
Newbury Racecourse	d				
Thatcham	d				
Midgham	d				
Aldermaston	d				
Theale	d				
Reading West	d				
Reading 7	a	00 07		01 12	
	d			01 15	
Twyford 8	a			01 21	
Maidenhead 8	a			01 29	
Slough 8	a			01 37	
Ealing Broadway ⊖	a			01 53	
London Paddington 15 ⊖	a			02 05	

Mondays to Fridays
from 17 September

		GW	GW	GW	GW	GW	GW	GW	GW	GW	GW	GW	GW	CH	GW	GW	GW	GW	GW	GW	GW	GW	GW
		MO	MO	MO	MO	MX	MX	MO	MO	MO	MX	MO	MX	MX	MO	MX	MO	MO					
		◇1	◇1	◇1	◇1	◇1	◇1	1	1		◇1	◇1	1			1	1	1	1	◇1	1	1	1
		A	B	B	A												C	D					
				☕	☕		☕			🚌					🚌					☕			
Birmingham New Street 12	d																						
Birmingham International	d																						
Coventry	d																						
Leamington Spa 8	d													23p38									
Banbury	d												23p45	23p57									
Kings Sutton	d												23p50										
Heyford	d												23p58										
Tackley	d												00 03										
Bicester Town	d																						
Islip	d																						
Oxford	a												00 13	00 21									
	d	22p46	22p46			23p09				00 05	00 07		00 27		03 38	04 00			05 03		05 24		05 43
Radley	d												00 33						05 09				05 49
Culham	d												00 37										
Appleford	d												00 39										
Didcot Parkway	a	22p58	22p58			23p23				00 30	00 20		00 46		04 03	04 12			05 17		05 36		05 58
	d	22p59	22p59	23p11	23p11	23p23	23p35	23p50			00 21	00 35	00 46			04 12	04 12	04 12	05 18	05 41	05 46		06 00
Cholsey	d							23p56					00 52			04 18	04 18	04 18	05 23		05 52		
Goring & Streatley	d							00 01					00 57			04 23	04 23	04 23	05 28		05 57		
Pangbourne	d												01 01			04 28	04 28	04 28	05 33		06 02		
Tilehurst	d							00 08					01 06			04 32	04 32	04 32	05 37		06 06		
Bedwyn	d																						
Hungerford	d																						
Kintbury	d																						
Newbury	a																						
	d								23p45													05 40	
Newbury Racecourse	d								23p47													05 42	
Thatcham	d								23p52													05 47	
Midgham	d								23p57													05 51	
Aldermaston	d								00 01													05 55	
Theale	d								00 06													06 00	
Reading West	d								00s13													06 07	
Reading 7	a	23p17	23p17	23p28	23p28	23p40	23p53	00 15	00 17		00 38	00 52	01 12			04 38	04 38	04 39	05 43	05 56	06 12	06 12	06 16
	d	23p22	23p22	23p30	23p30	23p41	23p55	00 15			00 39	00 53	01 15			04 39	04 39	04 39	05 44	05 57	06 15		06 16
Twyford 8	a							00 22				01 00	01 21			04 45	04 45	04 46	05 50		06 21		06 23
Maidenhead 8	a					23p54		00 30				01 07	01 29			04 53	04 53	04 54	05 58		06 28		06 31
Slough 8	a	23p43	23p43			00 01		00 37			00 55	01 17	01 37			05 00	05 00	05 02	06 10		06 40		
Ealing Broadway ⊖	a							01 00				01 34	01 53			05 25	05 25	05 26	06 35		07 05		
London Paddington 15 ⊖	a	00 05	00 06	00 12	00 13	00 28	00 33	01 12			01 17	01 43	02 05			05 41	05 41	05 41	06 46	06 24	07 17		06 54

A from 29 October
B from 17 September until 22 October
C from 17 September until 15 October
D from 22 October

Table 116

Birmingham, Banbury, Bicester, Oxford and Bedwyn - Reading and London

Mondays to Fridays
from 17 September

Network Diagram - see first Page of Table 116

		GW	GW	GW	GW	GW	GW	GW	GW	GW	GW	GW	GW	GW	GW	GW	GW	CH	GW	GW	GW	GW	GW
		1	◇1	1	1	◇1	1	1	1	◇1	1	◇1	1	1	◇1	◇1	1		◇1	1	◇1	1	◇1
						☕				☕		☕			☕	☕			☕				☕
Birmingham New Street 12	d																						
Birmingham International	d																						
Coventry	d																						
Leamington Spa 8	d																						
Banbury	d																06 07						
Kings Sutton	d																06 11						
Heyford	d																06 21						
Tackley	d																06 25						
Bicester Town	d																	06 17					
Islip	d																	06 28					
Oxford	a																06 35	06 43					
	d		05 59					06 07		06 27							06 36		06 56				
Radley	d							06 13									06 42						
Culham	d							06 17									06 46						
Appleford	d							06 19									06 48						
Didcot Parkway	a		06 12					06 25		06 39							06 56		07 07				
	d		06 13		06 20	06 30		06 31	06 37	06 39		06 47			06 59		07 01		07 09		07 14		07 20
Cholsey	d				06 25			06 37	06 43								07 07				07 20		
Goring & Streatley	d				06 30			06 42	06 48								07 12				07 26		
Pangbourne	d				06 35			06 47	06 53								07 17				07 33		
Tilehurst	d				06 40			06 51	06 58								07 21				07 40		
Bedwyn	d			05 55									06 13										
Hungerford	d			06 01									06 18			06 40							
Kintbury	d			06 05									06 23										
Newbury	a			06 12									06 30			06 49							
	d	05 58		06 12									06 30			06 50				06 56			
Newbury Racecourse	d												06 32							06 58			
Thatcham	d	06 02		06 17									06 37			06 57				07 03			
Midgham	d												06 42							07 07			
Aldermaston	d												06 45							07 11			
Theale	d	06 10		06 25									06 50			07 07				07 16			
Reading West	d	06 17		06 32			←				←		06 57	←						07 23		←	
Reading 7	a	06 21	06 30	06 36	06 46	06 43	06 46	06 58	07 05	06 54	06 58	07 00	07 02	07 05	07 14	07 19	07 28		07 25	07 29		07 28	07 34
	d	06 22	06 31	06 36	06 46	06 44	06 46	06 59	07 07	06 56	06 59	07 01		07 07	07 16	07 21	07 30		07 27			07 30	07 36
Twyford 8	a			06 43	→		06 53	→	→		07 05						→					07 37	
Maidenhead 8	a		06 42				07 02			07 07	07 13			07 18							07 59	07 45	
Slough 8	a	06 40	06 50			06 58					07 20											07 55	
Ealing Broadway ⊖	a																					08 18	
London Paddington 15 ⊖	a	07 01	07 08	07 14		07 16	07 29			07 30	07 49	07 32		07 43	07 44	07 53			07 59		08 26	08 32	08 07

		GW	GW	XC	GW	GW	GW	GW	GW	GW	GW	XC	GW	GW	GW	GW	GW	GW	GW	GW	XC	GW
		◇1	1	◇1	◇1	1	1	1	◇1	◇1	◇1	◇1	◇1	◇1	1	◇1	1	1	1	1	◇1	◇1
											A					A						B
		☕		T	☕				T	☕	☕⊘		☕	☕		☕⊘					T	☕
Birmingham New Street 12	d			06 04								06 33									07 04	
Birmingham International	d			06 14																	07 14	
Coventry	d			06 25																	07 25	
Leamington Spa 8	d			06 38								07 00									07 38	
Banbury	d		06 27	06 57								07 22							07 26		07 55	
Kings Sutton	d		06 33																07 31			
Heyford	d		06 41																07 40			
Tackley	d		06 46																07 44			
Bicester Town	d																					
Islip	d																					
Oxford	a		06 58	07 14								07 41							07 55		08 14	
	d		07 00	07 16				07 21	07 33			07 43				07 52			07 56	08 06	08 16	
Radley	d		07 06					07 27											08 02			
Culham	d		07 10					07 31											08 06			
Appleford	d		07 12					07 33											08 09			
Didcot Parkway	a		07 19					07 40											08 15	08 18		
	d		07 28		07 29			07 49		07 47			07 55	08 01					08 15	08 20		08 29
Cholsey	d		07 34					07 55											08 22			
Goring & Streatley	d		07 39					08 00											08 27			
Pangbourne	d		07 44					08 04											08 32			
Tilehurst	d		07 48					08 09											08 37			
Bedwyn	d	06 47					07 07											07 56				
Hungerford	d	06 54					07 12				07 34							08 01				
Kintbury	d	07 00					07 17											08 06				
Newbury	a	07 08					07 24				07 46							08 14				
	d	07 09					07 24				07 49						07 55					
Newbury Racecourse	d						07 26										07 57					
Thatcham	d	07 16					07 32										08 02					
Midgham	d						07 36										08 07					
Aldermaston	d						07 40										08 10					
Theale	d	07 25					07 45										08 16					
Reading West	d	07 34				←	07 52								←		08 23					
Reading 7	a	07 37	07 53	07 39	07 43	07 53	07 56	08 17	07 57	08 00	08 06	08 10	08 12	08 16	08 17	08 21	08 27		08 46	08 35	08 39	08 44
	d	07 39	07 55		07 45	07 55		08 19	07 58	08 02	08 08		08 14	08 17	08 19	08 23			08 48	08 35		08 45
Twyford 8	a		→			08 02		→							08 25				→			
Maidenhead 8	a					08 10									08 33							
Slough 8	a					08 20																
Ealing Broadway ⊖	a																					
London Paddington 15 ⊖	a	08 09			08 14	08 48			08 31	08 33	08 38		08 40	08 44	08 58	08 51				09 06		09 14

A ☕ from Reading ⊘ to Reading
B The Bristolian

Birmingham, Banbury, Bicester, Oxford and Bedwyn - Reading and London

Network Diagram - see first Page of Table 116

Station		GW ■	GW ◇■ 🛒	GW ■	CH	GW ◇■ A 🛒⊘	GW ■	GW ◇■ 🛒	GW ■	GW ■	XC ◇■	GW ◇■ 🛒	GW ◇■ B 🛒⊘	GW ■	GW ■	GW ◇■	GW ■	XC ◇■ 🍴	GW ◇■ 🛒	GW ■	GW ◇■	GW ■	CH
Birmingham New Street 12	d										07 33							08 04					
Birmingham International	d																	08 14					
Coventry	d																	08 25					
Leamington Spa 8	d										08 04							08 38					
Banbury	d										08 21							08 55					
Kings Sutton	d																						
Heyford	d																						
Tackley	d																						
Bicester Town	d				08 02																		09 07
Islip	d				08 13																		09 18
Oxford	a				08 28						08 41							09 14					09 32
	d			08 21						08 37	08 44		08 51			09 01	09 07	09 16			09 31		
Radley	d			08 27													09 13						
Culham	d																09 17						
Appleford	d									08 45													
Didcot Parkway	a			08 36						08 51						09 14	09 24						
	d			08 37		08 47		08 53		09 01		08 59				09 15	09 31		09 29				
Cholsey	d			08 43						09 07							09 37						
Goring & Streatley	d			08 48						09 12							09 42						
Pangbourne	d			08 53						09 17							09 47						
Tilehurst	d			08 57						09 21							09 51						
Bedwyn	d													08 41									
Hungerford	d													08 46									
Kintbury	d													08 51									
Newbury	a													08 58									
	d		08 29						08 38					08 58						09 22			
Newbury Racecourse	d								08 40											09 25			
Thatcham	d								08 45					09 03						09 30			
Midgham	d								08 49											09 34			
Aldermaston	d								08 53											09 38			
Theale	d								08 58					09 11						09 43			
Reading West	d	←					←		09 05						←					09 50		←	
Reading 7	a	08 46	08 50	09 03		09 01	09 03	09 07	09 10	09 28	09 11	09 14	09 14	09 20	09 28	09 32	09 57	09 39	09 44	09 54	09 54	09 57	
	d	08 48	08 52	09 03		09 02	09 03	09 08		09 33		09 16	09 18	09 21	09 33	09 37	10 03		09 46		09 55	10 03	
Twyford 3	a	08 54		→			09 09			→					09 39		→					10 09	
Maidenhead 3	a	09 02					09 17								09 47							10 17	
Slough 3	a						09 29								09 54	09 52					10 10	10 24	
Ealing Broadway ⊖	a						09 54								10 19							10 49	
London Paddington 15 ⊖	a	09 27	09 21			09 29	10 03	09 39				09 44	09 47	09 56	10 31	10 12			10 15		10 30	11 01	

Station		GW ◇■ 🛒	GW ■	XC ◇■ 🍴	GW ■	GW ◇■ 🍴	GW ◇■ 🛒	GW ■	GW ■	XC ◇■ 🍴	GW ■	GW ◇■ 🛒	GW ◇■	GW ◇■ C 🛒	GW ■	GW ■	XC ◇■ 🍴	CH	GW ■	GW ◇■ 🍴	GW ◇■ 🛒	GW ■
Birmingham New Street 12	d			08 33						09 04							09 33					
Birmingham International	d									09 14												
Coventry	d									09 25												
Leamington Spa 8	d			09 00						09 38							10 00					
Banbury	d			09 19					09 39	09 55							10 19					
Kings Sutton	d								09 45													
Heyford	d								09 53													
Tackley	d								09 58													
Bicester Town	d																	10 30				
Islip	d																	10 41				
Oxford	a			09 41					10 08	10 14							10 41	10 56				
	d		09 36	09 43		10 01			10 08	10 16			10 31			10 36	10 43			11 01		
Radley	d								10 14													
Culham	d																					
Appleford	d		09 44													10 44						
Didcot Parkway	a		09 50						10 23							10 51						
	d	09 53	10 01				10 16		10 31			10 29		10 47		11 01					11 17	
Cholsey	d		10 07						10 37							11 07						
Goring & Streatley	d		10 12						10 42							11 12						
Pangbourne	d		10 17						10 47							11 17						
Tilehurst	d		10 21						10 51							11 21						
Bedwyn	d				09 36														10 38			
Hungerford	d				09 41														10 43			
Kintbury	d				09 46														10 48			
Newbury	a				09 53														10 55			
	d				09 53						10 13								10 55			
Newbury Racecourse	d										10 15											
Thatcham	d				09 58						10 20								11 00			
Midgham	d										10 24											
Aldermaston	d										10 28											
Theale	d				10 06						10 33								11 08			
Reading West	d							←			10 40				←							←
Reading 7	a	10 06	10 28	10 10	10 16	10 25	10 31	10 28	10 58	10 39	10 45	10 44	10 54	11 00	10 58	11 28	11 07		11 20	11 24	11 30	11 28
	d	10 08	10 33		10 18	10 26	10 32	10 33	11 03			10 45	10 55	11 02	11 03	11 33			11 20	11 26	11 32	11 33
Twyford 3	a		→					10 39	→						11 09	→						11 39
Maidenhead 3	a							10 47							11 17							11 47
Slough 3	a					10 39		10 54					11 09		11 24					11 39		11 54
Ealing Broadway ⊖	a							11 18							11 49							12 19
London Paddington 15 ⊖	a	10 37			10 56	11 00	11 07	11 32				11 14	11 29	11 32	12 01				11 54	11 59	12 00	12 31

A 🛒 from Reading ⊘ to Reading

B The Cathedrals Express. 🛒 from Reading ⊘ to Reading

C The Red Dragon

Table 116

Mondays to Fridays

from 17 September

Birmingham, Banbury, Bicester, Oxford and Bedwyn - Reading and London

Network Diagram - see first Page of Table 116

Station		GW ■	XC ◇■ 🍴	GW ◇■ 🛒	GW ■	GW ◇■ 🍴	GW ■	GW ◇■ 🛒	GW ■	XC ◇■ 🍴	CH	GW ■	GW ◇■ 🍴	GW ◇■ 🛒	GW ■	GW ■	XC ◇■ 🍴	GW ■	GW ◇■ 🛒	GW ◇■ 🍴	GW ◇■ 🛒	GW ■	GW ■
Birmingham New Street 12	d		10 04							10 33							11 04						
Birmingham International	d		10 14														11 14						
Coventry	d		10 25														11 25						
Leamington Spa 8	d		10 38							11 00							11 38						
Banbury	d		10 55							11 19							11 55						
Kings Sutton	d																						
Heyford	d																						
Tackley	d																						
Bicester Town	d										11 30												
Islip	d										11 41												
Oxford	a		11 14							11 40	11 56						12 14						
	d	11 07	11 16			11 31			11 37	11 43			12 01			12 07	12 16			12 31			12 37
Radley	d	11 13														12 13							
Culham	d																						
Appleford	d															12 17							
Didcot Parkway	a	11 22							11 51							12 24							12 49
	d	11 31		11 29				11 53	12 01					12 16		12 31			12 29		12 47		13 01
Cholsey	d	11 37							12 07							12 37							13 07
Goring & Streatley	d	11 42							12 12							12 42							13 12
Pangbourne	d	11 47							12 17							12 47							13 17
Tilehurst	d	11 51							12 21							12 51							13 21
Bedwyn	d											11 38											
Hungerford	d											11 43											
Kintbury	d											11 48											
Newbury	a											11 55											
	d				11 13							11 55						12 13					
Newbury Racecourse	d				11 15													12 15					
Thatcham	d				11 20							12 00						12 20					
Midgham	d				11 24													12 24					
Aldermaston	d				11 28													12 28					
Theale	d				11 33							12 08						12 33					
Reading West	d				11 40		←								←			12 40				←	
Reading 7	a	11 58	11 39	11 43	11 45	11 54	11 58	12 06	12 27	12 10		12 17	12 24	12 30	12 27	12 57	12 39	12 45	12 44	12 54	13 00	12 57	13 29
	d	12 03		11 44		11 55	12 03	12 08	12 33			12 18	12 26	12 32	12 33	13 03			12 45	12 55	13 02	13 03	13 33
Twyford 3	a	→					12 09		→						12 39	→						13 09	→
Maidenhead 3	a						12 17								12 47							13 17	
Slough 3	a					12 09	12 24						12 39		12 54					13 09		13 24	
Ealing Broadway ⊖	a						12 49								13 19							13 49	
London Paddington 15 ⊖	a			12 14		12 29	13 02	12 37				12 54	13 06	13 00	13 31				13 14	13 29	13 32	14 01	

Station		XC ◇■ 🍴	GW ◇■ 🍴	GW ■	GW ◇■ 🛒	GW ■	GW ■	GW ■	XC ◇■ 🍴	GW ◇■ 🛒	GW ■	GW ◇■ 🍴	GW ■	GW ◇■ 🛒	GW ■	XC ◇■ 🍴	GW ◇■ 🛒	GW ◇■ 🍴	GW ◇■ 🛒	GW ■	GW ■	XC ◇■ 🍴	CH
Birmingham New Street 12	d	11 33							12 04							12 33						13 04	
Birmingham International	d								12 14													13 14	
Coventry	d								12 25													13 25	
Leamington Spa 8	d	12 00							12 38							13 00						13 38	
Banbury	d	12 19						12 42	12 55							13 21						13 55	
Kings Sutton	d							12 48															
Heyford	d							12 56															
Tackley	d							13 01															
Bicester Town	d																						14 00
Islip	d																						14 11
Oxford	a	12 40						13 11	13 14							13 40						14 14	14 28
	d	12 43	13 01				13 07		13 16			13 31			13 37	13 43		14 01			14 07	14 16	
Radley	d						13 13														14 13		
Culham	d						13 17																
Appleford	d																				14 17		
Didcot Parkway	a						13 24								13 49						14 24		
	d				13 16		13 31			13 29				13 53	14 01				14 16		14 31		
Cholsey	d						13 37								14 07						14 37		
Goring & Streatley	d						13 42								14 12						14 42		
Pangbourne	d						13 47								14 17						14 47		
Tilehurst	d						13 51								14 21						14 51		
Bedwyn	d			12 38													13 32						
Hungerford	d			12 43													13 39						
Kintbury	d			12 48																			
Newbury	a			12 55													13 48						
	d			13 03							13 13						13 48						
Newbury Racecourse	d										13 15												
Thatcham	d			13 08							13 20						13 55						
Midgham	d										13 24												
Aldermaston	d										13 28												
Theale	d			13 16							13 33						14 04						
Reading West	d					←					13 40		←							←			
Reading 7	a	13 07	13 24	13 27	13 31	13 29	13 58		13 39	13 43	13 45	13 54	13 58	14 06	14 27	14 10	14 15	14 24	14 31	14 27	14 58	14 39	
	d		13 26	13 29	13 32	13 33	14 03			13 44		13 55	14 03	14 08	14 33		14 17	14 26	14 32	14 33	15 03		
Twyford 3	a					13 39	→						14 09		→					14 39	→		
Maidenhead 3	a					13 47							14 17							14 47			
Slough 3	a		13 39			13 54						14 09	14 24					14 39		14 54			
Ealing Broadway ⊖	a					14 19							14 49							15 19			
London Paddington 15 ⊖	a		14 01	14 09	14 06	14 31				14 14		14 29	15 01	14 37			14 44	15 00	15 08	15 32			

Birmingham, Banbury, Bicester, Oxford and Bedwyn - Reading and London

Network Diagram - see first Page of Table 116

		GW		GW	GW	GW	GW	GW	XC	GW	GW	GW		GW	GW	XC	GW	GW	GW	GW	GW	GW		GW	XC
		◇1		1	◇1	◇1	1	1	◇1	1	◇1	◇1		1	1	◇1	◇1	1	◇1	1	◇1	1		1	◇1
		☕				A ☕⊘			🛒		🛒	☕				🛒	☕		☕		B ☕				🛒
Birmingham New Street 12	d								13 33							14 04									14 33
Birmingham International	d															14 14									
Coventry	d															14 25									
Leamington Spa 8	d								14 00							14 38									15 00
Banbury	d								14 19							14 55								15 08	15 19
Kings Sutton	d																							15 14	
Heyford	d																							15 22	
Tackley	d																							15 27	
Bicester Town	d																								
Islip	d																								
Oxford	a								14 40							15 14								15 39	15 41
	d				14 31			14 37	14 43		15 01				15 07	15 16			15 31			15 37			15 43
Radley	d														15 13							15 43			
Culham	d														15 17										
Appleford	d																								
Didcot Parkway	a							14 51							15 24							15 51			
	d	14 29				14 47		15 01				15 16			15 31		15 29				15 53	16 01			
Cholsey	d							15 07							15 37							16 07			
Goring & Streatley	d							15 12							15 42							16 12			
Pangbourne	d							15 17							15 47							16 17			
Tilehurst	d							15 21							15 51							16 21			
Bedwyn	d									14 38															
Hungerford	d									14 43															
Kintbury	d									14 48															
Newbury	a									14 55															
	d			14 13						14 55								15 13							
Newbury Racecourse	d			14 15														15 15							
Thatcham	d			14 20						15 00								15 20							
Midgham	d			14 24														15 24							
Aldermaston	d			14 28														15 28							
Theale	d			14 33						15 08								15 33							
Reading West	d			14 40			←							←				15 40		←					
Reading 7	a	14 43		14 45	14 54	15 00	14 58	15 27	15 07	15 20	15 24	15 31		15 27	15 58	15 39	15 43	15 45	15 54	15 58	16 06	16 27			16 10
	d	14 44			14 55	15 02	15 03	15 33		15 20	15 26	15 32		15 33	16 03		15 44		15 55	16 03	16 08	16 33			
Twyford 3	a						15 09	→						15 39	→					16 09		→			
Maidenhead 3	a						15 17							15 47						16 17					
Slough 3	a				15 09		15 24				15 39			15 54					16 09	16 24					
Ealing Broadway ⊖	a						15 49							16 19						16 49					
London Paddington 15 ⊖	a	15 14			15 29	15 32	16 02			15 54	16 01	16 09		16 31			16 14		16 27	17 02	16 39				

		CH	GW	GW	GW	GW	GW	XC		GW	GW	GW	GW	GW	GW	XC	GW	GW		GW	GW	GW	GW	GW	XC
			1	◇1	1	◇1	1	◇1		◇1	1	◇1	◇1	1	1	◇1	◇1	1			1	◇1	1	1	◇1
				🛒		☕		🛒		☕			☕			🛒	☕				🛒	☕			🛒
Birmingham New Street 12	d							15 04								15 33									16 04
Birmingham International	d							15 14																	16 14
Coventry	d							15 25																	16 25
Leamington Spa 8	d							15 38								16 00									16 38
Banbury	d							15 55								16 19									16 55
Kings Sutton	d																								
Heyford	d																								
Tackley	d																								
Bicester Town	d	15 30																							
Islip	d	15 41																							
Oxford	a	15 56						16 14								16 40									17 14
	d			16 01			16 07	16 16				16 31			16 37	16 43				16 51	17 01			17 06	17 16
Radley	d						16 13								16 43									17 12	
Culham	d																							17 16	
Appleford	d						16 17																		
Didcot Parkway	a						16 24								16 51					17 04				17 23	
	d					16 16	16 31			16 29			16 47		17 05							17 16		17 31	
Cholsey	d						16 37								17 11									17 37	
Goring & Streatley	d						16 42								17 16									17 42	
Pangbourne	d						16 47								17 20									17 47	
Tilehurst	d						16 51								17 25									17 51	
Bedwyn	d		15 36															16 44							
Hungerford	d		15 41														16 39	16 49							
Kintbury	d		15 46															16 54							
Newbury	a		15 53														16 48	17 03							
	d		15 53								16 13						16 48								
Newbury Racecourse	d										16 15														
Thatcham	d		15 58								16 20						16 55								
Midgham	d										16 24														
Aldermaston	d										16 28														
Theale	d		16 06								16 33						17 04								
Reading West	d				←						16 40			←										←	
Reading 7	a		16 16	16 24	16 27	16 31	16 59	16 39		16 43	16 45	16 54	17 00	16 59	17 31	17 07	17 15				17 24	17 31	17 31	17 57	17 39
	d		16 19	16 26	16 33	16 34	17 03			16 44		16 55	17 02	17 03	17 33		17 17				17 26	17 32	17 33	18 00	
Twyford 3	a				16 39		→							17 09	→								17 39	→	
Maidenhead 3	a				16 47									17 17			17 28						17 47		
Slough 3	a			16 39	16 54							17 09		17 24							17 39		17 54		
Ealing Broadway ⊖	a				17 21									17 49									18 19		
London Paddington 15 ⊖	a		16 57	17 00	17 31	17 09				17 14		17 34	17 30	18 01			17 54				17 59	18 02	18 31		

A ☕ from Reading ⊘ to Reading

B The Cheltenham Spa Express

Birmingham, Banbury, Bicester, Oxford and Bedwyn - Reading and London

Network Diagram - see first Page of Table 116

		CH	GW	GW		GW	GW	GW	GW	XC	GW	GW	GW	GW		GW	GW	XC	GW	GW	GW	GW	GW	GW	
			1	◇1		◇1	1	◇1	1	◇1	1	1	1	◇1		1	1	◇1	1	◇1	1	◇1	1	1	
				☕		☕		☕		🛒			🛒	☕				🛒		☕		A ☕⊘			
Birmingham New Street 12	d									16 33								17 04							
Birmingham International	d																	17 14							
Coventry	d																	17 25							
Leamington Spa 8	d									17 00								17 38							
Banbury	d									17 19	17 23							17 55							
Kings Sutton	d										17 27														
Heyford	d										17 36														
Tackley	d										17 40														
Bicester Town	d	16 57																							
Islip	d	17 08																							
Oxford	a	17 23								17 39	17 52							18 14							
	d					17 31			17 37	17 43			18 01				18 07	18 16			18 31			18 37	
Radley	d								17 43								18 13							18 43	
Culham	d																18 17								
Appleford	d								17 47															18 47	
Didcot Parkway	a								17 54								18 24							18 56	
	d			17 29				17 53	18 01					18 16			18 31			18 29		18 47		19 01	
Cholsey	d								18 07								18 37							19 07	
Goring & Streatley	d								18 12								18 42							19 12	
Pangbourne	d								18 17								18 47							19 17	
Tilehurst	d								18 21								18 51							19 21	
Bedwyn	d											17 36							17 55						
Hungerford	d											17 41							18 00						
Kintbury	d											17 46							18 05						
Newbury	a											17 53							18 12						
	d		17 13									17 53							18 13						
Newbury Racecourse	d		17 15																18 15						
Thatcham	d		17 20									17 58							18 20						
Midgham	d		17 24																18 24						
Aldermaston	d		17 28									18 04							18 28						
Theale	d		17 33									18 09							18 33						
Reading West	d		17 40				←									←			18 40				←		
Reading 7	a		17 45	17 44		17 54	17 57	18 06	18 27	18 09		18 21	18 24	18 31		18 27	19 00	18 39	18 45	18 46	18 55	19 01	19 00	19 27	
	d			17 46		17 56	18 00	18 08	18 33			18 22	18 26	18 32		18 33	19 03			18 47	18 57	19 02	19 03	19 33	
Twyford 3	a						18 06		→							18 39	→						19 09	→	
Maidenhead 3	a						18 17									18 47							19 21		
Slough 3	a					18 10	18 24						18 39			18 54					19 09		19 29		
Ealing Broadway ⊖	a						18 41									19 19							19 53		
London Paddington 15 ⊖	a			18 14		18 28	18 52	18 39				18 54	18 59	19 02		19 33				19 14	19 31	19 32	20 02		

		XC	CH	GW	GW	GW	GW	GW	GW	XC		GW	GW	GW	GW	GW	GW	XC	GW	GW		GW	GW	GW	GW
		◇1		1	1	1	◇1	1	1	◇1		◇1	◇1	1	◇1	◇1	1	◇1	◇1	◇1		1	1	1	1
		🛒					🛒			🛒		☕			☕	☕		🛒	☕						
Birmingham New Street 12	d	17 33								18 04								18 33							
Birmingham International	d									18 14															
Coventry	d									18 25															
Leamington Spa 8	d	18 00								18 38								19 00							
Banbury	d	18 19							18 37	18 55								19 19							
Kings Sutton	d								18 43																
Heyford	d								18 51																
Tackley	d								18 56																
Bicester Town	d		18 18																						
Islip	d		18 29																						
Oxford	a	18 40	18 44						19 08	19 14								19 39							
	d	18 43				19 01	19 06			19 16			19 31				19 37	19 42		20 01					20 07
Radley	d					19 07																			20 13
Culham	d																								20 17
Appleford	d																								
Didcot Parkway	a					19 16											19 49								20 24
	d					19 32						19 29			19 47		20 01		20 00						20 31
Cholsey	d					19 37											20 07								20 37
Goring & Streatley	d					19 42											20 12								20 42
Pangbourne	d					19 47											20 17								20 47
Tilehurst	d					19 51											20 21								20 51
Bedwyn	d				19 03																			19 55	
Hungerford	d				19 08																			20 00	
Kintbury	d				19 13																			20 05	
Newbury	a				19 22																			20 12	
	d			18 53												19 49							19 55	20 12	
Newbury Racecourse	d																						19 57		
Thatcham	d			18 58																			20 02	20 17	
Midgham	d																						20 06		
Aldermaston	d																						20 10		
Theale	d			19 06																			20 15	20 25	
Reading West	d							←						←								←	20 21		
Reading 7	a	19 07		19 16		19 57	19 32	19 27		19 39		19 44	19 54	19 57	20 00	20 06	20 27	20 10	20 14	20 24		20 27	20 27	20 34	20 58
	d			19 18		19 58	19 32	19 33				19 45	19 55	19 58	20 02	20 08	20 33		20 15	20 26		20 33		20 34	21 14
Twyford 3	a					→		19 42						20 04			→					20 39			→
Maidenhead 3	a							19 50						20 12								20 47			
Slough 3	a						19 47	19 57					20 09	20 19						20 39		20 54			
Ealing Broadway ⊖	a							20 22						20 49								21 19			
London Paddington 15 ⊖	a			19 54			20 06	20 31				20 14	20 30	20 59	20 32	20 39			20 46	21 01		21 30		21 07	

A ☕ from Reading ⊘ to Reading

Birmingham, Banbury, Bicester, Oxford and Bedwyn - Reading and London

Network Diagram - see first Page of Table 116

		XC	CH	GW	GW	GW		GW	GW	GW	XC	GW	GW	GW	XC	GW		GW	GW	GW	GW FX	GW FO	XC	GW	CH
		◇1 🍴		◇1 ☕	◇1 ☕	1		◇1 ☕	1	1	◇1 🍴	1	◇1	1	◇1	◇1 ☕		1	◇1 ☕	1	◇1 ☕	◇1 ☕	◇1	1	
Birmingham New Street 12	d	19 04									19 33				20 04								20 33		
Birmingham International	d	19 14													20 14										
Coventry	d	19 25													20 25										
Leamington Spa 8	d	19 38									20 05				20 38								21 00		
Banbury	d	19 55				20 01					20 23				20 55								21 19		
Kings Sutton	d					20 07																			
Heyford	d					20 15																			
Tackley	d					20 20																			
Bicester Town	d		20 00																						21 30
Islip	d		20 11																						21 41
Oxford	a	20 14	20 26			20 32					20 40				21 14								21 40		21 56
	d	20 16			20 31					20 37	20 42		21 01		21 16					21 21			21 43	21 51	
Radley	d																			21 27				21 57	
Culham	d																			21 31					
Appleford	d									20 45															
Didcot Parkway	a									20 51										21 38				22 06	
	d			20 29				20 47		21 01						21 29				21 44	21 53	21 53		22 08	
Cholsey	d									21 08										21 50				22 14	
Goring & Streatley	d									21 13										21 55				22 19	
Pangbourne	d									21 19										21 59				22 24	
Tilehurst	d									21 22										22 02				22 27	
Bedwyn	d											20 33						21 06							
Hungerford	d											20 38						21 11							
Kintbury	d											20 43						21 16							
Newbury	a											20 50						21 23							
	d											20 50						21 23	21 42						
Newbury Racecourse	d											20 52						21 25							
Thatcham	d											20 57						21 30							
Midgham	d											21 02						21 35							
Aldermaston	d											21 05						21 38							
Theale	d											21 10						21 43							
Reading West	d								←			21 17		←				21 50							
Reading 7	a	20 39		20 44	20 54			21 00	20 58	21 29	21 07	21 22	21 24	21 29	21 40	21 43		21 55	21 59	22 12	22 11	22 11	22 17	22 37	
	d			20 45	20 55			21 02	21 14	21 33			21 26	21 33		21 44			22 01		22 12	22 12			
Twyford 3	a								21 20	→				21 39											
Maidenhead 3	a								21 28					21 47											
Slough 3	a				21 09				21 40				21 39	21 58											
Ealing Broadway ⊖	a								22 04					22 21											
London Paddington 15 ⊖	a			21 14	21 29			21 32	22 16				22 00	22 33		22 14			22 30		22 44	22 45			

		GW		XC	GW	GW FO	GW FX	GW	GW	GW FX	GW FO	GW		GW	XC	GW	CH FO	GW	CH
		◇		◇1	1	◇1	◇1	◇1 ☕	1	1	1	◇1		1	◇1	◇1 ☕		1	
Birmingham New Street 12	d			21 04											22 04				
Birmingham International	d			21 14											22 14				
Coventry	d			21 25											22 25				
Leamington Spa 8	d			21 38											22 38				23 38
Banbury	d	21 38		21 55						22 25	22 25				22 55			23 45	23 57
Kings Sutton	d	21 42								22 31	22 31							23 50	
Heyford	d	21 51								22 38	22 39							23 58	
Tackley	d	21 55								22 44	22 44							00 03	
Bicester Town	d																23 42		
Islip	d																23 53		
Oxford	a	22 05		22 14						22 56	22 56				23 14		00 08	00 13	00 21
	d	22 11		22 16		22 34	22 34		22 52			23 09			23 15			00 27	
Radley	d								22 58									00 33	
Culham	d								23 02									00 37	
Appleford	d								23 04									00 39	
Didcot Parkway	a	22 24							23 11			23 23						00 46	
	d	22 27						22 52	23 11			23 23				23 35		00 46	
Cholsey	d								23 18									00 52	
Goring & Streatley	d								23 23									00 57	
Pangbourne	d								23 26									01 01	
Tilehurst	d								23 30									01 06	
Bedwyn	d				21 55									23 00					
Hungerford	d				22 00									23 05					
Kintbury	d				22 05									23 10					
Newbury	a				22 12									23 17					
	d				22 13									23 17					
Newbury Racecourse	d				22 15									23 19					
Thatcham	d				22 20									23 24					
Midgham	d				22 24									23 29					
Aldermaston	d				22 28									23 32					
Theale	d				22 33									23 37					
Reading West	d				22 40									23 44					
Reading 7	a	22 44		22 41	22 45	22 58	22 58	23 06	23 40			23 40		23 49	23 52	23 53		01 12	
	d	22 44				22 59	22 59	23 08				23 41				23 55		01 15	
Twyford 3	a																	01 21	
Maidenhead 3	a											23 54						01 29	
Slough 3	a	23 01				23 12	23 15					00 01						01 37	
Ealing Broadway ⊖	a																	01 53	
London Paddington 15 ⊖	a	23 25				23 36	23 36	23 41				00 28				00 33		02 05	

Birmingham, Banbury, Bicester, Oxford and Bedwyn - Reading and London

Network Diagram - see first Page of Table 116

		GW	GW	GW	CH	GW	CH	GW	GW	GW		GW	GW	GW	GW	GW	GW	GW	GW	GW		GW	GW	GW	XC
		◇1	◇1 ☕	◇1		1		1	1	1		◇1 ☕	1	1	◇1	1	◇1 ☕	1	1	◇1		◇1 ☕	1	1	◇1 🍴
Birmingham New Street 12	d																								06 04
Birmingham International	d																								06 14
Coventry	d																								06 25
Leamington Spa 8	d						23p38																		06 38
Banbury	d					23p45	23p57																		06 55
Kings Sutton	d					23p50																			
Heyford	d					23p58																			
Tackley	d					00 03																			
Bicester Town	d				23p42																				
Islip	d				23p53																				
Oxford	a				00 08	00 13	00 21																		07 14
	d	23p09		00 07		00 27		03 59	05 14	05 49				06 07	06 31				06 42	07 01				07 07	07 16
Radley	d					00 33			05 20					06 13										07 13	
Culham	d					00 37			05 24															07 17	
Appleford	d					00 39								06 17											
Didcot Parkway	a	23p23		00 20		00 46		04 10	05 31	06 01				06 24					06 54					07 24	
	d	23p23	23p35	00 21		00 46		04 10	05 31	06 01		06 29		06 31			06 59		07 01			07 17		07 31	
Cholsey	d					00 52			05 37	06 07				06 37					07 07					07 37	
Goring & Streatley	d					00 57			05 42	06 12				06 42					07 12					07 42	
Pangbourne	d					01 01			05 47	06 17				06 47					07 17					07 47	
Tilehurst	d					01 06			05 51	06 21				06 51					07 21					07 51	
Bedwyn	d												06 05					06 39							
Hungerford	d												06 11					06 43							
Kintbury	d												06 15					06 48							
Newbury	a												06 22					06 55							
	d												06 22					06 55							
Newbury Racecourse	d												06 24												
Thatcham	d												06 29					07 00							
Midgham	d												06 34												
Aldermaston	d												06 37												
Theale	d												06 42					07 08							
Reading West	d												06 49			←							←		
Reading 7	a	23p40	23p53	00 38		01 12		04 27	05 57	06 27		06 43	06 52	06 57	07 00	06 57	07 14	07 20	07 27	07 27		07 31	07 27	07 59	07 39
	d	23p41	23p55	00 39		01 15		04 40	06 03	06 33		06 45	06 52	07 03	07 00	07 03	07 15	07 21	07 33	07 27		07 32	07 33	08 03	
Twyford 3	a					01 21		04 46	06 09	06 39				→		07 09			→				07 39	→	
Maidenhead 3	a	23p54				01 29		04 54	06 17	06 47						07 17							07 47		
Slough 3	a	00 01		00 55		01 37		05 01	06 24	06 54					07 16	07 24				07 42			07 54		
Ealing Broadway ⊖	a					01 53		05 19	06 49	07 19						07 49							08 19		
London Paddington 15 ⊖	a	00 28	00 33	01 17		02 05		05 31	07 01	07 31		07 14	07 22		07 37	08 01	07 44	07 54		08 01		08 07	08 31		

		GW	GW	GW	GW	GW		GW	GW	XC	GW	GW	GW	CH	GW	GW		GW	XC	GW	GW	GW	GW	GW	GW
		1	◇1 ☕	◇1 ☕	1	◇1 ☕		1	1	◇1	◇1 ☕	1	◇1		◇1 ☕	1		1	◇1 🍴	1	◇1 ☕	◇1 ☕	◇1 ☕	◇1 ☕	1
Birmingham New Street 12	d									06 33									07 04						
Birmingham International	d																		07 14						
Coventry	d																		07 25						
Leamington Spa 8	d									07 00									07 38						
Banbury	d				07 02					07 19									07 55						
Kings Sutton	d				07 08																				
Heyford	d				07 17																				
Tackley	d				07 21																				
Bicester Town	d													07 36											
Islip	d													07 47											
Oxford	a				07 32					07 40				08 02					08 14						
	d			07 31					07 37	07 43			08 01					08 07	08 16				08 31		
Radley	d																	08 13							
Culham	d																								
Appleford	d																	08 17							
Didcot Parkway	a								07 49									08 24							
	d		07 29			07 47			08 01		07 59				08 17			08 31			08 29			08 47	
Cholsey	d								08 07									08 37							
Goring & Streatley	d								08 12									08 42							
Pangbourne	d								08 17									08 47							
Tilehurst	d								08 21									08 51							
Bedwyn	d											07 37													
Hungerford	d											07 41													
Kintbury	d											07 46													
Newbury	a											07 53													
	d	07 13										07 53								08 13		08 34			
Newbury Racecourse	d	07 15																		08 15					
Thatcham	d	07 20										07 58								08 20					
Midgham	d	07 24																		08 24					
Aldermaston	d	07 28																		08 28					
Theale	d	07 33										08 06								08 33					
Reading West	d	07 42						←								←				08 40					←
Reading 7	a	07 45	07 44	07 54		08 00		07 59	08 27	08 06	08 14	08 19	08 25		08 31	08 27		08 57	08 39	08 44	08 44	08 52	08 54	09 00	08 57
	d		07 46	07 54		08 02		08 03	08 33		08 16	08 20	08 26		08 32	08 33		09 03			08 46	08 52	08 55	09 02	09 03
Twyford 3	a							08 09	→							08 39		→							09 09
Maidenhead 3	a							08 17								08 47									09 17
Slough 3	a			08 09				08 24					08 40			08 54							09 09		09 24
Ealing Broadway ⊖	a							08 49								09 19									09 49
London Paddington 15 ⊖	a		08 14	08 29		08 32		09 01			08 44	08 52	08 59		09 02	09 31					09 14	09 21	09 29	09 32	10 01

Birmingham, Banbury, Bicester, Oxford and Bedwyn - Reading and London

Network Diagram - see first Page of Table 116

		GW ◇1 ⊡	GW 1	XC ◇1 ⚒	GW ◇1 ⊡	GW 1	GW ◇1 ⚒	GW ◇1 A ⊡⊘	GW 1	GW 1	GW 1	CH	XC ◇1 ⚒	GW ◇1 ⊡	GW ◇1 A ⊡⊘	GW 1	GW ◇1 A ⊡⊘	GW 1	GW 1	XC ◇1 ⚒	GW 1	GW ◇1 ⚒
Birmingham New Street 12	d			07 33									08 04							08 33		
Birmingham International	d												08 14									
Coventry	d												08 25									
Leamington Spa 8	d			08 00									08 38							09 00		
Banbury	d			08 19									08 55			09 02				09 19		
Kings Sutton	d															09 08						
Heyford	d															09 17						
Tackley	d															09 21						
Bicester Town	d											08 45										
Islip	d											08 56										
Oxford	a			08 40								09 11	09 14			09 32				09 40		
	d		08 37	08 43			09 01				09 07		09 16		09 31				09 37	09 43		10 01
Radley	d										09 13											
Culham	d										09 17											
Appleford	d																					
Didcot Parkway	a		08 49								09 24								09 49			
	d	08 52	09 01		08 59			09 17			09 31			09 29			09 47		10 01			
Cholsey	d		09 07								09 37								10 07			
Goring & Streatley	d		09 12								09 42								10 12			
Pangbourne	d		09 17								09 47								10 17			
Tilehurst	d		09 21								09 51								10 21			
Bedwyn	d					08 38															09 37	
Hungerford	d					08 43															09 41	
Kintbury	d					08 48															09 46	
Newbury	a					08 55															09 53	
	d					08 55				09 03											09 53	
Newbury Racecourse	d									09 06												
Thatcham	d					09 00				09 11											09 58	
Midgham	d									09 16												
Aldermaston	d									09 19												
Theale	d					09 08				09 24											10 06	
Reading West	d								←	09 31								←				
Reading 7	a	09 07	09 27	09 11	09 14	09 20	09 24	09 32	09 27	09 35	09 57		09 39	09 45	09 54		10 00	09 57	10 27	10 07	10 17	10 25
	d	09 09	09 33		09 16	09 20	09 24	09 33	09 33		10 03			09 46	09 55		10 02	10 03	10 33		10 18	10 25
Twyford 3	a		→						09 39		→							10 09	→			
Maidenhead 3	a								09 47									10 17				
Slough 3	a						09 40		09 54						10 09			10 24				10 40
Ealing Broadway	⊖ a								10 19									10 49				
London Paddington 15	⊖ a	09 37			09 44	09 52	09 59	10 02	10 31					10 14	10 29		10 32	11 01			10 52	10 59

		GW 1	GW ◇1 ⊡	GW 1	XC ◇1 ⚒	CH	GW 1	GW ◇1 ⊡	GW ◇1 ⊡	GW ◇1 ⊡	GW 1	GW 1	XC ◇1 ⚒	GW 1	GW ◇1	GW 1	GW 1	XC ◇1 ⚒	GW 1	GW ◇1 ⊡	GW ◇1 ⚒	GW 1	GW ◇1 ⊡
Birmingham New Street 12	d				09 04								09 33					10 04					
Birmingham International	d				09 14													10 14					
Coventry	d				09 25													10 25					
Leamington Spa 8	d				09 38								10 00					10 38					
Banbury	d				09 55								10 19					10 55				11 02	
Kings Sutton	d																					11 08	
Heyford	d																					11 17	
Tackley	d																					11 21	
Bicester Town	d					09 57																	
Islip	d					10 08																	
Oxford	a				10 14	10 23							10 40					11 14				11 32	
	d			10 07	10 16				10 31			10 37	10 43		11 01		11 07	11 16			11 31		
Radley	d			10 13													11 13						
Culham	d																						
Appleford	d			10 17																			
Didcot Parkway	a			10 23								10 49					11 24						
	d		10 22	10 31				10 29		10 47		11 01					11 31			11 29			11 47
Cholsey	d			10 37								11 07					11 37						
Goring & Streatley	d			10 42								11 12					11 42						
Pangbourne	d			10 47								11 17					11 47						
Tilehurst	d			10 51								11 21					11 51						
Bedwyn	d													10 40									
Hungerford	d													10 46									
Kintbury	d													10 50									
Newbury	a													10 57									
	d						10 13							10 57					11 13				
Newbury Racecourse	d						10 15												11 15				
Thatcham	d						10 20							11 02					11 20				
Midgham	d						10 24												11 24				
Aldermaston	d						10 28												11 28				
Theale	d						10 33							11 10					11 33				
Reading West	d	←					10 40				←					←			11 40				
Reading 7	a	10 27	10 36	10 58	10 39		10 44	10 45	10 54	11 01	10 58	11 27	11 09	11 21	11 24	11 27	11 58	11 39	11 44	11 44	11 54		12 00
	d	10 33	10 39	11 03				10 46	10 55	11 02	11 03	11 33		11 21	11 25	11 33	12 03			11 45	11 55		12 02
Twyford 3	a	10 39		→							11 09	→				11 39	→						
Maidenhead 3	a	10 47									11 17					11 47							
Slough 3	a	10 54							11 09		11 24				11 39	11 54					12 09		
Ealing Broadway	⊖ a	11 19									11 49					12 19							
London Paddington 15	⊖ a	11 31	11 08					11 14	11 29	11 33	12 01			11 52	11 59	12 31				12 14	12 29		12 32

A ⊡ from Reading ⊘ to Reading

Birmingham, Banbury, Bicester, Oxford and Bedwyn - Reading and London

Network Diagram - see first Page of Table 116

		GW 1	GW 1	XC ◇1 ⚒	CH	GW 1	GW ◇1 ⚒	GW 1	GW ◇1 ⊡	GW 1	XC ◇1 ⚒	GW ◇1 ⊡	GW 1	GW ◇1 ⚒	GW 1	GW ◇1 ⊡	GW 1	GW 1	XC ◇1 ⚒	GW ◇1 ⚒	GW 1	GW 1
Birmingham New Street 12	d			10 33							11 04								11 33			
Birmingham International	d										11 14											
Coventry	d										11 25											
Leamington Spa 8	d			11 00							11 38								12 00			
Banbury	d			11 19							11 55								12 19			
Kings Sutton	d																					
Heyford	d																					
Tackley	d																					
Bicester Town	d				11 30																	
Islip	d				11 41																	
Oxford	a			11 40	11 56						12 14								12 40			
	d		11 37	11 43			12 01			12 07	12 16			12 31				12 37	12 43	13 01		13 07
Radley	d									12 13												13 13
Culham	d																					13 17
Appleford	d									12 17												
Didcot Parkway	a		11 49							12 24								12 49				13 24
	d		12 01						12 22	12 31		12 29				12 47		13 01				13 31
Cholsey	d		12 07							12 37								13 07				13 37
Goring & Streatley	d		12 12							12 42								13 12				13 42
Pangbourne	d		12 17							12 47								13 17				13 47
Tilehurst	d		12 21							12 51								13 21				13 51
Bedwyn	d					11 38									12 32							
Hungerford	d					11 43									12 38							
Kintbury	d					11 48									12 42							
Newbury	a					11 55									12 50							
	d					11 55							12 24									
Newbury Racecourse	d												12 26									
Thatcham	d					12 00							12 31									
Midgham	d												12 36									
Aldermaston	d												12 39									
Theale	d					12 08							12 44									
Reading West	d	←						←					12 51				←				←	
Reading 7	a	11 58	12 28	12 07		12 17	12 25	12 28	12 37	12 57	12 39	12 45	12 55	12 53		13 00	12 57	13 27	13 06	13 25	13 27	13 59
	d	12 03	12 33			12 18	12 25	12 33	12 39	13 03		12 47		12 55		13 02	13 03	13 33		13 25	13 33	14 03
Twyford 3	a	12 09	→					12 39		→							13 09	→			13 39	→
Maidenhead 3	a	12 17						12 47									13 17				13 47	
Slough 3	a	12 24					12 40	12 54						13 09			13 24			13 40	13 54	
Ealing Broadway	⊖ a	12 49						13 19									13 49				14 19	
London Paddington 15	⊖ a	13 01				12 52	12 59	13 31	13 07			13 13		13 30		13 33	14 01			13 59	14 31	

		XC ◇1 ⚒	CH	GW 1	GW ◇1 ⊡	GW 1	GW ◇1	GW 1	GW ◇1 ⊡	GW 1	GW 1	XC ◇1 ⚒	GW 1	GW ◇1 ⚒	GW 1	GW ◇1 ⊡	GW 1	XC ◇1 ⚒	GW 1	GW ◇1 ⊡	GW ◇1 ⊡	GW ◇1 ⊡	GW 1
Birmingham New Street 12	d	12 04										12 33						13 04					
Birmingham International	d	12 14																13 14					
Coventry	d	12 25																13 25					
Leamington Spa 8	d	12 38										13 02						13 38					
Banbury	d	12 55						13 02				13 21						13 55					
Kings Sutton	d							13 08															
Heyford	d							13 17															
Tackley	d							13 21															
Bicester Town	d		13 00																				
Islip	d		13 11																				
Oxford	a	13 14	13 26					13 32				13 40						14 14					
	d	13 16					13 31				13 37	13 43		14 01			14 07	14 16			14 31		
Radley	d																14 13						
Culham	d																						
Appleford	d																14 17						
Didcot Parkway	a										13 51						14 24						
	d				13 29				13 47		14 01					14 22	14 31			14 29		14 47	
Cholsey	d										14 07						14 37						
Goring & Streatley	d										14 12						14 42						
Pangbourne	d										14 17						14 47						
Tilehurst	d										14 21						14 51						
Bedwyn	d												13 40										
Hungerford	d												13 46										
Kintbury	d												13 50										
Newbury	a												13 57										
	d			13 12		13 28							13 57						14 13				
Newbury Racecourse	d			13 15															14 15				
Thatcham	d			13 20		13 33							14 02						14 20				
Midgham	d			13 24															14 24				
Aldermaston	d			13 28															14 28				
Theale	d			13 33		13 41							14 10						14 33				
Reading West	d			13 40						←					←				14 40				←
Reading 7	a	13 39		13 44	13 44	13 51	13 54		14 00	13 59	14 27	14 07	14 18	14 25	14 27	14 38	14 58	14 39	14 44	14 44	14 53	15 00	14 58
	d				13 45	13 51	13 55		14 02	14 03	14 33		14 18	14 25	14 33	14 39	15 03			14 45	14 55	15 02	15 03
Twyford 3	a									14 09	→				14 39		→						15 09
Maidenhead 3	a									14 17					14 47								15 17
Slough 3	a						14 09			14 24				14 40	14 54						15 10		15 24
Ealing Broadway	⊖ a									14 49					15 19								15 49
London Paddington 15	⊖ a				14 14	14 23	14 29		14 32	15 01			14 54	14 59	15 31	15 09				15 14	15 29	15 32	16 01

Birmingham, Banbury, Bicester, Oxford and Bedwyn - Reading and London

Network Diagram - see first Page of Table 116

Station		GW 1	XC ◇1	CH	GW 1	GW ◇1	GW 1	GW 1	XC ◇1	GW 1	GW ◇1	GW ◇1	GW 1	GW ◇1	GW 1	GW 1	XC ◇1	CH	GW 1	GW ◇1	GW ◇1	GW 1	GW ◇1
Birmingham New Street 12	d		13 33						14 04								14 33						
Birmingham International	d								14 14														
Coventry	d								14 25														
Leamington Spa 8	d		14 00						14 38								15 00						
Banbury	d		14 19						14 55				15 02				15 20						
Kings Sutton	d												15 08										
Heyford	d												15 17										
Tackley	d												15 21										
Bicester Town	d			14 18														15 28					
Islip	d			14 29														15 39					
Oxford	a		14 40	14 44					15 14				15 32				15 41	15 54					
	d	14 37	14 43			15 01		15 07	15 16			15 31				15 37	15 43			16 01			
Radley	d							15 13															
Culham	d							15 17															
Appleford	d																						
Didcot Parkway	a	14 49						15 24								15 49							
	d	15 01						15 31			15 29			15 47		16 01							16 22
Cholsey	d	15 07						15 37								16 07							
Goring & Streatley	d	15 12						15 42								16 12							
Pangbourne	d	15 17						15 47								16 17							
Tilehurst	d	15 21						15 51								16 21							
Bedwyn	d				14 38														15 38				
Hungerford	d				14 43														15 43				
Kintbury	d				14 48														15 48				
Newbury	a				14 55														15 55				
	d				14 55					15 13									15 55		16 06		
Newbury Racecourse	d									15 15													
Thatcham	d				15 00					15 20									16 00				
Midgham	d									15 24													
Aldermaston	d									15 28													
Theale	d				15 08					15 33									16 08				
Reading West	d						←			15 40					←							←	
Reading 7	a	15 27	15 07		15 17	15 25	15 27	15 59	15 39	15 44	15 44	15 54		16 01	15 59	16 29	16 08		16 17	16 25	16 25	16 29	16 38
	d	15 33			15 19	15 25	15 33	16 03			15 45	15 55		16 02	16 03	16 33			16 18	16 26	16 28	16 33	16 39
Twyford 3	a	→					15 39	→							16 09	→						16 39	
Maidenhead 3	a						15 47								16 17							16 47	
Slough 3	a					15 40	15 54					16 10			16 24					16 40		16 54	
Ealing Broadway ⊖	a						16 19								16 49							17 19	
London Paddington 15 ⊖	a				15 54	15 59	16 31				16 14	16 29		16 37	17 01				16 52	16 59	17 02	17 31	17 07

Station		GW 1	XC ◇1	GW 1	GW ◇1	GW ◇1	GW ◇1	GW 1	GW 1	XC ◇1	CH	GW 1	GW ◇1	GW 1	GW 1	XC ◇1	GW ◇1	GW 1	GW ◇1	GW ◇1	GW 1	GW 1
Birmingham New Street 12	d		15 04							15 33						16 04						
Birmingham International	d		15 14													16 14						
Coventry	d		15 25													16 25						
Leamington Spa 8	d		15 38							16 02						16 38						
Banbury	d		15 55							16 20						16 55						
Kings Sutton	d																					
Heyford	d																					
Tackley	d																					
Bicester Town	d										16 30											
Islip	d										16 41											
Oxford	a		16 14							16 40	16 56					17 14						
	d	16 07	16 16			16 31			16 37	16 43			17 01		17 07	17 16			17 31			17 37
Radley	d	16 13													17 13							
Culham	d														17 17							
Appleford	d	16 17																				
Didcot Parkway	a	16 24							16 49						17 24							17 49
	d	16 31			16 29		16 47		17 01						17 31		17 29			17 47		18 01
Cholsey	d	16 37							17 07						17 37							18 07
Goring & Streatley	d	16 42							17 12						17 42							18 12
Pangbourne	d	16 47							17 17						17 47							18 17
Tilehurst	d	16 51							17 21						17 51							18 21
Bedwyn	d											16 43										
Hungerford	d											16 49										
Kintbury	d											16 53										
Newbury	a											17 00										
	d			16 13								17 01						17 15				
Newbury Racecourse	d			16 15														17 17				
Thatcham	d			16 20								17 06						17 22				
Midgham	d			16 24														17 27				
Aldermaston	d			16 28														17 30				
Theale	d			16 33								17 14						17 35				
Reading West	d			16 40				←						←				17 42			←	
Reading 7	a	16 58	16 39	16 44	16 44	16 55	17 00	16 58	17 27	17 07		17 22	17 26	17 27	17 57	17 39	17 44	17 46	17 55	18 00	17 57	18 27
	d	17 03			16 45	16 55	17 02	17 03	17 33			17 22	17 27	17 33	18 03		17 45		17 57	18 02	18 03	18 33
Twyford 3	a	→						17 09	→					17 39	→						18 09	→
Maidenhead 3	a							17 17						17 47							18 17	
Slough 3	a					17 10		17 24					17 41	17 54					18 10		18 24	
Ealing Broadway ⊖	a							17 49						18 19							18 49	
London Paddington 15 ⊖	a				17 14	17 29	17 32	18 01				17 54	18 00	18 31			18 14		18 29	18 32	19 01	

Birmingham, Banbury, Bicester, Oxford and Bedwyn - Reading and London

Network Diagram - see first Page of Table 116

Station		XC ◇1	GW 1	GW 1	GW ◇1	GW 1	GW ◇1	GW 1	XC ◇1	CH	GW 1	GW ◇1	GW ◇1	GW ◇1	GW 1	GW 1	XC ◇1	GW 1	GW ◇1	GW 1	GW 1	XC ◇1	GW 1
Birmingham New Street 12	d	16 33							17 04								17 33					18 04	
Birmingham International	d								17 14													18 14	
Coventry	d								17 25													18 25	
Leamington Spa 8	d	17 00							17 38								18 02					18 38	
Banbury	d	17 19	17 23						17 55								18 19					18 55	
Kings Sutton	d		17 29																				
Heyford	d		17 38																				
Tackley	d		17 42																				
Bicester Town	d									18 04													
Islip	d									18 15													
Oxford	a	17 41	17 53						18 14	18 30							18 40					19 14	
	d	17 43			18 01			18 07	18 16				18 31			18 37	18 43		19 01		19 07	19 16	
Radley	d							18 13													19 13		
Culham	d																				19 17		
Appleford	d							18 17															
Didcot Parkway	a							18 24								18 49					19 24		
	d						18 22	18 31				18 29		18 47		19 01					19 31		
Cholsey	d							18 37								19 07					19 37		
Goring & Streatley	d							18 42								19 12					19 42		
Pangbourne	d							18 47								19 17					19 47		
Tilehurst	d							18 51								19 21					19 51		
Bedwyn	d			17 38														18 38					
Hungerford	d			17 43														18 43					
Kintbury	d			17 48														18 48					
Newbury	a			17 55														18 55					
	d			17 55							18 13							18 55					19 13
Newbury Racecourse	d										18 15												19 15
Thatcham	d			18 00							18 20							19 00					19 20
Midgham	d										18 24												19 24
Aldermaston	d										18 28												19 28
Theale	d			18 08							18 33							19 08					19 33
Reading West	d					←					18 40				←					←			19 40
Reading 7	a	18 07		18 18	18 25	18 27	18 38	18 58	18 39		18 44	18 44	18 55	19 00	18 58	19 29	19 07	19 17	19 25	19 29	19 57	19 39	19 44
	d			18 19	18 25	18 33	18 39	19 03				18 45	18 56	19 02	19 03	19 33		19 20	19 25	19 33	20 03		
Twyford 3	a					18 39		→							19 09	→				19 39	→		
Maidenhead 3	a					18 47									19 17					19 47			
Slough 3	a				18 40	18 54							19 10		19 24				19 40	19 54			
Ealing Broadway ⊖	a					19 19									19 49					20 19			
London Paddington 15 ⊖	a			18 52	18 59	19 31	19 08					19 14	19 29	19 32	20 01			19 52	19 59	20 31			

Station		GW ◇1	GW ◇1	GW 1	GW ◇1	GW 1	GW ◇1	GW 1	XC ◇1	CH	GW ◇1	GW 1	GW 1	GW ◇1	GW 1	XC ◇1	GW ◇1	GW ◇1	GW 1	GW ◇1	GW 1	XC ◇1
Birmingham New Street 12	d								18 33							19 04						19 33
Birmingham International	d															19 14						
Coventry	d															19 25						
Leamington Spa 8	d								19 00							19 38						20 03
Banbury	d			19 02					19 19							19 55						20 21
Kings Sutton	d			19 08																		
Heyford	d			19 17																		
Tackley	d			19 21																		
Bicester Town	d									19 17												
Islip	d									19 28												
Oxford	a			19 32					19 40	19 43						20 14						20 40
	d		19 31					19 37	19 43		20 01				20 07	20 16		20 31			20 37	20 43
Radley	d														20 13							
Culham	d																					
Appleford	d														20 17							
Didcot Parkway	a							19 49							20 24						20 49	
	d	19 29			19 47			20 01						20 23	20 31		20 29			20 47	21 01	
Cholsey	d							20 07							20 37						21 07	
Goring & Streatley	d							20 12							20 42						21 12	
Pangbourne	d							20 17							20 47						21 17	
Tilehurst	d							20 21							20 51						21 21	
Bedwyn	d											19 41										
Hungerford	d											19 47										
Kintbury	d											19 51										
Newbury	a											19 58										
	d						19 46					19 58										
Newbury Racecourse	d											20 00										
Thatcham	d											20 05										
Midgham	d											20 10										
Aldermaston	d											20 13										
Theale	d											20 18										
Reading West	d					←						20 25	←						←			
Reading 7	a	19 44	19 55		20 00	19 57	20 07	20 29	20 10		20 25	20 28	20 29	20 38	20 57	20 39	20 44	20 54	20 57	21 06	21 27	21 10
	d	19 45	19 55		20 03	20 03	20 09	20 33			20 25		20 33	20 39	21 03		20 45	20 54	21 03	21 08	21 33	
Twyford 3	a					20 09		→					20 39		→				21 09		→	
Maidenhead 3	a					20 17							20 47						21 17			
Slough 3	a		20 10			20 24					20 40		20 54					21 09	21 24			
Ealing Broadway ⊖	a					20 49							21 19						21 49			
London Paddington 15 ⊖	a	20 14	20 29		20 32	21 01	20 37				20 59		21 31	21 07			21 14	21 29	22 02	21 36		

Table 116

Saturdays
until 23 June

Birmingham, Banbury, Bicester, Oxford and Bedwyn - Reading and London

Network Diagram - see first Page of Table 116

		CH	GW	GW	GW	GW	XC	GW	GW	GW	GW	XC	GW	GW	GW	CH	XC	GW	GW	GW	GW	GW	GW
			◇1	1	1	1	◇1	◇1	◇1	◇1	◇1	◇1	1	◇1	1		◇1	1	1	◇1	◇1	◇1	◇1
										A	B												
Birmingham New Street	d						20 04					20 33					21 04						
Birmingham International	d						20 14										21 14						
Coventry	d						20 25										21 25						
Leamington Spa	d						20 38					21 00					21 38						
Banbury	d				20 38		20 55					21 20					21 55	22 00					
Kings Sutton	d				20 44													22 06					
Heyford	d				20 53													22 15					
Tackley	d				20 57													22 19					
Bicester Town	d	20 28														21 37							
Islip	d	20 39														21 48							
Oxford	a	20 54			21 08		21 14					21 41				22 03	22 16	22 30					
	d		21 01				21 16		21 31			21 43	21 50	22 01			22 18			22 35			23 01
Radley	d												21 56										
Culham	d																						
Appleford	d																						
Didcot Parkway	a								21 43				22 04	22 12						22 47			23 13
	d							21 34	21 45	21 47	21 47		22 04	22 13						22 48	22 49		23 14
Cholsey	d												22 10										
Goring & Streatley	d												22 15										
Pangbourne	d												22 21										
Tilehurst	d												22 24										
Bedwyn	d					20 48													22 00				
Hungerford	d					20 54													22 06				
Kintbury	d					20 58													22 10				
Newbury	a					21 05													22 17				
	d					21 05													22 17				
Newbury Racecourse	d					21 07													22 19				
Thatcham	d					21 12													22 24				
Midgham	d					21 17													22 29				
Aldermaston	d					21 20													22 32				
Theale	d					21 25													22 37				
Reading West	d			←		21 32									←				22 44			←	
Reading	a		21 25	21 27		21 36	21 40	21 48	21 59	21 59	21 59	22 10	22 31	22 28	22 31		22 41		22 48	23 08	23 04	23 08	23 29
	d		21 25	21 33				21 50	22 01	22 03	22 03		22 33	22 29	22 33					23 09	23 05	23 09	23 29
Twyford	a			21 39									→		22 39					→			
Maidenhead	a			21 47											22 47								
Slough	a		21 40	21 54					22 11					22 43	22 54							23 26	23 45
Ealing Broadway	a			22 19											23 19								
London Paddington	a		21 59	22 31				22 16	22 34	22 30	22 37			23 02	23 28						23 36	23 46	00 10

		GW	GW	GW	CH
		1	◇1	1	
Birmingham New Street	d				
Birmingham International	d				
Coventry	d				
Leamington Spa	d				
Banbury	d				
Kings Sutton	d				
Heyford	d				
Tackley	d				
Bicester Town	d				22 55
Islip	d				23 06
Oxford	a				23 21
	d			23 07	
Radley	d			23 13	
Culham	d			23 17	
Appleford	d			23 20	
Didcot Parkway	a			23 25	
	d		23 30	23 36	
Cholsey	d			23 42	
Goring & Streatley	d			23 49	
Pangbourne	d				
Tilehurst	d			23 56	
Bedwyn	d	23 00			
Hungerford	d	23 06			
Kintbury	d	23 10			
Newbury	a	23 17			
	d	23 17			
Newbury Racecourse	d	23 19			
Thatcham	d	23 24			
Midgham	d	23 29			
Aldermaston	d	23 32			
Theale	d	23 37			
Reading West	d	23 44			
Reading	a	23 48	23 49	00 02	
	d		23 51	00 03	
Twyford	a			00 10	
Maidenhead	a			00 18	
Slough	a			00 30	
Ealing Broadway	a			00 54	
London Paddington	a		00 33	01 03	

A not 19 May

B 19 May

Table 116

Saturdays
30 June to 8 September

Birmingham, Banbury, Bicester, Oxford and Bedwyn - Reading and London

Network Diagram - see first Page of Table 116

		GW	GW	XC	GW	CH	GW	CH	GW	GW	GW	GW	GW	GW	GW	GW	GW	GW	GW	GW	GW	GW	GW
		◇1	◇1	◇1	◇1		1		1	1	1	◇1	1	1	◇1	1	◇1	1	1	◇1	◇1	1	1
Birmingham New Street	d			22p04																			
Birmingham International	d																						
Coventry	d																						
Leamington Spa	d			22p53				23p38															
Banbury	d			23p16			23p45	23p57															
Kings Sutton	d						23p50																
Heyford	d						23p58																
Tackley	d						00 03																
Bicester Town	d					23p42																	
Islip	d					23p53																	
Oxford	a			23p35		00 08	00 13	00 21															
	d	23p09		23p36	00 07		00 27		03 59	05 14	05 49			06 07	06 31				06 42	07 01			07 07
Radley	d						00 33			05 20				06 13									07 13
Culham	d						00 37			05 24													07 17
Appleford	d						00 39							06 17									
Didcot Parkway	a	23p23			00 20		00 46		04 10	05 31	06 01			06 24					06 54				07 24
	d	23p23	23p35		00 21		00 46		04 10	05 31	06 01	06 29		06 31			06 59		07 01		07 17		07 31
Cholsey	d						00 52			05 37	06 07			06 37					07 07				07 37
Goring & Streatley	d						00 57			05 42	06 12			06 42					07 12				07 42
Pangbourne	d						01 01			05 47	06 17			06 47					07 17				07 47
Tilehurst	d						01 06			05 51	06 21			06 51					07 21				07 51
Bedwyn	d												06 05					06 39					
Hungerford	d												06 11					06 43					
Kintbury	d												06 15					06 48					
Newbury	a												06 22					06 55					
	d												06 22					06 55					
Newbury Racecourse	d												06 24										
Thatcham	d												06 29					07 00					
Midgham	d												06 34										
Aldermaston	d												06 37										
Theale	d												06 42					07 08					
Reading West	d												06 49			←						←	
Reading	a	23p40	23p53	00 07	00 38		01 12		04 27	05 57	06 27	06 43	06 52	06 57	07 00	06 57	07 14	07 20	07 27	07 27	07 31	07 27	07 59
	d	23p41	23p55		00 39		01 15		04 40	06 03	06 33	06 45	06 52	07 03	07 00	07 03	07 15	07 21	07 33	07 27	07 32	07 33	08 03
Twyford	a						01 21		04 46	06 09	06 39			→		07 09			→			07 39	→
Maidenhead	a	23p54					01 29		04 54	06 17	06 47					07 17						07 47	
Slough	a	00 01			00 55		01 37		05 01	06 24	06 54				07 16	07 24				07 42		07 54	
Ealing Broadway	a						01 53		05 19	06 49	07 19					07 49						08 19	
London Paddington	a	00 28	00 33		01 17		02 05		05 31	07 01	07 31	07 14	07 22		07 37	08 01	07 44	07 54		08 01	08 07	08 31	

		XC	GW	GW	GW	GW	GW	GW	GW	XC	GW	GW	GW	CH	GW	GW	GW	XC	GW	GW	GW	GW	GW
		◇1	1	◇1	◇1	1	◇1	1	1	◇1	◇1	1	◇1		◇1	1	1	◇1	1	◇1	◇1	◇1	◇1
Birmingham New Street	d	06 04								06 33								07 04					
Birmingham International	d	06 14																07 14					
Coventry	d	06 25																07 25					
Leamington Spa	d	06 38								07 00								07 38					
Banbury	d	06 55				07 02				07 19								07 55					
Kings Sutton	d					07 08																	
Heyford	d					07 17																	
Tackley	d					07 21																	
Bicester Town	d													07 36									
Islip	d													07 47									
Oxford	a	07 14				07 32				07 40				08 02				08 14					
	d	07 16			07 31				07 37	07 43			08 01				08 07	08 16				08 31	
Radley	d																08 13						
Culham	d																						
Appleford	d																08 17						
Didcot Parkway	a								07 49								08 24						
	d			07 29			07 47		08 01		07 59				08 17		08 31			08 29			08 47
Cholsey	d								08 07								08 37						
Goring & Streatley	d								08 12								08 42						
Pangbourne	d								08 17								08 47						
Tilehurst	d								08 21								08 51						
Bedwyn	d											07 37											
Hungerford	d											07 41											
Kintbury	d											07 46											
Newbury	a											07 53											
	d		07 13									07 53							08 13		08 34		
Newbury Racecourse	d		07 15																08 15				
Thatcham	d		07 20									07 58							08 20				
Midgham	d		07 24																08 24				
Aldermaston	d		07 28																08 28				
Theale	d		07 33									08 06							08 33				
Reading West	d		07 42					←								←			08 40				
Reading	a	07 39	07 45	07 44	07 54		08 00	07 59	08 27	08 06	08 14	08 19	08 25		08 31	08 27	08 57	08 39	08 44	08 44	08 52	08 54	09 00
	d			07 46	07 54		08 02	08 03	08 33		08 16	08 20	08 26		08 32	08 33	09 03			08 46	08 52	08 55	09 02
Twyford	a							08 09	→							08 39	→						
Maidenhead	a							08 17								08 47							
Slough	a				08 09			08 24					08 40			08 54						09 09	
Ealing Broadway	a							08 49								09 19							
London Paddington	a			08 14	08 29		08 32	09 01			08 44	08 52	08 59		09 02	09 31				09 14	09 21	09 29	09 32

Birmingham, Banbury, Bicester, Oxford and Bedwyn - Reading and London

Network Diagram - see first Page of Table 116

		GW ■	GW ◇■ ᴨ	GW ■	XC ◇■ ⌶	GW ◇■ ᴨ	GW ■	GW ◇■ ⌶	GW ◇■ A ᴨ⊘	GW ■	GW ■	GW ■	CH	XC ◇■ ⌶	GW ◇■ ᴨ	GW ◇■ A ᴨ⊘	GW ■	GW ◇■ A ᴨ⊘	GW ■	GW ■	XC ◇■ ⌶	GW ■
Birmingham New Street ■12	d				07 33									08 04							08 33	
Birmingham International	d													08 14								
Coventry	d													08 25								
Leamington Spa ■8	d				08 00									08 38							09 00	
Banbury	d				08 19									08 55			09 02				09 19	
Kings Sutton	d																09 08					
Heyford	d																09 17					
Tackley	d																09 21					
Bicester Town	d												08 45									
Islip	d												08 56									
Oxford	a				08 40								09 11	09 14			09 32				09 40	
	d			08 37	08 43			09 01				09 07		09 16		09 31				09 37	09 43	
Radley	d											09 13										
Culham	d											09 17										
Appleford	d																					
Didcot Parkway	a			08 49								09 24								09 49		
	d		08 52	09 01		08 59			09 17			09 31			09 29			09 47		10 01		
Cholsey	d			09 07								09 37								10 07		
Goring & Streatley	d			09 12								09 42								10 12		
Pangbourne	d			09 17								09 47								10 17		
Tilehurst	d			09 21								09 51								10 21		
Bedwyn	d						08 38															09 37
Hungerford	d						08 43															09 41
Kintbury	d						08 48															09 46
Newbury	a						08 55															09 53
	d						08 55				09 03											09 53
Newbury Racecourse	d										09 06											
Thatcham	d						09 00				09 11											09 58
Midgham	d										09 16											
Aldermaston	d										09 19											
Theale	d						09 08				09 24											10 06
Reading West	d	←								←	09 31								←			
Reading ■7	a	08 57	09 07	09 27	09 11	09 14	09 20	09 24	09 32	09 27	09 35	09 57		09 39	09 45	09 54		10 00	09 57	10 27	10 07	10 17
	d	09 03	09 09	09 33		09 16	09 20	09 24	09 33	09 33		10 03			09 46	09 55		10 02	10 03	10 33		10 18
Twyford ■3	a	09 09		→						09 39		→							10 09	→		
Maidenhead ■3	a	09 17								09 47									10 17			
Slough ■3	a	09 24						09 40		09 54						10 09			10 24			
Ealing Broadway ⊖	a	09 49								10 19									10 49			
London Paddington ■15 ⊖	a	10 01	09 37			09 44	09 52	09 59	10 02	10 31					10 14	10 29		10 32	11 01			10 52

		GW ◇■ ⌶	GW ■	GW ◇■ ᴨ	GW ■	XC ◇■ ⌶	CH	GW ■	GW ◇■ ᴨ	GW ◇■ ᴨ	GW ◇■ ᴨ	GW ■	GW ■	XC ◇■ ⌶	GW ■	GW ◇■	GW ■	GW ■	XC ◇■ ⌶	GW ■	GW ◇■ ᴨ	GW ◇■ ⌶	GW ■
Birmingham New Street ■12	d					09 04								09 33					10 04				
Birmingham International	d					09 14													10 14				
Coventry	d					09 25													10 25				
Leamington Spa ■8	d					09 38								10 00					10 38				
Banbury	d					09 55								10 19					10 55				11 02
Kings Sutton	d																						11 08
Heyford	d																						11 17
Tackley	d																						11 21
Bicester Town	d						09 57																
Islip	d						10 08																
Oxford	a					10 14	10 23							10 40					11 14				11 32
	d	10 01			10 07	10 16				10 31			10 37	10 43		11 01		11 07	11 16			11 31	
Radley	d				10 13													11 13					
Culham	d																						
Appleford	d				10 17																		
Didcot Parkway	a				10 23								10 49					11 24					
	d			10 22	10 31				10 29		10 47		11 01					11 31			11 29		
Cholsey	d				10 37								11 07					11 37					
Goring & Streatley	d				10 42								11 12					11 42					
Pangbourne	d				10 47								11 17					11 47					
Tilehurst	d				10 51								11 21					11 51					
Bedwyn	d														10 40								
Hungerford	d														10 46								
Kintbury	d														10 50								
Newbury	a														10 57								
	d							10 13							10 57					11 13			
Newbury Racecourse	d							10 15												11 15			
Thatcham	d							10 20							11 02					11 20			
Midgham	d							10 24												11 24			
Aldermaston	d							10 28												11 28			
Theale	d							10 33							11 10					11 33			
Reading West	d		←					10 40				←					←			11 40			
Reading ■7	a	10 25	10 27	10 36	10 58	10 39		10 44	10 45	10 54	11 01	10 58	11 27	11 09	11 21	11 24	11 27	11 58	11 39	11 44	11 44	11 54	
	d	10 25	10 33	10 39	11 03				10 46	10 55	11 02	11 03	11 33		11 21	11 25	11 33	12 03			11 45	11 55	
Twyford ■3	a		10 39		→							11 09	→				11 39	→					
Maidenhead ■3	a		10 47									11 17					11 47						
Slough ■3	a	10 40	10 54							11 09		11 24				11 39	11 54					12 09	
Ealing Broadway ⊖	a		11 19									11 49					12 19						
London Paddington ■15 ⊖	a	10 59	11 31	11 08					11 14	11 29	11 33	12 01			11 52	11 59	12 31				12 14	12 29	

A ᴨ from Reading ⊘ to Reading

		GW ◇■ ᴨ	GW ■	GW ■	XC ◇■ ⌶	CH	GW ■	GW ◇■ ⌶	GW ■	GW ◇■ ᴨ	GW ■	XC ◇■ ⌶	GW ◇■ ᴨ	GW ■	GW ◇■ ⌶	GW ■	GW ◇■ ᴨ	GW ■	GW ■	XC ◇■ ⌶	GW ◇■ ⌶	GW ■
Birmingham New Street ■12	d				10 33							11 04								11 33		
Birmingham International	d											11 14										
Coventry	d											11 25										
Leamington Spa ■8	d				11 00							11 38								12 00		
Banbury	d				11 19							11 55								12 19		
Kings Sutton	d																					
Heyford	d																					
Tackley	d																					
Bicester Town	d					11 30																
Islip	d					11 41																
Oxford	a				11 40	11 56						12 14								12 40		
	d			11 37	11 43			12 01			12 07	12 16			12 31				12 37	12 43	13 01	
Radley	d										12 13											
Culham	d																					
Appleford	d										12 17											
Didcot Parkway	a			11 49							12 24								12 49			
	d	11 47		12 01						12 22	12 31		12 29				12 47		13 01			
Cholsey	d			12 07							12 37								13 07			
Goring & Streatley	d			12 12							12 42								13 12			
Pangbourne	d			12 17							12 47								13 17			
Tilehurst	d			12 21							12 51								13 21			
Bedwyn	d						11 38									12 32						
Hungerford	d						11 43									12 38						
Kintbury	d						11 48									12 42						
Newbury	a						11 55									12 50						
	d						11 55							12 24								
Newbury Racecourse	d													12 26								
Thatcham	d						12 00							12 31								
Midgham	d													12 36								
Aldermaston	d													12 39								
Theale	d						12 08							12 44								
Reading West	d		←						←					12 51				←				←
Reading ■7	a	12 00	11 58	12 28	12 07		12 17	12 25	12 28	12 37	12 57	12 39	12 45	12 55	12 53		13 00	12 57	13 27	13 06	13 25	13 27
	d	12 02	12 03	12 33			12 18	12 25	12 33	12 39	13 03		12 47		12 55		13 02	13 03	13 33		13 25	13 33
Twyford ■3	a		12 09	→					12 39		→							13 09	→			13 39
Maidenhead ■3	a		12 17						12 47									13 17				13 47
Slough ■3	a		12 24					12 40	12 54						13 09			13 24			13 40	13 54
Ealing Broadway ⊖	a		12 49						13 19									13 49				14 19
London Paddington ■15 ⊖	a	12 32	13 01				12 52	12 59	13 31	13 07			13 13		13 30		13 33	14 01			13 59	14 31

		GW ■	XC ◇■ ⌶	CH	GW ■	GW ◇■ ᴨ	GW ■	GW ◇■	GW ■	GW ◇■ ᴨ	GW ■	GW ■	XC ◇■ ⌶	GW ■	GW ◇■ ⌶	GW ■	GW ◇■ ᴨ	GW ■	XC ◇■ ⌶	GW ■	GW ◇■ ᴨ	GW ◇■ ᴨ	GW ◇■ ᴨ
Birmingham New Street ■12	d		12 04										12 33						13 04				
Birmingham International	d		12 14																13 14				
Coventry	d		12 25																13 25				
Leamington Spa ■8	d		12 38										13 02						13 38				
Banbury	d		12 55						13 02				13 21						13 55				
Kings Sutton	d								13 08														
Heyford	d								13 17														
Tackley	d								13 21														
Bicester Town	d			13 00																			
Islip	d			13 11																			
Oxford	a		13 14	13 26					13 32				13 40						14 14				
	d	13 07	13 16					13 31				13 37	13 43		14 01			14 07	14 16			14 31	
Radley	d	13 13																14 13					
Culham	d	13 17																					
Appleford	d																	14 17					
Didcot Parkway	a	13 24										13 51						14 24					
	d	13 31				13 29				13 47		14 01					14 22	14 31			14 29		14 47
Cholsey	d	13 37										14 07						14 37					
Goring & Streatley	d	13 42										14 12						14 42					
Pangbourne	d	13 47										14 17						14 47					
Tilehurst	d	13 51										14 21						14 51					
Bedwyn	d													13 40									
Hungerford	d													13 46									
Kintbury	d													13 50									
Newbury	a													13 57									
	d				13 12		13 28							13 57						14 13			
Newbury Racecourse	d				13 15															14 15			
Thatcham	d				13 20		13 33							14 02						14 20			
Midgham	d				13 24															14 24			
Aldermaston	d				13 28															14 28			
Theale	d				13 33		13 41							14 10						14 33			
Reading West	d				13 40						←					←				14 40			
Reading ■7	a	13 59	13 39		13 44	13 44	13 51	13 54		14 00	13 59	14 27	14 07	14 18	14 25	14 27	14 38	14 58	14 39	14 44	14 44	14 53	15 00
	d	14 03				13 45	13 51	13 55		14 02	14 03	14 33		14 18	14 25	14 33	14 39	15 03			14 45	14 55	15 02
Twyford ■3	a	→									14 09	→				14 39		→					
Maidenhead ■3	a										14 17					14 47							
Slough ■3	a							14 09			14 24				14 40	14 54						15 10	
Ealing Broadway ⊖	a										14 49					15 19							
London Paddington ■15 ⊖	a					14 14	14 23	14 29		14 32	15 01			14 54	14 59	15 31	15 09				15 14	15 29	15 32

Table 116

Saturdays

30 June to 8 September

Birmingham, Banbury, Bicester, Oxford and Bedwyn - Reading and London

Network Diagram - see first Page of Table 116

		GW 1	GW 1	XC ◇1 ✠	CH	GW 1		GW ◇1	GW 1	GW 1	XC ◇1 ✠	GW 1	GW ◇1 ⊏	GW ◇1 ✠	GW 1	GW ◇1 ⊏		GW 1	GW 1	XC ◇1 ✠	CH	GW 1	GW ◇1	GW ◇1 ⊏	GW 1
Birmingham New Street 12	d			13 33							14 04									14 33					
Birmingham International	d										14 14														
Coventry	d										14 25														
Leamington Spa 8	d			14 00							14 38									15 00					
Banbury	d			14 19							14 55				15 02					15 20					
Kings Sutton	d														15 08										
Heyford	d														15 17										
Tackley	d														15 21										
Bicester Town	d				14 18																15 28				
Islip	d				14 29																15 39				
Oxford	a			14 40	14 44						15 14				15 32					15 41	15 54				
	d		14 37	14 43				15 01		15 07	15 16			15 31					15 37	15 43			16 01		
Radley	d									15 13															
Culham	d									15 17															
Appleford	d																								
Didcot Parkway	a		14 49							15 24									15 49						
	d		15 01							15 31			15 29			15 47			16 01						
Cholsey	d		15 07							15 37									16 07						
Goring & Streatley	d		15 12							15 42									16 12						
Pangbourne	d		15 17							15 47									16 17						
Tilehurst	d		15 21							15 51									16 21						
Bedwyn	d					14 38																15 38			
Hungerford	d					14 43																15 43			
Kintbury	d					14 48																15 48			
Newbury	a					14 55																15 55			
	d					14 55						15 13										15 55		16 06	
Newbury Racecourse	d											15 15													
Thatcham	d					15 00						15 20										16 00			
Midgham	d											15 24													
Aldermaston	d											15 28													
Theale	d					15 08						15 33										16 08			
Reading West	d	←							←			15 40						←							←
Reading 7	a	14 58	15 27	15 07		15 17		15 25	15 27	15 59	15 39	15 44	15 44	15 54		16 01		15 59	16 29	16 08		16 17	16 25	16 25	16 29
	d	15 03	15 33			15 19		15 25	15 33	16 03			15 45	15 55		16 02		16 03	16 33			16 18	16 26	16 28	16 33
Twyford 3	a	15 09	→						15 39	→								16 09	→						16 39
Maidenhead 3	a	15 17							15 47									16 17							16 47
Slough 3	a	15 24						15 40	15 54					16 10				16 24					16 40		16 54
Ealing Broadway ⊖	a	15 49							16 19									16 49							17 19
London Paddington 15 ⊖	a	16 01				15 54		15 59	16 31				16 14	16 29		16 37		17 01				16 52	16 59	17 02	17 31

		GW ◇1 ⊏		GW 1	XC ◇1 ✠	GW 1	GW ◇1 ⊏	GW ◇1 ✠	GW ◇1 ⊏	GW 1	GW 1	XC ◇1 ✠		CH	GW 1	GW ◇1	GW 1	GW 1	XC ◇1 ✠	GW ◇1 ⊏	GW 1	GW ◇1 ⊏		GW ◇1 ⊏	GW 1
Birmingham New Street 12	d				15 04							15 33							16 04						
Birmingham International	d				15 14														16 14						
Coventry	d				15 25														16 25						
Leamington Spa 8	d				15 38							16 02							16 38						
Banbury	d				15 55							16 20							16 55						
Kings Sutton	d																								
Heyford	d																								
Tackley	d																								
Bicester Town	d													16 30											
Islip	d													16 41											
Oxford	a				16 14							16 40		16 56					17 14						
	d			16 07	16 16			16 31			16 37	16 43				17 01		17 07	17 16			17 31			
Radley	d			16 13														17 13							
Culham	d																	17 17							
Appleford	d			16 17																					
Didcot Parkway	a			16 24							16 49							17 24							
	d	16 22		16 31			16 29		16 47		17 01							17 31		17 29				17 47	
Cholsey	d			16 37							17 07							17 37							
Goring & Streatley	d			16 42							17 12							17 42							
Pangbourne	d			16 47							17 17							17 47							
Tilehurst	d			16 51							17 21							17 51							
Bedwyn	d														16 43										
Hungerford	d														16 49										
Kintbury	d														16 53										
Newbury	a														17 00										
	d					16 13									17 01						17 15				
Newbury Racecourse	d					16 15															17 17				
Thatcham	d					16 20									17 06						17 22				
Midgham	d					16 24															17 27				
Aldermaston	d					16 28															17 30				
Theale	d					16 33									17 14						17 35				
Reading West	d					16 40				←							←				17 42				←
Reading 7	a	16 38		16 58	16 39	16 44	16 44	16 55	17 00	16 58	17 27	17 07			17 22	17 26	17 27	17 57	17 39	17 44	17 46	17 55		18 00	17 57
	d	16 39		17 03			16 45	16 55	17 02	17 03	17 33				17 22	17 27	17 33	18 03		17 45		17 57		18 02	18 03
Twyford 3	a			→						17 09	→						17 39	→							18 09
Maidenhead 3	a									17 17							17 47								18 17
Slough 3	a							17 10		17 24						17 41	17 54					18 10			18 24
Ealing Broadway ⊖	a									17 49							18 19								18 49
London Paddington 15 ⊖	a	17 07					17 14	17 29	17 32	18 01					17 54	18 00	18 31			18 14		18 29		18 32	19 01

Table 116

Saturdays

30 June to 8 September

Birmingham, Banbury, Bicester, Oxford and Bedwyn - Reading and London

Network Diagram - see first Page of Table 116

		GW 1	XC ◇1 ✠	GW 1	GW 1	GW ◇1	GW 1	GW ◇1 ⊏		GW 1	XC ◇1 ✠	CH	GW 1	GW ◇1 ⊏	GW ◇1 ✠	GW ◇1 ⊏	GW 1	GW 1		XC ◇1 ✠	GW 1	GW ◇1	GW 1	GW 1	XC ◇1 ✠
Birmingham New Street 12	d		16 33								17 04									17 33					18 04
Birmingham International	d										17 14														18 14
Coventry	d										17 25														18 25
Leamington Spa 8	d		17 00								17 38									18 02					18 38
Banbury	d		17 19	17 23							17 55									18 19					18 55
Kings Sutton	d			17 29																					
Heyford	d			17 38																					
Tackley	d			17 42																					
Bicester Town	d											18 04													
Islip	d											18 15													
Oxford	a		17 41	17 53							18 14	18 30								18 40					19 14
	d	17 37	17 43			18 01				18 07	18 16				18 31			18 37		18 43		19 01		19 07	19 16
Radley	d									18 13														19 13	
Culham	d																							19 17	
Appleford	d									18 17															
Didcot Parkway	a	17 49								18 24								18 49						19 24	
	d	18 01						18 22		18 31				18 29		18 47		19 01						19 31	
Cholsey	d	18 07								18 37								19 07						19 37	
Goring & Streatley	d	18 12								18 42								19 12						19 42	
Pangbourne	d	18 17								18 47								19 17						19 47	
Tilehurst	d	18 21								18 51								19 21						19 51	
Bedwyn	d				17 38																18 38				
Hungerford	d				17 43																18 43				
Kintbury	d				17 48																18 48				
Newbury	a				17 55																18 55				
	d				17 55								18 13								18 55				
Newbury Racecourse	d												18 15												
Thatcham	d				18 00								18 20								19 00				
Midgham	d												18 24												
Aldermaston	d												18 28												
Theale	d				18 08								18 33								19 08				
Reading West	d						←						18 40				←						←		
Reading 7	a	18 27	18 07		18 18	18 25	18 27	18 38		18 58	18 39		18 44	18 44	18 55	19 00	18 58	19 29		19 07	19 17	19 25	19 29	19 57	19 39
	d	18 33			18 19	18 25	18 33	18 39		19 03				18 45	18 56	19 02	19 03	19 33			19 20	19 25	19 33	20 03	
Twyford 3	a	→					18 39			→							19 09	→					19 39	→	
Maidenhead 3	a						18 47										19 17						19 47		
Slough 3	a					18 40	18 54								19 10		19 24					19 40	19 54		
Ealing Broadway ⊖	a						19 19										19 49						20 19		
London Paddington 15 ⊖	a				18 52	18 59	19 31	19 08						19 14	19 29	19 32	20 01					19 52	19 59	20 31	

		GW 1	GW ◇1 ⊏	GW ◇1 ✠		GW 1	GW ◇1	GW ◇1 ⊏	GW ◇1 ⊏	GW 1	XC ◇1 ✠	CH	GW ◇1	GW 1		GW 1	GW ◇1 ⊏	GW 1	XC ◇1 ✠	GW ◇1 ⊏	GW 1	GW 1	GW ◇1 ⊏	GW 1
Birmingham New Street 12	d										18 33								19 04					
Birmingham International	d																		19 14					
Coventry	d																		19 25					
Leamington Spa 8	d										19 00								19 38					
Banbury	d					19 02					19 19								19 55					
Kings Sutton	d					19 08																		
Heyford	d					19 17																		
Tackley	d					19 21																		
Bicester Town	d											19 17												
Islip	d											19 28												
Oxford	a					19 32					19 40	19 43							20 14					
	d			19 31						19 37	19 43		20 01					20 07	20 16		20 31			20 37
Radley	d																	20 13						
Culham	d																							
Appleford	d																	20 17						
Didcot Parkway	a									19 49								20 24						20 49
	d		19 29				19 47			20 01							20 23	20 31		20 29			20 47	21 01
Cholsey	d									20 07								20 37						21 07
Goring & Streatley	d									20 12								20 42						21 12
Pangbourne	d									20 17								20 47						21 17
Tilehurst	d									20 21								20 51						21 21
Bedwyn	d													19 41										
Hungerford	d													19 47										
Kintbury	d													19 51										
Newbury	a													19 58										
	d	19 13							19 46					19 58										
Newbury Racecourse	d	19 15												20 00										
Thatcham	d	19 20												20 05										
Midgham	d	19 24												20 10										
Aldermaston	d	19 28												20 13										
Theale	d	19 33												20 18										
Reading West	d	19 40						←						20 25		←						←		
Reading 7	a	19 44	19 44	19 55			20 00	19 57	20 07	20 29	20 10		20 25	20 28		20 29	20 38	20 57	20 39	20 44	20 54	20 57	21 06	21 27
	d		19 45	19 55			20 03	20 03	20 09	20 33			20 25			20 33	20 39	21 03		20 45	20 54	21 03	21 08	21 33
Twyford 3	a							20 09		→						20 39		→				21 09		→
Maidenhead 3	a							20 17								20 47						21 17		
Slough 3	a			20 10				20 24					20 40			20 54					21 09	21 24		
Ealing Broadway ⊖	a							20 49								21 19						21 49		
London Paddington 15 ⊖	a		20 14	20 29			20 32	21 01	20 37				20 59			21 31	21 07			21 14	21 29	22 02	21 36	

30 June to 8 September

Birmingham, Banbury, Bicester, Oxford and Bedwyn - Reading and London

Network Diagram - see first Page of Table 116

		XC ◇1 ⊼	CH	GW ◇1	GW 1	GW 1	GW 1	XC ◇1 ⊼	GW ◇1 ꟼ	GW ◇1	GW ◇1 ꟼ	XC ◇1 ⊼	GW 1	GW ◇1	GW 1	CH	XC ◇1	GW 1	GW 1	GW ◇1	GW ◇1 ꟼ	GW ◇1	GW 1
Birmingham New Street 12	d	19 33						20 04				20 33					21 04						
Birmingham International	d							20 14									21 14						
Coventry	d							20 25									21 25						
Leamington Spa 8	d	20 03						20 38				21 00					21 38						
Banbury	d	20 21				20 38		20 55				21 20					21 55	22 00					
Kings Sutton	d					20 44												22 06					
Heyford	d					20 53												22 15					
Tackley	d					20 57												22 19					
Bicester Town	d		20 28													21 37							
Islip	d		20 39													21 48							
Oxford	a	20 40	20 54			21 08		21 14				21 41				22 03	22 16	22 30					
	d	20 43		21 01				21 16		21 31		21 43	21 50	22 01			22 18			22 35		23 01	
Radley	d												21 56										
Culham	d																						
Appleford	d																						
Didcot Parkway	a									21 43			22 04	22 12						22 47		23 13	
	d								21 34	21 45	21 47		22 04	22 13						22 48	22 49	23 14	
Cholsey	d												22 10										
Goring & Streatley	d												22 15										
Pangbourne	d												22 21										
Tilehurst	d												22 24										
Bedwyn	d						20 48												22 00				23 00
Hungerford	d						20 54												22 06				23 06
Kintbury	d						20 58												22 10				23 10
Newbury	a						21 05												22 17				23 17
	d						21 05												22 17				23 17
Newbury Racecourse	d						21 07												22 19				23 19
Thatcham	d						21 12												22 24				23 24
Midgham	d						21 17												22 29				23 29
Aldermaston	d						21 20												22 32				23 32
Theale	d						21 25												22 37				23 37
Reading West	d				←		21 32								←				22 44				23 44
Reading 7	a	21 10		21 25	21 27		21 36	21 40	21 48	21 59	21 59	22 10	22 31	22 28	22 31		22 41		22 48	23 04	23 04	23 30	23 48
	d			21 25	21 33				21 50	22 01	22 03		22 33	22 29	22 33					23 05	23 05	23 31	
Twyford 3	a				21 39								→		22 39								
Maidenhead 3	a				21 47										22 47								
Slough 3	a			21 40	21 54					22 11				22 43	22 54					23 23		23 45	
Ealing Broadway ⊖	a				22 19										23 19								
London Paddington 15 ⊖	a			21 59	22 31				22 16	22 34	22 30			23 02	23 28					23 43	23 36	00 10	

		GW ◇1 ꟼ	GW 1	CH
Birmingham New Street 12	d			
Birmingham International	d			
Coventry	d			
Leamington Spa 8	d			
Banbury	d			
Kings Sutton	d			
Heyford	d			
Tackley	d			
Bicester Town	d			22 55
Islip	d			23 06
Oxford	a			23 21
	d		23 07	
Radley	d		23 13	
Culham	d		23 17	
Appleford	d		23 20	
Didcot Parkway	a		23 25	
	d	23 30	23 36	
Cholsey	d		23 42	
Goring & Streatley	d		23 47	
Pangbourne	d		23 51	
Tilehurst	d		23 56	
Bedwyn	d			
Hungerford	d			
Kintbury	d			
Newbury	a			
	d			
Newbury Racecourse	d			
Thatcham	d			
Midgham	d			
Aldermaston	d			
Theale	d			
Reading West	d			
Reading 7	a	23 51	00 01	
	d	23 51	00 03	
Twyford 3	a		00 09	
Maidenhead 3	a		00 17	
Slough 3	a		00 28	
Ealing Broadway ⊖	a		00 52	
London Paddington 15 ⊖	a	00 34	01 02	

15 September to 20 October

Birmingham, Banbury, Bicester, Oxford and Bedwyn - Reading and London

Network Diagram - see first Page of Table 116

		GW ◇1	GW ◇1 ꟼ	XC ◇1 A	GW ◇1	CH	GW 1	CH	GW 1	GW 1	GW 1	GW ◇1 ꟼ	GW 1	GW 1	GW ◇1	GW 1	GW ◇1 ꟼ	GW 1	GW 1	GW ◇1	GW ◇1 ꟼ	GW 1	GW 1
Birmingham New Street 12	d			22p04																			
Birmingham International	d																						
Coventry	d																						
Leamington Spa 8	d			22p53				23p38															
Banbury	d			23p16			23p45	23p57															
Kings Sutton	d						23p50																
Heyford	d						23p58																
Tackley	d						00 03																
Bicester Town	d					23p42																	
Islip	d					23p53																	
Oxford	a			23p35		00 08	00 13	00 21															
	d	23p09		23p36	00 07		00 27		03 59	05 14	05 49			06 07	06 31				06 42	07 01			07 07
Radley	d						00 33			05 20				06 13									07 13
Culham	d						00 37			05 24													07 17
Appleford	d						00 39							06 17									
Didcot Parkway	a	23p23			00 20		00 46		04 10	05 31	06 01			06 24					06 54				07 24
	d	23p23	23p35		00 21		00 46		04 10	05 31	06 01	06 29		06 31			06 59		07 01		07 17		07 31
Cholsey	d						00 52			05 37	06 07			06 37					07 07				07 37
Goring & Streatley	d						00 57			05 42	06 12			06 42					07 12				07 42
Pangbourne	d						01 01			05 47	06 17			06 47					07 17				07 47
Tilehurst	d						01 06			05 51	06 21			06 51					07 21				07 51
Bedwyn	d												06 05					06 39					
Hungerford	d												06 11					06 43					
Kintbury	d												06 15					06 48					
Newbury	a												06 22					06 55					
	d												06 22					06 55					
Newbury Racecourse	d												06 24										
Thatcham	d												06 29					07 00					
Midgham	d												06 34										
Aldermaston	d												06 37										
Theale	d												06 42					07 08					
Reading West	d												06 49			←						←	
Reading 7	a	23p40	23p53	00 07	00 38		01 12		04 27	05 57	06 27	06 43	06 52	06 57	07 00	06 57	07 14	07 20	07 27	07 27	07 31	07 27	07 59
	d	23p41	23p55		00 39		01 15		04 40	06 03	06 33	06 45	06 52	07 03	07 00	07 03	07 15	07 21	07 33	07 27	07 32	07 33	08 03
Twyford 3	a						01 21		04 46	06 09	06 39			→		07 09			→			07 39	→
Maidenhead 3	a	23p54					01 29		04 54	06 17	06 47					07 17						07 47	
Slough 3	a	00 01			00 55		01 37		05 01	06 24	06 54				07 16	07 24				07 42		07 54	
Ealing Broadway ⊖	a						01 53		05 19	06 49	07 19					07 49						08 19	
London Paddington 15 ⊖	a	00 28	00 33		01 17		02 05		05 31	07 01	07 31	07 14	07 22		07 37	08 01	07 44	07 54		08 01	08 07	08 31	

		XC ◇1 ⊼	GW 1	GW ◇1 ꟼ	GW ◇1 ꟼ	GW 1	GW ◇1 ꟼ	GW 1	GW 1	XC ◇1	GW ◇1 ꟼ	GW 1	GW ◇1	CH	GW ◇1 ꟼ	GW 1	GW 1	XC ◇1 ⊼	GW 1	GW ◇1 ꟼ	GW ◇1 ꟼ	GW ◇1 ꟼ	GW ◇1 ꟼ
Birmingham New Street 12	d	06 04								06 33								07 04					
Birmingham International	d	06 14																07 14					
Coventry	d	06 25																07 25					
Leamington Spa 8	d	06 38								07 00								07 38					
Banbury	d	06 55				07 02				07 19								07 55					
Kings Sutton	d					07 08																	
Heyford	d					07 17																	
Tackley	d					07 21																	
Bicester Town	d													07 36									
Islip	d													07 47									
Oxford	a	07 14				07 32				07 40				08 02				08 14					
	d	07 16			07 31				07 37	07 43			08 01				08 07	08 16				08 31	
Radley	d																08 13						
Culham	d																						
Appleford	d																08 17						
Didcot Parkway	a								07 49								08 24						
	d			07 29			07 47		08 01		07 59				08 17		08 31			08 29			08 47
Cholsey	d								08 07								08 37						
Goring & Streatley	d								08 12								08 42						
Pangbourne	d								08 17								08 47						
Tilehurst	d								08 21								08 51						
Bedwyn	d											07 37											
Hungerford	d											07 41											
Kintbury	d											07 46											
Newbury	a											07 53											
	d		07 13									07 53							08 13		08 34		
Newbury Racecourse	d		07 15																08 15				
Thatcham	d		07 20									07 58							08 20				
Midgham	d		07 24																08 24				
Aldermaston	d		07 28																08 28				
Theale	d		07 33									08 06							08 33				
Reading West	d		07 42					←								←			08 40				
Reading 7	a	07 39	07 45	07 44	07 54		08 00	07 59	08 27	08 06	08 14	08 19	08 25		08 31	08 27	08 57	08 39	08 44	08 44	08 52	08 54	09 00
	d			07 46	07 54		08 02	08 03	08 33		08 16	08 20	08 26		08 32	08 33	09 03			08 46	08 52	08 55	09 02
Twyford 3	a							08 09	→							08 39	→						
Maidenhead 3	a							08 17								08 47							
Slough 3	a				08 09			08 24					08 40			08 54						09 09	
Ealing Broadway ⊖	a							08 49								09 19							
London Paddington 15 ⊖	a			08 14	08 29		08 32	09 01			08 44	08 52	08 59		09 02	09 31				09 14	09 21	09 29	09 32

A 15 September

15 September to 20 October

Birmingham, Banbury, Bicester, Oxford and Bedwyn - Reading and London

Network Diagram - see first Page of Table 116

		GW ■		GW ◇■ ⊡	GW ■	XC ◇■ ⊼	GW ◇■ ⊡	GW ■	GW ◇■ ⊼	GW ◇■ A ⊡⊘	GW ■	GW ■		GW ■	CH	XC ◇■ ⊼	GW ◇■ ⊡	GW ◇■ A ⊡⊘	GW ■	GW ◇■ A ⊡⊘	GW ■	GW ■		XC ◇■ ⊼	GW ■
Birmingham New Street 12	d					07 33										08 04								08 33	
Birmingham International	d															08 14									
Coventry	d															08 25									
Leamington Spa 8	d					08 00										08 38								09 00	
Banbury	d					08 19										08 55			09 02					09 19	
Kings Sutton	d																		09 08						
Heyford	d																		09 17						
Tackley	d																		09 21						
Bicester Town	d														08 45										
Islip	d														08 56										
Oxford	a					08 40									09 11	09 14			09 32					09 40	
	d				08 37	08 43			09 01					09 07		09 16		09 31				09 37		09 43	
Radley	d													09 13											
Culham	d													09 17											
Appleford	d																								
Didcot Parkway	a				08 49									09 24								09 49			
	d			08 52	09 01		08 59			09 17				09 31			09 29			09 47		10 01			
Cholsey	d				09 07									09 37								10 07			
Goring & Streatley	d				09 12									09 42								10 12			
Pangbourne	d				09 17									09 47								10 17			
Tilehurst	d				09 21									09 51								10 21			
Bedwyn	d							08 38																	09 37
Hungerford	d							08 43																	09 41
Kintbury	d							08 48																	09 46
Newbury	a							08 55																	09 53
	d							08 55				09 03													09 53
Newbury Racecourse	d											09 06													
Thatcham	d							09 00				09 11													09 58
Midgham	d											09 16													
Aldermaston	d											09 19													
Theale	d							09 08				09 24													10 06
Reading West	d	←									←	09 31									←				
Reading 7	a	08 57		09 07	09 27	09 11	09 14	09 20	09 24	09 32	09 27	09 35		09 57		09 39	09 45	09 54		10 00	09 57	10 27		10 07	10 17
	d	09 03		09 09	09 33		09 16	09 20	09 24	09 33	09 33			10 03			09 46	09 55		10 02	10 03	10 33			10 18
Twyford 3	a	09 09			→						09 39			→							10 09	→			
Maidenhead 3	a	09 17									09 47										10 17				
Slough 3	a	09 24							09 40		09 54							10 09			10 24				
Ealing Broadway ⊖	a	09 49									10 19										10 49				
London Paddington 15 ⊖	a	10 01		09 37			09 44	09 52	09 59	10 02	10 31						10 14	10 29		10 32	11 01				10 52

		GW ◇■ ⊼	GW ◇■ ⊡	GW ■	GW ◇■ ⊡	GW ■	XC ◇■ ⊼	CH		GW ■	GW ◇■ ⊡	GW ◇■ ⊡	GW ◇■ ⊡	GW ■	GW ■	XC ◇■ ⊼	GW ■	GW ◇■		GW ■	GW ■	XC ◇■ ⊼	GW ■	GW ◇■ ⊡	GW ◇■ ⊼
Birmingham New Street 12	d						09 04									09 33						10 04			
Birmingham International	d						09 14															10 14			
Coventry	d						09 25															10 25			
Leamington Spa 8	d						09 38									10 00						10 38			
Banbury	d						09 55									10 19						10 55			
Kings Sutton	d																								
Heyford	d																								
Tackley	d																								
Bicester Town	d							09 57																	
Islip	d							10 08																	
Oxford	a						10 14	10 23								10 40						11 14			
	d	10 01				10 07	10 16					10 31			10 37	10 43		11 01			11 07	11 16			11 31
Radley	d					10 13															11 13				
Culham	d																								
Appleford	d					10 17																			
Didcot Parkway	a					10 23									10 49						11 24				
	d		10 17		10 22	10 31					10 29		10 47		11 01						11 31			11 29	
Cholsey	d					10 37									11 07						11 37				
Goring & Streatley	d					10 42									11 12						11 42				
Pangbourne	d					10 47									11 17						11 47				
Tilehurst	d					10 51									11 21						11 51				
Bedwyn	d																10 40								
Hungerford	d																10 46								
Kintbury	d																10 50								
Newbury	a																10 57								
	d									10 13							10 57						11 13		
Newbury Racecourse	d									10 15													11 15		
Thatcham	d									10 20							11 02						11 20		
Midgham	d									10 24													11 24		
Aldermaston	d									10 28													11 28		
Theale	d									10 33							11 10						11 33		
Reading West	d			←						10 40				←						←			11 40		
Reading 7	a	10 25	10 32	10 27	10 36	10 58	10 39			10 44	10 45	10 54	11 01	10 58	11 27	11 09	11 21	11 24		11 27	11 58	11 39	11 44	11 44	11 54
	d	10 25	10 33	10 33	10 39	11 03					10 46	10 55	11 02	11 03	11 33		11 21	11 25		11 33	12 03			11 45	11 55
Twyford 3	a			10 39		→								11 09	→					11 39	→				
Maidenhead 3	a			10 47										11 17						11 47					
Slough 3	a	10 40		10 54								11 09		11 24				11 39		11 54					12 09
Ealing Broadway ⊖	a			11 19										11 49						12 19					
London Paddington 15 ⊖	a	10 59	11 02	11 31	11 08						11 14	11 29	11 33	12 01			11 52	11 59		12 31				12 14	12 29

A ⊡ from Reading ⊘ to Reading

15 September to 20 October

Birmingham, Banbury, Bicester, Oxford and Bedwyn - Reading and London

Network Diagram - see first Page of Table 116

		GW ■	GW ◇■ ⊡	GW ■		GW ■	XC ◇■ ⊼	CH	GW ■	GW ◇■ ⊼	GW ■	GW ◇■ ⊡	GW ■	XC ◇■ ⊼		GW ■	GW ◇■ ⊡	GW ◇■ ⊼	GW ◇■ ⊡	GW ■	GW ■	XC ◇■ ⊼	GW ◇■ ⊼	GW ■
Birmingham New Street 12	d						10 33							11 04								11 33		
Birmingham International	d													11 14										
Coventry	d													11 25										
Leamington Spa 8	d						11 00							11 38								12 00		
Banbury	d	11 02					11 19							11 55								12 19		
Kings Sutton	d	11 08																						
Heyford	d	11 17																						
Tackley	d	11 21																						
Bicester Town	d							11 30																
Islip	d							11 41																
Oxford	a	11 32					11 40	11 56						12 14								12 40		
	d					11 37	11 43			12 01			12 07	12 16				12 31			12 37	12 43	13 01	
Radley	d												12 13											
Culham	d																							
Appleford	d												12 17											
Didcot Parkway	a					11 49							12 24								12 49			
	d		11 47			12 01						12 22	12 31				12 29		12 47		13 01			
Cholsey	d					12 07							12 37								13 07			
Goring & Streatley	d					12 12							12 42								13 12			
Pangbourne	d					12 17							12 47								13 17			
Tilehurst	d					12 21							12 51								13 21			
Bedwyn	d								11 38															
Hungerford	d								11 43															
Kintbury	d								11 48															
Newbury	a								11 55															
	d								11 55							12 13								
Newbury Racecourse	d															12 15								
Thatcham	d								12 00							12 20								
Midgham	d															12 24								
Aldermaston	d															12 28								
Theale	d								12 08							12 33								
Reading West	d			←							←					12 40				←				←
Reading 7	a		12 00	11 58		12 28	12 07		12 17	12 25	12 28	12 37	12 57	12 39		12 44	12 44	12 53	13 00	12 57	13 27	13 06	13 25	13 27
	d		12 02	12 03		12 33			12 18	12 25	12 33	12 39	13 03				12 45	12 55	13 02	13 03	13 33		13 25	13 33
Twyford 3	a			12 09		→					12 39		→							13 09	→			13 39
Maidenhead 3	a			12 17							12 47									13 17				13 47
Slough 3	a			12 24						12 40	12 54							13 09		13 24			13 40	13 54
Ealing Broadway ⊖	a			12 49							13 19									13 49				14 19
London Paddington 15 ⊖	a		12 32	13 01					12 52	12 59	13 31	13 07					13 12	13 30	13 33	14 01			13 59	14 31

		GW ■	XC ◇■ ⊼	CH	GW ■	GW ◇■ ⊡	GW ■	GW ◇■	GW ■	GW ◇■ ⊡		GW ■	GW ■	XC ◇■ ⊼	GW ◇■ ⊡	GW ◇■ ⊼	GW ■	GW ◇■ ⊡	GW ■	XC ◇■ ⊼		GW ■	GW ◇■ ⊡	GW ◇■ ⊡	GW ◇■ ⊡
Birmingham New Street 12	d		12 04											12 33						13 04					
Birmingham International	d		12 14																	13 14					
Coventry	d		12 25																	13 25					
Leamington Spa 8	d		12 38											13 02						13 38					
Banbury	d		12 55						13 02					13 21						13 55					
Kings Sutton	d								13 08																
Heyford	d								13 17																
Tackley	d								13 21																
Bicester Town	d			13 00																					
Islip	d			13 11																					
Oxford	a		13 14	13 26					13 32					13 40						14 14					
	d	13 07	13 16					13 31					13 37	13 43		14 01			14 07	14 16				14 31	
Radley	d	13 13																	14 13						
Culham	d	13 17																							
Appleford	d																		14 17						
Didcot Parkway	a	13 24											13 51						14 24						
	d	13 31				13 29				13 47			14 01					14 22	14 31				14 29		14 47
Cholsey	d	13 37											14 07						14 37						
Goring & Streatley	d	13 42											14 12						14 42						
Pangbourne	d	13 47											14 17						14 47						
Tilehurst	d	13 51											14 21						14 51						
Bedwyn	d						13 07								13 33										
Hungerford	d						13 13								13 40										
Kintbury	d						13 17																		
Newbury	a						13 24								13 49										
	d				13 13		13 28								13 50							14 13			
Newbury Racecourse	d				13 15																	14 15			
Thatcham	d				13 20		13 33								13 57							14 20			
Midgham	d				13 24																	14 24			
Aldermaston	d				13 28																	14 28			
Theale	d				13 33		13 41								14 06							14 33			
Reading West	d				13 40							←					←					14 40			
Reading 7	a	13 59	13 39		13 44	13 44	13 51	13 54		14 00		13 59	14 27	14 07	14 19	14 25	14 27	14 38	14 58	14 39		14 44	14 44	14 53	15 00
	d	14 03				13 45	13 51	13 55		14 02		14 03	14 33		14 19	14 25	14 33	14 39	15 03				14 45	14 55	15 02
Twyford 3	a	→										14 09	→				14 39		→						
Maidenhead 3	a											14 17					14 47								
Slough 3	a							14 09				14 24				14 40	14 54							15 10	
Ealing Broadway ⊖	a											14 49					15 19								
London Paddington 15 ⊖	a					14 14	14 23	14 29		14 32		15 01			14 45	14 59	15 31	15 09					15 14	15 29	15 32

Table 116

Saturdays

15 September to 20 October

Birmingham, Banbury, Bicester, Oxford and Bedwyn - Reading and London

Network Diagram - see first Page of Table 116

		GW ■1	GW ■1	XC ◇■1	CH	GW ■1	GW ◇■1	GW ■1	GW ■1	XC ◇■1	GW ■1	GW ◇■1	GW ◇■1	GW ■1	GW ◇■1	GW ■1	GW ■1	XC ◇■1	CH	GW ■1	GW ◇■1	GW ■1	GW ◇■1
Birmingham New Street ■12	d			13 33						14 04								14 33					
Birmingham International	d									14 14													
Coventry	d									14 25													
Leamington Spa ■8	d			14 00						14 38								15 00					
Banbury	d			14 19						14 55				15 02				15 20					
Kings Sutton	d													15 08									
Heyford	d													15 17									
Tackley	d													15 21									
Bicester Town	d				14 18														15 28				
Islip	d				14 29														15 39				
Oxford	a			14 40	14 44					15 14				15 32				15 41	15 54				
	d		14 37	14 43			15 01		15 07	15 16			15 31				15 37	15 43			16 01		
Radley	d								15 13														
Culham	d								15 17														
Appleford	d																						
Didcot Parkway	a		14 49						15 24								15 49						
	d		15 01						15 31			15 29			15 47		16 01						16 22
Cholsey	d		15 07						15 37								16 07						
Goring & Streatley	d		15 12						15 42								16 12						
Pangbourne	d		15 17						15 47								16 17						
Tilehurst	d		15 21						15 51								16 21						
Bedwyn	d					14 38														15 38			
Hungerford	d					14 43														15 43			
Kintbury	d					14 48														15 48			
Newbury	a					14 55														15 55			
	d					14 55					15 13									15 55			
Newbury Racecourse	d										15 15												
Thatcham	d					15 00					15 20									16 00			
Midgham	d										15 24												
Aldermaston	d										15 28												
Theale	d					15 08					15 33									16 08			
Reading West	d	←						←			15 40					←						←	
Reading ■7	a	14 58	15 27	15 07		15 17	15 25	15 27	15 59	15 39	15 44	15 44	15 54		16 00	15 59	16 29	16 08		16 17	16 25	16 29	16 38
	d	15 03	15 33			15 19	15 25	15 33	16 03			15 45	15 55		16 01	16 03	16 33			16 18	16 26	16 33	16 39
Twyford ■3	a	15 09	→					15 39	→							16 09	→					16 39	
Maidenhead ■3	a	15 17						15 47								16 17						16 47	
Slough ■3	a	15 24					15 40	15 54					16 10			16 24					16 40	16 54	
Ealing Broadway ⊖	a	15 49						16 19								16 49						17 19	
London Paddington ■15 ⊖	a	16 01				15 54	15 59	16 31				16 14	16 29		16 32	17 01				16 52	16 59	17 31	17 07

		GW ■1	XC ◇■1	GW ■1	GW ◇■1	GW ◇■1	GW ◇■1	GW ■1	GW ■1	XC ◇■1	CH	GW ◇■1	GW ◇■1	GW ■1	GW ■1	XC ◇■1	GW ■1	GW ◇■1	GW ◇■1	GW ◇■1	GW ■1	GW ■1
Birmingham New Street ■12	d		15 04							15 33						16 04						
Birmingham International	d		15 14													16 14						
Coventry	d		15 25													16 25						
Leamington Spa ■8	d		15 38							16 02						16 38						
Banbury	d		15 55							16 20						16 55						
Kings Sutton	d																					
Heyford	d																					
Tackley	d																					
Bicester Town	d										16 30											
Islip	d										16 41											
Oxford	a		16 14							16 40	16 56					17 14						
	d	16 07	16 16			16 31			16 37	16 43			17 01		17 07	17 16			17 31			17 37
Radley	d	16 13													17 13							
Culham	d														17 17							
Appleford	d	16 17																				
Didcot Parkway	a	16 24							16 49						17 24							17 49
	d	16 31			16 29		16 47		17 01						17 31			17 29		17 47		18 01
Cholsey	d	16 37							17 07						17 37							18 07
Goring & Streatley	d	16 42							17 12						17 42							18 12
Pangbourne	d	16 47							17 17						17 47							18 17
Tilehurst	d	16 51							17 21						17 51							18 21
Bedwyn	d											16 35					16 56					
Hungerford	d											16 42					17 00					
Kintbury	d																17 05					
Newbury	a											16 52					17 13					
	d			16 13								16 53					17 13					
Newbury Racecourse	d			16 15													17 15					
Thatcham	d			16 20								16 59					17 20					
Midgham	d			16 24													17 25					
Aldermaston	d			16 28													17 28					
Theale	d			16 33								17 08					17 33					
Reading West	d			16 40				←						←			17 40				←	
Reading ■7	a	16 58	16 39	16 44	16 44	16 55	17 00	16 58	17 27	17 07		17 17	17 26	17 27	17 57	17 39	17 44	17 44	17 55	18 00	17 57	18 27
	d	17 03			16 45	16 55	17 02	17 03	17 33			17 18	17 27	17 33	18 03			17 45	17 57	18 02	18 03	18 33
Twyford ■3	a	→						17 09	→					17 39	→						18 09	→
Maidenhead ■3	a							17 17						17 47							18 17	
Slough ■3	a					17 10		17 24					17 41	17 54					18 10		18 24	
Ealing Broadway ⊖	a							17 49						18 19							18 49	
London Paddington ■15 ⊖	a				17 14	17 29	17 32	18 01				17 51	18 00	18 31				18 14	18 29	18 32	19 01	

Table 116

Saturdays

15 September to 20 October

Birmingham, Banbury, Bicester, Oxford and Bedwyn - Reading and London

Network Diagram - see first Page of Table 116

		XC ◇■1	GW ■1	GW ■1	GW ◇■1	GW ■1	GW ◇■1	GW ■1	XC ◇■1	CH	GW ■1	GW ◇■1	GW ◇■1	GW ◇■1	GW ■1	GW ■1	XC ◇■1	GW ■1	GW ◇■1	GW ■1	GW ■1	XC ◇■1	GW ■1
Birmingham New Street ■12	d	16 33							17 04								17 33					18 04	
Birmingham International	d								17 14													18 14	
Coventry	d								17 25													18 25	
Leamington Spa ■8	d	17 00							17 38								18 02					18 38	
Banbury	d	17 19	17 23						17 55								18 19					18 55	
Kings Sutton	d		17 29																				
Heyford	d		17 38																				
Tackley	d		17 42																				
Bicester Town	d									18 04													
Islip	d									18 15													
Oxford	a	17 41	17 53						18 14	18 30							18 40					19 14	
	d	17 43			18 01			18 07	18 16				18 31			18 37	18 43		19 01		19 07	19 16	
Radley	d							18 13													19 13		
Culham	d																				19 17		
Appleford	d							18 17															
Didcot Parkway	a							18 24								18 49					19 24		
	d						18 22	18 31				18 29		18 47		19 01					19 31		
Cholsey	d							18 37								19 07					19 37		
Goring & Streatley	d							18 42								19 12					19 42		
Pangbourne	d							18 47								19 17					19 47		
Tilehurst	d							18 51								19 21					19 51		
Bedwyn	d			17 38														18 38					
Hungerford	d			17 43														18 43					
Kintbury	d			17 48														18 48					
Newbury	a			17 55														18 55					
	d			17 55							18 13							18 55					19 13
Newbury Racecourse	d										18 15												19 15
Thatcham	d			18 00							18 20							19 00					19 20
Midgham	d										18 24												19 24
Aldermaston	d										18 28												19 28
Theale	d			18 08							18 33							19 08					19 33
Reading West	d					←					18 40				←					←			19 40
Reading ■7	a	18 07		18 18	18 25	18 27	18 38	18 58	18 39		18 44	18 44	18 55	19 00	18 58	19 29	19 07	19 17	19 25	19 29	19 57	19 39	19 44
	d			18 19	18 25	18 33	18 39	19 03				18 45	18 56	19 02	19 03	19 33		19 20	19 25	19 33	20 03		
Twyford ■3	a					18 39		→							19 09	→				19 39	→		
Maidenhead ■3	a					18 47									19 17					19 47			
Slough ■3	a				18 40	18 54							19 10		19 24				19 40	19 54			
Ealing Broadway ⊖	a					19 19									19 49					20 19			
London Paddington ■15 ⊖	a			18 52	18 59	19 31	19 08					19 14	19 29	19 32	20 01			19 52	19 59	20 31			

		GW ◇■1	GW ◇■1	GW ■1	GW ◇■1	GW ■1	GW ◇■1	GW ■1	XC ◇■1	CH	GW ◇■1	GW ■1	GW ■1	GW ◇■1	GW ■1	XC ◇■1	GW ◇■1	GW ◇■1	GW ■1	GW ◇■1	GW ■1	XC ◇■1
Birmingham New Street ■12	d								18 33							19 04						19 33
Birmingham International	d															19 14						
Coventry	d															19 25						
Leamington Spa ■8	d								19 00							19 38						20 03
Banbury	d			19 02					19 19							19 55						20 21
Kings Sutton	d			19 08																		
Heyford	d			19 17																		
Tackley	d			19 21																		
Bicester Town	d									19 17												
Islip	d									19 28												
Oxford	a			19 32					19 40	19 43						20 14						20 40
	d		19 31					19 37	19 43		20 01				20 07	20 16		20 31			20 37	20 43
Radley	d														20 13							
Culham	d																					
Appleford	d														20 17							
Didcot Parkway	a							19 49							20 24						20 49	
	d	19 29			19 47			20 01						20 23	20 31		20 29			20 47	21 01	
Cholsey	d							20 07							20 37						21 07	
Goring & Streatley	d							20 12							20 42						21 12	
Pangbourne	d							20 17							20 47						21 17	
Tilehurst	d							20 21							20 51						21 21	
Bedwyn	d											19 41										
Hungerford	d											19 47										
Kintbury	d											19 51										
Newbury	a											19 58										
	d						19 46					19 58										
Newbury Racecourse	d											20 00										
Thatcham	d											20 05										
Midgham	d											20 10										
Aldermaston	d											20 13										
Theale	d											20 18										
Reading West	d					←						20 25	←						←			
Reading ■7	a	19 44	19 55		20 00	19 57	20 07	20 29	20 10		20 25	20 28	20 29	20 38	21 04	20 39	20 44	20 54	21 04	21 07	21 29	21 18
	d	19 45	19 55		20 03	20 03	20 09	20 33			20 25		20 33	20 39	21 05		20 45	20 54	21 05	21 09	21 33	
Twyford ■3	a					20 09		→					20 39		→				21 12		→	
Maidenhead ■3	a					20 17							20 47						21 20			
Slough ■3	a		20 10			20 24					20 40		20 54					21 09	21 27			
Ealing Broadway ⊖	a					20 49							21 19						21 52			
London Paddington ■15 ⊖	a	20 14	20 29		20 32	21 01	20 37				20 59		21 31	21 07			21 14	21 29	22 02	21 36		

Table 116

Saturdays
15 September to 20 October

Birmingham, Banbury, Bicester, Oxford and Bedwyn - Reading and London

Network Diagram - see first Page of Table 116

		CH	GW ◇1	GW 1	GW 1	GW 1	XC ◇1 🍴	GW ◇1 ☕	GW ◇1	GW ◇1 ☕	XC ◇1 🍴	GW 1	GW ◇1	GW 1	CH	XC ◇1	GW 1	GW 1	GW ◇1 ☕	GW ◇1	GW ◇1	GW 1	GW ◇1 ☕
Birmingham New Street 12	d						20 04				20 33					21 04							
Birmingham International	d						20 14									21 14							
Coventry	d						20 25									21 25							
Leamington Spa 8	d						20 38				21 00					21 38							
Banbury	d				20 38		20 55				21 20					21 55	22 00						
Kings Sutton	d				20 44												22 06						
Heyford	d				20 53												22 15						
Tackley	d				20 57												22 19						
Bicester Town	d	20 28													21 37								
Islip	d	20 39													21 48								
Oxford	a	20 54			21 08		21 14				21 41				22 03	22 16	22 30						
	d		21 01				21 16		21 31		21 43	21 50	22 01			22 18				22 35	23 01		
Radley	d											21 56											
Culham	d																						
Appleford	d																						
Didcot Parkway	a								21 43			22 04	22 12							22 47	23 13		
	d							21 34	21 45	21 47		22 04	22 13						22 49	22 51	23 13		23 30
Cholsey	d											22 10											
Goring & Streatley	d											22 15											
Pangbourne	d											22 21											
Tilehurst	d											22 24											
Bedwyn	d					20 48												22 00				23 00	
Hungerford	d					20 54												22 06				23 06	
Kintbury	d					20 58												22 10				23 10	
Newbury	a					21 05												22 17				23 17	
	d					21 05												22 17				23 17	
Newbury Racecourse	d					21 07												22 19				23 19	
Thatcham	d					21 12												22 24				23 24	
Midgham	d					21 17												22 29				23 29	
Aldermaston	d					21 20												22 32				23 32	
Theale	d					21 25												22 37				23 37	
Reading West	d			←		21 32								←				22 44				23 44	
Reading 7	a		21 25	21 29		21 36	21 40	21 51	21 59	22 01	22 10	22 35	22 31	22 35		22 41		22 48	23 04	23 08	23 30	23 48	23 51
	d		21 25	21 33				21 53	22 02	22 06		22 36	22 32	22 36					23 05	23 09	23 31		23 51
Twyford 3	a			21 40								→		22 43									
Maidenhead 3	a			21 48										22 51									
Slough 3	a		21 40	21 55					22 15				22 46	22 58						23 26	23 45		
Ealing Broadway ⊖	a			22 20										23 23									
London Paddington 15 ⊖	a		21 59	22 32				22 22	22 33	22 37			23 05	23 32					23 36	23 46	00 10		00 34

		GW 1	CH
Birmingham New Street 12	d		
Birmingham International	d		
Coventry	d		
Leamington Spa 8	d		
Banbury	d		
Kings Sutton	d		
Heyford	d		
Tackley	d		
Bicester Town	d		22 55
Islip	d		23 06
Oxford	a		23 21
	d	23 07	
Radley	d	23 13	
Culham	d	23 17	
Appleford	d	23 20	
Didcot Parkway	a	23 25	
	d	23 36	
Cholsey	d	23 42	
Goring & Streatley	d	23 47	
Pangbourne	d		
Tilehurst	d	23 56	
Bedwyn	d		
Hungerford	d		
Kintbury	d		
Newbury	a		
	d		
Newbury Racecourse	d		
Thatcham	d		
Midgham	d		
Aldermaston	d		
Theale	d		
Reading West	d		
Reading 7	a	00 02	
	d	00 03	
Twyford 3	a	00 10	
Maidenhead 3	a	00 18	
Slough 3	a	00 29	
Ealing Broadway ⊖	a	00 53	
London Paddington 15 ⊖	a	01 04	

Table 116

Saturdays
from 27 October

Birmingham, Banbury, Bicester, Oxford and Bedwyn - Reading and London

Network Diagram - see first Page of Table 116

		GW ◇1	GW ◇1 ☕	GW ◇1	CH	GW 1	CH	GW 1	GW 1	GW 1	GW ◇1 ☕	GW 1	GW 1	GW ◇1	GW 1	GW ◇1 ☕	GW 1	GW 1	GW ◇1	GW ◇1 ☕	GW 1	GW 1	XC ◇1 🍴
Birmingham New Street 12	d																						06 04
Birmingham International	d																						06 14
Coventry	d																						06 25
Leamington Spa 8	d						23p38																06 38
Banbury	d					23p45	23p57																06 55
Kings Sutton	d					23p50																	
Heyford	d					23p58																	
Tackley	d					00 03																	
Bicester Town	d				23p42																		
Islip	d				23p53																		
Oxford	a				00 08	00 13	00 21																07 14
	d	23p09		00 07		00 27		03 59	05 14	05 49			06 07	06 31				06 42	07 01			07 07	07 16
Radley	d					00 33			05 20				06 13									07 13	
Culham	d					00 37			05 24													07 17	
Appleford	d					00 39							06 17										
Didcot Parkway	a	23p23		00 20		00 46		04 10	05 31	06 01			06 24					06 54				07 24	
	d	23p23	23p35	00 21		00 46		04 10	05 31	06 01	06 29		06 31			06 59		07 01		07 17		07 31	
Cholsey	d					00 52			05 37	06 07			06 37					07 07				07 37	
Goring & Streatley	d					00 57			05 42	06 12			06 42					07 12				07 42	
Pangbourne	d					01 01			05 47	06 17			06 47					07 17				07 47	
Tilehurst	d					01 06			05 51	06 21			06 51					07 21				07 51	
Bedwyn	d											06 05					06 39						
Hungerford	d											06 11					06 43						
Kintbury	d											06 15					06 48						
Newbury	a											06 22					06 55						
	d											06 22					06 55						
Newbury Racecourse	d											06 24											
Thatcham	d											06 29					07 00						
Midgham	d											06 34											
Aldermaston	d											06 37											
Theale	d											06 42					07 08						
Reading West	d											06 49			←						←		
Reading 7	a	23p40	23p53	00 38		01 12		04 27	05 57	06 27	06 43	06 52	06 57	07 00	06 57	07 14	07 20	07 27	07 27	07 31	07 27	07 59	07 39
	d	23p41	23p55	00 39		01 15		04 40	06 03	06 33	06 45	06 52	07 03	07 00	07 03	07 15	07 21	07 33	07 27	07 32	07 33	08 03	
Twyford 3	a					01 21		04 46	06 09	06 39			→		07 09			→			07 39	→	
Maidenhead 3	a	23p54				01 29		04 54	06 17	06 47					07 17						07 47		
Slough 3	a	00 01		00 55		01 37		05 01	06 24	06 54				07 16	07 24				07 42		07 54		
Ealing Broadway ⊖	a					01 53		05 19	06 49	07 19					07 49						08 19		
London Paddington 15 ⊖	a	00 28	00 33	01 17		02 05		05 31	07 01	07 31	07 14	07 22		07 37	08 01	07 44	07 54		08 01	08 07	08 31		

		GW 1	GW ◇1 ☕	GW ◇1 ☕	GW 1	GW ◇1 ☕	GW 1	GW 1	XC ◇1	GW ◇1 ☕	GW 1	GW ◇1	CH	GW ◇1 ☕	GW 1	GW 1	XC ◇1 🍴	GW 1	GW ◇1 ☕	GW ◇1 ☕	GW ◇1 ☕	GW ◇1 ☕	GW 1
Birmingham New Street 12	d								06 33								07 04						
Birmingham International	d																07 14						
Coventry	d																07 25						
Leamington Spa 8	d								07 00								07 38						
Banbury	d				07 02				07 19								07 55						
Kings Sutton	d				07 08																		
Heyford	d				07 17																		
Tackley	d				07 21																		
Bicester Town	d												07 36										
Islip	d												07 47										
Oxford	a				07 32				07 40				08 02				08 14						
	d			07 31				07 37	07 43			08 01				08 07	08 16				08 31		
Radley	d															08 13							
Culham	d																						
Appleford	d															08 17							
Didcot Parkway	a							07 49								08 24							
	d		07 29			07 47		08 01		07 59				08 17		08 31			08 29			08 47	
Cholsey	d							08 07								08 37							
Goring & Streatley	d							08 12								08 42							
Pangbourne	d							08 17								08 47							
Tilehurst	d							08 21								08 51							
Bedwyn	d										07 37												
Hungerford	d										07 41												
Kintbury	d										07 46												
Newbury	a										07 53												
	d	07 13									07 53							08 13		08 34			
Newbury Racecourse	d	07 15																08 15					
Thatcham	d	07 20									07 58							08 20					
Midgham	d	07 24																08 24					
Aldermaston	d	07 28																08 28					
Theale	d	07 33									08 06							08 33					
Reading West	d	07 42					←								←			08 40					←
Reading 7	a	07 45	07 44	07 54		08 00	07 59	08 27	08 06	08 14	08 19	08 25		08 31	08 27	08 57	08 39	08 44	08 44	08 52	08 54	09 00	08 57
	d		07 46	07 54		08 02	08 03	08 33		08 16	08 20	08 26		08 32	08 33	09 03			08 46	08 52	08 55	09 02	09 03
Twyford 3	a						08 09	→							08 39	→							09 09
Maidenhead 3	a						08 17								08 47								09 17
Slough 3	a			08 09			08 24					08 40			08 54						09 09		09 24
Ealing Broadway ⊖	a						08 49								09 19								09 49
London Paddington 15 ⊖	a		08 14	08 29		08 32	09 01			08 44	08 52	08 59		09 02	09 31				09 14	09 21	09 29	09 32	10 01

Table 116

Saturdays
from 27 October

Birmingham, Banbury, Bicester, Oxford and Bedwyn - Reading and London

Network Diagram - see first Page of Table 116

		GW		GW	XC	GW	GW	GW	GW	GW	GW	GW		CH	XC	GW	GW	GW	GW	GW	GW	XC		GW	GW
		◇1 ⊡		1	◇1 ⊼	◇1 ⊡	1	◇1 ⊼	◇1 A ⊡⊘	1	1	1			◇1 ⊼	◇1 ⊡	◇1 A ⊡⊘	1	◇1 A ⊡⊘	1	1	◇1 ⊼		1	◇1 ⊼
Birmingham New Street 12	d				07 33										08 04							08 33			
Birmingham International	d														08 14										
Coventry	d														08 25										
Leamington Spa 8	d				08 00										08 38							09 00			
Banbury	d				08 19										08 55			09 02				09 19			
Kings Sutton	d																	09 08							
Heyford	d																	09 17							
Tackley	d																	09 21							
Bicester Town	d													08 45											
Islip	d													08 56											
Oxford	a				08 40									09 11	09 14			09 32				09 40			
	d			08 37	08 43			09 01				09 07			09 16		09 31				09 37	09 43			10 01
Radley	d											09 13													
Culham	d											09 17													
Appleford	d																								
Didcot Parkway	a			08 49								09 24									09 49				
	d	08 52		09 01		08 59			09 17			09 31				09 29			09 47		10 01				
Cholsey	d			09 07								09 37									10 07				
Goring & Streatley	d			09 12								09 42									10 12				
Pangbourne	d			09 17								09 47									10 17				
Tilehurst	d			09 21								09 51									10 21				
Bedwyn	d						08 38																	09 37	
Hungerford	d						08 43																	09 41	
Kintbury	d						08 48																	09 46	
Newbury	a						08 55																	09 53	
	d						08 55				09 03													09 53	
Newbury Racecourse	d										09 06														
Thatcham	d						09 00				09 11													09 58	
Midgham	d										09 16														
Aldermaston	d										09 19														
Theale	d						09 08				09 24													10 06	
Reading West	d									←	09 31									←					
Reading 7	a	09 07		09 27	09 11	09 14	09 20	09 24	09 32	09 27	09 35	09 57			09 39	09 45	09 54		10 00	09 57	10 27	10 07		10 17	10 25
	d	09 09		09 33		09 16	09 20	09 24	09 33	09 33		10 03				09 46	09 55		10 02	10 03	10 33			10 18	10 25
Twyford 3	a			→						09 39		→								10 09	→				
Maidenhead 3	a									09 47										10 17					
Slough 3	a							09 40		09 54							10 09			10 24					10 40
Ealing Broadway ⊖	a									10 19										10 49					
London Paddington 15 ⊖	a	09 37				09 44	09 52	09 59	10 02	10 31						10 14	10 29		10 32	11 01				10 52	10 59

		GW	GW	GW	GW	XC	CH	GW		GW	GW	GW	GW	GW	XC	GW	GW	GW		GW	XC	GW	GW	GW	GW
		◇1 ⊡	1	◇1 ⊡	1	◇1 ⊼		1		◇1 ⊡	◇1 ⊡	◇1 ⊡	1	1	◇1 ⊼	1	◇1	1		1	◇1 ⊼	1	◇1 ⊡	◇1 ⊼	1
Birmingham New Street 12	d					09 04									09 33						10 04				
Birmingham International	d					09 14															10 14				
Coventry	d					09 25															10 25				
Leamington Spa 8	d					09 38									10 00						10 38				
Banbury	d					09 55									10 19						10 55				11 02
Kings Sutton	d																								11 08
Heyford	d																								11 17
Tackley	d																								11 21
Bicester Town	d						09 57																		
Islip	d						10 08																		
Oxford	a					10 14	10 23								10 40						11 14				11 32
	d				10 07	10 16					10 31			10 37	10 43		11 01			11 07	11 16			11 31	
Radley	d				10 13															11 13					
Culham	d																								
Appleford	d				10 17																				
Didcot Parkway	a				10 23									10 49						11 24					
	d	10 17		10 22	10 31					10 29		10 47		11 01						11 31			11 29		
Cholsey	d				10 37									11 07						11 37					
Goring & Streatley	d				10 42									11 12						11 42					
Pangbourne	d				10 47									11 17						11 47					
Tilehurst	d				10 51									11 21						11 51					
Bedwyn	d															10 40									
Hungerford	d															10 46									
Kintbury	d															10 50									
Newbury	a															10 57									
	d							10 13								10 57						11 13			
Newbury Racecourse	d							10 15														11 15			
Thatcham	d							10 20								11 02						11 20			
Midgham	d							10 24														11 24			
Aldermaston	d							10 28														11 28			
Theale	d							10 33								11 10						11 33			
Reading West	d		←					10 40					←					←				11 40			
Reading 7	a	10 32	10 27	10 36	10 58	10 39		10 44		10 45	10 54	11 01	10 58	11 27	11 09	11 21	11 24	11 27		11 58	11 39	11 44	11 44	11 54	
	d	10 33	10 33	10 39	11 03					10 46	10 55	11 02	11 03	11 33		11 21	11 25	11 33		12 03			11 45	11 55	
Twyford 3	a		10 39		→								11 09	→				11 39		→					
Maidenhead 3	a		10 47										11 17					11 47							
Slough 3	a		10 54								11 09		11 24				11 39	11 54						12 09	
Ealing Broadway ⊖	a		11 19										11 49					12 19							
London Paddington 15 ⊖	a	11 02	11 31	11 08						11 14	11 29	11 33	12 01			11 52	11 59	12 31					12 14	12 29	

A ⊡ from Reading ⊘ to Reading

Table 116

Saturdays
from 27 October

Birmingham, Banbury, Bicester, Oxford and Bedwyn - Reading and London

Network Diagram - see first Page of Table 116

		GW	GW	GW		XC	CH	GW	GW	GW	GW	GW	XC	GW		GW	GW	GW	GW	GW	XC	GW	GW	GW
		◇1 ⊡	1	1		◇1 ⊼		1	◇1 ⊼	1	◇1 ⊡	1	◇1 ⊼	1		◇1 ⊡	◇1 ⊼	◇1 ⊡	1	1	◇1 ⊼	◇1 ⊼	1	1
Birmingham New Street 12	d					10 33							11 04								11 33			
Birmingham International	d												11 14											
Coventry	d												11 25											
Leamington Spa 8	d					11 00							11 38								12 00			
Banbury	d					11 19							11 55								12 19			
Kings Sutton	d																							
Heyford	d																							
Tackley	d																							
Bicester Town	d						11 30																	
Islip	d						11 41																	
Oxford	a					11 40	11 56						12 14								12 40			
	d			11 37		11 43			12 01			12 07	12 16				12 31			12 37	12 43	13 01		13 07
Radley	d											12 13												13 13
Culham	d																							13 17
Appleford	d											12 17												
Didcot Parkway	a			11 49								12 24								12 49				13 24
	d	11 47		12 01							12 22	12 31				12 29		12 47		13 01				13 31
Cholsey	d			12 07								12 37								13 07				13 37
Goring & Streatley	d			12 12								12 42								13 12				13 42
Pangbourne	d			12 17								12 47								13 17				13 47
Tilehurst	d			12 21								12 51								13 21				13 51
Bedwyn	d							11 38																
Hungerford	d							11 43																
Kintbury	d							11 48																
Newbury	a							11 55																
	d							11 55						12 13										
Newbury Racecourse	d													12 15										
Thatcham	d							12 00						12 20										
Midgham	d													12 24										
Aldermaston	d													12 28										
Theale	d							12 08						12 33										
Reading West	d		←							←				12 40					←				←	
Reading 7	a	12 00	11 58	12 28		12 07		12 17	12 25	12 28	12 37	12 57	12 39	12 44		12 44	12 53	13 00	12 57	13 27	13 06	13 25	13 27	13 59
	d	12 02	12 03	12 33				12 18	12 25	12 33	12 39	13 03				12 45	12 55	13 02	13 03	13 33		13 25	13 33	14 03
Twyford 3	a		12 09	→						12 39		→							13 09	→			13 39	→
Maidenhead 3	a		12 17							12 47									13 17				13 47	
Slough 3	a		12 24						12 40	12 54							13 09		13 24			13 40	13 54	
Ealing Broadway ⊖	a		12 49							13 19									13 49				14 19	
London Paddington 15 ⊖	a	12 32	13 01					12 52	12 59	13 31	13 07					13 12	13 30	13 33	14 01			13 59	14 31	

		XC	CH	GW	GW	GW	GW	GW	GW	GW		GW	XC	GW	GW	GW	GW	GW	XC	GW		GW	GW	GW	GW
		◇1 ⊼		1	◇1 ⊡	1	◇1	1	◇1 ⊡	1		1	◇1 ⊼	◇1 ⊡	◇1 ⊼	1	◇1 ⊡	1	◇1 ⊼	1		◇1 ⊡	◇1 ⊡	◇1 ⊡	1
Birmingham New Street 12	d	12 04											12 33						13 04						
Birmingham International	d	12 14																	13 14						
Coventry	d	12 25																	13 25						
Leamington Spa 8	d	12 38											13 02						13 38						
Banbury	d	12 55						13 02					13 21						13 55						
Kings Sutton	d							13 08																	
Heyford	d							13 17																	
Tackley	d							13 21																	
Bicester Town	d		13 00																						
Islip	d		13 11																						
Oxford	a	13 14	13 26					13 32					13 40						14 14						
	d	13 16					13 31					13 37	13 43		14 01			14 07	14 16				14 31		
Radley	d																	14 13							
Culham	d																								
Appleford	d																	14 17							
Didcot Parkway	a											13 51						14 24							
	d				13 29				13 47			14 01					14 22	14 31				14 29		14 47	
Cholsey	d											14 07						14 37							
Goring & Streatley	d											14 12						14 42							
Pangbourne	d											14 17						14 47							
Tilehurst	d											14 21						14 51							
Bedwyn	d					13 07								13 33											
Hungerford	d					13 13								13 40											
Kintbury	d					13 17																			
Newbury	a					13 24								13 49											
	d			13 13		13 28								13 50						14 13					
Newbury Racecourse	d			13 15																14 15					
Thatcham	d			13 20		13 33								13 57						14 20					
Midgham	d			13 24																14 24					
Aldermaston	d			13 28																14 28					
Theale	d			13 33		13 41								14 06						14 33					
Reading West	d			13 40						←						←				14 40					←
Reading 7	a	13 39		13 44	13 44	13 51	13 54		14 00	13 59		14 27	14 07	14 19	14 25	14 27	14 38	14 58	14 39	14 44		14 44	14 53	15 00	14 58
	d				13 45	13 51	13 55		14 02	14 03		14 33		14 19	14 25	14 33	14 39	15 03				14 45	14 55	15 02	15 03
Twyford 3	a									14 09		→				14 39		→							15 09
Maidenhead 3	a									14 17						14 47									15 17
Slough 3	a						14 09			14 24					14 40	14 54							15 10		15 24
Ealing Broadway ⊖	a									14 49						15 19									15 49
London Paddington 15 ⊖	a				14 14	14 23	14 29		14 32	15 01				14 45	14 59	15 31	15 09					15 14	15 29	15 32	16 01

Birmingham, Banbury, Bicester, Oxford and Bedwyn - Reading and London

Network Diagram - see first Page of Table 116

		GW	XC	CH	GW	GW		GW	GW	XC	GW	GW	GW	GW	GW	GW		GW	XC	CH	GW	GW	GW	GW	GW
		1	◇1 🛒		1	◇1		1	1	◇1 🛒	1	◇1 ☕	◇1 🛒	1	◇1 ☕	1		1	◇1 🛒		1	◇1	1	◇1 ☕	1
Birmingham New Street 12	d		13 33							14 04									14 33						
Birmingham International	d									14 14															
Coventry	d									14 25															
Leamington Spa 8	d		14 00							14 38									15 00						
Banbury	d		14 19							14 55				15 02					15 20						
Kings Sutton	d													15 08											
Heyford	d													15 17											
Tackley	d													15 21											
Bicester Town	d			14 18																15 28					
Islip	d			14 29																15 39					
Oxford	a		14 40	14 44						15 14				15 32					15 41	15 54					
	d	14 37	14 43			15 01			15 07	15 16			15 31					15 37	15 43			16 01			16 07
Radley	d								15 13																16 13
Culham	d								15 17																
Appleford	d																								16 17
Didcot Parkway	a	14 49							15 24									15 49							16 24
	d	15 01							15 31			15 29			15 47			16 01						16 22	16 31
Cholsey	d	15 07							15 37									16 07							16 37
Goring & Streatley	d	15 12							15 42									16 12							16 42
Pangbourne	d	15 17							15 47									16 17							16 47
Tilehurst	d	15 21							15 51									16 21							16 51
Bedwyn	d				14 38																15 38				
Hungerford	d				14 43																15 43				
Kintbury	d				14 48																15 48				
Newbury	a				14 55																15 55				
	d				14 55						15 13										15 55				
Newbury Racecourse	d										15 15														
Thatcham	d				15 00						15 20										16 00				
Midgham	d										15 24														
Aldermaston	d										15 28														
Theale	d				15 08						15 33										16 08				
Reading West	d							←			15 40					←							←		
Reading 7	a	15 27	15 07		15 17	15 25		15 27	15 59	15 39	15 44	15 44	15 54		16 00	15 59		16 29	16 08		16 17	16 25	16 29	16 38	16 58
	d	15 33			15 19	15 25		15 33	16 03			15 45	15 55		16 01	16 03		16 33			16 18	16 26	16 33	16 39	17 03
Twyford 3	a	→						15 39	→							16 09		→					16 39		→
Maidenhead 3	a							15 47								16 17							16 47		
Slough 3	a					15 40		15 54					16 10			16 24						16 40	16 54		
Ealing Broadway ⊖	a							16 19								16 49							17 19		
London Paddington 15 ⊖	a				15 54	15 59		16 31				16 14	16 29		16 32	17 01					16 52	16 59	17 31	17 07	

		XC		GW	GW	GW	GW	GW	GW	XC	CH	GW		GW	GW	GW	XC	GW	GW	GW	GW	GW		GW	XC
		◇1 🛒		1	◇1 ☕	◇1 🛒	◇1 ☕	1	1	◇1 🛒		◇1 ☕		◇1	1	1	◇1 🛒	1	◇1 ☕	◇1 ☕	◇1 ☕	1		1	◇1 🛒
Birmingham New Street 12	d	15 04								15 33							16 04								16 33
Birmingham International	d	15 14															16 14								
Coventry	d	15 25															16 25								
Leamington Spa 8	d	15 38								16 02							16 38								17 00
Banbury	d	15 55								16 20							16 55								17 19
Kings Sutton	d																								
Heyford	d																								
Tackley	d																								
Bicester Town	d										16 30														
Islip	d										16 41														
Oxford	a	16 14								16 40	16 56						17 14								17 41
	d	16 16				16 31			16 37	16 43				17 01		17 07	17 16			17 31				17 37	17 43
Radley	d															17 13									
Culham	d															17 17									
Appleford	d																								
Didcot Parkway	a								16 49							17 24								17 49	
	d				16 29		16 47		17 01							17 31			17 29		17 47			18 01	
Cholsey	d								17 07							17 37								18 07	
Goring & Streatley	d								17 12							17 42								18 12	
Pangbourne	d								17 17							17 47								18 17	
Tilehurst	d								17 21							17 51								18 21	
Bedwyn	d											16 35						16 56							
Hungerford	d											16 42						17 00							
Kintbury	d																	17 05							
Newbury	a											16 52						17 13							
	d			16 13								16 53						17 13							
Newbury Racecourse	d			16 15														17 15							
Thatcham	d			16 20								16 59						17 20							
Midgham	d			16 24														17 25							
Aldermaston	d			16 28														17 28							
Theale	d			16 33								17 08						17 33							
Reading West	d			16 40				←							←			17 40				←			
Reading 7	a	16 39		16 44	16 44	16 55	17 00	16 58	17 27	17 07		17 17		17 26	17 27	17 57	17 39	17 44	17 44	17 55	18 00	17 57		18 27	18 07
	d				16 45	16 55	17 02	17 03	17 33			17 18		17 27	17 33	18 03			17 45	17 57	18 02	18 03		18 33	
Twyford 3	a							17 09	→						17 39	→						18 09		→	
Maidenhead 3	a							17 17							17 47							18 17			
Slough 3	a					17 10		17 24						17 41	17 54					18 10		18 24			
Ealing Broadway ⊖	a							17 49							18 19							18 49			
London Paddington 15 ⊖	a				17 14	17 29	17 32	18 01				17 51		18 00	18 31				18 14	18 29	18 32	19 01			

Table 116

Saturdays
from 27 October

Birmingham, Banbury, Bicester, Oxford and Bedwyn - Reading and London

Network Diagram - see first Page of Table 116

		GW	GW	GW	GW	GW	GW	XC		CH	GW	GW	GW	GW	GW	GW	XC	GW		GW	GW	GW	XC	GW	GW
		1	1	◇1	1	◇1 ☕	1	◇1 🛒			1	◇1 ☕	◇1 🛒	◇1 ☕	1	1	◇1 🛒	1		◇1	1	1	◇1 🛒	1	◇1 ☕
Birmingham New Street 12	d							17 04									17 33						18 04		
Birmingham International	d							17 14															18 14		
Coventry	d							17 25															18 25		
Leamington Spa 8	d							17 38									18 02						18 38		
Banbury	d	17 23						17 55									18 19						18 55		
Kings Sutton	d	17 29																							
Heyford	d	17 38																							
Tackley	d	17 42																							
Bicester Town	d									18 04															
Islip	d									18 15															
Oxford	a	17 53						18 14		18 30							18 40						19 14		
	d			18 01			18 07	18 16					18 31			18 37	18 43			19 01		19 07	19 16		
Radley	d						18 13															19 13			
Culham	d																					19 17			
Appleford	d						18 17																		
Didcot Parkway	a						18 24									18 49						19 24			
	d					18 22	18 31					18 29		18 47		19 01						19 31			19 29
Cholsey	d						18 37									19 07						19 37			
Goring & Streatley	d						18 42									19 12						19 42			
Pangbourne	d						18 47									19 17						19 47			
Tilehurst	d						18 51									19 21						19 51			
Bedwyn	d		17 38															18 38							
Hungerford	d		17 43															18 43							
Kintbury	d		17 48															18 48							
Newbury	a		17 55															18 55							
	d		17 55								18 13							18 55						19 13	
Newbury Racecourse	d										18 15													19 15	
Thatcham	d		18 00								18 20							19 00						19 20	
Midgham	d										18 24													19 24	
Aldermaston	d										18 28													19 28	
Theale	d		18 08								18 33							19 08						19 33	
Reading West	d				←						18 40				←						←			19 40	
Reading 7	a		18 18	18 25	18 27	18 38	18 58	18 39			18 44	18 44	18 55	19 00	18 58	19 29	19 07	19 17		19 25	19 29	19 57	19 39	19 44	19 44
	d		18 19	18 25	18 33	18 39	19 03					18 45	18 56	19 02	19 03	19 33		19 20		19 25	19 33	20 03			19 45
Twyford 3	a				18 39		→								19 09	→					19 39	→			
Maidenhead 3	a				18 47										19 17						19 47				
Slough 3	a			18 40	18 54								19 10		19 24					19 40	19 54				
Ealing Broadway ⊖	a				19 19										19 49						20 19				
London Paddington 15 ⊖	a		18 52	18 59	19 31	19 08						19 14	19 29	19 32	20 01			19 52		19 59	20 31				20 14

		GW	GW	GW		GW	GW	GW	XC	CH	GW	GW	GW	GW		GW	XC	GW	GW	GW	GW	GW	XC	CH	
		◇1 🛒	1	◇1 ☕		1	◇1 ☕	1	◇1 🛒		◇1	1	1	◇1 ☕		1	◇1 🛒	◇1 ☕	◇1	1	◇1 ☕	1	◇1 🛒		
Birmingham New Street 12	d								18 33								19 04						19 33		
Birmingham International	d																19 14								
Coventry	d																19 25								
Leamington Spa 8	d								19 00								19 38						20 03		
Banbury	d		19 02						19 19								19 55						20 21		
Kings Sutton	d		19 08																						
Heyford	d		19 17																						
Tackley	d		19 21																						
Bicester Town	d									19 17														20 28	
Islip	d									19 28														20 39	
Oxford	a		19 32						19 40	19 43							20 14						20 40	20 54	
	d	19 31						19 37	19 43		20 01					20 07	20 16		20 31			20 37	20 43		
Radley	d															20 13									
Culham	d																								
Appleford	d															20 17									
Didcot Parkway	a							19 49								20 24						20 49			
	d			19 47				20 01						20 23		20 31		20 29			20 47	21 01			
Cholsey	d							20 07								20 37						21 07			
Goring & Streatley	d							20 12								20 42						21 12			
Pangbourne	d							20 17								20 47						21 17			
Tilehurst	d							20 21								20 51						21 21			
Bedwyn	d											19 41													
Hungerford	d											19 47													
Kintbury	d											19 51													
Newbury	a											19 58													
	d						19 46					19 58													
Newbury Racecourse	d											20 00													
Thatcham	d											20 05													
Midgham	d											20 10													
Aldermaston	d											20 13													
Theale	d											20 18													
Reading West	d					←						20 25	←							←					
Reading 7	a	19 55		20 00		19 57	20 07	20 29	20 10		20 25	20 28	20 29	20 38		21 04	20 39	20 44	20 54	21 04	21 07	21 29	21 18		
	d	19 55		20 03		20 03	20 09	20 33			20 25		20 33	20 39		21 05		20 45	20 54	21 05	21 09	21 33			
Twyford 3	a					20 09		→					20 39			→				21 12		→			
Maidenhead 3	a					20 17							20 47							21 20					
Slough 3	a	20 10				20 24					20 40		20 54						21 09	21 27					
Ealing Broadway ⊖	a					20 49							21 19							21 52					
London Paddington 15 ⊖	a	20 29		20 32		21 01	20 37				20 59		21 31	21 07				21 14	21 29	22 02	21 36				

Birmingham, Banbury, Bicester, Oxford and Bedwyn - Reading and London

Network Diagram - see first Page of Table 116

		GW	GW	GW	GW	XC	GW	GW	GW	XC	GW	GW	GW	CH	XC	GW	GW	GW	GW	GW	GW	GW	GW
		◇1	1	1	1	◇1	◇1	◇1	◇1	◇1	1	◇1	1		◇1	1	1	◇1	◇1	◇1	1	◇1	1
Birmingham New Street 12	d					20 04				20 33					21 04								
Birmingham International	d					20 14									21 14								
Coventry	d					20 25									21 25								
Leamington Spa 8	d					20 38				21 00					21 38								
Banbury	d			20 38		20 55				21 20					21 55	22 00							
Kings Sutton	d			20 44												22 06							
Heyford	d			20 53												22 15							
Tackley	d			20 57												22 19							
Bicester Town	d													21 37									
Islip	d													21 48									
Oxford	a			21 08		21 14				21 41				22 03	22 16	22 30							
	d	21 01				21 16		21 31		21 43	21 50	22 01			22 18				22 35	23 01			23 07
Radley	d										21 56												23 13
Culham	d																						23 17
Appleford	d																						23 20
Didcot Parkway	a							21 43			22 04	22 12							22 47	23 12			23 25
	d						21 34	21 45	21 47		22 04	22 13						22 49	22 51	23 13		23 30	23 36
Cholsey	d										22 10												23 42
Goring & Streatley	d										22 15												23 47
Pangbourne	d										22 21												23 51
Tilehurst	d										22 24												23 56
Bedwyn	d				20 48												22 00				23 00		
Hungerford	d				20 54												22 06				23 06		
Kintbury	d				20 58												22 10				23 10		
Newbury	a				21 05												22 17				23 17		
	d				21 05												22 17				23 17		
Newbury Racecourse	d				21 07												22 19				23 19		
Thatcham	d				21 12												22 24				23 24		
Midgham	d				21 17												22 29				23 29		
Aldermaston	d				21 20												22 32				23 32		
Theale	d				21 25												22 37				23 37		
Reading West	d		←		21 32								←				22 44				23 44		
Reading 7	a	21 25	21 29		21 36	21 40	21 51	21 59	22 01	22 10	22 35	22 31	22 35		22 41		22 48	23 04	23 08	23 29	23 48	23 52	00 02
	d	21 25	21 33				21 53	22 02	22 06		22 36	22 32	22 36					23 05	23 09	23 29		23 53	00 03
Twyford 3	a		21 40								→		22 43										00 10
Maidenhead 3	a		21 48										22 51										00 18
Slough 3	a	21 40	21 55					22 15				22 46	22 58						23 26	23 45			00 29
Ealing Broadway ⊖	a		22 20										23 23										00 53
London Paddington 15 ⊖	a	21 59	22 32				22 22	22 33	22 37			23 05	23 32					23 36	23 46	00 10		00 33	01 04

		CH
Birmingham New Street 12	d	
Birmingham International	d	
Coventry	d	
Leamington Spa 8	d	
Banbury	d	
Kings Sutton	d	
Heyford	d	
Tackley	d	
Bicester Town	d	22 55
Islip	d	23 06
Oxford	a	23 21
	d	
Radley	d	
Culham	d	
Appleford	d	
Didcot Parkway	a	
	d	
Cholsey	d	
Goring & Streatley	d	
Pangbourne	d	
Tilehurst	d	
Bedwyn	d	
Hungerford	d	
Kintbury	d	
Newbury	a	
	d	
Newbury Racecourse	d	
Thatcham	d	
Midgham	d	
Aldermaston	d	
Theale	d	
Reading West	d	
Reading 7	a	
	d	
Twyford 3	a	
Maidenhead 3	a	
Slough 3	a	
Ealing Broadway ⊖	a	
London Paddington 15 ⊖	a	

Birmingham, Banbury, Bicester, Oxford and Bedwyn - Reading and London

Network Diagram - see first Page of Table 116

		GW	GW	GW	GW	GW	GW	GW	GW	GW	GW	GW	GW	GW	GW	GW	GW	XC	CH	GW	GW	GW	GW
		◇1	◇1	1	1		1	◇1	◇1	◇1		1	◇1	◇1		1	1	◇1		◇1	◇1	◇1	
Birmingham New Street 12	d																	09 04					
Birmingham International	d																	09 14					
Coventry	d																	09 25					
Leamington Spa 8	d																	09 38					
Banbury	d																	09 55					
Kings Sutton	d																						
Heyford	d																						
Tackley	d																						
Bicester Town	d																		10 05				
Islip	d																		10 16				
Oxford	a																	10 14	10 32				
	d	23p01		23p07		07 45	08 05		08 50			09 01		09 48			10 05	10 16			10 44	10 55	
Radley	d			23p13			08 11					09 07					10 11						
Culham	d			23p17																			
Appleford	d			23p20													10 16						
Didcot Parkway	a	23p13		23p25		08 10	08 19		09 02			09 16		10 00			10 20				10 58	11 07	
	d	23p14	23p30	23p36	07 45		08 21	08 43	09 03	09 14		09 16	09 45	10 01			10 21			10 38	10 58	11 07	
Cholsey	d			23p42			08 27					09 22					10 27						
Goring & Streatley	d			23p49	07 53		08 32					09 27					10 32						
Pangbourne	d						08 37					09 32					10 36						
Tilehurst	d			23p56			08 42					09 36					10 41						
Bedwyn	d															09 51							
Hungerford	d															09 57							
Kintbury	d															10 01							
Newbury	a															10 08							
	d										08 35				09 15								10 19
Newbury Racecourse	d														09 20								10 24
Thatcham	d										08 46				09 30								10 34
Midgham	d														09 40								10 44
Aldermaston	d														09 47								10 51
Theale	d										09 04				09 59								11 03
Reading West	d														10 14								11 18
Reading 7	a	23p29	23p49	00 02	08 03		08 51	09 01	09 22	09 28	09 30	09 42	09 58	10 21	10 30		10 45	10 38		10 53	11 13	11 23	11 34
	d	23p29	23p51	00 03	08 03		08 52	09 03	09 23	09 29		09 52	10 00	10 22			10 52			10 54	11 14	11 23	
Twyford 3	a			00 10			08 58					09 58					10 58				11 20		
Maidenhead 3	a			00 18			09 06					10 06					11 06				11 28		
Slough 3	a	23p45		00 30	08 22		09 14		09 38			10 14		10 37			11 16				11 35	11 37	
Ealing Broadway ⊖	a			00 54			09 42					10 42					11 42						
London Paddington 15 ⊖	a	00 10	00 33	01 03	08 44		09 52	09 44	10 00	10 07		10 51	10 44	10 58			11 51			11 29	11 58	12 01	

		GW	GW	XC	GW	GW	GW	GW	GW	CH	GW	GW	XC	GW	GW	GW	XC	GW	GW	GW	GW	GW	XC
		1	1	◇1	1	◇1	1	◇1	◇1			1	◇1	◇1	1	◇1	◇1	◇1	◇1		1	1	◇1
Birmingham New Street 12	d			10 04									11 04				11 33						12 04
Birmingham International	d			10 14									11 14										12 14
Coventry	d			10 25									11 25										12 25
Leamington Spa 8	d			10 38									11 38				12 00						12 38
Banbury	d			10 55	11 00								11 55				12 19						12 55
Kings Sutton	d				11 05																		
Heyford	d				11 14																		
Tackley	d				11 19																		
Bicester Town	d									11 33													
Islip	d									11 44													
Oxford	a			11 14	11 29					12 00			12 14				12 38						13 14
	d		11 05	11 16					11 50			12 05	12 16				12 43		12 50			13 05	13 16
Radley	d		11 11									12 11										13 11	
Culham	d																						
Appleford	d											12 16										13 16	
Didcot Parkway	a		11 19						12 02			12 21							13 02			13 21	
	d		11 21			11 29		11 50	12 03			12 21		12 29		12 47		12 59	13 03			13 21	
Cholsey	d		11 27									12 27										13 27	
Goring & Streatley	d		11 32									12 32										13 32	
Pangbourne	d		11 36									12 36										13 36	
Tilehurst	d		11 41									12 41										13 41	
Bedwyn	d	11 11																			13 11		
Hungerford	d	11 17																			13 17		
Kintbury	d	11 21																			13 21		
Newbury	a	11 28																			13 28		
	d										11 38									12 19			
Newbury Racecourse	d																			12 24			
Thatcham	d										11 49									12 34			
Midgham	d																			12 44			
Aldermaston	d																			12 51			
Theale	d										12 07									13 03			
Reading West	d						←								←					13 18			
Reading 7	a		11 44	11 42		11 45	11 44	12 05	12 21		12 33	12 46	12 42	12 44	12 46	13 00	13 09	13 17	13 23	13 34		13 46	13 42
	d		11 52			11 47	11 52	12 05	12 23			12 52		12 44	12 52	13 02		13 19	13 25			13 52	
Twyford 3	a		→				11 58					→			12 58							→	
Maidenhead 3	a						12 06								13 06								
Slough 3	a						12 14		12 38						13 14				13 41				
Ealing Broadway ⊖	a						12 42								13 42								
London Paddington 15 ⊖	a					12 22	12 51	12 42	13 03					13 22	13 51	13 42		13 59	14 05				

Birmingham, Banbury, Bicester, Oxford and Bedwyn - Reading and London

Network Diagram - see first Page of Table 116

		CH		GW	GW	GW	XC	GW	GW	GW	XC	GW		GW	XC	GW	GW	CH	GW	GW	XC	GW		GW	GW
				◇1	1	◇1	◇1	◇1	🚌	1	◇1	◇1		◇1	◇1	◇1	🚌		1	1	◇1	◇1		1	◇1
				☕		☕	🍴				☕	☕		☕	🍴						☕	☕			☕
Birmingham New Street 12	d						12 33				13 04				13 33						14 04				
Birmingham International	d										13 14										14 14				
Coventry	d										13 25										14 25				
Leamington Spa 8	d						13 00				13 38				14 00						14 38				
Banbury	d						13 19				13 55				14 19						14 55				
Kings Sutton	d																								
Heyford	d																								
Tackley	d																								
Bicester Town	d	13 03																14 33							
Islip	d	13 14																14 44							
Oxford	a	13 30					13 41				14 14				14 38			15 00			15 14				
	d						13 43	13 50		14 05	14 17				14 42	14 50				15 05	15 16				
Radley	d									14 11										15 11					
Culham	d																								
Appleford	d									14 16															
Didcot Parkway	a							14 02		14 20						15 03				15 19					
	d			13 33		13 51		14 03		14 21		14 34		14 52		15 08				15 21		15 32			15 47
Cholsey	d									14 27										15 27					
Goring & Streatley	d									14 32										15 32					
Pangbourne	d									14 36										15 36					
Tilehurst	d									14 41										15 41					
Bedwyn	d																		15 11						
Hungerford	d																		15 17						
Kintbury	d																		15 21						
Newbury	a																		15 28						
	d								13 38								14 19								
Newbury Racecourse	d																14 24								
Thatcham	d								13 49								14 34								
Midgham	d																14 44								
Aldermaston	d																14 51								
Theale	d								14 07								15 03								
Reading West	d				←												15 18							←	
Reading 7	a			13 45	13 46	14 05	14 13	14 21	14 33	14 46	14 42	14 46		15 05	15 09	15 25	15 34			15 43	15 42	15 47		15 43	16 00
	d			13 47	13 52	14 06		14 21		14 52		14 48		15 07		15 26				15 52		15 49		15 52	16 02
Twyford 3	a				13 58					14 58										→				15 58	
Maidenhead 3	a				14 06					15 06														16 06	
Slough 3	a				14 14			14 37		15 15						15 41								16 15	
Ealing Broadway ⊖	a				14 42					15 42														16 42	
London Paddington 15 ⊖	a			14 22	14 51	14 43		14 59		15 51		15 21		15 43		16 03						16 22		16 51	16 42

		XC	GW	GW	GW	XC	CH	GW		GW	GW	GW	GW	XC	GW	GW	GW	GW		GW	XC	GW	GW	GW	XC
		◇1	◇1	🚌	1	◇1		1		◇1	1	◇1	◇1	◇1	◇1	◇1	🚌	1		1	◇1	◇1	1	◇1	◇1
		🍴	☕			☕				☕		☕		🍴	☕	☕					☕	☕		☕	🍴
Birmingham New Street 12	d	14 33				15 04								15 33							16 04				16 33
Birmingham International	d					15 14															16 14				
Coventry	d					15 25															16 25				
Leamington Spa 8	d	15 00				15 38								16 00							16 38				17 00
Banbury	d	15 19				15 55		16 00						16 19							16 55				17 19
Kings Sutton	d							16 05																	
Heyford	d							16 14																	
Tackley	d							16 18																	
Bicester Town	d						16 03																		
Islip	d						16 14																		
Oxford	a	15 41				16 14	16 30	16 33						16 41							17 14				17 38
	d	15 43	15 50		16 05	16 16							16 37	16 43		16 50				17 05	17 16				17 43
Radley	d				16 11															17 11					
Culham	d																								
Appleford	d				16 16															17 16					
Didcot Parkway	a		16 02		16 20											17 02				17 21					
	d		16 03		16 21					16 32		16 51			17 02	17 10				17 21		17 29		17 47	
Cholsey	d				16 27															17 27					
Goring & Streatley	d				16 33															17 32					
Pangbourne	d				16 38															17 36					
Tilehurst	d				16 42															17 43					
Bedwyn	d																	17 21							
Hungerford	d																	17 27							
Kintbury	d																	17 31							
Newbury	a																	17 38							
	d			15 38													16 19								
Newbury Racecourse	d																16 24								
Thatcham	d			15 49													16 34								
Midgham	d																16 44								
Aldermaston	d																16 51								
Theale	d			16 07													17 03								
Reading West	d										←						17 18						←		
Reading 7	a	16 09	16 22	16 33	16 48	16 42				16 46	16 48	17 05	17 11	17 13	17 16	17 27	17 34			17 46	17 41	17 44	17 46	18 00	18 16
	d		16 23		16 52					16 47	16 52	17 06	17 11		17 18	17 29				17 52		17 47	17 52	18 02	
Twyford 3	a				→						16 58		17 18							→			17 58		
Maidenhead 3	a										17 06		17 26										18 06		
Slough 3	a		16 36								17 17		17 34			17 43							18 16		
Ealing Broadway ⊖	a										17 42												18 43		
London Paddington 15 ⊖	a		17 04							17 22	17 51	17 43	17 58		18 03	18 13						18 22	18 51	18 43	

Birmingham, Banbury, Bicester, Oxford and Bedwyn - Reading and London

Network Diagram - see first Page of Table 116

		GW	GW	CH		GW	GW	XC	GW	GW	XC	GW	GW	GW		GW	GW	XC	CH	XC	GW	GW	GW	GW
		◇1	◇1			🚌	1	◇1	1	◇1	◇1	◇1	◇1	🚌		◇1	1	◇1		◇1	◇1	🚌	1	◇1
		☕	☕					☕		☕	🍴	☕	☕			☕		☕		🍴	☕			
Birmingham New Street 12	d							17 04			17 33							18 04		18 33				
Birmingham International	d							17 14										18 14						
Coventry	d							17 25										18 25						
Leamington Spa 8	d							17 38			18 01							18 38		19 00				
Banbury	d							17 55	18 00		18 20							18 55		19 19				
Kings Sutton	d								18 07															
Heyford	d								18 16															
Tackley	d								18 20															
Bicester Town	d			17 33															19 07					
Islip	d			17 44															19 18					
Oxford	a			18 00				18 14	18 31		18 41							19 14	19 34	19 38				
	d		17 50				18 05	18 16			18 42		18 50				19 05	19 16		19 43				19 50
Radley	d						18 12										19 11							
Culham	d																							
Appleford	d																19 16							
Didcot Parkway	a		18 02				18 18						19 02				19 21							20 04
	d	18 01	18 05				18 20			18 49		18 59	19 08			19 19	19 25				19 59			20 06
Cholsey	d						18 26										19 32							
Goring & Streatley	d						18 31										19 37							
Pangbourne	d						18 35										19 42							
Tilehurst	d						18 40										19 46							
Bedwyn	d																						19 45	
Hungerford	d																						19 51	
Kintbury	d																						19 55	
Newbury	a																						20 02	
	d					17 45								18 19								19 31		
Newbury Racecourse	d													18 24										
Thatcham	d					17 56								18 34								19 42		
Midgham	d													18 44										
Aldermaston	d													18 51										
Theale	d					18 14								19 03								20 00		
Reading West	d													19 18										
Reading 7	a	18 19	18 27			18 40	18 45	18 41		19 02	19 13	19 12	19 27	19 34		19 36	19 52	19 42		20 10	20 15	20 26		20 24
	d	18 21	18 27				18 52			19 05		19 14	19 30			19 38	19 52				20 17			20 27
Twyford 3	a						18 58										19 58							
Maidenhead 3	a						19 06										20 06							
Slough 3	a		18 41				19 16						19 44				20 15							20 43
Ealing Broadway ⊖	a						19 42										20 42							
London Paddington 15 ⊖	a	18 59	19 07				19 51			19 42		19 59	20 07			20 14	20 51				20 59			21 05

		GW	GW	XC	XC	GW	GW	CH	GW	GW		GW	GW	XC	GW	GW	XC	GW	GW	XC		GW	GW	GW	CH
		◇1	1	◇1	◇1	◇1	◇1		◇1	🚌		1	1	◇1	◇1	1	◇1	◇1	◇1	◇1		🚌	1	🚌	
		☕		☕	🍴	☕			☕					☕	☕		🍴	☕							
Birmingham New Street 12	d			19 04	19 33									20 04			20 33			21 04					
Birmingham International	d			19 14										20 14						21 14					
Coventry	d			19 25										20 25						21 24					
Leamington Spa 8	d			19 38	20 00									20 38			21 00			21 35					
Banbury	d			19 55	20 19									20 55			21 19								
Kings Sutton	d																								
Heyford	d																								
Tackley	d																								
Bicester Town	d							20 33																	22 03
Islip	d							20 44																	22 14
Oxford	a			20 14	20 40			21 00						21 14			21 38			22 08					22 30
	d		20 05	20 16	20 43		20 50						21 05	21 16			21 40		21 50	22 10			22 17		
Radley	d		20 11										21 11										22 23		
Culham	d																								
Appleford	d																								
Didcot Parkway	a		20 19				21 00						21 19						22 01				22 32		
	d	20 17	20 21			20 59	21 04		21 17				21 21		21 29			22 00	22 03				22 32		
Cholsey	d		20 27										21 27										22 38		
Goring & Streatley	d		20 32										21 32										22 43		
Pangbourne	d		20 36										21 36										22 48		
Tilehurst	d		20 41										21 41										22 52		
Bedwyn	d											21 23													
Hungerford	d											21 29													
Kintbury	d											21 33													
Newbury	a											21 40													
	d									20 19												21 50		21 53	
Newbury Racecourse	d									20 24														21 58	
Thatcham	d									20 34												22 01		22 08	
Midgham	d									20 44														22 18	
Aldermaston	d									20 51														22 25	
Theale	d									21 03												22 19		22 37	
Reading West	d									21 18						←								22 52	
Reading 7	a	20 42	20 46	20 43	21 13	21 15	21 24		21 32	21 34			21 46	21 43	21 47	21 46	22 07	22 16	22 20	22 35		22 45	22 57	23 08	
	d	20 43	20 52			21 17	21 24		21 32				21 52		21 49	21 52		22 18	22 23				22 58		
Twyford 3	a		20 57										→			21 58							23 04		
Maidenhead 3	a		21 06				21 38									22 06							23 12		
Slough 3	a		21 16				21 44									22 16			22 40				23 18		
Ealing Broadway ⊖	a		21 42													22 42							23 42		
London Paddington 15 ⊖	a	21 19	21 52			21 57	22 07		22 14						22 27	22 51		22 59	23 01				23 51		

Sundays
until 24 June

Birmingham, Banbury, Bicester, Oxford and Bedwyn - Reading and London

Network Diagram - see first Page of Table 116

		GW	GW	GW	GW	GW	GW	GW
		◇1	1	◇1 ☕	bus	1	bus	bus
Birmingham New Street 12	d							
Birmingham International	d							
Coventry	d							
Leamington Spa 8	d							
Banbury	d							
Kings Sutton	d							
Heyford	d							
Tackley	d							
Bicester Town	d							
Islip	d							
Oxford	a							
	d	22 46			23 00			
Radley	d				23 15			
Culham	d							
Appleford	d							
Didcot Parkway	a	22 58			23 25			
	d	22 59		23 12		23 50		
Cholsey	d					23 56		
Goring & Streatley	d					00 01		
Pangbourne	d					00 06		
Tilehurst	d					00 10		
Bedwyn	d		23 05					
Hungerford	d		23 11					
Kintbury	d		23 15					
Newbury	a		23 22					
	d						23 30	23 50
Newbury Racecourse	d							23 55
Thatcham	d						23 41	00 05
Midgham	d							00 15
Aldermaston	d							00 22
Theale	d						23 59	00 34
Reading West	d							00 49
Reading 7	a	23 17		23 28		00 16	00 25	01 05
	d	23 22		23 30		00 16		
Twyford 3	a					00 22		
Maidenhead 3	a					00 30		
Slough 3	a	23 43				00 38		
Ealing Broadway ⊖	a					01 01		
London Paddington 15 ⊖	a	00 05		00 13		01 10		

Sundays
1 July to 9 September

		GW	GW	GW	GW	GW	GW	GW	GW	GW	GW	GW	GW	GW	GW	GW	XC	CH	GW	GW	GW	GW	GW
		◇1	◇1 ☕	1	1	bus	1	◇1 ☕	◇1	◇1 ☕	1	1	◇1 ☕	◇1	1	1	◇1 🍴		◇1 ☕	◇1 ☕	◇1	◇1	1
Birmingham New Street 12	d																09 04						
Birmingham International	d																						
Coventry	d																						
Leamington Spa 8	d																09 38						
Banbury	d																09 55						
Kings Sutton	d																						
Heyford	d																						
Tackley	d																						
Bicester Town	d																	10 05					
Islip	d																	10 16					
Oxford	a																10 14	10 32					
	d	23p01		23p07		07 45	08 05		08 50			09 01		09 50		10 05	10 16				10 44	10 55	
Radley	d			23p13			08 11					09 07				10 11							
Culham	d			23p17																			
Appleford	d			23p20												10 16							
Didcot Parkway	a	23p13		23p25		08 10	08 19		09 02			09 16		10 02		10 21					10 56	11 07	
	d	23p14	23p30	23p36	07 47		08 21	08 43	09 03	09 14		09 16	09 45	10 03		10 21				10 46	10 57	11 07	
Cholsey	d			23p42			08 27					09 22				10 27							
Goring & Streatley	d			23p47	07 55		08 32					09 27				10 33							
Pangbourne	d			23p51			08 37					09 32				10 37							
Tilehurst	d			23p56			08 42					09 36				10 42							
Bedwyn	d														09 35								10 54
Hungerford	d														09 41								11 00
Kintbury	d														09 46								11 04
Newbury	a														09 52								11 11
	d										09 05				09 53				10 32				11 11
Newbury Racecourse	d										09 07				09 55								
Thatcham	d										09 12				10 00								11 16
Midgham	d										09 17				10 05								
Aldermaston	d										09 20				10 08								
Theale	d										09 25				10 13								11 24
Reading West	d										09 32				10 20								
Reading 7	a	23p30	23p51	00 01	08 05		08 46	08 59	09 19	09 29	09 35	09 42	09 58	10 18	10 25	10 49	10 42		10 48	11 00	11 13	11 22	11 34
	d	23p31	23p51	00 03	08 05		08 52	09 01	09 19	09 31	09 35	09 52	10 00	10 20	10 26	10 52			10 49	11 02	11 13	11 22	11 34
Twyford 3	a			00 09			08 58					09 58				10 58					11 20		
Maidenhead 3	a			00 17			09 06				09 47	10 06			10 37	11 06					11 28		11 52
Slough 3	a	23p45		00 28	08 23		09 14		09 35		09 55	10 14		10 35	10 44	11 14					11 35	11 38	11 59
Ealing Broadway ⊖	a			00 52			09 36					10 36				11 36							
London Paddington 15 ⊖	a	00 10	00 34	01 02	08 44		09 45	09 29	09 54	09 59	10 23	10 46	10 29	10 55	11 17	11 46			11 21	11 29	11 55	12 00	12 22

Table 116

Sundays
1 July to 9 September

Birmingham, Banbury, Bicester, Oxford and Bedwyn - Reading and London

Network Diagram - see first Page of Table 116

		GW	XC	GW	GW	GW	GW	GW	GW	CH	GW	GW	XC	GW	GW	GW	XC	GW	GW	GW	GW	XC	CH
		1	◇1 🍴	1	◇1 ☕	◇1 ☕	1	◇1 ☕	◇1		1	1	◇1 🍴	◇1 ☕	1	◇1 ☕	◇1 🍴	◇1 ☕	◇1	1	1	◇1 🍴	
Birmingham New Street 12	d		10 04										11 04				11 33					12 04	
Birmingham International	d																						
Coventry	d																						
Leamington Spa 8	d		10 38										11 38				12 00					12 38	
Banbury	d		10 55	11 00									11 55				12 19					12 55	
Kings Sutton	d			11 05																			
Heyford	d			11 14																			
Tackley	d			11 19																			
Bicester Town	d									11 33													13 03
Islip	d									11 44													13 14
Oxford	a		11 14	11 29						12 00			12 14				12 38					13 14	13 30
	d	11 05	11 16						11 50			12 05	12 16				12 43		12 50		13 05	13 16	
Radley	d	11 11										12 11									13 11		
Culham	d																						
Appleford	d											12 16											
Didcot Parkway	a	11 21							12 02			12 21							13 02		13 21		
	d	11 21			11 29			11 47	12 03			12 21		12 29		12 47		12 59	13 03		13 21		
Cholsey	d	11 27										12 27									13 27		
Goring & Streatley	d	11 33										12 33									13 33		
Pangbourne	d	11 37										12 37									13 37		
Tilehurst	d	11 42										12 42									13 42		
Bedwyn	d																			12 45			
Hungerford	d																			12 51			
Kintbury	d																			12 55			
Newbury	a																			13 02			
	d					11 26					12 03									13 03			
Newbury Racecourse	d										12 05												
Thatcham	d										12 10									13 08			
Midgham	d										12 15												
Aldermaston	d										12 18												
Theale	d										12 23									13 16			
Reading West	d						←				12 30				←								
Reading 7	a	11 49	11 42		11 44	11 46	11 49	12 01	12 18		12 33	12 51	12 39	12 44	12 51	13 01	13 09	13 14	13 20	13 25	13 49	13 42	
	d	11 52			11 44	11 48	11 52	12 02	12 19		12 33	12 52		12 44	12 52	13 02		13 15	13 20	13 26	13 52		
Twyford 3	a	→					11 58					→			12 58						→		
Maidenhead 3	a						12 06				12 45				13 06					13 37			
Slough 3	a						12 14		12 32		12 53				13 14				13 36	13 45			
Ealing Broadway ⊖	a						12 36								13 36								
London Paddington 15 ⊖	a				12 14	12 17	12 46	12 29	12 51		13 26			13 14	13 45	13 29		13 41	13 56	14 08			

		GW	GW	GW	GW	XC	GW	GW	GW	XC	GW	GW	GW	XC	GW	CH	GW	GW	XC	GW	GW	GW
		◇1 ☕	◇1 ☕	1	◇1 ☕	◇1 🍴	◇1	1	1	◇1 🍴	◇1 ☕	1	◇1 ☕	◇1 🍴	◇1		1	1	◇1 🍴	◇1 ☕	1	◇1 ☕
Birmingham New Street 12	d					12 33				13 04				13 33					14 04			
Birmingham International	d																		14 14			
Coventry	d																		14 25			
Leamington Spa 8	d					13 00				13 38				14 00					14 38			
Banbury	d					13 19				13 55				14 19					14 55			
Kings Sutton	d																					
Heyford	d																					
Tackley	d																					
Bicester Town	d															14 33						
Islip	d															14 44						
Oxford	a					13 41				14 14				14 38		15 00			15 14			
	d					13 43	13 50		14 05	14 17				14 43	14 50			15 05	15 16			
Radley	d								14 11									15 11				
Culham	d																					
Appleford	d								14 16													
Didcot Parkway	a						14 02		14 21						15 04			15 21				
	d	13 33			13 47		14 03		14 21		14 29		14 47		15 05			15 21		15 29		15 47
Cholsey	d								14 27									15 27				
Goring & Streatley	d								14 33									15 33				
Pangbourne	d								14 37									15 37				
Tilehurst	d								14 42									15 42				
Bedwyn	d																14 45					
Hungerford	d																14 51					
Kintbury	d																14 55					
Newbury	a																15 02					
	d		13 31					14 03									15 03					
Newbury Racecourse	d							14 05														
Thatcham	d							14 10									15 08					
Midgham	d							14 15														
Aldermaston	d							14 18														
Theale	d							14 23									15 16					
Reading West	d			←				14 31				←									←	
Reading 7	a	13 45	13 48	13 49	14 01	14 09	14 20	14 34	14 49	14 43	14 44	14 49	15 00	15 07	15 21		15 25	15 49	15 42	15 44	15 49	16 00
	d	13 47	13 51	13 52	14 02		14 20	14 34	14 52		14 44	14 52	15 02		15 22		15 26	15 52		15 44	15 52	16 02
Twyford 3	a			13 58					→			14 58						→			15 58	
Maidenhead 3	a			14 06				14 45				15 06					15 37				16 06	
Slough 3	a			14 14			14 36	14 54				15 14			15 36		15 45				16 14	
Ealing Broadway ⊖	a			14 36								15 36									16 36	
London Paddington 15 ⊖	a	14 14	14 21	14 45	14 29		14 55	15 25			15 14	15 45	15 29		15 55		16 17			16 14	16 47	16 29

Table 116

Sundays

1 July to 9 September

Birmingham, Banbury, Bicester, Oxford and Bedwyn - Reading and London

Network Diagram - see first Page of Table 116

Station		GW	GW	GW	XC	CH	GW	GW	GW	GW	GW	XC	GW	GW	GW	GW	GW	XC	GW	GW	GW	XC	GW
		◇■ ⊏⊐	■	■	◇■ ⊏⊐		■	◇■ ⊏⊐	◇■ ⊏⊐	■	◇■ ⊏⊐	◇■ ℸ	◇■ ⊏⊐	◇■ ⊏⊐	◇■	■	■	◇■ ⊏⊐	◇■ ⊏⊐	■	◇■ ⊏⊐	◇■ ℸ	◇■ ⊏⊐
Birmingham New Street 12	d				15 04							15 33						16 04				16 33	
Birmingham International	d				15 14													16 14					
Coventry	d				15 25													16 25					
Leamington Spa 8	d				15 38							16 00						16 38				17 00	
Banbury	d				15 55		16 00					16 19						16 55				17 19	
Kings Sutton	d						16 05																
Heyford	d						16 14																
Tackley	d						16 18																
Bicester Town	d					16 03																	
Islip	d					16 14																	
Oxford	a				16 14	16 30	16 33					16 41						17 14				17 38	
	d	15 50		16 05	16 16							16 43		16 50	16 54		17 05	17 16				17 43	
Radley	d			16 11													17 11						
Culham	d																						
Appleford	d			16 16																			
Didcot Parkway	a	16 02		16 21										17 02	17 07		17 21						
	d	16 03		16 21				16 33			16 47		16 59	17 04	17 08		17 21		17 29		17 47		17 59
Cholsey	d			16 27													17 27						
Goring & Streatley	d			16 33													17 33						
Pangbourne	d			16 37													17 37						
Tilehurst	d			16 42													17 42						
Bedwyn	d															16 54							
Hungerford	d															17 00							
Kintbury	d															17 04							
Newbury	a															17 11							
	d		16 03						16 31							17 11							
Newbury Racecourse	d		16 05																				
Thatcham	d		16 10													17 16							
Midgham	d		16 15																				
Aldermaston	d		16 18																				
Theale	d		16 23													17 24							
Reading West	d		16 31							←										←			
Reading 7	a	16 20	16 34	16 49	16 43			16 45	16 49	16 49	17 00	17 11	17 12	17 21	17 23	17 33	17 49	17 38	17 42	17 49	18 00	18 13	18 12
	d	16 20	16 34	16 52				16 47	16 51	16 52	17 02		17 14	17 21	17 24	17 34	17 52		17 44	17 52	18 02		18 14
Twyford 3	a			→						16 58					17 30		→			17 58			
Maidenhead 3	a		16 45							17 06					17 38	17 45				18 06			
Slough 3	a	16 33	16 54							17 14				17 38	17 45	17 52				18 14			
Ealing Broadway ⊖	a									17 36										18 36			
London Paddington 15 ⊖	a	16 51	17 23					17 14	17 21	17 47	17 29		17 41	17 59	18 07	18 11			18 14	18 47	18 29		18 42

Station		GW	CH	GW	GW	XC	GW	GW	GW	XC	GW	GW	GW	GW	GW	XC	CH	XC	GW	GW	GW	GW
		◇■ ⊏⊐		■	■	◇■ ⊏⊐	■	◇■ ⊏⊐	◇■ ⊏⊐	◇■ ℸ	◇■ ⊏⊐	◇■ ⊏⊐	◇■ ⊏⊐	■	■	◇■ ⊏⊐		◇■ ℸ	◇■ ⊏⊐	◇■	■	◇■ ⊏⊐
Birmingham New Street 12	d					17 04				17 33						18 04		18 33				
Birmingham International	d					17 14										18 14						
Coventry	d					17 25										18 25						
Leamington Spa 8	d					17 38				18 01						18 38		19 00				
Banbury	d					17 55	18 00			18 20						18 55		19 19				
Kings Sutton	d						18 07															
Heyford	d						18 16															
Tackley	d						18 20															
Bicester Town	d		17 33														19 07					
Islip	d		17 44														19 18					
Oxford	a		18 00			18 14	18 31			18 41						19 14	19 34	19 38				
	d	17 50			18 05	18 16				18 42		18 50			19 05	19 16		19 43		19 53		
Radley	d				18 11										19 11							
Culham	d																					
Appleford	d														19 16							
Didcot Parkway	a	18 02			18 18							19 03			19 21					20 04		
	d	18 03			18 21				18 45		18 59	19 04	19 17		19 21				19 59	20 06		20 17
Cholsey	d				18 27										19 27							
Goring & Streatley	d				18 33										19 33							
Pangbourne	d				18 37										19 36							
Tilehurst	d				18 42										19 42							
Bedwyn	d													18 54								
Hungerford	d													19 00								
Kintbury	d													19 04								
Newbury	a													19 11								
	d			18 03				18 34						19 11							19 53	
Newbury Racecourse	d			18 05																	19 55	
Thatcham	d			18 10										19 16							20 00	
Midgham	d			18 15																	20 05	
Aldermaston	d			18 18																	20 08	
Theale	d			18 23										19 24							20 13	
Reading West	d			18 31																	20 21	
Reading 7	a	18 20		18 34	18 49	18 40		18 52	18 58	19 07	19 12	19 20	19 32	19 36	19 47	19 40		20 13	20 12	20 23	20 24	20 32
	d	18 20		18 34	18 52			18 53	19 02		19 14	19 24	19 32	19 37	19 52				20 14	20 23		20 32
Twyford 3	a				18 58										19 58							
Maidenhead 3	a			18 46	19 06									19 48	20 06							
Slough 3	a	18 35		18 54	19 14							19 38		20 01	20 14					20 42		
Ealing Broadway ⊖	a				19 36										20 36							
London Paddington 15 ⊖	a	18 53		19 23	19 47			19 21	19 30		19 42	19 56	20 01	20 22	20 47				20 46	21 02		21 01

Table 116

Sundays

1 July to 9 September

Birmingham, Banbury, Bicester, Oxford and Bedwyn - Reading and London

Network Diagram - see first Page of Table 116

Station		GW	GW	XC	XC	GW	GW	CH	GW	GW	XC	GW	GW	XC	GW	GW	GW	XC	GW	GW	CH	GW	GW
		◇■ ⊏⊐	■	◇■ ⊏⊐	◇■ ℸ	◇■ ⊏⊐	◇■		◇■ ⊏⊐	■	◇■ ⊏⊐	◇■ ⊏⊐	■	◇■ ℸ	◇■ ⊏⊐	◇■	■	◇■	◇■ ⊏⊐	■		■	◇■
Birmingham New Street 12	d			19 04	19 33						20 04			20 33				21 04					
Birmingham International	d			19 14							20 14							21 14					
Coventry	d			19 25							20 25							21 24					
Leamington Spa 8	d			19 38	20 00						20 38			21 00				21 35					
Banbury	d			19 55	20 19						20 55			21 19									
Kings Sutton	d																						
Heyford	d																						
Tackley	d																						
Bicester Town	d							20 33													22 03		
Islip	d							20 44													22 14		
Oxford	a			20 14	20 40			21 00			21 14			21 38				22 08			22 30		
	d		20 05	20 16	20 43		20 50				21 16		21 21	21 40		21 50		22 10		22 21			22 46
Radley	d		20 11										21 27							22 27			
Culham	d																						
Appleford	d																						
Didcot Parkway	a		20 21				21 00						21 35			22 00				22 35			22 58
	d		20 21			20 59	21 01		21 17			21 31	21 35		22 01	22 02				22 35			22 59
Cholsey	d		20 27										21 41							22 41			
Goring & Streatley	d		20 33										21 46							22 46			
Pangbourne	d		20 37										21 51							22 51			
Tilehurst	d		20 42										21 55							22 55			
Bedwyn	d									20 54												22 35	
Hungerford	d									21 00												22 41	
Kintbury	d									21 04												22 45	
Newbury	a									21 11												22 52	
	d	20 24								21 12							21 53		22 19			22 53	
Newbury Racecourse	d																21 55						
Thatcham	d									21 17							22 00					22 58	
Midgham	d																22 05						
Aldermaston	d																22 08						
Theale	d									21 25							22 13					23 06	
Reading West	d																22 21						
Reading 7	a	20 42	20 49	20 42	21 11	21 15	21 17		21 32	21 33	21 43	21 47	22 02	22 07	22 17	22 20	22 24	22 33	22 36	23 00		23 15	23 15
	d	20 47	20 52			21 17	21 20		21 32			21 49	22 10		22 19	22 24			22 36	23 00			23 22
Twyford 3	a		20 58										22 16							23 06			
Maidenhead 3	a		21 06				21 32						22 24							23 14			
Slough 3	a		21 14				21 38						22 33			22 41				23 22			23 42
Ealing Broadway ⊖	a		21 36										22 56							23 44			
London Paddington 15 ⊖	a	21 14	21 47			21 44	21 59		22 02			22 29	23 05		22 46	23 00			23 06	23 54			00 02

Station		GW	GW	GW	GW
		◇■ ⊏⊐		■	■
Birmingham New Street 12	d				
Birmingham International	d				
Coventry	d				
Leamington Spa 8	d				
Banbury	d				
Kings Sutton	d				
Heyford	d				
Tackley	d				
Bicester Town	d				
Islip	d				
Oxford	a				
	d			23 15	
Radley	d			23 22	
Culham	d				
Appleford	d				
Didcot Parkway	a			23 30	
	d	23 12		23 30	
Cholsey	d			23 36	
Goring & Streatley	d			23 42	
Pangbourne	d			23 46	
Tilehurst	d			23 50	
Bedwyn	d				
Hungerford	d				
Kintbury	d				
Newbury	a				
	d		23 23		23 45
Newbury Racecourse	d				23 47
Thatcham	d		23 28		23 52
Midgham	d				23 57
Aldermaston	d				00 01
Theale	d		23 36		00 06
Reading West	d				00s13
Reading 7	a	23 28	23 44	23 56	00 17
	d	23 30		23 56	
Twyford 3	a			00 02	
Maidenhead 3	a			00 10	
Slough 3	a			00 20	
Ealing Broadway ⊖	a			00 43	
London Paddington 15 ⊖	a	00 05		00 52	

Birmingham, Banbury, Bicester, Oxford and Bedwyn - Reading and London

Network Diagram - see first Page of Table 116

		GW ◇1	GW ◇1 ☕	GW 1	GW 1	GW 🚌	GW 1	GW ◇1 ☕	GW 1	GW ◇1	GW 1	GW ◇1 ☕	GW ◇1	GW 1	GW 1	XC ◇1 🍴	CH	GW ◇1 ☕	GW ◇1 ☕	GW ◇1	GW 1	GW ◇1	GW 1
Birmingham New Street 12	d														09 04							
Birmingham International	d														09 14							
Coventry	d														09 25							
Leamington Spa 8	d														09 38							
Banbury	d														09 55							
Kings Sutton	d																					
Heyford	d																					
Tackley	d																					
Bicester Town	d															10 05						
Islip	d															10 16						
Oxford	a														10 14	10 32						
	d	23p01		23p07		07 45				08 50	09 05		09 50		10 05	10 16				10 44		10 55	11 05
Radley	d		23p13								09 11				10 11								11 11
Culham	d		23p17																			
Appleford	d		23p20												10 16								
Didcot Parkway	a	23p13		23p25		08 10				09 02	09 20		10 02		10 21					10 57		11 07	11 20
	d	23p13	23p30	23p36	08 00		08 21	08 45		09 03	09 21	09 45	10 03		10 21				10 45	10 58		11 07	11 21
Cholsey	d		23p42			08 27				09 27				10 27								11 27
Goring & Streatley	d		23p47	08 08		08 32				09 33				10 33								11 33
Pangbourne	d					08 36				09 37				10 37								11 37
Tilehurst	d		23p56			08 44				09 42				10 42								11 46
Bedwyn	d												09 35						10 42		
Hungerford	d												09 41						10 48		
Kintbury	d												09 46						10 52		
Newbury	a												09 52						10 59		
	d							08 46					09 53				10 32			11 00		
Newbury Racecourse	d							08 48					09 55									
Thatcham	d							08 53					10 00							11 05		
Midgham	d							08 58					10 05									
Aldermaston	d							09 01					10 08									
Theale	d							09 06					10 13							11 13		
Reading West	d							09 14					10 21									
Reading 7	a	23p30	23p51	00 02	08 19		08 52	09 02	09 17	09 22	09 48	10 02	10 20	10 24	10 50	10 38		10 48	11 01	11 13	11 21	11 25	11 52
	d	23p31	23p51	00 03	08 20		08 52	09 03		09 23	09 53	10 03	10 21		10 53			10 49	11 03	11 15		11 25	11 53
Twyford 3	a		00 10			08 58				09 59				10 59					11 21			→
Maidenhead 3	a		00 18			09 06				10 07				11 07					11 29			
Slough 3	a	23p45		00 29	08 38		09 15			09 38	10 15		10 36		11 15					11 36		11 42	
Ealing Broadway ⊖	a		00 53			09 42				10 42				11 42								
London Paddington 15 ⊖	a	00 10	00 34	01 04	09 00		09 51	09 44		10 00	10 52	10 44	10 59		11 50			11 29	11 44	11 59		12 06	

		XC ◇1 ☕	GW ◇1 ☕	GW ◇1 ☕	GW 1	GW ◇1 ☕	GW ◇1	CH	GW 1	GW 1	XC ◇1 ☕	GW ◇1 ☕	GW 1	GW 1	GW ◇1 ☕	GW ◇1	GW 1	XC ◇1 ☕	CH	GW ◇1 ☕	GW ◇1 ☕	GW 1	XC ◇1 🍴
Birmingham New Street 12	d	10 04								11 04						12 04				12 33
Birmingham International	d	10 14								11 14						12 14				
Coventry	d	10 25								11 25						12 25				
Leamington Spa 8	d	10 38								11 38						12 38				13 00
Banbury	d	10 55								11 55						12 55				13 19
Kings Sutton	d																					
Heyford	d																					
Tackley	d																					
Bicester Town	d						11 33										13 03			
Islip	d						11 44										13 14			
Oxford	a	11 14						12 00			12 14						13 14	13 30				13 38
	d	11 16					11 50			12 05	12 16					12 50	13 05	13 16					13 43
Radley	d								12 11						13 11					
Culham	d																					
Appleford	d								12 16												
Didcot Parkway	a					12 02			12 21						13 02	13 20					
	d		11 33			11 45	12 03			12 21		12 33			12 59	13 03	13 21			13 33			
Cholsey	d								12 27						13 27					
Goring & Streatley	d								12 33						13 33					
Pangbourne	d								12 37						13 37					
Tilehurst	d								12 42						13 45					
Bedwyn	d												12 42								
Hungerford	d												12 48								
Kintbury	d												12 52								
Newbury	a												12 59								
	d		11 26					11 53					13 00							13 31		
Newbury Racecourse	d							11 55													
Thatcham	d							12 00					13 05								
Midgham	d							12 05													
Aldermaston	d							12 08													
Theale	d							12 13					13 13								
Reading West	d			←				12 21				←							VITE		←	
Reading 7	a	11 42	11 47	11 49	11 52	12 01	12 21		12 24	12 52	12 42	12 47	12 52	13 21	13 19	13 23	13 52	13 42		13 47	13 49	13 52	14 13
	d		11 49	11 51	11 53	12 03	12 23			12 53		12 49	12 53		13 21	13 24	13 53			13 49	13 51	13 53	
Twyford 3	a			11 59					→			12 59				→					13 59	
Maidenhead 3	a			12 07								13 07										14 07	
Slough 3	a			12 15		12 38						13 15			13 41						14 15	
Ealing Broadway ⊖	a			12 42								13 42										14 42	
London Paddington 15 ⊖	a		12 22	12 29	12 51	12 43	13 03					13 22	13 52		13 59	14 03				14 22	14 29	14 50	

Birmingham, Banbury, Bicester, Oxford and Bedwyn - Reading and London

Network Diagram - see first Page of Table 116

		GW ◇1 ☕	GW 1	GW ◇1	GW 1	XC ◇1 ☕	GW ◇1 ☕	GW 1	XC ◇1 🍴	XC ◇1 🍴	GW 1	GW ◇1 ☕	GW ◇1	CH	GW 1	XC ◇1 ☕	XC ◇1 🍴	XC ◇1 🍴	GW ◇1 ☕	GW ◇1 ☕	GW 1	GW 1
Birmingham New Street 12	d				13 04			13 33	13 33						14 04	14 33	14 33				
Birmingham International	d				13 14											14 14						
Coventry	d				13 25											14 25						
Leamington Spa 8	d				13 38			14 00	14 00						14 38	15 00	15 00				
Banbury	d				13 55			14 19	14 19						14 55	15 19	15 19				
Kings Sutton	d																				
Heyford	d																				
Tackley	d																				
Bicester Town	d												14 33								
Islip	d												14 44								
Oxford	a				14 14			14 38	14 38				15 00		15 14	15 41	15 41				
	d		13 50	14 05	14 17			14 43	14 43			14 50		15 05	15 16	15 43	15 43		15 50		16 05
Radley	d			14 11										15 11						16 11
Culham	d																				
Appleford	d			14 16																	16 16
Didcot Parkway	a		14 02	14 20									15 03		15 20					16 02		16 20
	d	14 00		14 03	14 21		14 33					14 59	15 03		15 21				15 59	16 03		16 21
Cholsey	d			14 27										15 27						16 27
Goring & Streatley	d			14 33										15 33						16 33
Pangbourne	d			14 37										15 37						16 37
Tilehurst	d			14 45										15 47						16 46
Bedwyn	d									14 42											
Hungerford	d									14 48											
Kintbury	d									14 52											
Newbury	a									14 59											
	d		13 53								15 00										15 53	
Newbury Racecourse	d		13 55																		15 55	
Thatcham	d		14 00								15 05										16 00	
Midgham	d		14 05																		16 05	
Aldermaston	d		14 08																		16 08	
Theale	d		14 13								15 13										16 13	
Reading West	d		14 21					←														16 21	
Reading 7	a	14 19	14 24	14 25	14 53	14 43	14 47	14 53	15 07	15 13	15 21	15 19	15 25		15 53	15 45	16 07	16 13	16 19	16 22	16 24	16 53
	d	14 21		14 25	14 53		14 49	14 53				15 21	15 26		15 53				16 21	16 28		16 53
Twyford 3	a				→			14 59							15 59							→
Maidenhead 3	a							15 07							16 07							
Slough 3	a			14 41				15 15					15 41		16 15					16 36		
Ealing Broadway ⊖	a							15 42							16 42							
London Paddington 15 ⊖	a	14 57		15 04			15 22	15 51				15 58	16 03		16 52				17 01	17 07		

		XC ◇1 ☕	CH	GW ◇1 ☕	GW ◇1 ☕	GW 1	GW ◇1 ☕	GW ◇1	XC ◇1 🍴	GW ◇1 ☕	GW 1	GW ◇1 ☕	GW 1	XC ◇1 ☕	GW ◇1 ☕	GW 1	GW ◇1 ☕	XC ◇1 🍴	GW ◇1 ☕	GW 1	GW ◇1 ☕	CH	GW 1
Birmingham New Street 12	d	15 04							15 33					16 04				16 33					
Birmingham International	d	15 14												16 14									
Coventry	d	15 25												16 25									
Leamington Spa 8	d	15 38							16 00					16 38				17 00					
Banbury	d	15 55							16 19					16 55				17 19					
Kings Sutton	d																					
Heyford	d																					
Tackley	d																					
Bicester Town	d		16 03																			17 33	
Islip	d		16 14																			17 44	
Oxford	a	16 14	16 30						16 41					17 14				17 38				18 00	
	d	16 16						16 37	16 43			16 50	17 05	17 16				17 43			17 50		18 05
Radley	d												17 11										18 11
Culham	d																					
Appleford	d																					
Didcot Parkway	a							16 49				17 02	17 20								18 02		18 18
	d			16 32			16 47	16 50		16 59		17 04	17 21		17 29		17 47		17 59		18 03		18 21
Cholsey	d												17 27										18 27
Goring & Streatley	d												17 33										18 33
Pangbourne	d												17 37										18 37
Tilehurst	d												17 46										18 42
Bedwyn	d										16 42												
Hungerford	d										16 48												
Kintbury	d										16 52												
Newbury	a										16 59												
	d				16 31						17 00									17 53			
Newbury Racecourse	d																			17 55			
Thatcham	d										17 05									18 00			
Midgham	d																			18 05			
Aldermaston	d																			18 08			
Theale	d										17 13									18 13			
Reading West	d					←										←				18 21			
Reading 7	a	16 43		16 46	16 49	16 53	17 04	17 10	17 13	17 16	17 21	17 27	17 53	17 43	17 46	17 53	18 01	18 15	18 19	18 24	18 27		18 53
	d			16 48	16 51	16 53	17 06	17 11		17 18		17 28	17 53		17 48	17 53	18 03		18 21		18 28		18 53
Twyford 3	a					16 59		17 17					→			17 59								18 59
Maidenhead 3	a					17 07		17 25								18 07							19 07
Slough 3	a					17 15		17 33				17 43				18 18					18 41		19 18
Ealing Broadway ⊖	a					17 42										18 42							19 42
London Paddington 15 ⊖	a			17 22	17 30	17 52	17 43	17 58		18 01		18 07			18 22	18 52	18 44		18 59		19 07		19 52

16 September to 21 October

Birmingham, Banbury, Bicester, Oxford and Bedwyn - Reading and London

Network Diagram - see first Page of Table 116

		XC	GW	GW	XC	GW	GW	GW	GW	GW	XC	CH	XC	GW	GW	GW	GW	GW	XC	GW	XC	GW
		◇1	◇1	◇1	◇1	1	◇1	◇1	◇1	1	◇1		◇1	◇1	◇1	1	◇1	1	◇1	◇1	◇1	◇1
		🛒	🛒	🛒	🍴		🛒	🛒	🛒		🛒		🍴	🛒			🛒		🛒	🛒	🍴	🛒
Birmingham New Street 12	d	17 04			17 33						18 04		18 33						19 04		19 33	
Birmingham International	d	17 14									18 14								19 14			
Coventry	d	17 25									18 25								19 25			
Leamington Spa 8	d	17 38			18 01						18 38		19 00						19 38		20 00	
Banbury	d	17 55			18 20						18 55		19 19						19 55		20 19	
Kings Sutton	d																					
Heyford	d																					
Tackley	d																					
Bicester Town	d											19 07										
Islip	d											19 18										
Oxford	a	18 14			18 39						19 14	19 34	19 38						20 14		20 40	
	d	18 16			18 43			18 50		19 05	19 16		19 43		19 50			20 05	20 16		20 43	
Radley	d									19 11								20 11				
Culham	d																					
Appleford	d									19 16												
Didcot Parkway	a							19 02		19 21					20 04			20 20				
	d			18 47			18 59	19 08	19 17	19 23				19 59	20 06		20 17	20 21				20 59
Cholsey	d									19 27								20 27				
Goring & Streatley	d									19 33								20 33				
Pangbourne	d									19 37								20 37				
Tilehurst	d									19 46								20 42				
Bedwyn	d					18 42																
Hungerford	d					18 48																
Kintbury	d					18 52																
Newbury	a					18 59																
	d		18 34			19 00										19 53				20 25		
Newbury Racecourse	d															19 55						
Thatcham	d					19 05										20 00						
Midgham	d															20 05						
Aldermaston	d															20 08						
Theale	d					19 13										20 13						
Reading West	d															20 21						
Reading 7	a	18 45	18 49	19 01	19 13	19 21	19 19	19 27	19 33	19 53	19 45		20 15	20 19	20 24	20 24	20 33	20 53	20 43	20 50	21 15	21 20
	d		18 51	19 03			19 21	19 28	19 34	19 53				20 21	20 24		20 34	20 53		20 51		21 24
Twyford 3	a									19 59								20 59				
Maidenhead 3	a									20 07								21 07				
Slough 3	a							19 44		20 18					20 43			21 18				
Ealing Broadway ⊖	a									20 42								21 42				
London Paddington 15 ⊖	a		19 29	19 44			19 59	20 07	20 14	20 52				20 59	21 05		21 13	21 52		21 29		22 02

		GW	CH	GW	GW	XC	GW	GW	XC	GW	GW	GW	GW	XC	GW	CH	GW	GW	GW	GW	GW	GW	GW
		◇1		1	◇1	◇1	◇1	1	◇1	◇1	◇1	1	◇1	◇1	1		1	◇1	◇1			1	1
					🛒	🛒	🛒		🍴	🛒			🛒						🛒	🚌			
Birmingham New Street 12	d					20 04			20 33					21 04									
Birmingham International	d					20 14								21 14									
Coventry	d					20 25								21 24									
Leamington Spa 8	d					20 38			21 00					21 35									
Banbury	d					20 55			21 19														
Kings Sutton	d																						
Heyford	d																						
Tackley	d																						
Bicester Town	d		20 33													22 03							
Islip	d		20 44													22 14							
Oxford	a		21 00			21 14			21 38					22 08		22 30							
	d	20 50				21 16		21 21	21 40		21 50			22 10	22 17			22 46		23 00			
Radley	d							21 27							22 23					23 15			
Culham	d																						
Appleford	d																						
Didcot Parkway	a	21 00						21 35			22 00				22 31			22 58		23 35			
	d	21 09			21 17		21 31	21 35		22 01	22 03				22 31			22 59	23 11			23 50	
Cholsey	d							21 41							22 37							23 56	
Goring & Streatley	d							21 46							22 42							00 01	
Pangbourne	d							21 51							22 47								
Tilehurst	d							21 55							22 51							00 08	
Bedwyn	d			20 54													22 35						
Hungerford	d			21 00													22 41						
Kintbury	d			21 04													22 45						
Newbury	a			21 11													22 52						
	d			21 12								21 53	22 19				22 53				23 23		23 45
Newbury Racecourse	d											21 55											23 47
Thatcham	d			21 17								22 00					22 58				23 28		23 52
Midgham	d											22 05											23 57
Aldermaston	d											22 08											00 01
Theale	d			21 25								22 13					23 06				23 36		00 06
Reading West	d											22 21											00s13
Reading 7	a	21 24		21 33	21 33	21 43	21 47	22 02	22 08	22 17	22 21	22 24	22 36	22 38	22 59		23 15	23 17	23 28		23 44	00 15	00 17
	d	21 28			21 34		21 49	22 03		22 18	22 22		22 37		23 00			23 22	23 30			00 15	
Twyford 3	a							22 10							23 07							00 22	
Maidenhead 3	a	21 40						22 24							23 15							00 30	
Slough 3	a	21 44						22 34			22 43				23 22			23 43				00 37	
Ealing Broadway ⊖	a							22 57							23 44							01 00	
London Paddington 15 ⊖	a	22 07			22 15		22 29	23 07		22 58	23 13		23 16		23 53			00 06	00 12			01 12	

from 28 October

Birmingham, Banbury, Bicester, Oxford and Bedwyn - Reading and London

Network Diagram - see first Page of Table 116

		GW	GW	GW	GW	GW	GW	GW	GW	GW	GW	GW	GW	GW	GW	XC	CH	GW	GW	GW	GW	GW	GW
		◇1	◇1	1	1		1	◇1	1	◇1	1	◇1	◇1	1	1	◇1		◇1	◇1	◇1	1	◇1	1
			🛒			🚌		🛒				🛒				🍴		🛒	🛒				
Birmingham New Street 12	d															09 04							
Birmingham International	d															09 14							
Coventry	d															09 25							
Leamington Spa 8	d															09 38							
Banbury	d															09 55							
Kings Sutton	d																						
Heyford	d																						
Tackley	d																						
Bicester Town	d																10 05						
Islip	d																10 16						
Oxford	a															10 14	10 32						
	d	23p01		23p07		07 45				08 50	09 05		09 50		10 05	10 16				10 44		10 55	11 05
Radley	d			23p13							09 11				10 11								11 11
Culham	d			23p17																			
Appleford	d			23p20											10 16								
Didcot Parkway	a	23p12		23p25		08 10				09 02	09 20		10 02		10 21					10 57		11 07	11 20
	d	23p13	23p30	23p36	08 00		08 21	08 43		09 03	09 21	09 45	10 03		10 21				10 46	10 58		11 07	11 21
Cholsey	d			23p42			08 27				09 27				10 27								11 27
Goring & Streatley	d			23p47	08 08		08 32				09 33				10 33								11 33
Pangbourne	d			23p51			08 36				09 37				10 37								11 37
Tilehurst	d			23p56			08 43				09 42				10 42								11 42
Bedwyn	d													09 35							10 42		
Hungerford	d													09 41							10 48		
Kintbury	d													09 46							10 52		
Newbury	a													09 52							10 59		
	d								08 46					09 53				10 32			11 00		
Newbury Racecourse	d								08 48					09 55									
Thatcham	d								08 53					10 00							11 05		
Midgham	d								08 58					10 05									
Aldermaston	d								09 01					10 08									
Theale	d								09 06					10 13							11 13		
Reading West	d								09 14					10 21									
Reading 7	a	23p29	23p52	00 02	08 19		08 51	09 01	09 17	09 22	09 49	10 00	10 20	10 24	10 52	10 38		10 48	11 00	11 13	11 21	11 25	11 52
	d	23p29	23p53	00 03	08 20		08 52	09 03		09 23	09 53	10 02	10 21		10 53			10 49	11 02	11 15		11 25	11 53
Twyford 3	a			00 10			08 58				09 59				10 59					11 21			→
Maidenhead 3	a			00 18			09 06				10 07				11 07					11 29			
Slough 3	a	23p45		00 29	08 38		09 15			09 38	10 15		10 36		11 15					11 36		11 42	
Ealing Broadway ⊖	a			00 53			09 42				10 42				11 42								
London Paddington 15 ⊖	a	00 10	00 33	01 04	08 59		09 51	09 44		10 00	10 51	10 44	10 59		11 50			11 29	11 44	11 59		12 06	

		XC	GW	GW	GW	GW	GW	CH	GW	GW	XC	GW	GW	GW	GW	GW	GW	XC	CH	GW	GW	GW	GW
		◇1	◇1	◇1	1	◇1	◇1		1	1	◇1	◇1	1	◇1	1	◇1	1	◇1		◇1	◇1	1	◇1
		🛒	🛒	🛒		🛒					🛒	🛒		🛒				🛒		🛒	🛒		🛒
Birmingham New Street 12	d	10 04									11 04							12 04					
Birmingham International	d	10 14									11 14							12 14					
Coventry	d	10 25									11 25							12 25					
Leamington Spa 8	d	10 38									11 38							12 38					
Banbury	d	10 55									11 55							12 55					
Kings Sutton	d																						
Heyford	d																						
Tackley	d																						
Bicester Town	d							11 33											13 03				
Islip	d							11 44											13 14				
Oxford	a	11 14						12 00			12 14							13 14	13 30				
	d	11 16					11 50			12 05	12 16					12 50	13 05	13 16					
Radley	d									12 11							13 11						
Culham	d																						
Appleford	d									12 16													
Didcot Parkway	a						12 02			12 21						13 02	13 20						
	d		11 29			11 47	12 03			12 21		12 29		12 47		13 03	13 21			13 29			13 47
Cholsey	d									12 27							13 27						
Goring & Streatley	d									12 33							13 33						
Pangbourne	d									12 37							13 37						
Tilehurst	d									12 42							13 45						
Bedwyn	d														12 42								
Hungerford	d														12 48								
Kintbury	d														12 52								
Newbury	a														12 59								
	d			11 26					11 53						13 00						13 31		
Newbury Racecourse	d								11 55														
Thatcham	d								12 00						13 05								
Midgham	d								12 05														
Aldermaston	d								12 08														
Theale	d								12 13						13 13								
Reading West	d				←				12 21				←									←	
Reading 7	a	11 43	11 45	11 49	11 52	12 01	12 21		12 24	12 52	12 42	12 42	12 52	13 01	13 21	13 23	13 52	13 42		13 47	13 49	13 52	14 01
	d		11 47	11 51	11 53	12 02	12 23			12 53		12 44	12 53	13 02		13 24	13 53			13 49	13 51	13 53	14 02
Twyford 3	a				11 59					→			12 59				→					13 59	
Maidenhead 3	a				12 07								13 07									14 07	
Slough 3	a				12 15		12 38						13 15			13 37						14 15	
Ealing Broadway ⊖	a				12 42								13 42									14 42	
London Paddington 15 ⊖	a		12 21	12 29	12 51	12 44	13 03					13 22	13 52	13 44		14 00				14 22	14 29	14 50	14 44

Table 116

Birmingham, Banbury, Bicester, Oxford and Bedwyn - Reading and London

Sundays from 28 October

Network Diagram - see first Page of Table 116

		XC		GW	GW	GW	XC	GW	GW	GW	XC	GW		GW	CH	GW	XC	GW	GW	GW	XC	GW		GW	GW
		◇1		◇1	1	1	◇1	◇1	1	◇1	◇1	1		◇1		1	◇1	◇1	1	◇1	◇1	◇1		1	1
		⊼					⊏	⊏		⊏	⊼						⊏	⊏		⊏	⊼	⊏			
Birmingham New Street 12	d	12 33					13 04				13 33						14 04				14 33				
Birmingham International	d						13 14										14 14								
Coventry	d						13 25										14 25								
Leamington Spa 8	d	13 00					13 38				14 00						14 38				15 00				
Banbury	d	13 19					13 55				14 19						14 55				15 19				
Kings Sutton	d																								
Heyford	d																								
Tackley	d																								
Bicester Town	d														14 33										
Islip	d														14 44										
Oxford	a	13 41					14 14				14 38				15 00		15 14				15 41				
	d	13 43		13 50		14 05	14 17				14 43			14 50		15 05	15 16				15 43	15 50			16 05
Radley	d					14 11										15 11									16 11
Culham	d																								
Appleford	d					14 16																			16 16
Didcot Parkway	a			14 02		14 20								15 03		15 20						16 02			16 20
	d			14 03		14 21		14 29		14 47				15 03		15 21		15 29		15 47		16 03			16 21
Cholsey	d					14 27										15 27									16 27
Goring & Streatley	d					14 33										15 33									16 33
Pangbourne	d					14 37										15 37									16 37
Tilehurst	d					14 45										15 46									16 44
Bedwyn	d											14 42													
Hungerford	d											14 48													
Kintbury	d											14 52													
Newbury	a											14 59													
	d				13 53							15 00												15 53	
Newbury Racecourse	d				13 55																			15 55	
Thatcham	d				14 00							15 05												16 00	
Midgham	d				14 05																			16 05	
Aldermaston	d				14 08																			16 08	
Theale	d				14 13							15 13												16 13	
Reading West	d				14 21				←										←					16 21	
Reading 7	a	14 13		14 21	14 24	14 53	14 43	14 47	14 53	15 01	15 13	15 21		15 21		15 53	15 45	15 47	15 53	16 01	16 13	16 22		16 24	16 53
	d			14 21		14 53		14 49	14 53	15 02				15 22		15 53		15 49	15 53	16 02		16 23			16 53
Twyford 3	a					→			14 59							→			15 59						→
Maidenhead 3	a								15 07										16 07						
Slough 3	a			14 37					15 15					15 36					16 15			16 36			
Ealing Broadway ⊖	a								15 42										16 42						
London Paddington 15 ⊖	a			14 59				15 22	15 51	15 44				15 59				16 22	16 52	16 44		17 00			

		XC	CH	GW	GW	GW	GW	GW		XC	GW	GW	GW	GW	XC	GW	GW	GW		XC	GW	GW	GW	CH	GW
		◇1		◇1	◇1	1	◇1	◇1		◇1	1	◇1	◇1	1	◇1	◇1	1	◇1		◇1	◇1	1	◇1		1
		⊏		⊏	⊏		⊏			⊼		⊏	⊏		⊏	⊏		⊏		⊼	⊏		⊏		
Birmingham New Street 12	d	15 04								15 33					16 04					16 33					
Birmingham International	d	15 14													16 14										
Coventry	d	15 25													16 25										
Leamington Spa 8	d	15 38								16 00					16 38					17 00					
Banbury	d	15 55								16 19					16 55					17 19					
Kings Sutton	d																								
Heyford	d																								
Tackley	d																								
Bicester Town	d		16 03																					17 33	
Islip	d		16 14																					17 44	
Oxford	a	16 14	16 30							16 41					17 14					17 38				18 00	
	d	16 16						16 37		16 43			16 50	17 05	17 16					17 43			17 50		18 05
Radley	d													17 11											18 11
Culham	d																								
Appleford	d																								
Didcot Parkway	a							16 49					17 02	17 20									18 02		18 18
	d			16 31			16 47	16 50				16 59	17 04	17 21		17 29		17 47			17 59		18 03		18 21
Cholsey	d													17 27											18 27
Goring & Streatley	d													17 33											18 33
Pangbourne	d													17 37											18 37
Tilehurst	d													17 42											18 42
Bedwyn	d										16 42														
Hungerford	d										16 48														
Kintbury	d										16 52														
Newbury	a										16 59														
	d				16 31						17 00											17 53			
Newbury Racecourse	d																					17 55			
Thatcham	d										17 05											18 00			
Midgham	d																					18 05			
Aldermaston	d																					18 08			
Theale	d										17 13											18 13			
Reading West	d					←											←					18 21			
Reading 7	a	16 43		16 47	16 49	16 53	17 01	17 06		17 13	17 21	17 19	17 27	17 53	17 43	17 46	17 53	18 01		18 15	18 20	18 24	18 27		18 53
	d			16 49	16 51	16 53	17 01	17 07				17 21	17 28	17 53		17 49	17 53	18 03			18 22		18 28		18 53
Twyford 3	a					16 59		17 14						→			17 59								18 59
Maidenhead 3	a					17 07		17 22									18 07								19 07
Slough 3	a					17 15		17 39					17 43				18 18						18 41		19 18
Ealing Broadway ⊖	a					17 42											18 42								19 42
London Paddington 15 ⊖	a			17 22	17 30	17 52	17 43	18 03				17 58	18 07			18 22	18 52	18 44			18 59		19 07		19 52

Table 116

Birmingham, Banbury, Bicester, Oxford and Bedwyn - Reading and London

Sundays from 28 October

Network Diagram - see first Page of Table 116

		XC	GW	GW		XC	GW	GW	GW	GW	GW	XC	CH	XC		GW	GW	GW	GW	GW	XC	GW	XC	GW	
		◇1	◇1	◇1		◇1	1	◇1	◇1	◇1	1	◇1		◇1		◇1	◇1	1	◇1	1	◇1	◇1	◇1	◇1	
		⊏	⊏	⊏		⊼		⊏	⊏	⊏		⊏		⊼		⊏			⊏		⊏	⊏	⊼	⊏	
Birmingham New Street 12	d	17 04				17 33						18 04		18 33							19 04		19 33		
Birmingham International	d	17 14										18 14									19 14				
Coventry	d	17 25										18 25									19 25				
Leamington Spa 8	d	17 38				18 01						18 38		19 00							19 38		20 00		
Banbury	d	17 55				18 20						18 55		19 19							19 55		20 19		
Kings Sutton	d																								
Heyford	d																								
Tackley	d																								
Bicester Town	d												19 07												
Islip	d												19 18												
Oxford	a	18 14				18 41						19 14	19 34	19 38							20 14		20 40		
	d	18 16				18 43			18 50		19 05	19 16		19 43			19 50			20 05	20 16		20 43		
Radley	d										19 11									20 11					
Culham	d																								
Appleford	d										19 16														
Didcot Parkway	a								19 02		19 21						20 04			20 20					
	d			18 47				18 59	19 08	19 17	19 21					19 59	20 06		20 17	20 21				20 59	
Cholsey	d										19 27									20 27					
Goring & Streatley	d										19 33									20 33					
Pangbourne	d										19 37									20 37					
Tilehurst	d										19 43									20 42					
Bedwyn	d						18 42																		
Hungerford	d						18 48																		
Kintbury	d						18 52																		
Newbury	a						18 59																		
	d		18 34				19 00											19 53				20 25			
Newbury Racecourse	d																	19 55							
Thatcham	d						19 05											20 00							
Midgham	d																	20 05							
Aldermaston	d																	20 08							
Theale	d						19 13											20 13							
Reading West	d																	20 21							
Reading 7	a	18 45	18 49	19 01		19 13	19 21	19 19	19 27	19 32	19 53	19 45		20 15		20 19	20 24	20 24	20 33	20 53	20 43	20 47	21 13	21 22	
	d		18 51	19 03				19 21	19 28	19 34	19 53					20 21	20 24		20 34	20 53		20 49		21 24	
Twyford 3	a										19 59									20 59					
Maidenhead 3	a										20 07									21 07					
Slough 3	a								19 44		20 18						20 43			21 15					
Ealing Broadway ⊖	a										20 42									21 42					
London Paddington 15 ⊖	a		19 29	19 44				19 59	20 07	20 14	20 51					20 59	21 05		21 13	21 52		21 29		22 02	

		GW	CH	GW	GW	XC	GW	GW	XC	GW		GW	GW	GW	XC	GW	CH	GW	GW	GW		GW	GW	GW	GW
		◇1		1	◇1	◇1	◇1	1	◇1	◇1		◇1	1	◇1	◇1	1		1	◇1	◇1		🚌		1	1
					⊏	⊏	⊏		⊼	⊏				⊏						⊏					
Birmingham New Street 12	d					20 04			20 33						21 04										
Birmingham International	d					20 14									21 14										
Coventry	d					20 25									21 24										
Leamington Spa 8	d					20 38			21 00						21 35										
Banbury	d					20 55			21 19																
Kings Sutton	d																								
Heyford	d																								
Tackley	d																								
Bicester Town	d		20 33														22 03								
Islip	d		20 44														22 14								
Oxford	a		21 00			21 14			21 38						22 08		22 30								
	d	20 50				21 16		21 21	21 40			21 50			22 10	22 17			22 46			23 00			
Radley	d							21 27								22 23						23 15			
Culham	d																								
Appleford	d																								
Didcot Parkway	a	21 00						21 35				22 00				22 31			22 58			23 35			
	d	21 09			21 17		21 31	21 35		22 01		22 03				22 31			22 59	23 11				23 50	
Cholsey	d							21 41								22 37								23 56	
Goring & Streatley	d							21 46								22 42								00 01	
Pangbourne	d							21 51								22 47									
Tilehurst	d							21 55								22 51								00 08	
Bedwyn	d			20 54														22 35							
Hungerford	d			21 00														22 41							
Kintbury	d			21 04														22 45							
Newbury	a			21 11														22 52							
	d			21 12									21 53	22 19				22 53					23 23		23 45
Newbury Racecourse	d												21 55												23 47
Thatcham	d			21 17									22 00					22 58					23 28		23 52
Midgham	d												22 05												23 57
Aldermaston	d												22 08												00 01
Theale	d			21 25									22 13					23 06					23 36		00 06
Reading West	d												22 21												00s13
Reading 7	a	21 24		21 33	21 33	21 43	21 47	22 03	22 07	22 18		22 24	22 24	22 36	22 44	22 59		23 15	23 17	23 28			23 44	00 15	00 17
	d	21 28			21 34		21 49	22 06		22 20		22 24		22 36		23 00			23 22	23 30				00 15	
Twyford 3	a							22 15								23 07								00 22	
Maidenhead 3	a	21 40						22 24								23 15								00 30	
Slough 3	a	21 44						22 34				22 43				23 22			23 43					00 37	
Ealing Broadway ⊖	a							22 57								23 44								01 00	
London Paddington 15 ⊖	a	22 07			22 13		22 29	23 07		22 58		23 13		23 16		23 53			00 05	00 13				01 12	

London - Greenford and Reading

Network Diagram - see first Page of Table 116

Miles	Miles	Miles	Station	GW MX [1]	GW MO [1] A	GW MX ◇[1]	GW [1] A	GW MX [1]	GW MX [1]	GW MX ◇[1] ⊡	GW MO ◇[1] A ⊡	GW MO ◇[1] A	GW MX [1]	GW MO [1] A	GW MX [1]	GW MX ◇[1]	GW MO [1]	GW MX [1]	GW [1]	GW [1]	HC	HC
0	0	0	London Paddington [15] ⊖ d	22p45	23p15	23p18			23p29	23p30	23p37	23p47	23p48	23p53		00 22	00 34	00 34	01 34	03 34	04 42	05 13
4¼	4¼	4¼	Acton Main Line d	22p51									23p54									
5¾	5¾	5¾	Ealing Broadway ⊖ d	22p54	23p24				23p37			23p55	23p57	00 02			00 42	00 42	01 42	03 42	04 50	05 21
6½	6½	6½	West Ealing d										23p59									
—	7¼	—	Drayton Green d																			
—	7½	—	Castle Bar Park d																			
—	8¼	—	South Greenford d																			
—	9¼	—	Greenford ⊖ a																			
7¼	—	7¼	Hanwell d										00 02									
9	—	9	Southall d		23p29								00 06	00 07			00 47	00 47	01 47	03 48	04 54	05 25
10¾	—	10¾	Hayes & Harlington d	23p01	23p33				23p44				00 10	00 11			00 51	00 51	01 51	03 52	04 58	05 29
—	—	14¾	Heathrow Terminal 1-2-3 [2] ✈ a																		05 04	05 35
—	—	16½	Heathrow Terminal 4 ✈ a																		05 10	05 41
13¼	—	—	West Drayton d		23p37								00 14	00 15			00 55	00 55	01 55	03 56		
14¾	—	—	Iver d										00 17									
16¼	—	—	Langley d		23p42		←						00 21	00 20	←		01 00	01 00				
18½	—	—	Slough [3] a	23p11	23p46	23p36	23p46		23p53		00 02	00 09	00 26	00 24	00 26	00 39	01 05	01 05	02 04	04 04		
—	—	—	d	23p12	23p46	23p36	23p46		23p54		00 03	00 10	00 26	00 24	00 26	00 39	01 05	01 05	02 04	04 05		
21	—	—	Burnham d	23p16	→		23p51						→	00 28	00 30		01 09	01 09				
22½	—	—	Taplow d	23p20											00 34			01 13				
24¼	—	—	Maidenhead [3] d	23p24		23p44	23p56		00 01			00 17		00 34	00 41		01 15	01 16	02 11	04 12		
31	—	—	Twyford [3] d	23p32			00 04	00 07	00 09					00 42	00 48		01 23	01 24	02 19	04 20		
36	—	—	Reading [7] a	23p41		23p58	00 14	00 16	00 19	00 03	00 14	00 29		00 49	00 57	01 00	01 32	01 35	02 29	04 30		
—	—	—	Oxford a	00 26		00 28			01 15							01 34						

Station	GW [1]	GW [1]	GW ◇[1] ⊡	HC	GW ◇[1] ⊡	GW [1]	GW [1]	GW [1]	GW ◇[1]	GW [1]	GW [1]	HC	GW [1]	GW [1]	GW [1]	GW [1]	GW [1]	GW ◇[1] ⊡	HC	GW [1]	GW [1]	GW ◇[1] ⊡
London Paddington [15] ⊖ d	05 18	05 22	05 27	05 33	05 36		05 42	05 45	05 48		05 57	06 03	06 12	06 15	06 20		06 27	06 30	06 33	06 42	06 45	06 45
Acton Main Line d								05 51						06 21							06 51	
Ealing Broadway ⊖ d		05 30		05 41			05 50	05 54			06 05	06 11	06 20	06 24			06 35		06 41	06 50	06 54	
West Ealing d				05 43				05 57				06 13		06 27					06 43		06 57	
Drayton Green d								05 59						06 29							06 59	
Castle Bar Park d								06 01						06 31							07 01	
South Greenford d								06 04						06 34							07 04	
Greenford ⊖ a								06 09						06 39							07 09	
Hanwell d				05 45								06 15							06 45			
Southall d		05 35		05 49			05 58				06 10	06 19	06 28				06 41		06 49	06 58		
Hayes & Harlington d		05 39		05 53			06 02				06 14	06 23	06 32				06 45		06 53	07 02		
Heathrow Terminal 1-2-3 [2] ✈ a				06 05								06 35							07 05			
Heathrow Terminal 4 ✈ a																						
West Drayton d		05 43					06 06				06 18		06 40				06 49			07 06		
Iver d		05 46									06 21						06 52					
Langley d		05 50				←				←	06 25					←	06 56					
Slough [3] a	05 34	05 54			05 51	05 54	06 13		06 05	06 13	06 29		06 47		06 34	06 47	07 00			07 13		
d	05 34	05 54			05 52	05 54	06 13		06 05	06 13	06 29		06 47		06 35	06 47	07 00			07 13		
Burnham d		→					→			06 17			→			06 51				→		
Taplow d										06 21						06 54						
Maidenhead [3] d						06 02				06 28	06 37					06 58	07 08					
Twyford [3] d						06 10				06 35	06 45					07 06	07 16					
Reading [7] a	05 52		05 55		06 05	06 20			06 20	06 45	06 53				06 49	07 15	07 27	06 54				07 09
Oxford a	06 22					07 02			06 56		07 46				07 22							

Station	GW [1]	GW [1]	GW [1]	GW ◇[1] ⊡	HC	GW ◇[1] B ⊡	GW [1]	GW [1]	GW [1]	GW ◇[1] ⊡	GW [1]	GW [1]	GW [1]	GW [1]	GW ◇[1] C ⊘	HC	GW [1]	GW [1]	GW ◇[1] D ⊡	GW ◇[1] ⊡	GW [1]	GW [1]
London Paddington [15] ⊖ d	06 48		06 57	07 00	07 03	07 06	07 12	07 12	07 15	07 15	07 18	07 21		07 27	07 30	07 33	07 42	07 45	07 45	07 48	07 50	07 57
Acton Main Line d									07 21									07 51				
Ealing Broadway ⊖ d			07 05		07 11			07 20	07 24					07 35		07 41	07 50	07 54				08 05
West Ealing d					07 13				07 27							07 43		07 57				
Drayton Green d									07 29									07 59				
Castle Bar Park d									07 31									08 01				
South Greenford d									07 34									08 04				
Greenford ⊖ a									07 39									08 09				
Hanwell d					07 15											07 45						
Southall d			07 10		07 19			07 28						07 40		07 49	07 59					08 10
Hayes & Harlington d			07 14		07 23			07 32						07 44		07 53	08 02					08 14
Heathrow Terminal 1-2-3 [2] ✈ a					07 35											08 05						
Heathrow Terminal 4 ✈ a																						
West Drayton d			07 18					07 36						07 48			08 06					08 18
Iver d			07 21											07 51								08 21
Langley d		←	07 25										←	07 55								08 25
Slough [3] a	07 04	07 13	07 29					07 43				07 36	07 43	07 59			08 13				08 06	08 29
d	07 04	07 13	07 29					07 43				07 36	07 43	07 59			08 13				08 06	08 29
Burnham d		07 17						→					07 47				→					→
Taplow d		07 21											07 51									
Maidenhead [3] d		07 25	07 37				07 43						07 55	08 07								
Twyford [3] d		07 33	07 45				07 51						08 03	08 15								
Reading [7] a	07 19	07 45	07 52	07 24		07 30	08 02			07 40	07 47	07 51	08 14	08 23	07 57				08 09	08 14	08 21	
Oxford a	08 02		08 43									08 19		09 15							08 49	

A from 21 May until 18 June
E The Devon Express
C The Merchant Venturer
D The St. David

London - Greenford and Reading

Network Diagram - see first Page of Table 116

Station	GW ◇[1] ⊡	GW [1]	HC	GW [1]	GW [1]	GW [1]	GW ◇[1] ⊡	GW [1]	GW [1]	GW ◇[1] ⊡	GW [1]	GW [1]	GW ◇[1] ⊡	HC	GW [1]	GW [1]	GW ◇[1] ⊘	GW [1]	GW [1]	GW [1]	GW [1]
London Paddington [15] ⊖ d	08 00		08 03	08 06	08 12	08 15	08 15	08 18		08 22		08 27	08 30	08 33	08 38	08 45	08 45	08 47	08 51		
Acton Main Line d						08 21										08 51					
Ealing Broadway ⊖ d			08 11		08 20	08 24						08 35		08 41	08 47	08 54		08 59			
West Ealing d			08 13			08 27								08 43		08 57		09 01			
Drayton Green d						08 29										08 59					
Castle Bar Park d						08 31										09 01					
South Greenford d						08 34										09 04					
Greenford ⊖ a						08 39										09 09					
Hanwell d			08 15											08 45	08 50						
Southall d			08 19		08 28							08 40		08 49							
Hayes & Harlington d			08 23		08 32							08 44		08 53	08 56			09 08			
Heathrow Terminal 1-2-3 [2] ✈ a			08 35											09 05							
Heathrow Terminal 4 ✈ a																					
West Drayton d					08 36							08 48			09 00						
Iver d												08 51			09 03						
Langley d		←							←		←	08 55			09 06					←	←
Slough [3] a		08 13		08 24	08 43				08 29	08 36	08 43	08 59			09 11			09 16	09 06	09 11	09 16
d		08 13		08 24	08 43				08 29	08 36	08 43	08 59			09 11			09 16	09 06	09 11	09 16
Burnham d		08 17			→						08 47				→			→			09 20
Taplow d		08 21									08 51										09 24
Maidenhead [3] d		08 25		08 32					08 38		08 55	09 06								09 18	09 28
Twyford [3] d		08 33		08a42					08 46		09 03	09 16								09a29	09 36
Reading [7] a	08 25	08 44					08 39	08 48	08 55	08 51	09 13	09 23	08 56				09 09		09 20		09 46
Oxford a									09 43	09 20		10 14							09 53		

Station	GW [1]	GW ◇[1] ⊡	HC	GW ◇[1] ⊡	GW [1]	GW [1]	GW ◇[1] ⊡	GW [1]	GW ◇[1] H	GW [1]	GW [1]	GW ◇[1] ⊘	HC	GW [1]	GW [1]	GW ◇[1] ⊘	GW ◇[1] ⊡	GW ◇[1]	GW [1]	GW [1]	GW ◇[1] A ⊡
London Paddington [15] ⊖ d	08 55	09 00	09 03	09 06	09 12	09 15	09 15	09 18	09 21		09 27	09 30	09 33	09 42	09 45	09 45	09 48	09 50		09 57	10 00
Acton Main Line d						09 21									09 51						
Ealing Broadway ⊖ d	09 03		09 11		09 20	09 24					09 35		09 41	09 50	09 54					10 05	
West Ealing d			09 13			09 27							09 43		09 57						
Drayton Green d						09 29									09 59						
Castle Bar Park d						09 31									10 01						
South Greenford d						09 34									10 04						
Greenford ⊖ a						09 39									10 09						
Hanwell d			09 15										09 45								
Southall d	09 08		09 19		09 28								09 49	09 58							
Hayes & Harlington d	09 12		09 23		09 32						09 42		09 53	10 02						10 12	
Heathrow Terminal 1-2-3 [2] ✈ a			09 35										10 05								
Heathrow Terminal 4 ✈ a																					
West Drayton d	09 16				09 36						09 46			10 06						10 16	
Iver d	09 19										09 49									10 19	
Langley d	09 23									←	09 52								←	10 22	
Slough [3] a	09 27				09 43				09 36	09 43	09 57			10 13				10 06	10 13	10 27	
d	09 27				09 43				09 36	09 43	09 57			10 13				10 06	10 13	10 27	
Burnham d					→					09 45				→					10 17		
Taplow d										09 51									10 21		
Maidenhead [3] d	09 35									09 55	10 04								10 25	10 34	
Twyford [3] d	09 43									10 03	10 12								10 33	10 42	
Reading [7] a	09 52	09 25		09 30			09 39	09 48	09 52	10 17	10 22	09 56				10 09	10 14	10 21	10 45	10 52	10 25
Oxford a	10 41								10 18		11 14							10 47		11 41	

Station	HC	GW ◇[1] B ⊘	GW [1]	GW [1]	GW ◇[1] ⊡	GW [1]	GW ◇[1] ⊡	GW [1]	GW [1]	GW ◇[1] ⊘	HC	GW [1]	GW [1]	GW ◇[1] ⊘	GW ◇[1]	GW [1]	GW [1]	GW ◇[1] ⊡	HC	GW FX ◇[1] C ⊘
London Paddington [15] ⊖ d	10 03	10 06	10 12	10 15	10 15	10 18	10 22		10 27	10 30	10 33	10 42	10 45	10 45	10 50		10 57	11 00	11 03	11 06
Acton Main Line d				10 21									10 51							
Ealing Broadway ⊖ d	10 11		10 20	10 24					10 35		10 41	10 50	10 54				11 05		11 11	
West Ealing d	10 13			10 27							10 43		10 57						11 13	
Drayton Green d				10 29									10 59							
Castle Bar Park d				10 31									11 01							
South Greenford d				10 34									11 04							
Greenford ⊖ a				10 39									11 09							
Hanwell d	10 15										10 45								11 15	
Southall d	10 19		10 28								10 49	10 58							11 19	
Hayes & Harlington d	10 23		10 32						10 42		10 53	11 02					11 12		11 23	
Heathrow Terminal 1-2-3 [2] ✈ a	10 35										11 05								11 35	
Heathrow Terminal 4 ✈ a																				
West Drayton d			10 36						10 46			11 06					11 16			
Iver d									10 49								11 19			
Langley d								←	10 52							←	11 22			
Slough [3] a			10 43				10 36	10 43	10 57			11 13			11 06	11 13	11 27			
d			10 43				10 36	10 43	10 57			11 13			11 06	11 13	11 27			
Burnham d			→					10 47				→				11 17				
Taplow d								10 51								11 21				
Maidenhead [3] d								10 55	11 04							11 25	11 34			
Twyford [3] d								11 03	11 12							11 33	11 42			
Reading [7] a		10 30			10 39	10 48	10 51	11 13	11 22	10 56				11 09	11 21	11 45	11 52	11 25		11 30
Oxford a							11 18		12 14						11 50		12 41			

A The Torbay Express
B The Cornish Riveira
C The Mayflower

Table 117

London - Greenford and Reading

Mondays to Fridays

until 22 June

Network Diagram - see first Page of Table 116

		GW	GW	GW	GW	GW	GW	GW	GW	HC	GW	GW	GW	GW	GW	GW	GW	GW	HC	GW	GW
		1	1	◇1 ☕	1	◇1 🍴	1	1	◇1 ☕		1	1	◇1 ⊘	◇1 B ☕	◇1 🍴	1	1	◇1 ☕		FX ◇1 C ⊘	1
London Paddington 15 ⊖	d	11 12	11 15	11 15	11 18	11 20		11 27	11 30	11 33	11 42	11 45	11 45	11 48	11 50		11 57	12 00	12 03	12 06	12 12
Acton Main Line	d		11 21									11 51									
Ealing Broadway ⊖	d	11 20	11 24					11 35		11 41	11 50	11 54					12 05		12 11		12 20
West Ealing	d		11 27							11 43		11 57							12 13		
Drayton Green	d		11 29									11 59									
Castle Bar Park	d		11 31									12 01									
South Greenford	d		11 34									12 04									
Greenford ⊖	a		11 39									12 09									
Hanwell	d									11 45									12 15		
Southall	d	11 28								11 49	11 58								12 19		12 28
Hayes & Harlington	d	11 32						11 42		11 53	12 02						12 12		12 23		12 32
Heathrow Terminal 1-2-3 2 ✈	a									12 05									12 35		
Heathrow Terminal 4 ✈	a																				
West Drayton	d	11 36						11 46			12 06						12 16				12 36
Iver	d							11 49									12 19				
Langley	d						←	11 52								←	12 22				
Slough 3	a	11 43				11 36	11 43	11 57			12 13				12 06	12 13	12 27				12 43
	d	11 43				11 36	11 43	11 57			12 13				12 06	12 13	12 27				12 43
Burnham	d	→					11 47				→					12 17					→
Taplow	d						11 51									12 21					
Maidenhead 3	d						11 55	12 04								12 25	12 34				
Twyford 3	d						12 03	12 12								12 33	12 42				
Reading 7	a			11 39	11 47	11 52	12 17	12 22	11 56				12 09	12 14	12 22	12 45	12 50	12 25		12 30	
Oxford	a					12 18		13 14							12 48		13 41				

		GW	GW	GW	GW	GW	GW	GW	HC	GW	GW	GW	GW	GW	GW	GW	HC	GW	GW	GW	GW	GW
		1	◇1 ☕	◇1 ☕	◇1 🍴	1	1	◇1 ☕		1	1	◇1 ⊘	◇1 🍴	1	1	◇1 ☕		◇1 ⊘	1	1	◇1 ☕	1
London Paddington 15 ⊖	d	12 15	12 15	12 18	12 21		12 27	12 30	12 33	12 42	12 45	12 45	12 50		12 57	13 00	13 03	13 06	13 12	13 15	13 15	13 18
Acton Main Line	d	12 21									12 51									13 21		
Ealing Broadway ⊖	d	12 24					12 35		12 41	12 50	12 54				13 05		13 11		13 20	13 24		
West Ealing	d	12 27							12 43		12 57						13 13			13 27		
Drayton Green	d	12 29									12 59									13 29		
Castle Bar Park	d	12 31									13 01									13 31		
South Greenford	d	12 34									13 04									13 34		
Greenford ⊖	a	12 39									13 10									13 39		
Hanwell	d								12 45								13 15					
Southall	d								12 49	12 58							13 19		13 28			
Hayes & Harlington	d						12 42		12 53	13 02					13 12		13 23		13 32			
Heathrow Terminal 1-2-3 2 ✈	a								13 05								13 35					
Heathrow Terminal 4 ✈	a																					
West Drayton	d						12 46			13 06					13 16				13 36			
Iver	d						12 49								13 19							
Langley	d					←	12 52							←	13 22							
Slough 3	a				12 36	12 43	12 57			13 13			13 06	13 13	13 27				13 43			
	d				12 36	12 43	12 57			13 13			13 06	13 13	13 27				13 43			
Burnham	d					12 47				→				13 17					→			
Taplow	d					12 51								13 21								
Maidenhead 3	d					12 55	13 04							13 25	13 34							
Twyford 3	d					13 03	13 12							13 33	13 42							
Reading 7	a		12 39	12 46	12 51	13 14	13 22	12 56				13 09	13 22	13 45	13 51	13 25		13 30			13 39	13 47
Oxford	a				13 18		14 14						13 50		14 42							

		GW	GW	GW	GW	HC	GW	GW	GW	GW	GW	GW	GW	GW	HC	GW	GW	GW	GW	GW	GW
		◇1 🍴	1	1	◇1 ☕		1	1	◇1 ☕	◇1 ☕	◇1 🍴	1	1	◇1 ☕		◇1 ⊘	1	1	◇1 ☕	1	◇1 🍴
London Paddington 15 ⊖	d	13 21		13 27	13 30	13 33	13 42	13 45	13 45	13 48	13 50		13 57	14 00	14 03	14 06	14 12	14 15	14 15	14 18	14 21
Acton Main Line	d							13 51										14 21			
Ealing Broadway ⊖	d			13 35		13 41	13 50	13 54					14 05		14 11		14 20	14 24			
West Ealing	d					13 43		13 57							14 13			14 27			
Drayton Green	d							13 59										14 29			
Castle Bar Park	d							14 01										14 31			
South Greenford	d							14 04										14 34			
Greenford ⊖	a							14 09										14 39			
Hanwell	d					13 45									14 15						
Southall	d					13 49	13 58								14 19		14 28				
Hayes & Harlington	d			13 42		13 53	14 02						14 12		14 23		14 32				
Heathrow Terminal 1-2-3 2 ✈	a					14 05									14 35						
Heathrow Terminal 4 ✈	a																				
West Drayton	d			13 46			14 06						14 16				14 36				
Iver	d			13 49									14 19								
Langley	d		←	13 52								←	14 22								
Slough 3	a	13 36	13 43	13 57			14 13				14 06	14 13	14 27				14 43				14 36
	d	13 36	13 43	13 57			14 13				14 06	14 13	14 27				14 43				14 36
Burnham	d		13 47				→					14 17					→				
Taplow	d		13 51									14 21									
Maidenhead 3	d		13 55	14 04								14 25	14 34								
Twyford 3	d		14 03	14 12								14 33	14 42								
Reading 7	a	13 52	14 12	14 21	13 56				14 09	14 14	14 21	14 45	14 52	14 25		14 30			14 39	14 47	14 52
Oxford	a	14 18		15 14							14 48		15 41								15 18

A The Mayflower   B The Cheltenham Spa Express   C The Royal Duchy

Table 117

London - Greenford and Reading

Mondays to Fridays

until 22 June

Network Diagram - see first Page of Table 116

		GW	GW	GW	HC	GW	GW	GW	GW	GW	GW	GW	HC	GW	GW	GW	GW	GW	GW	GW	GW	GW
		1	1	◇1 ☕		1	1	◇1 ☕	◇1 🍴	1	1	◇1 ☕		◇1 A ⊘	1	1	◇1 ☕	1	◇1 🍴	1	1	◇1 ☕
London Paddington 15 ⊖	d		14 27	14 30	14 33	14 42	14 45	14 45	14 50		14 57	15 00	15 03	15 06	15 12	15 15	15 15	15 18	15 22		15 27	15 30
Acton Main Line	d						14 51									15 21						
Ealing Broadway ⊖	d		14 35		14 41	14 50	14 54				15 05		15 11		15 20	15 24					15 35	
West Ealing	d				14 43		14 57						15 13			15 27						
Drayton Green	d						14 59									15 29						
Castle Bar Park	d						15 01									15 31						
South Greenford	d						15 04									15 34						
Greenford ⊖	a						15 09									15 39						
Hanwell	d				14 45								15 15									
Southall	d				14 49	14 58							15 19		15 28						15 40	
Hayes & Harlington	d		14 42		14 53	15 02					15 12		15 23		15 32						15 44	
Heathrow Terminal 1-2-3 2 ✈	a				15 05								15 35									
Heathrow Terminal 4 ✈	a																					
West Drayton	d		14 46			15 06					15 16				15 36						15 48	
Iver	d		14 49								15 19										15 51	
Langley	d	←	14 52							←	15 22									←	15 55	
Slough 3	a	14 43	14 57			15 13			15 06	15 13	15 27				15 43				15 36	15 43	15 59	
	d	14 43	14 57			15 13			15 06	15 13	15 27				15 43				15 36	15 43	15 59	
Burnham	d	14 47				→				15 17					→					15 47		
Taplow	d	14 51								15 21										15 51		
Maidenhead 3	d	14 55	15 04							15 25	15 34									15 55	16 07	
Twyford 3	d	15 03	15 12							15 33	15 42									16 03	16 15	
Reading 7	a	15 13	15 22	14 56				15 09	15 22	15 44	15 52	15 25		15 30			15 39	15 47	15 51	16 13	16 23	15 56
Oxford	a		16 14						15 50		16 43								16 18		17 15	

		HC	GW	GW	GW	GW	GW	GW	GW	GW	HC	GW	GW	GW	GW	GW	GW	GW	GW	GW	HC
			1	1	◇1 ☕	◇1 ☕	◇1 ☕	1	1	◇1 ☕		◇1 ☕	1	1	◇1 ☕	1	◇1 🍴	1	1	◇1 ☕	
London Paddington 15 ⊖	d	15 33	15 42	15 45	15 45	15 48	15 51		15 57	16 00	16 03	16 06	16 12	16 15	16 15	16 18	16 22		16 27	16 30	16 33
Acton Main Line	d			15 51										16 21							
Ealing Broadway ⊖	d	15 41	15 50	15 54					16 05		16 11		16 20	16 24					16 35		16 41
West Ealing	d	15 43		15 57							16 13			16 27							16 43
Drayton Green	d			15 59										16 29							
Castle Bar Park	d			16 01										16 31							
South Greenford	d			16 04										16 34							
Greenford ⊖	a			16 09										16 39							
Hanwell	d	15 45									16 15										16 45
Southall	d	15 49	15 58								16 19		16 28						16 40		16 49
Hayes & Harlington	d	15 53	16 02						16 11		16 23		16 32						16 44		16 53
Heathrow Terminal 1-2-3 2 ✈	a	16 05									16 35										17 05
Heathrow Terminal 4 ✈	a																				
West Drayton	d		16 06						16 16				16 36								
Iver	d								16 19										16 49		
Langley	d							←	16 22									←	16 52		
Slough 3	a		16 13				16 06	16 13	16 27				16 44				16 37	16 44	16 57		
	d		16 13				16 06	16 13	16 27				16 45				16 38	16 45	16 57		
Burnham	d		→					16 17					→					16 50			
Taplow	d							16 21										16 54			
Maidenhead 3	d							16 25	16 34									16 59	17 04		
Twyford 3	d							16 33	16 42									17 07	17 12		
Reading 7	a				16 09	16 14	16 20	16 44	16 52	16 25		16 30			16 39	16 47	16 52	17 18	17 21	16 56	
Oxford	a						16 47		17 44								17 24		18 12		

		GW	GW	GW	GW	GW	GW	GW	GW	HC	GW	GW	GW	GW	GW	GW	GW	GW	GW	GW	GW	HC
		◇1 ☕	1	1	◇1 B ☕	◇1	1	1	◇1 ☕		◇1 ☕	◇1 ☕	1	1	1	◇1 C ⊘	1	1	◇1 ☕	1	◇1 ☕	
London Paddington 15 ⊖	d	16 36	16 42	16 45	16 45	16 49		16 55	17 00	17 03	17 03	17 06		17 12	17 15	17 15	17 18	17 18	17 22	17 25	17 30	17 33
Acton Main Line	d			16 51													17 24					
Ealing Broadway ⊖	d		16 50	16 54				17 04		17 11					17 23		17 27			17 33		17 41
West Ealing	d			16 57						17 13							17 30					17 43
Drayton Green	d			16 59													17 32					
Castle Bar Park	d			17 01													17 34					
South Greenford	d			17 04													17 37					
Greenford ⊖	a			17 09													17 42					
Hanwell	d									17 15												17 45
Southall	d		16 58							17 19					17 29					17 38		17 49
Hayes & Harlington	d		17 02					17 11		17 23					17 33					17 42		17 53
Heathrow Terminal 1-2-3 2 ✈	a									17 35												18 05
Heathrow Terminal 4 ✈	a																					
West Drayton	d		17 07					17 16							17 38					17 47		
Iver	d		17 10					17 20							17 41					17 50		
Langley	d		17 14				←	17 24							17 44					17 54		
Slough 3	a		17 18			17 04	17 18	17 27						17 32	17 49					17 58		
	d		17 18			17 04	17 18	17 28						17 35	17 49					17 58		
Burnham	d		→				17 22	17 33						17 40	17 53					18 02		
Taplow	d						17 26	17 36						17 43	17 57					18 06		
Maidenhead 3	d						17 30	17 43					←	17 47	18a05			17 40		18 10		
Twyford 3	d						17 38	17 51				17 28	17 38	17a57				17 48		18 17		
Reading 7	a	17 01			17 09	17 19	→	→	17 24		17 29	17 35	17 46			17 40		17 56	17 49	→	17 54	
Oxford	a					17 50												18 45	18 15			

A The Cornishman   B The Capitals United   C The Red Dragon

Table 117

Mondays to Fridays
until 22 June

London - Greenford and Reading

Network Diagram - see first Page of Table 116

	GW ◇1 ⊏	GW 1	GW 1	GW 1		GW ◇1 ⊏	GW 1	GW 1	GW ◇1 ⊏	GW ◇1 ⊏	GW 1	GW ◇1 A ⊏	GW 1	HC		GW ◇1 B ✕		GW ◇1 ⊏	GW 1	GW 1	GW ◇1 ⊏	GW 1	GW 1	GW 1
London Paddington 15 ⊖ d	17 33		17 36	17 42		17 45	17 45	17 48	17 48	17 50	17 57	18 00		18 03		18 03		18 06		18 12	18 15	18 15	18 18	18 18
Acton Main Line d								17 54															18 24	
Ealing Broadway ⊖ d							17 53	17 57			18 05			18 11								18 23	18 27	
West Ealing d								18 00						18 13									18 30	
Drayton Green d								18 02															18 32	
Castle Bar Park d								18 04															18 34	
South Greenford d								18 07															18 37	
Greenford ⊖ a								18 12															18 42	
Hanwell d														18 15										
Southall d							17 59				18 10			18 19								18 29		
Hayes & Harlington d							18 03				18 14			18 23								18 33		
Heathrow Terminal 1-2-3 2 ✈ a														18 35										
Heathrow Terminal 4 ✈ a																								
West Drayton d							18 08				18 19											18 38		
Iver d											18 22													
Langley d							18 12				18 26											18 42		
Slough 3 a				18 04			18 16				18 30									18 35		18 47		
d				18 05			18 16				18 30									18 36		18 47		
Burnham d							18 21				18 35											18 51		
Taplow d											18 39													
Maidenhead 3 d		←	17 58	18a13			18 26			18 09	18 45		←						←	18 49		18 57		18 40
Twyford 3 d		17 51	18 07				18 34				18 52		18 17					18 28	18 34	18a58		19 05		18 48
Reading 7 a	17 59	18 00	18 15			18 09	→		18 14	18 20	→	18 25	18 26			18 30		18 35	18 44		18 40	→		18 56
Oxford a			19 04							18 47			19 16											19 43

		GW ◇1 C ⊏	GW FO 1	GW FX 1	GW ◇1 ⊏	HC	GW ◇1 ⊏	GW 1	GW 1	GW ◇1 ⊏		GW 1	GW 1	GW ◇1 ⊏	GW FO 1	GW FX 1	GW 1	GW ◇1 ⊼	GW 1	GW 1		GW ◇1 ⊏		HC
London Paddington 15 ⊖ d		18 22	18 25	18 25	18 30	18 33	18 33		18 36	18 45			18 45	18 47			18 48	18 51		18 57		19 00		19 03
Acton Main Line d																	18 54							
Ealing Broadway ⊖ d			18 33	18 33		18 41							18 53				18 57			19 05				19 11
West Ealing d						18 43											19 00							19 13
Drayton Green d																	19 02							
Castle Bar Park d																	19 04							
South Greenford d																	19 07							
Greenford ⊖ a																	19 12							
Hanwell d						18 45																		19 15
Southall d			18 38	18 38		18 49							18 59							19 10				19 19
Hayes & Harlington d			18 42	18 42		18 53							19 03							19 14				19 23
Heathrow Terminal 1-2-3 2 ✈ a						19 05																		19 35
Heathrow Terminal 4 ✈ a																								
West Drayton d			18 46	18 46																19 19				
Iver d			18 49	18 49																19 22				
Langley d			18 52	18 52											←	←			←	19 26				
Slough 3 a			18 59	18 59					18 54				19 11		18 59	18 59		19 06	19 11	19 30				
d			18 59	18 59					18 55				19 11		18 59	18 59		19 06	19 11	19 30				
Burnham d			→	→									→		19 03	19 03			19 15	19 34				
Taplow d															19 06	19 06				19 38				
Maidenhead 3 d								←	19a03			←			19 10	19 10			19 21	19 43				
Twyford 3 d								18 52				19 05		19 09	19 18	19 18			19 38	19 51				
Reading 7 a		18 49			18 54		18 59	19 01		19 09		19 13		19 17	19 26	19 26		19 22	19 47	→		19 27		
Oxford a		19 19										20 13			20 18	20 27		19 48						

A The Bristolian
B The Golden Hind
C The Cathedrals Express
D The Armada

Table 117

Mondays to Fridays
until 22 June

London - Greenford and Reading

Network Diagram - see first Page of Table 116

	GW FX 1 A ✕	GW 1	GW FO 1	GW 1	GW 1	GW ◇1 ⊏			GW 1	GW FX ◇1 ⊏	GW FO ◇1 ⊏	GW 1	GW 1	GW 1	GW ◇1 ⊏	HC		GW 1	GW 1	GW ◇1 ⊏	GW ◇1 ⊏	GW ◇1 ⊼	GW 1	GW 1
London Paddington 15 ⊖ d	19 03	19 06	19 12	19 12	19 15	19 15			19 18	19 22	19 22			19 27	19 30	19 33		19 42	19 45	19 45	19 48	19 50		19 57
Acton Main Line d					19 21														19 51					
Ealing Broadway ⊖ d				19 20	19 24									19 35		19 41		19 50	19 54					20 05
West Ealing d					19 27											19 43			19 57					
Drayton Green d					19 29														19 59					
Castle Bar Park d					19 31														20 01					
South Greenford d					19 34														20 04					
Greenford ⊖ a					19 39														20 09					
Hanwell d																19 45								
Southall d				19 28										19 40		19 49		19 58						
Hayes & Harlington d				19 32										19 44		19 53		20 02						20 12
Heathrow Terminal 1-2-3 2 ✈ a																20 05								
Heathrow Terminal 4 ✈ a																								
West Drayton d														19 48				20 06						20 16
Iver d														19 51				20 09						20 19
Langley d													←	19 55				20 13					←	20 22
Slough 3 a				19 41						19 36	19 36		19 41	19 59				20 17				20 06	20 17	20 27
d				19 41						19 36	19 36		19 41	19 59				20 17				20 06	20 17	20 27
Burnham d				→									19 45	20 03				→					20 20	
Taplow d													19 48										20 25	
Maidenhead 3 d		19 27							19 40			←	19 52	20 09							20 06		20 29	20 34
Twyford 3 d		19a38							19 48			19 51	20 00	20 17									20 37	20 42
Reading 7 a	19 32		19 41			19 39			19 56	19 51	19 51	20 00	20 11	20 23	19 56					20 09	20 17	20 22	20 45	20 52
Oxford a			20 28						20 45	20 18	20 21			21 14								20 47		21 43

	GW ◇1 ⊏	HC		GW 1	GW 1	GW ◇1 Ø	GW ◇1 ⊼	GW 1	GW 1	HC	GW ◇1 ⊏	GW 1		GW 1	GW ◇1 ⊏	GW ◇1	GW 1	GW 1	HC	GW 1	GW ◇1 ⊏	GW 1		GW ◇1
London Paddington 15 ⊖ d	20 00	20 03		20 12	20 15	20 15	20 20		20 27	20 33	20 35	20 42		20 45	20 45	20 48		20 57	21 03	21 12	21 15	21 15		21 18
Acton Main Line d					20 21									20 51								21 21		
Ealing Broadway ⊖ d		20 11		20 20	20 24				20 35	20 41		20 50		20 54				21 05	21 11	21 20		21 24		
West Ealing d		20 13			20 27					20 43				20 57					21 13			21 27		
Drayton Green d					20 29									20 59								21 29		
Castle Bar Park d					20 31									21 01								21 31		
South Greenford d					20 34									21 04								21 34		
Greenford ⊖ a					20 39									21 09								21 39		
Hanwell d		20 15								20 45									21 15					
Southall d		20 19		20 28						20 49		20 58							21 19	21 28				
Hayes & Harlington d		20 23		20 32					20 42	20 53		21 02						21 12	21 23	21 32				
Heathrow Terminal 1-2-3 2 ✈ a		20 35								21 05									21 35					
Heathrow Terminal 4 ✈ a																								
West Drayton d				20 36					20 46			21 06						21 16		21 36				
Iver d									20 49									21 19						
Langley d								←	20 52								←	21 22						
Slough 3 a				20 43			20 35	20 43	20 57			21 13				21 04	21 13	21 27		21 43				21 34
d				20 43			20 36	20 43	20 57			21 13				21 05	21 13	21 27		21 43				21 35
Burnham d				→				20 47				→					21 17			→				
Taplow d								20 51									21 21							
Maidenhead 3 d								20 55	21 04								21 25	21 34						
Twyford 3 d								21 03	21 12								21 33	21 42						
Reading 7 a	20 25					20 39	20 50	21 13	21 20		20 59				21 09	21 20	21 45	21 51			21 39			21 50
Oxford a							21 19		22 14							21 51		22 41						22 18

	GW 1	HC	GW 1	GW ◇1 ⊏	GW 1	GW FX ◇1 ⊏	GW FO ◇1 ⊼	GW 1		GW 1	HC	GW FO ◇1 ⊏	GW 1	GW FX ◇1 ⊏	GW FO 1	GW FX 1	GW ◇1	GW 1		HC	GW FO ◇1 ⊏	GW FO 1	GW FX 1	GW FX ◇1 ⊏
London Paddington 15 ⊖ d	21 27	21 33	21 42	21 45		21 48	21 48			21 58	22 03	22 15		22 15	22 16	22 16	22 18			22 33	22 45			22 45
Acton Main Line d			21 48																					
Ealing Broadway ⊖ d	21 35	21 41	21 51							22 06	22 11				22 24	22 24				22 41				
West Ealing d		21 43									22 13									22 43				
Drayton Green d																								
Castle Bar Park d																								
South Greenford d																								
Greenford ⊖ a																								
Hanwell d		21 45									22 15									22 45				
Southall d	21 42	21 49	21 58								22 19				22 29	22 29				22 49				
Hayes & Harlington d	21 46	21 53	22 02							22 13	22 23				22 33	22 33				22 53				
Heathrow Terminal 1-2-3 2 ✈ a		22 05									22 35									23 05				
Heathrow Terminal 4 ✈ a																								
West Drayton d	21 50		22 06							22 17					22 37	22 37								
Iver d	21 53									22 20														
Langley d	21 57				←			←		22 23			←					←				←	←	
Slough 3 a	22 02		22 14		21 43	22 03	22 03	22 02		22 28			22 14		22 45	22 45	22 35	22 28				22 45	22 45	
d	22 07		22 15		21 43	22 03	22 03	22 07		22 39			22 15		22 45	22 45	22 36	22 39				22 45	22 45	
Burnham d	→		→		21 47					→			22 18		→	→						22 49	22 49	
Taplow d					21 51								22 22									22 53	22 53	
Maidenhead 3 d					21 55			22 14					22 26				22 44	22 47				22 57	22 57	
Twyford 3 d					22 03			22 22					22 34					22 55				23 05	23 05	
Reading 7 a				22 09	22 15	22 22	22 22	22 30				22 39	22 46	22 48			22 58	23 04			23 09	23 14	23 16	23 18
Oxford a						22 47	22 47	23 21									23 28	23 48						

A The Armada

Table 117

London - Greenford and Reading

Mondays to Fridays

until 22 June

Network Diagram - see first Page of Table 116

Station		GW ■	GW ◇■	GW ■	GW ■	HC	GW ◇■	GW FX ■	GW FO ■	GW FX ◇■ ⊡	GW FO ◇■ ⊡	GW FO ■	GW ■
London Paddington ■15 ⊖	d	22 45	22 48		22 59	23 03	23 18	23 29	23 29	23 30	23 30	23 42	23 48
Acton Main Line	d	22 51											23 54
Ealing Broadway ⊖	d	22 54			23 07	23 11		23 37	23 37				23 57
West Ealing	d					23 13							23 59
Drayton Green	d												
Castle Bar Park	d												
South Greenford	d												
Greenford ⊖	a												
Hanwell	d					23 15							00 02
Southall	d				23 12	23 19							00 06
Hayes & Harlington	d	23 01			23 16	23 23		23 44	23 44				00 10
Heathrow Terminal 1-2-3 ■2 ✈	a					23 35							
Heathrow Terminal 4 ✈	a					23 41							
West Drayton	d				23 20								00 14
Iver	d				23 23								00 17
Langley	d			←	23 27								00 21
Slough ■3	a	23 11	23 06	23 11	23 32		23 36	23 53	23 53			23 58	00 26
	d	23 12	23 06	23 12	23 32		23 36	23 54	23 54			23 58	00 26
Burnham	d	→		23 16									00 30
Taplow	d			23 20									00 34
Maidenhead ■3	d		23 14	23 24	23 40		23 44	00 01	00 01			00 08	00 41
Twyford ■3	d			23 32	23 48			00 09	00 09				00 48
Reading ■7	a		23 28	23 41	23 58		23 58	00 19	00 19	00 03	00 05	00 21	00 57
Oxford	a		23 56	00 26			00 28	01 15	01 16			01 02	

Mondays to Fridays

25 June to 14 September

Station		GW MO ■ B	GW MX ■	GW MO ■ B	GW MO ■	GW MX ◇■	GW MO ■	GW MX ■	GW MX ■	GW MX ◇■ ⊡	GW MO ◇■ B ⊡	GW ◇■ C ⊡	GW MO ◇■ B	GW ◇■ C	GW MX ■	GW MO ■	GW MX ■	GW MX ◇■	GW MO ■	GW MX ■	GW ■	GW ■	HC
London Paddington ■15 ⊖	d	22p43	22p45		23p15	23p18			23p29	23p30	23p37	23p37	23p47	23p47	23p48	23p53		00 22	00 34	00 34	01 34	03 34	04 42
Acton Main Line	d		22p51												23p54								
Ealing Broadway ⊖	d	22p50	22p54		23p24				23p37				23p55	23p55	23p57	00 02			00 42	00 42	01 42	03 42	04 50
West Ealing	d														23p59								
Drayton Green	d																						
Castle Bar Park	d																						
South Greenford	d																						
Greenford ⊖	a																						
Hanwell	d														00 02								
Southall	d	22p56			23p29										00 06	00 07			00 47	00 47	01 47	03 48	04 54
Hayes & Harlington	d	23p02	23p01		23p33				23p44						00 10	00 11			00 51	00 51	01 51	03 52	04 58
Heathrow Terminal 1-2-3 ■2 ✈	a																						05 04
Heathrow Terminal 4 ✈	a																						05 10
West Drayton	d	23p06			23p37										00 14	00 15			00 55	00 55	01 55	03 56	
Iver	d														00 17								
Langley	d	23p10		←	23p42		←								00 21	00 20	←		01 00	01 00			
Slough ■3	a	23p14	23p11	23p14	23p46	23p36	23p46		23p53		23p54	00 02	00 08	00 09	00 26	00 24	00 26	00 39	01 05	01 05	02 04	04 04	
	d	23p16	23p12	23p16	23p46	23p36	23p46		23p54		23p55	00 03	00 08	00 10	00 26	00 24	00 26	00 39	01 05	01 05	02 04	04 05	
Burnham	d	→	23p16	23p20	→		23p51								→	00 28	00 30		01 09	01 09			
Taplow	d		23p20														00 34			01 13			
Maidenhead ■3	d		23p24	23p25		23p44	23p56		00 01				00 16	00 17		00 34	00 41		01 15	01 16	02 11	04 12	
Twyford ■3	d		23p32	23p32			00 04	00 07	00 09							00 42	00 48		01 23	01 24	02 19	04 20	
Reading ■7	a		23p41	23p43		23p58	00 14	00 16	00 19	00 03	00 14	00 14	00 28	00 29		00 49	00 57	01 00	01 32	01 35	02 29	04 30	
Oxford	a		00 26	00 35		00 28			01 15				00 57					01 34					

B from 2 July until 10 September C 25 June

Table 117

London - Greenford and Reading

Mondays to Fridays

25 June to 14 September

Network Diagram - see first Page of Table 116

Station		HC	GW ■	GW ■	GW ◇■ ⊡	HC	GW ◇■ ⊡	GW ■	GW ■	GW ■	GW ◇■	GW ■	GW ■	HC	GW ■	GW ■	GW ■	GW ■	GW ■	GW ◇■ ⊡	HC	GW ■	GW ■
London Paddington ■15 ⊖	d	05 13	05 18	05 22	05 27	05 33	05 36		05 42	05 45	05 48		05 57	06 03	06 12	06 15	06 20		06 27	06 30	06 33	06 42	06 45
Acton Main Line	d									05 51						06 21							06 51
Ealing Broadway ⊖	d	05 21		05 30		05 41			05 50	05 54			06 05	06 11	06 20	06 24			06 35		06 41	06 50	06 54
West Ealing	d					05 43				05 57				06 13		06 27					06 43		06 57
Drayton Green	d									05 59						06 29							06 59
Castle Bar Park	d									06 01						06 31							07 01
South Greenford	d									06 04						06 34							07 04
Greenford ⊖	a									06 09						06 39							07 09
Hanwell	d					05 45								06 15							06 45		
Southall	d	05 25		05 35		05 49			05 58				06 10	06 19	06 28				06 41		06 49	06 58	
Hayes & Harlington	d	05 29		05 39		05 53			06 02				06 14	06 23	06 32				06 45		06 53	07 02	
Heathrow Terminal 1-2-3 ■2 ✈	a	05 35				06 05								06 35							07 05		
Heathrow Terminal 4 ✈	a	05 41																					
West Drayton	d			05 43					06 06				06 18		06 40				06 49			07 06	
Iver	d			05 46									06 21						06 52				
Langley	d			05 50				←				←	06 25					←	06 56				
Slough ■3	a		05 34	05 54			05 51	05 54	06 13		06 05	06 13	06 29		06 47		06 34	06 47	07 00			07 13	
	d		05 34	05 54			05 52	05 54	06 13		06 05	06 13	06 29		06 47		06 35	06 47	07 00			07 13	
Burnham	d			→					→			06 17			→			06 51				→	
Taplow	d											06 21						06 54					
Maidenhead ■3	d							06 02				06 28	06 37					06 58	07 08				
Twyford ■3	d							06 10				06 35	06 45					07 06	07 16				
Reading ■7	a		05 52		05 55		06 05	06 20			06 20	06 45	06 53				06 49	07 15	07 27	06 54			
Oxford	a		06 22					07 02			06 56		07 46				07 22						

Station		GW ◇■ ⊡	GW ■	GW ■	GW ■	GW ◇■ ⊡	HC	GW ◇■ A ⊡	GW ■	GW ■	GW ■	GW ◇■ ⊡	GW ■	GW ■	GW ■	GW ■	GW ◇■ B ⊘	HC	GW ■	GW ■	GW ◇■ C ⊡	GW ◇■ ⊡
London Paddington ■15 ⊖	d	06 45	06 48		06 57	07 00	07 03	07 06	07 12	07 12	07 15	07 15	07 18	07 21		07 27	07 30	07 33	07 42	07 45	07 45	07 48
Acton Main Line	d										07 21									07 51		
Ealing Broadway ⊖	d				07 05		07 11			07 20	07 24					07 35		07 41	07 50	07 54		
West Ealing	d						07 13				07 27							07 43		07 57		
Drayton Green	d										07 29									07 59		
Castle Bar Park	d										07 31									08 01		
South Greenford	d										07 34									08 04		
Greenford ⊖	a										07 39									08 09		
Hanwell	d						07 15											07 45				
Southall	d				07 10		07 19			07 28						07 40		07 49	07 59			
Hayes & Harlington	d				07 14		07 23			07 32						07 44		07 53	08 02			
Heathrow Terminal 1-2-3 ■2 ✈	a						07 35											08 05				
Heathrow Terminal 4 ✈	a																					
West Drayton	d				07 18					07 36						07 48			08 06			
Iver	d				07 21											07 51						
Langley	d			←	07 25										←	07 55						
Slough ■3	a		07 04	07 13	07 29					07 43				07 36	07 43	07 59			08 13			
	d		07 04	07 13	07 29					07 43				07 36	07 43	07 59			08 13			
Burnham	d			07 17						→					07 47				→			
Taplow	d			07 21											07 51							
Maidenhead ■3	d			07 25	07 37				07 43						07 55	08 07						
Twyford ■3	d			07 33	07 45				07 51						08 03	08 15						
Reading ■7	a	07 09	07 19	07 45	07 52	07 24		07 30	08 02			07 40	07 47	07 51	08 14	08 23	07 57				08 09	08 14
Oxford	a		08 02		08 43									08 19		09 15						

Station		GW ■	GW ■	GW ◇■ ⊡	GW ■	HC	GW ■	GW ■	GW ■	GW ◇■ ⊡	GW ■	GW ■	GW ◇■ ⊡	GW ■	GW ■	GW ◇■ ⊡	HC	GW ■	GW ■	GW ◇■ ⊘	GW ■	GW ■	GW ■
London Paddington ■15 ⊖	d	07 50	07 57	08 00		08 03	08 06	08 12	08 15	08 15	08 18		08 22		08 27	08 30	08 33	08 38	08 45	08 45	08 47	08 51	
Acton Main Line	d								08 21										08 51				
Ealing Broadway ⊖	d		08 05			08 11		08 20	08 24						08 35		08 41	08 47	08 54		08 59		
West Ealing	d					08 13			08 27								08 43		08 57		09 01		
Drayton Green	d								08 29										08 59				
Castle Bar Park	d								08 31										09 01				
South Greenford	d								08 34										09 04				
Greenford ⊖	a								08 39										09 09				
Hanwell	d					08 15											08 45	08 50					
Southall	d		08 10			08 19		08 28							08 40		08 49						
Hayes & Harlington	d		08 14			08 23		08 32							08 44		08 53	08 56			09 08		
Heathrow Terminal 1-2-3 ■2 ✈	a					08 35											09 05						
Heathrow Terminal 4 ✈	a																						
West Drayton	d		08 18					08 36							08 48			09 00					
Iver	d		08 21												08 51			09 03					
Langley	d		08 25		←							←		←	08 55			09 06					←
Slough ■3	a	08 06	08 29		08 13		08 24	08 43				08 29	08 36	08 43	08 59			09 11			09 16	09 06	09 11
	d	08 06	08 29		08 13		08 24	08 43				08 29	08 36	08 43	08 59			09 11			09 16	09 06	09 11
Burnham	d		→		08 17			→						08 47				→			→		
Taplow	d				08 21									08 51									
Maidenhead ■3	d				08 25		08 32					08 38		08 55	09 06								09 18
Twyford ■3	d				08 33		08a42					08 46		09 03	09 16								09a29
Reading ■7	a	08 21		08 25	08 44					08 39	08 48	08 55	08 51	09 13	09 23	08 56				09 09		09 20	
Oxford	a	08 49										09 43	09 20		10 14							09 53	

A The Devon Express B The Merchant Venturer C The St. David

Table 117

London - Greenford and Reading

Mondays to Fridays

25 June to 14 September

Network Diagram - see first Page of Table 116

	GW 1	GW 1	GW ◇1 ⌷	HC	GW ◇1 A ⌷	GW ◇1 C ⌷	GW 1	GW 1	GW ◇1 ⌷	GW 1	GW ◇1 ⌶	GW 1	GW 1	GW ◇1 ∅	HC	GW 1	GW 1	GW ◇1 ∅	GW ◇1 ⌷
London Paddington 15 ⊖ d		08 55	09 00	09 03	09 06	09 06	09 12	09 15	09 15	09 18	09 21		09 27	09 30	09 33	09 42	09 45	09 45	09 48
Acton Main Line d								09 21									09 51		
Ealing Broadway ⊖ d		09 03		09 11			09 20	09 24					09 35		09 41	09 50	09 54		
West Ealing d				09 13				09 27							09 43		09 57		
Drayton Green d								09 29									09 59		
Castle Bar Park d								09 31									10 01		
South Greenford d								09 34									10 04		
Greenford ⊖ a								09 39									10 09		
Hanwell d				09 15											09 45				
Southall d		09 08		09 19			09 28								09 49	09 58			
Hayes & Harlington d		09 12		09 23			09 32						09 42		09 53	10 02			
Heathrow Terminal 1-2-3 2 ✈ a				09 35											10 05				
Heathrow Terminal 4 ✈ a																			
West Drayton d		09 16					09 36						09 46			10 06			
Iver d		09 19											09 49						
Langley d	←	09 23										←	09 52						
Slough 3 a	09 16	09 27					09 43				09 36	09 43	09 57			10 13			
d	09 16	09 27					09 43				09 36	09 43	09 57			10 13			
Burnham d	09 20						→					09 45				→			
Taplow d	09 24											09 51							
Maidenhead 3 d	09 28	09 35										09 55	10 04						
Twyford 3 d	09 36	09 43										10 03	10 12						
Reading 7 a	09 46	09 52	09 25		09 30	09 30			09 39	09 48	09 52	10 17	10 22	09 56				10 09	10 14
Oxford a		10 41									10 18		11 14						

	GW ◇1	GW 1	GW 1	GW ◇1 E ⌷	HC	GW ◇1 F ∅	GW 1	GW 1	GW ◇1 ⌷	GW 1	GW ◇1 ⌷	GW 1	GW 1	GW ◇1 ∅	HC	GW 1	GW 1	GW ◇1 ∅	GW ◇1	GW 1	GW 1
London Paddington 15 ⊖ d	09 50		09 57	10 00	10 03	10 06	10 12	10 15	10 15	10 18	10 22		10 27	10 30	10 33	10 42	10 45	10 45	10 50		10 57
Acton Main Line d								10 21									10 51				
Ealing Broadway ⊖ d			10 05		10 11		10 20	10 24					10 35		10 41	10 50	10 54				11 05
West Ealing d					10 13			10 27							10 43		10 57				
Drayton Green d								10 29									10 59				
Castle Bar Park d								10 31									11 01				
South Greenford d								10 34									11 04				
Greenford ⊖ a								10 39									11 09				
Hanwell d					10 15										10 45						
Southall d					10 19		10 28								10 49	10 58					
Hayes & Harlington d			10 12		10 23		10 32						10 42		10 53	11 02					11 12
Heathrow Terminal 1-2-3 2 ✈ a					10 35										11 05						
Heathrow Terminal 4 ✈ a																					
West Drayton d			10 16				10 36						10 46			11 06					11 16
Iver d			10 19										10 49								11 19
Langley d		←	10 22									←	10 52							←	11 22
Slough 3 a	10 06	10 13	10 27				10 43				10 36	10 43	10 57			11 13			11 06	11 13	11 27
d	10 06	10 13	10 27				10 43				10 36	10 43	10 57			11 13			11 06	11 13	11 27
Burnham d		10 17					→					10 47				→				11 17	
Taplow d		10 21										10 51								11 21	
Maidenhead 3 d		10 25	10 34									10 55	11 04							11 25	11 34
Twyford 3 d		10 33	10 42									11 03	11 12							11 33	11 42
Reading 7 a	10 21	10 45	10 52	10 25		10 30			10 39	10 48	10 51	11 13	11 22	10 56				11 09	11 21	11 45	11 52
Oxford a	10 47		11 41								11 18		12 14						11 50		12 41

A until 29 June, from 3 September

C from 6 July until 31 August. The Atlantic Coast Express

E The Torbay Express

F The Cornish Riveira

Table 117

London - Greenford and Reading

Mondays to Fridays

25 June to 14 September

Network Diagram - see first Page of Table 116

	GW ◇1 ⌷	HC	GW ◇1 A ∅	GW 1	GW 1	GW ◇1 ⌷	GW 1	GW ◇1 ⌶	GW 1	GW 1	GW ◇1 ⌷	HC	GW 1	GW 1	GW ◇1 ∅	GW ◇1 B ⌷	GW ◇1 ⌶	GW 1	GW 1	GW ◇1 ⌷	HC
London Paddington 15 ⊖ d	11 00	11 03	11 06	11 12	11 15	11 15	11 18	11 20		11 27	11 30	11 33	11 42	11 45	11 45	11 48	11 50		11 57	12 00	12 03
Acton Main Line d					11 21									11 51							
Ealing Broadway ⊖ d		11 11		11 20	11 24					11 35		11 41	11 50	11 54					12 05		12 11
West Ealing d		11 13			11 27							11 43		11 57							12 13
Drayton Green d					11 29									11 59							
Castle Bar Park d					11 31									12 01							
South Greenford d					11 34									12 04							
Greenford ⊖ a					11 39									12 09							
Hanwell d		11 15										11 45									12 15
Southall d		11 19		11 28								11 49	11 58								12 19
Hayes & Harlington d		11 23		11 32						11 42		11 53	12 02						12 12		12 23
Heathrow Terminal 1-2-3 2 ✈ a		11 35										12 05									12 35
Heathrow Terminal 4 ✈ a																					
West Drayton d				11 36						11 46			12 06						12 16		
Iver d										11 49									12 19		
Langley d									←	11 52								←	12 22		
Slough 3 a				11 43				11 36	11 43	11 57			12 13				12 06	12 13	12 27		
d				11 43				11 36	11 43	11 57			12 13				12 06	12 13	12 27		
Burnham d				→					11 47				→					12 17			
Taplow d									11 51									12 21			
Maidenhead 3 d									11 55	12 04								12 25	12 34		
Twyford 3 d									12 03	12 12								12 33	12 42		
Reading 7 a	11 25		11 30			11 39	11 47	11 52	12 17	12 22	11 56				12 09	12 14	12 22	12 45	12 50	12 25	
Oxford a								12 18		13 14							12 48		13 41		

	GW ◇1 C ∅	GW 1	GW 1	GW ◇1 ⌷	GW ◇1 ⌷	GW ◇1 ⌶	GW 1	GW 1	GW ◇1 ⌷	HC	GW 1	GW 1	GW ◇1 ∅	GW ◇1 ⌶	GW 1	GW 1	GW ◇1 ⌷	HC	GW ◇1 ∅
London Paddington 15 ⊖ d	12 06	12 12	12 15	12 15	12 18	12 21		12 27	12 30	12 33	12 42	12 45	12 45	12 50		12 57	13 00	13 03	13 06
Acton Main Line d			12 21									12 51							
Ealing Broadway ⊖ d		12 20	12 24					12 35		12 41	12 50	12 54				13 05		13 11	
West Ealing d			12 27							12 43		12 57						13 13	
Drayton Green d			12 29									12 59							
Castle Bar Park d			12 31									13 01							
South Greenford d			12 34									13 04							
Greenford ⊖ a			12 39									13 10							
Hanwell d										12 45								13 15	
Southall d		12 28								12 49	12 58							13 19	
Hayes & Harlington d		12 32						12 42		12 53	13 02					13 12		13 23	
Heathrow Terminal 1-2-3 2 ✈ a										13 05								13 35	
Heathrow Terminal 4 ✈ a																			
West Drayton d		12 36						12 46			13 06					13 16			
Iver d								12 49								13 19			
Langley d							←	12 52							←	13 22			
Slough 3 a		12 43				12 36	12 43	12 57			13 13			13 06	13 13	13 27			
d		12 43				12 36	12 43	12 57			13 13			13 06	13 13	13 27			
Burnham d		→					12 47				→				13 17				
Taplow d							12 51								13 21				
Maidenhead 3 d							12 55	13 04							13 25	13 34			
Twyford 3 d							13 03	13 12							13 33	13 42			
Reading 7 a	12 30			12 39	12 46	12 51	13 14	13 22	12 56				13 09	13 22	13 45	13 51	13 25		13 30
Oxford a						13 18		14 14						13 50		14 42			

	GW 1	GW 1	GW ◇1 ⌷	GW 1	GW ◇1 ⌶	GW 1	GW 1	GW ◇1 ⌷	HC	GW 1	GW 1	GW ◇1 ⌷	GW ◇1 ⌷	GW ◇1 ⌶	GW 1	GW 1	GW ◇1 ⌷	HC	GW ◇1 ∅	GW 1	GW 1
London Paddington 15 ⊖ d	13 12	13 15	13 15	13 18	13 21		13 27	13 30	13 33	13 42	13 45	13 45	13 48	13 50		13 57	14 00	14 03	14 06	14 12	14 15
Acton Main Line d		13 21									13 51										14 21
Ealing Broadway ⊖ d	13 20	13 24					13 35		13 41	13 50	13 54					14 05		14 11		14 20	14 24
West Ealing d		13 27							13 43		13 57							14 13			14 27
Drayton Green d		13 29									13 59										14 29
Castle Bar Park d		13 31									14 01										14 31
South Greenford d		13 34									14 04										14 34
Greenford ⊖ a		13 39									14 09										14 39
Hanwell d									13 45									14 15			
Southall d	13 28								13 49	13 58								14 19		14 28	
Hayes & Harlington d	13 32						13 42		13 53	14 02						14 12		14 23		14 32	
Heathrow Terminal 1-2-3 2 ✈ a									14 05									14 35			
Heathrow Terminal 4 ✈ a																					
West Drayton d	13 36						13 46			14 06						14 16				14 36	
Iver d							13 49									14 19					
Langley d						←	13 52								←	14 22					
Slough 3 a	13 43				13 36	13 43	13 57			14 13				14 06	14 13	14 27				14 43	
d	13 43				13 36	13 43	13 57			14 13				14 06	14 13	14 27				14 43	
Burnham d	→					13 47				→					14 17					→	
Taplow d						13 51									14 21						
Maidenhead 3 d						13 55	14 04								14 25	14 34					
Twyford 3 d						14 03	14 12								14 33	14 42					
Reading 7 a			13 39	13 47	13 52	14 12	14 21	13 56				14 09	14 14	14 21	14 45	14 52	14 25		14 30		
Oxford a					14 18		15 14							14 48		15 41					

A The Mayflower

B The Cheltenham Spa Express

C The Royal Duchy

London - Greenford and Reading

25 June to 14 September

Network Diagram - see first Page of Table 116

		GW ◇1 ☕	GW 1	GW ◇1 trolley	GW 1	GW 1	GW ◇1 ☕	HC	GW FO ◇1 A ☕	GW 1	GW 1	GW ◇1 ☕	GW ◇1 trolley	GW 1	GW 1	GW ◇1 ☕	HC	GW ◇1 B ∅	GW 1	GW 1	GW ◇1 ☕
London Paddington 15 ⊖	d	14 15	14 18	14 21		14 27	14 30	14 33	14 36	14 42	14 45	14 45	14 50		14 57	15 00	15 03	15 06	15 12	15 15	15 15
Acton Main Line	d										14 51									15 21	
Ealing Broadway ⊖	d					14 35		14 41		14 50	14 54				15 05		15 11		15 20	15 24	
West Ealing	d							14 43			14 57						15 13			15 27	
Drayton Green	d										14 59									15 29	
Castle Bar Park	d										15 01									15 31	
South Greenford	d										15 04									15 34	
Greenford ⊖	a										15 09									15 39	
Hanwell	d							14 45									15 15				
Southall	d							14 49		14 58							15 19		15 28		
Hayes & Harlington	d					14 42		14 53		15 02					15 12		15 23		15 32		
Heathrow Terminal 1-2-3 2 ✈	a							15 05									15 35				
Heathrow Terminal 4 ✈	a																				
West Drayton	d					14 46				15 06					15 16				15 36		
Iver	d					14 49									15 19						
Langley	d				←	14 52								←	15 22						
Slough 3	a			14 36	14 43	14 57				15 13			15 06	15 13	15 27				15 43		
	d			14 36	14 43	14 57				15 13			15 06	15 13	15 27				15 43		
Burnham	d				14 47					→				15 17					→		
Taplow	d				14 51									15 21							
Maidenhead 3	d				14 55	15 04								15 25	15 34						
Twyford 3	d				15 03	15 12								15 33	15 42						
Reading 7	a	14 39	14 47	14 52	15 13	15 22	14 56					15 09	15 22	15 44	15 52	15 25		15 30			15 39
Oxford	a			15 18		16 14							15 50		16 43						

		GW 1	GW ◇1 trolley	GW 1	GW 1	GW ◇1 ☕	HC	GW 1	GW 1	GW ◇1 ☕	GW ◇1 ☕	GW ◇1 ☕	GW 1	GW 1	GW ◇1 ☕	HC	GW ◇1 ☕	GW 1	GW 1	GW ◇1 ☕	GW 1	GW ◇1 trolley
London Paddington 15 ⊖	d	15 18	15 22		15 27	15 30	15 33	15 42	15 45	15 45	15 48	15 51		15 57	16 00	16 03	16 06	16 12	16 15	16 15	16 18	16 22
Acton Main Line	d								15 51										16 21			
Ealing Broadway ⊖	d				15 35		15 41	15 50	15 54					16 05		16 11		16 20	16 24			
West Ealing	d						15 43		15 57							16 13			16 27			
Drayton Green	d								15 59										16 29			
Castle Bar Park	d								16 01										16 31			
South Greenford	d								16 04										16 34			
Greenford ⊖	a								16 09										16 39			
Hanwell	d						15 45									16 15						
Southall	d				15 40		15 49	15 58								16 19		16 28				
Hayes & Harlington	d				15 44		15 53	16 02						16 11		16 23		16 32				
Heathrow Terminal 1-2-3 2 ✈	a						16 05									16 35						
Heathrow Terminal 4 ✈	a																					
West Drayton	d				15 48			16 06						16 16				16 36				
Iver	d				15 51									16 19								
Langley	d			←	15 55								←	16 22								
Slough 3	a		15 36	15 43	15 59			16 13				16 06	16 13	16 27				16 44				16 37
	d		15 36	15 43	15 59			16 13				16 06	16 13	16 27				16 45				16 38
Burnham	d			15 47				→					16 17					→				
Taplow	d			15 51									16 21									
Maidenhead 3	d			15 55	16 07								16 25	16 34								
Twyford 3	d			16 03	16 15								16 33	16 42								
Reading 7	a	15 47	15 51	16 13	16 23	15 56				16 09	16 14	16 20	16 44	16 52	16 25		16 30			16 39	16 47	16 52
Oxford	a		16 18		17 15							16 47		17 44								17 24

		GW 1	GW 1	GW ◇1 ☕	HC	GW ◇1 ☕	GW 1	GW 1	GW ◇1 C ☕	GW ◇1	GW 1	GW 1	GW ◇1 ☕	HC	GW ◇1 ☕	GW ◇1 ☕	GW 1	GW 1	GW 1	GW ◇1 D ∅	GW 1	GW 1
London Paddington 15 ⊖	d		16 27	16 30	16 33	16 36	16 42	16 45	16 45	16 49		16 55	17 00	17 03	17 03	17 06		17 12	17 15	17 15	17 18	17 18
Acton Main Line	d							16 51													17 24	
Ealing Broadway ⊖	d		16 35		16 41		16 50	16 54				17 04		17 11					17 23		17 27	
West Ealing	d				16 43			16 57						17 13							17 30	
Drayton Green	d							16 59													17 32	
Castle Bar Park	d							17 01													17 34	
South Greenford	d							17 04													17 37	
Greenford ⊖	a							17 09													17 42	
Hanwell	d				16 45									17 15								
Southall	d		16 40		16 49		16 58							17 19					17 29			
Hayes & Harlington	d		16 44		16 53		17 02					17 11		17 23					17 33			
Heathrow Terminal 1-2-3 2 ✈	a				17 05									17 35								
Heathrow Terminal 4 ✈	a																					
West Drayton	d						17 07					17 16							17 38			
Iver	d		16 49				17 10					17 20							17 41			
Langley	d	←	16 52				17 14				←	17 24							17 44			
Slough 3	a	16 44	16 57				17 18			17 04	17 18	17 27						17 32	17 49			
	d	16 45	16 57				17 18			17 04	17 18	17 28						17 35	17 49			
Burnham	d	16 50					→				17 22	17 33						17 40	17 53			
Taplow	d	16 54									17 26	17 36						17 43	17 57			
Maidenhead 3	d	16 59	17 04								17 30	17 43					←	17 47	18a05			17 40
Twyford 3	d	17 07	17 12								17 38	17 51				17 28	17 38	17a57				17 48
Reading 7	a	17 18	17 21	16 56		17 01			17 09	17 19	→	→	17 24		17 29	17 35	17 46			17 40		17 56
Oxford	a		18 12							17 50												18 45

A from 6 July until 31 August
B The Cornishman
C The Capitals United
D The Red Dragon

London - Greenford and Reading

25 June to 14 September

Network Diagram - see first Page of Table 116

		GW ◇1 ☕	GW 1	GW ◇1 ☕	HC	GW ◇1 ☕	GW 1	GW 1	GW 1	GW ◇1 ☕	GW 1	GW 1	GW ◇1 ☕	GW ◇1 ☕	GW 1	GW ◇1 A ☕	GW 1	HC	GW ◇1 B ✕	GW ◇1 ☕	GW 1
London Paddington 15 ⊖	d	17 22	17 25	17 30	17 33	17 33		17 36	17 42	17 45	17 45	17 48	17 48	17 50	17 57	18 00		18 03	18 03	18 06	
Acton Main Line	d											17 54									
Ealing Broadway ⊖	d		17 33		17 41						17 53	17 57			18 05			18 11			
West Ealing	d				17 43							18 00						18 13			
Drayton Green	d											18 02									
Castle Bar Park	d											18 04									
South Greenford	d											18 07									
Greenford ⊖	a											18 12									
Hanwell	d				17 45													18 15			
Southall	d		17 38		17 49						17 59				18 10			18 19			
Hayes & Harlington	d		17 42		17 53						18 03				18 14			18 23			
Heathrow Terminal 1-2-3 2 ✈	a				18 05													18 35			
Heathrow Terminal 4 ✈	a																				
West Drayton	d		17 47								18 08				18 19						
Iver	d		17 50												18 22						
Langley	d		17 54								18 12				18 26						
Slough 3	a		17 58						18 04		18 16				18 30						
	d		17 58						18 05		18 16				18 30						
Burnham	d		18 02								18 21				18 35						
Taplow	d		18 06												18 39						
Maidenhead 3	d		18 10				←	17 58	18a13		18 26			18 09	18 45		←				←
Twyford 3	d		18 17				17 51	18 07			18 34				18 52		18 17			18 28	18 34
Reading 7	a	17 49	→	17 54		17 59	18 00	18 15		18 09	→		18 14	18 20	→	18 25	18 26		18 30	18 35	18 44
Oxford	a	18 15						19 04						18 47			19 16				

		GW 1	GW ◇1 ☕	GW 1	GW 1	GW 1	GW ◇1 C ☕	GW FO 1	GW FX 1	GW ◇1 ☕	HC	GW ◇1 ☕	GW 1	GW 1	GW ◇1 ☕	GW 1	GW 1	GW ◇1 ☕	GW FO 1	GW FX 1	GW 1	GW ◇1 trolley	GW 1
London Paddington 15 ⊖	d	18 12	18 15	18 15	18 18	18 18	18 22	18 25	18 25	18 30	18 33	18 33		18 36	18 45		18 45	18 47			18 48	18 51	
Acton Main Line	d				18 24																18 54		
Ealing Broadway ⊖	d			18 23	18 27			18 33	18 33		18 41						18 53				18 57		
West Ealing	d				18 30						18 43										19 00		
Drayton Green	d				18 32																19 02		
Castle Bar Park	d				18 34																19 04		
South Greenford	d				18 37																19 07		
Greenford ⊖	a				18 42																19 12		
Hanwell	d										18 45												
Southall	d			18 29				18 38	18 38		18 49						18 59						
Hayes & Harlington	d			18 33				18 42	18 42		18 53						19 03						
Heathrow Terminal 1-2-3 2 ✈	a										19 05												
Heathrow Terminal 4 ✈	a																						
West Drayton	d			18 38				18 46	18 46														
Iver	d							18 49	18 49														
Langley	d			18 42				18 52	18 52										←	←			←
Slough 3	a	18 35		18 47				18 59	18 59					18 54			19 11		18 59	18 59		19 06	19 11
	d	18 36		18 47				18 59	18 59					18 55			19 11		18 59	18 59		19 06	19 11
Burnham	d			18 51				→	→								→		19 03	19 03			19 15
Taplow	d																		19 06	19 06			
Maidenhead 3	d	18 49		18 57		18 40							←	19a03		←			19 10	19 10			19 21
Twyford 3	d	18a58		19 05		18 48							18 52			19 05		19 09	19 18	19 18			19 38
Reading 7	a		18 40	→		18 56	18 49			18 54		18 59	19 01		19 09	19 13		19 17	19 26	19 26		19 22	19 47
Oxford	a					19 43	19 19									20 13			20 18	20 27		19 48	

A The Bristolian
B The Golden Hind
C The Cathedrals Express

London - Greenford and Reading

Mondays to Fridays

25 June to 14 September

Network Diagram - see first Page of Table 116

		GW [1]	GW ◇[1] ☕			HC	GW [1] A ✕	GW [1]	GW FO [1]	GW [1]	GW [1]	GW FX ◇[1] ☕	GW FO ◇[1] ☕	GW [1]		GW FX ◇[1] ☕	GW FO ◇[1] ☕	GW [1]	GW [1]	GW [1]	GW ◇[1] ☕	HC	GW [1]	GW [1]
London Paddington [15] ⊖	d	18 57	19 00			19 03	19 03	19 06	19 12	19 12	19 15	19 15	19 15	19 18		19 22	19 22			19 27	19 30	19 33	19 42	19 45
Acton Main Line	d										19 21													19 51
Ealing Broadway ⊖	d	19 05				19 11				19 20	19 24									19 35		19 41	19 50	19 54
West Ealing	d					19 13					19 27											19 43		19 57
Drayton Green	d										19 29													19 59
Castle Bar Park	d										19 31													20 01
South Greenford	d										19 34													20 04
Greenford ⊖	a										19 39													20 09
Hanwell	d					19 15																19 45		
Southall	d	19 10				19 19				19 28										19 40		19 49	19 58	
Hayes & Harlington	d	19 14				19 23				19 32										19 44		19 53	20 02	
Heathrow Terminal 1-2-3 [2] ✈	a					19 35																20 05		
Heathrow Terminal 4 ✈	a																							
West Drayton	d	19 19																		19 48			20 06	
Iver	d	19 22																		19 51			20 09	
Langley	d	19 26																	←	19 55			20 13	
Slough [3]	a	19 30								19 41						19 36	19 36		19 41	19 59			20 17	
	d	19 30								19 41						19 36	19 36		19 41	19 59			20 17	
Burnham	d	19 34								→									19 45	20 03			→	
Taplow	d	19 38																	19 48					
Maidenhead [3]	d	19 43						19 27						19 40				←	19 52	20 09				
Twyford [3]	d	19 51						19a38						19 48				19 51	20 00	20 17				
Reading [7]	a	→	19 27				19 32		19 41			19 39		19 56		19 51	19 51	20 00	20 11	20 23	19 56			
Oxford	a								20 28					20 45		20 18	20 21			21 14				

		GW ◇[1] ☕	GW ◇[1] ☕	GW ◇[1] H	GW [1]	GW [1]	GW ◇[1] ☕	HC	GW [1]	GW [1]		GW ◇[1] Ø	GW ◇[1] H	GW [1]	GW [1]	HC	GW ◇[1] ☕	GW [1]	GW [1]	GW ◇[1] ☕		GW ◇[1]	GW [1]	GW [1]	HC
London Paddington [15] ⊖	d	19 45	19 48	19 50		19 57	20 00	20 03	20 12	20 15		20 15	20 20		20 27	20 33	20 35	20 42	20 45	20 45		20 48		20 57	21 03
Acton Main Line	d									20 21									20 51						
Ealing Broadway ⊖	d					20 05		20 11	20 20	20 24					20 35	20 41		20 50	20 54					21 05	21 11
West Ealing	d							20 13		20 27						20 43			20 57						21 13
Drayton Green	d									20 29									20 59						
Castle Bar Park	d									20 31									21 01						
South Greenford	d									20 34									21 04						
Greenford ⊖	a									20 39									21 09						
Hanwell	d							20 15								20 45									21 15
Southall	d							20 19	20 28							20 49		20 58							21 19
Hayes & Harlington	d					20 12		20 23	20 32						20 42	20 53		21 02						21 12	21 23
Heathrow Terminal 1-2-3 [2] ✈	a							20 35								21 05									21 35
Heathrow Terminal 4 ✈	a																								
West Drayton	d					20 16			20 36						20 46			21 06						21 16	
Iver	d					20 19									20 49									21 19	
Langley	d				←	20 22								←	20 52								←	21 22	
Slough [3]	a			20 06	20 17	20 27			20 43				20 35	20 43	20 57			21 13				21 04	21 13	21 27	
	d			20 06	20 17	20 27			20 43				20 36	20 43	20 57			21 13				21 05	21 13	21 27	
Burnham	d				20 20				→					20 47				→					21 17		
Taplow	d				20 25									20 51									21 21		
Maidenhead [3]	d		20 06		20 29	20 34								20 55	21 04								21 25	21 34	
Twyford [3]	d				20 37	20 42								21 03	21 12								21 33	21 42	
Reading [7]	a	20 09	20 17	20 22	20 45	20 52	20 25					20 39	20 50	21 13	21 20		20 59			21 09		21 20	21 45	21 51	
Oxford	a			20 47		21 43							21 19		22 14							21 51		22 41	

		GW [1]	GW ◇[1] ☕	GW [1]	GW ◇[1]	GW [1]		HC	GW [1]	GW ◇[1] ☕	GW [1]	GW FO ◇[1] H	GW FX ◇[1] ☕	GW [1]	GW [1]	HC		GW FO ◇[1] ☕	GW [1]	GW FX ◇[1] ☕	GW FO [1]	GW FX [1]	GW ◇[1]	GW [1]	HC
London Paddington [15] ⊖	d	21 12	21 15	21 15	21 18	21 27		21 33	21 42	21 45		21 48	21 48		21 58	22 03		22 15		22 15	22 16	22 16	22 18		22 33
Acton Main Line	d			21 21					21 48																
Ealing Broadway ⊖	d	21 20		21 24		21 35		21 41	21 51						22 06	22 11					22 24	22 24			22 41
West Ealing	d			21 27				21 43								22 13									22 43
Drayton Green	d			21 29																					
Castle Bar Park	d			21 31																					
South Greenford	d			21 34																					
Greenford ⊖	a			21 39																					
Hanwell	d							21 45								22 15									22 45
Southall	d	21 28				21 42		21 49	21 58							22 19					22 29	22 29			22 49
Hayes & Harlington	d	21 32				21 46		21 53	22 02						22 13	22 23					22 33	22 33			22 53
Heathrow Terminal 1-2-3 [2] ✈	a							22 05								22 35									23 05
Heathrow Terminal 4 ✈	a																								
West Drayton	d	21 36				21 50			22 06						22 17						22 37	22 37			
Iver	d					21 53									22 20										
Langley	d					21 57					←			←	22 23				←					←	
Slough [3]	a	21 43			21 34	22 02			22 14		21 43	22 03	22 03	22 02	22 28				22 14		22 45	22 45	22 35	22 28	
	d	21 43			21 35	22 07			22 15		21 43	22 03	22 03	22 07	22 39				22 15		22 45	22 45	22 36	22 39	
Burnham	d	→				→			→		21 47				→				22 18		→	→			
Taplow	d										21 51								22 22						
Maidenhead [3]	d										21 55			22 14					22 26				22 44	22 47	
Twyford [3]	d										22 03			22 22					22 34					22 55	
Reading [7]	a		21 39		21 50					22 09	22 15	22 22	22 22	22 30				22 39	22 46	22 48			22 58	23 04	
Oxford	a				22 18							22 47	22 47	23 21									23 28	23 48	

▲ The Armada

London - Greenford and Reading

Mondays to Fridays

25 June to 14 September

Network Diagram - see first Page of Table 116

		GW FO ◇[1] ☕		GW FO [1]	GW FX [1]	GW FX ◇[1] ☕	GW [1]	GW ◇[1]	GW [1]	GW [1]	HC	GW ◇[1]		GW FX [1]	GW FO [1]	GW FX ◇[1] ☕	GW FO ◇[1] ☕	GW FO [1]		GW [1]
London Paddington [15] ⊖	d	22 45				22 45	22 45	22 48		22 59	23 03	23 18		23 29	23 29	23 30	23 30	23 42		23 48
Acton Main Line	d						22 51													23 54
Ealing Broadway ⊖	d						22 54			23 07	23 11			23 37	23 37					23 57
West Ealing	d										23 13									23 59
Drayton Green	d																			
Castle Bar Park	d																			
South Greenford	d																			
Greenford ⊖	a																			
Hanwell	d										23 15									00 02
Southall	d									23 12	23 19									00 06
Hayes & Harlington	d						23 01			23 16	23 23			23 44	23 44					00 10
Heathrow Terminal 1-2-3 [2] ✈	a										23 35									
Heathrow Terminal 4 ✈	a										23 41									
West Drayton	d									23 20										00 14
Iver	d									23 23										00 17
Langley	d			←	←				←	23 27										00 21
Slough [3]	a			22 45	22 45		23 11	23 06	23 11	23 32		23 36		23 53	23 53			23 58		00 26
	d			22 45	22 45		23 12	23 06	23 12	23 32		23 36		23 54	23 54			23 58		00 26
Burnham	d			22 49	22 49		→		23 16											00 30
Taplow	d			22 53	22 53				23 20											00 34
Maidenhead [3]	d			22 57	22 57			23 14	23 24	23 40		23 44		00 01	00 01			00 08		00 41
Twyford [3]	d			23 05	23 05				23 32	23 48				00 09	00 09					00 48
Reading [7]	a	23 09		23 14	23 16	23 18		23 28	23 41	23 58		23 58		00 19	00 19	00 03	00 05	00 21		00 57
Oxford	a							23 56	00 26			00 28		01 15	01 16			01 02		

Mondays to Fridays

from 17 September

		GW MX [1]	GW MO [1]	GW MX ◇[1]	GW MO [1]	GW MX [1]	GW MX [1]	GW MX ◇[1] ☕	GW MO ◇[1] ☕	GW MO ◇[1]		GW MX [1]	GW MO [1]	GW MX [1]	GW MX ◇[1]	GW MO [1]	GW MX [1]	GW [1]	GW [1]	HC		HC	GW [1]	GW [1]	GW ◇[1] ☕
London Paddington [15] ⊖	d	22p45	23p15	23p18			23p29	23p30	23p37	23p47		23p48	23p53		00 22	00 34	00 34	01 34	03 34	04 42		05 13	05 18	05 22	05 27
Acton Main Line	d	22p51										23p54													
Ealing Broadway ⊖	d	22p54	23p24				23p37			23p55		23p57	00 02			00 42	00 42	01 42	03 42	04 50		05 21		05 30	
West Ealing	d											23p59													
Drayton Green	d																								
Castle Bar Park	d																								
South Greenford	d																								
Greenford ⊖	a																								
Hanwell	d											00 02													
Southall	d		23p29									00 06	00 07			00 47	00 47	01 47	03 48	04 54		05 25		05 35	
Hayes & Harlington	d	23p01	23p33				23p44					00 10	00 11			00 51	00 51	01 51	03 52	04 58		05 29		05 39	
Heathrow Terminal 1-2-3 [2] ✈	a																			05 04		05 35			
Heathrow Terminal 4 ✈	a																			05 10		05 41			
West Drayton	d		23p37									00 14	00 15			00 55	00 55	01 55	03 56					05 43	
Iver	d											00 17												05 46	
Langley	d		23p42		←							00 21	00 20	←		01 00	01 00							05 50	
Slough [3]	a	23p11	23p46	23p36	23p46		23p53		00 01	00 09		00 26	00 24	00 26	00 39	01 05	01 05	02 04	04 04				05 34	05 54	
	d	23p12	23p46	23p36	23p46		23p54		00 02	00 10		00 26	00 24	00 26	00 39	01 05	01 05	02 04	04 05				05 34	05 54	
Burnham	d	23p16	→		23p50							→	00 28	00 30		01 09	01 09							→	
Taplow	d	23p20												00 34			01 13								
Maidenhead [3]	d	23p24		23p44	23p56		00 01			00 17			00 34	00 41		01 15	01 16	02 11	04 12						
Twyford [3]	d	23p32			00 03	00 07	00 09						00 42	00 48		01 23	01 24	02 19	04 20						
Reading [7]	a	23p41		23p58	00 11	00 16	00 19	00 03	00 14	00 30			00 49	00 57	01 00	01 32	01 35	02 29	04 30				05 52		05 55
Oxford	a	00 26		00 28			01 15								01 34								06 22		

Mondays to Fridays

from 17 September

London - Greenford and Reading

Network Diagram - see first Page of Table 116

		HC	GW ◇1 ⊡	GW 1	GW 1	GW 1		GW ◇1	GW 1	GW 1	HC	GW 1	GW 1	GW 1	GW 1	GW 1		GW ◇1 ⊡	HC	GW 1	GW 1	GW ◇1 ⊡	GW 1	GW 1	GW 1
London Paddington 15 ⊖	d	05 33	05 36		05 42	05 45		05 48		05 57	06 03	06 12	06 15	06 20		06 27		06 30	06 33	06 42	06 45	06 45	06 48		06 57
Acton Main Line	d					05 51							06 21								06 51				
Ealing Broadway ⊖	d	05 41			05 50	05 54				06 05	06 11	06 20	06 24			06 35			06 41	06 50	06 54				07 05
West Ealing	d	05 43				05 57					06 13		06 27						06 43		06 57				
Drayton Green	d					05 59							06 29								06 59				
Castle Bar Park	d					06 01							06 31								07 01				
South Greenford	d					06 04							06 34								07 04				
Greenford ⊖	a					06 09							06 39								07 09				
Hanwell	d	05 45									06 15								06 45						
Southall	d	05 49			05 58					06 10	06 19	06 28				06 41			06 49	06 58					07 10
Hayes & Harlington	d	05 53			06 02					06 14	06 23	06 32				06 45			06 53	07 02					07 14
Heathrow Terminal 1-2-3 2 ✈	a	06 05									06 35								07 05						
Heathrow Terminal 4 ✈	a																								
West Drayton	d				06 06					06 18		06 40				06 49				07 06					07 18
Iver	d									06 21						06 52									07 21
Langley	d			←					←	06 25					←	06 56								←	07 25
Slough 3	a		05 51	05 54	06 13			06 05	06 13	06 29		06 47		06 34	06 47	07 00				07 13			07 04	07 13	07 29
	d		05 52	05 54	06 13			06 05	06 13	06 29		06 47		06 35	06 47	07 00				07 13			07 04	07 13	07 29
Burnham	d				→				06 17			→			06 51					→				07 17	
Taplow	d								06 21						06 54									07 21	
Maidenhead 3	d			06 02					06 28	06 37					06 58	07 08								07 25	07 37
Twyford 3	d			06 10					06 35	06 45					07 06	07 16								07 33	07 45
Reading 7	a		06 05	06 20				06 20	06 45	06 53				06 49	07 15	07 27		06 54				07 09	07 19	07 45	07 52
Oxford	a			07 02				06 56		07 46				07 22									08 02		08 43

		GW ◇1 ⊡		HC	GW ◇1 A ⊡	GW 1	GW 1	GW 1	GW ◇1 ⊡	GW 1	GW 1	GW 1		GW 1	GW ◇1 B Ø	HC	GW 1	GW 1	GW ◇1 C ⊡	GW ◇1 ⊡	GW 1	GW 1		GW ◇1 ⊡	GW 1
London Paddington 15 ⊖	d	07 00		07 03	07 06	07 12	07 12	07 15	07 15	07 18	07 21			07 27	07 30	07 33	07 42	07 45	07 45	07 48	07 50	07 57		08 00	
Acton Main Line	d							07 21										07 51							
Ealing Broadway ⊖	d			07 11			07 20	07 24						07 35		07 41	07 50	07 54				08 05			
West Ealing	d			07 13				07 27								07 43		07 57							
Drayton Green	d							07 29										07 59							
Castle Bar Park	d							07 31										08 01							
South Greenford	d							07 34										08 04							
Greenford ⊖	a							07 39										08 09							
Hanwell	d			07 15												07 45									
Southall	d			07 19			07 28							07 40		07 49	07 59					08 10			
Hayes & Harlington	d			07 23			07 32							07 44		07 53	08 02					08 14			
Heathrow Terminal 1-2-3 2 ✈	a			07 35												08 05									
Heathrow Terminal 4 ✈	a																								
West Drayton	d						07 36							07 48			08 06					08 18			
Iver	d													07 51								08 21			
Langley	d											←		07 55								08 25			←
Slough 3	a						07 43				07 36	07 43		07 59			08 13				08 06	08 29			08 13
	d						07 43				07 36	07 43		07 59			08 13				08 06	08 29			08 13
Burnham	d						→					07 47					→					→			08 17
Taplow	d											07 51													08 21
Maidenhead 3	d					07 43						07 55		08 07											08 25
Twyford 3	d					07 51						08 03		08 15											08 33
Reading 7	a	07 24			07 30	08 02			07 40	07 47	07 51	08 14		08 23	07 57				08 09	08 14	08 21			08 25	08 44
Oxford	a										08 19			09 15							08 49				

		HC	GW 1	GW 1	GW 1	GW ◇1 ⊡	GW 1	GW 1		GW ◇1 ⊡	GW 1	GW 1	GW ◇1 ⊡	HC	GW 1	GW ◇1 Ø	GW 1	GW 1		GW 1	GW 1	GW 1	GW 1	GW ◇1 ⊡	HC
London Paddington 15 ⊖	d	08 03	08 06	08 12	08 15	08 15	08 18			08 22		08 27	08 30	08 33	08 38	08 45	08 46	08 47		08 51			08 55	09 00	09 03
Acton Main Line	d				08 21												08 51								
Ealing Broadway ⊖	d	08 11		08 20	08 24							08 35		08 41	08 47		08 54	08 59					09 03		09 11
West Ealing	d	08 13			08 27									08 43			08 57	09 01							09 13
Drayton Green	d				08 29												08 59								
Castle Bar Park	d				08 31												09 01								
South Greenford	d				08 34												09 04								
Greenford ⊖	a				08 39												09 10								
Hanwell	d	08 15												08 45	08 50										09 15
Southall	d	08 19		08 28								08 40		08 49									09 08		09 19
Hayes & Harlington	d	08 23		08 32								08 44		08 53	08 56			09 08					09 12		09 23
Heathrow Terminal 1-2-3 2 ✈	a	08 35												09 05											09 35
Heathrow Terminal 4 ✈	a																								
West Drayton	d			08 36								08 48			09 00								09 16		
Iver	d											08 51			09 03								09 19		
Langley	d							←			←	08 55			09 06						←	←	09 23		
Slough 3	a		08 27	08 43				08 29		08 36	08 43	08 59			09 11			09 16		09 06	09 11	09 16	09 27		
	d		08 27	08 43				08 29		08 36	08 43	08 59			09 11			09 16		09 06	09 11	09 16	09 27		
Burnham	d			→							08 47				→			→				09 20			
Taplow	d										08 51											09 24			
Maidenhead 3	d		08 35					08 39			08 55	09 06									09 18	09 28	09 35		
Twyford 3	d		08a45					08 48			09 03	09 16									09a29	09 36	09 43		
Reading 7	a					08 39	08 48	08 56		08 51	09 15	09 24	08 56			09 09				09 20		09 46	09 52	09 25	
Oxford	a							09 43		09 20		10 14								09 53			10 41		

A The Devon Express B The Merchant Venturer C The St. David

Mondays to Fridays

from 17 September

London - Greenford and Reading

Network Diagram - see first Page of Table 116

		GW ◇1 ⊡		GW 1		GW 1	GW ◇1 ⊡	GW 1	GW ◇1 ✗	GW 1	GW 1	GW ◇1 Ø	HC	GW 1		GW 1	GW ◇1 Ø	GW ◇1 ⊡	GW ◇1	GW 1	GW 1	GW ◇1 A ⊡	HC		
London Paddington 15 ⊖	d	09 06		09 12		09 15	09 15	09 18	09 21		09 27	09 30	09 33	09 42		09 45	09 45	09 48	09 50		09 57	10 00	10 03		
Acton Main Line	d					09 21										09 51									
Ealing Broadway ⊖	d			09 20		09 24					09 35		09 41	09 50		09 54					10 05		10 11		
West Ealing	d					09 27							09 43			09 57							10 13		
Drayton Green	d					09 29										09 59									
Castle Bar Park	d					09 31										10 01									
South Greenford	d					09 34										10 04									
Greenford ⊖	a					09 39										10 09									
Hanwell	d												09 45										10 15		
Southall	d			09 28									09 49	09 58									10 19		
Hayes & Harlington	d			09 32							09 42		09 53	10 02							10 12		10 23		
Heathrow Terminal 1-2-3 2 ✈	a												10 05										10 35		
Heathrow Terminal 4 ✈	a																								
West Drayton	d			09 36							09 46			10 06							10 16				
Iver	d										09 49										10 19				
Langley	d									←	09 52									←	10 22				
Slough 3	a			09 43					09 36	09 43	09 57			10 13					10 06	10 13	10 27				
	d			09 43					09 36	09 43	09 57			10 13					10 06	10 13	10 27				
Burnham	d			→						09 45				→						10 17					
Taplow	d									09 51										10 21					
Maidenhead 3	d									09 55	10 04									10 25	10 34				
Twyford 3	d									10 03	10 12									10 33	10 42				
Reading 7	a	09 30					09 39	09 48	09 52	10 17	10 22	09 56					10 09	10 14	10 21	10 44	10 52	10 25			
Oxford	a								10 18		11 14								10 47		11 41				

		GW ◇1 B Ø	GW 1	GW 1	GW ◇1 ⊡	GW 1	GW ◇1 ⊡	GW 1	GW 1	GW ◇1 Ø		HC	GW 1	GW 1	GW ◇1 Ø	GW ◇1	GW 1	GW 1	GW ◇1 ⊡	HC		GW ◇1 C Ø		GW 1	GW 1
London Paddington 15 ⊖	d	10 06	10 12	10 15	10 15	10 18	10 22		10 27	10 30		10 33	10 42	10 45	10 45	10 50		10 57	11 00	11 03		11 06		11 12	11 15
Acton Main Line	d			10 21										10 51											11 21
Ealing Broadway ⊖	d		10 20	10 24					10 35			10 41	10 50	10 54				11 05		11 11				11 20	11 24
West Ealing	d			10 27								10 43		10 57						11 13					11 27
Drayton Green	d			10 29										10 59											11 29
Castle Bar Park	d			10 31										11 01											11 31
South Greenford	d			10 34										11 04											11 34
Greenford ⊖	a			10 39										11 09											11 39
Hanwell	d											10 45								11 15					
Southall	d		10 28									10 49	10 58							11 19				11 28	
Hayes & Harlington	d		10 32						10 42			10 53	11 02					11 12		11 23				11 32	
Heathrow Terminal 1-2-3 2 ✈	a											11 05								11 35					
Heathrow Terminal 4 ✈	a																								
West Drayton	d		10 36						10 46				11 06					11 16						11 36	
Iver	d								10 49									11 19							
Langley	d							←	10 52								←	11 22							
Slough 3	a		10 43				10 36	10 43	10 57				11 13			11 06	11 13	11 27						11 43	
	d		10 43				10 36	10 43	10 57				11 13			11 06	11 13	11 27						11 43	
Burnham	d		→					10 47					→				11 17							→	
Taplow	d							10 51									11 21								
Maidenhead 3	d							10 55	11 04								11 25	11 34							
Twyford 3	d							11 03	11 12								11 33	11 42							
Reading 7	a	10 30			10 39	10 48	10 51	11 13	11 22	10 56					11 09	11 21	11 45	11 52	11 25			11 30			
Oxford	a						11 18		12 14							11 50		12 41							

		GW ◇1 ⊡	GW 1	GW ◇1 ✗	GW 1	GW 1		GW ◇1 ⊡	HC	GW 1	GW 1	GW ◇1 Ø	GW ◇1 D ⊡	GW ◇1 ✗	GW 1	GW 1		GW ◇1 ⊡	HC	GW ◇1 E Ø		GW 1	GW 1	GW ◇1 ⊡	GW ◇1 ⊡
London Paddington 15 ⊖	d	11 15	11 18	11 20		11 27		11 30	11 33	11 42	11 45	11 45	11 48	11 50		11 57		12 00	12 03	12 06		12 12	12 15	12 15	12 18
Acton Main Line	d										11 51												12 21		
Ealing Broadway ⊖	d					11 35			11 41	11 50	11 54					12 05			12 11			12 20	12 24		
West Ealing	d								11 43		11 57								12 13				12 27		
Drayton Green	d										11 59												12 29		
Castle Bar Park	d										12 01												12 31		
South Greenford	d										12 04												12 34		
Greenford ⊖	a										12 09												12 39		
Hanwell	d								11 45										12 15						
Southall	d								11 49	11 58									12 19			12 28			
Hayes & Harlington	d					11 42			11 53	12 02						12 12			12 23			12 32			
Heathrow Terminal 1-2-3 2 ✈	a								12 05										12 35						
Heathrow Terminal 4 ✈	a																								
West Drayton	d					11 46				12 06						12 16						12 36			
Iver	d					11 49										12 19									
Langley	d				←	11 52									←	12 22									
Slough 3	a			11 36	11 43	11 57				12 13				12 06	12 13	12 27						12 43			
	d			11 36	11 43	11 57				12 13				12 06	12 13	12 27						12 43			
Burnham	d				11 47					→					12 17							→			
Taplow	d				11 51										12 21										
Maidenhead 3	d				11 55	12 04									12 25	12 34									
Twyford 3	d				12 03	12 12									12 33	12 42									
Reading 7	a	11 39	11 47	11 52	12 17	12 22		11 56				12 09	12 14	12 22	12 45	12 50		12 25		12 30				12 39	12 46
Oxford	a			12 18		13 14								12 48		13 41									

A The Torbay Express
B The Cornish Riveira
C The Mayflower
D The Cheltenham Spa Express
E The Royal Duchy

London - Greenford and Reading

Network Diagram - see first Page of Table 116

		GW ◇■ ⊼	GW ■	GW ■	GW ◇■ ☐	HC	GW ■	GW ■	GW ◇■ Ø	GW ◇■ ⊼	GW ■	GW ■	GW ◇■ ☐	HC	GW FX ◇■ Ø	GW FO ◇■ Ø	GW ■	GW ■	GW ◇■ ☐	GW ■	GW ◇■ ⊼	GW ■
London Paddington 15 ⊖	d	12 21		12 27	12 30	12 33	12 42	12 45	12 45	12 50		12 57	13 00	13 03	13 06	13 06	13 12	13 15	13 15	13 18	13 21	
Acton Main Line	d							12 51										13 21				
Ealing Broadway ⊖	d			12 35		12 41	12 50	12 54				13 05		13 11			13 20	13 24				
West Ealing	d					12 43		12 57						13 13				13 27				
Drayton Green	d							12 59										13 29				
Castle Bar Park	d							13 01										13 31				
South Greenford	d							13 04										13 34				
Greenford ⊖	a							13 10										13 39				
Hanwell	d					12 45								13 15								
Southall	d					12 49	12 58							13 19			13 28					
Hayes & Harlington	d			12 42		12 53	13 02					13 12		13 23			13 32					
Heathrow Terminal 1-2-3 2 ✈	a					13 05								13 35								
Heathrow Terminal 4 ✈	a																					
West Drayton	d			12 46			13 06					13 16					13 36					
Iver	d			12 49								13 19										
Langley	d		←	12 52							←	13 22										←
Slough 3	a	12 36	12 43	12 57			13 13			13 06	13 13	13 27					13 43				13 36	13 43
	d	12 36	12 43	12 57			13 13			13 06	13 13	13 27					13 43				13 36	13 43
Burnham	d		12 47				→				13 17						→					13 47
Taplow	d		12 51								13 21											13 51
Maidenhead 3	d		12 55	13 04							13 25	13 34										13 55
Twyford 3	d		13 03	13 12							13 33	13 42										14 03
Reading 7	a	12 51	13 14	13 22	12 56				13 09	13 22	13 45	13 51	13 25		13 30				13 39	13 47	13 52	14 12
Oxford	a	13 18		14 14						13 50		14 42									14 18	

		GW ■	GW ◇■ ☐	HC	GW ■	GW ■	GW ◇■ ☐	GW ◇■ ☐	GW ◇■ ⊼	GW ■	GW ■	GW ◇■ ☐	HC	GW ◇■ Ø	GW ■	GW ■	GW ◇■ ☐	GW ■	GW ◇■ ⊼	GW ■	GW ■	GW ◇■ ☐
London Paddington 15 ⊖	d	13 27	13 30	13 33	13 42	13 45	13 45	13 48	13 50		13 57	14 00	14 03	14 06	14 12	14 15	14 15	14 18	14 21		14 27	14 30
Acton Main Line	d					13 51										14 21						
Ealing Broadway ⊖	d	13 35		13 41	13 50	13 54					14 05		14 11		14 20	14 24					14 35	
West Ealing	d			13 43		13 57							14 13			14 27						
Drayton Green	d					13 59										14 29						
Castle Bar Park	d					14 01										14 31						
South Greenford	d					14 04										14 34						
Greenford ⊖	a					14 09										14 39						
Hanwell	d			13 45									14 15									
Southall	d			13 49	13 58								14 19		14 28							
Hayes & Harlington	d	13 42		13 53	14 02						14 12		14 23		14 32						14 42	
Heathrow Terminal 1-2-3 2 ✈	a			14 05									14 35									
Heathrow Terminal 4 ✈	a																					
West Drayton	d	13 46			14 06						14 16				14 36						14 46	
Iver	d	13 49									14 19										14 49	
Langley	d	13 52								←	14 22									←	14 52	
Slough 3	a	13 57			14 13				14 06	14 13	14 27				14 43				14 36	14 43	14 57	
	d	13 57			14 13				14 06	14 13	14 27				14 43				14 36	14 43	14 57	
Burnham	d				→					14 17					→					14 47		
Taplow	d									14 21										14 51		
Maidenhead 3	d	14 04								14 25	14 34									14 55	15 04	
Twyford 3	d	14 12								14 33	14 42									15 03	15 12	
Reading 7	a	14 21	13 56				14 09	14 14	14 21	14 45	14 52	14 25		14 30			14 39	14 47	14 52	15 13	15 22	14 56
Oxford	a	15 14							14 48		15 41								15 18		16 14	

		HC	GW ■	GW ■	GW ◇■ ☐	GW ◇■ ⊼	GW ■	GW ■	GW ◇■ ☐	HC	GW ◇■ A Ø	GW ■	GW ■	GW ◇■ ☐	GW ■	GW ◇■ ⊼	GW ■	GW ■	GW ◇■ ☐	HC	GW ■
London Paddington 15 ⊖	d	14 33	14 42	14 45	14 45	14 50		14 57	15 00	15 03	15 06	15 12	15 15	15 15	15 18	15 22		15 27	15 30	15 33	15 42
Acton Main Line	d			14 51									15 21								
Ealing Broadway ⊖	d	14 41	14 50	14 54				15 05		15 11		15 20	15 24					15 35		15 41	15 50
West Ealing	d	14 43		14 57						15 13			15 27							15 43	
Drayton Green	d			14 59									15 29								
Castle Bar Park	d			15 01									15 31								
South Greenford	d			15 04									15 34								
Greenford ⊖	a			15 09									15 39								
Hanwell	d	14 45								15 15										15 45	
Southall	d	14 49	14 58							15 19		15 28						15 40		15 49	15 58
Hayes & Harlington	d	14 53	15 02					15 12		15 23		15 32						15 44		15 53	16 02
Heathrow Terminal 1-2-3 2 ✈	a	15 05								15 35										16 05	
Heathrow Terminal 4 ✈	a																				
West Drayton	d		15 06					15 16				15 36						15 48			16 06
Iver	d							15 19										15 51			
Langley	d						←	15 22									←	15 55			
Slough 3	a		15 13			15 06	15 13	15 27				15 43				15 36	15 43	15 59			16 13
	d		15 13			15 06	15 13	15 27				15 43				15 36	15 43	15 59			16 13
Burnham	d		→				15 17					→					15 47				→
Taplow	d						15 21										15 51				
Maidenhead 3	d						15 25	15 34									15 55	16 07			
Twyford 3	d						15 33	15 42									16 03	16 15			
Reading 7	a				15 09	15 22	15 44	15 52	15 25		15 30			15 39	15 47	15 51	16 13	16 23	15 56		
Oxford	a					15 50		16 47								16 18		17 15			

A The Cornishman

London - Greenford and Reading

Network Diagram - see first Page of Table 116

		GW ■	GW ◇■ ☐	GW ◇■ ☐	GW ◇■ ☐	GW ■	GW ■	GW ◇■ ☐	HC	GW FX ◇■ ☐	GW FO ◇■ ☐	GW ■	GW ■	GW ◇■ ☐	GW ■	GW ◇■ ⊼	GW ■	GW ■	GW ◇■ ☐	HC	GW ◇■ ☐	GW ■	GW ■
London Paddington 15 ⊖	d	15 45	15 45	15 48	15 51		15 57	16 00	16 03	16 06	16 06	16 12	16 15	16 15	16 18	16 22		16 27	16 30	16 33	16 33	16 42	16 45
Acton Main Line	d	15 51											16 21										16 51
Ealing Broadway ⊖	d	15 54					16 05		16 11			16 20	16 24					16 35		16 41		16 50	16 54
West Ealing	d	15 57							16 13				16 27							16 43			16 57
Drayton Green	d	15 59											16 29										16 59
Castle Bar Park	d	16 01											16 31										17 01
South Greenford	d	16 04											16 34										17 04
Greenford ⊖	a	16 09											16 39										17 09
Hanwell	d								16 15											16 45			
Southall	d								16 19			16 28						16 40		16 49		16 58	
Hayes & Harlington	d						16 11		16 23			16 32						16 44		16 53		17 02	
Heathrow Terminal 1-2-3 2 ✈	a								16 35											17 05			
Heathrow Terminal 4 ✈	a																						
West Drayton	d						16 16					16 36										17 07	
Iver	d						16 19											16 49				17 10	
Langley	d					←	16 22										←	16 52				17 14	
Slough 3	a				16 06	16 13	16 27					16 44				16 37	16 44	16 57				17 18	
	d				16 06	16 13	16 27					16 45				16 38	16 45	16 57				17 18	
Burnham	d					16 17						→					16 50					→	
Taplow	d					16 21											16 54						
Maidenhead 3	d					16 25	16 34										16 59	17 04					
Twyford 3	d					16 33	16 42										17 07	17 12					
Reading 7	a		16 09	16 14	16 20	16 44	16 52	16 25		16 30				16 39	16 47	16 52	17 18	17 21	16 56		17 01		
Oxford	a				16 47		17 44									17 24		18 12					

		GW ◇■ A ☐	GW ◇■	GW ■	GW ■	GW ◇■ ☐	HC	GW ◇■ ☐	GW ◇■ ☐	GW ■	GW ■	GW ■	GW ◇■ B Ø	GW ■	GW ■	GW ◇■ ☐	GW ■	GW ◇■ ☐	HC	GW ◇■ ☐	GW ■	GW ■
London Paddington 15 ⊖	d	16 45	16 49		16 55	17 00	17 03	17 03	17 06		17 12	17 15	17 15	17 18	17 18	17 22	17 25	17 30	17 33	17 33		17 36
Acton Main Line	d													17 24								
Ealing Broadway ⊖	d				17 04		17 11					17 23		17 27			17 33		17 41			
West Ealing	d						17 13							17 30					17 43			
Drayton Green	d													17 32								
Castle Bar Park	d													17 34								
South Greenford	d													17 37								
Greenford ⊖	a													17 42								
Hanwell	d						17 15												17 45			
Southall	d						17 19					17 29					17 38		17 49			
Hayes & Harlington	d				17 11		17 23					17 33					17 42		17 53			
Heathrow Terminal 1-2-3 2 ✈	a						17 35												18 05			
Heathrow Terminal 4 ✈	a																					
West Drayton	d				17 16							17 38					17 47					
Iver	d				17 20							17 41					17 50					
Langley	d			←	17 24							17 44					17 54					
Slough 3	a		17 04	17 18	17 27						17 32	17 49					17 58					
	d		17 04	17 18	17 28						17 35	17 49					17 58					
Burnham	d			17 22	17 33						17 40	17 53					18 02					
Taplow	d			17 26	17 36						17 43	17 57					18 06					
Maidenhead 3	d			17 30	17 43					←	17 47	18a05			17 40		18 10				←	17 58
Twyford 3	d			17 38	17 51				17 28	17 38	17a57				17 48		18 17				17 51	18 07
Reading 7	a	17 09	17 19	→	→	17 24		17 29	17 35	17 46			17 40		17 56	17 49	→	17 54		17 59	18 00	18 15
Oxford	a		17 50												18 45	18 15						19 04

		GW ■	GW ◇■ ☐	GW ■	GW ■	GW ◇■ ☐	GW ◇■ ☐	GW ■	GW ◇■ C ☐	GW ■	HC	GW FX ◇■ D ✕	GW ◇■ ☐	GW ■	GW ■	GW ◇■ ☐	GW ■	GW ■	GW ■	GW ◇■ E ☐	GW FO ■
London Paddington 15 ⊖	d	17 42	17 45	17 45	17 48	17 48	17 50	17 57	18 00		18 03	18 03	18 06		18 12	18 15	18 15	18 18	18 18	18 22	18 25
Acton Main Line	d				17 54													18 24			
Ealing Broadway ⊖	d			17 53	17 57			18 05			18 11						18 23	18 27			18 33
West Ealing	d				18 00						18 13							18 30			
Drayton Green	d				18 02													18 32			
Castle Bar Park	d				18 04													18 34			
South Greenford	d				18 07													18 37			
Greenford ⊖	a				18 12													18 42			
Hanwell	d										18 15										
Southall	d			17 59				18 10			18 19						18 29				18 38
Hayes & Harlington	d			18 03				18 14			18 23						18 33				18 42
Heathrow Terminal 1-2-3 2 ✈	a										18 35										
Heathrow Terminal 4 ✈	a																				
West Drayton	d			18 08				18 19									18 38				18 46
Iver	d							18 22													18 49
Langley	d			18 12				18 26									18 42				18 52
Slough 3	a	18 04		18 16				18 30							18 35		18 47				18 59
	d	18 05		18 16				18 30							18 36		18 47				18 59
Burnham	d			18 21				18 35									18 51				→
Taplow	d							18 39													
Maidenhead 3	d	18a13		18 26			18 09	18 45		←				←	18 49		18 57		18 40		
Twyford 3	d			18 34				18 52		18 17			18 28	18 34	18a58		19 05		18 48		
Reading 7	a		18 09	→		18 14	18 20	→	18 25	18 26		18 30	18 35	18 44		18 40	→		18 56	18 49	
Oxford	a						18 47			19 17									19 43	19 20	

A The Capitals United
B The Red Dragon
C The Bristolian
D The Golden Hind
E The Cathedrals Express

London - Greenford and Reading

Network Diagram - see first Page of Table 116

		GW	GW	HC	GW	GW	GW	GW		GW	GW	GW	GW	GW	GW	GW	GW	GW		GW		HC	GW	GW	GW
		FX											FO	FX											FO
		■1	◇■1 ☕		◇■1 ☕	■1	■1	◇■1 ☕		■1	■1	◇■1 ☕	■1	■1	■1	◇■1 ⌶	■1	■1		◇■1 ☕			■1 A ✕	■1	■1
London Paddington 15 ⊖	d	18 25	18 30	18 33	18 33		18 36	18 45			18 45	18 47			18 48	18 51		18 57		19 00		19 03	19 03	19 06	19 12
Acton Main Line	d														18 54										
Ealing Broadway ⊖	d	18 33		18 41							18 53				18 57			19 05				19 11			
West Ealing	d			18 43											19 00							19 13			
Drayton Green	d														19 02										
Castle Bar Park	d														19 04										
South Greenford	d														19 07										
Greenford ⊖	a														19 12										
Hanwell	d			18 45																		19 15			
Southall	d	18 38		18 49							18 59							19 10				19 19			
Hayes & Harlington	d	18 42		18 53							19 03							19 14				19 23			
Heathrow Terminal 1-2-3 2 ✈	a			19 05																		19 35			
Heathrow Terminal 4 ✈	a																								
West Drayton	d	18 46																19 19							
Iver	d	18 49																19 22							
Langley	d	18 52											←	←			←	19 26							
Slough 3	a	18 59					18 54				19 11		18 59	18 59		19 06	19 11	19 30							
	d	18 59					18 55				19 11		18 59	18 59		19 06	19 11	19 30							
Burnham	d	→									→		19 03	19 03			19 15	19 34							
Taplow	d												19 06	19 06				19 38							
Maidenhead 3	d					←	19a03			←			19 10	19 10			19 21	19 43						19 27	
Twyford 3	d					18 52				19 05		19 09	19 18	19 18			19 38	19 51						19a38	
Reading 7	a		18 54		18 59	19 01		19 09		19 13		19 17	19 26	19 26		19 22	19 47	→		19 27			19 32		19 41
Oxford	a									20 13			20 18	20 27		19 48									20 28

		GW	GW	GW		GW	GW	GW	GW	GW	GW	GW	GW	HC		GW	GW	GW	GW	GW	GW	GW	GW	HC	
				FX		FO		FX	FO																
		■1	■1	◇■1 ☕		◇■1 ☕	■1	◇■1 ☕	◇■1 ☕	■1	■1	■1	◇■1 ☕			■1	■1	◇■1 ☕	◇■1 ☕	◇■1 ⌶	■1	■1	◇■1 ☕		
London Paddington 15 ⊖	d	19 12	19 15	19 15		19 15	19 18	19 22	19 22			19 27	19 30	19 33		19 42	19 45	19 45	19 48	19 50		19 57	20 00	20 03	
Acton Main Line	d		19 21														19 51								
Ealing Broadway ⊖	d	19 20	19 24									19 35		19 41		19 50	19 54					20 05		20 11	
West Ealing	d		19 27											19 43			19 57							20 13	
Drayton Green	d		19 29														19 59								
Castle Bar Park	d		19 31														20 01								
South Greenford	d		19 34														20 04								
Greenford ⊖	a		19 39														20 09								
Hanwell	d													19 45										20 15	
Southall	d	19 28										19 40		19 49		19 58								20 19	
Hayes & Harlington	d	19 32										19 44		19 53		20 02						20 12		20 23	
Heathrow Terminal 1-2-3 2 ✈	a													20 05										20 35	
Heathrow Terminal 4 ✈	a																								
West Drayton	d											19 48				20 06						20 16			
Iver	d											19 51				20 09						20 19			
Langley	d										←	19 55				20 13					←	20 22			
Slough 3	a	19 41						19 36	19 36		19 41	19 59				20 17				20 06	20 17	20 27			
	d	19 41						19 36	19 36		19 41	19 59				20 17				20 06	20 17	20 27			
Burnham	d	→									19 45	20 03				→					20 20				
Taplow	d										19 48										20 25				
Maidenhead 3	d						19 40			←	19 52	20 09							20 06		20 29	20 34			
Twyford 3	d						19 48			19 51	20 00	20 17									20 37	20 42			
Reading 7	a			19 39			19 56	19 51	19 51	20 00	20 11	20 23	19 56					20 09	20 17	20 22	20 45	20 52	20 25		
Oxford	a						20 45	20 18	20 21			21 14								20 47		21 43			

		GW	GW	GW	GW	GW	GW	HC	GW	GW		GW	GW	GW	GW	GW	HC	GW	GW	GW		GW	GW	HC	GW
		■1	■1	◇■1 Ø	◇■1 ⌶	■1	■1		◇■1 ☕	■1		■1	◇■1 ☕	◇■1	■1	■1		■1	◇■1 ☕	■1		◇■1	■1		■1
London Paddington 15 ⊖	d	20 12	20 15	20 15	20 20		20 27	20 33	20 35	20 42		20 45	20 45	20 48		20 57	21 03	21 12	21 15	21 15		21 18	21 27	21 33	21 42
Acton Main Line	d		20 21									20 51								21 21					21 48
Ealing Broadway ⊖	d	20 20	20 24				20 35	20 41		20 50		20 54				21 05	21 11	21 20		21 24			21 35	21 41	21 51
West Ealing	d		20 27					20 43				20 57					21 13			21 27				21 43	
Drayton Green	d		20 29									20 59								21 29					
Castle Bar Park	d		20 31									21 01								21 31					
South Greenford	d		20 34									21 04								21 34					
Greenford ⊖	a		20 39									21 09								21 39					
Hanwell	d							20 45									21 15							21 45	
Southall	d	20 28						20 49		20 58							21 19	21 28					21 42	21 49	21 58
Hayes & Harlington	d	20 32					20 42	20 53		21 02						21 12	21 23	21 32					21 46	21 53	22 02
Heathrow Terminal 1-2-3 2 ✈	a							21 05									21 35							22 05	
Heathrow Terminal 4 ✈	a																								
West Drayton	d	20 36					20 46			21 06						21 16		21 36					21 50		22 06
Iver	d						20 49									21 19							21 53		
Langley	d					←	20 52								←	21 22							21 57		
Slough 3	a	20 43			20 35	20 43	20 57			21 13				21 04	21 13	21 27		21 43				21 34	22 02		22 14
	d	20 43			20 36	20 43	20 57			21 13				21 05	21 13	21 27		21 43				21 35	22 07		22 15
Burnham	d	→				20 47				→					21 17			→					→		→
Taplow	d					20 51									21 21										
Maidenhead 3	d					20 55	21 04								21 25	21 34									
Twyford 3	d					21 03	21 12								21 33	21 42									
Reading 7	a			20 39	20 50	21 13	21 20		20 59				21 09	21 20	21 44	21 51			21 39			21 50			
Oxford	a				21 19		22 14							21 51		22 41						22 18			

A The Armada

Table 117

Mondays to Fridays

from 17 September

London - Greenford and Reading

Network Diagram - see first Page of Table 116

		GW	GW	GW	GW	GW		GW	HC	GW	GW	GW	GW	GW	GW	GW		GW	HC	GW	GW	GW	GW	GW	GW
				FO	FX					FO		FX	FO	FX	FO	FX				FO	FO	FX	FX		
		◇■1 ☕	■1	◇■1 ⌶	◇■1 ☕	■1		■1		◇■1 ☕	■1	◇■1 ☕	■1	■1	◇■1	◇■1		■1		◇■1 ☕	■1	■1	◇■1 ☕	■1	◇■1
London Paddington 15 ⊖	d	21 45		21 48	21 48			21 58	22 03	22 15		22 15	22 16	22 16	22 18	22 18			22 33	22 45			22 45	22 45	22 48
Acton Main Line	d																							22 51	
Ealing Broadway ⊖	d							22 06	22 11				22 24	22 24					22 41					22 54	
West Ealing	d								22 13										22 43						
Drayton Green	d																								
Castle Bar Park	d																								
South Greenford	d																								
Greenford ⊖	a																								
Hanwell	d								22 15										22 45						
Southall	d								22 19				22 29	22 29					22 49						
Hayes & Harlington	d							22 13	22 23				22 33	22 33					22 53					23 01	
Heathrow Terminal 1-2-3 2 ✈	a								22 35										23 05						
Heathrow Terminal 4 ✈	a																								
West Drayton	d							22 17					22 37	22 37											
Iver	d							22 20																	
Langley	d		←			←		22 23			←							←			←	←			
Slough 3	a		21 43	22 03	22 03	22 02		22 28			22 14		22 45	22 45	22 35	22 36		22 28			22 45	22 45		23 11	23 06
	d		21 43	22 03	22 03	22 07		22 39			22 15		22 45	22 45	22 36	22 37		22 39			22 45	22 45		23 12	23 06
Burnham	d		21 47					→			22 18		→	→							22 49	22 49		→	
Taplow	d		21 51								22 22										22 53	22 53			
Maidenhead 3	d		21 55			22 14					22 26				22 44	22 45		22 47			22 57	22 57			23 14
Twyford 3	d		22 03			22 22					22 34							22 55			23 05	23 05			
Reading 7	a	22 09	22 15	22 22	22 22	22 30				22 39	22 46	22 48			22 58	22 58		23 04		23 09	23 14	23 16	23 18		23 28
Oxford	a			22 47	22 47	23 21									23 28	23 28		23 48							23 56

		GW		GW	HC	GW	GW	GW	GW	GW	GW			GW
							FX	FO	FX	FO	FO			
		■1		■1		◇■1	■1	■1	◇■1 ☕	◇■1 ☕	■1			■1
London Paddington 15 ⊖	d			22 59	23 03	23 18	23 29	23 29	23 30	23 30	23 42			23 48
Acton Main Line	d													23 54
Ealing Broadway ⊖	d			23 07	23 11		23 37	23 37						23 57
West Ealing	d				23 13									23 59
Drayton Green	d													
Castle Bar Park	d													
South Greenford	d													
Greenford ⊖	a													
Hanwell	d				23 15									00 02
Southall	d			23 12	23 19									00 06
Hayes & Harlington	d			23 16	23 23		23 44	23 44						00 10
Heathrow Terminal 1-2-3 2 ✈	a				23 35									
Heathrow Terminal 4 ✈	a				23 41									
West Drayton	d			23 20										00 14
Iver	d			23 23										00 17
Langley	d	←		23 27										00 21
Slough 3	a	23 11		23 32		23 36	23 53	23 53			23 58			00 26
	d	23 12		23 32		23 36	23 54	23 54			23 58			00 26
Burnham	d	23 16												00 30
Taplow	d	23 20												00 34
Maidenhead 3	d	23 24		23 40		23 44	00 01	00 01			00 08			00 41
Twyford 3	d	23 32		23 48			00 09	00 09						00 48
Reading 7	a	23 41		23 58		23 58	00 19	00 19	00 03	00 05	00 21			00 57
Oxford	a	00 26				00 28	01 15	01 16			01 02			

Table 117

London - Greenford and Reading

Saturdays until 23 June

Network Diagram - see first Page of Table 116

	GW	GW	GW	GW	GW	GW	GW	GW	GW	GW	GW	HC	HC	GW	GW	HC	GW	GW	GW	HC	GW	GW
	1	◇1	1	1	◇1 ⊡	1	1	◇1	1	1	1			◇1	1		1	◇1	1		1	1
London Paddington 15 ⊖ d	22p45	23p18		23p29	23p30	23p42	23p48	00 22	00 34	01 44	03 34	04 42	05 13	05 21	05 25	05 33	05 45	05 50	05 57	06 03	06 12	06 15
Acton Main Line d	22p51						23p54										05 51					06 21
Ealing Broadway ⊖ d	22p54			23p37			23p57		00 42	01 52	03 42	04 50	05 21		05 33	05 41	05 54		06 05	06 11	06 20	06 24
West Ealing d							23p59									05 43	05 57			06 13		06 27
Drayton Green d																	05 59					06 29
Castle Bar Park d																	06 01					06 31
South Greenford d																	06 04					06 34
Greenford ⊖ a																	06 09					06 39
Hanwell d							00 02									05 45				06 15		
Southall d							00 06		00 47	01 57	03 47	04 54	05 25		05 38	05 49			06 10	06 19	06 28	
Hayes & Harlington d	23p01			23p44			00 10		00 51	02 01	03 51	04 58	05 29		05 42	05 53			06 14	06 23	06 32	
Heathrow Terminal 1-2-3 2 ✈ a												05 04	05 35			06 05				06 35		
Heathrow Terminal 4 ✈ a												05 10	05 41									
West Drayton d							00 14		00 55	02 05	03 55								06 18		06 36	
Iver d							00 17												06 21			
Langley d							00 21		01 00										06 25			
Slough 3 a	23p11	23p36		23p53		23p58	00 26	00 38	01 05	02 13	04 03			05 37	05 50			06 06	06 30		06 43	
d	23p12	23p36		23p54		23p58	00 26	00 39	01 05	02 13	04 03			05 38	05 51			06 06	06 31		06 43	
Burnham d	23p16						00 30		01 09						05 55				06 35		→	
Taplow d	23p20						00 34		01 13						05 58				06 38			
Maidenhead 3 d	23p24	23p44		00 01		00 08	00 41		01 16	02 21	04 11				06 02				06 42			
Twyford 3 d	23p32		00 07	00 09			00 48		01 24	02 29	04 19				06 10				06 50			
Reading 7 a	23p41	23p58	00 16	00 19	00 05	00 21	00 57	00 55	01 35	02 38	04 30			05 52	06 17			06 22	06 56			
Oxford a	00 26	00 28		01 16		01 02		01 28						06 22	07 03			06 52	07 43			

	GW	GW	GW	GW	HC	GW	GW	GW	GW	GW	GW	HC	GW	GW	GW	GW	GW	GW	HC	GW	GW	GW
	◇1	1	1	◇1 ⊡		1	1	◇1	1	1	◇1 ⊡		1	1	◇1	1	1	▪1 ⊡		▪1 ⊡	1	1
London Paddington 15 ⊖ d	06 21		06 27	06 30	06 33	06 42	06 45	06 50		06 57	07 00	07 03	07 12	07 15	07 21		07 27	07 30	07 33	07 36	07 42	07 45
Acton Main Line d							06 51							07 21								07 51
Ealing Broadway ⊖ d			06 35		06 41	06 50	06 54			07 05		07 11	07 20	07 24			07 35		07 41		07 50	07 54
West Ealing d					06 43		06 57					07 13		07 27					07 43			07 57
Drayton Green d							06 59							07 29								07 59
Castle Bar Park d							07 01							07 31								08 01
South Greenford d							07 04							07 34								08 04
Greenford ⊖ a							07 09							07 39								08 09
Hanwell d					06 45							07 15							07 45			
Southall d					06 49	06 58						07 19	07 28						07 49		07 58	
Hayes & Harlington d			06 42		06 53	07 02				07 12		07 23	07 32				07 42		07 53		08 02	
Heathrow Terminal 1-2-3 2 ✈ a					07 05							07 35							08 05			
Heathrow Terminal 4 ✈ a																						
West Drayton d			06 46			07 06				07 16			07 36				07 46				08 06	
Iver d			06 49							07 19							07 49					
Langley d		←	06 52						←	07 22						←	07 52					
Slough 3 a	06 37	06 43	06 57			07 13		07 06	07 13	07 27			07 43		07 37	07 43	07 57				08 13	
d	06 38	06 43	06 57			07 13		07 06	07 13	07 27			07 43		07 38	07 43	07 57				08 13	
Burnham d		06 47				→			07 17				→			07 47					→	
Taplow d		06 51							07 21							07 51						
Maidenhead 3 d		06 55	07 04						07 25	07 34						07 55	08 04					
Twyford 3 d		07 03	07 12						07 33	07 42						08 03	08 12					
Reading 7 a	06 53	07 13	07 20	06 57				07 22	07 43	07 52	07 26				07 53	08 13	08 22	07 57				
Oxford a	07 18		08 09					07 48		08 40					08 19		09 14					

	GW	GW	GW	GW	GW	HC	GW	GW	GW	GW	GW	GW	GW	GW	HC	GW	GW	GW	GW	GW	GW
	◇1 ⊡	◇1	1	1	◇1 ⊡		1	1	◇1 ⊡	1	◇1 ⊡	1	1	◇1 ⊡		▪1 A ⊡	1	1	◇1 ⊡	◇1	1
London Paddington 15 ⊖ d	07 45	07 50		07 57	08 00	08 03	08 12	08 15	08 15	08 18	08 21		08 27	08 30	08 33	08 35	08 42	08 45	08 45	08 50	
Acton Main Line d								08 21										08 51			
Ealing Broadway ⊖ d				08 05		08 11	08 20	08 24					08 35		08 41		08 50	08 54			
West Ealing d						08 13		08 27							08 43			08 57			
Drayton Green d								08 29										08 59			
Castle Bar Park d								08 31										09 01			
South Greenford d								08 34										09 04			
Greenford ⊖ a								08 39										09 09			
Hanwell d						08 15									08 45						
Southall d						08 19	08 28								08 49		08 58				
Hayes & Harlington d				08 12		08 23	08 32						08 42		08 53		09 02				
Heathrow Terminal 1-2-3 2 ✈ a						08 35									09 05						
Heathrow Terminal 4 ✈ a																					
West Drayton d				08 16			08 36						08 46				09 06				
Iver d				08 19									08 49								
Langley d			←	08 22								←	08 52								←
Slough 3 a		08 06	08 13	08 27			08 43				08 38	08 43	08 57				09 13			09 06	09 13
d		08 06	08 13	08 27			08 43				08 39	08 43	08 57				09 13			09 06	09 13
Burnham d			08 17				→					08 47					→				09 17
Taplow d			08 21									08 51									09 21
Maidenhead 3 d			08 25	08 34								08 55	09 04								09 25
Twyford 3 d			08 33	08 42								09 03	09 12								09 33
Reading 7 a	08 09	08 22	08 43	08 52	08 26				08 40	08 48	08 53	09 13	09 23	08 56					09 10	09 22	09 43
Oxford a		08 48		09 40							09 18		10 14							09 48	

A The Torbay Express

Table 117

London - Greenford and Reading

Saturdays until 23 June

Network Diagram - see first Page of Table 116

	GW	GW	HC	GW	GW	GW	GW	GW	GW	GW	GW	HC	GW	GW	GW	GW	GW	GW	GW	HC	GW	GW
	1	◇1 ⊡		▪1 ⌀	1	1	1	◇1	1	1	◇1 ⊡		1	1	◇1 ⊡	◇1	1	1	◇1 ⊡		▪1 ⌀	1
London Paddington 15 ⊖ d	08 57	09 00	09 03	09 06	09 12	09 15	09 18	09 21		09 27	09 30	09 33	09 42	09 45	09 45	09 50		09 57	10 00	10 03	10 06	10 12
Acton Main Line d						09 21								09 51								
Ealing Broadway ⊖ d	09 05		09 11		09 20	09 24				09 35		09 41	09 50	09 54				10 05		10 11		10 20
West Ealing d			09 13			09 27						09 43		09 57						10 13		
Drayton Green d						09 29								09 59								
Castle Bar Park d						09 31								10 01								
South Greenford d						09 34								10 04								
Greenford ⊖ a						09 39								10 09								
Hanwell d			09 15									09 45								10 15		
Southall d			09 19		09 28							09 49	09 58							10 19		10 28
Hayes & Harlington d	09 12		09 23		09 32					09 42		09 53	10 02					10 12		10 23		10 32
Heathrow Terminal 1-2-3 2 ✈ a			09 35									10 05								10 35		
Heathrow Terminal 4 ✈ a																						
West Drayton d	09 16				09 36					09 46			10 06					10 16				10 36
Iver d	09 19									09 49								10 19				
Langley d	09 22								←	09 52							←	10 22				
Slough 3 a	09 27				09 43			09 38	09 43	09 57			10 13			10 06	10 13	10 27				10 43
d	09 27				09 43			09 39	09 43	09 57			10 13			10 06	10 13	10 27				10 43
Burnham d					→				09 47				→				10 17					→
Taplow d									09 51								10 21					
Maidenhead 3 d	09 34								09 55	10 04							10 25	10 34				
Twyford 3 d	09 42								10 03	10 12							10 33	10 42				
Reading 7 a	09 52	09 26		09 31			09 48	09 54	10 13	10 22	09 57				10 09	10 22	10 43	10 52	10 26		10 31	
Oxford a	10 40							10 19		11 14						10 48		11 40				

	GW	GW	GW	GW	GW	GW	GW	HC	GW	GW	GW	GW	GW	GW	GW	GW	HC	GW	GW	GW	GW
	1	◇1 ⊡	1	◇1 ⊡	1	1	◇1 ⊡		▪1 ⊡	1	1	◇1 ⌀	◇1 ✕	1	1	◇1 ⊡		▪1 ⌀	1	1	1
London Paddington 15 ⊖ d	10 15	10 15	10 18	10 21		10 27	10 30	10 33	10 35	10 42	10 45	10 45	10 50		10 57	11 00	11 03	11 06	11 12	11 15	11 18
Acton Main Line d	10 21										10 51									11 21	
Ealing Broadway ⊖ d	10 24					10 35		10 41		10 52	10 54				11 05		11 11		11 20	11 24	
West Ealing d	10 27							10 43			10 57						11 13			11 27	
Drayton Green d	10 29										10 59									11 29	
Castle Bar Park d	10 31										11 01									11 31	
South Greenford d	10 34										11 04									11 34	
Greenford ⊖ a	10 39										11 09									11 39	
Hanwell d								10 45									11 15				
Southall d								10 49		10 58							11 19		11 28		
Hayes & Harlington d						10 42		10 53		11 02					11 12		11 23		11 32		
Heathrow Terminal 1-2-3 2 ✈ a								11 05									11 35				
Heathrow Terminal 4 ✈ a																					
West Drayton d						10 46				11 06					11 16				11 36		
Iver d						10 49									11 19						
Langley d					←	10 52								←	11 22						
Slough 3 a				10 38	10 43	10 57				11 13			11 06	11 13	11 27				11 43		
d				10 39	10 43	10 57				11 13			11 06	11 13	11 27				11 43		
Burnham d					10 47					→				11 17					→		
Taplow d					10 51									11 21							
Maidenhead 3 d					10 55	11 04								11 25	11 34						
Twyford 3 d					11 03	11 12								11 33	11 42						
Reading 7 a		10 40	10 48	10 53	11 13	11 22	10 57		11 02			11 09	11 22	11 43	11 52	11 26		11 31			11 48
Oxford a				11 19		12 14							11 48		12 40						

	GW	GW	GW	GW	HC	GW	GW	GW	GW	GW	GW	GW	GW	HC	GW	GW	GW	GW	GW	GW	GW	GW
	◇1 ✕	1	1	◇1 ⌀		▪1 ⊡	1	1	◇1 ⌀	◇1	1	1	◇1 ⊡		▪1 ⌀	1	1	◇1 ⊡	1	◇1	1	1
London Paddington 15 ⊖ d	11 21		11 27	11 30	11 33	11 35	11 42	11 45	11 45	11 50		11 57	12 00	12 03	12 06	12 12	12 15	12 15	12 18	12 21		12 27
Acton Main Line d								11 51									12 21					
Ealing Broadway ⊖ d			11 35		11 41		11 50	11 54				12 05		12 11		12 20	12 24					12 35
West Ealing d					11 43			11 57						12 13			12 27					
Drayton Green d								11 59									12 29					
Castle Bar Park d								12 01									12 31					
South Greenford d								12 04									12 34					
Greenford ⊖ a								12 09									12 39					
Hanwell d					11 45									12 15								
Southall d					11 49		11 58							12 19		12 28						
Hayes & Harlington d			11 42		11 53		12 02					12 12		12 23		12 32						12 42
Heathrow Terminal 1-2-3 2 ✈ a					12 05									12 35								
Heathrow Terminal 4 ✈ a																						
West Drayton d			11 46				12 06					12 16				12 36						12 46
Iver d			11 49									12 19										12 49
Langley d		←	11 52								←	12 22									←	12 52
Slough 3 a	11 38	11 43	11 57				12 13			12 06	12 13	12 27				12 43				12 38	12 43	12 57
d	11 39	11 43	11 57				12 13			12 06	12 13	12 27				12 43				12 39	12 43	12 57
Burnham d		11 47					→				12 17					→					12 47	
Taplow d		11 51									12 21										12 51	
Maidenhead 3 d		11 55	12 04								12 25	12 34									12 55	13 04
Twyford 3 d		12 03	12 12								12 33	12 42									13 03	13 12
Reading 7 a	11 54	12 13	12 22	11 57		12 03			12 09	12 22	12 43	12 52	12 26		12 31			12 40	12 48	12 54	13 13	13 22
Oxford a	12 20		13 14							12 48		13 40								13 19		14 14

London - Greenford and Reading

Network Diagram - see first Page of Table 116

		GW	HC	GW	GW	GW	GW	GW	GW	GW	GW	HC	GW	GW	GW	GW	GW	GW	GW	GW	HC	GW	GW
		◇1 ⊡		1 ⊡	1	1	◇1 ⊡	◇1 ✕	1	1	◇1 ⊡		1 ⊡	1	1	1	◇1 ✕	1	1	◇1 ⊡		1	1
London Paddington 15 ⊖	d	12 30	12 33	12 35	12 42	12 45	12 45	12 50		12 57	13 00	13 03	13 06	13 12	13 15	13 18	13 21		13 27	13 30	13 33	13 42	13 45
Acton Main Line	d					12 51									13 21								13 51
Ealing Broadway ⊖	d		12 41		12 50	12 54				13 05		13 11		13 20	13 24				13 35		13 41	13 50	13 54
West Ealing	d		12 43			12 57						13 13			13 27						13 43		13 57
Drayton Green	d					12 59									13 29								13 59
Castle Bar Park	d					13 01									13 31								14 01
South Greenford	d					13 04									13 34								14 04
Greenford ⊖	a					13 09									13 39								14 09
Hanwell	d		12 45									13 15									13 45		
Southall	d		12 49		12 58							13 19		13 28							13 49	13 58	
Hayes & Harlington	d		12 53		13 02					13 12		13 23		13 32					13 42		13 53	14 02	
Heathrow Terminal 1-2-3 2 ✈	a		13 05									13 35									14 05		
Heathrow Terminal 4 ✈	a																						
West Drayton	d				13 06					13 16				13 36					13 46			14 06	
Iver	d									13 19									13 49				
Langley	d								←	13 22								←	13 52				
Slough 3	a				13 13			13 06	13 13	13 27				13 43			13 38	13 43	13 57			14 13	
	d				13 13			13 06	13 13	13 27				13 43			13 39	13 43	13 57			14 13	
Burnham	d				→				13 17					→				13 47				→	
Taplow	d								13 21									13 51					
Maidenhead 3	d								13 25	13 34								13 55	14 04				
Twyford 3	d								13 33	13 42								14 03	14 12				
Reading 7	a	12 57		13 02			13 09	13 22	13 43	13 52	13 26		13 31			13 48	13 54	14 13	14 22	13 58			
Oxford	a							13 48		14 40							14 19		15 14				

		GW	GW	GW	GW	GW	HC	GW	GW	GW	GW	GW	GW	GW	GW	GW	HC	GW	GW	GW	GW	GW
		◇1 ⊡	◇1 ✕	1	1	◇1 ⊡		◇1 ⊡	1	1	◇1 ⊡	1	◇1 ✕	1	1	◇1 ⊡		1	1	◇1 ⊡	◇1	1
London Paddington 15 ⊖	d	13 45	13 50		13 57	14 00	14 03	14 06	14 12	14 15	14 15	14 18	14 21		14 27	14 30	14 33	14 42	14 45	14 45	14 50	
Acton Main Line	d									14 21									14 51			
Ealing Broadway ⊖	d				14 05		14 11		14 20	14 24					14 35		14 41	14 50	14 54			
West Ealing	d						14 13			14 27							14 43		14 57			
Drayton Green	d									14 29									14 59			
Castle Bar Park	d									14 31									15 01			
South Greenford	d									14 34									15 04			
Greenford ⊖	a									14 39									15 09			
Hanwell	d						14 15										14 45					
Southall	d						14 19		14 28								14 49	14 58				
Hayes & Harlington	d				14 12		14 23		14 32						14 42		14 53	15 02				
Heathrow Terminal 1-2-3 2 ✈	a						14 35										15 05					
Heathrow Terminal 4 ✈	a																					
West Drayton	d				14 16				14 36						14 46			15 06				
Iver	d				14 19										14 49							
Langley	d			←	14 22									←	14 52							←
Slough 3	a		14 06	14 13	14 27				14 43				14 38	14 43	14 57			15 13			15 06	15 13
	d		14 06	14 13	14 27				14 43				14 39	14 43	14 57			15 13			15 06	15 13
Burnham	d			14 17					→					14 47				→				15 17
Taplow	d			14 21										14 51								15 21
Maidenhead 3	d			14 25	14 34									14 55	15 04							15 25
Twyford 3	d			14 33	14 42									15 03	15 12							15 33
Reading 7	a	14 09	14 22	14 43	14 52	14 26		14 31			14 40	14 48	14 53	15 13	15 22	14 57				15 09	15 22	15 43
Oxford	a		14 48		15 40								15 18		16 14						15 48	

		GW	GW	HC	GW	GW	GW	GW	GW	GW	GW	GW	HC	GW	GW	GW	GW	GW	GW	GW	HC	GW	GW
		1	◇1 ⊡		◇1 ⊡	1	1	1	◇1 ✕	1	1	◇1 ⊡		1	1	◇1 ⊡	◇1	1	1	◇1 ⊡		◇1 ⊡	1
London Paddington 15 ⊖	d	14 57	15 00	15 03	15 06	15 12	15 15	15 18	15 21		15 27	15 30	15 33	15 42	15 45	15 45	15 50		15 57	16 00	16 03	16 06	16 12
Acton Main Line	d						15 21								15 51								
Ealing Broadway ⊖	d	15 05		15 11		15 20	15 24				15 35		15 41	15 50	15 54				16 05		16 11		16 20
West Ealing	d			15 13			15 27						15 43		15 57						16 13		
Drayton Green	d						15 29								15 59								
Castle Bar Park	d						15 31								16 01								
South Greenford	d						15 34								16 04								
Greenford ⊖	a						15 39								16 09								
Hanwell	d			15 15									15 45								16 15		
Southall	d			15 19		15 28							15 49	15 58							16 19		16 28
Hayes & Harlington	d	15 12		15 23		15 32					15 42		15 53	16 02					16 12		16 23		16 32
Heathrow Terminal 1-2-3 2 ✈	a			15 35									16 05								16 35		
Heathrow Terminal 4 ✈	a																						
West Drayton	d	15 16				15 36					15 46			16 06					16 16				16 36
Iver	d	15 19									15 49								16 19				
Langley	d	15 22								←	15 52							←	16 22				
Slough 3	a	15 27				15 43			15 38	15 43	15 57			16 13			16 06	16 13	16 27				16 43
	d	15 27				15 43			15 39	15 43	15 57			16 13			16 06	16 13	16 27				16 43
Burnham	d					→				15 47				→				16 17					→
Taplow	d									15 51								16 21					
Maidenhead 3	d	15 34								15 55	16 04							16 25	16 34				
Twyford 3	d	15 42								16 03	16 12							16 33	16 42				
Reading 7	a	15 52	15 26		15 31			15 48	15 54	16 13	16 22	15 58				16 09	16 22	16 43	16 52	16 26		16 31	
Oxford	a	16 40							16 19		17 14						16 48		17 40				

		GW	GW	GW	GW	GW	GW	GW	HC	GW	GW	GW	GW	GW	GW	GW	HC	GW	GW	GW	GW	GW
		1	◇1 ⊡	1	◇1 ⊡	1	1	◇1 ⊡		1	1	◇1 ⊡	◇1 ✕	1	1	◇1 ⊡		◇1 ⊡	1	1	1	◇1 ⊡
London Paddington 15 ⊖	d	16 15	16 15	16 18	16 21		16 27	16 30	16 33	16 42	16 45	16 45	16 50		16 57	17 00	17 03	17 06	17 12	17 15	17 18	17 21
Acton Main Line	d	16 21									16 51									17 21		
Ealing Broadway ⊖	d	16 24					16 35		16 41	16 50	16 54				17 05		17 11		17 20	17 24		
West Ealing	d	16 27							16 43		16 57						17 13			17 27		
Drayton Green	d	16 29									16 59									17 29		
Castle Bar Park	d	16 31									17 01									17 31		
South Greenford	d	16 34									17 04									17 34		
Greenford ⊖	a	16 39									17 09									17 39		
Hanwell	d								16 45								17 15					
Southall	d								16 49	16 58							17 19		17 28			
Hayes & Harlington	d						16 42		16 53	17 02					17 12		17 23		17 32			
Heathrow Terminal 1-2-3 2 ✈	a								17 05								17 35					
Heathrow Terminal 4 ✈	a																					
West Drayton	d						16 46			17 06					17 16				17 36			
Iver	d						16 49								17 19							
Langley	d					←	16 52							←	17 22							
Slough 3	a				16 38	16 43	16 57			17 13			17 06	17 13	17 27				17 43			17 38
	d				16 39	16 43	16 57			17 13			17 06	17 13	17 27				17 43			17 39
Burnham	d					16 47				→				17 17					→			
Taplow	d					16 51								17 21								
Maidenhead 3	d					16 55	17 04							17 25	17 34							
Twyford 3	d					17 03	17 12							17 33	17 42							
Reading 7	a		16 40	16 48	16 53	17 13	17 22	16 57				17 09	17 22	17 43	17 52	17 26		17 31			17 48	17 53
Oxford	a				17 18		18 14						17 48		18 40							18 18

		GW	GW	GW	HC	GW	GW	GW	GW	GW	GW	GW	HC	GW	GW	GW	GW	GW	GW	GW	GW	GW	HC
		1	1	◇1 ⊡		1	1	◇1 ⊡	◇1 ✕	1	1	◇1 ⊡		◇1 ⊡	1	1	◇1 ⊡	1	◇1 ⊡	1	1	◇1 ⊡	
London Paddington 15 ⊖	d		17 27	17 30	17 33	17 42	17 45	17 45	17 50		17 57	18 00	18 03	18 06	18 12	18 15	18 15	18 18	18 21		18 27	18 30	18 33
Acton Main Line	d						17 51									18 21							
Ealing Broadway ⊖	d		17 35		17 41	17 50	17 54				18 05		18 11		18 20	18 24					18 35		18 41
West Ealing	d				17 43		17 57						18 13			18 27							18 43
Drayton Green	d						17 59									18 29							
Castle Bar Park	d						18 01									18 31							
South Greenford	d						18 04									18 34							
Greenford ⊖	a						18 09									18 39							
Hanwell	d				17 45								18 15										18 45
Southall	d				17 49	17 58							18 19		18 28								18 49
Hayes & Harlington	d		17 42		17 53	18 02					18 12		18 23		18 32						18 42		18 53
Heathrow Terminal 1-2-3 2 ✈	a				18 05								18 35										19 05
Heathrow Terminal 4 ✈	a																						
West Drayton	d		17 46			18 06					18 16				18 36						18 46		
Iver	d		17 49								18 19										18 49		
Langley	d	←	17 52							←	18 22									←	18 52		
Slough 3	a	17 43	17 57			18 13			18 06	18 13	18 27				18 43				18 38	18 43	18 57		
	d	17 43	17 57			18 13			18 06	18 13	18 27				18 43				18 39	18 43	18 57		
Burnham	d	17 47				→				18 17					→					18 47			
Taplow	d	17 51								18 21										18 51			
Maidenhead 3	d	17 55	18 04							18 25	18 34									18 55	19 04		
Twyford 3	d	18 03	18 12							18 33	18 42									19 03	19 12		
Reading 7	a	18 13	18 22	17 57				18 09	18 22	18 43	18 52	18 27		18 31			18 40	18 48	18 53	19 13	19 23	18 57	
Oxford	a		19 14						18 48		19 40								19 18		20 14		

		GW	GW	GW	GW	GW	GW	GW	HC	GW	GW	GW	GW	GW	GW	GW	HC	GW	GW	GW	GW	GW	GW
		1	1	◇1 ⊡	◇1	1	1	◇1 ⊡		◇1 ⊡	1	1	◇1	1	1	◇1 ⊡		1	1	◇1 ⊡	◇1 ✕	1	1
London Paddington 15 ⊖	d	18 42	18 45	18 45	18 50		18 57	19 00	19 03	19 06	19 12	19 15	19 21		19 27	19 30	19 33	19 42	19 45	19 45	19 50		19 57
Acton Main Line	d		18 51									19 21							19 51				
Ealing Broadway ⊖	d	18 50	18 54				19 05		19 11		19 20	19 24			19 35		19 41	19 50	19 54				20 05
West Ealing	d		18 57						19 13			19 27					19 43		19 57				
Drayton Green	d		18 59									19 29							19 59				
Castle Bar Park	d		19 01									19 31							20 01				
South Greenford	d		19 04									19 34							20 04				
Greenford ⊖	a		19 09									19 39							20 09				
Hanwell	d								19 15								19 45						
Southall	d	18 58							19 19		19 28						19 49	19 58					
Hayes & Harlington	d	19 02					19 12		19 23		19 32				19 42		19 53	20 02					20 12
Heathrow Terminal 1-2-3 2 ✈	a								19 35								20 05						
Heathrow Terminal 4 ✈	a																						
West Drayton	d	19 06					19 16				19 36				19 46			20 06					20 16
Iver	d						19 19								19 49								20 19
Langley	d					←	19 22							←	19 52							←	20 22
Slough 3	a	19 13			19 06	19 13	19 27				19 43		19 37	19 43	19 57			20 13			20 06	20 13	20 27
	d	19 13			19 06	19 13	19 27				19 43		19 38	19 43	19 57			20 13			20 06	20 13	20 27
Burnham	d	→				19 17					→			19 47				→				20 17	
Taplow	d					19 21								19 51								20 21	
Maidenhead 3	d					19 25	19 34							19 55	20 04							20 25	20 34
Twyford 3	d					19 33	19 42							20 03	20 12							20 33	20 42
Reading 7	a			19 09	19 22	19 43	19 52	19 26		19 30			19 52	20 13	20 23	19 57				20 09	20 21	20 43	20 52
Oxford	a				19 48		20 40						20 20		21 14						20 47		21 40

Table 117

London - Greenford and Reading

Saturdays
until 23 June

Network Diagram - see first Page of Table 116

		GW		HC	GW	GW	GW	GW	GW	GW	GW	GW		HC	GW	GW	GW	GW	GW	GW	HC	GW		GW	GW
		◇1			◇1	1	1	◇1	◇1	1	1	◇1			1	◇1	1	◇1	1	1		1		1	◇1
		☕			☕			☕				☕				☕		✕							
London Paddington 15 ⊖	d	20 00		20 03	20 06	20 12	20 15	20 15	20 20		20 27	20 30		20 33	20 42	20 45	20 45	20 50		20 57	21 03	21 12		21 15	21 17
Acton Main Line	d						20 21										20 51							21 21	
Ealing Broadway ⊖	d			20 11		20 20	20 24				20 35			20 41	20 50		20 54			21 05	21 11	21 20		21 24	
West Ealing	d			20 13			20 27							20 43			20 57				21 13			21 27	
Drayton Green	d						20 29										20 59							21 29	
Castle Bar Park	d						20 31										21 01							21 31	
South Greenford	d						20 34										21 04							21 34	
Greenford ⊖	a						20 39										21 09							21 39	
Hanwell	d			20 15										20 45							21 15				
Southall	d			20 19		20 28								20 49	20 58						21 19	21 28			
Hayes & Harlington	d			20 23		20 32					20 42			20 53	21 02					21 12	21 23	21 32			
Heathrow Terminal 1-2-3 2 ✈	a			20 35										21 05							21 35				
Heathrow Terminal 4 ✈	a																								
West Drayton	d					20 36					20 46				21 06					21 16		21 36			
Iver	d										20 49									21 19					
Langley	d									←	20 52								←	21 22					
Slough 3	a					20 43			20 35	20 43	20 57				21 13			21 06	21 13	21 27		21 43			21 34
	d					20 43			20 35	20 43	20 57				21 13			21 06	21 13	21 27		21 43			21 35
Burnham	d					→				20 47					→				21 17			→			
Taplow	d									20 51									21 21						
Maidenhead 3	d									20 55	21 04								21 25	21 34					
Twyford 3	d									21 06	21 12								21 33	21 42					
Reading 7	a	20 27			20 31			20 40	20 51	21 14	21 22	20 57				21 09		21 22	21 43	21 52					21 51
Oxford	a								21 19		22 14							21 53		22 43					22 20

		GW	GW	HC	GW	GW	GW	GW		GW	HC	GW	GW	HC	GW	GW	GW	GW		GW	HC	GW	GW	GW	GW
		◇1	1		1	◇1	1	1		◇1		1	◇1		◇1	1	1	◇1		1		1	◇1	◇1	1
		☕								☕					☕								☕		
London Paddington 15 ⊖	d	21 30		21 33	21 42	21 50		21 57		22 00	22 03	22 12	22 15	22 33	22 35		22 45	23 00			23 03	23 20	23 30	23 33	
Acton Main Line	d				21 48												22 51								
Ealing Broadway ⊖	d			21 41	21 52			22 05			22 11	22 20		22 41			22 55				23 11	23 28			
West Ealing	d			21 43							22 13			22 43							23 13				
Drayton Green	d																								
Castle Bar Park	d																								
South Greenford	d																								
Greenford ⊖	a																								
Hanwell	d			21 45							22 15			22 45							23 15				
Southall	d			21 49	21 58						22 19	22 28		22 49			23 00				23 19	23 33			
Hayes & Harlington	d			21 53	22 02			22 12			22 23	22 32		22 53			23 04				23 23	23 37			
Heathrow Terminal 1-2-3 2 ✈	a			22 05							22 35			23 05							23 35				
Heathrow Terminal 4 ✈	a																				23 41				
West Drayton	d				22 06			22 16				22 36					23 08					23 41			
Iver	d							22 19									23 11					23 44			
Langley	d		←				←	22 22								←	23 14			←		23 48			←
Slough 3	a		21 43		22 13	22 06	22 13	22 27				22 43	22 31			22 43	23 19	23 16		23 19		23 53		23 49	23 53
	d		21 43		22 13	22 06	22 13	22 27				22 43	22 32			22 43	23 21	23 17		23 21		23 54		23 50	23 54
Burnham	d		21 47		→		22 17					→				22 47	→			23 25		→			23 57
Taplow	d		21 51				22 21									22 51									00 01
Maidenhead 3	d		21 55				22 25	22 34								22 55				23 32					00 05
Twyford 3	d		22 03				22 33	22 42								23 03				23 39					00 13
Reading 7	a	21 55	22 13			22 22	22 41	22 54		22 27			22 48		23 00	23 13		23 33		23 46			23 59	00 06	00 20
Oxford	a					22 50		23 38					23 20					00 04		00 32				00 38	01 05

		GW
		1
London Paddington 15 ⊖	d	23 42
Acton Main Line	d	
Ealing Broadway ⊖	d	23 50
West Ealing	d	
Drayton Green	d	
Castle Bar Park	d	
South Greenford	d	
Greenford ⊖	a	
Hanwell	d	
Southall	d	23 56
Hayes & Harlington	d	00 01
Heathrow Terminal 1-2-3 2 ✈	a	
Heathrow Terminal 4 ✈	a	
West Drayton	d	00 06
Iver	d	
Langley	d	
Slough 3	a	00 13
	d	00 14
Burnham	d	00 18
Taplow	d	00 21
Maidenhead 3	d	00 25
Twyford 3	d	00 33
Reading 7	a	00 43
Oxford	a	

Table 117

London - Greenford and Reading

Saturdays
30 June to 8 September

Network Diagram - see first Page of Table 116

		GW	GW	GW	GW	GW	GW	GW	GW	GW		GW	GW	HC	HC	GW	GW	HC	GW	GW		GW	HC	GW	GW
		1	◇1	1	1	◇1	1	1	◇1	1		1	1			◇1	1		1	◇1		1		1	1
						☕																			
London Paddington 15 ⊖	d	22p45	23p18		23p29	23p30	23p42	23p48	00 22	00 34		01 44	03 34	04 42	05 13	05 21	05 25	05 33	05 45	05 50		05 57	06 03	06 12	06 15
Acton Main Line	d	22p51						23p54											05 51						06 21
Ealing Broadway ⊖	d	22p54			23p37			23p57		00 42		01 52	03 42	04 50	05 21		05 33	05 41	05 54			06 05	06 11	06 20	06 24
West Ealing	d							23p59										05 43	05 57				06 13		06 27
Drayton Green	d																		05 59						06 29
Castle Bar Park	d																		06 01						06 31
South Greenford	d																		06 04						06 34
Greenford ⊖	a																		06 09						06 39
Hanwell	d							00 02										05 45					06 15		
Southall	d							00 06		00 47		01 57	03 47	04 54	05 25		05 38	05 49				06 10	06 19	06 28	
Hayes & Harlington	d	23p01			23p44			00 10		00 51		02 01	03 51	04 58	05 29		05 42	05 53				06 14	06 23	06 32	
Heathrow Terminal 1-2-3 2 ✈	a													05 04	05 35			06 05					06 35		
Heathrow Terminal 4 ✈	a													05 10	05 41										
West Drayton	d							00 14		00 55		02 05	03 55									06 18		06 36	
Iver	d							00 17														06 21			
Langley	d							00 21		01 00												06 25			
Slough 3	a	23p11	23p36		23p53		23p58	00 26	00 38	01 05		02 13	04 03			05 37	05 50			06 06		06 30		06 43	
	d	23p12	23p36		23p54		23p58	00 26	00 39	01 05		02 13	04 03			05 38	05 51			06 06		06 31		06 43	
Burnham	d	23p16						00 30		01 09							05 55					06 35		→	
Taplow	d	23p20						00 34		01 13							05 58					06 38			
Maidenhead 3	d	23p24	23p44		00 01		00 08	00 41		01 16		02 21	04 11				06 02					06 42			
Twyford 3	d	23p32		00 07	00 09			00 48		01 24		02 29	04 19				06 10					06 50			
Reading 7	a	23p41	23p58	00 16	00 19	00 05	00 21	00 57	00 55	01 35		02 38	04 30			05 52	06 17			06 22		06 56			
Oxford	a	00 26	00 28		01 16		01 02		01 28							06 22	07 03			06 52		07 43			

		GW	GW	GW	GW	HC		GW	GW	GW	GW	GW	GW	HC	GW	GW		GW	GW	GW	GW	HC	GW	GW	GW
		◇1	1	1	◇1			1	1	◇1	1	1	◇1		1	1		◇1	1	1	1		1	1	1
					☕								☕								☕		☕		
London Paddington 15 ⊖	d	06 21		06 27	06 30	06 33		06 42	06 45	06 50		06 57	07 00	07 03	07 12	07 15		07 21		07 27	07 30	07 33	07 36	07 42	07 45
Acton Main Line	d								06 51							07 21									07 51
Ealing Broadway ⊖	d			06 35		06 41		06 50	06 54			07 05		07 11	07 20	07 24				07 35		07 41		07 50	07 54
West Ealing	d					06 43			06 57					07 13		07 27						07 43			07 57
Drayton Green	d								06 59							07 29									07 59
Castle Bar Park	d								07 01							07 31									08 01
South Greenford	d								07 04							07 34									08 04
Greenford ⊖	a								07 09							07 39									08 09
Hanwell	d					06 45								07 15								07 45			
Southall	d					06 49		06 58						07 19	07 28							07 49		07 58	
Hayes & Harlington	d			06 42		06 53		07 02				07 12		07 23	07 32					07 42		07 53		08 02	
Heathrow Terminal 1-2-3 2 ✈	a					07 05								07 35								08 05			
Heathrow Terminal 4 ✈	a																								
West Drayton	d			06 46				07 06				07 16			07 36					07 46				08 06	
Iver	d			06 49								07 19								07 49					
Langley	d		←	06 52							←	07 22							←	07 52					
Slough 3	a	06 37	06 43	06 57				07 13		07 06	07 13	07 27			07 43			07 37	07 43	07 57				08 13	
	d	06 38	06 43	06 57				07 13		07 06	07 13	07 27			07 43			07 38	07 43	07 57				08 13	
Burnham	d		06 47					→			07 17				→				07 47					→	
Taplow	d		06 51								07 21								07 51						
Maidenhead 3	d		06 55	07 04							07 25	07 34							07 55	08 04					
Twyford 3	d		07 03	07 12							07 33	07 42							08 03	08 12					
Reading 7	a	06 53	07 13	07 20	06 57					07 22	07 43	07 52	07 26					07 53	08 13	08 22	07 57		08 02		
Oxford	a	07 18		08 09						07 48		08 40						08 19		09 14					

		GW		GW	GW	GW	GW	HC	GW	GW	GW	GW		GW	GW	GW	GW	HC	GW	GW	GW	GW		GW	GW
		◇1		◇1	1	1	◇1		1	1	◇1	1		◇1	1	1	◇1		1	1	1	◇1		◇1	1
																			A						
		☕					☕				☕			☕			☕		☕			☕			
London Paddington 15 ⊖	d	07 45		07 50		07 57	08 00	08 03	08 12	08 15	08 15	08 18		08 21		08 27	08 30	08 33	08 35	08 42	08 45	08 45		08 50	
Acton Main Line	d									08 21											08 51				
Ealing Broadway ⊖	d					08 05		08 11	08 20	08 24						08 35		08 41		08 50	08 54				
West Ealing	d							08 13		08 27								08 43			08 57				
Drayton Green	d									08 29											08 59				
Castle Bar Park	d									08 31											09 01				
South Greenford	d									08 34											09 04				
Greenford ⊖	a									08 39											09 09				
Hanwell	d							08 15										08 45							
Southall	d							08 19	08 28									08 49		08 58					
Hayes & Harlington	d					08 12		08 23	08 32							08 42		08 53		09 02					
Heathrow Terminal 1-2-3 2 ✈	a							08 35										09 05							
Heathrow Terminal 4 ✈	a																								
West Drayton	d					08 16			08 36							08 46				09 06					
Iver	d					08 19										08 49									
Langley	d				←	08 22									←	08 52									←
Slough 3	a			08 06	08 13	08 27			08 43					08 38	08 43	08 57				09 13				09 06	09 13
	d			08 06	08 13	08 27			08 43					08 39	08 43	08 57				09 13				09 06	09 13
Burnham	d				08 17				→						08 47					→					09 17
Taplow	d				08 21										08 51										09 21
Maidenhead 3	d				08 25	08 34									08 55	09 04									09 25
Twyford 3	d				08 33	08 42									09 03	09 12									09 33
Reading 7	a	08 09		08 22	08 43	08 52	08 26				08 40	08 48		08 53	09 13	09 23	08 56					09 10		09 22	09 43
Oxford	a			08 48		09 40								09 18		10 14								09 48	

A The Torbay Express

Table 117

London - Greenford and Reading

Saturdays

30 June to 8 September

Network Diagram - see first Page of Table 116

	GW	GW	HC	GW	GW	GW	GW	GW	GW	GW	GW	HC	GW	GW	GW	GW	GW	GW	GW	HC	GW	GW
	1	◇1 ☕		▪1 ∅	1	1	1	◇1	1	1	◇1 ☕		1	1	◇1 ☕	◇1	1	1	◇1 ☕		▪1 ∅	1
London Paddington 15 ⊖ d	08 57	09 00	09 03	09 06	09 12	09 15	09 18	09 21		09 27	09 30	09 33	09 42	09 45	09 45	09 50		09 57	10 00	10 03	10 06	10 12
Acton Main Line d						09 21								09 51								
Ealing Broadway ⊖ d	09 05		09 11		09 20	09 24				09 35		09 41	09 50	09 54				10 05		10 11		10 20
West Ealing d			09 13			09 27						09 43		09 57						10 13		
Drayton Green d						09 29								09 59								
Castle Bar Park d						09 31								10 01								
South Greenford d						09 34								10 04								
Greenford ⊖ a						09 39								10 09								
Hanwell d			09 15									09 45								10 15		
Southall d			09 19		09 28							09 49	09 58							10 19		10 28
Hayes & Harlington d	09 12		09 23		09 32					09 42		09 53	10 02					10 12		10 23		10 32
Heathrow Terminal 1-2-3 2 ✈ a			09 35									10 05								10 35		
Heathrow Terminal 4 ✈ a																						
West Drayton d	09 16				09 36					09 46			10 06					10 16				10 36
Iver d	09 19									09 49								10 19				
Langley d	09 22								←	09 52							←	10 22				
Slough 3 a	09 27				09 43			09 38	09 43	09 57			10 13			10 06	10 13	10 27				10 43
d	09 27				09 43			09 39	09 43	09 57			10 13			10 06	10 13	10 27				10 43
Burnham d					→				09 47				→				10 17					→
Taplow d									09 51								10 21					
Maidenhead 3 d	09 34								09 55	10 04							10 25	10 34				
Twyford 3 d	09 42								10 03	10 12							10 33	10 42				
Reading 7 a	09 52	09 26		09 31			09 48	09 54	10 13	10 22	09 57				10 09	10 22	10 43	10 52	10 26		10 31	
Oxford a	10 40							10 19		11 14						10 48		11 40				

	GW	GW	GW	GW	GW	GW	GW	HC	GW	GW	GW	GW	GW	GW	GW	GW	HC	GW	GW	GW	GW
	1	◇1 ☕	1	◇1 ☕	1	1	◇1 ☕		▪1 ☕	1	1	◇1 ∅	◇1 ✕	1	1	◇1 ☕		▪1 ∅	1	1	1
London Paddington 15 ⊖ d	10 15	10 15	10 18	10 21		10 27	10 30	10 33	10 35	10 42	10 45	10 45	10 50		10 57	11 00	11 03	11 06	11 12	11 15	11 18
Acton Main Line d	10 21										10 51									11 21	
Ealing Broadway ⊖ d	10 24					10 35		10 41		10 52	10 54				11 05		11 11		11 20	11 24	
West Ealing d	10 27							10 43			10 57						11 13			11 27	
Drayton Green d	10 29										10 59									11 29	
Castle Bar Park d	10 31										11 01									11 31	
South Greenford d	10 34										11 04									11 34	
Greenford ⊖ a	10 39										11 09									11 39	
Hanwell d								10 45									11 15				
Southall d								10 49		10 58							11 19		11 28		
Hayes & Harlington d						10 42		10 53		11 02					11 12		11 23		11 32		
Heathrow Terminal 1-2-3 2 ✈ a								11 05									11 35				
Heathrow Terminal 4 ✈ a																					
West Drayton d						10 46				11 06					11 16				11 36		
Iver d						10 49									11 19						
Langley d					←	10 52								←	11 22						
Slough 3 a				10 38	10 43	10 57				11 13			11 06	11 13	11 27				11 43		
d				10 39	10 43	10 57				11 13			11 06	11 13	11 27				11 43		
Burnham d					10 47					→				11 17					→		
Taplow d					10 51									11 21							
Maidenhead 3 d					10 55	11 04								11 25	11 34						
Twyford 3 d					11 03	11 12								11 33	11 42						
Reading 7 a		10 40	10 48	10 53	11 13	11 22	10 57					11 09	11 22	11 43	11 52	11 26		11 31			11 48
Oxford a				11 19		12 14							11 48		12 40						

	GW	GW	GW	GW	HC	GW	GW	GW	GW	GW	GW	GW	GW	HC	GW	GW	GW	GW	GW	GW	GW	GW
	◇1 ✕	1	1	◇1 ∅		▪1 ☕	1	1	◇1 ∅	◇1	1	1	◇1 ☕		▪1 ∅	1	1	◇1 ☕	1	◇1	1	1
London Paddington 15 ⊖ d	11 21		11 27	11 30	11 33	11 35	11 42	11 45	11 45	11 50		11 57	12 00	12 03	12 06	12 12	12 15	12 15	12 18	12 21		12 27
Acton Main Line d								11 51									12 21					
Ealing Broadway ⊖ d			11 35		11 41		11 50	11 54				12 05		12 11		12 20	12 24					12 35
West Ealing d					11 43			11 57						12 13			12 27					
Drayton Green d								11 59									12 29					
Castle Bar Park d								12 01									12 31					
South Greenford d								12 04									12 34					
Greenford ⊖ a								12 09									12 39					
Hanwell d					11 45									12 15								
Southall d					11 49		11 58							12 19		12 28						
Hayes & Harlington d			11 42		11 53		12 02					12 12		12 23		12 32						12 42
Heathrow Terminal 1-2-3 2 ✈ a					12 05									12 35								
Heathrow Terminal 4 ✈ a																						
West Drayton d			11 46				12 06					12 16				12 36						12 46
Iver d			11 49									12 19										12 49
Langley d		←	11 52								←	12 22									←	12 52
Slough 3 a	11 38	11 43	11 57				12 13			12 06	12 13	12 27				12 43				12 38	12 43	12 57
d	11 39	11 43	11 57				12 13			12 06	12 13	12 27				12 43				12 39	12 43	12 57
Burnham d		11 47					→				12 17					→					12 47	
Taplow d		11 51									12 21										12 51	
Maidenhead 3 d		11 55	12 04								12 25	12 34									12 55	13 04
Twyford 3 d		12 03	12 12								12 33	12 42									13 03	13 12
Reading 7 a	11 54	12 13	12 22	11 57					12 09	12 22	12 43	12 52	12 26		12 31			12 40	12 48	12 54	13 13	13 22
Oxford a	12 20		13 14							12 48		13 40								13 19		14 14

Table 117

London - Greenford and Reading

Saturdays

30 June to 8 September

Network Diagram - see first Page of Table 116

	GW	HC	GW	GW	GW	GW	GW	GW	GW	GW	HC	GW	GW	GW	GW	GW	GW	GW	GW	HC	GW	GW
	◇1 ☕		▪1 ☕	1	1	◇1 ☕	◇1 ✕	1	1	◇1 ☕		▪1 ☕	1	1	1	◇1 ✕	1	1	◇1 ☕		1	1
London Paddington 15 ⊖ d	12 30	12 33	12 35	12 42	12 45	12 45	12 50		12 57	13 00	13 03	13 06	13 12	13 15	13 18	13 21		13 27	13 30	13 33	13 42	13 45
Acton Main Line d					12 51									13 21								13 51
Ealing Broadway ⊖ d		12 41		12 50	12 54				13 05		13 11		13 20	13 24				13 35		13 41	13 50	13 54
West Ealing d		12 43			12 57						13 13			13 27						13 43		13 57
Drayton Green d					12 59									13 29								13 59
Castle Bar Park d					13 01									13 31								14 01
South Greenford d					13 04									13 34								14 04
Greenford ⊖ a					13 09									13 39								14 09
Hanwell d		12 45									13 15									13 45		
Southall d		12 49		12 58							13 19		13 28							13 49	13 58	
Hayes & Harlington d		12 53		13 02					13 12		13 23		13 32					13 42		13 53	14 02	
Heathrow Terminal 1-2-3 2 ✈ a		13 05									13 35									14 05		
Heathrow Terminal 4 ✈ a																						
West Drayton d				13 06					13 16				13 36					13 46			14 06	
Iver d									13 19									13 49				
Langley d								←	13 22								←	13 52				
Slough 3 a				13 13			13 06	13 13	13 27				13 43			13 38	13 43	13 57			14 13	
d				13 13			13 06	13 13	13 27				13 43			13 39	13 43	13 57			14 13	
Burnham d				→				13 17					→				13 47				→	
Taplow d								13 21									13 51					
Maidenhead 3 d								13 25	13 34								13 55	14 04				
Twyford 3 d								13 33	13 42								14 03	14 12				
Reading 7 a	12 57		13 02			13 09	13 22	13 43	13 52	13 26		13 31			13 48	13 54	14 13	14 22	13 58			
Oxford a							13 48		14 40							14 19		15 14				

	GW	GW	GW	GW	GW	HC	GW	GW	GW	GW	GW	GW	GW	GW	GW	HC	GW	GW	GW	GW	GW
	◇1 ☕	◇1 ✕	1	1	◇1 ☕		◇1 ☕	1	1	◇1 ☕	1	◇1 ✕	1	1	◇1 ☕		1	1	◇1 ☕	◇1	1
London Paddington 15 ⊖ d	13 45	13 50		13 57	14 00	14 03	14 06	14 12	14 15	14 15	14 18	14 21		14 27	14 30	14 33	14 42	14 45	14 45	14 50	
Acton Main Line d									14 21									14 51			
Ealing Broadway ⊖ d				14 05		14 11		14 20	14 24					14 35		14 41	14 50	14 54			
West Ealing d						14 13			14 27							14 43		14 57			
Drayton Green d									14 29									14 59			
Castle Bar Park d									14 31									15 01			
South Greenford d									14 34									15 04			
Greenford ⊖ a									14 39									15 09			
Hanwell d						14 15										14 45					
Southall d						14 19		14 28								14 49	14 58				
Hayes & Harlington d				14 12		14 23		14 32						14 42		14 53	15 02				
Heathrow Terminal 1-2-3 2 ✈ a						14 35										15 05					
Heathrow Terminal 4 ✈ a																					
West Drayton d				14 16				14 36						14 46			15 06				
Iver d				14 19										14 49							
Langley d			←	14 22									←	14 52							←
Slough 3 a		14 06	14 13	14 27				14 43				14 38	14 43	14 57			15 13			15 06	15 13
d		14 06	14 13	14 27				14 43				14 39	14 43	14 57			15 13			15 06	15 13
Burnham d			14 17					→					14 47				→				15 17
Taplow d			14 21										14 51								15 21
Maidenhead 3 d			14 25	14 34									14 55	15 04							15 25
Twyford 3 d			14 33	14 42									15 03	15 12							15 33
Reading 7 a	14 09	14 22	14 43	14 52	14 26					14 40	14 48	14 53	15 13	15 22	14 57				15 09	15 22	15 43
Oxford a		14 48		15 40								15 18		16 14						15 48	

	GW	GW	HC	GW	GW	GW	GW	GW	GW	GW	GW	HC	GW	GW	GW	GW	GW	GW	GW	HC	GW	GW
	1	◇1 ☕		◇1 ☕	1	1	1	◇1 ✕	1	1	◇1 ☕		1	1	◇1 ☕	◇1	1	1	◇1 ☕		◇1 ☕	1
London Paddington 15 ⊖ d	14 57	15 00	15 03	15 06	15 12	15 15	15 18	15 21		15 27	15 30	15 33	15 42	15 45	15 45	15 50		15 57	16 00	16 03	16 06	16 12
Acton Main Line d						15 21								15 51								
Ealing Broadway ⊖ d	15 05		15 11		15 20	15 24				15 35		15 41	15 50	15 54				16 05		16 11		16 20
West Ealing d			15 13			15 27						15 43		15 57						16 13		
Drayton Green d						15 29								15 59								
Castle Bar Park d						15 31								16 01								
South Greenford d						15 34								16 04								
Greenford ⊖ a						15 39								16 09								
Hanwell d			15 15									15 45								16 15		
Southall d			15 19		15 28							15 49	15 58							16 19		16 28
Hayes & Harlington d	15 12		15 23		15 32					15 42		15 53	16 02					16 12		16 23		16 32
Heathrow Terminal 1-2-3 2 ✈ a			15 35									16 05								16 35		
Heathrow Terminal 4 ✈ a																						
West Drayton d	15 16				15 36					15 46			16 06					16 16				16 36
Iver d	15 19									15 49								16 19				
Langley d	15 22								←	15 52							←	16 22				
Slough 3 a	15 27				15 43			15 38	15 43	15 57			16 13			16 06	16 13	16 27				16 43
d	15 27				15 43			15 39	15 43	15 57			16 13			16 06	16 13	16 27				16 43
Burnham d					→				15 47				→				16 17					→
Taplow d									15 51								16 21					
Maidenhead 3 d	15 34								15 55	16 04							16 25	16 34				
Twyford 3 d	15 42								16 03	16 12							16 33	16 42				
Reading 7 a	15 52	15 26		15 31			15 48	15 54	16 13	16 22	15 58				16 09	16 22	16 43	16 52	16 26		16 31	
Oxford a	16 40							16 19		17 14						16 48		17 40				

Table 117

London - Greenford and Reading

Saturdays

30 June to 8 September

Network Diagram - see first Page of Table 116

		GW	GW	GW	GW	GW	GW	GW	HC	GW	GW	GW	GW	GW	GW	GW	HC	GW	GW	GW	GW	GW
		■1	◇■1	■1	◇■1	■1	■1	◇■1		■1	■1	◇■1	◇■1	■1	■1	◇■1		◇■1	■1	■1	■1	◇■1
			☕		☕			☕				☕	🍴			☕		☕				☕
London Paddington 15 ⊖	d	16 15	16 15	16 18	16 21		16 27	16 30	16 33	16 42	16 45	16 45	16 50		16 57	17 00	17 03	17 06	17 12	17 15	17 18	17 21
Acton Main Line	d	16 21									16 51									17 21		
Ealing Broadway ⊖	d	16 24					16 35		16 41	16 50	16 54				17 05		17 11		17 20	17 24		
West Ealing	d	16 27							16 43		16 57						17 13			17 27		
Drayton Green	d	16 29									16 59									17 29		
Castle Bar Park	d	16 31									17 01									17 31		
South Greenford	d	16 34									17 04									17 34		
Greenford ⊖	a	16 39									17 09									17 39		
Hanwell	d								16 45								17 15					
Southall	d								16 49	16 58							17 19		17 28			
Hayes & Harlington	d						16 42		16 53	17 02					17 12		17 23		17 32			
Heathrow Terminal 1-2-3 2 ✈	a								17 05								17 35					
Heathrow Terminal 4 ✈	a																					
West Drayton	d						16 46			17 06					17 16				17 36			
Iver	d						16 49								17 19							
Langley	d					←	16 52							←	17 22							
Slough 3	a				16 38	16 43	16 57			17 13			17 06	17 13	17 27				17 43			17 38
	d				16 39	16 43	16 57			17 13			17 06	17 13	17 27				17 43			17 39
Burnham	d					16 47				→				17 17					→			
Taplow	d					16 51								17 21								
Maidenhead 3	d					16 55	17 04							17 25	17 34							
Twyford 3	d					17 03	17 12							17 33	17 42							
Reading 7	a		16 40	16 48	16 53	17 13	17 22	16 57				17 09	17 22	17 43	17 52	17 26		17 31			17 48	17 53
Oxford	a				17 18		18 14						17 48		18 40							18 18

		GW	GW	GW	HC	GW	GW	GW	GW	GW	GW	GW	HC	GW	GW	GW	GW	GW	GW	GW	GW	GW	HC
		■1	■1	◇■1		■1	■1	◇■1	◇■1	■1	■1	◇■1		◇■1	■1	■1	◇■1	■1	◇■1	■1	■1	◇■1	
				☕				☕	🍴			☕		☕			☕		☕			☕	
London Paddington 15 ⊖	d		17 27	17 30	17 33	17 42	17 45	17 45	17 50		17 57	18 00	18 03	18 06	18 12	18 15	18 15	18 18	18 21		18 27	18 30	18 33
Acton Main Line	d						17 51									18 21							
Ealing Broadway ⊖	d		17 35		17 41	17 50	17 54				18 05		18 11		18 20	18 24					18 35		18 41
West Ealing	d				17 43		17 57						18 13			18 27							18 43
Drayton Green	d						17 59									18 29							
Castle Bar Park	d						18 01									18 31							
South Greenford	d						18 04									18 34							
Greenford ⊖	a						18 09									18 39							
Hanwell	d				17 45								18 15										18 45
Southall	d				17 49	17 58							18 19		18 28								18 49
Hayes & Harlington	d		17 42		17 53	18 02					18 12		18 23		18 32						18 42		18 53
Heathrow Terminal 1-2-3 2 ✈	a				18 05								18 35										19 05
Heathrow Terminal 4 ✈	a																						
West Drayton	d		17 46			18 06					18 16				18 36						18 46		
Iver	d		17 49								18 19										18 49		
Langley	d	←	17 52							←	18 22									←	18 52		
Slough 3	a	17 43	17 57			18 13			18 06	18 13	18 27				18 43				18 38	18 43	18 57		
	d	17 43	17 57			18 13			18 06	18 13	18 27				18 43				18 39	18 43	18 57		
Burnham	d	17 47				→				18 17					→					18 47			
Taplow	d	17 51								18 21										18 51			
Maidenhead 3	d	17 55	18 04							18 25	18 34									18 55	19 04		
Twyford 3	d	18 03	18 12							18 33	18 42									19 03	19 12		
Reading 7	a	18 13	18 22	17 57				18 09	18 22	18 43	18 52	18 27		18 06			18 40	18 48	18 53	19 13	19 23	18 57	
Oxford	a		19 14						18 48		19 40								19 18		20 14		

		GW	GW	GW	GW	GW	GW	GW	HC	GW	GW	GW	GW	GW	GW	GW	HC	GW	GW	GW	GW	GW	GW
		■1	■1	◇■1	◇■1	■1	■1	◇■1		◇■1	■1	■1	◇■1	■1	■1	◇■1		■1	■1	◇■1	◇■1	■1	■1
				☕				☕		☕						☕				☕	🍴		
London Paddington 15 ⊖	d	18 42	18 45	18 45	18 50		18 57	19 00	19 03	19 06	19 12	19 15	19 21		19 27	19 30	19 33	19 42	19 45	19 45	19 50		19 57
Acton Main Line	d		18 51									19 21							19 51				
Ealing Broadway ⊖	d	18 50	18 54				19 05		19 11		19 20	19 24			19 35		19 41	19 50	19 54				20 05
West Ealing	d		18 57						19 13			19 27					19 43		19 57				
Drayton Green	d		18 59									19 29							19 59				
Castle Bar Park	d		19 01									19 31							20 01				
South Greenford	d		19 04									19 34							20 04				
Greenford ⊖	a		19 09									19 39							20 09				
Hanwell	d								19 15								19 45						
Southall	d	18 58							19 19		19 28						19 49	19 58					
Hayes & Harlington	d	19 02					19 12		19 23		19 32				19 42		19 53	20 02					20 12
Heathrow Terminal 1-2-3 2 ✈	a								19 35								20 05						
Heathrow Terminal 4 ✈	a																						
West Drayton	d	19 06					19 16				19 36				19 46			20 06					20 16
Iver	d						19 19								19 49								20 19
Langley	d					←	19 22							←	19 52							←	20 22
Slough 3	a	19 13			19 06	19 13	19 27				19 43		19 37	19 43	19 57			20 13			20 06	20 13	20 27
	d	19 13			19 06	19 13	19 27				19 43		19 38	19 43	19 57			20 13			20 06	20 13	20 27
Burnham	d	→				19 17					→			19 47				→				20 17	
Taplow	d					19 21								19 51								20 21	
Maidenhead 3	d					19 25	19 34							19 55	20 04							20 25	20 34
Twyford 3	d					19 33	19 42							20 03	20 12							20 33	20 42
Reading 7	a			19 09	19 22	19 43	19 52	19 26		19 30			19 52	20 13	20 23	19 57				20 09	20 21	20 43	20 52
Oxford	a				19 48		20 40						20 20		21 14						20 47		21 40

Table 117

London - Greenford and Reading

Saturdays

30 June to 8 September

Network Diagram - see first Page of Table 116

		GW	HC	GW	GW	GW	GW	GW	GW	GW	GW	HC	GW	GW	GW	GW	GW	GW	HC	GW	GW	GW
		◇■1		◇■1	■1	■1	◇■1	◇■1	■1	■1	◇■1		■1	◇■1	■1	◇■1	■1	■1		■1	■1	◇■1
		☕		☕			☕				☕			☕		🍴						
London Paddington 15 ⊖	d	20 00	20 03	20 06	20 12	20 15	20 15	20 20		20 27	20 30	20 33	20 42	20 45	20 45	20 50		20 57	21 03	21 12	21 15	21 17
Acton Main Line	d					20 21									20 51						21 21	
Ealing Broadway ⊖	d		20 11		20 20	20 24				20 35		20 41	20 50		20 54			21 05	21 11	21 20	21 24	
West Ealing	d		20 13			20 27						20 43			20 57				21 13		21 27	
Drayton Green	d					20 29									20 59						21 29	
Castle Bar Park	d					20 31									21 01						21 31	
South Greenford	d					20 34									21 04						21 34	
Greenford ⊖	a					20 39									21 09						21 39	
Hanwell	d		20 15									20 45							21 15			
Southall	d		20 19		20 28							20 49	20 58						21 19	21 28		
Hayes & Harlington	d		20 23		20 32					20 42		20 53	21 02					21 12	21 23	21 32		
Heathrow Terminal 1-2-3 2 ✈	a		20 35									21 05							21 35			
Heathrow Terminal 4 ✈	a																					
West Drayton	d				20 36					20 46			21 06					21 16		21 36		
Iver	d									20 49								21 19				
Langley	d								←	20 52							←	21 22				
Slough 3	a				20 43			20 35	20 43	20 57			21 13			21 06	21 13	21 27		21 43		21 34
	d				20 43			20 35	20 43	20 57			21 13			21 06	21 13	21 27		21 43		21 35
Burnham	d				→				20 47				→				21 17			→		
Taplow	d								20 51								21 21					
Maidenhead 3	d								20 55	21 04							21 25	21 34				
Twyford 3	d								21 06	21 12							21 33	21 42				
Reading 7	a	20 27		20 31			20 40	20 51	21 14	21 22	20 57			21 09		21 22	21 43	21 52				21 51
Oxford	a							21 19		22 14						21 53		22 43				22 20

		GW	GW	HC	GW	GW	GW	GW	GW	HC	GW	GW	HC	GW	GW	GW	GW	GW	HC	GW	GW	GW	GW
		◇■1	■1		■1	◇■1	■1	■1	◇■1		■1	◇■1		◇■1	■1	■1	◇■1	■1		■1	◇■1	◇■1	■1
		☕							☕					☕							☕		
London Paddington 15 ⊖	d	21 30		21 33	21 42	21 50		21 57	22 00	22 03	22 12	22 15	22 33	22 35		22 45	23 00		23 03	23 20	23 30	23 33	
Acton Main Line	d				21 48											22 51							
Ealing Broadway ⊖	d			21 41	21 52			22 05		22 11	22 20		22 41			22 55			23 11	23 28			
West Ealing	d			21 43						22 13			22 43						23 13				
Drayton Green	d																						
Castle Bar Park	d																						
South Greenford	d																						
Greenford ⊖	a																						
Hanwell	d			21 45						22 15			22 45						23 15				
Southall	d			21 49	21 58					22 19	22 28		22 49			23 00			23 19	23 33			
Hayes & Harlington	d			21 53	22 02			22 12		22 23	22 32		22 53			23 04			23 23	23 37			
Heathrow Terminal 1-2-3 2 ✈	a			22 05						22 35			23 05						23 35				
Heathrow Terminal 4 ✈	a																		23 41				
West Drayton	d				22 06			22 16			22 36					23 08				23 41			
Iver	d							22 19								23 11				23 44			
Langley	d		←				←	22 22							←	23 14		←		23 48			←
Slough 3	a		21 43		22 13	22 06	22 13	22 27			22 43	22 31			22 43	23 19	23 16	23 19		23 53		23 49	23 53
	d		21 43		22 13	22 06	22 13	22 27			22 43	22 32			22 43	23 21	23 17	23 21		23 54		23 50	23 54
Burnham	d		21 47		→		22 17				→				22 47	→		23 25		→			23 57
Taplow	d		21 51				22 21								22 51								00 01
Maidenhead 3	d		21 55				22 25	22 34							22 55			23 32					00 05
Twyford 3	d		22 03				22 33	22 42							23 03			23 39					00 13
Reading 7	a	21 55	22 13			22 22	22 41	22 52	22 27			22 48		23 00	23 13		23 33	23 46			23 59	00 06	00 20
Oxford	a					22 50		23 38				23 20					00 04	00 32				00 38	01 05

		GW
		■1
London Paddington 15 ⊖	d	23 42
Acton Main Line	d	
Ealing Broadway ⊖	d	23 50
West Ealing	d	
Drayton Green	d	
Castle Bar Park	d	
South Greenford	d	
Greenford ⊖	a	
Hanwell	d	
Southall	d	23 56
Hayes & Harlington	d	00 01
Heathrow Terminal 1-2-3 2 ✈	a	
Heathrow Terminal 4 ✈	a	
West Drayton	d	00 06
Iver	d	
Langley	d	
Slough 3	a	00 13
	d	00 14
Burnham	d	00 18
Taplow	d	00 21
Maidenhead 3	d	00 25
Twyford 3	d	00 33
Reading 7	a	00 43
Oxford	a	

London - Greenford and Reading

Network Diagram - see first Page of Table 116

	GW	GW	GW	GW	GW	GW	GW	GW	GW	GW	GW	HC	HC	GW	GW	HC	GW	GW	GW	HC	GW	GW
	■	◇■	■	■	◇■ ⊡	■	■	◇■	■	■	■			◇■	■		■	◇■	■		■	■
London Paddington ⊖ d	22p45	23p18		23p29	23p30	23p42	23p48	00 22	00 34	01 44	03 34	04 42	05 13	05 21	05 25	05 33	05 45	05 50	05 57	06 03	06 12	06 15
Acton Main Line d	22p51						23p54										05 51					06 21
Ealing Broadway ⊖ d	22p54			23p37			23p57		00 42	01 52	03 42	04 50	05 21		05 33	05 41	05 54		06 05	06 11	06 20	06 24
West Ealing d							23p59									05 43	05 57			06 13		06 27
Drayton Green d																	05 59					06 29
Castle Bar Park d																	06 01					06 31
South Greenford d																	06 04					06 34
Greenford ⊖ a																	06 09					06 39
Hanwell d							00 02									05 45				06 15		
Southall d							00 06		00 47	01 57	03 47	04 54	05 25		05 38	05 49			06 10	06 19	06 28	
Hayes & Harlington d	23p01			23p44			00 10		00 51	02 01	03 51	04 58	05 29		05 42	05 53			06 14	06 23	06 32	
Heathrow Terminal 1-2-3 ✈ a												05 04	05 35			06 05				06 35		
Heathrow Terminal 4 ✈ a												05 10	05 41									
West Drayton d							00 14		00 55	02 05	03 55								06 18		06 36	
Iver d							00 17												06 21			
Langley d							00 21		01 00										06 25			
Slough a	23p11	23p36		23p53		23p58	00 26	00 38	01 05	02 13	04 03			05 37	05 50			06 06	06 30		06 43	
d	23p12	23p36		23p54		23p58	00 26	00 39	01 05	02 13	04 03			05 38	05 51			06 06	06 31		06 43	
Burnham d	23p16						00 30		01 09						05 55				06 35		→	
Taplow d	23p20						00 34		01 13						05 58				06 38			
Maidenhead d	23p24	23p44		00 01		00 08	00 41		01 16	02 21	04 11				06 02				06 42			
Twyford d	23p32		00 07	00 09			00 48		01 24	02 29	04 19				06 10				06 50			
Reading a	23p41	23p58	00 16	00 19	00 05	00 21	00 57	00 55	01 35	02 38	04 30			05 52	06 17			06 22	06 56			
Oxford a	00 26	00 28		01 16		01 02		01 28						06 22	07 03			06 52	07 43			

	GW	GW	GW	GW	HC	GW	GW	GW	GW	GW	GW	HC	GW	GW	GW	GW	GW	GW	HC	GW	GW	GW
	◇■	■	■	◇■ ⊡		■	■	◇■	■	■	◇■ ⊡		■	■	◇■	■	■	■ ⊡		■	■	◇■ ⊡
London Paddington ⊖ d	06 21		06 27	06 30	06 33	06 42	06 45	06 50		06 57	07 00	07 03	07 12	07 15	07 21		07 27	07 30	07 33	07 42	07 45	07 45
Acton Main Line d							06 51							07 21							07 51	
Ealing Broadway ⊖ d			06 35		06 41	06 50	06 54			07 05		07 11	07 20	07 24			07 35		07 41	07 50	07 54	
West Ealing d					06 43		06 57					07 13		07 27					07 43		07 57	
Drayton Green d							06 59							07 29							07 59	
Castle Bar Park d							07 01							07 31							08 01	
South Greenford d							07 04							07 34							08 04	
Greenford ⊖ a							07 09							07 39							08 09	
Hanwell d					06 45							07 15							07 45			
Southall d					06 49	06 58						07 19	07 28						07 49	07 58		
Hayes & Harlington d			06 42		06 53	07 02				07 12		07 23	07 32				07 42		07 53	08 02		
Heathrow Terminal 1-2-3 ✈ a					07 05							07 35							08 05			
Heathrow Terminal 4 ✈ a																						
West Drayton d			06 46			07 06				07 16			07 36				07 46			08 06		
Iver d			06 49							07 19							07 49					
Langley d		←	06 52						←	07 22						←	07 52					
Slough a	06 37	06 43	06 57			07 13		07 06	07 13	07 27			07 43		07 37	07 43	07 57			08 13		
d	06 38	06 43	06 57			07 13		07 06	07 13	07 27			07 43		07 38	07 43	07 57			08 13		
Burnham d		06 47				→			07 17				→			07 47				→		
Taplow d		06 51							07 21							07 51						
Maidenhead d		06 55	07 04						07 25	07 34						07 55	08 04					
Twyford d		07 03	07 12						07 33	07 42						08 03	08 12					
Reading a	06 53	07 13	07 20	06 57				07 22	07 43	07 52	07 26				07 53	08 13	08 22	07 57				08 09
Oxford a	07 18		08 09					07 48		08 40					08 19		09 14					

	GW	GW	GW	GW	HC	GW	GW	GW	GW	GW	GW	GW	GW	HC	GW	GW	GW	GW	GW	GW	GW
	◇■	■	■	◇■ ⊡		■	■	◇■ ⊡	◇■ ⊡	◇■ ⊡	■	■	◇■ ⊡		■	■	◇■ ⊡	◇■	■	■	◇■ ⊡
London Paddington ⊖ d	07 50		07 57	08 00	08 03	08 12	08 15	08 15	08 18	08 21		08 27	08 30	08 33	08 42	08 45	08 45	08 50		08 57	09 00
Acton Main Line d							08 21									08 51					
Ealing Broadway ⊖ d			08 05		08 11	08 20	08 24					08 35		08 41	08 50	08 54				09 05	
West Ealing d					08 13		08 27							08 43		08 57					
Drayton Green d							08 29									08 59					
Castle Bar Park d							08 31									09 01					
South Greenford d							08 34									09 04					
Greenford ⊖ a							08 39									09 09					
Hanwell d					08 15									08 45							
Southall d					08 19	08 28								08 49	08 58						
Hayes & Harlington d			08 12		08 23	08 32						08 42		08 53	09 02					09 12	
Heathrow Terminal 1-2-3 ✈ a					08 35									09 05							
Heathrow Terminal 4 ✈ a																					
West Drayton d			08 16			08 36						08 46			09 06					09 16	
Iver d			08 19									08 49								09 19	
Langley d		←	08 22								←	08 52							←	09 22	
Slough a	08 06	08 13	08 27			08 43				08 38	08 43	08 57			09 13			09 06	09 13	09 27	
d	08 06	08 13	08 27			08 43				08 39	08 43	08 57			09 13			09 06	09 13	09 27	
Burnham d		08 17				→					08 47				→				09 17		
Taplow d		08 21									08 51								09 21		
Maidenhead d		08 25	08 34								08 55	09 04							09 25	09 34	
Twyford d		08 33	08 42								09 03	09 12							09 33	09 42	
Reading a	08 22	08 43	08 52	08 26				08 40	08 46	08 53	09 13	09 23	08 56				09 09	09 22	09 43	09 52	09 26
Oxford a	08 48		09 40							09 18		10 14						09 48		10 40	

Table 117

Saturdays

London - Greenford and Reading

15 September to 20 October

Network Diagram - see first Page of Table 116

	HC	GW	GW	GW	GW	GW	GW	GW	GW	HC	GW	GW	GW	GW	GW	GW	GW	HC	GW	GW	GW	GW
		◇■ ⊘	■	■	■	◇■	■	■	◇■ ⊡		■	■	◇■ ⊡	◇■	■	■	◇■ ⊡		◇■ ⊘	■	■	◇■ ⊡
London Paddington ⊖ d	09 03	09 06	09 12	09 15	09 18	09 21		09 27	09 30	09 33	09 42	09 45	09 45	09 50		09 57	10 00	10 03	10 06	10 12	10 15	10 15
Acton Main Line d				09 21								09 51									10 21	
Ealing Broadway ⊖ d	09 11		09 20	09 24				09 35		09 41	09 50	09 54				10 05		10 11		10 20	10 24	
West Ealing d	09 13			09 27						09 43		09 57						10 13			10 27	
Drayton Green d				09 29								09 59									10 29	
Castle Bar Park d				09 31								10 01									10 31	
South Greenford d				09 34								10 04									10 34	
Greenford ⊖ a				09 39								10 09									10 39	
Hanwell d	09 15									09 45								10 15				
Southall d	09 19		09 28							09 49	09 58							10 19		10 28		
Hayes & Harlington d	09 23		09 32					09 42		09 53	10 02					10 12		10 23		10 32		
Heathrow Terminal 1-2-3 ✈ a	09 35									10 05								10 35				
Heathrow Terminal 4 ✈ a																						
West Drayton d			09 36					09 46			10 06					10 16				10 36		
Iver d								09 49								10 19						
Langley d							←	09 52							←	10 22						
Slough a			09 43			09 38	09 43	09 57			10 13			10 06	10 13	10 27				10 43		
d			09 43			09 39	09 43	09 57			10 13			10 06	10 13	10 27				10 43		
Burnham d			→				09 47				→				10 17					→		
Taplow d							09 51								10 21							
Maidenhead d							09 55	10 04							10 25	10 34						
Twyford d							10 03	10 12							10 33	10 42						
Reading a		09 30			09 48	09 54	10 13	10 22	09 57				10 09	10 22	10 43	10 52	10 26		10 30			10 40
Oxford a						10 19		11 14						10 48		11 40						

	GW	GW	GW	GW	GW	HC	GW	GW	GW	GW	GW	GW	GW	HC	GW	GW	GW	GW	GW	GW	GW
	■	◇■ ⊡	■	■	◇■ ⊡		■	■	◇■ ⊘	◇■ ⊼	■	■	◇■ ⊡		◇■ ⊘	■	■	■	◇■ ⊼	■	■
London Paddington ⊖ d	10 18	10 21		10 27	10 30	10 33	10 42	10 45	10 45	10 50		10 57	11 00	11 03	11 06	11 12	11 15	11 18	11 21		11 27
Acton Main Line d								10 51									11 21				
Ealing Broadway ⊖ d				10 35		10 41	10 52	10 54				11 05		11 11		11 20	11 24				11 35
West Ealing d						10 43		10 57						11 13			11 27				
Drayton Green d								10 59									11 29				
Castle Bar Park d								11 01									11 31				
South Greenford d								11 04									11 34				
Greenford ⊖ a								11 09									11 39				
Hanwell d						10 45								11 15							
Southall d						10 49	10 58							11 19		11 28					
Hayes & Harlington d				10 42		10 53	11 02					11 12		11 23		11 32					11 42
Heathrow Terminal 1-2-3 ✈ a						11 05								11 35							
Heathrow Terminal 4 ✈ a																					
West Drayton d				10 46			11 06					11 16				11 36					11 46
Iver d				10 49								11 19									11 49
Langley d			←	10 52							←	11 22								←	11 52
Slough a		10 38	10 43	10 57			11 13			11 06	11 13	11 27				11 43			11 38	11 43	11 57
d		10 39	10 43	10 57			11 13			11 06	11 13	11 27				11 43			11 39	11 43	11 57
Burnham d			10 47				→				11 17					→				11 47	
Taplow d			10 51								11 21									11 51	
Maidenhead d			10 55	11 04							11 25	11 34								11 55	12 04
Twyford d			11 03	11 12							11 33	11 42								12 03	12 12
Reading a	10 48	10 53	11 13	11 22	10 57				11 09	11 22	11 43	11 52	11 26		11 30			11 48	11 54	12 13	12 22
Oxford a		11 19		12 14						11 48		12 40							12 20		13 14

	GW	HC	GW	GW	GW	GW	GW	GW	GW	HC	GW	GW	GW	GW	GW	GW	GW	GW	GW	HC	GW	GW
	◇■ ⊘		■	■	◇■ ⊘	◇■	■	■	◇■ ⊡		◇■ ⊘	■	■	◇■ ⊡	◇■ ⊡	◇■	■	■	◇■ ⊡		■	■
London Paddington ⊖ d	11 30	11 33	11 42	11 45	11 45	11 50		11 57	12 00	12 03	12 06	12 12	12 15	12 15	12 18	12 21		12 27	12 30	12 33	12 42	12 45
Acton Main Line d				11 51									12 21									12 51
Ealing Broadway ⊖ d		11 41	11 50	11 54				12 05		12 11		12 20	12 24					12 35		12 41	12 50	12 54
West Ealing d		11 43		11 57						12 13			12 27							12 43		12 57
Drayton Green d				11 59									12 29									12 59
Castle Bar Park d				12 01									12 31									13 01
South Greenford d				12 04									12 34									13 04
Greenford ⊖ a				12 09									12 39									13 09
Hanwell d		11 45								12 15										12 45		
Southall d		11 49	11 58							12 19		12 28								12 49	12 58	
Hayes & Harlington d		11 53	12 02					12 12		12 23		12 32						12 42		12 53	13 02	
Heathrow Terminal 1-2-3 ✈ a		12 05								12 35										13 05		
Heathrow Terminal 4 ✈ a																						
West Drayton d			12 06					12 16				12 36						12 46			13 06	
Iver d								12 19										12 49				
Langley d							←	12 22									←	12 52				
Slough a			12 13			12 06	12 13	12 27				12 43				12 38	12 43	12 57			13 13	
d			12 13			12 06	12 13	12 27				12 43				12 39	12 43	12 57			13 13	
Burnham d			→				12 17					→					12 47				→	
Taplow d							12 21										12 51					
Maidenhead d							12 25	12 34									12 55	13 04				
Twyford d							12 33	12 42									13 03	13 12				
Reading a	11 57				12 09	12 22	12 43	12 52	12 26		12 30			12 40	12 45	12 54	13 13	13 22	12 57			
Oxford a						12 48		13 40								13 19		14 14				

London - Greenford and Reading

Network Diagram - see first Page of Table 116

	GW	GW	GW	GW	GW	HC	GW	GW	GW	GW	GW	GW	GW	GW	HC	GW	GW	GW	GW	GW	GW	GW
London Paddington d	12 45	12 50		12 57	13 00	13 03	13 06	13 12	13 15	13 18	13 21		13 27	13 30	13 33	13 42	13 45	13 45	13 50		13 57	14 00
Acton Main Line d									13 21								13 51					
Ealing Broadway d				13 05		13 11		13 20	13 24				13 35		13 41	13 50	13 54				14 05	
West Ealing d						13 13			13 27						13 43		13 57					
Drayton Green d									13 29								13 59					
Castle Bar Park d									13 31								14 01					
South Greenford d									13 34								14 04					
Greenford a									13 39								14 09					
Hanwell d						13 15									13 45							
Southall d						13 19		13 28							13 49	13 58						
Hayes & Harlington d				13 12		13 23		13 32					13 42		13 53	14 02					14 12	
Heathrow Terminal 1-2-3 a						13 35									14 05							
Heathrow Terminal 4 a																						
West Drayton d				13 16				13 36					13 46			14 06					14 16	
Iver d				13 19									13 49								14 19	
Langley d			←	13 22								←	13 52							←	14 22	
Slough a		13 06	13 13	13 27				13 43			13 38	13 43	13 57			14 13			14 06	14 13	14 27	
Slough d		13 06	13 13	13 27				13 43			13 39	13 43	13 57			14 13			14 06	14 13	14 27	
Burnham d			13 17					→				13 47				→				14 17		
Taplow d			13 21									13 51								14 21		
Maidenhead d			13 25	13 34								13 55	14 04							14 25	14 34	
Twyford d			13 33	13 42								14 03	14 12							14 33	14 42	
Reading a	13 09	13 22	13 43	13 52	13 26		13 30			13 48	13 54	14 13	14 22	13 58				14 09	14 22	14 43	14 52	14 26
Oxford a		13 48		14 40							14 19		15 14						14 48		15 40	

	HC	GW	GW	GW	GW	GW	GW	GW	GW	GW	HC	GW	GW	GW	GW	GW	GW	GW	HC	GW	GW
London Paddington d	14 03	14 06	14 12	14 15	14 15	14 18	14 21		14 27	14 30	14 33	14 42	14 45	14 45	14 50		14 57	15 00	15 03	15 06	15 12
Acton Main Line d				14 21									14 51								
Ealing Broadway d	14 11		14 20	14 24					14 35		14 41	14 50	14 54				15 05		15 11		15 20
West Ealing d	14 13			14 27							14 43		14 57						15 13		
Drayton Green d				14 29									14 59								
Castle Bar Park d				14 31									15 01								
South Greenford d				14 34									15 04								
Greenford a				14 39									15 09								
Hanwell d	14 15										14 45								15 15		
Southall d	14 19		14 28								14 49	14 58							15 19		15 28
Hayes & Harlington d	14 23		14 32						14 42		14 53	15 02					15 12		15 23		15 32
Heathrow Terminal 1-2-3 a	14 35										15 05								15 35		
Heathrow Terminal 4 a																					
West Drayton d			14 36						14 46			15 06					15 16				15 36
Iver d									14 49								15 19				
Langley d								←	14 52							←	15 22				
Slough a			14 43				14 38	14 43	14 57			15 13			15 06	15 13	15 27				15 43
Slough d			14 43				14 39	14 43	14 57			15 13			15 06	15 13	15 27				15 43
Burnham d			→					14 47				→				15 17					→
Taplow d								14 51								15 21					
Maidenhead d								14 55	15 04							15 25	15 34				
Twyford d								15 03	15 12							15 33	15 42				
Reading a		14 30			14 40	14 48	14 53	15 13	15 22	14 57				15 09	15 22	15 43	15 52	15 26		15 29	
Oxford a							15 18		16 14						15 48		16 40				

	GW	GW	GW	GW	GW	GW	HC	GW	GW	GW	GW	GW	GW	GW	HC	GW	GW	GW	GW	GW	GW	GW
London Paddington d	15 15	15 18	15 21		15 27	15 30	15 33	15 42	15 45	15 45	15 50		15 57	16 00	16 03	16 06	16 12	16 15	16 15	16 18	16 21	
Acton Main Line d	15 21								15 51									16 21				
Ealing Broadway d	15 24				15 35		15 41	15 50	15 54				16 05		16 11		16 20	16 24				
West Ealing d	15 27						15 43		15 57						16 13			16 27				
Drayton Green d	15 29								15 59									16 29				
Castle Bar Park d	15 31								16 01									16 31				
South Greenford d	15 34								16 04									16 34				
Greenford a	15 39								16 09									16 39				
Hanwell d							15 45								16 15							
Southall d							15 49	15 58							16 19		16 28					
Hayes & Harlington d					15 42		15 53	16 02					16 12		16 23		16 32					
Heathrow Terminal 1-2-3 a							16 05								16 35							
Heathrow Terminal 4 a																						
West Drayton d					15 46			16 06					16 16				16 36					
Iver d					15 49								16 19									
Langley d				←	15 52							←	16 22									←
Slough a			15 38	15 43	15 57			16 13			16 06	16 13	16 27				16 43				16 38	16 43
Slough d			15 39	15 43	15 57			16 13			16 06	16 13	16 27				16 43				16 39	16 43
Burnham d				15 47				→				16 17					→					16 47
Taplow d				15 51								16 21										16 51
Maidenhead d				15 55	16 04							16 25	16 34									16 55
Twyford d				16 03	16 12							16 33	16 42									17 03
Reading a		15 48	15 54	16 13	16 22	15 58				16 09	16 22	16 43	16 52	16 26		16 31			16 40	16 48	16 53	17 13
Oxford a			16 19		17 14						16 48		17 40								17 18	

London - Greenford and Reading

Network Diagram - see first Page of Table 116

	GW	GW	HC	GW	GW	GW	GW	GW	GW	GW	HC	GW	GW	GW	GW	GW	GW	GW	GW	HC	GW
London Paddington d	16 27	16 30	16 33	16 42	16 45	16 45	16 50		16 57	17 00	17 03	17 06	17 12	17 15	17 18	17 21		17 27	17 30	17 33	17 42
Acton Main Line d					16 51									17 21							
Ealing Broadway d	16 35		16 41	16 50	16 54				17 05		17 11		17 20	17 24				17 35		17 41	17 50
West Ealing d			16 43		16 57						17 13			17 27						17 43	
Drayton Green d					16 59									17 29							
Castle Bar Park d					17 01									17 31							
South Greenford d					17 04									17 34							
Greenford a					17 09									17 39							
Hanwell d			16 45								17 15									17 45	
Southall d			16 49	16 58							17 19		17 28							17 49	17 58
Hayes & Harlington d	16 42		16 53	17 02					17 12		17 23		17 32					17 42		17 53	18 02
Heathrow Terminal 1-2-3 a			17 05								17 35									18 05	
Heathrow Terminal 4 a																					
West Drayton d	16 46			17 06					17 16				17 36					17 46			18 06
Iver d	16 49								17 19									17 49			
Langley d	16 52							←	17 22								←	17 52			
Slough a	16 57			17 13			17 06	17 13	17 27				17 43			17 38	17 43	17 57			18 13
Slough d	16 57			17 13			17 06	17 13	17 27				17 43			17 39	17 43	17 57			18 13
Burnham d				→				17 17					→				17 47				→
Taplow d								17 21									17 51				
Maidenhead d	17 04							17 25	17 34								17 55	18 04			
Twyford d	17 12							17 33	17 42								18 03	18 12			
Reading a	17 22	16 57				17 09	17 22	17 43	17 52	17 26		17 30			17 48	17 53	18 13	18 22	17 57		
Oxford a	18 14						17 48		18 40							18 18		19 14			

	GW	GW	GW	GW	GW	GW	HC	GW	GW	GW	GW	GW	GW	GW	GW	GW	HC	GW	GW	GW	GW	GW
London Paddington d	17 45	17 45	17 50		17 57	18 00	18 03	18 06	18 12	18 15	18 15	18 18	18 21		18 27	18 30	18 33	18 42	18 45	18 45	18 50	
Acton Main Line d	17 51									18 21									18 51			
Ealing Broadway d	17 54				18 05		18 11		18 20	18 24					18 35		18 41	18 50	18 54			
West Ealing d	17 57						18 13			18 27							18 43		18 57			
Drayton Green d	17 59									18 29									18 59			
Castle Bar Park d	18 01									18 31									19 01			
South Greenford d	18 04									18 34									19 04			
Greenford a	18 09									18 39									19 09			
Hanwell d							18 15										18 45					
Southall d							18 19		18 28								18 49	18 58				
Hayes & Harlington d					18 12		18 23		18 32						18 42		18 53	19 02				
Heathrow Terminal 1-2-3 a							18 35										19 05					
Heathrow Terminal 4 a																						
West Drayton d					18 16				18 36						18 46			19 06				
Iver d					18 19										18 49							
Langley d				←	18 22									←	18 52							←
Slough a			18 06	18 13	18 27				18 43				18 38	18 43	18 57			19 13			19 06	19 13
Slough d			18 06	18 13	18 27				18 43				18 39	18 43	18 57			19 13			19 06	19 13
Burnham d				18 17					→					18 47				→				19 17
Taplow d				18 21										18 51								19 21
Maidenhead d				18 25	18 34									18 55	19 04							19 25
Twyford d				18 33	18 42									19 03	19 12							19 33
Reading a		18 09	18 22	18 43	18 52	18 27		18 30			18 40	18 48	18 53	19 13	19 22	18 57				19 09	19 22	19 43
Oxford a			18 48		19 40								19 18		20 14						19 48	

	GW	GW	HC	GW	GW	GW	GW	GW	GW	GW	GW	HC	GW	GW	GW	GW	GW	GW	GW	HC	GW	GW
London Paddington d	18 57	19 00	19 03	19 06	19 12	19 15	19 15	19 21		19 27	19 30	19 33	19 42	19 45	19 45	19 50		19 57	20 00	20 03	20 06	20 12
Acton Main Line d						19 21								19 51								
Ealing Broadway d	19 05		19 11		19 20	19 24				19 35		19 41	19 50	19 54				20 05		20 11		20 20
West Ealing d			19 13			19 27						19 43		19 57						20 13		
Drayton Green d						19 29								19 59								
Castle Bar Park d						19 31								20 01								
South Greenford d						19 34								20 04								
Greenford a						19 39								20 09								
Hanwell d			19 15									19 45								20 15		
Southall d			19 19		19 28							19 49	19 58							20 19		20 28
Hayes & Harlington d	19 12		19 23		19 32					19 42		19 53	20 02					20 12		20 23		20 32
Heathrow Terminal 1-2-3 a			19 35									20 05								20 35		
Heathrow Terminal 4 a																						
West Drayton d	19 16				19 36					19 46			20 06					20 16				20 36
Iver d	19 19									19 49								20 19				
Langley d	19 22								←	19 52							←	20 22				
Slough a	19 27				19 43			19 37	19 43	19 57			20 13			20 06	20 13	20 27				20 43
Slough d	19 27				19 43			19 38	19 43	19 57			20 13			20 06	20 13	20 27				20 43
Burnham d					→				19 47				→				20 17					→
Taplow d									19 51								20 21					
Maidenhead d	19 34								19 55	20 04							20 25	20 34				
Twyford d	19 42								20 03	20 12							20 33	20 42				
Reading a	19 52	19 26		19 30			19 39	19 52	20 13	20 20	19 57				20 09	20 21	20 43	20 52	20 27		20 31	
Oxford a	20 40							20 20		21 14						20 47		21 40				

Table 117

Saturdays

15 September to 20 October

London - Greenford and Reading

Network Diagram - see first Page of Table 116

	GW 1	GW ◇1 ☕	GW ◇1	GW 1	GW 1	GW ◇1 ☕	HC	GW 1	GW ◇1 ☕	GW 1	GW ◇1 🚲	GW 1	GW 1	HC	GW 1	GW 1	GW ◇1	GW ◇1 ☕	GW 1	HC	GW 1
London Paddington 15 ⊖ d	20 15	20 15	20 20		20 27	20 30	20 33	20 42	20 45	20 45	20 50		20 57	21 03	21 12	21 15	21 17	21 30		21 33	21 42
Acton Main Line d										20 51						21 21					21 48
Ealing Broadway ⊖ d	20 24				20 35		20 41	20 50		20 54			21 05	21 11	21 20	21 24				21 41	21 52
West Ealing d	20 27						20 43			20 57				21 13		21 27				21 43	
Drayton Green d	20 29									20 59						21 29					
Castle Bar Park d	20 31									21 01						21 31					
South Greenford d	20 34									21 04						21 34					
Greenford ⊖ a	20 39									21 09						21 39					
Hanwell d							20 45							21 15						21 45	
Southall d							20 49	20 58						21 19	21 28					21 49	21 58
Hayes & Harlington d					20 42		20 53	21 02					21 12	21 23	21 32					21 53	22 02
Heathrow Terminal 1-2-3 2 ✈ a							21 05							21 35						22 05	
Heathrow Terminal 4 ✈ a																					
West Drayton d					20 46			21 06					21 16		21 36						22 06
Iver d					20 49								21 19								
Langley d				←	20 52							←	21 22						←		
Slough 3 a			20 35	20 43	20 57			21 13			21 06	21 13	21 27		21 43		21 34		21 43		22 13
d			20 35	20 43	20 57			21 13			21 06	21 13	21 27		21 43		21 35		21 43		22 13
Burnham d				20 47				→				21 17			→				21 47		→
Taplow d				20 51								21 21							21 51		
Maidenhead 3 d				20 55	21 04							21 25	21 34						21 55		
Twyford 3 d				21 06	21 12							21 33	21 46						22 06		
Reading 7 a		20 40	20 51	21 14	21 22	20 57			21 10		21 24	21 41	21 55				21 51	21 58	22 14		
Oxford a			21 19		22 14						21 55		22 43				22 20				

	GW ◇1	GW 1	GW 1	GW ◇1 ☕	HC	GW 1	GW ◇1	HC	GW ◇1 ☕	GW 1	GW 1	GW ◇1	GW 1	HC	GW 1	GW ◇1 ☕	GW ◇1	GW 1	GW 1
London Paddington 15 ⊖ d	21 50		21 57	22 00	22 03	22 12	22 15	22 33	22 35		22 45	23 00		23 03	23 20	23 30	23 33		23 42
Acton Main Line d											22 51								
Ealing Broadway ⊖ d			22 05		22 11	22 20		22 41			22 55			23 11	23 28				23 50
West Ealing d					22 13			22 43						23 13					
Drayton Green d																			
Castle Bar Park d																			
South Greenford d																			
Greenford ⊖ a																			
Hanwell d					22 15			22 45						23 15					
Southall d					22 19	22 28		22 49			23 00			23 19	23 33				23 56
Hayes & Harlington d			22 12		22 23	22 32		22 53			23 04			23 23	23 37				00 01
Heathrow Terminal 1-2-3 2 ✈ a					22 35			23 05						23 35					
Heathrow Terminal 4 ✈ a														23 41					
West Drayton d			22 16			22 36					23 08				23 41				00 06
Iver d			22 19								23 11				23 44				
Langley d		←	22 22							←	23 14		←		23 48			←	
Slough 3 a	22 06	22 13	22 27			22 43	22 31			22 43	23 19	23 16	23 19		23 53		23 49	23 53	00 13
d	22 06	22 13	22 27			22 43	22 32			22 43	23 21	23 17	23 21		23 54		23 50	23 54	00 14
Burnham d		22 17				→				22 47	→		23 25		→			23 57	00 18
Taplow d		22 21								22 51								00 01	00 21
Maidenhead 3 d		22 25	22 34							22 55			23 32					00 05	00 25
Twyford 3 d		22 33	22 45							23 03			23 39					00 13	00a34
Reading 7 a	22 22	22 41	22 56	22 27			22 48		23 00	23 13		23 33	23 46			23 59	00 06	00 20	
Oxford a	22 50		23 38				23 20					00 04	00 32				00 39	01 07	

Saturdays

from 27 October

	GW 1	GW ◇1	GW 1	GW 1	GW ◇1 ☕	GW 1	GW 1	GW ◇1	GW 1	GW 1	GW 1	HC	HC	GW ◇1	GW 1	HC	GW 1	GW ◇1	GW 1	HC	GW 1	GW 1
London Paddington 15 ⊖ d	22p45	23p18		23p29	23p30	23p42	23p48	00 22	00 34	01 44	03 34	04 42	05 13	05 21	05 25	05 33	05 45	05 50	05 57	06 03	06 12	06 15
Acton Main Line d	22p51						23p54										05 51					06 21
Ealing Broadway ⊖ d	22p54			23p37			23p57		00 42	01 52	03 42	04 50	05 21		05 33	05 41	05 54		06 05	06 11	06 20	06 24
West Ealing d							23p59									05 43	05 57			06 13		06 27
Drayton Green d																	05 59					06 29
Castle Bar Park d																	06 01					06 31
South Greenford d																	06 04					06 34
Greenford ⊖ a																	06 09					06 39
Hanwell d							00 02									05 45				06 15		
Southall d							00 06		00 47	01 57	03 47	04 54	05 25		05 38	05 49			06 10	06 19	06 28	
Hayes & Harlington d	23p01			23p44			00 10		00 51	02 01	03 51	04 58	05 29		05 42	05 53			06 14	06 23	06 32	
Heathrow Terminal 1-2-3 2 ✈ a												05 04	05 35			06 05				06 35		
Heathrow Terminal 4 ✈ a												05 10	05 41									
West Drayton d							00 14		00 55	02 05	03 55								06 18		06 36	
Iver d							00 17												06 21			
Langley d							00 21		01 00										06 25			
Slough 3 a	23p11	23p36		23p53		23p58	00 26	00 38	01 05	02 13	04 03			05 37	05 50			06 06	06 30		06 43	
d	23p12	23p36		23p54		23p58	00 26	00 39	01 05	02 13	04 03			05 38	05 51			06 06	06 31		06 43	
Burnham d	23p16						00 30		01 09						05 55				06 35		→	
Taplow d	23p20						00 34		01 13						05 58				06 38			
Maidenhead 3 d	23p24	23p44		00 01		00 08	00 41		01 16	02 21	04 11				06 02				06 42			
Twyford 3 d	23p32		00 07	00 09			00 48		01 24	02 29	04 19				06 10				06 50			
Reading 7 a	23p41	23p58	00 16	00 19	00 05	00 21	00 57	00 55	01 35	02 38	04 30			05 52	06 17			06 22	06 56			
Oxford a	00 26	00 28		01 16		01 02		01 28						06 22	07 03			06 52	07 43			

Table 117

Saturdays

from 27 October

London - Greenford and Reading

Network Diagram - see first Page of Table 116

	GW ◇1	GW 1	GW 1	GW ◇1 ☕	HC	GW 1	GW 1	GW ◇1	GW 1	GW 1	GW ◇1 ☕	HC	GW 1	GW 1	GW ◇1	GW 1	GW 1	GW 1 ☕	HC	GW 1	GW 1	GW ◇1 ☕
London Paddington 15 ⊖ d	06 21		06 27	06 30	06 33	06 42	06 45	06 50		06 57	07 00	07 03	07 12	07 15	07 21		07 27	07 30	07 33	07 42	07 45	07 45
Acton Main Line d							06 51							07 21							07 51	
Ealing Broadway ⊖ d			06 35		06 41	06 50	06 54			07 05		07 11	07 20	07 24			07 35		07 41	07 50	07 54	
West Ealing d					06 43		06 57					07 13		07 27					07 43		07 57	
Drayton Green d							06 59							07 29							07 59	
Castle Bar Park d							07 01							07 31							08 01	
South Greenford d							07 04							07 34							08 04	
Greenford ⊖ a							07 09							07 39							08 09	
Hanwell d					06 45							07 15							07 45			
Southall d					06 49	06 58						07 19	07 28						07 49	07 58		
Hayes & Harlington d			06 42		06 53	07 02				07 12		07 23	07 32				07 42		07 53	08 02		
Heathrow Terminal 1-2-3 2 ✈ a					07 05							07 35							08 05			
Heathrow Terminal 4 ✈ a																						
West Drayton d			06 46			07 06				07 16			07 36				07 46			08 06		
Iver d			06 49							07 19							07 49					
Langley d		←	06 52						←	07 22						←	07 52					
Slough 3 a	06 37	06 43	06 57			07 13		07 06	07 13	07 27			07 43		07 37	07 43	07 57			08 13		
d	06 38	06 43	06 57			07 13		07 06	07 13	07 27			07 43		07 38	07 43	07 57			08 13		
Burnham d		06 47				→			07 17				→			07 47				→		
Taplow d		06 51							07 21							07 51						
Maidenhead 3 d		06 55	07 04						07 25	07 34						07 55	08 04					
Twyford 3 d		07 03	07 12						07 33	07 42						08 03	08 12					
Reading 7 a	06 53	07 13	07 20	06 57				07 22	07 43	07 52	07 26				07 53	08 13	08 22	07 57				08 09
Oxford a	07 18		08 09					07 48		08 40					08 19		09 14					

	GW ◇1	GW 1	GW 1	GW ◇1 ☕	HC	GW 1	GW 1	GW ◇1 ☕	GW ◇1 ☕	GW ◇1 ☕	GW 1	GW 1	GW ◇1 ☕	HC	GW 1	GW 1	GW ◇1 ☕	GW ◇1	GW 1	GW 1	GW ◇1 ☕
London Paddington 15 ⊖ d	07 50		07 57	08 00	08 03	08 12	08 15	08 15	08 18	08 21		08 27	08 30	08 33	08 42	08 45	08 45	08 50		08 57	09 00
Acton Main Line d							08 21									08 51					
Ealing Broadway ⊖ d			08 05		08 11	08 20	08 24					08 35		08 41	08 50	08 54				09 05	
West Ealing d					08 13		08 27							08 43		08 57					
Drayton Green d							08 29									08 59					
Castle Bar Park d							08 31									09 01					
South Greenford d							08 34									09 04					
Greenford ⊖ a							08 39									09 09					
Hanwell d					08 15									08 45							
Southall d					08 19	08 28								08 49	08 58						
Hayes & Harlington d			08 12		08 23	08 32						08 42		08 53	09 02					09 12	
Heathrow Terminal 1-2-3 2 ✈ a					08 35									09 05							
Heathrow Terminal 4 ✈ a																					
West Drayton d			08 16			08 36						08 46			09 06					09 16	
Iver d			08 19									08 49								09 19	
Langley d		←	08 22								←	08 52							←	09 22	
Slough 3 a	08 06	08 13	08 27			08 43				08 38	08 43	08 57			09 13			09 06	09 13	09 27	
d	08 06	08 13	08 27			08 43				08 39	08 43	08 57			09 13			09 06	09 13	09 27	
Burnham d		08 17				→					08 47				→				09 17		
Taplow d		08 21									08 51								09 21		
Maidenhead 3 d		08 25	08 34								08 55	09 04							09 25	09 34	
Twyford 3 d		08 33	08 42								09 03	09 12							09 33	09 42	
Reading 7 a	08 22	08 43	08 52	08 26				08 40	08 46	08 53	09 13	09 23	08 56				09 09	09 22	09 43	09 52	09 26
Oxford a	08 48		09 40							09 18		10 14						09 48		10 40	

	HC	GW ◇1 Ø	GW 1	GW 1	GW 1	GW ◇1	GW 1	GW 1	GW ◇1 ☕	HC	GW 1	GW 1	GW ◇1 ☕	GW ◇1	GW 1	GW 1	GW ◇1 ☕	HC	GW ◇1 Ø	GW 1	GW 1	GW ◇1 ☕
London Paddington 15 ⊖ d	09 03	09 06	09 12	09 15	09 18	09 21		09 27	09 30	09 33	09 42	09 45	09 45	09 50		09 57	10 00	10 03	10 06	10 12	10 15	10 15
Acton Main Line d				09 21								09 51									10 21	
Ealing Broadway ⊖ d	09 11		09 20	09 24				09 35		09 41	09 50	09 54				10 05		10 11		10 20	10 24	
West Ealing d	09 13			09 27						09 43		09 57						10 13			10 27	
Drayton Green d				09 29								09 59									10 29	
Castle Bar Park d				09 31								10 01									10 31	
South Greenford d				09 34								10 04									10 34	
Greenford ⊖ a				09 39								10 09									10 39	
Hanwell d	09 15									09 45								10 15				
Southall d	09 19		09 28							09 49	09 58							10 19		10 28		
Hayes & Harlington d	09 23		09 32					09 42		09 53	10 02					10 12		10 23		10 32		
Heathrow Terminal 1-2-3 2 ✈ a	09 35									10 05								10 35				
Heathrow Terminal 4 ✈ a																						
West Drayton d			09 36					09 46			10 06					10 16				10 36		
Iver d								09 49								10 19						
Langley d							←	09 52							←	10 22						
Slough 3 a			09 43			09 38	09 43	09 57			10 13			10 06	10 13	10 27				10 43		
d			09 43			09 39	09 43	09 57			10 13			10 06	10 13	10 27				10 43		
Burnham d			→				09 47				→				10 17					→		
Taplow d							09 51								10 21							
Maidenhead 3 d							09 55	10 04							10 25	10 34						
Twyford 3 d							10 03	10 12							10 33	10 42						
Reading 7 a		09 30			09 48	09 54	10 13	10 22	09 57				10 09	10 22	10 43	10 52	10 26		10 30			10 40
Oxford a						10 19		11 14						10 48		11 40						

Table 117

London - Greenford and Reading

Saturdays

from 27 October

Network Diagram - see first Page of Table 116

	GW 1	GW ◇1 ⊐	GW 1	GW 1	GW ◇1 ⊐	HC	GW 1	GW 1	GW ◇1 Ø	GW ◇1 ⌶	GW 1	GW 1	GW ◇1 ⊐	HC	GW ◇1 Ø	GW 1	GW 1	GW 1	GW ◇1 ⌶	GW 1	GW 1
London Paddington ⊖ d	10 18	10 21		10 27	10 30	10 33	10 42	10 45	10 45	10 50		10 57	11 00	11 03	11 06	11 12	11 15	11 18	11 21		11 27
Acton Main Line d								10 51									11 21				
Ealing Broadway ⊖ d				10 35		10 41	10 52	10 54				11 05		11 11		11 20	11 24				11 35
West Ealing d						10 43		10 57						11 13			11 27				
Drayton Green d								10 59									11 29				
Castle Bar Park d								11 01									11 31				
South Greenford d								11 04									11 34				
Greenford ⊖ a								11 09									11 39				
Hanwell d						10 45								11 15							
Southall d						10 49	10 58							11 19		11 28					
Hayes & Harlington d				10 42		10 53	11 02					11 12		11 23		11 32					11 42
Heathrow Terminal 1-2-3 ✈ a						11 05								11 35							
Heathrow Terminal 4 ✈ a																					
West Drayton d				10 46			11 06					11 16				11 36					11 46
Iver d				10 49								11 19									11 49
Langley d			←	10 52							←	11 22								←	11 52
Slough a		10 38	10 43	10 57			11 13			11 06	11 13	11 27				11 43			11 38	11 43	11 57
Slough d		10 39	10 43	10 57			11 13			11 06	11 13	11 27				11 43			11 39	11 43	11 57
Burnham d			10 47				→				11 17					→				11 47	
Taplow d			10 51								11 21									11 51	
Maidenhead d			10 55	11 04							11 25	11 34								11 55	12 04
Twyford d			11 03	11 12							11 33	11 42								12 03	12 12
Reading a	10 48	10 53	11 13	11 22	10 57				11 09	11 22	11 43	11 52	11 26		11 30			11 48	11 54	12 13	12 22
Oxford a		11 19		12 14						11 48		12 40							12 20		13 14

	GW ◇1 Ø	HC	GW 1	GW 1	GW ◇1 Ø	GW ◇1	GW 1	GW 1	GW ◇1 ⊐	HC	GW ◇1 Ø	GW 1	GW 1	GW ◇1 ⊐	GW ◇1 ⊐	GW ◇1	GW 1	GW 1	GW ◇1 ⊐	HC	GW 1	GW 1
London Paddington ⊖ d	11 30	11 33	11 42	11 45	11 45	11 50		11 57	12 00	12 03	12 06	12 12	12 15	12 15	12 18	12 21		12 27	12 30	12 33	12 42	12 45
Acton Main Line d				11 51									12 21									12 51
Ealing Broadway ⊖ d		11 41	11 50	11 54				12 05		12 11		12 20	12 24					12 35		12 41	12 50	12 54
West Ealing d		11 43		11 57						12 13			12 27							12 43		12 57
Drayton Green d				11 59									12 29									12 59
Castle Bar Park d				12 01									12 31									13 01
South Greenford d				12 04									12 34									13 04
Greenford ⊖ a				12 09									12 39									13 09
Hanwell d		11 45								12 15										12 45		
Southall d		11 49	11 58							12 19		12 28								12 49	12 58	
Hayes & Harlington d		11 53	12 02					12 12		12 23		12 32						12 42		12 53	13 02	
Heathrow Terminal 1-2-3 ✈ a		12 05								12 35										13 05		
Heathrow Terminal 4 ✈ a																						
West Drayton d			12 06					12 16				12 36						12 46			13 06	
Iver d								12 19										12 49				
Langley d							←	12 22									←	12 52				
Slough a			12 13			12 06	12 13	12 27				12 43				12 38	12 43	12 57			13 13	
Slough d			12 13			12 06	12 13	12 27				12 43				12 39	12 43	12 57			13 13	
Burnham d			→				12 17					→					12 47				→	
Taplow d							12 21										12 51					
Maidenhead d							12 25	12 34									12 55	13 04				
Twyford d							12 33	12 42									13 03	13 12				
Reading a	11 57				12 09	12 22	12 43	12 52	12 26		12 30			12 40	12 45	12 54	13 13	13 22	12 57			
Oxford a						12 48		13 40								13 19		14 14				

	GW ◇1 ⊐	GW ◇1 ⌶	GW 1	GW 1	GW ◇1 ⊐	HC	GW 1 ⊐	GW 1	GW 1	GW 1	GW ◇1 ⌶	GW 1	GW 1	GW ◇1 ⊐	HC	GW 1	GW 1	GW ◇1 ⊐	GW ◇1 ⌶	GW 1	GW 1	GW ◇1 ⊐
London Paddington ⊖ d	12 45	12 50		12 57	13 00	13 03	13 06	13 12	13 15	13 18	13 21		13 27	13 30	13 33	13 42	13 45	13 45	13 50		13 57	14 00
Acton Main Line d									13 21								13 51					
Ealing Broadway ⊖ d				13 05		13 11		13 20	13 24				13 35		13 41	13 50	13 54				14 05	
West Ealing d						13 13			13 27						13 43		13 57					
Drayton Green d									13 29								13 59					
Castle Bar Park d									13 31								14 01					
South Greenford d									13 34								14 04					
Greenford ⊖ a									13 39								14 09					
Hanwell d						13 15									13 45							
Southall d						13 19		13 28							13 49	13 58						
Hayes & Harlington d				13 12		13 23		13 32					13 42		13 53	14 02					14 12	
Heathrow Terminal 1-2-3 ✈ a						13 35									14 05							
Heathrow Terminal 4 ✈ a																						
West Drayton d				13 16				13 36					13 46			14 06					14 16	
Iver d				13 19									13 49								14 19	
Langley d			←	13 22								←	13 52							←	14 22	
Slough a		13 06	13 13	13 27				13 43			13 38	13 43	13 57			14 13			14 06	14 13	14 27	
Slough d		13 06	13 13	13 27				13 43			13 39	13 43	13 57			14 13			14 06	14 13	14 27	
Burnham d			13 17					→				13 47				→				14 17		
Taplow d			13 21									13 51								14 21		
Maidenhead d			13 25	13 34								13 55	14 04							14 25	14 34	
Twyford d			13 33	13 42								14 03	14 12							14 33	14 42	
Reading a	13 09	13 22	13 43	13 52	13 26		13 30			13 48	13 54	14 13	14 22	13 58				14 09	14 22	14 43	14 52	14 26
Oxford a		13 48		14 40							14 19		15 14						14 48		15 40	

Table 117

London - Greenford and Reading

Saturdays

from 27 October

Network Diagram - see first Page of Table 116

	HC	GW ◇1 ⊐	GW 1	GW 1	GW ◇1 ⊐	GW 1	GW ◇1 ⌶	GW 1	GW 1	GW ◇1 ⊐	HC	GW 1	GW 1	GW ◇1 ⊐	GW ◇1	GW 1	GW 1	GW ◇1 ⊐	HC	GW ◇1 ⊐	GW 1
London Paddington ⊖ d	14 03	14 06	14 12	14 15	14 15	14 18	14 21		14 27	14 30	14 33	14 42	14 45	14 45	14 50		14 57	15 00	15 03	15 06	15 12
Acton Main Line d				14 21									14 51								
Ealing Broadway ⊖ d	14 11		14 20	14 24					14 35		14 41	14 50	14 54				15 05		15 11		15 20
West Ealing d	14 13			14 27							14 43		14 57						15 13		
Drayton Green d				14 29									14 59								
Castle Bar Park d				14 31									15 01								
South Greenford d				14 34									15 04								
Greenford ⊖ a				14 39									15 09								
Hanwell d	14 15										14 45								15 15		
Southall d	14 19		14 28								14 49	14 58							15 19		15 28
Hayes & Harlington d	14 23		14 32						14 42		14 53	15 02					15 12		15 23		15 32
Heathrow Terminal 1-2-3 ✈ a	14 35										15 05								15 35		
Heathrow Terminal 4 ✈ a																					
West Drayton d			14 36						14 46			15 06					15 16				15 36
Iver d									14 49								15 19				
Langley d								←	14 52							←	15 22				
Slough a			14 43				14 38	14 43	14 57			15 13			15 06	15 13	15 27				15 43
Slough d			14 43				14 39	14 43	14 57			15 13			15 06	15 13	15 27				15 43
Burnham d			→					14 47				→				15 17					→
Taplow d								14 51								15 21					
Maidenhead d								14 55	15 04							15 25	15 34				
Twyford d								15 03	15 12							15 33	15 42				
Reading a		14 30			14 40	14 48	14 53	15 13	15 22	14 57				15 09	15 22	15 43	15 52	15 26		15 29	
Oxford a							15 18		16 14						15 48		16 40				

	GW 1	GW 1	GW ◇1 ⌶	GW 1	GW 1	GW ◇1 ⊐	HC	GW 1	GW 1	GW ◇1 ⊐	GW ◇1	GW 1	GW 1	GW ◇1 ⊐	HC	GW ◇1 ⊐	GW 1	GW 1	GW ◇1 ⊐	GW 1	GW ◇1 ⊐	GW 1
London Paddington ⊖ d	15 15	15 18	15 21		15 27	15 30	15 33	15 42	15 45	15 45	15 50		15 57	16 00	16 03	16 06	16 12	16 15	16 15	16 18	16 21	
Acton Main Line d	15 21								15 51									16 21				
Ealing Broadway ⊖ d	15 24				15 35		15 41	15 50	15 54				16 05		16 11		16 20	16 24				
West Ealing d	15 27						15 43		15 57						16 13			16 27				
Drayton Green d	15 29								15 59									16 29				
Castle Bar Park d	15 31								16 01									16 31				
South Greenford d	15 34								16 04									16 34				
Greenford ⊖ a	15 39								16 09									16 39				
Hanwell d							15 45								16 15							
Southall d							15 49	15 58							16 19		16 28					
Hayes & Harlington d					15 42		15 53	16 02					16 12		16 23		16 32					
Heathrow Terminal 1-2-3 ✈ a							16 05								16 35							
Heathrow Terminal 4 ✈ a																						
West Drayton d					15 46			16 06					16 16				16 36					
Iver d					15 49								16 19									
Langley d				←	15 52							←	16 22									←
Slough a			15 38	15 43	15 57			16 13			16 06	16 13	16 27				16 43				16 38	16 43
Slough d			15 39	15 43	15 57			16 13			16 06	16 13	16 27				16 43				16 39	16 43
Burnham d				15 47				→				16 17					→					16 47
Taplow d				15 51								16 21										16 51
Maidenhead d				15 55	16 04							16 25	16 34									16 55
Twyford d				16 03	16 12							16 33	16 42									17 03
Reading a		15 48	15 54	16 13	16 22	15 58				16 09	16 22	16 43	16 52	16 26		16 31			16 40	16 48	16 53	17 13
Oxford a			16 19		17 14						16 48		17 40								17 18	

	GW 1	GW ◇1 ⊐	HC	GW 1	GW 1	GW ◇1 ⊐	GW ◇1 ⌶	GW 1	GW 1	GW ◇1 ⊐	HC	GW ◇1 ⊐	GW 1	GW 1	GW 1	GW ◇1 ⊐	GW 1	GW 1	GW ◇1 ⊐	HC	GW 1
London Paddington ⊖ d	16 27	16 30	16 33	16 42	16 45	16 45	16 50		16 57	17 00	17 03	17 06	17 12	17 15	17 18	17 21		17 27	17 30	17 33	17 42
Acton Main Line d					16 51									17 21							
Ealing Broadway ⊖ d	16 35		16 41	16 50	16 54				17 05		17 11		17 20	17 24				17 35		17 41	17 50
West Ealing d			16 43		16 57						17 13			17 27						17 43	
Drayton Green d					16 59									17 29							
Castle Bar Park d					17 01									17 31							
South Greenford d					17 04									17 34							
Greenford ⊖ a					17 09									17 39							
Hanwell d			16 45								17 15									17 45	
Southall d			16 49	16 58							17 19		17 28							17 49	17 58
Hayes & Harlington d	16 42		16 53	17 02					17 12		17 23		17 32					17 42		17 53	18 02
Heathrow Terminal 1-2-3 ✈ a			17 05								17 35									18 05	
Heathrow Terminal 4 ✈ a																					
West Drayton d	16 46			17 06					17 16				17 36					17 46			18 06
Iver d	16 49								17 19									17 49			
Langley d	16 52							←	17 22								←	17 52			
Slough a	16 57			17 13			17 06	17 13	17 27				17 43			17 38	17 43	17 57			18 13
Slough d	16 57			17 13			17 06	17 13	17 27				17 43			17 39	17 43	17 57			18 13
Burnham d				→				17 17					→				17 47				→
Taplow d								17 21									17 51				
Maidenhead d	17 04							17 25	17 34								17 55	18 04			
Twyford d	17 12							17 33	17 42								18 03	18 12			
Reading a	17 22	16 57				17 09	17 22	17 43	17 52	17 26		17 30			17 48	17 53	18 13	18 22	17 57		
Oxford a	18 14						17 48		18 40							18 18		19 14			

Table 117

London - Greenford and Reading

Saturdays from 27 October

Network Diagram - see first Page of Table 116

		GW	GW	GW	GW	GW	GW	HC	GW	GW	GW	GW	GW	GW	GW	GW	GW	HC	GW	GW	GW	GW	GW
		■	◇■	◇■	■	■	◇■		◇■	■	■	◇■	■	◇■	■	■	◇■		■	■	◇■	◇■	■
London Paddington 15 ⊖	d	17 45	17 45	17 50		17 57	18 00	18 03	18 06	18 12	18 15	18 15	18 18	18 21		18 27	18 30	18 33	18 42	18 45	18 45	18 50	
Acton Main Line	d	17 51									18 21									18 51			
Ealing Broadway ⊖	d	17 54				18 05		18 11		18 20	18 24					18 35		18 41	18 50	18 54			
West Ealing	d	17 57						18 13			18 27							18 43		18 57			
Drayton Green	d	17 59									18 29									18 59			
Castle Bar Park	d	18 01									18 31									19 01			
South Greenford	d	18 04									18 34									19 04			
Greenford ⊖	a	18 09									18 39									19 09			
Hanwell	d							18 15										18 45					
Southall	d							18 19		18 28								18 49	18 58				
Hayes & Harlington	d					18 12		18 23		18 32						18 42		18 53	19 02				
Heathrow Terminal 1-2-3 2 ✈	a							18 35										19 05					
Heathrow Terminal 4 ✈	a																						
West Drayton	d					18 16				18 36						18 46			19 06				
Iver	d					18 19										18 49							
Langley	d				←	18 22									←	18 52							←
Slough 3	a			18 06	18 13	18 27				18 43				18 38	18 43	18 57			19 13			19 06	19 13
	d			18 06	18 13	18 27				18 43				18 39	18 43	18 57			19 13			19 06	19 13
Burnham	d				18 17					→					18 47				→				19 17
Taplow	d				18 21										18 51								19 21
Maidenhead 3	d				18 25	18 34									18 55	19 04							19 25
Twyford 3	d				18 33	18 42									19 03	19 12							19 33
Reading 7	a		18 09	18 22	18 43	18 52	18 27		18 30			18 40	18 48	18 53	19 13	19 22	18 57				19 09	19 22	19 43
Oxford	a			18 48		19 40								19 18		20 14						19 48	

		GW	GW	HC	GW	GW	GW	GW	GW	GW	GW	GW	HC	GW	GW	GW	GW	GW	GW	GW	HC	GW	GW
		■	◇■		◇■	■	■	◇■	◇■	■	■	◇■		■	■	◇■	◇■	■	■	◇■		◇■	■
London Paddington 15 ⊖	d	18 57	19 00	19 03	19 06	19 12	19 15	19 15	19 21		19 27	19 30	19 33	19 42	19 45	19 45	19 50		19 57	20 00	20 03	20 06	20 12
Acton Main Line	d						19 21								19 51								
Ealing Broadway ⊖	d	19 05		19 11		19 20	19 24				19 35		19 41	19 50	19 54				20 05		20 11		20 20
West Ealing	d			19 13			19 27						19 43		19 57						20 13		
Drayton Green	d						19 29								19 59								
Castle Bar Park	d						19 31								20 01								
South Greenford	d						19 34								20 04								
Greenford ⊖	a						19 39								20 09								
Hanwell	d			19 15									19 45								20 15		
Southall	d			19 19		19 28							19 49	19 58							20 19		20 28
Hayes & Harlington	d	19 12		19 23		19 32					19 42		19 53	20 02					20 12		20 23		20 32
Heathrow Terminal 1-2-3 2 ✈	a			19 35									20 05								20 35		
Heathrow Terminal 4 ✈	a																						
West Drayton	d	19 16				19 36					19 46			20 06					20 16				20 36
Iver	d	19 19									19 49								20 19				
Langley	d	19 22								←	19 52							←	20 22				
Slough 3	a	19 27				19 43			19 37	19 43	19 57			20 13			20 06	20 13	20 27				20 43
	d	19 27				19 43			19 38	19 43	19 57			20 13			20 06	20 13	20 27				20 43
Burnham	d					→				19 47				→				20 17					→
Taplow	d									19 51								20 21					
Maidenhead 3	d	19 34								19 55	20 04							20 25	20 34				
Twyford 3	d	19 42								20 03	20 12							20 33	20 42				
Reading 7	a	19 52	19 26		19 30			19 39	19 52	20 13	20 20	19 57				20 09	20 21	20 43	20 52	20 27		20 31	
Oxford	a	20 40							20 20		21 14						20 47		21 40				

		GW	GW	GW	GW	GW	GW	HC	GW	GW	GW	GW	GW	GW	HC	GW	GW	GW	GW	GW	HC	GW
		■	◇■	◇■	■	■	◇■		■	◇■	■	◇■	■	■		■	■	◇■	◇■	■		■
London Paddington 15 ⊖	d	20 15	20 15	20 20		20 27	20 30	20 33	20 42	20 45	20 45	20 50		20 57	21 03	21 12	21 15	21 17	21 30		21 33	21 42
Acton Main Line	d	20 21									20 51						21 21					21 48
Ealing Broadway ⊖	d	20 24				20 35		20 41	20 50		20 54			21 05	21 11	21 20	21 24				21 41	21 52
West Ealing	d	20 27						20 43			20 57				21 13		21 27				21 43	
Drayton Green	d	20 29									20 59						21 29					
Castle Bar Park	d	20 31									21 01						21 31					
South Greenford	d	20 34									21 04						21 34					
Greenford ⊖	a	20 39									21 09						21 39					
Hanwell	d							20 45							21 15						21 45	
Southall	d							20 49	20 58						21 19	21 28					21 49	21 58
Hayes & Harlington	d					20 42		20 53	21 02					21 12	21 23	21 32					21 53	22 02
Heathrow Terminal 1-2-3 2 ✈	a							21 05							21 35						22 05	
Heathrow Terminal 4 ✈	a																					
West Drayton	d					20 46			21 06					21 16		21 36						22 06
Iver	d					20 49								21 19								
Langley	d				←	20 52							←	21 22						←		
Slough 3	a			20 35	20 43	20 57			21 13			21 06	21 13	21 27		21 43		21 34		21 43		22 13
	d			20 35	20 43	20 57			21 13			21 06	21 13	21 27		21 43		21 35		21 43		22 13
Burnham	d				20 47				→				21 17			→				21 47		→
Taplow	d				20 51								21 21							21 51		
Maidenhead 3	d				20 55	21 04							21 25	21 34						21 55		
Twyford 3	d				21 06	21 12							21 33	21 46						22 06		
Reading 7	a		20 40	20 51	21 14	21 22	20 57			21 10		21 24	21 41	21 55				21 51	21 58	22 14		
Oxford	a			21 19		22 14						21 55		22 43				22 20				

Table 117

London - Greenford and Reading

Saturdays from 27 October

Network Diagram - see first Page of Table 116

		GW	GW	GW	GW	HC	GW	GW	HC	GW	GW	GW	GW	GW	HC	GW	GW	GW	GW	GW
		◇■	■	■	◇■		■	◇■		◇■	■	■	◇■	■		■	◇■	◇■	■	■
London Paddington 15 ⊖	d	21 50		21 57	22 00	22 03	22 12	22 15	22 33	22 35		22 45	23 00		23 03	23 20	23 30	23 33		23 42
Acton Main Line	d											22 51								
Ealing Broadway ⊖	d			22 05		22 11	22 20		22 41			22 55			23 11	23 28				23 50
West Ealing	d					22 13			22 43						23 13					
Drayton Green	d																			
Castle Bar Park	d																			
South Greenford	d																			
Greenford ⊖	a																			
Hanwell	d					22 15			22 45						23 15					
Southall	d					22 19	22 28		22 49			23 00			23 19	23 33				23 56
Hayes & Harlington	d			22 12		22 23	22 32		22 53			23 04			23 23	23 37				00 01
Heathrow Terminal 1-2-3 2 ✈	a					22 35			23 05						23 35					
Heathrow Terminal 4 ✈	a														23 41					
West Drayton	d			22 16			22 36					23 08				23 41				00 06
Iver	d			22 19								23 11				23 44				
Langley	d		←	22 22							←	23 14		←		23 48			←	
Slough 3	a	22 06	22 13	22 27			22 43	22 31			22 43	23 19	23 16	23 19		23 53		23 49	23 53	00 13
	d	22 06	22 13	22 27			22 43	22 32			22 43	23 21	23 17	23 21		23 54		23 50	23 54	00 14
Burnham	d		22 17				→				22 47	→		23 25		→			23 57	00 18
Taplow	d		22 21								22 51								00 01	00 21
Maidenhead 3	d		22 25	22 34							22 55			23 32					00 05	00 25
Twyford 3	d		22 33	22 45							23 03			23 39					00 13	00a34
Reading 7	a	22 22	22 41	22 56	22 27			22 48		23 00	23 13		23 33	23 46			23 59	00 06	00 20	
Oxford	a	22 50		23 41				23 20					00 04	00 35				00 39	01 07	

Sundays until 24 June

		GW	GW	GW	GW	GW	GW	GW	GW	GW	GW	HC	HC	GW	HC	GW	GW	GW	HC	GW	GW	GW	GW
		■	◇■	■	■	◇■	■	■	■	■	■			■		■	◇■	◇■		■	◇■	◇■	◇■
London Paddington 15 ⊖	d	22p45	23p00		23p20	23p33		23p42	00 05	00 30	01 00		06 12	06 43	07 12	07 29	08 00	08 03	08 12	08 15	08 30	08 37	08 42
Acton Main Line	d	22p51																					
Ealing Broadway ⊖	d	22p55			23p28			23p50	00 13	00 38	01 08	05 20	06 20	06 52	07 20	07 36			08 20	08 24			
West Ealing	d																						
Drayton Green	d																						
Castle Bar Park	d																						
South Greenford	d																						
Greenford ⊖	a																						
Hanwell	d																						
Southall	d	23p00			23p33			23p56	00 19	00 44	01 13	05 24	06 24	06 58	07 24	07 42			08 24	08 29			
Hayes & Harlington	d	23p04			23p37			00 01	00 23	00 48	01 17	05 28	06 28	07 02	07 28	07 46			08 28	08 33			
Heathrow Terminal 1-2-3 2 ✈	a											05 34	06 34		07 34				08 34				
Heathrow Terminal 4 ✈	a											05 40	06 41		07 41				08 41				
West Drayton	d	23p08			23p41			00 06	00 27	00 52				07 06		07 50				08 37			
Iver	d	23p11			23p44				00 30														
Langley	d	23p14		←	23p48		←		00 33	00 56				07 11		07 55				08 42			
Slough 3	a	23p19	23p16	23p19	23p53	23p49	23p53	00 13	00 37	01 00	01 25			07 16		07 58		08 25		08 46			09 03
	d	23p21	23p17	23p21	23p54	23p50	23p54	00 14	00 38	01 01	01 26			07 16		07 58		08 25		08 46			09 04
Burnham	d	→		23p25	→		23p57	00 18	00 42					07 20		08 03							
Taplow	d						00 01	00 21	00 45														
Maidenhead 3	d			23p32			00 05	00 25	00 49	01 08	01 33			07 25		08 08		08 33		08 54			
Twyford 3	d			23p39			00 13	00 33	00 57	01 16	01 41			07 33		08 17				09 02			
Reading 7	a		23p33	23p46		00 06	00 20	00 43	01 05	01 24	01 50			07 42		08 25	08 33	08 44		09 10	09 05	09 14	09 20
Oxford	a		00 04	00 32		00 38	01 05									09 30		09 12					09 51

		GW	GW	GW	HC	GW	GW	GW	GW	GW	GW	HC	GW	GW	GW	GW	GW	GW	GW	HC	GW	GW	GW
		■	◇■	◇■		■	◇■	◇■	◇■	■	◇■		■	◇■	◇■	◇■	■	◇■	◇■		■	◇■	◇■
London Paddington 15 ⊖	d	08 43	08 57	09 03	09 12	09 15	09 30	09 35	09 42	09 43	10 03	10 12	10 15	10 30	10 37	10 42	10 43	10 57	11 03	11 12	11 15	11 30	11 37
Acton Main Line	d																						
Ealing Broadway ⊖	d	08 50			09 20	09 24				09 50		10 20	10 24				10 50			11 20	11 24		
West Ealing	d																						
Drayton Green	d																						
Castle Bar Park	d																						
South Greenford	d																						
Greenford ⊖	a																						
Hanwell	d																						
Southall	d	08 56			09 24	09 29				09 56		10 24	10 29				10 56			11 24	11 29		
Hayes & Harlington	d	09 02			09 28	09 33				10 02		10 28	10 33				11 02			11 28	11 33		
Heathrow Terminal 1-2-3 2 ✈	a				09 34							10 34								11 34			
Heathrow Terminal 4 ✈	a				09 41							10 41								11 41			
West Drayton	d	09 06				09 37				10 06			10 37				11 06				11 37		
Iver	d																						
Langley	d	09 10				09 42				10 10			10 42				11 10				11 43		
Slough 3	a	09 14				09 46		09 58		10 14			10 46			11 05	11 14				11 47		
	d	09 16				09 46		09 59		10 16			10 46			11 06	11 16				11 48		
Burnham	d	09 20								10 20							11 20						
Taplow	d																						
Maidenhead 3	d	09 27				09 54				10 27			10 54				11 27				11 55		
Twyford 3	d	09 35				10 02				10 35			11 02				11 35				12 03		
Reading 7	a	09 42	09 30	09 36		10 10	10 03	10 11	10 15	10 42	10 36		11 10	11 03	11 10	11 20	11 43	11 30	11 36		12 11	12 03	12 12
Oxford	a	10 28						10 43		11 27						11 50	12 27						

Table 117

London - Greenford and Reading

Sundays until 24 June

Network Diagram - see first Page of Table 116

	GW	GW	GW	HC	GW	GW	GW	GW	GW	GW	GW	HC	GW	GW	GW	GW	GW	GW	HC	GW	GW
London Paddington ⊖ d	11 42	11 43	12 03	12 12	12 15	12 30	12 37	12 42	12 43	12 57	13 03	13 12	13 15	13 30	13 37	13 42	13 43	14 03	14 12	14 15	14 30
Acton Main Line d																					
Ealing Broadway ⊖ d		11 50		12 20	12 24				12 50			13 20	13 24				13 50		14 20	14 24	
West Ealing d																					
Drayton Green d																					
Castle Bar Park d																					
South Greenford d																					
Greenford ⊖ a																					
Hanwell d																					
Southall d		11 56		12 24	12 29				12 56			13 24	13 29				13 56		14 24	14 29	
Hayes & Harlington d		12 02		12 28	12 33				13 02			13 28	13 33				14 02		14 28	14 33	
Heathrow Terminal 1-2-3 a				12 34								13 34							14 34		
Heathrow Terminal 4 a				12 41								13 41							14 41		
West Drayton d		12 06			12 37				13 06				13 37				14 06			14 37	
Iver d																					
Langley d		12 10			12 42				13 10				13 42				14 10			14 42	
Slough a	12 02	12 14			12 46			13 06	13 14				13 47			14 05	14 14			14 46	
Slough d	12 03	12 16			12 46			13 07	13 16				13 48			14 06	14 16			14 46	
Burnham d		12 20							13 20								14 20				
Taplow d																					
Maidenhead d		12 27			12 54				13 27				13 55				14 27			14 54	
Twyford d		12 35			13 02				13 35				14 03				14 35			15 02	
Reading a	12 18	12 43	12 36		13 10	13 03	13 11	13 21	13 43	13 30	13 36		14 11	14 03	14 10	14 21	14 42	14 37		15 11	15 03
Oxford a	12 48	13 28						13 50	14 28							14 50	15 27				

	GW	GW	GW	GW	GW	HC	GW	GW	GW	GW	GW	GW	GW	HC	GW	GW	GW	GW	GW	GW	GW	HC
London Paddington ⊖ d	14 37	14 42	14 43	14 57	15 03	15 12	15 15	15 27	15 30	15 37	15 42	15 43	16 03	16 12	16 15	16 30	16 37	16 42	16 43	16 57	17 03	17 12
Acton Main Line d																						
Ealing Broadway ⊖ d			14 50			15 20	15 24					15 50		16 20	16 24				16 50			17 20
West Ealing d																						
Drayton Green d																						
Castle Bar Park d																						
South Greenford d																						
Greenford ⊖ a																						
Hanwell d																						
Southall d			14 56			15 24	15 29					15 56		16 24	16 29				16 56			17 24
Hayes & Harlington d			15 02			15 28	15 33					16 02		16 28	16 33				17 02			17 28
Heathrow Terminal 1-2-3 a						15 34								16 34								17 34
Heathrow Terminal 4 a						15 41								16 41								17 41
West Drayton d			15 06				15 37					16 06			16 37				17 06			
Iver d																						
Langley d			15 10				15 42					16 10			16 42				17 10			
Slough a		15 02	15 14				15 46	15 49			16 04	16 14			16 46			17 03	17 14			
Slough d		15 03	15 16				15 46	15 50			16 05	16 16			16 46			17 04	17 16			
Burnham d			15 20				15 51					16 20			16 51				17 20			
Taplow d																						
Maidenhead d			15 27				15 56	16 01				16 27			16 56			17 11	17 27			
Twyford d			15 35				16 04	16 10				16 35			17 04				17 35			
Reading a	15 10	15 19	15 43	15 30	15 36		16 12	16 16	16 03	16 10	16 19	16 43	16 36		17 12	17 03	17 09	17 22	17 43	17 31	17 36	
Oxford a		15 50	16 25					16 41			16 50	17 25						17 50	18 27			

	GW	GW	GW	GW	GW	GW	GW	HC	GW	GW	GW	GW	GW	GW	GW	HC	GW	GW	GW	GW	GW
London Paddington ⊖ d	17 15	17 30	17 37	17 42	17 43	17 57	18 03	18 12	18 15	18 30	18 37	18 42	18 43	18 57	19 03	19 12	19 15	19 33	19 37	19 42	19 43
Acton Main Line d																					
Ealing Broadway ⊖ d	17 24				17 51			18 20	18 24				18 50			19 20	19 24				19 50
West Ealing d																					
Drayton Green d																					
Castle Bar Park d																					
South Greenford d																					
Greenford ⊖ a																					
Hanwell d																					
Southall d	17 29				17 56			18 24	18 29				18 56			19 24	19 29				19 56
Hayes & Harlington d	17 33				18 02			18 28	18 33				19 02			19 28	19 33				20 02
Heathrow Terminal 1-2-3 a								18 34								19 34					
Heathrow Terminal 4 a								18 41								19 41					
West Drayton d	17 37				18 06				18 37				19 06				19 37				20 06
Iver d																					
Langley d	17 42				18 10				18 42				19 10				19 42				20 10
Slough a	17 46			18 04	18 14				18 46			19 06	19 14				19 46			20 05	20 14
Slough d	17 46			18 04	18 16				18 46			19 07	19 16				19 46			20 06	20 16
Burnham d	17 51				18 20				18 51				19 20				19 51				20 20
Taplow d																					
Maidenhead d	17 56			18 14	18 27				18 56			19 14	19 27				19 56				20 27
Twyford d	18 04				18 35				19 04				19 35				20 04				20 35
Reading a	18 12	18 04	18 11	18 24	18 43	18 30	18 36		19 12	19 04	19 10	19 25	19 43	19 30	19 37		20 12	20 06	20 10	20 20	20 43
Oxford a				18 50	19 25							19 55	20 25							20 50	21 30

Table 117

London - Greenford and Reading

Sundays until 24 June

Network Diagram - see first Page of Table 116

	GW	GW	HC	GW	GW	GW	GW	GW	GW	GW	HC	GW	GW	GW	GW	GW	HC	GW	GW	GW	GW	GW
London Paddington ⊖ d	19 57	20 03	20 12	20 15	20 30	20 37	20 42	20 43	20 57	21 03	21 12	21 15	21 37	21 42	21 43	22 03	22 12	22 15	22 37	22 42	22 43	23 03
Acton Main Line d																						
Ealing Broadway ⊖ d			20 20	20 24				20 50			21 20	21 24			21 50		22 20	22 24			22 50	
West Ealing d																						
Drayton Green d																						
Castle Bar Park d																						
South Greenford d																						
Greenford ⊖ a																						
Hanwell d																						
Southall d			20 24	20 29				20 56			21 24	21 29			21 56		22 24	22 29			22 56	
Hayes & Harlington d			20 28	20 33				21 02			21 28	21 33			22 02		22 28	22 33			23 02	
Heathrow Terminal 1-2-3 a			20 34								21 34						22 34					
Heathrow Terminal 4 a			20 41								21 41						22 41					
West Drayton d				20 37				21 06				21 37			22 06			22 37			23 06	
Iver d																						
Langley d				20 42				21 10				21 42			22 10			22 42			23 10	
Slough a				20 46			21 01	21 14				21 46		22 05	22 14			22 46		23 01	23 14	
Slough d				20 46			21 01	21 16				21 46		22 06	22 16			22 46		23 02	23 16	
Burnham d				20 50				21 20				21 51			22 20			22 51			23 20	
Taplow d																						
Maidenhead d				20 56				21 27				21 56			22 31			22 56			23 24	
Twyford d				21 04				21 35				22 04			22 41			23 04			23 32	
Reading a	20 30	20 36		21 11	21 04	21 11	21 23	21 44	21 30	21 36		22 12	22 12	22 20	22 48	22 42		23 13	23 17	23 21	23 43	23 45
Oxford a							21 53	22 30						22 51								

	HC	GW	GW	GW	GW
London Paddington ⊖ d	23 12	23 15	23 37	23 47	23 53
Acton Main Line d					
Ealing Broadway ⊖ d	23 20	23 24		23 55	00 02
West Ealing d					
Drayton Green d					
Castle Bar Park d					
South Greenford d					
Greenford ⊖ a					
Hanwell d					
Southall d	23 24	23 29			00 07
Hayes & Harlington d	23 28	23 33			00 11
Heathrow Terminal 1-2-3 a	23 34				
Heathrow Terminal 4 a	23 41				
West Drayton d		23 37			00 15
Iver d					
Langley d		23 42			00 20
Slough a		23 46	00 02	00 09	00 24
Slough d		23 46	00 03	00 10	00 24
Burnham d		23 51			00 28
Taplow d					
Maidenhead d		23 56		00 17	00 34
Twyford d		00 04			00 42
Reading a		00 14	00 14	00 29	00 49
Oxford a					

Sundays 1 July to 9 September

	GW	GW	GW	GW	GW	GW	GW	GW	GW	GW	HC	HC	GW	HC	GW	GW	GW	HC	GW	GW	GW	GW
London Paddington ⊖ d	22p45	23p00		23p20	23p33		23p42	00 05	00 30	01 00		06 12	06 43	07 12	07 29	08 00	08 03	08 12	08 15	08 30	08 37	08 42
Acton Main Line d	22p51																					
Ealing Broadway ⊖ d	22p55			23p28			23p50	00 13	00 38	01 08	05 20	06 20	06 52	07 20	07 36			08 20	08 24			
West Ealing d																						
Drayton Green d																						
Castle Bar Park d																						
South Greenford d																						
Greenford ⊖ a																						
Hanwell d																						
Southall d	23p00			23p33			23p56	00 19	00 44	01 13	05 24	06 24	06 58	07 24	07 42			08 24	08 29			
Hayes & Harlington d	23p04			23p37			00 01	00 23	00 48	01 17	05 28	06 28	07 02	07 28	07 46			08 28	08 33			
Heathrow Terminal 1-2-3 a											05 34	06 34		07 34				08 34				
Heathrow Terminal 4 a											05 40	06 41		07 41				08 41				
West Drayton d	23p08			23p41			00 06	00 27	00 52				07 06		07 50				08 37			
Iver d	23p11			23p44				00 30														
Langley d	23p14		←	23p48		←		00 33	00 56				07 11		07 55				08 42			
Slough a	23p19	23p16	23p19	23p53	23p49	23p53	00 13	00 37	01 00	01 25			07 16		07 58		08 21		08 46			08 58
Slough d	23p21	23p17	23p21	23p54	23p50	23p54	00 14	00 38	01 01	01 26			07 16		07 58		08 21		08 46			08 59
Burnham d	→		23p25	→		23p57	00 18	00 42					07 20		08 03							
Taplow d						00 01	00 21	00 45														
Maidenhead d			23p32			00 05	00 25	00 49	01 08	01 33			07 25		08 08		08 28		08 54			
Twyford d			23p39			00 13	00 33	00 57	01 16	01 41			07 33		08 16				09 02			
Reading a		23p33	23p46		00 06	00 20	00 43	01 05	01 24	01 50			07 42		08 25	08 26	08 41		09 10	09 01	09 09	09 14
Oxford a		00 04	00 32		00 38	01 05									09 30		09 13					09 48

Sundays

1 July to 9 September

London - Greenford and Reading

Network Diagram - see first Page of Table 116

		GW 1	GW ◇1 ☕	GW ◇1 ☕	GW 1	HC	GW 1	HC	GW ◇1 ☕	GW ◇1 ☕	GW 1	GW ◇1 ☕	GW ◇1 ☕	GW 1	HC	GW 1	GW ◇1 ☕	HC	GW ◇1 ☕	GW ◇1 ☕	GW 1	GW ◇1 ☕	GW ◇1 ☕
London Paddington 15 ⊖	d	08 43	08 57	09 03	09 03	09 07	09 15	09 37	09 37	09 42	09 43	09 57	10 03	10 03	10 07	10 15	10 30	10 37	10 37	10 42	10 43	10 57	11 03
Acton Main Line	d																						
Ealing Broadway ⊖	d	08 51				09 15	09 24	09 45			09 50				10 15	10 24		10 45			10 50		
West Ealing	d																						
Drayton Green	d																						
Castle Bar Park	d																						
South Greenford	d																						
Greenford ⊖	a																						
Hanwell	d																						
Southall	d	08 56				09 19	09 29	09 49			09 56				10 19	10 29		10 49			10 56		
Hayes & Harlington	d	09 02				09 24	09 33	09 54			10 02				10 24	10 33		10 54			11 02		
Heathrow Terminal 1-2-3 2 ✈	a					09 29		09 59							10 29			10 59					
Heathrow Terminal 4 ✈	a					09 39		10 09							10 39			11 09					
West Drayton	d	09 06					09 37				10 06					10 37					11 06		
Iver	d																						
Langley	d	09 10					09 42				10 10					10 42					11 10		
Slough 3	a	09 14			09 23		09 46			09 58	10 14			10 23		10 46				10 59	11 14		
	d	09 16			09 23		09 46			09 59	10 16			10 23		10 46				11 00	11 16		
Burnham	d	09 20									10 20										11 20		
Taplow	d																						
Maidenhead 3	d	09 27			09 30		09 54				10 27			10 30		10 54					11 27		
Twyford 3	d	09 35					10 02				10 35					11 02					11 35		
Reading 7	a	09 42	09 25	09 36	09 43		10 10		10 01	10 11	10 43	10 24	10 36	10 43		11 10	10 55		11 02	11 17	11 43	11 24	11 36
Oxford	a	10 28								10 43	11 27									11 50	12 27		

		GW 1	HC	GW 1	GW ◇1 ☕	HC	GW ◇1 ☕	GW ◇1	GW 1	GW ◇1 ☕	GW ◇1 ☕	GW 1	HC	GW 1	GW ◇1 ☕	HC	GW ◇1 ☕	GW ◇1 ☕	GW 1	GW ◇1 ☕	GW ◇1 ☕	GW 1
London Paddington 15 ⊖	d	11 03	11 07	11 15	11 35	11 37	11 37	11 42	11 43	11 57	12 03	12 03	12 07	12 15	12 30	12 37	12 37	12 42	12 43	12 57	13 03	13 03
Acton Main Line	d																					
Ealing Broadway ⊖	d		11 15	11 24		11 45			11 50				12 15	12 24		12 45			12 50			
West Ealing	d																					
Drayton Green	d																					
Castle Bar Park	d																					
South Greenford	d																					
Greenford ⊖	a																					
Hanwell	d																					
Southall	d		11 19	11 29		11 49			11 56				12 19	12 29		12 49			12 56			
Hayes & Harlington	d		11 24	11 33		11 54			12 02				12 24	12 33		12 54			13 02			
Heathrow Terminal 1-2-3 2 ✈	a		11 29			11 59							12 29			12 59						
Heathrow Terminal 4 ✈	a		11 39			12 09							12 39			13 09						
West Drayton	d			11 37					12 06					12 37					13 06			
Iver	d																					
Langley	d			11 42					12 10					12 42					13 10			
Slough 3	a	11 23		11 46				11 58	12 14			12 23		12 46				13 00	13 14			13 23
	d	11 23		11 46				12 00	12 16			12 23		12 46				13 01	13 16			13 23
Burnham	d								12 20										13 20			
Taplow	d																					
Maidenhead 3	d	11 30		11 54					12 27			12 30		12 54					13 27			13 30
Twyford 3	d			12 02					12 35					13 02					13 35			
Reading 7	a	11 43		12 10	12 01		12 07	12 17	12 43	12 24	12 36	12 43		13 10	12 54		13 04	13 18	13 43	13 24	13 37	13 43
Oxford	a							12 49	13 28									13 50	14 27			

		HC	GW 1	HC	GW ◇1 ☕	GW ◇1 ☕	GW 1	GW ◇1 ☕	GW ◇1 ☕	GW 1	HC	GW 1	GW ◇1 ☕	HC	GW ◇1 ☕	GW ◇1	GW 1	GW ◇1 ☕	GW ◇1 ☕	GW 1	HC	GW 1	GW ◇1
London Paddington 15 ⊖	d	13 07	13 15	13 37	13 37	13 42	13 43	13 57	14 03	14 03	14 07	14 15	14 30	14 37	14 37	14 42	14 43	14 57	15 03	15 03	15 07	15 15	15 27
Acton Main Line	d																						
Ealing Broadway ⊖	d	13 15	13 24	13 45			13 50				14 15	14 24		14 45			14 50				15 15	15 24	
West Ealing	d																						
Drayton Green	d																						
Castle Bar Park	d																						
South Greenford	d																						
Greenford ⊖	a																						
Hanwell	d																						
Southall	d	13 19	13 29	13 49			13 56				14 19	14 29		14 49			14 56				15 19	15 29	
Hayes & Harlington	d	13 24	13 33	13 54			14 02				14 24	14 33		14 54			15 02				15 24	15 33	
Heathrow Terminal 1-2-3 2 ✈	a	13 29		13 59							14 29			14 59							15 29		
Heathrow Terminal 4 ✈	a	13 39		14 09							14 39			15 09							15 39		
West Drayton	d		13 37				14 06					14 37					15 06					15 37	
Iver	d																						
Langley	d		13 42				14 10					14 42					15 10					15 42	
Slough 3	a		13 46			13 59	14 14			14 23		14 46				15 00	15 14			15 23		15 46	15 49
	d		13 46			14 00	14 16			14 23		14 46				15 00	15 16			15 23		15 46	15 50
Burnham	d						14 20										15 20					15 51	
Taplow	d																						
Maidenhead 3	d		13 54				14 27			14 30		14 54					15 27			15 30		15 56	16 01
Twyford 3	d		14 02				14 35					15 02					15 35					16 04	16 10
Reading 7	a		14 10		14 03	14 19	14 43	14 26	14 36	14 43		15 10	14 55		15 05	15 17	15 43	15 25	15 36	15 43		16 12	16 16
Oxford	a					14 50	15 27									15 50	16 25						16 41

Table 117

Sundays

1 July to 9 September

London - Greenford and Reading

Network Diagram - see first Page of Table 116

		HC	GW ◇1 ☕	GW ◇1	GW 1	GW ◇1 ☕	GW ◇1 ☕	GW 1	HC	GW 1	GW ◇1 ☕	HC	GW ◇1 ☕	GW ◇1	GW 1	GW ◇1 ☕	GW ◇1 ☕	GW 1	HC	GW 1	GW ◇1 ☕	HC
London Paddington 15 ⊖	d	15 37	15 37	15 42	15 43	15 57	16 03	16 03	16 07	16 15	16 30	16 37	16 37	16 42	16 43	16 57	17 03	17 03	17 07	17 15	17 33	17 37
Acton Main Line	d																					
Ealing Broadway ⊖	d	15 45			15 50				16 15	16 24		16 45			16 50				17 15	17 24		17 45
West Ealing	d																					
Drayton Green	d																					
Castle Bar Park	d																					
South Greenford	d																					
Greenford ⊖	a																					
Hanwell	d																					
Southall	d	15 49			15 56				16 19	16 29		16 49			16 56				17 19	17 29		17 49
Hayes & Harlington	d	15 54			16 02				16 24	16 33		16 54			17 02				17 24	17 33		17 54
Heathrow Terminal 1-2-3 2 ✈	a	15 59							16 29			16 59							17 29			17 59
Heathrow Terminal 4 ✈	a	16 09							16 39			17 09							17 39			18 09
West Drayton	d				16 06					16 37					17 06					17 37		
Iver	d																					
Langley	d				16 10					16 42					17 10					17 42		
Slough 3	a			16 00	16 14			16 23		16 46				17 00	17 14			17 23		17 46		
	d			16 00	16 16			16 23		16 46				17 00	17 16			17 23		17 46		
Burnham	d				16 20					16 51					17 20					17 51		
Taplow	d																					
Maidenhead 3	d				16 27			16 30		16 56				17 07	17 27			17 30		17 56		
Twyford 3	d				16 35					17 04					17 35					18 04		
Reading 7	a		16 04	16 16	16 43	16 26	16 36	16 43		17 12	16 55		17 09	17 19	17 43	17 25	17 36	17 43		18 12	17 59	
Oxford	a			16 50	17 25									17 50	18 27							

		GW ◇1 ☕	GW ◇1 ☕	GW 1	GW ◇1 ☕	GW ◇1 ☕	HC	GW 1	GW 1	GW ◇1 ☕	HC	GW ◇1 ☕	GW ◇1	GW 1	GW ◇1 ☕	GW ◇1 ☕	GW 1	HC	GW 1	GW ◇1 ☕	HC	GW ◇1 ☕	GW ◇1 ☕
London Paddington 15 ⊖	d	17 37	17 42	17 43	17 57	18 03	18 07	18 11	18 15	18 30	18 37	18 37	18 42	18 43	18 57	19 03	19 03	19 07	19 15	19 33	19 37	19 37	19 42
Acton Main Line	d																						
Ealing Broadway ⊖	d			17 50			18 15		18 24		18 45			18 50				19 15	19 24		19 45		
West Ealing	d																						
Drayton Green	d																						
Castle Bar Park	d																						
South Greenford	d																						
Greenford ⊖	a																						
Hanwell	d																						
Southall	d			17 56			18 19		18 29		18 49			18 56				19 19	19 29		19 49		
Hayes & Harlington	d			18 02			18 24		18 33		18 54			19 02				19 24	19 33		19 54		
Heathrow Terminal 1-2-3 2 ✈	a						18 29				18 59							19 29			19 59		
Heathrow Terminal 4 ✈	a						18 39				19 09							19 39			20 09		
West Drayton	d			18 06					18 37					19 06					19 37				
Iver	d																						
Langley	d			18 10					18 42					19 10					19 42				
Slough 3	a		17 57	18 14				18 28	18 46				19 01	19 14			19 23		19 46				19 59
	d		17 58	18 16				18 29	18 46				19 02	19 16			19 23		19 46				20 00
Burnham	d			18 20					18 51					19 20					19 51				
Taplow	d																						
Maidenhead 3	d		18 07	18 27				18 36	18 56				19 09	19 27			19 30		19 56				
Twyford 3	d			18 35					19 04					19 35					20 04				
Reading 7	a	18 10	18 20	18 43	18 25	18 36		18 48	19 12	18 54		19 10	19 21	19 43	19 26	19 36	19 43		20 12	20 06		20 10	20 19
Oxford	a		18 50	19 25									19 50	20 25									20 50

		GW 1	GW ◇1 ☕	GW ◇1 ☕	HC	GW 1	GW ◇1 ☕	HC	GW ◇1 ☕	GW ◇1	GW 1	GW ◇1 ☕	GW ◇1 ☕	HC	GW 1	GW ◇1 ☕	GW ◇1	GW 1	GW ◇1 ☕	HC	GW 1	GW ◇1	GW 1
London Paddington 15 ⊖	d	19 43	19 57	20 03	20 07	20 15	20 30	20 37	20 37	20 42	20 43	20 57	21 03	21 07	21 15	21 37	21 42	21 43	22 03	22 12	22 15	22 42	22 43
Acton Main Line	d																						
Ealing Broadway ⊖	d	19 50			20 15	20 24		20 45			20 50			21 15	21 24			21 50		22 20	22 24		22 50
West Ealing	d																						
Drayton Green	d																						
Castle Bar Park	d																						
South Greenford	d																						
Greenford ⊖	a																						
Hanwell	d																						
Southall	d	19 56			20 19	20 29		20 49			20 56			21 19	21 29			21 56		22 24	22 29		22 56
Hayes & Harlington	d	20 02			20 24	20 33		20 54			21 02			21 24	21 33			22 02		22 28	22 33		23 02
Heathrow Terminal 1-2-3 2 ✈	a				20 29			20 59						21 29						22 34			
Heathrow Terminal 4 ✈	a				20 39			21 09						21 39						22 41			
West Drayton	d	20 06				20 37					21 06				21 37			22 06			22 37		23 06
Iver	d																						
Langley	d	20 10				20 42					21 10				21 42			22 10			22 42		23 10
Slough 3	a	20 14				20 46				20 58	21 14				21 46		21 58	22 14			22 46	22 58	23 14
	d	20 16				20 46				20 58	21 16				21 46		21 59	22 16			22 46	22 58	23 16
Burnham	d	20 20				20 51					21 20				21 51			22 20			22 50		23 20
Taplow	d																						
Maidenhead 3	d	20 27				20 56					21 27				21 56			22 31			22 56		23 25
Twyford 3	d	20 35				21 04					21 35				22 04			22 39			23 04		23 32
Reading 7	a	20 43	20 26	20 36		21 12	20 55		21 02	21 17	21 43	21 28	21 36		22 11	22 09	22 18	22 46	22 47		23 11	23 19	23 43
Oxford	a	21 31								21 49	22 29						22 50	23 36				23 51	00 35

Table 117

Sundays

1 July to 9 September

London - Greenford and Reading

Network Diagram - see first Page of Table 116

		GW	HC	GW	GW	GW	GW
		◇1 ☕		1	◇1 ☕	◇1	1
London Paddington 15 ⊖	d	23 03	23 12	23 15	23 37	23 47	23 53
Acton Main Line	d						
Ealing Broadway ⊖	d		23 20	23 24		23 55	00 02
West Ealing	d						
Drayton Green	d						
Castle Bar Park	d						
South Greenford	d						
Greenford ⊖	a						
Hanwell	d						
Southall	d		23 24	23 29			00 07
Hayes & Harlington	d		23 28	23 33			00 11
Heathrow Terminal 1-2-3 2 ✈	a		23 34				
Heathrow Terminal 4 ✈	a		23 41				
West Drayton	d			23 37			00 15
Iver	d						
Langley	d			23 42			00 20
Slough 3	a			23 46	23 54	00 08	00 24
	d			23 46	23 55	00 08	00 24
Burnham	d			23 51			00 28
Taplow	d						
Maidenhead 3	d			23 56		00 16	00 34
Twyford 3	d			00 04			00 42
Reading 7	a	23 41		00 14	00 14	00 28	00 49
Oxford	a					00 57	

Sundays

16 September to 21 October

		GW	GW	GW	GW	GW	GW	GW	GW	GW	GW	GW	GW	GW	GW	HC	HC	GW	HC	GW	GW	GW	HC
		1	◇1	1	1	◇1	1	1	bus	1	bus	1	bus	1	bus			1		1	◇1 ☕	◇1	
London Paddington 15 ⊖	d	22p45	23p00		23p20	23p33		23p42		00 05		00 30		01 00			06 12	06 43	07 12	07 29	07 57	08 03	08 12
Acton Main Line	d	22p51																					
Ealing Broadway ⊖	d	22p55			23p28			23p50		00 13		00 38		01 08		05 20	06 20	06 52	07 20	07 36			08 20
West Ealing	d																						
Drayton Green	d																						
Castle Bar Park	d																						
South Greenford	d																						
Greenford ⊖	a																						
Hanwell	d																						
Southall	d	23p00			23p33			23p56		00 19		00 44		01 13		05 24	06 24	06 58	07 24	07 42			08 24
Hayes & Harlington	d	23p04			23p37			00 01		00 23		00 48		01 17		05 28	06 28	07 02	07 28	07 46			08 28
Heathrow Terminal 1-2-3 2 ✈	a															05 34	06 34		07 34				08 34
Heathrow Terminal 4 ✈	a															05 40	06 41		07 41				08 41
West Drayton	d	23p08			23p41			00 06		00 27		00 52						07 06		07 50			
Iver	d	23p11			23p44					00 30													
Langley	d	23p14		←	23p48		←			00 33		00 56						07 11		07 55			
Slough 3	a	23p19	23p16	23p19	23p53	23p49	23p53	00 13		00 37		01 00		01 25				07 16		07 58		08 24	
	d	23p21	23p17	23p21	23p54	23p50	23p54	00 14		00 38		01 01		01 26				07 16		07 58		08 25	
Burnham	d	→		23p25	→		23p57	00 18		00 42								07 20		08 03			
Taplow	d						00 01	00 21		00 45													
Maidenhead 3	d			23p32			00 05	00 25		00 49		01 08		01 33				07 25		08 08		08 32	
Twyford 3	d			23p39			00 13	00a34	00 41	00a58	01 05	01a17	01 24	01a42	01 49			07a36		08 16			
Reading 7	a		23p33	23p46		00 06	00 20		01 14		01 38		01 57		02 22					08 25	08 30	08 43	
Oxford	a		00 04	00 32		00 39	01 07													09 30		09 12	

		GW	GW	GW	GW	GW	GW	HC	GW	GW	GW	GW	GW	GW	HC	GW	GW	GW	GW	GW	GW	HC	GW
		1	◇1 ☕	◇1	1	◇1 ☕	◇1 ☕		1	◇1 ☕	◇1 ☕	1	◇1 ☕	◇1 ☕		1	◇1 ☕	◇1 ☕	1	◇1 ☕	◇1 ☕		1
London Paddington 15 ⊖	d	08 15	08 30	08 42	08 43	08 57	09 03	09 12	09 15	09 30	09 35	09 43	09 57	10 03	10 12	10 15	10 37	10 42	10 43	10 57	11 03	11 12	11 15
Acton Main Line	d																						
Ealing Broadway ⊖	d	08 24			08 50			09 20	09 24			09 50			10 20	10 24			10 50			11 20	11 24
West Ealing	d																						
Drayton Green	d																						
Castle Bar Park	d																						
South Greenford	d																						
Greenford ⊖	a																						
Hanwell	d																						
Southall	d	08 29			08 56			09 24	09 29			09 56			10 24	10 29			10 56			11 24	11 29
Hayes & Harlington	d	08 33			09 02			09 28	09 33			10 02			10 28	10 33			11 02			11 28	11 33
Heathrow Terminal 1-2-3 2 ✈	a							09 34							10 34							11 34	
Heathrow Terminal 4 ✈	a							09 41							10 41							11 41	
West Drayton	d	08 37			09 06				09 37			10 06				10 37			11 06				11 37
Iver	d																						
Langley	d	08 42			09 10				09 42			10 10				10 42			11 10				11 42
Slough 3	a	08 46		09 04	09 14				09 46		09 58	10 14				10 46		11 05	11 14				11 46
	d	08 46		09 05	09 16				09 46		09 59	10 16				10 46		11 06	11 16				11 46
Burnham	d				09 20							10 20							11 20				
Taplow	d																						
Maidenhead 3	d	08 54			09 27				09 54			10 27				11 08			11 27				11 54
Twyford 3	d	09 02			09 35				10 02			10 35				11 16			11 35				12 02
Reading 7	a	09 10	09 05	09 20	09 42	09 31	09 36		10 10	10 02	10 11	10 42	10 31	10 36		11 24	11 12	11 21	11 42	11 31	11 36		12 10
Oxford	a			09 51	10 29						10 43	11 28						11 50	12 27				

Table 117

Sundays

16 September to 21 October

London - Greenford and Reading

Network Diagram - see first Page of Table 116

		GW	GW	GW	GW	GW	GW	HC	GW	GW	GW	GW	GW	GW	HC	GW	GW	GW	GW	GW	GW	HC
		◇1 ☕	◇1 ☕	◇1	1	◇1 ☕	◇1 ☕		1	◇1 ☕	◇1 ☕	1	◇1 ☕	◇1 ☕		1	◇1 ☕	◇1 ☕	1	◇1 ☕	◇1 ☕	
London Paddington 15 ⊖	d	11 27	11 37	11 42	11 43	11 57	12 03	12 12	12 15	12 37	12 42	12 43	12 57	13 03	13 12	13 15	13 37	13 42	13 43	13 57	14 03	14 12
Acton Main Line	d																					
Ealing Broadway ⊖	d				11 50			12 20	12 24			12 50			13 20	13 24			13 50			14 20
West Ealing	d																					
Drayton Green	d																					
Castle Bar Park	d																					
South Greenford	d																					
Greenford ⊖	a																					
Hanwell	d																					
Southall	d				11 56			12 24	12 29			12 56			13 24	13 29			13 56			14 24
Hayes & Harlington	d				12 02			12 28	12 33			13 02			13 28	13 33			14 02			14 28
Heathrow Terminal 1-2-3 2 ✈	a							12 34							13 34							14 34
Heathrow Terminal 4 ✈	a							12 41							13 41							14 41
West Drayton	d				12 06				12 37			13 06				13 37			14 05			
Iver	d																					
Langley	d				12 10				12 42			13 10				13 42			14 10			
Slough 3	a			12 01	12 14				12 46		13 06	13 14				13 46		14 05	14 14			
	d			12 03	12 16				12 46		13 07	13 16				13 46		14 06	14 16			
Burnham	d				12 20							13 20							14 20			
Taplow	d																					
Maidenhead 3	d				12 27				12 54			13 27				13 54			14 27			
Twyford 3	d				12 35				13 02			13 35				14 02			14 35			
Reading 7	a	12 01	12 12	12 19	12 42	12 31	12 36		13 10	13 12	13 21	13 42	13 31	13 36		14 10	14 12	14 21	14 42	14 31	14 36	
Oxford	a			12 50	13 29						13 50	14 30						14 50	15 30			

		GW	GW	GW	GW	GW	GW	HC	GW	GW	GW	GW	GW	GW	GW	HC	GW	GW	GW	GW	GW	GW	GW
		1	◇1 ☕	◇1	1	◇1 ☕	◇1 ☕		1	◇1	◇1 ☕	◇1	1	◇1 ☕	◇1 ☕		1	◇1 ☕	◇1 ☕	◇1	1	◇1 ☕	◇1 ☕
London Paddington 15 ⊖	d	14 15	14 37	14 42	14 43	14 57	15 03	15 12	15 15	15 27	15 37	15 42	15 43	15 57	16 03	16 12	16 15	16 30	16 37	16 42	16 43	16 57	17 03
Acton Main Line	d																						
Ealing Broadway ⊖	d	14 24			14 50			15 20	15 24				15 50			16 20	16 24				16 50		
West Ealing	d																						
Drayton Green	d																						
Castle Bar Park	d																						
South Greenford	d																						
Greenford ⊖	a																						
Hanwell	d																						
Southall	d	14 29			14 56			15 24	15 29				15 56			16 24	16 29				16 56		
Hayes & Harlington	d	14 33			15 02			15 28	15 33				16 02			16 28	16 33				17 02		
Heathrow Terminal 1-2-3 2 ✈	a							15 34								16 34							
Heathrow Terminal 4 ✈	a							15 41								16 41							
West Drayton	d	14 37			15 06				15 37				16 06				16 37				17 06		
Iver	d																						
Langley	d	14 42			15 10				15 42				16 10				16 42				17 10		
Slough 3	a	14 46		15 04	15 14				15 46	15 49		16 04	16 14				16 46			17 03	17 14		
	d	14 46		15 05	15 16				15 46	15 50		16 05	16 16				16 46			17 04	17 16		
Burnham	d				15 20				15 50				16 20				16 50				17 20		
Taplow	d																						
Maidenhead 3	d	14 54			15 27				15 56	16 01			16 27				17 04			17 11	17 27		
Twyford 3	d	15 02			15 35				16 03	16 10			16 35				17 11				17 35		
Reading 7	a	15 10	15 12	15 21	15 42	15 31	15 36		16 11	16 18	16 12	16 21	16 42	16 30	16 36		17 19	17 03	17 12	17 25	17 42	17 31	17 36
Oxford	a			15 50	16 31					16 45		16 50	17 30							17 50	18 31		

		HC	GW	GW	GW	GW	GW	GW	GW	HC	GW	GW	GW	GW	GW	GW	GW	HC	GW	GW	GW	GW
			1	◇1 ☕	◇1 ☕	◇1 ☕	1	◇1 ☕	◇1 ☕		1	◇1 ☕	◇1 ☕	◇1	1	◇1 ☕	◇1 ☕		1	◇1 ☕	◇1 ☕	◇1 ☕
London Paddington 15 ⊖	d	17 12	17 15	17 33	17 37	17 42	17 43	17 57	18 03	18 12	18 15	18 30	18 37	18 42	18 43	18 57	19 03	19 12	19 15	19 33	19 37	19 42
Acton Main Line	d																					
Ealing Broadway ⊖	d	17 20	17 24				17 50			18 20	18 24				18 50			19 20	19 24			
West Ealing	d																					
Drayton Green	d																					
Castle Bar Park	d																					
South Greenford	d																					
Greenford ⊖	a																					
Hanwell	d																					
Southall	d	17 24	17 29				17 56			18 24	18 29				18 56			19 24	19 29			
Hayes & Harlington	d	17 28	17 33				18 02			18 28	18 33				19 02			19 28	19 33			
Heathrow Terminal 1-2-3 2 ✈	a	17 34								18 34								19 34				
Heathrow Terminal 4 ✈	a	17 41								18 41								19 41				
West Drayton	d		17 37				18 06				18 37				19 06				19 37			
Iver	d																					
Langley	d		17 42				18 10				18 42				19 10				19 42			
Slough 3	a		17 46			18 03	18 14				18 46			19 06	19 14				19 46			20 04
	d		17 46			18 04	18 16				18 46			19 07	19 16				19 46			20 04
Burnham	d		17 50				18 20				18 50				19 20				19 50			
Taplow	d																					
Maidenhead 3	d		17 56			18 13	18 27				18 56			19 14	19 27				19 56			
Twyford 3	d		18 03				18 35				19 03				19 35				20 03			
Reading 7	a		18 12	18 03	18 14	18 23	18 42	18 31	18 36		19 11	19 03	19 14	19 26	19 42	19 31	19 36		20 11	20 06	20 14	20 21
Oxford	a					18 50	19 31							19 55	20 31							20 50

London - Greenford and Reading

Sundays
16 September to 21 October

Network Diagram - see first Page of Table 116

	GW 1	GW ◇1 🍴	GW ◇1 🍴	HC	GW 1	GW ◇1 🍴	GW ◇1 🍴	GW ◇1	GW 1	GW ◇1 🍴	GW ◇1 🍴	HC	GW 1	GW ◇1 🍴	GW ◇1	GW 1	GW ◇1 🍴	HC	GW 1	GW ◇1 🍴	GW ◇1	GW 1
London Paddington ⊖ d	19 43	19 57	20 03	20 12	20 15	20 30	20 37	20 42	20 43	20 57	21 03	21 12	21 15	21 37	21 42	21 43	22 03	22 12	22 15	22 37	22 42	22 43
Acton Main Line d																						
Ealing Broadway ⊖ d	19 50			20 20	20 24				20 50			21 20	21 24			21 50		22 20	22 24			22 50
West Ealing d																						
Drayton Green d																						
Castle Bar Park d																						
South Greenford d																						
Greenford ⊖ a																						
Hanwell d																						
Southall d	19 56			20 24	20 29				20 56			21 24	21 29			21 56		22 24	22 29			22 56
Hayes & Harlington d	20 02			20 28	20 33				21 02			21 28	21 33			22 02		22 28	22 33			23 02
Heathrow Terminal 1-2-3 ✈ a				20 34								21 34						22 34				
Heathrow Terminal 4 ✈ a				20 41								21 41						22 41				
West Drayton d	20 06				20 37				21 06				21 37			22 06			22 37			23 06
Iver d																						
Langley d	20 10				20 42				21 10				21 42			22 10			22 42			23 10
Slough a	20 14				20 46			21 03	21 14				21 46		22 05	22 14			22 46		23 02	23 14
Slough d	20 16				20 46			21 04	21 16				21 46		22 06	22 16			22 46		23 02	23 16
Burnham d	20 20				20 50				21 20				21 50			22 20			22 51			23 20
Taplow d																						
Maidenhead d	20 27				20 56				21 27				22 09			22 31			22 56			23 24
Twyford d	20 35				21 03				21 35				22 18			22 39			23 04			23 32
Reading a	20 42	20 31	20 36		21 11	21 03	21 14	21 24	21 42	21 31	21 36		22 25	22 12	22 20	22 46	22 47		23 11	23 15	23 19	23 43
Oxford a	21 30							21 56	22 29						22 51							

	GW ◇1 🍴	HC	GW 1	GW ◇1 🍴	GW ◇1	GW 1
London Paddington ⊖ d	23 03	23 12	23 15	23 37	23 47	23 53
Acton Main Line d						
Ealing Broadway ⊖ d		23 20	23 24		23 55	00 02
West Ealing d						
Drayton Green d						
Castle Bar Park d						
South Greenford d						
Greenford ⊖ a						
Hanwell d						
Southall d		23 24	23 29			00 07
Hayes & Harlington d		23 28	23 33			00 11
Heathrow Terminal 1-2-3 ✈ a		23 34				
Heathrow Terminal 4 ✈ a		23 41				
West Drayton d			23 37			00 15
Iver d						
Langley d			23 42			00 20
Slough a			23 46	00 01	00 09	00 24
Slough d			23 46	00 02	00 10	00 24
Burnham d			23 50			00 28
Taplow d						
Maidenhead d			23 56		00 17	00 34
Twyford d			00 03			00 42
Reading a	23 45		00 11	00 14	00 30	00 49
Oxford a						

Sundays
from 28 October

	GW 1	GW ◇1	GW 1	GW 1	GW ◇1	GW 1	GW 1	GW 🚌	GW 1	GW 🚌	GW 1	GW 🚌	GW 1	GW 🚌	HC	HC	GW 1	HC	GW 1	GW ◇1 🍴	GW ◇1	HC
London Paddington ⊖ d	22p45	23p00		23p20	23p33		23p42		00 05		00 30		01 00			06 12	06 43	07 12	07 29	08 00	08 03	08 12
Acton Main Line d	22p51																					
Ealing Broadway ⊖ d	22p55			23p28			23p50		00 13		00 38		01 08		05 20	06 20	06 52	07 20	07 36			08 20
West Ealing d																						
Drayton Green d																						
Castle Bar Park d																						
South Greenford d																						
Greenford ⊖ a																						
Hanwell d																						
Southall d	23p00			23p33			23p56		00 19		00 44		01 13		05 24	06 24	06 58	07 24	07 42			08 24
Hayes & Harlington d	23p04			23p37			00 01		00 23		00 48		01 17		05 27	06 28	07 02	07 28	07 46			08 28
Heathrow Terminal 1-2-3 ✈ a															05 34	06 34		07 34				08 34
Heathrow Terminal 4 ✈ a															05 40	06 41		07 41				08 41
West Drayton d	23p08			23p41			00 06		00 27		00 52						07 06		07 50			
Iver d	23p11			23p44					00 30													
Langley d	23p14		←	23p48		←			00 33		00 56						07 11		07 55			
Slough a	23p19	23p16	23p19	23p53	23p49	23p53	00 13		00 37		01 00		01 25				07 16		07 58		08 24	
Slough d	23p21	23p17	23p21	23p54	23p50	23p54	00 14		00 38		01 01		01 26				07 16		07 58		08 25	
Burnham d	→		23p25	→		23p57	00 18		00 42								07 20		08 03			
Taplow d						00 01	00 21		00 45													
Maidenhead d			23p32			00 05	00 25		00 49		01 08		01 33				07 25		08 08		08 32	
Twyford d			23p39			00 13	00a34	00 41	00a58	01 05	01a17	01 24	01a42	01 49			07a36		08 16			
Reading a		23p33	23p46		00 06	00 20		01 14		01 38		01 57		02 22					08 25	08 33	08 43	
Oxford a		00 04	00 35		00 39	01 07													09 30		09 12	

London - Greenford and Reading

Sundays
from 28 October

Network Diagram - see first Page of Table 116

	GW 1	GW ◇1 🍴	GW ◇1	GW 1	GW ◇1 🍴	GW ◇1 🍴	HC	GW 1	GW ◇1 🍴	GW ◇1 🍴	GW 1	GW ◇1 🍴	GW ◇1 🍴	HC	GW 1	GW ◇1 🍴	GW ◇1 🍴	GW 1	GW ◇1 🍴	GW ◇1 🍴	HC	GW 1
London Paddington ⊖ d	08 15	08 30	08 42	08 43	08 57	09 03	09 12	09 15	09 30	09 35	09 43	09 57	10 03	10 12	10 15	10 37	10 42	10 43	10 57	11 03	11 12	11 15
Acton Main Line d																						
Ealing Broadway ⊖ d	08 24			08 50			09 20	09 24			09 50			10 20	10 24			10 50			11 20	11 24
West Ealing d																						
Drayton Green d																						
Castle Bar Park d																						
South Greenford d																						
Greenford ⊖ a																						
Hanwell d																						
Southall d	08 29			08 56			09 24	09 29			09 56			10 24	10 29			10 56			11 24	11 29
Hayes & Harlington d	08 33			09 02			09 28	09 33			10 02			10 28	10 33			11 02			11 28	11 33
Heathrow Terminal 1-2-3 ✈ a							09 34							10 34							11 34	
Heathrow Terminal 4 ✈ a							09 41							10 41							11 41	
West Drayton d	08 37			09 06				09 37			10 06				10 37			11 06				11 37
Iver d																						
Langley d	08 42			09 10				09 42			10 10				10 42			11 10				11 42
Slough a	08 46		09 04	09 14				09 46		09 58	10 14				10 46		11 05	11 14				11 46
Slough d	08 46		09 05	09 16				09 46		09 59	10 16				10 46		11 06	11 16				11 46
Burnham d				09 20							10 20							11 20				
Taplow d																						
Maidenhead d	08 54			09 27				09 54			10 27				11 08			11 27				11 54
Twyford d	09 02			09 35				10 02			10 35				11 16			11 35				12 02
Reading a	09 10	09 05	09 20	09 42	09 31	09 36		10 10	10 03	10 11	10 42	10 31	10 36		11 24	11 12	11 21	11 42	11 31	11 36		12 10
Oxford a			09 51	10 29						10 43	11 29						11 50	12 27				

	GW ◇1 🍴	GW ◇1 🍴	GW ◇1	GW 1	GW ◇1 🍴	GW ◇1 🍴	HC	GW 1	GW ◇1 🍴	GW ◇1 🍴	GW 1	GW ◇1 🍴	GW ◇1 🍴	HC	GW 1	GW ◇1 🍴	GW ◇1 🍴	GW 1	GW ◇1 🍴	GW ◇1 🍴	HC
London Paddington ⊖ d	11 27	11 37	11 42	11 43	11 57	12 03	12 12	12 15	12 37	12 42	12 43	12 57	13 03	13 12	13 15	13 37	13 42	13 43	13 57	14 03	14 12
Acton Main Line d																					
Ealing Broadway ⊖ d				11 50			12 20	12 24			12 50			13 20	13 24			13 50			14 20
West Ealing d																					
Drayton Green d																					
Castle Bar Park d																					
South Greenford d																					
Greenford ⊖ a																					
Hanwell d																					
Southall d				11 56			12 24	12 29			12 56			13 24	13 29			13 56			14 24
Hayes & Harlington d				12 02			12 28	12 33			13 02			13 28	13 33			14 02			14 28
Heathrow Terminal 1-2-3 ✈ a							12 34							13 34							14 34
Heathrow Terminal 4 ✈ a							12 41							13 41							14 41
West Drayton d				12 06				12 37			13 06				13 37			14 05			
Iver d																					
Langley d				12 10				12 42			13 10				13 42			14 10			
Slough a			12 01	12 14				12 46		13 06	13 14				13 46		14 05	14 14			
Slough d			12 03	12 16				12 46		13 07	13 16				13 46		14 06	14 16			
Burnham d				12 20							13 20							14 20			
Taplow d																					
Maidenhead d				12 27				12 54			13 27				13 54			14 27			
Twyford d				12 35				13 02			13 35				14 02			14 35			
Reading a	12 01	12 12	12 19	12 42	12 31	12 36		13 10	13 12	13 21	13 42	13 31	13 36		14 10	14 12	14 21	14 42	14 31	14 36	
Oxford a			12 50	13 29						13 50	14 30						14 50	15 30			

	GW 1	GW ◇1 🍴	GW ◇1	GW 1	GW ◇1 🍴	GW ◇1 🍴	HC	GW 1	GW ◇1	GW ◇1 🍴	GW ◇1	GW 1	GW ◇1 🍴	GW ◇1 🍴	HC	GW 1	GW ◇1 🍴	GW ◇1 🍴	GW ◇1	GW 1	GW ◇1 🍴	GW ◇1 🍴
London Paddington ⊖ d	14 15	14 37	14 42	14 43	14 57	15 03	15 12	15 15	15 27	15 37	15 42	15 43	15 57	16 03	16 12	16 15	16 30	16 37	16 42	16 43	16 57	17 03
Acton Main Line d																						
Ealing Broadway ⊖ d	14 24			14 50			15 20	15 24				15 50			16 20	16 24				16 50		
West Ealing d																						
Drayton Green d																						
Castle Bar Park d																						
South Greenford d																						
Greenford ⊖ a																						
Hanwell d																						
Southall d	14 29			14 56			15 24	15 29				15 56			16 24	16 29				16 56		
Hayes & Harlington d	14 33			15 02			15 28	15 33				16 02			16 28	16 33				17 02		
Heathrow Terminal 1-2-3 ✈ a							15 34								16 34							
Heathrow Terminal 4 ✈ a							15 41								16 41							
West Drayton d	14 37			15 06				15 37				16 06				16 37				17 06		
Iver d																						
Langley d	14 42			15 10				15 42				16 10				16 42				17 10		
Slough a	14 46		15 04	15 14				15 46	15 49		16 04	16 14				16 46			17 03	17 14		
Slough d	14 46		15 05	15 16				15 46	15 50		16 05	16 16				16 46			17 04	17 16		
Burnham d				15 20				15 50				16 20				16 50				17 20		
Taplow d																						
Maidenhead d	14 54			15 27				15 56	16 01			16 27				16 56			17 11	17 27		
Twyford d	15 02			15 35				16 03	16 10			16 35				17 03				17 35		
Reading a	15 10	15 12	15 21	15 42	15 31	15 36		16 11	16 18	16 12	16 21	16 43	16 30	16 36		17 11	17 03	17 12	17 25	17 42	17 31	17 36
Oxford a			15 50	16 31					16 45		16 50	17 30							17 50	18 31		

Table 117

Sundays from 28 October

London - Greenford and Reading

Network Diagram - see first Page of Table 116

	HC	GW	GW	GW	GW	GW	GW	GW	HC	GW	GW	GW	GW	GW	GW	GW	HC	GW	GW	GW	GW
		1	◇1 🍽	◇1 🍽	◇1 🍽	1	◇1 🍽	◇1 🍽		1	◇1 🍽	◇1 🍽	◇1	1	◇1 🍽	◇1 🍽		1	◇1 🍽	◇1 🍽	◇1 🍽
London Paddington 15 ⊖ d	17 12	17 15	17 33	17 37	17 42	17 43	17 57	18 03	18 12	18 15	18 30	18 37	18 42	18 43	18 57	19 03	19 12	19 15	19 33	19 37	19 42
Acton Main Line d																					
Ealing Broadway ⊖ d	17 20	17 24				17 50			18 20	18 24				18 50			19 20	19 24			
West Ealing d																					
Drayton Green d																					
Castle Bar Park d																					
South Greenford d																					
Greenford ⊖ a																					
Hanwell d																					
Southall d	17 24	17 29				17 56			18 24	18 29				18 56			19 24	19 29			
Hayes & Harlington d	17 28	17 33				18 02			18 28	18 33				19 02			19 28	19 33			
Heathrow Terminal 1-2-3 2 ✈ a	17 34								18 34								19 34				
Heathrow Terminal 4 ✈ a	17 41								18 41								19 41				
West Drayton d		17 37				18 06				18 37				19 06				19 37			
Iver d																					
Langley d		17 42				18 10				18 42				19 10				19 42			
Slough 3 a		17 46			18 03	18 14				18 46			19 06	19 14				19 46			20 04
d		17 46			18 04	18 16				18 46			19 07	19 16				19 46			20 04
Burnham d		17 50				18 20				18 50				19 20				19 50			
Taplow d																					
Maidenhead 3 d		17 56			18 13	18 27				18 56			19 15	19 27				19 56			
Twyford 3 d		18 03				18 35				19 03				19 35				20 03			
Reading 7 a		18 12	18 03	18 14	18 23	18 42	18 31	18 36		19 11	19 03	19 14	19 26	19 42	19 31	19 36		20 11	20 06	20 14	20 21
Oxford a					18 50	19 31							19 55	20 31							20 50

	GW	GW	GW	HC	GW	GW	GW	GW	GW	GW	GW	HC	GW	GW	GW	GW	GW	HC	GW	GW	GW	GW
	1	◇1 🍽	◇1 🍽		1	◇1 🍽	◇1 🍽	◇1	1	◇1 🍽	◇1 🍽		1	◇1 🍽	◇1	1	◇1 🍽		1	◇1 🍽	◇1	1
London Paddington 15 ⊖ d	19 43	19 57	20 03	20 12	20 15	20 30	20 37	20 42	20 43	20 57	21 03	21 12	21 15	21 37	21 42	21 43	22 03	22 12	22 15	22 37	22 42	22 43
Acton Main Line d																						
Ealing Broadway ⊖ d	19 50			20 20	20 24				20 50			21 20	21 24			21 50		22 20	22 24			22 50
West Ealing d																						
Drayton Green d																						
Castle Bar Park d																						
South Greenford d																						
Greenford ⊖ a																						
Hanwell d																						
Southall d	19 56			20 24	20 29				20 56			21 24	21 29			21 56		22 24	22 29			22 56
Hayes & Harlington d	20 02			20 28	20 33				21 02			21 28	21 33			22 02		22 28	22 33			23 02
Heathrow Terminal 1-2-3 2 ✈ a				20 34								21 34						22 34				
Heathrow Terminal 4 ✈ a				20 41								21 41						22 41				
West Drayton d	20 06				20 37				21 06				21 37			22 06			22 37			23 06
Iver d																						
Langley d	20 10				20 42				21 10				21 42			22 10			22 42			23 10
Slough 3 a	20 14				20 46			21 03	21 14				21 46		22 05	22 14			22 46		23 02	23 14
d	20 16				20 46			21 04	21 16				21 46		22 06	22 16			22 46		23 02	23 16
Burnham d	20 20				20 50				21 20				21 50			22 20			22 51			23 20
Taplow d																						
Maidenhead 3 d	20 27				20 56				21 27				22 09			22 31			22 56			23 24
Twyford 3 d	20 35				21 04				21 35				22 18			22 39			23 04			23 32
Reading 7 a	20 42	20 31	20 36		21 11	21 03	21 14	21 24	21 42	21 31	21 36		22 25	22 12	22 20	22 46	22 47		23 11	23 15	23 19	23 43
Oxford a	21 30							21 54	22 29						22 51							

	GW	HC	GW	GW	GW	GW
	◇1 🍽		1	◇1 🍽	◇1	1
London Paddington 15 ⊖ d	23 03	23 12	23 15	23 37	23 47	23 53
Acton Main Line d						
Ealing Broadway ⊖ d		23 20	23 24		23 55	00 02
West Ealing d						
Drayton Green d						
Castle Bar Park d						
South Greenford d						
Greenford ⊖ a						
Hanwell d						
Southall d		23 24	23 29			00 07
Hayes & Harlington d		23 28	23 33			00 11
Heathrow Terminal 1-2-3 2 ✈ a		23 34				
Heathrow Terminal 4 ✈ a		23 41				
West Drayton d			23 37			00 15
Iver d						
Langley d			23 42			00 20
Slough 3 a			23 46	00 01	00 09	00 24
d			23 46	00 02	00 10	00 24
Burnham d			23 50			00 28
Taplow d						
Maidenhead 3 d			23 56		00 17	00 34
Twyford 3 d			00 03			00 42
Reading 7 a	23 45		00 11	00 14	00 30	00 49
Oxford a						

Table 117

Mondays to Fridays until 22 June

Reading and Greenford - London

Network Diagram - see first Page of Table 116

Miles	Miles	Miles		GW MX	GW MX	GW MO	GW MO	HC MX	HC MO	GW MO	GW MX	GW MX	GW MX	GW MO	GW MX	GW MX	GW MO	GW MX	GW	GW
				1	1	◇1 A	◇1 A 🍽			1 A	◇1	◇1 🍽	1	1 A	1	◇1	◇1	1	1	1
—	—	—	Oxford d			22p46					23p09					00 07		00 27		
0	—	—	Reading 7 d	22p48	23p15	23p22	23p30			23p36	23p41	23p55	00 15	00 16		00 39	00 53	01 15	02 24	03 54
5	—	—	Twyford 3 d	22p54	23p22					23p42			00 21	00 23			00 59	01 21	02 30	04 00
11¾	—	—	Maidenhead 3 d	23p02	23p29					23p50	23p54		00 29	00 31			01 07	01 29	02 38	04 08
13½	—	—	Taplow d	23p05	23p33								00 32							
15	—	—	Burnham d	23p08	23p36					23p55			00 35		←					
17½	—	—	Slough 3 a	23p13	23p41	23p43				23p59	00 01		00 40	00 38	00 40	00 55	01 14	01 37	02 45	04 15
—	—	—	d	23p27	23p41	23p43				00 01	00 02		00 40	00 38	00 40	00 56	01 14	01 37	02 45	04 15
19¾	—	—	Langley d	23p31	23p45					00 05			→	00 42	00 44					
21¼	—	—	Iver d	23p34	23p48															
22¾	—	—	West Drayton d	23p38	23p51					00 10				00 47	00 49				02 52	04 22
—	—	0	Heathrow Terminal 4 ✈ d					00 01	00 01											
—	—	1¾	Heathrow Terminal 1-2-3 2 ✈ d					00 07	00 07											
25¼	—	5¾	Hayes & Harlington d	23p43	23p56			00 13	00 13	00 16				00 52	00 54		01 23	01 46	02 57	04 27
27	—	7½	Southall d	23p47	23p59			00 16	00 16	00 20				00 56	00 57				03 00	04 30
28¾	—	9¼	Hanwell d																	
—	0	—	Greenford ⊖ d																	
—	1	—	South Greenford d																	
—	1¾	—	Castle Bar Park d																	
—	2	—	Drayton Green d																	
29½	2¾	10	West Ealing d																	
30¼	3½	11	Ealing Broadway ⊖ d	23p52	00 06			00 22	00 21	00 25				01 01	01 03		01 30	01 53	03 06	04 36
31¾	5	12¼	Acton Main Line d																	
36	9¾	16½	London Paddington 15 ⊖ a	00 02	00 17	00 05	00 13	00 30	00 30	00 34	00 28	00 33		01 10	01 16	01 17	01 39	02 05	03 18	04 47

	GW MX	GW MO	HC	GW	HC	GW	GW	GW	GW	GW	HC	GW	GW	GW	GW	GW	GW	HC	GW	GW	GW	GW
	1	1		1		1	1	1	◇1 🍽	1		1	1	1	1	1	◇1		1	1	1	◇1 🍽
Oxford d	04 00							05 03						05 24	05 43		05 59					
Reading 7 d	04 39	04 39		05 14		05 39		05 44	05 57	05 59		06 07		06 15	06 16	06 22	06 31		06 31	06 36	06 36	06 44
Twyford 3 d	04 45	04 45		05 20		05 45		05 50				06 13		06 21	06 23				06 37	06 42	06 44	
Maidenhead 3 d	04 53	04 53		05 28		05 53		05 58		06 10		06 21		06 29	06 31		06 43		06 46	06 53		
Taplow d				05 32				06 02				06 24		06 32						06 57		
Burnham d				05 35				06 05				06 27		06 35					06 50	07 01		
Slough 3 a	05 00	05 00		05 40		06 01		06 10		06 17		06 32		06 40		06 40	06 50		06 55	07 06		06 58
d	05 00	05 00		05 40		06 01		06 10		06 17		06 32		06 40		06 41	06 50		06 56	07 06		06 59
Langley d	05 04	05 04		05 44				06 14				06 36		06 44					06 59	→		
Iver d	05 07	05 07		05 47				06 17						06 47					07 03			
West Drayton d	05 11	05 11		05 51				06 21				06 41		06 51					07 07			
Heathrow Terminal 4 ✈ d			05 23		05 51																	
Heathrow Terminal 1-2-3 2 ✈ d			05 29		05 57						06 27							06 57				
Hayes & Harlington d	05 16	05 16	05 35	05 56	06 03	06 10		06 26			06 33	06 46		06 56				07 03	07 11			
Southall d	05 19	05 19	05 38	05 59	06 06	06 13		06 29			06 36	06 50		07 00				07 06	07 15			
Hanwell d			05 41		06 09						06 39							07 09				
Greenford ⊖ d							06 16						06 46									
South Greenford d							06 19						06 49									
Castle Bar Park d							06 22						06 52									
Drayton Green d							06 24						06 54									
West Ealing d			05 43		06 11		06 26				06 41		06 56					07 11				
Ealing Broadway ⊖ d	05 28	05 28	05 46	06 05	06 14	06 19	06 29	06 35			06 44	06 55	06 59	07 05				07 14	07 21			
Acton Main Line d	05 31	05 31		06 08			06 33	06 38					07 03									
London Paddington 15 ⊖ a	05 41	05 41	05 56	06 16	06 24	06 31	06 42	06 46	06 24	06 36	06 54	07 09	07 12	07 17	06 54	07 01	07 08	07 24	07 32		07 14	07 16

	GW	GW	GW	GW	GW	GW	HC	GW	GW	GW	GW	GW	GW	GW	GW	GW	HC	GW	GW	GW	GW	GW
	1	◇1 🍽	1	1	1	◇1 🍽		1	1	1	1	◇1 🍽	◇1 🍽	1	◇1 🍽	1		1	◇1 🍽	1	◇1 🍽	◇1 🍽
Oxford d		06 27									06 07				06 56			06 36				
Reading 7 d	06 46	06 56			06 57	07 01		07 02	07 07		07 10	07 16	07 21		07 27			07 30	07 33	07 34	07 36	07 39
Twyford 3 d	06 53				07 03			07 08			07 16			07 22				07 37		07 41		
Maidenhead 3 d	07 03	07 08			07 11			07 16	07 18		07 24			07 31		07 41		07 45		07 49		
Taplow d											07 28									07 53		
Burnham d				←				07 21			07 31							07 51		07 56		
Slough 3 a				07 06	07 19			07 26			07 36					07 49		07 55		08 01		
d				07 06	07 20			07 26			07 36					07 50		07 56		08 01		
Langley d				07 11				07 31			07 41							08 00		08 06		
Iver d				07 14							07 44									08 09		
West Drayton d				07 18				07 36			07 48							08 04		08 13		
Heathrow Terminal 4 ✈ d																						
Heathrow Terminal 1-2-3 2 ✈ d							07 27										07 57					
Hayes & Harlington d				07 23			07 33	07 41			07 53						08 03	08 10		08 17		
Southall d				07 27			07 36	07 45			07 57						08 06	08 13				
Hanwell d							07 39										08 09					
Greenford ⊖ d			07 16							07 46												
South Greenford d			07 19							07 49												
Castle Bar Park d			07 22							07 52												
Drayton Green d			07 24							07 54												
West Ealing d			07 26				07 41			07 56							08 11					
Ealing Broadway ⊖ d			07 29	07 33			07 44	07 52		07 59	08 03						08 14	08 18		08 24		
Acton Main Line d			07 33							08 03												
London Paddington 15 ⊖ a	07 29	07 30	07 42	07 44	07 49	07 32	07 54	08 04	07 43	08 12	08 16	07 44	07 53	07 57	07 59	08 21	08 24	08 32	08 02	08 36	08 07	08 09

A from 21 May until 18 June

Reading and Greenford - London

until 22 June

Network Diagram - see first Page of Table 116

	GW ◇1 ☕	GW ◇1	GW 1	GW 1	GW ◇1 🍽	GW ◇1 ☕	GW 1	GW ◇1 ☕	GW 1	HC	GW 1	GW 1	GW 1	GW ◇1 ☕	GW ◇1 ☕	GW 1	GW ◇1 A ☕⊘	GW 1	HC
Oxford d				07 00	07 33											07 21	07 52		
Reading 7 d	07 45			07 55	07 58	08 02	08 06	08 08					08 12	08 14	08 17	08 19	08 23		
Twyford 3 d			07 56	08 02			08a12						08 17			08 26			
Maidenhead 3 d		08 00	08 04	08 11									08 26			08 34		08 41	
Taplow d													08 29						
Burnham d				08 15									08 32						
Slough 3 a				08 20									08 38					08 49	
d				08 20							08 26		08 38					08 50	
Langley d											08 30		08 42						
Iver d													08 44						
West Drayton d											08 35		08 50						
Heathrow Terminal 4 ✈ d																			
Heathrow Terminal 1-2-3 2 ✈ d										08 27									08 57
Hayes & Harlington d										08 33	08 39		08 53						09 03
Southall d				08 30						08 36	08 43							09 00	09 06
Hanwell d										08 39									09 09
Greenford ⊖ d									08 16			08 46							
South Greenford d									08 19			08 49							
Castle Bar Park d									08 22			08 52							
Drayton Green d									08 24			08 54							
West Ealing d									08 26	08 41		08 56							09 11
Ealing Broadway ⊖ d									08 29	08 44	08 49	08 59	09 04						09 14
Acton Main Line d									08 33			09 03							
London Paddington 15 ⊖ a	08 14	08 26	08 28	08 48	08 31	08 33		08 38	08 42	08 54	09 03	09 12	09 16	08 40	08 44	08 58	08 51	09 21	09 24

	GW 1	GW ◇1 B ☕	GW 1	GW ◇1 C ☕	GW 1	GW ◇1 ☕	GW ◇1 ☕	GW 1	GW 1	HC	GW 1	GW ◇1 ☕	GW ◇1 ☕	GW 1	GW 1	GW ◇1 D ☕⊘	GW 1	GW ◇1 ☕	GW 1	GW ◇1 E ☕	GW ◇1
Oxford d			08 06		07 56						08 21					08 51			08 36		09 01
Reading 7 d	08 31	08 34	08 35	08 45	08 48	08 52	09 02				09 03	09 08	09 16		09 17	09 18	09 21	09 27	09 33	09 34	09 37
Twyford 3 d	08 37				08 54						09 09				09 24				09 39		
Maidenhead 3 d	08 45				09 03						09 17				09 35				09 47		
Taplow d	08 49										09 21				09 36						
Burnham d	08 50										09 24				09 39						
Slough 3 a	08 57										09 29				09 44				09 54		09 52
d	08 57								09 14		09 30				09 44				09 54		09 52
Langley d	09 01										09 33										
Iver d	09 04										09 36								→		
West Drayton d	09 08								09 21		09 40				09 51						
Heathrow Terminal 4 ✈ d																					
Heathrow Terminal 1-2-3 2 ✈ d										09 27											
Hayes & Harlington d	09 13								09 26	09 33	09 45				09 56						
Southall d	09 17								09 30	09 36	09 48										
Hanwell d										09 39											
Greenford ⊖ d								09 16						09 46							
South Greenford d								09 19						09 49							
Castle Bar Park d								09 22						09 52							
Drayton Green d								09 24						09 54							
West Ealing d								09 26		09 41				09 56							
Ealing Broadway ⊖ d	09 23							09 29	09 36	09 44	09 54			09 59	10 03						
Acton Main Line d								09 33						10 03							
London Paddington 15 ⊖ a	09 35	09 00	09 06	09 14	09 27	09 21	09 29	09 42	09 48	09 54	10 03	09 39	09 44	10 12	10 16	09 47	09 56	09 59		10 02	10 12

	GW ◇1 ☕	HC	GW 1	GW 1	GW ◇1	GW ◇1 ☕	GW 1	GW 1	HC	GW 1	GW ◇1 ☕	GW ◇1 ☕	GW 1	GW 1	GW ◇1 🍽	GW ◇1 ☕	GW 1	GW 1	HC	GW 1
Oxford d					09 31					09 07					10 01					09 36
Reading 7 d	09 46			09 48	09 55	10 02				10 03	10 08	10 12	10 18	10 18	10 26	10 32				10 33
Twyford 3 d				09 54						10 09				10 24						10 39
Maidenhead 3 d				10 02						10 17				10 32						10 47
Taplow d				10 06										10 36						
Burnham d			←	10 09				←						10 39				←		
Slough 3 a			09 54	10 14	10 10			10 14		10 24				10 44	10 39			10 44		10 54
d			09 54	10 14	10 11			10 14		10 24				10 44	10 40			10 44		10 54
Langley d			09 58	→						10 28				→						10 58
Iver d			10 01							10 31										11 01
West Drayton d			10 05					10 21		10 35								10 51		11 05
Heathrow Terminal 4 ✈ d																				
Heathrow Terminal 1-2-3 2 ✈ d		09 57							10 27										10 57	
Hayes & Harlington d		10 03	10 10					10 26	10 33	10 40								10 56	11 03	11 10
Southall d		10 06	10 13						10 36	10 43									11 06	11 13
Hanwell d		10 09							10 39										11 09	
Greenford ⊖ d							10 16										10 46			
South Greenford d							10 19										10 49			
Castle Bar Park d							10 22										10 52			
Drayton Green d							10 24										10 54			
West Ealing d		10 11					10 26		10 41								10 56		11 11	
Ealing Broadway ⊖ d		10 14	10 19				10 29	10 33	10 44	10 49							10 59	11 03	11 14	11 19
Acton Main Line d							10 33										11 03			
London Paddington 15 ⊖ a	10 15	10 24	10 31		10 30	10 32	10 42	10 46	10 54	11 01	10 37	10 39	10 56		11 00	11 07	11 12	11 16	11 24	11 32

A ☕ from Reading ⊘ to Reading
B The Armada
C The Bristolian
D The Cathedrals Express. ☕ from Reading ⊘ to Reading
E The Golden Hind

Table 117

Mondays to Fridays

Reading and Greenford - London

until 22 June

Network Diagram - see first Page of Table 116

	GW ◇1 ☕	GW 1	GW ◇1 ☕	GW ◇1	GW ◇1 A ☕	GW 1	GW 1	HC	GW 1	GW ◇1 ☕	GW 1	GW 1	GW ◇1 🍽	GW ◇1 ☕	GW 1	GW 1	HC	GW 1	GW ◇1 ☕	GW 1
Oxford d				10 31					10 08				11 01					10 36		
Reading 7 d	10 45	10 48	10 52	10 55	11 02				11 03	11 11	11 18	11 20	11 26	11 32				11 33	11 44	11 48
Twyford 3 d		10 54							11 09		11 24							11 39		11 54
Maidenhead 3 d		11 02							11 17		11 32							11 47		12 02
Taplow d		11 06									11 36									12 06
Burnham d		11 09					←				11 39					←				12 09
Slough 3 a		11 14		11 09			11 14		11 24		11 44		11 39			11 44		11 54		12 14
d		11 14		11 10			11 14		11 24		11 44		11 40			11 44		11 54		12 14
Langley d		→							11 28		→							11 58		→
Iver d									11 31									12 01		
West Drayton d							11 21		11 35							11 51		12 05		
Heathrow Terminal 4 ✈ d																				
Heathrow Terminal 1-2-3 2 ✈ d								11 27									11 57			
Hayes & Harlington d							11 26	11 33	11 40							11 56	12 03	12 10		
Southall d								11 36	11 43								12 06	12 13		
Hanwell d								11 39									12 09			
Greenford ⊖ d						11 16									11 46					
South Greenford d						11 19									11 49					
Castle Bar Park d						11 22									11 52					
Drayton Green d						11 24									11 54					
West Ealing d						11 26		11 41							11 56		12 11			
Ealing Broadway ⊖ d						11 29	11 33	11 44	11 49						11 59	12 03	12 14	12 19		
Acton Main Line d						11 33									12 03					
London Paddington 15 ⊖ a	11 14		11 24	11 29	11 32	11 42	11 46	11 54	12 01	11 38		11 55	11 59	12 00	12 12	12 16	12 24	12 31	12 14	

	GW ◇1 ☕	GW ◇1 🍽	GW ◇1 ☕	GW 1	GW 1	HC	GW 1	GW ◇1 ☕	GW ◇1 ☕	GW 1	GW 1	GW ◇1 🍽	GW ◇1 ☕	GW 1	GW 1	HC	GW 1	GW ◇1 ☕	GW 1	GW ◇1 🍽
Oxford d		11 31					11 07					12 01					11 37			12 31
Reading 7 d	11 52	11 55	12 02				12 03	12 08	12 12	12 18	12 18	12 26	12 32				12 33	12 45	12 48	12 55
Twyford 3 d							12 09				12 24						12 39		12 54	
Maidenhead 3 d							12 17				12 32						12 47		13 02	
Taplow d											12 36								13 06	
Burnham d					←						12 39				←				13 09	
Slough 3 a		12 09			12 14		12 24				12 44	12 39			12 44		12 54		13 14	13 09
d		12 10			12 14		12 24				12 44	12 40			12 44		12 54		13 14	13 10
Langley d							12 28				→						12 58		→	
Iver d							12 31										13 01			
West Drayton d					12 21		12 35								12 51		13 05			
Heathrow Terminal 4 ✈ d																				
Heathrow Terminal 1-2-3 2 ✈ d						12 27										12 57				
Hayes & Harlington d					12 26	12 33	12 40								12 56	13 03	13 10			
Southall d						12 36	12 43									13 06	13 13			
Hanwell d						12 39										13 09				
Greenford ⊖ d				12 16										12 46						
South Greenford d				12 19										12 49						
Castle Bar Park d				12 22										12 52						
Drayton Green d				12 24										12 54						
West Ealing d				12 26		12 41								12 56		13 11				
Ealing Broadway ⊖ d				12 29	12 33	12 44	12 49							12 59	13 03	13 14	13 19			
Acton Main Line d				12 33										13 03						
London Paddington 15 ⊖ a	12 23	12 29	12 32	12 42	12 46	12 54	13 02	12 37	12 40	12 52		13 06	13 00	13 12	13 16	13 24	13 31	13 14		13 29

	GW ◇1 ☕	GW 1	GW 1	HC	GW 1	GW ◇1 ☕	GW 1 B ☕	GW 1	GW ◇1 🍽	GW 1	GW ◇1 ☕	GW 1	GW 1	HC	GW 1	GW ◇1 ☕	GW 1	GW ◇1 🍽	GW ◇1 C ☕	GW 1
Oxford d					12 07				13 01						12 37			13 31		
Reading 7 d	13 02				13 03	13 11	13 17	13 18	13 26	13 29	13 32				13 33	13 44	13 48	13 55	14 01	
Twyford 3 d					13 09			13 24							13 39		13 54			
Maidenhead 3 d					13 17			13 32							13 47		14 02			
Taplow d								13 36									14 06			
Burnham d			←					13 39					←				14 09			
Slough 3 a			13 14		13 24			13 44	13 39				13 44		13 54		14 14	14 09		
d			13 14		13 24			13 44	13 40				13 44		13 54		14 14	14 10		
Langley d					13 28			→							13 58		→			
Iver d					13 31										14 01					
West Drayton d			13 21		13 35								13 51		14 05					
Heathrow Terminal 4 ✈ d																				
Heathrow Terminal 1-2-3 2 ✈ d				13 27										13 57						
Hayes & Harlington d			13 26	13 33	13 40								13 56	14 03	14 10					
Southall d				13 36	13 43									14 06	14 13					
Hanwell d				13 39										14 09						
Greenford ⊖ d		13 16										13 46								14 16
South Greenford d		13 19										13 49								14 19
Castle Bar Park d		13 22										13 52								14 22
Drayton Green d		13 24										13 54								14 24
West Ealing d		13 26		13 41								13 56		14 11						14 26
Ealing Broadway ⊖ d		13 29	13 33	13 44	13 49							13 59	14 03	14 14	14 19					14 29
Acton Main Line d		13 33										14 03								14 33
London Paddington 15 ⊖ a	13 32	13 42	13 46	13 54	14 01	13 38	13 44		14 01	14 09	14 06	14 12	14 16	14 24	14 31	14 14		14 29	14 32	14 42

A The Red Dragon
B The Cornish Riviera
C The St. David

until 22 June

Reading and Greenford - London

Network Diagram - see first Page of Table 116

		GW	HC	GW	GW	GW	GW	GW	GW	GW	GW	GW	HC	GW	GW	GW	GW	GW	GW	GW	GW
		■		■	◇■ R	◇■ R	◇■ R	■	◇■ X	◇■ R	■	■		■	◇■ R	■	■ A R	◇■	◇■ R	■	■
Oxford	d			13 07					14 01					13 37				14 31			
Reading 7	d			14 03	14 08	14 12	14 17	14 18	14 26	14 32				14 33	14 44	14 48	14 52	14 55	15 02		
Twyford 3	d			14 09				14 24						14 39		14 54					
Maidenhead 3	d			14 17				14 32						14 47		15 02					
Taplow	d							14 36								15 06					
Burnham	d	←						14 39				←				15 09					←
Slough 3	a	14 14		14 24				14 44	14 39			14 44		14 54		15 14		15 09			15 14
	d	14 14		14 24				14 44	14 40			14 44		14 54		15 14		15 10			15 14
Langley	d			14 28				→						14 58		→					
Iver	d			14 31										15 01							
West Drayton	d	14 21		14 35								14 51		15 05							15 21
Heathrow Terminal 4 ✈	d																				
Heathrow Terminal 1-2-3 2 ✈	d		14 27										14 57								
Hayes & Harlington	d	14 26	14 33	14 40								14 56	15 03	15 10							15 26
Southall	d		14 36	14 43									15 06	15 13							
Hanwell	d		14 39										15 09								
Greenford ⊖	d										14 46									15 16	
South Greenford	d										14 49									15 19	
Castle Bar Park	d										14 52									15 22	
Drayton Green	d										14 54									15 24	
West Ealing	d		14 41								14 56		15 11							15 26	
Ealing Broadway ⊖	d	14 33	14 44	14 49							14 59	15 03	15 14	15 19						15 29	15 33
Acton Main Line	d										15 03									15 33	
London Paddington 15 ⊖	a	14 46	14 54	15 01	14 37	14 40	14 44		15 00	15 08	15 12	15 16	15 24	15 32	15 14		15 24	15 29	15 32	15 42	15 46

		HC	GW	GW	GW	GW	GW	GW	GW	GW	HC	GW	GW	GW	GW	GW	GW	GW	GW	HC	GW
			■	◇■ R	■	■	◇■ X	◇■ R	■	■		■	◇■ R	■	◇■ R	◇■ R	◇■ R	■	■		■
Oxford	d		14 07				15 01					14 37				15 31					15 07
Reading 7	d		15 03	15 11	15 18	15 20	15 26	15 32				15 33	15 44	15 48	15 52	15 55	16 02				16 03
Twyford 3	d		15 09		15 24							15 39		15 54							16 09
Maidenhead 3	d		15 17		15 32							15 47		16 02							16 17
Taplow	d				15 36									16 06							
Burnham	d				15 39					←				16 09					←		
Slough 3	a		15 24		15 44		15 39			15 44		15 54		16 14		16 09			16 14		16 24
	d		15 24		15 44		15 40			15 44		15 54		16 14		16 10			16 14		16 24
Langley	d		15 28		→							15 58		→							16 28
Iver	d		15 31									16 01									16 31
West Drayton	d		15 35							15 51		16 05							16 21		16 35
Heathrow Terminal 4 ✈	d																				
Heathrow Terminal 1-2-3 2 ✈	d	15 27									15 57									16 27	
Hayes & Harlington	d	15 33	15 40							15 56	16 03	16 10							16 26	16 33	16 40
Southall	d	15 36	15 43								16 06	16 13								16 36	16 43
Hanwell	d	15 39									16 09									16 39	
Greenford ⊖	d								15 46									16 16			
South Greenford	d								15 49									16 19			
Castle Bar Park	d								15 52									16 22			
Drayton Green	d								15 54									16 24			
West Ealing	d	15 41							15 56		16 11							16 26		16 41	
Ealing Broadway ⊖	d	15 44	15 49						15 59	16 03	16 14	16 19						16 29	16 33	16 44	16 49
Acton Main Line	d								16 03									16 33			
London Paddington 15 ⊖	a	15 54	16 02	15 38		15 54	16 01	16 09	16 12	16 17	16 24	16 31	16 14		16 22	16 27	16 30	16 42	16 46	16 54	17 02

		GW	GW	GW	GW	GW	GW	GW	HC	GW	GW	GW	GW	GW	GW	GW	GW	GW	HC	GW
		◇■ C R	◇■ R	■	■	◇■ X	■	■		■	◇■ R	◇■ R	■	◇■ D R	◇■	◇■ R	■	■		■
Oxford	d					16 01				15 37					16 31					16 07
Reading 7	d	16 08	16 15	16 18	16 19	16 26				16 33	16 34	16 44	16 48	16 51	16 55	17 02				17 03
Twyford 3	d			16 24						16 39			16 54							17 09
Maidenhead 3	d			16 32						16 47			17 02							17 17
Taplow	d			16 36									17 06							
Burnham	d			16 39				←					17 09					←		
Slough 3	a			16 44		16 39		16 44		16 54			17 14		17 09			17 14		17 24
	d			16 44		16 40		16 44		16 54			17 14		17 10			17 14		17 24
Langley	d			→						16 58			→							17 28
Iver	d									17 01										17 31
West Drayton	d							16 51		17 05								17 21		17 35
Heathrow Terminal 4 ✈	d																			
Heathrow Terminal 1-2-3 2 ✈	d								16 57										17 27	
Hayes & Harlington	d							16 56	17 03	17 10								17 26	17 33	17 40
Southall	d								17 06	17 13									17 36	17 43
Hanwell	d								17 09										17 39	
Greenford ⊖	d						16 46										17 16			
South Greenford	d						16 49										17 19			
Castle Bar Park	d						16 52										17 22			
Drayton Green	d						16 54										17 24			
West Ealing	d						16 56		17 11								17 26		17 41	
Ealing Broadway ⊖	d						16 59	17 03	17 14	17 21							17 29	17 33	17 44	17 49
Acton Main Line	d						17 03										17 33			
London Paddington 15 ⊖	a	16 39	16 44		16 57	17 00	17 12	17 19	17 24	17 31	17 09	17 14		17 24	17 34	17 30	17 42	17 48	17 54	18 01

A The Cornishman

C The Cheltenham Spa Express

D The Torbay Express

Table 117

Mondays to Fridays

until 22 June

Reading and Greenford - London

Network Diagram - see first Page of Table 116

		GW	GW	GW	GW	GW	GW	GW	HC	GW	GW	GW	GW	GW	GW	GW	GW	HC	GW	GW	GW	GW
		◇■ A R	■	◇■ R	■ X	◇■ R	■	■		■	■	◇■ R	◇■ B R	■	◇■ R	■	■		■	◇■ R	◇■ R	◇■ R
Oxford	d				17 01					16 37					17 31				17 07			
Reading 7	d	17 11	17 14	17 17	17 26	17 32				17 33	17 42	17 46	17 51	17 54	17 56				18 00	18 01	18 08	18 12
Twyford 3	d		17 24							17 39	17 48								18 10			
Maidenhead 3	d		17 32	17 29						17 47	17 56			18 08					18 17			
Taplow	d		17 36								18 00											
Burnham	d		17 39					←			18 02						←					
Slough 3	a		17 44		17 39			17 44		17 54	18 07			18 14	18 10		18 14		18 24			
	d		17 44		17 40			17 44		17 54	18 07			18 14	18 11		18 14		18 24			
Langley	d		→							17 58				→					18 28			
Iver	d									18 01									18 32			
West Drayton	d							17 51		18 05	18 14								18 35			
Heathrow Terminal 4 ✈	d																					
Heathrow Terminal 1-2-3 2 ✈	d								17 57									18 27				
Hayes & Harlington	d							17 56	18 03	18 10	18 19						18 26	18 33	18 40			
Southall	d								18 06	18 13								18 36	18 43			
Hanwell	d								18 09									18 39				
Greenford ⊖	d						17 46									18 16						
South Greenford	d						17 49									18 19						
Castle Bar Park	d						17 52									18 22						
Drayton Green	d						17 54									18 24						
West Ealing	d						17 56		18 11							18 26		18 41				
Ealing Broadway ⊖	d						17 59	18 03	18 14	18 19	18 26					18 29	18 33	18 44	18 49			
Acton Main Line	d						18 03									18 33						
London Paddington 15 ⊖	a	17 39		17 54	17 59	18 02	18 12	18 14	18 24	18 31	18 37	18 14	18 21		18 28	18 42	18 46	18 54	19 00	18 30	18 39	18 44

		GW	GW	GW	GW	GW	GW	GW	HC	GW	GW	GW	GW	GW	GW	GW	GW	HC	GW	GW
		■	■	■	■ X	◇■ R	■	■		■	◇■ R	■	◇■ C R	■	◇■ R	■	■		■	◇■ R
Oxford	d				18 01					17 37				18 31					18 07	
Reading 7	d		18 18	18 22	18 26	18 32				18 33	18 47	18 48	18 51	18 57	19 02				19 03	19 11
Twyford 3	d		18 24							18 39		18 54							19 09	
Maidenhead 3	d	18 26	18 32							18 48		19 05							19 21	
Taplow	d		18 35									19 09								
Burnham	d		18 39					←				19 12					←			
Slough 3	a	18 33	18 44		18 39			18 44		18 54		19 17		19 09			19 17		19 29	
	d	18 33	18 44		18 40			18 44		18 54		19 17		19 10			19 17		19 29	
Langley	d		→							18 58		→							19 33	
Iver	d									19 01									19 36	
West Drayton	d							18 51		19 05							19 24		19 39	
Heathrow Terminal 4 ✈	d																			
Heathrow Terminal 1-2-3 2 ✈	d								18 57									19 27		
Hayes & Harlington	d	18 45						18 56	19 03	19 10							19 29	19 33	19 44	
Southall	d								19 06	19 13								19 36	19 47	
Hanwell	d								19 09									19 39		
Greenford ⊖	d						18 46									19 16				
South Greenford	d						18 49									19 19				
Castle Bar Park	d						18 52									19 22				
Drayton Green	d						18 54									19 24				
West Ealing	d						18 56		19 11							19 26		19 41		
Ealing Broadway ⊖	d	18 54					18 59	19 05	19 14	19 19						19 29	19 36	19 44	19 53	
Acton Main Line	d						19 03									19 33				
London Paddington 15 ⊖	a	19 04		18 54	18 59	19 02	19 12	19 18	19 24	19 31	19 14		19 24	19 31	19 32	19 42	19 45	19 54	20 02	19 38

		GW	GW	GW	GW	GW	HC	GW	GW	GW	GW FO	GW FX	GW	GW	HC	GW	GW	GW	GW	GW	GW	GW
		■	■	■	◇■ R	◇■ X		■	◇■ R	■	◇■	◇■	■	■		■	◇■ R	◇■ R	◇■ R	■	◇■	■
Oxford	d					19 06		18 37			19 31	19 31				19 01					20 01	
Reading 7	d	19 18		19 18	19 25	19 32		19 33	19 45	19 48	19 55	19 55				19 58	20 02	20 08	20 15	20 18	20 26	
Twyford 3	d			19 24				19 42		19 54						20 04				20 24		
Maidenhead 3	d			19 32				19 50		20 02						20 12				20 32		
Taplow	d			19 36						20 05										20 36		
Burnham	d			19 39						20 09				←						20 39		
Slough 3	a			19 44		19 47		19 57		20 14	20 09	20 09		20 14		20 19				20 44	20 39	
	d			19 44		19 47		19 57		20 14	20 10	20 10		20 14		20 24				20 44	20 40	
Langley	d							20 01		→						20 28				→		
Iver	d							20 04								20 31						
West Drayton	d			19 51				20 08						20 21		20 35						
Heathrow Terminal 4 ✈	d																					
Heathrow Terminal 1-2-3 2 ✈	d						19 57								20 27							
Hayes & Harlington	d			19 56			20 03	20 13						20 26	20 33	20 40						
Southall	d						20 06	20 16							20 36	20 43						
Hanwell	d						20 09								20 39							
Greenford ⊖	d		19 46										20 16									20 46
South Greenford	d		19 49										20 19									20 49
Castle Bar Park	d		19 52										20 22									20 52
Drayton Green	d		19 54										20 24									20 54
West Ealing	d		19 56				20 11						20 26		20 41							20 56
Ealing Broadway ⊖	d		19 59	20 03			20 14	20 22					20 29	20 33	20 44	20 49						20 59
Acton Main Line	d		20 03										20 33									21 03
London Paddington 15 ⊖	a	19 54	20 12	20 16	19 54	20 06	20 24	20 31	20 14		20 30	20 31	20 42	20 49	20 54	20 59	20 32	20 39	20 46		21 01	21 12

A The Merchant Venturer

B The Mayflower

C The Royal Duchy

Reading and Greenford - London

Mondays to Fridays

until 22 June

Network Diagram - see first Page of Table 116

		GW ■	HC	GW ■	GW ■	GW ◇■ 🍴	GW ■	GW ◇■ 🍴	GW ◇■ 🍴	GW ◇■ 🍴	GW ■	GW ■	HC	GW ■	GW ■	GW ◇■	HC	GW ■	GW ◇■ 🍴	GW ◇■
Oxford	d			19 37					20 31						20 07	21 01		20 37		21 32
Reading [7]	d			20 33	20 34	20 45	20 48	20 52	20 55	21 02					21 14	21 26		21 33	21 44	21 56
Twyford [5]	d			20 39			20 54								21 20			21 39		
Maidenhead [3]	d			20 47			21 02								21 28			21 47		
Taplow	d						21 06								21 32			21 50		
Burnham	d	←					21 09					←			21 35			21 53		
Slough [3]	a	20 44		20 54			21 13		21 09			21 13			21 40	21 39		21 58		22 13
	d	20 44		20 54			21 14		21 10			21 14			21 40	21 40		21 59		22 13
Langley	d			20 58			→					21 17			21 44			22 02		
Iver	d			21 01								21 20			21 47			22 05		
West Drayton	d	20 51		21 05								21 24			21 51			22 09		
Heathrow Terminal 4 ✈	d																			
Heathrow Terminal 1-2-3 [2] ✈	d		20 57										21 27				21 57			
Hayes & Harlington	d	20 56	21 03	21 10								21 28	21 33		21 56		22 03	22 14		
Southall	d		21 06	21 13									21 36		21 59		22 06			
Hanwell	d		21 09										21 39				22 09			
Greenford ⊖	d										21 16			21 46						
South Greenford	d										21 19			21 49						
Castle Bar Park	d										21 22			21 52						
Drayton Green	d										21 24			21 54						
West Ealing	d		21 11								21 26		21 41	21 56			22 11			
Ealing Broadway ⊖	d	21 03	21 14	21 19							21 29	21 35	21 44	21 59	22 05		22 14	22 21		
Acton Main Line	d										21 33			22 03						
London Paddington [15] ⊖	a	21 15	21 24	21 31	21 08	21 14		21 21	21 29	21 32	21 42	21 48	21 54	22 13	22 16	22 00	22 24	22 33	22 14	22 39

		GW ◇■ 🍴	GW FX ◇■ 🍴	GW FO ◇■ 🍴	HC	GW ■	HC	GW ◇	GW ■	GW FX ◇■	GW FO ◇■	GW ◇■ 🍴	GW ◇■ 🍴	HC	GW ■	GW ■	GW ◇■	GW ◇■ 🍴
Oxford	d							22 11		22 34	22 34						23 09	
Reading [7]	d	22 01	22 12	22 12		22 16		22 44	22 48	22 59	22 59	23 04	23 08			23 15	23 41	23 55
Twyford [5]	d					22 22			22 54							23 22		
Maidenhead [3]	d					22 31			23 02							23 29	23 54	
Taplow	d					22 34			23 05							23 33		
Burnham	d					22 37			23 08						←	23 36		
Slough [3]	a					22 42		23 01	23 13	23 15	23 12				23 13	23 41	00 01	
	d					22 42		23 01	23 27	23 16	23 16				23 27	23 41	00 02	
Langley	d					22 46			→						23 31	23 45		
Iver	d					22 49									23 34	23 48		
West Drayton	d					22 53									23 38	23 51		
Heathrow Terminal 4 ✈	d																	
Heathrow Terminal 1-2-3 [2] ✈	d				22 27		22 57							23 27				
Hayes & Harlington	d				22 33	22 57	23 03							23 33	23 43	23 56		
Southall	d				22 36	23 01	23 06							23 36	23 47	23 59		
Hanwell	d				22 39		23 09							23 39				
Greenford ⊖	d																	
South Greenford	d																	
Castle Bar Park	d																	
Drayton Green	d																	
West Ealing	d				22 41		23 11							23 41				
Ealing Broadway ⊖	d				22 44	23 06	23 14							23 44	23 52	00 06		
Acton Main Line	d																	
London Paddington [15] ⊖	a	22 30	22 44	22 45	22 54	23 18	23 24	23 25		23 36	23 36	23 38	23 41	23 54	00 02	00 17	00 28	00 33

Mondays to Fridays

25 June to 14 September

		GW MX ■	GW MX ■	GW MO ◇■ A	GW ◇■ B	GW MO ◇■ A 🍴	GW ◇■ B 🍴	HC MO	HC MX	GW MO ■ A	GW ■ B	GW MX ◇■	GW MX ◇■ 🍴	GW MO ■ A	GW MO ■ A	GW MX ■	GW ■ B	GW MO ■ A	GW MX ■	GW MO ◇■ A	GW MX ◇■	GW ◇■ B	GW MX ■
Oxford	d			22p46	22p46							23p09		23p15						00≀01	00 07		00 27
Reading [7]	d	22p48	23p15	23p22	23p22	23p30	23p30			23p35	23p36	23p41	23p55	23p56	00≀15	00 15	00≀16			00≀32	00 39	00≀53	01 15
Twyford [5]	d	22p54	23p22	≀	≀	≀	≀			23p41	23p42			00≀03	00≀21	00 21	00≀23			00≀38		00≀59	01 21
Maidenhead [3]	d	23p02	23p29	≀	≀	≀	≀			23p49	23p50	23p54		00≀11	00≀29	00 29	00≀31			00≀46		01≀07	01 29
Taplow	d	23p05	23p33	≀	≀	≀	≀			≀	≀			≀	≀	00 32	≀			≀		≀	
Burnham	d	23p08	23p36	≀	≀	≀	≀			23p54	23p55			00≀15	≀	00 35	≀	←	←	≀		≀	
Slough [3]	a	23p13	23p41	23p42	23p43	≀	≀			23p58	23p59	00 01		00≀20	00≀36	00 40	00≀38	00≀36	00 40	00≀53	00 55	01≀14	01 37
	d	23p27	23p41	23p42	23p43	≀	≀			23p59	00≀01	00 02		00≀20	00≀40	00 40	00≀38	00≀40	00 40	00≀53	00 56	01≀14	01 37
Langley	d	23p31	23p45	≀	≀	≀	≀			00≀03	00≀05			00≀24	→	→	00≀42	00≀44	00 44	≀		≀	
Iver	d	23p34	23p48	≀	≀	≀	≀			≀	≀			≀			≀	≀		≀		≀	
West Drayton	d	23p38	23p51	≀	≀	≀	≀			00≀08	00≀10			00≀29			00≀47	00≀49	00 49	≀		≀	
Heathrow Terminal 4 ✈	d			≀	≀	≀	≀	00 01	00 01	≀	≀			≀			≀	≀		≀		≀	
Heathrow Terminal 1-2-3 [2] ✈	d			≀	≀	≀	≀	00 07	00 07	≀	≀			≀			≀	≀		≀		≀	
Hayes & Harlington	d	23p43	23p56	≀	≀	≀	≀	00 13	00 13	00≀16	00≀16			00≀34			00≀52	00≀54	00 54	01≀02		01≀23	01 46
Southall	d	23p47	23p59	≀	≀	≀	≀	00 16	00 16	00≀20	00≀20			00≀38			00≀56	00≀57	00 57	≀		≀	
Hanwell	d			≀	≀	≀	≀			≀	≀			≀			≀	≀		≀		≀	
Greenford ⊖	d			≀	≀	≀	≀			≀	≀			≀			≀	≀		≀		≀	
South Greenford	d			≀	≀	≀	≀			≀	≀			≀			≀	≀		≀		≀	
Castle Bar Park	d			≀	≀	≀	≀			≀	≀			≀			≀	≀		≀		≀	
Drayton Green	d			≀	≀	≀	≀			≀	≀			≀			≀	≀		≀		≀	
West Ealing	d			≀	≀	≀	≀			≀	≀			≀			≀	≀		≀		≀	
Ealing Broadway ⊖	d	23p52	00 06	≀	≀	≀	≀	00 21	00 22	00≀25	00≀25			00≀43			01≀01	01≀03	01 03	01≀09		01≀30	01 53
Acton Main Line	d			≀	≀	≀	≀			≀	≀			≀			≀	≀		≀		≀	
London Paddington [15] ⊖	a	00 02	00 17	00≀02	00≀05	00≀05	00≀13	00 30	00 30	00≀34	00≀34	00 28	00 33	00≀52			01≀10	01≀14	01 16	01≀18	01 17	01≀39	02 05

A from 2 July until 10 September

B 25 June

Reading and Greenford - London

Mondays to Fridays

25 June to 14 September

Network Diagram - see first Page of Table 116

		GW ■	GW ■	GW ■ B	GW ■ C	HC	GW ■	HC	GW ■	GW ■	GW ■	GW ◇■ 🍴	GW ■	HC	GW ■	GW ■	GW ■	GW ■	GW ■	GW ◇■	HC
Oxford	d			04≀00							05 03						05 24	05 43		05 59	
Reading [7]	d	02 24	03 54	04≀39	04≀39		05 14		05 39		05 44	05 57	05 59		06 07		06 15	06 16	06 22	06 31	
Twyford [5]	d	02 30	04 00	04≀45	04≀45		05 20		05 45		05 50				06 13		06 21	06 23			
Maidenhead [3]	d	02 38	04 08	04≀53	04≀53		05 28		05 53		05 58		06 10		06 21		06 29	06 31		06 43	
Taplow	d			≀	≀		05 32				06 02				06 24		06 32				
Burnham	d			≀	≀		05 35				06 05				06 27		06 35				
Slough [3]	a	02 45	04 15	05≀00	05≀00		05 40		06 01		06 10		06 17		06 32		06 40		06 40	06 50	
	d	02 45	04 15	05≀00	05≀00		05 40		06 01		06 10		06 17		06 32		06 40		06 41	06 50	
Langley	d			05≀04	05≀04		05 44				06 14				06 36		06 44				
Iver	d			05≀07	05≀07		05 47				06 17						06 47				
West Drayton	d	02 52	04 22	05≀11	05≀11		05 51				06 21				06 41		06 51				
Heathrow Terminal 4 ✈	d			≀	≀	05 23		05 51													
Heathrow Terminal 1-2-3 [2] ✈	d			≀	≀	05 29		05 57						06 27							06 57
Hayes & Harlington	d	02 57	04 27	05≀16	05≀16	05 35	05 56	06 03	06 10		06 26			06 33	06 46		06 56				07 03
Southall	d	03 00	04 30	05≀19	05≀19	05 38	05 59	06 06	06 13		06 29			06 36	06 50		07 00				07 06
Hanwell	d			≀	≀	05 41		06 09						06 39							07 09
Greenford ⊖	d			≀	≀					06 16						06 46					
South Greenford	d			≀	≀					06 19						06 49					
Castle Bar Park	d			≀	≀					06 22						06 52					
Drayton Green	d			≀	≀					06 24						06 54					
West Ealing	d			≀	≀	05 43		06 11		06 26				06 41		06 56					07 11
Ealing Broadway ⊖	d	03 06	04 36	05≀28	05≀28	05 46	06 05	06 14	06 19	06 29	06 35			06 44	06 55	06 59	07 05				07 14
Acton Main Line	d			05≀31	05≀31		06 08			06 33	06 38					07 03					
London Paddington [15] ⊖	a	03 18	04 47	05≀41	05≀41	05 56	06 16	06 24	06 31	06 42	06 46	06 24	06 36	06 54	07 09	07 12	07 17	06 54	07 01	07 08	07 24

		GW ■	GW ■	GW ■	GW ◇■ 🍴	GW ■	GW ◇■ 🍴	GW ■	GW ■	GW ■	GW ◇■ 🍴	HC	GW ■	GW ■	GW ■	GW ■	GW ◇■ 🍴	GW ◇■ 🍴	GW ■	GW ◇■ 🍴	GW ■	HC
Oxford	d						06 27									06 07				06 56		
Reading [7]	d	06 31	06 36	06 36	06 44	06 46	06 56			06 57	07 01		07 02	07 07		07 10	07 16	07 21		07 27		
Twyford [5]	d	06 37	06 42	06 44		06 53				07 03			07 08			07 16			07 22			
Maidenhead [3]	d	06 46	06 53			07 03	07 08			07 11			07 16	07 18		07 24			07 31		07 41	
Taplow	d		06 57													07 28						
Burnham	d	06 50	07 01						←				07 21			07 31						
Slough [3]	a	06 55	07 06		06 58				07 06	07 19			07 26			07 36					07 49	
	d	06 56	07 06		06 59				07 06	07 20			07 26			07 36					07 50	
Langley	d	06 59	→						07 11				07 31			07 41						
Iver	d	07 03							07 14							07 44						
West Drayton	d	07 07							07 18				07 36			07 48						
Heathrow Terminal 4 ✈	d																					
Heathrow Terminal 1-2-3 [2] ✈	d											07 27										07 57
Hayes & Harlington	d	07 11							07 23			07 33	07 41			07 53						08 03
Southall	d	07 15							07 27			07 36	07 45			07 57						08 06
Hanwell	d											07 39										08 09
Greenford ⊖	d							07 16							07 46							
South Greenford	d							07 19							07 49							
Castle Bar Park	d							07 22							07 52							
Drayton Green	d							07 24							07 54							
West Ealing	d							07 26				07 41			07 56							08 11
Ealing Broadway ⊖	d	07 21						07 29	07 33			07 44	07 52		07 59	08 03						08 14
Acton Main Line	d							07 33							08 03							
London Paddington [15] ⊖	a	07 32		07 14	07 16	07 29	07 30	07 42	07 44	07 49	07 32	07 54	08 04	07 43	08 12	08 16	07 44	07 53	07 57	07 59	08 21	08 24

		GW ■	GW ◇■ 🍴	GW ■	GW ◇■ 🍴	GW ◇■ 🍴	GW ◇■ 🍴	GW ◇■	GW ■	GW ■	GW ◇■ ✕	GW ◇■ 🍴	GW ■	GW ◇■ 🍴	GW ■	HC	GW ■	GW ■	GW ■	GW ◇■ 🍴	GW ◇■ 🍴	GW ■
Oxford	d	06 36								07 00	07 33											07 21
Reading [7]	d	07 30	07 33	07 34	07 36	07 39	07 45			07 55	07 58	08 02	08 06	08 08					08 12	08 14	08 17	08 19
Twyford [5]	d	07 37		07 41					07 56	08 02			08a12						08 17			08 26
Maidenhead [3]	d	07 45		07 49				08 00	08 04	08 11									08 26			08 34
Taplow	d			07 53															08 29			
Burnham	d	07 51		07 56						08 15									08 32			
Slough [3]	a	07 55		08 01						08 20									08 38			
	d	07 56		08 01						08 20							08 26		08 38			
Langley	d	08 00		08 06													08 30		08 42			
Iver	d			08 09															08 44			
West Drayton	d	08 04		08 13													08 35		08 50			
Heathrow Terminal 4 ✈	d																					
Heathrow Terminal 1-2-3 [2] ✈	d															08 27						
Hayes & Harlington	d	08 10		08 17												08 33	08 39		08 53			
Southall	d	08 13								08 30						08 36	08 43					
Hanwell	d															08 39						
Greenford ⊖	d														08 16			08 46				
South Greenford	d														08 19			08 49				
Castle Bar Park	d														08 22			08 52				
Drayton Green	d														08 24			08 54				
West Ealing	d														08 26	08 41		08 56				
Ealing Broadway ⊖	d	08 18		08 24											08 29	08 44	08 49	08 59	09 04			
Acton Main Line	d														08 33			09 03				
London Paddington [15] ⊖	a	08 32	08 02	08 36	08 07	08 09	08 14	08 26	08 28	08 48	08 31	08 33		08 38	08 42	08 54	09 03	09 12	09 16	08 40	08 44	08 58

B not 25 June

C 25 June

Table 117

Mondays to Fridays

25 June to 14 September

Reading and Greenford - London

Network Diagram - see first Page of Table 116

		GW ◇■ A ⊡⊘	GW ■	HC	GW ■	GW ◇■ B ⊡	GW ■	GW ◇■ C ⊡	GW ■	XC ◇■ H	GW ◇■ ⊡	GW ◇■ ⊡	GW ■	GW ■	HC	GW ■	GW ◇■ ⊡	GW ◇■ ⊡	GW ■	GW ■	GW ◇■ D ⊡⊘
Oxford	d	07 52					08 06		07 56	08 16						08 21					08 51
Reading [7]	d	08 23			08 31	08 34	08 35	08 45	08 48	08a39	08 52	09 02				09 03	09 08	09 16		09 17	09 18
Twyford [3]	d				08 37				08 54							09 09				09 24	
Maidenhead [3]	d		08 41		08 45				09 03							09 17				09 35	
Taplow	d				08 49											09 21				09 36	
Burnham	d				08 50											09 24				09 39	
Slough [3]	a		08 49		08 57											09 29				09 44	
	d		08 50		08 57									09 14		09 30				09 44	
Langley	d				09 01											09 33					
Iver	d				09 04											09 36					
West Drayton	d				09 08									09 21		09 40				09 51	
Heathrow Terminal 4 ✈	d																				
Heathrow Terminal 1-2-3 [2] ✈	d			08 57											09 27						
Hayes & Harlington	d			09 03	09 13									09 26	09 33	09 45				09 56	
Southall	d		09 00	09 06	09 17									09 30	09 36	09 48					
Hanwell	d			09 09											09 39						
Greenford ⊖	d												09 16						09 46		
South Greenford	d												09 19						09 49		
Castle Bar Park	d												09 22						09 52		
Drayton Green	d												09 24						09 54		
West Ealing	d			09 11									09 26		09 41				09 56		
Ealing Broadway ⊖	d			09 14	09 23								09 29	09 36	09 44	09 54			09 59	10 03	
Acton Main Line	d												09 33						10 03		
London Paddington [15] ⊖	a	08 51	09 21	09 24	09 35	09 00	09 06	09 14	09 27		09 21	09 29	09 42	09 48	09 54	10 03	09 39	09 44	10 12	10 16	09 47

		GW ■	GW ◇■ ⊡	GW ■	GW ◇■ E ⊡	GW ◇■	GW ◇■ ⊡	HC	GW ■	GW ■	GW ◇■	GW ◇■ ⊡	GW ■	GW ■	HC	GW ■	GW ◇■ ⊡	GW ◇■ ⊡	GW ■	GW ■	GW ◇■ H	GW ◇■ ⊡
Oxford	d			08 36		09 01					09 31					09 07					10 01	
Reading [7]	d	09 21	09 27	09 33	09 34	09 37	09 46			09 48	09 55	10 02				10 03	10 08	10 12	10 18	10 18	10 26	10 32
Twyford [3]	d			09 39						09 54						10 09				10 24		
Maidenhead [3]	d			09 47						10 02						10 17				10 32		
Taplow	d									10 06										10 36		
Burnham	d								←	10 09				←						10 39		
Slough [3]	a			09 54		09 52			09 54	10 14	10 10			10 14		10 24				10 44	10 39	
	d			09 54		09 52			09 54	10 14	10 11			10 14		10 24				10 44	10 40	
Langley	d			→					09 58	→						10 28				→		
Iver	d								10 01							10 31						
West Drayton	d								10 05					10 21		10 35						
Heathrow Terminal 4 ✈	d																					
Heathrow Terminal 1-2-3 [2] ✈	d							09 57							10 27							
Hayes & Harlington	d							10 03	10 10					10 26	10 33	10 40						
Southall	d							10 06	10 13						10 36	10 43						
Hanwell	d							10 09							10 39							
Greenford ⊖	d												10 16									
South Greenford	d												10 19									
Castle Bar Park	d												10 22									
Drayton Green	d												10 24									
West Ealing	d							10 11					10 26		10 41							
Ealing Broadway ⊖	d							10 14	10 19				10 29	10 33	10 44	10 49						
Acton Main Line	d												10 33									
London Paddington [15] ⊖	a	09 56	09 59		10 02	10 12	10 15	10 24	10 31		10 30	10 32	10 42	10 46	10 54	11 01	10 37	10 39	10 56		11 00	11 07

		GW ■	GW ■	HC	GW ■	GW ◇■ ⊡	GW ■	GW ◇■ ⊡	GW ◇■	GW ◇■ F ⊡	GW ■	GW ■	HC	GW ■	GW ◇■ ⊡	GW ■	GW ■	GW ◇■ H	GW ◇■ ⊡	GW ■	GW ■
Oxford	d				09 36				10 31					10 08				11 01			
Reading [7]	d				10 33	10 45	10 48	10 52	10 55	11 02				11 03	11 11	11 18	11 20	11 26	11 32		
Twyford [3]	d				10 39		10 54							11 09		11 24					
Maidenhead [3]	d				10 47		11 02							11 17		11 32					
Taplow	d						11 06									11 36					
Burnham	d		←				11 09					←				11 39					←
Slough [3]	a		10 44		10 54		11 14		11 09			11 14		11 24		11 44		11 39			11 44
	d		10 44		10 54		11 14		11 10			11 14		11 24		11 44		11 40			11 44
Langley	d				10 58		→							11 28		→					
Iver	d				11 01									11 31							
West Drayton	d		10 51		11 05							11 21		11 35							11 51
Heathrow Terminal 4 ✈	d																				
Heathrow Terminal 1-2-3 [2] ✈	d			10 57									11 27								
Hayes & Harlington	d		10 56	11 03	11 10							11 26	11 33	11 40							11 56
Southall	d			11 06	11 13								11 36	11 43							
Hanwell	d			11 09									11 39								
Greenford ⊖	d	10 46									11 16									11 46	
South Greenford	d	10 49									11 19									11 49	
Castle Bar Park	d	10 52									11 22									11 52	
Drayton Green	d	10 54									11 24									11 54	
West Ealing	d	10 56		11 11							11 26		11 41							11 56	
Ealing Broadway ⊖	d	10 59	11 03	11 14	11 19						11 29	11 33	11 44	11 49						11 59	12 03
Acton Main Line	d	11 03									11 33									12 03	
London Paddington [15] ⊖	a	11 12	11 16	11 24	11 32	11 14		11 24	11 29	11 32	11 42	11 46	11 54	12 01	11 38		11 55	11 59	12 00	12 12	12 16

A ⊡ from Reading ⊘ to Reading
B The Armada
C The Bristolian
D The Cathedrals Express. ⊡ from Reading ⊘ to Reading
E The Golden Hind
F The Red Dragon

Table 117

Mondays to Fridays

25 June to 14 September

Reading and Greenford - London

Network Diagram - see first Page of Table 116

		HC	GW ■	GW ◇■ ⊡	GW ■	GW ◇■ ⊡	GW ◇■ H	GW ◇■ ⊡	GW ■	GW ■	HC	GW ■	GW ◇■ ⊡	GW ◇■ ⊡	GW ■	GW ■	GW ◇■ H	GW ◇■ ⊡	GW ■	GW ■	HC
Oxford	d		10 36				11 31					11 07					12 01				
Reading [7]	d		11 33	11 44	11 48	11 52	11 55	12 02				12 03	12 08	12 12	12 18	12 18	12 26	12 32			
Twyford [3]	d		11 39		11 54							12 09				12 24					
Maidenhead [3]	d		11 47		12 02							12 17				12 32					
Taplow	d				12 06											12 36					
Burnham	d				12 09					←						12 39				←	
Slough [3]	a		11 54		12 14		12 09			12 14		12 24				12 44	12 39			12 44	
	d		11 54		12 14		12 10			12 14		12 24				12 44	12 40			12 44	
Langley	d		11 58		→							12 28				→					
Iver	d		12 01									12 31									
West Drayton	d		12 05							12 21		12 35								12 51	
Heathrow Terminal 4 ✈	d																				
Heathrow Terminal 1-2-3 [2] ✈	d	11 57									12 27										12 57
Hayes & Harlington	d	12 03	12 10							12 26	12 33	12 40								12 56	13 03
Southall	d	12 06	12 13								12 36	12 43									13 06
Hanwell	d	12 09									12 39										13 09
Greenford ⊖	d								12 16										12 46		
South Greenford	d								12 19										12 49		
Castle Bar Park	d								12 22										12 52		
Drayton Green	d								12 24										12 54		
West Ealing	d	12 11							12 26		12 41								12 56		13 11
Ealing Broadway ⊖	d	12 14	12 19						12 29	12 33	12 44	12 49							12 59	13 03	13 14
Acton Main Line	d								12 33										13 03		
London Paddington [15] ⊖	a	12 24	12 31	12 14		12 23	12 29	12 32	12 42	12 46	12 54	13 02	12 37	12 40	12 52		13 06	13 00	13 12	13 16	13 24

		GW ■	GW ◇■ ⊡	GW ■	GW ◇■ H	GW ◇■ ⊡	GW ■	GW ■	HC	GW ■	XC ◇■ H	GW ◇■ ⊡	GW ■ ■ A ⊡	GW ■	GW ◇■ H	GW ■	GW ◇■ ⊡	GW ■	GW ■	HC	GW ■	GW ◇■ ⊡
Oxford	d	11 37			12 31					12 07	12 16				13 01						12 37	
Reading [7]	d	12 33	12 45	12 48	12 55	13 02				13 03	12a39	13 11	13 17	13 18	13 26	13 29	13 32				13 33	13 44
Twyford [3]	d	12 39		12 54						13 09				13 24							13 39	
Maidenhead [3]	d	12 47		13 02						13 17				13 32							13 47	
Taplow	d			13 06										13 36								
Burnham	d			13 09				←						13 39					←			
Slough [3]	a	12 54		13 14	13 09			13 14		13 24				13 44	13 39				13 44		13 54	
	d	12 54		13 14	13 10			13 14		13 24				13 44	13 40				13 44		13 54	
Langley	d	12 58		→						13 28				→							13 58	
Iver	d	13 01								13 31											14 01	
West Drayton	d	13 05						13 21		13 35									13 51		14 05	
Heathrow Terminal 4 ✈	d																					
Heathrow Terminal 1-2-3 [2] ✈	d								13 27											13 57		
Hayes & Harlington	d	13 10						13 26	13 33	13 40									13 56	14 03	14 10	
Southall	d	13 13							13 36	13 43										14 06	14 13	
Hanwell	d								13 39											14 09		
Greenford ⊖	d						13 16											13 46				
South Greenford	d						13 19											13 49				
Castle Bar Park	d						13 22											13 52				
Drayton Green	d						13 24											13 54				
West Ealing	d						13 26		13 41									13 56		14 11		
Ealing Broadway ⊖	d	13 19					13 29	13 33	13 44	13 49								13 59	14 03	14 14	14 19	
Acton Main Line	d						13 33											14 03				
London Paddington [15] ⊖	a	13 31	13 14		13 29	13 32	13 42	13 46	13 54	14 01		13 38	13 44		14 01	14 09	14 06	14 12	14 16	14 24	14 31	14 14

		GW ■	GW ◇■ H	GW ◇■ B ⊡	GW ■	GW ■	HC	GW ■	GW ◇■ ⊡	GW ◇■ ⊡	GW ◇■ ⊡	GW ■	GW ◇■ H	GW ◇■ ⊡	GW ■	GW ■	HC	GW ■	GW ◇■ ⊡	GW ■
Oxford	d		13 31					13 07					14 01					13 37		
Reading [7]	d	13 48	13 55	14 01				14 03	14 08	14 12	14 17	14 18	14 26	14 32				14 33	14 44	14 48
Twyford [3]	d	13 54						14 09				14 24						14 39		14 54
Maidenhead [3]	d	14 02						14 17				14 32						14 47		15 02
Taplow	d	14 06										14 36								15 06
Burnham	d	14 09				←						14 39				←				15 09
Slough [3]	a	14 14	14 09			14 14		14 24				14 44	14 39			14 44		14 54		15 14
	d	14 14	14 10			14 14		14 24				14 44	14 40			14 44		14 54		15 14
Langley	d	→						14 28				→						14 58		→
Iver	d							14 31										15 01		
West Drayton	d					14 21		14 35								14 51		15 05		
Heathrow Terminal 4 ✈	d																			
Heathrow Terminal 1-2-3 [2] ✈	d						14 27										14 57			
Hayes & Harlington	d					14 26	14 33	14 40								14 56	15 03	15 10		
Southall	d						14 36	14 43									15 06	15 13		
Hanwell	d						14 39										15 09			
Greenford ⊖	d				14 16										14 46					
South Greenford	d				14 19										14 49					
Castle Bar Park	d				14 22										14 52					
Drayton Green	d				14 24										14 54					
West Ealing	d				14 26		14 41								14 56		15 11			
Ealing Broadway ⊖	d				14 29	14 33	14 44	14 49							14 59	15 03	15 14	15 19		
Acton Main Line	d				14 33										15 03					
London Paddington [15] ⊖	a		14 29	14 32	14 42	14 46	14 54	15 01	14 37	14 40	14 44		15 00	15 08	15 12	15 16	15 24	15 32	15 14	

A The Cornish Riviera
B The St. David

Reading and Greenford - London

Mondays to Fridays

25 June to 14 September

Network Diagram - see first Page of Table 116

		GW	GW	GW	GW	GW	HC	GW	GW	GW	GW	GW	GW	GW	GW	HC	GW	GW	GW	GW	GW	GW
		A																				
Oxford	d		14 31					14 07				15 01					14 37				15 31	
Reading	d	14 52	14 55	15 02				15 03	15 11	15 18	15 20	15 26	15 32				15 33	15 44	15 48	15 52	15 55	16 02
Twyford	d							15 09		15 24							15 39		15 54			
Maidenhead	d							15 17		15 32							15 47		16 02			
Taplow	d									15 36									16 06			
Burnham	d					←				15 39					←				16 09			
Slough	a		15 09			15 14		15 24		15 44		15 39			15 44		15 54		16 14		16 09	
	d		15 10			15 14		15 24		15 44		15 40			15 44		15 54		16 14		16 10	
Langley	d							15 28		→							15 58		→			
Iver	d							15 31									16 01					
West Drayton	d					15 21		15 35							15 51		16 05					
Heathrow Terminal 4	d																					
Heathrow Terminal 1-2-3	d						15 27									15 57						
Hayes & Harlington	d					15 26	15 33	15 40							15 56	16 03	16 10					
Southall	d						15 36	15 43								16 06	16 13					
Hanwell	d						15 39									16 09						
Greenford	d				15 16									15 46								
South Greenford	d				15 19									15 49								
Castle Bar Park	d				15 22									15 52								
Drayton Green	d				15 24									15 54								
West Ealing	d				15 26		15 41							15 56		16 11						
Ealing Broadway	d				15 29	15 33	15 44	15 49						15 59	16 03	16 14	16 19					
Acton Main Line	d				15 33									16 03								
London Paddington	a	15 24	15 29	15 32	15 42	15 46	15 54	16 02	15 38		15 54	16 01	16 09	16 12	16 17	16 24	16 31	16 14		16 22	16 27	16 30

		GW	GW	HC	GW	GW	GW	GW	GW	GW	GW	GW	HC	GW	GW	GW	GW	GW	GW	GW	GW
						C												D			
Oxford	d				15 07					16 01				15 37					16 31		
Reading	d				16 03	16 08	16 15	16 18	16 19	16 26				16 33	16 34	16 44	16 48	16 51	16 55	17 02	
Twyford	d				16 09			16 24						16 39			16 54				
Maidenhead	d				16 17			16 32						16 47			17 02				
Taplow	d							16 36									17 06				
Burnham	d		←					16 39				←					17 09				
Slough	a		16 14		16 24			16 44		16 39		16 44		16 54			17 14		17 09		
	d		16 14		16 24			16 44		16 40		16 44		16 54			17 14		17 10		
Langley	d				16 28			→						16 58			→				
Iver	d				16 31									17 01							
West Drayton	d		16 21		16 35							16 51		17 05							
Heathrow Terminal 4	d																				
Heathrow Terminal 1-2-3	d			16 27									16 57								
Hayes & Harlington	d		16 26	16 33	16 40							16 56	17 03	17 10							
Southall	d			16 36	16 43								17 06	17 13							
Hanwell	d			16 39									17 09								
Greenford	d	16 16									16 46										17 16
South Greenford	d	16 19									16 49										17 19
Castle Bar Park	d	16 22									16 52										17 22
Drayton Green	d	16 24									16 54										17 24
West Ealing	d	16 26		16 41							16 56		17 11								17 26
Ealing Broadway	d	16 29	16 33	16 44	16 49						16 59	17 03	17 14	17 21							17 29
Acton Main Line	d	16 33									17 03										17 33
London Paddington	a	16 42	16 46	16 54	17 02	16 39	16 44		16 57	17 00	17 12	17 19	17 24	17 31	17 09	17 14		17 24	17 34	17 30	17 42

		GW	HC	GW	GW	GW	GW	GW	GW	GW	GW	HC	GW	GW	GW	GW	GW	GW	GW	GW	HC
					E											F					
Oxford	d			16 07				17 01					16 37					17 31			
Reading	d			17 03	17 11	17 14	17 17	17 26	17 32				17 33	17 42	17 46	17 51	17 54	17 56			
Twyford	d			17 09		17 24							17 39	17 48							
Maidenhead	d			17 17		17 32	17 29						17 47	17 56			18 08				
Taplow	d					17 36								18 00							
Burnham	d	←				17 39					←			18 02						←	
Slough	a	17 14		17 24		17 44		17 39			17 44		17 54	18 07			18 14	18 10		18 14	
	d	17 14		17 24		17 44		17 40			17 44		17 54	18 07			18 14	18 11		18 14	
Langley	d			17 28		→							17 58				→				
Iver	d			17 31									18 01								
West Drayton	d	17 21		17 35							17 51		18 05	18 14							
Heathrow Terminal 4	d																				
Heathrow Terminal 1-2-3	d		17 27									17 57									18 27
Hayes & Harlington	d	17 26	17 33	17 40							17 56	18 03	18 10	18 19						18 26	18 33
Southall	d		17 36	17 43								18 06	18 13								18 36
Hanwell	d		17 39									18 09									18 39
Greenford	d									17 46									18 16		
South Greenford	d									17 49									18 19		
Castle Bar Park	d									17 52									18 22		
Drayton Green	d									17 54									18 24		
West Ealing	d		17 41							17 56		18 11							18 26		18 41
Ealing Broadway	d	17 33	17 44	17 49						17 59	18 03	18 14	18 19	18 26					18 29	18 33	18 44
Acton Main Line	d									18 03									18 33		
London Paddington	a	17 48	17 54	18 01	17 39		17 54	17 59	18 02	18 12	18 14	18 24	18 31	18 37	18 14	18 21		18 28	18 42	18 46	18 54

A The Cornishman
C The Cheltenham Spa Express
D The Torbay Express
E The Merchant Venturer
F The Mayflower

Table 117

Reading and Greenford - London

Mondays to Fridays

25 June to 14 September

Network Diagram - see first Page of Table 116

		GW	GW	GW	GW	GW	GW	GW	GW	GW	GW	GW	HC	GW	GW	GW	GW	GW	GW	GW	GW
																	A				
Oxford	d	17 07							18 01					17 37				18 31			
Reading	d	18 00	18 01	18 08	18 12		18 18	18 22	18 26	18 32				18 33	18 47	18 48	18 51	18 57	19 02		
Twyford	d	18 10					18 24							18 39		18 54					
Maidenhead	d	18 17				18 26	18 32							18 48		19 05					
Taplow	d						18 35									19 09					
Burnham	d						18 39					←				19 12					←
Slough	a	18 24				18 33	18 44		18 39			18 44		18 54		19 17		19 09			19 17
	d	18 24				18 33	18 44		18 40			18 44		18 54		19 17		19 10			19 17
Langley	d	18 28					→							18 58		→					
Iver	d	18 32												19 01							
West Drayton	d	18 35										18 51		19 05							19 24
Heathrow Terminal 4	d																				
Heathrow Terminal 1-2-3	d												18 57								
Hayes & Harlington	d	18 40				18 45						18 56	19 03	19 10							19 29
Southall	d	18 43											19 06	19 13							
Hanwell	d												19 09								
Greenford	d										18 46									19 16	
South Greenford	d										18 49									19 19	
Castle Bar Park	d										18 52									19 22	
Drayton Green	d										18 54									19 24	
West Ealing	d										18 56		19 11							19 26	
Ealing Broadway	d	18 49				18 54					18 59	19 05	19 14	19 19						19 29	19 36
Acton Main Line	d										19 03									19 33	
London Paddington	a	19 00	18 30	18 39	18 44	19 04		18 54	18 59	19 02	19 12	19 18	19 24	19 31	19 14		19 24	19 31	19 32	19 42	19 45

		HC	GW	GW	GW	GW	GW	GW	GW	HC	GW	GW	GW	GW	GW	GW	GW	HC	GW	GW
														FO	FX					
Oxford	d		18 07						19 06		18 37			19 31	19 31				19 01	
Reading	d		19 03	19 11	19 18		19 18	19 25	19 32		19 33	19 45	19 48	19 55	19 55				19 58	20 02
Twyford	d		19 09				19 24				19 42		19 54						20 04	
Maidenhead	d		19 21				19 32				19 50		20 02						20 12	
Taplow	d						19 36						20 05							
Burnham	d						19 39						20 09				←			
Slough	a		19 29				19 44		19 47		19 57		20 14	20 09	20 09		20 14		20 19	
	d		19 29				19 44		19 47		19 57		20 14	20 10	20 10		20 14		20 24	
Langley	d		19 33								20 01		→						20 28	
Iver	d		19 36								20 04								20 31	
West Drayton	d		19 39				19 51				20 08						20 21		20 35	
Heathrow Terminal 4	d																			
Heathrow Terminal 1-2-3	d	19 27								19 57								20 27		
Hayes & Harlington	d	19 33	19 44				19 56			20 03	20 13						20 26	20 33	20 40	
Southall	d	19 36	19 47							20 06	20 16							20 36	20 43	
Hanwell	d	19 39								20 09								20 39		
Greenford	d					19 46										20 16				
South Greenford	d					19 49										20 19				
Castle Bar Park	d					19 52										20 22				
Drayton Green	d					19 54										20 24				
West Ealing	d	19 41				19 56				20 11						20 26		20 41		
Ealing Broadway	d	19 44	19 53			19 59	20 03			20 14	20 22					20 29	20 33	20 44	20 49	
Acton Main Line	d					20 03										20 33				
London Paddington	a	19 54	20 02	19 38	19 54	20 12	20 16	19 54	20 06	20 24	20 31	20 14		20 30	20 31	20 42	20 49	20 54	20 59	20 32

		GW	GW	GW	GW	GW	GW	GW	GW	HC	GW	GW	GW	GW	GW	GW	GW	GW	GW	HC	GW	GW
		B	C			D																
Oxford	d						20 01				19 37					20 31						20 07
Reading	d	20 08	20 08	20 15	20 18	20 21	20 26				20 33	20 34	20 45	20 48	20 52	20 55	21 02					21 14
Twyford	d				20 24						20 39			20 54								21 20
Maidenhead	d				20 32						20 47			21 02								21 28
Taplow	d				20 36									21 06								21 32
Burnham	d				20 39				←					21 09					←			21 35
Slough	a				20 44		20 39		20 44		20 54			21 13		21 09			21 13			21 40
	d				20 44		20 40		20 44		20 54			21 14		21 10			21 14			21 40
Langley	d				→						20 58			→					21 17			21 44
Iver	d										21 01								21 20			21 47
West Drayton	d								20 51		21 05								21 24			21 51
Heathrow Terminal 4	d																					
Heathrow Terminal 1-2-3	d									20 57										21 27		
Hayes & Harlington	d								20 56	21 03	21 10								21 28	21 33		21 56
Southall	d									21 06	21 13									21 36		21 59
Hanwell	d									21 09										21 39		
Greenford	d							20 46										21 16			21 46	
South Greenford	d							20 49										21 19			21 49	
Castle Bar Park	d							20 52										21 22			21 52	
Drayton Green	d							20 54										21 24			21 54	
West Ealing	d							20 56		21 11								21 26		21 41	21 56	
Ealing Broadway	d							20 59	21 03	21 14	21 19							21 29	21 35	21 44	21 59	22 05
Acton Main Line	d							21 03										21 33			22 03	
London Paddington	a	20 39	20 39	20 46		20 52	21 01	21 12	21 15	21 24	21 31	21 08	21 14		21 21	21 29	21 32	21 42	21 48	21 54	22 13	22 16

A The Royal Duchy
B from 2 July until 31 August. The Atlantic Coast Express
C from 25 June until 29 June, from 3 September until 14 September
D FO from 6 July until 31 August

Table 117

Reading and Greenford - London

Mondays to Fridays

25 June to 14 September

Network Diagram - see first Page of Table 116

		GW	HC	GW	GW	GW	GW	GW	GW	HC	GW	HC	GW	GW	GW	GW	GW	GW	HC	GW
								FX	FO						FX	FO				
		◇1		1	◇1 🍴	◇1	◇1 🍴	◇1 🍴	◇1 🍴		1		◇	1	◇1	◇1	◇1 🍴	◇1 🍴		1
Oxford	d	21 01		20 37		21 32							22 11		22 34	22 34				
Reading 7	d	21 26		21 33	21 44	21 56	22 01	22 12	22 12		22 16		22 44	22 48	22 59	22 59	23 04	23 08		
Twyford 3	d			21 39							22 22			22 54						
Maidenhead 3	d			21 47							22 31			23 02						
Taplow	d			21 50							22 34			23 05						
Burnham	d			21 53							22 37			23 08						←
Slough 3	a	21 39		21 58		22 13					22 42		23 01	23 13	23 15	23 12				23 13
	d	21 40		21 59		22 13					22 42		23 01	23 27	23 16	23 16				23 27
Langley	d			22 02							22 46			→						23 31
Iver	d			22 05							22 49									23 34
West Drayton	d			22 09							22 53									23 38
Heathrow Terminal 4 ✈	d																			
Heathrow Terminal 1-2-3 2 ✈	d		21 57							22 27		22 57							23 27	
Hayes & Harlington	d		22 03	22 14						22 33	22 57	23 03							23 33	23 43
Southall	d		22 06							22 36	23 01	23 06							23 36	23 47
Hanwell	d		22 09							22 39		23 09							23 39	
Greenford ⊖	d																			
South Greenford	d																			
Castle Bar Park	d																			
Drayton Green	d																			
West Ealing	d		22 11							22 41		23 11							23 41	
Ealing Broadway ⊖	d		22 14	22 21						22 44	23 06	23 14							23 44	23 52
Acton Main Line	d																			
London Paddington 15 ⊖	a	22 00	22 24	22 33	22 14	22 39	22 30	22 44	22 45	22 54	23 18	23 24	23 25		23 36	23 36	23 38	23 41	23 54	00 02

		GW	GW	GW
		1	◇1	◇1 🍴
Oxford	d		23 09	
Reading 7	d	23 15	23 41	23 55
Twyford 3	d	23 22		
Maidenhead 3	d	23 29	23 54	
Taplow	d	23 33		
Burnham	d	23 36		
Slough 3	a	23 41	00 01	
	d	23 41	00 02	
Langley	d	23 45		
Iver	d	23 48		
West Drayton	d	23 51		
Heathrow Terminal 4 ✈	d			
Heathrow Terminal 1-2-3 2 ✈	d			
Hayes & Harlington	d	23 56		
Southall	d	23 59		
Hanwell	d			
Greenford ⊖	d			
South Greenford	d			
Castle Bar Park	d			
Drayton Green	d			
West Ealing	d			
Ealing Broadway ⊖	d	00 06		
Acton Main Line	d			
London Paddington 15 ⊖	a	00 17	00 28	00 33

Table 117

Reading and Greenford - London

Mondays to Fridays

from 17 September

Network Diagram - see first Page of Table 116

		GW	GW	GW	GW	GW	GW	HC	HC	GW	GW	GW	GW	GW	GW	GW	GW	GW	GW	GW	GW	GW	GW
		MX	MX	MO	MO	MO	MO	MO	MX	MO	MX	MX	MX	MO	MO	MX	MX	MO	MX		MO		
		1	1	◇1	◇1	◇1	◇1			1	◇1	◇1	1	1	1	1	◇1	◇1	1	1	1	1	1
				A	B	B 🍴	A 🍴					🍴		A	B					C	D	E	F
Oxford	d			22p46	22p46						23p09						00 07		00 27				
Reading 7	d	22p48	23p15	23p22	23p22	23p30	23p30			23p36	23p41	23p55	00 15	00 15	00 15		00 39	00 53	01 15	02 24	02 24	03 53	03 54
Twyford 3	d	22p54	23p22							23p43			00 21	00 22	00 22			01 00	01 21	02 30	02 31	04 00	04 00
Maidenhead 3	d	23p02	23p29							23p51	23p54		00 29	00 30	00 30			01 08	01 29	02 38	02 39	04 08	04 08
Taplow	d	23p05	23p33										00 32										
Burnham	d	23p08	23p36							23p56			00 35			←							
Slough 3	a	23p13	23p41	23p43	23p43					00 01	00 01		00 40	00 37	00 37	00 40	00 55	01 17	01 37	02 45	02 46	04 15	04 15
	d	23p27	23p41	23p44	23p44					00 02	00 02		00 40	00 37	00 37	00 40	00 56	01 17	01 37	02 45	02 46	04 15	04 15
Langley	d	23p31	23p45							00 06			→	00 41	00 41	00 44							
Iver	d	23p34	23p48																				
West Drayton	d	23p38	23p51							00 11				00 46	00 47	00 49				02 52	02 53	04 22	04 22
Heathrow Terminal 4 ✈	d							00 01	00 01														
Heathrow Terminal 1-2-3 2 ✈	d							00 07	00 07														
Hayes & Harlington	d	23p43	23p56					00 13	00 13	00 16				00 51	00 52	00 54		01 27	01 46	02 57	02 58	04 27	04 27
Southall	d	23p47	23p59					00 16	00 16	00 20				00 54	00 55	00 57				03 00	03 01	04 30	04 30
Hanwell	d																						
Greenford ⊖	d																						
South Greenford	d																						
Castle Bar Park	d																						
Drayton Green	d																						
West Ealing	d																						
Ealing Broadway ⊖	d	23p52	00 06					00 21	00 22	00 25				01 00	01 00	01 03		01 34	01 53	03 06	03 07	04 36	04 36
Acton Main Line	d																						
London Paddington 15 ⊖	a	00 02	00 17	00 05	00 06	00 12	00 13	00 30	00 30	00 34	00 28	00 33		01 12	01 12	01 16	01 17	01 43	02 05	03 18	03 18	04 47	04 47

		GW	GW	GW	HC	GW	HC	GW	GW	GW	GW	GW	HC	GW	GW	GW	GW	GW	GW	HC	GW
		MX	MO	MO																	
		1	1	1		1		1	1	1	◇1	1		1	1	1	1	1	◇1		1
			H	D							🍴										
Oxford	d	04 00								05 03						05 24	05 43		05 59		
Reading 7	d	04 39	04 39	04 39		05 14		05 39		05 44	05 57	05 59		06 07		06 15	06 16	06 22	06 31		06 32
Twyford 3	d	04 45	04 45	04 47		05 20		05 45		05 50				06 13		06 21	06 23				06 38
Maidenhead 3	d	04 53	04 53	04 55		05 28		05 53		05 58		06 10		06 21		06 29	06 31		06 43		06 46
Taplow	d					05 32				06 02				06 24		06 32					
Burnham	d					05 35				06 05				06 27		06 35					06 50
Slough 3	a	05 00	05 00	05 02		05 40		06 01		06 10		06 17		06 32		06 40		06 40	06 50		06 55
	d	05 00	05 00	05 03		05 40		06 01		06 10		06 17		06 32		06 40		06 41	06 50		06 56
Langley	d	05 04	05 04	05 05		05 44				06 14				06 36		06 44					06 59
Iver	d	05 07	05 07	05 08		05 47				06 17						06 47					07 03
West Drayton	d	05 11	05 11	05 14		05 51				06 21				06 41		06 51					07 07
Heathrow Terminal 4 ✈	d				05 23		05 51														
Heathrow Terminal 1-2-3 2 ✈	d				05 29		05 57						06 27							06 57	
Hayes & Harlington	d	05 16	05 16	05 18	05 35	05 56	06 03	06 10		06 26			06 33	06 46		06 56				07 03	07 11
Southall	d	05 19	05 19	05 20	05 38	05 59	06 06	06 13		06 29			06 36	06 50		07 00				07 06	07 15
Hanwell	d				05 41		06 09						06 39							07 09	
Greenford ⊖	d								06 16						06 46						
South Greenford	d								06 19						06 49						
Castle Bar Park	d								06 22						06 52						
Drayton Green	d								06 24						06 54						
West Ealing	d				05 43		06 11		06 26				06 41		06 56					07 11	
Ealing Broadway ⊖	d	05 28	05 28	05 28	05 46	06 05	06 14	06 19	06 29	06 35			06 44	06 55	06 59	07 05				07 14	07 21
Acton Main Line	d	05 31	05 31	05 31		06 08			06 33	06 38					07 03						
London Paddington 15 ⊖	a	05 41	05 41	05 41	05 56	06 16	06 24	06 31	06 42	06 46	06 24	06 36	06 54	07 09	07 12	07 17	06 54	07 01	07 08	07 24	07 32

A from 29 October
B from 17 September until 22 October
C from 17 September until 19 October, MX from 23 October
D from 22 October
E from 22 October
F from 17 September until 19 October
H from 17 September until 15 October

Reading and Greenford - London

Network Diagram - see first Page of Table 116

		GW 1	GW 1	GW ◇1 ☕	GW 1	GW ◇1 ☕	GW 1	GW 1	GW 1	GW ◇1 ☕	HC	GW 1	GW 1	GW 1	GW 1	GW ◇1 ☕	GW ◇1 ☕	GW 1	GW ◇1 ☕	GW 1	HC	GW 1
Oxford	d					06 27			06 07										06 56			06 36
Reading 7	d	06 36	06 36	06 44	06 46	06 56			06 59	07 01		07 02	07 07		07 10	07 16	07 21		07 27			07 30
Twyford 3	d	06 42	06 44		06 53				07 05			07 09			07 16			07 22				07 37
Maidenhead 3	d	06 53			07 03	07 08			07 13			07 17	07 18		07 24			07 31		07 41		07 45
Taplow	d	06 57													07 28							
Burnham	d	07 01						←				07 21			07 31							07 51
Slough 3	a	07 06		06 58				07 06	07 20			07 26			07 36					07 49		07 55
	d	07 06		06 59				07 06	07 21			07 27			07 36					07 50		07 56
Langley	d	→						07 11				07 31			07 41							08 00
Iver	d							07 14							07 44							
West Drayton	d							07 18				07 36			07 48							08 04
Heathrow Terminal 4 ✈	d																					
Heathrow Terminal 1-2-3 2 ✈	d										07 27										07 57	
Hayes & Harlington	d							07 23			07 33	07 41			07 53						08 03	08 10
Southall	d							07 27			07 36	07 45			07 57						08 06	08 13
Hanwell	d										07 39										08 09	
Greenford ⊖	d						07 16							07 46								
South Greenford	d						07 19							07 49								
Castle Bar Park	d						07 22							07 52								
Drayton Green	d						07 24							07 54								
West Ealing	d						07 26				07 41			07 56							08 11	
Ealing Broadway ⊖	d						07 29	07 33			07 44	07 52		07 59	08 03						08 14	08 18
Acton Main Line	d						07 33							08 03								
London Paddington 15 ⊖	a		07 14	07 16	07 29	07 30	07 42	07 44	07 49	07 32	07 54	08 04	07 43	08 12	08 16	07 44	07 53	07 57	07 59	08 21	08 24	08 32

		GW ◇1 ☕	GW 1	GW ◇1 ☕	GW ◇1 ☕	GW ◇1 ☕	GW ◇1	GW 1	GW 1	GW ◇1 🍴	GW ◇1 ☕	GW 1	GW ◇1 ☕	GW 1	HC	GW 1	GW 1	GW 1	GW ◇1 ☕	GW ◇1 ☕	GW 1
Oxford	d								07 00	07 33											07 21
Reading 7	d	07 33	07 34	07 36	07 39	07 45			07 55	07 58	08 02	08 06	08 08					08 12	08 14	08 17	08 19
Twyford 3	d		07 41					07 56	08 02			08a12						08 17			08 26
Maidenhead 3	d		07 49				08 00	08 04	08 11									08 26			08 34
Taplow	d		07 53															08 29			
Burnham	d		07 56						08 15									08 32			
Slough 3	a		08 01						08 20									08 38			
	d		08 01						08 20									08 38			
Langley	d		08 06													08 29		08 42			
Iver	d		08 09													08 32		08 44			
West Drayton	d		08 13													08 38		08 50			
Heathrow Terminal 4 ✈	d																				
Heathrow Terminal 1-2-3 2 ✈	d														08 27						
Hayes & Harlington	d		08 17												08 33	08 42		08 53			
Southall	d								08 30						08 36	08 46					
Hanwell	d														08 39						
Greenford ⊖	d													08 16			08 46				
South Greenford	d													08 19			08 49				
Castle Bar Park	d													08 22			08 52				
Drayton Green	d													08 24			08 54				
West Ealing	d													08 26	08 41		08 56				
Ealing Broadway ⊖	d		08 24											08 29	08 44	08 52	08 59	09 04			
Acton Main Line	d													08 33			09 03				
London Paddington 15 ⊖	a	08 02	08 36	08 07	08 09	08 14	08 26	08 28	08 48	08 31	08 33		08 38	08 42	08 54	09 03	09 12	09 16	08 40	08 44	08 58

		GW ◇1 A ☕⊘	GW 1	HC	GW 1	GW ◇1 B ☕	GW 1	GW ◇1 C ☕	GW 1	GW ◇1 ☕	GW ◇1 ☕	GW 1	GW 1	HC	GW 1	GW ◇1 ☕	GW ◇1 ☕	GW 1	GW 1	GW ◇1 D ☕⊘	GW 1
Oxford	d	07 52					08 06		07 56						08 21					08 51	
Reading 7	d	08 23			08 31	08 34	08 35	08 45	08 48	08 52	09 02				09 03	09 08	09 16		09 17	09 18	09 21
Twyford 3	d				08 37				08 54						09 09				09 24		
Maidenhead 3	d		08 41		08 45				09 03						09 17				09 35		
Taplow	d				08 49										09 21				09 36		
Burnham	d				08 50										09 24				09 39		
Slough 3	a		08 49		08 57										09 29				09 44		
	d		08 50		08 57								09 14		09 30				09 44		
Langley	d				09 01										09 33						
Iver	d				09 04										09 36						
West Drayton	d				09 08								09 21		09 40				09 51		
Heathrow Terminal 4 ✈	d																				
Heathrow Terminal 1-2-3 2 ✈	d			08 57										09 27							
Hayes & Harlington	d			09 03	09 13								09 26	09 33	09 45				09 56		
Southall	d		09 00	09 06	09 17								09 30	09 36	09 48						
Hanwell	d			09 09										09 39							
Greenford ⊖	d											09 16						09 46			
South Greenford	d											09 19						09 49			
Castle Bar Park	d											09 22						09 52			
Drayton Green	d											09 24						09 54			
West Ealing	d			09 11								09 26		09 41				09 56			
Ealing Broadway ⊖	d			09 14	09 23							09 29	09 36	09 44	09 54			09 59	10 03		
Acton Main Line	d											09 33						10 03			
London Paddington 15 ⊖	a	08 51	09 21	09 24	09 35	09 00	09 06	09 14	09 27	09 21	09 29	09 42	09 48	09 54	10 03	09 39	09 44	10 12	10 18	09 47	09 56

A ☕ from Reading ⊘ to Reading
B The Armada
C The Bristolian
D The Cathedrals Express. ☕ from Reading ⊘ to Reading

Table 117

Reading and Greenford - London

Mondays to Fridays
from 17 September

Network Diagram - see first Page of Table 116

		GW ◇1 ☕	GW 1	GW ◇1 A ☕	GW ◇1	GW ◇1 ☕	HC	GW 1	GW 1	GW ◇1	GW ◇1 ☕	GW 1	GW 1	HC	GW 1	GW ◇1 ☕	GW ◇1 ☕	GW 1	GW 1	GW ◇1 🍴	GW ◇1 ☕	GW 1
Oxford	d		08 37		09 01					09 31					09 07					10 01		
Reading 7	d	09 27	09 33	09 34	09 37	09 46			09 48	09 55	10 02				10 03	10 08	10 12	10 18	10 18	10 26	10 32	
Twyford 3	d		09 39						09 54						10 09				10 24			
Maidenhead 3	d		09 47						10 02						10 17				10 32			
Taplow	d								10 06										10 36			
Burnham	d							←	10 09				←						10 39			
Slough 3	a		09 54		09 52			09 54	10 14	10 10			10 14		10 24				10 44	10 39		
	d		09 54		09 52			09 54	10 14	10 11			10 14		10 24				10 44	10 40		
Langley	d		→					09 58	→						10 28				→			
Iver	d							10 01							10 31							
West Drayton	d							10 05					10 21		10 35							
Heathrow Terminal 4 ✈	d																					
Heathrow Terminal 1-2-3 2 ✈	d						09 57							10 27								
Hayes & Harlington	d						10 03	10 10					10 26	10 33	10 40							
Southall	d						10 06	10 13						10 36	10 43							
Hanwell	d						10 09							10 39								
Greenford ⊖	d											10 16										10 46
South Greenford	d											10 19										10 49
Castle Bar Park	d											10 22										10 52
Drayton Green	d											10 24										10 54
West Ealing	d						10 11					10 26		10 41								10 56
Ealing Broadway ⊖	d						10 14	10 19				10 29	10 33	10 44	10 49							10 59
Acton Main Line	d											10 33										11 03
London Paddington 15 ⊖	a	09 59		10 02	10 12	10 15	10 24	10 31		10 30	10 32	10 42	10 46	10 54	11 01	10 37	10 39	10 56		11 00	11 07	11 12

		GW 1	HC	GW 1	GW ◇1 ☕	GW 1	GW ◇1 ☕	GW ◇1	GW ◇1 B ☕	GW 1	GW 1	HC	GW 1	GW ◇1 ☕	GW 1	GW 1	GW ◇1 🍴	GW ◇1 ☕	GW 1	GW 1	HC
Oxford	d			09 36				10 31					10 08				11 01				
Reading 7	d			10 33	10 45	10 48	10 52	10 55	11 02				11 03	11 11	11 18	11 20	11 26	11 32			
Twyford 3	d			10 39		10 54							11 09		11 24						
Maidenhead 3	d			10 47		11 02							11 17		11 32						
Taplow	d					11 06									11 36						
Burnham	d	←				11 09					←				11 39					←	
Slough 3	a	10 44		10 54		11 14		11 09			11 14		11 24		11 44		11 39			11 44	
	d	10 44		10 54		11 14		11 10			11 14		11 24		11 44		11 40			11 44	
Langley	d			10 58		→							11 28		→						
Iver	d			11 01									11 31								
West Drayton	d	10 51		11 05							11 21		11 35							11 51	
Heathrow Terminal 4 ✈	d																				
Heathrow Terminal 1-2-3 2 ✈	d		10 57									11 27									11 57
Hayes & Harlington	d	10 56	11 03	11 10							11 26	11 33	11 40							11 56	12 03
Southall	d		11 06	11 13								11 36	11 43								12 06
Hanwell	d		11 09									11 39									12 09
Greenford ⊖	d									11 16									11 46		
South Greenford	d									11 19									11 49		
Castle Bar Park	d									11 22									11 52		
Drayton Green	d									11 24									11 54		
West Ealing	d		11 11							11 26		11 41							11 56		12 11
Ealing Broadway ⊖	d	11 03	11 14	11 19						11 29	11 33	11 44	11 49						11 59	12 03	12 14
Acton Main Line	d									11 33									12 03		
London Paddington 15 ⊖	a	11 16	11 24	11 32	11 14		11 24	11 29	11 32	11 42	11 46	11 54	12 01	11 38		11 54	11 59	12 00	12 12	12 16	12 24

		GW 1	GW ◇1 ☕	GW 1	GW ◇1 ☕	GW ◇1 🍴	GW ◇1 ☕	GW 1	GW 1	HC	GW 1	GW ◇1 ☕	GW ◇1 ☕	GW 1	GW 1	GW ◇1 🍴	GW ◇1 ☕	GW 1	GW 1	HC	GW 1
Oxford	d	10 36				11 31					11 07					12 01					11 37
Reading 7	d	11 33	11 44	11 48	11 52	11 55	12 02				12 03	12 08	12 12	12 18	12 18	12 26	12 32				12 33
Twyford 3	d	11 39		11 54							12 09				12 24						12 39
Maidenhead 3	d	11 47		12 02							12 17				12 32						12 47
Taplow	d			12 06											12 36						
Burnham	d			12 09					←						12 39				←		
Slough 3	a	11 54		12 14		12 09			12 14		12 24				12 44	12 39			12 44		12 54
	d	11 54		12 14		12 10			12 14		12 24				12 44	12 40			12 44		12 54
Langley	d	11 58		→							12 28				→						12 58
Iver	d	12 01									12 31										13 01
West Drayton	d	12 05							12 21		12 35								12 51		13 05
Heathrow Terminal 4 ✈	d																				
Heathrow Terminal 1-2-3 2 ✈	d									12 27										12 57	
Hayes & Harlington	d	12 10							12 26	12 33	12 40								12 56	13 03	13 10
Southall	d	12 13								12 36	12 43									13 06	13 13
Hanwell	d									12 39										13 09	
Greenford ⊖	d							12 16										12 46			
South Greenford	d							12 19										12 49			
Castle Bar Park	d							12 22										12 52			
Drayton Green	d							12 24										12 54			
West Ealing	d							12 26		12 41								12 56		13 11	
Ealing Broadway ⊖	d	12 19						12 29	12 33	12 44	12 49							12 59	13 03	13 14	13 19
Acton Main Line	d							12 33										13 03			
London Paddington 15 ⊖	a	12 31	12 14		12 23	12 29	12 32	12 42	12 46	12 54	13 02	12 37	12 40	12 54		13 06	13 00	13 12	13 16	13 24	13 31

A The Golden Hind
B The Red Dragon

Reading and Greenford - London

Network Diagram - see first Page of Table 116

		GW	GW	GW	GW	GW	GW	HC	GW	GW	GW	GW	GW	GW	GW	GW	GW	HC	GW	GW	GW
		◇■ ⊡	■	◇■ ✕	◇■ ⊡	■	■		■	◇■ ⊡	■ A ⊡	■	◇■ ✕	■	◇■ ⊡	■	■		■	◇■ ⊡	■
Oxford	d			12 31					12 07				13 01						12 37		
Reading	d	12 45	12 48	12 55	13 02				13 03	13 11	13 17	13 18	13 26	13 29	13 32				13 33	13 44	13 48
Twyford	d		12 54						13 09			13 24							13 39		13 54
Maidenhead	d		13 02						13 17			13 32							13 47		14 02
Taplow	d		13 06									13 36									14 06
Burnham	d		13 09				←					13 39					←				14 09
Slough	a		13 14	13 09			13 14		13 24			13 44	13 39				13 44		13 54		14 14
	d		13 14	13 10			13 14		13 24			13 44	13 40				13 44		13 54		14 14
Langley	d		→						13 28			→							13 58		→
Iver	d								13 31										14 01		
West Drayton	d						13 21		13 35								13 51		14 05		
Heathrow Terminal 4	d																				
Heathrow Terminal 1-2-3	d							13 27										13 57			
Hayes & Harlington	d						13 26	13 33	13 40								13 56	14 03	14 10		
Southall	d							13 36	13 43									14 06	14 13		
Hanwell	d							13 39										14 09			
Greenford	d					13 16										13 46					
South Greenford	d					13 19										13 49					
Castle Bar Park	d					13 22										13 52					
Drayton Green	d					13 24										13 54					
West Ealing	d					13 26		13 41								13 56		14 11			
Ealing Broadway	d					13 29	13 33	13 44	13 49							13 59	14 03	14 14	14 19		
Acton Main Line	d					13 33										14 03					
London Paddington	a	13 14		13 29	13 32	13 42	13 46	13 54	14 01	13 38	13 44		14 01	14 09	14 06	14 12	14 16	14 24	14 31	14 14	

		GW	GW	GW	GW	HC	GW	GW	GW	GW	GW	GW	GW	GW	GW	HC	GW	GW	GW	GW
		◇■ ✕	◇■ B ⊡	■	■		■	◇■ ⊡	◇■ ⊡	◇■ ⊡	■	◇■ ✕	◇■ ⊡	■	■		■	◇■ ⊡	■	■ C ⊡
Oxford	d	13 31					13 07					14 01					13 37			
Reading	d	13 55	14 01				14 03	14 08	14 12	14 17	14 18	14 26	14 32				14 33	14 44	14 48	14 52
Twyford	d						14 09				14 24						14 39		14 54	
Maidenhead	d						14 17				14 32						14 47		15 02	
Taplow	d										14 36								15 06	
Burnham	d				←						14 39				←				15 09	
Slough	a	14 09			14 14		14 24				14 44	14 39			14 44		14 54		15 14	
	d	14 10			14 14		14 24				14 44	14 40			14 44		14 54		15 14	
Langley	d						14 28				→						14 58		→	
Iver	d						14 31										15 01			
West Drayton	d				14 21		14 35								14 51		15 05			
Heathrow Terminal 4	d																			
Heathrow Terminal 1-2-3	d					14 27										14 57				
Hayes & Harlington	d				14 26	14 33	14 40								14 56	15 03	15 10			
Southall	d					14 36	14 43									15 06	15 13			
Hanwell	d					14 39										15 09				
Greenford	d			14 16										14 46						
South Greenford	d			14 19										14 49						
Castle Bar Park	d			14 22										14 52						
Drayton Green	d			14 24										14 54						
West Ealing	d			14 26		14 41								14 56		15 11				
Ealing Broadway	d			14 29	14 33	14 44	14 49							14 59	15 03	15 14	15 19			
Acton Main Line	d			14 33										15 03						
London Paddington	a	14 29	14 32	14 42	14 46	14 54	15 01	14 37	14 40	14 44		15 00	15 08	15 12	15 16	15 24	15 32	15 14		15 24

		GW	GW	GW	GW	HC	GW	GW	GW	GW	GW	GW	GW	GW	HC	GW	GW	GW	GW	GW	GW	GW
		◇■	◇■ ⊡	■	■		■	◇■ ⊡	■	■	◇■ ✕	◇■ ⊡	■	■		■	◇■ ⊡	■	◇■ ⊡	◇■ ⊡	◇■ ⊡	■
Oxford	d	14 31					14 07				15 01					14 37				15 31		
Reading	d	14 55	15 02				15 03	15 11	15 18	15 20	15 26	15 32				15 33	15 44	15 48	15 52	15 55	16 02	
Twyford	d						15 09		15 24							15 39		15 54				
Maidenhead	d						15 17		15 32							15 47		16 02				
Taplow	d								15 36									16 06				
Burnham	d				←				15 39					←				16 09				
Slough	a	15 09			15 14		15 24		15 44		15 39			15 44		15 54		16 14		16 09		
	d	15 10			15 14		15 24		15 44		15 40			15 44		15 54		16 14		16 10		
Langley	d						15 28		→							15 58		→				
Iver	d						15 31									16 01						
West Drayton	d				15 21		15 35							15 51		16 05						
Heathrow Terminal 4	d																					
Heathrow Terminal 1-2-3	d					15 27									15 57							
Hayes & Harlington	d				15 26	15 33	15 40							15 56	16 03	16 10						
Southall	d					15 36	15 43								16 06	16 13						
Hanwell	d					15 39									16 09							
Greenford	d			15 16									15 46									16 16
South Greenford	d			15 19									15 49									16 19
Castle Bar Park	d			15 22									15 52									16 22
Drayton Green	d			15 24									15 54									16 24
West Ealing	d			15 26		15 41							15 56		16 11							16 26
Ealing Broadway	d			15 29	15 33	15 44	15 49						15 59	16 03	16 14	16 19						16 29
Acton Main Line	d			15 33									16 03									16 33
London Paddington	a	15 29	15 32	15 42	15 46	15 54	16 02	15 38		15 54	16 01	16 09	16 12	16 17	16 24	16 31	16 14		16 24	16 27	16 30	16 42

A The Cornish Riviera
B The St. David
C The Cornishman

Table 117 Mondays to Fridays
from 17 September

Reading and Greenford - London

Network Diagram - see first Page of Table 116

		GW	HC	GW	GW	GW	GW	GW	GW	GW	GW	HC	GW	GW	GW	GW	GW	GW	GW	GW	GW
		■		■	◇■ A ⊡	◇■ ⊡	■	■	◇■ ✕	■	■		■	◇■ ⊡	◇■ ⊡	■	◇■ B ⊡	◇■	◇■ ⊡	■	■
Oxford	d			15 07					16 01				15 37					16 31			
Reading	d			16 03	16 08	16 15	16 18	16 19	16 26				16 33	16 34	16 44	16 48	16 51	16 55	17 02		
Twyford	d			16 09			16 24						16 39			16 54					
Maidenhead	d			16 17			16 32						16 47			17 02					
Taplow	d						16 36									17 06					
Burnham	d	←					16 39				←					17 09					←
Slough	a	16 14		16 24			16 44		16 39		16 44		16 54			17 14		17 09			17 14
	d	16 14		16 24			16 44		16 40		16 44		16 54			17 14		17 10			17 14
Langley	d			16 28			→						16 58			→					
Iver	d			16 31									17 01								
West Drayton	d	16 21		16 35							16 51		17 05								17 21
Heathrow Terminal 4	d																				
Heathrow Terminal 1-2-3	d		16 27									16 57									
Hayes & Harlington	d	16 26	16 33	16 40							16 56	17 03	17 10								17 26
Southall	d		16 36	16 43								17 06	17 13								
Hanwell	d		16 39									17 09									
Greenford	d									16 46										17 16	
South Greenford	d									16 49										17 19	
Castle Bar Park	d									16 52										17 22	
Drayton Green	d									16 54										17 24	
West Ealing	d		16 41							16 56		17 11								17 26	
Ealing Broadway	d	16 33	16 44	16 49						16 59	17 03	17 14	17 21							17 29	17 33
Acton Main Line	d									17 03										17 33	
London Paddington	a	16 46	16 54	17 02	16 39	16 44		16 57	17 00	17 12	17 19	17 24	17 31	17 09	17 14		17 24	17 34	17 30	17 42	17 48

		HC	GW	GW	GW	GW	GW	GW	GW	GW	HC	GW	GW	GW	GW	GW	GW	GW	GW	HC	GW
			■	◇■ C ⊡	■	◇■ ⊡	■ ✕	◇■ ⊡	■	■		■	■	◇■ ⊡	◇■ D ⊡	■	◇■ ⊡	■	■		■
Oxford	d		16 07				17 01					16 37					17 31				17 06
Reading	d		17 03	17 11	17 14	17 17	17 26	17 32				17 33	17 42	17 46	17 51	17 54	17 56				18 00
Twyford	d		17 09		17 24							17 39	17 48								18 10
Maidenhead	d		17 17		17 32	17 29						17 47	17 56			18 08					18 17
Taplow	d				17 36								18 00								
Burnham	d				17 39					←			18 02						←		
Slough	a		17 24		17 44		17 39			17 44		17 54	18 07			18 14	18 10		18 14		18 24
	d		17 24		17 44		17 40			17 44		17 54	18 07			18 14	18 11		18 14		18 24
Langley	d		17 28		→							17 58				→					
Iver	d		17 31									18 01									
West Drayton	d		17 35							17 51		18 05	18 14								
Heathrow Terminal 4	d																				
Heathrow Terminal 1-2-3	d	17 27									17 57									18 27	
Hayes & Harlington	d	17 33	17 40							17 56	18 03	18 10	18 19						18 26	18 33	18 34
Southall	d	17 36	17 43								18 06	18 13								18 36	
Hanwell	d	17 39									18 09									18 39	
Greenford	d								17 46									18 16			
South Greenford	d								17 49									18 19			
Castle Bar Park	d								17 52									18 22			
Drayton Green	d								17 54									18 24			
West Ealing	d	17 41							17 56		18 11							18 26		18 41	
Ealing Broadway	d	17 44	17 49						17 59	18 03	18 14	18 19	18 26					18 29	18 33	18 44	18 41
Acton Main Line	d								18 03									18 33			
London Paddington	a	17 54	18 01	17 39		17 54	17 59	18 02	18 12	18 14	18 24	18 31	18 37	18 14	18 21		18 28	18 42	18 46	18 54	18 52

		GW	GW	GW	GW	GW	GW	GW	GW	GW	GW	HC	GW	GW	GW	GW	GW	GW	GW	GW	HC
		◇■ ⊡	◇■ ⊡	◇■ ⊡	■	■	■	■ ✕	◇■ ⊡	■	■		■	◇■ ⊡	■	◇■ E ⊡	■	◇■ ⊡	■	■	
Oxford	d							18 01					17 37				18 31				
Reading	d	18 01	18 08	18 12		18 18	18 22	18 26	18 32				18 33	18 47	18 48	18 51	18 57	19 02			
Twyford	d					18 24							18 39		18 54						
Maidenhead	d				18 26	18 32							18 48		19 05						
Taplow	d					18 35									19 09						
Burnham	d					18 39					←				19 12					←	
Slough	a				18 33	18 44		18 39			18 44		18 54		19 17		19 09			19 17	
	d				18 33	18 44		18 40			18 44		18 54		19 17		19 10			19 17	
Langley	d					→							18 58		→						
Iver	d												19 01								
West Drayton	d										18 51		19 05							19 24	
Heathrow Terminal 4	d																				
Heathrow Terminal 1-2-3	d											18 57									19 27
Hayes & Harlington	d				18 45						18 56	19 03	19 10							19 29	19 33
Southall	d											19 06	19 13								19 36
Hanwell	d											19 09									19 39
Greenford	d									18 46									19 16		
South Greenford	d									18 49									19 19		
Castle Bar Park	d									18 52									19 22		
Drayton Green	d									18 54									19 24		
West Ealing	d									18 56		19 11							19 26		19 41
Ealing Broadway	d				18 54					18 59	19 05	19 14	19 19						19 29	19 36	19 44
Acton Main Line	d									19 03									19 33		
London Paddington	a	18 30	18 39	18 44	19 04		18 54	18 59	19 02	19 12	19 18	19 24	19 33	19 14		19 24	19 31	19 32	19 42	19 45	19 54

A The Cheltenham Spa Express
B The Torbay Express
C The Merchant Venturer
D The Mayflower
E The Royal Duchy

Table 117

Reading and Greenford - London

Mondays to Fridays

from 17 September

Network Diagram - see first Page of Table 116

		GW	GW	GW	GW	GW	GW	GW	HC	GW	GW	GW	GW	GW	GW	HC	GW	GW	GW	GW
		1	◇1 ☕	1	1	1	◇1 ☕	◇1 ✕		1	◇1 ☕	1	◇1	1	1		1	◇1 ☕	◇1 ☕	◇1 ☕
Oxford	d	18 07						19 06		18 37			19 31				19 01			
Reading 7	d	19 03	19 11	19 18		19 18	19 25	19 32		19 33	19 45	19 48	19 55				19 58	20 02	20 08	20 15
Twyford 3	d	19 09				19 24				19 42		19 54					20 04			
Maidenhead 3	d	19 21				19 32				19 50		20 02					20 12			
Taplow	d					19 36						20 05								
Burnham	d					19 39						20 09			←					
Slough 3	a	19 29				19 44		19 47		19 57		20 14	20 09		20 14		20 19			
	d	19 29				19 44		19 47		19 57		20 14	20 10		20 14		20 24			
Langley	d	19 33								20 01		→					20 28			
Iver	d	19 36								20 04							20 31			
West Drayton	d	19 39				19 51				20 08					20 21		20 35			
Heathrow Terminal 4 ✈	d																			
Heathrow Terminal 1-2-3 2 ✈	d								19 57							20 27				
Hayes & Harlington	d	19 44				19 56			20 03	20 13					20 26	20 33	20 40			
Southall	d	19 47							20 06	20 16						20 36	20 43			
Hanwell	d								20 09							20 39				
Greenford ⊖	d				19 46									20 16						
South Greenford	d				19 49									20 19						
Castle Bar Park	d				19 52									20 22						
Drayton Green	d				19 54									20 24						
West Ealing	d				19 56				20 11					20 26		20 41				
Ealing Broadway ⊖	d	19 53			19 59	20 03			20 14	20 22				20 29	20 33	20 44	20 49			
Acton Main Line	d				20 03									20 33						
London Paddington 15 ⊖	a	20 02	19 38	19 54	20 12	20 16	19 59	20 06	20 24	20 31	20 14		20 30	20 42	20 49	20 54	20 59	20 32	20 39	20 46

		GW	GW	GW	GW	HC	GW	GW	GW	GW	GW	GW	GW	GW	GW	HC	GW	GW	GW	HC	GW
		1	◇1	1	1		1	1	◇1 ☕	1	◇1 ☕	◇1 ☕	◇1 ☕	1	1		1	1	◇1		1
Oxford	d		20 01				19 37					20 31						20 07	21 01		20 37
Reading 7	d	20 18	20 26				20 33	20 34	20 45	20 48	20 52	20 55	21 02					21 14	21 26		21 33
Twyford 3	d	20 24					20 39			20 54								21 20			21 39
Maidenhead 3	d	20 32					20 47			21 02								21 28			21 47
Taplow	d	20 36								21 06								21 32			21 50
Burnham	d	20 39			←					21 09					←			21 35			21 53
Slough 3	a	20 44	20 39		20 44		20 54			21 13		21 09			21 13			21 40	21 39		21 58
	d	20 44	20 40		20 44		20 54			21 14		21 10			21 14			21 40	21 40		21 59
Langley	d	→					20 58			→					21 17			21 44			22 02
Iver	d						21 01								21 20			21 47			22 05
West Drayton	d				20 51		21 05								21 24			21 51			22 09
Heathrow Terminal 4 ✈	d																				
Heathrow Terminal 1-2-3 2 ✈	d					20 57										21 27				21 57	
Hayes & Harlington	d				20 56	21 03	21 10								21 28	21 33		21 56		22 03	22 14
Southall	d					21 06	21 13									21 36		21 59		22 06	
Hanwell	d					21 09										21 39				22 09	
Greenford ⊖	d			20 46										21 16			21 46				
South Greenford	d			20 49										21 19			21 49				
Castle Bar Park	d			20 52										21 22			21 52				
Drayton Green	d			20 54										21 24			21 54				
West Ealing	d			20 56		21 11								21 26		21 41	21 56			22 11	
Ealing Broadway ⊖	d			20 59	21 03	21 14	21 19							21 29	21 35	21 44	21 59	22 05		22 14	22 21
Acton Main Line	d			21 03										21 33			22 03				
London Paddington 15 ⊖	a		21 01	21 12	21 16	21 24	21 30	21 07	21 14		21 21	21 29	21 32	21 42	21 47	21 54	22 13	22 16	22 00	22 24	22 33

		GW	GW	GW	GW	HC	GW	HC	GW	GW	GW	GW	GW	GW	HC	GW	GW	GW	GW
				FX	FO						FX	FO							
		◇1 ☕	◇1 ☕	◇1 ☕	◇1 ☕		1		◇	1	◇1	◇1	◇1 ☕	◇1 ☕		1	1	◇1	◇1 ☕
Oxford	d								22 11		22 34	22 34						23 09	
Reading 7	d	21 44	22 01	22 12	22 12		22 16		22 44	22 48	22 59	22 59	23 04	23 08			23 15	23 41	23 55
Twyford 3	d						22 22			22 54							23 22		
Maidenhead 3	d						22 31			23 02							23 29	23 54	
Taplow	d						22 34			23 05							23 33		
Burnham	d						22 37			23 08						←	23 36		
Slough 3	a						22 42		23 01	23 13	23 15	23 12				23 13	23 41	00 01	
	d						22 42		23 01	23 27	23 16	23 16				23 27	23 41	00 02	
Langley	d						22 46			→						23 31	23 45		
Iver	d						22 49									23 34	23 48		
West Drayton	d						22 53									23 38	23 51		
Heathrow Terminal 4 ✈	d																		
Heathrow Terminal 1-2-3 2 ✈	d					22 27		22 57							23 27				
Hayes & Harlington	d					22 33	22 57	23 03							23 33	23 43	23 56		
Southall	d					22 36	23 01	23 06							23 36	23 47	23 59		
Hanwell	d					22 39		23 09							23 39				
Greenford ⊖	d																		
South Greenford	d																		
Castle Bar Park	d																		
Drayton Green	d																		
West Ealing	d					22 41		23 11							23 41				
Ealing Broadway ⊖	d					22 44	23 06	23 14							23 44	23 52	00 06		
Acton Main Line	d																		
London Paddington 15 ⊖	a	22 14	22 30	22 44	22 45	22 54	23 18	23 24	23 25		23 36	23 36	23 38	23 41	23 54	00 02	00 17	00 28	00 33

Table 117

Reading and Greenford - London

Saturdays

until 23 June

Network Diagram - see first Page of Table 116

		GW	GW	GW	HC	GW	GW	GW	GW	GW	GW	HC	GW	HC	GW	GW	GW	HC	GW	GW	GW	HC
		1	1	◇1		◇1 ☕	1	◇1	1	1	1		1		1	1	1		1	1	1	
Oxford	d			23p09				00 07	00 27		03 59								05 14			
Reading 7	d	22p48	23p15	23p41		23p55	00 15	00 39	01 15	04 10	04 40		05 10		05 33		05 48		06 03		06 18	
Twyford 3	d	22p54	23p22				00 21		01 21	04 16	04 46		05 16		05 39		05 54		06 09		06 24	
Maidenhead 3	d	23p02	23p29	23p54			00 29		01 29	04 24	04 54		05 24		05 47		06 02		06 17		06 32	
Taplow	d	23p05	23p33				00 32						05 28				06 06				06 36	
Burnham	d	23p08	23p36				00 35						05 31				06 09				06 39	
Slough 3	a	23p13	23p41	00 01			00 40	00 55	01 37	04 31	05 01		05 35		05 54		06 14		06 24		06 44	
	d	23p27	23p41	00 02			00 40	00 56	01 37	04 32	05 02		05 36		05 54		06 14		06 24		06 44	
Langley	d	23p31	23p45				00 44						05 40		05 58				06 28			
Iver	d	23p34	23p48										05 43		06 01				06 31			
West Drayton	d	23p38	23p51				00 49			04 38			05 45		06 05		06 21		06 35		06 51	
Heathrow Terminal 4 ✈	d				00 01							05 23		05 51								
Heathrow Terminal 1-2-3 2 ✈	d				00 07							05 29		05 57				06 27				06 57
Hayes & Harlington	d	23p43	23p56		00 14		00 54		01 46	04 43	05 11	05 35	05 51	06 03	06 10		06 26	06 33	06 40		06 56	07 03
Southall	d	23p47	23p59		00 17		00 57			04 46	05 13	05 38	05 54	06 06	06 13			06 36	06 43			07 06
Hanwell	d											05 41		06 09				06 39				07 09
Greenford ⊖	d															06 16				06 46		
South Greenford	d															06 19				06 49		
Castle Bar Park	d															06 22				06 52		
Drayton Green	d															06 24				06 54		
West Ealing	d											05 43		06 11		06 26		06 41		06 56		07 11
Ealing Broadway ⊖	d	23p52	00 06		00 22		01 03		01 53	04 52	05 19	05 46	06 00	06 14	06 19	06 29	06 33	06 44	06 49	06 59	07 03	07 14
Acton Main Line	d										05 23		06 03			06 33				07 03		
London Paddington 15 ⊖	a	00 02	00 17	00 28	00 30	00 33	01 14	01 17	02 05	05 01	05 31	05 56	06 11	06 24	06 31	06 42	06 46	06 54	07 01	07 12	07 16	07 24

		GW	GW	GW	GW	GW	GW	HC	GW	GW	GW	GW	GW	GW	GW	GW	HC	GW	GW	GW	GW	GW	GW
		1	◇1 ☕	1	1	1	◇1		1	◇1 ☕	1	1	◇1	◇1 ☕	1	1		1	◇1 ☕	1	◇1 ☕	◇1 ☕	1
Oxford	d	05 49					06 31		06 07				07 01					06 42			07 31		
Reading 7	d	06 33	06 45		06 48	06 52	07 00		07 03	07 15	07 18	07 21	07 27	07 32				07 33	07 46	07 48	07 54	08 02	
Twyford 3	d	06 39			06 54				07 09		07 24							07 39		07 54			
Maidenhead 3	d	06 47			07 02				07 17		07 32							07 47		08 02			
Taplow	d				07 06						07 36									08 06			
Burnham	d				07 09						07 39					←				08 09			
Slough 3	a	06 54			07 14		07 16		07 24		07 44		07 42			07 44		07 54		08 14	08 09		
	d	06 54			07 14		07 17		07 24		07 44		07 42			07 44		07 54		08 14	08 09		
Langley	d	06 58							07 28		→							07 58		→			
Iver	d	07 01							07 31									08 01					
West Drayton	d	07 05			07 21				07 35							07 51		08 05					
Heathrow Terminal 4 ✈	d																						
Heathrow Terminal 1-2-3 2 ✈	d							07 27									07 57						
Hayes & Harlington	d	07 10			07 26			07 33	07 40							07 56	08 03	08 10					
Southall	d	07 13						07 36	07 43								08 06	08 13					
Hanwell	d							07 39									08 09						
Greenford ⊖	d			07 16											07 46								08 16
South Greenford	d			07 19											07 49								08 19
Castle Bar Park	d			07 22											07 52								08 22
Drayton Green	d			07 24											07 54								08 24
West Ealing	d			07 26				07 41							07 56		08 11						08 26
Ealing Broadway ⊖	d	07 19		07 29	07 33			07 44	07 49						07 59	08 03	08 14	08 19					08 29
Acton Main Line	d			07 33											08 03								08 33
London Paddington 15 ⊖	a	07 31	07 14	07 42	07 46	07 22	07 37	07 54	08 01	07 44		07 54	08 01	08 07	08 12	08 16	08 24	08 31	08 14		08 29	08 32	08 42

		GW	HC	GW	GW	GW	GW	GW	GW	GW	GW	HC	GW	GW	GW	GW	GW	GW	GW	GW
		1		1	◇1 ☕	1	1	◇1	◇1 ☕	1	1		1	◇1 ☕	1	◇1 ☕	◇1 ☕	◇1 ☕	1	1
Oxford	d			07 07				08 01					07 37				08 31			
Reading 7	d			08 03	08 16	08 18	08 20	08 26	08 32				08 33	08 46	08 48	08 52	08 55	09 02		
Twyford 3	d			08 09		08 24							08 39		08 54					
Maidenhead 3	d			08 17		08 32							08 47		09 02					
Taplow	d					08 36									09 06					
Burnham	d	←				08 39					←				09 09					←
Slough 3	a	08 14		08 24		08 44		08 40			08 44		08 54		09 14		09 09			09 14
	d	08 14		08 24		08 44		08 41			08 44		08 54		09 14		09 11			09 14
Langley	d			08 28		→							08 58		→					
Iver	d			08 31									09 01							
West Drayton	d	08 21		08 35							08 51		09 05							09 21
Heathrow Terminal 4 ✈	d																			
Heathrow Terminal 1-2-3 2 ✈	d		08 27									08 57								
Hayes & Harlington	d	08 26	08 33	08 40							08 56	09 03	09 10							09 26
Southall	d		08 36	08 43								09 06	09 13							
Hanwell	d		08 39									09 09								
Greenford ⊖	d									08 46									09 16	
South Greenford	d									08 49									09 19	
Castle Bar Park	d									08 52									09 22	
Drayton Green	d									08 54									09 24	
West Ealing	d		08 41							08 56		09 11							09 26	
Ealing Broadway ⊖	d	08 33	08 44	08 49						08 59	09 03	09 14	09 19						09 29	09 33
Acton Main Line	d									09 03									09 33	
London Paddington 15 ⊖	a	08 46	08 54	09 01	08 44		08 52	08 59	09 02	09 12	09 16	09 24	09 31	09 14		09 21	09 29	09 32	09 42	09 46

Table 117

Saturdays until 23 June

Reading and Greenford - London

Network Diagram - see first Page of Table 116

		HC	GW	GW	GW	GW	GW	GW	GW	GW	GW	HC	GW	GW	GW	GW	GW	GW	GW	GW	HC	GW
			■	◇■ ☕	◇■ ☕	■	■	◇■ 🍴	◇■ ☕	■	■		■	◇■ ☕	◇■ ☕	■	◇■ A ☕②	◇■ ☕	■	■		■
Oxford	d		08 07					09 01					08 37				09 31					09 07
Reading ■	d		09 03	09 09	09 16	09 18	09 20	09 24	09 33				09 33	09 42	09 46	09 48	09 55	10 02				10 03
Twyford ■	d		09 09			09 24							09 39			09 54						10 09
Maidenhead ■	d		09 17			09 32							09 47			10 02						10 17
Taplow	d					09 36										10 06						
Burnham	d					09 39					←					10 09				←		
Slough ■	a		09 24			09 44		09 40			09 44		09 54			10 14	10 09			10 14		10 24
	d		09 24			09 44		09 40			09 44		09 54			10 14	10 10			10 14		10 24
Langley	d		09 28			→							09 58			→						10 28
Iver	d		09 31										10 01									10 31
West Drayton	d		09 35								09 51		10 05							10 21		10 35
Heathrow Terminal 4 ✈	d																					
Heathrow Terminal 1-2-3 ■ ✈	d	09 27										09 57									10 27	
Hayes & Harlington	d	09 33	09 40								09 56	10 03	10 10							10 26	10 33	10 40
Southall	d	09 36	09 43									10 06	10 13								10 36	10 43
Hanwell	d	09 39										10 09									10 39	
Greenford ⊖	d									09 46									10 16			
South Greenford	d									09 49									10 19			
Castle Bar Park	d									09 52									10 22			
Drayton Green	d									09 54									10 24			
West Ealing	d	09 41								09 56		10 11							10 26		10 41	
Ealing Broadway ⊖	d	09 44	09 49							09 59	10 03	10 14	10 19						10 29	10 33	10 44	10 49
Acton Main Line	d									10 03									10 33			
London Paddington ■ ⊖	a	09 54	10 01	09 37	09 44		09 52	09 59	10 02	10 12	10 16	10 24	10 31	10 11	10 14		10 29	10 32	10 42	10 46	10 54	11 01

		GW	GW	GW	GW	GW	GW	HC	GW	GW	GW	GW	GW	GW	GW	GW	GW	HC	GW
		◇■ ☕	■	■	◇■ 🍴	■	■		■	◇■ ☕	◇■ ☕	■	◇■ ☕	◇■ ☕	◇■ ☕	■	■		■
Oxford	d				10 01				09 37					10 31					10 07
Reading ■	d	10 13	10 18	10 18	10 25				10 33	10 39	10 46	10 48	10 53	10 55	11 02				11 03
Twyford ■	d			10 24					10 39			10 54							11 09
Maidenhead ■	d			10 32					10 47			11 02							11 17
Taplow	d			10 36								11 06							
Burnham	d			10 39			←					11 09					←		
Slough ■	a			10 44	10 40		10 44		10 54			11 14		11 09			11 14		11 24
	d			10 44	10 40		10 44		10 54			11 14		11 10			11 14		11 24
Langley	d			→					10 58			→							11 28
Iver	d								11 01										11 31
West Drayton	d						10 51		11 05								11 21		11 35
Heathrow Terminal 4 ✈	d																		
Heathrow Terminal 1-2-3 ■ ✈	d							10 57										11 27	
Hayes & Harlington	d						10 56	11 03	11 10								11 26	11 33	11 40
Southall	d							11 06	11 13									11 36	11 43
Hanwell	d							11 09										11 39	
Greenford ⊖	d					10 46										11 16			
South Greenford	d					10 49										11 19			
Castle Bar Park	d					10 52										11 22			
Drayton Green	d					10 54										11 24			
West Ealing	d					10 56		11 11								11 26		11 41	
Ealing Broadway ⊖	d					10 59	11 03	11 14	11 19							11 29	11 33	11 44	11 49
Acton Main Line	d					11 03										11 33			
London Paddington ■ ⊖	a	10 39	10 52		10 59	11 12	11 16	11 24	11 31	11 08	11 14		11 24	11 29	11 33	11 42	11 46	11 54	12 01

		GW	GW	GW	GW	GW	GW	HC	GW	GW	GW	GW	GW	GW	GW	GW	HC	GW	GW	GW	GW	GW
		◇■ ☕	■	■	◇■	■	■		■	◇■ ☕	■	■2 ■1 ☕	◇■ 🍴	◇■ ☕	■	■		■	◇■ ☕	■	■	◇■ 🍴
Oxford	d				11 01				10 37				11 31					11 07				12 01
Reading ■	d	11 14	11 18	11 21	11 25				11 33	11 45	11 48	11 53	11 55	12 02				12 03	12 13	12 18	12 18	12 25
Twyford ■	d		11 24						11 39		11 54							12 09			12 24	
Maidenhead ■	d		11 32						11 47		12 02							12 17			12 32	
Taplow	d		11 36								12 06										12 36	
Burnham	d		11 39				←				12 09					←					12 39	
Slough ■	a		11 44		11 39		11 44		11 54		12 14		12 09			12 14		12 24			12 44	12 40
	d		11 44		11 40		11 44		11 54		12 14		12 11			12 14		12 24			12 44	12 40
Langley	d		→						11 58		→							12 28			→	
Iver	d								12 01									12 31				
West Drayton	d						11 51		12 05							12 21		12 35				
Heathrow Terminal 4 ✈	d																					
Heathrow Terminal 1-2-3 ■ ✈	d							11 57									12 27					
Hayes & Harlington	d						11 56	12 03	12 10							12 26	12 33	12 40				
Southall	d							12 06	12 13								12 36	12 43				
Hanwell	d							12 09									12 39					
Greenford ⊖	d					11 46									12 16							
South Greenford	d					11 49									12 19							
Castle Bar Park	d					11 52									12 22							
Drayton Green	d					11 54									12 24							
West Ealing	d					11 56		12 11							12 26		12 41					
Ealing Broadway ⊖	d					11 59	12 03	12 14	12 19						12 29	12 33	12 44	12 49				
Acton Main Line	d					12 03									12 33							
London Paddington ■ ⊖	a	11 40		11 52	11 59	12 12	12 16	12 24	12 31	12 14		12 23	12 29	12 32	12 42	12 46	12 54	13 01	12 39	12 52		12 59

A ☕ from Reading ② to Reading

Table 117

Saturdays until 23 June

Reading and Greenford - London

Network Diagram - see first Page of Table 116

		GW	GW	HC	GW	GW	GW	GW	GW	GW	GW	GW	GW	HC	GW	GW	GW	GW	GW	GW	GW
		■	■		■	◇■ ☕	■2 ■1 ☕	◇■ ☕	■	◇■ 🍴	◇■ ☕	■	■		■	◇■ ☕	■	■2 ■1 ☕	◇■ 🍴	■	■
Oxford	d				11 37					12 31					12 07				13 01		
Reading ■	d				12 33	12 39	12 42	12 47	12 48	12 55	13 02				13 03	13 12	13 18	13 19	13 25		
Twyford ■	d				12 39				12 54						13 09		13 24				
Maidenhead ■	d				12 47				13 02						13 17		13 32				
Taplow	d								13 06								13 36				
Burnham	d		←						13 09				←				13 39				←
Slough ■	a		12 44		12 54				13 14	13 09			13 14		13 24		13 44		13 40		13 44
	d		12 44		12 54				13 14	13 11			13 14		13 24		13 44		13 40		13 44
Langley	d				12 58				→						13 28		→				
Iver	d				13 01										13 31						
West Drayton	d		12 51		13 05								13 21		13 35						13 51
Heathrow Terminal 4 ✈	d																				
Heathrow Terminal 1-2-3 ■ ✈	d			12 57										13 27							
Hayes & Harlington	d		12 56	13 03	13 10								13 26	13 33	13 40						13 56
Southall	d			13 06	13 13									13 36	13 43						
Hanwell	d			13 09										13 39							
Greenford ⊖	d	12 46										13 16								13 46	
South Greenford	d	12 49										13 19								13 49	
Castle Bar Park	d	12 52										13 22								13 52	
Drayton Green	d	12 54										13 24								13 54	
West Ealing	d	12 56		13 11								13 26		13 41						13 56	
Ealing Broadway ⊖	d	12 59	13 03	13 14	13 19							13 29	13 33	13 44	13 49					13 59	14 03
Acton Main Line	d	13 03										13 33								14 03	
London Paddington ■ ⊖	a	13 12	13 16	13 24	13 31	13 07	13 09	13 13		13 30	13 33	13 42	13 46	13 54	14 01	13 41		13 46	13 59	14 12	14 16

		HC	GW	GW	GW	GW	GW	GW	GW	GW	HC	GW	GW	GW	GW	GW	GW	GW	HC	GW
			■	◇■ ☕	■	■	◇■	◇■ ☕	■	■		■	◇■ ☕	■	■	◇■ 🍴	■	■		■
Oxford	d		12 37				13 31					13 07				14 01				13 37
Reading ■	d		13 33	13 45	13 48	13 51	13 55	14 02				14 03	14 13	14 18	14 18	14 25				14 33
Twyford ■	d		13 39		13 54							14 09			14 24					14 39
Maidenhead ■	d		13 47		14 02							14 17			14 32					14 47
Taplow	d				14 06										14 36					
Burnham	d				14 09					←					14 39			←		
Slough ■	a		13 54		14 14		14 09			14 14		14 24			14 44	14 40		14 44		14 54
	d		13 54		14 14		14 10			14 14		14 24			14 44	14 40		14 44		14 54
Langley	d		13 58		→							14 28			→					14 58
Iver	d		14 01									14 31								15 01
West Drayton	d		14 05							14 21		14 35						14 51		15 05
Heathrow Terminal 4 ✈	d																			
Heathrow Terminal 1-2-3 ■ ✈	d	13 57									14 27								14 57	
Hayes & Harlington	d	14 03	14 10							14 26	14 33	14 40						14 56	15 03	15 10
Southall	d	14 06	14 13								14 36	14 43							15 06	15 13
Hanwell	d	14 09									14 39								15 09	
Greenford ⊖	d								14 16								14 46			
South Greenford	d								14 19								14 49			
Castle Bar Park	d								14 22								14 52			
Drayton Green	d								14 24								14 54			
West Ealing	d	14 11							14 26		14 41						14 56		15 11	
Ealing Broadway ⊖	d	14 14	14 19						14 29	14 33	14 44	14 49					14 59	15 03	15 14	15 19
Acton Main Line	d								14 33								15 03			
London Paddington ■ ⊖	a	14 24	14 31	14 14		14 23	14 29	14 32	14 42	14 46	14 54	15 01	14 39	14 54		14 59	15 12	15 16	15 24	15 31

		GW	GW	GW	GW	GW	GW	GW	GW	HC	GW	GW	GW	GW	GW	GW	GW	HC	GW	GW	GW	GW
		◇■ ☕	◇■ ☕	■	■2 ■1 ☕	◇■ ☕	◇■ ☕	■	■		■	◇■ ☕	■	■	◇■	■	■		■	◇■ ☕	■	■2 ■1 ☕
Oxford	d					14 31					14 07				15 01				14 37			
Reading ■	d	14 39	14 45	14 48	14 53	14 55	15 02				15 03	15 12	15 18	15 19	15 25				15 33	15 45	15 48	15 53
Twyford ■	d			14 54							15 09		15 24						15 39		15 54	
Maidenhead ■	d			15 02							15 17		15 32						15 47		16 02	
Taplow	d			15 06									15 36								16 06	
Burnham	d			15 09					←				15 39				←				16 09	
Slough ■	a			15 14		15 10			15 14		15 24		15 44		15 40		15 44		15 54		16 14	
	d			15 14		15 11			15 14		15 24		15 44		15 40		15 44		15 54		16 14	
Langley	d			→							15 28		→						15 58		→	
Iver	d										15 31								16 01			
West Drayton	d								15 21		15 35						15 51		16 05			
Heathrow Terminal 4 ✈	d																					
Heathrow Terminal 1-2-3 ■ ✈	d									15 27								15 57				
Hayes & Harlington	d								15 26	15 33	15 40						15 56	16 03	16 10			
Southall	d									15 36	15 43							16 06	16 13			
Hanwell	d									15 39								16 09				
Greenford ⊖	d							15 16								15 46						
South Greenford	d							15 19								15 49						
Castle Bar Park	d							15 22								15 52						
Drayton Green	d							15 24								15 54						
West Ealing	d							15 26		15 41						15 56		16 11				
Ealing Broadway ⊖	d							15 29	15 33	15 44	15 49					15 59	16 03	16 14	16 19			
Acton Main Line	d							15 33								16 03						
London Paddington ■ ⊖	a	15 09	15 14		15 23	15 29	15 32	15 42	15 46	15 54	16 01	15 39		15 54	15 59	16 12	16 16	16 24	16 31	16 14		16 23

Table 117

Reading and Greenford - London

Network Diagram - see first Page of Table 116

		GW	GW	GW	GW	GW	HC	GW	GW	GW	GW	GW	GW	GW	GW	HC	GW	GW	GW	GW
		◇[1] 🛒	[8] [1] ⊡	◇[1] ⊡	[1]	[1]		[1]	◇[1] ⊡	[1]	[1]	◇[1]	◇[1] ⊡	[1]	[1]		[1]	◇[1] ⊡	◇[1] ⊡	[1]
Oxford	d	15 31						15 07				16 01					15 37			
Reading [7]	d	15 55	16 01	16 02				16 03	16 13	16 18	16 18	16 26	16 28				16 33	16 39	16 45	16 48
Twyford [3]	d							16 09			16 24						16 39			16 54
Maidenhead [3]	d							16 17			16 32						16 47			17 02
Taplow	d										16 36									17 06
Burnham	d					←					16 39				←					17 09
Slough [3]	a	16 10				16 14		16 24			16 44	16 40			16 44		16 54			17 14
	d	16 11				16 14		16 24			16 44	16 41			16 44		16 54			17 14
Langley	d							16 28			→						16 58			→
Iver	d							16 31									17 01			
West Drayton	d					16 21		16 35							16 51		17 05			
Heathrow Terminal 4 ✈	d																			
Heathrow Terminal 1-2-3 [2] ✈	d						16 27									16 57				
Hayes & Harlington	d					16 26	16 33	16 40							16 56	17 03	17 10			
Southall	d						16 36	16 43								17 06	17 13			
Hanwell	d						16 39									17 09				
Greenford ⊖	d				16 16									16 46						
South Greenford	d				16 19									16 49						
Castle Bar Park	d				16 22									16 52						
Drayton Green	d				16 24									16 54						
West Ealing	d				16 26		16 41							16 56		17 11				
Ealing Broadway ⊖	d				16 29	16 33	16 44	16 49						16 59	17 03	17 14	17 19			
Acton Main Line	d				16 33									17 03						
London Paddington [15] ⊖	a	16 29	16 32	16 37	16 42	16 46	16 54	17 01	16 39	16 52		16 59	17 02	17 12	17 16	17 24	17 31	17 07	17 14	

		GW	GW	GW	GW	GW	HC	GW	GW	GW	GW	GW	GW	GW	HC	GW	GW	GW	GW	GW	GW	GW
		[8] [1] ⊡	◇[1] 🛒	◇[1] ⊡	[1]	[1]		[1]	◇[1] ⊡	[1]	[1]	◇[1]	[1]	[1]		[1]	◇[1] ⊡	◇[1] ⊡	[1]	[8] [1] ⊡	◇[1] ⊡	◇[1] ⊡
Oxford	d		16 31					16 07				17 01				16 37					17 31	
Reading [7]	d	16 51	16 55	17 02				17 03	17 12	17 18	17 22	17 27				17 33	17 36	17 45	17 48	17 54	17 57	18 02
Twyford [3]	d							17 09		17 24						17 39			17 54			
Maidenhead [3]	d							17 17		17 32						17 47			18 02			
Taplow	d									17 36									18 06			
Burnham	d					←				17 39				←					18 09			
Slough [3]	a		17 10			17 14		17 24		17 44		17 41		17 44		17 54			18 14		18 10	
	d		17 11			17 14		17 24		17 44		17 42		17 44		17 54			18 14		18 11	
Langley	d							17 28		→						17 58			→			
Iver	d							17 31								18 01						
West Drayton	d					17 21		17 35						17 51		18 05						
Heathrow Terminal 4 ✈	d																					
Heathrow Terminal 1-2-3 [2] ✈	d						17 27								17 57							
Hayes & Harlington	d					17 26	17 33	17 40						17 56	18 03	18 10						
Southall	d						17 36	17 43							18 06	18 13						
Hanwell	d						17 39								18 09							
Greenford ⊖	d				17 16								17 46									
South Greenford	d				17 19								17 49									
Castle Bar Park	d				17 22								17 52									
Drayton Green	d				17 24								17 54									
West Ealing	d				17 26		17 41						17 56		18 11							
Ealing Broadway ⊖	d				17 29	17 33	17 44	17 49					17 59	18 03	18 14	18 19						
Acton Main Line	d				17 33								18 03									
London Paddington [15] ⊖	a	17 21	17 29	17 32	17 42	17 46	17 54	18 01	17 38		17 54	18 00	18 12	18 16	18 24	18 31	18 08	18 14		18 23	18 29	18 32

		GW	GW	HC	GW	GW	GW	GW	GW	GW	GW	HC	GW	GW	GW	GW	GW	GW	GW	GW	GW
		[1]	[1]		[1]	◇[1] ⊡	[1]	[1]	◇[1]	[1]	[1]		[1]	◇[1] ⊡	◇[1] ⊡	[1]	◇[1] ⊡	◇[1] 🛒	◇[1] ⊡	[1]	[1]
Oxford	d				17 07				18 01				17 37					18 31			
Reading [7]	d				18 03	18 13	18 18	18 19	18 25				18 33	18 39	18 45	18 48	18 50	18 56	19 02		
Twyford [3]	d				18 09		18 24						18 39			18 54					
Maidenhead [3]	d				18 17		18 32						18 47			19 02					
Taplow	d						18 36									19 06					
Burnham	d		←				18 39				←					19 09					←
Slough [3]	a		18 14		18 24		18 44		18 40		18 44		18 54			19 14		19 10			19 14
	d		18 14		18 24		18 44		18 40		18 44		18 54			19 14		19 11			19 14
Langley	d				18 28		→						18 58			→					
Iver	d				18 31								19 01								
West Drayton	d		18 21		18 35						18 51		19 05								19 21
Heathrow Terminal 4 ✈	d																				
Heathrow Terminal 1-2-3 [2] ✈	d			18 27								18 57									
Hayes & Harlington	d		18 26	18 33	18 40						18 56	19 03	19 10								19 26
Southall	d			18 36	18 43							19 06	19 13								
Hanwell	d			18 39								19 09									
Greenford ⊖	d	18 16								18 46										19 16	
South Greenford	d	18 19								18 49										19 19	
Castle Bar Park	d	18 22								18 52										19 22	
Drayton Green	d	18 24								18 54										19 24	
West Ealing	d	18 26		18 41						18 56		19 11								19 26	
Ealing Broadway ⊖	d	18 29	18 33	18 44	18 49					18 59	19 03	19 14	19 19							19 29	19 33
Acton Main Line	d	18 33								19 03										19 33	
London Paddington [15] ⊖	a	18 42	18 46	18 54	19 01	18 39		18 52	18 59	19 12	19 16	19 24	19 31	19 08	19 14		19 22	19 29	19 32	19 42	19 46

		HC	GW	GW	GW	GW	GW	GW	GW	HC	GW	GW	GW	GW	GW	GW	GW	HC	GW	GW
			[1]	◇[1] ⊡	[1]	[1]	◇[1]	[1]	[1]		[1]	◇[1] ⊡	[1]	◇[1] 🛒	◇[1] ⊡	[1]	[1]		[1]	◇[1] ⊡
Oxford	d		18 07				19 01				18 37			19 31					19 07	
Reading [7]	d		19 03	19 12	19 18	19 20	19 25				19 33	19 45	19 48	19 55	20 03				20 03	20 09
Twyford [3]	d		19 09		19 24						19 39		19 54						20 09	
Maidenhead [3]	d		19 17		19 32						19 47		20 02						20 17	
Taplow	d				19 36								20 06							
Burnham	d				19 39				←				20 09				←			
Slough [3]	a		19 24		19 44		19 40		19 44		19 54		20 14	20 10			20 14		20 24	
	d		19 24		19 44		19 40		19 44		19 54		20 14	20 10			20 14		20 24	
Langley	d		19 28		→						19 58		→						20 28	
Iver	d		19 31								20 01								20 31	
West Drayton	d		19 35						19 51		20 05						20 21		20 35	
Heathrow Terminal 4 ✈	d																			
Heathrow Terminal 1-2-3 [2] ✈	d	19 27								19 57								20 27		
Hayes & Harlington	d	19 33	19 40						19 56	20 03	20 10						20 26	20 33	20 40	
Southall	d	19 36	19 43							20 06	20 13							20 36	20 43	
Hanwell	d	19 39								20 09								20 39		
Greenford ⊖	d							19 46								20 16				
South Greenford	d							19 49								20 19				
Castle Bar Park	d							19 52								20 22				
Drayton Green	d							19 54								20 24				
West Ealing	d	19 41						19 56		20 11						20 26		20 41		
Ealing Broadway ⊖	d	19 44	19 49					19 59	20 03	20 14	20 19					20 29	20 33	20 44	20 49	
Acton Main Line	d							20 03								20 33				
London Paddington [15] ⊖	a	19 54	20 01	19 39		19 52	19 59	20 12	20 16	20 24	20 31	20 14		20 29	20 32	20 42	20 46	20 54	21 01	20 37

		GW	GW	GW	GW	HC	GW	GW	GW	GW	GW	GW	GW	GW	HC	GW	GW	GW	GW	GW	GW	HC
		[1]	◇[1]	[1]	[1]		[1]	◇[1] ⊡	◇[1] ⊡	[1]	◇[1]	◇[1] ⊡	[1]	[1]		[1]	◇[1] ⊡	[1]	◇[1]	[1]	[1]	
Oxford	d		20 01				19 37				20 31					20 07			21 01			
Reading [7]	d	20 18	20 25				20 33	20 39	20 45	20 48	20 54	21 01				21 03	21 08	21 18	21 25			
Twyford [3]	d	20 24					20 39			20 54						21 09		21 24				
Maidenhead [3]	d	20 32					20 47			21 02						21 17		21 32				
Taplow	d	20 36								21 06								21 36				
Burnham	d	20 39			←					21 09				←				21 39			←	
Slough [3]	a	20 44	20 40		20 44		20 54			21 14	21 09			21 14		21 24		21 44	21 40		21 44	
	d	20 44	20 40		20 44		20 54			21 14	21 09			21 14		21 24		21 44	21 40		21 44	
Langley	d	→					20 58			→						21 28		→				
Iver	d						21 01									21 31						
West Drayton	d				20 51		21 05							21 21		21 35					21 51	
Heathrow Terminal 4 ✈	d																					
Heathrow Terminal 1-2-3 [2] ✈	d					20 57									21 27							21 57
Hayes & Harlington	d				20 56	21 03	21 10							21 26	21 33	21 40					21 56	22 03
Southall	d					21 06	21 13								21 36	21 43						22 06
Hanwell	d					21 09									21 39							22 09
Greenford ⊖	d			20 46									21 16							21 46		
South Greenford	d			20 49									21 19							21 49		
Castle Bar Park	d			20 52									21 22							21 52		
Drayton Green	d			20 54									21 24							21 54		
West Ealing	d			20 56		21 11							21 26		21 41					21 56		22 11
Ealing Broadway ⊖	d			20 59	21 03	21 14	21 19						21 29	21 33	21 44	21 49				21 59	22 03	22 14
Acton Main Line	d			21 03									21 33							22 03		
London Paddington [15] ⊖	a		20 59	21 12	21 16	21 24	21 31	21 07	21 14		21 29	21 32	21 42	21 46	21 54	22 02	21 36		21 59	22 12	22 16	22 24

		GW	GW	GW	GW	GW	GW	GW	GW	HC	GW	GW	HC	GW	GW	GW	GW	HC	GW
		[1]	[1]	◇[1] ⊡	[8] [1] ⊡	◇[1]	◇[1] A ⊡	◇[1] B ⊡	[1]		[1]	◇[1]		[1]	[1]	◇[1] ⊡	◇[1]		[1]
Oxford	d	20 37				21 31						22 01		21 50			22 35		
Reading [7]	d	21 33	21 48	21 50	22 00	22 01	22 03	22 03			22 18	22 29		22 33	22 48	23 05	23 09		23 18
Twyford [3]	d	21 39	21 54								22 24			22 39	22 54				23 24
Maidenhead [3]	d	21 47	22 02								22 32			22 47	23 02				23 32
Taplow	d		22 06								22 36				23 06				23 36
Burnham	d		22 09						←		22 39				23 09				23 39
Slough [3]	a	21 54	22 14			22 11			22 14		22 44	22 43		22 54	23 14		23 26		23 44
	d	21 54	22 14			22 12			22 14		22 44	22 44		22 54	23 14		23 27		23 44
Langley	d	21 58	→											22 58					
Iver	d	22 01												23 01					
West Drayton	d	22 05							22 21		22 51			23 05	23 21				23 51
Heathrow Terminal 4 ✈	d																		
Heathrow Terminal 1-2-3 [2] ✈	d									22 27			22 57					23 27	
Hayes & Harlington	d	22 10							22 26	22 33	22 56		23 03	23 10	23 26			23 33	23 56
Southall	d	22 13								22 36			23 06	23 13				23 36	
Hanwell	d									22 39			23 09					23 39	
Greenford ⊖	d																		
South Greenford	d																		
Castle Bar Park	d																		
Drayton Green	d																		
West Ealing	d									22 41			23 11					23 41	
Ealing Broadway ⊖	d	22 19							22 33	22 44	23 03		23 14	23 19	23 33			23 44	00 03
Acton Main Line	d																		
London Paddington [15] ⊖	a	22 31		22 16	22 26	22 34	22 30	22 37	22 46	22 54	23 16	23 02	23 24	23 28	23 46	23 36	23 46	23 54	00 16

A not 19 May

B 19 May

Table 117

Reading and Greenford - London

Saturdays
until 23 June

Network Diagram - see first Page of Table 116

		GW ◇1	GW ◇1 ⊐	GW 1
Oxford	d	23 01		23 07
Reading 7	d	23 29	23 51	00 03
Twyford 3	d			00 10
Maidenhead 3	d			00 18
Taplow	d			00 22
Burnham	d			00 25
Slough 3	a	23 45		00 30
	d	23 46		00 30
Langley	d			00 34
Iver	d			00 37
West Drayton	d			00 40
Heathrow Terminal 4 ✈	d			
Heathrow Terminal 1-2-3 2 ✈	d			
Hayes & Harlington	d			00 45
Southall	d			00 48
Hanwell	d			
Greenford ⊖	d			
South Greenford	d			
Castle Bar Park	d			
Drayton Green	d			
West Ealing	d			
Ealing Broadway ⊖	d			00 54
Acton Main Line	d			
London Paddington 15 ⊖	a	00 10	00 33	01 03

Saturdays
30 June to 8 September

		GW 1	GW 1	GW ◇1	HC	GW ◇1 ⊐	GW 1	GW ◇1	GW 1	GW 1	GW 1	HC	GW 1	HC	GW 1	GW 1	GW 1	HC	GW 1	GW 1	GW 1	HC
Oxford	d			23p09				00 07	00 27		03 59								05 14			
Reading 7	d	22p48	23p15	23p41		23p55	00 15	00 39	01 15	04 10	04 40		05 10		05 33		05 48		06 03		06 18	
Twyford 3	d	22p54	23p22				00 21		01 21	04 16	04 46		05 16		05 39		05 54		06 09		06 24	
Maidenhead 3	d	23p02	23p29	23p54			00 29		01 29	04 24	04 54		05 24		05 47		06 02		06 17		06 32	
Taplow	d	23p05	23p33				00 32						05 28				06 06				06 36	
Burnham	d	23p08	23p36				00 35						05 31				06 09				06 39	
Slough 3	a	23p13	23p41	00 01			00 40	00 55	01 37	04 31	05 01		05 35		05 54		06 14		06 24		06 44	
	d	23p27	23p41	00 02			00 40	00 56	01 37	04 32	05 02		05 36		05 54		06 14		06 24		06 44	
Langley	d	23p31	23p45				00 44						05 40		05 58				06 28			
Iver	d	23p34	23p48										05 43		06 01				06 31			
West Drayton	d	23p38	23p51				00 49			04 38			05 45		06 05		06 21		06 35		06 51	
Heathrow Terminal 4 ✈	d				00 01							05 23		05 51								
Heathrow Terminal 1-2-3 2 ✈	d				00 07							05 29		05 57				06 27				06 57
Hayes & Harlington	d	23p43	23p56		00 14		00 54		01 46	04 43	05 11	05 35	05 51	06 03	06 10		06 26	06 33	06 40		06 56	07 03
Southall	d	23p47	23p59		00 17		00 57			04 46	05 13	05 38	05 54	06 06	06 13			06 36	06 43			07 06
Hanwell	d											05 41		06 09				06 39				07 09
Greenford ⊖	d															06 16				06 46		
South Greenford	d															06 19				06 49		
Castle Bar Park	d															06 22				06 52		
Drayton Green	d															06 24				06 54		
West Ealing	d											05 43		06 11		06 26		06 41		06 56		07 11
Ealing Broadway ⊖	d	23p52	00 06		00 22		01 03		01 53	04 52	05 19	05 46	06 00	06 14	06 19	06 29	06 33	06 44	06 49	06 59	07 03	07 14
Acton Main Line	d										05 23		06 03			06 33				07 03		
London Paddington 15 ⊖	a	00 02	00 17	00 28	00 30	00 33	01 14	01 17	02 05	05 01	05 31	05 56	06 11	06 24	06 31	06 42	06 46	06 54	07 01	07 12	07 16	07 24

		GW 1	GW ◇1 ⊐	GW 1	GW 1	GW 1	GW ◇1	HC	GW 1	GW ◇1 ⊐	GW 1	GW 1	GW ◇1	GW ◇1 ⊐	GW 1	GW 1	HC	GW 1	GW ◇1 ⊐	GW 1	GW ◇1 ⊐	GW ◇1 ⊐	GW 1
Oxford	d	05 49					06 31		06 07				07 01					06 42			07 31		
Reading 7	d	06 33	06 45		06 48	06 52	07 00		07 03	07 15	07 18	07 21	07 27	07 32				07 33	07 46	07 48	07 54	08 02	
Twyford 3	d	06 39			06 54				07 09		07 24							07 39		07 54			
Maidenhead 3	d	06 47			07 02				07 17		07 32							07 47		08 02			
Taplow	d				07 06						07 36									08 06			
Burnham	d				07 09						07 39					←				08 09			
Slough 3	a	06 54			07 14		07 16		07 24		07 44		07 42			07 44		07 54		08 14	08 09		
	d	06 54			07 14		07 17		07 24		07 44		07 42			07 44		07 54		08 14	08 09		
Langley	d	06 58							07 28		→							07 58		→			
Iver	d	07 01							07 31									08 01					
West Drayton	d	07 05			07 21				07 35							07 51		08 05					
Heathrow Terminal 4 ✈	d																						
Heathrow Terminal 1-2-3 2 ✈	d							07 27									07 57						
Hayes & Harlington	d	07 10			07 26			07 33	07 40							07 56	08 03	08 10					
Southall	d	07 13						07 36	07 43								08 06	08 13					
Hanwell	d							07 39									08 09						
Greenford ⊖	d			07 16											07 46								08 16
South Greenford	d			07 19											07 49								08 19
Castle Bar Park	d			07 22											07 52								08 22
Drayton Green	d			07 24											07 54								08 24
West Ealing	d			07 26				07 41							07 56		08 11						08 26
Ealing Broadway ⊖	d	07 19		07 29	07 33			07 44	07 49						07 59	08 03	08 14	08 19					08 29
Acton Main Line	d			07 33											08 03								08 33
London Paddington 15 ⊖	a	07 31	07 14	07 42	07 46	07 22	07 37	07 54	08 01	07 44		07 54	08 01	08 07	08 12	08 16	08 24	08 31	08 14		08 29	08 32	08 42

Table 117

Reading and Greenford - London

Saturdays
30 June to 8 September

Network Diagram - see first Page of Table 116

		GW 1	HC	GW 1	GW ◇1 ⊐	GW 1	GW 1	GW ◇1	GW ◇1 ⊐	GW 1	GW 1	HC	GW 1	GW ◇1 ⊐	GW 1	GW ◇1 ⊐	GW ◇1 ⊐	GW ◇1 ⊐	GW 1	GW 1
Oxford	d			07 07				08 01					07 37				08 31			
Reading 7	d			08 03	08 16	08 18	08 20	08 26	08 32				08 33	08 46	08 48	08 52	08 55	09 02		
Twyford 3	d			08 09		08 24							08 39		08 54					
Maidenhead 3	d			08 17		08 32							08 47		09 02					
Taplow	d					08 36									09 06					
Burnham	d	←				08 39					←				09 09					←
Slough 3	a	08 14		08 24		08 44		08 40			08 44		08 54		09 14		09 09			09 14
	d	08 14		08 24		08 44		08 41			08 44		08 54		09 14		09 11			09 14
Langley	d			08 28		→							08 58		→					
Iver	d			08 31									09 01							
West Drayton	d	08 21		08 35							08 51		09 05							09 21
Heathrow Terminal 4 ✈	d																			
Heathrow Terminal 1-2-3 2 ✈	d		08 27									08 57								
Hayes & Harlington	d	08 26	08 33	08 40							08 56	09 03	09 10							09 26
Southall	d		08 36	08 43								09 06	09 13							
Hanwell	d		08 39									09 09								
Greenford ⊖	d									08 46									09 16	
South Greenford	d									08 49									09 19	
Castle Bar Park	d									08 52									09 22	
Drayton Green	d									08 54									09 24	
West Ealing	d		08 41							08 56		09 11							09 26	
Ealing Broadway ⊖	d	08 33	08 44	08 49						08 59	09 03	09 14	09 19						09 29	09 33
Acton Main Line	d									09 03									09 33	
London Paddington 15 ⊖	a	08 46	08 54	09 01	08 44		08 52	08 59	09 02	09 12	09 16	09 24	09 31	09 14		09 21	09 29	09 32	09 42	09 46

		HC	GW 1	GW ◇1 ⊐	GW ◇1 ⊐	GW 1	GW 1	GW ◇1 Ⱶ	GW ◇1 ⊐	GW 1	GW 1	HC	GW 1	GW ◇1 ⊐	GW ◇1 ⊐	GW 1	GW ◇1 A ⊐⊘	GW ◇1 ⊐	GW 1	GW 1	HC	GW 1
Oxford	d		08 07					09 01					08 37				09 31					09 07
Reading 7	d		09 03	09 09	09 16	09 18	09 20	09 24	09 33				09 33	09 42	09 46	09 48	09 55	10 02				10 03
Twyford 3	d		09 09			09 24							09 39			09 54						10 09
Maidenhead 3	d		09 17			09 32							09 47			10 02						10 17
Taplow	d					09 36										10 06						
Burnham	d					09 39					←					10 09				←		
Slough 3	a		09 24			09 44		09 40			09 44		09 54			10 14	10 09			10 14		10 24
	d		09 24			09 44		09 40			09 44		09 54			10 14	10 10			10 14		10 24
Langley	d		09 28			→							09 58			→						10 28
Iver	d		09 31										10 01									10 31
West Drayton	d		09 35								09 51		10 05							10 21		10 35
Heathrow Terminal 4 ✈	d																					
Heathrow Terminal 1-2-3 2 ✈	d	09 27										09 57									10 27	
Hayes & Harlington	d	09 33	09 40								09 56	10 03	10 10							10 26	10 33	10 40
Southall	d	09 36	09 43									10 06	10 13								10 36	10 43
Hanwell	d	09 39										10 09									10 39	
Greenford ⊖	d									09 46									10 16			
South Greenford	d									09 49									10 19			
Castle Bar Park	d									09 52									10 22			
Drayton Green	d									09 54									10 24			
West Ealing	d	09 41								09 56		10 11							10 26		10 41	
Ealing Broadway ⊖	d	09 44	09 49							09 59	10 03	10 14	10 19						10 29	10 33	10 44	10 49
Acton Main Line	d									10 03									10 33			
London Paddington 15 ⊖	a	09 54	10 01	09 37	09 44		09 52	09 59	10 02	10 12	10 16	10 24	10 31	10 11	10 14		10 29	10 32	10 42	10 46	10 54	11 01

		GW ◇1 ⊐	GW 1	GW 1	GW ◇1 Ⱶ	GW 1	GW 1	HC	GW 1	GW ◇1 ⊐	GW ◇1 ⊐	GW 1	GW ◇1 ⊐	GW ◇1 ⊐	GW ◇1 ⊐	GW 1	GW 1	HC	GW 1
Oxford	d				10 01				09 37					10 31					10 07
Reading 7	d	10 13	10 18	10 18	10 25				10 33	10 39	10 46	10 48	10 53	10 55	11 02				11 03
Twyford 3	d			10 24					10 39			10 54							11 09
Maidenhead 3	d			10 32					10 47			11 02							11 17
Taplow	d			10 36								11 06							
Burnham	d			10 39			←					11 09					←		
Slough 3	a			10 44	10 40		10 44		10 54			11 14		11 09			11 14		11 24
	d			10 44	10 40		10 44		10 54			11 14		11 10			11 14		11 24
Langley	d			→					10 58			→							11 28
Iver	d								11 01										11 31
West Drayton	d						10 51		11 05								11 21		11 35
Heathrow Terminal 4 ✈	d																		
Heathrow Terminal 1-2-3 2 ✈	d							10 57										11 27	
Hayes & Harlington	d						10 56	11 03	11 10								11 26	11 33	11 40
Southall	d							11 06	11 13									11 36	11 43
Hanwell	d							11 09										11 39	
Greenford ⊖	d					10 46										11 16			
South Greenford	d					10 49										11 19			
Castle Bar Park	d					10 52										11 22			
Drayton Green	d					10 54										11 24			
West Ealing	d					10 56		11 11								11 26		11 41	
Ealing Broadway ⊖	d					10 59	11 03	11 14	11 19							11 29	11 33	11 44	11 49
Acton Main Line	d					11 03										11 33			
London Paddington 15 ⊖	a	10 39	10 52		10 59	11 12	11 16	11 24	11 31	11 08	11 14		11 24	11 29	11 33	11 42	11 46	11 54	12 01

A ⊐ from Reading ⊘ to Reading

Reading and Greenford - London

Network Diagram - see first Page of Table 116

		GW	GW	GW	GW	GW	GW	HC	GW	GW	GW	GW	GW	GW	GW	GW	HC	GW	GW	GW	GW	GW
		◇1 ⊐	1	1	◇1	1	1		1	◇1 ⊐	1	■1 ⊐	◇1 ✕	◇1 ⊐	1	1		1	◇1 ⊐	1	1	◇1 ✕
Oxford	d				11 01				10 37				11 31					11 07				12 01
Reading 7	d	11 14	11 18	11 21	11 25				11 33	11 45	11 48	11 53	11 55	12 02				12 03	12 13	12 18	12 18	12 25
Twyford 3	d		11 24						11 39		11 54							12 09			12 24	
Maidenhead 3	d		11 32						11 47		12 02							12 17			12 32	
Taplow	d		11 36								12 06										12 36	
Burnham	d		11 39				←				12 09					←					12 39	
Slough 3	a		11 44		11 39		11 44		11 54		12 14		12 09			12 14		12 24			12 44	12 40
	d		11 44		11 40		11 44		11 54		12 14		12 11			12 14		12 24			12 44	12 40
Langley	d		→						11 58		→							12 28			→	
Iver	d								12 01									12 31				
West Drayton	d						11 51		12 05							12 21		12 35				
Heathrow Terminal 4 ✈	d																					
Heathrow Terminal 1-2-3 2 ✈	d							11 57									12 27					
Hayes & Harlington	d						11 56	12 03	12 10							12 26	12 33	12 40				
Southall	d							12 06	12 13								12 36	12 43				
Hanwell	d							12 09									12 39					
Greenford ⊖	d					11 46									12 16							
South Greenford	d					11 49									12 19							
Castle Bar Park	d					11 52									12 22							
Drayton Green	d					11 54									12 24							
West Ealing	d					11 56		12 11							12 26		12 41					
Ealing Broadway ⊖	d					11 59	12 03	12 14	12 19						12 29	12 33	12 44	12 49				
Acton Main Line	d					12 03									12 33							
London Paddington 15 ⊖	a	11 40		11 52	11 59	12 12	12 16	12 24	12 31	12 14		12 23	12 29	12 32	12 42	12 46	12 54	13 01	12 39	12 52		12 59

		GW	GW	HC	GW	GW	GW	GW	GW	GW	GW	GW	GW	HC	GW	GW	GW	GW	GW	GW	GW
		1	1		1	◇1 ⊐	■1 ⊐	◇1 ⊐	1	◇1 ✕	◇1 ⊐	1	1		1	◇1 ⊐	1	■1 ⊐	◇1 ✕	1	1
Oxford	d				11 37					12 31					12 07				13 01		
Reading 7	d				12 33	12 39	12 42	12 47	12 48	12 55	13 02				13 03	13 12	13 18	13 19	13 25		
Twyford 3	d				12 39				12 54						13 09		13 24				
Maidenhead 3	d				12 47				13 02						13 17		13 32				
Taplow	d								13 06								13 36				
Burnham	d		←						13 09				←				13 39				←
Slough 3	a		12 44		12 54				13 14	13 09			13 14		13 24		13 44		13 40		13 44
	d		12 44		12 54				13 14	13 11			13 14		13 24		13 44		13 40		13 44
Langley	d				12 58				→						13 28		→				
Iver	d				13 01										13 31						
West Drayton	d		12 51		13 05								13 21		13 35						13 51
Heathrow Terminal 4 ✈	d																				
Heathrow Terminal 1-2-3 2 ✈	d			12 57										13 27							
Hayes & Harlington	d		12 56	13 03	13 10								13 26	13 33	13 40						13 56
Southall	d			13 06	13 13									13 36	13 43						
Hanwell	d			13 09										13 39							
Greenford ⊖	d	12 46										13 16								13 46	
South Greenford	d	12 49										13 19								13 49	
Castle Bar Park	d	12 52										13 22								13 52	
Drayton Green	d	12 54										13 24								13 54	
West Ealing	d	12 56		13 11								13 26		13 41						13 56	
Ealing Broadway ⊖	d	12 59	13 03	13 14	13 19							13 29	13 33	13 44	13 49					13 59	14 03
Acton Main Line	d	13 03										13 33								14 03	
London Paddington 15 ⊖	a	13 12	13 16	13 24	13 31	13 07	13 09	13 13		13 30	13 33	13 42	13 46	13 54	14 01	13 41		13 46	13 59	14 12	14 16

		HC	GW	GW	GW	GW	GW	GW	GW	GW	HC	GW	GW	GW	GW	GW	GW	GW	HC	GW
			1	◇1 ⊐	1	1	◇1	◇1 ⊐	1	1		1	◇1 ⊐	1	1	◇1 ✕	1	1		1
Oxford	d		12 37				13 31					13 07				14 01				13 37
Reading 7	d		13 33	13 45	13 48	13 51	13 55	14 02				14 03	14 13	14 18	14 18	14 25				14 33
Twyford 3	d		13 39		13 54							14 09			14 24					14 39
Maidenhead 3	d		13 47		14 02							14 17			14 32					14 47
Taplow	d				14 06										14 36					
Burnham	d				14 09					←					14 39			←		
Slough 3	a		13 54		14 14		14 09			14 14		14 24			14 44	14 40		14 44		14 54
	d		13 54		14 14		14 10			14 14		14 24			14 44	14 40		14 44		14 54
Langley	d		13 58		→							14 28			→					14 58
Iver	d		14 01									14 31								15 01
West Drayton	d		14 05							14 21		14 35						14 51		15 05
Heathrow Terminal 4 ✈	d																			
Heathrow Terminal 1-2-3 2 ✈	d	13 57									14 27								14 57	
Hayes & Harlington	d	14 03	14 10							14 26	14 33	14 40						14 56	15 03	15 10
Southall	d	14 06	14 13								14 36	14 43							15 06	15 13
Hanwell	d	14 09									14 39								15 09	
Greenford ⊖	d								14 16								14 46			
South Greenford	d								14 19								14 49			
Castle Bar Park	d								14 22								14 52			
Drayton Green	d								14 24								14 54			
West Ealing	d	14 11							14 26		14 41						14 56		15 11	
Ealing Broadway ⊖	d	14 14	14 19						14 29	14 33	14 44	14 49					14 59	15 03	15 14	15 19
Acton Main Line	d								14 33								15 03			
London Paddington 15 ⊖	a	14 24	14 31	14 14		14 23	14 29	14 32	14 42	14 46	14 54	15 01	14 39	14 54		14 59	15 12	15 16	15 24	15 31

Reading and Greenford - London

Network Diagram - see first Page of Table 116

		GW	GW	GW	GW	GW	GW	GW	GW	HC	GW	GW	GW	GW	GW	GW	GW	HC	GW	GW	GW	GW
		◇1 ⊐	◇1 ⊐	1	■1 ⊐	◇1 ⊐	◇1 ⊐	1	1		1	◇1 ⊐	1	1	◇1	1	1		1	◇1 ⊐	1	■1 ⊐
Oxford	d					14 31					14 07				15 01				14 37			
Reading 7	d	14 39	14 45	14 48	14 53	14 55	15 02				15 03	15 12	15 18	15 19	15 25				15 33	15 45	15 48	15 53
Twyford 3	d			14 54							15 09		15 24						15 39		15 54	
Maidenhead 3	d			15 02							15 17		15 32						15 47		16 02	
Taplow	d			15 06									15 36								16 06	
Burnham	d			15 09					←				15 39				←				16 09	
Slough 3	a			15 14		15 10			15 14		15 24		15 44		15 40		15 44		15 54		16 14	
	d			15 14		15 11			15 14		15 24		15 44		15 40		15 44		15 54		16 14	
Langley	d			→							15 28		→						15 58		→	
Iver	d										15 31								16 01			
West Drayton	d								15 21		15 35						15 51		16 05			
Heathrow Terminal 4 ✈	d																					
Heathrow Terminal 1-2-3 2 ✈	d									15 27								15 57				
Hayes & Harlington	d								15 26	15 33	15 40						15 56	16 03	16 10			
Southall	d									15 36	15 43							16 06	16 13			
Hanwell	d									15 39								16 09				
Greenford ⊖	d							15 16								15 46						
South Greenford	d							15 19								15 49						
Castle Bar Park	d							15 22								15 52						
Drayton Green	d							15 24								15 54						
West Ealing	d							15 26		15 41						15 56		16 11				
Ealing Broadway ⊖	d							15 29	15 33	15 44	15 49					15 59	16 03	16 14	16 19			
Acton Main Line	d							15 33								16 03						
London Paddington 15 ⊖	a	15 09	15 14		15 23	15 29	15 32	15 42	15 46	15 54	16 01	15 39		15 54	15 59	16 12	16 16	16 24	16 31	16 14		16 23

		GW	GW	GW	GW	GW	HC	GW	GW	GW	GW	GW	GW	GW	GW	HC	GW	GW	GW	GW
		◇1 ✕	■1 ⊐	◇1 ⊐	1	1		1	◇1 ⊐	1	1	◇1	◇1 ⊐	1	1		1	◇1 ⊐	◇1 ⊐	1
Oxford	d	15 31						15 07				16 01					15 37			
Reading 7	d	15 55	16 01	16 02				16 03	16 13	16 18	16 18	16 26	16 28				16 33	16 39	16 45	16 48
Twyford 3	d							16 09			16 24						16 39			16 54
Maidenhead 3	d							16 17			16 32						16 47			17 02
Taplow	d										16 36									17 06
Burnham	d					←					16 39				←					17 09
Slough 3	a	16 10				16 14		16 24			16 44	16 40			16 44		16 54			17 14
	d	16 11				16 14		16 24			16 44	16 41			16 44		16 54			17 14
Langley	d							16 28			→						16 58			→
Iver	d							16 31									17 01			
West Drayton	d					16 21		16 35							16 51		17 05			
Heathrow Terminal 4 ✈	d																			
Heathrow Terminal 1-2-3 2 ✈	d						16 27									16 57				
Hayes & Harlington	d					16 26	16 33	16 40							16 56	17 03	17 10			
Southall	d						16 36	16 43								17 06	17 13			
Hanwell	d						16 39									17 09				
Greenford ⊖	d				16 16									16 46						
South Greenford	d				16 19									16 49						
Castle Bar Park	d				16 22									16 52						
Drayton Green	d				16 24									16 54						
West Ealing	d				16 26		16 41							16 56		17 11				
Ealing Broadway ⊖	d				16 29	16 33	16 44	16 49						16 59	17 03	17 14	17 19			
Acton Main Line	d				16 33									17 03						
London Paddington 15 ⊖	a	16 29	16 32	16 37	16 42	16 46	16 54	17 01	16 39	16 52		16 59	17 02	17 12	17 16	17 24	17 31	17 07	17 14	

		GW	GW	GW	GW	GW	HC	GW	GW	GW	GW	GW	GW	GW	HC	GW	GW	GW	GW	GW	GW	GW
		■1 ⊐	◇1 ✕	◇1 ⊐	1	1		1	◇1 ⊐	1	1	◇1	1	1		1	◇1 ⊐	◇1 ⊐	1	■1 ⊐	◇1 ⊐	◇1 ⊐
Oxford	d		16 31					16 07				17 01				16 37					17 31	
Reading 7	d	16 51	16 55	17 02				17 03	17 12	17 18	17 22	17 27				17 33	17 36	17 45	17 48	17 54	17 57	18 02
Twyford 3	d							17 09		17 24						17 39			17 54			
Maidenhead 3	d							17 17		17 32						17 47			18 02			
Taplow	d									17 36									18 06			
Burnham	d					←				17 39				←					18 09			
Slough 3	a		17 10			17 14		17 24		17 44		17 41		17 44		17 54			18 14		18 10	
	d		17 11			17 14		17 24		17 44		17 42		17 44		17 54			18 14		18 11	
Langley	d							17 28		→						17 58			→			
Iver	d							17 31								18 01						
West Drayton	d					17 21		17 35						17 51		18 05						
Heathrow Terminal 4 ✈	d																					
Heathrow Terminal 1-2-3 2 ✈	d						17 27								17 57							
Hayes & Harlington	d					17 26	17 33	17 40						17 56	18 03	18 10						
Southall	d						17 36	17 43							18 06	18 13						
Hanwell	d						17 39								18 09							
Greenford ⊖	d				17 16								17 46									
South Greenford	d				17 19								17 49									
Castle Bar Park	d				17 22								17 52									
Drayton Green	d				17 24								17 54									
West Ealing	d				17 26		17 41						17 56		18 11							
Ealing Broadway ⊖	d				17 29	17 33	17 44	17 49					17 59	18 03	18 14	18 19						
Acton Main Line	d				17 33								18 03									
London Paddington 15 ⊖	a	17 21	17 29	17 32	17 42	17 46	17 54	18 01	17 38		17 54	18 00	18 12	18 16	18 24	18 31	18 08	18 14		18 23	18 29	18 32

Table 117

Reading and Greenford - London

Saturdays

30 June to 8 September

Network Diagram - see first Page of Table 116

	GW	GW	HC	GW	GW	GW	GW	GW	GW	GW	HC	GW	GW	GW	GW	GW	GW	GW	GW	GW
	1	1		1	◇1 ⊏	1	1	◇1	1	1		1	◇1 ⊏	◇1 ⊏	1	◇1 ⊏	◇1 ✕	◇1 ⊏	1	1
Oxford d				17 07				18 01				17 37					18 31			
Reading 7 d				18 03	18 13	18 18	18 19	18 25				18 33	18 39	18 45	18 48	18 50	18 56	19 02		
Twyford 3 d				18 09		18 24						18 39			18 54					
Maidenhead 3 d				18 17		18 32						18 47			19 02					
Taplow d						18 36									19 06					
Burnham d		←				18 39				←					19 09					←
Slough 3 a		18 14		18 24		18 44		18 40		18 44		18 54			19 14		19 10			19 14
d		18 14		18 24		18 44		18 40		18 44		18 54			19 14		19 11			19 14
Langley d				18 28		→						18 58			→					
Iver d				18 31								19 01								
West Drayton d		18 21		18 35						18 51		19 05								19 21
Heathrow Terminal 4 ✈ d																				
Heathrow Terminal 1-2-3 2 ✈ d			18 27								18 57									
Hayes & Harlington d		18 26	18 33	18 40						18 56	19 03	19 10								19 26
Southall d			18 36	18 43							19 06	19 13								
Hanwell d			18 39								19 09									
Greenford ⊖ d	18 16								18 46										19 16	
South Greenford d	18 19								18 49										19 19	
Castle Bar Park d	18 22								18 52										19 22	
Drayton Green d	18 24								18 54										19 24	
West Ealing d	18 26		18 41						18 56		19 11								19 26	
Ealing Broadway ⊖ d	18 29	18 33	18 44	18 49					18 59	19 03	19 14	19 19							19 29	19 33
Acton Main Line d	18 33								19 03										19 33	
London Paddington 15 ⊖ a	18 42	18 46	18 54	19 01	18 39		18 52	18 59	19 12	19 16	19 24	19 31	19 08	19 14		19 22	19 29	19 32	19 42	19 46

	HC	GW	GW	GW	GW	GW	GW	GW	HC	GW	GW	GW	GW	GW	GW	GW	HC	GW	GW
		1	◇1 ⊏	1	1	◇1	1	1		1	◇1 ⊏	1	◇1 ✕	◇1 ⊏	1	1		1	◇1 ⊏
Oxford d		18 07				19 01				18 37			19 31					19 07	
Reading 7 d		19 03	19 12	19 18	19 20	19 25				19 33	19 45	19 48	19 55	20 03				20 03	20 09
Twyford 3 d		19 09		19 24						19 39		19 54						20 09	
Maidenhead 3 d		19 17		19 32						19 47		20 02						20 17	
Taplow d				19 36								20 06							
Burnham d				19 39				←				20 09				←			
Slough 3 a		19 24		19 44		19 40		19 44		19 54		20 14	20 10			20 14		20 24	
d		19 24		19 44		19 40		19 44		19 54		20 14	20 10			20 14		20 24	
Langley d		19 28		→						19 58		→						20 28	
Iver d		19 31								20 01								20 31	
West Drayton d		19 35						19 51		20 05						20 21		20 35	
Heathrow Terminal 4 ✈ d																			
Heathrow Terminal 1-2-3 2 ✈ d	19 27								19 57								20 27		
Hayes & Harlington d	19 33	19 40						19 56	20 03	20 10						20 26	20 33	20 40	
Southall d	19 36	19 43							20 06	20 13							20 36	20 43	
Hanwell d	19 39								20 09								20 39		
Greenford ⊖ d							19 46								20 16				
South Greenford d							19 49								20 19				
Castle Bar Park d							19 52								20 22				
Drayton Green d							19 54								20 24				
West Ealing d	19 41						19 56		20 11						20 26		20 41		
Ealing Broadway ⊖ d	19 44	19 49					19 59	20 03	20 14	20 19					20 29	20 33	20 44	20 49	
Acton Main Line d							20 03								20 33				
London Paddington 15 ⊖ a	19 54	20 01	19 39		19 52	19 59	20 12	20 16	20 24	20 31	20 14		20 29	20 32	20 42	20 46	20 54	21 01	20 37

	GW	GW	GW	GW	HC	GW	GW	GW	GW	GW	GW	GW	GW	HC	GW	GW	GW	GW	GW	GW	HC
	1	◇1	1	1		1	◇1 ⊏	◇1 ⊏	1	◇1	◇1 ⊏	1	1		1	◇1 ⊏	1	◇1	1	1	
Oxford d		20 01				19 37				20 31					20 07			21 01			
Reading 7 d	20 18	20 25				20 33	20 39	20 45	20 48	20 54	21 01				21 03	21 08	21 18	21 25			
Twyford 3 d	20 24					20 39			20 54						21 09		21 24				
Maidenhead 3 d	20 32					20 47			21 02						21 17		21 32				
Taplow d	20 36								21 06								21 36				
Burnham d	20 39			←					21 09				←				21 39			←	
Slough 3 a	20 44	20 40		20 44		20 54			21 14	21 09			21 14		21 24		21 44	21 40		21 44	
d	20 44	20 40		20 44		20 54			21 14	21 09			21 14		21 24		21 44	21 40		21 44	
Langley d	→					20 58			→						21 28		→				
Iver d						21 01									21 31						
West Drayton d				20 51		21 05							21 21		21 35					21 51	
Heathrow Terminal 4 ✈ d																					
Heathrow Terminal 1-2-3 2 ✈ d					20 57									21 27							21 57
Hayes & Harlington d				20 56	21 03	21 10							21 26	21 33	21 40					21 56	22 03
Southall d					21 06	21 13								21 36	21 43						22 06
Hanwell d					21 09									21 39							22 09
Greenford ⊖ d			20 46									21 16							21 46		
South Greenford d			20 49									21 19							21 49		
Castle Bar Park d			20 52									21 22							21 52		
Drayton Green d			20 54									21 24							21 54		
West Ealing d			20 56		21 11							21 26		21 41					21 56		22 11
Ealing Broadway ⊖ d			20 59	21 03	21 14	21 19						21 29	21 33	21 44	21 49				21 59	22 03	22 14
Acton Main Line d			21 03									21 33							22 03		
London Paddington 15 ⊖ a		20 59	21 12	21 16	21 24	21 31	21 07	21 14		21 29	21 32	21 42	21 46	21 54	22 02	21 36		21 59	22 12	22 16	22 24

Table 117

Reading and Greenford - London

Saturdays

30 June to 8 September

Network Diagram - see first Page of Table 116

	GW	GW	GW	GW	GW	GW	GW	HC	GW	GW	HC	GW	GW	GW	GW	HC	GW	GW
	1	1	◇1 ⊏	1 ⊏	◇1	◇1 ⊏	1		1	◇1		1	1	◇1 ⊏	◇1		1	◇1
Oxford d	20 37				21 31					22 01		21 50			22 35			23 01
Reading 7 d	21 33	21 48	21 50	22 00	22 01	22 03			22 18	22 29		22 33	22 48	23 05	23 05		23 18	23 31
Twyford 3 d	21 39	21 54							22 24			22 39	22 54				23 24	
Maidenhead 3 d	21 47	22 02							22 32			22 47	23 02				23 32	
Taplow d		22 06							22 36				23 06				23 36	
Burnham d		22 09					←		22 39				23 09				23 39	
Slough 3 a	21 54	22 14			22 11		22 14		22 44	22 43		22 54	23 14		23 23		23 44	23 45
d	21 54	22 14			22 12		22 14		22 44	22 44		22 54	23 14		23 24		23 44	23 46
Langley d	21 58	→										22 58						
Iver d	22 01											23 01						
West Drayton d	22 05						22 21		22 51			23 05	23 21				23 51	
Heathrow Terminal 4 ✈ d																		
Heathrow Terminal 1-2-3 2 ✈ d								22 27			22 57					23 27		
Hayes & Harlington d	22 10						22 26	22 33	22 56		23 03	23 10	23 26			23 33	23 56	
Southall d	22 13							22 36			23 06	23 13				23 36		
Hanwell d								22 39			23 09					23 39		
Greenford ⊖ d																		
South Greenford d																		
Castle Bar Park d																		
Drayton Green d																		
West Ealing d								22 41			23 11					23 41		
Ealing Broadway ⊖ d	22 19						22 33	22 44	23 03		23 14	23 19	23 33			23 44	00 03	
Acton Main Line d																		
London Paddington 15 ⊖ a	22 31		22 16	22 26	22 34	22 30	22 46	22 54	23 16	23 02	23 24	23 28	23 46	23 36	23 43	23 54	00 16	00 10

	GW	GW
	◇1 ⊏	1
Oxford d		23 07
Reading 7 d	23 51	00 03
Twyford 3 d		00 09
Maidenhead 3 d		00 17
Taplow d		00 21
Burnham d		00 24
Slough 3 a		00 28
d		00 29
Langley d		00 33
Iver d		00 36
West Drayton d		00 39
Heathrow Terminal 4 ✈ d		
Heathrow Terminal 1-2-3 2 ✈ d		
Hayes & Harlington d		00 44
Southall d		00 47
Hanwell d		
Greenford ⊖ d		
South Greenford d		
Castle Bar Park d		
Drayton Green d		
West Ealing d		
Ealing Broadway ⊖ d		00 53
Acton Main Line d		
London Paddington 15 ⊖ a	00 34	01 02

Saturdays

15 September to 20 October

	GW	GW	GW	HC	GW	GW	GW	GW	GW	GW	HC	GW	HC	GW	GW	GW	HC	GW	GW	GW	HC
	1	1	◇1		◇1 ⊏	1	◇1	1	1	1		1		1	1	1		1	1	1	
Oxford d			23p09				00 07	00 27		03 59								05 14			
Reading 7 d	22p48	23p15	23p41		23p55	00 15	00 39	01 15	04 10	04 40		05 10		05 33		05 48		06 03		06 18	
Twyford 3 d	22p54	23p22				00 21		01 21	04 16	04 46		05 16		05 39		05 54		06 09		06 24	
Maidenhead 3 d	23p02	23p29	23p54			00 29		01 29	04 24	04 54		05 24		05 47		06 02		06 17		06 32	
Taplow d	23p05	23p33				00 32						05 28				06 06				06 36	
Burnham d	23p08	23p36				00 35						05 31				06 09				06 39	
Slough 3 a	23p13	23p41	00 01			00 40	00 55	01 37	04 31	05 01		05 35		05 54		06 14		06 24		06 44	
d	23p27	23p41	00 02			00 40	00 56	01 37	04 32	05 02		05 36		05 54		06 14		06 24		06 44	
Langley d	23p31	23p45				00 44						05 40		05 58				06 28			
Iver d	23p34	23p48										05 43		06 01				06 31			
West Drayton d	23p38	23p51				00 49			04 38			05 45		06 05		06 21		06 35		06 51	
Heathrow Terminal 4 ✈ d				00 01							05 23		05 51								
Heathrow Terminal 1-2-3 2 ✈ d				00 07							05 29		05 57				06 27				06 57
Hayes & Harlington d	23p43	23p56		00 14		00 54		01 46	04 43	05 11	05 35	05 51	06 03	06 10		06 26	06 33	06 40		06 56	07 03
Southall d	23p47	23p59		00 17		00 57			04 46	05 13	05 38	05 54	06 06	06 13			06 36	06 43			07 06
Hanwell d											05 41		06 09				06 39				07 09
Greenford ⊖ d															06 16				06 46		
South Greenford d															06 19				06 49		
Castle Bar Park d															06 22				06 52		
Drayton Green d															06 24				06 54		
West Ealing d											05 43		06 11		06 26		06 41		06 56		07 11
Ealing Broadway ⊖ d	23p52	00 06		00 22		01 03		01 53	04 52	05 19	05 46	06 00	06 14	06 19	06 29	06 33	06 44	06 49	06 59	07 03	07 14
Acton Main Line d										05 23		06 03			06 33				07 03		
London Paddington 15 ⊖ a	00 02	00 17	00 28	00 30	00 33	01 14	01 17	02 05	05 01	05 31	05 56	06 11	06 24	06 31	06 42	06 46	06 54	07 01	07 12	07 16	07 24

Reading and Greenford - London

Saturdays

15 September to 20 October

Network Diagram - see first Page of Table 116

	GW	GW	GW	GW	GW	GW	HC	GW	GW	GW	GW	GW	GW	GW	GW	HC	GW	GW	GW	GW	GW	GW
	1	◇1 ☕	1	1	1	◇1		1	◇1 ☕	1	1	◇1	◇1 ☕	1	1		1	◇1 ☕	1	◇1 ☕	◇1 ☕	1
Oxford d	05 49					06 31		06 07				07 01					06 42			07 31		
Reading 7 d	06 33	06 45		06 48	06 52	07 00		07 03	07 15	07 18	07 21	07 27	07 32				07 33	07 46	07 48	07 54	08 02	
Twyford 3 d	06 39			06 54				07 09		07 24							07 39		07 54			
Maidenhead 3 d	06 47			07 02				07 17		07 32							07 47		08 02			
Taplow d				07 06						07 36									08 06			
Burnham d				07 09						07 39					←				08 09			
Slough 3 a	06 54			07 14		07 16		07 24		07 44		07 42			07 44		07 54		08 14	08 09		
d	06 54			07 14		07 17		07 24		07 44		07 42			07 44		07 54		08 14	08 09		
Langley d	06 58							07 28		→							07 58		→			
Iver d	07 01							07 31									08 01					
West Drayton d	07 05			07 21				07 35							07 51		08 05					
Heathrow Terminal 4 ✈ d																						
Heathrow Terminal 1-2-3 2 ✈ d							07 27									07 57						
Hayes & Harlington d	07 10			07 26			07 33	07 40							07 56	08 03	08 10					
Southall d	07 13						07 36	07 43								08 06	08 13					
Hanwell d							07 39									08 09						
Greenford ⊖ d			07 16											07 46								08 16
South Greenford d			07 19											07 49								08 19
Castle Bar Park d			07 22											07 52								08 22
Drayton Green d			07 24											07 54								08 24
West Ealing d			07 26				07 41							07 56		08 11						08 26
Ealing Broadway ⊖ d	07 19		07 29	07 33			07 44	07 49						07 59	08 03	08 14	08 19					08 29
Acton Main Line d			07 33											08 03								08 33
London Paddington 15 ⊖ a	07 31	07 14	07 42	07 46	07 22	07 37	07 54	08 01	07 44		07 54	08 01	08 07	08 12	08 16	08 24	08 31	08 14		08 29	08 32	08 42

	GW	HC	GW	XC	GW	GW	GW	GW	GW	GW	GW	HC	GW	GW	GW	GW	GW	GW	GW	GW
	1		1	◇1 🍴	◇1 ☕	1	1	◇1	◇1 ☕	1	1		1	◇1 ☕	1	◇1 ☕	◇1 ☕	◇1 ☕	1	1
Oxford d			07 07	07 16				08 01					07 37				08 31			
Reading 7 d			08 03	07a39	08 16	08 18	08 20	08 26	08 32				08 33	08 46	08 48	08 52	08 55	09 02		
Twyford 3 d			08 09			08 24							08 39		08 54					
Maidenhead 3 d			08 17			08 32							08 47		09 02					
Taplow d						08 36									09 06					
Burnham d	←					08 39					←				09 09					←
Slough 3 a	08 14		08 24			08 44		08 40			08 44		08 54		09 14		09 09			09 14
d	08 14		08 24			08 44		08 41			08 44		08 54		09 14		09 11			09 14
Langley d			08 28			→							08 58		→					
Iver d			08 31										09 01							
West Drayton d	08 21		08 35								08 51		09 05							09 21
Heathrow Terminal 4 ✈ d																				
Heathrow Terminal 1-2-3 2 ✈ d		08 27										08 57								
Hayes & Harlington d	08 26	08 33	08 40								08 56	09 03	09 10							09 26
Southall d		08 36	08 43									09 06	09 13							
Hanwell d		08 39										09 09								
Greenford ⊖ d										08 46									09 16	
South Greenford d										08 49									09 19	
Castle Bar Park d										08 52									09 22	
Drayton Green d										08 54									09 24	
West Ealing d		08 41								08 56		09 11							09 26	
Ealing Broadway ⊖ d	08 33	08 44	08 49							08 59	09 03	09 14	09 19						09 29	09 33
Acton Main Line d										09 03									09 33	
London Paddington 15 ⊖ a	08 46	08 54	09 01		08 44		08 52	08 59	09 02	09 12	09 16	09 24	09 31	09 14		09 21	09 29	09 32	09 42	09 46

	HC	GW	GW	GW	GW	GW	GW	GW	GW	GW	HC	GW	GW	GW	GW	GW	GW	GW	GW	HC	GW
		1	◇1 ☕	◇1 ☕	1	1	◇1 🍴	◇1 ☕	1	1		1	◇1 ☕	◇1 ☕	1	◇1 A ☕⊘	◇1 ☕	1	1		1
Oxford d		08 07					09 01					08 37				09 31					09 07
Reading 7 d		09 03	09 09	09 16	09 18	09 20	09 24	09 33				09 33	09 42	09 46	09 48	09 55	10 02				10 03
Twyford 3 d		09 09			09 24							09 39			09 54						10 09
Maidenhead 3 d		09 17			09 32							09 47			10 02						10 17
Taplow d					09 36										10 06						
Burnham d					09 39					←					10 09				←		
Slough 3 a		09 24			09 44		09 40			09 44		09 54			10 14	10 09			10 14		10 24
d		09 24			09 44		09 40			09 44		09 54			10 14	10 10			10 14		10 24
Langley d		09 28			→							09 58			→						10 28
Iver d		09 31										10 01									10 31
West Drayton d		09 35								09 51		10 05							10 21		10 35
Heathrow Terminal 4 ✈ d																					
Heathrow Terminal 1-2-3 2 ✈ d	09 27										09 57									10 27	
Hayes & Harlington d	09 33	09 40								09 56	10 03	10 10							10 26	10 33	10 40
Southall d	09 36	09 43									10 06	10 13								10 36	10 43
Hanwell d	09 39										10 09									10 39	
Greenford ⊖ d									09 46									10 16			
South Greenford d									09 49									10 19			
Castle Bar Park d									09 52									10 22			
Drayton Green d									09 54									10 24			
West Ealing d	09 41								09 56		10 11							10 26		10 41	
Ealing Broadway ⊖ d	09 44	09 49							09 59	10 03	10 14	10 19						10 29	10 33	10 44	10 49
Acton Main Line d									10 03									10 33			
London Paddington 15 ⊖ a	09 54	10 01	09 37	09 44		09 52	09 59	10 02	10 12	10 16	10 24	10 31	10 11	10 14		10 29	10 32	10 42	10 46	10 54	11 01

A ☕ from Reading ⊘ to Reading

Table 117

Reading and Greenford - London

Saturdays

15 September to 20 October

Network Diagram - see first Page of Table 116

	GW	GW	GW	GW	GW	GW	GW	HC	GW	GW	GW	GW	GW	GW	GW	GW	GW	HC	GW
	◇1 ☕	1	1	◇1 🍴	◇1 ☕	1	1		1	◇1 ☕	◇1 ☕	1	◇1 ☕	◇1 ☕	◇1 ☕	1	1		1
Oxford d				10 01					09 37					10 31					10 07
Reading 7 d	10 13	10 18	10 18	10 25	10 33				10 33	10 39	10 46	10 48	10 53	10 55	11 02				11 03
Twyford 3 d			10 24						10 39			10 54							11 09
Maidenhead 3 d			10 32						10 47			11 02							11 17
Taplow d			10 36									11 06							
Burnham d			10 39				←					11 09					←		
Slough 3 a			10 44	10 40			10 44		10 54			11 14		11 09			11 14		11 24
d			10 44	10 40			10 44		10 54			11 14		11 10			11 14		11 24
Langley d			→						10 58			→							11 28
Iver d									11 01										11 31
West Drayton d							10 51		11 05								11 21		11 35
Heathrow Terminal 4 ✈ d																			
Heathrow Terminal 1-2-3 2 ✈ d								10 57										11 27	
Hayes & Harlington d							10 56	11 03	11 10								11 26	11 33	11 40
Southall d								11 06	11 13									11 36	11 43
Hanwell d								11 09										11 39	
Greenford ⊖ d						10 46										11 16			
South Greenford d						10 49										11 19			
Castle Bar Park d						10 52										11 22			
Drayton Green d						10 54										11 24			
West Ealing d						10 56		11 11								11 26		11 41	
Ealing Broadway ⊖ d						10 59	11 03	11 14	11 19							11 29	11 33	11 44	11 49
Acton Main Line d						11 03										11 33			
London Paddington 15 ⊖ a	10 39	10 52		10 59	11 02	11 12	11 16	11 24	11 31	11 08	11 14		11 24	11 29	11 33	11 42	11 46	11 54	12 01

	GW	GW	GW	GW	GW	GW	HC	GW	GW	GW	GW	GW	GW	GW	GW	HC	GW	GW	GW	GW
	◇1 ☕	1	1	◇1	1	1		1	◇1 ☕	1	1 ☕	◇1 🍴	◇1 ☕	1	1		1	◇1 ☕	1	1
Oxford d				11 01				10 37				11 31					11 07			
Reading 7 d	11 14	11 18	11 21	11 25				11 33	11 45	11 48	11 53	11 55	12 02				12 03	12 13	12 18	12 18
Twyford 3 d		11 24						11 39		11 54							12 09			12 24
Maidenhead 3 d		11 32						11 47		12 02							12 17			12 32
Taplow d		11 36								12 06										12 36
Burnham d		11 39				←				12 09					←					12 39
Slough 3 a		11 44		11 39		11 44		11 54		12 14		12 09			12 14		12 24			12 44
d		11 44		11 40		11 44		11 54		12 14		12 11			12 14		12 24			12 44
Langley d		→						11 58		→							12 28			→
Iver d								12 01									12 31			
West Drayton d						11 51		12 05							12 21		12 35			
Heathrow Terminal 4 ✈ d																				
Heathrow Terminal 1-2-3 2 ✈ d							11 57									12 27				
Hayes & Harlington d						11 56	12 03	12 10							12 26	12 33	12 40			
Southall d							12 06	12 13								12 36	12 43			
Hanwell d							12 09									12 39				
Greenford ⊖ d					11 46									12 16						
South Greenford d					11 49									12 19						
Castle Bar Park d					11 52									12 22						
Drayton Green d					11 54									12 24						
West Ealing d					11 56		12 11							12 26		12 41				
Ealing Broadway ⊖ d					11 59	12 03	12 14	12 19						12 29	12 33	12 44	12 49			
Acton Main Line d					12 03									12 33						
London Paddington 15 ⊖ a	11 40		11 52	11 59	12 12	12 16	12 24	12 31	12 14		12 23	12 29	12 32	12 42	12 46	12 54	13 01	12 39	12 52	

	GW	GW	GW	HC	GW	GW	GW	GW	GW	GW	GW	GW	GW	HC	GW	GW	GW	GW	GW	GW
	◇1 🍴	1	1		1	◇1 ☕	◇1 ☕	1	◇1 ☕	◇1 🍴	◇1 ☕	1	1		1	◇1 ☕	1	◇1 ☕	◇1 🍴	1
Oxford d	12 01				11 37					12 31					12 07				13 01	
Reading 7 d	12 25				12 33	12 39	12 45	12 48	12 54	12 55	13 02				13 03	13 12	13 18	13 20	13 25	
Twyford 3 d					12 39			12 54							13 09		13 24			
Maidenhead 3 d					12 47			13 02							13 17		13 32			
Taplow d								13 06									13 36			
Burnham d			←					13 09					←				13 39			
Slough 3 a	12 40		12 44		12 54			13 14		13 09			13 14		13 24		13 44		13 40	
d	12 40		12 44		12 54			13 14		13 11			13 14		13 24		13 44		13 40	
Langley d					12 58			→							13 28		→			
Iver d					13 01										13 31					
West Drayton d			12 51		13 05								13 21		13 35					
Heathrow Terminal 4 ✈ d																				
Heathrow Terminal 1-2-3 2 ✈ d				12 57										13 27						
Hayes & Harlington d			12 56	13 03	13 10								13 26	13 33	13 40					
Southall d				13 06	13 13									13 36	13 43					
Hanwell d				13 09										13 39						
Greenford ⊖ d		12 46										13 16								13 46
South Greenford d		12 49										13 19								13 49
Castle Bar Park d		12 52										13 22								13 52
Drayton Green d		12 54										13 24								13 54
West Ealing d		12 56		13 11								13 26		13 41						13 56
Ealing Broadway ⊖ d		12 59	13 03	13 14	13 19							13 29	13 33	13 44	13 49					13 59
Acton Main Line d		13 03										13 33								14 03
London Paddington 15 ⊖ a	12 59	13 12	13 16	13 24	13 31	13 07	13 12		13 21	13 30	13 33	13 42	13 46	13 54	14 01	13 41		13 46	13 59	14 12

Reading and Greenford - London

15 September to 20 October

Network Diagram - see first Page of Table 116

	GW 1	HC	GW 1	GW ◇1 ☕	GW 1	GW 1	GW ◇1	GW ◇1 ☕	GW 1	GW 1	HC	GW 1	GW ◇1 ☕	GW 1	GW ◇1 ☕	GW ◇1 🍴	GW 1	GW 1	HC	GW 1
Oxford d			12 37				13 31					13 07				14 01				13 37
Reading 7 d			13 33	13 45	13 48	13 51	13 55	14 02				14 03	14 13	14 18	14 19	14 25				14 33
Twyford 3 d			13 39		13 54							14 09		14 24						14 39
Maidenhead 3 d			13 47		14 02							14 17		14 32						14 47
Taplow d					14 06									14 36						
Burnham d	←				14 09					←				14 39				←		
Slough 3 a	13 44		13 54		14 14		14 09			14 14		14 24		14 44		14 40		14 44		14 54
Slough 3 d	13 44		13 54		14 14		14 10			14 14		14 24		14 44		14 40		14 44		14 54
Langley d			13 58		→							14 28		→						14 58
Iver d			14 01									14 31								15 01
West Drayton d	13 51		14 05							14 21		14 35						14 51		15 05
Heathrow Terminal 4 ✈ d																				
Heathrow Terminal 1-2-3 2 ✈ d		13 57									14 27								14 57	
Hayes & Harlington d	13 56	14 03	14 10							14 26	14 33	14 40						14 56	15 03	15 10
Southall d		14 06	14 13								14 36	14 43							15 06	15 13
Hanwell d		14 09									14 39								15 09	
Greenford ⊖ d									14 16								14 46			
South Greenford d									14 19								14 49			
Castle Bar Park d									14 22								14 52			
Drayton Green d									14 24								14 54			
West Ealing d		14 11							14 26		14 41						14 56		15 11	
Ealing Broadway ⊖ d	14 03	14 14	14 19						14 29	14 33	14 44	14 49					14 59	15 03	15 14	15 19
Acton Main Line d									14 33								15 03			
London Paddington 15 ⊖ a	14 16	14 24	14 31	14 14		14 23	14 29	14 32	14 42	14 46	14 54	15 01	14 39		14 45	14 59	15 12	15 16	15 24	15 31

	GW ◇1 ☕	GW ◇1 ☕	GW 1	GW ◇1 ☕	GW ◇1 ☕	GW ◇1 ☕	GW 1	GW 1	HC	GW 1	GW ◇1 ☕	GW 1	GW 1	GW ◇1	GW 1	GW 1	HC	GW 1	GW ◇1 ☕	GW 1
Oxford d					14 31					14 07				15 01				14 37		
Reading 7 d	14 39	14 45	14 48	14 53	14 55	15 02				15 03	15 12	15 18	15 19	15 25				15 33	15 45	15 48
Twyford 3 d			14 54							15 09		15 24						15 39		15 54
Maidenhead 3 d			15 02							15 17		15 32						15 47		16 02
Taplow d			15 06									15 36								16 06
Burnham d			15 09					←				15 39				←				16 09
Slough 3 a			15 14		15 10			15 14		15 24		15 44		15 40		15 44		15 54		16 14
Slough 3 d			15 14		15 11			15 14		15 24		15 44		15 40		15 44		15 54		16 14
Langley d			→							15 28		→						15 58		→
Iver d										15 31								16 01		
West Drayton d								15 21		15 35						15 51		16 05		
Heathrow Terminal 4 ✈ d																				
Heathrow Terminal 1-2-3 2 ✈ d									15 27								15 57			
Hayes & Harlington d								15 26	15 33	15 40						15 56	16 03	16 10		
Southall d									15 36	15 43							16 06	16 13		
Hanwell d									15 39								16 09			
Greenford ⊖ d							15 16								15 46					
South Greenford d							15 19								15 49					
Castle Bar Park d							15 22								15 52					
Drayton Green d							15 24								15 54					
West Ealing d							15 26		15 41						15 56		16 11			
Ealing Broadway ⊖ d							15 29	15 33	15 44	15 49					15 59	16 03	16 14	16 19		
Acton Main Line d							15 33								16 03					
London Paddington 15 ⊖ a	15 09	15 14		15 22	15 29	15 32	15 42	15 46	15 54	16 01	15 39		15 54	15 59	16 12	16 16	16 24	16 31	16 14	

	GW ◇1 ☕	GW ◇1 🍴	GW ◇1 ☕	GW 1	GW 1	HC	GW 1	GW ◇1 ☕	GW 1	GW 1	GW ◇1	GW 1	GW 1	HC	GW 1	GW ◇1 ☕	GW ◇1 ☕	GW 1	GW ◇1 ☕
Oxford d		15 31					15 07				16 01				15 37				
Reading 7 d	15 53	15 55	16 01				16 03	16 13	16 18	16 18	16 26				16 33	16 39	16 45	16 48	16 51
Twyford 3 d							16 09			16 24					16 39			16 54	
Maidenhead 3 d							16 17			16 32					16 47			17 02	
Taplow d										16 36								17 06	
Burnham d					←					16 39			←					17 09	
Slough 3 a		16 10			16 14		16 24			16 44	16 40		16 44		16 54			17 14	
Slough 3 d		16 11			16 14		16 24			16 44	16 41		16 44		16 54			17 14	
Langley d							16 28			→					16 58			→	
Iver d							16 31								17 01				
West Drayton d					16 21		16 35						16 51		17 05				
Heathrow Terminal 4 ✈ d																			
Heathrow Terminal 1-2-3 2 ✈ d						16 27								16 57					
Hayes & Harlington d					16 26	16 33	16 40						16 56	17 03	17 10				
Southall d						16 36	16 43							17 06	17 13				
Hanwell d						16 39								17 09					
Greenford ⊖ d				16 16								16 46							
South Greenford d				16 19								16 49							
Castle Bar Park d				16 22								16 52							
Drayton Green d				16 24								16 54							
West Ealing d				16 26		16 41						16 56		17 11					
Ealing Broadway ⊖ d				16 29	16 33	16 44	16 49					16 59	17 03	17 14	17 19				
Acton Main Line d				16 33								17 03							
London Paddington 15 ⊖ a	16 23	16 29	16 32	16 42	16 46	16 54	17 01	16 39	16 52		16 59	17 12	17 16	17 24	17 31	17 07	17 14		17 21

Table 117

Reading and Greenford - London

Saturdays

15 September to 20 October

Network Diagram - see first Page of Table 116

	GW ◇1 🍴	GW ◇1 ☕	GW 1	GW 1	HC	GW 1	GW ◇1 ☕	GW ◇1 ☕	GW 1	GW ◇1	GW 1	GW 1	HC	GW 1	GW ◇1 ☕	GW 1	GW ◇1 ☕	GW ◇1 ☕	GW ◇1 ☕	GW 1	GW 1
Oxford d	16 31					16 07				17 01				16 37				17 31			
Reading 7 d	16 55	17 02				17 03	17 12	17 18	17 18	17 27				17 33	17 45	17 48	17 54	17 57	18 02		
Twyford 3 d						17 09			17 24					17 39		17 54					
Maidenhead 3 d						17 17			17 32					17 47		18 02					
Taplow d									17 36							18 06					
Burnham d				←					17 39			←				18 09					←
Slough 3 a	17 10			17 14		17 24			17 44	17 41		17 44		17 54		18 14		18 10			18 14
Slough 3 d	17 11			17 14		17 24			17 44	17 42		17 44		17 54		18 14		18 11			18 14
Langley d						17 28			→					17 58		→					
Iver d						17 31								18 01							
West Drayton d				17 21		17 35						17 51		18 05							18 21
Heathrow Terminal 4 ✈ d																					
Heathrow Terminal 1-2-3 2 ✈ d					17 27								17 57								
Hayes & Harlington d				17 26	17 33	17 40						17 56	18 03	18 10							18 26
Southall d					17 36	17 43							18 06	18 13							
Hanwell d					17 39								18 09								
Greenford ⊖ d			17 16								17 46									18 16	
South Greenford d			17 19								17 49									18 19	
Castle Bar Park d			17 22								17 52									18 22	
Drayton Green d			17 24								17 54									18 24	
West Ealing d			17 26		17 41						17 56		18 11							18 26	
Ealing Broadway ⊖ d			17 29	17 33	17 44	17 49					17 59	18 03	18 14	18 19						18 29	18 33
Acton Main Line d			17 33								18 03									18 33	
London Paddington 15 ⊖ a	17 29	17 32	17 42	17 46	17 54	18 01	17 38	17 51		18 00	18 12	18 16	18 24	18 31	18 14		18 21	18 29	18 32	18 42	18 46

	HC	GW 1	GW ◇1 ☕	GW 1	GW 1	GW ◇1	GW 1	GW 1	HC	GW 1	GW ◇1 ☕	GW ◇1 ☕	GW 1	GW ◇1 ☕	GW ◇1 🍴	GW ◇1 ☕	GW 1	GW 1	HC	GW 1
Oxford d		17 07				18 01				17 37					18 31					18 07
Reading 7 d		18 03	18 13	18 18	18 19	18 25				18 33	18 39	18 45	18 48	18 50	18 56	19 02				19 03
Twyford 3 d		18 09		18 24						18 39			18 54							19 09
Maidenhead 3 d		18 17		18 32						18 47			19 02							19 17
Taplow d				18 36									19 06							
Burnham d				18 39				←					19 09					←		
Slough 3 a		18 24		18 44		18 40		18 44		18 54			19 14		19 10			19 14		19 24
Slough 3 d		18 24		18 44		18 40		18 44		18 54			19 14		19 11			19 14		19 24
Langley d		18 28		→						18 58			→							19 28
Iver d		18 31								19 01										19 31
West Drayton d		18 35						18 51		19 05								19 21		19 35
Heathrow Terminal 4 ✈ d																				
Heathrow Terminal 1-2-3 2 ✈ d	18 27								18 57										19 27	
Hayes & Harlington d	18 33	18 40						18 56	19 03	19 10								19 26	19 33	19 40
Southall d	18 36	18 43							19 06	19 13									19 36	19 43
Hanwell d	18 39								19 09										19 39	
Greenford ⊖ d							18 46										19 16			
South Greenford d							18 49										19 19			
Castle Bar Park d							18 52										19 22			
Drayton Green d							18 54										19 24			
West Ealing d	18 41						18 56		19 11								19 26		19 41	
Ealing Broadway ⊖ d	18 44	18 49					18 59	19 03	19 14	19 19							19 29	19 33	19 44	19 49
Acton Main Line d							19 03										19 33			
London Paddington 15 ⊖ a	18 54	19 01	18 39		18 52	18 59	19 12	19 16	19 24	19 31	19 08	19 14		19 22	19 29	19 32	19 42	19 46	19 54	20 01

	GW ◇1 ☕	GW 1	GW 1	GW ◇1	GW 1	GW 1	HC	GW 1	GW ◇1 ☕	GW 1	GW ◇1 🍴	GW ◇1 ☕	GW 1	GW 1	HC	GW 1	GW ◇1 ☕	GW 1	GW ◇1
Oxford d				19 01				18 37			19 31					19 07			20 01
Reading 7 d	19 12	19 18	19 20	19 25				19 33	19 45	19 48	19 55	20 03				20 03	20 09	20 18	20 25
Twyford 3 d		19 24						19 39		19 54						20 09		20 24	
Maidenhead 3 d		19 32						19 47		20 02						20 17		20 32	
Taplow d		19 36								20 06								20 36	
Burnham d		19 39				←				20 09				←				20 39	
Slough 3 a		19 44		19 40		19 44		19 54		20 14	20 10			20 14		20 24		20 44	20 40
Slough 3 d		19 44		19 40		19 44		19 54		20 14	20 10			20 14		20 24		20 44	20 40
Langley d		→						19 58		→						20 28		→	
Iver d								20 01								20 31			
West Drayton d						19 51		20 05						20 21		20 35			
Heathrow Terminal 4 ✈ d																			
Heathrow Terminal 1-2-3 2 ✈ d							19 57								20 27				
Hayes & Harlington d						19 56	20 03	20 10						20 26	20 33	20 40			
Southall d							20 06	20 13							20 36	20 43			
Hanwell d							20 09								20 39				
Greenford ⊖ d					19 46								20 16						
South Greenford d					19 49								20 19						
Castle Bar Park d					19 52								20 22						
Drayton Green d					19 54								20 24						
West Ealing d					19 56		20 11						20 26		20 41				
Ealing Broadway ⊖ d					19 59	20 03	20 14	20 19					20 29	20 33	20 44	20 49			
Acton Main Line d					20 03								20 33						
London Paddington 15 ⊖ a	19 39		19 52	19 59	20 12	20 16	20 24	20 31	20 14		20 29	20 32	20 42	20 46	20 54	21 01	20 37		20 59

Reading and Greenford - London

Saturdays
15 September to 20 October

Network Diagram - see first Page of Table 116

Station		GW ■	GW ■	HC	GW ■	GW ◇■ 🍴	GW ◇■ 🍴	GW ■	GW ◇■	GW ◇■ 🍴	GW ■	GW ■	HC	GW ■	GW ◇■ 🍴	GW ■	GW ◇■	GW ■	GW ■	HC	GW ■
Oxford	d				19 37				20 31					20 07			21 01				20 37
Reading ■	d				20 33	20 39	20 45	20 48	20 54	21 01				21 05	21 09	21 21	21 25				21 33
Twyford ■	d				20 39			20 54						21 12		21 28					21 40
Maidenhead ■	d				20 47			21 02						21 20		21 36					21 48
Taplow	d							21 06								21 40					
Burnham	d		←					21 09				←				21 43			←		
Slough ■	a		20 44		20 54			21 14	21 09			21 14		21 27		21 47	21 40		21 47		21 55
	d		20 44		20 54			21 14	21 09			21 14		21 27		21 48	21 40		21 48		21 55
Langley	d				20 58			→						21 31		→					21 59
Iver	d				21 01									21 34							22 02
West Drayton	d		20 51		21 05							21 21		21 38					21 54		22 06
Heathrow Terminal 4 ✈	d																				
Heathrow Terminal 1-2-3 ✈	d			20 57									21 27							21 57	
Hayes & Harlington	d		20 56	21 03	21 10							21 26	21 33	21 43					21 59	22 03	22 11
Southall	d			21 06	21 13								21 36	21 46						22 06	22 14
Hanwell	d			21 09									21 39							22 09	
Greenford ⊖	d	20 46									21 16							21 46			
South Greenford	d	20 49									21 19							21 49			
Castle Bar Park	d	20 52									21 22							21 52			
Drayton Green	d	20 54									21 24							21 54			
West Ealing	d	20 56		21 11							21 26		21 41					21 56		22 11	
Ealing Broadway ⊖	d	20 59	21 03	21 14	21 19						21 29	21 33	21 44	21 52				21 59	22 06	22 14	22 20
Acton Main Line	d	21 03									21 33							22 03			
London Paddington ⊖	a	21 12	21 16	21 24	21 31	21 07	21 14		21 29	21 32	21 42	21 46	21 54	22 02	21 36		21 59	22 12	22 16	22 24	22 32

Station		GW ■	GW ◇■ 🍴	GW ◇■	GW ◇■ 🍴	HC	GW ■	GW ◇■	HC	GW ■	GW ■	GW ◇■ 🍴	GW ◇■	HC	GW ■	GW ◇■	GW ◇■ 🍴	GW ■
Oxford	d			21 31				22 01		21 50			22 35			23 01		23 07
Reading ■	d	21 48	21 53	22 02	22 06		22 20	22 32		22 36	22 48	23 05	23 09		23 18	23 31	23 51	00 03
Twyford ■	d	21 55					22 27			22 43	22 55				23 24			00 10
Maidenhead ■	d	22 03					22 34			22 51	23 03				23 32			00 18
Taplow	d	22 07					22 38				23 07				23 36			00 22
Burnham	d	22 10					22 41				23 10				23 39			00 25
Slough ■	a	22 14		22 15			22 46	22 46		22 58	23 15		23 26		23 44	23 45		00 29
	d	22 15		22 16			22 46	22 47		22 58	23 15		23 27		23 44	23 46		00 30
Langley	d									23 02								00 34
Iver	d									23 05								00 37
West Drayton	d	22 22					22 53			23 09	23 22				23 51			00 40
Heathrow Terminal 4 ✈	d																	
Heathrow Terminal 1-2-3 ✈	d					22 27			22 57					23 27				
Hayes & Harlington	d	22 26				22 33	22 58		23 03	23 14	23 27			23 33	23 56			00 45
Southall	d					22 36			23 06	23 17				23 36				00 48
Hanwell	d					22 39			23 09					23 39				
Greenford ⊖	d																	
South Greenford	d																	
Castle Bar Park	d																	
Drayton Green	d																	
West Ealing	d					22 41			23 11					23 41				
Ealing Broadway ⊖	d	22 33				22 44	23 05		23 14	23 23	23 34			23 44	00 03			00 54
Acton Main Line	d																	
London Paddington ⊖	a	22 46	22 22	22 33	22 37	22 54	23 17	23 05	23 24	23 32	23 46	23 36	23 46	23 54	00 16	00 10	00 34	01 04

Saturdays
from 27 October

Station		GW ■	GW ■	GW ◇■	HC	GW ◇■ 🍴	GW ■	GW ◇■	GW ■	GW ■	GW ■	HC	GW ■	HC	GW ■	GW ■	GW ■	HC	GW ■	GW ■	GW ■	HC
Oxford	d			23p09				00 07	00 27		03 59								05 14			
Reading ■	d	22p48	23p15	23p41		23p55	00 15	00 39	01 15	04 10	04 40		05 10		05 33		05 48		06 03		06 18	
Twyford ■	d	22p54	23p22				00 21		01 21	04 16	04 46		05 16		05 39		05 54		06 09		06 24	
Maidenhead ■	d	23p02	23p29	23p54			00 29		01 29	04 24	04 54		05 24		05 47		06 02		06 17		06 32	
Taplow	d	23p05	23p33				00 32						05 28				06 06				06 36	
Burnham	d	23p08	23p36				00 35						05 31				06 09				06 39	
Slough ■	a	23p13	23p41	00 01			00 40	00 55	01 37	04 31	05 01		05 35		05 54		06 14		06 24		06 44	
	d	23p27	23p41	00 02			00 40	00 56	01 37	04 32	05 02		05 36		05 54		06 14		06 24		06 44	
Langley	d	23p31	23p45				00 44						05 40		05 58				06 28			
Iver	d	23p34	23p48										05 43		06 01				06 31			
West Drayton	d	23p38	23p51				00 49			04 38			05 45		06 05		06 21		06 35		06 51	
Heathrow Terminal 4 ✈	d				00 01							05 23		05 51								
Heathrow Terminal 1-2-3 ✈	d				00 07							05 29		05 57				06 27				06 57
Hayes & Harlington	d	23p43	23p56		00 14		00 54		01 46	04 43	05 11	05 35	05 51	06 03	06 10		06 26	06 33	06 40		06 56	07 03
Southall	d	23p47	23p59		00 17		00 57			04 46	05 13	05 38	05 54	06 06	06 13			06 36	06 43			07 06
Hanwell	d											05 41		06 09				06 39				07 09
Greenford ⊖	d															06 16				06 46		
South Greenford	d															06 19				06 49		
Castle Bar Park	d															06 22				06 52		
Drayton Green	d															06 24				06 54		
West Ealing	d											05 43		06 11		06 26		06 41		06 56		07 11
Ealing Broadway ⊖	d	23p52	00 06		00 22		01 03		01 53	04 52	05 19	05 46	06 00	06 14	06 19	06 29	06 33	06 44	06 49	06 59	07 03	07 14
Acton Main Line	d										05 23		06 03			06 33				07 03		
London Paddington ⊖	a	00 02	00 17	00 28	00 30	00 33	01 14	01 17	02 05	05 01	05 31	05 56	06 11	06 24	06 31	06 42	06 46	06 54	07 01	07 12	07 16	07 24

Reading and Greenford - London

Saturdays
from 27 October

Network Diagram - see first Page of Table 116

Station		GW ■	GW ◇■ 🍴	GW ■	GW ■	GW ■	GW ◇■	HC	GW ■	GW ◇■ 🍴	GW ■	GW ■	GW ◇■	GW ◇■ 🍴	GW ■	GW ■	HC	GW ■	GW ◇■ 🍴	GW ■	GW ◇■ 🍴	GW ◇■ 🍴	GW ■
Oxford	d	05 49					06 31		06 07				07 01					06 42			07 31		
Reading ■	d	06 33	06 45		06 48	06 52	07 00		07 03	07 15	07 18	07 21	07 27	07 32				07 33	07 46	07 48	07 54	08 02	
Twyford ■	d	06 39			06 54				07 09		07 24							07 39		07 54			
Maidenhead ■	d	06 47			07 02				07 17		07 32							07 47		08 02			
Taplow	d				07 06						07 36									08 06			
Burnham	d				07 09						07 39					←				08 09			
Slough ■	a	06 54			07 14		07 16		07 24		07 44		07 42			07 44		07 54		08 14	08 09		
	d	06 54			07 14		07 17		07 24		07 44		07 42			07 44		07 54		08 14	08 09		
Langley	d	06 58							07 28		→							07 58		→			
Iver	d	07 01							07 31									08 01					
West Drayton	d	07 05			07 21				07 35							07 51		08 05					
Heathrow Terminal 4 ✈	d																						
Heathrow Terminal 1-2-3 ✈	d							07 27									07 57						
Hayes & Harlington	d	07 10			07 26			07 33	07 40							07 56	08 03	08 10					
Southall	d	07 13						07 36	07 43								08 06	08 13					
Hanwell	d							07 39									08 09						
Greenford ⊖	d			07 16											07 46								08 16
South Greenford	d			07 19											07 49								08 19
Castle Bar Park	d			07 22											07 52								08 22
Drayton Green	d			07 24											07 54								08 24
West Ealing	d			07 26				07 41							07 56		08 11						08 26
Ealing Broadway ⊖	d	07 19		07 29	07 33			07 44	07 49						07 59	08 03	08 14	08 19					08 29
Acton Main Line	d			07 33											08 03								08 33
London Paddington ⊖	a	07 31	07 14	07 42	07 46	07 22	07 37	07 54	08 01	07 44		07 54	08 01	08 07	08 12	08 16	08 24	08 31	08 14		08 29	08 32	08 42

Station		GW ■	HC	GW ■	GW ◇■ 🍴	GW ■	GW ■	GW ◇■	GW ◇■ 🍴	GW ■	GW ■	HC	GW ■	GW ◇■ 🍴	GW ■	GW ◇■ 🍴	GW ◇■ 🍴	GW ◇■ 🍴	GW ■	GW ■
Oxford	d			07 07				08 01					07 37				08 31			
Reading ■	d			08 03	08 16	08 18	08 20	08 26	08 32				08 33	08 46	08 48	08 52	08 55	09 02		
Twyford ■	d			08 09		08 24							08 39		08 54					
Maidenhead ■	d			08 17		08 32							08 47		09 02					
Taplow	d					08 36									09 06					
Burnham	d	←				08 39					←				09 09					←
Slough ■	a	08 14		08 24		08 44		08 40			08 44		08 54		09 14		09 09			09 14
	d	08 14		08 24		08 44		08 41			08 44		08 54		09 14		09 11			09 14
Langley	d			08 28		→							08 58		→					
Iver	d			08 31									09 01							
West Drayton	d	08 21		08 35							08 51		09 05							09 21
Heathrow Terminal 4 ✈	d																			
Heathrow Terminal 1-2-3 ✈	d		08 27									08 57								
Hayes & Harlington	d	08 26	08 33	08 40							08 56	09 03	09 10							09 26
Southall	d		08 36	08 43								09 06	09 13							
Hanwell	d		08 39									09 09								
Greenford ⊖	d									08 46									09 16	
South Greenford	d									08 49									09 19	
Castle Bar Park	d									08 52									09 22	
Drayton Green	d									08 54									09 24	
West Ealing	d		08 41							08 56		09 11							09 26	
Ealing Broadway ⊖	d	08 33	08 44	08 49						08 59	09 03	09 14	09 19						09 29	09 33
Acton Main Line	d									09 03									09 33	
London Paddington ⊖	a	08 46	08 54	09 01	08 44		08 52	08 59	09 02	09 12	09 16	09 24	09 31	09 14		09 21	09 29	09 32	09 42	09 46

Station		HC	GW ■	GW ◇■ 🍴	GW ◇■ 🍴	GW ■	GW ■	GW ◇■ trolley	GW ◇■ 🍴	GW ■	GW ■	HC	GW ■	GW ◇■ 🍴	GW ◇■ 🍴	GW ■	GW ◇■ A 🍴⊘	GW ◇■ 🍴	GW ■	GW ■	HC	GW ■
Oxford	d		08 07					09 01					08 37				09 31					09 07
Reading ■	d		09 03	09 09	09 16	09 18	09 20	09 24	09 33				09 33	09 42	09 46	09 48	09 55	10 02				10 03
Twyford ■	d		09 09			09 24							09 39			09 54						10 09
Maidenhead ■	d		09 17			09 32							09 47			10 02						10 17
Taplow	d					09 36										10 06						
Burnham	d					09 39					←					10 09				←		
Slough ■	a		09 24			09 44		09 40			09 44		09 54			10 14	10 09			10 14		10 24
	d		09 24			09 44		09 40			09 44		09 54			10 14	10 10			10 14		10 24
Langley	d		09 28			→							09 58			→						10 28
Iver	d		09 31										10 01									10 31
West Drayton	d		09 35								09 51		10 05							10 21		10 35
Heathrow Terminal 4 ✈	d																					
Heathrow Terminal 1-2-3 ✈	d	09 27										09 57									10 27	
Hayes & Harlington	d	09 33	09 40								09 56	10 03	10 10							10 26	10 33	10 40
Southall	d	09 36	09 43									10 06	10 13								10 36	10 43
Hanwell	d	09 39										10 09									10 39	
Greenford ⊖	d									09 46									10 16			
South Greenford	d									09 49									10 19			
Castle Bar Park	d									09 52									10 22			
Drayton Green	d									09 54									10 24			
West Ealing	d	09 41								09 56		10 11							10 26		10 41	
Ealing Broadway ⊖	d	09 44	09 49							09 59	10 03	10 14	10 19						10 29	10 33	10 44	10 49
Acton Main Line	d									10 03									10 33			
London Paddington ⊖	a	09 54	10 01	09 37	09 44		09 52	09 59	10 02	10 12	10 16	10 24	10 31	10 11	10 14		10 29	10 32	10 42	10 46	10 54	11 01

A 🍴 from Reading ⊘ to Reading

Table 117

Saturdays
from 27 October

Reading and Greenford - London

Network Diagram - see first Page of Table 116

	GW	GW	GW	GW	GW	GW	GW	HC	GW	GW	GW	GW	GW	GW	GW	GW	GW	HC	GW
	◇■1 ⊡	■1	■1	◇■1 ⌶	◇■1 ⊡	■1	■1		■1	◇■1 ⊡	◇■1 ⊡	■1	◇■1 ⊡	◇■1 ⊡	◇■1 ⊡	■1	■1		■1
Oxford d				10 01					09 37					10 31					10 07
Reading ■7 d	10 13	10 18	10 18	10 25	10 33				10 33	10 39	10 46	10 48	10 53	10 55	11 02				11 03
Twyford ■3 d			10 24						10 39			10 54							11 09
Maidenhead ■3 d			10 32						10 47			11 02							11 17
Taplow d			10 36									11 06							
Burnham d			10 39				←					11 09					←		
Slough ■3 a			10 44	10 40			10 44		10 54			11 14		11 09			11 14		11 24
d			10 44	10 40			10 44		10 54			11 14		11 10			11 14		11 24
Langley d			→						10 58			→							11 28
Iver d									11 01										11 31
West Drayton d							10 51		11 05								11 21		11 35
Heathrow Terminal 4 ✈ d																			
Heathrow Terminal 1-2-3 ■2✈ d								10 57										11 27	
Hayes & Harlington d							10 56	11 03	11 10								11 26	11 33	11 40
Southall d								11 06	11 13									11 36	11 43
Hanwell d								11 09										11 39	
Greenford ⊖ d						10 46										11 16			
South Greenford d						10 49										11 19			
Castle Bar Park d						10 52										11 22			
Drayton Green d						10 54										11 24			
West Ealing d						10 56		11 11								11 26		11 41	
Ealing Broadway ⊖ d						10 59	11 03	11 14	11 19							11 29	11 33	11 44	11 49
Acton Main Line d						11 03										11 33			
London Paddington ■15 ⊖ a	10 39	10 52		10 59	11 02	11 12	11 16	11 24	11 31	11 08	11 14		11 24	11 29	11 33	11 42	11 46	11 54	12 01

	GW	GW	GW	GW	GW	GW	HC	GW	GW	GW	GW	GW	GW	GW	GW	HC	GW	GW	GW	GW
	◇■1 ⊡	■1	■1	◇■1	■1	■1		■1	◇■1 ⊡	■1	■2 ■1 ⊡	◇■1 ⌶	◇■1 ⊡	■1	■1		■1	◇■1 ⊡	■1	■1
Oxford d				11 01				10 37				11 31					11 07			
Reading ■7 d	11 14	11 18	11 21	11 25				11 33	11 45	11 48	11 53	11 55	12 02				12 03	12 13	12 18	12 18
Twyford ■3 d		11 24						11 39		11 54							12 09			12 24
Maidenhead ■3 d		11 32						11 47		12 02							12 17			12 32
Taplow d		11 36								12 06										12 36
Burnham d		11 39				←				12 09					←					12 39
Slough ■3 a		11 44		11 39		11 44		11 54		12 14		12 09			12 14		12 24			12 44
d		11 44		11 40		11 44		11 54		12 14		12 11			12 14		12 24			12 44
Langley d		→						11 58		→							12 28			→
Iver d								12 01									12 31			
West Drayton d						11 51		12 05							12 21		12 35			
Heathrow Terminal 4 ✈ d																				
Heathrow Terminal 1-2-3 ■2✈ d							11 57									12 27				
Hayes & Harlington d						11 56	12 03	12 10							12 26	12 33	12 40			
Southall d							12 06	12 13								12 36	12 43			
Hanwell d							12 09									12 39				
Greenford ⊖ d					11 46									12 16						
South Greenford d					11 49									12 19						
Castle Bar Park d					11 52									12 22						
Drayton Green d					11 54									12 24						
West Ealing d					11 56		12 11							12 26		12 41				
Ealing Broadway ⊖ d					11 59	12 03	12 14	12 19						12 29	12 33	12 44	12 49			
Acton Main Line d					12 03									12 33						
London Paddington ■15 ⊖ a	11 40		11 52	11 59	12 12	12 16	12 24	12 31	12 14		12 23	12 29	12 32	12 42	12 46	12 54	13 01	12 39	12 52	

	GW	GW	GW	HC	GW	GW	GW	GW	GW	GW	GW	GW	GW	HC	GW	GW	GW	GW	GW	GW
	◇■1 ⌶	■1	■1		■1	◇■1 ⊡	◇■1 ⊡	■1	◇■1 ⊡	◇■1 ⌶	◇■1 ⊡	■1	■1		■1	◇■1 ⊡	■1	◇■1 ⊡	◇■1 ⌶	■1
Oxford d	12 01				11 37					12 31					12 07				13 01	
Reading ■7 d	12 25				12 33	12 39	12 45	12 48	12 54	12 55	13 02				13 03	13 12	13 18	13 20	13 25	
Twyford ■3 d					12 39			12 54							13 09		13 24			
Maidenhead ■3 d					12 47			13 02							13 17		13 32			
Taplow d								13 06									13 36			
Burnham d			←					13 09					←				13 39			
Slough ■3 a	12 40		12 44		12 54			13 14		13 09			13 14		13 24		13 44		13 40	
d	12 40		12 44		12 54			13 14		13 11			13 14		13 24		13 44		13 40	
Langley d					12 58			→							13 28		→			
Iver d					13 01										13 31					
West Drayton d			12 51		13 05								13 21		13 35					
Heathrow Terminal 4 ✈ d																				
Heathrow Terminal 1-2-3 ■2✈ d				12 57										13 27						
Hayes & Harlington d			12 56	13 03	13 10								13 26	13 33	13 40					
Southall d				13 06	13 13									13 36	13 43					
Hanwell d				13 09										13 39						
Greenford ⊖ d		12 46										13 16								13 46
South Greenford d		12 49										13 19								13 49
Castle Bar Park d		12 52										13 22								13 52
Drayton Green d		12 54										13 24								13 54
West Ealing d		12 56		13 11								13 26		13 41						13 56
Ealing Broadway ⊖ d		12 59	13 03	13 14	13 19							13 29	13 33	13 44	13 49					13 59
Acton Main Line d		13 03										13 33								14 03
London Paddington ■15 ⊖ a	12 59	13 12	13 16	13 24	13 31	13 07	13 12		13 21	13 30	13 33	13 42	13 46	13 54	14 01	13 41		13 46	13 59	14 12

Table 117

Saturdays
from 27 October

Reading and Greenford - London

Network Diagram - see first Page of Table 116

	GW	HC	GW	GW	GW	GW	GW	GW	GW	GW	HC	GW	GW	GW	GW	GW	GW	GW	HC	GW
	■1		■1	◇■1 ⊡	■1	■1	◇■1	◇■1 ⊡	■1	■1		■1	◇■1 ⊡	■1	◇■1 ⊡	◇■1 ⌶	■1	■1		■1
Oxford d			12 37				13 31					13 07				14 01				13 37
Reading ■7 d			13 33	13 45	13 48	13 51	13 55	14 02				14 03	14 13	14 18	14 19	14 25				14 33
Twyford ■3 d			13 39		13 54							14 09		14 24						14 39
Maidenhead ■3 d			13 47		14 02							14 17		14 32						14 47
Taplow d					14 06									14 36						
Burnham d	←				14 09					←				14 39				←		
Slough ■3 a	13 44		13 54		14 14		14 09			14 14		14 24		14 44		14 40		14 44		14 54
d	13 44		13 54		14 14		14 10			14 14		14 24		14 44		14 40		14 44		14 54
Langley d			13 58		→							14 28		→						14 58
Iver d			14 01									14 31								15 01
West Drayton d	13 51		14 05							14 21		14 35						14 51		15 05
Heathrow Terminal 4 ✈ d																				
Heathrow Terminal 1-2-3 ■2✈ d		13 57									14 27								14 57	
Hayes & Harlington d	13 56	14 03	14 10							14 26	14 33	14 40						14 56	15 03	15 10
Southall d		14 06	14 13								14 36	14 43							15 06	15 13
Hanwell d		14 09									14 39								15 09	
Greenford ⊖ d									14 16								14 46			
South Greenford d									14 19								14 49			
Castle Bar Park d									14 22								14 52			
Drayton Green d									14 24								14 54			
West Ealing d		14 11							14 26		14 41						14 56		15 11	
Ealing Broadway ⊖ d	14 03	14 14	14 19						14 29	14 33	14 44	14 49					14 59	15 03	15 14	15 19
Acton Main Line d									14 33								15 03			
London Paddington ■15 ⊖ a	14 16	14 24	14 31	14 14		14 23	14 29	14 32	14 42	14 46	14 54	15 01	14 39		14 45	14 59	15 12	15 16	15 24	15 31

	GW	GW	GW	GW	GW	GW	GW	GW	HC	GW	GW	GW	GW	GW	GW	GW	HC	GW	GW	GW
	◇■1 ⊡	◇■1 ⊡	■1	◇■1 ⊡	◇■1 ⊡	◇■1 ⊡	■1	■1		■1	◇■1 ⊡	■1	■1	◇■1	■1	■1		■1	◇■1 ⊡	■1
Oxford d					14 31					14 07				15 01				14 37		
Reading ■7 d	14 39	14 45	14 48	14 53	14 55	15 02				15 03	15 12	15 18	15 19	15 25				15 33	15 45	15 48
Twyford ■3 d			14 54							15 09		15 24						15 39		15 54
Maidenhead ■3 d			15 02							15 17		15 32						15 47		16 02
Taplow d			15 06									15 36								16 06
Burnham d			15 09					←				15 39				←				16 09
Slough ■3 a			15 14		15 10			15 14		15 24		15 44		15 40		15 44		15 54		16 14
d			15 14		15 11			15 14		15 24		15 44		15 40		15 44		15 54		16 14
Langley d			→							15 28		→						15 58		→
Iver d										15 31								16 01		
West Drayton d								15 21		15 35						15 51		16 05		
Heathrow Terminal 4 ✈ d																				
Heathrow Terminal 1-2-3 ■2✈ d									15 27								15 57			
Hayes & Harlington d								15 26	15 33	15 40						15 56	16 03	16 10		
Southall d									15 36	15 43							16 06	16 13		
Hanwell d									15 39								16 09			
Greenford ⊖ d							15 16								15 46					
South Greenford d							15 19								15 49					
Castle Bar Park d							15 22								15 52					
Drayton Green d							15 24								15 54					
West Ealing d							15 26		15 41						15 56		16 11			
Ealing Broadway ⊖ d							15 29	15 33	15 44	15 49					15 59	16 03	16 14	16 19		
Acton Main Line d							15 33								16 03					
London Paddington ■15 ⊖ a	15 09	15 14		15 22	15 29	15 32	15 42	15 46	15 54	16 01	15 39		15 54	15 59	16 12	16 16	16 24	16 31	16 14	

	GW	GW	GW	GW	GW	HC	GW	GW	GW	GW	GW	GW	GW	HC	GW	GW	GW	GW	GW
	◇■1 ⊡	◇■1 ⌶	◇■1 ⊡	■1	■1		■1	◇■1 ⊡	■1	■1	◇■1	■1	■1		■1	◇■1 ⊡	◇■1 ⊡	■1	◇■1 ⊡
Oxford d		15 31					15 07				16 01				15 37				
Reading ■7 d	15 53	15 55	16 01				16 03	16 13	16 18	16 18	16 26				16 33	16 39	16 45	16 48	16 51
Twyford ■3 d							16 09			16 24					16 39			16 54	
Maidenhead ■3 d							16 17			16 32					16 47			17 02	
Taplow d										16 36								17 06	
Burnham d					←					16 39			←					17 09	
Slough ■3 a		16 10			16 14		16 24			16 44	16 40		16 44		16 54			17 14	
d		16 11			16 14		16 24			16 44	16 41		16 44		16 54			17 14	
Langley d							16 28			→					16 58			→	
Iver d							16 31								17 01				
West Drayton d					16 21		16 35						16 51		17 05				
Heathrow Terminal 4 ✈ d																			
Heathrow Terminal 1-2-3 ■2✈ d						16 27								16 57					
Hayes & Harlington d					16 26	16 33	16 40						16 56	17 03	17 10				
Southall d						16 36	16 43							17 06	17 13				
Hanwell d						16 39								17 09					
Greenford ⊖ d				16 16								16 46							
South Greenford d				16 19								16 49							
Castle Bar Park d				16 22								16 52							
Drayton Green d				16 24								16 54							
West Ealing d				16 26		16 41						16 56		17 11					
Ealing Broadway ⊖ d				16 29	16 33	16 44	16 49					16 59	17 03	17 14	17 19				
Acton Main Line d				16 33								17 03							
London Paddington ■15 ⊖ a	16 23	16 29	16 32	16 42	16 46	16 54	17 01	16 39	16 52		16 59	17 12	17 16	17 24	17 31	17 07	17 14		17 21

Reading and Greenford - London

Saturdays from 27 October

Network Diagram - see first Page of Table 116

		GW ◇1 🍴	GW ◇1 ☕	GW 1	GW 1	HC	GW 1		GW ◇1 ☕	GW ◇1 ☕		GW 1	GW ◇1	GW 1	GW 1	HC	GW 1	GW ◇1 ☕	GW 1	GW ◇1 ☕		GW ◇1 ☕	GW ◇1 ☕	GW 1	GW 1
Oxford	d	16 31					16 07						17 01				16 37					17 31			
Reading 7	d	16 55	17 02				17 03		17 12	17 18		17 18	17 27				17 33	17 45	17 48	17 54		17 57	18 02		
Twyford 3	d						17 09					17 24					17 39		17 54						
Maidenhead 3	d						17 17					17 32					17 47		18 02						
Taplow	d											17 36							18 06						
Burnham	d				←							17 39			←				18 09						←
Slough 3	a	17 10			17 14		17 24					17 44	17 41		17 44		17 54		18 14			18 10			18 14
	d	17 11			17 14		17 24					17 44	17 42		17 44		17 54		18 14			18 11			18 14
Langley	d						17 28					→					17 58		→						
Iver	d						17 31										18 01								
West Drayton	d				17 21		17 35								17 51		18 05								18 21
Heathrow Terminal 4 ✈	d																								
Heathrow Terminal 1-2-3 2 ✈	d					17 27										17 57									
Hayes & Harlington	d				17 26	17 33	17 40								17 56	18 03	18 10								18 26
Southall	d					17 36	17 43									18 06	18 13								
Hanwell	d					17 39										18 09									
Greenford ⊖	d			17 16										17 46										18 16	
South Greenford	d			17 19										17 49										18 19	
Castle Bar Park	d			17 22										17 52										18 22	
Drayton Green	d			17 24										17 54										18 24	
West Ealing	d			17 26		17 41								17 56		18 11								18 26	
Ealing Broadway ⊖	d			17 29	17 33	17 44	17 49							17 59	18 03	18 14	18 19							18 29	18 33
Acton Main Line	d			17 33										18 03										18 33	
London Paddington 15 ⊖	a	17 29	17 32	17 42	17 46	17 54	18 01		17 38	17 51			18 00	18 12	18 16	18 24	18 31	18 14		18 21		18 29	18 32	18 42	18 46

		HC	GW 1		GW ◇1 ☕	GW 1		GW 1	GW ◇1	GW 1	GW 1	HC	GW 1		GW ◇1 ☕	GW ◇1 ☕		GW 1	GW ◇1 ☕	GW ◇1 🍴	GW ◇1 ☕	GW 1	GW 1	HC	GW 1
Oxford	d		17 07						18 01				17 37							18 31					18 07
Reading 7	d		18 03		18 13	18 18		18 19	18 25				18 33		18 39	18 45		18 48	18 50	18 56	19 02				19 03
Twyford 3	d		18 09			18 24							18 39					18 54							19 09
Maidenhead 3	d		18 17			18 32							18 47					19 02							19 17
Taplow	d					18 36												19 06							
Burnham	d					18 39					←							19 09					←		
Slough 3	a		18 24			18 44			18 40		18 44		18 54					19 14		19 10			19 14		19 24
	d		18 24			18 44			18 40		18 44		18 54					19 14		19 11			19 14		19 24
Langley	d		18 28			→							18 58					→							19 28
Iver	d		18 31										19 01												19 31
West Drayton	d		18 35								18 51		19 05										19 21		19 35
Heathrow Terminal 4 ✈	d																								
Heathrow Terminal 1-2-3 2 ✈	d	18 27										18 57												19 27	
Hayes & Harlington	d	18 33	18 40								18 56	19 03	19 10										19 26	19 33	19 40
Southall	d	18 36	18 43									19 06	19 13											19 36	19 43
Hanwell	d	18 39										19 09												19 39	
Greenford ⊖	d									18 46												19 16			
South Greenford	d									18 49												19 19			
Castle Bar Park	d									18 52												19 22			
Drayton Green	d									18 54												19 24			
West Ealing	d	18 41								18 56		19 11										19 26		19 41	
Ealing Broadway ⊖	d	18 44	18 49							18 59	19 03	19 14	19 19									19 29	19 33	19 44	19 49
Acton Main Line	d									19 03												19 33			
London Paddington 15 ⊖	a	18 54	19 01		18 39			18 52	18 59	19 12	19 16	19 24	19 31		19 08	19 14			19 22	19 29	19 32	19 42	19 46	19 54	20 01

				GW ◇1 ☕	GW 1	GW 1	GW ◇1	GW 1	GW 1	HC	GW 1	GW ◇1 ☕		GW 1	GW ◇1 🍴	GW ◇1 ☕	GW 1	GW 1	HC	GW 1		GW ◇1 ☕		GW 1	GW ◇1
Oxford	d						19 01				18 37				19 31					19 07					20 01
Reading 7	d			19 12	19 18	19 20	19 25				19 33	19 45		19 48	19 55	20 03				20 03		20 09		20 18	20 25
Twyford 3	d				19 24						19 39			19 54						20 09				20 24	
Maidenhead 3	d				19 32						19 47			20 02						20 17				20 32	
Taplow	d				19 36									20 06										20 36	
Burnham	d				19 39				←					20 09				←						20 39	
Slough 3	a				19 44		19 40		19 44		19 54			20 14	20 10			20 14		20 24				20 44	20 40
	d				19 44		19 40		19 44		19 54			20 14	20 10			20 14		20 24				20 44	20 40
Langley	d				→						19 58			→						20 28				→	
Iver	d										20 01									20 31					
West Drayton	d								19 51		20 05							20 21		20 35					
Heathrow Terminal 4 ✈	d																								
Heathrow Terminal 1-2-3 2 ✈	d									19 57									20 27						
Hayes & Harlington	d								19 56	20 03	20 10							20 26	20 33	20 40					
Southall	d									20 06	20 13								20 36	20 43					
Hanwell	d									20 09									20 39						
Greenford ⊖	d							19 46									20 16								
South Greenford	d							19 49									20 19								
Castle Bar Park	d							19 52									20 22								
Drayton Green	d							19 54									20 24								
West Ealing	d							19 56		20 11							20 26		20 41						
Ealing Broadway ⊖	d							19 59	20 03	20 14	20 19						20 29	20 33	20 44	20 49					
Acton Main Line	d							20 03									20 33								
London Paddington 15 ⊖	a			19 39		19 52	19 59	20 12	20 16	20 24	20 31	20 14			20 29	20 32	20 42	20 46	20 54	21 01		20 37			20 59

Reading and Greenford - London

Saturdays from 27 October

Network Diagram - see first Page of Table 116

		GW 1	GW 1	HC	GW 1	GW ◇1 ☕	GW ◇1 ☕	GW 1		GW ◇1	GW ◇1 ☕	GW 1	GW 1	HC	GW 1		GW ◇1 ☕	GW 1		GW ◇1	GW 1	GW 1	HC	GW 1	
Oxford	d				19 37					20 31					20 07					21 01				20 37	
Reading 7	d				20 33	20 39	20 45	20 48		20 54	21 01				21 05		21 09	21 21		21 25				21 33	
Twyford 3	d				20 39			20 54							21 12			21 28						21 40	
Maidenhead 3	d				20 47			21 02							21 20			21 36						21 48	
Taplow	d							21 06										21 40							
Burnham	d		←					21 09					←					21 43				←			
Slough 3	a		20 44		20 54			21 14		21 09			21 14		21 27			21 47		21 40		21 47		21 55	
	d		20 44		20 54			21 14		21 09			21 14		21 27			21 48		21 40		21 48		21 55	
Langley	d				20 58			→							21 31			→						21 59	
Iver	d				21 01										21 34									22 02	
West Drayton	d		20 51		21 05								21 21		21 38							21 54		22 06	
Heathrow Terminal 4 ✈	d																								
Heathrow Terminal 1-2-3 2 ✈	d			20 57										21 27									21 57		
Hayes & Harlington	d		20 56	21 03	21 10								21 26	21 33	21 43							21 59	22 03	22 11	
Southall	d			21 06	21 13									21 36	21 46								22 06	22 14	
Hanwell	d			21 09										21 39									22 09		
Greenford ⊖	d	20 46										21 16									21 46				
South Greenford	d	20 49										21 19									21 49				
Castle Bar Park	d	20 52										21 22									21 52				
Drayton Green	d	20 54										21 24									21 54				
West Ealing	d	20 56		21 11								21 26		21 41							21 56		22 11		
Ealing Broadway ⊖	d	20 59	21 03	21 14	21 19							21 29	21 33	21 44	21 52						21 59	22 06	22 14	22 20	
Acton Main Line	d	21 03										21 33									22 03				
London Paddington 15 ⊖	a	21 12	21 16	21 24	21 31	21 07	21 14			21 29	21 32	21 42	21 46	21 54	22 02		21 36			21 59	22 12	22 16	22 24	22 32	

		GW 1	GW ◇1 ☕	GW ◇1			GW ◇1 ☕	HC	GW 1	GW ◇1	HC	GW 1		GW 1		GW ◇1 ☕	GW ◇1	HC	GW 1	GW ◇1	GW ◇1 ☕	GW 1			
Oxford	d			21 31						22 01		21 50					22 35			23 01		23 07			
Reading 7	d	21 48	21 53	22 02			22 06		22 20	22 32		22 36		22 48		23 05	23 09		23 18	23 29	23 53	00 03			
Twyford 3	d	21 55							22 27			22 43		22 55					23 24			00 10			
Maidenhead 3	d	22 03							22 34			22 51		23 03					23 32			00 18			
Taplow	d	22 07							22 38					23 07					23 36			00 22			
Burnham	d	22 10							22 41					23 10					23 39			00 25			
Slough 3	a	22 14		22 15					22 46	22 46		22 58		23 15			23 26		23 44	23 45		00 29			
	d	22 15		22 16					22 46	22 47		22 58		23 15			23 27		23 44	23 46		00 30			
Langley	d											23 02										00 34			
Iver	d											23 05										00 37			
West Drayton	d	22 22							22 53			23 09		23 22					23 51			00 40			
Heathrow Terminal 4 ✈	d																								
Heathrow Terminal 1-2-3 2 ✈	d							22 27			22 57							23 27							
Hayes & Harlington	d	22 26						22 33	22 58		23 03	23 14		23 27				23 33	23 56			00 45			
Southall	d							22 36			23 06	23 17						23 36				00 48			
Hanwell	d							22 39			23 09							23 39							
Greenford ⊖	d																								
South Greenford	d																								
Castle Bar Park	d																								
Drayton Green	d																								
West Ealing	d							22 41			23 11							23 41							
Ealing Broadway ⊖	d	22 33						22 44	23 05		23 14	23 23		23 34				23 44	00 03			00 54			
Acton Main Line	d																								
London Paddington 15 ⊖	a	22 46	22 22	22 33			22 37	22 54	23 17	23 05	23 24	23 32		23 46		23 36	23 46	23 54	00 16	00 10	00 33	01 04			

Sundays until 24 June

		GW 1	GW ◇1	HC	GW ◇1 ☕	GW 1	HC	GW 1	HC	GW 1		HC	GW 1	GW 1	HC	GW 1	GW ◇1 ☕	GW 1	GW ◇1	GW ◇1 ☕		GW 1	GW ◇1 ☕	HC	GW 1
Oxford	d		23p01			23p07										08 05			08 50						09 01
Reading 7	d	23p18	23p29		23p51	00 03		06 22		07 22			08 03	08 18		08 52	09 03	09 18	09 23	09 29			09 47		09 52
Twyford 3	d	23p24				00 10		06 28		07 28				08 24		08 58		09 24							09 58
Maidenhead 3	d	23p32				00 18		06 36		07 36				08 36		09 06		09 36							10 06
Taplow	d	23p36				00 22																			
Burnham	d	23p39				00 25		06 40		07 40				08 40				09 40				←			
Slough 3	a	23p44	23p45			00 30		06 45		07 45			08 22	08 45		09 14		09 45	09 38			09 45			10 14
	d	23p44	23p46			00 30		06 46		07 46			08 23	08 46		09 18		09 48	09 38			09 48			10 18
Langley	d					00 34		06 50		07 50				08 50		09 23		→				09 50			10 23
Iver	d					00 37																			
West Drayton	d	23p51				00 40		06 55		07 55				08 55		09 30						09 56			10 30
Heathrow Terminal 4 ✈	d			00 01			06 07		07 07			08 07			09 07									10 07	
Heathrow Terminal 1-2-3 2 ✈	d			00 07			06 13		07 13			08 13			09 13									10 13	
Hayes & Harlington	d	23p56		00 13		00 45	06 19	07 02	07 19	08 02		08 19		09 02	09 19	09 34						10 01		10 19	10 34
Southall	d			00 16		00 48	06 22	07 05	07 22	08 05		08 22		09 05	09 22	09 37								10 23	10 37
Hanwell	d																								
Greenford ⊖	d																								
South Greenford	d																								
Castle Bar Park	d																								
Drayton Green	d																								
West Ealing	d																								
Ealing Broadway ⊖	d	00 03		00 21		00 54	06 27	07 11	07 27	08 11		08 27		09 11	09 27	09 42						10 08		10 28	10 42
Acton Main Line	d																								
London Paddington 15 ⊖	a	00 16	00 10	00 30	00 33	01 03	06 36	07 20	07 36	08 20		08 36	08 44	09 20	09 36	09 52	09 44		10 00	10 07		10 18	10 22	10 36	10 51

Table 117

Reading and Greenford - London

Sundays until 24 June

Network Diagram - see first Page of Table 116

	GW ◇1 ⊡	GW 1	GW ◇1	GW 1	GW ◇1 ⊡	HC	GW 1	GW ◇1 ⊡	GW ◇1 ⊡	GW ◇1	GW 1	GW ◇1	GW 1	GW ◇1 ⊡	GW ◇1 ⊡	HC	GW 1	GW ◇1 ⊡	GW 1	GW ◇1
Oxford d			09 48				10 05			10 44		10 55					11 05			11 50
Reading 7 d	10 00	10 19	10 22		10 44		10 52	10 54	11 02	11 14	11 18	11 23		11 47	11 51		11 52	12 05	12 18	12 23
Twyford 3 d		10 25					10 58			11 21	11 24						11 58		12 24	
Maidenhead 3 d		10 38					11 06			11 29	11 32						12 06		12 36	
Taplow d																				
Burnham d		10 43		←							11 37		←						12 40	
Slough 3 a		10 47	10 37	10 47			11 16			11 35	11 41	11 37	11 41				12 14		12 45	12 38
d		10 48	10 37	10 48			11 18			11 36	11 48	11 38	11 48				12 18		12 48	12 39
Langley d		→		10 50			11 23				→		11 50				12 23		→	
Iver d																				
West Drayton d				10 56			11 30						11 56				12 30			
Heathrow Terminal 4 ✈ d						11 07										12 07				
Heathrow Terminal 1-2-3 2 ✈ d						11 13										12 13				
Hayes & Harlington d				11 01		11 19	11 34						12 01			12 19	12 34			
Southall d						11 22	11 37									12 22	12 37			
Hanwell d																				
Greenford ⊖ d																				
South Greenford d																				
Castle Bar Park d																				
Drayton Green d																				
West Ealing d																				
Ealing Broadway ⊖ d				11 08		11 27	11 42						12 08			12 27	12 42			
Acton Main Line d																				
London Paddington 15 ⊖ a	10 44		10 58	11 18	11 22	11 36	11 51	11 29	11 44	11 58		12 01	12 18	12 22	12 29	12 36	12 51	12 42		13 03

	GW 1	GW ◇1 ⊡	HC	GW 1	GW ◇1 ⊡	GW 1	GW ◇1 ⊡	GW ◇1 ⊡	GW ◇1	GW 1	GW ◇1 ⊡	HC	GW 1	GW ◇1 ⊡	GW ◇1 ⊡	GW 1	GW ◇1	GW 1	GW ◇1 ⊡
Oxford d				12 05					12 50				13 05				13 50		
Reading 7 d		12 44		12 52	13 02	13 18	13 19	13 21	13 25		13 47		13 52	13 56	14 06	14 18	14 21		14 48
Twyford 3 d				12 58		13 24							13 58			14 24			
Maidenhead 3 d				13 06		13 36							14 06			14 36			
Taplow d																			
Burnham d	←					13 40				←						14 40		←	
Slough 3 a	12 45			13 14		13 45			13 41	13 45			14 14			14 45	14 37	14 45	
d	12 48			13 18		13 48			13 41	13 48			14 18			14 48	14 37	14 48	
Langley d	12 50			13 23		→				13 50			14 23			→		14 50	
Iver d																			
West Drayton d	12 56			13 30						13 56			14 30					14 56	
Heathrow Terminal 4 ✈ d			13 07									14 07							
Heathrow Terminal 1-2-3 2 ✈ d			13 13									14 13							
Hayes & Harlington d	13 01		13 19	13 34						14 01		14 19	14 34					15 01	
Southall d			13 22	13 37								14 22	14 37						
Hanwell d																			
Greenford ⊖ d																			
South Greenford d																			
Castle Bar Park d																			
Drayton Green d																			
West Ealing d																			
Ealing Broadway ⊖ d	13 08		13 27	13 42						14 08		14 27	14 42					15 08	
Acton Main Line d																			
London Paddington 15 ⊖ a	13 18	13 22	13 36	13 51	13 42		13 59	14 02	14 05	14 19	14 22	14 36	14 51	14 33	14 43		14 59	15 18	15 21

	HC	GW 1	GW ◇1 ⊡	GW ◇1 ⊡	GW 1	GW ◇1 ⊡	GW ◇1	GW 1	GW ◇1 ⊡	HC	GW 1	GW ◇1 ⊡	GW 1	GW ◇1 ⊡	GW ◇1 ⊡	GW 1	GW ◇1 ⊡	HC	GW 1
Oxford d		14 05					14 50				15 05				15 50				16 05
Reading 7 d		14 52	14 54	15 07	15 18	15 20	15 26		15 49		15 52	16 02	16 18	16 20	16 23		16 47		16 52
Twyford 3 d		14 58			15 24						15 58		16 26						16 58
Maidenhead 3 d		15 06			15 36						16 06		16 36						17 06
Taplow d																			
Burnham d					15 40			←			16 11		16 40			←			17 11
Slough 3 a		15 15			15 45		15 41	15 45			16 15		16 45		16 36	16 45			17 17
d		15 18			15 48		15 41	15 48			16 18		16 48		16 37	16 48			17 18
Langley d		15 25			→			15 50			16 23		→			16 50			17 23
Iver d																			
West Drayton d		15 30						15 56			16 30					16 56			17 30
Heathrow Terminal 4 ✈ d	15 07									16 07								17 07	
Heathrow Terminal 1-2-3 2 ✈ d	15 13									16 13								17 13	
Hayes & Harlington d	15 19	15 34						16 01		16 19	16 34					17 01		17 19	17 34
Southall d	15 22	15 37								16 22	16 37							17 22	17 37
Hanwell d																			
Greenford ⊖ d																			
South Greenford d																			
Castle Bar Park d																			
Drayton Green d																			
West Ealing d																			
Ealing Broadway ⊖ d	15 27	15 42						16 08		16 27	16 42					17 08		17 27	17 42
Acton Main Line d																			
London Paddington 15 ⊖ a	15 36	15 51	15 29	15 43		15 57	16 03	16 18	16 22	16 36	16 51	16 42		17 01	17 04	17 19	17 22	17 36	17 51

Table 117

Reading and Greenford - London

Sundays until 24 June

Network Diagram - see first Page of Table 116

	GW ◇1 ⊡	GW ◇1 ⊡	GW ◇1	GW ◇1 ⊡	GW 1	GW ◇1 ⊡	GW ◇1 ⊡	GW 1	GW ◇1 ⊡	GW ◇1 ⊡	HC	GW 1	GW ◇1 ⊡	GW 1	GW ◇1 ⊡	GW ◇1 ⊡	GW 1	GW ◇1 ⊡	HC	GW 1
Oxford d			16 37				16 50					17 05				17 50				18 05
Reading 7 d	16 55	17 06	17 11	17 18	17 18	17 23	17 29		17 47	17 50		17 52	18 02	18 18	18 21	18 27		18 50		18 52
Twyford 3 d			17 18		17 24							17 58		18 25						18 58
Maidenhead 3 d			17 26		17 36							18 06		18 36						19 06
Taplow d																				
Burnham d					17 41			←				18 12		18 40			←			19 11
Slough 3 a			17 34		17 46		17 43	17 46				18 16		18 45		18 41	18 45			19 16
d			17 34		17 52		17 47	17 52				18 18		18 48		18 41	18 48			19 18
Langley d					→			17 56				18 23		→			18 50			19 23
Iver d																				
West Drayton d								17 59				18 30					18 56			19 30
Heathrow Terminal 4 ✈ d											18 07								19 07	
Heathrow Terminal 1-2-3 2 ✈ d											18 13								19 13	
Hayes & Harlington d								18 04			18 19	18 34					19 01		19 19	19 34
Southall d											18 22	18 37							19 22	19 37
Hanwell d																				
Greenford ⊖ d																				
South Greenford d																				
Castle Bar Park d																				
Drayton Green d																				
West Ealing d																				
Ealing Broadway ⊖ d								18 10			18 27	18 43					19 08		19 27	19 42
Acton Main Line d																				
London Paddington 15 ⊖ a	17 32	17 43	17 58	18 03		18 06	18 13	18 19	18 22	18 27	18 36	18 51	18 43		18 59	19 07	19 18	19 22	19 36	19 51

	GW ◇1 ⊡	GW ◇1 ⊡	GW ◇1 ⊡	GW 1	GW ◇1 ⊡	GW ◇1 ⊡	GW ◇1 ⊡	GW 1	GW ◇1 ⊡	HC	GW 1	GW ◇1 ⊡	GW 1	GW ◇1 ⊡	GW ◇1	GW 1	GW ◇1 ⊡	HC	GW 1
Oxford d						18 50					19 05				19 50				20 05
Reading 7 d	18 56	19 05	19 14	19 18	19 25	19 30	19 38		19 49		19 52	20 17	20 18	20 23	20 27		20 43		20 52
Twyford 3 d				19 25							19 58		20 25						20 58
Maidenhead 3 d				19 36							20 06		20 36						21 06
Taplow d																			
Burnham d				19 40				←			20 11		20 40			←			21 11
Slough 3 a				19 45		19 44		19 45			20 15		20 46		20 43	20 46			21 16
d				19 53		19 44		19 53			20 18		20 48		20 43	20 48			21 19
Langley d				→				19 57			20 23		→			20 50			21 25
Iver d																			
West Drayton d								20 01			20 30					20 56			21 29
Heathrow Terminal 4 ✈ d										20 07								21 07	
Heathrow Terminal 1-2-3 2 ✈ d										20 13								21 13	
Hayes & Harlington d								20 06		20 19	20 34					21 01		21 19	21 33
Southall d										20 22	20 37							21 22	21 37
Hanwell d																			
Greenford ⊖ d																			
South Greenford d																			
Castle Bar Park d																			
Drayton Green d																			
West Ealing d																			
Ealing Broadway ⊖ d								20 12		20 27	20 42					21 08		21 27	21 42
Acton Main Line d																			
London Paddington 15 ⊖ a	19 31	19 42	19 59		20 02	20 07	20 14	20 21	20 27	20 36	20 51	20 59		21 01	21 05	21 17	21 19	21 36	21 52

	GW ◇1 ⊡	GW ◇1 ⊡	GW 1	GW ◇1 ⊡	GW ◇1	GW ◇1 ⊡	GW 1	GW ◇1 ⊡	HC	GW 1	GW ◇1 ⊡	GW ◇1	HC	GW 1	GW ◇1 ⊡	GW ◇1 ⊡	GW 1	GW ◇1	GW ◇1 ⊡	GW 1
Oxford d					20 50					21 05		21 50					22 17	22 46		
Reading 7 d	21 01	21 17	21 18	21 20	21 24	21 32		21 49		21 52	22 18	22 23		22 29	22 39	22 45	22 58	23 22	23 30	23 36
Twyford 3 d			21 24							21 58				22 38			23 04			23 42
Maidenhead 3 d			21 36		21 38					22 06				22 46			23 12			23 50
Taplow d																				
Burnham d			21 41				←			22 11				22 50						23 55
Slough 3 a			21 45		21 44		21 45			22 16		22 40		22 56			23 18	23 43		23 59
d			21 52		21 44		21 52			22 18		22 41		23 08			23 18	23 43		00 01
Langley d			→				21 56			22 23				23 12			23 23			00 05
Iver d																				
West Drayton d							21 59			22 30				23 17			23 29			00 10
Heathrow Terminal 4 ✈ d									22 07				23 07							
Heathrow Terminal 1-2-3 2 ✈ d									22 13				23 13							
Hayes & Harlington d							22 04		22 19	22 34			23 19	23 23			23 34			00 16
Southall d							22 08		22 22	22 37			23 22				23 37			00 20
Hanwell d																				
Greenford ⊖ d																				
South Greenford d																				
Castle Bar Park d																				
Drayton Green d																				
West Ealing d																				
Ealing Broadway ⊖ d							22 13		22 27	22 42			23 27	23 31			23 42			00 25
Acton Main Line d																				
London Paddington 15 ⊖ a	21 43	21 57		22 01	22 07	22 14	22 21	22 27	22 36	22 51	22 59	23 01	23 36	23 40	23 15	23 28	23 51	00 05	00 13	00 34

Reading and Greenford - London

Network Diagram - see first Page of Table 116

	GW 1	GW ◇1	HC	GW ◇1 ☕	GW 1	HC	GW 1	HC	GW 1	HC	GW 1	GW 1	GW 1	GW ◇1 ☕	HC	GW 1	GW ◇1	GW ◇1 ☕	GW 1	GW 1	GW ◇1 ☕	HC
Oxford d		23p01			23p07								08 05				08 50					
Reading 7 d	23p18	23p31		23p51	00 03		06 22		07 22		08 05	08 22	08 52	09 01		09 18	09 19	09 31		09 35	09 45	
Twyford 3 d	23p24				00 09		06 28		07 28			08 28	08 58			09 24						
Maidenhead 3 d	23p32				00 17		06 36		07 36			08 36	09 06			09 32				09 47		
Taplow d	23p36				00 21																	
Burnham d	23p39				00 24		06 40		07 40			08 40				09 37			←			
Slough 3 a	23p44	23p45			00 28		06 45		07 45		08 23	08 45	09 14			09 41	09 35		09 41	09 55		
d	23p44	23p46			00 29		06 46		07 46		08 24	08 46	09 14			09 42	09 35		09 42	09 56		
Langley d					00 33		06 50		07 50			08 50	09 18			→			09 44			
Iver d					00 36																	
West Drayton d	23p51				00 39		06 55		07 55			08 55	09 24						09 49			
Heathrow Terminal 4 ✈ d			00 01			06 07		07 07		08 07					09 21							09 51
Heathrow Terminal 1-2-3 2 ✈ d			00 07			06 13		07 13		08 13					09 27							09 57
Hayes & Harlington d	23p56		00 13		00 44	06 19	07 02	07 19	08 02	08 19		09 02	09 28		09 33				09 55			10 03
Southall d			00 16		00 47	06 22	07 05	07 22	08 05	08 22		09 05	09 31		09 36				09 59			10 06
Hanwell d																						
Greenford ⊖ d																						
South Greenford d																						
Castle Bar Park d																						
Drayton Green d																						
West Ealing d																						
Ealing Broadway ⊖ d	00 03		00 21		00 53	06 27	07 11	07 27	08 11	08 27		09 11	09 37		09 41				10 03			10 11
Acton Main Line d																						
London Paddington 15 ⊖ a	00 16	00 10	00 30	00 34	01 02	06 36	07 20	07 36	08 20	08 36	08 44	09 20	09 45	09 29	09 50		09 54	09 59	10 13	10 23	10 14	10 20

	GW 1	GW ◇1 ☕	HC	GW 1	GW ◇1	GW 1	GW 1	GW ◇1 ☕	HC	GW ◇1 ☕	GW 1	GW ◇1 ☕	HC	GW ◇1	GW 1	GW ◇1	GW 1	GW 1	GW ◇1 ☕	GW ◇1 ☕	HC
Oxford d	09 01				09 50						10 05			10 44		10 55					
Reading 7 d	09 52	10 00		10 18	10 20		10 26	10 44		10 49	10 52	11 02		11 13	11 18	11 22		11 34	11 44	11 48	
Twyford 3 d	09 58			10 24							10 58			11 20	11 24						
Maidenhead 3 d	10 06			10 32			10 37				11 06			11 28	11 32			11 52			
Taplow d																					
Burnham d				10 37		←									11 37		←				
Slough 3 a	10 14			10 41	10 35	10 41	10 44				11 14			11 35	11 41	11 38	11 41	11 59			
d	10 14			10 42	10 35	10 42	10 46				11 14			11 35	11 42	11 39	11 42	12 00			
Langley d	10 18			→		10 44					11 18				→		11 44				
Iver d																					
West Drayton d	10 23					10 50					11 23						11 50				
Heathrow Terminal 4 ✈ d			10 21						10 51				11 21								11 51
Heathrow Terminal 1-2-3 2 ✈ d			10 27						10 57				11 27								11 57
Hayes & Harlington d	10 27		10 33			10 54			11 03		11 27		11 33				11 54				12 03
Southall d	10 31		10 36			10 59			11 06		11 31		11 36				11 59				12 06
Hanwell d																					
Greenford ⊖ d																					
South Greenford d																					
Castle Bar Park d																					
Drayton Green d																					
West Ealing d																					
Ealing Broadway ⊖ d	10 36		10 41			11 03			11 11		11 36		11 41				12 03				12 11
Acton Main Line d																					
London Paddington 15 ⊖ a	10 46	10 29	10 50		10 55	11 13	11 17	11 14	11 20	11 21	11 46	11 29	11 50	11 55		12 00	12 13	12 22	12 14	12 17	12 20

	GW 1	GW ◇1 ☕	HC	GW 1	GW ◇1	GW 1	GW 1	GW ◇1 ☕	HC	GW 1	GW ◇1 ☕	GW ◇1 ☕	HC	GW 1	GW ◇1	GW 1	GW 1	GW ◇1 ☕	GW ◇1 ☕
Oxford d	11 05				11 50					12 05					12 50				
Reading 7 d	11 52	12 02		12 18	12 19		12 33	12 44		12 52	13 02	13 15		13 18	13 20		13 26	13 28	13 47
Twyford 3 d	11 58			12 24						12 59				13 24					
Maidenhead 3 d	12 06			12 32			12 45			13 07				13 32			13 38		
Taplow d																			
Burnham d				12 37		←								13 37		←			
Slough 3 a	12 14			12 41	12 32	12 41	12 53			13 14				13 41	13 36	13 41	13 45		
d	12 14			12 42	12 33	12 42	12 54			13 14				13 42	13 36	13 42	13 45		
Langley d	12 18			→		12 46				13 18				→		13 46			
Iver d																			
West Drayton d	12 23					12 50				13 23						13 50			
Heathrow Terminal 4 ✈ d			12 21						12 51				13 21						
Heathrow Terminal 1-2-3 2 ✈ d			12 27						12 57				13 27						
Hayes & Harlington d	12 27		12 33			12 54			13 03	13 27			13 33			13 54			
Southall d	12 31		12 36			12 59			13 06	13 31			13 36			13 59			
Hanwell d																			
Greenford ⊖ d																			
South Greenford d																			
Castle Bar Park d																			
Drayton Green d																			
West Ealing d																			
Ealing Broadway ⊖ d	12 36		12 41			13 03			13 11	13 36			13 41			14 03			
Acton Main Line d																			
London Paddington 15 ⊖ a	12 46	12 29	12 50		12 51	13 13	13 26	13 14	13 20	13 45	13 29	13 41	13 50		13 56	14 13	14 08	13 59	14 14

Table 117

Reading and Greenford - London

Sundays
1 July to 9 September

Network Diagram - see first Page of Table 116

	HC	GW ◇1 ☕	GW 1	GW ◇1 ☕	HC	GW 1	GW ◇1	GW 1	GW 1	GW ◇1 ☕	HC	GW ◇1 ☕	GW 1	GW ◇1 ☕	HC	GW 1	GW ◇1	GW 1	GW 1	GW ◇1 ☕
Oxford d			13 05				13 50						14 05				14 50			
Reading 7 d		13 51	13 52	14 02		14 18	14 20		14 34	14 44		14 50	14 52	15 02		15 18	15 22		15 26	15 30
Twyford 3 d			13 58			14 24							14 58			15 24				
Maidenhead 3 d			14 06			14 32			14 46				15 06			15 32			15 38	
Taplow d																				
Burnham d						14 37		←								15 37		←		
Slough 3 a			14 14			14 41	14 36	14 41	14 54				15 14			15 41	15 36	15 41	15 45	
d			14 14			14 42	14 36	14 42	14 54				15 14			15 42	15 37	15 42	15 46	
Langley d			14 18			→		14 46					15 18			→		15 46		
Iver d																				
West Drayton d			14 23					14 50					15 23					15 50		
Heathrow Terminal 4 ✈ d	13 51				14 21						14 51				15 21					
Heathrow Terminal 1-2-3 2 ✈ d	13 57				14 27						14 57				15 27					
Hayes & Harlington d	14 03		14 27		14 33			14 54			15 03		15 27		15 33			15 55		
Southall d	14 06		14 31		14 36			14 59			15 06		15 31		15 36			15 59		
Hanwell d																				
Greenford ⊖ d																				
South Greenford d																				
Castle Bar Park d																				
Drayton Green d																				
West Ealing d																				
Ealing Broadway ⊖ d	14 11		14 36		14 41			15 03			15 11		15 36		15 41			16 03		
Acton Main Line d																				
London Paddington 15 ⊖ a	14 20	14 21	14 45	14 29	14 50		14 55	15 13	15 25	15 14	15 20	15 21	15 45	15 29	15 50		15 55	16 13	16 17	15 58

	GW ◇1 ☕	HC	GW ◇1 ☕	GW 1	GW ◇1 ☕	HC	GW 1	GW ◇1 ☕	GW 1	GW 1	GW ◇1 ☕	HC	GW ◇1 ☕	GW 1	GW ◇1 ☕	GW ◇1 ☕	HC	GW 1	GW ◇1 ☕
Oxford d				15 05				15 50						16 05					
Reading 7 d	15 44		15 50	15 52	16 02		16 18	16 20		16 34	16 47		16 51	16 52	17 02	17 14		17 18	17 21
Twyford 3 d				15 58			16 24							16 58				17 24	
Maidenhead 3 d				16 06			16 33			16 46				17 06				17 33	
Taplow d																			
Burnham d				16 11			16 38		←					17 11				17 38	
Slough 3 a				16 14			16 42	16 33	16 42	16 54				17 14				17 42	
d				16 14			16 43	16 33	16 43	16 54				17 14				17 43	
Langley d				16 18			→		16 47					17 18				→	
Iver d																			
West Drayton d				16 23					16 51					17 23					
Heathrow Terminal 4 ✈ d		15 51				16 21						16 51					17 21		
Heathrow Terminal 1-2-3 2 ✈ d		15 57				16 27						16 57					17 27		
Hayes & Harlington d		16 03		16 27		16 33			16 55			17 03		17 27			17 33		
Southall d		16 06		16 31		16 36			17 00			17 06		17 31			17 36		
Hanwell d																			
Greenford ⊖ d																			
South Greenford d																			
Castle Bar Park d																			
Drayton Green d																			
West Ealing d																			
Ealing Broadway ⊖ d		16 11		16 36		16 42			17 04			17 11		17 36			17 41		
Acton Main Line d																			
London Paddington 15 ⊖ a	16 14	16 20	16 21	16 47	16 29	16 50		16 51	17 15	17 23	17 14	17 20	17 21	17 47	17 29	17 41	17 50		17 51

	GW ◇1 ☕	GW 1	GW ◇1	GW 1	GW ◇1 ☕	HC	GW ◇1 ☕	GW 1	GW ◇1 ☕	GW ◇1 ☕	HC	GW 1	GW ◇1 ☕	GW 1	GW 1	GW ◇1 ☕	HC	GW 1	GW ◇1 ☕	GW ◇1 ☕
Oxford d	16 50		16 54					17 05					17 50					18 05		
Reading 7 d	17 21		17 24	17 34	17 44		17 49	17 52	18 02	18 14		18 18	18 20		18 34	18 47		18 52	18 53	19 02
Twyford 3 d			17 30					17 58				18 24						18 58		
Maidenhead 3 d			17 38	17 45				18 06				18 34			18 46			19 06		
Taplow d																				
Burnham d		←						18 11				18 38		←				19 11		
Slough 3 a	17 38	17 42	17 45	17 52				18 14				18 43	18 35	18 43	18 54			19 14		
d	17 38	17 43	17 45	17 52				18 14				18 43	18 35	18 43	18 54			19 14		
Langley d		17 47						18 18				→		18 47				19 18		
Iver d																				
West Drayton d		17 51						18 23						18 51				19 23		
Heathrow Terminal 4 ✈ d						17 51					18 21						18 51			
Heathrow Terminal 1-2-3 2 ✈ d						17 57					18 27						18 57			
Hayes & Harlington d		17 55				18 03		18 27			18 33			18 56			19 03	19 27		
Southall d		18 00				18 06		18 31			18 36			19 00			19 06	19 31		
Hanwell d																				
Greenford ⊖ d																				
South Greenford d																				
Castle Bar Park d																				
Drayton Green d																				
West Ealing d																				
Ealing Broadway ⊖ d		18 04				18 11		18 36			18 42			19 05			19 11	19 36		
Acton Main Line d																				
London Paddington 15 ⊖ a	17 59	18 14	18 07	18 11	18 14	18 20	18 21	18 47	18 29	18 42	18 50		18 53	19 15	19 23	19 13	19 20	19 47	19 21	19 30

Table 117

Reading and Greenford - London

Sundays

1 July to 9 September

Network Diagram - see first Page of Table 116

		GW ◇1 🍴	HC	GW 1	GW ◇1 🍴	GW ◇1 🍴	GW ◇1 🍴	GW 1	GW 1	GW ◇1 🍴	HC	GW 1	GW ◇1 🍴	GW ◇1 🍴	HC	GW 1	GW ◇1	GW ◇1 🍴	GW ◇1 🍴	HC	GW 1
Oxford	d					18 50						19 05					19 53				20 05
Reading 7	d	19 14		19 18	19 21	19 24	19 32		19 37	19 45		19 52	19 59	20 14		20 18	20 23	20 32	20 47		20 52
Twyford 3	d			19 24								19 58				20 24					20 58
Maidenhead 3	d			19 34					19 49			20 06				20 34					21 06
Taplow	d																				
Burnham	d			19 38				←				20 11				20 38					21 11
Slough 3	a			19 43		19 38		19 43	20 01			20 14				20 42	20 42				21 14
	d			19 43		19 38		19 43	20 01			20 14				20 43	20 42				21 14
Langley	d			→				19 47				20 18				20 47					21 18
Iver	d																				
West Drayton	d							19 51				20 23				20 51					21 23
Heathrow Terminal 4 ✈	d		19 21								19 51				20 21					20 51	
Heathrow Terminal 1-2-3 2 ✈	d		19 27								19 57				20 27					20 57	
Hayes & Harlington	d		19 33					19 56			20 03	20 27			20 33	20 56				21 03	21 27
Southall	d		19 36					20 00			20 06	20 31			20 36	21 00				21 06	21 31
Hanwell	d																				
Greenford ⊖	d																				
South Greenford	d																				
Castle Bar Park	d																				
Drayton Green	d																				
West Ealing	d																				
Ealing Broadway ⊖	d		19 42					20 05			20 11	20 36			20 42	21 05				21 11	21 36
Acton Main Line	d																				
London Paddington 15 ⊖	a	19 42	19 50		19 51	19 56	20 01	20 15	20 22	20 14	20 20	20 47	20 25	20 46	20 50	21 17	21 02	21 01	21 14	21 20	21 47

		GW ◇1 🍴	GW ◇1 🍴	HC	GW ◇1	GW 1	GW ◇1 🍴	GW ◇1 🍴	HC	GW 1	GW ◇1 🍴	GW ◇1	GW ◇1 🍴	GW ◇1 🍴	HC	GW 1	GW 1	GW ◇1	GW ◇1 🍴	GW 1
Oxford	d				20 50					21 21		21 50					22 21	22 46		
Reading 7	d	21 13	21 17		21 20	21 24	21 32	21 49		22 10	22 19	22 24	22 36	22 39		22 40	23 00	23 22	23 30	23 35
Twyford 3	d					21 30				22 16						22 49	23 07			23 41
Maidenhead 3	d				21 32	21 38				22 24						22 57	23 15			23 49
Taplow	d																			
Burnham	d					21 43				22 29						23 01				23 54
Slough 3	a				21 38	21 48				22 33		22 41				23 06	23 22	23 42		23 58
	d				21 38	21 48				22 34		22 42				23 06	23 22	23 42		23 59
Langley	d					21 52				22 38						23 10	23 26			00 03
Iver	d																			
West Drayton	d					21 56				22 43						23 15	23 31			00 08
Heathrow Terminal 4 ✈	d			21 21					22 07						23 07					
Heathrow Terminal 1-2-3 2 ✈	d			21 27					22 13						23 13					
Hayes & Harlington	d			21 33		22 01			22 19	22 47					23 19	23 24	23 36			00 16
Southall	d			21 36		22 05			22 22	22 51					23 22	23 27	23 39			00 20
Hanwell	d																			
Greenford ⊖	d																			
South Greenford	d																			
Castle Bar Park	d																			
Drayton Green	d																			
West Ealing	d																			
Ealing Broadway ⊖	d			21 42		22 11			22 27	22 56					23 27	23 33	23 45			00 25
Acton Main Line	d																			
London Paddington 15 ⊖	a	21 40	21 44	21 50	21 59	22 20	22 02	22 29	22 36	23 05	22 46	23 00	23 06	23 13	23 36	23 42	23 54	00 02	00 05	00 34

		GW 1
Oxford	d	23 15
Reading 7	d	23 56
Twyford 3	d	00 03
Maidenhead 3	d	00 11
Taplow	d	
Burnham	d	00 15
Slough 3	a	00 20
	d	00 20
Langley	d	00 24
Iver	d	
West Drayton	d	00 29
Heathrow Terminal 4 ✈	d	
Heathrow Terminal 1-2-3 2 ✈	d	
Hayes & Harlington	d	00 34
Southall	d	00 38
Hanwell	d	
Greenford ⊖	d	
South Greenford	d	
Castle Bar Park	d	
Drayton Green	d	
West Ealing	d	
Ealing Broadway ⊖	d	00 43
Acton Main Line	d	
London Paddington 15 ⊖	a	00 52

Table 117

Reading and Greenford - London

Sundays

16 September to 21 October

Network Diagram - see first Page of Table 116

		GW 1	GW ◇1	HC	GW ◇1 🍴	GW 1	GW 🚌	HC	GW 1	GW 🚌	HC	GW 1	HC	GW 1	GW 1	GW 1	HC	GW 1	GW ◇1 🍴	GW 1	GW ◇1	GW ◇1 🍴	GW 1
Oxford	d		23p01			23p07															08 50		
Reading 7	d	23p18	23p31		23p51	00 03	05 52			06 52				08 17	08 20			08 52	09 03	09 18	09 23	09 33	
Twyford 3	d	23p24				00 10	06a20		06 30	07a20		07 30		08 25				08 58		09 25			
Maidenhead 3	d	23p32				00 18			06 38			07 38		08 36				09 06		09 36			
Taplow	d	23p36				00 22																	
Burnham	d	23p39				00 25			06 41			07 41		08 40		←				09 40			←
Slough 3	a	23p44	23p45			00 29			06 47			07 47		08 45	08 38	08 45		09 15		09 45	09 38		09 45
	d	23p44	23p46			00 30			06 48			07 48		08 46	08 38	08 46		09 18		09 48	09 38		09 48
Langley	d					00 34			06 52			07 52		→		08 50		09 23		→			09 52
Iver	d					00 37																	
West Drayton	d	23p51				00 40			06 56			07 56				08 55		09 29					09 58
Heathrow Terminal 4 ✈	d			00 01				06 07			07 07		08 07				09 07						
Heathrow Terminal 1-2-3 2 ✈	d			00 07				06 13			07 13		08 13				09 13						
Hayes & Harlington	d	23p56		00 13		00 45		06 19	07 03		07 19	08 03	08 19			09 03	09 19	09 33					10 00
Southall	d			00 16		00 48		06 22	07 07		07 22	08 07	08 22			09 06	09 22	09 37					
Hanwell	d																						
Greenford ⊖	d																						
South Greenford	d																						
Castle Bar Park	d																						
Drayton Green	d																						
West Ealing	d																						
Ealing Broadway ⊖	d	00 03		00 21		00 54		06 27	07 13		07 27	08 13	08 27			09 12	09 27	09 42					10 08
Acton Main Line	d																						
London Paddington 15 ⊖	a	00 16	00 10	00 30	00 34	01 04		06 36	07 22		07 36	08 22	08 36		09 00	09 20	09 36	09 51	09 44		10 00	10 07	10 20

		HC	GW 1	GW ◇1 🍴	GW 1	GW ◇1	GW 1	GW ◇1 🍴	GW ◇1 🍴	HC	GW 1	GW ◇1 🍴	GW ◇1	GW 1	GW ◇1	GW 1	GW ◇1 🍴	GW ◇1 🍴	HC	GW 1	GW ◇1 🍴
Oxford	d		09 05			09 50					10 05		10 44		10 55					11 05	
Reading 7	d		09 53	10 03	10 17	10 21		10 44	10 49		10 53	11 03	11 15	11 18	11 25		11 49	11 51		11 53	12 03
Twyford 3	d		09 59		10 25						10 59		11 22	11 25						11 59	
Maidenhead 3	d		10 07		10 36						11 07		11 30	11 36						12 07	
Taplow	d																				
Burnham	d				10 40		←							11 40		←					
Slough 3	a		10 15		10 45	10 36	10 45				11 15		11 36	11 45	11 42	11 45				12 15	
	d		10 18		10 48	10 36	10 48				11 18		11 37	11 48	11 42	11 48				12 18	
Langley	d		10 23		→		10 52				11 23			→		11 52				12 23	
Iver	d																				
West Drayton	d		10 29				10 58				11 29					11 58				12 29	
Heathrow Terminal 4 ✈	d	10 07								11 07									12 07		
Heathrow Terminal 1-2-3 2 ✈	d	10 13								11 13									12 13		
Hayes & Harlington	d	10 19	10 33				11 00			11 19	11 33					12 00			12 19	12 33	
Southall	d	10 23	10 37							11 22	11 37								12 22	12 37	
Hanwell	d																				
Greenford ⊖	d																				
South Greenford	d																				
Castle Bar Park	d																				
Drayton Green	d																				
West Ealing	d																				
Ealing Broadway ⊖	d	10 28	10 42				11 08			11 27	11 42					12 08			12 27	12 42	
Acton Main Line	d																				
London Paddington 15 ⊖	a	10 36	10 52	10 44		10 59	11 19	11 22	11 29	11 36	11 50	11 44	11 59		12 06	12 19	12 22	12 29	12 36	12 51	12 43

		GW 1	GW ◇1	GW 1	GW ◇1 🍴	HC	GW 1	GW 1	GW ◇1 🍴	GW ◇1	GW 1	GW ◇1 🍴	GW ◇1 🍴	HC	GW 1	GW 1	GW ◇1 🍴	GW ◇1	GW 1	GW ◇1 🍴
Oxford	d		11 50				12 05			12 50					13 05			13 50		
Reading 7	d	12 18	12 23		12 49		12 53	13 17	13 21	13 24		13 49	13 51		13 53	14 17	14 21	14 25		14 49
Twyford 3	d	12 25					12 59	13 25							13 59	14 25				
Maidenhead 3	d	12 36					13 07	13 36							14 07	14 36				
Taplow	d																			
Burnham	d	12 40		←				13 40			←					14 40			←	
Slough 3	a	12 45	12 38	12 45			13 15	13 45		13 41	13 45				14 15	14 45		14 41	14 45	
	d	12 48	12 39	12 48			13 18	13 48		13 41	13 48				14 18	14 48		14 41	14 48	
Langley	d	→		12 52			13 23	→			13 52				14 23	→			14 52	
Iver	d																			
West Drayton	d			12 58			13 31				13 58				14 29				14 58	
Heathrow Terminal 4 ✈	d					13 07								14 07						
Heathrow Terminal 1-2-3 2 ✈	d					13 13								14 13						
Hayes & Harlington	d			13 00		13 19	13 33				14 00			14 19	14 33				15 00	
Southall	d					13 23	13 37							14 22	14 37					
Hanwell	d																			
Greenford ⊖	d																			
South Greenford	d																			
Castle Bar Park	d																			
Drayton Green	d																			
West Ealing	d																			
Ealing Broadway ⊖	d			13 08		13 28	13 42				14 08			14 27	14 42				15 08	
Acton Main Line	d																			
London Paddington 15 ⊖	a		13 03	13 20	13 22	13 36	13 52		13 59	14 03	14 20	14 22	14 29	14 36	14 50		14 57	15 04	15 20	15 22

Reading and Greenford - London

Sundays

16 September to 21 October

Network Diagram - see first Page of Table 116

		GW ◇1 ⊡	HC	GW 1	GW 1	GW ◇1 ⊡	GW ◇1	GW 1	GW ◇1 ⊡	GW ◇1 ⊡	HC	GW 1	GW 1	GW ◇1 ⊡	GW ◇1 ⊡	GW 1	GW ◇1 ⊡	GW ◇1 ⊡	HC	GW 1
Oxford	d			14 05			14 50					15 05			15 50					16 05
Reading 7	d	14 51		14 53	15 17	15 21	15 26		15 49	15 51		15 53	16 18	16 21	16 28		16 48	16 51		16 53
Twyford 3	d			14 59	15 25							15 59	16 25							16 59
Maidenhead 3	d			15 07	15 36							16 07	16 36							17 07
Taplow	d																			
Burnham	d				15 40			←				16 13	16 40			←				17 13
Slough 3	a			15 15	15 45		15 41	15 45				16 15	16 45		16 36	16 45				17 15
	d			15 18	15 48		15 41	15 48				16 18	16 48		16 41	16 48				17 18
Langley	d			15 23	→			15 52				16 23	→			16 52				17 23
Iver	d																			
West Drayton	d			15 29				15 58				16 29				16 58				17 29
Heathrow Terminal 4 ✈	d		15 07								16 07								17 07	
Heathrow Terminal 1-2-3 2 ✈	d		15 13								16 13								17 13	
Hayes & Harlington	d		15 19	15 33				16 00			16 19	16 33				17 00			17 19	17 33
Southall	d		15 22	15 37							16 22	16 37							17 22	17 37
Hanwell	d																			
Greenford ⊖	d																			
South Greenford	d																			
Castle Bar Park	d																			
Drayton Green	d																			
West Ealing	d																			
Ealing Broadway ⊖	d		15 27	15 42				16 08			16 27	16 42				17 08			17 27	17 42
Acton Main Line	d																			
London Paddington 15 ⊖	a	15 29	15 36	15 51		15 58	16 03	16 20	16 23	16 30	16 36	16 52		17 01	17 07	17 20	17 22	17 30	17 36	17 52

		GW 1	GW ◇1 ⊡	GW ◇1	GW ◇1 ⊡	GW ◇1 ⊡	GW ◇1 ⊡	GW 1	GW ◇1 ⊡	GW ◇1 ⊡	HC	GW 1	GW ◇1 ⊡	GW 1	GW ◇1 ⊡	GW ◇1 ⊡	GW 1	GW ◇1 ⊡	GW ◇1 ⊡	HC	GW 1
Oxford	d			16 37			16 50					17 05				17 50					18 05
Reading 7	d	17 01	17 06	17 11	17 18	17 24	17 28		17 48	17 51		17 53	18 03	18 18	18 21	18 28		18 48	18 51		18 53
Twyford 3	d	17 10		17 18								17 59		18 25							18 59
Maidenhead 3	d	17 36		17 26								18 07		18 36							19 07
Taplow	d																				
Burnham	d	17 40						←				18 13		18 40			←				19 13
Slough 3	a	17 45		17 33			17 43	17 45				18 18		18 45		18 41	18 45				19 18
	d	17 48		17 34			17 43	17 48				18 18		18 48		18 41	18 48				19 18
Langley	d	→						17 52				18 23		→			18 52				19 23
Iver	d																				
West Drayton	d							17 58				18 29					18 58				19 29
Heathrow Terminal 4 ✈	d										18 07									19 07	
Heathrow Terminal 1-2-3 2 ✈	d										18 13									19 13	
Hayes & Harlington	d							18 00			18 19	18 33					19 00			19 19	19 33
Southall	d										18 22	18 37								19 22	19 37
Hanwell	d																				
Greenford ⊖	d																				
South Greenford	d																				
Castle Bar Park	d																				
Drayton Green	d																				
West Ealing	d																				
Ealing Broadway ⊖	d							18 08			18 27	18 42					19 08			19 27	19 42
Acton Main Line	d																				
London Paddington 15 ⊖	a		17 43	17 58	18 01	18 04	18 07	18 19	18 22	18 29	18 36	18 52	18 44		18 59	19 07	19 19	19 23	19 29	19 36	19 52

		GW ◇1 ⊡	GW 1	GW ◇1 ⊡	GW ◇1 ⊡	GW ◇1 ⊡	GW ◇1 ⊡	GW 1	GW ◇1 ⊡	GW ◇1 ⊡	HC	GW 1	GW 1	GW ◇1 ⊡	GW ◇1	GW ◇1 ⊡	GW 1	GW ◇1 ⊡	HC	GW 1
Oxford	d					18 50						19 05			19 50					20 05
Reading 7	d	19 03	19 18	19 21	19 25	19 28	19 34		19 48	19 51		19 53	20 18	20 21	20 24	20 34		20 51		20 53
Twyford 3	d		19 25									19 59	20 25							20 59
Maidenhead 3	d		19 36									20 07	20 36							21 07
Taplow	d																			
Burnham	d		19 40					←				20 13	20 40				←			21 13
Slough 3	a		19 45			19 44		19 45				20 18	20 45		20 43		20 45			21 18
	d		19 48			19 45		19 48				20 18	20 48		20 43		20 48			21 18
Langley	d		→					19 52				20 23	→				20 52			21 23
Iver	d																			
West Drayton	d							19 58				20 29					20 58			21 29
Heathrow Terminal 4 ✈	d										20 07								21 07	
Heathrow Terminal 1-2-3 2 ✈	d										20 13								21 13	
Hayes & Harlington	d							20 00			20 19	20 33					21 00		21 19	21 33
Southall	d										20 22	20 37					21 06		21 22	21 37
Hanwell	d																			
Greenford ⊖	d																			
South Greenford	d																			
Castle Bar Park	d																			
Drayton Green	d																			
West Ealing	d																			
Ealing Broadway ⊖	d							20 08			20 27	20 42					21 12		21 27	21 42
Acton Main Line	d																			
London Paddington 15 ⊖	a	19 44		19 59	20 02	20 07	20 14	20 20	20 23	20 29	20 36	20 52		20 59	21 05	21 13	21 21	21 29	21 36	21 52

Table 117

Reading and Greenford - London

Sundays

16 September to 21 October

Network Diagram - see first Page of Table 116

		GW 1	GW ◇1 ⊡	GW ◇1 ⊡	GW ◇1	GW ◇1 ⊡	GW 1	GW ◇1 ⊡	HC	GW 1	GW ◇1 ⊡	GW ◇1	GW 1	GW ◇1 ⊡	GW ◇1 ⊡	HC	GW 1	GW ◇1	GW ◇1 ⊡	GW 1
Oxford	d				20 50					21 21		21 50					22 17	22 46		
Reading 7	d	21 18	21 21	21 24	21 28	21 34		21 49		22 03	22 18	22 22	22 29	22 37	22 41		23 00	23 22	23 30	23 36
Twyford 3	d	21 25								22 17			22 39				23 07			23 43
Maidenhead 3	d	21 36			21 40					22 25			22 47				23 15			23 51
Taplow	d																			
Burnham	d	21 40					←			22 29			22 51							23 56
Slough 3	a	21 47			21 44		21 47			22 34		22 43	22 56				23 22	23 43		00 01
	d	21 48			21 46		21 48			22 34		22 44	23 01				23 23	23 44		00 02
Langley	d	→					21 52			22 39			23 06				23 27			00 06
Iver	d																			
West Drayton	d						21 58			22 44			23 11				23 31			00 11
Heathrow Terminal 4 ✈	d								22 07							23 07				
Heathrow Terminal 1-2-3 2 ✈	d								22 13							23 13				
Hayes & Harlington	d						22 00		22 19	22 49			23 16			23 19	23 35			00 16
Southall	d						22 06		22 22	22 52						23 22	23 39			00 20
Hanwell	d																			
Greenford ⊖	d																			
South Greenford	d																			
Castle Bar Park	d																			
Drayton Green	d																			
West Ealing	d																			
Ealing Broadway ⊖	d						22 11		22 27	22 58			23 23			23 27	23 44			00 25
Acton Main Line	d																			
London Paddington 15 ⊖	a		21 59	22 02	22 07	22 15	22 21	22 29	22 36	23 07	22 58	23 13	23 33	23 16	23 22	23 36	23 53	00 06	00 12	00 34

Sundays

from 28 October

		GW 1	GW ◇1	HC	GW ◇1 ⊡	GW 1	GW (bus)	HC	GW 1	GW (bus)	HC	GW 1	HC	GW 1	GW 1	GW 1	HC	GW 1	GW ◇1 ⊡	GW 1	GW ◇1	GW ◇1 ⊡	GW 1
Oxford	d		23p01			23p07															08 50		
Reading 7	d	23p18	23p29		23p53	00 03	05 52			06 52				08 17	08 20			08 52	09 03	09 18	09 23	09 33	
Twyford 3	d	23p24				00 10	06a20		06 30	07a20		07 30		08 25				08 58		09 25			
Maidenhead 3	d	23p32				00 18			06 38			07 38		08 36				09 06		09 36			
Taplow	d	23p36				00 22																	
Burnham	d	23p39				00 25			06 41			07 41		08 40		←				09 40			←
Slough 3	a	23p44	23p45			00 29			06 47			07 47		08 45	08 38	08 45		09 15		09 45	09 38		09 45
	d	23p44	23p46			00 30			06 48			07 48		08 46	08 38	08 46		09 18		09 48	09 38		09 48
Langley	d					00 34			06 52			07 52		→		08 50		09 23		→			09 52
Iver	d					00 37																	
West Drayton	d	23p51				00 40			06 56			07 56				08 55		09 29					09 58
Heathrow Terminal 4 ✈	d			00 01				06 07			07 07		08 07				09 07						
Heathrow Terminal 1-2-3 2 ✈	d			00 07				06 13			07 13		08 13				09 13						
Hayes & Harlington	d	23p56		00 13		00 45		06 19	07 03		07 19	08 03	08 19			09 03	09 19	09 33					10 00
Southall	d			00 16		00 48		06 22	07 07		07 22	08 07	08 22			09 06	09 22	09 37					
Hanwell	d																						
Greenford ⊖	d																						
South Greenford	d																						
Castle Bar Park	d																						
Drayton Green	d																						
West Ealing	d																						
Ealing Broadway ⊖	d	00 03		00 21		00 54		06 27	07 13		07 27	08 13	08 27			09 12	09 27	09 42					10 08
Acton Main Line	d																						
London Paddington 15 ⊖	a	00 16	00 10	00 30	00 33	01 04		06 36	07 22		07 36	08 22	08 36		08 59	09 20	09 36	09 51	09 44		10 00	10 07	10 20

		HC	GW 1	GW ◇1 ⊡	GW 1	GW ◇1	GW 1	GW ◇1 ⊡	GW ◇1 ⊡	HC	GW 1	GW ◇1 ⊡	GW ◇1	GW 1	GW ◇1	GW 1	GW ◇1 ⊡	GW ◇1 ⊡	HC	GW 1	GW ◇1 ⊡
Oxford	d		09 05			09 50					10 05		10 44		10 55					11 05	
Reading 7	d		09 53	10 02	10 17	10 21		10 44	10 49		10 53	11 02	11 15	11 18	11 25		11 47	11 51		11 53	12 02
Twyford 3	d		09 59		10 25						10 59		11 22	11 25						11 59	
Maidenhead 3	d		10 07		10 36						11 07		11 30	11 36						12 07	
Taplow	d																				
Burnham	d				10 40		←							11 40		←					
Slough 3	a		10 15		10 45	10 36	10 45				11 15		11 36	11 45	11 42	11 45				12 15	
	d		10 18		10 49	10 36	10 49				11 18		11 37	11 48	11 42	11 48				12 18	
Langley	d		10 23		→		10 52				11 23			→		11 52				12 23	
Iver	d																				
West Drayton	d		10 29				10 58				11 29					11 58				12 29	
Heathrow Terminal 4 ✈	d	10 07								11 07									12 07		
Heathrow Terminal 1-2-3 2 ✈	d	10 13								11 13									12 13		
Hayes & Harlington	d	10 20	10 33				11 00			11 19	11 33					12 00			12 19	12 33	
Southall	d	10 23	10 37							11 22	11 37								12 22	12 37	
Hanwell	d																				
Greenford ⊖	d																				
South Greenford	d																				
Castle Bar Park	d																				
Drayton Green	d																				
West Ealing	d																				
Ealing Broadway ⊖	d	10 28	10 42				11 08			11 27	11 42					12 08			12 27	12 42	
Acton Main Line	d																				
London Paddington 15 ⊖	a	10 36	10 51	10 44		10 59	11 19	11 22	11 29	11 36	11 50	11 44	11 59		12 06	12 19	12 21	12 29	12 36	12 51	12 44

Table 117

Sundays from 28 October

Reading and Greenford - London

Network Diagram - see first Page of Table 116

		GW ■	GW ◇■	GW ■	GW ◇■ ⟂	HC	GW ■	GW ◇■ ⟂	GW ■	GW ◇■	GW ■	GW ◇■ ⟂	GW ◇■ ⟂	HC	GW ■	GW ◇■ ⟂	GW ■	GW ◇■	GW ■	GW ◇■ ⟂
Oxford	d		11 50				12 05			12 50					13 05			13 50		
Reading	d	12 18	12 23		12 44		12 53	13 02	13 17	13 24		13 49	13 51		13 53	14 02	14 17	14 21		14 49
Twyford	d	12 25					12 59		13 25						13 59		14 25			
Maidenhead	d	12 36					13 07		13 36						14 07		14 36			
Taplow	d																			
Burnham	d	12 40		←					13 40		←						14 40		←	
Slough	a	12 45	12 38	12 45			13 15		13 45	13 37	13 45				14 15		14 45	14 37	14 45	
	d	12 48	12 39	12 48			13 18		13 49	13 37	13 49				14 18		14 48	14 37	14 48	
Langley	d	→		12 52			13 23		→		13 52				14 23		→		14 52	
Iver	d																			
West Drayton	d			12 58			13 29				13 58				14 29				14 58	
Heathrow Terminal 4	d					13 07								14 07						
Heathrow Terminal 1-2-3	d					13 13								14 13						
Hayes & Harlington	d			13 00		13 19	13 33				14 00			14 19	14 33				15 00	
Southall	d					13 22	13 37							14 22	14 37					
Hanwell	d																			
Greenford ⊖	d																			
South Greenford	d																			
Castle Bar Park	d																			
Drayton Green	d																			
West Ealing	d																			
Ealing Broadway ⊖	d			13 08		13 27	13 42				14 08			14 27	14 42				15 08	
Acton Main Line	d																			
London Paddington ⊖	a		13 03	13 18	13 22	13 36	13 52	13 44		14 00	14 19	14 22	14 29	14 36	14 50	14 44		14 59	15 20	15 22

		GW ◇■ ⟂	HC	GW ■	GW ◇■ ⟂	GW ■	GW ◇■	GW ■	GW ◇■ ⟂	GW ◇■ ⟂	HC	GW ■	GW ◇■ ⟂	GW ■	GW ◇■ ⟂	GW ■	GW ◇■ ⟂	GW ◇■ ⟂	HC	GW ■
Oxford	d			14 05			14 50					15 05			15 50					16 05
Reading	d	14 51		14 53	15 02	15 17	15 22		15 49	15 51		15 53	16 02	16 18	16 23		16 49	16 51		16 53
Twyford	d			14 59		15 25						15 59		16 25						16 59
Maidenhead	d			15 07		15 36						16 07		16 36						17 07
Taplow	d																			
Burnham	d					15 40		←				16 13		16 40		←				17 13
Slough	a			15 15		15 45	15 36	15 45				16 15		16 45	16 36	16 45				17 15
	d			15 18		15 48	15 37	15 48				16 18		16 48	16 36	16 48				17 18
Langley	d			15 23		→		15 52				16 23		→		16 52				17 23
Iver	d																			
West Drayton	d			15 29				15 58				16 29				16 58				17 29
Heathrow Terminal 4	d		15 07								16 07								17 07	
Heathrow Terminal 1-2-3	d		15 13								16 13								17 13	
Hayes & Harlington	d		15 19	15 33				16 00			16 19	16 33				17 00			17 19	17 33
Southall	d		15 22	15 37							16 22	16 37							17 22	17 37
Hanwell	d																			
Greenford ⊖	d																			
South Greenford	d																			
Castle Bar Park	d																			
Drayton Green	d																			
West Ealing	d																			
Ealing Broadway ⊖	d		15 27	15 42				16 08			16 27	16 42				17 08			17 27	17 42
Acton Main Line	d																			
London Paddington ⊖	a	15 29	15 36	15 51	15 44		15 59	16 20	16 22	16 30	16 36	16 52	16 44		17 00	17 20	17 22	17 30	17 36	17 52

		GW ◇■ ⟂	GW ◇■	GW ■	GW ◇■ ⟂	GW ◇■ ⟂	GW ◇■ ⟂	GW ■	GW ◇■ ⟂	GW ◇■ ⟂	HC	GW ■	GW ◇■ ⟂	GW ■	GW ◇■ ⟂	GW ◇■ ⟂	GW ■	GW ◇■ ⟂	GW ◇■ ⟂	HC	GW ■
Oxford	d		16 37				16 50					17 05				17 50					18 05
Reading	d	17 01	17 07	17 18	17 21	17 25	17 28		17 49	17 51		17 53	18 03	18 18	18 22	18 28		18 50	18 51		18 53
Twyford	d		17 14	17 25								17 59		18 25							18 59
Maidenhead	d		17 28	17 36								18 07		18 36							19 07
Taplow	d																				
Burnham	d			17 40				←				18 13		18 40			←				19 13
Slough	a		17 39	17 45			17 43	17 45				18 18		18 45		18 41	18 45				19 18
	d		17 39	17 48			17 43	17 48				18 18		18 48		18 41	18 48				19 18
Langley	d			→				17 52				18 23		→			18 52				19 23
Iver	d																				
West Drayton	d							17 58				18 29					18 58				19 29
Heathrow Terminal 4	d										18 07									19 07	
Heathrow Terminal 1-2-3	d										18 13									19 13	
Hayes & Harlington	d							18 00			18 19	18 33					19 00			19 19	19 33
Southall	d										18 22	18 37								19 22	19 37
Hanwell	d																				
Greenford ⊖	d																				
South Greenford	d																				
Castle Bar Park	d																				
Drayton Green	d																				
West Ealing	d																				
Ealing Broadway ⊖	d							18 08			18 27	18 42					19 08			19 27	19 42
Acton Main Line	d																				
London Paddington ⊖	a	17 43	18 03		17 58	18 01	18 07	18 19	18 22	18 29	18 36	18 52	18 44		18 59	19 07	19 18	19 22	19 29	19 36	19 52

		GW ◇■ ⟂	GW ■	GW ◇■ ⟂	GW ◇■ ⟂	GW ◇■ ⟂	GW ◇■ ⟂	GW ■	GW ◇■ ⟂	GW ◇■ ⟂	HC	GW ■	GW ■	GW ◇■ ⟂	GW ◇■	GW ◇■ ⟂	GW ■	GW ◇■ ⟂	HC	GW ■
Oxford	d					18 50						19 05			19 50					20 05
Reading	d	19 03	19 18	19 21	19 25	19 28	19 34		19 48	19 51		19 53	20 18	20 21	20 24	20 34		20 49		20 53
Twyford	d		19 25									19 59	20 25							20 59
Maidenhead	d		19 36									20 07	20 36							21 07
Taplow	d																			
Burnham	d		19 40					←				20 13	20 40				←			21 13
Slough	a		19 45			19 44		19 45				20 18	20 45		20 43		20 45			21 15
	d		19 48			19 44		19 48				20 18	20 48		20 43		20 48			21 18
Langley	d		→					19 52				20 23	→				20 52			21 23
Iver	d																			
West Drayton	d							19 58				20 29					20 58			21 29
Heathrow Terminal 4	d										20 07								21 07	
Heathrow Terminal 1-2-3	d										20 13								21 13	
Hayes & Harlington	d							20 00			20 19	20 33					21 00		21 19	21 33
Southall	d										20 22	20 37					21 06		21 22	21 37
Hanwell	d																			
Greenford ⊖	d																			
South Greenford	d																			
Castle Bar Park	d																			
Drayton Green	d																			
West Ealing	d																			
Ealing Broadway ⊖	d							20 08			20 27	20 42					21 12		21 27	21 42
Acton Main Line	d																			
London Paddington ⊖	a	19 44		19 59	20 02	20 07	20 14	20 18	20 22	20 29	20 36	20 51		20 59	21 05	21 13	21 21	21 29	21 36	21 52

		GW ■	GW ◇■ ⟂	GW ◇■ ⟂	GW ◇■	GW ◇■ ⟂	GW ■	GW ◇■ ⟂	HC	GW ■	GW ◇■ ⟂	GW ◇■	GW ■	GW ◇■ ⟂	GW ◇■ ⟂	HC	GW ■	GW ◇■	GW ◇■ ⟂	GW ■
Oxford	d				20 50					21 21		21 50					22 17	22 46		
Reading	d	21 18	21 21	21 24	21 28	21 34		21 49		22 06	22 20	22 24	22 29	22 36	22 41		23 00	23 22	23 30	23 36
Twyford	d	21 25								22 17			22 39				23 07			23 43
Maidenhead	d	21 36			21 40					22 25			22 47				23 15			23 51
Taplow	d																			
Burnham	d	21 40					←			22 29			22 51							23 56
Slough	a	21 45			21 44		21 45			22 34		22 43	22 56				23 22	23 43		00 01
	d	21 48			21 46		21 48			22 34		22 44	23 01				23 23	23 44		00 02
Langley	d	→					21 52			22 39			23 05				23 27			00 06
Iver	d																			
West Drayton	d						21 58			22 44			23 10				23 31			00 11
Heathrow Terminal 4	d								22 07							23 07				
Heathrow Terminal 1-2-3	d								22 13							23 13				
Hayes & Harlington	d						22 00		22 19	22 49			23 16			23 19	23 35			00 16
Southall	d						22 06		22 22	22 52						23 22	23 39			00 20
Hanwell	d																			
Greenford ⊖	d																			
South Greenford	d																			
Castle Bar Park	d																			
Drayton Green	d																			
West Ealing	d																			
Ealing Broadway ⊖	d						22 11		22 27	22 58			23 23			23 27	23 44			00 25
Acton Main Line	d																			
London Paddington ⊖	a		21 59	22 02	22 07	22 13	22 21	22 29	22 36	23 07	22 58	23 13	23 33	23 16	23 22	23 36	23 53	00 05	00 13	00 34

Mondays to Fridays

London - Heathrow Airport

Network Diagram - see first Page of Table 116

Miles		HC	HX	HX [1]	HC	HX [1]	HX	HX [1]	HX	HX [1]		HX	HX [1]	HX	HX [1]	HX	HX [1]	HX	HX [1]	HX		HX [1]	HX	HX [1]
0	London Paddington [15] ⊖ d	04 42		05 10	05 13	05 25		05 40		05 55			06 10		06 25		06 40		06 55			07 10		07 25
14¾	Heathrow Terminals 1-2-3 [2] ✈ a	05 04		05 26	05 35	05 40		05 55		06 10			06 25		06 40		06 55		07 10			07 25		07 40
—	d	05 05	05 16	05 29	05 36	05 41	05 44	05 56	06 03	06 11		06 18	06 26	06 33	06 41	06 48	06 56	07 03	07 11	07 18		07 26	07 33	07 41
—	Heathrow Terminal 4 ✈ a	05 10	05 20		05 41		05 48		06 07			06 22		06 37		06 52		07 07		07 22			07 37	
16¼	Heathrow Terminal 5 ✈ a			05 33		05 46		06 01		06 16			06 31		06 46		07 01		07 16			07 31		07 46

	HX	HX [1]	HX	HX [1]	HX	HX [1]		HX	HX [1]	HX	HX [1]	HX	HX [1]	HX	HX [1]	HX		HX [1]	HX	HX [1]	HX	HX [1]	HX	HX [1]
London Paddington [15] ⊖ d		07 40		07 55		08 10			08 25		08 40		08 55		09 10			09 25		09 40		09 55		10 10
Heathrow Terminals 1-2-3 [2] ✈ a		07 55		08 10		08 25			08 40		08 55		09 10		09 25			09 40		09 55		10 10		10 25
d	07 48	07 56	08 03	08 11	08 18	08 26		08 33	08 41	08 48	08 56	09 03	09 11	09 18	09 26	09 33		09 41	09 48	09 56	10 03	10 11	10 18	10 26
Heathrow Terminal 4 ✈ a	07 52		08 07		08 22			08 37		08 52		09 07		09 22		09 37			09 52		10 07		10 22	
Heathrow Terminal 5 ✈ a		08 01		08 16		08 31			08 46		09 01		09 16		09 31			09 46		10 01		10 16		10 31

	HX	HX [1]		HX	HX [1]	HX	HX [1]	HX	HX [1]	HX	HX [1]	HX		HX [1]	HX	HX [1]	HX	HX [1]	HX	HX [1]	HX	HX [1]		HX
London Paddington [15] ⊖ d		10 25			10 40		10 55		11 10		11 25			11 40		11 55		12 10		12 25		12 40		
Heathrow Terminals 1-2-3 [2] ✈ a		10 40			10 55		11 10		11 25		11 40			11 55		12 10		12 25		12 40		12 55		
d	10 33	10 41		10 48	10 56	11 03	11 11	11 18	11 26	11 33	11 41	11 48		11 56	12 03	12 11	12 18	12 26	12 33	12 41	12 48	12 56		13 03
Heathrow Terminal 4 ✈ a	10 37			10 52		11 07		11 22		11 37		11 52			12 07		12 22		12 37		12 52			13 07
Heathrow Terminal 5 ✈ a		10 46			11 01		11 16		11 31		11 46			12 01		12 16		12 31		12 46		13 01		

	HX [1]	HX	HX [1]	HX	HX [1]	HX	HX [1]	HX		HX [1]	HX	HX [1]	HX	HX [1]	HX	HX [1]	HX	HX [1]		HX	HX [1]	HX	HX [1]	HX
London Paddington [15] ⊖ d	12 55		13 10		13 25		13 40			13 55		14 10		14 25		14 40		14 55			15 10		15 25	
Heathrow Terminals 1-2-3 [2] ✈ a	13 10		13 25		13 40		13 55			14 10		14 25		14 40		14 55		15 10			15 25		15 40	
d	13 11	13 18	13 26	13 33	13 41	13 48	13 56	14 03		14 11	14 18	14 26	14 33	14 41	14 48	14 56	15 03	15 11		15 18	15 26	15 33	15 41	15 48
Heathrow Terminal 4 ✈ a		13 22		13 37		13 52		14 07			14 22		14 37		14 52		15 07			15 22		15 37		15 52
Heathrow Terminal 5 ✈ a	13 16		13 31		13 46		14 01			14 16		14 31		14 46		15 01		15 16			15 31		15 46	

	HX [1]	HX	HX [1]	HX		HX [1]	HX	HX [1]	HX	HX [1]	HX	HX [1]	HX	HX [1]		HX	HX [1]	HX	HX [1]	HX	HX [1]	HX	HX [1]	HX
London Paddington [15] ⊖ d	15 40		15 55			16 10		16 25		16 40		16 55		17 10			17 25		17 40		17 55		18 10	
Heathrow Terminals 1-2-3 [2] ✈ a	15 55		16 10			16 25		16 40		16 55		17 10		17 25			17 40		17 55		18 10		18 25	
d	15 56	16 03	16 11	16 18		16 26	16 33	16 41	16 48	16 56	17 03	17 11	17 18	17 26		17 33	17 41	17 48	17 56	18 03	18 11	18 18	18 26	18 33
Heathrow Terminal 4 ✈ a		16 07		16 22			16 37		16 52		17 07		17 22			17 37		17 52		18 07		18 22		18 37
Heathrow Terminal 5 ✈ a	16 01		16 16			16 31		16 46		17 01		17 16		17 31			17 46		18 01		18 16		18 31	

		HX [1]	HX	HX [1]	HX	HX [1]	HX	HX [1]	HX	HX [1]		HX	HX [1]	HX	HX [1]	HX	HX [1]	HX	HX [1]	HX		HX [1]	HX	HX [1]
London Paddington [15] ⊖ d		18 25		18 40		18 55		19 10		19 25			19 40		19 55		20 10		20 25			20 40		20 55
Heathrow Terminals 1-2-3 [2] ✈ a		18 40		18 55		19 10		19 25		19 40			19 55		20 10		20 25		20 40			20 55		21 10
d		18 41	18 48	18 56	19 03	19 11	19 18	19 26	19 33	19 41		19 48	19 56	20 03	20 11	20 18	20 26	20 33	20 41	20 48		20 56	21 03	21 11
Heathrow Terminal 4 ✈ a			18 52		19 07		19 22		19 37			19 52		20 07		20 22		20 37		20 52			21 07	
Heathrow Terminal 5 ✈ a		18 46		19 01		19 16		19 31		19 46			20 01		20 16		20 31		20 46			21 01		21 16

	HX	HX [1]	HX	HX [1]	HX	HX [1]		HX	HX [1]	HX	HX [1]	HX	HX [1]	HX	HX [1]	HX		HX [1]	HX	HX [1]	HX	HC	HX [1]	HX
London Paddington [15] ⊖ d		21 10		21 25		21 40			21 55		22 10		22 25		22 40			22 55		23 10		23 03	23 25	
Heathrow Terminals 1-2-3 [2] ✈ a		21 25		21 40		21 55			22 10		22 25		22 40		22 55			23 10		23 25		23 35	23 40	
d	21 18	21 26	21 33	21 41	21 48	21 56		22 03	22 11	22 18	22 26	22 33	22 41	22 48	22 56	23 03		23 11	23 18	23 26	23 33	23 37	23 41	23 48
Heathrow Terminal 4 ✈ a	21 22		21 37		21 52			22 07		22 22		22 37		22 52		23 07			23 22		23 37	23 41		23 52
Heathrow Terminal 5 ✈ a		21 31		21 46		22 01			22 16		22 31		22 46		23 01			23 16		23 31			23 46	

Saturdays

	HC	HX	HX [1]	HC	HX [1]	HX	HX [1]	HX	HX [1]		HX	HX [1]	HX	HX [1]	HX	HX [1]	HX	HX [1]	HX		HX [1]	HX	HX [1]	HX
London Paddington [15] ⊖ d	04 42		05 10	05 13	05 25		05 40		05 55			06 10		06 25		06 40		06 55			07 10		07 25	
Heathrow Terminals 1-2-3 [2] ✈ a	05 04		05 26	05 35	05 40		05 55		06 10			06 25		06 40		06 55		07 10			07 25		07 40	
d	05 05	05 16	05 29	05 36	05 41	05 44	05 56	06 03	06 11		06 18	06 26	06 33	06 41	06 48	06 56	07 03	07 11	07 18		07 26	07 33	07 41	07 48
Heathrow Terminal 4 ✈ a	05 10	05 20		05 41		05 48		06 07			06 22		06 37		06 52		07 07		07 22			07 37		07 52
Heathrow Terminal 5 ✈ a			05 33		05 46		06 01		06 16			06 31		06 46		07 01		07 16			07 31		07 46	

	HX [1]	HX	HX [1]	HX	HX [1]		HX	HX [1]	HX	HX [1]	HX	HX [1]	HX	HX [1]	HX		HX [1]	HX	HX [1]	HX	HX [1]	HX	HX [1]	HX
London Paddington [15] ⊖ d	07 40		07 55		08 10			08 25		08 40		08 55		09 10			09 25		09 40		09 55		10 10	
Heathrow Terminals 1-2-3 [2] ✈ a	07 55		08 10		08 25			08 40		08 55		09 10		09 25			09 40		09 55		10 10		10 25	
d	07 56	08 03	08 11	08 18	08 26		08 33	08 41	08 48	08 56	09 03	09 11	09 18	09 26	09 33		09 41	09 48	09 56	10 03	10 11	10 18	10 26	10 33
Heathrow Terminal 4 ✈ a		08 07		08 22			08 37		08 52		09 07		09 22		09 37			09 52		10 07		10 22		10 37
Heathrow Terminal 5 ✈ a	08 01		08 16		08 31			08 46		09 01		09 16		09 31			09 46		10 01		10 16		10 31	

	HX [1]		HX	HX [1]	HX	HX [1]	HX	HX [1]	HX	HX [1]	HX		HX [1]	HX	HX [1]	HX	HX [1]	HX	HX [1]	HX	HX [1]		HX	HX [1]
London Paddington [15] ⊖ d	10 25			10 40		10 55		11 10		11 25			11 40		11 55		12 10		12 25		12 40			12 55
Heathrow Terminals 1-2-3 [2] ✈ a	10 40			10 55		11 10		11 25		11 40			11 55		12 10		12 25		12 40		12 55			13 10
d	10 41		10 48	10 56	11 03	11 11	11 18	11 26	11 33	11 41	11 48		11 56	12 03	12 11	12 18	12 26	12 33	12 41	12 48	12 56		13 03	13 11
Heathrow Terminal 4 ✈ a			10 52		11 07		11 22		11 37		11 52			12 07		12 22		12 37		12 52			13 07	
Heathrow Terminal 5 ✈ a	10 46			11 01		11 16		11 31		11 46			12 01		12 16		12 31		12 46		13 01			13 16

Saturdays

London - Heathrow Airport

Network Diagram - see first Page of Table 116

	HX	HX [1]	HX	HX [1]	HX	HX [1]	HX		HX [1]	HX	HX [1]	HX	HX [1]	HX	HX [1]	HX	HX [1]		HX	HX [1]	HX	HX [1]	HX	HX [1]
London Paddington [15] ⊖ d		13 10		13 25		13 40			13 55		14 10		14 25		14 40		14 55			15 10		15 25		15 40
Heathrow Terminals 1-2-3 [2] ✈ a		13 25		13 40		13 55			14 10		14 25		14 40		14 55		15 10			15 25		15 40		15 55
d	13 18	13 26	13 33	13 41	13 48	13 56	14 03		14 11	14 18	14 26	14 33	14 41	14 48	14 56	15 03	15 11		15 18	15 26	15 33	15 41	15 48	15 56
Heathrow Terminal 4 ✈ a	13 22		13 37		13 52		14 07			14 22		14 37		14 52		15 07			15 22		15 37		15 52	
Heathrow Terminal 5 ✈ a		13 31		13 46		14 01			14 16		14 31		14 46		15 01		15 16			15 31		15 46		16 01

	HX	HX [1]	HX		HX [1]	HX	HX [1]	HX	HX [1]	HX	HX [1]	HX	HX [1]		HX	HX [1]	HX	HX [1]	HX	HX [1]	HX	HX [1]	HX	
London Paddington [15] ⊖ d		15 55			16 10		16 25		16 40		16 55		17 10			17 25		17 40		17 55		18 10		
Heathrow Terminals 1-2-3 [2] ✈ a		16 10			16 25		16 40		16 55		17 10		17 25			17 40		17 55		18 10		18 25		
d	16 03	16 11	16 18		16 26	16 33	16 41	16 48	16 56	17 03	17 11	17 18	17 26		17 33	17 41	17 48	17 56	18 03	18 11	18 18	18 26	18 33	
Heathrow Terminal 4 ✈ a	16 07		16 22			16 37		16 52		17 07		17 22			17 37		17 52		18 07		18 22		18 37	
Heathrow Terminal 5 ✈ a		16 16			16 31		16 46		17 01		17 16		17 31			17 46		18 01		18 16		18 31		

	HX [1]	HX	HX [1]	HX	HX [1]	HX	HX [1]	HX	HX [1]		HX	HX [1]	HX	HX [1]	HX	HX [1]	HX	HX [1]	HX		HX [1]	HX	HX [1]	HX
London Paddington [15] ⊖ d	18 25		18 40		18 55		19 10		19 25			19 40		19 55		20 10		20 25			20 40		20 55	
Heathrow Terminals 1-2-3 [2] ✈ a	18 40		18 55		19 10		19 25		19 40			19 55		20 10		20 25		20 40			20 55		21 10	
d	18 41	18 48	18 56	19 03	19 11	19 18	19 26	19 33	19 41		19 48	19 56	20 03	20 11	20 18	20 26	20 33	20 41	20 48		20 56	21 03	21 11	21 18
Heathrow Terminal 4 ✈ a		18 52		19 07		19 22		19 37			19 52		20 07		20 22		20 37		20 52			21 07		21 22
Heathrow Terminal 5 ✈ a	18 46		19 01		19 16		19 31		19 46			20 01		20 16		20 31		20 46			21 01		21 16	

	HX [1]	HX	HX [1]	HX	HX [1]		HX	HX [1]	HX	HX [1]	HX	HX [1]	HX	HX [1]	HX		HX [1]	HX	HX [1]	HX	HC	HX [1]	HX	
London Paddington [15] ⊖ d	21 10		21 25		21 40			21 55		22 10		22 25		22 40			22 55		23 10		23 03	23 25		
Heathrow Terminals 1-2-3 [2] ✈ a	21 25		21 40		21 55			22 10		22 25		22 40		22 55			23 10		23 25		23 35	23 40		
d	21 26	21 33	21 41	21 48	21 56		22 03	22 11	22 18	22 26	22 33	22 41	22 48	22 56	23 03		23 11	23 18	23 26	23 33	23 37	23 41	23 48	
Heathrow Terminal 4 ✈ a		21 37		21 52			22 07		22 22		22 37		22 52		23 07			23 22		23 37	23 41		23 52	
Heathrow Terminal 5 ✈ a	21 31		21 46		22 01			22 16		22 31		22 46		23 01			23 16		23 31			23 46		

Sundays

until 24 June

	HX [1]	HC	HX [1]	HC	HX [1]	HX	HX [1]	HX	HX		HX	HC	HX [1]	HX	HX [1]	HX	HX [1]	HX	HX [1]		HX	HC	HX [1]	HX
London Paddington [15] ⊖ d	05 10		05 25		05 40		05 55		06 10			06 12	06 25		06 40		06 55		07 10			07 12	07 25	
Heathrow Terminals 1-2-3 [2] ✈ a	05 26		05 41		05 56		06 11		06 26			06 34	06 41		06 56		07 11		07 26			07 34	07 41	
d	05 27	05 36	05 42	05 47	05 59	06 01	06 13	06 19	06 31		06 33	06 37	06 47	06 49	06 59	07 01	07 13	07 19	07 31		07 33	07 37	07 47	07 49
Heathrow Terminal 4 ✈ a		05 40		05 51		06 05		06 23			06 37	06 41		06 53		07 05		07 23			07 37	07 41		07 53
Heathrow Terminal 5 ✈ a	05 32		05 47		06 03		06 17		06 35				06 51		07 03		07 17		07 35				07 51	

	HX [1]	HX	HX [1]	HX	HX [1]		HX	HC	HX [1]	HX	HX [1]	HX	HX [1]	HX	HX [1]		HX	HC	HX [1]	HX	HX [1]	HX	HX [1]	HX
London Paddington [15] ⊖ d	07 40		07 55		08 10			08 12	08 25		08 40		08 55		09 10			09 12	09 25		09 40		09 55	
Heathrow Terminals 1-2-3 [2] ✈ a	07 56		08 11		08 26			08 34	08 41		08 56		09 11		09 26			09 34	09 41		09 56		10 11	
d	07 59	08 01	08 13	08 19	08 31		08 33	08 37	08 47	08 49	08 59	09 01	09 13	09 19	09 31		09 33	09 37	09 47	09 49	09 59	10 01	10 13	10 19
Heathrow Terminal 4 ✈ a		08 05		08 23			08 37	08 41		08 53		09 05		09 23			09 37	09 41		09 53		10 05		10 23
Heathrow Terminal 5 ✈ a	08 03		08 17		08 35				08 51		09 03		09 17		09 35				09 51		10 03		10 17	

	HX [1]		HX	HC	HX [1]	HX	HX [1]	HX	HX [1]	HX	HX [1]		HX	HC	HX [1]	HX	HX [1]	HX	HX [1]	HX	HX		HX	HC
London Paddington [15] ⊖ d	10 10			10 12	10 25		10 40		10 55		11 10			11 12	11 25		11 40		11 55		12 10			12 12
Heathrow Terminals 1-2-3 [2] ✈ a	10 26			10 34	10 41		10 56		11 11		11 26			11 34	11 41		11 56		12 11		12 26			12 34
d	10 31		10 33	10 37	10 47	10 49	10 59	11 01	11 13	11 19	11 31		11 33	11 37	11 47	11 49	11 59	12 01	12 13	12 19	12 31		12 33	12 37
Heathrow Terminal 4 ✈ a			10 37	10 41		10 53		11 05		11 23			11 37	11 41		11 53		12 05		12 23			12 37	12 41
Heathrow Terminal 5 ✈ a	10 35				10 51		11 03		11 17		11 35				11 51		12 03		12 17		12 35			

	HX	HX	HX [1]	HX	HX [1]	HX	HX [1]		HX	HC	HX [1]	HX	HX [1]	HX	HX [1]	HX	HX [1]		HX	HC	HX [1]	HX	HX [1]	HX
London Paddington [15] ⊖ d	12 25		12 40		12 55		13 10			13 12	13 25		13 40		13 55		14 10			14 12	14 25		14 40	
Heathrow Terminals 1-2-3 [2] ✈ a	12 41		12 56		13 11		13 26			13 34	13 41		13 56		14 11		14 26			14 34	14 41		14 56	
d	12 47	12 49	12 59	13 01	13 13	13 19	13 31		13 33	13 37	13 47	13 49	13 59	14 01	14 13	14 19	14 31		14 33	14 37	14 47	14 49	14 59	15 01
Heathrow Terminal 4 ✈ a		12 53		13 05		13 23			13 37	13 41		13 53		14 05		14 23			14 37	14 41		14 53		15 05
Heathrow Terminal 5 ✈ a	12 51		13 03		13 17		13 35				13 51		14 03		14 17		14 35				14 51		15 03	

	HX [1]	HX	HX [1]		HX	HC	HX [1]	HX	HX [1]	HX	HX [1]	HX	HX [1]		HX	HC	HX [1]	HX	HX [1]	HX	HX [1]	HX	HX	
London Paddington [15] ⊖ d	14 55		15 10			15 12	15 25		15 40		15 55		16 10			16 12	16 25		16 40		16 55		17 10	
Heathrow Terminals 1-2-3 [2] ✈ a	15 11		15 26			15 34	15 41		15 56		16 11		16 26			16 34	16 41		16 56		17 11		17 26	
d	15 13	15 19	15 31		15 33	15 37	15 47	15 49	15 59	16 01	16 13	16 19	16 31		16 33	16 37	16 47	16 49	16 59	17 01	17 13	17 19	17 31	
Heathrow Terminal 4 ✈ a		15 23			15 37	15 41		15 53		16 05		16 23			16 37	16 41		16 53		17 05		17 23		
Heathrow Terminal 5 ✈ a	15 17		15 35				15 51		16 03		16 17		16 35				16 51		17 03		17 17		17 35	

	HX	HC	HX	HX	HX	HX	HX	HX	HX		HX	HC	HX	HX	HX	HX	HX	HX	HX		HX	HC	HX	HX
London Paddington [15] ⊖ d		17 12	17 25		17 40		17 55		18 10			18 12	18 25		18 40		18 55		19 10			19 12	19 25	
Heathrow Terminals 1-2-3 [2] ✈ a		17 34	17 41		17 56		18 11		18 26			18 34	18 41		18 56		19 11		19 26			19 34	19 41	
d	17 33	17 37	17 47	17 49	17 59	18 01	18 13	18 19	18 31		18 33	18 37	18 47	18 49	18 59	19 01	19 13	19 19	19 31		19 33	19 37	19 47	19 49
Heathrow Terminal 4 ✈ a	17 37	17 41		17 53		18 05		18 23			18 37	18 41		18 53		19 05		19 23			19 37	19 41		19 53
Heathrow Terminal 5 ✈ a			17 51		18 03		18 17		18 35				18 51		19 03		19 17		19 35				19 51	

Table 118

Sundays
until 24 June

London - Heathrow Airport

Network Diagram - see first Page of Table 116

	HX	HX	HX	HX	HX	HX	HC	HX	HX	HX	HX	HX	HX	HX	HX	HC	HX	HX	HX	HX	HX	HX
London Paddington [15] ⊖ d	19 40		19 55		20 10		20 12	20 25		20 40		20 55		21 10		21 12	21 25		21 40		21 55	
Heathrow Terminals 1-2-3 [2] ✈ a	19 56		20 11		20 26		20 34	20 41		20 56		21 11		21 26		21 34	21 41		21 56		22 11	
d	19 59	20 01	20 13	20 19	20 31	20 33	20 37	20 47	20 49	20 59	21 01	21 13	21 19	21 31	21 33	21 37	21 47	21 49	21 59	22 01	22 13	22 19
Heathrow Terminal 4 ✈ a		20 05		20 23		20 37	20 41		20 53		21 05		21 23		21 37	21 41		21 53		22 05		22 23
Heathrow Terminal 5 ✈ a	20 03		20 17		20 35			20 51		21 03		21 17		21 35			21 51		22 03		22 17	

	HX	HX	HC	HX	HX	HX	HX	HX	HX	HX	HX	HC	HX	HX
London Paddington [15] ⊖ d	22 10		22 12	22 25		22 40		22 55		23 10		23 12	23 25	
Heathrow Terminals 1-2-3 [2] ✈ a	22 26		22 34	22 41		22 56		23 11		23 26		23 34	23 41	
d	22 31	22 33	22 37	22 47	22 49	22 59	23 01	23 13	23 19	23 31	23 33	23 37	23 47	23 49
Heathrow Terminal 4 ✈ a		22 37	22 41		22 53		23 05		23 23		23 37	23 41		23 53
Heathrow Terminal 5 ✈ a	22 35			22 51		23 03		23 17		23 35			23 51	

Sundays
1 July to 9 September

	HX [1]	HC	HX [1]	HC	HX [1]	HX	HX [1]	HX	HX	HX	HC	HX [1]	HX	HX [1]	HX	HX [1]	HX	HX [1]	HX	HC	HX [1]	HX
London Paddington [15] ⊖ d	05 10		05 25		05 40		05 55		06 10		06 12	06 25		06 40		06 55		07 10		07 12	07 25	
Heathrow Terminals 1-2-3 [2] ✈ a	05 26		05 41		05 56		06 11		06 26		06 34	06 41		06 56		07 11		07 26		07 34	07 41	
d	05 27	05 36	05 42	05 47	05 59	06 01	06 13	06 19	06 31	06 33	06 37	06 47	06 49	06 59	07 01	07 13	07 19	07 31	07 33	07 37	07 47	07 49
Heathrow Terminal 4 ✈ a		05 40		05 51		06 05		06 23		06 37	06 41		06 53		07 05		07 23		07 37	07 41		07 53
Heathrow Terminal 5 ✈ a	05 32		05 47		06 03		06 17		06 35			06 51		07 03		07 17		07 35			07 51	

	HX [1]	HX	HX [1]	HX	HX [1]	HX	HC	HX [1]	HX	HX [1]	HX	HX [1]	HX	HX [1]	HC	HX [1]	HX	HX [1]	HC	HX [1]	HX	HX [1]
London Paddington [15] ⊖ d	07 40		07 55		08 10		08 12	08 25		08 40		08 55		09 10	09 07	09 25		09 40	09 37	09 55		10 10
Heathrow Terminals 1-2-3 [2] ✈ a	07 56		08 11		08 26		08 34	08 41		08 56		09 11		09 25	09 29	09 40		09 55	09 59	10 10		10 25
d	07 59	08 01	08 13	08 19	08 31	08 33	08 37	08 47	08 49	08 59	09 01	09 13	09 15	09 26	09 35	09 41	09 44	09 56	10 05	10 11	10 14	10 26
Heathrow Terminal 4 ✈ a		08 05		08 23		08 37	08 41		08 53		09 05		09 19		09 39		09 48		10 09		10 18	
Heathrow Terminal 5 ✈ a	08 03		08 17		08 35			08 51		09 03		09 17		09 31		09 46		10 01		10 16		10 31

	HC	HX [1]	HX	HX [1]	HC	HX [1]	HX	HX [1]	HC	HX [1]	HX	HX [1]	HC	HX [1]	HX	HX	HC	HX [1]	HX	HX [1]	HC
London Paddington [15] ⊖ d	10 07	10 25		10 40	10 37	10 55		11 10	11 07	11 25		11 40	11 37	11 55		12 10	12 07	12 25		12 40	12 37
Heathrow Terminals 1-2-3 [2] ✈ a	10 29	10 40		10 55	10 59	11 10		11 25	11 29	11 40		11 55	11 59	12 10		12 25	12 29	12 40		12 55	12 59
d	10 35	10 41	10 44	10 56	11 05	11 11	11 14	11 26	11 35	11 41	11 44	11 56	12 05	12 11	12 14	12 26	12 35	12 41	12 44	12 56	13 05
Heathrow Terminal 4 ✈ a	10 39		10 48		11 09		11 18		11 39		11 48		12 09		12 18		12 39		12 48		13 09
Heathrow Terminal 5 ✈ a		10 46		11 01		11 16		11 31		11 46		12 01		12 16		12 31		12 46		13 01	

	HX [1]	HX	HX [1]	HC	HX [1]	HX	HX [1]	HC	HX [1]	HX	HX [1]	HC	HX [1]	HX	HX [1]	HC	HX [1]	HX	HX [1]	HC	HX [1]	HX
London Paddington [15] ⊖ d	12 55		13 10	13 07	13 25		13 40	13 37	13 55		14 10	14 07	14 25		14 40	14 37	14 55		15 10	15 07	15 25	
Heathrow Terminals 1-2-3 [2] ✈ a	13 10		13 25	13 29	13 40		13 55	13 59	14 10		14 25	14 29	14 40		14 55	14 59	15 10		15 25	15 29	15 40	
d	13 11	13 14	13 26	13 35	13 41	13 44	13 56	14 05	14 11	14 14	14 26	14 35	14 41	14 44	14 56	15 05	15 11	15 14	15 26	15 35	15 41	15 44
Heathrow Terminal 4 ✈ a		13 18		13 39		13 48		14 09		14 18		14 39		14 48		15 09		15 18		15 39		15 48
Heathrow Terminal 5 ✈ a	13 16		13 31		13 46		14 01		14 16		14 31		14 46		15 01		15 16		15 31		15 46	

	HX [1]	HC	HX [1]	HX	HX [1]	HC	HX [1]	HX	HX [1]	HC	HX	HX	HX	HC	HX	HX	HX	HC	HX	HX	HX
London Paddington [15] ⊖ d	15 40	15 37	15 55		16 10	16 07	16 25		16 40	16 37	16 55		17 10	17 07	17 25		17 40	17 37	17 55		18 10
Heathrow Terminals 1-2-3 [2] ✈ a	15 55	15 59	16 10		16 25	16 29	16 40		16 55	16 59	17 10		17 25	17 29	17 40		17 55	17 59	18 10		18 25
d	15 56	16 05	16 11	16 14	16 26	16 35	16 41	16 44	16 56	17 05	17 11	17 14	17 26	17 35	17 41	17 44	17 56	18 05	18 11	18 14	18 26
Heathrow Terminal 4 ✈ a		16 09		16 18		16 39		16 48		17 09		17 18		17 39		17 48		18 09		18 18	
Heathrow Terminal 5 ✈ a	16 01		16 16		16 31		16 46		17 01		17 16		17 31		17 46		18 01		18 16		18 31

	HC	HX	HX	HX	HC	HX	HX	HX	HC	HX	HX	HX	HC	HX	HX	HX	HC	HX	HX	HX	HX	HC
London Paddington [15] ⊖ d	18 07	18 25		18 40	18 37	18 55		19 10	19 07	19 25		19 40	19 37	19 55		20 10	20 07	20 25			20 40	20 37
Heathrow Terminals 1-2-3 [2] ✈ a	18 29	18 40		18 55	18 59	19 10		19 25	19 29	19 40		19 55	19 59	20 10		20 25	20 29	20 40			20 55	20 59
d	18 35	18 41	18 44	18 56	19 05	19 11	19 14	19 26	19 35	19 41	19 44	19 56	20 05	20 11	20 14	20 26	20 35	20 41	20 44	20 49	20 56	21 05
Heathrow Terminal 4 ✈ a	18 39		18 48		19 09		19 18		19 39		19 48		20 09		20 18		20 39		20 48	20 53		21 09
Heathrow Terminal 5 ✈ a		18 46		19 01		19 16		19 31		19 46		20 01		20 16		20 31		20 46			21 01	

	HX	HX	HX	HC	HX	HX	HX	HX	HX	HX	HX	HX	HC	HX	HX	HX	HX	HX	HX	HX	HX	HC
London Paddington [15] ⊖ d	20 55		21 10	21 07	21 25		21 40		21 55		22 10		22 12	22 25		22 40		22 55		23 10		23 12
Heathrow Terminals 1-2-3 [2] ✈ a	21 10		21 25	21 29	21 40		21 56		22 11		22 26		22 34	22 41		22 56		23 11		23 26		23 34
d	21 11	21 14	21 26	21 35	21 41	21 49	21 59	22 01	22 13	22 19	22 31	22 33	22 37	22 47	22 49	22 59	23 01	23 13	23 19	23 31	23 33	23 37
Heathrow Terminal 4 ✈ a		21 18		21 39		21 53		22 05		22 23		22 37	22 41		22 53		23 05		23 23		23 37	23 41
Heathrow Terminal 5 ✈ a	21 16		21 31		21 46		22 03		22 17		22 35			22 51		23 03		23 17		23 35		

	HX	HX
London Paddington [15] ⊖ d	23 25	
Heathrow Terminals 1-2-3 [2] ✈ a	23 41	
d	23 47	23 49
Heathrow Terminal 4 ✈ a		23 53
Heathrow Terminal 5 ✈ a	23 51	

Table 118

Sundays
16 September to 21 October

London - Heathrow Airport

Network Diagram - see first Page of Table 116

	HX [1]	HC	HX [1]	HC	HX [1]	HX	HX [1]	HX	HX	HX	HC	HX [1]	HX	HX [1]	HX	HX [1]	HX	HX [1]	HX	HC	HX [1]	HX
London Paddington [15] ⊖ d	05 10		05 25		05 40		05 55		06 10		06 12	06 25		06 40		06 55		07 10		07 12	07 25	
Heathrow Terminals 1-2-3 [2] ✈ a	05 26		05 41		05 56		06 11		06 26		06 34	06 41		06 56		07 11		07 26		07 34	07 41	
d	05 27	05 36	05 42	05 47	05 59	06 01	06 13	06 19	06 31	06 33	06 37	06 47	06 49	06 59	07 01	07 13	07 19	07 31	07 33	07 37	07 47	07 49
Heathrow Terminal 4 ✈ a		05 40		05 51		06 05		06 23		06 37	06 41		06 53		07 05		07 23		07 37	07 41		07 53
Heathrow Terminal 5 ✈ a	05 32		05 47		06 03		06 17		06 35			06 51		07 03		07 17		07 35			07 51	

	HX [1]	HX	HX [1]	HX	HX [1]	HX	HC	HX [1]	HX	HX [1]	HX	HX [1]	HX	HX [1]	HX	HC	HX [1]	HX	HX [1]	HX	HX [1]	HX
London Paddington [15] ⊖ d	07 40		07 55		08 10		08 12	08 25		08 40		08 55		09 10		09 12	09 25		09 40		09 55	
Heathrow Terminals 1-2-3 [2] ✈ a	07 56		08 11		08 26		08 34	08 41		08 56		09 11		09 26		09 34	09 41		09 56		10 11	
d	07 59	08 01	08 13	08 19	08 31	08 33	08 37	08 47	08 49	08 59	09 01	09 13	09 19	09 31	09 33	09 37	09 47	09 49	09 59	10 01	10 13	10 19
Heathrow Terminal 4 ✈ a		08 05		08 23		08 37	08 41		08 53		09 05		09 23		09 37	09 41		09 53		10 05		10 23
Heathrow Terminal 5 ✈ a	08 03		08 17		08 35			08 51		09 03		09 17		09 35			09 51		10 03		10 17	

	HX [1]	HX	HC	HX [1]	HX	HX [1]	HX	HX [1]	HX	HX [1]	HX	HC	HX [1]	HX	HX [1]	HX	HX [1]	HX	HX	HX	HC
London Paddington [15] ⊖ d	10 10		10 12	10 25		10 40		10 55		11 10		11 12	11 25		11 40		11 55		12 10		12 12
Heathrow Terminals 1-2-3 [2] ✈ a	10 26		10 34	10 41		10 56		11 11		11 26		11 34	11 41		11 56		12 11		12 26		12 34
d	10 31	10 33	10 37	10 47	10 49	10 59	11 01	11 13	11 19	11 31	11 33	11 37	11 47	11 49	11 59	12 01	12 13	12 19	12 31	12 33	12 37
Heathrow Terminal 4 ✈ a		10 37	10 41		10 53		11 05		11 23		11 37	11 41		11 53		12 05		12 23		12 37	12 41
Heathrow Terminal 5 ✈ a	10 35			10 51		11 03		11 17		11 35			11 51		12 03		12 17		12 35		

	HX	HX	HX [1]	HX	HX [1]	HX	HX [1]	HX	HC	HX [1]	HX	HX [1]	HX	HX [1]	HX	HX [1]	HX	HC	HX [1]	HX	HX [1]	HX
London Paddington [15] ⊖ d	12 25		12 40		12 55		13 10		13 12	13 25		13 40		13 55		14 10		14 12	14 25		14 40	
Heathrow Terminals 1-2-3 [2] ✈ a	12 41		12 56		13 11		13 26		13 34	13 41		13 56		14 11		14 26		14 34	14 41		14 56	
d	12 47	12 49	12 59	13 01	13 13	13 19	13 31	13 33	13 37	13 47	13 49	13 59	14 01	14 13	14 19	14 31	14 33	14 37	14 47	14 49	14 59	15 01
Heathrow Terminal 4 ✈ a		12 53		13 05		13 23		13 37	13 41		13 53		14 05		14 23		14 37	14 41		14 53		15 05
Heathrow Terminal 5 ✈ a	12 51		13 03		13 17		13 35			13 51		14 03		14 17		14 35			14 51		15 03	

	HX [1]	HX	HX [1]	HX	HC	HX [1]	HX	HX [1]	HX	HX [1]	HX	HX [1]	HX	HC	HX [1]	HX	HX [1]	HX	HX [1]	HX	HX
London Paddington [15] ⊖ d	14 55		15 10		15 12	15 25		15 40		15 55		16 10		16 12	16 25		16 40		16 55		17 10
Heathrow Terminals 1-2-3 [2] ✈ a	15 11		15 26		15 34	15 41		15 56		16 11		16 26		16 34	16 41		16 56		17 11		17 26
d	15 13	15 19	15 31	15 33	15 37	15 47	15 49	15 59	16 01	16 13	16 19	16 31	16 33	16 37	16 47	16 49	16 59	17 01	17 13	17 19	17 31
Heathrow Terminal 4 ✈ a		15 23		15 37	15 41		15 53		16 05		16 23		16 37	16 41		16 53		17 05		17 23	
Heathrow Terminal 5 ✈ a	15 17		15 35			15 51		16 03		16 17		16 35			16 51		17 03		17 17		17 35

	HX	HC	HX	HX	HX	HX	HX	HX	HX	HX	HC	HX	HX	HX	HX	HX	HX	HX	HX	HC	HX	HX
London Paddington [15] ⊖ d		17 12	17 25		17 40		17 55		18 10		18 12	18 25		18 40		18 55		19 10		19 12	19 25	
Heathrow Terminals 1-2-3 [2] ✈ a		17 34	17 41		17 56		18 11		18 26		18 34	18 41		18 56		19 11		19 26		19 34	19 41	
d	17 33	17 37	17 47	17 49	17 59	18 01	18 13	18 19	18 31	18 33	18 37	18 47	18 49	18 59	19 01	19 13	19 19	19 31	19 33	19 37	19 47	19 49
Heathrow Terminal 4 ✈ a	17 37	17 41		17 53		18 05		18 23		18 37	18 41		18 53		19 05		19 23		19 37	19 41		19 53
Heathrow Terminal 5 ✈ a			17 51		18 03		18 17		18 35			18 51		19 03		19 17		19 35			19 51	

	HX	HX	HX	HX	HX	HX	HC	HX	HX	HX	HX	HX	HX	HX	HX	HC	HX	HX	HX	HX	HX	HX
London Paddington [15] ⊖ d	19 40		19 55		20 10		20 12	20 25		20 40		20 55		21 10		21 12	21 25		21 40		21 55	
Heathrow Terminals 1-2-3 [2] ✈ a	19 56		20 11		20 26		20 34	20 41		20 56		21 11		21 26		21 34	21 41		21 56		22 11	
d	19 59	20 01	20 13	20 19	20 31	20 33	20 37	20 47	20 49	20 59	21 01	21 13	21 19	21 31	21 33	21 37	21 47	21 49	21 59	22 01	22 13	22 19
Heathrow Terminal 4 ✈ a		20 05		20 23		20 37	20 41		20 53		21 05		21 23		21 37	21 41		21 53		22 05		22 23
Heathrow Terminal 5 ✈ a	20 03		20 17		20 35			20 51		21 03		21 17		21 35			21 51		22 03		22 17	

	HX	HX	HC	HX	HX	HX	HX	HX	HX	HX	HX	HC	HX	HX
London Paddington [15] ⊖ d	22 10		22 12	22 25		22 40		22 55		23 10		23 12	23 25	
Heathrow Terminals 1-2-3 [2] ✈ a	22 26		22 34	22 41		22 56		23 11		23 26		23 34	23 41	
d	22 31	22 33	22 37	22 47	22 49	22 59	23 01	23 13	23 19	23 31	23 33	23 37	23 47	23 49
Heathrow Terminal 4 ✈ a		22 37	22 41		22 53		23 05		23 23		23 37	23 41		23 53
Heathrow Terminal 5 ✈ a	22 35			22 51		23 03		23 17		23 35			23 51	

Sundays
from 28 October

	HX [1]	HC	HX [1]	HC	HX [1]	HX	HX [1]	HX	HX	HX	HC	HX [1]	HX	HX [1]	HX	HX [1]	HX	HX [1]	HX	HC	HX [1]	HX
London Paddington [15] ⊖ d	05 10		05 25		05 40		05 55		06 10		06 12	06 25		06 40		06 55		07 10		07 12	07 25	
Heathrow Terminals 1-2-3 [2] ✈ a	05 26		05 41		05 56		06 11		06 26		06 34	06 41		06 56		07 11		07 26		07 34	07 41	
d	05 27	05 36	05 42	05 47	05 59	06 01	06 13	06 19	06 31	06 33	06 37	06 47	06 49	06 59	07 01	07 13	07 19	07 31	07 33	07 37	07 47	07 49
Heathrow Terminal 4 ✈ a		05 40		05 51		06 05		06 23		06 37	06 41		06 53		07 05		07 23		07 37	07 41		07 53
Heathrow Terminal 5 ✈ a	05 32		05 47		06 03		06 17		06 35			06 51		07 03		07 17		07 35			07 51	

	HX [1]	HX	HX [1]	HX	HX [1]	HX	HC	HX [1]	HX	HX [1]	HX	HX [1]	HX	HX [1]	HX	HC	HX [1]	HX	HX [1]	HX	HX [1]	HX
London Paddington [15] ⊖ d	07 40		07 55		08 10		08 12	08 25		08 40		08 55		09 10		09 12	09 25		09 40		09 55	
Heathrow Terminals 1-2-3 [2] ✈ a	07 56		08 11		08 26		08 34	08 41		08 56		09 11		09 26		09 34	09 41		09 56		10 11	
d	07 59	08 01	08 13	08 19	08 31	08 33	08 37	08 47	08 49	08 59	09 01	09 13	09 19	09 31	09 33	09 37	09 47	09 49	09 59	10 01	10 13	10 19
Heathrow Terminal 4 ✈ a		08 05		08 23		08 37	08 41		08 53		09 05		09 23		09 37	09 41		09 53		10 05		10 23
Heathrow Terminal 5 ✈ a	08 03		08 17		08 35			08 51		09 03		09 17		09 35			09 51		10 03		10 17	

Table 118

London - Heathrow Airport

Sundays

from 28 October

Network Diagram - see first Page of Table 116

	HX ■		HX	HC	HX ■	HX	HX ■	HX	HX ■	HX	HX ■		HX	HC	HX ■	HX	HX ■	HX	HX ■	HX	HX ■		HX	HC
London Paddington 15 ⊖ d	10 10			10 12	10 25		10 40		10 55		11 10			11 12	11 25		11 40		11 55		12 10			12 12
HeathrowTerminals 1-2-3 2 ✈ a	10 26			10 34	10 41		10 56		11 11		11 26			11 34	11 41		11 56		12 11		12 26			12 34
d	10 31		10 33	10 37	10 47	10 49	10 59	11 01	11 13	11 19	11 31		11 33	11 37	11 47	11 49	11 59	12 01	12 13	12 19	12 31		12 33	12 37
Heathrow Terminal 4 ✈ a			10 37	10 41		10 53		11 05		11 23			11 37	11 41		11 53		12 05		12 23			12 37	12 41
Heathrow Terminal 5 ✈ a	10 35				10 51		11 03		11 17		11 35				11 51		12 03		12 17		12 35			

	HX	HX	HX ■	HX	HX ■	HX	HX ■		HX	HC	HX ■	HX	HX ■	HX	HX ■	HX	HX ■		HX	HC	HX ■	HX	HX ■	HX
London Paddington 15 ⊖ d	12 25		12 40		12 55		13 10			13 12	13 25		13 40		13 55		14 10			14 12	14 25		14 40	
HeathrowTerminals 1-2-3 2 ✈ a	12 41		12 56		13 11		13 26			13 34	13 41		13 56		14 11		14 26			14 34	14 41		14 56	
d	12 47	12 49	12 59	13 01	13 13	13 19	13 31		13 33	13 37	13 47	13 49	13 59	14 01	14 13	14 19	14 31		14 33	14 37	14 47	14 49	14 59	15 01
Heathrow Terminal 4 ✈ a		12 53		13 05		13 23			13 37	13 41		13 53		14 05		14 23			14 37	14 41		14 53		15 05
Heathrow Terminal 5 ✈ a	12 51		13 03		13 17		13 35				13 51		14 03		14 17		14 35				14 51		15 03	

	HX ■	HX	HX ■		HX	HC	HX ■	HX	HX ■	HX	HX ■	HX	HX ■		HX	HC	HX ■	HX	HX ■	HX	HX ■	HX	HX ■	
London Paddington 15 ⊖ d	14 55		15 10			15 12	15 25		15 40		15 55		16 10			16 12	16 25		16 40		16 55		17 10	
HeathrowTerminals 1-2-3 2 ✈ a	15 11		15 26			15 34	15 41		15 56		16 11		16 26			16 34	16 41		16 56		17 11		17 26	
d	15 13	15 19	15 31		15 33	15 37	15 47	15 49	15 59	16 01	16 13	16 19	16 31		16 33	16 37	16 47	16 49	16 59	17 01	17 13	17 19	17 31	
Heathrow Terminal 4 ✈ a		15 23			15 37	15 41		15 53		16 05		16 23			16 37	16 41		16 53		17 05		17 23		
Heathrow Terminal 5 ✈ a	15 17		15 35				15 51		16 03		16 17		16 35				16 51		17 03		17 17		17 35	

	HX	HC	HX ■	HX	HX ■	HX	HX ■	HX	HX ■		HX	HC	HX ■	HX	HX ■	HX	HX ■	HX	HX ■		HX	HC	HX ■	HX
London Paddington 15 ⊖ d		17 12	17 25		17 40		17 55		18 10			18 12	18 25		18 40		18 55		19 10			19 12	19 25	
HeathrowTerminals 1-2-3 2 ✈ a		17 34	17 41		17 56		18 11		18 26			18 34	18 41		18 56		19 11		19 26			19 34	19 41	
d	17 33	17 37	17 47	17 49	17 59	18 01	18 13	18 19	18 31		18 33	18 37	18 47	18 49	18 59	19 01	19 13	19 19	19 31		19 33	19 37	19 47	19 49
Heathrow Terminal 4 ✈ a	17 37	17 41		17 53		18 05		18 23			18 37	18 41		18 53		19 05		19 23			19 37	19 41		19 53
Heathrow Terminal 5 ✈ a			17 51		18 03		18 17		18 35				18 51		19 03		19 17		19 35				19 51	

	HX ■	HX	HX ■	HX	HX ■		HX	HC	HX ■	HX	HX ■	HX	HX ■	HX	HX ■		HX	HC	HX ■	HX	HX ■	HX	HX ■	HX
London Paddington 15 ⊖ d	19 40		19 55		20 10			20 12	20 25		20 40		20 55		21 10			21 12	21 25		21 40		21 55	
HeathrowTerminals 1-2-3 2 ✈ a	19 56		20 11		20 26			20 34	20 41		20 56		21 11		21 26			21 34	21 41		21 56		22 11	
d	19 59	20 01	20 13	20 19	20 31		20 33	20 37	20 47	20 49	20 59	21 01	21 13	21 19	21 31		21 33	21 37	21 47	21 49	21 59	22 01	22 13	22 19
Heathrow Terminal 4 ✈ a		20 05		20 23			20 37	20 41		20 53		21 05		21 23			21 37	21 41		21 53		22 05		22 23
Heathrow Terminal 5 ✈ a	20 03		20 17		20 35				20 51		21 03		21 17		21 35				21 51		22 03		22 17	

	HX ■		HX	HC	HX ■	HX	HX ■	HX	HX ■	HX	HX ■		HX	HC	HX ■	HX
London Paddington 15 ⊖ d	22 10			22 12	22 25		22 40		22 55		23 10			23 12	23 25	
HeathrowTerminals 1-2-3 2 ✈ a	22 26			22 34	22 41		22 56		23 11		23 26			23 34	23 41	
d	22 31		22 33	22 37	22 47	22 49	22 59	23 01	23 13	23 19	23 31		23 33	23 37	23 47	23 49
Heathrow Terminal 4 ✈ a			22 37	22 41		22 53		23 05		23 23			23 37	23 41		23 53
Heathrow Terminal 5 ✈ a	22 35				22 51		23 03		23 17		23 35				23 51	

Table 118

Mondays to Fridays

Heathrow Airport - London

Network Diagram - see first Page of Table 116

Miles		HX MX ■	HX MO ■ A	HX MO A	HC	HX ■	HC	HX ■	HX	HX ■		HC	HX	HX ■	HX	HX ■	HX	HX ■	HX	HX ■		HX	HX ■	HX
0	Heathrow Terminal 5 ✈ d	23p42	23p48	23p58		05 07		05 27		05 42				05 57		06 12		06 27		06 42			06 57	
—	Heathrow Terminal 4 ✈ d				00 01		05 23		05 32			05 51	05 57		06 12		06 27		06 42			06 57		07 12
1½	HeathrowTerminals 1-2-3 2 ✈ a	23p46	23p52	00 02	00 05	05 11	05 27	05 31	05 36	05 46		05 55	06 01	06 01	06 16	06 16	06 31	06 31	06 46	06 46		07 01	07 01	07 16
—	d				00 07	05 12	05 29	05 33		05 48		05 57		06 03		06 18		06 33		06 48			07 03	
16¼	London Paddington 15 ⊖ a				00 30	05 28	05 56	05 49		06 04		06 24		06 19		06 34		06 49		07 05			07 19	

	HX ■	HX	HX ■	HX	HX ■	HX		HX ■	HX	HX ■	HX	HX ■	HX	HX ■	HX	HX ■		HX	HX ■	HX	HX ■	HX	HX ■	HX
Heathrow Terminal 5 ✈ d	07 12		07 27		07 42			07 57		08 12		08 27		08 42		08 57			09 12		09 27		09 42	
Heathrow Terminal 4 ✈ d		07 27		07 42		07 57			08 12		08 27		08 42		08 57			09 12		09 27		09 42		09 57
HeathrowTerminals 1-2-3 2 ✈ a	07 16	07 31	07 31	07 46	07 46	08 01		08 01	08 16	08 16	08 31	08 31	08 46	08 46	09 01	09 01		09 16	09 16	09 31	09 31	09 46	09 46	10 01
d	07 18		07 33		07 48			08 03		08 18		08 33		08 48		09 03			09 18		09 33		09 48	
London Paddington 15 ⊖ a	07 35		07 49		08 04			08 19		08 35		08 49		09 04		09 19			09 35		09 49		10 05	

	HX ■	HX		HX ■	HX	HX ■	HX	HX ■	HX	HX ■	HX	HX ■		HX	HX ■	HX	HX ■	HX	HX ■	HX	HX ■	HX		HX ■
Heathrow Terminal 5 ✈ d	09 57			10 12		10 27		10 42		10 57		11 12			11 27		11 42		11 57		12 12			12 27
Heathrow Terminal 4 ✈ d		10 12			10 27		10 42		10 57		11 12			11 27		11 42		11 57		12 12		12 27		
HeathrowTerminals 1-2-3 2 ✈ a	10 01	10 16		10 16	10 31	10 31	10 46	10 46	11 01	11 01	11 16	11 16		11 31	11 31	11 46	11 46	12 01	12 01	12 16	12 16	12 31		12 31
d	10 03			10 18		10 33		10 48		11 03		11 18			11 33		11 48		12 03		12 18			12 33
London Paddington 15 ⊖ a	10 19			10 34		10 49		11 04		11 19		11 34			11 49		12 04		12 19		12 34			12 49

	HX	HX ■	HX	HX ■	HX	HX ■	HX	HX ■		HX	HX ■	HX	HX ■	HX	HX ■	HX	HX ■	HX		HX ■	HX	HX ■	HX	HX ■
Heathrow Terminal 5 ✈ d		12 42		12 57		13 12		13 27			13 42		13 57		14 12		14 27			14 42		14 57		15 12
Heathrow Terminal 4 ✈ d	12 42		12 57		13 12		13 27			13 42		13 57		14 12		14 27		14 42			14 57		15 12	
HeathrowTerminals 1-2-3 2 ✈ a	12 46	12 46	13 01	13 01	13 16	13 16	13 31	13 31		13 46	13 46	14 01	14 01	14 16	14 16	14 31	14 31	14 46		14 46	15 01	15 01	15 16	15 16
d		12 48		13 03		13 18		13 33			13 48		14 03		14 18		14 33			14 48		15 03		15 18
London Paddington 15 ⊖ a		13 04		13 19		13 35		13 49			14 04		14 19		14 34		14 49			15 04		15 19		15 35

	HX	HX ■	HX	HX ■		HX	HX ■	HX	HX ■	HX	HX ■	HX	HX ■	HX		HX ■	HX	HX ■	HX	HX ■	HX	HX ■	HX	HX ■
Heathrow Terminal 5 ✈ d		15 27		15 42			15 57		16 12		16 27		16 42			16 57		17 12		17 27		17 42		17 57
Heathrow Terminal 4 ✈ d	15 27		15 42			15 57		16 12		16 27		16 42		16 57			17 12		17 27		17 42		17 57	
HeathrowTerminals 1-2-3 2 ✈ a	15 31	15 31	15 46	15 46		16 01	16 01	16 16	16 16	16 31	16 31	16 46	16 46	17 01		17 01	17 16	17 16	17 31	17 31	17 46	17 46	18 01	18 01
d		15 33		15 48			16 03		16 18		16 33		16 48			17 03		17 18		17 33		17 48		18 03
London Paddington 15 ⊖ a		15 49		16 05			16 19		16 35		16 49		17 05			17 19		17 35		17 49		18 05		18 19

		HX	HX ■	HX	HX ■	HX	HX ■	HX	HX ■	HX		HX ■	HX	HX ■	HX	HX ■	HX	HX ■	HX	HX ■		HX	HX ■	HX
Heathrow Terminal 5 ✈ d			18 12		18 27		18 42		18 57			19 12		19 27		19 42		19 57		20 12			20 27	
Heathrow Terminal 4 ✈ d		18 12		18 27		18 42		18 57		19 12			19 27		19 42		19 57		20 12			20 27		20 42
HeathrowTerminals 1-2-3 2 ✈ a		18 16	18 16	18 31	18 31	18 46	18 46	19 01	19 01	19 16		19 16	19 31	19 31	19 46	19 46	20 01	20 01	20 16	20 16		20 31	20 31	20 46
d			18 18		18 33		18 48		19 03			19 18		19 33		19 48		20 03		20 18			20 33	
London Paddington 15 ⊖ a			18 35		18 49		19 05		19 19			19 35		19 49		20 04		20 19		20 34			20 49	

	HX ■	HX	HX ■	HX	HX ■	HX		HX ■	HX	HX ■	HX	HX ■	HX	HX ■	HX	HX ■		HX	HX ■	HX	HX ■	HX	HX ■	HX
Heathrow Terminal 5 ✈ d	20 42		20 57		21 12			21 27		21 42		21 57		22 12		22 27			22 42		22 57		23 12	
Heathrow Terminal 4 ✈ d		20 57		21 12		21 27			21 42		21 57		22 12		22 27			22 42		22 57		23 12		23 27
HeathrowTerminals 1-2-3 2 ✈ a	20 46	21 01	21 01	21 16	21 16	21 31		21 31	21 46	21 46	22 01	22 01	22 16	22 16	22 31	22 31		22 46	22 46	23 01	23 01	23 16	23 16	23 31
d	20 48		21 03		21 18			21 33		21 48		22 03		22 18		22 33			22 48		23 03		23 18	
London Paddington 15 ⊖ a	21 04		21 19		21 34			21 49		22 04		22 19		22 34		22 49			23 04		23 19		23 34	

	HX ■	HX ■		HX	HX
Heathrow Terminal 5 ✈ d	23 27	23 42			23 53
Heathrow Terminal 4 ✈ d				23 42	
HeathrowTerminals 1-2-3 2 ✈ a	23 31	23 46		23 46	23 57
d	23 33	23 48			
London Paddington 15 ⊖ a	23 49	00 04			

Saturdays

	HX ■	HC	HX ■	HC	HX ■	HX	HX ■	HC	HX		HX ■	HX	HX ■	HX	HX ■	HX	HX ■	HX	HX ■		HX	HX ■	HX	HX ■
Heathrow Terminal 5 ✈ d	23p42		05 07		05 27		05 42				05 57		06 12		06 27		06 42		06 57			07 12		07 27
Heathrow Terminal 4 ✈ d		00 01		05 23		05 32		05 51	05 57			06 12		06 27		06 42		06 57			07 12		07 27	
HeathrowTerminals 1-2-3 2 ✈ a	23p46	00 05	05 11	05 27	05 31	05 36	05 46	05 55	06 01		06 01	06 16	06 16	06 31	06 31	06 46	06 46	07 01	07 01		07 16	07 16	07 31	07 31
d		00 07	05 12	05 29	05 33		05 48	05 57			06 03		06 18		06 33		06 48		07 03			07 18		07 33
London Paddington 15 ⊖ a		00 30	05 28	05 56	05 49		06 04	06 24			06 19		06 34		06 49		07 04		07 19			07 34		07 49

	HX	HX ■	HX	HX ■	HX		HX ■	HX	HX ■	HX	HX ■	HX	HX ■	HX	HX ■		HX	HX ■	HX	HX ■	HX	HX ■	HX	HX ■
Heathrow Terminal 5 ✈ d		07 42		07 57			08 12		08 27		08 42		08 57		09 12			09 27		09 42		09 57		10 12
Heathrow Terminal 4 ✈ d	07 42		07 57		08 12			08 27		08 42		08 57		09 12			09 27		09 42		09 57		10 12	
HeathrowTerminals 1-2-3 2 ✈ a	07 46	07 46	08 01	08 01	08 16		08 16	08 31	08 31	08 46	08 46	09 01	09 01	09 16	09 16		09 31	09 31	09 46	09 46	10 01	10 01	10 16	10 16
d		07 48		08 03			08 18		08 33		08 48		09 03		09 18			09 33		09 48		10 03		10 18
London Paddington 15 ⊖ a		08 04		08 19			08 34		08 49		09 04		09 19		09 34			09 49		10 04		10 19		10 34

A from 21 May

Table 118

Saturdays

Heathrow Airport - London

Network Diagram - see first Page of Table 116

	HX		HX ■	HX	HX ■	HX	HX ■	HX	HX ■	HX	HX ■		HX	HX ■	HX	HX ■	HX	HX ■	HX	HX ■	HX		HX ■	HX
Heathrow Terminal 5 ✈ d			10 27		10 42		10 57		11 12		11 27			11 42		11 57		12 12		12 27			12 42	
Heathrow Terminal 4 ✈ d	10 27			10 42		10 57		11 12		11 27			11 42		11 57		12 12		12 27		12 42			12 57
HeathrowTerminals 1-2-3 ■ ✈ a	10 31		10 31	10 46	10 46	11 01	11 01	11 16	11 16	11 31	11 31		11 46	11 46	12 01	12 01	12 16	12 16	12 31	12 31	12 46		12 46	13 01
d			10 33		10 48		11 03		11 18		11 33			11 48		12 03		12 18		12 33			12 48	
London Paddington ■ ⊖ a			10 49		11 04		11 19		11 34		11 49			12 04		12 19		12 34		12 49			13 04	

	HX ■	HX	HX ■	HX	HX ■	HX	HX ■		HX	HX ■	HX	HX ■	HX	HX ■	HX	HX ■	HX		HX ■	HX	HX ■	HX	HX ■	HX
Heathrow Terminal 5 ✈ d	12 57		13 12		13 27		13 42			13 57		14 12		14 27		14 42			14 57		15 12		15 27	
Heathrow Terminal 4 ✈ d		13 12		13 27		13 42			13 57		14 12		14 27		14 42		14 57			15 12		15 27		15 42
HeathrowTerminals 1-2-3 ■ ✈ a	13 01	13 16	13 16	13 31	13 31	13 46	13 46		14 01	14 01	14 16	14 16	14 31	14 31	14 46	14 46	15 01		15 01	15 16	15 16	15 31	15 31	15 46
d	13 03		13 18		13 33		13 48			14 03		14 18		14 33		14 48			15 03		15 18		15 33	
London Paddington ■ ⊖ a	13 19		13 35		13 49		14 04			14 19		14 34		14 49		15 04			15 19		15 34		15 49	

	HX ■	HX	HX ■		HX	HX ■	HX	HX ■	HX	HX ■	HX	HX ■	HX		HX ■	HX	HX ■	HX	HX ■	HX	HX ■	HX	HX ■	
Heathrow Terminal 5 ✈ d	15 42		15 57			16 12		16 27		16 42		16 57			17 12		17 27		17 42		17 57		18 12	
Heathrow Terminal 4 ✈ d		15 57			16 12		16 27		16 42		16 57		17 12			17 27		17 42		17 57		18 12		
HeathrowTerminals 1-2-3 ■ ✈ a	15 46	16 01	16 01		16 16	16 16	16 31	16 31	16 46	16 46	17 01	17 01	17 16		17 16	17 31	17 31	17 46	17 46	18 01	18 01	18 16	18 16	
d	15 48		16 03			16 18		16 33		16 48		17 03			17 18		17 33		17 48		18 03		18 18	
London Paddington ■ ⊖ a	16 04		16 19			16 34		16 49		17 04		17 19			17 34		17 49		18 04		18 19		18 34	

	HX	HX ■	HX	HX ■	HX	HX ■	HX	HX ■	HX		HX ■	HX	HX ■	HX	HX ■	HX	HX ■	HX	HX ■		HX	HX ■	HX	HX ■
Heathrow Terminal 5 ✈ d		18 27		18 42		18 57		19 12			19 27		19 42		19 57		20 12		20 27			20 42		20 57
Heathrow Terminal 4 ✈ d	18 27		18 42		18 57		19 12		19 27			19 42		19 57		20 12		20 27			20 42		20 57	
HeathrowTerminals 1-2-3 ■ ✈ a	18 31	18 31	18 46	18 46	19 01	19 01	19 16	19 16	19 31		19 31	19 46	19 46	20 01	20 01	20 16	20 16	20 31	20 31		20 46	20 46	21 01	21 01
d		18 33		18 48		19 03		19 18			19 33		19 48		20 03		20 18		20 33			20 48		21 03
London Paddington ■ ⊖ a		18 49		19 04		19 19		19 34			19 49		20 04		20 19		20 34		20 49			21 04		21 19

	HX	HX ■	HX	HX ■	HX		HX ■	HX	HX ■	HX	HX ■	HX	HX ■	HX	HX ■		HX	HX ■	HX	HX ■	HX	HX ■	HX ■	HX
Heathrow Terminal 5 ✈ d		21 12		21 27			21 42		21 57		22 12		22 27		22 42			22 57		23 12		23 27	23 42	
Heathrow Terminal 4 ✈ d	21 12		21 27		21 42			21 57		22 12		22 27		22 42			22 57		23 12		23 27			23 42
HeathrowTerminals 1-2-3 ■ ✈ a	21 16	21 16	21 31	21 31	21 46		21 46	22 01	22 01	22 16	22 16	22 31	22 31	22 46	22 46		23 01	23 01	23 16	23 16	23 31	23 31	23 46	23 46
d		21 18		21 33			21 48		22 03		22 18		22 33		22 48			23 03		23 18		23 33		
London Paddington ■ ⊖ a		21 34		21 49			22 04		22 19		22 35		22 49		23 05			23 19		23 34		23 49		

	HX
Heathrow Terminal 5 ✈ d	23 53
Heathrow Terminal 4 ✈ d	
HeathrowTerminals 1-2-3 ■ ✈ a	23 57
d	
London Paddington ■ ⊖ a	

Sundays
until 24 June

	HC	HX ■	HX ■	HX ■	HX ■	HX	HX ■	HC	HX		HX ■	HX	HX ■	HX	HX ■	HX	HX ■	HC	HX		HX ■	HX	HX ■	HX
Heathrow Terminal 5 ✈ d		05 03	05 18	05 33	05 48		06 03				06 18		06 33		06 48		07 03				07 18		07 33	
Heathrow Terminal 4 ✈ d	00 01					05 53		06 07	06 13			06 25		06 41		06 53		07 07	07 13			07 25		07 41
HeathrowTerminals 1-2-3 ■ ✈ a	00 05	05 07	05 22	05 37	05 52	05 57	06 07	06 11	06 17		06 22	06 29	06 37	06 45	06 52	06 57	07 07	07 11	07 17		07 22	07 29	07 37	07 45
d	00 07	05 08	05 23	05 38	05 53		06 08	06 13			06 23		06 38		06 53		07 08	07 13			07 23		07 38	
London Paddington ■ ⊖ a	00 30	05 24	05 39	05 54	06 09		06 24	06 36			06 39		06 54		07 09		07 24	07 36			07 39		07 54	

	HX ■	HX	HX ■	HC	HX		HX ■	HX	HX ■	HX	HX ■	HX	HX ■	HC	HX		HX ■	HX	HX ■	HX	HX ■	HX	HX ■	HC
Heathrow Terminal 5 ✈ d	07 48		08 03				08 18		08 33		08 48		09 03				09 18		09 33		09 48		10 03	
Heathrow Terminal 4 ✈ d		07 53		08 07	08 13			08 25		08 41		08 53		09 07	09 13			09 25		09 41		09 53		10 07
HeathrowTerminals 1-2-3 ■ ✈ a	07 52	07 57	08 07	08 11	08 17		08 22	08 29	08 37	08 45	08 52	08 57	09 07	09 11	09 17		09 22	09 29	09 37	09 45	09 52	09 57	10 07	10 11
d	07 53		08 08	08 13			08 23		08 38		08 53		09 08	09 13			09 23		09 38		09 53		10 08	10 13
London Paddington ■ ⊖ a	08 09		08 24	08 36			08 39		08 54		09 09		09 24	09 36			09 39		09 54		10 09		10 24	10 36

	HX		HX ■	HX	HX ■	HX	HX ■	HX	HX ■	HC	HX		HX ■	HX	HX ■	HX	HX ■	HX	HX ■	HC	HX		HX ■	HX
Heathrow Terminal 5 ✈ d			10 18		10 33		10 48		11 03				11 18		11 33		11 48		12 03				12 18	
Heathrow Terminal 4 ✈ d	10 13			10 25		10 41		10 53		11 07	11 13			11 25		11 41		11 53		12 07	12 13			12 25
HeathrowTerminals 1-2-3 ■ ✈ a	10 17		10 22	10 29	10 37	10 45	10 52	10 57	11 07	11 11	11 17		11 22	11 29	11 37	11 45	11 52	11 57	12 07	12 11	12 17		12 22	12 29
d			10 23		10 38		10 53		11 08	11 13			11 23		11 38		11 53		12 08	12 13			12 23	
London Paddington ■ ⊖ a			10 39		10 54		11 09		11 24	11 36			11 39		11 54		12 09		12 24	12 36			12 39	

	HX ■	HX	HX ■	HX	HX ■	HC	HX		HX ■	HX	HX ■	HX	HX ■	HX	HX ■	HC	HX		HX ■	HX	HX ■	HX	HX ■	HX
Heathrow Terminal 5 ✈ d	12 33		12 48		13 03				13 18		13 33		13 48		14 03				14 18		14 33		14 48	
Heathrow Terminal 4 ✈ d		12 41		12 53		13 07	13 13			13 25		13 41		13 53		14 07	14 13			14 25		14 41		14 53
HeathrowTerminals 1-2-3 ■ ✈ a	12 37	12 45	12 52	12 57	13 07	13 11	13 17		13 22	13 29	13 37	13 45	13 52	13 57	14 07	14 11	14 17		14 22	14 29	14 37	14 45	14 52	14 57
d	12 38		12 53		13 08	13 13			13 23		13 38		13 53		14 08	14 13			14 23		14 38		14 53	
London Paddington ■ ⊖ a	12 54		13 09		13 24	13 36			13 39		13 54		14 09		14 24	14 36			14 39		14 54		15 09	

Table 118

Sundays
until 24 June

Heathrow Airport - London

Network Diagram - see first Page of Table 116

	HX ■	HC	HX		HX ■	HX	HX ■	HX	HX ■	HX	HX ■	HC	HX		HX ■	HX	HX ■	HX	HX ■	HX	HX ■	HC	HX	
Heathrow Terminal 5 ✈ d	15 03				15 18		15 33		15 48		16 03				16 18		16 33		16 48		17 03			
Heathrow Terminal 4 ✈ d		15 07	15 13			15 25		15 41		15 53		16 07	16 13			16 25		16 41		16 53		17 07	17 13	
HeathrowTerminals 1-2-3 ■ ✈ a	15 07	15 11	15 17		15 22	15 29	15 37	15 45	15 52	15 57	16 07	16 11	16 17		16 22	16 29	16 37	16 45	16 52	16 57	17 07	17 11	17 17	
d	15 08	15 13			15 23		15 38		15 53		16 08	16 13			16 23		16 38		16 53		17 08	17 13		
London Paddington ■ ⊖ a	15 24	15 36			15 39		15 54		16 09		16 24	16 36			16 39		16 54		17 09		17 24	17 36		

	HX ■	HX	HX ■	HX	HX ■	HX	HX ■	HC	HX		HX ■	HX	HX ■	HX	HX ■	HX	HX ■	HC	HX		HX ■	HX	HX ■	HX
Heathrow Terminal 5 ✈ d	17 18		17 33		17 48		18 03				18 18		18 33		18 48		19 03				19 18		19 33	
Heathrow Terminal 4 ✈ d		17 25		17 41		17 53		18 07	18 13			18 25		18 41		18 53		19 07	19 13			19 25		19 41
HeathrowTerminals 1-2-3 ■ ✈ a	17 22	17 29	17 37	17 45	17 52	17 57	18 07	18 11	18 17		18 22	18 29	18 37	18 45	18 52	18 57	19 07	19 11	19 17		19 22	19 29	19 37	19 45
d	17 23		17 38		17 53		18 08	18 13			18 23		18 38		18 53		19 08	19 13			19 23		19 38	
London Paddington ■ ⊖ a	17 39		17 54		18 09		18 24	18 36			18 39		18 54		19 09		19 24	19 36			19 39		19 54	

	HX ■	HX	HX ■	HC	HX		HX ■	HX	HX ■	HX	HX ■	HX	HX ■	HC	HX		HX ■	HX	HX ■	HX	HX ■	HX	HX ■	HC
Heathrow Terminal 5 ✈ d	19 48		20 03				20 18		20 33		20 48		21 03				21 18		21 33		21 48		22 03	
Heathrow Terminal 4 ✈ d		19 53		20 07	20 13			20 25		20 41		20 53		21 07	21 13			21 25		21 41		21 53		22 07
HeathrowTerminals 1-2-3 ■ ✈ a	19 52	19 57	20 07	20 11	20 17		20 22	20 29	20 37	20 45	20 52	20 57	21 07	21 11	21 17		21 22	21 29	21 37	21 45	21 52	21 57	22 07	22 11
d	19 53		20 08	20 13			20 23		20 38		20 53		21 08	21 13			21 23		21 38		21 53		22 08	22 13
London Paddington ■ ⊖ a	20 09		20 24	20 36			20 39		20 54		21 09		21 24	21 36			21 39		21 54		22 09		22 24	22 36

	HX		HX ■	HX	HX ■	HX	HX ■	HX	HX ■	HC	HX		HX ■	HX	HX ■	HX	HX ■	HX
Heathrow Terminal 5 ✈ d			22 18		22 33		22 48		23 03				23 18		23 33		23 48	23 58
Heathrow Terminal 4 ✈ d	22 13			22 25		22 41		22 53		23 07	23 13			23 25		23 41		
HeathrowTerminals 1-2-3 ■ ✈ a	22 17		22 22	22 29	22 37	22 45	22 52	22 57	23 07	23 11	23 17		23 22	23 29	23 37	23 45	23 52	00 02
d			22 23		22 38		22 53		23 08	23 13			23 23		23 38		23 53	
London Paddington ■ ⊖ a			22 39		22 54		23 09		23 24	23 36			23 43		23 56		00 09	

Sundays
1 July to 9 September

	HC	HX ■	HX ■	HX ■	HX ■	HX	HX ■	HC	HX		HX ■	HX	HX ■	HX	HX ■	HX	HX ■	HC	HX		HX ■	HX	HX ■	HX
Heathrow Terminal 5 ✈ d		05 03	05 18	05 33	05 48		06 03				06 18		06 33		06 48		07 03				07 18		07 33	
Heathrow Terminal 4 ✈ d	00 01					05 53		06 07	06 13			06 25		06 41		06 53		07 07	07 13			07 25		07 41
HeathrowTerminals 1-2-3 ■ ✈ a	00 05	05 07	05 22	05 37	05 52	05 57	06 07	06 11	06 17		06 22	06 29	06 37	06 45	06 52	06 57	07 07	07 11	07 17		07 22	07 29	07 37	07 45
d	00 07	05 08	05 23	05 38	05 53		06 08	06 13			06 23		06 38		06 53		07 08	07 13			07 23		07 38	
London Paddington ■ ⊖ a	00 30	05 24	05 39	05 54	06 09		06 24	06 36			06 39		06 54		07 09		07 24	07 36			07 39		07 54	

	HX ■	HX	HX ■	HC	HX		HX ■	HX	HX ■	HX	HX ■	HX	HX ■	HX	HX ■		HC	HX ■	HX	HX ■	HC	HX ■	HX	HX ■
Heathrow Terminal 5 ✈ d	07 48		08 03				08 18		08 33		08 48		09 00		09 13			09 27		09 42		09 57		10 12
Heathrow Terminal 4 ✈ d		07 53		08 07	08 13			08 25		08 41		08 53		09 06			09 21		09 31		09 51		10 01	
HeathrowTerminals 1-2-3 ■ ✈ a	07 52	07 57	08 07	08 11	08 17		08 22	08 29	08 37	08 45	08 52	08 57	09 04	09 10	09 17		09 25	09 31	09 35	09 46	09 55	10 01	10 05	10 16
d	07 53		08 08	08 13			08 23		08 38		08 53		09 06		09 19		09 27	09 33		09 48	09 57	10 03		10 18
London Paddington ■ ⊖ a	08 09		08 24	08 36			08 39		08 54		09 09		09 22		09 34		09 50	09 49		10 04	10 20	10 19		10 34

	HC		HX ■	HX	HX ■	HC	HX ■	HX	HX ■	HC	HX ■		HX	HX ■	HC	HX ■	HX	HX ■	HC	HX ■	HX		HX ■	HC
Heathrow Terminal 5 ✈ d			10 27		10 42		10 57		11 12		11 27			11 42		11 57		12 12		12 27			12 42	
Heathrow Terminal 4 ✈ d	10 21			10 31		10 51		11 01		11 21			11 31		11 51		12 01		12 21		12 31			12 51
HeathrowTerminals 1-2-3 ■ ✈ a	10 25		10 31	10 35	10 46	10 55	11 01	11 05	11 16	11 25	11 31		11 35	11 46	11 55	12 01	12 05	12 16	12 25	12 31	12 35		12 46	12 55
d	10 27		10 33		10 48	10 57	11 03		11 18	11 27	11 33			11 48	11 57	12 03		12 18	12 27	12 33			12 48	12 57
London Paddington ■ ⊖ a	10 50		10 49		11 04	11 20	11 19		11 34	11 50	11 49			12 04	12 20	12 19		12 34	12 50	12 49			13 04	13 20

	HX ■	HX	HX ■	HC	HX ■	HX	HX ■		HC	HX ■	HX	HX ■	HC	HX ■	HX	HX ■	HC		HX ■	HX	HX ■	HC	HX ■	HX
Heathrow Terminal 5 ✈ d	12 57		13 12		13 27		13 42			13 57		14 12		14 27		14 42			14 57		15 12		15 27	
Heathrow Terminal 4 ✈ d		13 01		13 21		13 31			13 51		14 01		14 21		14 31		14 51			15 01		15 21		15 31
HeathrowTerminals 1-2-3 ■ ✈ a	13 01	13 05	13 16	13 25	13 31	13 35	13 46		13 55	14 01	14 05	14 16	14 25	14 31	14 35	14 46	14 55		15 01	15 05	15 16	15 25	15 31	15 35
d	13 03		13 18	13 27	13 33		13 48		13 57	14 03		14 18	14 27	14 33		14 48	14 57		15 03		15 18	15 27	15 33	
London Paddington ■ ⊖ a	13 19		13 34	13 50	13 49		14 04		14 20	14 19		14 34	14 50	14 49		15 04	15 20		15 19		15 34	15 50	15 49	

	HX ■	HC	HX ■		HX	HX ■	HC	HX ■	HX	HX ■	HC	HX ■	HX		HX ■	HC	HX ■	HX	HX ■	HC	HX ■	HX	HX ■	
Heathrow Terminal 5 ✈ d	15 42		15 57			16 12		16 27		16 42		16 57			17 12		17 27		17 42		17 57		18 12	
Heathrow Terminal 4 ✈ d		15 51			16 01		16 21		16 31		16 51		17 01			17 21		17 31		17 51		18 01		
HeathrowTerminals 1-2-3 ■ ✈ a	15 46	15 55	16 01		16 05	16 16	16 25	16 31	16 35	16 46	16 55	17 01	17 05		17 16	17 25	17 31	17 35	17 46	17 55	18 01	18 05	18 16	
d	15 48	15 57	16 03			16 18	16 27	16 33		16 48	16 57	17 03			17 18	17 27	17 33		17 48	17 57	18 03		18 18	
London Paddington ■ ⊖ a	16 04	16 20	16 19			16 34	16 50	16 49		17 04	17 20	17 19			17 34	17 50	17 49		18 04	18 20	18 19		18 34	

	HC	HX ■	HX	HX ■	HC	HX ■	HX	HX ■	HC		HX ■	HX	HX ■	HC	HX ■	HX	HX ■	HC	HX ■		HX	HX	HX ■	HC
Heathrow Terminal 5 ✈ d		18 27		18 42		18 57		19 12			19 27		19 42		19 57		20 12		20 27				20 42	
Heathrow Terminal 4 ✈ d	18 21		18 31		18 51		19 01		19 21			19 31		19 51		20 01		20 21			20 31	20 41		20 51
HeathrowTerminals 1-2-3 ■ ✈ a	18 25	18 31	18 35	18 46	18 55	19 01	19 05	19 16	19 25		19 31	19 35	19 46	19 55	20 01	20 05	20 16	20 25	20 31		20 35	20 45	20 46	20 55
d	18 27	18 33		18 48	18 57	19 03		19 18	19 27		19 33		19 48	19 57	20 03		20 18	20 27	20 33				20 48	20 57
London Paddington ■ ⊖ a	18 50	18 49		19 04	19 20	19 19		19 34	19 50		19 49		20 04	20 20	20 19		20 34	20 50	20 49				21 04	21 20

Table 118

Sundays

1 July to 9 September

Heathrow Airport - London

Network Diagram - see first Page of Table 116

	HX	HX	HX	HC	HX		HX	HX	HX	HX	HC	HX	HX	HX	HX		HX	HX	HX	HX	HC	HX	HX	HX
Heathrow Terminal 5 ✈ d	20 57		21 12		21 27			21 48		22 03			22 18		22 33			22 48		23 03			23 18	
Heathrow Terminal 4 ✈ d		21 01		21 21			21 41		21 53		22 07	22 13		22 25			22 41		22 53		23 07	23 13		23 25
HeathrowTerminals 1-2-3 ✈ a	21 01	21 05	21 16	21 25	21 31		21 45	21 52	21 57	22 07	22 11	22 17	22 22	22 29	22 37		22 45	22 52	22 57	23 07	23 11	23 17	23 22	23 29
d	21 03		21 18	21 27	21 33			21 53		22 08	22 13		22 23		22 38			22 53		23 08	23 13		23 23	
London Paddington ⊖ a	21 19		21 34	21 50	21 49			22 09		22 24	22 36		22 39		22 54			23 09		23 24	23 36		23 43	

	HX		HX	HX	HX
Heathrow Terminal 5 ✈ d	23 33			23 48	23 58
Heathrow Terminal 4 ✈ d			23 41		
HeathrowTerminals 1-2-3 ✈ a	23 37		23 45	23 52	00 02
d	23 38			23 53	
London Paddington ⊖ a	23 56			00 09	

Sundays

from 16 September

	HC	HX	HX	HX	HX	HX	HX	HC	HX		HX	HX	HX	HX	HX	HX	HX	HC	HX		HX	HX	HX	HX
Heathrow Terminal 5 ✈ d		05 03	05 18	05 33	05 48		06 03				06 18		06 33		06 48		07 03				07 18		07 33	
Heathrow Terminal 4 ✈ d	00 01					05 53		06 07	06 13			06 25		06 41		06 53		07 07	07 13			07 25		07 41
HeathrowTerminals 1-2-3 ✈ a	00 05	05 07	05 22	05 37	05 52	05 57	06 07	06 11	06 17		06 22	06 29	06 37	06 45	06 52	06 57	07 07	07 11	07 17		07 22	07 29	07 37	07 45
d	00 07	05 08	05 23	05 38	05 53		06 08	06 13			06 23		06 38		06 53		07 08	07 13			07 23		07 38	
London Paddington ⊖ a	00 30	05 24	05 39	05 54	06 09		06 24	06 36			06 39		06 54		07 09		07 24	07 36			07 39		07 54	

	HX	HX	HX	HC	HX		HX	HX	HX	HX	HX	HX	HX	HC	HX		HX	HX	HX	HX	HX	HX	HX	HC
Heathrow Terminal 5 ✈ d	07 48		08 03				08 18		08 33		08 48		09 03				09 18		09 33		09 48		10 03	
Heathrow Terminal 4 ✈ d		07 53		08 07	08 13			08 25		08 41		08 53		09 07	09 13			09 25		09 41		09 53		10 07
HeathrowTerminals 1-2-3 ✈ a	07 52	07 57	08 07	08 11	08 17		08 22	08 29	08 37	08 45	08 52	08 57	09 07	09 11	09 17		09 22	09 29	09 37	09 45	09 52	09 57	10 07	10 11
d	07 53		08 08	08 13			08 23		08 38		08 53		09 08	09 13			09 23		09 38		09 53		10 08	10 13
London Paddington ⊖ a	08 09		08 24	08 36			08 39		08 54		09 09		09 24	09 36			09 39		09 54		10 09		10 24	10 36

	HX		HX	HX	HX	HX	HX	HX	HX	HC	HX		HX	HX	HX	HX	HX	HX	HX	HC	HX		HX	HX
Heathrow Terminal 5 ✈ d			10 18		10 33		10 48		11 03				11 18		11 33		11 48		12 03				12 18	
Heathrow Terminal 4 ✈ d	10 13			10 25		10 41		10 53		11 07	11 13			11 25		11 41		11 53		12 07	12 13			12 25
HeathrowTerminals 1-2-3 ✈ a	10 17		10 22	10 29	10 37	10 45	10 52	10 57	11 07	11 11	11 17		11 22	11 29	11 37	11 45	11 52	11 57	12 07	12 11	12 17		12 22	12 29
d			10 23		10 38		10 53		11 08	11 13			11 23		11 38		11 53		12 08	12 13			12 23	
London Paddington ⊖ a			10 39		10 54		11 09		11 24	11 36			11 39		11 54		12 09		12 24	12 36			12 39	

	HX	HX	HX	HX	HX	HC	HX		HX	HX	HX	HX	HX	HX	HX	HC	HX		HX	HX	HX	HX	HX	HX
Heathrow Terminal 5 ✈ d	12 33		12 48		13 03				13 18		13 33		13 48		14 03				14 18		14 33		14 48	
Heathrow Terminal 4 ✈ d		12 41		12 53		13 07	13 13			13 25		13 41		13 53		14 07	14 13			14 25		14 41		14 53
HeathrowTerminals 1-2-3 ✈ a	12 37	12 45	12 52	12 57	13 07	13 11	13 17		13 22	13 29	13 37	13 45	13 52	13 57	14 07	14 11	14 17		14 22	14 29	14 37	14 45	14 52	14 57
d	12 38		12 53		13 08	13 13			13 23		13 38		13 53		14 08	14 13			14 23		14 38		14 53	
London Paddington ⊖ a	12 54		13 09		13 24	13 36			13 39		13 54		14 09		14 24	14 36			14 39		14 54		15 09	

	HX	HC	HX		HX	HX	HX	HX	HX	HX	HX	HC	HX		HX	HX	HX	HX	HX	HX	HX	HC	HX	
Heathrow Terminal 5 ✈ d	15 03				15 18		15 33		15 48		16 03				16 18		16 33		16 48		17 03			
Heathrow Terminal 4 ✈ d		15 07	15 13			15 25		15 41		15 53		16 07	16 13			16 25		16 41		16 53		17 07	17 13	
HeathrowTerminals 1-2-3 ✈ a	15 07	15 11	15 17		15 22	15 29	15 37	15 45	15 52	15 57	16 07	16 11	16 17		16 22	16 29	16 37	16 45	16 52	16 57	17 07	17 11	17 17	
d	15 08	15 13			15 23		15 38		15 53		16 08	16 13			16 23		16 38		16 53		17 08	17 13		
London Paddington ⊖ a	15 24	15 36			15 39		15 54		16 09		16 24	16 36			16 39		16 54		17 09		17 24	17 36		

	HX	HX	HX	HX	HX	HX	HX	HC	HX		HX	HX	HX	HX	HX	HX	HX	HC	HX		HX	HX	HX	HX
Heathrow Terminal 5 ✈ d	17 18		17 33		17 48		18 03				18 18		18 33		18 48		19 03				19 18		19 33	
Heathrow Terminal 4 ✈ d		17 25		17 41		17 53		18 07	18 13			18 25		18 41		18 53		19 07	19 13			19 25		19 41
HeathrowTerminals 1-2-3 ✈ a	17 22	17 29	17 37	17 45	17 52	17 57	18 07	18 11	18 17		18 22	18 29	18 37	18 45	18 52	18 57	19 07	19 11	19 17		19 22	19 29	19 37	19 45
d	17 23		17 38		17 53		18 08	18 13			18 23		18 38		18 53		19 08	19 13			19 23		19 38	
London Paddington ⊖ a	17 39		17 54		18 09		18 24	18 36			18 39		18 54		19 09		19 24	19 36			19 39		19 54	

	HX	HX	HX	HC	HX		HX	HX	HX	HX	HX	HX	HX	HC	HX		HX	HX	HX	HX	HX	HX	HX	HC
Heathrow Terminal 5 ✈ d	19 48		20 03				20 18		20 33		20 48		21 03				21 18		21 33		21 48		22 03	
Heathrow Terminal 4 ✈ d		19 53		20 07	20 13			20 25		20 41		20 53		21 07	21 13			21 25		21 41		21 53		22 07
HeathrowTerminals 1-2-3 ✈ a	19 52	19 57	20 07	20 11	20 17		20 22	20 29	20 37	20 45	20 52	20 57	21 07	21 11	21 17		21 22	21 29	21 37	21 45	21 52	21 57	22 07	22 11
d	19 53		20 08	20 13			20 23		20 38		20 53		21 08	21 13			21 23		21 38		21 53		22 08	22 13
London Paddington ⊖ a	20 09		20 24	20 36			20 39		20 54		21 09		21 24	21 36			21 39		21 54		22 09		22 24	22 36

	HX		HX	HX	HX	HX	HX	HX	HX	HC	HX		HX	HX	HX	HX	HX	HX
Heathrow Terminal 5 ✈ d			22 18		22 33		22 48		23 03				23 18		23 33		23 48	23 58
Heathrow Terminal 4 ✈ d	22 13			22 25		22 41		22 53		23 07	23 13			23 25		23 41		
HeathrowTerminals 1-2-3 ✈ a	22 17		22 22	22 29	22 37	22 45	22 52	22 57	23 07	23 11	23 17		23 22	23 29	23 37	23 45	23 52	00 02
d			22 23		22 38		22 53		23 08	23 13			23 23		23 38		23 53	
London Paddington ⊖ a			22 39		22 54		23 09		23 24	23 36			23 43		23 56		00 09	

Table 119

Mondays to Fridays

Slough - Windsor & Eton

Network Diagram - see first Page of Table 116

Miles		GW	GW	GW	GW	GW	GW	GW	GW	GW		GW	GW	GW	GW	GW	GW	GW	GW	GW		GW	GW	GW
0	Slough d	05 38	05 58	06 18	06 37	06 55	07 13	07 31	07 54	08 13		08 31	08 54	09 14	09 33	09 53	10 11	10 30	10 50	11 10		11 30	11 50	12 10
2¼	Windsor & Eton Central a	05 44	06 04	06 24	06 43	07 01	07 19	07 37	08 00	08 19		08 37	09 00	09 20	09 39	09 59	10 17	10 36	10 56	11 16		11 36	11 56	12 16

	GW	GW	GW	GW	GW	GW		GW	GW	GW	GW	GW	GW	GW	GW	GW		GW	GW	GW	GW	GW	GW	GW
Slough d	12 30	12 50	13 10	13 30	13 50	14 10		14 30	14 50	15 10	15 30	15 50	16 21	16 43	17 01	17 21		17 40	17 58	18 16	18 40	18 58	19 16	19 40
Windsor & Eton Central a	12 36	12 56	13 16	13 36	13 56	14 16		14 36	14 56	15 16	15 36	15 56	16 27	16 49	17 07	17 27		17 46	18 04	18 22	18 46	19 04	19 22	19 46

	GW	GW		GW	GW	GW	GW	GW	GW	GW	GW	GW
Slough d	20 00	20 20		20 40	21 00	21 20	21 40	22 00	22 20	22 40	23 00	23 20
Windsor & Eton Central a	20 06	20 26		20 46	21 06	21 26	21 46	22 06	22 26	22 46	23 06	23 26

Saturdays

	GW	GW	GW	GW	GW	GW	GW	GW	GW		GW	GW	GW	GW	GW	GW	GW	GW	GW		GW	GW	GW	GW
Slough d	06 17	06 47	07 17	07 47	08 17	08 47	09 17	09 47	10 17		10 37	10 57	11 17	11 37	11 57	12 17	12 37	12 57	13 17		13 37	13 57	14 17	14 37
Windsor & Eton Central a	06 23	06 53	07 23	07 53	08 23	08 53	09 23	09 53	10 23		10 43	11 03	11 23	11 43	12 03	12 23	12 43	13 03	13 23		13 43	14 03	14 23	14 43

	GW	GW	GW	GW	GW		GW	GW	GW	GW	GW	GW	GW	GW	GW	GW	GW	GW	GW	GW	GW	GW	GW	GW
Slough d	14 57	15 17	15 37	15 57	16 17		16 37	16 57	17 17	17 37	17 57	18 17	18 37	18 57	19 17	19 47	20 17	20 47	21 17	21 47	22 17	22 53	23 22	23 56
Windsor & Eton Central a	15 03	15 23	15 43	16 03	16 23		16 43	17 03	17 23	17 43	18 03	18 23	18 43	19 03	19 23	19 53	20 23	20 53	21 23	21 53	22 23	22 59	23 28	00 02

Sundays

	GW	GW	GW	GW	GW	GW	GW	GW	GW		GW	GW	GW	GW	GW	GW	GW	GW	GW		GW	GW	GW	GW
Slough d	23p56	08 22	08 52	09 22	09 52	10 12	10 32	10 52	11 12		11 32	11 52	12 12	12 32	12 52	13 12	13 32	13 52	14 12		14 32	14 52	15 12	15 32
Windsor & Eton Central a	00 02	08 28	08 58	09 28	09 58	10 18	10 38	10 58	11 18		11 38	11 58	12 18	12 38	12 58	13 18	13 38	13 58	14 18		14 38	14 58	15 18	15 38

	GW	GW	GW	GW	GW		GW	GW	GW	GW	GW	GW	GW	GW	GW		GW	GW	GW	GW	GW
Slough d	15 52	16 12	16 32	16 52	17 12		17 32	17 52	18 12	18 32	18 52	19 22	19 52	20 22	20 52		21 22	21 52	22 22	22 52	23 22
Windsor & Eton Central a	15 58	16 18	16 38	16 58	17 18		17 38	17 58	18 18	18 38	18 58	19 28	19 58	20 28	20 58		21 28	21 58	22 28	22 58	23 28

Table 119

Mondays to Fridays

Windsor & Eton - Slough

Network Diagram - see first Page of Table 116

Miles		GW	GW	GW	GW	GW	GW	GW	GW	GW		GW	GW	GW	GW	GW	GW	GW	GW	GW		GW	GW	GW
0	Windsor & Eton Central d	05 48	06 08	06 28	06 46	07 04	07 22	07 40	08 04	08 22		08 40	09 04	09 24	09 42	10 02	10 20	10 40	11 00	11 20		11 40	12 00	12 20
2¼	Slough a	05 54	06 14	06 34	06 52	07 10	07 28	07 46	08 10	08 28		08 46	09 10	09 30	09 48	10 08	10 26	10 46	11 06	11 26		11 46	12 06	12 26

	GW	GW	GW	GW	GW	GW		GW	GW	GW	GW	GW	GW	GW	GW	GW		GW	GW	GW	GW	GW	GW	GW
Windsor & Eton Central d	12 40	13 00	13 20	13 40	14 00	14 20		14 40	15 00	15 20	15 40	16 00	16 30	16 52	17 10	17 30		17 49	18 07	18 28	18 49	19 07	19 27	19 50
Slough a	12 46	13 06	13 26	13 46	14 06	14 26		14 46	15 06	15 26	15 46	16 06	16 36	16 58	17 16	17 36		17 55	18 13	18 34	18 55	19 13	19 33	19 56

	GW	GW		GW	GW	GW	GW	GW	GW	GW	GW	GW
Windsor & Eton Central d	20 10	20 30		20 50	21 10	21 30	21 50	22 10	22 30	22 50	23 10	23 30
Slough a	20 16	20 36		20 56	21 16	21 36	21 56	22 16	22 36	22 56	23 16	23 36

Saturdays

	GW	GW	GW	GW	GW	GW	GW	GW	GW		GW	GW	GW	GW	GW	GW	GW	GW	GW		GW	GW	GW	GW
Windsor & Eton Central d	06 27	06 57	07 27	07 57	08 27	08 57	09 27	09 57	10 27		10 47	11 07	11 27	11 47	12 07	12 27	12 47	13 07	13 27		13 47	14 07	14 27	14 47
Slough a	06 33	07 03	07 33	08 03	08 33	09 03	09 33	10 03	10 33		10 53	11 13	11 33	11 53	12 13	12 33	12 53	13 13	13 33		13 53	14 13	14 33	14 53

	GW	GW	GW	GW	GW		GW	GW	GW	GW	GW	GW	GW	GW	GW		GW	GW	GW	GW	GW	GW	GW	GW
Windsor & Eton Central d	15 07	15 27	15 47	16 07	16 27		16 47	17 07	17 27	17 47	18 07	18 27	18 47	19 07	19 27		19 57	20 27	20 57	21 26	21 57	22 27	23 02	23 32
Slough a	15 13	15 33	15 53	16 13	16 33		16 53	17 13	17 33	17 53	18 13	18 33	18 53	19 13	19 33		20 03	20 33	21 03	21 32	22 03	22 33	23 08	23 38

Sundays

	GW	GW	GW	GW	GW	GW	GW	GW	GW		GW	GW	GW	GW	GW	GW	GW	GW	GW		GW	GW	GW	GW
Windsor & Eton Central d	00 05	08 32	09 02	09 32	10 02	10 22	10 42	11 02	11 22		11 42	12 02	12 22	12 42	13 02	13 22	13 42	14 02	14 22		14 42	15 02	15 22	15 42
Slough a	00 11	08 38	09 08	09 38	10 08	10 28	10 48	11 08	11 28		11 48	12 08	12 28	12 48	13 08	13 28	13 48	14 08	14 28		14 48	15 08	15 28	15 48

	GW	GW	GW	GW	GW		GW	GW	GW	GW	GW	GW	GW	GW	GW		GW	GW	GW	GW	GW
Windsor & Eton Central d	16 02	16 22	16 42	17 02	17 22		17 42	18 02	18 22	18 42	19 02	19 32	20 02	20 32	21 02		21 32	22 02	22 32	23 02	23 32
Slough a	16 08	16 28	16 48	17 08	17 28		17 48	18 08	18 28	18 48	19 08	19 38	20 08	20 38	21 08		21 38	22 08	22 38	23 08	23 38

Table 120

Mondays to Fridays

Maidenhead - Marlow

Network Diagram - see first Page of Table 116

Miles			GW MX 1	GW 1	GW 1	GW 1	GW 1	GW 1	GW 1	GW 1	GW 1	GW 1	GW 1	GW 1	GW 1	GW 1	GW 1	GW 1	GW 1	GW 1	GW 1	GW 1	GW 1
—	London Paddington 15 ⊖	d																					
0	**Maidenhead 3**	d	23p49	05 25	05 49		06 31		07 09		07 41		08 11		09 02	09 38	10 38	11 38	12 38	13 38	14 38	15 38	16 40
1¼	Furze Platt	d	23p53	05 29	05 53		06 35		07 13		07 45		08 15		09 06	09 42	10 42	11 42	12 42	13 42	14 42	15 42	16 44
3	Cookham	d	23p56	05 32							07 48		08 18		09 09	09 45	10 45	11 45	12 45	13 45	14 45	15 45	16 47
4½	Bourne End 3	a	23p59	05 36	06 01		06 43		07 21		07 52		08 22		09 13	09 49	10 49	11 49	12 49	13 49	14 49	15 49	16 51
—		d	00 04	05 40		06 18		06 49		07 28		07 57		08 25		09 53	10 53	11 53	12 53	13 53	14 53	15 53	16 55
7¼	**Marlow**	a	00 12	05 48		06 25		06 56		07 35		08 04		08 32		10 01	11 01	12 01	13 01	14 01	15 01	16 01	17 03

		GW 1	GW 1	GW 1	GW 1	GW 1	GW 1	GW 1	GW 1	GW 1	GW 1	GW 1	GW 1	GW 1
London Paddington 15 ⊖	d		17 42				18 36							
Maidenhead 3	d	17 46	18 14		18 46		19 14		19 47		20 42	21 39	22 49	23 49
Furze Platt	d	17 50	18 18		18 49		19 18		19 51		20 46	21 43	22 53	23 53
Cookham	d	17 53	18 22		18 53		19 22		19 54		20 49	21 46	22 56	23 56
Bourne End 3	a	17 57	18 28		18 57		19 26		19 58		20 53	21 50	23 00	23 59
	d	18 01		18 31		19 02		19 31		20 01	20 57	21 54	23 04	00 04
Marlow	a	18 09		18 38		19 09		19 38		20 08	21 05	22 02	23 12	00 12

Saturdays

		GW 1	GW 1	GW 1	GW 1	GW 1	GW 1	GW 1	GW 1	GW 1	GW 1	GW 1	GW 1	GW 1	GW 1	GW 1	GW 1	GW 1	GW 1	GW 1
London Paddington 15 ⊖	d																			
Maidenhead 3	d	23p49	06 38	07 38	08 38	09 38	10 38	11 38	12 38	13 38	14 38	15 38	16 38	17 38	18 38	19 38	20 38	21 38	22 38	23 38
Furze Platt	d	23p53	06 42	07 42	08 42	09 42	10 42	11 42	12 42	13 42	14 42	15 42	16 42	17 42	18 42	19 42	20 42	21 42	22 42	23 42
Cookham	d	23p56	06 45	07 45	08 45	09 45	10 45	11 45	12 45	13 45	14 45	15 45	16 45	17 45	18 45	19 45	20 45	21 45	22 45	23 45
Bourne End 3	a	23p59	06 49	07 49	08 49	09 49	10 49	11 49	12 49	13 49	14 49	15 49	16 49	17 49	18 49	19 49	20 49	21 49	22 49	23 49
	d	00 04	06 53	07 53	08 53	09 53	10 53	11 53	12 53	13 53	14 53	15 53	16 53	17 53	18 53	19 53	20 53	21 53	22 53	23 53
Marlow	a	00 12	07 01	08 01	09 01	10 01	11 01	12 01	13 01	14 01	15 01	16 01	17 01	18 01	19 01	20 01	21 01	22 01	23 01	00 01

Sundays

		GW 1	GW 1	GW 1	GW 1	GW 1	GW 1	GW 1	GW 1	GW 1	GW 1	GW 1	GW 1	GW 1	GW 1	GW 1
London Paddington 15 ⊖	d															
Maidenhead 3	d	23p38	08 35	09 35	10 35	11 35	12 35	13 35	14 35	15 35	16 35	17 35	18 35	19 35	20 35	21 40
Furze Platt	d	23p42	08 39	09 39	10 39	11 39	12 39	13 39	14 39	15 39	16 39	17 39	18 39	19 39	20 39	21 44
Cookham	d	23p45	08 42	09 42	10 42	11 42	12 42	13 42	14 42	15 42	16 42	17 42	18 42	19 42	20 42	21 47
Bourne End 3	a	23p49	08 47	09 47	10 47	11 47	12 47	13 47	14 47	15 47	16 47	17 47	18 47	19 47	20 47	21 52
	d	23p53	08 51	09 51	10 51	11 51	12 51	13 51	14 51	15 51	16 51	17 51	18 51	19 51	20 51	21 56
Marlow	a	00 01	08 58	09 58	10 58	11 58	12 58	13 58	14 58	15 58	16 58	17 58	18 58	19 58	20 58	22 03

Table 120

Mondays to Fridays

Marlow - Maidenhead

Network Diagram - see first Page of Table 116

Miles			GW MX 1	GW 1	GW 1	GW 1	GW 1	GW 1	GW 1	GW 1	GW 1	GW 1	GW 1	GW 1	GW 1	GW 1	GW 1	GW 1	GW 1	GW 1	GW 1	GW 1	GW 1
0	**Marlow**	d	00 15	06 04		06 39		07 17		07 46		08 15		08 35		10 06	11 06	12 06	13 06	14 06	15 06	16 06	17 06
2¾	Bourne End 3	a	00 22	06 11		06 46		07 24		07 53		08 22		08 42		10 13	11 13	12 13	13 13	14 13	15 13	16 13	17 13
—		d	00 26		06 14		06 49		07 27		07 56		08 28	08 46	09 17	10 17	11 17	12 17	13 17	14 17	15 17	16 17	17 17
4¼	Cookham	d	00 30		06 17		06 52		07 30		07 59		08 31	08 50	09 20	10 21	11 21	12 21	13 21	14 21	15 21	16 21	17 21
6	Furze Platt	d	00 33		06 21		06 56		07 34		08 03		08 35	08 53	09 24	10 24	11 24	12 24	13 24	14 24	15 24	16 24	17 24
7¼	**Maidenhead 3**	a	00 38		06 25		07 00		07 38		08 07		08 39	08 58	09 28	10 29	11 29	12 29	13 29	14 29	15 29	16 29	17 29
—	London Paddington 15 ⊖	a							08 21				09 21										

		GW 1	GW 1	GW 1	GW 1	GW 1	GW 1	GW 1	GW 1	GW 1	GW 1	GW 1	GW 1
Marlow	d	18 21		18 51		19 21		19 51		20 15	21 08	22 05	23 15
Bourne End 3	a	18 28		18 58		19 28		19 58		20 22	21 15	22 12	23 22
	d		18 31		19 01		19 32		20 05	20 26	21 19	22 16	23 26
Cookham	d		18 34		19 04		19 35		20 08	20 30	21 23	22 20	23 30
Furze Platt	d		18 37		19 07		19 38		20 12	20 33	21 26	22 23	23 33
Maidenhead 3	a		18 42		19 12		19 43		20 16	20 38	21 31	22 28	23 38
London Paddington 15 ⊖	a												

Saturdays

		GW 1	GW 1	GW 1	GW 1	GW 1	GW 1	GW 1	GW 1	GW 1	GW 1	GW 1	GW 1	GW 1	GW 1	GW 1	GW 1	GW 1	GW 1
Marlow	d	00 15	07 06	08 06	09 06	10 06	11 06	12 06	13 06	14 06	15 06	16 06	17 06	18 06	19 06	20 06	21 06	22 06	23 06
Bourne End 3	a	00 22	07 13	08 13	09 13	10 13	11 13	12 13	13 13	14 13	15 13	16 13	17 13	18 13	19 13	20 13	21 13	22 13	23 13
	d	00 26	07 17	08 17	09 17	10 17	11 17	12 17	13 17	14 17	15 17	16 17	17 17	18 17	19 17	20 17	21 17	22 17	23 17
Cookham	d	00 30	07 21	08 21	09 21	10 21	11 21	12 21	13 21	14 21	15 21	16 21	17 21	18 21	19 21	20 21	21 21	22 21	23 21
Furze Platt	d	00 33	07 24	08 24	09 24	10 24	11 24	12 24	13 24	14 24	15 24	16 24	17 24	18 24	19 24	20 24	21 24	22 24	23 24
Maidenhead 3	a	00 38	07 29	08 29	09 29	10 29	11 29	12 29	13 29	14 29	15 29	16 29	17 29	18 29	19 29	20 29	21 29	22 29	23 29
London Paddington 15 ⊖	a																		

Sundays

		GW 1	GW 1	GW 1	GW 1	GW 1	GW 1	GW 1	GW 1	GW 1	GW 1	GW 1	GW 1	GW 1	GW 1	GW 1
Marlow	d	00 06	09 01	10 01	11 01	12 01	13 01	14 01	15 01	16 01	17 01	18 01	19 01	20 01	21 01	22 06
Bourne End 3	a	00 13	09 08	10 08	11 08	12 08	13 08	14 08	15 08	16 08	17 08	18 08	19 08	20 08	21 08	22 13
	d	00 17	09 12	10 12	11 12	12 12	13 12	14 12	15 12	16 12	17 12	18 12	19 12	20 12	21 12	22 17
Cookham	d	00 21	09 16	10 16	11 16	12 16	13 16	14 16	15 16	16 16	17 16	18 16	19 16	20 16	21 16	22 20
Furze Platt	d	00 24	09 20	10 20	11 20	12 20	13 20	14 20	15 20	16 20	17 20	18 20	19 20	20 20	21 20	22 24
Maidenhead 3	a	00 29	09 24	10 24	11 24	12 24	13 24	14 24	15 24	16 24	17 24	18 24	19 24	20 24	21 24	22 28
London Paddington 15 ⊖	a															

Table 121

Mondays to Fridays

Twyford - Henley-on-Thames

Network Diagram - see first Page of Table 116

Miles			GW 1	GW 1	GW 1	GW 1	GW 1	GW 1	GW 1	GW 1	GW 1	GW 1	GW 1	GW 1	GW 1	GW 1	GW 1	GW 1	GW 1	GW 1	GW 1	GW 1	GW 1
—	London Paddington 15 ⊖	d																			17 12		18 12
—	Reading 7	d					08 06																
0	**Twyford 3**	d	05 42	06 21	06 50	07 27	08 14	08 45	09 21	09 53	10 36	11 21	12 06	12 51	13 36	14 21	15 06	15 48	16 48	17 31	17 58	18 31	18 58
1¾	Wargrave	d	05 46	06 25	06 54	07 31	08 19	08 49	09 25	09 57	10 40	11 25	12 10	12 55	13 40	14 25	15 10	15 52	16 52	17 35	18 03	18 35	19 03
2¾	Shiplake	d	05 49	06 28	06 57	07 34	08 22	08 52	09 28	10 00	10 43	11 28	12 13	12 58	13 43	14 28	15 13	15 55	16 55	17 38	18 06	18 38	19 06
4½	**Henley-on-Thames**	a	05 54	06 33	07 02	07 39	08 26	08 57	09 33	10 05	10 48	11 33	12 18	13 03	13 48	14 33	15 18	16 00	17 00	17 43	18 13	18 43	19 13

		GW 1	GW 1	GW 1	GW 1	GW 1	GW 1
London Paddington 15 ⊖	d	19 06					
Reading 7	d						
Twyford 3	d	19 38	20 09	20 47	21 50	23 00	23 37
Wargrave	d	19 42	20 13	20 51	21 54	23 04	23 41
Shiplake	d	19 45	20 16	20 54	21 57	23 07	23 44
Henley-on-Thames	a	19 52	20 21	20 59	22 02	23 12	23 49

Saturdays

		GW 1	GW 1	GW 1	GW 1	GW 1	GW 1	GW 1	GW 1	GW 1	GW 1	GW 1	GW 1	GW 1	GW 1	GW 1	GW 1	GW 1	GW 1
London Paddington 15 ⊖	d																		
Reading 7	d																		
Twyford 3	d	06 57	07 50	08 50	09 50	10 50	11 50	12 50	13 50	14 50	15 50	16 50	17 50	18 50	19 50	20 50	21 50	22 50	23 50
Wargrave	d	07 01	07 54	08 54	09 54	10 54	11 54	12 54	13 54	14 54	15 54	16 54	17 54	18 54	19 54	20 54	21 54	22 54	23 54
Shiplake	d	07 04	07 57	08 57	09 57	10 57	11 57	12 57	13 57	14 57	15 57	16 57	17 57	18 57	19 57	20 57	21 57	22 57	23 57
Henley-on-Thames	a	07 09	08 02	09 02	10 02	11 02	12 02	13 02	14 02	15 02	16 02	17 02	18 02	19 02	20 02	21 02	22 02	23 02	00 02

Sundays

		GW 1	GW 1	GW 1	GW 1	GW 1	GW 1	GW 1	GW 1	GW 1	GW 1	GW 1	GW 1	GW 1	GW 1
London Paddington 15 ⊖	d														
Reading 7	d														
Twyford 3	d	23p50	09 43	10 43	11 43	12 43	13 43	14 43	15 43	16 43	17 43	18 43	19 43	20 43	21 43
Wargrave	d	23p54	09 47	10 47	11 47	12 47	13 47	14 47	15 47	16 47	17 47	18 47	19 47	20 47	21 47
Shiplake	d	23p57	09 50	10 50	11 50	12 50	13 50	14 50	15 50	16 50	17 50	18 50	19 50	20 50	21 50
Henley-on-Thames	a	00 02	09 55	10 55	11 55	12 55	13 55	14 55	15 55	16 55	17 55	18 55	19 55	20 55	21 55

Table 121

Mondays to Fridays

Henley-on-Thames - Twyford

Network Diagram - see first Page of Table 116

Miles			GW MX 1	GW 1	GW 1	GW 1	GW 1	GW 1	GW 1	GW 1	GW 1	GW 1	GW 1	GW 1	GW 1	GW 1	GW 1	GW 1	GW 1	GW 1	GW 1	GW 1	GW 1
0	**Henley-on-Thames**	d	23p52	06 06	06 36	07 09	07 44	08 29	09 01	09 36	10 09	10 54	11 39	12 24	13 09	13 54	14 39	15 24	16 20	17 09	17 46	18 17	18 46
1¾	Shiplake	d	23p56	06 10	06 40	07 13	07 48	08 33	09 05	09 40	10 13	10 58	11 43	12 28	13 13	13 58	14 43	15 28	16 24	17 13	17 50	18 21	18 50
2¾	Wargrave	d	23p59	06 13	06 43	07 16	07 51	08 36	09 08	09 43	10 16	11 01	11 46	12 31	13 16	14 01	14 46	15 31	16 27	17 16	17 53	18 24	18 53
4½	**Twyford 3**	a	00 04	06 18	06 48	07 21	07 56	08 41	09 13	09 48	10 21	11 06	11 51	12 36	13 21	14 06	14 51	15 36	16 32	17 21	17 58	18 29	18 58
—	Reading 7	a	00 16																				
—	London Paddington 15 ⊖	a				07 57	08 28																

		GW 1	GW 1	GW 1	GW 1	GW 1	GW 1	GW 1
Henley-on-Thames	d	19 16	19 55	20 24	21 02	22 06	23 15	23 52
Shiplake	d	19 20	19 59	20 28	21 06	22 10	23 19	23 56
Wargrave	d	19 23	20 02	20 31	21 09	22 13	23 22	23 59
Twyford 3	a	19 28	20 07	20 36	21 14	22 18	23 27	00 04
Reading 7	a							00 16
London Paddington 15 ⊖	a							

Saturdays

		GW 1	GW 1	GW 1	GW 1	GW 1	GW 1	GW 1	GW 1	GW 1	GW 1	GW 1	GW 1	GW 1	GW 1	GW 1	GW 1	GW 1	GW 1
Henley-on-Thames	d	23p52	07 24	08 24	09 24	10 24	11 24	12 24	13 24	14 24	15 24	16 24	17 24	18 24	19 24	20 24	21 24	22 24	23 08
Shiplake	d	23p56	07 28	08 28	09 28	10 28	11 28	12 28	13 28	14 28	15 28	16 28	17 28	18 28	19 28	20 28	21 28	22 28	23 12
Wargrave	d	23p59	07 31	08 31	09 31	10 31	11 31	12 31	13 31	14 31	15 31	16 31	17 31	18 31	19 31	20 31	21 31	22 31	23 15
Twyford 3	a	00 04	07 36	08 36	09 36	10 36	11 36	12 36	13 36	14 36	15 36	16 36	17 36	18 36	19 36	20 36	21 36	22 36	23 20
Reading 7	a	00 16																	
London Paddington 15 ⊖	a																		

Sundays

		GW 1	GW 1	GW 1	GW 1	GW 1	GW 1	GW 1	GW 1	GW 1	GW 1	GW 1	GW 1	GW 1	GW 1
Henley-on-Thames	d	00 08	10 03	11 03	12 03	13 03	14 03	15 03	16 03	17 03	18 03	19 03	20 03	21 03	22 01
Shiplake	d	00 12	10 07	11 07	12 07	13 07	14 07	15 07	16 07	17 07	18 07	19 07	20 07	21 07	22 05
Wargrave	d	00 15	10 10	11 10	12 10	13 10	14 10	15 10	16 10	17 10	18 10	19 10	20 10	21 10	22 08
Twyford 3	a	00 20	10 15	11 15	12 15	13 15	14 15	15 15	16 15	17 15	18 15	19 15	20 15	21 15	22 13
Reading 7	a														
London Paddington 15 ⊖	a														

Mondays to Fridays

Reading - Basingstoke

Network Diagram - see first Page of Table 116

Miles			GW MO A	GW	GW	GW	GW	GW	XC	GW	XC	GW	XC	GW	GW	XC	GW	XC	GW	XC	GW	GW	XC
0	**Reading**	d	23p37	05 39	06 05	06 39	07 07	07 39	07 46	08 07	08 15	08 38	08 46	09 05	09 39	09 46	10 07	10 15	10 39	10 46	11 07	11 39	11 46
1	Reading West	d	23p40	05 42	06 08	06 42	07 10	07 42		08 10		08 41		09 08	09 42		10 10		10 42		11 10	11 42	
7¼	Mortimer	d	23p48	05 50	06 16	06 50	07 18	07 50		08 18		08 49		09 16	09 50		10 18		10 50		11 18	11 50	
10½	Bramley (Hants)	d	23p53	05 55	06 21	06 55	07 23	07 55		08 23		08 54		09 21	09 55		10 23		10 55		11 23	11 55	
15½	**Basingstoke**	a	00 01	06 04	06 30	07 04	07 32	08 04	08 08	08 32	08 40	09 03	09 08	09 30	10 04	10 08	10 32	10 39	11 04	11 08	11 32	12 04	12 08

		GW	XC	GW	XC	GW	GW	XC	GW	XC	GW	XC	GW	GW	XC	GW	XC	GW	XC	GW	GW	XC	GW
Reading	d	12 07	12 15	12 39	12 46	13 07	13 39	13 46	14 07	14 15	14 39	14 46	15 07	15 39	15 46	16 07	16 15	16 39	16 46	17 07	17 41	17 46	18 07
Reading West	d	12 10		12 42		13 10	13 42		14 10		14 42		15 10	15 42		16 10		16 42		17 10	17 42		18 10
Mortimer	d	12 18		12 50		13 18	13 50		14 18		14 50		15 18	15 50		16 18		16 50		17 18	17 50		18 18
Bramley (Hants)	d	12 23		12 55		13 23	13 55		14 23		14 55		15 23	15 55		16 23		16 55		17 23	17 55		18 23
Basingstoke	a	12 32	12 39	13 04	13 08	13 32	14 04	14 08	14 32	14 39	15 04	15 08	15 32	16 04	16 08	16 32	16 39	17 04	17 08	17 32	18 06	18 08	18 32

		XC	GW	XC	GW	GW	XC	GW	GW	XC	GW	GW	XC	GW	XC	GW	GW
Reading	d	18 15	18 41	18 46	19 07	19 38	19 46	20 07	20 37	20 46	21 07	21 39	21 46	22 10	22 48	22 55	23 34
Reading West	d		18 42		19 10	19 41		20 10	20 40		21 10	21 42		22 13		22 58	23 37
Mortimer	d		18 50		19 18	19 49		20 18	20 48		21 18	21 50		22 21		23 06	23 45
Bramley (Hants)	d		18 55		19 23	19 54		20 23	20 53		21 23	21 55		22 26		23 11	23 50
Basingstoke	a	18 47	19 06	19 08	19 32	20 03	20 09	20 32	21 02	21 09	21 31	22 03	22 09	22 34	23 06	23 19	23 58

Saturdays
until 8 September

		GW	GW	GW	GW	XC	GW	XC	GW	XC	GW	GW	XC	GW	XC	GW	XC	GW	GW	XC	GW	XC	GW
Reading	d	06 07	06 39	07 07	07 39	07 46	08 10	08 23	08 39	08 46	09 09	09 39	09 46	10 07	10 15	10 39	10 46	11 09	11 39	11 46	12 09	12 15	12 39
Reading West	d	06 10	06 42	07 10	07 42		08 13		08 42		09 12	09 42		10 10		10 42		11 12	11 42		12 12		12 42
Mortimer	d	06 18	06 50	07 18	07 50		08 21		08 50		09 20	09 50		10 18		10 50		11 20	11 50		12 20		12 50
Bramley (Hants)	d	06 23	06 55	07 23	07 55		08 26		08 55		09 25	09 55		10 23		10 55		11 25	11 55		12 25		12 55
Basingstoke	a	06 32	07 03	07 32	08 03	08 08	08 34	08 40	09 03	09 08	09 33	10 03	10 08	10 31	10 39	11 03	11 08	11 33	12 03	12 08	12 33	12 40	13 03

		XC	GW	GW	XC	GW	XC	GW	XC	GW	GW	XC	GW	XC	GW	XC	GW	GW	XC	GW	XC	GW	XC
Reading	d	12 46	13 09	13 39	13 46	14 07	14 15	14 39	14 46	15 07	15 39	15 46	16 07	16 15	16 39	16 46	17 07	17 39	17 46	18 07	18 15	18 39	18 46
Reading West	d		13 12	13 42		14 10		14 42		15 10	15 42		16 10		16 42		17 10	17 42		18 10		18 42	
Mortimer	d		13 20	13 50		14 18		14 50		15 18	15 50		16 18		16 50		17 18	17 50		18 18		18 50	
Bramley (Hants)	d		13 25	13 55		14 23		14 55		15 23	15 55		16 23		16 55		17 23	17 55		18 23		18 55	
Basingstoke	a	13 08	13 33	14 03	14 08	14 31	14 40	15 03	15 08	15 31	16 03	16 08	16 31	16 40	17 03	17 08	17 31	18 03	18 08	18 31	18 40	19 03	19 08

		GW	GW	XC	GW	GW	XC	GW	GW	XC	GW	GW	XC	GW
Reading	d	19 07	19 39	19 46	20 07	20 39	20 46	21 07	21 39	21 47	22 07	22 39	22 49	23 07
Reading West	d	19 10	19 42		20 10	20 42		21 10	21 42		22 10	22 42		23 10
Mortimer	d	19 18	19 50		20 18	20 50		21 18	21 50		22 18	22 50		23 18
Bramley (Hants)	d	19 23	19 55		20 23	20 55		21 23	21 55		22 23	22 55		23 23
Basingstoke	a	19 31	20 03	20 08	20 31	21 03	21 08	21 31	22 03	22 09	22 31	23 03	23 07	23 31

Saturdays
from 15 September

		GW	GW	GW	GW	XC	GW	XC	GW	XC	GW	GW	XC	GW	XC	GW	XC	GW	GW	XC	GW	XC	GW
Reading	d	06 07	06 39	07 07	07 39	07 46	08 07	08 23	08 39	08 46	09 07	09 39	09 46	10 07	10 15	10 39	10 46	11 07	11 39	11 46	12 07	12 15	12 39
Reading West	d	06 10	06 42	07 10	07 42		08 10		08 42		09 10	09 42		10 10		10 42		11 10	11 42		12 10		12 42
Mortimer	d	06 18	06 50	07 18	07 50		08 18		08 50		09 18	09 50		10 18		10 50		11 18	11 50		12 18		12 50
Bramley (Hants)	d	06 23	06 55	07 23	07 55		08 23		08 55		09 23	09 55		10 23		10 55		11 23	11 55		12 23		12 55
Basingstoke	a	06 32	07 03	07 32	08 03	08 08	08 31	08 40	09 03	09 08	09 31	10 03	10 08	10 31	10 39	11 03	11 08	11 31	12 03	12 08	12 31	12 40	13 03

		XC	GW	GW	XC	GW	XC	GW	XC	GW	GW	XC	GW	XC	GW	XC	GW	GW	XC	GW	XC	GW	XC
Reading	d	12 46	13 07	13 39	13 46	14 07	14 15	14 39	14 46	15 07	15 39	15 46	16 07	16 15	16 39	16 46	17 07	17 39	17 46	18 07	18 15	18 39	18 46
Reading West	d		13 10	13 42		14 10		14 42		15 10	15 42		16 10		16 42		17 10	17 42		18 10		18 42	
Mortimer	d		13 18	13 50		14 18		14 50		15 18	15 50		16 18		16 50		17 18	17 50		18 18		18 50	
Bramley (Hants)	d		13 23	13 55		14 23		14 55		15 23	15 55		16 23		16 55		17 23	17 55		18 23		18 55	
Basingstoke	a	13 08	13 31	14 03	14 08	14 31	14 40	15 03	15 08	15 31	16 03	16 08	16 31	16 40	17 03	17 08	17 31	18 03	18 08	18 31	18 40	19 03	19 08

A from 21 May

Table 122

Saturdays
from 15 September

Reading - Basingstoke

Network Diagram - see first Page of Table 116

		GW	GW	XC	GW	GW	XC	GW	GW	XC	GW	GW	XC	GW
Reading	d	19 07	19 39	19 46	20 07	20 39	20 46	21 07	21 39	21 47	22 07	22 39	22 49	23 07
Reading West	d	19 10	19 42		20 10	20 42		21 10	21 42		22 10	22 42		23 10
Mortimer	d	19 18	19 50		20 18	20 50		21 18	21 50		22 18	22 50		23 18
Bramley (Hants)	d	19 23	19 55		20 23	20 55		21 23	21 55		22 23	22 55		23 23
Basingstoke	a	19 31	20 03	20 08	20 31	21 03	21 08	21 31	22 03	22 08	22 31	23 03	23 07	23 31

Sundays
until 24 June

		GW	GW	GW	XC	GW	XC	GW	XC	GW	XC	GW	XC	GW	XC	GW	XC	GW	XC	GW	XC	GW	XC
Reading	d	07 37	08 37	09 37	09 53	10 37	10 53	11 37	11 53	12 37	12 53	13 37	13 53	14 37	14 53	15 37	15 53	16 37	16 53	17 37	17 53	18 37	18 53
Reading West	d	07 40	08 40	09 40		10 40		11 40		12 40		13 40		14 40		15 40		16 40		17 40		18 40	
Mortimer	d	07 48	08 48	09 48		10 48		11 48		12 48		13 48		14 48		15 48		16 48		17 48		18 48	
Bramley (Hants)	d	07 53	08 53	09 53		10 53		11 53		12 53		13 53		14 53		15 53		16 53		17 53		18 53	
Basingstoke	a	08 01	09 01	10 01	10 09	11 01	11 09	12 01	12 09	13 01	13 09	14 01	14 09	15 01	15 09	16 01	16 09	17 01	17 09	18 01	18 09	19 01	19 09

		GW	XC	GW	XC	GW	XC	GW	GW
Reading	d	19 37	19 53	20 37	20 53	21 37	21 53	22 37	23 37
Reading West	d	19 40		20 40		21 40		22 41	23 40
Mortimer	d	19 48		20 48		21 48		22 49	23 48
Bramley (Hants)	d	19 53		20 53		21 53		22 54	23 53
Basingstoke	a	20 01	20 09	21 01	21 09	22 01	22 09	23 02	00 01

Sundays
1 July to 9 September

		GW	GW	GW	XC	GW	XC	GW	XC	GW	XC	GW	XC	GW	XC	GW	XC	GW	XC	GW	XC	GW	XC
Reading	d	07 37	08 37	09 37	09 53	10 37	10 53	11 37	11 53	12 37	12 53	13 37	13 53	14 37	14 53	15 37	15 53	16 37	16 53	17 37	17 53	18 37	18 53
Reading West	d	07 40	08 40	09 40		10 40		11 40		12 40		13 40		14 40		15 40		16 40		17 40		18 40	
Mortimer	d	07 48	08 48	09 48		10 48		11 48		12 48		13 48		14 48		15 48		16 48		17 48		18 48	
Bramley (Hants)	d	07 53	08 53	09 53		10 53		11 53		12 53		13 53		14 53		15 53		16 53		17 53		18 53	
Basingstoke	a	08 01	09 01	10 01	10 09	11 01	11 09	12 01	12 09	13 01	13 09	14 01	14 09	15 01	15 09	16 01	16 09	17 01	17 09	18 01	18 09	19 01	19 09

		GW	XC	GW	XC	GW	XC	GW	GW
Reading	d	19 37	19 53	20 37	20 53	21 37	21 53	22 37	23 37
Reading West	d	19 40		20 40		21 40		22 41	23 40
Mortimer	d	19 48		20 48		21 48		22 49	23 48
Bramley (Hants)	d	19 53		20 53		21 53		22 54	23 53
Basingstoke	a	20 01	20 09	21 01	21 09	22 01	22 09	23 02	00 01

Sundays
from 16 September

		GW	GW	GW	XC	GW	XC	GW	XC	GW	XC	GW	XC	GW	XC	GW	XC	GW	XC	GW	XC	GW	XC
Reading	d	07 37	08 37	09 37	09 53	10 37	10 53	11 37	11 53	12 37	12 53	13 37	13 53	14 37	14 53	15 37	15 53	16 37	16 53	17 37	17 53	18 37	18 53
Reading West	d	07 40	08 40	09 40		10 40		11 40		12 40		13 40		14 40		15 40		16 40		17 40		18 40	
Mortimer	d	07 48	08 48	09 48		10 48		11 48		12 48		13 48		14 48		15 48		16 48		17 48		18 48	
Bramley (Hants)	d	07 53	08 53	09 53		10 53		11 53		12 53		13 53		14 53		15 53		16 53		17 53		18 53	
Basingstoke	a	08 01	09 01	10 01	10 09	11 01	11 09	12 01	12 09	13 01	13 09	14 01	14 09	15 01	15 09	16 01	16 09	17 01	17 09	18 01	18 09	19 01	19 09

		GW	XC	GW	XC	GW	XC	GW	GW
Reading	d	19 37	19 53	20 37	20 53	21 37	21 53	22 37	23 37
Reading West	d	19 40		20 40		21 40		22 41	23 40
Mortimer	d	19 48		20 48		21 48		22 49	23 48
Bramley (Hants)	d	19 53		20 53		21 53		22 54	23 53
Basingstoke	a	20 01	20 09	21 01	21 09	22 01	22 09	23 02	00 01

Table 122

Mondays to Fridays

Basingstoke - Reading

Network Diagram - see first Page of Table 116

Miles			GW MX 1	GW MO 1	XC ◇1	GW	GW	XC ◇1 ⊼	GW	GW	XC ◇1 ⊼	GW	XC ◇1 ⊼	GW	XC ◇1 ⊼	GW	GW	XC ◇1 ⊼	GW	XC ◇1 ⊼	GW	XC ◇1 ⊼	GW
0	**Basingstoke**	d	00 02	00 07	05 47	06 07	06 33	06 47	07 08	07 36	07 47	08 07	08 18	08 36	08 47	09 06	09 36	09 47	10 07	10 19	10 36	10 47	11 07
5	Bramley (Hants)	d	00 09	00 14		06 14	06 40		07 14	07 43		08 14		08 43		09 13	09 43		10 14		10 43		11 14
8¼	Mortimer	d	00 14	00 19		06 19	06 45		07 19	07 48		08 19		08 48		09 18	09 48		10 19		10 48		11 19
14½	Reading West	d	00 22	00 26		06 28	06 54		07 28	07 57		08 28		08 57		09 27	09 57		10 28		10 57		11 28
15½	**Reading 7**	a	00 26	00 30	06 04	06 32	06 57	07 04	07 32	08 00	08 04	08 31	08 36	09 00	09 04	09 30	10 00	10 04	10 31	10 36	11 00	11 04	11 31

		GW	XC ◇1 ⊼	GW	XC ◇1 ⊼	GW	XC ◇1 ⊼	GW	GW	XC ◇1 ⊼	GW	XC ◇1	GW	XC ◇1 ⊼	GW	GW	XC ◇1 ⊼	GW	XC ◇1 ⊼	GW	XC ◇1 ⊼	GW	GW
Basingstoke	d	11 36	11 47	12 07	12 18	12 36	12 47	13 07	13 36	13 47	14 07	14 19	14 36	14 47	15 07	15 36	15 47	16 07	16 18	16 36	16 47	17 07	17 36
Bramley (Hants)	d	11 43		12 14		12 43		13 14	13 43		14 14		14 43		15 14	15 43		16 14		16 43		17 14	17 43
Mortimer	d	11 48		12 19		12 48		13 19	13 48		14 19		14 48		15 19	15 48		16 19		16 48		17 19	17 48
Reading West	d	11 57		12 28		12 57		13 28	13 57		14 28		14 57		15 28	15 57		16 28		16 57		17 28	17 57
Reading 7	a	12 00	12 04	12 31	12 36	13 00	13 04	13 31	14 00	14 04	14 31	14 36	15 00	15 04	15 31	16 00	16 04	16 31	16 35	17 00	17 03	17 31	18 00

		XC ◇1 ⊼	GW	XC ◇1 ⊼	GW	XC ◇1 ⊼	GW	GW	XC ◇1 ⊼	GW	GW	XC ◇1	GW	GW 1	GW 1	GW 1	GW 1
Basingstoke	d	17 47	18 08	18 18	18 36	18 47	19 09	19 36	19 47	20 06	20 36	20 47	21 06	21 42	22 24	22 55	23 30
Bramley (Hants)	d		18 15		18 43		19 16	19 43		20 13	20 43		21 13	21 49	22 31	23 02	23 37
Mortimer	d		18 20		18 48		19 21	19 48		20 18	20 48		21 18	21 54	22 36	23 07	23 42
Reading West	d		18 29		18 57		19 30	19 57		20 27	20 57		21 27	22 02	22 44	23 15	23 50
Reading 7	a	18 04	18 32	18 36	19 00	19 04	19 33	20 00	20 04	20 30	21 01	21 04	21 30	22 05	22 47	23 18	23 53

Saturdays

		GW 1	XC ◇1	GW 1	XC ◇1 ⊼	GW 1	XC ◇1 ⊼	GW 1	XC ◇1 ⊼	GW 1	XC ◇1 ⊼	GW 1	XC ◇1 ⊼	GW 1	GW 1	XC ◇1 ⊼	GW 1	XC ◇1 ⊼	GW 1	XC ◇1 ⊼	GW 1	GW 1	XC ◇1 ⊼
Basingstoke	d	00 02	05 41	06 37	06 47	07 07	07 25	07 37	07 47	08 07	08 19	08 37	08 47	09 07	09 37	09 47	10 07	10 19	10 37	10 47	11 07	11 37	11 47
Bramley (Hants)	d	00 09		06 44		07 14		07 44		08 14		08 44		09 14	09 44		10 14		10 44		11 14	11 44	
Mortimer	d	00 14		06 49		07 19		07 49		08 19		08 49		09 19	09 49		10 19		10 49		11 19	11 49	
Reading West	d	00 22		06 57		07 27		07 57		08 27		08 57		09 27	09 57		10 27		10 57		11 27	11 57	
Reading 7	a	00 26	05 59	07 00	07 04	07 31	07 42	08 00	08 04	08 31	08 35	09 00	09 04	09 31	10 00	10 04	10 31	10 34	11 00	11 04	11 31	12 00	12 04

		GW 1	XC ◇1 ⊼	GW 1	XC ◇1 ⊼	GW 1	GW 1	XC ◇1 ⊼	GW 1	XC ◇1 ⊼	GW 1	XC ◇1 ⊼	GW 1	GW 1	XC ◇1 ⊼	GW 1	XC ◇1 ⊼	GW 1	XC ◇1 ⊼	GW 1	GW 1	XC ◇1 ⊼	GW 1
Basingstoke	d	12 07	12 19	12 37	12 47	13 07	13 37	13 47	14 07	14 19	14 37	14 47	15 07	15 37	15 47	16 07	16 19	16 37	16 47	17 07	17 37	17 47	18 07
Bramley (Hants)	d	12 14		12 44		13 14	13 44		14 14		14 44		15 14	15 44		16 14		16 44		17 14	17 44		18 14
Mortimer	d	12 19		12 49		13 19	13 49		14 19		14 49		15 19	15 49		16 19		16 49		17 19	17 49		18 19
Reading West	d	12 27		12 57		13 27	13 57		14 27		14 57		15 27	15 57		16 27		16 57		17 27	17 57		18 27
Reading 7	a	12 31	12 35	13 00	13 04	13 31	14 00	14 04	14 31	14 35	15 00	15 04	15 31	16 00	16 05	16 31	16 35	17 00	17 04	17 31	18 00	18 04	18 31

		XC ◇1 ⊼	GW 1	XC ◇1 ⊼	GW 1	GW 1	XC ◇1 ⊼	GW 1	GW 1	XC ◇1	GW 1	GW 1	GW 1	GW 1	GW 1	GW 1
Basingstoke	d	18 19	18 37	18 47	19 07	19 37	19 47	20 08	20 37	20 47	21 07	21 39	22 07	22 37	23 07	23 37
Bramley (Hants)	d		18 44		19 14	19 44		20 14	20 44		21 14	21 44	22 14	22 44	23 14	23 44
Mortimer	d		18 49		19 19	19 49		20 19	20 49		21 19	21 49	22 19	22 49	23 19	23 49
Reading West	d		18 57		19 27	19 57		20 27	20 57		21 27	21 57	22 27	22 57	23 27	23 57
Reading 7	a	18 35	19 00	19 04	19 31	20 01	20 04	20 32	21 01	21 04	21 31	22 02	22 31	23 00	23 31	00 01

Sundays
until 24 June

		GW 1	GW 1	GW 1	XC ◇1 ⊼	GW 1	XC ◇1 ⊼	GW 1	XC ◇1 ⊼	GW 1	XC ◇1 ⊼	GW 1	XC ◇1 ⊼	GW 1	XC ◇1 ⊼	GW 1	XC ◇1 ⊼	GW 1	XC ◇1 ⊼	GW 1	XC ◇1 ⊼	GW 1	XC ◇1 ⊼
Basingstoke	d	23p37	08 07	09 07	09 47	10 07	10 47	11 07	11 47	12 07	12 47	13 07	13 47	14 07	14 47	15 07	15 47	16 07	16 47	17 07	17 47	18 07	18 47
Bramley (Hants)	d	23p44	08 14	09 14		10 14		11 14		12 14		13 14		14 14		15 14		16 14		17 14		18 14	
Mortimer	d	23p49	08 19	09 19		10 19		11 19		12 19		13 19		14 19		15 19		16 19		17 19		18 19	
Reading West	d	23p57	08 27	09 27		10 27		11 27		12 27		13 27		14 27		15 27		16 27		17 27		18 27	
Reading 7	a	00 01	08 30	09 30	10 04	10 30	11 04	11 30	12 03	12 30	13 04	13 30	14 04	14 30	15 04	15 30	16 04	16 30	17 04	17 30	18 04	18 30	19 04

		GW 1	XC ◇1 ⊼	GW 1	XC ◇1	GW 1	GW 1	GW 1
Basingstoke	d	19 07	19 47	20 07	20 47	21 07	22 07	23 07
Bramley (Hants)	d	19 14		20 14		21 14	22 15	23 14
Mortimer	d	19 19		20 19		21 19	22 20	23 19
Reading West	d	19 28		20 27		21 27	22 30	23 27
Reading 7	a	19 31	20 04	20 30	21 03	21 30	22 33	23 30

Table 122

Sundays
1 July to 9 September

Basingstoke - Reading

Network Diagram - see first Page of Table 116

		GW 1	GW 1	GW 1	XC ◇1 ⊼	GW 1	XC ◇1 ⊼	GW 1	XC ◇1 ⊼	GW 1	XC ◇1 ⊼	GW 1	XC ◇1 ⊼	GW 1	XC ◇1 ⊼	GW 1	XC ◇1 ⊼	GW 1	XC ◇1 ⊼	GW 1	XC ◇1 ⊼	GW 1	XC ◇1 ⊼
Basingstoke	d	23p37	08 07	09 07	09 47	10 07	10 47	11 07	11 47	12 07	12 47	13 07	13 47	14 07	14 47	15 07	15 47	16 07	16 47	17 07	17 47	18 07	18 47
Bramley (Hants)	d	23p44	08 14	09 14		10 14		11 14		12 14		13 14		14 14		15 14		16 14		17 14		18 14	
Mortimer	d	23p49	08 19	09 19		10 19		11 19		12 19		13 19		14 19		15 19		16 19		17 19		18 19	
Reading West	d	23p57	08 27	09 27		10 27		11 27		12 27		13 27		14 27		15 27		16 27		17 27		18 27	
Reading 7	a	00 01	08 30	09 30	10 04	10 30	11 04	11 30	12 04	12 30	13 04	13 30	14 03	14 30	15 04	15 30	16 04	16 30	17 04	17 30	18 04	18 30	19 03

		GW 1	XC ◇1 ⊼	GW 1	XC ◇1	GW 1	GW 1	GW 1
Basingstoke	d	19 07	19 47	20 07	20 47	21 07	22 07	23 07
Bramley (Hants)	d	19 14		20 14		21 14	22 15	23 14
Mortimer	d	19 19		20 19		21 19	22 20	23 19
Reading West	d	19 28		20 27		21 27	22 30	23 27
Reading 7	a	19 31	20 04	20 30	21 03	21 30	22 33	23 30

Sundays
from 16 September

		GW 1	GW 1	GW 1	XC ◇1 ⊼	GW 1	XC ◇1 ⊼	GW 1	XC ◇1 ⊼	GW 1	XC ◇1 ⊼	GW 1	XC ◇1 ⊼	GW 1	XC ◇1 ⊼	GW 1	XC ◇1 ⊼	GW 1	XC ◇1 ⊼	GW 1	XC ◇1 ⊼	GW 1	XC ◇1 ⊼
Basingstoke	d	23p37	08 07	09 07	09 47	10 07	10 47	11 07	11 47	12 07	12 47	13 07	13 47	14 07	14 47	15 07	15 47	16 07	16 47	17 07	17 47	18 07	18 47
Bramley (Hants)	d	23p44	08 14	09 14		10 14		11 14		12 14		13 14		14 14		15 14		16 14		17 14		18 14	
Mortimer	d	23p49	08 19	09 19		10 19		11 19		12 19		13 19		14 19		15 19		16 19		17 19		18 19	
Reading West	d	23p57	08 27	09 27		10 27		11 27		12 27		13 27		14 27		15 27		16 27		17 27		18 27	
Reading 7	a	00 01	08 30	09 30	10 03	10 30	11 04	11 30	12 04	12 30	13 04	13 30	14 02	14 30	15 04	15 30	16 02	16 30	17 04	17 30	18 04	18 30	19 02

		GW 1	XC ◇1 ⊼	GW 1	XC ◇1	GW 1	GW 1	GW 1
Basingstoke	d	19 07	19 47	20 07	20 47	21 07	22 07	23 07
Bramley (Hants)	d	19 14		20 14		21 14	22 15	23 14
Mortimer	d	19 19		20 19		21 19	22 20	23 19
Reading West	d	19 28		20 27		21 27	22 30	23 27
Reading 7	a	19 31	20 04	20 30	21 03	21 30	22 33	23 30

Network Diagram for Table 123

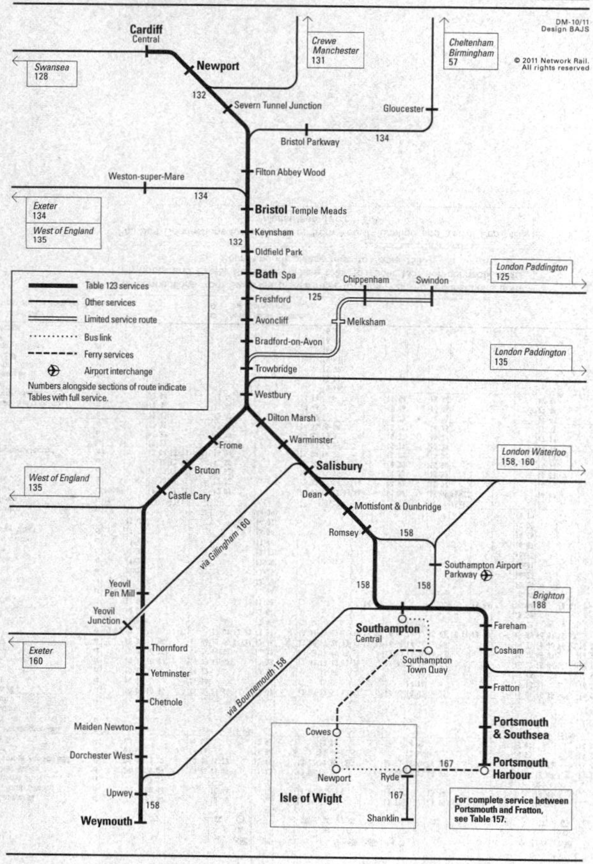

Table 123

Mondays to Fridays

until 29 June

South Wales and Bristol - Weymouth and Portsmouth

Network Diagram - see first Page of Table 123

Miles	Miles	Miles			GW MX	GW MX	GW	GW	GW	GW	GW	GW	GW		GW	GW	GW	GW	GW	GW	SW	GW	GW		GW
						■ A ⊡			◇1 ⊡		◇					◇ H	◇1 B ⊡		■ H	◇	◇1		◇ H		◇1 ⊡
0	0	—	**Cardiff Central** 7	d												06 28			07 30				08 30		
11¾	11¾	—	Newport (South Wales)	d												06 42			07 44				08 44		
21¾	21¾	—	Severn Tunnel Jn	d												06 53			07 55				08 55		
33¾	33¾	—	Filton Abbey Wood	d												07 09		07 28	08 09	08 23			09 09		
38¼	38¼	—	**Bristol Temple Meads** 10	d	23p20				05 20		05 44				06 48	07 22		07 49	08 22	08 41	08 51	09 05	09 22		
42¾	42¾	—	Keynsham	d	23p27						05 51				06 55			07 56		08 48	08 58				
48¾	48¾	—	Oldfield Park	d	23p34						05 58				07 02			08 03		08 55		09 17			
—	—	—	London Paddington 15 ⊖	d		23p45											07 06								09 06
—	—	0	Swindon	d									06 12												
—	—	16¾	Chippenham	d									06 28												
—	—	23	Melksham	d									06 37												
49¾	49¾	—	**Bath Spa** 7	d	23p38						06 02				07 06	07 35		08 07	08 35	08 59	09 07	09 21	09 35		
56¾	56¾	—	Freshford	d	23p47						06 12				07 15			08 16		09 08					
57¾	57¾	—	Avoncliff	d	23p50						06 14				07 18			08 19		09 11					
59	59	—	Bradford-on-Avon	d	23p54				05 44		06 18				07 22	07 47		08 23	08 47	09 15	09 20	09 33			
62¼	62¼	28½	Trowbridge	d	23p59				05 52		06 25		06 47		07 28	07 53		08 29	08 53	09 21	09 27	09 39	09 51		
66¼	66¼	32½	**Westbury**	a	00 07	01 35			05 59		06 32		06 55		07 35	08 00	08 25	08 36	09 00	09 28	09 33	09 49	09 58		
—	—	—		d	00 08		05 24	05 49		06 25	06 37	06 47	07 01			08 01			09 01	09 31	09 39		09 59		
—	72	—	Frome	d	00a19					06a35		06 56								09 40					
—	82½	—	Bruton	d								07 08								09 52					
—	86	—	Castle Cary	a								07 13								09 59					10 31
—	—	—		d								07 14								10 00					
—	97¾	—	Yeovil Pen Mill	d								07 35								10 14					
—	101	—	Thornford	d								07x39								10x18					
—	102	—	Yetminster	d								07x42								10x21					
—	104	—	Chetnole	d								07x46								10x25					
—	110½	—	Maiden Newton	d								07 58								10 37					
—	118¼	—	Dorchester West	d								08 09								10 48					
—	122¾	—	Upwey	a								08 16								10 55					
—	125¼	—	**Weymouth**	a								08 24								11 03					
67¾	—	—	Dilton Marsh	d									07x03												
71	—	—	Warminster	d			05 32	05 57			06 45		07 12			08 09			09 09		09 46		10 07		
90¾	—	—	**Salisbury**	a			05 55	06 18			07 10		07 36			08 32			09 32		10 09		10 29		
—	—	—		d				06 19			07 11		07 36			08 32			09 32				10 30		
107¼	—	—	Romsey	d				06 38			07 30		07 56			08 50			09 50				10 50		
115½	—	—	**Southampton Central**	a				06 49			07 40		08 09			09 04			10 04				11 04		
130	—	—	Fareham	a				07 14			08 05					09 27			10 27				11 27		
—	—	—		d				07 15			08 06					09 27			10 27				11 27		
135¾	—	—	Cosham	a				07 23			08 13					09 35			10 35				11 35		
139½	—	—	Fratton	a				07 34			08 20					09 42			10 42				11 42		
140½	—	—	Portsmouth & Southsea	a				07 38			08 24					09 46			10 46				11 46		
141¼	—	—	**Portsmouth Harbour**	a				07 45			08 30					09 55			10 54				11 54		
—	—	—	Havant	a																					
—	—	—	**Chichester** 4	a																					
—	—	—	Barnham	a																					
—	—	—	Worthing 4	a																					
—	—	—	Shoreham-by-Sea	a																					
—	—	—	Hove 2	a																					
—	—	—	Brighton 10	a																					

A The Night Riviera

B The Devon Express

For connections from Swansea please refer to Table 128. For connections from Plymouth and Exeter St Davids please refer to Table 135. For connections to Bournemouth please refer to Table 158

For Bus Connections for either to or from Yeovil Junction and Yeovil Pen Mill please see Table 123A

Table 123

Mondays to Fridays
until 29 June

South Wales and Bristol - Weymouth and Portsmouth

Network Diagram - see first Page of Table 123

		GW	GW	GW	GW	GW	GW	GW	GW	GW	GW	SW	GW	GW	GW	GW	GW	GW FO	GW	GW	GW	GW	SW
			◇	◇ 🍴			◇ 🍴	◇■ A Ø	◇	◇ 🍴	■ B 🍴	◇■ C 🍴	◇■ ☕	◇ 🍴		◇ 🍴		◇	◇	◇ 🍴	◇■ D Ø		◇■
Cardiff Central ■	d			09 30			10 30			11 30				12 30		13 30				14 30			
Newport (South Wales)	d			09 44			10 44			11 44				12 44		13 44				14 44			
Severn Tunnel Jn.	d			09 55																			
Filton Abbey Wood	d		09 23	10 09		10 25	11 09		11 23	12 09	12 25			13 09	13 23	14 09			14 25	15 09		15 23	
Bristol Temple Meads ■	d		09 49	10 22		10 49	11 22		11 49	12 22	12 39	12 51		13 22	13 49	14 22			14 48	15 22		15 44	15 51
Keynsham	d		09 56			10 56			11 56		12 46	12 58			13 56				14 55			15 51	15 58
Oldfield Park	d		10 03			11 03			12 03		12 53				14 03				15 02			15 58	
London Paddington ■ ⊖	d							11 06					12 18								15 06		
Swindon	d																						
Chippenham	d																						
Melksham	d																						
Bath Spa ■	d		10 07	10 35		11 07	11 35		12 07	12 35	12 57	13 07		13 35	14 07	14 35			15 06	15 35		16 02	16 07
Freshford	d		10 16			11 16			12 16		13 06				14 16				15 15			16 11	
Avoncliff	d		10 18			11 19			12 19		13 08				14 19				15 18			16 13	
Bradford-on-Avon	d		10 22	10 47		11 23	11 47		12 23	12 47	13 12	13 20		13 47	14 23	14 47			15 22	15 47		16 17	16 22
Trowbridge	d		10 29	10 53		11 29	11 53		12 29	12 53	13 19	13 27		13 53	14 29	14 53			15 28	15 53		16 24	16 28
Westbury	a		10 36	11 00		11 36	12 00	12 21	12 36	13 00	13 26	13 33	13 57	14 00	14 36	15 00			15 35	16 00	16 22	16 33	16 36
	d	10 08	10 37	11 01	11 11		12 01	12 22	12 37	13 01	13 27	13 39	13 59	14 01	14 37	15 01	15 11	15 20	15 38	16 01	16 23		16 39
Frome	d		10 46						12 49						14a50				15 47				
Bruton	d		10 58						13 01										15 58				
Castle Cary	a		11 03					12 39	13 06				14 16					15 46	16 04		16 41		
	d		11 03						13 06										16 09				
Yeovil Pen Mill	d		11 17						13 20										16 24				
Thornford	d		11x22						13x25										16x28				
Yetminster	d		11x25						13x28										16x31				
Chetnole	d		11x29						13x32										16x35				
Maiden Newton	d		11 41						13 44										16 47				
Dorchester West	d		11 54						13 54										16 58				
Upwey	a		12 02						14 02										17 05				
Weymouth	a		12 09						14 09										17 10				
Dilton Marsh	d	10x10			11x13						13x29						15x13						
Warminster	d	10a19		11 09	11 21		12 09			13 09	13 36	13 46		14 09		15 09	15a22			16 09			16 47
Salisbury	a			11 32	11 41		12 32			13 32	13 58	14 10		14 32		15 32				16 32			17 09
	d			11 32	11 42		12 32			13 32	13 59			14 32		15 32				16 32			
Romsey	d			11 50	12 10		12 50			13 50	14 19			14 50		15 50				16 50			
Southampton Central	a			12 04	12 22		13 04			14 04	14 32			15 04		16 04				17 04			
Fareham	a			12 27			13 27			14 27	14 55			15 27		16 27				17 27			
	d			12 27			13 27			14 27	14 56			15 27		16 27				17 27			
Cosham	a			12 35			13 35			14 35	15 04			15 35		16 35				17 35			
Fratton	a			12 42			13 42			14 42				15 42		16 42				17 42			
Portsmouth & Southsea	a			12 46			13 46			14 46				15 46		16 46				17 46			
Portsmouth Harbour	a			12 54			13 54			14 54				15 54		16 54				17 54			
Havant	a										15 10												
Chichester ■	a										15 21												
Barnham	a										15 29												
Worthing ■	a										15 45												
Shoreham-by-Sea	a										15 56												
Hove ■	a										16 07												
Brighton ■	a										16 14												

A The Mayflower
B 🍴 from Bristol Temple Meads
C not 4 June, 5 June
D The Cornishman

For connections from Swansea please refer to Table 128. For connections from Plymouth and Exeter St Davids please refer to Table 135. For connections to Bournemouth please refer to Table 158

For Bus Connections for either to or from Yeovil Junction and Yeovil Pen Mill please see Table 123A

Table 123

Mondays to Fridays
until 29 June

South Wales and Bristol - Weymouth and Portsmouth

Network Diagram - see first Page of Table 123

		GW	GW	GW	GW	GW	GW	GW	GW	GW	GW	GW	GW	GW	GW	GW	GW	GW	GW	GW	GW	GW	GW
		◇ 🍴		◇			◇■ ☕	■ 🍴	◇		◇■ ☕	■ 🍴	◇		◇■ ☕	◇ 🍴	◇■ ☕		◇	◇■ ☕		◇■ ☕	◇
Cardiff Central ■	d	15 30						16 30				17 30				18 30			19 30				20 30
Newport (South Wales)	d	15 44						16 44				17 44				18 44			19 44				20 44
Severn Tunnel Jn.	d							16 55				17 55				18 55							
Filton Abbey Wood	d	16 09		16 25	16 49	16 55		17 09	17 23	17 49		18 09		18 25		19 09		19 23	20 09				21 08
Bristol Temple Meads ■	d	16 22		16 49	17 07	17 14		17 22	17 49	18 07		18 22		18 49		19 22		19 49	20 22		20 49		21 23
Keynsham	d			16 56	17 14				17 56	18 14				18 56				19 56			20 56		
Oldfield Park	d			17 03	17 21	17 26			18 03	18 21				19 03				20 03			21 03		
London Paddington ■ ⊖	d						16 36				17 33				18 06		18 33			19 45		20 35	
Swindon	d												18 44										
Chippenham	d												19 01										
Melksham	d												19 11										
Bath Spa ■	d	16 35		17 07	17 25	17 31		17 37	18 07	18 25		18 35		19 07		19 35		20 07	20 35		21 07		21 36
Freshford	d			17 16		17 40			18 16	18 34				19 16				20 16			21 16		
Avoncliff	d			17 19					18 19	18 37				19 19				20 19			21 19		
Bradford-on-Avon	d	16 47		17 23	17 37	17 45		17 50	18 23	18 41		18 47		19 23		19 47		20 23	20 47		21 23		21 48
Trowbridge	d	16 53		17 30	17 44	17 51		17 57	18 29	18 47		18 53	19 20	19 29		19 53		20 29	20 53		21 29		21 55
Westbury	a	17 00		17 36	17 51	17 58	18 02	18 05	18 36	18 56	18 59	19 00	19 27	19 36	19 52	20 00	20 04	20 36	21 00	21 06	21 36	21 56	22 03
	d	17 01	17 11	17 39	17 54		18 04	18 05	18 40		19 01	19 02	19 41		19 53	20 01	20 05	20 37	21 01	21 06	21 38	21 57	22 03
Frome	d			17 48					18 49						20a04			20a48			21 49		
Bruton	d			18 00					19 01												22 01		
Castle Cary	a			18 05			18 20		19 06		19 17						20 23			21 24	22 06	22 14	
	d			18 06					19 06												22 06		
Yeovil Pen Mill	d			18 21					19 19												22 20		
Thornford	d			18x26					19x25												22x25		
Yetminster	d			18x29					19x28												22x28		
Chetnole	d			18x33					19x32												22x32		
Maiden Newton	d			18 45					19 44												22 44		
Dorchester West	d			18 58					19 54												22 54		
Upwey	a			19 06					20 02												23 02		
Weymouth	a			19 14					20 10												23 10		
Dilton Marsh	d		17x13		17x56								19x43										22x06
Warminster	d	17 09	17a22		18a05			18 13				19 09	19 51			20 09			21 09				22 11
Salisbury	a	17 32						18 35				19 32	20 13			20 32			21 32				22 32
	d	17 32						18 35				19 32	20 14			20 32			21 32				22 32
Romsey	d	17 50						18 54				19 50	20 35			20 50			21 50				22 53
Southampton Central	a	18 04						19 04				20 04	20 48			21 04			22 02				23 04
Fareham	a	18 27						19 27				20 27				21 27			22 42				23 27
	d	18 27						19 27				20 27				21 27			22 42				23 27
Cosham	a	18 35						19 34															
Fratton	a	18 48						19 42				20 42				21 41			22 56				23 44
Portsmouth & Southsea	a	18 52						19 46				20 46				21 45			22 59				23 48
Portsmouth Harbour	a	19 00						19 54				20 54				21 52			23 04				23 54
Havant	a																						
Chichester ■	a																						
Barnham	a																						
Worthing ■	a																						
Shoreham-by-Sea	a																						
Hove ■	a																						
Brighton ■	a																						

For connections from Swansea please refer to Table 128. For connections from Plymouth and Exeter St Davids please refer to Table 135. For connections to Bournemouth please refer to Table 158

For Bus Connections for either to or from Yeovil Junction and Yeovil Pen Mill please see Table 123A

Table 123

Mondays to Fridays

until 29 June

South Wales and Bristol - Weymouth and Portsmouth

Network Diagram - see first Page of Table 123

		GW	SW	GW	GW
			■		■ A
Cardiff Central	d	21 00			
Newport (South Wales)	d	21 15			
Severn Tunnel Jn.	d	21 25			
Filton Abbey Wood	d	21 42			
Bristol Temple Meads	d	22 00	22 25	23 20	
Keynsham	d	22 07		23 27	
Oldfield Park	d	22 14		23 34	
London Paddington ⊖	d				23 45
Swindon	d				
Chippenham	d				
Melksham	d				
Bath Spa	d	22 18	22 38	23 38	
Freshford	d	22 27		23 47	
Avoncliff	d	22 30		23 50	
Bradford-on-Avon	d	22 34	22 51	23 54	
Trowbridge	d	22 40	22 57	23 59	
Westbury	a	22 47	23 04	00 07	01 35
	d		23 08	00 08	
Frome	d			00a19	
Bruton	d				
Castle Cary	a				
	d				
Yeovil Pen Mill	d				
Thornford	d				
Yetminster	d				
Chetnole	d				
Maiden Newton	d				
Dorchester West	d				
Upwey	a				
Weymouth	a				
Dilton Marsh	d				
Warminster	d		23 15		
Salisbury	a		23 35		
	d				
Romsey	d				
Southampton Central	a				
Fareham	a				
	d				
Cosham	a				
Fratton	a				
Portsmouth & Southsea	a				
Portsmouth Harbour	a				
Havant	a				
Chichester	a				
Barnham	a				
Worthing	a				
Shoreham-by-Sea	a				
Hove	a				
Brighton	a				

A The Night Riviera

For connections from Swansea please refer to Table 128. For connections from Plymouth and Exeter St Davids please refer to Table 135. For connections to Bournemouth please refer to Table 158

For Bus Connections for either to or from Yeovil Junction and Yeovil Pen Mill please see Table 123A

Table 123

Mondays to Fridays

2 July to 31 August

South Wales and Bristol - Weymouth and Portsmouth

Network Diagram - see first Page of Table 123

		GW MX	GW MX	GW	GW	GW	GW	GW	GW	GW	GW	GW	GW	GW	GW	GW	SW	GW	GW	GW	GW	GW	GW
			■ A			◇■		◇				◇	◇■ B		■	◇	◇■		◇	◇■ C		◇	◇
Cardiff Central	d											06 28			07 30				08 30				09 30
Newport (South Wales)	d											06 42			07 44				08 44				09 44
Severn Tunnel Jn.	d											06 53			07 55				08 55				09 55
Filton Abbey Wood	d											07 09		07 28	08 09	08 23			09 09			09 23	10 09
Bristol Temple Meads	d	23p20				05 20		05 44			06 48	07 22		07 49	08 22	08 41	08 51	09 05	09 22			09 49	10 22
Keynsham	d	23p27						05 51			06 55			07 56		08 48	08 58					09 56	
Oldfield Park	d	23p34						05 58			07 02			08 03		08 55		09 17				10 03	
London Paddington ⊖	d		23p45										07 06							09 06			
Swindon	d									06 12													
Chippenham	d									06 28													
Melksham	d									06 37													
Bath Spa	d	23p38						06 02			07 06	07 35		08 07	08 35	08 59	09 07	09 21	09 35			10 07	10 35
Freshford	d	23p47						06 12			07 15			08 16		09 08						10 16	
Avoncliff	d	23p50						06 14			07 18			08 19		09 11						10 18	
Bradford-on-Avon	d	23p54				05 44		06 18			07 22	07 47		08 23	08 47	09 15	09 20	09 33				10 22	10 47
Trowbridge	d	23p59				05 52		06 25		06 47	07 28	07 53		08 29	08 53	09 21	09 27	09 39	09 51			10 29	10 53
Westbury	a	00 07	01 35			05 59		06 32		06 55	07 35	08 00	08 25	08 36	09 00	09 28	09 33	09 49	09 58			10 36	11 00
	d	00 08		05 24	05 49		06 25	06 37	06 47	07 01		08 01			09 01	09 31	09 39		09 59		10 08	10 37	11 01
Frome	d	00a19					06a35		06 56							09 40						10 46	
Bruton	d								07 08							09 52						10 58	
Castle Cary	a								07 13							09 59				10 31		11 03	
	d								07 14							10 00						11 03	
Yeovil Pen Mill	d								07 35							10 14						11 17	
Thornford	d								07x39							10x18						11x22	
Yetminster	d								07x42							10x21						11x25	
Chetnole	d								07x46							10x25						11x29	
Maiden Newton	d								07 58							10 37						11 41	
Dorchester West	d								08 09							10 48						11 54	
Upwey	a								08 16							10 55						12 02	
Weymouth	a								08 24							11 03						12 09	
Dilton Marsh	d									07x03											10x10		
Warminster	d			05 32	05 57			06 45		07 12		08 09			09 09		09 46		10 07		10a19		11 09
Salisbury	a			05 55	06 18			07 10		07 36		08 32			09 32		10 09		10 29				11 32
	d				06 19			07 11		07 36		08 32			09 32				10 30				11 32
Romsey	d				06 38			07 30		07 56		08 50			09 50				10 50				11 50
Southampton Central	a				06 49			07 40		08 09		09 04			10 04				11 04				12 04
Fareham	a				07 14			08 05				09 27			10 27				11 27				12 27
	d				07 15			08 06				09 27			10 27				11 27				12 27
Cosham	a				07 23			08 13				09 35			10 35				11 35				12 35
Fratton	a				07 34			08 20				09 42			10 42				11 42				12 42
Portsmouth & Southsea	a				07 38			08 24				09 46			10 46				11 46				12 46
Portsmouth Harbour	a				07 45			08 30				09 55			10 54				11 54				12 54
Havant	a																						
Chichester	a																						
Barnham	a																						
Worthing	a																						
Shoreham-by-Sea	a																						
Hove	a																						
Brighton	a																						

A The Night Riviera   B The Devon Express   C The Atlantic Coast Express

For connections from Swansea please refer to Table 128. For connections from Plymouth and Exeter St Davids please refer to Table 135. For connections to Bournemouth please refer to Table 158

For Bus Connections for either to or from Yeovil Junction and Yeovil Pen Mill please see Table 123A

Table 123

Mondays to Fridays
2 July to 31 August

South Wales and Bristol - Weymouth and Portsmouth

Network Diagram - see first Page of Table 123

		GW	GW	GW	GW	GW	GW	GW	SW	GW	GW	GW	GW	GW	GW	GW	GW	GW	GW	GW	SW	GW	GW
															FO			FO					
				◇ ⊼	◇1 A ⌀	◇	◇ ⊼	■ B ⊼	◇1 ⊼	◇1 ⊡	◇ ⊼		◇ ⊼		◇	◇	◇ ⊼	◇1 ⊡	◇1 C ⌀		◇1	◇ ⊼	
Cardiff Central 7	d			10 30			11 30				12 30		13 30				14 30					15 30	
Newport (South Wales)	d			10 44			11 44				12 44		13 44				14 44					15 44	
Severn Tunnel Jn.	d																						
Filton Abbey Wood	d		10 25	11 09		11 23	12 09	12 25			13 09	13 23	14 09			14 25	15 09			15 23		16 09	
Bristol Temple Meads 10	d		10 49	11 22		11 49	12 22	12 39	12 51		13 22	13 49	14 22			14 48	15 22			15 44	15 51	16 22	
Keynsham	d		10 56			11 56		12 46	12 58			13 56				14 55				15 51	15 58		
Oldfield Park	d		11 03			12 03		12 53				14 03				15 02				15 58			
London Paddington 15 ⊖	d				11 06					12 18								14 36	15 06				
Swindon	d																						
Chippenham	d																						
Melksham	d																						
Bath Spa 7	d		11 07	11 35		12 07	12 35	12 57	13 07		13 35	14 07	14 35			15 06	15 35			16 02	16 07	16 35	
Freshford	d		11 16			12 16		13 06				14 16				15 15				16 11			
Avoncliff	d		11 19			12 19		13 08				14 19				15 18				16 13			
Bradford-on-Avon	d		11 23	11 47		12 23	12 47	13 12	13 20		13 47	14 23	14 47			15 22	15 47			16 17	16 22	16 47	
Trowbridge	d		11 29	11 53		12 29	12 53	13 19	13 27		13 53	14 29	14 53			15 28	15 53			16 24	16 28	16 53	
Westbury	a		11 36	12 00	12 21	12 36	13 00	13 26	13 33	13 57	14 00	14 36	15 00			15 35	16 00	16 14	16 22	16 33	16 36	17 00	
	d	11 11		12 01	12 22	12 37	13 01	13 27	13 39	13 59	14 01	14 37	15 01	15 11	15 20	15 38	16 01	16 15	16 23		16 39	17 01	17 11
Frome	d					12 49						14a50				15 47							
Bruton	d					13 01										15 58							
Castle Cary	a				12 39	13 06				14 16					15 46	16 04		16 32	16 41				
	d					13 06										16 09							
Yeovil Pen Mill	d					13 20										16 24							
Thornford	d					13x25										16x28							
Yetminster	d					13x28										16x31							
Chetnole	d					13x32										16x35							
Maiden Newton	d					13 44										16 47							
Dorchester West	d					13 54										16 58							
Upwey	a					14 02										17 05							
Weymouth	a					14 09										17 10							
Dilton Marsh	d	11x13						13x29						15x13									17x13
Warminster	d	11 21		12 09			13 09	13 36	13 46		14 09		15 09	15a22			16 09				16 47	17 09	17a22
Salisbury	a	11 41		12 32			13 32	13 58	14 10		14 32		15 32				16 32				17 09	17 32	
	d	11 42		12 32			13 32	13 59			14 32		15 32				16 32					17 32	
Romsey	d	12 10		12 50			13 50	14 19			14 50		15 50				16 50					17 50	
Southampton Central	a	12 22		13 04			14 04	14 32			15 04		16 04				17 04					18 04	
Fareham	a			13 27			14 27	14 55			15 27		16 27				17 27					18 27	
	d			13 27			14 27	14 56			15 27		16 27				17 27					18 27	
Cosham	a			13 35			14 35	15 04			15 35		16 35				17 35					18 35	
Fratton	a			13 42			14 42				15 42		16 42				17 42					18 48	
Portsmouth & Southsea	a			13 46			14 46				15 46		16 46				17 46					18 52	
Portsmouth Harbour	a			13 54			14 54				15 54		16 54				17 54					19 00	
Havant	a							15 10															
Chichester 4	a							15 21															
Barnham	a							15 29															
Worthing 4	a							15 45															
Shoreham-by-Sea	a							15 56															
Hove 2	a							16 07															
Brighton 10	a							16 14															

A The Mayflower

B ⊼ from Bristol Temple Meads

C The Cornishman

For connections from Swansea please refer to Table 128. For connections from Plymouth and Exeter St Davids please refer to Table 135. For connections to Bournemouth please refer to Table 158

For Bus Connections for either to or from Yeovil Junction and Yeovil Pen Mill please see Table 123A

Table 123

Mondays to Fridays
2 July to 31 August

South Wales and Bristol - Weymouth and Portsmouth

Network Diagram - see first Page of Table 123

		GW	GW	GW	GW	GW	GW	GW	GW	GW	GW	GW	GW	GW	GW	GW	GW	GW	GW	GW	GW	GW
		◇			◇1 ⊡	■ ⊼	◇		◇1 ⊡	■ ⊼	◇		◇1 ⊡	◇ ⊼	◇1 ⊡		◇	◇1 ⊡		◇1 ⊡	◇	
Cardiff Central 7	d					16 30				17 30				18 30			19 30				20 30	21 00
Newport (South Wales)	d					16 44				17 44				18 44			19 44				20 44	21 15
Severn Tunnel Jn.	d					16 55				17 55				18 55								21 25
Filton Abbey Wood	d	16 25	16 49	16 55		17 09	17 23	17 49		18 09		18 25		19 09		19 23	20 09				21 08	21 42
Bristol Temple Meads 10	d	16 49	17 07	17 14		17 22	17 49	18 07		18 22		18 49		19 22		19 49	20 22		20 49		21 23	22 00
Keynsham	d	16 56	17 14				17 56	18 14				18 56				19 56			20 56			22 07
Oldfield Park	d	17 03	17 21	17 26			18 03	18 21				19 03				20 03			21 03			22 14
London Paddington 15 ⊖	d				16 36				17 33				18 06		18 33			19 45		20 35		
Swindon	d										18 44											
Chippenham	d										19 01											
Melksham	d										19 11											
Bath Spa 7	d	17 07	17 25	17 31		17 37	18 07	18 25		18 35		19 07		19 35		20 07	20 35		21 07		21 36	22 18
Freshford	d	17 16		17 40			18 16	18 34				19 16				20 16			21 16			22 27
Avoncliff	d	17 19					18 19	18 37				19 19				20 19			21 19			22 30
Bradford-on-Avon	d	17 23	17 37	17 45		17 50	18 23	18 41		18 47		19 23		19 47		20 23	20 47		21 23		21 48	22 34
Trowbridge	d	17 30	17 44	17 51		17 57	18 29	18 47		18 53	19 20	19 29		19 53		20 29	20 53		21 29		21 55	22 40
Westbury	a	17 36	17 51	17 58	18 02	18 05	18 36	18 56	18 59	19 00	19 27	19 36	19 52	20 00	20 04	20 36	21 00	21 06	21 36	21 56	22 03	22 47
	d	17 39	17 54		18 04	18 05	18 40		19 01	19 02	19 41		19 53	20 01	20 05	20 37	21 01	21 06	21 38	21 57	22 03	
Frome	d	17 48					18 49						20a04			20a48			21 49			
Bruton	d	18 00					19 01												22 01			
Castle Cary	a	18 05			18 20		19 06		19 17						20 23			21 24	22 06	22 14		
	d	18 06					19 06												22 06			
Yeovil Pen Mill	d	18 21					19 19												22 20			
Thornford	d	18x26					19x25												22x25			
Yetminster	d	18x29					19x28												22x28			
Chetnole	d	18x33					19x32												22x32			
Maiden Newton	d	18 45					19 44												22 44			
Dorchester West	d	18 58					19 54												22 54			
Upwey	a	19 06					20 02												23 02			
Weymouth	a	19 14					20 10												23 10			
Dilton Marsh	d		17x56								19x43										22x06	
Warminster	d		18a05			18 13				19 09	19 51			20 09			21 09				22 11	
Salisbury	a					18 35				19 32	20 13			20 32			21 32				22 32	
	d					18 35				19 32	20 14			20 32			21 32				22 32	
Romsey	d					18 54				19 50	20 35			20 50			21 50				22 53	
Southampton Central	a					19 04				20 04	20 48			21 04			22 02				23 04	
Fareham	a					19 27				20 27				21 27			22 42				23 27	
	d					19 27				20 27				21 27			22 42				23 27	
Cosham	a					19 34																
Fratton	a					19 42				20 42				21 41			22 56				23 44	
Portsmouth & Southsea	a					19 46				20 46				21 45			22 59				23 48	
Portsmouth Harbour	a					19 54				20 54				21 52			23 04				23 54	
Havant	a																					
Chichester 4	a																					
Barnham	a																					
Worthing 4	a																					
Shoreham-by-Sea	a																					
Hove 2	a																					
Brighton 10	a																					

For connections from Swansea please refer to Table 128. For connections from Plymouth and Exeter St Davids please refer to Table 135. For connections to Bournemouth please refer to Table 158

For Bus Connections for either to or from Yeovil Junction and Yeovil Pen Mill please see Table 123A

Table 123

Mondays to Fridays

2 July to 31 August

South Wales and Bristol - Weymouth and Portsmouth

Network Diagram - see first Page of Table 123

		SW	GW	GW
		◼1		■ A
Cardiff Central 7	d			
Newport (South Wales)	d			
Severn Tunnel Jn.	d			
Filton Abbey Wood	d			
Bristol Temple Meads 10	d	22 25	23 20	
Keynsham	d		23 27	
Oldfield Park	d		23 34	
London Paddington 15 ⊖	d			23 45
Swindon	d			
Chippenham	d			
Melksham	d			
Bath Spa 7	d	22 38	23 38	
Freshford	d		23 47	
Avoncliff	d		23 50	
Bradford-on-Avon	d	22 51	23 54	
Trowbridge	d	22 57	23 59	
Westbury	a	23 04	00 07	01 35
	d	23 08	00 08	
Frome	d		00a19	
Bruton	d			
Castle Cary	a			
	d			
Yeovil Pen Mill	d			
Thornford	d			
Yetminster	d			
Chetnole	d			
Maiden Newton	d			
Dorchester West	d			
Upwey	a			
Weymouth	a			
Dilton Marsh	d			
Warminster	d	23 15		
Salisbury	a	23 35		
	d			
Romsey	d			
Southampton Central	a			
Fareham	a			
	d			
Cosham	a			
Fratton	a			
Portsmouth & Southsea	a			
Portsmouth Harbour	a			
Havant	a			
Chichester 4	a			
Barnham	a			
Worthing 4	a			
Shoreham-by-Sea	a			
Hove 2	a			
Brighton 10	a			

A The Night Riviera

For connections from Swansea please refer to Table 128. For connections from Plymouth and Exeter St Davids please refer to Table 135. For connections to Bournemouth please refer to Table 158

For Bus Connections for either to or from Yeovil Junction and Yeovil Pen Mill please see Table 123A

Table 123

Mondays to Fridays

3 September to 14 September

South Wales and Bristol - Weymouth and Portsmouth

Network Diagram - see first Page of Table 123

		GW	GW	GW	GW	GW	GW	GW	GW	GW	GW	GW	GW	GW	GW	GW	SW	GW	GW	GW	GW	GW	GW
		A	■ B			◇1		◇				◇	◇1 C		■	◇	◇1		◇	◇1		◇	◇
Cardiff Central 7	d											06 28			07 30				08 30				09 30
Newport (South Wales)	d											06 42			07 44				08 44				09 44
Severn Tunnel Jn.	d											06 53			07 55				08 55				09 55
Filton Abbey Wood	d											07 09		07 28	08 09	08 23			09 09			09 23	10 09
Bristol Temple Meads 10	d	23p20				05 20		05 44			06 48	07 22		07 49	08 22	08 41	08 51	09 05	09 22			09 49	10 22
Keynsham	d	23p27						05 51			06 55			07 56		08 48	08 58					09 56	
Oldfield Park	d	23p34						05 58			07 02			08 03		08 55		09 17				10 03	
London Paddington 15 ⊖	d		23p45										07 06							09 06			
Swindon	d									06 12													
Chippenham	d									06 28													
Melksham	d									06 37													
Bath Spa 7	d	23p38						06 02			07 06	07 35		08 07	08 35	08 59	09 07	09 21	09 35			10 07	10 35
Freshford	d	23p47						06 12			07 15			08 16		09 08						10 16	
Avoncliff	d	23p50						06 14			07 18			08 19		09 11						10 18	
Bradford-on-Avon	d	23p54				05 44		06 18			07 22	07 47		08 23	08 47	09 15	09 20	09 33				10 22	10 47
Trowbridge	d	23p59				05 52		06 25		06 47	07 28	07 53		08 29	08 53	09 21	09 27	09 39	09 51			10 29	10 53
Westbury	a	00 07	01 35			05 59		06 32		06 55	07 35	08 00	08 25	08 36	09 00	09 28	09 33	09 49	09 58			10 36	11 00
	d	00 08		05 24	05 49		06 25	06 37	06 47	07 01		08 01			09 01	09 31	09 39		09 59		10 08	10 37	11 01
Frome	d	00a19					06a35		06 56							09 40						10 46	
Bruton	d								07 08							09 52						10 58	
Castle Cary	a								07 13							09 59				10 31		11 03	
	d								07 14							10 00						11 03	
Yeovil Pen Mill	d								07 35							10 14						11 17	
Thornford	d								07x39							10x18						11x22	
Yetminster	d								07x42							10x21						11x25	
Chetnole	d								07x46							10x25						11x29	
Maiden Newton	d								07 58							10 37						11 41	
Dorchester West	d								08 09							10 48						11 54	
Upwey	a								08 16							10 55						12 02	
Weymouth	a								08 24							11 03						12 09	
Dilton Marsh	d									07x03											10x10		
Warminster	d			05 32	05 57			06 45		07 12		08 09			09 09		09 46		10 07		10a19		11 09
Salisbury	a			05 55	06 18			07 10		07 36		08 32			09 32		10 09		10 29				11 32
	d				06 19			07 11		07 36		08 32			09 32				10 30				11 32
Romsey	d				06 38			07 30		07 56		08 50			09 50				10 50				11 50
Southampton Central	a				06 49			07 40		08 09		09 04			10 04				11 04				12 04
Fareham	a				07 14			08 05				09 27			10 27				11 27				12 27
	d				07 15			08 06				09 27			10 27				11 27				12 27
Cosham	a				07 23			08 13				09 35			10 35				11 35				12 35
Fratton	a				07 34			08 20				09 42			10 42				11 42				12 42
Portsmouth & Southsea	a				07 38			08 24				09 46			10 46				11 46				12 46
Portsmouth Harbour	a				07 45			08 30				09 55			10 54				11 54				12 54
Havant	a																						
Chichester 4	a																						
Barnham	a																						
Worthing 4	a																						
Shoreham-by-Sea	a																						
Hove 2	a																						
Brighton 10	a																						

A not 3 September, 10 September B not 3 September, 10 September. The Night Riviera C The Devon Express

For connections from Swansea please refer to Table 128. For connections from Plymouth and Exeter St Davids please refer to Table 135. For connections to Bournemouth please refer to Table 158

For Bus Connections for either to or from Yeovil Junction and Yeovil Pen Mill please see Table 123A

South Wales and Bristol - Weymouth and Portsmouth

Network Diagram - see first Page of Table 123

		GW	GW	GW	GW	GW	GW	GW	SW	GW	GW	GW	GW	GW	GW FO	GW	GW	GW	GW	SW	GW	GW	GW
				◇ ⊼	◇1 A ⊘	◇	◇ ⊼	■ B ⊼	◇1 ⊼	◇1 ⊡	◇ ⊼		◇ ⊼		◇	◇	◇ ⊼	◇1 C ⊘		◇1	◇ ⊼		◇
Cardiff Central 7	d			10 30			11 30				12 30		13 30				14 30				15 30		
Newport (South Wales)	d			10 44			11 44				12 44		13 44				14 44				15 44		
Severn Tunnel Jn.	d																						
Filton Abbey Wood	d		10 25	11 09		11 23	12 09	12 25			13 09	13 23	14 09			14 25	15 09		15 23		16 09		16 25
Bristol Temple Meads 10	d		10 49	11 22		11 49	12 22	12 39	12 51		13 22	13 49	14 22			14 48	15 22		15 44	15 51	16 22		16 49
Keynsham	d		10 56			11 56		12 46	12 58			13 56				14 55			15 51	15 58			16 56
Oldfield Park	d		11 03			12 03		12 53				14 03				15 02			15 58				17 03
London Paddington 15 ⊖	d				11 06					12 18								15 06					
Swindon	d																						
Chippenham	d																						
Melksham	d																						
Bath Spa 7	d		11 07	11 35		12 07	12 35	12 57	13 07		13 35	14 07	14 35			15 06	15 35		16 02	16 07	16 35		17 07
Freshford	d		11 16			12 16		13 06				14 16				15 15			16 11				17 16
Avoncliff	d		11 19			12 19		13 08				14 19				15 18			16 13				17 19
Bradford-on-Avon	d		11 23	11 47		12 23	12 47	13 12	13 20		13 47	14 23	14 47			15 22	15 47		16 17	16 22	16 47		17 23
Trowbridge	d		11 29	11 53		12 29	12 53	13 19	13 27		13 53	14 29	14 53			15 28	15 53		16 24	16 28	16 53		17 30
Westbury	a		11 36	12 00	12 21	12 36	13 00	13 26	13 33	13 57	14 00	14 36	15 00			15 35	16 00	16 22	16 33	16 36	17 00		17 36
	d	11 11		12 01	12 22	12 37	13 01	13 27	13 39	13 59	14 01	14 37	15 01	15 11	15 20	15 38	16 01	16 23		16 39	17 01	17 11	17 39
Frome	d					12 49						14a50				15 47							17 48
Bruton	d					13 01										15 58							18 00
Castle Cary	a				12 39	13 06				14 16					15 46	16 04		16 41					18 05
	d					13 06										16 09							18 06
Yeovil Pen Mill	d					13 20										16 24							18 21
Thornford	d					13x25										16x28							18x26
Yetminster	d					13x28										16x31							18x29
Chetnole	d					13x32										16x35							18x33
Maiden Newton	d					13 44										16 47							18 45
Dorchester West	d					13 54										16 58							18 58
Upwey	a					14 02										17 05							19 06
Weymouth	a					14 09										17 10							19 14
Dilton Marsh	d	11x13						13x29						15x13								17x13	
Warminster	d	11 21		12 09			13 09	13 36	13 46		14 09		15 09	15a22			16 09			16 47	17 09	17a22	
Salisbury	a	11 41		12 32			13 32	13 58	14 10		14 32		15 32				16 32			17 09	17 32		
	d	11 42		12 32			13 32	13 59			14 32		15 32				16 32				17 32		
Romsey	d	12 10		12 50			13 50	14 19			14 50		15 50				16 50				17 50		
Southampton Central	a	12 22		13 04			14 04	14 32			15 04		16 04				17 04				18 04		
Fareham	a			13 27			14 27	14 55			15 27		16 27				17 27				18 27		
	d			13 27			14 27	14 56			15 27		16 27				17 27				18 27		
Cosham	a			13 35			14 35	15 04			15 35		16 35				17 35				18 35		
Fratton	a			13 42			14 42				15 42		16 42				17 42				18 48		
Portsmouth & Southsea	a			13 46			14 46				15 46		16 46				17 46				18 52		
Portsmouth Harbour	a			13 54			14 54				15 54		16 54				17 54				19 00		
Havant	a							15 10															
Chichester 4	a							15 21															
Barnham	a							15 29															
Worthing 4	a							15 45															
Shoreham-by-Sea	a							15 56															
Hove 2	a							16 07															
Brighton 10	a							16 14															

A The Mayflower

B ⊼ from Bristol Temple Meads

C The Cornishman

For connections from Swansea please refer to Table 128. For connections from Plymouth and Exeter St Davids please refer to Table 135. For connections to Bournemouth please refer to Table 158

For Bus Connections for either to or from Yeovil Junction and Yeovil Pen Mill please see Table 123A

South Wales and Bristol - Weymouth and Portsmouth

Network Diagram - see first Page of Table 123

		GW	GW	GW	GW	GW	GW	GW	GW	GW	GW	GW	GW	GW	GW	GW	GW	GW	GW	GW	GW	SW
				◇1 ⊡	■ ⊼	◇		◇1 ⊡	■ ⊼	◇		◇1 ⊡	◇ ⊼	◇1 ⊡		◇	◇1 ⊡		◇1 ⊡	◇		1
Cardiff Central 7	d				16 30				17 30				18 30			19 30				20 30	21 00	
Newport (South Wales)	d				16 44				17 44				18 44			19 44				20 44	21 15	
Severn Tunnel Jn.	d				16 55				17 55				18 55								21 25	
Filton Abbey Wood	d	16 49	16 55		17 09	17 23	17 49		18 09		18 25		19 09		19 23	20 09				21 08	21 42	
Bristol Temple Meads 10	d	17 07	17 14		17 22	17 49	18 07		18 22		18 49		19 22		19 49	20 22		20 49		21 23	22 00	22 25
Keynsham	d	17 14				17 56	18 14				18 56				19 56			20 56			22 07	
Oldfield Park	d	17 21	17 26			18 03	18 21				19 03				20 03			21 03			22 14	
London Paddington 15 ⊖	d			16 36				17 33				18 06		18 33			19 45		20 35			
Swindon	d									18 44												
Chippenham	d									19 01												
Melksham	d									19 11												
Bath Spa 7	d	17 25	17 31		17 37	18 07	18 25		18 35		19 07		19 35		20 07	20 35		21 07		21 36	22 18	22 38
Freshford	d		17 40			18 16	18 34				19 16				20 16			21 16			22 27	
Avoncliff	d					18 19	18 37				19 19				20 19			21 19			22 30	
Bradford-on-Avon	d	17 37	17 45		17 50	18 23	18 41		18 47		19 23		19 47		20 23	20 47		21 23		21 48	22 34	22 51
Trowbridge	d	17 44	17 51		17 57	18 29	18 47		18 53	19 20	19 29		19 53		20 29	20 53		21 29		21 55	22 40	22 57
Westbury	a	17 51	17 58	18 02	18 05	18 36	18 56	18 59	19 00	19 27	19 36	19 52	20 00	20 04	20 36	21 00	21 06	21 36	21 56	22 03	22 47	23 04
	d	17 54		18 04	18 05	18 40		19 01	19 02	19 41		19 53	20 01	20 05	20 37	21 01	21 06	21 38	21 57	22 03		23 08
Frome	d					18 49						20a04			20a48			21 49				
Bruton	d					19 01												22 01				
Castle Cary	a			18 20		19 06		19 17						20 23			21 24	22 06	22 14			
	d					19 06												22 06				
Yeovil Pen Mill	d					19 19												22 20				
Thornford	d					19x25												22x25				
Yetminster	d					19x28												22x28				
Chetnole	d					19x32												22x32				
Maiden Newton	d					19 44												22 44				
Dorchester West	d					19 54												22 54				
Upwey	a					20 02												23 02				
Weymouth	a					20 10												23 10				
Dilton Marsh	d	17x56								19x43										22x06		
Warminster	d	18a05			18 13				19 09	19 51			20 09			21 09				22 11		23 15
Salisbury	a				18 35				19 32	20 13			20 32			21 32				22 32		23 35
	d				18 35				19 32	20 14			20 32			21 32				22 32		
Romsey	d				18 54				19 50	20 35			20 50			21 50				22 53		
Southampton Central	a				19 04				20 04	20 48			21 04			22 02				23 04		
Fareham	a				19 27				20 27				21 27			22 42				23 27		
	d				19 27				20 27				21 27			22 42				23 27		
Cosham	a				19 34																	
Fratton	a				19 42				20 42				21 41			22 56				23 44		
Portsmouth & Southsea	a				19 46				20 46				21 45			22 59				23 48		
Portsmouth Harbour	a				19 54				20 54				21 52			23 04				23 54		
Havant	a																					
Chichester 4	a																					
Barnham	a																					
Worthing 4	a																					
Shoreham-by-Sea	a																					
Hove 2	a																					
Brighton 10	a																					

For connections from Swansea please refer to Table 128. For connections from Plymouth and Exeter St Davids please refer to Table 135. For connections to Bournemouth please refer to Table 158

For Bus Connections for either to or from Yeovil Junction and Yeovil Pen Mill please see Table 123A

Table 123

Mondays to Fridays

3 September to 14 September

South Wales and Bristol - Weymouth and Portsmouth

Network Diagram - see first Page of Table 123

		GW	GW
			🛏 A 🛋 ☕
Cardiff Central	d		
Newport (South Wales)	d		
Severn Tunnel Jn.	d		
Filton Abbey Wood	d		
Bristol Temple Meads	d	23 20	
Keynsham	d	23 27	
Oldfield Park	d	23 34	
London Paddington ⊖	d		23 45
Swindon	d		
Chippenham	d		
Melksham	d		
Bath Spa	d	23 38	
Freshford	d	23 47	
Avoncliff	d	23 50	
Bradford-on-Avon	d	23 54	
Trowbridge	d	23 59	
Westbury	a	00 07	01 35
	d	00 08	
Frome	d	00a19	
Bruton	d		
Castle Cary	a		
	d		
Yeovil Pen Mill	d		
Thornford	d		
Yetminster	d		
Chetnole	d		
Maiden Newton	d		
Dorchester West	d		
Upwey	a		
Weymouth	a		
Dilton Marsh	d		
Warminster	d		
Salisbury	a		
	d		
Romsey	d		
Southampton Central	a		
Fareham	a		
	d		
Cosham	a		
Fratton	a		
Portsmouth & Southsea	a		
Portsmouth Harbour	a		
Havant	a		
Chichester	a		
Barnham	a		
Worthing	a		
Shoreham-by-Sea	a		
Hove	a		
Brighton	a		

A The Night Riviera

For connections from Swansea please refer to Table 128. For connections from Plymouth and Exeter St Davids please refer to Table 135. For connections to Bournemouth please refer to Table 158

For Bus Connections for either to or from Yeovil Junction and Yeovil Pen Mill please see Table 123A

Table 123

Mondays to Fridays

from 17 September

South Wales and Bristol - Weymouth and Portsmouth

Network Diagram - see first Page of Table 123

		GW MO	GW MX	GW MX	GW	GW	GW	GW	GW	GW		GW	GW	GW	GW	GW	GW	GW	SW	GW		GW	GW	GW	GW
		A ✕		🛏 B 🛋 ☕			◇■ ☕		◇					◇ ✕	◇■ C ☕		🛏 ✕	◇	◇■			◇ ✕	◇■ ☕		◇
Cardiff Central	d	22p00												06 28			07 30					08 30			
Newport (South Wales)	d	22p19												06 42			07 44					08 44			
Severn Tunnel Jn.	d	22p36												06 53			07 55					08 55			
Filton Abbey Wood	d	22p53												07 09		07 28	08 09	08 23				09 09			09 23
Bristol Temple Meads	d	23p10	23p20				05 20		05 44				06 48	07 22		07 49	08 22	08 41	08 51	09 05		09 22			09 49
Keynsham	d		23p27						05 51				06 55			07 56		08 48	08 58						09 56
Oldfield Park	d		23p34						05 58				07 02			08 03		08 55		09 17					10 03
London Paddington ⊖	d			23p45											07 06								09 06		
Swindon	d											06 12													
Chippenham	d											06 28													
Melksham	d											06 37													
Bath Spa	d	23p30	23p38						06 02				07 06	07 35		08 07	08 35	08 59	09 07	09 21		09 35			10 07
Freshford	d		23p47						06 12				07 15			08 16		09 08							10 16
Avoncliff	d		23p50						06 14				07 18			08 19		09 11							10 18
Bradford-on-Avon	d	23p43	23p54				05 44		06 18				07 22	07 47		08 23	08 47	09 15	09 20	09 33					10 22
Trowbridge	d	23p50	23p59				05 52		06 25			06 47	07 28	07 53		08 29	08 53	09 21	09 27	09 39		09 51			10 29
Westbury	a	23p57	00 07	01 35			05 59		06 32			06 55	07 35	08 00	08 25	08 36	09 00	09 28	09 33	09 49		09 58			10 36
	d	23p58	00 08		05 24	05 49		06 25	06 37	06 47		07 01		08 01			09 01	09 31	09 39			09 59		10 08	10 37
Frome	d		00a19					06a35		06 56								09 40							10 46
Bruton	d									07 08								09 52							10 58
Castle Cary	a									07 13								09 59					10 31		11 03
	d									07 14								10 00							11 03
Yeovil Pen Mill	d									07 35								10 14							11 17
Thornford	d									07x39								10x18							11x22
Yetminster	d									07x42								10x21							11x25
Chetnole	d									07x46								10x25							11x29
Maiden Newton	d									07 58								10 37							11 41
Dorchester West	d									08 09								10 48							11 54
Upwey	a									08 16								10 55							12 02
Weymouth	a									08 24								11 03							12 09
Dilton Marsh	d	00x01										07x03												10x10	
Warminster	d	00a07			05 32	05 57			06 45			07 12		08 09			09 09		09 46			10 07		10a19	
Salisbury	a				05 55	06 18			07 10			07 36		08 32			09 32		10 09			10 29			
	d					06 19			07 11			07 36		08 32			09 32					10 30			
Romsey	d					06 38			07 30			07 56		08 50			09 50					10 50			
Southampton Central	a					06 49			07 40			08 09		09 04			10 04					11 04			
Fareham	a					07 14			08 05					09 27			10 27					11 27			
	d					07 15			08 06					09 27			10 27					11 27			
Cosham	a					07 23			08 13					09 35			10 35					11 35			
Fratton	a					07 34			08 20					09 42			10 42					11 42			
Portsmouth & Southsea	a					07 38			08 24					09 46			10 46					11 46			
Portsmouth Harbour	a					07 45			08 30					09 55			10 54					11 54			
Havant	a																								
Chichester	a																								
Barnham	a																								
Worthing	a																								
Shoreham-by-Sea	a																								
Hove	a																								
Brighton	a																								

A from 17 September until 22 October B The Night Riviera C The Devon Express

For connections from Swansea please refer to Table 128. For connections from Plymouth and Exeter St Davids please refer to Table 135. For connections to Bournemouth please refer to Table 158

For Bus Connections for either to or from Yeovil Junction and Yeovil Pen Mill please see Table 123A

Table 123

Mondays to Fridays
from 17 September

South Wales and Bristol - Weymouth and Portsmouth

Network Diagram - see first Page of Table 123

		GW	GW	GW	GW	GW	GW	GW	GW	SW	GW	GW	GW	GW	GW	GW FO	GW	GW	GW	GW	SW	GW	GW
		◇ ✠			◇ ✠	◇■1 A ⊘	◇	◇ ✠	■ B ✠	◇■1 ✠	◇■1 ⊐	◇ ✠		◇ ✠		◇	◇	◇ ✠	◇■1 C ⊘		◇■1	◇ ✠	
Cardiff Central 7	d	09 30			10 30			11 30				12 30		13 30				14 30				15 30	
Newport (South Wales)	d	09 44			10 44			11 44				12 44		13 44				14 44				15 44	
Severn Tunnel Jn.	d	09 55																					
Filton Abbey Wood	d	10 09		10 25	11 09		11 23	12 09	12 25			13 09	13 23	14 09			14 25	15 09		15 23		16 09	
Bristol Temple Meads 10	d	10 22		10 49	11 22		11 49	12 22	12 39	12 51		13 22	13 49	14 22			14 48	15 22		15 44	15 51	16 22	
Keynsham	d			10 56			11 56		12 46	12 58			13 56				14 55			15 51	15 58		
Oldfield Park	d			11 03			12 03		12 53				14 03				15 02			15 58			
London Paddington 15 ⊖	d					11 06					12 18								15 06				
Swindon	d																						
Chippenham	d																						
Melksham	d																						
Bath Spa 7	d	10 35		11 07	11 35		12 07	12 35	12 57	13 07		13 35	14 07	14 35			15 06	15 35		16 02	16 07	16 35	
Freshford	d			11 16			12 16		13 06				14 16				15 15			16 11			
Avoncliff	d			11 19			12 19		13 08				14 19				15 18			16 13			
Bradford-on-Avon	d	10 47		11 23	11 47		12 23	12 47	13 12	13 20		13 47	14 23	14 47			15 22	15 47		16 17	16 22	16 47	
Trowbridge	d	10 53		11 29	11 53		12 29	12 53	13 19	13 27		13 53	14 29	14 53			15 28	15 53		16 24	16 28	16 53	
Westbury	a	11 00		11 36	12 00	12 21	12 36	13 00	13 26	13 33	13 57	14 00	14 36	15 00			15 35	16 00	16 22	16 33	16 36	17 00	
	d	11 01	11 11		12 01	12 22	12 37	13 01	13 27	13 39	13 59	14 01	14 37	15 01	15 11	15 20	15 38	16 01	16 23		16 39	17 01	17 11
Frome	d						12 49						14a50				15 47						
Bruton	d						13 01										15 58						
Castle Cary	a					12 39	13 06				14 16					15 46	16 04		16 41				
	d						13 06										16 09						
Yeovil Pen Mill	d						13 20										16 24						
Thornford	d						13x25										16x28						
Yetminster	d						13x28										16x31						
Chetnole	d						13x32										16x35						
Maiden Newton	d						13 44										16 47						
Dorchester West	d						13 54										16 58						
Upwey	a						14 02										17 05						
Weymouth	a						14 09										17 10						
Dilton Marsh	d		11x13						13x29						15x13								17x13
Warminster	d	11 09	11 21		12 09			13 09	13 36	13 46		14 09		15 09	15a22			16 09			16 47	17 09	17a22
Salisbury	a	11 32	11 41		12 32			13 32	13 58	14 10		14 32		15 32				16 32			17 09	17 32	
	d	11 32	11 42		12 32			13 32	13 59			14 32		15 32				16 32				17 32	
Romsey	d	11 50	12 10		12 50			13 50	14 19			14 50		15 50				16 50				17 50	
Southampton Central	a	12 04	12 22		13 04			14 04	14 32			15 04		16 04				17 04				18 04	
Fareham	a	12 27			13 27			14 27	14 55			15 27		16 27				17 27				18 27	
	d	12 27			13 27			14 27	14 56			15 27		16 27				17 27				18 27	
Cosham	a	12 35			13 35			14 35	15 04			15 35		16 35				17 35				18 35	
Fratton	a	12 42			13 42			14 42				15 42		16 42				17 42				18 48	
Portsmouth & Southsea	a	12 46			13 46			14 46				15 46		16 46				17 46				18 52	
Portsmouth Harbour	a	12 54			13 54			14 54				15 54		16 54				17 54				19 00	
Havant	a								15 10														
Chichester 4	a								15 21														
Barnham	a								15 29														
Worthing 4	a								15 45														
Shoreham-by-Sea	a								15 56														
Hove 2	a								16 07														
Brighton 10	a								16 14														

A The Mayflower

B ✠ from Bristol Temple Meads

C The Cornishman

For connections from Swansea please refer to Table 128. For connections from Plymouth and Exeter St Davids please refer to Table 135. For connections to Bournemouth please refer to Table 158

For Bus Connections for either to or from Yeovil Junction and Yeovil Pen Mill please see Table 123A

Table 123

Mondays to Fridays
from 17 September

South Wales and Bristol - Weymouth and Portsmouth

Network Diagram - see first Page of Table 123

		GW	GW	GW	GW	GW	GW	GW	GW	GW	GW	GW	GW	GW	GW	GW	GW	GW	GW	GW	GW	GW
		◇			◇■1 ⊐	■ ✠	◇		◇■1 ⊐	■ ✠	◇		◇■1 ⊐	◇ ✠	◇■1 ⊐		◇	◇■1 ⊐		◇■1 ⊐	◇	
Cardiff Central 7	d					16 30				17 30				18 30			19 30				20 30	21 00
Newport (South Wales)	d					16 44				17 44				18 44			19 44				20 44	21 15
Severn Tunnel Jn.	d					16 55				17 55				18 55								21 25
Filton Abbey Wood	d	16 25	16 49	16 55		17 09	17 23	17 49		18 09		18 25		19 09		19 23	20 09				21 08	21 42
Bristol Temple Meads 10	d	16 49	17 07	17 14		17 22	17 49	18 07		18 22		18 49		19 22		19 49	20 22		20 49		21 23	22 00
Keynsham	d	16 56	17 14				17 56	18 14				18 56				19 56			20 56			22 07
Oldfield Park	d	17 03	17 21	17 26			18 03	18 21				19 03				20 03			21 03			22 14
London Paddington 15 ⊖	d				16 33				17 33				18 06		18 33			19 45		20 35		
Swindon	d										18 44											
Chippenham	d										19 01											
Melksham	d										19 11											
Bath Spa 7	d	17 07	17 25	17 31		17 37	18 07	18 25		18 35		19 07		19 35		20 07	20 35		21 07		21 36	22 18
Freshford	d	17 16		17 40			18 16	18 34				19 16				20 16			21 16			22 27
Avoncliff	d	17 19					18 19	18 37				19 19				20 19			21 19			22 30
Bradford-on-Avon	d	17 23	17 37	17 45		17 50	18 23	18 41		18 47		19 23		19 47		20 23	20 47		21 23		21 48	22 34
Trowbridge	d	17 30	17 44	17 51		17 57	18 29	18 47		18 53	19 20	19 29		19 53		20 29	20 53		21 29		21 55	22 40
Westbury	a	17 36	17 51	17 58	18 02	18 05	18 36	18 56	18 59	19 00	19 27	19 36	19 52	20 00	20 04	20 36	21 00	21 06	21 36	21 56	22 03	22 47
	d	17 39	17 54		18 04	18 05	18 40		19 01	19 02	19 41		19 53	20 01	20 05	20 37	21 01	21 06	21 40	21 57	22 03	
Frome	d	17 48					18 49						20a04			20a48			21 50			
Bruton	d	18 00					19 01												22 02			
Castle Cary	a	18 05			18 20		19 06		19 17						20 23			21 24	22 07	22 14		
	d	18 06					19 06												22 08			
Yeovil Pen Mill	d	18 21					19 19												22 23			
Thornford	d	18x26					19x25												22x28			
Yetminster	d	18x29					19x28												22x31			
Chetnole	d	18x33					19x32												22x35			
Maiden Newton	d	18 45					19 44												22 47			
Dorchester West	d	18 58					19 54												22 58			
Upwey	a	19 06					20 02												23 05			
Weymouth	a	19 14					20 10												23 13			
Dilton Marsh	d		17x56								19x43										22x06	
Warminster	d		18a05			18 13				19 09	19 51			20 09			21 09				22 11	
Salisbury	a					18 35				19 32	20 13			20 32			21 32				22 32	
	d					18 35				19 32	20 14			20 32			21 32				22 32	
Romsey	d					18 54				19 50	20 35			20 50			21 50				22 53	
Southampton Central	a					19 04				20 04	20 48			21 04			22 02				23 04	
Fareham	a					19 27				20 27				21 27			22 42				23 27	
	d					19 27				20 27				21 27			22 42				23 27	
Cosham	a					19 34																
Fratton	a					19 42				20 42				21 41			22 56				23 44	
Portsmouth & Southsea	a					19 46				20 46				21 45			22 59				23 48	
Portsmouth Harbour	a					19 54				20 54				21 52			23 04				23 54	
Havant	a																					
Chichester 4	a																					
Barnham	a																					
Worthing 4	a																					
Shoreham-by-Sea	a																					
Hove 2	a																					
Brighton 10	a																					

For connections from Swansea please refer to Table 128. For connections from Plymouth and Exeter St Davids please refer to Table 135. For connections to Bournemouth please refer to Table 158

For Bus Connections for either to or from Yeovil Junction and Yeovil Pen Mill please see Table 123A

Table 123

Mondays to Fridays
from 17 September

South Wales and Bristol - Weymouth and Portsmouth

Network Diagram - see first Page of Table 123

		SW	GW	GW
				A
Cardiff Central 7	d			
Newport (South Wales)	d			
Severn Tunnel Jn.	d			
Filton Abbey Wood	d			
Bristol Temple Meads 10	d	22 25	23 20	
Keynsham	d		23 27	
Oldfield Park	d		23 34	
London Paddington 15 ⊖	d			23 45
Swindon	d			
Chippenham	d			
Melksham	d			
Bath Spa 7	d	22 38	23 38	
Freshford	d		23 47	
Avoncliff	d		23 50	
Bradford-on-Avon	d	22 51	23 54	
Trowbridge	d	22 57	23 59	
Westbury	a	23 04	00 07	01 35
	d	23 08	00 08	
Frome	d		00a19	
Bruton	d			
Castle Cary	a			
	d			
Yeovil Pen Mill	d			
Thornford	d			
Yetminster	d			
Chetnole	d			
Maiden Newton	d			
Dorchester West	d			
Upwey	a			
Weymouth	a			
Dilton Marsh	d			
Warminster	d	23 15		
Salisbury	a	23 35		
	d			
Romsey	d			
Southampton Central	a			
Fareham	a			
	d			
Cosham	a			
Fratton	a			
Portsmouth & Southsea	a			
Portsmouth Harbour	a			
Havant	a			
Chichester 4	a			
Barnham	a			
Worthing 4	a			
Shoreham-by-Sea	a			
Hove 2	a			
Brighton 10	a			

A The Night Riviera

For connections from Swansea please refer to Table 128. For connections from Plymouth and Exeter St Davids please refer to Table 135. For connections to Bournemouth please refer to Table 158

For Bus Connections for either to or from Yeovil Junction and Yeovil Pen Mill please see Table 123A

Table 123

Saturdays
until 8 September

South Wales and Bristol - Weymouth and Portsmouth

Network Diagram - see first Page of Table 123

		GW	GW	GW	GW	GW	GW	GW	GW	GW		GW	GW	GW	SW	GW	GW	GW	GW	GW		GW	GW	GW	GW
			A			◇				◇			◇	◇	◇	B	◇ C	◇ D	◇			◇	◇ E		
Cardiff Central 7	d									06 30			07 30						08 30				09 30		
Newport (South Wales)	d									06 44			07 44						08 44				09 44		
Severn Tunnel Jn.	d									06 55			07 55						08 55				09 55		
Filton Abbey Wood	d									07 09			08 09	08 23					09 09			09 23	10 09		10 28
Bristol Temple Meads 10	d	23p20				05 49			06 49	07 22		07 49	08 22	08 39	08 51		09 09	09 09	09 22			09 49	10 22		10 49
Keynsham	d	23p27				05 56			06 56			07 56		08 46	08 58		09 16	09 16				09 56			10 56
Oldfield Park	d	23p34				06 03			07 03			08 03		08 53			09 24	09 24				10 03			11 03
London Paddington 15 ⊖	d		23p45													08 35									
Swindon	d																								
Chippenham	d																								
Melksham	d																								
Bath Spa 7	d	23p38				06 07			07 07	07 35		08 07	08 35	08 57	09 07		09 28	09 28	09 35			10 07	10 35		11 07
Freshford	d	23p47				06 16			07 16			08 16		09 06								10 16			11 16
Avoncliff	d	23p50				06 18			07 18			08 19		09 08								10 18			11 18
Bradford-on-Avon	d	23p54				06 22			07 22	07 47		08 23	08 47	09 13	09 20		09 40	09 40	09 47			10 22	10 47		11 22
Trowbridge	d	23p59				06 28			07 29	07 53		08 29	08 53	09 19	09 27		09 46	09 46	09 53			10 29	10 53		11 29
Westbury	a	00 07	01 35			06 36			07 36	08 01		08 36	09 01	09 27	09 34	09 56	09 53	09 53	10 01			10 36	11 01		11 36
	d	00 08		05 26	06 01	06 43	06 47	07 03		08 01			09 01	09 27	09 39	09 58	10 02	10 02	10 01	10 10		10 37	11 01	11 11	
Frome	d	00a19					06 56							09 36			10 16	10 16				10 46			
Bruton	d						07 08							09 48			10 34	10 34				10 58			
Castle Cary	a						07 14							09 53		10 14	10 39	10 39				11 03			
	d						07 15							09 53			10 40	10 40				11 03			
Yeovil Pen Mill	d						07 29							10 07			10 54	10 55				11 17			
Thornford	d						07x33							10x12								11x22			
Yetminster	d						07x36							10x15								11x25			
Chetnole	d						07x40							10x19								11x29			
Maiden Newton	d						07 52							10 31			11 15	11 15				11 41			
Dorchester West	d						08 03							10 38			11 29	11 29				11 54			
Upwey	a						08 10							10 49								12 02			
Weymouth	a						08 17							10 57			11 42	11 42				12 09			
Dilton Marsh	d							07x06												10x13				11x13	
Warminster	d			05 34	06 09	06 51		07 13		08 09			09 09		09 46				10 09	10a19			11 09	11 21	
Salisbury	a			05 58	06 31	07 12		07 34		08 32			09 31		10 09				10 31				11 32	11 42	
	d				06 32	07 24		07 36		08 32			09 32						10 32				11 32	11 43	
Romsey	d				06 50	07 44		07 55		08 50			09 50						10 50				11 50	12 04	
Southampton Central	a				07 02	08 02		08 07		09 03			10 03						11 03				12 03	12 20	
Fareham	a				07 27	08 27				09 27			10 27						11 27				12 27		
	d				07 27	08 27				09 27			10 27						11 27				12 27		
Cosham	a				07 35	08 35				09 35			10 35						11 35				12 35		
Fratton	a				07 42	08 42				09 42			10 42						11 42				12 42		
Portsmouth & Southsea	a				07 46	08 46				09 46			10 46						11 46				12 46		
Portsmouth Harbour	a				07 52	08 52				09 52			10 52						11 52				12 52		
Havant	a																								
Chichester 4	a																								
Barnham	a																								
Worthing 4	a																								
Shoreham-by-Sea	a																								
Hove 2	a																								
Brighton 10	a																								

A The Night Riviera
B The Torbay Express
C 4 August, 11 August, 1 September
D not 4 August, 11 August, 1 September
E from Bristol Temple Meads

For connections from Swansea please refer to Table 128. For connections from Plymouth and Exeter St Davids please refer to Table 135. For connections to Bournemouth please refer to Table 158

For Bus Connections for either to or from Yeovil Junction and Yeovil Pen Mill please see Table 123A

Table 123

Saturdays
until 8 September

South Wales and Bristol - Weymouth and Portsmouth

Network Diagram - see first Page of Table 123

		GW	GW	GW	GW	GW	SW	GW	GW	GW	GW	GW	GW	GW	GW	GW	GW	SW	GW	GW	GW	GW	GW
		■ 1 ⊡	◇ A ✕	◇	◇ A ✕	■ ◇	◇1 ✕	■ 1 ⊡	◇		◇		◇	◇		◇1 ⊡		◇1	◇	◇	■	◇1 ⊡	◇
Cardiff Central 7	d		10 30		11 30				12 30		13 30			14 30					15 30		16 30		
Newport (South Wales)	d		10 44		11 44				12 44		13 44			14 44					15 44		16 44		
Severn Tunnel Jn.	d																				16 55		
Filton Abbey Wood	d		11 09	11 23	12 09	12 28			13 09	13 23	14 09		14 25	15 09			15 22		16 09	16 28	17 09		17 23
Bristol Temple Meads 10	d		11 22	11 49	12 22	12 43	12 51		13 22	13 49	14 22		14 49	15 22			15 38	15 51	16 22	16 49	17 22		17 49
Keynsham	d			11 56		12 50	12 58			13 56			14 56				15 45	15 58		16 56			17 56
Oldfield Park	d			12 03		12 57				14 03			15 03				15 52			17 03			18 03
London Paddington 15 ⊖	d	10 35						12 35								15 06						17 06	
Swindon	d														15 22								
Chippenham	d														15 38								
Melksham	d														15 48								
Bath Spa 7	d		11 35	12 07	12 35	13 00	13 07		13 35	14 07	14 35		15 07	15 35			15 56	16 07	16 35	17 07	17 35		18 07
Freshford	d			12 16						14 16			15 16				16 05			17 16			18 16
Avoncliff	d			12 18						14 18			15 18				16 08			17 19			18 19
Bradford-on-Avon	d		11 47	12 22	12 47	13 13	13 20		13 47	14 22	14 47		15 22	15 47			16 12	16 24	16 47	17 23	17 47		18 23
Trowbridge	d		11 53	12 29	12 53	13 20	13 27		13 53	14 29	14 53		15 29	15 53	15 58		16 18	16 30	16 53	17 29	17 53		18 29
Westbury	a	11 53	12 01	12 36	13 01	13 27	13 33	13 59	14 01	14 36	15 01		15 36	16 01	16 05	16 22	16 25	16 37	17 01	17 36	18 01	18 22	18 36
	d	11 54	12 01	12 37	13 01	13 28	13 39	13 59	14 01	14 37	15 01	15 11	15 37	16 01	16 08	16 23		16 39	17 01	17 38	18 01	18 22	18 39
Frome	d			12 47						14a49			15 46							17 47			18 49
Bruton	d			12 57									15 57							17 59			19 00
Castle Cary	a	12 11		13 03				14 16					16 02			16 40				18 04		18 40	19 05
	d			13 04									16 02							18 05			19 06
Yeovil Pen Mill	d			13 17									16 17							18 21			19 19
Thornford	d			13x22									16x22							18x26			19x24
Yetminster	d			13x25									16x25							18x29			19x27
Chetnole	d			13x29									16x29							18x33			19x31
Maiden Newton	d			13 41									16 47							18 44			19 43
Dorchester West	d			13 54									16 58							18 54			19 54
Upwey	a			14 02									17 05							19 02			20 01
Weymouth	a			14 08									17 10							19 10			20 09
Dilton Marsh	d					13x31						15x14			16x11								
Warminster	d		12 09		13 09	13 37	13 46		14 09		15 09	15a23		16 09	16a17			16 47	17 09		18 09		
Salisbury	a		12 32		13 32	13 59	14 10		14 32		15 32			16 32				17 09	17 32		18 32		
	d		12 32		13 32	14 00			14 32		15 32			16 32					17 32		18 32		
Romsey	d		12 50		13 50	14 20			14 50		15 50			16 50					17 50		18 50		
Southampton Central	a		13 03		14 03	14 32			15 03		16 03			17 03					18 03		19 03		
Fareham	a		13 27		14 27	14 54			15 27		16 27			17 27					18 27		19 27		
	d		13 27		14 27	14 55			15 27		16 27			17 27					18 27		19 27		
Cosham	a		13 35		14 35	15 03			15 35		16 35			17 35					18 35		19 35		
Fratton	a		13 42		14 42				15 42		16 42			17 42					18 42		19 42		
Portsmouth & Southsea	a		13 46		14 46				15 46		16 46			17 46					18 46		19 46		
Portsmouth Harbour	a		13 52		14 52				15 52		16 52			17 52					18 52		19 52		
Havant	a					15 10																	
Chichester 4	a					15 21																	
Barnham	a					15 29																	
Worthing 4	a					15 44																	
Shoreham-by-Sea	a					15 55																	
Hove 2	a					16 07																	
Brighton 10	a					16 14																	

A ✕ from Bristol Temple Meads

For connections from Swansea please refer to Table 128. For connections from Plymouth and Exeter St Davids please refer to Table 135. For connections to Bournemouth please refer to Table 158

For Bus Connections for either to or from Yeovil Junction and Yeovil Pen Mill please see Table 123A

Table 123

Saturdays
until 8 September

South Wales and Bristol - Weymouth and Portsmouth

Network Diagram - see first Page of Table 123

		GW	GW	GW	GW	GW	GW	GW	GW	GW	GW	GW	GW	SW	GW
		◇			◇	◇1 ⊡		◇	◇1 ⊡			◇		1	
Cardiff Central 7	d	17 30			18 30			19 30				20 30			
Newport (South Wales)	d	17 44			18 44			19 44				20 44			
Severn Tunnel Jn.	d	17 55													
Filton Abbey Wood	d	18 09		18 28	19 09		19 24	20 09				21 08			
Bristol Temple Meads 10	d	18 22		18 49	19 22		19 49	20 22		20 49		21 22	22 00	22 23	23 11
Keynsham	d			18 56			19 56			20 56			22 07		23 18
Oldfield Park	d			19 03			20 03			21 03			22 14		23 25
London Paddington 15 ⊖	d					19 06			20 06						
Swindon	d										21 08				
Chippenham	d										21 24				
Melksham	d										21 34				
Bath Spa 7	d	18 35		19 07	19 35		20 07	20 35		21 07		21 35	22 18	22 36	23 29
Freshford	d			19 16			20 16			21 16			22 27		23 38
Avoncliff	d			19 18			20 18			21 19			22 30		23 40
Bradford-on-Avon	d	18 47		19 22	19 47		20 22	20 47		21 23		21 47	22 34	22 47	23 44
Trowbridge	d	18 53		19 29	19 53		20 29	20 53		21 29	21 43	21 53	22 40	22 53	23 50
Westbury	a	19 01		19 36	20 01	20 26	20 36	21 01	21 25	21 36	21 51	22 01	22 47	23 00	23 57
	d	19 01	19 09		20 01	20 27	20 37	21 01	21 26	21 39		22 01		23 04	23 58
Frome	d						20a48			21 49					00a08
Bruton	d									22 01					
Castle Cary	a					20 44			21 43	22 06					
	d									22 06					
Yeovil Pen Mill	d									22 20					
Thornford	d									22x25					
Yetminster	d									22x28					
Chetnole	d									22x32					
Maiden Newton	d									22 44					
Dorchester West	d									22 54					
Upwey	a									23 02					
Weymouth	a									23 10					
Dilton Marsh	d		19x12									22x05			
Warminster	d	19 09	19 19		20 09			21 09				22 10		23 11	
Salisbury	a	19 32	19 40		20 32			21 32				22 32		23 34	
	d	19 32	19 41		20 32			21 32				22 32			
Romsey	d	19 50	20 04		20 50			21 50				22 50			
Southampton Central	a	20 02	20 18		21 03			22 03				23 03			
Fareham	a	20 27			21 27			22 26				23 26			
	d	20 28			21 27			22 27				23 27			
Cosham	a														
Fratton	a	20 42			21 42			22 42				23 40			
Portsmouth & Southsea	a	20 46			21 46			22 46				23 44			
Portsmouth Harbour	a	20 52			21 52			22 52				23 52			
Havant	a														
Chichester 4	a														
Barnham	a														
Worthing 4	a														
Shoreham-by-Sea	a														
Hove 2	a														
Brighton 10	a														

For connections from Swansea please refer to Table 128. For connections from Plymouth and Exeter St Davids please refer to Table 135. For connections to Bournemouth please refer to Table 158

For Bus Connections for either to or from Yeovil Junction and Yeovil Pen Mill please see Table 123A

Table 123

Saturdays
from 15 September

South Wales and Bristol - Weymouth and Portsmouth

Network Diagram - see first Page of Table 123

		GW	GW	GW	GW	GW	GW	GW	GW	GW	GW	GW	GW	SW	GW	GW	GW	GW	GW	GW	GW	GW	GW
			■ A			◇				◇		◇	◇	◇1	◇1	◇		◇	◇ B			◇ B	◇1
Cardiff Central 7	d									06 30		07 30				08 30			09 30			10 30	
Newport (South Wales)	d									06 44		07 44				08 44			09 44			10 44	
Severn Tunnel Jn.	d									06 55		07 55				08 55			09 55				
Filton Abbey Wood	d									07 09		08 09	08 23			09 09		09 23	10 09		10 28	11 09	
Bristol Temple Meads 10	d	23p20				05 49			06 49	07 22	07 49	08 22	08 39	08 51		09 22		09 49	10 22		10 49	11 22	
Keynsham	d	23p27				05 56			06 56		07 56		08 46	08 58				09 56			10 56		
Oldfield Park	d	23p34				06 03			07 03		08 03		08 53					10 03			11 03		
London Paddington 15 ⊖	d		23p45												08 18								11 06
Swindon	d																						
Chippenham	d																						
Melksham	d																						
Bath Spa 7	d	23p38				06 07			07 07	07 35	08 07	08 35	08 57	09 07		09 35		10 07	10 35		11 07	11 35	
Freshford	d	23p47				06 16			07 16		08 16		09 06					10 16			11 16		
Avoncliff	d	23p50				06 18			07 18		08 19		09 08					10 18			11 18		
Bradford-on-Avon	d	23p54				06 22			07 22	07 47	08 23	08 47	09 13	09 20		09 47		10 22	10 47		11 22	11 47	
Trowbridge	d	23p59				06 28			07 29	07 53	08 29	08 53	09 19	09 27		09 53		10 29	10 53		11 29	11 53	
Westbury	a	00 07	01 35			06 36			07 36	08 01	08 36	09 01	09 27	09 34	09 59	10 01		10 36	11 01		11 36	12 01	12 22
	d	00 08		05 26	06 01	06 43	06 47	07 03		08 01		09 01	09 27	09 39	10 00	10 01	10 10	10 37	11 01	11 11		12 01	12 22
Frome	d	00a19					06 56						09 36					10 46					
Bruton	d						07 08						09 48					10 58					
Castle Cary	a						07 14						09 53		10 17			11 03					12 40
	d						07 15						09 53					11 03					
Yeovil Pen Mill	d						07 29						10 07					11 17					
Thornford	d						07x33						10x12					11x22					
Yetminster	d						07x36						10x15					11x25					
Chetnole	d						07x40						10x19					11x29					
Maiden Newton	d						07 52						10 31					11 41					
Dorchester West	d						08 03						10 38					11 54					
Upwey	a						08 10						10 49					12 02					
Weymouth	a						08 17						10 57					12 09					
Dilton Marsh	d							07x06									10x13			11x13			
Warminster	d			05 34	06 09	06 51		07 13		08 09		09 09		09 46		10 09	10a19		11 09	11 21		12 09	
Salisbury	a			05 58	06 31	07 12		07 34		08 32		09 31		10 09		10 31			11 32	11 42		12 32	
	d				06 32	07 24		07 36		08 32		09 32				10 32			11 32	11 43		12 32	
Romsey	d				06 50	07 44		07 55		08 50		09 50				10 50			11 50	12 04		12 50	
Southampton Central	a				07 02	08 02		08 07		09 03		10 03				11 03			12 03	12 20		13 03	
Fareham	a				07 27	08 27				09 27		10 27				11 27			12 27			13 27	
	d				07 27	08 27				09 27		10 27				11 27			12 27			13 27	
Cosham	a				07 35	08 35				09 35		10 35				11 35			12 35			13 35	
Fratton	a				07 42	08 42				09 42		10 42				11 42			12 42			13 42	
Portsmouth & Southsea	a				07 46	08 46				09 46		10 46				11 46			12 46			13 46	
Portsmouth Harbour	a				07 52	08 52				09 52		10 52				11 52			12 52			13 52	
Havant	a																						
Chichester 4	a																						
Barnham	a																						
Worthing 4	a																						
Shoreham-by-Sea	a																						
Hove 2	a																						
Brighton 10	a																						

A The Night Riviera

B from Bristol Temple Meads

For connections from Swansea please refer to Table 128. For connections from Plymouth and Exeter St Davids please refer to Table 135. For connections to Bournemouth please refer to Table 158

For Bus Connections for either to or from Yeovil Junction and Yeovil Pen Mill please see Table 123A

Table 123

Saturdays
from 15 September

South Wales and Bristol - Weymouth and Portsmouth

Network Diagram - see first Page of Table 123

		GW	GW	GW	SW	GW	GW	GW	GW	GW	GW	GW	GW	GW	GW	SW	GW	GW	GW	GW	GW	GW	GW
		◇	◇ A	■ ◇	◇1	◇1	◇		◇		◇	◇		◇1		◇1	◇		◇	■	◇1	◇	◇
Cardiff Central 7	d		11 30				12 30		13 30			14 30					15 30			16 30			17 30
Newport (South Wales)	d		11 44				12 44		13 44			14 44					15 44			16 44			17 44
Severn Tunnel Jn.	d																			16 55			17 55
Filton Abbey Wood	d	11 23	12 09	12 28			13 09	13 23	14 09		14 25	15 09			15 22		16 09		16 28	17 09		17 23	18 09
Bristol Temple Meads 10	d	11 49	12 22	12 43	12 51		13 22	13 49	14 22		14 49	15 22			15 38	15 51	16 22		16 49	17 22		17 49	18 22
Keynsham	d	11 56		12 50	12 58			13 56			14 56				15 45	15 58			16 56			17 56	
Oldfield Park	d	12 03		12 57				14 03			15 03				15 52				17 03			18 03	
London Paddington 15 ⊖	d					12 18								15 06							17 06		
Swindon	d												15 22										
Chippenham	d												15 38										
Melksham	d												15 48										
Bath Spa 7	d	12 07	12 35	13 00	13 07		13 35	14 07	14 35		15 07	15 35			15 56	16 07	16 35		17 07	17 35		18 07	18 35
Freshford	d	12 16						14 16			15 16				16 05				17 16			18 16	
Avoncliff	d	12 18						14 18			15 18				16 08				17 19			18 19	
Bradford-on-Avon	d	12 22	12 47	13 13	13 20		13 47	14 22	14 47		15 22	15 47			16 12	16 24	16 47		17 23	17 47		18 23	18 47
Trowbridge	d	12 29	12 53	13 20	13 27		13 53	14 29	14 53		15 29	15 53	15 58		16 18	16 30	16 53		17 29	17 53		18 29	18 53
Westbury	a	12 36	13 01	13 27	13 33	13 57	14 01	14 36	15 01		15 36	16 01	16 05	16 22	16 25	16 37	17 01		17 36	18 01	18 22	18 36	19 01
	d	12 37	13 01	13 28	13 39	13 58	14 01	14 37	15 01	15 11	15 37	16 01		16 23		16 39	17 01	17 08	17 38	18 01	18 22	18 39	19 01
Frome	d	12 47						14a49			15 46								17 47			18 49	
Bruton	d	12 57									15 57								17 59			19 00	
Castle Cary	a	13 03				14 14					16 03			16 40					18 04		18 40	19 05	
	d	13 04									16 09								18 05			19 06	
Yeovil Pen Mill	d	13 17									16 24								18 21			19 19	
Thornford	d	13x22									16x28								18x26			19x24	
Yetminster	d	13x25									16x31								18x29			19x27	
Chetnole	d	13x29									16x35								18x33			19x31	
Maiden Newton	d	13 41									16 47								18 44			19 43	
Dorchester West	d	13 54									16 58								18 54			19 54	
Upwey	a	14 02									17 05								19 02			20 01	
Weymouth	a	14 08									17 10								19 10			20 09	
Dilton Marsh	d			13x31						15x14								17x10					
Warminster	d		13 09	13 37	13 46		14 09		15 09	15a23		16 09				16 47	17 09	17a19		18 09			19 09
Salisbury	a		13 32	13 59	14 10		14 32		15 32			16 32				17 09	17 32			18 32			19 32
	d		13 32	14 00			14 32		15 32			16 32					17 32			18 32			19 32
Romsey	d		13 50	14 20			14 50		15 50			16 50					17 50			18 50			19 50
Southampton Central	a		14 03	14 32			15 03		16 03			17 03					18 03			19 03			20 02
Fareham	a		14 27	14 54			15 27		16 27			17 27					18 27			19 27			20 27
	d		14 27	14 55			15 27		16 27			17 27					18 27			19 27			20 28
Cosham	a		14 35	15 03			15 35		16 35			17 35					18 35			19 35			
Fratton	a		14 42				15 42		16 42			17 42					18 42			19 42			20 42
Portsmouth & Southsea	a		14 46				15 46		16 46			17 46					18 46			19 46			20 46
Portsmouth Harbour	a		14 52				15 52		16 52			17 52					18 52			19 52			20 52
Havant	a			15 10																			
Chichester 4	a			15 21																			
Barnham	a			15 29																			
Worthing 4	a			15 44																			
Shoreham-by-Sea	a			15 55																			
Hove 2	a			16 07																			
Brighton 10	a			16 14																			

A from Bristol Temple Meads

For connections from Swansea please refer to Table 128. For connections from Plymouth and Exeter St Davids please refer to Table 135. For connections to Bournemouth please refer to Table 158

For Bus Connections for either to or from Yeovil Junction and Yeovil Pen Mill please see Table 123A

Table 123

Saturdays
from 15 September

South Wales and Bristol - Weymouth and Portsmouth

Network Diagram - see first Page of Table 123

		GW	GW	GW	GW	GW	GW	GW	GW	GW	GW	GW	SW	GW
				◇	◇1 🚌		◇	◇1 🚌			◇		1	
Cardiff Central 7	d			18 30			19 30				20 30			
Newport (South Wales)	d			18 44			19 44				20 44			
Severn Tunnel Jn.	d													
Filton Abbey Wood	d		18 28	19 09		19 24	20 09				21 09			
Bristol Temple Meads 10	d		18 49	19 22		19 49	20 22		20 49		21 22	22 00	22 23	23 11
Keynsham	d		18 56			19 56			20 56			22 07		23 18
Oldfield Park	d		19 03			20 03			21 03			22 14		23 25
London Paddington 15 ⊖	d				19 06			20 06						
Swindon	d									21 08				
Chippenham	d									21 24				
Melksham	d									21 34				
Bath Spa 7	d		19 07	19 35		20 07	20 35		21 07		21 35	22 18	22 36	23 29
Freshford	d		19 16			20 16			21 16			22 27		23 38
Avoncliff	d		19 18			20 18			21 19			22 30		23 40
Bradford-on-Avon	d		19 22	19 47		20 22	20 47		21 23		21 47	22 34	22 47	23 44
Trowbridge	d		19 29	19 53		20 29	20 53		21 29	21 43	21 53	22 40	22 53	23 50
Westbury	a		19 36	20 01	20 26	20 36	21 01	21 25	21 36	21 51	22 01	22 47	23 00	23 57
	d	19 09		20 01	20 27	20 37	21 01	21 26	21 41		22 01		23 04	23 58
Frome	d					20a48			21 50					00a08
Bruton	d								22 02					
Castle Cary	a				20 44			21 43	22 07					
	d								22 08					
Yeovil Pen Mill	d								22 23					
Thornford	d								22x28					
Yetminster	d								22x31					
Chetnole	d								22x35					
Maiden Newton	d								22 47					
Dorchester West	d								22 58					
Upwey	a								23 05					
Weymouth	a								23 13					
Dilton Marsh	d	19x12									22x05			
Warminster	d	19 19		20 09			21 09				22 10		23 11	
Salisbury	a	19 40		20 32			21 32				22 32		23 34	
	d	19 41		20 32			21 32				22 32			
Romsey	d	20 04		20 50			21 50				22 50			
Southampton Central	a	20 18		21 03			22 03				23 03			
Fareham	a			21 27			22 26				23 26			
	d			21 27			22 27				23 27			
Cosham	a													
Fratton	a			21 42			22 42				23 40			
Portsmouth & Southsea	a			21 46			22 46				23 44			
Portsmouth Harbour	a			21 52			22 52				23 52			
Havant	a													
Chichester 4	a													
Barnham	a													
Worthing 4	a													
Shoreham-by-Sea	a													
Hove 2	a													
Brighton 10	a													

For connections from Swansea please refer to Table 128. For connections from Plymouth and Exeter St Davids please refer to Table 135. For connections to Bournemouth please refer to Table 158

For Bus Connections for either to or from Yeovil Junction and Yeovil Pen Mill please see Table 123A

Table 123

Sundays
until 24 June

South Wales and Bristol - Weymouth and Portsmouth

Network Diagram - see first Page of Table 123

		GW	GW	GW	GW	GW	GW	GW	GW	GW	GW	GW	GW	GW	GW	SW	GW	GW	GW	GW	GW	GW	GW
			◇		◇	◇1 🚌	◇	■ ◇ A ⌶	◇1 🚌	◇	◇1 🚌		◇	◇1 🚌	◇	◇1	◇	◇1 🚌	◇	◇	◇	◇	
Cardiff Central 7	d		08 05		09 15		10 08	11 08		12 08			13 08		14 08		15 08		16 08	16 35		17 08	
Newport (South Wales)	d		08 23		09 29		10 22	11 22		12 22			13 22		14 22		15 22		16 22	16 49		17 22	
Severn Tunnel Jn.	d		08 40		09 46		10 39	11 39		12 39			13 39		14 39		15 39		16 39			17 39	
Filton Abbey Wood	d		08 55		10 03		10 54	11 54		12 57			13 54		14 55		15 55		16 55	17 20		17 54	
Bristol Temple Meads 10	d		09 10	09 20	10 15		11 10	12 15		13 10			14 15		15 10	16 04	16 15		17 15	17 40	17 44	18 10	
Keynsham	d		09 17	09 27			11 17			13 17					15 17	16 11			17 22		17 51	18 17	
Oldfield Park	d		09 24	09 35			11 24			13 24					15 24				17 29		17 58	18 24	
London Paddington 15 ⊖	d					09 30			11 30		12 30			13 30				15 30					
Swindon	d					10 35			12 35		13 35												18 19
Chippenham	d																						18 35
Melksham	d																						18 45
Bath Spa 7	d		09 27	09 39	10 29		11 27	12 27		13 27			14 27		15 27	16 20	16 27		17 33	17 52	18 01	18 27	
Freshford	d			09 48	10 40			12 38					14 38				16 38				18 11		
Avoncliff	d			09 50	10 42			12 40					14 40				16 40				18 13		
Bradford-on-Avon	d		09 40	09 54	10 46		11 40	12 44		13 40			14 44		15 40	16 31	16 44		17 47	18 05	18 17	18 40	
Trowbridge	d		09 46	10 01	10 53		11 47	12 51		13 47			14 51		15 47	16 37	16 51		17 53	18 12	18 24	18 46	18 54
Westbury	a		09 53	10 08	11 00	11 08	11 54	13 00	13 09	13 54	14 07		14 58		15 57	16 44	16 58	17 03	18 00	18 19	18 31	18 53	19 06
	d	09 05	09 59	10 09	11 01	11 18	12 01	13 01		14 03		14 25	15 00		15 58	16 46	16 59	17 04	18 01	18 20	18 31	18 56	
Frome	d	09 15		10 19								14 34									18 39		
Bruton	d	09 27		10 31								14 46									18 52		
Castle Cary	a	09 32		10 35		11 34						14 51		15 23				17 21			18 57		
	d	09 40		10 37								14 51									18 58		
Yeovil Pen Mill	d	09 54		10 51								15 05									19 12		
Thornford	d	09x59		10x56								15 11									19x17		
Yetminster	d	10x02		10x59								15 14									19x20		
Chetnole	d	10x06		11x03								15 18									19x24		
Maiden Newton	d	10 18		11 15								15 29									19 36		
Dorchester West	d	10 26		11 30								15 40									19 47		
Upwey	a	10 36		11 37								15 49									19 55		
Weymouth	a	10 42		11 43								15 54									20 01		
Dilton Marsh	d		10x02				12x04			14x06					16x02		17x02			18x23			
Warminster	d		10 08		11 09		12 10	13 09		14 12			15 08		16 08	16 53	17 08		18 09	18 29		19 04	
Salisbury	a		10 32		11 32		12 32	13 32		14 34			15 32		16 32	17 16	17 32		18 33	18 52		19 32	
	d		10 32		11 33		12 33	13 33		14 48			15 33		16 33		17 33		18 33	18 56		19 32	
Romsey	d		10 50		11 51		12 52	13 51		15 10			15 51		16 51		17 51		18 51	19 14		19 50	
Southampton Central	a		11 02		12 03		13 05	14 03		15 21			16 03		17 03		18 03		19 03	19 25		20 02	
Fareham	a		11 26		12 28		13 33	14 26		15 50			16 27		17 27		18 27		19 28	19 48		20 26	
	d		11 26		12 28		13 34	14 27		15 51			16 27		17 27		18 27		19 28	19 49		20 26	
Cosham	a		11 33		12 35		13 42	14 34		16 01			16 35		17 34		18 34		19 35	19 57			
Fratton	a		11 40		12 42			14 41					16 42		17 41		18 41		19 42			20 41	
Portsmouth & Southsea	a		11 45		12 46			14 45					16 46		17 46		18 45		19 46			20 45	
Portsmouth Harbour	a		11 52		12 52			14 55					16 52		17 52		18 52		19 53			20 51	
Havant	a						14 03			16 11										20 09			
Chichester 4	a						14 19			16 22										20 20			
Barnham	a						14 27			16 30										20 28			
Worthing 4	a						14 45			16 45										20 50			
Shoreham-by-Sea	a						14 51			16 52										20 56			
Hove 2	a						15 00			16 58										21 03			
Brighton 10	a						15 06			17 06										21 09			

A ⌶ from Bristol Temple Meads

For connections from Swansea please refer to Table 128. For connections from Plymouth and Exeter St Davids please refer to Table 135. For connections to Bournemouth please refer to Table 158

For Bus Connections for either to or from Yeovil Junction and Yeovil Pen Mill please see Table 123A

South Wales and Bristol - Weymouth and Portsmouth

Sundays until 24 June

Network Diagram - see first Page of Table 123

		GW	GW	GW	GW	GW	GW	GW	GW	SW	GW	GW
		■	◇1 ⊡	◇	◇1 ⊡	◇	◇1 ⊡		◇	1		⊼
Cardiff Central [7]	d	17 40		18 08		19 08			20 18			22 00
Newport (South Wales)	d	17 54		18 22		19 22			20 31			22 19
Severn Tunnel Jn.	d			18 39		19 40			20 48			22 36
Filton Abbey Wood	d	18 23		18 56		19 55			21 05			22 53
Bristol Temple Meads [10]	d	18 50		19 10		20 15		20 50	21 25	21 35	22 15	23 10
Keynsham	d			19 17				20 57			22 22	
Oldfield Park	d			19 24				21 04			22 29	
London Paddington [15] ⊖	d		17 57		18 57		19 57					
Swindon	d		19 01		20u00		21 01					
Chippenham	d				20u16							
Melksham	d											
Bath Spa [7]	d	19 02		19 27		20 27		21 07	21 38	21 49	22 32	23 22
Freshford	d					20 38		21 17			22 42	
Avoncliff	d					20 40		21 20			22 45	
Bradford-on-Avon	d	19 15		19 40		20 44		21 24	21 50	22 00	22 49	23 35
Trowbridge	d	19 22		19 46		20 51		21 30	21 57	22 06	22 55	23 42
Westbury	a	19 29	19 32	19 53	20 38	20 58	21 35	21 37	22 04	22 13	23 02	23 49
	d	19 31		19 54	20 41	20 59	21 36	21 38	22 05	22 15		23 50
Frome	d							21 48				
Bruton	d							21 59				
Castle Cary	a				20 58		21 53	22 04				
	d							22 05				
Yeovil Pen Mill	d							22 19				
Thornford	d							22x23				
Yetminster	d							22x26				
Chetnole	d							22x30				
Maiden Newton	d							22 42				
Dorchester West	d							22 53				
Upwey	a							23 00				
Weymouth	a							23 06				
Dilton Marsh	d			19x58								23x53
Warminster	d	19 38		20 04		21 07			22 13	22 22		23a59
Salisbury	a	20 00		20 25		21 28			22 34	22 46		
	d	20 01		20 30		21 33			22 36			
Romsey	d	20 19		20 48		21 51			22 54			
Southampton Central	a	20 29		20 59		22 03			23 05			
Fareham	a	20 54		21 24		22 26			23 29			
	d	20 55		21 25		22 26			23 30			
Cosham	a											
Fratton	a	21 09		21 38		22 40			23 43			
Portsmouth & Southsea	a	21 15		21 41		22 43			23 46			
Portsmouth Harbour	a	21 26		21 48		22 50			23 54			
Havant	a											
Chichester [4]	a											
Barnham	a											
Worthing [4]	a											
Shoreham-by-Sea	a											
Hove [2]	a											
Brighton [10]	a											

For connections from Swansea please refer to Table 128. For connections from Plymouth and Exeter St Davids please refer to Table 135. For connections to Bournemouth please refer to Table 158

For Bus Connections for either to or from Yeovil Junction and Yeovil Pen Mill please see Table 123A

South Wales and Bristol - Weymouth and Portsmouth

Sundays 1 July to 9 September

Network Diagram - see first Page of Table 123

		GW	GW	GW	GW	GW	GW	GW	GW	GW	GW	GW	GW	GW	GW	GW	SW	GW	GW	GW	GW	GW	GW
			◇		◇1 ⊡	◇	◇1 ⊡	◇	■ ◇ A ⊼	◇1 ⊡	◇	◇1 ⊡		◇	◇1 ⊡	◇	◇1	◇	◇1 ⊡	◇	◇	◇	◇
Cardiff Central [7]	d		08 05			09 15		10 08	11 08		12 08			13 08		14 08		15 08		16 08	16 35		17 08
Newport (South Wales)	d		08 23			09 29		10 22	11 22		12 22			13 22		14 22		15 22		16 22	16 49		17 22
Severn Tunnel Jn.	d		08 40			09 46		10 39	11 39		12 39			13 39		14 39		15 39		16 39			17 39
Filton Abbey Wood	d		08 55			10 03		10 54	11 54		12 57			13 54		14 55		15 55		16 55	17 20		17 54
Bristol Temple Meads [10]	d		09 10	09 20		10 15		11 10	12 15		13 10			14 15		15 10	16 04	16 15		17 15	17 40	17 44	18 10
Keynsham	d		09 17	09 27				11 17			13 17					15 17	16 11			17 22		17 51	18 17
Oldfield Park	d		09 24	09 35				11 24			13 24					15 24				17 29		17 58	18 24
London Paddington [15] ⊖	d				08 57		09 57			11 35		12 57			13 57				15 57				
Swindon	d																						
Chippenham	d																						
Melksham	d																						
Bath Spa [7]	d		09 27	09 39		10 29		11 27	12 27		13 27			14 27		15 27	16 20	16 27		17 33	17 52	18 01	18 27
Freshford	d			09 48		10 40			12 38					14 38				16 38				18 11	
Avoncliff	d			09 50		10 42			12 40					14 40				16 40				18 13	
Bradford-on-Avon	d		09 40	09 54		10 46		11 40	12 44		13 40			14 44		15 40	16 31	16 44		17 47	18 05	18 17	18 40
Trowbridge	d		09 46	10 01		10 53		11 47	12 51		13 47			14 51		15 47	16 37	16 51		17 53	18 12	18 24	18 46
Westbury	a		09 53	10 08	10 23	11 00		11 54	13 00	13 05	13 54	14 18		14 58		15 57	16 44	16 58	17 23	18 00	18 19	18 31	18 53
	d	09 12	09 59	10 09		11 01		12 01	13 01	13 06	14 03		14 25	15 00		15 58	16 46	16 59	17 25	18 01	18 20	18 31	18 56
Frome	d	09 22		10 19									14 34									18 39	
Bruton	d	09 34		10 31									14 46									18 52	
Castle Cary	a	09 38		10 35			11 34			13 24			14 51		15 35				17 41			18 57	
	d	09 40		10 37									14 51									18 58	
Yeovil Pen Mill	d	09 54		10 51									15 05									19 12	
Thornford	d	09x59		10x56									15 11									19x17	
Yetminster	d	10x02		10x59									15 14									19x20	
Chetnole	d	10x06		11x03									15 18									19x24	
Maiden Newton	d	10 18		11 15									15 29									19 36	
Dorchester West	d	10 26		11 30									15 40									19 47	
Upwey	a	10 36		11 37									15 49									19 55	
Weymouth	a	10 42		11 43									15 54									20 01	
Dilton Marsh	d		10x02					12x04			14x06					16x02		17x02			18x23		
Warminster	d		10 08			11 09		12 10	13 09		14 12			15 08		16 08	16 53	17 08		18 09	18 29		19 04
Salisbury	a		10 32			11 32		12 32	13 32		14 34			15 32		16 32	17 16	17 32		18 33	18 52		19 32
	d		10 32			11 33		12 33	13 33		14 48			15 33		16 33		17 33		18 33	18 56		19 32
Romsey	d		10 50			11 51		12 52	13 51		15 10			15 51		16 51		17 51		18 51	19 14		19 50
Southampton Central	a		11 02			12 03		13 05	14 03		15 21			16 03		17 03		18 03		19 03	19 25		20 02
Fareham	a		11 26			12 28		13 33	14 26		15 50			16 27		17 27		18 27		19 28	19 48		20 26
	d		11 26			12 28		13 34	14 27		15 51			16 27		17 27		18 27		19 28	19 49		20 26
Cosham	a		11 33			12 35		13 42	14 34		16 01			16 35		17 34		18 34		19 35	19 57		
Fratton	a		11 40			12 42			14 41					16 42		17 41		18 41		19 42			20 41
Portsmouth & Southsea	a		11 45			12 46			14 45					16 46		17 46		18 45		19 46			20 45
Portsmouth Harbour	a		11 52			12 52			14 55					16 52		17 52		18 52		19 53			20 51
Havant	a							14 03			16 11										20 09		
Chichester [4]	a							14 19			16 22										20 20		
Barnham	a							14 27			16 30										20 28		
Worthing [4]	a							14 45			16 45										20 50		
Shoreham-by-Sea	a							14 51			16 52										20 56		
Hove [2]	a							15 00			16 58										21 03		
Brighton [10]	a							15 06			17 06										21 09		

A ⊼ from Bristol Temple Meads

For connections from Swansea please refer to Table 128. For connections from Plymouth and Exeter St Davids please refer to Table 135. For connections to Bournemouth please refer to Table 158

For Bus Connections for either to or from Yeovil Junction and Yeovil Pen Mill please see Table 123A

Table 123

Sundays

1 July to 9 September

South Wales and Bristol - Weymouth and Portsmouth

Network Diagram - see first Page of Table 123

		GW	GW	GW	GW	GW	GW	GW	GW	GW	SW	GW	GW
			◇1 ⚏	■	◇	◇1 ⚏	◇	◇1 ⚏		◇	1		🚌
Cardiff Central 7	d			17 40	18 08		19 08			20 18			22 00
Newport (South Wales)	d			17 54	18 22		19 22			20 31			22 19
Severn Tunnel Jn.	d				18 39		19 40			20 48			22 36
Filton Abbey Wood	d			18 23	18 56		19 55			21 05			22 53
Bristol Temple Meads 10	d			18 50	19 10		20 15		20 50	21 25	21 35	22 15	23 10
Keynsham	d				19 17				20 57			22 22	
Oldfield Park	d				19 24				21 04			22 29	
London Paddington 15 ⊖	d		17 57			18 57		19 57					
Swindon	d	18 19											
Chippenham	d	18 35											
Melksham	d	18 45											
Bath Spa 7	d			19 02	19 27		20 27		21 07	21 38	21 49	22 32	23 22
Freshford	d						20 38		21 17			22 42	
Avoncliff	d						20 40		21 20			22 45	
Bradford-on-Avon	d			19 15	19 40		20 44		21 24	21 50	22 00	22 49	23 35
Trowbridge	d	18 54		19 22	19 46		20 51		21 30	21 57	22 06	22 55	23 42
Westbury	a	19 06	19 27	19 29	19 53		20 58	21 28	21 37	22 04	22 13	23 02	23 49
	d			19 31	19 54		20 59	21 29	21 38	22 05	22 15		23 50
Frome	d								21 48				
Bruton	d								21 59				
Castle Cary	a					20 30		21 46	22 04				
	d								22 05				
Yeovil Pen Mill	d								22 19				
Thornford	d								22x23				
Yetminster	d								22x26				
Chetnole	d								22x30				
Maiden Newton	d								22 42				
Dorchester West	d								22 53				
Upwey	a								23 00				
Weymouth	a								23 06				
Dilton Marsh	d				19x58								23x53
Warminster	d			19 38	20 04		21 07			22 13	22 22		23a59
Salisbury	a			20 00	20 25		21 28			22 34	22 46		
	d			20 01	20 30		21 33			22 36			
Romsey	d			20 19	20 48		21 51			22 54			
Southampton Central	a			20 29	20 59		22 03			23 05			
Fareham	a			20 54	21 24		22 26			23 29			
	d			20 55	21 25		22 26			23 30			
Cosham	a												
Fratton	a			21 09	21 38		22 40			23 43			
Portsmouth & Southsea	a			21 15	21 41		22 43			23 46			
Portsmouth Harbour	a			21 26	21 48		22 50			23 54			
Havant	a												
Chichester 4	a												
Barnham	a												
Worthing 4	a												
Shoreham-by-Sea	a												
Hove 2	a												
Brighton 10	a												

For connections from Swansea please refer to Table 128. For connections from Plymouth and Exeter St Davids please refer to Table 135. For connections to Bournemouth please refer to Table 158

For Bus Connections for either to or from Yeovil Junction and Yeovil Pen Mill please see Table 123A

Table 123

Sundays

16 September to 21 October

South Wales and Bristol - Weymouth and Portsmouth

Network Diagram - see first Page of Table 123

		GW	GW	GW	GW	GW	GW	GW	GW	GW	GW	GW
		◇	◇1 ⚏	◇1 ⚏	◇	◇	■ ◇ A 🚌	◇1 ⚏	◇	◇1 ⚏	◇	
Cardiff Central 7	d						10 55		11 55		12 55	
Newport (South Wales)	d						11 09		12 08		13 10	
Severn Tunnel Jn.	d						11 26		12 25		13 28	
Filton Abbey Wood	d						11 41		12 42		13 43	
Bristol Temple Meads 10	d						12 00		13 00		14 00	
Keynsham	d						12 08		13 08		14 08	
Oldfield Park	d						12 19		13 19		14 19	
London Paddington 15 ⊖	d		08 57	09 57				11 27		12 57		
Swindon	d											
Chippenham	d											
Melksham	d											
Bath Spa 7	d	09 30			10 30	11 34	12 23		13 27		14 25	
Freshford	d				10 40		12 33				14 35	
Avoncliff	d				10 42		12 36				14 38	
Bradford-on-Avon	d	09 42			10 46	11 49	12 40		13 40		14 42	
Trowbridge	d	09 49			10 53	11 55	12 46		13 47		14 48	
Westbury	a	09 57	10 23		10 59	12 02	12 59	13 05	13 54	14 18	14 55	
	d	09 59			11 01	12 03	13 01	13 06	14 03		15 03	15 00
Frome	d											15 08
Bruton	d											15 20
Castle Cary	a			11 34				13 24				15 24
	d											15 25
Yeovil Pen Mill	d											15 40
Thornford	d											15 46
Yetminster	d											15 49
Chetnole	d											15 53
Maiden Newton	d											16 04
Dorchester West	d											16 15
Upwey	a											16 24
Weymouth	a											16 29
Dilton Marsh	d	10x02				12x07			14x06			
Warminster	d	10 08			11 09	12 13	13 09		14 12		15 11	
Salisbury	a	10 32			11 32	12 34	13 32		14 34		15 32	
	d	10 32			11 33	12 36	13 33		14 48		15 33	
Romsey	d	10 50			11 51	12 54	13 51		15 10		15 51	
Southampton Central	a	11 02			12 03	13 05	14 03		15 21		16 03	
Fareham	a	11 26			12 28	13 33	14 26		15 50		16 27	
	d	11 26			12 28	13 34	14 27		15 51		16 27	
Cosham	a	11 33			12 35	13 42	14 34		16 01		16 35	
Fratton	a	11 40			12 42		14 41				16 42	
Portsmouth & Southsea	a	11 45			12 46		14 45				16 46	
Portsmouth Harbour	a	11 52			12 52		14 55				16 52	
Havant	a					14 03			16 11			
Chichester 4	a					14 19			16 22			
Barnham	a					14 27			16 30			
Worthing 4	a					14 45			16 45			
Shoreham-by-Sea	a					14 51			16 52			
Hove 2	a					15 00			16 58			
Brighton 10	a					15 06			17 06			

		GW	GW	SW	GW	GW	GW	GW	GW	GW	GW	GW
		◇1 ⚏	◇	◇1	◇	◇1 ⚏	◇	◇	◇	◇		◇1 ⚏
Cardiff Central 7	d		14 08		15 08		16 08	16 35		17 08		
Newport (South Wales)	d		14 23		15 22		16 22	16 49		17 22		
Severn Tunnel Jn.	d		14 40		15 39		16 39			17 39		
Filton Abbey Wood	d		14 56		15 55		16 55	17 20		17 54		
Bristol Temple Meads 10	d		15 10	16 04	16 15		17 15	17 40	17 44	18 10		
Keynsham	d		15 18	16 11			17 22		17 51	18 17		
Oldfield Park	d		15 29				17 29		17 58	18 24		
London Paddington 15 ⊖	d	13 57				15 57						17 57
Swindon	d										18 19	
Chippenham	d										18 35	
Melksham	d										18 45	
Bath Spa 7	d		15 33	16 20	16 27		17 33	17 52	18 01	18 27		
Freshford	d				16 38				18 11			
Avoncliff	d				16 40				18 13			
Bradford-on-Avon	d		15 46	16 31	16 44		17 47	18 05	18 17	18 40		
Trowbridge	d		15 52	16 37	16 51		17 53	18 12	18 24	18 46	18 54	
Westbury	a		15 59	16 44	16 58	17 23	18 00	18 19	18 31	18 53	19 06	19 28
	d		16 05	16 46	16 59	17 25	18 01	18 20	18 31	18 56		
Frome	d								18 39			
Bruton	d								18 52			
Castle Cary	a	15 35				17 41			18 57			
	d								18 58			
Yeovil Pen Mill	d								19 12			
Thornford	d								19x17			
Yetminster	d								19x20			
Chetnole	d								19x24			
Maiden Newton	d								19 36			
Dorchester West	d								19 47			
Upwey	a								19 55			
Weymouth	a								20 01			
Dilton Marsh	d		16x08		17x02			18x23				
Warminster	d		16 14	16 53	17 08		18 09	18 29		19 04		
Salisbury	a		16 35	17 16	17 32		18 33	18 52		19 32		
	d		16 35		17 33		18 33	18 56		19 32		
Romsey	d		16 53		17 51		18 51	19 14		19 50		
Southampton Central	a		17 04		18 03		19 03	19 25		20 02		
Fareham	a		17 27		18 27		19 28	19 48		20 26		
	d		17 27		18 27		19 28	19 49		20 26		
Cosham	a		17 35		18 34		19 35	19 57				
Fratton	a		17 42		18 41		19 42			20 41		
Portsmouth & Southsea	a		17 47		18 45		19 46			20 45		
Portsmouth Harbour	a		17 52		18 52		19 53			20 51		
Havant	a							20 09				
Chichester 4	a							20 20				
Barnham	a							20 28				
Worthing 4	a							20 50				
Shoreham-by-Sea	a							20 56				
Hove 2	a							21 03				
Brighton 10	a							21 09				

A 🚌 from Bristol Temple Meads

For connections from Swansea please refer to Table 128. For connections from Plymouth and Exeter St Davids please refer to Table 135. For connections to Bournemouth please refer to Table 158

For Bus Connections for either to or from Yeovil Junction and Yeovil Pen Mill please see Table 123A

Table 123

Sundays
16 September to 21 October

South Wales and Bristol - Weymouth and Portsmouth

Network Diagram - see first Page of Table 123

		GW	GW	GW	GW	GW	GW	GW	SW	GW	GW
		■	◇	◇■ ☕	◇	◇■ ☕		◇	■		✕
Cardiff Central [7]	d	17 40	18 08		19 08			20 18			22 00
Newport (South Wales)	d	17 54	18 22		19 22			20 31			22 19
Severn Tunnel Jn.	d		18 39		19 40			20 48			22 36
Filton Abbey Wood	d	18 23	18 56		19 55			21 05			22 53
Bristol Temple Meads [10]	d	18 50	19 10		20 15		20 50	21 25	21 35	22 15	23 10
Keynsham	d		19 17				20 57			22 22	
Oldfield Park	d		19 24				21 04			22 29	
London Paddington [15] ⊖	d			18 57		19 57					
Swindon	d										
Chippenham	d										
Melksham	d										
Bath Spa [7]	d	19 02	19 27		20 27		21 07	21 38	21 49	22 32	23 30
Freshford	d				20 38		21 17			22 42	
Avoncliff	d				20 40		21 20			22 45	
Bradford-on-Avon	d	19 15	19 40		20 44		21 24	21 50	22 00	22 49	23 43
Trowbridge	d	19 22	19 46		20 51		21 30	21 57	22 06	22 55	23 50
Westbury	a	19 29	19 57		20 58	21 28	21 37	22 04	22 13	23 02	23 57
	d	19 31	19 58		20 59	21 29	21 38	22 05	22 15		23 58
Frome	d						21 48				
Bruton	d						21 59				
Castle Cary	a			20 30		21 46	22 04				
	d						22 05				
Yeovil Pen Mill	d						22 19				
Thornford	d						22x23				
Yetminster	d						22x26				
Chetnole	d						22x30				
Maiden Newton	d						22 42				
Dorchester West	d						22 53				
Upwey	a						23 00				
Weymouth	a						23 06				
Dilton Marsh	d		20x01								00x01
Warminster	d	19 38	20 07		21 07			22 13	22 22		00a07
Salisbury	a	20 00	20 29		21 28			22 34	22 46		
	d	20 01	20 30		21 33			22 36			
Romsey	d	20 19	20 48		21 51			22 54			
Southampton Central	a	20 29	20 59		22 03			23 05			
Fareham	a	20 54	21 24		22 26			23 29			
	d	20 55	21 25		22 26			23 30			
Cosham	a										
Fratton	a	21 09	21 38		22 40			23 43			
Portsmouth & Southsea	a	21 15	21 41		22 43			23 46			
Portsmouth Harbour	a	21 26	21 48		22 50			23 54			
Havant	a										
Chichester [4]	a										
Barnham	a										
Worthing [4]	a										
Shoreham-by-Sea	a										
Hove [2]	a										
Brighton [10]	a										

For connections from Swansea please refer to Table 128. For connections from Plymouth and Exeter St Davids please refer to Table 135. For connections to Bournemouth please refer to Table 158

For Bus Connections for either to or from Yeovil Junction and Yeovil Pen Mill please see Table 123A

Table 123

Sundays
from 28 October

South Wales and Bristol - Weymouth and Portsmouth

Network Diagram - see first Page of Table 123

		GW	GW	GW	GW	GW	GW	GW	GW	GW
		◇	◇■ ☕	◇	◇■ ☕	◇	■ ◇ A ✕	◇■ ☕	◇	◇■ ☕
Cardiff Central [7]	d	08 05		09 15		10 08	11 08		12 08	
Newport (South Wales)	d	08 23		09 29		10 22	11 22		12 22	
Severn Tunnel Jn.	d	08 40		09 46		10 39	11 39		12 39	
Filton Abbey Wood	d	08 55		10 03		10 54	11 54		12 57	
Bristol Temple Meads [10]	d	09 10		10 15		11 10	12 15		13 10	
Keynsham	d	09 17				11 17			13 17	
Oldfield Park	d	09 24				11 24			13 24	
London Paddington [15] ⊖	d		08 57		09 57			11 27		12 57
Swindon	d									
Chippenham	d									
Melksham	d									
Bath Spa [7]	d	09 27		10 29		11 27	12 27		13 27	
Freshford	d			10 40			12 38			
Avoncliff	d			10 42			12 40			
Bradford-on-Avon	d	09 40		10 46		11 40	12 44		13 40	
Trowbridge	d	09 46		10 53		11 47	12 51		13 47	
Westbury	a	09 53	10 23	11 00		11 54	13 00	13 05	13 54	14 18
	d	09 59		11 01		12 01	13 01	13 06	14 03	
Frome	d									
Bruton	d									
Castle Cary	a				11 34			13 24		
	d									
Yeovil Pen Mill	d									
Thornford	d									
Yetminster	d									
Chetnole	d									
Maiden Newton	d									
Dorchester West	d									
Upwey	a									
Weymouth	a									
Dilton Marsh	d	10x02				12x04			14x06	
Warminster	d	10 08		11 09		12 10	13 09		14 12	
Salisbury	a	10 32		11 32		12 32	13 32		14 34	
	d	10 32		11 33		12 33	13 33		14 48	
Romsey	d	10 50		11 51		12 52	13 51		15 10	
Southampton Central	a	11 02		12 03		13 05	14 03		15 21	
Fareham	a	11 26		12 28		13 33	14 26		15 50	
	d	11 26		12 28		13 34	14 27		15 51	
Cosham	a	11 33		12 35		13 42	14 34		16 01	
Fratton	a	11 40		12 42			14 41			
Portsmouth & Southsea	a	11 45		12 46			14 45			
Portsmouth Harbour	a	11 52		12 52			14 55			
Havant	a					14 03			16 11	
Chichester [4]	a					14 19			16 22	
Barnham	a					14 27			16 30	
Worthing [4]	a					14 45			16 45	
Shoreham-by-Sea	a					14 51			16 52	
Hove [2]	a					15 00			16 58	
Brighton [10]	a					15 06			17 06	

		GW	GW	GW	GW	SW	GW	GW	GW	GW	GW	GW	GW	GW
			◇	◇■ ☕	◇	◇■	◇	◇■ ☕	◇	◇	◇	◇		◇■ ☕
Cardiff Central [7]	d		13 08		14 08		15 08		16 08	16 35		17 08		
Newport (South Wales)	d		13 22		14 22		15 22		16 22	16 49		17 22		
Severn Tunnel Jn.	d		13 39		14 39		15 39		16 39			17 39		
Filton Abbey Wood	d		13 54		14 55		15 55		16 55	17 20		17 54		
Bristol Temple Meads [10]	d	13 55	14 15		15 10	16 04	16 15		17 15	17 40	17 44	18 10		
Keynsham	d	14 02			15 17	16 11			17 22		17 51	18 17		
Oldfield Park	d	14 09			15 24				17 29		17 58	18 24		
London Paddington [15] ⊖	d			13 57				15 57						17 57
Swindon	d												18 19	
Chippenham	d												18 35	
Melksham	d												18 45	
Bath Spa [7]	d	14 13	14 27		15 27	16 20	16 27		17 33	17 52	18 01	18 27		
Freshford	d	14 23	14 38				16 38				18 11			
Avoncliff	d	14 25	14 40				16 40				18 13			
Bradford-on-Avon	d	14 29	14 44		15 40	16 31	16 44		17 47	18 05	18 17	18 40		
Trowbridge	d	14 36	14 51		15 47	16 37	16 51		17 53	18 12	18 24	18 46	18 54	
Westbury	a	14 43	14 58		15 57	16 44	16 58	17 23	18 00	18 19	18 31	18 53	19 06	19 28
	d	14 45	15 00		16 05	16 46	16 59	17 25	18 01	18 20	18 31	18 56		
Frome	d	14 54									18 39			
Bruton	d	15 06									18 52			
Castle Cary	a	15 10		15 35				17 41			18 57			
	d	15 11									18 58			
Yeovil Pen Mill	d	15 26									19 12			
Thornford	d	15 32									19x17			
Yetminster	d	15 35									19x20			
Chetnole	d	15 39									19x24			
Maiden Newton	d	15 50									19 36			
Dorchester West	d	16 01									19 47			
Upwey	a	16 10									19 55			
Weymouth	a	16 15									20 01			
Dilton Marsh	d				16x08		17x02			18x23				
Warminster	d		15 08		16 14	16 53	17 08		18 09	18 29		19 04		
Salisbury	a		15 32		16 34	17 16	17 32		18 33	18 52		19 32		
	d		15 33		16 35		17 33		18 33	18 56		19 32		
Romsey	d		15 51		16 53		17 51		18 51	19 14		19 50		
Southampton Central	a		16 03		17 04		18 03		19 03	19 25		20 02		
Fareham	a		16 27		17 27		18 27		19 28	19 48		20 26		
	d		16 27		17 27		18 27		19 28	19 49		20 26		
Cosham	a		16 35		17 35		18 34		19 35	19 57				
Fratton	a		16 42		17 42		18 41		19 42			20 41		
Portsmouth & Southsea	a		16 46		17 47		18 45		19 46			20 45		
Portsmouth Harbour	a		16 52		17 52		18 52		19 53			20 51		
Havant	a									20 09				
Chichester [4]	a									20 20				
Barnham	a									20 28				
Worthing [4]	a									20 50				
Shoreham-by-Sea	a									20 56				
Hove [2]	a									21 03				
Brighton [10]	a									21 09				

A ✕ from Bristol Temple Meads

For connections from Swansea please refer to Table 128. For connections from Plymouth and Exeter St Davids please refer to Table 135. For connections to Bournemouth please refer to Table 158

For Bus Connections for either to or from Yeovil Junction and Yeovil Pen Mill please see Table 123A

Table 123

Sundays
from 28 October

South Wales and Bristol - Weymouth and Portsmouth

Network Diagram - see first Page of Table 123

		GW	GW	GW	GW	GW	GW	GW	SW	GW	GW
		■	◇	◇1 ⊡	◇	◇1 ⊡		◇	1		✕
Cardiff Central 7	d	17 40	18 08		19 08			20 18			22 00
Newport (South Wales)	d	17 54	18 22		19 22			20 31			22 19
Severn Tunnel Jn.	d		18 39		19 40			20 48			22 36
Filton Abbey Wood	d	18 23	18 56		19 55			21 05			22 53
Bristol Temple Meads 10	d	18 50	19 10		20 15		20 50	21 25	21 35	22 15	23 10
Keynsham	d		19 17				20 57			22 22	
Oldfield Park	d		19 24				21 04			22 29	
London Paddington 15 ⊖	d			18 57		19 57					
Swindon	d										
Chippenham	d										
Melksham	d										
Bath Spa 7	d	19 02	19 27		20 27		21 07	21 38	21 49	22 32	23 22
Freshford	d				20 38		21 17			22 42	
Avoncliff	d				20 40		21 20			22 45	
Bradford-on-Avon	d	19 15	19 40		20 44		21 24	21 50	22 00	22 49	23 35
Trowbridge	d	19 22	19 46		20 51		21 30	21 57	22 06	22 55	23 42
Westbury	a	19 29	19 57		20 58	21 28	21 37	22 04	22 13	23 02	23 49
	d	19 31	19 58		20 59	21 29	21 38	22 05	22 15		23 50
Frome	d						21 48				
Bruton	d						21 59				
Castle Cary	a			20 30		21 46	22 04				
	d						22 05				
Yeovil Pen Mill	d						22 19				
Thornford	d						22x23				
Yetminster	d						22x26				
Chetnole	d						22x30				
Maiden Newton	d						22 42				
Dorchester West	d						22 53				
Upwey	a						23 00				
Weymouth	a						23 06				
Dilton Marsh	d		20x01								23x53
Warminster	d	19 38	20 07		21 07			22 13	22 22		23a59
Salisbury	a	20 00	20 29		21 28			22 34	22 46		
	d	20 01	20 30		21 33			22 36			
Romsey	d	20 19	20 48		21 51			22 54			
Southampton Central	a	20 29	20 59		22 03			23 05			
Fareham	a	20 54	21 24		22 26			23 29			
	d	20 55	21 25		22 26			23 30			
Cosham	a										
Fratton	a	21 09	21 38		22 40			23 43			
Portsmouth & Southsea	a	21 15	21 41		22 43			23 46			
Portsmouth Harbour	a	21 26	21 48		22 50			23 54			
Havant	a										
Chichester 4	a										
Barnham	a										
Worthing 4	a										
Shoreham-by-Sea	a										
Hove 2	a										
Brighton 10	a										

For connections from Swansea please refer to Table 128. For connections from Plymouth and Exeter St Davids please refer to Table 135. For connections to Bournemouth please refer to Table 158

For Bus Connections for either to or from Yeovil Junction and Yeovil Pen Mill please see Table 123A

Table 123

Mondays to Fridays
until 29 June

Portsmouth and Weymouth - Bristol and South Wales

Network Diagram - see first Page of Table 123

Miles	Miles	Miles			GW	GW	GW	GW	GW	GW	GW	GW	SW	GW	GW	GW	GW	GW	GW	GW	GW	GW	GW
						◇1 ⊡	◇1 ⊡			◇	◇1 A ⊘		1	◇		◇1 ⊡	■ ✕	◇		◇ ✕	◇	◇1 A ⊘	◇ ✕
—	—	—	Brighton 10	d																			
—	—	—	Hove 2	d																			
—	—	—	Shoreham-by-Sea	d																			
—	—	—	Worthing 4	d																			
—	—	—	Barnham	d																			
—	—	—	**Chichester 4**	d																			
—	—	—	Havant	d																			
0	—	—	**Portsmouth Harbour** ⛴	d													06 00			07 05			08 23
0¾	—	—	Portsmouth & Southsea	d													06 04			07 09			08 27
1¾	—	—	Fratton	d													06 08			07 13			08 31
5½	—	—	Cosham	d													06 15			07 21			08 39
11¼	—	—	Fareham	a													06 23			07 28			08 46
—	—	—		d													06 24			07 29			08 47
25¾	—	—	**Southampton Central** ⛴	d													06 46			07 52	08 23		09 10
34	—	—	Romsey	d													07 00			08 11	08 35		09 21
50½	—	—	**Salisbury**	a													07 18			08 29	09 00		09 39
—	—	—		d				06 02					06 40				07 19			08 30	09 03		09 40
70¼	—	—	Warminster	d				06 24					07 00		07 23		07 39			08 52	09 25		10 01
73½	—	—	Dilton Marsh	d				06x28							07x27		07x43				09x29		
—	0	—	**Weymouth**	d										05 33				06 40					
—	2½	—	Upwey	d										05 37				06 45					
—	7	—	Dorchester West	d										05 45				06 53					
—	14¾	—	Maiden Newton	d										05 57				07 05					
—	21¼	—	Chetnole	d										06x06				07x13					
—	23¼	—	Yetminster	d										06x08				07x16					
—	24¼	—	Thornford	d										06x10				07x18					
—	27½	—	Yeovil Pen Mill	d										06 20				07 30					
—	39¼	—	Castle Cary	a										06 33				07 43					
—	—	—		d							06 38			06 45		07 27		07 44				09 42	
—	42¾	—	Bruton	d										06 51				07 49					
—	53¼	—	Frome	d			06 07			06 45				07 04				08 02					
75	59	—	**Westbury**	a			06 17	06 33		06 54	06 59		07 08	07 12	07 32	07 45	07 47	08 09		09 01	09 35	10 00	10 09
—	—	—		d	05 58	06 06	06 18		06 38	06 55	07 01	07 04	07 09	07 18	07 38	07 51	07 53	08 17	08 45	09 10	09 38	10 01	10 10
79	63	4	Trowbridge	d	06 04				06 44	07 02		07 10	07 15	07 24	07 44		08 00	08 23	08 51	09 16	09 44		10 16
82¼	66¼	—	Bradford-on-Avon	d	06 10				06 50	07 08			07 21	07 30	07 50		08 06	08 29	08 57	09 22	09 50		10 22
83½	67½	—	Avoncliff	d	06 13				06 53	07 11				07 33	07 53			08 32	09 00		09 53		
84½	68½	—	Freshford	d	06 16				06 56	07 13				07 36	07 56		08 10	08 35	09 03		09 56		
91½	75½	—	Bath Spa 7	a	06 26				07 06	07 24			07 33	07 46	08 06		08 21	08 45	09 13	09 35	10 06		10 34
—	—	9½	Melksham	d								07 20											
—	—	15¾	Chippenham	a								07 30											
—	—	32½	Swindon	a								07 48											
—	—	—	London Paddington 15 ⊖	a		07 53	08 09				08 38					09 21						11 24	
92½	76½	—	Oldfield Park	a	06 30				07 10	07 28			07 37	07 50	08 10		08 25	08 49	09 17		10 10		
98½	82½	—	Keynsham	a	06 37				07 18	07 35			07 44	07 58	08 18		08 32	08 56	09 25	09 44	10 18		
103	87	—	**Bristol Temple Meads 10**	a	06 46				07 27	07 46			07 52	08 06	08 29		08 41	09 05	09 35	09 52	10 28		10 48
107½	91½	—	Filton Abbey Wood	a	07 01				07 42	08 01				08 21	08 48		09 01	09 21	09 48	10 03	10 48		11 01
119½	119½	—	Severn Tunnel Jn	a	07 14																		
129½	113½	—	Newport (South Wales)	a	07 25					08 27							09 25			10 26			11 26
141¼	125¼	—	**Cardiff Central 7**	a	07 44					08 46							09 43			10 43			11 43

A ⊘ to Westbury

For connections to Swansea please refer to Table 128. For connections to Exeter St Davids and Plymouth please refer to Table 135. For connections from Bournemouth please refer to Table 158

For Bus Connections for either to or from Yeovil Junction and Yeovil Pen Mill please see Table 123A

Portsmouth and Weymouth - Bristol and South Wales

Network Diagram - see first Page of Table 123

		GW	GW	GW	GW	SW	GW	GW	GW	GW	GW	GW	GW	SW	GW	GW	GW	GW	GW	GW	GW	GW	GW
		◇		◇1	◇ T	◇1	◇ A T	◇ T		◇1 B	◇ T	◇	◇ T	◇1		◇	◇1 X B		◇ T		◇1 C B	◇1 B	■ T
Brighton 10	d						08 59																
Hove 2	d						09 03																
Shoreham-by-Sea	d						09 13																
Worthing 4	d						09 22																
Barnham	d						09 38																
Chichester 4	d						09 47																
Havant	d						09 59																
Portsmouth Harbour ⛴	d				09 23			10 23			11 23		12 23						13 23				14 23
Portsmouth & Southsea	d				09 27			10 27			11 27		12 27						13 27				14 27
Fratton	d				09 31			10 31			11 31		12 31						13 31				14 31
Cosham	d				09 39		10 05	10 39			11 39		12 39						13 39				14 39
Fareham	a				09 46		10 14	10 46			11 46		12 46						13 46				14 46
	d				09 47		10 15	10 47			11 47		12 47						13 47				14 47
Southampton Central ⛴	d				10 10		10 42	11 10			12 10	12 27	13 10						14 10				15 10
Romsey	d				10 21		10 54	11 21			12 21	12 39	13 21						14 21				15 21
Salisbury	a				10 39		11 13	11 39			12 39	13 02	13 39						14 39				15 39
	d				10 40	10 52	11 13	11 40			12 40	13 06	13 40	13 52					14 40				15 40
Warminster	d		10 25		11 01	11 12	11 34	12 01			13 01	13 34	14 01	14 12					15 01	15 28			16 01
Dilton Marsh	d		10x29									13x38								15x32			
Weymouth	d	08 53							11 10							13 10							
Upwey	d	08 58							11 15							13 15							
Dorchester West	d	09 06							11 23							13 23							
Maiden Newton	d	09 18							11 43							13 46							
Chetnole	d	09x26							11x50							13x53							
Yetminster	d	09x29							11x53							13x56							
Thornford	d	09x31							11x55							13x59							
Yeovil Pen Mill	d	09 41							12 05							14 08							
Castle Cary	a	09 54							12 19							14 22							
	d	09 55							12 23	12 45						14 22	14 44				15 51		
Bruton	d	10 01							12 29							14 28							
Frome	d	10 15							12 42							14 41		14 59				15 55	
Westbury	a	10 24	10 33		11 09	11 20	11 42	12 09	12 48	13 04	13 09	13 42	14 09	14 20		14 48	15 02	15 08	15 09	15 36		16 05	16 09
	d	10 38		11 05	11 10	11 21	11 43	12 10	12 52	13 05	13 10	13 44	14 10	14 21	14 38	14 51	15 03		15 10	15 38		16 08	16 10
Trowbridge	d	10 44			11 16	11 27	11 49	12 16	12 58		13 16	13 50	14 16	14 27	14 44	14 57			15 16	15 44			16 16
Bradford-on-Avon	d	10 50			11 22	11 33	11 55	12 22	13 04		13 22	13 56	14 22	14 33	14 50	15 03			15 22	15 50			16 22
Avoncliff	d	10 53					11 58		13 07			13 59			14 53	15 06				15 53			
Freshford	d	10 56					12 01		13 10			14 02			14 56	15 09				15 56			
Bath Spa 7	a	11 06			11 34	11 46	12 11	12 34	13 20		13 34	14 12	14 34	14 46	15 06	15 19			15 34	16 06			16 34
Melksham	d																						
Chippenham	a																						
Swindon	a																						
London Paddington 15 ⊖	a			12 23						14 44							16 22				17 24	17 54	
Oldfield Park	a	11 10					12 15		13 24			14 16			15 10					16 10			
Keynsham	a	11 18				11 54	12 22		13 32			14 24		14 54	15 18					16 18			
Bristol Temple Meads 10	a	11 28			11 48	12 05	12 31	12 48	13 41		13 48	14 35	14 48	15 05	15 28	15 34			15 48	16 29			16 48
Filton Abbey Wood	a	11 48			12 01		12 48	13 01			14 01	14 47	15 01			15 48			16 01	16 48			17 01
Severn Tunnel Jn.	a																						17 13
Newport (South Wales)	a				12 25			13 26			14 26		15 25						16 25				17 25
Cardiff Central 7	a				12 43			13 43			14 43		15 43						16 43				17 43

A T to Southampton Central

C The Torbay Express

For connections to Swansea please refer to Table 128. For connections to Exeter St Davids and Plymouth please refer to Table 135. For connections from Bournemouth please refer to Table 158

For Bus Connections for either to or from Yeovil Junction and Yeovil Pen Mill please see Table 123A

Table 123

Mondays to Fridays

until 29 June

Portsmouth and Weymouth - Bristol and South Wales

Network Diagram - see first Page of Table 123

		GW	GW	GW	GW	GW	GW	GW	GW	GW	GW	GW	GW	GW	GW	GW	GW	GW FO	GW FX	GW	SW	GW	GW FO
		◇	■ T		■ T			◇ T	◇	◇1 B	◇	◇	◇ T	◇ T	1		◇1 B	◇	◇		◇1		◇
Brighton 10	d												16 59										
Hove 2	d												17 03										
Shoreham-by-Sea	d												17 13										
Worthing 4	d												17 22										
Barnham	d												17 39										
Chichester 4	d												17 47										
Havant	d												17 58										
Portsmouth Harbour ⛴	d		15 23		16 23			17 23						18 23				19 23	19 23				20 23
Portsmouth & Southsea	d		15 27		16 27			17 27						18 27				19 27	19 27				20 27
Fratton	d		15 31		16 31			17 31						18 31				19 31	19 31				20 31
Cosham	d		15 39		16 39			17 39					18 05	18 39				19 39	19 39				
Fareham	a		15 46		16 46			17 46					18 12	18 46				19 46	19 46				20 46
	d		15 47		16 47			17 47					18 13	18 47				19 47	19 47				20 47
Southampton Central ⛴	d		16 10		17 10			18 10					18 42	19 10				20 10	20 10				21 10
Romsey	d		16 21		17 21			18 21					18 54	19 21				20 21	20 21				21 21
Salisbury	a		16 39		17 39			18 39					19 12	19 39				20 39	20 39				21 39
	d		16 40		17 40			18 40					19 13	19 40				20 40	20 40		20 57		21 40
Warminster	d		17 01	17 28	18 01	18 18		19 01					19 32	20 01				21 01	21 01		21 17		22 01
Dilton Marsh	d			17x32		18x22							19x37										
Weymouth	d	15 08							17 30													20 21	
Upwey	d	15 13							17 35													20 26	
Dorchester West	d	15 21							17 43													20 34	
Maiden Newton	d	15 33							17 54													20 44	
Chetnole	d	15x42							18x03													20x52	
Yetminster	d	15x45							18x06													20x56	
Thornford	d	15x47							18x08													20x58	
Yeovil Pen Mill	d	15 56							18 23													21 06	
Castle Cary	a	16 09							18 36													21 18	
	d	16 10							18 37	18 54							20 46					21 18	
Bruton	d	16 16							18 43													21 24	
Frome	d	16 29							19 06		←				20 15					21 02		21 37	
Westbury	a	16 38	17 09	17 36	18 09	18 28		19 09	19 17	19 12	19 17		19 40	20 09	20 26		21 04	21 08	21 08	21 12	21 25	21 46	22 09
	d	16 38	17 10	17 38	18 10		18 38	19 10	19 19	19 12	19 19	19 32	19 41	20 10		20 38	21 05	21 10	21 10		21 25	21 55	22 10
Trowbridge	d	16 44	17 16	17 44	18 16		18 44	19 16	→		19 25	19 38	19 48	20 16		20 44		21 17	21 17		21 31	22 02	22 16
Bradford-on-Avon	d	16 50	17 22	17 50	18 22		18 50	19 22			19 31		19 54	20 22		20 50		21 23	21 23		21 37	22 08	22 22
Avoncliff	d	16 53		17 53			18 54				19 34		19 56			20 53						22 11	
Freshford	d	16 56		17 56			18 56				19 37		19 58			20 56						22 13	
Bath Spa 7	a	17 06	17 34	18 06	18 34		19 06	19 34			19 47		20 12	20 34		21 06		21 34	21 34		21 50	22 24	22 34
Melksham	d											19 48											
Chippenham	a											20 01											
Swindon	a											20 21											
London Paddington 15 ⊖	a									20 39							22 30						
Oldfield Park	a	17 10		18 10			19 10				19 51		20 14			21 10						22 28	
Keynsham	a	17 18		18 18			19 18				19 59		20 21			21 18					21 58	22 35	
Bristol Temple Meads 10	a	17 29	17 48	18 28	18 48		19 29	19 48			20 08		20 30	20 48		21 28		21 48	21 48		22 06	22 43	22 50
Filton Abbey Wood	a	17 48	18 01	18 48	19 01		19 48	20 01						21 01				22 01	22 01				23 01
Severn Tunnel Jn.	a		18 13		19 13			20 16						21 13				22 17	22 17				23 16
Newport (South Wales)	a		18 25		19 26			20 27						21 26				22 29	22 36				23 34
Cardiff Central 7	a		18 43		19 46			20 43						21 44				22 52	23 00				23 56

For connections to Swansea please refer to Table 128. For connections to Exeter St Davids and Plymouth please refer to Table 135. For connections from Bournemouth please refer to Table 158

For Bus Connections for either to or from Yeovil Junction and Yeovil Pen Mill please see Table 123A

Table 123

Mondays to Fridays
until 29 June

Portsmouth and Weymouth - Bristol and South Wales

Network Diagram - see first Page of Table 123

		GW	GW	GW	GW
		FX ◇			
Brighton 10	d				
Hove 2	d				
Shoreham-by-Sea	d				
Worthing 4	d				
Barnham	d				
Chichester 4	d				
Havant	d				
Portsmouth Harbour ⛴	d	20 23			21 23
Portsmouth & Southsea	d	20 27			21 27
Fratton	d	20 31			21 31
Cosham	d				
Fareham	a	20 46			21 47
	d	20 47			21 48
Southampton Central ⛴	d	21 10	21 20		22 22
Romsey	d	21 21	21 31		22 34
Salisbury	a	21 39	21 51		22 58
	d	21 40	21 53		23 00
Warminster	d	22 01	22 15		23 20
Dilton Marsh	d		22x19		23x24
Weymouth	d				
Upwey	d				
Dorchester West	d				
Maiden Newton	d				
Chetnole	d				
Yetminster	d				
Thornford	d				
Yeovil Pen Mill	d				
Castle Cary	a				
	d				
Bruton	d				
Frome	d				
Westbury	a	22 09	22 26		23 31
	d	22 10		22 32	
Trowbridge	d	22 16		22 38	
Bradford-on-Avon	d	22 22		22 44	
Avoncliff	d			22 46	
Freshford	d			22 50	
Bath Spa 7	a	22 34		23 00	
Melksham	d				
Chippenham	a				
Swindon	a				
London Paddington 15 ⊖	a				
Oldfield Park	a			23 04	
Keynsham	a			23 12	
Bristol Temple Meads 10	a	22 48		23 23	
Filton Abbey Wood	a	23 01			
Severn Tunnel Jn.	a	23 16			
Newport (South Wales)	a	23 34			
Cardiff Central 7	a	23 56			

For connections to Swansea please refer to Table 128. For connections to Exeter St Davids and Plymouth please refer to Table 135. For connections from Bournemouth please refer to Table 158

For Bus Connections for either to or from Yeovil Junction and Yeovil Pen Mill please see Table 123A

Table 123

Mondays to Fridays
2 July to 31 August

Portsmouth and Weymouth - Bristol and South Wales

Network Diagram - see first Page of Table 123

		GW	GW	GW	GW	GW	GW	GW	GW	SW		GW	GW	GW	GW	GW	GW	GW	GW	GW		GW	GW	GW	GW
			◇1 🍽	◇1 🍽			◇	◇1 A ⊘		1		◇		◇1 🍽	■ ≖	◇		◇ ≖	◇	◇1 A ⊘		◇ ≖	◇		◇1
Brighton 10	d																								
Hove 2	d																								
Shoreham-by-Sea	d																								
Worthing 4	d																								
Barnham	d																								
Chichester 4	d																								
Havant	d																								
Portsmouth Harbour ⛴	d														06 00			07 05				08 23			
Portsmouth & Southsea	d														06 04			07 09				08 27			
Fratton	d														06 08			07 13				08 31			
Cosham	d														06 15			07 21				08 39			
Fareham	a														06 23			07 28				08 46			
	d														06 24			07 29				08 47			
Southampton Central ⛴	d														06 46			07 52	08 23			09 10			
Romsey	d														07 00			08 11	08 35			09 21			
Salisbury	a														07 18			08 29	09 00			09 39			
	d				06 02					06 40					07 19			08 30	09 03			09 40			
Warminster	d				06 24					07 00			07 23		07 39			08 52	09 25			10 01		10 25	
Dilton Marsh	d				06x28								07x27		07x43				09x29					10x29	
Weymouth	d											05 33				06 40							08 53		
Upwey	d											05 37				06 45							08 58		
Dorchester West	d											05 45				06 53							09 06		
Maiden Newton	d											05 57				07 05							09 18		
Chetnole	d											06x06				07x13							09x26		
Yetminster	d											06x08				07x16							09x29		
Thornford	d											06x10				07x18							09x31		
Yeovil Pen Mill	d											06 20				07 30							09 41		
Castle Cary	a											06 33				07 43							09 54		
	d							06 38				06 45		07 27		07 44				09 42			09 55		
Bruton	d											06 51				07 49							10 01		
Frome	d			06 07			06 45					07 04				08 02							10 15		
Westbury	a			06 17	06 33		06 54	06 59		07 08		07 12	07 32	07 45	07 47	08 09		09 01	09 35	10 00		10 09	10 24	10 33	
	d	05 58	06 06	06 18		06 38	06 55	07 01	07 04	07 09		07 18	07 38	07 51	07 53	08 17	08 45	09 10	09 38	10 01		10 10	10 38		11 05
Trowbridge	d	06 04				06 44	07 02		07 10	07 15		07 24	07 44		08 00	08 23	08 51	09 16	09 44			10 16	10 44		
Bradford-on-Avon	d	06 10				06 50	07 08			07 21		07 30	07 50		08 06	08 29	08 57	09 22	09 50			10 22	10 50		
Avoncliff	d	06 13				06 53	07 11					07 33	07 53			08 32	09 00		09 53				10 53		
Freshford	d	06 16				06 56	07 13					07 36	07 56		08 10	08 35	09 03		09 56				10 56		
Bath Spa 7	a	06 26				07 06	07 24			07 33		07 46	08 06		08 21	08 45	09 13	09 35	10 06			10 34	11 06		
Melksham	d								07 20																
Chippenham	a								07 30																
Swindon	a								07 48																
London Paddington 15 ⊖	a		07 53	08 09				08 38						09 21						11 24					12 23
Oldfield Park	a	06 30				07 10	07 28			07 37		07 50	08 10		08 25	08 49	09 17		10 10				11 10		
Keynsham	a	06 37				07 18	07 35			07 44		07 58	08 18		08 32	08 56	09 25	09 44	10 18				11 18		
Bristol Temple Meads 10	a	06 46				07 27	07 46			07 52		08 06	08 29		08 41	09 05	09 35	09 52	10 28			10 48	11 28		
Filton Abbey Wood	a	07 01				07 42	08 01					08 21	08 48		09 01	09 21	09 48	10 03	10 48			11 01	11 48		
Severn Tunnel Jn.	a	07 14																							
Newport (South Wales)	a	07 25					08 27								09 25			10 26				11 26			
Cardiff Central 7	a	07 44					08 46								09 43			10 43				11 43			

A ⊘ to Westbury

For connections to Swansea please refer to Table 128. For connections to Exeter St Davids and Plymouth please refer to Table 135. For connections from Bournemouth please refer to Table 158

For Bus Connections for either to or from Yeovil Junction and Yeovil Pen Mill please see Table 123A

Table 123

Mondays to Fridays

2 July to 31 August

Portsmouth and Weymouth - Bristol and South Wales

Network Diagram - see first Page of Table 123

		GW	SW	GW	GW	GW		GW	GW	GW	GW	SW	GW	GW	GW	GW		GW	GW	GW	GW	GW	GW	GW	GW
				A																C					
		◇ ☕	◇1	◇ ☕	◇ ☕			◇1 🚌	◇ ☕	◇	◇ ☕	◇1		◇	◇1 ✕🚌			◇ ☕		◇1 🚌	◇1 🚌	1 ☕	◇	1 ☕	
Brighton 10	d			08 59																					
Hove 2	d			09 03																					
Shoreham-by-Sea	d			09 13																					
Worthing 4	d			09 22																					
Barnham	d			09 38																					
Chichester 4	d			09 47																					
Havant	d			09 59																					
Portsmouth Harbour ⛴	d	09 23			10 23				11 23		12 23							13 23				14 23		15 23	
Portsmouth & Southsea	d	09 27			10 27				11 27		12 27							13 27				14 27		15 27	
Fratton	d	09 31			10 31				11 31		12 31							13 31				14 31		15 31	
Cosham	d	09 39		10 05	10 39				11 39		12 39							13 39				14 39		15 39	
Fareham	a	09 46		10 14	10 46				11 46		12 46							13 46				14 46		15 46	
	d	09 47		10 15	10 47				11 47		12 47							13 47				14 47		15 47	
Southampton Central ⛴	d	10 10		10 42	11 10				12 10	12 27	13 10							14 10				15 10		16 10	
Romsey	d	10 21		10 54	11 21				12 21	12 39	13 21							14 21				15 21		16 21	
Salisbury	a	10 39		11 13	11 39				12 39	13 02	13 39							14 39				15 39		16 39	
	d	10 40	10 52	11 13	11 40				12 40	13 06	13 40	13 52						14 40				15 40		16 40	
Warminster	d	11 01	11 12	11 33	12 01				13 01	13 34	14 01	14 12						15 01	15 28			16 01		17 01	17 28
Dilton Marsh	d									13x38									15x32						17x32
Weymouth	d					11 10								13 10									15 08		
Upwey	d					11 15								13 15									15 13		
Dorchester West	d					11 23								13 23									15 21		
Maiden Newton	d					11 43								13 46									15 33		
Chetnole	d					11x50								13x53									15x42		
Yetminster	d					11x53								13x56									15x45		
Thornford	d					11x55								13x59									15x47		
Yeovil Pen Mill	d					12 05								14 08									15 56		
Castle Cary	a					12 19								14 22									16 09		
	d					12 23		12 45						14 22	14 44					15 51			16 10		
Bruton	d					12 29								14 28									16 16		
Frome	d					12 42								14 41		14 59					15 55		16 29		
Westbury	a	11 09	11 20	11 38	12 09	12 48		13 04	13 09	13 42	14 09	14 20		14 48	15 02	15 08		15 09	15 36		16 05	16 09	16 38	17 09	17 36
	d	11 10	11 21	11 39	12 10	12 52		13 05	13 10	13 44	14 10	14 21	14 38	14 51	15 03			15 10	15 38		16 08	16 10	16 38	17 10	17 38
Trowbridge	d	11 16	11 27	11 45	12 16	12 58			13 16	13 50	14 16	14 27	14 44	14 57				15 16	15 44			16 16	16 44	17 16	17 44
Bradford-on-Avon	d	11 22	11 33	11 51	12 22	13 04			13 22	13 56	14 22	14 33	14 50	15 03				15 22	15 50			16 22	16 50	17 22	17 50
Avoncliff	d			11 53		13 07				13 59			14 53	15 06					15 53				16 53		17 53
Freshford	d			11 56		13 10				14 02			14 56	15 09					15 56				16 56		17 56
Bath Spa 7	a	11 34	11 46	12 07	12 34	13 20			13 34	14 12	14 34	14 46	15 06	15 19				15 34	16 06			16 34	17 06	17 34	18 06
Melksham	d																								
Chippenham	a																								
Swindon	a																								
London Paddington 15 ⊖	a							14 44							16 22					17 24	17 54				
Oldfield Park	a			12 11		13 24				14 16			15 10						16 10				17 10		18 10
Keynsham	a		11 54	12 18		13 32				14 24		14 54	15 18						16 18				17 18		18 18
Bristol Temple Meads 10	a	11 48	12 05	12 31	12 48	13 41			13 48	14 35	14 48	15 05	15 28	15 34				15 48	16 29			16 48	17 29	17 48	18 28
Filton Abbey Wood	a	12 01		12 48	13 01				14 01	14 47	15 01			15 48				16 01	16 48			17 01	17 48	18 01	18 48
Severn Tunnel Jn.	a																					17 13		18 13	
Newport (South Wales)	a	12 25			13 26				14 26		15 25							16 25				17 25		18 25	
Cardiff Central 7	a	12 43			13 43				14 43		15 43							16 43				17 43		18 43	

A ☕ to Southampton Central

C The Torbay Express

For connections to Swansea please refer to Table 128. For connections to Exeter St Davids and Plymouth please refer to Table 135. For connections from Bournemouth please refer to Table 158

For Bus Connections for either to or from Yeovil Junction and Yeovil Pen Mill please see Table 123A

Table 123

Mondays to Fridays

2 July to 31 August

Portsmouth and Weymouth - Bristol and South Wales

Network Diagram - see first Page of Table 123

		GW		GW	GW	GW	GW	GW	GW	GW	GW	GW		GW	GW	GW	GW	GW	GW	SW	GW	GW		GW	GW
								A									FO	FX				FO		FX	
		1 ☕				◇ ☕	◇	◇1 🚌	◇	◇	◇ ☕	◇ ☕		1		◇1 🚌	◇	◇		◇1		◇		◇	
Brighton 10	d										16 59														
Hove 2	d										17 03														
Shoreham-by-Sea	d										17 13														
Worthing 4	d										17 22														
Barnham	d										17 39														
Chichester 4	d										17 47														
Havant	d										17 58														
Portsmouth Harbour ⛴	d	16 23				17 23						18 23					19 23	19 23				20 23		20 23	
Portsmouth & Southsea	d	16 27				17 27						18 27					19 27	19 27				20 27		20 27	
Fratton	d	16 31				17 31						18 31					19 31	19 31				20 31		20 31	
Cosham	d	16 39				17 39					18 05	18 39					19 39	19 39							
Fareham	a	16 46				17 46					18 12	18 46					19 46	19 46				20 46		20 46	
	d	16 47				17 47					18 13	18 47					19 47	19 47				20 47		20 47	
Southampton Central ⛴	d	17 10				18 10					18 42	19 10					20 10	20 10				21 10		21 10	21 20
Romsey	d	17 21				18 21					18 54	19 21					20 21	20 21				21 21		21 21	21 31
Salisbury	a	17 39				18 39					19 12	19 39					20 39	20 39				21 39		21 39	21 51
	d	17 40				18 40					19 13	19 40					20 40	20 40		20 57		21 40		21 40	21 53
Warminster	d	18 01		18 18		19 01					19 32	20 01					21 01	21 01		21 17		22 01		22 01	22 15
Dilton Marsh	d			18x22							19x37														22x19
Weymouth	d						17 30														20 21				
Upwey	d						17 35														20 26				
Dorchester West	d						17 43														20 34				
Maiden Newton	d						17 54														20 44				
Chetnole	d						18x03														20x52				
Yetminster	d						18x06														20x56				
Thornford	d						18x08														20x58				
Yeovil Pen Mill	d						18 23														21 06				
Castle Cary	a						18 36														21 18				
	d						18 37	18 54								20 46					21 18				
Bruton	d						18 43														21 24				
Frome	d						19 06		←					20 15					21 02		21 37				
Westbury	a	18 09		18 28		19 09	19 17	19 12	19 17		19 40	20 09		20 26		21 04	21 08	21 08	21 12	21 25	21 46	22 09		22 09	22 26
	d	18 10			18 38	19 10	19 19	19 12	19 19	19 32	19 41	20 10			20 38	21 05	21 10	21 10		21 25	21 55	22 10		22 10	
Trowbridge	d	18 16			18 44	19 16	→		19 25	19 38	19 48	20 16			20 44		21 17	21 17		21 31	22 02	22 16		22 16	
Bradford-on-Avon	d	18 22			18 50	19 22			19 31		19 54	20 22			20 50		21 23	21 23		21 37	22 08	22 22		22 22	
Avoncliff	d				18 54				19 34		19 56				20 53						22 11				
Freshford	d				18 56				19 37		19 58				20 56						22 13				
Bath Spa 7	a	18 34			19 06	19 34			19 47		20 12	20 34			21 06		21 34	21 34		21 50	22 24	22 34		22 34	
Melksham	d									19 48															
Chippenham	a									20 01															
Swindon	a									20 21															
London Paddington 15 ⊖	a							20 39								22 30									
Oldfield Park	a				19 10				19 51		20 14				21 10						22 28				
Keynsham	a				19 18				19 59		20 21				21 18					21 58	22 35				
Bristol Temple Meads 10	a	18 48			19 29	19 48			20 08		20 30	20 48			21 28		21 48	21 48		22 06	22 43	22 50		22 48	
Filton Abbey Wood	a	19 01			19 48	20 01						21 01					22 01	22 01				23 01		23 01	
Severn Tunnel Jn.	a	19 13				20 16						21 13					22 17	22 17				23 16		23 16	
Newport (South Wales)	a	19 26				20 27						21 26					22 29	22 36				23 34		23 34	
Cardiff Central 7	a	19 46				20 43						21 44					22 52	23 00				23 56		23 56	

A The Atlantic Coast Express

For connections to Swansea please refer to Table 128. For connections to Exeter St Davids and Plymouth please refer to Table 135. For connections from Bournemouth please refer to Table 158

For Bus Connections for either to or from Yeovil Junction and Yeovil Pen Mill please see Table 123A

Table 123

Mondays to Fridays

2 July to 31 August

Portsmouth and Weymouth - Bristol and South Wales

Network Diagram - see first Page of Table 123

		GW	GW
Brighton 10	d		
Hove 2	d		
Shoreham-by-Sea	d		
Worthing 4	d		
Barnham	d		
Chichester 4	d		
Havant	d		
Portsmouth Harbour ⛴	d		21 23
Portsmouth & Southsea	d		21 27
Fratton	d		21 31
Cosham	d		
Fareham	a		21 47
	d		21 48
Southampton Central ⛴	d		22 22
Romsey	d		22 34
Salisbury	a		22 58
	d		23 00
Warminster	d		23 20
Dilton Marsh	d		23x24
Weymouth	d		
Upwey	d		
Dorchester West	d		
Maiden Newton	d		
Chetnole	d		
Yetminster	d		
Thornford	d		
Yeovil Pen Mill	d		
Castle Cary	a		
	d		
Bruton	d		
Frome	d		
Westbury	a		23 31
	d	22 32	
Trowbridge	d	22 38	
Bradford-on-Avon	d	22 44	
Avoncliff	d	22 46	
Freshford	d	22 50	
Bath Spa 7	a	23 00	
Melksham	d		
Chippenham	a		
Swindon	a		
London Paddington 15 ⊖	a		
Oldfield Park	a	23 04	
Keynsham	a	23 12	
Bristol Temple Meads 10	a	23 23	
Filton Abbey Wood	a		
Severn Tunnel Jn.	a		
Newport (South Wales)	a		
Cardiff Central 7	a		

For connections to Swansea please refer to Table 128. For connections to Exeter St Davids and Plymouth please refer to Table 135. For connections from Bournemouth please refer to Table 158

For Bus Connections for either to or from Yeovil Junction and Yeovil Pen Mill please see Table 123A

Table 123

Mondays to Fridays

3 September to 14 September

Portsmouth and Weymouth - Bristol and South Wales

Network Diagram - see first Page of Table 123

		GW	GW	GW	GW	GW	GW	GW	GW	SW		GW	GW	GW	GW	GW	GW	GW	GW	GW		GW	GW	GW	GW
			◇■ ⊡	◇■ ⊡			◇	◇■ A ⊘		■		◇		◇■ ⊡	■ ⌶	◇		◇ ⌶	◇	◇■ A ⊘		◇ ⌶	◇		◇■
Brighton 10	d																								
Hove 2	d																								
Shoreham-by-Sea	d																								
Worthing 4	d																								
Barnham	d																								
Chichester 4	d																								
Havant	d																								
Portsmouth Harbour ⛴	d														06 00			07 05				08 23			
Portsmouth & Southsea	d														06 04			07 09				08 27			
Fratton	d														06 08			07 13				08 31			
Cosham	d														06 15			07 21				08 39			
Fareham	a														06 23			07 28				08 46			
	d														06 24			07 29				08 47			
Southampton Central ⛴	d														06 46			07 52	08 23			09 10			
Romsey	d														07 00			08 11	08 35			09 21			
Salisbury	a														07 18			08 29	09 00			09 39			
	d				06 02					06 40					07 19			08 30	09 03			09 40			
Warminster	d				06 24					07 00			07 23		07 39			08 52	09 25			10 01		10 25	
Dilton Marsh	d				06x28								07x27		07x43				09x29					10x29	
Weymouth	d											05 33				06 40							08 53		
Upwey	d											05 37				06 45							08 58		
Dorchester West	d											05 45				06 53							09 06		
Maiden Newton	d											05 57				07 05							09 18		
Chetnole	d											06x06				07x13							09x26		
Yetminster	d											06x08				07x16							09x29		
Thornford	d											06x10				07x18							09x31		
Yeovil Pen Mill	d											06 20				07 30							09 41		
Castle Cary	a											06 33				07 43							09 54		
	d							06 38				06 45		07 27		07 44				09 42			09 55		
Bruton	d											06 51				07 49							10 01		
Frome	d			06 07			06 45					07 04				08 02							10 15		
Westbury	a			06 17	06 33		06 54	06 59		07 08		07 12	07 32	07 45	07 47	08 09		09 01	09 35	10 00		10 09	10 24	10 33	
	d	05 58	06 06	06 18		06 38	06 55	07 01	07 04	07 09		07 18	07 38	07 51	07 53	08 17	08 45	09 10	09 38	10 01		10 10	10 38		11 05
Trowbridge	d	06 04				06 44	07 02		07 10	07 15		07 24	07 44		08 00	08 23	08 51	09 16	09 44			10 16	10 44		
Bradford-on-Avon	d	06 10				06 50	07 08			07 21		07 30	07 50		08 06	08 29	08 57	09 22	09 50			10 22	10 50		
Avoncliff	d	06 13				06 53	07 11					07 33	07 53			08 32	09 00		09 53				10 53		
Freshford	d	06 16				06 56	07 13					07 36	07 56		08 10	08 35	09 03		09 56				10 56		
Bath Spa 7	a	06 26				07 06	07 24			07 33		07 46	08 06		08 21	08 45	09 13	09 35	10 06			10 34	11 06		
Melksham	d								07 20																
Chippenham	a								07 30																
Swindon	a								07 48																
London Paddington 15 ⊖	a		07 53	08 09				08 38						09 21						11 24					12 23
Oldfield Park	a	06 30				07 10	07 28			07 37		07 50	08 10		08 25	08 49	09 17		10 10				11 10		
Keynsham	a	06 37				07 18	07 35			07 44		07 58	08 18		08 32	08 56	09 25	09 44	10 18				11 18		
Bristol Temple Meads 10	a	06 46				07 27	07 46			07 52		08 06	08 29		08 41	09 05	09 35	09 52	10 28			10 48	11 28		
Filton Abbey Wood	a	07 01				07 42	08 01					08 21	08 48		09 01	09 21	09 48	10 03	10 48			11 01	11 48		
Severn Tunnel Jn.	a	07 14																							
Newport (South Wales)	a	07 25					08 27								09 25			10 26				11 26			
Cardiff Central 7	a	07 44					08 46								09 43			10 43				11 43			

A ⊘ to Westbury

For connections to Swansea please refer to Table 128. For connections to Exeter St Davids and Plymouth please refer to Table 135. For connections from Bournemouth please refer to Table 158

For Bus Connections for either to or from Yeovil Junction and Yeovil Pen Mill please see Table 123A

Table 123

Mondays to Fridays
3 September to 14 September

Portsmouth and Weymouth - Bristol and South Wales

Network Diagram - see first Page of Table 123

		GW	SW	GW	GW	GW	GW	GW	GW	GW	SW	GW	GW	GW	GW	GW	GW	GW	GW	GW	GW	GW	GW
		◇ ⊼	◇■	◇ A ⊼	◇ ⊼		◇■ ⊡	◇ ⊼	◇	◇ ⊼	◇■		◇	◇■ ✕⊡		◇ ⊼		◇■ C ⊡	◇■ ⊡	■ ⊼	◇	■ ⊼	
Brighton 10	d			08 59																			
Hove 2	d			09 03																			
Shoreham-by-Sea	d			09 13																			
Worthing 4	d			09 22																			
Barnham	d			09 38																			
Chichester 4	d			09 47																			
Havant	d			09 59																			
Portsmouth Harbour ⛴	d	09 23			10 23			11 23		12 23						13 23				14 23		15 23	
Portsmouth & Southsea	d	09 27			10 27			11 27		12 27						13 27				14 27		15 27	
Fratton	d	09 31			10 31			11 31		12 31						13 31				14 31		15 31	
Cosham	d	09 39		10 05	10 39			11 39		12 39						13 39				14 39		15 39	
Fareham	a	09 46		10 14	10 46			11 46		12 46						13 46				14 46		15 46	
	d	09 47		10 15	10 47			11 47		12 47						13 47				14 47		15 47	
Southampton Central ⛴	d	10 10		10 42	11 10			12 10	12 27	13 10						14 10				15 10		16 10	
Romsey	d	10 21		10 54	11 21			12 21	12 39	13 21						14 21				15 21		16 21	
Salisbury	a	10 39		11 13	11 39			12 39	13 02	13 39						14 39				15 39		16 39	
	d	10 40	10 52	11 13	11 40			12 40	13 06	13 40	13 52					14 40				15 40		16 40	
Warminster	d	11 01	11 12	11 34	12 01			13 01	13 34	14 01	14 12					15 01	15 28			16 01		17 01	17 28
Dilton Marsh	d								13x38								15x32						17x32
Weymouth	d					11 10							13 10								15 08		
Upwey	d					11 15							13 15								15 13		
Dorchester West	d					11 23							13 23								15 21		
Maiden Newton	d					11 43							13 46								15 33		
Chetnole	d					11x50							13x53								15x42		
Yetminster	d					11x53							13x56								15x45		
Thornford	d					11x55							13x59								15x47		
Yeovil Pen Mill	d					12 05							14 08								15 56		
Castle Cary	a					12 19							14 22								16 09		
	d					12 23	12 45						14 22	14 44				15 51			16 10		
Bruton	d					12 29							14 28								16 16		
Frome	d					12 42							14 41		14 59				15 55		16 29		
Westbury	a	11 09	11 20	11 42	12 09	12 48	13 04	13 09	13 42	14 09	14 20		14 48	15 02	15 08	15 09	15 36		16 05	16 09	16 38	17 09	17 36
	d	11 10	11 21	11 43	12 10	12 52	13 05	13 10	13 44	14 10	14 21	14 38	14 51	15 03		15 10	15 38		16 08	16 10	16 38	17 10	17 38
Trowbridge	d	11 16	11 27	11 49	12 16	12 58		13 16	13 50	14 16	14 27	14 44	14 57			15 16	15 44			16 16	16 44	17 16	17 44
Bradford-on-Avon	d	11 22	11 33	11 55	12 22	13 04		13 22	13 56	14 22	14 33	14 50	15 03			15 22	15 50			16 22	16 50	17 22	17 50
Avoncliff	d			11 58		13 07			13 59			14 53	15 06				15 53				16 53		17 53
Freshford	d			12 01		13 10			14 02			14 56	15 09				15 56				16 56		17 56
Bath Spa 7	a	11 34	11 46	12 11	12 34	13 20		13 34	14 12	14 34	14 46	15 06	15 19			15 34	16 06			16 34	17 06	17 34	18 06
Melksham	d																						
Chippenham	a																						
Swindon	a																						
London Paddington 15 ⊖	a						14 44							16 22				17 24	17 54				
Oldfield Park	a			12 15		13 24			14 16			15 10					16 10				17 10		18 10
Keynsham	a		11 54	12 22		13 32			14 24		14 54	15 18					16 18				17 18		18 18
Bristol Temple Meads 10	a	11 48	12 05	12 31	12 48	13 41		13 48	14 35	14 48	15 05	15 28	15 34			15 48	16 29			16 48	17 29	17 48	18 28
Filton Abbey Wood	a	12 01		12 48	13 01			14 01	14 47	15 01			15 48			16 01	16 48			17 01	17 48	18 01	18 48
Severn Tunnel Jn.	a																			17 13		18 13	
Newport (South Wales)	a	12 25			13 26			14 26		15 25						16 25				17 25		18 25	
Cardiff Central 7	a	12 43			13 43			14 43		15 43						16 43				17 43		18 43	

A ⊼ to Southampton Central

C The Torbay Express

For connections to Swansea please refer to Table 128. For connections to Exeter St Davids and Plymouth please refer to Table 135. For connections from Bournemouth please refer to Table 158

For Bus Connections for either to or from Yeovil Junction and Yeovil Pen Mill please see Table 123A

Table 123

Mondays to Fridays
3 September to 14 September

Portsmouth and Weymouth - Bristol and South Wales

Network Diagram - see first Page of Table 123

		GW	GW	GW	GW	GW	GW	GW	GW	GW	GW	GW	GW	GW	GW FO	GW	GW	SW	GW	GW FO	GW	GW
		■ ⊼			◇ ⊼	◇	◇■ ⊡	◇	◇	◇ ⊼	◇ ⊼	■		◇■ ⊡	◇	◇ A		◇■		◇	◇ A	
Brighton 10	d									16 59												
Hove 2	d									17 03												
Shoreham-by-Sea	d									17 13												
Worthing 4	d									17 22												
Barnham	d									17 39												
Chichester 4	d									17 47												
Havant	d									17 58												
Portsmouth Harbour ⛴	d	16 23			17 23						18 23				19 23	19 23				20 23	20 23	
Portsmouth & Southsea	d	16 27			17 27						18 27				19 27	19 27				20 27	20 27	
Fratton	d	16 31			17 31						18 31				19 31	19 31				20 31	20 31	
Cosham	d	16 39			17 39					18 05	18 39				19 39	19 39						
Fareham	a	16 46			17 46					18 12	18 46				19 46	19 46				20 46	20 46	
	d	16 47			17 47					18 13	18 47				19 47	19 47				20 47	20 47	
Southampton Central ⛴	d	17 10			18 10					18 42	19 10				20 10	20 10				21 10	21 10	21 20
Romsey	d	17 21			18 21					18 54	19 21				20 21	20 21				21 21	21 21	21 31
Salisbury	a	17 39			18 39					19 12	19 39				20 39	20 39				21 39	21 39	21 51
	d	17 40			18 40					19 13	19 40				20 40	20 40		20 57		21 40	21 40	21 53
Warminster	d	18 01	18 18		19 01					19 32	20 01				21 01	21 01		21 17		22 01	22 01	22 15
Dilton Marsh	d		18x22							19x37												22x19
Weymouth	d					17 30													20 21			
Upwey	d					17 35													20 26			
Dorchester West	d					17 43													20 34			
Maiden Newton	d					17 54													20 44			
Chetnole	d					18x03													20x52			
Yetminster	d					18x06													20x56			
Thornford	d					18x08													20x58			
Yeovil Pen Mill	d					18 23													21 06			
Castle Cary	a					18 36													21 18			
	d					18 37	18 54							20 46					21 18			
Bruton	d					18 43													21 24			
Frome	d					19 06		←				20 15					21 02		21 37			
Westbury	a	18 09	18 28		19 09	19 17	19 12	19 17		19 40	20 09	20 26		21 04	21 08	21 08	21 12	21 25	21 46	22 09	22 09	22 26
	d	18 10		18 38	19 10	19 19	19 12	19 19	19 32	19 41	20 10		20 38	21 05	21 10	21 10		21 25	21 55	22 10	22 10	
Trowbridge	d	18 16		18 44	19 16	→		19 25	19 38	19 48	20 16		20 44		21 17	21 17		21 31	22 02	22 16	22 16	
Bradford-on-Avon	d	18 22		18 50	19 22			19 31		19 54	20 22		20 50		21 23	21 23		21 37	22 08	22 22	22 22	
Avoncliff	d			18 54				19 34		19 56			20 53						22 11			
Freshford	d			18 56				19 37		19 58			20 56						22 13			
Bath Spa 7	a	18 34		19 06	19 34			19 47		20 12	20 34		21 06		21 34	21 34		21 50	22 24	22 34	22 34	
Melksham	d								19 48													
Chippenham	a								20 01													
Swindon	a								20 21													
London Paddington 15 ⊖	a						20 39							22 30								
Oldfield Park	a			19 10				19 51		20 14			21 10						22 28			
Keynsham	a			19 18				19 59		20 21			21 18					21 58	22 35			
Bristol Temple Meads 10	a	18 48		19 29	19 48			20 08		20 30	20 48		21 28		21 48	21 48		22 06	22 43	22 50	22 48	
Filton Abbey Wood	a	19 01		19 48	20 01						21 01				22 01	22 01				23 01	23 01	
Severn Tunnel Jn.	a	19 13			20 16						21 13				22 17	22 17				23 16	23 16	
Newport (South Wales)	a	19 26			20 27						21 26				22 29	22 36				23 34	23 34	
Cardiff Central 7	a	19 46			20 43						21 44				22 52	23 00				23 56	23 56	

A not 7 September, 14 September

For connections to Swansea please refer to Table 128. For connections to Exeter St Davids and Plymouth please refer to Table 135. For connections from Bournemouth please refer to Table 158

For Bus Connections for either to or from Yeovil Junction and Yeovil Pen Mill please see Table 123A

Table 123

Mondays to Fridays

3 September to 14 September

Portsmouth and Weymouth - Bristol and South Wales

Network Diagram - see first Page of Table 123

		GW	GW
Brighton 10	d		
Hove 2	d		
Shoreham-by-Sea	d		
Worthing 4	d		
Barnham	d		
Chichester 4	d		
Havant	d		
Portsmouth Harbour ⛴	d		21 23
Portsmouth & Southsea	d		21 27
Fratton	d		21 31
Cosham	d		
Fareham	a		21 47
	d		21 48
Southampton Central ⛴	d		22 22
Romsey	d		22 34
Salisbury	a		22 58
	d		23 00
Warminster	d		23 20
Dilton Marsh	d		23x24
Weymouth	d		
Upwey	d		
Dorchester West	d		
Maiden Newton	d		
Chetnole	d		
Yetminster	d		
Thornford	d		
Yeovil Pen Mill	d		
Castle Cary	a		
	d		
Bruton	d		
Frome	d		
Westbury	a		23 31
	d	22 32	
Trowbridge	d	22 38	
Bradford-on-Avon	d	22 44	
Avoncliff	d	22 46	
Freshford	d	22 50	
Bath Spa 7	a	23 00	
Melksham	d		
Chippenham	a		
Swindon	a		
London Paddington 15 ⊖	a		
Oldfield Park	a	23 04	
Keynsham	a	23 12	
Bristol Temple Meads 10	a	23 23	
Filton Abbey Wood	a		
Severn Tunnel Jn.	a		
Newport (South Wales)	a		
Cardiff Central 7	a		

For connections to Swansea please refer to Table 128. For connections to Exeter St Davids and Plymouth please refer to Table 135. For connections from Bournemouth please refer to Table 158

For Bus Connections for either to or from Yeovil Junction and Yeovil Pen Mill please see Table 123A

Table 123

Mondays to Fridays

from 17 September

Portsmouth and Weymouth - Bristol and South Wales

Network Diagram - see first Page of Table 123

		GW	GW	GW	GW	GW	GW	GW	GW	SW	GW	GW	GW	GW	GW	GW	GW	GW	GW	GW	GW	GW	GW
			◇1 ⊡	◇1 ⊡			◇	◇1 A ⊘		1	◇		◇1 ⊡	■ 工	◇		◇ 工	◇	◇1 A ⊘	◇ 工	◇		◇1
Brighton 10	d																						
Hove 2	d																						
Shoreham-by-Sea	d																						
Worthing 4	d																						
Barnham	d																						
Chichester 4	d																						
Havant	d																						
Portsmouth Harbour ⛴	d													06 00			07 05			08 23			
Portsmouth & Southsea	d													06 04			07 09			08 27			
Fratton	d													06 08			07 13			08 31			
Cosham	d													06 15			07 21			08 39			
Fareham	a													06 23			07 28			08 46			
	d													06 24			07 29			08 47			
Southampton Central ⛴	d													06 46			07 52	08 23		09 10			
Romsey	d													07 00			08 11	08 35		09 21			
Salisbury	a													07 18			08 29	09 00		09 39			
	d				06 02					06 40				07 19			08 30	09 03		09 40			
Warminster	d				06 24					07 00		07 23		07 39			08 52	09 25		10 01		10 25	
Dilton Marsh	d				06x28							07x27		07x43				09x29				10x29	
Weymouth	d										05 33				06 40						08 53		
Upwey	d										05 37				06 45						08 58		
Dorchester West	d										05 45				06 53						09 06		
Maiden Newton	d										05 57				07 05						09 18		
Chetnole	d										06x06				07x13						09x26		
Yetminster	d										06x08				07x16						09x29		
Thornford	d										06x10				07x18						09x31		
Yeovil Pen Mill	d										06 20				07 30						09 41		
Castle Cary	a										06 33				07 43						09 54		
	d							06 38			06 45		07 27		07 44				09 42		09 55		
Bruton	d										06 51				07 49						10 01		
Frome	d			06 07			06 45				07 04				08 02						10 15		
Westbury	a			06 17	06 33		06 54	06 59		07 08	07 12	07 32	07 45	07 47	08 09		09 01	09 35	10 00	10 09	10 24	10 33	
	d	05 58	06 06	06 18		06 38	06 55	07 01	07 04	07 09	07 18	07 38	07 51	07 53	08 17	08 45	09 10	09 38	10 01	10 10	10 38		11 05
Trowbridge	d	06 04				06 44	07 02		07 10	07 15	07 24	07 44		08 00	08 23	08 51	09 16	09 44		10 16	10 44		
Bradford-on-Avon	d	06 10				06 50	07 08			07 21	07 30	07 50		08 06	08 29	08 57	09 22	09 50		10 22	10 50		
Avoncliff	d	06 13				06 53	07 11				07 33	07 53			08 32	09 00		09 53			10 53		
Freshford	d	06 16				06 56	07 13				07 36	07 56		08 10	08 35	09 03		09 56			10 56		
Bath Spa 7	a	06 26				07 06	07 24			07 33	07 46	08 06		08 21	08 45	09 13	09 35	10 06		10 34	11 06		
Melksham	d								07 20														
Chippenham	a								07 30														
Swindon	a								07 48														
London Paddington 15 ⊖	a		07 53	08 09				08 38					09 21						11 24				12 23
Oldfield Park	a	06 30				07 10	07 28			07 37	07 50	08 10		08 25	08 49	09 17		10 10			11 10		
Keynsham	a	06 37				07 18	07 35			07 44	07 58	08 18		08 32	08 56	09 25	09 44	10 18			11 18		
Bristol Temple Meads 10	a	06 46				07 27	07 46			07 52	08 06	08 29		08 41	09 05	09 35	09 52	10 28		10 48	11 28		
Filton Abbey Wood	a	07 01				07 42	08 01				08 21	08 48		09 01	09 21	09 48	10 03	10 48		11 01	11 48		
Severn Tunnel Jn.	a	07 14																					
Newport (South Wales)	a	07 25					08 27							09 25			10 26			11 26			
Cardiff Central 7	a	07 44					08 46							09 43			10 43			11 43			

A ⊘ to Westbury

For connections to Swansea please refer to Table 128. For connections to Exeter St Davids and Plymouth please refer to Table 135. For connections from Bournemouth please refer to Table 158

For Bus Connections for either to or from Yeovil Junction and Yeovil Pen Mill please see Table 123A

Table 123

Mondays to Fridays
from 17 September

Portsmouth and Weymouth - Bristol and South Wales

Network Diagram - see first Page of Table 123

		GW	SW	GW	GW	GW	GW	GW	GW	GW	SW	GW	GW	GW	GW	GW	GW	GW	GW	GW	GW	GW	GW
		◇	◇[1]	◇	◇		◇[1]	◇	◇	◇	◇[1]		◇	◇[1]		◇		◇[1]	◇[1]	[2]	◇	[2]	
				A														C					
		🛒		🛒	🛒		☕	🛒		🛒				✕☕		🛒		☕	☕	🛒		🛒	
Brighton [10]	d			08 59																			
Hove [2]	d			09 03																			
Shoreham-by-Sea	d			09 13																			
Worthing [4]	d			09 22																			
Barnham	d			09 38																			
Chichester [4]	d			09 47																			
Havant	d			09 59																			
Portsmouth Harbour ⛴	d	09 23			10 23			11 23		12 23						13 23				14 23		15 23	
Portsmouth & Southsea	d	09 27			10 27			11 27		12 27						13 27				14 27		15 27	
Fratton	d	09 31			10 31			11 31		12 31						13 31				14 31		15 31	
Cosham	d	09 39		10 05	10 39			11 39		12 39						13 39				14 39		15 39	
Fareham	a	09 46		10 14	10 46			11 46		12 46						13 46				14 46		15 46	
	d	09 47		10 15	10 47			11 47		12 47						13 47				14 47		15 47	
Southampton Central ⛴	d	10 10		10 42	11 10			12 10	12 27	13 10						14 10				15 10		16 10	
Romsey	d	10 21		10 54	11 21			12 21	12 39	13 21						14 21				15 21		16 21	
Salisbury	a	10 39		11 13	11 39			12 39	13 02	13 39						14 39				15 39		16 39	
	d	10 40	10 52	11 13	11 40			12 40	13 06	13 40	13 52					14 40				15 40		16 40	
Warminster	d	11 01	11 12	11 34	12 01			13 01	13 34	14 01	14 12					15 01	15 28			16 01		17 01	17 28
Dilton Marsh	d								13x38								15x32						17x32
Weymouth	d					11 10							13 10								15 08		
Upwey	d					11 15							13 15								15 13		
Dorchester West	d					11 23							13 23								15 21		
Maiden Newton	d					11 43							13 46								15 33		
Chetnole	d					11x50							13x53								15x42		
Yetminster	d					11x53							13x56								15x45		
Thornford	d					11x55							13x59								15x47		
Yeovil Pen Mill	d					12 05							14 08								15 56		
Castle Cary	a					12 19							14 22								16 09		
	d					12 23	12 45						14 22	14 44				15 51			16 10		
Bruton	d					12 29							14 28								16 16		
Frome	d					12 42							14 41		14 59				15 55		16 29		
Westbury	a	11 09	11 20	11 42	12 09	12 48	13 04	13 09	13 42	14 09	14 20		14 48	15 02	15 08	15 09	15 36		16 05	16 09	16 38	17 09	17 36
	d	11 10	11 21	11 43	12 10	12 52	13 05	13 10	13 44	14 10	14 21	14 38	14 51	15 03		15 10	15 38		16 08	16 10	16 38	17 10	17 38
Trowbridge	d	11 16	11 27	11 49	12 16	12 58		13 16	13 50	14 16	14 27	14 44	14 57			15 16	15 44			16 16	16 44	17 16	17 44
Bradford-on-Avon	d	11 22	11 33	11 55	12 22	13 04		13 22	13 56	14 22	14 33	14 50	15 03			15 22	15 50			16 22	16 50	17 22	17 50
Avoncliff	d			11 58		13 07			13 59			14 53	15 06				15 53				16 53		17 53
Freshford	d			12 01		13 10			14 02			14 56	15 09				15 56				16 56		17 56
Bath Spa [7]	a	11 34	11 46	12 11	12 34	13 20		13 34	14 12	14 34	14 46	15 06	15 19			15 34	16 06			16 34	17 06	17 34	18 06
Melksham	d																						
Chippenham	a																						
Swindon	a																						
London Paddington [15] ⊖	a						14 44							16 24				17 24	17 54				
Oldfield Park	a			12 15		13 24			14 16			15 10					16 10				17 10		18 10
Keynsham	a		11 54	12 22		13 32			14 24		14 54	15 18					16 18				17 18		18 18
Bristol Temple Meads [10]	a	11 48	12 05	12 31	12 48	13 41		13 48	14 35	14 48	15 05	15 28	15 34			15 48	16 29			16 48	17 29	17 48	18 28
Filton Abbey Wood	a	12 01		12 48	13 01			14 01	14 47	15 01			15 48			16 01	16 48			17 01	17 48	18 01	18 48
Severn Tunnel Jn.	a																			17 13		18 13	
Newport (South Wales)	a	12 25			13 26			14 26		15 25						16 25				17 25		18 25	
Cardiff Central [7]	a	12 43			13 43			14 43		15 43						16 43				17 43		18 43	

A 🛒 to Southampton Central

C The Torbay Express

For connections to Swansea please refer to Table 128. For connections to Exeter St Davids and Plymouth please refer to Table 135. For connections from Bournemouth please refer to Table 158

For Bus Connections for either to or from Yeovil Junction and Yeovil Pen Mill please see Table 123A

Table 123

Mondays to Fridays
from 17 September

Portsmouth and Weymouth - Bristol and South Wales

Network Diagram - see first Page of Table 123

		GW	GW	GW	GW	GW	GW	GW	GW	GW	GW	GW	GW	GW	GW FO	GW FX	GW	SW	GW	GW FO	GW FX	GW
		[2]			◇	◇	◇[1]	◇	◇	◇	◇	[1]		◇[1]	◇	◇		◇[1]		◇	◇	
		🛒			🛒		☕			🛒	🛒			☕								
Brighton [10]	d									16 59												
Hove [2]	d									17 03												
Shoreham-by-Sea	d									17 13												
Worthing [4]	d									17 22												
Barnham	d									17 39												
Chichester [4]	d									17 47												
Havant	d									17 58												
Portsmouth Harbour ⛴	d	16 23			17 23						18 23				19 23	19 23				20 23	20 23	
Portsmouth & Southsea	d	16 27			17 27						18 27				19 27	19 27				20 27	20 27	
Fratton	d	16 31			17 31						18 31				19 31	19 31				20 31	20 31	
Cosham	d	16 39			17 39					18 05	18 39				19 39	19 39						
Fareham	a	16 46			17 46					18 12	18 46				19 46	19 46				20 46	20 46	
	d	16 47			17 47					18 13	18 47				19 47	19 47				20 47	20 47	
Southampton Central ⛴	d	17 10			18 10					18 42	19 10				20 10	20 10				21 10	21 10	21 20
Romsey	d	17 21			18 21					18 54	19 21				20 21	20 21				21 21	21 21	21 31
Salisbury	a	17 39			18 39					19 12	19 39				20 39	20 39				21 39	21 39	21 51
	d	17 40			18 40					19 13	19 40				20 40	20 40		20 57		21 40	21 40	21 53
Warminster	d	18 01	18 18		19 01					19 32	20 01				21 01	21 01		21 17		22 01	22 01	22 15
Dilton Marsh	d		18x22							19x37												22x19
Weymouth	d					17 30													20 21			
Upwey	d					17 35													20 26			
Dorchester West	d					17 43													20 34			
Maiden Newton	d					17 54													20 44			
Chetnole	d					18x03													20x52			
Yetminster	d					18x06													20x56			
Thornford	d					18x08													20x58			
Yeovil Pen Mill	d					18 23													21 06			
Castle Cary	a					18 36													21 18			
	d					18 37	18 54							20 46					21 18			
Bruton	d					18 43													21 24			
Frome	d					19 06		←				20 15					21 02		21 37			
Westbury	a	18 09	18 28		19 09	19 17	19 12	19 17		19 40	20 09	20 26		21 04	21 08	21 08	21 12	21 25	21 46	22 09	22 09	22 26
	d	18 10		18 38	19 10	19 19	19 12	19 19	19 32	19 41	20 10		20 38	21 05	21 10	21 10		21 25	21 55	22 10	22 10	
Trowbridge	d	18 16		18 44	19 16	→		19 25	19 38	19 48	20 16		20 44		21 17	21 17		21 31	22 02	22 16	22 16	
Bradford-on-Avon	d	18 22		18 50	19 22			19 31		19 54	20 22		20 50		21 23	21 23		21 37	22 08	22 22	22 22	
Avoncliff	d			18 54				19 34		19 56			20 53						22 11			
Freshford	d			18 56				19 37		19 58			20 56						22 13			
Bath Spa [7]	a	18 34		19 06	19 34			19 47		20 12	20 34		21 06		21 34	21 34		21 50	22 24	22 34	22 34	
Melksham	d								19 48													
Chippenham	a								20 01													
Swindon	a								20 21													
London Paddington [15] ⊖	a						20 39							22 30								
Oldfield Park	a			19 10				19 51		20 14			21 10						22 28			
Keynsham	a			19 18				19 59		20 21			21 18					21 58	22 35			
Bristol Temple Meads [10]	a	18 48		19 29	19 48			20 08		20 30	20 48		21 28		21 48	21 48		22 06	22 43	22 50	22 48	
Filton Abbey Wood	a	19 01		19 48	20 01						21 01				22 01	22 01				23 01	23 01	
Severn Tunnel Jn.	a	19 13			20 16						21 13				22 17	22 17				23 16	23 16	
Newport (South Wales)	a	19 26			20 27						21 26				22 29	22 36				23 34	23 34	
Cardiff Central [7]	a	19 46			20 43						21 44				22 52	23 00				23 56	23 56	

For connections to Swansea please refer to Table 128. For connections to Exeter St Davids and Plymouth please refer to Table 135. For connections from Bournemouth please refer to Table 158

For Bus Connections for either to or from Yeovil Junction and Yeovil Pen Mill please see Table 123A

Table 123

Mondays to Fridays

from 17 September

Portsmouth and Weymouth - Bristol and South Wales

Network Diagram - see first Page of Table 123

		GW	GW
Brighton 10	d		
Hove 2	d		
Shoreham-by-Sea	d		
Worthing 4	d		
Barnham	d		
Chichester 4	d		
Havant	d		
Portsmouth Harbour ⛴	d		21 23
Portsmouth & Southsea	d		21 27
Fratton	d		21 31
Cosham	d		
Fareham	a		21 47
	d		21 48
Southampton Central ⛴	d		22 22
Romsey	d		22 34
Salisbury	a		22 58
	d		23 00
Warminster	d		23 20
Dilton Marsh	d		23x24
Weymouth	d		
Upwey	d		
Dorchester West	d		
Maiden Newton	d		
Chetnole	d		
Yetminster	d		
Thornford	d		
Yeovil Pen Mill	d		
Castle Cary	a		
	d		
Bruton	d		
Frome	d		
Westbury	a		23 31
	d	22 32	
Trowbridge	d	22 38	
Bradford-on-Avon	d	22 44	
Avoncliff	d	22 46	
Freshford	d	22 50	
Bath Spa 7	a	23 00	
Melksham	d		
Chippenham	a		
Swindon	a		
London Paddington 15 ⊖	a		
Oldfield Park	a	23 04	
Keynsham	a	23 12	
Bristol Temple Meads 10	a	23 23	
Filton Abbey Wood	a		
Severn Tunnel Jn.	a		
Newport (South Wales)	a		
Cardiff Central 7	a		

For connections to Swansea please refer to Table 128. For connections to Exeter St Davids and Plymouth please refer to Table 135. For connections from Bournemouth please refer to Table 158

For Bus Connections for either to or from Yeovil Junction and Yeovil Pen Mill please see Table 123A

Table 123

Saturdays

until 8 September

Portsmouth and Weymouth - Bristol and South Wales

Network Diagram - see first Page of Table 123

		GW	GW	GW	SW	GW	GW	GW	GW	GW		GW	GW	GW	GW	GW	GW	GW	GW	GW		SW	GW	GW	GW
					1		◇1 ⊡	◇	◇				◇ A ⫫	◇	◇1 ⊡	◇ A ⫫	◇		1 ⊡	◇ A ⫫		◇1	1 ⊡	◇	◇
Brighton 10	d																							09 00	
Hove 2	d																							09 04	
Shoreham-by-Sea	d																							09 13	
Worthing 4	d																							09 22	
Barnham	d																							09 41	
Chichester 4	d																							09 49	
Havant	d																							10 00	
Portsmouth Harbour ⛴	d							06 00					07 23			08 23				09 23					10 23
Portsmouth & Southsea	d							06 04					07 27			08 27				09 27					10 27
Fratton	d							06 08					07 31			08 31				09 31					10 31
Cosham	d							06 19					07 39			08 39				09 39				10 06	10 39
Fareham	a							06 27					07 46			08 46				09 46				10 15	10 46
	d							06 28					07 47			08 47				09 47				10 16	10 47
Southampton Central ⛴	d							06 53					08 10	08 27		09 10				10 10				10 42	11 10
Romsey	d							07 11					08 21	08 38		09 21				10 21				10 53	11 21
Salisbury	a							07 29					08 40	09 02		09 39				10 39				11 12	11 39
	d	06 03			06 40			07 30					08 40	09 03		09 40				10 40		10 52		11 13	11 40
Warminster	d	06 25			07 00	07 23		07 50					09 01	09 25		10 01		10 25		11 01		11 12		11 35	12 01
Dilton Marsh	d	06x29				07x27		07x54						09x29				10x29							
Weymouth	d								06 38								08 46								
Upwey	d								06 43								08 51								
Dorchester West	d								06 51								08 59								
Maiden Newton	d								07 03								09 11								
Chetnole	d								07x11								09x19								
Yetminster	d								07x14								09x22								
Thornford	d								07x16								09x24								
Yeovil Pen Mill	d								07 30								09 34								
Castle Cary	a								07 43								09 47								
	d						07 33		07 44						09 40		09 48						11 24		
Bruton	d								07 49								09 54								
Frome	d			06 49					08 02								10 07								
Westbury	a	06 33		06 58	07 08	07 31	07 51	07 59	08 11				09 09	09 35	09 58	10 09	10 16	10 33		11 09		11 20	11 42	11 43	12 09
	d		06 38		07 09	07 38	07 56	08 02	08 17	08 38		09 05	09 10	09 38	09 59	10 10	10 38		11 02	11 10		11 21	11 45	11 47	12 10
Trowbridge	d		06 45		07 15	07 44		08 08	08 23	08 44		09 11	09 16	09 44		10 16	10 44			11 16		11 27		11 53	12 16
Bradford-on-Avon	d		06 51		07 21	07 50		08 14	08 29	08 50			09 22	09 50		10 22	10 50			11 22		11 33		11 59	12 22
Avoncliff	d		06 53			07 53			08 32	08 53				09 53			10 53							12 02	
Freshford	d		06 56			07 56			08 35	08 56				09 56			10 56							12 05	
Bath Spa 7	a		07 06		07 33	08 06		08 30	08 45	09 06			09 34	10 06		10 34	11 06			11 34		11 46		12 15	12 34
Melksham	d											09 20													
Chippenham	a											09 30													
Swindon	a											09 49													
London Paddington 15 ⊖	a						09 21								11 24				12 23				13 09		
Oldfield Park	a		07 11		07 37	08 11			08 49	09 11				10 11			11 10							12 19	
Keynsham	a		07 18		07 44	08 18			08 56	09 18				10 18			11 18					11 54		12 26	
Bristol Temple Meads 10	a		07 29		07 52	08 29		08 44	09 05	09 27			09 48	10 29		10 48	11 29			11 48		12 05		12 35	12 48
Filton Abbey Wood	a		07 48			08 48		09 01		09 48			10 01	10 48		11 01	11 48			12 01				12 48	13 01
Severn Tunnel Jn.	a																								
Newport (South Wales)	a							09 25					10 24			11 24				12 24					13 25
Cardiff Central 7	a							09 43					10 43			11 43				12 43					13 43

A ⫫ to Bristol Temple Meads

For connections to Swansea please refer to Table 128. For connections to Exeter St Davids and Plymouth please refer to Table 135. For connections from Bournemouth please refer to Table 158

For Bus Connections for either to or from Yeovil Junction and Yeovil Pen Mill please see Table 123A

Table 123

Saturdays
until 8 September

Portsmouth and Weymouth - Bristol and South Wales

Network Diagram - see first Page of Table 123

		GW	GW	GW	GW	SW	GW	GW	GW	GW	GW	GW	GW	GW	GW	GW	GW	GW	GW	GW	GW	GW	GW
		◇	◇	◇	◇	◇■	◇			◇	◇■ ☕		◇	■ ■	◇■ ☕		◇	◇	■	◇	◇	◇	◇■ ☕
Brighton 10	d																						
Hove 2	d																						
Shoreham-by-Sea	d																						
Worthing 4	d																						
Barnham	d																						
Chichester 4	d																						
Havant	d																						
Portsmouth Harbour ⛴	d		11 23		12 23					13 23			14 23				15 23		16 23		17 23		
Portsmouth & Southsea	d		11 27		12 27					13 27			14 27				15 27		16 27		17 27		
Fratton	d		11 31		12 31					13 31			14 31				15 31		16 31		17 31		
Cosham	d		11 39		12 39					13 39			14 39				15 39		16 39		17 39		
Fareham	a		11 46		12 46					13 46			14 46				15 46		16 46		17 46		
	d		11 47		12 47					13 47			14 47				15 47		16 47		17 47		
Southampton Central ⛴	d		12 10	12 27	13 10					14 10			15 10				16 10		17 10		18 10		
Romsey	d		12 21	12 38	13 21					14 21			15 21				16 21		17 21		18 21		
Salisbury	a		12 39	13 02	13 39					14 39			15 39				16 39		17 39		18 39		
	d		12 40	13 04	13 40	13 52				14 40			15 40				16 40		17 40		18 40		
Warminster	d		13 01	13 26	14 01	14 12				15 01		15 28	16 01			16 28	17 01		18 01		19 01		
Dilton Marsh	d			13x30								15x33				16x33							
Weymouth	d	11 10					13 10											16 08		16 55		17 28	
Upwey	d	11 15					13 15											16 13				17 33	
Dorchester West	d	11 26					13 23											16 23		17 08		17 41	
Maiden Newton	d	11 43					13 43											16 42		17 20		17 52	
Chetnole	d	11x50					13x51											16 51				18x01	
Yetminster	d	11x53					13x54											16 54				18x04	
Thornford	d	11x56					13x56											16 56				18x06	
Yeovil Pen Mill	d	12 05					14 06											17 05		17 39		18 18	
Castle Cary	a	12 19					14 19											17 18		17 53		18 31	
	d	12 22					14 20				15 08			15 50	16 19			17 19		17 56		18 32	18 53
Bruton	d	12 27					14 26											17 25		18 02		18 38	
Frome	d	12 39					14 39		14 59									17 38		18 15		19 05	
Westbury	a	12 48	13 09	13 34	14 09	14 20	14 48		15 08	15 09	15 26	15 36	16 09		16 36	16 36	17 09	17 47	18 09	18 24	19 09	19 13	19 11
	d	12 49	13 10	13 38	14 10	14 21	14 48	15 06		15 10	15 28	15 38	16 10		16 38	16 38	17 10	17 48	18 10	18 38	19 10	19 17	19 12
Trowbridge	d	12 56	13 16	13 44	14 16	14 27	14 55	15 12		15 16		15 44	16 16			16 44	17 16	17 54	18 16	18 44	19 16	→	
Bradford-on-Avon	d	13 02	13 22	13 50	14 22	14 33	15 01			15 22		15 50	16 22			16 50	17 22	18 00	18 22	18 50	19 22		
Avoncliff	d	13 05		13 53			15 04					15 53				16 53		18 03					
Freshford	d	13 07		13 56			15 06					15 56				16 56		18 06					
Bath Spa 7	a	13 18	13 34	14 06	14 34	14 46	15 17			15 35		16 06	16 34			17 06	17 34	18 16	18 34	19 06	19 34		
Melksham	d							15 21															
Chippenham	a							15 29															
Swindon	a							15 50															
London Paddington 15 ⊖	a										17 02			17 21	18 08								20 37
Oldfield Park	a	13 22		14 11			15 21					16 11				17 11		18 20		19 10			
Keynsham	a	13 28		14 18		14 54	15 28					16 18				17 18		18 27		19 18			
Bristol Temple Meads 10	a	13 37	13 48	14 28	14 48	15 05	15 36			15 49		16 29	16 48			17 28	17 48	18 36	18 48	19 26	19 48		
Filton Abbey Wood	a	13 48	14 01	14 48	15 01		15 48			16 01		16 48	17 01			17 48	18 01	18 48	19 01		20 01		
Severn Tunnel Jn.	a												17 14				18 13						
Newport (South Wales)	a		14 24		15 25					16 24			17 26				18 25		19 26		20 25		
Cardiff Central 7	a		14 43		15 43					16 43			17 43				18 43		19 43		20 43		

For connections to Swansea please refer to Table 128. For connections to Exeter St Davids and Plymouth please refer to Table 135. For connections from Bournemouth please refer to Table 158

For Bus Connections for either to or from Yeovil Junction and Yeovil Pen Mill please see Table 123A

Table 123

Saturdays
until 8 September

Portsmouth and Weymouth - Bristol and South Wales

Network Diagram - see first Page of Table 123

		GW	GW	GW	GW	GW	GW	GW	SW	GW	GW	GW
		◇	◇	◇■ ☕	◇			◇	◇■		◇	
Brighton 10	d		17 00									
Hove 2	d		17 04									
Shoreham-by-Sea	d		17 13									
Worthing 4	d		17 22									
Barnham	d		17 38									
Chichester 4	d		17 46									
Havant	d		18 00									
Portsmouth Harbour ⛴	d				18 23			19 23			20 23	
Portsmouth & Southsea	d				18 27			19 27			20 27	
Fratton	d				18 31			19 31			20 31	
Cosham	d		18 06		18 39			19 39				
Fareham	a		18 14		18 46			19 46			20 45	
	d		18 15		18 47			19 47			20 47	
Southampton Central ⛴	d		18 45		19 10			20 10			21 10	21 27
Romsey	d		18 56		19 21			20 21			21 21	21 38
Salisbury	a		19 14		19 39			20 39			21 40	22 02
	d		19 15		19 40			20 40	20 57		21 40	22 04
Warminster	d		19 36		20 01			21 01	21 17		22 01	22 26
Dilton Marsh	d		19x41									22x30
Weymouth	d									20 21		
Upwey	d									20 26		
Dorchester West	d									20 34		
Maiden Newton	d									20 45		
Chetnole	d									20x54		
Yetminster	d									20x57		
Thornford	d									20x59		
Yeovil Pen Mill	d									21 09		
Castle Cary	a									21 22		
	d			19 47						21 23		
Bruton	d									21 29		
Frome	d	←					20 53			21 42		
Westbury	a	19 13	19 45	20 05	20 09		21 02	21 09	21 25	21 51	22 10	22 34
	d	19 17	19 46	20 06	20 10	20 38		21 10	21 25	21 55	22 10	22 38
Trowbridge	d	19 23	19 52		20 16	20 44		21 16	21 31	22 02	22 16	22 44
Bradford-on-Avon	d	19 29	19 58		20 22	20 50		21 22	21 37	22 08	22 22	22 50
Avoncliff	d	19 32	20 01			20 53				22 11		22 53
Freshford	d	19 35	20 04			20 56				22 13		22 56
Bath Spa 7	a	19 45	20 14		20 34	21 07		21 37	21 50	22 24	22 34	23 07
Melksham	d											
Chippenham	a											
Swindon	a											
London Paddington 15 ⊖	a			21 32								
Oldfield Park	a	19 49	20 18			21 11				22 28		23 11
Keynsham	a	19 57	20 25			21 18			21 58	22 35		23 18
Bristol Temple Meads 10	a	20 05	20 33		20 48	21 29		21 51	22 06	22 44	22 50	23 31
Filton Abbey Wood	a				21 01			22 01			23 01	
Severn Tunnel Jn.	a							22 17			23 17	
Newport (South Wales)	a				21 25			22 38			23 35	
Cardiff Central 7	a				21 43			22 58			23 55	

For connections to Swansea please refer to Table 128. For connections to Exeter St Davids and Plymouth please refer to Table 135. For connections from Bournemouth please refer to Table 158

For Bus Connections for either to or from Yeovil Junction and Yeovil Pen Mill please see Table 123A

Table 123

Saturdays
from 15 September

Portsmouth and Weymouth - Bristol and South Wales

Network Diagram - see first Page of Table 123

		GW	GW	GW	SW	GW	GW	GW	GW	GW	GW	GW	GW	GW	GW	GW	GW	GW	GW	SW	GW	GW	GW
					■1		◇■1 ⌸	◇	◇			◇ A ⌶	◇	◇■1 ⌸	◇ A ⌶	◇		■ ■1 ⌸	◇ A ⌶	◇■1	◇	◇	◇
Brighton ■10	d																				09 00		
Hove ■2	d																				09 04		
Shoreham-by-Sea	d																				09 13		
Worthing ■4	d																				09 22		
Barnham	d																				09 41		
Chichester ■4	d																				09 49		
Havant	d																				10 00		
Portsmouth Harbour ⛴	d							06 00				07 23			08 23				09 23			10 23	
Portsmouth & Southsea	d							06 04				07 27			08 27				09 27			10 27	
Fratton	d							06 08				07 31			08 31				09 31			10 31	
Cosham	d							06 19				07 39			08 39				09 39		10 06	10 39	
Fareham	a							06 27				07 46			08 46				09 46		10 15	10 46	
	d							06 28				07 47			08 47				09 47		10 16	10 47	
Southampton Central ⛴	d							06 53				08 10	08 27		09 10				10 10		10 42	11 10	
Romsey	d							07 11				08 21	08 38		09 21				10 21		10 53	11 21	
Salisbury	a							07 29				08 40	09 02		09 39				10 39		11 12	11 39	
	d	06 03			06 40			07 30				08 40	09 03		09 40				10 40	10 52	11 13	11 40	
Warminster	d	06 25			07 00	07 23		07 50				09 01	09 25		10 01		10 25		11 01	11 12	11 35	12 01	
Dilton Marsh	d	06x29				07x27		07x54					09x29				10x29						
Weymouth	d								06 38							08 46							11 10
Upwey	d								06 43							08 51							11 15
Dorchester West	d								06 51							08 59							11 26
Maiden Newton	d								07 03							09 11							11 43
Chetnole	d								07x11							09x19							11x50
Yetminster	d								07x14							09x22							11x53
Thornford	d								07x16							09x24							11x56
Yeovil Pen Mill	d								07 30							09 34							12 05
Castle Cary	a								07 43							09 47							12 19
	d						07 33		07 44					09 40		09 48							12 22
Bruton	d								07 49							09 54							12 27
Frome	d			06 49					08 02							10 07							12 39
Westbury	a	06 33		06 58	07 08	07 31	07 51	07 59	08 11			09 09	09 35	09 58	10 09	10 16	10 33		11 09	11 20	11 43	12 09	12 48
	d		06 38		07 09	07 38	07 56	08 02	08 17	08 38	09 05	09 10	09 38	09 59	10 10	10 38		11 02	11 10	11 21	11 47	12 10	12 49
Trowbridge	d		06 45		07 15	07 44		08 08	08 23	08 44	09 11	09 16	09 44		10 16	10 44			11 16	11 27	11 53	12 16	12 56
Bradford-on-Avon	d		06 51		07 21	07 50		08 14	08 29	08 50		09 22	09 50		10 22	10 50			11 22	11 33	11 59	12 22	13 02
Avoncliff	d		06 53			07 53			08 32	08 53			09 53			10 53					12 02		13 05
Freshford	d		06 56			07 56			08 35	08 56			09 56			10 56					12 05		13 07
Bath Spa ■7	a		07 06		07 33	08 06		08 30	08 45	09 06		09 34	10 06		10 34	11 06			11 34	11 46	12 15	12 34	13 18
Melksham	d										09 20												
Chippenham	a										09 30												
Swindon	a										09 49												
London Paddington ■15 ⊖	a						09 21							11 24				12 23					
Oldfield Park	a		07 11		07 37	08 11			08 49	09 11			10 11			11 10					12 19		13 22
Keynsham	a		07 18		07 44	08 18			08 56	09 18			10 18			11 18				11 54	12 26		13 28
Bristol Temple Meads ■10	a		07 29		07 52	08 29		08 44	09 05	09 27		09 48	10 29		10 48	11 29			11 48	12 05	12 35	12 48	13 37
Filton Abbey Wood	a		07 48			08 48		09 01		09 48		10 01	10 48		11 01	11 48			12 01		12 48	13 01	13 48
Severn Tunnel Jn.	a																						
Newport (South Wales)	a							09 25				10 24			11 24				12 24			13 25	
Cardiff Central ■7	a							09 43				10 43			11 43				12 43			13 43	

A ⌶ to Bristol Temple Meads

For connections to Swansea please refer to Table 128. For connections to Exeter St Davids and Plymouth please refer to Table 135. For connections from Bournemouth please refer to Table 158

For Bus Connections for either to or from Yeovil Junction and Yeovil Pen Mill please see Table 123A

Table 123

Saturdays
from 15 September

Portsmouth and Weymouth - Bristol and South Wales

Network Diagram - see first Page of Table 123

		GW	GW	GW	GW	SW	GW	GW	GW	GW	GW	GW	GW	GW	GW	GW	GW	GW	GW	GW	GW	GW	GW
		◇■1 ⌸	◇	◇	◇	◇■1	◇	◇■1 A ⊘			◇		◇■1	◇■1 ⌸	◇	◇	◇		■		◇	◇	◇■1 ⌸
Brighton ■10	d																						
Hove ■2	d																						
Shoreham-by-Sea	d																						
Worthing ■4	d																						
Barnham	d																						
Chichester ■4	d																						
Havant	d																						
Portsmouth Harbour ⛴	d		11 23		12 23						13 23				14 23		15 23		16 23		17 23		
Portsmouth & Southsea	d		11 27		12 27						13 27				14 27		15 27		16 27		17 27		
Fratton	d		11 31		12 31						13 31				14 31		15 31		16 31		17 31		
Cosham	d		11 39		12 39						13 39				14 39		15 39		16 39		17 39		
Fareham	a		11 46		12 46						13 46				14 46		15 46		16 46		17 46		
	d		11 47		12 47						13 47				14 47		15 47		16 47		17 47		
Southampton Central ⛴	d		12 10	12 27	13 10						14 10				15 10		16 10		17 10		18 10		
Romsey	d		12 21	12 38	13 21						14 21				15 21		16 21		17 21		18 21		
Salisbury	a		12 39	13 02	13 39						14 39				15 39		16 39		17 39		18 39		
	d		12 40	13 04	13 40	13 52					14 40				15 40		16 40		17 40		18 40		
Warminster	d		13 01	13 26	14 01	14 12					15 01	15 28			16 01		17 01	17 28	18 01		19 01		
Dilton Marsh	d			13x30								15x33						17 32					
Weymouth	d						13 10									15 08						17 28	
Upwey	d						13 15									15 13						17 33	
Dorchester West	d						13 23									15 21						17 41	
Maiden Newton	d						13 43									15 33						17 52	
Chetnole	d						13x51									15x42						18x01	
Yetminster	d						13x54									15x45						18x04	
Thornford	d						13x56									15x47						18x06	
Yeovil Pen Mill	d						14 06									15 56						18 18	
Castle Cary	a						14 19									16 09						18 31	
	d	12 45					14 20	14 44					15 49			16 10						18 32	18 53
Bruton	d						14 26									16 16						18 38	
Frome	d						14 39			14 59				15 55		16 29						19 05	
Westbury	a	13 03	13 09	13 34	14 09	14 20	14 48	15 02		15 08	15 09	15 36		16 05	16 09	16 38	17 09	17 36	18 09		19 09	19 13	19 11
	d	13 05	13 10	13 38	14 10	14 21	14 48	15 03	15 06		15 10	15 38		16 07	16 10	16 38	17 10	17 38	18 10	18 38	19 10	19 17	19 12
Trowbridge	d		13 16	13 44	14 16	14 27	14 55		15 12		15 16	15 44			16 16	16 44	17 16	17 44	18 16	18 44	19 16	→	
Bradford-on-Avon	d		13 22	13 50	14 22	14 33	15 01				15 22	15 50			16 22	16 50	17 22	17 50	18 22	18 50	19 22		
Avoncliff	d			13 53			15 04					15 53				16 53		17 53		18 53			
Freshford	d			13 56			15 06					15 56				16 56		17 56		18 56			
Bath Spa ■7	a		13 34	14 06	14 34	14 46	15 17				15 35	16 06			16 34	17 06	17 34	18 06	18 34	19 07	19 34		
Melksham	d								15 21														
Chippenham	a								15 29														
Swindon	a								15 50														
London Paddington ■15 ⊖	a	14 45						16 23					17 21	17 51									20 37
Oldfield Park	a			14 11			15 21					16 11				17 11		18 10		19 11			
Keynsham	a			14 18		14 54	15 28					16 18				17 18		18 18		19 18			
Bristol Temple Meads ■10	a		13 48	14 28	14 48	15 05	15 36				15 49	16 29			16 48	17 29	17 48	18 29	18 48	19 29	19 48		
Filton Abbey Wood	a		14 01	14 48	15 01		15 48				16 01	16 48			17 01	17 48	18 01	18 48	19 01	19 48	20 01		
Severn Tunnel Jn.	a														17 14		18 13						
Newport (South Wales)	a		14 24		15 25						16 24				17 26		18 25		19 26		20 25		
Cardiff Central ■7	a		14 43		15 43						16 43				17 43		18 43		19 43		20 43		

A ⊘ to Westbury

For connections to Swansea please refer to Table 128. For connections to Exeter St Davids and Plymouth please refer to Table 135. For connections from Bournemouth please refer to Table 158

For Bus Connections for either to or from Yeovil Junction and Yeovil Pen Mill please see Table 123A

Portsmouth and Weymouth - Bristol and South Wales

Saturdays from 15 September

Network Diagram - see first Page of Table 123

		GW		GW	GW	GW	GW	GW	GW	SW	GW	GW		GW
		◇		◇	◇■ ☕	◇			◇	◇■		◇		
Brighton 10	d			17 00										
Hove 2	d			17 04										
Shoreham-by-Sea	d			17 13										
Worthing 4	d			17 22										
Barnham	d			17 38										
Chichester 4	d			17 46										
Havant	d			18 00										
Portsmouth Harbour ⛴	d					18 23			19 23			20 23		
Portsmouth & Southsea	d					18 27			19 27			20 27		
Fratton	d					18 31			19 31			20 31		
Cosham	d			18 06		18 39			19 39					
Fareham	a			18 14		18 46			19 46			20 45		
	d			18 15		18 47			19 47			20 47		
Southampton Central ⛴	d			18 45		19 10			20 10			21 10		21 27
Romsey	d			18 56		19 21			20 21			21 21		21 38
Salisbury	a			19 14		19 39			20 39			21 40		22 02
	d			19 15		19 40			20 40	20 57		21 40		22 04
Warminster	d			19 36		20 01			21 01	21 17		22 01		22 26
Dilton Marsh	d			19x41										22x30
Weymouth	d										20 21			
Upwey	d										20 26			
Dorchester West	d										20 34			
Maiden Newton	d										20 45			
Chetnole	d										20x54			
Yetminster	d										20x57			
Thornford	d										20x59			
Yeovil Pen Mill	d										21 09			
Castle Cary	a										21 22			
	d				19 47						21 23			
Bruton	d										21 29			
Frome	d	⟵						20 53			21 42			
Westbury	a	19 13		19 45	20 05	20 09		21 02	21 09	21 25	21 51	22 10		22 34
	d	19 17		19 46	20 06	20 10	20 38		21 10	21 25	21 55	22 10		22 38
Trowbridge	d	19 23		19 52		20 16	20 44		21 16	21 31	22 02	22 16		22 44
Bradford-on-Avon	d	19 29		19 58		20 22	20 50		21 22	21 37	22 08	22 22		22 50
Avoncliff	d	19 32		20 01			20 53				22 11			22 53
Freshford	d	19 35		20 04			20 56				22 13			22 56
Bath Spa 7	a	19 45		20 14		20 34	21 07		21 37	21 50	22 24	22 34		23 07
Melksham	d													
Chippenham	a													
Swindon	a													
London Paddington 15 ⊖	a				21 32									
Oldfield Park	a	19 49		20 18			21 11				22 28			23 11
Keynsham	a	19 57		20 25			21 18			21 58	22 35			23 18
Bristol Temple Meads 10	a	20 05		20 33		20 48	21 29		21 51	22 06	22 44	22 50		23 31
Filton Abbey Wood	a					21 01			22 01			23 01		
Severn Tunnel Jn.	a								22 17			23 17		
Newport (South Wales)	a					21 25			22 38			23 35		
Cardiff Central 7	a					21 43			22 58			23 55		

For connections to Swansea please refer to Table 128. For connections to Exeter St Davids and Plymouth please refer to Table 135. For connections from Bournemouth please refer to Table 158

For Bus Connections for either to or from Yeovil Junction and Yeovil Pen Mill please see Table 123A

Portsmouth and Weymouth - Bristol and South Wales

Sundays until 24 June

Network Diagram - see first Page of Table 123

		GW	GW	GW	GW	GW	GW	GW	GW	GW		GW	SW	GW	GW	GW	GW	GW	GW	GW		GW	GW	GW	GW
		◇■ ☕		◇■ ☕	■		◇	◇■ ☕	◇	◇■ ☕		◇	◇■	◇	◇	◇■ ☕	◇	■		◇		◇■ ☕	◇	◇	◇
Brighton 10	d											11 10												15 46	
Hove 2	d											11 14												15 50	
Shoreham-by-Sea	d											11 20												15 56	
Worthing 4	d											11 29												16 08	
Barnham	d											11 46												16 25	
Chichester 4	d											11 54												16 34	
Havant	d											12 10												16 48	
Portsmouth Harbour ⛴	d				09 08				11 08					13 08			14 08	15 08					16 08		17 08
Portsmouth & Southsea	d				09 12				11 12					13 12			14 12	15 12					16 12		17 12
Fratton	d				09 16				11 16					13 16			14 16	15 16					16 16		17 16
Cosham	d				09 23				11 23			12 23		13 23			14 23	15 23					16 23	16 55	17 23
Fareham	a				09 31				11 31			12 31		13 31			14 31	15 31					16 31	17 02	17 31
	d				09 32				11 32			12 32		13 32			14 32	15 32					16 32	17 03	17 32
Southampton Central ⛴	d				09 54				11 54			12 54		13 54			14 54	15 54					16 54	17 26	17 54
Romsey	d				10 06				12 06			13 06		14 06			15 06	16 06					17 06	17 39	18 06
Salisbury	a				10 24				12 24			13 24		14 24			15 24	16 24					17 24	18 00	18 24
	d				10 29				12 27			13 26	13 55	14 27			15 27	16 27					17 27	18 01	18 27
Warminster	d				10 50				12 48			13 46	14 15	14 48			15 48	16 48					17 48	18 21	18 48
Dilton Marsh	d				10x55									14x53			15x53	16x53						18x26	
Weymouth	d						11 14								14 15					16 10					
Upwey	d						11 19								14 20					16 15					
Dorchester West	d						11 28								14 28					16 23					
Maiden Newton	d						11 40								14 40					16 35					
Chetnole	d						11x48								14x48					16x43					
Yetminster	d						11x51								14x51					16x46					
Thornford	d						11x53								14x53					16x48					
Yeovil Pen Mill	d						12 03								15 04					16 58					
Castle Cary	a						12 15								15 16					17 10					
	d	09 21					12 17	12 34							15 18	15 34				17 13		17 31			
Bruton	d						12 22								15 24					17 18					
Frome	d		09 25				12 35								15 37					17 31					
Westbury	a	09 38	09 33		10 58		12 44	12 52	12 54			13 55	14 23	14 56	15 46	15 51	15 56	16 56		17 40		17 48	17 57	18 30	18 55
	d	09 41	09 45	10 51	11 00	11 50		12 53	12 56	13 54		13 58	14 24	15 02	15 47	15 52	15 59	17 00	17 10	17 41		17 51	18 02	18 32	19 01
Trowbridge	d		09 51		11 06	11 56			13 03			14 04	14 30	15 08	15 53		16 05	17 06	17 16	17 48			18 08	18 38	19 07
Bradford-on-Avon	d		09 57		11 12	12 02			13 09			14 10	14 36	15 14	15 59		16 11	17 12		17 54			18 14	18 44	19 13
Avoncliff	d		10 00			12 05						14 13			16 02		16 14			17 57				18 47	
Freshford	d		10 02			12 07						14 16			16 05		16 17			17 59				18 50	
Bath Spa 7	a		10 15		11 25	12 19			13 23			14 26	14 49	15 27	16 16		16 29	17 25		18 10			18 27	19 00	19 26
Melksham	d																		17 25						
Chippenham	a																		17 35						
Swindon	a	10 18																	17 53			18 26			
London Paddington 15 ⊖	a	11 29		12 29				14 33		15 29						17 32						19 31			
Oldfield Park	a		10 19		11 28	12 23			13 26			14 29			16 19			17 28		18 13				19 04	
Keynsham	a		10 26		11 35	12 30			13 33			14 37	14 57		16 27			17 35		18 21				19 11	
Bristol Temple Meads 10	a		10 33		11 44	12 38			13 42			14 46	15 05	15 40	16 35		16 42	17 44		18 33			18 40	19 20	19 39
Filton Abbey Wood	a				11 55				13 55			14 57		15 55			16 55	17 55					18 55		19 55
Severn Tunnel Jn.	a				12 10				14 07			15 09		16 07			17 10	18 07					19 07		20 10
Newport (South Wales)	a				12 29				14 27			15 28		16 26			17 29	18 26					19 26		20 28
Cardiff Central 7	a				12 44				14 51			15 43		16 44			17 46	18 44					19 42		20 46

For connections to Swansea please refer to Table 128. For connections to Exeter St Davids and Plymouth please refer to Table 135. For connections from Bournemouth please refer to Table 158

For Bus Connections for either to or from Yeovil Junction and Yeovil Pen Mill please see Table 123A

Table 123

Sundays until 24 June

Portsmouth and Weymouth - Bristol and South Wales

Network Diagram - see first Page of Table 123

		GW ◇	GW	GW ◇1	GW ◇	SW ◇1	GW ◇	GW ◇	GW	GW ◇1	GW	GW ◇	GW
Brighton 10	d						17 46						
Hove 2	d						17 50						
Shoreham-by-Sea	d						17 56						
Worthing 4	d						18 08						
Barnham	d						18 25						
Chichester 4	d						18 34						
Havant	d						18 48						
Portsmouth Harbour ⛴	d				18 08			19 08				20 08	22 03
Portsmouth & Southsea	d				18 12			19 12				20 12	22 12
Fratton	d				18 16			19 16				20 16	22 16
Cosham	d				18 23		18 55	19 23					
Fareham	a				18 31		19 02	19 31				20 31	22 31
	d				18 32		19 03	19 32				20 32	22 32
Southampton Central ⛴	d				18 54		19 30	19 54				20 54	22 57
Romsey	d				19 06		19 42	20 06				21 06	23 09
Salisbury	a				19 24		20 00	20 24				21 24	23 27
	d				19 25	19 55	20 03	20 27				21 27	23 28
Warminster	d				19 48	20 15	20 23	20 48				21 48	23 48
Dilton Marsh	d						20x28					21x53	23x53
Weymouth	d	17 56							20 09				
Upwey	d	18 01							20 14				
Dorchester West	d	18 09							20 22				
Maiden Newton	d	18 21							20 34				
Chetnole	d	18x29							20x42				
Yetminster	d	18x32							20x45				
Thornford	d	18x34							20x47				
Yeovil Pen Mill	d	18 44							20 57				
Castle Cary	a	18 56							21 09				
	d	18 59		19 35					21 10	21 19			
Bruton	d	19 05							21 16				
Frome	d	19 18							21 34		←		
Westbury	a	19 27		19 53	19 55	20 23	20 32	20 56	21 43	21 39	21 43	21 56	23 57
	d	19 30	19 35	19 54	20 01	20 23	20 36	21 02	21 45	21 40	21 45	22 00	
Trowbridge	d	19 36	19 42		20 07	20 29	20 42	21 08	→		21 51	22 06	
Bradford-on-Avon	d	19 42			20 13	20 35	20 48	21 14			21 57	22 12	
Avoncliff	d	19 45					20 51				22 00		
Freshford	d	19 48					20 54				22 03		
Bath Spa 7	a	19 59			20 26	20 48	21 10	21 27			22 14	22 25	
Melksham	d		19 53										
Chippenham	a		20 03										
Swindon	a		20 21	20 31						22 15			
London Paddington 15 ⊖	a			21 43						23 28			
Oldfield Park	a	20 02					21 13				22 17		
Keynsham	a	20 10				20 56	21 21				22 25		
Bristol Temple Meads 10	a	20 18			20 39	21 04	21 30	21 40			22 33	22 38	
Filton Abbey Wood	a				20 55			21 55				22 55	
Severn Tunnel Jn.	a				21 07			22 14				23 08	
Newport (South Wales)	a				21 26			22 31				23 26	
Cardiff Central 7	a				21 42			22 53				23 47	

For connections to Swansea please refer to Table 128. For connections to Exeter St Davids and Plymouth please refer to Table 135. For connections from Bournemouth please refer to Table 158

For Bus Connections for either to or from Yeovil Junction and Yeovil Pen Mill please see Table 123A

Table 123

Sundays 1 July to 9 September

Portsmouth and Weymouth - Bristol and South Wales

Network Diagram - see first Page of Table 123

		GW ◇1	GW	GW ◇1	GW ■	GW	GW ◇	GW ◇1	GW ◇	GW ◇
Brighton 10	d									11 10
Hove 2	d									11 14
Shoreham-by-Sea	d									11 20
Worthing 4	d									11 29
Barnham	d									11 46
Chichester 4	d									11 54
Havant	d									12 10
Portsmouth Harbour ⛴	d				09 08				11 08	
Portsmouth & Southsea	d				09 12				11 12	
Fratton	d				09 16				11 16	
Cosham	d				09 23				11 23	12 23
Fareham	a				09 31				11 31	12 31
	d				09 32				11 32	12 32
Southampton Central ⛴	d				09 54				11 54	12 54
Romsey	d				10 06				12 06	13 06
Salisbury	a				10 24				12 24	13 24
	d				10 29				12 27	13 26
Warminster	d				10 50				12 48	13 46
Dilton Marsh	d				10x55					
Weymouth	d						11 14			
Upwey	d						11 19			
Dorchester West	d						11 28			
Maiden Newton	d						11 40			
Chetnole	d						11x48			
Yetminster	d						11x51			
Thornford	d						11x53			
Yeovil Pen Mill	d						12 03			
Castle Cary	a						12 15			
	d	09 34					12 17	12 34		
Bruton	d						12 22			
Frome	d		09 39				12 35			
Westbury	a	09 51	09 48		10 58		12 44	12 52	12 54	13 55
	d	09 54	09 58	10 51	11 00	11 50		12 53	12 56	13 56
Trowbridge	d		10 04		11 06	11 56			13 02	14 02
Bradford-on-Avon	d		10 10		11 12	12 02			13 08	14 08
Avoncliff	d		10 13			12 05				14 11
Freshford	d		10 15			12 07				14 14
Bath Spa 7	a		10 26		11 25	12 19			13 22	14 24
Melksham	d									
Chippenham	a									
Swindon	a									
London Paddington 15 ⊖	a	11 21		12 17				14 21		
Oldfield Park	a		10 30		11 28	12 23			13 25	14 27
Keynsham	a		10 37		11 35	12 30			13 32	14 35
Bristol Temple Meads 10	a		10 45		11 44	12 38			13 41	14 44
Filton Abbey Wood	a				11 55				13 55	14 55
Severn Tunnel Jn.	a				12 10				14 07	15 07
Newport (South Wales)	a				12 29				14 27	15 26
Cardiff Central 7	a				12 44				14 51	15 41

		GW ◇1	SW ◇1	GW ◇	GW ◇	GW ◇1	GW ◇	GW ■	GW	GW ◇	GW ◇1	GW ◇	GW ◇	GW ◇
Brighton 10	d												15 46	
Hove 2	d												15 50	
Shoreham-by-Sea	d												15 56	
Worthing 4	d												16 08	
Barnham	d												16 25	
Chichester 4	d												16 34	
Havant	d												16 48	
Portsmouth Harbour ⛴	d			13 08			14 08	15 08				16 08		17 08
Portsmouth & Southsea	d			13 12			14 12	15 12				16 12		17 12
Fratton	d			13 16			14 16	15 16				16 16		17 16
Cosham	d			13 23			14 23	15 23				16 23	16 55	17 23
Fareham	a			13 31			14 31	15 31				16 31	17 02	17 31
	d			13 32			14 32	15 32				16 32	17 03	17 32
Southampton Central ⛴	d			13 54			14 54	15 54				16 54	17 26	17 54
Romsey	d			14 06			15 06	16 06				17 06	17 39	18 06
Salisbury	a			14 24			15 24	16 24				17 24	18 00	18 24
	d		13 55	14 27			15 27	16 27				17 27	18 01	18 27
Warminster	d		14 15	14 48			15 48	16 48				17 48	18 21	18 48
Dilton Marsh	d			14x53			15x53	16x53					18x26	
Weymouth	d				14 15					16 10				
Upwey	d				14 20					16 15				
Dorchester West	d				14 28					16 23				
Maiden Newton	d				14 40					16 35				
Chetnole	d				14x48					16x43				
Yetminster	d				14x51					16x46				
Thornford	d				14x53					16x48				
Yeovil Pen Mill	d				15 04					16 58				
Castle Cary	a				15 16					17 10				
	d				15 18	15 34				17 13	17 37			
Bruton	d				15 24					17 18				
Frome	d				15 37					17 31				
Westbury	a		14 23	14 56	15 46	15 51	15 56	16 56		17 40	17 54	17 57	18 30	18 55
	d	13 59	14 24	15 02	15 47	15 52	15 59	17 00	17 10	17 41	17 56	18 02	18 32	19 01
Trowbridge	d		14 30	15 08	15 53		16 05	17 06	17 16	17 48		18 08	18 38	19 07
Bradford-on-Avon	d		14 36	15 14	15 59		16 11	17 12		17 54		18 14	18 44	19 13
Avoncliff	d				16 02		16 14			17 57			18 47	
Freshford	d				16 05		16 17			17 59			18 50	
Bath Spa 7	a		14 49	15 27	16 16		16 29	17 25		18 10		18 27	19 00	19 26
Melksham	d								17 25					
Chippenham	a								17 35					
Swindon	a								17 53					
London Paddington 15 ⊖	a	15 21				17 21					19 21			
Oldfield Park	a				16 19			17 28		18 13			19 04	
Keynsham	a		14 57		16 27			17 35		18 21			19 11	
Bristol Temple Meads 10	a		15 05	15 40	16 35		16 42	17 44		18 33		18 40	19 20	19 39
Filton Abbey Wood	a			15 55			16 55	17 55				18 55		19 55
Severn Tunnel Jn.	a			16 07			17 10	18 07				19 07		20 10
Newport (South Wales)	a			16 26			17 29	18 26				19 26		20 28
Cardiff Central 7	a			16 44			17 46	18 44				19 42		20 46

For connections to Swansea please refer to Table 128. For connections to Exeter St Davids and Plymouth please refer to Table 135. For connections from Bournemouth please refer to Table 158

For Bus Connections for either to or from Yeovil Junction and Yeovil Pen Mill please see Table 123A

Table 123

Sundays

1 July to 9 September

Portsmouth and Weymouth - Bristol and South Wales

Network Diagram - see first Page of Table 123

Station		GW ◇1 ☕	GW ◇	GW	GW ◇	SW ◇1	GW ◇1 ☕	GW ◇	GW ◇	GW	GW ◇1 ☕	GW	GW ◇	GW
Brighton 10	d							17 46						
Hove 2	d							17 50						
Shoreham-by-Sea	d							17 56						
Worthing 4	d							18 08						
Barnham	d							18 25						
Chichester 4	d							18 34						
Havant	d							18 48						
Portsmouth Harbour ⛴	d				18 08				19 08				20 08	22 03
Portsmouth & Southsea	d				18 12				19 12				20 12	22 12
Fratton	d				18 16				19 16				20 16	22 16
Cosham	d				18 23			18 55	19 23					
Fareham	a				18 31			19 02	19 31				20 31	22 31
	d				18 32			19 03	19 32				20 32	22 32
Southampton Central ⛴	d				18 54			19 30	19 54				20 54	22 57
Romsey	d				19 06			19 42	20 06				21 06	23 09
Salisbury	a				19 24			20 00	20 24				21 24	23 27
	d				19 25	19 55		20 03	20 27				21 27	23 28
Warminster	d				19 48	20 15		20 23	20 48				21 48	23 48
Dilton Marsh	d							20x28					21x53	23x53
Weymouth	d		17 56							20 09				
Upwey	d		18 01							20 14				
Dorchester West	d		18 09							20 22				
Maiden Newton	d		18 21							20 34				
Chetnole	d		18x29							20x42				
Yetminster	d		18x32							20x45				
Thornford	d		18x34							20x47				
Yeovil Pen Mill	d		18 44							20 57				
Castle Cary	a		18 56							21 09				
	d		18 59				20 06			21 10	21 19			
Bruton	d		19 05							21 16				
Frome	d		19 18							21 34		←		
Westbury	a		19 27		19 55	20 23	20 25	20 32	20 56	21 43	21 39	21 43	21 56	23 57
	d	19 11	19 30	19 35	20 01	20 23	20 26	20 36	21 02	21 45	21 40	21 45	22 00	
Trowbridge	d		19 36	19 42	20 07	20 29		20 44	21 08	→		21 51	22 06	
Bradford-on-Avon	d		19 42		20 13	20 35		20 50	21 14			21 57	22 12	
Avoncliff	d		19 45					20 53				22 00		
Freshford	d		19 48					20 56				22 03		
Bath Spa 7	a		19 59		20 26	20 48		21 09	21 27			22 14	22 25	
Melksham	d			19 53										
Chippenham	a			20 03										
Swindon	a			20 21										
London Paddington 15 ⊖	a	20 25					21 40				23 06			
Oldfield Park	a		20 02					21 12				22 17		
Keynsham	a		20 10			20 56		21 20				22 25		
Bristol Temple Meads 10	a		20 18		20 39	21 04		21 29	21 40			22 33	22 38	
Filton Abbey Wood	a				20 55				21 55				22 55	
Severn Tunnel Jn.	a				21 07				22 14				23 08	
Newport (South Wales)	a				21 26				22 31				23 26	
Cardiff Central 7	a				21 42				22 53				23 47	

For connections to Swansea please refer to Table 128. For connections to Exeter St Davids and Plymouth please refer to Table 135. For connections from Bournemouth please refer to Table 158

For Bus Connections for either to or from Yeovil Junction and Yeovil Pen Mill please see Table 123A

Table 123

Sundays

16 September to 21 October

Portsmouth and Weymouth - Bristol and South Wales

Network Diagram - see first Page of Table 123

Station		GW	GW ◇1 ☕	GW ◇1 ☕	GW ■	GW	GW ◇1 ☕	GW ◇	GW ◇	GW ◇1 ☕	SW ◇1
Brighton 10	d								11 10		
Hove 2	d								11 14		
Shoreham-by-Sea	d								11 20		
Worthing 4	d								11 29		
Barnham	d								11 46		
Chichester 4	d								11 54		
Havant	d								12 10		
Portsmouth Harbour ⛴	d				09 08			11 08			
Portsmouth & Southsea	d				09 12			11 12			
Fratton	d				09 16			11 16			
Cosham	d				09 23			11 23	12 23		
Fareham	a				09 31			11 31	12 31		
	d				09 32			11 32	12 32		
Southampton Central ⛴	d				09 54			11 54	12 54		
Romsey	d				10 06			12 06	13 06		
Salisbury	a				10 24			12 24	13 24		
	d				10 29			12 27	13 26		13 55
Warminster	d				10 50			12 48	13 46		14 15
Dilton Marsh	d				10x55						
Weymouth	d										
Upwey	d										
Dorchester West	d										
Maiden Newton	d										
Chetnole	d										
Yetminster	d										
Thornford	d										
Yeovil Pen Mill	d										
Castle Cary	a										
	d		09 34				12 33				
Bruton	d										
Frome	d	09 25									
Westbury	a	09 34	09 51		10 58		12 52	12 54	13 55		14 23
	d	09 44	09 54	10 51	11 00	11 50	12 53	12 56	13 56	13 59	14 24
Trowbridge	d	09 50			11 06	11 56		13 02	14 02		14 30
Bradford-on-Avon	d	09 56			11 12	12 02		13 08	14 08		14 36
Avoncliff	d	09 59				12 05			14 11		
Freshford	d	10 01				12 07			14 14		
Bath Spa 7	a	10 12			11 26	12 18		13 23	14 24		14 49
Melksham	d										
Chippenham	a										
Swindon	a										
London Paddington 15 ⊖	a		11 29	12 29			14 29			15 29	
Oldfield Park	a				11 33	12 24		13 27	14 27		
Keynsham	a				11 40	12 31		13 34	14 35		14 57
Bristol Temple Meads 10	a				11 52	12 42		13 45	14 46		15 05
Filton Abbey Wood	a				12 03			13 58	14 58		
Severn Tunnel Jn.	a				12 18			14 10	15 10		
Newport (South Wales)	a				12 37			14 30	15 29		
Cardiff Central 7	a				12 52			14 54	15 44		

Station		GW ◇	GW ◇	GW ◇1 ☕	GW ◇	GW ■	GW	GW ◇1 ☕	GW ◇	GW ◇	GW ◇	GW ◇	GW
Brighton 10	d									15 46			
Hove 2	d									15 50			
Shoreham-by-Sea	d									15 56			
Worthing 4	d									16 08			
Barnham	d									16 25			
Chichester 4	d									16 34			
Havant	d									16 48			
Portsmouth Harbour ⛴	d	13 08			14 08	15 08			16 08		17 08		
Portsmouth & Southsea	d	13 12			14 12	15 12			16 12		17 12		
Fratton	d	13 16			14 16	15 16			16 16		17 16		
Cosham	d	13 23			14 23	15 23			16 23	16 55	17 23		
Fareham	a	13 31			14 31	15 31			16 31	17 02	17 31		
	d	13 32			14 32	15 32			16 32	17 03	17 32		
Southampton Central ⛴	d	13 54			14 54	15 54			16 54	17 26	17 54		
Romsey	d	14 06			15 06	16 06			17 06	17 39	18 06		
Salisbury	a	14 24			15 24	16 24			17 24	18 00	18 24		
	d	14 27			15 27	16 27			17 27	18 01	18 27		
Warminster	d	14 48			15 48	16 48			17 48	18 21	18 48		
Dilton Marsh	d	14x53			15x53	16x53				18x26			
Weymouth	d		14 00									17 56	
Upwey	d		14 05									18 01	
Dorchester West	d		14 13									18 09	
Maiden Newton	d		14 25									18 21	
Chetnole	d		14x33									18x29	
Yetminster	d		14x36									18x32	
Thornford	d		14x38									18x34	
Yeovil Pen Mill	d		14 48									18 44	
Castle Cary	a		15 00									18 56	
	d		15 03	15 34				17 37				18 59	
Bruton	d		15 08									19 05	
Frome	d		15 21									19 18	
Westbury	a	14 56	15 30	15 51	15 56	16 56		17 54	17 57	18 30	18 55	19 27	
	d	15 02	15 31	15 52	15 59	17 00	17 10	17 56	18 02	18 32	19 01	19 30	19 35
Trowbridge	d	15 08	15 37		16 05	17 06	17 16		18 08	18 38	19 07	19 36	19 42
Bradford-on-Avon	d	15 14	15 43		16 11	17 12			18 14	18 44	19 13	19 42	
Avoncliff	d		15 46		16 14					18 47		19 45	
Freshford	d		15 49		16 17					18 50		19 48	
Bath Spa 7	a	15 27	16 00		16 29	17 25			18 27	19 00	19 26	19 59	
Melksham	d						17 25						19 53
Chippenham	a						17 35						20 03
Swindon	a						17 53						20 21
London Paddington 15 ⊖	a			17 30				19 29					
Oldfield Park	a		16 03			17 28				19 04		20 02	
Keynsham	a		16 11			17 35				19 11		20 10	
Bristol Temple Meads 10	a	15 43	16 23		16 42	17 44			18 40	19 20	19 39	20 18	
Filton Abbey Wood	a	15 55			16 55	17 55			18 55		19 55		
Severn Tunnel Jn.	a	16 07			17 10	18 07			19 07		20 10		
Newport (South Wales)	a	16 26			17 29	18 26			19 26		20 28		
Cardiff Central 7	a	16 44			17 46	18 44			19 42		20 46		

For connections to Swansea please refer to Table 128. For connections to Exeter St Davids and Plymouth please refer to Table 135. For connections from Bournemouth please refer to Table 158

For Bus Connections for either to or from Yeovil Junction and Yeovil Pen Mill please see Table 123A

Table 123

Sundays

16 September to 21 October

Portsmouth and Weymouth - Bristol and South Wales

Network Diagram - see first Page of Table 123

		GW	GW	SW	GW	GW	GW	GW	GW	GW	GW	GW
		◇1	◇	◇1	◇1	◇	◇		◇1		◇	
Brighton 10	d					17 46						
Hove 2	d					17 50						
Shoreham-by-Sea	d					17 56						
Worthing 4	d					18 08						
Barnham	d					18 25						
Chichester 4	d					18 34						
Havant	d					18 48						
Portsmouth Harbour ⛴	d		18 08				19 08				20 08	22 03
Portsmouth & Southsea	d		18 12				19 12				20 12	22 12
Fratton	d		18 16				19 16				20 16	22 16
Cosham	d		18 23			18 55	19 23					
Fareham	a		18 31			19 02	19 31				20 31	22 31
	d		18 32			19 03	19 32				20 32	22 32
Southampton Central ⛴	d		18 54			19 30	19 54				20 54	22 57
Romsey	d		19 06			19 42	20 06				21 06	23 09
Salisbury	a		19 24			20 00	20 24				21 24	23 27
	d		19 25	19 55		20 03	20 27				21 27	23 28
Warminster	d		19 48	20 15		20 23	20 48				21 48	23 48
Dilton Marsh	d					20x28					21x53	23x53
Weymouth	d							20 09				
Upwey	d							20 14				
Dorchester West	d							20 22				
Maiden Newton	d							20 34				
Chetnole	d							20x42				
Yetminster	d							20x45				
Thornford	d							20x47				
Yeovil Pen Mill	d							20 57				
Castle Cary	a							21 09				
	d				20 07			21 10	21 19			
Bruton	d							21 16				
Frome	d							21 34		←		
Westbury	a		19 55	20 23	20 26	20 32	20 56	21 43	21 39	21 43	21 56	23 57
	d	19 51	20 01	20 23	20 27	20 36	21 02	21 45	21 40	21 45	22 00	
Trowbridge	d		20 07	20 29		20 42	21 08	→		21 51	22 06	
Bradford-on-Avon	d		20 13	20 35		20 48	21 14			21 57	22 12	
Avoncliff	d					20 51				22 00		
Freshford	d					20 54				22 03		
Bath Spa 7	a		20 26	20 48		21 09	21 27			22 14	22 25	
Melksham	d											
Chippenham	a											
Swindon	a											
London Paddington 15 ⊖	a	21 29			21 59				23 16			
Oldfield Park	a					21 12				22 17		
Keynsham	a			20 56		21 20				22 25		
Bristol Temple Meads 10	a		20 39	21 04		21 29	21 40			22 33	22 38	
Filton Abbey Wood	a		20 55				21 55				22 55	
Severn Tunnel Jn.	a		21 07				22 14				23 08	
Newport (South Wales)	a		21 26				22 31				23 26	
Cardiff Central 7	a		21 42				22 53				23 47	

For connections to Swansea please refer to Table 128. For connections to Exeter St Davids and Plymouth please refer to Table 135. For connections from Bournemouth please refer to Table 158

For Bus Connections for either to or from Yeovil Junction and Yeovil Pen Mill please see Table 123A

Table 123

Sundays

from 28 October

Portsmouth and Weymouth - Bristol and South Wales

Network Diagram - see first Page of Table 123

		GW	GW	GW	GW	GW	GW	GW	GW	GW	SW
		◇1		◇1	■		◇1	◇	◇	◇1	◇1
Brighton 10	d								11 10		
Hove 2	d								11 14		
Shoreham-by-Sea	d								11 20		
Worthing 4	d								11 29		
Barnham	d								11 46		
Chichester 4	d								11 54		
Havant	d								12 10		
Portsmouth Harbour ⛴	d				09 08			11 08			
Portsmouth & Southsea	d				09 12			11 12			
Fratton	d				09 16			11 16			
Cosham	d				09 23			11 23	12 23		
Fareham	a				09 31			11 31	12 31		
	d				09 32			11 32	12 32		
Southampton Central ⛴	d				09 54			11 54	12 54		
Romsey	d				10 06			12 06	13 06		
Salisbury	a				10 24			12 24	13 24		
	d				10 29			12 27	13 26		13 55
Warminster	d				10 50			12 48	13 46		14 15
Dilton Marsh	d				10x55						
Weymouth	d										
Upwey	d										
Dorchester West	d										
Maiden Newton	d										
Chetnole	d										
Yetminster	d										
Thornford	d										
Yeovil Pen Mill	d										
Castle Cary	a										
	d	09 34					12 33				
Bruton	d										
Frome	d		09 39								
Westbury	a	09 51	09 48		10 58		12 52	12 54	13 55		14 23
	d	09 54	09 58	10 51	11 00	11 50	12 53	12 56	13 56	13 59	14 24
Trowbridge	d		10 04		11 06	11 56		13 02	14 02		14 30
Bradford-on-Avon	d		10 10		11 12	12 02		13 08	14 08		14 36
Avoncliff	d		10 13			12 05			14 11		
Freshford	d		10 15			12 07			14 14		
Bath Spa 7	a		10 26		11 25	12 19		13 22	14 24		14 49
Melksham	d										
Chippenham	a										
Swindon	a										
London Paddington 15 ⊖	a	11 29		12 29			14 29			15 29	
Oldfield Park	a		10 30		11 28	12 23		13 25	14 27		
Keynsham	a		10 37		11 35	12 30		13 32	14 35		14 57
Bristol Temple Meads 10	a		10 45		11 44	12 38		13 41	14 44		15 05
Filton Abbey Wood	a				11 55			13 55	14 55		
Severn Tunnel Jn.	a				12 10			14 07	15 07		
Newport (South Wales)	a				12 29			14 27	15 26		
Cardiff Central 7	a				12 44			14 51	15 41		

		GW	GW	GW	GW	GW	GW	GW	GW	GW	GW	GW	GW
		◇	◇	◇1	◇	■		◇1	◇	◇	◇	◇	
Brighton 10	d									15 46			
Hove 2	d									15 50			
Shoreham-by-Sea	d									15 56			
Worthing 4	d									16 08			
Barnham	d									16 25			
Chichester 4	d									16 34			
Havant	d									16 48			
Portsmouth Harbour ⛴	d	13 08			14 08	15 08			16 08		17 08		
Portsmouth & Southsea	d	13 12			14 12	15 12			16 12		17 12		
Fratton	d	13 16			14 16	15 16			16 16		17 16		
Cosham	d	13 23			14 23	15 23			16 23	16 55	17 23		
Fareham	a	13 31			14 31	15 31			16 31	17 02	17 31		
	d	13 32			14 32	15 32			16 32	17 03	17 32		
Southampton Central ⛴	d	13 54			14 54	15 54			16 54	17 26	17 54		
Romsey	d	14 06			15 06	16 06			17 06	17 39	18 06		
Salisbury	a	14 24			15 24	16 24			17 24	18 00	18 24		
	d	14 27			15 27	16 27			17 27	18 01	18 27		
Warminster	d	14 48			15 48	16 48			17 48	18 21	18 48		
Dilton Marsh	d	14x53			15x53	16x53				18x26			
Weymouth	d		14 00									17 56	
Upwey	d		14 05									18 01	
Dorchester West	d		14 13									18 09	
Maiden Newton	d		14 25									18 21	
Chetnole	d		14x33									18x29	
Yetminster	d		14x36									18x32	
Thornford	d		14x38									18x34	
Yeovil Pen Mill	d		14 48									18 44	
Castle Cary	a		15 00									18 56	
	d		15 03	15 34				17 37				18 59	
Bruton	d		15 08									19 05	
Frome	d		15 21									19 18	
Westbury	a	14 56	15 30	15 51	15 56	16 56		17 54	17 57	18 30	18 55	19 27	
	d	15 02	15 31	15 52	15 59	17 00	17 10	17 56	18 02	18 32	19 01	19 30	19 35
Trowbridge	d	15 08	15 37		16 05	17 06	17 16		18 08	18 38	19 07	19 36	19 42
Bradford-on-Avon	d	15 14	15 43		16 11	17 12			18 14	18 44	19 13	19 42	
Avoncliff	d		15 46		16 14					18 47		19 45	
Freshford	d		15 49		16 17					18 50		19 48	
Bath Spa 7	a	15 27	16 00		16 29	17 25			18 27	19 00	19 26	19 59	
Melksham	d						17 25						19 53
Chippenham	a						17 35						20 03
Swindon	a						17 53						20 21
London Paddington 15 ⊖	a			17 30				19 29					
Oldfield Park	a		16 03			17 28				19 04		20 02	
Keynsham	a		16 11			17 35				19 11		20 10	
Bristol Temple Meads 10	a	15 40	16 23		16 42	17 44			18 40	19 20	19 39	20 18	
Filton Abbey Wood	a	15 55			16 55	17 55			18 55		19 55		
Severn Tunnel Jn.	a	16 07			17 10	18 07			19 07		20 10		
Newport (South Wales)	a	16 26			17 29	18 26			19 26		20 28		
Cardiff Central 7	a	16 44			17 46	18 44			19 42		20 46		

For connections to Swansea please refer to Table 128. For connections to Exeter St Davids and Plymouth please refer to Table 135. For connections from Bournemouth please refer to Table 158

For Bus Connections for either to or from Yeovil Junction and Yeovil Pen Mill please see Table 123A

Table 123

Sundays
from 28 October

Portsmouth and Weymouth - Bristol and South Wales

Network Diagram - see first Page of Table 123

		GW	GW	SW	GW	GW		GW	GW	GW	GW	GW	GW
		◇1 ꟷP	◇	◇1	◇1 ꟷP	◇		◇		◇1 ꟷP		◇	
Brighton 10	d					17 46							
Hove 2	d					17 50							
Shoreham-by-Sea	d					17 56							
Worthing 4	d					18 08							
Barnham	d					18 25							
Chichester 4	d					18 34							
Havant	d					18 48							
Portsmouth Harbour	d		18 08					19 08				20 08	22 03
Portsmouth & Southsea	d		18 12					19 12				20 12	22 12
Fratton	d		18 16					19 16				20 16	22 16
Cosham	d		18 23			18 55		19 23					
Fareham	a		18 31			19 02		19 31				20 31	22 31
	d		18 32			19 03		19 32				20 32	22 32
Southampton Central	d		18 54			19 30		19 54				20 54	22 57
Romsey	d		19 06			19 42		20 06				21 06	23 09
Salisbury	a		19 24			20 00		20 24				21 24	23 27
	d		19 25	19 55		20 03		20 27				21 27	23 28
Warminster	d		19 48	20 15		20 23		20 48				21 48	23 48
Dilton Marsh	d					20x28						21x53	23x53
Weymouth	d								20 09				
Upwey	d								20 14				
Dorchester West	d								20 22				
Maiden Newton	d								20 34				
Chetnole	d								20x42				
Yetminster	d								20x45				
Thornford	d								20x47				
Yeovil Pen Mill	d								20 57				
Castle Cary	a								21 09				
	d				20 07				21 10	21 19			
Bruton	d								21 16				
Frome	d								21 34		←		
Westbury	a		19 55	20 23	20 26	20 32		20 56	21 43	21 39	21 43	21 56	23 57
	d	19 51	20 01	20 23	20 27	20 36		21 02	21 45	21 40	21 45	22 00	
Trowbridge	d		20 07	20 29		20 42		21 08	→		21 51	22 06	
Bradford-on-Avon	d		20 13	20 35		20 48		21 14			21 57	22 12	
Avoncliff	d					20 51					22 00		
Freshford	d					20 54					22 03		
Bath Spa 7	a		20 26	20 48		21 09		21 27			22 14	22 25	
Melksham	d												
Chippenham	a												
Swindon	a												
London Paddington 15 ⊖	a	21 29			21 59					23 16			
Oldfield Park	a					21 12					22 17		
Keynsham	a			20 56		21 20					22 25		
Bristol Temple Meads 10	a		20 39	21 04		21 29		21 40			22 33	22 38	
Filton Abbey Wood	a		20 55					21 55				22 55	
Severn Tunnel Jn.	a		21 07					22 14				23 08	
Newport (South Wales)	a		21 26					22 31				23 26	
Cardiff Central 7	a		21 42					22 53				23 47	

For connections to Swansea please refer to Table 128. For connections to Exeter St Davids and Plymouth please refer to Table 135. For connections from Bournemouth please refer to Table 158

For Bus Connections for either to or from Yeovil Junction and Yeovil Pen Mill please see Table 123A

Table 123A

Mondays to Fridays

Yeovil Pen Mill - Yeovil Junction

		GW BHX	GW BHX	GW BHX	GW BHX	GW BHX	GW BHX	GW BHX	GW BHX	GW BHX	GW BHX	GW BHX	GW BHX	GW BHX	GW BHX	GW BHX	GW BHX	GW BHX	GW BHX	GW BHX	GW BHX	GW BHX	GW BHX
Yeovil Pen Mill	d	07 20	07 50	08 20	08 50	09 20	09 50	10 20	10 50	11 20	11 50	12 20	12 50	13 20	13 50	14 20	14 50	15 20	15 50	16 20	16 50	17 20	17 50
Yeovil Bus Station	d	07 30	08 00	08 30	09 00	09 30	10 00	10 30	11 00	11 30	12 00	12 30	13 00	13 30	14 00	14 30	15 00	15 30	16 00	16 30	17 00	17 30	18 00
Yeovil Junction	a	07 35	08 05	08 35	09 05	09 35	10 05	10 35	11 05	11 35	12 05	12 35	13 05	13 35	14 05	14 35	15 05	15 35	16 05	16 35	17 05	17 35	18 05

		GW BHX	GW BHX	GW BHX	GW BHX
Yeovil Pen Mill	d	18 20	18 50	19 20	19 50
Yeovil Bus Station	d	18 30	19 00	19a30	20a00
Yeovil Junction	a	18 35	19 05		

Saturdays

		GW	GW	GW	GW	GW	GW	GW	GW	GW	GW	GW	GW	GW	GW	GW	GW	GW	GW	GW	GW	GW	GW
Yeovil Pen Mill	d	07 20	07 50	08 20	08 50	09 20	09 50	10 20	10 50	11 20	11 50	12 20	12 50	13 20	13 50	14 20	14 50	15 20	15 50	16 20	16 50	17 20	17 50
Yeovil Bus Station	d	07 30	08 00	08 30	09 00	09 30	10 00	10 30	11 00	11 30	12 00	12 30	13 00	13 30	14 00	14 30	15 00	15 30	16 00	16 30	17 00	17 30	18 00
Yeovil Junction	a	07 35	08 05	08 35	09 05	09 35	10 05	10 35	11 05	11 35	12 05	12 35	13 05	13 35	14 05	14 35	15 05	15 35	16 05	16 35	17 05	17 35	18 05

		GW	GW	GW	GW
Yeovil Pen Mill	d	18 20	18 50	19 20	19 50
Yeovil Bus Station	d	18 30	19 00	19a30	20a00
Yeovil Junction	a	18 35	19 05		

Table 123A

Mondays to Fridays

Yeovil Junction - Yeovil Pen Mill

		GW BHX	GW BHX	GW BHX	GW BHX	GW BHX	GW BHX	GW BHX	GW BHX	GW BHX	GW BHX	GW BHX	GW BHX	GW BHX	GW BHX	GW BHX	GW BHX	GW BHX	GW BHX	GW BHX	GW BHX	GW BHX	GW BHX
Yeovil Junction	d	06 50	07 20	07 50	08 20	08 50	09 20	09 50	10 20	10 50	11 20	11 50	12 20	12 50	13 20	13 50	14 20	14 50	15 20	15 50	16 20	16 50	17 20
Yeovil Bus Station	d	06 57	07 27	07 57	08 27	08 57	09 27	09 57	10 27	10 57	11 27	11 57	12 27	12 57	13 27	13 57	14 27	14 57	15 27	15 57	16 27	16 57	17 27
Yeovil Pen Mill	a	07 02	07 32	08 02	08 32	09 02	09 32	10 02	10 32	11 02	11 32	12 02	12 32	13 02	13 32	14 02	14 32	15 02	15 32	16 02	16 32	17 02	17 32

		GW BHX	GW BHX	GW BHX	GW BHX
Yeovil Junction	d	17 50	18 20	18 50	19 20
Yeovil Bus Station	d	17 57	18 27	18 57	19 27
Yeovil Pen Mill	a	18 02	18 32	19 02	19 32

Saturdays

		GW	GW	GW	GW	GW	GW	GW	GW	GW	GW	GW	GW	GW	GW	GW	GW	GW	GW	GW	GW	GW	GW
Yeovil Junction	d	06 50	07 20	07 50	08 20	08 50	09 20	09 50	10 20	10 50	11 20	11 50	12 20	12 50	13 20	13 50	14 20	14 50	15 20	15 50	16 20	16 50	17 20
Yeovil Bus Station	d	06 57	07 27	07 57	08 27	08 57	09 27	09 57	10 27	10 57	11 27	11 57	12 27	12 57	13 27	13 57	14 27	14 57	15 27	15 57	16 27	16 57	17 27
Yeovil Pen Mill	a	07 02	07 32	08 02	08 32	09 02	09 32	10 02	10 32	11 02	11 32	12 02	12 32	13 02	13 32	14 02	14 32	15 02	15 32	16 02	16 32	17 02	17 32

		GW	GW	GW	GW
Yeovil Junction	d	17 50	18 20	18 50	19 20
Yeovil Bus Station	d	17 57	18 27	18 57	19 27
Yeovil Pen Mill	a	18 02	18 32	19 02	19 32

No Sunday Service

Route Diagram for Table 125

DM-11/11
Design BAJS

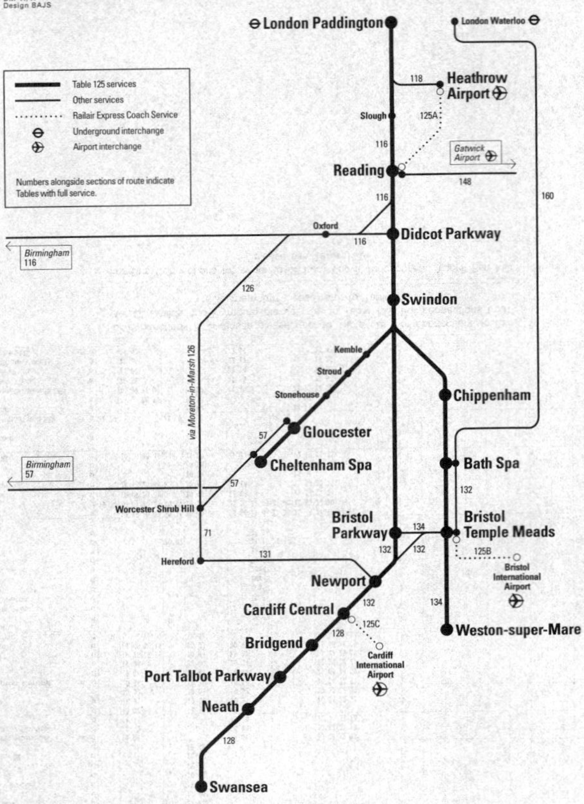

London - Swindon, Cheltenham Spa, Bristol, Weston-super-Mare and South Wales

Route Diagram - see first Page of Table 125

Miles	Miles	Miles			GW MX ◇1 ⊡	GW MO ◇1 A ⊡	GW MX ◇1 ⊡	GW MO A	GW MO ◇1 A ⊡	GW MX ◇1 ⊡	GW MX	GW MO ◇1 A ⊡	GW MX ◇1 ⊡		GW MO ◇1 A ⊡	GW MX ◇1 ⊡	GW MO ◇1 A ⊡	GW	GW ◇1 ⊡	GW ◇1 ⊡	GW ◇	GW ◇1	GW ◇1 ⊡		GW ◇1 ⊡
—	—	—	London Paddington [15] ⊖	d	21p15	21p37	21p45		22p03	22p15		22p37	22p45		23p03	23p30	23p37		05 27	05 36		05 48	06 30		06 45
18½	18½	18½	Slough [3]	d													00 03			05 52		06 05			
36	36	36	Reading [7]	d	21p41	22p12	22p11		22p45	22p49		23p17	23p19		23p47	00 08	00 14		05 56	06 07		06 22	06 56		07 11
53¼	53¼	53¼	Didcot Parkway	d	22p00	22p28	22p31		22p59	23p09		23b32	23p39		00s01	00 25	00s30			06 21		06 39	07 12		
77¼	77¼	77¼	Swindon	a	22p18	22p45	22p48		23p17	23p26		23b51	23p55		00s19	00 44	00s48		06 23	06 41			07 28		07 38
—	—	—		d	22p19	22p46	22p49	22p57	23p17	23p27	23p33		23p57			00 45		06 12	06 25	06 50			07 30		07 38
—	—	91	Kemble	d				23p11			23p47									07 07					
—	—	102¼	Stroud	d				23p26			00 02									07 22					
—	—	105	Stonehouse	d				23p31			00 07									07 28					
—	—	113¾	Gloucester [7]	a				23p48			00 24									07 45					
—	—	120¼	Cheltenham Spa	a				00 05												08 01					
—	—	—	Worcester Shrub Hill	d																	06 49	08a10			
—	94	—	Chippenham	d			23p03		23p33	23p40					00s34	00 59	01s04	06a28	06 39				07 44		
—	107	—	Bath Spa [7]	a			23p17		23p46	23p54					00s49	01 13	01s18		06 52				07 57		
111¾	—	—	Bristol Parkway [7]	a	22p45	23p11						00s21	00 21								08 19				08 04
—	—	—		d	22p45	23p12							00 23								08 19				08 07
117¾	118½	—	Bristol Temple Meads [10]	a			23p32		00 01	00 10		00 35			01 03	01 29	01 32		07 07		08 36		08 17		
—	137½	—	Weston-super-Mare	a			00s05																		
133½	—	—	Newport (South Wales)	a	23p19	23p41							00 51			02s10			07 44						08 32
145¼	—	—	Cardiff Central [7]	a	23p40	00 01							01 11			02 31			08 00						08 46
165½	—	—	Bridgend	a	00 02	00 23							01 36						08 23						09 09
177¾	—	—	Port Talbot Parkway	a	00 15	00 36							01 49						08 36						09 22
183¼	—	—	Neath	a	00 22	00 44							01 57						08 44						09 30
192¾	—	—	Swansea	a	00 37	00 57							02 10						08 57						09 45

		GW	GW	GW 1	GW ◇1 ⊡	GW ◇1 ⊡	GW ◇1 B ⊘	GW ◇1 C ⊡	GW ◇1 ⊡		GW ◇1 ⊡	GW ◇1 ⊡	GW ◇1 ⊡	GW ◇1 ⊡	GW ◇1 D ⊡⊘	GW ◇1 ⊡	GW	GW ◇1 ⊡	GW ■		GW ◇1 Ħ	GW ◇1 E ⊡⊘	GW ◇1 D ⊡⊘	GW ◇1 ⊡	GW ◇1 F ⊡
London Paddington [15] ⊖	d			06 48	07 00	07 15	07 30	07 45	07 48		08 00	08 15	08 22	08 30	08 45	09 00		09 15			09 21	09 30	09 45	09 48	10 00
Slough [3]	d			07 04									08 36								09 36				
Reading [7]	d			07 22	07 26	07 42	07 57	08 11	08 16		08 27	08 42	08 52	08 57	09 11	09 27		09 42			09 52	09 57	10 11	10 16	10 27
Didcot Parkway	d			07 49	07 42	07 57			08 33		08 41	08 57		09 12				09 57				10 12		10 33	
Swindon	a				07 58	08 14	08 27	08 38	08 53		08 59	09 14		09 30	09 38	09 54		10 14				10 30	10 38	10 53	10 55
	d	07 54			08 00	08 15	08 27	08 38	08 54		09 00	09 15		09 31	09 38	09 55	09 54	10 15				10 31	10 38	10 54	10 55
Kemble	d	08 07							09 07								10 07							11 07	
Stroud	d	08 22							09 22								10 22							11 22	
Stonehouse	d	08 28							09 28								10 28							11 28	
Gloucester [7]	a	08 50							09 44								10 50							11 44	
Cheltenham Spa	a	09 05							10 03								11 05							12 03	
Worcester Shrub Hill	d		09 06	09a15									10a44						11 06		11a34				
Chippenham	d				08 14		08 42				09 14			09 45		10 09						10 44			11 09
Bath Spa [7]	a				08 27		08 55				09 29			09 59		10 23						10 59			11 24
Bristol Parkway [7]	a		10 22			08 40		09 04				09 40			10 04			10 40	12 22				11 04		
	d		10 22			08 41		09 07				09 41			10 07			10 41	12 22				11 07		
Bristol Temple Meads [10]	a		10 37		08 45		09 10				09 45			10 15		10 38			12 34			11 15			11 40
Weston-super-Mare	a																								12 06
Newport (South Wales)	a					09 07		09 31				10 04			10 31			11 06					11 31		
Cardiff Central [7]	a					09 24		09 48				10 21			10 46			11 23					11 46		
Bridgend	a							10 09							11 09								12 09		
Port Talbot Parkway	a							10 22							11 22								12 22		
Neath	a							10 30							11 30								12 30		
Swansea	a							10 44							11 43								12 43		

		GW ◇1 ⊡	GW ◇1 ⊡	GW ◇1 E ⊡⊘	GW ◇1 D ⊡⊘		GW	GW ◇1 ⊡	GW ◇1 ⊡	GW ◇	GW ◇1 Ħ	GW ◇1 ⊡	GW ◇1 D ⊡⊘	GW ◇1 G ⊡	GW ◇1 ⊡		GW ◇1 ⊡	GW ◇1 Ħ	GW ◇1 ⊡	GW ◇1 D ⊡⊘	GW ◇1 ⊡	GW	GW ◇1 ⊡	GW ◇1 ⊡	GW ◇1 ⊡
London Paddington [15] ⊖	d	10 15	10 22	10 30	10 45			11 00	11 15		11 20	11 30	11 45	11 48	12 00		12 15	12 21	12 30	12 45	13 00		13 15	13 30	13 45
Slough [3]	d		10 36								11 36							12 36							
Reading [7]	d	10 42	10 52	10 57	11 11			11 27	11 42		11 52	11 57	12 11	12 16	12 27		12 42	12 52	12 57	13 11	13 27		13 42	13 57	14 11
Didcot Parkway	d	10 57		11 12					11 57			12 12		12 33			12 57		13 12				13 57	14 12	
Swindon	a	11 14		11 30	11 38			11 55	12 14			12 30	12 38	12 53	12 55		13 14		13 30	13 38	13 54		14 14	14 30	14 38
	d	11 15		11 30	11 38		11 54	11 55	12 15			12 30	12 38	12 54	12 55		13 15		13 32	13 38	13 55	13 54	14 15	14 30	14 38
Kemble	d						12 07							13 07								14 07			
Stroud	d						12 22							13 22								14 22			
Stonehouse	d						12 28							13 28								14 28			
Gloucester [7]	a						12 50							13 44								14 50			
Cheltenham Spa	a						13 05							14 03								15 05			
Worcester Shrub Hill	d		12a44							13 06	13a31							14a46							
Chippenham	d			11 44				12 09				12 44			13 09				13 44		14 09			14 44	
Bath Spa [7]	a			11 59				12 23				12 59			13 24				13 59		14 23			14 59	
Bristol Parkway [7]	a	11 40			12 04				12 40	14 22			13 04				13 40			14 04			14 40		15 04
	d	11 41			12 07				12 41	14 22			13 07				13 41			14 07			14 41		15 07
Bristol Temple Meads [10]	a			12 15				12 39		14 38		13 15			13 44				14 15		14 39			15 15	
Weston-super-Mare	a																								
Newport (South Wales)	a	12 04			12 31				13 06				13 31				14 04			14 30			15 06		15 31
Cardiff Central [7]	a	12 21			12 46				13 22				13 46				14 22			14 46			15 22		15 46
Bridgend	a				13 09								14 09							15 09					16 09
Port Talbot Parkway	a				13 22								14 22							15 22					16 22
Neath	a				13 30								14 30							15 30					16 30
Swansea	a				13 44								14 43							15 43					16 43

A from 21 May until 18 June
B The Merchant Venturer
C The St. David
D ⊡ from Bridgend ⊘ to Bridgend
E ⊡ from Chippenham ⊘ to Chippenham
F The Torbay Express
G The Cheltenham Spa Express
b Previous night, stops to set down only

For connections from Heathrow Airport, Gatwick Airport and Oxford please refer to Tables 125A, 148 and 116. For connections to Birmingham New Street and Hereford please refer to Tables 57 and 131

until 22 June

London - Swindon, Cheltenham Spa, Bristol, Weston-super-Mare and South Wales

Route Diagram - see first Page of Table 125

		GW	GW	GW	GW	GW	GW	GW	GW	GW	GW	GW	GW	GW	GW	GW	GW	GW	GW	GW	GW	GW
		◇1 ⊐	◇1 ⊐	◇1 ⊐	◇	◇1 A ✗	◇1 ⊐	◇1 ⊐		◇1 ⊐	◇1 ⊐	◇1 ⊐	◇1 ⊐	◇1 ⊐		◇1 ⊐	◇1 ⊐	◇1 ⊐	◇1 ⊐	◇1 B ⊐	◇	◇1 ⊐
London Paddington ⊖	d	13 48	14 00	14 15		14 21	14 30	14 45		15 00	15 15	15 30	15 45	15 48		15 51	16 00	16 15	16 30	16 45		17 00
Slough	d					14 36										16 06						
Reading	d	14 16	14 27	14 42		14 52	14 57	15 11		15 27	15 42	15 57	16 11	16 16		16 22	16 27	16 41	16 57	17 11		17 26
Didcot Parkway	d	14 33		14 57			15 12				15 57	16 12		16 33				16 56	17 12			17 42
Swindon	a	14 54	14 55	15 14			15 30	15 38		15 55	16 14	16 30	16 38	16 53			16 55	17 13	17 30	17 38		17 58
	d	14 54	14 55	15 15			15 30	15 38	15 54	15 55	16 15	16 30	16 38	16 54			16 55	17 15	17 30	17 38	17 54	18 00
Kemble	d	15 07							16 07					17 07							18 07	
Stroud	d	15 22							16 22					17 22							18 22	
Stonehouse	d	15 28							16 28					17 28							18 28	
Gloucester	a	15 44							16 50					17 46							18 49	
Cheltenham Spa	a	16 03							17 05					18 03							19 05	
Worcester Shrub Hill	d				15 06	16a39									17 06	18a08						
Chippenham	d		15 09				15 44			16 10		16 45					17 13		17 45			18 14
Bath Spa	a		15 24				15 59			16 24		16 59					17 26		17 59			18 27
Bristol Parkway	a			15 40	16 22			16 05			16 40		17 04		18 22			17 40		18 04		
	d			15 41	16 22			16 07			16 41		17 07		18 22			17 41		18 07		
Bristol Temple Meads	a		15 40		16 37		16 15			16 39		17 15			18 38		17 41		18 14			18 44
Weston-super-Mare	a						16 52					17 52							18 51			
Newport (South Wales)	a			16 05				16 30			17 06		17 31					18 04		18 30		
Cardiff Central	a			16 22				16 46			17 22		17 46					18 19		18 48		
Bridgend	a							17 09					18 09					18 44		19 09		
Port Talbot Parkway	a							17 22					18 22					18 57		19 22		
Neath	a							17 30					18 30					19 04		19 30		
Swansea	a							17 43					18 48					19 18		19 46		

		GW	GW	GW	GW	GW	GW	GW	GW	GW	GW	GW	GW	GW	GW	GW	GW FX	GW FO	GW	GW	GW	GW	GW FX
		◇1 C ⊐⊘		◇1 ⊐	◇1 ⊐	◇1 ⊐	◇	◇1 ⊐	◇1 ⊐	◇1 D ⊐	◇1 ⊐	◇1 E ⊐	◇1 ⊐	◇1 ⊐	◇1 ⊐	◇1 ⊐	◇1 ⊐	◇1 ⊐	◇		◇1 ⊐	◇1 ⊐	◇1 ⊐
London Paddington ⊖	d	17 15		17 22	17 30	17 45		17 48	17 50	18 00	18 15	18 22	18 30	18 45	18 47	19 00	19 15	19 15			19 22	19 30	19 48
Slough	d																				19 36		
Reading	d	17 43		17 50	17 56	18 11		18 16	18 22	18 27	18 43	18 50	18 56	19 11	19 18	19 27	19 41	19u48			19 52	19 57	20 18
Didcot Parkway	d	17 57			18 11			18 33		18 42	18 57		19 12		19 33	19 42	19 57					20 12	20 33
Swindon	a	18 14			18 28	18 38		18 53		18 59	19 15		19 28	19 38	19 52	20 00	20 13	20 15				20 30	20 52
	d	18 15			18 30	18 38	18 44	18 54		19 00	19 17		19 30	19 38	19 54	20 00	20 15	20 16	20 25			20 30	20 54
Kemble	d							19 07							20 07				20 38				21 11
Stroud	d							19 22							20 22				20 53				21 26
Stonehouse	d							19 28							20 28				20 59				21 31
Gloucester	a							19 45							20 45				21 14				21 46
Cheltenham Spa	a							20 03							21 02				21 33				22 02
Worcester Shrub Hill	d		19 07	19a34					20a03			20a41								21 32	21a46		22a24
Chippenham	d				18 44		19a01			19 14			19 44			20 15						20 44	
Bath Spa	a				18 57					19 28			19 57			20 29						20 59	
Bristol Parkway	a	18 40	20 22			19 04					19 42			20 04			20 40	20 42		23 04			
	d	18 41	20 22			19 07					19 44			20 07			20 42	20 43		23 05			
Bristol Temple Meads	a		20 38		19 12					19 43			20 13			20 44				23 19		21 15	
Weston-super-Mare	a				19 48								20 53									21 50	
Newport (South Wales)	a	19 11				19 31					20 07			20 31			21 04	21 05					
Cardiff Central	a	19 26				19 48					20 22			20 48			21 19	21 19					
Bridgend	a	19 49				20 10					20 45			21 15			21 45	21 45					
Port Talbot Parkway	a	20 02				20 26					20 58			21 28			21 58	21 58					
Neath	a	20 10				20 33					21 05			21 36			22 06	22 06					
Swansea	a	20 23				20 47					21 19			21 49			22 19	22 19					

		GW FO	GW	GW	GW	GW	GW	GW	GW	GW FX	GW FO	GW FO	GW FX	GW	GW FO	GW FX	GW FO	GW FX
		◇1 ⊐	◇1 ⊐	◇1 F ⊐⊘	◇1 A ✗	◇1 ⊐		◇1 ⊐	◇1 ⊐	◇1 ⊐	◇1 A ✗	◇1 ⊐	◇1 ⊐		◇1 ⊐	◇1 ⊐	◇1 ⊐	◇1 ⊐
London Paddington ⊖	d	19 48	20 00	20 15	20 20	20 45		21 15	21 45	21 48	21 48	22 15	22 15		22 45	22 45	23 30	23 30
Slough	d				20 36					22 03	22 03							
Reading	d	20 18	20 27	20 41	20 52	21 11		21 41	22 11	22 22	22 22	22 41	22 49		23 11	23 19	00 08	00 08
Didcot Parkway	d	20 33	20 42	20 57		21 26		22 00	22 31			23 01	23 09		23 30	23 39	00 25	00 25
Swindon	a	20 48	21 00	21 14		21 43		22 18	22 48			23 19	23 26		23 48	23 55	00 44	00 44
	d	20 54	21 00	21 15		21 44	22 04	22 19	22 49			23 21	23 27	23 33	23 49	23 57	00 45	00 45
Kemble	d	21 11					22 21							23 47				
Stroud	d	21 26					22 36							00 02				
Stonehouse	d	21 31					22 41							00 07				
Gloucester	a	21 46					22 56							00 24				
Cheltenham Spa	a	22 02					23 11											
Worcester Shrub Hill	d	22a24			22a40					00a12	00a13							
Chippenham	d		21 16			21 58			23 03			23 33	23 40				00 59	00 59
Bath Spa	a		21 29			22 11			23 17			23 47	23 54				01 13	01 13
Bristol Parkway	a			21 40				22 45							00 14	00 21		
	d			21 41				22 45							00 16	00 23		
Bristol Temple Meads	a		21 44			22 30			23 32			00 03	00 10				01 29	01 29
Weston-super-Mare	a								00s05									
Newport (South Wales)	a			22 03				23 19							00 38	00 51	02s02	02s10
Cardiff Central	a			22 23				23 40							00 53	01 11	02 19	02 31
Bridgend	a			22 46				00 02							01 19	01 36		
Port Talbot Parkway	a			22 59				00 15							01 32	01 49		
Neath	a			23 07				00 22							01 39	01 57		
Swansea	a			23 20				00 37							01 53	02 10		

A ✗ to Reading
B The Capitals United
C The Red Dragon. ⊐ from Bridgend ⊘ to Bridgend
D The Bristolian
E The Cathedrals Express
F ⊐ from Bridgend ⊘ to Bridgend

For connections from Heathrow Airport, Gatwick Airport and Oxford please refer to Tables 125A, 148 and 116. For connections to Birmingham New Street and Hereford please refer to Tables 57 and 131

25 June to 14 September

London - Swindon, Cheltenham Spa, Bristol, Weston-super-Mare and South Wales

Route Diagram - see first Page of Table 125

		GW MX	GW	GW MX	GW MO	GW MO	GW	GW MO	GW MX	GW MX	GW	GW MX	GW	GW MO	GW MX	GW	GW MO	GW	GW	GW	GW	GW	GW
		◇1 ⊐	◇1 A ⊐	◇1 ⊐	◇1 B ⊐		◇1 A ⊐	◇1 B ⊐	◇1 ⊐		◇1 A ⊐	◇1 ⊐	◇1 A ⊐	◇1 B ⊐	◇1 ⊐	◇1 A ⊐	◇1 B ⊐		◇1 ⊐	◇1 ⊐	◇	◇1	◇1 ⊐
London Paddington ⊖	d	21p15	21p37	21p45	21p37		22p03	22p03	22p15		22p37	22p45	23p03	23p03	23p30	23p37	23p37		05 27	05 36		05 48	06 30
Slough	d															00 03	23p55			05 52		06 05	
Reading	d	21p41	22p12	22p11	22p12		22p45	22p50	22p49		23p17	23p19	23p47	23p47	00 08	00 14	00 14		05 56	06 07		06 22	06 56
Didcot Parkway	d	22p00	22p28	22p31	22p30		22p59	23p05	23p09		23b32	23p39	00s01	00s02	00 25	00s30	00s32			06 21		06 39	07 12
Swindon	a	22p18	22p45	22p48	22p49		23p17	23p25	23p26		23b51	23p55	00s19	00s21	00 44	00s48	00s51		06 23	06 41			07 28
	d	22p19	22p46	22p49	22p51	22p57	23p17	23p25	23p27	23p33		23p57			00 45			06 12	06 25	06 50			07 30
Kemble	d					23p11				23p47										07 07			
Stroud	d					23p26				00 02										07 22			
Stonehouse	d					23p31				00 07										07 28			
Gloucester	a					23p48				00 24										07 45			
Cheltenham Spa	a					00 05														08 01			
Worcester Shrub Hill	d																				06 49	08a10	
Chippenham	d			23p03			23p33	23p41	23p40				00s34	00s37	00 59	01s04	01s07	06a28	06 39				07 44
Bath Spa	a			23p17			23p46	23p54	23p54				00s49	00s51	01 13	01s18	01s21		06 52				07 57
Bristol Parkway	a	22p45	23p11		23p15						00s21	00 21									08 19		
	d	22p45	23p12		23p17							00 23									08 19		
Bristol Temple Meads	a			23p32			00 01	00 09	00 10		00 35		01 03	01 05	01 29	01 32	01 35		07 07		08 36		08 17
Weston-super-Mare	a			00s05																			
Newport (South Wales)	a	23p19	23p41		23p43							00 51			02s10				07 44				
Cardiff Central	a	23p40	00 01		00 04							01 11			02 31				08 00				
Bridgend	a	00 02	00 23		00 27							01 36							08 23				
Port Talbot Parkway	a	00 15	00 36		00 40							01 49							08 36				
Neath	a	00 22	00 44		00 48							01 57							08 44				
Swansea	a	00 37	00 57		01 01							02 10							08 57				

		GW	GW	GW	GW	GW	GW	GW	GW	GW	GW	GW	GW	GW	GW	GW	GW	GW	GW	GW	GW	GW	GW
		◇1 ⊐			1	◇1 ⊐	◇1 ⊐	◇1 C ⊘	◇1 D ⊐	◇1 ⊐	◇1 ⊐	◇1 ⊐	◇1 ⊐	◇1 ⊐	◇1 E ⊐⊘	◇1 ⊐		◇1 ⊐	■	◇1 ✗	◇1 F ⊐⊘	◇1 E ⊐⊘	◇1 ⊐
London Paddington ⊖	d	06 45			06 48	07 00	07 15	07 30	07 45	07 48	08 00	08 15	08 22	08 30	08 45	09 00		09 15		09 21	09 30	09 45	09 48
Slough	d				07 04								08 36							09 36			
Reading	d	07 11			07 22	07 26	07 42	07 57	08 11	08 16	08 27	08 42	08 52	08 57	09 11	09 27		09 42		09 52	09 57	10 11	10 16
Didcot Parkway	d				07 49	07 42	07 57			08 33	08 41	08 57		09 12				09 57			10 12		10 33
Swindon	a	07 38				07 58	08 14	08 27	08 38	08 53	08 59	09 14		09 30	09 38	09 54		10 14			10 30	10 38	10 53
	d	07 38	07 54			08 00	08 15	08 27	08 38	08 54	09 00	09 15		09 31	09 38	09 55	09 54	10 15			10 31	10 38	10 54
Kemble	d		08 07							09 07							10 07						11 07
Stroud	d		08 22							09 22							10 22						11 22
Stonehouse	d		08 28							09 28							10 28						11 28
Gloucester	a		08 50							09 44							10 50						11 44
Cheltenham Spa	a		09 05							10 03							11 05						12 03
Worcester Shrub Hill	d			09 06	09a15								10a44						11 06	11a34			
Chippenham	d					08 14		08 42			09 14			09 45		10 09					10 44		
Bath Spa	a					08 27		08 55			09 29			09 59		10 23					10 59		
Bristol Parkway	a	08 04		10 22			08 40		09 04			09 40			10 04			10 40	12 22			11 04	
	d	08 07		10 22			08 41		09 07			09 41			10 07			10 41	12 22			11 07	
Bristol Temple Meads	a			10 37		08 45		09 10			09 45			10 15		10 38			12 34		11 15		
Weston-super-Mare	a																						
Newport (South Wales)	a	08 32					09 07		09 31			10 04			10 31			11 06				11 31	
Cardiff Central	a	08 46					09 24		09 48			10 21			10 46			11 23				11 46	
Bridgend	a	09 09							10 09						11 09							12 09	
Port Talbot Parkway	a	09 22							10 22						11 22							12 22	
Neath	a	09 30							10 30						11 30							12 30	
Swansea	a	09 45							10 44						11 43							12 43	

		GW	GW	GW	GW	GW	GW	GW	GW	GW	GW	GW	GW	GW	GW	GW	GW	GW	GW	GW	GW	GW
		◇1 G ⊐	◇1 ⊐	◇1 ⊐	◇1 F ⊐⊘	◇1 E ⊐⊘		◇1 ⊐	◇1 ⊐	◇	◇1 ✗	◇1 ⊐	◇1 E ⊐⊘	◇1 H ⊐	◇1 ⊐	◇1 ⊐	◇1 ✗	◇1 ⊐	◇1 E ⊐⊘	◇1 ⊐		◇1 ⊐
London Paddington ⊖	d	10 00	10 15	10 22	10 30	10 45		11 00	11 15		11 20	11 30	11 45	11 48	12 00	12 15	12 21	12 30	12 45	13 00		13 15
Slough	d			10 36							11 36						12 36					
Reading	d	10 27	10 42	10 52	10 57	11 11		11 27	11 42		11 52	11 57	12 11	12 16	12 27	12 42	12 52	12 57	13 11	13 27		13 42
Didcot Parkway	d		10 57		11 12				11 57			12 12		12 33		12 57		13 12				13 57
Swindon	a	10 55	11 14		11 30	11 38		11 55	12 14			12 30	12 38	12 53	12 55	13 14		13 30	13 38	13 54		14 14
	d	10 55	11 15		11 30	11 38	11 54	11 55	12 15			12 30	12 38	12 54	12 55	13 15		13 32	13 38	13 55	13 54	14 15
Kemble	d						12 07							13 07							14 07	
Stroud	d						12 22							13 22							14 22	
Stonehouse	d						12 28							13 28							14 28	
Gloucester	a						12 50							13 44							14 50	
Cheltenham Spa	a						13 05							14 03							15 05	
Worcester Shrub Hill	d			12a44						13 06	13a31						14a46					
Chippenham	d	11 09			11 44			12 09				12 44			13 09			13 44		14 09		
Bath Spa	a	11 24			11 59			12 23				12 59			13 24			13 59		14 23		
Bristol Parkway	a		11 40			12 04			12 40	14 22			13 04			13 40			14 04			14 40
	d		11 41			12 07			12 41	14 22			13 07			13 41			14 07			14 41
Bristol Temple Meads	a	11 40			12 15			12 39		14 38		13 15			13 44			14 15		14 39		
Weston-super-Mare	a	12 06																				
Newport (South Wales)	a		12 04			12 31			13 06				13 31			14 04			14 30			15 06
Cardiff Central	a		12 21			12 46			13 22				13 46			14 22			14 46			15 22
Bridgend	a					13 09							14 09						15 09			
Port Talbot Parkway	a					13 22							14 22						15 22			
Neath	a					13 30							14 30						15 30			
Swansea	a					13 44							14 43						15 43			

A 25 June
B from 2 July until 10 September
C The Merchant Venturer
D The St. David
E ⊐ from Bridgend ⊘ to Bridgend
F ⊐ from Chippenham ⊘ to Chippenham
G The Torbay Express
H The Cheltenham Spa Express
b Previous night, stops to set down only

For connections from Heathrow Airport, Gatwick Airport and Oxford please refer to Tables 125A, 148 and 116. For connections to Birmingham New Street and Hereford please refer to Tables 57 and 131

25 June to 14 September

London - Swindon, Cheltenham Spa, Bristol, Weston-super-Mare and South Wales

Route Diagram - see first Page of Table 125

		GW ◇1 ⊡	GW ◇1 ⊡	GW ◇1 ⊡	GW ◇1 ⊡	GW ◇1 ⊡	GW ◇	GW ◇1 A ⊼	GW ◇1 ⊡	GW FO G	GW ◇1 ⊡	GW	GW ◇1 ⊡	GW ◇1 ⊡	GW ◇1 ⊡	GW ◇1 ⊡	GW ◇1 ⊡	GW	GW ◇1 ⊡	GW ◇1 ⊡	GW ◇1 ⊡	GW ◇1 ⊡	GW ◇1 B ⊡	GW ◇
London Paddington 15 ⊖	d	13 30	13 45	13 48	14 00	14 15		14 21	14 30	14 36	14 45		15 00	15 15	15 30	15 45	15 48		15 51	16 00	16 15	16 30	16 45	
Slough 3	d							14 36											16 06					
Reading 7	d	13 57	14 11	14 16	14 27	14 42		14 52	14 57	15 08	15 11		15 27	15 42	15 57	16 11	16 16		16 22	16 27	16 41	16 57	17 11	
Didcot Parkway	d	14 12		14 33		14 57			15 12					15 57	16 12		16 33				16 56	17 12		
Swindon	a	14 30	14 38	14 54	14 55	15 14			15 30		15 38		15 55	16 14	16 30	16 38	16 53			16 55	17 13	17 30	17 38	
	d	14 30	14 38	14 54	14 55	15 15			15 30		15 38	15 54	15 55	16 15	16 30	16 38	16 54			16 55	17 15	17 30	17 38	17 54
Kemble	d			15 07								16 07					17 07							18 07
Stroud	d			15 22								16 22					17 22							18 22
Stonehouse	d			15 28								16 28					17 28							18 28
Gloucester 7	a			15 44								16 50					17 46							18 49
Cheltenham Spa	a			16 03								17 05					18 03							19 05
Worcester Shrub Hill	d						15 06	16a39										17 06	18a08					
Chippenham	d	14 44			15 09				15 44				16 10		16 45					17 13		17 45		
Bath Spa 7	a	14 59			15 24				15 59				16 24		16 59					17 26		17 59		
Bristol Parkway 7	a		15 04			15 40	16 22				16 05			16 40		17 04		18 22			17 40		18 04	
	d		15 07			15 41	16 22				16 07			16 41		17 07		18 22			17 41		18 07	
Bristol Temple Meads 10	a	15 15			15 40		16 37		16 15				16 39		17 15			18 38		17 41		18 14		
Weston-super-Mare	a								16 52						17 52							18 51		
Newport (South Wales)	a		15 31			16 05					16 30			17 06		17 31					18 04		18 30	
Cardiff Central 7	a		15 46			16 22					16 46			17 22		17 46					18 19		18 48	
Bridgend	a		16 09								17 09					18 09					18 44		19 09	
Port Talbot Parkway	a		16 22								17 22					18 22					18 57		19 22	
Neath	a		16 30								17 30					18 30					19 04		19 30	
Swansea	a		16 43								17 43					18 48					19 18		19 46	

		GW ◇1 ⊡	GW ◇1 C ⊡Ø	GW	GW ◇1 ⊡	GW ◇1 ⊡	GW ◇1 ⊡	GW ◇	GW ◇1 ⊡	GW ◇1 ⊡	GW ◇1 D ⊡	GW ◇1 ⊡	GW ◇1 E ⊡	GW ◇1 ⊡	GW ◇1 ⊡	GW ◇1 ⊡	GW ◇1 ⊡	GW FX ◇1 ⊡	GW FO ◇1 ⊡	GW ◇	GW	GW ◇1 ⊡
London Paddington 15 ⊖	d	17 00	17 15		17 22	17 30	17 45		17 48	17 50	18 00	18 15	18 22	18 30	18 45	18 47	19 00	19 15	19 15			19 22
Slough 3	d																					19 36
Reading 7	d	17 26	17 43		17 50	17 56	18 11		18 16	18 22	18 27	18 43	18 50	18 56	19 11	19 18	19 27	19 41	19u48			19 52
Didcot Parkway	d	17 42	17 57			18 11			18 33		18 42	18 57		19 12		19 33	19 42	19 57				
Swindon	a	17 58	18 14			18 28	18 38		18 53		18 59	19 15		19 28	19 38	19 52	20 00	20 13	20 15			
	d	18 00	18 15			18 30	18 38	18 44	18 54		19 00	19 17		19 30	19 38	19 54	20 00	20 15	20 16	20 25		
Kemble	d								19 07							20 07				20 38		
Stroud	d								19 22							20 22				20 53		
Stonehouse	d								19 28							20 28				20 59		
Gloucester 7	a								19 45							20 45				21 14		
Cheltenham Spa	a								20 03							21 02				21 33		
Worcester Shrub Hill	d			19 07	19a34					20a03			20a41								21 32	21a46
Chippenham	d	18 14				18 44		19a01			19 14			19 44			20 15					
Bath Spa 7	a	18 27				18 57					19 28			19 57			20 29					
Bristol Parkway 7	a		18 40	20 22			19 04					19 42			20 04			20 40	20 42		23 04	
	d		18 41	20 22			19 07					19 44			20 07			20 42	20 43		23 05	
Bristol Temple Meads 10	a	18 44		20 38		19 12					19 43			20 13			20 44				23 19	
Weston-super-Mare	a					19 48								20 53								
Newport (South Wales)	a		19 11				19 31					20 07			20 31			21 04	21 05			
Cardiff Central 7	a		19 26				19 48					20 22			20 48			21 19	21 19			
Bridgend	a		19 49				20 10					20 45			21 15			21 45	21 45			
Port Talbot Parkway	a		20 02				20 26					20 58			21 28			21 58	21 58			
Neath	a		20 10				20 33					21 05			21 36			22 06	22 06			
Swansea	a		20 23				20 47					21 19			21 49			22 19	22 19			

		GW ◇1 ⊡	GW FX ◇1 ⊡	GW FO ◇1 ⊡	GW ◇1 ⊡	GW ◇1 F ⊡Ø	GW ◇1 A ⊼	GW ◇1 ⊡	GW	GW ◇1 ⊡	GW ◇1 ⊡	GW FO ◇1 A ⊼	GW FX ◇1 ⊡	GW FO ◇1 ⊡	GW FX ◇1 ⊡	GW	GW FO ◇1 ⊡	GW FX ◇1 ⊡	GW FO ◇1 ⊡	GW FX ◇1 ⊡
London Paddington 15 ⊖	d	19 30	19 48	19 48	20 00	20 15	20 20	20 45		21 15	21 45	21 48	21 48	22 15	22 15		22 45	22 45	23 30	23 30
Slough 3	d						20 36					22 03	22 03							
Reading 7	d	19 57	20 18	20 18	20 27	20 41	20 52	21 11		21 41	22 11	22 22	22 22	22 41	22 49		23 11	23 19	00 08	00 08
Didcot Parkway	d	20 12	20 33	20 33	20 42	20 57		21 26		22 00	22 31			23 01	23 09		23 30	23 39	00 25	00 25
Swindon	a	20 30	20 52	20 48	21 00	21 14		21 43		22 18	22 48			23 19	23 26		23 48	23 55	00 44	00 44
	d	20 30	20 54	20 54	21 00	21 15		21 44	22 04	22 19	22 49			23 21	23 27	23 33	23 49	23 57	00 45	00 45
Kemble	d		21 11	21 11					22 21							23 47				
Stroud	d		21 26	21 26					22 36							00 02				
Stonehouse	d		21 31	21 31					22 41							00 07				
Gloucester 7	a		21 46	21 46					22 56							00 24				
Cheltenham Spa	a		22 02	22 02					23 11											
Worcester Shrub Hill	d		22a24	22a24			22a40					00a12	00a12							
Chippenham	d	20 44			21 16			21 58			23 03			23 33	23 40				00 59	00 59
Bath Spa 7	a	20 59			21 29			22 11			23 17			23 47	23 54				01 13	01 13
Bristol Parkway 7	a					21 40				22 45							00 14	00 21		
	d					21 41				22 45							00 16	00 23		
Bristol Temple Meads 10	a	21 15			21 44			22 30			23 32			00 03	00 10				01 29	01 29
Weston-super-Mare	a	21 50									00s05									
Newport (South Wales)	a					22 03				23 19							00 38	00 51	02s02	02s10
Cardiff Central 7	a					22 23				23 40							00 53	01 11	02 19	02 31
Bridgend	a					22 46				00 02							01 19	01 36		
Port Talbot Parkway	a					22 59				00 15							01 32	01 49		
Neath	a					23 07				00 22							01 39	01 57		
Swansea	a					23 20				00 37							01 53	02 10		

A ⊼ to Reading
B The Capitals United
C The Red Dragon. ⊡ from Bridgend Ø to Bridgend
D The Bristolian
E The Cathedrals Express
F ⊡ from Bridgend Ø to Bridgend
G from 06 July to 31 August

For connections from Heathrow Airport, Gatwick Airport and Oxford please refer to Tables 125A, 148 and 116. For connections to Birmingham New Street and Hereford please refer to Tables 57 and 131

from 17 September

London - Swindon, Cheltenham Spa, Bristol, Weston-super-Mare and South Wales

Route Diagram - see first Page of Table 125

		GW MX ◇1 ⊡	GW MX ◇1 ⊡	GW MO ◇1 ⊡	GW MO	GW MO ◇1 ⊡	GW MX ◇1 ⊡	GW MX	GW MO ◇1 A ⊡	GW MO ◇1 B ⊡	GW MX ◇1 ⊡	GW MO ◇1 B ⊡	GW MO ◇1 A ⊡	GW B 🚌	GW MX ◇1 ⊡	GW MO ◇1 B ⊡	GW MO ◇1 A ⊡	GW B 🚌	GW B 🚌	GW	GW ◇1 ⊡	GW ◇1 ⊡	GW ◇
London Paddington 15 ⊖	d	21p15	21p45	21p37		22p03	22p15		22p37	22p37	22p45	23p03	23p03		23p30	23p37	23p37				05 27	05 36	
Slough 3	d															00 02	00 02					05 52	
Reading 7	d	21p41	22p11	22p14		22p50	22p49		23p17	23p17	23p19	23p46	23p46		00 08	00 14	00 14				05 56	06 07	
Didcot Parkway	d	22p00	22p31	22p29		23p07	23p09		23b32	23b32	23p39	00s04	00s04		00 25	00s31	00s33					06 21	
Swindon	a	22p18	22p48	22p49		23p27	23p26		23b51	23b51	23p55	00s23	00s23		00 44	00s51	00s53				06 23	06 41	
	d	22p19	22p49	22p50	22p57	23p27	23p27	23p33			23p57			00 33	00 45			01 00	01 01	06 12	06 25	06 50	
Kemble	d				23p11			23p47														07 07	
Stroud	d				23p26			00 02														07 22	
Stonehouse	d				23p31			00 07														07 28	
Gloucester 7	a				23p48			00 24														07 45	
Cheltenham Spa	a				00 05																	08 01	
Worcester Shrub Hill	d																						06 49
Chippenham	d		23p03			23p43	23p40						00s39	01s08	00 59		01s08	01s35	01s36	06a28	06 39		
Bath Spa 7	a		23p17			23p56	23p54						00s53	01 43	01 13		01s23	02 10	02 11		06 52		
Bristol Parkway 7	a	22p45		23p15					00s18	00s21	00 21												08 19
	d	22p45		23p16							00 23												08 19
Bristol Temple Meads 10	a		23p32			00 11	00 10		00 35	00 35		01 01	01 07		01 29	01 25	01 37				07 07		08 36
Weston-super-Mare	a		00s05																				
Newport (South Wales)	a	23p19		23p40							00 51				02s10						07 44		
Cardiff Central 7	a	23p40		00 05							01 11				02 31						08 00		
Bridgend	a	00 02		00 28							01 36										08 23		
Port Talbot Parkway	a	00 15		00 40							01 49										08 36		
Neath	a	00 22		00 48							01 57										08 44		
Swansea	a	00 37		01 02							02 10										08 57		

		GW ◇1	GW ◇1 ⊡	GW ◇1 ⊡	GW	GW	GW 1	GW ◇1 ⊡	GW ◇1 ⊡	GW ◇1 C Ø	GW ◇1 D ⊡	GW ◇1 ⊡	GW ◇1 ⊡	GW ◇1 ⊡	GW ◇1 ⊡	GW ◇1 ⊡	GW ◇1 E ⊡Ø	GW ◇1 ⊡	GW	GW ◇1 ⊡	GW 1 ⊼	GW ◇1	GW ◇1 F ⊡Ø
London Paddington 15 ⊖	d	05 48	06 30	06 45			06 48	07 00	07 15	07 30	07 45	07 48	08 00	08 15	08 22	08 30	08 45	09 00		09 15		09 21	09 30
Slough 3	d	06 05					07 04								08 36							09 36	
Reading 7	d	06 22	06 56	07 11			07 22	07 26	07 42	07 57	08 11	08 16	08 27	08 42	08 52	08 57	09 11	09 27		09 42		09 52	09 57
Didcot Parkway	d	06 39	07 12				07 49	07 42	07 57			08 33	08 41	08 57		09 12				09 57			10 12
Swindon	a		07 28	07 38				07 58	08 14	08 27	08 38	08 53	08 59	09 14		09 30	09 38	09 54		10 14			10 30
	d		07 30	07 38	07 54			08 00	08 15	08 27	08 38	08 54	09 00	09 15		09 31	09 38	09 55	09 54	10 15			10 31
Kemble	d				08 07							09 07							10 07				
Stroud	d				08 22							09 22							10 22				
Stonehouse	d				08 28							09 28							10 28				
Gloucester 7	a				08 50							09 44							10 50				
Cheltenham Spa	a				09 05							10 03							11 05				
Worcester Shrub Hill	d	08a10				09 06	09a15								10a44						11 06	11a34	
Chippenham	d		07 44					08 14		08 42			09 14			09 45		10 09					10 44
Bath Spa 7	a		07 57					08 27		08 55			09 29			09 59		10 23					10 59
Bristol Parkway 7	a			08 04		10 22			08 40		09 04			09 40			10 04			10 40	12 22		
	d			08 07		10 22			08 41		09 07			09 41			10 07			10 41	12 22		
Bristol Temple Meads 10	a		08 17			10 37		08 45		09 10			09 45			10 15		10 38			12 34		11 15
Weston-super-Mare	a																						
Newport (South Wales)	a			08 32					09 07		09 31			10 04			10 31			11 06			
Cardiff Central 7	a			08 46					09 24		09 48			10 21			10 46			11 23			
Bridgend	a			09 09							10 09						11 09						
Port Talbot Parkway	a			09 22							10 22						11 22						
Neath	a			09 30							10 30						11 30						
Swansea	a			09 45							10 44						11 43						

		GW ◇1 E ⊡Ø	GW ◇1 ⊡	GW ◇1 G ⊡	GW ◇1 ⊡	GW ◇1 ⊡	GW ◇1 F ⊡Ø	GW ◇1 E ⊡Ø	GW	GW ◇1 ⊡	GW ◇1 ⊡	GW ◇	GW ◇1 ⊼	GW ◇1 ⊡	GW ◇1 E ⊡Ø	GW ◇1 H ⊡	GW ◇1 ⊡	GW ◇1 ⊡	GW ◇1 ⊼	GW ◇1 ⊡	GW ◇1 E ⊡Ø	GW ◇1 ⊡
London Paddington 15 ⊖	d	09 45	09 48	10 00	10 15	10 22	10 30	10 45		11 00	11 15		11 20	11 30	11 45	11 48	12 00	12 15	12 21	12 30	12 45	13 00
Slough 3	d					10 36							11 36						12 36			
Reading 7	d	10 11	10 16	10 27	10 42	10 52	10 57	11 11		11 27	11 42		11 52	11 57	12 11	12 16	12 27	12 42	12 52	12 57	13 11	13 27
Didcot Parkway	d		10 33		10 57		11 12				11 57			12 12		12 33		12 57		13 12		
Swindon	a	10 38	10 53	10 55	11 14		11 30	11 38		11 55	12 14			12 30	12 38	12 53	12 55	13 14		13 30	13 38	13 54
	d	10 38	10 54	10 55	11 15		11 30	11 38	11 54	11 55	12 15			12 30	12 38	12 54	12 55	13 15		13 32	13 38	13 55
Kemble	d		11 07						12 07							13 07						
Stroud	d		11 22						12 22							13 22						
Stonehouse	d		11 28						12 28							13 28						
Gloucester 7	a		11 44						12 50							13 44						
Cheltenham Spa	a		12 03						13 05							14 03						
Worcester Shrub Hill	d					12a44						13 06	13a31						14a46			
Chippenham	d			11 09			11 44			12 09				12 44			13 09			13 44		14 09
Bath Spa 7	a			11 24			11 59			12 23				12 59			13 24			13 59		14 23
Bristol Parkway 7	a	11 04			11 40			12 04			12 40	14 22			13 04			13 40			14 04	
	d	11 07			11 41			12 07			12 41	14 22			13 07			13 41			14 07	
Bristol Temple Meads 10	a			11 40			12 15			12 39		14 38		13 15			13 44			14 15		14 39
Weston-super-Mare	a			12 06																		
Newport (South Wales)	a	11 31			12 04			12 31			13 06				13 31			14 04			14 30	
Cardiff Central 7	a	11 46			12 21			12 46			13 22				13 46			14 22			14 46	
Bridgend	a	12 09						13 09							14 09						15 09	
Port Talbot Parkway	a	12 22						13 22							14 22						15 22	
Neath	a	12 30						13 30							14 30						15 30	
Swansea	a	12 43						13 44							14 43						15 43	

A from 29 October
B from 17 September until 22 October
C The Merchant Venturer
D The St. David
E ⊡ from Bridgend Ø to Bridgend
F ⊡ from Chippenham Ø to Chippenham
G The Torbay Express
H The Cheltenham Spa Express
b Previous night, stops to set down only

For connections from Heathrow Airport, Gatwick Airport and Oxford please refer to Tables 125A, 148 and 116. For connections to Birmingham New Street and Hereford please refer to Tables 57 and 131

London - Swindon, Cheltenham Spa, Bristol, Weston-super-Mare and South Wales

Route Diagram - see first Page of Table 125

		GW	GW ◇1 ⊡	GW ◇1 ⊡	GW ◇1 ⊡	GW ◇1 ⊡	GW ◇1 ⊡	GW ◇1 ⊡	GW ◇	GW ◇1 A ⌶	GW ◇1 ⊡	GW ◇1 ⊡	GW	GW ◇1 ⊡	GW ◇1 ⊡	GW ◇1 ⊡	GW ◇1 ⊡	GW ◇1 ⊡	GW	GW ◇1 ⊡	GW ◇1 ⊡	GW ◇1 ⊡	GW ◇1 ⊡
London Paddington 15 ⊖	d		13 15	13 30	13 45	13 48	14 00	14 15		14 21	14 30	14 45		15 00	15 15	15 30	15 45	15 48		15 51	16 00	16 15	16 30
Slough 3	d									14 36										16 06			
Reading 7	d		13 42	13 57	14 11	14 16	14 27	14 42		14 52	14 57	15 11		15 27	15 42	15 57	16 11	16 16		16 22	16 27	16 41	16 57
Didcot Parkway	d		13 57	14 12		14 33		14 57			15 12				15 57	16 12		16 33				16 56	17 12
Swindon	a		14 14	14 30	14 38	14 54	14 55	15 14			15 30	15 38		15 55	16 14	16 30	16 38	16 53			16 55	17 13	17 30
	d	13 54	14 15	14 30	14 38	14 54	14 55	15 15			15 30	15 38	15 54	15 55	16 15	16 30	16 38	16 54			16 55	17 15	17 30
Kemble	d	14 07				15 07							16 07					17 07					
Stroud	d	14 22				15 22							16 22					17 22					
Stonehouse	d	14 28				15 28							16 28					17 28					
Gloucester 7	a	14 50				15 44							16 50					17 46					
Cheltenham Spa	a	15 05				16 03							17 05					18 03					
Worcester Shrub Hill	d								15 06	16a39									17 06	18a08			
Chippenham	d			14 44			15 09				15 44			16 10		16 45					17 13		17 45
Bath Spa 7	a			14 59			15 24				15 59			16 24		16 59					17 26		17 59
Bristol Parkway 7	a		14 40		15 04			15 40	16 22			16 05			16 40		17 04		18 22			17 40	
	d		14 41		15 07			15 41	16 22			16 07			16 41		17 07		18 22			17 41	
Bristol Temple Meads 10	a			15 15			15 40		16 37		16 15			16 39		17 15			18 38		17 41		18 14
Weston-super-Mare	a										16 52					17 52							18 51
Newport (South Wales)	a		15 06		15 31			16 05				16 30			17 06		17 31					18 04	
Cardiff Central 7	a		15 22		15 46			16 22				16 46			17 22		17 46					18 19	
Bridgend	a				16 09							17 09					18 09					18 44	
Port Talbot Parkway	a				16 22							17 22					18 22					18 57	
Neath	a				16 30							17 30					18 30					19 04	
Swansea	a				16 43							17 43					18 48					19 18	

		GW ◇1 B ⊡	GW ◇	GW ◇1 ⊡	GW ◇1 C ⊡⊘	GW	GW ◇1 ⊡	GW ◇1 ⊡	GW ◇1 ⊡	GW ◇	GW ◇1 ⊡	GW ◇1 ⊡	GW ◇1 D ⊡	GW ◇1 ⊡	GW ◇1 E ⊡	GW ◇1 ⊡	GW ◇1 ⊡	GW ◇1 ⊡	GW ◇1 ⊡	GW FX ◇1 ⊡	GW FO ◇1 ⊡	GW ◇
London Paddington 15 ⊖	d	16 45		17 00	17 15		17 22	17 30	17 45		17 48	17 50	18 00	18 15	18 22	18 30	18 45	18 47	19 00	19 15	19 15	
Slough 3	d																					
Reading 7	d	17 11		17 26	17 43		17 50	17 56	18 11		18 16	18 22	18 27	18 43	18 50	18 56	19 11	19 18	19 27	19 41	19u48	
Didcot Parkway	d			17 42	17 57			18 11			18 33		18 42	18 57		19 12		19 33	19 42	19 57		
Swindon	a	17 38		17 58	18 14			18 28	18 38		18 53		18 59	19 15		19 28	19 38	19 52	20 00	20 13	20 15	
	d	17 38	17 54	18 00	18 15			18 30	18 38	18 44	18 54		19 00	19 17		19 30	19 38	19 54	20 00	20 15	20 16	20 25
Kemble	d		18 07								19 07							20 07				20 38
Stroud	d		18 22								19 22							20 22				20 53
Stonehouse	d		18 28								19 28							20 28				20 59
Gloucester 7	a		18 49								19 45							20 45				21 14
Cheltenham Spa	a		19 05								20 03							21 02				21 33
Worcester Shrub Hill	d					19 07	19a34					20a03			20a41							
Chippenham	d			18 14				18 44		19a01			19 14			19 44			20 15			
Bath Spa 7	a			18 27				18 57					19 28			19 57			20 29			
Bristol Parkway 7	a	18 04			18 40	20 22			19 04					19 42			20 04			20 40	20 42	
	d	18 07			18 41	20 22			19 07					19 44			20 07			20 42	20 43	
Bristol Temple Meads 10	a			18 44		20 38		19 12					19 43			20 13			20 44			
Weston-super-Mare	a							19 48								20 53						
Newport (South Wales)	a	18 30			19 11				19 31					20 07			20 31			21 04	21 05	
Cardiff Central 7	a	18 48			19 26				19 48					20 22			20 48			21 19	21 19	
Bridgend	a	19 09			19 49				20 10					20 45			21 15			21 45	21 45	
Port Talbot Parkway	a	19 22			20 02				20 26					20 58			21 28			21 58	21 58	
Neath	a	19 30			20 10				20 33					21 05			21 36			22 06	22 06	
Swansea	a	19 46			20 23				20 47					21 19			21 49			22 19	22 19	

		GW	GW ◇1 ⊡	GW ◇1 ⊡	GW FX ◇1 ⊡	GW FO ◇1 ⊡	GW ◇1 ⊡	GW ◇1 F ⊡⊘	GW ◇1 A ⌶	GW ◇1 ⊡	GW	GW ◇1 ⊡	GW ◇1 ⊡	GW FO ◇1 A ⌶	GW FX ◇1 ⊡	GW FO ◇1 ⊡	GW FX ◇1 ⊡	GW	GW FO ◇1 ⊡	GW FX ◇1 ⊡	GW FO ◇1 ⊡	GW FX ◇1 ⊡
London Paddington 15 ⊖	d		19 22	19 30	19 48	19 48	20 00	20 15	20 20	20 45		21 15	21 45	21 48	21 48	22 15	22 15		22 45	22 45	23 30	23 30
Slough 3	d		19 36						20 36					22 03	22 03							
Reading 7	d		19 52	19 57	20 18	20 18	20 27	20 41	20 52	21 11		21 41	22 11	22 22	22 22	22 41	22 49		23 11	23 19	00 08	00 08
Didcot Parkway	d			20 12	20 33	20 33	20 42	20 57		21 26		22 00	22 31			23 01	23 09		23 30	23 39	00 25	00 25
Swindon	a			20 30	20 52	20 48	21 00	21 14		21 43		22 18	22 48			23 19	23 26		23 48	23 55	00 44	00 44
	d			20 30	20 54	20 54	21 00	21 15		21 44	22 04	22 19	22 49			23 21	23 27	23 33	23 49	23 57	00 45	00 45
Kemble	d				21 11	21 11					22 21							23 47				
Stroud	d				21 26	21 26					22 36							00 02				
Stonehouse	d				21 31	21 31					22 41							00 07				
Gloucester 7	a				21 46	21 46					22 56							00 24				
Cheltenham Spa	a				22 02	22 02					23 11											
Worcester Shrub Hill	d	21 32	21a46		22a24	22a24			22a40					00a12	00a12							
Chippenham	d			20 44			21 16			21 58			23 03			23 33	23 40				00 59	00 59
Bath Spa 7	a			20 59			21 29			22 11			23 17			23 47	23 54				01 13	01 13
Bristol Parkway 7	a	23 04						21 40				22 45							00 14	00 21		
	d	23 05						21 41				22 45							00 16	00 23		
Bristol Temple Meads 10	a	23 19		21 15			21 44			22 30			23 32			00 03	00 10				01 29	01 29
Weston-super-Mare	a			21 50									00s05									
Newport (South Wales)	a							22 03				23 19							00 38	00 51	02s02	02s10
Cardiff Central 7	a							22 23				23 40							00 53	01 11	02 19	02 31
Bridgend	a							22 46				00 02							01 19	01 36		
Port Talbot Parkway	a							22 59				00 15							01 32	01 49		
Neath	a							23 07				00 22							01 39	01 57		
Swansea	a							23 20				00 37							01 53	02 10		

A ⌶ to Reading
B The Capitals United
C The Red Dragon. ⊡ from Bridgend ⊘ to Bridgend
D The Bristolian
E The Cathedrals Express
F ⊡ from Bridgend ⊘ to Bridgend

For connections from Heathrow Airport, Gatwick Airport and Oxford please refer to Tables 125A, 148 and 116. For connections to Birmingham New Street and Hereford please refer to Tables 57 and 131

London - Swindon, Cheltenham Spa, Bristol, Weston-super-Mare and South Wales

Route Diagram - see first Page of Table 125

		GW ◇1 ⊡	GW ◇1 ⊡	GW ◇1 ⊡	GW	GW ◇1 ⊡	GW ◇1 ⊡	GW ◇	GW ◇1	GW ◇1	GW	GW ◇1 ⊡	GW ◇1 ⊡	GW	GW ◇1	GW ■ 1 ⊡	GW ◇1 ⊡	GW ◇1 ⊡	GW ◇1 ⊡	GW ◇1 ⊡	GW ◇1 ⊡	GW ◇1 ⊡	GW ◇1 ⊡
London Paddington 15 ⊖	d	21p15	21p45	22p15		22p45	23p30		05 21	06 21		06 30	07 00		07 21	07 30	07 45	08 00	08 15	08 21	08 30	08 45	09 00
Slough 3	d								05 38	06 38					07 38					08 39			
Reading 7	d	21p41	22p11	22p41		23p11	00 08		05 54	06 54		06 59	07 27		07 53	07 57	08 11	08 27	08 42	08 54	08 57	09 11	09 27
Didcot Parkway	d	22p00	22p31	23p01		23p30	00 25		06 08			07 12				08 12			08 56		09 12		
Swindon	a	22p18	22p48	23p19		23p48	00 44					07 30	07 54			08 30	08 38	08 55	09 15		09 30	09 38	09 54
	d	22p19	22p49	23p21	23p33	23p49	00 45				07 16	07 30	07 55			08 30	08 38	08 55	09 15		09 30	09 38	09 55
Kemble	d				23p47						07 30								09 31				
Stroud	d				00 02						07 45								09 46				
Stonehouse	d				00 07						07 50								09 51				
Gloucester 7	a				00 24						08 06								10 06				
Cheltenham Spa	a										08 24								10 22				
Worcester Shrub Hill	d							06 47	07a44	08a40				09 08	09a40					10a44			
Chippenham	d		23p03	23p33			00 59					07 44	08 09			08 44		09 09			09 44		10 09
Bath Spa 7	a		23p17	23p47			01 13					08 00	08 24			09 00		09 24			10 00		10 24
Bristol Parkway 7	a	22p45				00 14		08 19						10 24			09 04					10 05	
	d	22p45				00 16		08 19						10 25			09 07					10 07	
Bristol Temple Meads 10	a		23p32	00 03			01 29	08 34				08 15	08 39	10 39		09 15		09 39			10 15		10 39
Weston-super-Mare	a		00s05																				11 06
Newport (South Wales)	a	23p19				00 38	02s02										09 30					10 31	
Cardiff Central 7	a	23p40				00 53	02 19										09 47					10 47	
Bridgend	a	00 02				01 19											10 09					11 09	
Port Talbot Parkway	a	00 15				01 32											10 22					11 22	
Neath	a	00 22				01 39											10 30					11 30	
Swansea	a	00 37				01 53											10 43					11 43	

		GW	GW ◇1 ⊡	GW ◇1 ⊡	GW ◇1 ⊡	GW ◇1 ⊡	GW ■	GW ◇1 ⊡	GW ◇1 ⊡	GW ◇1 A ⊡⊘	GW ◇1 ⊡	GW	GW ◇	GW ◇1 ⌶	GW ◇1 B ⊡⊘	GW ◇1 A ⊡⊘	GW ◇1 ⊡	GW ◇1 ⊡	GW ◇1 ⊡	GW ◇1 ⊡	GW ◇1 ⊡	GW	GW ◇
London Paddington 15 ⊖	d		09 30	09 45	10 00	10 15		10 21	10 30	10 45	11 00			11 21	11 30	11 45	12 00	12 15	12 30	12 45	13 00		
Slough 3	d							10 39						11 39									
Reading 7	d		09 57	10 11	10 27	10 42		10 54	10 57	11 11	11 27			11 54	11 58	12 11	12 27	12 42	12 57	13 11	13 27		
Didcot Parkway	d		10 12			10 56			11 12						12 12			12 56	13 12				
Swindon	a		10 30	10 38	10 54	11 15			11 30	11 38	11 54				12 30	12 38	12 54	13 15	13 30	13 38	13 55		
	d	10 14	10 30	10 38	10 55	11 15			11 30	11 38	11 55	12 14			12 30	12 38	12 55	13 15	13 30	13 38	13 55	14 14	
Kemble	d	10 28				11 31						12 28						13 31				14 28	
Stroud	d	10 43				11 46						12 43						13 46				14 43	
Stonehouse	d	10 48				11 51						12 48						13 51				14 48	
Gloucester 7	a	11 07				12 07						13 03						14 06				15 03	
Cheltenham Spa	a	11 23				12 22						13 24						14 22				15 25	
Worcester Shrub Hill	d						11 06	12a39					12 54	13a40									15 06
Chippenham	d		10 44		11 09				11 44		12 09				12 44		13 09		13 44		14 09		
Bath Spa 7	a		11 00		11 24				12 00		12 24				12 59		13 24		14 00		14 24		
Bristol Parkway 7	a			11 04			12 24			12 04			14 20			13 04				14 04			16 24
	d			11 07			12 25			12 07			14 20			13 07				14 07			16 25
Bristol Temple Meads 10	a		11 15		11 39		12 39		12 15		12 39		14 36		13 14		13 42		14 15		14 39		16 39
Weston-super-Mare	a								12 35										14 35				
Newport (South Wales)	a			11 31						12 31						13 31				14 31			
Cardiff Central 7	a			11 46						12 46						13 47				14 46			
Bridgend	a			12 09						13 09						14 09				15 09			
Port Talbot Parkway	a			12 22						13 22						14 22				15 22			
Neath	a			12 30						13 30						14 30				15 30			
Swansea	a			12 43						13 43						14 43				15 43			

		GW ◇1 ⌶	GW ◇1 ⊡	GW ◇1 ⊡	GW ◇1 ⊡	GW ◇1 ⊡	GW ◇1 ⌶	GW	GW ◇1 ⊡	GW ◇1 ⊡	GW ◇1 ⊡	GW	GW	GW ◇1 C ⌶	GW ◇1 ⊡	GW ◇1 ⊡	GW ◇1 ⊡	GW ◇1 ⊡	GW ◇1 ⊡	GW ◇1 ⊡	GW ◇1 ⊡	GW ◇1 ⊡
London Paddington 15 ⊖	d	13 21	13 30	13 45	14 00	14 15	14 21		14 30	14 45	15 00			15 21	15 30	15 45	16 00	16 15	16 21	16 30	16 45	17 00
Slough 3	d	13 39					14 39							15 39					16 39			
Reading 7	d	13 54	13 59	14 11	14 27	14 42	14 54		14 57	15 11	15 27			15 54	15 59	16 11	16 27	16 42	16 54	16 57	17 11	17 27
Didcot Parkway	d		14 12			14 56			15 12						16 12			16 56		17 12		
Swindon	a		14 30	14 38	14 54	15 15			15 30	15 38	15 54				16 30	16 38	16 54	17 15		17 30	17 38	17 54
	d		14 30	14 38	14 55	15 15		15 22	15 30	15 38	15 55	16 14			16 30	16 38	16 55	17 15		17 30	17 38	17 55
Kemble	d					15 31						16 28						17 31				
Stroud	d					15 46						16 43						17 46				
Stonehouse	d					15 51						16 48						17 51				
Gloucester 7	a					16 06						17 03						18 06				
Cheltenham Spa	a					16 22						17 25						18 22				
Worcester Shrub Hill	d	15a40					16a40						17 08	17a40					18a43			
Chippenham	d		14 44		15 09			15a38	15 44		16 09				16 44		17 09			17 44		18 09
Bath Spa 7	a		15 00		15 24				16 00		16 24				17 00		17 24			18 00		18 24
Bristol Parkway 7	a			15 04						16 04			18 24			17 04					18 04	
	d			15 07						16 07			18 25			17 07					18 07	
Bristol Temple Meads 10	a		15 15		15 41				16 15		16 39		18 39		17 15		17 39			18 15		18 39
Weston-super-Mare	a								16 35						17 35					18 36		
Newport (South Wales)	a			15 31						16 31						17 29					18 30	
Cardiff Central 7	a			15 46						16 47						17 46					18 46	
Bridgend	a			16 09						17 09						18 09					19 09	
Port Talbot Parkway	a			16 22						17 22						18 22					19 22	
Neath	a			16 30						17 30						18 30					19 30	
Swansea	a			16 43						17 43						18 46					19 43	

A ⊡ from Bridgend ⊘ to Bridgend
B ⊡ from Chippenham ⊘ to Chippenham
C ⌶ to Reading

For connections from Heathrow Airport, Gatwick Airport and Oxford please refer to Tables 125A, 148 and 116. For connections to Birmingham New Street and Hereford please refer to Tables 57 and 131

Saturdays
until 23 June

London - Swindon, Cheltenham Spa, Bristol, Weston-super-Mare and South Wales

Route Diagram - see first Page of Table 125

		GW	GW	GW	GW	GW	GW	GW	GW	GW	GW	GW	GW	GW	GW	GW	GW	GW	GW	GW	GW	GW	GW
				◇1 ⊏⊐	◇1 ⊏⊐	◇1 ⊏⊐	◇1 ⊏⊐	◇1 ⊏⊐	◇1 ⊏⊐	◇1 ⊏⊐	◇1 ⊏⊐	◇1 ⊏⊐		◇1 ⊏⊐	◇1 ⊏⊐	◇1 A ✕	◇1 ⊏⊐		◇1 ⊏⊐	◇1 ⊏⊐	◇1 ⊏⊐	◇1 ⊏⊐	◇1
London Paddington 15 ⊖	d			17 21	17 30	17 45	18 00	18 15	18 21	18 30	18 45	19 00		19 30	19 45	19 50	20 00		20 15	20 30	20 45	21 30	21 50
Slough 3	d			17 39					18 39							20 06							22 06
Reading 7	d			17 54	17 57	18 11	18 27	18 42	18 54	18 57	19 11	19 27		19 57	20 11	20 22	20 27		20 42	20 57	21 13	21 57	22 23
Didcot Parkway	d				18 12			18 56		19 12				20 12			20 42		20 56	21 12		22 12	22 38
Swindon	a				18 30	18 38	18 54	19 15		19 29	19 38	19 54		20 30	20 38		21 00		21 15	21 30	21 40	22 30	
	d	18 14			18 30	18 38	18 55	19 15		19 30	19 38	19 55	20 00	20 30	20 38		21 00	21 08	21 15	21 30	21 41	22 30	
Kemble	d	18 28						19 31					20 15						21 31				
Stroud	d	18 43						19 46					20 30						21 46				
Stonehouse	d	18 48						19 51					20 35						21 51				
Gloucester 7	a	19 03						20 06					20 50						22 05				
Cheltenham Spa	a	19 25						20 22					21 03						22 20				
Worcester Shrub Hill	d		19 07	19a40					20a42							22a02							00a07
Chippenham	d				18 44		19 09			19 44		20 09		20 45			21 14	21a24		21 45		22 44	
Bath Spa 7	a				19 00		19 24			19 59		20 24		21 00			21 29			21 58		23 00	
Bristol Parkway 7	a		20 24			19 05					20 05				21 04						22 06		
	d		20 25			19 07					20 07				21 07						22 11		
Bristol Temple Meads 10	a		20 39		19 15		19 38			20 15		20 40		21 16			21 45			22 14		23 15	
Weston-super-Mare	a				19 50					20 36		21 26								22s47			
Newport (South Wales)	a					19 30					20 30				21 30						22 46		
Cardiff Central 7	a					19 46					20 44				21 47						23 06		
Bridgend	a					20 09					21 09				22 09						23 28		
Port Talbot Parkway	a					20 22					21 22				22 22						23 41		
Neath	a					20 30					21 30				22 30						23 49		
Swansea	a					20 43					21 43				22 43						00 02		

		GW	GW	GW	GW
			◇1 ⊏⊐	◇1 ⊏⊐	◇1 ⊏⊐
London Paddington 15 ⊖	d		22 00	22 35	23 30
Slough 3	d				
Reading 7	d		22 27	23 02	23 59
Didcot Parkway	d		22 41	23 23	00 18
Swindon	a		22 59	23 39	00 38
	d	22 35	22 59	23 41	00 38
Kemble	d	22 49			
Stroud	d	23 04			
Stonehouse	d	23 09			
Gloucester 7	a	23 25			
Cheltenham Spa	a				
Worcester Shrub Hill	d				
Chippenham	d			23 55	00 53
Bath Spa 7	a			00 11	01 08
Bristol Parkway 7	a		23 27		
	d		23 28		
Bristol Temple Meads 10	a			00 25	01 23
Weston-super-Mare	a				
Newport (South Wales)	a		23 57		
Cardiff Central 7	a		00 18		
Bridgend	a				
Port Talbot Parkway	a				
Neath	a				
Swansea	a				

Saturdays
30 June to 8 September

		GW	GW	GW	GW	GW	GW	GW	GW	GW	GW	GW	GW	GW	GW	GW	GW	GW	GW	GW	GW	GW	GW
		◇1 ⊏⊐	◇1 ⊏⊐	◇1 ⊏⊐		◇1 ⊏⊐	◇1 ⊏⊐	◇	◇1	◇1		◇1 ⊏⊐	◇1 ⊏⊐		◇1	■ 1 ⊏⊐	◇1 ⊏⊐	◇1 ⊏⊐	◇1 ⊏⊐	◇1 ⊏⊐	◇1 ⊏⊐	◇1 ⊏⊐	◇1 ⊏⊐
London Paddington 15 ⊖	d	21p15	21p45	22p15		22p45	23p30		05 21	06 21		06 30	07 00		07 21	07 30	07 45	08 00	08 15	08 21	08 30	08 45	09 00
Slough 3	d								05 38	06 38					07 38					08 39			
Reading 7	d	21p41	22p11	22p41		23p11	00 08		05 54	06 54		06 59	07 27		07 53	07 57	08 11	08 27	08 42	08 54	08 57	09 11	09 27
Didcot Parkway	d	22p00	22p31	23p01		23p30	00 25		06 08			07 12				08 12			08 56		09 12		
Swindon	a	22p18	22p48	23p19		23p48	00 44					07 30	07 54			08 30	08 38	08 55	09 15		09 30	09 38	09 54
	d	22p19	22p49	23p21	23p33	23p49	00 45				07 16	07 30	07 55			08 30	08 38	08 55	09 15		09 30	09 38	09 55
Kemble	d				23p47						07 30								09 31				
Stroud	d				00 02						07 45								09 46				
Stonehouse	d				00 07						07 50								09 51				
Gloucester 7	a				00 24						08 06								10 06				
Cheltenham Spa	a										08 24								10 22				
Worcester Shrub Hill	d							06 47	07a44	08a40				09 08	09a40					10a44			
Chippenham	d		23p03	23p33			00 59					07 44	08 09			08 44		09 09			09 44		10 09
Bath Spa 7	a		23p17	23p47			01 13					08 00	08 24			09 00		09 24			10 00		10 24
Bristol Parkway 7	a	22p45				00 14		08 19						10 24			09 04					10 05	
	d	22p45				00 16		08 19						10 25			09 07					10 07	
Bristol Temple Meads 10	a		23p32	00 03			01 29	08 34				08 15	08 39	10 39		09 15		09 39			10 15		10 39
Weston-super-Mare	a		00s05																				11 06
Newport (South Wales)	a	23p19				00 38	02s02										09 30					10 31	
Cardiff Central 7	a	23p40				00 53	02 19										09 47					10 47	
Bridgend	a	00 02				01 19											10 09					11 09	
Port Talbot Parkway	a	00 15				01 32											10 22					11 22	
Neath	a	00 22				01 39											10 30					11 30	
Swansea	a	00 37				01 53											10 43					11 43	

A ✕ to Reading

For connections from Heathrow Airport, Gatwick Airport and Oxford please refer to Tables 125A, 148 and 116. For connections to Birmingham New Street and Hereford please refer to Tables 57 and 131

Saturdays
30 June to 8 September

London - Swindon, Cheltenham Spa, Bristol, Weston-super-Mare and South Wales

Route Diagram - see first Page of Table 125

		GW	GW	GW	GW	GW	GW	GW	GW	GW	GW	GW	GW	GW	GW	GW	GW	GW	GW	GW	GW	GW	GW
			◇1 ⊏⊐	◇1 ⊏⊐	◇1 ⊏⊐	◇1 ⊏⊐	■	◇1 ⊏⊐	◇1 ⊏⊐	◇1 A ⊏⊐⊘	◇1 ⊏⊐		◇	◇1 ✕	◇1 B ⊏⊐⊘	◇1 A ⊏⊐⊘	◇1 ⊏⊐	◇1 ⊏⊐	◇1 ⊏⊐	◇1 ⊏⊐	◇1 ⊏⊐		◇
London Paddington 15 ⊖	d		09 30	09 45	10 00	10 15		10 21	10 30	10 45	11 00			11 21	11 30	11 45	12 00	12 15	12 30	12 45	13 00		
Slough 3	d							10 39						11 39									
Reading 7	d		09 57	10 11	10 27	10 42		10 54	10 57	11 11	11 27			11 54	11 58	12 11	12 27	12 42	12 57	13 11	13 27		
Didcot Parkway	d		10 12			10 56			11 12						12 12			12 56	13 12				
Swindon	a		10 30	10 38	10 54	11 15			11 30	11 38	11 54				12 30	12 38	12 54	13 15	13 30	13 38	13 55		
	d	10 14	10 30	10 38	10 55	11 15			11 30	11 38	11 55	12 14			12 30	12 38	12 55	13 15	13 30	13 38	13 55	14 14	
Kemble	d	10 28				11 31						12 28						13 31				14 28	
Stroud	d	10 43				11 46						12 43						13 46				14 43	
Stonehouse	d	10 48				11 51						12 48						13 51				14 48	
Gloucester 7	a	11 07				12 07						13 03						14 06				15 03	
Cheltenham Spa	a	11 23				12 22						13 24						14 22				15 25	
Worcester Shrub Hill	d						11 06	12a39					12 54	13a40									15 06
Chippenham	d		10 44		11 09				11 44		12 09				12 44		13 09		13 44		14 09		
Bath Spa 7	a		11 00		11 24				12 00		12 24				12 59		13 24		14 00		14 24		
Bristol Parkway 7	a			11 04			12 24			12 04			14 20			13 04				14 04			16 24
	d			11 07			12 25			12 07			14 20			13 07				14 07			16 25
Bristol Temple Meads 10	a		11 15		11 39		12 39		12 15		12 39		14 36		13 14		13 42		14 15		14 39		16 39
Weston-super-Mare	a								12 35										14 35				
Newport (South Wales)	a			11 31						12 31						13 31				14 31			
Cardiff Central 7	a			11 46						12 46						13 47				14 46			
Bridgend	a			12 09						13 09						14 09				15 09			
Port Talbot Parkway	a			12 22						13 22						14 22				15 22			
Neath	a			12 30						13 30						14 30				15 30			
Swansea	a			12 43						13 43						14 43				15 43			

		GW	GW	GW	GW	GW	GW	GW	GW	GW	GW	GW	GW	GW	GW	GW	GW	GW	GW	GW	GW	GW
		◇1 ✕	◇1 ⊏⊐	◇1 ⊏⊐	◇1 ⊏⊐	◇1 ⊏⊐	◇1 ✕		◇1 ⊏⊐	◇1 ⊏⊐	◇1 ⊏⊐			◇1 C ✕	◇1 ⊏⊐	◇1 ⊏⊐	◇1 ⊏⊐	◇1 ⊏⊐	◇1 ⊏⊐	◇1 ⊏⊐	◇1 ⊏⊐	◇1 ⊏⊐
London Paddington 15 ⊖	d	13 21	13 30	13 45	14 00	14 15	14 21		14 30	14 45	15 00			15 21	15 30	15 45	16 00	16 15	16 21	16 30	16 45	17 00
Slough 3	d	13 39					14 39							15 39					16 39			
Reading 7	d	13 54	13 59	14 11	14 27	14 42	14 54		14 57	15 11	15 27			15 54	15 59	16 11	16 27	16 42	16 54	16 57	17 11	17 27
Didcot Parkway	d		14 12			14 56			15 12						16 12			16 56		17 12		
Swindon	a		14 30	14 38	14 54	15 15			15 30	15 38	15 54				16 30	16 38	16 54	17 15		17 30	17 38	17 54
	d		14 30	14 38	14 55	15 15		15 22	15 30	15 38	15 55	16 14			16 30	16 38	16 55	17 15		17 30	17 38	17 55
Kemble	d					15 31						16 28						17 31				
Stroud	d					15 46						16 43						17 46				
Stonehouse	d					15 51						16 48						17 51				
Gloucester 7	a					16 06						17 03						18 06				
Cheltenham Spa	a					16 22						17 25						18 22				
Worcester Shrub Hill	d	15a40					16a40						17 08	17a40					18a43			
Chippenham	d		14 44		15 09			15a38	15 44		16 09				16 44		17 09			17 44		18 09
Bath Spa 7	a		15 00		15 24				16 00		16 24				17 00		17 24			18 00		18 24
Bristol Parkway 7	a			15 04						16 04			18 24			17 04					18 04	
	d			15 07						16 07			18 25			17 07					18 07	
Bristol Temple Meads 10	a		15 15		15 41				16 15		16 39		18 39		17 15		17 39			18 15		18 39
Weston-super-Mare	a								16 35						17 35					18 36		
Newport (South Wales)	a			15 31						16 31						17 29					18 30	
Cardiff Central 7	a			15 46						16 47						17 46					18 46	
Bridgend	a			16 09						17 09						18 09					19 09	
Port Talbot Parkway	a			16 22						17 22						18 22					19 22	
Neath	a			16 30						17 30						18 30					19 30	
Swansea	a			16 43						17 43						18 46					19 43	

		GW	GW	GW	GW	GW	GW	GW	GW	GW	GW	GW	GW	GW	GW	GW	GW	GW	GW	GW	GW	GW	GW
				◇1 ⊏⊐	◇1 ⊏⊐	◇1 ⊏⊐	◇1 ⊏⊐	◇1 ⊏⊐	◇1 ⊏⊐	◇1 ⊏⊐	◇1 ⊏⊐	◇1 ⊏⊐		◇1 ⊏⊐	◇1 ⊏⊐	◇1 C ✕	◇1 ⊏⊐		◇1 ⊏⊐	◇1 ⊏⊐	◇1 ⊏⊐	◇1 ⊏⊐	◇1
London Paddington 15 ⊖	d			17 21	17 30	17 45	18 00	18 15	18 21	18 30	18 45	19 00		19 30	19 45	19 50	20 00		20 15	20 30	20 45	21 30	21 50
Slough 3	d			17 39					18 39							20 06							22 06
Reading 7	d			17 54	17 57	18 11	18 27	18 42	18 54	18 57	19 11	19 27		19 57	20 11	20 22	20 27		20 42	20 57	21 13	21 57	22 23
Didcot Parkway	d				18 12			18 56		19 12				20 12			20 42		20 56	21 12		22 12	22 38
Swindon	a				18 30	18 38	18 54	19 15		19 29	19 38	19 54		20 30	20 38		21 00		21 15	21 30	21 40	22 30	
	d	18 14			18 30	18 38	18 55	19 15		19 30	19 38	19 55	20 00	20 30	20 38		21 00	21 08	21 15	21 30	21 41	22 30	
Kemble	d	18 28						19 31					20 15						21 31				
Stroud	d	18 43						19 46					20 30						21 46				
Stonehouse	d	18 48						19 51					20 35						21 51				
Gloucester 7	a	19 03						20 06					20 50						22 05				
Cheltenham Spa	a	19 25						20 22					21 03						22 20				
Worcester Shrub Hill	d		19 07	19a40					20a42							22a02							00a07
Chippenham	d				18 44		19 09			19 44		20 09		20 45			21 14	21a24		21 45		22 44	
Bath Spa 7	a				19 00		19 24			19 59		20 24		21 00			21 29			21 58		23 00	
Bristol Parkway 7	a		20 24			19 05					20 05				21 04						22 06		
	d		20 25			19 07					20 07				21 07						22 11		
Bristol Temple Meads 10	a		20 39		19 15		19 38			20 15		20 40		21 16			21 45			22 14		23 15	
Weston-super-Mare	a				19 50					20 36		21 26								22s47			
Newport (South Wales)	a					19 30					20 30				21 30						22 46		
Cardiff Central 7	a					19 46					20 44				21 47						23 06		
Bridgend	a					20 09					21 09				22 09						23 28		
Port Talbot Parkway	a					20 22					21 22				22 22						23 41		
Neath	a					20 30					21 30				22 30						23 49		
Swansea	a					20 43					21 43				22 43						00 02		

A ⊏⊐ from Bridgend ⊘ to Bridgend
B ⊏⊐ from Chippenham ⊘ to Chippenham
C ✕ to Reading

For connections from Heathrow Airport, Gatwick Airport and Oxford please refer to Tables 125A, 148 and 116. For connections to Birmingham New Street and Hereford please refer to Tables 57 and 131

Saturdays
30 June to 8 September

London - Swindon, Cheltenham Spa, Bristol, Weston-super-Mare and South Wales

Route Diagram - see first Page of Table 125

Station		GW	GW ◇■ ☕	GW ◇■ ☕	GW ◇■ ☕
London Paddington 15 ⊖	d		22 00	22 35	23 30
Slough 3	d				
Reading 7	d		22 27	23 02	23 59
Didcot Parkway	d		22 41	23 23	00 18
Swindon	a		22 59	23 39	00 37
	d	22 35	22 59	23 41	00 38
Kemble	d	22 49			
Stroud	d	23 04			
Stonehouse	d	23 09			
Gloucester 7	a	23 25			
Cheltenham Spa	a				
Worcester Shrub Hill	d				
Chippenham	d			23 55	00 53
Bath Spa 7	a			00 11	01 08
Bristol Parkway 7	a		23 27		
	d		23 28		
Bristol Temple Meads 10	a			00 25	01 22
Weston-super-Mare	a				
Newport (South Wales)	a		23 57		
Cardiff Central 7	a		00 18		
Bridgend	a				
Port Talbot Parkway	a				
Neath	a				
Swansea	a				

Saturdays
from 15 September

Station		GW ◇■ ☕	GW ◇■ ☕	GW ◇■ ☕	GW	GW ◇■ ☕	GW ◇■ ☕	GW ◇	GW ◇■	GW ◇■	GW	GW ◇■ ☕
London Paddington 15 ⊖	d	21p15	21p45	22p15		22p45	23p30		05 21	06 21		06 30
Slough 3	d								05 38	06 38		
Reading 7	d	21p41	22p11	22p41		23p11	00 08		05 54	06 54		06 59
Didcot Parkway	d	22p00	22p31	23p01		23p30	00 25		06 08			07 12
Swindon	a	22p18	22p48	23p19		23p48	00 44					07 30
	d	22p19	22p49	23p21	23p33	23p49	00 45				07 16	07 30
Kemble	d				23p47						07 30	
Stroud	d				00 02						07 45	
Stonehouse	d				00 07						07 50	
Gloucester 7	a				00 24						08 06	
Cheltenham Spa	a										08 24	
Worcester Shrub Hill	d							06 47	07a44	08a40		
Chippenham	d		23p03	23p33			00 59					07 44
Bath Spa 7	a		23p17	23p47			01 13					08 00
Bristol Parkway 7	a	22p45				00 14		08 19				
	d	22p45				00 16		08 19				
Bristol Temple Meads 10	a		23p32	00 03			01 29	08 34				08 15
Weston-super-Mare	a		00s05									
Newport (South Wales)	a	23p19				00 38	02s02					
Cardiff Central 7	a	23p40				00 53	02 19					
Bridgend	a	00 02				01 19						
Port Talbot Parkway	a	00 15				01 32						
Neath	a	00 22				01 39						
Swansea	a	00 37				01 53						

Station		GW ◇■ ☕	GW	GW ◇■	GW ■ 1 ☕	GW ◇■ ☕	GW ◇■ ☕	GW ◇■ ☕	GW ◇■ ☕	GW ◇■ ☕	GW ◇■ ☕	GW ◇■ ☕
London Paddington 15 ⊖	d	07 00		07 21	07 30	07 45	08 00	08 15	08 21	08 30	08 45	09 00
Slough 3	d			07 38					08 39			
Reading 7	d	07 27		07 53	07 57	08 11	08 27	08 42	08 54	08 57	09 11	09 27
Didcot Parkway	d				08 12			08 56		09 12		
Swindon	a	07 54			08 30	08 38	08 55	09 15		09 30	09 38	09 54
	d	07 55			08 30	08 38	08 55	09 15		09 30	09 38	09 55
Kemble	d							09 31				
Stroud	d							09 46				
Stonehouse	d							09 51				
Gloucester 7	a							10 06				
Cheltenham Spa	a							10 22				
Worcester Shrub Hill	d		09 08	09a40					10a44			
Chippenham	d	08 09			08 44		09 09			09 44		10 09
Bath Spa 7	a	08 24			09 00		09 24			10 00		10 24
Bristol Parkway 7	a		10 24			09 04					10 04	
	d		10 25			09 07					10 07	
Bristol Temple Meads 10	a	08 39	10 39		09 15		09 39			10 15		10 39
Weston-super-Mare	a											
Newport (South Wales)	a					09 30					10 31	
Cardiff Central 7	a					09 47					10 46	
Bridgend	a					10 09					11 09	
Port Talbot Parkway	a					10 22					11 22	
Neath	a					10 30					11 30	
Swansea	a					10 43					11 43	

Station		GW	GW ◇■ ☕	GW ◇■ ☕	GW ◇■ ☕	GW ◇■ ☕	GW ■	GW ◇■ ☕	GW ◇■ ☕	GW ◇■ A ☕⊘	GW ◇■ ☕	GW
London Paddington 15 ⊖	d		09 30	09 45	10 00	10 15		10 21	10 30	10 45	11 00	
Slough 3	d							10 39				
Reading 7	d		09 57	10 11	10 27	10 42		10 54	10 57	11 11	11 27	
Didcot Parkway	d		10 12			10 56			11 12			
Swindon	a		10 30	10 38	10 54	11 15			11 30	11 38	11 54	
	d	10 14	10 30	10 38	10 55	11 15			11 30	11 38	11 55	12 14
Kemble	d	10 28				11 31						12 28
Stroud	d	10 43				11 46						12 43
Stonehouse	d	10 48				11 51						12 48
Gloucester 7	a	11 07				12 07						13 03
Cheltenham Spa	a	11 23				12 22						13 24
Worcester Shrub Hill	d						11 06	12a39				
Chippenham	d		10 44		11 09				11 44		12 09	
Bath Spa 7	a		11 00		11 24				12 00		12 24	
Bristol Parkway 7	a			11 04			12 24			12 04		
	d			11 07			12 25			12 07		
Bristol Temple Meads 10	a		11 15		11 39		12 39		12 15		12 39	
Weston-super-Mare	a											
Newport (South Wales)	a			11 31						12 31		
Cardiff Central 7	a			11 46						12 46		
Bridgend	a			12 09						13 09		
Port Talbot Parkway	a			12 22						13 22		
Neath	a			12 30						13 30		
Swansea	a			12 43						13 43		

Station		GW ◇	GW ◇■ ⌶	GW ◇■ B ☕⊘	GW ◇■ A ☕⊘	GW ◇■ ☕	GW ◇■ ☕	GW ◇■ ☕	GW ◇■ ☕	GW ◇■ ☕	GW	GW ◇
London Paddington 15 ⊖	d		11 21	11 30	11 45	12 00	12 15	12 30	12 45	13 00		
Slough 3	d		11 39									
Reading 7	d		11 54	11 58	12 11	12 27	12 42	12 57	13 11	13 27		
Didcot Parkway	d			12 12			12 56	13 12				
Swindon	a			12 30	12 38	12 54	13 15	13 30	13 38	13 55		
	d			12 30	12 38	12 55	13 15	13 30	13 38	13 55	14 14	
Kemble	d						13 31				14 28	
Stroud	d						13 46				14 43	
Stonehouse	d						13 51				14 48	
Gloucester 7	a						14 06				15 03	
Cheltenham Spa	a						14 22				15 25	
Worcester Shrub Hill	d	12 54	13a40									15 06
Chippenham	d			12 44		13 09		13 44		14 09		
Bath Spa 7	a			12 59		13 24		14 00		14 24		
Bristol Parkway 7	a	14 20			13 04				14 04			16 24
	d	14 20			13 07				14 07			16 25
Bristol Temple Meads 10	a	14 36		13 14		13 42		14 15		14 39		16 39
Weston-super-Mare	a											
Newport (South Wales)	a				13 31				14 31			
Cardiff Central 7	a				13 47				14 46			
Bridgend	a				14 09				15 09			
Port Talbot Parkway	a				14 22				15 22			
Neath	a				14 30				15 30			
Swansea	a				14 43				15 43			

A ☕ from Bridgend ⊘ to Bridgend

B ☕ from Chippenham ⊘ to Chippenham

For connections from Heathrow Airport, Gatwick Airport and Oxford please refer to Tables 125A, 148 and 116. For connections to Birmingham New Street and Hereford please refer to Tables 57 and 131

Saturdays
from 15 September

London - Swindon, Cheltenham Spa, Bristol, Weston-super-Mare and South Wales

Route Diagram - see first Page of Table 125

Station		GW ◇■ ⌶	GW ◇■ ☕	GW ◇■ ☕	GW ◇■ ☕	GW ◇■ ☕	GW ◇■ ⌶	GW	GW ◇■ ☕	GW ◇■ ☕	GW ◇■ ☕
London Paddington 15 ⊖	d	13 21	13 30	13 45	14 00	14 15	14 21		14 30	14 45	15 00
Slough 3	d	13 39					14 39				
Reading 7	d	13 54	13 59	14 11	14 27	14 42	14 54		14 57	15 11	15 27
Didcot Parkway	d		14 12			14 56			15 12		
Swindon	a		14 30	14 38	14 54	15 15			15 30	15 38	15 54
	d		14 30	14 38	14 55	15 15		15 22	15 30	15 38	15 55
Kemble	d					15 31					
Stroud	d					15 46					
Stonehouse	d					15 51					
Gloucester 7	a					16 06					
Cheltenham Spa	a					16 22					
Worcester Shrub Hill	d	15a40					16a40				
Chippenham	d		14 44		15 09			15a38	15 44		16 09
Bath Spa 7	a		15 00		15 24				16 00		16 24
Bristol Parkway 7	a			15 04						16 04	
	d			15 07						16 07	
Bristol Temple Meads 10	a		15 15		15 41				16 15		16 39
Weston-super-Mare	a										
Newport (South Wales)	a			15 31						16 31	
Cardiff Central 7	a			15 46						16 47	
Bridgend	a			16 09						17 09	
Port Talbot Parkway	a			16 22						17 22	
Neath	a			16 30						17 30	
Swansea	a			16 43						17 43	

Station		GW	GW	GW ◇■ A ⌶	GW ◇■ ☕	GW ◇■ ☕	GW ◇■ ☕	GW ◇■ ☕	GW ◇■ ☕	GW ◇■ ☕	GW ◇■ ☕	GW ◇■ ☕
London Paddington 15 ⊖	d			15 21	15 30	15 45	16 00	16 15	16 21	16 30	16 45	17 00
Slough 3	d			15 39					16 39			
Reading 7	d			15 54	15 59	16 11	16 27	16 42	16 54	16 57	17 11	17 27
Didcot Parkway	d				16 12			16 56		17 12		
Swindon	a				16 30	16 38	16 54	17 15		17 30	17 38	17 54
	d	16 14			16 30	16 38	16 55	17 15		17 30	17 38	17 55
Kemble	d	16 28						17 31				
Stroud	d	16 43						17 46				
Stonehouse	d	16 48						17 51				
Gloucester 7	a	17 03						18 06				
Cheltenham Spa	a	17 25						18 22				
Worcester Shrub Hill	d		17 08	17a40					18a43			
Chippenham	d				16 44		17 09			17 44		18 09
Bath Spa 7	a				17 00		17 24			18 00		18 24
Bristol Parkway 7	a		18 24			17 04					18 04	
	d		18 25			17 07					18 07	
Bristol Temple Meads 10	a		18 39		17 15		17 39			18 15		18 39
Weston-super-Mare	a									18 36		
Newport (South Wales)	a					17 29					18 30	
Cardiff Central 7	a					17 46					18 46	
Bridgend	a					18 09					19 09	
Port Talbot Parkway	a					18 22					19 22	
Neath	a					18 30					19 30	
Swansea	a					18 46					19 43	

Station		GW	GW	GW ◇■ ☕	GW ◇■ ☕	GW ◇■ ☕	GW ◇■ ☕	GW ◇■ ☕	GW ◇■ ☕	GW ◇■ ☕	GW ◇■ ☕	GW ◇■ ☕
London Paddington 15 ⊖	d			17 21	17 30	17 45	18 00	18 15	18 21	18 30	18 45	19 00
Slough 3	d			17 39					18 39			
Reading 7	d			17 54	17 57	18 11	18 27	18 42	18 54	18 57	19 11	19 27
Didcot Parkway	d				18 12			18 56		19 12		
Swindon	a				18 30	18 38	18 54	19 15		19 29	19 38	19 54
	d	18 14			18 30	18 38	18 55	19 15		19 30	19 38	19 55
Kemble	d	18 28						19 31				
Stroud	d	18 43						19 46				
Stonehouse	d	18 48						19 51				
Gloucester 7	a	19 03						20 06				
Cheltenham Spa	a	19 25						20 22				
Worcester Shrub Hill	d		19 07	19a40					20a42			
Chippenham	d				18 44		19 09			19 44		20 09
Bath Spa 7	a				19 00		19 24			19 59		20 24
Bristol Parkway 7	a		20 24			19 05					20 05	
	d		20 25			19 07					20 07	
Bristol Temple Meads 10	a		20 39		19 15		19 38			20 15		20 40
Weston-super-Mare	a				19 50					20 36		21 26
Newport (South Wales)	a					19 30					20 30	
Cardiff Central 7	a					19 46					20 44	
Bridgend	a					20 09					21 09	
Port Talbot Parkway	a					20 22					21 22	
Neath	a					20 30					21 30	
Swansea	a					20 43					21 43	

Station		GW	GW ◇■ ☕	GW ◇■ ☕	GW ◇■ ☕	GW ◇■ A ⌶	GW ◇■ ☕	GW	GW ◇■ ☕	GW ◇■ ☕	GW ◇■ ☕	GW ◇■ ☕
London Paddington 15 ⊖	d		19 15	19 30	19 45	19 50	20 00		20 15	20 30	20 45	21 30
Slough 3	d					20 06						
Reading 7	d		19 42	19 57	20 11	20 22	20 27		20 42	20 57	21 13	21 58
Didcot Parkway	d		19 56	20 12			20 42		20 56	21 12		22 13
Swindon	a		20 14	20 30	20 38		21 00		21 15	21 30	21 40	22 30
	d	20 00	20 14	20 30	20 38		21 00	21 08	21 15	21 30	21 41	22 31
Kemble	d	20 15							21 31			
Stroud	d	20 30							21 46			
Stonehouse	d	20 35							21 51			
Gloucester 7	a	20 50							22 05			
Cheltenham Spa	a	21 03							22 20			
Worcester Shrub Hill	d					22a02						
Chippenham	d			20 45			21 14	21a24		21 45		22 45
Bath Spa 7	a			21 00			21 29			21 58		23 01
Bristol Parkway 7	a		20 40		21 04						22 06	
	d		20 40		21 07						22 11	
Bristol Temple Meads 10	a			21 16			21 45			22 14		23 15
Weston-super-Mare	a									22s47		
Newport (South Wales)	a		21 05		21 30						22 46	
Cardiff Central 7	a		21 23		21 47						23 06	
Bridgend	a		21 46		22 09						23 28	
Port Talbot Parkway	a		21 59		22 22						23 41	
Neath	a		22 07		22 30						23 49	
Swansea	a		22 19		22 43						00 02	

Station		GW ◇■ B	GW ◇■ C	GW	GW ◇■ ☕	GW ◇■ B ☕	GW ◇■ C ☕	GW B 🚌	GW ◇■ B ☕	GW ◇■ C ☕
London Paddington 15 ⊖	d	21 50	21 50		22 00	22 35	22 35		23 30	23 30
Slough 3	d	22 06	22 06							
Reading 7	d	22 23	22 22		22 27	23 02	23 02		23 59	23 59
Didcot Parkway	d	22 38	22 37		22 41	23 24	23 27		00 18	00 18
Swindon	a				22 59	23 40	23 43		00 37	00 37
	d			22 35	22 59	23 41	23 45	23 50	00 38	00 38
Kemble	d			22 49						
Stroud	d			23 04						
Stonehouse	d			23 09						
Gloucester 7	a			23 25						
Cheltenham Spa	a									
Worcester Shrub Hill	d	00a07	00a07							
Chippenham	d						23 59	00 25		00 53
Bath Spa 7	a						00 14	01 00		01 07
Bristol Parkway 7	a				23 27					
	d				23 28					
Bristol Temple Meads 10	a					00 15	00 28	01 30	01 11	01 22
Weston-super-Mare	a									
Newport (South Wales)	a				23 57					
Cardiff Central 7	a				00 18					
Bridgend	a									
Port Talbot Parkway	a									
Neath	a									
Swansea	a									

A ⌶ to Reading

B from 15 September until 20 October

C from 27 October

For connections from Heathrow Airport, Gatwick Airport and Oxford please refer to Tables 125A, 148 and 116. For connections to Birmingham New Street and Hereford please refer to Tables 57 and 131

Table 125

Sundays
until 24 June

London - Swindon, Cheltenham Spa, Bristol, Weston-super-Mare and South Wales

Route Diagram - see first Page of Table 125

		GW	GW	GW	GW	GW	GW	GW	GW	GW	GW	GW	GW	GW	GW	GW	GW	GW	GW	GW	GW	GW	GW
		◇1	◇1	◇1	◇1	◇1	◇1	◇1	◇1	◇1	◇1	◇1	◇1		◇1	◇1	◇1	◇1	◇1	◇1	◇1	◇1	◇1
		⊡	⊡	⊡	⊡	⊡		⊡	⊡	⊡	⊡	⊡	⊡		⊡	⊡	⊡	⊡	⊡	⊡	⊡	⊡	⊡
London Paddington 15 ⊖	d	20p45	22p00	22p35	23p30	08 00	08 03	08 30	08 37	08 57	09 03	09 30	09 35		09 42	10 03	10 37	10 42	10 57	11 03	11 30	11 37	12 03
Slough 3	d						08 25						09 59					11 06					
Reading 7	d	21p13	22p27	23p02	23p59	08 35	08 44	09 06	09 15	09 31	09 38	10 05	10 12		10 18	10 38	11 12	11 21	11 32	11 38	12 05	12 12	12 38
Didcot Parkway	d		22p41	23p23	00 18	08 49	09 00	09 21			09 52		10 28		10 33	10 53	11 26	11 37		11 52		12 26	12 52
Swindon	a	21p40	22p59	23p39	00 38	09 06		09 41	09 47	10 01	10 10	10 33			10 50	11 11	11 43		12 01	12 10	12 33	12 45	13 10
	d	21p41	22p59	23p41	00 38	09 08		09 43		10 02	10 11			10 47	10 52	11 11	11 45		12 02	12 11		12 45	13 11
Kemble	d									10 15				11 01					12 15				
Stroud	d									10 30				11 16					12 30				
Stonehouse	d									10 35				11 21					12 35				
Gloucester 7	a									10 51				11 36					12 51				
Cheltenham Spa	a									11 16				11 49					13 16				
Worcester Shrub Hill	d						10a31						12a05					13a09					
Chippenham	d			23p55	00 53	09 22					10 26					11 26				12 26			13 26
Bath Spa 7	a			00 11	01 08	09 35					10 39					11 39				12 40			13 39
Bristol Parkway 7	a	22p06	23p27					10 07							11 16		12 10					13 11	
	d	22p11	23p28					10 09							11 18		12 11					13 11	
Bristol Temple Meads 10	a			00 25	01 23	09 50					10 54					11 54				12 54			13 54
Weston-super-Mare	a															12 31				13 16			14 26
Newport (South Wales)	a	22p46	23p57					10 33							11 43		12 37					13 37	
Cardiff Central 7	a	23p06	00 18					10 51							12 01		12 56					13 56	
Bridgend	a	23p28						11 14							12 24		13 18					14 18	
Port Talbot Parkway	a	23p41						11 27							12 37		13 31					14 31	
Neath	a	23p49						11 36							12 44		13 38					14 38	
Swansea	a	00 02						11 49							12 58		13 52					14 52	

		GW	GW	GW	GW	GW	GW	GW	GW	GW	GW	GW	GW	GW	GW	GW	GW	GW	GW	GW	GW	GW	GW
		◇1	◇1		◇1	◇1	◇1		◇1	◇1	◇1	◇1		◇1	◇1	◇1	◇1	◇1	◇1	◇1	◇1		
		⊡	⊡		⊡	⊡	⊡		⊡	⊡	⊡	⊡			⊡	⊡	⊡		⊡	⊡	⊡		
London Paddington 15 ⊖	d	12 30	12 37		12 42	12 57	13 03		13 37	13 42	14 03	14 37		14 42	14 57	15 03	15 37	15 42	16 03	16 30	16 37		
Slough 3	d				13 07					14 06				15 03				16 05					
Reading 7	d	13 05	13 13		13 21	13 31	13 38		14 13	14 21	14 38	15 13		15 21	15 31	15 38	16 12	16 21	16 38	17 05	17 13		
Didcot Parkway	d		13 26		13 38		13 52		14 27	14 37	14 52	15 27		15 36		15 52	16 26	16 39	16 52		17 27		
Swindon	a	13 33	13 43			14 01	14 10		14 44		15 10	15 44			16 01	16 10	16 43		17 10	17 33	17 44		
	d		13 45			14 04	14 11	14 21	14 46		15 11	15 46			16 02	16 11	16 45		17 11		17 46	17 49	
Kemble	d					14 17		14 36							16 15							18 03	
Stroud	d					14 32		14 51							16 30							18 17	
Stonehouse	d					14 37		14 56							16 35							18 22	
Gloucester 7	a					14 53		15 19							16 51							18 49	
Cheltenham Spa	a					15 16		15 33							17 16								
Worcester Shrub Hill	d			14 36	15a09					16a08			16 40	17a09				18a08					18 40
Chippenham	d						14 26				15 26					16 26			17 26				
Bath Spa 7	a						14 39				15 39					16 39			17 39				
Bristol Parkway 7	a		14 10	15 49					15 11			16 11	17 57				17 10				18 11		19 57
	d		14 11	15 55					15 12			16 12	17 58				17 11				18 12		19 58
Bristol Temple Meads 10	a			16 09			14 53				15 54		18 10			16 53			17 54				20 11
Weston-super-Mare	a			16 56												17 26							
Newport (South Wales)	a		14 37						15 38			16 38					17 40				18 38		
Cardiff Central 7	a		14 56						15 57			16 57					17 58				18 57		
Bridgend	a		15 18						16 19			17 19					18 21				19 19		
Port Talbot Parkway	a		15 31						16 32			17 32					18 35				19 32		
Neath	a		15 38						16 38			17 39					18 43				19 39		
Swansea	a		15 52						16 53			17 54					18 58				19 53		

		GW	GW	GW	GW	GW	GW	GW	GW	GW	GW	GW	GW	GW	GW	GW	GW	GW	GW	GW	GW	GW
		◇1	◇1	◇1		◇1	◇1	◇1	◇1	◇1	◇1	◇1		◇1	◇1	◇1		◇1	◇1	◇1	◇1	◇1
			⊡	⊡		⊡	⊡	⊡	⊡	⊡	⊡	⊡			⊡	⊡		⊡	⊡	⊡	⊡	⊡
London Paddington 15 ⊖	d	16 42	16 57	17 03		17 30	17 37	17 42	17 57	18 03	18 30	18 37		18 42	18 57	19 03		19 33	19 37	19 42	19 57	20 03
Slough 3	d	17 04						18 04						19 07						20 06		
Reading 7	d	17 25	17 32	17 37		18 08	18 13	18 24	18 32	18 38	19 04	19 12		19 28	19 32	19 38		20 08	20 13	20 21	20 33	20 38
Didcot Parkway	d	17 39	17 47	17 51			18 27	18 39		18 52		19 26		19 44		19 52			20 27	20 37		20 52
Swindon	a		18 08	18 10		18 34	18 43		19 00	19 10	19 35	19 43				20 10		20 35	20 46		20 59	21 10
	d		18 10	18 11	18 19	18 34	18 45			19 11	19 36	19 45				20 11	20 28	20 35	20 46			21 11
Kemble	d		18 23								19 50						20 42					
Stroud	d		18 38								20 05						20 57					
Stonehouse	d		18 43								20 09						21 02					
Gloucester 7	a		18 57								20 32						21 17					
Cheltenham Spa	a		19 18								20 49						21 33					
Worcester Shrub Hill	d	19a10						20a12					20 37	21a13						22a10		
Chippenham	d			18 26	18a35	18 49				19 26						20 26		20 50				21 26
Bath Spa 7	a			18 39		19 06				19 39						20 39		21 03				21 39
Bristol Parkway 7	a						19 14					20 10	21 53						21 11			
	d						19 15					20 11	21 55						21 12			
Bristol Temple Meads 10	a			18 54		19 25				19 54			22 07			20 54		21 18				21 53
Weston-super-Mare	a					19 58										21 26						22 28
Newport (South Wales)	a						19 41					20 37							21 38			
Cardiff Central 7	a						19 59					20 56							22 00			
Bridgend	a						20 22					21 18							22 23			
Port Talbot Parkway	a						20 35					21 31							22 36			
Neath	a						20 43					21 38							22 44			
Swansea	a						20 56					21 53							22 57			

For connections from Heathrow Airport, Gatwick Airport and Oxford please refer to Tables 125A, 148 and 116. For connections to Birmingham New Street and Hereford please refer to Tables 57 and 131

Table 125

Sundays
until 24 June

London - Swindon, Cheltenham Spa, Bristol, Weston-super-Mare and South Wales

Route Diagram - see first Page of Table 125

		GW	GW	GW	GW	GW	GW	GW	GW	GW	GW
		◇1	◇1	◇1	◇1	◇1		◇1	◇1	◇1	◇1
		⊡	⊡	⊡	⊡			⊡	⊡	⊡	⊡
London Paddington 15 ⊖	d	20 30	20 37	21 03	21 37	21 42		22 03	22 37	23 03	23 37
Slough 3	d					22 06					00 03
Reading 7	d	21 06	21 13	21 38	22 12	22 22		22 45	23 17	23 47	00 14
Didcot Parkway	d		21 27	21 52	22 28	22 40		22 59	23s32	00s01	00s30
Swindon	a	21 35	21 44	22 10	22 45			23 17	23s51	00s19	00s48
	d	21 36	21 46	22 11	22 46		22 57	23 17			
Kemble	d	21 50					23 11				
Stroud	d	22 05					23 26				
Stonehouse	d	22 10					23 31				
Gloucester 7	a	22 25					23 48				
Cheltenham Spa	a	22 41					00 05				
Worcester Shrub Hill	d					00a12					
Chippenham	d			22 26				23 33		00s34	01s04
Bath Spa 7	a			22 42				23 46		00s49	01s18
Bristol Parkway 7	a		22 11		23 11				00s21		
	d		22 12		23 12						
Bristol Temple Meads 10	a			22 57				00 01	00 35	01 03	01 32
Weston-super-Mare	a										
Newport (South Wales)	a		22 37		23 41						
Cardiff Central 7	a		23 00		00 01						
Bridgend	a		23 21		00 23						
Port Talbot Parkway	a		23 35		00 36						
Neath	a		23 43		00 44						
Swansea	a		23 57		00 57						

Sundays
1 July to 9 September

		GW	GW	GW	GW	GW	GW	GW	GW	GW	GW	GW	GW	GW	GW	GW	GW	GW	GW	GW	GW	GW	GW
		◇1	◇1	◇1	◇1	◇1	◇1	◇1	◇1	◇1	◇1	◇1		◇1	◇1	◇1	◇1	◇1	◇1	◇1	◇1	◇1	
		⊡	⊡	⊡	⊡	⊡		⊡	⊡	⊡	⊡	⊡		⊡	⊡	⊡	⊡	⊡	⊡	⊡	⊡	⊡	
London Paddington 15 ⊖	d	20p45	22p00	22p35	23p30	08 00	08 03	08 30	08 37	09 03	09 37	09 42		10 03	10 30	10 37	10 42	11 03	11 37	12 03	12 30	12 37	
Slough 3	d						08 21					09 59					11 00						
Reading 7	d	21p13	22p27	23p02	23p59	08 34	08 44	09 06	09 11	09 38	10 06	10 11		10 38	10 56	11 12	11 21	11 38	12 12	12 38	12 56	13 12	
Didcot Parkway	d		22p41	23p23	00 18	08 49	09 02	09 23		09 52	10 20	10 28		10 52		11 26	11 37	11 52	12 26	12 52		13 26	
Swindon	a	21p40	22p59	23p39	00 37	09 08		09 41	09 46	10 10	10 38			11 11	11 26	11 43		12 10	12 45	13 10	13 26	13 43	
	d	21p41	22p59	23p41	00 38	09 09		09 42	09 47	10 11	10 39		10 47	11 11	11 26	11 45		12 11	12 45	13 11	13 26	13 45	
Kemble	d								10 00				11 01		11 40						13 40		
Stroud	d								10 15				11 16		11 55						13 55		
Stonehouse	d								10 20				11 21		12 00						14 00		
Gloucester 7	a								10 39				11 36		12 15						14 15		
Cheltenham Spa	a								10 55				11 49		12 31						14 31		
Worcester Shrub Hill	d						10a32					12a05					13a09						14 36
Chippenham	d			23p55	00 53	09 25				10 26				11 26				12 26		13 26			
Bath Spa 7	a			00 11	01 08	09 37				10 39				11 39				12 39		13 39			
Bristol Parkway 7	a	22p06	23p27					10 07			11 04					12 10			13 11			14 10	15 49
	d	22p11	23p28					10 08			11 05					12 11			13 11			14 11	15 55
Bristol Temple Meads 10	a			00 25	01 22	09 52				10 54				11 55				12 54		13 54			16 09
Weston-super-Mare	a													12 31						14 26			16 56
Newport (South Wales)	a	22p46	23p57					10 33			11 32					12 37			13 37			14 37	
Cardiff Central 7	a	23p06	00 18					10 51			11 50					12 56			13 56			14 56	
Bridgend	a	23p28						11 14			12 13					13 18			14 18			15 18	
Port Talbot Parkway	a	23p41						11 27			12 26					13 31			14 31			15 31	
Neath	a	23p49						11 35			12 33					13 38			14 38			15 38	
Swansea	a	00 02						11 49			12 47					13 52			14 52			15 52	

		GW	GW	GW	GW	GW	GW	GW	GW	GW	GW	GW	GW	GW	GW	GW	GW	GW	GW	GW	GW	GW	GW
		◇1	◇1		◇1	◇1	◇1	◇1	◇1		◇1	◇1	◇1	◇1	◇1	◇1	◇1		◇1	◇1			◇1
		⊡	⊡		⊡	⊡	⊡	⊡	⊡			⊡	⊡		⊡	⊡	⊡			⊡			⊡
London Paddington 15 ⊖	d	12 42	13 03		13 37	13 42	14 03	14 30	14 37		14 42	15 03	15 37	15 42	16 03	16 30	16 37		16 42	17 03			17 33
Slough 3	d	13 01				14 00					15 00			16 00					17 00				
Reading 7	d	13 21	13 38		14 12	14 21	14 38	14 56	15 12		15 21	15 38	16 12	16 21	16 38	16 56	17 12		17 22	17 38			18 08
Didcot Parkway	d	13 37	13 52		14 26	14 37	14 52		15 26		15 36	15 52	16 26	16 37	16 52		17 26		17 37	17 52			
Swindon	a		14 10		14 43		15 10	15 26	15 43			16 10	16 43		17 10	17 26	17 43			18 10			18 34
	d		14 11	14 21	14 45		15 11	15 26	15 45			16 11	16 45		17 11	17 34	17 45			18 11	18 19	18 22	18 34
Kemble	d			14 36				15 40								17 48						18 36	
Stroud	d			14 51				15 55								18 03						18 50	
Stonehouse	d			14 56				16 00								18 08						18 55	
Gloucester 7	a			15 19				16 15								18 25						19 21	
Cheltenham Spa	a			15 33				16 32								18 46							
Worcester Shrub Hill	d	15a09				16a08				16 40	17a09			18a08				18 40	19a10				
Chippenham	d		14 26				15 26					16 26			17 26					18 26	18a35		18 49
Bath Spa 7	a		14 39				15 39					16 40			17 39					18 39			19 07
Bristol Parkway 7	a				15 10				16 10	17 57			17 10				18 10	19 57					
	d				15 11				16 11	17 58			17 11				18 11	19 58					
Bristol Temple Meads 10	a		14 54				15 54			18 10		16 54			17 54			20 11		18 54			19 25
Weston-super-Mare	a											17 26											19 58
Newport (South Wales)	a				15 37				16 37				17 40				18 37						
Cardiff Central 7	a				15 56				16 56				17 58				18 56						
Bridgend	a				16 18				17 18				18 21				19 18						
Port Talbot Parkway	a				16 31				17 31				18 35				19 31						
Neath	a				16 38				17 38				18 43				19 38						
Swansea	a				16 52				17 53				18 58				19 52						

For connections from Heathrow Airport, Gatwick Airport and Oxford please refer to Tables 125A, 148 and 116. For connections to Birmingham New Street and Hereford please refer to Tables 57 and 131

Table 125

London - Swindon, Cheltenham Spa, Bristol, Weston-super-Mare and South Wales

Sundays

1 July to 9 September

Route Diagram - see first Page of Table 125

		GW ◇1 ☕	GW ◇1 ☕	GW ◇1 ☕	GW ◇1 ☕	GW ◇1 ☕	GW	GW ◇1	GW ◇1 ☕	GW	GW ◇1 ☕	GW ◇1 ☕	GW ◇1 ☕	GW ◇1 ☕	GW ◇1 ☕	GW ◇1 ☕	GW ◇1 ☕	GW ◇1 ☕	GW ◇1	GW	GW ◇1 ☕	GW ◇1 ☕
London Paddington 15 ⊖	d	17 37	17 42	18 03	18 30	18 37		18 42	19 03		19 33	19 37	19 42	20 03	20 30	20 37	21 03	21 37	21 42		22 03	23 03
Slough 3	d		17 58					19 02					20 00						21 59			
Reading 7	d	18 12	18 21	18 38	18 55	19 12		19 22	19 38		20 08	20 12	20 21	20 38	20 56	21 06	21 38	22 12	22 22		22 50	23 47
Didcot Parkway	d	18 26	18 36	18 52		19 26		19 38	19 52			20 26	20 37	20 52		21 20	21 52	22 30	22 38		23 05	00s02
Swindon	a	18 43		19 10	19 25	19 43			20 10		20 35	20 45		21 10	21 26	21 37	22 14	22 49			23 25	00s21
	d	18 45		19 11	19 25	19 45			20 11	20 28	20 35	20 45		21 11	21 26	21 39	22 14	22 51		22 57	23 25	
Kemble	d				19 39					20 42					21 40					23 11		
Stroud	d				19 54					20 57					21 55					23 26		
Stonehouse	d				19 58					21 02					22 00					23 31		
Gloucester 7	a				20 17					21 17					22 17					23 48		
Cheltenham Spa	a				20 33					21 33					22 33					00 05		
Worcester Shrub Hill	d		20a12				20 37	21a10					22a10						00a12			
Chippenham	d			19 26					20 26		20 50			21 26			22 28				23 41	00s37
Bath Spa 7	a			19 39					20 39		21 03			21 39			22 42				23 54	00s51
Bristol Parkway 7	a	19 14				20 10	21 53					21 10				22 04		23 15				
	d	19 15				20 11	21 55					21 11				22 05		23 17				
Bristol Temple Meads 10	a			19 54			22 07		20 54		21 18			21 54			22 57				00 09	01 05
Weston-super-Mare	a								21 26					22 27								
Newport (South Wales)	a	19 41				20 37						21 37				22 37		23 43				
Cardiff Central 7	a	19 59				20 56						21 59				23 00		00 04				
Bridgend	a	20 22				21 18						22 22				23 21		00 27				
Port Talbot Parkway	a	20 35				21 31						22 35				23 35		00 40				
Neath	a	20 43				21 38						22 43				23 43		00 48				
Swansea	a	20 56				21 53						22 56				23 57		01 01				

		GW ◇1 ☕
London Paddington 15 ⊖	d	23 37
Slough 3	d	23 55
Reading 7	d	00 14
Didcot Parkway	d	00s32
Swindon	a	00s51
Kemble	d	
Stroud	d	
Stonehouse	d	
Gloucester 7	a	
Cheltenham Spa	a	
Worcester Shrub Hill	d	
Chippenham	d	01s07
Bath Spa 7	a	01s21
Bristol Parkway 7	a	
	d	
Bristol Temple Meads 10	a	01 35
Weston-super-Mare	a	
Newport (South Wales)	a	
Cardiff Central 7	a	
Bridgend	a	
Port Talbot Parkway	a	
Neath	a	
Swansea	a	

Sundays

16 September to 21 October

		GW ◇1 ☕	GW ◇1 ☕	GW ◇1 ☕	GW 🚌	GW ◇1 ☕	GW 🚌	GW ◇1 ☕	GW ◇1	GW	GW ◇1 ☕	GW ◇1 ☕	GW ◇1 ☕	GW	GW ◇1 ☕	GW ◇1 ☕	GW	GW ◇1 ☕	GW ◇1 ☕	GW ◇1 ☕	GW	GW	GW ◇1 ☕
London Paddington 15 ⊖	d	20p45	22p00	22p35		23p30		07 57	08 03		08 30		09 03		09 30	09 35		10 03	10 37	10 42			11 03
Slough 3	d								08 25							09 59				11 06			
Reading 7	d	21p13	22p27	23p02		23p59		08 32	08 44		09 06		09 38		10 06	10 12		10 38	11 13	11 21			11 38
Didcot Parkway	d		22p41	23p24		00 18		08 46	09 00		09 22		09 52		10 20	10 28		10 52	11 27	11 37			11 52
Swindon	a	21p40	22p59	23p40		00 37		09 05			09 42		10 10		10 38			11 10	11 44				12 10
	d	21p41	22p59	23p41	23p50	00 38	00 47	09 15		09 11	09 45	09 50	10 11	10 30	10 39		10 43	11 11	11 46		11 49	12 04	12 11
Kemble	d											10 04					10 57				12 04		
Stroud	d											10 19					11 12				12 19		
Stonehouse	d											10 24					11 17				12 24		
Gloucester 7	a											10 39					11 32				12 39		
Cheltenham Spa	a											10 52					11 45				12 51		
Worcester Shrub Hill	d								10a31							12a05				13a09			
Chippenham	d				00 25		01 22			09 26				10 45								12 19	
Bath Spa 7	a				01 00		01 57			09 40				10 59								12 33	
Bristol Parkway 7	a	22p06	23p27								10 09				11 04				12 12				
	d	22p11	23p28								10 11				11 05				12 13				
Bristol Temple Meads 10	a			00 15	01 30	01 11	02 27	09 48					10 47					11 45					12 44
Weston-super-Mare	a																	12 31					
Newport (South Wales)	a	22p46	23p57								10 36				11 32				12 38				
Cardiff Central 7	a	23p06	00 18								10 53				11 50				12 58				
Bridgend	a	23p28									11 16				12 13				13 19				
Port Talbot Parkway	a	23p41									11 29				12 26				13 32				
Neath	a	23p49									11 38				12 33				13 39				
Swansea	a	00 02									11 51				12 47				13 53				

For connections from Heathrow Airport, Gatwick Airport and Oxford please refer to Tables 125A, 148 and 116. For connections to Birmingham New Street and Hereford please refer to Tables 57 and 131

Table 125

London - Swindon, Cheltenham Spa, Bristol, Weston-super-Mare and South Wales

Sundays

16 September to 21 October

Route Diagram - see first Page of Table 125

		GW ◇1 ☕	GW 🚌	GW ◇1 ☕	GW	GW ◇1 ☕	GW ◇1 ☕	GW 🚌	GW ◇1 ☕	GW	GW ◇1 ☕	GW ◇1 ☕	GW ◇1 ☕	GW ◇1 ☕	GW ◇1	GW	GW ◇1 ☕	GW ◇1 ☕	GW ◇1	GW ◇1 ☕	GW ◇1 ☕	GW ◇1 ☕	GW ◇1
London Paddington 15 ⊖	d	11 37		12 03		12 37	12 42		13 03		13 37	13 42	14 03	14 37	14 42		15 03	15 37	15 42	16 03	16 30	16 37	16 42
Slough 3	d						13 07					14 06			15 05				16 05				17 04
Reading 7	d	12 13		12 38		13 13	13 21		13 38		14 13	14 21	14 38	15 13	15 21		15 38	16 13	16 21	16 38	17 05	17 13	17 25
Didcot Parkway	d	12 27		12 52		13 27	13 38		13 52		14 27	14 37	14 52	15 27	15 36		15 52	16 27	16 39	16 52		17 27	17 39
Swindon	a	12 45		13 10		13 45			14 09		14 45		15 10	15 45			16 10	16 45		17 10	17 35	17 45	
	d	12 46	12 55	13 11	13 25	13 46		13 55	14 11	14 14	14 46		15 11	15 46		16 01	16 11	16 46		17 11	17 36	17 46	
Kemble	d				13 39					14 27						16 16					17 50		
Stroud	d				13 54					14 42						16 31					18 05		
Stonehouse	d				13 59					14 47						16 36					18 10		
Gloucester 7	a				14 18					15 03						16 50					18 25		
Cheltenham Spa	a				14 31					15 19						17 04					18 46		
Worcester Shrub Hill	d						15a09					16a08			17a09				18a08				19a10
Chippenham	d		13a30					14a30					15 26				16 26			17 26			
Bath Spa 7	a												15 39				16 39			17 39			
Bristol Parkway 7	a	13 12				14 12					15 12			16 12				17 12				18 12	
	d	13 13				14 13					15 13			16 13				17 13				18 13	
Bristol Temple Meads 10	a			13 45					14 44				15 53				16 53			17 53			
Weston-super-Mare	a			14 27													17 26						
Newport (South Wales)	a	13 38				14 38					15 38			16 38				17 40				18 40	
Cardiff Central 7	a	13 58				14 58					15 58			16 58				17 58				19 00	
Bridgend	a	14 19				15 17					16 19			17 19				18 21				19 21	
Port Talbot Parkway	a	14 32				15 31					16 32			17 32				18 35				19 35	
Neath	a	14 39				15 39					16 39			17 38				18 43				19 43	
Swansea	a	14 53				15 53					16 53			17 54				18 58				19 56	

		GW ◇1 ☕	GW	GW	GW ◇1 ☕	GW ◇1 ☕	GW ◇1 ☕	GW ◇1 ☕	GW ◇1 ☕	GW ◇1 ☕	GW ◇1	GW ◇1 ☕	GW	GW ◇1 ☕	GW ◇1 ☕	GW ◇1 ☕	GW ◇1 ☕	GW ◇1 ☕	GW ◇1 ☕	GW ◇1 ☕	GW ◇1 ☕	GW ◇1
London Paddington 15 ⊖	d	17 03			17 33	17 37	17 42	18 03	18 30	18 37	18 42	19 03		19 33	19 37	19 42	20 03	20 30	20 37	21 03	21 37	21 42
Slough 3	d						18 04				19 07					20 04						22 06
Reading 7	d	17 38			18 08	18 15	18 24	18 38	19 05	19 15	19 28	19 38		20 07	20 15	20 21	20 38	21 05	21 15	21 38	22 14	22 22
Didcot Parkway	d	17 52				18 29	18 39	18 52		19 29	19 44	19 52			20 29	20 37	20 52		21 29	21 54	22 29	22 40
Swindon	a	18 10			18 34	18 46		19 10	19 35	19 46		20 10		20 35	20 46		21 10	21 35	21 46	22 14	22 49	
	d	18 11	18 19	18 22	18 34	18 48		19 11	19 36	19 47		20 11	20 28	20 35	20 47		21 11	21 36	21 47	22 15	22 50	
Kemble	d			18 36					19 50				20 42					21 50				
Stroud	d			18 50					20 05				20 57					22 05				
Stonehouse	d			18 55					20 09				21 02					22 10				
Gloucester 7	a			19 15					20 32				21 17					22 25				
Cheltenham Spa	a								20 49				21 33					22 48				
Worcester Shrub Hill	d						20a12				21a13					22a10						00a12
Chippenham	d	18 26	18a35		18 49			19 26				20 26		20 50			21 26			22 29		
Bath Spa 7	a	18 39			19 06			19 39				20 39		21 03			21 39			22 43		
Bristol Parkway 7	a					19 14				20 12					21 12				22 12		23 15	
	d					19 15				20 13					21 13				22 13		23 16	
Bristol Temple Meads 10	a	18 54			19 25			19 53				20 54		21 18			21 53			22 58		
Weston-super-Mare	a				19 58							21 26					22 27					
Newport (South Wales)	a					19 40				20 38					21 38				22 38		23 40	
Cardiff Central 7	a					20 00				20 59					21 59				23 00		00 05	
Bridgend	a					20 21				21 21					22 21				23 21		00 28	
Port Talbot Parkway	a					20 35				21 35					22 35				23 35		00 40	
Neath	a					20 43				21 41					22 41				23 41		00 48	
Swansea	a					20 56				21 56					22 58				23 59		01 02	

		GW	GW ◇1 ☕	GW ◇1 ☕	GW ◇1 ☕	GW ◇1 ☕
London Paddington 15 ⊖	d		22 03	22 37	23 03	23 37
Slough 3	d					00 02
Reading 7	d		22 50	23 17	23 46	00 14
Didcot Parkway	d		23 07	23s32	00s04	00s31
Swindon	a		23 27	23s51	00s23	00s51
	d	22 57	23 27			
Kemble	d	23 11				
Stroud	d	23 26				
Stonehouse	d	23 31				
Gloucester 7	a	23 48				
Cheltenham Spa	a	00 05				
Worcester Shrub Hill	d					
Chippenham	d		23 43			
Bath Spa 7	a		23 56			
Bristol Parkway 7	a			00s21		
	d					
Bristol Temple Meads 10	a		00 11	00 35	01 01	01 25
Weston-super-Mare	a					
Newport (South Wales)	a					
Cardiff Central 7	a					
Bridgend	a					
Port Talbot Parkway	a					
Neath	a					
Swansea	a					

For connections from Heathrow Airport, Gatwick Airport and Oxford please refer to Tables 125A, 148 and 116. For connections to Birmingham New Street and Hereford please refer to Tables 57 and 131

Table 125

Sundays
from 28 October

London - Swindon, Cheltenham Spa, Bristol, Weston-super-Mare and South Wales

Route Diagram - see first Page of Table 125

	GW ◇1 ⊡	GW ◇1 ⊡	GW ◇1 ⊡	GW ◇1 ⊡	GW ◇1 ⊡	GW ◇1	GW ◇1 ⊡	GW ◇1 ⊡	GW ◇1 ⊡		GW ◇1 ⊡	GW ◇1 ⊡	GW	GW ◇1 ⊡	GW ◇1 ⊡	GW ◇1 ⊡	GW	GW ◇1 ⊡	GW ◇1 ⊡		GW ◇1 ⊡	GW	GW ◇1 ⊡	GW ◇1 ⊡
London Paddington [15] ⊖ d	20p45	22p00	22p35	23p30	08 00	08 03	08 30		09 03		09 30	09 35		10 03	10 37	10 42		11 03	11 37		12 03		12 37	12 42
Slough [3] d						08 25						09 59				11 06								13 07
Reading [7] d	21p13	22p27	23p02	23p59	08 34	08 44	09 06		09 38		10 06	10 12		10 38	11 13	11 21		11 38	12 13		12 38		13 13	13 21
Didcot Parkway d		22p41	23p27	00 18	08 52	09 00	09 25		09 52		10 20	10 28		10 52	11 27	11 37		11 52	12 27		12 52		13 27	13 38
Swindon a	21p40	22p59	23p43	00 37	09 11		09 43		10 09		10 38			11 10	11 44			12 10	12 45		13 10		13 45	
d	21p41	22p59	23p45	00 38	09 11		09 44	09 50	10 11		10 39		10 43	11 11	11 46		11 49	12 11	12 46		13 11	13 25	13 46	
Kemble d								10 03					10 57				12 04					13 39		
Stroud d								10 18					11 12				12 19					13 54		
Stonehouse d								10 23					11 17				12 24					13 59		
Gloucester [7] a								10 40					11 32				12 39					14 18		
Cheltenham Spa a								10 55					11 45				12 51					14 31		
Worcester Shrub Hill d						10a31						12a05				13a09								15a09
Chippenham d			23p59	00 53	09 28				10 26					11 26				12 26			13 26			
Bath Spa [7] a			00 14	01 07	09 40				10 39					11 39				12 39			13 39			
Bristol Parkway [7] a	22p06	23p27					10 09				11 04				12 11				13 12				14 12	
d	22p11	23p28					10 10				11 05				12 12				13 13				14 13	
Bristol Temple Meads [10] a			00 28	01 22	09 55				10 57					11 54				12 54			13 54			
Weston-super-Mare a														12 31							14 26			
Newport (South Wales) a	22p46	23p57					10 35				11 32				12 38				13 38				14 38	
Cardiff Central [7] a	23p06	00 18					10 53				11 50				12 57				13 58				14 58	
Bridgend a	23p28						11 16				12 13				13 19				14 19				15 18	
Port Talbot Parkway a	23p41						11 29				12 26				13 32				14 32				15 31	
Neath a	23p49						11 37				12 33				13 39				14 39				15 39	
Swansea a	00 02						11 51				12 47				13 53				14 53				15 53	

	GW ◇1 ⊡	GW	GW ◇1 ⊡	GW	GW ◇1 ⊡		GW ◇1 ⊡	GW ◇1 ⊡	GW	GW	GW ◇1	GW ◇1 ⊡	GW ◇1 ⊡	GW ◇1	GW ◇1 ⊡		GW ◇1 ⊡	GW ◇1 ⊡	GW	GW ◇1	GW ◇1 ⊡	GW	GW	GW ◇1 ⊡
London Paddington [15] ⊖ d	13 03		13 37		13 42		14 03	14 37			14 42	15 03	15 37	15 42	16 03		16 30	16 37		16 42	17 03			17 33
Slough [3] d					14 06						15 05			16 05						17 04				
Reading [7] d	13 38		14 13		14 21		14 38	15 13			15 21	15 38	16 13	16 21	16 38		17 05	17 13		17 25	17 38			18 08
Didcot Parkway d	13 52		14 27		14 37		14 52	15 27			15 36	15 52	16 27	16 39	16 52			17 27		17 39	17 52			
Swindon a	14 10		14 45				15 10	15 45				16 10	16 45		17 10		17 35	17 45			18 10			18 34
d	14 11	14 21	14 46				15 11	15 46	16 01			16 11	16 46		17 11		17 36	17 46			18 11	18 19	18 22	18 34
Kemble d		14 36							16 16								17 50						18 36	
Stroud d		14 51							16 31								18 05						18 50	
Stonehouse d		14 56							16 36								18 10						18 55	
Gloucester [7] a		15 19							16 50								18 25						19 15	
Cheltenham Spa a		15 33							17 04								18 46							
Worcester Shrub Hill d				15 36	16a08					16 40	17a09			18a08					18 40	19a10				
Chippenham d	14 26						15 26					16 26			17 26						18 26	18a35		18 49
Bath Spa [7] a	14 39						15 39					16 39			17 39						18 39			19 06
Bristol Parkway [7] a			15 12	16 49				16 12		17 57			17 12					18 12	19 57					
d			15 13	16 55				16 13		17 58			17 13					18 13	19 58					
Bristol Temple Meads [10] a	14 54			17 09			15 53			18 10		16 53			17 53				20 11		18 54			19 25
Weston-super-Mare a												17 26												19 58
Newport (South Wales) a			15 38					16 38					17 40					18 40						
Cardiff Central [7] a			15 58					16 58					17 58					19 00						
Bridgend a			16 19					17 19					18 21					19 21						
Port Talbot Parkway a			16 32					17 32					18 35					19 35						
Neath a			16 39					17 39					18 43					19 43						
Swansea a			16 53					17 53					18 58					19 56						

	GW ◇1 ⊡		GW ◇1 ⊡	GW ◇1 ⊡	GW ◇1 ⊡	GW ◇1 ⊡	GW	GW ◇1	GW ◇1 ⊡	GW	GW ◇1 ⊡		GW ◇1 ⊡	GW ◇1 ⊡	GW ◇1 ⊡	GW ◇1 ⊡	GW ◇1 ⊡	GW ◇1 ⊡	GW ◇1 ⊡	GW ◇1	GW		GW ◇1 ⊡	GW ◇1 ⊡
London Paddington [15] ⊖ d	17 37		17 42	18 03	18 30	18 37		18 42	19 03		19 33		19 37	19 42	20 03	20 30	20 37	21 03	21 37	21 42			22 03	22 37
Slough [3] d			18 04					19 07						20 04						22 06				
Reading [7] d	18 15		18 24	18 38	19 05	19 15		19 28	19 38		20 07		20 15	20 21	20 38	21 05	21 15	21 38	22 14	22 22			22 50	23 17
Didcot Parkway d	18 29		18 39	18 52		19 29		19 44	19 52				20 29	20 37	20 52		21 29	21 54	22 29	22 40			23 07	23s32
Swindon a	18 46			19 10	19 35	19 46			20 10		20 35		20 46		21 10	21 35	21 46	22 14	22 49				23 27	23s51
d	18 48			19 11	19 36	19 47			20 11	20 28	20 35		20 47		21 11	21 36	21 47	22 15	22 50		22 57		23 27	
Kemble d					19 50					20 42						21 50					23 11			
Stroud d					20 05					20 57						22 05					23 26			
Stonehouse d					20 09					21 02						22 10					23 31			
Gloucester [7] a					20 32					21 17						22 25					23 48			
Cheltenham Spa a					20 49					21 33						22 41					00 05			
Worcester Shrub Hill d			20a12				20 37	21a13						22a10						00a12				
Chippenham d				19 26					20 26		20 50				21 26			22 29					23 43	
Bath Spa [7] a				19 39					20 39		21 03				21 39			22 43					23 56	
Bristol Parkway [7] a	19 14					20 12	21 53						21 12				22 12		23 15					00s18
d	19 15					20 13	21 55						21 13				22 13		23 16					
Bristol Temple Meads [10] a				19 53			22 07		20 54		21 18				21 53			22 58					00 11	00 35
Weston-super-Mare a									21 26						22 27									
Newport (South Wales) a	19 40					20 38							21 38				22 38		23 40					
Cardiff Central [7] a	20 00					20 59							21 59				23 00		00 05					
Bridgend a	20 21					21 21							22 21				23 21		00 28					
Port Talbot Parkway a	20 35					21 35							22 35				23 35		00 40					
Neath a	20 42					21 41							22 41				23 41		00 48					
Swansea a	20 56					21 56							22 58				23 59		01 02					

For connections from Heathrow Airport, Gatwick Airport and Oxford please refer to Tables 125A, 148 and 116. For connections to Birmingham New Street and Hereford please refer to Tables 57 and 131

Table 125

Sundays
from 28 October

London - Swindon, Cheltenham Spa, Bristol, Weston-super-Mare and South Wales

Route Diagram - see first Page of Table 125

	GW ◇1 ⊡	GW ◇1 ⊡
London Paddington [15] ⊖ d	23 03	23 37
Slough [3] d		00 02
Reading [7] d	23 46	00 14
Didcot Parkway d	00s04	00s33
Swindon a	00s23	00s53
d		
Kemble d		
Stroud d		
Stonehouse d		
Gloucester [7] a		
Cheltenham Spa a		
Worcester Shrub Hill d		
Chippenham d	00s39	01s08
Bath Spa [7] a	00s53	01s23
Bristol Parkway [7] a		
d		
Bristol Temple Meads [10] a	01 07	01 37
Weston-super-Mare a		
Newport (South Wales) a		
Cardiff Central [7] a		
Bridgend a		
Port Talbot Parkway a		
Neath a		
Swansea a		

For connections from Heathrow Airport, Gatwick Airport and Oxford please refer to Tables 125A, 148 and 116. For connections to Birmingham New Street and Hereford please refer to Tables 57 and 131

South Wales, Weston-super-Mare, Bristol, Cheltenham Spa and Swindon - London

Route Diagram - see first Page of Table 125

Miles	Miles	Miles			GW MO	GW MO	GW MX	GW MX	GW	GW	GW	GW	GW		AW	GW	GW	GW	GW	XC	GW	AW	GW		GW
					◇1 A	◇1 A ⊡	◇1 ⊡	◇1	◇1 ⊡		◇1 ⊡	◇1 ⊡	◇1 ⊡			◇1 ⊡	◇1 ⊡	◇1 ⊡	◇1 ⊡	◇1			◇1 ⊡		◇1 ⊡
0	—	—	Swansea	d									03 57				04 58								
9½	—	—	Neath	d									04 09				05 10								
15	—	—	Port Talbot Parkway	d									04 17				05 18								
27¼	—	—	Bridgend	d									04 30				05 30								
47½	—	—	Cardiff Central 7	d									05 14				05 55					06 12			
59¼	—	—	Newport (South Wales)	d									05 32				06 09					06 28			
—	0	—	Weston-super-Mare	d			22p01																		
—	19	—	Bristol Temple Meads 10	d		22p10	22p35		04 47		05 30					06 00							06 30		06 40
81	—	—	Bristol Parkway 7	a									05 59				06 29								
—	—	—		d					04u57				06 01				06 31								
—	30½	—	Bath Spa 7	d		22p23	22p47				05 43					06 13							06 43		06 52
—	43½	—	Chippenham	d		22p35	23p00				05 55					06 25							06 55		07 05
—	—	—	Worcester Shrub Hill	d	21p34			22p43				05 11						05 21	05 37						
—	—	0	Cheltenham Spa	d											05 37			05 54		06 03	06 24				
—	—	6½	Gloucester 7	d						05 18					05a48			06 09		06a16	06a34	07a20			
—	—	15½	Stonehouse	d						05 31								06 23							
—	—	18	Stroud	d						05 36								06 29							
—	—	29¼	Kemble	d						05 51								06 43							
115½	60¼	43	Swindon	a		22p50	23p14		05 22	06 06	06 10		06 27			06 40	06 57	06 58					07 10		07 19
—	—	—		d		22p53	23p16		05 23		06 11		06 28			06 41	06 58	07 01					07 11		07 20
139½	84¼	67	Didcot Parkway	a	22p58	23p08	23p33	00 20	05 41		06 29	06 39	06 46			06 58		07 19	07 07				07 28		
156¾	101½	84½	Reading 7	a	23p17	23p28	23p53	00 38	05 56		06 43	06 54	07 00			07 14	07 31	07 34	07 25				07 43		
174¼	119	101¾	Slough 3	a	23p43			00 55			06 58														
192¾	137½	120¼	London Paddington 15 ⊖	a	00 05	00 13	00 33	01 17	06 24		07 16	07 30	07 32			07 44	08 02	08 07	07 59				08 14		08 16

		GW	GW	GW	GW	XC	GW	XC	GW		GW	GW	AW	GW	GW	GW	GW	AW	XC		XC	GW	GW	GW	GW
		◇1 ⊡	◇1 ⊡	◇1 ⊡	◇1 B ⊡⊘	◇1	◇	◇1			◇1 C ⊘	◇1 D ⊡		◇1 B ⊡⊘	◇1 ⊡	◇1 ⊡	◇1 E ⊡⊘		◇1 ⌶		◇1 F ⌶	◇1 B ⊡⊘		◇1 ⊡	
Swansea	d	05 27									05 58			06 28								06 58			
Neath	d	05 39									06 10			06 40								07 10			
Port Talbot Parkway	d	05 47									06 18			06 48								07 18			
Bridgend	d	05 59									06 30			07 00								07 30			
Cardiff Central 7	d	06 24						06 40			06 55		07 12	07 25							07 45	07 55			
Newport (South Wales)	d	06 38						06 55			07 09		07 27	07 39							08 02	08 09			
Weston-super-Mare	d			06 20								06 49				07 25								07 49	
Bristol Temple Meads 10	d			07 00								07 30				08 00							08 12	08 30	08 41
Bristol Parkway 7	a	06 58									07 29			07 59								08 30			08 52
	d	07 01									07 31			08 01								08 31			08 52
Bath Spa 7	d			07 13								07 43				08 13							08 30	08 43	
Chippenham	d			07 25					07 31			07 55				08 25							08 44	08 55	
Worcester Shrub Hill	d				06 33		06 49								07 09		07 34								
Cheltenham Spa	d		06 31			06 43	07 16								07 30			07 45	08 16						
Gloucester 7	d		06 46			06a53	07a26	07a44					08a20		07 45			07a57	08a27		08a44				09a33
Stonehouse	d		06 59												07 59										
Stroud	d		07 05												08 05										
Kemble	d		07 19												08 19										
Swindon	a	07 27	07 35	07 40					07 48		07 57	08 10		08 27	08 33	08 40						08 57	09 03	09 10	
	d	07 28	07 35	07 41							07 58	08 11		08 28	08 35	08 41						08 59		09 11	
Didcot Parkway	a	07 45	07 53	08 00								08 28		08 46	08 52	08 58								09 28	
Reading 7	a	08 00	08 12	08 16	08 21							08 44		09 01	09 07	09 14	09 14					09 25		09 44	
Slough 3	a																								
London Paddington 15 ⊖	a	08 33	08 40	08 44	08 51						08 54	09 14		09 29	09 39	09 44	09 47					09 59		10 15	

		GW	GW	AW	GW		GW	XC	GW	XC	AW	GW	GW	GW	GW		GW	XC	XC	GW	AW	GW	GW	GW	GW
		◇1 B ⊡⊘	◇1 ⊡		◇1 ⊡		◇1 ⌶	◇1 ⌶		◇1 F ⌶		◇1 ⊡	◇1 ⊡	◇1 G ⊡	◇1 ⊡			◇1 ⌶	◇1 F ⌶	◇1 ⊡		◇1 ⊡	◇1 ⌶	◇	◇1 ⊡
Swansea	d	07 28										07 58		08 28											09 28
Neath	d	07 40										08 10		08 40											09 40
Port Talbot Parkway	d	07 48										08 18		08 48											09 48
Bridgend	d	08 00									08 21	08 30		09 00							09 38				10 00
Cardiff Central 7	d	08 25								08 45	09 12	08 55		09 25					09 45	09 55	10 12				10 25
Newport (South Wales)	d	08 39								09 02	09 27	09 09		09 39					10 00	10 09	10 27				10 39
Weston-super-Mare	d														09 29										
Bristol Temple Meads 10	d				09 00								09 30		10 00							10 30		10 41	
Bristol Parkway 7	a	08 59										09 30		09 59						10 30				10 52	10 59
	d	09 01										09 31		10 01						10 31				10 52	11 01
Bath Spa 7	d				09 13								09 43		10 13							10 43			
Chippenham	d				09 25								09 55		10 25							10 55			
Worcester Shrub Hill	d						08 39		09 06														10 08		
Cheltenham Spa	d		08 31	08 45				09 12	09 34								09 40	10 11							
Gloucester 7	d		08 46	08a58				09a22	09a42	09a44	10a20						09 54	10a22	10a44		11a20			11a34	
Stonehouse	d		08 59														10 06								
Stroud	d		09 05														10 11								
Kemble	d		09 19														10 27								
Swindon	a	09 27	09 33		09 40							09 57	10 10	10 27	10 40		10 44			10 57		11 10			11 27
	d	09 29	09 35		09 41							09 59	10 11	10 29	10 41					10 59		11 11			11 29
Didcot Parkway	a		09 52									10 16	10 28	10 46						11 17		11 28			
Reading 7	a	09 59	10 06		10 10		10 25					10 31	10 44	11 00	11 09					11 30		11 43	11 54		11 59
Slough 3	a						10 39																12 09		
London Paddington 15 ⊖	a	10 32	10 37		10 39		11 00					11 07	11 14	11 32	11 38					12 00		12 14	12 29		12 32

A from 21 May until 18 June
B ⊡ from Reading ⊘ to Reading
C The Capitals United
D The Bristolian
E The Cathedrals Express. ⊡ from Reading ⊘ to Reading
F ⌶ from Newport (South Wales)
G The Red Dragon

For connections from Hereford and Birmingham New Street please refer to Tables 131 and 57. For connections to Oxford, Gatwick Airport and Heathrow Airport please refer to Tables 116, 148 and 125A

South Wales, Weston-super-Mare, Bristol, Cheltenham Spa and Swindon - London

Route Diagram - see first Page of Table 125

			GW	AW	GW	XC	GW	XC	GW	GW	GW		GW	GW	AW	XC	XC	GW	AW	GW	GW		GW	GW	GW
			◇1 ⊡		◇1 ⊡	◇1 ⌶	■	◇1 A ⌶	◇1 ⊡	◇1 ⊡	◇1 ⊡		◇1 ⊡			◇1 ⌶	◇1 A ⌶	◇1 ⊡		◇1 ⊡	◇1 ⌶		◇	◇1 B ⊡	◇1 ⊡
Swansea	d										10 28													11 28	
Neath	d										10 40													11 40	
Port Talbot Parkway	d										10 48													11 48	
Bridgend	d										11 00								11 38					12 00	
Cardiff Central 7	d							10 45	10 55		11 25						11 45	11 55	12 12					12 25	
Newport (South Wales)	d							11 00	11 09		11 39						12 02	12 09	12 28					12 39	
Weston-super-Mare	d																								
Bristol Temple Meads 10	d				11 00					11 30			12 00							12 30			12 41		
Bristol Parkway 7	a								11 30		11 59							12 30					12 52	12 59	
	d								11 31		12 01							12 31					12 52	13 01	
Bath Spa 7	d				11 13					11 43			12 13							12 43					
Chippenham	d				11 25					11 55			12 25							12 55					
Worcester Shrub Hill	d						11 06														12 08				
Cheltenham Spa	d		10 31	10 45		11 11	11 32							11 40	11 45	12 11									12 31
Gloucester 7	d		10 46	10a57		11a22	11a42	11a44						11 54	11a57	12a22	12a44		13a20				13a31		12 46
Stonehouse	d		10 59											12 06											12 59
Stroud	d		11 05											12 11											13 05
Kemble	d		11 19											12 27											13 19
Swindon	a		11 33		11 40				11 57	12 10	12 27		12 40	12 44				12 57		13 10				13 27	13 33
	d		11 35		11 41				11 59	12 11	12 29		12 41					12 59		13 11				13 29	13 35
Didcot Parkway	a		11 52						12 16	12 28	12 46							13 16		13 28					13 52
Reading 7	a		12 06		12 10				12 30	12 44	13 00		13 09					13 31		13 43	13 54			13 59	14 06
Slough 3	a																				14 09				
London Paddington 15 ⊖	a		12 37		12 40				13 00	13 14	13 32		13 38					14 06		14 14	14 29			14 32	14 37

		GW	XC	GW	XC	GW	AW		GW	GW	GW	GW	AW	XC	XC	GW	GW		GW	GW	GW	GW	AW	GW	GW
		◇1 ⊡	◇1 ⌶	◇	◇1 A ⌶	◇1 ⊡	⌶		◇1 ⊡	◇1 C ⊡⊘	◇1 ⊡			◇1 ⌶	◇1 A ⌶	◇1 ⊡	◇1 ⊡		◇1 ⊡	◇	◇1 C ⊡⊘	◇1 D ⊡	⌶	◇1 ⊡	◇1 ⌶
Swansea	d									12 28											13 28				
Neath	d									12 40											13 40				
Port Talbot Parkway	d									12 48											13 48				
Bridgend	d						12 38			13 00											14 00				
Cardiff Central 7	d				12 45	12 55	13 12			13 25					13 45	13 55					14 25				
Newport (South Wales)	d				13 01	13 09	13 28			13 39					14 00	14 09					14 39				
Weston-super-Mare	d																								
Bristol Temple Meads 10	d	13 00							13 30		14 00						14 30			14 41				15 00	
Bristol Parkway 7	a					13 30				13 59						14 30				14 51	15 00				
	d					13 31				14 01						14 31				14 52	15 01				
Bath Spa 7	d	13 13							13 43		14 13						14 43							15 13	
Chippenham	d	13 25							13 55		14 25						14 55							15 25	
Worcester Shrub Hill	d			13 06															14 09						14 41
Cheltenham Spa	d		13 11	13 34								13 40	13 45	14 11								14 31	14 45		
Gloucester 7	d		13a22	13a42	13a44		14a20					13 54	13a57	14a22	14a44					15a32		14 46	14a56		
Stonehouse	d											14 06										14 59			
Stroud	d											14 11										15 05			
Kemble	d											14 27										15 19			
Swindon	a	13 40				13 57			14 10	14 27	14 40	14 44				14 57	15 10				15 27	15 33		15 40	
	d	13 41				13 59			14 11	14 29	14 41					14 59	15 11				15 29	15 35		15 41	
Didcot Parkway	a					14 15			14 28	14 46						15 15	15 28					15 52			
Reading 7	a	14 10				14 31			14 43	15 00	15 09					15 31	15 43		15 54		16 00	16 06		16 13	16 24
Slough 3	a																		16 09						16 39
London Paddington 15 ⊖	a	14 40				15 08			15 14	15 32	15 38					16 09	16 14		16 27		16 30	16 39		16 44	17 00

		XC	GW		XC	GW	AW	GW	GW	GW	GW	XC	XC		GW	AW	GW	GW	GW	GW	GW	AW	GW		XC
		◇1 ⌶	◇		◇1 A ⌶	◇1 ⊡		◇1 ⊡	◇1 ⊡	◇1 E ⊡		◇1 ⌶	◇1		◇1 ⊡	■ ⌶	◇1 ⊡	◇1 ⊡		◇1 ⊡	◇1 ⊡		◇1 ⊡		◇1
Swansea	d								14 28											15 28					
Neath	d								14 40											15 40					
Port Talbot Parkway	d								14 48											15 48					
Bridgend	d						14 38		15 00											16 00					
Cardiff Central 7	d				14 45	14 55	15 12		15 25				15 45		15 55	16 05				16 25					
Newport (South Wales)	d				15 01	15 09	15 28		15 39				16 00		16 09	16 21				16 39					
Weston-super-Mare	d																								
Bristol Temple Meads 10	d							15 30		16 00							16 30		16 41				17 00		
Bristol Parkway 7	a					15 30			15 59						16 30				16 52	16 59					
	d					15 31			16 01						16 31				16 52	17 01					
Bath Spa 7	d							15 43		16 13							16 43						17 13		
Chippenham	d							15 55		16 25							16 55						17 25		
Worcester Shrub Hill	d		15 06															16 03							
Cheltenham Spa	d	15 11	15 34								15 40	16 11									16 31	16 45			17 15
Gloucester 7	d	15a22	15a42		15a44		16a21				15 54	16a22	16a44			17a14			17a33		16 46	16a56			17a26
Stonehouse	d										16 06										16 59				
Stroud	d										16 11										17 05				
Kemble	d										16 27										17 19				
Swindon	a					15 57		16 10	16 27	16 40	16 44				16 57		17 10			17 27	17 33		17 40		
	d					15 59		16 11	16 29	16 41					16 59		17 11			17 29	17 35		17 41		
Didcot Parkway	a					16 16		16 28	16 46						17 16		17 28				17 52				
Reading 7	a					16 31		16 43	17 00	17 09					17 31		17 44	17 54		18 00	18 06		18 12		
Slough 3	a																	18 10							
London Paddington 15 ⊖	a					17 09		17 14	17 30	17 39					18 02		18 14	18 28		18 30	18 39		18 44		

A ⌶ from Newport (South Wales)
B The St. David
C ⊡ from Reading ⊘ to Reading
D The Cheltenham Spa Express
E The Merchant Venturer

For connections from Hereford and Birmingham New Street please refer to Tables 131 and 57. For connections to Oxford, Gatwick Airport and Heathrow Airport please refer to Tables 116, 148 and 125A

until 22 June

South Wales, Weston-super-Mare, Bristol, Cheltenham Spa and Swindon - London

Route Diagram - see first Page of Table 125

	GW	XC ◇1	GW ◇1 ☕	AW	GW ◇1 ☕	GW ◇1 A ☕⊘	GW ◇	AW	GW ◇1 ☕	XC ◇1	XC ◇1 B ⊼	GW ◇1 ☕	GW ◇1 ⊼	AW	GW ◇1 ☕	GW	GW ◇1 ☕	GW ◇1 ☕	AW	XC ◇1	GW ◇1 ☕	GW ◇1 ☕
Swansea d						16 28											17 28					
Neath d						16 40											17 40					
Port Talbot Parkway d						16 48											17 48					
Bridgend d				16 38		17 00								17 38			18 00					
Cardiff Central 7 d		16 45	16 55	17 12		17 25					17 45	17 55		18 12			18 25					
Newport (South Wales) d		17 00	17 09	17 28		17 39					18 00	18 09		18 27			18 39					
Weston-super-Mare d					17 10										18 08							
Bristol Temple Meads 10 d					17 30				18 00						18 30	18 41					19 30	
Bristol Parkway 7 a			17 30			17 59						18 30				18 52	18 59					
d			17 31			18 01						18 31				18 52	19 01					
Bath Spa 7 d					17 43				18 13						18 43						19 43	
Chippenham d					17 55				18 25						18 55						19 55	
Worcester Shrub Hill d	17 06												17 31									18 55
Cheltenham Spa d	17 33						17 40	17 45		18 18								18 34	18 45	19 15		
Gloucester 7 d	17a42	17a44		18a21			17 54	17a57		18a29	18a44			19a20		19a30		18 51	18a56	19a27		
Stonehouse d							18 06											19 04				
Stroud d							18 11											19 09				
Kemble d							18 25											19 23				
Swindon a			17 57		18 10	18 27	18 41		18 40			18 57			19 10		19 27	19 38			20 10	
d			17 59		18 11	18 29			18 41			18 59			19 11		19 29	19 41			20 11	
Didcot Parkway a			18 16		18 28	18 46									19 28		19 46	19 58			20 28	
Reading 7 a			18 31		18 46	19 01			19 09			19 25	19 32		19 44		20 00	20 14			20 44	20 54
Slough 3 a													19 47									21 09
London Paddington 15 ⊖ a			19 02		19 14	19 32			19 38			19 54	20 06		20 14		20 32	20 46			21 14	21 29

	GW	XC ◇1	AW	GW	GW ◇	GW ◇1 ☕	GW	XC ◇1	XC ◇1	XC ◇1	GW ◇1 ☕	GW ◇1	GW 1	GW	GW FX ◇1 ☕	GW FO ◇1 ☕	GW	GW FO ◇1	GW FX ◇1	XC ◇1	XC ◇1	XC ◇1
Swansea d						18 28									19 29	19 29						
Neath d						18 40									19 40	19 40						
Port Talbot Parkway d						18 48									19 48	19 48						
Bridgend d						19 00									20 00	20 00						
Cardiff Central 7 d		18 45				19 25				19 50					20 25	20 25						21 05
Newport (South Wales) d		19 01				19 39				20 05					20 39	20 39						21 21
Weston-super-Mare d																						
Bristol Temple Meads 10 d				19 41					20 00		20 30			20 41								
Bristol Parkway 7 a				19 52		19 59			20 08					20 52	21 01	21 01						
d				19 52		20 01			20 10					20 52	21 01	21 01						
Bath Spa 7 d											20 43											
Chippenham d					20 02						20 55											
Worcester Shrub Hill d	19 07											20 03						21 03	21 03			
Cheltenham Spa d	19 34		19 45				20 01	20 11					20 48				21 00			21 11	21 52	
Gloucester 7 d	19a42	19a45	19a56	20a32			20 13	20a22	20a38	20a53			20a58	21a31			21 21			21a22	22a01	22a02
Stonehouse d							20 25										21 33					
Stroud d							20 30										21 39					
Kemble d							20 44										21 54					
Swindon a					20 21	20 27	21 03				21 10				21 29	21 29	22 09					
d						20 29					21 11				21 33	21 33						
Didcot Parkway a						20 46					21 28				21 52	21 52						
Reading 7 a						21 00					21 43	21 55			22 11	22 11		22 58	22 58			
Slough 3 a												22 13						23 12	23 15			
London Paddington 15 ⊖ a						21 32					22 14	22 39			22 44	22 45		23 36	23 36			

	AW	GW ◇1 ☕	GW ◇1 ☕	GW	GW	XC ◇1	GW ◇1 ☕	AW	GW	GW ◇1	LM FO	AW FO	AW FX
Swansea d		20 28											
Neath d		20 40											
Port Talbot Parkway d		20 48											
Bridgend d	20 38	21 00										22 38	22 38
Cardiff Central 7 d	21 12	21 25				21 50						23 20	23 19
Newport (South Wales) d	21 27	21 39				22 05						23 40	23 40
Weston-super-Mare d							22 01						
Bristol Temple Meads 10 d			21 50				22 35						
Bristol Parkway 7 a		21 59											
d		22 01											
Bath Spa 7 d			22 02				22 47						
Chippenham d			22 15				23 00						
Worcester Shrub Hill d					21 32				22 28	22 43	23 46		
Cheltenham Spa d				22 01	22 07			23 00	23 05		00 09		
Gloucester 7 d	22a21			22 14	22a21	22a46		23a12	23a17		00a20	00a39	00a39
Stonehouse d				22 26									
Stroud d				22 31									
Kemble d				22 46									
Swindon a		22 27	22 33	23 05			23 14						
d		22 28	22 34				23 16						
Didcot Parkway a			22 50				23 33			00 20			
Reading 7 a		23 02	23 06				23 53			00 38			
Slough 3 a										00 55			
London Paddington 15 ⊖ a		23 38	23 41				00 33			01 17			

A ☕ from Reading ⊘ to Reading

B ⊼ from Newport (South Wales)

For connections from Hereford and Birmingham New Street please refer to Tables 131 and 57. For connections to Oxford, Gatwick Airport and Heathrow Airport please refer to Tables 116, 148 and 125A

Table 125

Mondays to Fridays

25 June to 14 September

South Wales, Weston-super-Mare, Bristol, Cheltenham Spa and Swindon - London

Route Diagram - see first Page of Table 125

	GW MO ◇1 A	GW ◇1 B	GW MO ◇1 A ☕	GW ◇1 B ☕	GW MX ◇1 ☕	GW MX ◇1	GW ◇1 ☕	GW	GW ◇1 ☕	GW ◇1 ☕	GW ◇1 ☕	AW	GW ◇1 ☕	GW ◇1 ☕	GW ◇1 ☕	GW ◇1 ☕	XC ◇1	GW	AW	GW ◇1 ☕	GW ◇1 C ☕	GW ◇1 ☕
Swansea d											03 57			04 58								05 27
Neath d											04 09			05 10								05 39
Port Talbot Parkway d											04 17			05 18								05 47
Bridgend d											04 30			05 30								05 59
Cardiff Central 7 d											05 14			05 55					06 12			06 24
Newport (South Wales) d											05 32			06 09					06 28			06 38
Weston-super-Mare d					22p01																	
Bristol Temple Meads 10 d			22p10	22p10	22p35		04 47		05 30				06 00							06 30	06 40	
Bristol Parkway 7 a											05 59			06 29								06 58
d							04u57				06 01			06 31								07 01
Bath Spa 7 d			22p23	22p23	22p47				05 43				06 13							06 43	06 52	
Chippenham d			22p35	22p35	23p00				05 55				06 25							06 55	07 05	
Worcester Shrub Hill d	21p34	21p34				22p43				05 11					05 21	05 37						
Cheltenham Spa d												05 37			05 54		06 03	06 24				
Gloucester 7 d								05 18				05a48			06 09		06a16	06a34	07a20			
Stonehouse d								05 31							06 23							
Stroud d								05 36							06 29							
Kemble d								05 51							06 43							
Swindon a			22p50	22p50	23p14		05 22	06 06	06 10		06 27		06 40	06 57	06 58					07 10	07 19	07 27
d			22p53	22p53	23p16		05 23		06 11		06 28		06 41	06 58	07 01					07 11	07 20	07 28
Didcot Parkway a	22p58	22p58	23p10	23p08	23p33	00 20	05 41		06 29	06 39	06 46		06 58		07 19	07 07				07 28		07 45
Reading 7 a	23p15	23p17	23p28	23p28	23p53	00 38	05 56		06 43	06 54	07 00		07 14	07 31	07 34	07 25				07 43		08 00
Slough 3 a	23p42	23p43				00 55			06 58													
London Paddington 15 ⊖ a	00 02	00 05	00 05	00 13	00 33	01 17	06 24		07 16	07 30	07 32		07 44	08 02	08 07	07 59				08 14	08 16	08 33

	GW ◇1 ☕	GW ◇1 ☕	GW ◇1 D ☕⊘	XC ◇1	GW ◇	XC ◇1	GW	GW ◇1 E ⊘	GW ◇1 F ☕	AW	GW ◇1 D ☕⊘	GW ◇1 ☕	GW ◇1 ☕	GW ◇1 G ☕⊘	AW	XC ◇1 ⊼	XC ◇1 H ⊼	GW ◇1 D ☕⊘	GW	GW ◇1 ☕	GW	GW ◇1 D ☕⊘
Swansea d								05 58			06 28							06 58				07 28
Neath d								06 10			06 40							07 10				07 40
Port Talbot Parkway d								06 18			06 48							07 18				07 48
Bridgend d								06 30			07 00							07 30				08 00
Cardiff Central 7 d						06 40		06 55		07 12	07 25						07 45	07 55				08 25
Newport (South Wales) d						06 55		07 09		07 27	07 39						08 02	08 09				08 39
Weston-super-Mare d		06 20							06 49				07 25							07 49		
Bristol Temple Meads 10 d		07 00							07 30				08 00						08 12	08 30	08 41	
Bristol Parkway 7 a								07 29			07 59							08 30			08 52	08 59
d								07 31			08 01							08 31			08 52	09 01
Bath Spa 7 d		07 13							07 43				08 13						08 30	08 43		
Chippenham d		07 25					07 31		07 55				08 25						08 44	08 55		
Worcester Shrub Hill d			06 33		06 49							07 09		07 34								
Cheltenham Spa d	06 31			06 43	07 16							07 30			07 45	08 16						
Gloucester 7 d	06 46			06a53	07a26	07a44				08a20		07 45			07a57	08a27	08a44				09a33	
Stonehouse d	06 59											07 59										
Stroud d	07 05											08 05										
Kemble d	07 19											08 19										
Swindon a	07 35	07 40					07 48	07 57	08 10		08 27	08 33	08 40					08 57	09 03	09 10		09 27
d	07 35	07 41						07 58	08 11		08 28	08 35	08 41					08 59		09 11		09 29
Didcot Parkway a	07 53	08 00							08 28		08 46	08 52	08 58							09 28		
Reading 7 a	08 12	08 16	08 21						08 44		09 01	09 07	09 14	09 14				09 25		09 44		09 59
Slough 3 a																						
London Paddington 15 ⊖ a	08 40	08 44	08 51					08 54	09 14		09 29	09 39	09 44	09 47				09 59		10 15		10 32

	GW ◇1 ☕	AW	GW ◇1 ☕	GW ◇1 ⊼	XC ◇1 ⊼	GW	XC ◇1 H ⊼	AW	GW ◇1 ☕	GW ◇1 ☕	GW ◇1 I ☕	GW ◇1 ☕	GW	XC ◇1 ⊼	XC ◇1 H ⊼	GW ◇1 ☕	AW	GW ◇1 ☕	GW ◇1 ⊼	GW ◇	GW ◇1 ☕
Swansea d									07 58		08 28										09 28
Neath d									08 10		08 40										09 40
Port Talbot Parkway d									08 18		08 48										09 48
Bridgend d								08 21	08 30		09 00						09 38				10 00
Cardiff Central 7 d							08 45	09 12	08 55		09 25				09 45	09 55	10 12				10 25
Newport (South Wales) d							09 02	09 27	09 09		09 39				10 00	10 09	10 27				10 39
Weston-super-Mare d												09 29									
Bristol Temple Meads 10 d			09 00							09 30		10 00						10 30		10 41	
Bristol Parkway 7 a									09 30		09 59					10 30				10 52	10 59
d									09 31		10 01					10 31				10 52	11 01
Bath Spa 7 d			09 13							09 43		10 13						10 43			
Chippenham d			09 25							09 55		10 25						10 55			
Worcester Shrub Hill d				08 39		09 06													10 08		
Cheltenham Spa d	08 31	08 45			09 12	09 34							09 40	10 11							
Gloucester 7 d	08 46	08a58			09a22	09a42	09a44	10a20					09 54	10a22	10a44		11a20			11a34	
Stonehouse d	08 59												10 06								
Stroud d	09 05												10 11								
Kemble d	09 19												10 27								
Swindon a	09 33		09 40						09 57	10 10	10 27	10 40	10 44			10 57		11 10			11 27
d	09 35		09 41						09 59	10 11	10 29	10 41				10 59		11 11			11 29
Didcot Parkway a	09 52								10 16	10 28	10 46					11 17		11 28			
Reading 7 a	10 06		10 10	10 25					10 31	10 44	11 00	11 09				11 30		11 43	11 54		11 59
Slough 3 a				10 39															12 09		
London Paddington 15 ⊖ a	10 37		10 39	11 00					11 07	11 14	11 32	11 38				12 00		12 14	12 29		12 32

A from 2 July until 10 September

B 25 June

C from 25 June until 29 June, from 3 September until 14 September

D ☕ from Reading ⊘ to Reading

E The Capitals United

F The Bristolian

G The Cathedrals Express. ☕ from Reading ⊘ to Reading

H ⊼ from Newport (South Wales)

I The Red Dragon

For connections from Hereford and Birmingham New Street please refer to Tables 131 and 57. For connections to Oxford, Gatwick Airport and Heathrow Airport please refer to Tables 116, 148 and 125A

Table 125

25 June to 14 September

South Wales, Weston-super-Mare, Bristol, Cheltenham Spa and Swindon - London

Route Diagram - see first Page of Table 125

		GW	AW	GW	XC	GW	XC	GW	GW	GW	GW	GW	AW	XC	XC	GW	AW	GW	GW	GW	GW	GW	GW
		◇1 ⊏		◇1 ⊏	◇1 Ħ	■	◇1 A Ħ	◇1 ⊏	◇1 ⊏	◇1 ⊏	◇1 ⊏			◇1 Ħ	◇1 A Ħ	◇1 ⊏		◇1 ⊏	◇1 Ħ	◇	◇1 B ⊏	◇1 ⊏	◇1 ⊏
Swansea	d									10 28											11 28		
Neath	d									10 40											11 40		
Port Talbot Parkway	d									10 48											11 48		
Bridgend	d									11 00							11 38				12 00		
Cardiff Central 7	d						10 45	10 55		11 25					11 45	11 55	12 12				12 25		
Newport (South Wales)	d						11 00	11 09		11 39					12 02	12 09	12 28				12 39		
Weston-super-Mare	d																						
Bristol Temple Meads 10	d			11 00					11 30		12 00							12 30		12 41			13 00
Bristol Parkway 7	a							11 30		11 59						12 30				12 52	12 59		
	d							11 31		12 01						12 31				12 52	13 01		
Bath Spa 7	d			11 13					11 43		12 13							12 43					13 13
Chippenham	d			11 25					11 55		12 25							12 55					13 25
Worcester Shrub Hill	d					11 06													12 08				
Cheltenham Spa	d	10 31	10 45		11 11	11 32						11 40	11 45	12 11								12 31	
Gloucester 7	d	10 46	10a57		11a22	11a42	11a44					11 54	11a57	12a22	12a44		13a20			13a31		12 46	
Stonehouse	d	10 59										12 06										12 59	
Stroud	d	11 05										12 11										13 05	
Kemble	d	11 19										12 27										13 19	
Swindon	a	11 33		11 40				11 57	12 10	12 27	12 40	12 44				12 57		13 10			13 27	13 33	13 40
	d	11 35		11 41				11 59	12 11	12 29	12 41					12 59		13 11			13 29	13 35	13 41
Didcot Parkway	a	11 52						12 16	12 28	12 46						13 16		13 28				13 52	
Reading 7	a	12 06		12 10				12 30	12 44	13 00	13 09					13 31		13 43	13 54		13 59	14 06	14 10
Slough 3	a																		14 09				
London Paddington 15 ⊖	a	12 37		12 40				13 00	13 14	13 32	13 38					14 06		14 14	14 29		14 32	14 37	14 40

		XC	GW	XC	GW	AW	GW	GW	GW	GW	AW	XC	XC	GW	GW	GW	GW	GW	GW	AW	GW	GW
		◇1 Ħ	◇	◇1 A Ħ	◇1 ⊏	Ħ	◇1 ⊏	◇1 C ⊏⊘	◇1 ⊏			◇1 Ħ	◇1 A Ħ	◇1 ⊏	◇1 ⊏	◇1 ⊏	◇	◇1 C ⊏⊘	◇1 D ⊏	Ħ	◇1 ⊏	◇1 Ħ
Swansea	d							12 28										13 28				
Neath	d							12 40										13 40				
Port Talbot Parkway	d							12 48										13 48				
Bridgend	d					12 38		13 00										14 00				
Cardiff Central 7	d			12 45	12 55	13 12		13 25					13 45	13 55				14 25				
Newport (South Wales)	d			13 01	13 09	13 28		13 39					14 00	14 09				14 39				
Weston-super-Mare	d																					
Bristol Temple Meads 10	d						13 30		14 00						14 30		14 41				15 00	
Bristol Parkway 7	a				13 30			13 59						14 30			14 51	15 00				
	d				13 31			14 01						14 31			14 52	15 01				
Bath Spa 7	d						13 43		14 13						14 43						15 13	
Chippenham	d						13 55		14 25						14 55						15 25	
Worcester Shrub Hill	d		13 06													14 09						14 41
Cheltenham Spa	d	13 11	13 34							13 40	13 45	14 11							14 31	14 45		
Gloucester 7	d	13a22	13a42	13a44		14a20				13 54	13a57	14a22	14a44				15a32		14 46	14a56		
Stonehouse	d									14 06									14 59			
Stroud	d									14 11									15 05			
Kemble	d									14 27									15 19			
Swindon	a				13 57		14 10	14 27	14 40	14 44				14 57	15 10			15 27	15 33		15 40	
	d				13 59		14 11	14 29	14 41					14 59	15 11			15 29	15 35		15 41	
Didcot Parkway	a				14 15		14 28	14 46						15 15	15 28				15 52			
Reading 7	a				14 31		14 43	15 00	15 09					15 31	15 43	15 54		16 00	16 06		16 13	16 24
Slough 3	a															16 09						16 39
London Paddington 15 ⊖	a				15 08		15 14	15 32	15 38					16 09	16 14	16 27		16 30	16 39		16 44	17 00

		XC	GW	XC	GW	AW	GW	GW	GW	GW	XC	XC	GW	AW	GW	GW	GW	GW	GW	AW	GW	XC	GW
		◇1 Ħ	◇	◇1 A Ħ	◇1 ⊏		◇1 ⊏	◇1 ⊏	◇1 E ⊏		◇1 Ħ	◇1	◇1 ⊏	■ Ħ	◇1 ⊏	◇1 ⊏		◇1 ⊏	◇1 ⊏		◇1 ⊏	◇1	
Swansea	d							14 28										15 28					
Neath	d							14 40										15 40					
Port Talbot Parkway	d							14 48										15 48					
Bridgend	d					14 38		15 00										16 00					
Cardiff Central 7	d			14 45	14 55	15 12		15 25				15 45	15 55	16 05				16 25					
Newport (South Wales)	d			15 01	15 09	15 28		15 39				16 00	16 09	16 21				16 39					
Weston-super-Mare	d																						
Bristol Temple Meads 10	d						15 30		16 00						16 30		16 41				17 00		
Bristol Parkway 7	a				15 30			15 59					16 30				16 52	16 59					
	d				15 31			16 01					16 31				16 52	17 01					
Bath Spa 7	d						15 43		16 13						16 43						17 13		
Chippenham	d						15 55		16 25						16 55						17 25		
Worcester Shrub Hill	d		15 06													16 03							17 06
Cheltenham Spa	d	15 11	15 34							15 40	16 11								16 31	16 45		17 15	17 33
Gloucester 7	d	15a22	15a42	15a44		16a21				15 54	16a22	16a44		17a14			17a33		16 46	16a56		17a26	17a42
Stonehouse	d									16 06									16 59				
Stroud	d									16 11									17 05				
Kemble	d									16 27									17 19				
Swindon	a				15 57		16 10	16 27	16 40	16 44			16 57		17 10			17 27	17 33		17 40		
	d				15 59		16 11	16 29	16 41				16 59		17 11			17 29	17 35		17 41		
Didcot Parkway	a				16 16		16 28	16 46					17 16		17 28				17 52				
Reading 7	a				16 31		16 43	17 00	17 09				17 31		17 44	17 54		18 00	18 06		18 12		
Slough 3	a															18 10							
London Paddington 15 ⊖	a				17 09		17 14	17 30	17 39				18 02		18 14	18 28		18 30	18 39		18 44		

A Ħ from Newport (South Wales)
B The St. David
C ⊏ from Reading ⊘ to Reading
D The Cheltenham Spa Express
E The Merchant Venturer

For connections from Hereford and Birmingham New Street please refer to Tables 131 and 57. For connections to Oxford, Gatwick Airport and Heathrow Airport please refer to Tables 116, 148 and 125A

Table 125

Mondays to Fridays

25 June to 14 September

South Wales, Weston-super-Mare, Bristol, Cheltenham Spa and Swindon - London

Route Diagram - see first Page of Table 125

		XC	GW	AW	GW	GW	GW	AW	GW	XC	XC	GW	GW	AW	GW	GW	GW	GW	AW	XC	GW	GW	GW
		◇1	◇1 ⊏		◇1 ⊏	◇1 A ⊏⊘	◇		◇1 ⊏	◇1	◇1 B Ħ	◇1 ⊏	◇1 Ħ		◇1 ⊏		◇1 ⊏	◇1 ⊏		◇1	◇1 ⊏	◇1 ⊏	
Swansea	d					16 28											17 28						
Neath	d					16 40											17 40						
Port Talbot Parkway	d					16 48											17 48						
Bridgend	d			16 38		17 00								17 38			18 00						
Cardiff Central 7	d	16 45	16 55	17 12		17 25					17 45	17 55		18 12			18 25						
Newport (South Wales)	d	17 00	17 09	17 28		17 39					18 00	18 09		18 27			18 39						
Weston-super-Mare	d				17 10										18 08								
Bristol Temple Meads 10	d				17 30				18 00						18 30	18 41					19 30		
Bristol Parkway 7	a		17 30			17 59						18 30				18 52	18 59						
	d		17 31			18 01						18 31				18 52	19 01						
Bath Spa 7	d				17 43				18 13						18 43						19 43		
Chippenham	d				17 55				18 25						18 55						19 55		
Worcester Shrub Hill	d												17 31									18 55	19 07
Cheltenham Spa	d						17 40	17 45		18 18								18 34	18 45	19 15			19 34
Gloucester 7	d	17a44		18a21			17 54	17a57		18a29	18a44			19a20		19a30		18 51	18a56	19a27			19a42
Stonehouse	d						18 06											19 04					
Stroud	d						18 11											19 09					
Kemble	d						18 25											19 23					
Swindon	a		17 57		18 10	18 27	18 41		18 40			18 57			19 10		19 27	19 38			20 10		
	d		17 59		18 11	18 29			18 41			18 59			19 11		19 29	19 41			20 11		
Didcot Parkway	a		18 16		18 28	18 46									19 28		19 46	19 58			20 28		
Reading 7	a		18 31		18 46	19 01			19 09			19 25	19 32		19 44		20 00	20 14			20 44	20 54	
Slough 3	a												19 47									21 09	
London Paddington 15 ⊖	a		19 02		19 14	19 32			19 38			19 54	20 06		20 14		20 32	20 46			21 14	21 29	

		XC	AW	GW	GW	GW	GW	XC	XC	XC	GW	GW	GW	GW	GW	GW	GW	GW	GW	XC	XC	XC
															FX	FO		FO	FX			
		◇1			◇	◇1 ⊏		◇1	◇1	◇1	◇1 ⊏	◇1	1		◇1 ⊏	◇1 ⊏		◇1	◇1	◇1	◇1	◇1
Swansea	d					18 28									19 29	19 29						
Neath	d					18 40									19 40	19 40						
Port Talbot Parkway	d					18 48									19 48	19 48						
Bridgend	d					19 00									20 00	20 00						
Cardiff Central 7	d	18 45				19 25				19 50					20 25	20 25						21 05
Newport (South Wales)	d	19 01				19 39				20 05					20 39	20 39						21 21
Weston-super-Mare	d																					
Bristol Temple Meads 10	d			19 41					20 00		20 30			20 41								
Bristol Parkway 7	a			19 52		19 59			20 08					20 52	21 01	21 01						
	d			19 52		20 01			20 10					20 52	21 01	21 01						
Bath Spa 7	d										20 43											
Chippenham	d				20 02						20 55											
Worcester Shrub Hill	d											20 03						21 03	21 03			
Cheltenham Spa	d		19 45				20 01	20 11					20 48				21 00			21 11	21 52	
Gloucester 7	d	19a45	19a56	20a32			20 13	20a22	20a38	20a53			20a58	21a31			21 21			21a22	22a01	22a02
Stonehouse	d						20 25										21 33					
Stroud	d						20 30										21 39					
Kemble	d						20 44										21 54					
Swindon	a				20 21	20 27	21 03				21 10				21 29	21 29	22 09					
	d					20 29					21 11				21 33	21 33						
Didcot Parkway	a					20 46					21 28				21 52	21 52						
Reading 7	a					21 00					21 43	21 55			22 11	22 11		22 58	22 58			
Slough 3	a											22 13						23 12	23 15			
London Paddington 15 ⊖	a					21 32					22 14	22 39			22 44	22 45		23 36	23 36			

		AW	GW	GW	GW	GW	XC	GW	AW	GW	GW	LM	AW	AW
												FO	FO	FX
			◇1 ⊏	◇1 ⊏			◇1	◇1 ⊏			◇1			
Swansea	d		20 28											
Neath	d		20 40											
Port Talbot Parkway	d		20 48											
Bridgend	d	20 38	21 00										22 38	22 38
Cardiff Central 7	d	21 12	21 25				21 50						23 20	23 19
Newport (South Wales)	d	21 27	21 39				22 05						23 40	23 40
Weston-super-Mare	d							22 01						
Bristol Temple Meads 10	d			21 50				22 35						
Bristol Parkway 7	a		21 59											
	d		22 01											
Bath Spa 7	d			22 02				22 47						
Chippenham	d			22 15				23 00						
Worcester Shrub Hill	d					21 32				22 28	22 43	23 46		
Cheltenham Spa	d				22 01	22 07			23 00	23 05		00 09		
Gloucester 7	d	22a21			22 14	22a21	22a46		23a12	23a17		00a20	00a39	00a39
Stonehouse	d				22 26									
Stroud	d				22 31									
Kemble	d				22 46									
Swindon	a		22 27	22 33	23 05			23 14						
	d		22 28	22 34				23 16						
Didcot Parkway	a			22 50				23 33			00 20			
Reading 7	a		23 02	23 06				23 53			00 38			
Slough 3	a										00 55			
London Paddington 15 ⊖	a		23 38	23 41				00 33			01 17			

A ⊏ from Reading ⊘ to Reading
B Ħ from Newport (South Wales)

For connections from Hereford and Birmingham New Street please refer to Tables 131 and 57. For connections to Oxford, Gatwick Airport and Heathrow Airport please refer to Tables 116, 148 and 125A

Table 125

Mondays to Fridays
from 17 September

South Wales, Weston-super-Mare, Bristol, Cheltenham Spa and Swindon - London

Route Diagram - see first Page of Table 125

		GW MO	GW MO	GW MO	GW MO	GW MX	GW MX	GW	GW	GW		GW	GW	AW	GW	GW	GW	GW	XC	GW		AW	GW	GW	GW
		◇■	◇■	◇■	◇■	◇■	◇■	◇■		◇■		◇■	◇■		◇■	◇■	◇■	◇■	◇■				◇■	◇■	◇■
		A	B	A	B																				
				🍴	🍴	🍴		🍴		🍴		🍴	🍴		🍴	🍴	🍴	🍴					🍴	🍴	🍴
Swansea	d												03 57			04 58									05 27
Neath	d												04 09			05 10									05 39
Port Talbot Parkway	d												04 17			05 18									05 47
Bridgend	d												04 30			05 30									05 59
Cardiff Central ■	d												05 14			05 55						06 12			06 24
Newport (South Wales)	d												05 32			06 09						06 28			06 38
Weston-super-Mare	d					22p01																			
Bristol Temple Meads ■	d			22p10	22p10	22p35		04 47		05 30					06 00								06 30	06 40	
Bristol Parkway ■	a												05 59			06 29									06 58
	d							04u57					06 01			06 31									07 01
Bath Spa ■	d			22p23	22p23	22p47				05 43					06 13								06 43	06 52	
Chippenham	d			22p35	22p35	23p00				05 55					06 25								06 55	07 05	
Worcester Shrub Hill	d	21p28	21p34				22p43					05 11					05 21	05 37							
Cheltenham Spa	d													05 37			05 54		06 03	06 24					
Gloucester ■	d								05 18					05a48			06 09		06a16	06a34		07a20			
Stonehouse	d								05 31								06 23								
Stroud	d								05 36								06 29								
Kemble	d								05 51								06 43								
Swindon	a			22p50	22p50	23p14		05 22	06 06	06 10			06 27		06 40	06 57	06 58						07 10	07 19	07 27
	d			22p53	22p53	23p16		05 23		06 11			06 28		06 41	06 58	07 01						07 11	07 20	07 28
Didcot Parkway	a	22p58	22p58	23p09	23p09	23p33	00 20	05 41		06 29		06 39	06 46		06 58		07 19	07 07					07 28		07 45
Reading ■	a	23p17	23p17	23p28	23p28	23p53	00 38	05 56		06 43		06 54	07 00		07 14	07 31	07 34	07 25					07 43		08 00
Slough ■	a	23p43	23p43				00 55			06 58															
London Paddington ■ ⊖	a	00 06	00 05	00 12	00 13	00 33	01 17	06 24		07 16		07 30	07 32		07 44	08 02	08 07	07 59					08 14	08 16	08 33

		GW	GW	GW	XC	GW		XC	GW	GW	GW	AW	GW	GW	GW	GW		AW	XC	XC	GW	GW	GW	GW	GW
		◇■	◇■	◇■	◇■	◇		◇■		◇■	◇■		◇■	◇■	◇■	◇■			◇■	◇■	◇■		◇■		◇■
				C						D	E		C			F				G	C				C
		🍴	🍴	🍴Ø						Ø	🍴		🍴Ø	🍴	🍴	🍴Ø			🛒	🛒	🍴Ø		🍴		🍴Ø
Swansea	d									05 58			06 28								06 58				07 28
Neath	d									06 10			06 40								07 10				07 40
Port Talbot Parkway	d									06 18			06 48								07 18				07 48
Bridgend	d									06 30			07 00								07 30				08 00
Cardiff Central ■	d							06 40		06 55		07 12	07 25							07 45	07 55				08 25
Newport (South Wales)	d							06 55		07 09		07 27	07 39							08 02	08 09				08 39
Weston-super-Mare	d		06 20								06 49				07 25								07 49		
Bristol Temple Meads ■	d		07 00								07 30				08 00							08 12	08 30	08 41	
Bristol Parkway ■	a									07 29			07 59								08 30			08 52	08 59
	d									07 31			08 01								08 31			08 52	09 01
Bath Spa ■	d		07 13								07 43				08 13							08 30	08 43		
Chippenham	d		07 25						07 31		07 55				08 25							08 44	08 55		
Worcester Shrub Hill	d			06 30		06 49								07 09		07 34									
Cheltenham Spa	d	06 31			06 43	07 16								07 30				07 45	08 16						
Gloucester ■	d	06 46			06a53	07a26		07a44				08a20		07 45				07a57	08a27	08a44				09a33	
Stonehouse	d	06 59												07 59											
Stroud	d	07 05												08 05											
Kemble	d	07 19												08 19											
Swindon	a	07 35	07 40						07 48	07 57	08 10		08 27	08 33	08 40						08 57	09 03	09 10		09 27
	d	07 35	07 41							07 58	08 11		08 28	08 35	08 41						08 59		09 11		09 29
Didcot Parkway	a	07 53	08 00								08 28		08 46	08 52	08 58								09 28		
Reading ■	a	08 12	08 16	08 21							08 44		09 01	09 07	09 14	09 14					09 25		09 44		09 59
Slough ■	a																								
London Paddington ■ ⊖	a	08 40	08 44	08 51						08 54	09 14		09 29	09 39	09 44	09 47					09 59		10 15		10 32

		GW		AW	GW	GW	XC	GW	XC	AW	GW	GW		GW	GW	GW	XC	XC	GW	AW	GW	GW		GW	GW
		◇■			◇■	◇■	◇■		◇■		◇■	◇■		◇■	◇■		◇■	◇■	◇■		◇■	◇■		◇	◇■
									G					H				G							
		🍴			🍴	🛒	🛒		🛒		🍴	🍴		🍴	🍴		🛒	🛒	🍴		🍴	🛒			🍴
Swansea	d										07 58			08 28											09 28
Neath	d										08 10			08 40											09 40
Port Talbot Parkway	d										08 18			08 48											09 48
Bridgend	d									08 21	08 30			09 00						09 38					10 00
Cardiff Central ■	d								08 45	09 12	08 55			09 25				09 45	09 55	10 12					10 25
Newport (South Wales)	d								09 02	09 27	09 09			09 39				10 00	10 09	10 27					10 39
Weston-super-Mare	d														09 29									10 41	
Bristol Temple Meads ■	d				09 00							09 30			10 00						10 30				
Bristol Parkway ■	a										09 30			09 59					10 30					10 52	10 59
	d										09 31			10 01					10 31					10 52	11 01
Bath Spa ■	d				09 13							09 43			10 13						10 43				
Chippenham	d				09 25							09 55			10 25						10 55				
Worcester Shrub Hill	d					08 39		09 06														10 08			
Cheltenham Spa	d	08 31		08 45			09 12	09 34								09 40	10 11								
Gloucester ■	d	08 46		08a58			09a22	09a42	09a44	10a20						09 54	10a22	10a44		11a20				11a34	
Stonehouse	d	08 59														10 06									
Stroud	d	09 05														10 11									
Kemble	d	09 19														10 27									
Swindon	a	09 33			09 40						09 57	10 10		10 27	10 40	10 44			10 57		11 10				11 27
	d	09 35			09 41						09 59	10 11		10 29	10 41				10 59		11 11				11 29
Didcot Parkway	a	09 52									10 16	10 28		10 46					11 17		11 28				
Reading ■	a	10 06			10 10	10 25					10 31	10 44		11 00	11 09				11 30		11 43	11 54			11 59
Slough ■	a					10 39																12 09			
London Paddington ■ ⊖	a	10 37			10 39	11 00					11 07	11 14		11 32	11 38				12 00		12 14	12 29			12 32

A from 17 September until 22 October
B from 29 October
C 🍴 from Reading Ø to Reading
D The Capitals United
E The Bristolian
F The Cathedrals Express. 🍴 from Reading Ø to Reading
G 🛒 from Newport (South Wales)
H The Red Dragon

For connections from Hereford and Birmingham New Street please refer to Tables 131 and 57. For connections to Oxford, Gatwick Airport and Heathrow Airport please refer to Tables 116, 148 and 125A

Table 125

Mondays to Fridays
from 17 September

South Wales, Weston-super-Mare, Bristol, Cheltenham Spa and Swindon - London

Route Diagram - see first Page of Table 125

		GW	AW	GW	XC	GW	XC	GW		GW	GW	GW	GW	AW	XC	XC	GW	AW		GW	GW	GW	GW	GW	GW
						■																			
		◇■		◇■	◇■		◇■	◇■		◇■	◇■	◇■			◇■	◇■	◇■			◇■	◇■	◇	◇■	◇■	◇■
							A									A							B		
		🍴		🍴	🛒		🛒	🍴		🍴	🍴	🍴			🛒	🛒	🍴			🍴	🛒		🍴	🍴	🍴
Swansea	d										10 28												11 28		
Neath	d										10 40												11 40		
Port Talbot Parkway	d										10 48												11 48		
Bridgend	d										11 00							11 38					12 00		
Cardiff Central ■	d						10 45	10 55			11 25					11 45	11 55	12 12					12 25		
Newport (South Wales)	d						11 00	11 09			11 39					12 02	12 09	12 28					12 39		
Weston-super-Mare	d																								
Bristol Temple Meads ■	d			11 00						11 30		12 00								12 30		12 41			13 00
Bristol Parkway ■	a							11 30			11 59						12 30					12 52	12 59		
	d							11 31			12 01						12 31					12 52	13 01		
Bath Spa ■	d			11 13						11 43		12 13								12 43					13 13
Chippenham	d			11 25						11 55		12 25								12 55					13 25
Worcester Shrub Hill	d					11 06															12 08				
Cheltenham Spa	d	10 31	10 45		11 11	11 32							11 40	11 45	12 11									12 31	
Gloucester ■	d	10 46	10a57		11a22	11a42	11a44						11 54	11a57	12a22	12a44		13a20				13a31		12 46	
Stonehouse	d	10 59											12 06											12 59	
Stroud	d	11 05											12 11											13 05	
Kemble	d	11 19											12 27											13 19	
Swindon	a	11 33		11 40				11 57		12 10	12 27	12 40	12 44				12 57			13 10			13 27	13 33	13 40
	d	11 35		11 41				11 59		12 11	12 29	12 41					12 59			13 11			13 29	13 35	13 41
Didcot Parkway	a	11 52						12 16		12 28	12 46						13 16			13 28				13 52	
Reading ■	a	12 06		12 10				12 30		12 44	13 00	13 09					13 31			13 43	13 54		13 59	14 06	14 10
Slough ■	a																				14 09				
London Paddington ■ ⊖	a	12 37		12 40				13 00		13 14	13 32	13 38					14 06			14 14	14 29		14 32	14 37	14 40

		XC	GW	XC		GW	AW	GW	GW	GW	GW	AW	XC	XC		GW	GW	GW	GW	GW	GW	AW	GW	GW	
		◇■	◇	◇■		◇■		◇■	◇■	◇■			◇■	◇■		◇■	◇■	◇■	◇	◇■	◇■		◇■	◇■	
				A					C					A						C	D				
		🛒		🛒		🍴	🛒	🍴	🍴Ø	🍴			🛒	🛒		🍴	🍴	🍴		🍴Ø	🍴	🛒	🍴	🛒	
Swansea	d								12 28											13 28					
Neath	d								12 40											13 40					
Port Talbot Parkway	d								12 48											13 48					
Bridgend	d						12 38		13 00											14 00					
Cardiff Central ■	d			12 45		12 55	13 12		13 25					13 45		13 55				14 25					
Newport (South Wales)	d			13 01		13 09	13 28		13 39					14 00		14 09				14 39					
Weston-super-Mare	d																								
Bristol Temple Meads ■	d							13 30		14 00							14 30		14 41				15 00		
Bristol Parkway ■	a					13 30			13 59							14 30			14 51	15 00					
	d					13 31			14 01							14 31			14 52	15 01					
Bath Spa ■	d							13 43		14 13							14 43						15 13		
Chippenham	d							13 55		14 25							14 55						15 25		
Worcester Shrub Hill	d		13 06															14 09						14 41	
Cheltenham Spa	d	13 11	13 34								13 40	13 45	14 11								14 31	14 45			
Gloucester ■	d	13a22	13a42	13a44			14a20				13 54	13a57	14a22	14a44					15a32		14 46	14a56			
Stonehouse	d										14 06										14 59				
Stroud	d										14 11										15 05				
Kemble	d										14 27										15 19				
Swindon	a					13 57		14 10	14 27	14 40	14 44					14 57	15 10			15 27	15 33		15 40		
	d					13 59		14 11	14 29	14 41						14 59	15 11			15 29	15 35		15 41		
Didcot Parkway	a					14 15		14 28	14 46							15 15	15 28				15 52				
Reading ■	a					14 31		14 43	15 00	15 09						15 31	15 43	15 54		16 00	16 06		16 13	16 24	
Slough ■	a																	16 09						16 39	
London Paddington ■ ⊖	a					15 08		15 14	15 32	15 38						16 09	16 14	16 27		16 30	16 39		16 44	17 00	

		XC	GW	XC	GW	AW	GW	GW	GW	GW		XC	XC	GW	AW	GW	GW	GW	GW	GW		AW	GW	XC	GW
															■										
		◇■	◇	◇■	◇■		◇■	◇■	◇■			◇■	◇■	◇■		◇■	◇■		◇■	◇■			◇■	◇■	
				A					E																
		🛒		🛒	🍴		🍴	🍴	🍴			🛒		🍴	🛒	🍴	🍴		🍴	🍴			🍴		
Swansea	d							14 28											15 28						
Neath	d							14 40											15 40						
Port Talbot Parkway	d							14 48											15 48						
Bridgend	d					14 38		15 00											16 00						
Cardiff Central ■	d			14 45	14 55	15 12		15 25					15 45	15 55	16 05				16 25						
Newport (South Wales)	d			15 01	15 09	15 28		15 39					16 00	16 09	16 21				16 39						
Weston-super-Mare	d																								
Bristol Temple Meads ■	d						15 30		16 00							16 30		16 41					17 00		
Bristol Parkway ■	a				15 30			15 59						16 30				16 52	16 59						
	d				15 31			16 01						16 31				16 52	17 01						
Bath Spa ■	d						15 43		16 13							16 43							17 13		
Chippenham	d						15 55		16 25							16 55							17 25		
Worcester Shrub Hill	d		15 06														16 03								17 06
Cheltenham Spa	d	15 11	15 34							15 40		16 11								16 31		16 45		17 15	17 33
Gloucester ■	d	15a22	15a42	15a44		16a21				15 54		16a22	16a44		17a14			17a33		16 46		16a56		17a26	17a42
Stonehouse	d									16 06										16 59					
Stroud	d									16 11										17 05					
Kemble	d									16 27										17 19					
Swindon	a				15 57		16 10	16 27	16 40	16 44				16 57		17 10			17 27	17 33			17 40		
	d				15 59		16 11	16 29	16 41					16 59		17 11			17 29	17 35			17 41		
Didcot Parkway	a				16 16		16 28	16 46						17 16		17 28				17 52					
Reading ■	a				16 31		16 43	17 00	17 09					17 31		17 44	17 54		18 00	18 06			18 12		
Slough ■	a																18 10								
London Paddington ■ ⊖	a				17 09		17 14	17 30	17 39					18 02		18 14	18 28		18 30	18 39			18 44		

A 🛒 from Newport (South Wales)
B The St. David
C 🍴 from Reading Ø to Reading
D The Cheltenham Spa Express
E The Merchant Venturer

For connections from Hereford and Birmingham New Street please refer to Tables 131 and 57. For connections to Oxford, Gatwick Airport and Heathrow Airport please refer to Tables 116, 148 and 125A

Table 125

South Wales, Weston-super-Mare, Bristol, Cheltenham Spa and Swindon - London

Mondays to Fridays
from 17 September

Route Diagram - see first Page of Table 125

		XC ◇1	GW ◇1 🛒	AW	GW ◇1 🛒	GW ◇1 A 🛒⊘		GW ◇	AW	GW ◇1 🛒	XC ◇1	XC ◇1 B 🍴	GW ◇1 🛒	GW ◇1 🍴	AW	GW ◇1 🛒		GW	GW ◇1 🛒	GW ◇1 🛒	AW	XC ◇1	GW ◇1 🛒	GW ◇1 🛒	GW
Swansea	d					16 28													17 28						
Neath	d					16 40													17 40						
Port Talbot Parkway	d					16 48													17 48						
Bridgend	d			16 38		17 00									17 38				18 00						
Cardiff Central 7	d	16 45	16 55	17 12		17 25						17 45	17 55		18 12				18 25						
Newport (South Wales)	d	17 00	17 09	17 28		17 39						18 00	18 09		18 27				18 39						
Weston-super-Mare	d				17 10											18 08									
Bristol Temple Meads 10	d				17 30					18 00						18 30		18 41					19 30		
Bristol Parkway 7	a		17 30			17 59							18 30					18 52	18 59						
	d		17 31			18 01							18 31					18 52	19 01						
Bath Spa 7	d				17 43					18 13						18 43							19 43		
Chippenham	d				17 55					18 25						18 55							19 55		
Worcester Shrub Hill	d													17 31										18 55	19 07
Cheltenham Spa	d							17 40	17 45		18 18									18 34	18 45	19 15			19 34
Gloucester 7	d	17a44		18a21				17 54	17a57		18a29	18a44			19a20			19a30		18 51	18a56	19a27			19a42
Stonehouse	d							18 06												19 04					
Stroud	d							18 11												19 09					
Kemble	d							18 25												19 23					
Swindon	a		17 57		18 10	18 27		18 41		18 40			18 57			19 10			19 27	19 38			20 10		
	d		17 59		18 11	18 29				18 41			18 59			19 11			19 29	19 41			20 11		
Didcot Parkway	a		18 16		18 28	18 46										19 28			19 46	19 58			20 28		
Reading 7	a		18 31		18 46	19 01				19 09			19 25	19 32		19 44			20 00	20 14			20 44	20 54	
Slough 3	a													19 47										21 09	
London Paddington 15 ⊖	a		19 02		19 14	19 32				19 38			19 59	20 06		20 14			20 32	20 46			21 14	21 29	

		XC ◇1		AW	GW	GW ◇	GW ◇1 🛒	GW	XC ◇1	XC ◇1	XC ◇1	GW ◇1 🛒		GW 1	GW	GW FX ◇1 🛒	GW FO ◇1 🛒	GW	GW FO ◇1	GW FX ◇1	XC ◇1	XC ◇1		XC ◇1	AW
Swansea	d						18 28									19 29	19 29								
Neath	d						18 40									19 40	19 40								
Port Talbot Parkway	d						18 48									19 48	19 48								
Bridgend	d						19 00									20 00	20 00								20 38
Cardiff Central 7	d	18 45					19 25				19 50					20 25	20 25							21 05	21 12
Newport (South Wales)	d	19 01					19 39				20 05					20 39	20 39							21 21	21 27
Weston-super-Mare	d																								
Bristol Temple Meads 10	d				19 41					20 00		20 30			20 41										
Bristol Parkway 7	a				19 52		19 59			20 08					20 52	21 01	21 01								
	d				19 52		20 01			20 10					20 52	21 01	21 01								
Bath Spa 7	d											20 43													
Chippenham	d					20 02						20 55													
Worcester Shrub Hill	d																		21 03	21 03					
Cheltenham Spa	d			19 45				20 01	20 11					20 48				21 00			21 11	21 52			
Gloucester 7	d	19a45		19a56	20a32			20 13	20a22	20a38	20a53			20a58	21a31			21 21			21a22	22a01		22a02	22a21
Stonehouse	d							20 25										21 33							
Stroud	d							20 30										21 39							
Kemble	d							20 44										21 54							
Swindon	a					20 21	20 27	21 03				21 10				21 29	21 29	22 09							
	d						20 29					21 11				21 33	21 33								
Didcot Parkway	a						20 46					21 28				21 52	21 52								
Reading 7	a						21 00					21 43				22 11	22 11		22 58	22 58					
Slough 3	a																		23 12	23 15					
London Paddington 15 ⊖	a						21 32					22 14				22 44	22 45		23 36	23 36					

		GW ◇1 🛒	GW ◇1 🛒	GW	GW	XC ◇1	GW ◇1 🛒	AW		GW	GW ◇1	LM FO	AW FO	AW FX
Swansea	d	20 28												
Neath	d	20 40												
Port Talbot Parkway	d	20 48												
Bridgend	d	21 00											22 38	22 38
Cardiff Central 7	d	21 25				21 50							23 20	23 19
Newport (South Wales)	d	21 39				22 05							23 40	23 40
Weston-super-Mare	d						22 01							
Bristol Temple Meads 10	d		21 50				22 35							
Bristol Parkway 7	a	21 59												
	d	22 01												
Bath Spa 7	d		22 02				22 47							
Chippenham	d		22 15				23 00							
Worcester Shrub Hill	d				21 32					22 28	22 43	23 46		
Cheltenham Spa	d			22 01	22 07			23 00		23 05		00 09		
Gloucester 7	d			22 14	22a21	22a46		23a12		23a17		00a20	00a39	00a39
Stonehouse	d			22 26										
Stroud	d			22 31										
Kemble	d			22 46										
Swindon	a	22 27	22 33	23 05			23 14							
	d	22 28	22 34				23 16							
Didcot Parkway	a		22 50				23 33				00 20			
Reading 7	a	23 02	23 06				23 53				00 38			
Slough 3	a										00 55			
London Paddington 15 ⊖	a	23 38	23 41				00 33				01 17			

A 🛒 from Reading ⊘ to Reading

B 🍴 from Newport (South Wales)

For connections from Hereford and Birmingham New Street please refer to Tables 131 and 57. For connections to Oxford, Gatwick Airport and Heathrow Airport please refer to Tables 116, 148 and 125A

Table 125

South Wales, Weston-super-Mare, Bristol, Cheltenham Spa and Swindon - London

Saturdays
until 23 June

Route Diagram - see first Page of Table 125

		GW ◇1 🛒	GW ◇1	LM	GW ◇1 🛒	GW	GW ◇1 🛒	XC ◇1	XC ◇1 🍴	GW ◇1 🛒		GW ◇1 🛒	GW ◇1 🛒	XC ◇1	GW	AW	GW ◇1 🛒	GW ◇1 🛒	GW ◇	XC ◇1		GW ◇1 🛒	AW	GW ◇1 🛒	GW ◇1 🛒
Swansea	d						03 58			04 58							05 28					05 58			
Neath	d						04 10			05 10							05 40					06 10			
Port Talbot Parkway	d						04 18			05 18							05 48					06 18			
Bridgend	d						04 30			05 30							06 00					06 30			
Cardiff Central 7	d						04 55			05 55						06 12	06 25			06 40		06 55	07 12		
Newport (South Wales)	d						05 09			06 09						06 28	06 39			06 55		07 09	07 27		
Weston-super-Mare	d	22p01																06 24							
Bristol Temple Meads 10	d	22p35			05 30		06 00		06 15			06 30						07 00						07 30	
Bristol Parkway 7	a								06 23	06 29							06 59					07 29			
	d								06 25	06 31							07 01					07 31			
Bath Spa 7	d	22p47			05 43		06 13					06 43						07 13						07 43	
Chippenham	d	23p00			05 55		06 25					06 55						07 25						07 55	
Worcester Shrub Hill	d		22p43	23p46									06 12						06 47						07 08
Cheltenham Spa	d			00 09		05 30		06 04						06 43	06 48				07 13						
Gloucester 7	d			00a20		05 44		06a13	06a54					06a54	06a58	07a20			07a24	07a44			08a21		
Stonehouse	d					05 56																			
Stroud	d					06 01																			
Kemble	d					06 16																			
Swindon	a	23p14			06 09	06 32	06 39			06 57		07 09					07 27	07 40				07 57		08 09	
	d	23p16			06 11		06 41			06 59		07 11					07 29	07 41				07 59		08 11	
Didcot Parkway	a	23p33	00 20		06 28		06 58			07 16		07 28					07 46	07 59				08 16		08 28	
Reading 7	a	23p53	00 38		06 43		07 14			07 31		07 44	07 54				08 00	08 14				08 31		08 44	08 54
Slough 3	a		00 55										08 09												09 09
London Paddington 15 ⊖	a	00 33	01 17		07 14		07 44			08 07		08 14	08 29				08 32	08 44				09 02		09 14	09 29

		GW ◇1 🛒	GW ◇1 🛒	GW ◇1 🛒	AW	XC ◇1 🍴		XC ◇1 A 🍴	GW ◇1 B 🛒⊘	GW ◇1 🛒	GW ◇1 B 🛒⊘	AW	GW	GW ◇1 B 🛒⊘	GW ◇1 🛒	GW		GW ◇1 🛒	XC ◇1 🍴	XC ◇1 A 🍴	GW ◇1 🛒	GW ◇1 🛒	GW	AW	GW ◇1 🛒
Swansea	d	06 28							06 58					07 28											08 28
Neath	d	06 40							07 10					07 40											08 40
Port Talbot Parkway	d	06 48							07 18					07 48											08 48
Bridgend	d	07 00							07 30					08 00										08 23	09 00
Cardiff Central 7	d	07 25						07 45	07 55					08 25						08 45				09 12	09 25
Newport (South Wales)	d	07 39						08 00	08 09					08 39						09 00				09 26	09 39
Weston-super-Mare	d			07 24											08 30										
Bristol Temple Meads 10	d			08 00						08 30			08 41		09 00						09 30				
Bristol Parkway 7	a	07 59							08 30				08 52	08 59											09 59
	d	08 01							08 31				08 52	09 01											10 01
Bath Spa 7	d			08 13						08 43					09 13						09 43				
Chippenham	d			08 25						08 55					09 25	09 31					09 55				
Worcester Shrub Hill	d										08 04											09 02	09 08		
Cheltenham Spa	d		07 30		07 45	08 11						08 45						09 00	09 11				09 35		
Gloucester 7	d		07 46		07a57	08a22		08a45				08a57	09a33					09 16	09a22	09a44			09a44	10a19	
Stonehouse	d		07 58															09 29							
Stroud	d		08 03															09 34							
Kemble	d		08 17															09 48							
Swindon	a	08 27	08 33	08 39					08 58	09 09				09 27	09 40	09 49		10 02			10 10				10 28
	d	08 29	08 35	08 41					08 59	09 11				09 29	09 41			10 04			10 11				10 29
Didcot Parkway	a	08 46	08 51	08 58					09 16	09 28				09 46				10 21			10 28				10 47
Reading 7	a	09 00	09 07	09 14					09 32	09 45	09 54			10 00	10 11			10 36			10 45	10 54			11 01
Slough 3	a										10 09											11 09			
London Paddington 15 ⊖	a	09 32	09 37	09 44					10 02	10 14	10 29			10 32	10 39			11 08			11 14	11 29			11 33

		GW ◇1 🛒		GW	XC ◇1 🍴	XC ◇1 A 🍴	GW ◇1 🛒	GW ◇1 🍴	AW	AW	GW ◇	GW ◇1 🛒		GW ◇1 🛒	GW ◇1 🛒	XC ◇1 🍴	XC ◇1 A 🍴	GW ■	GW ◇1 🛒	GW ◇1 🍴	GW ◇1 🛒	GW ◇1 🛒		AW	GW
Swansea	d											09 28									10 28				
Neath	d											09 40									10 40				
Port Talbot Parkway	d											09 48									10 48				
Bridgend	d									09 40		10 00									11 00				
Cardiff Central 7	d					09 45				10 12		10 25					10 45				11 25				
Newport (South Wales)	d					10 00				10 27		10 39					11 00				11 39				
Weston-super-Mare	d																					11 30			
Bristol Temple Meads 10	d	10 00					10 30				10 41			11 00					11 30			12 00			
Bristol Parkway 7	a										10 52	10 59									11 59				
	d										10 52	11 01									12 01				
Bath Spa 7	d	10 13					10 43							11 13					11 43			12 13			
Chippenham	d	10 25					10 55							11 25					11 55			12 25			
Worcester Shrub Hill	d							10 08										11 06		11 15					
Cheltenham Spa	d			10 01	10 11				10 45						11 00	11 11		11 34						11 45	12 01
Gloucester 7	d			10 15	10a22	10a44			10a56	11a21	11a32				11 16	11a22	11a44	11a44						11a57	12 15
Stonehouse	d			10 27											11 29										12 27
Stroud	d			10 32											11 34										12 32
Kemble	d			10 47											11 48										12 47
Swindon	a	10 39		11 04			11 09					11 27		11 39	12 02				12 09		12 27	12 40			13 04
	d	10 41					11 11					11 29		11 41	12 04				12 11		12 29	12 41			
Didcot Parkway	a						11 28					11 46			12 21				12 28		12 46				
Reading 7	a	11 12					11 44	11 54				12 00		12 11	12 37				12 45	12 53	13 00	13 10			
Slough 3	a							12 09												13 09					
London Paddington 15 ⊖	a	11 40					12 14	12 29				12 32		12 39	13 07				13 13	13 30	13 33	13 41			

A 🍴 from Newport (South Wales)

B 🛒 from Reading ⊘ to Reading

For connections from Hereford and Birmingham New Street please refer to Tables 131 and 57. For connections to Oxford, Gatwick Airport and Heathrow Airport please refer to Tables 116, 148 and 125A

South Wales, Weston-super-Mare, Bristol, Cheltenham Spa and Swindon - London

Route Diagram - see first Page of Table 125

	XC	XC	AW	GW	GW	GW	GW		GW	GW	XC	GW
	◇1 ⊼	◇1 A ⊼		◇1 ⊏	◇	◇1 ⊏	◇1 ⊏		◇1 ⊏	◇1 ⊏	◇1 ⊼	◇
Swansea d						11 28						
Neath d						11 40						
Port Talbot Parkway d						11 48						
Bridgend d			11 38			12 00						
Cardiff Central d		11 45	12 12			12 25						
Newport (South Wales) d		12 00	12 27			12 39						
Weston-super-Mare d										13 01		
Bristol Temple Meads d				12 30	12 41		13 00			13 30		
Bristol Parkway a					12 52	12 59						
d					12 52	13 01						
Bath Spa d				12 43			13 13			13 43		
Chippenham d				12 55			13 25			13 55		
Worcester Shrub Hill d												12 54
Cheltenham Spa d	12 11								13 00		13 11	13 20
Gloucester d	12a22	12a44	13a21		13a34				13 16		13a22	13a32
Stonehouse d									13 29			
Stroud d									13 34			
Kemble d									13 48			
Swindon a				13 09		13 27	13 39		14 02	14 09		
d				13 11		13 29	13 41		14 04	14 11		
Didcot Parkway a				13 28		13 46			14 21	14 28		
Reading a				13 44		14 00	14 11		14 38	14 44		
Slough a												
London Paddington ⊖ a				14 14		14 32	14 39		15 09	15 14		

	XC	GW	AW	AW	GW		GW	GW	XC	XC	GW	AW
	◇1 A ⊼	◇1 ⊏		⊼	◇1 ⊏		◇1 ⊏		◇1 ⊼	◇1 A ⊼	◇1 ⊏	⊼
Swansea d					12 28							
Neath d					12 40							
Port Talbot Parkway d					12 48							
Bridgend d				12 40	13 00							
Cardiff Central d	12 45			13 12	13 25					13 45		
Newport (South Wales) d	13 00			13 27	13 39					14 00		
Weston-super-Mare d												
Bristol Temple Meads d							14 00				14 30	
Bristol Parkway a					13 59							
d					14 01							
Bath Spa d							14 13				14 43	
Chippenham d							14 25				14 55	
Worcester Shrub Hill d		13 04										
Cheltenham Spa d			13 45					14 01	14 11			14 45
Gloucester d	13a44		13a57	14a21				14 15	14a22	14a44		14a56
Stonehouse d								14 27				
Stroud d								14 32				
Kemble d								14 47				
Swindon a					14 27		14 39	15 04			15 09	
d					14 29		14 41				15 11	
Didcot Parkway a					14 46						15 28	
Reading a		14 53			15 00		15 10				15 44	
Slough a		15 10										
London Paddington ⊖ a		15 29			15 32		15 39				16 14	

	GW	GW	GW		GW	GW	GW	GW	XC	GW	XC	AW
	◇	◇1 ⊏	◇1 ⊏			◇1 ⊏	◇1 ⊏	◇1 ⊼	◇1 ⊼	◇	◇1 A ⊼	
Swansea d		13 28										
Neath d		13 40										
Port Talbot Parkway d		13 48										
Bridgend d		14 00										14 38
Cardiff Central d		14 25									14 45	15 12
Newport (South Wales) d		14 39									15 00	15 27
Weston-super-Mare d							15 01					
Bristol Temple Meads d	14 41		15 00				15 30					
Bristol Parkway a	14 52	14 59										
d	14 52	15 01										
Bath Spa d			15 13				15 43					
Chippenham d			15 25		15 30		15 55					
Worcester Shrub Hill d								15 01		15 06		
Cheltenham Spa d						15 00			15 11	15 34		
Gloucester d	15a32					15 16			15a22	15a42	15a44	16a19
Stonehouse d						15 29						
Stroud d						15 34						
Kemble d						15 48						
Swindon a		15 27	15 39		15 50	16 02	16 09					
d		15 29	15 41			16 04	16 11					
Didcot Parkway a		15 46				16 21	16 28					
Reading a		16 01	16 11			16 38	16 44	16 55				
Slough a								17 10				
London Paddington ⊖ a		16 37	16 39			17 07	17 14	17 29				

	GW		GW	GW	XC	XC	GW	GW	AW	AW	GW	
	◇1 ⊏		◇1 ⊏		◇1 ⊼	◇1	◇1 ⊏	◇1 ⊏				
Swansea d	14 28											
Neath d	14 40											
Port Talbot Parkway d	14 48											
Bridgend d	15 00									15 40		
Cardiff Central d	15 25					15 45				16 12		
Newport (South Wales) d	15 39					16 00				16 26		
Weston-super-Mare d												
Bristol Temple Meads d			16 00				16 30				16 41	
Bristol Parkway a	15 59										16 52	
d	16 01										16 52	
Bath Spa d			16 13				16 43					
Chippenham d			16 25				16 55					
Worcester Shrub Hill d								16 04				
Cheltenham Spa d				16 01	16 11				16 45			
Gloucester d				16 15	16a22	16a44			16a56	17a19	17a33	
Stonehouse d				16 27								
Stroud d				16 32								
Kemble d				16 47								
Swindon a	16 27		16 39	17 04			17 09					
d	16 29		16 41				17 11					
Didcot Parkway a	16 46						17 28					
Reading a	17 00		17 10				17 44	17 55				
Slough a								18 10				
London Paddington ⊖ a	17 32		17 38				18 14	18 29				

	GW	GW	GW	GW	GW	XC	XC	GW	AW		AW	GW
	◇1 ⊏	◇1 ⊏	◇1 ⊏	◇1 ⊏	◇1 ⊼	◇1 ⊼	◇1					◇1 ⊏
Swansea d	15 28											16 28
Neath d	15 40											16 40
Port Talbot Parkway d	15 48											16 48
Bridgend d	16 00										16 38	17 00
Cardiff Central d	16 25						16 45				17 12	17 25
Newport (South Wales) d	16 39						17 00				17 27	17 39
Weston-super-Mare d				17 01								
Bristol Temple Meads d		17 00		17 30								
Bristol Parkway a	16 59											17 59
d	17 01											18 01
Bath Spa d		17 13		17 43								
Chippenham d		17 25		17 55								
Worcester Shrub Hill d					17 02			17 08				
Cheltenham Spa d			17 00			17 11		17 34	17 45			
Gloucester d			17 16			17a22	17a44	17a44	17a56		18a20	
Stonehouse d			17 29									
Stroud d			17 34									
Kemble d			17 48									
Swindon a	17 27	17 39	18 02	18 09								18 27
d	17 29	17 41	18 04	18 11								18 29
Didcot Parkway a	17 46		18 21	18 28								18 46
Reading a	18 00	18 11	18 38	18 44	18 55							19 00
Slough a					19 10							
London Paddington ⊖ a	18 32	18 39	19 08	19 14	19 29							19 32

	GW	GW	GW	GW	XC	XC	AW		AW	GW	GW	GW
	◇1 ⊏		◇1 ⊏	◇1 ⊼	◇1	◇1 A ⊼				◇	◇1 ⊏	◇1 ⊏
Swansea d											17 28	
Neath d											17 40	
Port Talbot Parkway d											17 48	
Bridgend d									17 38		18 00	
Cardiff Central d						17 45			18 12		18 25	
Newport (South Wales) d						18 00			18 27		18 39	
Weston-super-Mare d			18 01									
Bristol Temple Meads d	18 00		18 30							18 41		
Bristol Parkway a										18 52	18 59	
d										18 52	19 01	
Bath Spa d	18 13		18 43									
Chippenham d	18 25		18 55									
Worcester Shrub Hill d				18 06								
Cheltenham Spa d		18 01			18 18		18 45					19 00
Gloucester d		18 15			18a29	18a44	18a56		19a20	19a33		19 16
Stonehouse d		18 27										19 29
Stroud d		18 32										19 34
Kemble d		18 47										19 48
Swindon a	18 39	19 04	19 09								19 27	20 03
d	18 41		19 11								19 29	20 05
Didcot Parkway a			19 28								19 46	20 22
Reading a	19 10		19 44	19 55							20 00	20 38
Slough a				20 10								
London Paddington ⊖ a	19 39		20 14	20 29							20 32	21 07

A ⊼ from Newport (South Wales)

For connections from Hereford and Birmingham New Street please refer to Tables 131 and 57. For connections to Oxford, Gatwick Airport and Heathrow Airport please refer to Tables 116, 148 and 125A

South Wales, Weston-super-Mare, Bristol, Cheltenham Spa and Swindon - London

Route Diagram - see first Page of Table 125

	XC	GW	GW	GW	XC		AW	GW	GW	GW	GW	GW
	◇1	◇1 ⊏	◇1		◇1				◇1 ⊏		◇1 ⊏	◇1
Swansea d									18 28			
Neath d									18 40			
Port Talbot Parkway d									18 48			
Bridgend d									19 00			
Cardiff Central d					18 45				19 25			
Newport (South Wales) d					19 00				19 39			
Weston-super-Mare d											20 10	
Bristol Temple Meads d		19 30						19 41			20 33	
Bristol Parkway a								19 52	19 59			
d								19 52	20 01			
Bath Spa d		19 43									20 46	
Chippenham d		19 55									20 58	
Worcester Shrub Hill d			19 02	19 07								20 06
Cheltenham Spa d	19 11			19 34			19 45			20 01		
Gloucester d	19a22			19a42	19a44		19a56	20a33		20 15		
Stonehouse d										20 27		
Stroud d										20 32		
Kemble d										20 47		
Swindon a		20 09							20 27	21 03	21 13	
d		20 11							20 29		21 14	
Didcot Parkway a		20 28							20 46		21 31	21 43
Reading a		20 44	20 54						21 06		21 48	21 59
Slough a			21 09									22 11
London Paddington ⊖ a		21 14	21 29						21 36		22 16	22 34

	XC	XC	GW		XC	GW	GW	GW	GW	GW	XC	GW
	◇1	◇1			◇1		◇1 A ⊏	◇1 B ⊏	◇1		◇1	◇1 ⊏
Swansea d							19 28	19 28				
Neath d							19 40	19 40				
Port Talbot Parkway d							19 48	19 48				
Bridgend d							20 00	20 00				
Cardiff Central d		20 00					20 25	20 25			20 50	
Newport (South Wales) d		20 15					20 39	20 39			21 05	
Weston-super-Mare d												
Bristol Temple Meads d						20 43						21 47
Bristol Parkway a						20 52	21 01	21 01				
d						20 52	21 01	21 01				
Bath Spa d												22 02
Chippenham d												22 15
Worcester Shrub Hill d									21 15			
Cheltenham Spa d	20 11		21 02		21 11					21 19		
Gloucester d	20a22	21a04	21a12		21a22	21a34				21 35	21a48	
Stonehouse d										21 47		
Stroud d										21 52		
Kemble d										22 07		
Swindon a							21 29	21 29		22 24		22 29
d							21 29	21 29				22 31
Didcot Parkway a							21 47	21 47	22 47			22 48
Reading a							21 59	21 59	23 08			23 04
Slough a									23 26			
London Paddington ⊖ a							22 30	22 37	23 46			23 36

	XC		GW	GW
	◇1			◇1 ⊏
Swansea d				
Neath d				
Port Talbot Parkway d				
Bridgend d				
Cardiff Central d				
Newport (South Wales) d				
Weston-super-Mare d				21 53
Bristol Temple Meads d				22 30
Bristol Parkway a				
d				
Bath Spa d				22 43
Chippenham d				22 55
Worcester Shrub Hill d			21 31	
Cheltenham Spa d	21 50		22 01	
Gloucester d	21a59		22a10	
Stonehouse d				
Stroud d				
Kemble d				
Swindon a				23 10
d				23 11
Didcot Parkway a				23 28
Reading a				23 49
Slough a				
London Paddington ⊖ a				00 33

Saturdays
30 June to 8 September

	GW	GW	LM	GW	GW	GW	XC	XC	GW		GW	GW
	◇1 ⊏	◇1		◇1 ⊏		◇1 ⊏	◇1	◇1 ⊼	◇1 ⊏		◇1 ⊏	◇1 ⊏
Swansea d						03 58			04 58			
Neath d						04 10			05 10			
Port Talbot Parkway d						04 18			05 18			
Bridgend d						04 30			05 30			
Cardiff Central d						04 55			05 55			
Newport (South Wales) d						05 09			06 09			
Weston-super-Mare d	22p01											
Bristol Temple Meads d	22p35			05 30		06 00		06 15			06 30	
Bristol Parkway a								06 23	06 29			
d								06 25	06 31			
Bath Spa d	22p47			05 43		06 13					06 43	
Chippenham d	23p00			05 55		06 25					06 55	
Worcester Shrub Hill d		22p43	23p46									06 12
Cheltenham Spa d			00 09		05 30		06 04					
Gloucester d			00a20		05 44		06a13	06a54				
Stonehouse d					05 56							
Stroud d					06 01							
Kemble d					06 16							
Swindon a	23p14			06 09	06 32	06 39			06 57		07 09	
d	23p16			06 11		06 41			06 59		07 11	
Didcot Parkway a	23p33	00 20		06 28		06 58			07 16		07 28	
Reading a	23p53	00 38		06 43		07 14			07 31		07 44	07 54
Slough a		00 55										08 09
London Paddington ⊖ a	00 33	01 17		07 14		07 44			08 07		08 14	08 29

	XC	GW	AW	GW	GW	GW	XC		GW	AW	GW	GW
	◇1			◇1 ⊏	◇1 ⊏	◇	◇1		◇1 ⊏		◇1 ⊏	◇1 ⊏
Swansea d				05 28					05 58			
Neath d				05 40					06 10			
Port Talbot Parkway d				05 48					06 18			
Bridgend d				06 00					06 30			
Cardiff Central d			06 12	06 25			06 40		06 55	07 12		
Newport (South Wales) d			06 28	06 39			06 55		07 09	07 27		
Weston-super-Mare d					06 24							
Bristol Temple Meads d					07 00						07 30	
Bristol Parkway a				06 59					07 29			
d				07 01					07 31			
Bath Spa d					07 13						07 43	
Chippenham d					07 25						07 55	
Worcester Shrub Hill d						06 47						07 08
Cheltenham Spa d	06 43	06 48				07 13						
Gloucester d	06a54	06a58	07a20			07a24	07a44			08a21		
Stonehouse d												
Stroud d												
Kemble d												
Swindon a				07 27	07 40				07 57		08 09	
d				07 29	07 41				07 59		08 11	
Didcot Parkway a				07 46	07 59				08 16		08 28	
Reading a				08 00	08 14				08 31		08 44	08 54
Slough a												09 09
London Paddington ⊖ a				08 32	08 44				09 02		09 14	09 29

A not 19 May

B 19 May

For connections from Hereford and Birmingham New Street please refer to Tables 131 and 57. For connections to Oxford, Gatwick Airport and Heathrow Airport please refer to Tables 116, 148 and 125A

South Wales, Weston-super-Mare, Bristol, Cheltenham Spa and Swindon - London

Route Diagram - see first Page of Table 125

		GW	GW	GW	AW	XC	XC	GW	GW	GW	AW	GW	GW	GW	GW	GW	XC	XC	GW	GW	GW	AW	GW
		◇1	◇1	◇1		◇1	◇1	◇1	◇1	◇1			◇1	◇1		◇1	◇1	◇1	◇1	◇1			◇1
		☕	☕	☕		🛒	A 🛒	B ☕⊘	☕	B ☕⊘			B ☕⊘	☕		☕	🛒	A 🛒	☕	☕			☕
Swansea	d	06 28						06 58					07 28										08 28
Neath	d	06 40						07 10					07 40										08 40
Port Talbot Parkway	d	06 48						07 18					07 48										08 48
Bridgend	d	07 00						07 30					08 00									08 23	09 00
Cardiff Central 7	d	07 25					07 45	07 55					08 25					08 45				09 12	09 25
Newport (South Wales)	d	07 39					08 00	08 09					08 39					09 00				09 26	09 39
Weston-super-Mare	d			07 24										08 30									
Bristol Temple Meads 10	d			08 00					08 30			08 41		09 00					09 30				
Bristol Parkway 7	a	07 59						08 30				08 52	08 59										09 59
	d	08 01						08 31				08 52	09 01										10 01
Bath Spa 7	d			08 13					08 43					09 13					09 43				
Chippenham	d			08 25					08 55					09 25	09 31				09 55				
Worcester Shrub Hill	d									08 04										09 02	09 08		
Cheltenham Spa	d		07 30		07 45	08 11					08 45					09 00	09 11				09 35		
Gloucester 7	d		07 46		07a57	08a22	08a45				08a57	09a33				09 16	09a22	09a44			09a44	10a19	
Stonehouse	d		07 58													09 29							
Stroud	d		08 03													09 34							
Kemble	d		08 17													09 48							
Swindon	a	08 27	08 33	08 39				08 58	09 09				09 27	09 40	09 49	10 02			10 10				10 28
	d	08 29	08 35	08 41				08 59	09 11				09 29	09 41		10 04			10 11				10 29
Didcot Parkway	a	08 46	08 51	08 58				09 16	09 28				09 46			10 21			10 28				10 47
Reading 7	a	09 00	09 07	09 14				09 32	09 45	09 54			10 00	10 11		10 36			10 45	10 54			11 01
Slough 3	a									10 09										11 09			
London Paddington 15 ⊖	a	09 32	09 37	09 44				10 02	10 14	10 29			10 32	10 39		11 08			11 14	11 29			11 33

		GW	GW	XC	XC	GW	GW	AW	AW	GW	GW	GW	GW	XC	XC	GW	GW	GW	GW	GW	AW	GW
		◇1		◇1	◇1	◇1	◇1			◇	◇1	◇1	◇1	◇1	◇1	■	◇1	◇1	◇1	◇1		
		☕		🛒	A 🛒	☕	🛒				☕	☕	☕	🛒	A 🛒		☕	🛒	☕	☕		
Swansea	d										09 28								10 28			
Neath	d										09 40								10 40			
Port Talbot Parkway	d										09 48								10 48			
Bridgend	d								09 40		10 00								11 00			
Cardiff Central 7	d				09 45				10 12		10 25				10 45				11 25			
Newport (South Wales)	d				10 00				10 27		10 39				11 00				11 39			
Weston-super-Mare	d																			11 30		
Bristol Temple Meads 10	d	10 00				10 30				10 41		11 00					11 30			12 00		
Bristol Parkway 7	a									10 52	10 59								11 59			
	d									10 52	11 01								12 01			
Bath Spa 7	d	10 13				10 43						11 13					11 43			12 13		
Chippenham	d	10 25				10 55						11 25					11 55			12 25		
Worcester Shrub Hill	d						10 08									11 06		11 15				
Cheltenham Spa	d		10 01	10 11				10 45					11 00	11 11		11 34					11 45	12 01
Gloucester 7	d		10 15	10a22	10a44			10a56	11a21	11a32			11 16	11a22	11a44	11a44					11a57	12 15
Stonehouse	d		10 27										11 29									12 27
Stroud	d		10 32										11 34									12 32
Kemble	d		10 47										11 48									12 47
Swindon	a	10 39	11 04			11 09					11 27	11 39	12 02				12 09		12 27	12 40		13 04
	d	10 41				11 11					11 29	11 41	12 04				12 11		12 29	12 41		
Didcot Parkway	a					11 28					11 46		12 21				12 28		12 46			
Reading 7	a	11 12				11 44	11 54				12 00	12 11	12 37				12 45	12 53	13 00	13 10		
Slough 3	a						12 09											13 09				
London Paddington 15 ⊖	a	11 40				12 14	12 29				12 32	12 39	13 07				13 13	13 30	13 33	13 41		

		XC	XC	AW	GW	GW	GW	GW	GW	GW	XC	GW	XC	GW	AW	AW	GW	GW	GW	XC	XC	GW	AW
		◇1	◇1		◇1	◇	◇1	◇1	◇1	◇1	◇1	◇	◇1	◇1			◇1	◇1		◇1	◇1	◇1	
		🛒	A 🛒		☕		☕	☕	☕	☕	🛒		A 🛒	☕		🛒	☕	☕		🛒	A 🛒	☕	🛒
Swansea	d						11 28										12 28						
Neath	d						11 40										12 40						
Port Talbot Parkway	d						11 48										12 48						
Bridgend	d			11 38			12 00									12 40	13 00						
Cardiff Central 7	d		11 45	12 12			12 25						12 45			13 12	13 25				13 45		
Newport (South Wales)	d		12 00	12 27			12 39						13 00			13 27	13 39				14 00		
Weston-super-Mare	d									13 01													
Bristol Temple Meads 10	d				12 30	12 41		13 00		13 30								14 00				14 30	
Bristol Parkway 7	a					12 52	12 59										13 59						
	d					12 52	13 01										14 01						
Bath Spa 7	d				12 43			13 13		13 43								14 13				14 43	
Chippenham	d				12 55			13 25		13 55								14 25				14 55	
Worcester Shrub Hill	d											12 54		13 04									
Cheltenham Spa	d	12 11							13 00		13 11	13 20			13 45				14 01	14 11			14 45
Gloucester 7	d	12a22	12a44	13a21		13a34			13 16		13a22	13a32	13a44		13a57	14a21			14 15	14a22	14a44		14a56
Stonehouse	d								13 29										14 27				
Stroud	d								13 34										14 32				
Kemble	d								13 48										14 47				
Swindon	a				13 09		13 27	13 39	14 02	14 09							14 27	14 39	15 04			15 09	
	d				13 11		13 29	13 41	14 04	14 11							14 29	14 41				15 11	
Didcot Parkway	a				13 28		13 46		14 21	14 28							14 46					15 28	
Reading 7	a				13 44		14 00	14 11	14 38	14 44				14 53			15 00	15 10				15 44	
Slough 3	a													15 10									
London Paddington 15 ⊖	a				14 14		14 32	14 39	15 09	15 14				15 29			15 32	15 39				16 14	

A 🛒 from Newport (South Wales)

B ☕ from Reading ⊘ to Reading

For connections from Hereford and Birmingham New Street please refer to Tables 131 and 57. For connections to Oxford, Gatwick Airport and Heathrow Airport please refer to Tables 116, 148 and 125A

Table 125

Saturdays
30 June to 8 September

South Wales, Weston-super-Mare, Bristol, Cheltenham Spa and Swindon - London

Route Diagram - see first Page of Table 125

		GW	GW	GW	GW	GW	GW	GW	XC	GW	XC	AW	GW	GW	GW	XC	XC	GW	GW	AW	AW	GW
		◇	◇1	◇1		◇1	◇1	◇1	◇1	◇	◇1		◇1	◇1		◇1	◇1	◇1	◇1			
			☕	☕		☕	☕	🛒	🛒		A 🛒		☕	☕		🛒		☕	☕			
Swansea	d		13 28										14 28									
Neath	d		13 40										14 40									
Port Talbot Parkway	d		13 48										14 48									
Bridgend	d		14 00									14 38	15 00								15 40	
Cardiff Central 7	d		14 25								14 45	15 12	15 25				15 45				16 12	
Newport (South Wales)	d		14 39								15 00	15 27	15 39				16 00				16 26	
Weston-super-Mare	d						15 01															
Bristol Temple Meads 10	d	14 41		15 00			15 30							16 00				16 30				16 41
Bristol Parkway 7	a	14 52	14 59										15 59									16 52
	d	14 52	15 01										16 01									16 52
Bath Spa 7	d			15 13			15 43							16 13				16 43				
Chippenham	d			15 25	15 30		15 55							16 25				16 55				
Worcester Shrub Hill	d							15 01		15 06									16 04			
Cheltenham Spa	d					15 00			15 11	15 34					16 01	16 11				16 45		
Gloucester 7	d	15a32				15 16			15a22	15a42	15a44	16a19			16 15	16a22	16a44			16a56	17a19	17a33
Stonehouse	d					15 29									16 27							
Stroud	d					15 34									16 32							
Kemble	d					15 48									16 47							
Swindon	a		15 27	15 39	15 50	16 02	16 09						16 27	16 39	17 04			17 09				
	d		15 29	15 41		16 04	16 11						16 29	16 41				17 11				
Didcot Parkway	a		15 46			16 21	16 28						16 46					17 28				
Reading 7	a		16 01	16 11		16 38	16 44	16 55					17 00	17 10				17 44	17 55			
Slough 3	a							17 10											18 10			
London Paddington 15 ⊖	a		16 37	16 39		17 07	17 14	17 29					17 32	17 38				18 14	18 29			

		GW	GW	GW	GW	GW	XC	XC	GW	AW	AW	GW	GW	GW	GW	GW	XC	XC	AW	AW	GW	GW	GW
		◇1	◇1	◇1	◇1	◇1	◇1	◇1				◇1	◇1		◇1	◇1	◇1	◇1			◇	◇1	◇1
		☕	☕	☕	☕	🛒	🛒					☕	☕		☕	🛒		A 🛒				☕	☕
Swansea	d	15 28										16 28										17 28	
Neath	d	15 40										16 40										17 40	
Port Talbot Parkway	d	15 48										16 48										17 48	
Bridgend	d	16 00									16 38	17 00								17 38		18 00	
Cardiff Central 7	d	16 25						16 45			17 12	17 25						17 45		18 12		18 25	
Newport (South Wales)	d	16 39						17 00			17 27	17 39						18 00		18 27		18 39	
Weston-super-Mare	d				17 01										18 01								
Bristol Temple Meads 10	d		17 00		17 30								18 00		18 30						18 41		
Bristol Parkway 7	a	16 59										17 59									18 52	18 59	
	d	17 01										18 01									18 52	19 01	
Bath Spa 7	d		17 13		17 43								18 13		18 43								
Chippenham	d		17 25		17 55								18 25		18 55								
Worcester Shrub Hill	d					17 02			17 08							18 06							
Cheltenham Spa	d			17 00			17 11		17 34	17 45				18 01			18 18		18 45				19 00
Gloucester 7	d			17 16			17a22	17a44	17a44	17a56	18a20			18 15			18a29	18a44	18a56	19a20	19a33		19 16
Stonehouse	d			17 29										18 27									19 29
Stroud	d			17 34										18 32									19 34
Kemble	d			17 48										18 47									19 48
Swindon	a	17 27	17 39	18 02	18 09							18 27	18 39	19 04	19 09							19 27	20 03
	d	17 29	17 41	18 04	18 11							18 29	18 41		19 11							19 29	20 05
Didcot Parkway	a	17 46		18 21	18 28							18 46			19 28							19 46	20 22
Reading 7	a	18 00	18 11	18 38	18 44	18 55						19 00	19 10		19 44	19 55						20 00	20 38
Slough 3	a					19 10										20 10							
London Paddington 15 ⊖	a	18 32	18 39	19 08	19 14	19 29						19 32	19 39		20 14	20 29						20 32	21 07

		XC	GW	GW	GW	XC	AW	GW	GW	GW	GW	GW	XC	XC	GW	XC	GW	GW	GW	GW	XC	GW	XC
		◇1	◇1	◇1		◇1			◇1		◇1	◇1	◇1	◇1		◇1		◇1	◇1		◇1	◇1	◇1
			☕						☕		☕							☕				☕	
Swansea	d								18 28									19 28					
Neath	d								18 40									19 40					
Port Talbot Parkway	d								18 48									19 48					
Bridgend	d								19 00									20 00					
Cardiff Central 7	d					18 45			19 25					20 00				20 25			20 50		
Newport (South Wales)	d					19 00			19 39					20 15				20 39			21 05		
Weston-super-Mare	d										20 10												
Bristol Temple Meads 10	d		19 30					19 41			20 33						20 43					21 47	
Bristol Parkway 7	a							19 52	19 59								20 52	21 01					
	d							19 52	20 01								20 52	21 01					
Bath Spa 7	d		19 43								20 46											22 02	
Chippenham	d		19 55								20 58											22 15	
Worcester Shrub Hill	d			19 02	19 07							20 06							21 15				
Cheltenham Spa	d	19 11			19 34		19 45			20 01			20 11		21 02	21 11				21 19			21 50
Gloucester 7	d	19a22			19a42	19a44	19a56	20a33		20 15			20a22	21a04	21a12	21a22	21a34			21 35	21a48		21a59
Stonehouse	d									20 27										21 47			
Stroud	d									20 32										21 52			
Kemble	d									20 47										22 07			
Swindon	a		20 09						20 27	21 03	21 13							21 29		22 24		22 29	
	d		20 11						20 29		21 14							21 29				22 31	
Didcot Parkway	a		20 28						20 46		21 31	21 43						21 47	22 47			22 48	
Reading 7	a		20 44	20 54					21 06		21 48	21 59						21 59	23 04			23 04	
Slough 3	a			21 09								22 11							23 23				
London Paddington 15 ⊖	a		21 14	21 29					21 36		22 16	22 34						22 30	23 43			23 36	

A 🛒 from Newport (South Wales)

For connections from Hereford and Birmingham New Street please refer to Tables 131 and 57. For connections to Oxford, Gatwick Airport and Heathrow Airport please refer to Tables 116, 148 and 125A

Table 125

Saturdays
30 June to 8 September

South Wales, Weston-super-Mare, Bristol, Cheltenham Spa and Swindon - London

Route Diagram - see first Page of Table 125

		GW	GW
			◇■
Swansea	d		
Neath	d		
Port Talbot Parkway	d		
Bridgend	d		
Cardiff Central	d		
Newport (South Wales)	d		
Weston-super-Mare	d		21 53
Bristol Temple Meads	d		22 30
Bristol Parkway	a		
	d		
Bath Spa	d		22 43
Chippenham	d		22 55
Worcester Shrub Hill	d	21 31	
Cheltenham Spa	d	22 01	
Gloucester	d	22a10	
Stonehouse	d		
Stroud	d		
Kemble	d		
Swindon	a		23 10
	d		23 11
Didcot Parkway	a		23 28
Reading	a		23 51
Slough	a		
London Paddington	a		00 34

Saturdays
from 15 September

		GW	GW	LM	GW	GW	GW	XC	XC	GW	GW	GW	XC	GW	AW	GW	GW	GW	XC	GW	AW	GW	GW
		◇■	◇■		◇■		◇■	◇■	◇■	◇■	◇■	◇■	◇■			◇■	◇■	◇	◇■	◇■		◇■	◇■
Swansea	d						03 58			04 58						05 28				05 58			
Neath	d						04 10			05 10						05 40				06 10			
Port Talbot Parkway	d						04 18			05 18						05 48				06 18			
Bridgend	d						04 30			05 30						06 00				06 30			
Cardiff Central	d						04 55			05 55					06 12	06 25			06 40	06 55	07 12		
Newport (South Wales)	d						05 09			06 09					06 28	06 39			06 55	07 09	07 27		
Weston-super-Mare	d	22p01															06 24						
Bristol Temple Meads	d	22p35			05 30		06 00		06 15		06 30						07 00					07 30	
Bristol Parkway	a								06 23	06 29						06 59				07 29			
	d								06 25	06 31						07 01				07 31			
Bath Spa	d	22p47			05 43		06 13				06 43						07 13					07 43	
Chippenham	d	23p00			05 55		06 25				06 55						07 25					07 55	
Worcester Shrub Hill	d		22p43	23p46								06 12						06 47					07 08
Cheltenham Spa	d			00 09		05 30		06 04					06 43	06 48				07 13					
Gloucester	d			00a20		05 44		06a13	06a54				06a54	06a58	07a20			07a24	07a44		08a21		
Stonehouse	d					05 56																	
Stroud	d					06 01																	
Kemble	d					06 16																	
Swindon	a	23p14			06 09	06 32	06 39			06 57	07 09					07 27	07 40			07 57		08 09	
	d	23p16			06 11		06 41			06 59	07 11					07 29	07 41			07 59		08 11	
Didcot Parkway	a	23p33	00 20		06 28		06 58			07 16	07 28					07 46	07 59			08 16		08 28	
Reading	a	23p53	00 38		06 43		07 14			07 31	07 44	07 54				08 00	08 14			08 31		08 44	08 54
Slough	a		00 55									08 09											09 09
London Paddington	a	00 33	01 17		07 14		07 44			08 07	08 14	08 29				08 32	08 44			09 02		09 14	09 29

		GW	GW	GW	AW	XC	XC	GW	GW	GW	AW	GW	GW	GW	XC	AW	GW	GW	GW	XC	GW	GW	GW
		◇■	◇■	◇■		◇■	◇■ A	◇■ B	◇■	◇■ B			◇■ B	◇■	◇■ A			◇■	◇■	◇■	◇■	◇■	◇■
Swansea	d	06 28						06 58					07 28					07 58					08 28
Neath	d	06 40						07 10					07 40					08 10					08 40
Port Talbot Parkway	d	06 48						07 18					07 48					08 18					08 48
Bridgend	d	07 00						07 30					08 00			08 23		08 30					09 00
Cardiff Central	d	07 25					07 45	07 55					08 25		08 45	09 12		08 55					09 25
Newport (South Wales)	d	07 39					08 00	08 09					08 39		09 00	09 26		09 09					09 39
Weston-super-Mare	d			07 24										08 30									
Bristol Temple Meads	d			08 00					08 30			08 41		09 00							09 30		
Bristol Parkway	a	07 59						08 30				08 52	08 59					09 30					09 59
	d	08 01						08 31				08 52	09 01					09 31					10 01
Bath Spa	d			08 13					08 43					09 13							09 43		
Chippenham	d			08 25					08 55					09 25			09 31				09 55		
Worcester Shrub Hill	d									08 04												09 02	
Cheltenham Spa	d		07 30		07 45	08 11					08 45								09 00	09 11			
Gloucester	d		07 46		07a57	08a22	08a45				08a57	09a33			09a44	10a19			09 16	09a22			
Stonehouse	d		07 58																09 29				
Stroud	d		08 03																09 34				
Kemble	d		08 17																09 48				
Swindon	a	08 27	08 33	08 39				08 58	09 09				09 27	09 40			09 49	09 57	10 02		10 10		10 28
	d	08 29	08 35	08 41				08 59	09 11				09 29	09 41				09 59	10 04		10 11		10 29
Didcot Parkway	a	08 46	08 51	08 58				09 16	09 28				09 46					10 16	10 21		10 28		10 47
Reading	a	09 00	09 07	09 14				09 32	09 45	09 54			10 00	10 11				10 32	10 36		10 45	10 54	11 01
Slough	a									10 09												11 09	
London Paddington	a	09 32	09 37	09 44				10 02	10 14	10 29			10 32	10 39				11 02	11 08		11 14	11 29	11 33

A from Newport (South Wales)

B from Reading, to Reading

For connections from Hereford and Birmingham New Street please refer to Tables 131 and 57. For connections to Oxford, Gatwick Airport and Heathrow Airport please refer to Tables 116, 148 and 125A

Table 125

Saturdays
from 15 September

South Wales, Weston-super-Mare, Bristol, Cheltenham Spa and Swindon - London

Route Diagram - see first Page of Table 125

		GW	GW	GW	XC	XC	GW	GW	AW	AW	GW	GW	GW	GW	XC	XC	GW	GW	GW	GW	AW	GW
			◇■		◇■	◇■ A	◇■	◇■			◇	◇■	◇■	◇■	◇■	◇■ A	■	◇■	◇■	◇■		◇■
Swansea	d											09 28								10 28		
Neath	d											09 40								10 40		
Port Talbot Parkway	d											09 48								10 48		
Bridgend	d									09 40		10 00								11 00		
Cardiff Central	d					09 45				10 12		10 25				10 45				11 25		
Newport (South Wales)	d					10 00				10 27		10 39				11 00				11 39		
Weston-super-Mare	d																					
Bristol Temple Meads	d		10 00				10 30				10 41		11 00					11 30				12 00
Bristol Parkway	a										10 52	10 59								11 59		
	d										10 52	11 01								12 01		
Bath Spa	d		10 13				10 43						11 13					11 43				12 13
Chippenham	d		10 25				10 55						11 25					11 55				12 25
Worcester Shrub Hill	d	09 08						10 08									11 06		11 15			
Cheltenham Spa	d	09 35		10 01	10 11				10 45					11 00	11 11		11 34				11 45	
Gloucester	d	09a44		10 15	10a22	10a44			10a56	11a21	11a32			11 16	11a22	11a44	11a44				11a57	
Stonehouse	d			10 27										11 29								
Stroud	d			10 32										11 34								
Kemble	d			10 47										11 48								
Swindon	a		10 39	11 04			11 09					11 27	11 39	12 02				12 09		12 27		12 40
	d		10 41				11 11					11 29	11 41	12 04				12 11		12 29		12 41
Didcot Parkway	a						11 28					11 46		12 21				12 28		12 46		
Reading	a		11 12				11 44	11 54				12 00	12 11	12 37				12 44	12 53	13 00		13 10
Slough	a							12 09											13 09			
London Paddington	a		11 40				12 14	12 29				12 32	12 39	13 07				13 12	13 30	13 33		13 41

		GW	XC	XC	AW	GW	GW	GW	GW	GW	XC	GW	XC	GW	GW	AW	AW	GW	GW	GW	XC	XC	GW
			◇■	◇■ A		◇■	◇	◇■	◇■	◇■	◇■	◇	◇■ A	◇■	◇■			◇■	◇■		◇■	◇■ A	◇■
Swansea	d							11 28										12 28					
Neath	d							11 40										12 40					
Port Talbot Parkway	d							11 48										12 48					
Bridgend	d				11 38			12 00									12 40	13 00					
Cardiff Central	d			11 45	12 12			12 25					12 45				13 12	13 25				13 45	
Newport (South Wales)	d			12 00	12 27			12 39					13 00				13 27	13 39				14 00	
Weston-super-Mare	d																						
Bristol Temple Meads	d					12 30	12 41		13 00					13 30					14 00				14 30
Bristol Parkway	a						12 52	12 59										13 59					
	d						12 52	13 01										14 01					
Bath Spa	d					12 43			13 13					13 43					14 13				14 43
Chippenham	d					12 55			13 25					13 55					14 25				14 55
Worcester Shrub Hill	d											12 54			13 04								
Cheltenham Spa	d	12 01	12 11							13 00	13 11	13 20				13 45				14 01	14 11		
Gloucester	d	12 15	12a22	12a44	13a21		13a34			13 16	13a22	13a32	13a44			13a57	14a21			14 15	14a22	14a44	
Stonehouse	d	12 27								13 29										14 27			
Stroud	d	12 32								13 34										14 32			
Kemble	d	12 47								13 48										14 47			
Swindon	a	13 04				13 09		13 27	13 39	14 02				14 09				14 27	14 39	15 04			15 09
	d					13 11		13 29	13 41	14 04				14 11				14 29	14 41				15 11
Didcot Parkway	a					13 28		13 46		14 21				14 28				14 46					15 28
Reading	a					13 44		14 00	14 11	14 38				14 44	14 53			15 00	15 10				15 44
Slough	a														15 10								
London Paddington	a					14 14		14 32	14 39	15 09				15 14	15 29			15 32	15 39				16 14

		AW	GW	GW	GW	GW	GW	XC	GW	GW	GW	XC	AW	GW	GW	GW	XC	XC	GW	GW	AW	AW
			◇	◇■	◇■		◇■	◇■	◇■	◇■	◇	◇■ A		◇■	◇■		◇■	◇■	◇■	◇■		
Swansea	d			13 28										14 28								
Neath	d			13 40										14 40								
Port Talbot Parkway	d			13 48										14 48								
Bridgend	d			14 00									14 38	15 00								15 40
Cardiff Central	d			14 25								14 45	15 12	15 25				15 45				16 12
Newport (South Wales)	d			14 39								15 00	15 27	15 39				16 00				16 26
Weston-super-Mare	d																					
Bristol Temple Meads	d		14 41		15 00				15 30						16 00				16 30			
Bristol Parkway	a		14 52	14 59										15 59								
	d		14 52	15 01										16 01								
Bath Spa	d				15 13				15 43						16 13				16 43			
Chippenham	d				15 25	15 30			15 55						16 25				16 55			
Worcester Shrub Hill	d									15 01	15 06									16 04		
Cheltenham Spa	d	14 45					15 00	15 11			15 34					16 01	16 11				16 45	
Gloucester	d	14a56	15a32				15 16	15a22			15a42	15a44	16a19			16 15	16a22	16a44			16a56	17a19
Stonehouse	d						15 29									16 27						
Stroud	d						15 34									16 32						
Kemble	d						15 48									16 47						
Swindon	a			15 27	15 39	15 50	16 02		16 09					16 27	16 39	17 04			17 09			
	d			15 29	15 41		16 04		16 11					16 29	16 41				17 11			
Didcot Parkway	a			15 46			16 21		16 28					16 46					17 28			
Reading	a			16 00	16 11		16 38		16 44	16 55				17 00	17 10				17 44	17 55		
Slough	a									17 10										18 10		
London Paddington	a			16 32	16 39		17 07		17 14	17 29				17 32	17 38				18 14	18 29		

A from Newport (South Wales)

For connections from Hereford and Birmingham New Street please refer to Tables 131 and 57. For connections to Oxford, Gatwick Airport and Heathrow Airport please refer to Tables 116, 148 and 125A

Table 125

Saturdays from 15 September

South Wales, Weston-super-Mare, Bristol, Cheltenham Spa and Swindon - London

Route Diagram - see first Page of Table 125

		GW	GW	GW	GW	XC	XC	GW	GW	GW		AW	AW	GW	GW	GW	XC	XC	GW	GW		AW	AW	GW	GW
			◇1 ☕	◇1 ☕	◇1 ☕	◇1 ⊼	◇1	◇1 ☕	◇1 ⊼					◇1 ☕	◇1 ☕		◇1	◇1 A ⊼	◇1 ☕	◇1 ⊼					◇1 ☕
Swansea	d		15 28											16 28											17 28
Neath	d		15 40											16 40											17 40
Port Talbot Parkway	d		15 48											16 48											17 48
Bridgend	d		16 00										16 38	17 00									17 38		18 00
Cardiff Central	d		16 25				16 45						17 12	17 25				17 45					18 12		18 25
Newport (South Wales)	d		16 39				17 00						17 27	17 39				18 00					18 27		18 39
Weston-super-Mare	d																								
Bristol Temple Meads	d	16 41		17 00				17 30							18 00				18 30					18 41	
Bristol Parkway	a	16 52	16 59											17 59										18 52	18 59
	d	16 52	17 01											18 01										18 52	19 01
Bath Spa	d			17 13				17 43							18 13				18 43						
Chippenham	d			17 25				17 55							18 25				18 55						
Worcester Shrub Hill	d								17 02	17 08										18 06					
Cheltenham Spa	d				17 00	17 11				17 34		17 45				18 01	18 18					18 45			
Gloucester	d	17a33			17 16	17a22	17a44			17a44		17a56	18a20			18 15	18a29	18a44				18a56	19a20	19a33	
Stonehouse	d				17 29											18 27									
Stroud	d				17 34											18 32									
Kemble	d				17 48											18 47									
Swindon	a		17 27	17 39	18 02			18 09						18 27	18 39	19 04			19 09						19 27
	d		17 29	17 41	18 04			18 11						18 29	18 41				19 11						19 29
Didcot Parkway	a		17 46		18 21			18 28						18 46					19 28						19 46
Reading	a		18 00	18 11	18 38			18 44	18 55					19 00	19 10				19 44	19 55					20 00
Slough	a								19 10											20 10					
London Paddington ⊖	a		18 32	18 39	19 08			19 14	19 29					19 32	19 39				20 14	20 29					20 32

		GW	XC	GW	GW	GW		XC	AW	GW	GW	GW	GW	GW	XC	XC		GW	XC	GW	GW	GW	XC	GW	GW
		◇1 ☕	◇1	◇1 ☕	◇1			◇1			◇1 ☕		◇1 ☕	◇1	◇1	◇1			◇1		◇1 ☕		◇1	◇1 ☕	◇1
Swansea	d										18 28										19 28				
Neath	d										18 40										19 40				
Port Talbot Parkway	d										18 48										19 48				
Bridgend	d										19 00										20 00				
Cardiff Central	d							18 45			19 25					20 00					20 25		20 50		
Newport (South Wales)	d							19 00			19 39					20 15					20 39		21 05		
Weston-super-Mare	d												20 10												
Bristol Temple Meads	d			19 30						19 41			20 33							20 43				21 47	
Bristol Parkway	a									19 52	19 59									20 52	21 01				
	d									19 52	20 01									20 52	21 01				
Bath Spa	d			19 43									20 46											22 02	
Chippenham	d			19 55									20 58											22 15	
Worcester Shrub Hill	d				19 02	19 07								20 06											21 15
Cheltenham Spa	d	19 00	19 11			19 34			19 45			20 01			20 11			21 02	21 11			21 19			
Gloucester	d	19 16	19a22			19a42		19a44	19a56	20a33		20 15			20a22	21a04		21a12	21a22	21a34		21 35	21a48		
Stonehouse	d	19 29										20 27										21 47			
Stroud	d	19 34										20 32										21 52			
Kemble	d	19 48										20 47										22 07			
Swindon	a	20 03		20 09							20 27	21 03	21 13								21 29	22 24		22 29	
	d	20 05		20 11							20 29		21 14								21 29			22 31	
Didcot Parkway	a	20 22		20 28							20 46		21 31	21 43							21 47			22 48	22 47
Reading	a	20 38		20 44	20 54						21 07		21 51	21 59							22 01			23 04	23 08
Slough	a				21 09									22 15											23 26
London Paddington ⊖	a	21 07		21 14	21 29						21 36		22 22	22 33							22 37			23 36	23 46

		XC		GW	GW	GW
		◇1			◇1 B ☕	◇1 C ☕
Swansea	d					
Neath	d					
Port Talbot Parkway	d					
Bridgend	d					
Cardiff Central	d					
Newport (South Wales)	d					
Weston-super-Mare	d				21 53	21 53
Bristol Temple Meads	d				22 30	22 30
Bristol Parkway	a					
	d					
Bath Spa	d				22 43	22 43
Chippenham	d				22 55	22 55
Worcester Shrub Hill	d			21 31		
Cheltenham Spa	d	21 50		22 01		
Gloucester	d	21a59		22a10		
Stonehouse	d					
Stroud	d					
Kemble	d					
Swindon	a				23 10	23 10
	d				23 11	23 11
Didcot Parkway	a				23 28	23 28
Reading	a				23 51	23 52
Slough	a					
London Paddington ⊖	a				00 34	00 33

A ⊼ from Newport (South Wales) B from 15 September until 20 October C from 27 October

For connections from Hereford and Birmingham New Street please refer to Tables 131 and 57. For connections to Oxford, Gatwick Airport and Heathrow Airport please refer to Tables 116, 148 and 125A

Table 125

Sundays until 24 June

South Wales, Weston-super-Mare, Bristol, Cheltenham Spa and Swindon - London

Route Diagram - see first Page of Table 125

		GW	GW	GW	GW	GW	XC	GW	GW	GW		GW	GW	GW	GW	GW	GW	XC	AW	XC		GW	GW	GW	GW
		◇1 ☕	◇1 ☕	◇1 ☕	◇1 ☕	◇1 ☕	◇1 ⊼	◇1 ☕	◇1 ☕					◇1 ☕	◇1	◇1 ☕	◇1 ☕	◇1 ⊼		◇1 A ⊼		◇1 ☕	◇1 ☕	◇1 ☕	◇1 ☕
Swansea	d							08 07									09 21						10 21		
Neath	d							08 19									09 33						10 33		
Port Talbot Parkway	d							08 26									09 40						10 40		
Bridgend	d							08 38									09 52						10 52		
Cardiff Central	d				07 55			09 05									10 15		10 23	10 45			11 15		
Newport (South Wales)	d				08 13			09 19									10 32		10 38	10 59			11 32		
Weston-super-Mare	d	21p53				08 11										09 56									
Bristol Temple Meads	d	22p30	07 45	08 15		08 45	09 15						09 41	09 48		10 30						11 30		12 00	
Bristol Parkway	a				08 42		09 23	09 46					09 53				10 59						11 59		
	d				08 43		09 25	09 48					09 53				11 01						12 01		
Bath Spa	d	22p43	07 58	08 28		08 58								10 00		10 43						11 43		12 13	
Chippenham	d	22p55	08 10	08 40		09 10								10 12		10 55						11 55		12 25	
Worcester Shrub Hill	d														09 35										
Cheltenham Spa	d									09 24		10 05						10 53							11 46
Gloucester	d						09a54			09 38		10a15	10a32					11a03	11a42	11a49					12 02
Stonehouse	d									09 50															12 15
Stroud	d									09 55															12 20
Kemble	d									10 15															12 35
Swindon	a	23p10	08 25	08 55	09 08	09 24		10 13		10 30				10 27		11 10	11 29					12 10	12 27	12 40	12 48
	d	23p11	08 26	08 55	09 09	09 29		10 14	10 20					10 35		11 11	11 29					12 11	12 29	12 41	12 51
Didcot Parkway	a	23p28	08 43	09 13		09 45			10 37						11 07	11 28	11 49					12 29	12 46	12 58	
Reading	a	23p49	09 01	09 28	09 45	09 58		10 42	10 53					11 01	11 23	11 45	12 05					12 44	13 00	13 17	13 19
Slough	a														11 37										
London Paddington ⊖	a	00 33	09 44	10 07	10 22	10 44		11 22	11 29					11 44	12 01	12 22	12 42					13 22	13 42	13 59	14 02

		GW	XC	GW	AW	XC		GW	GW	GW	GW	GW	XC	AW	XC	GW		GW	GW	XC	AW	XC	GW	GW	GW
		◇1	◇1 ⊼			◇1 A ⊼		◇1 ☕		◇1 ☕		◇1 ☕	◇1 ⊼		◇1 A ⊼	◇1 ☕		◇1 ☕	◇1	◇1 ⊼		◇1 A ⊼	◇1 ☕	◇1 ☕	
Swansea	d									11 21						12 21									
Neath	d									11 33						12 33									
Port Talbot Parkway	d									11 40						12 40									
Bridgend	d									11 52						12 52									
Cardiff Central	d					11 45				12 15				12 23	12 45	13 15						13 45			
Newport (South Wales)	d					11 59				12 32				12 38	12 59	13 32						13 59			
Weston-super-Mare	d											12 51													
Bristol Temple Meads	d							12 30	12 41			13 30											14 30		
Bristol Parkway	a								12 52	12 59						13 59									
	d								12 52	13 02						14 01									
Bath Spa	d							12 43				13 43											14 43		
Chippenham	d							12 55				13 55											14 55		
Worcester Shrub Hill	d	11 30																	13 30					14 30	14 36
Cheltenham Spa	d		11 53	12 00	12 18						13 01		13 11					13 46		14 12	14 18				15 01
Gloucester	d		12a03	12a11	12a28	12a46			13a31		13 15		13a21	13a34	13a47			14 02		14a22	14a29	14a46			15a10
Stonehouse	d										13 27							14 15							
Stroud	d										13 32							14 20							
Kemble	d										13 46							14 35							
Swindon	a							13 10		13 29	14 01	14 10				14 29		14 50					15 10		
	d							13 11		13 29		14 11				14 29		14 51					15 11		
Didcot Parkway	a	13 02						13 32		13 50		14 33				14 51			15 03				15 31	16 02	
Reading	a	13 23						13 45		14 05		14 46				15 05		15 17	15 25				15 47	16 22	
Slough	a	13 41																	15 41					16 36	
London Paddington ⊖	a	14 05						14 22		14 43		15 21				15 43		15 57	16 03				16 22	17 04	

		XC		GW	GW	AW	XC	GW	GW	GW	GW	GW		XC	AW	XC	GW	GW	GW	GW	GW	GW		GW	XC
		◇1 ⊼			◇1 ☕		◇1 A ⊼	◇1 ☕	◇1 ☕	◇1 ☕	◇1 ☕	◇1 ☕		◇1 ⊼		◇1	◇1 ☕		◇1 ☕		◇1 ☕	◇1 ☕			◇1 ⊼
Swansea	d				13 21				14 21										15 21						
Neath	d				13 33				14 33										15 33						
Port Talbot Parkway	d				13 40				14 40										15 40						
Bridgend	d				13 52				14 52										15 52						
Cardiff Central	d				14 15	14 23	14 45		15 15							15 45			16 15						
Newport (South Wales)	d				14 32	14 38	14 59		15 32							15 59			16 32						
Weston-super-Mare	d							14 51																	
Bristol Temple Meads	d			14 41				15 30		16 00							16 30	16 41			17 00				
Bristol Parkway	a			14 52	14 59				15 59									16 52	16 59						
	d			14 53	15 01				16 01									16 52	17 01						
Bath Spa	d							15 43		16 13							16 43				17 13				
Chippenham	d							15 55		16 25							16 55				17 25				
Worcester Shrub Hill	d											15 27										16 27		16 40	
Cheltenham Spa	d	15 11									15 46			16 11	16 18					16 33				17 08	17 11
Gloucester	d	15a21		15a35		15a37	15a46				16 02			16a21	16a29	16a46		17a32		16 47				17a16	17a21
Stonehouse	d										16 15									16 59					
Stroud	d										16 20									17 04					
Kemble	d										16 35									17 19					
Swindon	a				15 29			16 10	16 29	16 40	16 50						17 10		17 27	17 34	17 40				
	d				15 29			16 11	16 29	16 41	16 51						17 11		17 29		17 41				
Didcot Parkway	a				15 46			16 31	16 50	17 00		17 02					17 28		17 46		18 00	18 02			
Reading	a				16 00			16 46	17 05	17 16	17 20	17 27					17 44		18 00		18 19	18 27			
Slough	a											17 43										18 41			
London Paddington ⊖	a				16 42			17 22	17 43	18 03	18 06	18 13					18 22		18 43		18 59	19 07			

A ⊼ from Newport (South Wales)

For connections from Hereford and Birmingham New Street please refer to Tables 131 and 57. For connections to Oxford, Gatwick Airport and Heathrow Airport please refer to Tables 116, 148 and 125A

Table 125

Sundays until 24 June

South Wales, Weston-super-Mare, Bristol, Cheltenham Spa and Swindon - London

Route Diagram - see first Page of Table 125

Station	AW	XC ◇■	GW	GW ◇■ ⊡	GW ◇■ ⊡	GW ◇■ ⊡	GW ◇■ ⊡	GW ◇■ ⊡	GW ◇■ ⊡	XC ◇■ ✕	XC ◇■	GW ◇■ ⊡	GW ◇■ ⊡	GW ◇■	AW	GW	XC ◇■ ✕	GW	AW	XC ◇■	GW ◇■ ⊡	GW ◇■ ⊡
Swansea d						16 21						16 51										17 51
Neath d						16 33						17 03										18 03
Port Talbot Parkway d						16 40						17 10										18 10
Bridgend d						16 52						17 22										18 22
Cardiff Central d	16 23	16 45				17 15					17 45	17 50							18 23	18 45		18 50
Newport (South Wales) d	16 38	16 59				17 30					17 59	18 04							18 38	18 59		19 04
Weston-super-Mare d				17 02			17 29															
Bristol Temple Meads d				17 30			18 00						18 30					18 41			19 00	
Bristol Parkway a						17 59						18 31						18 52				19 31
Bristol Parkway d						18 01						18 33						18 52				19 33
Bath Spa d				17 43			18 13						18 43								19 13	
Chippenham d			17 35	17 55			18 25						18 55								19 25	
Worcester Shrub Hill d									17 27					18 27		18 40						
Cheltenham Spa d								17 46		18 11					18 35	19 06	19 13					
Gloucester d	17a37	17a46						18 02		18a22	18a46				18a46	19a17	19a26	19a33	19a38	19a47		
Stonehouse d								18 15														
Stroud d								18 20														
Kemble d								18 35														
Swindon a			17 53	18 10		18 31	18 39	18 49				18 59	19 11								19 39	19 58
Swindon d				18 11	18 27	18 31	18 41	18 50				19 01	19 11								19 41	19 59
Didcot Parkway a						18 48	18 59		19 02			19 18		20 04							19 58	20 16
Reading a				18 46	18 55	19 02	19 12	19 22	19 27			19 36	19 47	20 24							20 15	20 42
Slough a									19 44					20 43								
London Paddington ⊖ a				19 22	19 31	19 42	19 59	20 02	20 07			20 14	20 27	21 05							20 59	21 19

Station	GW	GW	XC ◇■	GW ◇■ ⊡	GW ◇■ ⊡	GW ◇■	GW ◇■ ⊡	GW ◇■ ⊡	XC ◇■	AW	GW ◇■	GW	GW	GW ◇■ ⊡	XC ◇■	GW ◇■ ⊡	GW ◇■ ⊡	GW ◇■	GW	XC ◇■	GW ◇■ ⊡
Swansea d							18 51									19 59					
Neath d							19 03									20 11					
Port Talbot Parkway d							19 10									20 18					
Bridgend d							19 22									20 30					
Cardiff Central d			19 45				19 50								20 45	20 55					
Newport (South Wales) d			20 00				20 04								20 59	21 09					
Weston-super-Mare d					19 27									20 26							
Bristol Temple Meads d					20 00								20 41	21 00							22 10
Bristol Parkway a							20 31						20 52			21 36					
Bristol Parkway d							20 33						20 52			21 38					
Bath Spa d					20 13									21 13							22 23
Chippenham d	20 05				20 25									21 25							22 35
Worcester Shrub Hill d						19 32					20 30	20 37						21 34			
Cheltenham Spa d								20 05	20 11	20 18		21 03							21 46	21 52	
Gloucester d		19 34	20a49					20 23	20a21	20a29		21a13	21a33		21a47				21 59	22a02	
Stonehouse d		19 48						20 36											22 12		
Stroud d		19 53						20 42											22 17		
Kemble d		20 07						20 57											22 32		
Swindon a	20 21	20 23			20 39		20 59	21 11						21 40		22 04			22 47		22 50
Swindon d				20 33	20 41		20 59	21 11						21 41		22 05	22 17				22 53
Didcot Parkway a					20 58	21 00	21 16	21 28			22 01			21 58				22 58			23 08
Reading a				20 59	21 15	21 24	21 32	21 47			22 20			22 16		22 37	22 44	23 17			23 28
Slough a						21 44					22 40							23 43			
London Paddington ⊖ a				21 43	21 57	22 07	22 14	22 27			23 01			22 59		23 15	23 28	00 05			00 13

Sundays 1 July to 9 September

Station	GW ◇■ ⊡	GW ◇■ ⊡	GW ◇■ ⊡	GW ◇■ ⊡	GW ◇■ ⊡	XC ◇■ ✕	GW ◇■ ⊡	GW	GW	GW	GW ◇■ ⊡	GW ◇■	GW ◇■ ⊡	GW ◇■ ⊡	XC ◇■ ✕	AW	XC ◇■ A ✕	GW ◇■ ⊡	GW ◇■ ⊡	GW ◇■ ⊡	GW ◇■	GW ◇■ ⊡
Swansea d							08 07							09 21					10 21			
Neath d							08 19							09 33					10 33			
Port Talbot Parkway d							08 26							09 40					10 40			
Bridgend d							08 38							09 52					10 52			
Cardiff Central d				07 55			09 05							10 15		10 23	10 45		11 15			
Newport (South Wales) d				08 13			09 19							10 32		10 38	10 59		11 32			
Weston-super-Mare d	21p53				08 11								09 56									
Bristol Temple Meads d	22p30	07 45	08 15		08 45	09 15				09 41	09 48		10 30					11 30		12 00		
Bristol Parkway a				08 42		09 23	09 46			09 53				10 59					11 59			
Bristol Parkway d				08 43		09 25	09 48			09 53				11 01					12 01			
Bath Spa d	22p43	07 58	08 28		08 58						10 00		10 43					11 43		12 13		
Chippenham d	22p55	08 10	08 40		09 10						10 12		10 55					11 55		12 25		
Worcester Shrub Hill d												09 35									11 30	
Cheltenham Spa d								09 24	10 05						10 53							11 46
Gloucester d						09a54		09 38	10a15	10a32					11a03	11a42	11a49					12 02
Stonehouse d								09 50														12 15
Stroud d								09 55														12 20
Kemble d								10 09														12 35
Swindon a	23p10	08 25	08 55	09 08	09 24		10 13	10 24			10 27		11 10	11 27				12 10	12 27	12 40		12 48
Swindon d	23p11	08 26	08 55	09 09	09 29		10 14				10 29		11 11	11 29				12 11	12 29	12 41		12 51
Didcot Parkway a	23p28	08 43	09 13		09 45						10 45	11 07	11 29	11 46				12 29	12 46	12 58	13 02	
Reading a	23p51	08 59	09 29	09 43	09 58		10 42				11 00	11 22	11 44	12 01				12 44	13 01	13 14	13 20	13 26
Slough a												11 38									13 36	
London Paddington ⊖ a	00 34	09 29	09 59	10 14	10 29		11 14				11 29	12 00	12 14	12 29				13 14	13 29	13 41	13 56	13 59

A ✕ from Newport (South Wales)

For connections from Hereford and Birmingham New Street please refer to Tables 131 and 57. For connections to Oxford, Gatwick Airport and Heathrow Airport please refer to Tables 116, 148 and 125A

Table 125

Sundays 1 July to 9 September

South Wales, Weston-super-Mare, Bristol, Cheltenham Spa and Swindon - London

Route Diagram - see first Page of Table 125

Station	GW	XC ◇■ ✕	AW	XC ◇■ A ✕	GW ◇■ ⊡	GW	GW ◇■ ⊡	GW	GW ◇■ ⊡	XC ◇■ ✕	AW	XC ◇■ A ✕	GW ◇■ ⊡	GW ◇■	GW ◇■ ⊡	XC ◇■ ✕	AW	XC ◇■ A ✕	GW ◇■ ⊡	GW ◇■ ⊡	GW	XC ◇■ ✕
Swansea d							11 21						12 21									
Neath d							11 33						12 33									
Port Talbot Parkway d							11 40						12 40									
Bridgend d							11 52						12 52									
Cardiff Central d				11 45			12 15				12 23	12 45	13 15					13 45				
Newport (South Wales) d				11 59			12 32				12 38	12 59	13 32					13 59				
Weston-super-Mare d									12 51													
Bristol Temple Meads d					12 30	12 41			13 30										14 30			
Bristol Parkway a						12 52	12 59						13 59									
Bristol Parkway d						12 52	13 01						14 01									
Bath Spa d					12 43				13 43										14 43			
Chippenham d					12 55				13 55										14 55			
Worcester Shrub Hill d														13 30						14 30	14 36	
Cheltenham Spa d	12 00	12 11	12 18					13 01		13 11					13 46	14 12	14 18				15 01	15 11
Gloucester d	12a11	12a21	12a28	12a46		13a31		13 15		13a21	13a34	13a47			14 02	14a22	14a29	14a46			15a10	15a21
Stonehouse d								13 27							14 15							
Stroud d								13 32							14 20							
Kemble d								13 46							14 35							
Swindon a					13 10		13 27	14 01	14 10				14 27		14 50				15 10			
Swindon d					13 11		13 29		14 11				14 29		14 51				15 11			
Didcot Parkway a					13 32		13 46		14 29				14 46	15 04					15 29	16 02		
Reading a					13 45		14 01		14 44				15 00	15 21	15 27				15 44	16 20		
Slough a														15 36						16 33		
London Paddington ⊖ a					14 14		14 29		15 14				15 29	15 55	15 58				16 14	16 51		

Station	GW	GW ◇■ ⊡	AW	XC ◇■ A ✕	GW ◇■ ⊡	GW ◇■ ⊡	GW ◇■ ⊡	GW ◇■ ⊡	GW ◇■ ⊡	XC ◇■ ✕	AW	GW ◇■ ⊡	GW	GW ◇■ ⊡	GW	GW ◇■ ⊡	GW ◇■ ⊡	GW	XC ◇■ ✕	AW	XC ◇■
Swansea d		13 21				14 21								15 21							
Neath d		13 33				14 33								15 33							
Port Talbot Parkway d		13 40				14 40								15 40							
Bridgend d		13 52				14 52								15 52							
Cardiff Central d		14 15	14 23	14 45		15 15								16 15						16 23	16 45
Newport (South Wales) d		14 32	14 38	14 59		15 32								16 32						16 38	16 59
Weston-super-Mare d					14 51																
Bristol Temple Meads d	14 41				15 30		16 00					16 30	16 41			17 00					
Bristol Parkway a	14 52	14 59				15 59							16 52	16 59							
Bristol Parkway d	14 53	15 01				16 01							16 52	17 01							
Bath Spa d					15 43		16 13					16 43				17 13					
Chippenham d					15 55		16 25					16 55				17 25					
Worcester Shrub Hill d									15 27								16 27	16 40			
Cheltenham Spa d								15 46		16 11	16 18				16 33			17 08	17 11		
Gloucester d	15a35		15a37	15a46				16 02		16a21	16a29		17a32		16 47			17a16	17a21	17a37	17a46
Stonehouse d								16 15							16 59						
Stroud d								16 20							17 04						
Kemble d								16 35							17 19						
Swindon a		15 27			16 10	16 27	16 40	16 50				17 10		17 27	17 34	17 40					
Swindon d		15 29			16 11	16 29	16 41	16 51				17 11		17 29		17 41					
Didcot Parkway a		15 46			16 32	16 46	16 58		17 02			17 28		17 46		17 58	18 02				
Reading a		16 00			16 45	17 00	17 12	17 18	17 21			17 42		18 00		18 12	18 20				
Slough a									17 38								18 35				
London Paddington ⊖ a		16 29			17 14	17 29	17 41	17 51	17 59			18 14		18 29		18 42	18 53				

Station	GW	GW ◇■ ⊡	GW ◇■ ⊡	GW ◇■ ⊡	GW ◇■ ⊡	GW ◇■ ⊡	XC ◇■ ✕	XC ◇■	GW ◇■ ⊡	GW ◇■ ⊡	GW ◇■	AW	GW	XC ◇■ ✕	GW	AW	XC ◇■	GW ◇■ ⊡	GW ◇■ ⊡	GW	GW	GW ◇■ ⊡
Swansea d			16 21						16 51										17 51			
Neath d			16 33						17 03										18 03			
Port Talbot Parkway d			16 40						17 10										18 10			
Bridgend d			16 52						17 22										18 22			
Cardiff Central d			17 15					17 45	17 50							18 23	18 45		18 50			
Newport (South Wales) d			17 32					17 59	18 04							18 38	18 59		19 04			
Weston-super-Mare d		17 02		17 29																		19 27
Bristol Temple Meads d		17 30		18 00						18 30					18 41			19 00				20 00
Bristol Parkway a			17 59						18 31						18 52				19 31			
Bristol Parkway d			18 01						18 33						18 52				19 33			
Bath Spa d		17 43		18 13						18 43								19 13				20 13
Chippenham d	17 35	17 55		18 25						18 55								19 25		20 05		20 25
Worcester Shrub Hill d						17 27					18 27		18 40									
Cheltenham Spa d					17 46		18 11					18 35	19 06	19 13								
Gloucester d					18 02		18a22	18a46				18a46	19a17	19a26	19a33	19a38	19a47				19 34	
Stonehouse d					18 15																19 48	
Stroud d					18 20																19 53	
Kemble d					18 35																20 07	
Swindon a	17 53	18 10	18 27	18 39	18 49				18 59	19 11								19 39	19 58	20 21	20 23	20 39
Swindon d		18 11	18 29	18 41	18 51				18 59	19 11								19 41	19 59			20 41
Didcot Parkway a			18 44	18 59		19 03			19 16		20 04							19 58	20 16			20 58
Reading a		18 42	18 58	19 12	19 18	19 20			19 32	19 43	20 23							20 12	20 32			21 15
Slough a						19 38					20 42											
London Paddington ⊖ a		19 13	19 30	19 42	19 51	19 56			20 01	20 14	21 02							20 46	21 01			21 44

A ✕ from Newport (South Wales)

For connections from Hereford and Birmingham New Street please refer to Tables 131 and 57. For connections to Oxford, Gatwick Airport and Heathrow Airport please refer to Tables 116, 148 and 125A

Table 125

Sundays

1 July to 9 September

South Wales, Weston-super-Mare, Bristol, Cheltenham Spa and Swindon - London

Route Diagram - see first Page of Table 125

		GW ◇1	XC ◇1	GW ◇1 ⊒		GW ◇1 ⊒	AW	GW ◇1	GW	GW	GW ◇1 ⊒	GW ◇1 ⊒	GW ◇1	GW		XC ◇1	GW ◇1 ⊒
Swansea	d			18 51								19 59					
Neath	d			19 03								20 11					
Port Talbot Parkway	d			19 10								20 18					
Bridgend	d			19 22								20 30					
Cardiff Central 7	d		19 45	19 50								20 55					
Newport (South Wales)	d		20 00	20 04								21 09					
Weston-super-Mare	d										20 26						
Bristol Temple Meads 10	d									20 41	21 00						22 10
Bristol Parkway 7	a			20 31						20 52		21 36					
	d			20 33						20 52		21 38					
Bath Spa 7	d										21 13						22 23
Chippenham	d										21 25						22 35
Worcester Shrub Hill	d	19 32						20 30	20 37				21 34				
Cheltenham Spa	d					20 05	20 18		21 03					21 46		21 52	
Gloucester 7	d		20a49			20 23	20a29		21a13	21a33				21 59		22a02	
Stonehouse	d					20 36								22 12			
Stroud	d					20 42								22 17			
Kemble	d					20 57								22 32			
Swindon	a			20 59		21 11					21 40	22 04		22 47			22 50
	d			20 59		21 11					21 42	22 05					22 53
Didcot Parkway	a	21 00		21 16		21 30		22 00			22 00		22 58				23 10
Reading 7	a	21 17		21 32		21 47		22 20			22 17	22 37	23 15				23 28
Slough 3	a	21 38						22 41					23 42				
London Paddington 15 ⊖	a	21 59		22 02		22 29		23 00			22 46	23 13	00 02				00 05

Sundays

16 September to 21 October

		GW ◇1 ⊒	GW 🚌	GW 🚌	GW ◇1 ⊒	GW 1 ⊒	GW ◇1 ⊒	GW 🚌	GW 🚌	GW 🚌		GW ◇1 ⊒	GW 🚌	XC ◇1 ⌶	GW ◇1 ⊒	GW	GW	XC ◇1 ⌶	GW ◇1 ⊒	GW ◇1		XC ◇1 ⌶	GW ◇1 ⊒	GW	GW ◇1 ⊒
Swansea	d														08 07								09 07		
Neath	d														08 19								09 19		
Port Talbot Parkway	d														08 26								09 26		
Bridgend	d														08 38								09 38		
Cardiff Central 7	d						07 45								09 05								10 05		
Newport (South Wales)	d						08 03								09 19								10 19		
Weston-super-Mare	d	21p53										08 20													10 20
Bristol Temple Meads 10	d	22p30			07 55	08 20		07 35				08 55		09 20					09 55			10 00			10 55
Bristol Parkway 7	a						08 31							09 28	09 46							10 08	10 46		
	d						08 32							09 33	09 48							10 17	10 48		
Bath Spa 7	d	22p43	07 30					08 10	08 30							09 50									
Chippenham	d	22p55		07 45				08 45		08 45						10 03									
Worcester Shrub Hill	d																			09 35					
Cheltenham Spa	d												08 45				09 24	09 52						10 24	
Gloucester 7	d												09a05	10a28			09 38	10a01				11a14		10 38	
Stonehouse	d																09 50							10 50	
Stroud	d																09 55							10 55	
Kemble	d																10 09							11 09	
Swindon	a	23p10	08 20	08 20	08 26	08 52	08 58	09 20	09 20	09 20		09 26			10 13	10 18	10 24		10 26				11 13	11 24	11 26
	d	23p11			08 29		08 59					09 29			10 14				10 29				11 14		11 29
Didcot Parkway	a	23p28			08 45							09 45							10 45	11 07			11 32		11 45
Reading 7	a	23p51			09 02		09 31					10 02			10 42				11 01	11 25			11 47		12 01
Slough 3	a																			11 42					
London Paddington 15 ⊖	a	00 34			09 44		10 07					10 44			11 22				11 44	12 06			12 22		12 43

		XC ◇1 ⌶	XC ◇1 ⌶	AW	XC ◇1 A ⌶	GW		XC ◇1 ⌶	GW ◇1 ⊒	GW	GW ◇1 ⊒	GW ◇1	XC ◇1 ⌶	XC ◇1 ⌶	AW	XC ◇1 A ⌶		GW	GW ◇1 ⊒	XC ◇1 ⌶	XC ◇1 ⌶	GW ◇1 ⊒	GW	XC ◇1 ⌶	AW
Swansea	d								10 07										11 07						
Neath	d								10 19										11 19						
Port Talbot Parkway	d								10 26										11 26						
Bridgend	d								10 38										11 38						
Cardiff Central 7	d			10 23	10 45				11 05							11 45			12 05						12 23
Newport (South Wales)	d			10 38	10 59				11 19							11 59			12 19						12 38
Weston-super-Mare	d																								
Bristol Temple Meads 10	d							11 30			11 50										12 30	12 52			
Bristol Parkway 7	a							11 38	11 46										12 46		12 39				
	d							11 43	11 48										12 48		12 49				
Bath Spa 7	d					11 20					12 13							12 42				13 13			
Chippenham	d					11 34					12 25							12 55				13 26			
Worcester Shrub Hill	d											11 30													
Cheltenham Spa	d	10 53	11 11							11 24			11 53	12 10	12 18					12 51			13 01	13 11	
Gloucester 7	d	11a03	11a20	11a42	11a49			12a55		11 38			12a03	12a19	12a28	12a46				13a02	13a52		13 15	13a21	13a34
Stonehouse	d									11 50													13 27		
Stroud	d									11 55													13 32		
Kemble	d									12 09													13 46		
Swindon	a					11 52			12 13	12 24	12 40							13 10	13 13			13 41	14 01		
	d								12 14		12 41								13 14			13 42			
Didcot Parkway	a								12 32		12 58	13 02							13 32			13 59			
Reading 7	a								12 47		13 19	13 23							13 47			14 19			
Slough 3	a											13 41													
London Paddington 15 ⊖	a								13 22		13 59	14 03							14 22			14 57			

A ⌶ from Newport (South Wales)

For connections from Hereford and Birmingham New Street please refer to Tables 131 and 57. For connections to Oxford, Gatwick Airport and Heathrow Airport please refer to Tables 116, 148 and 125A

Table 125

Sundays

16 September to 21 October

South Wales, Weston-super-Mare, Bristol, Cheltenham Spa and Swindon - London

Route Diagram - see first Page of Table 125

		XC ◇1 A ⌶		XC ◇1 ⌶	XC ◇1 ⌶	AW	XC ◇1 ⌶	GW ◇1 ⊒	GW ◇1 ⊒	GW ◇1	XC ◇1 A ⌶	XC ◇1 ⌶		GW ◇1 ⊒	GW ◇1 ⊒	GW ◇1 ⊒	GW	GW ◇1 ⊒	XC ◇1 ⌶	GW	XC ◇1 ⌶	AW		XC ◇1 A ⌶	XC ◇1 ⌶
Swansea	d							12 07						13 07											
Neath	d							12 19						13 19											
Port Talbot Parkway	d							12 26						13 26											
Bridgend	d							12 38						13 38											
Cardiff Central 7	d	12 45						13 05			13 45			14 05								14 23		14 45	
Newport (South Wales)	d	12 59						13 19			13 59			14 19								14 38		14 59	
Weston-super-Mare	d								13 15									14 51							
Bristol Temple Meads 10	d						13 30		13 50			14 30			14 50			15 30							15 30
Bristol Parkway 7	a						13 38	13 46				14 38		14 48											15 39
	d						13 43	13 48				14 45		14 50											15 47
Bath Spa 7	d								14 13						15 13			15 43							
Chippenham	d								14 25						15 25			15 55							
Worcester Shrub Hill	d									13 30						14 30				14 36					
Cheltenham Spa	d			13 51	14 12	14 18											14 46		14 52	15 01	15 11				
Gloucester 7	d	13a47		14a02	14a22	14a29	14a54				14a46	15a56					15 03		15a09	15a12	15a21	15a37		15a46	16a54
Stonehouse	d																15 17								
Stroud	d																15 22								
Kemble	d																15 36								
Swindon	a							14 13	14 40					15 15	15 40		15 51	16 10							
	d							14 14	14 41					15 18	15 41			16 11							
Didcot Parkway	a							14 32	14 58	15 03					15 58	16 02		16 31							
Reading 7	a							14 47	15 19	15 25				15 47	16 19	16 22		16 46							
Slough 3	a									15 41						16 36									
London Paddington 15 ⊖	a							15 22	15 58	16 03				16 23	17 01	17 07		17 22							

		GW ◇1 ⊒	GW ◇1 ⊒	GW ◇1 ⊒	GW ◇1 ⊒	XC ◇1 ⌶	XC ◇1 ⌶	AW		XC ◇1	XC ◇1 ⌶	GW ◇1 ⊒	GW ◇1 ⊒	GW	XC ◇1 ⌶	GW ◇1 ⊒	GW ◇1 ⊒	GW		XC ◇1 ⌶	AW	XC ◇1	XC ◇1 ⌶	GW	GW ◇1 ⊒
Swansea	d	14 21											15 21												
Neath	d	14 33											15 33												
Port Talbot Parkway	d	14 40											15 40												
Bridgend	d	14 52											15 52												
Cardiff Central 7	d	15 15								15 45			16 15								16 23	16 45			
Newport (South Wales)	d	15 32								15 59			16 32								16 38	16 59			
Weston-super-Mare	d																								17 02
Bristol Temple Meads 10	d		16 00								16 30	16 30				17 00							17 30		17 30
Bristol Parkway 7	a	15 59									16 38		16 59										17 39		
	d	16 01									16 45		17 01										18 02		
Bath Spa 7	d		16 13									16 43				17 13									17 43
Chippenham	d		16 25									16 55				17 25								17 35	17 55
Worcester Shrub Hill	d				15 27												16 27	16 40							
Cheltenham Spa	d			15 46		15 52	16 11	16 18						16 32	16 52			17 08		17 11					
Gloucester 7	d			16 02		16a02	16a21	16a29		16a46	17a58			16 46	17a01			17a17		17a21	17a37	17a46	18a58		
Stonehouse	d			16 15										16 58											
Stroud	d			16 20										17 03											
Kemble	d			16 35										17 18											
Swindon	a	16 26	16 40	16 50								17 10	17 26	17 33		17 40								17 53	18 10
	d	16 29	16 41	16 51								17 11	17 29			17 41									18 11
Didcot Parkway	a	16 46	16 58		17 02							17 28	17 46			17 58	18 02								
Reading 7	a	17 04	17 16	17 21	17 27							17 46	18 01			18 19	18 27								18 46
Slough 3	a				17 43												18 41								
London Paddington 15 ⊖	a	17 43	18 01	18 04	18 07							18 22	18 44			18 59	19 07								19 23

		GW ◇1 ⊒	GW ◇1 ⊒	GW ◇1 ⊒		GW ◇1 ⊒	XC ◇1 ⌶	XC ◇1 ⌶	XC ◇1	GW ◇1 ⊒	GW ◇1 ⊒	GW ◇1	AW	XC ◇1 ⌶		GW	AW	XC ◇1	XC ◇1 ⌶	GW ◇1 ⊒	GW ◇1 ⊒	GW	GW	XC ◇1 ⌶
Swansea	d	16 21								16 51											17 51			
Neath	d	16 33								17 03											18 03			
Port Talbot Parkway	d	16 40								17 10											18 10			
Bridgend	d	16 52								17 22											18 22			
Cardiff Central 7	d	17 15							17 45	17 50							18 23	18 45			18 50			
Newport (South Wales)	d	17 32							17 59	18 04							18 38	18 59			19 04			
Weston-super-Mare	d		17 29																					
Bristol Temple Meads 10	d		18 00								18 30								18 30	19 00				
Bristol Parkway 7	a	17 59								18 31									18 42		19 31			
	d	18 01								18 33									19 00		19 33			
Bath Spa 7	d		18 13								18 43									19 13				
Chippenham	d		18 25								18 55									19 25		20 05		
Worcester Shrub Hill	d					17 27						18 27				18 40								
Cheltenham Spa	d			17 46			17 52	18 11					18 35	18 52		19 07								19 52
Gloucester 7	d			18 02			18a01	18a22	18a46				18a46	19a01		19a18	19a38	19a47	19a58				19 34	20a01
Stonehouse	d			18 15																			19 48	
Stroud	d			18 20																			19 53	
Kemble	d			18 34																			20 07	
Swindon	a	18 26	18 40	18 48						18 57	19 10									19 40	19 57	20 21	20 23	
	d	18 29	18 41	18 49						18 59	19 11									19 41	19 59			
Didcot Parkway	a	18 46	18 58			19 02				19 16		20 04								19 58	20 16			
Reading 7	a	19 01	19 19	19 22		19 27				19 33	19 46	20 24								20 19	20 33			
Slough 3	a					19 44						20 43												
London Paddington 15 ⊖	a	19 44	19 59	20 02		20 07				20 14	20 23	21 05								20 59	21 13			

A ⌶ from Newport (South Wales)

For connections from Hereford and Birmingham New Street please refer to Tables 131 and 57. For connections to Oxford, Gatwick Airport and Heathrow Airport please refer to Tables 116, 148 and 125A

Sundays
16 September to 21 October

South Wales, Weston-super-Mare, Bristol, Cheltenham Spa and Swindon - London

Route Diagram - see first Page of Table 125

		XC	XC	GW	GW	GW	GW	XC	AW	XC	XC	GW	GW	GW	GW	GW	XC	GW	GW	XC	XC
		◇1	◇1 H	◇1 ⊏	◇1	◇1 ⊏	◇1 ⊏	◇1		◇1 H	◇1 H	◇1 ⊏	◇1	◇1 ⊏	◇1		◇1		◇1 ⊏	◇1	◇1
Swansea	d					18 51								19 59							
Neath	d					19 03								20 11							
Port Talbot Parkway	d					19 10								20 18							
Bridgend	d					19 22								20 30							
Cardiff Central	d	19 45				19 50								20 55							
Newport (South Wales)	d	20 00				20 04								21 09							
Weston-super-Mare	d			19 27								20 26									
Bristol Temple Meads	d		19 30	20 00							20 30	21 00							22 10		22 10
Bristol Parkway	a		19 38			20 31					20 38			21 36							22 19
	d		19 45			20 33					20 43			21 38							22 24
Bath Spa	d			20 13								21 13							22 23		
Chippenham	d			20 25								21 24							22 35		
Worcester Shrub Hill	d				19 32								20 30		21 28			21 36			
Cheltenham Spa	d						20 05	20 11	20 18	20 52						21 46	21 52	22 02		22 52	
Gloucester	d	20a49	20a56				20 23	20a21	20a29	21a01	21a55					21 59	22a05	22a13		23a03	23a19
Stonehouse	d						20 36									22 12					
Stroud	d						20 42									22 17					
Kemble	d						20 57									22 32					
Swindon	a			20 40		20 57	21 11					21 40		22 04		22 47			22 50		
	d			20 41		20 59	21 11					21 41		22 05					22 53		
Didcot Parkway	a			20 58	21 00	21 16	21 30					22 00	22 00		22 58				23 09		
Reading	a			21 20	21 24	21 33	21 47					22 17	22 21	22 40	23 17				23 28		
Slough	a				21 44								22 43		23 43						
London Paddington ⊖	a			22 02	22 07	22 15	22 29					22 58	23 13	23 22	00 06				00 12		

Sundays
from 28 October

		GW	GW	GW	GW	GW	GW	GW	GW	GW	GW	GW	GW	GW	GW	GW	GW	AW	XC	GW	GW	GW	AW
		◇1 ⊏	◇1 ⊏	◇1 ⊏	1 ⊏	◇1 ⊏	◇1 ⊏				◇1 ⊏	◇1	◇1 ⊏		◇1 ⊏	◇1 ⊏			◇1 H	◇1 ⊏	◇1		
Swansea	d						08 07								09 21					10 21			
Neath	d						08 19								09 33					10 33			
Port Talbot Parkway	d						08 26								09 40					10 40			
Bridgend	d						08 38								09 52					10 52			
Cardiff Central	d			07 45			09 05								10 15			10 23		11 15			
Newport (South Wales)	d			08 03			09 19								10 32			10 38		11 32			
Weston-super-Mare	d	21p53				08 11							09 56										
Bristol Temple Meads	d	22p30	07 45		08 20	08 45				09 41	09 48		10 30			11 30			11 30				
Bristol Parkway	a			08 31			09 46			09 53					10 59				11 38	11 59			
	d			08 32			09 48			09 53					11 01				11 40	12 01			
Bath Spa	d	22p43	07 58		08 33	08 58					10 00		10 43			11 43							
Chippenham	d	22p55	08 10		08 45	09 10					10 12		10 55			11 55							
Worcester Shrub Hill	d											09 35									11 30		
Cheltenham Spa	d							09 24	10 05					10 24			11 24					12 08	12 18
Gloucester	d							09 38	10a15	10a32				10 38			11 38	11a42	12a07			12a19	12a28
Stonehouse	d							09 50						10 50			11 50						
Stroud	d							09 55						10 55			11 55						
Kemble	d							10 09						11 09			12 09						
Swindon	a	23p10	08 25	08 58	09 00	09 24	10 13	10 24			10 27		11 10	11 24	11 26	12 10	12 24			12 26			
	d	23p11	08 26	08 59		09 29	10 14				10 29		11 11		11 29	12 11				12 29			
Didcot Parkway	a	23p28	08 43			09 45					10 45	11 07	11 28		11 46	12 29				12 46	13 02		
Reading	a	23p52	09 01	09 31		10 00	10 42				11 00	11 25	11 45		12 01	12 42				13 01	13 23		
Slough	a											11 42									13 37		
London Paddington ⊖	a	00 33	09 44	10 07		10 44	11 22				11 44	12 06	12 21		12 44	13 22				13 44	14 00		

		GW	GW	GW	AW	GW	XC	AW	GW	GW	GW	XC	GW	GW	GW	GW	GW	GW	XC	AW	XC	GW	GW
		◇1 ⊏	◇1 ⊏			◇1 ⊏	◇1 H			◇1 ⊏	◇1	◇1 H	◇1 ⊏		◇1 ⊏	◇1 ⊏		◇1 ⊏	◇1 H		◇1 A H	◇1 ⊏	◇1 ⊏
Swansea	d		11 21							12 21					13 21							14 21	
Neath	d		11 33							12 33					13 33							14 33	
Port Talbot Parkway	d		11 40							12 40					13 40							14 40	
Bridgend	d		11 52							12 52					13 52							14 52	
Cardiff Central	d		12 15		12 23					13 15					14 15					14 23	14 45	15 15	
Newport (South Wales)	d		12 32		12 38					13 32					14 32					14 38	14 59	15 32	
Weston-super-Mare	d					12 51												14 51					
Bristol Temple Meads	d	12 30				13 30	13 30		13 41				14 30	14 41				15 30					16 00
Bristol Parkway	a		12 59				13 38		13 52	13 59				14 52	14 59							15 59	
	d		13 01				13 40		13 52	14 01				14 53	15 01							16 01	
Bath Spa	d	12 43				13 43							14 43					15 43					16 13
Chippenham	d	12 55				13 55							14 55					15 55					16 25
Worcester Shrub Hill	d										13 30					14 30							
Cheltenham Spa	d			13 01				14 18				14 27					14 46		15 11				
Gloucester	d			13 14	13a34		14a08	14a29	14a31			14a43		15a35			15 03		15a21	15a37	15a46		
Stonehouse	d			13 27													15 17						
Stroud	d			13 32													15 22						
Kemble	d			13 46													15 36						
Swindon	a	13 10	13 26	14 01		14 10				14 26			15 10		15 26		15 51	16 10				16 26	16 40
	d	13 11	13 29			14 11				14 29			15 11		15 29			16 11				16 29	16 41
Didcot Parkway	a	13 28	13 46			14 28				14 46	15 03		15 28		15 46	16 02		16 30				16 46	16 58
Reading	a	13 47	14 01			14 47				15 01	15 21		15 47		16 01	16 22		16 47				17 01	17 19
Slough	a										15 36					16 36							
London Paddington ⊖	a	14 22	14 44			15 22				15 44	15 59		16 22		16 44	17 00		17 22				17 43	17 58

A H from Newport (South Wales)

For connections from Hereford and Birmingham New Street please refer to Tables 131 and 57. For connections to Oxford, Gatwick Airport and Heathrow Airport please refer to Tables 116, 148 and 125A

Sundays
from 28 October

South Wales, Weston-super-Mare, Bristol, Cheltenham Spa and Swindon - London

Route Diagram - see first Page of Table 125

		GW	GW	GW	XC	AW	XC	GW	GW	GW	GW	GW	GW	GW	XC	AW	XC	GW	GW	GW	GW	GW
		◇1 ⊏	◇1 ⊏		◇1 H		◇1	◇1 ⊏		◇1 ⊏		◇1 ⊏	◇1 ⊏		◇1 H		◇1		◇1 ⊏	◇1 ⊏	◇1 ⊏	◇1 ⊏
Swansea	d									15 21										16 21		
Neath	d									15 33										16 33		
Port Talbot Parkway	d									15 40										16 40		
Bridgend	d									15 52										16 52		
Cardiff Central	d						15 45			16 15						16 23	16 45			17 15		
Newport (South Wales)	d						15 59			16 32						16 38	16 59			17 32		
Weston-super-Mare	d																		17 02		17 29	
Bristol Temple Meads	d							16 30	16 41			17 00							17 30		18 00	
Bristol Parkway	a								16 52	16 59										17 59		
	d								16 52	17 01										17 59		
Bath Spa	d							16 43				17 13							17 43		18 13	
Chippenham	d							16 55				17 25						17 35	17 55		18 25	
Worcester Shrub Hill	d		15 27	15 36									16 27	16 40								
Cheltenham Spa	d	15 46		16 01	16 11	16 18					16 32			17 08	17 11							17 46
Gloucester	d	16 02		16a10	16a21	16a29	16a46		17a32		16 46			17a16	17a21	17a37	17a46					18 02
Stonehouse	d	16 15									16 58											18 15
Stroud	d	16 20									17 03											18 20
Kemble	d	16 35									17 18											18 34
Swindon	a	16 50						17 10		17 26	17 33	17 40						17 53	18 10	18 26	18 40	18 48
	d	16 51						17 11		17 29		17 41							18 11	18 29	18 41	18 49
Didcot Parkway	a		17 02					17 28		17 46		17 58	18 02							18 46	18 58	
Reading	a	17 22	17 27					17 46		18 01		18 20	18 27						18 46	19 01	19 19	19 22
Slough	a		17 43										18 41									
London Paddington ⊖	a	18 01	18 07					18 22		18 44		18 59	19 07						19 22	19 44	19 59	20 02

		GW	XC	XC	GW	GW	GW	AW	GW	GW	AW	XC	GW	GW	GW	GW	GW	GW	XC	GW	GW	XC	AW
		◇1 ⊏	◇1 H	◇1	◇1 ⊏	◇1 ⊏	◇1					◇1	◇1 ⊏	◇1 ⊏			◇1 ⊏	◇1	◇1	◇1 ⊏	◇1 ⊏	◇1	
Swansea	d				16 51									17 51						18 51			
Neath	d				17 03									18 03						19 03			
Port Talbot Parkway	d				17 10									18 10						19 10			
Bridgend	d				17 22									18 22						19 22			
Cardiff Central	d			17 45	17 50						18 23	18 45		18 50					19 45	19 50			
Newport (South Wales)	d			17 59	18 04						18 38	18 59		19 04					20 00	20 04			
Weston-super-Mare	d																19 27						
Bristol Temple Meads	d					18 30				18 41			19 00				20 00						
Bristol Parkway	a				18 31					18 52				19 31						20 31			
	d				18 33					18 52				19 33						20 33			
Bath Spa	d					18 43							19 13				20 13						
Chippenham	d					18 55							19 25		20 05		20 25						
Worcester Shrub Hill	d	17 27					18 27		18 40									19 32					
Cheltenham Spa	d		18 11					18 35	19 06												20 05	20 11	20 18
Gloucester	d		18a22	18a46				18a46	19a17	19a33	19a38	19a47				19 34			20a49		20 23	20a21	20a29
Stonehouse	d															19 48					20 36		
Stroud	d															19 53					20 42		
Kemble	d															20 07					20 57		
Swindon	a				18 57	19 10							19 40	19 57	20 21	20 23	20 40			20 57	21 11		
	d				18 59	19 11							19 41	19 59			20 41			20 59	21 11		
Didcot Parkway	a	19 02			19 16		20 04						19 58	20 16			20 58	21 00		21 16	21 30		
Reading	a	19 27			19 32	19 46	20 24						20 19	20 33			21 22	21 24		21 33	21 47		
Slough	a	19 44					20 43											21 44					
London Paddington ⊖	a	20 07			20 14	20 22	21 05						20 59	21 13			22 02	22 07		22 13	22 29		

		GW	GW	GW	GW	GW	GW	GW	XC	GW
		◇1			◇1 ⊏	◇1 ⊏	◇1		◇1	◇1 ⊏
Swansea	d					19 59				
Neath	d					20 11				
Port Talbot Parkway	d					20 18				
Bridgend	d					20 30				
Cardiff Central	d					20 55				
Newport (South Wales)	d					21 09				
Weston-super-Mare	d				20 26					
Bristol Temple Meads	d			20 41	21 00					22 10
Bristol Parkway	a			20 52		21 36				
	d			20 52		21 38				
Bath Spa	d				21 13					22 23
Chippenham	d				21 24					22 35
Worcester Shrub Hill	d	20 30	20 37				21 34			
Cheltenham Spa	d		21 03					21 46	21 52	
Gloucester	d		21a13	21a33				21 59	22a02	
Stonehouse	d							22 12		
Stroud	d							22 17		
Kemble	d							22 32		
Swindon	a				21 40	22 04		22 47		22 50
	d				21 40	22 05				22 53
Didcot Parkway	a	22 00			22 00		22 58			23 09
Reading	a	22 24			22 18	22 40	23 17			23 28
Slough	a	22 43					23 43			
London Paddington ⊖	a	23 13			22 58	23 22	00 05			00 13

For connections from Hereford and Birmingham New Street please refer to Tables 131 and 57. For connections to Oxford, Gatwick Airport and Heathrow Airport please refer to Tables 116, 148 and 125A

Reading - Heathrow Railair Link

Express Coach Service

		GW	GW	GW	GW	GW	GW	GW	GW	GW		GW	GW	GW	GW	GW	GW	GW	GW	GW		GW	GW	GW	GW
Reading 7	d	04 00	05 00	05 30	05 55	06 08	06 20	06 40	07 00	07 20	...	07 40	08 00	08 20	08 40	09 05	09 25	09 45	10 05	10 25	...	10 45	11 05	11 25	11 45
Heathrow Terminal 5 Bus	a	04 38	05 38	06 08	06 33	06 48	07 15	07 35	07 55	08 15		08 35	08 55	09 15	09 35	09 45	10 05	10 25	10 45	11 05		11 25	11 45	12 05	12 25
Heathrow Terminal 1 Bus	a	04 46	05 46	06 16	06 41	06 58	07 25	07 45	08 05	08 25	...	08 45	09 05	09 25	09 45	09 55	10 15	10 35	10 55	11 15	...	11 35	11 55	12 15	12 35
Heathrow Terminal 2 Bus	a																								
Heathrow Terminal 3 Bus	a	04 51	05 51	06 21	06 46	07 04	07 31	07 51	08 11	08 31	...	08 51	09 11	09 31	09 51	10 01	10 21	10 41	11 01	11 21	...	11 41	12 01	12 21	12 41

		GW	GW	GW	GW	GW		GW	GW	GW	GW	GW	GW	GW	GW	GW		GW	GW	GW	GW	GW	GW	GW	GW
Reading 7	d	12 05	12 25	12 45	13 05	13 25	...	13 45	14 05	14 25	14 45	15 05	15 25	15 45	16 05	16 25	...	16 45	17 05	17 25	17 45	18 05	18 35	19 05	19 35
Heathrow Terminal 5 Bus	a	12 45	13 05	13 25	13 45	14 05		14 25	14 45	15 05	15 25	15 45	16 05	16 25	16 45	17 05		17 25	17 45	18 05	18 25	18 45	19 15	19 45	20 15
Heathrow Terminal 1 Bus	a	12 55	13 15	13 35	13 55	14 15	...	14 35	14 55	15 15	15 35	15 55	16 15	16 35	16 55	17 15	...	17 35	17 55	18 15	18 35	18 55	19 25	19 55	20 25
Heathrow Terminal 2 Bus	a																								
Heathrow Terminal 3 Bus	a	13 01	13 21	13 41	14 01	14 21	...	14 41	15 01	15 21	15 41	16 01	16 21	16 41	17 01	17 21	...	17 41	18 01	18 21	18 41	19 01	19 31	20 01	20 31

		GW		GW	GW	GW	GW
Reading 7	d	20 05	...	20 35	21 05	22 05	23 05
Heathrow Terminal 5 Bus	a	20 43		21 13	21 43	22 43	23 43
Heathrow Terminal 1 Bus	a	20 51	...	21 21	21 51	22 51	23 51
Heathrow Terminal 2 Bus	a						
Heathrow Terminal 3 Bus	a	20 56	...	21 26	21 56	22 56	23 56

Saturdays

		GW	GW	GW	GW	GW	GW	GW	GW	GW		GW	GW	GW	GW	GW	GW	GW	GW	GW		GW	GW	GW	GW
Reading 7	d	04 00	05 00	05 45	06 15	06 45	07 15	07 45	08 15	08 45	...	09 15	09 45	10 15	10 45	11 15	11 45	12 15	12 45	13 15	...	13 45	14 15	14 45	15 15
Heathrow Terminal 5 Bus	a	04 38	05 38	06 25	06 55	07 25	07 55	08 25	08 55	09 25		09 55	10 25	10 55	11 25	11 55	12 25	12 55	13 25	13 55		14 25	14 55	15 25	15 55
Heathrow Terminal 1 Bus	a	04 46	05 46	06 35	07 05	07 35	08 05	08 35	09 05	09 35	...	10 05	10 35	11 05	11 35	12 05	12 35	13 05	13 35	14 05	...	14 35	15 05	15 35	16 05
Heathrow Terminal 2 Bus	a																								
Heathrow Terminal 3 Bus	a	04 51	05 51	06 41	07 11	07 41	08 11	08 41	09 11	09 41	...	10 11	10 41	11 11	11 41	12 11	12 41	13 11	13 41	14 11	...	14 41	15 11	15 41	16 11

		GW	GW	GW	GW	GW		GW	GW	GW	GW	GW	GW	GW	GW
Reading 7	d	15 45	16 15	16 45	17 15	17 45	...	18 15	18 45	19 15	19 45	20 25	20 55	22 05	23 05
Heathrow Terminal 5 Bus	a	16 25	16 55	17 25	17 55	18 25		18 55	19 25	19 55	20 25	21 05	21 35	22 43	23 43
Heathrow Terminal 1 Bus	a	16 35	17 05	17 35	18 05	18 35	...	19 05	19 35	20 05	20 35	21 15	21 45	22 51	23 51
Heathrow Terminal 2 Bus	a														
Heathrow Terminal 3 Bus	a	16 41	17 11	17 41	18 11	18 41	...	19 11	19 41	20 11	20 41	21 21	21 51	22 56	23 56

Sundays

		GW	GW	GW	GW	GW	GW	GW	GW	GW		GW	GW	GW	GW	GW	GW	GW	GW	GW		GW	GW	GW	GW
Reading 7	d	04 00	05 00	05 45	06 15	06 45	07 15	07 45	08 15	08 45	...	09 15	09 45	10 15	10 45	11 15	11 45	12 15	12 45	13 15	...	13 45	14 15	14 45	15 15
Heathrow Terminal 5 Bus	a	04 38	05 38	06 25	06 55	07 25	07 55	08 25	08 55	09 25		09 55	10 25	10 55	11 25	11 55	12 25	12 55	13 25	13 55		14 25	14 55	15 25	15 55
Heathrow Terminal 1 Bus	a	04 46	05 46	06 35	07 05	07 35	08 05	08 35	09 05	09 35	...	10 05	10 35	11 05	11 35	12 05	12 35	13 05	13 35	14 05	...	14 35	15 05	15 35	16 05
Heathrow Terminal 2 Bus	a																								
Heathrow Terminal 3 Bus	a	04 51	05 51	06 41	07 11	07 41	08 11	08 41	09 11	09 41	...	10 11	10 41	11 11	11 41	12 11	12 41	13 11	13 41	14 11	...	14 41	15 11	15 41	16 11

		GW	GW	GW	GW	GW		GW	GW	GW	GW	GW	GW	GW	GW
Reading 7	d	15 45	16 15	16 45	17 15	17 45	...	18 15	18 45	19 15	19 45	20 25	20 55	22 05	23 05
Heathrow Terminal 5 Bus	a	16 25	16 55	17 25	17 55	18 25		18 55	19 25	19 55	20 25	21 05	21 35	22 43	23 43
Heathrow Terminal 1 Bus	a	16 35	17 05	17 35	18 05	18 35	...	19 05	19 35	20 05	20 35	21 15	21 45	22 51	23 51
Heathrow Terminal 2 Bus	a														
Heathrow Terminal 3 Bus	a	16 41	17 11	17 41	18 11	18 41	...	19 11	19 41	20 11	20 41	21 21	21 51	22 56	23 56

Heathrow - Reading Railair Link

Express Coach Service

		GW	GW	GW	GW	GW	GW	GW	GW	GW		GW	GW	GW	GW	GW	GW	GW	GW	GW		GW	GW	GW	GW
Heathrow Central Bus Stn	d	00 05	05 00	06 00	06 30	06 57	07 20	07 40	08 00	08 20	...	08 40	09 00	09 20	09 40	10 00	10 15	10 35	10 55	11 15	...	11 35	11 55	12 15	12 35
Heathrow Terminal 5 Bus	d	00 13	05 08	06 08	06 38	07 05	07 28	07 50	08 10	08 30		08 50	09 10	09 30	09 50	10 10	10 25	10 45	11 05	11 25		11 45	12 05	12 25	12 45
Reading 7	a	00 51	05 46	06 46	07 21	07 48	08 21	08 46	09 06	09 26	...	09 39	09 59	10 13	10 33	10 53	11 08	11 28	11 48	12 08	...	12 28	12 48	13 08	13 28

		GW	GW	GW	GW	GW		GW	GW	GW	GW	GW	GW	GW	GW	GW		GW	GW	GW	GW	GW	GW	GW	GW
Heathrow Central Bus Stn	d	12 55	13 15	13 35	13 55	14 15	...	14 35	14 55	15 15	15 35	15 55	16 15	16 35	16 55	17 15	...	17 35	17 55	18 15	18 35	18 55	19 15	19 40	20 10
Heathrow Terminal 5 Bus	d	13 05	13 25	13 45	14 05	14 25		14 45	15 05	15 25	15 45	16 05	16 25	16 45	17 05	17 25		17 45	18 05	18 25	18 45	19 05	19 25	19 50	20 20
Reading 7	a	13 48	14 08	14 28	14 48	15 08	...	15 28	15 48	16 08	16 28	16 48	17 14	17 34	17 54	18 14	...	18 34	18 54	19 14	19 34	19 54	20 14	20 31	21 01

		GW		GW	GW	GW	GW
Heathrow Central Bus Stn	d	20 40	...	21 10	21 40	22 15	23 05
Heathrow Terminal 5 Bus	d	20 50		21 20	21 50	22 23	23 13
Reading 7	a	21 31	...	22 01	22 31	23 01	23 51

Saturdays

		GW	GW	GW	GW	GW	GW	GW	GW	GW		GW	GW	GW	GW	GW	GW	GW	GW	GW		GW	GW	GW	GW
Heathrow Central Bus Stn	d	00 05	05 00	06 00	07 00	07 30	08 00	08 30	09 00	09 30	...	10 00	10 30	11 00	11 30	12 00	12 30	13 00	13 30	14 00	...	14 30	15 00	15 30	16 00
Heathrow Terminal 5 Bus	d	00 13	05 08	06 08	07 10	07 40	08 10	08 40	09 10	09 40		10 10	10 40	11 10	11 40	12 10	12 40	13 10	13 40	14 10		14 40	15 10	15 40	16 10
Reading 7	a	00 51	05 46	06 46	07 53	08 23	08 53	09 23	09 53	10 23	...	10 53	11 23	11 53	12 23	12 53	13 23	13 53	14 23	14 53	...	15 23	15 53	16 23	16 53

		GW	GW	GW	GW	GW		GW	GW	GW	GW	GW	GW	GW	GW
Heathrow Central Bus Stn	d	16 30	17 00	17 30	18 00	18 30	...	19 00	19 20	19 50	20 20	20 50	21 30	22 00	23 05
Heathrow Terminal 5 Bus	d	16 40	17 10	17 40	18 10	18 40		19 10	19 30	20 00	20 30	21 00	21 38	22 08	23 13
Reading 7	a	17 23	17 53	18 23	18 53	19 23	...	19 53	20 13	20 43	21 13	21 43	22 19	22 49	23 51

Sundays

		GW	GW	GW	GW	GW	GW	GW	GW	GW		GW	GW	GW	GW	GW	GW	GW	GW	GW		GW	GW	GW	GW
Heathrow Central Bus Stn	d	00 05	05 00	06 00	07 00	07 30	08 00	08 30	09 00	09 30	...	10 00	10 30	11 00	11 30	12 00	12 30	13 00	13 30	14 00	...	14 30	15 00	15 30	16 00
Heathrow Terminal 5 Bus	d	00 13	05 08	06 08	07 10	07 40	08 10	08 40	09 10	09 40		10 10	10 40	11 10	11 40	12 10	12 40	13 10	13 40	14 10		14 40	15 10	15 40	16 10
Reading 7	a	00 51	05 46	06 46	07 53	08 23	08 53	09 23	09 53	10 23	...	10 53	11 23	11 53	12 23	12 53	13 23	13 53	14 23	14 53	...	15 23	15 53	16 23	16 53

		GW	GW	GW	GW	GW		GW	GW	GW	GW	GW	GW	GW	GW
Heathrow Central Bus Stn	d	16 30	17 00	17 30	18 00	18 30	...	19 00	19 20	19 50	20 20	20 50	21 30	22 00	23 05
Heathrow Terminal 5 Bus	d	16 40	17 10	17 40	18 10	18 40		19 10	19 30	20 00	20 30	21 00	21 38	22 08	23 13
Reading 7	a	17 23	17 53	18 23	18 53	19 23	...	19 53	20 13	20 43	21 13	21 43	22 19	22 49	23 51

Table 125B

Bristol - Bristol International Airport

Bus Service

		GW A	GW	GW	GW	GW	GW	GW	GW	GW		GW	GW	GW	GW	GW	GW	GW	GW	GW		GW	GW	GW	GW
Bristol Temple Meads 10	d	23p52	00 12	02 42	03 57	04 52	05 12	05 32	05 52	06 12	...	06 22	06 32	06 42	06 52	07 02	07 12	07 22	07 32	07 46	...	07 56	08 06	08 16	08 26
Bristol Internatl Airport ✈	a	00 11	00 31	03 01	04 16	05 11	05 31	05 51	06 11	06 31		06 41	06 51	07 01	07 11	07 21	07 31	07 43	07 56	08 10		08 20	08 30	08 40	08 50

		GW	GW	GW	GW	GW		GW	GW	GW	GW	GW	GW	GW	GW	GW		GW	GW	GW	GW	GW	GW	GW	GW
Bristol Temple Meads 10	d	08 36	08 46	08 56	09 06	09 16	...	09 26	09 36	09 45	09 55	10 05	10 15	10 25	10 35	10 45	...	10 55	11 05	11 15	11 25	11 35	11 45	11 55	12 05
Bristol Internatl Airport ✈	a	09 00	09 10	09 20	09 30	09 40		09 49	09 58	10 07	10 17	10 27	10 37	10 47	10 57	11 07		11 17	11 27	11 37	11 47	11 57	12 07	12 17	12 27

		GW		GW	GW	GW	GW	GW	GW	GW	GW	GW		GW	GW	GW	GW	GW	GW	GW	GW	GW		GW	GW
Bristol Temple Meads 10	d	12 15	...	12 25	12 35	12 45	12 55	13 05	13 15	13 25	13 35	13 45	...	13 55	14 05	14 15	14 25	14 35	14 45	14 55	15 05	15 15	...	15 25	15 35
Bristol Internatl Airport ✈	a	12 37		12 47	12 57	13 07	13 17	13 27	13 37	13 47	13 57	14 07		14 17	14 27	14 37	14 47	14 57	15 07	15 17	15 27	15 37		15 49	16 01

		GW	GW	GW	GW	GW	GW	GW		GW	GW	GW	GW	GW	GW	GW	GW	GW		GW	GW	GW	GW	GW	GW
Bristol Temple Meads 10	d	15 48	15 58	16 08	16 18	16 28	16 38	16 48	...	16 58	17 08	17 18	17 28	17 38	17 48	17 58	18 08	18 15	...	18 25	18 35	18 45	18 55	19 05	19 15
Bristol Internatl Airport ✈	a	16 14	16 24	16 34	16 44	16 54	17 04	17 14		17 24	17 34	17 44	17 54	18 04	18 12	18 22	18 30	18 37		18 47	18 57	19 07	19 17	19 27	19 37

		GW	GW	GW		GW	GW	GW	GW	GW	GW	GW	GW	GW		GW	GW
Bristol Temple Meads 10	d	19 35	19 55	20 12	...	20 32	20 52	21 12	21 32	21 52	22 12	22 32	22 52	23 12	...	23 32	23 52
Bristol Internatl Airport ✈	a	19 57	20 17	20 31		20 51	21 11	21 31	21 51	22 11	22 31	22 51	23 11	23 31		23 51	00 11

Saturdays

		GW	GW	GW	GW	GW	GW	GW	GW	GW		GW	GW	GW	GW	GW	GW	GW	GW	GW		GW	GW	GW	GW
Bristol Temple Meads 10	d	23p52	00 12	02 42	03 57	04 52	05 12	05 32	05 52	06 12	...	06 22	06 32	06 42	06 52	07 02	07 12	07 22	07 32	07 43	...	07 53	08 03	08 13	08 23
Bristol Internatl Airport ✈	a	00 11	00 31	03 01	04 16	05 11	05 31	05 51	06 11	06 31		06 41	06 51	07 01	07 11	07 21	07 31	07 42	07 52	08 03		08 13	08 23	08 33	08 43

		GW	GW	GW	GW	GW		GW	GW	GW	GW	GW	GW	GW	GW	GW		GW	GW	GW	GW	GW	GW	GW	GW
Bristol Temple Meads 10	d	08 33	08 43	08 53	09 03	09 13	...	09 23	09 33	09 45	09 55	10 05	10 15	10 25	10 35	10 45	...	10 55	11 05	11 15	11 25	11 35	11 45	11 55	12 05
Bristol Internatl Airport ✈	a	08 53	09 03	09 13	09 23	09 33		09 43	09 55	10 07	10 17	10 27	10 37	10 47	10 57	11 07		11 17	11 27	11 37	11 47	11 57	12 07	12 17	12 27

		GW		GW	GW	GW	GW	GW	GW	GW	GW	GW		GW	GW	GW	GW	GW	GW	GW	GW	GW		GW	GW
Bristol Temple Meads 10	d	12 15	...	12 25	12 35	12 45	12 55	13 05	13 15	13 25	13 35	13 45	...	13 55	14 05	14 15	14 25	14 35	14 45	14 55	15 05	15 15	...	15 25	15 35
Bristol Internatl Airport ✈	a	12 37		12 47	12 57	13 07	13 17	13 27	13 37	13 47	13 57	14 07		14 17	14 27	14 37	14 47	14 57	15 07	15 17	15 27	15 37		15 47	15 56

		GW	GW	GW	GW	GW	GW	GW		GW	GW	GW	GW	GW	GW	GW	GW	GW		GW	GW	GW	GW	GW	GW
Bristol Temple Meads 10	d	15 46	15 56	16 16	16 36	16 56	17 16	17 36	...	17 56	18 15	18 35	18 55	19 15	19 35	19 55	20 12	20 32	...	20 52	21 12	21 32	21 52	22 12	22 32
Bristol Internatl Airport ✈	a	16 07	16 17	16 37	16 57	17 17	17 37	17 57		18 17	18 37	18 57	19 17	19 37	19 57	20 17	20 31	20 51		21 11	21 31	21 51	22 11	22 31	22 51

		GW	GW	GW		GW
Bristol Temple Meads 10	d	22 52	23 12	23 32	...	23 52
Bristol Internatl Airport ✈	a	23 11	23 31	23 51		00 11

Sundays

		GW	GW	GW	GW	GW	GW	GW	GW	GW		GW	GW	GW	GW	GW	GW	GW	GW	GW		GW	GW	GW	GW
Bristol Temple Meads 10	d	23p52	00 12	02 42	03 57	04 52	05 12	05 32	05 52	06 12	...	06 32	06 52	07 12	07 32	07 53	08 13	08 33	08 53	09 13	...	09 33	09 55	10 15	10 35
Bristol Internatl Airport ✈	a	00 11	00 31	03 01	04 16	05 11	05 31	05 51	06 11	06 31		06 51	07 11	07 31	07 51	08 12	08 32	08 52	09 12	09 32		09 54	10 16	10 36	10 56

		GW	GW	GW	GW	GW		GW	GW	GW	GW	GW	GW	GW	GW	GW		GW	GW	GW	GW	GW	GW	GW	GW
Bristol Temple Meads 10	d	10 55	11 15	11 25	11 35	11 45	...	11 55	12 05	12 15	12 25	12 35	12 45	12 55	13 05	13 15	...	13 25	13 35	13 45	13 55	14 05	14 15	14 25	14 35
Bristol Internatl Airport ✈	a	11 16	11 36	11 46	11 56	12 06		12 16	12 26	12 36	12 46	12 56	13 06	13 16	13 26	13 36		13 46	13 56	14 06	14 16	14 26	14 36	14 46	14 56

		GW		GW	GW	GW	GW	GW	GW	GW	GW	GW		GW	GW	GW	GW	GW	GW	GW	GW	GW		GW	GW
Bristol Temple Meads 10	d	14 45	...	14 55	15 05	15 15	15 25	15 35	15 45	15 55	16 15	16 35	...	16 55	17 15	17 35	17 55	18 15	18 35	18 55	19 15	19 35	...	19 55	20 12
Bristol Internatl Airport ✈	a	15 06		15 16	15 26	15 36	15 46	15 56	16 06	16 16	16 36	16 56		17 16	17 36	17 56	18 16	18 36	18 56	19 16	19 36	19 56		20 16	20 31

		GW	GW	GW	GW	GW	GW	GW		GW	GW	GW	GW
Bristol Temple Meads 10	d	20 32	20 52	21 12	21 32	21 52	22 12	22 32	...	22 52	23 12	23 32	23 52
Bristol Internatl Airport ✈	a	20 51	21 11	21 31	21 51	22 11	22 31	22 51		23 11	23 31	23 51	00 11

A not 14 May

Table 125B

Bristol International Airport - Bristol

Bus Service

		GW MX	GW MO A	GW	GW	GW	GW	GW	GW	GW		GW	GW	GW	GW	GW	GW	GW	GW	GW		GW	GW	GW	GW
Bristol Internatl Airport ✈	d	23p50	23p50	00 50	03 05	04 20	05 20	06 00	06 20	06 40	...	06 50	07 00	07 10	07 20	07 30	07 40	07 50	08 00	08 10	...	08 20	08 30	08 40	08 50
Bristol Temple Meads 10	a	00 14	00 16	01 14	03 28	04 43	05 43	06 23	06 43	07 03		07 13	07 23	07 33	07 48	08 02	08 12	08 22	08 32	08 42		08 52	09 02	09 12	09 22

		GW	GW	GW	GW	GW		GW	GW	GW	GW	GW	GW	GW	GW	GW		GW	GW	GW	GW	GW	GW	GW	GW
Bristol Internatl Airport ✈	d	09 00	09 10	09 20	09 30	09 40	...	09 50	10 00	10 10	10 20	10 30	10 40	10 50	11 00	11 10	...	11 20	11 30	11 40	11 50	12 00	12 10	12 20	12 30
Bristol Temple Meads 10	a	09 32	09 42	09 52	10 00	10 10		10 20	10 30	10 40	10 50	11 00	11 10	11 20	11 30	11 40		11 50	12 00	12 10	12 20	12 30	12 40	12 50	13 00

		GW		GW	GW	GW	GW	GW	GW	GW	GW	GW		GW	GW	GW	GW	GW	GW	GW	GW	GW		GW	GW
Bristol Internatl Airport ✈	d	12 40	...	12 50	13 00	13 10	13 20	13 30	13 40	13 50	14 00	14 10	...	14 20	14 30	14 40	14 50	15 00	15 10	15 20	15 30	15 40	...	15 50	16 00
Bristol Temple Meads 10	a	13 10		13 20	13 30	13 40	13 50	14 00	14 10	14 20	14 30	14 40		14 50	15 00	15 10	15 20	15 30	15 40	15 51	16 02	16 12		16 22	16 32

		GW	GW	GW	GW	GW	GW	GW		GW	GW	GW	GW	GW	GW	GW	GW	GW		GW	GW	GW	GW	GW	GW
Bristol Internatl Airport ✈	d	16 10	16 20	16 30	16 40	16 50	17 00	17 10	...	17 20	17 30	17 40	17 50	18 00	18 10	18 20	18 30	18 40	...	18 50	19 00	19 10	19 20	19 30	19 50
Bristol Temple Meads 10	a	16 42	16 52	17 02	17 12	17 22	17 32	17 42		17 52	18 02	18 12	18 21	18 30	18 40	18 50	19 00	19 10		19 20	19 30	19 40	19 50	20 00	20 16

		GW	GW	GW		GW	GW	GW	GW	GW	GW	GW	GW	GW
Bristol Internatl Airport ✈	d	20 10	20 30	20 50	...	21 10	21 30	21 50	22 10	22 30	22 50	23 10	23 30	23 50
Bristol Temple Meads 10	a	20 34	20 54	21 14		21 34	21 54	22 14	22 34	22 54	23 14	23 34	23 54	00 14

Saturdays

		GW	GW	GW	GW	GW	GW	GW	GW	GW		GW	GW	GW	GW	GW	GW	GW	GW	GW		GW	GW	GW	GW
Bristol Internatl Airport ✈	d	23p50	00 50	03 05	04 20	05 20	05 40	06 00	06 20	06 40	...	06 50	07 00	07 10	07 20	07 30	07 40	07 50	08 00	08 10	...	08 20	08 30	08 40	08 50
Bristol Temple Meads 10	a	00 14	01 14	03 28	04 43	05 43	06 04	06 24	06 44	07 04		07 14	07 24	07 34	07 45	07 56	08 06	08 16	08 26	08 36		08 46	08 56	09 06	09 16

		GW	GW	GW	GW	GW		GW	GW	GW	GW	GW	GW	GW	GW	GW		GW	GW	GW	GW	GW	GW	GW	GW
Bristol Internatl Airport ✈	d	09 00	09 10	09 20	09 30	09 40	...	09 50	10 00	10 10	10 20	10 30	10 40	10 50	11 00	11 10	...	11 20	11 30	11 40	11 50	12 00	12 10	12 20	12 30
Bristol Temple Meads 10	a	09 26	09 36	09 48	09 59	10 09		10 19	10 29	10 39	10 49	10 59	11 09	11 19	11 29	11 39		11 49	11 59	12 09	12 19	12 29	12 39	12 49	12 59

		GW		GW	GW	GW	GW	GW	GW	GW	GW	GW		GW	GW	GW	GW	GW	GW	GW	GW	GW		GW	GW
Bristol Internatl Airport ✈	d	12 40	...	12 50	13 00	13 10	13 20	13 30	13 40	13 50	14 00	14 10	...	14 20	14 30	14 40	14 50	15 00	15 10	15 20	15 30	15 40	...	15 50	16 00
Bristol Temple Meads 10	a	13 09		13 19	13 29	13 39	13 49	13 59	14 09	14 19	14 29	14 39		14 49	14 59	15 09	15 19	15 29	15 39	15 50	16 00	16 10		16 20	16 30

		GW	GW	GW	GW	GW	GW	GW		GW	GW	GW	GW	GW	GW	GW	GW	GW		GW	GW	GW	GW	GW	GW
Bristol Internatl Airport ✈	d	16 10	16 20	16 30	16 50	17 10	17 30	17 50	...	18 10	18 30	18 50	19 10	19 30	19 50	20 10	20 30	20 50	...	21 10	21 30	21 50	22 10	22 30	22 50
Bristol Temple Meads 10	a	16 40	16 50	17 00	17 20	17 40	18 00	18 19		18 39	18 59	19 19	19 39	19 59	20 17	20 36	20 56	21 16		21 36	21 56	22 16	22 36	22 56	23 16

		GW	GW	GW
Bristol Internatl Airport ✈	d	23 10	23 30	23 50
Bristol Temple Meads 10	a	23 36	23 56	00 16

Sundays

		GW	GW	GW	GW	GW	GW	GW	GW	GW		GW	GW	GW	GW	GW	GW	GW	GW	GW		GW	GW	GW	GW
Bristol Internatl Airport ✈	d	23p50	00 50	03 05	04 20	05 20	05 50	06 10	06 30	06 50	...	07 10	07 30	07 50	08 10	08 30	08 50	09 10	09 30	09 50	...	10 10	10 30	10 50	11 10
Bristol Temple Meads 10	a	00 16	01 16	03 29	04 44	05 44	06 14	06 34	06 54	07 14		07 34	07 55	08 15	08 35	08 55	09 15	09 35	09 57	10 17		10 37	10 57	11 17	11 37

		GW	GW	GW	GW	GW		GW	GW	GW	GW	GW	GW	GW	GW	GW		GW	GW	GW	GW	GW	GW	GW	GW
Bristol Internatl Airport ✈	d	11 20	11 30	11 40	11 50	12 00	...	12 10	12 20	12 30	12 40	12 50	13 00	13 10	13 20	13 30	...	13 40	13 50	14 00	14 10	14 20	14 30	14 40	14 50
Bristol Temple Meads 10	a	11 47	11 57	12 07	12 17	12 27		12 37	12 47	12 57	13 07	13 17	13 27	13 37	13 47	13 57		14 07	14 17	14 27	14 37	14 47	14 57	15 07	15 17

		GW		GW	GW	GW	GW	GW	GW	GW	GW	GW		GW	GW	GW	GW	GW	GW	GW	GW	GW		GW	GW
Bristol Internatl Airport ✈	d	15 00	...	15 10	15 20	15 30	15 40	15 50	16 00	16 10	16 20	16 30	...	16 50	17 10	17 30	17 50	18 10	18 30	18 50	19 10	19 30	...	19 50	20 10
Bristol Temple Meads 10	a	15 27		15 37	15 49	16 00	16 10	16 20	16 30	16 40	16 50	17 00		17 20	17 40	18 00	18 18	18 37	18 57	19 17	19 37	19 57		20 16	20 36

		GW	GW	GW	GW	GW	GW	GW		GW	GW	GW	GW
Bristol Internatl Airport ✈	d	20 30	20 50	21 10	21 30	21 50	22 10	22 30	...	22 50	23 10	23 30	23 50
Bristol Temple Meads 10	a	20 56	21 16	21 36	21 56	22 16	22 36	22 56		23 16	23 36	23 56	00 16

A from 21 May

London and Oxford - Worcester and Hereford

Mondays to Fridays

Network Diagram - see first Page of Table 116

Miles			GW MX ◇1 ☐	GW MO ◇1 A	GW MO ◇1 B	GW 1	GW ◇1 C ═	GW 1 C ═	GW 1	GW ◇1 ☐	GW ◇1 ═
0	**London Paddington** [15] ⊖	d	21p48	21p42	21p42		05 48	06 48		08 22	09 21
18½	Slough [3]	d	22p03	21p59	22p06		06 05	07 04		08 36	09 36
36	Reading [7]	d	22p22	22p22	22p22		06 22	07 22		08 52	09 52
53¼	Didcot Parkway	d		22p38	22p40		06 39	07 49			
63½	**Oxford**	d	22p52	22p51	22p51		06 56	08 04	08 58	09 21	10 25
70½	Hanborough	d	23p03	23p04	23p05		07 06	08 14	09 07	09 32	10 35
71½	Combe	d									
75	Finstock	d									
76¾	Charlbury	a	23p10	23p11	23p12		07 13	08 21	09 14	09 39	10 42
—		d	23p11	23p12	23p13		07 13	08 21	09 14	09 40	10 42
80½	Ascott-under-Wychwood	d									
81¾	Shipton	d	23p18								
84¾	Kingham	d	23p24	23p21	23p22		07 22	08 30	09 23	09 49	10 51
91¾	Moreton-in-Marsh	a	23p31	23p29	23p30		07 30	08 38	09 35	09 57	10 59
—		d	23p32	23p32	23p32	05 46	07 30	08 38		09 58	10 59
101¾	Honeybourne	d	23p44	23p43	23p43		07 41	08 49		10 09	
106¾	Evesham	a	23p50	23p50	23p50	06 00	07 48	08 56		10 17	11 14
—		d	23p52	23p52	23p52	06 00	07 51	08 56		10 24	11 14
112¾	Pershore	d	23p59	00 01	00 01	06 08	07 58	09 03		10 32	11 21
120½	**Worcester Shrub Hill** [7]	a	00 12	00 12	00 12	06 19	08 10	09 15		10 44	11 34
121¼	**Worcester Foregate Street** [7]	a				06 39	08 17	09 18		10 48	11 40
128	Malvern Link	a						09 27		11 02	
128¾	Great Malvern	a						09 32		11 06	
131¾	Colwall	a								11 14	
136	Ledbury	a								11 22	
149¾	**Hereford** [7]	a								11 42	

		GW ◇1	GW ◇1 ☐	GW ◇1 ═	GW ◇1 D ═	GW ◇1 E ═	GW ◇1 ═	GW ◇1 F ═	GW ◇1 ☐	GW 1 E	GW ◇1 ☐	GW ◇1 ☐	GW ◇1 G ☐
London Paddington [15] ⊖	d	09 50	10 22	11 20	12 21	12 21	13 21	14 21	15 51		17 22	17 50	18 22
Slough [3]	d	10 06	10 36	11 36	12 36	12 36	13 36	14 36	16 06				
Reading [7]	d	10 22	10 52	11 52	12 52	12 52	13 52	14 52	16 22		17 50	18 22	18 50
Didcot Parkway	d												
Oxford	d	10 48	11 19	12 19	13 21	13 21	14 19	15 19	16 49	17 32	18 17	18 49	19 22
Hanborough	d	10 57	11 30	12 29	13 31	13 30	14 29	15 29	16 59	17 41	18 27		19 33
Combe	d									17 43			
Finstock	d									17 48			
Charlbury	a	11 04	11 37	12 36	13 38	13 38	14 36	15 36	17 07	17 52	18 34	19 02	19 40
	d	11 04	11 38	12 36	13 38	13 38	14 36	15 36	17 08	17 52	18 35	19 03	19 41
Ascott-under-Wychwood	d									17 57			
Shipton	d									18 00		19 11	
Kingham	d	11 13	11 47	12 45	13 47	13 47	14 45	15 45	17 18	18 05	18 45	19 18	19 51
Moreton-in-Marsh	a	11 22	11 55	12 53	13 55	13 55	14 54	15 53	17 26	18 13	18 53	19 26	19 59
	d		11 56	12 53	13 55	13 55		15 53	17 27	18 13	18 54	19 27	20 00
Honeybourne	d		12 07	13 04	14 06	14 06		16 04	17 39	18 24	19 06		20 12
Evesham	a		12 15	13 11	14 12	14 12		16 11	17 46	18 31	19 13	19 43	20 19
	d		12 24	13 11	14 26	14 26		16 20	17 47	18 40	19 14	19 44	20 20
Pershore	d		12 32	13 18	14 33	14 33		16 27	17 56	18 48	19 22	19 52	20 28
Worcester Shrub Hill [7]	a		12 44	13 31	14 46	14 46		16 39	18 08	18 59	19 34	20 03	20 41
Worcester Foregate Street [7]	a		12 48	13 35	14 51	14 51		16 43		19 11	19 38		20 45
Malvern Link	a		12 58	13 50	15 05	15 05				19 20	19 48		20 54
Great Malvern	a		13 02	13 56	15 09	15 09				19 24	19 52		20 58
Colwall	a		13 16								19 58		21 04
Ledbury	a		13 24								20 06		21 12
Hereford [7]	a		13 48								20 27		21 33

		GW FX ◇1 ☐	GW FO ◇1 ☐	GW ◇1 F ═	GW FO ◇1 H ═	GW FX ◇1 ☐	GW FO ◇1 I ═	GW FO ◇1 J ═
London Paddington [15] ⊖	d	19 22	19 22	20 20	21 48	21 48	21 48	21 48
Slough [3]	d	19 36	19 36	20 36	22 03	22 03	22 03	22 03
Reading [7]	d	19 52	19 52	20 52	22 22	22 22	22 22	22 22
Didcot Parkway	d							
Oxford	d	20 19	20 24	21 21	22 52	22 52	22 52	22 52
Hanborough	d	20 30	20 35	21 31	23 03	23 03	23 03	23 03
Combe	d							
Finstock	d							
Charlbury	a	20 37	20 42	21 38	23 10	23 10	23 10	23 10
	d	20 38	20 43	21 39	23 11	23 11	23 11	23 11
Ascott-under-Wychwood	d							
Shipton	d				23 18	23 18	23 18	23 18
Kingham	d	20 47	20 52	21 48	23 24	23 24	23 24	23 24
Moreton-in-Marsh	a	20 55	21 00	21 56	23 31	23 31	23 31	23 33
	d	20 56	21 01	21 57	23 32	23 32	23 32	23 35
Honeybourne	d	21 07	21 12	22 08	23 44	23 44	23 44	23 46
Evesham	a	21 15	21 19	22 16	23 50	23 50	23 50	23 55
	d	21 19	21 19	22 16	23 52	23 52	23 52	23 56
Pershore	d	21 27	21 27	22 24	23 59	23 59	23 59	00 05
Worcester Shrub Hill [7]	a	21 46	21 46	22 40	00 12	00 12	00 13	00 18
Worcester Foregate Street [7]	a	21 50	21 50	22 44				
Malvern Link	a	22 02	22 02	22 53				
Great Malvern	a	22 06	22 06	22 59				
Colwall	a	22 25	22 25					
Ledbury	a	22 33	22 33					
Hereford [7]	a	22 54	22 54					

A from 2 July until 10 September
B from 21 May until 25 June, from 17 September
C ═ from Oxford
D from 17 September
E until 14 September
F ═ to Oxford
G The Cathedrals Express
H 29 June, from 7 September. ═ to Oxford
I until 22 June. ═ to Oxford
J from 6 July until 31 August

London and Oxford - Worcester and Hereford

Saturdays

Network Diagram - see first Page of Table 116

		GW ◇1 A ═	GW ◇1 B ═	GW ◇1 C ═	GW ◇1	GW ◇1 D ═	GW ◇1 D ═	GW ◇1 ☐	GW ◇1 ☐	GW ◇1 ═
London Paddington [15] ⊖	d	21p48	21p48	21p48	05 21	06 21	07 21	08 21	10 21	11 21
Slough [3]	d	22p03	22p03	22p03	05 38	06 38	07 38	08 39	10 39	11 39
Reading [7]	d	22p22	22p22	22p22	05 54	06 54	07 53	08 54	10 54	11 54
Didcot Parkway	d				06 08					
Oxford	d	22p52	22p52	22p52	06 23	07 23	08 23	09 23	11 23	12 23
Hanborough	d	23p03	23p03	23p03	06 34	07 32	08 32	09 34	11 33	12 33
Combe	d									
Finstock	d									
Charlbury	a	23p10	23p10	23p10	06 41	07 39	08 39	09 41	11 40	12 40
	d	23p11	23p11	23p11	06 42	07 39	08 39	09 42	11 41	12 40
Ascott-under-Wychwood	d									
Shipton	d	23p18	23p18	23p18						
Kingham	d	23p24	23p24	23p24	06 51	07 48	08 48	09 51	11 50	12 49
Moreton-in-Marsh	a	23p31	23p31	23p33	07 00	07 56	08 56	10 00	11 59	12 58
	d	23p32	23p32	23p35	07 00	07 56	08 56	10 00	11 59	12 58
Honeybourne	d	23p44	23p44	23p46	07 12	08 07	09 07	10 12	12 11	13 09
Evesham	a	23p50	23p50	23p55	07 20	08 15	09 15	10 20	12 19	13 17
	d	23p52	23p52	23p56	07 25	08 21	09 21	10 25	12 20	13 21
Pershore	d	23p59	23p59	00 05	07 32	08 28	09 28	10 32	12 27	13 28
Worcester Shrub Hill [7]	a	00 12	00 13	00 18	07 44	08 40	09 40	10 44	12 39	13 40
Worcester Foregate Street [7]	a				07 48	08 44	09 44	10 48	12 47	13 44
Malvern Link	a				07 58	08 54	09 54	10 58	12 57	13 54
Great Malvern	a				08 03	09 00	10 00	11 05	13 02	14 00
Colwall	a							11 12	13 13	
Ledbury	a							11 20	13 21	
Hereford [7]	a							11 41	13 40	

		GW ◇1 ═	GW ◇1 ═	GW ◇1 E ═	GW ◇1 ☐	GW ◇1 ☐	GW ◇1 ☐	GW ◇1 E ═	GW ◇1 F	GW ◇1 G
London Paddington [15] ⊖	d	13 21	14 21	15 21	16 21	17 21	18 21	19 50	21 50	21 50
Slough [3]	d	13 39	14 39	15 39	16 39	17 39	18 39	20 06	22 06	22 06
Reading [7]	d	13 54	14 54	15 54	16 54	17 54	18 54	20 22	22 22	22 23
Didcot Parkway	d								22 37	22 38
Oxford	d	14 23	15 23	16 23	17 23	18 23	19 23	20 49	22 50	22 50
Hanborough	d	14 32	15 32	16 32	17 33	18 33	19 33	20 58	23 00	23 00
Combe	d									
Finstock	d									
Charlbury	a	14 39	15 39	16 39	17 40	18 40	19 40	21 05	23 07	23 07
	d	14 39	15 39	16 39	17 41	18 41	19 41	21 05	23 07	23 07
Ascott-under-Wychwood	d									
Shipton	d	14 46			17 48			21 12	23 14	23 14
Kingham	d	14 51	15 48	16 48	17 54	18 50	19 50	21 17	23 19	23 19
Moreton-in-Marsh	a	14 59	15 57	16 57	18 03	18 59	19 59	21 25	23 27	23 27
	d	14 59	15 57	16 57	18 03	18 59	19 59	21 25	23 27	23 27
Honeybourne	d	15 10	16 08	17 08	18 15	19 11	20 11	21 36	23 38	23 38
Evesham	a	15 18	16 16	17 16	18 23	19 19	20 19	21 43	23 45	23 45
	d	15 21	16 21	17 21	18 24	19 21	20 23	21 43	23 45	23 45
Pershore	d	15 28	16 28	17 28	18 31	19 28	20 30	21 50	23 53	23 53
Worcester Shrub Hill [7]	a	15 40	16 40	17 40	18 43	19 40	20 42	22 02	00 07	00 07
Worcester Foregate Street [7]	a	15 44	16 44	17 44	18 55	19 44	20 48	22 06		
Malvern Link	a	15 54	16 55	17 54	19 05		20 58	22 16		
Great Malvern	a	16 00	17 00	18 00	19 09		21 02	22 22		
Colwall	a				19 15		21 08			
Ledbury	a				19 23		21 16			
Hereford [7]	a				19 45		21 34			

Sundays
until 24 June

		GW ◇1	GW ◇1	GW ◇1 ☐	GW ◇1 ☐	GW ◇1 ☐	GW ◇1 ☐	GW ◇1	GW ◇1	GW ◇1	GW ◇1 ☐	GW ◇1	GW ◇1 ☐	GW ◇1
London Paddington [15] ⊖	d	21p50	08 03	09 35	10 42	12 42	13 42	14 42	15 42	16 42	17 42	18 42	19 42	21 42
Slough [3]	d	22p06	08 25	09 59	11 06	13 07	14 06	15 03	16 05	17 04	18 04	19 07	20 06	22 06
Reading [7]	d	22p23	08 44	10 12	11 21	13 21	14 21	15 21	16 21	17 25	18 24	19 28	20 21	22 22
Didcot Parkway	d	22p38	09 00	10 28	11 37	13 38	14 37	15 36	16 39	17 39	18 39	19 44	20 37	22 40
Oxford	d	22p50	09 18	10 45	11 51	13 51	14 51	15 51	16 51	17 55	18 51	19 59	20 51	22 51
Hanborough	d	23p00	09 27	10 58	12 01	14 01		16 00		18 06	19 04	20 09	21 02	23 05
Combe	d													
Finstock	d													
Charlbury	a	23p07	09 34	11 05	12 09	14 09	15 04	16 08	17 08	18 13	19 11	20 16	21 09	23 12
	d	23p07	09 35	11 06	12 09	14 09	15 06	16 09	17 09	18 13	19 12	20 17	21 10	23 13
Ascott-under-Wychwood	d													
Shipton	d	23p14												
Kingham	d	23p19	09 44	11 16	12 19	14 19	15 15	16 19	17 18	18 22	19 21	20 26	21 19	23 22
Moreton-in-Marsh	a	23p27	09 52	11 24	12 27	14 26	15 25	16 27	17 25	18 30	19 28	20 34	21 27	23 30
	d	23p27	09 52	11 25	12 28	14 28	15 25	16 28	17 25	18 31	19 29	20 34	21 29	23 32
Honeybourne	d	23p38	10 03	11 36	12 39		15 38	16 39		18 42	19 40	20 45	21 41	23 43
Evesham	a	23p45	10 12	11 44	12 47	14 48	15 47	16 48	17 42	18 48	19 48	20 53	21 48	23 50
	d	23p45	10 12	11 46	12 48	14 48	15 47	16 48	17 48	18 51	19 51	20 53	21 48	23 52
Pershore	d	23p53	10 20	11 54	12 56	14 56	15 56	16 57	17 56	18 58	19 59	21 03	21 57	00 01
Worcester Shrub Hill [7]	a	00 07	10 31	12 05	13 09	15 09	16 08	17 09	18 08	19 10	20 12	21 13	22 10	00 12
Worcester Foregate Street [7]	a		10 34	12 09	13 12	15 12		17 12	18 10	19 13	20 16		22 13	
Malvern Link	a		10 46	12 19	13 22	15 22		17 22		19 23	20 24		22 23	
Great Malvern	a		10 50	12 22	13 26	15 26		17 26		19 27	20 29		22 27	
Colwall	a			12 28	13 32	15 32		17 32			20 37			
Ledbury	a			12 36	13 41	15 41		17 41			20 45			
Hereford [7]	a			12 54	14 06	16 05		17 58			21 03			

A 30 June, from 8 September. ═ to Oxford
B until 23 June. ═ to Oxford
C from 7 July until 1 September
D ═ from Oxford
E ═ to Oxford
F from 27 October
G until 20 October

Table 126

London and Oxford - Worcester and Hereford

Sundays

1 July to 9 September

Network Diagram - see first Page of Table 116

		GW	GW	GW	GW	GW	GW	GW	GW	GW	GW	GW	GW	GW
		◇■	◇■	◇■	◇■	◇■	◇■	◇■	◇■	◇■	◇■	◇■	◇■	◇■
				🛒	🛒	🛒	🛒				🛒		🛒	
London Paddington ■ ⊖	d	21p50	08 03	09 42	10 42	12 42	13 42	14 42	15 42	16 42	17 42	18 42	19 42	21 42
Slough ■	d	22p06	08 21	09 59	11 00	13 01	14 00	15 00	16 00	17 00	17 58	19 02	20 00	21 59
Reading ■	d	22p23	08 44	10 11	11 21	13 21	14 21	15 21	16 21	17 22	18 21	19 22	20 21	22 22
Didcot Parkway	d	22p38	09 02	10 28	11 37	13 37	14 37	15 36	16 37	17 37	18 36	19 38	20 37	22 38
Oxford	d	22p50	09 18	10 45	11 51	13 50	14 50	15 54	16 54	17 54	18 53	19 56	20 51	22 51
Hanborough	d	23p00	09 28	10 58	12 02	14 02		16 00		18 03	19 04	20 06	21 02	23 04
Combe	d													
Finstock	d													
Charlbury	a	23p07	09 35	11 05	12 09	14 09	15 04	16 08	17 04	18 10	19 11	20 13	21 09	23 11
	d	23p07	09 35	11 06	12 10	14 10	15 05	16 09	17 05	18 11	19 12	20 14	21 10	23 12
Ascott-under-Wychwood	d													
Shipton	d	23p14												
Kingham	d	23p19	09 44	11 16	12 19	14 19	15 15	16 19	17 13	18 20	19 21	20 23	21 18	23 21
Moreton-in-Marsh	a	23p27	09 52	11 24	12 27	14 26	15 25	16 27	17 23	18 28	19 28	20 31	21 26	23 29
	d	23p27	09 53	11 25	12 28	14 28	15 25	16 28	17 24	18 28	19 29	20 31	21 29	23 32
Honeybourne	d	23p38	10 04	11 36	12 39		15 38	16 40		18 39	19 40	20 42	21 40	23 43
Evesham	a	23p45	10 10	11 44	12 47	14 48	15 47	16 48	17 41	18 46	19 48	20 50	21 48	23 50
	d	23p45	10 13	11 46	12 48	14 48	15 47	16 48	17 48	18 50	19 51	20 50	21 48	23 52
Pershore	d	23p53	10 20	11 54	12 56	14 56	15 56	16 57	17 56	18 58	19 59	21 00	21 57	00 01
Worcester Shrub Hill ■	a	00 07	10 32	12 05	13 09	15 09	16 08	17 09	18 08	19 10	20 12	21 10	22 10	00 12
Worcester Foregate Street ■	a		10 35	12 09	13 12	15 12		17 12	18 10	19 13	20 16		22 13	
Malvern Link	a		10 47	12 19	13 22	15 22		17 22		19 23	20 24		22 23	
Great Malvern	a		10 50	12 22	13 26	15 26		17 26		19 26	20 29		22 27	
Colwall	a			12 28	13 32	15 32		17 32			20 37			
Ledbury	a			12 36	13 41	15 41		17 41			20 45			
Hereford ■	a			12 54	14 06	16 05		17 58			21 03			

Sundays

16 September to 21 October

		GW	GW	GW	GW	GW	GW	GW	GW	GW	GW	GW	GW	GW
		◇■	◇■	◇■	◇■	◇■	◇■	◇■	◇■	◇■	◇■	◇■	◇■	◇■
				🛒	🛒	🛒	🛒				🛒		🛒	
London Paddington ■ ⊖	d	21p50	08 03	09 35	10 42	12 42	13 42	14 42	15 42	16 42	17 42	18 42	19 42	21 42
Slough ■	d	22p06	08 25	09 59	11 06	13 07	14 06	15 05	16 05	17 04	18 04	19 07	20 04	22 06
Reading ■	d	22p23	08 44	10 12	11 21	13 21	14 21	15 21	16 21	17 25	18 24	19 28	20 21	22 22
Didcot Parkway	d	22p38	09 00	10 28	11 37	13 38	14 37	15 36	16 39	17 39	18 39	19 44	20 37	22 40
Oxford	d	22p50	09 18	10 45	11 51	13 51	14 51	15 51	16 51	17 55	18 51	19 59	20 51	22 51
Hanborough	d	23p00	09 27	10 58	12 01	14 01		16 00		18 06	19 04	20 09	21 02	23 05
Combe	d													
Finstock	d													
Charlbury	a	23p07	09 34	11 05	12 09	14 09	15 04	16 08	17 08	18 13	19 11	20 16	21 09	23 12
	d	23p07	09 35	11 06	12 09	14 09	15 06	16 09	17 09	18 13	19 12	20 17	21 10	23 13
Ascott-under-Wychwood	d													
Shipton	d	23p14												
Kingham	d	23p19	09 44	11 16	12 19	14 19	15 15	16 19	17 18	18 22	19 21	20 26	21 19	23 22
Moreton-in-Marsh	a	23p27	09 52	11 24	12 27	14 26	15 25	16 27	17 25	18 30	19 28	20 34	21 27	23 30
	d	23p27	09 52	11 25	12 28	14 28	15 25	16 28	17 25	18 31	19 29	20 34	21 29	23 32
Honeybourne	d	23p38	10 03	11 36	12 39		15 38	16 39		18 42	19 40	20 45	21 41	23 43
Evesham	a	23p45	10 12	11 44	12 47	14 48	15 47	16 48	17 42	18 48	19 48	20 53	21 48	23 50
	d	23p45	10 12	11 46	12 48	14 48	15 47	16 48	17 48	18 51	19 51	20 53	21 48	23 52
Pershore	d	23p53	10 20	11 54	12 56	14 56	15 56	16 57	17 56	18 58	19 59	21 03	21 57	00 01
Worcester Shrub Hill ■	a	00 07	10 31	12 05	13 09	15 09	16 08	17 09	18 08	19 10	20 12	21 13	22 10	00 12
Worcester Foregate Street ■	a		10 34	12 09	13 12	15 12		17 12	18 10	19 13	20 16		22 13	
Malvern Link	a		10 46	12 19	13 22	15 22		17 22		19 23	20 24		22 23	
Great Malvern	a		10 50	12 22	13 26	15 26		17 26		19 27	20 29		22 27	
Colwall	a			12 28	13 32	15 32		17 32			20 37			
Ledbury	a			12 36	13 41	15 41		17 41			20 45			
Hereford ■	a			12 54	14 06	16 05		17 58			21 03			

Sundays

from 28 October

		GW	GW	GW	GW	GW	GW	GW	GW	GW	GW	GW	GW	GW
		◇■	◇■	◇■	◇■	◇■	◇■	◇■	◇■	◇■	◇■	◇■	◇■	◇■
				🛒	🛒	🛒	🛒				🛒		🛒	
London Paddington ■ ⊖	d	21p50	08 03	09 35	10 42	12 42	13 42	14 42	15 42	16 42	17 42	18 42	19 42	21 42
Slough ■	d	22p06	08 25	09 59	11 06	13 07	14 06	15 05	16 05	17 04	18 04	19 07	20 04	22 06
Reading ■	d	22p22	08 44	10 12	11 21	13 21	14 21	15 21	16 21	17 25	18 24	19 28	20 21	22 22
Didcot Parkway	d	22p37	09 00	10 28	11 37	13 38	14 37	15 36	16 39	17 39	18 39	19 44	20 37	22 40
Oxford	d	22p50	09 18	10 45	11 51	13 51	14 51	15 51	16 51	17 55	18 51	19 59	20 51	22 51
Hanborough	d	23p00	09 27	10 58	12 01	14 01		16 00		18 06	19 04	20 09	21 02	23 05
Combe	d													
Finstock	d													
Charlbury	a	23p07	09 34	11 05	12 09	14 09	15 04	16 08	17 08	18 13	19 11	20 16	21 09	23 12
	d	23p07	09 35	11 06	12 09	14 09	15 06	16 09	17 09	18 13	19 12	20 17	21 10	23 13
Ascott-under-Wychwood	d													
Shipton	d	23p14												
Kingham	d	23p19	09 44	11 16	12 19	14 19	15 15	16 19	17 18	18 22	19 21	20 26	21 19	23 22
Moreton-in-Marsh	a	23p27	09 52	11 24	12 27	14 26	15 25	16 27	17 25	18 30	19 28	20 34	21 27	23 30
	d	23p27	09 52	11 25	12 28	14 28	15 25	16 28	17 25	18 31	19 29	20 34	21 29	23 32
Honeybourne	d	23p38	10 03	11 36	12 39		15 38	16 39		18 42	19 40	20 45	21 41	23 43
Evesham	a	23p45	10 12	11 44	12 47	14 48	15 47	16 48	17 42	18 48	19 48	20 53	21 48	23 50
	d	23p45	10 12	11 46	12 48	14 48	15 47	16 48	17 48	18 51	19 51	20 53	21 48	23 52
Pershore	d	23p53	10 20	11 54	12 56	14 56	15 56	16 57	17 56	18 58	19 59	21 03	21 57	00 01
Worcester Shrub Hill ■	a	00 07	10 31	12 05	13 09	15 09	16 08	17 09	18 08	19 10	20 12	21 13	22 10	00 12
Worcester Foregate Street ■	a		10 34	12 09	13 12	15 12		17 12	18 10	19 13	20 16		22 13	
Malvern Link	a		10 46	12 19	13 22	15 22		17 22		19 23	20 24		22 23	
Great Malvern	a		10 50	12 22	13 26	15 26		17 26		19 27	20 29		22 27	
Colwall	a			12 28	13 32	15 32		17 32			20 37			
Ledbury	a			12 36	13 41	15 41		17 41			20 45			
Hereford ■	a			12 54	14 06	16 05		17 58			21 03			

Table 126

Mondays to Fridays

Hereford and Worcester - Oxford and London

Network Diagram - see first Page of Table 116

Miles			GW MO	GW MO	GW MO	GW MX	GW	GW	GW	GW	GW	GW	GW	GW	GW	GW	GW	GW	GW	GW	GW	GW	GW
			◇■	◇■	◇■	◇■	◇■	◇■	◇■	◇■	◇■	■	◇■	◇■	◇■	◇■	◇■	◇■	◇■	◇■	◇■	■	■
			A	B	C					D	E		F									G	H
							🛒	🛒	🍴	🛒⊘	🛒⊘		🛒⊘	🍴		🍴	🍴	🍴	🛒	🍴			
0	**Hereford** ■	d				21p51				05 35	05 35		06 44						13 14				
13¾	Ledbury	d				22p09				05 52	05 52		07 01						13 31				
18	Colwall	d				22p17				05 59	05 59		07 08						13 39				
20¾	Great Malvern	d				22p22		05 18		06 04	06 04		07 15			09 54			13 44	14 26		15 22	15 22
21¾	Malvern Link	d						05 21		06 08	06 08		07 19			09 56			13 49	14 28		|	|
28½	**Worcester Foregate Street** ■	d				22p34		05 32		06 19	06 19	06 53	07 30	08 26		10 05		12 06	13 59	14 38		15 34	15 34
29¾	**Worcester Shrub Hill** ■	d	21p28	21p34	21p34	22p43	05 11	05 37		06 30	06 33	06 56	07 34	08 39		10 08		12 08	14 09	14 41		15 42	15 42
37	Pershore	d	21p38	21p44	21p44	22p52		05 46		06 38	06 41	07 05	07 43	08 48		10 17		12 17	14 18	14 50		15 51	15 51
43	Evesham	a	21p46	21p48	21p48	23p00	05 24	05 54		06 46	06 49	07 13	07 51	08 56		10 25		12 25	14 26	14 58		15 59	15 59
—		d	21p49	21p49	21p49	23p01	05 29	05 54		06 51	06 51	07 13	07 52	09 04		10 31		12 31	14 30	15 06		15 59	15 59
48	Honeybourne	d	21p57	21p57	21p57	23p08	05 36			06 58	06 58		07 59	09 11		10 37		12 38	14 37	15 12		|	|
58	Moreton-in-Marsh	a	22p09	22p09	22p09	23p19	05 47	06 09		07 09	07 09	07 28	08 11	09 23		10 49		12 50	14 48	15 24		16 14	16 14
—		d	22p10	22p10	22p10	23p27	05 48	06 10		07 10	07 10	07 28	08 12	09 23	09 51	10 49	11 51	12 50	14 49	15 24	15 53	16 14	16 14
65	Kingham	d	22p19	22p19	22p19	23p36	05 56	06 18		07 19	07 19	07 36	08 21	09 31	09 58	10 57	11 58	12 58	14 57	15 32	16 00	16 22	16 22
68	Shipton	d	|	|	|					|	|	07 41										|	|
69¾	Ascott-under-Wychwood	d	|	|	|					|	|	07 43										|	|
73	Charlbury	a	22p29	22p29	22p29	23p45	06 05	06 27		07 28	07 28	07 49	08 30	09 40	10 07	11 06	12 07	13 06	15 06	15 41	16 08	16 31	16 31
—		d	22p29	22p29	22p29	23p45	06 06	06 28	07 15	07 30	07 30	07 49	08 31	09 40	10 07	11 06	12 07	13 06	15 07	15 41	16 09	16 31	16 31
74¾	Finstock	d	|	|	|					|	|	07 53										|	|
78¾	Combe	d	|	|	|					|	|	07 58										|	|
79¾	Hanborough	d	22p37	22p37	22p37		06 14	06 36	07 23	07 39	07 39	08 01	08 39	09 47	10 15	11 14	12 15	13 14	15 15	15 49	16 17	|	|
86¾	**Oxford**	a	22p46	22p46	22p46	23p58	06 24	06 46	07 32	07 47	07 49	08 12	08 49	09 58	10 25	11 28	12 29	13 25	15 25	15 59	16 27	16 46	16 49
96¾	Didcot Parkway	a	22p58	22p58	22p58	00 20	06 39	07 07		|	|												
113¾	Reading ■	a	23p17	23p15	23p17	00 38	06 54	07 25	07 57	08 21	08 21		09 14	10 25	10 54	11 54	12 54	13 54	15 54	16 24	16 54		
131¾	Slough ■	a	23p43	23p42	23p43	00 55				|	|			10 39	11 09	12 09	13 09	14 09	16 09	16 39	17 09		
149¾	**London Paddington** ■ ⊖	a	00 06	00 02	00 05	01 17	07 30	07 59	08 31	08 51	08 51		09 47	11 00	11 29	12 29	13 29	14 29	16 27	17 00	17 34		

		GW	GW	GW	GW	GW FO	GW FX	GW
		◇■	◇■	◇■	◇■	◇■	◇■	◇■
					G			
		🛒	🍴	🛒				
Hereford ■	d	15 14						21 51
Ledbury	d	15 31						22 09
Colwall	d	15 38						22 17
Great Malvern	d	15 44			19 44			22 22
Malvern Link	d	15 48			19 46			
Worcester Foregate Street ■	d	15 59	17 28	18 49	19 54	20 59	20 59	22 34
Worcester Shrub Hill ■	d	16 03	17 31	18 55	20 03	21 03	21 03	22 43
Pershore	d	16 13	17 40	19 04	20 12	21 12	21 12	22 52
Evesham	a	16 21	17 48	19 12	20 20	21 20	21 20	23 00
	d	16 21	17 48	19 12	20 20	21 21	21 21	23 01
Honeybourne	d	16 28	17 54	19 20	20 27	21 28	21 28	23 08
Moreton-in-Marsh	a	16 40	18 06	19 31	20 39	21 39	21 39	23 19
	d	16 40	18 06	19 48	20 48	21 40	21 40	23 27
Kingham	d	16 49	18 14	19 56	20 56	21 48	21 48	23 36
Shipton	d	16 55			|			
Ascott-under-Wychwood	d				|			
Charlbury	a	17 01	18 23	20 05	21 05	21 57	21 57	23 45
	d	17 11	18 37	20 06	21 05	22 07	22 07	23 45
Finstock	d				|			
Combe	d				|			
Hanborough	d	17 19	18 44	20 14	21 12	22 15	22 15	
Oxford	a	17 29	19 02	20 24	21 27	22 27	22 27	23 58
Didcot Parkway	a				|			00 20
Reading ■	a	17 54	19 32	20 54	21 55	22 58	22 58	00 38
Slough ■	a	18 10	19 47	21 09	22 13	23 12	23 15	00 55
London Paddington ■ ⊖	a	18 28	20 06	21 29	22 39	23 36	23 36	01 17

A from 17 September until 22 October
B from 2 July until 10 September
C from 21 May until 25 June, MO from 29 October
D from 17 September. 🛒 from Reading ⊘ to Reading
E until 14 September. 🛒 from Reading ⊘ to Reading
F The Cathedrals Express. 🛒 from Reading ⊘ to Reading
G until 14 September
H from 17 September

Table 126

Hereford and Worcester - Oxford and London

Network Diagram - see first Page of Table 116

Saturdays

		GW	GW	GW	GW	GW	GW	GW	GW	GW	GW	GW	GW	GW	GW	GW	GW	GW	GW
		◇1	◇1	◇1	◇1	◇1	◇1	◇1	◇1	◇1	◇1	◇1	◇1	◇1	◇1	◇1	◇1	◇1	1
					A										B	C	D	E	
			☕	☕	☕⊘	☕	🛒	🛒	☕	🛒	🛒	☕	🛒	🛒					
Hereford 7	d	21p51		06 17	07 10				12 13			15 13						20 20	20 20	
Ledbury	d	22p09		06 34	07 30				12 31			15 31						20 40	20 40	
Colwall	d	22p17		06 41	07 37				12 38			15 38						20 47	20 47	
Great Malvern	d	22p22	05 56	06 49	07 43	08 43	09 51	10 58	12 44	14 34		15 44	16 34	17 49	18 35			20 53	20 53	22 41
Malvern Link	d		05 59	06 53	07 46	08 47	09 54	11 01	12 48	14 37		15 48	16 37	17 52	18 38			20 57	20 57	22 44
Worcester Foregate Street 7	d	22p34	06 09	07 04	07 59	08 58	10 04	11 11	12 59	14 57		15 59	16 55	18 02	18 48	20 02	20 02	21 11	21 11	22 53
Worcester Shrub Hill 7	d	22p43	06 12	07 08	08 04	09 02	10 08	11 15	13 04	15 01		16 04	17 02	18 06	19 02	20 06	20 06	21 15	21 15	22 57
Pershore	d	22p52	06 21	07 17	08 13	09 11	10 16	11 23	13 13	15 09		16 12	17 10	18 15	19 10	20 15	20 15	21 24	21 24	23 06
Evesham	a	23p00	06 29	07 25	08 21	09 19	10 25	11 32	13 21	15 18		16 21	17 19	18 23	19 19	20 23	20 23	21 32	21 32	23 15
	d	23p01	06 30	07 26	08 26	09 32	10 32	11 32	13 30	15 26		16 22	17 26	18 27	19 27	20 24	20 24	21 33	21 33	
Honeybourne	d	23p08	06 36	07 33	08 33	09 39	10 38	11 38	13 37	15 32		16 28	17 32	18 33	19 33	20 31	20 31	21 39	21 39	
Moreton-in-Marsh	a	23p19	06 48	07 45	08 45	09 51	10 50	11 51	13 49	15 45		16 40	17 45	18 46	19 46	20 43	20 43	21 51	21 51	
	d	23p27	06 48	07 45	08 45	09 51	10 50	11 51	13 49	15 45		16 41	17 45	18 46	19 46	20 43	20 43	21 51	21 51	
Kingham	d	23p36	06 56	07 54	08 54	10 00	10 58	11 59	13 58	15 53		16 49	17 53	18 54	19 54	20 52	20 52	22 00	22 00	
Shipton	d			07 59	08 59							16 55						22 05	22 05	
Ascott-under-Wychwood	d																			
Charlbury	a	23p45	07 06	08 06	09 06	10 09	11 08	12 08	14 07	16 02		17 02	18 02	19 03	20 03	21 01	21 01	22 12	22 12	
	d	23p45	07 06	08 07	09 07	10 10	11 08	12 08	14 08	16 02		17 02	18 02	19 03	20 03	21 06	21 06	22 12	22 12	
Finstock	d																			
Combe	d																			
Hanborough	d		07 13	08 15	09 15	10 18	11 15	12 16	14 16	16 10		17 10	18 10	19 11	20 11	21 14	21 14	22 20	22 20	
Oxford	a	23p58	07 24	08 26	09 25	10 29	11 26	12 28	14 26	16 21		17 21	18 21	19 21	20 21	21 25	21 25	22 34	22 34	
Didcot Parkway	a	00 20														21 43	21 43	22 47	22 47	
Reading 7	a	00 38	07 54	08 54	09 54	10 54	11 54	12 53	14 53	16 55		17 55	18 55	19 55	20 54	21 59	21 59	23 04	23 08	
Slough 3	a	00 55	08 09	09 09	10 09	11 09	12 09	13 09	15 10	17 10		18 10	19 10	20 10	21 09	22 11	22 15	23 23	23 26	
London Paddington 15 ⊖	a	01 17	08 29	09 29	10 29	11 29	12 29	13 30	15 29	17 29		18 29	19 29	20 29	21 29	22 34	22 33	23 43	23 46	

Sundays

until 24 June

		GW	GW	GW	GW	GW	GW	GW	GW	GW		GW	GW
		◇1	◇1	◇1	◇1	◇1	◇1	◇1	◇1	◇1		◇1	◇1
					☕	☕	☕	☕					
Hereford 7	d				13 32	14 32		16 35		18 30			
Ledbury	d				13 50	14 55		16 52		18 48			
Colwall	d				13 57	15 02		17 00		18 55			
Great Malvern	d	09 20	11 15	13 15	14 11	15 08		17 05		19 11		20 15	
Malvern Link	d	09 23	11 18	13 18	14 15	15 12		17 09		19 14		20 18	
Worcester Foregate Street 7	d	09 31	11 27	13 26	14 26	15 23		17 22	18 25	19 29		20 26	
Worcester Shrub Hill 7	d	09 35	11 30	13 30	14 30	15 27	16 27	17 27	18 27	19 32		20 30	21 34
Pershore	d	09 44	11 39	13 39	14 40	15 36	16 36	17 36	18 36	19 42		20 39	21 44
Evesham	a	09 52	11 48	13 47	14 48	15 45	16 45	17 45	18 45	19 49		20 48	21 48
	d	09 52	11 49	13 49	14 49	15 49	16 49	17 49	18 49	19 49		20 49	21 49
Honeybourne	d	09 58	11 56	13 56		15 57	16 57	17 57	18 57	19 57		20 55	21 57
Moreton-in-Marsh	a	10 10	12 06	14 08	15 06	16 09	17 09	18 09	19 09	20 09		21 09	22 09
	d	10 10	12 08	14 08	15 08	16 10	17 10	18 10	19 10	20 10		21 10	22 10
Kingham	d	10 18	12 16	14 16	15 16	16 19	17 19	18 19	19 19	20 19		21 19	22 19
Shipton	d												
Ascott-under-Wychwood	d												
Charlbury	a	10 28	12 25	14 25	15 25	16 29	17 29	18 29	19 29	20 29		21 29	22 29
	d	10 29	12 25	14 25	15 25	16 29	17 29	18 29	19 29	20 29		21 29	22 29
Finstock	d												
Combe	d												
Hanborough	d	10 36	12 33	14 32	15 34	16 37	17 37		19 37	20 37		21 37	22 37
Oxford	a	10 51	12 47	14 47	15 49	16 49	17 49	18 49	19 49	20 48		21 49	22 46
Didcot Parkway	a	11 07	13 02	15 03	16 02	17 02	18 02	19 02	20 04	21 00		22 01	22 58
Reading 7	a	11 23	13 23	15 25	16 22	17 27	18 27	19 27	20 24	21 24		22 20	23 17
Slough 3	a	11 37	13 41	15 41	16 36	17 43	18 41	19 44	20 43	21 44		22 40	23 43
London Paddington 15 ⊖	a	12 01	14 05	16 03	17 04	18 13	19 07	20 07	21 05	22 07		23 01	00 05

A ☕ from Reading ⊘ to Reading
B until 8 September
C from 15 September
D from 30 June until 8 September
E until 23 June, from 15 September

Table 126

Hereford and Worcester - Oxford and London

Network Diagram - see first Page of Table 116

Sundays

1 July to 9 September

		GW	GW	GW	GW	GW	GW	GW	GW	GW		GW	GW
		◇1	◇1	◇1	◇1	◇1	◇1	◇1	◇1	◇1		◇1	◇1
					☕	☕	☕	☕					
Hereford 7	d				13 32	14 32		16 35		18 30			
Ledbury	d				13 50	14 55		16 52		18 48			
Colwall	d				13 57	15 02		17 00		18 55			
Great Malvern	d	09 20	11 15	13 15	14 11	15 08		17 05		19 11		20 15	
Malvern Link	d	09 23	11 18	13 18	14 15	15 12		17 09		19 14		20 18	
Worcester Foregate Street 7	d	09 31	11 27	13 26	14 26	15 23		17 22	18 25	19 29		20 26	
Worcester Shrub Hill 7	d	09 35	11 30	13 30	14 30	15 27	16 27	17 27	18 27	19 32		20 30	21 34
Pershore	d	09 44	11 39	13 39	14 40	15 36	16 36	17 36	18 36	19 42		20 39	21 44
Evesham	a	09 52	11 48	13 47	14 48	15 45	16 45	17 45	18 45	19 49		20 48	21 48
	d	09 52	11 49	13 49	14 49	15 49	16 49	17 49	18 49	19 49		20 49	21 49
Honeybourne	d	09 58	11 56	13 54		15 57	16 55	17 57	18 57	19 57		20 55	21 57
Moreton-in-Marsh	a	10 10	12 06	14 08	15 06	16 09	17 09	18 09	19 09	20 09		21 09	22 09
	d	10 10	12 08	14 08	15 08	16 10	17 10	18 10	19 10	20 10		21 10	22 10
Kingham	d	10 18	12 16	14 16	15 16	16 19	17 19	18 19	19 19	20 19		21 19	22 19
Shipton	d												
Ascott-under-Wychwood	d												
Charlbury	a	10 28	12 25	14 24	15 26	16 29	17 29	18 29	19 28	20 29		21 27	22 29
	d	10 29	12 25	14 24	15 26	16 29	17 29	18 29	19 28	20 29		21 27	22 29
Finstock	d												
Combe	d												
Hanborough	d	10 36	12 33	14 32	15 34	16 37	17 37		19 37	20 37		21 36	22 37
Oxford	a	10 51	12 47	14 48	15 49	16 49	17 47	18 49	19 48	20 48		21 48	22 46
Didcot Parkway	a	11 07	13 02	15 04	16 02	17 02	18 02	19 03	20 04	21 00		22 00	22 58
Reading 7	a	11 22	13 20	15 21	16 20	17 21	18 20	19 20	20 23	21 17		22 20	23 15
Slough 3	a	11 38	13 36	15 36	16 33	17 38	18 35	19 38	20 42	21 38		22 41	23 42
London Paddington 15 ⊖	a	12 00	13 56	15 55	16 51	17 59	18 53	19 56	21 02	21 59		23 00	00 02

Sundays

16 September to 21 October

		GW	GW	GW	GW	GW	GW	GW	GW	GW		GW	GW
		◇1	◇1	◇1	◇1	◇1	◇1	◇1	◇1	◇1		◇1	◇1
					☕	☕	☕	☕					
Hereford 7	d				13 32	14 32		16 35		18 30			
Ledbury	d				13 50	14 55		16 52		18 48			
Colwall	d				13 57	15 02		17 00		18 55			
Great Malvern	d	09 20	11 15	13 15	14 11	15 08		17 05		19 11		20 15	
Malvern Link	d	09 23	11 18	13 18	14 15	15 12		17 09		19 14		20 18	
Worcester Foregate Street 7	d	09 31	11 27	13 26	14 26	15 23		17 22	18 25	19 29		20 26	
Worcester Shrub Hill 7	d	09 35	11 30	13 30	14 30	15 27	16 27	17 27	18 27	19 32		20 30	21 28
Pershore	d	09 44	11 39	13 39	14 40	15 36	16 36	17 36	18 36	19 42		20 39	21 38
Evesham	a	09 52	11 48	13 47	14 48	15 45	16 45	17 45	18 45	19 49		20 48	21 46
	d	09 52	11 49	13 49	14 49	15 49	16 49	17 49	18 49	19 49		20 49	21 49
Honeybourne	d	09 58	11 56	13 56		15 57	16 57	17 57	18 57	19 57		20 57	21 57
Moreton-in-Marsh	a	10 10	12 06	14 06	15 06	16 09	17 09	18 09	19 09	20 09		21 09	22 09
	d	10 10	12 08	14 08	15 08	16 10	17 10	18 10	19 10	20 10		21 10	22 10
Kingham	d	10 18	12 16	14 16	15 16	16 19	17 19	18 19	19 19	20 19		21 19	22 19
Shipton	d												
Ascott-under-Wychwood	d												
Charlbury	a	10 28	12 25	14 25	15 25	16 29	17 29	18 29	19 29	20 29		21 29	22 29
	d	10 29	12 25	14 25	15 25	16 29	17 29	18 29	19 29	20 29		21 29	22 29
Finstock	d												
Combe	d												
Hanborough	d	10 36	12 33	14 33	15 34	16 37	17 37		19 37	20 37		21 37	22 37
Oxford	a	10 51	12 47	14 47	15 49	16 49	17 49	18 49	19 49	20 48		21 49	22 46
Didcot Parkway	a	11 07	13 02	15 03	16 02	17 02	18 02	19 02	20 04	21 00		22 00	22 58
Reading 7	a	11 25	13 23	15 25	16 22	17 27	18 27	19 27	20 24	21 24		22 21	23 17
Slough 3	a	11 42	13 41	15 41	16 36	17 43	18 41	19 44	20 43	21 44		22 43	23 43
London Paddington 15 ⊖	a	12 06	14 03	16 03	17 07	18 07	19 07	20 07	21 05	22 07		23 13	00 06

Sundays

from 28 October

		GW	GW	GW	GW	GW	GW	GW	GW	GW		GW	GW
		◇1	◇1	◇1	◇1	◇1	◇1	◇1	◇1	◇1		◇1	◇1
					☕	☕	☕	☕					
Hereford 7	d				13 32	14 32		16 35		18 30			
Ledbury	d				13 50	14 55		16 52		18 48			
Colwall	d				13 57	15 02		17 00		18 55			
Great Malvern	d	09 20	11 15	13 15	14 11	15 08		17 05		19 11		20 15	
Malvern Link	d	09 23	11 18	13 18	14 15	15 12		17 09		19 14		20 18	
Worcester Foregate Street 7	d	09 31	11 27	13 26	14 26	15 23		17 22	18 25	19 29		20 26	
Worcester Shrub Hill 7	d	09 35	11 30	13 30	14 30	15 27	16 27	17 27	18 27	19 32		20 30	21 34
Pershore	d	09 44	11 39	13 39	14 40	15 36	16 36	17 36	18 36	19 42		20 39	21 44
Evesham	a	09 52	11 48	13 47	14 48	15 45	16 45	17 45	18 45	19 49		20 48	21 48
	d	09 52	11 49	13 49	14 49	15 49	16 49	17 49	18 49	19 49		20 49	21 49
Honeybourne	d	09 58	11 56	13 56		15 57	16 57	17 57	18 57	19 57		20 57	21 57
Moreton-in-Marsh	a	10 10	12 06	14 06	15 06	16 09	17 09	18 09	19 09	20 09		21 09	22 09
	d	10 10	12 08	14 08	15 08	16 10	17 10	18 10	19 10	20 10		21 10	22 10
Kingham	d	10 18	12 16	14 16	15 16	16 19	17 19	18 19	19 19	20 19		21 19	22 19
Shipton	d												
Ascott-under-Wychwood	d												
Charlbury	a	10 28	12 25	14 25	15 25	16 29	17 29	18 29	19 29	20 29		21 29	22 29
	d	10 29	12 25	14 25	15 25	16 29	17 29	18 29	19 29	20 29		21 29	22 29
Finstock	d												
Combe	d												
Hanborough	d	10 36	12 33	14 33	15 34	16 37	17 37		19 37	20 37		21 37	22 37
Oxford	a	10 51	12 47	14 47	15 49	16 49	17 49	18 49	19 49	20 48		21 49	22 46
Didcot Parkway	a	11 07	13 02	15 03	16 02	17 02	18 02	19 02	20 04	21 00		22 00	22 58
Reading 7	a	11 25	13 23	15 21	16 22	17 27	18 27	19 27	20 24	21 24		22 24	23 17
Slough 3	a	11 42	13 37	15 36	16 36	17 43	18 41	19 44	20 43	21 44		22 43	23 43
London Paddington 15 ⊖	a	12 06	14 00	15 59	17 00	18 07	19 07	20 07	21 05	22 07		23 13	00 05

Table 126A

Mondays to Fridays

Kingham - Chipping Norton
Bus Service

		GW BHX A	GW BHX	GW BHX	GW BHX B	GW BHX A	GW BHX	GW BHX A	GW BHX	GW BHX	GW B	GW BHX	GW BHX A	GW BHX	GW BHX	GW B	GW BHX	GW BHX	GW B	GW BHX	GW BHX A	GW BHX B	GW BHX B
Kingham	d	06 30	07 00	07 30	08 30	08 35	09 55	10 55	11 55	12 55	13 23	13 55	14 55	15 50	16 40	17 17	17 20	18 10	18 22	18 50	19 20	19 25	19 50
Chipping Norton West St.	a	06 43	07 13	07 43	08 43	08 48	10 08	11 08	12 08	13 08	13 35	14 08	15 08	16 03	16 53	17 29	17 33	18 23	18 34	19 03	19x33	19 38	20 03

		GW BHX A
Kingham	d	19 52
Chipping Norton West St.	a	20x05

Saturdays

		GW	GW	GW	GW	GW	GW	GW	GW	GW	GW	GW	GW	GW
Kingham	d	08 15	08 55	09 55	10 55	11 55	12 55	13 55	14 55	15 50	16 50	17 55	18 50	19 50
Chipping Norton West St.	a	08 28	09 08	10 08	11 08	12 08	13 08	14 08	15 08	16 03	17 03	18 08	19 03	20x03

Sundays

		GW	GW	GW
Kingham	d	13 23	17 17	18 22
Chipping Norton West St.	a	13 35	17 29	18 34

Table 126A

Mondays to Fridays

Chipping Norton - Kingham
Bus Service

		GW BHX A	GW BHX B	GW BHX A	GW BHX A	GW BHX A	GW B	GW BHX	GW BHX	GW BHX	GW BHX	GW BHX	GW B	GW BHX	GW BHX A	GW BHX B	GW BHX	GW BHX	GW BHX	GW B	GW BHX	GW BHX A	GW BHX B
Chipping Norton West St.	d	06 00	06 07	06 45	07 15	08 00	09 25	09 30	10 35	11 35	12 35	13 35	1339	14 35	15 30	15 30	16 20	16 55	17 45	18 03	18 25	19 05	19 10
Kingham	a	06 12	06 19	06 58	07 28	08 14	09 37	09 44	10 50	11 50	12 50	13 50	1351	14 50	15 44	15 45	16 35	17 10	18 00	18 15	18 40	19 20	19 25

Saturdays

		GW	GW	GW	GW	GW	GW	GW	GW	GW	GW	GW	GW	GW
Chipping Norton West St.	d	08 00	08 30	09 30	10 35	11 35	12 35	13 35	14 35	15 30	16 30	17 30	18 25	19 10
Kingham	a	08 14	08 44	09 44	10 50	11 50	12 50	13 50	14 50	15 44	16 45	17 45	18 40	19 25

Sundays

		GW	GW	GW
Chipping Norton West St.	d	09 25	13 39	18 03
Kingham	a	09 37	13 51	18 15

Route Diagram for Tables 127, 128

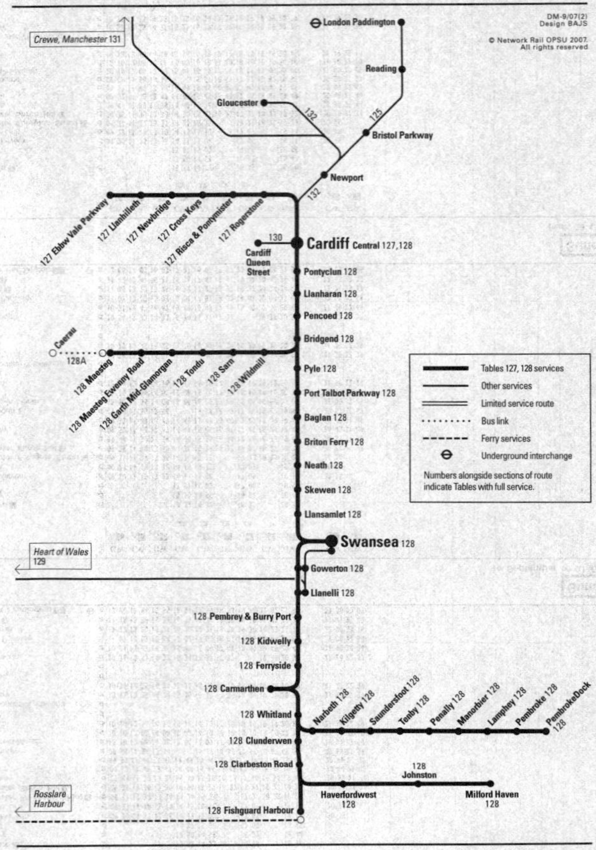

Table 127

Mondays to Fridays

Cardiff Central - Ebbw Vale Parkway

Route Diagram - see first Page of Table 127

Miles			AW MX	AW A	AW	AW	AW	AW	AW	AW	AW	AW	AW	AW	AW	AW	AW	AW	AW	AW	AW FX	AW FO	AW B	AW C
0	Cardiff Central 7	d	23p05	23p53	06 35	07 35	08 35	09 35	10 35	11 35	12 35	13 35	14 35	15 35	16 35	17 35	18 35	19 35	20 35	21 35	23 05	23 05	23 53	23 53
14	Rogerstone	d	23p27	00 16	06 57	07 57	08 57	09 57	10 57	11 57	12 57	13 57	14 57	15 57	16 57	17 57	18 57	19 57	20 57	21 57	23 27	23 29	00 14	00 16
15¼	Risca & Pontymister	d	23p30	00 22	07 00	08 00	09 00	10 00	11 00	12 00	13 00	14 00	15 00	16 00	17 00	18 00	19 00	20 00	21 00	22 00	23 30	23 32	00 20	00 22
17¼	Cross Keys	d	23p36	00 26	07 06	08 06	09 06	10 06	11 06	12 06	13 06	14 06	15 06	16 06	17 06	18 06	19 06	20 06	21 06	22 06	23 36	23 38	00 24	00 26
20¾	Newbridge (Ebbw Vale)	d	23p44	00 34	07 14	08 14	09 14	10 14	11 14	12 14	13 14	14 14	15 14	16 14	17 14	18 14	19 14	20 14	21 14	22 14	23 44	23 46	00 32	00 34
23½	Llanhilleth	d	23p50	00 41	07 20	08 20	09 20	10 20	11 20	12 20	13 20	14 20	15 20	16 20	17 20	18 20	19 20	20 20	21 20	22 20	23 50	23 52	00 39	00 41
28¾	**Ebbw Vale Parkway**	a	00 02	00 52	07 31	08 31	09 31	10 31	11 31	12 31	13 31	14 31	15 31	16 31	17 31	18 31	19 31	20 34	21 31	22 31	00 02	00 05	00 50	00 52

Saturdays

		AW	AW D	AW	AW	AW	AW	AW	AW	AW	AW	AW	AW	AW	AW	AW	AW	AW	AW	AW	AW E
Cardiff Central 7	d	23p05	23p53	06 35	07 39	08 35	09 35	10 35	11 35	12 35	13 35	14 35	15 35	16 35	17 35	18 35	19 35	20 35	21 35	23 05	23 35
Rogerstone	d	23p29	00 14	06 57	08 00	08 57	09 57	10 57	11 57	12 57	13 57	14 57	15 57	16 57	17 57	18 57	19 57	20 57	21 57	23 27	23 56
Risca & Pontymister	d	23p32	00 20	07 00	08 04	09 00	10 00	11 00	12 00	13 00	14 00	15 00	16 00	17 00	18 00	19 00	20 00	21 00	22 00	23 30	00 02
Cross Keys	d	23p38	00 24	07 06	08 09	09 06	10 06	11 06	12 06	13 06	14 06	15 06	16 06	17 06	18 06	19 06	20 06	21 06	22 06	23 36	00 06
Newbridge (Ebbw Vale)	d	23p46	00 32	07 14	08 17	09 14	10 14	11 14	12 14	13 14	14 14	15 14	16 14	17 14	18 14	19 14	20 14	21 14	22 14	23 44	00 14
Llanhilleth	d	23p52	00 39	07 20	08 23	09 20	10 20	11 20	12 20	13 20	14 20	15 20	16 20	17 20	18 20	19 20	20 20	21 20	22 20	23 50	00 21
Ebbw Vale Parkway	a	00 05	00 50	07 31	08 35	09 31	10 31	11 31	12 31	13 31	14 31	15 31	16 31	17 31	18 31	19 31	20 34	21 31	22 31	00 02	00 32

Sundays

		AW	AW F	AW	AW	AW	AW	AW	AW	AW
Cardiff Central 7	d	23p05	23p35	07 40	09 24	11 30	13 30	15 32	17 30	19 30
Rogerstone	d	23p27	23p56	08 03	09 45	11 51	13 51	15 53	17 51	19 51
Risca & Pontymister	d	23p30	00 02	08 07	09 49	11 55	13 55	15 57	17 55	19 55
Cross Keys	d	23p36	00 06	08 13	09 55	12 01	14 01	16 03	18 01	20 01
Newbridge (Ebbw Vale)	d	23p44	00 14	08 21	10 03	12 09	14 09	16 11	18 09	20 09
Llanhilleth	d	23p50	00 21	08 28	10 10	12 16	14 16	16 18	18 16	20 16
Ebbw Vale Parkway	a	00 02	00 32	08 39	10 21	12 27	14 27	16 29	18 27	20 27

A 26 July, 27 July, 2 August
B 10 August
C 25 July, 26 July, 1 August
D 11 August
E 4 August
F 5 August

Table 127

Mondays to Fridays

Ebbw Vale Parkway - Cardiff Central

Route Diagram - see first Page of Table 127

Miles			AW	AW	AW	AW	AW	AW	AW	AW	AW	AW	AW	AW	AW	AW	AW	AW FX	AW FO	AW
0	**Ebbw Vale Parkway**	d	06 40	07 40	08 40	09 40	10 40	11 40	12 40	13 40	14 40	15 40	16 40	17 40	18 40	19 40	20 40	21 40	21 40	22 40
5¼	Llanhilleth	d	06 48	07 48	08 48	09 48	10 48	11 48	12 48	13 48	14 48	15 48	16 48	17 48	18 48	19 48	20 48	21 48	21 48	22 48
8	Newbridge (Ebbw Vale)	d	06 54	07 54	08 54	09 54	10 54	11 54	12 54	13 54	14 54	15 54	16 54	17 54	18 54	19 54	20 54	21 54	21 54	22 54
11½	Cross Keys	d	07 02	08 02	09 02	10 02	11 02	12 02	13 02	14 02	15 02	16 02	17 02	18 02	19 02	20 02	21 02	22 02	22 02	23 02
13½	Risca & Pontymister	d	07 07	08 07	09 07	10 07	11 07	12 07	13 07	14 07	15 07	16 07	17 07	18 07	19 07	20 07	21 07	22 07	22 07	23 07
14¾	Rogerstone	d	07 11	08 11	09 11	10 11	11 11	12 11	13 11	14 11	15 11	16 11	17 11	18 11	19 11	20 11	21 11	22 11	22 11	23 11
28¾	**Cardiff Central 7**	a	07 37	08 37	09 37	10 37	11 37	12 37	13 37	14 37	15 37	16 37	17 37	18 37	19 39	20 39	21 38	22 40	22 41	23 37

Saturdays

		AW	AW	AW	AW	AW	AW	AW	AW	AW	AW	AW	AW	AW	AW	AW	AW	AW
Ebbw Vale Parkway	d	06 40	07 40	08 40	09 40	10 40	11 40	12 40	13 40	14 40	15 40	16 40	17 40	18 40	19 40	20 40	21 40	22 40
Llanhilleth	d	06 48	07 48	08 48	09 48	10 48	11 48	12 48	13 48	14 48	15 48	16 48	17 48	18 48	19 48	20 48	21 48	22 48
Newbridge (Ebbw Vale)	d	06 54	07 54	08 54	09 54	10 54	11 54	12 54	13 54	14 54	15 54	16 54	17 54	18 54	19 54	20 54	21 54	22 54
Cross Keys	d	07 02	08 02	09 02	10 02	11 02	12 02	13 02	14 02	15 02	16 02	17 02	18 02	19 02	20 02	21 02	22 02	23 02
Risca & Pontymister	d	07 07	08 07	09 07	10 07	11 07	12 07	13 07	14 07	15 07	16 07	17 07	18 07	19 07	20 07	21 07	22 07	23 07
Rogerstone	d	07 11	08 11	09 11	10 11	11 11	12 11	13 11	14 11	15 11	16 11	17 11	18 11	19 11	20 11	21 11	22 11	23 11
Cardiff Central 7	a	07 37	08 37	09 37	10 37	11 37	12 37	13 37	14 37	15 37	16 37	17 36	18 37	19 37	20 37	21 37	22 41	23 37

Sundays

		AW	AW	AW	AW	AW	AW	AW
Ebbw Vale Parkway	d	08 40	10 27	12 27	14 30	16 30	18 30	20 40
Llanhilleth	d	08 48	10 35	12 35	14 38	16 38	18 38	20 48
Newbridge (Ebbw Vale)	d	08 54	10 41	12 41	14 44	16 44	18 44	20 54
Cross Keys	d	09 02	10 49	12 49	14 52	16 52	18 52	21 02
Risca & Pontymister	d	09 07	10 54	12 54	14 57	16 57	18 57	21 07
Rogerstone	d	09 11	10 58	12 58	15 01	17 01	19 01	21 11
Cardiff Central 7	a	09 37	11 24	13 24	15 23	17 25	19 23	21 37

Table 128

Mondays to Fridays

until 22 June

Cardiff - Maesteg, Swansea and West Wales

Route Diagram - see first Page of Table 127

Miles	Miles			AW MX	AW MO	AW MX	AW MO	AW MX	GW MX	GW	GW MX	AW	AW	AW	AW	AW	AW	AW	AW	AW	AW	AW	AW
					◇ A	◇	◇ A		◇1	◇1 A	◇1		◇							◇		◇	
—	—	London Paddington 15 ⊖	d						21p15	21p37	22p45												
—	—	Reading 7	d						21p41	22p12	23p19												
—	—	Manchester Piccadilly 10	d																				
—	—	Gloucester 7	d																				05 50
—	—	Bristol Parkway 7	d						22p45	23p12	00 23												
—	—	Newport (South Wales)	d						23p19	23p42	00 52											06 17	06 44
0	—	**Cardiff Central 7**	d	21p04	22p30			23p15	23p43	00 04	01 13								05 39	05 51		06 42	07 03
11	—	Pontyclun	d					23p29											05 51				07 15
14	—	Llanharan	d					23p34											05 56				07 20
16¼	—	Pencoed	d					23p39											06 01				07 24
20¼	0	Bridgend	d	21p27	22p51			23p45	00 02	00 24	01 36								06 07	06 13		07 02	07 32
—	1	Wildmill	d																	06 15			07 34
—	2¼	Sarn	d																	06 18			07 37
—	3	Tondu	d																	06 22			07 41
—	7	Garth (Mid Glamorgan)	d																	06 31			07 50
—	7¾	Maesteg (Ewenny Road)	d																	06 34			07 53
—	8¼	Maesteg	a																	06 39			07 57
26¼	—	Pyle	d	21p34				23p53											06 15			07 10	
32½	—	Port Talbot Parkway	d	21p45	23p05			00 01	00 15	00 37	01 49								06 23			07 18	
34½	—	Baglan	d					00 05											06 27			07 22	
36¼	—	Briton Ferry	d					00 09											06 30			07 25	
38	—	Neath	d	21p52	23p13			00 13	00 22	00 45	01 57								06 34			07 29	
41¾	—	Skewen	d					00 16											06 38			07 33	
43½	—	Llansamlet	d					00 20											06 42			07 37	
47½	—	**Swansea**	a	22p04	23p25			00 28	00 37	00 57	02 10								06 51			07 45	
—	—		d	22p27	23p38	23p45		00 45					04 36					05 50		06 53		07 50	
53	—	Gowerton	d	22b41	23b49	23b56		00c55										06x00		07x03		08x00	
58¾	—	Llanelli	a	22p47	23p56	00 01		01s02					04 52					06 07		07 10		08 07	
—	—		d	22p49	23p58	00 03												06 09		07 11		08 08	
62¾	—	Pembrey & Burry Port	d	22p54	00 04	00 08		01s09										06 15		07 17		08 14	
68	—	Kidwelly	d	23b00	00x11			01c15										06x22		07x23		08x20	
72¼	—	Ferryside	d	23b06	00x17		←	01c21										06x28		07x29		08x26	
79¼	—	**Carmarthen**	a	23p18	00 30	00 28	00 30	01 40										06 42		07 43		08 40	
—	—		d	23p21	00 34	00 31	00 34							04 53	05 38	05 50	05 58	06 43		07 46		08 45	
93¾	—	Whitland	a	23p35	→	00 46	00 50							05 06	05 54	06 05	06 13	07 00		08 00		08 59	
—	—		d	23p36		00 46	00 50							05 06	05 54	06 05	06 13	07 00		08 00		09 02	
—	5¼	Narberth	d												06x03			07x09				09x11	
—	10¾	Kilgetty	d												06x13			07x19				09x21	
—	11½	Saundersfoot	d												06x15			07x21				09x23	
—	15¾	**Tenby**	a												06 22			07 28				09 30	
—	—		d												06 25			07 42				09 43	
—	17	Penally	d												06x28			07x45				09x46	
—	20¼	Manorbier	d												06 35			07 52				09 53	
—	23¾	Lamphey	d												06x42			07x59				10x00	
—	25¼	Pembroke	d												06 45			08 02				10 03	
—	27¼	**Pembroke Dock**	a												07 00			08 17				10 18	
98¾	—	Clunderwen	d	23b42										05x13		06x12	06x19			08 07			
105¼	0	Clarbeston Road	d	23b51		01x00	01x03							05x21		06x20	06x27		07 34	08x14			
—	5¼	Haverfordwest	d	23p59										05 32			06 35			08 23			
—	10	Johnston	d	00x07										05x40			06x43			08x31			
—	14	**Milford Haven**	a	00 22										05 55			06 58			08 48			
—	—	Fishguard & Goodwick	a			01 20										06 38			07 52				
121	—	**Fishguard Harbour** ⛴	a			01 28	01 30									06 44			07 58				
—	—		d									02 45											
—	—	Rosslare Harbour ⛴	a									06 15											

A from 21 May until 18 June
b Previous night, stops on request
c Stops to set down only, stops on request

When events are being held at the Millenium Stadium, services are subject to alteration. Please check times before travelling.

Table 128

Mondays to Fridays

until 22 June

Cardiff - Maesteg, Swansea and West Wales

Route Diagram - see first Page of Table 127

		AW	AW ◇	GW ◇1	AW ◇	AW ◇	GW ◇1	AW ◇		AW	AW	GW ◇1 A	AW	AW ◇	AW	AW ◇	GW ◇1 B	AW ◇	AW ■	AW	AW	AW	AW ◇	GW ◇1 B	AW
London Paddington ⊖	d			05 27			06 45					07 45					08 45							09 45	
Reading	d			05 56			07 11					08 11					09 11							10 11	
Manchester Piccadilly	d													06 30		07 30							08 30		
Gloucester	d										07 58				08 58										10 58
Bristol Parkway	d						08 07					09 07					10 07							11 07	
Newport (South Wales)	d		07 35	07 44		08 01	08 32	08 38			08 52	09 32		09 37	09 52	10 22	10 31						11 22	11 31	11 51
Cardiff Central	d		07 58	08 02	08 09	08 20	08 48	09 04		09 14	09 18	09 48		10 04	10 18	10 40	10 48	10 57			11 14	11 18	11 39	11 48	12 18
Pontyclun	d					08 32					09 30				10 30							11 30			12 30
Llanharan	d					08 37					09 35				10 35							11 35			12 35
Pencoed	d					08 41					09 39				10 39							11 39			12 39
Bridgend	d		08 17	08 23	08 29	08 49	09 09	09 23		09 34	09 46	10 09		10 23	10 46	10 59	11 09				11 34	11 46	12 00	12 09	12 46
Wildmill	d					08 51					09 49				10 49							11 49			12 49
Sarn	d					08 54					09 52				10 52							11 52			12 52
Tondu	d					08 58					09 55				10 55							11 55			12 55
Garth (Mid Glamorgan)	d					09 07					10 05				11 05							12 05			13 05
Maesteg (Ewenny Road)	d					09 10					10 07				11 07							12 07			13 07
Maesteg	a					09 15					10 12				11 12							12 14			13 12
Pyle	d				08 37					09 43											11 42				
Port Talbot Parkway	d		08 30	08 36	08 45		09 22	09 36		09 52		10 22		10 36		11 12	11 22				11 50		12 12	12 22	
Baglan	d				08 49					09 55											11 54				
Briton Ferry	d				08 52					09 59											11 57				
Neath	d		08 37	08 44	08 56		09 30	09 43		10 03		10 30		10 43		11 19	11 30				12 01		12 19	12 30	
Skewen	d				09 00					10 06											12 05				
Llansamlet	d				09 04					10 10											12 09				
Swansea	a		08 50	08 57	09 12		09 45	09 55		10 21		10 44		10 55		11 34	11 43				12 20		12 33	12 43	
	d		09 01		09 16			10 00						11 00		11 38				12 00			12 37		
Gowerton	d		09x17					10x11												12x11					
Llanelli	a		09 24		09 32			10 17						11 18		11 52		12 01		12 18			13 01		
	d		09 25					10 19						11 18		11 54		12 03		12 20			13 03		
Pembrey & Burry Port	d		09 31					10 25						11 24		12 00				12 26			13 09		
Kidwelly	d		09x37					10x31								12x06									
Ferryside	d		09x43					10x36								12x11									
Carmarthen	a		09 55					10 51						11 44		12 26				12 49			13 26		
	d		09 57										10 58	11 48						12 51			13 30		
Whitland	a		10 13										11 12	12 01				12 45		13 06			13 45		
	d	09 07	10 14										11 13	12 01				12 45		13 06			13 45		
Narberth	d												11x22							13x15					
Kilgetty	d												11x32							13x25					
Saundersfoot	d												11x34							13x27					
Tenby	a												11 41							13 34					
	d												11 49							13 45					
Penally	d												11x52							13x48					
Manorbier	d												11 58							13 54					
Lamphey	d												12x06							14x02					
Pembroke	d												12 09							14 05					
Pembroke Dock	a												12 23							14 19					
Clunderwen	d	09x14	10x20											12x07									13x52		
Clarbeston Road	d	09x22	10x28											12x15				12 59					13x59		
Haverfordwest	d		10 36											12 23									14 08		
Johnston	d		10x44											12x31									14x16		
Milford Haven	a		10 57											12 48									14 31		
Fishguard & Goodwick	a	09 41																13 17							
Fishguard Harbour ⛴	a	09 47																13 27							
	d																		14 30						
Rosslare Harbour ⛴	a																		18 00						

A The St. David

B from Bridgend, to Bridgend

When events are being held at the Millenium Stadium, services are subject to alteration. Please check times before travelling.

Table 128

Mondays to Fridays

until 22 June

Cardiff - Maesteg, Swansea and West Wales

Route Diagram - see first Page of Table 127

		AW ◇	AW ◇	GW ◇1 A		AW	AW	AW	AW ◇	GW ◇1 A	AW	AW ◇	GW ◇1 A			AW	AW	AW	GW ◇1	AW ■	AW	AW	GW ◇1	AW ■	
London Paddington ⊖	d			10 45						11 45			12 45						13 45				14 45		
Reading	d			11 11						12 11			13 11						14 11				15 11		
Manchester Piccadilly	d		09 30						10 30			11 30								12 30				13 30	
Gloucester	d							11 58										13 58			14 58				
Bristol Parkway	d			12 07						13 07			14 07						15 07				16 07		
Newport (South Wales)	d		12 23	12 32				12 52	13 23	13 31		14 22	14 31					14 52	15 32	15 37	15 52		16 31	16 40	
Cardiff Central	d		12 39	12 48			13 14	13 18	13 40	13 48	14 21	14 39	14 48				15 14	15 18	15 48	16 04	16 18		16 48	17 04	
Pontyclun	d							13 30			14 33							15 30			16 30				
Llanharan	d							13 35			14 38							15 35			16 35				
Pencoed	d							13 39			14 42							15 39			16 39				
Bridgend	d		12 58	13 09			13 34	13 46	14 04	14 09	14 49	14 58	15 09				15 34	15 46	16 09	16 25	16 46		17 09	17 25	
Wildmill	d							13 49			14 52							15 49			16 49				
Sarn	d							13 52			14 55							15 52			16 52				
Tondu	d							13 55			14 58							15 55			16 55				
Garth (Mid Glamorgan)	d							14 05			15 08							16 05			17 05				
Maesteg (Ewenny Road)	d							14 07			15 10							16 07			17 07				
Maesteg	a							14 12			15 15							16 12			17 12				
Pyle	d						13 42										15 42			16 33				17 32	
Port Talbot Parkway	d		13 11	13 22			13 50		14 18	14 22		15 11	15 22				15 50		16 22	16 41			17 22	17 40	
Baglan	d						13 54										15 54							17 42	
Briton Ferry	d						13 57										15 57							17 46	
Neath	d		13 18	13 30			14 01		14 25	14 30		15 18	15 30				16 01		16 30	16 48			17 30	17 50	
Skewen	d						14 05										16 05							17 54	
Llansamlet	d						14 09										16 09							17 58	
Swansea	a		13 33	13 44			14 20		14 34	14 43		15 34	15 43				16 20		16 43	17 01			17 43	18 05	
	d	13 14	13 37			14 00			14 37			15 37				16 00	16 40			17 05		17 35		18 09	
Gowerton	d					14x10										16x10	16 51			17x16		17x45		18 20	
Llanelli	a	13 31	13 52			14 17			14 53			15 52				16 17	16 58			17 22		17 52		18 26	
	d		13 54			14 19			14 54			15 54				16 19	16 59			17 24		17 54		18 28	
Pembrey & Burry Port	d		14 00			14 25			15 00			16 00				16 25	17 05			17 30		18 00		18 33	
Kidwelly	d		14x06									16x06					17x12			17x36		18x08		18 39	
Ferryside	d		14x11									16x11					17x18			17x41		18x14		18 45	
Carmarthen	a		14 28			14 48			15 20			16 28				16 48	17 30			17 53		18 30		18 57	
	d					14 51			15 28							16 51	17 35			17 56				19 02	
Whitland	a					15 05			15 43							17 05	17 50			18 13				19 18	
	d					15 06			15 43							17 06	17 50			18 14				19 18	
Narberth	d					15x15										17x15								19 28	
Kilgetty	d					15x25										17x25								19 38	
Saundersfoot	d					15x27										17x27								19 40	
Tenby	a					15 34										17 34								19 52	
	d					15 45										17 45									
Penally	d					15x48										17x48									
Manorbier	d					15 54										17 54									
Lamphey	d					16x02										18x02									
Pembroke	d					16 05										18 05									
Pembroke Dock	a					16 19										18 19									
Clunderwen	d								15x50								17x57			18x20					
Clarbeston Road	d								15x57								18x05			18x28					
Haverfordwest	d								16 06											18 36					
Johnston	d								16x14											18x44					
Milford Haven	a								16 29											18 59					
Fishguard & Goodwick	a																18 26								
Fishguard Harbour ⛴	a																18 29								
	d																								
Rosslare Harbour ⛴	a																								

A from Bridgend, to Bridgend

When events are being held at the Millenium Stadium, services are subject to alteration. Please check times before travelling.

Table 128

Mondays to Fridays

until 22 June

Cardiff - Maesteg, Swansea and West Wales

Route Diagram - see first Page of Table 127

		AW	AW	AW	GW	AW	GW	AW	AW	GW	AW	AW	GW	AW	AW	GW	AW	GW	GW	AW	AW	GW	GW
																						FX	FO
				■							■				■								
		◇	◇		◇1		◇1			◇1			◇1			◇1		◇1	◇1			◇1	◇1
										A			B										
		🛒		🛒	☕		☕			☕	🛒		☕⊘		🛒	☕		☕	☕			☕	☕
London Paddington [15] ⊖	d				15 45		16 15			16 45			17 15			17 45		18 15	18 45			19 15	19 15
Reading [7]	d				16 11		16 41			17 11			17 43			18 11		18 43	19 11			19 41	19u48
Manchester Piccadilly [10]	d			14 30							15 30				16 30								
Gloucester [7]	d							16 58				17 59					18 58				19 58		
Bristol Parkway [7]	d				17 07		17 41			18 07			18 41			19 07		19 44	20 07			20 42	20 43
Newport (South Wales)	d	17 01		17 22	17 31		18 04	17 52		18 31	18 41	18 53	19 11		19 22	19 31	19 52	20 08	20 33		20 52	21 04	21 07
Cardiff Central [7]	d	17 18		17 39	17 48	18 04	18 22	18 12		18 50	19 04	19 12	19 28		19 46	19 51	20 13	20 24	20 54	21 04	21 10	21 22	21 22
Pontyclun	d	17 32						18 24				19 28					20 25				21 22		
Llanharan	d	17 36						18 29				19 33					20 30				21 27		
Pencoed	d	17 40						18 33				19 37					20 34				21 32		
Bridgend	d	17 46		17 59	18 09	18 24	18 44	18 49		19 09	19 23	19 45	19 49		20 05	20 10	20 41	20 45	21 15	21 27	21 41	21 45	21 45
Wildmill	d	17 48						18 52				19 48					20 44				21 43		
Sarn	d	17 51						18 55				19 51					20 47				21 46		
Tondu	d	17 55						18 58				19 54					20 50				21 50		
Garth (Mid Glamorgan)	d	18 04						19 08				20 04					21 00				21 59		
Maesteg (Ewenny Road)	d	18 07						19 10				20 06					21 02				22 02		
Maesteg	a	18 15						19 15				20 11					21 07				22 06		
Pyle	d			18 07		18 33					19 30									21 34			
Port Talbot Parkway	d			18 17	18 22	18 41	18 57			19 22	19 38		20 02		20 21	20 26		20 58	21 28	21 45		21 58	21 58
Baglan	d					18 45					19 41												
Briton Ferry	d					18 48					19 44												
Neath	d			18 25	18 30	18 52	19 04			19 30	19 48		20 10		20 28	20 33		21 05	21 36	21 52		22 06	22 06
Skewen	d					18 56					19 53												
Llansamlet	d					19 00					19 57												
Swansea	a			18 37	18 48	19 11	19 18			19 46	20 04		20 23		20 42	20 47		21 19	21 49	22 04		22 19	22 19
	d		18 21	18 41					19 35		20 08		20 32		20 52					22 27			
Gowerton	d			18x52							20x19									22x41			
Llanelli	a		18 35	18 59					19 51		20 25		20 48		21 07					22 47			
	d			19 00					19 52		20 27		20 49		21 09					22 49			
Pembrey & Burry Port	d			19 06					19 59		20 32		20 56		21 14					22 54			
Kidwelly	d								20x06											23x00			
Ferryside	d								20x12											23x06			
Carmarthen	a			19 27					20 28		20 55		21 20		21 35					23 18			
	d			19 30							21 00				21 38					23 21			
Whitland	a			19 45							21 15				21 52					23 35			
	d			19 46							21 15				21 53					23 36			
Narberth	d										21x24												
Kilgetty	d										21x33												
Saundersfoot	d										21x35												
Tenby	a										21 42												
	d										21 43												
Penally	d										21x46												
Manorbier	d										21 52												
Lamphey	d										22x00												
Pembroke	d										22 03												
Pembroke Dock	a										22 18												
Clunderwen	d			19x53											21x59					23x42			
Clarbeston Road	d			20x00										20 05	22x07					23x51			
Haverfordwest	d			20 09											22 20					23 59			
Johnston	d			20x17											22x28					00x07			
Milford Haven	a			20 32											22 43					00 22			
Fishguard & Goodwick	a													20 23									
Fishguard Harbour ⛴	a													20 29									
	d																						
Rosslare Harbour ⛴	a																						

A The Capitals United

B The Red Dragon. ☕ from Bridgend ⊘ to Bridgend

When events are being held at the Millenium Stadium, services are subject to alteration. Please check times before travelling.

Table 128

Mondays to Fridays

until 22 June

Cardiff - Maesteg, Swansea and West Wales

Route Diagram - see first Page of Table 127

		AW	AW	GW	AW	AW	AW	GW	GW	GW
		FX	FO						FO	FX
		◇	◇	◇1		◇		◇1	◇1	◇1
				A						
		🛒	🛒	☕⊘				☕	☕	☕
London Paddington [15] ⊖	d			20 15				21 15	22 45	22 45
Reading [7]	d			20 41				21 41	23 11	23 19
Manchester Piccadilly [10]	d	18 30	18 30							
Gloucester [7]	d									
Bristol Parkway [7]	d			21 41				22 45	00 16	00 23
Newport (South Wales)	d	21 52	21 52	22 05				23 19	00 38	00 52
Cardiff Central [7]	d	22 09	22 09	22 26	22 35		23 15	23 43	00 55	01 13
Pontyclun	d	22 21	22 21				23 29			
Llanharan	d	22 25	22 25				23 34			
Pencoed	d	22 29	22 29				23 39			
Bridgend	d	22 35	22 35	22 46	22 59		23 45	00 02	01 19	01 36
Wildmill	d				23 01					
Sarn	d				23 04					
Tondu	d				23 08					
Garth (Mid Glamorgan)	d				23 17					
Maesteg (Ewenny Road)	d				23 20					
Maesteg	a				23 24					
Pyle	d						23 53			
Port Talbot Parkway	d	22 47	22 47	22 59			00 01	00 15	01 32	01 49
Baglan	d						00 05			
Briton Ferry	d						00 09			
Neath	d		22 54	23 07			00 13	00 22	01 39	01 57
Skewen	d						00 16			
Llansamlet	d						00 20			
Swansea	a		23 07	23 20			00 28	00 37	01 53	02 10
	d		23 11			23 45	00 45			
Gowerton	d		23x22			23x56	00b55			
Llanelli	a	23 16	23 29			00 01	01s02			
	d	23 18	23 30			00 03				
Pembrey & Burry Port	d	23 23	23 36			00 08	01s09			
Kidwelly	d	23x29	23x42				01b15			
Ferryside	d	23x35	23x47				01b21			
Carmarthen	a	23 56	00 04			00 28	01 40			
	d					00 31				
Whitland	a					00 46				
	d					00 46				
Narberth	d									
Kilgetty	d									
Saundersfoot	d									
Tenby	a									
	d									
Penally	d									
Manorbier	d									
Lamphey	d									
Pembroke	d									
Pembroke Dock	a									
Clunderwen	d									
Clarbeston Road	d					01x00				
Haverfordwest	d									
Johnston	d									
Milford Haven	a									
Fishguard & Goodwick	a					01 20				
Fishguard Harbour ⛴	a					01 28				
	d									
Rosslare Harbour ⛴	a									

A ☕ from Bridgend ⊘ to Bridgend

b Stops to set down only, stops on request

When events are being held at the Millenium Stadium, services are subject to alteration. Please check times before travelling.

Table 128

Mondays to Fridays

25 June to 20 July

Cardiff - Maesteg, Swansea and West Wales

Route Diagram - see first Page of Table 127

		AW MX	AW MO ◇	AW MX ◇	AW MO ◇	AW MX	GW MX ◇■ ☕	GW ◇■ A ☕	GW ◇■ B ☕	GW MX ◇■ ☕	AW B	AW ◇	AW	AW	AW	AW 🛒	AW 🛒	AW	AW ◇ 🛒	AW	AW ◇ C		AW
London Paddington [15] ⊖	d						21p15	21p37	21p37	22p45													
Reading [7]	d						21p41	22p12	22p12	23p19													
Manchester Piccadilly [10]	d																						
Gloucester [7]	d																						05 50
Bristol Parkway [7]	d						22p45	23p12	23p17	00 23													
Newport (South Wales)	d						23p19	23p42	23p43	00 52											06 17		06 44
Cardiff Central [7]	d	21p04	22p30			23p15	23p43	00 04	00 08	01 13									05 39	05 51	06 42		07 03
Pontyclun	d					23p29													05 51				07 15
Llanharan	d					23p34													05 56				07 20
Pencoed	d					23p39													06 01				07 24
Bridgend	d	21p27	22p51			23p45	00 02	00 24	00 28	01 36									06 07	06 13	07 02		07 32
Wildmill	d																			06 15			07 34
Sarn	d																			06 18			07 37
Tondu	d																			06 22			07 41
Garth (Mid Glamorgan)	d																			06 31			07 50
Maesteg (Ewenny Road)	d																			06 34			07 53
Maesteg	a																			06 39			07 57
Pyle	d	21p34				23p53													06 15		07 10		
Port Talbot Parkway	d	21p45	23p05			00 01	00 15	00 37	00 41	01 49									06 23		07 18		
Baglan	d					00 05													06 27		07 22		
Briton Ferry	d					00 09													06 30		07 25		
Neath	d	21p52	23p13			00 13	00 22	00 45	00 49	01 57									06 34		07 29		
Skewen	d					00 16													06 38		07 33		
Llansamlet	d					00 20													06 42		07 37		
Swansea	a	22p04	23p25			00 28	00 37	00 57	01 01	02 10									06 51		07 45		
	d	22p27	23p38	23p45		00 45						04 36					05 50		06 53		07 50		
Gowerton	d	22b41	23b49	23b56		00c55											06x00		07x03		08x00		
Llanelli	a	22p47	23p56	00 01		01s02						04 52					06 07		07 10		08 07		
	d	22p49	23p58	00 03													06 09		07 11		08 08		
Pembrey & Burry Port	d	22p54	00 04	00 08		01s09											06 15		07 17		08 14		
Kidwelly	d	23b00	00x11			01c15											06x22		07x23		08x20		
Ferryside	d	23b06	00x17		←	01c21											06x28		07x29		08x26		
Carmarthen	a	23p18	00 30	00 28	00 30	01 40											06 42		07 43		08 40		
	d	23p21	00 34	00 31	00 34								04 53	05 38	05 50	05 58	06 43		07 46		08 45		
Whitland	a	23p35	↦	00 46	00 50								05 06	05 54	06 05	06 13	07 00		08 00		08 59		
	d	23p36		00 46	00 50								05 06	05 54	06 05	06 13	07 00		08 00		09 07	09 02	
Narberth	d													06x03			07x09					09x11	
Kilgetty	d													06x13			07x19					09x21	
Saundersfoot	d													06x15			07x21					09x23	
Tenby	a													06 22			07 28					09 30	
	d													06 25			07 42					09 43	
Penally	d													06x28			07x45					09x46	
Manorbier	d													06 35			07 52					09 53	
Lamphey	d													06x42			07x59					10x00	
Pembroke	d													06 45			08 02					10 03	
Pembroke Dock	a													07 00			08 17					10 18	
Clunderwen	d	23b42											05x13		06x12	06x19			08 07		09x14		
Clarbeston Road	d	23b51		01x00	01x03								05x21		06x20	06x27		07 34	08x14		09x22		
Haverfordwest	d	23p59											05 32			06 35			08 23				
Johnston	d	00x07											05x40			06x43			08x31				
Milford Haven	a	00 22											05 55			06 58			08 48				
Fishguard & Goodwick	a			01 20											06 38			07 52			09 41		
Fishguard Harbour ⛴	a			01 28	01 30										06 44			07 58			09 47		
	d										02 45												
Rosslare Harbour ⛴	a										06 15												

A 25 June
B 2 July, 9 July, 16 July

C ◇ to Whitland

b Previous night, stops on request
c Stops to set down only, stops on request

When events are being held at the Millenium Stadium, services are subject to alteration. Please check times before travelling.

Table 128

Mondays to Fridays

25 June to 20 July

Cardiff - Maesteg, Swansea and West Wales

Route Diagram - see first Page of Table 127

		AW ◇ 🛒	GW ◇■ ☕	AW ◇ 🛒	AW ◇	GW ◇■ ☕	AW ◇ 🛒	AW	AW	GW ◇■ A ☕	AW 🛒	AW ◇ 🛒	AW	AW ◇ 🛒	GW ◇■ B ☕⊘	AW ◇ 🛒	AW B	AW 🛒	AW	AW	AW ◇ 🛒	GW ◇■ B ☕⊘	AW	AW ◇
London Paddington [15] ⊖	d		05 27			06 45				07 45					08 45							09 45		
Reading [7]	d		05 56			07 11				08 11					09 11							10 11		
Manchester Piccadilly [10]	d											06 30		07 30							08 30			
Gloucester [7]	d								07 58				08 58										10 58	
Bristol Parkway [7]	d					08 07				09 07					10 07							11 07		
Newport (South Wales)	d	07 35	07 44		08 01	08 32	08 38		08 52	09 32		09 37	09 52	10 22	10 31						11 22	11 31	11 51	
Cardiff Central [7]	d	07 58	08 02	08 09	08 20	08 48	09 04	09 14	09 18	09 48		10 04	10 18	10 40	10 48	10 57			11 14	11 18	11 39	11 48	12 18	
Pontyclun	d				08 32				09 30				10 30							11 30			12 30	
Llanharan	d				08 37				09 35				10 35							11 35			12 35	
Pencoed	d				08 41				09 39				10 39							11 39			12 39	
Bridgend	d	08 17	08 23	08 29	08 49	09 09	09 23	09 34	09 46	10 09		10 23	10 46	10 59	11 09				11 34	11 46	12 00	12 09	12 46	
Wildmill	d				08 51				09 49				10 49							11 49			12 49	
Sarn	d				08 54				09 52				10 52							11 52			12 52	
Tondu	d				08 58				09 55				10 55							11 55			12 55	
Garth (Mid Glamorgan)	d				09 07				10 05				11 05							12 05			13 05	
Maesteg (Ewenny Road)	d				09 10				10 07				11 07							12 07			13 07	
Maesteg	a				09 15				10 12				11 12							12 14			13 12	
Pyle	d			08 37				09 43											11 42					
Port Talbot Parkway	d	08 30	08 36	08 45		09 22	09 36	09 52		10 22		10 36		11 12	11 22				11 50		12 12	12 22		
Baglan	d			08 49				09 55											11 54					
Briton Ferry	d			08 52				09 59											11 57					
Neath	d	08 37	08 44	08 56		09 30	09 43	10 03		10 30		10 43		11 19	11 30				12 01		12 19	12 30		
Skewen	d			09 00				10 06											12 05					
Llansamlet	d			09 04				10 10											12 09					
Swansea	a	08 50	08 57	09 12		09 45	09 55	10 21		10 44		10 55		11 34	11 43				12 20		12 33	12 43		
	d	09 01		09 16			10 00					11 00		11 38				12 00			12 37			13 14
Gowerton	d	09x17					10x11											12x11						
Llanelli	a	09 24		09 32			10 17					11 18		11 52		12 01		12 18			13 01			13 31
	d	09 25					10 19					11 18		11 54		12 03		12 20			13 03			
Pembrey & Burry Port	d	09 31					10 25					11 24		12 00				12 26			13 09			
Kidwelly	d	09x37					10x31							12x06										
Ferryside	d	09x43					10x36							12x11										
Carmarthen	a	09 55					10 51					11 44		12 26				12 49			13 26			
	d	09 57									10 58	11 48						12 51			13 30			
Whitland	a	10 13									11 12	12 01				12 45		13 06			13 45			
	d	10 14									11 13	12 01				12 45		13 06			13 45			
Narberth	d										11x22							13x15						
Kilgetty	d										11x32							13x25						
Saundersfoot	d										11x34							13x27						
Tenby	a										11 41							13 34						
	d										11 49							13 45						
Penally	d										11x52							13x48						
Manorbier	d										11 58							13 54						
Lamphey	d										12x06							14x02						
Pembroke	d										12 09							14 05						
Pembroke Dock	a										12 23							14 19						
Clunderwen	d	10x20										12x07									13x52			
Clarbeston Road	d	10x28										12x15				12 59					13x59			
Haverfordwest	d	10 36										12 23									14 08			
Johnston	d	10x44										12x31									14x16			
Milford Haven	a	10 57										12 48									14 31			
Fishguard & Goodwick	a															13 17								
Fishguard Harbour ⛴	a															13 27								
	d																14 30							
Rosslare Harbour ⛴	a																18 00							

A The St. David

B ☕ from Bridgend ⊘ to Bridgend

When events are being held at the Millenium Stadium, services are subject to alteration. Please check times before travelling.

Table 128

Cardiff - Maesteg, Swansea and West Wales

Mondays to Fridays

25 June to 20 July

Route Diagram - see first Page of Table 127

		AW	GW	AW	AW	AW	AW	GW	AW	AW	GW	AW	AW	AW	GW	AW	AW	AW	GW	AW	AW
		◇ ⊥	◇1 A ⊏⊘				◇ ⊥	◇1 A ⊏⊘		◇ ⊥	◇1 A ⊏⊘				◇1 ⊏	■ ⊥	⊥	⊥	◇1 ⊏	■ ⊥	◇ ⊥
London Paddington 15 ⊖	d		10 45					11 45			12 45				13 45				14 45		
Reading 7	d		11 11					12 11			13 11				14 11				15 11		
Manchester Piccadilly 10	d	09 30					10 30			11 30						12 30				13 30	
Gloucester 7	d					11 58								13 58			14 58				
Bristol Parkway 7	d		12 07					13 07			14 07				15 07				16 07		
Newport (South Wales)	d	12 23	12 32			12 52	13 23	13 31		14 22	14 31			14 52	15 32	15 37	15 52		16 31	16 40	17 01
Cardiff Central 7	d	12 39	12 48		13 14	13 18	13 40	13 48	14 21	14 39	14 48		15 14	15 18	15 48	16 04	16 18		16 48	17 04	17 18
Pontyclun	d					13 30			14 33					15 30			16 30				17 32
Llanharan	d					13 35			14 38					15 35			16 35				17 36
Pencoed	d					13 39			14 42					15 39			16 39				17 40
Bridgend	d	12 58	13 09		13 34	13 46	14 04	14 09	14 49	14 58	15 09		15 34	15 46	16 09	16 25	16 46		17 09	17 25	17 46
Wildmill	d					13 49			14 52					15 49			16 49				17 48
Sarn	d					13 52			14 55					15 52			16 52				17 51
Tondu	d					13 55			14 58					15 55			16 55				17 55
Garth (Mid Glamorgan)	d					14 05			15 08					16 05			17 05				18 04
Maesteg (Ewenny Road)	d					14 07			15 10					16 07			17 07				18 07
Maesteg	a					14 12			15 15					16 12			17 12				18 15
Pyle	d				13 42								15 42			16 33				17 32	
Port Talbot Parkway	d	13 11	13 22		13 50		14 18	14 22		15 11	15 22		15 50		16 22	16 41			17 22	17 40	
Baglan	d				13 54								15 54							17 42	
Briton Ferry	d				13 57								15 57							17 46	
Neath	d	13 18	13 30		14 01		14 25	14 30		15 18	15 30		16 01		16 30	16 48			17 30	17 50	
Skewen	d				14 05								16 05							17 54	
Llansamlet	d				14 09								16 09							17 58	
Swansea	a	13 33	13 44		14 20		14 34	14 43		15 34	15 43		16 20		16 43	17 01			17 43	18 05	
	d	13 37		14 00			14 37			15 37		16 00	16 40			17 05		17 35		18 09	
Gowerton	d			14x10								16x10	16 51			17x16		17x45		18 20	
Llanelli	a	13 52		14 17			14 53			15 52		16 17	16 58			17 22		17 52		18 26	
	d	13 54		14 19			14 54			15 54		16 19	16 59			17 24		17 54		18 28	
Pembrey & Burry Port	d	14 00		14 25			15 00			16 00		16 25	17 05			17 30		18 00		18 33	
Kidwelly	d	14x06								16x06			17x12			17x36		18x08		18 39	
Ferryside	d	14x11								16x11			17x18			17x41		18x14		18 45	
Carmarthen	a	14 28		14 48			15 20			16 28		16 48	17 30			17 53		18 30		18 57	
	d			14 51			15 28					16 51	17 35			17 56				19 02	
Whitland	a			15 05			15 43					17 05	17 50			18 13				19 18	
	d			15 06			15 43					17 06	17 50			18 14				19 18	
Narberth	d			15x15								17x15								19 28	
Kilgetty	d			15x25								17x25								19 38	
Saundersfoot	d			15x27								17x27								19 40	
Tenby	a			15 34								17 34								19 52	
	d			15 45								17 45									
Penally	d			15x48								17x48									
Manorbier	d			15 54								17 54									
Lamphey	d			16x02								18x02									
Pembroke	d			16 05								18 05									
Pembroke Dock	a			16 19								18 19									
Clunderwen	d						15x50						17x57			18x20					
Clarbeston Road	d						15x57						18x05			18x28					
Haverfordwest	d						16 06									18 36					
Johnston	d						16x14									18x44					
Milford Haven	a						16 29									18 59					
Fishguard & Goodwick	a												18 26								
Fishguard Harbour ⛴	a												18 29								
	d																				
Rosslare Harbour ⛴	a																				

A ⊏ from Bridgend ⊘ to Bridgend

When events are being held at the Millenium Stadium, services are subject to alteration. Please check times before travelling.

Table 128

Cardiff - Maesteg, Swansea and West Wales

Mondays to Fridays

25 June to 20 July

Route Diagram - see first Page of Table 127

		AW	AW	GW	AW	GW	AW	AW	GW	AW	AW	GW	AW	AW	GW	AW	GW	GW	AW	AW	GW FX	GW FO	AW FX
		◇	■ ⊥	◇1 ⊏		◇1 ⊏			◇1 A ⊏	■ ⊥		◇1 B ⊏⊘		■ ⊥	◇1 ⊏		◇1 ⊏	◇1 ⊏			◇1 ⊏	◇1 ⊏	◇ ⊥
London Paddington 15 ⊖	d			15 45		16 15			16 45			17 15			17 45		18 15	18 45			19 15	19 15	
Reading 7	d			16 11		16 41			17 11			17 43			18 11		18 43	19 11			19 41	19u48	
Manchester Piccadilly 10	d		14 30							15 30				16 30									18 30
Gloucester 7	d						16 58				17 59					18 58				19 58			
Bristol Parkway 7	d			17 07		17 41			18 07			18 41			19 07		19 44	20 07			20 42	20 43	
Newport (South Wales)	d		17 22	17 31		18 04	17 52		18 31	18 41	18 53	19 11		19 22	19 31	19 52	20 08	20 33		20 52	21 04	21 07	21 52
Cardiff Central 7	d		17 39	17 48	18 04	18 22	18 12		18 50	19 04	19 12	19 28		19 46	19 51	20 13	20 24	20 54	21 04	21 10	21 22	21 22	22 09
Pontyclun	d						18 24				19 28					20 25				21 22			22 21
Llanharan	d						18 29				19 33					20 30				21 27			22 25
Pencoed	d						18 33				19 37					20 34				21 32			22 29
Bridgend	d		17 59	18 09	18 24	18 44	18 49		19 09	19 23	19 45	19 49		20 05	20 10	20 41	20 45	21 15	21 27	21 41	21 45	21 45	22 35
Wildmill	d						18 52				19 48					20 44				21 43			
Sarn	d						18 55				19 51					20 47				21 46			
Tondu	d						18 58				19 54					20 50				21 50			
Garth (Mid Glamorgan)	d						19 08				20 04					21 00				21 59			
Maesteg (Ewenny Road)	d						19 10				20 06					21 02				22 02			
Maesteg	a						19 15				20 11					21 07				22 06			
Pyle	d		18 07		18 33					19 30									21 34				
Port Talbot Parkway	d		18 17	18 22	18 41	18 57			19 22	19 38		20 02		20 21	20 26		20 58	21 28	21 45		21 58	21 58	22 47
Baglan	d				18 45					19 41													
Briton Ferry	d				18 48					19 44													
Neath	d		18 25	18 30	18 52	19 04			19 30	19 48		20 10		20 28	20 33		21 05	21 36	21 52		22 06	22 06	
Skewen	d				18 56					19 53													
Llansamlet	d				19 00					19 57													
Swansea	a		18 37	18 48	19 11	19 18			19 46	20 04		20 23		20 42	20 47		21 19	21 49	22 04		22 19	22 19	
	d	18 21	18 41					19 35		20 08		20 32		20 52					22 27				
Gowerton	d		18x52							20x19									22x41				
Llanelli	a	18 35	18 59					19 51		20 25		20 48		21 07					22 47				23 16
	d		19 00					19 52		20 27		20 49		21 09					22 49				23 18
Pembrey & Burry Port	d		19 06					19 59		20 32		20 56		21 14					22 54				23 23
Kidwelly	d							20x06											23x00				23x29
Ferryside	d							20x12											23x06				23x35
Carmarthen	a		19 27					20 28		20 55		21 20		21 35					23 18				23 56
	d		19 30							21 00				21 38					23 21				
Whitland	a		19 45							21 15				21 52					23 35				
	d		19 46							21 15				21 53					23 36				
Narberth	d									21x24													
Kilgetty	d									21x33													
Saundersfoot	d									21x35													
Tenby	a									21 42													
	d									21 43													
Penally	d									21x46													
Manorbier	d									21 52													
Lamphey	d									22x00													
Pembroke	d									22 03													
Pembroke Dock	a									22 18													
Clunderwen	d		19x53											21x59					23x42				
Clarbeston Road	d		20x00										20 05	22x07					23x51				
Haverfordwest	d		20 09											22 20					23 59				
Johnston	d		20x17											22x28					00x07				
Milford Haven	a		20 32											22 43					00 22				
Fishguard & Goodwick	a												20 23										
Fishguard Harbour ⛴	a												20 29										
	d																						
Rosslare Harbour ⛴	a																						

A The Capitals United

B The Red Dragon. ⊏ from Bridgend ⊘ to Bridgend

When events are being held at the Millenium Stadium, services are subject to alteration. Please check times before travelling.

Table 128

Mondays to Fridays

25 June to 20 July

Cardiff - Maesteg, Swansea and West Wales

Route Diagram - see first Page of Table 127

		AW FO ◇	GW ◇ A	AW	AW ◇	AW	GW ◇	GW FO ◇	GW FX ◇
London Paddington	d		20 15				21 15	22 45	22 45
Reading	d		20 41				21 41	23 11	23 19
Manchester Piccadilly	d	18 30							
Gloucester	d								
Bristol Parkway	d		21 41				22 45	00 16	00 23
Newport (South Wales)	d	21 52	22 05				23 19	00 38	00 52
Cardiff Central	d	22 09	22 26	22 35		23 15	23 43	00 55	01 13
Pontyclun	d	22 21				23 29			
Llanharan	d	22 25				23 34			
Pencoed	d	22 29				23 39			
Bridgend	d	22 35	22 46	22 59		23 45	00 02	01 19	01 36
Wildmill	d			23 01					
Sarn	d			23 04					
Tondu	d			23 08					
Garth (Mid Glamorgan)	d			23 17					
Maesteg (Ewenny Road)	d			23 20					
Maesteg	a			23 24					
Pyle	d					23 53			
Port Talbot Parkway	d	22 47	22 59			00 01	00 15	01 32	01 49
Baglan	d					00 05			
Briton Ferry	d					00 09			
Neath	d	22 54	23 07			00 13	00 22	01 39	01 57
Skewen	d					00 16			
Llansamlet	d					00 20			
Swansea	a	23 07	23 20			00 28	00 37	01 53	02 10
	d	23 11			23 45	00 45			
Gowerton	d	23x22			23x56	00b55			
Llanelli	a	23 29			00 01	01s02			
	d	23 30			00 03				
Pembrey & Burry Port	d	23 36			00 08	01s09			
Kidwelly	d	23x42				01b15			
Ferryside	d	23x47				01b21			
Carmarthen	a	00 04			00 28	01 40			
	d				00 31				
Whitland	a				00 46				
	d				00 46				
Narberth	d								
Kilgetty	d								
Saundersfoot	d								
Tenby	a								
	d								
Penally	d								
Manorbier	d								
Lamphey	d								
Pembroke	d								
Pembroke Dock	a								
Clunderwen	d								
Clarbeston Road	d				01x00				
Haverfordwest	d								
Johnston	d								
Milford Haven	a								
Fishguard & Goodwick	a				01 20				
Fishguard Harbour	a				01 28				
	d								
Rosslare Harbour	a								

A from Bridgend to Bridgend

b Stops to set down only, stops on request

When events are being held at the Millenium Stadium, services are subject to alteration. Please check times before travelling.

Table 128

Mondays to Fridays

3 September to 14 September

Cardiff - Maesteg, Swansea and West Wales

Route Diagram - see first Page of Table 127

		AW A	AW MO ◇	AW ◇ A	AW MO ◇	AW A	GW ◇ A	GW MO ◇	GW ◇ A	AW
London Paddington	d						21p15	21p37	22p45	
Reading	d						21p41	22p12	23p19	
Manchester Piccadilly	d									
Gloucester	d									
Bristol Parkway	d						22p45	23p17	00 23	
Newport (South Wales)	d						23p19	23p43	00 52	
Cardiff Central	d	21p04	22p30			23p15	23p43	00 08	01 13	
Pontyclun	d					23p29				
Llanharan	d					23p34				
Pencoed	d					23p39				
Bridgend	d	21p27	22p51			23p45	00 02	00 28	01 36	
Wildmill	d									
Sarn	d									
Tondu	d									
Garth (Mid Glamorgan)	d									
Maesteg (Ewenny Road)	d									
Maesteg	a									
Pyle	d	21p34				23p53				
Port Talbot Parkway	d	21p45	23p05			00 01	00 15	00 41	01 49	
Baglan	d					00 05				
Briton Ferry	d					00 09				
Neath	d	21p52	23p13			00 13	00 22	00 49	01 57	
Skewen	d					00 16				
Llansamlet	d					00 20				
Swansea	a	22p04	23p25			00 28	00 37	01 01	02 10	
	d	22p27	23p38	23p45		00 45				
Gowerton	d	22b41	23b49	23b56		00c55				
Llanelli	a	22p47	23p56	00 01		01s02				
	d	22p49	23p58	00 03						
Pembrey & Burry Port	d	22p54	00 04	00 08		01s09				
Kidwelly	d	23b00	00x11			01c15				
Ferryside	d	23b06	00x17		←	01c21				
Carmarthen	a	23p18	00 30	00 28	00 30	01 40				
	d	23p21	00 34	00 31	00 34					
Whitland	a	23p35	→	00 46	00 50					
	d	23p36		00 46	00 50					
Narberth	d									
Kilgetty	d									
Saundersfoot	d									
Tenby	a									
	d									
Penally	d									
Manorbier	d									
Lamphey	d									
Pembroke	d									
Pembroke Dock	a									
Clunderwen	d	23b42								
Clarbeston Road	d	23b51		01x00	01x03					
Haverfordwest	d	23p59								
Johnston	d	00x07								
Milford Haven	a	00 22								
Fishguard & Goodwick	a			01 20						
Fishguard Harbour	a			01 28	01 30					
	d									02 45
Rosslare Harbour	a									06 15

		AW ◇	AW	AW	AW	AW	AW	AW	AW ◇	AW	AW ◇ B		AW	AW ◇
London Paddington	d													
Reading	d													
Manchester Piccadilly	d													
Gloucester	d												05 50	
Bristol Parkway	d													
Newport (South Wales)	d										06 17		06 44	07 35
Cardiff Central	d								05 39	05 51	06 42		07 03	07 58
Pontyclun	d								05 51				07 15	
Llanharan	d								05 56				07 20	
Pencoed	d								06 01				07 24	
Bridgend	d								06 07	06 13	07 02		07 32	08 17
Wildmill	d									06 15			07 34	
Sarn	d									06 18			07 37	
Tondu	d									06 22			07 41	
Garth (Mid Glamorgan)	d									06 31			07 50	
Maesteg (Ewenny Road)	d									06 34			07 53	
Maesteg	a									06 39			07 57	
Pyle	d								06 15		07 10			
Port Talbot Parkway	d								06 23		07 18			08 30
Baglan	d								06 27		07 22			
Briton Ferry	d								06 30		07 25			
Neath	d								06 34		07 29			08 37
Skewen	d								06 38		07 33			
Llansamlet	d								06 42		07 37			
Swansea	a								06 51		07 45			08 50
	d	04 36					05 50		06 53		07 50			09 01
Gowerton	d						06x00		07x03		08x00			09x17
Llanelli	a	04 52					06 07		07 10		08 07			09 24
	d						06 09		07 11		08 08			09 25
Pembrey & Burry Port	d						06 15		07 17		08 14			09 31
Kidwelly	d						06x22		07x23		08x20			09x37
Ferryside	d						06x28		07x29		08x26			09x43
Carmarthen	a						06 42		07 43		08 40			09 55
	d		04 53	05 38	05 50	05 58	06 43		07 46		08 45			09 57
Whitland	a		05 06	05 54	06 05	06 13	07 00		08 00		08 59			10 13
	d		05 06	05 54	06 05	06 13	07 00		08 00		09 07	09 02		10 14
Narberth	d			06x03			07x09					09x11		
Kilgetty	d			06x13			07x19					09x21		
Saundersfoot	d			06x15			07x21					09x23		
Tenby	a			06 22			07 28					09 30		
	d			06 25			07 42					09 43		
Penally	d			06x28			07x45					09x46		
Manorbier	d			06 35			07 52					09 53		
Lamphey	d			06x42			07x59					10x00		
Pembroke	d			06 45			08 02					10 03		
Pembroke Dock	a			07 00			08 17					10 18		
Clunderwen	d		05x13		06x12	06x19			08 07		09x14			10x20
Clarbeston Road	d		05x21		06x20	06x27		07 34	08x14		09x22			10x28
Haverfordwest	d		05 32			06 35			08 23					10 36
Johnston	d		05x40			06x43			08x31					10x44
Milford Haven	a		05 55			06 58			08 48					10 57
Fishguard & Goodwick	a				06 38			07 52			09 41			
Fishguard Harbour	a				06 44			07 58			09 47			
	d													
Rosslare Harbour	a													

A not 3 September, 10 September

B ◇ to Whitland

b Previous night, stops on request

c Stops to set down only, stops on request

When events are being held at the Millenium Stadium, services are subject to alteration. Please check times before travelling.

Table 128

Mondays to Fridays

Cardiff - Maesteg, Swansea and West Wales

3 September to 14 September

Route Diagram - see first Page of Table 127

		GW	AW	AW	GW	AW		AW	AW	GW	AW	AW	AW	AW	GW	AW	AW	AW	AW	AW	AW	GW	AW	AW	AW
		◇1 ⊐	◇ ⊤	◇	◇1 ⊐	◇ ⊤				◇1 A ⊐	⊤	◇ ⊤		◇ ⊤	◇1 B ⊐⌀	◇ ⊤	■	⊤			◇ ⊤	◇1 B ⊐⌀		◇	◇ ⊤
London Paddington ⊖	d	05 27			06 45					07 45					08 45							09 45			
Reading	d	05 56			07 11					08 11					09 11							10 11			
Manchester Piccadilly	d											06 30		07 30							08 30				09 30
Gloucester	d								07 58				08 58										10 58		
Bristol Parkway	d				08 07					09 07					10 07							11 07			
Newport (South Wales)	d	07 44		08 01	08 32	08 38			08 52	09 32		09 37	09 52	10 22	10 31						11 22	11 31	11 51		12 23
Cardiff Central	d	08 02	08 09	08 20	08 48	09 04		09 14	09 18	09 48		10 04	10 18	10 40	10 48	10 57			11 14	11 18	11 39	11 48	12 18		12 39
Pontyclun	d			08 32					09 30				10 30							11 30			12 30		
Llanharan	d			08 37					09 35				10 35							11 35			12 35		
Pencoed	d			08 41					09 39				10 39							11 39			12 39		
Bridgend	d	08 23	08 29	08 49	09 09	09 23		09 34	09 46	10 09		10 23	10 46	10 59	11 09				11 34	11 46	12 00	12 09	12 46		12 58
Wildmill	d			08 51					09 49				10 49							11 49			12 49		
Sarn	d			08 54					09 52				10 52							11 52			12 52		
Tondu	d			08 58					09 55				10 55							11 55			12 55		
Garth (Mid Glamorgan)	d			09 07					10 05				11 05							12 05			13 05		
Maesteg (Ewenny Road)	d			09 10					10 07				11 07							12 07			13 07		
Maesteg	a			09 15					10 12				11 12							12 14			13 12		
Pyle	d		08 37					09 43											11 42						
Port Talbot Parkway	d	08 36	08 45		09 22	09 36		09 52		10 22		10 36		11 12	11 22				11 50		12 12	12 22			13 11
Baglan	d		08 49					09 55											11 54						
Briton Ferry	d		08 52					09 59											11 57						
Neath	d	08 44	08 56		09 30	09 43		10 03		10 30		10 43		11 19	11 30				12 01		12 19	12 30			13 18
Skewen	d		09 00					10 06											12 05						
Llansamlet	d		09 04					10 10											12 09						
Swansea	a	08 57	09 12		09 45	09 55		10 21		10 44		10 55		11 34	11 43				12 20		12 33	12 43			13 33
	d		09 16			10 00						11 00		11 38				12 00			12 37			13 14	13 37
Gowerton	d					10x11												12x11							
Llanelli	a		09 32			10 17						11 18		11 52		12 01		12 18			13 01			13 31	13 52
	d					10 19						11 18		11 54		12 03		12 20			13 03				13 54
Pembrey & Burry Port	d					10 25						11 24		12 00				12 26			13 09				14 00
Kidwelly	d					10x31								12x06											14x06
Ferryside	d					10x36								12x11											14x11
Carmarthen	a					10 51						11 44		12 26				12 49			13 26				14 28
	d										10 58	11 48						12 51			13 30				
Whitland	a										11 12	12 01				12 45		13 06			13 45				
	d										11 13	12 01				12 45		13 06			13 45				
Narberth	d										11x22							13x15							
Kilgetty	d										11x32							13x25							
Saundersfoot	d										11x34							13x27							
Tenby	a										11 41							13 34							
	d										11 49							13 45							
Penally	d										11x52							13x48							
Manorbier	d										11 58							13 54							
Lamphey	d										12x06							14x02							
Pembroke	d										12 09							14 05							
Pembroke Dock	a										12 23							14 19							
Clunderwen	d											12x07									13x52				
Clarbeston Road	d											12x15				12 59					13x59				
Haverfordwest	d											12 23									14 08				
Johnston	d											12x31									14x16				
Milford Haven	a											12 48									14 31				
Fishguard & Goodwick	a															13 17									
Fishguard Harbour ⛴	a															13 27									
	d																14 30								
Rosslare Harbour ⛴	a																18 00								

A The St. David

B ⊐ from Bridgend ⌀ to Bridgend

When events are being held at the Millenium Stadium, services are subject to alteration. Please check times before travelling.

Table 128

Mondays to Fridays

Cardiff - Maesteg, Swansea and West Wales

3 September to 14 September

Route Diagram - see first Page of Table 127

		GW		AW	AW	AW	AW	GW	AW	AW	GW			AW	AW	AW	GW	AW	AW	AW	GW	AW		AW	AW
		◇1 A ⊐⌀					◇ ⊤	◇1 A ⊐⌀		◇ ⊤	◇1 A ⊐⌀						◇1 ⊐	■ ⊤	⊤	⊤	◇1 ⊐	■ ⊤		◇ ⊤	◇
London Paddington ⊖	d	10 45						11 45			12 45						13 45				14 45				
Reading	d	11 11						12 11			13 11						14 11				15 11				
Manchester Piccadilly	d						10 30			11 30								12 30				13 30			
Gloucester	d					11 58										13 58			14 58						
Bristol Parkway	d	12 07						13 07			14 07						15 07				16 07				
Newport (South Wales)	d	12 32				12 52	13 23	13 31		14 22	14 31					14 52	15 32	15 37	15 52		16 31	16 40		17 01	
Cardiff Central	d	12 48			13 14	13 18	13 40	13 48	14 21	14 39	14 48				15 14	15 18	15 48	16 04	16 18		16 48	17 04		17 18	
Pontyclun	d					13 30			14 33							15 30			16 30					17 32	
Llanharan	d					13 35			14 38							15 35			16 35					17 36	
Pencoed	d					13 39			14 42							15 39			16 39					17 40	
Bridgend	d	13 09			13 34	13 46	14 04	14 09	14 49	14 58	15 09				15 34	15 46	16 09	16 25	16 46		17 09	17 25		17 46	
Wildmill	d					13 49			14 52							15 49			16 49					17 48	
Sarn	d					13 52			14 55							15 52			16 52					17 51	
Tondu	d					13 55			14 58							15 55			16 55					17 55	
Garth (Mid Glamorgan)	d					14 05			15 08							16 05			17 05					18 04	
Maesteg (Ewenny Road)	d					14 07			15 10							16 07			17 07					18 07	
Maesteg	a					14 12			15 15							16 12			17 12					18 15	
Pyle	d				13 42										15 42			16 33				17 32			
Port Talbot Parkway	d	13 22			13 50		14 18	14 22		15 11	15 22				15 50		16 22	16 41			17 22	17 40			
Baglan	d				13 54										15 54							17 42			
Briton Ferry	d				13 57										15 57							17 46			
Neath	d	13 30			14 01		14 25	14 30		15 18	15 30				16 01		16 30	16 48			17 30	17 50			
Skewen	d				14 05										16 05							17 54			
Llansamlet	d				14 09										16 09							17 58			
Swansea	a	13 44			14 20		14 34	14 43		15 34	15 43				16 20		16 43	17 01			17 43	18 05			
	d			14 00			14 37			15 37				16 00	16 40			17 05		17 35		18 09			18 21
Gowerton	d			14x10										16x10	16 51			17x16		17x45		18 20			
Llanelli	a			14 17			14 53			15 52				16 17	16 58			17 22		17 52		18 26			18 35
	d			14 19			14 54			15 54				16 19	16 59			17 24		17 54		18 28			
Pembrey & Burry Port	d			14 25			15 00			16 00				16 25	17 05			17 30		18 00		18 33			
Kidwelly	d									16x06					17x12			17x36		18x08		18 39			
Ferryside	d									16x11					17x18			17x41		18x14		18 45			
Carmarthen	a			14 48			15 20			16 28				16 48	17 30			17 53		18 30		18 57			
	d			14 51			15 28							16 51	17 35			17 56				19 02			
Whitland	a			15 05			15 43							17 05	17 50			18 13				19 18			
	d			15 06			15 43							17 06	17 50			18 14				19 18			
Narberth	d			15x15										17x15								19 28			
Kilgetty	d			15x25										17x25								19 38			
Saundersfoot	d			15x27										17x27								19 40			
Tenby	a			15 34										17 34								19 52			
	d			15 45										17 45											
Penally	d			15x48										17x48											
Manorbier	d			15 54										17 54											
Lamphey	d			16x02										18x02											
Pembroke	d			16 05										18 05											
Pembroke Dock	a			16 19										18 19											
Clunderwen	d						15x50								17x57			18x20							
Clarbeston Road	d						15x57								18x05			18x28							
Haverfordwest	d						16 06											18 36							
Johnston	d						16x14											18x44							
Milford Haven	a						16 29											18 59							
Fishguard & Goodwick	a														18 26										
Fishguard Harbour ⛴	a														18 29										
	d																								
Rosslare Harbour ⛴	a																								

A ⊐ from Bridgend ⌀ to Bridgend

When events are being held at the Millenium Stadium, services are subject to alteration. Please check times before travelling.

Table 128

Mondays to Fridays

3 September to 14 September

Cardiff - Maesteg, Swansea and West Wales

Route Diagram - see first Page of Table 127

	AW	GW	AW	GW	AW	AW	GW		AW	AW	GW	AW	AW	GW	AW	GW	GW		AW	AW	GW	GW FO	AW	AW FO
	■ ⊼	◇■ ⊐		◇■ ⊐			◇■ A ⊐		■ ⊼		◇■ B ⊐⊘		■ ⊼	◇■ ⊐		◇■ ⊐	◇■ ⊐				◇■ C ⊐	◇■ ⊐	◇ C ⊼	◇ ⊼
London Paddington ⊖ d		15 45		16 15			16 45				17 15			17 45		18 15	18 45				19 15	19 15		
Reading d		16 11		16 41			17 11				17 43			18 11		18 43	19 11				19 41	19u48		
Manchester Piccadilly d	14 30								15 30				16 30										18 30	18 30
Gloucester d					16 58					17 59					18 58					19 58				
Bristol Parkway d		17 07		17 41			18 07				18 41			19 07		19 44	20 07				20 42	20 43		
Newport (South Wales) d	17 22	17 31		18 04	17 52		18 31		18 41	18 53	19 11		19 22	19 31	19 52	20 08	20 33			20 52	21 04	21 07	21 52	21 52
Cardiff Central d	17 39	17 48	18 04	18 22	18 12		18 50		19 04	19 12	19 28		19 46	19 51	20 13	20 24	20 54		21 04	21 10	21 22	21 22	22 09	22 09
Pontyclun d					18 24					19 28					20 25					21 22			22 21	22 21
Llanharan d					18 29					19 33					20 30					21 27			22 25	22 25
Pencoed d					18 33					19 37					20 34					21 32			22 29	22 29
Bridgend d	17 59	18 09	18 24	18 44	18 49		19 09		19 23	19 45	19 49		20 05	20 10	20 41	20 45	21 15		21 27	21 41	21 45	21 45	22 35	22 35
Wildmill d					18 52					19 48					20 44					21 43				
Sarn d					18 55					19 51					20 47					21 46				
Tondu d					18 58					19 54					20 50					21 50				
Garth (Mid Glamorgan) d					19 08					20 04					21 00					21 59				
Maesteg (Ewenny Road) d					19 10					20 06					21 02					22 02				
Maesteg a					19 15					20 11					21 07					22 06				
Pyle d	18 07		18 33						19 30										21 34					
Port Talbot Parkway d	18 17	18 22	18 41	18 57			19 22		19 38		20 02		20 21	20 26		20 58	21 28		21 45		21 58	21 58	22 47	22 47
Baglan d			18 45						19 41															
Briton Ferry d			18 48						19 44															
Neath d	18 25	18 30	18 52	19 04			19 30		19 48		20 10		20 28	20 33		21 05	21 36		21 52		22 06	22 06		22 54
Skewen d			18 56						19 53															
Llansamlet d			19 00						19 57															
Swansea a	18 37	18 48	19 11	19 18			19 46		20 04		20 23		20 42	20 47		21 19	21 49		22 04		22 19	22 19		23 07
d	18 41					19 35			20 08		20 32		20 52						22 27					23 11
Gowerton d	18x52								20x19										22x41					23x22
Llanelli a	18 59					19 51			20 25		20 48		21 07						22 47				23 16	23 29
d	19 00					19 52			20 27		20 49		21 09						22 49				23 18	23 30
Pembrey & Burry Port d	19 06					19 59			20 32		20 56		21 14						22 54				23 23	23 36
Kidwelly d						20x06													23x00				23x29	23x42
Ferryside d						20x12													23x06				23x35	23x47
Carmarthen a	19 27					20 28			20 55		21 20		21 35						23 18				23 56	00 04
d	19 30								21 00				21 38						23 21					
Whitland a	19 45								21 15				21 52						23 35					
d	19 46								21 15				21 53						23 36					
Narberth d									21x24															
Kilgetty d									21x33															
Saundersfoot d									21x35															
Tenby a									21 42															
d									21 43															
Penally d									21x46															
Manorbier d									21 52															
Lamphey d									22x00															
Pembroke d									22 03															
Pembroke Dock a									22 18															
Clunderwen d	19x53												21x59						23x42					
Clarbeston Road d	20x00											20 05	22x07						23x51					
Haverfordwest d	20 09												22 20						23 59					
Johnston d	20x17												22x28						00x07					
Milford Haven a	20 32												22 43						00 22					
Fishguard & Goodwick a												20 23												
Fishguard Harbour ⛴ a												20 29												
d																								
Rosslare Harbour ⛴ a																								

A The Capitals United

B The Red Dragon. ⊐ from Bridgend ⊘ to Bridgend

C not 7 September, 14 September

When events are being held at the Millenium Stadium, services are subject to alteration. Please check times before travelling.

Table 128

Mondays to Fridays

3 September to 14 September

Cardiff - Maesteg, Swansea and West Wales

Route Diagram - see first Page of Table 127

	GW	AW	AW		AW	GW	GW FO	GW
	◇■ A ⊐⊘		◇			◇■ ⊐	◇■ ⊐	◇■ B ⊐
London Paddington ⊖ d	20 15					21 15	22 45	22 45
Reading d	20 41					21 41	23 11	23 19
Manchester Piccadilly d								
Gloucester d								
Bristol Parkway d	21 41					22 45	00 16	00 23
Newport (South Wales) d	22 05					23 19	00 38	00 52
Cardiff Central d	22 26	22 35			23 15	23 43	00 55	01 13
Pontyclun d					23 29			
Llanharan d					23 34			
Pencoed d					23 39			
Bridgend d	22 46	22 59			23 45	00 02	01 19	01 36
Wildmill d		23 01						
Sarn d		23 04						
Tondu d		23 08						
Garth (Mid Glamorgan) d		23 17						
Maesteg (Ewenny Road) d		23 20						
Maesteg a		23 24						
Pyle d					23 53			
Port Talbot Parkway d	22 59				00 01	00 15	01 32	01 49
Baglan d					00 05			
Briton Ferry d					00 09			
Neath d	23 07				00 13	00 22	01 39	01 57
Skewen d					00 16			
Llansamlet d					00 20			
Swansea a	23 20				00 28	00 37	01 53	02 10
d			23 45		00 45			
Gowerton d			23x56		00b55			
Llanelli a			00 01		01s02			
d			00 03					
Pembrey & Burry Port d			00 08		01s09			
Kidwelly d					01b15			
Ferryside d					01b21			
Carmarthen a			00 28		01 40			
d			00 31					
Whitland a			00 46					
d			00 46					
Narberth d								
Kilgetty d								
Saundersfoot d								
Tenby a								
d								
Penally d								
Manorbier d								
Lamphey d								
Pembroke d								
Pembroke Dock a								
Clunderwen d								
Clarbeston Road d			01x00					
Haverfordwest d								
Johnston d								
Milford Haven a								
Fishguard & Goodwick a			01 20					
Fishguard Harbour ⛴ a			01 28					
d								
Rosslare Harbour ⛴ a								

A ⊐ from Bridgend ⊘ to Bridgend

B not 7 September, 14 September

b Stops to set down only, stops on request

When events are being held at the Millenium Stadium, services are subject to alteration. Please check times before travelling.

from 17 September

Cardiff - Maesteg, Swansea and West Wales

Route Diagram - see first Page of Table 127

		AW MX	AW MO ◇	AW MX ◇	AW MO ◇	AW MX	GW MX ◇1 ⊏	GW MO ◇1 ⊏	GW MX ◇1 ⊏	AW B		AW ◇	AW	AW	AW	AW ⊼	AW	AW	AW ◇ ⊼	AW		AW ◇ A	AW	AW ◇ ⊼
London Paddington 15 ⊖	d						21p15	21p37	22p45															
Reading 7	d						21p41	22p14	23p19															
Manchester Piccadilly 10	d																							
Gloucester 7	d																						05 50	
Bristol Parkway 7	d						22p45	23p16	00 23															
Newport (South Wales)	d						23p19	23p43	00 52													06 17	06 44	07 35
Cardiff Central 7	d	21p04	22p30			23p15	23p43	00 05	01 13										05 39	05 51		06 42	07 03	07 58
Pontyclun	d					23p29													05 51				07 15	
Llanharan	d					23p34													05 56				07 20	
Pencoed	d					23p39													06 01				07 24	
Bridgend	d	21p27	22p51			23p45	00 02	00 28	01 36										06 07	06 13		07 02	07 32	08 17
Wildmill	d																			06 15			07 34	
Sarn	d																			06 18			07 37	
Tondu	d																			06 22			07 41	
Garth (Mid Glamorgan)	d																			06 31			07 50	
Maesteg (Ewenny Road)	d																			06 34			07 53	
Maesteg	a																			06 39			07 57	
Pyle	d	21p34				23p53													06 15			07 10		
Port Talbot Parkway	d	21p45	23p05			00 01	00 15	00 41	01 49										06 23			07 18		08 30
Baglan	d					00 05													06 27			07 22		
Briton Ferry	d					00 09													06 30			07 25		
Neath	d	21p52	23p13			00 13	00 22	00 49	01 57										06 34			07 29		08 37
Skewen	d					00 16													06 38			07 33		
Llansamlet	d					00 20													06 42			07 37		
Swansea	a	22p04	23p25			00 28	00 37	01 02	02 10										06 51			07 45		08 50
	d	22p27	23p38	23p45		00 45						04 36					05 50		06 53			07 50		09 01
Gowerton	d	22b41	23b49	23b56		00c55											06x00		07x03			08x00		09x17
Llanelli	a	22p47	23p56	00 01		01s02						04 52					06 07		07 10			08 07		09 24
	d	22p49	23p58	00 03													06 09		07 11			08 08		09 25
Pembrey & Burry Port	d	22p54	00 04	00 08		01s09											06 15		07 17			08 14		09 31
Kidwelly	d	23b00	00x11			01c15											06x22		07x23			08x20		09x37
Ferryside	d	23b06	00x17		←	01c21											06x28		07x29			08x26		09x43
Carmarthen	a	23p18	00 30	00 28	00 30	01 40											06 42		07 43			08 40		09 55
	d	23p21	00 34	00 31	00 34								04 53	05 38	05 50	05 58	06 43		07 46			08 45		09 57
Whitland	a	23p35	→	00 46	00 50								05 06	05 54	06 05	06 13	07 00		08 00			08 59		10 13
	d	23p36		00 46	00 50								05 06	05 54	06 05	06 13	07 00		08 00			09 07 09 02		10 14
Narberth	d													06x03			07x09					09x11		
Kilgetty	d													06x13			07x19					09x21		
Saundersfoot	d													06x15			07x21					09x23		
Tenby	a													06 22			07 28					09 30		
	d													06 25			07 42					09 43		
Penally	d													06x28			07x45					09x46		
Manorbier	d													06 35			07 52					09 53		
Lamphey	d													06x42			07x59					10x00		
Pembroke	d													06 45			08 02					10 03		
Pembroke Dock	a													07 00			08 17					10 18		
Clunderwen	d	23b42											05x13		06x12	06x19			08 07			09x14		10x20
Clarbeston Road	d	23b51		01x00	01x03								05x21		06x20	06x27		07 34	08x14			09x22		10x28
Haverfordwest	d	23p59											05 32			06 35			08 23					10 36
Johnston	d	00x07											05x40			06x43			08x31					10x44
Milford Haven	a	00 22											05 55			06 58			08 48					10 57
Fishguard & Goodwick	a			01 20											06 38			07 52				09 41		
Fishguard Harbour ⛴	a			01 28	01 30										06 44			07 58				09 47		
	d									02 45														
Rosslare Harbour ⛴	a									06 15														

A ◇ to Whitland

b Previous night, stops on request

c Stops to set down only, stops on request

When events are being held at the Millenium Stadium, services are subject to alteration. Please check times before travelling.

from 17 September

Cardiff - Maesteg, Swansea and West Wales

Route Diagram - see first Page of Table 127

		GW ◇1 ⊏	AW ◇ ⊼	AW ◇	GW ◇1 ⊏	AW ◇ ⊼		AW	AW	GW ◇1 A ⊏	AW	AW ◇ ⊼	AW	AW ◇ ⊼	GW ◇1 B ⊏⊘	AW ◇ ⊼	AW B	AW	AW	AW	AW ◇ ⊼	GW ◇1 B ⊏⊘	AW	AW ◇	AW ◇ ⊼
London Paddington 15 ⊖	d	05 27			06 45					07 45					08 45							09 45			
Reading 7	d	05 56			07 11					08 11					09 11							10 11			
Manchester Piccadilly 10	d											06 30		07 30							08 30				09 30
Gloucester 7	d								07 58				08 58										10 58		
Bristol Parkway 7	d				08 07					09 07					10 07							11 07			
Newport (South Wales)	d	07 44		08 01	08 32	08 38			08 52	09 32		09 37	09 52	10 22	10 31						11 22	11 31	11 51		12 23
Cardiff Central 7	d	08 02	08 09	08 20	08 48	09 04		09 14	09 18	09 48		10 04	10 18	10 40	10 48	10 57			11 14	11 18	11 39	11 48	12 18		12 39
Pontyclun	d			08 32					09 30				10 30							11 30			12 30		
Llanharan	d			08 37					09 35				10 35							11 35			12 35		
Pencoed	d			08 41					09 39				10 39							11 39			12 39		
Bridgend	d	08 23	08 29	08 49	09 09	09 23		09 34	09 46	10 09		10 23	10 46	10 59	11 09				11 34	11 46	12 00	12 09	12 46		12 58
Wildmill	d			08 51					09 49				10 49							11 49			12 49		
Sarn	d			08 54					09 52				10 52							11 52			12 52		
Tondu	d			08 58					09 55				10 55							11 55			12 55		
Garth (Mid Glamorgan)	d			09 07					10 05				11 05							12 05			13 05		
Maesteg (Ewenny Road)	d			09 10					10 07				11 07							12 07			13 07		
Maesteg	a			09 15					10 12				11 12							12 14			13 12		
Pyle	d		08 37					09 43											11 42						
Port Talbot Parkway	d	08 36	08 45		09 22	09 36		09 52		10 22		10 36		11 12	11 22				11 50		12 12	12 22			13 11
Baglan	d		08 49					09 55											11 54						
Briton Ferry	d		08 52					09 59											11 57						
Neath	d	08 44	08 56		09 30	09 43		10 03		10 30		10 43		11 19	11 30				12 01		12 19	12 30			13 18
Skewen	d		09 00					10 06											12 05						
Llansamlet	d		09 04					10 10											12 09						
Swansea	a	08 57	09 12		09 45	09 55		10 21		10 44		10 55		11 34	11 43				12 20		12 33	12 43			13 33
	d		09 16			10 00						11 00		11 38				12 00			12 37			13 14	13 37
Gowerton	d					10x11												12x11							
Llanelli	a		09 32			10 17						11 18		11 52		12 01		12 18			13 01			13 31	13 52
	d					10 19						11 18		11 54		12 03		12 20			13 03				13 54
Pembrey & Burry Port	d					10 25						11 24		12 00				12 26			13 09				14 00
Kidwelly	d					10x31								12x06											14x06
Ferryside	d					10x36								12x11											14x11
Carmarthen	a					10 51						11 44		12 26				12 49			13 26				14 28
	d										10 58	11 48						12 51			13 30				
Whitland	a										11 12	12 01				12 45		13 06			13 45				
	d										11 13	12 01				12 45		13 06			13 45				
Narberth	d										11x22							13x15							
Kilgetty	d										11x32							13x25							
Saundersfoot	d										11x34							13x27							
Tenby	a										11 41							13 34							
	d										11 49							13 45							
Penally	d										11x52							13x48							
Manorbier	d										11 58							13 54							
Lamphey	d										12x06							14x02							
Pembroke	d										12 09							14 05							
Pembroke Dock	a										12 23							14 19							
Clunderwen	d											12x07									13x52				
Clarbeston Road	d											12x15				12 59					13x59				
Haverfordwest	d											12 23									14 08				
Johnston	d											12x31									14x16				
Milford Haven	a											12 48									14 31				
Fishguard & Goodwick	a															13 17									
Fishguard Harbour ⛴	a															13 27									
	d																14 30								
Rosslare Harbour ⛴	a																18 00								

A The St. David

B ⊏ from Bridgend ⊘ to Bridgend

When events are being held at the Millenium Stadium, services are subject to alteration. Please check times before travelling.

Table 128

Mondays to Fridays

from 17 September

Cardiff - Maesteg, Swansea and West Wales

Route Diagram - see first Page of Table 127

		GW	AW	AW	AW	AW	GW	AW	AW	GW	AW	AW	AW	GW	AW	AW	AW	GW	AW	AW	AW
		◇1 A ⊓⊘				◇ ⊼	◇1 A ⊓⊘		◇ ⊼	◇1 A ⊓⊘				◇1 ⊓	■ ⊼	⊼		◇1 ⊓	■ ⊼	◇ ⊼	◇
London Paddington 15 ⊖	d	10 45					11 45			12 45				13 45				14 45			
Reading 7	d	11 11					12 11			13 11				14 11				15 11			
Manchester Piccadilly 10	d					10 30			11 30						12 30				13 30		
Gloucester 7	d				11 58								13 58			14 58					
Bristol Parkway 7	d	12 07					13 07			14 07				15 07				16 07			
Newport (South Wales)	d	12 32			12 52	13 23	13 31		14 22	14 31			14 52	15 32	15 37	15 52		16 31	16 40	17 01	
Cardiff Central 7	d	12 48		13 14	13 18	13 40	13 48	14 21	14 39	14 48		15 14	15 18	15 48	16 04	16 18		16 48	17 04	17 18	
Pontyclun	d				13 30			14 33					15 30			16 30				17 32	
Llanharan	d				13 35			14 38					15 35			16 35				17 36	
Pencoed	d				13 39			14 42					15 39			16 39				17 40	
Bridgend	d	13 09		13 34	13 46	14 04	14 09	14 49	14 58	15 09		15 34	15 46	16 09	16 25	16 46		17 09	17 25	17 46	
Wildmill	d				13 49			14 52					15 49			16 49				17 48	
Sarn	d				13 52			14 55					15 52			16 52				17 51	
Tondu	d				13 55			14 58					15 55			16 55				17 55	
Garth (Mid Glamorgan)	d				14 05			15 08					16 05			17 05				18 04	
Maesteg (Ewenny Road)	d				14 07			15 10					16 07			17 07				18 07	
Maesteg	a				14 12			15 15					16 12			17 12				18 15	
Pyle	d			13 42								15 42			16 33				17 32		
Port Talbot Parkway	d	13 22		13 50		14 18	14 22		15 11	15 22		15 50		16 22	16 41			17 22	17 40		
Baglan	d			13 54								15 54							17 42		
Briton Ferry	d			13 57								15 57							17 46		
Neath	d	13 30		14 01		14 25	14 30		15 18	15 30		16 01		16 30	16 48			17 30	17 50		
Skewen	d			14 05								16 05							17 54		
Llansamlet	d			14 09								16 09							17 58		
Swansea	a	13 44		14 20		14 34	14 43		15 34	15 43		16 20		16 43	17 01			17 43	18 05		
	d		14 00			14 37			15 37		16 00	16 40			17 05		17 35		18 09		18 21
Gowerton	d		14x10								16x10	16 51			17x16		17x45		18 20		
Llanelli	a		14 17			14 53			15 52		16 17	16 58			17 22		17 52		18 26		18 35
	d		14 19			14 54			15 54		16 19	16 59			17 24		17 54		18 28		
Pembrey & Burry Port	d		14 25			15 00			16 00		16 25	17 05			17 30		18 00		18 33		
Kidwelly	d								16x06			17x12			17x36		18x08		18 39		
Ferryside	d								16x11			17x18			17x41		18x14		18 45		
Carmarthen	a		14 48			15 20			16 28		16 48	17 30			17 53		18 30		18 57		
	d		14 51			15 28					16 51	17 35			17 56				19 02		
Whitland	a		15 05			15 43					17 05	17 50			18 13				19 18		
	d		15 06			15 43					17 06	17 50			18 14				19 18		
Narberth	d		15x15								17x15								19 28		
Kilgetty	d		15x25								17x25								19 38		
Saundersfoot	d		15x27								17x27								19 40		
Tenby	a		15 34								17 34								19 52		
	d		15 45								17 45										
Penally	d		15x48								17x48										
Manorbier	d		15 54								17 54										
Lamphey	d		16x02								18x02										
Pembroke	d		16 05								18 05										
Pembroke Dock	a		16 19								18 19										
Clunderwen	d					15x50						17x57			18x20						
Clarbeston Road	d					15x57						18x05			18x28						
Haverfordwest	d					16 06									18 36						
Johnston	d					16x14									18x44						
Milford Haven	a					16 29									18 59						
Fishguard & Goodwick	a											18 26									
Fishguard Harbour ⛴	a											18 29									
	d																				
Rosslare Harbour ⛴	a																				

A ⊓ from Bridgend ⊘ to Bridgend

When events are being held at the Millenium Stadium, services are subject to alteration. Please check times before travelling.

Table 128

Mondays to Fridays

from 17 September

Cardiff - Maesteg, Swansea and West Wales

Route Diagram - see first Page of Table 127

		AW	GW	AW	GW	AW	AW	GW	AW	AW	GW	AW	AW	GW	AW	GW	GW	AW	AW	GW FX	GW FO	AW FX	AW FO
		■ ⊼	◇1 ⊓		◇1 ⊓			◇1 A ⊓	■ ⊼		◇1 B ⊓⊘		■ ⊼	◇1 ⊓		◇1 ⊓	◇1 ⊓			◇1 ⊓	◇1 ⊓	◇ ⊼	◇ ⊼
London Paddington 15 ⊖	d		15 45		16 15			16 45			17 15			17 45		18 15	18 45			19 15	19 15		
Reading 7	d		16 11		16 41			17 11			17 43			18 11		18 43	19 11			19 41	19u48		
Manchester Piccadilly 10	d	14 30							15 30				16 30									18 30	18 30
Gloucester 7	d					16 58				17 59					18 58				19 58				
Bristol Parkway 7	d		17 07		17 41			18 07			18 41			19 07		19 44	20 07			20 42	20 43		
Newport (South Wales)	d	17 22	17 31		18 04	17 52		18 31	18 41	18 53	19 11		19 22	19 31	19 52	20 08	20 33		20 52	21 04	21 07	21 52	21 52
Cardiff Central 7	d	17 39	17 48	18 04	18 22	18 12		18 50	19 04	19 12	19 28		19 46	19 51	20 13	20 24	20 54	21 04	21 10	21 22	21 22	22 09	22 09
Pontyclun	d					18 24				19 28					20 25				21 22			22 21	22 21
Llanharan	d					18 29				19 33					20 30				21 27			22 25	22 25
Pencoed	d					18 33				19 37					20 34				21 32			22 29	22 29
Bridgend	d	17 59	18 09	18 24	18 44	18 49		19 09	19 23	19 45	19 49		20 05	20 10	20 41	20 45	21 15	21 27	21 41	21 45	21 45	22 35	22 35
Wildmill	d					18 52				19 48					20 44				21 43				
Sarn	d					18 55				19 51					20 47				21 46				
Tondu	d					18 58				19 54					20 50				21 50				
Garth (Mid Glamorgan)	d					19 08				20 04					21 00				21 59				
Maesteg (Ewenny Road)	d					19 10				20 06					21 02				22 02				
Maesteg	a					19 15				20 11					21 07				22 06				
Pyle	d	18 07		18 33					19 30									21 34					
Port Talbot Parkway	d	18 17	18 22	18 41	18 57			19 22	19 38		20 02		20 21	20 26		20 58	21 28	21 45		21 58	21 58	22 47	22 47
Baglan	d			18 45					19 41														
Briton Ferry	d			18 48					19 44														
Neath	d	18 25	18 30	18 52	19 04			19 30	19 48		20 10		20 28	20 33		21 05	21 36	21 52		22 06	22 06		22 54
Skewen	d			18 56					19 53														
Llansamlet	d			19 00					19 57														
Swansea	a	18 37	18 48	19 11	19 18			19 46	20 04		20 23		20 42	20 47		21 19	21 49	22 04		22 19	22 19		23 07
	d	18 41					19 35		20 08		20 32		20 52					22 27					23 11
Gowerton	d	18x52							20x19									22x41					23x22
Llanelli	a	18 59					19 51		20 25		20 48		21 07					22 47				23 16	23 29
	d	19 00					19 52		20 27		20 49		21 09					22 49				23 18	23 30
Pembrey & Burry Port	d	19 06					19 59		20 32		20 56		21 14					22 54				23 23	23 36
Kidwelly	d						20x06											23x00				23x29	23x42
Ferryside	d						20x12											23x06				23x35	23x47
Carmarthen	a	19 27					20 28		20 55		21 20		21 35					23 18				23 56	00 04
	d	19 30							21 00				21 38					23 21					
Whitland	a	19 45							21 15				21 52					23 35					
	d	19 46							21 15				21 53					23 36					
Narberth	d								21x24														
Kilgetty	d								21x33														
Saundersfoot	d								21x35														
Tenby	a								21 42														
	d								21 43														
Penally	d								21x46														
Manorbier	d								21 52														
Lamphey	d								22x00														
Pembroke	d								22 03														
Pembroke Dock	a								22 18														
Clunderwen	d	19x53											21x59					23x42					
Clarbeston Road	d	20x00										20 05	22x07					23x51					
Haverfordwest	d	20 09											22 20					23 59					
Johnston	d	20x17											22x28					00x07					
Milford Haven	a	20 32											22 43					00 22					
Fishguard & Goodwick	a											20 23											
Fishguard Harbour ⛴	a											20 29											
	d																						
Rosslare Harbour ⛴	a																						

A The Capitals United

B The Red Dragon. ⊓ from Bridgend ⊘ to Bridgend

When events are being held at the Millenium Stadium, services are subject to alteration. Please check times before travelling.

Mondays to Fridays

from 17 September

Cardiff - Maesteg, Swansea and West Wales

Route Diagram - see first Page of Table 127

		GW	AW	AW	AW	GW	GW FO	GW FX
		◇1 A 🍴⊘		◇		◇1 🍴	◇1 🍴	◇1 🍴
London Paddington 15 ⊖	d	20 15				21 15	22 45	22 45
Reading 7	d	20 41				21 41	23 11	23 19
Manchester Piccadilly 10	d							
Gloucester 7	d							
Bristol Parkway 7	d	21 41				22 45	00 16	00 23
Newport (South Wales)	d	22 05				23 19	00 38	00 52
Cardiff Central 7	d	22 26	22 35		23 15	23 43	00 55	01 13
Pontyclun	d				23 29			
Llanharan	d				23 34			
Pencoed	d				23 39			
Bridgend	d	22 46	22 59		23 45	00 02	01 19	01 36
Wildmill	d		23 01					
Sarn	d		23 04					
Tondu	d		23 08					
Garth (Mid Glamorgan)	d		23 17					
Maesteg (Ewenny Road)	d		23 20					
Maesteg	a		23 24					
Pyle	d				23 53			
Port Talbot Parkway	d	22 59			00 01	00 15	01 32	01 49
Baglan	d				00 05			
Briton Ferry	d				00 09			
Neath	d	23 07			00 13	00 22	01 39	01 57
Skewen	d				00 16			
Llansamlet	d				00 20			
Swansea	a	23 20			00 28	00 37	01 53	02 10
	d			23 45	00 45			
Gowerton	d			23x56	00b55			
Llanelli	a			00 01	01s02			
	d			00 03				
Pembrey & Burry Port	d			00 08	01s09			
Kidwelly	d				01b15			
Ferryside	d				01b21			
Carmarthen	a			00 28	01 40			
	d			00 31				
Whitland	a			00 46				
	d			00 46				
Narberth	d							
Kilgetty	d							
Saundersfoot	d							
Tenby	a							
	d							
Penally	d							
Manorbier	d							
Lamphey	d							
Pembroke	d							
Pembroke Dock	a							
Clunderwen	d							
Clarbeston Road	d			01x00				
Haverfordwest	d							
Johnston	d							
Milford Haven	a							
Fishguard & Goodwick	a			01 20				
Fishguard Harbour ⛴	a			01 28				
	d							
Rosslare Harbour ⛴	a							

A 🍴 from Bridgend ⊘ to Bridgend

b Stops to set down only, stops on request

When events are being held at the Millenium Stadium, services are subject to alteration. Please check times before travelling.

Saturdays

until 23 June

Cardiff - Maesteg, Swansea and West Wales

Route Diagram - see first Page of Table 127

		AW	AW	AW	AW	AW	GW	GW	AW	AW	AW	AW	AW	AW	AW	AW	AW	AW	GW	AW	AW	GW	GW
			◇ 🚌	◇			◇1 🍴	◇1 🍴	8	◇				🚌	🚌		◇ 🚌		◇1	◇		1	◇1
London Paddington 15 ⊖	d						21p15	22p45															
Reading 7	d						21p41	23p11															
Manchester Piccadilly 10	d		18p30																				
Gloucester 7	d																				05 50		
Bristol Parkway 7	d						22p45	00 16															07 11
Newport (South Wales)	d		21p52				23p19	00 38													06 44		07 31
Cardiff Central 7	d	21p04	22p09			23p15	23p43	00 55									05 39	05 51		06 42	07 04		07 48
Pontyclun	d		22p21			23p29											05 51	06 03			07 16		
Llanharan	d		22p25			23p34											05 56	06 08			07 21		
Pencoed	d		22p29			23p39											06 01	06 12			07 25		
Bridgend	d	21p27	22p35			23p45	00 02	01 19									06 07	06 20		07 02	07 32		08 09
Wildmill	d																	06 22			07 35		
Sarn	d																	06 25			07 38		
Tondu	d																	06 29			07 41		
Garth (Mid Glamorgan)	d																	06 38			07 51		
Maesteg (Ewenny Road)	d																	06 41			07 53		
Maesteg	a																	06 45			07 58		
Pyle	d	21p34				23p53											06 15			07 10			
Port Talbot Parkway	d	21p45	22p47			00 01	00 15	01 32									06 23			07 18			08 22
Baglan	d					00 05											06 27			07 22			
Briton Ferry	d					00 09											06 30			07 25			
Neath	d	21p52	22p54			00 13	00 22	01 39									06 34			07 29			08 30
Skewen	d					00 16											06 38			07 33			
Llansamlet	d					00 20											06 42			07 37			
Swansea	a	22p04	23p07			00 28	00 37	01 53									06 51			07 45			08 44
	d	22p27	23p11	23p45	00 05	00 45				04 36					05 50		06 53		07 24	07 50		08 15	
Gowerton	d	22b41	23b22	23b56	00x16	00c55									06x00		07x03			08x00			
Llanelli	a	22p47	23p29	00 01	00 23	01s02				04 52					06 07		07 10		07 42	08 07		08 31	
	d	22p49	23p30	00 03	00 25										06 09		07 11		07 43	08 08		08 36	
Pembrey & Burry Port	d	22p54	23p36	00 08	00 31	01s09									06 15		07 17		07 50	08 14		08 43	
Kidwelly	d	23b00	23b42		00x38	01c15									06x22		07x23			08x20			
Ferryside	d	23b06	23b47		00x44	01c21									06x28		07x29			08x26			
Carmarthen	a	23p18	00 04	00 28	01 00	01 40									06 42		07 43		08 11	08 42		09 08	
	d	23p21		00 31							04 53	05 38	05 50	05 58	06 43		07 46		08 18	08 45			
Whitland	a	23p35		00 46							05 06	05 54	06 05	06 13	07 00		08 00		08 35	09 00			
	d	23p36		00 46							05 06	05 54	06 05	06 13	07 00		08 00		08 37	09 00			
Narberth	d											06x03			07x09				08x46				
Kilgetty	d											06x13			07x19				08x55				
Saundersfoot	d											06x15			07x21				08x58				
Tenby	a											06 22			07 28				09 06				
	d											06 25			07 42				09 10				
Penally	d											06x28			07x45				09x14				
Manorbier	d											06 35			07 52				09 22				
Lamphey	d											06x42			07x59				09x31				
Pembroke	d											06 45			08 02				09 36				
Pembroke Dock	a											07 00			08 17				09 43				
Clunderwen	d	23b42									05x13		06x12	06x19			08 07			09x07			
Clarbeston Road	d	23b51		01x00							05x21		06x20	06x27		07 34	08x14			09x15			
Haverfordwest	d	23p59									05 32			06 35			08 23						
Johnston	d	00x07									05x40			06x43			08x31						
Milford Haven	a	00 22									05 55			06 58			08 48						
Fishguard & Goodwick	a			01 20									06 38			07 52				09 33			
Fishguard Harbour ⛴	a			01 28									06 44			07 58				09 43			
	d								02 45														
Rosslare Harbour ⛴	a								06 15														

b Previous night, stops on request

c Stops to set down only, stops on request

When events are being held at the Millenium Stadium, services are subject to alteration. Please check times before travelling.

Table 128

Saturdays until 23 June

Cardiff - Maesteg, Swansea and West Wales

Route Diagram - see first Page of Table 127

		AW	AW	AW	AW	AW	AW	AW	GW	AW	AW	AW	AW	AW	GW	AW	AW	AW	AW	GW	AW	AW	AW	AW
			◇ ⌶	◇ ⌶		◇ ⌶			◇1 ⊒	⌶	◇ ⌶		◇ ⌶	B	◇1 ⊒	◇ ⌶			⌶	◇1 ⊒	◇ ⌶		◇	
London Paddington ⊖	d								07 45						08 45					09 45				
Reading	d								08 11						09 11					10 11				
Manchester Piccadilly	d										06 30					07 30					08 30			
Gloucester	d							07 58				08 58										10 58		
Bristol Parkway	d								09 07						10 07					11 07				
Newport (South Wales)	d		07 38		08 01	08 33		08 52	09 31		09 38	09 52			10 31	10 36				11 31	11 37	11 52		
Cardiff Central	d		07 58	08 09	08 22	09 04	09 14	09 18	09 48		10 04	10 18	10 54		10 48	11 04	11 14	11 21		11 48	12 04	12 18		
Pontyclun	d				08 34			09 30				10 30						11 33				12 30		
Llanharan	d				08 39			09 35				10 35						11 38				12 35		
Pencoed	d				08 43			09 39				10 39						11 42				12 39		
Bridgend	d		08 17	08 29	08 51	09 23	09 34	09 46	10 09		10 23	10 46			11 09	11 23	11 34	11 49		12 09	12 23	12 46		
Wildmill	d				08 53			09 49				10 49						11 52				12 49		
Sarn	d				08 56			09 52				10 52						11 55				12 52		
Tondu	d				09 00			09 55				10 55						11 58				12 55		
Garth (Mid Glamorgan)	d				09 09			10 05				11 05						12 08				13 05		
Maesteg (Ewenny Road)	d				09 12			10 07				11 07						12 10				13 07		
Maesteg	a				09 16			10 12				11 12						12 15				13 12		
Pyle	d			08 37			09 43										11 42							
Port Talbot Parkway	d		08 30	08 45		09 38	09 52		10 22		10 35				11 22	11 36	11 50			12 22	12 36			
Baglan	d			08 49			09 55										11 54							
Briton Ferry	d			08 52			09 59										11 57							
Neath	d		08 37	08 56		09 45	10 03		10 30		10 42				11 30	11 43	12 01			12 30	12 43			
Skewen	d			09 00			10 06										12 05							
Llansamlet	d			09 04			10 10										12 09							
Swansea	a		08 51	09 13		09 57	10 21		10 43		10 55				11 43	11 56	12 20			12 43	12 55			
	d		09 02	09 16		10 04					11 00				11 50	12 05			12 35		13 03		13 16	13 35
Gowerton	d		09x18			10x15													12x52					13x48
Llanelli	a		09 25	09 32		10 22					11 15		11 58		12 06	12 21			12 59		13 19		13 32	13 55
	d		09 26			10 22					11 17		11 58		12 08	12 22			13 01		13 20			13 56
Pembrey & Burry Port	d		09 32			10 28					11 23				12 14	12 28			13 07		13 26			14 02
Kidwelly	d		09x38			10x34										12x34								
Ferryside	d		09x44			10x40										12x40								
Carmarthen	a		09 56			10 51					11 42				12 39	12 51			13 33		13 46			14 25
	d	09 40	09 58							10 56	11 47				12 46						13 49			14 38
Whitland	a	09 54	10 14							11 10	12 01		12 34		13 03						14 03			14 54
	d	09 54	10 15							11 11	12 02		12 34		13 05						14 04			14 54
Narberth	d	10x03								11x20														15x03
Kilgetty	d	10x13								11x30														15x13
Saundersfoot	d	10x15								11x32					13 25									15x15
Tenby	a	10 24								11 39					13 33									15 22
	d									11 45					13 41									15 34
Penally	d									11x48														15x37
Manorbier	d									11 54					13 51									15 43
Lamphey	d									12x02														15x51
Pembroke	d									12 05					14 03									15 54
Pembroke Dock	a									12 20					14 14									16 09
Clunderwen	d		10x21								12x08										14x10			
Clarbeston Road	d		10x29								12x16										14x18			
Haverfordwest	d		10 37								12 24										14 26			
Johnston	d		10x45								12x32										14x34			
Milford Haven	a		10 58								12 47										14 49			
Fishguard & Goodwick	a												13 07											
Fishguard Harbour ⛴	a												13 17											
	d													14 30										
Rosslare Harbour ⛴	a													18 00										

When events are being held at the Millenium Stadium, services are subject to alteration. Please check times before travelling.

Table 128

Saturdays until 23 June

Cardiff - Maesteg, Swansea and West Wales

Route Diagram - see first Page of Table 127

		GW	AW	AW	AW	GW	AW	AW	GW	AW	AW	AW	AW	GW	AW	AW	AW	GW	AW	AW	AW
		◇1 A ⊒⊘	◇ ⌶			◇1 A ⊒⊘	◇ ⌶		◇1 ⊒	◇ ⌶				◇1 ⊒	■ ⌶	⌶		◇1 ⊒	⌶	■ ⌶	◇ ⌶
London Paddington ⊖	d	10 45				11 45			12 45					13 45				14 45			
Reading	d	11 11				12 11			13 11					14 11				15 11			
Manchester Piccadilly	d		09 30				10 30			11 30					12 30					13 30	
Gloucester	d				11 58								13 58			14 58					
Bristol Parkway	d	12 07				13 07			14 07					15 07				16 07			
Newport (South Wales)	d	12 31	12 37		12 52	13 31	13 37		14 31	14 37			14 52	15 31	15 22	15 52		16 31		16 37	16 56
Cardiff Central	d	12 48	13 04	13 14	13 18	13 48	14 04	14 21	14 48	15 04		15 14	15 18	15 48	15 42	16 18	16 37	16 48		17 04	17 18
Pontyclun	d				13 30			14 33					15 30			16 30	16 49				17 30
Llanharan	d				13 35			14 38					15 35			16 35					17 35
Pencoed	d				13 39			14 42					15 39			16 39	16 56				17 39
Bridgend	d	13 09	13 23	13 34	13 46	14 09	14 23	14 49	15 09	15 23		15 34	15 46	16 09	16 01	16 46	17a03	17 09		17 25	17 46
Wildmill	d				13 49			14 52					15 49			16 49					17 48
Sarn	d				13 52			14 55					15 52			16 52					17 51
Tondu	d				13 55			14 58					15 55			16 55					17 55
Garth (Mid Glamorgan)	d				14 05			15 08					16 05			17 05					18 04
Maesteg (Ewenny Road)	d				14 07			15 10					16 07			17 07					18 07
Maesteg	a				14 12			15 15					16 12			17 12					18 15
Pyle	d			13 42								15 42								17 32	
Port Talbot Parkway	d	13 22	13 36	13 50		14 22	14 36		15 22	15 36		15 50		16 22	16 19			17 22		17 40	
Baglan	d			13 54								15 54								17 42	
Briton Ferry	d			13 57								15 57								17 46	
Neath	d	13 30	13 43	14 01		14 30	14 43		15 30	15 43		16 01		16 30	16 26			17 30		17 50	
Skewen	d			14 05								16 05								17 54	
Llansamlet	d			14 09								16 09								17 58	
Swansea	a	13 43	13 55	14 20		14 43	14 55		15 43	15 55		16 20		16 43	16 37			17 43		18 05	
	d		14 05				15 00			16 00	16 05	16 40			16 40				17 51	18 09	
Gowerton	d										16x16	16 51			16x51				18x01	18x20	
Llanelli	a		14 20				15 20			16 15	16 23	16 58			16 57				18 08	18 26	
	d		14 22				15 22			16 17	16 24	16 59			16 59				18 10	18 28	
Pembrey & Burry Port	d		14 28				15 28			16 23	16 30	17 05			10 05				18 16	18 33	
Kidwelly	d		14x34							16x29	16x37	17x12			17x11				18x24	18x39	
Ferryside	d		14x39							16x34	16x43	17x18			17x16				18x30	18x45	
Carmarthen	a		14 51				15 46			16 51	16 57	17 30			17 28				18 46	18 57	
	d						15 49				17 06	17 35			17 31					19 02	
Whitland	a						16 03				17 22	17 50			17 45					19 18	
	d						16 04				17 32	17 50			17 48					19 18	
Narberth	d										17x41									19x28	
Kilgetty	d										17x51									19x38	
Saundersfoot	d										17x53									19x40	
Tenby	a										18 00									19 50	
	d										18 05									19 50	
Penally	d										18x08									19x53	
Manorbier	d										18 14									20 00	
Lamphey	d										18x22									20x07	
Pembroke	d										18 25									20 10	
Pembroke Dock	a										18 40									20 20	
Clunderwen	d						16x10					17x57			17x52						
Clarbeston Road	d						16x18					18x05			18x00						
Haverfordwest	d						16 26								18 08						
Johnston	d						16x34								18x16						
Milford Haven	a						16 49								18 31						
Fishguard & Goodwick	a											18 24									
Fishguard Harbour ⛴	a											18 29									
	d																				
Rosslare Harbour ⛴	a																				

A ⊒ from Bridgend ⊘ to Bridgend

When events are being held at the Millenium Stadium, services are subject to alteration. Please check times before travelling.

Table 128

Cardiff - Maesteg, Swansea and West Wales

Saturdays

until 23 June

Route Diagram - see first Page of Table 127

		AW	AW	GW	AW	AW	AW	GW	AW	AW	AW	GW	AW	GW	AW	GW	AW	AW	GW	AW	AW	AW	GW
		◇		◇1 ⊡	B 🛒			◇1 ⊡	B 🛒			◇1 ⊡	B 🛒	◇1 ⊡		◇1 ⊡			◇1 ⊡	◇ 🛒			◇1 ⊡
London Paddington 15 ⊖	d			15 45				16 45				17 45				18 45			19 45				20 45
Reading 7	d			16 11				17 11				18 11				19 11			20 11				21 13
Manchester Piccadilly 10	d				14 30				15 30				16 30							18 30			
Gloucester 7	d					16 58				17 58					18 58			19 58					
Bristol Parkway 7	d			17 07				18 07				19 07				20 07			21 07				22 11
Newport (South Wales)	d			17 31	17 37	17 52		18 31	18 37	18 52		19 31	19 41		19 52	20 31		20 52	21 31	21 45			22 46
Cardiff Central 7	d		17 38	17 48	18 04	18 18		18 48	19 04	19 16		19 48	20 04		20 13	20 48	21 04	21 10	21 48	22 07		22 43	23 07
Pontyclun	d					18 30				19 28					20 25			21 22		22 19		22 57	
Llanharan	d					18 35				19 33					20 30			21 27		22 23		23 02	
Pencoed	d					18 39				19 37					20 34			21 30		22 27		23 07	
Bridgend	d		17 58	18 09	18 25	18 46		19 09	19 23	19 45		20 09	20 23		20 41	21 09	21 23	21 41	22 09	22 33		23 13	23 28
Wildmill	d					18 49				19 48					20 44			21 43					
Sarn	d					18 52				19 51					20 47			21 46					
Tondu	d					18 55				19 54					20 50			21 50					
Garth (Mid Glamorgan)	d					19 05				20 04					21 00			21 59					
Maesteg (Ewenny Road)	d					19 07				20 06					21 02			22 02					
Maesteg	a					19 13				20 11					21 07			22 06					
Pyle	d		18 06		18 33				19 30								21 31					23 21	
Port Talbot Parkway	d		18 14	18 22	18 41			19 22	19 38			20 22	20 36			21 22	21 39		22 22	22 45		23 30	23 41
Baglan	d		18 18						19 41													23 34	
Briton Ferry	d		18 21						19 44													23 37	
Neath	d		18 25	18 30	18 49			19 30	19 48			20 30				21 30	21 46		22 30	22 52		23 41	23 49
Skewen	d		18 29						19 53													23 45	
Llansamlet	d		18 33						19 57													23 49	
Swansea	a		18 44	18 46	19 02			19 43	20 04			20 43				21 43	21 57		22 43	23 05		23 57	00 02
	d	18 21			19 05		19 35		20 08			21 00					22 25			23 10	23 45	00 09	
Gowerton	d				19x16				20x19					←			22x36			23x22		00s20	
Llanelli	a	18 37			19 23		19 51		20 25			21 16	21 05	21 16			22 42			23 29	00 01	00s28	
	d				19 24		19 52		20 27			21 16	21 06	21 16			22 44			23 30	00 02		
Pembrey & Burry Port	d				19 30		19 59		20 32			→	21 12	21 23			22 50			23 36	00 07	00s34	
Kidwelly	d						20x06										22x56			23x42		00s40	
Ferryside	d						20x12										23x01			23x47		00s46	
Carmarthen	a				19 51		20 28		20 55				21 31	21 48			23 18			00 04	00 30	01 04	
	d				19 55				21 00				22 05								00 31		
Whitland	a				20 10				21 15				22 19								00 44		
	d				20 10				21 15				22 20								00 44		
Narberth	d								21x24														
Kilgetty	d								21x33														
Saundersfoot	d								21x35														
Tenby	a								21 42														
	d								21 43														
Penally	d								21x46														
Manorbier	d								21 52														
Lamphey	d								22x00														
Pembroke	d								22 03														
Pembroke Dock	a								22 18														
Clunderwen	d				20x17								22x26										
Clarbeston Road	d				20x25						20 30		22x34										
Haverfordwest	d				20 33								22 42								00x58		
Johnston	d				20x41								22x50										
Milford Haven	a				20 56								23 05										
Fishguard & Goodwick	a										20 48										01 18		
Fishguard Harbour ⛴	a										20 54										01 26		
	d																						
Rosslare Harbour ⛴	a																						

When events are being held at the Millenium Stadium, services are subject to alteration. Please check times before travelling.

Table 128

Cardiff - Maesteg, Swansea and West Wales

Saturdays

30 June to 8 September

Route Diagram - see first Page of Table 127

		AW	AW	AW	AW	AW	GW	AW	GW	AW	AW	AW	AW	AW	AW	AW	AW	AW	AW	GW	AW	AW	GW
			◇ 🛒	◇			◇1 ⊡	A	◇1 ⊡	B	◇				🛒	🛒		◇ 🛒		◇1	◇		1
London Paddington 15 ⊖	d						21p15		22p45														
Reading 7	d						21p41		23p11														
Manchester Piccadilly 10	d		18p30																				
Gloucester 7	d																					05 50	
Bristol Parkway 7	d						22p45		00 16														
Newport (South Wales)	d		21p52				23p19		00 38													06 44	
Cardiff Central 7	d	21p04	22p09			23p15	23p43	00 11	00 55									05 39	05 51		06 42	07 04	
Pontyclun	d		22p21			23p29		00 23										05 51	06 03			07 16	
Llanharan	d		22p25			23p34		00 29										05 56	06 08			07 21	
Pencoed	d		22p29			23p39		00 34										06 01	06 12			07 25	
Bridgend	d	21p27	22p35			23p45	00 02	00 40	01 19									06 07	06 20		07 02	07 32	
Wildmill	d																		06 22			07 35	
Sarn	d																		06 25			07 38	
Tondu	d																		06 29			07 41	
Garth (Mid Glamorgan)	d																		06 38			07 51	
Maesteg (Ewenny Road)	d																		06 41			07 53	
Maesteg	a																		06 45			07 58	
Pyle	d	21p34				23p53		00 48										06 15			07 10		
Port Talbot Parkway	d	21p45	22p47			00 01	00 15	00 57	01 32									06 23			07 18		
Baglan	d					00 05		01 01										06 27			07 22		
Briton Ferry	d					00 09		01 05										06 30			07 25		
Neath	d	21p52	22p54			00 13	00 22	01 09	01 39									06 34			07 29		
Skewen	d					00 16		01 13										06 38			07 33		
Llansamlet	d					00 20		01 17										06 42			07 37		
Swansea	a	22p04	23p07			00 28	00 37	01 26	01 53									06 51			07 45		
	d	22p27	23p11	23p45	00 05	00 45		01 31			04 36					05 50		06 53		07 24	07 50		08 15
Gowerton	d	22b41	23b22	23b56	00x16	00c55		01x42								06x00		07x03			08x00		
Llanelli	a	22p47	23p29	00 01	00 23	01s02		01s48			04 52					06 07		07 10		07 42	08 07		08 31
	d	22p49	23p30	00 03	00 25											06 09		07 11		07 43	08 08		08 36
Pembrey & Burry Port	d	22p54	23p36	00 08	00 31	01s09		01s55								06 15		07 17		07 50	08 14		08 43
Kidwelly	d	23b00	23b42		00x38	01c15		02x03								06x22		07x23			08x20		
Ferryside	d	23b06	23b47		00x44	01c21		02x10								06x28		07x29			08x26		
Carmarthen	a	23p18	00 04	00 28	01 00	01 40		02 27								06 42		07 43		08 11	08 42		09 08
	d	23p21		00 31								04 53	05 38	05 50	05 58	06 43		07 46		08 18	08 45		
Whitland	a	23p35		00 46								05 06	05 54	06 05	06 13	07 00		08 00		08 35	09 00		
	d	23p36		00 46								05 06	05 54	06 05	06 13	07 00		08 00		08 37	09 00		
Narberth	d												06x03			07x09				08x46			
Kilgetty	d												06x13			07x19				08x55			
Saundersfoot	d												06x15			07x21				08x58			
Tenby	a												06 22			07 28				09 06			
	d												06 25			07 42				09 10			
Penally	d												06x28			07x45				09x14			
Manorbier	d												06 35			07 52				09 22			
Lamphey	d												06x42			07x59				09x31			
Pembroke	d												06 45			08 02				09 36			
Pembroke Dock	a												07 00			08 17				09 43			
Clunderwen	d	23b42										05x13		06x12	06x19			08 07			09x07		
Clarbeston Road	d	23b51		01x00								05x21		06x20	06x27		07 34	08x14			09x15		
Haverfordwest	d	23p59										05 32			06 35			08 23					
Johnston	d	00x07										05x40			06x43			08x31					
Milford Haven	a	00 22										05 55			06 58			08 48					
Fishguard & Goodwick	a			01 20										06 38			07 52				09 33		
Fishguard Harbour ⛴	a			01 28										06 44			07 58				09 43		
	d									02 45													
Rosslare Harbour ⛴	a									06 15													

A 11 August

b Previous night, stops on request

c Stops to set down only, stops on request

When events are being held at the Millenium Stadium, services are subject to alteration. Please check times before travelling.

Table 128

Saturdays

30 June to 8 September

Cardiff - Maesteg, Swansea and West Wales

Route Diagram - see first Page of Table 127

		GW	AW	AW	AW	AW		AW	AW	AW	GW	AW	AW	AW	AW	AW	GW	AW	AW	AW	AW	GW	AW	AW	AW
		◇1		◇ H	◇ H			◇ H			◇1 ⊏	H	◇ H		◇ H	B	◇1 ⊏	◇ H			H	◇1 ⊏	◇ H		◇
London Paddington 15 ⊖	d										07 45						08 45					09 45			
Reading 7	d										08 11						09 11					10 11			
Manchester Piccadilly 10	d												06 30					07 30					08 30		
Gloucester 7	d									07 58				08 58										10 58	
Bristol Parkway 7	d	07 11									09 07						10 07					11 07			
Newport (South Wales)	d	07 31		07 38		08 01		08 33		08 52	09 31		09 38	09 52			10 31	10 36				11 31	11 37	11 52	
Cardiff Central 7	d	07 48		07 58	08 09	08 22		09 04	09 14	09 18	09 48		10 04	10 18	10 54		10 48	11 04	11 14	11 21		11 48	12 04	12 18	
Pontyclun	d					08 34				09 30				10 30						11 33				12 30	
Llanharan	d					08 39				09 35				10 35						11 38				12 35	
Pencoed	d					08 43				09 39				10 39						11 42				12 39	
Bridgend	d	08 09		08 17	08 29	08 51		09 23	09 34	09 46	10 09		10 23	10 46			11 09	11 23	11 34	11 49		12 09	12 23	12 46	
Wildmill	d					08 53				09 49				10 49						11 52				12 49	
Sarn	d					08 56				09 52				10 52						11 55				12 52	
Tondu	d					09 00				09 55				10 55						11 58				12 55	
Garth (Mid Glamorgan)	d					09 09				10 05				11 05						12 08				13 05	
Maesteg (Ewenny Road)	d					09 12				10 07				11 07						12 10				13 07	
Maesteg	a					09 16				10 12				11 12						12 15				13 12	
Pyle	d				08 37				09 43										11 42						
Port Talbot Parkway	d	08 22		08 30	08 45			09 38	09 52		10 22		10 35				11 22	11 36	11 50			12 22	12 36		
Baglan	d				08 49				09 55										11 54						
Briton Ferry	d				08 52				09 59										11 57						
Neath	d	08 30		08 37	08 56			09 45	10 03		10 30		10 42				11 30	11 43	12 01			12 30	12 43		
Skewen	d				09 00				10 06										12 05						
Llansamlet	d				09 04				10 10										12 09						
Swansea	a	08 44		08 51	09 13			09 57	10 21		10 43		10 55				11 43	11 56	12 20			12 43	12 55		
	d			09 02	09 16			10 04					11 00				11 50	12 05			12 35		13 03		13 16
Gowerton	d			09x18				10x15													12x52				
Llanelli	a			09 25	09 32			10 22					11 15		11 58		12 06	12 21			12 59		13 19		13 32
	d			09 26				10 22					11 17		11 58		12 08	12 22			13 01		13 20		
Pembrey & Burry Port	d			09 32				10 28					11 23				12 14	12 28			13 07		13 26		
Kidwelly	d			09x38				10x34										12x34							
Ferryside	d			09x44				10x40										12x40							
Carmarthen	a			09 56				10 51					11 42				12 39	12 51			13 33		13 46		
	d		09 40	09 58								10 56	11 47				12 46						13 49		
Whitland	a		09 54	10 14								11 10	12 01		12 34		13 03						14 03		
	d		09 54	10 15								11 11	12 02		12 34		13 05						14 04		
Narberth	d		10x03									11x20													
Kilgetty	d		10x13									11x30													
Saundersfoot	d		10x15									11x32					13 25								
Tenby	a		10 24									11 39					13 33								
	d											11 45					13 41								
Penally	d											11x48													
Manorbier	d											11 54					13 51								
Lamphey	d											12x02													
Pembroke	d											12 05					14 03								
Pembroke Dock	a											12 20					14 14								
Clunderwen	d			10x21									12x08										14x10		
Clarbeston Road	d			10x29									12x16										14x18		
Haverfordwest	d			10 37									12 24										14 26		
Johnston	d			10x45									12x32										14x34		
Milford Haven	a			10 58									12 47										14 49		
Fishguard & Goodwick	a														13 07										
Fishguard Harbour ⛴	a														13 17										
	d															14 30									
Rosslare Harbour ⛴	a															18 00									

When events are being held at the Millenium Stadium, services are subject to alteration. Please check times before travelling.

Table 128

Saturdays

30 June to 8 September

Cardiff - Maesteg, Swansea and West Wales

Route Diagram - see first Page of Table 127

		AW		GW	AW	AW	AW	GW	AW	AW	GW	AW			AW	AW	AW	GW	AW	AW	AW	GW		AW	AW
				◇1 A ⊏⊘	◇ H			◇1 A ⊏⊘	◇ H		◇1 ⊏	◇ H						◇1 ⊏	■ H	H		◇1 ⊏		H	■ H
London Paddington 15 ⊖	d			10 45				11 45			12 45							13 45				14 45			
Reading 7	d			11 11				12 11			13 11							14 11				15 11			
Manchester Piccadilly 10	d				09 30				10 30			11 30							12 30						13 30
Gloucester 7	d						11 58										13 58			14 58					
Bristol Parkway 7	d			12 07				13 07			14 07							15 07				16 07			
Newport (South Wales)	d			12 31	12 37		12 52	13 31	13 37		14 31	14 37					14 52	15 31	15 22	15 52		16 31			16 37
Cardiff Central 7	d			12 48	13 04	13 14	13 18	13 48	14 04	14 21	14 48	15 04				15 14	15 18	15 48	15 42	16 18	16 37	16 48			17 04
Pontyclun	d						13 30			14 33							15 30			16 30	16 49				
Llanharan	d						13 35			14 38							15 35			16 35					
Pencoed	d						13 39			14 42							15 39			16 39	16 56				
Bridgend	d			13 09	13 23	13 34	13 46	14 09	14 23	14 49	15 09	15 23				15 34	15 46	16 09	16 01	16 46	17a03	17 09			17 25
Wildmill	d						13 49			14 52							15 49			16 49					
Sarn	d						13 52			14 55							15 52			16 52					
Tondu	d						13 55			14 58							15 55			16 55					
Garth (Mid Glamorgan)	d						14 05			15 08							16 05			17 05					
Maesteg (Ewenny Road)	d						14 07			15 10							16 07			17 07					
Maesteg	a						14 12			15 15							16 12			17 12					
Pyle	d					13 42										15 42									17 32
Port Talbot Parkway	d			13 22	13 36	13 50		14 22	14 36		15 22	15 36				15 50		16 22	16 19			17 22			17 40
Baglan	d					13 54										15 54									17 42
Briton Ferry	d					13 57										15 57									17 46
Neath	d			13 30	13 43	14 01		14 30	14 43		15 30	15 43				16 01		16 30	16 26			17 30			17 50
Skewen	d					14 05										16 05									17 54
Llansamlet	d					14 09										16 09									17 58
Swansea	a			13 43	13 55	14 20		14 43	14 55		15 43	15 55				16 20		16 43	16 37			17 43			18 05
	d	13 35			14 05				15 00			16 00			16 05	16 40			16 40					17 51	18 09
Gowerton	d	13x48													16x16	16 51			16x51					18x01	18x20
Llanelli	a	13 55			14 20				15 20			16 15			16 23	16 58			16 57					18 08	18 26
	d	13 56			14 22				15 22			16 17			16 24	16 59			16 59					18 10	18 28
Pembrey & Burry Port	d	14 02			14 28				15 28			16 23			16 30	17 05			10 05					18 16	18 33
Kidwelly	d				14x34							16x29			16x37	17x12			17x11					18x24	18x39
Ferryside	d				14x39							16x34			16x43	17x18			17x16					18x30	18x45
Carmarthen	a	14 25			14 51				15 46			16 51			16 57	17 30			17 28					18 46	18 57
	d	14 38							15 49						17 06	17 35			17 31						19 02
Whitland	a	14 54							16 03						17 22	17 50			17 45						19 18
	d	14 54							16 04						17 32	17 50			17 48						19 18
Narberth	d	15x03													17x41										19x28
Kilgetty	d	15x13													17x51										19x38
Saundersfoot	d	15x15													17x53										19x40
Tenby	a	15 22													18 00										19 50
	d	15 34													18 05										19 50
Penally	d	15x37													18x08										19x53
Manorbier	d	15 43													18 14										20 00
Lamphey	d	15x51													18x22										20x07
Pembroke	d	15 54													18 25										20 10
Pembroke Dock	a	16 09													18 40										20 20
Clunderwen	d								16x10							17x57			17x52						
Clarbeston Road	d								16x18							18x05			18x00						
Haverfordwest	d								16 26										18 08						
Johnston	d								16x34										18x16						
Milford Haven	a								16 49										18 31						
Fishguard & Goodwick	a															18 24									
Fishguard Harbour ⛴	a															18 29									
	d																								
Rosslare Harbour ⛴	a																								

A ⊏ from Bridgend ⊘ to Bridgend

When events are being held at the Millenium Stadium, services are subject to alteration. Please check times before travelling.

Table 128

Saturdays

30 June to 8 September

Cardiff - Maesteg, Swansea and West Wales

Route Diagram - see first Page of Table 127

		AW	AW	AW	GW	AW	AW	AW		GW	AW	AW	AW	GW	AW	GW	AW	GW		AW	AW	GW	AW	AW	AW
		◇ ✕	◇		◇1 ☕	■ ✕				◇1 ☕	■ ✕			◇1 ☕	■ ✕	◇1 ☕		◇1 ☕				◇1 ☕	◇ ✕	A	
London Paddington 15 ⊖	d				15 45					16 45				17 45				18 45				19 45			
Reading 7	d				16 11					17 11				18 11				19 11				20 11			
Manchester Piccadilly 10	d					14 30					15 30				16 30								18 30		
Gloucester 7	d						16 58					17 58					18 58				19 58				
Bristol Parkway 7	d				17 07					18 07				19 07				20 07				21 07			
Newport (South Wales)	d	16 56			17 31	17 37	17 52			18 31	18 37	18 52		19 31	19 41		19 52	20 31			20 52	21 31	21 45		
Cardiff Central 7	d	17 18		17 38	17 48	18 04	18 18			18 48	19 04	19 16		19 48	20 04		20 13	20 48		21 04	21 10	21 48	22 07	22 36	
Pontyclun	d	17 30					18 30					19 28					20 25				21 22		22 19	22 48	
Llanharan	d	17 35					18 35					19 33					20 30				21 27		22 23	22 54	
Pencoed	d	17 39					18 39					19 37					20 34				21 30		22 27	22 59	
Bridgend	d	17 46		17 58	18 09	18 25	18 46			19 09	19 23	19 45		20 09	20 23		20 41	21 09		21 23	21 41	22 09	22 33	23 06	
Wildmill	d	17 48					18 49					19 48					20 44				21 43			23 09	
Sarn	d	17 51					18 52					19 51					20 47				21 46			23 12	
Tondu	d	17 55					18 55					19 54					20 50				21 50			23 17	
Garth (Mid Glamorgan)	d	18 04					19 05					20 04					21 00				21 59			23 27	
Maesteg (Ewenny Road)	d	18 07					19 07					20 06					21 02				22 02			23 30	
Maesteg	a	18 15					19 13					20 11					21 07				22 06			23 35	
Pyle	d			18 06		18 33					19 30									21 31					
Port Talbot Parkway	d			18 14	18 22	18 41				19 22	19 38			20 22	20 36			21 22		21 39		22 22	22 45		
Baglan	d			18 18							19 41														
Briton Ferry	d			18 21							19 44														
Neath	d			18 25	18 30	18 49				19 30	19 48			20 30				21 30		21 46		22 30	22 52		
Skewen	d			18 29							19 53														
Llansamlet	d			18 33							19 57														
Swansea	a			18 44	18 46	19 02				19 43	20 04			20 43				21 43		21 57		22 43	23 05		
	d		18 21			19 05		19 35			20 08			21 00						22 25			23 10		23 45
Gowerton	d					19x16					20x19									22x36			23x22		
Llanelli	a		18 37			19 23		19 51			20 25			21 16	21 05	← 21 16				22 42			23 29		00 01
	d					19 24		19 52			20 27			21 16	21 06	21 16				22 44			23 30		00 02
Pembrey & Burry Port	d					19 30		19 59			20 32			→	21 12	21 23				22 50			23 36		00 07
Kidwelly	d							20x06												22x56			23x42		
Ferryside	d							20x12												23x01			23x47		
Carmarthen	a					19 51		20 28			20 55				21 31	21 48				23 18			00 04		00 30
	d					19 55					21 00				22 05										00 31
Whitland	a					20 10					21 15				22 19										00 44
	d					20 10					21 15				22 20										00 44
Narberth	d										21x24														
Kilgetty	d										21x33														
Saundersfoot	d										21x35														
Tenby	a										21 42														
	d										21 43														
Penally	d										21x46														
Manorbier	d										21 52														
Lamphey	d										22x00														
Pembroke	d										22 03														
Pembroke Dock	a										22 18														
Clunderwen	d					20x17									22x26										
Clarbeston Road	d					20x25							20 30		22x34										00x58
Haverfordwest	d					20 33									22 42										
Johnston	d					20x41									22x50										
Milford Haven	a					20 56									23 05										
Fishguard & Goodwick	a												20 48												01 18
Fishguard Harbour ⛴	a												20 54												01 26
	d																								
Rosslare Harbour ⛴	a																								

A 28 July, 4 August

When events are being held at the Millenium Stadium, services are subject to alteration. Please check times before travelling.

Table 128

Saturdays

30 June to 8 September

Cardiff - Maesteg, Swansea and West Wales

Route Diagram - see first Page of Table 127

		AW	GW
			◇1 ☕
London Paddington 15 ⊖	d		20 45
Reading 7	d		21 13
Manchester Piccadilly 10	d		
Gloucester 7	d		
Bristol Parkway 7	d		22 11
Newport (South Wales)	d		22 46
Cardiff Central 7	d	22 43	23 07
Pontyclun	d	22 57	
Llanharan	d	23 02	
Pencoed	d	23 07	
Bridgend	d	23 13	23 28
Wildmill	d		
Sarn	d		
Tondu	d		
Garth (Mid Glamorgan)	d		
Maesteg (Ewenny Road)	d		
Maesteg	a		
Pyle	d	23 21	
Port Talbot Parkway	d	23 30	23 41
Baglan	d	23 34	
Briton Ferry	d	23 37	
Neath	d	23 41	23 49
Skewen	d	23 45	
Llansamlet	d	23 49	
Swansea	a	23 57	00 02
	d	00 09	
Gowerton	d	00s20	
Llanelli	a	00s28	
	d		
Pembrey & Burry Port	d	00s34	
Kidwelly	d	00s40	
Ferryside	d	00s46	
Carmarthen	a	01 04	
	d		
Whitland	a		
	d		
Narberth	d		
Kilgetty	d		
Saundersfoot	d		
Tenby	a		
	d		
Penally	d		
Manorbier	d		
Lamphey	d		
Pembroke	d		
Pembroke Dock	a		
Clunderwen	d		
Clarbeston Road	d		
Haverfordwest	d		
Johnston	d		
Milford Haven	a		
Fishguard & Goodwick	a		
Fishguard Harbour ⛴	a		
	d		
Rosslare Harbour ⛴	a		

When events are being held at the Millenium Stadium, services are subject to alteration. Please check times before travelling.

Table 128

Saturdays

15 September to 20 October

Cardiff - Maesteg, Swansea and West Wales

Route Diagram - see first Page of Table 127

		AW	AW	AW	AW	AW	GW	GW	AW	AW	AW	AW	AW	AW	AW	AW	AW	AW	AW		AW	GW	GW
			◇ ⊼	◇			◇1 ⊡	◇1 ⊡	B	◇							◇ ⊼		◇ A			1	◇1
London Paddington 15 ⊖	d						21p15	22p45															
Reading 7	d						21p41	23p11															
Manchester Piccadilly 10	d		18p30																				
Gloucester 7	d																				05 50		
Bristol Parkway 7	d						22p45	00 16															07 11
Newport (South Wales)	d		21p52				23p19	00 38													06 44		07 31
Cardiff Central 7	d	21p04	22p09			23p15	23p43	00 55									05 39	05 51	06 42		07 04		07 48
Pontyclun	d		22p21			23p29											05 51	06 03			07 16		
Llanharan	d		22p25			23p34											05 56	06 08			07 21		
Pencoed	d		22p29			23p39											06 01	06 12			07 25		
Bridgend	d	21p27	22p35			23p45	00 02	01 19									06 07	06 20	07 02		07 32		08 09
Wildmill	d																	06 22			07 35		
Sarn	d																	06 25			07 38		
Tondu	d																	06 29			07 41		
Garth (Mid Glamorgan)	d																	06 38			07 51		
Maesteg (Ewenny Road)	d																	06 41			07 53		
Maesteg	a																	06 45			07 58		
Pyle	d	21p34				23p53											06 15		07 10				
Port Talbot Parkway	d	21p45	22p47			00 01	00 15	01 32									06 23		07 18				08 22
Baglan	d					00 05											06 27		07 22				
Briton Ferry	d					00 09											06 30		07 25				
Neath	d	21p52	22p54			00 13	00 22	01 39									06 34		07 29				08 30
Skewen	d					00 16											06 38		07 33				
Llansamlet	d					00 20											06 42		07 37				
Swansea	a	22p04	23p07			00 28	00 37	01 53									06 51		07 45				08 44
	d	22p27	23p11	23p45	00 05	00 45				04 36					05 50		06 53		07 50			08 15	
Gowerton	d	22b41	23b22	23b56	00x16	00c55									06x00		07x03		08x00				
Llanelli	a	22p47	23p29	00 01	00 23	01s02				04 52					06 07		07 10		08 07			08 31	
	d	22p49	23p30	00 03	00 25										06 09		07 11		08 08			08 36	
Pembrey & Burry Port	d	22p54	23p36	00 08	00 31	01s09									06 15		07 17		08 14			08 43	
Kidwelly	d	23b00	23b42		00x38	01c15									06x22		07x23		08x20				
Ferryside	d	23b06	23b47		00x44	01c21									06x28		07x29		08x26				
Carmarthen	a	23p18	00 04	00 28	01 00	01 40									06 42		07 43		08 40			09 08	
	d	23p21		00 31							04 53	05 38	05 50	05 58	06 43		07 46		08 43				
Whitland	a	23p35		00 46							05 06	05 54	06 05	06 13	07 00		08 00		08 59				
	d	23p36		00 46							05 06	05 54	06 05	06 13	07 00		08 00		09 07	09 02			
Narberth	d											06x03			07x09					09x11			
Kilgetty	d											06x13			07x19					09x21			
Saundersfoot	d											06x15			07x21					09x23			
Tenby	a											06 22			07 28					09 30			
	d											06 25			07 42					09 43			
Penally	d											06x28			07x45					09x46			
Manorbier	d											06 35			07 52					09 53			
Lamphey	d											06x42			07x59					10x00			
Pembroke	d											06 45			08 02					10 03			
Pembroke Dock	a											07 00			08 17					10 17			
Clunderwen	d	23b42									05x13		06x12	06x19			08 07		09x14				
Clarbeston Road	d	23b51		01x00							05x21		06x20	06x27		07 34	08x14		09x22				
Haverfordwest	d	23p59									05 32			06 35			08 23						
Johnston	d	00x07									05x40			06x43			08x31						
Milford Haven	a	00 22									05 55			06 58			08 48						
Fishguard & Goodwick	a			01 20									06 38			07 52			09 41				
Fishguard Harbour ⛴	a			01 28									06 44			07 58			09 47				
	d								02 45														
Rosslare Harbour ⛴	a								06 15														

A ◇ to Whitland

b Previous night, stops on request

c Stops to set down only, stops on request

When events are being held at the Millenium Stadium, services are subject to alteration. Please check times before travelling.

Table 128

Saturdays

15 September to 20 October

Cardiff - Maesteg, Swansea and West Wales

Route Diagram - see first Page of Table 127

		AW	AW	AW	AW	AW	AW	GW	AW	AW	AW	GW	AW	AW	AW	AW	AW	AW	GW	AW	AW	AW	GW	AW
		◇ ⊼	◇ ⊼		◇ ⊼			◇1 ⊡		◇ ⊼		◇1 ⊡	◇ ⊼	B		◇ ⊼			◇1 ⊡	◇ ⊼		◇	◇1 A ⊡⊘	
London Paddington 15 ⊖	d							07 45				08 45							09 45				10 45	
Reading 7	d							08 11				09 11							10 11				11 11	
Manchester Piccadilly 10	d									06 30						07 30				08 30				
Gloucester 7	d						07 58				08 58										10 58			
Bristol Parkway 7	d							09 07				10 07							11 07				12 07	
Newport (South Wales)	d	07 38		08 01	08 33		08 52	09 31		09 38	09 52	10 31				10 36			11 31	11 37	11 52		12 31	
Cardiff Central 7	d	07 58	08 09	08 22	09 04	09 14	09 18	09 48		10 04	10 18	10 48	10 54			11 04	11 14	11 21	11 48	12 04	12 18		12 48	
Pontyclun	d			08 34			09 30				10 30							11 33			12 30			
Llanharan	d			08 39			09 35				10 35							11 38			12 35			
Pencoed	d			08 43			09 39				10 39							11 42			12 39			
Bridgend	d	08 17	08 29	08 51	09 23	09 34	09 46	10 09		10 23	10 46	11 09				11 23	11 34	11 49	12 09	12 23	12 46		13 09	
Wildmill	d			08 53			09 49				10 49							11 52			12 49			
Sarn	d			08 56			09 52				10 52							11 55			12 52			
Tondu	d			09 00			09 55				10 55							11 58			12 55			
Garth (Mid Glamorgan)	d			09 09			10 05				11 05							12 08			13 05			
Maesteg (Ewenny Road)	d			09 12			10 07				11 07							12 10			13 07			
Maesteg	a			09 16			10 12				11 12							12 15			13 12			
Pyle	d		08 37			09 43											11 42							
Port Talbot Parkway	d	08 30	08 45		09 38	09 52		10 22		10 35		11 22				11 36	11 50		12 22	12 36			13 22	
Baglan	d		08 49			09 55											11 54							
Briton Ferry	d		08 52			09 59											11 57							
Neath	d	08 37	08 56		09 45	10 03		10 30		10 42		11 30				11 43	12 01		12 30	12 43			13 30	
Skewen	d		09 00			10 06											12 05							
Llansamlet	d		09 04			10 10											12 09							
Swansea	a	08 51	09 13		09 57	10 21		10 43		10 55		11 43				11 56	12 20		12 43	12 55			13 43	
	d	09 02	09 16		10 04					11 00					11 50	12 05				13 03		13 16		13 50
Gowerton	d	09x18			10x15										12x01									14x00
Llanelli	a	09 25	09 32		10 22					11 15			11 58		12 08	12 21				13 19		13 32		14 07
	d	09 26			10 22					11 17			11 58		12 10	12 22				13 20				14 09
Pembrey & Burry Port	d	09 32			10 28					11 23					12 16	12 28				13 26				14 15
Kidwelly	d	09x38			10x34											12x34								
Ferryside	d	09x44			10x40											12x40								
Carmarthen	a	09 56			10 51					11 42					12 39	12 51				13 46				14 39
	d	09 58							10 56	11 47					12 56					13 49				14 56
Whitland	a	10 14							11 10	12 01			12 34		13 11					14 03				15 10
	d	10 15							11 11	12 02			12 34		13 11					14 04				15 10
Narberth	d								11x20						13x20									15x19
Kilgetty	d								11x30						13x30									15x29
Saundersfoot	d								11x32						13x32									15x31
Tenby	a								11 39						13 39									15 38
	d								11 45						13 45									15 45
Penally	d								11x48						13x48									15x48
Manorbier	d								11 54						13 54									15 54
Lamphey	d								12x02						14x02									16x02
Pembroke	d								12 05						14 05									16 05
Pembroke Dock	a								12 20						14 19									16 19
Clunderwen	d	10x21								12x08										14x10				
Clarbeston Road	d	10x29								12x16										14x18				
Haverfordwest	d	10 37								12 24										14 26				
Johnston	d	10x45								12x32										14x34				
Milford Haven	a	10 58								12 47										14 49				
Fishguard & Goodwick	a												13 07											
Fishguard Harbour ⛴	a												13 17											
	d													14 30										
Rosslare Harbour ⛴	a													18 00										

A ⊡ from Bridgend ⊘ to Bridgend

When events are being held at the Millenium Stadium, services are subject to alteration. Please check times before travelling.

Table 128

Cardiff - Maesteg, Swansea and West Wales

15 September to 20 October

Route Diagram - see first Page of Table 127

		AW	AW	AW	GW	AW	AW	GW	AW	AW	AW	AW	GW	AW	AW	AW	GW	AW	AW	AW	AW
		◇ 🛒			◇1 A 🍴⊘	◇ 🛒		◇1 🍴	◇ 🛒				◇1 🍴	■ 🛒	🛒		◇1 🍴		■ 🛒	◇ 🛒	◇
London Paddington 15 ⊖	d				11 45			12 45					13 45				14 45				
Reading 7	d				12 11			13 11					14 11				15 11				
Manchester Piccadilly 10	d	09 30				10 30			11 30					12 30					13 30		
Gloucester 7	d			11 58								13 58			14 58						
Bristol Parkway 7	d				13 07			14 07					15 07				16 07				
Newport (South Wales)	d	12 37		12 52	13 31	13 37		14 31	14 37			14 52	15 31	15 22	15 52		16 31		16 37	16 56	
Cardiff Central 7	d	13 04	13 14	13 18	13 48	14 04	14 21	14 48	15 04		15 14	15 18	15 48	15 42	16 18	16 37	16 48		17 04	17 18	
Pontyclun	d			13 30			14 33					15 30			16 30	16 49				17 30	
Llanharan	d			13 35			14 38					15 35			16 35					17 35	
Pencoed	d			13 39			14 42					15 39			16 39	16 56				17 39	
Bridgend	d	13 23	13 34	13 46	14 09	14 23	14 49	15 09	15 23		15 34	15 46	16 09	16 01	16 46	17a03	17 09		17 25	17 46	
Wildmill	d			13 49			14 52					15 49			16 49					17 48	
Sarn	d			13 52			14 55					15 52			16 52					17 51	
Tondu	d			13 55			14 58					15 55			16 55					17 55	
Garth (Mid Glamorgan)	d			14 05			15 08					16 05			17 05					18 04	
Maesteg (Ewenny Road)	d			14 07			15 10					16 07			17 07					18 07	
Maesteg	a			14 12			15 15					16 12			17 12					18 15	
Pyle	d		13 42								15 42								17 32		
Port Talbot Parkway	d	13 36	13 50		14 22	14 36		15 22	15 36		15 50		16 22	16 19			17 22		17 40		
Baglan	d		13 54								15 54								17 42		
Briton Ferry	d		13 57								15 57								17 46		
Neath	d	13 43	14 01		14 30	14 43		15 30	15 43		16 01		16 30	16 26			17 30		17 50		
Skewen	d		14 05								16 05								17 54		
Llansamlet	d		14 09								16 09								17 58		
Swansea	a	13 55	14 20		14 43	14 55		15 43	15 55		16 20		16 43	16 37			17 43		18 05		
	d	14 05				15 00			16 00	16 05	16 40			16 40				17 51	18 09		18 21
Gowerton	d									16x16	16 51			16x51				18x01	18x20		
Llanelli	a	14 20				15 20			16 15	16 23	16 58			16 57				18 08	18 26		18 37
	d	14 22				15 22			16 17	16 25	16 59			16 59				18 10	18 28		
Pembrey & Burry Port	d	14 28				15 28			16 23	16 31	17 05			10 05				18 16	18 33		
Kidwelly	d	14x34							16x29		17x12			17x11				18x24	18x39		
Ferryside	d	14x39							16x34		17x18			17x16				18x30	18x45		
Carmarthen	a	14 51				15 46			16 51	16 54	17 30			17 28				18 46	18 57		
	d					15 49				16 56	17 35			17 31					19 02		
Whitland	a					16 03				17 10	17 50			17 45					19 18		
	d					16 04				17 11	17 50			17 48					19 18		
Narberth	d									17x20									19x28		
Kilgetty	d									17x29									19x38		
Saundersfoot	d									17x31									19x40		
Tenby	a									17 38									19 50		
	d									17 43									19 50		
Penally	d									17x46									19x53		
Manorbier	d									17 53									20 00		
Lamphey	d									18x00									20x07		
Pembroke	d									18 03									20 10		
Pembroke Dock	a									18 18									20 20		
Clunderwen	d					16x10					17x57			17x52							
Clarbeston Road	d					16x18					18x05			18x00							
Haverfordwest	d					16 26								18 08							
Johnston	d					16x34								18x16							
Milford Haven	a					16 49								18 31							
Fishguard & Goodwick	a										18 24										
Fishguard Harbour ⛴	a										18 29										
	d																				
Rosslare Harbour ⛴	a																				

A 🍴 from Bridgend ⊘ to Bridgend

When events are being held at the Millenium Stadium, services are subject to alteration. Please check times before travelling.

Table 128

Cardiff - Maesteg, Swansea and West Wales

15 September to 20 October

Route Diagram - see first Page of Table 127

		AW	GW	AW	AW	AW	GW	AW	AW	AW	GW	AW	GW	AW	GW	AW	AW	GW	GW	AW	AW	AW	GW
			◇1 🍴	■ 🛒			◇1 🍴	■ 🛒			◇1 🍴	■ 🛒	◇1 🍴		◇1 🍴			◇1 🍴	◇1 🍴	◇ 🛒			◇1 🍴
London Paddington 15 ⊖	d		15 45				16 45				17 45				18 45			19 15	19 45				20 45
Reading 7	d		16 11				17 11				18 11				19 11			19 42	20 11				21 13
Manchester Piccadilly 10	d			14 30				15 30				16 30								18 30			
Gloucester 7	d				16 58				17 58					18 58			19 58						
Bristol Parkway 7	d		17 07				18 07				19 07				20 07			20 40	21 07				22 11
Newport (South Wales)	d		17 31	17 37	17 52		18 31	18 37	18 52		19 31	19 41		19 52	20 31		20 52	21 07	21 31	21 45			22 46
Cardiff Central 7	d	17 38	17 48	18 04	18 18		18 48	19 04	19 16		19 48	20 04		20 13	20 48	21 04	21 10	21 23	21 48	22 07		22 43	23 07
Pontyclun	d				18 30				19 28					20 25			21 22			22 19		22 57	
Llanharan	d				18 35				19 33					20 30			21 27			22 23		23 02	
Pencoed	d				18 39				19 37					20 34			21 30			22 27		23 07	
Bridgend	d	17 58	18 09	18 25	18 46		19 09	19 23	19 45		20 09	20 23		20 41	21 09	21 23	21 41	21 46	22 09	22 33		23 13	23 28
Wildmill	d				18 49				19 48					20 44			21 43						
Sarn	d				18 52				19 51					20 47			21 46						
Tondu	d				18 55				19 54					20 50			21 50						
Garth (Mid Glamorgan)	d				19 05				20 04					21 00			21 59						
Maesteg (Ewenny Road)	d				19 07				20 06					21 02			22 02						
Maesteg	a				19 13				20 11					21 07			22 06						
Pyle	d	18 06		18 33				19 30								21 31						23 21	
Port Talbot Parkway	d	18 14	18 22	18 41			19 22	19 38			20 22	20 36			21 22	21 39		21 59	22 22	22 45		23 30	23 41
Baglan	d	18 18						19 41														23 34	
Briton Ferry	d	18 21						19 44														23 37	
Neath	d	18 25	18 30	18 49			19 30	19 48			20 30				21 30	21 46		22 07	22 30	22 52		23 41	23 49
Skewen	d	18 29						19 53														23 45	
Llansamlet	d	18 33						19 57														23 49	
Swansea	a	18 44	18 46	19 02			19 43	20 04			20 43				21 43	21 57		22 19	22 43	23 05		23 57	00 02
	d			19 05		19 35		20 08			21 00					22 25				23 10	23 45	00 09	
Gowerton	d			19x16				20x19					←			22x36				23x22		00s20	
Llanelli	a			19 23		19 51		20 25			21 16	21 05	21 16			22 42				23 29	00 01	00s28	
	d			19 24		19 52		20 27			21 16	21 06	21 16			22 44				23 30	00 02		
Pembrey & Burry Port	d			19 30		19 59		20 32			→	21 12	21 23			22 50				23 36	00 07	00s34	
Kidwelly	d					20x06										22x56				23x42		00s40	
Ferryside	d					20x12										23x01				23x47		00s46	
Carmarthen	a			19 51		20 28		20 55				21 31	21 48			23 18				00 04	00 30	01 04	
	d			19 55				21 00				22 05									00 31		
Whitland	a			20 10				21 15				22 19									00 44		
	d			20 10				21 15				22 20									00 44		
Narberth	d							21x24															
Kilgetty	d							21x33															
Saundersfoot	d							21x35															
Tenby	a							21 42															
	d							21 43															
Penally	d							21x46															
Manorbier	d							21 52															
Lamphey	d							22x00															
Pembroke	d							22 03															
Pembroke Dock	a							22 18															
Clunderwen	d			20x17								22x26											
Clarbeston Road	d			20x25						20 30		22x34									00x58		
Haverfordwest	d			20 33								22 42											
Johnston	d			20x41								22x50											
Milford Haven	a			20 56								23 05											
Fishguard & Goodwick	a									20 48											01 18		
Fishguard Harbour ⛴	a									20 54											01 26		
	d																						
Rosslare Harbour ⛴	a																						

When events are being held at the Millenium Stadium, services are subject to alteration. Please check times before travelling.

Table 128

Saturdays from 27 October

Cardiff - Maesteg, Swansea and West Wales

Route Diagram - see first Page of Table 127

		AW	AW	AW	AW	AW	GW	GW	AW	AW		AW	AW	AW	AW	AW	AW	AW	AW	AW			AW	GW	GW
			◇ 🛒	◇			◇■ 🍴	◇■ 🍴	B	◇								◇ 🛒		◇ A				■	◇■
London Paddington 15 ⊖	d						21p15	22p45																	
Reading 7	d						21p41	23p11																	
Manchester Piccadilly 10	d		18p30																						
Gloucester 7	d																						05 50		
Bristol Parkway 7	d						22p45	00 16																	07 11
Newport (South Wales)	d		21p52				23p19	00 38															06 44		07 31
Cardiff Central 7	d	21p04	22p09			23p15	23p43	00 55										05 39	05 51	06 42			07 04		07 48
Pontyclun	d		22p21			23p29												05 51	06 03				07 16		
Llanharan	d		22p25			23p34												05 56	06 08				07 21		
Pencoed	d		22p29			23p39												06 01	06 12				07 25		
Bridgend	d	21p27	22p35			23p45	00 02	01 19										06 07	06 20	07 02			07 32		08 09
Wildmill	d																		06 22				07 35		
Sarn	d																		06 25				07 38		
Tondu	d																		06 29				07 41		
Garth (Mid Glamorgan)	d																		06 38				07 51		
Maesteg (Ewenny Road)	d																		06 41				07 53		
Maesteg	a																		06 45				07 58		
Pyle	d	21p34				23p53												06 15		07 10					
Port Talbot Parkway	d	21p45	22p47			00 01	00 15	01 32										06 23		07 18					08 22
Baglan	d					00 05												06 27		07 22					
Briton Ferry	d					00 09												06 30		07 25					
Neath	d	21p52	22p54			00 13	00 22	01 39										06 34		07 29					08 30
Skewen	d					00 16												06 38		07 33					
Llansamlet	d					00 20												06 42		07 37					
Swansea	a	22p04	23p07			00 28	00 37	01 53										06 51		07 45					08 44
	d	22p27	23p11	23p45	00 05	00 45				04 36						05 50		06 53		07 50				08 15	
Gowerton	d	22b41	23b22	23b56	00x16	00c55										06x00		07x03		08x00					
Llanelli	a	22p47	23p29	00 01	00 23	01s02				04 52						06 07		07 10		08 07				08 31	
	d	22p49	23p30	00 03	00 25											06 09		07 11		08 08				08 36	
Pembrey & Burry Port	d	22p54	23p36	00 08	00 31	01s09										06 15		07 17		08 14				08 43	
Kidwelly	d	23b00	23b42		00x38	01c15										06x22		07x23		08x20					
Ferryside	d	23b06	23b47		00x44	01c21										06x28		07x29		08x26					
Carmarthen	a	23p18	00 04	00 28	01 00	01 40										06 42		07 43		08 40				09 08	
	d	23p21		00 31								04 53	05 38	05 50	05 58	06 43		07 46		08 43					
Whitland	a	23p35		00 46								05 06	05 54	06 05	06 13	07 00		08 00		08 59					
	d	23p36		00 46								05 06	05 54	06 05	06 13	07 00		08 00		09 07	09 02				
Narberth	d												06x03			07x09					09x11				
Kilgetty	d												06x13			07x19					09x21				
Saundersfoot	d												06x15			07x21					09x23				
Tenby	a												06 22			07 28					09 30				
	d												06 25			07 42					09 43				
Penally	d												06x28			07x45					09x46				
Manorbier	d												06 35			07 52					09 53				
Lamphey	d												06x42			07x59					10x00				
Pembroke	d												06 45			08 02					10 03				
Pembroke Dock	a												07 00			08 17					10 17				
Clunderwen	d	23b42										05x13		06x12	06x19			08 07		09x14					
Clarbeston Road	d	23b51		01x00								05x21		06x20	06x27		07 34	08x14		09x22					
Haverfordwest	d	23p59										05 32			06 35			08 23							
Johnston	d	00x07										05x40			06x43			08x31							
Milford Haven	a	00 22										05 55			06 58			08 48							
Fishguard & Goodwick	a			01 20										06 38			07 52			09 41					
Fishguard Harbour ⛴	a			01 28										06 44			07 58			09 47					
	d								02 45																
Rosslare Harbour ⛴	a								06 15																

A ◇ to Whitland

b Previous night, stops on request

c Stops to set down only, stops on request

When events are being held at the Millenium Stadium, services are subject to alteration. Please check times before travelling.

Table 128

Saturdays from 27 October

Cardiff - Maesteg, Swansea and West Wales

Route Diagram - see first Page of Table 127

		AW	AW	AW	AW	AW	AW		GW	AW	AW	AW	GW	AW	AW	AW	AW	AW	AW	GW	AW	AW	AW	GW	AW
		◇ 🛒	◇ 🛒		◇ 🛒				◇■ 🍴		◇ 🛒		◇■ 🍴	◇ 🛒	B		◇ 🛒			◇■ 🍴	◇ 🛒		◇	◇■ A 🍴⊘	
London Paddington 15 ⊖	d								07 45				08 45							09 45				10 45	
Reading 7	d								08 11				09 11							10 11				11 11	
Manchester Piccadilly 10	d										06 30						07 30				08 30				
Gloucester 7	d						07 58					08 58										10 58			
Bristol Parkway 7	d								09 07				10 07							11 07				12 07	
Newport (South Wales)	d	07 38		08 01	08 33		08 52		09 31		09 38	09 52	10 31				10 36			11 31	11 37	11 52		12 31	
Cardiff Central 7	d	07 58	08 09	08 22	09 04	09 14	09 18		09 48		10 04	10 18	10 48	10 54			11 04	11 14	11 21	11 48	12 04	12 18		12 48	
Pontyclun	d			08 34			09 30					10 30							11 33			12 30			
Llanharan	d			08 39			09 35					10 35							11 38			12 35			
Pencoed	d			08 43			09 39					10 39							11 42			12 39			
Bridgend	d	08 17	08 29	08 51	09 23	09 34	09 46		10 09		10 23	10 46	11 09				11 23	11 34	11 49	12 09	12 23	12 46		13 09	
Wildmill	d			08 53			09 49					10 49							11 52			12 49			
Sarn	d			08 56			09 52					10 52							11 55			12 52			
Tondu	d			09 00			09 55					10 55							11 58			12 55			
Garth (Mid Glamorgan)	d			09 09			10 05					11 05							12 08			13 05			
Maesteg (Ewenny Road)	d			09 12			10 07					11 07							12 10			13 07			
Maesteg	a			09 16			10 12					11 12							12 15			13 12			
Pyle	d		08 37			09 43												11 42							
Port Talbot Parkway	d	08 30	08 45		09 38	09 52			10 22		10 35		11 22				11 36	11 50		12 22	12 36			13 22	
Baglan	d		08 49			09 55												11 54							
Briton Ferry	d		08 52			09 59												11 57							
Neath	d	08 37	08 56		09 45	10 03			10 30		10 42		11 30				11 43	12 01		12 30	12 43			13 30	
Skewen	d		09 00			10 06												12 05							
Llansamlet	d		09 04			10 10												12 09							
Swansea	a	08 51	09 13		09 57	10 21			10 43		10 55		11 43				11 56	12 20		12 43	12 55			13 43	
	d	09 02	09 16		10 04						11 00					11 50	12 05				13 03		13 16		13 50
Gowerton	d	09x18			10x15											12x01									14x00
Llanelli	a	09 25	09 32		10 22						11 15			11 58		12 08	12 21				13 19		13 32		14 07
	d	09 26			10 22						11 17			11 58		12 10	12 22				13 20				14 09
Pembrey & Burry Port	d	09 32			10 28						11 23					12 16	12 28				13 26				14 15
Kidwelly	d	09x38			10x34												12x34								
Ferryside	d	09x44			10x40												12x40								
Carmarthen	a	09 56			10 51						11 42					12 39	12 51				13 46				14 39
	d	09 58								10 56	11 47					12 56					13 49				14 56
Whitland	a	10 14								11 10	12 01			12 34		13 11					14 03				15 10
	d	10 15								11 11	12 02			12 34		13 11					14 04				15 10
Narberth	d									11x20						13x20									15x19
Kilgetty	d									11x30						13x30									15x29
Saundersfoot	d									11x32						13x32									15x31
Tenby	a									11 39						13 39									15 38
	d									11 45						13 45									15 45
Penally	d									11x48						13x48									15x48
Manorbier	d									11 54						13 54									15 54
Lamphey	d									12x02						14x02									16x02
Pembroke	d									12 05						14 05									16 05
Pembroke Dock	a									12 20						14 19									16 19
Clunderwen	d	10x21									12x08										14x10				
Clarbeston Road	d	10x29									12x16										14x18				
Haverfordwest	d	10 37									12 24										14 26				
Johnston	d	10x45									12x32										14x34				
Milford Haven	a	10 58									12 47										14 49				
Fishguard & Goodwick	a													13 07											
Fishguard Harbour ⛴	a													13 17											
	d														14 30										
Rosslare Harbour ⛴	a														18 00										

A 🍴 from Bridgend ⊘ to Bridgend

When events are being held at the Millenium Stadium, services are subject to alteration. Please check times before travelling.

Table 128

Cardiff - Maesteg, Swansea and West Wales

Route Diagram - see first Page of Table 127

		AW	AW		AW	GW	AW	AW	GW	AW		AW	AW		AW	GW	AW	AW	AW	GW	AW	AW	AW		AW
		◇ ✠				◇1 A ⊡Ø	◇ ✠		◇1 ⊡	◇ ✠						◇1 ⊡	■ ✠	✠		◇1 ⊡		■ ✠	◇ ✠		◇
London Paddington 15 ⊖	d					11 45			12 45							13 45				14 45					
Reading 7	d					12 11			13 11							14 11				15 11					
Manchester Piccadilly 10	d	09 30					10 30			11 30							12 30					13 30			
Gloucester 7	d				11 58										13 58			14 58							
Bristol Parkway 7	d					13 07			14 07							15 07				16 07					
Newport (South Wales)	d	12 37			12 52	13 31	13 37		14 31	14 37					14 52	15 31	15 22	15 52		16 31		16 37	16 56		
Cardiff Central 7	d	13 04	13 14		13 18	13 48	14 04	14 21	14 48	15 04			15 14		15 18	15 48	15 42	16 18	16 37	16 48		17 04	17 18		
Pontyclun	d				13 30			14 33							15 30			16 30	16 49				17 30		
Llanharan	d				13 35			14 38							15 35			16 35					17 35		
Pencoed	d				13 39			14 42							15 39			16 39	16 56				17 39		
Bridgend	d	13 23	13 34		13 46	14 09	14 23	14 49	15 09	15 23			15 34		15 46	16 09	16 01	16 46	17a03	17 09		17 25	17 46		
Wildmill	d				13 49			14 52							15 49			16 49					17 48		
Sarn	d				13 52			14 55							15 52			16 52					17 51		
Tondu	d				13 55			14 58							15 55			16 55					17 55		
Garth (Mid Glamorgan)	d				14 05			15 08							16 05			17 05					18 04		
Maesteg (Ewenny Road)	d				14 07			15 10							16 07			17 07					18 07		
Maesteg	a				14 12			15 15							16 12			17 12					18 15		
Pyle	d		13 42										15 42									17 32			
Port Talbot Parkway	d	13 36	13 50			14 22	14 36		15 22	15 36			15 50			16 22	16 19			17 22		17 40			
Baglan	d		13 54										15 54									17 42			
Briton Ferry	d		13 57										15 57									17 46			
Neath	d	13 43	14 01			14 30	14 43		15 30	15 43			16 01			16 30	16 26			17 30		17 50			
Skewen	d		14 05										16 05									17 54			
Llansamlet	d		14 09										16 09									17 58			
Swansea	a	13 55	14 20			14 43	14 55		15 43	15 55			16 20			16 43	16 37			17 43		18 05			
	d	14 05					15 00			16 00		16 05	16 40				16 40				17 51	18 09			18 21
Gowerton	d											16x16	16 51				16x51				18x01	18x20			
Llanelli	a	14 20					15 20			16 15		16 23	16 58				16 57				18 08	18 26			18 37
	d	14 22					15 22			16 17		16 25	16 59				16 59				18 10	18 28			
Pembrey & Burry Port	d	14 28					15 28			16 23		16 31	17 05				10 05				18 16	18 33			
Kidwelly	d	14x34								16x29			17x12				17x11				18x24	18x39			
Ferryside	d	14x39								16x34			17x18				17x16				18x30	18x45			
Carmarthen	a	14 51					15 46			16 51		16 54	17 30				17 28				18 46	18 57			
	d						15 49					16 56	17 35				17 31					19 02			
Whitland	a						16 03					17 10	17 50				17 45					19 18			
	d						16 04					17 11	17 50				17 48					19 18			
Narberth	d											17x20										19x28			
Kilgetty	d											17x29										19x38			
Saundersfoot	d											17x31										19x40			
Tenby	a											17 38										19 50			
	d											17 43										19 50			
Penally	d											17x46										19x53			
Manorbier	d											17 53										20 00			
Lamphey	d											18x00										20x07			
Pembroke	d											18 03										20 10			
Pembroke Dock	a											18 18										20 20			
Clunderwen	d						16x10						17x57				17x52								
Clarbeston Road	d						16x18						18x05				18x00								
Haverfordwest	d						16 26										18 08								
Johnston	d						16x34										18x16								
Milford Haven	a						16 49										18 31								
Fishguard & Goodwick	a												18 24												
Fishguard Harbour ⛴	a												18 29												
	d																								
Rosslare Harbour ⛴	a																								

A ⊡ from Bridgend Ø to Bridgend

When events are being held at the Millenium Stadium, services are subject to alteration. Please check times before travelling.

Table 128

Cardiff - Maesteg, Swansea and West Wales

Route Diagram - see first Page of Table 127

		AW	GW	AW	AW	AW	GW	AW	AW		AW	GW	AW	GW	AW	GW	AW	AW	GW		GW	AW	AW	AW	GW
			◇1 ⊡	■ ✠			◇1 ⊡	■ ✠				◇1 ⊡	■ ✠	◇1 ⊡		◇1 ⊡			◇1 ⊡		◇1 ⊡	◇ ✠			◇1 ⊡
London Paddington 15 ⊖	d		15 45				16 45					17 45				18 45			19 15		19 45				20 45
Reading 7	d		16 11				17 11					18 11				19 11			19 42		20 11				21 13
Manchester Piccadilly 10	d			14 30				15 30					16 30									18 30			
Gloucester 7	d				16 58				17 58						18 58			19 58							
Bristol Parkway 7	d		17 07				18 07					19 07				20 07			20 40		21 07				22 11
Newport (South Wales)	d		17 31	17 37	17 52		18 31	18 37	18 52			19 31	19 41		19 52	20 31		20 52	21 07		21 31	21 45			22 46
Cardiff Central 7	d	17 38	17 48	18 04	18 18		18 48	19 04	19 16			19 48	20 04		20 13	20 48	21 04	21 10	21 23		21 48	22 07		22 43	23 07
Pontyclun	d				18 30				19 28						20 25			21 22				22 19		22 57	
Llanharan	d				18 35				19 33						20 30			21 27				22 23		23 02	
Pencoed	d				18 39				19 37						20 34			21 30				22 27		23 07	
Bridgend	d	17 58	18 09	18 25	18 46		19 09	19 23	19 45			20 09	20 23		20 41	21 09	21 23	21 41	21 46		22 09	22 33		23 13	23 28
Wildmill	d				18 49				19 48						20 44			21 43							
Sarn	d				18 52				19 51						20 47			21 46							
Tondu	d				18 55				19 54						20 50			21 50							
Garth (Mid Glamorgan)	d				19 05				20 04						21 00			21 59							
Maesteg (Ewenny Road)	d				19 07				20 06						21 02			22 02							
Maesteg	a				19 13				20 11						21 07			22 06							
Pyle	d	18 06		18 33				19 30									21 31							23 21	
Port Talbot Parkway	d	18 14	18 22	18 41			19 22	19 38				20 22	20 36			21 22	21 39		21 59		22 22	22 45		23 30	23 41
Baglan	d	18 18						19 41																23 34	
Briton Ferry	d	18 21						19 44																23 37	
Neath	d	18 25	18 30	18 49			19 30	19 48				20 30				21 30	21 46		22 07		22 30	22 52		23 41	23 49
Skewen	d	18 29						19 53																23 45	
Llansamlet	d	18 33						19 57																23 49	
Swansea	a	18 44	18 46	19 02			19 43	20 04				20 43				21 43	21 57		22 19		22 43	23 05		23 57	00 02
	d			19 05		19 35		20 08				21 00					22 25					23 10	23 45	00 09	
Gowerton	d			19x16				20x19						←			22x36					23x22		00s20	
Llanelli	a			19 23		19 51		20 25				21 16	21 05	21 16			22 42					23 29	00 01	00s28	
	d			19 24		19 52		20 27				21 16	21 06	21 16			22 44					23 30	00 02		
Pembrey & Burry Port	d			19 30		19 59		20 32				→	21 12	21 23			22 50					23 36	00 07	00s34	
Kidwelly	d					20x06											22x56					23x42		00s40	
Ferryside	d					20x12											23x01					23x47		00s46	
Carmarthen	a			19 51		20 28		20 55					21 31	21 48			23 18					00 04	00 30	01 04	
	d			19 55				21 00					22 05										00 31		
Whitland	a			20 10				21 15					22 19										00 44		
	d			20 10				21 15					22 20										00 44		
Narberth	d							21x24																	
Kilgetty	d							21x33																	
Saundersfoot	d							21x35																	
Tenby	a							21 42																	
	d							21 43																	
Penally	d							21x46																	
Manorbier	d							21 52																	
Lamphey	d							22x00																	
Pembroke	d							22 03																	
Pembroke Dock	a							22 18																	
Clunderwen	d			20x17									22x26												
Clarbeston Road	d			20x25							20 30		22x34										00x58		
Haverfordwest	d			20 33									22 42												
Johnston	d			20x41									22x50												
Milford Haven	a			20 56									23 05												
Fishguard & Goodwick	a										20 48												01 18		
Fishguard Harbour ⛴	a										20 54												01 26		
	d																								
Rosslare Harbour ⛴	a																								

When events are being held at the Millenium Stadium, services are subject to alteration. Please check times before travelling.

Table 128

Sundays until 24 June

Cardiff - Maesteg, Swansea and West Wales

Route Diagram - see first Page of Table 127

		AW	AW	AW	GW	AW	AW	AW	AW	AW	AW	AW	GW	AW	AW	GW	AW	GW	GW	AW	GW	AW	AW
		◇ H			◇1 ⊏	B		◇ H			◇ H	◇	◇1 ⊏	◇	B	◇1 ⊏	H	◇1 ⊏	◇1 ⊏		◇1 ⊏	■ H	◇
London Paddington ⊖	d				20p45								08 30			09 42			10 37		11 37		
Reading	d				21p13								09 06			10 18			11 12		12 12		
Manchester Piccadilly	d	18p30																				10 30	
Gloucester	d																						
Bristol Parkway	d				22p11								10 09			11 18			12 11		13 11		
Newport (South Wales)	d	21p45			22p46						09 27		10 33	11 00		11 43			12 37		13 37	13 29	
Cardiff Central	d	22p07		22p43	23p07			07 10			09 50		10 55	11 25		12 04	12 10		12 57		13 57	14 03	
Pontyclun	d	22p19		22p57							10 03											14 16	
Llanharan	d	22p23		23p02							10 08											14 21	
Pencoed	d	22p27		23p07							10 13											14 26	
Bridgend	d	22p33		23p13	23p28			07 31			10 20		11 15	11 45		12 25	12 31		13 19		14 19	14 33	
Wildmill	d																						
Sarn	d																						
Tondu	d																						
Garth (Mid Glamorgan)	d																						
Maesteg (Ewenny Road)	d																						
Maesteg	a																						
Pyle	d			23p21							10 28						12 39					14 41	
Port Talbot Parkway	d	22p45		23p30	23p41			07 45			10 37		11 28	11 59		12 38	12 48		13 32		14 32	14 49	
Baglan	d			23p34																			
Briton Ferry	d			23p37																			
Neath	d	22p52		23p41	23p49			07 53			10 45		11 37	12 07		12 45			13 39		14 39	14 57	
Skewen	d			23p45																			
Llansamlet	d			23p49																			
Swansea	a	23p05		23p57	00 02			08 06			10 58		11 49	12 19		12 58			13 52		14 52	15 10	
	d	23p10	23p45	00 09				08 15			11 01	11 07		12 25		13 08				14 11	14 58	15 13	15 26
Gowerton	d	23b22		00s20				08x26				11x16		12x35				←		14x22			15x36
Llanelli	a	23p29	00 01	00s28				08 33			11 17	11 23		12 42		13 24	13 17	13 24		14 29	15 14	15 29	15 48
	d	23p30	00 02					08 35			11 19			12 43		13 30	13 17	13 30		14 31	15 15	15 30	
Pembrey & Burry Port	d	23p36	00 07	00s34				08 41			11 25			12 49		↪	13 23	13 36		14 37	15 22	15 36	
Kidwelly	d	23b42		00s40				08x48			11x32			12x55						14x43			
Ferryside	d	23b47		00s46				08x54			11x38			13x01						14x49			
Carmarthen	a	00 04	00 30	01 04				09 07			11 51			13 15			13 47	13 58		15 04	15 43	15 59	
	d		00 31				08 20	09 10	09 55	10 19	11 55			13 20			14 04			15 07		16 03	
Whitland	a		00 44				08 36	09 26	10 11	10 34	12 11			13 35			14 20			15 21		16 19	
	d		00 44				08 36	09 26	10 11	10 34	12 11			13 36			14 20			15 22		16 20	
Narberth	d							09x35		10x43										15x31			
Kilgetty	d							09x45		10x52										15x41			
Saundersfoot	d							09x47		10x54										15x43			
Tenby	a							09 54		11 01										15 50			
	d							09 56		11 11										15 54			
Penally	d							09x59		11x14										15x57			
Manorbier	d							10 06		11 20										16 03			
Lamphey	d							10x14		11x28										16x11			
Pembroke	d							10 17		11 31										16 14			
Pembroke Dock	a							10 32		11 44										16 29			
Clunderwen	d						08x44		10x19		12x19						14x28					16x28	
Clarbeston Road	d		00x58				08x52		10x27		12x27						14x36					16x36	
Haverfordwest	d						09 00		10 35		12 35						14 44					16 44	
Johnston	d						09x09		10x44		12x44						14x53					16x53	
Milford Haven	a						09 20		10 55		12 55						15 08					17 08	
Fishguard & Goodwick	a		01 18																				
Fishguard Harbour ⛴	a		01 26											14 10									
	d					02 45									14 30								
Rosslare Harbour ⛴	a					06 15									18 00								

b Previous night, stops on request

When events are being held at the Millenium Stadium, services are subject to alteration. Please check times before travelling.

Table 128

Sundays until 24 June

Cardiff - Maesteg, Swansea and West Wales

Route Diagram - see first Page of Table 127

		GW	AW	GW	AW	GW	AW	GW	AW	GW	AW	AW	GW	AW	GW	GW	AW	GW	GW
		◇1 ⊏		◇1 ⊏	■ H	◇1 ⊏		◇1 ⊏	■ H	◇1 ⊏			◇1 ⊏	◇ H	◇1 ⊏	◇1 ⊏	◇	◇1 ⊏	◇1 ⊏
London Paddington ⊖	d	12 37		13 37		14 37		15 37		16 37			17 37		18 37	19 37		20 37	21 37
Reading	d	13 13		14 13		15 13		16 12		17 13			18 13		19 12	20 13		21 13	22 12
Manchester Piccadilly	d				12 30				14 30										
Gloucester	d																		
Bristol Parkway	d	14 11		15 12		16 12		17 11		18 12			19 15		20 11	21 12		22 12	23 12
Newport (South Wales)	d	14 37		15 38	15 46	16 38		17 41	17 34	18 38			19 41		20 37	21 38		22 37	23 42
Cardiff Central	d	14 57		15 57	16 16	16 58		18 01	18 06	18 58			20 01	20 15	20 57	22 02	22 30	23 01	00 04
Pontyclun	d								18 21										
Llanharan	d								18 26										
Pencoed	d								18 30										
Bridgend	d	15 19		16 20	16 37	17 20		18 22	18 38	19 20			20 22	20 37	21 19	22 23	22 51	23 22	00 24
Wildmill	d																		
Sarn	d																		
Tondu	d																		
Garth (Mid Glamorgan)	d																		
Maesteg (Ewenny Road)	d																		
Maesteg	a																		
Pyle	d				16 45				18 46					20 45					
Port Talbot Parkway	d	15 32		16 33	16 54	17 33		18 35	18 54	19 33			20 35	20 54	21 32	22 36	23 05	23 37	00 37
Baglan	d																		
Briton Ferry	d																		
Neath	d	15 39		16 39	17 02	17 40		18 43	19 02	19 40			20 43	21 02	21 39	22 44	23 13	23 44	00 45
Skewen	d																		
Llansamlet	d																		
Swansea	a	15 52		16 53	17 14	17 54		18 58	19 15	19 53			20 56	21 14	21 53	22 57	23 25	23 57	00 57
	d		16 26	17 05	17 25		18 11		19 20			20 35		21 18			23 38		
Gowerton	d		16x37				18x22					20x46					23x49		
Llanelli	a		16 44	17 21	17 41		18 29		19 36			20 54		21 34			23 56		
	d		16 46	17 22	17 41		18 31		19 36			20 55		21 34			23 58		
Pembrey & Burry Port	d		16 52	17 29	17 48		18 37		19 43			21 01		21 41			00 04		
Kidwelly	d		16x59				18x44					21x08					00x11		
Ferryside	d		17x05				18x50					21x14					00x17		
Carmarthen	a		17 19	17 50	18 14		19 03		20 05			21 32		22 04			00 30		
	d		17 32		18 20		19 06		20 07					22 05			00 34		
Whitland	a		17 48		18 36		19 22		20 23					22 21			00 50		
	d		17 48		18 37		19 22		20 30		20 30			22 22			00 50		
Narberth	d		17x57								20x37								
Kilgetty	d		18x07								20x46								
Saundersfoot	d		18x09								20x48								
Tenby	a		18 16								20 55								
	d		18 19								20 59								
Penally	d		18x22								21x02								
Manorbier	d		18 29								21 08								
Lamphey	d		18x36								21x16								
Pembroke	d		18 40								21 19								
Pembroke Dock	a		18 55								21 34								
Clunderwen	d				18x45		19x30		20x37					22x29					
Clarbeston Road	d				18x53		19x38		20x45					22x37			01x03		
Haverfordwest	d				19 01		19a46		20 54					22 46					
Johnston	d				19x10				21x02					22x54					
Milford Haven	a				19 25				21 19					23 10					
Fishguard & Goodwick	a																		
Fishguard Harbour ⛴	a																01 30		
	d																		
Rosslare Harbour ⛴	a																		

When events are being held at the Millenium Stadium, services are subject to alteration. Please check times before travelling.

Table 128

Sundays

1 July to 9 September

Cardiff - Maesteg, Swansea and West Wales

Route Diagram - see first Page of Table 127

		AW	AW	AW	GW	AW	AW	AW	AW	AW	AW	AW	AW
		◇			◇1	A	B		◇			◇	◇
London Paddington 15 ⊖	d				20p45								
Reading 7	d				21p13								
Manchester Piccadilly 10	d	18p30											
Gloucester 7	d												
Bristol Parkway 7	d				22p11								
Newport (South Wales)	d	21p45			22p46							09 27	
Cardiff Central 7	d	22p07		22p43	23p07	00 08			07 10			09 50	
Pontyclun	d	22p19		22p57		00 20						10 03	
Llanharan	d	22p23		23p02		00 26						10 08	
Pencoed	d	22p27		23p07		00 31						10 13	
Bridgend	d	22p33		23p13	23p28	00 37			07 31			10 20	
Wildmill	d												
Sarn	d												
Tondu	d												
Garth (Mid Glamorgan)	d												
Maesteg (Ewenny Road)	d												
Maesteg	a												
Pyle	d			23p21		00 45						10 28	
Port Talbot Parkway	d	22p45		23p30	23p41	00 54			07 45			10 37	
Baglan	d			23p34		00 58							
Briton Ferry	d			23p37		01 02							
Neath	d	22p52		23p41	23p49	01 06			07 53			10 45	
Skewen	d			23p45		01 10							
Llansamlet	d			23p49		01 14							
Swansea	a	23p05		23p57	00 02	01 23			08 06			10 58	
	d	23p10	23p45	00 09		01 28			08 15			11 01	11 07
Gowerton	d	23b22		00s20		01x39			08x26				11x16
Llanelli	a	23p29	00 01	00s28		01s45			08 33			11 17	11 23
	d	23p30	00 02						08 35			11 19	
Pembrey & Burry Port	d	23p36	00 07	00s34		01s52			08 41			11 25	
Kidwelly	d	23b42		00s40		02x00			08x48			11x32	
Ferryside	d	23b47		00s46		02x07			08x54			11x38	
Carmarthen	a	00 04	00 30	01 04		02 24			09 07			11 51	
	d		00 31					08 20	09 10	09 55	10 19	11 55	
Whitland	a		00 44					08 36	09 26	10 11	10 34	12 11	
	d		00 44					08 36	09 26	10 11	10 34	12 11	
Narberth	d								09x35		10x43		
Kilgetty	d								09x45		10x52		
Saundersfoot	d								09x47		10x54		
Tenby	a								09 54		11 01		
	d								09 56		11 11		
Penally	d								09x59		11x14		
Manorbier	d								10 06		11 20		
Lamphey	d								10x14		11x28		
Pembroke	d								10 17		11 31		
Pembroke Dock	a								10 32		11 44		
Clunderwen	d							08x44		10x19		12x19	
Clarbeston Road	d		00x58					08x52		10x27		12x27	
Haverfordwest	d							09 00		10 35		12 35	
Johnston	d							09x09		10x44		12x44	
Milford Haven	a							09 20		10 55		12 55	
Fishguard & Goodwick	a		01 18										
Fishguard Harbour ⛴	a		01 26										
	d						02 45						
Rosslare Harbour ⛴	a						06 15						

		GW	AW	AW	GW	AW	GW	AW		GW	AW		AW
		◇1	◇	B	◇1		◇1			◇1	■		◇
London Paddington 15 ⊖	d	08 30			09 37		10 37			11 37			
Reading 7	d	09 06			10 06		11 12			12 12			
Manchester Piccadilly 10	d										10 30		
Gloucester 7	d												
Bristol Parkway 7	d	10 08			11 05		12 11			13 11			
Newport (South Wales)	d	10 33	11 00		11 32		12 37			13 37	13 29		
Cardiff Central 7	d	10 54	11 25		11 53	12 05	12 57			13 57	14 03		
Pontyclun	d										14 16		
Llanharan	d										14 21		
Pencoed	d										14 26		
Bridgend	d	11 15	11 45		12 14	12 26	13 19			14 19	14 33		
Wildmill	d												
Sarn	d												
Tondu	d												
Garth (Mid Glamorgan)	d												
Maesteg (Ewenny Road)	d												
Maesteg	a												
Pyle	d					12 34					14 41		
Port Talbot Parkway	d	11 28	11 59		12 27	12 43	13 32			14 32	14 49		
Baglan	d												
Briton Ferry	d												
Neath	d	11 36	12 07		12 34		13 39			14 39	14 57		
Skewen	d												
Llansamlet	d												
Swansea	a	11 49	12 19		12 47		13 52			14 52	15 10		
	d		12 25		12 58			14 11		14 58	15 13		15 26
Gowerton	d		12x35					14x22					15x36
Llanelli	a		12 42		13 15	13 23		14 29		15 14	15 29		15 48
	d		12 43		13 16	13 23		14 31		15 15	15 30		
Pembrey & Burry Port	d		12 49		13 23	13 29		14 37		15 22	15 36		
Kidwelly	d		12x55					14x43					
Ferryside	d		13x01					14x49					
Carmarthen	a		13 15		13 44	13 56		15 04		15 43	15 59		
	d		13 20			14 04		15 07			16 03		
Whitland	a		13 35			14 20		15 21			16 19		
	d		13 36			14 20		15 22			16 20		
Narberth	d							15x31					
Kilgetty	d							15x41					
Saundersfoot	d							15x43					
Tenby	a							15 50					
	d							15 54					
Penally	d							15x57					
Manorbier	d							16 03					
Lamphey	d							16x11					
Pembroke	d							16 14					
Pembroke Dock	a							16 29					
Clunderwen	d					14x28					16x28		
Clarbeston Road	d					14x36					16x36		
Haverfordwest	d					14 44					16 44		
Johnston	d					14x53					16x53		
Milford Haven	a					15 08					17 08		
Fishguard & Goodwick	a												
Fishguard Harbour ⛴	a		14 10										
	d			14 30									
Rosslare Harbour ⛴	a			18 00									

A 5 August

b Previous night, stops on request

When events are being held at the Millenium Stadium, services are subject to alteration. Please check times before travelling.

Table 128

Sundays

1 July to 9 September

Cardiff - Maesteg, Swansea and West Wales

Route Diagram - see first Page of Table 127

		GW	AW	GW	AW	GW		AW	GW	AW	GW
		◇1		◇1	■	◇1			◇1	■	◇1
London Paddington 15 ⊖	d	12 37		13 37		14 37			15 37		16 37
Reading 7	d	13 12		14 12		15 12			16 12		17 12
Manchester Piccadilly 10	d				12 30					14 30	
Gloucester 7	d										
Bristol Parkway 7	d	14 11		15 11		16 11			17 11		18 11
Newport (South Wales)	d	14 37		15 37	15 46	16 37			17 41	17 34	18 37
Cardiff Central 7	d	14 57		15 57	16 16	16 57			18 01	18 06	18 57
Pontyclun	d									18 21	
Llanharan	d									18 26	
Pencoed	d									18 30	
Bridgend	d	15 19		16 19	16 37	17 19			18 22	18 38	19 19
Wildmill	d										
Sarn	d										
Tondu	d										
Garth (Mid Glamorgan)	d										
Maesteg (Ewenny Road)	d										
Maesteg	a										
Pyle	d				16 45					18 46	
Port Talbot Parkway	d	15 32		16 32	16 54	17 32			18 35	18 54	19 32
Baglan	d										
Briton Ferry	d										
Neath	d	15 39		16 39	17 02	17 39			18 43	19 02	19 39
Skewen	d										
Llansamlet	d										
Swansea	a	15 52		16 52	17 14	17 53			18 58	19 15	19 52
	d		16 26	17 05	17 25			18 11		19 20	
Gowerton	d		16x37					18x22			
Llanelli	a		16 44	17 21	17 41			18 29		19 36	
	d		16 46	17 22	17 41			18 31		19 36	
Pembrey & Burry Port	d		16 52	17 29	17 48			18 37		19 43	
Kidwelly	d		16x59					18x44			
Ferryside	d		17x05					18x50			
Carmarthen	a		17 19	17 50	18 14			19 03		20 05	
	d		17 32		18 20			19 06		20 07	
Whitland	a		17 48		18 36			19 22		20 23	
	d		17 48		18 37			19 22		20 30	
Narberth	d		17x57								
Kilgetty	d		18x07								
Saundersfoot	d		18x09								
Tenby	a		18 16								
	d		18 19								
Penally	d		18x22								
Manorbier	d		18 29								
Lamphey	d		18x36								
Pembroke	d		18 40								
Pembroke Dock	a		18 55								
Clunderwen	d				18x45			19x30		20x37	
Clarbeston Road	d				18x53			19x38		20x45	
Haverfordwest	d				19 01			19a46		20 54	
Johnston	d				19x10					21x02	
Milford Haven	a				19 25					21 19	
Fishguard & Goodwick	a										
Fishguard Harbour ⛴	a										
	d										
Rosslare Harbour ⛴	a										

		AW	AW	GW	AW	GW		GW	AW	GW	GW
				◇1	◇	◇1		◇1	◇	◇1	◇1
London Paddington 15 ⊖	d			17 37		18 37		19 37		20 37	21 37
Reading 7	d			18 12		19 12		20 12		21 06	22 12
Manchester Piccadilly 10	d										
Gloucester 7	d										
Bristol Parkway 7	d			19 15		20 11		21 11		22 05	23 17
Newport (South Wales)	d			19 41		20 37		21 37		22 38	23 43
Cardiff Central 7	d			20 01	20 15	20 57		22 01	22 30	23 01	00 08
Pontyclun	d										
Llanharan	d										
Pencoed	d										
Bridgend	d			20 22	20 37	21 19		22 22	22 51	23 22	00 28
Wildmill	d										
Sarn	d										
Tondu	d										
Garth (Mid Glamorgan)	d										
Maesteg (Ewenny Road)	d										
Maesteg	a										
Pyle	d				20 45						
Port Talbot Parkway	d			20 35	20 54	21 32		22 35	23 05	23 37	00 41
Baglan	d										
Briton Ferry	d										
Neath	d			20 43	21 02	21 39		22 43	23 13	23 44	00 49
Skewen	d										
Llansamlet	d										
Swansea	a			20 56	21 14	21 53		22 56	23 25	23 57	01 01
	d		20 35		21 18				23 38		
Gowerton	d		20x46						23x49		
Llanelli	a		20 54		21 34				23 56		
	d		20 55		21 34				23 58		
Pembrey & Burry Port	d		21 01		21 41				00 04		
Kidwelly	d		21x08						00x11		
Ferryside	d		21x14						00x17		
Carmarthen	a		21 32		22 04				00 30		
	d				22 05				00 34		
Whitland	a				22 21				00 50		
	d	20 30			22 22				00 50		
Narberth	d	20x37									
Kilgetty	d	20x46									
Saundersfoot	d	20x48									
Tenby	a	20 55									
	d	20 59									
Penally	d	21x02									
Manorbier	d	21 08									
Lamphey	d	21x16									
Pembroke	d	21 19									
Pembroke Dock	a	21 34									
Clunderwen	d				22x29						
Clarbeston Road	d				22x37				01x03		
Haverfordwest	d				22 46						
Johnston	d				22x54						
Milford Haven	a				23 10						
Fishguard & Goodwick	a										
Fishguard Harbour ⛴	a								01 30		
	d										
Rosslare Harbour ⛴	a										

When events are being held at the Millenium Stadium, services are subject to alteration. Please check times before travelling.

Table 128

Sundays

16 September to 21 October

Cardiff - Maesteg, Swansea and West Wales

Route Diagram - see first Page of Table 127

		AW	AW	AW	GW	AW	AW	AW	AW	AW	GW	AW	AW
		◇ 🛒			◇1 ☕	B			◇ 🛒	◇	◇1 ☕	◇	B
London Paddington 15 ⊖	d				20p45						08 30		
Reading 7	d				21p13						09 06		
Manchester Piccadilly 10	d	18p30											
Gloucester 7	d												
Bristol Parkway 7	d				22p11						10 11		
Newport (South Wales)	d	21p45			22p46				09 27		10 36	11 00	
Cardiff Central 7	d	22p07		22p43	23p07				09 50		10 57	11 18	
Pontyclun	d	22p19		22p57					10 03				
Llanharan	d	22p23		23p02					10 08				
Pencoed	d	22p27		23p07					10 13				
Bridgend	d	22p33		23p13	23p28				10 20		11 17	11 38	
Wildmill	d												
Sarn	d												
Tondu	d												
Garth (Mid Glamorgan)	d												
Maesteg (Ewenny Road)	d												
Maesteg	a												
Pyle	d			23p21					10 28				
Port Talbot Parkway	d	22p45		23p30	23p41				10 35		11 30	11 52	
Baglan	d			23p34									
Briton Ferry	d			23p37									
Neath	d	22p52		23p41	23p49				10 43		11 39	12 00	
Skewen	d			23p45									
Llansamlet	d			23p49									
Swansea	a	23p05		23p57	00 02				10 55		11 51	12 13	
	d	23p10	23p45	00 09					10 58	11 04		12 15	
Gowerton	d	23b22		00s20						11x16		12x26	
Llanelli	a	23p29	00 01	00s28					11 15	11 23		12 32	
	d	23p30	00 02						11 17			12 34	
Pembrey & Burry Port	d	23p36	00 07	00s34					11 25			12 39	
Kidwelly	d	23b42		00s40					11x32			12x46	
Ferryside	d	23b47		00s46					11x38			12x52	
Carmarthen	a	00 04	00 30	01 04					11 51			13 05	
	d		00 31				09 55	10 19	11 55			13 08	
Whitland	a		00 44				10 11	10 34	12 11			13 23	
	d		00 44				10 11	10 34	12 11			13 23	
Narberth	d							10x43					
Kilgetty	d							10x52					
Saundersfoot	d							10x54					
Tenby	a							11 01					
	d							11 11					
Penally	d							11x14					
Manorbier	d							11 20					
Lamphey	d							11x28					
Pembroke	d							11 31					
Pembroke Dock	a							11 44					
Clunderwen	d						10x19		12x19				
Clarbeston Road	d		00x58				10x27		12x27				
Haverfordwest	d						10 35		12 35				
Johnston	d						10x44		12x44				
Milford Haven	a						10 55		12 55				
Fishguard & Goodwick	a		01 18										
Fishguard Harbour ⛴	a		01 26									13 59	
	d					02 45							14 30
Rosslare Harbour ⛴	a					06 15							18 00

		GW	AW	GW	AW	GW	AW		AW	GW	AW	GW
		◇1 ☕	🛒	◇1 ☕		◇1 ☕	■ 🛒		◇	◇1 ☕		◇1 ☕
London Paddington 15 ⊖	d	09 30		10 37		11 37				12 37		13 37
Reading 7	d	10 06		11 13		12 13				13 13		14 13
Manchester Piccadilly 10	d						10 31					
Gloucester 7	d											
Bristol Parkway 7	d	11 05		12 13		13 13				14 13		15 13
Newport (South Wales)	d	11 32		12 38		13 38	13 29			14 38		15 38
Cardiff Central 7	d	11 53	12 05	12 58		13 58	14 03			14 58		15 58
Pontyclun	d						14 16					
Llanharan	d						14 21					
Pencoed	d						14 26					
Bridgend	d	12 14	12 26	13 19		14 19	14 33			15 19		16 19
Wildmill	d											
Sarn	d											
Tondu	d											
Garth (Mid Glamorgan)	d											
Maesteg (Ewenny Road)	d											
Maesteg	a											
Pyle	d		12 34				14 41					
Port Talbot Parkway	d	12 27	12 43	13 33		14 32	14 49			15 32		16 32
Baglan	d											
Briton Ferry	d											
Neath	d	12 34		13 40		14 40	14 57			15 40		16 40
Skewen	d											
Llansamlet	d											
Swansea	a	12 47		13 53		14 53	15 10			15 53		16 53
	d	12 58			14 11	14 58	15 13		15 26		16 26	17 05
Gowerton	d				14x22				15x36		16x37	
Llanelli	a	13 15	13 23		14 29	15 14	15 29		15 48		16 44	17 21
	d	13 16	13 23		14 31	15 15	15 30				16 46	17 22
Pembrey & Burry Port	d	13 23	13 29		14 37	15 22	15 36				16 52	17 29
Kidwelly	d				14x43						16x59	
Ferryside	d				14x49						17x05	
Carmarthen	a	13 44	13 56		15 04	15 43	15 59				17 19	17 50
	d		14 04		15 07		16 03				17 32	
Whitland	a		14 20		15 21		16 19				17 48	
	d		14 20		15 22		16 20				17 48	
Narberth	d				15x31						17x57	
Kilgetty	d				15x41						18x07	
Saundersfoot	d				15x43						18x09	
Tenby	a				15 50						18 16	
	d				15 54						18 19	
Penally	d				15x57						18x22	
Manorbier	d				16 03						18 29	
Lamphey	d				16x11						18x36	
Pembroke	d				16 14						18 40	
Pembroke Dock	a				16 29						18 55	
Clunderwen	d		14x28				16x28					
Clarbeston Road	d		14x36				16x36					
Haverfordwest	d		14 44				16 44					
Johnston	d		14x53				16x53					
Milford Haven	a		15 08				17 08					
Fishguard & Goodwick	a											
Fishguard Harbour ⛴	a											
	d											
Rosslare Harbour ⛴	a											

b Previous night, stops on request

When events are being held at the Millenium Stadium, services are subject to alteration. Please check times before travelling.

Table 128

Sundays

16 September to 21 October

Cardiff - Maesteg, Swansea and West Wales

Route Diagram - see first Page of Table 127

		AW	GW	AW	GW	AW		GW	AW	AW
		■ 🛒	◇1 ☕		◇1 ☕	■ 🛒		◇1 ☕		
London Paddington 15 ⊖	d		14 37		15 37			16 37		
Reading 7	d		15 13		16 13			17 13		
Manchester Piccadilly 10	d	12 30				14 30				
Gloucester 7	d									
Bristol Parkway 7	d		16 13		17 13			18 13		
Newport (South Wales)	d	15 46	16 38		17 40	17 34		18 40		
Cardiff Central 7	d	16 16	16 58		18 01	18 06		19 01		
Pontyclun	d					18 21				
Llanharan	d					18 26				
Pencoed	d					18 30				
Bridgend	d	16 37	17 19		18 22	18 38		19 22		
Wildmill	d									
Sarn	d									
Tondu	d									
Garth (Mid Glamorgan)	d									
Maesteg (Ewenny Road)	d									
Maesteg	a									
Pyle	d	16 45				18 46				
Port Talbot Parkway	d	16 54	17 32		18 35	18 54		19 35		
Baglan	d									
Briton Ferry	d									
Neath	d	17 02	17 39		18 43	19 02		19 43		
Skewen	d									
Llansamlet	d									
Swansea	a	17 14	17 54		18 58	19 15		19 56		
	d	17 25		18 11		19 20				20 35
Gowerton	d			18x22						20x46
Llanelli	a	17 41		18 29		19 36				20 54
	d	17 41		18 31		19 36				20 55
Pembrey & Burry Port	d	17 48		18 37		19 43				21 01
Kidwelly	d			18x44						21x08
Ferryside	d			18x50						21x14
Carmarthen	a	18 14		19 03		20 05				21 32
	d	18 20		19 06		20 07				
Whitland	a	18 36		19 22		20 23				
	d	18 37		19 22		20 30			20 30	
Narberth	d								20x37	
Kilgetty	d								20x46	
Saundersfoot	d								20x48	
Tenby	a								20 55	
	d								20 59	
Penally	d								21x02	
Manorbier	d								21 08	
Lamphey	d								21x16	
Pembroke	d								21 19	
Pembroke Dock	a								21 34	
Clunderwen	d	18x45		19x30		20x37				
Clarbeston Road	d	18x53		19x38		20x45				
Haverfordwest	d	19 01		19a46		20 54				
Johnston	d	19x10				21x02				
Milford Haven	a	19 25				21 19				
Fishguard & Goodwick	a									
Fishguard Harbour ⛴	a									
	d									
Rosslare Harbour ⛴	a									

		GW	AW	GW	GW	AW	GW		GW
		◇1 ☕	◇ 🛒	◇1 ☕	◇1 ☕	◇	◇1 ☕		◇1 ☕
London Paddington 15 ⊖	d	17 37		18 37	19 37		20 37		21 37
Reading 7	d	18 15		19 15	20 15		21 15		22 14
Manchester Piccadilly 10	d								
Gloucester 7	d								
Bristol Parkway 7	d	19 15		20 13	21 13		22 13		23 16
Newport (South Wales)	d	19 40		20 38	21 38		22 38		23 43
Cardiff Central 7	d	20 01	20 15	21 00	22 00	22 30	23 00		00 05
Pontyclun	d								
Llanharan	d								
Pencoed	d								
Bridgend	d	20 22	20 37	21 22	22 22	22 51	23 22		00 28
Wildmill	d								
Sarn	d								
Tondu	d								
Garth (Mid Glamorgan)	d								
Maesteg (Ewenny Road)	d								
Maesteg	a								
Pyle	d		20 45						
Port Talbot Parkway	d	20 35	20 54	21 35	22 35	23 05	23 35		00 41
Baglan	d								
Briton Ferry	d								
Neath	d	20 43	21 02	21 42	22 42	23 13	23 42		00 49
Skewen	d								
Llansamlet	d								
Swansea	a	20 56	21 14	21 56	22 58	23 25	23 59		01 02
	d		21 18			23 38			
Gowerton	d					23x49			
Llanelli	a		21 34			23 56			
	d		21 34			23 58			
Pembrey & Burry Port	d		21 41			00 04			
Kidwelly	d					00x11			
Ferryside	d					00x17			
Carmarthen	a		22 04			00 30			
	d		22 05			00 34			
Whitland	a		22 21			00 50			
	d		22 22			00 50			
Narberth	d								
Kilgetty	d								
Saundersfoot	d								
Tenby	a								
	d								
Penally	d								
Manorbier	d								
Lamphey	d								
Pembroke	d								
Pembroke Dock	a								
Clunderwen	d		22x29						
Clarbeston Road	d		22x37			01x03			
Haverfordwest	d		22 46						
Johnston	d		22x54						
Milford Haven	a		23 10						
Fishguard & Goodwick	a								
Fishguard Harbour ⛴	a					01 30			
	d								
Rosslare Harbour ⛴	a								

When events are being held at the Millenium Stadium, services are subject to alteration. Please check times before travelling.

Sundays
from 28 October

Cardiff - Maesteg, Swansea and West Wales

Route Diagram - see first Page of Table 127

		AW	AW	AW	GW	AW	AW	AW	AW	AW	GW	AW	AW	GW	AW	GW	AW	GW	AW			AW	GW	AW	GW
		◇ 🛒			◇■1 ☕	B			◇ 🛒	◇	◇■1 ☕	◇	B	◇■1 ☕	🛒	◇■1 ☕		◇■1 ☕	■ 🛒			◇	◇■1 ☕		◇■1 ☕
London Paddington ■15 ⊖	d				20p45						08 30			09 30		10 37		11 37					12 37		13 37
Reading ■7	d				21p13						09 06			10 06		11 13		12 13					13 13		14 13
Manchester Piccadilly ■10	d	18p30																	10 31						
Gloucester ■7	d																								
Bristol Parkway ■7	d				22p11						10 10			11 05		12 12		13 13					14 13		15 13
Newport (South Wales)	d	21p45			22p46				09 27		10 35	11 00		11 32		12 38		13 38	13 29				14 38		15 38
Cardiff Central ■7	d	22p07		22p43	23p07				09 50		10 56	11 18		11 53	12 05	12 58		13 58	14 03				14 58		15 58
Pontyclun	d	22p19		22p57					10 03										14 16						
Llanharan	d	22p23		23p02					10 08										14 21						
Pencoed	d	22p27		23p07					10 13										14 26						
Bridgend	d	22p33		23p13	23p28				10 20		11 17	11 38		12 14	12 26	13 19		14 19	14 33				15 19		16 19
Wildmill	d																								
Sarn	d																								
Tondu	d																								
Garth (Mid Glamorgan)	d																								
Maesteg (Ewenny Road)	d																								
Maesteg	a																								
Pyle	d			23p21					10 28						12 34				14 41						
Port Talbot Parkway	d	22p45		23p30	23p41				10 37		11 30	11 52		12 27	12 43	13 33		14 32	14 49				15 32		16 33
Baglan	d			23p34																					
Briton Ferry	d			23p37																					
Neath	d	22p52		23p41	23p49				10 45		11 38	12 00		12 34		13 40		14 40	14 57				15 40		16 40
Skewen	d			23p45																					
Llansamlet	d			23p49																					
Swansea	a	23p05		23p57	00 02				10 58		11 51	12 13		12 47		13 53		14 53	15 10				15 53		16 53
	d	23p10	23p45	00 09					11 01	11 07		12 15		12 58			14 11	14 58	15 13			15 26		16 26	17 05
Gowerton	d	23b22		00s20						11x16		12x26					14x22					15x36		16x37	
Llanelli	a	23p29	00 01	00s28					11 17	11 23		12 32		13 15	13 23		14 29	15 14	15 29			15 48		16 44	17 21
	d	23p30	00 02						11 19			12 34		13 16	13 23		14 31	15 15	15 30					16 46	17 22
Pembrey & Burry Port	d	23p36	00 07	00s34					11 25			12 39		13 23	13 29		14 37	15 22	15 36					16 52	17 29
Kidwelly	d	23b42		00s40					11x32			12x46					14x43							16x59	
Ferryside	d	23b47		00s46					11x38			12x52					14x49							17x05	
Carmarthen	a	00 04	00 30	01 04					11 51			13 05		13 44	13 56		15 04	15 43	15 59					17 19	17 50
	d		00 31				09 55	10 19	11 55			13 08			14 04		15 07		16 03					17 32	
Whitland	a		00 44				10 11	10 34	12 11			13 23			14 20		15 21		16 19					17 48	
	d		00 44				10 11	10 34	12 11			13 23			14 20		15 22		16 20					17 48	
Narberth	d							10x43									15x31							17x57	
Kilgetty	d							10x52									15x41							18x07	
Saundersfoot	d							10x54									15x43							18x09	
Tenby	a							11 01									15 50							18 16	
	d							11 11									15 54							18 19	
Penally	d							11x14									15x57							18x22	
Manorbier	d							11 20									16 03							18 29	
Lamphey	d							11x28									16x11							18x36	
Pembroke	d							11 31									16 14							18 40	
Pembroke Dock	a							11 44									16 29							18 55	
Clunderwen	d						10x19		12x19						14x28				16x28						
Clarbeston Road	d		00x58				10x27		12x27						14x36				16x36						
Haverfordwest	d						10 35		12 35						14 44				16 44						
Johnston	d						10x44		12x44						14x53				16x53						
Milford Haven	a						10 55		12 55						15 08				17 08						
Fishguard & Goodwick	a		01 18																						
Fishguard Harbour ⛴	a		01 26									13 59													
	d					02 45							14 30												
Rosslare Harbour ⛴	a					06 15							18 00												

b Previous night, stops on request

When events are being held at the Millenium Stadium, services are subject to alteration. Please check times before travelling.

Sundays
from 28 October

Cardiff - Maesteg, Swansea and West Wales

Route Diagram - see first Page of Table 127

		AW	GW	AW	GW	AW		GW	AW	AW	GW	AW	GW	GW	AW	GW		GW
		■ 🛒	◇■1 ☕		◇■1 ☕	■ 🛒		◇■1 ☕			◇■1 ☕	◇ 🛒	◇■1 ☕	◇■1 ☕	◇	◇■1 ☕		◇■1 ☕
London Paddington ■15 ⊖	d		14 37		15 37			16 37			17 37		18 37	19 37		20 37		21 37
Reading ■7	d		15 13		16 13			17 13			18 15		19 15	20 15		21 15		22 14
Manchester Piccadilly ■10	d	12 30				14 30												
Gloucester ■7	d																	
Bristol Parkway ■7	d		16 13		17 13			18 13			19 15		20 13	21 13		22 13		23 16
Newport (South Wales)	d	15 46	16 38		17 40	17 34		18 40			19 40		20 38	21 38		22 38		23 43
Cardiff Central ■7	d	16 16	16 58		18 01	18 06		19 01			20 01	20 15	21 00	22 00	22 30	23 00		00 05
Pontyclun	d					18 21												
Llanharan	d					18 26												
Pencoed	d					18 30												
Bridgend	d	16 37	17 19		18 22	18 38		19 22			20 22	20 37	21 22	22 22	22 51	23 22		00 28
Wildmill	d																	
Sarn	d																	
Tondu	d																	
Garth (Mid Glamorgan)	d																	
Maesteg (Ewenny Road)	d																	
Maesteg	a																	
Pyle	d	16 45				18 46						20 45						
Port Talbot Parkway	d	16 54	17 32		18 35	18 54		19 35			20 35	20 54	21 35	22 35	23 05	23 35		00 41
Baglan	d																	
Briton Ferry	d																	
Neath	d	17 02	17 40		18 43	19 02		19 43			20 42	21 02	21 42	22 42	23 13	23 42		00 49
Skewen	d																	
Llansamlet	d																	
Swansea	a	17 14	17 53		18 58	19 15		19 56			20 56	21 14	21 56	22 58	23 25	23 59		01 02
	d	17 25		18 11		19 20				20 35		21 18			23 38			
Gowerton	d			18x22						20x46					23x49			
Llanelli	a	17 41		18 29		19 36				20 54		21 34			23 56			
	d	17 41		18 31		19 36				20 55		21 34			23 58			
Pembrey & Burry Port	d	17 48		18 37		19 43				21 01		21 41			00 04			
Kidwelly	d			18x44						21x08					00x11			
Ferryside	d			18x50						21x14					00x17			
Carmarthen	a	18 14		19 03		20 05				21 32		22 04			00 30			
	d	18 20		19 06		20 07						22 05			00 34			
Whitland	a	18 36		19 22		20 23						22 21			00 50			
	d	18 37		19 22		20 30			20 30			22 22			00 50			
Narberth	d								20x37									
Kilgetty	d								20x46									
Saundersfoot	d								20x48									
Tenby	a								20 55									
	d								20 59									
Penally	d								21x02									
Manorbier	d								21 08									
Lamphey	d								21x16									
Pembroke	d								21 19									
Pembroke Dock	a								21 34									
Clunderwen	d	18x45		19x30		20x37						22x29						
Clarbeston Road	d	18x53		19x38		20x45						22x37			01x03			
Haverfordwest	d	19 01		19a46		20 54						22 46						
Johnston	d	19x10				21x02						22x54						
Milford Haven	a	19 25				21 19						23 10						
Fishguard & Goodwick	a																	
Fishguard Harbour ⛴	a														01 30			
	d																	
Rosslare Harbour ⛴	a																	

When events are being held at the Millenium Stadium, services are subject to alteration. Please check times before travelling.

until 22 June

West Wales, Swansea and Maesteg - Cardiff

Route Diagram - see first Page of Table 127

Miles	Miles			AW MO	AW MX	AW	AW	AW MX	AW MX	AW	GW	GW		GW	AW	GW	GW	AW	AW	GW	AW	GW		AW	AW
				A		◇ B	B			◇	◇■ ☕	◇■ ☕		◇■ ☕	◇ 🛒	◇■ C ⊘	◇■ D ☕⊘		🛒	◇■ D ☕⊘	◇ 🛒	◇■ D ☕⊘			◇ 🛒
—	—	Rosslare Harbour ⛴	d	21p00																					
0	—	**Fishguard Harbour** ⛴	a	00 30																					
—	—		d							01 50															
—	—	Fishguard & Goodwick	d							01 53															
—	0	**Milford Haven**	d			21p35	23p15	23p18	00 18																06 00
—	4	Johnston	d			21b43	23b23	23b26	00x26																06x08
—	8¾	Haverfordwest	d			21p51	23p30	23p33	00 33																06 15
15¾	14	Clarbeston Road	d			21b59	23b39	23b41	00x41	02x12															06x23
22¼	—	Clunderwen	d			22b07	23b46	23b48	00x48																06x30
—	0	**Pembroke Dock**	d																						
—	2	Pembroke	d																						
—	3½	Lamphey	d																						
—	7	Manorbier	d																						
—	10¼	Penally	d																						
—	11½	**Tenby**	a																						
—	—		d																						
—	15¾	Saundersfoot	d																						
—	16½	Kilgetty	d																						
—	22	Narberth	d																						
27¾	27¼	Whitland	a			22p13	23p53	23p54	00 54	02 24															06 36
—	—		d			22p14	23p53	23p54	00 54	02 24															06 36
41¾	—	**Carmarthen**	a			22p31	00 14	00 16	01 16	02 41															06 52
—	—		d			22p34				02 44					05 03				05 50		06 15				06 57
48¾	—	Ferryside	d			22b44													06x00		06x25				
53	—	Kidwelly	d			22b50													06x05		06x30				
58¼	—	Pembrey & Burry Port	d			22p58									05 21				06 12		06 37				07 15
62¼	—	Llanelli	a			23p04				03 06					05 26				06 17		06 42				07 20
—	—		d			23p04				03 06					05 28				06 18		06 44				07 22
68	—	Gowerton	d			23b12													06x24		06x50				07x28
73½	—	**Swansea**	a			23p27				03 29									06 38		07 04				07 41
—	—		d			23p31					03 57	04 58		05 27		05 58	06 28		06 42	06 58	07 06	07 28			07 45
77½	—	Llansamlet	d																06 46						
79¼	—	Skewen	d																06 50						
83	—	Neath	d			23p43					04 09	05 10		05 39		06 10	06 40		06 54	07 10	07 17	07 40			07 56
84¾	—	Briton Ferry	d																06 58						
86½	—	Baglan	d																07 01						
88½	—	Port Talbot Parkway	d			23p50					04 17	05 18		05 47	06 01	06 18	06 48		07 05	07 18	07 24	07 48			08 03
94¾	—	Pyle	d			23p57									06 08				07 12		07 31				08 09
—	0	Maesteg	d		22p15													06 42							
—	0½	Maesteg (Ewenny Road)	d		22p17													06 44							
—	1¼	Garth (Mid Glamorgan)	d		22p20													06 47							
—	5¼	Tondu	d		22p29													06 56							
—	6	Sarn	d		22p32													06 59							
—	7¼	Wildmill	d		22p34													07 01							
100¾	8¼	Bridgend	d		22p38	00 05					04 30	05 30		05 59	06 15	06 30	07 00	07 05	07 20	07 30	07 39	08 00		08 07	08 17
104¾	—	Pencoed	d		22p44										06 21			07 11	07 26					08 13	
107	—	Llanharan	d		22p48										06 25			07 15			07 46				08 24
110	—	Pontyclun	d		22p52										06 30			07 20	07 33					08 21	
121	—	**Cardiff Central** 7	a		23p08	00 30					05 02	05 52		06 21	06 43	06 52	07 22	07 34	07 48	07 52	08 02	08 22		08 34	08 43
—	—	Newport (South Wales)	a		23p39						05 30	06 09		06 37	07 02	07 09	07 39			08 09	08 17	08 39			09 02
—	—	Bristol Parkway 7	a								05 59	06 29		06 58		07 29	07 59			08 30		08 59			
—	—	Gloucester 7	a		00 39																				
—	—	Manchester Piccadilly 10	a												10 15						11 15				12 15
—	—	Reading 7	a								07 00	07 31		08 00			09 01			09 25		09 59			
—	—	London Paddington 15 ⊖	a								07 32	08 02		08 33		08 54	09 29			09 59		10 32			

A not 14 May
B from 21 May until 18 June
C The Capitals United
D ☕ from Reading ⊘ to Reading
b Previous night, stops on request

When events are being held at the Millenium Stadium, services are subject to alteration. Please check times before travelling.

until 22 June

West Wales, Swansea and Maesteg - Cardiff

Route Diagram - see first Page of Table 127

		AW	AW	GW	GW	AW	AW	AW		AW	GW	AW	AW	GW	AW	AW	AW	AW		AW		GW	AW	AW	GW
				◇■ ☕	◇■ A ☕	◇ 🛒		◇			◇■ ☕	◇ 🛒		◇■ ☕	◇ 🛒							◇■ B ☕	◇ 🛒	🛒	◇■ C ☕⊘
Rosslare Harbour ⛴	d																								
Fishguard Harbour ⛴	a																								
	d	06 53										08 04								09 56					
Fishguard & Goodwick	d	06 56										08 07								09 59					
Milford Haven	d					07 05									09 08										
Johnston	d					07x13									09x16										
Haverfordwest	d					07 20									09 23										
Clarbeston Road	d	07a16				07x28						08x25			09x31					10x17					
Clunderwen	d					07x35						08x33			09x38					10x25					
Pembroke Dock	d									07 09								09 09							
Pembroke	d									07 17								09 17							
Lamphey	d									07x20								09x20							
Manorbier	d									07 28								09 29							
Penally	d									07x34								09x34							
Tenby	a									07 35								09 37							
	d									07 38								09 38							
Saundersfoot	d									07x44								09x46							
Kilgetty	d									07x46								09x48							
Narberth	d									07x56								09x58							
Whitland	a					07 41				08 04		08 37			09 44			10 06		10 31					
	d					07 41				08 05		08 38			09 44			10 07		10 32					
Carmarthen	a					07 55				08 25		08 55			10 02			10 24		10 49					
	d				07 30	08 01				08 30		09 00			10 04			10 31					11 02		
Ferryside	d				07 42	08x11				08x40		09x10											11x12		
Kidwelly	d				07 49	08x16				08x46		09x15											11x17		
Pembrey & Burry Port	d				07 56	08 23				08 53		09 18			10 24			10 50					11 23		
Llanelli	a				08 02	08 28				08 59		09 24			10 29			10 56					11 29		
	d				08 04	08 30		08 45		09 00		09 25			10 31			10 57					11 30		
Gowerton	d					08x36		08x53		09x08								11x04					11x37		
Swansea	a				08 21	08 49		09 08		09 23		09 48			10 48			11 22					11 49		
	d			07 58	08 28	08 55		09 11			09 28	09 55		10 28	10 55		11 10					11 28	11 55		12 28
Llansamlet	d							09 18									11 17								
Skewen	d							09 22									11 21								
Neath	d			08 10	08 40	09 06		09 26			09 40	10 06		10 40	11 06		11 25					11 40	12 06		12 40
Briton Ferry	d							09 30									11 28								
Baglan	d							09 33									11 32								
Port Talbot Parkway	d			08 18	08 48	09 13		09 37			09 48	10 13		10 48	11 13		11 36					11 48	12 13		12 48
Pyle	d							09 44									11 43								
Maesteg	d		07 58				09 15						10 15			11 15								12 15	
Maesteg (Ewenny Road)	d		08 00				09 17						10 17			11 17								12 17	
Garth (Mid Glamorgan)	d		08 03				09 20						10 20			11 20								12 20	
Tondu	d		08 12				09 29						10 29			11 29								12 29	
Sarn	d		08 15				09 32						10 32			11 32								12 32	
Wildmill	d		08 17				09 34						10 34			11 34								12 34	
Bridgend	d		08 21	08 30	09 00	09 25	09 38	09 53			10 00	10 25	10 38	11 00	11 25	11 38	11 55					12 00	12 25	12 38	13 00
Pencoed	d		08 27				09 44						10 44			11 44								12 44	
Llanharan	d						09 48						10 48			11 48								12 48	
Pontyclun	d		08 34				09 52						10 52			11 52								12 52	
Cardiff Central 7	a		08 48	08 52	09 22	09 46	10 07	10 17			10 22	10 47	11 09	11 22	11 48	12 08	12 18					12 22	12 47	13 07	13 22
Newport (South Wales)	a		09 25	09 09	09 39	10 17	10 25				10 39	11 02		11 39	12 17	12 25						12 39	13 02	13 25	13 39
Bristol Parkway 7	a			09 30	09 59						10 59			11 59								12 59			13 59
Gloucester 7	a		10 20				11 20									13 20								14 20	
Manchester Piccadilly 10	a					13 15						14 15			15 15								16 15		
Reading 7	a			10 31	11 00						11 59			13 00								13 59			15 00
London Paddington 15 ⊖	a			11 07	11 32						12 32			13 32								14 32			15 32

A The Red Dragon
B The St. David
C ☕ from Reading ⊘ to Reading

When events are being held at the Millenium Stadium, services are subject to alteration. Please check times before travelling.

West Wales, Swansea and Maesteg - Cardiff

until 22 June

Route Diagram - see first Page of Table 127

		AW	AW	AW	AW	AW	GW	AW	AW	GW	AW	AW	AW	AW	AW	AW	GW	AW	AW	GW	AW	AW	AW
		◇	◇		◇		◇1 A ⊏⊘	◇		◇1 ⊏	B	■	■				◇1 ⊏	■		◇1 A ⊏⊘	■		
Rosslare Harbour	d										09 00												
Fishguard Harbour	a										12 30												
	d												13 30										
Fishguard & Goodwick	d												13 33										
Milford Haven	d	11 08										13 08									15 08		
Johnston	d	11x16										13x16									15x16		
Haverfordwest	d	11 23										13 23									15 23		
Clarbeston Road	d	11x31										13x31									15x31		
Clunderwen	d	11x38										13x38									15x38		
Pembroke Dock	d					11 09										13 09							
Pembroke	d					11 17										13 17							
Lamphey	d					11x20										13x20							
Manorbier	d					11 29										13 29							
Penally	d					11x34										13x34							
Tenby	a					11 37										13 37							
	d					11 43										13 41							
Saundersfoot	d					11x51										13x49							
Kilgetty	d					11x53										13x51							
Narberth	d					12x03										14x01							
Whitland	a	11 44				12 11						13 44	14 04			14 09					15 44		
	d	11 44				12 11						13 44	14 04			14 09					15 44		
Carmarthen	a	12 00				12 29						14 00	14 21			14 29					16 00		
	d	12 05				12 33		13 02				14 05	14 25			14 34		15 05			16 05		
Ferryside	d							13x12										15x15					
Kidwelly	d							13x17										15x20					
Pembrey & Burry Port	d	12 23				12 52		13 23				14 23				14 53		15 27			16 23		
Llanelli	a	12 28				12 58		13 29				14 28	14 47			14 59		15 32			16 28		
	d	12 30	12 42			12 59		13 30				14 30	14 47			14 59		15 34			16 30		
Gowerton	d					13x06						14x36									16x36		
Swansea	a	12 47	13 04			13 22		13 51				14 49				15 22		15 51			16 49		
	d	12 54			13 10		13 28	13 55		14 28		14 55			15 10		15 28	15 55		16 28	16 55		17 10
Llansamlet	d				13 17										15 17								17 17
Skewen	d				13 21										15 21								17 21
Neath	d	13 05			13 25		13 40	14 06		14 40		15 06			15 25		15 40	16 06		16 40	17 06		17 25
Briton Ferry	d				13 28										15 28								17 28
Baglan	d				13 32										15 32								17 32
Port Talbot Parkway	d	13 12			13 36		13 48	14 13		14 48		15 13			15 36		15 48	16 13		16 48	17 13		17 36
Pyle	d				13 43										15 43								17 43
Maesteg	d			13 15					14 15					15 17					16 15			17 15	
Maesteg (Ewenny Road)	d			13 17					14 17					15 19					16 17			17 17	
Garth (Mid Glamorgan)	d			13 20					14 20					15 22					16 20			17 20	
Tondu	d			13 29					14 29					15 31					16 29			17 29	
Sarn	d			13 32					14 32					15 34					16 32			17 32	
Wildmill	d			13 34					14 34					15 36					16 34			17 34	
Bridgend	d	13 24		13 38	13 52		14 00	14 25	14 38	15 00		15 25		15 40	15 52		16 00	16 25	16 38	17 00	17 25	17 38	17 54
Pencoed	d			13 44					14 44					15 46					16 44			17 44	
Llanharan	d			13 48					14 48					15 50					16 48			17 48	
Pontyclun	d			13 52					14 52					15 54					16 52			17 52	
Cardiff Central 7	a	13 47		14 07	14 15		14 22	14 47	15 07	15 22		15 47	16 04	16 09	16 15		16 22	16 46	17 07	17 22	17 47	18 07	18 20
Newport (South Wales)	a	14 17					14 39	15 02	15 26	15 39		16 02	16 18				16 39	17 02	17 25	17 39	18 02	18 25	
Bristol Parkway 7	a						15 00			15 59							16 59			17 59			
Gloucester 7	a								16 21				17 14						18 21			19 20	
Manchester Piccadilly 10	a	17 14						18 13				19 15						20 15			21 05		
Reading 7	a						16 00			17 00							18 00			19 01			
London Paddington 15 ⊖	a						16 30			17 30							18 30			19 32			

A ⊏ from Reading ⊘ to Reading

When events are being held at the Millenium Stadium, services are subject to alteration. Please check times before travelling.

West Wales, Swansea and Maesteg - Cardiff

until 22 June

Route Diagram - see first Page of Table 127

		AW	GW	AW	AW	AW	GW	AW	AW	AW	AW	AW	GW FX	GW FO	AW	AW	GW	AW	AW	AW	AW	AW	AW
			◇1 ⊏	◇	◇		◇1 ⊏	◇					◇1 ⊏	◇1 ⊏	◇		◇1 ⊏	◇					B
Rosslare Harbour	d																						21 00
Fishguard Harbour	a																						00 30
	d								19 00													20 50	
Fishguard & Goodwick	d								19 03													20 53	
Milford Haven	d							17 08										19 08			20 36		
Johnston	d							17x16										19x16			20x44		
Haverfordwest	d							17 23										19 23			20 51		
Clarbeston Road	d							17x31	19a21									19x31			20x59	21x12	
Clunderwen	d							17x38										19x38			21x06	21x19	
Pembroke Dock	d	15 09										17 09											
Pembroke	d	15 17										17 17											
Lamphey	d	15x20										17x20											
Manorbier	d	15 29										17 29											
Penally	d	15x34										17x34											
Tenby	a	15 37										17 37											
	d	15 41										17 38								19 57			
Saundersfoot	d	15x49										17x46								20x05			
Kilgetty	d	15x51										17x48								20x07			
Narberth	d	16x01										17x58								20x17			
Whitland	a	16 09						17 44				18 06						19 44		20 25	21 12	21 26	
	d	16 09						17 45				18 07						19 44		20 27	21 12	21 26	
Carmarthen	a	16 27						18 02				18 24						20 00		20 45	21 34	21 47	
	d	16 31		17 04				18 07				18 31			18 59			20 05		20 47			
Ferryside	d			17x14				18x17							19x09					20x58			
Kidwelly	d			17x19				18x23							19x15					21x04			
Pembrey & Burry Port	d	16 50		17 25				18 30				18 50			19 23			20 23		21 11			
Llanelli	a	16 56		17 31				18 35				18 56			19 29			20 28		21 17			
	d	16 57		17 32	17 48			18 36				18 57			19 30			20 29		21 17			
Gowerton	d	17x04			17x57							19x04											
Swansea	a	17 22		17 49	18 18			18 54				19 22			19 49			20 47		21 39			
	d		17 28	17 55			18 28	19 00			19 10		19 29	19 29	19 52		20 28	20 57		21 45			
Llansamlet	d										19 17									21 52			
Skewen	d										19 21									21 56			
Neath	d		17 40	18 06			18 40	19 11			19 25		19 40	19 40	20 03		20 40	21 08		22 00			
Briton Ferry	d										19 28									22 03			
Baglan	d										19 32									22 07			
Port Talbot Parkway	d		17 48	18 13			18 48	19 19			19 36		19 48	19 48	20 10		20 48	21 15		22 11			
Pyle	d										19 43									22 18			
Maesteg	d					18 20				19 17						20 15			21 15				
Maesteg (Ewenny Road)	d					18 22				19 19						20 17			21 17				
Garth (Mid Glamorgan)	d					18 25				19 22						20 20			21 20				
Tondu	d					18 34				19 31						20 29			21 29				
Sarn	d					18 37				19 34						20 32			21 32				
Wildmill	d					18 39				19 36						20 34			21 34				
Bridgend	d		18 00	18 25		18 43	19 00	19 32		19 40	19 51		20 00	20 00	20 24	20 38	21 00	21 27	21 38	22 26			
Pencoed	d					18 49				19 46						20 44			21 44				
Llanharan	d					18 53				19 49						20 48			21 48				
Pontyclun	d					18 57				19 54						20 52			21 52				
Cardiff Central 7	a		18 22	18 46		19 13	19 22	19 57		20 10	20 17		20 22	20 22	20 46	21 08	21 22	21 50	22 10	22 49			
Newport (South Wales)	a		18 39	19 03			19 39						20 38	20 38		21 25	21 38						
Bristol Parkway 7	a		18 59				19 59						21 01	21 01			21 59						
Gloucester 7	a															22 21							
Manchester Piccadilly 10	a			22 13																			
Reading 7	a		20 00				21 00						22 11	22 11			23 02						
London Paddington 15 ⊖	a		20 32				21 32						22 44	22 45			23 38						

When events are being held at the Millenium Stadium, services are subject to alteration. Please check times before travelling.

Table 128

Mondays to Fridays

until 22 June

West Wales, Swansea and Maesteg - Cardiff

Route Diagram - see first Page of Table 127

		AW	AW	AW	AW	AW	AW	AW	AW
			FO	FX	FX				
		◇							
Rosslare Harbour ⛴	d								
Fishguard Harbour ⛴	a								
	d								
Fishguard & Goodwick	d								
Milford Haven	d								23 18
Johnston	d								23x26
Haverfordwest	d								23 33
Clarbeston Road	d								23x41
Clunderwen	d								23x48
Pembroke Dock	d						21 09	22 23	
Pembroke	d						21 17	22 31	
Lamphey	d						21x20	22x34	
Manorbier	d						21 29	22 42	
Penally	d						21x34	22x48	
Tenby	a						21 37	22 50	
	d						21 42	22 50	
Saundersfoot	d						21x50	22x58	
Kilgetty	d						21x52	23x00	
Narberth	d						22x02	23x09	
Whitland	a						22 10	23 17	23 54
	d						22 10	23 20	23 54
Carmarthen	a						22 28	23 39	00 16
	d						22 35		
Ferryside	d						22x45		
Kidwelly	d						22x51		
Pembrey & Burry Port	d						22 58		
Llanelli	a						23 04		
	d	21 43					23 05		
Gowerton	d	21x50					23x12		
Swansea	a	22 08					23 32		
	d					22 32			
Llansamlet	d					22 39			
Skewen	d					22 43			
Neath	d					22 47			
Briton Ferry	d					22 50			
Baglan	d					22 54			
Port Talbot Parkway	d					22 58			
Pyle	d					23 05			
Maesteg	d		22 15	22 15					
Maesteg (Ewenny Road)	d		22 17	22 17					
Garth (Mid Glamorgan)	d		22 20	22 20					
Tondu	d		22 29	22 29					
Sarn	d		22 32	22 32					
Wildmill	d		22 34	22 34					
Bridgend	d		22 38	22 38	22 52	23 13			
Pencoed	d		22 44	22 44					
Llanharan	d		22 48	22 48					
Pontyclun	d		22 52	22 52					
Cardiff Central 7	a		23 08	23 08	23 18	23 38			
Newport (South Wales)	a		23 38	23 39					
Bristol Parkway 7	a								
Gloucester 7	a		00 39	00 39					
Manchester Piccadilly 10	a								
Reading 7	a								
London Paddington 15 ⊖	a								

When events are being held at the Millenium Stadium, services are subject to alteration. Please check times before travelling.

Table 128

Mondays to Fridays

25 June to 14 September

West Wales, Swansea and Maesteg - Cardiff

Route Diagram - see first Page of Table 127

		AW	AW	AW	AW	AW	AW	AW	GW	GW	GW	AW	GW	GW	AW	AW	GW	AW	GW	AW	AW	AW	AW
			MX	MO	MO	MX	MX																
		B		◇				◇	◇1	◇1	◇1	◇	◇1	◇1			◇1	◇	◇1		◇		
													A	B			B		B				
									⊡	⊡	⊡	ᕼ	⊘	⊡⊘		ᕼ	⊡⊘	ᕼ	⊡⊘		ᕼ		
Rosslare Harbour ⛴	d	21p00																					
Fishguard Harbour ⛴	a	00 30																					
	d							01 50														06 53	
Fishguard & Goodwick	d							01 53														06 56	
Milford Haven	d			21p35	23p15	23p18	00 18														06 00		
Johnston	d			21b43	23b23	23b26	00x26														06x08		
Haverfordwest	d			21p51	23p30	23p33	00 33														06 15		
Clarbeston Road	d			21b59	23b39	23b41	00x41	02x12													06x23	07a16	
Clunderwen	d			22b07	23b46	23b48	00x48														06x30		
Pembroke Dock	d																						
Pembroke	d																						
Lamphey	d																						
Manorbier	d																						
Penally	d																						
Tenby	a																						
	d																						
Saundersfoot	d																						
Kilgetty	d																						
Narberth	d																						
Whitland	a			22p13	23p53	23p54	00 54	02 24													06 36		
	d			22p14	23p53	23p54	00 54	02 24													06 36		
Carmarthen	a			22p31	00 14	00 16	01 16	02 41													06 52		
	d			22p34				02 44				05 03				05 50		06 15			06 57		
Ferryside	d			22b44												06x00		06x25					
Kidwelly	d			22b50												06x05		06x30					
Pembrey & Burry Port	d			22p58								05 21				06 12		06 37			07 15		
Llanelli	a			23p04				03 06				05 26				06 17		06 42			07 20		
	d			23p04				03 06				05 28				06 18		06 44			07 22		
Gowerton	d			23b12												06x24		06x50			07x28		
Swansea	a			23p27				03 29								06 38		07 04			07 41		
	d			23p31					03 57	04 58	05 27		05 58	06 28		06 42	06 58	07 06	07 28		07 45		
Llansamlet	d															06 46							
Skewen	d															06 50							
Neath	d			23p43					04 09	05 10	05 39		06 10	06 40		06 54	07 10	07 17	07 40		07 56		
Briton Ferry	d															06 58							
Baglan	d															07 01							
Port Talbot Parkway	d			23p50					04 17	05 18	05 47	06 01	06 18	06 48		07 05	07 18	07 24	07 48		08 03		
Pyle	d			23p57								06 08				07 12		07 31			08 09		
Maesteg	d		22p15												06 42								07 58
Maesteg (Ewenny Road)	d		22p17												06 44								08 00
Garth (Mid Glamorgan)	d		22p20												06 47								08 03
Tondu	d		22p29												06 56								08 12
Sarn	d		22p32												06 59								08 15
Wildmill	d		22p34												07 01								08 17
Bridgend	d		22p38	00 05					04 30	05 30	05 59	06 15	06 30	07 00	07 05	07 20	07 30	07 39	08 00	08 07	08 17		08 21
Pencoed	d		22p44									06 21			07 11	07 26				08 13			08 27
Llanharan	d		22p48									06 25			07 15			07 46			08 24		
Pontyclun	d		22p52									06 30			07 20	07 33				08 21			08 34
Cardiff Central 7	a		23p08	00 30					05 02	05 52	06 21	06 43	06 52	07 22	07 34	07 48	07 52	08 02	08 22	08 34	08 43		08 48
Newport (South Wales)	a		23p39						05 30	06 09	06 37	07 02	07 09	07 39			08 09	08 17	08 39		09 02		09 25
Bristol Parkway 7	a								05 59	06 29	06 58		07 29	07 59			08 30		08 59				
Gloucester 7	a		00 39																				10 20
Manchester Piccadilly 10	a											10 15						11 15			12 15		
Reading 7	a								07 00	07 31	08 00			09 01			09 25		09 59				
London Paddington 15 ⊖	a								07 32	08 02	08 33		08 54	09 29			09 59		10 32				

A The Capitals United

B ⊡ from Reading ⊘ to Reading

b Previous night, stops on request

When events are being held at the Millenium Stadium, services are subject to alteration. Please check times before travelling.

West Wales, Swansea and Maesteg - Cardiff

25 June to 14 September

Route Diagram - see first Page of Table 127

	GW	GW	AW	AW	AW	AW	GW	AW	AW	GW	AW	AW	AW	AW	AW	GW	AW	AW	GW	AW	AW
	◇■	◇■ A	◇		◇		◇■	◇		◇■	◇					◇■ B	◇		◇■ C	◇	◇
	🍴	🍴	🛒			🛒	🍴	🛒		🍴	🛒			🛒		🍴	🛒	🛒	🍴⊘	🛒	🛒
Rosslare Harbour ⛴ d																					
Fishguard Harbour ⛴ a																					
d								08 04							09 56						
Fishguard & Goodwick d								08 07							09 59						
Milford Haven d			07 05								09 08									11 08	
Johnston d			07x13								09x16									11x16	
Haverfordwest d			07 20								09 23									11 23	
Clarbeston Road d			07x28					08x25			09x31				10x17					11x31	
Clunderwen d			07x35					08x33			09x38				10x25					11x38	
Pembroke Dock d						07 09								09 09							
Pembroke d						07 17								09 17							
Lamphey d						07x20								09x20							
Manorbier d						07 28								09 29							
Penally d						07x34								09x34							
Tenby a						07 35								09 37							
d						07 38								09 38							
Saundersfoot d						07x44								09x46							
Kilgetty d						07x46								09x48							
Narberth d						07x56								09x58							
Whitland a			07 41			08 04		08 37			09 44			10 06	10 31					11 44	
d			07 41			08 05		08 38			09 44			10 07	10 32					11 44	
Carmarthen a			07 55			08 25		08 55			10 02			10 24	10 49					12 00	
d		07 30	08 01			08 30		09 00			10 04			10 31			11 02			12 05	
Ferryside d		07 42	08x11			08x40		09x10									11x12				
Kidwelly d		07 49	08x16			08x46		09x15									11x17				
Pembrey & Burry Port d		07 56	08 23			08 53		09 18			10 24			10 50			11 23			12 23	
Llanelli a		08 02	08 28			08 59		09 24			10 29			10 56			11 29			12 28	
d		08 04	08 30		08 45	09 00		09 25			10 31			10 57			11 30			12 30	12 42
Gowerton d			08x36		08x53	09x08								11x04			11x37				
Swansea a		08 21	08 49		09 08	09 23		09 48			10 48			11 22			11 49			12 47	13 04
d	07 58	08 28	08 55		09 11		09 28	09 55		10 28	10 55		11 10			11 28	11 55		12 28	12 54	
Llansamlet d					09 18								11 17								
Skewen d					09 22								11 21								
Neath d	08 10	08 40	09 06		09 26		09 40	10 06		10 40	11 06		11 25			11 40	12 06		12 40	13 05	
Briton Ferry d					09 30								11 28								
Baglan d					09 33								11 32								
Port Talbot Parkway d	08 18	08 48	09 13		09 37		09 48	10 13		10 48	11 13		11 36			11 48	12 13		12 48	13 12	
Pyle d					09 44								11 43								
Maesteg d				09 15					10 15			11 15						12 15			
Maesteg (Ewenny Road) d				09 17					10 17			11 17						12 17			
Garth (Mid Glamorgan) d				09 20					10 20			11 20						12 20			
Tondu d				09 29					10 29			11 29						12 29			
Sarn d				09 32					10 32			11 32						12 32			
Wildmill d				09 34					10 34			11 34						12 34			
Bridgend d	08 30	09 00	09 25	09 38	09 53		10 00	10 25	10 38	11 00	11 25	11 38	11 55			12 00	12 25	12 38	13 00	13 24	
Pencoed d				09 44					10 44			11 44						12 44			
Llanharan d				09 48					10 48			11 48						12 48			
Pontyclun d				09 52					10 52			11 52						12 52			
Cardiff Central ■ a	08 52	09 22	09 46	10 07	10 17		10 22	10 47	11 09	11 22	11 48	12 08	12 18			12 22	12 47	13 07	13 22	13 47	
Newport (South Wales) a	09 09	09 39	10 17	10 25			10 39	11 02		11 39	12 17	12 25				12 39	13 02	13 25	13 39	14 17	
Bristol Parkway ■ a	09 30	09 59					10 59			11 59						12 59			13 59		
Gloucester ■ a				11 20								13 20						14 20			
Manchester Piccadilly ■ a			13 15					14 15			15 15						16 15			17 14	
Reading ■ a	10 31	11 00					11 59			13 00						13 59			15 00		
London Paddington ■ ⊖ a	11 07	11 32					12 32			13 32						14 32			15 32		

A The Red Dragon

B The St. David

C 🍴 from Reading ⊘ to Reading

When events are being held at the Millenium Stadium, services are subject to alteration. Please check times before travelling.

West Wales, Swansea and Maesteg - Cardiff

25 June to 14 September

Route Diagram - see first Page of Table 127

	AW	AW	AW	GW	AW	AW	GW	AW	AW	AW	AW	AW	AW	GW	AW	AW	GW	AW	AW	AW	AW	GW
								▣	■	■					■			■				
		◇		◇■ A	◇		◇■							◇■			◇■ A					◇■
		🛒		🍴⊘	🛒		🍴		🛒	🛒			🛒	🍴	🛒		🍴⊘	🛒				🍴
Rosslare Harbour ⛴ d								09 00														
Fishguard Harbour ⛴ a								12 30														
d										13 30												
Fishguard & Goodwick d										13 33												
Milford Haven d									13 08									15 08				
Johnston d									13x16									15x16				
Haverfordwest d									13 23									15 23				
Clarbeston Road d									13x31									15x31				
Clunderwen d									13x38									15x38				
Pembroke Dock d			11 09										13 09								15 09	
Pembroke d			11 17										13 17								15 17	
Lamphey d			11x20										13x20								15x20	
Manorbier d			11 29										13 29								15 29	
Penally d			11x34										13x34								15x34	
Tenby a			11 37										13 37								15 37	
d			11 43										13 41								15 41	
Saundersfoot d			11x51										13x49								15x49	
Kilgetty d			11x53										13x51								15x51	
Narberth d			12x03										14x01								16x01	
Whitland a			12 11						13 44	14 04			14 09					15 44			16 09	
d			12 11						13 44	14 04			14 09					15 44			16 09	
Carmarthen a			12 29						14 00	14 21			14 29					16 00			16 27	
d			12 33		13 02				14 05	14 25			14 34		15 05			16 05			16 31	
Ferryside d					13x12										15x15							
Kidwelly d					13x17										15x20							
Pembrey & Burry Port d			12 52		13 23				14 23				14 53		15 27			16 23			16 50	
Llanelli a			12 58		13 29				14 28	14 47			14 59		15 32			16 28			16 56	
d			12 59		13 30				14 30	14 47			14 59		15 34			16 30			16 57	
Gowerton d			13x06						14x36									16x36			17x04	
Swansea a			13 22		13 51				14 49				15 22		15 51			16 49			17 22	
d		13 10		13 28	13 55		14 28		14 55			15 10		15 28	15 55		16 28	16 55		17 10		17 28
Llansamlet d		13 17										15 17								17 17		
Skewen d		13 21										15 21								17 21		
Neath d		13 25		13 40	14 06		14 40		15 06			15 25		15 40	16 06		16 40	17 06		17 25		17 40
Briton Ferry d		13 28										15 28								17 28		
Baglan d		13 32										15 32								17 32		
Port Talbot Parkway d		13 36		13 48	14 13		14 48		15 13			15 36		15 48	16 13		16 48	17 13		17 36		17 48
Pyle d		13 43										15 43								17 43		
Maesteg d	13 15					14 15					15 17					16 15			17 15			
Maesteg (Ewenny Road) d	13 17					14 17					15 19					16 17			17 17			
Garth (Mid Glamorgan) d	13 20					14 20					15 22					16 20			17 20			
Tondu d	13 29					14 29					15 31					16 29			17 29			
Sarn d	13 32					14 32					15 34					16 32			17 32			
Wildmill d	13 34					14 34					15 36					16 34			17 34			
Bridgend d	13 38	13 52		14 00	14 25	14 38	15 00		15 25		15 40	15 52		16 00	16 25	16 38	17 00	17 25	17 38	17 54		18 00
Pencoed d	13 44					14 44					15 46					16 44			17 44			
Llanharan d	13 48					14 48					15 50					16 48			17 48			
Pontyclun d	13 52					14 52					15 54					16 52			17 52			
Cardiff Central ■ a	14 07	14 15		14 22	14 47	15 07	15 22		15 47	16 04	16 09	16 15		16 22	16 46	17 07	17 22	17 47	18 07	18 20		18 22
Newport (South Wales) a				14 39	15 02	15 26	15 39		16 02	16 18				16 39	17 02	17 25	17 39	18 02	18 25			18 39
Bristol Parkway ■ a				15 00			15 59							16 59			17 59					18 59
Gloucester ■ a						16 21				17 14						18 21			19 20			
Manchester Piccadilly ■ a					18 13				19 15						20 15			21 05				
Reading ■ a				16 00			17 00							18 00			19 01					20 00
London Paddington ■ ⊖ a				16 30			17 30							18 30			19 32					20 32

A 🍴 from Reading ⊘ to Reading

When events are being held at the Millenium Stadium, services are subject to alteration. Please check times before travelling.

Table 128

Mondays to Fridays

25 June to 14 September

West Wales, Swansea and Maesteg - Cardiff

Route Diagram - see first Page of Table 127

		AW	AW	AW	GW	AW	AW	AW	AW	AW	GW FX	GW FO	AW	AW	GW	AW	AW	AW	AW	AW	AW	AW	AW FO
		◇	◇		◇1	◇					◇1	◇1	◇		◇1	◇					B	◇	
Rosslare Harbour	d																				21 00		
Fishguard Harbour	a																				00 30		
	d						19 00													20 50			
Fishguard & Goodwick	d						19 03													20 53			
Milford Haven	d					17 08										19 08			20 36				
Johnston	d					17x16										19x16			20x44				
Haverfordwest	d					17 23										19 23			20 51				
Clarbeston Road	d					17x31	19a21									19x31			20x59	21x12			
Clunderwen	d					17x38										19x38			21x06	21x19			
Pembroke Dock	d									17 09													
Pembroke	d									17 17													
Lamphey	d									17x20													
Manorbier	d									17 29													
Penally	d									17x34													
Tenby	a									17 37													
	d									17 38								19 57					
Saundersfoot	d									17x46								20x05					
Kilgetty	d									17x48								20x07					
Narberth	d									17x58								20x17					
Whitland	a					17 44				18 06						19 44		20 25	21 12	21 26			
	d					17 45				18 07						19 44		20 27	21 12	21 26			
Carmarthen	a					18 02				18 24						20 00		20 45	21 34	21 47			
	d	17 04				18 07				18 31			18 59			20 05		20 47					
Ferryside	d	17x14				18x17							19x09					20x58					
Kidwelly	d	17x19				18x23							19x15					21x04					
Pembrey & Burry Port	d	17 25				18 30				18 50			19 23			20 23		21 11					
Llanelli	a	17 31				18 35				18 56			19 29			20 28		21 17					
	d	17 32	17 48			18 36				18 57			19 30			20 29		21 17				21 43	
Gowerton	d		17x57							19x04												21x50	
Swansea	a	17 49	18 18			18 54				19 22			19 49			20 47		21 39				22 08	
	d	17 55			18 28	19 00			19 10		19 29	19 29	19 52		20 28	20 57		21 45					
Llansamlet	d								19 17									21 52					
Skewen	d								19 21									21 56					
Neath	d	18 06			18 40	19 11			19 25		19 40	19 40	20 03		20 40	21 08		22 00					
Briton Ferry	d								19 28									22 03					
Baglan	d								19 32									22 07					
Port Talbot Parkway	d	18 13			18 48	19 19			19 36		19 48	19 48	20 10		20 48	21 15		22 11					
Pyle	d								19 43									22 18					
Maesteg	d			18 20				19 17						20 15			21 15						22 15
Maesteg (Ewenny Road)	d			18 22				19 19						20 17			21 17						22 17
Garth (Mid Glamorgan)	d			18 25				19 22						20 20			21 20						22 20
Tondu	d			18 34				19 31						20 29			21 29						22 29
Sarn	d			18 37				19 34						20 32			21 32						22 32
Wildmill	d			18 39				19 36						20 34			21 34						22 34
Bridgend	d	18 25		18 43	19 00	19 32		19 40	19 51		20 00	20 00	20 24	20 38	21 00	21 27	21 38	22 26					22 38
Pencoed	d			18 49				19 46						20 44			21 44						22 44
Llanharan	d			18 53				19 49						20 48			21 48						22 48
Pontyclun	d			18 57				19 54						20 52			21 52						22 52
Cardiff Central 7	a	18 46		19 13	19 22	19 57		20 10	20 17		20 22	20 22	20 46	21 08	21 22	21 50	22 10	22 49					23 08
Newport (South Wales)	a	19 03			19 39						20 38	20 38		21 25	21 38								23 38
Bristol Parkway 7	a				19 59						21 01	21 01			21 59								
Gloucester 7	a													22 21									00 39
Manchester Piccadilly 10	a	22 13																					
Reading 7	a				21 00						22 11	22 11			23 02								
London Paddington 15 ⊖	a				21 32						22 44	22 45			23 38								

When events are being held at the Millenium Stadium, services are subject to alteration. Please check times before travelling.

Table 128

Mondays to Fridays

25 June to 14 September

West Wales, Swansea and Maesteg - Cardiff

Route Diagram - see first Page of Table 127

		AW FX	AW FX	AW	AW	AW	AW
Rosslare Harbour	d						
Fishguard Harbour	a						
	d						
Fishguard & Goodwick	d						
Milford Haven	d						23 18
Johnston	d						23x26
Haverfordwest	d						23 33
Clarbeston Road	d						23x41
Clunderwen	d						23x48
Pembroke Dock	d				21 09	22 23	
Pembroke	d				21 17	22 31	
Lamphey	d				21x20	22x34	
Manorbier	d				21 29	22 42	
Penally	d				21x34	22x48	
Tenby	a				21 37	22 50	
	d				21 42	22 50	
Saundersfoot	d				21x50	22x58	
Kilgetty	d				21x52	23x00	
Narberth	d				22x02	23x09	
Whitland	a				22 10	23 17	23 54
	d				22 10	23 20	23 54
Carmarthen	a				22 28	23 39	00 16
	d				22 35		
Ferryside	d				22x45		
Kidwelly	d				22x51		
Pembrey & Burry Port	d				22 58		
Llanelli	a				23 04		
	d				23 05		
Gowerton	d				23x12		
Swansea	a				23 32		
	d			22 32			
Llansamlet	d			22 39			
Skewen	d			22 43			
Neath	d			22 47			
Briton Ferry	d			22 50			
Baglan	d			22 54			
Port Talbot Parkway	d			22 58			
Pyle	d			23 05			
Maesteg	d	22 15					
Maesteg (Ewenny Road)	d	22 17					
Garth (Mid Glamorgan)	d	22 20					
Tondu	d	22 29					
Sarn	d	22 32					
Wildmill	d	22 34					
Bridgend	d	22 38	22 52	23 13			
Pencoed	d	22 44					
Llanharan	d	22 48					
Pontyclun	d	22 52					
Cardiff Central 7	a	23 08	23 18	23 38			
Newport (South Wales)	a	23 39					
Bristol Parkway 7	a						
Gloucester 7	a	00 39					
Manchester Piccadilly 10	a						
Reading 7	a						
London Paddington 15 ⊖	a						

When events are being held at the Millenium Stadium, services are subject to alteration. Please check times before travelling.

Table 128

Mondays to Fridays

from 17 September

West Wales, Swansea and Maesteg - Cardiff

Route Diagram - see first Page of Table 127

		AW	AW MX	AW MO ◇	AW MO	AW MX	AW MX	AW ◇	GW ◇1 ⊏P	GW ◇1 ⊏P		GW ◇1 ⊏P	AW ◇ 🛒	GW ◇1 A ⊘	GW ◇1 B ⊏P⊘	AW	AW 🛒	GW ◇1 B ⊏P⊘	AW ◇ 🛒	GW ◇1 B ⊏P⊘		AW	AW ◇ 🛒	AW	AW
Rosslare Harbour ⛴	d	21p00																							
Fishguard Harbour ⛴	a	00 30																							
	d							01 50																06 53	
Fishguard & Goodwick	d							01 53																06 56	
Milford Haven	d			21p35	23p15	23p18	00 18																06 00		
Johnston	d			21b43	23b23	23b26	00x26																06x08		
Haverfordwest	d			21p51	23p30	23p33	00 33																06 15		
Clarbeston Road	d			21b59	23b39	23b41	00x41	02x12															06x23	07a16	
Clunderwen	d			22b07	23b46	23b48	00x48																06x30		
Pembroke Dock	d																								
Pembroke	d																								
Lamphey	d																								
Manorbier	d																								
Penally	d																								
Tenby	a																								
	d																								
Saundersfoot	d																								
Kilgetty	d																								
Narberth	d																								
Whitland	a			22p13	23p53	23p54	00 54	02 24															06 36		
	d			22p14	23p53	23p54	00 54	02 24															06 36		
Carmarthen	a			22p31	00 14	00 16	01 16	02 41															06 52		
	d			22p34				02 44					05 03				05 50		06 15				06 57		
Ferryside	d			22b44													06x00		06x25						
Kidwelly	d			22b50													06x05		06x30						
Pembrey & Burry Port	d			22p58									05 21				06 12		06 37				07 15		
Llanelli	a			23p04				03 06					05 26				06 17		06 42				07 20		
	d			23p04				03 06					05 28				06 18		06 44				07 22		
Gowerton	d			23b12													06x24		06x50				07x28		
Swansea	a			23p27				03 29									06 38		07 04				07 41		
	d			23p31					03 57	04 58		05 27		05 58	06 28		06 42	06 58	07 06	07 28			07 45		
Llansamlet	d																06 46								
Skewen	d																06 50								
Neath	d			23p43					04 09	05 10		05 39		06 10	06 40		06 54	07 10	07 17	07 40			07 56		
Briton Ferry	d																06 58								
Baglan	d																07 01								
Port Talbot Parkway	d			23p50					04 17	05 18		05 47	06 01	06 18	06 48		07 05	07 18	07 24	07 48			08 03		
Pyle	d			23p57									06 08				07 12		07 31				08 09		
Maesteg	d		22p15													06 42									07 58
Maesteg (Ewenny Road)	d		22p17													06 44									08 00
Garth (Mid Glamorgan)	d		22p20													06 47									08 03
Tondu	d		22p29													06 56									08 12
Sarn	d		22p32													06 59									08 15
Wildmill	d		22p34													07 01									08 17
Bridgend	d		22p38	00 05					04 30	05 30		05 59	06 15	06 30	07 00	07 05	07 20	07 30	07 39	08 00		08 07	08 17		08 21
Pencoed	d		22p44										06 21			07 11	07 26					08 13			08 27
Llanharan	d		22p48										06 25			07 15			07 46				08 24		
Pontyclun	d		22p52										06 30			07 20	07 33					08 21			08 34
Cardiff Central 7	a		23p08	00 30					05 02	05 52		06 21	06 43	06 52	07 22	07 34	07 48	07 52	08 02	08 22		08 34	08 43		08 48
Newport (South Wales)	a		23p39						05 30	06 09		06 37	07 02	07 09	07 39			08 09	08 17	08 39			09 02		09 25
Bristol Parkway 7	a								05 59	06 29		06 58		07 29	07 59			08 30		08 59					
Gloucester 7	a		00 39																						10 20
Manchester Piccadilly 10	a												10 15						11 15				12 15		
Reading 7	a								07 00	07 31		08 00			09 01			09 25		09 59					
London Paddington 15 ⊖	a								07 32	08 02		08 33		08 54	09 29			09 59		10 32					

A The Capitals United

B ⊏P from Reading ⊘ to Reading

b Previous night, stops on request

When events are being held at the Millenium Stadium, services are subject to alteration. Please check times before travelling.

Table 128

Mondays to Fridays

from 17 September

West Wales, Swansea and Maesteg - Cardiff

Route Diagram - see first Page of Table 127

		GW ◇1 ⊏P	GW ◇1 A ⊏P	AW ◇ 🛒	AW	AW ◇		AW	GW ◇1 ⊏P	AW ◇ 🛒	AW	GW ◇1 ⊏P	AW ◇ 🛒	AW	AW	AW		AW		GW ◇1 B ⊏P	AW ◇ 🛒	AW 🛒	GW ◇1 C ⊏P⊘	AW ◇ 🛒	AW ◇ 🛒
Rosslare Harbour ⛴	d																								
Fishguard Harbour ⛴	a																								
	d									08 04								09 56							
Fishguard & Goodwick	d									08 07								09 59							
Milford Haven	d			07 05									09 08											11 08	
Johnston	d			07x13									09x16											11x16	
Haverfordwest	d			07 20									09 23											11 23	
Clarbeston Road	d			07x28						08x25			09x31					10x17						11x31	
Clunderwen	d			07x35						08x33			09x38					10x25						11x38	
Pembroke Dock	d							07 09								09 09									
Pembroke	d							07 17								09 17									
Lamphey	d							07x20								09x20									
Manorbier	d							07 28								09 29									
Penally	d							07x34								09x34									
Tenby	a							07 35								09 37									
	d							07 38								09 38									
Saundersfoot	d							07x44								09x46									
Kilgetty	d							07x46								09x48									
Narberth	d							07x56								09x58									
Whitland	a			07 41				08 04		08 37			09 44			10 06		10 31						11 44	
	d			07 41				08 05		08 38			09 44			10 07		10 32						11 44	
Carmarthen	a			07 55				08 25		08 55			10 02			10 24		10 49						12 00	
	d		07 30	08 01				08 30		09 00			10 04			10 31					11 02			12 05	
Ferryside	d		07 42	08x11				08x40		09x10											11x12				
Kidwelly	d		07 49	08x16				08x46		09x15											11x17				
Pembrey & Burry Port	d		07 56	08 23				08 53		09 18			10 24			10 50					11 23			12 23	
Llanelli	a		08 02	08 28				08 59		09 24			10 29			10 56					11 29			12 28	
	d		08 04	08 30		08 45		09 00		09 25			10 31			10 57					11 30			12 30	12 42
Gowerton	d			08x36		08x53		09x08								11x04					11x37				
Swansea	a		08 21	08 49		09 08		09 23		09 48			10 48			11 22					11 49			12 47	13 04
	d	07 58	08 28	08 55		09 11			09 28	09 55		10 28	10 55		11 10					11 28	11 55		12 28	12 54	
Llansamlet	d					09 18									11 17										
Skewen	d					09 22									11 21										
Neath	d	08 10	08 40	09 06		09 26			09 40	10 06		10 40	11 06		11 25					11 40	12 06		12 40	13 05	
Briton Ferry	d					09 30									11 28										
Baglan	d					09 33									11 32										
Port Talbot Parkway	d	08 18	08 48	09 13		09 37			09 48	10 13		10 48	11 13		11 36					11 48	12 13		12 48	13 12	
Pyle	d					09 44									11 43										
Maesteg	d				09 15						10 15			11 15								12 15			
Maesteg (Ewenny Road)	d				09 17						10 17			11 17								12 17			
Garth (Mid Glamorgan)	d				09 20						10 20			11 20								12 20			
Tondu	d				09 29						10 29			11 29								12 29			
Sarn	d				09 32						10 32			11 32								12 32			
Wildmill	d				09 34						10 34			11 34								12 34			
Bridgend	d	08 30	09 00	09 25	09 38	09 53			10 00	10 25	10 38	11 00	11 25	11 38	11 55					12 00	12 25	12 38	13 00	13 24	
Pencoed	d				09 44						10 44			11 44								12 44			
Llanharan	d				09 48						10 48			11 48								12 48			
Pontyclun	d				09 52						10 52			11 52								12 52			
Cardiff Central 7	a	08 52	09 22	09 46	10 07	10 17			10 22	10 47	11 09	11 22	11 48	12 08	12 18					12 22	12 47	13 07	13 22	13 47	
Newport (South Wales)	a	09 09	09 39	10 17	10 25				10 39	11 02		11 39	12 17	12 25						12 39	13 02	13 25	13 39	14 17	
Bristol Parkway 7	a	09 30	09 59						10 59			11 59								12 59			13 59		
Gloucester 7	a				11 20									13 20								14 20			
Manchester Piccadilly 10	a			13 15						14 15			15 15								16 15			17 14	
Reading 7	a	10 31	11 00						11 59			13 00								13 59			15 00		
London Paddington 15 ⊖	a	11 07	11 32						12 32			13 32								14 32			15 32		

A The Red Dragon

B The St. David

C ⊏P from Reading ⊘ to Reading

When events are being held at the Millenium Stadium, services are subject to alteration. Please check times before travelling.

Table 128

Mondays to Fridays

from 17 September

West Wales, Swansea and Maesteg - Cardiff

Route Diagram - see first Page of Table 127

		AW		AW	AW	GW	AW	AW	GW	AW	AW	AW	AW	AW	AW	GW	AW	AW	GW	AW	AW	AW		AW	GW
				◇ ✠		◇1 A ☕⊘	◇ ✠		◇1 ☕	B	■ ✠	■ ✠			✠	◇1 ☕	■ ✠		◇1 A ☕⊘	■ ✠					◇1 ☕
Rosslare Harbour ⛴	d									09 00															
Fishguard Harbour ⛴	a									12 30															
	d											13 30													
Fishguard & Goodwick	d											13 33													
Milford Haven	d										13 08									15 08					
Johnston	d										13x16									15x16					
Haverfordwest	d										13 23									15 23					
Clarbeston Road	d										13x31									15x31					
Clunderwen	d										13x38									15x38					
Pembroke Dock	d				11 09										13 09									15 09	
Pembroke	d				11 17										13 17									15 17	
Lamphey	d				11x20										13x20									15x20	
Manorbier	d				11 29										13 29									15 29	
Penally	d				11x34										13x34									15x34	
Tenby	a				11 37										13 37									15 37	
	d				11 43										13 41									15 41	
Saundersfoot	d				11x51										13x49									15x49	
Kilgetty	d				11x53										13x51									15x51	
Narberth	d				12x03										14x01									16x01	
Whitland	a				12 11						13 44	14 04			14 09					15 44				16 09	
	d				12 11						13 44	14 04			14 09					15 44				16 09	
Carmarthen	a				12 29						14 00	14 21			14 29					16 00				16 27	
	d				12 33		13 02				14 05	14 25			14 34		15 05			16 05				16 31	
Ferryside	d						13x12										15x15								
Kidwelly	d						13x17										15x20								
Pembrey & Burry Port	d				12 52		13 23				14 23				14 53		15 27			16 23				16 50	
Llanelli	a				12 58		13 29				14 28	14 47			14 59		15 32			16 28				16 56	
	d				12 59		13 30				14 30	14 47			14 59		15 34			16 30				16 57	
Gowerton	d				13x06						14x36									16x36				17x04	
Swansea	a				13 22		13 51				14 49				15 22		15 51			16 49				17 22	
	d			13 10		13 28	13 55		14 28		14 55			15 10		15 28	15 55		16 28	16 55		17 10			17 28
Llansamlet	d			13 17										15 17								17 17			
Skewen	d			13 21										15 21								17 21			
Neath	d			13 25		13 40	14 06		14 40		15 06			15 25		15 40	16 06		16 40	17 06		17 25			17 40
Briton Ferry	d			13 28										15 28								17 28			
Baglan	d			13 32										15 32								17 32			
Port Talbot Parkway	d			13 36		13 48	14 13		14 48		15 13			15 36		15 48	16 13		16 48	17 13		17 36			17 48
Pyle	d			13 43										15 43								17 43			
Maesteg	d	13 15						14 15					15 17					16 15			17 15				
Maesteg (Ewenny Road)	d	13 17						14 17					15 19					16 17			17 17				
Garth (Mid Glamorgan)	d	13 20						14 20					15 22					16 20			17 20				
Tondu	d	13 29						14 29					15 31					16 29			17 29				
Sarn	d	13 32						14 32					15 34					16 32			17 32				
Wildmill	d	13 34						14 34					15 36					16 34			17 34				
Bridgend	d	13 38		13 52		14 00	14 25	14 38	15 00		15 25		15 40	15 52		16 00	16 25	16 38	17 00	17 25	17 38	17 54			18 00
Pencoed	d	13 44						14 44					15 46					16 44			17 44				
Llanharan	d	13 48						14 48					15 50					16 48			17 48				
Pontyclun	d	13 52						14 52					15 54					16 52			17 52				
Cardiff Central 7	a	14 07		14 15		14 22	14 47	15 07	15 22		15 47	16 04	16 09	16 15		16 22	16 46	17 07	17 22	17 47	18 07	18 20			18 22
Newport (South Wales)	a					14 39	15 02	15 26	15 39		16 02	16 18				16 39	17 02	17 25	17 39	18 02	18 25				18 39
Bristol Parkway 7	a					15 00			15 59							16 59			17 59						18 59
Gloucester 7	a							16 21				17 14						18 21			19 20				
Manchester Piccadilly 10	a						18 13				19 15						20 15			21 05					
Reading 7	a					16 00			17 00							18 00			19 01						20 00
London Paddington 15 ⊖	a					16 30			17 30							18 30			19 32						20 32

A ☕ from Reading ⊘ to Reading

When events are being held at the Millenium Stadium, services are subject to alteration. Please check times before travelling.

Table 128

Mondays to Fridays

from 17 September

West Wales, Swansea and Maesteg - Cardiff

Route Diagram - see first Page of Table 127

		AW	AW	AW	GW	AW	AW	AW		AW	AW	GW FX	GW FO	AW	AW	GW	AW	AW		AW	AW	AW	AW	AW	AW FO
		◇ ✠	◇		◇1 ☕	◇						◇1 ☕	◇1 ☕	◇		◇1 ☕	◇						B	◇	
Rosslare Harbour ⛴	d																						21 00		
Fishguard Harbour ⛴	a																						00 30		
	d						19 00															20 50			
Fishguard & Goodwick	d						19 03															20 53			
Milford Haven	d					17 08											19 08				20 36				
Johnston	d					17x16											19x16				20x44				
Haverfordwest	d					17 23											19 23				20 51				
Clarbeston Road	d					17x31	19a21										19x31				20x59	21x12			
Clunderwen	d					17x38											19x38				21x06	21x19			
Pembroke Dock	d										17 09														
Pembroke	d										17 17														
Lamphey	d										17x20														
Manorbier	d										17 29														
Penally	d										17x34														
Tenby	a										17 37														
	d										17 38									19 57					
Saundersfoot	d										17x46									20x05					
Kilgetty	d										17x48									20x07					
Narberth	d										17x58									20x17					
Whitland	a					17 44					18 06						19 44			20 25	21 12	21 26			
	d					17 45					18 07						19 44			20 27	21 12	21 26			
Carmarthen	a					18 02					18 24						20 00			20 45	21 34	21 47			
	d	17 04				18 07					18 31			18 59			20 05			20 47					
Ferryside	d	17x14				18x17								19x09						20x58					
Kidwelly	d	17x19				18x23								19x15						21x04					
Pembrey & Burry Port	d	17 25				18 30					18 50			19 23			20 23			21 11					
Llanelli	a	17 31				18 35					18 56			19 29			20 28			21 17					
	d	17 32	17 48			18 36					18 57			19 30			20 29			21 17				21 43	
Gowerton	d		17x57								19x04													21x50	
Swansea	a	17 49	18 18			18 54					19 22			19 49			20 47			21 39				22 08	
	d	17 55			18 28	19 00				19 10		19 29	19 29	19 52		20 28	20 57			21 45					
Llansamlet	d									19 17										21 52					
Skewen	d									19 21										21 56					
Neath	d	18 06			18 40	19 11				19 25		19 40	19 40	20 03		20 40	21 08			22 00					
Briton Ferry	d									19 28										22 03					
Baglan	d									19 32										22 07					
Port Talbot Parkway	d	18 13			18 48	19 19				19 36		19 48	19 48	20 10		20 48	21 15			22 11					
Pyle	d									19 43										22 18					
Maesteg	d			18 20				19 17							20 15			21 15							22 15
Maesteg (Ewenny Road)	d			18 22				19 19							20 17			21 17							22 17
Garth (Mid Glamorgan)	d			18 25				19 22							20 20			21 20							22 20
Tondu	d			18 34				19 31							20 29			21 29							22 29
Sarn	d			18 37				19 34							20 32			21 32							22 32
Wildmill	d			18 39				19 36							20 34			21 34							22 34
Bridgend	d	18 25		18 43	19 00	19 32		19 40		19 51		20 00	20 00	20 24	20 38	21 00	21 27	21 38		22 26					22 38
Pencoed	d			18 49				19 46							20 44			21 44							22 44
Llanharan	d			18 53				19 49							20 48			21 48							22 48
Pontyclun	d			18 57				19 54							20 52			21 52							22 52
Cardiff Central 7	a	18 46		19 13	19 22	19 57		20 10		20 17		20 22	20 22	20 46	21 08	21 22	21 50	22 10		22 49					23 08
Newport (South Wales)	a	19 03			19 39							20 38	20 38		21 25	21 38									23 38
Bristol Parkway 7	a				19 59							21 01	21 01			21 59									
Gloucester 7	a														22 21										00 39
Manchester Piccadilly 10	a	22 13																							
Reading 7	a				21 00							22 11	22 11			23 02									
London Paddington 15 ⊖	a				21 32							22 44	22 45			23 38									

When events are being held at the Millenium Stadium, services are subject to alteration. Please check times before travelling.

Table 128

Mondays to Fridays

from 17 September

West Wales, Swansea and Maesteg - Cardiff

Route Diagram - see first Page of Table 127

		AW FX	AW FX	AW	AW	AW	AW
Rosslare Harbour ⛴	d						
Fishguard Harbour ⛴	a						
	d						
Fishguard & Goodwick	d						
Milford Haven	d						23 18
Johnston	d						23x26
Haverfordwest	d						23 33
Clarbeston Road	d						23x41
Clunderwen	d						23x48
Pembroke Dock	d				21 09	22 23	
Pembroke	d				21 17	22 31	
Lamphey	d				21x20	22x34	
Manorbier	d				21 29	22 42	
Penally	d				21x34	22x48	
Tenby	a				21 37	22 50	
	d				21 42	22 50	
Saundersfoot	d				21x50	22x58	
Kilgetty	d				21x52	23x00	
Narberth	d				22x02	23x09	
Whitland	a				22 10	23 17	23 54
	d				22 10	23 20	23 54
Carmarthen	a				22 28	23 39	00 16
	d				22 35		
Ferryside	d				22x45		
Kidwelly	d				22x51		
Pembrey & Burry Port	d				22 58		
Llanelli	a				23 04		
	d				23 05		
Gowerton	d				23x12		
Swansea	a				23 32		
	d			22 32			
Llansamlet	d			22 39			
Skewen	d			22 43			
Neath	d			22 47			
Briton Ferry	d			22 50			
Baglan	d			22 54			
Port Talbot Parkway	d			22 58			
Pyle	d			23 05			
Maesteg	d	22 15					
Maesteg (Ewenny Road)	d	22 17					
Garth (Mid Glamorgan)	d	22 20					
Tondu	d	22 29					
Sarn	d	22 32					
Wildmill	d	22 34					
Bridgend	d	22 38	22 52	23 13			
Pencoed	d	22 44					
Llanharan	d	22 48					
Pontyclun	d	22 52					
Cardiff Central 7	a	23 08	23 18	23 38			
Newport (South Wales)	a	23 39					
Bristol Parkway 7	a						
Gloucester 7	a	00 39					
Manchester Piccadilly 10	a						
Reading 7	a						
London Paddington 15 ⊖	a						

When events are being held at the Millenium Stadium, services are subject to alteration. Please check times before travelling.

Table 128

Saturdays

until 23 June

West Wales, Swansea and Maesteg - Cardiff

Route Diagram - see first Page of Table 127

		AW	AW	AW	AW	AW	GW	GW	GW	AW	GW	GW	AW	AW	GW	AW	GW	AW	AW	AW	GW	AW	AW
		B																					
						◇	◇1	◇1	◇1	◇	◇1	◇1		◇	◇1		◇1	◇			◇1	◇	
															A		A						
							☕	☕	☕	🛒	☕	☕		🛒	☕⊘	🛒	☕⊘	🛒			☕	🛒	
Rosslare Harbour ⛴	d	21p00																					
Fishguard Harbour ⛴	a	00 30																					
	d					01 50													06 53				
Fishguard & Goodwick	d					01 53													06 56				
Milford Haven	d			23p18	00 18													06 00				07 05	
Johnston	d			23b26	00x26													06x08				07x13	
Haverfordwest	d			23p33	00 33													06 15				07 20	
Clarbeston Road	d			23b41	00x41	02x12												06x23	07a16			07x28	
Clunderwen	d			23b48	00x48													06x30				07x35	
Pembroke Dock	d																						
Pembroke	d																						
Lamphey	d																						
Manorbier	d																						
Penally	d																						
Tenby	a																						
	d																						
Saundersfoot	d																						
Kilgetty	d																						
Narberth	d																						
Whitland	a			23p54	00 54	02 24												06 36				07 41	
	d			23p54	00 54	02 24												06 36				07 41	
Carmarthen	a			00 16	01 16	02 41												06 52				07 55	
	d					02 44				05 04				05 55		06 20		06 57				08 01	
Ferryside	d													06x05		06x30						08x11	
Kidwelly	d													06x10		06x35						08x16	
Pembrey & Burry Port	d									05 22				06 17		06 42		07 15				08 23	
Llanelli	a					03 06				05 27				06 22		06 47		07 20				08 28	
	d					03 06				05 29				06 24		06 48		07 22				08 30	
Gowerton	d													06x30		06x55		07x28				08x36	
Swansea	a					03 29								06 43		07 10		07 41				08 49	
	d						03 58	04 58	05 28		05 58	06 28		06 47	06 58	07 13	07 28	07 45			08 28	08 55	
Llansamlet	d															07 20							
Skewen	d															07 24							
Neath	d						04 10	05 10	05 40		06 10	06 40		06 58	07 10	07 28	07 40	07 56			08 40	09 06	
Briton Ferry	d															07 31							
Baglan	d															07 35							
Port Talbot Parkway	d						04 18	05 18	05 48	06 02	06 18	06 48		07 05	07 18	07 39	07 48	08 03			08 48	09 13	
Pyle	d									06 08				07 11		07 46		08 09				09 20	
Maesteg	d		22p15										06 46							08 00			09 17
Maesteg (Ewenny Road)	d		22p17										06 48							08 02			09 19
Garth (Mid Glamorgan)	d		22p20										06 51							08 05			09 22
Tondu	d		22p29										07 00							08 14			09 31
Sarn	d		22p32										07 03							08 17			09 34
Wildmill	d		22p34										07 05							08 19			09 36
Bridgend	d		22p38				04 30	05 30	06 00	06 16	06 30	07 00	07 09	07 19	07 30	07 54	08 00	08 17		08 23	09 00	09 27	09 40
Pencoed	d		22p44							06 22			07 15			08 07		08 23					09 46
Llanharan	d		22p48							06 25				07 26		08 11				08 31			09 50
Pontyclun	d		22p52							06 30			07 22			08 15		08 30					09 54
Cardiff Central 7	a		23p08				04 52	05 52	06 22	06 43	06 52	07 22	07 36	07 42	07 52	08 34	08 22	08 44		08 47	09 22	09 46	10 09
Newport (South Wales)	a		23p38				05 09	06 09	06 38	07 02	07 08	07 39		08 02	08 08		08 38	09 02		09 24	09 39	10 07	10 25
Bristol Parkway 7	a						05 36	06 29	06 59		07 29	07 59			08 30		08 59				09 59		
Gloucester 7	a		00 39																	10 19			11 21
Manchester Piccadilly 10	a									10 14				11 15				12 15				13 15	
Reading 7	a						07 14	07 31	08 00		08 31	09 00			09 32		10 00				11 01		
London Paddington 15 ⊖	a						07 44	08 07	08 32		09 02	09 32			10 02		10 32				11 33		

A ☕ from Reading ⊘ to Reading

b Previous night, stops on request

When events are being held at the Millenium Stadium, services are subject to alteration. Please check times before travelling.

Saturdays until 23 June

West Wales, Swansea and Maesteg - Cardiff

Route Diagram - see first Page of Table 127

		AW	AW	GW	AW	AW		AW	GW	AW	AW	AW	AW	AW		GW		AW	AW	GW	AW	AW	AW	AW	AW
		◇	🛒	◇1 🍽	◇ 🛒	🛒			◇1 🍽	◇ 🛒						◇1 🍽		◇ 🛒	🛒	◇1 🍽	◇ 🛒	◇ 🛒		◇ 🛒	
Rosslare Harbour ⛴	d																								
Fishguard Harbour ⛴	a																								
	d				08 04									09 53											
Fishguard & Goodwick	d				08 07									09 56											
Milford Haven	d									09 08											11 08				
Johnston	d									09x16											11x16				
Haverfordwest	d									09 23											11 23				
Clarbeston Road	d				08x25					09x31				10x14							11x31				
Clunderwen	d				08x33					09x38				10x22							11x38				
Pembroke Dock	d		07 09			08 35														10 00					
Pembroke	d		07 17			08 43														10 10					
Lamphey	d		07x20			08x46																			
Manorbier	d		07 28			08 55														10 23					
Penally	d		07x34			09x00																			
Tenby	a		07 37			09 03														10 32					
	d		07 38			09 08														10 36					11 41
Saundersfoot	d		07x44			09x16														10 46					11x49
Kilgetty	d		07x46			09x18																			11x51
Narberth	d		07x56			09x28																			12x01
Whitland	a		08 04		08 37	09 38				09 44				10 28						11 06	11 44				12 09
	d		08 05		08 38					09 44			10 07	10 29						11 07	11 44				12 09
Carmarthen	a		08 25		08 55					10 02			10 26	10 46						11 25	12 00				12 27
	d		08 30		09 00				09 35	10 04			10 29					11 02		11 35	12 05				12 31
Ferryside	d		08x40		09x10													11x12							
Kidwelly	d		08x45		09x15													11x17							
Pembrey & Burry Port	d		08 51		09 21				09 56	10 24			10 48					11 23		11 56	12 23				12 50
Llanelli	a		08 56		09 27				10 01	10 29			10 54					11 29		12 01	12 28				12 56
	d	08 45	08 58		09 28				10 03	10 31			10 55					11 37		12 03	12 30	12 37			12 57
Gowerton	d	08x53	09x09										11x02					11x37							13x04
Swansea	a	09 08	09 23		09 45				10 21	10 48			11 22					11 49		12 21	12 47	13 06			13 23
	d	09 11		09 28	09 55				10 28	10 55		11 10				11 28		11 55		12 28	12 55			13 10	
Llansamlet	d	09 19										11 17												13 17	
Skewen	d	09 23										11 21												13 21	
Neath	d	09 27	09 46	09 40	10 06				10 40	11 06		11 25				11 40		12 06		12 40	13 06			13 25	
Briton Ferry	d	09 31										11 28												13 28	
Baglan	d	09 34										11 32												13 32	
Port Talbot Parkway	d	09 38	09 53	09 48	10 13				10 48	11 13		11 36				11 48		12 13		12 48	13 13			13 36	
Pyle	d	09 46	10 05		10 19					11 20		11 43									13 20			13 43	
Maesteg	d							10 15			11 15								12 17				13 15		
Maesteg (Ewenny Road)	d							10 17			11 17								12 19				13 17		
Garth (Mid Glamorgan)	d							10 20			11 20								12 22				13 20		
Tondu	d							10 29			11 29								12 31				13 29		
Sarn	d							10 32			11 32								12 34				13 32		
Wildmill	d							10 34			11 34								12 36				13 34		
Bridgend	d	09 54	10s13	10 00	10 27			10 38	11 00	11 27	11 38	11 55				12 00		12 25	12 40	13 00	13 27		13 38	13 52	
Pencoed	d							10 44			11 44								12 46				13 44		
Llanharan	d							10 48			11 48								12 50				13 48		
Pontyclun	d							10 52			11 52								12 54				13 52		
Cardiff Central 7	a	10 20	10 43	10 22	10 48			11 13	11 22	11 48	12 07	12 18				12 22		12 50	13 09	13 22	13 48		14 09	14 15	
Newport (South Wales)	a			10 39	11 07				11 39	12 07	12 25					12 39		13 04	13 25	13 38	14 07				
Bristol Parkway 7	a			10 59					11 59							12 59				13 59					
Gloucester 7	a										13 21								14 21						
Manchester Piccadilly 10	a				14 15					15 15								16 15			17 15				
Reading 7	a			12 00					13 00							14 00				15 00					
London Paddington 15 ⊖	a			12 32					13 33							14 32				15 32					

When events are being held at the Millenium Stadium, services are subject to alteration. Please check times before travelling.

Table 128

Saturdays until 23 June

West Wales, Swansea and Maesteg - Cardiff

Route Diagram - see first Page of Table 127

		GW		AW	AW	GW	AW	AW	AW	AW	AW	AW	GW	AW	AW	GW	AW	AW	AW	GW	AW	AW		AW	GW
							B	■	■					■			■								
		◇1 🍽		◇ 🛒		◇1 🍽		🛒	🛒			🛒	◇1 🍽	🛒		◇1 🍽	🛒			◇1 🍽	◇ 🛒	◇			◇1 🍽
Rosslare Harbour ⛴	d						09 00																		
Fishguard Harbour ⛴	a						12 30																		
	d								13 30																
Fishguard & Goodwick	d								13 33																
Milford Haven	d							13 08									15 08								
Johnston	d							13x16									15x16								
Haverfordwest	d							13 23									15 23								
Clarbeston Road	d							13x31									15x31								
Clunderwen	d							13x38									15x38								
Pembroke Dock	d											13 09								14 55					
Pembroke	d											13 17								15 05					
Lamphey	d											13x20								15x08					
Manorbier	d											13 29								15 20					
Penally	d											13x34								15x26					
Tenby	a											13 37								15 29					
	d											13 42								15 36					
Saundersfoot	d											13x50								15 46					
Kilgetty	d											13x52								15x49					
Narberth	d											14x02								15x58					
Whitland	a							13 44	14 04			14 10					15 44			16 08					
	d							13 44	14 04			14 11					15 44			16 09					
Carmarthen	a							14 00	14 21			14 28					16 00			16 27					
	d			13 02				14 05	14 23			14 33		15 05			16 05			16 33	17 04				
Ferryside	d			13x12										15x15						16x45	17x14				
Kidwelly	d			13x17										15x20						16x50	17x19				
Pembrey & Burry Port	d			13 23				14 23				14 52		15 27			16 23			16 58	17 25				
Llanelli	a			13 29				14 28	14 45			14 58		15 32			16 28			17 03	17 31				
	d			13 30				14 30	14 45			14 58		15 34			16 30			17 05	17 32	17 41			
Gowerton	d							14x36									16x36					17x51			
Swansea	a			13 48				14 49				15 22		15 51			16 49			17 21	17 49	18 10			
	d	13 28		14 00		14 28		14 55			15 10		15 28	15 55		16 28	16 55		17 10	17 28	17 55				18 28
Llansamlet	d										15 17								17 17						
Skewen	d										15 21								17 21						
Neath	d	13 40		14 11		14 40		15 06			15 25		15 40	16 06		16 40	17 06		17 25	17 40	18 06				18 40
Briton Ferry	d										15 28								17 28						
Baglan	d										15 32								17 32						
Port Talbot Parkway	d	13 48		14 18		14 48		15 13			15 36		15 48	16 13		16 48	17 13		17 36	17 48	18 13				18 48
Pyle	d										15 43			16 20			17 20		17 43						
Maesteg	d				14 15					15 17					16 15			17 15						18 20	
Maesteg (Ewenny Road)	d				14 17					15 19					16 17			17 17						18 22	
Garth (Mid Glamorgan)	d				14 20					15 22					16 20			17 20						18 25	
Tondu	d				14 29					15 31					16 29			17 29						18 34	
Sarn	d				14 32					15 34					16 32			17 32						18 37	
Wildmill	d				14 34					15 36					16 34			17 34						18 39	
Bridgend	d	14 00		14 30	14 38	15 00		15 25		15 40	15 52		16 00	16 27	16 38	17 00	17 27	17 38	17 54	18 00	18 25			18 43	19 00
Pencoed	d				14 44					15 46					16 44			17 44						18 49	
Llanharan	d				14 48					15 50					16 48			17 48						18 53	
Pontyclun	d				14 52					15 54					16 52			17 52						18 57	
Cardiff Central 7	a	14 22		14 52	15 07	15 22		15 47	15 54	16 09	16 15		16 22	16 48	17 07	17 22	17 48	18 07	18 20	18 22	18 46			19 13	19 22
Newport (South Wales)	a	14 39		15 07	15 25	15 39		16 07		16 23	16 32		16 39	17 07	17 27	17 39	18 07	18 25		18 39	19 03				19 39
Bristol Parkway 7	a	14 59				15 59							16 59			17 59				18 59					19 59
Gloucester 7	a				16 19					17 19					18 20			19 20							
Manchester Piccadilly 10	a			18 15				19 15						20 15			21 15				22 15				
Reading 7	a	16 01				17 00							18 00			19 00				20 00					21 06
London Paddington 15 ⊖	a	16 37				17 32							18 32			19 32				20 32					21 36

When events are being held at the Millenium Stadium, services are subject to alteration. Please check times before travelling.

Table 128

West Wales, Swansea and Maesteg - Cardiff

Saturdays
until 23 June

Route Diagram - see first Page of Table 127

		AW	AW	AW	AW	AW	AW	GW	GW	AW	AW	AW	AW	AW	AW	AW	AW	AW	AW	AW	AW	AW	AW
			◇		◇			◇1 A ⊐	◇1 B ⊐	◇		◇				🛏		◇					
Rosslare Harbour ⛴	d															21 00							
Fishguard Harbour ⛴	a															00 30							
	d			19 00											21 00								
Fishguard & Goodwick	d			19 03											21 03								
Milford Haven	d		17 08									19 08					21 16						23 18
Johnston	d		17x16									19x16					21x24						23x26
Haverfordwest	d		17 23									19 23					21 31						23 33
Clarbeston Road	d		17x31	19a21								19x31			21x22		21x39						23x41
Clunderwen	d		17x38									19x38			21x29		21x46						23x48
Pembroke Dock	d	16 25												19 09							21 09	22 23	
Pembroke	d	16 33												19 17							21 17	22 31	
Lamphey	d	16x36												19 21							21x20	22x34	
Manorbier	d	16 45												19 29							21 29	22 42	
Penally	d	16x50												19 34							21x34	22x48	
Tenby	a	16 53												19 37							21 37	22 50	
	d	16 55												19 49							21 42	22 50	
Saundersfoot	d	17x03												19x57							21x50	22x58	
Kilgetty	d	17x05												19x59							21x52	23x00	
Narberth	d	17x15												20x09							22x02	23x09	
Whitland	a	17 26	17 44				←					19 44		20 17	21 36		21 52				22 10	23 17	23 54
	d	17 26	17 45									19 44		20 19	21 36		21 52				22 11	23 20	23 54
Carmarthen	a	17 44	18 03				17 44					20 04		20 37	22 00		22 14				22 28	23 39	00 16
	d	18 33	18 07				18 33			18 59		20 07		20 47							22 35		
Ferryside	d	→	18x17							19x09				20x58							22x45		
Kidwelly	d		18x23							19x15				21x04							22x51		
Pembrey & Burry Port	d		18 30				18 52			19 23		20 25		21 11							22 58		
Llanelli	a		18 35				18 58			19 29		20 30		21 17							23 04		
	d		18 36				18 59			19 30		20 31		21 17				21 40			23 05		
Gowerton	d						19x06											21x47			23x12		
Swansea	a		18 54				19 23			19 49		20 50		21 39				22 10			23 30		
	d		19 00			19 10		19 28	19 28	19 52		20 55		21 43						22 20			
Llansamlet	d					19 17								21 50						22 27			
Skewen	d					19 21								21 54						22 31			
Neath	d		19 11			19 25		19 40	19 40	20 03		21 06		21 58						22 35			
Briton Ferry	d					19 28								22 02						22 38			
Baglan	d					19 32								22 05						22 42			
Port Talbot Parkway	d		19 19			19 36		19 48	19 48	20 10		21 13		22 09						22 46			
Pyle	d					19 43								22 16						22 53			
Maesteg	d				19 15						20 15		21 15						22 15				
Maesteg (Ewenny Road)	d				19 17						20 17		21 17						22 17				
Garth (Mid Glamorgan)	d				19 20						20 20		21 20						22 20				
Tondu	d				19 29						20 29		21 29						22 29				
Sarn	d				19 32						20 32		21 32						22 32				
Wildmill	d				19 34						20 34		21 34						22 34				
Bridgend	d		19 32		19 38	19 51		20 00	20 00	20 23	20 38	21 25	21 38	22 25					22 38	23 01			
Pencoed	d				19 44						20 44		21 44						22 44				
Llanharan	d				19 47						20 48		21 48						22 48				
Pontyclun	d				19 52						20 52		21 52						22 52				
Cardiff Central 7	a		19 57		20 05	20 17		20 23	20 23	20 46	21 07	21 46	22 09	22 47					23 08	23 26			
Newport (South Wales)	a				20 24			20 39	20 39		21 25	22 05							23 37				
Bristol Parkway 7	a							21 01	21 01														
Gloucester 7	a										22 22												
Manchester Piccadilly 10	a				23 50																		
Reading 7	a							21 59	21 59														
London Paddington 15 ⊖	a							22 30	22 37														

A not 19 May

B 19 May

When events are being held at the Millenium Stadium, services are subject to alteration. Please check times before travelling.

Table 128

West Wales, Swansea and Maesteg - Cardiff

Saturdays
30 June to 8 September

Route Diagram - see first Page of Table 127

		AW	AW	AW	AW	AW	GW	GW	GW	AW	GW	GW	AW	AW	GW	AW	GW	AW	AW	AW	GW	AW	AW
		🛏				◇	◇1 ⊐	◇1 ⊐	◇1 ⊐	◇ ✕	◇1 ⊐	◇1 ⊐		◇ ✕	◇1 A ⊐⊘	✕	◇1 A ⊐⊘	◇ ✕			◇1 ⊐	◇ ✕	
Rosslare Harbour ⛴	d	21p00																					
Fishguard Harbour ⛴	a	00 30																					
	d					01 50													06 53				
Fishguard & Goodwick	d					01 53													06 56				
Milford Haven	d			23p18	00 18													06 00				07 05	
Johnston	d			23b26	00x26													06x08				07x13	
Haverfordwest	d			23p33	00 33													06 15				07 20	
Clarbeston Road	d			23b41	00x41	02x12												06x23	07a16			07x28	
Clunderwen	d			23b48	00x48													06x30				07x35	
Pembroke Dock	d																						
Pembroke	d																						
Lamphey	d																						
Manorbier	d																						
Penally	d																						
Tenby	a																						
	d																						
Saundersfoot	d																						
Kilgetty	d																						
Narberth	d																						
Whitland	a			23p54	00 54	02 24												06 36				07 41	
	d			23p54	00 54	02 24												06 36				07 41	
Carmarthen	a			00 16	01 16	02 41												06 52				07 55	
	d					02 44				05 04				05 55		06 20		06 57				08 01	
Ferryside	d													06x05		06x30						08x11	
Kidwelly	d													06x10		06x35						08x16	
Pembrey & Burry Port	d									05 22				06 17		06 42		07 15				08 23	
Llanelli	a					03 06				05 27				06 22		06 47		07 20				08 28	
	d					03 06				05 29				06 24		06 48		07 22				08 30	
Gowerton	d													06x30		06x55		07x28				08x36	
Swansea	a					03 29								06 43		07 10		07 41				08 49	
	d						03 58	04 58	05 28		05 58	06 28		06 47	06 58	07 13	07 28	07 45			08 28	08 55	
Llansamlet	d															07 20							
Skewen	d															07 24							
Neath	d						04 10	05 10	05 40		06 10	06 40		06 58	07 10	07 28	07 40	07 56			08 40	09 06	
Briton Ferry	d															07 31							
Baglan	d															07 35							
Port Talbot Parkway	d						04 18	05 18	05 48	06 02	06 18	06 48		07 05	07 18	07 39	07 48	08 03			08 48	09 13	
Pyle	d									06 08				07 11		07 46		08 09				09 20	
Maesteg	d		22p15										06 46							08 00			09 17
Maesteg (Ewenny Road)	d		22p17										06 48							08 02			09 19
Garth (Mid Glamorgan)	d		22p20										06 51							08 05			09 22
Tondu	d		22p29										07 00							08 14			09 31
Sarn	d		22p32										07 03							08 17			09 34
Wildmill	d		22p34										07 05							08 19			09 36
Bridgend	d		22p38				04 30	05 30	06 00	06 16	06 30	07 00	07 09	07 19	07 30	07 54	08 00	08 17		08 23	09 00	09 27	09 40
Pencoed	d		22p44							06 22			07 15			08 07		08 23					09 46
Llanharan	d		22p48							06 25				07 26		08 11				08 31			09 50
Pontyclun	d		22p52							06 30			07 22			08 15		08 30					09 54
Cardiff Central 7	a		23p08				04 52	05 52	06 22	06 43	06 52	07 22	07 36	07 42	07 52	08 34	08 22	08 44		08 47	09 22	09 46	10 09
Newport (South Wales)	a		23p38				05 09	06 09	06 38	07 02	07 08	07 39		08 02	08 08		08 38	09 02		09 24	09 39	10 07	10 25
Bristol Parkway 7	a						05 36	06 29	06 59		07 29	07 59			08 30		08 59				09 59		
Gloucester 7	a		00 39																	10 19			11 21
Manchester Piccadilly 10	a									10 14				11 15				12 15				13 15	
Reading 7	a						07 14	07 31	08 00		08 31	09 00			09 32		10 00				11 01		
London Paddington 15 ⊖	a						07 44	08 07	08 32		09 02	09 32			10 02		10 32				11 33		

A ⊐ from Reading ⊘ to Reading

b Previous night, stops on request

When events are being held at the Millenium Stadium, services are subject to alteration. Please check times before travelling.

Table 128

Saturdays

30 June to 8 September

West Wales, Swansea and Maesteg - Cardiff

Route Diagram - see first Page of Table 127

	AW	AW	GW	AW	AW		AW	GW	AW	AW	AW	AW	AW		GW		AW	AW	GW	AW	AW	AW	AW	AW
	◇	H	◇1 ⊡	◇ H	H			◇1 ⊡	◇ H						◇1 ⊡		◇ H	H	◇1 ⊡	◇ H	◇ H		◇ H	
Rosslare Harbour ⛴ d																								
Fishguard Harbour ⛴ a																								
d				08 04									09 53											
Fishguard & Goodwick d				08 07									09 56											
Milford Haven d									09 08											11 08				
Johnston d									09x16											11x16				
Haverfordwest d									09 23											11 23				
Clarbeston Road d				08x25					09x31				10x14							11x31				
Clunderwen d				08x33					09x38				10x22							11x38				
Pembroke Dock d		07 09			08 35														10 00					
Pembroke d		07 17			08 43														10 10					
Lamphey d		07x20			08x46																			
Manorbier d		07 28			08 55														10 23					
Penally d		07x34			09x00																			
Tenby a		07 37			09 03														10 32					
d		07 38			09 08														10 36					11 41
Saundersfoot d		07x44			09x16														10 46					11x49
Kilgetty d		07x46			09x18																			11x51
Narberth d		07x56			09x28																			12x01
Whitland a		08 04		08 37	09 38				09 44				10 28						11 06	11 44				12 09
d		08 05		08 38					09 44			10 07	10 29						11 07	11 44				12 09
Carmarthen a		08 25		08 55					10 02			10 26	10 46						11 25	12 00				12 27
d		08 30		09 00				09 35	10 04			10 29					11 02		11 35	12 05				12 31
Ferryside d		08x40		09x10													11x12							
Kidwelly d		08x45		09x15													11x17							
Pembrey & Burry Port d		08 51		09 21				09 56	10 24			10 48					11 23		11 56	12 23				12 50
Llanelli a		08 56		09 27				10 01	10 29			10 54					11 29		12 01	12 28				12 56
d	08 45	08 58		09 28				10 03	10 31			10 55					11 37		12 03	12 30	12 37			12 57
Gowerton d	08x53	09x09										11x02					11x37							13x04
Swansea a	09 08	09 23		09 45				10 21	10 48			11 22					11 49		12 21	12 47	13 06			13 23
d	09 11		09 28	09 55				10 28	10 55		11 10				11 28		11 55		12 28	12 55			13 10	
Llansamlet d	09 19										11 17												13 17	
Skewen d	09 23										11 21												13 21	
Neath d	09 27	09 46	09 40	10 06				10 40	11 06		11 25				11 40		12 06		12 40	13 06			13 25	
Briton Ferry d	09 31										11 28												13 28	
Baglan d	09 34										11 32												13 32	
Port Talbot Parkway d	09 38	09 53	09 48	10 13				10 48	11 13		11 36				11 48		12 13		12 48	13 13			13 36	
Pyle d	09 46	10 05		10 19					11 20		11 43									13 20			13 43	
Maesteg d							10 15			11 15								12 17				13 15		
Maesteg (Ewenny Road) d							10 17			11 17								12 19				13 17		
Garth (Mid Glamorgan) d							10 20			11 20								12 22				13 20		
Tondu d							10 29			11 29								12 31				13 29		
Sarn d							10 32			11 32								12 34				13 32		
Wildmill d							10 34			11 34								12 36				13 34		
Bridgend d	09 54	10s13	10 00	10 27			10 38	11 00	11 27	11 38	11 55				12 00		12 25	12 40	13 00	13 27		13 38	13 52	
Pencoed d							10 44			11 44								12 46				13 44		
Llanharan d							10 48			11 48								12 50				13 48		
Pontyclun d							10 52			11 52								12 54				13 52		
Cardiff Central 7 a	10 20	10 43	10 22	10 48			11 13	11 22	11 48	12 07	12 18				12 22		12 50	13 09	13 22	13 48		14 09	14 15	
Newport (South Wales) a			10 39	11 07				11 39	12 07	12 25					12 39		13 04	13 25	13 38	14 07				
Bristol Parkway 7 a			10 59					11 59							12 59				13 59					
Gloucester 7 a										13 21								14 21						
Manchester Piccadilly 10 a				14 15					15 15								16 15			17 15				
Reading 7 a			12 00					13 00							14 00				15 00					
London Paddington 15 ⊖ a			12 32					13 33							14 32				15 32					

When events are being held at the Millenium Stadium, services are subject to alteration. Please check times before travelling.

Table 128

Saturdays

30 June to 8 September

West Wales, Swansea and Maesteg - Cardiff

Route Diagram - see first Page of Table 127

	GW		AW	AW	GW	AW	AW	AW	AW	AW	AW	GW	AW	AW	GW	AW	AW	AW	GW	AW	AW		AW	GW
	◇1 ⊡		◇ H		◇1 ⊡	B	■ H	■ H			H	◇1 ⊡	■ H	H	◇1 ⊡	■ H			◇1 ⊡	◇ H	◇			◇1 ⊡
Rosslare Harbour ⛴ d						09 00																		
Fishguard Harbour ⛴ a						12 30																		
d								13 30																
Fishguard & Goodwick d								13 33																
Milford Haven d							13 08									15 08								
Johnston d							13x16									15x16								
Haverfordwest d							13 23									15 23								
Clarbeston Road d							13x31									15x31								
Clunderwen d							13x38									15x38								
Pembroke Dock d											13 09								14 55					
Pembroke d											13 17								15 05					
Lamphey d											13x20								15x08					
Manorbier d											13 29								15 20					
Penally d											13x34								15x26					
Tenby a											13 37								15 29					
d											13 42								15 36					
Saundersfoot d											13x50								15 46					
Kilgetty d											13x52								15x49					
Narberth d											14x02								15x58					
Whitland a							13 44	14 04			14 10					15 44			16 08					
d							13 44	14 04			14 11					15 44			16 09					
Carmarthen a							14 00	14 21			14 28					16 00			16 27					
d			13 02				14 05	14 23			14 33		15 05			16 05			16 33	17 04				
Ferryside d			13x12										15x15						16x45	17x14				
Kidwelly d			13x17										15x20						16x50	17x19				
Pembrey & Burry Port d			13 23				14 23				14 52		15 27			16 23			16 58	17 25				
Llanelli a			13 29				14 28	14 45			14 58		15 32			16 28			17 03	17 31				
d			13 30				14 30	14 45			14 58		15 34			16 30			17 05	17 32	17 41			
Gowerton d							14x36									16x36					17x51			
Swansea a			13 48				14 49				15 22		15 51			16 49			17 21	17 49	18 10			
d	13 28		14 00		14 28		14 55			15 10		15 28	15 55		16 28	16 55		17 10	17 28	17 55				18 28
Llansamlet d										15 17								17 17						
Skewen d										15 21								17 21						
Neath d	13 40		14 11		14 40		15 06			15 25		15 40	16 06		16 40	17 06		17 25	17 40	18 06				18 40
Briton Ferry d										15 28								17 28						
Baglan d										15 32								17 32						
Port Talbot Parkway d	13 48		14 18		14 48		15 13			15 36		15 48	16 13		16 48	17 13		17 36	17 48	18 13				18 48
Pyle d										15 43			16 20			17 20		17 43						
Maesteg d				14 15					15 17					16 15			17 15						18 20	
Maesteg (Ewenny Road) d				14 17					15 19					16 17			17 17						18 22	
Garth (Mid Glamorgan) d				14 20					15 22					16 20			17 20						18 25	
Tondu d				14 29					15 31					16 29			17 29						18 34	
Sarn d				14 32					15 34					16 32			17 32						18 37	
Wildmill d				14 34					15 36					16 34			17 34						18 39	
Bridgend d	14 00		14 30	14 38	15 00		15 25		15 40	15 52		16 00	16 27	16 38	17 00	17 27	17 38	17 54	18 00	18 25			18 43	19 00
Pencoed d				14 44					15 46					16 44			17 44						18 49	
Llanharan d				14 48					15 50					16 48			17 48						18 53	
Pontyclun d				14 52					15 54					16 52			17 52						18 57	
Cardiff Central 7 a	14 22		14 52	15 07	15 22		15 47	15 54	16 09	16 15		16 22	16 48	17 07	17 22	17 48	18 07	18 20	18 22	18 46			19 13	19 22
Newport (South Wales) a	14 39		15 07	15 25	15 39		16 07		16 23	16 32		16 39	17 07	17 27	17 39	18 07	18 25		18 39	19 03				19 39
Bristol Parkway 7 a	14 59				15 59							16 59			17 59				18 59					19 59
Gloucester 7 a				16 19					17 19					18 20			19 20							
Manchester Piccadilly 10 a			18 15				19 15						20 15			21 15				22 15				
Reading 7 a	16 01				17 00							18 00			19 00				20 00					21 06
London Paddington 15 ⊖ a	16 37				17 32							18 32			19 32				20 32					21 36

When events are being held at the Millenium Stadium, services are subject to alteration. Please check times before travelling.

West Wales, Swansea and Maesteg - Cardiff

Saturdays

30 June to 8 September

Route Diagram - see first Page of Table 127

		AW	AW	AW	AW	AW	AW	GW		AW	AW	AW	AW	AW	AW	AW	AW	AW		AW	AW	AW	AW	AW
			◇		◇			◇1 🛒		◇		◇				🚌		◇						
Rosslare Harbour ⛴	d															21 00								
Fishguard Harbour ⛴	a															00 30								
	d			19 00											21 00									
Fishguard & Goodwick	d			19 03											21 03									
Milford Haven	d		17 08									19 08					21 16							23 18
Johnston	d		17x16									19x16					21x24							23x26
Haverfordwest	d		17 23									19 23					21 31							23 33
Clarbeston Road	d		17x31	19a21								19x31			21x22		21x39							23x41
Clunderwen	d		17x38									19x38			21x29		21x46							23x48
Pembroke Dock	d	16 25												19 09								21 09	22 23	
Pembroke	d	16 33												19 17								21 17	22 31	
Lamphey	d	16x36												19 21								21x20	22x34	
Manorbier	d	16 45												19 29								21 29	22 42	
Penally	d	16x50												19 34								21x34	22x48	
Tenby	a	16 53												19 37								21 37	22 50	
	d	16 55												19 49								21 42	22 50	
Saundersfoot	d	17x03												19x57								21x50	22x58	
Kilgetty	d	17x05												19x59								21x52	23x00	
Narberth	d	17x15												20x09								22x02	23x09	
Whitland	a	17 26	17 44				←					19 44		20 17	21 36		21 52					22 10	23 17	23 54
	d	17 26	17 45									19 44		20 19	21 36		21 52					22 11	23 20	23 54
Carmarthen	a	17 44	18 03				17 44					20 04		20 37	22 00		22 14					22 28	23 39	00 16
	d	18 33	18 07				18 33			18 59		20 07		20 47								22 35		
Ferryside	d	→	18x17							19x09				20x58								22x45		
Kidwelly	d		18x23							19x15				21x04								22x51		
Pembrey & Burry Port	d		18 30				18 52			19 23		20 25		21 11								22 58		
Llanelli	a		18 35				18 58			19 29		20 30		21 17								23 04		
	d		18 36				18 59			19 30		20 31		21 17				21 40				23 05		
Gowerton	d						19x06											21x47				23x12		
Swansea	a		18 54				19 23			19 49		20 50		21 39				22 10				23 30		
	d		19 00			19 10		19 28		19 52		20 55		21 43							22 20			
Llansamlet	d					19 17								21 50							22 27			
Skewen	d					19 21								21 54							22 31			
Neath	d		19 11			19 25		19 40		20 03		21 06		21 58							22 35			
Briton Ferry	d					19 28								22 02							22 38			
Baglan	d					19 32								22 05							22 42			
Port Talbot Parkway	d		19 19			19 36		19 48		20 10		21 13		22 09							22 46			
Pyle	d					19 43								22 16							22 53			
Maesteg	d				19 15						20 15		21 15							22 15				
Maesteg (Ewenny Road)	d				19 17						20 17		21 17							22 17				
Garth (Mid Glamorgan)	d				19 20						20 20		21 20							22 20				
Tondu	d				19 29						20 29		21 29							22 29				
Sarn	d				19 32						20 32		21 32							22 32				
Wildmill	d				19 34						20 34		21 34							22 34				
Bridgend	d		19 32		19 38	19 51		20 00		20 23	20 38	21 25	21 38	22 25						22 38	23 01			
Pencoed	d				19 44						20 44		21 44							22 44				
Llanharan	d				19 47						20 48		21 48							22 48				
Pontyclun	d				19 52						20 52		21 52							22 52				
Cardiff Central 7	a		19 57		20 05	20 17		20 23		20 46	21 07	21 46	22 09	22 47						23 08	23 26			
Newport (South Wales)	a				20 24			20 39			21 25	22 05								23 36				
Bristol Parkway 7	a							21 01																
Gloucester 7	a										22 22													
Manchester Piccadilly 10	a				23 50															00 40				
Reading 7	a							21 59																
London Paddington 15 ⊖	a							22 30																

When events are being held at the Millenium Stadium, services are subject to alteration. Please check times before travelling.

Table 128

West Wales, Swansea and Maesteg - Cardiff

Saturdays

15 September to 20 October

Route Diagram - see first Page of Table 127

		AW	AW	AW	AW	AW	GW	GW	GW	AW		GW	GW	AW	AW	GW	AW	GW	AW	AW		AW	GW	GW	AW
		🚌				◇	◇1 🛒	◇1 🛒	◇1 🛒	◇ 🍴		◇1 🛒	◇1 🛒		◇ 🍴	◇1 A 🛒⊘		◇1 A 🛒⊘	◇ 🍴				◇1 🛒	◇1 🛒	◇ 🍴
Rosslare Harbour ⛴	d	21p00																							
Fishguard Harbour ⛴	a	00 30																							
	d					01 50														06 53					
Fishguard & Goodwick	d					01 53														06 56					
Milford Haven	d			23p18	00 18														06 00						07 05
Johnston	d			23b26	00x26														06x08						07x13
Haverfordwest	d			23p33	00 33														06 15						07 20
Clarbeston Road	d			23b41	00x41	02x12													06x23	07a16					07x28
Clunderwen	d			23b48	00x48														06x30						07x35
Pembroke Dock	d																								
Pembroke	d																								
Lamphey	d																								
Manorbier	d																								
Penally	d																								
Tenby	a																								
	d																								
Saundersfoot	d																								
Kilgetty	d																								
Narberth	d																								
Whitland	a			23p54	00 54	02 24													06 36						07 41
	d			23p54	00 54	02 24													06 36						07 41
Carmarthen	a			00 16	01 16	02 41													06 52						07 55
	d					02 44				05 04					05 55		06 20		06 57						08 01
Ferryside	d														06x05		06x30								08x11
Kidwelly	d														06x10		06x35								08x16
Pembrey & Burry Port	d									05 22					06 17		06 42		07 15						08 23
Llanelli	a					03 06				05 27					06 22		06 47		07 20						08 28
	d					03 06				05 29					06 24		06 48		07 22						08 30
Gowerton	d														06x30		06x55		07x28						08x36
Swansea	a					03 29									06 43		07 10		07 41						08 49
	d						03 58	04 58	05 28			05 58	06 28		06 47	06 58	07 13	07 28	07 45				07 58	08 28	08 55
Llansamlet	d																07 20								
Skewen	d																07 24								
Neath	d						04 10	05 10	05 40			06 10	06 40		06 58	07 10	07 28	07 40	07 56				08 10	08 40	09 06
Briton Ferry	d																07 31								
Baglan	d																07 35								
Port Talbot Parkway	d						04 18	05 18	05 48	06 02		06 18	06 48		07 05	07 18	07 39	07 48	08 03				08 18	08 48	09 13
Pyle	d									06 08					07 11		07 46		08 09						09 20
Maesteg	d		22p15											06 46								08 00			
Maesteg (Ewenny Road)	d		22p17											06 48								08 02			
Garth (Mid Glamorgan)	d		22p20											06 51								08 05			
Tondu	d		22p29											07 00								08 14			
Sarn	d		22p32											07 03								08 17			
Wildmill	d		22p34											07 05								08 19			
Bridgend	d		22p38				04 30	05 30	06 00	06 16		06 30	07 00	07 09	07 19	07 30	07 54	08 00	08 17			08 23	08 30	09 00	09 27
Pencoed	d		22p44							06 22				07 15			08 07		08 23						
Llanharan	d		22p48							06 25					07 26		08 11					08 31			
Pontyclun	d		22p52							06 30				07 22			08 15		08 30						
Cardiff Central 7	a		23p08				04 52	05 52	06 22	06 43		06 52	07 22	07 36	07 42	07 52	08 34	08 22	08 44			08 47	08 52	09 22	09 46
Newport (South Wales)	a		23p38				05 09	06 09	06 38	07 02		07 08	07 39		08 02	08 08		08 38	09 02			09 24	09 08	09 39	10 07
Bristol Parkway 7	a						05 36	06 29	06 59			07 29	07 59			08 30		08 59					09 30	09 59	
Gloucester 7	a		00 39																			10 19			
Manchester Piccadilly 10	a									10 14					11 15				12 15						13 15
Reading 7	a						07 14	07 31	08 00			08 31	09 00			09 32		10 00					10 32	11 01	
London Paddington 15 ⊖	a						07 44	08 07	08 32			09 02	09 32			10 02		10 32					11 02	11 33	

A 🛒 from Reading ⊘ to Reading

b Previous night, stops on request

When events are being held at the Millenium Stadium, services are subject to alteration. Please check times before travelling.

Table 128

West Wales, Swansea and Maesteg - Cardiff

Saturdays

15 September to 20 October

Route Diagram - see first Page of Table 127

		AW	AW	AW	GW	AW	AW	GW	AW	AW	AW	AW	AW	GW	AW	AW	GW	AW	AW	AW	AW	AW
			◇		◇1	◇		◇1	◇					◇1	◇		◇1	◇	◇		◇	
Rosslare Harbour ⛴	d																					
Fishguard Harbour ⛴	a																					
	d					08 04							09 53									
Fishguard & Goodwick	d					08 07							09 56									
Milford Haven	d								09 08									11 08				
Johnston	d								09x16									11x16				
Haverfordwest	d								09 23									11 23				
Clarbeston Road	d					08x25			09x31				10x14					11x31				
Clunderwen	d					08x33			09x38				10x22					11x38				
Pembroke Dock	d			07 09								09 09										11 09
Pembroke	d			07 17								09 17										11 17
Lamphey	d			07x20								09x20										11x20
Manorbier	d			07 28								09 29										11 29
Penally	d			07x34								09x34										11x34
Tenby	a			07 35								09 37										11 37
	d			07 38								09 37										11 41
Saundersfoot	d			07x44								09x45										11x49
Kilgetty	d			07x46								09x47										11x51
Narberth	d			07x56								09x57										12x01
Whitland	a			08 04		08 37			09 44			10 05	10 28					11 44				12 09
	d			08 05		08 38			09 44			10 05	10 29					11 44				12 09
Carmarthen	a			08 25		08 55			10 02			10 23	10 46					12 00				12 27
	d			08 30		09 00		09 35	10 04			10 28			11 02			12 05				12 31
Ferryside	d			08x40		09x10									11x12							
Kidwelly	d			08x46		09x15									11x17							
Pembrey & Burry Port	d			08 53		09 21		09 56	10 24			10 47			11 23			12 23				12 50
Llanelli	a			08 59		09 27		10 01	10 29			10 53			11 29			12 28				12 56
	d		08 45	09 00		09 28		10 03	10 31			10 53			11 37			12 30	12 37			12 57
Gowerton	d		08x53	09x08								11x01			11x37							13x04
Swansea	a		09 08	09 23		09 45		10 21	10 48			11 21			11 49			12 47	13 06			13 23
	d		09 11		09 28	09 55		10 28	10 55		11 10			11 28	11 55		12 28	12 55			13 10	
Llansamlet	d		09 19								11 17										13 17	
Skewen	d		09 23								11 21										13 21	
Neath	d		09 27	09 46	09 40	10 06		10 40	11 06		11 25			11 40	12 06		12 40	13 06			13 25	
Briton Ferry	d		09 31								11 28										13 28	
Baglan	d		09 34								11 32										13 32	
Port Talbot Parkway	d		09 38	09 53	09 48	10 13		10 48	11 13		11 36			11 48	12 13		12 48	13 13			13 36	
Pyle	d		09 46	10 05		10 19			11 20		11 43							13 20			13 43	
Maesteg	d	09 17					10 15			11 15						12 17				13 15		
Maesteg (Ewenny Road)	d	09 19					10 17			11 17						12 19				13 17		
Garth (Mid Glamorgan)	d	09 22					10 20			11 20						12 22				13 20		
Tondu	d	09 31					10 29			11 29						12 31				13 29		
Sarn	d	09 34					10 32			11 32						12 34				13 32		
Wildmill	d	09 36					10 34			11 34						12 36				13 34		
Bridgend	d	09 40	09 54	10s13	10 00	10 27	10 38	11 00	11 27	11 38	11 55			12 00	12 25	12 40	13 00	13 27		13 38	13 52	
Pencoed	d	09 46					10 44			11 44						12 46				13 44		
Llanharan	d	09 50					10 48			11 48						12 50				13 48		
Pontyclun	d	09 54					10 52			11 52						12 54				13 52		
Cardiff Central 7	a	10 09	10 20	10 43	10 22	10 48	11 13	11 22	11 48	12 07	12 18			12 22	12 50	13 09	13 22	13 48		14 09	14 15	
Newport (South Wales)	a	10 25			10 39	11 07		11 39	12 07	12 25				12 39	13 04	13 25	13 38	14 07				
Bristol Parkway 7	a				10 59			11 59						12 59			13 59					
Gloucester 7	a	11 21								13 21						14 21						
Manchester Piccadilly 10	a					14 15			15 15						16 15			17 15				
Reading 7	a				12 00			13 00						14 00			15 00					
London Paddington 15 ⊖	a				12 32			13 33						14 32			15 32					

When events are being held at the Millenium Stadium, services are subject to alteration. Please check times before travelling.

Table 128

West Wales, Swansea and Maesteg - Cardiff

Saturdays

15 September to 20 October

Route Diagram - see first Page of Table 127

		GW	AW	AW	GW	AW	AW	AW	AW	AW	AW	GW	AW	AW	GW	AW	AW	AW	AW	GW	AW	AW	AW
		◇1	◇		◇1	B	■	■				◇1	■		◇1	■				◇1	◇	◇	
Rosslare Harbour ⛴	d					09 00																	
Fishguard Harbour ⛴	a					12 30																	
	d							13 30															
Fishguard & Goodwick	d							13 33															
Milford Haven	d						13 08									15 08							
Johnston	d						13x16									15x16							
Haverfordwest	d						13 23									15 23							
Clarbeston Road	d						13x31									15x31							
Clunderwen	d						13x38									15x38							
Pembroke Dock	d										13 09								15 09				
Pembroke	d										13 17								15 17				
Lamphey	d										13x20								15x20				
Manorbier	d										13 29								15 29				
Penally	d										13x34								15x34				
Tenby	a										13 37								15 37				
	d										13 42								15 40				
Saundersfoot	d										13x50								15x48				
Kilgetty	d										13x52								15x50				
Narberth	d										14x02								16x00				
Whitland	a						13 44	14 04			14 10					15 44			16 08				
	d						13 44	14 04			14 11					15 44			16 09				
Carmarthen	a						14 00	14 21			14 28					16 00			16 26				
	d		13 02				14 05	14 23			14 33		15 05			16 05			16 31		17 04		
Ferryside	d		13x12										15x15								17x14		
Kidwelly	d		13x17										15x20								17x19		
Pembrey & Burry Port	d		13 23				14 23				14 52		15 27			16 23			16 50		17 25		
Llanelli	a		13 29				14 28	14 45			14 58		15 32			16 28			16 56		17 31		
	d		13 30				14 30	14 45			14 58		15 34			16 30			16 57		17 32	17 41	
Gowerton	d						14x36									16x36			17x04			17x51	
Swansea	a		13 48				14 49				15 22		15 51			16 49			17 22		17 49	18 10	
	d	13 28	14 00		14 28		14 55			15 10		15 28	15 55		16 28	16 55		17 10		17 28	17 55		
Llansamlet	d									15 17								17 17					
Skewen	d									15 21								17 21					
Neath	d	13 40	14 11		14 40		15 06			15 25		15 40	16 06		16 40	17 06		17 25		17 40	18 06		
Briton Ferry	d									15 28								17 28					
Baglan	d									15 32								17 32					
Port Talbot Parkway	d	13 48	14 18		14 48		15 13			15 36		15 48	16 13		16 48	17 13		17 36		17 48	18 13		
Pyle	d									15 43			16 20			17 20		17 43					
Maesteg	d			14 15					15 17					16 15			17 15						18 20
Maesteg (Ewenny Road)	d			14 17					15 19					16 17			17 17						18 22
Garth (Mid Glamorgan)	d			14 20					15 22					16 20			17 20						18 25
Tondu	d			14 29					15 31					16 29			17 29						18 34
Sarn	d			14 32					15 34					16 32			17 32						18 37
Wildmill	d			14 34					15 36					16 34			17 34						18 39
Bridgend	d	14 00	14 30	14 38	15 00		15 25		15 40	15 52		16 00	16 27	16 38	17 00	17 27	17 38	17 54		18 00	18 25		18 43
Pencoed	d			14 44					15 46					16 44			17 44						18 49
Llanharan	d			14 48					15 50					16 48			17 48						18 53
Pontyclun	d			14 52					15 54					16 52			17 52						18 57
Cardiff Central 7	a	14 22	14 52	15 07	15 22		15 47	15 54	16 09	16 15		16 22	16 48	17 07	17 22	17 48	18 07	18 20		18 22	18 46		19 13
Newport (South Wales)	a	14 39	15 07	15 25	15 39		16 07		16 23	16 32		16 39	17 07	17 27	17 39	18 07	18 25			18 39	19 03		
Bristol Parkway 7	a	14 59			15 59							16 59			17 59					18 59			
Gloucester 7	a			16 19					17 19					18 20			19 20						
Manchester Piccadilly 10	a		18 15				19 15						20 15			21 15					22 15		
Reading 7	a	16 00			17 00							18 00			19 00					20 00			
London Paddington 15 ⊖	a	16 32			17 32							18 32			19 32					20 32			

When events are being held at the Millenium Stadium, services are subject to alteration. Please check times before travelling.

Table 128

West Wales, Swansea and Maesteg - Cardiff

Saturdays

15 September to 20 October

Route Diagram - see first Page of Table 127

		GW	AW	AW	AW	AW	AW	GW		AW	AW	AW	AW	AW	AW	AW	AW	AW		AW	AW	AW	AW	AW
		◇1 ⊟	◇		◇			◇1 ⊟		◇		◇				🚌		◇						
Rosslare Harbour ⛴	d															21 00								
Fishguard Harbour ⛴	a															00 30								
	d			19 00											21 00									
Fishguard & Goodwick	d			19 03											21 03									
Milford Haven	d		17 08									19 08					21 16							23 18
Johnston	d		17x16									19x16					21x24							23x26
Haverfordwest	d		17 23									19 23					21 31							23 33
Clarbeston Road	d		17x31	19a21								19x31			21x22		21x39							23x41
Clunderwen	d		17x38									19x38			21x29		21x46							23x48
Pembroke Dock	d						17 09							19 09								21 09	22 23	
Pembroke	d						17 17							19 17								21 17	22 31	
Lamphey	d						17x20							19 21								21x20	22x34	
Manorbier	d						17 29							19 29								21 29	22 42	
Penally	d						17x34							19 34								21x34	22x48	
Tenby	a						17 37							19 37								21 37	22 50	
	d						17 41							19 49								21 42	22 50	
Saundersfoot	d						17x49							19x57								21x50	22x58	
Kilgetty	d						17x51							19x59								21x52	23x00	
Narberth	d						18x01							20x09								22x02	23x09	
Whitland	a		17 44				18 11					19 44		20 17	21 36		21 52					22 10	23 17	23 54
	d		17 45				18 11					19 44		20 19	21 36		21 52					22 11	23 20	23 54
Carmarthen	a		18 03				18 29					20 04		20 37	22 00		22 14					22 28	23 39	00 16
	d		18 07				18 33			18 59		20 07		20 47								22 35		
Ferryside	d		18x17							19x09				20x58								22x45		
Kidwelly	d		18x23							19x15				21x04								22x51		
Pembrey & Burry Port	d		18 30				18 52			19 23		20 25		21 11								22 58		
Llanelli	a		18 35				18 58			19 29		20 30		21 17								23 04		
	d		18 36				18 59			19 30		20 31		21 17				21 40				23 05		
Gowerton	d						19x06											21x47				23x12		
Swansea	a		18 54				19 23			19 49		20 50		21 39				22 10				23 30		
	d	18 28	19 00			19 10		19 28		19 52		20 55		21 43							22 20			
Llansamlet	d					19 17								21 50							22 27			
Skewen	d					19 21								21 54							22 31			
Neath	d	18 40	19 11			19 25		19 40		20 03		21 06		21 58							22 35			
Briton Ferry	d					19 28								22 02							22 38			
Baglan	d					19 32								22 05							22 42			
Port Talbot Parkway	d	18 48	19 19			19 36		19 48		20 10		21 13		22 09							22 46			
Pyle	d					19 43								22 16							22 53			
Maesteg	d				19 15						20 15		21 15							22 15				
Maesteg (Ewenny Road)	d				19 17						20 17		21 17							22 17				
Garth (Mid Glamorgan)	d				19 20						20 20		21 20							22 20				
Tondu	d				19 29						20 29		21 29							22 29				
Sarn	d				19 32						20 32		21 32							22 32				
Wildmill	d				19 34						20 34		21 34							22 34				
Bridgend	d	19 00	19 32		19 38	19 51		20 00		20 23	20 38	21 25	21 38	22 25						22 38	23 01			
Pencoed	d				19 44						20 44		21 44							22 44				
Llanharan	d				19 47						20 48		21 48							22 48				
Pontyclun	d				19 52						20 52		21 52							22 52				
Cardiff Central 7	a	19 22	19 57		20 05	20 17		20 23		20 46	21 07	21 46	22 09	22 47						23 08	23 26			
Newport (South Wales)	a	19 39			20 24			20 39			21 25	22 05								23 37				
Bristol Parkway 7	a	19 59						21 01																
Gloucester 7	a										22 22													
Manchester Piccadilly 10	a				23 50																			
Reading 7	a	21 07						22 01																
London Paddington 15 ⊖	a	21 36						22 37																

When events are being held at the Millenium Stadium, services are subject to alteration. Please check times before travelling.

Table 128

West Wales, Swansea and Maesteg - Cardiff

Saturdays

from 27 October

Route Diagram - see first Page of Table 127

		AW	AW	AW	AW	AW	GW	GW	GW	AW		GW	GW	AW	AW	GW	AW	GW	AW	AW		AW	GW	GW	AW
		🚌				◇	◇1 ⊟	◇1 ⊟	◇1 ⊟	◇ ⌶		◇1 ⊟	◇1 ⊟		◇ ⌶	◇1 A ⊟⊘		◇1 A ⊟⊘	◇ ⌶				◇1 ⊟	◇1 ⊟	◇ ⌶
Rosslare Harbour ⛴	d	21p00																							
Fishguard Harbour ⛴	a	00 30																							
	d					01 50														06 53					
Fishguard & Goodwick	d					01 53														06 56					
Milford Haven	d			23p18	00 18														06 00						07 05
Johnston	d			23b26	00x26														06x08						07x13
Haverfordwest	d			23p33	00 33														06 15						07 20
Clarbeston Road	d			23b41	00x41	02x12													06x23	07a16					07x28
Clunderwen	d			23b48	00x48														06x30						07x35
Pembroke Dock	d																								
Pembroke	d																								
Lamphey	d																								
Manorbier	d																								
Penally	d																								
Tenby	a																								
	d																								
Saundersfoot	d																								
Kilgetty	d																								
Narberth	d																								
Whitland	a			23p54	00 54	02 24													06 36						07 41
	d			23p54	00 54	02 24													06 36						07 41
Carmarthen	a			00 16	01 16	02 41													06 52						07 55
	d					02 44				05 04					05 55		06 20		06 57						08 01
Ferryside	d														06x05		06x30								08x11
Kidwelly	d														06x10		06x35								08x16
Pembrey & Burry Port	d									05 22					06 17		06 42		07 15						08 23
Llanelli	a					03 06				05 27					06 22		06 47		07 20						08 28
	d					03 06				05 29					06 24		06 48		07 22						08 30
Gowerton	d														06x30		06x55		07x28						08x36
Swansea	a					03 29									06 43		07 10		07 41						08 49
	d						03 58	04 58	05 28			05 58	06 28		06 47	06 58	07 13	07 28	07 45				07 58	08 28	08 55
Llansamlet	d																07 20								
Skewen	d																07 24								
Neath	d						04 10	05 10	05 40			06 10	06 40		06 58	07 10	07 28	07 40	07 56				08 10	08 40	09 06
Briton Ferry	d																07 31								
Baglan	d																07 35								
Port Talbot Parkway	d						04 18	05 18	05 48	06 02		06 18	06 48		07 05	07 18	07 39	07 48	08 03				08 18	08 48	09 13
Pyle	d									06 08					07 11		07 46		08 09						09 20
Maesteg	d		22p15											06 46								08 00			
Maesteg (Ewenny Road)	d		22p17											06 48								08 02			
Garth (Mid Glamorgan)	d		22p20											06 51								08 05			
Tondu	d		22p29											07 00								08 14			
Sarn	d		22p32											07 03								08 17			
Wildmill	d		22p34											07 05								08 19			
Bridgend	d		22p38				04 30	05 30	06 00	06 16		06 30	07 00	07 09	07 19	07 30	07 54	08 00	08 17			08 23	08 30	09 00	09 27
Pencoed	d		22p44							06 22				07 15			08 07		08 23						
Llanharan	d		22p48							06 25					07 26		08 11					08 31			
Pontyclun	d		22p52							06 30				07 22			08 15		08 30						
Cardiff Central 7	a		23p08				04 52	05 52	06 22	06 43		06 52	07 22	07 36	07 42	07 52	08 34	08 22	08 44			08 47	08 52	09 22	09 46
Newport (South Wales)	a		23p38				05 09	06 09	06 38	07 02		07 08	07 39		08 02	08 08		08 38	09 02			09 24	09 08	09 39	10 07
Bristol Parkway 7	a						05 36	06 29	06 59			07 29	07 59			08 30		08 59					09 30	09 59	
Gloucester 7	a		00 39																			10 19			
Manchester Piccadilly 10	a									10 14					11 15				12 15						13 15
Reading 7	a						07 14	07 31	08 00			08 31	09 00			09 32		10 00					10 32	11 01	
London Paddington 15 ⊖	a						07 44	08 07	08 32			09 02	09 32			10 02		10 32					11 02	11 33	

A ⊟ from Reading ⊘ to Reading

b Previous night, stops on request

When events are being held at the Millenium Stadium, services are subject to alteration. Please check times before travelling.

Table 128

Saturdays
from 27 October

West Wales, Swansea and Maesteg - Cardiff

Route Diagram - see first Page of Table 127

		AW	AW	AW	GW	AW	AW	GW	AW	AW	AW	AW	AW	GW	AW	AW	GW	AW	AW	AW	AW	AW
			◇		◇1 ⊡	◇ ✕		◇1 ⊡	◇ ✕					◇1 ⊡	◇ ✕	✕	◇1 ⊡	◇ ✕	◇ ✕		◇ ✕	
Rosslare Harbour ⛴	d																					
Fishguard Harbour ⛴	a																					
	d					08 04							09 53									
Fishguard & Goodwick	d					08 07							09 56									
Milford Haven	d								09 08									11 08				
Johnston	d								09x16									11x16				
Haverfordwest	d								09 23									11 23				
Clarbeston Road	d					08x25			09x31				10x14					11x31				
Clunderwen	d					08x33			09x38				10x22					11x38				
Pembroke Dock	d			07 09								09 09										11 09
Pembroke	d			07 17								09 17										11 17
Lamphey	d			07x20								09x20										11x20
Manorbier	d			07 28								09 29										11 29
Penally	d			07x34								09x34										11x34
Tenby	a			07 35								09 37										11 37
	d			07 38								09 37										11 41
Saundersfoot	d			07x44								09x45										11x49
Kilgetty	d			07x46								09x47										11x51
Narberth	d			07x56								09x57										12x01
Whitland	a			08 04		08 37			09 44			10 05	10 28					11 44				12 09
	d			08 05		08 38			09 44			10 05	10 29					11 44				12 09
Carmarthen	a			08 25		08 55			10 02			10 23	10 46					12 00				12 27
	d			08 30		09 00		09 35	10 04			10 28			11 02			12 05				12 31
Ferryside	d			08x40		09x10									11x12							
Kidwelly	d			08x46		09x15									11x17							
Pembrey & Burry Port	d			08 53		09 21		09 56	10 24			10 47			11 23			12 23				12 50
Llanelli	a			08 59		09 27		10 01	10 29			10 53			11 29			12 28				12 56
	d		08 45	09 00		09 28		10 03	10 31			10 53			11 37			12 30	12 37			12 57
Gowerton	d		08x53	09x08								11x01			11x37							13x04
Swansea	a		09 08	09 23		09 45		10 21	10 48			11 21			11 49			12 47	13 06			13 23
	d		09 11		09 28	09 55		10 28	10 55		11 10			11 28	11 55		12 28	12 55			13 10	
Llansamlet	d		09 19								11 17										13 17	
Skewen	d		09 23								11 21										13 21	
Neath	d		09 27	09 46	09 40	10 06		10 40	11 06		11 25			11 40	12 06		12 40	13 06			13 25	
Briton Ferry	d		09 31								11 28										13 28	
Baglan	d		09 34								11 32										13 32	
Port Talbot Parkway	d		09 38	09 53	09 48	10 13		10 48	11 13		11 36			11 48	12 13		12 48	13 13			13 36	
Pyle	d		09 46	10 05		10 19			11 20		11 43							13 20			13 43	
Maesteg	d	09 17					10 15			11 15						12 17				13 15		
Maesteg (Ewenny Road)	d	09 19					10 17			11 17						12 19				13 17		
Garth (Mid Glamorgan)	d	09 22					10 20			11 20						12 22				13 20		
Tondu	d	09 31					10 29			11 29						12 31				13 29		
Sarn	d	09 34					10 32			11 32						12 34				13 32		
Wildmill	d	09 36					10 34			11 34						12 36				13 34		
Bridgend	d	09 40	09 54	10s13	10 00	10 27	10 38	11 00	11 27	11 38	11 55			12 00	12 25	12 40	13 00	13 27		13 38	13 52	
Pencoed	d	09 46					10 44			11 44						12 46				13 44		
Llanharan	d	09 50					10 48			11 48						12 50				13 48		
Pontyclun	d	09 54					10 52			11 52						12 54				13 52		
Cardiff Central 7	a	10 09	10 20	10 43	10 22	10 48	11 13	11 22	11 48	12 07	12 18			12 22	12 50	13 09	13 22	13 48		14 09	14 15	
Newport (South Wales)	a	10 25			10 39	11 07		11 39	12 07	12 25				12 39	13 04	13 25	13 38	14 07				
Bristol Parkway 7	a				10 59			11 59						12 59			13 59					
Gloucester 7	a	11 21								13 21						14 21						
Manchester Piccadilly 10	a					14 15			15 15						16 15			17 15				
Reading 7	a				12 00			13 00						14 00			15 00					
London Paddington 15 ⊖	a				12 32			13 33						14 32			15 32					

When events are being held at the Millenium Stadium, services are subject to alteration. Please check times before travelling.

Table 128

Saturdays
from 27 October

West Wales, Swansea and Maesteg - Cardiff

Route Diagram - see first Page of Table 127

		GW	AW	AW	GW	AW	AW	AW	AW	AW	AW	GW	AW	AW	GW	AW	AW	AW	AW	GW	AW	AW	AW
		◇1 ⊡	◇ ✕		◇1 ⊡	B	■ ✕	■ ✕			✕	◇1 ⊡	■ ✕		◇1 ⊡	■ ✕				◇1 ⊡	◇ ✕	◇	
Rosslare Harbour ⛴	d					09 00																	
Fishguard Harbour ⛴	a					12 30																	
	d							13 30															
Fishguard & Goodwick	d							13 33															
Milford Haven	d						13 08									15 08							
Johnston	d						13x16									15x16							
Haverfordwest	d						13 23									15 23							
Clarbeston Road	d						13x31									15x31							
Clunderwen	d						13x38									15x38							
Pembroke Dock	d										13 09								15 09				
Pembroke	d										13 17								15 17				
Lamphey	d										13x20								15x20				
Manorbier	d										13 29								15 29				
Penally	d										13x34								15x34				
Tenby	a										13 37								15 37				
	d										13 42								15 40				
Saundersfoot	d										13x50								15x48				
Kilgetty	d										13x52								15x50				
Narberth	d										14x02								16x00				
Whitland	a						13 44	14 04			14 10					15 44			16 08				
	d						13 44	14 04			14 11					15 44			16 09				
Carmarthen	a						14 00	14 21			14 28					16 00			16 26				
	d		13 02				14 05	14 23			14 33		15 05			16 05			16 31		17 04		
Ferryside	d		13x12										15x15								17x14		
Kidwelly	d		13x17										15x20								17x19		
Pembrey & Burry Port	d		13 23				14 23				14 52		15 27			16 23			16 50		17 25		
Llanelli	a		13 29				14 28	14 45			14 58		15 32			16 28			16 56		17 31		
	d		13 30				14 30	14 45			14 58		15 34			16 30			16 57		17 32	17 41	
Gowerton	d						14x36									16x36			17x04			17x51	
Swansea	a		13 48				14 49				15 22		15 51			16 49			17 22		17 49	18 10	
	d	13 28	14 00		14 28		14 55			15 10		15 28	15 55		16 28	16 55		17 10		17 28	17 55		
Llansamlet	d									15 17								17 17					
Skewen	d									15 21								17 21					
Neath	d	13 40	14 11		14 40		15 06			15 25		15 40	16 06		16 40	17 06		17 25		17 40	18 06		
Briton Ferry	d									15 28								17 28					
Baglan	d									15 32								17 32					
Port Talbot Parkway	d	13 48	14 18		14 48		15 13			15 36		15 48	16 13		16 48	17 13		17 36		17 48	18 13		
Pyle	d									15 43			16 20			17 20		17 43					
Maesteg	d			14 15					15 17					16 15			17 15						18 20
Maesteg (Ewenny Road)	d			14 17					15 19					16 17			17 17						18 22
Garth (Mid Glamorgan)	d			14 20					15 22					16 20			17 20						18 25
Tondu	d			14 29					15 31					16 29			17 29						18 34
Sarn	d			14 32					15 34					16 32			17 32						18 37
Wildmill	d			14 34					15 36					16 34			17 34						18 39
Bridgend	d	14 00	14 30	14 38	15 00		15 25		15 40	15 52		16 00	16 27	16 38	17 00	17 27	17 38	17 54		18 00	18 25		18 43
Pencoed	d			14 44					15 46					16 44			17 44						18 49
Llanharan	d			14 48					15 50					16 48			17 48						18 53
Pontyclun	d			14 52					15 54					16 52			17 52						18 57
Cardiff Central 7	a	14 22	14 52	15 07	15 22		15 47	15 54	16 09	16 15		16 22	16 48	17 07	17 22	17 48	18 07	18 20		18 22	18 46		19 13
Newport (South Wales)	a	14 39	15 07	15 25	15 39		16 07		16 23	16 32		16 39	17 07	17 27	17 39	18 07	18 25			18 39	19 03		
Bristol Parkway 7	a	14 59			15 59							16 59			17 59					18 59			
Gloucester 7	a			16 19					17 19					18 20			19 20						
Manchester Piccadilly 10	a		18 15				19 15						20 15			21 15					22 15		
Reading 7	a	16 00			17 00							18 00			19 00					20 00			
London Paddington 15 ⊖	a	16 32			17 32							18 32			19 32					20 32			

When events are being held at the Millenium Stadium, services are subject to alteration. Please check times before travelling.

Table 128

West Wales, Swansea and Maesteg - Cardiff

Saturdays
from 27 October

Route Diagram - see first Page of Table 127

		GW	AW	AW	AW	AW	AW	GW	AW	AW	AW	AW	AW	AW	AW	AW	AW	AW	AW	AW	AW	AW
		◇1 ☕	◇		◇			◇1 ☕	◇		◇				B		◇					
Rosslare Harbour ⛴	d														21 00							
Fishguard Harbour ⛴	a														00 30							
	d			19 00										21 00								
Fishguard & Goodwick	d			19 03										21 03								
Milford Haven	d		17 08								19 08					21 16						23 18	
Johnston	d		17x16								19x16					21x24						23x26	
Haverfordwest	d		17 23								19 23					21 31						23 33	
Clarbeston Road	d		17x31	19a21							19x31			21x22		21x39						23x41	
Clunderwen	d		17x38								19x38			21x29		21x46						23x48	
Pembroke Dock	d						17 09						19 09							21 09	22 23	
Pembroke	d						17 17						19 17							21 17	22 31	
Lamphey	d						17x20						19 21							21x20	22x34	
Manorbier	d						17 29						19 29							21 29	22 42	
Penally	d						17x34						19 34							21x34	22x48	
Tenby	a						17 37						19 37							21 37	22 50	
	d						17 41						19 49							21 42	22 50	
Saundersfoot	d						17x49						19x57							21x50	22x58	
Kilgetty	d						17x51						19x59							21x52	23x00	
Narberth	d						18x01						20x09							22x02	23x09	
Whitland	a		17 44				18 11				19 44		20 17	21 36		21 52				22 10	23 17	23 54
	d		17 45				18 11				19 44		20 19	21 36		21 52				22 11	23 20	23 54
Carmarthen	a		18 03				18 29				20 04		20 37	22 00		22 14				22 28	23 39	00 16
	d		18 07				18 33		18 59		20 07		20 47							22 35		
Ferryside	d		18x17						19x09				20x58							22x45		
Kidwelly	d		18x23						19x15				21x04							22x51		
Pembrey & Burry Port	d		18 30				18 52		19 23		20 25		21 11							22 58		
Llanelli	a		18 35				18 58		19 29		20 30		21 17							23 04		
	d		18 36				18 59		19 30		20 31		21 17				21 40			23 05		
Gowerton	d						19x06										21x47			23x12		
Swansea	a		18 54				19 23		19 49		20 50		21 39				22 10			23 30		
	d	18 28	19 00			19 10		19 28	19 52		20 55		21 43						22 20			
Llansamlet	d					19 17							21 50						22 27			
Skewen	d					19 21							21 54						22 31			
Neath	d	18 40	19 11			19 25		19 40	20 03		21 06		21 58						22 35			
Briton Ferry	d					19 28							22 02						22 38			
Baglan	d					19 32							22 05						22 42			
Port Talbot Parkway	d	18 48	19 19			19 36		19 48	20 10		21 13		22 09						22 46			
Pyle	d					19 43							22 16						22 53			
Maesteg	d				19 15					20 15		21 15						22 15				
Maesteg (Ewenny Road)	d				19 17					20 17		21 17						22 17				
Garth (Mid Glamorgan)	d				19 20					20 20		21 20						22 20				
Tondu	d				19 29					20 29		21 29						22 29				
Sarn	d				19 32					20 32		21 32						22 32				
Wildmill	d				19 34					20 34		21 34						22 34				
Bridgend	d	19 00	19 32		19 38	19 51		20 00	20 23	20 38	21 25	21 38	22 25					22 38	23 01			
Pencoed	d				19 44					20 44		21 44						22 44				
Llanharan	d				19 47					20 48		21 48						22 48				
Pontyclun	d				19 52					20 52		21 52						22 52				
Cardiff Central 7	a	19 22	19 57		20 05	20 17		20 23	20 46	21 07	21 46	22 09	22 47					23 08	23 26			
Newport (South Wales)	a	19 39			20 24			20 39		21 25	22 05							23 36				
Bristol Parkway 7	a	19 59						21 01														
Gloucester 7	a									22 22												
Manchester Piccadilly 10	a				23 50													00 40				
Reading 7	a	21 07						22 01														
London Paddington 15 ⊖	a	21 36						22 37														

When events are being held at the Millenium Stadium, services are subject to alteration. Please check times before travelling.

Table 128

West Wales, Swansea and Maesteg - Cardiff

Sundays
until 24 June

Route Diagram - see first Page of Table 127

		AW	AW	AW	AW	GW	AW	GW	AW	GW	AW	GW	AW	AW	AW	GW	GW	AW	AW	GW	GW	AW	AW
		B		◇	🚌	◇1 ☕	B	◇1 ☕	◇ ⌶	◇1 ☕		◇1 ☕	◇ ⌶		⌶	◇1 ☕	◇1 ☕	■ ⌶		◇1 ☕	◇1 ☕	■ ⌶	◇
Rosslare Harbour ⛴	d	21p00					09 00																
Fishguard Harbour ⛴	a	00 30					12 30																
	d			01 50																			
Fishguard & Goodwick	d																						
Milford Haven	d		23p18										09 28					11 28				13 23	
Johnston	d		23b26										09 36					11x36				13x29	
Haverfordwest	d		23p33										09 43					11 43				13 36	
Clarbeston Road	d		23b41										09 52					11x52				13x45	
Clunderwen	d		23b48										09 59					11x59				13x52	
Pembroke Dock	d														10 40				11 55				
Pembroke	d														10 48				12 03				
Lamphey	d														10x51				12x06				
Manorbier	d														11 00				12 15				
Penally	d														11x05				12x20				
Tenby	a														11 08				12 23				
	d														11 14				12 23				
Saundersfoot	d														11x22				12x31				
Kilgetty	d														11x24				12x33				
Narberth	d														11x34				12x43				
Whitland	a		23p54	02s22									10 06		11 42			12 06	12 51			13 59	
	d		23p54										10 08		11 45			12 08	12 54			14 02	
Carmarthen	a		00 16	02s40									10 26		12 05			12 26	13 14			14 20	
	d				02 50				08 40		09 40		10 30	11 07				12 29	13 17			14 23	
Ferryside	d										09x50			11x17					13x27				
Kidwelly	d										09x56			11x23					13x33				
Pembrey & Burry Port	d								08 59		10 03		10 49	11 31				12 49	13 40			14 42	
Llanelli	a			03s06					09 05		10 09		10 54	11 37				12 55	13 46			14 48	
	d								09 07		10 10		10 56	11 37				12 55	13 47			14 49	15 41
Gowerton	d										10x17			11x45					13x54				
Swansea	a				03 50				09 27		10 35		11 15	12 01				13 15	14 12			15 08	16 04
	d					08 07		09 21	09 32	10 21		11 21	11 32			12 21	13 21	13 43		14 21	15 21	15 33	
Llansamlet	d																						
Skewen	d																						
Neath	d					08 19		09 33	09 43	10 33		11 33	11 43			12 33	13 33	13 54		14 33	15 33	15 44	
Briton Ferry	d																						
Baglan	d																						
Port Talbot Parkway	d					08 26		09 40	09 50	10 40		11 40	11 50			12 40	13 40	14 01		14 40	15 40	15 51	
Pyle	d								09 57				11 57					14 09				15 58	
Maesteg	d																						
Maesteg (Ewenny Road)	d																						
Garth (Mid Glamorgan)	d																						
Tondu	d																						
Sarn	d																						
Wildmill	d																						
Bridgend	d					08 38		09 52	10 05	10 52		11 52	12 05			12 52	13 52	14 17		14 52	15 52	16 06	
Pencoed	d												12 11									16 12	
Llanharan	d												12 15									16 16	
Pontyclun	d												12 20									16 21	
Cardiff Central 7	a			04 10		09 01		10 14	10 29	11 14		12 14	12 35			13 14	14 14	14 40		15 14	16 14	16 36	
Newport (South Wales)	a					09 18		10 31	10 48	11 31		12 31	12 52			13 31	14 31	15 12		15 31	16 31	16 52	
Bristol Parkway 7	a					09 46		10 59		11 59		12 59				13 59	14 59			15 59	16 59		
Gloucester 7	a																						
Manchester Piccadilly 10	a								14 19				16 15					18 17				20 17	
Reading 7	a					10 42		12 05		13 00		14 05				15 05	16 00			17 05	18 00		
London Paddington 15 ⊖	a					11 22		12 42		13 42		14 43				15 43	16 42			17 43	18 43		

b Previous night, stops on request

When events are being held at the Millenium Stadium, services are subject to alteration. Please check times before travelling.

Table 128

Sundays

until 24 June

West Wales, Swansea and Maesteg - Cardiff

Route Diagram - see first Page of Table 127

		AW	GW	GW	AW	GW		GW	AW	AW	GW	AW	AW	AW	AW	AW		AW	AW	AW
		⊼	◇■ 🍽	◇■ 🍽	■ ⊼	◇■ 🍽		◇■ 🍽			◇■ 🍽	◇			B	◇		◇		
Rosslare Harbour	d														21 00					
Fishguard Harbour	a														00 30					
	d	14 23																		
Fishguard & Goodwick	d																			
Milford Haven	d				15 28					17 30				19 38				21 35		23 15
Johnston	d				15x36					17x38				19x46				21x43		23x23
Haverfordwest	d				15 43					17 45				19 53				21 51		23 30
Clarbeston Road	d				15x52					17x53				20x01				21x59		23x39
Clunderwen	d				15x59					18x00				20x08				22x07		23x46
Pembroke Dock	d								16 45				19 00						21 45	
Pembroke	d								16 53				19 08						21 53	
Lamphey	d								16x56				19x11						21x56	
Manorbier	d								17 05				19 20						22 05	
Penally	d								17x10				19x25						22x10	
Tenby	a								17 13				19 28						22 13	
	d								17 13				19 28						22 13	
Saundersfoot	d								17x21				19x36						22x21	
Kilgetty	d								17x23				19x38						22x23	
Narberth	d								17x33				19x48						22x33	
Whitland	a	14 55			16 06				17 41	18 06			19 56	20 14				22 13	22 41	23 53
	d	14 55			16 09				17 44	18 08			19 59	20 17				22 14	22 44	23 53
Carmarthen	a	15 13			16 26				18 04	18 29			20 16	20 36				22 31	23 05	00 14
	d	15 16	15 30		16 31	16 55			18 07		19 09		20 19			21 05		22 34		
Ferryside	d	15x26			16x41				18x17				20x30					22x44		
Kidwelly	d	15x32			16x47				18x23				20x36					22x50		
Pembrey & Burry Port	d	15 39	15 50		16 55	17 15			18 31		19 29		20 43			21 24		22 58		
Llanelli	a	15 47	15 56		17 01	17 21			18 37		19 35		20 49			21 30		23 04		
	d	15 47	15 58		17 01	17 22			18 38		19 36	19 55	20 51			21 31		23 04		
Gowerton	d	15x55							18x46			20x02	20x58					23x12		
Swansea	a	16 14	16 14		17 20	17 39			19 06		19 53	20 16	21 17			21 48		23 27		
	d		16 21	16 51	17 30	17 51		18 51			19 59	20 40				21 52		23 31		
Llansamlet	d																			
Skewen	d																			
Neath	d		16 33	17 03	17 41	18 03		19 03			20 11	20 51				22 03		23 43		
Briton Ferry	d																			
Baglan	d																			
Port Talbot Parkway	d		16 40	17 10	17 48	18 10		19 10			20 18	20 58				22 10		23 50		
Pyle	d				17 55											22 17		23 57		
Maesteg	d																			
Maesteg (Ewenny Road)	d																			
Garth (Mid Glamorgan)	d																			
Tondu	d																			
Sarn	d																			
Wildmill	d																			
Bridgend	d		16 52	17 22	18 03	18 22		19 22			20 30	21 11				22 25		00 05		
Pencoed	d				18 09															
Llanharan	d				18 13															
Pontyclun	d				18 18															
Cardiff Central 7	a		17 14	17 45	18 34	18 45		19 45			20 53	21 36				22 49		00 30		
Newport (South Wales)	a		17 29	18 03	18 52	19 03		20 03			21 08					23 18				
Bristol Parkway 7	a		17 59	18 31		19 31		20 31			21 36									
Gloucester 7	a																			
Manchester Piccadilly 10	a				22 19															
Reading 7	a		19 02	19 36		20 42		21 32			22 37									
London Paddington 15 ⊖	a		19 42	20 14		21 19		22 14			23 15									

When events are being held at the Millenium Stadium, services are subject to alteration. Please check times before travelling.

Table 128

Sundays

1 July to 9 September

West Wales, Swansea and Maesteg - Cardiff

Route Diagram - see first Page of Table 127

		AW	AW	AW	AW	AW	GW	AW	GW	AW		GW	AW	GW	AW	AW	AW	GW	GW	AW		AW	GW	GW	AW
		B			◇	🚌	◇■ 🍽	B	◇■ 🍽	◇ ⊼		◇■ 🍽		◇■ 🍽	◇ ⊼		⊼	◇■ 🍽	◇■ 🍽	■ ⊼			◇■ 🍽	◇■ 🍽	■ ⊼
Rosslare Harbour	d	21p00						09 00																	
Fishguard Harbour	a	00 30						12 30																	
	d				01 50																				
Fishguard & Goodwick	d																								
Milford Haven	d			23p18											09 28					11 28					13 23
Johnston	d			23b26											09 36					11x36					13x29
Haverfordwest	d			23p33											09 43					11 43					13 36
Clarbeston Road	d			23b41											09 52					11x52					13x45
Clunderwen	d			23b48											09 59					11x59					13x52
Pembroke Dock	d																10 40					11 55			
Pembroke	d																10 48					12 03			
Lamphey	d																10x51					12x06			
Manorbier	d																11 00					12 15			
Penally	d																11x05					12x20			
Tenby	a																11 08					12 23			
	d																11 14					12 23			
Saundersfoot	d																11x22					12x31			
Kilgetty	d																11x24					12x33			
Narberth	d																11x34					12x43			
Whitland	a			23p54	02s22										10 06		11 42			12 06		12 51			13 59
	d			23p54											10 08		11 45			12 08		12 54			14 02
Carmarthen	a			00 16	02s40										10 26		12 05			12 26		13 14			14 20
	d					02 50				08 40			09 40		10 30	11 07				12 29		13 17			14 23
Ferryside	d												09x50			11x17						13x27			
Kidwelly	d												09x56			11x23						13x33			
Pembrey & Burry Port	d									08 59			10 03		10 49	11 31				12 49		13 40			14 42
Llanelli	a				03s06					09 05			10 09		10 54	11 37				12 55		13 46			14 48
	d									09 07			10 10		10 56	11 37				12 55		13 47			14 49
Gowerton	d												10x17			11x45						13x54			
Swansea	a					03 50				09 27			10 35		11 15	12 01				13 15		14 12			15 08
	d						08 07		09 21	09 32		10 21		11 21	11 32			12 21	13 21	13 43			14 21	15 21	15 33
Llansamlet	d																								
Skewen	d																								
Neath	d						08 19		09 33	09 43		10 33		11 33	11 43			12 33	13 33	13 54			14 33	15 33	15 44
Briton Ferry	d																								
Baglan	d																								
Port Talbot Parkway	d						08 26		09 40	09 50		10 40		11 40	11 50			12 40	13 40	14 01			14 40	15 40	15 51
Pyle	d									09 57					11 57					14 09					15 58
Maesteg	d		22p15																						
Maesteg (Ewenny Road)	d		22p17																						
Garth (Mid Glamorgan)	d		22p20																						
Tondu	d		22p29																						
Sarn	d		22p32																						
Wildmill	d		22p34																						
Bridgend	d		22p38				08 38		09 52	10 05		10 52		11 52	12 05			12 52	13 52	14 17			14 52	15 52	16 06
Pencoed	d		22p44												12 11										16 12
Llanharan	d		22p48												12 15										16 16
Pontyclun	d		22p52												12 20										16 21
Cardiff Central 7	a		23p08		04 10		09 01		10 14	10 29		11 14		12 14	12 35			13 14	14 14	14 40			15 14	16 14	16 36
Newport (South Wales)	a		23p36				09 18		10 31	10 48		11 31		12 31	12 52			13 31	14 31	15 12			15 31	16 31	16 52
Bristol Parkway 7	a						09 46		10 59			11 59		12 59				13 59	14 59				15 59	16 59	
Gloucester 7	a		00 40																						
Manchester Piccadilly 10	a									14 19					16 15					18 17					20 17
Reading 7	a						10 42		12 01			13 01		14 01				15 00	16 00				17 00	18 00	
London Paddington 15 ⊖	a						11 14		12 29			13 29		14 29				15 29	16 29				17 29	18 29	

b Previous night, stops on request

When events are being held at the Millenium Stadium, services are subject to alteration. Please check times before travelling.

Table 128

Sundays

1 July to 9 September

West Wales, Swansea and Maesteg - Cardiff

Route Diagram - see first Page of Table 127

		AW	AW	GW	GW	AW	GW	GW	AW	AW	GW	AW	AW	AW	AW	AW	AW	AW	AW
		◇		◇1	◇1	■	◇1	◇1			◇1	◇			B	◇	◇		
Rosslare Harbour	d														21 00				
Fishguard Harbour	a														00 30				
	d		14 23																
Fishguard & Goodwick	d																		
Milford Haven	d					15 28				17 30				19 38			21 35		23 15
Johnston	d					15x36				17x38				19x46			21x43		23x23
Haverfordwest	d					15 43				17 45				19 53			21 51		23 30
Clarbeston Road	d					15x52				17x53				20x01			21x59		23x39
Clunderwen	d					15x59				18x00				20x08			22x07		23x46
Pembroke Dock	d								16 45				19 00					21 45	
Pembroke	d								16 53				19 08					21 53	
Lamphey	d								16x56				19x11					21x56	
Manorbier	d								17 05				19 20					22 05	
Penally	d								17x10				19x25					22x10	
Tenby	a								17 13				19 28					22 13	
	d								17 13				19 28					22 13	
Saundersfoot	d								17x21				19x36					22x21	
Kilgetty	d								17x23				19x38					22x23	
Narberth	d								17x33				19x48					22x33	
Whitland	a		14 55			16 06			17 41	18 06			19 56	20 14			22 13	22 41	23 53
	d		14 55			16 09			17 44	18 08			19 59	20 17			22 14	22 44	23 53
Carmarthen	a		15 13			16 26			18 04	18 29			20 16	20 36			22 31	23 05	00 14
	d		15 16	15 30		16 31	16 55		18 07		19 09		20 19			21 05	22 34		
Ferryside	d		15x26			16x41			18x17				20x30				22x44		
Kidwelly	d		15x32			16x47			18x23				20x36				22x50		
Pembrey & Burry Port	d		15 39	15 50		16 55	17 15		18 31		19 29		20 43			21 24	22 58		
Llanelli	a		15 47	15 56		17 01	17 21		18 37		19 35		20 49			21 30	23 04		
	d	15 41	15 47	15 58		17 01	17 22		18 38		19 36	19 55	20 51			21 31	23 04		
Gowerton	d		15x55						18x46			20x02	20x58				23x12		
Swansea	a	16 04	16 14	16 14		17 20	17 39		19 06		19 53	20 16	21 17			21 48	23 27		
	d			16 21	16 51	17 30	17 51	18 51			19 59	20 40				21 52	23 31		
Llansamlet	d																		
Skewen	d																		
Neath	d			16 33	17 03	17 41	18 03	19 03			20 11	20 51				22 03	23 43		
Briton Ferry	d																		
Baglan	d																		
Port Talbot Parkway	d			16 40	17 10	17 48	18 10	19 10			20 18	20 58				22 10	23 50		
Pyle	d					17 55										22 17	23 57		
Maesteg	d																		
Maesteg (Ewenny Road)	d																		
Garth (Mid Glamorgan)	d																		
Tondu	d																		
Sarn	d																		
Wildmill	d																		
Bridgend	d			16 52	17 22	18 03	18 22	19 22			20 30	21 11				22 25	00 05		
Pencoed	d					18 09													
Llanharan	d					18 13													
Pontyclun	d					18 18													
Cardiff Central 7	a			17 12	17 45	18 34	18 45	19 45			20 53	21 36				22 49	00 30		
Newport (South Wales)	a			17 31	18 03	18 52	19 03	20 03			21 08					23 18			
Bristol Parkway 7	a			17 59	18 31		19 31	20 31			21 36								
Gloucester 7	a																		
Manchester Piccadilly 10	a					22 19													
Reading 7	a			18 58	19 32		20 32	21 32			22 37								
London Paddington 15 ⊖	a			19 30	20 01		21 01	22 02			23 13								

When events are being held at the Millenium Stadium, services are subject to alteration. Please check times before travelling.

Table 128

Sundays

16 September to 21 October

West Wales, Swansea and Maesteg - Cardiff

Route Diagram - see first Page of Table 127

		AW	AW	AW	AW	GW	AW	GW	GW	AW	GW	AW	AW	GW	GW	AW	AW	GW	GW	AW	AW	AW	GW
		B		◇		◇1	B	◇1	◇1		◇1	◇		◇1	◇1	■		◇1	◇1	■	◇		◇1
Rosslare Harbour	d	21p00					09 00																
Fishguard Harbour	a	00 30					12 30																
	d			01 50																		14 23	
Fishguard & Goodwick	d																						
Milford Haven	d		23p18													11 10				13 23			
Johnston	d		23b26													11x18				13x29			
Haverfordwest	d		23p33													11 25				13 36			
Clarbeston Road	d		23b41													11x34				13x45			
Clunderwen	d		23b48													11x41				13x52			
Pembroke Dock	d																11 55						
Pembroke	d																12 03						
Lamphey	d																12x06						
Manorbier	d																12 15						
Penally	d																12x20						
Tenby	a																12 23						
	d																12 23						
Saundersfoot	d																12x31						
Kilgetty	d																12x33						
Narberth	d																12x43						
Whitland	a		23p54	02s22												11 48	12 51			13 59		14 55	
	d		23p54													11 50	12 54			14 02		14 55	
Carmarthen	a		00 16	02s40												12 08	13 14			14 20		15 13	
	d				02 50					09 40		10 30	11 07			12 11	13 17			14 23		15 16	15 30
Ferryside	d									09x50			11x17				13x27					15x26	
Kidwelly	d									09x56			11x23				13x33					15x32	
Pembrey & Burry Port	d									10 03		10 49	11 31			12 31	13 40			14 42		15 39	15 50
Llanelli	a			03s06						10 09		10 54	11 37			12 37	13 46			14 48		15 47	15 56
	d									10 10		10 56	11 37			12 37	13 47			14 49	15 41	15 47	15 58
Gowerton	d									10x17			11x45				13x54					15x55	
Swansea	a				03 50					10 35		11 15	12 01			12 57	14 12			15 08	16 04	16 14	16 14
	d					08 07		09 07	10 07		11 07	11 32		12 07	13 07	13 43		14 21	15 21	15 33			16 21
Llansamlet	d																						
Skewen	d																						
Neath	d					08 19		09 19	10 19		11 19	11 43		12 19	13 19	13 54		14 33	15 33	15 44			16 33
Briton Ferry	d																						
Baglan	d																						
Port Talbot Parkway	d					08 26		09 26	10 26		11 26	11 50		12 26	13 26	14 01		14 40	15 40	15 51			16 40
Pyle	d											11 57				14 09				15 58			
Maesteg	d																						
Maesteg (Ewenny Road)	d																						
Garth (Mid Glamorgan)	d																						
Tondu	d																						
Sarn	d																						
Wildmill	d																						
Bridgend	d					08 38		09 38	10 38		11 38	12 05		12 38	13 38	14 17		14 52	15 52	16 06			16 52
Pencoed	d											12 11								16 12			
Llanharan	d											12 15								16 16			
Pontyclun	d											12 20								16 21			
Cardiff Central 7	a			04 10		09 00		10 00	11 00		12 00	12 35		13 00	14 00	14 40		15 14	16 14	16 36			17 12
Newport (South Wales)	a					09 18		10 18	11 18		12 18	12 52		13 18	14 18	15 12		15 31	16 31	16 52			17 31
Bristol Parkway 7	a					09 46		10 46	11 46		12 46			13 46	14 48			15 59	16 59				17 59
Gloucester 7	a																						
Manchester Piccadilly 10	a											16 15				18 17				20 17			
Reading 7	a					10 42		11 47	12 47		13 47			14 47	15 47			17 04	18 01				19 01
London Paddington 15 ⊖	a					11 22		12 22	13 22		14 22			15 22	16 23			17 43	18 44				19 44

b Previous night, stops on request

When events are being held at the Millenium Stadium, services are subject to alteration. Please check times before travelling.

Sundays

16 September to 21 October

West Wales, Swansea and Maesteg - Cardiff

Route Diagram - see first Page of Table 127

		GW	AW	GW	GW	AW		AW	GW	AW	AW	AW	AW	AW	AW	AW		AW
		◇1 ⊡	■ ⌶	◇1 ⊡	◇1 ⊡				◇1 ⊡	◇			B	◇	◇			
Rosslare Harbour ⛴	d												21 00					
Fishguard Harbour ⛴	a												00 30					
	d																	
Fishguard & Goodwick	d																	
Milford Haven	d		15 28					17 30				19 38			21 35			23 15
Johnston	d		15x36					17x38				19x46			21x43			23x23
Haverfordwest	d		15 43					17 45				19 53			21 51			23 30
Clarbeston Road	d		15x52					17x53				20x01			21x59			23x39
Clunderwen	d		15x59					18x00				20x08			22x07			23x46
Pembroke Dock	d					16 45					19 00					21 45		
Pembroke	d					16 53					19 08					21 53		
Lamphey	d					16x56					19x11					21x56		
Manorbier	d					17 05					19 20					22 05		
Penally	d					17x10					19x25					22x10		
Tenby	a					17 13					19 28					22 13		
	d					17 13					19 28					22 13		
Saundersfoot	d					17x21					19x36					22x21		
Kilgetty	d					17x23					19x38					22x23		
Narberth	d					17x33					19x48					22x33		
Whitland	a		16 06			17 41		18 06			19 56	20 14			22 13	22 41		23 53
	d		16 09			17 44		18 08			19 59	20 17			22 14	22 44		23 53
Carmarthen	a		16 26			18 04		18 29			20 16	20 36			22 31	23 05		00 14
	d		16 31	16 55		18 07			19 09		20 19			21 05	22 34			
Ferryside	d		16x41			18x17					20x30				22x44			
Kidwelly	d		16x47			18x23					20x36				22x50			
Pembrey & Burry Port	d		16 55	17 15		18 31			19 29		20 43			21 24	22 58			
Llanelli	a		17 01	17 21		18 37			19 35		20 49			21 30	23 04			
	d		17 01	17 22		18 38			19 36	19 55	20 51			21 31	23 04			
Gowerton	d					18x46				20x02	20x58				23x12			
Swansea	a		17 20	17 39		19 06			19 53	20 16	21 17			21 48	23 27			
	d	16 51	17 30	17 51	18 51				19 59	20 40				21 52	23 31			
Llansamlet	d																	
Skewen	d																	
Neath	d	17 03	17 41	18 03	19 03				20 11	20 51				22 03	23 43			
Briton Ferry	d																	
Baglan	d																	
Port Talbot Parkway	d	17 10	17 48	18 10	19 10				20 18	20 58				22 10	23 50			
Pyle	d		17 55											22 17	23 57			
Maesteg	d																	
Maesteg (Ewenny Road)	d																	
Garth (Mid Glamorgan)	d																	
Tondu	d																	
Sarn	d																	
Wildmill	d																	
Bridgend	d	17 22	18 03	18 22	19 22				20 30	21 11				22 25	00 05			
Pencoed	d		18 09															
Llanharan	d		18 13															
Pontyclun	d		18 18															
Cardiff Central 7	a	17 45	18 34	18 45	19 45				20 53	21 36				22 49	00 30			
Newport (South Wales)	a	18 03	18 52	19 03	20 03				21 08					23 18				
Bristol Parkway 7	a	18 31		19 31	20 31				21 36									
Gloucester 7	a																	
Manchester Piccadilly 10	a		22 19															
Reading 7	a	19 33		20 33	21 33				22 40									
London Paddington 15 ⊖	a	20 14		21 13	22 15				23 22									

When events are being held at the Millenium Stadium, services are subject to alteration. Please check times before travelling.

Table 128

Sundays

from 28 October

West Wales, Swansea and Maesteg - Cardiff

Route Diagram - see first Page of Table 127

		AW	AW	AW	AW	AW	GW	GW	GW		AW	GW	AW	AW	GW	GW	AW	AW	GW		GW	AW	AW	AW	AW
		B			◇	🚌	◇1 ⊡	◇1 ⊡	◇1 ⊡			◇1 ⊡	◇ ⌶		◇1 ⊡	◇1 ⊡	■ ⌶		◇1 ⊡		◇1 ⊡	■ ⌶	◇	B	⌶
Rosslare Harbour ⛴	d	21p00																						09 00	
Fishguard Harbour ⛴	a	00 30																						12 30	
	d				01 50																				14 23
Fishguard & Goodwick	d																								
Milford Haven	d			23p18													11 28					13 23			
Johnston	d			23b26													11x36					13x29			
Haverfordwest	d			23p33													11 43					13 36			
Clarbeston Road	d			23b41													11x52					13x45			
Clunderwen	d			23b48													11x59					13x52			
Pembroke Dock	d																	11 55							
Pembroke	d																	12 03							
Lamphey	d																	12x06							
Manorbier	d																	12 15							
Penally	d																	12x20							
Tenby	a																	12 23							
	d																	12 23							
Saundersfoot	d																	12x31							
Kilgetty	d																	12x33							
Narberth	d																	12x43							
Whitland	a			23p54	02s22												12 06	12 51				13 59			14 55
	d			23p54													12 08	12 54				14 02			14 55
Carmarthen	a			00 16	02s40												12 26	13 14				14 20			15 13
	d					02 50					09 40		10 30	11 07			12 29	13 17				14 23			15 16
Ferryside	d										09x50			11x17				13x27							15x26
Kidwelly	d										09x56			11x23				13x33							15x32
Pembrey & Burry Port	d										10 03		10 49	11 31			12 49	13 40				14 42			15 39
Llanelli	a				03s06						10 09		10 54	11 37			12 55	13 46				14 48			15 47
	d										10 10		10 56	11 37			12 55	13 47				14 49	15 41		15 47
Gowerton	d										10x17			11x45				13x54							15x55
Swansea	a					03 50					10 35		11 15	12 01			13 15	14 12				15 08	16 04		16 14
	d						08 07	09 21	10 21			11 21	11 32		12 21	13 21	13 43		14 21		15 21	15 33			
Llansamlet	d																								
Skewen	d																								
Neath	d						08 19	09 33	10 33			11 33	11 43		12 33	13 33	13 54		14 33		15 33	15 44			
Briton Ferry	d																								
Baglan	d																								
Port Talbot Parkway	d						08 26	09 40	10 40			11 40	11 50		12 40	13 40	14 01		14 40		15 40	15 51			
Pyle	d												11 57				14 09					15 58			
Maesteg	d		22p15																						
Maesteg (Ewenny Road)	d		22p17																						
Garth (Mid Glamorgan)	d		22p20																						
Tondu	d		22p29																						
Sarn	d		22p32																						
Wildmill	d		22p34																						
Bridgend	d		22p38				08 38	09 52	10 52			11 52	12 05		12 52	13 52	14 17		14 52		15 52	16 06			
Pencoed	d		22p44										12 11									16 12			
Llanharan	d		22p48										12 15									16 16			
Pontyclun	d		22p52										12 20									16 21			
Cardiff Central 7	a		23p08		04 10		09 00	10 14	11 14			12 14	12 35		13 14	14 14	14 40		15 14		16 14	16 36			
Newport (South Wales)	a		23p36				09 18	10 31	11 31			12 31	12 52		13 31	14 31	15 12		15 31		16 31	16 52			
Bristol Parkway 7	a						09 46	10 59	11 59			12 59			13 59	14 59			15 59		16 59				
Gloucester 7	a		00 40																						
Manchester Piccadilly 10	a												16 15				18 17					20 17			
Reading 7	a						10 42	12 01	13 01			14 01			15 01	16 01			17 01		18 01				
London Paddington 15 ⊖	a						11 22	12 44	13 44			14 44			15 44	16 44			17 43		18 44				

b Previous night, stops on request

When events are being held at the Millenium Stadium, services are subject to alteration. Please check times before travelling.

Table 128

West Wales, Swansea and Maesteg - Cardiff

Sundays

from 28 October

Route Diagram - see first Page of Table 127

		GW	GW	AW	GW	GW		AW	AW	GW	AW	AW	AW	AW	AW	AW		AW	AW
				■										B					
		◇1	◇1		◇1	◇1				◇1	◇				◇	◇			
		R	R	H	R	R				R									
Rosslare Harbour	d													21 00					
Fishguard Harbour	a													00 30					
	d																		
Fishguard & Goodwick	d																		
Milford Haven	d			15 28					17 30				19 38			21 35			23 15
Johnston	d			15x36					17x38				19x46			21x43			23x23
Haverfordwest	d			15 43					17 45				19 53			21 51			23 30
Clarbeston Road	d			15x52					17x53				20x01			21x59			23x39
Clunderwen	d			15x59					18x00				20x08			22x07			23x46
Pembroke Dock	d							16 45				19 00						21 45	
Pembroke	d							16 53				19 08						21 53	
Lamphey	d							16x56				19x11						21x56	
Manorbier	d							17 05				19 20						22 05	
Penally	d							17x10				19x25						22x10	
Tenby	a							17 13				19 28						22 13	
	d							17 13				19 28						22 13	
Saundersfoot	d							17x21				19x36						22x21	
Kilgetty	d							17x23				19x38						22x23	
Narberth	d							17x33				19x48						22x33	
Whitland	a			16 06				17 41	18 06			19 56	20 14			22 13		22 41	23 53
	d			16 09				17 44	18 08			19 59	20 17			22 14		22 44	23 53
Carmarthen	a			16 26				18 04	18 29			20 16	20 36			22 31		23 05	00 14
	d	15 30		16 31	16 55			18 07		19 09		20 19			21 05	22 34			
Ferryside	d			16x41				18x17				20x30				22x44			
Kidwelly	d			16x47				18x23				20x36				22x50			
Pembrey & Burry Port	d	15 50		16 55	17 15			18 31		19 29		20 43			21 24	22 58			
Llanelli	a	15 56		17 01	17 21			18 37		19 35		20 49			21 30	23 04			
	d	15 58		17 01	17 22			18 38		19 36	19 55	20 51			21 31	23 04			
Gowerton	d							18x46			20x02	20x58				23x12			
Swansea	a	16 14		17 20	17 39			19 06		19 53	20 16	21 17			21 48	23 27			
	d	16 21	16 51	17 30	17 51	18 51				19 59	20 40				21 52	23 31			
Llansamlet	d																		
Skewen	d																		
Neath	d	16 33	17 03	17 41	18 03	19 03				20 11	20 51				22 03	23 43			
Briton Ferry	d																		
Baglan	d																		
Port Talbot Parkway	d	16 40	17 10	17 48	18 10	19 10				20 18	20 58				22 10	23 50			
Pyle	d			17 55											22 17	23 57			
Maesteg	d																		
Maesteg (Ewenny Road)	d																		
Garth (Mid Glamorgan)	d																		
Tondu	d																		
Sarn	d																		
Wildmill	d																		
Bridgend	d	16 52	17 22	18 03	18 22	19 22				20 30	21 11				22 25	00 05			
Pencoed	d			18 09															
Llanharan	d			18 13															
Pontyclun	d			18 18															
Cardiff Central 7	a	17 12	17 45	18 34	18 45	19 45				20 53	21 36				22 49	00 30			
Newport (South Wales)	a	17 31	18 03	18 52	19 03	20 03				21 08					23 18				
Bristol Parkway 7	a	17 59	18 31		19 31	20 31				21 36									
Gloucester 7	a																		
Manchester Piccadilly 10	a			22 19															
Reading 7	a	19 01	19 32		20 33	21 33				22 40									
London Paddington 15 ⊖	a	19 44	20 14		21 13	22 13				23 22									

When events are being held at the Millenium Stadium, services are subject to alteration. Please check times before travelling.

Network Diagram for Tables 129, 131

DM-12/11
Design BAJS

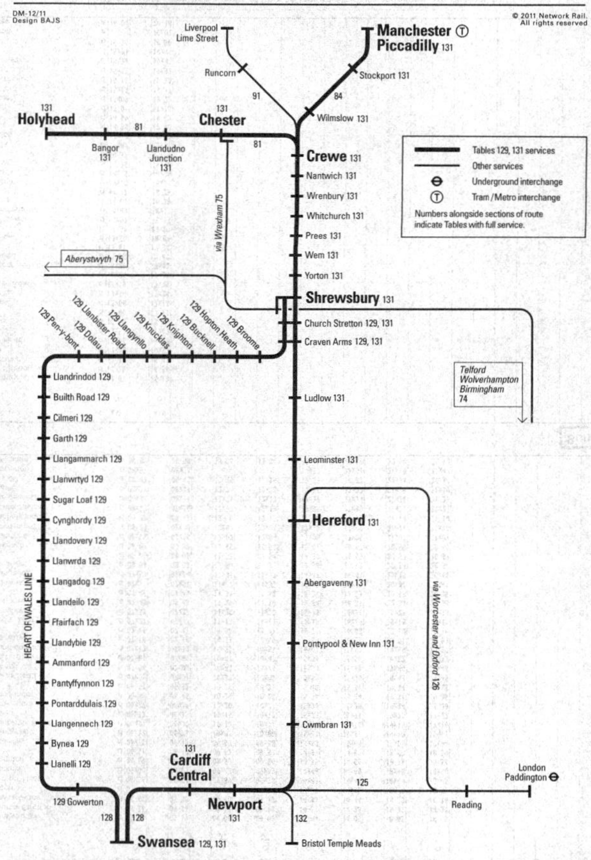

Swansea - Shrewsbury

HEART OF WALES LINE

Route Diagram - see first Page of Table 129

Miles			AW SO ◇	AW SX ◇	AW SO ◇ H	AW SX ◇ H	AW SO ◇	AW SX ◇	AW SX ◇	AW SO ◇
0	**Swansea**	d	04 36	04 36	09 16	09 16	13 16	13 14	18 21	18 21
5½	Gowerton	d								
11¼	Llanelli	d	04 53	04 53	09 34	09 34	13 35	13 35	18 39	18 39
14	Bynea	d	04x58	04x58	09x39	09x39	13x39	13x40	18x44	18x44
16	Llangennech	d	05x01	05x01	09x43	09x43	13x43	13x44	18x47	18x47
18¼	Pontarddulais	d	05x05	05x05	09x47	09x47	13x48	13x48	18x51	18x51
23	Pantyffynnon	d	05 13	05 13	09 55	09 55	13 55	13 56	18 59	18 59
24¼	Ammanford	d	05 16	05 16	09 58	09 58	13 58	13 59	19 02	19 02
26	Llandybie	d	05 20	05 20	10 02	10 02	14 03	14 03	19 06	19 06
30	Ffairfach	d	05x27	05x27	10x10	10x10	14x10	14x11	19x13	19x13
30¾	Llandeilo	a	05 30	05 30	10 12	10 12	14 12	14 13	19 16	19 16
—		d	05 32	05 32	10 15	10 15	14 15	14 16	19 18	19 18
36½	Llangadog	d	05 42	05 42	10 24	10 24	14 24	14 25	19 28	19 28
38¼	Llanwrda	d	05 45	05 45	10 28	10 28	14 28	14 29	19 31	19 31
42	Llandovery	a	05 52	05 52	10 34	10 34	14 34	14 35	19 38	19 38
—		d	05 54	05 54	10 37	10 37	14 37	14 38	19 40	19 40
46¾	Cynghordy	d	06x02	06x02	10x45	10x45	14x45	14x46	19x48	19x48
49½	Sugar Loaf	d	06x10	06x10	10x54	10x54	14x53	14x55	19x56	19x56
53½	Llanwrtyd	a	06 16	06 16	11 00	11 00	14 59	15 01	20 02	20 02
—		d	06 19	06 19	11 05	11 05	15 01	15 03	20 07	20 07
56¾	Llangammarch	d	06x24	06x24	11x11	11x11	15x07	15x09	20x12	20x13
58½	Garth (Powys)	d	06x28	06x28	11x15	11x17	15x11	15x13	20x16	20x16
62	Cilmeri	d	06x33	06x33	11x20	11x21	15x16	15x19	20x21	20x21
64	Builth Road	d	06x36	06x36	11x23	11x24	15x19	15x22	20x24	20x24
69¾	Llandrindod	a	06 47	06 47	11 35	11 36	15 31	15 34	20 36	20 36
—		d	06 55	06 55	11 39	11 40	15 40	15 40	20 40	20 40
73¼	Pen-y-bont	d	07x02	07x02	11x46	11x48	15x47	15x48	20x47	20x47
76¼	Dolau	d	07x07	07 07	11 51	11 53	15 52	15 53	20 52	20 52
79¾	Llanbister Road	d	07x12	07x13	11x57	11x59	15x57	15x59	20x58	20x58
82¾	Llangynllo	d	07x17	07x18	12x02	12x05	16x02	16x04	21x03	21x03
86¾	Knucklas	d	07x23	07x24	12x08	12x11	16x08	16x11	21x09	21x09
89¾	Knighton	a	07 29	07 30	12 13	12 16	16 14	16 16	21 14	21 14
—		d	07 32	07 32	12 16	12 18	16 16	16 19	21 17	21 17
93½	Bucknell	d	07 38	07 38	12 22	12 24	16 22	16 25	21 23	21 23
96½	Hopton Heath	d	07x42	07x42	12x26	12x28	16x26	16x29	21x27	21x27
99	Broome	d	07x46	07x46	12x30	12x32	16x30	16x34	21x31	21x31
101½	Craven Arms	a	07 53	07 53	12 37	12 39	16 37	16 40	21 38	21 38
108¾	Church Stretton	a	08 06	08 06	12 51	12 52	16 51	16 53	21 51	21 51
121½	**Shrewsbury**	a	08 22	08 22	13 09	13 08	17 11	17 09	22 08	22 08

Sundays

		AW ◇ A	AW ◇ B	AW ◇ C	AW ◇ D
Swansea	d	11 04	11 07	15 26	15 26
Gowerton	d	11x16	11x16	15x36	15x36
Llanelli	d	11 29	11 29	15 51	15 55
Bynea	d	11x34	11x34	15x56	16x00
Llangennech	d	11x38	11x38	16x00	16x04
Pontarddulais	d	11x42	11x42	16x04	16x08
Pantyffynnon	d	11 50	11 50	16 11	16 15
Ammanford	d	11 53	11 53	16 14	16 18
Llandybie	d	11 57	11 57	16 19	16 23
Ffairfach	d	12x05	12x05	16x26	16x30
Llandeilo	a	12 07	12 07	16 29	16 33
	d	12 10	12 10	16 31	16 35
Llangadog	d	12 19	12 19	16 41	16 45
Llanwrda	d	12 23	12 23	16 44	16 48
Llandovery	a	12 29	12 29	16 51	16 55
	d	12 32	12 32	16 53	16 57
Cynghordy	d	12x40	12x40	17x02	17x06
Sugar Loaf	d	12x49	12x49	17x10	17x14
Llanwrtyd	a	12 55	12 55	17 16	17 20
	d	12 57	12 57	17 19	17 23
Llangammarch	d	13x03	13x03	17x25	17x29
Garth (Powys)	d	13x07	13x07	17x29	17x33
Cilmeri	d	13x13	13x13	17x34	17x38
Builth Road	d	13x16	13x16	17x38	17x42
Llandrindod	a	13 28	13 28	17 49	17 53
	d	13 43	13 43	18 00	18 00
Pen-y-bont	d	13x51	13x51	18x08	18x08
Dolau	d	13 56	13 56	18 13	18 13
Llanbister Road	d	14x02	14x02	18x19	18x19
Llangynllo	d	14x07	14x07	18x24	18x24
Knucklas	d	14x14	14x14	18x31	18x31
Knighton	a	14 19	14 19	18 36	18 36
	d	14 22	14 22	18 39	18 39
Bucknell	d	14 28	14 28	18 45	18 45
Hopton Heath	d	14x32	14x32	18x49	18x49
Broome	d	14x37	14x37	18x54	18x54
Craven Arms	a	14 44	14 44	19 01	19 01
Church Stretton	a	14 57	14 57	19 15	19 15
Shrewsbury	a	15 15	15 15	19 31	19 31

A from 16 September until 21 October
B until 9 September, from 28 October
C until 9 September
D from 16 September

When events are being held at the Millenium Stadium, services are subject to alteration. Please check times before travelling.

Shrewsbury - Swansea

HEART OF WALES LINE

Route Diagram - see first Page of Table 129

Miles			AW SO ◇	AW SX ◇	AW SO ◇ H	AW SX ◇ H	AW SX ◇	AW SO ◇	AW SX ◇	AW SO ◇
0	**Shrewsbury**	d	05 19	05 19	09 00	09 00	14 04	14 05	18 05	18 05
12¾	Church Stretton	d	05 36	05 36	09 17	09 18	14 22	14 23	18 22	18 23
20	Craven Arms	d	05 47	05 50	09 30	09 28	14 33	14 36	18 35	18 36
22½	Broome	d	05x52	05x55	09x35	09x34	14x39	14x42	18x40	18x42
25	Hopton Heath	d	05x56	05x59	09x39	09x38	14x43	14x45	18x44	18x45
28	Bucknell	d	06x00	06x03	09x43	09x43	14x48	14x50	18x48	18x50
32¼	Knighton	a	06 09	06 10	09 50	09 50	14 55	14 56	18 55	18 56
—		d	06 11	06 12	09 52	09 52	14 57	14 59	18 57	18 59
34¾	Knucklas	d	06x15	06x17	09x57	09x58	15x03	15x04	19x02	19x04
38¾	Llangynllo	d	06x22	06x25	10x05	10x06	15x11	15x11	19x10	19x11
41¾	Llanbister Road	d	06x27	06x30	10x10	10x11	15x16	15x16	19x15	19x16
45¼	Dolau	d	06x33	06x35	10x15	10x17	15x22	15x21	19x20	19x22
48½	Pen-y-bont	d	06x37	06x39	10x20	10x21	15x26	15x25	19x24	19x26
51¾	Llandrindod	a	06 48	06 46	10 29	10 28	15 35	15 34	19 31	19 35
—		d	06 52	06 52	10 29	10 31	15 40	15 37	19 34	19 35
57½	Builth Road	d	07x01	07x01	10x39	10x40	15x50	15x46	19x43	19x45
59½	Cilmeri	d	07x04	07x04	10x42	10x44	15x53	15x50	19x46	19x48
63	Garth (Powys)	d	07x09	07x09	10x47	10x49	15x59	15x55	19x52	19x53
64¾	Llangammarch	d	07x12	07x12	10x51	10x53	16x03	15x59	19x55	19x57
68	Llanwrtyd	a	07 18	07 18	10 57	10 59	16 09	16 05	20 01	20 03
—		d	07 21	07 21	11 06	11 07	16 11	16 08	20 10	20 10
70¾	Sugar Loaf	d	07x27	07x27	11x13	11x13	16x18	16x14	20x16	20x16
74¾	Cynghordy	d	07x33	07x33	11x20	11x20	16x25	16x21	20x23	20x23
79½	Llandovery	a	07 43	07 43	11 29	11 30	16 34	16 31	20 33	20 33
—		d	07 45	07 45	11 32	11 32	16 37	16 33	20 35	20 35
83¼	Llanwrda	d	07x51	07x51	11x37	11x38	16x43	16x39	20x41	20x41
85	Llangadog	d	07x54	07x54	11x41	11x42	16x47	16x43	20x45	20x45
90¾	Llandeilo	a	08 03	08 03	11 50	11 51	16 56	16 52	20 54	20 54
—		d	08 06	08 06	11 53	11 54	16 58	16 55	20 57	20 57
91½	Ffairfach	d	08 08	08 08	11 55	11 56	17 01	16 57	20 59	20 59
95½	Llandybie	d	08x15	08x15	12x02	12x04	17x08	17x05	21x07	21x07
97¼	Ammanford	d	08x20	08x20	12x07	12x08	17x13	17x09	21x11	21x11
98½	Pantyffynnon	d	08 23	08 23	12 10	12 11	17 16	17 12	21 14	21 14
103¼	Pontarddulais	d	08x30	08x30	12x17	12x18	17x23	17x19	21x21	21x21
105½	Llangennech	d	08x34	08x34	12x21	12x23	17x27	17x24	21x26	21x26
107½	Bynea	d	08x37	08x37	12x24	12x26	17x31	17x27	21x29	21x29
110¼	Llanelli	a	08 42	08 42	12 29	12 35	17 38	17 32	21 34	21 34
116	Gowerton	a	08x53	08x53			17x57	17x51	21x50	21x47
121½	**Swansea**	a	09 08	09 08	13 06	13 04	18 18	18 10	22 08	22 10

Sundays

		AW ◇	AW ◇
Shrewsbury	d	12 07	16 18
Church Stretton	d	12 25	16 36
Craven Arms	d	12 36	16 47
Broome	d	12x42	16x53
Hopton Heath	d	12x46	16x57
Bucknell	d	12x51	17x02
Knighton	a	12 58	17 08
	d	13 00	17 11
Knucklas	d	13x06	17x16
Llangynllo	d	13x14	17x24
Llanbister Road	d	13x19	17x29
Dolau	d	13x25	17x35
Pen-y-bont	d	13x29	17x40
Llandrindod	a	13 38	17 49
	d	13 41	17 54
Builth Road	d	13x50	18x04
Cilmeri	d	13x54	18x07
Garth (Powys)	d	13x59	18x13
Llangammarch	d	14x03	18x17
Llanwrtyd	a	14 09	18 23
	d	14 12	18 25
Sugar Loaf	d	14x18	18x32
Cynghordy	d	14x25	18x39
Llandovery	a	14 35	18 48
	d	14 37	18 51
Llanwrda	d	14x43	18x57
Llangadog	d	14x47	19x01
Llandeilo	a	14 56	19 10
	d	14 59	19 12
Ffairfach	d	15 01	19 15
Llandybie	d	15x09	19x22
Ammanford	d	15x13	19x27
Pantyffynnon	d	15 16	19 30
Pontarddulais	d	15x23	19x37
Llangennech	d	15x28	19x41
Bynea	d	15x31	19x45
Llanelli	a	15 36	19 50
Gowerton	a		20x02
Swansea	a	16 04	20 16

When events are being held at the Millenium Stadium, services are subject to alteration. Please check times before travelling.

Network Diagram for Table 130

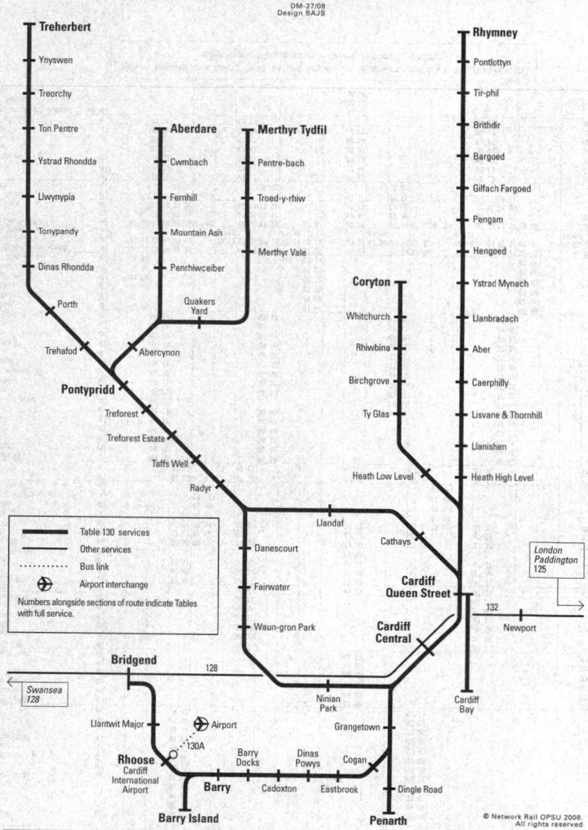

Table 130

Mondays to Fridays

until 14 September

Treherbert, Aberdare, Merthyr, Pontypridd, Rhymney and Coryton - Cardiff, Penarth, Barry, Barry Island and Bridgend

Network Diagram - see first Page of Table 130

Miles	Miles	Miles	Miles	Miles			AW MX	AW MX	AW	AW	AW	AW	AW	AW	AW		AW	AW	AW	AW	AW	AW	AW	AW	AW
									A	A															
0	—	—	—	—	**Treherbert**	d															05 47				
0½	—	—	—	—	Ynyswen	d															05 49				
1¼	—	—	—	—	Treorchy	d															05 51				
2¾	—	—	—	—	Ton Pentre	d															05 53				
3¼	—	—	—	—	Ystrad Rhondda	a															05 56				
—	—	—	—	—		d															05 58				
4½	—	—	—	—	Llwynypia	d															06 00				
5½	—	—	—	—	Tonypandy	d															06 03				
6	—	—	—	—	Dinas Rhondda	d															06 05				
7½	—	—	—	—	Porth	a															06 08				
—	—	—	—	—		d															06 09				
8¾	—	—	—	—	Trehafod	d															06 12				
—	—	0	—	—	**Merthyr Tydfil**	d			22p38																
—	—	1½	—	—	Pentre-bach	d			22p42																
—	—	2¾	—	—	Troed Y Rhiw	d			22p45																
—	—	4½	—	—	Merthyr Vale	a			22p48																
—	—	—	—	—		d			22p50																
—	—	6¾	—	—	Quakers Yard	d			22p55																
—	—	—	—	0	**Aberdare** 3	d																			
—	—	—	—	1½	Cwmbach	d																			
—	—	—	—	2¾	Fernhill	d																			
—	—	—	—	3¾	Mountain Ash	a																			
—	—	—	—	—		d																			
—	—	—	—	5	Penrhiwceiber	d																			
—	—	8¼	—	7¾	Abercynon	d			22p59																
10¾	—	11½	—	11	**Pontypridd** 3	a			23p07												06 17				
—	—	—	—	—		d			23p09					05 24							06 18				
11½	—	—	—	—	Trefforest	d			23p12					05 27							06 21				
14	—	—	—	—	Trefforest Estate	d			23p16					05 31											
16¼	—	—	—	—	Taffs Well 3	d			23p20					05 34							06 28				
18¼	—	—	0	—	Radyr 3	a			23p23					05 37							06 31				
—	—	—	—	—		d		23p10	23p23					05 37							06 31				
—	—	—	1½	—	Danescourt	d																			
—	—	—	2	—	Fairwater	d																			
—	—	—	2¼	—	Waun-gron Park	d																			
—	—	—	3¾	—	Ninian Park	d																			
19¼	—	—	—	—	Llandaf	d		23p12	23p26					05 40							06 34				
21¾	—	—	—	—	Cathays	d		23p16	23p31					05 45							06 39				
—	0	—	—	—	**Rhymney** 3	d																			
—	1	—	—	—	Pontlottyn	d																			
—	3½	—	—	—	Tir-phil	d																			
—	4½	—	—	—	Brithdir	d																			
—	6	—	—	—	Bargoed	a																			
—	—	—	—	—		d																			
—	6½	—	—	—	Gilfach Fargoed	d																			
—	7½	—	—	—	Pengam	d																			
—	9¼	—	—	—	Hengoed	d																			
—	10½	—	—	—	Ystrad Mynach 3	d																			
—	13	—	—	—	Llanbradach	d																			
—	15	—	—	—	Aber	d																			
—	15¾	—	—	—	Caerphilly 3	d													06 10						
—	18¼	—	—	—	Lisvane & Thornhill	d													06 14						
—	19¼	—	—	—	Llanishen	d													06 16						
—	20¼	—	—	—	Heath High Level	d													06 19						
—	—	0	—	—	**Coryton**	d																			
—	—	0½	—	—	Whitchurch (Cardiff)	d																			
—	—	0¾	—	—	Rhiwbina	d																			
—	—	1¼	—	—	Birchgrove	d																			
—	—	1½	—	—	Ty Glas	d																			
—	—	2¼	—	—	Heath Low Level	d																			
22½	22¾	4¾	—	—	**Cardiff Queen Street** 3	a		23p20	23p34					05 49					06 25		06 42				
—	—	—	—	—		d		23p20	23p36					05 51					06 26	06 36	06 43	06 48		07 00	
—	—	5¾	—	—	**Cardiff Bay**	a														06 40		06 52		07 04	
23	23¼	—	4¾	—	**Cardiff Central** 7	a		23p25	23p39					05 54					06 29		06 48				
—	—	—	—	—		d		23p30	23p41	00 26	05 20	05 41	05 46	05 55	06 16		06 25	06 36	06 41				06 55		07 01
24	24¼	—	—	—	Grangetown	d		23p34	23p45	00 30	05 24	05 45	05 50	05 59	06 20		06 29	06 40	06 45				06 59		07 05
—	26¾	—	—	—	Dingle Road	d							05 54		06 24			06 44							07 11
—	27	—	—	—	**Penarth**	a							05 59		06 29			06 49							07 16
25¾	—	—	—	—	Cogan	d		23p37	23p48	00 34	05 28	05 48		06 03			06 33		06 48				07 03		
26½	—	—	—	—	Eastbrook	d		23p40	23p51	00 36	05 30	05 51		06 05			06 35		06 51				07 05		
27½	—	—	—	—	Dinas Powys	d		23p42	23p54	00 39	05 32	05 53		06 07			06 37		06 53				07 07		
29½	—	—	—	—	Cadoxton	d		23p46	23p58	00 44	05 37	05 57		06 12			06 42		06 57				07 12		
30¼	—	—	—	—	Barry Docks	d		23p49	00 03	00 47	05 40	06 00		06 15			06 45		07 00				07 15		
31½	—	0	—	—	**Barry** 3	d	23p15	23p54	00 08	00 52	05 44	06 05		06 19			06 49		07 05				07 19		
32¼	—	—	—	—	**Barry Island**	a		00 01		00 58	05 50			06 25			06 55						07 25		
—	—	3¼	—	—	Rhoose Cardiff Int Airport ✈	d	23p30		00 15			06 12							07 12						
—	—	9¾	—	—	Llantwit Major	d	23p45		00 25			06 22							07 22						
—	—	19	—	—	**Bridgend**	a	00 10		00 43			06 39							07 39						

A 26 July, 27 July, 2 August

When events are being held at the Millenium Stadium, services are subject to alteration. Please check times before travelling.

Table 130

Mondays to Fridays

until 14 September

Treherbert, Aberdare, Merthyr, Pontypridd, Rhymney and Coryton - Cardiff, Penarth, Barry, Barry Island and Bridgend

Network Diagram - see first Page of Table 130

			AW	AW	AW	AW	AW	AW	AW	AW	AW		AW	AW	AW	AW	AW	AW	AW	AW	AW		AW	AW	AW
Treherbert	d				06 17											06 47									
Ynyswen	d				06 19											06 49									
Treorchy	d				06 21											06 51									
Ton Pentre	d				06 23											06 53									
Ystrad Rhondda	a				06 26											06 56									
	d				06 28											06 58									
Llwynypia	d				06 30											07 00									
Tonypandy	d				06 33											07 03									
Dinas Rhondda	d				06 35											07 05									
Porth	a				06 38											07 08									
	d				06 39											07 09									
Trehafod	d				06 42											07 12									
Merthyr Tydfil	d												06 38											07 08	
Pentre-bach	d												06 42											07 12	
Troed Y Rhiw	d												06 45											07 15	
Merthyr Vale	a												06 48											07 18	
	d												06 50											07 20	
Quakers Yard	d												06 55											07 25	
Aberdare 3	d							06 22											06 52						
Cwmbach	d							06 25											06 55						
Fernhill	d							06 28											06 58						
Mountain Ash	a							06 31											07 01						
	d							06 34											07 04						
Penrhiwceiber	d							06 37											07 07						
Abercynon	d							06 43					06 59						07 13					07 29	
Pontypridd 3	a				06 47			06 52					07 07			07 17			07 22					07 37	
	d				06 48			06 54					07 09			07 18			07 24					07 39	
Trefforest	d				06 51			06 57					07 12			07 21			07 27					07 42	
Trefforest Estate	d												07 16											07 46	
Taffs Well 3	d				06 58	06 53		07 04					07 20			07 28			07 34					07 50	
Radyr 3	a				07 01	06 56		07 07					07 23			07 31			07 37					07 53	
	d				07 01	07 04		07 07					07 23			07 31	07 34		07 37					07 53	
Danescourt	d					07 08											07 38								
Fairwater	d					07 10											07 40								
Waun-gron Park	d					07 12											07 42								
Ninian Park	d					07 15											07 45								
Llandaf	d				07 04			07 10					07 26			07 34			07 40					07 56	
Cathays	d				07 09			07 15					07 31			07 39			07 45					08 01	
Rhymney 3	d			06 10					06 34											07 02					
Pontlottyn	d			06 13					06 37											07 05					
Tir-phil	d			06 17					06 41											07 09					
Brithdir	d			06 20					06 44											07 12					
Bargoed	a			06 23					06 47											07 15					
	d			06 27					06 48						07 02					07 17					07 32
Gilfach Fargoed	d			06 29											07 04					07 19					
Pengam	d			06 32					06 52						07 07					07 22					07 37
Hengoed	d			06 35					06 56						07 10					07 25					07 40
Ystrad Mynach 3	d			06 38					06 58						07 13					07 28					07 43
Llanbradach	d			06 43					07 03						07 18					07 33					07 48
Aber	d			06 47					07 07						07 22					07 37					07 52
Caerphilly 3	d			06 50					07 10						07 25					07 40					07 55
Lisvane & Thornhill	d			06 54					07 14						07 29					07 44					07 59
Llanishen	d			06 56					07 16						07 31					07 46					08 01
Heath High Level	d			06 59					07 19						07 34					07 49					08 04
Coryton	d		06 45								07 15										07 45				
Whitchurch (Cardiff)	d		06 46								07 16										07 46				
Rhiwbina	d		06 48								07 18										07 48				
Birchgrove	d		06 50								07 20										07 50				
Ty Glas	d		06 51								07 21										07 51				
Heath Low Level	d		06 54								07 24										07 54				
Cardiff Queen Street 3	a		06 59	07 04	07 12			07 19	07 24		07 29		07 34		07 39	07 44			07 49	07 54	07 59			08 04	08 09
	d		07 01	07 06	07 13		07 12	07 21	07 26	07 24	07 31		07 36	07 36	07 41	07 46		07 48	07 51	07 56	08 01		08 00	08 06	08 11
Cardiff Bay	a						07 16			07 28				07 40				07 52					08 04		
Cardiff Central 7	a		07 04	07 09	07 16	07 20		07 24	07 29		07 34		07 39		07 44	07 52	07 50		07 54	07 59	08 04			08 09	08 14
	d			07 10	07 16			07 25	07 31				07 41		07 46				07 55	08 01				08 10	08 16
Grangetown	d			07 14	07 20			07 29	07 35				07 45		07 50				07 59	08 05				08 14	08 20
Dingle Road	d				07 26				07 41						07 56					08 11					08 26
Penarth	a				07 31				07 46						08 01					08 16					08 31
Cogan	d			07 18				07 33					07 48						08 03					08 18	
Eastbrook	d			07 20				07 35					07 51						08 05					08 20	
Dinas Powys	d			07 22				07 37					07 53						08 07					08 22	
Cadoxton	d			07 27				07 42					07 57						08 12					08 27	
Barry Docks	d			07 30				07 45					08 00						08 15					08 30	
Barry 3	d			07 34				07 49					08 05						08 19					08 34	
Barry Island	a			07 40				07 55											08 25					08 40	
Rhoose Cardiff Int Airport ✈	d												08 12												
Llantwit Major	d												08 22												
Bridgend	a												08 39												

When events are being held at the Millenium Stadium, services are subject to alteration. Please check times before travelling.

Table 130

Mondays to Fridays

until 14 September

Treherbert, Aberdare, Merthyr, Pontypridd, Rhymney and Coryton - Cardiff, Penarth, Barry, Barry Island and Bridgend

Network Diagram - see first Page of Table 130

		AW	AW	AW	AW	AW	AW		AW	AW	AW	AW	AW	AW	AW	AW	AW		AW	AW	AW	AW	AW	AW	AW
Treherbert	d		07 17										07 45											08 17	
Ynyswen	d		07 19										07 47											08 19	
Treorchy	d		07 21										07 49											08 21	
Ton Pentre	d		07 23										07 51											08 23	
Ystrad Rhondda	a		07 26										07 54											08 26	
	d		07 28										07 58											08 28	
Llwynypia	d		07 30										08 00											08 30	
Tonypandy	d		07 33										08 03											08 33	
Dinas Rhondda	d		07 35										08 05											08 35	
Porth	a		07 38										08 08											08 38	
	d		07 39										08 09											08 39	
Trehafod	d		07 42										08 12											08 42	
Merthyr Tydfil	d									07 38											08 08				
Pentre-bach	d									07 42											08 12				
Troed Y Rhiw	d									07 45											08 15				
Merthyr Vale	a									07 48											08 18				
	d									07 50											08 20				
Quakers Yard	d									07 55											08 25				
Aberdare 3	d				07 22											07 52									
Cwmbach	d				07 25											07 55									
Fernhill	d				07 28											07 58									
Mountain Ash	a				07 31											08 01									
	d				07 34											08 04									
Penrhiwceiber	d				07 37											08 07									
Abercynon	d				07 43					07 59						08 13					08 29				
Pontypridd 3	a		07 47		07 52					08 07			08 17			08 22					08 37			08 47	
	d		07 48		07 54					08 09			08 18			08 24					08 39			08 48	
Trefforest	d		07 51		07 57					08 12			08 21			08 27					08 42			08 51	
Trefforest Estate	d									08 16											08 46				
Taffs Well 3	d		07 58		08 04					08 20			08 28			08 34					08 50			08 58	
Radyr 3	a		08 01		08 07					08 23			08 31			08 37					08 53			09 01	
	d		08 01	08 04	08 07					08 23			08 31	08 34		08 37					08 53			09 01	09 04
Danescourt	d			08 08										08 38											09 08
Fairwater	d			08 10										08 40											09 10
Waun-gron Park	d			08 12										08 42											09 12
Ninian Park	d			08 15										08 45											09 15
Llandaf	d		08 04		08 10					08 26			08 34			08 40					08 56			09 04	
Cathays	d		08 09		08 15					08 31			08 39			08 45					09 01			09 09	
Rhymney 3	d					07 24						07 44													
Pontlottyn	d					07 27						07 47													
Tir-phil	d					07 31						07 51													
Brithdir	d					07 34						07 54													
Bargoed	a					07 37						08 00													
	d					07 45						08 02					08 17					08 32			
Gilfach Fargoed	d					07 47											08 19								
Pengam	d					07 50						08 07					08 22					08 37			
Hengoed	d					07 54						08 10					08 25					08 40			
Ystrad Mynach 3	d					07 57						08 13					08 28					08 43			
Llanbradach	d					08 02						08 18					08 33					08 48			
Aber	d					08 07						08 22					08 37					08 52			
Caerphilly 3	d					08 10						08 25					08 40					08 55			
Lisvane & Thornhill	d					08 14						08 29					08 44					08 59			
Llanishen	d					08 16						08 31					08 46					09 01			
Heath High Level	d					08 19						08 34					08 49					09 04			
Coryton	d								08 15										08 45						
Whitchurch (Cardiff)	d								08 16										08 46						
Rhiwbina	d								08 18										08 48						
Birchgrove	d								08 20										08 50						
Ty Glas	d								08 21										08 51						
Heath Low Level	d								08 24										08 54						
Cardiff Queen Street 3	a		08 14		08 19	08 24			08 29	08 34		08 39	08 44			08 49	08 54		08 59		09 04	09 09		09 14	
	d	08 12	08 16		08 21	08 26	08 24		08 31	08 36	08 36	08 41	08 46		08 48	08 51	08 56		09 01	09 00	09 06	09 11	09 12	09 16	
Cardiff Bay	a	08 16					08 28				08 40				08 52					09 04			09 16		
Cardiff Central 7	a		08 22	08 20	08 24	08 29			08 34	08 39		08 47	08 52	08 50		08 54	08 59		09 04		09 09	09 14		09 22	09 20
	d				08 25	08 31				08 41						08 55	09 01				09 10	09 16			
Grangetown	d				08 29	08 35				08 45						08 59	09 05				09 14	09 20			
Dingle Road	d					08 41											09 11					09 26			
Penarth	a					08 46											09 16					09 31			
Cogan	d				08 33					08 48						09 03					09 18				
Eastbrook	d				08 35					08 51						09 05					09 20				
Dinas Powys	d				08 37					08 53						09 07					09 22				
Cadoxton	d				08 42					08 57						09 12					09 27				
Barry Docks	d				08 45					08 59						09 15					09 30				
Barry 3	d				08 49					09 03						09 19					09 34				
Barry Island	a				08 55											09 25					09 40				
Rhoose Cardiff Int Airport ✈	d									09 10															
Llantwit Major	d									09 19															
Bridgend	a									09 36															

When events are being held at the Millenium Stadium, services are subject to alteration. Please check times before travelling.

Mondays to Fridays

until 14 September

Treherbert, Aberdare, Merthyr, Pontypridd, Rhymney and Coryton - Cardiff, Penarth, Barry, Barry Island and Bridgend

Network Diagram - see first Page of Table 130

		AW	AW		AW	AW	AW	AW	AW	AW	AW	AW	AW		AW	AW	AW	AW	AW	AW	AW	AW	AW		AW
Treherbert	d									08 47											09 17				
Ynyswen	d									08 49											09 19				
Treorchy	d									08 51											09 21				
Ton Pentre	d									08 53											09 23				
Ystrad Rhondda	a									08 56											09 26				
	d									08 58											09 28				
Llwynypia	d									09 00											09 30				
Tonypandy	d									09 03											09 33				
Dinas Rhondda	d									09 05											09 35				
Porth	a									09 08											09 38				
	d									09 09											09 39				
Trehafod	d									09 12											09 42				
Merthyr Tydfil	d						08 38											09 08							
Pentre-bach	d						08 42											09 12							
Troed Y Rhiw	d						08 45											09 15							
Merthyr Vale	a						08 48											09 18							
	d						08 50											09 20							
Quakers Yard	d						08 55											09 25							
Aberdare [3]	d	08 22											08 52										09 22		
Cwmbach	d	08 25											08 55										09 25		
Fernhill	d	08 28											08 58										09 28		
Mountain Ash	a	08 31											09 01										09 31		
	d	08 34											09 04										09 34		
Penrhiwceiber	d	08 37											09 07										09 37		
Abercynon	d	08 43					08 59						09 13					09 29					09 43		
Pontypridd [3]	a	08 52					09 07			09 17			09 22					09 37			09 47		09 52		
	d	08 54					09 09			09 18			09 24					09 39			09 48		09 54		
Trefforest	d	08 57					09 12			09 21			09 27					09 42			09 51		09 57		
Trefforest Estate	d						09 16											09 46							
Taffs Well [3]	d	09 04					09 20			09 28			09 34					09 50			09 58		10 04		
Radyr [3]	a	09 07					09 23			09 31			09 37					09 53			10 01		10 07		
	d	09 07					09 23			09 31	09 34		09 37					09 53			10 01	10 04	10 07		
Danescourt	d										09 38											10 08			
Fairwater	d										09 40											10 10			
Waun-gron Park	d										09 42											10 12			
Ninian Park	d										09 45											10 15			
Llandaf	d	09 10					09 26			09 34			09 40					09 56			10 04		10 10		
Cathays	d	09 15					09 31			09 39			09 45					10 01			10 09		10 15		
Rhymney [3]	d		08 30																						09 25
Pontlottyn	d		08 33																						09 28
Tir-phil	d		08 37																						09 32
Brithdir	d		08 40																						09 35
Bargoed	a		08 44																						09 38
	d		08 47						09 02						09 17				09 32						09 40
Gilfach Fargoed	d														09 19										
Pengam	d		08 52						09 07						09 22				09 37						09 45
Hengoed	d		08 55						09 10						09 25				09 40						09 49
Ystrad Mynach [3]	d		08 58						09 13						09 28				09 43						09 54
Llanbradach	d		09 03						09 18						09 33				09 48						09 59
Aber	d		09 07						09 22						09 37				09 52						10 04
Caerphilly [3]	d		09 10						09 25						09 40				09 55						10 10
Lisvane & Thornhill	d		09 14						09 29						09 44				09 59						10 14
Llanishen	d		09 16						09 31						09 46				10 01						10 16
Heath High Level	d		09 19						09 34						09 49				10 04						10 19
Coryton	d					09 15										09 45									
Whitchurch (Cardiff)	d					09 16										09 46									
Rhiwbina	d					09 18										09 48									
Birchgrove	d					09 20										09 50									
Ty Glas	d					09 21										09 51									
Heath Low Level	d					09 24										09 54									
Cardiff Queen Street [3]	a	09 19	09 24			09 29	09 34		09 39	09 44			09 49		09 54	09 59		10 04	10 09		10 14		10 19		10 24
	d	09 21	09 26		09 24	09 31	09 36	09 36	09 41	09 46		09 48	09 51		09 56	10 01	10 00	10 06	10 11	10 12	10 16		10 21		10 26
Cardiff Bay	a				09 28			09 40				09 52					10 04			10 16					
Cardiff Central [7]	a	09 24	09 29			09 34	09 39		09 44	09 52	09 50		09 54		09 59	10 04		10 09	10 14		10 22	10 20	10 24		10 29
	d	09 25	09 31				09 41		09 46				09 55		10 01			10 10	10 16				10 25		10 31
Grangetown	d	09 29	09 35				09 45		09 50				09 59		10 05			10 14	10 20				10 29		10 35
Dingle Road	d		09 41						09 56						10 11				10 26						10 41
Penarth	a		09 46						10 02						10 16				10 31						10 46
Cogan	d	09 33					09 48						10 03					10 18					10 33		
Eastbrook	d	09 35					09 51						10 05					10 20					10 35		
Dinas Powys	d	09 37					09 53						10 07					10 22					10 37		
Cadoxton	d	09 42					09 57						10 12					10 27					10 42		
Barry Docks	d	09 45					09 59						10 15					10 30					10 45		
Barry [3]	d	09 49					10 03						10 19					10 34					10 49		
Barry Island	a	09 55											10 25					10 40					10 55		
Rhoose Cardiff Int Airport ✈	d						10 10																		
Llantwit Major	d						10 19																		
Bridgend	a						10 36																		

When events are being held at the Millenium Stadium, services are subject to alteration. Please check times before travelling.

Mondays to Fridays

until 14 September

Treherbert, Aberdare, Merthyr, Pontypridd, Rhymney and Coryton - Cardiff, Penarth, Barry, Barry Island and Bridgend

Network Diagram - see first Page of Table 130

		AW	AW	AW	AW	AW	AW	AW	AW		AW	AW	AW	AW	AW	AW	AW	AW	AW		AW	AW	AW	AW	AW
Treherbert	d						09 47																10 17		
Ynyswen	d						09 49																10 19		
Treorchy	d						09 51																10 21		
Ton Pentre	d						09 53																10 23		
Ystrad Rhondda	a						09 56																10 26		
	d						09 58																10 28		
Llwynypia	d						10 00																10 30		
Tonypandy	d						10 03																10 33		
Dinas Rhondda	d						10 05																10 35		
Porth	a						10 08																10 38		
	d						10 09																10 52		
Trehafod	d						10 12																10 55		
Merthyr Tydfil	d			09 38								10 04													
Pentre-bach	d			09 42								10 08													
Troed Y Rhiw	d			09 45								10 11													
Merthyr Vale	a			09 48								10 14													
	d			09 50								10 16													
Quakers Yard	d			09 55								10 22													
Aberdare [3]	d										09 52										10 22				
Cwmbach	d										09 55										10 25				
Fernhill	d										09 58										10 28				
Mountain Ash	a										10 01										10 31				
	d										10 04										10 34				
Penrhiwceiber	d										10 07										10 37				
Abercynon	d			09 59							10 13	10 26									10 43				
Pontypridd [3]	a			10 07			10 17				10 22	10 32									10 52		11 00		
	d			10 09			10 18				10 24					10 39					10 54		11 04		
Trefforest	d			10 12			10 21				10 27					10 42					10 57		11 07		
Trefforest Estate	d			10 16																					
Taffs Well [3]	d			10 20			10 28				10 34					10 50					11 04		11 13		
Radyr [3]	a			10 23			10 31				10 37					10 53					11 07		11 17		
	d			10 23			10 31	10 34			10 37					10 53		11 04			11 07		11 17		
Danescourt	d							10 38										11 08							
Fairwater	d							10 40										11 10							
Waun-gron Park	d							10 42										11 12							
Ninian Park	d							10 45										11 15							
Llandaf	d			10 26			10 34				10 40					10 56					11 10				
Cathays	d			10 31			10 39				10 45					11 01					11 15				
Rhymney [3]	d																					10 25			
Pontlottyn	d																					10 28			
Tir-phil	d																					10 32			
Brithdir	d																					10 35			
Bargoed	a																					10 38			
	d					10 02							10 17				10 32					10 40			
Gilfach Fargoed	d												10 19												
Pengam	d					10 07							10 22				10 37					10 45			
Hengoed	d					10 10							10 25				10 40					10 49			
Ystrad Mynach [3]	d					10 13							10 28				10 43					10 54			
Llanbradach	d					10 18							10 33				10 48					10 59			
Aber	d					10 22							10 37				10 52					11 04			
Caerphilly [3]	d					10 25							10 40				10 55					11 10			
Lisvane & Thornhill	d					10 29							10 44				10 59					11 14			
Llanishen	d					10 31							10 46				11 01					11 16			
Heath High Level	d					10 34							10 49				11 04					11 19			
Coryton	d		10 15											10 45											11 15
Whitchurch (Cardiff)	d		10 16											10 46											11 16
Rhiwbina	d		10 18											10 48											11 18
Birchgrove	d		10 20											10 50											11 20
Ty Glas	d		10 21											10 51											11 21
Heath Low Level	d		10 24											10 54											11 24
Cardiff Queen Street [3]	a		10 29	10 34		10 39	10 44				10 49		10 54	10 59		11 04	11 09				11 19	11 24			11 29
	d	10 24	10 31	10 36	10 36	10 41	10 46		10 48		10 51		10 56	11 01	11 00	11 06	11 11		11 12		11 21	11 26		11 24	11 31
Cardiff Bay	a	10 28			10 40				10 52						11 04				11 16					11 28	
Cardiff Central [7]	a		10 34	10 39		10 44	10 52	10 50			10 54		10 59	11 04		11 09	11 14	11 20			11 24	11 29	11 34		11 34
	d			10 41		10 46					10 55		11 01			11 10	11 16				11 25	11 31			
Grangetown	d			10 45		10 50					10 59		11 05			11 14	11 20				11 29	11 35			
Dingle Road	d					10 56							11 11				11 26					11 41			
Penarth	a					11 01							11 16				11 31					11 46			
Cogan	d			10 48							11 03					11 18					11 33				
Eastbrook	d			10 51							11 05					11 20					11 35				
Dinas Powys	d			10 53							11 07					11 22					11 37				
Cadoxton	d			10 57							11 12					11 27					11 42				
Barry Docks	d			11 00							11 15					11 30					11 45				
Barry [3]	d			11 05							11 19					11 34					11 49				
Barry Island	a										11 25					11 40					11 55				
Rhoose Cardiff Int Airport ✈	d			11 12																					
Llantwit Major	d			11 22																					
Bridgend	a			11 39																					

When events are being held at the Millenium Stadium, services are subject to alteration. Please check times before travelling.

Table 130

Mondays to Fridays
until 14 September

Treherbert, Aberdare, Merthyr, Pontypridd, Rhymney and Coryton - Cardiff, Penarth, Barry, Barry Island and Bridgend

Network Diagram - see first Page of Table 130

		AW	AW	AW	AW	AW	AW	AW	AW	AW	AW	AW	AW	AW	AW	AW	AW	AW	AW	AW	AW	AW	AW
Treherbert	d				10 47										11 17								
Ynyswen	d				10 49										11 19								
Treorchy	d				10 51										11 21								
Ton Pentre	d				10 53										11 23								
Ystrad Rhondda	a				10 56										11 26								
	d				10 58										11 28								
Llwynypia	d				11 00										11 30								
Tonypandy	d				11 03										11 33								
Dinas Rhondda	d				11 05										11 35								
Porth	a				11 08										11 38								
	d				11 09										11 39								
Trehafod	d				11 12										11 42								
Merthyr Tydfil	d	10 38										11 08									11 38		
Pentre-bach	d	10 42										11 12									11 42		
Troed Y Rhiw	d	10 45										11 15									11 45		
Merthyr Vale	a	10 48										11 18									11 48		
	d	10 50										11 20									11 50		
Quakers Yard	d	10 55										11 25									11 55		
Aberdare 3	d							10 52									11 22						
Cwmbach	d							10 55									11 25						
Fernhill	d							10 58									11 28						
Mountain Ash	a							11 01									11 31						
	d							11 04									11 34						
Penrhiwceiber	d							11 07									11 37						
Abercynon	d	10 59						11 13				11 29					11 43				11 59		
Pontypridd 3	a	11 07			11 17			11 22				11 37			11 47		11 52				12 07		
	d	11 09			11 18			11 24				11 39			11 48		11 54				12 09		
Trefforest	d	11 12			11 21			11 27				11 42			11 51		11 57				12 12		
Trefforest Estate	d	11 16										11 46									12 16		
Taffs Well 3	d	11 20			11 28			11 34				11 50			11 58		12 04				12 20		
Radyr 3	a	11 23			11 31			11 37				11 53			12 01		12 07				12 23		
	d	11 23			11 31	11 34		11 37				11 53			12 01	12 04	12 07				12 23		
Danescourt	d					11 38										12 08							
Fairwater	d					11 40										12 10							
Waun-gron Park	d					11 42										12 12							
Ninian Park	d					11 45										12 15							
Llandaf	d	11 26			11 34			11 40				11 56			12 04		12 10				12 26		
Cathays	d	11 31			11 39			11 45				12 01			12 09		12 15				12 31		
Rhymney 3	d																	11 29					
Pontlottyn	d																	11 32					
Tir-phil	d																	11 36					
Brithdir	d																	11 39					
Bargoed	a																	11 42					
	d			11 02					11 17				11 32					11 47					12 02
Gilfach Fargoed	d								11 19														
Pengam	d			11 07					11 22				11 37					11 52					12 07
Hengoed	d			11 10					11 25				11 40					11 55					12 10
Ystrad Mynach 3	d			11 13					11 28				11 43					11 58					12 13
Llanbradach	d			11 18					11 33				11 48					12 03					12 18
Aber	d			11 22					11 37				11 52					12 07					12 22
Caerphilly 3	d			11 25					11 40				11 55					12 10					12 25
Lisvane & Thornhill	d			11 29					11 44				11 59					12 14					12 29
Llanishen	d			11 31					11 46				12 01					12 16					12 31
Heath High Level	d			11 34					11 49				12 04					12 19					12 34
Coryton	d									11 45										12 15			
Whitchurch (Cardiff)	d									11 46										12 16			
Rhiwbina	d									11 48										12 18			
Birchgrove	d									11 50										12 20			
Ty Glas	d									11 51										12 21			
Heath Low Level	d									11 54										12 24			
Cardiff Queen Street 3	a	11 34		11 39	11 44			11 49	11 54	11 59		12 04	12 09		12 14		12 19	12 24		12 29	12 34		12 39
	d	11 36	11 36	11 41	11 46		11 48	11 51	11 56	12 01	12 00	12 06	12 11	12 12	12 16		12 21	12 26	12 24	12 31	12 36	12 36	12 41
Cardiff Bay	a		11 40				11 52				12 04			12 16					12 28			12 40	
Cardiff Central 7	a	11 39		11 44	11 52	11 50		11 54	11 59	12 04		12 09	12 14		12 22	12 20	12 24	12 29		12 34	12 39		12 44
	d	11 41		11 46				11 55	12 01			12 10	12 16				12 25	12 31			12 41		12 46
Grangetown	d	11 45		11 50				11 59	12 05			12 14	12 20				12 29	12 35			12 45		12 50
Dingle Road	d			11 56					12 11				12 26					12 41					12 56
Penarth	a			12 01					12 16				12 31					12 46					13 01
Cogan	d	11 48						12 03				12 18					12 33				12 48		
Eastbrook	d	11 51						12 05				12 20					12 35				12 51		
Dinas Powys	d	11 53						12 07				12 22					12 37				12 53		
Cadoxton	d	11 57						12 12				12 27					12 42				12 57		
Barry Docks	d	12 00						12 15				12 30					12 45				13 00		
Barry 3	d	12 05						12 19				12 34					12 49				13 05		
Barry Island	a							12 25				12 40					12 55						
Rhoose Cardiff Int Airport ✈	d	12 12																			13 12		
Llantwit Major	d	12 22																			13 22		
Bridgend	a	12 39																			13 39		

When events are being held at the Millenium Stadium, services are subject to alteration. Please check times before travelling.

Table 130

Mondays to Fridays
until 14 September

Treherbert, Aberdare, Merthyr, Pontypridd, Rhymney and Coryton - Cardiff, Penarth, Barry, Barry Island and Bridgend

Network Diagram - see first Page of Table 130

		AW	AW	AW	AW	AW	AW	AW	AW	AW	AW	AW	AW	AW	AW	AW	AW	AW	AW	AW	AW	AW
Treherbert	d	11 47										12 17									12 47	
Ynyswen	d	11 49										12 19									12 49	
Treorchy	d	11 51										12 21									12 51	
Ton Pentre	d	11 53										12 23									12 53	
Ystrad Rhondda	a	11 56										12 26									12 56	
	d	11 58										12 28									12 58	
Llwynypia	d	12 00										12 30									13 00	
Tonypandy	d	12 03										12 33									13 03	
Dinas Rhondda	d	12 05										12 35									13 05	
Porth	a	12 08										12 38									13 08	
	d	12 09										12 39									13 09	
Trehafod	d	12 12										12 42									13 12	
Merthyr Tydfil	d								12 08									12 38				
Pentre-bach	d								12 12									12 42				
Troed Y Rhiw	d								12 15									12 45				
Merthyr Vale	a								12 18									12 48				
	d								12 20									12 50				
Quakers Yard	d								12 25									12 55				
Aberdare 3	d													12 22								
Cwmbach	d													12 25								
Fernhill	d													12 28								
Mountain Ash	a													12 31								
	d													12 34								
Penrhiwceiber	d													12 37								
Abercynon	d								12 29					12 43				12 59				
Pontypridd 3	a	12 17							12 37			12 48		12 52				13 07			13 17	
	d	12 18							12 39			12 48		12 54				13 09			13 18	
Trefforest	d	12 21							12 42			12 51		12 57				13 12			13 21	
Trefforest Estate	d								12 46									13 16				
Taffs Well 3	d	12 28							12 50			12 58		13 04				13 20			13 28	
Radyr 3	a	12 31							12 53			13 01		13 07				13 23			13 31	
	d	12 31	12 34						12 53			13 01	13 04	13 07				13 23			13 31	13 34
Danescourt	d		12 38										13 08									13 38
Fairwater	d		12 40										13 10									13 40
Waun-gron Park	d		12 42										13 12									13 42
Ninian Park	d		12 45										13 15									13 45
Llandaf	d	12 34							12 56			13 04		13 10				13 26			13 34	
Cathays	d	12 39							13 01			13 09		13 15				13 31			13 39	
Rhymney 3	d														12 29							
Pontlottyn	d														12 32							
Tir-phil	d														12 36							
Brithdir	d														12 39							
Bargoed	a														12 42							
	d					12 17				12 32					12 47					13 02		
Gilfach Fargoed	d					12 19																
Pengam	d					12 22				12 37					12 52					13 07		
Hengoed	d					12 25				12 40					12 55					13 10		
Ystrad Mynach 3	d					12 28				12 43					12 58					13 13		
Llanbradach	d					12 33				12 48					13 03					13 18		
Aber	d					12 37				12 52					13 07					13 22		
Caerphilly 3	d					12 40				12 55					13 10					13 25		
Lisvane & Thornhill	d					12 44				12 59					13 14					13 29		
Llanishen	d					12 46				13 01					13 16					13 31		
Heath High Level	d					12 49				13 04					13 19					13 34		
Coryton	d						12 45										13 15					
Whitchurch (Cardiff)	d						12 46										13 16					
Rhiwbina	d						12 48										13 18					
Birchgrove	d						12 50										13 20					
Ty Glas	d						12 51										13 21					
Heath Low Level	d						12 54										13 24					
Cardiff Queen Street 3	a	12 44				12 54	12 59		13 04	13 09		13 14		13 19	13 24		13 29	13 34		13 39	13 44	
	d	12 46		12 48		12 56	13 01	13 00	13 06	13 11	13 12	13 16		13 21	13 26	13 24	13 31	13 36	13 36	13 41	13 46	
Cardiff Bay	a			12 52				13 04			13 16					13 28			13 40			
Cardiff Central 7	a	12 52	12 50			12 59	13 04		13 09	13 14		13 22	13 20	13 24	13 29		13 34	13 39		13 44	13 52	13 50
	d				12 55	13 01			13 10	13 16				13 25	13 31			13 41		13 46		
Grangetown	d				12 59	13 05			13 14	13 20				13 29	13 35			13 45		13 50		
Dingle Road	d					13 11				13 26					13 41					13 56		
Penarth	a					13 16				13 31					13 46					14 01		
Cogan	d				13 03				13 18					13 33				13 48				
Eastbrook	d				13 05				13 20					13 35				13 51				
Dinas Powys	d				13 07				13 22					13 37				13 53				
Cadoxton	d				13 12				13 27					13 42				13 57				
Barry Docks	d				13 15				13 30					13 45				14 00				
Barry 3	d				13 19				13 34					13 49				14 05				
Barry Island	a				13 25				13 40					13 55								
Rhoose Cardiff Int Airport ✈	d																	14 12				
Llantwit Major	d																	14 22				
Bridgend	a																	14 39				

When events are being held at the Millenium Stadium, services are subject to alteration. Please check times before travelling.

Table 130

Mondays to Fridays
until 14 September

Treherbert, Aberdare, Merthyr, Pontypridd, Rhymney and Coryton - Cardiff, Penarth, Barry, Barry Island and Bridgend

Network Diagram - see first Page of Table 130

		AW	AW	AW	AW	AW	AW		AW	AW	AW	AW	AW	AW	AW	AW	AW		AW	AW	AW	AW	AW	AW	AW
Treherbert	d									13 17										13 47				
Ynyswen	d									13 19										13 49				
Treorchy	d									13 21										13 51				
Ton Pentre	d									13 23										13 53				
Ystrad Rhondda	a									13 26										13 56				
	d									13 28										13 58				
Llwynypia	d									13 30										14 00				
Tonypandy	d									13 33										14 03				
Dinas Rhondda	d									13 35										14 05				
Porth	a									13 38										14 08				
	d									13 39										14 09				
Trehafod	d									13 42										14 12				
Merthyr Tydfil	d						13 08										13 38								
Pentre-bach	d						13 12										13 42								
Troed Y Rhiw	d						13 15										13 45								
Merthyr Vale	a						13 18										13 48								
	d						13 20										13 50								
Quakers Yard	d						13 25										13 55								
Aberdare 3	d		12 52																					13 52	
Cwmbach	d		12 55																					13 55	
Fernhill	d		12 58																					13 58	
Mountain Ash	a		13 01																					14 01	
	d		13 04																					14 04	
Penrhiwceiber	d		13 07																					14 07	
Abercynon	d		13 13				13 29						13 45				13 59							14 13	
Pontypridd 3	a		13 22				13 37				13 47		13 52				14 07				14 17			14 22	
	d		13 24				13 39				13 48		13 54				14 09				14 18			14 24	
Trefforest	d		13 27				13 42				13 51		13 57				14 12				14 21			14 27	
Trefforest Estate	d						13 46										14 16								
Taffs Well 3	d		13 34				13 50				13 58		14 04				14 20				14 28			14 34	
Radyr 3	a		13 37				13 53				14 01		14 07				14 23				14 31			14 37	
	d		13 37				13 53				14 01	14 04	14 07				14 23				14 31	14 34		14 37	
Danescourt	d											14 08										14 38			
Fairwater	d											14 10										14 40			
Waun-gron Park	d											14 12										14 42			
Ninian Park	d											14 15										14 45			
Llandaf	d		13 40				13 56				14 04		14 10				14 26				14 34			14 40	
Cathays	d		13 45				14 01				14 09		14 15				14 31				14 39			14 45	
Rhymney 3	d													13 29											
Pontlottyn	d													13 32											
Tir-phil	d													13 36											
Brithdir	d													13 39											
Bargoed	a													13 42											
	d			13 17					13 32					13 47						14 02					14 17
Gilfach Fargoed	d			13 19																					14 19
Pengam	d			13 22					13 37					13 52						14 07					14 22
Hengoed	d			13 25					13 40					13 55						14 10					14 25
Ystrad Mynach 3	d			13 28					13 43					13 58						14 13					14 28
Llanbradach	d			13 33					13 48					14 03						14 18					14 33
Aber	d			13 37					13 52					14 07						14 22					14 37
Caerphilly 3	d			13 40					13 55					14 10						14 25					14 40
Lisvane & Thornhill	d			13 44					13 59					14 14						14 29					14 44
Llanishen	d			13 46					14 01					14 16						14 31					14 46
Heath High Level	d			13 49					14 04					14 19						14 34					14 49
Coryton	d				13 45											14 15									
Whitchurch (Cardiff)	d				13 46											14 16									
Rhiwbina	d				13 48											14 18									
Birchgrove	d				13 50											14 20									
Ty Glas	d				13 51											14 21									
Heath Low Level	d				13 54											14 24									
Cardiff Queen Street 3	a		13 49	13 54	13 59		14 04		14 09		14 14		14 19	14 24		14 29	14 34			14 39	14 44			14 49	14 54
	d	13 48	13 51	13 56	14 01	14 00	14 06		14 11	14 12	14 16		14 21	14 26	14 24	14 31	14 36		14 36	14 41	14 46		14 48	14 51	14 56
Cardiff Bay	a	13 52				14 04				14 16					14 28				14 40				14 52		
Cardiff Central 7	a		13 54	13 59	14 04		14 09		14 14		14 22	14 20	14 24	14 29		14 34	14 39			14 44	14 52	14 50		14 54	14 59
	d		13 55	14 01			14 10		14 16				14 25	14 31			14 41			14 46				14 55	15 01
Grangetown	d		13 59	14 05			14 14		14 20				14 29	14 35			14 45			14 50				14 59	15 05
Dingle Road	d			14 11					14 26					14 41						14 56					15 11
Penarth	a			14 16					14 31					14 46						15 01					15 16
Cogan	d		14 03				14 18						14 33				14 48							15 03	
Eastbrook	d		14 05				14 20						14 35				14 51							15 05	
Dinas Powys	d		14 07				14 22						14 37				14 53							15 07	
Cadoxton	d		14 12				14 27						14 42				14 57							15 12	
Barry Docks	d		14 15				14 30						14 45				15 00							15 15	
Barry 3	d		14 19				14 34						14 49				15 05							15 19	
Barry Island	a		14 25				14 40						14 55											15 25	
Rhoose Cardiff Int Airport ✈	d																15 12								
Llantwit Major	d																15 22								
Bridgend	a																15 39								

When events are being held at the Millenium Stadium, services are subject to alteration. Please check times before travelling.

Table 130

Mondays to Fridays
until 14 September

Treherbert, Aberdare, Merthyr, Pontypridd, Rhymney and Coryton - Cardiff, Penarth, Barry, Barry Island and Bridgend

Network Diagram - see first Page of Table 130

		AW	AW		AW	AW	AW	AW	AW	AW	AW	AW	AW		AW	AW	AW	AW	AW	AW	AW	AW	AW		AW
Treherbert	d										14 17							14 47							
Ynyswen	d										14 19							14 49							
Treorchy	d										14 21							14 51							
Ton Pentre	d										14 23							14 53							
Ystrad Rhondda	a										14 26							14 56							
	d										14 28							14 58							
Llwynypia	d										14 30							15 00							
Tonypandy	d										14 33							15 03							
Dinas Rhondda	d										14 35							15 05							
Porth	a										14 38							15 08							
	d										14 52							15 09							
Trehafod	d										14 55							15 12							
Merthyr Tydfil	d				14 08										14 38										
Pentre-bach	d				14 12										14 42										
Troed Y Rhiw	d				14 15										14 45										
Merthyr Vale	a				14 18										14 48										
	d				14 20										14 50										
Quakers Yard	d				14 25										14 55										
Aberdare 3	d								14 22												14 52				
Cwmbach	d								14 25												14 55				
Fernhill	d								14 28												14 58				
Mountain Ash	a								14 31												15 01				
	d								14 34												15 04				
Penrhiwceiber	d								14 37												15 07				
Abercynon	d				14 29				14 43						14 59						15 13				
Pontypridd 3	a				14 37				14 52		15 00				15 07			15 17			15 22				
	d				14 39				14 54		15 04				15 09			15 18			15 24				
Trefforest	d				14 42				14 57		15 07				15 12			15 21			15 27				
Trefforest Estate	d				14 46										15 16										
Taffs Well 3	d				14 50				15 04		15 13				15 20			15 28			15 34				
Radyr 3	a				14 53				15 07		15 17				15 23			15 31			15 37				
	d				14 53		15 04		15 07		15 17				15 23			15 31	15 34		15 37				
Danescourt	d						15 08												15 38						
Fairwater	d						15 10												15 40						
Waun-gron Park	d						15 12												15 42						
Ninian Park	d						15 15												15 45						
Llandaf	d				14 56				15 10						15 26			15 34			15 40				
Cathays	d				15 01				15 15						15 31			15 39			15 45				
Rhymney 3	d									14 25															
Pontlottyn	d									14 28															
Tir-phil	d									14 32															
Brithdir	d									14 35															
Bargoed	a									14 38															
	d					14 32				14 40							15 02					15 17			
Gilfach Fargoed	d																					15 19			
Pengam	d					14 37				14 45							15 07					15 22			
Hengoed	d					14 40				14 49							15 10					15 25			
Ystrad Mynach 3	d					14 43				14 54							15 13					15 28			
Llanbradach	d					14 48				14 59							15 18					15 33			
Aber	d					14 52				15 04							15 22					15 37			
Caerphilly 3	d					14 55				15 10							15 25					15 40			
Lisvane & Thornhill	d					14 59				15 14							15 29					15 44			
Llanishen	d					15 01				15 16							15 31					15 46			
Heath High Level	d					15 04				15 19							15 34					15 49			
Coryton	d	14 45											15 15										15 45		
Whitchurch (Cardiff)	d	14 46											15 16										15 46		
Rhiwbina	d	14 48											15 18										15 48		
Birchgrove	d	14 50											15 20										15 50		
Ty Glas	d	14 51											15 21										15 51		
Heath Low Level	d	14 54											15 24										15 54		
Cardiff Queen Street 3	a	14 59			15 04	15 09			15 19	15 24			15 29		15 34		15 39	15 44			15 49	15 54	15 59		
	d	15 01	15 00		15 06	15 11		15 12	15 21	15 26		15 24	15 31		15 36	15 36	15 41	15 46		15 48	15 51	15 56	16 01		16 00
Cardiff Bay	a		15 04					15 16				15 28				15 40				15 52					16 04
Cardiff Central 7	a	15 04			15 09	15 14	15 20		15 24	15 29	15 34		15 34		15 39		15 44	15 52	15 50		15 54	15 59	16 04		
	d				15 10	15 16			15 25	15 31					15 41		15 46				15 55	16 01			
Grangetown	d				15 14	15 20			15 29	15 35					15 45		15 50				15 59	16 05			
Dingle Road	d					15 26				15 41							15 56					16 11			
Penarth	a					15 31				15 46							16 01					16 16			
Cogan	d				15 18				15 33						15 48						16 03				
Eastbrook	d				15 20				15 35						15 51						16 05				
Dinas Powys	d				15 22				15 37						15 53						16 07				
Cadoxton	d				15 27				15 42						15 57						16 12				
Barry Docks	d				15 30				15 45						16 00						16 15				
Barry 3	d				15 34				15 49						16 05						16 19				
Barry Island	a				15 40				15 55												16 25				
Rhoose Cardiff Int Airport ✈	d														16 12										
Llantwit Major	d														16 22										
Bridgend	a														16 39										

When events are being held at the Millenium Stadium, services are subject to alteration. Please check times before travelling.

Treherbert, Aberdare, Merthyr, Pontypridd, Rhymney and Coryton - Cardiff, Penarth, Barry, Barry Island and Bridgend

Network Diagram - see first Page of Table 130

		AW	AW	AW	AW	AW	AW	AW	AW		AW	AW	AW	AW	AW	AW	AW	AW	AW		AW	AW	AW	AW	AW
Treherbert	d				15 13										15 47										
Ynyswen	d				15 15										15 49										
Treorchy	d				15 21										15 51										
Ton Pentre	d				15 23										15 53										
Ystrad Rhondda	a				15 26										15 56										
	d				15 28										15 58										
Llwynypia	d				15 30										16 00										
Tonypandy	d				15 33										16 03										
Dinas Rhondda	d				15 35										16 05										
Porth	a				15 38										16 08										
	d				15 39										16 09										
Trehafod	d				15 42										16 12										
Merthyr Tydfil	d	15 08										15 38											16 08		
Pentre-bach	d	15 12										15 42											16 12		
Troed Y Rhiw	d	15 15										15 45											16 15		
Merthyr Vale	a	15 18										15 48											16 18		
	d	15 20										15 50											16 20		
Quakers Yard	d	15 25										15 55											16 25		
Aberdare 3	d						15 22										15 52								
Cwmbach	d						15 25										15 55								
Fernhill	d						15 28										15 58								
Mountain Ash	a						15 31										16 01								
	d						15 34										16 04								
Penrhiwceiber	d						15 37										16 07								
Abercynon	d	15 29					15 43					15 59					16 13						16 29		
Pontypridd 3	a	15 37			15 47		15 52					16 07			16 17			16 22					16 37		
	d	15 39			15 48		15 54					16 09			16 18			16 24					16 39		
Trefforest	d	15 42			15 51		15 57					16 12			16 21			16 27					16 42		
Trefforest Estate	d	15 46										16 16											16 46		
Taffs Well 3	d	15 50			15 58		16 04					16 20			16 28			16 34					16 50		
Radyr 3	a	15 53			16 01		16 07					16 23			16 31			16 37					16 53		
	d	15 53			16 01	16 04	16 07					16 23			16 31	16 34		16 37					16 53		
Danescourt	d					16 08										16 38									
Fairwater	d					16 10										16 40									
Waun-gron Park	d					16 12										16 42									
Ninian Park	d					16 15										16 45									
Llandaf	d	15 56			16 04		16 10					16 26			16 34			16 40					16 56		
Cathays	d	16 01			16 09		16 15					16 31			16 39			16 45					17 01		
Rhymney 3	d							15 25																	
Pontlottyn	d							15 28																	
Tir-phil	d							15 32																	
Brithdir	d							15 35																	
Bargoed	a							15 38																	
	d		15 32					15 40						16 02					16 17					16 32	
Gilfach Fargoed	d																		16 19						
Pengam	d		15 37					15 45						16 07					16 22					16 37	
Hengoed	d		15 40					15 49						16 10					16 25					16 40	
Ystrad Mynach 3	d		15 43					15 54						16 13					16 28					16 43	
Llanbradach	d		15 48					15 59						16 18					16 33					16 48	
Aber	d		15 52					16 04						16 22					16 37					16 52	
Caerphilly 3	d		15 55					16 10						16 25					16 40					16 55	
Lisvane & Thornhill	d		15 59					16 14						16 29					16 44					16 59	
Llanishen	d		16 01					16 16						16 31					16 46					17 01	
Heath High Level	d		16 04					16 19						16 34					16 49					17 04	
Coryton	d										16 15										16 45				
Whitchurch (Cardiff)	d										16 16										16 46				
Rhiwbina	d										16 18										16 48				
Birchgrove	d										16 20										16 50				
Ty Glas	d										16 21										16 51				
Heath Low Level	d										16 24										16 54				
Cardiff Queen Street 3	a	16 04	16 09		16 14		16 19	16 24			16 29	16 34		16 39	16 44			16 49	16 54		16 59		17 04	17 09	
	d	16 06	16 11	16 12	16 16		16 21	16 26	16 24		16 31	16 36	16 36	16 41	16 46		16 48	16 51	16 56		17 01	17 00	17 06	17 11	17 12
Cardiff Bay	a			16 16					16 28				16 40				16 52					17 04			17 16
Cardiff Central 7	a	16 09	16 14		16 22	16 20	16 24	16 32			16 34	16 39		16 44	16 52	16 50		16 54	16 59		17 04		17 09	17 14	
	d	16 10	16 16				16 25					16 41		16 46				16 55	17 01				17 10	17 16	
Grangetown	d	16 14	16 20				16 29					16 45		16 50				16 59	17 05				17 14	17 20	
Dingle Road	d		16 26											16 56					17 11					17 26	
Penarth	a		16 31											17 01					17 16					17 31	
Cogan	d	16 18					16 33					16 48						17 03					17 18		
Eastbrook	d	16 20					16 35					16 51						17 05					17 20		
Dinas Powys	d	16 22					16 37					16 53						17 07					17 22		
Cadoxton	d	16 27					16 42					16 57						17 12					17 27		
Barry Docks	d	16 30					16 45					17 00						17 15					17 30		
Barry 3	d	16 34					16 49					17 05						17 19					17 34		
Barry Island	a	16 40					16 55											17 25					17 40		
Rhoose Cardiff Int Airport ✈	d											17 12													
Llantwit Major	d											17 22													
Bridgend	a											17 39													

When events are being held at the Millenium Stadium, services are subject to alteration. Please check times before travelling.

Treherbert, Aberdare, Merthyr, Pontypridd, Rhymney and Coryton - Cardiff, Penarth, Barry, Barry Island and Bridgend

Network Diagram - see first Page of Table 130

		AW	AW	AW	AW		AW	AW	AW	AW	AW	AW	AW	AW	AW		AW	AW	AW	AW	AW	AW	AW	AW	AW
Treherbert	d	16 17										16 47											17 17		
Ynyswen	d	16 19										16 49											17 19		
Treorchy	d	16 21										16 51											17 21		
Ton Pentre	d	16 23										16 53											17 23		
Ystrad Rhondda	a	16 26										16 56											17 26		
	d	16 28										16 58											17 28		
Llwynypia	d	16 30										17 00											17 30		
Tonypandy	d	16 33										17 03											17 33		
Dinas Rhondda	d	16 35										17 05											17 35		
Porth	a	16 38										17 08											17 38		
	d	16 39										17 09											17 39		
Trehafod	d	16 42										17 12											17 42		
Merthyr Tydfil	d								16 38											17 08					
Pentre-bach	d								16 42											17 12					
Troed Y Rhiw	d								16 45											17 15					
Merthyr Vale	a								16 48											17 18					
	d								16 50											17 20					
Quakers Yard	d								16 55											17 25					
Aberdare 3	d			16 22											16 52										17 22
Cwmbach	d			16 25											16 55										17 25
Fernhill	d			16 28											16 58										17 28
Mountain Ash	a			16 31											17 01										17 31
	d			16 34											17 04										17 34
Penrhiwceiber	d			16 37											17 07										17 37
Abercynon	d			16 43					16 59						17 13					17 29					17 43
Pontypridd 3	a	16 47		16 52					17 07			17 17			17 22					17 37			17 47		17 52
	d	16 48		16 54					17 09			17 18			17 24					17 39			17 48		17 54
Trefforest	d	16 51		16 57					17 12			17 21			17 27					17 42			17 51		17 57
Trefforest Estate	d								17 16											17 46					
Taffs Well 3	d	16 58		17 04					17 20			17 28			17 34					17 50			17 58		18 04
Radyr 3	a	17 01		17 07					17 23			17 31			17 37					17 53			18 01		18 07
	d	17 01	17 04	17 07					17 23			17 31	17 34		17 37					17 53			18 01	18 04	18 07
Danescourt	d		17 08										17 38											18 08	
Fairwater	d		17 10										17 40											18 10	
Waun-gron Park	d		17 12										17 42											18 12	
Ninian Park	d		17 15										17 45											18 15	
Llandaf	d	17 04		17 10					17 26			17 34			17 40					17 56			18 04		18 10
Cathays	d	17 09		17 15					17 31			17 39			17 45					18 01			18 09		18 15
Rhymney 3	d				16 29																				
Pontlottyn	d				16 32																				
Tir-phil	d				16 36																				
Brithdir	d				16 39																				
Bargoed	a				16 42																				
	d				16 47						17 02						17 17				17 32				
Gilfach Fargoed	d																17 19								
Pengam	d				16 52						17 07						17 22				17 37				
Hengoed	d				16 55						17 10						17 25				17 40				
Ystrad Mynach 3	d				16 58						17 13						17 28				17 43				
Llanbradach	d				17 03						17 18						17 33				17 48				
Aber	d				17 07						17 22						17 37				17 52				
Caerphilly 3	d				17 10						17 25						17 40				17 55				
Lisvane & Thornhill	d				17 14						17 29						17 44				17 59				
Llanishen	d				17 16						17 31						17 46				18 01				
Heath High Level	d				17 19						17 34						17 49				18 04				
Coryton	d							17 15										17 45							
Whitchurch (Cardiff)	d							17 16										17 46							
Rhiwbina	d							17 18										17 48							
Birchgrove	d							17 20										17 50							
Ty Glas	d							17 21										17 51							
Heath Low Level	d							17 24										17 54							
Cardiff Queen Street 3	a	17 14		17 19	17 24			17 29	17 34		17 39	17 44			17 49		17 54	17 59		18 04	18 09		18 14		18 19
	d	17 16		17 21	17 26		17 24	17 31	17 36	17 36	17 41	17 46		17 48	17 51		17 56	18 01	18 00	18 06	18 11	18 12	18 16		18 21
Cardiff Bay	a						17 28			17 40				17 52					18 04			18 16			
Cardiff Central 7	a	17 22	17 20	17 24	17 29			17 34	17 39		17 44	17 52	17 50		17 54		17 59	18 04		18 09	18 14		18 22	18 20	18 24
	d			17 25	17 31				17 41		17 46				17 55		18 01			18 10	18 16				18 25
Grangetown	d			17 29	17 35				17 45		17 50				17 59		18 05			18 14	18 20				18 29
Dingle Road	d				17 41						17 56						18 11				18 26				
Penarth	a				17 46						18 01						18 16				18 31				
Cogan	d			17 33					17 48						18 03					18 18					18 33
Eastbrook	d			17 35					17 51						18 05					18 20					18 35
Dinas Powys	d			17 37					17 53						18 07					18 22					18 37
Cadoxton	d			17 42					17 57						18 12					18 27					18 42
Barry Docks	d			17 45					18 00						18 15					18 30					18 45
Barry 3	d			17 49					18 05						18 19					18 34					18 49
Barry Island	a			17 55											18 25					18 40					18 55
Rhoose Cardiff Int Airport ✈	d								18 12																
Llantwit Major	d								18 22																
Bridgend	a								18 39																

When events are being held at the Millenium Stadium, services are subject to alteration. Please check times before travelling.

Treherbert, Aberdare, Merthyr, Pontypridd, Rhymney and Coryton - Cardiff, Penarth, Barry, Barry Island and Bridgend

Network Diagram - see first Page of Table 130

		AW	AW	AW	AW	AW	AW	AW	AW	AW	AW	AW	AW	AW	AW	AW	AW	AW	AW	AW	AW	AW
Treherbert	d						17 47									18 17						
Ynyswen	d						17 49									18 19						
Treorchy	d						17 51									18 21						
Ton Pentre	d						17 53									18 23						
Ystrad Rhondda	a						17 56									18 26						
	d						17 58									18 28						
Llwynypia	d						18 00									18 30						
Tonypandy	d						18 03									18 33						
Dinas Rhondda	d						18 05									18 35						
Porth	a						18 08									18 38						
	d						18 09									18 39						
Trehafod	d						18 12									18 42						
Merthyr Tydfil	d				17 38									18 08								18 38
Pentre-bach	d				17 42									18 12								18 42
Troed Y Rhiw	d				17 45									18 15								18 45
Merthyr Vale	a				17 48									18 18								18 48
	d				17 50									18 20								18 50
Quakers Yard	d				17 55									18 25								18 55
Aberdare	d									17 52								18 22				
Cwmbach	d									17 55								18 25				
Fernhill	d									17 58								18 28				
Mountain Ash	a									18 01								18 31				
	d									18 04								18 34				
Penrhiwceiber	d									18 07								18 37				
Abercynon	d				17 59					18 13				18 29				18 43				18 59
Pontypridd	a				18 07		18 17			18 22				18 37		18 47		18 52				19 07
	d				18 09		18 18			18 24				18 39		18 48		18 54				19 09
Trefforest	d				18 12		18 21			18 27				18 42		18 51		18 57				19 12
Trefforest Estate	d				18 16									18 46								19 16
Taffs Well	d				18 20		18 28			18 34				18 50		18 58		19 04				19 20
Radyr	a				18 23		18 31			18 37				18 53		19 01		19 07				19 23
	d				18 23		18 31	18 34		18 37				18 53		19 01	19 04	19 07				19 23
Danescourt	d							18 38									19 08					
Fairwater	d							18 40									19 10					
Waun-gron Park	d							18 42									19 12					
Ninian Park	d							18 45									19 15					
Llandaf	d				18 26		18 34			18 40				18 56		19 04		19 10				19 26
Cathays	d				18 31		18 39			18 45				19 01		19 09		19 15				19 31
Rhymney	d	17 29																				
Pontlottyn	d	17 32																				
Tir-phil	d	17 36																				
Brithdir	d	17 39																				
Bargoed	a	17 42																				
	d	17 47									18 17								18 48			
Gilfach Fargoed	d										18 19								18 50			
Pengam	d	17 52									18 22								18 53			
Hengoed	d	17 55									18 25								18 56			
Ystrad Mynach	d	17 58									18 28								18 59			
Llanbradach	d	18 03									18 33								19 04			
Aber	d	18 07									18 37								19 08			
Caerphilly	d	18 10									18 40								19 11			
Lisvane & Thornhill	d	18 14									18 44								19 15			
Llanishen	d	18 16									18 46								19 17			
Heath High Level	d	18 19									18 49								19 20			
Coryton	d			18 15								18 45									19 15	
Whitchurch (Cardiff)	d			18 16								18 46									19 16	
Rhiwbina	d			18 18								18 48									19 18	
Birchgrove	d			18 20								18 50									19 20	
Ty Glas	d			18 21								18 51									19 21	
Heath Low Level	d			18 24								18 54									19 24	
Cardiff Queen Street	a	18 24		18 29	18 34		18 44			18 49	18 54	18 59		19 04		19 14		19 19	19 24		19 29	19 34
	d	18 26	18 24	18 31	18 36	18 36	18 46		18 48	18 51	18 56	19 01	19 00	19 06	19 12	19 16		19 21	19 26	19 24	19 31	19 36
Cardiff Bay	a		18 28			18 40			18 52				19 04		19 16					19 28		
Cardiff Central	a	18 29		18 34	18 39		18 52	18 50		18 54	18 59	19 06		19 10		19 22	19 22	19 24	19 29		19 34	19 39
	d	18 31			18 41					18 55	19 01							19 25	19 31			19 41
Grangetown	d	18 35			18 45					18 59	19 05							19 29	19 35			19 45
Dingle Road	d	18 41									19 11								19 41			
Penarth	a	18 46									19 16								19 46			
Cogan	d				18 48					19 03								19 33				19 48
Eastbrook	d				18 51					19 05								19 35				19 51
Dinas Powys	d				18 53					19 07								19 37				19 53
Cadoxton	d				18 57					19 12								19 42				19 57
Barry Docks	d				19 00					19 15								19 45				20 00
Barry	d				19 05					19 19								19 49				20 05
Barry Island	a									19 25								19 55				
Rhoose Cardiff Int Airport ✈	d				19 12																	20 12
Llantwit Major	d				19 22																	20 22
Bridgend	a				19 39																	20 39

When events are being held at the Millenium Stadium, services are subject to alteration. Please check times before travelling.

Treherbert, Aberdare, Merthyr, Pontypridd, Rhymney and Coryton - Cardiff, Penarth, Barry, Barry Island and Bridgend

Network Diagram - see first Page of Table 130

		AW	AW	AW	AW	AW	AW	AW	AW	AW	AW	AW	AW	AW	AW	AW	AW	AW	AW	AW	AW	AW	AW
Treherbert	d		18 47						19 17							19 47					
Ynyswen	d		18 49						19 19							19 49					
Treorchy	d		18 51						19 21							19 51					
Ton Pentre	d		18 53						19 23							19 53					
Ystrad Rhondda	a		18 56						19 26							19 56					
	d		18 58						19 28							19 58					
Llwynypia	d		19 00						19 30							20 00					
Tonypandy	d		19 03						19 33							20 03					
Dinas Rhondda	d		19 05						19 35							20 05					
Porth	a		19 08						19 38							20 08					
	d		19 09						19 39							20 09					
Trehafod	d		19 12						19 42							20 12					
Merthyr Tydfil	d							19 08							19 38								
Pentre-bach	d							19 12							19 42								
Troed Y Rhiw	d							19 15							19 45								
Merthyr Vale	a							19 18							19 48								
	d							19 20							19 50								
Quakers Yard	d							19 25							19 55								
Aberdare	d				18 52															19 52			
Cwmbach	d				18 55															19 55			
Fernhill	d				18 58															19 58			
Mountain Ash	a				19 01															20 01			
	d				19 04															20 04			
Penrhiwceiber	d				19 07															20 07			
Abercynon	d				19 13			19 29				19 43			19 59					20 13			
Pontypridd	a		19 17		19 22			19 37		19 47		19 52			20 07			20 18		20 22			
	d		19 18		19 24			19 39		19 48		19 54			20 09			20 18		20 24			
Trefforest	d		19 21		19 27			19 42		19 51		19 57			20 12			20 21		20 27			
Trefforest Estate	d							19 46							20 16								
Taffs Well	d		19 28		19 34			19 50		19 58		20 04			20 20			20 28		20 34			
Radyr	a		19 31		19 37			19 53		20 01		20 07			20 23			20 31		20 37			
	d		19 31		19 37			19 53		20 01	20 04	20 07			20 23			20 31		20 37			
Danescourt	d										20 08												
Fairwater	d										20 10												
Waun-gron Park	d										20 12												
Ninian Park	d										20 15												
Llandaf	d		19 34		19 40			19 56		20 04		20 10			20 26			20 34		20 40			
Cathays	d		19 39		19 45			20 01		20 09		20 15			20 31			20 39		20 45			
Rhymney	d																19 45						
Pontlottyn	d																19 48						
Tir-phil	d																19 52						
Brithdir	d																19 55						
Bargoed	a																19 58						
	d																19 59						
Gilfach Fargoed	d																20 01						
Pengam	d																20 04						
Hengoed	d																20 07						
Ystrad Mynach	d																20 10						
Llanbradach	d																20 15						
Aber	d																20 19						
Caerphilly	d					19 40											20 22				20 40		
Lisvane & Thornhill	d					19 44											20 26				20 44		
Llanishen	d					19 46											20 28				20 46		
Heath High Level	d					19 49											20 31				20 49		
Coryton	d													20 15									
Whitchurch (Cardiff)	d													20 16									
Rhiwbina	d													20 18									
Birchgrove	d													20 20									
Ty Glas	d													20 21									
Heath Low Level	d													20 24									
Cardiff Queen Street	a		19 44		19 49	19 54		20 04		20 14		20 19		20 29	20 34		20 39	20 44		20 49	20 54		
	d	19 36	19 46	19 48	19 51	19 56	20 00	20 06	20 12	20 16		20 21	20 24	20 31	20 36	20 36	20 41	20 46	20 48	20 51	20 56	21 00	21 12
Cardiff Bay	a	19 40		19 52			20 04		20 16				20 28			20 40			20 52			21 04	21 16
Cardiff Central	a		19 52		19 57	19 59		20 09		20 22	20 24	20 24		20 34	20 39		20 47	20 52		20 57	20 59		
	d					20 06		20 10				20 31			20 41					21 06	21 10		
Grangetown	d					20 10		20 14				20 35			20 45					21 10	21 14		
Dingle Road	d					20 14						20 41								21 14			
Penarth	a					20 19						20 46								21 19			
Cogan	d							20 18							20 48						21 18		
Eastbrook	d							20 20							20 51						21 20		
Dinas Powys	d							20 22							20 53						21 22		
Cadoxton	d							20 27							20 57						21 27		
Barry Docks	d							20 30							21 00						21 30		
Barry	d							20 34							21 05						21 34		
Barry Island	a							20 40													21 40		
Rhoose Cardiff Int Airport ✈	d														21 12								
Llantwit Major	d														21 22								
Bridgend	a														21 39								

When events are being held at the Millenium Stadium, services are subject to alteration. Please check times before travelling.

Table 130

Mondays to Fridays
until 14 September

Treherbert, Aberdare, Merthyr, Pontypridd, Rhymney and Coryton - Cardiff, Penarth, Barry, Barry Island and Bridgend

Network Diagram - see first Page of Table 130

		AW	AW		AW	AW	AW	AW	AW FO	AW FX	AW	AW	AW		AW	AW	AW	AW	AW	AW	AW	AW	AW FX		AW FO
Treherbert	d	20 17																	21 17						
Ynyswen	d	20 19																	21 19						
Treorchy	d	20 21																	21 21						
Ton Pentre	d	20 23																	21 23						
Ystrad Rhondda	a	20 26																	21 26						
	d	20 28																	21 28						
Llwynypia	d	20 30																	21 30						
Tonypandy	d	20 33																	21 33						
Dinas Rhondda	d	20 35																	21 35						
Porth	a	20 38																	21 38						
	d	20 39																	21 39						
Trehafod	d	20 42																	21 42						
Merthyr Tydfil	d								20 38	20 38													21 38		21 38
Pentre-bach	d								20 42	20 42													21 42		21 42
Troed Y Rhiw	d								20 45	20 45													21 45		21 45
Merthyr Vale	a								20 48	20 48													21 48		21 48
	d								20 50	20 50													21 50		21 50
Quakers Yard	d								20 55	20 55													21 55		21 55
Aberdare ■	d				20 22										20 54										
Cwmbach	d				20 25										20 57										
Fernhill	d				20 28										21 00										
Mountain Ash	a				20 31										21 03										
	d				20 34										21 04										
Penrhiwceiber	d				20 37										21 07										
Abercynon	d				20 43				20 59	20 59					21 13								21 59		21 59
Pontypridd ■	a	20 47			20 52				21 07	21 07					21 22				21 47				22 07		22 07
	d	20 48			20 54				21 09	21 09					21 24				21 48				22 09		22 09
Trefforest	d	20 51			20 57				21 12	21 12					21 27				21 51				22 12		22 12
Trefforest Estate	d								21 16	21 16													22 16		22 16
Taffs Well ■	d	20 58			21 04				21 20	21 20					21 34				21 58				22 20		22 20
Radyr ■	a	21 01			21 07				21 23	21 23					21 37				22 01				22 23		22 23
	d	21 01	21 04		21 07				21 23	21 23					21 37				22 01	22 04			22 23		22 23
Danescourt	d		21 08																	22 08					
Fairwater	d		21 10																	22 10					
Waun-gron Park	d		21 12																	22 12					
Ninian Park	d		21 15																	22 15					
Llandaf	d	21 04			21 10				21 26	21 26					21 40				22 04				22 26		22 26
Cathays	d	21 09			21 15				21 31	21 31					21 45				22 09				22 31		22 31
Rhymney ■	d											20 48									21 33				
Pontlottyn	d											20 51									21 36				
Tir-phil	d											20 55									21 40				
Brithdir	d											20 58									21 43				
Bargoed	a											21 01									21 46				
	d											21 02									21 47				
Gilfach Fargoed	d											21 04									21 49				
Pengam	d											21 07									21 52				
Hengoed	d											21 10									21 55				
Ystrad Mynach ■	d											21 13					21 39				21 58				
Llanbradach	d											21 18					21 44				22 03				
Aber	d											21 22					21 48				22 07				
Caerphilly ■	d											21 25					21 51				22 10				
Lisvane & Thornhill	d											21 29					21 55				22 14				
Llanishen	d											21 31					21 57				22 16				
Heath High Level	d											21 34					22 00				22 19				
Coryton	d							21 15																	
Whitchurch (Cardiff)	d							21 16																	
Rhiwbina	d							21 18																	
Birchgrove	d							21 20																	
Ty Glas	d							21 21																	
Heath Low Level	d							21 24																	
Cardiff Queen Street ■	a	21 14			21 19			21 29	21 34	21 34		21 42			21 49		22 05		22 14		22 24		22 34		22 34
	d	21 16			21 21	21 24		21 31	21 36	21 36	21 36	21 44	21 48		21 51	22 00	22 06	22 12	22 16		22 26	22 24	22 36		22 36
Cardiff Bay	a					21 28					21 40		21 52			22 04		22 16				22 28			
Cardiff Central ■	a	21 22	21 25		21 27			21 34	21 39	21 39		21 47			21 54		22 09		22 22	22 20	22 29		22 39		22 39
	d						21 31		21 41	21 41					21 56		22 10				22 31		22 41		22 41
Grangetown	d						21 35		21 45	21 45					22 00		22 14				22 35		22 45		22 45
Dingle Road	d						21 41								22 04						22 41				
Penarth	a						21 46								22 09						22 46				
Cogan	d								21 48	21 48							22 18						22 48		22 48
Eastbrook	d								21 51	21 51							22 20						22 51		22 51
Dinas Powys	d								21 53	21 53							22 22						22 53		22 53
Cadoxton	d								21 57	21 57							22 27						22 57		22 57
Barry Docks	d								22 00	22 00							22 30						23 00		23 00
Barry ■	d								22 05	22 05							22 34						23a05		23 05
Barry Island	a																22 40								
Rhoose Cardiff Int Airport ✈	d								22 12	22 12															23 12
Llantwit Major	d								22 22	22 22															23 22
Bridgend	a								22 39	22 40															23 39

When events are being held at the Millenium Stadium, services are subject to alteration. Please check times before travelling.

Table 130

Mondays to Fridays
until 14 September

Treherbert, Aberdare, Merthyr, Pontypridd, Rhymney and Coryton - Cardiff, Penarth, Barry, Barry Island and Bridgend

Network Diagram - see first Page of Table 130

		AW	AW	AW	AW	AW	AW	AW	AW FX ═		AW	AW	AW A	AW B	AW	AW	AW
Treherbert	d																
Ynyswen	d																
Treorchy	d																
Ton Pentre	d																
Ystrad Rhondda	a																
	d																
Llwynypia	d																
Tonypandy	d																
Dinas Rhondda	d																
Porth	a																
	d																
Trehafod	d																
Merthyr Tydfil	d												22 38	22 38			
Pentre-bach	d												22 42	22 42			
Troed Y Rhiw	d												22 45	22 45			
Merthyr Vale	a												22 48	22 48			
	d												22 50	22 50			
Quakers Yard	d												22 55	22 55			
Aberdare ■	d				21 54										22 54		
Cwmbach	d				21 57										22 57		
Fernhill	d				22 00										23 00		
Mountain Ash	a				22 03										23 03		
	d				22 04										23 04		
Penrhiwceiber	d				22 07										23 07		
Abercynon	d				22 13								22 59	22 59	23 13		
Pontypridd ■	a				22 22								23 07	23 07	23 22		
	d				22 24								23 09	23 09			
Trefforest	d				22 27								23 12	23 12			
Trefforest Estate	d												23 16	23 16			
Taffs Well ■	d				22 34								23 20	23 20			
Radyr ■	a				22 37								23 23	23 23			
	d				22 37						23 10		23 23	23 23			
Danescourt	d																
Fairwater	d																
Waun-gron Park	d																
Ninian Park	d																
Llandaf	d				22 40						23 12		23 26	23 26			
Cathays	d				22 45						23 16		23 31	23 31			
Rhymney ■	d																
Pontlottyn	d																
Tir-phil	d																
Brithdir	d																
Bargoed	a																
	d																
Gilfach Fargoed	d																
Pengam	d																
Hengoed	d																
Ystrad Mynach ■	d																
Llanbradach	d																
Aber	d																
Caerphilly ■	d		22 28														
Lisvane & Thornhill	d																
Llanishen	d																
Heath High Level	d																
Coryton	d					22 45											
Whitchurch (Cardiff)	d					22 46											
Rhiwbina	d					22 48											
Birchgrove	d					22 50											
Ty Glas	d					22 51											
Heath Low Level	d					22 54											
Cardiff Queen Street ■	a		22 39		22 49	22 59					23 20		23 34	23 34			
	d	22 36	22 39	22 48	22 54	23 01	23 00	23 12			23 20	23 24	23 36	23 36		23 36	23 48
Cardiff Bay	a	22 40		22 52			23 04	23 16				23 28				23 40	23 52
Cardiff Central ■	a		22 43		23 00	23 06					23 25		23 39	23 42			
	d				23 12						23 30		23 41				
Grangetown	d				23 16						23 34		23 45				
Dingle Road	d				23 20												
Penarth	a				23 25												
Cogan	d										23 37		23 48				
Eastbrook	d										23 40		23 51				
Dinas Powys	d										23 42		23 54				
Cadoxton	d										23 46		23 58				
Barry Docks	d										23 49		00 03				
Barry ■	d								23 15		23 54		00 08				
Barry Island	a										00 01						
Rhoose Cardiff Int Airport ✈	d								23 30				00 15				
Llantwit Major	d								23 45				00 25				
Bridgend	a								00 10				00 43				

A 25 July, 26 July, 1 August, 10 August

B not 25 July, 26 July, 1 August, 10 August

When events are being held at the Millenium Stadium, services are subject to alteration. Please check times before travelling.

Treherbert, Aberdare, Merthyr, Pontypridd, Rhymney and Coryton - Cardiff, Penarth, Barry, Barry Island and Bridgend

Network Diagram - see first Page of Table 130

		AW MX	AW MX	AW	AW	AW	AW	AW	AW	AW		AW	AW	AW	AW	AW	AW	AW	AW	AW		AW	AW	AW	AW
Treherbert	d													05 47								06 17			
Ynyswen	d													05 49								06 19			
Treorchy	d													05 51								06 21			
Ton Pentre	d													05 53								06 23			
Ystrad Rhondda	a													05 56								06 26			
	d													05 58								06 28			
Llwynypia	d													06 00								06 30			
Tonypandy	d													06 03								06 33			
Dinas Rhondda	d													06 05								06 35			
Porth	a													06 08								06 38			
	d													06 09								06 39			
Trehafod	d													06 12								06 42			
Merthyr Tydfil	d																								
Pentre-bach	d																								
Troed Y Rhiw	d																								
Merthyr Vale	a																								
	d																								
Quakers Yard	d																								
Aberdare 3	d																								06 21
Cwmbach	d																								06 24
Fernhill	d																								06 28
Mountain Ash	a																								06 31
	d																								06 34
Penrhiwceiber	d																								06 38
Abercynon	d																								06 44
Pontypridd 3	a													06 17								06 47			06 52
	d						05 24							06 18								06 48			06 54
Trefforest	d						05 27							06 21								06 51			06 57
Trefforest Estate	d						05 31																		
Taffs Well 3	d						05 34							06 28								06 58	06 53		07 04
Radyr 3	a						05 37							06 31								07 01	06 56		07 07
	d		23p10				05 37							06 31								07 01	07 04		07 07
Danescourt	d																						07 08		
Fairwater	d																						07 10		
Waun-gron Park	d																						07 12		
Ninian Park	d																						07 15		
Llandaf	d		23p12				05 40							06 34								07 04			07 10
Cathays	d		23p16				05 45							06 39								07 09			07 15
Rhymney 3	d																			06 10					
Pontlottyn	d																			06 13					
Tir-phil	d																			06 17					
Brithdir	d																			06 20					
Bargoed	a																			06 23					
	d																			06 27					
Gilfach Fargoed	d																			06 29					
Pengam	d																			06 32					
Hengoed	d																			06 35					
Ystrad Mynach 3	d																			06 38					
Llanbradach	d																			06 43					
Aber	d																			06 47					
Caerphilly 3	d											06 10								06 50					
Lisvane & Thornhill	d											06 14								06 54					
Llanishen	d											06 16								06 56					
Heath High Level	d											06 19								06 59					
Coryton	d																		06 45						
Whitchurch (Cardiff)	d																		06 46						
Rhiwbina	d																		06 48						
Birchgrove	d																		06 50						
Ty Glas	d																		06 51						
Heath Low Level	d																		06 54						
Cardiff Queen Street 3	a		23p19				05 51					06 25		06 42					06 59	07 04		07 12			07 19
	d		23p20				05 51					06 26	06 36	06 43	06 48		07 00		07 01	07 06		07 13		07 12	07 21
Cardiff Bay	a												06 40		06 52		07 04							07 16	
Cardiff Central 7	a		23p25				05 54					06 29		06 48					07 05	07 09		07 16	07 20		07 24
	d		23p30	05 20	05 41	05 46	05 55	06 16	06 25	06 36		06 41				06 55		07 01		07 10		07 16			07 25
Grangetown	d		23p34	05 24	05 45	05 50	05 59	06 20	06 29	06 40		06 45				06 59		07 05		07 14		07 20			07 29
Dingle Road	d					05 54		06 24		06 44								07 11				07 26			
Penarth	a					06 00		06 30		06 50								07 17				07 32			
Cogan	d		23p37	05 28	05 48		06 03		06 33			06 48				07 03				07 18					07 33
Eastbrook	d		23p40	05 30	05 51		06 05		06 35			06 51				07 05				07 20					07 35
Dinas Powys	d		23p42	05 32	05 53		06 07		06 37			06 53				07 07				07 22					07 37
Cadoxton	d		23p46	05 37	05 57		06 12		06 42			06 57				07 12				07 27					07 42
Barry Docks	d		23p49	05 40	06 00		06 15		06 45			07 00				07 15				07 30					07 45
Barry 3	d	23p15	23p54	05 44	06 05		06 19		06 49			07 05				07 19				07 34					07 49
Barry Island	a		00 01	05 51			06 26		06 56							07 26				07 41					07 56
Rhoose Cardiff Int Airport ✈	d	23p30			06 12							07 12													
Llantwit Major	d	23p45			06 22							07 22													
Bridgend	a	00 10			06 40							07 40													

When events are being held at the Millenium Stadium, services are subject to alteration. Please check times before travelling.

Treherbert, Aberdare, Merthyr, Pontypridd, Rhymney and Coryton - Cardiff, Penarth, Barry, Barry Island and Bridgend

Network Diagram - see first Page of Table 130

		AW	AW	AW	AW	AW		AW	AW	AW	AW	AW	AW	AW	AW	AW		AW	AW	AW	AW	AW	AW	AW	AW
Treherbert	d								06 47											07 17					
Ynyswen	d								06 49											07 19					
Treorchy	d								06 51											07 21					
Ton Pentre	d								06 53											07 23					
Ystrad Rhondda	a								06 56											07 26					
	d								06 58											07 28					
Llwynypia	d								07 00											07 30					
Tonypandy	d								07 03											07 33					
Dinas Rhondda	d								07 05											07 35					
Porth	a								07 08											07 38					
	d								07 09											07 39					
Trehafod	d								07 12											07 42					
Merthyr Tydfil	d				06 38											07 08									
Pentre-bach	d				06 42											07 12									
Troed Y Rhiw	d				06 45											07 15									
Merthyr Vale	a				06 48											07 18									
	d				06 50											07 20									
Quakers Yard	d				06 55											07 25									
Aberdare 3	d											06 51										07 21			
Cwmbach	d											06 54										07 24			
Fernhill	d											06 58										07 28			
Mountain Ash	a											07 01										07 31			
	d											07 04										07 34			
Penrhiwceiber	d											07 08										07 38			
Abercynon	d				06 59							07 14				07 29						07 44			
Pontypridd 3	a				07 07				07 17			07 22				07 37				07 47		07 52			
	d				07 09				07 18			07 24				07 39				07 48		07 54			
Trefforest	d				07 12				07 21			07 27				07 42				07 51		07 57			
Trefforest Estate	d				07 16											07 46									
Taffs Well 3	d				07 20				07 28			07 34				07 50				07 58		08 04			
Radyr 3	a				07 23				07 31			07 37				07 53				08 01		08 07			
	d				07 23				07 31	07 34		07 37				07 53				08 01	08 04	08 07			
Danescourt	d									07 38											08 08				
Fairwater	d									07 40											08 10				
Waun-gron Park	d									07 42											08 12				
Ninian Park	d									07 45											08 15				
Llandaf	d				07 26				07 34			07 40				07 56				08 04		08 10			
Cathays	d				07 31				07 39			07 45				08 01				08 09		08 15			
Rhymney 3	d	06 34											07 02										07 24		
Pontlottyn	d	06 37											07 05										07 27		
Tir-phil	d	06 41											07 09										07 31		
Brithdir	d	06 44											07 12										07 34		
Bargoed	a	06 47											07 15										07 37		
	d	06 48						07 02					07 17					07 32					07 45		
Gilfach Fargoed	d							07 04					07 19										07 47		
Pengam	d	06 52						07 07					07 22					07 37					07 50		
Hengoed	d	06 56						07 10					07 25					07 40					07 54		
Ystrad Mynach 3	d	06 58						07 13					07 28					07 43					07 57		
Llanbradach	d	07 03						07 18					07 33					07 48					08 02		
Aber	d	07 07						07 22					07 37					07 52					08 07		
Caerphilly 3	d	07 10						07 25					07 40					07 55					08 10		
Lisvane & Thornhill	d	07 14						07 29					07 44					07 59					08 14		
Llanishen	d	07 16						07 31					07 46					08 01					08 16		
Heath High Level	d	07 19						07 34					07 49					08 04					08 19		
Coryton	d			07 15										07 45											08 15
Whitchurch (Cardiff)	d			07 16										07 46											08 16
Rhiwbina	d			07 18										07 48											08 18
Birchgrove	d			07 20										07 50											08 20
Ty Glas	d			07 21										07 51											08 21
Heath Low Level	d			07 24										07 54											08 24
Cardiff Queen Street 3	a	07 24		07 29	07 34			07 39	07 44			07 49	07 54	07 59		08 04		08 09		08 14		08 19	08 24		08 29
	d	07 26	07 24	07 31	07 36	07 36		07 41	07 46		07 48	07 51	07 56	08 01	08 00	08 06		08 11	08 12	08 16		08 21	08 26	08 24	08 31
Cardiff Bay	a		07 28			07 40					07 52				08 04				08 16					08 28	
Cardiff Central 7	a	07 29		07 34	07 39			07 44	07 53	07 50		07 54	07 59	08 04		08 09		08 14		08 23	08 20	08 24	08 29		08 34
	d	07 31			07 41			07 46				07 55	08 01			08 10		08 16				08 25	08 31		
Grangetown	d	07 35			07 45			07 50				07 59	08 05			08 14		08 20				08 29	08 35		
Dingle Road	d	07 41						07 56					08 11					08 26					08 41		
Penarth	a	07 47						08 02					08 17					08 32					08 47		
Cogan	d				07 48							08 03				08 18						08 33			
Eastbrook	d				07 51							08 05				08 20						08 35			
Dinas Powys	d				07 53							08 07				08 22						08 37			
Cadoxton	d				07 57							08 12				08 27						08 42			
Barry Docks	d				08 00							08 15				08 30						08 45			
Barry 3	d				08 05							08 19				08 34						08 49			
Barry Island	a											08 26				08 41						08 56			
Rhoose Cardiff Int Airport ✈	d				08 12																				
Llantwit Major	d				08 22																				
Bridgend	a				08 40																				

When events are being held at the Millenium Stadium, services are subject to alteration. Please check times before travelling.

Table 130

Mondays to Fridays
from 17 September

Treherbert, Aberdare, Merthyr, Pontypridd, Rhymney and Coryton - Cardiff, Penarth, Barry, Barry Island and Bridgend

Network Diagram - see first Page of Table 130

		AW		AW	AW	AW	AW	AW	AW	AW	AW	AW		AW	AW	AW	AW	AW	AW	AW	AW	AW		AW	AW
Treherbert	d					07 45											08 17								
Ynyswen	d					07 47											08 19								
Treorchy	d					07 49											08 21								
Ton Pentre	d					07 51											08 23								
Ystrad Rhondda	a					07 54											08 26								
	d					07 58											08 28								
Llwynypia	d					08 00											08 30								
Tonypandy	d					08 03											08 33								
Dinas Rhondda	d					08 05											08 35								
Porth	a					08 08											08 38								
	d					08 09											08 39								
Trehafod	d					08 12											08 42								
Merthyr Tydfil	d	07 38												08 08										08 38	
Pentre-bach	d	07 42												08 12										08 42	
Troed Y Rhiw	d	07 45												08 15										08 45	
Merthyr Vale	a	07 48												08 18										08 48	
	d	07 50												08 20										08 50	
Quakers Yard	d	07 55												08 25										08 55	
Aberdare ■	d								07 51										08 21						
Cwmbach	d								07 54										08 24						
Fernhill	d								07 58										08 28						
Mountain Ash	a								08 01										08 31						
	d								08 04										08 34						
Penrhiwceiber	d								08 08										08 38						
Abercynon	d	07 59							08 14					08 29					08 44					08 59	
Pontypridd ■	a	08 07				08 17			08 22					08 37			08 47		08 52					09 07	
	d	08 09				08 18			08 24					08 39			08 48		08 54					09 09	
Trefforest	d	08 12				08 21			08 27					08 42			08 51		08 57					09 12	
Trefforest Estate	d	08 16												08 46										09 16	
Taffs Well ■	d	08 20				08 28			08 34					08 50			08 58		09 04					09 20	
Radyr ■	a	08 23				08 31			08 37					08 53			09 01		09 07					09 23	
	d	08 23				08 31	08 34		08 37					08 53			09 01	09 04	09 07					09 23	
Danescourt	d						08 38											09 08							
Fairwater	d						08 40											09 10							
Waun-gron Park	d						08 42											09 12							
Ninian Park	d						08 45											09 15							
Llandaf	d	08 26				08 34			08 40					08 56			09 04		09 10					09 26	
Cathays	d	08 31				08 39			08 45					09 01			09 09		09 15					09 31	
Rhymney ■	d				07 44															08 30					
Pontlottyn	d				07 47															08 33					
Tir-phil	d				07 51															08 37					
Brithdir	d				07 54															08 40					
Bargoed	a				08 00															08 44					
	d				08 02					08 17					08 32					08 47					
Gilfach Fargoed	d									08 19															
Pengam	d				08 07					08 22					08 37					08 52					
Hengoed	d				08 10					08 25					08 40					08 55					
Ystrad Mynach ■	d				08 13					08 28					08 43					08 58					
Llanbradach	d				08 18					08 33					08 48					09 03					
Aber	d				08 22					08 37					08 52					09 07					
Caerphilly ■	d				08 25					08 40					08 55					09 10					
Lisvane & Thornhill	d				08 29					08 44					08 59					09 14					
Llanishen	d				08 31					08 46					09 01					09 16					
Heath High Level	d				08 34					08 49					09 04					09 19					
Coryton	d										08 45											09 15			
Whitchurch (Cardiff)	d										08 46											09 16			
Rhiwbina	d										08 48											09 18			
Birchgrove	d										08 50											09 20			
Ty Glas	d										08 51											09 21			
Heath Low Level	d										08 54											09 24			
Cardiff Queen Street ■	a	08 34			08 39	08 44			08 49	08 54	08 59			09 04	09 09		09 14		09 19	09 24		09 29		09 34	
	d	08 36		08 36	08 41	08 46		08 48	08 51	08 56	09 01	09 00		09 06	09 11	09 12	09 16		09 21	09 26	09 24	09 31		09 36	09 36
Cardiff Bay	a			08 40				08 52				09 04				09 16					09 28				09 40
Cardiff Central ■	a	08 39			08 48	08 53	08 50		08 54	08 59	09 04			09 09	09 14		09 23	09 20	09 24	09 29		09 34		09 39	
	d	08 41							08 55	09 01				09 10	09 16				09 25	09 31				09 41	
Grangetown	d	08 45							08 59	09 05				09 14	09 20				09 29	09 35				09 45	
Dingle Road	d									09 11					09 26					09 41					
Penarth	a									09 17					09 32					09 47					
Cogan	d	08 48							09 03					09 18					09 33					09 48	
Eastbrook	d	08 51							09 05					09 20					09 35					09 51	
Dinas Powys	d	08 53							09 07					09 22					09 37					09 53	
Cadoxton	d	08 57							09 12					09 27					09 42					09 57	
Barry Docks	d	08 59							09 15					09 30					09 45					09 59	
Barry ■	d	09 03							09 19					09 34					09 49					10 03	
Barry Island	a								09 26					09 41					09 56						
Rhoose Cardiff Int Airport ✈	d	09 10																						10 10	
Llantwit Major	d	09 19																						10 19	
Bridgend	a	09 37																						10 37	

When events are being held at the Millenium Stadium, services are subject to alteration. Please check times before travelling.

Table 130

Mondays to Fridays
from 17 September

Treherbert, Aberdare, Merthyr, Pontypridd, Rhymney and Coryton - Cardiff, Penarth, Barry, Barry Island and Bridgend

Network Diagram - see first Page of Table 130

		AW	AW	AW	AW	AW	AW	AW		AW	AW	AW	AW	AW	AW	AW	AW	AW		AW	AW	AW	AW	AW	AW
Treherbert	d		08 47											09 17										09 47	
Ynyswen	d		08 49											09 19										09 49	
Treorchy	d		08 51											09 21										09 51	
Ton Pentre	d		08 53											09 23										09 53	
Ystrad Rhondda	a		08 56											09 26										09 56	
	d		08 58											09 28										09 58	
Llwynypia	d		09 00											09 30										10 00	
Tonypandy	d		09 03											09 33										10 03	
Dinas Rhondda	d		09 05											09 35										10 05	
Porth	a		09 08											09 38										10 08	
	d		09 09											09 39										10 09	
Trehafod	d		09 12											09 42										10 12	
Merthyr Tydfil	d										09 08										09 38				
Pentre-bach	d										09 12										09 42				
Troed Y Rhiw	d										09 15										09 45				
Merthyr Vale	a										09 18										09 48				
	d										09 20										09 50				
Quakers Yard	d										09 25										09 55				
Aberdare ■	d					08 51										09 21									
Cwmbach	d					08 54										09 24									
Fernhill	d					08 58										09 28									
Mountain Ash	a					09 01										09 31									
	d					09 04										09 34									
Penrhiwceiber	d					09 08										09 38									
Abercynon	d					09 14					09 29					09 44					09 59				
Pontypridd ■	a		09 17			09 22					09 37			09 47		09 52					10 07			10 17	
	d		09 18			09 24					09 39			09 48		09 54					10 09			10 18	
Trefforest	d		09 21			09 27					09 42			09 51		09 57					10 12			10 21	
Trefforest Estate	d										09 46										10 16				
Taffs Well ■	d		09 28			09 34					09 50			09 58		10 04					10 20			10 28	
Radyr ■	a		09 31			09 37					09 53			10 01		10 07					10 23			10 31	
	d		09 31	09 34		09 37					09 53			10 01	10 04	10 07					10 23			10 31	10 34
Danescourt	d			09 38											10 08										10 38
Fairwater	d			09 40											10 10										10 40
Waun-gron Park	d			09 42											10 12										10 42
Ninian Park	d			09 45											10 15										10 45
Llandaf	d		09 34			09 40					09 56			10 04		10 10					10 26			10 34	
Cathays	d		09 39			09 45					10 01			10 09		10 15					10 31			10 39	
Rhymney ■	d																09 25								
Pontlottyn	d																09 28								
Tir-phil	d																09 32								
Brithdir	d																09 35								
Bargoed	a																09 38								
	d	09 02										09 25					09 40						10 02		
Gilfach Fargoed	d											09 27													
Pengam	d	09 07										09 30					09 45						10 07		
Hengoed	d	09 10										09 33					09 49						10 10		
Ystrad Mynach ■	d	09 13					09 28					09 43					09 54						10 13		
Llanbradach	d	09 18					09 33					09 48					09 59						10 18		
Aber	d	09 22					09 37					09 52					10 04						10 22		
Caerphilly ■	d	09 25					09 40					09 55					10 10						10 25		
Lisvane & Thornhill	d	09 29					09 44					09 59					10 14						10 29		
Llanishen	d	09 31					09 46					10 01					10 16						10 31		
Heath High Level	d	09 34					09 49					10 04					10 19						10 34		
Coryton	d							09 45												10 15					
Whitchurch (Cardiff)	d							09 46												10 16					
Rhiwbina	d							09 48												10 18					
Birchgrove	d							09 50												10 20					
Ty Glas	d							09 51												10 21					
Heath Low Level	d							09 54												10 24					
Cardiff Queen Street ■	a	09 39	09 44			09 49	09 54	09 59			10 04	10 09		10 14		10 19	10 24			10 29	10 34		10 39	10 44	
	d	09 41	09 46		09 48	09 51	09 56	10 01		10 00	10 06	10 11	10 12	10 16		10 21	10 26	10 24		10 31	10 36	10 36	10 41	10 46	
Cardiff Bay	a				09 52					10 04			10 16					10 28				10 40			
Cardiff Central ■	a	09 44	09 53	09 50		09 54	09 59	10 04			10 09	10 14		10 23	10 20	10 24	10 29			10 34	10 39		10 44	10 53	10 50
	d	09 46				09 55	10 01				10 10	10 16				10 25	10 31				10 41		10 46		
Grangetown	d	09 50				09 59	10 05				10 14	10 20				10 29	10 35				10 45		10 50		
Dingle Road	d	09 56					10 11					10 26					10 41						10 56		
Penarth	a	10 02					10 17					10 32					10 47						11 02		
Cogan	d					10 03					10 18					10 33					10 48				
Eastbrook	d					10 05					10 20					10 35					10 51				
Dinas Powys	d					10 07					10 22					10 37					10 53				
Cadoxton	d					10 12					10 27					10 42					10 57				
Barry Docks	d					10 15					10 30					10 45					11 00				
Barry ■	d					10 19					10 34					10 49					11 05				
Barry Island	a					10 26					10 41					10 56									
Rhoose Cardiff Int Airport ✈	d																				11 12				
Llantwit Major	d																				11 22				
Bridgend	a																				11 40				

When events are being held at the Millenium Stadium, services are subject to alteration. Please check times before travelling.

Table 130

Mondays to Fridays

from 17 September

Treherbert, Aberdare, Merthyr, Pontypridd, Rhymney and Coryton - Cardiff, Penarth, Barry, Barry Island and Bridgend

Network Diagram - see first Page of Table 130

		AW	AW	AW		AW	AW	AW	AW	AW	AW	AW	AW	AW		AW	AW	AW	AW	AW	AW	AW	AW	AW
Treherbert	d															10 17						10 47		
Ynyswen	d															10 19						10 49		
Treorchy	d															10 21						10 51		
Ton Pentre	d															10 23						10 53		
Ystrad Rhondda	a															10 26						10 56		
	d															10 28						10 58		
Llwynypia	d															10 30						11 00		
Tonypandy	d															10 33						11 03		
Dinas Rhondda	d															10 35						11 05		
Porth	a															10 38						11 08		
	d															10 52						11 09		
Trehafod	d															10 55						11 12		
Merthyr Tydfil	d			10 04															10 38					
Pentre-bach	d			10 08															10 42					
Troed Y Rhiw	d			10 11															10 45					
Merthyr Vale	a			10 14															10 48					
	d			10 16															10 50					
Quakers Yard	d			10 22															10 55					
Aberdare 3	d		09 51										10 21											
Cwmbach	d		09 54										10 24											
Fernhill	d		09 58										10 28											
Mountain Ash	a		10 01										10 31											
	d		10 04										10 34											
Penrhiwceiber	d		10 08										10 38											
Abercynon	d		10 14	10 26									10 44						10 59					
Pontypridd 3	a		10 22	10 32									10 52			11 00			11 07					
	d		10 24						10 39				10 54			11 04			11 09			11 17		
Trefforest	d		10 27						10 42				10 57			11 07			11 12			11 18		
Trefforest Estate	d																		11 16					
Taffs Well 3	d		10 34						10 50				11 04			11 13			11 20			11 28		
Radyr 3	a		10 37						10 53				11 07			11 17			11 23			11 31		
	d		10 37						10 53		11 04		11 07			11 17			11 23			11 31	11 34	
Danescourt	d										11 08												11 38	
Fairwater	d										11 10												11 40	
Waun-gron Park	d										11 12												11 42	
Ninian Park	d										11 15												11 45	
Llandaf	d		10 40						10 56				11 10						11 26			11 34		
Cathays	d		10 45						11 01				11 15						11 31			11 39		
Rhymney 3	d													10 25										
Pontlottyn	d													10 28										
Tir-phil	d													10 32										
Brithdir	d													10 35										
Bargoed	a													10 38										
	d									10 25				10 40							11 02			
Gilfach Fargoed	d									10 27														
Pengam	d									10 30				10 45							11 07			
Hengoed	d									10 33				10 49							11 10			
Ystrad Mynach 3	d					10 28				10 43				10 54							11 13			
Llanbradach	d					10 33				10 48				10 59							11 18			
Aber	d					10 37				10 52				11 04							11 22			
Caerphilly 3	d					10 40				10 55				11 10							11 25			
Lisvane & Thornhill	d					10 44				10 59				11 14							11 29			
Llanishen	d					10 46				11 01				11 16							11 31			
Heath High Level	d					10 49				11 04				11 19							11 34			
Coryton	d						10 45											11 15						
Whitchurch (Cardiff)	d						10 46											11 16						
Rhiwbina	d						10 48											11 18						
Birchgrove	d						10 50											11 20						
Ty Glas	d						10 51											11 21						
Heath Low Level	d						10 54											11 24						
Cardiff Queen Street 3	a		10 49			10 54	10 59		11 04	11 09			11 19	11 24				11 29	11 34		11 39	11 44		
	d	10 48	10 51			10 56	11 01	11 00	11 06	11 11		11 12	11 21	11 26			11 24	11 31	11 36	11 36	11 41	11 46		11 48
Cardiff Bay	a	10 52						11 04				11 16					11 28			11 40				11 52
Cardiff Central 7	a		10 54			10 59	11 04		11 09	11 14	11 20		11 24	11 29		11 34		11 34	11 39		11 44	11 53	11 50	
	d		10 55			11 01			11 10	11 16			11 25	11 31					11 41		11 46			
Grangetown	d		10 59			11 05			11 14	11 20			11 29	11 35					11 45		11 50			
Dingle Road	d					11 11				11 26				11 41							11 56			
Penarth	a					11 17				11 32				11 47							12 02			
Cogan	d		11 03						11 18				11 33						11 48					
Eastbrook	d		11 05						11 20				11 35						11 51					
Dinas Powys	d		11 07						11 22				11 37						11 53					
Cadoxton	d		11 12						11 27				11 42						11 57					
Barry Docks	d		11 15						11 30				11 45						12 00					
Barry 3	d		11 19						11 34				11 49						12 05					
Barry Island	a		11 26						11 41				11 56											
Rhoose Cardiff Int Airport ✈	d																		12 12					
Llantwit Major	d																		12 22					
Bridgend	a																		12 40					

When events are being held at the Millenium Stadium, services are subject to alteration. Please check times before travelling.

Table 130

Mondays to Fridays

from 17 September

Treherbert, Aberdare, Merthyr, Pontypridd, Rhymney and Coryton - Cardiff, Penarth, Barry, Barry Island and Bridgend

Network Diagram - see first Page of Table 130

		AW	AW	AW	AW	AW	AW	AW	AW	AW		AW	AW	AW	AW	AW	AW	AW	AW	AW		AW	AW	AW	AW
Treherbert	d														11 17				11 47						
Ynyswen	d														11 19				11 49						
Treorchy	d														11 21				11 51						
Ton Pentre	d														11 23				11 53						
Ystrad Rhondda	a														11 26				11 56						
	d														11 28				11 58						
Llwynypia	d														11 30				12 00						
Tonypandy	d														11 33				12 03						
Dinas Rhondda	d														11 35				12 05						
Porth	a														11 38				12 08						
	d														11 52				12 09						
Trehafod	d														11 55				12 12						
Merthyr Tydfil	d					11 08										11 38									
Pentre-bach	d					11 12										11 42									
Troed Y Rhiw	d					11 15										11 45									
Merthyr Vale	a					11 18										11 48									
	d					11 20										11 50									
Quakers Yard	d					11 25										11 55									
Aberdare 3	d	10 51								11 21															
Cwmbach	d	10 54								11 24															
Fernhill	d	10 58								11 28															
Mountain Ash	a	11 01								11 31															
	d	11 04								11 34															
Penrhiwceiber	d	11 08								11 38															
Abercynon	d	11 14				11 29				11 44						11 59									
Pontypridd 3	a	11 22				11 37				11 52					12 00	12 07			12 17						
	d	11 24				11 39				11 54					12 04	12 09			12 18						
Trefforest	d	11 27				11 42				11 57					12 07	12 12			12 21						
Trefforest Estate	d					11 46										12 16									
Taffs Well 3	d	11 34				11 50				12 04					12 13	12 20			12 28						
Radyr 3	a	11 37				11 53				12 07					12 17	12 23			12 31						
	d	11 37				11 53		12 04		12 07					12 17	12 23			12 31	12 34					
Danescourt	d							12 08												12 38					
Fairwater	d							12 10												12 40					
Waun-gron Park	d							12 12												12 42					
Ninian Park	d							12 15												12 45					
Llandaf	d	11 40				11 56				12 10						12 26			12 34						
Cathays	d	11 45				12 01				12 15						12 31			12 39						
Rhymney 3	d											11 29													
Pontlottyn	d											11 32													
Tir-phil	d											11 36													
Brithdir	d											11 39													
Bargoed	a											11 42													
	d						11 25					11 47						12 02							
Gilfach Fargoed	d						11 27																		
Pengam	d						11 30					11 52						12 07							
Hengoed	d						11 33					11 55						12 10							
Ystrad Mynach 3	d		11 28				11 39					11 58						12 13						12 28	
Llanbradach	d		11 33				11 43					12 03						12 18						12 33	
Aber	d		11 37				11 48					12 07						12 22						12 37	
Caerphilly 3	d		11 40				11 55					12 10						12 25						12 40	
Lisvane & Thornhill	d		11 44				11 59					12 14						12 29						12 44	
Llanishen	d		11 46				12 01					12 16						12 31						12 46	
Heath High Level	d		11 49				12 04					12 19						12 34						12 49	
Coryton	d			11 45										12 15											12 45
Whitchurch (Cardiff)	d			11 46										12 16											12 46
Rhiwbina	d			11 48										12 18											12 48
Birchgrove	d			11 50										12 20											12 50
Ty Glas	d			11 51										12 21											12 51
Heath Low Level	d			11 54										12 24											12 54
Cardiff Queen Street 3	a	11 49	11 54	11 59		12 04	12 09			12 19		12 24		12 29		12 34		12 39	12 44					12 54	12 59
	d	11 51	11 56	12 01	12 00	12 06	12 11		12 12	12 21		12 26	12 24	12 31		12 36	12 36	12 41	12 46			12 48		12 56	13 01
Cardiff Bay	a				12 04				12 16				12 28				12 40					12 52			
Cardiff Central 7	a	11 54	11 59	12 04		12 09	12 14	12 20		12 24		12 29		12 34	12 39	12 39		12 44	12 53	12 50				12 59	13 04
	d	11 55	12 01			12 10	12 16			12 25		12 31				12 41		12 46					12 55	13 01	
Grangetown	d	11 59	12 05			12 14	12 20			12 29		12 35				12 45		12 50					12 59	13 05	
Dingle Road	d		12 11				12 26					12 41						12 56						13 11	
Penarth	a		12 17				12 32					12 47						13 02						13 17	
Cogan	d	12 03				12 18				12 33						12 48							13 03		
Eastbrook	d	12 05				12 20				12 35						12 51							13 05		
Dinas Powys	d	12 07				12 22				12 37						12 53							13 07		
Cadoxton	d	12 12				12 27				12 42						12 57							13 12		
Barry Docks	d	12 15				12 30				12 45						13 00							13 15		
Barry 3	d	12 19				12 34				12 49						13 05							13 19		
Barry Island	a	12 26				12 41				12 56													13 26		
Rhoose Cardiff Int Airport ✈	d															13 12									
Llantwit Major	d															13 22									
Bridgend	a															13 40									

When events are being held at the Millenium Stadium, services are subject to alteration. Please check times before travelling.

Table 130

Mondays to Fridays
from 17 September

Treherbert, Aberdare, Merthyr, Pontypridd, Rhymney and Coryton - Cardiff, Penarth, Barry, Barry Island and Bridgend

Network Diagram - see first Page of Table 130

		AW	AW	AW	AW	AW		AW	AW	AW	AW	AW	AW	AW	AW	AW		AW	AW	AW	AW	AW	AW	AW	AW
Treherbert	d					12 17										12 47									
Ynyswen	d					12 19										12 49									
Treorchy	d					12 21										12 51									
Ton Pentre	d					12 23										12 53									
Ystrad Rhondda	a					12 26										12 56									
	d					12 28										12 58									
Llwynypia	d					12 30										13 00									
Tonypandy	d					12 33										13 03									
Dinas Rhondda	d					12 35										13 05									
Porth	a					12 38										13 08									
	d					12 39										13 09									
Trehafod	d					12 42										13 12									
Merthyr Tydfil	d		12 08										12 38											13 08	
Pentre-bach	d		12 12										12 42											13 12	
Troed Y Rhiw	d		12 15										12 45											13 15	
Merthyr Vale	a		12 18										12 48											13 18	
	d		12 20										12 50											13 20	
Quakers Yard	d		12 25										12 55											13 25	
Aberdare 3	d								12 21											12 51					
Cwmbach	d								12 24											12 54					
Fernhill	d								12 28											12 58					
Mountain Ash	a								12 31											13 01					
	d								12 34											13 04					
Penrhiwceiber	d								12 38											13 08					
Abercynon	d		12 29						12 44				12 59							13 14				13 29	
Pontypridd 3	a		12 37			12 48			12 52				13 07			13 17				13 22				13 37	
	d		12 39			12 48			12 54				13 09			13 18				13 24				13 39	
Trefforest	d		12 42			12 51			12 57				13 12			13 21				13 27				13 42	
Trefforest Estate	d		12 46										13 16											13 46	
Taffs Well 3	d		12 50			12 58			13 04				13 20			13 28				13 34				13 50	
Radyr 3	a		12 53			13 01			13 07				13 23			13 31				13 37				13 53	
	d		12 53			13 01		13 04	13 07				13 23			13 31		13 34		13 37				13 53	
Danescourt	d							13 08										13 38							
Fairwater	d							13 10										13 40							
Waun-gron Park	d							13 12										13 42							
Ninian Park	d							13 15										13 45							
Llandaf	d		12 56			13 04			13 10				13 26			13 34				13 40				13 56	
Cathays	d		13 01			13 09			13 15				13 31			13 39				13 45				14 01	
Rhymney 3	d									12 29															
Pontlottyn	d									12 32															
Tir-phil	d									12 36															
Brithdir	d									12 39															
Bargoed	a									12 42															
	d			12 25						12 47					13 02										13 25
Gilfach Fargoed	d			12 27																					13 27
Pengam	d			12 30						12 52					13 07										13 30
Hengoed	d			12 33						12 55					13 10										13 33
Ystrad Mynach 3	d			12 43						12 58					13 13						13 28				13 43
Llanbradach	d			12 48						13 03					13 18						13 33				13 48
Aber	d			12 52						13 07					13 22						13 37				13 52
Caerphilly 3	d			12 55						13 10					13 25						13 40				13 55
Lisvane & Thornhill	d			12 59						13 14					13 29						13 44				13 59
Llanishen	d			13 01						13 16					13 31						13 46				14 01
Heath High Level	d			13 04						13 19					13 34						13 49				14 04
Coryton	d											13 15										13 45			
Whitchurch (Cardiff)	d											13 16										13 46			
Rhiwbina	d											13 18										13 48			
Birchgrove	d											13 20										13 50			
Ty Glas	d											13 21										13 51			
Heath Low Level	d											13 24										13 54			
Cardiff Queen Street 3	a		13 04	13 09		13 14			13 19	13 24		13 29	13 34		13 39	13 44				13 49	13 54	13 59		14 04	14 09
	d	13 00	13 06	13 11	13 12	13 16			13 21	13 26	13 24	13 31	13 36	13 36	13 41	13 46			13 48	13 51	13 56	14 01	14 00	14 06	14 11
Cardiff Bay	a	13 04			13 16						13 28			13 40					13 52				14 04		
Cardiff Central 7	a		13 09	13 14		13 23		13 20	13 24	13 29		13 34	13 39		13 44	13 53		13 50		13 54	13 59	14 04		14 09	14 14
	d		13 10	13 16					13 25	13 31			13 41		13 46					13 55	14 01			14 10	14 16
Grangetown	d		13 14	13 20					13 29	13 35			13 45		13 50					13 59	14 05			14 14	14 20
Dingle Road	d			13 26						13 41					13 56						14 11				14 26
Penarth	a			13 32						13 47					14 02						14 17				14 32
Cogan	d		13 18						13 33				13 48							14 03				14 18	
Eastbrook	d		13 20						13 35				13 51							14 05				14 20	
Dinas Powys	d		13 22						13 37				13 53							14 07				14 22	
Cadoxton	d		13 27						13 42				13 57							14 12				14 27	
Barry Docks	d		13 30						13 45				14 00							14 15				14 30	
Barry 3	d		13 34						13 49				14 05							14 19				14 34	
Barry Island	a		13 41						13 56											14 26				14 41	
Rhoose Cardiff Int Airport ✈	d												14 12												
Llantwit Major	d												14 22												
Bridgend	a												14 40												

When events are being held at the Millenium Stadium, services are subject to alteration. Please check times before travelling.

Table 130

Mondays to Fridays
from 17 September

Treherbert, Aberdare, Merthyr, Pontypridd, Rhymney and Coryton - Cardiff, Penarth, Barry, Barry Island and Bridgend

Network Diagram - see first Page of Table 130

		AW		AW	AW	AW	AW	AW	AW	AW	AW	AW		AW	AW	AW	AW	AW	AW	AW	AW	AW		AW	AW
Treherbert	d			13 17										13 47											
Ynyswen	d			13 19										13 49											
Treorchy	d			13 21										13 51											
Ton Pentre	d			13 23										13 53											
Ystrad Rhondda	a			13 26										13 56											
	d			13 28										13 58											
Llwynypia	d			13 30										14 00											
Tonypandy	d			13 33										14 03											
Dinas Rhondda	d			13 35										14 05											
Porth	a			13 38										14 08											
	d			13 39										14 09											
Trehafod	d			13 42										14 12											
Merthyr Tydfil	d									13 38											14 08				
Pentre-bach	d									13 42											14 12				
Troed Y Rhiw	d									13 45											14 15				
Merthyr Vale	a									13 48											14 18				
	d									13 50											14 20				
Quakers Yard	d									13 55											14 25				
Aberdare 3	d																13 51								
Cwmbach	d																13 54								
Fernhill	d																13 58								
Mountain Ash	a																14 01								
	d																14 04								
Penrhiwceiber	d																14 08								
Abercynon	d					13 45				13 59							14 14				14 29				
Pontypridd 3	a			13 47		13 52				14 07				14 17			14 22				14 37				
	d			13 48		13 54				14 09				14 18			14 24				14 39				
Trefforest	d			13 51		13 57				14 12				14 21			14 27				14 42				
Trefforest Estate	d									14 16											14 46				
Taffs Well 3	d			13 58		14 04				14 20				14 28			14 34				14 50				
Radyr 3	a			14 01		14 07				14 23				14 31			14 37				14 53				
	d			14 01	14 04	14 07				14 23				14 31	14 34		14 37				14 53			15 04	
Danescourt	d				14 08										14 38									15 08	
Fairwater	d				14 10										14 40									15 10	
Waun-gron Park	d				14 12										14 42									15 12	
Ninian Park	d				14 15										14 45									15 15	
Llandaf	d			14 04		14 10				14 26				14 34			14 40				14 56				
Cathays	d			14 09		14 15				14 31				14 39			14 45				15 01				
Rhymney 3	d						13 29																		
Pontlottyn	d						13 32																		
Tir-phil	d						13 36																		
Brithdir	d						13 39																		
Bargoed	a						13 42																		
	d						13 47					14 02										14 25			
Gilfach Fargoed	d																					14 27			
Pengam	d						13 52					14 07										14 30			
Hengoed	d						13 55					14 10										14 33			
Ystrad Mynach 3	d						13 58					14 13						14 28				14 43			
Llanbradach	d						14 03					14 18						14 33				14 48			
Aber	d						14 07					14 22						14 37				14 52			
Caerphilly 3	d						14 10					14 25						14 40				14 55			
Lisvane & Thornhill	d						14 14					14 29						14 44				14 59			
Llanishen	d						14 16					14 31						14 46				15 01			
Heath High Level	d						14 19					14 34						14 49				15 04			
Coryton	d								14 15										14 45						
Whitchurch (Cardiff)	d								14 16										14 46						
Rhiwbina	d								14 18										14 48						
Birchgrove	d								14 20										14 50						
Ty Glas	d								14 21										14 51						
Heath Low Level	d								14 24										14 54						
Cardiff Queen Street 3	a			14 14		14 19	14 24		14 29	14 34		14 39		14 44			14 49	14 54	14 59		15 04	15 09			
	d	14 12		14 16		14 21	14 26	14 24	14 31	14 36	14 36	14 41		14 46		14 48	14 51	14 56	15 01	15 00	15 06	15 11			15 12
Cardiff Bay	a	14 16						14 28			14 40					14 52				15 04					15 16
Cardiff Central 7	a			14 23	14 20	14 24	14 29		14 34	14 39		14 44		14 53	14 50		14 54	14 59	15 04		15 09	15 14		15 20	
	d					14 25	14 31			14 41		14 46					14 55	15 01			15 10	15 16			
Grangetown	d					14 29	14 35			14 45		14 50					14 59	15 05			15 14	15 20			
Dingle Road	d						14 41					14 56						15 11				15 26			
Penarth	a						14 47					15 02						15 17				15 32			
Cogan	d					14 33				14 48							15 03				15 18				
Eastbrook	d					14 35				14 51							15 05				15 20				
Dinas Powys	d					14 37				14 53							15 07				15 22				
Cadoxton	d					14 42				14 57							15 12				15 27				
Barry Docks	d					14 45				15 00							15 15				15 30				
Barry 3	d					14 49				15 05							15 19				15 34				
Barry Island	a					14 56											15 26				15 41				
Rhoose Cardiff Int Airport ✈	d									15 12															
Llantwit Major	d									15 22															
Bridgend	a									15 40															

When events are being held at the Millenium Stadium, services are subject to alteration. Please check times before travelling.

Table 130

Mondays to Fridays
from 17 September

Treherbert, Aberdare, Merthyr, Pontypridd, Rhymney and Coryton - Cardiff, Penarth, Barry, Barry Island and Bridgend

Network Diagram - see first Page of Table 130

		AW	AW	AW	AW	AW	AW	AW		AW	AW	AW	AW	AW	AW	AW	AW	AW		AW	AW	AW	AW	AW	AW
Treherbert	d			14 17							14 47											15 13			
Ynyswen	d			14 19							14 49											15 15			
Treorchy	d			14 21							14 51											15 21			
Ton Pentre	d			14 23							14 53											15 23			
Ystrad Rhondda	a			14 26							14 56											15 26			
	d			14 28							14 58											15 28			
Llwynypia	d			14 30							15 00											15 30			
Tonypandy	d			14 33							15 03											15 33			
Dinas Rhondda	d			14 35							15 05											15 35			
Porth	a			14 38							15 08											15 38			
	d			14 52							15 09											15 39			
Trehafod	d			14 55							15 12											15 42			
Merthyr Tydfil	d						14 38											15 08							
Pentre-bach	d						14 42											15 12							
Troed Y Rhiw	d						14 45											15 15							
Merthyr Vale	a						14 48											15 18							
	d						14 50											15 20							
Quakers Yard	d						14 55											15 25							
Aberdare [3]	d	14 21												14 51										15 21	
Cwmbach	d	14 24												14 54										15 24	
Fernhill	d	14 28												14 58										15 28	
Mountain Ash	a	14 31												15 01										15 31	
	d	14 34												15 04										15 34	
Penrhiwceiber	d	14 38												15 08										15 38	
Abercynon	d	14 44					14 59							15 14				15 29						15 44	
Pontypridd [3]	a	14 52		15 00			15 07				15 17			15 22				15 37				15 47		15 52	
	d	14 54		15 04			15 09				15 18			15 24				15 39				15 48		15 54	
Trefforest	d	14 57		15 07			15 12				15 21			15 27				15 42				15 51		15 57	
Trefforest Estate	d						15 16											15 46							
Taffs Well [3]	d	15 04		15 13			15 20				15 28			15 34				15 50				15 58		16 04	
Radyr [3]	a	15 07		15 17			15 23				15 31			15 37				15 53				16 01		16 07	
	d	15 07		15 17			15 23				15 31	15 34		15 37				15 53				16 01	16 04	16 07	
Danescourt	d											15 38											16 08		
Fairwater	d											15 40											16 10		
Waun-gron Park	d											15 42											16 12		
Ninian Park	d											15 45											16 15		
Llandaf	d	15 10					15 26				15 34			15 40				15 56				16 04		16 10	
Cathays	d	15 15					15 31				15 39			15 45				16 01				16 09		16 15	
Rhymney [3]	d		14 25																						15 25
Pontlottyn	d		14 28																						15 28
Tir-phil	d		14 32																						15 32
Brithdir	d		14 35																						15 35
Bargoed	a		14 38																						15 38
	d		14 40							15 02										15 25					15 40
Gilfach Fargoed	d																			15 27					
Pengam	d		14 45							15 07										15 30					15 45
Hengoed	d		14 49							15 10										15 33					15 49
Ystrad Mynach [3]	d		14 54							15 13					15 28					15 43					15 54
Llanbradach	d		14 59							15 18					15 33					15 48					15 59
Aber	d		15 04							15 22					15 37					15 52					16 04
Caerphilly [3]	d		15 10							15 25					15 40					15 55					16 10
Lisvane & Thornhill	d		15 14							15 29					15 44					15 59					16 14
Llanishen	d		15 16							15 31					15 46					16 01					16 16
Heath High Level	d		15 19							15 34					15 49					16 04					16 19
Coryton	d					15 15										15 45									
Whitchurch (Cardiff)	d					15 16										15 46									
Rhiwbina	d					15 18										15 48									
Birchgrove	d					15 20										15 50									
Ty Glas	d					15 21										15 51									
Heath Low Level	d					15 24										15 54									
Cardiff Queen Street [3]	a	15 19	15 24			15 29	15 34			15 39	15 44			15 49	15 54	15 59		16 04		16 09		16 14		16 19	16 24
	d	15 21	15 26		15 24	15 31	15 36	15 36		15 41	15 46		15 48	15 51	15 56	16 01	16 00	16 06		16 11	16 12	16 16		16 21	16 26
Cardiff Bay	a				15 28			15 40					15 52				16 04				16 16				
Cardiff Central [7]	a	15 24	15 29	15 34		15 34	15 39			15 44	15 53	15 50		15 54	15 59	16 04		16 09		16 14		16 23	16 20	16 24	16 33
	d	15 25	15 31				15 41			15 46				15 55	16 01			16 10		16 16				16 25	
Grangetown	d	15 29	15 35				15 45			15 50				15 59	16 05			16 14		16 20				16 29	
Dingle Road	d		15 41							15 56					16 11					16 26					
Penarth	a		15 47							16 02					16 17					16 32					
Cogan	d	15 33					15 48							16 03				16 18						16 33	
Eastbrook	d	15 35					15 51							16 05				16 20						16 35	
Dinas Powys	d	15 37					15 53							16 07				16 22						16 37	
Cadoxton	d	15 42					15 57							16 12				16 27						16 42	
Barry Docks	d	15 45					16 00							16 15				16 30						16 45	
Barry [3]	d	15 49					16 05							16 19				16 34						16 49	
Barry Island	a	15 56												16 26				16 41						16 56	
Rhoose Cardiff Int Airport ✈	d						16 12																		
Llantwit Major	d						16 22																		
Bridgend	a						16 40																		

When events are being held at the Millenium Stadium, services are subject to alteration. Please check times before travelling.

Table 130

Mondays to Fridays
from 17 September

Treherbert, Aberdare, Merthyr, Pontypridd, Rhymney and Coryton - Cardiff, Penarth, Barry, Barry Island and Bridgend

Network Diagram - see first Page of Table 130

		AW	AW	AW		AW	AW	AW	AW	AW	AW	AW	AW	AW		AW	AW	AW	AW	AW	AW	AW	AW	AW	
Treherbert	d							15 47											16 17						
Ynyswen	d							15 49											16 19						
Treorchy	d							15 51											16 21						
Ton Pentre	d							15 53											16 23						
Ystrad Rhondda	a							15 56											16 26						
	d							15 58											16 28						
Llwynypia	d							16 00											16 30						
Tonypandy	d							16 03											16 33						
Dinas Rhondda	d							16 05											16 35						
Porth	a							16 08											16 38						
	d							16 09											16 39						
Trehafod	d							16 12											16 42						
Merthyr Tydfil	d			15 38												16 08									
Pentre-bach	d			15 42												16 12									
Troed Y Rhiw	d			15 45												16 15									
Merthyr Vale	a			15 48												16 18									
	d			15 50												16 20									
Quakers Yard	d			15 55												16 25									
Aberdare [3]	d										15 51										16 21				
Cwmbach	d										15 54										16 24				
Fernhill	d										15 58										16 28				
Mountain Ash	a										16 01										16 31				
	d										16 04										16 34				
Penrhiwceiber	d										16 08										16 38				
Abercynon	d			15 59							16 14					16 29					16 44				
Pontypridd [3]	a			16 07				16 17			16 22					16 37			16 47		16 52				
	d			16 09				16 18			16 24					16 39			16 48		16 54				
Trefforest	d			16 12				16 21			16 27					16 42			16 51		16 57				
Trefforest Estate	d			16 16												16 46									
Taffs Well [3]	d			16 20				16 28			16 34					16 50			16 58		17 04				
Radyr [3]	a			16 23				16 31			16 37					16 53			17 01		17 07				
	d			16 23				16 31	16 34		16 37					16 53			17 01	17 04	17 07				
Danescourt	d								16 38											17 08					
Fairwater	d								16 40											17 10					
Waun-gron Park	d								16 42											17 12					
Ninian Park	d								16 45											17 15					
Llandaf	d			16 26				16 34			16 40					16 56			17 04		17 10				
Cathays	d			16 31				16 39			16 45					17 01			17 09		17 15				
Rhymney [3]	d																					16 29			
Pontlottyn	d																					16 32			
Tir-phil	d																					16 36			
Brithdir	d																					16 39			
Bargoed	a																					16 42			
	d						16 02					16 17					16 32					16 47			
Gilfach Fargoed	d											16 19													
Pengam	d						16 07					16 22					16 37					16 52			
Hengoed	d						16 10					16 25					16 40					16 55			
Ystrad Mynach [3]	d						16 13					16 28					16 43					16 58			
Llanbradach	d						16 18					16 33					16 48					17 03			
Aber	d						16 22					16 37					16 52					17 07			
Caerphilly [3]	d						16 25					16 40					16 55					17 10			
Lisvane & Thornhill	d						16 29					16 44					16 59					17 14			
Llanishen	d						16 31					16 46					17 01					17 16			
Heath High Level	d						16 34					16 49					17 04					17 19			
Coryton	d		16 15										16 45											17 15	
Whitchurch (Cardiff)	d		16 16										16 46											17 16	
Rhiwbina	d		16 18										16 48											17 18	
Birchgrove	d		16 20										16 50											17 20	
Ty Glas	d		16 21										16 51											17 21	
Heath Low Level	d		16 24										16 54											17 24	
Cardiff Queen Street [3]	a		16 29	16 34			16 39	16 44			16 49	16 54	16 59			17 04	17 09		17 14		17 19	17 24		17 29	
	d	16 24	16 31	16 36		16 36	16 41	16 46		16 48	16 51	16 56	17 01	17 00		17 06	17 11	17 12	17 16		17 21	17 26	17 24	17 31	
Cardiff Bay	a	16 28				16 40				16 52				17 04				17 16					17 28		
Cardiff Central [7]	a		16 34	16 39			16 44	16 53	16 50		16 54	16 59	17 04			17 09	17 14		17 23	17 20	17 24	17 29		17 34	
	d			16 41			16 46				16 55	17 01				17 10	17 16				17 25	17 31			
Grangetown	d			16 45			16 50				16 59	17 05				17 14	17 20				17 29	17 35			
Dingle Road	d						16 56					17 11					17 26					17 41			
Penarth	a						17 02					17 17					17 32					17 47			
Cogan	d			16 48							17 03					17 18					17 33				
Eastbrook	d			16 51							17 05					17 20					17 35				
Dinas Powys	d			16 53							17 07					17 22					17 37				
Cadoxton	d			16 57							17 12					17 27					17 42				
Barry Docks	d			17 00							17 15					17 30					17 45				
Barry [3]	d			17 05							17 19					17 34					17 49				
Barry Island	a										17 26					17 41					17 56				
Rhoose Cardiff Int Airport ✈	d			17 12																					
Llantwit Major	d			17 22																					
Bridgend	a			17 40																					

When events are being held at the Millenium Stadium, services are subject to alteration. Please check times before travelling.

Table 130

Mondays to Fridays
from 17 September

Treherbert, Aberdare, Merthyr, Pontypridd, Rhymney and Coryton - Cardiff, Penarth, Barry, Barry Island and Bridgend

Network Diagram - see first Page of Table 130

		AW	AW	AW	AW	AW	AW	AW	AW	AW		AW	AW	AW	AW	AW	AW	AW	AW	AW		AW	AW	AW	AW
Treherbert	d				16 47											17 17									17 47
Ynyswen	d				16 49											17 19									17 49
Treorchy	d				16 51											17 21									17 51
Ton Pentre	d				16 53											17 23									17 53
Ystrad Rhondda	a				16 56											17 26									17 56
	d				16 58											17 28									17 58
Llwynypia	d				17 00											17 30									18 00
Tonypandy	d				17 03											17 33									18 03
Dinas Rhondda	d				17 05											17 35									18 05
Porth	a				17 08											17 38									18 08
	d				17 09											17 39									18 09
Trehafod	d				17 12											17 42									18 12
Merthyr Tydfil	d	16 38											17 08										17 38		
Pentre-bach	d	16 42											17 12										17 42		
Troed Y Rhiw	d	16 45											17 15										17 45		
Merthyr Vale	a	16 48											17 18										17 48		
	d	16 50											17 20										17 50		
Quakers Yard	d	16 55											17 25										17 55		
Aberdare	d							16 51										17 21							
Cwmbach	d							16 54										17 24							
Fernhill	d							16 58										17 28							
Mountain Ash	a							17 01										17 31							
	d							17 04										17 34							
Penrhiwceiber	d							17 08										17 38							
Abercynon	d	16 59						17 14					17 29					17 44					17 59		
Pontypridd	a	17 07			17 17			17 22					17 37			17 47		17 52					18 07		18 17
	d	17 09			17 18			17 24					17 39			17 48		17 54					18 09		18 18
Trefforest	d	17 12			17 21			17 27					17 42			17 51		17 57					18 12		18 21
Trefforest Estate	d	17 16											17 46										18 16		
Taffs Well	d	17 20			17 28			17 34					17 50			17 58		18 04					18 20		18 28
Radyr	a	17 23			17 31			17 37					17 53			18 01		18 07					18 23		18 31
	d	17 23			17 31	17 34		17 37					17 53			18 01	18 04	18 07					18 23		18 31
Danescourt	d					17 38											18 08								
Fairwater	d					17 40											18 10								
Waun-gron Park	d					17 42											18 12								
Ninian Park	d					17 45											18 15								
Llandaf	d	17 26			17 34			17 40					17 56			18 04		18 10					18 26		18 34
Cathays	d	17 31			17 39			17 45					18 01			18 09		18 15					18 31		18 39
Rhymney	d																		17 29						
Pontlottyn	d																		17 32						
Tir-phil	d																		17 36						
Brithdir	d																		17 39						
Bargoed	a																		17 42						
	d			17 02					17 17					17 32					17 47						
Gilfach Fargoed	d								17 19																
Pengam	d			17 07					17 22					17 37					17 52						
Hengoed	d			17 10					17 25					17 40					17 55						
Ystrad Mynach	d			17 13					17 28					17 43					17 58						
Llanbradach	d			17 18					17 33					17 48					18 03						
Aber	d			17 22					17 37					17 52					18 07						
Caerphilly	d			17 25					17 40					17 55					18 10						
Lisvane & Thornhill	d			17 29					17 44					17 59					18 14						
Llanishen	d			17 31					17 46					18 01					18 16						
Heath High Level	d			17 34					17 49					18 04					18 19						
Coryton	d									17 45												18 15			
Whitchurch (Cardiff)	d									17 46												18 16			
Rhiwbina	d									17 48												18 18			
Birchgrove	d									17 50												18 20			
Ty Glas	d									17 51												18 21			
Heath Low Level	d									17 54												18 24			
Cardiff Queen Street	a	17 34		17 39	17 44			17 49	17 54	17 59			18 04	18 09		18 14		18 19	18 24			18 29	18 34		18 44
	d	17 36	17 36	17 41	17 46		17 48	17 51	17 56	18 01		18 00	18 06	18 11	18 12	18 16		18 21	18 26	18 24		18 31	18 36	18 36	18 46
Cardiff Bay	a		17 40				17 52					18 04			18 16					18 28				18 40	
Cardiff Central	a	17 39		17 44	17 53	17 50		17 54	17 59	18 04			18 09	18 14		18 23	18 20	18 24	18 29			18 34	18 39		18 53
	d	17 41		17 46				17 55	18 01				18 10	18 16				18 25	18 31				18 41		
Grangetown	d	17 45		17 50				17 59	18 05				18 14	18 20				18 29	18 35				18 45		
Dingle Road	d			17 56					18 11					18 26					18 41						
Penarth	a			18 02					18 17					18 32					18 47						
Cogan	d	17 48						18 03					18 18					18 33					18 48		
Eastbrook	d	17 51						18 05					18 20					18 35					18 51		
Dinas Powys	d	17 53						18 07					18 22					18 37					18 53		
Cadoxton	d	17 57						18 12					18 27					18 42					18 57		
Barry Docks	d	18 00						18 15					18 30					18 45					19 00		
Barry	d	18 05						18 19					18 34					18 49					19 05		
Barry Island	a							18 26					18 41					18 56							
Rhoose Cardiff Int Airport ✈	d	18 12																					19 12		
Llantwit Major	d	18 22																					19 22		
Bridgend	a	18 40																					19 40		

When events are being held at the Millenium Stadium, services are subject to alteration. Please check times before travelling.

Table 130

Mondays to Fridays
from 17 September

Treherbert, Aberdare, Merthyr, Pontypridd, Rhymney and Coryton - Cardiff, Penarth, Barry, Barry Island and Bridgend

Network Diagram - see first Page of Table 130

		AW	AW	AW	AW	AW		AW	AW	AW	AW	AW	AW	AW	AW	AW		AW	AW	AW	AW	AW	AW	AW	AW
Treherbert	d										18 17									18 47					
Ynyswen	d										18 19									18 49					
Treorchy	d										18 21									18 51					
Ton Pentre	d										18 23									18 53					
Ystrad Rhondda	a										18 26									18 56					
	d										18 28									18 58					
Llwynypia	d										18 30									19 00					
Tonypandy	d										18 33									19 03					
Dinas Rhondda	d										18 35									19 05					
Porth	a										18 38									19 08					
	d										18 39									19 09					
Trehafod	d										18 42									19 12					
Merthyr Tydfil	d								18 08									18 38							19 08
Pentre-bach	d								18 12									18 42							19 12
Troed Y Rhiw	d								18 15									18 45							19 15
Merthyr Vale	a								18 18									18 48							19 18
	d								18 20									18 50							19 20
Quakers Yard	d								18 25									18 55							19 25
Aberdare	d			17 51									18 21									18 51			
Cwmbach	d			17 54									18 24									18 54			
Fernhill	d			17 58									18 28									18 58			
Mountain Ash	a			18 01									18 31									19 01			
	d			18 04									18 34									19 04			
Penrhiwceiber	d			18 08									18 38									19 08			
Abercynon	d			18 14					18 29				18 44					18 59				19 14			19 29
Pontypridd	a			18 22					18 37		18 47		18 52					19 07		19 17		19 22			19 37
	d			18 24					18 39		18 48		18 54					19 09		19 18		19 24			19 39
Trefforest	d			18 27					18 42		18 51		18 57					19 12		19 21		19 27			19 42
Trefforest Estate	d								18 46									19 16							19 46
Taffs Well	d			18 34					18 50		18 58		19 04					19 20		19 28		19 34			19 50
Radyr	a			18 37					18 53		19 01		19 07					19 23		19 31		19 37			19 53
	d	18 34		18 37					18 53		19 01	19 04	19 07					19 23		19 31		19 37			19 53
Danescourt	d	18 38										19 08													
Fairwater	d	18 40										19 10													
Waun-gron Park	d	18 42										19 12													
Ninian Park	d	18 45										19 15													
Llandaf	d			18 40					18 56		19 04		19 10					19 26		19 34		19 40			19 56
Cathays	d			18 45					19 01		19 09		19 15					19 31		19 39		19 45			20 01
Rhymney	d																								
Pontlottyn	d																								
Tir-phil	d																								
Brithdir	d																								
Bargoed	a																								
	d				18 17									18 48											
Gilfach Fargoed	d				18 19									18 50											
Pengam	d				18 22									18 53											
Hengoed	d				18 25									18 56											
Ystrad Mynach	d				18 28									18 59											
Llanbradach	d				18 33									19 04											
Aber	d				18 37									19 08											
Caerphilly	d				18 40									19 11									19 40		
Lisvane & Thornhill	d				18 44									19 15									19 44		
Llanishen	d				18 46									19 17									19 46		
Heath High Level	d				18 49									19 20									19 49		
Coryton	d					18 45										19 15									
Whitchurch (Cardiff)	d					18 46										19 16									
Rhiwbina	d					18 48										19 18									
Birchgrove	d					18 50										19 20									
Ty Glas	d					18 51										19 21									
Heath Low Level	d					18 54										19 24									
Cardiff Queen Street	a			18 49	18 54	18 59			19 04		19 14		19 19	19 24		19 29		19 34		19 44		19 49	19 54		20 04
	d		18 48	18 51	18 56	19 01		19 00	19 06	19 12	19 16		19 21	19 26	19 24	19 31		19 36	19 36	19 46	19 48	19 51	19 56	20 00	20 06
Cardiff Bay	a		18 52					19 04		19 16					19 28				19 40		19 52			20 04	
Cardiff Central	a	18 50		18 54	18 59	19 07			19 10		19 23	19 22	19 24	19 29		19 34		19 39		19 53		19 57	19 59		20 09
	d			18 55	19 01								19 25	19 31				19 41					20 06		20 10
Grangetown	d			18 59	19 05								19 29	19 35				19 45					20 10		20 14
Dingle Road	d				19 11									19 41									20 14		
Penarth	a				19 17									19 47									20 20		
Cogan	d			19 03									19 33					19 48							20 18
Eastbrook	d			19 05									19 35					19 51							20 20
Dinas Powys	d			19 07									19 37					19 53							20 22
Cadoxton	d			19 12									19 42					19 57							20 27
Barry Docks	d			19 15									19 45					20 00							20 30
Barry	d			19 19									19 49					20 05							20 34
Barry Island	a			19 26									19 56												20 41
Rhoose Cardiff Int Airport ✈	d																	20 12							
Llantwit Major	d																	20 22							
Bridgend	a																	20 40							

When events are being held at the Millenium Stadium, services are subject to alteration. Please check times before travelling.

Treherbert, Aberdare, Merthyr, Pontypridd, Rhymney and Coryton - Cardiff, Penarth, Barry, Barry Island and Bridgend

Network Diagram - see first Page of Table 130

		AW		AW	AW	AW	AW	AW	AW	AW	AW	AW		AW	AW	AW	AW	AW	AW	AW	AW	AW		AW	AW
Treherbert	d			19 17								19 47							20 17						
Ynyswen	d			19 19								19 49							20 19						
Treorchy	d			19 21								19 51							20 21						
Ton Pentre	d			19 23								19 53							20 23						
Ystrad Rhondda	a			19 26								19 56							20 26						
	d			19 28								19 58							20 28						
Llwynypia	d			19 30								20 00							20 30						
Tonypandy	d			19 33								20 03							20 33						
Dinas Rhondda	d			19 35								20 05							20 35						
Porth	a			19 38								20 08							20 38						
	d			19 39								20 09							20 39						
Trehafod	d			19 42								20 12							20 42						
Merthyr Tydfil	d								19 38																
Pentre-bach	d								19 42																
Troed Y Rhiw	d								19 45																
Merthyr Vale	a								19 48																
	d								19 50																
Quakers Yard	d								19 55																
Aberdare 3	d														19 51						20 21				
Cwmbach	d														19 54						20 24				
Fernhill	d														19 58						20 28				
Mountain Ash	a														20 01						20 31				
	d														20 04						20 34				
Penrhiwceiber	d														20 08						20 38				
Abercynon	d					19 43			19 59						20 14						20 44				
Pontypridd 3	a			19 47		19 52			20 07			20 17			20 22				20 47		20 52				
	d			19 48		19 54			20 09			20 18			20 24				20 48		20 54				
Trefforest	d			19 51		19 57			20 12			20 21			20 27				20 51		20 57				
Trefforest Estate	d								20 16																
Taffs Well 3	d			19 58		20 04			20 20			20 28			20 34				20 58		21 04				
Radyr 3	a			20 01		20 07			20 23			20 31			20 37				21 01		21 07				
	d			20 01	20 04	20 07			20 23			20 31			20 37				21 01	21 04	21 07				
Danescourt	d				20 08															21 08					
Fairwater	d				20 10															21 10					
Waun-gron Park	d				20 12															21 12					
Ninian Park	d				20 15															21 15					
Llandaf	d			20 04		20 10			20 26			20 34			20 40				21 04		21 10				
Cathays	d			20 09		20 15			20 31			20 39			20 45				21 09		21 15				
Rhymney 3	d										19 45														
Pontlottyn	d										19 48														
Tir-phil	d										19 52														
Brithdir	d										19 55														
Bargoed	a										19 58														
	d										19 59														
Gilfach Fargoed	d										20 01														
Pengam	d										20 04														
Hengoed	d										20 07														
Ystrad Mynach 3	d										20 10														
Llanbradach	d										20 15														
Aber	d										20 19														
Caerphilly 3	d										20 22					20 40									
Lisvane & Thornhill	d										20 26					20 44									
Llanishen	d										20 28					20 46									
Heath High Level	d										20 31					20 49									
Coryton	d							20 15																	21 15
Whitchurch (Cardiff)	d							20 16																	21 16
Rhiwbina	d							20 18																	21 18
Birchgrove	d							20 20																	21 20
Ty Glas	d							20 21																	21 21
Heath Low Level	d							20 24																	21 24
Cardiff Queen Street 3	a			20 14		20 19		20 29	20 34		20 39	20 44			20 49	20 54			21 14		21 19				21 29
	d	20 12		20 16		20 21	20 24	20 31	20 36	20 36	20 41	20 46		20 48	20 51	20 56	21 00	21 12	21 16		21 21	21 24			21 31
Cardiff Bay	a	20 16					20 28			20 40				20 52			21 04	21 16				21 28			
Cardiff Central 7	a			20 23	20 24	20 24		20 34	20 39		20 48	20 53			20 57	20 59			21 23	21 25	21 28				21 34
	d					20 31			20 41						21 06	21 10								21 31	
Grangetown	d					20 35			20 45						21 10	21 14								21 35	
Dingle Road	d					20 41									21 14									21 41	
Penarth	a					20 47									21 20									21 47	
Cogan	d								20 48							21 18									
Eastbrook	d								20 51							21 20									
Dinas Powys	d								20 53							21 22									
Cadoxton	d								20 57							21 27									
Barry Docks	d								21 00							21 30									
Barry 3	d								21 05							21 34									
Barry Island	a															21 41									
Rhoose Cardiff Int Airport ✈	d								21 12																
Llantwit Major	d								21 22																
Bridgend	a								21 40																

When events are being held at the Millenium Stadium, services are subject to alteration. Please check times before travelling.

Treherbert, Aberdare, Merthyr, Pontypridd, Rhymney and Coryton - Cardiff, Penarth, Barry, Barry Island and Bridgend

Network Diagram - see first Page of Table 130

		AW	AW	AW	AW	AW	AW	AW		AW	AW	AW	AW	AW	AW FO	AW FX	AW	AW		AW	AW	AW	AW	AW	AW FX
Treherbert	d										21 17														
Ynyswen	d										21 19														
Treorchy	d										21 21														
Ton Pentre	d										21 23														
Ystrad Rhondda	a										21 26														
	d										21 28														
Llwynypia	d										21 30														
Tonypandy	d										21 33														
Dinas Rhondda	d										21 35														
Porth	a										21 38														
	d										21 39														
Trehafod	d										21 42														
Merthyr Tydfil	d	20 38													21 38	21 38									
Pentre-bach	d	20 42													21 42	21 42									
Troed Y Rhiw	d	20 45													21 45	21 45									
Merthyr Vale	a	20 48													21 48	21 48									
	d	20 50													21 50	21 50									
Quakers Yard	d	20 55													21 55	21 55									
Aberdare 3	d					20 51															21 51				
Cwmbach	d					20 54															21 54				
Fernhill	d					20 58															21 58				
Mountain Ash	a					21 01															22 01				
	d					21 04															22 04				
Penrhiwceiber	d					21 08															22 08				
Abercynon	d	20 59				21 14									21 59	21 59					22 14				
Pontypridd 3	a	21 07				21 22					21 47				22 07	22 07					22 22				
	d	21 09				21 24					21 48				22 09	22 09					22 24				
Trefforest	d	21 12				21 27					21 51				22 12	22 12					22 27				
Trefforest Estate	d	21 16													22 16	22 16									
Taffs Well 3	d	21 20				21 34					21 58				22 20	22 20					22 33				
Radyr 3	a	21 23				21 37					22 01				22 23	22 23					22 37				
	d	21 23				21 37					22 01	22 04			22 23	22 23					22 37				
Danescourt	d											22 08													
Fairwater	d											22 10													
Waun-gron Park	d											22 12													
Ninian Park	d											22 15													
Llandaf	d	21 26				21 40					22 04				22 26	22 26					22 40				
Cathays	d	21 31				21 45					22 09				22 31	22 31					22 44				
Rhymney 3	d			20 48									21 33												
Pontlottyn	d			20 51									21 36												
Tir-phil	d			20 55									21 40												
Brithdir	d			20 58									21 43												
Bargoed	a			21 01									21 46												
	d			21 02									21 47												
Gilfach Fargoed	d			21 04									21 49												
Pengam	d			21 07									21 52												
Hengoed	d			21 10									21 55												
Ystrad Mynach 3	d			21 13				21 39					21 58												
Llanbradach	d			21 18				21 44					22 03												
Aber	d			21 22				21 48					22 07												
Caerphilly 3	d			21 25				21 51					22 10					22 28							
Lisvane & Thornhill	d			21 29				21 55					22 14												
Llanishen	d			21 31				21 57					22 16												
Heath High Level	d			21 34				22 00					22 19												
Coryton	d																					22 45			
Whitchurch (Cardiff)	d																					22 46			
Rhiwbina	d																					22 48			
Birchgrove	d																					22 50			
Ty Glas	d																					22 51			
Heath Low Level	d																					22 54			
Cardiff Queen Street 3	a	21 34		21 42		21 49		22 05			22 14		22 24		22 34	22 34		22 39			22 53	22 59			
	d	21 36	21 36	21 44	21 48	21 51	22 00	22 06		22 12	22 16		22 26	22 24	22 36	22 36	22 36	22 39		22 48	22 53	23 01	23 00	23 12	
Cardiff Bay	a		21 40		21 52		22 04			22 16				22 28			22 40			22 52			23 04	23 16	
Cardiff Central 7	a	21 39		21 51		21 54		22 09			22 23	22 20	22 29		22 39	22 39		22 43			23 00	23 07			
	d	21 41				21 56		22 10					22 31		22 41	22 41					23 12				
Grangetown	d	21 45				22 00		22 14					22 35		22 45	22 45					23 16				
Dingle Road	d					22 04							22 41								23 20				
Penarth	a					22 10							22 47								23 26				
Cogan	d	21 48						22 18							22 48	22 49									
Eastbrook	d	21 51						22 20							22 51	22 51									
Dinas Powys	d	21 53						22 22							22 53	22 53									
Cadoxton	d	21 57						22 27							22 57	22 57									
Barry Docks	d	22 00						22 30							23 00	23 00									
Barry 3	d	22 05						22 34							23 05	23a05									23 15
Barry Island	a							22 41																	
Rhoose Cardiff Int Airport ✈	d	22 12													23 12										23 30
Llantwit Major	d	22 22													23 22										23 45
Bridgend	a	22 40													23 40										00 10

When events are being held at the Millenium Stadium, services are subject to alteration. Please check times before travelling.

Mondays to Fridays
from 17 September

Treherbert, Aberdare, Merthyr, Pontypridd, Rhymney and Coryton - Cardiff, Penarth, Barry, Barry Island and Bridgend

Network Diagram - see first Page of Table 130

		AW	AW	AW	AW	AW	AW
Treherbert	d						
Ynyswen	d						
Treorchy	d						
Ton Pentre	d						
Ystrad Rhondda	a						
	d						
Llwynypia	d						
Tonypandy	d						
Dinas Rhondda	d						
Porth	a						
	d						
Trehafod	d						
Merthyr Tydfil	d			22 38			
Pentre-bach	d			22 42			
Troed Y Rhiw	d			22 45			
Merthyr Vale	a			22 48			
	d			22 50			
Quakers Yard	d			22 55			
Aberdare ■	d				22 51		
Cwmbach	d				22 54		
Fernhill	d				22 58		
Mountain Ash	a				23 01		
	d				23 04		
Penrhiwceiber	d				23 08		
Abercynon	d			22 59	23 14		
Pontypridd ■	a			23 07	23 22		
	d			23 09			
Trefforest	d			23 12			
Trefforest Estate	d			23 16			
Taffs Well ■	d			23 20			
Radyr ■	a			23 23			
	d	23 10		23 23			
Danescourt	d						
Fairwater	d						
Waun-gron Park	d						
Ninian Park	d						
Llandaf	d	23 12		23 26			
Cathays	d	23 16		23 31			
Rhymney ■	d						
Pontlottyn	d						
Tir-phil	d						
Brithdir	d						
Bargoed	a						
	d						
Gilfach Fargoed	d						
Pengam	d						
Hengoed	d						
Ystrad Mynach ■	d						
Llanbradach	d						
Aber	d						
Caerphilly ■	d						
Lisvane & Thornhill	d						
Llanishen	d						
Heath High Level	d						
Coryton	d						
Whitchurch (Cardiff)	d						
Rhiwbina	d						
Birchgrove	d						
Ty Glas	d						
Heath Low Level	d						
Cardiff Queen Street ■	a	23 19		23 34			
	d	23 20	23 24	23 36		23 36	23 48
Cardiff Bay	a		23 28			23 40	23 52
Cardiff Central ■	a	23 25		23 43			
	d	23 30					
Grangetown	d	23 34					
Dingle Road	d						
Penarth	a						
Cogan	d	23 37					
Eastbrook	d	23 40					
Dinas Powys	d	23 42					
Cadoxton	d	23 46					
Barry Docks	d	23 49					
Barry ■	d	23 54					
Barry Island	a	00 01					
Rhoose Cardiff Int Airport ✈	d						
Llantwit Major	d						
Bridgend	a						

When events are being held at the Millenium Stadium, services are subject to alteration. Please check times before travelling.

Saturdays
until 8 September

Treherbert, Aberdare, Merthyr, Pontypridd, Rhymney and Coryton - Cardiff, Penarth, Barry, Barry Island and Bridgend

Network Diagram - see first Page of Table 130

		AW	AW A	AW A	AW	AW	AW	AW	AW	AW	AW	AW	AW	AW	AW	AW	AW	AW	AW	AW	AW	AW	AW
Treherbert	d													05 47							06 17		
Ynyswen	d													05 49							06 19		
Treorchy	d													05 51							06 21		
Ton Pentre	d													05 53							06 23		
Ystrad Rhondda	a													05 56							06 26		
	d													05 58							06 28		
Llwynypia	d													06 00							06 30		
Tonypandy	d													06 03							06 33		
Dinas Rhondda	d													06 05							06 35		
Porth	a													06 08							06 38		
	d													06 09							06 39		
Trehafod	d													06 12							06 42		
Merthyr Tydfil	d		22p38																				
Pentre-bach	d		22p42																				
Troed Y Rhiw	d		22p45																				
Merthyr Vale	a		22p48																				
	d		22p50																				
Quakers Yard	d		22p55																				
Aberdare ■	d																						
Cwmbach	d																						
Fernhill	d																						
Mountain Ash	a																						
	d																						
Penrhiwceiber	d																						
Abercynon	d		22p59																				
Pontypridd ■	a		23p07											06 17							06 47		
	d		23p09					05 24						06 18							06 48		
Trefforest	d		23p12					05 27						06 21							06 51		
Trefforest Estate	d		23p16					05 31															
Taffs Well ■	d		23p20					05 34						06 28							06 58	06 53	
Radyr ■	a		23p23					05 37						06 31							07 01	06 56	
	d	23p10	23p23					05 37						06 31							07 01	07 04	
Danescourt	d																					07 08	
Fairwater	d																					07 10	
Waun-gron Park	d																					07 12	
Ninian Park	d																					07 15	
Llandaf	d	23p12	23p26					05 40						06 34							07 04		
Cathays	d	23p16	23p31					05 45						06 39							07 09		
Rhymney ■	d																			06 10			
Pontlottyn	d																			06 13			
Tir-phil	d																			06 17			
Brithdir	d																			06 20			
Bargoed	a																			06 23			
	d																			06 27			
Gilfach Fargoed	d																			06 29			
Pengam	d																			06 32			
Hengoed	d																			06 35			
Ystrad Mynach ■	d																			06 38			
Llanbradach	d																			06 43			
Aber	d																			06 47			
Caerphilly ■	d											06 10								06 50			
Lisvane & Thornhill	d											06 14								06 54			
Llanishen	d											06 16								06 56			
Heath High Level	d											06 19								06 59			
Coryton	d																		06 45				
Whitchurch (Cardiff)	d																		06 46				
Rhiwbina	d																		06 48				
Birchgrove	d																		06 50				
Ty Glas	d																		06 51				
Heath Low Level	d																		06 54				
Cardiff Queen Street ■	a	23p20	23p34					05 49				06 25		06 42					06 59	07 04	07 12		
	d	23p20	23p36					05 51				06 26	06 36	06 43	06 48		07 00		07 01	07 06	07 13		07 12
Cardiff Bay	a												06 40		06 52		07 04						07 16
Cardiff Central ■	a	23p25	23p39					05 54				06 29		06 48					07 04	07 09	07 16	07 20	
	d	23p30	23p41	00 26	05 20	05 41	05 46	05 55	06 16	06 25	06 36	06 41				06 55		07 01		07 10	07 16		
Grangetown	d	23p34	23p45	00 30	05 24	05 45	05 50	05 59	06 20	06 29	06 40	06 45				06 59		07 05		07 14	07 20		
Dingle Road	d						05 54		06 24		06 44							07 11			07 26		
Penarth	a						05 59		06 29		06 49							07 16			07 31		
Cogan	d	23p37	23p48	00 34	05 28	05 48		06 03		06 33		06 48				07 03				07 18			
Eastbrook	d	23p40	23p51	00 36	05 30	05 51		06 05		06 35		06 51				07 05				07 20			
Dinas Powys	d	23p42	23p54	00 39	05 32	05 53		06 07		06 37		06 53				07 07				07 22			
Cadoxton	d	23p46	23p58	00 44	05 37	05 57		06 12		06 42		06 57				07 12				07 27			
Barry Docks	d	23p49	00 03	00 47	05 40	06 00		06 15		06 45		07 00				07 15				07 30			
Barry ■	d	23p54	00 08	00 52	05 44	06 05		06 19		06 49		07 05				07 19				07 34			
Barry Island	a	00 01		00 58	05 50			06 25		06 55						07 25				07 40			
Rhoose Cardiff Int Airport ✈	d		00 15			06 12						07 12											
Llantwit Major	d		00 25			06 22						07 22											
Bridgend	a		00 43			06 39						07 39											

A 11 August

When events are being held at the Millenium Stadium, services are subject to alteration. Please check times before travelling.

Table 130

Saturdays
until 8 September

Treherbert, Aberdare, Merthyr, Pontypridd, Rhymney and Coryton - Cardiff, Penarth, Barry, Barry Island and Bridgend

Network Diagram - see first Page of Table 130

		AW	AW	AW	AW	AW		AW	AW	AW	AW	AW	AW	AW	AW	AW		AW	AW	AW	AW	AW	AW	AW	AW
Treherbert	d									06 47											07 17				
Ynyswen	d									06 49											07 19				
Treorchy	d									06 51											07 21				
Ton Pentre	d									06 53											07 23				
Ystrad Rhondda	a									06 56											07 26				
	d									06 58											07 28				
Llwynypia	d									07 00											07 30				
Tonypandy	d									07 03											07 33				
Dinas Rhondda	d									07 05											07 35				
Porth	a									07 08											07 38				
	d									07 09											07 39				
Trehafod	d									07 12											07 42				
Merthyr Tydfil	d					06 38												07 08							
Pentre-bach	d					06 42												07 12							
Troed Y Rhiw	d					06 45												07 15							
Merthyr Vale	a					06 48												07 18							
	d					06 50												07 20							
Quakers Yard	d					06 55												07 25							
Aberdare	d	06 22											06 52										07 22		
Cwmbach	d	06 25											06 55										07 25		
Fernhill	d	06 28											06 58										07 28		
Mountain Ash	a	06 31											07 01										07 31		
	d	06 34											07 04										07 34		
Penrhiwceiber	d	06 37											07 07										07 37		
Abercynon	d	06 43				06 59							07 13					07 29					07 43		
Pontypridd	a	06 52				07 07				07 17			07 22					07 37			07 47		07 52		
	d	06 54				07 09				07 18			07 24					07 39			07 48		07 54		
Trefforest	d	06 57				07 12				07 21			07 27					07 42			07 51		07 57		
Trefforest Estate	d					07 16												07 46							
Taffs Well	d	07 04				07 20				07 28			07 34					07 50			07 58		08 04		
Radyr	a	07 07				07 23				07 31			07 37					07 53			08 01		08 07		
	d	07 07				07 23				07 31	07 34		07 37					07 53			08 01	08 04	08 07		
Danescourt	d										07 38											08 08			
Fairwater	d										07 40											08 10			
Waun-gron Park	d										07 42											08 12			
Ninian Park	d										07 45											08 15			
Llandaf	d	07 10				07 26				07 34			07 40					07 56			08 04		08 10		
Cathays	d	07 15				07 31				07 39			07 45					08 01			08 09		08 15		
Rhymney	d		06 34											07 02										07 24	
Pontlottyn	d		06 37											07 05										07 27	
Tir-phil	d		06 41											07 09										07 31	
Brithdir	d		06 44											07 12										07 34	
Bargoed	a		06 47											07 15										07 37	
	d		06 48						07 02					07 17					07 32					07 45	
Gilfach Fargoed	d								07 04					07 19										07 47	
Pengam	d		06 52						07 07					07 22					07 37					07 50	
Hengoed	d		06 56						07 10					07 25					07 40					07 54	
Ystrad Mynach	d		06 58						07 13					07 28					07 43					07 57	
Llanbradach	d		07 03						07 18					07 33					07 48					08 02	
Aber	d		07 07						07 22					07 37					07 52					08 07	
Caerphilly	d		07 10						07 25					07 40					07 55					08 10	
Lisvane & Thornhill	d		07 14						07 29					07 44					07 59					08 14	
Llanishen	d		07 16						07 31					07 46					08 01					08 16	
Heath High Level	d		07 19						07 34					07 49					08 04					08 19	
Coryton	d				07 15										07 45										
Whitchurch (Cardiff)	d				07 16										07 46										
Rhiwbina	d				07 18										07 48										
Birchgrove	d				07 20										07 50										
Ty Glas	d				07 21										07 51										
Heath Low Level	d				07 24										07 54										
Cardiff Queen Street	a	07 19	07 24		07 29	07 34			07 39	07 44			07 49	07 54	07 59			08 04	08 09		08 14		08 19	08 24	
	d	07 21	07 26	07 24	07 31	07 36		07 36	07 41	07 46		07 48	07 51	07 56	08 01	08 00		08 06	08 11	08 12	08 16		08 21	08 26	08 24
Cardiff Bay	a			07 28				07 40				07 52				08 04				08 16					08 28
Cardiff Central	a	07 24	07 29		07 34	07 39			07 44	07 52	07 50		07 54	07 59	08 04			08 09	08 14		08 22	08 20	08 24	08 29	
	d	07 25	07 31			07 41			07 46				07 55	08 01				08 10	08 16				08 25	08 31	
Grangetown	d	07 29	07 35			07 45			07 50				07 59	08 05				08 14	08 20				08 29	08 35	
Dingle Road	d		07 41						07 56					08 11					08 26					08 41	
Penarth	a		07 46						08 01					08 16					08 31					08 46	
Cogan	d	07 33				07 48							08 03					08 18					08 33		
Eastbrook	d	07 35				07 51							08 05					08 20					08 35		
Dinas Powys	d	07 37				07 53							08 07					08 22					08 37		
Cadoxton	d	07 42				07 57							08 12					08 27					08 42		
Barry Docks	d	07 45				08 00							08 15					08 30					08 45		
Barry	d	07 49				08 05							08 19					08 34					08 49		
Barry Island	a	07 55											08 25					08 40					08 55		
Rhoose Cardiff Int Airport ✈	d					08 12																			
Llantwit Major	d					08 22																			
Bridgend	a					08 39																			

When events are being held at the Millenium Stadium, services are subject to alteration. Please check times before travelling.

Table 130

Saturdays
until 8 September

Treherbert, Aberdare, Merthyr, Pontypridd, Rhymney and Coryton - Cardiff, Penarth, Barry, Barry Island and Bridgend

Network Diagram - see first Page of Table 130

		AW		AW	AW	AW	AW	AW	AW	AW	AW	AW		AW	AW	AW	AW	AW	AW	AW	AW	AW		AW	AW
Treherbert	d						07 45											08 17							
Ynyswen	d						07 47											08 19							
Treorchy	d						07 49											08 21							
Ton Pentre	d						07 51											08 23							
Ystrad Rhondda	a						07 54											08 26							
	d						07 58											08 28							
Llwynypia	d						08 00											08 30							
Tonypandy	d						08 03											08 33							
Dinas Rhondda	d						08 05											08 35							
Porth	a						08 08											08 38							
	d						08 09											08 39							
Trehafod	d						08 12											08 42							
Merthyr Tydfil	d			07 38											08 08										08 38
Pentre-bach	d			07 42											08 12										08 42
Troed Y Rhiw	d			07 45											08 15										08 45
Merthyr Vale	a			07 48											08 18										08 48
	d			07 50											08 20										08 50
Quakers Yard	d			07 55											08 25										08 55
Aberdare	d									07 52										08 22					
Cwmbach	d									07 55										08 25					
Fernhill	d									07 58										08 28					
Mountain Ash	a									08 01										08 31					
	d									08 04										08 34					
Penrhiwceiber	d									08 07										08 37					
Abercynon	d			07 59						08 13					08 29					08 43					08 59
Pontypridd	a			08 07			08 17			08 22					08 37			08 47		08 52					09 07
	d			08 09			08 18			08 24					08 39			08 48		08 54					09 09
Trefforest	d			08 12			08 21			08 27					08 42			08 51		08 57					09 12
Trefforest Estate	d			08 16											08 46										09 16
Taffs Well	d			08 20			08 28			08 34					08 50			08 58		09 04					09 20
Radyr	a			08 23			08 31			08 37					08 53			09 01		09 07					09 23
	d			08 23			08 31	08 34		08 37					08 53			09 01	09 04	09 07					09 23
Danescourt	d							08 38											09 08						
Fairwater	d							08 40											09 10						
Waun-gron Park	d							08 42											09 12						
Ninian Park	d							08 45											09 15						
Llandaf	d			08 26			08 34			08 40					08 56			09 04		09 10					09 26
Cathays	d			08 31			08 39			08 45					09 01			09 09		09 15					09 31
Rhymney	d					07 44															08 30				
Pontlottyn	d					07 47															08 33				
Tir-phil	d					07 51															08 37				
Brithdir	d					07 54															08 40				
Bargoed	a					08 00															08 44				
	d					08 02					08 17					08 32					08 47				
Gilfach Fargoed	d										08 19														
Pengam	d					08 07					08 22					08 37					08 52				
Hengoed	d					08 10					08 25					08 40					08 55				
Ystrad Mynach	d					08 13					08 28					08 43					08 58				
Llanbradach	d					08 18					08 33					08 48					09 03				
Aber	d					08 22					08 37					08 52					09 07				
Caerphilly	d					08 25					08 40					08 55					09 10				
Lisvane & Thornhill	d					08 29					08 44					08 59					09 14				
Llanishen	d					08 31					08 46					09 01					09 16				
Heath High Level	d					08 34					08 49					09 04					09 19				
Coryton	d	08 15										08 45												09 15	
Whitchurch (Cardiff)	d	08 16										08 46												09 16	
Rhiwbina	d	08 18										08 48												09 18	
Birchgrove	d	08 20										08 50												09 20	
Ty Glas	d	08 21										08 51												09 21	
Heath Low Level	d	08 24										08 54												09 24	
Cardiff Queen Street	a	08 29		08 34		08 39	08 44			08 49	08 54	08 59			09 04	09 09		09 14		09 19	09 24			09 29	09 34
	d	08 31		08 36	08 36	08 41	08 46		08 48	08 51	08 56	09 01		09 00	09 06	09 11	09 12	09 16		09 21	09 26	09 24		09 31	09 36
Cardiff Bay	a				08 40				08 52					09 04			09 16					09 28			
Cardiff Central	a	08 34		08 39		08 47	08 52	08 50		08 54	08 59	09 04			09 09	09 14		09 22	09 20	09 24	09 29			09 34	09 39
	d			08 41						08 55	09 01				09 10	09 16				09 25	09 31				09 41
Grangetown	d			08 45						08 59	09 05				09 14	09 20				09 29	09 35				09 45
Dingle Road	d										09 11					09 26					09 41				
Penarth	a										09 16					09 31					09 46				
Cogan	d			08 48						09 03					09 18					09 33					09 48
Eastbrook	d			08 51						09 05					09 20					09 35					09 51
Dinas Powys	d			08 53						09 07					09 22					09 37					09 53
Cadoxton	d			08 57						09 12					09 27					09 42					09 57
Barry Docks	d			09 00						09 15					09 30					09 45					10 00
Barry	d			09 05						09 19					09 34					09 49					10 05
Barry Island	a									09 25					09 40					09 55					
Rhoose Cardiff Int Airport ✈	d			09 12																					10 12
Llantwit Major	d			09 22																					10 22
Bridgend	a			09 39																					10 39

When events are being held at the Millenium Stadium, services are subject to alteration. Please check times before travelling.

Saturdays
until 8 September

Treherbert, Aberdare, Merthyr, Pontypridd, Rhymney and Coryton - Cardiff, Penarth, Barry, Barry Island and Bridgend

Network Diagram - see first Page of Table 130

		AW	AW	AW	AW	AW	AW	AW		AW	AW	AW	AW	AW	AW	AW	AW	AW		AW	AW	AW	AW	AW	AW
Treherbert	d			08 47											09 17										09 47
Ynyswen	d			08 49											09 19										09 49
Treorchy	d			08 51											09 21										09 51
Ton Pentre	d			08 53											09 23										09 53
Ystrad Rhondda	a			08 56											09 26										09 56
	d			08 58											09 28										09 58
Llwynypia	d			09 00											09 30										10 00
Tonypandy	d			09 03											09 33										10 03
Dinas Rhondda	d			09 05											09 35										10 05
Porth	a			09 08											09 38										10 08
	d			09 09											09 39										10 09
Trehafod	d			09 12											09 42										10 12
Merthyr Tydfil	d												09 08										09 38			
Pentre-bach	d												09 12										09 42			
Troed Y Rhiw	d												09 15										09 45			
Merthyr Vale	a												09 18										09 48			
	d												09 20										09 50			
Quakers Yard	d												09 25										09 55			
Aberdare 3	d						08 52										09 22								
Cwmbach	d						08 55										09 25								
Fernhill	d						08 58										09 28								
Mountain Ash	a						09 01										09 31								
	d						09 04										09 34								
Penrhiwceiber	d						09 07										09 37								
Abercynon	d						09 13					09 29					09 43					09 59			
Pontypridd 3	a			09 17			09 22					09 37			09 47		09 52					10 07			10 17
	d			09 18			09 24					09 39			09 48		09 54					10 09			10 18
Trefforest	d			09 21			09 27					09 42			09 51		09 57					10 12			10 21
Trefforest Estate	d												09 46										10 16			
Taffs Well 3	d			09 28			09 34					09 50			09 58		10 04					10 20			10 28
Radyr 3	a			09 31			09 37					09 53			10 01		10 07					10 23			10 31
	d			09 31	09 34		09 37					09 53			10 01	10 04	10 07					10 23			10 31
Danescourt	d				09 38											10 08									
Fairwater	d				09 40											10 10									
Waun-gron Park	d				09 42											10 12									
Ninian Park	d				09 45											10 15									
Llandaf	d			09 34			09 40					09 56			10 04		10 10					10 26			10 34
Cathays	d			09 39			09 45					10 01			10 09		10 15					10 31			10 39
Rhymney 3	d																		09 29							
Pontlottyn	d																		09 32							
Tir-phil	d																		09 36							
Brithdir	d																		09 39							
Bargoed	a																		09 42							
	d		09 02					09 17					09 32					09 47						10 02		
Gilfach Fargoed	d							09 19																	
Pengam	d		09 07					09 22					09 37					09 52						10 07		
Hengoed	d		09 10					09 25					09 40					09 55						10 10		
Ystrad Mynach 3	d		09 13					09 28					09 43					09 58						10 13		
Llanbradach	d		09 18					09 33					09 48					10 03						10 18		
Aber	d		09 22					09 37					09 52					10 07						10 22		
Caerphilly 3	d		09 25					09 40					09 55					10 10						10 25		
Lisvane & Thornhill	d		09 29					09 44					09 59					10 14						10 29		
Llanishen	d		09 31					09 46					10 01					10 16						10 31		
Heath High Level	d		09 34					09 49					10 04					10 19						10 34		
Coryton	d									09 45											10 15				
Whitchurch (Cardiff)	d									09 46											10 16				
Rhiwbina	d									09 48											10 18				
Birchgrove	d									09 50											10 20				
Ty Glas	d									09 51											10 21				
Heath Low Level	d									09 54											10 24				
Cardiff Queen Street 3	a		09 39	09 44			09 49	09 54		09 59		10 04	10 09		10 14		10 19	10 24			10 29	10 34		10 39	10 44
	d	09 36	09 41	09 46		09 48	09 51	09 56		10 01	10 00	10 06	10 11	10 12	10 16		10 21	10 26		10 24	10 31	10 36	10 36	10 41	10 46
Cardiff Bay	a	09 40				09 52					10 04			10 16						10 28			10 40		
Cardiff Central 7	a		09 44	09 52	09 50		09 54	09 59		10 04		10 09	10 14		10 22	10 20	10 24	10 29			10 34	10 39		10 44	10 52
	d		09 46				09 55	10 01				10 10	10 16				10 25	10 31				10 41		10 46	
Grangetown	d		09 50				09 59	10 05				10 14	10 20				10 29	10 35				10 45		10 50	
Dingle Road	d		09 56					10 11					10 26					10 41						10 56	
Penarth	a		10 02					10 16					10 31					10 46						11 01	
Cogan	d						10 03					10 18					10 33					10 48			
Eastbrook	d						10 05					10 20					10 35					10 51			
Dinas Powys	d						10 07					10 22					10 37					10 53			
Cadoxton	d						10 12					10 27					10 42					10 57			
Barry Docks	d						10 15					10 30					10 45					11 00			
Barry 3	d						10 19					10 34					10 49					11 05			
Barry Island	a						10 25					10 40					10 55									
Rhoose Cardiff Int Airport ✈	d																					11 12			
Llantwit Major	d																					11 22			
Bridgend	a																					11 39			

When events are being held at the Millenium Stadium, services are subject to alteration. Please check times before travelling.

Saturdays
until 8 September

Treherbert, Aberdare, Merthyr, Pontypridd, Rhymney and Coryton - Cardiff, Penarth, Barry, Barry Island and Bridgend

Network Diagram - see first Page of Table 130

		AW	AW	AW		AW	AW	AW	AW	AW	AW	AW	AW	AW		AW	AW	AW	AW	AW	AW	AW	AW	AW
Treherbert	d															10 17						10 47		
Ynyswen	d															10 19						10 49		
Treorchy	d															10 21						10 51		
Ton Pentre	d															10 23						10 53		
Ystrad Rhondda	a															10 26						10 56		
	d															10 28						10 58		
Llwynypia	d															10 30						11 00		
Tonypandy	d															10 33						11 03		
Dinas Rhondda	d															10 35						11 05		
Porth	a															10 38						11 08		
	d															10 52						11 09		
Trehafod	d															10 55						11 12		
Merthyr Tydfil	d					10 04														10 38					
Pentre-bach	d					10 08														10 42					
Troed Y Rhiw	d					10 11														10 45					
Merthyr Vale	a					10 14														10 48					
	d					10 16														10 50					
Quakers Yard	d					10 22														10 55					
Aberdare 3	d			09 52										10 22										
Cwmbach	d			09 55										10 25										
Fernhill	d			09 58										10 28										
Mountain Ash	a			10 01										10 31										
	d			10 04										10 34										
Penrhiwceiber	d			10 07										10 37										
Abercynon	d			10 13		10 26								10 43						10 59					
Pontypridd 3	a			10 22		10 32								10 52			11 00			11 07			11 17		
	d			10 24						10 39				10 54			11 04			11 09			11 18		
Trefforest	d			10 27						10 42				10 57			11 07			11 12			11 21		
Trefforest Estate	d																			11 16					
Taffs Well 3	d			10 34						10 50				11 04			11 13			11 20			11 28		
Radyr 3	a			10 37						10 53				11 07			11 17			11 23			11 31		
	d	10 34		10 37						10 53		11 04		11 07			11 17			11 23			11 31	11 34	
Danescourt	d	10 38										11 08												11 38	
Fairwater	d	10 40										11 10												11 40	
Waun-gron Park	d	10 42										11 12												11 42	
Ninian Park	d	10 45										11 15												11 45	
Llandaf	d			10 40						10 56				11 10						11 26			11 34		
Cathays	d			10 45						11 01				11 15						11 31			11 39		
Rhymney 3	d															10 29									
Pontlottyn	d															10 32									
Tir-phil	d															10 36									
Brithdir	d															10 39									
Bargoed	a															10 42									
	d						10 17				10 32					10 47						11 02			
Gilfach Fargoed	d						10 19																		
Pengam	d						10 22				10 37					10 52						11 07			
Hengoed	d						10 25				10 40					10 55						11 10			
Ystrad Mynach 3	d						10 28				10 43					10 58						11 13			
Llanbradach	d						10 33				10 48					11 03						11 18			
Aber	d						10 37				10 52					11 07						11 22			
Caerphilly 3	d						10 40				10 55					11 10						11 25			
Lisvane & Thornhill	d						10 44				10 59					11 14						11 29			
Llanishen	d						10 46				11 01					11 16						11 31			
Heath High Level	d						10 49				11 04					11 19						11 34			
Coryton	d							10 45											11 15					
Whitchurch (Cardiff)	d							10 46											11 16					
Rhiwbina	d							10 48											11 18					
Birchgrove	d							10 50											11 20					
Ty Glas	d							10 51											11 21					
Heath Low Level	d							10 54											11 24					
Cardiff Queen Street 3	a			10 49			10 54	10 59		11 04	11 09			11 19		11 24			11 29	11 34		11 39	11 44		
	d		10 48	10 51			10 56	11 01	11 00	11 06	11 11		11 12	11 21		11 26		11 24	11 31	11 36	11 36	11 41	11 46		
Cardiff Bay	a		10 52						11 04				11 16					11 28			11 40			
Cardiff Central 7	a	10 50		10 54			10 59	11 04		11 09	11 14	11 20		11 24		11 29	11 34		11 34	11 39		11 44	11 52	11 50
	d			10 55			11 01			11 10	11 16			11 25		11 31				11 41		11 46		
Grangetown	d			10 59			11 05			11 14	11 20			11 29		11 35				11 45		11 50		
Dingle Road	d						11 11				11 26					11 41						11 56			
Penarth	a						11 16				11 31					11 46						12 01			
Cogan	d			11 03						11 18				11 33						11 48					
Eastbrook	d			11 05						11 20				11 35						11 51					
Dinas Powys	d			11 07						11 22				11 37						11 53					
Cadoxton	d			11 12						11 27				11 42						11 57					
Barry Docks	d			11 15						11 30				11 45						12 00					
Barry 3	d			11 19						11 34				11 49						12 05					
Barry Island	a			11 25						11 40				11 55											
Rhoose Cardiff Int Airport ✈	d																			12 12					
Llantwit Major	d																			12 22					
Bridgend	a																			12 39					

When events are being held at the Millenium Stadium, services are subject to alteration. Please check times before travelling.

Treherbert, Aberdare, Merthyr, Pontypridd, Rhymney and Coryton - Cardiff, Penarth, Barry, Barry Island and Bridgend

Network Diagram - see first Page of Table 130

		AW	AW	AW	AW	AW	AW	AW	AW	AW	AW	AW	AW	AW	AW	AW	AW	AW	AW	AW	AW	AW	AW
Treherbert	d									11 17									11 47				
Ynyswen	d									11 19									11 49				
Treorchy	d									11 21									11 51				
Ton Pentre	d									11 23									11 53				
Ystrad Rhondda	a									11 26									11 56				
	d									11 28									11 58				
Llwynypia	d									11 30									12 00				
Tonypandy	d									11 33									12 03				
Dinas Rhondda	d									11 35									12 05				
Porth	a									11 38									12 08				
	d									11 39									12 09				
Trehafod	d									11 42									12 12				
Merthyr Tydfil	d						11 08									11 38							
Pentre-bach	d						11 12									11 42							
Troed Y Rhiw	d						11 15									11 45							
Merthyr Vale	a						11 18									11 48							
	d						11 20									11 50							
Quakers Yard	d						11 25									11 55							
Aberdare 3	d		10 52									11 22											
Cwmbach	d		10 55									11 25											
Fernhill	d		10 58									11 28											
Mountain Ash	a		11 01									11 31											
	d		11 04									11 34											
Penrhiwceiber	d		11 07									11 37											
Abercynon	d		11 13				11 29					11 43				11 59							
Pontypridd 3	a		11 22				11 37			11 47		11 52				12 07			12 17				
	d		11 24				11 39			11 48		11 54				12 09			12 18				
Trefforest	d		11 27				11 42			11 51		11 57				12 12			12 21				
Trefforest Estate	d						11 46									12 16							
Taffs Well 3	d		11 34				11 50			11 58		12 04				12 20			12 28				
Radyr 3	a		11 37				11 53			12 01		12 07				12 23			12 31				
	d		11 37				11 53			12 01	12 04	12 07				12 23			12 31	12 34			
Danescourt	d										12 08									12 38			
Fairwater	d										12 10									12 40			
Waun-gron Park	d										12 12									12 42			
Ninian Park	d										12 15									12 45			
Llandaf	d		11 40				11 56			12 04		12 10				12 26			12 34				
Cathays	d		11 45				12 01			12 09		12 15				12 31			12 39				
Rhymney 3	d												11 29										
Pontlottyn	d												11 32										
Tir-phil	d												11 36										
Brithdir	d												11 39										
Bargoed	a												11 42										
	d			11 17				11 32					11 47					12 02				12 17	
Gilfach Fargoed	d			11 19																		12 19	
Pengam	d			11 22				11 37					11 52					12 07				12 22	
Hengoed	d			11 25				11 40					11 55					12 10				12 25	
Ystrad Mynach 3	d			11 28				11 43					11 58					12 13				12 28	
Llanbradach	d			11 33				11 48					12 03					12 18				12 33	
Aber	d			11 37				11 52					12 07					12 22				12 37	
Caerphilly 3	d			11 40				11 55					12 10					12 25				12 40	
Lisvane & Thornhill	d			11 44				11 59					12 14					12 29				12 44	
Llanishen	d			11 46				12 01					12 16					12 31				12 46	
Heath High Level	d			11 49				12 04					12 19					12 34				12 49	
Coryton	d				11 45										12 15								12 45
Whitchurch (Cardiff)	d				11 46										12 16								12 46
Rhiwbina	d				11 48										12 18								12 48
Birchgrove	d				11 50										12 20								12 50
Ty Glas	d				11 51										12 21								12 51
Heath Low Level	d				11 54										12 24								12 54
Cardiff Queen Street 3	a		11 49	11 54	11 59		12 04	12 09		12 14		12 19	12 24		12 29	12 34		12 39	12 44			12 54	12 59
	d	11 48	11 51	11 56	12 01	12 00	12 06	12 11	12 12	12 16		12 21	12 26	12 24	12 31	12 36	12 36	12 41	12 46		12 48	12 56	13 01
Cardiff Bay	a	11 52				12 04			12 16					12 28			12 40				12 52		
Cardiff Central 7	a		11 54	11 59	12 04		12 09	12 14		12 22	12 20	12 24	12 29		12 34	12 39		12 44	12 52	12 50		12 59	13 04
	d		11 55	12 01			12 10	12 16				12 25	12 31			12 41		12 46	12 55			13 01	
Grangetown	d		11 59	12 05			12 14	12 20				12 29	12 35			12 45		12 50	12 59			13 05	
Dingle Road	d			12 11				12 26					12 41					12 56				13 11	
Penarth	a			12 16				12 31					12 46					13 01				13 16	
Cogan	d		12 03				12 18					12 33				12 48			13 03				
Eastbrook	d		12 05				12 20					12 35				12 51			13 05				
Dinas Powys	d		12 07				12 22					12 37				12 53			13 07				
Cadoxton	d		12 12				12 27					12 42				12 57			13 12				
Barry Docks	d		12 15				12 30					12 45				13 00			13 15				
Barry 3	d		12 19				12 34					12 49				13 05			13 19				
Barry Island	a		12 25				12 40					12 55							13 25				
Rhoose Cardiff Int Airport ✈	d															13 12							
Llantwit Major	d															13 22							
Bridgend	a															13 39							

When events are being held at the Millenium Stadium, services are subject to alteration. Please check times before travelling.

Treherbert, Aberdare, Merthyr, Pontypridd, Rhymney and Coryton - Cardiff, Penarth, Barry, Barry Island and Bridgend

Network Diagram - see first Page of Table 130

		AW	AW	AW	AW	AW	AW	AW	AW	AW	AW	AW	AW	AW	AW	AW	AW	AW	AW	AW	AW	AW	AW
Treherbert	d					12 17									12 47								
Ynyswen	d					12 19									12 49								
Treorchy	d					12 21									12 51								
Ton Pentre	d					12 23									12 53								
Ystrad Rhondda	a					12 26									12 56								
	d					12 28									12 58								
Llwynypia	d					12 30									13 00								
Tonypandy	d					12 33									13 03								
Dinas Rhondda	d					12 35									13 05								
Porth	a					12 38									13 08								
	d					12 39									13 09								
Trehafod	d					12 42									13 12								
Merthyr Tydfil	d		12 08									12 38										13 08	
Pentre-bach	d		12 12									12 42										13 12	
Troed Y Rhiw	d		12 15									12 45										13 15	
Merthyr Vale	a		12 18									12 48										13 18	
	d		12 20									12 50										13 20	
Quakers Yard	d		12 25									12 55										13 25	
Aberdare 3	d							12 22										12 52					
Cwmbach	d							12 25										12 55					
Fernhill	d							12 28										12 58					
Mountain Ash	a							12 31										13 01					
	d							12 34										13 04					
Penrhiwceiber	d							12 37										13 07					
Abercynon	d		12 29					12 43				12 59						13 13				13 29	
Pontypridd 3	a		12 37			12 48		12 52				13 07			13 17			13 22				13 37	
	d		12 39			12 48		12 54				13 09			13 18			13 24				13 39	
Trefforest	d		12 42			12 51		12 57				13 12			13 21			13 27				13 42	
Trefforest Estate	d		12 46									13 16										13 46	
Taffs Well 3	d		12 50			12 58		13 04				13 20			13 28			13 34				13 50	
Radyr 3	a		12 53			13 01		13 07				13 23			13 31			13 37				13 53	
	d		12 53			13 01	13 04	13 07				13 23			13 31	13 34		13 37				13 53	
Danescourt	d						13 08									13 38							
Fairwater	d						13 10									13 40							
Waun-gron Park	d						13 12									13 42							
Ninian Park	d						13 15									13 45							
Llandaf	d		12 56			13 04		13 10				13 26			13 34			13 40				13 56	
Cathays	d		13 01			13 09		13 15				13 31			13 39			13 45				14 01	
Rhymney 3	d								12 29														
Pontlottyn	d								12 32														
Tir-phil	d								12 36														
Brithdir	d								12 39														
Bargoed	a								12 42														
	d			12 32					12 47					13 02					13 17				13 32
Gilfach Fargoed	d																		13 19				
Pengam	d			12 37					12 52					13 07					13 22				13 37
Hengoed	d			12 40					12 55					13 10					13 25				13 40
Ystrad Mynach 3	d			12 43					12 58					13 13					13 28				13 43
Llanbradach	d			12 48					13 03					13 18					13 33				13 48
Aber	d			12 52					13 07					13 22					13 37				13 52
Caerphilly 3	d			12 55					13 10					13 25					13 40				13 55
Lisvane & Thornhill	d			12 59					13 14					13 29					13 44				13 59
Llanishen	d			13 01					13 16					13 31					13 46				14 01
Heath High Level	d			13 04					13 19					13 34					13 49				14 04
Coryton	d										13 15									13 45			
Whitchurch (Cardiff)	d										13 16									13 46			
Rhiwbina	d										13 18									13 48			
Birchgrove	d										13 20									13 50			
Ty Glas	d										13 21									13 51			
Heath Low Level	d										13 24									13 54			
Cardiff Queen Street 3	a		13 04	13 09		13 14		13 19	13 24		13 29	13 34		13 39	13 44			13 49	13 54	13 59		14 04	14 09
	d	13 00	13 06	13 11	13 12	13 16		13 21	13 26	13 24	13 31	13 36	13 36	13 41	13 46		13 48	13 51	13 56	14 01	14 00	14 06	14 11
Cardiff Bay	a	13 04			13 16					13 28			13 40				13 52				14 04		
Cardiff Central 7	a		13 09	13 14		13 22	13 20	13 24	13 29		13 34	13 39		13 44	13 52	13 50		13 54	13 59	14 04		14 09	14 14
	d		13 10	13 16				13 25	13 31			13 41		13 46				13 55	14 01			14 10	14 16
Grangetown	d		13 14	13 20				13 29	13 35			13 45		13 50				13 59	14 05			14 14	14 20
Dingle Road	d			13 26					13 41					13 56					14 11				14 26
Penarth	a			13 31					13 46					14 01					14 16				14 31
Cogan	d		13 18					13 33				13 48						14 03				14 18	
Eastbrook	d		13 20					13 35				13 51						14 05				14 20	
Dinas Powys	d		13 22					13 37				13 53						14 07				14 22	
Cadoxton	d		13 27					13 42				13 57						14 12				14 27	
Barry Docks	d		13 30					13 45				14 00						14 15				14 30	
Barry 3	d		13 34					13 49				14 05						14 19				14 34	
Barry Island	a		13 40					13 55										14 25				14 40	
Rhoose Cardiff Int Airport ✈	d											14 12											
Llantwit Major	d											14 22											
Bridgend	a											14 39											

When events are being held at the Millenium Stadium, services are subject to alteration. Please check times before travelling.

Table 130

Saturdays until 8 September

Treherbert, Aberdare, Merthyr, Pontypridd, Rhymney and Coryton - Cardiff, Penarth, Barry, Barry Island and Bridgend

Network Diagram - see first Page of Table 130

		AW		AW	AW	AW	AW	AW	AW	AW	AW	AW		AW	AW	AW	AW	AW	AW	AW	AW	AW		AW	AW
Treherbert	d			13 17										13 47											
Ynyswen	d			13 19										13 49											
Treorchy	d			13 21										13 51											
Ton Pentre	d			13 23										13 53											
Ystrad Rhondda	a			13 26										13 56											
	d			13 28										13 58											
Llwynypia	d			13 30										14 00											
Tonypandy	d			13 33										14 03											
Dinas Rhondda	d			13 35										14 05											
Porth	a			13 38										14 08											
	d			13 39										14 09											
Trehafod	d			13 42										14 12											
Merthyr Tydfil	d									13 38											14 08				
Pentre-bach	d									13 42											14 12				
Troed Y Rhiw	d									13 45											14 15				
Merthyr Vale	a									13 48											14 18				
	d									13 50											14 20				
Quakers Yard	d									13 55											14 25				
Aberdare	d																13 52								
Cwmbach	d																13 55								
Fernhill	d																13 58								
Mountain Ash	a																14 01								
	d																14 04								
Penrhiwceiber	d																14 07								
Abercynon	d					13 45				13 59							14 13				14 29				
Pontypridd	a			13 47		13 52				14 07				14 17			14 22				14 37				
	d			13 48		13 54				14 09				14 18			14 24				14 39				
Trefforest	d			13 51		13 57				14 12				14 21			14 27				14 42				
Trefforest Estate	d									14 16											14 46				
Taffs Well	d			13 58		14 04				14 20				14 28			14 34				14 50				
Radyr	a			14 01		14 07				14 23				14 31			14 37				14 53				
	d			14 01	14 04	14 07				14 23				14 31	14 34		14 37				14 53			15 04	
Danescourt	d				14 08										14 38									15 08	
Fairwater	d				14 10										14 40									15 10	
Waun-gron Park	d				14 12										14 42									15 12	
Ninian Park	d				14 15										14 45									15 15	
Llandaf	d			14 04		14 10				14 26				14 34			14 40				14 56				
Cathays	d			14 09		14 15				14 31				14 39			14 45				15 01				
Rhymney	d						13 29																		
Pontlottyn	d						13 32																		
Tir-phil	d						13 36																		
Brithdir	d						13 39																		
Bargoed	a						13 42																		
	d						13 47					14 02						14 17				14 32			
Gilfach Fargoed	d																	14 19							
Pengam	d						13 52					14 07						14 22				14 37			
Hengoed	d						13 55					14 10						14 25				14 40			
Ystrad Mynach	d						13 58					14 13						14 28				14 43			
Llanbradach	d						14 03					14 18						14 33				14 48			
Aber	d						14 07					14 22						14 37				14 52			
Caerphilly	d						14 10					14 25						14 40				14 55			
Lisvane & Thornhill	d						14 14					14 29						14 44				14 59			
Llanishen	d						14 16					14 31						14 46				15 01			
Heath High Level	d						14 19					14 34						14 49				15 04			
Coryton	d								14 15										14 45						
Whitchurch (Cardiff)	d								14 16										14 46						
Rhiwbina	d								14 18										14 48						
Birchgrove	d								14 20										14 50						
Ty Glas	d								14 21										14 51						
Heath Low Level	d								14 24										14 54						
Cardiff Queen Street	a			14 14		14 19	14 24		14 29	14 34		14 39		14 44			14 49	14 54	14 59		15 04	15 09			
	d	14 12		14 16		14 21	14 26	14 24	14 31	14 36	14 36	14 41		14 46		14 48	14 51	14 56	15 01	15 00	15 06	15 11			15 12
Cardiff Bay	a	14 16						14 28			14 40					14 52				15 04					15 16
Cardiff Central	a			14 22	14 20	14 24	14 29		14 34	14 39		14 44		14 52	14 50		14 54	14 59	15 04		15 09	15 14		15 20	
	d					14 25	14 31			14 41		14 46					14 55	15 01			15 10	15 16			
Grangetown	d					14 29	14 35			14 45		14 50					14 59	15 05			15 14	15 20			
Dingle Road	d						14 41					14 56						15 11				15 26			
Penarth	a						14 46					15 01						15 16				15 31			
Cogan	d					14 33				14 48							15 03				15 18				
Eastbrook	d					14 35				14 51							15 05				15 20				
Dinas Powys	d					14 37				14 53							15 07				15 22				
Cadoxton	d					14 42				14 57							15 12				15 27				
Barry Docks	d					14 45				15 00							15 15				15 30				
Barry	d					14 49				15 05							15 19				15 34				
Barry Island	a					14 55											15 25				15 40				
Rhoose Cardiff Int Airport ✈	d									15 12															
Llantwit Major	d									15 22															
Bridgend	a									15 39															

When events are being held at the Millenium Stadium, services are subject to alteration. Please check times before travelling.

Table 130

Saturdays until 8 September

Treherbert, Aberdare, Merthyr, Pontypridd, Rhymney and Coryton - Cardiff, Penarth, Barry, Barry Island and Bridgend

Network Diagram - see first Page of Table 130

		AW	AW	AW	AW	AW	AW	AW		AW	AW	AW	AW	AW	AW	AW	AW	AW		AW	AW	AW	AW	AW	AW
Treherbert	d			14 17							14 47											15 13			
Ynyswen	d			14 19							14 49											15 15			
Treorchy	d			14 21							14 51											15 21			
Ton Pentre	d			14 23							14 53											15 23			
Ystrad Rhondda	a			14 26							14 56											15 26			
	d			14 28							14 58											15 28			
Llwynypia	d			14 30							15 00											15 30			
Tonypandy	d			14 33							15 03											15 33			
Dinas Rhondda	d			14 35							15 05											15 35			
Porth	a			14 38							15 08											15 38			
	d			14 52							15 09											15 39			
Trehafod	d			14 55							15 12											15 42			
Merthyr Tydfil	d						14 38											15 08							
Pentre-bach	d						14 42											15 12							
Troed Y Rhiw	d						14 45											15 15							
Merthyr Vale	a						14 48											15 18							
	d						14 50											15 20							
Quakers Yard	d						14 55											15 25							
Aberdare	d	14 22												14 52										15 22	
Cwmbach	d	14 25												14 55										15 25	
Fernhill	d	14 28												14 58										15 28	
Mountain Ash	a	14 31												15 01										15 31	
	d	14 34												15 04										15 34	
Penrhiwceiber	d	14 37												15 07										15 37	
Abercynon	d	14 43					14 59							15 13				15 29						15 43	
Pontypridd	a	14 52		15 00			15 07				15 17			15 22				15 37				15 47		15 52	
	d	14 54		15 04			15 09				15 18			15 24				15 39				15 48		15 54	
Trefforest	d	14 57		15 07			15 12				15 21			15 27				15 42				15 51		15 57	
Trefforest Estate	d						15 16											15 46							
Taffs Well	d	15 04		15 13			15 20				15 28			15 34				15 50				15 58		16 04	
Radyr	a	15 07		15 17			15 23				15 31			15 37				15 53				16 01		16 07	
	d	15 07		15 17			15 23				15 31	15 34		15 37				15 53				16 01	16 04	16 07	
Danescourt	d											15 38											16 08		
Fairwater	d											15 40											16 10		
Waun-gron Park	d											15 42											16 12		
Ninian Park	d											15 45											16 15		
Llandaf	d	15 10					15 26				15 34			15 40				15 56				16 04		16 10	
Cathays	d	15 15					15 31				15 39			15 45				16 01				16 09		16 15	
Rhymney	d		14 29																						15 29
Pontlottyn	d		14 32																						15 32
Tir-phil	d		14 36																						15 36
Brithdir	d		14 39																						15 39
Bargoed	a		14 42																						15 42
	d		14 47							15 02					15 17					15 32					15 47
Gilfach Fargoed	d														15 19										
Pengam	d		14 52							15 07					15 22					15 37					15 52
Hengoed	d		14 55							15 10					15 25					15 40					15 55
Ystrad Mynach	d		14 58							15 13					15 28					15 43					15 58
Llanbradach	d		15 03							15 18					15 33					15 48					16 03
Aber	d		15 07							15 22					15 37					15 52					16 07
Caerphilly	d		15 10							15 25					15 40					15 55					16 10
Lisvane & Thornhill	d		15 14							15 29					15 44					15 59					16 14
Llanishen	d		15 16							15 31					15 46					16 01					16 16
Heath High Level	d		15 19							15 34					15 49					16 04					16 19
Coryton	d					15 15										15 45									
Whitchurch (Cardiff)	d					15 16										15 46									
Rhiwbina	d					15 18										15 48									
Birchgrove	d					15 20										15 50									
Ty Glas	d					15 21										15 51									
Heath Low Level	d					15 24										15 54									
Cardiff Queen Street	a	15 19	15 24			15 29	15 34			15 39	15 44			15 49	15 54	15 59		16 04		16 09		16 14		16 19	16 24
	d	15 21	15 26		15 24	15 31	15 36	15 36		15 41	15 46		15 48	15 51	15 56	16 01	16 00	16 06		16 11	16 12	16 16		16 21	16 26
Cardiff Bay	a				15 28			15 40					15 52				16 04				16 16				
Cardiff Central	a	15 24	15 29	15 34		15 34	15 39			15 44	15 52	15 50		15 54	15 59	16 04		16 09		16 14		16 22	16 20	16 24	16 32
	d	15 25	15 31				15 41			15 46				15 55	16 01			16 10		16 16				16 25	
Grangetown	d	15 29	15 35				15 45			15 50				15 59	16 05			16 14		16 20				16 29	
Dingle Road	d		15 41							15 56					16 11					16 26					
Penarth	a		15 46							16 01					16 16					16 31					
Cogan	d	15 33					15 48							16 03				16 18						16 33	
Eastbrook	d	15 35					15 51							16 05				16 20						16 35	
Dinas Powys	d	15 37					15 53							16 07				16 22						16 37	
Cadoxton	d	15 42					15 57							16 12				16 27						16 42	
Barry Docks	d	15 45					16 00							16 15				16 30						16 45	
Barry	d	15 49					16 05							16 19				16 34						16 49	
Barry Island	a	15 55												16 25				16 40						16 55	
Rhoose Cardiff Int Airport ✈	d						16 12																		
Llantwit Major	d						16 22																		
Bridgend	a						16 39																		

When events are being held at the Millenium Stadium, services are subject to alteration. Please check times before travelling.

Table 130

Saturdays until 8 September

Treherbert, Aberdare, Merthyr, Pontypridd, Rhymney and Coryton - Cardiff, Penarth, Barry, Barry Island and Bridgend

Network Diagram - see first Page of Table 130

		AW	AW	AW		AW	AW	AW	AW	AW	AW	AW	AW	AW		AW	AW	AW	AW	AW	AW	AW	AW	AW
Treherbert	d							15 47											16 17					
Ynyswen	d							15 49											16 19					
Treorchy	d							15 51											16 21					
Ton Pentre	d							15 53											16 23					
Ystrad Rhondda	a							15 56											16 26					
	d							15 58											16 28					
Llwynypia	d							16 00											16 30					
Tonypandy	d							16 03											16 33					
Dinas Rhondda	d							16 05											16 35					
Porth	a							16 08											16 38					
	d							16 09											16 39					
Trehafod	d							16 12											16 42					
Merthyr Tydfil	d			15 38												16 08								
Pentre-bach	d			15 42												16 12								
Troed Y Rhiw	d			15 45												16 15								
Merthyr Vale	a			15 48												16 18								
	d			15 50												16 20								
Quakers Yard	d			15 55												16 25								
Aberdare ■	d										15 52										16 22			
Cwmbach	d										15 55										16 25			
Fernhill	d										15 58										16 28			
Mountain Ash	a										16 01										16 31			
	d										16 04										16 34			
Penrhiwceiber	d										16 07										16 37			
Abercynon	d			15 59							16 13					16 29					16 43			
Pontypridd ■	a			16 07				16 17			16 22					16 37			16 47		16 52			
	d			16 09				16 18			16 24					16 39			16 48		16 54			
Trefforest	d			16 12				16 21			16 27					16 42			16 51		16 57			
Trefforest Estate	d			16 16												16 46								
Taffs Well ■	d			16 20				16 28			16 34					16 50			16 58		17 04			
Radyr ■	a			16 23				16 31			16 37					16 53			17 01		17 07			
	d			16 23				16 32	16 34		16 37					16 53			17 01	17 04	17 07			
Danescourt	d								16 38											17 08				
Fairwater	d								16 40											17 10				
Waun-gron Park	d								16 42											17 12				
Ninian Park	d								16 45											17 15				
Llandaf	d			16 26				16 34			16 40					16 56			17 04		17 10			
Cathays	d			16 31				16 39			16 45					17 01			17 09		17 15			
Rhymney ■	d																					16 29		
Pontlottyn	d																					16 32		
Tir-phil	d																					16 36		
Brithdir	d																					16 39		
Bargoed	a																					16 42		
	d						16 02					16 17					16 32					16 47		
Gilfach Fargoed	d											16 19												
Pengam	d						16 07					16 22					16 37					16 52		
Hengoed	d						16 10					16 25					16 40					16 55		
Ystrad Mynach ■	d						16 13					16 28					16 43					16 58		
Llanbradach	d						16 18					16 33					16 48					17 03		
Aber	d						16 22					16 37					16 52					17 07		
Caerphilly ■	d						16 25					16 40					16 55					17 10		
Lisvane & Thornhill	d						16 29					16 44					16 59					17 14		
Llanishen	d						16 31					16 46					17 01					17 16		
Heath High Level	d						16 34					16 49					17 04					17 19		
Coryton	d		16 15										16 45											17 15
Whitchurch (Cardiff)	d		16 16										16 46											17 16
Rhiwbina	d		16 18										16 48											17 18
Birchgrove	d		16 20										16 50											17 20
Ty Glas	d		16 21										16 51											17 21
Heath Low Level	d		16 24										16 54											17 24
Cardiff Queen Street ■	a		16 29	16 34			16 39	16 44			16 49	16 54	16 59			17 04	17 09		17 14		17 19	17 24		17 29
	d	16 24	16 31	16 36		16 36	16 41	16 46		16 48	16 51	16 56	17 01	17 00		17 06	17 11	17 12	17 16		17 21	17 26	17 24	17 31
Cardiff Bay	a	16 28				16 40				16 52				17 04				17 16					17 28	
Cardiff Central ■	a		16 34	16 39			16 44	16 53	16 50		16 54	16 59	17 04			17 09	17 14		17 22	17 20	17 24	17 29		17 34
	d			16 41			16 46				16 55	17 01				17 10	17 16				17 25	17 31		
Grangetown	d			16 45			16 50				16 59	17 05				17 14	17 20				17 29	17 35		
Dingle Road	d						16 56					17 11					17 26					17 41		
Penarth	a						17 01					17 16					17 31					17 46		
Cogan	d			16 48							17 03					17 18					17 33			
Eastbrook	d			16 51							17 05					17 20					17 35			
Dinas Powys	d			16 53							17 07					17 22					17 37			
Cadoxton	d			16 57							17 12					17 27					17 42			
Barry Docks	d			17 00							17 15					17 30					17 45			
Barry ■	d			17 05							17 19					17 34					17 49			
Barry Island	a										17 25					17 40					17 55			
Rhoose Cardiff Int Airport ✈	d			17 12																				
Llantwit Major	d			17 22																				
Bridgend	a			17 39																				

When events are being held at the Millenium Stadium, services are subject to alteration. Please check times before travelling.

Table 130

Saturdays until 8 September

Treherbert, Aberdare, Merthyr, Pontypridd, Rhymney and Coryton - Cardiff, Penarth, Barry, Barry Island and Bridgend

Network Diagram - see first Page of Table 130

		AW	AW	AW	AW	AW	AW	AW	AW	AW		AW	AW	AW	AW	AW	AW	AW	AW	AW		AW	AW	AW	AW
Treherbert	d				16 47											17 17									17 47
Ynyswen	d				16 49											17 19									17 49
Treorchy	d				16 51											17 21									17 51
Ton Pentre	d				16 53											17 23									17 53
Ystrad Rhondda	a				16 56											17 26									17 56
	d				16 58											17 28									17 58
Llwynypia	d				17 00											17 30									18 00
Tonypandy	d				17 03											17 33									18 03
Dinas Rhondda	d				17 05											17 35									18 05
Porth	a				17 08											17 38									18 08
	d				17 09											17 39									18 09
Trehafod	d				17 12											17 42									18 12
Merthyr Tydfil	d	16 38											17 08										17 38		
Pentre-bach	d	16 42											17 12										17 42		
Troed Y Rhiw	d	16 45											17 15										17 45		
Merthyr Vale	a	16 48											17 18										17 48		
	d	16 50											17 20										17 50		
Quakers Yard	d	16 55											17 25										17 55		
Aberdare ■	d							16 52										17 22							
Cwmbach	d							16 55										17 25							
Fernhill	d							16 58										17 28							
Mountain Ash	a							17 01										17 31							
	d							17 04										17 34							
Penrhiwceiber	d							17 07										17 37							
Abercynon	d	16 59						17 13					17 29					17 43					17 59		
Pontypridd ■	a	17 07			17 17			17 22					17 37			17 47		17 52					18 07		18 17
	d	17 09			17 18			17 24					17 39			17 48		17 54					18 09		18 18
Trefforest	d	17 12			17 21			17 27					17 42			17 51		17 57					18 12		18 21
Trefforest Estate	d	17 16											17 46										18 16		
Taffs Well ■	d	17 20			17 28			17 34					17 50			17 58		18 04					18 20		18 28
Radyr ■	a	17 23			17 31			17 37					17 53			18 01		18 07					18 23		18 31
	d	17 23			17 31	17 34		17 37					17 53			18 01	18 04	18 07					18 23		18 31
Danescourt	d					17 38											18 08								
Fairwater	d					17 40											18 10								
Waun-gron Park	d					17 42											18 12								
Ninian Park	d					17 45											18 15								
Llandaf	d	17 26			17 34			17 40					17 56			18 04		18 10					18 26		18 34
Cathays	d	17 31			17 39			17 45					18 01			18 09		18 15					18 31		18 39
Rhymney ■	d																		17 29						
Pontlottyn	d																		17 32						
Tir-phil	d																		17 36						
Brithdir	d																		17 39						
Bargoed	a																		17 42						
	d			17 02					17 17					17 32					17 47						
Gilfach Fargoed	d								17 19																
Pengam	d			17 07					17 22					17 37					17 52						
Hengoed	d			17 10					17 25					17 40					17 55						
Ystrad Mynach ■	d			17 13					17 28					17 43					17 58						
Llanbradach	d			17 18					17 33					17 48					18 03						
Aber	d			17 22					17 37					17 52					18 07						
Caerphilly ■	d			17 25					17 40					17 55					18 10						
Lisvane & Thornhill	d			17 29					17 44					17 59					18 14						
Llanishen	d			17 31					17 46					18 01					18 16						
Heath High Level	d			17 34					17 49					18 04					18 19						
Coryton	d									17 45												18 15			
Whitchurch (Cardiff)	d									17 46												18 16			
Rhiwbina	d									17 48												18 18			
Birchgrove	d									17 50												18 20			
Ty Glas	d									17 51												18 21			
Heath Low Level	d									17 54												18 24			
Cardiff Queen Street ■	a	17 34		17 39	17 44			17 49	17 54	17 59			18 04	18 09		18 14		18 19	18 24			18 29	18 34		18 44
	d	17 36	17 36	17 41	17 46		17 48	17 51	17 56	18 01		18 00	18 06	18 11	18 12	18 16		18 21	18 26	18 24		18 31	18 36	18 36	18 46
Cardiff Bay	a		17 40				17 52					18 04			18 16					18 28				18 40	
Cardiff Central ■	a	17 39		17 44	17 52	17 50		17 54	17 59	18 04			18 09	18 14		18 22	18 20	18 24	18 29			18 34	18 39		18 52
	d	17 41		17 46				17 55	18 01				18 10	18 16				18 25	18 31				18 41		
Grangetown	d	17 45		17 50				17 59	18 05				18 14	18 20				18 29	18 35				18 45		
Dingle Road	d			17 56					18 11					18 26					18 41						
Penarth	a			18 01					18 16					18 31					18 46						
Cogan	d	17 48						18 03					18 18					18 33					18 48		
Eastbrook	d	17 51						18 05					18 20					18 35					18 51		
Dinas Powys	d	17 53						18 07					18 22					18 37					18 53		
Cadoxton	d	17 57						18 12					18 27					18 42					18 57		
Barry Docks	d	18 00						18 15					18 30					18 45					19 00		
Barry ■	d	18 05						18 19					18 34					18 49					19 05		
Barry Island	a							18 25					18 40					18 55							
Rhoose Cardiff Int Airport ✈	d	18 12																					19 12		
Llantwit Major	d	18 22																					19 22		
Bridgend	a	18 39																					19 39		

When events are being held at the Millenium Stadium, services are subject to alteration. Please check times before travelling.

Table 130

Saturdays until 8 September

Treherbert, Aberdare, Merthyr, Pontypridd, Rhymney and Coryton - Cardiff, Penarth, Barry, Barry Island and Bridgend

Network Diagram - see first Page of Table 130

Station		AW	AW	AW	AW	AW		AW	AW	AW	AW	AW	AW	AW	AW	AW		AW	AW	AW	AW	AW	AW	AW	AW
Treherbert	d										18 17									18 47					
Ynyswen	d										18 19									18 49					
Treorchy	d										18 21									18 51					
Ton Pentre	d										18 23									18 53					
Ystrad Rhondda	a										18 26									18 56					
	d										18 28									18 58					
Llwynypia	d										18 30									19 00					
Tonypandy	d										18 33									19 03					
Dinas Rhondda	d										18 35									19 05					
Porth	a										18 38									19 08					
	d										18 39									19 09					
Trehafod	d										18 42									19 12					
Merthyr Tydfil	d								18 08									18 38							19 08
Pentre-bach	d								18 12									18 42							19 12
Troed Y Rhiw	d								18 15									18 45							19 15
Merthyr Vale	a								18 18									18 48							19 18
	d								18 20									18 50							19 20
Quakers Yard	d								18 25									18 55							19 25
Aberdare ■	d			17 52									18 22									18 52			
Cwmbach	d			17 55									18 25									18 55			
Fernhill	d			17 58									18 28									18 58			
Mountain Ash	a			18 01									18 31									19 01			
	d			18 04									18 34									19 04			
Penrhiwceiber	d			18 07									18 37									19 07			
Abercynon	d			18 13					18 29				18 43					18 59				19 13			19 29
Pontypridd ■	a			18 22					18 37		18 47		18 52					19 07		19 17		19 22			19 37
	d			18 24					18 39		18 48		18 54					19 09		19 18		19 24			19 39
Trefforest	d			18 27					18 42		18 51		18 57					19 12		19 21		19 27			19 42
Trefforest Estate	d								18 46									19 16							19 46
Taffs Well ■	d			18 34					18 50		18 58		19 04					19 20		19 28		19 34			19 50
Radyr ■	a			18 37					18 53		19 01		19 07					19 23		19 31		19 37			19 53
	d	18 34		18 37					18 53		19 01	19 04	19 07					19 23		19 31		19 37			19 53
Danescourt	d	18 38										19 08													
Fairwater	d	18 40										19 10													
Waun-gron Park	d	18 42										19 12													
Ninian Park	d	18 45										19 15													
Llandaf	d			18 40					18 56		19 04		19 10					19 26		19 34		19 40			19 56
Cathays	d			18 45					19 01		19 09		19 15					19 31		19 39		19 45			20 01
Rhymney ■	d																								
Pontlottyn	d																								
Tir-phil	d																								
Brithdir	d																								
Bargoed	a																								
	d				18 17									18 48											
Gilfach Fargoed	d				18 19									18 50											
Pengam	d				18 22									18 53											
Hengoed	d				18 25									18 56											
Ystrad Mynach ■	d				18 28									18 59											
Llanbradach	d				18 33									19 04											
Aber	d				18 37									19 08											
Caerphilly ■	d				18 40									19 11									19 40		
Lisvane & Thornhill	d				18 44									19 15									19 44		
Llanishen	d				18 46									19 17									19 46		
Heath High Level	d				18 49									19 20									19 49		
Coryton	d					18 45										19 15									
Whitchurch (Cardiff)	d					18 46										19 16									
Rhiwbina	d					18 48										19 18									
Birchgrove	d					18 50										19 20									
Ty Glas	d					18 51										19 21									
Heath Low Level	d					18 54										19 24									
Cardiff Queen Street ■	a			18 49	18 54	18 59			19 04		19 14		19 19	19 24		19 29		19 34		19 44		19 49	19 54		20 04
	d		18 48	18 51	18 56	19 01		19 00	19 06	19 12	19 16		19 21	19 26	19 24	19 31		19 36	19 36	19 46	19 48	19 51	19 56	20 00	20 06
Cardiff Bay	a		18 52					19 04		19 16					19 28				19 40		19 52			20 04	
Cardiff Central ■	a	18 50		18 54	18 59	19 06			19 10		19 22	19 22	19 24	19 29		19 34		19 39		19 52		19 57	19 59		20 09
	d			18 55	19 01								19 25	19 31				19 41					20 06		20 10
Grangetown	d			18 59	19 05								19 29	19 35				19 45					20 10		20 14
Dingle Road	d				19 11									19 41									20 14		
Penarth	a				19 16									19 46									20 19		
Cogan	d			19 03									19 33					19 48							20 18
Eastbrook	d			19 05									19 35					19 51							20 20
Dinas Powys	d			19 07									19 37					19 53							20 22
Cadoxton	d			19 12									19 42					19 57							20 27
Barry Docks	d			19 15									19 45					20 00							20 30
Barry ■	d			19 19									19 49					20 05							20 34
Barry Island	a			19 25									19 55												20 40
Rhoose Cardiff Int Airport ✈	d																	20 12							
Llantwit Major	d																	20 22							
Bridgend	a																	20 39							

When events are being held at the Millenium Stadium, services are subject to alteration. Please check times before travelling.

Table 130

Saturdays until 8 September

Treherbert, Aberdare, Merthyr, Pontypridd, Rhymney and Coryton - Cardiff, Penarth, Barry, Barry Island and Bridgend

Network Diagram - see first Page of Table 130

Station		AW		AW	AW	AW	AW	AW	AW	AW	AW	AW		AW	AW	AW	AW	AW	AW	AW	AW	AW		AW	AW
Treherbert	d			19 17								19 47							20 17						
Ynyswen	d			19 19								19 49							20 19						
Treorchy	d			19 21								19 51							20 21						
Ton Pentre	d			19 23								19 53							20 23						
Ystrad Rhondda	a			19 26								19 56							20 26						
	d			19 28								19 58							20 28						
Llwynypia	d			19 30								20 00							20 30						
Tonypandy	d			19 33								20 03							20 33						
Dinas Rhondda	d			19 35								20 05							20 35						
Porth	a			19 38								20 08							20 38						
	d			19 39								20 09							20 39						
Trehafod	d			19 42								20 12							20 42						
Merthyr Tydfil	d								19 38																
Pentre-bach	d								19 42																
Troed Y Rhiw	d								19 45																
Merthyr Vale	a								19 48																
	d								19 50																
Quakers Yard	d								19 55																
Aberdare ■	d														19 52						20 22				
Cwmbach	d														19 55						20 25				
Fernhill	d														19 58						20 28				
Mountain Ash	a														20 01						20 31				
	d														20 04						20 34				
Penrhiwceiber	d														20 07						20 37				
Abercynon	d					19 43			19 59						20 13						20 43				
Pontypridd ■	a			19 47		19 52			20 07			20 18			20 22				20 47		20 52				
	d			19 48		19 54			20 09			20 18			20 24				20 48		20 54				
Trefforest	d			19 51		19 57			20 12			20 21			20 27				20 51		20 57				
Trefforest Estate	d								20 16																
Taffs Well ■	d			19 58		20 04			20 20			20 28			20 34				20 58		21 04				
Radyr ■	a			20 01		20 07			20 23			20 31			20 37				21 01		21 07				
	d			20 01	20 04	20 07			20 23			20 31			20 37				21 01	21 04	21 07				
Danescourt	d				20 08															21 08					
Fairwater	d				20 10															21 10					
Waun-gron Park	d				20 12															21 12					
Ninian Park	d				20 15															21 15					
Llandaf	d			20 04		20 10			20 26			20 34			20 40				21 04		21 10				
Cathays	d			20 09		20 15			20 31			20 39			20 45				21 09		21 15				
Rhymney ■	d										19 45														
Pontlottyn	d										19 48														
Tir-phil	d										19 52														
Brithdir	d										19 55														
Bargoed	a										19 58														
	d										19 59														
Gilfach Fargoed	d										20 01														
Pengam	d										20 04														
Hengoed	d										20 07														
Ystrad Mynach ■	d										20 10														
Llanbradach	d										20 15														
Aber	d										20 19														
Caerphilly ■	d										20 22					20 40									
Lisvane & Thornhill	d										20 26					20 44									
Llanishen	d										20 28					20 46									
Heath High Level	d										20 31					20 49									
Coryton	d							20 15																	21 15
Whitchurch (Cardiff)	d							20 16																	21 16
Rhiwbina	d							20 18																	21 18
Birchgrove	d							20 20																	21 20
Ty Glas	d							20 21																	21 21
Heath Low Level	d							20 24																	21 24
Cardiff Queen Street ■	a			20 14		20 19		20 29	20 34		20 39	20 44			20 49	20 54			21 14		21 19				21 29
	d	20 12		20 16		20 21	20 24	20 31	20 36	20 36	20 41	20 46		20 48	20 51	20 56	21 00	21 12	21 16		21 21	21 24			21 31
Cardiff Bay	a	20 16					20 28			20 40				20 52			21 04	21 16				21 28			
Cardiff Central ■	a			20 22	20 24	20 24		20 34	20 39		20 47	20 52			20 57	20 59			21 22	21 25	21 27				21 34
	d					20 31			20 41						21 06	21 10								21 31	
Grangetown	d					20 35			20 45						21 10	21 14								21 35	
Dingle Road	d					20 41									21 14									21 41	
Penarth	a					20 46									21 19									21 46	
Cogan	d								20 48							21 18									
Eastbrook	d								20 51							21 20									
Dinas Powys	d								20 53							21 22									
Cadoxton	d								20 57							21 27									
Barry Docks	d								21 00							21 30									
Barry ■	d								21 05							21 34									
Barry Island	a															21 40									
Rhoose Cardiff Int Airport ✈	d								21 12																
Llantwit Major	d								21 22																
Bridgend	a								21 39																

When events are being held at the Millenium Stadium, services are subject to alteration. Please check times before travelling.

Saturdays
until 8 September

Treherbert, Aberdare, Merthyr, Pontypridd, Rhymney and Coryton - Cardiff, Penarth, Barry, Barry Island and Bridgend

Network Diagram - see first Page of Table 130

		AW	AW	AW	AW	AW	AW	AW		AW	AW	AW	AW	AW	AW	AW	AW	AW		AW	AW	AW	AW	AW	AW
Treherbert	d										21 17														
Ynyswen	d										21 19														
Treorchy	d										21 21														
Ton Pentre	d										21 23														
Ystrad Rhondda	a										21 26														
	d										21 28														
Llwynypia	d										21 30														
Tonypandy	d										21 33														
Dinas Rhondda	d										21 35														
Porth	a										21 38														
	d										21 39														
Trehafod	d										21 42														
Merthyr Tydfil	d	20 38													21 38										
Pentre-bach	d	20 42													21 42										
Troed Y Rhiw	d	20 45													21 45										
Merthyr Vale	a	20 48													21 48										
	d	20 50													21 50										
Quakers Yard	d	20 55													21 55										
Aberdare 3	d					20 54														21 54					
Cwmbach	d					20 57														21 57					
Fernhill	d					21 00														22 00					
Mountain Ash	a					21 03														22 03					
	d					21 04														22 04					
Penrhiwceiber	d					21 07														22 07					
Abercynon	d	20 59				21 13									21 59					22 13					
Pontypridd 3	a	21 07				21 22					21 47				22 07					22 22					
	d	21 09				21 24					21 48				22 09					22 24					
Trefforest	d	21 12				21 27					21 51				22 12					22 27					
Trefforest Estate	d	21 16													22 16										
Taffs Well 3	d	21 20				21 34					21 58				22 20					22 34					
Radyr 3	a	21 23				21 37					22 01				22 23					22 37					
	d	21 23				21 37					22 01	22 04			22 23					22 37				23 14	
Danescourt	d											22 08													
Fairwater	d											22 10													
Waun-gron Park	d											22 12													
Ninian Park	d											22 15													
Llandaf	d	21 26				21 40					22 04				22 26					22 40				23 16	
Cathays	d	21 31				21 45					22 09				22 31					22 45				23 20	
Rhymney 3	d			20 48									21 33												
Pontlottyn	d			20 51									21 36												
Tir-phil	d			20 55									21 40												
Brithdir	d			20 58									21 43												
Bargoed	a			21 01									21 46												
	d			21 02									21 47												
Gilfach Fargoed	d			21 04									21 49												
Pengam	d			21 07									21 52												
Hengoed	d			21 10									21 55												
Ystrad Mynach 3	d			21 13				21 39					21 58												
Llanbradach	d			21 18				21 44					22 03												
Aber	d			21 22				21 48					22 07												
Caerphilly 3	d			21 25				21 51					22 10				22 28								
Lisvane & Thornhill	d			21 29				21 55					22 14												
Llanishen	d			21 31				21 57					22 16												
Heath High Level	d			21 34				22 00					22 19												
Coryton	d																				22 45				
Whitchurch (Cardiff)	d																				22 46				
Rhiwbina	d																				22 48				
Birchgrove	d																				22 50				
Ty Glas	d																				22 51				
Heath Low Level	d																				22 54				
Cardiff Queen Street 3	a	21 34		21 42		21 49		22 05			22 14		22 24		22 34		22 39			22 49	22 59			23 24	
	d	21 36	21 36	21 44	21 48	21 51	22 00	22 06		22 12	22 16		22 26	22 24	22 36	22 36	22 39	22 48		22 54	23 01	23 00	23 12	23 25	23 24
Cardiff Bay	a		21 40		21 52		22 04			22 16				22 28		22 40		22 52				23 04	23 16		23 28
Cardiff Central 7	a	21 39		21 47		21 54		22 09			22 22	22 20	22 29		22 41		22 43			23 00	23 06			23 28	
	d	21 41				22 06		22 10					22 31							23 12				23 30	
Grangetown	d	21 45				22 10		22 14					22 35							23 16				23 34	
Dingle Road	d					22 14							22 41							23 20					
Penarth	a					22 19							22 46							23 25					
Cogan	d	21 48						22 18																23 37	
Eastbrook	d	21 51						22 20																23 40	
Dinas Powys	d	21 53						22 22																23 42	
Cadoxton	d	21 57						22 27																23 46	
Barry Docks	d	22 00						22 30																23 49	
Barry 3	d	22 05						22 34																23 54	
Barry Island	a							22 40																00 01	
Rhoose Cardiff Int Airport ✈	d	22 12																							
Llantwit Major	d	22 22																							
Bridgend	a	22 39																							

When events are being held at the Millenium Stadium, services are subject to alteration. Please check times before travelling.

Saturdays
until 8 September

Treherbert, Aberdare, Merthyr, Pontypridd, Rhymney and Coryton - Cardiff, Penarth, Barry, Barry Island and Bridgend

Network Diagram - see first Page of Table 130

		AW A	AW B	AW C		AW	AW	AW
Treherbert	d							
Ynyswen	d							
Treorchy	d							
Ton Pentre	d							
Ystrad Rhondda	a							
	d							
Llwynypia	d							
Tonypandy	d							
Dinas Rhondda	d							
Porth	a							
	d							
Trehafod	d							
Merthyr Tydfil	d	22 38	22 38	22 38				
Pentre-bach	d	22 42	22 42	22 42				
Troed Y Rhiw	d	22 45	22 45	22 45				
Merthyr Vale	a	22 48	22 48	22 48				
	d	22 50	22 50	22 50				
Quakers Yard	d	22 55	22 55	22 55				
Aberdare 3	d					22 54		
Cwmbach	d					22 57		
Fernhill	d					23 00		
Mountain Ash	a					23 03		
	d					23 04		
Penrhiwceiber	d					23 07		
Abercynon	d	22 59	22 59	22 59		23 13		
Pontypridd 3	a	23 07	23 07	23 07		23 22		
	d	23 09	23 09	23 09				
Trefforest	d	23 12	23 12	23 12				
Trefforest Estate	d	23 16	23 16	23 16				
Taffs Well 3	d	23 20	23 20	23 20				
Radyr 3	a	23 23	23 23	23 23				
	d	23 23	23 24	23 23				
Danescourt	d							
Fairwater	d							
Waun-gron Park	d							
Ninian Park	d							
Llandaf	d	23 26	23 27	23 26				
Cathays	d	23 31	23 31	23 31				
Rhymney 3	d							
Pontlottyn	d							
Tir-phil	d							
Brithdir	d							
Bargoed	a							
	d							
Gilfach Fargoed	d							
Pengam	d							
Hengoed	d							
Ystrad Mynach 3	d							
Llanbradach	d							
Aber	d							
Caerphilly 3	d							
Lisvane & Thornhill	d							
Llanishen	d							
Heath High Level	d							
Coryton	d							
Whitchurch (Cardiff)	d							
Rhiwbina	d							
Birchgrove	d							
Ty Glas	d							
Heath Low Level	d							
Cardiff Queen Street 3	a	23 34	23 34	23 34				
	d	23 36	23 36	23 36			23 36	23 48
Cardiff Bay	a						23 40	23 52
Cardiff Central 7	a	23 39	23 39	23 42				
	d	23 41	23 41					
Grangetown	d	23 45	23 45					
Dingle Road	d							
Penarth	a							
Cogan	d	23 48	23 48					
Eastbrook	d	23 51	23 51					
Dinas Powys	d	23 54	23 54					
Cadoxton	d	23 58	23 58					
Barry Docks	d	00 03	00 03					
Barry 3	d	00 08	00 08					
Barry Island	a							
Rhoose Cardiff Int Airport ✈	d	00 15	00 15					
Llantwit Major	d	00 25	00 25					
Bridgend	a	00 43	00 43					

A 28 July B 4 August C not from 28 July until 4 August

When events are being held at the Millenium Stadium, services are subject to alteration. Please check times before travelling.

Table 130

Saturdays from 15 September

Treherbert, Aberdare, Merthyr, Pontypridd, Rhymney and Coryton - Cardiff, Penarth, Barry, Barry Island and Bridgend

Network Diagram - see first Page of Table 130

		AW A	AW B	AW	AW	AW	AW	AW	AW	AW		AW	AW	AW	AW	AW	AW	AW	AW	AW		AW	AW	AW	AW
Treherbert	d													05 47								06 17			
Ynyswen	d													05 49								06 19			
Treorchy	d													05 51								06 21			
Ton Pentre	d													05 53								06 23			
Ystrad Rhondda	a													05 56								06 26			
	d													05 58								06 28			
Llwynypia	d													06 00								06 30			
Tonypandy	d													06 03								06 33			
Dinas Rhondda	d													06 05								06 35			
Porth	a													06 08								06 38			
	d													06 09								06 39			
Trehafod	d													06 12								06 42			
Merthyr Tydfil	d																								
Pentre-bach	d																								
Troed Y Rhiw	d																								
Merthyr Vale	a																								
	d																								
Quakers Yard	d																								
Aberdare 3	d																								06 21
Cwmbach	d																								06 24
Fernhill	d																								06 28
Mountain Ash	a																								06 31
	d																								06 34
Penrhiwceiber	d																								06 38
Abercynon	d																								06 44
Pontypridd 3	a													06 17								06 47			06 52
	d						05 24							06 18								06 48			06 54
Trefforest	d						05 27							06 21								06 51			06 57
Trefforest Estate	d						05 31																		
Taffs Well 3	d						05 34							06 28								06 58	06 53		07 04
Radyr 3	a						05 37							06 31								07 01	06 56		07 07
	d	23p10	23p10				05 37							06 31								07 01	07 04		07 07
Danescourt	d																						07 08		
Fairwater	d																						07 10		
Waun-gron Park	d																						07 12		
Ninian Park	d																						07 15		
Llandaf	d	23p12	23p12				05 40							06 34								07 04			07 10
Cathays	d	23p16	23p16				05 45							06 39								07 09			07 15
Rhymney 3	d																			06 10					
Pontlottyn	d																			06 13					
Tir-phil	d																			06 17					
Brithdir	d																			06 20					
Bargoed	a																			06 23					
	d																			06 27					
Gilfach Fargoed	d																			06 29					
Pengam	d																			06 32					
Hengoed	d																			06 35					
Ystrad Mynach 3	d																			06 38					
Llanbradach	d																			06 43					
Aber	d																			06 47					
Caerphilly 3	d											06 10								06 50					
Lisvane & Thornhill	d											06 14								06 54					
Llanishen	d											06 16								06 56					
Heath High Level	d											06 19								06 59					
Coryton	d																		06 45						
Whitchurch (Cardiff)	d																		06 46						
Rhiwbina	d																		06 48						
Birchgrove	d																		06 50						
Ty Glas	d																		06 51						
Heath Low Level	d																		06 54						
Cardiff Queen Street 3	a	23p20	23p19				05 49					06 25		06 42					06 59	07 04		07 12			07 19
	d	23p20	23p20				05 51					06 26	06 36	06 43	06 48		07 00		07 01	07 06		07 13		07 12	07 21
Cardiff Bay	a												06 40		06 52		07 04							07 16	
Cardiff Central 7	a	23p25	23p25				05 54					06 29		06 48					07 04	07 09		07 16	07 20		07 24
	d	23p30	23p30	05 20	05 41	05 46	05 55	06 16	06 25	06 36		06 41				06 55		07 01		07 10		07 16			07 25
Grangetown	d	23p34	23p34	05 24	05 45	05 50	05 59	06 20	06 29	06 40		06 45				06 59		07 05		07 14		07 20			07 29
Dingle Road	d					05 54		06 24		06 44								07 11				07 26			
Penarth	a					06 00		06 30		06 50								07 17				07 32			
Cogan	d	23p37	23p37	05 28	05 48		06 03		06 33			06 48				07 03				07 18					07 33
Eastbrook	d	23p40	23p40	05 30	05 51		06 05		06 35			06 51				07 05				07 20					07 35
Dinas Powys	d	23p42	23p42	05 32	05 53		06 07		06 37			06 53				07 07				07 22					07 37
Cadoxton	d	23p46	23p46	05 37	05 57		06 12		06 42			06 57				07 12				07 27					07 42
Barry Docks	d	23p49	23p49	05 40	06 00		06 15		06 45			07 00				07 15				07 30					07 45
Barry 3	d	23p54	23p54	05 44	06 05		06 19		06 49			07 05				07 19				07 34					07 49
Barry Island	a	00 01	00 01	05 51			06 26		06 56							07 26				07 41					07 56
Rhoose Cardiff Int Airport ✈	d				06 12							07 12													
Llantwit Major	d				06 22							07 22													
Bridgend	a				06 40							07 40													

A 15 September

B not 15 September

When events are being held at the Millenium Stadium, services are subject to alteration. Please check times before travelling.

Table 130

Saturdays from 15 September

Treherbert, Aberdare, Merthyr, Pontypridd, Rhymney and Coryton - Cardiff, Penarth, Barry, Barry Island and Bridgend

Network Diagram - see first Page of Table 130

		AW	AW	AW	AW	AW		AW	AW	AW	AW	AW	AW	AW	AW	AW		AW	AW	AW	AW	AW	AW	AW	AW
Treherbert	d								06 47											07 17					
Ynyswen	d								06 49											07 19					
Treorchy	d								06 51											07 21					
Ton Pentre	d								06 53											07 23					
Ystrad Rhondda	a								06 56											07 26					
	d								06 58											07 28					
Llwynypia	d								07 00											07 30					
Tonypandy	d								07 03											07 33					
Dinas Rhondda	d								07 05											07 35					
Porth	a								07 08											07 38					
	d								07 09											07 39					
Trehafod	d								07 12											07 42					
Merthyr Tydfil	d				06 38											07 08									
Pentre-bach	d				06 42											07 12									
Troed Y Rhiw	d				06 45											07 15									
Merthyr Vale	a				06 48											07 18									
	d				06 50											07 20									
Quakers Yard	d				06 55											07 25									
Aberdare 3	d											06 51										07 21			
Cwmbach	d											06 54										07 24			
Fernhill	d											06 58										07 28			
Mountain Ash	a											07 01										07 31			
	d											07 04										07 34			
Penrhiwceiber	d											07 08										07 38			
Abercynon	d				06 59							07 14				07 29						07 44			
Pontypridd 3	a				07 07				07 17			07 22				07 37				07 47		07 52			
	d				07 09				07 18			07 24				07 39				07 48		07 54			
Trefforest	d				07 12				07 21			07 27				07 42				07 51		07 57			
Trefforest Estate	d				07 16											07 46									
Taffs Well 3	d				07 20				07 28			07 34				07 50				07 58		08 04			
Radyr 3	a				07 23				07 31			07 37				07 53				08 01		08 07			
	d				07 23				07 31	07 34		07 37				07 53				08 01	08 04	08 07			
Danescourt	d									07 38											08 08				
Fairwater	d									07 40											08 10				
Waun-gron Park	d									07 42											08 12				
Ninian Park	d									07 45											08 15				
Llandaf	d				07 26				07 34			07 40				07 56				08 04		08 10			
Cathays	d				07 31				07 39			07 45				08 01				08 09		08 15			
Rhymney 3	d	06 34											07 02										07 24		
Pontlottyn	d	06 37											07 05										07 27		
Tir-phil	d	06 41											07 09										07 31		
Brithdir	d	06 44											07 12										07 34		
Bargoed	a	06 47											07 15										07 37		
	d	06 48						07 02					07 17					07 32					07 45		
Gilfach Fargoed	d							07 04					07 19										07 47		
Pengam	d	06 52						07 07					07 22					07 37					07 50		
Hengoed	d	06 56						07 10					07 25					07 40					07 54		
Ystrad Mynach 3	d	06 58						07 13					07 28					07 43					07 57		
Llanbradach	d	07 03						07 18					07 33					07 48					08 02		
Aber	d	07 07						07 22					07 37					07 52					08 07		
Caerphilly 3	d	07 10						07 25					07 40					07 55					08 10		
Lisvane & Thornhill	d	07 14						07 29					07 44					07 59					08 14		
Llanishen	d	07 16						07 31					07 46					08 01					08 16		
Heath High Level	d	07 19						07 34					07 49					08 04					08 19		
Coryton	d			07 15										07 45											08 15
Whitchurch (Cardiff)	d			07 16										07 46											08 16
Rhiwbina	d			07 18										07 48											08 18
Birchgrove	d			07 20										07 50											08 20
Ty Glas	d			07 21										07 51											08 21
Heath Low Level	d			07 24										07 54											08 24
Cardiff Queen Street 3	a	07 24		07 29	07 34			07 39	07 44			07 49	07 54	07 59		08 04		08 09		08 14		08 19	08 24		08 29
	d	07 26	07 24	07 31	07 36	07 36		07 41	07 46		07 48	07 51	07 56	08 01	08 00	08 06		08 11	08 12	08 16		08 21	08 26	08 24	08 31
Cardiff Bay	a		07 28			07 40					07 52				08 04				08 16					08 28	
Cardiff Central 7	a	07 29		07 34	07 39			07 44	07 53	07 50		07 54	07 59	08 04		08 09		08 14		08 23	08 20	08 24	08 29		08 34
	d	07 31			07 41			07 46				07 55	08 01			08 10		08 16				08 25	08 31		
Grangetown	d	07 35			07 45			07 50				07 59	08 05			08 14		08 20				08 29	08 35		
Dingle Road	d	07 41						07 56					08 11					08 26					08 41		
Penarth	a	07 47						08 02					08 17					08 32					08 47		
Cogan	d				07 48							08 03				08 18						08 33			
Eastbrook	d				07 51							08 05				08 20						08 35			
Dinas Powys	d				07 53							08 07				08 22						08 37			
Cadoxton	d				07 57							08 12				08 27						08 42			
Barry Docks	d				08 00							08 15				08 30						08 45			
Barry 3	d				08 05							08 19				08 34						08 49			
Barry Island	a											08 26				08 41						08 56			
Rhoose Cardiff Int Airport ✈	d				08 12																				
Llantwit Major	d				08 22																				
Bridgend	a				08 40																				

When events are being held at the Millenium Stadium, services are subject to alteration. Please check times before travelling.

Treherbert, Aberdare, Merthyr, Pontypridd, Rhymney and Coryton - Cardiff, Penarth, Barry, Barry Island and Bridgend

Network Diagram - see first Page of Table 130

		AW		AW	AW	AW	AW	AW	AW	AW	AW	AW		AW	AW	AW	AW	AW	AW	AW	AW	AW		AW	AW
Treherbert	d					07 45											08 17								
Ynyswen	d					07 47											08 19								
Treorchy	d					07 49											08 21								
Ton Pentre	d					07 51											08 23								
Ystrad Rhondda	a					07 54											08 26								
	d					07 58											08 28								
Llwynypia	d					08 00											08 30								
Tonypandy	d					08 03											08 33								
Dinas Rhondda	d					08 05											08 35								
Porth	a					08 08											08 38								
	d					08 09											08 39								
Trehafod	d					08 12											08 42								
Merthyr Tydfil	d	07 38												08 08										08 38	
Pentre-bach	d	07 42												08 12										08 42	
Troed Y Rhiw	d	07 45												08 15										08 45	
Merthyr Vale	a	07 48												08 18										08 48	
	d	07 50												08 20										08 50	
Quakers Yard	d	07 55												08 25										08 55	
Aberdare 3	d								07 51										08 21						
Cwmbach	d								07 54										08 24						
Fernhill	d								07 58										08 28						
Mountain Ash	a								08 01										08 31						
	d								08 04										08 34						
Penrhiwceiber	d								08 08										08 38						
Abercynon	d	07 59							08 14					08 29					08 44					08 59	
Pontypridd 3	a	08 07				08 17			08 22					08 37			08 47		08 52					09 07	
	d	08 09				08 18			08 24					08 39			08 48		08 54					09 09	
Trefforest	d	08 12				08 21			08 27					08 42			08 51		08 57					09 12	
Trefforest Estate	d	08 16												08 46										09 16	
Taffs Well 3	d	08 20				08 28			08 34					08 50			08 58		09 04					09 20	
Radyr 3	a	08 23				08 31			08 37					08 53			09 01		09 07					09 23	
	d	08 23				08 31	08 34		08 37					08 53			09 01	09 04	09 07					09 23	
Danescourt	d						08 38											09 08							
Fairwater	d						08 40											09 10							
Waun-gron Park	d						08 42											09 12							
Ninian Park	d						08 45											09 15							
Llandaf	d	08 26				08 34			08 40					08 56			09 04		09 10					09 26	
Cathays	d	08 31				08 39			08 45					09 01			09 09		09 15					09 31	
Rhymney 3	d				07 44															08 30					
Pontlottyn	d				07 47															08 33					
Tir-phil	d				07 51															08 37					
Brithdir	d				07 54															08 40					
Bargoed	a				08 00															08 44					
	d				08 02					08 17					08 32					08 47					
Gilfach Fargoed	d									08 19															
Pengam	d				08 07					08 22					08 37					08 52					
Hengoed	d				08 10					08 25					08 40					08 55					
Ystrad Mynach 3	d				08 13					08 28					08 43					08 58					
Llanbradach	d				08 18					08 33					08 48					09 03					
Aber	d				08 22					08 37					08 52					09 07					
Caerphilly 3	d				08 25					08 40					08 55					09 10					
Lisvane & Thornhill	d				08 29					08 44					08 59					09 14					
Llanishen	d				08 31					08 46					09 01					09 16					
Heath High Level	d				08 34					08 49					09 04					09 19					
Coryton	d										08 45											09 15			
Whitchurch (Cardiff)	d										08 46											09 16			
Rhiwbina	d										08 48											09 18			
Birchgrove	d										08 50											09 20			
Ty Glas	d										08 51											09 21			
Heath Low Level	d										08 54											09 24			
Cardiff Queen Street 3	a	08 34			08 39	08 44			08 49	08 54	08 59			09 04	09 09		09 14		09 19	09 24		09 29		09 34	
	d	08 36		08 36	08 41	08 46		08 48	08 51	08 56	09 01	09 00		09 06	09 11	09 12	09 16		09 21	09 26	09 24	09 31		09 36	09 36
Cardiff Bay	a			08 40				08 52				09 04				09 16					09 28				09 40
Cardiff Central 7	a	08 39			08 48	08 53	08 50		08 54	08 59	09 04			09 09	09 14		09 23	09 20	09 24	09 29		09 34		09 39	
	d	08 41							08 55	09 01				09 10	09 16				09 25	09 31				09 41	
Grangetown	d	08 45							08 59	09 05				09 14	09 20				09 29	09 35				09 45	
Dingle Road	d									09 11					09 26					09 41					
Penarth	a									09 17					09 32					09 47					
Cogan	d	08 48							09 03					09 18					09 33					09 48	
Eastbrook	d	08 51							09 05					09 20					09 35					09 51	
Dinas Powys	d	08 53							09 07					09 22					09 37					09 53	
Cadoxton	d	08 57							09 12					09 27					09 42					09 57	
Barry Docks	d	09 00							09 15					09 30					09 45					10 00	
Barry 3	d	09 05							09 19					09 34					09 49					10 05	
Barry Island	a								09 26					09 41					09 56						
Rhoose Cardiff Int Airport ✈	d	09 12																						10 12	
Llantwit Major	d	09 22																						10 22	
Bridgend	a	09 40																						10 40	

When events are being held at the Millenium Stadium, services are subject to alteration. Please check times before travelling.

Treherbert, Aberdare, Merthyr, Pontypridd, Rhymney and Coryton - Cardiff, Penarth, Barry, Barry Island and Bridgend

Network Diagram - see first Page of Table 130

		AW	AW	AW	AW	AW	AW	AW		AW	AW	AW	AW	AW	AW	AW	AW	AW		AW	AW	AW	AW	AW	AW
Treherbert	d		08 47											09 17										09 47	
Ynyswen	d		08 49											09 19										09 49	
Treorchy	d		08 51											09 21										09 51	
Ton Pentre	d		08 53											09 23										09 53	
Ystrad Rhondda	a		08 56											09 26										09 56	
	d		08 58											09 28										09 58	
Llwynypia	d		09 00											09 30										10 00	
Tonypandy	d		09 03											09 33										10 03	
Dinas Rhondda	d		09 05											09 35										10 05	
Porth	a		09 08											09 38										10 08	
	d		09 09											09 39										10 09	
Trehafod	d		09 12											09 42										10 12	
Merthyr Tydfil	d										09 08										09 38				
Pentre-bach	d										09 12										09 42				
Troed Y Rhiw	d										09 15										09 45				
Merthyr Vale	a										09 18										09 48				
	d										09 20										09 50				
Quakers Yard	d										09 25										09 55				
Aberdare 3	d					08 51										09 21									
Cwmbach	d					08 54										09 24									
Fernhill	d					08 58										09 28									
Mountain Ash	a					09 01										09 31									
	d					09 04										09 34									
Penrhiwceiber	d					09 08										09 38									
Abercynon	d					09 14					09 29					09 44					09 59				
Pontypridd 3	a		09 17			09 22					09 37			09 47		09 52					10 07			10 17	
	d		09 18			09 24					09 39			09 48		09 54					10 09			10 18	
Trefforest	d		09 21			09 27					09 42			09 51		09 57					10 12			10 21	
Trefforest Estate	d										09 46										10 16				
Taffs Well 3	d		09 28			09 34					09 50			09 58		10 04					10 20			10 28	
Radyr 3	a		09 31			09 37					09 53			10 01		10 07					10 23			10 31	
	d		09 31	09 34		09 37					09 53			10 01	10 04	10 07					10 23			10 31	10 34
Danescourt	d			09 38											10 08										10 38
Fairwater	d			09 40											10 10										10 40
Waun-gron Park	d			09 42											10 12										10 42
Ninian Park	d			09 45											10 15										10 45
Llandaf	d		09 34			09 40					09 56			10 04		10 10					10 26			10 34	
Cathays	d		09 39			09 45					10 01			10 09		10 15					10 31			10 39	
Rhymney 3	d																09 29								
Pontlottyn	d																09 32								
Tir-phil	d																09 36								
Brithdir	d																09 39								
Bargoed	a																09 42								
	d	09 02										09 25					09 47						10 02		
Gilfach Fargoed	d											09 27													
Pengam	d	09 07										09 30					09 52						10 07		
Hengoed	d	09 10										09 33					09 55						10 10		
Ystrad Mynach 3	d	09 13					09 28					09 43					09 58						10 13		
Llanbradach	d	09 18					09 33					09 48					10 03						10 18		
Aber	d	09 22					09 37					09 52					10 07						10 22		
Caerphilly 3	d	09 25					09 40					09 55					10 10						10 25		
Lisvane & Thornhill	d	09 29					09 44					09 59					10 14						10 29		
Llanishen	d	09 31					09 46					10 01					10 16						10 31		
Heath High Level	d	09 34					09 49					10 04					10 19						10 34		
Coryton	d							09 45												10 15					
Whitchurch (Cardiff)	d							09 46												10 16					
Rhiwbina	d							09 48												10 18					
Birchgrove	d							09 50												10 20					
Ty Glas	d							09 51												10 21					
Heath Low Level	d							09 54												10 24					
Cardiff Queen Street 3	a	09 39	09 44			09 49	09 54	09 59			10 04	10 09		10 14		10 19	10 24			10 29	10 34		10 39	10 44	
	d	09 41	09 46		09 48	09 51	09 56	10 01		10 00	10 06	10 11	10 12	10 16		10 21	10 26	10 24		10 31	10 36	10 36	10 41	10 46	
Cardiff Bay	a				09 52					10 04			10 16					10 28				10 40			
Cardiff Central 7	a	09 44	09 53	09 50		09 54	09 59	10 04			10 09	10 14		10 23	10 20	10 24	10 29			10 34	10 39		10 44	10 53	10 50
	d	09 46				09 55	10 01				10 10	10 16				10 25	10 31				10 41		10 46		
Grangetown	d	09 50				09 59	10 05				10 14	10 20				10 29	10 35				10 45		10 50		
Dingle Road	d	09 56					10 11					10 26					10 41						10 56		
Penarth	a	10 02					10 17					10 32					10 47						11 02		
Cogan	d					10 03					10 18					10 33					10 48				
Eastbrook	d					10 05					10 20					10 35					10 51				
Dinas Powys	d					10 07					10 22					10 37					10 53				
Cadoxton	d					10 12					10 27					10 42					10 57				
Barry Docks	d					10 15					10 30					10 45					11 00				
Barry 3	d					10 19					10 34					10 49					11 05				
Barry Island	a					10 26					10 41					10 56									
Rhoose Cardiff Int Airport ✈	d																				11 12				
Llantwit Major	d																				11 22				
Bridgend	a																				11 40				

When events are being held at the Millenium Stadium, services are subject to alteration. Please check times before travelling.

Table 130

Saturdays
from 15 September

Treherbert, Aberdare, Merthyr, Pontypridd, Rhymney and Coryton - Cardiff, Penarth, Barry, Barry Island and Bridgend

Network Diagram - see first Page of Table 130

Station		AW	AW	AW	AW	AW	AW	AW	AW	AW	AW	AW	AW	AW	AW	AW	AW	AW	AW	AW	AW	AW
Treherbert	d													10 17						10 47		
Ynyswen	d													10 19						10 49		
Treorchy	d													10 21						10 51		
Ton Pentre	d													10 23						10 53		
Ystrad Rhondda	a													10 26						10 56		
	d													10 28						10 58		
Llwynypia	d													10 30						11 00		
Tonypandy	d													10 33						11 03		
Dinas Rhondda	d													10 35						11 05		
Porth	a													10 38						11 08		
	d													10 52						11 09		
Trehafod	d													10 55						11 12		
Merthyr Tydfil	d			10 04													10 38					
Pentre-bach	d			10 08													10 42					
Troed Y Rhiw	d			10 11													10 45					
Merthyr Vale	a			10 14													10 48					
	d			10 16													10 50					
Quakers Yard	d			10 22													10 55					
Aberdare ■	d		09 51									10 21										
Cwmbach	d		09 54									10 24										
Fernhill	d		09 58									10 28										
Mountain Ash	a		10 01									10 31										
	d		10 04									10 34										
Penrhiwceiber	d		10 08									10 38										
Abercynon	d		10 14	10 26								10 44					10 59					
Pontypridd ■	a		10 22	10 32								10 52		11 00			11 07			11 17		
	d		10 24					10 39				10 54		11 04			11 09			11 18		
Trefforest	d		10 27					10 42				10 57		11 07			11 12			11 21		
Trefforest Estate	d																11 16					
Taffs Well ■	d		10 34					10 50				11 04		11 13			11 20			11 28		
Radyr ■	a		10 37					10 53				11 07		11 17			11 23			11 31		
	d		10 37					10 53		11 04		11 07		11 17			11 23			11 31	11 34	
Danescourt	d									11 08											11 38	
Fairwater	d									11 10											11 40	
Waun-gron Park	d									11 12											11 42	
Ninian Park	d									11 15											11 45	
Llandaf	d		10 40					10 56				11 10					11 26			11 34		
Cathays	d		10 45					11 01				11 15					11 31			11 39		
Rhymney ■	d												10 29									
Pontlottyn	d												10 32									
Tir-phil	d												10 36									
Brithdir	d												10 39									
Bargoed	a												10 42									
	d								10 25				10 47						11 02			
Gilfach Fargoed	d								10 27													
Pengam	d								10 30				10 52						11 07			
Hengoed	d								10 33				10 55						11 10			
Ystrad Mynach ■	d				10 28				10 43				10 58						11 13			
Llanbradach	d				10 33				10 48				11 03						11 18			
Aber	d				10 37				10 52				11 07						11 22			
Caerphilly ■	d				10 40				10 55				11 10						11 25			
Lisvane & Thornhill	d				10 44				10 59				11 14						11 29			
Llanishen	d				10 46				11 01				11 16						11 31			
Heath High Level	d				10 49				11 04				11 19						11 34			
Coryton	d					10 45										11 15						
Whitchurch (Cardiff)	d					10 46										11 16						
Rhiwbina	d					10 48										11 18						
Birchgrove	d					10 50										11 20						
Ty Glas	d					10 51										11 21						
Heath Low Level	d					10 54										11 24						
Cardiff Queen Street ■	a		10 49		10 54	10 59		11 04	11 09			11 19	11 24			11 29	11 34		11 39	11 44		
	d	10 48	10 51		10 56	11 01	11 00	11 06	11 11		11 12	11 21	11 26		11 24	11 31	11 36	11 36	11 41	11 46		11 48
Cardiff Bay	a	10 52					11 04				11 16				11 28			11 40				11 52
Cardiff Central ■	a		10 54		10 59	11 04		11 09	11 14	11 20		11 24	11 29	11 34		11 34	11 39		11 44	11 53	11 50	
	d		10 55		11 01			11 10	11 16			11 25	11 31				11 41		11 46			
Grangetown	d		10 59		11 05			11 14	11 20			11 29	11 35				11 45		11 50			
Dingle Road	d				11 11				11 26				11 41						11 56			
Penarth	a				11 17				11 32				11 47						12 02			
Cogan	d		11 03					11 18				11 33					11 48					
Eastbrook	d		11 05					11 20				11 35					11 51					
Dinas Powys	d		11 07					11 22				11 37					11 53					
Cadoxton	d		11 12					11 27				11 42					11 57					
Barry Docks	d		11 15					11 30				11 45					12 00					
Barry ■	d		11 19					11 34				11 49					12 05					
Barry Island	a		11 26					11 41				11 56										
Rhoose Cardiff Int Airport ✈	d																12 12					
Llantwit Major	d																12 22					
Bridgend	a																12 40					

When events are being held at the Millenium Stadium, services are subject to alteration. Please check times before travelling.

Table 130

Saturdays
from 15 September

Treherbert, Aberdare, Merthyr, Pontypridd, Rhymney and Coryton - Cardiff, Penarth, Barry, Barry Island and Bridgend

Network Diagram - see first Page of Table 130

Station		AW	AW	AW	AW	AW	AW	AW	AW	AW	AW	AW	AW	AW	AW	AW	AW	AW	AW	AW	AW	AW	AW
Treherbert	d								11 17									11 47					
Ynyswen	d								11 19									11 49					
Treorchy	d								11 21									11 51					
Ton Pentre	d								11 23									11 53					
Ystrad Rhondda	a								11 26									11 56					
	d								11 28									11 58					
Llwynypia	d								11 30									12 00					
Tonypandy	d								11 33									12 03					
Dinas Rhondda	d								11 35									12 05					
Porth	a								11 38									12 08					
	d								11 39									12 09					
Trehafod	d								11 42									12 12					
Merthyr Tydfil	d					11 08									11 38								
Pentre-bach	d					11 12									11 42								
Troed Y Rhiw	d					11 15									11 45								
Merthyr Vale	a					11 18									11 48								
	d					11 20									11 50								
Quakers Yard	d					11 25									11 55								
Aberdare ■	d	10 51									11 21												
Cwmbach	d	10 54									11 24												
Fernhill	d	10 58									11 28												
Mountain Ash	a	11 01									11 31												
	d	11 04									11 34												
Penrhiwceiber	d	11 08									11 38												
Abercynon	d	11 14				11 29					11 44				11 59								
Pontypridd ■	a	11 22				11 37			11 47		11 52				12 07			12 17					
	d	11 24				11 39			11 48		11 54				12 09			12 18					
Trefforest	d	11 27				11 42			11 51		11 57				12 12			12 21					
Trefforest Estate	d					11 46									12 16								
Taffs Well ■	d	11 34				11 50			11 58		12 04				12 20			12 28					
Radyr ■	a	11 37				11 53			12 01		12 07				12 23			12 31					
	d	11 37				11 53			12 01	12 04	12 07				12 23			12 31	12 34				
Danescourt	d									12 08									12 38				
Fairwater	d									12 10									12 40				
Waun-gron Park	d									12 12									12 42				
Ninian Park	d									12 15									12 45				
Llandaf	d	11 40				11 56			12 04		12 10				12 26			12 34					
Cathays	d	11 45				12 01			12 09		12 15				12 31			12 39					
Rhymney ■	d											11 29											
Pontlottyn	d											11 32											
Tir-phil	d											11 36											
Brithdir	d											11 39											
Bargoed	a											11 42											
	d						11 25					11 47					12 02						
Gilfach Fargoed	d						11 27																
Pengam	d						11 30					11 52					12 07						
Hengoed	d						11 33					11 55					12 10						
Ystrad Mynach ■	d		11 28				11 43					11 58					12 13				12 28		
Llanbradach	d		11 33				11 48					12 03					12 18				12 33		
Aber	d		11 37				11 52					12 07					12 22				12 37		
Caerphilly ■	d		11 40				11 55					12 10					12 25				12 40		
Lisvane & Thornhill	d		11 44				11 59					12 14					12 29				12 44		
Llanishen	d		11 46				12 01					12 16					12 31				12 46		
Heath High Level	d		11 49				12 04					12 19					12 34				12 49		
Coryton	d			11 45										12 15								12 45	
Whitchurch (Cardiff)	d			11 46										12 16								12 46	
Rhiwbina	d			11 48										12 18								12 48	
Birchgrove	d			11 50										12 20								12 50	
Ty Glas	d			11 51										12 21								12 51	
Heath Low Level	d			11 54										12 24								12 54	
Cardiff Queen Street ■	a	11 49	11 54	11 59		12 04	12 09		12 14		12 19	12 24		12 29	12 34		12 39	12 44			12 54	12 59	
	d	11 51	11 56	12 01	12 00	12 06	12 11	12 12	12 16		12 21	12 26	12 24	12 31	12 36	12 36	12 41	12 46		12 48	12 56	13 01	13 00
Cardiff Bay	a				12 04			12 16					12 28			12 40				12 52			13 04
Cardiff Central ■	a	11 54	11 59	12 04		12 09	12 14		12 23	12 20	12 24	12 29		12 34	12 39		12 44	12 53	12 50		12 59	13 04	
	d	11 55	12 01			12 10	12 16				12 25	12 31			12 41		12 46	12 55			13 01		
Grangetown	d	11 59	12 05			12 14	12 20				12 29	12 35			12 45		12 50	12 59			13 05		
Dingle Road	d		12 11				12 26					12 41					12 56				13 11		
Penarth	a		12 17				12 32					12 47					13 02				13 17		
Cogan	d	12 03				12 18					12 33				12 48			13 03					
Eastbrook	d	12 05				12 20					12 35				12 51			13 05					
Dinas Powys	d	12 07				12 22					12 37				12 53			13 07					
Cadoxton	d	12 12				12 27					12 42				12 57			13 12					
Barry Docks	d	12 15				12 30					12 45				13 00			13 15					
Barry ■	d	12 19				12 34					12 49				13 05			13 19					
Barry Island	a	12 26				12 41					12 56							13 26					
Rhoose Cardiff Int Airport ✈	d														13 12								
Llantwit Major	d														13 22								
Bridgend	a														13 40								

When events are being held at the Millenium Stadium, services are subject to alteration. Please check times before travelling.

Saturdays
from 15 September

Treherbert, Aberdare, Merthyr, Pontypridd, Rhymney and Coryton - Cardiff, Penarth, Barry, Barry Island and Bridgend

Network Diagram - see first Page of Table 130

		AW	AW	AW	AW	AW		AW	AW	AW	AW	AW	AW	AW	AW	AW		AW	AW	AW	AW	AW	AW	AW	AW
Treherbert	d				12 17										12 47										
Ynyswen	d				12 19										12 49										
Treorchy	d				12 21										12 51										
Ton Pentre	d				12 23										12 53										
Ystrad Rhondda	a				12 26										12 56										
	d				12 28										12 58										
Llwynypia	d				12 30										13 00										
Tonypandy	d				12 33										13 03										
Dinas Rhondda	d				12 35										13 05										
Porth	a				12 38										13 08										
	d				12 39										13 09										
Trehafod	d				12 42										13 12										
Merthyr Tydfil	d	12 08										12 38											13 08		
Pentre-bach	d	12 12										12 42											13 12		
Troed Y Rhiw	d	12 15										12 45											13 15		
Merthyr Vale	a	12 18										12 48											13 18		
	d	12 20										12 50											13 20		
Quakers Yard	d	12 25										12 55											13 25		
Aberdare	d							12 21											12 51						
Cwmbach	d							12 24											12 54						
Fernhill	d							12 28											12 58						
Mountain Ash	a							12 31											13 01						
	d							12 34											13 04						
Penrhiwceiber	d							12 38											13 08						
Abercynon	d	12 29						12 44				12 59							13 14				13 29		
Pontypridd	a	12 37			12 48			12 52				13 07			13 17				13 22				13 37		
	d	12 39			12 48			12 54				13 09			13 18				13 24				13 39		
Trefforest	d	12 42			12 51			12 57				13 12			13 21				13 27				13 42		
Trefforest Estate	d	12 46										13 16											13 46		
Taffs Well	d	12 50			12 58			13 04				13 20			13 28				13 34				13 50		
Radyr	a	12 53			13 01			13 07				13 23			13 31				13 37				13 53		
	d	12 53			13 01	13 04		13 07				13 23			13 31	13 34			13 37				13 53		14 04
Danescourt	d					13 08										13 38									14 08
Fairwater	d					13 10										13 40									14 10
Waun-gron Park	d					13 12										13 42									14 12
Ninian Park	d					13 15										13 45									14 15
Llandaf	d	12 56			13 04			13 10				13 26			13 34				13 40				13 56		
Cathays	d	13 01			13 09			13 15				13 31			13 39				13 45				14 01		
Rhymney	d								12 29																
Pontlottyn	d								12 32																
Tir-phil	d								12 36																
Brithdir	d								12 39																
Bargoed	a								12 42																
	d		12 25						12 47					13 02										13 20	
Gilfach Fargoed	d		12 27																					13 22	
Pengam	d		12 30						12 52					13 07										13 25	
Hengoed	d		12 33						12 55					13 10										13 28	
Ystrad Mynach	d		12 43						12 58					13 13						13 28				13 39	
Llanbradach	d		12 48						13 03					13 18						13 33				13 43	
Aber	d		12 52						13 07					13 22						13 37				13 48	
Caerphilly	d		12 55						13 10					13 25						13 40				13 55	
Lisvane & Thornhill	d		12 59						13 14					13 29						13 44				13 59	
Llanishen	d		13 01						13 16					13 31						13 46				14 01	
Heath High Level	d		13 04						13 19					13 34						13 49				14 04	
Coryton	d										13 15										13 45				
Whitchurch (Cardiff)	d										13 16										13 46				
Rhiwbina	d										13 18										13 48				
Birchgrove	d										13 20										13 50				
Ty Glas	d										13 21										13 51				
Heath Low Level	d										13 24										13 54				
Cardiff Queen Street	a	13 04	13 09		13 14			13 19	13 24		13 29	13 34		13 39	13 44				13 49	13 54	13 59		14 04	14 09	
	d	13 06	13 11	13 12	13 16			13 21	13 26	13 24	13 31	13 36	13 36	13 41	13 46			13 48	13 51	13 56	14 01	14 00	14 06	14 11	
Cardiff Bay	a			13 16						13 28			13 40					13 52				14 04			
Cardiff Central	a	13 09	13 14		13 23	13 20		13 24	13 29		13 34	13 39		13 44	13 53	13 50			13 54	13 59	14 04		14 09	14 14	14 20
	d	13 10	13 16					13 25	13 31			13 41		13 46					13 55	14 01			14 10	14 16	
Grangetown	d	13 14	13 20					13 29	13 35			13 45		13 50					13 59	14 05			14 14	14 20	
Dingle Road	d		13 26						13 41					13 56						14 11				14 26	
Penarth	a		13 32						13 47					14 02						14 17				14 32	
Cogan	d	13 18						13 33				13 48							14 03				14 18		
Eastbrook	d	13 20						13 35				13 51							14 05				14 20		
Dinas Powys	d	13 22						13 37				13 53							14 07				14 22		
Cadoxton	d	13 27						13 42				13 57							14 12				14 27		
Barry Docks	d	13 30						13 45				14 00							14 15				14 30		
Barry	d	13 34						13 49				14 05							14 19				14 34		
Barry Island	a	13 41						13 56											14 26				14 41		
Rhoose Cardiff Int Airport	d											14 12													
Llantwit Major	d											14 22													
Bridgend	a											14 40													

When events are being held at the Millenium Stadium, services are subject to alteration. Please check times before travelling.

Saturdays
from 15 September

Treherbert, Aberdare, Merthyr, Pontypridd, Rhymney and Coryton - Cardiff, Penarth, Barry, Barry Island and Bridgend

Network Diagram - see first Page of Table 130

		AW		AW	AW	AW	AW	AW	AW	AW	AW	AW		AW	AW	AW	AW	AW	AW	AW	AW	AW		AW	AW
Treherbert	d							13 17				13 47													
Ynyswen	d							13 19				13 49													
Treorchy	d							13 21				13 51													
Ton Pentre	d							13 23				13 53													
Ystrad Rhondda	a							13 26				13 56													
	d							13 28				13 58													
Llwynypia	d							13 30				14 00													
Tonypandy	d							13 33				14 03													
Dinas Rhondda	d							13 35				14 05													
Porth	a							13 38				14 08													
	d							13 52				14 09													
Trehafod	d							13 55				14 12													
Merthyr Tydfil	d								13 38											14 08					
Pentre-bach	d								13 42											14 12					
Troed Y Rhiw	d								13 45											14 15					
Merthyr Vale	a								13 48											14 18					
	d								13 50											14 20					
Quakers Yard	d								13 55											14 25					
Aberdare	d															13 51									14 21
Cwmbach	d															13 54									14 24
Fernhill	d															13 58									14 28
Mountain Ash	a															14 01									14 31
	d															14 04									14 34
Penrhiwceiber	d															14 08									14 38
Abercynon	d			13 45					13 59							14 14				14 29					14 44
Pontypridd	a			13 52				14 00	14 07			14 17				14 22				14 37					14 52
	d			13 54				14 04	14 09			14 18				14 24				14 39					14 54
Trefforest	d			13 57				14 07	14 12			14 21				14 27				14 42					14 57
Trefforest Estate	d								14 16											14 46					
Taffs Well	d			14 04				14 13	14 20			14 28				14 34				14 50					15 04
Radyr	a			14 07				14 17	14 23			14 31				14 37				14 53					15 07
	d			14 07				14 17	14 23			14 31		14 34		14 37				14 53		15 04			15 07
Danescourt	d													14 38								15 08			
Fairwater	d													14 40								15 10			
Waun-gron Park	d													14 42								15 12			
Ninian Park	d													14 45								15 15			
Llandaf	d			14 10					14 26			14 34				14 40				14 56					15 10
Cathays	d			14 15					14 31			14 39				14 45				15 01					15 15
Rhymney	d				13 29																				
Pontlottyn	d				13 32																				
Tir-phil	d				13 36																				
Brithdir	d				13 39																				
Bargoed	a				13 42																				
	d				13 47						14 02										14 25				
Gilfach Fargoed	d																				14 27				
Pengam	d				13 52						14 07										14 30				
Hengoed	d				13 55						14 10										14 33				
Ystrad Mynach	d				13 58						14 13						14 28				14 43				
Llanbradach	d				14 03						14 18						14 33				14 48				
Aber	d				14 07						14 22						14 37				14 52				
Caerphilly	d				14 10						14 25						14 40				14 55				
Lisvane & Thornhill	d				14 14						14 29						14 44				14 59				
Llanishen	d				14 16						14 31						14 46				15 01				
Heath High Level	d				14 19						14 34						14 49				15 04				
Coryton	d						14 15											14 45							
Whitchurch (Cardiff)	d						14 16											14 46							
Rhiwbina	d						14 18											14 48							
Birchgrove	d						14 20											14 50							
Ty Glas	d						14 21											14 51							
Heath Low Level	d						14 24											14 54							
Cardiff Queen Street	a			14 19	14 24		14 29		14 34		14 39	14 44				14 49	14 54	14 59		15 04	15 09				15 19
	d	14 12		14 21	14 26	14 24	14 31		14 36	14 36	14 41	14 46			14 48	14 51	14 56	15 01	15 00	15 06	15 11			15 12	15 21
Cardiff Bay	a	14 16				14 28				14 40					14 52				15 04					15 16	
Cardiff Central	a			14 24	14 29		14 34	14 37	14 39		14 44	14 53		14 50		14 54	14 59	15 04		15 09	15 14	15 20			15 24
	d			14 25	14 31				14 41		14 46					14 55	15 01			15 10	15 16				15 25
Grangetown	d			14 29	14 35				14 45		14 50					14 59	15 05			15 14	15 20				15 29
Dingle Road	d				14 41						14 56						15 11				15 26				
Penarth	a				14 47						15 02						15 17				15 32				
Cogan	d			14 33					14 48							15 03				15 18					15 33
Eastbrook	d			14 35					14 51							15 05				15 20					15 35
Dinas Powys	d			14 37					14 53							15 07				15 22					15 37
Cadoxton	d			14 42					14 57							15 12				15 27					15 42
Barry Docks	d			14 45					15 00							15 15				15 30					15 45
Barry	d			14 49					15 05							15 19				15 34					15 49
Barry Island	a			14 56												15 26				15 41					15 56
Rhoose Cardiff Int Airport	d								15 12																
Llantwit Major	d								15 22																
Bridgend	a								15 40																

When events are being held at the Millenium Stadium, services are subject to alteration. Please check times before travelling.

Table 130

Saturdays from 15 September

Treherbert, Aberdare, Merthyr, Pontypridd, Rhymney and Coryton - Cardiff, Penarth, Barry, Barry Island and Bridgend

Network Diagram - see first Page of Table 130

		AW	AW	AW	AW	AW	AW	AW	AW	AW	AW	AW	AW	AW	AW	AW	AW	AW	AW	AW	AW	AW	AW
Treherbert	d		14 17						14 47										15 13				
Ynyswen	d		14 19						14 49										15 15				
Treorchy	d		14 21						14 51										15 21				
Ton Pentre	d		14 23						14 53										15 23				
Ystrad Rhondda	a		14 26						14 56										15 26				
	d		14 28						14 58										15 28				
Llwynypia	d		14 30						15 00										15 30				
Tonypandy	d		14 33						15 03										15 33				
Dinas Rhondda	d		14 35						15 05										15 35				
Porth	a		14 38						15 08										15 38				
	d		14 52						15 09										15 39				
Trehafod	d		14 55						15 12										15 42				
Merthyr Tydfil	d					14 38										15 08							
Pentre-bach	d					14 42										15 12							
Troed Y Rhiw	d					14 45										15 15							
Merthyr Vale	a					14 48										15 18							
	d					14 50										15 20							
Quakers Yard	d					14 55										15 25							
Aberdare ■	d											14 51									15 21		
Cwmbach	d											14 54									15 24		
Fernhill	d											14 58									15 28		
Mountain Ash	a											15 01									15 31		
	d											15 04									15 34		
Penrhiwceiber	d											15 08									15 38		
Abercynon	d					14 59						15 14				15 29					15 44		
Pontypridd ■	a		15 00			15 07			15 17			15 22				15 37			15 47		15 52		
	d		15 04			15 09			15 18			15 24				15 39			15 48		15 54		
Trefforest	d		15 07			15 12			15 21			15 27				15 42			15 51		15 57		
Trefforest Estate	d					15 16										15 46							
Taffs Well ■	d		15 13			15 20			15 28			15 34				15 50			15 58		16 04		
Radyr ■	a		15 17			15 23			15 31			15 37				15 53			16 01		16 07		
	d		15 17			15 23			15 31	15 34		15 37				15 53			16 01	16 04	16 07		
Danescourt	d									15 38										16 08			
Fairwater	d									15 40										16 10			
Waun-gron Park	d									15 42										16 12			
Ninian Park	d									15 45										16 15			
Llandaf	d					15 26			15 34			15 40				15 56			16 04		16 10		
Cathays	d					15 31			15 39			15 45				16 01			16 09		16 15		
Rhymney ■	d	14 29																				15 29	
Pontlottyn	d	14 32																				15 32	
Tir-phil	d	14 36																				15 36	
Brithdir	d	14 39																				15 39	
Bargoed	a	14 42																				15 42	
	d	14 47						15 02									15 25					15 47	
Gilfach Fargoed	d																15 27						
Pengam	d	14 52						15 07									15 30					15 52	
Hengoed	d	14 55						15 10									15 33					15 55	
Ystrad Mynach ■	d	14 58						15 13					15 28				15 43					15 58	
Llanbradach	d	15 03						15 18					15 33				15 48					16 03	
Aber	d	15 07						15 22					15 37				15 52					16 07	
Caerphilly ■	d	15 10						15 25					15 40				15 55					16 10	
Lisvane & Thornhill	d	15 14						15 29					15 44				15 59					16 14	
Llanishen	d	15 16						15 31					15 46				16 01					16 16	
Heath High Level	d	15 19						15 34					15 49				16 04					16 19	
Coryton	d				15 15									15 45									
Whitchurch (Cardiff)	d				15 16									15 46									
Rhiwbina	d				15 18									15 48									
Birchgrove	d				15 20									15 50									
Ty Glas	d				15 21									15 51									
Heath Low Level	d				15 24									15 54									
Cardiff Queen Street ■	a	15 24			15 29	15 34		15 39	15 44			15 49	15 54	15 59		16 04	16 09		16 14		16 19	16 24	
	d	15 26		15 24	15 31	15 36	15 36	15 41	15 46		15 48	15 51	15 56	16 01	16 00	16 06	16 11	16 12	16 16		16 21	16 26	16 24
Cardiff Bay	a			15 28			15 40				15 52				16 04			16 16					16 28
Cardiff Central ■	a	15 29	15 34		15 34	15 39		15 44	15 53	15 50		15 54	15 59	16 04		16 09	16 14		16 23	16 20	16 24	16 33	
	d	15 31				15 41		15 46				15 55	16 01			16 10	16 16				16 25		
Grangetown	d	15 35				15 45		15 50				15 59	16 05			16 14	16 20				16 29		
Dingle Road	d	15 41						15 56					16 11				16 26						
Penarth	a	15 47						16 02					16 17				16 32						
Cogan	d					15 48						16 03				16 18					16 33		
Eastbrook	d					15 51						16 05				16 20					16 35		
Dinas Powys	d					15 53						16 07				16 22					16 37		
Cadoxton	d					15 57						16 12				16 27					16 42		
Barry Docks	d					16 00						16 15				16 30					16 45		
Barry ■	d					16 05						16 19				16 34					16 49		
Barry Island	a											16 26				16 41					16 56		
Rhoose Cardiff Int Airport ✈	d					16 12																	
Llantwit Major	d					16 22																	
Bridgend	a					16 40																	

When events are being held at the Millenium Stadium, services are subject to alteration. Please check times before travelling.

Table 130

Saturdays from 15 September

Treherbert, Aberdare, Merthyr, Pontypridd, Rhymney and Coryton - Cardiff, Penarth, Barry, Barry Island and Bridgend

Network Diagram - see first Page of Table 130

		AW	AW	AW	AW	AW	AW	AW	AW	AW	AW	AW	AW	AW	AW	AW	AW	AW	AW	AW	AW	AW
Treherbert	d					15 47										16 17						
Ynyswen	d					15 49										16 19						
Treorchy	d					15 51										16 21						
Ton Pentre	d					15 53										16 23						
Ystrad Rhondda	a					15 56										16 26						
	d					15 58										16 28						
Llwynypia	d					16 00										16 30						
Tonypandy	d					16 03										16 33						
Dinas Rhondda	d					16 05										16 35						
Porth	a					16 08										16 38						
	d					16 09										16 39						
Trehafod	d					16 12										16 42						
Merthyr Tydfil	d		15 38										16 08									16 38
Pentre-bach	d		15 42										16 12									16 42
Troed Y Rhiw	d		15 45										16 15									16 45
Merthyr Vale	a		15 48										16 18									16 48
	d		15 50										16 20									16 50
Quakers Yard	d		15 55										16 25									16 55
Aberdare ■	d								15 51									16 21				
Cwmbach	d								15 54									16 24				
Fernhill	d								15 58									16 28				
Mountain Ash	a								16 01									16 31				
	d								16 04									16 34				
Penrhiwceiber	d								16 08									16 38				
Abercynon	d		15 59						16 14				16 29					16 44				16 59
Pontypridd ■	a		16 07			16 17			16 22				16 37			16 47		16 52				17 07
	d		16 09			16 18			16 24				16 39			16 48		16 54				17 09
Trefforest	d		16 12			16 21			16 27				16 42			16 51		16 57				17 12
Trefforest Estate	d		16 16										16 46									17 16
Taffs Well ■	d		16 20			16 28			16 34				16 50			16 58		17 04				17 20
Radyr ■	a		16 23			16 31			16 37				16 53			17 01		17 07				17 23
	d		16 23			16 32	16 34		16 37				16 53			17 01	17 04	17 07				17 23
Danescourt	d						16 38										17 08					
Fairwater	d						16 40										17 10					
Waun-gron Park	d						16 42										17 12					
Ninian Park	d						16 45										17 15					
Llandaf	d		16 26			16 34			16 40				16 56			17 04		17 10				17 26
Cathays	d		16 31			16 39			16 45				17 01			17 09		17 15				17 31
Rhymney ■	d																		16 29			
Pontlottyn	d																		16 32			
Tir-phil	d																		16 36			
Brithdir	d																		16 39			
Bargoed	a																		16 42			
	d				16 02					16 17				16 32					16 47			
Gilfach Fargoed	d									16 19												
Pengam	d				16 07					16 22				16 37					16 52			
Hengoed	d				16 10					16 25				16 40					16 55			
Ystrad Mynach ■	d				16 13					16 28				16 43					16 58			
Llanbradach	d				16 18					16 33				16 48					17 03			
Aber	d				16 22					16 37				16 52					17 07			
Caerphilly ■	d				16 25					16 40				16 55					17 10			
Lisvane & Thornhill	d				16 29					16 44				16 59					17 14			
Llanishen	d				16 31					16 46				17 01					17 16			
Heath High Level	d				16 34					16 49				17 04					17 19			
Coryton	d	16 15									16 45										17 15	
Whitchurch (Cardiff)	d	16 16									16 46										17 16	
Rhiwbina	d	16 18									16 48										17 18	
Birchgrove	d	16 20									16 50										17 20	
Ty Glas	d	16 21									16 51										17 21	
Heath Low Level	d	16 24									16 54										17 24	
Cardiff Queen Street ■	a	16 29	16 34		16 39	16 44			16 49	16 54	16 59		17 04	17 09		17 14		17 19	17 24		17 29	17 34
	d	16 31	16 36	16 36	16 41	16 46		16 48	16 51	16 56	17 01	17 00	17 06	17 11	17 12	17 16		17 21	17 26	17 24	17 31	17 36
Cardiff Bay	a			16 40				16 52				17 04			17 16					17 28		
Cardiff Central ■	a	16 34	16 39		16 44	16 53	16 50		16 54	16 59	17 04		17 09	17 14		17 23	17 20	17 24	17 29		17 34	17 39
	d		16 41		16 46				16 55	17 01			17 10	17 16				17 25	17 31			17 41
Grangetown	d		16 45		16 50				16 59	17 05			17 14	17 20				17 29	17 35			17 45
Dingle Road	d				16 56					17 11				17 26					17 41			
Penarth	a				17 02					17 17				17 32					17 47			
Cogan	d		16 48						17 03				17 18					17 33				17 48
Eastbrook	d		16 51						17 05				17 20					17 35				17 51
Dinas Powys	d		16 53						17 07				17 22					17 37				17 53
Cadoxton	d		16 57						17 12				17 27					17 42				17 57
Barry Docks	d		17 00						17 15				17 30					17 45				18 00
Barry ■	d		17 05						17 19				17 34					17 49				18 05
Barry Island	a								17 26				17 41					17 56				
Rhoose Cardiff Int Airport ✈	d		17 12																			18 12
Llantwit Major	d		17 22																			18 22
Bridgend	a		17 40																			18 40

When events are being held at the Millenium Stadium, services are subject to alteration. Please check times before travelling.

Table 130

Saturdays
from 15 September

Treherbert, Aberdare, Merthyr, Pontypridd, Rhymney and Coryton - Cardiff, Penarth, Barry, Barry Island and Bridgend

Network Diagram - see first Page of Table 130

		AW	AW	AW	AW	AW	AW	AW	AW	AW		AW	AW	AW	AW	AW	AW	AW	AW	AW		AW	AW	AW	AW
Treherbert	d			16 47											17 17									17 47	
Ynyswen	d			16 49											17 19									17 49	
Treorchy	d			16 51											17 21									17 51	
Ton Pentre	d			16 53											17 23									17 53	
Ystrad Rhondda	a			16 56											17 26									17 56	
	d			16 58											17 28									17 58	
Llwynypia	d			17 00											17 30									18 00	
Tonypandy	d			17 03											17 33									18 03	
Dinas Rhondda	d			17 05											17 35									18 05	
Porth	a			17 08											17 38									18 08	
	d			17 09											17 39									18 09	
Trehafod	d			17 12											17 42									18 12	
Merthyr Tydfil	d											17 08										17 38			
Pentre-bach	d											17 12										17 42			
Troed Y Rhiw	d											17 15										17 45			
Merthyr Vale	a											17 18										17 48			
	d											17 20										17 50			
Quakers Yard	d											17 25										17 55			
Aberdare 3	d						16 51										17 21								
Cwmbach	d						16 54										17 24								
Fernhill	d						16 58										17 28								
Mountain Ash	a						17 01										17 31								
	d						17 04										17 34								
Penrhiwceiber	d						17 08										17 38								
Abercynon	d						17 14					17 29					17 44					17 59			
Pontypridd 3	a			17 17			17 22					17 37			17 47		17 52					18 07		18 17	
	d			17 18			17 24					17 39			17 48		17 54					18 09		18 18	
Trefforest	d			17 21			17 27					17 42			17 51		17 57					18 12		18 21	
Trefforest Estate	d											17 46										18 16			
Taffs Well 3	d			17 28			17 34					17 50			17 58		18 04					18 20		18 28	
Radyr 3	a			17 31			17 37					17 53			18 01		18 07					18 23		18 31	
	d			17 31	17 34		17 37					17 53			18 01	18 04	18 07					18 23		18 31	18 34
Danescourt	d				17 38											18 08									18 38
Fairwater	d				17 40											18 10									18 40
Waun-gron Park	d				17 42											18 12									18 42
Ninian Park	d				17 45											18 15									18 45
Llandaf	d			17 34			17 40					17 56			18 04		18 10					18 26		18 34	
Cathays	d			17 39			17 45					18 01			18 09		18 15					18 31		18 39	
Rhymney 3	d																	17 29							
Pontlottyn	d																	17 32							
Tir-phil	d																	17 36							
Brithdir	d																	17 39							
Bargoed	a																	17 42							
	d		17 02					17 17					17 32					17 47							
Gilfach Fargoed	d							17 19																	
Pengam	d		17 07					17 22					17 37					17 52							
Hengoed	d		17 10					17 25					17 40					17 55							
Ystrad Mynach 3	d		17 13					17 28					17 43					17 58							
Llanbradach	d		17 18					17 33					17 48					18 03							
Aber	d		17 22					17 37					17 52					18 07							
Caerphilly 3	d		17 25					17 40					17 55					18 10							
Lisvane & Thornhill	d		17 29					17 44					17 59					18 14							
Llanishen	d		17 31					17 46					18 01					18 16							
Heath High Level	d		17 34					17 49					18 04					18 19							
Coryton	d								17 45											18 15					
Whitchurch (Cardiff)	d								17 46											18 16					
Rhiwbina	d								17 48											18 18					
Birchgrove	d								17 50											18 20					
Ty Glas	d								17 51											18 21					
Heath Low Level	d								17 54											18 24					
Cardiff Queen Street 3	a		17 39	17 44			17 49	17 54	17 59			18 04	18 09		18 14		18 19	18 24		18 29		18 34		18 44	
	d	17 36	17 41	17 46		17 48	17 51	17 56	18 01	18 00		18 06	18 11	18 12	18 16		18 21	18 26	18 24	18 31		18 36	18 36	18 46	
Cardiff Bay	a	17 40				17 52				18 04				18 16					18 28				18 40		
Cardiff Central 7	a		17 44	17 53	17 50		17 54	17 59	18 04			18 09	18 14		18 23	18 20	18 24	18 29		18 34		18 39		18 53	18 50
	d		17 46				17 55	18 01				18 10	18 16				18 25	18 31				18 41			
Grangetown	d		17 50				17 59	18 05				18 14	18 20				18 29	18 35				18 45			
Dingle Road	d		17 56					18 11					18 26					18 41							
Penarth	a		18 02					18 17					18 32					18 47							
Cogan	d						18 03					18 18					18 33					18 48			
Eastbrook	d						18 05					18 20					18 35					18 51			
Dinas Powys	d						18 07					18 22					18 37					18 53			
Cadoxton	d						18 12					18 27					18 42					18 57			
Barry Docks	d						18 15					18 30					18 45					19 00			
Barry 3	d						18 19					18 34					18 49					19 05			
Barry Island	a						18 26					18 41					18 56								
Rhoose Cardiff Int Airport ✈	d																					19 12			
Llantwit Major	d																					19 22			
Bridgend	a																					19 40			

When events are being held at the Millenium Stadium, services are subject to alteration. Please check times before travelling.

Table 130

Saturdays
from 15 September

Treherbert, Aberdare, Merthyr, Pontypridd, Rhymney and Coryton - Cardiff, Penarth, Barry, Barry Island and Bridgend

Network Diagram - see first Page of Table 130

		AW	AW	AW	AW	AW		AW	AW	AW	AW	AW	AW	AW	AW	AW		AW	AW	AW	AW	AW	AW	AW	AW
Treherbert	d									18 17									18 47						
Ynyswen	d									18 19									18 49						
Treorchy	d									18 21									18 51						
Ton Pentre	d									18 23									18 53						
Ystrad Rhondda	a									18 26									18 56						
	d									18 28									18 58						
Llwynypia	d									18 30									19 00						
Tonypandy	d									18 33									19 03						
Dinas Rhondda	d									18 35									19 05						
Porth	a									18 38									19 08						
	d									18 39									19 09						
Trehafod	d									18 42									19 12						
Merthyr Tydfil	d							18 08								18 38								19 08	
Pentre-bach	d							18 12								18 42								19 12	
Troed Y Rhiw	d							18 15								18 45								19 15	
Merthyr Vale	a							18 18								18 48								19 18	
	d							18 20								18 50								19 20	
Quakers Yard	d							18 25								18 55								19 25	
Aberdare 3	d		17 51									18 21									18 51				
Cwmbach	d		17 54									18 24									18 54				
Fernhill	d		17 58									18 28									18 58				
Mountain Ash	a		18 01									18 31									19 01				
	d		18 04									18 34									19 04				
Penrhiwceiber	d		18 08									18 38									19 08				
Abercynon	d		18 14					18 29				18 44				18 59					19 14			19 29	
Pontypridd 3	a		18 22					18 37		18 47		18 52				19 07			19 17		19 22			19 37	
	d		18 24					18 39		18 48		18 54				19 09			19 18		19 24			19 39	
Trefforest	d		18 27					18 42		18 51		18 57				19 12			19 21		19 27			19 42	
Trefforest Estate	d							18 46								19 16								19 46	
Taffs Well 3	d		18 34					18 50		18 58		19 04				19 20			19 28		19 34			19 50	
Radyr 3	a		18 37					18 53		19 01		19 07				19 23			19 31		19 37			19 53	
	d		18 37					18 53		19 01	19 04	19 07				19 23			19 31		19 37			19 53	
Danescourt	d										19 08														
Fairwater	d										19 10														
Waun-gron Park	d										19 12														
Ninian Park	d										19 15														
Llandaf	d		18 40					18 56		19 04		19 10				19 26			19 34		19 40			19 56	
Cathays	d		18 45					19 01		19 09		19 15				19 31			19 39		19 45			20 01	
Rhymney 3	d																								
Pontlottyn	d																								
Tir-phil	d																								
Brithdir	d																								
Bargoed	a																								
	d			18 17									18 48												
Gilfach Fargoed	d			18 19									18 50												
Pengam	d			18 22									18 53												
Hengoed	d			18 25									18 56												
Ystrad Mynach 3	d			18 28									18 59												
Llanbradach	d			18 33									19 04												
Aber	d			18 37									19 08												
Caerphilly 3	d			18 40									19 11									19 40			
Lisvane & Thornhill	d			18 44									19 15									19 44			
Llanishen	d			18 46									19 17									19 46			
Heath High Level	d			18 49									19 20									19 49			
Coryton	d				18 45										19 15										
Whitchurch (Cardiff)	d				18 46										19 16										
Rhiwbina	d				18 48										19 18										
Birchgrove	d				18 50										19 20										
Ty Glas	d				18 51										19 21										
Heath Low Level	d				18 54										19 24										
Cardiff Queen Street 3	a		18 49	18 54	18 59			19 04		19 14		19 19	19 24		19 29	19 34			19 44		19 49	19 54		20 04	
	d	18 48	18 51	18 56	19 01	19 00		19 06	19 12	19 16		19 21	19 26	19 24	19 31	19 36		19 36	19 46	19 48	19 51	19 56	20 00	20 06	20 12
Cardiff Bay	a	18 52				19 04			19 16					19 28				19 40		19 52			20 04		20 16
Cardiff Central 7	a		18 54	18 59	19 07			19 10		19 23	19 22	19 24	19 29		19 34	19 39			19 53		19 57	19 59		20 09	
	d		18 55	19 01								19 25	19 31			19 41						20 06		20 10	
Grangetown	d		18 59	19 05								19 29	19 35			19 45						20 10		20 14	
Dingle Road	d			19 11									19 41									20 14			
Penarth	a			19 17									19 47									20 20			
Cogan	d		19 03									19 33				19 48								20 18	
Eastbrook	d		19 05									19 35				19 51								20 20	
Dinas Powys	d		19 07									19 37				19 53								20 22	
Cadoxton	d		19 12									19 42				19 57								20 27	
Barry Docks	d		19 15									19 45				20 00								20 30	
Barry 3	d		19 19									19 49				20 05								20 34	
Barry Island	a		19 26									19 56												20 41	
Rhoose Cardiff Int Airport ✈	d															20 12									
Llantwit Major	d															20 22									
Bridgend	a															20 40									

When events are being held at the Millenium Stadium, services are subject to alteration. Please check times before travelling.

Table 130

Saturdays
from 15 September

Treherbert, Aberdare, Merthyr, Pontypridd, Rhymney and Coryton - Cardiff, Penarth, Barry, Barry Island and Bridgend

Network Diagram - see first Page of Table 130

		AW		AW	AW	AW	AW	AW	AW	AW	AW	AW		AW	AW	AW	AW	AW	AW	AW	AW	AW		AW	AW
Treherbert	d	19 17									19 47							20 17							
Ynyswen	d	19 19									19 49							20 19							
Treorchy	d	19 21									19 51							20 21							
Ton Pentre	d	19 23									19 53							20 23							
Ystrad Rhondda	a	19 26									19 56							20 26							
	d	19 28									19 58							20 28							
Llwynypia	d	19 30									20 00							20 30							
Tonypandy	d	19 33									20 03							20 33							
Dinas Rhondda	d	19 35									20 05							20 35							
Porth	a	19 38									20 08							20 38							
	d	19 39									20 09							20 39							
Trehafod	d	19 42									20 12							20 42							
Merthyr Tydfil	d							19 38																	20 38
Pentre-bach	d							19 42																	20 42
Troed Y Rhiw	d							19 45																	20 45
Merthyr Vale	a							19 48																	20 48
	d							19 50																	20 50
Quakers Yard	d							19 55																	20 55
Aberdare 3	d													19 51						20 21					
Cwmbach	d													19 54						20 24					
Fernhill	d													19 58						20 28					
Mountain Ash	a													20 01						20 31					
	d													20 04						20 34					
Penrhiwceiber	d													20 08						20 38					
Abercynon	d				19 43			19 59						20 14						20 44					20 59
Pontypridd 3	a	19 47			19 52			20 07			20 17			20 22				20 47		20 52					21 07
	d	19 48			19 54			20 09			20 18			20 24				20 48		20 54					21 09
Trefforest	d	19 51			19 57			20 12			20 21			20 27				20 51		20 57					21 12
Trefforest Estate	d							20 16																	21 16
Taffs Well 3	d	19 58			20 04			20 20			20 28			20 34				20 58		21 04					21 20
Radyr 3	a	20 01			20 07			20 23			20 31			20 37				21 01		21 07					21 23
	d	20 01		20 04	20 07			20 23			20 31			20 37				21 01	21 04	21 07					21 23
Danescourt	d			20 08															21 08						
Fairwater	d			20 10															21 10						
Waun-gron Park	d			20 12															21 12						
Ninian Park	d			20 15															21 15						
Llandaf	d	20 04			20 10			20 26			20 34			20 40				21 04		21 10					21 26
Cathays	d	20 09			20 15			20 31			20 39			20 45				21 09		21 15					21 31
Rhymney 3	d									19 45															
Pontlottyn	d									19 48															
Tir-phil	d									19 52															
Brithdir	d									19 55															
Bargoed	a									19 58															
	d									19 59															
Gilfach Fargoed	d									20 01															
Pengam	d									20 04															
Hengoed	d									20 07															
Ystrad Mynach 3	d									20 10															
Llanbradach	d									20 15															
Aber	d									20 19															
Caerphilly 3	d									20 22					20 40										
Lisvane & Thornhill	d									20 26					20 44										
Llanishen	d									20 28					20 46										
Heath High Level	d									20 31					20 49										
Coryton	d						20 15																	21 15	
Whitchurch (Cardiff)	d						20 16																	21 16	
Rhiwbina	d						20 18																	21 18	
Birchgrove	d						20 20																	21 20	
Ty Glas	d						20 21																	21 21	
Heath Low Level	d						20 24																	21 24	
Cardiff Queen Street 3	a	20 14			20 19		20 29	20 34		20 39	20 44			20 49	20 54			21 14		21 19				21 29	21 34
	d	20 16			20 21	20 24	20 31	20 36	20 36	20 41	20 46	20 48		20 51	20 56	21 00	21 12	21 16		21 21	21 24			21 31	21 36
Cardiff Bay	a					20 28			20 40			20 52				21 04	21 16				21 28				
Cardiff Central 7	a	20 23		20 24	20 24		20 34	20 39		20 48	20 53			20 57	20 59			21 23	21 25	21 28				21 34	21 39
	d				20 31			20 41						21 06	21 10							21 31			21 41
Grangetown	d				20 35			20 45						21 10	21 14							21 35			21 45
Dingle Road	d				20 41									21 14								21 41			
Penarth	a				20 47									21 20								21 47			
Cogan	d							20 48							21 18										21 48
Eastbrook	d							20 51							21 20										21 51
Dinas Powys	d							20 53							21 22										21 53
Cadoxton	d							20 57							21 27										21 57
Barry Docks	d							21 00							21 30										22 00
Barry 3	d							21 05							21 34										22 05
Barry Island	a														21 41										
Rhoose Cardiff Int Airport ✈	d							21 12																	22 12
Llantwit Major	d							21 22																	22 22
Bridgend	a							21 40																	22 40

When events are being held at the Millenium Stadium, services are subject to alteration. Please check times before travelling.

Table 130

Saturdays
from 15 September

Treherbert, Aberdare, Merthyr, Pontypridd, Rhymney and Coryton - Cardiff, Penarth, Barry, Barry Island and Bridgend

Network Diagram - see first Page of Table 130

		AW	AW	AW	AW	AW	AW	AW		AW	AW	AW	AW	AW	AW	AW	AW	AW		AW	AW	AW	AW	AW	AW
Treherbert	d									21 17															
Ynyswen	d									21 19															
Treorchy	d									21 21															
Ton Pentre	d									21 23															
Ystrad Rhondda	a									21 26															
	d									21 28															
Llwynypia	d									21 30															
Tonypandy	d									21 33															
Dinas Rhondda	d									21 35															
Porth	a									21 38															
	d									21 39															
Trehafod	d									21 42															
Merthyr Tydfil	d													21 38											22 38
Pentre-bach	d													21 42											22 42
Troed Y Rhiw	d													21 45											22 45
Merthyr Vale	a													21 48											22 48
	d													21 50											22 50
Quakers Yard	d													21 55											22 55
Aberdare 3	d				20 51												21 51								
Cwmbach	d				20 54												21 54								
Fernhill	d				20 58												21 58								
Mountain Ash	a				21 01												22 01								
	d				21 04												22 04								
Penrhiwceiber	d				21 08												22 08								
Abercynon	d				21 14									21 59			22 14								22 59
Pontypridd 3	a				21 22					21 47				22 07			22 22								23 07
	d				21 24					21 48				22 09			22 24								23 09
Trefforest	d				21 27					21 51				22 12			22 27								23 12
Trefforest Estate	d													22 16											23 16
Taffs Well 3	d				21 34					21 58				22 20			22 33								23 20
Radyr 3	a				21 37					22 01				22 23			22 37								23 23
	d				21 37					22 01	22 04			22 23			22 37						23 14		23 23
Danescourt	d										22 08														
Fairwater	d										22 10														
Waun-gron Park	d										22 12														
Ninian Park	d										22 15														
Llandaf	d				21 40					22 04				22 26			22 40						23 16		23 26
Cathays	d				21 45					22 09				22 31			22 44						23 20		23 31
Rhymney 3	d		20 48									21 33													
Pontlottyn	d		20 51									21 36													
Tir-phil	d		20 55									21 40													
Brithdir	d		20 58									21 43													
Bargoed	a		21 01									21 46													
	d		21 02									21 47													
Gilfach Fargoed	d		21 04									21 49													
Pengam	d		21 07									21 52													
Hengoed	d		21 10									21 55													
Ystrad Mynach 3	d		21 13				21 39					21 58													
Llanbradach	d		21 18				21 44					22 03													
Aber	d		21 22				21 48					22 07													
Caerphilly 3	d		21 25				21 51					22 10				22 28									
Lisvane & Thornhill	d		21 29				21 55					22 14													
Llanishen	d		21 31				21 57					22 16													
Heath High Level	d		21 34				22 00					22 19													
Coryton	d																			22 45					
Whitchurch (Cardiff)	d																			22 46					
Rhiwbina	d																			22 48					
Birchgrove	d																			22 50					
Ty Glas	d																			22 51					
Heath Low Level	d																			22 54					
Cardiff Queen Street 3	a		21 42		21 49		22 05			22 14		22 24		22 34		22 39	22 48			22 59			23 23		23 34
	d	21 36	21 44	21 48	21 51	22 00	22 06	22 12		22 16		22 26	22 24	22 36	22 36	22 39	22 54	22 48		23 01	23 00	23 12	23 24	23 24	23 36
Cardiff Bay	a	21 40		21 52		22 04		22 16					22 28		22 40			22 52			23 04	23 16		23 28	
Cardiff Central 7	a		21 51		21 54		22 09			22 23	22 20	22 29		22 41		22 43	22 57			23 07			23 27		23 43
	d				22 06		22 10					22 31					23 12						23 30		
Grangetown	d				22 10		22 14					22 35					23 16						23 34		
Dingle Road	d				22 14							22 41					23 20								
Penarth	a				22 20							22 47					23 26								
Cogan	d						22 18																23 37		
Eastbrook	d						22 20																23 40		
Dinas Powys	d						22 22																23 42		
Cadoxton	d						22 27																23 46		
Barry Docks	d						22 30																23 49		
Barry 3	d						22 34																23 54		
Barry Island	a						22 41																00 01		
Rhoose Cardiff Int Airport ✈	d																								
Llantwit Major	d																								
Bridgend	a																								

When events are being held at the Millenium Stadium, services are subject to alteration. Please check times before travelling.

Table 130 — Saturdays from 15 September

Treherbert, Aberdare, Merthyr, Pontypridd, Rhymney and Coryton - Cardiff, Penarth, Barry, Barry Island and Bridgend

Network Diagram - see first Page of Table 130

		AW	AW	AW
Treherbert	d			
Ynyswen	d			
Treorchy	d			
Ton Pentre	d			
Ystrad Rhondda	a			
	d			
Llwynypia	d			
Tonypandy	d			
Dinas Rhondda	d			
Porth	a			
	d			
Trehafod	d			
Merthyr Tydfil	d			
Pentre-bach	d			
Troed Y Rhiw	d			
Merthyr Vale	a			
	d			
Quakers Yard	d			
Aberdare	d	22 51		
Cwmbach	d	22 54		
Fernhill	d	22 58		
Mountain Ash	a	23 01		
	d	23 04		
Penrhiwceiber	d	23 08		
Abercynon	d	23 14		
Pontypridd	a	23 22		
	d			
Trefforest	d			
Trefforest Estate	d			
Taffs Well	d			
Radyr	a			
	d			
Danescourt	d			
Fairwater	d			
Waun-gron Park	d			
Ninian Park	d			
Llandaf	d			
Cathays	d			
Rhymney	d			
Pontlottyn	d			
Tir-phil	d			
Brithdir	d			
Bargoed	a			
	d			
Gilfach Fargoed	d			
Pengam	d			
Hengoed	d			
Ystrad Mynach	d			
Llanbradach	d			
Aber	d			
Caerphilly	d			
Lisvane & Thornhill	d			
Llanishen	d			
Heath High Level	d			
Coryton	d			
Whitchurch (Cardiff)	d			
Rhiwbina	d			
Birchgrove	d			
Ty Glas	d			
Heath Low Level	d			
Cardiff Queen Street	a			
	d		23 36	23 48
Cardiff Bay	a		23 40	23 52
Cardiff Central	a			
	d			
Grangetown	d			
Dingle Road	d			
Penarth	a			
Cogan	d			
Eastbrook	d			
Dinas Powys	d			
Cadoxton	d			
Barry Docks	d			
Barry	d			
Barry Island	a			
Rhoose Cardiff Int Airport ✈	d			
Llantwit Major	d			
Bridgend	a			

When events are being held at the Millenium Stadium, services are subject to alteration. Please check times before travelling.

Table 130 — Sundays until 24 June

Treherbert, Aberdare, Merthyr, Pontypridd, Rhymney and Coryton - Cardiff, Penarth, Barry, Barry Island and Bridgend

Network Diagram - see first Page of Table 130

		AW	AW	AW	AW	AW	AW	AW	AW	AW		AW	AW	AW	AW	AW	AW	AW	AW	AW		AW	AW	AW	AW
												A													
							🚌							🚌	🚌				🚌			🚌		🚌	
Treherbert	d				08 17															10 07					
Ynyswen	d				08 19															10 09					
Treorchy	d				08 21															10 11					
Ton Pentre	d				08 23															10 13					
Ystrad Rhondda	a				08 26															10 16					
	d				08 28															10 18					
Llwynypia	d				08 30															10 20					
Tonypandy	d				08 33															10 23					
Dinas Rhondda	d				08 35															10 25					
Porth	a				08 38															10 28					
	d				08 39															10 29					
Trehafod	d				08 42															10 32					
Merthyr Tydfil	d											09 38	09 38												
Pentre-bach	d											09 42	09 42												
Troed Y Rhiw	d											09 45	09 45												
Merthyr Vale	a											09 48	09 48												
	d											09 50	09 50												
Quakers Yard	d											09 55	09 55												
Aberdare	d															09 54							10 54		
Cwmbach	d															09 57							10 57		
Fernhill	d															10 00							11 00		
Mountain Ash	a															10 03							11 03		
	d															10 04							11 04		
Penrhiwceiber	d															10 07							11 07		
Abercynon	d											09 59	09 59			10 13							11 13		
Pontypridd	a				08 47							10 07	10 07			10 22				10 37			11 22		
	d				08 48							10 09	10 09			10 24				10 38			11 24		
Trefforest	d				08 51							10 12	10 12			10 27				10 41			11 27		
Trefforest Estate	d																								
Taffs Well	d				08 58							10 20	10 20			10 34				10 48			11 34		
Radyr	a				09 01							10 23	10 23			10 37				10 51			11 37		
	d	23p14			09 01		09 11					10 23	10 23		10 33	10 37			10 47	11 02		11 01	11 39	11 47	
Danescourt	d																								
Fairwater	d																								
Waun-gron Park	d																								
Ninian Park	d																								
Llandaf	d	23p16					09 21								10 43				10 57			11 11		11 57	
Cathays	d	23p20					09 36								10 58				11 12			11 26		12 12	
Rhymney	d													09 10											
Pontlottyn	d													09 18											
Tir-phil	d													09 23											
Brithdir	d													09 28											
Bargoed	a													09 33											
	d													09 33											
Gilfach Fargoed	d													09 38											
Pengam	d													09 43											
Hengoed	d													09 53											
Ystrad Mynach	d													09 58											
Llanbradach	d													10 08											
Aber	d													10 18											
Caerphilly	d													10 23											
Lisvane & Thornhill	d													10 33											
Llanishen	d													10 38											
Heath High Level	d													10 43											
Coryton	d																								
Whitchurch (Cardiff)	d																								
Rhiwbina	d																								
Birchgrove	d																								
Ty Glas	d																								
Heath Low Level	d																								
Cardiff Queen Street	a	23p24					09 41							10 58	11 03				11 17			11 31		12 17	
	d	23p25					09 41							10 58	11 03				11 17			11 31		12 17	12 24
Cardiff Bay	a																								12 28
Cardiff Central	a	23p28			09 15		09 49					10 41	10 36	11 06	11 11	10 51			11 25	11 13		11 39	11 50	12 25	
	d	23p30	08 25	08 41		09 25		09 55	10 25	10 37			10 41				10 55	11 16		11 25			11 55		
Grangetown	d	23p34	08 29	08 45		09 29		09 59	10 29	10 41			10 45				10 59			11 29			11 59		
Dingle Road	d									10 45															
Penarth	a									10 48															
Cogan	d	23p37	08 33	08 48		09 33		10 03	10 33				10 48				11 03			11 33			12 03		
Eastbrook	d	23p40	08 35	08 51		09 35		10 05	10 35				10 51				11 05			11 35			12 05		
Dinas Powys	d	23p42	08 37	08 53		09 37		10 07	10 37				10 53				11 07			11 37			12 07		
Cadoxton	d	23p46	08 42	08 57		09 42		10 12	10 42				10 57				11 12			11 42			12 12		
Barry Docks	d	23p49	08 45	09 00		09 45		10 15	10 45				11 00				11 15			11 45			12 15		
Barry	d	23p54	08 49	09 05		09 49		10 19	10 49				11 05				11 19	11 34		11 49			12 19		
Barry Island	a	00 01	08 55			09 55		10 25	10 55								11 25	11 41		11 55			12 25		
Rhoose Cardiff Int Airport ✈	d			09a11									11a11												
Llantwit Major	d																								
Bridgend	a																								

A 20 May

When events are being held at the Millenium Stadium, services are subject to alteration. Please check times before travelling.

Table 130

Sundays
until 24 June

Treherbert, Aberdare, Merthyr, Pontypridd, Rhymney and Coryton - Cardiff, Penarth, Barry, Barry Island and Bridgend

Network Diagram - see first Page of Table 130

		AW	AW	AW	AW	AW		AW	AW	AW	AW	AW	AW	AW	AW	AW		AW	AW	AW	AW	AW	AW	AW	AW
Treherbert	d										12 07														
Ynyswen	d										12 09														
Treorchy	d										12 11														
Ton Pentre	d										12 13														
Ystrad Rhondda	a										12 16														
	d										12 18														
Llwynypia	d										12 20														
Tonypandy	d										12 23														
Dinas Rhondda	d										12 25														
Porth	a										12 28														
	d										12 29														
Trehafod	d										12 32														
Merthyr Tydfil	d			11 38																			13 38		
Pentre-bach	d			11 42																			13 42		
Troed Y Rhiw	d			11 45																			13 45		
Merthyr Vale	a			11 48																			13 48		
	d			11 50																			13 50		
Quakers Yard	d			11 55																			13 55		
Aberdare 3	d															12 54									
Cwmbach	d															12 57									
Fernhill	d															13 00									
Mountain Ash	a															13 03									
	d															13 04									
Penrhiwceiber	d															13 07									
Abercynon	d			11 59												13 13							13 59		
Pontypridd 3	a			12 07							12 37					13 22							14 07		
	d			12 09							12 38					13 24							14 09		
Trefforest	d			12 12							12 41					13 27							14 12		
Trefforest Estate	d																								
Taffs Well 3	d			12 20							12 48					13 34							14 20		
Radyr 3	a			12 23							12 51					13 37							14 23		
	d			12 23							12 51					13 37							14 23		
Danescourt	d																								
Fairwater	d																								
Waun-gron Park	d																								
Ninian Park	d																								
Llandaf	d			12 26							12 54					13 40							14 26		
Cathays	d			12 31							12 59					13 45							14 31		
Rhymney 3	d								11 10																13 32
Pontlottyn	d								11 18																13 35
Tir-phil	d								11 23																13 39
Brithdir	d								11 28																13 42
Bargoed	a								11 33																13 45
	d								11 33																13 47
Gilfach Fargoed	d								11 38																13 51
Pengam	d								11 43																13 56
Hengoed	d								11 53																14 01
Ystrad Mynach 3	d								11 58																14 06
Llanbradach	d								12 08																14 13
Aber	d								12 18																14 19
Caerphilly 3	d								12 23																14 24
Lisvane & Thornhill	d								12 33																14 29
Llanishen	d								12 38																14 31
Heath High Level	d								12 43																14 34
Coryton	d																								
Whitchurch (Cardiff)	d																								
Rhiwbina	d																								
Birchgrove	d																								
Ty Glas	d																								
Heath Low Level	d																								
Cardiff Queen Street 3	a			12 34					12 58		13 02					13 49							14 34		14 39
	d			12 36	12 36	12 48			12 58	13 00	13 04	13 12	13 24	13 36	13 48	13 51		14 00	14 12	14 24			14 36	14 36	14 41
Cardiff Bay	a				12 40	12 52				13 04		13 16	13 28	13 40	13 52			14 04	14 16	14 28				14 40	
Cardiff Central 7	a			12 39					13 06		13 06					13 54							14 39		14 44
	d	12 25	12 31	12 41				12 55			13 25					13 55					14 25	14 31	14 41		
Grangetown	d	12 29	12 35	12 45				12 59			13 29					13 59					14 29	14 35	14 45		
Dingle Road	d		12 41																			14 41			
Penarth	a		12 46																			14 46			
Cogan	d	12 33		12 48				13 03			13 33					14 03					14 33		14 48		
Eastbrook	d	12 35		12 51				13 05			13 35					14 05					14 35		14 51		
Dinas Powys	d	12 37		12 53				13 07			13 37					14 07					14 37		14 53		
Cadoxton	d	12 42		12 57				13 12			13 42					14 12					14 42		14 57		
Barry Docks	d	12 45		13 00				13 15			13 45					14 15					14 45		15 00		
Barry 3	d	12 49		13 05				13 19			13 49					14 19					14 49		15 05		
Barry Island	a	12 55						13 25			13 55					14 25					14 55				
Rhoose Cardiff Int Airport ✈	d			13 12																			15 12		
Llantwit Major	d			13 26																			15 22		
Bridgend	a			13 49																			15 39		

When events are being held at the Millenium Stadium, services are subject to alteration. Please check times before travelling.

Table 130

Sundays
until 24 June

Treherbert, Aberdare, Merthyr, Pontypridd, Rhymney and Coryton - Cardiff, Penarth, Barry, Barry Island and Bridgend

Network Diagram - see first Page of Table 130

		AW		AW	AW	AW	AW	AW	AW	AW	AW	AW		AW	AW	AW	AW	AW	AW	AW	AW	AW		AW	AW
Treherbert	d						14 17																		16 17
Ynyswen	d						14 19																		16 19
Treorchy	d						14 21																		16 21
Ton Pentre	d						14 23																		16 23
Ystrad Rhondda	a						14 26																		16 26
	d						14 28																		16 28
Llwynypia	d						14 30																		16 30
Tonypandy	d						14 33																		16 33
Dinas Rhondda	d						14 35																		16 35
Porth	a						14 38																		16 38
	d						14 39																		16 39
Trehafod	d						14 42																		16 42
Merthyr Tydfil	d																	15 38							
Pentre-bach	d																	15 42							
Troed Y Rhiw	d																	15 45							
Merthyr Vale	a																	15 48							
	d																	15 50							
Quakers Yard	d																	15 55							
Aberdare 3	d										14 54														
Cwmbach	d										14 57														
Fernhill	d										15 00														
Mountain Ash	a										15 03														
	d										15 04														
Penrhiwceiber	d										15 07														
Abercynon	d										15 13							15 59							
Pontypridd 3	a						14 47				15 22							16 07							16 47
	d						14 48				15 24							16 09							16 48
Trefforest	d						14 51				15 27							16 12							16 51
Trefforest Estate	d																								
Taffs Well 3	d						14 58				15 34							16 20							16 58
Radyr 3	a						15 01				15 37							16 23							17 01
	d						15 01				15 37							16 23							17 01
Danescourt	d																								
Fairwater	d																								
Waun-gron Park	d																								
Ninian Park	d																								
Llandaf	d						15 04				15 40							16 26							17 04
Cathays	d						15 09				15 45							16 31							17 09
Rhymney 3	d														15 22										
Pontlottyn	d														15 25										
Tir-phil	d														15 29										
Brithdir	d														15 32										
Bargoed	a														15 35										
	d														15 37										
Gilfach Fargoed	d														15 39										
Pengam	d														15 42										
Hengoed	d														15 45										
Ystrad Mynach 3	d														15 48										
Llanbradach	d														15 53										
Aber	d														15 57										
Caerphilly 3	d														16 00										
Lisvane & Thornhill	d														16 04										
Llanishen	d														16 06										
Heath High Level	d														16 09										
Coryton	d																								
Whitchurch (Cardiff)	d																								
Rhiwbina	d																								
Birchgrove	d																								
Ty Glas	d																								
Heath Low Level	d																								
Cardiff Queen Street 3	a						15 14				15 49				16 14			16 34							17 14
	d	14 48			15 00	15 12	15 16	15 24	15 36	15 48	15 51	16 00		16 12	16 16	16 24		16 36	16 36	16 48		17 00		17 12	17 16
Cardiff Bay	a	14 52			15 04	15 16		15 28	15 40	15 52		16 04		16 16		16 28			16 40	16 52		17 04		17 16	
Cardiff Central 7	a						15 18				15 54				16 18			16 39							17 18
	d			14 55			15 25				15 55				16 25		16 31	16 41			16 55				17 25
Grangetown	d			14 59			15 29				15 59				16 29		16 35	16 45			16 59				17 29
Dingle Road	d																16 41								
Penarth	a																16 46								
Cogan	d			15 03			15 33				16 03				16 33			16 48			17 03				17 33
Eastbrook	d			15 05			15 35				16 05				16 35			16 51			17 05				17 35
Dinas Powys	d			15 07			15 37				16 07				16 37			16 53			17 07				17 37
Cadoxton	d			15 12			15 42				16 12				16 42			16 57			17 12				17 42
Barry Docks	d			15 15			15 45				16 15				16 45			17 00			17 15				17 45
Barry 3	d			15 19			15 49				16 19				16 49			17 05			17 19				17 49
Barry Island	a			15 25			15 55				16 25				16 55						17 25				17 55
Rhoose Cardiff Int Airport ✈	d																	17 12							
Llantwit Major	d																	17 22							
Bridgend	a																	17 39							

When events are being held at the Millenium Stadium, services are subject to alteration. Please check times before travelling.

Table 130

Sundays
until 24 June

Treherbert, Aberdare, Merthyr, Pontypridd, Rhymney and Coryton - Cardiff, Penarth, Barry, Barry Island and Bridgend

Network Diagram - see first Page of Table 130

		AW	AW	AW	AW	AW	AW	AW		AW	AW	AW	AW	AW	AW	AW	AW	AW		AW	AW	AW	AW	AW	AW
Treherbert	d															18 17							20 17		
Ynyswen	d															18 19							20 19		
Treorchy	d															18 21							20 21		
Ton Pentre	d															18 23							20 23		
Ystrad Rhondda	a															18 26							20 26		
	d															18 28							20 28		
Llwynypia	d															18 30							20 30		
Tonypandy	d															18 33							20 33		
Dinas Rhondda	d															18 35							20 35		
Porth	a															18 38							20 38		
	d															18 39							20 39		
Trehafod	d															18 42							20 42		
Merthyr Tydfil	d											17 38									19 38				
Pentre-bach	d											17 42									19 42				
Troed Y Rhiw	d											17 45									19 45				
Merthyr Vale	a											17 48									19 48				
	d											17 50									19 50				
Quakers Yard	d											17 55									19 55				
Aberdare 3	d				16 54												18 54							20 54	
Cwmbach	d				16 57												18 57							20 57	
Fernhill	d				17 00												19 00							21 00	
Mountain Ash	a				17 03												19 03							21 03	
	d				17 04												19 04							21 04	
Penrhiwceiber	d				17 07												19 07							21 07	
Abercynon	d				17 13							17 59					19 13				19 59			21 13	
Pontypridd 3	a				17 22							18 07				18 47	19 22				20 07		20 47	21 22	
	d				17 24							18 09				18 48	19 24				20 09		20 48	21 24	
Trefforest	d				17 27							18 12				18 51	19 27				20 12		20 51	21 27	
Trefforest Estate	d																								
Taffs Well 3	d				17 34							18 20				18 58	19 34				20 20		20 58	21 34	
Radyr 3	a				17 37							18 23				19 01	19 37				20 23		21 01	21 37	
	d				17 37							18 23				19 01	19 37				20 23		21 01	21 37	
Danescourt	d																								
Fairwater	d																								
Waun-gron Park	d																								
Ninian Park	d																								
Llandaf	d				17 40							18 26				19 04	19 40				20 26		21 04	21 40	
Cathays	d				17 45							18 31				19 09	19 45				20 31		21 09	21 45	
Rhymney 3	d							17 22										19 22							
Pontlottyn	d							17 25										19 25							
Tir-phil	d							17 29										19 29							
Brithdir	d							17 32										19 32							
Bargoed	a							17 35										19 35							
	d							17 37										19 37							
Gilfach Fargoed	d							17 39										19 39							
Pengam	d							17 42										19 42							
Hengoed	d							17 45										19 45							
Ystrad Mynach 3	d							17 48										19 48							
Llanbradach	d							17 53										19 53							
Aber	d							17 57										19 57							
Caerphilly 3	d							18 00										20 00							
Lisvane & Thornhill	d							18 04										20 04							
Llanishen	d							18 06										20 06							
Heath High Level	d							18 09										20 09							
Coryton	d																								
Whitchurch (Cardiff)	d																								
Rhiwbina	d																								
Birchgrove	d																								
Ty Glas	d																								
Heath Low Level	d																								
Cardiff Queen Street 3	a				17 49			18 14				18 34				19 14	19 48	20 14			20 34		21 14	21 49	
	d	17 24	17 36	17 48	17 51	18 00	18 12	18 16		18 24		18 36	18 36	18 48		19 16	19 51	20 16			20 36		21 16	21 51	
Cardiff Bay	a	17 28	17 40	17 52		18 04	18 16			18 28			18 40	18 52											
Cardiff Central 7	a				17 54			18 18				18 39				19 18	19 55	20 18			20 39		21 18	21 56	
	d				17 55			18 25			18 31	18 41			18 55	19 25	19 55	20 25		20 31	20 41	20 55	21 25		22 25
Grangetown	d				17 59			18 29			18 35	18 45			18 59	19 29	19 59	20 29		20 35	20 45	20 59	21 29		22 29
Dingle Road	d										18 41									20 41					
Penarth	a										18 46									20 46					
Cogan	d				18 03			18 33				18 48			19 03	19 33	20 03	20 33			20 48	21 03	21 33		22 33
Eastbrook	d				18 05			18 35				18 51			19 05	19 35	20 05	20 35			20 51	21 05	21 35		22 35
Dinas Powys	d				18 07			18 37				18 53			19 07	19 37	20 07	20 37			20 53	21 07	21 37		22 37
Cadoxton	d				18 12			18 42				18 57			19 12	19 42	20 12	20 42			20 57	21 12	21 42		22 42
Barry Docks	d				18 15			18 45				19 00			19 15	19 45	20 15	20 45			21 00	21 15	21 45		22 45
Barry 3	d				18 19			18 49				19 05			19 19	19 49	20 19	20 49			21 05	21 19	21 49		22 49
Barry Island	a				18 25			18 55							19 25	19 55	20 25	20 55				21 25	21 55		22 55
Rhoose Cardiff Int Airport ✈	d											19 12									21 12				
Llantwit Major	d											19 22									21 22				
Bridgend	a											19 39									21 39				

When events are being held at the Millenium Stadium, services are subject to alteration. Please check times before travelling.

Table 130

Sundays
until 24 June

Treherbert, Aberdare, Merthyr, Pontypridd, Rhymney and Coryton - Cardiff, Penarth, Barry, Barry Island and Bridgend

Network Diagram - see first Page of Table 130

		AW
Treherbert	d	
Ynyswen	d	
Treorchy	d	
Ton Pentre	d	
Ystrad Rhondda	a	
	d	
Llwynypia	d	
Tonypandy	d	
Dinas Rhondda	d	
Porth	a	
	d	
Trehafod	d	
Merthyr Tydfil	d	21 38
Pentre-bach	d	21 42
Troed Y Rhiw	d	21 45
Merthyr Vale	a	21 48
	d	21 50
Quakers Yard	d	21 55
Aberdare 3	d	
Cwmbach	d	
Fernhill	d	
Mountain Ash	a	
	d	
Penrhiwceiber	d	
Abercynon	d	21 59
Pontypridd 3	a	22 07
	d	22 09
Trefforest	d	22 12
Trefforest Estate	d	
Taffs Well 3	d	22 20
Radyr 3	a	22 23
	d	22 23
Danescourt	d	
Fairwater	d	
Waun-gron Park	d	
Ninian Park	d	
Llandaf	d	22 26
Cathays	d	22 31
Rhymney 3	d	
Pontlottyn	d	
Tir-phil	d	
Brithdir	d	
Bargoed	a	
	d	
Gilfach Fargoed	d	
Pengam	d	
Hengoed	d	
Ystrad Mynach 3	d	
Llanbradach	d	
Aber	d	
Caerphilly 3	d	
Lisvane & Thornhill	d	
Llanishen	d	
Heath High Level	d	
Coryton	d	
Whitchurch (Cardiff)	d	
Rhiwbina	d	
Birchgrove	d	
Ty Glas	d	
Heath Low Level	d	
Cardiff Queen Street 3	a	22 34
	d	22 36
Cardiff Bay	a	
Cardiff Central 7	a	22 42
	d	
Grangetown	d	
Dingle Road	d	
Penarth	a	
Cogan	d	
Eastbrook	d	
Dinas Powys	d	
Cadoxton	d	
Barry Docks	d	
Barry 3	d	
Barry Island	a	
Rhoose Cardiff Int Airport ✈	d	
Llantwit Major	d	
Bridgend	a	

When events are being held at the Millenium Stadium, services are subject to alteration. Please check times before travelling.

Table 130

Sundays

1 July to 9 September

Treherbert, Aberdare, Merthyr, Pontypridd, Rhymney and Coryton - Cardiff, Penarth, Barry, Barry Island and Bridgend

Network Diagram - see first Page of Table 130

Station		AW	AW A	AW B	AW B	AW	AW	AW	AW	AW		AW	AW	AW	AW	AW	AW	AW	AW	AW		AW	AW	AW	AW
Treherbert	d									08 17															
Ynyswen	d									08 19															
Treorchy	d									08 21															
Ton Pentre	d									08 23															
Ystrad Rhondda	a									08 26															
	d									08 28															
Llwynypia	d									08 30															
Tonypandy	d									08 33															
Dinas Rhondda	d									08 35															
Porth	a									08 38															
	d									08 39															
Trehafod	d									08 42															
Merthyr Tydfil	d		22p38	22p38																		09 38			
Pentre-bach	d		22p42	22p42																		09 42			
Troed Y Rhiw	d		22p45	22p45																		09 45			
Merthyr Vale	a		22p48	22p48																		09 48			
	d		22p50	22p50																		09 50			
Quakers Yard	d		22p55	22p55																		09 55			
Aberdare	d																								09 54
Cwmbach	d																								09 57
Fernhill	d																								10 00
Mountain Ash	a																								10 03
	d																								10 04
Penrhiwceiber	d																								10 07
Abercynon	d		22p59	22p59																		09 59			10 13
Pontypridd	a		23p07	23p07						08 47												10 07			10 22
	d		23p09	23p09						08 48												10 09			10 24
Trefforest	d		23p12	23p12						08 51												10 12			10 27
Trefforest Estate	d		23p16	23p16																					
Taffs Well	d		23p20	23p20						08 58												10 20			10 34
Radyr	a		23p23	23p23						09 01												10 23			10 37
	d	23p14	23p23	23p24						09 01												10 23			10 37
Danescourt	d																								
Fairwater	d																								
Waun-gron Park	d																								
Ninian Park	d																								
Llandaf	d	23p16	23p26	23p27						09 04												10 26			10 40
Cathays	d	23p20	23p31	23p31						09 09												10 31			10 45
Rhymney	d																09 10								
Pontlottyn	d																09 13								
Tir-phil	d																09 17								
Brithdir	d																09 20								
Bargoed	a																09 23								
	d																09 25								
Gilfach Fargoed	d																09 27								
Pengam	d																09 30								
Hengoed	d																09 33								
Ystrad Mynach	d																09 36								
Llanbradach	d																09 41								
Aber	d																09 45								
Caerphilly	d																09 48								
Lisvane & Thornhill	d																09 52								
Llanishen	d																09 54								
Heath High Level	d																09 57								
Coryton	d																								
Whitchurch (Cardiff)	d																								
Rhiwbina	d																								
Birchgrove	d																								
Ty Glas	d																								
Heath Low Level	d																								
Cardiff Queen Street	a	23p24	23p34	23p34						09 14							10 02					10 34			10 49
	d	23p25	23p36	23p36				09 00	09 12	09 16		09 24	09 36	09 48		10 00	10 04	10 12	10 24			10 36	10 36	10 48	10 51
Cardiff Bay	a							09 04	09 16			09 28	09 40	09 52		10 04		10 16	10 28				10 40	10 52	
Cardiff Central	a	23p28	23p39	23p39						09 19							10 07					10 39			10 54
	d	23p30	23p41	23p41	00 26	08 25	08 41			09 25					09 55		10 25			10 31		10 41			10 55
Grangetown	d	23p34	23p45	23p45	00 30	08 29	08 45			09 29					09 59		10 29			10 35		10 45			10 59
Dingle Road	d																			10 41					
Penarth	a																			10 46					
Cogan	d	23p37	23p48	23p48	00 34	08 33	08 48			09 33					10 03		10 33					10 48			11 03
Eastbrook	d	23p40	23p51	23p51	00 36	08 35	08 51			09 35					10 05		10 35					10 51			11 05
Dinas Powys	d	23p42	23p54	23p54	00 39	08 37	08 53			09 37					10 07		10 37					10 53			11 07
Cadoxton	d	23p46	23p58	23p58	00 44	08 42	08 57			09 42					10 12		10 42					10 57			11 12
Barry Docks	d	23p49	00 03	00 03	00 47	08 45	09 00			09 45					10 15		10 45					11 00			11 15
Barry	d	23p54	00 08	00 08	00 52	08 49	09 05			09 49					10 19		10 49					11 05			11 19
Barry Island	a	00 01			00 58	08 55				09 55					10 25		10 55								11 25
Rhoose Cardiff Int Airport	d		00 15	00 15			09 12															11 12			
Llantwit Major	d		00 25	00 25			09 22															11 22			
Bridgend	a		00 43	00 43			09 39															11 39			

A 29 July

B 5 August

When events are being held at the Millenium Stadium, services are subject to alteration. Please check times before travelling.

Table 130

Sundays

1 July to 9 September

Treherbert, Aberdare, Merthyr, Pontypridd, Rhymney and Coryton - Cardiff, Penarth, Barry, Barry Island and Bridgend

Network Diagram - see first Page of Table 130

Station		AW	AW	AW	AW	AW		AW	AW	AW	AW	AW	AW	AW	AW	AW		AW	AW	AW	AW	AW	AW	AW	AW
Treherbert	d			10 07																		12 07			
Ynyswen	d			10 09																		12 09			
Treorchy	d			10 11																		12 11			
Ton Pentre	d			10 13																		12 13			
Ystrad Rhondda	a			10 16																		12 16			
	d			10 18																		12 18			
Llwynypia	d			10 20																		12 20			
Tonypandy	d			10 23																		12 23			
Dinas Rhondda	d			10 25																		12 25			
Porth	a			10 28																		12 28			
	d			10 29																		12 29			
Trehafod	d			10 32																		12 32			
Merthyr Tydfil	d															11 38									
Pentre-bach	d															11 42									
Troed Y Rhiw	d															11 45									
Merthyr Vale	a															11 48									
	d															11 50									
Quakers Yard	d															11 55									
Aberdare	d									10 54															
Cwmbach	d									10 57															
Fernhill	d									11 00															
Mountain Ash	a									11 03															
	d									11 04															
Penrhiwceiber	d									11 07															
Abercynon	d									11 13						11 59									
Pontypridd	a			10 37						11 22						12 07						12 37			
	d			10 38						11 24						12 09						12 38			
Trefforest	d			10 41						11 27						12 12						12 41			
Trefforest Estate	d																								
Taffs Well	d			10 48						11 34						12 20						12 48			
Radyr	a			10 51						11 37						12 23						12 51			
	d			10 51						11 37						12 23						12 51			
Danescourt	d																								
Fairwater	d																								
Waun-gron Park	d																								
Ninian Park	d																								
Llandaf	d			10 54						11 40						12 26						12 54			
Cathays	d			10 59						11 45						12 31						12 59			
Rhymney	d											11 10													
Pontlottyn	d											11 13													
Tir-phil	d											11 17													
Brithdir	d											11 20													
Bargoed	a											11 23													
	d											11 25													
Gilfach Fargoed	d											11 27													
Pengam	d											11 30													
Hengoed	d											11 33													
Ystrad Mynach	d											11 36													
Llanbradach	d											11 41													
Aber	d											11 45													
Caerphilly	d											11 48													
Lisvane & Thornhill	d											11 52													
Llanishen	d											11 54													
Heath High Level	d											11 57													
Coryton	d																								
Whitchurch (Cardiff)	d																								
Rhiwbina	d																								
Birchgrove	d																								
Ty Glas	d																								
Heath Low Level	d																								
Cardiff Queen Street	a			11 02						11 49		12 02				12 34						13 02			
	d	11 00		11 04	11 12	11 24		11 36	11 48	11 51	12 00	12 04	12 12	12 24		12 36		12 36	12 48		13 00	13 04	13 12	13 24	13 36
Cardiff Bay	a	11 04			11 16	11 28		11 40	11 52		12 04		12 16	12 28				12 40	12 52		13 04		13 16	13 28	13 40
Cardiff Central	a			11 07						11 54		12 07				12 39						13 06			
	d		11 17	11 25						11 55		12 25			12 31	12 41				12 55		13 25			
Grangetown	d			11 29						11 59		12 29			12 35	12 45				12 59		13 29			
Dingle Road	d														12 41										
Penarth	a														12 46										
Cogan	d			11 33						12 03		12 33				12 48				13 03		13 33			
Eastbrook	d			11 35						12 05		12 35				12 51				13 05		13 35			
Dinas Powys	d			11 37						12 07		12 37				12 53				13 07		13 37			
Cadoxton	d			11 42						12 12		12 42				12 57				13 12		13 42			
Barry Docks	d			11 45						12 15		12 45				13 00				13 15		13 45			
Barry	d		11 34	11 49						12 19		12 49				13 05				13 19		13 49			
Barry Island	a		11 41	11 55						12 25		12 55								13 25		13 55			
Rhoose Cardiff Int Airport	d															13 12									
Llantwit Major	d															13 22									
Bridgend	a															13 39									

When events are being held at the Millenium Stadium, services are subject to alteration. Please check times before travelling.

Table 130

Sundays
1 July to 9 September

Treherbert, Aberdare, Merthyr, Pontypridd, Rhymney and Coryton - Cardiff, Penarth, Barry, Barry Island and Bridgend

Network Diagram - see first Page of Table 130

		AW		AW	AW	AW	AW	AW	AW	AW	AW	AW		AW	AW	AW	AW	AW	AW	AW	AW	AW		AW	AW
Treherbert	d															14 17									
Ynyswen	d															14 19									
Treorchy	d															14 21									
Ton Pentre	d															14 23									
Ystrad Rhondda	a															14 26									
	d															14 28									
Llwynypia	d															14 30									
Tonypandy	d															14 33									
Dinas Rhondda	d															14 35									
Porth	a															14 38									
	d															14 39									
Trehafod	d															14 42									
Merthyr Tydfil	d									13 38															
Pentre-bach	d									13 42															
Troed Y Rhiw	d									13 45															
Merthyr Vale	a									13 48															
	d									13 50															
Quakers Yard	d									13 55															
Aberdare 3	d			12 54																	14 54				
Cwmbach	d			12 57																	14 57				
Fernhill	d			13 00																	15 00				
Mountain Ash	a			13 03																	15 03				
	d			13 04																	15 04				
Penrhiwceiber	d			13 07																	15 07				
Abercynon	d			13 13						13 59											15 13				
Pontypridd 3	a			13 22						14 07							14 47				15 22				
	d			13 24						14 09							14 48				15 24				
Trefforest	d			13 27						14 12							14 51				15 27				
Trefforest Estate	d																								
Taffs Well 3	d			13 34						14 20							14 58				15 34				
Radyr 3	a			13 37						14 23							15 01				15 37				
	d			13 37						14 23							15 01				15 37				
Danescourt	d																								
Fairwater	d																								
Waun-gron Park	d																								
Ninian Park	d																								
Llandaf	d			13 40						14 26							15 04				15 40				
Cathays	d			13 45						14 31							15 09				15 45				
Rhymney 3	d					13 10																			15 22
Pontlottyn	d					13 13																			15 25
Tir-phil	d					13 17																			15 29
Brithdir	d					13 20																			15 32
Bargoed	a					13 23																			15 35
	d					13 25																			15 37
Gilfach Fargoed	d					13 27																			15 39
Pengam	d					13 30																			15 42
Hengoed	d					13 33																			15 45
Ystrad Mynach 3	d					13 36																			15 48
Llanbradach	d					13 41																			15 53
Aber	d					13 45																			15 57
Caerphilly 3	d					13 48																			16 00
Lisvane & Thornhill	d					13 52																			16 04
Llanishen	d					13 54																			16 06
Heath High Level	d					13 57																			16 09
Coryton	d																								
Whitchurch (Cardiff)	d																								
Rhiwbina	d																								
Birchgrove	d																								
Ty Glas	d																								
Heath Low Level	d																								
Cardiff Queen Street 3	a			13 49		14 02				14 34							15 14				15 49				16 14
	d	13 48		13 51	14 00	14 04	14 12	14 24		14 36	14 36	14 48			15 00	15 12	15 16	15 24	15 36	15 48	15 51	16 00		16 12	16 16
Cardiff Bay	a	13 52			14 04		14 16	14 28			14 40	14 52			15 04	15 16		15 28	15 40	15 52		16 04		16 16	
Cardiff Central 7	a			13 54		14 07				14 39							15 18				15 54				16 18
	d			13 55		14 25			14 31	14 41				14 55			15 25				15 55				16 25
Grangetown	d			13 59		14 29			14 35	14 45				14 59			15 29				15 59				16 29
Dingle Road	d								14 41																
Penarth	a								14 46																
Cogan	d			14 03		14 33				14 48				15 03			15 33				16 03				16 33
Eastbrook	d			14 05		14 35				14 51				15 05			15 35				16 05				16 35
Dinas Powys	d			14 07		14 37				14 53				15 07			15 37				16 07				16 37
Cadoxton	d			14 12		14 42				14 57				15 12			15 42				16 12				16 42
Barry Docks	d			14 15		14 45				15 00				15 15			15 45				16 15				16 45
Barry 3	d			14 19		14 49				15 05				15 19			15 49				16 19				16 49
Barry Island	a			14 25		14 55								15 25			15 55				16 25				16 55
Rhoose Cardiff Int Airport ✈	d									15 12															
Llantwit Major	d									15 22															
Bridgend	a									15 39															

When events are being held at the Millenium Stadium, services are subject to alteration. Please check times before travelling.

Table 130

Sundays
1 July to 9 September

Treherbert, Aberdare, Merthyr, Pontypridd, Rhymney and Coryton - Cardiff, Penarth, Barry, Barry Island and Bridgend

Network Diagram - see first Page of Table 130

		AW	AW	AW	AW	AW	AW	AW		AW	AW	AW	AW	AW	AW	AW	AW	AW		AW	AW	AW	AW	AW	AW
Treherbert	d										16 17														
Ynyswen	d										16 19														
Treorchy	d										16 21														
Ton Pentre	d										16 23														
Ystrad Rhondda	a										16 26														
	d										16 28														
Llwynypia	d										16 30														
Tonypandy	d										16 33														
Dinas Rhondda	d										16 35														
Porth	a										16 38														
	d										16 39														
Trehafod	d										16 42														
Merthyr Tydfil	d			15 38																		17 38			
Pentre-bach	d			15 42																		17 42			
Troed Y Rhiw	d			15 45																		17 45			
Merthyr Vale	a			15 48																		17 48			
	d			15 50																		17 50			
Quakers Yard	d			15 55																		17 55			
Aberdare 3	d														16 54										
Cwmbach	d														16 57										
Fernhill	d														17 00										
Mountain Ash	a														17 03										
	d														17 04										
Penrhiwceiber	d														17 07										
Abercynon	d			15 59											17 13							17 59			
Pontypridd 3	a			16 07							16 47				17 22							18 07			
	d			16 09							16 48				17 24							18 09			
Trefforest	d			16 12							16 51				17 27							18 12			
Trefforest Estate	d																								
Taffs Well 3	d			16 20							16 58				17 34							18 20			
Radyr 3	a			16 23							17 01				17 37							18 23			
	d			16 23							17 01				17 37							18 23			
Danescourt	d																								
Fairwater	d																								
Waun-gron Park	d																								
Ninian Park	d																								
Llandaf	d			16 26							17 04				17 40							18 26			
Cathays	d			16 31							17 09				17 45							18 31			
Rhymney 3	d																	17 22							
Pontlottyn	d																	17 25							
Tir-phil	d																	17 29							
Brithdir	d																	17 32							
Bargoed	a																	17 35							
	d																	17 37							
Gilfach Fargoed	d																	17 39							
Pengam	d																	17 42							
Hengoed	d																	17 45							
Ystrad Mynach 3	d																	17 48							
Llanbradach	d																	17 53							
Aber	d																	17 57							
Caerphilly 3	d																	18 00							
Lisvane & Thornhill	d																	18 04							
Llanishen	d																	18 06							
Heath High Level	d																	18 09							
Coryton	d																								
Whitchurch (Cardiff)	d																								
Rhiwbina	d																								
Birchgrove	d																								
Ty Glas	d																								
Heath Low Level	d																								
Cardiff Queen Street 3	a			16 34							17 14				17 49			18 14				18 34			
	d	16 24		16 36	16 36	16 48		17 00		17 12	17 16	17 24	17 36	17 48	17 51	18 00	18 12	18 16		18 24		18 36	18 36	18 48	
Cardiff Bay	a	16 28			16 40	16 52		17 04		17 16		17 28	17 40	17 52		18 04	18 16			18 28			18 40	18 52	
Cardiff Central 7	a			16 39							17 18				17 54			18 18				18 39			
	d		16 31	16 41			16 55				17 25				17 55			18 25			18 31	18 41			18 55
Grangetown	d		16 35	16 45			16 59				17 29				17 59			18 29			18 35	18 45			18 59
Dingle Road	d		16 41																		18 41				
Penarth	a		16 46																		18 46				
Cogan	d			16 48			17 03				17 33				18 03			18 33				18 48			19 03
Eastbrook	d			16 51			17 05				17 35				18 05			18 35				18 51			19 05
Dinas Powys	d			16 53			17 07				17 37				18 07			18 37				18 53			19 07
Cadoxton	d			16 57			17 12				17 42				18 12			18 42				18 57			19 12
Barry Docks	d			17 00			17 15				17 45				18 15			18 45				19 00			19 15
Barry 3	d			17 05			17 19				17 49				18 19			18 49				19 05			19 19
Barry Island	a						17 25				17 55				18 25			18 55							19 25
Rhoose Cardiff Int Airport ✈	d			17 12																		19 12			
Llantwit Major	d			17 22																		19 22			
Bridgend	a			17 39																		19 39			

When events are being held at the Millenium Stadium, services are subject to alteration. Please check times before travelling.

Table 130

Sundays

1 July to 9 September

Treherbert, Aberdare, Merthyr, Pontypridd, Rhymney and Coryton - Cardiff, Penarth, Barry, Barry Island and Bridgend

Network Diagram - see first Page of Table 130

		AW	AW	AW		AW	AW	AW	AW	AW	AW	AW
Treherbert	d	18 17							20 17			
Ynyswen	d	18 19							20 19			
Treorchy	d	18 21							20 21			
Ton Pentre	d	18 23							20 23			
Ystrad Rhondda	a	18 26							20 26			
	d	18 28							20 28			
Llwynypia	d	18 30							20 30			
Tonypandy	d	18 33							20 33			
Dinas Rhondda	d	18 35							20 35			
Porth	a	18 38							20 38			
	d	18 39							20 39			
Trehafod	d	18 42							20 42			
Merthyr Tydfil	d						19 38					21 38
Pentre-bach	d						19 42					21 42
Troed Y Rhiw	d						19 45					21 45
Merthyr Vale	a						19 48					21 48
	d						19 50					21 50
Quakers Yard	d						19 55					21 55
Aberdare 3	d		18 54							20 54		
Cwmbach	d		18 57							20 57		
Fernhill	d		19 00							21 00		
Mountain Ash	a		19 03							21 03		
	d		19 04							21 04		
Penrhiwceiber	d		19 07							21 07		
Abercynon	d		19 13				19 59			21 13		21 59
Pontypridd 3	a	18 47	19 22				20 07		20 47	21 22		22 07
	d	18 48	19 24				20 09		20 48	21 24		22 09
Trefforest	d	18 51	19 27				20 12		20 51	21 27		22 12
Trefforest Estate	d											
Taffs Well 3	d	18 58	19 34				20 20		20 58	21 34		22 20
Radyr 3	a	19 01	19 37				20 23		21 01	21 37		22 23
	d	19 01	19 37				20 23		21 01	21 37		22 23
Danescourt	d											
Fairwater	d											
Waun-gron Park	d											
Ninian Park	d											
Llandaf	d	19 04	19 40				20 26		21 04	21 40		22 26
Cathays	d	19 09	19 45				20 31		21 09	21 45		22 31
Rhymney 3	d			19 22								
Pontlottyn	d			19 25								
Tir-phil	d			19 29								
Brithdir	d			19 32								
Bargoed	a			19 35								
	d			19 37								
Gilfach Fargoed	d			19 39								
Pengam	d			19 42								
Hengoed	d			19 45								
Ystrad Mynach 3	d			19 48								
Llanbradach	d			19 53								
Aber	d			19 57								
Caerphilly 3	d			20 00								
Lisvane & Thornhill	d			20 04								
Llanishen	d			20 06								
Heath High Level	d			20 09								
Coryton	d											
Whitchurch (Cardiff)	d											
Rhiwbina	d											
Birchgrove	d											
Ty Glas	d											
Heath Low Level	d											
Cardiff Queen Street 3	a	19 14	19 48	20 14			20 34		21 14	21 49		22 34
	d	19 16	19 51	20 16			20 36		21 16	21 51		22 36
Cardiff Bay	a											
Cardiff Central 7	a	19 18	19 55	20 18			20 39		21 18	21 56		22 42
	d	19 25	19 55	20 25		20 31	20 41	20 55	21 25		22 25	
Grangetown	d	19 29	19 59	20 29		20 35	20 45	20 59	21 29		22 29	
Dingle Road	d					20 41						
Penarth	a					20 46						
Cogan	d	19 33	20 03	20 33			20 48	21 03	21 33		22 33	
Eastbrook	d	19 35	20 05	20 35			20 51	21 05	21 35		22 35	
Dinas Powys	d	19 37	20 07	20 37			20 53	21 07	21 37		22 37	
Cadoxton	d	19 42	20 12	20 42			20 57	21 12	21 42		22 42	
Barry Docks	d	19 45	20 15	20 45			21 00	21 15	21 45		22 45	
Barry 3	d	19 49	20 19	20 49			21 05	21 19	21 49		22 49	
Barry Island	a	19 55	20 25	20 55				21 25	21 55		22 55	
Rhoose Cardiff Int Airport ✈	d						21 12					
Llantwit Major	d						21 22					
Bridgend	a						21 39					

When events are being held at the Millenium Stadium, services are subject to alteration. Please check times before travelling.

Table 130

Sundays

16 September to 21 October

Treherbert, Aberdare, Merthyr, Pontypridd, Rhymney and Coryton - Cardiff, Penarth, Barry, Barry Island and Bridgend

Network Diagram - see first Page of Table 130

		AW	AW bus	AW bus	AW	AW bus	AW bus	AW bus	AW bus	AW		AW bus	AW bus	AW bus	AW	AW bus	AW	AW bus	AW bus	AW		AW bus	AW	AW	AW
Treherbert	d				08 17												10 07								
Ynyswen	d				08 19												10 09								
Treorchy	d				08 21												10 11								
Ton Pentre	d				08 23												10 13								
Ystrad Rhondda	a				08 26												10 16								
	d				08 28												10 18								
Llwynypia	d				08 30												10 20								
Tonypandy	d				08 33												10 23								
Dinas Rhondda	d				08 35												10 25								
Porth	a				08 38												10 28								
	d				08 39												10 29								
Trehafod	d				08 42												10 32								
Merthyr Tydfil	d									09 38															
Pentre-bach	d									09 42															
Troed Y Rhiw	d									09 45															
Merthyr Vale	a									09 48															
	d									09 50															
Quakers Yard	d									09 55															
Aberdare 3	d														09 53					10 53					
Cwmbach	d														09 56					10 56					
Fernhill	d														10 00					11 00					
Mountain Ash	a														10 03					11 03					
	d														10 03					11 03					
Penrhiwceiber	d														10 07					11 07					
Abercynon	d									09 59					10 13					11 13					
Pontypridd 3	a				08 47					10 07					10 22		10 37			11 22					
	d				08 48					10 09					10 24		10 38			11 24					
Trefforest	d				08 51					10 12					10 27		10 41			11 27					
Trefforest Estate	d																								
Taffs Well 3	d				08 58					10 20					10 34		10 48			11 34					
Radyr 3	a				09 01					10 23					10 37		10 51			11 37					
	d	23p14			09 02		09 11			10 27				10 33	10 37	10 47	10 51		11 01	11 37		11 47			
Danescourt	d																								
Fairwater	d																								
Waun-gron Park	d																								
Ninian Park	d																								
Llandaf	d	23p16					09 21							10 43		10 57			11 11			11 57			
Cathays	d	23p20					09 36							10 58		11 12			11 26			12 12			
Rhymney 3	d												09 10												
Pontlottyn	d												09 18												
Tir-phil	d												09 23												
Brithdir	d												09 28												
Bargoed	a												09 33												
	d												09 33												
Gilfach Fargoed	d												09 38												
Pengam	d												09 43												
Hengoed	d												09 53												
Ystrad Mynach 3	d												09 58												
Llanbradach	d												10 08												
Aber	d												10 18												
Caerphilly 3	d												10 23												
Lisvane & Thornhill	d												10 33												
Llanishen	d												10 38												
Heath High Level	d												10 43												
Coryton	d																								
Whitchurch (Cardiff)	d																								
Rhiwbina	d																								
Birchgrove	d																								
Ty Glas	d																								
Heath Low Level	d																								
Cardiff Queen Street 3	a	23p23					09 41						10 58	11 03		11 17			11 31			12 17			
	d	23p24					09 41						10 58	11 03		11 17			11 31			12 17	12 24		
Cardiff Bay	a																						12 28		
Cardiff Central 7	a	23p27			09 16		09 49			10 43			11 06	11 11	10 52	11 25	11 07		11 39	11 51		12 25			
	d	23p30	08 35	08 50		09 35		10 31	10 35			10 50						11 35						12 31	12 34
Grangetown	d	23p34	08 40	08 55		09 40		10 36	10 40			10 55						11 40						12 35	12 38
Dingle Road	d							10 46																12 41	
Penarth	a							10 51																12 47	
Cogan	d	23p37	08 45	09 00		09 45			10 45			11 00						11 45							12 42
Eastbrook	d	23p40	08 50	09 05		09 50			10 50			11 05						11 50							12 44
Dinas Powys	d	23p42	08 55	09 10		09 55			10 55			11 10						11 55							12 46
Cadoxton	d	23p46	09 05	09 20		10 05			11 05			11 20						12 05							12 51
Barry Docks	d	23p49	09 10	09 25		10 10			11 10			11 25						12 10							12 54
Barry 3	d	23p54	09 15	09 30		10 15			11 15			11 30						12 15							12 58
Barry Island	a	00 01	09 20			10 20			11 20									12 20							13 05
Rhoose Cardiff Int Airport ✈	d			09 45								11 45													
Llantwit Major	d			10 00								12 00													
Bridgend	a			10 25								12 25													

When events are being held at the Millenium Stadium, services are subject to alteration. Please check times before travelling.

Table 130

Sundays

16 September to 21 October

Treherbert, Aberdare, Merthyr, Pontypridd, Rhymney and Coryton - Cardiff, Penarth, Barry, Barry Island and Bridgend

Network Diagram - see first Page of Table 130

		AW	AW	AW	AW	AW 🚌		AW	AW	AW	AW	AW	AW	AW	AW	AW		AW	AW	AW	AW	AW	AW	AW	AW
Treherbert	d								12 07																
Ynyswen	d								12 09																
Treorchy	d								12 11																
Ton Pentre	d								12 13																
Ystrad Rhondda	a								12 16																
	d								12 18																
Llwynypia	d								12 20																
Tonypandy	d								12 23																
Dinas Rhondda	d								12 25																
Porth	a								12 28																
	d								12 29																
Trehafod	d								12 32																
Merthyr Tydfil	d	11 38																			13 38				
Pentre-bach	d	11 42																			13 42				
Troed Y Rhiw	d	11 45																			13 45				
Merthyr Vale	a	11 48																			13 48				
	d	11 50																			13 50				
Quakers Yard	d	11 55																			13 55				
Aberdare 3	d													12 53											
Cwmbach	d													12 56											
Fernhill	d													13 00											
Mountain Ash	a													13 03											
	d													13 03											
Penrhiwceiber	d													13 07											
Abercynon	d	11 59												13 13							13 59				
Pontypridd 3	a	12 07							12 37					13 22							14 07				
	d	12 09							12 38					13 24							14 09				
Trefforest	d	12 12							12 41					13 27							14 12				
Trefforest Estate	d																								
Taffs Well 3	d	12 20							12 48					13 34							14 20				
Radyr 3	a	12 23							12 51					13 37							14 23				
	d	12 23							12 51					13 37							14 23				
Danescourt	d																								
Fairwater	d																								
Waun-gron Park	d																								
Ninian Park	d																								
Llandaf	d	12 26							12 54					13 40							14 26				
Cathays	d	12 31							12 59					13 45							14 31				
Rhymney 3	d					11 10																	13 32		
Pontlottyn	d					11 18																	13 35		
Tir-phil	d					11 23																	13 39		
Brithdir	d					11 28																	13 42		
Bargoed	a					11 33																	13 45		
	d					11 33																	13 47		
Gilfach Fargoed	d					11 38																	13 51		
Pengam	d					11 43																	13 56		
Hengoed	d					11 53																	14 01		
Ystrad Mynach 3	d					11 58																	14 06		
Llanbradach	d					12 08																	14 13		
Aber	d					12 18																	14 19		
Caerphilly 3	d					12 23																	14 24		
Lisvane & Thornhill	d					12 33																	14 29		
Llanishen	d					12 38																	14 31		
Heath High Level	d					12 43																	14 34		
Coryton	d																								
Whitchurch (Cardiff)	d																								
Rhiwbina	d																								
Birchgrove	d																								
Ty Glas	d																								
Heath Low Level	d																								
Cardiff Queen Street 3	a	12 34				12 58			13 04					13 49							14 34		14 39		
	d	12 36	12 36	12 48		12 58		13 00	13 04	13 12	13 24	13 36	13 48	13 51	14 00	14 12		14 24			14 36	14 36	14 41	14 48	
Cardiff Bay	a		12 40	12 52				13 04		13 16	13 28	13 40	13 52		14 04	14 16		14 28				14 40		14 52	
Cardiff Central 7	a	12 39				13 06			13 06					13 54							14 39		14 48		
	d	12 41			12 55				13 25					13 55					14 25	14 31	14 41				14 55
Grangetown	d	12 45			12 59				13 29					13 59					14 29	14 35	14 45				14 59
Dingle Road	d																			14 41					
Penarth	a																			14 47					
Cogan	d	12 48			13 03				13 33					14 03					14 33		14 48				15 03
Eastbrook	d	12 51			13 05				13 35					14 05					14 35		14 51				15 05
Dinas Powys	d	12 53			13 07				13 37					14 07					14 37		14 53				15 07
Cadoxton	d	12 57			13 12				13 42					14 12					14 42		14 57				15 12
Barry Docks	d	13 00			13 15				13 45					14 15					14 45		15 00				15 15
Barry 3	d	13 05			13 19				13 49					14 19					14 49		15 05				15 19
Barry Island	a				13 26				13 56					14 26					14 56						15 26
Rhoose Cardiff Int Airport ✈	d	13 12																			15 12				
Llantwit Major	d	13 26																			15 22				
Bridgend	a	13 50																			15 40				

When events are being held at the Millenium Stadium, services are subject to alteration. Please check times before travelling.

Table 130

Sundays

16 September to 21 October

Treherbert, Aberdare, Merthyr, Pontypridd, Rhymney and Coryton - Cardiff, Penarth, Barry, Barry Island and Bridgend

Network Diagram - see first Page of Table 130

		AW		AW	AW	AW	AW	AW	AW	AW	AW	AW		AW	AW	AW	AW	AW	AW	AW	AW	AW		AW	AW
Treherbert	d				14 17																	16 17			
Ynyswen	d				14 19																	16 19			
Treorchy	d				14 21																	16 21			
Ton Pentre	d				14 23																	16 23			
Ystrad Rhondda	a				14 26																	16 26			
	d				14 28																	16 28			
Llwynypia	d				14 30																	16 30			
Tonypandy	d				14 33																	16 33			
Dinas Rhondda	d				14 35																	16 35			
Porth	a				14 38																	16 38			
	d				14 39																	16 39			
Trehafod	d				14 42																	16 42			
Merthyr Tydfil	d															15 38									
Pentre-bach	d															15 42									
Troed Y Rhiw	d															15 45									
Merthyr Vale	a															15 48									
	d															15 50									
Quakers Yard	d															15 55									
Aberdare 3	d								14 53																
Cwmbach	d								14 56																
Fernhill	d								15 00																
Mountain Ash	a								15 03																
	d								15 03																
Penrhiwceiber	d								15 07																
Abercynon	d								15 13							15 59									
Pontypridd 3	a				14 47				15 22							16 07						16 47			
	d				14 48				15 24							16 09						16 48			
Trefforest	d				14 51				15 27							16 12						16 51			
Trefforest Estate	d																								
Taffs Well 3	d				14 58				15 34							16 20						16 58			
Radyr 3	a				15 01				15 37							16 23						17 01			
	d				15 01				15 37							16 23						17 01			
Danescourt	d																								
Fairwater	d																								
Waun-gron Park	d																								
Ninian Park	d																								
Llandaf	d				15 04				15 40							16 26						17 04			
Cathays	d				15 09				15 45							16 31						17 09			
Rhymney 3	d											15 22													
Pontlottyn	d											15 25													
Tir-phil	d											15 29													
Brithdir	d											15 32													
Bargoed	a											15 35													
	d											15 37													
Gilfach Fargoed	d											15 39													
Pengam	d											15 42													
Hengoed	d											15 45													
Ystrad Mynach 3	d											15 48													
Llanbradach	d											15 53													
Aber	d											15 57													
Caerphilly 3	d											16 00													
Lisvane & Thornhill	d											16 04													
Llanishen	d											16 06													
Heath High Level	d											16 09													
Coryton	d																								
Whitchurch (Cardiff)	d																								
Rhiwbina	d																								
Birchgrove	d																								
Ty Glas	d																								
Heath Low Level	d																								
Cardiff Queen Street 3	a				15 14				15 49			16 14				16 34						17 14			
	d	15 00		15 12	15 16	15 24	15 36	15 48	15 51	16 00	16 12	16 16		16 24		16 36	16 36	16 48		17 00	17 12	17 16		17 24	17 36
Cardiff Bay	a	15 04		15 16		15 28	15 40	15 52		16 04	16 16			16 28			16 40	16 52		17 04	17 16			17 28	17 40
Cardiff Central 7	a				15 18				15 54			16 18				16 39						17 18			
	d				15 25				15 55			16 25			16 31	16 41			16 55			17 25			
Grangetown	d				15 29				15 59			16 29			16 35	16 45			16 59			17 29			
Dingle Road	d														16 41										
Penarth	a														16 47										
Cogan	d				15 33				16 03			16 33				16 48			17 03			17 33			
Eastbrook	d				15 35				16 05			16 35				16 51			17 05			17 35			
Dinas Powys	d				15 37				16 07			16 37				16 53			17 07			17 37			
Cadoxton	d				15 42				16 12			16 42				16 57			17 12			17 42			
Barry Docks	d				15 45				16 15			16 45				17 00			17 15			17 45			
Barry 3	d				15 49				16 19			16 49				17 05			17 19			17 49			
Barry Island	a				15 56				16 26			16 56							17 26			17 56			
Rhoose Cardiff Int Airport ✈	d															17 12									
Llantwit Major	d															17 22									
Bridgend	a															17 40									

When events are being held at the Millenium Stadium, services are subject to alteration. Please check times before travelling.

Table 130

Sundays

16 September to 21 October

Treherbert, Aberdare, Merthyr, Pontypridd, Rhymney and Coryton - Cardiff, Penarth, Barry, Barry Island and Bridgend

Network Diagram - see first Page of Table 130

		AW	AW	AW	AW	AW	AW	AW	AW	AW	AW	AW	AW	AW	AW	AW	AW	AW	AW	AW	AW	AW
Treherbert	d												18 17						20 17			
Ynyswen	d												18 19						20 19			
Treorchy	d												18 21						20 21			
Ton Pentre	d												18 23						20 23			
Ystrad Rhondda	a												18 26						20 26			
	d												18 28						20 28			
Llwynypia	d												18 30						20 30			
Tonypandy	d												18 33						20 33			
Dinas Rhondda	d												18 35						20 35			
Porth	a												18 38						20 38			
	d												18 39						20 39			
Trehafod	d												18 42						20 42			
Merthyr Tydfil	d								17 38								19 38					21 38
Pentre-bach	d								17 42								19 42					21 42
Troed Y Rhiw	d								17 45								19 45					21 45
Merthyr Vale	a								17 48								19 48					21 48
	d								17 50								19 50					21 50
Quakers Yard	d								17 55								19 55					21 55
Aberdare 3	d		16 53											18 53						20 53		
Cwmbach	d		16 56											18 56						20 56		
Fernhill	d		17 00											19 00						21 00		
Mountain Ash	a		17 03											19 03						21 03		
	d		17 03											19 03						21 03		
Penrhiwceiber	d		17 07											19 07						21 07		
Abercynon	d		17 13						17 59					19 13			19 59			21 13		21 59
Pontypridd 3	a		17 22						18 07				18 47	19 22			20 07		20 47	21 22		22 07
	d		17 24						18 09				18 48	19 24			20 09		20 48	21 24		22 09
Trefforest	d		17 27						18 12				18 51	19 27			20 12		20 51	21 27		22 12
Trefforest Estate	d																					
Taffs Well 3	d		17 34						18 20				18 58	19 34			20 20		20 58	21 34		22 20
Radyr 3	a		17 37						18 23				19 01	19 37			20 23		21 01	21 37		22 23
	d		17 37						18 23				19 01	19 37			20 23		21 01	21 37		22 23
Danescourt	d																					
Fairwater	d																					
Waun-gron Park	d																					
Ninian Park	d																					
Llandaf	d		17 40						18 26				19 04	19 40			20 26		21 04	21 40		22 26
Cathays	d		17 45						18 31				19 09	19 45			20 31		21 09	21 45		22 31
Rhymney 3	d					17 22									19 22							
Pontlottyn	d					17 25									19 25							
Tir-phil	d					17 29									19 29							
Brithdir	d					17 32									19 32							
Bargoed	a					17 35									19 35							
	d					17 37									19 37							
Gilfach Fargoed	d					17 39									19 39							
Pengam	d					17 42									19 42							
Hengoed	d					17 45									19 45							
Ystrad Mynach 3	d					17 48									19 48							
Llanbradach	d					17 53									19 53							
Aber	d					17 57									19 57							
Caerphilly 3	d					18 00									20 00							
Lisvane & Thornhill	d					18 04									20 04							
Llanishen	d					18 06									20 06							
Heath High Level	d					18 09									20 09							
Coryton	d																					
Whitchurch (Cardiff)	d																					
Rhiwbina	d																					
Birchgrove	d																					
Ty Glas	d																					
Heath Low Level	d																					
Cardiff Queen Street 3	a		17 49			18 14			18 34				19 14	19 49	20 14		20 34		21 14	21 49		22 34
	d	17 48	17 51	18 00	18 12	18 16	18 24		18 36	18 36	18 48		19 16	19 51	20 16		20 36		21 16	21 51		22 36
Cardiff Bay	a	17 52		18 04	18 16		18 28			18 40	18 52											
Cardiff Central 7	a		17 54			18 18			18 39				19 18	19 54	20 18		20 39		21 18	21 57		22 41
	d		17 55			18 25		18 31	18 41			18 55	19 25	19 55	20 25	20 31	20 41	20 55	21 25		22 25	
Grangetown	d		17 59			18 29		18 35	18 45			18 59	19 29	19 59	20 29	20 35	20 45	20 59	21 29		22 29	
Dingle Road	d							18 41								20 41						
Penarth	a							18 47								20 47						
Cogan	d		18 03			18 33			18 48			19 03	19 33	20 03	20 33		20 48	21 03	21 33		22 33	
Eastbrook	d		18 05			18 35			18 51			19 05	19 35	20 05	20 35		20 51	21 05	21 35		22 35	
Dinas Powys	d		18 07			18 37			18 53			19 07	19 37	20 07	20 37		20 53	21 07	21 37		22 37	
Cadoxton	d		18 12			18 42			18 57			19 12	19 42	20 12	20 42		20 57	21 12	21 42		22 42	
Barry Docks	d		18 15			18 45			19 00			19 15	19 45	20 15	20 45		21 00	21 15	21 45		22 45	
Barry 3	d		18 19			18 49			19 05			19 19	19 49	20 19	20 49		21 05	21 19	21 49		22 49	
Barry Island	a		18 26			18 56						19 26	19 56	20 26	20 56			21 26	21 56		22 56	
Rhoose Cardiff Int Airport ✈	d								19 12								21 12					
Llantwit Major	d								19 22								21 22					
Bridgend	a								19 40								21 40					

When events are being held at the Millenium Stadium, services are subject to alteration. Please check times before travelling.

Table 130

Sundays

from 28 October

Treherbert, Aberdare, Merthyr, Pontypridd, Rhymney and Coryton - Cardiff, Penarth, Barry, Barry Island and Bridgend

Network Diagram - see first Page of Table 130

		AW	AW	AW	AW	AW	AW	AW	AW	AW	AW	AW	AW	AW	AW	AW	AW	AW	AW	AW	AW	AW	AW
Treherbert	d						08 17															10 07	
Ynyswen	d						08 19															10 09	
Treorchy	d						08 21															10 11	
Ton Pentre	d						08 23															10 13	
Ystrad Rhondda	a						08 26															10 16	
	d						08 28															10 18	
Llwynypia	d						08 30															10 20	
Tonypandy	d						08 33															10 23	
Dinas Rhondda	d						08 35															10 25	
Porth	a						08 38															10 28	
	d						08 39															10 29	
Trehafod	d						08 42															10 32	
Merthyr Tydfil	d																09 38						
Pentre-bach	d																09 42						
Troed Y Rhiw	d																09 45						
Merthyr Vale	a																09 48						
	d																09 50						
Quakers Yard	d																09 55						
Aberdare 3	d																			09 53			
Cwmbach	d																			09 56			
Fernhill	d																			10 00			
Mountain Ash	a																			10 03			
	d																			10 03			
Penrhiwceiber	d																			10 07			
Abercynon	d																09 59			10 13			
Pontypridd 3	a						08 47										10 07			10 22		10 37	
	d						08 48										10 09			10 24		10 38	
Trefforest	d						08 51										10 12			10 27		10 41	
Trefforest Estate	d																						
Taffs Well 3	d						08 58										10 20			10 34		10 48	
Radyr 3	a						09 01										10 23			10 37		10 51	
	d	23p14					09 01										10 23			10 37		10 51	
Danescourt	d																						
Fairwater	d																						
Waun-gron Park	d																						
Ninian Park	d																						
Llandaf	d	23p16					09 04										10 26			10 40		10 54	
Cathays	d	23p20					09 09										10 31			10 45		10 59	
Rhymney 3	d												09 10										
Pontlottyn	d												09 13										
Tir-phil	d												09 17										
Brithdir	d												09 20										
Bargoed	a												09 23										
	d												09 25										
Gilfach Fargoed	d												09 27										
Pengam	d												09 30										
Hengoed	d												09 33										
Ystrad Mynach 3	d												09 36										
Llanbradach	d												09 41										
Aber	d												09 45										
Caerphilly 3	d												09 48										
Lisvane & Thornhill	d												09 52										
Llanishen	d												09 54										
Heath High Level	d												09 57										
Coryton	d																						
Whitchurch (Cardiff)	d																						
Rhiwbina	d																						
Birchgrove	d																						
Ty Glas	d																						
Heath Low Level	d																						
Cardiff Queen Street 3	a	23p23					09 14						10 02				10 34			10 49		11 02	
	d	23p24			09 00	09 12	09 16	09 24	09 36	09 48		10 00	10 04	10 12	10 24		10 36	10 36	10 48	10 51	11 00	11 04	11 12
Cardiff Bay	a				09 04	09 16		09 28	09 40	09 52		10 04		10 16	10 28			10 40	10 52		11 04		11 16
Cardiff Central 7	a	23p27					09 18						10 06				10 39			10 54		11 07	
	d	23p30	08 25	08 41			09 25				09 55		10 25			10 31	10 41			10 55		11 25	
Grangetown	d	23p34	08 29	08 45			09 29				09 59		10 29			10 35	10 45			10 59		11 29	
Dingle Road	d															10 41							
Penarth	a															10 47							
Cogan	d	23p37	08 33	08 48			09 33				10 03		10 33				10 48			11 03		11 33	
Eastbrook	d	23p40	08 35	08 51			09 35				10 05		10 35				10 51			11 05		11 35	
Dinas Powys	d	23p42	08 37	08 53			09 37				10 07		10 37				10 53			11 07		11 37	
Cadoxton	d	23p46	08 42	08 57			09 42				10 12		10 42				10 57			11 12		11 42	
Barry Docks	d	23p49	08 45	09 00			09 45				10 15		10 45				11 00			11 15		11 45	
Barry 3	d	23p54	08 49	09 05			09 49				10 19		10 49				11 05			11 19		11 49	
Barry Island	a	00 01	08 56				09 56				10 26		10 56							11 26		11 56	
Rhoose Cardiff Int Airport ✈	d			09 12													11 12						
Llantwit Major	d			09 22													11 22						
Bridgend	a			09 40													11 40						

When events are being held at the Millenium Stadium, services are subject to alteration. Please check times before travelling.

Table 130

Sundays from 28 October

Treherbert, Aberdare, Merthyr, Pontypridd, Rhymney and Coryton - Cardiff, Penarth, Barry, Barry Island and Bridgend

Network Diagram - see first Page of Table 130

		AW	AW	AW	AW	AW		AW	AW	AW	AW	AW	AW	AW	AW	AW		AW	AW	AW	AW	AW	AW	AW	AW
Treherbert	d																	12 07							
Ynyswen	d																	12 09							
Treorchy	d																	12 11							
Ton Pentre	d																	12 13							
Ystrad Rhondda	a																	12 16							
	d																	12 18							
Llwynypia	d																	12 20							
Tonypandy	d																	12 23							
Dinas Rhondda	d																	12 25							
Porth	a																	12 28							
	d																	12 29							
Trehafod	d																	12 32							
Merthyr Tydfil	d											11 38													
Pentre-bach	d											11 42													
Troed Y Rhiw	d											11 45													
Merthyr Vale	a											11 48													
	d											11 50													
Quakers Yard	d											11 55													
Aberdare ■	d				10 53																		12 53		
Cwmbach	d				10 56																		12 56		
Fernhill	d				11 00																		13 00		
Mountain Ash	a				11 03																		13 03		
	d				11 03																		13 03		
Penrhiwceiber	d				11 07																		13 07		
Abercynon	d				11 13							11 59											13 13		
Pontypridd ■	a				11 22							12 07						12 37					13 22		
	d				11 24							12 09						12 38					13 24		
Trefforest	d				11 27							12 12						12 41					13 27		
Trefforest Estate	d																								
Taffs Well ■	d				11 34							12 20						12 48					13 34		
Radyr ■	a				11 37							12 23						12 51					13 37		
	d				11 37							12 23						12 51					13 37		
Danescourt	d																								
Fairwater	d																								
Waun-gron Park	d																								
Ninian Park	d																								
Llandaf	d				11 40							12 26						12 54					13 40		
Cathays	d				11 45							12 31						12 59					13 45		
Rhymney ■	d							11 10																		13 10
Pontlottyn	d							11 13																		13 13
Tir-phil	d							11 17																		13 17
Brithdir	d							11 20																		13 20
Bargoed	a							11 23																		13 23
	d							11 25																		13 25
Gilfach Fargoed	d							11 27																		13 27
Pengam	d							11 30																		13 30
Hengoed	d							11 33																		13 33
Ystrad Mynach ■	d							11 36																		13 36
Llanbradach	d							11 41																		13 41
Aber	d							11 45																		13 45
Caerphilly ■	d							11 48																		13 48
Lisvane & Thornhill	d							11 52																		13 52
Llanishen	d							11 54																		13 54
Heath High Level	d							11 57																		13 57
Coryton	d																								
Whitchurch (Cardiff)	d																								
Rhiwbina	d																								
Birchgrove	d																								
Ty Glas	d																								
Heath Low Level	d																								
Cardiff Queen Street ■	a				11 49			12 02				12 34						13 04					13 49		14 02
	d	11 24	11 36	11 48	11 51	12 00		12 04	12 12	12 24		12 36	12 36	12 48		13 00		13 04	13 12	13 24	13 36	13 48	13 51	14 00	14 04
Cardiff Bay	a	11 28	11 40	11 52		12 04			12 16	12 28			12 40	12 52		13 04			13 16	13 28	13 40	13 52		14 04	
Cardiff Central ■	a				11 54			12 07				12 39						13 06					13 54		14 07
	d				11 55			12 25			12 31	12 41			12 55			13 25					13 55		14 25
Grangetown	d				11 59			12 29			12 35	12 45			12 59			13 29					13 59		14 29
Dingle Road	d										12 41														
Penarth	a										12 47														
Cogan	d				12 03			12 33				12 48			13 03			13 33					14 03		14 33
Eastbrook	d				12 05			12 35				12 51			13 05			13 35					14 05		14 35
Dinas Powys	d				12 07			12 37				12 53			13 07			13 37					14 07		14 37
Cadoxton	d				12 12			12 42				12 57			13 12			13 42					14 12		14 42
Barry Docks	d				12 15			12 45				13 00			13 15			13 45					14 15		14 45
Barry ■	d				12 19			12 49				13 05			13 19			13 49					14 19		14 49
Barry Island	a				12 26			12 56							13 26			13 56					14 26		14 56
Rhoose Cardiff Int Airport ✈	d											13 12													
Llantwit Major	d											13 22													
Bridgend	a											13 40													

When events are being held at the Millenium Stadium, services are subject to alteration. Please check times before travelling.

Table 130

Sundays from 28 October

Treherbert, Aberdare, Merthyr, Pontypridd, Rhymney and Coryton - Cardiff, Penarth, Barry, Barry Island and Bridgend

Network Diagram - see first Page of Table 130

		AW		AW	AW	AW	AW	AW	AW	AW	AW	AW		AW	AW	AW	AW	AW	AW	AW	AW	AW		AW	AW
Treherbert	d											14 17													
Ynyswen	d											14 19													
Treorchy	d											14 21													
Ton Pentre	d											14 23													
Ystrad Rhondda	a											14 26													
	d											14 28													
Llwynypia	d											14 30													
Tonypandy	d											14 33													
Dinas Rhondda	d											14 35													
Porth	a											14 38													
	d											14 39													
Trehafod	d											14 42													
Merthyr Tydfil	d					13 38																		15 38	
Pentre-bach	d					13 42																		15 42	
Troed Y Rhiw	d					13 45																		15 45	
Merthyr Vale	a					13 48																		15 48	
	d					13 50																		15 50	
Quakers Yard	d					13 55																		15 55	
Aberdare ■	d																14 53								
Cwmbach	d																14 56								
Fernhill	d																15 00								
Mountain Ash	a																15 03								
	d																15 03								
Penrhiwceiber	d																15 07								
Abercynon	d					13 59											15 13							15 59	
Pontypridd ■	a					14 07						14 47					15 22							16 07	
	d					14 09						14 48					15 24							16 09	
Trefforest	d					14 12						14 51					15 27							16 12	
Trefforest Estate	d																								
Taffs Well ■	d					14 20						14 58					15 34							16 20	
Radyr ■	a					14 23						15 01					15 37							16 23	
	d					14 23						15 01					15 37							16 23	
Danescourt	d																								
Fairwater	d																								
Waun-gron Park	d																								
Ninian Park	d																								
Llandaf	d					14 26						15 04					15 40							16 26	
Cathays	d					14 31						15 09					15 45							16 31	
Rhymney ■	d																			15 22					
Pontlottyn	d																			15 25					
Tir-phil	d																			15 29					
Brithdir	d																			15 32					
Bargoed	a																			15 35					
	d																			15 37					
Gilfach Fargoed	d																			15 39					
Pengam	d																			15 42					
Hengoed	d																			15 45					
Ystrad Mynach ■	d																			15 48					
Llanbradach	d																			15 53					
Aber	d																			15 57					
Caerphilly ■	d																			16 00					
Lisvane & Thornhill	d																			16 04					
Llanishen	d																			16 06					
Heath High Level	d																			16 09					
Coryton	d																								
Whitchurch (Cardiff)	d																								
Rhiwbina	d																								
Birchgrove	d																								
Ty Glas	d																								
Heath Low Level	d																								
Cardiff Queen Street ■	a					14 34						15 14					15 49			16 14				16 34	
	d	14 12		14 24		14 36	14 36	14 48		15 00	15 12	15 16		15 24	15 36	15 48	15 51	16 00	16 12	16 16	16 24			16 36	16 36
Cardiff Bay	a	14 16		14 28			14 40	14 52		15 04	15 16			15 28	15 40	15 52		16 04	16 16		16 28				16 40
Cardiff Central ■	a					14 39						15 18					15 54			16 18				16 39	
	d				14 31	14 41			14 55			15 25					15 55			16 25		16 31		16 41	
Grangetown	d				14 35	14 45			14 59			15 29					15 59			16 29		16 35		16 45	
Dingle Road	d				14 41																	16 41			
Penarth	a				14 47																	16 47			
Cogan	d					14 48			15 03			15 33					16 03			16 33				16 48	
Eastbrook	d					14 51			15 05			15 35					16 05			16 35				16 51	
Dinas Powys	d					14 53			15 07			15 37					16 07			16 37				16 53	
Cadoxton	d					14 57			15 12			15 42					16 12			16 42				16 57	
Barry Docks	d					15 00			15 15			15 45					16 15			16 45				17 00	
Barry ■	d					15 05			15 19			15 49					16 19			16 49				17 05	
Barry Island	a								15 26			15 56					16 26			16 56					
Rhoose Cardiff Int Airport ✈	d					15 12																		17 12	
Llantwit Major	d					15 22																		17 22	
Bridgend	a					15 40																		17 40	

When events are being held at the Millenium Stadium, services are subject to alteration. Please check times before travelling.

Table 130

Sundays
from 28 October

Treherbert, Aberdare, Merthyr, Pontypridd, Rhymney and Coryton - Cardiff, Penarth, Barry, Barry Island and Bridgend

Network Diagram - see first Page of Table 130

		AW	AW	AW	AW	AW	AW	AW		AW	AW	AW	AW	AW	AW	AW	AW	AW		AW	AW	AW	AW	AW	AW
Treherbert	d					16 17																18 17			
Ynyswen	d					16 19																18 19			
Treorchy	d					16 21																18 21			
Ton Pentre	d					16 23																18 23			
Ystrad Rhondda	a					16 26																18 26			
	d					16 28																18 28			
Llwynypia	d					16 30																18 30			
Tonypandy	d					16 33																18 33			
Dinas Rhondda	d					16 35																18 35			
Porth	a					16 38																18 38			
	d					16 39																18 39			
Trehafod	d					16 42																18 42			
Merthyr Tydfil	d																17 38								
Pentre-bach	d																17 42								
Troed Y Rhiw	d																17 45								
Merthyr Vale	a																17 48								
	d																17 50								
Quakers Yard	d																17 55								
Aberdare 3	d										16 53												18 53		
Cwmbach	d										16 56												18 56		
Fernhill	d										17 00												19 00		
Mountain Ash	a										17 03												19 03		
	d										17 03												19 03		
Penrhiwceiber	d										17 07												19 07		
Abercynon	d										17 13						17 59						19 13		
Pontypridd 3	a					16 47					17 22						18 07					18 47	19 22		
	d					16 48					17 24						18 09					18 48	19 24		
Trefforest	d					16 51					17 27						18 12					18 51	19 27		
Trefforest Estate	d																								
Taffs Well 3	d					16 58					17 34						18 20					18 58	19 34		
Radyr 3	a					17 01					17 37						18 23					19 01	19 37		
	d					17 01					17 37						18 23					19 01	19 37		
Danescourt	d																								
Fairwater	d																								
Waun-gron Park	d																								
Ninian Park	d																								
Llandaf	d					17 04					17 40						18 26					19 04	19 40		
Cathays	d					17 09					17 45						18 31					19 09	19 45		
Rhymney 3	d													17 22										19 22	
Pontlottyn	d													17 25										19 25	
Tir-phil	d													17 29										19 29	
Brithdir	d													17 32										19 32	
Bargoed	a													17 35										19 35	
	d													17 37										19 37	
Gilfach Fargoed	d													17 39										19 39	
Pengam	d													17 42										19 42	
Hengoed	d													17 45										19 45	
Ystrad Mynach 3	d													17 48										19 48	
Llanbradach	d													17 53										19 53	
Aber	d													17 57										19 57	
Caerphilly 3	d													18 00										20 00	
Lisvane & Thornhill	d													18 04										20 04	
Llanishen	d													18 06										20 06	
Heath High Level	d													18 09										20 09	
Coryton	d																								
Whitchurch (Cardiff)	d																								
Rhiwbina	d																								
Birchgrove	d																								
Ty Glas	d																								
Heath Low Level	d																								
Cardiff Queen Street 3	a					17 14					17 49			18 14			18 34					19 14	19 49	20 14	
	d	16 48		17 00	17 12	17 16	17 24	17 36		17 48	17 51	18 00	18 12	18 16	18 24		18 36	18 36		18 48		19 16	19 51	20 16	
Cardiff Bay	a	16 52		17 04	17 16		17 28	17 40		17 52		18 04	18 16		18 28			18 40		18 52					
Cardiff Central 7	a					17 18					17 54			18 18			18 39					19 18	19 54	20 18	
	d		16 55			17 25					17 55			18 25		18 31	18 41				18 55	19 25	19 55	20 25	20 31
Grangetown	d		16 59			17 29					17 59			18 29		18 35	18 45				18 59	19 29	19 59	20 29	20 35
Dingle Road	d															18 41									20 41
Penarth	a															18 47									20 47
Cogan	d		17 03			17 33					18 03			18 33			18 48				19 03	19 33	20 03	20 33	
Eastbrook	d		17 05			17 35					18 05			18 35			18 51				19 05	19 35	20 05	20 35	
Dinas Powys	d		17 07			17 37					18 07			18 37			18 53				19 07	19 37	20 07	20 37	
Cadoxton	d		17 12			17 42					18 12			18 42			18 57				19 12	19 42	20 12	20 42	
Barry Docks	d		17 15			17 45					18 15			18 45			19 00				19 15	19 45	20 15	20 45	
Barry 3	d		17 19			17 49					18 19			18 49			19 05				19 19	19 49	20 19	20 49	
Barry Island	a		17 26			17 56					18 26			18 56							19 26	19 56	20 26	20 56	
Rhoose Cardiff Int Airport ✈	d																19 12								
Llantwit Major	d																19 22								
Bridgend	a																19 40								

When events are being held at the Millenium Stadium, services are subject to alteration. Please check times before travelling.

Table 130

Sundays
from 28 October

Treherbert, Aberdare, Merthyr, Pontypridd, Rhymney and Coryton - Cardiff, Penarth, Barry, Barry Island and Bridgend

Network Diagram - see first Page of Table 130

		AW	AW	AW		AW	AW	AW
Treherbert	d			20 17				
Ynyswen	d			20 19				
Treorchy	d			20 21				
Ton Pentre	d			20 23				
Ystrad Rhondda	a			20 26				
	d			20 28				
Llwynypia	d			20 30				
Tonypandy	d			20 33				
Dinas Rhondda	d			20 35				
Porth	a			20 38				
	d			20 39				
Trehafod	d			20 42				
Merthyr Tydfil	d	19 38						21 38
Pentre-bach	d	19 42						21 42
Troed Y Rhiw	d	19 45						21 45
Merthyr Vale	a	19 48						21 48
	d	19 50						21 50
Quakers Yard	d	19 55						21 55
Aberdare 3	d					20 53		
Cwmbach	d					20 56		
Fernhill	d					21 00		
Mountain Ash	a					21 03		
	d					21 03		
Penrhiwceiber	d					21 07		
Abercynon	d	19 59				21 13		21 59
Pontypridd 3	a	20 07		20 47		21 22		22 07
	d	20 09		20 48		21 24		22 09
Trefforest	d	20 12		20 51		21 27		22 12
Trefforest Estate	d							
Taffs Well 3	d	20 20		20 58		21 34		22 20
Radyr 3	a	20 23		21 01		21 37		22 23
	d	20 23		21 01		21 37		22 23
Danescourt	d							
Fairwater	d							
Waun-gron Park	d							
Ninian Park	d							
Llandaf	d	20 26		21 04		21 40		22 26
Cathays	d	20 31		21 09		21 45		22 31
Rhymney 3	d							
Pontlottyn	d							
Tir-phil	d							
Brithdir	d							
Bargoed	a							
	d							
Gilfach Fargoed	d							
Pengam	d							
Hengoed	d							
Ystrad Mynach 3	d							
Llanbradach	d							
Aber	d							
Caerphilly 3	d							
Lisvane & Thornhill	d							
Llanishen	d							
Heath High Level	d							
Coryton	d							
Whitchurch (Cardiff)	d							
Rhiwbina	d							
Birchgrove	d							
Ty Glas	d							
Heath Low Level	d							
Cardiff Queen Street 3	a	20 34		21 14		21 49		22 34
	d	20 36		21 16		21 51		22 36
Cardiff Bay	a							
Cardiff Central 7	a	20 39		21 18		21 57		22 41
	d	20 41	20 55	21 25			22 25	
Grangetown	d	20 45	20 59	21 29			22 29	
Dingle Road	d							
Penarth	a							
Cogan	d	20 48	21 03	21 33			22 33	
Eastbrook	d	20 51	21 05	21 35			22 35	
Dinas Powys	d	20 53	21 07	21 37			22 37	
Cadoxton	d	20 57	21 12	21 42			22 42	
Barry Docks	d	21 00	21 15	21 45			22 45	
Barry 3	d	21 05	21 19	21 49			22 49	
Barry Island	a		21 26	21 56			22 56	
Rhoose Cardiff Int Airport ✈	d	21 12						
Llantwit Major	d	21 22						
Bridgend	a	21 40						

When events are being held at the Millenium Stadium, services are subject to alteration. Please check times before travelling.

Bridgend, Barry Island, Barry, Penarth and Cardiff - Coryton, Rhymney, Pontypridd, Merthyr, Aberdare and Treherbert

Network Diagram - see first Page of Table 130

Miles	Miles	Miles	Miles	Miles			AW A	AW A	AW A	AW A	AW A	AW		AW	AW	AW	AW	AW	AW	AW	AW	AW	AW	AW
—	—	0	—	—	**Bridgend**	d															05 37			
—	—	9¼	—	—	Llantwit Major	d															05 46			
—	—	15¾	—	—	Rhoose Cardiff Int Airport ✈	d															05 56			
0	—	—	—	—	**Barry Island**	d	22p45							05 15				05 51						
0¼	—	19	—	—	**Barry** 3	d	22p49							05 20				05 55			06 15			
2	—	—	—	—	Barry Docks	d	22p53							05 24				05 59			06 19			
2¾	—	—	—	—	Cadoxton	d	22p56							05 27				06 02			06 22			
4¼	—	—	—	—	Dinas Powys	d	23p00							05 31				06 06			06 26			
5¼	—	—	—	—	Eastbrook	d	23p03							05 33				06 08			06 28			
6½	—	—	—	—	Cogan	d	23p05							05 35				06 10			06 30			
—	0	—	—	—	**Penarth**	d											06 02						06 32	
—	0¼	—	—	—	Dingle Road	d											06 04						06 34	
8¼	2¼	—	—	—	Grangetown	d	23p09							05 39			06 08	06 14			06 34		06 38	
9¼	3¼	—	0	—	**Cardiff Central** 7	a	23p14							05 44			06 13	06 19			06 39		06 44	
—	—	—	—	—		d	23p26	23p40	23p56	00 05	00 20	05 26		05 46	05 56	06 11	06 15	06 21	06 26	06 36	06 41		06 46	06 51
—	—	0	—	—	**Cardiff Bay**	d																06 42		
9¾	4¼	1	—	—	**Cardiff Queen Street** 3	a	23p29					05 29		05 49	05 59	06 14	06 19	06 24	06 29	06 39	06 44	06 46	06 49	06 54
—	—	—	—	—		d	23p30					05 30		05 50	06 00	06 15	06 20	06 25	06 30	06 40	06 45		06 50	06 55
—	—	3½	—	—	Heath Low Level	d												06 30						07 00
—	4½	—	—	—	Ty Glas	d												06 33						07 03
—	—	4¾	—	—	Birchgrove	d												06 34						07 04
—	—	5¼	—	—	Rhiwbina	d												06 36						07 06
—	—	5½	—	—	Whitchurch (Cardiff)	d												06 38						07 08
—	—	6	—	—	**Coryton**	a												06 43						07 13
—	6¾	—	—	—	Heath High Level	d				00 12				05 55			06 25						06 55	
—	7¾	—	—	—	Llanishen	d				00 15				05 58			06 28						06 58	
—	8¾	—	—	—	Lisvane & Thornhill	d				00 17				06 00			06 30						07 00	
—	11¼	—	—	—	Caerphilly 3	d				00 23				06a08			06 36						07 06	
—	12	—	—	—	Aber	d				00 25							06 38						07 08	
—	14	—	—	—	Llanbradach	d				00 29							06 42						07 12	
—	16¾	—	—	—	Ystrad Mynach 3	d				00 34							06 47						07 17	
—	17¾	—	—	—	Hengoed	d				00 37							06 50						07 20	
—	19½	—	—	—	Pengam	d				00 40							06 53						07 23	
—	20½	—	—	—	Gilfach Fargoed	d				00 43														
—	21	—	—	—	Bargoed	a				00 47							07 01						07 31	
—	—	—	—	—		d				00 47														
—	22½	—	—	—	Brithdir	d				00 51														
—	23½	—	—	—	Tir-phil	d				00 54														
—	26	—	—	—	Pontlottyn	d				00 58														
—	27	—	—	—	**Rhymney** 3	a				01 05														
10½	—	—	—	—	Cathays	d	23p33	23p45	00 03		00 25	05 33			06 03	06 18			06 33	06 43	06 48			
13	—	—	—	—	Llandaf	d	23p37	23p49	00 07		00 29	05 37			06 07	06 22			06 37	06 47	06 52			
—	—	—	1	—	Ninian Park	d																		
—	—	—	2½	—	Waun-gron Park	d																		
—	—	—	3	—	Fairwater	d																		
—	—	—	3½	—	Danescourt	d																		
14	—	—	4¾	—	Radyr 3	a	23p40	23p53	00 10		00 32	05 40			06 10	06 24			06 40	06 50	06 54			
—	—	—	—	—		d	23p41	23p53	00 11		00 33	05 40			06 10	06 24			06 40	06 50	06 55			
16	—	—	—	—	Taffs Well 3	d	23p45	23p57	00 15		00 37	05 44			06 14	06 28			06 44	06 54	06 59			
18¼	—	—	—	—	Trefforest Estate	d	23p49					05 48			06 18				06 48					
20¾	—	—	—	—	Trefforest	d	23p53	00 03	00 21		00 43	05 52			06 22	06 35			06 52	07 01	07 06			
21¾	—	0	—	0	**Pontypridd** 3	a	23p56	00 06	00 24		00 48	05 55			06 25	06 38			06 55	07 04	07 09			
—	—	—	—	—		d	23p57	00 08	00 26			05 57	06 11		06 27	06 41			06 57	07 06	07 11			
—	—	3¼	—	3¼	Abercynon	d	00 07	00 17				06 04	06 19		06 34	06 49			07 04		07 19			
—	—	—	—	6	Penrhiwceiber	d		00 23					06 24			06 54					07 24			
—	—	—	—	7¼	Mountain Ash	a		00 26					06 28			06 58					07 28			
—	—	—	—	—		d		00 28					06 33			07 03					07 33			
—	—	—	—	8¼	Fernhill	d		00 30					06 35			07 05					07 35			
—	—	—	—	9½	Cwmbach	d		00 34					06 39			07 09					07 39			
—	—	—	—	11	**Aberdare** 3	a		00 41					06 46			07 16					07 46			
—	—	4¾	—	—	Quakers Yard	d	00 11					06 09			06 39				07 09					
—	—	7	—	—	Merthyr Vale	a	00 16					06 14			06 44				07 14					
—	—	—	—	—		d	00 19					06 17			06 47				07 17					
—	—	8¾	—	—	Troed Y Rhiw	d	00 22					06 20			06 50				07 20					
—	—	10	—	—	Pentre-bach	d	00 25					06 23			06 53				07 23					
—	—	11½	—	—	**Merthyr Tydfil**	a	00 30					06 31			07 01				07 31					
23½	—	—	—	—	Trehafod	d			00 31											07 11				
24¾	—	—	—	—	Porth	a			00 34											07 14				
—	—	—	—	—		d			00 35											07 15				
26¼	—	—	—	—	Dinas Rhondda	d			00 39											07 19				
26¾	—	—	—	—	Tonypandy	d			00 41											07 21				
27¾	—	—	—	—	Llwynypia	d			00 43											07 23				
29	—	—	—	—	Ystrad Rhondda	a			00 46											07 26				
—	—	—	—	—		d			00 47											07 29				
29½	—	—	—	—	Ton Pentre	d			00 49											07 31				
30¾	—	—	—	—	Treorchy	d			00 52											07 34				
31¾	—	—	—	—	Ynyswen	d			00 55											07 37				
32¼	—	—	—	—	**Treherbert**	a			01 02											07 43				

A 26 July, 27 July, 2 August

When events are being held at the Millenium Stadium, services are subject to alteration. Please check times before travelling.

Bridgend, Barry Island, Barry, Penarth and Cardiff - Coryton, Rhymney, Pontypridd, Merthyr, Aberdare and Treherbert

Network Diagram - see first Page of Table 130

		AW	AW	AW	AW	AW	AW	AW	AW	AW	AW	AW	AW	AW	AW	AW	AW	AW	AW	AW	AW	AW
Bridgend	d															06 42						
Llantwit Major	d															06 56						
Rhoose Cardiff Int Airport ✈	d															07 06						
Barry Island	d		06 25								06 55										07 25	
Barry 3	d		06 30								07 00					07 15					07 30	
Barry Docks	d		06 34								07 04					07 19					07 34	
Cadoxton	d		06 37								07 07					07 22					07 37	
Dinas Powys	d		06 41								07 11					07 26					07 41	
Eastbrook	d		06 43								07 13					07 28					07 43	
Cogan	d		06 45								07 15					07 30					07 45	
Penarth	d							07 02				07 17						07 32				07 47
Dingle Road	d							07 04				07 19						07 34				07 49
Grangetown	d		06 49					07 08			07 19	07 23				07 34		07 38			07 49	07 53
Cardiff Central 7	a		06 54					07 14			07 24	07 29				07 39		07 44			07 54	07 59
	d		06 56		07 06	07 06	07 11	07 16		07 21	07 26	07 31		07 36	07 36	07 41		07 46	07 51		07 56	08 01
Cardiff Bay	d	06 54		07 06					07 18				07 30				07 42			07 54		
Cardiff Queen Street 3	a	06 58	06 59	07 10	07 09		07 14	07 19	07 22	07 24	07 29	07 34	07 34	07 39		07 44	07 46	07 49	07 54	07 58	07 59	08 04
	d		07 00		07 10		07 15	07 20		07 25	07 30	07 35		07 40		07 45		07 50	07 55		08 00	08 05
Heath Low Level	d									07 30									08 00			
Ty Glas	d									07 33									08 03			
Birchgrove	d									07 34									08 04			
Rhiwbina	d									07 36									08 06			
Whitchurch (Cardiff)	d									07 38									08 08			
Coryton	a									07 43									08 13			
Heath High Level	d							07 25				07 40						07 55				08 10
Llanishen	d							07 28				07 43						07 58				08 13
Lisvane & Thornhill	d							07 30				07 45						08 00				08 15
Caerphilly 3	d							07 36				07 51						08 06				08 21
Aber	d							07 38				07 53						08 08				08 23
Llanbradach	d							07 42				07 57						08 12				08 27
Ystrad Mynach 3	d							07 47				08 02						08 17				08 32
Hengoed	d							07 50				08 05						08 20				08 35
Pengam	d							07 53				08 08						08 23				08 38
Gilfach Fargoed	d																					08 41
Bargoed	a							08 02				08 13						08 31				08 48
	d											08 14										
Brithdir	d											08 18										
Tir-phil	d											08 21										
Pontlottyn	d											08 25										
Rhymney 3	a											08 31										
Cathays	d		07 03		07 13		07 18				07 33			07 43		07 48					08 03	
Llandaf	d		07 07		07 17		07 22				07 37			07 47		07 52					08 07	
Ninian Park	d					07 10									07 40							
Waun-gron Park	d					07 13									07 43							
Fairwater	d					07 15									07 45							
Danescourt	d					07 17									07 47							
Radyr 3	a		07 10		07 20	07 24	07 25				07 40			07 50	07 54	07 55					08 10	
	d		07 10		07 20		07 25				07 40			07 50		07 55					08 10	
Taffs Well 3	d		07 14		07 24		07 29				07 44			07 54		07 59					08 14	
Trefforest Estate	d		07 18								07 48										08 18	
Trefforest	d		07 22		07 31		07 36				07 52			08 01		08 06					08 22	
Pontypridd 3	a		07 25		07 34		07 39				07 55			08 04		08 09					08 25	
	d		07 27		07 36		07 41				07 57			08 06		08 11					08 27	
Abercynon	d		07 34				07 49				08 04					08 19					08 34	
Penrhiwceiber	d						07 54									08 24						
Mountain Ash	a						07 58									08 28						
	d						08 03									08 33						
Fernhill	d						08 05									08 35						
Cwmbach	d						08 09									08 39						
Aberdare 3	a						08 16									08 46						
Quakers Yard	d		07 39								08 09										08 39	
Merthyr Vale	a		07 44								08 14										08 44	
	d		07 47								08 17										08 47	
Troed Y Rhiw	d		07 50								08 20										08 50	
Pentre-bach	d		07 53								08 23										08 53	
Merthyr Tydfil	a		08 01								08 31										09 01	
Trehafod	d				07 41									08 11								
Porth	a				07 44									08 14								
	d				07 45									08 15								
Dinas Rhondda	d				07 49									08 19								
Tonypandy	d				07 51									08 21								
Llwynypia	d				07 53									08 23								
Ystrad Rhondda	a				07 56									08 26								
	d				07 59									08 29								
Ton Pentre	d				08 01									08 31								
Treorchy	d				08 04									08 34								
Ynyswen	d				08 07									08 37								
Treherbert	a				08 13									08 43								

When events are being held at the Millenium Stadium, services are subject to alteration. Please check times before travelling.

Bridgend, Barry Island, Barry, Penarth and Cardiff - Coryton, Rhymney, Pontypridd, Merthyr, Aberdare and Treherbert

Network Diagram - see first Page of Table 130

		AW	AW	AW	AW	AW	AW	AW	AW	AW	AW	AW	AW	AW	AW	AW	AW	AW	AW	AW	AW	AW	AW
Bridgend	d													07 42									
Llantwit Major	d													07 56									
Rhoose Cardiff Int Airport ✈	d													08 06									
Barry Island	d				07 40				07 55										08 25				
Barry ■	d				07 45				08 00					08 15					08 30				
Barry Docks	d				07 49				08 04					08 19					08 34				
Cadoxton	d				07 52				08 07					08 22					08 37				
Dinas Powys	d				07 56				08 11					08 26					08 41				
Eastbrook	d				07 58				08 13					08 28					08 43				
Cogan	d				08 00				08 15					08 30					08 45				
Penarth	d					08 02				08 17						08 32				08 47			
Dingle Road	d					08 04				08 19						08 34				08 49			
Grangetown	d				08 04	08 08			08 19	08 23				08 34		08 38			08 49	08 53			
Cardiff Central ■	a				08 09	08 14			08 24	08 29				08 39		08 44			08 54	08 59			
	d		08 06	08 06	08 11	08 16		08 21	08 26	08 31		08 36	08 36	08 41		08 46	08 51		08 56	09 01		09 06	09 06
Cardiff Bay	d	08 06					08 18				08 30				08 42			08 54			09 06		
Cardiff Queen Street ■	a	08 10	08 09		08 14	08 19	08 22	08 24	08 29	08 34	08 34	08 39		08 44	08 46	08 49	08 54	08 58	08 59	09 04	09 10	09 09	
	d		08 10		08 15	08 20		08 25	08 30	08 35		08 40		08 45		08 50	08 55		09 00	09 05		09 10	
Heath Low Level	d							08 30									09 00						
Ty Glas	d							08 33									09 03						
Birchgrove	d							08 34									09 04						
Rhiwbina	d							08 36									09 06						
Whitchurch (Cardiff)	d							08 38									09 08						
Coryton	a							08 43									09 13						
Heath High Level	d					08 25				08 40						08 55				09 10			
Llanishen	d					08 28				08 43						08 58				09 13			
Lisvane & Thornhill	d					08 30				08 45						09 00				09 15			
Caerphilly ■	d					08 36				08 51						09 06				09 21			
Aber	d					08 38				08 53						09 08				09 23			
Llanbradach	d					08 42				08 57						09 12				09 27			
Ystrad Mynach ■	d					08 47				09 02						09 17				09 32			
Hengoed	d					08 50				09 05						09 20				09 35			
Pengam	d					08 53				09 08						09 23				09 38			
Gilfach Fargoed	d																			09 41			
Bargoed	a					08 58				09 16						09 31				09 48			
	d					08 59																	
Brithdir	d					09 03																	
Tir-phil	d					09 06																	
Pontlottyn	d					09 10																	
Rhymney ■	a					09 16																	
Cathays	d		08 13		08 18				08 33			08 43		08 48					09 03			09 13	
Llandaf	d		08 17		08 22				08 37			08 47		08 52					09 07			09 17	
Ninian Park	d			08 10									08 40										09 10
Waun-gron Park	d			08 13									08 43										09 13
Fairwater	d			08 15									08 45										09 15
Danescourt	d			08 17									08 47										09 17
Radyr ■	a		08 20	08 24	08 25				08 40			08 50	08 54	08 55					09 10			09 20	09 24
	d		08 20		08 25				08 40			08 50		08 55					09 10			09 20	
Taffs Well ■	d		08 24		08 29				08 44			08 54		08 59					09 14			09 24	
Trefforest Estate	d								08 48										09 18				
Trefforest	d		08 31		08 36				08 52			09 01		09 06					09 22			09 31	
Pontypridd ■	a		08 34		08 39				08 55			09 04		09 09					09 25			09 34	
	d		08 36		08 41				08 57			09 06		09 11					09 27			09 36	
Abercynon	d				08 49				09 04					09 19					09 34				
Penrhiwceiber	d				08 54									09 24									
Mountain Ash	a				08 58									09 28									
	d				09 03									09 33									
Fernhill	d				09 05									09 35									
Cwmbach	d				09 09									09 39									
Aberdare ■	a				09 16									09 46									
Quakers Yard	d								09 09										09 39				
Merthyr Vale	a								09 14										09 44				
	d								09 17										09 47				
Troed Y Rhiw	d								09 20										09 50				
Pentre-bach	d								09 23										09 53				
Merthyr Tydfil	a								09 31										10 01				
Trehafod	d		08 41									09 11										09 41	
Porth	a		08 44									09 14										09 44	
	d		08 45									09 15										09 45	
Dinas Rhondda	d		08 49									09 19										09 49	
Tonypandy	d		08 51									09 21										09 51	
Llwynypia	d		08 53									09 23										09 53	
Ystrad Rhondda	a		08 56									09 26										09 56	
	d		08 59									09 29										09 59	
Ton Pentre	d		09 01									09 31										10 01	
Treorchy	d		09 04									09 34										10 04	
Ynyswen	d		09 07									09 37										10 07	
Treherbert	a		09 13									09 43										10 13	

When events are being held at the Millenium Stadium, services are subject to alteration. Please check times before travelling.

Bridgend, Barry Island, Barry, Penarth and Cardiff - Coryton, Rhymney, Pontypridd, Merthyr, Aberdare and Treherbert

Network Diagram - see first Page of Table 130

		AW	AW	AW	AW	AW	AW	AW	AW	AW	AW	AW	AW	AW	AW	AW	AW	AW	AW	AW	AW	AW
Bridgend	d										08 42											
Llantwit Major	d										08 56											
Rhoose Cardiff Int Airport ✈	d										09 06											
Barry Island	d	08 40				08 55										09 25						09 40
Barry ■	d	08 45				09 00					09 15					09 30						09 45
Barry Docks	d	08 49				09 04					09 19					09 34						09 49
Cadoxton	d	08 52				09 07					09 22					09 37						09 52
Dinas Powys	d	08 56				09 11					09 26					09 41						09 56
Eastbrook	d	08 58				09 13					09 28					09 43						09 58
Cogan	d	09 00				09 15					09 30					09 45						10 00
Penarth	d						09 17						09 32				09 47					
Dingle Road	d						09 19						09 34				09 49					
Grangetown	d	09 04				09 19	09 23				09 34		09 38			09 49	09 53					10 04
Cardiff Central ■	a	09 09				09 24	09 29				09 39		09 44			09 54	09 59					10 09
	d	09 11	09 16		09 21	09 26	09 31		09 36	09 36	09 41		09 46	09 51		09 56	10 01		10 06	10 06		10 11
Cardiff Bay	d			09 18				09 30				09 42			09 54			10 06				
Cardiff Queen Street ■	a	09 14	09 19	09 22	09 24	09 29	09 34	09 34	09 39		09 44	09 46	09 49	09 54	09 58	09 59	10 04	10 10	10 09			10 14
	d	09 15	09 20		09 25	09 30	09 35		09 40		09 45		09 50	09 55		10 00	10 05		10 10			10 15
Heath Low Level	d				09 30									10 00								
Ty Glas	d				09 33									10 03								
Birchgrove	d				09 34									10 04								
Rhiwbina	d				09 36									10 06								
Whitchurch (Cardiff)	d				09 38									10 08								
Coryton	a				09 43									10 13								
Heath High Level	d		09 25				09 40						09 55				10 10					
Llanishen	d		09 28				09 43						09 58				10 13					
Lisvane & Thornhill	d		09 30				09 45						10 00				10 15					
Caerphilly ■	d		09 36				09 51						10 06				10 21					
Aber	d		09 38				09 53						10 08				10 23					
Llanbradach	d		09 42				09 57						10 12				10 27					
Ystrad Mynach ■	d		09 47				10 02						10 17				10 32					
Hengoed	d		09 50				10 05						10 20				10 35					
Pengam	d		09 53				10 08						10 23				10 38					
Gilfach Fargoed	d																10 41					
Bargoed	a		09 58				10 16						10 31				10 48					
	d		09 59																			
Brithdir	d		10 03																			
Tir-phil	d		10 06																			
Pontlottyn	d		10 10																			
Rhymney ■	a		10 16																			
Cathays	d	09 18				09 33			09 43		09 48					10 03			10 13			10 18
Llandaf	d	09 22				09 37			09 47		09 52					10 07			10 17			10 22
Ninian Park	d									09 40										10 10		
Waun-gron Park	d									09 43										10 13		
Fairwater	d									09 45										10 15		
Danescourt	d									09 47										10 17		
Radyr ■	a	09 25				09 40			09 50	09 54	09 55					10 10			10 20	10 24		10 25
	d	09 25				09 40			09 50		09 55					10 10			10 20			10 25
Taffs Well ■	d	09 29				09 44			09 54		09 59					10 14			10 24			10 29
Trefforest Estate	d					09 48																
Trefforest	d	09 36				09 52			10 01		10 06					10 22			10 31			10 36
Pontypridd ■	a	09 39				09 55			10 04		10 09					10 30			10 34			10 39
	d	09 41				09 57			10 06		10 11								10 36		10 35	10 41
Abercynon	d	09 49				10 04					10 19										10 41	10 49
Penrhiwceiber	d	09 54									10 24											10 54
Mountain Ash	a	09 58									10 28											10 58
	d	10 03									10 33											11 03
Fernhill	d	10 05									10 35											11 05
Cwmbach	d	10 09									10 39											11 09
Aberdare ■	a	10 16									10 46											11 16
Quakers Yard	d					10 09															10 45	
Merthyr Vale	a					10 14															10 50	
	d					10 17															10 52	
Troed Y Rhiw	d					10 20															10 55	
Pentre-bach	d					10 23															10 58	
Merthyr Tydfil	a					10 31															11 06	
Trehafod	d								10 11										10 41			
Porth	a								10 14										10 44			
	d								10 15										10 45			
Dinas Rhondda	d								10 19										10 49			
Tonypandy	d								10 21										10 51			
Llwynypia	d								10 23										10 53			
Ystrad Rhondda	a								10 26										10 56			
	d								10 29										10 59			
Ton Pentre	d								10 31										11 01			
Treorchy	d								10 34										11 04			
Ynyswen	d								10 37										11 07			
Treherbert	a								10 43										11 13			

When events are being held at the Millenium Stadium, services are subject to alteration. Please check times before travelling.

Table 130

Mondays to Fridays

until 7 September

Bridgend, Barry Island, Barry, Penarth and Cardiff - Coryton, Rhymney, Pontypridd, Merthyr, Aberdare and Treherbert

Network Diagram - see first Page of Table 130

		AW	AW	AW	AW	AW	AW	AW	AW		AW	AW	AW	AW	AW	AW	AW	AW	AW		AW	AW	AW	AW	AW
Bridgend	d										09 45														
Llantwit Major	d										09 58														
Rhoose Cardiff Int Airport ✈	d										10 08														
Barry Island	d				09 55											10 25						10 40			
Barry 3	d				10 00						10 16					10 30						10 45			
Barry Docks	d				10 04						10 19					10 34						10 49			
Cadoxton	d				10 07						10 22					10 37						10 52			
Dinas Powys	d				10 11						10 26					10 41						10 56			
Eastbrook	d				10 13						10 28					10 43						10 58			
Cogan	d				10 15						10 30					10 45						11 00			
Penarth	d	10 02				10 17							10 32					10 47					11 02		
Dingle Road	d	10 04				10 19							10 34					10 49					11 04		
Grangetown	d	10 08			10 19	10 23					10 34		10 38			10 49		10 53				11 04	11 08		
Cardiff Central 7	a	10 14			10 24	10 29					10 42		10 44			10 54		10 59				11 09	11 14		
	d	10 16		10 21	10 26	10 31		10 36	10 36				10 46	10 51		10 56	10 54	11 01	11 06			11 11	11 16		11 21
Cardiff Bay	d		10 18				10 30					10 42			10 54						11 06			11 18	
Cardiff Queen Street 3	a	10 19	10 22	10 24	10 29	10 34	10 34	10 39				10 46	10 49	10 54	10 58	10 59		11 04			11 10	11 14	11 19	11 22	11 24
	d	10 20		10 25	10 30	10 35		10 40					10 50	10 55		11 00		11 05				11 15	11 20		11 25
Heath Low Level	d			10 30										11 00											11 30
Ty Glas	d			10 33										11 03											11 33
Birchgrove	d			10 34										11 04											11 34
Rhiwbina	d			10 36										11 06											11 36
Whitchurch (Cardiff)	d			10 38										11 08											11 38
Coryton	a			10 43										11 13											11 43
Heath High Level	d	10 25				10 40							10 55					11 10					11 25		
Llanishen	d	10 28				10 43							10 58					11 13					11 28		
Lisvane & Thornhill	d	10 30				10 45							11 00					11 15					11 30		
Caerphilly 3	d	10 36				10 51							11 06					11 21					11 36		
Aber	d	10 38				10 53							11 08					11 23					11 38		
Llanbradach	d	10 42				10 57							11 12					11 27					11 42		
Ystrad Mynach 3	d	10 47				11 02							11 17					11 32					11 47		
Hengoed	d	10 50				11 05							11 20					11 35					11 50		
Pengam	d	10 53				11 08							11 23					11 38					11 53		
Gilfach Fargoed	d																	11 41							
Bargoed	a	10 58				11 16							11 31					11 48					11 58		
	d	10 59																					11 59		
Brithdir	d	11 03																					12 03		
Tir-phil	d	11 06																					12 06		
Pontlottyn	d	11 10																					12 10		
Rhymney 3	a	11 16																					12 16		
Cathays	d				10 33			10 43								11 03						11 18			
Llandaf	d				10 37			10 47								11 07						11 22			
Ninian Park	d								10 40										11 10						
Waun-gron Park	d								10 43										11 13						
Fairwater	d								10 45										11 15						
Danescourt	d								10 47										11 17						
Radyr 3	a				10 40			10 50	10 54							11 10	11 02		11 24			11 25			
	d				10 40			10 50								11 10	11 20					11 25			
Taffs Well 3	d				10 44			10 54								11 14	11 24					11 29			
Trefforest Estate	d				10 48											11 18									
Trefforest	d				10 52			11 01								11 22	11 31					11 36			
Pontypridd 3	a				10 55			11 04								11 25	11 34					11 39			
	d				10 57			11 06								11 27	11 36					11 41			
Abercynon	d				11 04											11 34						11 49			
Penrhiwceiber	d																					11 54			
Mountain Ash	a																					11 58			
	d																					12 03			
Fernhill	d																					12 05			
Cwmbach	d																					12 09			
Aberdare 3	a																					12 16			
Quakers Yard	d				11 09											11 39									
Merthyr Vale	a				11 14											11 44									
	d				11 17											11 47									
Troed Y Rhiw	d				11 20											11 50									
Pentre-bach	d				11 23											11 53									
Merthyr Tydfil	a				11 31											12 01									
Trehafod	d							11 11									11 41								
Porth	a							11 14									11 44								
	d							11 15									11 45								
Dinas Rhondda	d							11 19									11 49								
Tonypandy	d							11 21									11 51								
Llwynypia	d							11 23									11 53								
Ystrad Rhondda	a							11 26									11 56								
	d							11 29									11 59								
Ton Pentre	d							11 31									12 01								
Treorchy	d							11 34									12 04								
Ynyswen	d							11 37									12 07								
Treherbert	a							11 43									12 13								

When events are being held at the Millenium Stadium, services are subject to alteration. Please check times before travelling.

Table 130

Mondays to Fridays

until 7 September

Bridgend, Barry Island, Barry, Penarth and Cardiff - Coryton, Rhymney, Pontypridd, Merthyr, Aberdare and Treherbert

Network Diagram - see first Page of Table 130

		AW	AW	AW	AW		AW	AW	AW	AW	AW	AW	AW	AW	AW		AW	AW	AW	AW	AW	AW	AW	AW	AW
Bridgend	d							10 45																	
Llantwit Major	d							10 58																	
Rhoose Cardiff Int Airport ✈	d							11 08																	
Barry Island	d	10 55											11 25						11 40				11 55		
Barry 3	d	11 00						11 16					11 30						11 45				12 00		
Barry Docks	d	11 04						11 19					11 34						11 49				12 04		
Cadoxton	d	11 07						11 22					11 37						11 52				12 07		
Dinas Powys	d	11 11						11 26					11 41						11 56				12 11		
Eastbrook	d	11 13						11 28					11 43						11 58				12 13		
Cogan	d	11 15						11 30					11 45						12 00				12 15		
Penarth	d		11 17							11 32				11 47						12 02				12 17	
Dingle Road	d		11 19							11 34				11 49						12 04				12 19	
Grangetown	d	11 19	11 23					11 34		11 38			11 49	11 53					12 04	12 08			12 19	12 23	
Cardiff Central 7	a	11 24	11 29					11 39		11 44			11 54	11 59					12 09	12 14			12 24	12 29	
	d	11 26	11 31		11 36		11 36	11 41		11 46	11 51		11 56	12 01			12 06	12 06	12 11	12 16		12 21	12 26	12 31	
Cardiff Bay	d			11 30					11 42			11 54			12 06						12 18				12 30
Cardiff Queen Street 3	a	11 29	11 34	11 34	11 39			11 44	11 46	11 49	11 54	11 58	11 59	12 04	12 10		12 09		12 14	12 19	12 22	12 24	12 29	12 34	12 34
	d	11 30	11 35		11 40			11 45		11 50	11 55		12 00	12 05			12 10		12 15	12 20		12 25	12 30	12 35	
Heath Low Level	d										12 00											12 30			
Ty Glas	d										12 03											12 33			
Birchgrove	d										12 04											12 34			
Rhiwbina	d										12 06											12 36			
Whitchurch (Cardiff)	d										12 08											12 38			
Coryton	a										12 13											12 43			
Heath High Level	d		11 40							11 55				12 10						12 25				12 40	
Llanishen	d		11 43							11 58				12 13						12 28				12 43	
Lisvane & Thornhill	d		11 45							12 00				12 15						12 30				12 45	
Caerphilly 3	d		11 51							12 06				12 21						12 36				12 51	
Aber	d		11 53							12 08				12 23						12 38				12 53	
Llanbradach	d		11 57							12 12				12 27						12 42				12 57	
Ystrad Mynach 3	d		12 02							12 17				12 32						12 47				13 02	
Hengoed	d		12 05							12 20				12 35						12 50				13 05	
Pengam	d		12 08							12 23				12 38						12 53				13 08	
Gilfach Fargoed	d													12 41											
Bargoed	a		12 16							12 31				12 48						12 58				13 16	
	d																			12 59					
Brithdir	d																			13 03					
Tir-phil	d																			13 06					
Pontlottyn	d																			13 10					
Rhymney 3	a																			13 16					
Cathays	d	11 33			11 43			11 48					12 03				12 13		12 18				12 33		
Llandaf	d	11 37			11 47			11 52					12 07				12 17		12 22				12 37		
Ninian Park	d						11 40											12 10							
Waun-gron Park	d						11 43											12 13							
Fairwater	d						11 45											12 15							
Danescourt	d						11 47											12 17							
Radyr 3	a	11 40			11 50		11 54	11 55					12 10				12 20	12 24	12 25				12 40		
	d	11 40			11 50			11 55					12 10				12 20		12 25				12 40		
Taffs Well 3	d	11 44			11 54			11 59					12 14				12 24		12 29				12 44		
Trefforest Estate	d	11 48											12 18										12 48		
Trefforest	d	11 52			12 01			12 06					12 22				12 31		12 36				12 52		
Pontypridd 3	a	11 55			12 04			12 09					12 25				12 34		12 42				12 55		
	d	11 57			12 06			12 11					12 27				12 36						12 57		
Abercynon	d	12 04						12 19					12 34										13 04		
Penrhiwceiber	d							12 24																	
Mountain Ash	a							12 28																	
	d							12 33																	
Fernhill	d							12 35																	
Cwmbach	d							12 39																	
Aberdare 3	a							12 46																	
Quakers Yard	d	12 09											12 39										13 09		
Merthyr Vale	a	12 14											12 44										13 14		
	d	12 17											12 47										13 17		
Troed Y Rhiw	d	12 20											12 50										13 20		
Pentre-bach	d	12 23											12 53										13 23		
Merthyr Tydfil	a	12 31											13 01										13 31		
Trehafod	d				12 11												12 41								
Porth	a				12 14												12 44								
	d				12 15												12 45								
Dinas Rhondda	d				12 19												12 49								
Tonypandy	d				12 21												12 51								
Llwynypia	d				12 23												12 53								
Ystrad Rhondda	a				12 26												12 56								
	d				12 29												12 59								
Ton Pentre	d				12 31												13 01								
Treorchy	d				12 34												13 04								
Ynyswen	d				12 37												13 07								
Treherbert	a				12 43												13 13								

When events are being held at the Millenium Stadium, services are subject to alteration. Please check times before travelling.

Table 130

Mondays to Fridays
until 7 September

Bridgend, Barry Island, Barry, Penarth and Cardiff - Coryton, Rhymney, Pontypridd, Merthyr, Aberdare and Treherbert

Network Diagram - see first Page of Table 130

		AW	AW	AW	AW	AW	AW	AW	AW	AW	AW	AW	AW	AW	AW	AW	AW	AW	AW	AW	AW	AW
Bridgend	d				11 42																	
Llantwit Major	d				11 56																	
Rhoose Cardiff Int Airport ✈	d				12 06																	
Barry Island	d									12 25					12 40				12 55			
Barry	d				12 15					12 30					12 45				13 00			
Barry Docks	d				12 19					12 34					12 49				13 04			
Cadoxton	d				12 22					12 37					12 52				13 07			
Dinas Powys	d				12 26					12 41					12 56				13 11			
Eastbrook	d				12 28					12 43					12 58				13 13			
Cogan	d				12 30					12 45					13 00				13 15			
Penarth	d						12 32				12 47					13 02				13 17		
Dingle Road	d						12 34				12 49					13 04				13 19		
Grangetown	d				12 34		12 38			12 49	12 53				13 04	13 08			13 19	13 23		
Cardiff Central	a				12 44		12 44			12 54	12 59				13 09	13 14			13 24	13 29		
	d	12 36	12 36	12 41			12 46	12 51		12 56	13 01		13 06	13 06	13 11	13 16		13 21	13 26	13 31		13 36
Cardiff Bay	d					12 42			12 54			13 06					13 18				13 30	
Cardiff Queen Street	a	12 39		12 44		12 46	12 49	12 54	12 58	12 59	13 04	13 10	13 09		13 14	13 19	13 22	13 24	13 29	13 34	13 34	13 39
	d	12 40		12 45			12 50	12 55		13 00	13 05		13 10		13 15	13 20		13 25	13 30	13 35		13 40
Heath Low Level	d							13 00										13 30				
Ty Glas	d							13 03										13 33				
Birchgrove	d							13 04										13 34				
Rhiwbina	d							13 06										13 36				
Whitchurch (Cardiff)	d							13 08										13 38				
Coryton	a							13 13										13 43				
Heath High Level	d						12 55				13 10					13 25				13 40		
Llanishen	d						12 58				13 13					13 28				13 43		
Lisvane & Thornhill	d						13 00				13 15					13 30				13 45		
Caerphilly	d						13 06				13 21					13 36				13 51		
Aber	d						13 08				13 23					13 38				13 53		
Llanbradach	d						13 12				13 27					13 42				13 57		
Ystrad Mynach	d						13 17				13 32					13 47				14 02		
Hengoed	d						13 20				13 35					13 50				14 05		
Pengam	d						13 23				13 38					13 53				14 08		
Gilfach Fargoed	d										13 41											
Bargoed	a						13 31				13 48					13 58				14 16		
	d															13 59						
Brithdir	d															14 03						
Tir-phil	d															14 06						
Pontlottyn	d															14 10						
Rhymney	a															14 16						
Cathays	d	12 43		12 48						13 03			13 13		13 18				13 33			13 43
Llandaf	d	12 47		12 52						13 07			13 17		13 22				13 37			13 47
Ninian Park	d		12 40											13 10								
Waun-gron Park	d		12 43											13 13								
Fairwater	d		12 45											13 15								
Danescourt	d		12 47											13 17								
Radyr	a	12 50	12 54	12 55						13 10			13 20	13 24	13 25				13 40			13 50
	d	12 50		12 55						13 10			13 20		13 25				13 40			13 50
Taffs Well	d	12 54		12 59						13 14			13 24		13 29				13 44			13 54
Trefforest Estate	d									13 18									13 48			
Trefforest	d	13 01		13 06						13 22			13 31		13 36				13 52			14 01
Pontypridd	a	13 04		13 09						13 25			13 34		13 39				13 55			14 04
	d	13 06		13 11						13 27			13 36		13 41				13 57			14 06
Abercynon	d			13 19						13 34					13 49				14 04			
Penrhiwceiber	d			13 24											13 54							
Mountain Ash	a			13 28											13 58							
	d			13 33											14 03							
Fernhill	d			13 35											14 05							
Cwmbach	d			13 39											14 09							
Aberdare	a			13 46											14 16							
Quakers Yard	d									13 39									14 09			
Merthyr Vale	a									13 44									14 14			
	d									13 47									14 17			
Troed Y Rhiw	d									13 50									14 20			
Pentre-bach	d									13 53									14 23			
Merthyr Tydfil	a									14 01									14 31			
Trehafod	d	13 11											13 41									14 11
Porth	a	13 14											13 44									14 14
	d	13 15											13 45									14 15
Dinas Rhondda	d	13 19											13 49									14 19
Tonypandy	d	13 21											13 51									14 21
Llwynypia	d	13 23											13 53									14 23
Ystrad Rhondda	a	13 26											13 56									14 26
	d	13 29											13 59									14 29
Ton Pentre	d	13 31											14 01									14 31
Treorchy	d	13 34											14 04									14 34
Ynyswen	d	13 37											14 07									14 37
Treherbert	a	13 43											14 13									14 43

When events are being held at the Millenium Stadium, services are subject to alteration. Please check times before travelling.

Table 130

Mondays to Fridays
until 7 September

Bridgend, Barry Island, Barry, Penarth and Cardiff - Coryton, Rhymney, Pontypridd, Merthyr, Aberdare and Treherbert

Network Diagram - see first Page of Table 130

		AW	AW	AW	AW	AW	AW	AW	AW	AW	AW	AW	AW	AW	AW	AW	AW	AW	AW	AW	AW	AW	AW
Bridgend	d		12 42																			13 42	
Llantwit Major	d		12 56																			13 56	
Rhoose Cardiff Int Airport ✈	d		13 06																			14 06	
Barry Island	d							13 25					13 40				13 55						
Barry	d		13 15					13 30					13 45				14 00					14 15	
Barry Docks	d		13 19					13 34					13 49				14 04					14 19	
Cadoxton	d		13 22					13 37					13 52				14 07					14 22	
Dinas Powys	d		13 26					13 41					13 56				14 11					14 26	
Eastbrook	d		13 28					13 43					13 58				14 13					14 28	
Cogan	d		13 30					13 45					14 00				14 15					14 30	
Penarth	d				13 32				13 47					14 02				14 17					
Dingle Road	d				13 34				13 49					14 04				14 19					
Grangetown	d		13 34		13 38			13 49	13 53				14 04	14 08			14 19	14 23				14 34	
Cardiff Central	a		13 39		13 44			13 54	13 59				14 09	14 14			14 24	14 29				14 39	
	d	13 36	13 41		13 46	13 51		13 56	14 01		14 06	14 06	14 11	14 16		14 21	14 26	14 31		14 36	14 36	14 41	
Cardiff Bay	d			13 42			13 54			14 06					14 18				14 30				14 42
Cardiff Queen Street	a		13 44	13 46	13 49	13 54	13 58	13 59	14 04	14 10	14 09		14 14	14 19	14 22	14 24	14 29	14 34	14 34	14 39		14 44	14 46
	d		13 45		13 50	13 55		14 00	14 05		14 10		14 15	14 20		14 25	14 30	14 35		14 40		14 45	
Heath Low Level	d					14 00										14 30							
Ty Glas	d					14 03										14 33							
Birchgrove	d					14 04										14 34							
Rhiwbina	d					14 06										14 36							
Whitchurch (Cardiff)	d					14 08										14 38							
Coryton	a					14 13										14 43							
Heath High Level	d				13 55				14 10					14 25				14 40					
Llanishen	d				13 58				14 13					14 28				14 43					
Lisvane & Thornhill	d				14 00				14 15					14 30				14 45					
Caerphilly	d				14 06				14 21					14 36				14 51					
Aber	d				14 08				14 23					14 38				14 53					
Llanbradach	d				14 12				14 27					14 42				14 57					
Ystrad Mynach	d				14 17				14 32					14 47				15 02					
Hengoed	d				14 20				14 35					14 50				15 05					
Pengam	d				14 23				14 38					14 53				15 08					
Gilfach Fargoed	d								14 41														
Bargoed	a				14 31				14 48					14 58				15 16					
	d													14 59									
Brithdir	d													15 03									
Tir-phil	d													15 06									
Pontlottyn	d													15 10									
Rhymney	a													15 16									
Cathays	d		13 48					14 03			14 13		14 18				14 33			14 43		14 48	
Llandaf	d		13 52					14 07			14 17		14 22				14 37			14 47		14 52	
Ninian Park	d	13 40										14 10									14 40		
Waun-gron Park	d	13 43										14 13									14 43		
Fairwater	d	13 45										14 15									14 45		
Danescourt	d	13 47										14 17									14 47		
Radyr	a	13 54	13 55					14 10			14 20	14 24	14 25				14 40			14 50	14 54	14 55	
	d		13 55					14 10			14 20		14 25				14 40			14 50		14 55	
Taffs Well	d		13 59					14 14			14 24		14 29				14 44			14 54		14 59	
Trefforest Estate	d							14 18									14 48						
Trefforest	d		14 06					14 22			14 31		14 36				14 52			15 01		15 06	
Pontypridd	a		14 09					14 25			14 34		14 39				14 55			15 04		15 09	
	d		14 11					14 27			14 36		14 41				14 57			15 06		15 11	
Abercynon	d		14 19					14 34					14 49				15 04					15 19	
Penrhiwceiber	d		14 24										14 54									15 24	
Mountain Ash	a		14 28										14 58									15 28	
	d		14 33										15 03									15 33	
Fernhill	d		14 35										15 05									15 35	
Cwmbach	d		14 39										15 09									15 39	
Aberdare	a		14 46										15 16									15 46	
Quakers Yard	d							14 39									15 09						
Merthyr Vale	a							14 44									15 14						
	d							14 47									15 17						
Troed Y Rhiw	d							14 50									15 20						
Pentre-bach	d							14 53									15 23						
Merthyr Tydfil	a							15 01									15 31						
Trehafod	d										14 41									15 11			
Porth	a										14 44									15 14			
	d										14 45									15 15			
Dinas Rhondda	d										14 49									15 19			
Tonypandy	d										14 51									15 21			
Llwynypia	d										14 53									15 23			
Ystrad Rhondda	a										14 56									15 26			
	d										14 59									15 29			
Ton Pentre	d										15 01									15 31			
Treorchy	d										15 04									15 34			
Ynyswen	d										15 07									15 37			
Treherbert	a										15 13									15 43			

When events are being held at the Millenium Stadium, services are subject to alteration. Please check times before travelling.

Table 130

Mondays to Fridays
until 7 September

Bridgend, Barry Island, Barry, Penarth and Cardiff - Coryton, Rhymney, Pontypridd, Merthyr, Aberdare and Treherbert

Network Diagram - see first Page of Table 130

		AW	AW		AW	AW	AW	AW	AW	AW	AW	AW	AW		AW	AW	AW	AW	AW	AW	AW	AW	AW		AW
Bridgend	d																				14 42			
Llantwit Major	d																				14 56			
Rhoose Cardiff Int Airport ✈	d																				15 06			
Barry Island	d						14 25					14 40					14 55								
Barry [3]	d						14 30					14 45					15 00					15 15			
Barry Docks	d						14 34					14 49					15 04					15 19			
Cadoxton	d						14 37					14 52					15 07					15 22			
Dinas Powys	d						14 41					14 56					15 11					15 26			
Eastbrook	d						14 43					14 58					15 13					15 28			
Cogan	d						14 45					15 00					15 15					15 30			
Penarth	d	14 32							14 47				15 02					15 17							15 32
Dingle Road	d	14 34							14 49				15 04					15 19							15 34
Grangetown	d	14 38					14 49		14 53			15 04	15 08				15 19	15 23				15 34			15 38
Cardiff Central [7]	a	14 44					14 54		14 59			15 09	15 14				15 24	15 29				15 39			15 44
	d	14 46	14 51			14 51	14 56		15 01	15 06		15 11	15 16			15 21	15 26	15 31		15 36	15 36	15 41			15 46
Cardiff Bay	d				14 54						15 06				15 18				15 30				15 42		
Cardiff Queen Street [3]	a	14 49	14 54		14 58		14 59		15 04		15 10	15 14	15 19		15 22	15 24	15 29	15 34	15 34	15 39		15 44	15 46		15 49
	d	14 50	14 55				15 00		15 05			15 15	15 20			15 25	15 30	15 35		15 40		15 45			15 50
Heath Low Level	d		15 00													15 30									
Ty Glas	d		15 03													15 33									
Birchgrove	d		15 04													15 34									
Rhiwbina	d		15 06													15 36									
Whitchurch (Cardiff)	d		15 08													15 38									
Coryton	a		15 13													15 43									
Heath High Level	d	14 55							15 10				15 25					15 40							15 55
Llanishen	d	14 58							15 13				15 28					15 43							15 58
Lisvane & Thornhill	d	15 00							15 15				15 30					15 45							16 00
Caerphilly [3]	d	15 06							15 21				15 36					15 51							16 06
Aber	d	15 08							15 23				15 38					15 53							16 08
Llanbradach	d	15 12							15 27				15 42					15 57							16 12
Ystrad Mynach [3]	d	15 17							15 32				15 47					16 02							16 17
Hengoed	d	15 20							15 35				15 50					16 05							16 20
Pengam	d	15 23							15 38				15 53					16 08							16 23
Gilfach Fargoed	d								15 41																
Bargoed	a	15 31							15 48				15 58					16 16							16 31
	d												15 59												
Brithdir	d												16 03												
Tir-phil	d												16 06												
Pontlottyn	d												16 10												
Rhymney [3]	a												16 16												
Cathays	d						15 03					15 18					15 33			15 43		15 48			
Llandaf	d						15 07					15 22					15 37			15 47		15 52			
Ninian Park	d									15 10											15 40				
Waun-gron Park	d									15 13											15 43				
Fairwater	d									15 15											15 45				
Danescourt	d							←		15 17											15 47				
Radyr [3]	a					15 08	15 10	15 08		15 24		15 25					15 40			15 50	15 54	15 55			
	d					15 20	15 10	15 20				15 25					15 40			15 50		15 55			
Taffs Well [3]	d					→	15 14	15 24				15 29					15 44			15 54		15 59			
Trefforest Estate	d						15 18										15 48								
Trefforest	d						15 22	15 31				15 36					15 52			16 01		16 06			
Pontypridd [3]	a						15 25	15 34				15 39					15 55			16 04		16 09			
	d						15 27	15 36				15 41					15 57			16 06		16 11			
Abercynon	d						15 34					15 49					16 04					16 19			
Penrhiwceiber	d											15 54										16 24			
Mountain Ash	a											15 58										16 28			
	d											16 03										16 33			
Fernhill	d											16 05										16 35			
Cwmbach	d											16 09										16 39			
Aberdare [3]	a											16 16										16 46			
Quakers Yard	d						15 39										16 09								
Merthyr Vale	a						15 44										16 14								
	d						15 47										16 17								
Troed Y Rhiw	d						15 50										16 20								
Pentre-bach	d						15 53										16 23								
Merthyr Tydfil	a						16 01										16 31								
Trehafod	d							15 41												16 11					
Porth	a							15 44												16 14					
	d							15 45												16 15					
Dinas Rhondda	d							15 49												16 19					
Tonypandy	d							15 51												16 21					
Llwynypia	d							15 53												16 23					
Ystrad Rhondda	a							15 56												16 26					
	d							15 59												16 29					
Ton Pentre	d							16 01												16 31					
Treorchy	d							16 04												16 34					
Ynyswen	d							16 07												16 37					
Treherbert	a							16 13												16 43					

When events are being held at the Millenium Stadium, services are subject to alteration. Please check times before travelling.

Table 130

Mondays to Fridays
until 7 September

Bridgend, Barry Island, Barry, Penarth and Cardiff - Coryton, Rhymney, Pontypridd, Merthyr, Aberdare and Treherbert

Network Diagram - see first Page of Table 130

		AW	AW	AW	AW	AW	AW	AW	AW		AW	AW	AW	AW	AW	AW	AW	AW	AW		AW	AW	AW	AW	AW
Bridgend	d																		15 42						
Llantwit Major	d																		15 56						
Rhoose Cardiff Int Airport ✈	d																		16 06						
Barry Island	d			15 25					15 40					15 55											16 25
Barry [3]	d			15 30					15 45					16 00					16 15						16 30
Barry Docks	d			15 34					15 49					16 04					16 19						16 34
Cadoxton	d			15 37					15 52					16 07					16 22						16 37
Dinas Powys	d			15 41					15 56					16 11					16 26						16 41
Eastbrook	d			15 43					15 58					16 13					16 28						16 43
Cogan	d			15 45					16 00					16 15					16 30						16 45
Penarth	d				15 47						16 02				16 17							16 32			
Dingle Road	d				15 49						16 04				16 19							16 34			
Grangetown	d			15 49	15 53				16 04		16 08			16 19	16 23				16 34			16 38			16 49
Cardiff Central [7]	a			15 54	15 59				16 09		16 14			16 24	16 29				16 39			16 44			16 54
	d	15 51		15 56	16 01		16 06	16 06	16 11		16 16		16 21	16 26	16 31		16 36	16 36	16 41			16 46	16 51		16 56
Cardiff Bay	d		15 54			16 06						16 18				16 30					16 42			16 54	
Cardiff Queen Street [3]	a	15 54	15 58	15 59	16 04	16 10	16 09		16 14		16 19	16 22	16 24	16 29	16 34	16 34	16 39		16 44		16 46	16 49	16 54	16 58	16 59
	d	15 55		16 00	16 05		16 10		16 15		16 20		16 25	16 30	16 35		16 40		16 45			16 50	16 55		17 00
Heath Low Level	d	16 00											16 30										17 00		
Ty Glas	d	16 03											16 33										17 03		
Birchgrove	d	16 04											16 34										17 04		
Rhiwbina	d	16 06											16 36										17 06		
Whitchurch (Cardiff)	d	16 08											16 38										17 08		
Coryton	a	16 13											16 43										17 13		
Heath High Level	d				16 10						16 25				16 40							16 55			
Llanishen	d				16 13						16 28				16 43							16 58			
Lisvane & Thornhill	d				16 15						16 30				16 45							17 00			
Caerphilly [3]	d				16 21						16 36				16 51							17 06			
Aber	d				16 23						16 38				16 53							17 08			
Llanbradach	d				16 27						16 42				16 57							17 12			
Ystrad Mynach [3]	d				16 32						16 47				17 02							17 17			
Hengoed	d				16 35						16 50				17 05							17 20			
Pengam	d				16 38						16 53				17 08							17 23			
Gilfach Fargoed	d				16 41																				
Bargoed	a				16 48						16 58				17 16							17 31			
	d										16 59														
Brithdir	d										17 03														
Tir-phil	d										17 06														
Pontlottyn	d										17 10														
Rhymney [3]	a										17 16														
Cathays	d			16 03			16 13		16 18					16 33			16 43		16 48						17 03
Llandaf	d			16 07			16 17		16 22					16 37			16 47		16 52						17 07
Ninian Park	d							16 10										16 40							
Waun-gron Park	d							16 13										16 43							
Fairwater	d							16 15										16 45							
Danescourt	d							16 17										16 47							
Radyr [3]	a			16 10			16 20	16 24	16 25					16 40			16 50	16 54	16 55						17 10
	d			16 10			16 20		16 25					16 40			16 50		16 55						17 10
Taffs Well [3]	d			16 14			16 24		16 29					16 44			16 54		16 59						17 14
Trefforest Estate	d			16 18										16 48											17 18
Trefforest	d			16 22			16 31		16 36					16 52			17 01		17 06						17 22
Pontypridd [3]	a			16 25			16 34		16 39					16 55			17 04		17 09						17 25
	d			16 27			16 36		16 41					16 57			17 06		17 11						17 27
Abercynon	d			16 34					16 49					17 04					17 19						17 34
Penrhiwceiber	d								16 54										17 24						
Mountain Ash	a								16 58										17 28						
	d								17 03										17 33						
Fernhill	d								17 05										17 35						
Cwmbach	d								17 09										17 39						
Aberdare [3]	a								17 16										17 46						
Quakers Yard	d			16 39										17 09											17 39
Merthyr Vale	a			16 44										17 14											17 44
	d			16 47										17 17											17 47
Troed Y Rhiw	d			16 50										17 20											17 50
Pentre-bach	d			16 53										17 23											17 53
Merthyr Tydfil	a			17 01										17 31											18 01
Trehafod	d						16 41										17 11								
Porth	a						16 44										17 14								
	d						16 45										17 15								
Dinas Rhondda	d						16 49										17 19								
Tonypandy	d						16 51										17 21								
Llwynypia	d						16 53										17 23								
Ystrad Rhondda	a						16 56										17 26								
	d						16 59										17 29								
Ton Pentre	d						17 01										17 31								
Treorchy	d						17 04										17 34								
Ynyswen	d						17 07										17 37								
Treherbert	a						17 13										17 43								

When events are being held at the Millenium Stadium, services are subject to alteration. Please check times before travelling.

Table 130

Mondays to Fridays
until 7 September

Bridgend, Barry Island, Barry, Penarth and Cardiff - Coryton, Rhymney, Pontypridd, Merthyr, Aberdare and Treherbert

Network Diagram - see first Page of Table 130

		AW	AW	AW	AW		AW	AW	AW	AW	AW	AW	AW	AW	AW		AW	AW	AW	AW	AW	AW	AW	AW	AW
Bridgend	d																16 42								
Llantwit Major	d																16 56								
Rhoose Cardiff Int Airport ✈	d																17 06								
Barry Island	d						16 40				16 55											17 25			
Barry [3]	d						16 45				17 00						17 15					17 30			
Barry Docks	d						16 49				17 04						17 19					17 34			
Cadoxton	d						16 52				17 07						17 22					17 37			
Dinas Powys	d						16 56				17 11						17 26					17 41			
Eastbrook	d						16 58				17 13						17 28					17 43			
Cogan	d						17 00				17 15						17 30					17 45			
Penarth	d							17 02				17 17							17 32				17 47		
Dingle Road	d							17 04				17 19							17 34				17 49		
Grangetown	d						17 04	17 08			17 19	17 23					17 34		17 38			17 49	17 53		
Cardiff Central [7]	a						17 09	17 14			17 24	17 29					17 39		17 44			17 54	17 59		
	d	17 01		17 06	17 06		17 11	17 16		17 21	17 26	17 31		17 36	17 36		17 41		17 46	17 51		17 56	18 01		18 06
Cardiff Bay	d		17 06						17 18				17 30					17 42			17 54			18 06	
Cardiff Queen Street [3]	a	17 04	17 10	17 09			17 14	17 19	17 22	17 24	17 29	17 34	17 34	17 39			17 44	17 46	17 49	17 54	17 58	17 59	18 04	18 10	18 09
	d	17 05		17 10			17 15	17 20		17 25	17 30	17 35		17 40			17 45		17 50	17 55		18 00	18 05		18 10
Heath Low Level	d									17 30										18 00					
Ty Glas	d									17 33										18 03					
Birchgrove	d									17 34										18 04					
Rhiwbina	d									17 36										18 06					
Whitchurch (Cardiff)	d									17 38										18 08					
Coryton	a									17 43										18 13					
Heath High Level	d	17 10						17 25				17 40							17 55				18 10		
Llanishen	d	17 13						17 28				17 43							17 59				18 13		
Lisvane & Thornhill	d	17 15						17 30				17 45							18 02				18 15		
Caerphilly [3]	d	17 21						17 36				17 51							18 07				18 21		
Aber	d	17 23						17 38				17 53							18 10				18 23		
Llanbradach	d	17 27						17 42				17 57							18 14				18 27		
Ystrad Mynach [3]	d	17 33						17 47				18 02							18 20				18 32		
Hengoed	d	17 35						17 50				18 05							18 23				18 35		
Pengam	d	17 39						17 53				18 08							18 27				18 38		
Gilfach Fargoed	d	17 42										18 11							18 30				18 41		
Bargoed	a	17 45						18 01				18 14							18 34				18 48		
	d	17 47										18 16							18 44						
Brithdir	d	17 50										18 20							18 48						
Tir-phil	d	17 53										18 23							18 51						
Pontlottyn	d	17 58										18 27							18 55						
Rhymney [3]	a	18 04										18 33							19 01						
Cathays	d			17 13			17 18				17 33			17 43			17 48					18 03			18 13
Llandaf	d			17 17			17 22				17 37			17 47			17 52					18 07			18 17
Ninian Park	d				17 10										17 40										
Waun-gron Park	d				17 13										17 43										
Fairwater	d				17 15										17 45										
Danescourt	d				17 17										17 47										
Radyr [3]	a			17 20	17 24		17 25				17 40			17 50	17 54		17 55					18 10			18 20
	d			17 20			17 25				17 40			17 50			17 55					18 10			18 20
Taffs Well [3]	d			17 24			17 29				17 44			17 54			17 59					18 14			18 24
Trefforest Estate	d										17 48											18 18			
Trefforest	d			17 31			17 36				17 52			18 01			18 06					18 22			18 31
Pontypridd [3]	a			17 34			17 39				17 55			18 04			18 09					18 25			18 34
	d			17 36			17 41				17 57			18 06			18 11					18 27			18 36
Abercynon	d						17 49				18 04						18 19					18 34			
Penrhiwceiber	d						17 54										18 24								
Mountain Ash	a						17 58										18 28								
	d						18 03										18 33								
Fernhill	d						18 05										18 35								
Cwmbach	d						18 09										18 39								
Aberdare [3]	a						18 16										18 46								
Quakers Yard	d										18 09											18 39			
Merthyr Vale	a										18 14											18 44			
	d										18 17											18 47			
Troed Y Rhiw	d										18 20											18 50			
Pentre-bach	d										18 23											18 53			
Merthyr Tydfil	a										18 31											19 01			
Trehafod	d			17 41										18 11											18 41
Porth	a			17 44										18 14											18 44
	d			17 45										18 15											18 45
Dinas Rhondda	d			17 49										18 19											18 49
Tonypandy	d			17 51										18 21											18 51
Llwynypia	d			17 53										18 23											18 53
Ystrad Rhondda	a			17 56										18 26											18 56
	d			17 59										18 29											18 59
Ton Pentre	d			18 01										18 31											19 01
Treorchy	d			18 04										18 34											19 04
Ynyswen	d			18 07										18 37											19 07
Treherbert	a			18 13										18 43											19 13

When events are being held at the Millenium Stadium, services are subject to alteration. Please check times before travelling.

Table 130

Mondays to Fridays
until 7 September

Bridgend, Barry Island, Barry, Penarth and Cardiff - Coryton, Rhymney, Pontypridd, Merthyr, Aberdare and Treherbert

Network Diagram - see first Page of Table 130

			AW	AW	AW	AW	AW	AW	AW	AW			AW	AW	AW	AW	AW	AW	AW	AW	AW		AW	AW	AW
Bridgend	d													17 42											
Llantwit Major	d													17 56											
Rhoose Cardiff Int Airport ✈	d													18 06											
Barry Island	d			17 40				17 55										18 25						18 40	
Barry [3]	d			17 45				18 00						18 15				18 30						18 45	
Barry Docks	d			17 49				18 04						18 19				18 34						18 49	
Cadoxton	d			17 52				18 07						18 22				18 37						18 52	
Dinas Powys	d			17 56				18 11						18 26				18 41						18 56	
Eastbrook	d			17 58				18 13						18 28				18 43						18 58	
Cogan	d			18 00				18 15						18 30				18 45						19 00	
Penarth	d				18 02					18 17					18 32					18 47					
Dingle Road	d				18 04					18 19					18 34					18 49					
Grangetown	d			18 04	18 08			18 19		18 23				18 34	18 38			18 49		18 53				19 04	
Cardiff Central [7]	a			18 09	18 14			18 24		18 29				18 39	18 47			18 55		18 59				19 09	
	d		18 06	18 11	18 16		18 21	18 26		18 31	18 36		18 36	18 41			18 51			19 01			19 06	19 11	
Cardiff Bay	d					18 18			18 30							18 42			18 54		19 06				19 18
Cardiff Queen Street [3]	a			18 14	18 19	18 22	18 24	18 29	18 34	18 34	18 38			18 44		18 46	18 54		18 58	19 04	19 10		19 09	19 14	19 22
	d			18 15	18 20		18 25	18 30		18 35	18 40			18 50			18 55			19 05			19 10	19 15	
Heath Low Level	d						18 30										19 00								
Ty Glas	d						18 33										19 03								
Birchgrove	d						18 34										19 04								
Rhiwbina	d						18 36										19 06								
Whitchurch (Cardiff)	d						18 38										19 08								
Coryton	a						18 43										19 13								
Heath High Level	d				18 25					18 40										19 10					
Llanishen	d				18 28					18 43										19 13					
Lisvane & Thornhill	d				18 30					18 45										19 15					
Caerphilly [3]	d				18 36					18 51										19a23					
Aber	d				18 38					18 53															
Llanbradach	d				18 42					18 57															
Ystrad Mynach [3]	d				18a51					19 02															
Hengoed	d									19 05															
Pengam	d									19 08															
Gilfach Fargoed	d									19 11															
Bargoed	a									19 14															
	d									19 16															
Brithdir	d									19 20															
Tir-phil	d									19 23															
Pontlottyn	d									19 27															
Rhymney [3]	a									19 34															
Cathays	d			18 18				18 33			18 43			18 52									19 13	19 18	
Llandaf	d			18 22				18 37			18 47			18 56									19 17	19 22	
Ninian Park	d		18 10										18 40												
Waun-gron Park	d		18 13										18 43												
Fairwater	d		18 15										18 45												
Danescourt	d		18 17										18 47												
Radyr [3]	a		18 24	18 25				18 40			18 50		18 54	18 58									19 20	19 25	
	d			18 25				18 40			18 50			18 58									19 20	19 25	
Taffs Well [3]	d			18 29				18 44			18 54			19 03									19 24	19 29	
Trefforest Estate	d							18 48																	
Trefforest	d			18 36				18 52			19 01			19 10									19 31	19 36	
Pontypridd [3]	a			18 42				18 55			19 04			19 13									19 34	19 39	
	d							18 57			19 06			19 14									19 36	19 41	
Abercynon	d							19 04						19 21										19 49	
Penrhiwceiber	d													19 26										19 54	
Mountain Ash	a													19 30										19 56	
	d													19 33										20 03	
Fernhill	d													19 35										20 05	
Cwmbach	d													19 39										20 09	
Aberdare [3]	a													19 46										20 16	
Quakers Yard	d							19 09																	
Merthyr Vale	a							19 14																	
	d							19 17																	
Troed Y Rhiw	d							19 20																	
Pentre-bach	d							19 23																	
Merthyr Tydfil	a							19 31																	
Trehafod	d										19 11												19 41		
Porth	a										19 14												19 44		
	d										19 15												19 45		
Dinas Rhondda	d										19 19												19 49		
Tonypandy	d										19 21												19 51		
Llwynypia	d										19 23												19 53		
Ystrad Rhondda	a										19 26												19 56		
	d										19 29												19 59		
Ton Pentre	d										19 31												20 01		
Treorchy	d										19 34												20 04		
Ynyswen	d										19 37												20 07		
Treherbert	a										19 43												20 13		

When events are being held at the Millenium Stadium, services are subject to alteration. Please check times before travelling.

Table 130

Mondays to Fridays
until 7 September

Bridgend, Barry Island, Barry, Penarth and Cardiff - Coryton, Rhymney, Pontypridd, Merthyr, Aberdare and Treherbert

Network Diagram - see first Page of Table 130

		AW	AW	AW	AW	AW	AW	AW	AW	AW	AW	AW	AW	AW	AW	AW	AW	AW	AW	AW	AW	AW	AW
Bridgend	d					18 42												19 42					
Llantwit Major	d					18 56												19 56					
Rhoose Cardiff Int Airport ✈	d					19 06												20 06					
Barry Island	d	18 55								19 25				19 55									
Barry [3]	d	19 00				19 15				19 30				20 00				20 15					
Barry Docks	d	19 04				19 19				19 34				20 04				20 19					
Cadoxton	d	19 07				19 22				19 37				20 07				20 22					
Dinas Powys	d	19 11				19 26				19 41				20 11				20 26					
Eastbrook	d	19 13				19 28				19 43				20 13				20 28					
Cogan	d	19 15				19 30				19 45				20 15				20 30					
Penarth	d		19 17								19 47				20 20							20 47	
Dingle Road	d		19 19								19 49				20 22							20 49	
Grangetown	d	19 19	19 23			19 34				19 49	19 53			20 19	20 26			20 34				20 53	
Cardiff Central [7]	a	19 24	19 29			19 39				19 56	19 59			20 24	20 31			20 39				20 59	
	d	19 26	19 31		19 36	19 41		19 51		20 01	20 06			20 26	20 31		20 36	20 41		20 51		21 01	
Cardiff Bay	d			19 30			19 42		19 54			20 06	20 18			20 30			20 42		20 54		21 06
Cardiff Queen Street [3]	a	19 29	19 34	19 34		19 44	19 46	19 54	19 58	20 04	20 09	20 10	20 22	20 29	20 34	20 34		20 44	20 46	20 54	20 58	21 04	21 10
	d	19 30	19 35			19 45		19 55		20 05	20 10			20 30	20 35			20 45		20 55		21 05	
Heath Low Level	d							20 00												21 00			
Ty Glas	d							20 03												21 03			
Birchgrove	d							20 04												21 04			
Rhiwbina	d							20 06												21 06			
Whitchurch (Cardiff)	d							20 08												21 08			
Coryton	a							20 13												21 13			
Heath High Level	d		19 40							20 10					20 40							21 10	
Llanishen	d		19 43							20 13					20 43							21 13	
Lisvane & Thornhill	d		19 45							20 15					20 45							21 15	
Caerphilly [3]	d		19 51							20a27					20 51							21 21	
Aber	d		19 53												20 53							21 23	
Llanbradach	d		19 57												20 57							21 27	
Ystrad Mynach [3]	d		20 02												21 02							21a36	
Hengoed	d		20 05												21 05								
Pengam	d		20 08												21 08								
Gilfach Fargoed	d		20 11												21 11								
Bargoed	a		20 15												21 15								
	d		20 16												21 16								
Brithdir	d		20 20												21 20								
Tir-phil	d		20 23												21 23								
Pontlottyn	d		20 27												21 27								
Rhymney [3]	a		20 33												21 34								
Cathays	d	19 33				19 48					20 13			20 33				20 48					
Llandaf	d	19 37				19 52					20 17			20 37				20 52					
Ninian Park	d				19 40												20 40						
Waun-gron Park	d				19 43												20 43						
Fairwater	d				19 45												20 45						
Danescourt	d				19 47												20 47						
Radyr [3]	a	19 40			19 54	19 55					20 20			20 40			20 54	20 55					
	d	19 40				19 55					20 20			20 40				20 55					
Taffs Well [3]	d	19 44				19 59					20 24			20 44				20 59					
Trefforest Estate	d	19 48												20 48									
Trefforest	d	19 52				20 06					20 31			20 52				21 06					
Pontypridd [3]	a	19 55				20 09					20 34			20 55				21 09					
	d	19 57				20 11					20 36			20 57				21 11					
Abercynon	d	20 04				20 21								21 04				21 19					
Penrhiwceiber	d					20 26												21 24					
Mountain Ash	a					20 30												21 28					
	d					20 33												21 29					
Fernhill	d					20 35												21 31					
Cwmbach	d					20 39												21 35					
Aberdare [3]	a					20 46												21 42					
Quakers Yard	d	20 08												21 08									
Merthyr Vale	a	20 13												21 13									
	d	20 15												21 15									
Troed Y Rhiw	d	20 19												21 19									
Pentre-bach	d	20 22												21 22									
Merthyr Tydfil	a	20 30												21 30									
Trehafod	d										20 41												
Porth	a										20 44												
	d										20 45												
Dinas Rhondda	d										20 49												
Tonypandy	d										20 51												
Llwynypia	d										20 53												
Ystrad Rhondda	a										20 56												
	d										20 59												
Ton Pentre	d										21 01												
Treorchy	d										21 04												
Ynyswen	d										21 07												
Treherbert	a										21 13												

When events are being held at the Millenium Stadium, services are subject to alteration. Please check times before travelling.

Table 130

Mondays to Fridays
until 7 September

Bridgend, Barry Island, Barry, Penarth and Cardiff - Coryton, Rhymney, Pontypridd, Merthyr, Aberdare and Treherbert

Network Diagram - see first Page of Table 130

		AW	AW	AW	AW	AW	AW	AW	AW	AW	AW	AW	AW	AW	AW	AW	AW	AW	AW	AW	AW	AW
Bridgend	d								20 42											21 42		
Llantwit Major	d								20 56											21 56		
Rhoose Cardiff Int Airport ✈	d								21 06											22 06		
Barry Island	d			20 55													21 55					
Barry [3]	d			21 00					21 15								22 00			22 15		
Barry Docks	d			21 04					21 19								22 04			22 19		
Cadoxton	d			21 07					21 22								22 07			22 22		
Dinas Powys	d			21 11					21 26								22 11			22 26		
Eastbrook	d			21 13					21 28								22 13			22 28		
Cogan	d			21 15					21 30								22 15			22 30		
Penarth	d							21 20				21 47							22 20			
Dingle Road	d							21 22				21 49							22 22			
Grangetown	d			21 19				21 26	21 34			21 53					22 19		22 26	22 34		
Cardiff Central [7]	a			21 24				21 37	21 39			21 59					22 24		22 33	22 39		
	d	21 06		21 26		21 31	21 36		21 41			22 01		22 06		22 21	22 26		22 35	22 41		22 46
Cardiff Bay	d		21 18		21 30					21 42	21 54		22 06		22 18			22 30			22 42	
Cardiff Queen Street [3]	a	21 09	21 22	21 29	21 34	21 34			21 44	21 46	21 58	22 04	22 10	22 09	22 22	22 24	22 29	22 34	22 38	22 44	22 46	22 49
	d	21 10		21 30		21 35			21 45			22 05		22 10		22 25	22 30		22 39	22 45		22 50
Heath Low Level	d															22 30						
Ty Glas	d															22 33						
Birchgrove	d															22 34						
Rhiwbina	d															22 36						
Whitchurch (Cardiff)	d															22 38						
Coryton	a															22 43						
Heath High Level	d					21 40						22 10							22 44			
Llanishen	d					21 43						22 13							22 47			
Lisvane & Thornhill	d					21 45						22 15							22 49			
Caerphilly [3]	d					21 51						22a23							22 55			
Aber	d					21 53													22 57			
Llanbradach	d					21 57													23 01			
Ystrad Mynach [3]	d					22 02													23 06			
Hengoed	d					22 05													23 09			
Pengam	d					22 08													23 12			
Gilfach Fargoed	d					22 11													23 15			
Bargoed	a					22 15													23 19			
	d					22 16													23 20			
Brithdir	d					22 20													23 24			
Tir-phil	d					22 23													23 27			
Pontlottyn	d					22 27													23 31			
Rhymney [3]	a					22 34													23 37			
Cathays	d	21 13		21 33					21 48					22 13			22 33			22 48		22 53
Llandaf	d	21 17		21 37					21 52					22 17			22 37			22 52		22 57
Ninian Park	d						21 40															
Waun-gron Park	d						21 43															
Fairwater	d						21 45															
Danescourt	d						21 47															
Radyr [3]	a	21 20		21 40			21 54		21 55					22 20			22 40			22 55		22 59
	d	21 20		21 40					21 55					22 20			22 40			22 55		22 59
Taffs Well [3]	d	21 24		21 44					21 59					22 24			22 44			22 59		23 03
Trefforest Estate	d			21 48													22 48					
Trefforest	d	21 31		21 52					22 06					22 31			22 52			23 06		23 10
Pontypridd [3]	a	21 34		21 55					22 09					22 34			22 55			23 09		23 14
	d	21 36		21 57					22 11					22 36			22 57			23 11		23 15
Abercynon	d			22 04					22 19								23 04			23 19		
Penrhiwceiber	d								22 24											23 24		
Mountain Ash	a								22 28											23 28		
	d								22 29											23 29		
Fernhill	d								22 31											23 31		
Cwmbach	d								22 35											23 35		
Aberdare [3]	a								22 42											23 42		
Quakers Yard	d			22 08													23 08					
Merthyr Vale	a			22 13													23 13					
	d			22 15													23 15					
Troed Y Rhiw	d			22 19													23 19					
Pentre-bach	d			22 22													23 22					
Merthyr Tydfil	a			22 30													23 30					
Trehafod	d	21 41												22 41								23 20
Porth	a	21 44												22 44								23 23
	d	21 45												22 45								23 24
Dinas Rhondda	d	21 49												22 49								23 28
Tonypandy	d	21 51												22 51								23 30
Llwynypia	d	21 53												22 53								23 32
Ystrad Rhondda	a	21 56												22 56								23 35
	d	21 59												22 59								23 38
Ton Pentre	d	22 01												23 01								23 40
Treorchy	d	22 04												23 04								23 43
Ynyswen	d	22 07												23 07								23 46
Treherbert	a	22 13												23 13								23 52

When events are being held at the Millenium Stadium, services are subject to alteration. Please check times before travelling.

Bridgend, Barry Island, Barry, Penarth and Cardiff - Coryton, Rhymney, Pontypridd, Merthyr, Aberdare and Treherbert

Network Diagram - see first Page of Table 130

		AW	AW	AW	AW	AW	AW A	AW B	AW FX ⇌	AW	AW	AW A	AW FO	AW FX	AW	AW	AW A
Bridgend	d								22 15				22 42				
Llantwit Major	d								22 40				22 56				
Rhoose Cardiff Int Airport ✈	d								22 55				23 06				
Barry Island	d						22 45	22 44									
Barry 3	d						22 49	22 49	23a10				23 15	23 15			
Barry Docks	d						22 53	22 53					23 19	23 19			
Cadoxton	d						22 56	22 56					23 22	23 22			
Dinas Powys	d						23 00	23 00					23 26	23 26			
Eastbrook	d						23 03	23 02					23 28	23 28			
Cogan	d						23 05	23 04					23 30	23 30			
Penarth	d				22 47					23 26							
Dingle Road	d				22 49					23 28							
Grangetown	d				22 53		23 09	23 08		23 32			23 34	23 34			
Cardiff Central 7	a				23 00		23 14	23 13		23 40			23 42	23 42			
	d		22 55		23 15		23 26	23 26				23 40					23 56
Cardiff Bay	d	22 54		23 06		23 18					23 30				23 42	23 54	
Cardiff Queen Street 3	a	22 58		23 10	23 18	23 22	23 29	23 29			23 34				23 46	23 58	
	d				23 19		23 30	23 30									
Heath Low Level	d																
Ty Glas	d																
Birchgrove	d																
Rhiwbina	d																
Whitchurch (Cardiff)	d																
Coryton	a																
Heath High Level	d				23 24												
Llanishen	d				23 27												
Lisvane & Thornhill	d				23 29												
Caerphilly 3	d				23 35												
Aber	d				23 37												
Llanbradach	d				23 41												
Ystrad Mynach 3	d				23a50												
Hengoed	d																
Pengam	d																
Gilfach Fargoed	d																
Bargoed	a																
	d																
Brithdir	d																
Tir-phil	d																
Pontlottyn	d																
Rhymney 3	a																
Cathays	d						23 33	23 33				23 45					00 03
Llandaf	d						23 37	23 37				23 49					00 07
Ninian Park	d		22 59														
Waun-gron Park	d		23 02														
Fairwater	d		23 04														
Danescourt	d		23 06														
Radyr 3	a		23 14				23 40	23 40				23 53					00 10
	d						23 41	23 40				23 53					00 11
Taffs Well 3	d						23 45	23 44				23 57					00 15
Trefforest Estate	d						23 49										
Trefforest	d						23 53	23 52				00 03					00 21
Pontypridd 3	a						23 56	23 58				00 06					00 24
	d						23 57					00 08					00 26
Abercynon	d						00 07					00 17					
Penrhiwceiber	d											00 23					
Mountain Ash	a											00 26					
	d											00 28					
Fernhill	d											00 30					
Cwmbach	d											00 34					
Aberdare 3	a											00 41					
Quakers Yard	d						00 11										
Merthyr Vale	a						00 16										
	d						00 19										
Troed Y Rhiw	d						00 22										
Pentre-bach	d						00 25										
Merthyr Tydfil	a						00 30										
Trehafod	d																00 31
Porth	a																00 34
	d																00 35
Dinas Rhondda	d																00 39
Tonypandy	d																00 41
Llwynypia	d																00 43
Ystrad Rhondda	a																00 46
	d																00 47
Ton Pentre	d																00 49
Treorchy	d																00 52
Ynyswen	d																00 55
Treherbert	a																01 02

A 25 July, 26 July, 1 August, 10 August

B not 25 July, 26 July, 1 August, 10 August

When events are being held at the Millenium Stadium, services are subject to alteration. Please check times before travelling.

Bridgend, Barry Island, Barry, Penarth and Cardiff - Coryton, Rhymney, Pontypridd, Merthyr, Aberdare and Treherbert

Network Diagram - see first Page of Table 130

		AW	AW	AW	AW	AW	AW	AW	AW	AW	AW	AW	AW	AW	AW	AW	AW	AW	AW	AW	AW	AW
Bridgend	d									05 37												
Llantwit Major	d									05 46												
Rhoose Cardiff Int Airport ✈	d									05 56												
Barry Island	d		05 15				05 50								06 25							
Barry 3	d		05 20				05 55			06 15					06 30							
Barry Docks	d		05 24				05 59			06 19					06 34							
Cadoxton	d		05 27				06 02			06 22					06 37							
Dinas Powys	d		05 31				06 06			06 26					06 41							
Eastbrook	d		05 33				06 08			06 28					06 43							
Cogan	d		05 35				06 10			06 30					06 45							
Penarth	d					06 02						06 32								07 02		
Dingle Road	d					06 04						06 34								07 04		
Grangetown	d		05 39			06 08	06 14			06 34		06 38			06 49					07 08		
Cardiff Central 7	a		05 44			06 13	06 19			06 39		06 44			06 54					07 14		
	d	05 26	05 46	05 56	06 11	06 15	06 21	06 26	06 36	06 41		06 46	06 51		06 56		07 06	07 06	07 11	07 16		07 21
Cardiff Bay	d										06 42			06 54		07 06					07 18	
Cardiff Queen Street 3	a	05 29	05 49	05 59	06 14	06 19	06 24	06 29	06 39	06 44	06 46	06 49	06 54	06 58	06 59	07 10	07 09		07 14	07 19	07 22	07 24
	d	05 30	05 50	06 00	06 15	06 20	06 25	06 30	06 40	06 45		06 50	06 55		07 00		07 10		07 15	07 20		07 25
Heath Low Level	d						06 30						07 00									07 30
Ty Glas	d						06 33						07 03									07 33
Birchgrove	d						06 34						07 04									07 34
Rhiwbina	d						06 36						07 06									07 36
Whitchurch (Cardiff)	d						06 38						07 08									07 38
Coryton	a						06 44						07 14									07 44
Heath High Level	d		05 55			06 25						06 55								07 25		
Llanishen	d		05 58			06 28						06 58								07 28		
Lisvane & Thornhill	d		06 00			06 30						07 00								07 30		
Caerphilly 3	d		06a09			06 36						07 06								07 36		
Aber	d					06 38						07 08								07 38		
Llanbradach	d					06 42						07 12								07 42		
Ystrad Mynach 3	d					06 47						07 17								07 47		
Hengoed	d					06 50						07 20								07 50		
Pengam	d					06 53						07 23								07 53		
Gilfach Fargoed	d																					
Bargoed	a					07 02						07 32								08 03		
	d																					
Brithdir	d																					
Tir-phil	d																					
Pontlottyn	d																					
Rhymney 3	a																					
Cathays	d	05 33		06 03	06 18			06 33	06 43	06 48					07 03		07 13		07 18			
Llandaf	d	05 37		06 07	06 22			06 37	06 47	06 52					07 07		07 17		07 22			
Ninian Park	d																	07 10				
Waun-gron Park	d																	07 14				
Fairwater	d																	07 16				
Danescourt	d																	07 19				
Radyr 3	a	05 39		06 10	06 24			06 40	06 50	06 54					07 10		07 20	07 27	07 25			
	d	05 40		06 10	06 24			06 40	06 50	06 55					07 10		07 20		07 25			
Taffs Well 3	d	05 43		06 14	06 28			06 44	06 54	06 59					07 14		07 24		07 29			
Trefforest Estate	d	05 47		06 18				06 48							07 18							
Trefforest	d	05 52		06 22	06 35			06 52	07 01	07 06					07 22		07 31		07 36			
Pontypridd 3	a	05 55		06 25	06 38			06 55	07 04	07 09					07 25		07 34		07 39			
	d	05 57 / 06 11		06 27	06 41			06 57	07 06	07 11					07 27		07 36		07 41			
Abercynon	d	06 04 / 06 19		06 34	06 49			07 04		07 19					07 34				07 49			
Penrhiwceiber	d	06 25			06 55					07 25									07 55			
Mountain Ash	a	06 28			06 58					07 28									07 58			
	d	06 34			07 04					07 34									08 04			
Fernhill	d	06 37			07 07					07 37									08 07			
Cwmbach	d	06 41			07 11					07 41									08 11			
Aberdare 3	a	06 49			07 19					07 49									08 19			
Quakers Yard	d	06 09		06 39				07 09							07 39							
Merthyr Vale	a	06 14		06 44				07 14							07 44							
	d	06 17		06 47				07 17							07 47							
Troed Y Rhiw	d	06 21		06 51				07 21							07 51							
Pentre-bach	d	06 24		06 54				07 24							07 54							
Merthyr Tydfil	a	06 33		07 03				07 33							08 03							
Trehafod	d								07 11								07 41					
Porth	a								07 14								07 44					
	d								07 15								07 45					
Dinas Rhondda	d								07 19								07 49					
Tonypandy	d								07 21								07 51					
Llwynypia	d								07 23								07 53					
Ystrad Rhondda	a								07 26								07 56					
	d								07 29								07 59					
Ton Pentre	d								07 31								08 01					
Treorchy	d								07 34								08 04					
Ynyswen	d								07 37								08 07					
Treherbert	a								07 44								08 14					

When events are being held at the Millenium Stadium, services are subject to alteration. Please check times before travelling.

Table 130

Mondays to Fridays

from 17 September

Bridgend, Barry Island, Barry, Penarth and Cardiff - Coryton, Rhymney, Pontypridd, Merthyr, Aberdare and Treherbert

Network Diagram - see first Page of Table 130

		AW	AW	AW	AW	AW		AW	AW	AW	AW	AW	AW	AW	AW	AW		AW	AW	AW	AW	AW	AW	AW	AW
Bridgend	d							06 42																	
Llantwit Major	d							06 56																	
Rhoose Cardiff Int Airport ✈	d							07 06																	
Barry Island	d	06 55											07 25						07 40				07 55		
Barry	d	07 00						07 15					07 30						07 45				08 00		
Barry Docks	d	07 04						07 19					07 34						07 49				08 04		
Cadoxton	d	07 07						07 22					07 37						07 52				08 07		
Dinas Powys	d	07 11						07 26					07 41						07 56				08 11		
Eastbrook	d	07 13						07 28					07 43						07 58				08 13		
Cogan	d	07 15						07 30					07 45						08 00				08 15		
Penarth	d		07 17							07 32				07 47						08 02				08 17	
Dingle Road	d		07 19							07 34				07 49						08 04				08 19	
Grangetown	d	07 19	07 23					07 34		07 38			07 49	07 53					08 04	08 08			08 19	08 23	
Cardiff Central	a	07 24	07 29					07 39		07 44			07 54	07 59					08 09	08 14			08 24	08 29	
	d	07 26	07 31		07 36	07 36		07 41		07 46	07 51		07 56	08 01		08 06		08 06	08 11	08 16		08 21	08 26	08 31	
Cardiff Bay	d			07 30					07 42			07 54			08 06						08 18				08 30
Cardiff Queen Street	a	07 29	07 34	07 34	07 39			07 44	07 46	07 49	07 54	07 58	07 59	08 04	08 10	08 09			08 14	08 19	08 22	08 24	08 29	08 34	08 34
	d	07 30	07 35		07 40			07 45		07 50	07 55		08 00	08 05		08 10			08 15	08 20		08 25	08 30	08 35	
Heath Low Level	d										08 00											08 30			
Ty Glas	d										08 03											08 33			
Birchgrove	d										08 04											08 34			
Rhiwbina	d										08 06											08 36			
Whitchurch (Cardiff)	d										08 08											08 38			
Coryton	a										08 14											08 44			
Heath High Level	d		07 40							07 55				08 10						08 25				08 40	
Llanishen	d		07 43							07 58				08 13						08 28				08 43	
Lisvane & Thornhill	d		07 45							08 00				08 15						08 30				08 45	
Caerphilly	d		07 51							08 06				08 21						08 36				08 51	
Aber	d		07 53							08 08				08 23						08 38				08 53	
Llanbradach	d		07 57							08 12				08 27						08 42				08 57	
Ystrad Mynach	d		08 02							08 17				08 32						08 47				09 07	
Hengoed	d		08 05							08 20				08 35						08 50				09 10	
Pengam	d		08 08							08 23				08 38						08 53				09 13	
Gilfach Fargoed	d													08 41											
Bargoed	a		08 13							08 32				08 49						08 58				09 22	
	d		08 14																	08 59					
Brithdir	d		08 18																	09 03					
Tir-phil	d		08 21																	09 06					
Pontlottyn	d		08 25																	09 10					
Rhymney	a		08 32																	09 17					
Cathays	d	07 33			07 43			07 48					08 03			08 13			08 18				08 33		
Llandaf	d	07 37			07 47			07 52					08 07			08 17			08 22				08 37		
Ninian Park	d					07 40												08 10							
Waun-gron Park	d					07 44												08 14							
Fairwater	d					07 46												08 16							
Danescourt	d					07 49												08 19							
Radyr	a	07 40			07 50	07 57		07 55					08 10			08 20		08 27	08 25				08 40		
	d	07 40			07 50			07 55					08 10			08 20			08 25				08 40		
Taffs Well	d	07 44			07 54			07 59					08 14			08 24			08 29				08 44		
Trefforest Estate	d	07 48											08 18										08 48		
Trefforest	d	07 52			08 01			08 06					08 22			08 31			08 36				08 52		
Pontypridd	a	07 55			08 04			08 09					08 25			08 34			08 39				08 55		
	d	07 57			08 06			08 11					08 27			08 36			08 41				08 57		
Abercynon	d	08 04						08 19					08 34						08 49				09 04		
Penrhiwceiber	d							08 25											08 55						
Mountain Ash	a							08 28											08 58						
	d							08 34											09 04						
Fernhill	d							08 37											09 07						
Cwmbach	d							08 41											09 11						
Aberdare	a							08 49											09 19						
Quakers Yard	d	08 09											08 39										09 09		
Merthyr Vale	a	08 14											08 44										09 14		
	d	08 17											08 47										09 17		
Troed Y Rhiw	d	08 21											08 51										09 21		
Pentre-bach	d	08 24											08 54										09 24		
Merthyr Tydfil	a	08 33											09 03										09 33		
Trehafod	d				08 11											08 41									
Porth	a				08 14											08 44									
	d				08 15											08 45									
Dinas Rhondda	d				08 19											08 49									
Tonypandy	d				08 21											08 51									
Llwynypia	d				08 23											08 53									
Ystrad Rhondda	a				08 26											08 56									
	d				08 29											08 59									
Ton Pentre	d				08 31											09 01									
Treorchy	d				08 34											09 04									
Ynyswen	d				08 37											09 07									
Treherbert	a				08 44											09 14									

When events are being held at the Millenium Stadium, services are subject to alteration. Please check times before travelling.

Table 130

Mondays to Fridays

from 17 September

Bridgend, Barry Island, Barry, Penarth and Cardiff - Coryton, Rhymney, Pontypridd, Merthyr, Aberdare and Treherbert

Network Diagram - see first Page of Table 130

		AW		AW	AW	AW	AW	AW	AW	AW	AW	AW		AW	AW	AW	AW	AW	AW	AW	AW	AW		AW	AW
Bridgend	d				07 42																				
Llantwit Major	d				07 56																				
Rhoose Cardiff Int Airport ✈	d				08 06																				
Barry Island	d									08 25						08 40				08 55					
Barry	d				08 15					08 30						08 45				09 00					
Barry Docks	d				08 19					08 34						08 49				09 04					
Cadoxton	d				08 22					08 37						08 52				09 07					
Dinas Powys	d				08 26					08 41						08 56				09 11					
Eastbrook	d				08 28					08 43						08 58				09 13					
Cogan	d				08 30					08 45						09 00				09 15					
Penarth	d						08 32				08 47										09 17				
Dingle Road	d						08 34				08 49										09 19				
Grangetown	d				08 34		08 38			08 49	08 53					09 04				09 19	09 23				
Cardiff Central	a				08 39		08 44			08 54	08 59					09 09				09 24	09 29				
	d	08 36		08 36	08 41		08 46	08 51		08 56	09 01			09 06	09 06	09 11	09 16		09 21	09 26	09 31			09 36	09 36
Cardiff Bay	d					08 42			08 54			09 06						09 18				09 30			
Cardiff Queen Street	a	08 39			08 44	08 46	08 49	08 54	08 58	08 59	09 04	09 10		09 09		09 14	09 19	09 22	09 24	09 29	09 34	09 34		09 39	
	d	08 40			08 45		08 50	08 55		09 00	09 05			09 10		09 15	09 20		09 25	09 30	09 35			09 40	
Heath Low Level	d							09 00											09 30						
Ty Glas	d							09 03											09 33						
Birchgrove	d							09 04											09 34						
Rhiwbina	d							09 06											09 36						
Whitchurch (Cardiff)	d							09 08											09 38						
Coryton	a							09 14											09 44						
Heath High Level	d						08 55				09 10						09 25				09 40				
Llanishen	d						08 58				09 13						09 28				09 43				
Lisvane & Thornhill	d						09 00				09 15						09 30				09 45				
Caerphilly	d						09 06				09 21						09 36				09 51				
Aber	d						09 08				09 23						09 38				09 53				
Llanbradach	d						09 12				09 27						09 42				09 57				
Ystrad Mynach	d						09a22				09 32						09 47				10 07				
Hengoed	d										09 35						09 50				10 10				
Pengam	d										09 38						09 53				10 13				
Gilfach Fargoed	d										09 41														
Bargoed	a										09 49						09 58				10 22				
	d																09 59								
Brithdir	d																10 03								
Tir-phil	d																10 06								
Pontlottyn	d																10 10								
Rhymney	a																10 17								
Cathays	d	08 43			08 48					09 03				09 13		09 18				09 33				09 43	
Llandaf	d	08 47			08 52					09 07				09 17		09 22				09 37				09 47	
Ninian Park	d			08 40											09 10										09 40
Waun-gron Park	d			08 44											09 14										09 44
Fairwater	d			08 46											09 16										09 46
Danescourt	d			08 49											09 19										09 49
Radyr	a	08 50		08 57	08 55					09 10				09 20	09 27	09 25				09 40				09 50	09 57
	d	08 50			08 55					09 10				09 20		09 25				09 40				09 50	
Taffs Well	d	08 54			08 59					09 14				09 24		09 29				09 44				09 54	
Trefforest Estate	d									09 18										09 48					
Trefforest	d	09 01			09 06					09 22				09 31		09 36				09 52				10 01	
Pontypridd	a	09 04			09 09					09 25				09 34		09 39				09 55				10 04	
	d	09 06			09 11					09 27				09 36		09 41				09 57				10 06	
Abercynon	d				09 19					09 34						09 49				10 04					
Penrhiwceiber	d				09 25											09 55									
Mountain Ash	a				09 28											09 58									
	d				09 34											10 04									
Fernhill	d				09 37											10 07									
Cwmbach	d				09 41											10 11									
Aberdare	a				09 49											10 19									
Quakers Yard	d									09 39										10 09					
Merthyr Vale	a									09 44										10 14					
	d									09 47										10 17					
Troed Y Rhiw	d									09 51										10 21					
Pentre-bach	d									09 54										10 24					
Merthyr Tydfil	a									10 03										10 33					
Trehafod	d	09 11												09 41										10 11	
Porth	a	09 14												09 44										10 14	
	d	09 15												09 45										10 15	
Dinas Rhondda	d	09 19												09 49										10 19	
Tonypandy	d	09 21												09 51										10 21	
Llwynypia	d	09 23												09 53										10 23	
Ystrad Rhondda	a	09 26												09 56										10 26	
	d	09 29												09 59										10 29	
Ton Pentre	d	09 31												10 01										10 31	
Treorchy	d	09 34												10 04										10 34	
Ynyswen	d	09 37												10 07										10 37	
Treherbert	a	09 44												10 14										10 44	

When events are being held at the Millenium Stadium, services are subject to alteration. Please check times before travelling.

Table 130

Mondays to Fridays

from 17 September

Bridgend, Barry Island, Barry, Penarth and Cardiff - Coryton, Rhymney, Pontypridd, Merthyr, Aberdare and Treherbert

Network Diagram - see first Page of Table 130

Station		AW	AW	AW	AW	AW	AW	AW		AW	AW	AW	AW	AW	AW	AW	AW	AW		AW	AW	AW	AW	AW	AW
Bridgend	d	08 42																							09 45
Llantwit Major	d	08 56																							09 58
Rhoose Cardiff Int Airport ✈	d	09 06																							10 08
Barry Island	d						09 25							09 40						09 55					
Barry [3]	d	09 15					09 30							09 45						10 00					10 16
Barry Docks	d	09 19					09 34							09 49						10 04					10 19
Cadoxton	d	09 22					09 37							09 52						10 07					10 22
Dinas Powys	d	09 26					09 41							09 56						10 11					10 26
Eastbrook	d	09 28					09 43							09 58						10 13					10 28
Cogan	d	09 30					09 45							10 00						10 15					10 30
Penarth	d			09 32				09 47							10 02							10 17			
Dingle Road	d			09 34				09 49							10 04							10 19			
Grangetown	d	09 34		09 38			09 49	09 53						10 04	10 08					10 19		10 23			10 34
Cardiff Central [7]	a	09 39		09 44			09 54	09 59						10 09	10 14					10 24		10 29			10 42
	d	09 41		09 46	09 51		09 56	10 01			10 06	10 06		10 11	10 16		10 21	10 21		10 26		10 31		10 36	
Cardiff Bay	d		09 42			09 54				10 06						10 18							10 30		
Cardiff Queen Street [3]	a	09 44	09 46	09 49	09 54	09 58	09 59	10 04		10 10	10 09			10 14	10 19	10 22	10 24			10 29		10 34	10 34		
	d	09 45		09 50	09 55		10 00	10 05			10 10			10 15	10 20		10 25			10 30		10 35			
Heath Low Level	d				10 00												10 30								
Ty Glas	d				10 03												10 33								
Birchgrove	d				10 04												10 34								
Rhiwbina	d				10 06												10 36								
Whitchurch (Cardiff)	d				10 08												10 38								
Coryton	a				10 14												10 44								
Heath High Level	d			09 55				10 10							10 25							10 40			
Llanishen	d			09 58				10 13							10 28							10 43			
Lisvane & Thornhill	d			10 00				10 15							10 30							10 45			
Caerphilly [3]	d			10 06				10 21							10 36							10 51			
Aber	d			10 08				10 23							10 38							10 53			
Llanbradach	d			10 12				10 27							10 42							10 57			
Ystrad Mynach [3]	d			10a22				10 32							10 47							11 02			
Hengoed	d							10 35							10 50							11 05			
Pengam	d							10 38							10 53							11 08			
Gilfach Fargoed	d							10 41																	
Bargoed	a							10 49							10 58							11 17			
	d														10 59										
Brithdir	d														11 03										
Tir-phil	d														11 06										
Pontlottyn	d														11 10										
Rhymney [3]	a														11 17										
Cathays	d	09 48					10 03				10 13			10 18						10 33					
Llandaf	d	09 52					10 07				10 17			10 22						10 37					
Ninian Park	d											10 10												10 40	
Waun-gron Park	d											10 14												10 44	
Fairwater	d											10 16												10 46	
Danescourt	d											10 19									←			10 49	
Radyr [3]	a	09 55					10 10				10 20	10 27		10 25				10 43		10 40	10 43			10 57	
	d	09 55					10 10				10 20			10 25				10 50		10 40	10 50				
Taffs Well [3]	d	09 59					10 14				10 24			10 29				→		10 44	10 54				
Trefforest Estate	d																			10 48					
Trefforest	d	10 06					10 22				10 31			10 36						10 52	11 01				
Pontypridd [3]	a	10 09					10 30				10 34			10 39						10 55	11 04				
	d	10 11									10 36		10 35	10 41						10 57	11 06				
Abercynon	d	10 19											10 41	10 49						11 04					
Penrhiwceiber	d	10 25												10 55											
Mountain Ash	a	10 28												10 58											
	d	10 34												11 04											
Fernhill	d	10 37												11 07											
Cwmbach	d	10 41												11 11											
Aberdare [3]	a	10 49												11 19											
Quakers Yard	d												10 45							11 09					
Merthyr Vale	a												10 50							11 14					
	d												10 52							11 17					
Troed Y Rhiw	d												10 56							11 21					
Pentre-bach	d												10 59							11 24					
Merthyr Tydfil	a												11 08							11 33					
Trehafod	d										10 41										11 11				
Porth	a										10 44										11 14				
	d										10 45										11 15				
Dinas Rhondda	d										10 49										11 19				
Tonypandy	d										10 51										11 21				
Llwynypia	d										10 53										11 23				
Ystrad Rhondda	a										10 56										11 26				
	d										10 59										11 29				
Ton Pentre	d										11 01										11 31				
Treorchy	d										11 04										11 34				
Ynyswen	d										11 07										11 37				
Treherbert	a										11 14										11 44				

When events are being held at the Millenium Stadium, services are subject to alteration. Please check times before travelling.

Table 130

Mondays to Fridays

from 17 September

Bridgend, Barry Island, Barry, Penarth and Cardiff - Coryton, Rhymney, Pontypridd, Merthyr, Aberdare and Treherbert

Network Diagram - see first Page of Table 130

Station		AW	AW	AW		AW	AW	AW	AW	AW	AW	AW	AW	AW		AW	AW	AW	AW	AW	AW	AW	AW	AW
Bridgend	d																					10 45		
Llantwit Major	d																					10 58		
Rhoose Cardiff Int Airport ✈	d																					11 08		
Barry Island	d						10 25					10 40					10 55							
Barry [3]	d						10 30					10 45					11 00					11 16		
Barry Docks	d						10 34					10 49					11 04					11 19		
Cadoxton	d						10 37					10 52					11 07					11 22		
Dinas Powys	d						10 41					10 56					11 11					11 26		
Eastbrook	d						10 43					10 58					11 13					11 28		
Cogan	d						10 45					11 00					11 15					11 30		
Penarth	d		10 32						10 47				11 02					11 17						11 32
Dingle Road	d		10 34						10 49				11 04					11 19						11 34
Grangetown	d		10 38				10 49		10 53			11 04	11 08				11 19	11 23				11 34		11 38
Cardiff Central [7]	a		10 44				10 54		10 59			11 09	11 14				11 24	11 29				11 39		11 44
	d		10 46	10 51			10 56	10 54	11 01	11 06		11 11	11 16			11 21	11 26	11 31		11 36	11 36	11 41		11 46
Cardiff Bay	d	10 42				10 54					11 06			11 18					11 30				11 42	
Cardiff Queen Street [3]	a	10 46	10 49	10 54		10 58	10 59		11 04		11 10	11 14	11 19	11 22		11 24	11 29	11 34	11 34	11 39		11 44	11 46	11 49
	d		10 50	10 55			11 00		11 05			11 15	11 20			11 25	11 30	11 35		11 40		11 45		11 50
Heath Low Level	d			11 00												11 30								
Ty Glas	d			11 03												11 33								
Birchgrove	d			11 04												11 34								
Rhiwbina	d			11 06												11 36								
Whitchurch (Cardiff)	d			11 08												11 38								
Coryton	a			11 14												11 44								
Heath High Level	d		10 55						11 10				11 25					11 40						11 55
Llanishen	d		10 58						11 13				11 28					11 43						11 58
Lisvane & Thornhill	d		11 00						11 15				11 30					11 45						12 00
Caerphilly [3]	d		11 06						11 21				11 36					11 51						12 06
Aber	d		11 08						11 23				11 38					11 53						12 08
Llanbradach	d		11 12						11 27				11 42					11 57						12 12
Ystrad Mynach [3]	d		11a22						11 32				11 47					12 07						12a22
Hengoed	d								11 35				11 50					12 10						
Pengam	d								11 38				11 53					12 13						
Gilfach Fargoed	d								11 41															
Bargoed	a								11 49				11 58					12 22						
	d												11 59											
Brithdir	d												12 03											
Tir-phil	d												12 06											
Pontlottyn	d												12 10											
Rhymney [3]	a												12 17											
Cathays	d						11 03					11 18					11 33			11 43		11 48		
Llandaf	d						11 07					11 22					11 37			11 47		11 52		
Ninian Park	d									11 10											11 40			
Waun-gron Park	d									11 14											11 44			
Fairwater	d									11 16											11 46			
Danescourt	d									11 19											11 49			
Radyr [3]	a						11 10	11 02		11 27		11 25					11 40			11 50	11 57	11 55		
	d						11 10	11 20				11 25					11 40			11 50		11 55		
Taffs Well [3]	d						11 14	11 24				11 29					11 44			11 54		11 59		
Trefforest Estate	d						11 18										11 48							
Trefforest	d						11 22	11 31				11 36					11 52			12 01		12 06		
Pontypridd [3]	a						11 25	11 34				11 39					11 55			12 04		12 09		
	d						11 27	11 36				11 41					11 57			12 06		12 11		
Abercynon	d						11 34					11 49					12 04					12 19		
Penrhiwceiber	d											11 55										12 25		
Mountain Ash	a											11 58										12 28		
	d											12 04										12 34		
Fernhill	d											12 07										12 37		
Cwmbach	d											12 11										12 41		
Aberdare [3]	a											12 19										12 49		
Quakers Yard	d						11 39										12 09							
Merthyr Vale	a						11 44										12 14							
	d						11 47										12 17							
Troed Y Rhiw	d						11 51										12 21							
Pentre-bach	d						11 54										12 24							
Merthyr Tydfil	a						12 03										12 33							
Trehafod	d							11 41												12 11				
Porth	a							11 44												12 14				
	d							11 45												12 15				
Dinas Rhondda	d							11 49												12 19				
Tonypandy	d							11 51												12 21				
Llwynypia	d							11 53												12 23				
Ystrad Rhondda	a							11 56												12 26				
	d							11 59												12 29				
Ton Pentre	d							12 01												12 31				
Treorchy	d							12 04												12 34				
Ynyswen	d							12 07												12 37				
Treherbert	a							12 14												12 44				

When events are being held at the Millenium Stadium, services are subject to alteration. Please check times before travelling.

Table 130

Mondays to Fridays

from 17 September

Bridgend, Barry Island, Barry, Penarth and Cardiff - Coryton, Rhymney, Pontypridd, Merthyr, Aberdare and Treherbert

Network Diagram - see first Page of Table 130

		AW	AW	AW	AW	AW	AW	AW	AW	AW		AW	AW	AW	AW	AW	AW	AW	AW	AW		AW	AW	AW	AW
Bridgend	d																		11 42					
Llantwit Major	d																		11 56					
Rhoose Cardiff Int Airport ✈	d																		12 06					
Barry Island	d			11 25					11 40					11 55											
Barry 3	d			11 30					11 45					12 00						12 15					
Barry Docks	d			11 34					11 49					12 04						12 19					
Cadoxton	d			11 37					11 52					12 07						12 22					
Dinas Powys	d			11 41					11 56					12 11						12 26					
Eastbrook	d			11 43					11 58					12 13						12 28					
Cogan	d			11 45					12 00					12 15						12 30					
Penarth	d				11 47					12 02					12 17								12 32		
Dingle Road	d				11 49					12 04					12 19								12 34		
Grangetown	d			11 49	11 53				12 04	12 08				12 19	12 23					12 34			12 38		
Cardiff Central 7	a			11 54	11 59				12 09	12 14				12 24	12 29					12 44			12 44		
	d	11 51		11 56	12 01		12 06	12 06	12 11	12 16			12 21	12 26	12 31		12 36	12 36	12 41				12 46	12 51	
Cardiff Bay	d		11 54			12 06						12 18				12 30						12 42			12 54
Cardiff Queen Street 3	a	11 54	11 58	11 59	12 04	12 10	12 09		12 14	12 19		12 22	12 24	12 29	12 34	12 34	12 39		12 44			12 46	12 49	12 54	12 58
	d	11 55		12 00	12 05		12 10		12 15	12 20			12 25	12 30	12 35		12 40		12 45				12 50	12 55	
Heath Low Level	d	12 00											12 30											13 00	
Ty Glas	d	12 03											12 33											13 03	
Birchgrove	d	12 04											12 34											13 04	
Rhiwbina	d	12 06											12 36											13 06	
Whitchurch (Cardiff)	d	12 08											12 38											13 08	
Coryton	a	12 14											12 44											13 14	
Heath High Level	d				12 10					12 25					12 40								12 55		
Llanishen	d				12 13					12 28					12 43								12 58		
Lisvane & Thornhill	d				12 15					12 30					12 45								13 00		
Caerphilly 3	d				12 21					12 36					12 51								13 06		
Aber	d				12 23					12 38					12 53								13 08		
Llanbradach	d				12 27					12 42					12 57								13 12		
Ystrad Mynach 3	d				12 32					12 47					13 07								13a22		
Hengoed	d				12 35					12 50					13 10										
Pengam	d				12 38					12 53					13 13										
Gilfach Fargoed	d				12 41																				
Bargoed	a				12 49					12 58					13 22										
	d									12 59															
Brithdir	d									13 03															
Tir-phil	d									13 06															
Pontlottyn	d									13 10															
Rhymney 3	a									13 17															
Cathays	d			12 03			12 13		12 18					12 33			12 43		12 48						
Llandaf	d			12 07			12 17		12 22					12 37			12 47		12 52						
Ninian Park	d							12 10										12 40							
Waun-gron Park	d							12 14										12 44							
Fairwater	d							12 16										12 46							
Danescourt	d							12 19										12 49							
Radyr 3	a			12 10			12 20	12 27	12 25					12 40			12 50	12 57	12 55						
	d			12 10			12 20		12 25					12 40			12 50		12 55						
Taffs Well 3	d			12 14			12 24		12 29					12 44			12 54		12 59						
Trefforest Estate	d			12 18										12 48											
Trefforest	d			12 22			12 31		12 36					12 52			13 01		13 06						
Pontypridd 3	a			12 25			12 34		12 42					12 55			13 04		13 09						
	d			12 27			12 36							12 57			13 06		13 11						
Abercynon	d			12 34										13 04					13 19						
Penrhiwceiber	d																		13 25						
Mountain Ash	a																		13 28						
	d																		13 34						
Fernhill	d																		13 37						
Cwmbach	d																		13 41						
Aberdare 3	a																		13 49						
Quakers Yard	d			12 39										13 09											
Merthyr Vale	a			12 44										13 14											
	d			12 47										13 17											
Troed Y Rhiw	d			12 51										13 21											
Pentre-bach	d			12 54										13 24											
Merthyr Tydfil	a			13 03										13 33											
Trehafod	d						12 41										13 11								
Porth	a						12 44										13 14								
	d						12 45										13 15								
Dinas Rhondda	d						12 49										13 19								
Tonypandy	d						12 51										13 21								
Llwynypia	d						12 53										13 23								
Ystrad Rhondda	a						12 56										13 26								
	d						12 59										13 29								
Ton Pentre	d						13 01										13 31								
Treorchy	d						13 04										13 34								
Ynyswen	d						13 07										13 37								
Treherbert	a						13 14										13 44								

When events are being held at the Millenium Stadium, services are subject to alteration. Please check times before travelling.

Table 130

Mondays to Fridays

from 17 September

Bridgend, Barry Island, Barry, Penarth and Cardiff - Coryton, Rhymney, Pontypridd, Merthyr, Aberdare and Treherbert

Network Diagram - see first Page of Table 130

		AW	AW	AW	AW	AW		AW	AW	AW	AW	AW	AW	AW	AW	AW		AW	AW	AW	AW	AW	AW	AW	AW
Bridgend	d																	12 42							
Llantwit Major	d																	12 56							
Rhoose Cardiff Int Airport ✈	d																	13 06							
Barry Island	d	12 25						12 40				12 55											13 25		
Barry 3	d	12 30						12 45				13 00						13 15					13 30		
Barry Docks	d	12 34						12 49				13 04						13 19					13 34		
Cadoxton	d	12 37						12 52				13 07						13 22					13 37		
Dinas Powys	d	12 41						12 56				13 11						13 26					13 41		
Eastbrook	d	12 43						12 58				13 13						13 28					13 43		
Cogan	d	12 45						13 00				13 15						13 30					13 45		
Penarth	d		12 47						13 02				13 17							13 32				13 47	
Dingle Road	d		12 49						13 04				13 19							13 34				13 49	
Grangetown	d	12 49	12 53					13 04	13 08			13 19	13 23					13 34		13 38			13 49	13 53	
Cardiff Central 7	a	12 54	12 59					13 09	13 14			13 24	13 29					13 39		13 44			13 54	13 59	
	d	12 56	13 01		13 06	13 06		13 11	13 16		13 21	13 26	13 31		13 36	13 36		13 41		13 46	13 51		13 56	14 01	
Cardiff Bay	d			13 06						13 18				13 30					13 42			13 54			14 06
Cardiff Queen Street 3	a	12 59	13 04	13 10	13 09			13 14	13 19	13 22	13 24	13 29	13 34	13 34	13 39			13 44	13 46	13 49	13 54	13 58	13 59	14 04	14 10
	d	13 00	13 05		13 10			13 15	13 20		13 25	13 30	13 35		13 40			13 45		13 50	13 55		14 00	14 05	
Heath Low Level	d										13 30										14 00				
Ty Glas	d										13 33										14 03				
Birchgrove	d										13 34										14 04				
Rhiwbina	d										13 36										14 06				
Whitchurch (Cardiff)	d										13 38										14 08				
Coryton	a										13 44										14 14				
Heath High Level	d		13 10						13 25				13 40							13 55				14 10	
Llanishen	d		13 13						13 28				13 43							13 58				14 13	
Lisvane & Thornhill	d		13 15						13 30				13 45							14 00				14 15	
Caerphilly 3	d		13 21						13 36				13 51							14 06				14 21	
Aber	d		13 23						13 38				13 53							14 08				14 23	
Llanbradach	d		13 27						13 42				13 57							14 12				14 27	
Ystrad Mynach 3	d		13 32						13 47				14 07							14a22				14 32	
Hengoed	d		13 35						13 50				14 10											14 35	
Pengam	d		13 38						13 53				14 13											14 38	
Gilfach Fargoed	d		13 41																					14 41	
Bargoed	a		13 49						13 58				14 22											14 49	
	d								13 59																
Brithdir	d								14 03																
Tir-phil	d								14 06																
Pontlottyn	d								14 10																
Rhymney 3	a								14 17																
Cathays	d	13 03			13 13			13 18				13 33			13 43			13 48					14 03		
Llandaf	d	13 07			13 17			13 22				13 37			13 47			13 52					14 07		
Ninian Park	d					13 10										13 40									
Waun-gron Park	d					13 14										13 44									
Fairwater	d					13 16										13 46									
Danescourt	d					13 19										13 49									
Radyr 3	a	13 10			13 20	13 27		13 25				13 40			13 50	13 57		13 55					14 10		
	d	13 10			13 20			13 25				13 40			13 50			13 55					14 10		
Taffs Well 3	d	13 14			13 24			13 29				13 44			13 54			13 59					14 14		
Trefforest Estate	d	13 18										13 48											14 18		
Trefforest	d	13 22			13 31			13 36				13 52			14 01			14 06					14 22		
Pontypridd 3	a	13 25			13 34			13 39				13 55			14 04			14 09					14 25		
	d	13 27			13 36			13 41				13 57			14 06			14 11					14 27		
Abercynon	d	13 34						13 49				14 04						14 19					14 34		
Penrhiwceiber	d							13 55										14 25							
Mountain Ash	a							13 58										14 28							
	d							14 04										14 34							
Fernhill	d							14 07										14 37							
Cwmbach	d							14 11										14 41							
Aberdare 3	a							14 19										14 49							
Quakers Yard	d	13 39										14 09											14 39		
Merthyr Vale	a	13 44										14 14											14 44		
	d	13 47										14 17											14 47		
Troed Y Rhiw	d	13 51										14 21											14 51		
Pentre-bach	d	13 54										14 24											14 54		
Merthyr Tydfil	a	14 03										14 33											15 03		
Trehafod	d				13 41										14 11										
Porth	a				13 44										14 14										
	d				13 45										14 15										
Dinas Rhondda	d				13 49										14 19										
Tonypandy	d				13 51										14 21										
Llwynypia	d				13 53										14 23										
Ystrad Rhondda	a				13 56										14 26										
	d				13 59										14 29										
Ton Pentre	d				14 01										14 31										
Treorchy	d				14 04										14 34										
Ynyswen	d				14 07										14 37										
Treherbert	a				14 14										14 44										

When events are being held at the Millenium Stadium, services are subject to alteration. Please check times before travelling.

Table 130

Mondays to Fridays
from 17 September

Bridgend, Barry Island, Barry, Penarth and Cardiff - Coryton, Rhymney, Pontypridd, Merthyr, Aberdare and Treherbert

Network Diagram - see first Page of Table 130

Station		AW		AW	AW	AW	AW	AW	AW	AW	AW	AW		AW	AW	AW	AW	AW	AW	AW	AW	AW		AW	AW
Bridgend	d														13 42										
Llantwit Major	d														13 56										
Rhoose Cardiff Int Airport ✈	d														14 06										
Barry Island	d				13 40				13 55												14 25				
Barry 3	d				13 45				14 00						14 15						14 30				
Barry Docks	d				13 49				14 04						14 19						14 34				
Cadoxton	d				13 52				14 07						14 22						14 37				
Dinas Powys	d				13 56				14 11						14 26						14 41				
Eastbrook	d				13 58				14 13						14 28						14 43				
Cogan	d				14 00				14 15						14 30						14 45				
Penarth	d					14 02				14 17							14 32							14 47	
Dingle Road	d					14 04				14 19							14 34							14 49	
Grangetown	d				14 04	14 08			14 19	14 23					14 34		14 38				14 49			14 53	
Cardiff Central 7	a				14 09	14 14			14 24	14 29					14 39		14 44				14 54			14 59	
	d	14 06		14 06	14 11	14 16		14 21	14 26	14 31		14 36		14 36	14 41		14 46	14 51		14 51	14 56			15 01	15 06
Cardiff Bay	d						14 18				14 30					14 42			14 54						
Cardiff Queen Street 3	a	14 09			14 14	14 19	14 22	14 24	14 29	14 34	14 34	14 39			14 44	14 46	14 49	14 54	14 58		14 59			15 04	
	d	14 10			14 15	14 20		14 25	14 30	14 35		14 40			14 45		14 50	14 55			15 00			15 05	
Heath Low Level	d							14 30										15 00							
Ty Glas	d							14 33										15 03							
Birchgrove	d							14 34										15 04							
Rhiwbina	d							14 36										15 06							
Whitchurch (Cardiff)	d							14 38										15 08							
Coryton	a							14 44										15 14							
Heath High Level	d					14 25				14 40							14 55							15 10	
Llanishen	d					14 28				14 43							14 58							15 13	
Lisvane & Thornhill	d					14 30				14 45							15 00							15 15	
Caerphilly 3	d					14 36				14 51							15 06							15 21	
Aber	d					14 38				14 53							15 08							15 23	
Llanbradach	d					14 42				14 57							15 12							15 27	
Ystrad Mynach 3	d					14 47				15 07							15a22							15 32	
Hengoed	d					14 50				15 10														15 35	
Pengam	d					14 53				15 13														15 38	
Gilfach Fargoed	d																							15 41	
Bargoed	a					14 58				15 22														15 49	
	d					14 59																			
Brithdir	d					15 03																			
Tir-phil	d					15 06																			
Pontlottyn	d					15 10																			
Rhymney 3	a					15 17																			
Cathays	d	14 13			14 18				14 33			14 43			14 48						15 03				
Llandaf	d	14 17			14 22				14 37			14 47			14 52						15 07				
Ninian Park	d			14 10										14 40											15 10
Waun-gron Park	d			14 14										14 44											15 14
Fairwater	d			14 16										14 46											15 16
Danescourt	d			14 19										14 49								←			15 19
Radyr 3	a	14 20		14 27	14 25				14 40			14 50		14 57	14 55					15 08	15 10	15 08			15 27
	d	14 20			14 25				14 40			14 50			14 55					15 20	15 10	15 20			
Taffs Well 3	d	14 24			14 29				14 44			14 54			14 59					→	15 14	15 24			
Trefforest Estate	d								14 48												15 18				
Trefforest	d	14 31			14 36				14 52			15 01			15 06						15 22	15 31			
Pontypridd 3	a	14 34			14 39				14 55			15 04			15 09						15 25	15 34			
	d	14 36			14 41				14 57			15 06			15 11						15 27	15 36			
Abercynon	d				14 49				15 04						15 19						15 34				
Penrhiwceiber	d				14 55										15 25										
Mountain Ash	a				14 58										15 28										
	d				15 04										15 34										
Fernhill	d				15 07										15 37										
Cwmbach	d				15 11										15 41										
Aberdare 3	a				15 19										15 49										
Quakers Yard	d								15 09												15 39				
Merthyr Vale	a								15 14												15 44				
	d								15 17												15 47				
Troed Y Rhiw	d								15 21												15 51				
Pentre-bach	d								15 24												15 54				
Merthyr Tydfil	a								15 33												16 03				
Trehafod	d	14 41										15 11										15 41			
Porth	a	14 44										15 14										15 44			
	d	14 45										15 15										15 45			
Dinas Rhondda	d	14 49										15 19										15 49			
Tonypandy	d	14 51										15 21										15 51			
Llwynypia	d	14 53										15 23										15 53			
Ystrad Rhondda	a	14 56										15 26										15 56			
	d	14 59										15 29										15 59			
Ton Pentre	d	15 01										15 31										16 01			
Treorchy	d	15 04										15 34										16 04			
Ynyswen	d	15 07										15 37										16 07			
Treherbert	a	15 14										15 44										16 14			

When events are being held at the Millenium Stadium, services are subject to alteration. Please check times before travelling.

Table 130

Mondays to Fridays
from 17 September

Bridgend, Barry Island, Barry, Penarth and Cardiff - Coryton, Rhymney, Pontypridd, Merthyr, Aberdare and Treherbert

Network Diagram - see first Page of Table 130

Station		AW	AW	AW	AW	AW	AW	AW		AW	AW	AW	AW	AW	AW	AW	AW	AW		AW	AW	AW	AW	AW	AW
Bridgend	d												14 42												
Llantwit Major	d												14 56												
Rhoose Cardiff Int Airport ✈	d												15 06												
Barry Island	d		14 40				14 55											15 25						15 40	
Barry 3	d		14 45				15 00						15 15					15 30						15 45	
Barry Docks	d		14 49				15 04						15 19					15 34						15 49	
Cadoxton	d		14 52				15 07						15 22					15 37						15 52	
Dinas Powys	d		14 56				15 11						15 26					15 41						15 56	
Eastbrook	d		14 58				15 13						15 28					15 43						15 58	
Cogan	d		15 00				15 15						15 30					15 45						16 00	
Penarth	d			15 02				15 17							15 32					15 47					16 02
Dingle Road	d			15 04				15 19							15 34					15 49					16 04
Grangetown	d		15 04	15 08			15 19	15 23					15 34		15 38			15 49		15 53				16 04	16 08
Cardiff Central 7	a		15 09	15 14			15 24	15 29					15 39		15 45			15 54		15 59				16 09	16 14
	d		15 11	15 16		15 21	15 26	15 31			15 36	15 36	15 41		15 46	15 51		15 56		16 01		16 06	16 06	16 11	16 16
Cardiff Bay	d	15 06			15 18					15 30				15 42			15 54				16 06				
Cardiff Queen Street 3	a	15 10	15 14	15 19	15 22	15 24	15 29	15 34		15 34	15 39		15 44	15 46	15 49	15 54	15 58	15 59		16 04	16 10	16 09		16 14	16 19
	d		15 15	15 20		15 25	15 30	15 35			15 40		15 45		15 50	15 55		16 00		16 05		16 10		16 15	16 20
Heath Low Level	d					15 30										16 00									
Ty Glas	d					15 33										16 03									
Birchgrove	d					15 34										16 04									
Rhiwbina	d					15 36										16 06									
Whitchurch (Cardiff)	d					15 38										16 08									
Coryton	a					15 44										16 14									
Heath High Level	d			15 25				15 40							15 55					16 10					16 25
Llanishen	d			15 28				15 43							15 58					16 13					16 28
Lisvane & Thornhill	d			15 30				15 45							16 00					16 15					16 30
Caerphilly 3	d			15 36				15 51							16 06					16 21					16 36
Aber	d			15 38				15 53							16 08					16 23					16 38
Llanbradach	d			15 42				15 57							16 12					16 27					16 42
Ystrad Mynach 3	d			15 47				16 02							16 17					16 32					16 47
Hengoed	d			15 50				16 05							16 20					16 35					16 50
Pengam	d			15 53				16 08							16 23					16 38					16 53
Gilfach Fargoed	d																			16 41					
Bargoed	a			15 58				16 17							16 32					16 49					16 58
	d			15 59																					16 59
Brithdir	d			16 03																					17 03
Tir-phil	d			16 06																					17 06
Pontlottyn	d			16 10																					17 10
Rhymney 3	a			16 17																					17 17
Cathays	d		15 18				15 33				15 43		15 48					16 03				16 13		16 18	
Llandaf	d		15 22				15 37				15 47		15 52					16 07				16 17		16 22	
Ninian Park	d											15 40											16 10		
Waun-gron Park	d											15 44											16 14		
Fairwater	d											15 46											16 16		
Danescourt	d											15 49											16 19		
Radyr 3	a		15 25				15 40				15 50	15 57	15 55					16 10				16 20	16 27	16 25	
	d		15 25				15 40				15 50		15 55					16 10				16 20		16 25	
Taffs Well 3	d		15 29				15 44				15 54		15 59					16 14				16 24		16 29	
Trefforest Estate	d						15 48											16 18							
Trefforest	d		15 36				15 52				16 01		16 06					16 22				16 31		16 36	
Pontypridd 3	a		15 39				15 55				16 04		16 09					16 25				16 34		16 39	
	d		15 41				15 57				16 06		16 11					16 27				16 36		16 41	
Abercynon	d		15 49				16 04						16 19					16 34						16 49	
Penrhiwceiber	d		15 55										16 25											16 55	
Mountain Ash	a		15 58										16 28											16 58	
	d		16 04										16 34											17 04	
Fernhill	d		16 07										16 37											17 07	
Cwmbach	d		16 11										16 41											17 11	
Aberdare 3	a		16 19										16 49											17 19	
Quakers Yard	d						16 09											16 39							
Merthyr Vale	a						16 14											16 44							
	d						16 17											16 47							
Troed Y Rhiw	d						16 21											16 51							
Pentre-bach	d						16 24											16 54							
Merthyr Tydfil	a						16 33											17 03							
Trehafod	d										16 11											16 41			
Porth	a										16 14											16 44			
	d										16 15											16 45			
Dinas Rhondda	d										16 19											16 49			
Tonypandy	d										16 21											16 51			
Llwynypia	d										16 23											16 53			
Ystrad Rhondda	a										16 26											16 56			
	d										16 29											16 59			
Ton Pentre	d										16 31											17 01			
Treorchy	d										16 34											17 04			
Ynyswen	d										16 37											17 07			
Treherbert	a										16 44											17 14			

When events are being held at the Millenium Stadium, services are subject to alteration. Please check times before travelling.

Bridgend, Barry Island, Barry, Penarth and Cardiff - Coryton, Rhymney, Pontypridd, Merthyr, Aberdare and Treherbert

Network Diagram - see first Page of Table 130

		AW	AW	AW		AW	AW	AW	AW	AW	AW	AW	AW	AW		AW	AW	AW	AW	AW	AW	AW	AW	AW
Bridgend	d									15 42														
Llantwit Major	d									15 56														
Rhoose Cardiff Int Airport ✈	d									16 06														
Barry Island	d			15 55												16 25					16 40			
Barry 3	d			16 00						16 15						16 30					16 45			
Barry Docks	d			16 04						16 19						16 34					16 49			
Cadoxton	d			16 07						16 22						16 37					16 52			
Dinas Powys	d			16 11						16 26						16 41					16 56			
Eastbrook	d			16 13						16 28						16 43					16 58			
Cogan	d			16 15						16 30						16 45					17 00			
Penarth	d					16 17						16 32										17 02		
Dingle Road	d					16 19						16 34										17 04		
Grangetown	d			16 19		16 23				16 34		16 38				16 49					17 04	17 08		
Cardiff Central 7	a			16 24		16 29				16 39		16 44				16 54					17 09	17 14		
	d		16 21	16 26		16 31		16 36	16 36	16 41		16 46	16 51			16 56	17 01		17 06	17 06	17 11	17 16		17 21
Cardiff Bay	d	16 18					16 30				16 42			16 54				17 06					17 18	
Cardiff Queen Street 3	a	16 22	16 24	16 29		16 34	16 34	16 39		16 44	16 46	16 49	16 54	16 58		16 59	17 04	17 10	17 09		17 14	17 19	17 22	17 24
	d		16 25	16 30		16 35		16 40		16 45		16 50	16 55			17 00	17 05		17 10		17 15	17 20		17 25
Heath Low Level	d		16 30										17 00											17 30
Ty Glas	d		16 33										17 03											17 33
Birchgrove	d		16 34										17 04											17 34
Rhiwbina	d		16 36										17 06											17 36
Whitchurch (Cardiff)	d		16 38										17 08											17 38
Coryton	a		16 44										17 14											17 44
Heath High Level	d					16 40						16 55					17 10					17 25		
Llanishen	d					16 43						16 58					17 13					17 28		
Lisvane & Thornhill	d					16 45						17 00					17 15					17 30		
Caerphilly 3	d					16 51						17 06					17 21					17 36		
Aber	d					16 53						17 08					17 23					17 38		
Llanbradach	d					16 57						17 12					17 27					17 42		
Ystrad Mynach 3	d					17 02						17 17					17 33					17 47		
Hengoed	d					17 05						17 20					17 35					17 50		
Pengam	d					17 08						17 23					17 39					17 53		
Gilfach Fargoed	d																17 42							
Bargoed	a					17 17						17 32					17 45					18 02		
	d																17 47							
Brithdir	d																17 50							
Tir-phil	d																17 53							
Pontlottyn	d																17 58							
Rhymney 3	a																18 05							
Cathays	d			16 33				16 43		16 48						17 03			17 13		17 18			
Llandaf	d			16 37				16 47		16 52						17 07			17 17		17 22			
Ninian Park	d								16 40											17 10				
Waun-gron Park	d								16 44											17 14				
Fairwater	d								16 46											17 16				
Danescourt	d								16 49											17 19				
Radyr 3	a			16 40				16 50	16 57	16 55						17 10			17 20	17 27	17 25			
	d			16 40				16 50		16 55						17 10			17 20		17 25			
Taffs Well 3	d			16 44				16 54		16 59						17 14			17 24		17 29			
Trefforest Estate	d			16 48												17 18								
Trefforest	d			16 52				17 01		17 06						17 22			17 31		17 36			
Pontypridd 3	a			16 55				17 04		17 09						17 25			17 34		17 39			
	d			16 57				17 06		17 11						17 27			17 36		17 41			
Abercynon	d			17 04						17 19						17 34					17 49			
Penrhiwceiber	d									17 25											17 55			
Mountain Ash	a									17 28											17 58			
	d									17 34											18 04			
Fernhill	d									17 37											18 07			
Cwmbach	d									17 41											18 11			
Aberdare 3	a									17 49											18 19			
Quakers Yard	d			17 09												17 39								
Merthyr Vale	a			17 14												17 44								
	d			17 17												17 47								
Troed Y Rhiw	d			17 21												17 51								
Pentre-bach	d			17 24												17 54								
Merthyr Tydfil	a			17 33												18 03								
Trehafod	d							17 11											17 41					
Porth	a							17 14											17 44					
	d							17 15											17 45					
Dinas Rhondda	d							17 19											17 49					
Tonypandy	d							17 21											17 51					
Llwynypia	d							17 23											17 53					
Ystrad Rhondda	a							17 26											17 56					
	d							17 29											17 59					
Ton Pentre	d							17 31											18 01					
Treorchy	d							17 34											18 04					
Ynyswen	d							17 37											18 07					
Treherbert	a							17 44											18 14					

When events are being held at the Millenium Stadium, services are subject to alteration. Please check times before travelling.

Bridgend, Barry Island, Barry, Penarth and Cardiff - Coryton, Rhymney, Pontypridd, Merthyr, Aberdare and Treherbert

Network Diagram - see first Page of Table 130

		AW	AW	AW	AW	AW	AW	AW	AW	AW		AW	AW	AW	AW	AW	AW	AW	AW	AW		AW	AW	AW
Bridgend	d						16 42																	
Llantwit Major	d						16 56																	
Rhoose Cardiff Int Airport ✈	d						17 06																	
Barry Island	d	16 55											17 25					17 40					17 55	
Barry 3	d	17 00					17 15						17 30					17 45					18 00	
Barry Docks	d	17 04					17 19						17 34					17 49					18 04	
Cadoxton	d	17 07					17 22						17 37					17 52					18 07	
Dinas Powys	d	17 11					17 26						17 41					17 56					18 11	
Eastbrook	d	17 13					17 28						17 43					17 58					18 13	
Cogan	d	17 15					17 30						17 45					18 00					18 15	
Penarth	d		17 17						17 32					17 47					18 02					
Dingle Road	d		17 19						17 34					17 49					18 04					
Grangetown	d	17 19	17 23				17 34		17 38				17 49	17 53				18 04	18 08				18 19	
Cardiff Central 7	a	17 24	17 29				17 39		17 44				17 54	17 59				18 09	18 14				18 24	
	d	17 26	17 31		17 36	17 36	17 41		17 46	17 51			17 56	18 01		18 06	18 06	18 11	18 16			18 21	18 26	
Cardiff Bay	d			17 30				17 42				17 54			18 06					18 18				18 30
Cardiff Queen Street 3	a	17 29	17 34	17 34	17 39		17 44	17 46	17 49	17 54		17 58	17 59	18 04	18 10	18 09		18 14	18 19	18 22		18 24	18 29	18 34
	d	17 30	17 35		17 40		17 45		17 50	17 55			18 00	18 05		18 10		18 15	18 20			18 25	18 30	
Heath Low Level	d									18 00												18 30		
Ty Glas	d									18 03												18 33		
Birchgrove	d									18 04												18 34		
Rhiwbina	d									18 06												18 36		
Whitchurch (Cardiff)	d									18 08												18 38		
Coryton	a									18 14												18 44		
Heath High Level	d		17 40						17 55					18 10					18 25					
Llanishen	d		17 43						17 59					18 13					18 28					
Lisvane & Thornhill	d		17 45						18 02					18 15					18 30					
Caerphilly 3	d		17 51						18 07					18 21					18 36					
Aber	d		17 53						18 10					18 23					18 38					
Llanbradach	d		17 57						18 14					18 27					18 42					
Ystrad Mynach 3	d		18 02						18 20					18 32					18a52					
Hengoed	d		18 05						18 23					18 35										
Pengam	d		18 08						18 27					18 38										
Gilfach Fargoed	d		18 11						18 30					18 41										
Bargoed	a		18 14						18 34					18 49										
	d		18 16						18 44															
Brithdir	d		18 20						18 48															
Tir-phil	d		18 23						18 51															
Pontlottyn	d		18 27						18 55															
Rhymney 3	a		18 34						19 02															
Cathays	d	17 33			17 43		17 48						18 03			18 13		18 18					18 33	
Llandaf	d	17 37			17 47		17 52						18 07			18 17		18 22					18 37	
Ninian Park	d					17 40											18 10							
Waun-gron Park	d					17 44											18 14							
Fairwater	d					17 46											18 16							
Danescourt	d					17 49											18 19							
Radyr 3	a	17 40			17 50	17 57	17 55						18 10			18 20	18 27	18 25					18 40	
	d	17 40			17 50		17 55						18 10			18 20		18 25					18 40	
Taffs Well 3	d	17 44			17 54		17 59						18 14			18 24		18 29					18 44	
Trefforest Estate	d	17 48											18 18										18 48	
Trefforest	d	17 52			18 01		18 06						18 22			18 31		18 36					18 52	
Pontypridd 3	a	17 55			18 04		18 09						18 25			18 34		18 42					18 55	
	d	17 57			18 06		18 11						18 27			18 36							18 57	
Abercynon	d	18 04					18 19						18 34										19 04	
Penrhiwceiber	d						18 25																	
Mountain Ash	a						18 28																	
	d						18 34																	
Fernhill	d						18 37																	
Cwmbach	d						18 41																	
Aberdare 3	a						18 49																	
Quakers Yard	d	18 09											18 39										19 09	
Merthyr Vale	a	18 14											18 44										19 14	
	d	18 17											18 47										19 17	
Troed Y Rhiw	d	18 21											18 51										19 21	
Pentre-bach	d	18 24											18 54										19 24	
Merthyr Tydfil	a	18 33											19 03										19 33	
Trehafod	d				18 11											18 41								
Porth	a				18 14											18 44								
	d				18 15											18 45								
Dinas Rhondda	d				18 19											18 49								
Tonypandy	d				18 21											18 51								
Llwynypia	d				18 23											18 53								
Ystrad Rhondda	a				18 26											18 56								
	d				18 29											18 59								
Ton Pentre	d				18 31											19 01								
Treorchy	d				18 34											19 04								
Ynyswen	d				18 37											19 07								
Treherbert	a				18 44											19 14								

When events are being held at the Millenium Stadium, services are subject to alteration. Please check times before travelling.

Table 130

Mondays to Fridays
from 17 September

Bridgend, Barry Island, Barry, Penarth and Cardiff - Coryton, Rhymney, Pontypridd, Merthyr, Aberdare and Treherbert

Network Diagram - see first Page of Table 130

		AW		AW	AW	AW	AW	AW	AW	AW	AW	AW	AW	AW	AW	AW	AW	AW	AW	AW	AW	AW	AW
Bridgend	d				17 42															18 42			
Llantwit Major	d				17 56															18 56			
Rhoose Cardiff Int Airport ✈	d				18 06															19 06			
Barry Island	d								18 25					18 40		18 55							
Barry	d				18 15				18 30					18 45		19 00				19 15			
Barry Docks	d				18 19				18 34					18 49		19 04				19 19			
Cadoxton	d				18 22				18 37					18 52		19 07				19 22			
Dinas Powys	d				18 26				18 41					18 56		19 11				19 26			
Eastbrook	d				18 28				18 43					18 58		19 13				19 28			
Cogan	d				18 30				18 45					19 00		19 15				19 30			
Penarth	d	18 17				18 32					18 47						19 17						
Dingle Road	d	18 19				18 34					18 49						19 19						
Grangetown	d	18 23			18 34	18 38			18 49		18 53			19 04		19 19	19 23			19 34			
Cardiff Central	a	18 29			18 39	18 47			18 57		18 59			19 09		19 24	19 29			19 39			
	d	18 31	18 36	18 36	18 41			18 51			19 01		19 06	19 11		19 26	19 31		19 36	19 41		19 51	
Cardiff Bay	d						18 42			18 54		19 06			19 18			19 30			19 42		19 54
Cardiff Queen Street	a	18 34	18 38		18 44		18 46	18 54		18 58	19 04	19 10	19 09	19 14	19 22	19 29	19 34	19 34		19 44	19 46	19 54	19 58
	d	18 35	18 40		18 50			18 55			19 05		19 10	19 15		19 30	19 35			19 45		19 55	
Heath Low Level	d							19 00														20 00	
Ty Glas	d							19 03														20 03	
Birchgrove	d							19 04														20 04	
Rhiwbina	d							19 06														20 06	
Whitchurch (Cardiff)	d							19 08														20 08	
Coryton	a							19 14														20 14	
Heath High Level	d	18 40									19 10						19 40						
Llanishen	d	18 43									19 13						19 43						
Lisvane & Thornhill	d	18 45									19 15						19 45						
Caerphilly	d	18 51									19a24						19 51						
Aber	d	18 53															19 53						
Llanbradach	d	18 57															19 57						
Ystrad Mynach	d	19 02															20 02						
Hengoed	d	19 05															20 05						
Pengam	d	19 08															20 08						
Gilfach Fargoed	d	19 11															20 11						
Bargoed	a	19 14															20 15						
	d	19 16															20 16						
Brithdir	d	19 20															20 20						
Tir-phil	d	19 23															20 23						
Pontlottyn	d	19 27															20 27						
Rhymney	a	19 35															20 34						
Cathays	d		18 43		18 52								19 13	19 18		19 33				19 48			
Llandaf	d		18 47		18 56								19 17	19 22		19 37				19 52			
Ninian Park	d			18 40															19 40				
Waun-gron Park	d			18 44															19 44				
Fairwater	d			18 46															19 46				
Danescourt	d			18 49															19 49				
Radyr	a		18 50	18 57	18 59								19 20	19 25		19 40			19 57	19 55			
	d		18 50		18 59								19 20	19 25		19 40				19 55			
Taffs Well	d		18 54		19 03								19 24	19 29		19 44				19 59			
Trefforest Estate	d															19 48							
Trefforest	d		19 01		19 10								19 31	19 36		19 52				20 06			
Pontypridd	a		19 04		19 13								19 34	19 39		19 55				20 09			
	d		19 06		19 14								19 36	19 41		19 57				20 11			
Abercynon	d				19 21									19 49		20 04				20 21			
Penrhiwceiber	d				19 27									19 55						20 27			
Mountain Ash	a				19 30									19 59						20 31			
	d				19 34									20 04						20 34			
Fernhill	d				19 37									20 07						20 37			
Cwmbach	d				19 41									20 11						20 41			
Aberdare	a				19 49									20 19						20 49			
Quakers Yard	d															20 09							
Merthyr Vale	a															20 14							
	d															20 14							
Troed Y Rhiw	d															20 18							
Pentre-bach	d															20 22							
Merthyr Tydfil	a															20 31							
Trehafod	d		19 11										19 41										
Porth	a		19 14										19 44										
	d		19 15										19 45										
Dinas Rhondda	d		19 19										19 49										
Tonypandy	d		19 21										19 51										
Llwynypia	d		19 23										19 53										
Ystrad Rhondda	a		19 26										19 56										
	d		19 29										19 59										
Ton Pentre	d		19 31										20 01										
Treorchy	d		19 34										20 04										
Ynyswen	d		19 37										20 07										
Treherbert	a		19 44										20 14										

When events are being held at the Millenium Stadium, services are subject to alteration. Please check times before travelling.

Table 130

Mondays to Fridays
from 17 September

Bridgend, Barry Island, Barry, Penarth and Cardiff - Coryton, Rhymney, Pontypridd, Merthyr, Aberdare and Treherbert

Network Diagram - see first Page of Table 130

		AW	AW	AW	AW	AW	AW	AW	AW	AW	AW	AW	AW	AW	AW	AW	AW	AW	AW	AW	AW	AW
Bridgend	d									19 42												
Llantwit Major	d									19 56												
Rhoose Cardiff Int Airport ✈	d									20 06												
Barry Island	d	19 25				19 55												20 55				
Barry	d	19 30				20 00				20 15								21 00				
Barry Docks	d	19 34				20 04				20 19								21 04				
Cadoxton	d	19 37				20 07				20 22								21 07				
Dinas Powys	d	19 41				20 11				20 26								21 11				
Eastbrook	d	19 43				20 13				20 28								21 13				
Cogan	d	19 45				20 15				20 30								21 15				
Penarth	d		19 47				20 20							20 47								21 20
Dingle Road	d		19 49				20 22							20 49								21 22
Grangetown	d	19 49	19 53			20 19	20 26			20 34				20 53				21 19				21 26
Cardiff Central	a	19 54	19 59			20 24	20 31			20 39				20 59				21 24				21 37
	d	20 01	20 06			20 26	20 31		20 36	20 41		20 51		21 01		21 06		21 26		21 31	21 36	
Cardiff Bay	d			20 06	20 18			20 30			20 42		20 54		21 06		21 18		21 30			
Cardiff Queen Street	a	20 04	20 09	20 10	20 22	20 28	20 34	20 34		20 44	20 46	20 54	20 58	21 04	21 10	21 09	21 22	21 29	21 34	21 34		
	d	20 05	20 10			20 30	20 35			20 45		20 55		21 05		21 10		21 30		21 35		
Heath Low Level	d											21 00										
Ty Glas	d											21 03										
Birchgrove	d											21 04										
Rhiwbina	d											21 06										
Whitchurch (Cardiff)	d											21 08										
Coryton	a											21 14										
Heath High Level	d	20 10					20 40							21 10						21 40		
Llanishen	d	20 13					20 43							21 13						21 43		
Lisvane & Thornhill	d	20 15					20 45							21 15						21 45		
Caerphilly	d	20a25					20 51							21 21						21 51		
Aber	d						20 53							21 23						21 53		
Llanbradach	d						20 57							21 27						21 57		
Ystrad Mynach	d						21 02							21a36						22 02		
Hengoed	d						21 05													22 05		
Pengam	d						21 08													22 08		
Gilfach Fargoed	d						21 11													22 11		
Bargoed	a						21 15													22 15		
	d						21 16													22 16		
Brithdir	d						21 20													22 20		
Tir-phil	d						21 23													22 23		
Pontlottyn	d						21 27													22 27		
Rhymney	a						21 34													22 35		
Cathays	d		20 13			20 33				20 48						21 13		21 33				
Llandaf	d		20 17			20 37				20 52						21 17		21 37				
Ninian Park	d								20 40												21 40	
Waun-gron Park	d								20 44												21 44	
Fairwater	d								20 46												21 46	
Danescourt	d								20 49												21 49	
Radyr	a		20 20			20 39			20 57	20 55						21 20		21 40			21 57	
	d		20 20			20 40				20 55						21 20		21 40				
Taffs Well	d		20 24			20 44				20 59						21 24		21 44				
Trefforest Estate	d					20 48												21 48				
Trefforest	d		20 31			20 52				21 06						21 31		21 52				
Pontypridd	a		20 34			20 55				21 09						21 34		21 55				
	d		20 36			20 57				21 11						21 36		21 57				
Abercynon	d					21 04				21 19								22 04				
Penrhiwceiber	d									21 25												
Mountain Ash	a									21 28												
	d									21 29												
Fernhill	d									21 32												
Cwmbach	d									21 36												
Aberdare	a									21 44												
Quakers Yard	d					21 09												22 09				
Merthyr Vale	a					21 14												22 14				
	d					21 14												22 14				
Troed Y Rhiw	d					21 18												22 18				
Pentre-bach	d					21 22												22 22				
Merthyr Tydfil	a					21 31												22 31				
Trehafod	d		20 41													21 41						
Porth	a		20 44													21 44						
	d		20 45													21 45						
Dinas Rhondda	d		20 49													21 49						
Tonypandy	d		20 51													21 51						
Llwynypia	d		20 53													21 53						
Ystrad Rhondda	a		20 56													21 56						
	d		20 59													21 59						
Ton Pentre	d		21 01													22 01						
Treorchy	d		21 04													22 04						
Ynyswen	d		21 07													22 07						
Treherbert	a		21 14													22 14						

When events are being held at the Millenium Stadium, services are subject to alteration. Please check times before travelling.

Table 130

Mondays to Fridays

from 17 September

Bridgend, Barry Island, Barry, Penarth and Cardiff - Coryton, Rhymney, Pontypridd, Merthyr, Aberdare and Treherbert

Network Diagram - see first Page of Table 130

		AW	AW	AW	AW	AW	AW	AW	AW	AW	AW	AW	AW	AW	AW	AW	AW	AW	AW	AW	AW	AW FX	AW
Bridgend	d	20 42											21 42									22 15	
Llantwit Major	d	20 56											21 56									22 40	
Rhoose Cardiff Int Airport ✈	d	21 06											22 06									22 55	
Barry Island	d									21 55											22 44		
Barry 3	d	21 15								22 00			22 15								22 49	23a10	
Barry Docks	d	21 19								22 04			22 19								22 53		
Cadoxton	d	21 22								22 07			22 22								22 56		
Dinas Powys	d	21 26								22 11			22 26								23 00		
Eastbrook	d	21 28								22 13			22 28								23 03		
Cogan	d	21 30								22 15			22 30								23 05		
Penarth	d				21 47							22 20							22 47				23 26
Dingle Road	d				21 49							22 22							22 49				23 28
Grangetown	d	21 34			21 53					22 19		22 26	22 34						22 53		23 09		23 32
Cardiff Central 7	a	21 39			21 59					22 24		22 33	22 39						23 00		23 14		23 40
	d	21 41			22 01		22 06		22 21	22 26		22 35	22 41		22 46		22 55		23 15		23 26		
Cardiff Bay	d		21 42	21 54		22 06		22 18			22 30			22 42		22 54		23 06		23 18			
Cardiff Queen Street 3	a	21 44	21 46	21 58	22 04	22 10	22 09	22 22	22 24	22 29	22 34	22 38	22 44	22 46	22 49	22 58		23 10	23 18	23 22	23 29		
	d	21 45			22 05		22 10		22 25	22 30		22 39	22 45		22 50				23 19		23 30		
Heath Low Level	d								22 30														
Ty Glas	d								22 33														
Birchgrove	d								22 34														
Rhiwbina	d								22 36														
Whitchurch (Cardiff)	d								22 38														
Coryton	a								22 44														
Heath High Level	d				22 10							22 44							23 24				
Llanishen	d				22 13							22 47							23 27				
Lisvane & Thornhill	d				22 15							22 49							23 29				
Caerphilly 3	d				22a24							22 55							23 35				
Aber	d											22 57							23 37				
Llanbradach	d											23 01							23 41				
Ystrad Mynach 3	d											23 06							23a51				
Hengoed	d											23 09											
Pengam	d											23 12											
Gilfach Fargoed	d											23 15											
Bargoed	a											23 19											
	d											23 20											
Brithdir	d											23 24											
Tir-phil	d											23 27											
Pontlottyn	d											23 31											
Rhymney 3	a											23 38											
Cathays	d	21 48					22 13			22 33			22 48		22 53						23 33		
Llandaf	d	21 52					22 17			22 37			22 52		22 57						23 37		
Ninian Park	d																22 59						
Waun-gron Park	d																23 02						
Fairwater	d																23 04						
Danescourt	d																23 06						
Radyr 3	a	21 55					22 20			22 40			22 55		22 59		23 14				23 40		
	d	21 55					22 20			22 40			22 55		22 59						23 40		
Taffs Well 3	d	21 59					22 24			22 44			22 59		23 03						23 44		
Trefforest Estate	d									22 48													
Trefforest	d	22 06					22 31			22 52			23 06		23 10						23 52		
Pontypridd 3	a	22 09					22 34			22 55			23 09		23 14						23 58		
	d	22 11					22 36			22 57			23 11		23 15								
Abercynon	d	22 19								23 04			23 19										
Penrhiwceiber	d	22 25											23 25										
Mountain Ash	a	22 28											23 28										
	d	22 29											23 34										
Fernhill	d	22 32											23 37										
Cwmbach	d	22 36											23 41										
Aberdare 3	a	22 44											23 49										
Quakers Yard	d									23 09													
Merthyr Vale	a									23 14													
	d									23 14													
Troed Y Rhiw	d									23 18													
Pentre-bach	d									23 22													
Merthyr Tydfil	a									23 31													
Trehafod	d						22 41								23 20								
Porth	a						22 44								23 23								
	d						22 45								23 24								
Dinas Rhondda	d						22 49								23 28								
Tonypandy	d						22 51								23 30								
Llwynypia	d						22 53								23 32								
Ystrad Rhondda	a						22 56								23 35								
	d						22 59								23 38								
Ton Pentre	d						23 01								23 40								
Treorchy	d						23 04								23 43								
Ynyswen	d						23 07								23 46								
Treherbert	a						23 14								23 53								

When events are being held at the Millenium Stadium, services are subject to alteration. Please check times before travelling.

Table 130

Mondays to Fridays

from 17 September

Bridgend, Barry Island, Barry, Penarth and Cardiff - Coryton, Rhymney, Pontypridd, Merthyr, Aberdare and Treherbert

Network Diagram - see first Page of Table 130

		AW FO	AW FX	AW	AW	AW
Bridgend	d	22 42				
Llantwit Major	d	22 56				
Rhoose Cardiff Int Airport ✈	d	23 06				
Barry Island	d					
Barry 3	d	23 15	23 15			
Barry Docks	d	23 19	23 19			
Cadoxton	d	23 22	23 22			
Dinas Powys	d	23 26	23 26			
Eastbrook	d	23 28	23 28			
Cogan	d	23 30	23 30			
Penarth	d					
Dingle Road	d					
Grangetown	d	23 34	23 34			
Cardiff Central 7	a	23 42	23 42			
	d					
Cardiff Bay	d			23 30	23 42	23 54
Cardiff Queen Street 3	a			23 34	23 46	23 58
	d					
Heath Low Level	d					
Ty Glas	d					
Birchgrove	d					
Rhiwbina	d					
Whitchurch (Cardiff)	d					
Coryton	a					
Heath High Level	d					
Llanishen	d					
Lisvane & Thornhill	d					
Caerphilly 3	d					
Aber	d					
Llanbradach	d					
Ystrad Mynach 3	d					
Hengoed	d					
Pengam	d					
Gilfach Fargoed	d					
Bargoed	a					
	d					
Brithdir	d					
Tir-phil	d					
Pontlottyn	d					
Rhymney 3	a					
Cathays	d					
Llandaf	d					
Ninian Park	d					
Waun-gron Park	d					
Fairwater	d					
Danescourt	d					
Radyr 3	a					
	d					
Taffs Well 3	d					
Trefforest Estate	d					
Trefforest	d					
Pontypridd 3	a					
	d					
Abercynon	d					
Penrhiwceiber	d					
Mountain Ash	a					
	d					
Fernhill	d					
Cwmbach	d					
Aberdare 3	a					
Quakers Yard	d					
Merthyr Vale	a					
	d					
Troed Y Rhiw	d					
Pentre-bach	d					
Merthyr Tydfil	a					
Trehafod	d					
Porth	a					
	d					
Dinas Rhondda	d					
Tonypandy	d					
Llwynypia	d					
Ystrad Rhondda	a					
	d					
Ton Pentre	d					
Treorchy	d					
Ynyswen	d					
Treherbert	a					

When events are being held at the Millenium Stadium, services are subject to alteration. Please check times before travelling.

Table 130

Saturdays
until 8 September

Bridgend, Barry Island, Barry, Penarth and Cardiff - Coryton, Rhymney, Pontypridd, Merthyr, Aberdare and Treherbert

Network Diagram - see first Page of Table 130

		AW A	AW A	AW A	AW A	AW A	AW		AW	AW	AW	AW	AW
Bridgend	d												
Llantwit Major	d												
Rhoose Cardiff Int Airport ✈	d												
Barry Island	d	22p45							05 15				05 51
Barry	d	22p49							05 20				05 55
Barry Docks	d	22p53							05 24				05 59
Cadoxton	d	22p56							05 27				06 02
Dinas Powys	d	23p00							05 31				06 06
Eastbrook	d	23p03							05 33				06 08
Cogan	d	23p05							05 35				06 10
Penarth	d											06 02	
Dingle Road	d											06 04	
Grangetown	d	23p09							05 39			06 08	06 14
Cardiff Central	a	23p14							05 44			06 13	06 19
	d	23p26	23p40	23p56	00 05	00 20	05 26		05 46	05 56	06 11	06 15	06 21
Cardiff Bay	d												
Cardiff Queen Street	a	23p29					05 29		05 49	05 59	06 14	06 19	06 24
	d	23p30					05 30		05 50	06 00	06 15	06 20	06 25
Heath Low Level	d												06 30
Ty Glas	d												06 33
Birchgrove	d												06 34
Rhiwbina	d												06 36
Whitchurch (Cardiff)	d												06 38
Coryton	a												06 43
Heath High Level	d				00 12				05 55			06 25	
Llanishen	d				00 15				05 58			06 28	
Lisvane & Thornhill	d				00 17				06 00			06 30	
Caerphilly	d				00 23				06a08			06 36	
Aber	d				00 25							06 38	
Llanbradach	d				00 29							06 42	
Ystrad Mynach	d				00 34							06 47	
Hengoed	d				00 37							06 50	
Pengam	d				00 40							06 53	
Gilfach Fargoed	d				00 43								
Bargoed	a				00 47							07 01	
	d				00 47								
Brithdir	d				00 51								
Tir-phil	d				00 54								
Pontlottyn	d				00 58								
Rhymney	a				01 05								
Cathays	d	23p33	23p45	00 03		00 25	05 33			06 03	06 18		
Llandaf	d	23p37	23p49	00 07		00 29	05 37			06 07	06 22		
Ninian Park	d												
Waun-gron Park	d												
Fairwater	d												
Danescourt	d												
Radyr	a	23p40	23p53	00 10		00 32	05 40			06 10	06 24		
	d	23p41	23p53	00 11		00 33	05 40			06 10	06 24		
Taffs Well	d	23p45	23p57	00 15		00 37	05 44			06 14	06 28		
Trefforest Estate	d	23p49					05 48			06 18			
Trefforest	d	23p53	00 03	00 21		00 43	05 52			06 22	06 35		
Pontypridd	a	23p56	00 06	00 24		00 48	05 55			06 25	06 38		
	d	23p57	00 08	00 26			05 57	06 11		06 27	06 41		
Abercynon	d	00 07	00 17				06 04	06 19		06 34	06 49		
Penrhiwceiber	d		00 23					06 24			06 54		
Mountain Ash	a		00 26					06 28			06 58		
	d		00 28					06 33			07 03		
Fernhill	d		00 30					06 35			07 05		
Cwmbach	d		00 34					06 39			07 09		
Aberdare	a		00 41					06 46			07 16		
Quakers Yard	d	00 11					06 09			06 39			
Merthyr Vale	a	00 16					06 14			06 44			
	d	00 19					06 17			06 47			
Troed Y Rhiw	d	00 22					06 20			06 50			
Pentre-bach	d	00 25					06 23			06 53			
Merthyr Tydfil	a	00 30					06 31			07 01			
Trehafod	d			00 31									
Porth	a			00 34									
	d			00 35									
Dinas Rhondda	d			00 39									
Tonypandy	d			00 41									
Llwynypia	d			00 43									
Ystrad Rhondda	a			00 46									
	d			00 47									
Ton Pentre	d			00 49									
Treorchy	d			00 52									
Ynyswen	d			00 55									
Treherbert	a			01 02									

		AW	AW	AW	AW	AW	AW	AW	AW	AW	AW
Bridgend	d		05 37								
Llantwit Major	d		05 46								
Rhoose Cardiff Int Airport ✈	d		05 56								
Barry Island	d							06 25			
Barry	d		06 15					06 30			
Barry Docks	d		06 19					06 34			
Cadoxton	d		06 22					06 37			
Dinas Powys	d		06 26					06 41			
Eastbrook	d		06 28					06 43			
Cogan	d		06 30					06 45			
Penarth	d				06 32						
Dingle Road	d				06 34						
Grangetown	d		06 34		06 38			06 49			
Cardiff Central	a		06 39		06 44			06 54			
	d	06 26	06 41		06 46	06 51		06 56		07 06	07 06
Cardiff Bay	d			06 42			06 54		07 06		
Cardiff Queen Street	a	06 29	06 44	06 46	06 49	06 54	06 58	06 59	07 10	07 09	
	d	06 30	06 45		06 50	06 55		07 00		07 10	
Heath Low Level	d					07 00					
Ty Glas	d					07 03					
Birchgrove	d					07 04					
Rhiwbina	d					07 06					
Whitchurch (Cardiff)	d					07 08					
Coryton	a					07 13					
Heath High Level	d				06 55						
Llanishen	d				06 58						
Lisvane & Thornhill	d				07 00						
Caerphilly	d				07 06						
Aber	d				07 08						
Llanbradach	d				07 12						
Ystrad Mynach	d				07 17						
Hengoed	d				07 20						
Pengam	d				07 23						
Gilfach Fargoed	d										
Bargoed	a				07 31						
	d										
Brithdir	d										
Tir-phil	d										
Pontlottyn	d										
Rhymney	a										
Cathays	d	06 33	06 48					07 03		07 13	
Llandaf	d	06 37	06 52					07 07		07 17	
Ninian Park	d										07 10
Waun-gron Park	d										07 13
Fairwater	d										07 15
Danescourt	d										07 17
Radyr	a	06 40	06 54					07 10		07 20	07 24
	d	06 40	06 55					07 10		07 20	
Taffs Well	d	06 44	06 59					07 14		07 24	
Trefforest Estate	d	06 48						07 18			
Trefforest	d	06 52	07 06					07 22		07 31	
Pontypridd	a	06 55	07 09					07 25		07 34	
	d	06 57	07 11					07 27		07 36	
Abercynon	d	07 04	07 19					07 34			
Penrhiwceiber	d		07 24								
Mountain Ash	a		07 28								
	d		07 33								
Fernhill	d		07 35								
Cwmbach	d		07 39								
Aberdare	a		07 46								
Quakers Yard	d	07 09						07 39			
Merthyr Vale	a	07 14						07 44			
	d	07 17						07 47			
Troed Y Rhiw	d	07 20						07 50			
Pentre-bach	d	07 23						07 53			
Merthyr Tydfil	a	07 31						08 01			
Trehafod	d									07 41	
Porth	a									07 44	
	d									07 45	
Dinas Rhondda	d									07 49	
Tonypandy	d									07 51	
Llwynypia	d									07 53	
Ystrad Rhondda	a									07 56	
	d									07 59	
Ton Pentre	d									08 01	
Treorchy	d									08 04	
Ynyswen	d									08 07	
Treherbert	a									08 13	

A 11 August

When events are being held at the Millenium Stadium, services are subject to alteration. Please check times before travelling.

Table 130

Saturdays
until 8 September

Bridgend, Barry Island, Barry, Penarth and Cardiff - Coryton, Rhymney, Pontypridd, Merthyr, Aberdare and Treherbert

Network Diagram - see first Page of Table 130

		AW	AW	AW	AW	AW	AW	AW	AW	AW	AW
Bridgend	d										06 42
Llantwit Major	d										06 56
Rhoose Cardiff Int Airport ✈	d										07 06
Barry Island	d					06 55					
Barry	d					07 00					07 15
Barry Docks	d					07 04					07 19
Cadoxton	d					07 07					07 22
Dinas Powys	d					07 11					07 26
Eastbrook	d					07 13					07 28
Cogan	d					07 15					07 30
Penarth	d		07 02				07 17				
Dingle Road	d		07 04				07 19				
Grangetown	d		07 08			07 19	07 23				07 34
Cardiff Central	a		07 14			07 24	07 29				07 39
	d	07 11	07 16		07 21	07 26	07 31		07 36	07 36	07 41
Cardiff Bay	d			07 18				07 30			
Cardiff Queen Street	a	07 14	07 19	07 22	07 24	07 29	07 34	07 34	07 39		07 44
	d	07 15	07 20		07 25	07 30	07 35		07 40		07 45
Heath Low Level	d				07 30						
Ty Glas	d				07 33						
Birchgrove	d				07 34						
Rhiwbina	d				07 36						
Whitchurch (Cardiff)	d				07 38						
Coryton	a				07 43						
Heath High Level	d		07 25				07 40				
Llanishen	d		07 28				07 43				
Lisvane & Thornhill	d		07 30				07 45				
Caerphilly	d		07 36				07 51				
Aber	d		07 38				07 53				
Llanbradach	d		07 42				07 57				
Ystrad Mynach	d		07 47				08 02				
Hengoed	d		07 50				08 05				
Pengam	d		07 53				08 08				
Gilfach Fargoed	d										
Bargoed	a		08 02				08 13				
	d						08 14				
Brithdir	d						08 18				
Tir-phil	d						08 21				
Pontlottyn	d						08 25				
Rhymney	a						08 31				
Cathays	d	07 18				07 33			07 43		07 48
Llandaf	d	07 22				07 37			07 47		07 52
Ninian Park	d									07 40	
Waun-gron Park	d									07 43	
Fairwater	d									07 45	
Danescourt	d									07 47	
Radyr	a	07 25				07 40			07 50	07 54	07 55
	d	07 25				07 40			07 50		07 55
Taffs Well	d	07 29				07 44			07 54		07 59
Trefforest Estate	d					07 48					
Trefforest	d	07 36				07 52			08 01		08 06
Pontypridd	a	07 39				07 55			08 04		08 09
	d	07 41				07 57			08 06		08 11
Abercynon	d	07 49				08 04					08 19
Penrhiwceiber	d	07 54									08 24
Mountain Ash	a	07 58									08 28
	d	08 03									08 33
Fernhill	d	08 05									08 35
Cwmbach	d	08 09									08 39
Aberdare	a	08 16									08 46
Quakers Yard	d					08 09					
Merthyr Vale	a					08 14					
	d					08 17					
Troed Y Rhiw	d					08 20					
Pentre-bach	d					08 23					
Merthyr Tydfil	a					08 31					
Trehafod	d								08 11		
Porth	a								08 14		
	d								08 15		
Dinas Rhondda	d								08 19		
Tonypandy	d								08 21		
Llwynypia	d								08 23		
Ystrad Rhondda	a								08 26		
	d								08 29		
Ton Pentre	d								08 31		
Treorchy	d								08 34		
Ynyswen	d								08 37		
Treherbert	a								08 43		

		AW	AW	AW	AW	AW	AW	AW	AW	AW	AW	AW	AW
Bridgend	d												
Llantwit Major	d												
Rhoose Cardiff Int Airport ✈	d												
Barry Island	d					07 25					07 40		
Barry	d					07 30					07 45		
Barry Docks	d					07 34					07 49		
Cadoxton	d					07 37					07 52		
Dinas Powys	d					07 41					07 56		
Eastbrook	d					07 43					07 58		
Cogan	d					07 45					08 00		
Penarth	d		07 32				07 47					08 02	
Dingle Road	d		07 34				07 49					08 04	
Grangetown	d		07 38			07 49	07 53				08 04	08 08	
Cardiff Central	a		07 44			07 54	07 59				08 09	08 14	
	d		07 46	07 51		07 56	08 01		08 06	08 06	08 11	08 16	
Cardiff Bay	d	07 42			07 54			08 06					08 18
Cardiff Queen Street	a	07 46	07 49	07 54	07 58	07 59	08 04	08 10	08 09		08 14	08 19	08 22
	d		07 50	07 55		08 00	08 05		08 10		08 15	08 20	
Heath Low Level	d			08 00									
Ty Glas	d			08 03									
Birchgrove	d			08 04									
Rhiwbina	d			08 06									
Whitchurch (Cardiff)	d			08 08									
Coryton	a			08 13									
Heath High Level	d		07 55				08 10					08 25	
Llanishen	d		07 58				08 13					08 28	
Lisvane & Thornhill	d		08 00				08 15					08 30	
Caerphilly	d		08 06				08 21					08 36	
Aber	d		08 08				08 23					08 38	
Llanbradach	d		08 12				08 27					08 42	
Ystrad Mynach	d		08 17				08 32					08 47	
Hengoed	d		08 20				08 35					08 50	
Pengam	d		08 23				08 38					08 53	
Gilfach Fargoed	d						08 41						
Bargoed	a		08 31				08 48					08 58	
	d											08 59	
Brithdir	d											09 03	
Tir-phil	d											09 06	
Pontlottyn	d											09 10	
Rhymney	a											09 16	
Cathays	d					08 03			08 13		08 18		
Llandaf	d					08 07			08 17		08 22		
Ninian Park	d									08 10			
Waun-gron Park	d									08 13			
Fairwater	d									08 15			
Danescourt	d									08 17			
Radyr	a					08 10			08 20	08 24	08 25		
	d					08 10			08 20		08 25		
Taffs Well	d					08 14			08 24		08 29		
Trefforest Estate	d					08 18							
Trefforest	d					08 22			08 31		08 36		
Pontypridd	a					08 25			08 34		08 39		
	d					08 27			08 36		08 41		
Abercynon	d					08 34					08 49		
Penrhiwceiber	d										08 54		
Mountain Ash	a										08 58		
	d										09 03		
Fernhill	d										09 05		
Cwmbach	d										09 09		
Aberdare	a										09 16		
Quakers Yard	d					08 39							
Merthyr Vale	a					08 44							
	d					08 47							
Troed Y Rhiw	d					08 50							
Pentre-bach	d					08 53							
Merthyr Tydfil	a					09 01							
Trehafod	d								08 41				
Porth	a								08 44				
	d								08 45				
Dinas Rhondda	d								08 49				
Tonypandy	d								08 51				
Llwynypia	d								08 53				
Ystrad Rhondda	a								08 56				
	d								08 59				
Ton Pentre	d								09 01				
Treorchy	d								09 04				
Ynyswen	d								09 07				
Treherbert	a								09 13				

When events are being held at the Millenium Stadium, services are subject to alteration. Please check times before travelling.

Table 130

Saturdays
until 8 September

Bridgend, Barry Island, Barry, Penarth and Cardiff - Coryton, Rhymney, Pontypridd, Merthyr, Aberdare and Treherbert

Network Diagram - see first Page of Table 130

		AW	AW	AW	AW	AW	AW	AW	AW	AW	AW	AW	AW	AW	AW	AW	AW	AW	AW	AW	AW	AW
Bridgend	d							07 42														
Llantwit Major	d							07 56														
Rhoose Cardiff Int Airport ✈	d							08 06														
Barry Island	d		07 55										08 25					08 40				08 55
Barry 3	d		08 00					08 15					08 30					08 45				09 00
Barry Docks	d		08 04					08 19					08 34					08 49				09 04
Cadoxton	d		08 07					08 22					08 37					08 52				09 07
Dinas Powys	d		08 11					08 26					08 41					08 56				09 11
Eastbrook	d		08 13					08 28					08 43					08 58				09 13
Cogan	d		08 15					08 30					08 45					09 00				09 15
Penarth	d			08 17						08 32				08 47								
Dingle Road	d			08 19						08 34				08 49								
Grangetown	d		08 19	08 23				08 34		08 38			08 49	08 53				09 04				09 19
Cardiff Central 7	a		08 24	08 29				08 39		08 44			08 54	08 59				09 09				09 24
	d	08 21	08 26	08 31		08 36	08 36	08 41		08 46	08 51		08 56	09 01		09 06	09 06	09 11	09 16		09 21	09 26
Cardiff Bay	d				08 30				08 42			08 54			09 06					09 18		
Cardiff Queen Street 3	a	08 24	08 29	08 34	08 34	08 39		08 44	08 46	08 49	08 54	08 58	08 59	09 04	09 10	09 09		09 14	09 19	09 22	09 24	09 29
	d	08 25	08 30	08 35		08 40		08 45		08 50	08 55		09 00	09 05		09 10		09 15	09 20		09 25	09 30
Heath Low Level	d	08 30									09 00										09 30	
Ty Glas	d	08 33									09 03										09 33	
Birchgrove	d	08 34									09 04										09 34	
Rhiwbina	d	08 36									09 06										09 36	
Whitchurch (Cardiff)	d	08 38									09 08										09 38	
Coryton	a	08 43									09 13										09 43	
Heath High Level	d			08 40						08 55				09 10					09 25			
Llanishen	d			08 43						08 58				09 13					09 28			
Lisvane & Thornhill	d			08 45						09 00				09 15					09 30			
Caerphilly 3	d			08 51						09 06				09 21					09 36			
Aber	d			08 53						09 08				09 23					09 38			
Llanbradach	d			08 57						09 12				09 27					09 42			
Ystrad Mynach 3	d			09 02						09 17				09 32					09 47			
Hengoed	d			09 05						09 20				09 35					09 50			
Pengam	d			09 08						09 23				09 38					09 53			
Gilfach Fargoed	d													09 41								
Bargoed	a			09 16						09 31				09 48					09 58			
	d																		09 59			
Brithdir	d																		10 03			
Tir-phil	d																		10 06			
Pontlottyn	d																		10 10			
Rhymney 3	a																		10 16			
Cathays	d		08 33			08 43		08 48					09 03			09 13		09 18				09 33
Llandaf	d		08 37			08 47		08 52					09 07			09 17		09 22				09 37
Ninian Park	d						08 40										09 10					
Waun-gron Park	d						08 43										09 13					
Fairwater	d						08 45										09 15					
Danescourt	d						08 47										09 17					
Radyr 3	a		08 40			08 50	08 54	08 55					09 10			09 20	09 24	09 25				09 40
	d		08 40			08 50		08 55					09 10			09 20		09 25				09 40
Taffs Well 3	d		08 44			08 54		08 59					09 14			09 24		09 29				09 44
Trefforest Estate	d		08 48										09 18									09 48
Trefforest	d		08 52			09 01		09 06					09 22			09 31		09 36				09 52
Pontypridd 3	a		08 55			09 04		09 09					09 25			09 34		09 39				09 55
	d		08 57			09 06		09 11					09 27			09 36		09 41				09 57
Abercynon	d		09 04					09 19					09 34					09 49				10 04
Penrhiwceiber	d							09 24										09 54				
Mountain Ash	a							09 28										09 58				
	d							09 33										10 03				
Fernhill	d							09 35										10 05				
Cwmbach	d							09 39										10 09				
Aberdare 3	a							09 46										10 16				
Quakers Yard	d		09 09										09 39									10 09
Merthyr Vale	a		09 14										09 44									10 14
	d		09 17										09 47									10 17
Troed Y Rhiw	d		09 20										09 50									10 20
Pentre-bach	d		09 23										09 53									10 23
Merthyr Tydfil	a		09 31										10 01									10 31
Trehafod	d					09 11										09 41						
Porth	a					09 14										09 44						
	d					09 15										09 45						
Dinas Rhondda	d					09 19										09 49						
Tonypandy	d					09 21										09 51						
Llwynypia	d					09 23										09 53						
Ystrad Rhondda	a					09 26										09 56						
	d					09 29										09 59						
Ton Pentre	d					09 31										10 01						
Treorchy	d					09 34										10 04						
Ynyswen	d					09 37										10 07						
Treherbert	a					09 43										10 13						

When events are being held at the Millenium Stadium, services are subject to alteration. Please check times before travelling.

Table 130

Saturdays
until 8 September

Bridgend, Barry Island, Barry, Penarth and Cardiff - Coryton, Rhymney, Pontypridd, Merthyr, Aberdare and Treherbert

Network Diagram - see first Page of Table 130

		AW	AW	AW	AW	AW	AW	AW	AW	AW	AW	AW	AW	AW	AW	AW	AW	AW	AW	AW	AW	AW	AW
Bridgend	d					08 42																	
Llantwit Major	d					08 56																	
Rhoose Cardiff Int Airport ✈	d					09 06																	
Barry Island	d										09 25						09 40				09 55		
Barry 3	d					09 15					09 30						09 45				10 00		
Barry Docks	d					09 19					09 34						09 49				10 04		
Cadoxton	d					09 22					09 37						09 52				10 07		
Dinas Powys	d					09 26					09 41						09 56				10 11		
Eastbrook	d					09 28					09 43						09 58				10 13		
Cogan	d					09 30					09 45						10 00				10 15		
Penarth	d	09 17						09 32				09 47						10 02				10 17	
Dingle Road	d	09 19						09 34				09 49						10 04				10 19	
Grangetown	d	09 23				09 34		09 38			09 49	09 53					10 04	10 08			10 19	10 23	
Cardiff Central 7	a	09 29				09 39		09 44			09 54	09 59					10 09	10 14			10 24	10 29	
	d	09 31		09 36	09 36	09 41		09 46	09 51		09 56	10 01		10 06	10 06		10 11	10 16		10 21	10 26	10 31	
Cardiff Bay	d		09 30				09 42			09 54			10 06						10 18				10 30
Cardiff Queen Street 3	a	09 34	09 34	09 39		09 44	09 46	09 49	09 54	09 58	09 59	10 04	10 10	10 09			10 14	10 19	10 22	10 24	10 29	10 34	10 34
	d	09 35		09 40		09 45		09 50	09 55		10 00	10 05		10 10			10 15	10 20		10 25	10 30	10 35	
Heath Low Level	d								10 00											10 30			
Ty Glas	d								10 03											10 33			
Birchgrove	d								10 04											10 34			
Rhiwbina	d								10 06											10 36			
Whitchurch (Cardiff)	d								10 08											10 38			
Coryton	a								10 13											10 43			
Heath High Level	d	09 40						09 55				10 10						10 25				10 40	
Llanishen	d	09 43						09 58				10 13						10 28				10 43	
Lisvane & Thornhill	d	09 45						10 00				10 15						10 30				10 45	
Caerphilly 3	d	09 51						10 06				10 21						10 36				10 51	
Aber	d	09 53						10 08				10 23						10 38				10 53	
Llanbradach	d	09 57						10 12				10 27						10 42				10 57	
Ystrad Mynach 3	d	10 02						10 17				10 32						10 47				11 02	
Hengoed	d	10 05						10 20				10 35						10 50				11 05	
Pengam	d	10 08						10 23				10 38						10 53				11 08	
Gilfach Fargoed	d											10 41											
Bargoed	a	10 16						10 31				10 48						10 58				11 16	
	d																	10 59					
Brithdir	d																	11 03					
Tir-phil	d																	11 06					
Pontlottyn	d																	11 10					
Rhymney 3	a																	11 16					
Cathays	d			09 43		09 48					10 03			10 13			10 18				10 33		
Llandaf	d			09 47		09 52					10 07			10 17			10 22				10 37		
Ninian Park	d				09 40										10 10								
Waun-gron Park	d				09 43										10 13								
Fairwater	d				09 45										10 15								
Danescourt	d				09 47										10 17								
Radyr 3	a			09 50	09 54	09 55					10 10			10 20	10 24		10 25				10 40		
	d			09 50		09 55					10 10			10 20			10 25				10 40		
Taffs Well 3	d			09 54		09 59					10 14			10 24			10 29				10 44		
Trefforest Estate	d																				10 48		
Trefforest	d			10 01		10 06					10 22			10 31			10 36				10 52		
Pontypridd 3	a			10 04		10 09					10 30			10 34			10 39				10 55		
	d			10 06		10 11								10 36		10 35	10 41				10 57		
Abercynon	d					10 19										10 41	10 49				11 04		
Penrhiwceiber	d					10 24											10 54						
Mountain Ash	a					10 28											10 58						
	d					10 33											11 03						
Fernhill	d					10 35											11 05						
Cwmbach	d					10 39											11 09						
Aberdare 3	a					10 46											11 16						
Quakers Yard	d															10 45					11 09		
Merthyr Vale	a															10 50					11 14		
	d															10 52					11 17		
Troed Y Rhiw	d															10 55					11 20		
Pentre-bach	d															10 58					11 23		
Merthyr Tydfil	a															11 06					11 31		
Trehafod	d			10 11										10 41									
Porth	a			10 14										10 44									
	d			10 15										10 45									
Dinas Rhondda	d			10 19										10 49									
Tonypandy	d			10 21										10 51									
Llwynypia	d			10 23										10 53									
Ystrad Rhondda	a			10 26										10 56									
	d			10 29										10 59									
Ton Pentre	d			10 31										11 01									
Treorchy	d			10 34										11 04									
Ynyswen	d			10 37										11 07									
Treherbert	a			10 43										11 13									

When events are being held at the Millenium Stadium, services are subject to alteration. Please check times before travelling.

Table 130

Saturdays until 8 September

Bridgend, Barry Island, Barry, Penarth and Cardiff - Coryton, Rhymney, Pontypridd, Merthyr, Aberdare and Treherbert

Network Diagram - see first Page of Table 130

		AW	AW	AW	AW	AW	AW	AW	AW	AW	AW	AW	AW	AW	AW	AW	AW	AW	AW	AW	AW	AW
Bridgend	d			09 42																		
Llantwit Major	d			09 56																		
Rhoose Cardiff Int Airport ✈	d			10 06																		
Barry Island	d									10 25					10 40				10 55			
Barry 3	d			10 15						10 30					10 45				11 00			
Barry Docks	d			10 19						10 34					10 49				11 04			
Cadoxton	d			10 22						10 37					10 52				11 07			
Dinas Powys	d			10 26						10 41					10 56				11 11			
Eastbrook	d			10 28						10 43					10 58				11 13			
Cogan	d			10 30						10 45					11 00				11 15			
Penarth	d					10 32						10 47				11 02				11 17		
Dingle Road	d					10 34						10 49				11 04				11 19		
Grangetown	d			10 34		10 38				10 49		10 53			11 04	11 08			11 19	11 23		
Cardiff Central 7	a			10 42		10 44				10 54		10 59			11 09	11 14			11 24	11 29		
	d	10 36	10 36			10 46	10 51		10 51	10 56		11 01	11 06		11 11	11 16		11 21	11 26	11 31		11 36
Cardiff Bay	d				10 42			10 54						11 06			11 18				11 30	
Cardiff Queen Street 3	a	10 39			10 46	10 49	10 54	10 58		10 59		11 04		11 10	11 14	11 19	11 22	11 24	11 29	11 34	11 34	11 39
	d	10 40				10 50	10 55			11 00		11 05			11 15	11 20		11 25	11 30	11 35		11 40
Heath Low Level	d						11 00											11 30				
Ty Glas	d						11 03											11 33				
Birchgrove	d						11 04											11 34				
Rhiwbina	d						11 06											11 36				
Whitchurch (Cardiff)	d						11 08											11 38				
Coryton	a						11 13											11 43				
Heath High Level	d					10 55						11 10				11 25				11 40		
Llanishen	d					10 58						11 13				11 28				11 43		
Lisvane & Thornhill	d					11 00						11 15				11 30				11 45		
Caerphilly 3	d					11 06						11 21				11 36				11 51		
Aber	d					11 08						11 23				11 38				11 53		
Llanbradach	d					11 12						11 27				11 42				11 57		
Ystrad Mynach 3	d					11 17						11 32				11 47				12 02		
Hengoed	d					11 20						11 35				11 50				12 05		
Pengam	d					11 23						11 38				11 53				12 08		
Gilfach Fargoed	d											11 41										
Bargoed	a					11 31						11 48				11 58				12 16		
	d															11 59						
Brithdir	d															12 03						
Tir-phil	d															12 06						
Pontlottyn	d															12 10						
Rhymney 3	a															12 16						
Cathays	d	10 43								11 03					11 18				11 33			11 43
Llandaf	d	10 47								11 07					11 22				11 37			11 47
Ninian Park	d		10 40										11 10									
Waun-gron Park	d		10 43										11 13									
Fairwater	d		10 45										11 15									
Danescourt	d		10 47									←	11 17									
Radyr 3	a	10 50	10 54						11 02	11 10	11 02		11 24		11 25				11 40			11 50
	d	10 50							11 20	11 10	11 20				11 25				11 40			11 50
Taffs Well 3	d	10 54							→	11 14	11 24				11 29				11 44			11 54
Trefforest Estate	d									11 18									11 48			
Trefforest	d	11 01								11 22	11 31				11 36				11 52			12 01
Pontypridd 3	a	11 04								11 25	11 34				11 39				11 55			12 04
	d	11 06								11 27	11 36				11 41				11 57			12 06
Abercynon	d									11 34					11 49				12 04			
Penrhiwceiber	d														11 54							
Mountain Ash	a														11 58							
	d														12 03							
Fernhill	d														12 05							
Cwmbach	d														12 09							
Aberdare 3	a														12 16							
Quakers Yard	d									11 39									12 09			
Merthyr Vale	a									11 44									12 14			
	d									11 47									12 17			
Troed Y Rhiw	d									11 50									12 20			
Pentre-bach	d									11 53									12 23			
Merthyr Tydfil	a									12 01									12 31			
Trehafod	d	11 11									11 41											12 11
Porth	a	11 14									11 44											12 14
	d	11 15									11 45											12 15
Dinas Rhondda	d	11 19									11 49											12 19
Tonypandy	d	11 21									11 51											12 21
Llwynypia	d	11 23									11 53											12 23
Ystrad Rhondda	a	11 26									11 56											12 26
	d	11 29									11 59											12 29
Ton Pentre	d	11 31									12 01											12 31
Treorchy	d	11 34									12 04											12 34
Ynyswen	d	11 37									12 07											12 37
Treherbert	a	11 43									12 13											12 43

When events are being held at the Millenium Stadium, services are subject to alteration. Please check times before travelling.

Table 130

Saturdays until 8 September

Bridgend, Barry Island, Barry, Penarth and Cardiff - Coryton, Rhymney, Pontypridd, Merthyr, Aberdare and Treherbert

Network Diagram - see first Page of Table 130

		AW	AW	AW	AW	AW	AW	AW	AW	AW	AW	AW	AW	AW	AW	AW	AW	AW	AW	AW	AW	AW	AW
Bridgend	d		10 42																			11 42	
Llantwit Major	d		10 56																			11 56	
Rhoose Cardiff Int Airport ✈	d		11 06																			12 06	
Barry Island	d							11 25					11 40				11 55						
Barry 3	d		11 15					11 30					11 45				12 00					12 15	
Barry Docks	d		11 19					11 34					11 49				12 04					12 19	
Cadoxton	d		11 22					11 37					11 52				12 07					12 22	
Dinas Powys	d		11 26					11 41					11 56				12 11					12 26	
Eastbrook	d		11 28					11 43					11 58				12 13					12 28	
Cogan	d		11 30					11 45					12 00				12 15					12 30	
Penarth	d				11 32				11 47					12 02				12 17					
Dingle Road	d				11 34				11 49					12 04				12 19					
Grangetown	d		11 34		11 38			11 49	11 53				12 04	12 08			12 19	12 23				12 34	
Cardiff Central 7	a		11 39		11 44			11 54	11 59				12 09	12 14			12 24	12 29				12 39	
	d	11 36	11 41		11 46	11 51		11 56	12 01		12 06	12 06	12 11	12 16		12 21	12 26	12 31		12 36	12 36	12 41	
Cardiff Bay	d			11 42			11 54			12 06					12 18				12 30				12 42
Cardiff Queen Street 3	a		11 44	11 46	11 49	11 54	11 58	11 59	12 04	12 10	12 09		12 14	12 19	12 22	12 24	12 29	12 34	12 34	12 39		12 44	12 46
	d		11 45		11 50	11 55		12 00	12 05		12 10		12 15	12 20		12 25	12 30	12 35		12 40		12 45	
Heath Low Level	d					12 00										12 30							
Ty Glas	d					12 03										12 33							
Birchgrove	d					12 04										12 34							
Rhiwbina	d					12 06										12 36							
Whitchurch (Cardiff)	d					12 08										12 38							
Coryton	a					12 13										12 43							
Heath High Level	d				11 55				12 10					12 25				12 40					
Llanishen	d				11 58				12 13					12 28				12 43					
Lisvane & Thornhill	d				12 00				12 15					12 30				12 45					
Caerphilly 3	d				12 06				12 21					12 36				12 51					
Aber	d				12 08				12 23					12 38				12 53					
Llanbradach	d				12 12				12 27					12 42				12 57					
Ystrad Mynach 3	d				12 17				12 32					12 47				13 02					
Hengoed	d				12 20				12 35					12 50				13 05					
Pengam	d				12 23				12 38					12 53				13 08					
Gilfach Fargoed	d								12 41														
Bargoed	a				12 31				12 48					12 58				13 16					
	d													12 59									
Brithdir	d													13 03									
Tir-phil	d													13 06									
Pontlottyn	d													13 10									
Rhymney 3	a													13 16									
Cathays	d		11 48					12 03			12 13		12 18				12 33			12 43		12 48	
Llandaf	d		11 52					12 07			12 17		12 22				12 37			12 47		12 52	
Ninian Park	d	11 40										12 10									12 40		
Waun-gron Park	d	11 43										12 13									12 43		
Fairwater	d	11 45										12 15									12 45		
Danescourt	d	11 47										12 17									12 47		
Radyr 3	a	11 54	11 55					12 10			12 20	12 24	12 25				12 40			12 50	12 54	12 55	
	d		11 55					12 10			12 20		12 25				12 40			12 50		12 55	
Taffs Well 3	d		11 59					12 14			12 24		12 29				12 44			12 54		12 59	
Trefforest Estate	d							12 18									12 48						
Trefforest	d		12 06					12 22			12 31		12 36				12 52			13 01		13 06	
Pontypridd 3	a		12 09					12 25			12 34		12 42				12 55			13 04		13 09	
	d		12 11					12 27			12 36						12 57			13 06		13 11	
Abercynon	d		12 19					12 34									13 04					13 19	
Penrhiwceiber	d		12 24																			13 24	
Mountain Ash	a		12 28																			13 28	
	d		12 33																			13 33	
Fernhill	d		12 35																			13 35	
Cwmbach	d		12 39																			13 39	
Aberdare 3	a		12 46																			13 46	
Quakers Yard	d							12 39									13 09						
Merthyr Vale	a							12 44									13 14						
	d							12 47									13 17						
Troed Y Rhiw	d							12 50									13 20						
Pentre-bach	d							12 53									13 23						
Merthyr Tydfil	a							13 01									13 31						
Trehafod	d										12 41									13 11			
Porth	a										12 44									13 14			
	d										12 45									13 15			
Dinas Rhondda	d										12 49									13 19			
Tonypandy	d										12 51									13 21			
Llwynypia	d										12 53									13 23			
Ystrad Rhondda	a										12 56									13 26			
	d										12 59									13 29			
Ton Pentre	d										13 01									13 31			
Treorchy	d										13 04									13 34			
Ynyswen	d										13 07									13 37			
Treherbert	a										13 13									13 43			

When events are being held at the Millenium Stadium, services are subject to alteration. Please check times before travelling.

Saturdays until 8 September

Bridgend, Barry Island, Barry, Penarth and Cardiff - Coryton, Rhymney, Pontypridd, Merthyr, Aberdare and Treherbert

Network Diagram - see first Page of Table 130

Station		AW	AW	AW	AW	AW		AW	AW	AW	AW	AW	AW	AW	AW	AW		AW	AW	AW	AW	AW	AW	AW	AW
Bridgend	d																				12 42				
Llantwit Major	d																				12 56				
Rhoose Cardiff Int Airport ✈	d																				13 06				
Barry Island	d				12 25						12 40				12 55										
Barry ■3	d				12 30						12 45				13 00						13 15				
Barry Docks	d				12 34						12 49				13 04						13 19				
Cadoxton	d				12 37						12 52				13 07						13 22				
Dinas Powys	d				12 41						12 56				13 11						13 26				
Eastbrook	d				12 43						12 58				13 13						13 28				
Cogan	d				12 45						13 00				13 15						13 30				
Penarth	d	12 32				12 47						13 02				13 17							13 32		
Dingle Road	d	12 34				12 49						13 04				13 19							13 34		
Grangetown	d	12 38			12 49	12 53					13 04	13 08			13 19	13 23					13 34		13 38		
Cardiff Central ■7	a	12 44			12 54	12 59					13 09	13 14			13 24	13 29					13 39		13 44		
	d	12 46	12 51		12 56	13 01			13 06	13 06	13 11	13 16		13 21	13 26	13 31			13 36	13 36	13 41		13 46	13 51	
Cardiff Bay	d			12 54				13 06					13 18					13 30				13 42			13 54
Cardiff Queen Street ■3	a	12 49	12 54	12 58	12 59	13 04		13 10	13 09		13 14	13 19	13 22	13 24	13 29	13 34		13 34	13 39		13 44	13 46	13 49	13 54	13 58
	d	12 50	12 55		13 00	13 05			13 10		13 15	13 20		13 25	13 30	13 35			13 40		13 45		13 50	13 55	
Heath Low Level	d		13 00											13 30										14 00	
Ty Glas	d		13 03											13 33										14 03	
Birchgrove	d		13 04											13 34										14 04	
Rhiwbina	d		13 06											13 36										14 06	
Whitchurch (Cardiff)	d		13 08											13 38										14 08	
Coryton	a		13 13											13 43										14 13	
Heath High Level	d	12 55				13 10						13 25				13 40							13 55		
Llanishen	d	12 58				13 13						13 28				13 43							13 58		
Lisvane & Thornhill	d	13 00				13 15						13 30				13 45							14 00		
Caerphilly ■3	d	13 06				13 21						13 36				13 51							14 06		
Aber	d	13 08				13 23						13 38				13 53							14 08		
Llanbradach	d	13 12				13 27						13 42				13 57							14 12		
Ystrad Mynach ■3	d	13 17				13 32						13 47				14 02							14 17		
Hengoed	d	13 20				13 35						13 50				14 05							14 20		
Pengam	d	13 23				13 38						13 53				14 08							14 23		
Gilfach Fargoed	d					13 41																			
Bargoed	a	13 31				13 48						13 58				14 16							14 31		
	d											13 59													
Brithdir	d											14 03													
Tir-phil	d											14 06													
Pontlottyn	d											14 10													
Rhymney ■3	a											14 16													
Cathays	d				13 03				13 13		13 18				13 33				13 43		13 48				
Llandaf	d				13 07				13 17		13 22				13 37				13 47		13 52				
Ninian Park	d									13 10										13 40					
Waun-gron Park	d									13 13										13 43					
Fairwater	d									13 15										13 45					
Danescourt	d									13 17										13 47					
Radyr ■3	a				13 10				13 20	13 24	13 25				13 40				13 50	13 54	13 55				
	d				13 10				13 20		13 25				13 40				13 50		13 55				
Taffs Well ■3	d				13 14				13 24		13 29				13 44				13 54		13 59				
Trefforest Estate	d				13 18										13 48										
Trefforest	d				13 22				13 31		13 36				13 52				14 01		14 06				
Pontypridd ■3	a				13 25				13 34		13 39				13 55				14 04		14 09				
	d				13 27				13 36		13 41				13 57				14 06		14 11				
Abercynon	d				13 34						13 49				14 04						14 19				
Penrhiwceiber	d										13 54										14 24				
Mountain Ash	a										13 58										14 28				
	d										14 03										14 33				
Fernhill	d										14 05										14 35				
Cwmbach	d										14 09										14 39				
Aberdare ■3	a										14 16										14 46				
Quakers Yard	d				13 39										14 09										
Merthyr Vale	a				13 44										14 14										
	d				13 47										14 17										
Troed Y Rhiw	d				13 50										14 20										
Pentre-bach	d				13 53										14 23										
Merthyr Tydfil	a				14 01										14 31										
Trehafod	d								13 41										14 11						
Porth	a								13 44										14 14						
	d								13 45										14 15						
Dinas Rhondda	d								13 49										14 19						
Tonypandy	d								13 51										14 21						
Llwynypia	d								13 53										14 23						
Ystrad Rhondda	a								13 56										14 26						
	d								13 59										14 29						
Ton Pentre	d								14 01										14 31						
Treorchy	d								14 04										14 34						
Ynyswen	d								14 07										14 37						
Treherbert	a								14 13										14 43						

When events are being held at the Millenium Stadium, services are subject to alteration. Please check times before travelling.

Saturdays until 8 September

Bridgend, Barry Island, Barry, Penarth and Cardiff - Coryton, Rhymney, Pontypridd, Merthyr, Aberdare and Treherbert

Network Diagram - see first Page of Table 130

Station		AW		AW	AW	AW	AW	AW	AW	AW	AW	AW		AW	AW	AW	AW	AW	AW	AW	AW	AW		AW	AW
Bridgend	d																	13 42							
Llantwit Major	d																	13 56							
Rhoose Cardiff Int Airport ✈	d																	14 06							
Barry Island	d	13 25						13 40				13 55													14 25
Barry ■3	d	13 30						13 45				14 00						14 15							14 30
Barry Docks	d	13 34						13 49				14 04						14 19							14 34
Cadoxton	d	13 37						13 52				14 07						14 22							14 37
Dinas Powys	d	13 41						13 56				14 11						14 26							14 41
Eastbrook	d	13 43						13 58				14 13						14 28							14 43
Cogan	d	13 45						14 00				14 15						14 30							14 45
Penarth	d			13 47					14 02					14 17						14 32					
Dingle Road	d			13 49					14 04					14 19						14 34					
Grangetown	d	13 49		13 53				14 04	14 08			14 19		14 23				14 34		14 38					14 49
Cardiff Central ■7	a	13 54		13 59				14 09	14 14			14 24		14 29				14 39		14 44					14 54
	d	13 56		14 01		14 06	14 06	14 11	14 16		14 21	14 26		14 31		14 36	14 36	14 41		14 46	14 51			14 51	14 56
Cardiff Bay	d				14 06					14 18					14 30				14 42			14 54			
Cardiff Queen Street ■3	a	13 59		14 04	14 10	14 09		14 14	14 19	14 22	14 24	14 29		14 34	14 34	14 39		14 44	14 46	14 49	14 54	14 58			14 59
	d	14 00		14 05		14 10		14 15	14 20		14 25	14 30		14 35		14 40		14 45		14 50	14 55				15 00
Heath Low Level	d										14 30										15 00				
Ty Glas	d										14 33										15 03				
Birchgrove	d										14 34										15 04				
Rhiwbina	d										14 36										15 06				
Whitchurch (Cardiff)	d										14 38										15 08				
Coryton	a										14 43										15 13				
Heath High Level	d			14 10					14 25					14 40						14 55					
Llanishen	d			14 13					14 28					14 43						14 58					
Lisvane & Thornhill	d			14 15					14 30					14 45						15 00					
Caerphilly ■3	d			14 21					14 36					14 51						15 06					
Aber	d			14 23					14 38					14 53						15 08					
Llanbradach	d			14 27					14 42					14 57						15 12					
Ystrad Mynach ■3	d			14 32					14 47					15 02						15 17					
Hengoed	d			14 35					14 50					15 05						15 20					
Pengam	d			14 38					14 53					15 08						15 23					
Gilfach Fargoed	d			14 41																					
Bargoed	a			14 48					14 58					15 16						15 31					
	d								14 59																
Brithdir	d								15 03																
Tir-phil	d								15 06																
Pontlottyn	d								15 10																
Rhymney ■3	a								15 16																
Cathays	d	14 03				14 13		14 18				14 33				14 43		14 48							15 03
Llandaf	d	14 07				14 17		14 22				14 37				14 47		14 52							15 07
Ninian Park	d						14 10										14 40								
Waun-gron Park	d						14 13										14 43								
Fairwater	d						14 15										14 45								
Danescourt	d						14 17										14 47								
Radyr ■3	a	14 10				14 20	14 24	14 25				14 40				14 50	14 54	14 55						15 08	15 10
	d	14 10				14 20		14 25				14 40				14 50		14 55						15 20	15 10
Taffs Well ■3	d	14 14				14 24		14 29				14 44				14 54		14 59						→	15 14
Trefforest Estate	d	14 18										14 48													15 18
Trefforest	d	14 22				14 31		14 36				14 52				15 01		15 06							15 22
Pontypridd ■3	a	14 25				14 34		14 39				14 55				15 04		15 09							15 25
	d	14 27				14 36		14 41				14 57				15 06		15 11							15 27
Abercynon	d	14 34						14 49				15 04						15 19							15 34
Penrhiwceiber	d							14 54										15 24							
Mountain Ash	a							14 58										15 28							
	d							15 03										15 33							
Fernhill	d							15 05										15 35							
Cwmbach	d							15 09										15 39							
Aberdare ■3	a							15 16										15 46							
Quakers Yard	d	14 39										15 09													15 39
Merthyr Vale	a	14 44										15 14													15 44
	d	14 47										15 17													15 47
Troed Y Rhiw	d	14 50										15 20													15 50
Pentre-bach	d	14 53										15 23													15 53
Merthyr Tydfil	a	15 01										15 31													16 01
Trehafod	d					14 41										15 11									
Porth	a					14 44										15 14									
	d					14 45										15 15									
Dinas Rhondda	d					14 49										15 19									
Tonypandy	d					14 51										15 21									
Llwynypia	d					14 53										15 23									
Ystrad Rhondda	a					14 56										15 26									
	d					14 59										15 29									
Ton Pentre	d					15 01										15 31									
Treorchy	d					15 04										15 34									
Ynyswen	d					15 07										15 37									
Treherbert	a					15 13										15 43									

When events are being held at the Millenium Stadium, services are subject to alteration. Please check times before travelling.

Table 130

Saturdays
until 8 September

Bridgend, Barry Island, Barry, Penarth and Cardiff - Coryton, Rhymney, Pontypridd, Merthyr, Aberdare and Treherbert

Network Diagram - see first Page of Table 130

Station		AW	AW	AW	AW	AW	AW	AW	AW	AW	AW	AW	AW	AW	AW	AW	AW	AW	AW	AW	AW	AW	AW
Bridgend	d														14 42								
Llantwit Major	d														14 56								
Rhoose Cardiff Int Airport ✈	d														15 06								
Barry Island	d					14 40				14 55										15 25			
Barry 3	d					14 45				15 00					15 15					15 30			
Barry Docks	d					14 49				15 04					15 19					15 34			
Cadoxton	d					14 52				15 07					15 22					15 37			
Dinas Powys	d					14 56				15 11					15 26					15 41			
Eastbrook	d					14 58				15 13					15 28					15 43			
Cogan	d					15 00				15 15					15 30					15 45			
Penarth	d		14 47				15 02				15 17						15 32				15 47		
Dingle Road	d		14 49				15 04				15 19						15 34				15 49		
Grangetown	d		14 53			15 04	15 08			15 19	15 23				15 34		15 38			15 49	15 53		
Cardiff Central 7	a		14 59			15 09	15 14			15 24	15 29				15 39		15 44			15 54	15 59		
	d		15 01	15 06		15 11	15 16		15 21	15 26	15 31		15 36	15 36	15 41		15 46	15 51		15 56	16 01		16 06
Cardiff Bay	d				15 06			15 18				15 30				15 42			15 54			16 06	
Cardiff Queen Street 3	a		15 04		15 10	15 14	15 19	15 22	15 24	15 29	15 34	15 34	15 39		15 44	15 46	15 49	15 54	15 58	15 59	16 04	16 10	16 09
	d		15 05			15 15	15 20		15 25	15 30	15 35		15 40		15 45		15 50	15 55		16 00	16 05		16 10
Heath Low Level	d								15 30									16 00					
Ty Glas	d								15 33									16 03					
Birchgrove	d								15 34									16 04					
Rhiwbina	d								15 36									16 06					
Whitchurch (Cardiff)	d								15 38									16 08					
Coryton	a								15 43									16 13					
Heath High Level	d		15 10				15 25				15 40						15 55				16 10		
Llanishen	d		15 13				15 28				15 43						15 58				16 13		
Lisvane & Thornhill	d		15 15				15 30				15 45						16 00				16 15		
Caerphilly 3	d		15 21				15 36				15 51						16 06				16 21		
Aber	d		15 23				15 38				15 53						16 08				16 23		
Llanbradach	d		15 27				15 42				15 57						16 12				16 27		
Ystrad Mynach 3	d		15 32				15 47				16 02						16 17				16 32		
Hengoed	d		15 35				15 50				16 05						16 20				16 35		
Pengam	d		15 38				15 53				16 08						16 23				16 38		
Gilfach Fargoed	d		15 41																		16 41		
Bargoed	a		15 48				15 58				16 16						16 31				16 48		
	d						15 59																
Brithdir	d						16 03																
Tir-phil	d						16 06																
Pontlottyn	d						16 10																
Rhymney 3	a						16 16																
Cathays	d					15 18				15 33			15 43		15 48					16 03			16 13
Llandaf	d					15 22				15 37			15 47		15 52					16 07			16 17
Ninian Park	d			15 10										15 40									
Waun-gron Park	d			15 13										15 43									
Fairwater	d			15 15										15 45									
Danescourt	d	←		15 17										15 47									
Radyr 3	a	15 08		15 24		15 25				15 40			15 50	15 54	15 55					16 10			16 20
	d	15 20				15 25				15 40			15 50		15 55					16 10			16 20
Taffs Well 3	d	15 24				15 29				15 44			15 54		15 59					16 14			16 24
Trefforest Estate	d									15 48										16 18			
Trefforest	d	15 31				15 36				15 52			16 01		16 06					16 22			16 31
Pontypridd 3	a	15 34				15 39				15 55			16 04		16 09					16 25			16 34
	d	15 36				15 41				15 57			16 06		16 11					16 27			16 36
Abercynon	d					15 49				16 04					16 19					16 34			
Penrhiwceiber	d					15 54									16 24								
Mountain Ash	a					15 58									16 28								
	d					16 03									16 33								
Fernhill	d					16 05									16 35								
Cwmbach	d					16 09									16 39								
Aberdare 3	a					16 16									16 46								
Quakers Yard	d									16 09										16 39			
Merthyr Vale	a									16 14										16 44			
	d									16 17										16 47			
Troed Y Rhiw	d									16 20										16 50			
Pentre-bach	d									16 23										16 53			
Merthyr Tydfil	a									16 31										17 01			
Trehafod	d	15 41											16 11										16 41
Porth	a	15 44											16 14										16 44
	d	15 45											16 15										16 45
Dinas Rhondda	d	15 49											16 19										16 49
Tonypandy	d	15 51											16 21										16 51
Llwynypia	d	15 53											16 23										16 53
Ystrad Rhondda	a	15 56											16 26										16 56
	d	15 59											16 29										16 59
Ton Pentre	d	16 01											16 31										17 01
Treorchy	d	16 04											16 34										17 04
Ynyswen	d	16 07											16 37										17 07
Treherbert	a	16 13											16 43										17 13

When events are being held at the Millenium Stadium, services are subject to alteration. Please check times before travelling.

Table 130

Saturdays
until 8 September

Bridgend, Barry Island, Barry, Penarth and Cardiff - Coryton, Rhymney, Pontypridd, Merthyr, Aberdare and Treherbert

Network Diagram - see first Page of Table 130

Station		AW	AW	AW	AW	AW	AW	AW	AW	AW	AW	AW	AW	AW	AW	AW	AW	AW	AW	AW	AW	AW
Bridgend	d											15 42										
Llantwit Major	d											15 56										
Rhoose Cardiff Int Airport ✈	d											16 06										
Barry Island	d		15 40				15 55										16 25					16 40
Barry 3	d		15 45				16 00					16 15					16 30					16 45
Barry Docks	d		15 49				16 04					16 19					16 34					16 49
Cadoxton	d		15 52				16 07					16 22					16 37					16 52
Dinas Powys	d		15 56				16 11					16 26					16 41					16 56
Eastbrook	d		15 58				16 13					16 28					16 43					16 58
Cogan	d		16 00				16 15					16 30					16 45					17 00
Penarth	d			16 02				16 17						16 32								
Dingle Road	d			16 04				16 19						16 34								
Grangetown	d		16 04	16 08			16 19	16 23				16 34		16 38			16 49					17 04
Cardiff Central 7	a		16 09	16 14			16 24	16 29				16 39		16 44			16 54					17 09
	d	16 06	16 11	16 16		16 21	16 26	16 31		16 36	16 36	16 41		16 46	16 51		16 56	17 01		17 06	17 06	17 11
Cardiff Bay	d				16 18				16 30				16 42			16 54			17 06			
Cardiff Queen Street 3	a		16 14	16 19	16 22	16 24	16 29	16 34	16 34	16 39		16 44	16 46	16 49	16 54	16 58	16 59	17 04	17 10	17 09		17 14
	d		16 15	16 20		16 25	16 30	16 35		16 40		16 45		16 50	16 55		17 00	17 05		17 10		17 15
Heath Low Level	d					16 30									17 00							
Ty Glas	d					16 33									17 03							
Birchgrove	d					16 34									17 04							
Rhiwbina	d					16 36									17 06							
Whitchurch (Cardiff)	d					16 38									17 08							
Coryton	a					16 43									17 13							
Heath High Level	d			16 25				16 40						16 55				17 10				
Llanishen	d			16 28				16 43						16 58				17 13				
Lisvane & Thornhill	d			16 30				16 45						17 00				17 15				
Caerphilly 3	d			16 36				16 51						17 06				17 21				
Aber	d			16 38				16 53						17 08				17 23				
Llanbradach	d			16 42				16 57						17 12				17 27				
Ystrad Mynach 3	d			16 47				17 02						17 17				17 33				
Hengoed	d			16 50				17 05						17 20				17 35				
Pengam	d			16 53				17 08						17 23				17 39				
Gilfach Fargoed	d																	17 42				
Bargoed	a			16 58				17 16						17 31				17 45				
	d			16 59														17 47				
Brithdir	d			17 03														17 50				
Tir-phil	d			17 06														17 53				
Pontlottyn	d			17 10														17 58				
Rhymney 3	a			17 16														18 04				
Cathays	d		16 18				16 33			16 43		16 48					17 03			17 13		17 18
Llandaf	d		16 22				16 37			16 47		16 52					17 07			17 17		17 22
Ninian Park	d	16 10									16 40										17 10	
Waun-gron Park	d	16 13									16 43										17 13	
Fairwater	d	16 15									16 45										17 15	
Danescourt	d	16 17									16 47										17 17	
Radyr 3	a	16 24	16 25				16 40			16 50	16 54	16 55					17 10			17 20	17 24	17 25
	d		16 25				16 40			16 50		16 55					17 10			17 20		17 25
Taffs Well 3	d		16 29				16 44			16 54		16 59					17 14			17 24		17 29
Trefforest Estate	d						16 48										17 18					
Trefforest	d		16 36				16 52			17 01		17 06					17 22			17 31		17 36
Pontypridd 3	a		16 39				16 55			17 04		17 09					17 25			17 34		17 39
	d		16 41				16 57			17 06		17 11					17 27			17 36		17 41
Abercynon	d		16 49				17 04					17 19					17 34					17 49
Penrhiwceiber	d		16 54									17 24										17 54
Mountain Ash	a		16 58									17 28										17 58
	d		17 03									17 33										18 03
Fernhill	d		17 05									17 35										18 05
Cwmbach	d		17 09									17 39										18 09
Aberdare 3	a		17 16									17 46										18 16
Quakers Yard	d						17 09										17 39					
Merthyr Vale	a						17 14										17 44					
	d						17 17										17 47					
Troed Y Rhiw	d						17 20										17 50					
Pentre-bach	d						17 23										17 53					
Merthyr Tydfil	a						17 31										18 01					
Trehafod	d									17 11										17 41		
Porth	a									17 14										17 44		
	d									17 15										17 45		
Dinas Rhondda	d									17 19										17 49		
Tonypandy	d									17 21										17 51		
Llwynypia	d									17 23										17 53		
Ystrad Rhondda	a									17 26										17 56		
	d									17 29										17 59		
Ton Pentre	d									17 31										18 01		
Treorchy	d									17 34										18 04		
Ynyswen	d									17 37										18 07		
Treherbert	a									17 43										18 13		

When events are being held at the Millenium Stadium, services are subject to alteration. Please check times before travelling.

Bridgend, Barry Island, Barry, Penarth and Cardiff - Coryton, Rhymney, Pontypridd, Merthyr, Aberdare and Treherbert

Network Diagram - see first Page of Table 130

		AW	AW	AW	AW	AW	AW	AW	AW	AW		AW	AW	AW	AW	AW	AW	AW	AW	AW		AW	AW	AW	AW
Bridgend	d									16 42															
Llantwit Major	d									16 56															
Rhoose Cardiff Int Airport ✈	d									17 06															
Barry Island	d				16 55											17 25						17 40			
Barry 3	d				17 00					17 15						17 30						17 45			
Barry Docks	d				17 04					17 19						17 34						17 49			
Cadoxton	d				17 07					17 22						17 37						17 52			
Dinas Powys	d				17 11					17 26						17 41						17 56			
Eastbrook	d				17 13					17 28						17 43						17 58			
Cogan	d				17 15					17 30						17 45						18 00			
Penarth	d	17 02				17 17							17 32				17 47						18 02		
Dingle Road	d	17 04				17 19							17 34				17 49						18 04		
Grangetown	d	17 08			17 19	17 23				17 34			17 38			17 49	17 53					18 04	18 08		
Cardiff Central 7	a	17 14			17 24	17 29				17 39			17 44			17 54	17 59					18 09	18 14		
	d	17 16		17 21	17 26	17 31		17 36	17 36	17 41			17 46	17 51		17 56	18 01		18 06	18 06		18 11	18 16		18 21
Cardiff Bay	d		17 18				17 30					17 42			17 54			18 06						18 18	
Cardiff Queen Street 3	a	17 19	17 22	17 24	17 29	17 34	17 34	17 39		17 44		17 46	17 49	17 54	17 58	17 59	18 04	18 10	18 09			18 14	18 19	18 22	18 24
	d	17 20		17 25	17 30	17 35		17 40		17 45			17 50	17 55		18 00	18 05		18 10			18 15	18 20		18 25
Heath Low Level	d			17 30										18 00											18 30
Ty Glas	d			17 33										18 03											18 33
Birchgrove	d			17 34										18 04											18 34
Rhiwbina	d			17 36										18 06											18 36
Whitchurch (Cardiff)	d			17 38										18 08											18 38
Coryton	a			17 43										18 13											18 43
Heath High Level	d	17 25				17 40							17 55				18 10						18 25		
Llanishen	d	17 28				17 43							17 59				18 13						18 28		
Lisvane & Thornhill	d	17 30				17 45							18 02				18 15						18 30		
Caerphilly 3	d	17 36				17 51							18 07				18 21						18 36		
Aber	d	17 38				17 53							18 10				18 23						18 38		
Llanbradach	d	17 42				17 57							18 14				18 27						18 42		
Ystrad Mynach 3	d	17 47				18 02							18 20				18 32						18a51		
Hengoed	d	17 50				18 05							18 23				18 35								
Pengam	d	17 53				18 08							18 27				18 38								
Gilfach Fargoed	d					18 11							18 30				18 41								
Bargoed	a	18 01				18 14							18 34				18 48								
	d					18 16							18 44												
Brithdir	d					18 20							18 48												
Tir-phil	d					18 23							18 51												
Pontlottyn	d					18 27							18 55												
Rhymney 3	a					18 33							19 01												
Cathays	d				17 33			17 43		17 48						18 03			18 13			18 18			
Llandaf	d				17 37			17 47		17 52						18 07			18 17			18 22			
Ninian Park	d								17 40											18 10					
Waun-gron Park	d								17 43											18 13					
Fairwater	d								17 45											18 15					
Danescourt	d								17 47											18 17					
Radyr 3	a				17 40			17 50	17 54	17 55						18 10			18 20	18 24		18 25			
	d				17 40			17 50		17 55						18 10			18 20			18 25			
Taffs Well 3	d				17 44			17 54		17 59						18 14			18 24			18 29			
Trefforest Estate	d				17 48											18 18									
Trefforest	d				17 52			18 01		18 06						18 22			18 31			18 36			
Pontypridd 3	a				17 55			18 04		18 09						18 25			18 34			18 42			
	d				17 57			18 06		18 11						18 27			18 36						
Abercynon	d				18 04					18 19						18 34									
Penrhiwceiber	d									18 24															
Mountain Ash	a									18 28															
	d									18 33															
Fernhill	d									18 35															
Cwmbach	d									18 39															
Aberdare 3	a									18 46															
Quakers Yard	d				18 09											18 39									
Merthyr Vale	a				18 14											18 44									
	d				18 17											18 47									
Troed Y Rhiw	d				18 20											18 50									
Pentre-bach	d				18 23											18 53									
Merthyr Tydfil	a				18 31											19 01									
Trehafod	d							18 11											18 41						
Porth	a							18 14											18 44						
	d							18 15											18 45						
Dinas Rhondda	d							18 19											18 49						
Tonypandy	d							18 21											18 51						
Llwynypia	d							18 23											18 53						
Ystrad Rhondda	a							18 26											18 56						
	d							18 29											18 59						
Ton Pentre	d							18 31											19 01						
Treorchy	d							18 34											19 04						
Ynyswen	d							18 37											19 07						
Treherbert	a							18 43											19 13						

When events are being held at the Millenium Stadium, services are subject to alteration. Please check times before travelling.

Bridgend, Barry Island, Barry, Penarth and Cardiff - Coryton, Rhymney, Pontypridd, Merthyr, Aberdare and Treherbert

Network Diagram - see first Page of Table 130

		AW	AW	AW		AW		AW	AW	AW	AW	AW	AW	AW	AW	AW		AW	AW	AW	AW	AW	AW	AW	AW
Bridgend	d							17 42																18 42	
Llantwit Major	d							17 56																18 56	
Rhoose Cardiff Int Airport ✈	d							18 06																19 06	
Barry Island	d	17 55										18 25						18 40		18 55					
Barry 3	d	18 00						18 15				18 30						18 45		19 00				19 15	
Barry Docks	d	18 04						18 19				18 34						18 49		19 04				19 19	
Cadoxton	d	18 07						18 22				18 37						18 52		19 07				19 22	
Dinas Powys	d	18 11						18 26				18 41						18 56		19 11				19 26	
Eastbrook	d	18 13						18 28				18 43						18 58		19 13				19 28	
Cogan	d	18 15						18 30				18 45						19 00		19 15				19 30	
Penarth	d			18 17					18 32					18 47							19 17				
Dingle Road	d			18 19					18 34					18 49							19 19				
Grangetown	d	18 19		18 23				18 34	18 38			18 49		18 53				19 04		19 19	19 23			19 34	
Cardiff Central 7	a	18 24		18 29				18 39	18 47			18 55		18 59				19 09		19 24	19 29			19 39	
	d	18 26		18 31	18 36	18 36		18 41			18 51			19 01		19 06		19 11		19 26	19 31		19 36	19 41	
Cardiff Bay	d		18 30							18 42			18 54		19 06				19 18			19 30			19 42
Cardiff Queen Street 3	a	18 29	18 34	18 34	18 38			18 44		18 46	18 54		18 58	19 04	19 10	19 09		19 14	19 22	19 29	19 34	19 34		19 44	19 46
	d	18 30		18 35	18 40			18 50			18 55			19 05		19 10		19 15		19 30	19 35			19 45	
Heath Low Level	d										19 00														
Ty Glas	d										19 03														
Birchgrove	d										19 04														
Rhiwbina	d										19 06														
Whitchurch (Cardiff)	d										19 08														
Coryton	a										19 13														
Heath High Level	d			18 40										19 10							19 40				
Llanishen	d			18 43										19 13							19 43				
Lisvane & Thornhill	d			18 45										19 15							19 45				
Caerphilly 3	d			18 51										19a23							19 51				
Aber	d			18 53																	19 53				
Llanbradach	d			18 57																	19 57				
Ystrad Mynach 3	d			19 02																	20 02				
Hengoed	d			19 05																	20 05				
Pengam	d			19 08																	20 08				
Gilfach Fargoed	d			19 11																	20 11				
Bargoed	a			19 14																	20 15				
	d			19 16																	20 16				
Brithdir	d			19 20																	20 20				
Tir-phil	d			19 23																	20 23				
Pontlottyn	d			19 27																	20 27				
Rhymney 3	a			19 34																	20 33				
Cathays	d	18 33			18 43			18 52								19 13		19 18		19 33				19 48	
Llandaf	d	18 37			18 47			18 56								19 17		19 22		19 37				19 52	
Ninian Park	d					18 40																	19 40		
Waun-gron Park	d					18 43																	19 43		
Fairwater	d					18 45																	19 45		
Danescourt	d					18 47																	19 47		
Radyr 3	a	18 40			18 50	18 54		18 58								19 20		19 25		19 40			19 54	19 55	
	d	18 40			18 50			18 58								19 20		19 25		19 40				19 55	
Taffs Well 3	d	18 44			18 54			19 03								19 24		19 29		19 44				19 59	
Trefforest Estate	d	18 48																		19 48					
Trefforest	d	18 52			19 01			19 10								19 31		19 36		19 52				20 06	
Pontypridd 3	a	18 55			19 04			19 13								19 34		19 39		19 55				20 09	
	d	18 57			19 06			19 14								19 36		19 41		19 57				20 11	
Abercynon	d	19 04						19 21										19 49		20 04				20 21	
Penrhiwceiber	d							19 26										19 54						20 26	
Mountain Ash	a							19 30										19 56						20 30	
	d							19 33										20 03						20 33	
Fernhill	d							19 35										20 05						20 35	
Cwmbach	d							19 39										20 09						20 39	
Aberdare 3	a							19 46										20 16						20 46	
Quakers Yard	d	19 09																		20 08					
Merthyr Vale	a	19 14																		20 13					
	d	19 17																		20 15					
Troed Y Rhiw	d	19 20																		20 19					
Pentre-bach	d	19 23																		20 22					
Merthyr Tydfil	a	19 31																		20 30					
Trehafod	d				19 11											19 41									
Porth	a				19 14											19 44									
	d				19 15											19 45									
Dinas Rhondda	d				19 19											19 49									
Tonypandy	d				19 21											19 51									
Llwynypia	d				19 23											19 53									
Ystrad Rhondda	a				19 26											19 56									
	d				19 29											19 59									
Ton Pentre	d				19 31											20 01									
Treorchy	d				19 34											20 04									
Ynyswen	d				19 37											20 07									
Treherbert	a				19 43											20 13									

When events are being held at the Millenium Stadium, services are subject to alteration. Please check times before travelling.

Bridgend, Barry Island, Barry, Penarth and Cardiff - Coryton, Rhymney, Pontypridd, Merthyr, Aberdare and Treherbert

Network Diagram - see first Page of Table 130

		AW		AW	AW	AW	AW	AW	AW	AW	AW	AW		AW	AW	AW	AW	AW	AW	AW	AW	AW		AW	AW
Bridgend	d													19 42											
Llantwit Major	d													19 56											
Rhoose Cardiff Int Airport ✈	d													20 06											
Barry Island	d				19 25				19 55													20 55			
Barry	d				19 30				20 00					20 15								21 00			
Barry Docks	d				19 34				20 04					20 19								21 04			
Cadoxton	d				19 37				20 07					20 22								21 07			
Dinas Powys	d				19 41				20 11					20 26								21 11			
Eastbrook	d				19 43				20 13					20 28								21 13			
Cogan	d				19 45				20 15					20 30								21 15			
Penarth	d					19 47				20 20								20 47							
Dingle Road	d					19 49				20 22								20 49							
Grangetown	d				19 49	19 53			20 19	20 26				20 34				20 53				21 19			
Cardiff Central	a				19 54	19 59			20 24	20 31				20 39				20 59				21 24			
	d	19 51			20 01	20 06			20 26	20 31		20 36		20 41		20 51		21 01		21 06		21 26			21 31
Cardiff Bay	d			19 54			20 06	20 18			20 30				20 42		20 54		21 06		21 18			21 30	
Cardiff Queen Street	a	19 54		19 58	20 04	20 09	20 10	20 22	20 29	20 34	20 34			20 44	20 46	20 54	20 58	21 04	21 10	21 09	21 22	21 29		21 34	21 34
	d	19 55			20 05	20 10			20 30	20 35				20 45		20 55		21 05		21 10		21 30			21 35
Heath Low Level	d	20 00														21 00									
Ty Glas	d	20 03														21 03									
Birchgrove	d	20 04														21 04									
Rhiwbina	d	20 06														21 06									
Whitchurch (Cardiff)	d	20 08														21 08									
Coryton	a	20 13														21 13									
Heath High Level	d				20 10					20 40								21 10							21 40
Llanishen	d				20 13					20 43								21 13							21 43
Lisvane & Thornhill	d				20 15					20 45								21 15							21 45
Caerphilly	d				20a27					20 51								21 20							21 51
Aber	d									20 53								21 22							21 53
Llanbradach	d									20 57								21 26							21 57
Ystrad Mynach	d									21 02								21a36							22 02
Hengoed	d									21 05															22 05
Pengam	d									21 08															22 08
Gilfach Fargoed	d									21 11															22 11
Bargoed	a									21 15															22 15
	d									21 16															22 16
Brithdir	d									21 20															22 20
Tir-phil	d									21 23															22 23
Pontlottyn	d									21 27															22 27
Rhymney	a									21 34															22 34
Cathays	d					20 13			20 33					20 48						21 13		21 33			
Llandaf	d					20 17			20 37					20 52						21 17		21 37			
Ninian Park	d											20 40													
Waun-gron Park	d											20 43													
Fairwater	d											20 45													
Danescourt	d											20 47													
Radyr	a					20 20			20 40			20 54		20 55						21 20		21 40			
	d					20 20			20 40					20 55						21 20		21 40			
Taffs Well	d					20 24			20 44					20 59						21 24		21 44			
Trefforest Estate	d								20 48													21 48			
Trefforest	d					20 31			20 52					21 06						21 31		21 52			
Pontypridd	a					20 34			20 55					21 09						21 34		21 55			
	d					20 36			20 57					21 11						21 36		21 57			
Abercynon	d								21 04					21 19								22 04			
Penrhiwceiber	d													21 24											
Mountain Ash	a													21 28											
	d													21 29											
Fernhill	d													21 31											
Cwmbach	d													21 35											
Aberdare	a													21 42											
Quakers Yard	d								21 08													22 08			
Merthyr Vale	a								21 13													22 13			
	d								21 15													22 15			
Troed Y Rhiw	d								21 19													22 19			
Pentre-bach	d								21 22													22 22			
Merthyr Tydfil	a								21 30													22 30			
Trehafod	d					20 41														21 41					
Porth	a					20 44														21 44					
	d					20 45														21 45					
Dinas Rhondda	d					20 49														21 49					
Tonypandy	d					20 51														21 51					
Llwynypia	d					20 53														21 53					
Ystrad Rhondda	a					20 56														21 56					
	d					20 59														21 59					
Ton Pentre	d					21 01														22 01					
Treorchy	d					21 04														22 04					
Ynyswen	d					21 07														22 07					
Treherbert	a					21 13														22 13					

When events are being held at the Millenium Stadium, services are subject to alteration. Please check times before travelling.

Bridgend, Barry Island, Barry, Penarth and Cardiff - Coryton, Rhymney, Pontypridd, Merthyr, Aberdare and Treherbert

Network Diagram - see first Page of Table 130

		AW	AW	AW	AW	AW	AW	AW		AW	AW	AW	AW	AW	AW	AW	AW	AW		AW	AW	AW	AW	AW	AW A
Bridgend	d			20 42												21 42									
Llantwit Major	d			20 56												21 56									
Rhoose Cardiff Int Airport ✈	d			21 06												22 06									
Barry Island	d												21 55												22 44
Barry	d			21 15									22 00			22 15									22 48
Barry Docks	d			21 19									22 04			22 19									22 52
Cadoxton	d			21 22									22 07			22 22									22 55
Dinas Powys	d			21 26									22 11			22 26									22 59
Eastbrook	d			21 28									22 13			22 28									23 01
Cogan	d			21 30									22 15			22 30									23 03
Penarth	d		21 20				21 47								22 20								22 47		
Dingle Road	d		21 22				21 49								22 22								22 49		
Grangetown	d		21 26	21 34			21 53						22 19		22 26	22 34							22 53		23 07
Cardiff Central	a		21 37	21 39			21 59						22 24		22 33	22 39							23 00		23 12
	d	21 36		21 41			22 01			22 06		22 21	22 26		22 35	22 41		22 46			22 55		23 15		23 26
Cardiff Bay	d				21 42	21 54		22 06			22 18			22 30			22 42			22 54		23 06		23 18	
Cardiff Queen Street	a			21 44	21 46	21 58	22 04	22 10		22 09	22 22	22 24	22 29	22 34	22 38	22 44	22 46	22 49		22 58		23 10	23 18	23 22	23 29
	d			21 45			22 05			22 10		22 25	22 30		22 39	22 45		22 50					23 19		23 30
Heath Low Level	d											22 30													
Ty Glas	d											22 33													
Birchgrove	d											22 34													
Rhiwbina	d											22 36													
Whitchurch (Cardiff)	d											22 38													
Coryton	a											22 43													
Heath High Level	d						22 10								22 44								23 24		
Llanishen	d						22 13								22 47								23 27		
Lisvane & Thornhill	d						22 15								22 49								23 29		
Caerphilly	d						22a23								22 55								23 35		
Aber	d														22 57								23 37		
Llanbradach	d														23 01								23 41		
Ystrad Mynach	d														23 06								23a50		
Hengoed	d														23 09										
Pengam	d														23 12										
Gilfach Fargoed	d														23 15										
Bargoed	a														23 19										
	d														23 20										
Brithdir	d														23 24										
Tir-phil	d														23 27										
Pontlottyn	d														23 31										
Rhymney	a														23 37										
Cathays	d			21 48						22 13			22 33			22 48		22 53							23 33
Llandaf	d			21 52						22 17			22 37			22 52		22 57							23 37
Ninian Park	d	21 40																			22 59				
Waun-gron Park	d	21 43																			23 02				
Fairwater	d	21 45																			23 04				
Danescourt	d	21 47																			23 06				
Radyr	a	21 54		21 55						22 20			22 40			22 55		22 59			23 14				23 40
	d			21 55						22 20			22 40			22 55		22 59							23 41
Taffs Well	d			21 59						22 24			22 44			22 59		23 03							23 45
Trefforest Estate	d												22 48												23 49
Trefforest	d			22 06						22 31			22 52			23 06		23 10							23 53
Pontypridd	a			22 09						22 34			22 55			23 09		23 14							23 56
	d			22 11						22 36			22 57			23 11		23 15							23 57
Abercynon	d			22 19									23 04			23 19									00 07
Penrhiwceiber	d			22 24												23 24									
Mountain Ash	a			22 28												23 28									
	d			22 29												23 29									
Fernhill	d			22 31												23 31									
Cwmbach	d			22 35												23 35									
Aberdare	a			22 42												23 42									
Quakers Yard	d												23 08												00 11
Merthyr Vale	a												23 13												00 16
	d												23 15												00 19
Troed Y Rhiw	d												23 19												00 22
Pentre-bach	d												23 22												00 25
Merthyr Tydfil	a												23 30												00 30
Trehafod	d									22 41								23 20							
Porth	a									22 44								23 23							
	d									22 45								23 24							
Dinas Rhondda	d									22 49								23 28							
Tonypandy	d									22 51								23 30							
Llwynypia	d									22 53								23 32							
Ystrad Rhondda	a									22 56								23 35							
	d									22 59								23 38							
Ton Pentre	d									23 01								23 40							
Treorchy	d									23 04								23 43							
Ynyswen	d									23 07								23 46							
Treherbert	a									23 13								23 52							

A 4 August

When events are being held at the Millenium Stadium, services are subject to alteration. Please check times before travelling.

Table 130

Saturdays
until 8 September

Bridgend, Barry Island, Barry, Penarth and Cardiff - Coryton, Rhymney, Pontypridd, Merthyr, Aberdare and Treherbert

Network Diagram - see first Page of Table 130

		AW A	AW B	AW		AW	AW C	AW	AW	AW	AW C
Bridgend	d							22 42			
Llantwit Major	d							22 56			
Rhoose Cardiff Int Airport ✈	d							23 06			
Barry Island	d	22 45	22 44								
Barry 3	d	22 49	22 49					23 15			
Barry Docks	d	22 53	22 53					23 19			
Cadoxton	d	22 56	22 56					23 22			
Dinas Powys	d	23 00	23 00					23 26			
Eastbrook	d	23 03	23 02					23 28			
Cogan	d	23 05	23 04					23 30			
Penarth	d			23 26							
Dingle Road	d			23 28							
Grangetown	d	23 09	23 08	23 32				23 34			
Cardiff Central 7	a	23 14	23 13	23 40				23 42			
	d	23 26	23 26				23 40				23 56
Cardiff Bay	d					23 30			23 42	23 54	
Cardiff Queen Street 3	a	23 29	23 29			23 34			23 46	23 58	
	d	23 30	23 30								
Heath Low Level	d										
Ty Glas	d										
Birchgrove	d										
Rhiwbina	d										
Whitchurch (Cardiff)	d										
Coryton	a										
Heath High Level	d										
Llanishen	d										
Lisvane & Thornhill	d										
Caerphilly 3	d										
Aber	d										
Llanbradach	d										
Ystrad Mynach 3	d										
Hengoed	d										
Pengam	d										
Gilfach Fargoed	d										
Bargoed	a										
	d										
Brithdir	d										
Tir-phil	d										
Pontlottyn	d										
Rhymney 3	a										
Cathays	d	23 33	23 33				23 45				00 03
Llandaf	d	23 37	23 37				23 49				00 07
Ninian Park	d										
Waun-gron Park	d										
Fairwater	d										
Danescourt	d										
Radyr 3	a	23 40	23 40				23 53				00 10
	d	23 41	23 40				23 53				00 11
Taffs Well 3	d	23 45	23 44				23 57				00 15
Trefforest Estate	d	23 49									
Trefforest	d	23 53	23 52				00 03				00 21
Pontypridd 3	a	23 56	23 58				00 06				00 24
	d	23 57					00 08				00 26
Abercynon	d	00 07					00 17				
Penrhiwceiber	d						00 23				
Mountain Ash	a						00 26				
	d						00 28				
Fernhill	d						00 30				
Cwmbach	d						00 34				
Aberdare 3	a						00 41				
Quakers Yard	d	00 11									
Merthyr Vale	a	00 16									
	d	00 19									
Troed Y Rhiw	d	00 22									
Pentre-bach	d	00 25									
Merthyr Tydfil	a	00 30									
Trehafod	d										00 31
Porth	a										00 34
	d										00 35
Dinas Rhondda	d										00 39
Tonypandy	d										00 41
Llwynypia	d										00 43
Ystrad Rhondda	a										00 46
	d										00 47
Ton Pentre	d										00 49
Treorchy	d										00 52
Ynyswen	d										00 55
Treherbert	a										01 02

A 28 July

B not from 28 July until 4 August

C 4 August

When events are being held at the Millenium Stadium, services are subject to alteration. Please check times before travelling.

Table 130

Saturdays
from 15 September

Bridgend, Barry Island, Barry, Penarth and Cardiff - Coryton, Rhymney, Pontypridd, Merthyr, Aberdare and Treherbert

Network Diagram - see first Page of Table 130

		AW		AW	AW	AW	AW	AW	AW	AW		AW	AW	AW	AW	AW	AW	AW	AW	AW		AW	AW	AW	AW
Bridgend	d									05 37															
Llantwit Major	d									05 46															
Rhoose Cardiff Int Airport ✈	d									05 56															
Barry Island	d			05 15				05 50								06 25									06 55
Barry 3	d			05 20				05 55		06 15						06 30									07 00
Barry Docks	d			05 24				05 59		06 19						06 34									07 04
Cadoxton	d			05 27				06 02		06 22						06 37									07 07
Dinas Powys	d			05 31				06 06		06 26						06 41									07 11
Eastbrook	d			05 33				06 08		06 28						06 43									07 13
Cogan	d			05 35				06 10		06 30						06 45									07 15
Penarth	d						06 02						06 32									07 02			
Dingle Road	d						06 04						06 34									07 04			
Grangetown	d			05 39			06 08	06 14		06 34			06 38			06 49						07 08			07 19
Cardiff Central 7	a			05 44			06 13	06 19		06 39			06 44			06 54						07 14			07 24
	d	05 26		05 46	05 56	06 11	06 15	06 21	06 26	06 41			06 46	06 51		06 56		07 06	07 06	07 11		07 16		07 21	07 26
Cardiff Bay	d											06 42			06 54		07 06						07 18		
Cardiff Queen Street 3	a	05 29		05 49	05 59	06 14	06 19	06 24	06 29	06 44		06 46	06 49	06 54	06 58	06 59	07 10	07 09		07 14		07 19	07 22	07 24	07 29
	d	05 30		05 50	06 00	06 15	06 20	06 25	06 30	06 45			06 50	06 55		07 00		07 10		07 15		07 20		07 25	07 30
Heath Low Level	d							06 30						07 00										07 30	
Ty Glas	d							06 33						07 03										07 33	
Birchgrove	d							06 34						07 04										07 34	
Rhiwbina	d							06 36						07 06										07 36	
Whitchurch (Cardiff)	d							06 38						07 08										07 38	
Coryton	a							06 44						07 14										07 44	
Heath High Level	d			05 55			06 25						06 55									07 25			
Llanishen	d			05 58			06 28						06 58									07 28			
Lisvane & Thornhill	d			06 00			06 30						07 00									07 30			
Caerphilly 3	d			06a09			06 36						07 06									07 36			
Aber	d						06 38						07 08									07 38			
Llanbradach	d						06 42						07 12									07 42			
Ystrad Mynach 3	d						06 47						07 17									07 47			
Hengoed	d						06 50						07 20									07 50			
Pengam	d						06 53						07 23									07 53			
Gilfach Fargoed	d																								
Bargoed	a						07 02						07 32									08 03			
	d																								
Brithdir	d																								
Tir-phil	d																								
Pontlottyn	d																								
Rhymney 3	a																								
Cathays	d	05 33			06 03	06 18			06 33	06 48						07 03		07 13		07 18					07 33
Llandaf	d	05 37			06 07	06 22			06 37	06 52						07 07		07 17		07 22					07 37
Ninian Park	d																		07 10						
Waun-gron Park	d																		07 14						
Fairwater	d																		07 16						
Danescourt	d																		07 19						
Radyr 3	a	05 39			06 10	06 24			06 40	06 54						07 10		07 20	07 27	07 25					07 40
	d	05 40			06 10	06 24			06 40	06 55						07 10		07 20		07 25					07 40
Taffs Well 3	d	05 43			06 14	06 28			06 44	06 59						07 14		07 24		07 29					07 44
Trefforest Estate	d	05 47			06 18				06 48							07 18									07 48
Trefforest	d	05 52			06 22	06 35			06 52	07 06						07 22		07 31		07 36					07 52
Pontypridd 3	a	05 55			06 25	06 38			06 55	07 09						07 25		07 34		07 39					07 55
	d	05 57	06 11		06 27	06 41			06 57	07 11						07 27		07 36		07 41					07 57
Abercynon	d	06 04	06 19		06 34	06 49			07 04	07 19						07 34				07 49					08 04
Penrhiwceiber	d		06 25			06 55				07 25										07 55					
Mountain Ash	a		06 28			06 58				07 28										07 58					
	d		06 34			07 04				07 34										08 04					
Fernhill	d		06 37			07 07				07 37										08 07					
Cwmbach	d		06 41			07 11				07 41										08 11					
Aberdare 3	a		06 49			07 19				07 49										08 19					
Quakers Yard	d	06 09			06 39				07 09							07 39									08 09
Merthyr Vale	a	06 14			06 44				07 14							07 44									08 14
	d	06 17			06 47				07 17							07 47									08 17
Troed Y Rhiw	d	06 21			06 51				07 21							07 51									08 21
Pentre-bach	d	06 24			06 54				07 24							07 54									08 24
Merthyr Tydfil	a	06 33			07 03				07 33							08 03									08 33
Trehafod	d																	07 41							
Porth	a																	07 44							
	d																	07 45							
Dinas Rhondda	d																	07 49							
Tonypandy	d																	07 51							
Llwynypia	d																	07 53							
Ystrad Rhondda	a																	07 56							
	d																	07 59							
Ton Pentre	d																	08 01							
Treorchy	d																	08 04							
Ynyswen	d																	08 07							
Treherbert	a																	08 14							

When events are being held at the Millenium Stadium, services are subject to alteration. Please check times before travelling.

Table 130

Saturdays
from 15 September

Bridgend, Barry Island, Barry, Penarth and Cardiff - Coryton, Rhymney, Pontypridd, Merthyr, Aberdare and Treherbert

Network Diagram - see first Page of Table 130

		AW	AW	AW	AW	AW	AW	AW	AW	AW	AW	AW	AW	AW	AW	AW	AW	AW	AW	AW	AW	AW	AW
Bridgend	d					06 42																	
Llantwit Major	d					06 56																	
Rhoose Cardiff Int Airport ✈	d					07 06																	
Barry Island	d										07 25					07 40				07 55			
Barry 3	d					07 15					07 30					07 45				08 00			
Barry Docks	d					07 19					07 34					07 49				08 04			
Cadoxton	d					07 22					07 37					07 52				08 07			
Dinas Powys	d					07 26					07 41					07 56				08 11			
Eastbrook	d					07 28					07 43					07 58				08 13			
Cogan	d					07 30					07 45					08 00				08 15			
Penarth	d	07 17						07 32				07 47					08 02				08 17		
Dingle Road	d	07 19						07 34				07 49					08 04				08 19		
Grangetown	d	07 23				07 34		07 38			07 49	07 53				08 04	08 08			08 19	08 23		
Cardiff Central 7	a	07 29				07 39		07 44			07 54	07 59				08 09	08 14			08 24	08 29		
	d	07 31		07 36	07 36	07 41		07 46	07 51		07 56	08 01		08 06	08 06	08 11	08 16		08 21	08 26	08 31		08 36
Cardiff Bay	d		07 30				07 42			07 54			08 06					08 18				08 30	
Cardiff Queen Street 3	a	07 34	07 34	07 39		07 44	07 46	07 49	07 54	07 58	07 59	08 04	08 10	08 09		08 14	08 19	08 22	08 24	08 29	08 34	08 34	08 39
	d	07 35		07 40		07 45		07 50	07 55		08 00	08 05		08 10		08 15	08 20		08 25	08 30	08 35		08 40
Heath Low Level	d								08 00										08 30				
Ty Glas	d								08 03										08 33				
Birchgrove	d								08 04										08 34				
Rhiwbina	d								08 06										08 36				
Whitchurch (Cardiff)	d								08 08										08 38				
Coryton	a								08 14										08 44				
Heath High Level	d	07 40						07 55				08 10					08 25				08 40		
Llanishen	d	07 43						07 58				08 13					08 28				08 43		
Lisvane & Thornhill	d	07 45						08 00				08 15					08 30				08 45		
Caerphilly 3	d	07 51						08 06				08 21					08 36				08 51		
Aber	d	07 53						08 08				08 23					08 38				08 53		
Llanbradach	d	07 57						08 12				08 27					08 42				08 57		
Ystrad Mynach 3	d	08 02						08 17				08 32					08 47				09 07		
Hengoed	d	08 05						08 20				08 35					08 50				09 10		
Pengam	d	08 08						08 23				08 38					08 53				09 13		
Gilfach Fargoed	d											08 41											
Bargoed	a	08 13						08 32				08 49					08 58				09 22		
	d	08 14															08 59						
Brithdir	d	08 18															09 03						
Tir-phil	d	08 21															09 06						
Pontlottyn	d	08 25															09 10						
Rhymney 3	a	08 32															09 17						
Cathays	d			07 43		07 48					08 03			08 13		08 18				08 33			08 43
Llandaf	d			07 47		07 52					08 07			08 17		08 22				08 37			08 47
Ninian Park	d				07 40										08 10								
Waun-gron Park	d				07 44										08 14								
Fairwater	d				07 46										08 16								
Danescourt	d				07 49										08 19								
Radyr 3	a			07 50	07 57	07 55					08 10			08 20	08 27	08 25				08 40			08 50
	d			07 50		07 55					08 10			08 20		08 25				08 40			08 50
Taffs Well 3	d			07 54		07 59					08 14			08 24		08 29				08 44			08 54
Trefforest Estate	d										08 18									08 48			
Trefforest	d			08 01		08 06					08 22			08 31		08 36				08 52			09 01
Pontypridd 3	a			08 04		08 09					08 25			08 34		08 39				08 55			09 04
	d			08 06		08 11					08 27			08 36		08 41				08 57			09 06
Abercynon	d					08 19					08 34					08 49				09 04			
Penrhiwceiber	d					08 25										08 55							
Mountain Ash	a					08 28										08 58							
	d					08 34										09 04							
Fernhill	d					08 37										09 07							
Cwmbach	d					08 41										09 11							
Aberdare 3	a					08 49										09 19							
Quakers Yard	d										08 39									09 09			
Merthyr Vale	a										08 44									09 14			
	d										08 47									09 17			
Troed Y Rhiw	d										08 51									09 21			
Pentre-bach	d										08 54									09 24			
Merthyr Tydfil	a										09 03									09 33			
Trehafod	d			08 11										08 41									09 11
Porth	a			08 14										08 44									09 14
	d			08 15										08 45									09 15
Dinas Rhondda	d			08 19										08 49									09 19
Tonypandy	d			08 21										08 51									09 21
Llwynypia	d			08 23										08 53									09 23
Ystrad Rhondda	a			08 26										08 56									09 26
	d			08 29										08 59									09 29
Ton Pentre	d			08 31										09 01									09 31
Treorchy	d			08 34										09 04									09 34
Ynyswen	d			08 37										09 07									09 37
Treherbert	a			08 44										09 14									09 44

When events are being held at the Millenium Stadium, services are subject to alteration. Please check times before travelling.

Table 130

Saturdays
from 15 September

Bridgend, Barry Island, Barry, Penarth and Cardiff - Coryton, Rhymney, Pontypridd, Merthyr, Aberdare and Treherbert

Network Diagram - see first Page of Table 130

		AW	AW	AW	AW	AW	AW	AW	AW	AW	AW	AW	AW	AW	AW	AW	AW	AW	AW	AW	AW	AW
Bridgend	d		07 42																			08 42
Llantwit Major	d		07 56																			08 56
Rhoose Cardiff Int Airport ✈	d		08 06																			09 06
Barry Island	d							08 25					08 40				08 55					
Barry 3	d		08 15					08 30					08 45				09 00					09 15
Barry Docks	d		08 19					08 34					08 49				09 04					09 19
Cadoxton	d		08 22					08 37					08 52				09 07					09 22
Dinas Powys	d		08 26					08 41					08 56				09 11					09 26
Eastbrook	d		08 28					08 43					08 58				09 13					09 28
Cogan	d		08 30					08 45					09 00				09 15					09 30
Penarth	d				08 32				08 47									09 17				
Dingle Road	d				08 34				08 49									09 19				
Grangetown	d		08 34		08 38			08 49	08 53				09 04				09 19	09 23				09 34
Cardiff Central 7	a		08 39		08 44			08 54	08 59				09 09				09 24	09 29				09 39
	d	08 36	08 41		08 46	08 51		08 56	09 01		09 06	09 06	09 11	09 16		09 21	09 26	09 31		09 36	09 36	09 41
Cardiff Bay	d			08 42			08 54			09 06					09 18				09 30			
Cardiff Queen Street 3	a		08 44	08 46	08 49	08 54	08 58	08 59	09 04	09 10	09 09		09 14	09 19	09 22	09 24	09 29	09 34	09 34	09 39		09 44
	d		08 45		08 50	08 55		09 00	09 05		09 10		09 15	09 20		09 25	09 30	09 35		09 40		09 45
Heath Low Level	d					09 00										09 30						
Ty Glas	d					09 03										09 33						
Birchgrove	d					09 04										09 34						
Rhiwbina	d					09 06										09 36						
Whitchurch (Cardiff)	d					09 08										09 38						
Coryton	a					09 14										09 44						
Heath High Level	d				08 55				09 10					09 25				09 40				
Llanishen	d				08 58				09 13					09 28				09 43				
Lisvane & Thornhill	d				09 00				09 15					09 30				09 45				
Caerphilly 3	d				09 06				09 21					09 36				09 51				
Aber	d				09 08				09 23					09 38				09 53				
Llanbradach	d				09 12				09 27					09 42				09 57				
Ystrad Mynach 3	d				09a22				09 32					09 47				10 07				
Hengoed	d								09 35					09 50				10 10				
Pengam	d								09 38					09 53				10 13				
Gilfach Fargoed	d								09 41													
Bargoed	a								09 49					09 58				10 22				
	d													09 59								
Brithdir	d													10 03								
Tir-phil	d													10 06								
Pontlottyn	d													10 10								
Rhymney 3	a													10 17								
Cathays	d		08 48					09 03			09 13		09 18				09 33			09 43		09 48
Llandaf	d		08 52					09 07			09 17		09 22				09 37			09 47		09 52
Ninian Park	d	08 40										09 10									09 40	
Waun-gron Park	d	08 44										09 14									09 44	
Fairwater	d	08 46										09 16									09 46	
Danescourt	d	08 49										09 19									09 49	
Radyr 3	a	08 57	08 55					09 10			09 20	09 27	09 25				09 40			09 50	09 57	09 55
	d		08 55					09 10			09 20		09 25				09 40			09 50		09 55
Taffs Well 3	d		08 59					09 14			09 24		09 29				09 44			09 54		09 59
Trefforest Estate	d							09 18									09 48					
Trefforest	d		09 06					09 22			09 31		09 36				09 52			10 01		10 06
Pontypridd 3	a		09 09					09 25			09 34		09 39				09 55			10 04		10 09
	d		09 11					09 27			09 36		09 41				09 57			10 06		10 11
Abercynon	d		09 19					09 34					09 49				10 04					10 19
Penrhiwceiber	d		09 25										09 55									10 25
Mountain Ash	a		09 28										09 58									10 28
	d		09 34										10 04									10 34
Fernhill	d		09 37										10 07									10 37
Cwmbach	d		09 41										10 11									10 41
Aberdare 3	a		09 49										10 19									10 49
Quakers Yard	d							09 39									10 09					
Merthyr Vale	a							09 44									10 14					
	d							09 47									10 17					
Troed Y Rhiw	d							09 51									10 21					
Pentre-bach	d							09 54									10 24					
Merthyr Tydfil	a							10 03									10 33					
Trehafod	d										09 41									10 11		
Porth	a										09 44									10 14		
	d										09 45									10 15		
Dinas Rhondda	d										09 49									10 19		
Tonypandy	d										09 51									10 21		
Llwynypia	d										09 53									10 23		
Ystrad Rhondda	a										09 56									10 26		
	d										09 59									10 29		
Ton Pentre	d										10 01									10 31		
Treorchy	d										10 04									10 34		
Ynyswen	d										10 07									10 37		
Treherbert	a										10 14									10 44		

When events are being held at the Millenium Stadium, services are subject to alteration. Please check times before travelling.

Table 130

Saturdays from 15 September

Bridgend, Barry Island, Barry, Penarth and Cardiff - Coryton, Rhymney, Pontypridd, Merthyr, Aberdare and Treherbert

Network Diagram - see first Page of Table 130

		AW	AW	AW	AW	AW	AW	AW	AW	AW	AW	AW	AW	AW	AW	AW	AW	AW	AW	AW	AW	AW	AW
Bridgend	d																				09 42		
Llantwit Major	d																				09 56		
Rhoose Cardiff Int Airport ✈	d																				10 06		
Barry Island	d					09 25						09 40				09 55							
Barry ■	d					09 30						09 45				10 00					10 15		
Barry Docks	d					09 34						09 49				10 04					10 19		
Cadoxton	d					09 37						09 52				10 07					10 22		
Dinas Powys	d					09 41						09 56				10 11					10 26		
Eastbrook	d					09 43						09 58				10 13					10 28		
Cogan	d					09 45						10 00				10 15					10 30		
Penarth	d		09 32				09 47						10 02				10 17						10 32
Dingle Road	d		09 34				09 49						10 04				10 19						10 34
Grangetown	d		09 38			09 49	09 53					10 04	10 08			10 19	10 23				10 34		10 38
Cardiff Central ■	a		09 44			09 54	09 59					10 09	10 14			10 24	10 29				10 42		10 44
	d		09 46	09 51		09 56	10 01		10 06	10 06		10 11	10 16		10 21	10 26	10 31		10 36	10 36			10 46
Cardiff Bay	d	09 42			09 54			10 06						10 18				10 30				10 42	
Cardiff Queen Street ■	a	09 46	09 49	09 54	09 58	09 59	10 04	10 10	10 09			10 14	10 19	10 22	10 24	10 29	10 34	10 34	10 39			10 46	10 49
	d		09 50	09 55		10 00	10 05		10 10			10 15	10 20		10 25	10 30	10 35		10 40				10 50
Heath Low Level	d			10 00											10 30								
Ty Glas	d			10 03											10 33								
Birchgrove	d			10 04											10 34								
Rhiwbina	d			10 06											10 36								
Whitchurch (Cardiff)	d			10 08											10 38								
Coryton	a			10 14											10 44								
Heath High Level	d		09 55				10 10						10 25				10 40						10 55
Llanishen	d		09 58				10 13						10 28				10 43						10 58
Lisvane & Thornhill	d		10 00				10 15						10 30				10 45						11 00
Caerphilly ■	d		10 06				10 21						10 36				10 51						11 06
Aber	d		10 08				10 23						10 38				10 53						11 08
Llanbradach	d		10 12				10 27						10 42				10 57						11 12
Ystrad Mynach ■	d		10a22				10 32						10 47				11 07						11a22
Hengoed	d						10 35						10 50				11 10						
Pengam	d						10 38						10 53				11 13						
Gilfach Fargoed	d						10 41																
Bargoed	a						10 49						10 58				11 22						
	d												10 59										
Brithdir	d												11 03										
Tir-phil	d												11 06										
Pontlottyn	d												11 10										
Rhymney ■	a												11 17										
Cathays	d					10 03			10 13			10 18				10 33			10 43				
Llandaf	d					10 07			10 17			10 22				10 37			10 47				
Ninian Park	d									10 10										10 40			
Waun-gron Park	d									10 14										10 44			
Fairwater	d									10 16										10 46			
Danescourt	d									10 19										10 49			
Radyr ■	a					10 10			10 20	10 27		10 25				10 40			10 50	10 57			
	d					10 10			10 20			10 25				10 40			10 50				
Taffs Well ■	d					10 14			10 24			10 29				10 44			10 54				
Trefforest Estate	d															10 48							
Trefforest	d					10 22			10 31			10 36				10 52			11 01				
Pontypridd ■	a					10 30			10 34			10 39				10 55			11 04				
	d								10 36		10 35	10 41				10 57			11 06				
Abercynon	d										10 41	10 49				11 04							
Penrhiwceiber	d											10 55											
Mountain Ash	a											10 58											
	d											11 04											
Fernhill	d											11 07											
Cwmbach	d											11 11											
Aberdare ■	a											11 19											
Quakers Yard	d										10 45					11 09							
Merthyr Vale	a										10 50					11 14							
	d										10 52					11 17							
Troed Y Rhiw	d										10 56					11 21							
Pentre-bach	d										10 59					11 24							
Merthyr Tydfil	a										11 08					11 33							
Trehafod	d								10 41										11 11				
Porth	a								10 44										11 14				
	d								10 45										11 15				
Dinas Rhondda	d								10 49										11 19				
Tonypandy	d								10 51										11 21				
Llwynypia	d								10 53										11 23				
Ystrad Rhondda	a								10 56										11 26				
	d								10 59										11 29				
Ton Pentre	d								11 01										11 31				
Treorchy	d								11 04										11 34				
Ynyswen	d								11 07										11 37				
Treherbert	a								11 14										11 44				

When events are being held at the Millenium Stadium, services are subject to alteration. Please check times before travelling.

Table 130

Saturdays from 15 September

Bridgend, Barry Island, Barry, Penarth and Cardiff - Coryton, Rhymney, Pontypridd, Merthyr, Aberdare and Treherbert

Network Diagram - see first Page of Table 130

		AW	AW	AW	AW	AW	AW	AW	AW	AW	AW	AW	AW	AW	AW	AW	AW	AW	AW	AW	AW	AW
Bridgend	d																		10 42			
Llantwit Major	d																		10 56			
Rhoose Cardiff Int Airport ✈	d																		11 06			
Barry Island	d				10 25					10 40				10 55								
Barry ■	d				10 30					10 45				11 00					11 15			
Barry Docks	d				10 34					10 49				11 04					11 19			
Cadoxton	d				10 37					10 52				11 07					11 22			
Dinas Powys	d				10 41					10 56				11 11					11 26			
Eastbrook	d				10 43					10 58				11 13					11 28			
Cogan	d				10 45					11 00				11 15					11 30			
Penarth	d						10 47				11 02				11 17						11 32	
Dingle Road	d						10 49				11 04				11 19						11 34	
Grangetown	d				10 49		10 53			11 04	11 08			11 19	11 23				11 34		11 38	
Cardiff Central ■	a				10 54		10 59			11 09	11 14			11 24	11 29				11 39		11 44	
	d	10 51		10 51	10 56		11 01	11 06		11 11	11 16		11 21	11 26	11 31		11 36	11 36	11 41		11 46	11 51
Cardiff Bay	d		10 54						11 06			11 18				11 30				11 42		
Cardiff Queen Street ■	a	10 54	10 58		10 59		11 04		11 10	11 14	11 19	11 22	11 24	11 29	11 34	11 34	11 39		11 44	11 46	11 49	11 54
	d	10 55			11 00		11 05			11 15	11 20		11 25	11 30	11 35		11 40		11 45		11 50	11 55
Heath Low Level	d	11 00											11 30									12 00
Ty Glas	d	11 03											11 33									12 03
Birchgrove	d	11 04											11 34									12 04
Rhiwbina	d	11 06											11 36									12 06
Whitchurch (Cardiff)	d	11 08											11 38									12 08
Coryton	a	11 14											11 44									12 14
Heath High Level	d						11 10				11 25				11 40						11 55	
Llanishen	d						11 13				11 28				11 43						11 58	
Lisvane & Thornhill	d						11 15				11 30				11 45						12 00	
Caerphilly ■	d						11 21				11 36				11 51						12 06	
Aber	d						11 23				11 38				11 53						12 08	
Llanbradach	d						11 27				11 42				11 57						12 12	
Ystrad Mynach ■	d						11 32				11 47				12 07						12a22	
Hengoed	d						11 35				11 50				12 10							
Pengam	d						11 38				11 53				12 13							
Gilfach Fargoed	d						11 41															
Bargoed	a						11 49				11 58				12 22							
	d										11 59											
Brithdir	d										12 03											
Tir-phil	d										12 06											
Pontlottyn	d										12 10											
Rhymney ■	a										12 17											
Cathays	d				11 03					11 18				11 33			11 43		11 48			
Llandaf	d				11 07					11 22				11 37			11 47		11 52			
Ninian Park	d							11 10										11 40				
Waun-gron Park	d							11 14										11 44				
Fairwater	d							11 16										11 46				
Danescourt	d					←		11 19										11 49				
Radyr ■	a			11 02	11 10	11 02		11 27		11 25				11 40			11 50	11 57	11 55			
	d			11 20	11 10	11 20				11 25				11 40			11 50		11 55			
Taffs Well ■	d			→	11 14	11 24				11 29				11 44			11 54		11 59			
Trefforest Estate	d				11 18									11 48								
Trefforest	d				11 22	11 31				11 36				11 52			12 01		12 06			
Pontypridd ■	a				11 25	11 34				11 39				11 55			12 04		12 09			
	d				11 27	11 36				11 41				11 57			12 06		12 11			
Abercynon	d				11 34					11 49				12 04					12 19			
Penrhiwceiber	d									11 55									12 25			
Mountain Ash	a									11 58									12 28			
	d									12 04									12 34			
Fernhill	d									12 07									12 37			
Cwmbach	d									12 11									12 41			
Aberdare ■	a									12 19									12 49			
Quakers Yard	d				11 39									12 09								
Merthyr Vale	a				11 44									12 14								
	d				11 47									12 17								
Troed Y Rhiw	d				11 51									12 21								
Pentre-bach	d				11 54									12 24								
Merthyr Tydfil	a				12 03									12 33								
Trehafod	d					11 41											12 11					
Porth	a					11 44											12 14					
	d					11 45											12 15					
Dinas Rhondda	d					11 49											12 19					
Tonypandy	d					11 51											12 21					
Llwynypia	d					11 53											12 23					
Ystrad Rhondda	a					11 56											12 26					
	d					11 59											12 29					
Ton Pentre	d					12 01											12 31					
Treorchy	d					12 04											12 34					
Ynyswen	d					12 07											12 37					
Treherbert	a					12 14											12 44					

When events are being held at the Millenium Stadium, services are subject to alteration. Please check times before travelling.

Table 130

Saturdays
from 15 September

Bridgend, Barry Island, Barry, Penarth and Cardiff - Coryton, Rhymney, Pontypridd, Merthyr, Aberdare and Treherbert

Network Diagram - see first Page of Table 130

		AW	AW	AW	AW	AW	AW	AW	AW	AW	AW	AW	AW	AW	AW	AW	AW	AW	AW	AW	AW	AW	AW
Bridgend	d																	11 42					
Llantwit Major	d																	11 56					
Rhoose Cardiff Int Airport ✈	d																	12 06					
Barry Island	d		11 25					11 40					11 55										12 25
Barry	d		11 30					11 45					12 00					12 15					12 30
Barry Docks	d		11 34					11 49					12 04					12 19					12 34
Cadoxton	d		11 37					11 52					12 07					12 22					12 37
Dinas Powys	d		11 41					11 56					12 11					12 26					12 41
Eastbrook	d		11 43					11 58					12 13					12 28					12 43
Cogan	d		11 45					12 00					12 15					12 30					12 45
Penarth	d			11 47					12 02						12 17					12 32			
Dingle Road	d			11 49					12 04						12 19					12 34			
Grangetown	d		11 49	11 53				12 04	12 08				12 19		12 23			12 34		12 38			12 49
Cardiff Central	a		11 54	11 59				12 09	12 14				12 24		12 29			12 39		12 44			12 54
	d		11 56	12 01		12 06	12 06	12 11	12 16		12 21	12 21	12 26		12 31		12 36	12 41		12 46	12 51		12 56
Cardiff Bay	d	11 54			12 06					12 18						12 30			12 42			12 54	
Cardiff Queen Street	a	11 58	11 59	12 04	12 10	12 09		12 14	12 19	12 22	12 24		12 29		12 34	12 34		12 44	12 46	12 49	12 54	12 58	12 59
	d		12 00	12 05		12 10		12 15	12 20		12 25		12 30		12 35			12 45		12 50	12 55		13 00
Heath Low Level	d										12 30										13 00		
Ty Glas	d										12 33										13 03		
Birchgrove	d										12 34										13 04		
Rhiwbina	d										12 36										13 06		
Whitchurch (Cardiff)	d										12 38										13 08		
Coryton	a										12 44										13 14		
Heath High Level	d			12 10					12 25						12 40					12 55			
Llanishen	d			12 13					12 28						12 43					12 58			
Lisvane & Thornhill	d			12 15					12 30						12 45					13 00			
Caerphilly	d			12 21					12 36						12 51					13 06			
Aber	d			12 23					12 38						12 53					13 08			
Llanbradach	d			12 27					12 42						12 57					13 12			
Ystrad Mynach	d			12 32					12 47						13 02					13a22			
Hengoed	d			12 35					12 50						13 05								
Pengam	d			12 38					12 53						13 08								
Gilfach Fargoed	d			12 41																			
Bargoed	a			12 49					12 58						13 17								
	d								12 59														
Brithdir	d								13 03														
Tir-phil	d								13 06														
Pontlottyn	d								13 10														
Rhymney	a								13 17														
Cathays	d		12 03			12 13		12 18					12 33					12 48					13 03
Llandaf	d		12 07			12 17		12 22					12 37					12 52					13 07
Ninian Park	d						12 10										12 40						
Waun-gron Park	d						12 14										12 44						
Fairwater	d						12 16										12 46						
Danescourt	d						12 19							←			12 49						
Radyr	a		12 10			12 20	12 27	12 25				12 43	12 40	12 43			12 57	12 55					13 10
	d		12 10			12 20		12 25				12 50	12 40	12 50				12 55					13 10
Taffs Well	d		12 14			12 24		12 29				→	12 44	12 54				12 59					13 14
Trefforest Estate	d		12 18										12 48										13 18
Trefforest	d		12 22			12 31		12 36					12 52	13 01				13 06					13 22
Pontypridd	a		12 25			12 34		12 42					12 55	13 04				13 09					13 25
	d		12 27			12 36							12 57	13 06				13 11					13 27
Abercynon	d		12 34										13 04					13 19					13 34
Penrhiwceiber	d																	13 25					
Mountain Ash	a																	13 28					
	d																	13 34					
Fernhill	d																	13 37					
Cwmbach	d																	13 41					
Aberdare	a																	13 49					
Quakers Yard	d		12 39										13 09										13 39
Merthyr Vale	a		12 44										13 14										13 44
	d		12 47										13 17										13 47
Troed Y Rhiw	d		12 51										13 21										13 51
Pentre-bach	d		12 54										13 24										13 54
Merthyr Tydfil	a		13 03										13 33										14 03
Trehafod	d					12 41								13 11									
Porth	a					12 44								13 14									
	d					12 45								13 15									
Dinas Rhondda	d					12 49								13 19									
Tonypandy	d					12 51								13 21									
Llwynypia	d					12 53								13 23									
Ystrad Rhondda	a					12 56								13 26									
	d					12 59								13 29									
Ton Pentre	d					13 01								13 31									
Treorchy	d					13 04								13 34									
Ynyswen	d					13 07								13 37									
Treherbert	a					13 14								13 44									

When events are being held at the Millenium Stadium, services are subject to alteration. Please check times before travelling.

Table 130

Saturdays
from 15 September

Bridgend, Barry Island, Barry, Penarth and Cardiff - Coryton, Rhymney, Pontypridd, Merthyr, Aberdare and Treherbert

Network Diagram - see first Page of Table 130

		AW	AW	AW	AW	AW	AW	AW	AW	AW	AW	AW	AW	AW	AW	AW	AW	AW	AW	AW	AW	AW	AW
Bridgend	d														12 42								
Llantwit Major	d														12 56								
Rhoose Cardiff Int Airport ✈	d														13 06								
Barry Island	d					12 40				12 55										13 25			
Barry	d					12 45				13 00					13 15					13 30			
Barry Docks	d					12 49				13 04					13 19					13 34			
Cadoxton	d					12 52				13 07					13 22					13 37			
Dinas Powys	d					12 56				13 11					13 26					13 41			
Eastbrook	d					12 58				13 13					13 28					13 43			
Cogan	d					13 00				13 15					13 30					13 45			
Penarth	d	12 47					13 02				13 17						13 32				13 47		
Dingle Road	d	12 49					13 04				13 19						13 34				13 49		
Grangetown	d	12 53				13 04	13 08			13 19	13 23				13 34		13 38			13 49	13 53		
Cardiff Central	a	12 59				13 09	13 14			13 24	13 29				13 39		13 44			13 54	13 59		
	d	13 01		13 06	13 06	13 11	13 16		13 21	13 26	13 31		13 36	13 36	13 41		13 46	13 51		13 56	14 01		14 06
Cardiff Bay	d		13 06					13 18				13 30				13 42			13 54			14 06	
Cardiff Queen Street	a	13 04	13 10	13 09		13 14	13 19	13 22	13 24	13 29	13 34	13 34	13 39		13 44	13 46	13 49	13 54	13 58	13 59	14 04	14 10	14 09
	d	13 05		13 10		13 15	13 20		13 25	13 30	13 35		13 40		13 45		13 50	13 55		14 00	14 05		14 10
Heath Low Level	d								13 30									14 00					
Ty Glas	d								13 33									14 03					
Birchgrove	d								13 34									14 04					
Rhiwbina	d								13 36									14 06					
Whitchurch (Cardiff)	d								13 38									14 08					
Coryton	a								13 44									14 14					
Heath High Level	d	13 10					13 25				13 40						13 55				14 10		
Llanishen	d	13 13					13 28				13 43						13 58				14 13		
Lisvane & Thornhill	d	13 15					13 30				13 45						14 00				14 15		
Caerphilly	d	13 21					13 36				13 51						14 06				14 21		
Aber	d	13 23					13 38				13 53						14 08				14 23		
Llanbradach	d	13 27					13 42				13 57						14 12				14 27		
Ystrad Mynach	d	13 32					13 47				14 07						14a22				14 32		
Hengoed	d	13 35					13 50				14 10										14 35		
Pengam	d	13 38					13 53				14 13										14 38		
Gilfach Fargoed	d	13 41																			14 41		
Bargoed	a	13 49					13 58				14 22										14 49		
	d						13 59																
Brithdir	d						14 03																
Tir-phil	d						14 06																
Pontlottyn	d						14 10																
Rhymney	a						14 17																
Cathays	d			13 13		13 18				13 33			13 43		13 48					14 03			14 13
Llandaf	d			13 17		13 22				13 37			13 47		13 52					14 07			14 17
Ninian Park	d				13 10									13 40									
Waun-gron Park	d				13 14									13 44									
Fairwater	d				13 16									13 46									
Danescourt	d				13 19									13 49									
Radyr	a			13 20	13 27	13 25				13 40			13 50	13 57	13 55					14 10			14 20
	d			13 20		13 25				13 40			13 50		13 55					14 10			14 20
Taffs Well	d			13 24		13 29				13 44			13 54		13 59					14 14			14 24
Trefforest Estate	d									13 48										14 18			
Trefforest	d			13 31		13 36				13 52			14 01		14 06					14 22			14 31
Pontypridd	a			13 34		13 39				13 55			14 04		14 09					14 25			14 34
	d			13 36		13 41				13 57			14 06		14 11					14 27			14 36
Abercynon	d					13 49				14 04					14 19					14 34			
Penrhiwceiber	d					13 55									14 25								
Mountain Ash	a					13 58									14 28								
	d					14 04									14 34								
Fernhill	d					14 07									14 37								
Cwmbach	d					14 11									14 41								
Aberdare	a					14 19									14 49								
Quakers Yard	d									14 09										14 39			
Merthyr Vale	a									14 14										14 44			
	d									14 17										14 47			
Troed Y Rhiw	d									14 21										14 51			
Pentre-bach	d									14 24										14 54			
Merthyr Tydfil	a									14 33										15 03			
Trehafod	d			13 41									14 11										14 41
Porth	a			13 44									14 14										14 44
	d			13 45									14 15										14 45
Dinas Rhondda	d			13 49									14 19										14 49
Tonypandy	d			13 51									14 21										14 51
Llwynypia	d			13 53									14 23										14 53
Ystrad Rhondda	a			13 56									14 26										14 56
	d			13 59									14 29										14 59
Ton Pentre	d			14 01									14 31										15 01
Treorchy	d			14 04									14 34										15 04
Ynyswen	d			14 07									14 37										15 07
Treherbert	a			14 14									14 44										15 14

When events are being held at the Millenium Stadium, services are subject to alteration. Please check times before travelling.

Table 130

Saturdays
from 15 September

Bridgend, Barry Island, Barry, Penarth and Cardiff - Coryton, Rhymney, Pontypridd, Merthyr, Aberdare and Treherbert

Network Diagram - see first Page of Table 130

		AW		AW	AW	AW	AW	AW	AW	AW	AW	AW		AW	AW	AW	AW	AW	AW	AW	AW	AW		AW	AW
Bridgend	d													13 42											
Llantwit Major	d													13 56											
Rhoose Cardiff Int Airport ✈	d													14 06											
Barry Island	d			13 40				13 55												14 25					
Barry 3	d			13 45				14 00						14 15						14 30					
Barry Docks	d			13 49				14 04						14 19						14 34					
Cadoxton	d			13 52				14 07						14 22						14 37					
Dinas Powys	d			13 56				14 11						14 26						14 41					
Eastbrook	d			13 58				14 13						14 28						14 43					
Cogan	d			14 00				14 15						14 30						14 45					
Penarth	d				14 02				14 17							14 32						14 47			
Dingle Road	d				14 04				14 19							14 34						14 49			
Grangetown	d			14 04	14 08			14 19	14 23					14 34		14 38				14 49		14 53			
Cardiff Central 7	a			14 09	14 14			14 24	14 29					14 39		14 44				14 54		14 59			
	d	14 06		14 11	14 16		14 21	14 26	14 31		14 36	14 36		14 41		14 46	14 51		14 51	14 56		15 01		15 06	
Cardiff Bay	d					14 18				14 30					14 42			14 54							15 06
Cardiff Queen Street 3	a			14 14	14 19	14 22	14 24	14 29	14 34	14 34	14 39			14 44	14 46	14 49	14 54	14 58		14 59		15 04			15 10
	d			14 15	14 20		14 25	14 30	14 35		14 40			14 45		14 50	14 55			15 00		15 05			
Heath Low Level	d						14 30										15 00								
Ty Glas	d						14 33										15 03								
Birchgrove	d						14 34										15 04								
Rhiwbina	d						14 36										15 06								
Whitchurch (Cardiff)	d						14 38										15 08								
Coryton	a						14 44										15 14								
Heath High Level	d				14 25				14 40							14 55						15 10			
Llanishen	d				14 28				14 43							14 58						15 13			
Lisvane & Thornhill	d				14 30				14 45							15 00						15 15			
Caerphilly 3	d				14 36				14 51							15 06						15 21			
Aber	d				14 38				14 53							15 08						15 23			
Llanbradach	d				14 42				14 57							15 12						15 27			
Ystrad Mynach 3	d				14 47				15 07							15a22						15 32			
Hengoed	d				14 50				15 10													15 35			
Pengam	d				14 53				15 13													15 38			
Gilfach Fargoed	d																					15 41			
Bargoed	a				14 58				15 22													15 49			
	d				14 59																				
Brithdir	d				15 03																				
Tir-phil	d				15 06																				
Pontlottyn	d				15 10																				
Rhymney 3	a				15 17																				
Cathays	d			14 18				14 33			14 43			14 48						15 03					
Llandaf	d			14 22				14 37			14 47			14 52						15 07					
Ninian Park	d	14 10										14 40												15 10	
Waun-gron Park	d	14 14										14 44												15 14	
Fairwater	d	14 16										14 46												15 16	
Danescourt	d	14 19										14 49									←			15 19	
Radyr 3	a	14 27		14 25				14 40			14 50	14 57		14 55					15 08	15 10	15 08			15 27	
	d			14 25				14 40			14 50			14 55					15 20	15 10	15 20				
Taffs Well 3	d			14 29				14 44			14 54			14 59					→	15 14	15 24				
Trefforest Estate	d							14 48												15 18					
Trefforest	d			14 36				14 52			15 01			15 06						15 22	15 31				
Pontypridd 3	a			14 39				14 55			15 04			15 09						15 25	15 34				
	d			14 41				14 57			15 06			15 11						15 27	15 36				
Abercynon	d			14 49				15 04						15 19						15 34					
Penrhiwceiber	d			14 55										15 25											
Mountain Ash	a			14 58										15 28											
	d			15 04										15 34											
Fernhill	d			15 07										15 37											
Cwmbach	d			15 11										15 41											
Aberdare 3	a			15 19										15 49											
Quakers Yard	d							15 09												15 39					
Merthyr Vale	a							15 14												15 44					
	d							15 17												15 47					
Troed Y Rhiw	d							15 21												15 51					
Pentre-bach	d							15 24												15 54					
Merthyr Tydfil	a							15 33												16 03					
Trehafod	d										15 11										15 41				
Porth	a										15 14										15 44				
	d										15 15										15 45				
Dinas Rhondda	d										15 19										15 49				
Tonypandy	d										15 21										15 51				
Llwynypia	d										15 23										15 53				
Ystrad Rhondda	a										15 26										15 56				
	d										15 29										15 59				
Ton Pentre	d										15 31										16 01				
Treorchy	d										15 34										16 04				
Ynyswen	d										15 37										16 07				
Treherbert	a										15 44										16 14				

When events are being held at the Millenium Stadium, services are subject to alteration. Please check times before travelling.

Table 130

Saturdays
from 15 September

Bridgend, Barry Island, Barry, Penarth and Cardiff - Coryton, Rhymney, Pontypridd, Merthyr, Aberdare and Treherbert

Network Diagram - see first Page of Table 130

		AW	AW	AW	AW	AW	AW	AW		AW	AW	AW	AW	AW	AW	AW	AW	AW		AW	AW	AW	AW	AW	AW
Bridgend	d											14 42													
Llantwit Major	d											14 56													
Rhoose Cardiff Int Airport ✈	d											15 06													
Barry Island	d	14 40				14 55											15 25						15 40		
Barry 3	d	14 45				15 00						15 15					15 30						15 45		
Barry Docks	d	14 49				15 04						15 19					15 34						15 49		
Cadoxton	d	14 52				15 07						15 22					15 37						15 52		
Dinas Powys	d	14 56				15 11						15 26					15 41						15 56		
Eastbrook	d	14 58				15 13						15 28					15 43						15 58		
Cogan	d	15 00				15 15						15 30					15 45						16 00		
Penarth	d		15 02				15 17							15 32				15 47						16 02	
Dingle Road	d		15 04				15 19							15 34				15 49						16 04	
Grangetown	d	15 04	15 08			15 19	15 23					15 34		15 38			15 49	15 53					16 04	16 08	
Cardiff Central 7	a	15 09	15 14			15 24	15 29					15 39		15 44			15 54	15 59					16 09	16 14	
	d	15 11	15 16		15 21	15 26	15 31			15 36	15 36	15 41		15 46	15 51		15 56	16 01			16 06	16 06	16 11	16 16	
Cardiff Bay	d			15 18				15 30					15 42			15 54				16 06					16 18
Cardiff Queen Street 3	a	15 14	15 19	15 22	15 24	15 29	15 34	15 34		15 39		15 44	15 46	15 49	15 54	15 58	15 59	16 04		16 10	16 09		16 14	16 19	16 22
	d	15 15	15 20		15 25	15 30	15 35			15 40		15 45		15 50	15 55		16 00	16 05			16 10		16 15	16 20	
Heath Low Level	d				15 30										16 00										
Ty Glas	d				15 33										16 03										
Birchgrove	d				15 34										16 04										
Rhiwbina	d				15 36										16 06										
Whitchurch (Cardiff)	d				15 38										16 08										
Coryton	a				15 44										16 14										
Heath High Level	d		15 25				15 40							15 55				16 10						16 25	
Llanishen	d		15 28				15 43							15 58				16 13						16 28	
Lisvane & Thornhill	d		15 30				15 45							16 00				16 15						16 30	
Caerphilly 3	d		15 36				15 51							16 06				16 21						16 36	
Aber	d		15 38				15 53							16 08				16 23						16 38	
Llanbradach	d		15 42				15 57							16 12				16 27						16 42	
Ystrad Mynach 3	d		15 47				16 02							16 17				16 32						16 47	
Hengoed	d		15 50				16 05							16 20				16 35						16 50	
Pengam	d		15 53				16 08							16 23				16 38						16 53	
Gilfach Fargoed	d																	16 41							
Bargoed	a		15 58				16 17							16 32				16 49						16 58	
	d		15 59																					16 59	
Brithdir	d		16 03																					17 03	
Tir-phil	d		16 06																					17 06	
Pontlottyn	d		16 10																					17 10	
Rhymney 3	a		16 17																					17 17	
Cathays	d	15 18				15 33				15 43		15 48					16 03				16 13		16 18		
Llandaf	d	15 22				15 37				15 47		15 52					16 07				16 17		16 22		
Ninian Park	d										15 40											16 10			
Waun-gron Park	d										15 44											16 14			
Fairwater	d										15 46											16 16			
Danescourt	d										15 49											16 19			
Radyr 3	a	15 25				15 40				15 50	15 57	15 55					16 10				16 20	16 27	16 25		
	d	15 25				15 40				15 50		15 55					16 10				16 20		16 25		
Taffs Well 3	d	15 29				15 44				15 54		15 59					16 14				16 24		16 29		
Trefforest Estate	d					15 48											16 18								
Trefforest	d	15 36				15 52				16 01		16 06					16 22				16 31		16 36		
Pontypridd 3	a	15 39				15 55				16 04		16 09					16 25				16 34		16 39		
	d	15 41				15 57				16 06		16 11					16 27				16 36		16 41		
Abercynon	d	15 49				16 04						16 19					16 34						16 49		
Penrhiwceiber	d	15 55										16 25											16 55		
Mountain Ash	a	15 58										16 28											16 58		
	d	16 04										16 34											17 04		
Fernhill	d	16 07										16 37											17 07		
Cwmbach	d	16 11										16 41											17 11		
Aberdare 3	a	16 19										16 49											17 19		
Quakers Yard	d					16 09											16 39								
Merthyr Vale	a					16 14											16 44								
	d					16 17											16 47								
Troed Y Rhiw	d					16 21											16 51								
Pentre-bach	d					16 24											16 54								
Merthyr Tydfil	a					16 33											17 03								
Trehafod	d									16 11											16 41				
Porth	a									16 14											16 44				
	d									16 15											16 45				
Dinas Rhondda	d									16 19											16 49				
Tonypandy	d									16 21											16 51				
Llwynypia	d									16 23											16 53				
Ystrad Rhondda	a									16 26											16 56				
	d									16 29											16 59				
Ton Pentre	d									16 31											17 01				
Treorchy	d									16 34											17 04				
Ynyswen	d									16 37											17 07				
Treherbert	a									16 44											17 14				

When events are being held at the Millenium Stadium, services are subject to alteration. Please check times before travelling.

Table 130

Saturdays
from 15 September

Bridgend, Barry Island, Barry, Penarth and Cardiff - Coryton, Rhymney, Pontypridd, Merthyr, Aberdare and Treherbert

Network Diagram - see first Page of Table 130

		AW	AW	AW	AW	AW	AW	AW	AW	AW	AW	AW	AW	AW	AW	AW	AW	AW	AW	AW	AW	AW
Bridgend	d							15 42														
Llantwit Major	d							15 56														
Rhoose Cardiff Int Airport ✈	d							16 06														
Barry Island	d		15 55										16 25					16 40				16 55
Barry ❸	d		16 00					16 15					16 30					16 45				17 00
Barry Docks	d		16 04					16 19					16 34					16 49				17 04
Cadoxton	d		16 07					16 22					16 37					16 52				17 07
Dinas Powys	d		16 11					16 26					16 41					16 56				17 11
Eastbrook	d		16 13					16 28					16 43					16 58				17 13
Cogan	d		16 15					16 30					16 45					17 00				17 15
Penarth	d			16 17						16 32									17 02			
Dingle Road	d			16 19						16 34									17 04			
Grangetown	d		16 19	16 23				16 34		16 38			16 49					17 04	17 08			17 19
Cardiff Central ❼	a		16 24	16 29				16 39		16 44			16 54					17 09	17 14			17 24
	d	16 21	16 26	16 31		16 36	16 36	16 41		16 46	16 51		16 56	17 01		17 06	17 06	17 11	17 16		17 21	17 26
Cardiff Bay	d				16 30				16 42			16 54			17 06					17 18		
Cardiff Queen Street ❸	a	16 24	16 29	16 34	16 34	16 39		16 44	16 46	16 49	16 54	16 58	16 59	17 04	17 10	17 09		17 14	17 19	17 22	17 24	17 29
	d	16 25	16 30	16 35		16 40		16 45		16 50	16 55		17 00	17 05		17 10		17 15	17 20		17 25	17 30
Heath Low Level	d	16 30									17 00										17 30	
Ty Glas	d	16 33									17 03										17 33	
Birchgrove	d	16 34									17 04										17 34	
Rhiwbina	d	16 36									17 06										17 36	
Whitchurch (Cardiff)	d	16 38									17 08										17 38	
Coryton	a	16 44									17 14										17 44	
Heath High Level	d			16 40						16 55				17 10					17 25			
Llanishen	d			16 43						16 58				17 13					17 28			
Lisvane & Thornhill	d			16 45						17 00				17 15					17 30			
Caerphilly ❸	d			16 51						17 06				17 21					17 36			
Aber	d			16 53						17 08				17 23					17 38			
Llanbradach	d			16 57						17 12				17 27					17 42			
Ystrad Mynach ❸	d			17 02						17 17				17 33					17 47			
Hengoed	d			17 05						17 20				17 35					17 50			
Pengam	d			17 08						17 23				17 39					17 53			
Gilfach Fargoed	d													17 42								
Bargoed	a			17 17						17 32				17 45					18 02			
	d													17 47								
Brithdir	d													17 50								
Tir-phil	d													17 53								
Pontlottyn	d													17 58								
Rhymney ❸	a													18 05								
Cathays	d		16 33			16 43		16 48					17 03			17 13		17 18				17 33
Llandaf	d		16 37			16 47		16 52					17 07			17 17		17 22				17 37
Ninian Park	d						16 40										17 10					
Waun-gron Park	d						16 44										17 14					
Fairwater	d						16 46										17 16					
Danescourt	d						16 49										17 19					
Radyr ❸	a		16 40			16 50	16 57	16 55					17 10			17 20	17 27	17 25				17 40
	d		16 40			16 50		16 55					17 10			17 20		17 25				17 40
Taffs Well ❸	d		16 44			16 54		16 59					17 14			17 24		17 29				17 44
Trefforest Estate	d		16 48										17 18									17 48
Trefforest	d		16 52			17 01		17 06					17 22			17 31		17 36				17 52
Pontypridd ❸	a		16 55			17 04		17 09					17 25			17 34		17 39				17 55
	d		16 57			17 06		17 11					17 27			17 36		17 41				17 57
Abercynon	d		17 04					17 19					17 34					17 49				18 04
Penrhiwceiber	d							17 25										17 55				
Mountain Ash	a							17 28										17 58				
	d							17 34										18 04				
Fernhill	d							17 37										18 07				
Cwmbach	d							17 41										18 11				
Aberdare ❸	a							17 49										18 19				
Quakers Yard	d		17 09										17 39									18 09
Merthyr Vale	a		17 14										17 44									18 14
	d		17 17										17 47									18 17
Troed Y Rhiw	d		17 21										17 51									18 21
Pentre-bach	d		17 24										17 54									18 24
Merthyr Tydfil	a		17 33										18 03									18 33
Trehafod	d					17 11										17 41						
Porth	a					17 14										17 44						
	d					17 15										17 45						
Dinas Rhondda	d					17 19										17 49						
Tonypandy	d					17 21										17 51						
Llwynypia	d					17 23										17 53						
Ystrad Rhondda	a					17 26										17 56						
	d					17 29										17 59						
Ton Pentre	d					17 31										18 01						
Treorchy	d					17 34										18 04						
Ynyswen	d					17 37										18 07						
Treherbert	a					17 44										18 14						

When events are being held at the Millenium Stadium, services are subject to alteration. Please check times before travelling.

Table 130

Saturdays
from 15 September

Bridgend, Barry Island, Barry, Penarth and Cardiff - Coryton, Rhymney, Pontypridd, Merthyr, Aberdare and Treherbert

Network Diagram - see first Page of Table 130

		AW	AW	AW	AW	AW	AW	AW	AW	AW	AW	AW	AW	AW	AW	AW	AW	AW	AW	AW	AW	AW	
Bridgend	d					16 42																	
Llantwit Major	d					16 56																	
Rhoose Cardiff Int Airport ✈	d					17 06																	
Barry Island	d										17 25					17 40				17 55			
Barry ❸	d					17 15					17 30					17 45				18 00			
Barry Docks	d					17 19					17 34					17 49				18 04			
Cadoxton	d					17 22					17 37					17 52				18 07			
Dinas Powys	d					17 26					17 41					17 56				18 11			
Eastbrook	d					17 28					17 43					17 58				18 13			
Cogan	d					17 30					17 45					18 00				18 15			
Penarth	d	17 17						17 32				17 47					18 02					18 17	
Dingle Road	d	17 19						17 34				17 49					18 04					18 19	
Grangetown	d	17 23				17 34		17 38			17 49	17 53				18 04	18 08			18 19		18 23	
Cardiff Central ❼	a	17 29				17 39		17 44			17 54	17 59				18 09	18 14			18 24		18 29	
	d	17 31		17 36	17 36	17 41		17 46	17 51		17 56	18 01		18 06	18 06	18 11	18 16		18 21	18 26		18 31	18 36
Cardiff Bay	d		17 30				17 42			17 54			18 06					18 18			18 30		
Cardiff Queen Street ❸	a	17 34	17 34	17 39		17 44	17 46	17 49	17 54	17 58	17 59	18 04	18 10	18 09		18 14	18 19	18 22	18 24	18 29	18 34	18 34	18 38
	d	17 35		17 40		17 45		17 50	17 55		18 00	18 05		18 10		18 15	18 20		18 25	18 30		18 35	18 40
Heath Low Level	d								18 00										18 30				
Ty Glas	d								18 03										18 33				
Birchgrove	d								18 04										18 34				
Rhiwbina	d								18 06										18 36				
Whitchurch (Cardiff)	d								18 08										18 38				
Coryton	a								18 14										18 44				
Heath High Level	d	17 40						17 55				18 10					18 25					18 40	
Llanishen	d	17 43						17 59				18 13					18 28					18 43	
Lisvane & Thornhill	d	17 45						18 02				18 15					18 30					18 45	
Caerphilly ❸	d	17 51						18 07				18 21					18 36					18 51	
Aber	d	17 53						18 10				18 23					18 38					18 53	
Llanbradach	d	17 57						18 14				18 27					18 42					18 57	
Ystrad Mynach ❸	d	18 02						18 20				18 32					18a52					19 02	
Hengoed	d	18 05						18 23				18 35										19 05	
Pengam	d	18 08						18 27				18 38										19 08	
Gilfach Fargoed	d	18 11						18 30				18 41										19 11	
Bargoed	a	18 14						18 34				18 49										19 14	
	d	18 16						18 44														19 16	
Brithdir	d	18 20						18 48														19 20	
Tir-phil	d	18 23						18 51														19 23	
Pontlottyn	d	18 27						18 55														19 27	
Rhymney ❸	a	18 34						19 02														19 35	
Cathays	d			17 43		17 48					18 03			18 13		18 18				18 33			18 43
Llandaf	d			17 47		17 52					18 07			18 17		18 22				18 37			18 47
Ninian Park	d				17 40										18 10								
Waun-gron Park	d				17 44										18 14								
Fairwater	d				17 46										18 16								
Danescourt	d				17 49										18 19								
Radyr ❸	a			17 50	17 57	17 55					18 10			18 20	18 27	18 25				18 40			18 50
	d			17 50		17 55					18 10			18 20		18 25				18 40			18 50
Taffs Well ❸	d			17 54		17 59					18 14			18 24		18 29				18 44			18 54
Trefforest Estate	d										18 18									18 48			
Trefforest	d			18 01		18 06					18 22			18 31		18 36				18 52			19 01
Pontypridd ❸	a			18 04		18 09					18 25			18 34		18 42				18 55			19 04
	d			18 06		18 11					18 27			18 36						18 57			19 06
Abercynon	d					18 19					18 34									19 04			
Penrhiwceiber	d					18 25																	
Mountain Ash	a					18 28																	
	d					18 34																	
Fernhill	d					18 37																	
Cwmbach	d					18 41																	
Aberdare ❸	a					18 49																	
Quakers Yard	d										18 39									19 09			
Merthyr Vale	a										18 44									19 14			
	d										18 47									19 17			
Troed Y Rhiw	d										18 51									19 21			
Pentre-bach	d										18 54									19 24			
Merthyr Tydfil	a										19 03									19 33			
Trehafod	d			18 11										18 41									19 11
Porth	a			18 14										18 44									19 14
	d			18 15										18 45									19 15
Dinas Rhondda	d			18 19										18 49									19 19
Tonypandy	d			18 21										18 51									19 21
Llwynypia	d			18 23										18 53									19 23
Ystrad Rhondda	a			18 26										18 56									19 26
	d			18 29										18 59									19 29
Ton Pentre	d			18 31										19 01									19 31
Treorchy	d			18 34										19 04									19 34
Ynyswen	d			18 37										19 07									19 37
Treherbert	a			18 44										19 14									19 44

When events are being held at the Millenium Stadium, services are subject to alteration. Please check times before travelling.

Table 130

Saturdays
from 15 September

Bridgend, Barry Island, Barry, Penarth and Cardiff - Coryton, Rhymney, Pontypridd, Merthyr, Aberdare and Treherbert

Network Diagram - see first Page of Table 130

		AW	AW	AW	AW	AW		AW	AW	AW	AW	AW	AW	AW	AW	AW		AW	AW	AW	AW	AW	AW	AW	AW
Bridgend	d		17 42																	18 42					
Llantwit Major	d		17 56																	18 56					
Rhoose Cardiff Int Airport ✈	d		18 06																	19 06					
Barry Island	d							18 25					18 40		18 55									19 25	
Barry 3	d		18 15					18 30					18 45		19 00					19 15				19 30	
Barry Docks	d		18 19					18 34					18 49		19 04					19 19				19 34	
Cadoxton	d		18 22					18 37					18 52		19 07					19 22				19 37	
Dinas Powys	d		18 26					18 41					18 56		19 11					19 26				19 41	
Eastbrook	d		18 28					18 43					18 58		19 13					19 28				19 43	
Cogan	d		18 30					18 45					19 00		19 15					19 30				19 45	
Penarth	d			18 32						18 47						19 17									19 47
Dingle Road	d			18 34						18 49						19 19									19 49
Grangetown	d		18 34	18 38				18 49		18 53			19 04		19 19	19 23				19 34				19 49	19 53
Cardiff Central 7	a		18 39	18 47				18 57		18 59			19 09		19 24	19 29				19 39				19 54	19 59
	d	18 36	18 41			18 51				19 01		19 06	19 11		19 26	19 31			19 36	19 41		19 51		20 01	20 06
Cardiff Bay	d				18 42				18 54		19 06			19 18				19 30			19 42		19 54		
Cardiff Queen Street 3	a		18 44		18 46	18 54			18 58	19 04	19 10	19 09	19 14	19 22	19 29	19 34		19 34		19 44	19 46	19 54	19 58	20 04	20 09
	d		18 50			18 55				19 05		19 10	19 15		19 30	19 35				19 45		19 55		20 05	20 10
Heath Low Level	d					19 00																20 00			
Ty Glas	d					19 03																20 03			
Birchgrove	d					19 04																20 04			
Rhiwbina	d					19 06																20 06			
Whitchurch (Cardiff)	d					19 08																20 08			
Coryton	a					19 14																20 14			
Heath High Level	d									19 10						19 40								20 10	
Llanishen	d									19 13						19 43								20 13	
Lisvane & Thornhill	d									19 15						19 45								20 15	
Caerphilly 3	d									19a24						19 51								20a25	
Aber	d															19 53									
Llanbradach	d															19 57									
Ystrad Mynach 3	d															20 02									
Hengoed	d															20 05									
Pengam	d															20 08									
Gilfach Fargoed	d															20 11									
Bargoed	a															20 15									
	d															20 16									
Brithdir	d															20 20									
Tir-phil	d															20 23									
Pontlottyn	d															20 27									
Rhymney 3	a															20 34									
Cathays	d		18 52									19 13	19 18		19 33					19 48					20 13
Llandaf	d		18 56									19 17	19 22		19 37					19 52					20 17
Ninian Park	d	18 40																	19 40						
Waun-gron Park	d	18 44																	19 44						
Fairwater	d	18 46																	19 46						
Danescourt	d	18 49																	19 49						
Radyr 3	a	18 57	18 59									19 20	19 25		19 40				19 57	19 55					20 20
	d		18 59									19 20	19 25		19 40					19 55					20 20
Taffs Well 3	d		19 03									19 24	19 29		19 44					19 59					20 24
Trefforest Estate	d														19 48										
Trefforest	d		19 10									19 31	19 36		19 52					20 06					20 31
Pontypridd 3	a		19 13									19 34	19 39		19 55					20 09					20 34
	d		19 14									19 36	19 41		19 57					20 11					20 36
Abercynon	d		19 21										19 49		20 04					20 21					
Penrhiwceiber	d		19 27										19 55							20 27					
Mountain Ash	a		19 30										19 58							20 31					
	d		19 34										20 04							20 34					
Fernhill	d		19 37										20 07							20 37					
Cwmbach	d		19 41										20 11							20 41					
Aberdare 3	a		19 49										20 19							20 49					
Quakers Yard	d														20 09										
Merthyr Vale	a														20 14										
	d														20 14										
Troed Y Rhiw	d														20 18										
Pentre-bach	d														20 22										
Merthyr Tydfil	a														20 31										
Trehafod	d											19 41													20 41
Porth	a											19 44													20 44
	d											19 45													20 45
Dinas Rhondda	d											19 49													20 49
Tonypandy	d											19 51													20 51
Llwynypia	d											19 53													20 53
Ystrad Rhondda	a											19 56													20 56
	d											19 59													20 59
Ton Pentre	d											20 01													21 01
Treorchy	d											20 04													21 04
Ynyswen	d											20 07													21 07
Treherbert	a											20 14													21 14

When events are being held at the Millenium Stadium, services are subject to alteration. Please check times before travelling.

Table 130

Saturdays
from 15 September

Bridgend, Barry Island, Barry, Penarth and Cardiff - Coryton, Rhymney, Pontypridd, Merthyr, Aberdare and Treherbert

Network Diagram - see first Page of Table 130

		AW		AW	AW	AW	AW	AW	AW	AW	AW	AW		AW	AW	AW	AW	AW	AW	AW	AW	AW		AW	AW
Bridgend	d								19 42															20 42	
Llantwit Major	d								19 56															20 56	
Rhoose Cardiff Int Airport ✈	d								20 06															21 06	
Barry Island	d				19 55													20 55							
Barry 3	d				20 00				20 15									21 00						21 15	
Barry Docks	d				20 04				20 19									21 04						21 19	
Cadoxton	d				20 07				20 22									21 07						21 22	
Dinas Powys	d				20 11				20 26									21 11						21 26	
Eastbrook	d				20 13				20 28									21 13						21 28	
Cogan	d				20 15				20 30									21 15						21 30	
Penarth	d					20 20								20 47								21 20			
Dingle Road	d					20 22								20 49								21 22			
Grangetown	d				20 19	20 26			20 34					20 53				21 19				21 26		21 34	
Cardiff Central 7	a				20 24	20 31			20 39					20 59				21 24				21 37		21 39	
	d				20 26	20 31		20 36	20 41		20 51			21 01		21 06		21 26		21 31	21 36			21 41	
Cardiff Bay	d	20 06		20 18			20 30			20 42		20 54			21 06		21 18		21 30						21 42
Cardiff Queen Street 3	a	20 10		20 22	20 28	20 34	20 34		20 44	20 46	20 54	20 58		21 04	21 10	21 09	21 22	21 29	21 34	21 34				21 44	21 46
	d				20 30	20 35			20 45		20 55			21 05		21 10		21 30		21 35				21 45	
Heath Low Level	d										21 00														
Ty Glas	d										21 03														
Birchgrove	d										21 04														
Rhiwbina	d										21 06														
Whitchurch (Cardiff)	d										21 08														
Coryton	a										21 14														
Heath High Level	d					20 40								21 10						21 40					
Llanishen	d					20 43								21 13						21 43					
Lisvane & Thornhill	d					20 45								21 15						21 45					
Caerphilly 3	d					20 51								21 20						21 51					
Aber	d					20 53								21 22						21 53					
Llanbradach	d					20 57								21 26						21 57					
Ystrad Mynach 3	d					21 02								21a36						22 02					
Hengoed	d					21 05														22 05					
Pengam	d					21 08														22 08					
Gilfach Fargoed	d					21 11														22 11					
Bargoed	a					21 15														22 15					
	d					21 16														22 16					
Brithdir	d					21 20														22 20					
Tir-phil	d					21 23														22 23					
Pontlottyn	d					21 27														22 27					
Rhymney 3	a					21 34														22 35					
Cathays	d				20 33				20 48							21 13		21 33						21 48	
Llandaf	d				20 37				20 52							21 17		21 37						21 52	
Ninian Park	d							20 40													21 40				
Waun-gron Park	d							20 44													21 44				
Fairwater	d							20 46													21 46				
Danescourt	d							20 49													21 49				
Radyr 3	a				20 39			20 57	20 55							21 20		21 40			21 57			21 55	
	d				20 40				20 55							21 20		21 40						21 55	
Taffs Well 3	d				20 44				20 59							21 24		21 44						21 59	
Trefforest Estate	d				20 48													21 48							
Trefforest	d				20 52				21 06							21 31		21 52						22 06	
Pontypridd 3	a				20 55				21 09							21 34		21 55						22 09	
	d				20 57				21 11							21 36		21 57						22 11	
Abercynon	d				21 04				21 19									22 04						22 19	
Penrhiwceiber	d								21 25															22 25	
Mountain Ash	a								21 28															22 28	
	d								21 29															22 29	
Fernhill	d								21 32															22 32	
Cwmbach	d								21 36															22 36	
Aberdare 3	a								21 44															22 44	
Quakers Yard	d				21 09													22 09							
Merthyr Vale	a				21 14													22 14							
	d				21 14													22 14							
Troed Y Rhiw	d				21 18													22 18							
Pentre-bach	d				21 22													22 22							
Merthyr Tydfil	a				21 31													22 31							
Trehafod	d															21 41									
Porth	a															21 44									
	d															21 45									
Dinas Rhondda	d															21 49									
Tonypandy	d															21 51									
Llwynypia	d															21 53									
Ystrad Rhondda	a															21 56									
	d															21 59									
Ton Pentre	d															22 01									
Treorchy	d															22 04									
Ynyswen	d															22 07									
Treherbert	a															22 14									

When events are being held at the Millenium Stadium, services are subject to alteration. Please check times before travelling.

Table 130

Saturdays
from 15 September

Bridgend, Barry Island, Barry, Penarth and Cardiff - Coryton, Rhymney, Pontypridd, Merthyr, Aberdare and Treherbert

Network Diagram - see first Page of Table 130

		AW	AW	AW	AW	AW	AW	AW	AW	AW	AW	AW	AW	AW	AW	AW	AW	AW	AW	AW	AW	AW	AW
Bridgend	d										21 42										22 42		
Llantwit Major	d										21 56										22 56		
Rhoose Cardiff Int Airport ✈	d										22 06										23 06		
Barry Island	d							21 55											22 45				
Barry 3	d							22 00			22 15								22 49		23 15		
Barry Docks	d							22 04			22 19								22 53		23 19		
Cadoxton	d							22 07			22 22								22 56		23 22		
Dinas Powys	d							22 11			22 26								23 00		23 26		
Eastbrook	d							22 13			22 28								23 02		23 28		
Cogan	d							22 15			22 30								23 04		23 30		
Penarth	d		21 47							22 20							22 47			23 26			
Dingle Road	d		21 49							22 22							22 49			23 28			
Grangetown	d		21 53					22 19		22 26	22 34						22 53		23 08	23 32	23 34		
Cardiff Central 7	a		21 59					22 24		22 33	22 39						23 00		23 13	23 40	23 42		
	d		22 01		22 06		22 21	22 26		22 35	22 41		22 46		22 55		23 15		23 26				
Cardiff Bay	d	21 54		22 06		22 18			22 30			22 42		22 54		23 06		23 18				23 30	23 42
Cardiff Queen Street 3	a	21 58	22 04	22 10	22 09	22 22	22 24	22 29	22 34	22 38	22 44	22 46	22 49	22 58		23 10	23 18	23 22	23 29			23 34	23 46
	d		22 05		22 10		22 25	22 30		22 39	22 45		22 50				23 19		23 30				
Heath Low Level	d						22 30																
Ty Glas	d						22 33																
Birchgrove	d						22 34																
Rhiwbina	d						22 36																
Whitchurch (Cardiff)	d						22 38																
Coryton	a						22 44																
Heath High Level	d		22 10							22 44							23 24						
Llanishen	d		22 13							22 47							23 27						
Lisvane & Thornhill	d		22 15							22 49							23 29						
Caerphilly 3	d		22a24							22 55							23 35						
Aber	d									22 57							23 37						
Llanbradach	d									23 01							23 41						
Ystrad Mynach 3	d									23 06							23a51						
Hengoed	d									23 09													
Pengam	d									23 12													
Gilfach Fargoed	d									23 15													
Bargoed	a									23 19													
	d									23 20													
Brithdir	d									23 24													
Tir-phil	d									23 27													
Pontlottyn	d									23 31													
Rhymney 3	a									23 38													
Cathays	d				22 13			22 33			22 48		22 53						23 33				
Llandaf	d				22 17			22 37			22 52		22 57						23 37				
Ninian Park	d														22 59								
Waun-gron Park	d														23 02								
Fairwater	d														23 04								
Danescourt	d														23 06								
Radyr 3	a				22 20			22 40			22 55		22 59		23 14				23 40				
	d				22 20			22 40			22 55		22 59						23 40				
Taffs Well 3	d				22 24			22 44			22 59		23 03						23 44				
Trefforest Estate	d							22 48															
Trefforest	d				22 31			22 52			23 06		23 10						23 52				
Pontypridd 3	a				22 34			22 55			23 09		23 14						23 58				
	d				22 36			22 57			23 11		23 15										
Abercynon	d							23 04			23 19												
Penrhiwceiber	d										23 25												
Mountain Ash	a										23 28												
	d										23 34												
Fernhill	d										23 37												
Cwmbach	d										23 41												
Aberdare 3	a										23 49												
Quakers Yard	d							23 09															
Merthyr Vale	a							23 14															
	d							23 14															
Troed Y Rhiw	d							23 18															
Pentre-bach	d							23 22															
Merthyr Tydfil	a							23 31															
Trehafod	d				22 41								23 20										
Porth	a				22 44								23 23										
	d				22 45								23 24										
Dinas Rhondda	d				22 49								23 28										
Tonypandy	d				22 51								23 30										
Llwynypia	d				22 53								23 32										
Ystrad Rhondda	a				22 56								23 35										
	d				22 59								23 38										
Ton Pentre	d				23 01								23 40										
Treorchy	d				23 04								23 43										
Ynyswen	d				23 07								23 46										
Treherbert	a				23 14								23 53										

When events are being held at the Millenium Stadium, services are subject to alteration. Please check times before travelling.

Table 130

Saturdays
from 15 September

Bridgend, Barry Island, Barry, Penarth and Cardiff - Coryton, Rhymney, Pontypridd, Merthyr, Aberdare and Treherbert

Network Diagram - see first Page of Table 130

		AW
Bridgend	d	
Llantwit Major	d	
Rhoose Cardiff Int Airport ✈	d	
Barry Island	d	
Barry 3	d	
Barry Docks	d	
Cadoxton	d	
Dinas Powys	d	
Eastbrook	d	
Cogan	d	
Penarth	d	
Dingle Road	d	
Grangetown	d	
Cardiff Central 7	a	
	d	
Cardiff Bay	d	23 54
Cardiff Queen Street 3	a	23 58
	d	
Heath Low Level	d	
Ty Glas	d	
Birchgrove	d	
Rhiwbina	d	
Whitchurch (Cardiff)	d	
Coryton	a	
Heath High Level	d	
Llanishen	d	
Lisvane & Thornhill	d	
Caerphilly 3	d	
Aber	d	
Llanbradach	d	
Ystrad Mynach 3	d	
Hengoed	d	
Pengam	d	
Gilfach Fargoed	d	
Bargoed	a	
	d	
Brithdir	d	
Tir-phil	d	
Pontlottyn	d	
Rhymney 3	a	
Cathays	d	
Llandaf	d	
Ninian Park	d	
Waun-gron Park	d	
Fairwater	d	
Danescourt	d	
Radyr 3	a	
	d	
Taffs Well 3	d	
Trefforest Estate	d	
Trefforest	d	
Pontypridd 3	a	
	d	
Abercynon	d	
Penrhiwceiber	d	
Mountain Ash	a	
	d	
Fernhill	d	
Cwmbach	d	
Aberdare 3	a	
Quakers Yard	d	
Merthyr Vale	a	
	d	
Troed Y Rhiw	d	
Pentre-bach	d	
Merthyr Tydfil	a	
Trehafod	d	
Porth	a	
	d	
Dinas Rhondda	d	
Tonypandy	d	
Llwynypia	d	
Ystrad Rhondda	a	
	d	
Ton Pentre	d	
Treorchy	d	
Ynyswen	d	
Treherbert	a	

When events are being held at the Millenium Stadium, services are subject to alteration. Please check times before travelling.

Table 130

Sundays until 24 June

Bridgend, Barry Island, Barry, Penarth and Cardiff - Coryton, Rhymney, Pontypridd, Merthyr, Aberdare and Treherbert

Network Diagram - see first Page of Table 130

		AW (bus)	AW (bus)	AW	AW (bus)	AW	AW	AW (bus)	AW	AW	AW (bus)	AW (bus)	AW	AW (bus)	AW	AW	AW	AW	AW (bus)	AW	AW	AW	AW
Bridgend	d																						
Llantwit Major	d																						
Rhoose Cardiff Int Airport ✈	d														10 06								
Barry Island	d								08 55				09 55			10 25				10 55	11 25		
Barry 3	d								09 00				10 00		10 15	10 30				11 00	11 30		
Barry Docks	d								09 04				10 04		10 19	10 34				11 04	11 34		
Cadoxton	d								09 07				10 07		10 22	10 37				11 07	11 37		
Dinas Powys	d								09 11				10 11		10 26	10 41				11 11	11 41		
Eastbrook	d								09 13				10 13		10 28	10 43				11 13	11 43		
Cogan	d								09 15				10 15		10 30	10 45				11 15	11 45		
Penarth	d																	10 53					
Dingle Road	d																	10 55					
Grangetown	d								09 19				10 19		10 34	10 49		10 59		11 19	11 49		
Cardiff Central 7	a								09 27				10 24		10 42	10 56		11 04		11 34	12 01		
	d	07 52	08 07	08 26	08 26	08 45	09 00	09 07		09 41	09 52	10 06	10 30	10 26			11 00		11 07	11 40		12 10	12 18
Cardiff Bay	d																						
Cardiff Queen Street 3	a	08 00	08 15		08 34			09 15			10 00	10 14		10 34					11 15			12 13	12 21
	d	08 00	08 15		08 34			09 15			10 00	10 14		10 34					11 15			12 14	
Heath Low Level	d																						
Ty Glas	d																						
Birchgrove	d																						
Rhiwbina	d																						
Whitchurch (Cardiff)	d																						
Coryton	a																						
Heath High Level	d											10 29										12 19	
Llanishen	d											10 34										12 22	
Lisvane & Thornhill	d											10 39										12 24	
Caerphilly 3	d											10 49										12 30	
Aber	d											10 54										12 32	
Llanbradach	d											11 04										12 41	
Ystrad Mynach 3	d											11 14										12 51	
Hengoed	d											11 19										12 59	
Pengam	d											11 29										13 02	
Gilfach Fargoed	d											11 34										13 05	
Bargoed	a											11 39										13 08	
	d											11 39										13 08	
Brithdir	d											11 44										13 12	
Tir-phil	d											11 49										13 15	
Pontlottyn	d											11 54										13 19	
Rhymney 3	a											12 02										13 26	
Cathays	d	08 05	08 20		08 39			09 20			10 05			10 39					11 20				
Llandaf	d	08 20	08 35		08 54			09 35			10 20			10 54					11 35				
Ninian Park	d																						
Waun-gron Park	d																						
Fairwater	d																						
Danescourt	d																						
Radyr 3	a	08 30	08 45	08 40	09 04	08 55	09 11	09 45		09 52	10 30		10 40	11 04			11 11		11 45	11 51			
	d			08 40		08 55	09 14			09 55			10 40				11 14			11 55			
Taffs Well 3	d			08 44		08 59	09 18			09 59			10 44				11 18			11 59			
Trefforest Estate	d																						
Trefforest	d			08 52		09 06	09 25			10 06			10 52				11 25			12 06			
Pontypridd 3	a			08 55		09 09	09 28			10 09			10 55				11 28			12 09			
	d			08 57		09 11	09 30			10 11			10 57				11 30			12 11			
Abercynon	d			09 05		09 19				10 19			11 05							12 19			
Penrhiwceiber	d					09 24				10 24										12 24			
Mountain Ash	a					09 28				10 28										12 28			
	d					09 29				10 29										12 29			
Fernhill	d					09 31				10 31										12 31			
Cwmbach	d					09 35				10 35										12 35			
Aberdare 3	a					09 42				10 42										12 42			
Quakers Yard	d			09 09									11 09										
Merthyr Vale	a			09 14									11 14										
	d			09 16									11 16										
Troed Y Rhiw	d			09 20									11 20										
Pentre-bach	d			09 23									11 23										
Merthyr Tydfil	a			09 31									11 31										
Trehafod	d						09 35										11 35						
Porth	a						09 38										11 38						
	d						09 39										11 39						
Dinas Rhondda	d						09 43										11 43						
Tonypandy	d						09 45										11 45						
Llwynypia	d						09 47										11 47						
Ystrad Rhondda	a						09 50										11 50						
	d						09 53										11 53						
Ton Pentre	d						09 55										11 55						
Treorchy	d						09 58										11 58						
Ynyswen	d						10 01										12 01						
Treherbert	a						10 07										12 07						

When events are being held at the Millenium Stadium, services are subject to alteration. Please check times before travelling.

Table 130

Sundays until 24 June

Bridgend, Barry Island, Barry, Penarth and Cardiff - Coryton, Rhymney, Pontypridd, Merthyr, Aberdare and Treherbert

Network Diagram - see first Page of Table 130

		AW	AW	AW	AW	AW	AW	AW	AW	AW	AW	AW	AW	AW	AW	AW	AW	AW	AW	AW	AW	AW	AW
Bridgend	d																				13 52		
Llantwit Major	d																				14 12		
Rhoose Cardiff Int Airport ✈	d		12 06																		14 26		
Barry Island	d	11 55		12 25									12 55			13 25			13 55	14 25			
Barry 3	d	12 00	12 15	12 30									13 00			13 30			14 00	14 30	14 35		
Barry Docks	d	12 04	12 19	12 34									13 04			13 34			14 04	14 34	14 39		
Cadoxton	d	12 07	12 22	12 37									13 07			13 37			14 07	14 37	14 42		
Dinas Powys	d	12 11	12 26	12 41									13 11			13 41			14 11	14 41	14 46		
Eastbrook	d	12 13	12 28	12 43									13 13			13 43			14 13	14 43	14 48		
Cogan	d	12 15	12 30	12 45									13 15			13 45			14 15	14 45	14 50		
Penarth	d						12 47																
Dingle Road	d						12 49																
Grangetown	d	12 19	12 34	12 49			12 53						13 19			13 49			14 19	14 49	14 54		
Cardiff Central 7	a	12 24	12 42	12 56			12 59						13 24			13 54			14 24	14 56	15 02		
	d	12 26								13 06			13 41			14 06			14 26				
Cardiff Bay	d				12 30	12 42		12 54	13 06		13 18	13 30		13 42	13 54		14 06	14 18				14 30	14 42
Cardiff Queen Street 3	a	12 29			12 34	12 46		12 58	13 10	13 09	13 22	13 34	13 44	13 46	13 58	14 09	14 10	14 22	14 29			14 34	14 46
	d	12 30								13 10			13 45			14 10			14 30				
Heath Low Level	d																						
Ty Glas	d																						
Birchgrove	d																						
Rhiwbina	d																						
Whitchurch (Cardiff)	d																						
Coryton	a																						
Heath High Level	d															14 15							
Llanishen	d															14 18							
Lisvane & Thornhill	d															14 20							
Caerphilly 3	d															14 26							
Aber	d															14 28							
Llanbradach	d															14 32							
Ystrad Mynach 3	d															14 37							
Hengoed	d															14 40							
Pengam	d															14 43							
Gilfach Fargoed	d															14 46							
Bargoed	a															14 49							
	d															14 49							
Brithdir	d															14 53							
Tir-phil	d															14 56							
Pontlottyn	d															15 00							
Rhymney 3	a															15 07							
Cathays	d	12 33								13 13			13 48						14 33				
Llandaf	d	12 37								13 17			13 52						14 37				
Ninian Park	d																						
Waun-gron Park	d																						
Fairwater	d																						
Danescourt	d																						
Radyr 3	a	12 40								13 20			13 55						14 40				
	d	12 40								13 20			13 55						14 40				
Taffs Well 3	d	12 44								13 24			13 59						14 44				
Trefforest Estate	d																						
Trefforest	d	12 52								13 31			14 06						14 52				
Pontypridd 3	a	12 55								13 34			14 09						14 55				
	d	12 57								13 36			14 11						14 57				
Abercynon	d	13 05											14 19						15 05				
Penrhiwceiber	d												14 24										
Mountain Ash	a												14 28										
	d												14 29										
Fernhill	d												14 31										
Cwmbach	d												14 35										
Aberdare 3	a												14 42										
Quakers Yard	d	13 09																	15 09				
Merthyr Vale	a	13 14																	15 14				
	d	13 16																	15 16				
Troed Y Rhiw	d	13 20																	15 20				
Pentre-bach	d	13 23																	15 23				
Merthyr Tydfil	a	13 31																	15 31				
Trehafod	d									13 41													
Porth	a									13 44													
	d									13 45													
Dinas Rhondda	d									13 49													
Tonypandy	d									13 51													
Llwynypia	d									13 53													
Ystrad Rhondda	a									13 56													
	d									13 59													
Ton Pentre	d									14 01													
Treorchy	d									14 04													
Ynyswen	d									14 07													
Treherbert	a									14 13													

When events are being held at the Millenium Stadium, services are subject to alteration. Please check times before travelling.

Table 130

Sundays until 24 June

Bridgend, Barry Island, Barry, Penarth and Cardiff - Coryton, Rhymney, Pontypridd, Merthyr, Aberdare and Treherbert

Network Diagram - see first Page of Table 130

		AW		AW	AW	AW	AW	AW	AW	AW	AW	AW		AW	AW	AW	AW	AW	AW	AW	AW	AW		AW	AW
Bridgend	d																15 42								
Llantwit Major	d																15 56								
Rhoose Cardiff Int Airport ✈	d																16 06								
Barry Island	d								14 55			15 25				15 55		16 25				16 40			
Barry 3	d								15 00			15 30				16 00	16 15	16 30				16 45			
Barry Docks	d								15 04			15 34				16 04	16 19	16 34							
Cadoxton	d								15 07			15 37				16 07	16 22	16 37							
Dinas Powys	d								15 11			15 41				16 11	16 26	16 41							
Eastbrook	d								15 13			15 43				16 13	16 28	16 43							
Cogan	d								15 15			15 45				16 15	16 30	16 45							
Penarth	d	14 52																			16 47				
Dingle Road	d	14 54																			16 49				
Grangetown	d	14 58							15 19			15 49				16 19	16 34	16 49			16 53				
Cardiff Central 7	a	15 05							15 24			15 54				16 24	16 42	16 56			16 59	17 02			
	d					15 06			15 41			16 06				16 26									
Cardiff Bay	d			14 54	15 06		15 18	15 30		15 42	15 54			16 06	16 18				16 30	16 42				16 54	17 06
Cardiff Queen Street 3	a			14 58	15 10	15 09	15 22	15 34	15 44	15 46	15 58	16 09		16 10	16 22	16 29			16 34	16 46				16 58	17 10
	d					15 10			15 45			16 10				16 30									
Heath Low Level	d																								
Ty Glas	d																								
Birchgrove	d																								
Rhiwbina	d																								
Whitchurch (Cardiff)	d																								
Coryton	a																								
Heath High Level	d											16 15													
Llanishen	d											16 18													
Lisvane & Thornhill	d											16 20													
Caerphilly 3	d											16 26													
Aber	d											16 28													
Llanbradach	d											16 32													
Ystrad Mynach 3	d											16 37													
Hengoed	d											16 40													
Pengam	d											16 43													
Gilfach Fargoed	d											16 46													
Bargoed	a											16 49													
	d											16 49													
Brithdir	d											16 53													
Tir-phil	d											16 56													
Pontlottyn	d											17 00													
Rhymney 3	a											17 07													
Cathays	d					15 13			15 48							16 33									
Llandaf	d					15 17			15 52							16 37									
Ninian Park	d																								
Waun-gron Park	d																								
Fairwater	d																								
Danescourt	d																								
Radyr 3	a					15 20			15 55							16 40									
	d					15 20			15 55							16 40									
Taffs Well 3	d					15 24			15 59							16 44									
Trefforest Estate	d																								
Trefforest	d					15 31			16 06							16 52									
Pontypridd 3	a					15 34			16 09							16 55									
	d					15 36			16 11							16 57									
Abercynon	d								16 19							17 05									
Penrhiwceiber	d								16 24																
Mountain Ash	a								16 28																
	d								16 29																
Fernhill	d								16 31																
Cwmbach	d								16 35																
Aberdare 3	a								16 42																
Quakers Yard	d															17 09									
Merthyr Vale	a															17 14									
	d															17 16									
Troed Y Rhiw	d															17 20									
Pentre-bach	d															17 23									
Merthyr Tydfil	a															17 31									
Trehafod	d					15 41																			
Porth	a					15 44																			
	d					15 45																			
Dinas Rhondda	d					15 49																			
Tonypandy	d					15 51																			
Llwynypia	d					15 53																			
Ystrad Rhondda	a					15 56																			
	d					15 59																			
Ton Pentre	d					16 01																			
Treorchy	d					16 04																			
Ynyswen	d					16 07																			
Treherbert	a					16 13																			

When events are being held at the Millenium Stadium, services are subject to alteration. Please check times before travelling.

Table 130

Sundays until 24 June

Bridgend, Barry Island, Barry, Penarth and Cardiff - Coryton, Rhymney, Pontypridd, Merthyr, Aberdare and Treherbert

Network Diagram - see first Page of Table 130

		AW	AW	AW	AW	AW	AW	AW		AW	AW	AW	AW	AW	AW	AW	AW	AW		AW	AW	AW	AW	AW	AW
Bridgend	d												17 42											19 42	
Llantwit Major	d												17 56											19 56	
Rhoose Cardiff Int Airport ✈	d												18 06											20 06	
Barry Island	d				16 55			17 25				17 55		18 25							18 55	19 25	19 55		20 25
Barry 3	d				17 00			17 30				18 00	18 15	18 30							19 00	19 30	20 00	20 15	20 30
Barry Docks	d				17 04			17 34				18 04	18 19	18 34							19 04	19 34	20 04	20 19	20 34
Cadoxton	d				17 07			17 37				18 07	18 22	18 37							19 07	19 37	20 07	20 22	20 37
Dinas Powys	d				17 11			17 41				18 11	18 26	18 41							19 11	19 41	20 11	20 26	20 41
Eastbrook	d				17 13			17 43				18 13	18 28	18 43							19 13	19 43	20 13	20 28	20 43
Cogan	d				17 15			17 45				18 15	18 30	18 45							19 15	19 45	20 15	20 30	20 45
Penarth	d																18 47								
Dingle Road	d																18 49								
Grangetown	d				17 19			17 49				18 19	18 34	18 49			18 53				19 19	19 49	20 19	20 34	20 49
Cardiff Central 7	a				17 24			17 54				18 24	18 42	18 56			19 00				19 24	19 54	20 24	20 42	20 54
	d	17 06			17 41			18 06				18 26								19 06	19 41	20 06	20 26		21 06
Cardiff Bay	d		17 18	17 30		17 42	17 54			18 06	18 18				18 30	18 42		18 54							
Cardiff Queen Street 3	a	17 09	17 22	17 34	17 44	17 46	17 58	18 09		18 10	18 22	18 29			18 34	18 46		18 57		19 09	19 44	20 09	20 29		21 09
	d	17 10			17 45			18 10				18 30								19 10	19 45	20 10	20 30		21 10
Heath Low Level	d																								
Ty Glas	d																								
Birchgrove	d																								
Rhiwbina	d																								
Whitchurch (Cardiff)	d																								
Coryton	a																								
Heath High Level	d							18 15														20 15			
Llanishen	d							18 18														20 18			
Lisvane & Thornhill	d							18 20														20 20			
Caerphilly 3	d							18 26														20 26			
Aber	d							18 28														20 28			
Llanbradach	d							18 32														20 32			
Ystrad Mynach 3	d							18 37														20 37			
Hengoed	d							18 40														20 40			
Pengam	d							18 43														20 43			
Gilfach Fargoed	d							18 46														20 46			
Bargoed	a							18 49														20 49			
	d							18 49														20 49			
Brithdir	d							18 53														20 53			
Tir-phil	d							18 56														20 56			
Pontlottyn	d							19 00														21 00			
Rhymney 3	a							19 07														21 07			
Cathays	d	17 13			17 48							18 33								19 13	19 48		20 33		21 13
Llandaf	d	17 17			17 52							18 37								19 17	19 52		20 37		21 17
Ninian Park	d																								
Waun-gron Park	d																								
Fairwater	d																								
Danescourt	d																								
Radyr 3	a	17 20			17 55							18 40								19 20	19 55		20 40		21 20
	d	17 20			17 55							18 40								19 20	19 55		20 40		21 20
Taffs Well 3	d	17 24			17 59							18 44								19 24	19 59		20 44		21 24
Trefforest Estate	d																								
Trefforest	d	17 31			18 06							18 52								19 31	20 06		20 52		21 31
Pontypridd 3	a	17 34			18 09							18 55								19 34	20 09		20 55		21 34
	d	17 36			18 11							18 57								19 36	20 11		20 57		21 36
Abercynon	d				18 19							19 05									20 19		21 05		
Penrhiwceiber	d				18 24																20 24				
Mountain Ash	a				18 28																20 28				
	d				18 29																20 29				
Fernhill	d				18 31																20 31				
Cwmbach	d				18 35																20 35				
Aberdare 3	a				18 42																20 42				
Quakers Yard	d											19 09											21 09		
Merthyr Vale	a											19 14											21 14		
	d											19 16											21 16		
Troed Y Rhiw	d											19 20											21 20		
Pentre-bach	d											19 23											21 23		
Merthyr Tydfil	a											19 31											21 31		
Trehafod	d	17 41																		19 41					21 41
Porth	a	17 44																		19 44					21 44
	d	17 45																		19 45					21 45
Dinas Rhondda	d	17 49																		19 49					21 49
Tonypandy	d	17 51																		19 51					21 51
Llwynypia	d	17 53																		19 53					21 53
Ystrad Rhondda	a	17 56																		19 56					21 56
	d	17 59																		19 59					21 59
Ton Pentre	d	18 01																		20 01					22 01
Treorchy	d	18 04																		20 04					22 04
Ynyswen	d	18 07																		20 07					22 07
Treherbert	a	18 13																		20 13					22 13

When events are being held at the Millenium Stadium, services are subject to alteration. Please check times before travelling.

Table 130

Sundays
until 24 June

Bridgend, Barry Island, Barry, Penarth and Cardiff - Coryton, Rhymney, Pontypridd, Merthyr, Aberdare and Treherbert

Network Diagram - see first Page of Table 130

		AW	AW	AW	AW	AW	AW	AW
Bridgend	d						21 42	
Llantwit Major	d						21 56	
Rhoose Cardiff Int Airport ✈	d						22 06	
Barry Island	d			20 55	21 25	21 55		22 55
Barry 3	d			21 00	21 30	22 00	22 15	23 00
Barry Docks	d			21 04	21 34	22 04	22 19	23 04
Cadoxton	d			21 07	21 37	22 07	22 22	23 07
Dinas Powys	d			21 11	21 41	22 11	22 26	23 11
Eastbrook	d			21 13	21 43	22 13	22 28	23 13
Cogan	d			21 15	21 45	22 15	22 30	23 15
Penarth	d	20 47						
Dingle Road	d	20 49						
Grangetown	d	20 53		21 19	21 49	22 19	22 34	23 19
Cardiff Central 7	a	21 00		21 26	21 54	22 26	22 42	23 26
	d		21 16		22 06			
Cardiff Bay	d							
Cardiff Queen Street 3	a		21 19		22 09			
	d		21 20		22 10			
Heath Low Level	d							
Ty Glas	d							
Birchgrove	d							
Rhiwbina	d							
Whitchurch (Cardiff)	d							
Coryton	a							
Heath High Level	d		21 25					
Llanishen	d		21 28					
Lisvane & Thornhill	d		21 30					
Caerphilly 3	d		21 36					
Aber	d		21 38					
Llanbradach	d		21 42					
Ystrad Mynach 3	d		21 47					
Hengoed	d		21 50					
Pengam	d		21 53					
Gilfach Fargoed	d		21 56					
Bargoed	a		21 59					
	d		21 59					
Brithdir	d		22 03					
Tir-phil	d		22 06					
Pontlottyn	d		22 10					
Rhymney 3	a		22 17					
Cathays	d				22 13			
Llandaf	d				22 17			
Ninian Park	d							
Waun-gron Park	d							
Fairwater	d							
Danescourt	d							
Radyr 3	a				22 20			
	d				22 20			
Taffs Well 3	d				22 24			
Trefforest Estate	d							
Trefforest	d				22 31			
Pontypridd 3	a				22 34			
	d				22 36			
Abercynon	d							
Penrhiwceiber	d							
Mountain Ash	a							
	d							
Fernhill	d							
Cwmbach	d							
Aberdare 3	a							
Quakers Yard	d							
Merthyr Vale	a							
	d							
Troed Y Rhiw	d							
Pentre-bach	d							
Merthyr Tydfil	a							
Trehafod	d				22 41			
Porth	a				22 44			
	d				22 45			
Dinas Rhondda	d				22 49			
Tonypandy	d				22 51			
Llwynypia	d				22 53			
Ystrad Rhondda	a				22 56			
	d				22 59			
Ton Pentre	d				23 01			
Treorchy	d				23 04			
Ynyswen	d				23 07			
Treherbert	a				23 13			

When events are being held at the Millenium Stadium, services are subject to alteration. Please check times before travelling.

Table 130

Sundays
1 July to 9 September

Bridgend, Barry Island, Barry, Penarth and Cardiff - Coryton, Rhymney, Pontypridd, Merthyr, Aberdare and Treherbert

Network Diagram - see first Page of Table 130

		AW A	AW B	AW A	AW A	AW A	AW A	AW	AW	AW	AW	AW	AW	AW	AW	AW	AW	AW	AW	AW	AW	AW	AW
Bridgend	d																					09 42	
Llantwit Major	d																					09 56	
Rhoose Cardiff Int Airport ✈	d																					10 06	
Barry Island	d	22p44	22p45												08 55						09 55		10 25
Barry 3	d	22p48	22p49												09 00						10 00	10 15	10 30
Barry Docks	d	22p52	22p53												09 04						10 04	10 19	10 34
Cadoxton	d	22p55	22p56												09 07						10 07	10 22	10 37
Dinas Powys	d	22p59	23p00												09 11						10 11	10 26	10 41
Eastbrook	d	23p01	23p03												09 13						10 13	10 28	10 43
Cogan	d	23p03	23p05												09 15						10 15	10 30	10 45
Penarth	d																						
Dingle Road	d																						
Grangetown	d	23p07	23p09												09 19						10 19	10 34	10 49
Cardiff Central 7	a	23p12	23p14												09 24						10 24	10 42	10 56
	d	23p26	23p26	23p40	23p56	00 05	00 20	08 26	08 41	08 54	09 00				09 41				10 06		10 26		
Cardiff Bay	d											09 06	09 18	09 30		09 42	09 54	10 06		10 18			
Cardiff Queen Street 3	a	23p29	23p29					08 29	08 44	08 57	09 03	09 10	09 22	09 34	09 44	09 46	09 58	10 10	10 09	10 22	10 29		
	d	23p30	23p30					08 30	08 45		09 04				09 45				10 10		10 30		
Heath Low Level	d																						
Ty Glas	d																						
Birchgrove	d																						
Rhiwbina	d																						
Whitchurch (Cardiff)	d																						
Coryton	a																						
Heath High Level	d					00 12													10 15				
Llanishen	d					00 15													10 18				
Lisvane & Thornhill	d					00 17													10 20				
Caerphilly 3	d					00 23													10 26				
Aber	d					00 25													10 28				
Llanbradach	d					00 29													10 32				
Ystrad Mynach 3	d					00 34													10 37				
Hengoed	d					00 37													10 40				
Pengam	d					00 40													10 43				
Gilfach Fargoed	d					00 43													10 46				
Bargoed	a					00 47													10 49				
	d					00 47													10 49				
Brithdir	d					00 51													10 53				
Tir-phil	d					00 54													10 56				
Pontlottyn	d					00 58													11 00				
Rhymney 3	a					01 05													11 07				
Cathays	d	23p33	23p33	23p45	00 03		00 25	08 33	08 48		09 07				09 48						10 33		
Llandaf	d	23p37	23p37	23p49	00 07		00 29	08 37	08 52		09 11				09 52						10 37		
Ninian Park	d																						
Waun-gron Park	d																						
Fairwater	d																						
Danescourt	d																						
Radyr 3	a	23p40	23p40	23p53	00 10		00 32	08 40	08 55		09 14				09 55						10 40		
	d	23p41	23p41	23p53	00 11		00 33	08 40	08 55		09 14				09 55						10 40		
Taffs Well 3	d	23p45	23p45	23p57	00 15		00 37	08 44	08 59		09 18				09 59						10 44		
Trefforest Estate	d	23p49	23p49																				
Trefforest	d	23p53	23p53	00 03	00 21		00 43	08 52	09 06		09 25				10 06						10 52		
Pontypridd 3	a	23p56	23p56	00 06	00 24		00 48	08 55	09 09		09 28				10 09						10 55		
	d	23p57	23p57	00 08	00 26			08 57	09 11		09 30				10 11						10 57		
Abercynon	d	00 07	00 07	00 17				09 05	09 19						10 19						11 05		
Penrhiwceiber	d			00 23					09 24						10 24								
Mountain Ash	a			00 26					09 28						10 28								
	d			00 28					09 29						10 29								
Fernhill	d			00 30					09 31						10 31								
Cwmbach	d			00 34					09 35						10 35								
Aberdare 3	a			00 41					09 42						10 42								
Quakers Yard	d	00 11	00 11					09 09													11 09		
Merthyr Vale	a	00 16	00 16					09 14													11 14		
	d	00 19	00 19					09 16													11 16		
Troed Y Rhiw	d	00 22	00 22					09 20													11 20		
Pentre-bach	d	00 25	00 25					09 23													11 23		
Merthyr Tydfil	a	00 30	00 30					09 31													11 31		
Trehafod	d				00 31						09 35												
Porth	a				00 34						09 38												
	d				00 35						09 39												
Dinas Rhondda	d				00 39						09 43												
Tonypandy	d				00 41						09 45												
Llwynypia	d				00 43						09 47												
Ystrad Rhondda	a				00 46						09 50												
	d				00 47						09 53												
Ton Pentre	d				00 49						09 55												
Treorchy	d				00 52						09 58												
Ynyswen	d				00 55						10 01												
Treherbert	a				01 02						10 07												

A 5 August

B 29 July

When events are being held at the Millenium Stadium, services are subject to alteration. Please check times before travelling.

Table 130

Sundays

1 July to 9 September

Bridgend, Barry Island, Barry, Penarth and Cardiff - Coryton, Rhymney, Pontypridd, Merthyr, Aberdare and Treherbert

Network Diagram - see first Page of Table 130

		AW	AW	AW	AW	AW	AW	AW	AW	AW	AW	AW	AW	AW	AW	AW	AW	AW	AW	AW	AW	AW	AW
Bridgend	d																11 42						
Llantwit Major	d																11 56						
Rhoose Cardiff Int Airport ✈	d																12 06						
Barry Island	d									10 55			11 25			11 55		12 25					
Barry	d									11 00			11 30			12 00	12 15	12 30					
Barry Docks	d									11 04			11 34			12 04	12 19	12 34					
Cadoxton	d									11 07			11 37			12 07	12 22	12 37					
Dinas Powys	d									11 11			11 41			12 11	12 26	12 41					
Eastbrook	d									11 13			11 43			12 13	12 28	12 43					
Cogan	d									11 15			11 45			12 15	12 30	12 45					
Penarth	d			10 47																	12 47		
Dingle Road	d			10 49																	12 49		
Grangetown	d			10 53						11 19			11 49			12 19	12 34	12 49			12 53		
Cardiff Central	a			10 59						11 24			11 54			12 24	12 42	12 56			12 59		
	d					11 00				11 41			12 06			12 26							
Cardiff Bay	d	10 30	10 42		10 54		11 06	11 18	11 30		11 42	11 54		12 06	12 18				12 30	12 42		12 54	13 06
Cardiff Queen Street	a	10 34	10 46		10 58	11 03	11 10	11 22	11 34	11 44	11 46	11 58	12 09	12 10	12 22	12 29			12 34	12 46		12 58	13 10
	d					11 04				11 45			12 10			12 30							
Heath Low Level	d																						
Ty Glas	d																						
Birchgrove	d																						
Rhiwbina	d																						
Whitchurch (Cardiff)	d																						
Coryton	a																						
Heath High Level	d												12 15										
Llanishen	d												12 18										
Lisvane & Thornhill	d												12 20										
Caerphilly	d												12 26										
Aber	d												12 28										
Llanbradach	d												12 32										
Ystrad Mynach	d												12 37										
Hengoed	d												12 40										
Pengam	d												12 43										
Gilfach Fargoed	d												12 46										
Bargoed	a												12 49										
	d												12 49										
Brithdir	d												12 53										
Tir-phil	d												12 56										
Pontlottyn	d												13 00										
Rhymney	a												13 07										
Cathays	d					11 07				11 48						12 33							
Llandaf	d					11 11				11 52						12 37							
Ninian Park	d																						
Waun-gron Park	d																						
Fairwater	d																						
Danescourt	d																						
Radyr	a					11 14				11 55						12 40							
	d					11 14				11 55						12 40							
Taffs Well	d					11 18				11 59						12 44							
Trefforest Estate	d																						
Trefforest	d					11 25				12 06						12 52							
Pontypridd	a					11 28				12 09						12 55							
	d					11 30				12 11						12 57							
Abercynon	d									12 19						13 05							
Penrhiwceiber	d									12 24													
Mountain Ash	a									12 28													
	d									12 29													
Fernhill	d									12 31													
Cwmbach	d									12 35													
Aberdare	a									12 42													
Quakers Yard	d															13 09							
Merthyr Vale	a															13 14							
	d															13 16							
Troed Y Rhiw	d															13 20							
Pentre-bach	d															13 23							
Merthyr Tydfil	a															13 31							
Trehafod	d					11 35																	
Porth	a					11 38																	
	d					11 39																	
Dinas Rhondda	d					11 43																	
Tonypandy	d					11 45																	
Llwynypia	d					11 47																	
Ystrad Rhondda	a					11 50																	
	d					11 53																	
Ton Pentre	d					11 55																	
Treorchy	d					11 58																	
Ynyswen	d					12 01																	
Treherbert	a					12 07																	

When events are being held at the Millenium Stadium, services are subject to alteration. Please check times before travelling.

Table 130

Sundays

1 July to 9 September

Bridgend, Barry Island, Barry, Penarth and Cardiff - Coryton, Rhymney, Pontypridd, Merthyr, Aberdare and Treherbert

Network Diagram - see first Page of Table 130

		AW	AW	AW	AW	AW	AW	AW	AW	AW	AW	AW	AW	AW	AW	AW	AW	AW	AW	AW	AW	AW
Bridgend	d											13 42										
Llantwit Major	d											13 56										
Rhoose Cardiff Int Airport ✈	d											14 06										
Barry Island	d				12 55			13 25			13 55		14 25									14 55
Barry	d				13 00			13 30			14 00	14 15	14 30									15 00
Barry Docks	d				13 04			13 34			14 04	14 19	14 34									15 04
Cadoxton	d				13 07			13 37			14 07	14 22	14 37									15 07
Dinas Powys	d				13 11			13 41			14 11	14 26	14 41									15 11
Eastbrook	d				13 13			13 43			14 13	14 28	14 43									15 13
Cogan	d				13 15			13 45			14 15	14 30	14 45									15 15
Penarth	d															14 47						
Dingle Road	d															14 49						
Grangetown	d				13 19			13 49			14 19	14 34	14 49			14 53						15 19
Cardiff Central	a				13 24			13 54			14 24	14 42	14 56			15 01						15 24
	d	13 06			13 41			14 06			14 26								15 06			15 41
Cardiff Bay	d		13 18	13 30		13 42	13 54		14 06	14 18				14 30	14 42		14 54	15 06		15 18	15 30	
Cardiff Queen Street	a	13 09	13 22	13 34	13 44	13 46	13 58	14 09	14 10	14 22	14 29			14 34	14 46		14 58	15 10	15 09	15 22	15 34	15 44
	d	13 10			13 45			14 10			14 30								15 10			15 45
Heath Low Level	d																					
Ty Glas	d																					
Birchgrove	d																					
Rhiwbina	d																					
Whitchurch (Cardiff)	d																					
Coryton	a																					
Heath High Level	d							14 15														
Llanishen	d							14 18														
Lisvane & Thornhill	d							14 20														
Caerphilly	d							14 26														
Aber	d							14 28														
Llanbradach	d							14 32														
Ystrad Mynach	d							14 37														
Hengoed	d							14 40														
Pengam	d							14 43														
Gilfach Fargoed	d							14 46														
Bargoed	a							14 49														
	d							14 49														
Brithdir	d							14 53														
Tir-phil	d							14 56														
Pontlottyn	d							15 00														
Rhymney	a							15 07														
Cathays	d	13 13			13 48						14 33								15 13			15 48
Llandaf	d	13 17			13 52						14 37								15 17			15 52
Ninian Park	d																					
Waun-gron Park	d																					
Fairwater	d																					
Danescourt	d																					
Radyr	a	13 20			13 55						14 40								15 20			15 55
	d	13 20			13 55						14 40								15 20			15 55
Taffs Well	d	13 24			13 59						14 44								15 24			15 59
Trefforest Estate	d																					
Trefforest	d	13 31			14 06						14 52								15 31			16 06
Pontypridd	a	13 34			14 09						14 55								15 34			16 09
	d	13 36			14 11						14 57								15 36			16 11
Abercynon	d				14 19						15 05											16 19
Penrhiwceiber	d				14 24																	16 24
Mountain Ash	a				14 28																	16 28
	d				14 29																	16 29
Fernhill	d				14 31																	16 31
Cwmbach	d				14 35																	16 35
Aberdare	a				14 42																	16 42
Quakers Yard	d										15 09											
Merthyr Vale	a										15 14											
	d										15 16											
Troed Y Rhiw	d										15 20											
Pentre-bach	d										15 23											
Merthyr Tydfil	a										15 31											
Trehafod	d	13 41																	15 41			
Porth	a	13 44																	15 44			
	d	13 45																	15 45			
Dinas Rhondda	d	13 49																	15 49			
Tonypandy	d	13 51																	15 51			
Llwynypia	d	13 53																	15 53			
Ystrad Rhondda	a	13 56																	15 56			
	d	13 59																	15 59			
Ton Pentre	d	14 01																	16 01			
Treorchy	d	14 04																	16 04			
Ynyswen	d	14 07																	16 07			
Treherbert	a	14 13																	16 13			

When events are being held at the Millenium Stadium, services are subject to alteration. Please check times before travelling.

Table 130

Sundays
1 July to 9 September

Bridgend, Barry Island, Barry, Penarth and Cardiff - Coryton, Rhymney, Pontypridd, Merthyr, Aberdare and Treherbert

Network Diagram - see first Page of Table 130

		AW	AW	AW	AW	AW	AW	AW	AW	AW	AW	AW	AW	AW	AW	AW	AW	AW	AW	AW	AW	AW	AW
Bridgend	d							15 42															
Llantwit Major	d							15 56															
Rhoose Cardiff Int Airport ✈	d							16 06															
Barry Island	d			15 25			15 55		16 25				16 40						16 55			17 25	
Barry 3	d			15 30			16 00	16 15	16 30				16 45						17 00			17 30	
Barry Docks	d			15 34			16 04	16 19	16 34										17 04			17 34	
Cadoxton	d			15 37			16 07	16 22	16 37										17 07			17 37	
Dinas Powys	d			15 41			16 11	16 26	16 41										17 11			17 41	
Eastbrook	d			15 43			16 13	16 28	16 43										17 13			17 43	
Cogan	d			15 45			16 15	16 30	16 45										17 15			17 45	
Penarth	d											16 47											
Dingle Road	d											16 49											
Grangetown	d			15 49			16 19	16 34	16 49			16 53							17 19			17 49	
Cardiff Central 7	a			15 54			16 24	16 42	16 56			16 59	17 02						17 24			17 54	
	d			16 06			16 26									17 06			17 41			18 06	
Cardiff Bay	d	15 42	15 54		16 06	16 18				16 30	16 42			16 54	17 06		17 18	17 30		17 42	17 54		18 06
Cardiff Queen Street 3	a	15 46	15 58	16 09	16 10	16 22	16 29			16 34	16 46			16 58	17 10	17 09	17 22	17 34	17 44	17 46	17 58	18 09	18 10
	d			16 10			16 30									17 10			17 45			18 10	
Heath Low Level	d																						
Ty Glas	d																						
Birchgrove	d																						
Rhiwbina	d																						
Whitchurch (Cardiff)	d																						
Coryton	a																						
Heath High Level	d			16 15																		18 15	
Llanishen	d			16 18																		18 18	
Lisvane & Thornhill	d			16 20																		18 20	
Caerphilly 3	d			16 26																		18 26	
Aber	d			16 28																		18 28	
Llanbradach	d			16 32																		18 32	
Ystrad Mynach 3	d			16 37																		18 37	
Hengoed	d			16 40																		18 40	
Pengam	d			16 43																		18 43	
Gilfach Fargoed	d			16 46																		18 46	
Bargoed	a			16 49																		18 49	
	d			16 49																		18 49	
Brithdir	d			16 53																		18 53	
Tir-phil	d			16 56																		18 56	
Pontlottyn	d			17 00																		19 00	
Rhymney 3	a			17 07																		19 07	
Cathays	d						16 33									17 13			17 48				
Llandaf	d						16 37									17 17			17 52				
Ninian Park	d																						
Waun-gron Park	d																						
Fairwater	d																						
Danescourt	d																						
Radyr 3	a						16 40									17 20			17 55				
	d						16 40									17 20			17 55				
Taffs Well 3	d						16 44									17 24			17 59				
Trefforest Estate	d																						
Trefforest	d						16 52									17 31			18 06				
Pontypridd 3	a						16 55									17 34			18 09				
	d						16 57									17 36			18 11				
Abercynon	d						17 05												18 19				
Penrhiwceiber	d																		18 24				
Mountain Ash	a																		18 28				
	d																		18 29				
Fernhill	d																		18 31				
Cwmbach	d																		18 35				
Aberdare 3	a																		18 42				
Quakers Yard	d						17 09																
Merthyr Vale	a						17 14																
	d						17 16																
Troed Y Rhiw	d						17 20																
Pentre-bach	d						17 23																
Merthyr Tydfil	a						17 31																
Trehafod	d															17 41							
Porth	a															17 44							
	d															17 45							
Dinas Rhondda	d															17 49							
Tonypandy	d															17 51							
Llwynypia	d															17 53							
Ystrad Rhondda	a															17 56							
	d															17 59							
Ton Pentre	d															18 01							
Treorchy	d															18 04							
Ynyswen	d															18 07							
Treherbert	a															18 13							

When events are being held at the Millenium Stadium, services are subject to alteration. Please check times before travelling.

Table 130

Sundays
1 July to 9 September

Bridgend, Barry Island, Barry, Penarth and Cardiff - Coryton, Rhymney, Pontypridd, Merthyr, Aberdare and Treherbert

Network Diagram - see first Page of Table 130

		AW	AW	AW	AW	AW	AW	AW	AW	AW	AW	AW	AW	AW	AW	AW	AW	AW	AW	AW	AW	AW
Bridgend	d			17 42										19 42							21 42	
Llantwit Major	d			17 56										19 56							21 56	
Rhoose Cardiff Int Airport ✈	d			18 06										20 06							22 06	
Barry Island	d		17 55		18 25						18 55	19 25	19 55		20 25			20 55	21 25	21 55		22 55
Barry 3	d		18 00	18 15	18 30						19 00	19 30	20 00	20 15	20 30			21 00	21 30	22 00	22 15	23 00
Barry Docks	d		18 04	18 19	18 34						19 04	19 34	20 04	20 19	20 34			21 04	21 34	22 04	22 19	23 04
Cadoxton	d		18 07	18 22	18 37						19 07	19 37	20 07	20 22	20 37			21 07	21 37	22 07	22 22	23 07
Dinas Powys	d		18 11	18 26	18 41						19 11	19 41	20 11	20 26	20 41			21 11	21 41	22 11	22 26	23 11
Eastbrook	d		18 13	18 28	18 43						19 13	19 43	20 13	20 28	20 43			21 13	21 43	22 13	22 28	23 13
Cogan	d		18 15	18 30	18 45						19 15	19 45	20 15	20 30	20 45			21 15	21 45	22 15	22 30	23 15
Penarth	d							18 47								20 47						
Dingle Road	d							18 49								20 49						
Grangetown	d		18 19	18 34	18 49			18 53			19 19	19 49	20 19	20 34	20 49	20 53		21 19	21 49	22 19	22 34	23 19
Cardiff Central 7	a		18 24	18 42	18 56			19 00			19 24	19 54	20 24	20 42	20 54	21 00		21 26	21 54	22 26	22 42	23 26
	d		18 26							19 06	19 41	20 06	20 26		21 06		21 16		22 06			
Cardiff Bay	d	18 18				18 30	18 42		18 54													
Cardiff Queen Street 3	a	18 22	18 29			18 34	18 46		18 57	19 09	19 44	20 09	20 29		21 09		21 19		22 09			
	d		18 30							19 10	19 45	20 10	20 30		21 10		21 20		22 10			
Heath Low Level	d																					
Ty Glas	d																					
Birchgrove	d																					
Rhiwbina	d																					
Whitchurch (Cardiff)	d																					
Coryton	a																					
Heath High Level	d											20 15					21 25					
Llanishen	d											20 18					21 28					
Lisvane & Thornhill	d											20 20					21 30					
Caerphilly 3	d											20 26					21 36					
Aber	d											20 28					21 38					
Llanbradach	d											20 32					21 42					
Ystrad Mynach 3	d											20 37					21 47					
Hengoed	d											20 40					21 50					
Pengam	d											20 43					21 53					
Gilfach Fargoed	d											20 46					21 56					
Bargoed	a											20 49					21 59					
	d											20 49					21 59					
Brithdir	d											20 53					22 03					
Tir-phil	d											20 56					22 06					
Pontlottyn	d											21 00					22 10					
Rhymney 3	a											21 07					22 17					
Cathays	d		18 33							19 13	19 48		20 33		21 13				22 13			
Llandaf	d		18 37							19 17	19 52		20 37		21 17				22 17			
Ninian Park	d																					
Waun-gron Park	d																					
Fairwater	d																					
Danescourt	d																					
Radyr 3	a		18 40							19 20	19 55		20 40		21 20				22 20			
	d		18 40							19 20	19 55		20 40		21 20				22 20			
Taffs Well 3	d		18 44							19 24	19 59		20 44		21 24				22 24			
Trefforest Estate	d																					
Trefforest	d		18 52							19 31	20 06		20 52		21 31				22 31			
Pontypridd 3	a		18 55							19 34	20 09		20 55		21 34				22 34			
	d		18 57							19 36	20 11		20 57		21 36				22 36			
Abercynon	d		19 05								20 19		21 05									
Penrhiwceiber	d										20 24											
Mountain Ash	a										20 28											
	d										20 29											
Fernhill	d										20 31											
Cwmbach	d										20 35											
Aberdare 3	a										20 42											
Quakers Yard	d		19 09										21 09									
Merthyr Vale	a		19 14										21 14									
	d		19 16										21 16									
Troed Y Rhiw	d		19 20										21 20									
Pentre-bach	d		19 23										21 23									
Merthyr Tydfil	a		19 31										21 31									
Trehafod	d									19 41					21 41				22 41			
Porth	a									19 44					21 44				22 44			
	d									19 45					21 45				22 45			
Dinas Rhondda	d									19 49					21 49				22 49			
Tonypandy	d									19 51					21 51				22 51			
Llwynypia	d									19 53					21 53				22 53			
Ystrad Rhondda	a									19 56					21 56				22 56			
	d									19 59					21 59				22 59			
Ton Pentre	d									20 01					22 01				23 01			
Treorchy	d									20 04					22 04				23 04			
Ynyswen	d									20 07					22 07				23 07			
Treherbert	a									20 13					22 13				23 13			

When events are being held at the Millenium Stadium, services are subject to alteration. Please check times before travelling.

Table 130

Sundays

16 September to 21 October

Bridgend, Barry Island, Barry, Penarth and Cardiff - Coryton, Rhymney, Pontypridd, Merthyr, Aberdare and Treherbert

Network Diagram - see first Page of Table 130

		AW 🚌	AW 🚌	AW 🚌	AW	AW	AW	AW 🚌	AW 🚌	AW		AW 🚌	AW 🚌	AW 🚌	AW 🚌	AW	AW	AW 🚌	AW 🚌	AW 🚌		AW 🚌	AW	AW 🚌	AW
Bridgend	d																	09 30						10 30	
Llantwit Major	d																	09 55						10 55	
Rhoose Cardiff Int Airport ✈	d																	10 10						11 10	
Barry Island	d								08 30					09 30						10 30					
Barry ■	d								08 35					09 35				10 25		10 35				11 25	
Barry Docks	d								08 40					09 40				10 30		10 40				11 30	
Cadoxton	d								08 45					09 45				10 35		10 45				11 35	
Dinas Powys	d								08 55					09 55				10 45		10 55				11 45	
Eastbrook	d								09 00					10 00				10 50		11 00				11 50	
Cogan	d								09 05					10 05				10 55		11 05				11 55	
Penarth	d																					11 00			
Dingle Road	d																					11 05			
Grangetown	d								09 10					10 10				11 00		11 10		11 15		12 00	
Cardiff Central ■	a								09 15					10 15				11 05		11 15		11 20		12 05	
	d	07 52	08 07	08 26	08 30	08 41	09 00	09 07		09 45		09 52	10 06		10 26	10 30	11 00		11 07				11 41		12 10
Cardiff Bay	d																								
Cardiff Queen Street ■	a	08 00	08 15	08 34				09 15				10 00	10 14		10 34				11 15						12 13
	d	08 00	08 15	08 34				09 15				10 00	10 14		10 34				11 15						12 14
Heath Low Level	d																								
Ty Glas	d																								
Birchgrove	d																								
Rhiwbina	d																								
Whitchurch (Cardiff)	d																								
Coryton	a																								
Heath High Level	d												10 29												12 19
Llanishen	d												10 34												12 22
Lisvane & Thornhill	d												10 39												12 24
Caerphilly ■	d												10 49												12 30
Aber	d												10 54												12 32
Llanbradach	d												11 04												12 41
Ystrad Mynach ■	d												11 14												12 51
Hengoed	d												11 19												12 59
Pengam	d												11 29												13 02
Gilfach Fargoed	d												11 34												13 05
Bargoed	a												11 39												13 08
	d												11 39												13 08
Brithdir	d												11 44												13 12
Tir-phil	d												11 49												13 15
Pontlottyn	d												11 54												13 19
Rhymney ■	a												12 02												13 27
Cathays	d	08 05	08 20	08 39				09 20				10 05			10 39				11 20						
Llandaf	d	08 20	08 35	08 54				09 35				10 20			10 54				11 35						
Ninian Park	d																								
Waun-gron Park	d																								
Fairwater	d																								
Danescourt	d																								
Radyr ■	a	08 30	08 45	09 04	08 40	08 52	09 11	09 45		09 55		10 30			11 04	10 40	11 12		11 45				11 51		
	d				08 40	08 55	09 14			09 55						10 40	11 14						11 55		
Taffs Well ■	d				08 44	08 59	09 18			09 59						10 44	11 18						11 59		
Trefforest Estate	d																								
Trefforest	d				08 52	09 06	09 25			10 06						10 52	11 25						12 06		
Pontypridd ■	a				08 55	09 09	09 28			10 09						10 55	11 28						12 09		
	d				08 57	09 11	09 30			10 11						10 57	11 30						12 11		
Abercynon	d				09 05	09 19				10 19						11 05							12 19		
Penrhiwceiber	d					09 25				10 25													12 25		
Mountain Ash	a					09 28				10 28													12 28		
	d					09 29				10 29													12 29		
Fernhill	d					09 32				10 32													12 32		
Cwmbach	d					09 36				10 36													12 36		
Aberdare ■	a					09 44				10 44													12 44		
Quakers Yard	d				09 09											11 09									
Merthyr Vale	a				09 14											11 14									
	d				09 16											11 16									
Troed Y Rhiw	d				09 20											11 20									
Pentre-bach	d				09 23											11 23									
Merthyr Tydfil	a				09 32											11 32									
Trehafod	d						09 35										11 35								
Porth	a						09 38										11 38								
	d						09 39										11 39								
Dinas Rhondda	d						09 43										11 43								
Tonypandy	d						09 45										11 45								
Llwynypia	d						09 47										11 47								
Ystrad Rhondda	a						09 50										11 50								
	d						09 53										11 53								
Ton Pentre	d						09 55										11 55								
Treorchy	d						09 58										11 58								
Ynyswen	d						10 01										12 01								
Treherbert	a						10 08										12 08								

When events are being held at the Millenium Stadium, services are subject to alteration. Please check times before travelling.

Table 130

Sundays

16 September to 21 October

Bridgend, Barry Island, Barry, Penarth and Cardiff - Coryton, Rhymney, Pontypridd, Merthyr, Aberdare and Treherbert

Network Diagram - see first Page of Table 130

		AW 🚌	AW	AW	AW	AW		AW	AW	AW	AW	AW 🚌	AW	AW	AW	AW 🚌		AW	AW	AW	AW	AW	AW	AW	AW
Bridgend	d															12 30									13 52
Llantwit Major	d															12 55									14 12
Rhoose Cardiff Int Airport ✈	d															13 10									14 26
Barry Island	d	11 30										12 30			13 04					13 25			13 55	14 25	
Barry ■	d	11 35										12 35			13 09	13a25				13 30			14 00	14 30	14 35
Barry Docks	d	11 40										12 40			13 13					13 34			14 04	14 34	14 39
Cadoxton	d	11 45										12 45			13 16					13 37			14 07	14 37	14 42
Dinas Powys	d	11 55										12 55			13 20					13 41			14 11	14 41	14 46
Eastbrook	d	12 00										13 00			13 22					13 43			14 13	14 43	14 48
Cogan	d	12 05										13 05			13 24					13 45			14 15	14 45	14 50
Penarth	d							12 47																	
Dingle Road	d							12 49																	
Grangetown	d	12 10						12 53				13 10			13 28					13 49			14 19	14 49	14 54
Cardiff Central ■	a	12 15						13 00				13 15			13 33					13 54			14 24	14 57	15 02
	d		12 18	12 26							13 06				13 41					14 06			14 26		
Cardiff Bay	d				12 30	12 42			12 54	13 06			13 18	13 30				13 42	13 54		14 06	14 18			
Cardiff Queen Street ■	a		12 21	12 29	12 34	12 46			12 58	13 10	13 09		13 22	13 34	13 44			13 46	13 58	14 09	14 10	14 22	14 29		
	d			12 30							13 10				13 45					14 10			14 30		
Heath Low Level	d																								
Ty Glas	d																								
Birchgrove	d																								
Rhiwbina	d																								
Whitchurch (Cardiff)	d																								
Coryton	a																								
Heath High Level	d																			14 15					
Llanishen	d																			14 18					
Lisvane & Thornhill	d																			14 20					
Caerphilly ■	d																			14 26					
Aber	d																			14 28					
Llanbradach	d																			14 32					
Ystrad Mynach ■	d																			14 37					
Hengoed	d																			14 40					
Pengam	d																			14 43					
Gilfach Fargoed	d																			14 46					
Bargoed	a																			14 49					
	d																			14 49					
Brithdir	d																			14 53					
Tir-phil	d																			14 56					
Pontlottyn	d																			15 00					
Rhymney ■	a																			15 08					
Cathays	d			12 33							13 13				13 48								14 33		
Llandaf	d			12 37							13 17				13 52								14 37		
Ninian Park	d																								
Waun-gron Park	d																								
Fairwater	d																								
Danescourt	d																								
Radyr ■	a			12 40							13 20				13 55								14 40		
	d			12 40							13 20				13 55								14 40		
Taffs Well ■	d			12 44							13 24				13 59								14 44		
Trefforest Estate	d																								
Trefforest	d			12 52							13 31				14 06								14 52		
Pontypridd ■	a			12 55							13 34				14 09								14 55		
	d			12 57							13 36				14 11								14 57		
Abercynon	d			13 05											14 19								15 05		
Penrhiwceiber	d														14 25										
Mountain Ash	a														14 28										
	d														14 29										
Fernhill	d														14 32										
Cwmbach	d														14 36										
Aberdare ■	a														14 44										
Quakers Yard	d			13 09																			15 09		
Merthyr Vale	a			13 14																			15 14		
	d			13 16																			15 16		
Troed Y Rhiw	d			13 20																			15 20		
Pentre-bach	d			13 23																			15 23		
Merthyr Tydfil	a			13 32																			15 32		
Trehafod	d										13 41														
Porth	a										13 44														
	d										13 45														
Dinas Rhondda	d										13 49														
Tonypandy	d										13 51														
Llwynypia	d										13 53														
Ystrad Rhondda	a										13 56														
	d										13 59														
Ton Pentre	d										14 01														
Treorchy	d										14 04														
Ynyswen	d										14 07														
Treherbert	a										14 14														

When events are being held at the Millenium Stadium, services are subject to alteration. Please check times before travelling.

Table 130

Sundays

16 September to 21 October

Bridgend, Barry Island, Barry, Penarth and Cardiff - Coryton, Rhymney, Pontypridd, Merthyr, Aberdare and Treherbert

Network Diagram - see first Page of Table 130

		AW		AW	AW	AW	AW	AW	AW	AW	AW	AW		AW	AW	AW	AW	AW	AW	AW	AW	AW		AW	AW
Bridgend	d																	15 42						
Llantwit Major	d																	15 56						
Rhoose Cardiff Int Airport ✈	d																	16 06						
Barry Island	d									14 55				15 25			15 55		16 25					
Barry ■	d									15 00				15 30			16 00	16 15	16 30					
Barry Docks	d									15 04				15 34			16 04	16 19	16 34					
Cadoxton	d									15 07				15 37			16 07	16 22	16 37					
Dinas Powys	d									15 11				15 41			16 11	16 26	16 41					
Eastbrook	d									15 13				15 43			16 13	16 28	16 43					
Cogan	d									15 15				15 45			16 15	16 30	16 45					
Penarth	d				14 52																		16 47	
Dingle Road	d				14 54																		16 49	
Grangetown	d				14 58					15 19				15 49			16 19	16 34	16 49				16 53	
Cardiff Central ■	a				15 05					15 24				15 54			16 24	16 42	16 57				17 00	
	d							15 06			15 41				16 06			16 26							
Cardiff Bay	d	14 30		14 42		14 54	15 06		15 18	15 30		15 42		15 54		16 06	16 18				16 30	16 42			16 54
Cardiff Queen Street ■	a	14 34		14 46		14 58	15 10	15 09	15 22	15 34	15 44	15 46		15 58	16 09	16 10	16 22	16 29			16 34	16 46			16 58
	d							15 10			15 45				16 10			16 30							
Heath Low Level	d																								
Ty Glas	d																								
Birchgrove	d																								
Rhiwbina	d																								
Whitchurch (Cardiff)	d																								
Coryton	a																								
Heath High Level	d														16 15										
Llanishen	d														16 18										
Lisvane & Thornhill	d														16 20										
Caerphilly ■	d														16 26										
Aber	d														16 28										
Llanbradach	d														16 32										
Ystrad Mynach ■	d														16 37										
Hengoed	d														16 40										
Pengam	d														16 43										
Gilfach Fargoed	d														16 46										
Bargoed	a														16 49										
	d														16 49										
Brithdir	d														16 53										
Tir-phil	d														16 56										
Pontlottyn	d														17 00										
Rhymney ■	a														17 08										
Cathays	d							15 13			15 48							16 33							
Llandaf	d							15 17			15 52							16 37							
Ninian Park	d																								
Waun-gron Park	d																								
Fairwater	d																								
Danescourt	d																								
Radyr ■	a							15 20			15 55							16 40							
	d							15 20			15 55							16 40							
Taffs Well ■	d							15 24			15 59							16 44							
Trefforest Estate	d																								
Trefforest	d							15 31			16 06							16 52							
Pontypridd ■	a							15 34			16 09							16 55							
	d							15 36			16 11							16 57							
Abercynon	d										16 19							17 05							
Penrhiwceiber	d										16 25														
Mountain Ash	a										16 28														
	d										16 29														
Fernhill	d										16 32														
Cwmbach	d										16 36														
Aberdare ■	a										16 44														
Quakers Yard	d																	17 09							
Merthyr Vale	a																	17 14							
	d																	17 16							
Troed Y Rhiw	d																	17 20							
Pentre-bach	d																	17 23							
Merthyr Tydfil	a																	17 32							
Trehafod	d							15 41																	
Porth	a							15 44																	
	d							15 45																	
Dinas Rhondda	d							15 49																	
Tonypandy	d							15 51																	
Llwynypia	d							15 53																	
Ystrad Rhondda	a							15 56																	
	d							15 59																	
Ton Pentre	d							16 01																	
Treorchy	d							16 04																	
Ynyswen	d							16 07																	
Treherbert	a							16 14																	

When events are being held at the Millenium Stadium, services are subject to alteration. Please check times before travelling.

Table 130

Sundays

16 September to 21 October

Bridgend, Barry Island, Barry, Penarth and Cardiff - Coryton, Rhymney, Pontypridd, Merthyr, Aberdare and Treherbert

Network Diagram - see first Page of Table 130

		AW	AW	AW	AW	AW	AW	AW		AW	AW	AW	AW	AW	AW	AW	AW	AW		AW	AW	AW	AW	AW	AW
Bridgend	d													17 42											19 42
Llantwit Major	d													17 56											19 56
Rhoose Cardiff Int Airport ✈	d													18 06											20 06
Barry Island	d					16 55				17 25			17 55		18 25							18 55	19 25	19 55	
Barry ■	d					17 00				17 30			18 00	18 15	18 30							19 00	19 30	20 00	20 15
Barry Docks	d					17 04				17 34			18 04	18 19	18 34							19 04	19 34	20 04	20 19
Cadoxton	d					17 07				17 37			18 07	18 22	18 37							19 07	19 37	20 07	20 22
Dinas Powys	d					17 11				17 41			18 11	18 26	18 41							19 11	19 41	20 11	20 26
Eastbrook	d					17 13				17 43			18 13	18 28	18 43							19 13	19 43	20 13	20 28
Cogan	d					17 15				17 45			18 15	18 30	18 45							19 15	19 45	20 15	20 30
Penarth	d																	18 47							
Dingle Road	d																	18 49							
Grangetown	d					17 19				17 49			18 19	18 34	18 49			18 53				19 19	19 49	20 19	20 34
Cardiff Central ■	a					17 24				17 54			18 24	18 42	18 57			19 00				19 24	19 54	20 24	20 42
	d		17 06			17 41				18 06			18 26								19 06	19 41	20 06	20 26	
Cardiff Bay	d	17 06		17 18	17 30		17 42	17 54			18 06	18 18				18 30	18 42			18 54					
Cardiff Queen Street ■	a	17 10	17 09	17 22	17 34	17 44	17 46	17 58		18 09	18 10	18 22	18 29			18 34	18 46			18 57	19 09	19 44	20 09	20 29	
	d		17 10			17 45				18 10			18 30								19 10	19 45	20 10	20 30	
Heath Low Level	d																								
Ty Glas	d																								
Birchgrove	d																								
Rhiwbina	d																								
Whitchurch (Cardiff)	d																								
Coryton	a																								
Heath High Level	d									18 15													20 15		
Llanishen	d									18 18													20 18		
Lisvane & Thornhill	d									18 20													20 20		
Caerphilly ■	d									18 26													20 26		
Aber	d									18 28													20 28		
Llanbradach	d									18 32													20 32		
Ystrad Mynach ■	d									18 37													20 37		
Hengoed	d									18 40													20 40		
Pengam	d									18 43													20 43		
Gilfach Fargoed	d									18 46													20 46		
Bargoed	a									18 49													20 49		
	d									18 49													20 49		
Brithdir	d									18 53													20 53		
Tir-phil	d									18 56													20 56		
Pontlottyn	d									19 00													21 00		
Rhymney ■	a									19 08													21 08		
Cathays	d		17 13			17 48							18 33								19 13	19 48		20 33	
Llandaf	d		17 17			17 52							18 37								19 17	19 52		20 37	
Ninian Park	d																								
Waun-gron Park	d																								
Fairwater	d																								
Danescourt	d																								
Radyr ■	a		17 20			17 55							18 40								19 20	19 55		20 40	
	d		17 20			17 55							18 40								19 20	19 55		20 40	
Taffs Well ■	d		17 24			17 59							18 44								19 24	19 59		20 44	
Trefforest Estate	d																								
Trefforest	d		17 31			18 06							18 52								19 31	20 06		20 52	
Pontypridd ■	a		17 34			18 09							18 55								19 34	20 09		20 55	
	d		17 36			18 11							18 57								19 36	20 11		20 57	
Abercynon	d					18 19							19 05									20 19		21 05	
Penrhiwceiber	d					18 25																20 25			
Mountain Ash	a					18 28																20 28			
	d					18 29																20 29			
Fernhill	d					18 32																20 32			
Cwmbach	d					18 36																20 36			
Aberdare ■	a					18 44																20 44			
Quakers Yard	d												19 09											21 09	
Merthyr Vale	a												19 14											21 14	
	d												19 16											21 16	
Troed Y Rhiw	d												19 20											21 20	
Pentre-bach	d												19 23											21 23	
Merthyr Tydfil	a												19 32											21 32	
Trehafod	d		17 41																		19 41				
Porth	a		17 44																		19 44				
	d		17 45																		19 45				
Dinas Rhondda	d		17 49																		19 49				
Tonypandy	d		17 51																		19 51				
Llwynypia	d		17 53																		19 53				
Ystrad Rhondda	a		17 56																		19 56				
	d		17 59																		19 59				
Ton Pentre	d		18 01																		20 01				
Treorchy	d		18 04																		20 04				
Ynyswen	d		18 07																		20 07				
Treherbert	a		18 14																		20 14				

When events are being held at the Millenium Stadium, services are subject to alteration. Please check times before travelling.

Table 130

Sundays
16 September to 21 October

Bridgend, Barry Island, Barry, Penarth and Cardiff - Coryton, Rhymney, Pontypridd, Merthyr, Aberdare and Treherbert

Network Diagram - see first Page of Table 130

		AW	AW	AW	AW	AW	AW	AW	AW
Bridgend	d							21 42	
Llantwit Major	d							21 56	
Rhoose Cardiff Int Airport ✈	d							22 06	
Barry Island	d	20 25			20 55	21 25	21 55		22 55
Barry 3	d	20 30			21 00	21 30	22 00	22 15	23 00
Barry Docks	d	20 34			21 04	21 34	22 04	22 19	23 04
Cadoxton	d	20 37			21 07	21 37	22 07	22 22	23 07
Dinas Powys	d	20 41			21 11	21 41	22 11	22 26	23 11
Eastbrook	d	20 43			21 13	21 43	22 13	22 28	23 13
Cogan	d	20 45			21 15	21 45	22 15	22 30	23 15
Penarth	d		20 47						
Dingle Road	d		20 49						
Grangetown	d	20 49	20 53		21 19	21 49	22 19	22 34	23 19
Cardiff Central 7	a	20 54	21 00		21 27	21 54	22 27	22 42	23 27
	d	21 06		21 16		22 06			
Cardiff Bay	d								
Cardiff Queen Street 3	a	21 09		21 19		22 09			
	d	21 10		21 20		22 10			
Heath Low Level	d								
Ty Glas	d								
Birchgrove	d								
Rhiwbina	d								
Whitchurch (Cardiff)	d								
Coryton	a								
Heath High Level	d			21 25					
Llanishen	d			21 28					
Lisvane & Thornhill	d			21 30					
Caerphilly 3	d			21 36					
Aber	d			21 38					
Llanbradach	d			21 42					
Ystrad Mynach 3	d			21 47					
Hengoed	d			21 50					
Pengam	d			21 53					
Gilfach Fargoed	d			21 56					
Bargoed	a			21 59					
	d			21 59					
Brithdir	d			22 03					
Tir-phil	d			22 06					
Pontlottyn	d			22 10					
Rhymney 3	a			22 18					
Cathays	d	21 13				22 13			
Llandaf	d	21 17				22 17			
Ninian Park	d								
Waun-gron Park	d								
Fairwater	d								
Danescourt	d								
Radyr 3	a	21 20				22 20			
	d	21 20				22 20			
Taffs Well 3	d	21 24				22 24			
Trefforest Estate	d								
Trefforest	d	21 31				22 31			
Pontypridd 3	a	21 34				22 34			
	d	21 36				22 36			
Abercynon	d								
Penrhiwceiber	d								
Mountain Ash	a								
	d								
Fernhill	d								
Cwmbach	d								
Aberdare 3	a								
Quakers Yard	d								
Merthyr Vale	a								
	d								
Troed Y Rhiw	d								
Pentre-bach	d								
Merthyr Tydfil	a								
Trehafod	d	21 41				22 41			
Porth	a	21 44				22 44			
	d	21 45				22 45			
Dinas Rhondda	d	21 49				22 49			
Tonypandy	d	21 51				22 51			
Llwynypia	d	21 53				22 53			
Ystrad Rhondda	a	21 56				22 56			
	d	21 59				22 59			
Ton Pentre	d	22 01				23 01			
Treorchy	d	22 04				23 04			
Ynyswen	d	22 07				23 07			
Treherbert	a	22 14				23 14			

When events are being held at the Millenium Stadium, services are subject to alteration. Please check times before travelling.

Table 130

Sundays
from 28 October

Bridgend, Barry Island, Barry, Penarth and Cardiff - Coryton, Rhymney, Pontypridd, Merthyr, Aberdare and Treherbert

Network Diagram - see first Page of Table 130

		AW	AW	AW	AW	AW	AW	AW	AW	AW	AW	AW	AW	AW	AW	AW	AW	AW	AW	AW	AW	AW	AW
Bridgend	d															09 42							
Llantwit Major	d															09 56							
Rhoose Cardiff Int Airport ✈	d															10 06							
Barry Island	d								08 55						09 55		10 25						
Barry 3	d								09 00						10 00	10 15	10 30						
Barry Docks	d								09 04						10 04	10 19	10 34						
Cadoxton	d								09 07						10 07	10 22	10 37						
Dinas Powys	d								09 11						10 11	10 26	10 41						
Eastbrook	d								09 13						10 13	10 28	10 43						
Cogan	d								09 15						10 15	10 30	10 45						
Penarth	d																			10 47			
Dingle Road	d																			10 49			
Grangetown	d								09 19						10 19	10 34	10 49			10 53			
Cardiff Central 7	a								09 24						10 24	10 42	10 57			11 00			
	d	08 26	08 41	08 54	09 00				09 41				10 06		10 26							11 00	
Cardiff Bay	d					09 06	09 18	09 30		09 42	09 54	10 06		10 18				10 30	10 42		10 54		11 06
Cardiff Queen Street 3	a	08 29	08 44	08 57	09 03	09 10	09 22	09 34	09 44	09 46	09 58	10 10	10 09	10 22	10 29			10 34	10 46		10 58	11 03	11 10
	d	08 30	08 45		09 04				09 45				10 10		10 30							11 04	
Heath Low Level	d																						
Ty Glas	d																						
Birchgrove	d																						
Rhiwbina	d																						
Whitchurch (Cardiff)	d																						
Coryton	a																						
Heath High Level	d												10 15										
Llanishen	d												10 18										
Lisvane & Thornhill	d												10 20										
Caerphilly 3	d												10 26										
Aber	d												10 28										
Llanbradach	d												10 32										
Ystrad Mynach 3	d												10 37										
Hengoed	d												10 40										
Pengam	d												10 43										
Gilfach Fargoed	d												10 46										
Bargoed	a												10 49										
	d												10 49										
Brithdir	d												10 53										
Tir-phil	d												10 56										
Pontlottyn	d												11 00										
Rhymney 3	a												11 08										
Cathays	d	08 33	08 48		09 07				09 48						10 33							11 07	
Llandaf	d	08 37	08 52		09 11				09 52						10 37							11 11	
Ninian Park	d																						
Waun-gron Park	d																						
Fairwater	d																						
Danescourt	d																						
Radyr 3	a	08 40	08 55		09 14				09 55						10 40							11 14	
	d	08 40	08 55		09 14				09 55						10 40							11 14	
Taffs Well 3	d	08 44	08 59		09 18				09 59						10 44							11 18	
Trefforest Estate	d																						
Trefforest	d	08 52	09 06		09 25				10 06						10 52							11 25	
Pontypridd 3	a	08 55	09 09		09 28				10 09						10 55							11 28	
	d	08 57	09 11		09 30				10 11						10 57							11 30	
Abercynon	d	09 05	09 19						10 19						11 05								
Penrhiwceiber	d		09 25						10 25														
Mountain Ash	a		09 28						10 28														
	d		09 29						10 29														
Fernhill	d		09 32						10 32														
Cwmbach	d		09 36						10 36														
Aberdare 3	a		09 44						10 44														
Quakers Yard	d	09 09													11 09								
Merthyr Vale	a	09 14													11 14								
	d	09 16													11 16								
Troed Y Rhiw	d	09 20													11 20								
Pentre-bach	d	09 23													11 23								
Merthyr Tydfil	a	09 32													11 32								
Trehafod	d				09 35																	11 35	
Porth	a				09 38																	11 38	
	d				09 39																	11 39	
Dinas Rhondda	d				09 43																	11 43	
Tonypandy	d				09 45																	11 45	
Llwynypia	d				09 47																	11 47	
Ystrad Rhondda	a				09 50																	11 50	
	d				09 53																	11 53	
Ton Pentre	d				09 55																	11 55	
Treorchy	d				09 58																	11 58	
Ynyswen	d				10 01																	12 01	
Treherbert	a				10 08																	12 08	

When events are being held at the Millenium Stadium, services are subject to alteration. Please check times before travelling.

Sundays
from 28 October

Bridgend, Barry Island, Barry, Penarth and Cardiff - Coryton, Rhymney, Pontypridd, Merthyr, Aberdare and Treherbert

Network Diagram - see first Page of Table 130

		AW	AW	AW	AW	AW		AW	AW	AW	AW	AW	AW	AW	AW	AW		AW	AW	AW	AW	AW	AW	AW	AW
Bridgend	d											11 42													
Llantwit Major	d											11 56													
Rhoose Cardiff Int Airport ✈	d											12 06													
Barry Island	d			10 55				11 25			11 55		12 25										12 55		
Barry [3]	d			11 00				11 30			12 00	12 15	12 30										13 00		
Barry Docks	d			11 04				11 34			12 04	12 19	12 34										13 04		
Cadoxton	d			11 07				11 37			12 07	12 22	12 37										13 07		
Dinas Powys	d			11 11				11 41			12 11	12 26	12 41										13 11		
Eastbrook	d			11 13				11 43			12 13	12 28	12 43										13 13		
Cogan	d			11 15				11 45			12 15	12 30	12 45										13 15		
Penarth	d															12 47									
Dingle Road	d															12 49									
Grangetown	d			11 19				11 49			12 19	12 34	12 49			12 53							13 19		
Cardiff Central [7]	a			11 24				11 54			12 24	12 42	12 57			13 00							13 24		
	d			11 41				12 06			12 26									13 06			13 41		
Cardiff Bay	d	11 18	11 30		11 42	11 54			12 06	12 18				12 30	12 42			12 54	13 06		13 18	13 30		13 42	13 54
Cardiff Queen Street [3]	a	11 22	11 34	11 44	11 46	11 58		12 09	12 10	12 22	12 29			12 34	12 46			12 58	13 10	13 09	13 22	13 34	13 44	13 46	13 58
	d			11 45				12 10			12 30									13 10			13 45		
Heath Low Level	d																								
Ty Glas	d																								
Birchgrove	d																								
Rhiwbina	d																								
Whitchurch (Cardiff)	d																								
Coryton	a																								
Heath High Level	d							12 15																	
Llanishen	d							12 18																	
Lisvane & Thornhill	d							12 20																	
Caerphilly [3]	d							12 26																	
Aber	d							12 28																	
Llanbradach	d							12 32																	
Ystrad Mynach [3]	d							12 37																	
Hengoed	d							12 40																	
Pengam	d							12 43																	
Gilfach Fargoed	d							12 46																	
Bargoed	a							12 49																	
	d							12 49																	
Brithdir	d							12 53																	
Tir-phil	d							12 56																	
Pontlottyn	d							13 00																	
Rhymney [3]	a							13 08																	
Cathays	d			11 48							12 33									13 13			13 48		
Llandaf	d			11 52							12 37									13 17			13 52		
Ninian Park	d																								
Waun-gron Park	d																								
Fairwater	d																								
Danescourt	d																								
Radyr [3]	a			11 55							12 40									13 20			13 55		
	d			11 55							12 40									13 20			13 55		
Taffs Well [3]	d			11 59							12 44									13 24			13 59		
Trefforest Estate	d																								
Trefforest	d			12 06							12 52									13 31			14 06		
Pontypridd [3]	a			12 09							12 55									13 34			14 09		
	d			12 11							12 57									13 36			14 11		
Abercynon	d			12 19							13 05												14 19		
Penrhiwceiber	d			12 25																			14 25		
Mountain Ash	a			12 28																			14 28		
	d			12 29																			14 29		
Fernhill	d			12 32																			14 32		
Cwmbach	d			12 36																			14 36		
Aberdare [3]	a			12 44																			14 44		
Quakers Yard	d										13 09														
Merthyr Vale	a										13 14														
	d										13 16														
Troed Y Rhiw	d										13 20														
Pentre-bach	d										13 23														
Merthyr Tydfil	a										13 32														
Trehafod	d																			13 41					
Porth	a																			13 44					
	d																			13 45					
Dinas Rhondda	d																			13 49					
Tonypandy	d																			13 51					
Llwynypia	d																			13 53					
Ystrad Rhondda	a																			13 56					
	d																			13 59					
Ton Pentre	d																			14 01					
Treorchy	d																			14 04					
Ynyswen	d																			14 07					
Treherbert	a																			14 14					

When events are being held at the Millenium Stadium, services are subject to alteration. Please check times before travelling.

Sundays
from 28 October

Bridgend, Barry Island, Barry, Penarth and Cardiff - Coryton, Rhymney, Pontypridd, Merthyr, Aberdare and Treherbert

Network Diagram - see first Page of Table 130

		AW		AW	AW	AW	AW	AW	AW	AW	AW	AW		AW	AW	AW	AW	AW	AW	AW	AW	AW		AW	AW
Bridgend	d						13 42																		
Llantwit Major	d						13 56																		
Rhoose Cardiff Int Airport ✈	d						14 06																		
Barry Island	d	13 25				13 55		14 25										14 55			15 25				15 55
Barry [3]	d	13 30				14 00	14 15	14 30										15 00			15 30				16 00
Barry Docks	d	13 34				14 04	14 19	14 34										15 04			15 34				16 04
Cadoxton	d	13 37				14 07	14 22	14 37										15 07			15 37				16 07
Dinas Powys	d	13 41				14 11	14 26	14 41										15 11			15 41				16 11
Eastbrook	d	13 43				14 13	14 28	14 43										15 13			15 43				16 13
Cogan	d	13 45				14 15	14 30	14 45										15 15			15 45				16 15
Penarth	d										14 47														
Dingle Road	d										14 49														
Grangetown	d	13 49				14 19	14 34	14 49			14 53							15 19			15 49				16 19
Cardiff Central [7]	a	13 54				14 24	14 42	14 57			15 00							15 24			15 54				16 24
	d	14 06				14 26									15 06			15 41			16 06				16 26
Cardiff Bay	d			14 06	14 18				14 30	14 42		14 54		15 06		15 18	15 30		15 42	15 54		16 06		16 18	
Cardiff Queen Street [3]	a	14 09		14 10	14 22	14 29			14 34	14 46		14 58		15 10	15 09	15 22	15 34	15 44	15 46	15 58	16 09	16 10		16 22	16 29
	d	14 10				14 30									15 10			15 45			16 10				16 30
Heath Low Level	d																								
Ty Glas	d																								
Birchgrove	d																								
Rhiwbina	d																								
Whitchurch (Cardiff)	d																								
Coryton	a																								
Heath High Level	d	14 15																			16 15				
Llanishen	d	14 18																			16 18				
Lisvane & Thornhill	d	14 20																			16 20				
Caerphilly [3]	d	14 26																			16 26				
Aber	d	14 28																			16 28				
Llanbradach	d	14 32																			16 32				
Ystrad Mynach [3]	d	14 37																			16 37				
Hengoed	d	14 40																			16 40				
Pengam	d	14 43																			16 43				
Gilfach Fargoed	d	14 46																			16 46				
Bargoed	a	14 49																			16 49				
	d	14 49																			16 49				
Brithdir	d	14 53																			16 53				
Tir-phil	d	14 56																			16 56				
Pontlottyn	d	15 00																			17 00				
Rhymney [3]	a	15 08																			17 08				
Cathays	d					14 33									15 13			15 48							16 33
Llandaf	d					14 37									15 17			15 52							16 37
Ninian Park	d																								
Waun-gron Park	d																								
Fairwater	d																								
Danescourt	d																								
Radyr [3]	a					14 40									15 20			15 55							16 40
	d					14 40									15 20			15 55							16 40
Taffs Well [3]	d					14 44									15 24			15 59							16 44
Trefforest Estate	d																								
Trefforest	d					14 52									15 31			16 06							16 52
Pontypridd [3]	a					14 55									15 34			16 09							16 55
	d					14 57									15 36			16 11							16 57
Abercynon	d					15 05												16 19							17 05
Penrhiwceiber	d																	16 25							
Mountain Ash	a																	16 28							
	d																	16 29							
Fernhill	d																	16 32							
Cwmbach	d																	16 36							
Aberdare [3]	a																	16 44							
Quakers Yard	d					15 09																			17 09
Merthyr Vale	a					15 14																			17 14
	d					15 16																			17 16
Troed Y Rhiw	d					15 20																			17 20
Pentre-bach	d					15 23																			17 23
Merthyr Tydfil	a					15 32																			17 32
Trehafod	d														15 41										
Porth	a														15 44										
	d														15 45										
Dinas Rhondda	d														15 49										
Tonypandy	d														15 51										
Llwynypia	d														15 53										
Ystrad Rhondda	a														15 56										
	d														15 59										
Ton Pentre	d														16 01										
Treorchy	d														16 04										
Ynyswen	d														16 07										
Treherbert	a														16 14										

When events are being held at the Millenium Stadium, services are subject to alteration. Please check times before travelling.

Table 130

Sundays
from 28 October

Bridgend, Barry Island, Barry, Penarth and Cardiff - Coryton, Rhymney, Pontypridd, Merthyr, Aberdare and Treherbert

Network Diagram - see first Page of Table 130

		AW	AW	AW	AW	AW	AW	AW		AW	AW	AW	AW	AW	AW	AW	AW	AW		AW	AW	AW	AW	AW	AW
Bridgend	d	15 42																			17 42				
Llantwit Major	d	15 56																			17 56				
Rhoose Cardiff Int Airport	d	16 06																			18 06				
Barry Island	d		16 25										16 55			17 25				17 55		18 25			
Barry	d	16 15	16 30										17 00			17 30				18 00	18 15	18 30			
Barry Docks	d	16 19	16 34										17 04			17 34				18 04	18 19	18 34			
Cadoxton	d	16 22	16 37										17 07			17 37				18 07	18 22	18 37			
Dinas Powys	d	16 26	16 41										17 11			17 41				18 11	18 26	18 41			
Eastbrook	d	16 28	16 43										17 13			17 43				18 13	18 28	18 43			
Cogan	d	16 30	16 45										17 15			17 45				18 15	18 30	18 45			
Penarth	d					16 47																			18 47
Dingle Road	d					16 49																			18 49
Grangetown	d	16 34	16 49			16 53							17 19			17 49				18 19	18 34	18 49			18 53
Cardiff Central	a	16 42	16 57			17 00							17 24			17 54				18 24	18 42	18 57			19 00
	d									17 06			17 41			18 06				18 26					
Cardiff Bay	d			16 30	16 42		16 54	17 06			17 18	17 30		17 42	17 54		18 06	18 18					18 30	18 42	
Cardiff Queen Street	a			16 34	16 46		16 58	17 10		17 09	17 22	17 34	17 44	17 46	17 58	18 09	18 10	18 22		18 29			18 34	18 46	
	d									17 10			17 45			18 10				18 30					
Heath Low Level	d																								
Ty Glas	d																								
Birchgrove	d																								
Rhiwbina	d																								
Whitchurch (Cardiff)	d																								
Coryton	a																								
Heath High Level	d															18 15									
Llanishen	d															18 18									
Lisvane & Thornhill	d															18 20									
Caerphilly	d															18 26									
Aber	d															18 28									
Llanbradach	d															18 32									
Ystrad Mynach	d															18 37									
Hengoed	d															18 40									
Pengam	d															18 43									
Gilfach Fargoed	d															18 46									
Bargoed	a															18 49									
	d															18 49									
Brithdir	d															18 53									
Tir-phil	d															18 56									
Pontlottyn	d															19 00									
Rhymney	a															19 08									
Cathays	d									17 13			17 48							18 33					
Llandaf	d									17 17			17 52							18 37					
Ninian Park	d																								
Waun-gron Park	d																								
Fairwater	d																								
Danescourt	d																								
Radyr	a									17 20			17 55							18 40					
	d									17 20			17 55							18 40					
Taffs Well	d									17 24			17 59							18 44					
Trefforest Estate	d																								
Trefforest	d									17 31			18 06							18 52					
Pontypridd	a									17 34			18 09							18 55					
	d									17 36			18 11							18 57					
Abercynon	d												18 19							19 05					
Penrhiwceiber	d												18 25												
Mountain Ash	a												18 28												
	d												18 29												
Fernhill	d												18 32												
Cwmbach	d												18 36												
Aberdare	a												18 44												
Quakers Yard	d																			19 09					
Merthyr Vale	a																			19 14					
	d																			19 16					
Troed Y Rhiw	d																			19 20					
Pentre-bach	d																			19 23					
Merthyr Tydfil	a																			19 32					
Trehafod	d									17 41															
Porth	a									17 44															
	d									17 45															
Dinas Rhondda	d									17 49															
Tonypandy	d									17 51															
Llwynypia	d									17 53															
Ystrad Rhondda	a									17 56															
	d									17 59															
Ton Pentre	d									18 01															
Treorchy	d									18 04															
Ynyswen	d									18 07															
Treherbert	a									18 14															

When events are being held at the Millenium Stadium, services are subject to alteration. Please check times before travelling.

Table 130

Sundays
from 28 October

Bridgend, Barry Island, Barry, Penarth and Cardiff - Coryton, Rhymney, Pontypridd, Merthyr, Aberdare and Treherbert

Network Diagram - see first Page of Table 130

		AW	AW	AW		AW	AW	AW	AW	AW	AW	AW	AW	AW		AW	AW
Bridgend	d							19 42								21 42	
Llantwit Major	d							19 56								21 56	
Rhoose Cardiff Int Airport	d							20 06								22 06	
Barry Island	d			18 55		19 25	19 55		20 25			20 55	21 25	21 55			22 55
Barry	d			19 00		19 30	20 00	20 15	20 30			21 00	21 30	22 00		22 15	23 00
Barry Docks	d			19 04		19 34	20 04	20 19	20 34			21 04	21 34	22 04		22 19	23 04
Cadoxton	d			19 07		19 37	20 07	20 22	20 37			21 07	21 37	22 07		22 22	23 07
Dinas Powys	d			19 11		19 41	20 11	20 26	20 41			21 11	21 41	22 11		22 26	23 11
Eastbrook	d			19 13		19 43	20 13	20 28	20 43			21 13	21 43	22 13		22 28	23 13
Cogan	d			19 15		19 45	20 15	20 30	20 45			21 15	21 45	22 15		22 30	23 15
Penarth	d									20 47							
Dingle Road	d									20 49							
Grangetown	d			19 19		19 49	20 19	20 34	20 49	20 53		21 19	21 49	22 19		22 34	23 19
Cardiff Central	a			19 24		19 54	20 24	20 42	20 54	21 00		21 27	21 54	22 27		22 42	23 27
	d		19 06	19 41		20 06	20 26		21 06		21 16		22 06				
Cardiff Bay	d	18 54															
Cardiff Queen Street	a	18 57	19 09	19 44		20 09	20 29		21 09		21 19		22 09				
	d		19 10	19 45		20 10	20 30		21 10		21 20		22 10				
Heath Low Level	d																
Ty Glas	d																
Birchgrove	d																
Rhiwbina	d																
Whitchurch (Cardiff)	d																
Coryton	a																
Heath High Level	d					20 15					21 25						
Llanishen	d					20 18					21 28						
Lisvane & Thornhill	d					20 20					21 30						
Caerphilly	d					20 26					21 36						
Aber	d					20 28					21 38						
Llanbradach	d					20 32					21 42						
Ystrad Mynach	d					20 37					21 47						
Hengoed	d					20 40					21 50						
Pengam	d					20 43					21 53						
Gilfach Fargoed	d					20 46					21 56						
Bargoed	a					20 49					21 59						
	d					20 49					21 59						
Brithdir	d					20 53					22 03						
Tir-phil	d					20 56					22 06						
Pontlottyn	d					21 00					22 10						
Rhymney	a					21 08					22 18						
Cathays	d		19 13	19 48			20 33		21 13				22 13				
Llandaf	d		19 17	19 52			20 37		21 17				22 17				
Ninian Park	d																
Waun-gron Park	d																
Fairwater	d																
Danescourt	d																
Radyr	a		19 20	19 55			20 40		21 20				22 20				
	d		19 20	19 55			20 40		21 20				22 20				
Taffs Well	d		19 24	19 59			20 44		21 24				22 24				
Trefforest Estate	d																
Trefforest	d		19 31	20 06			20 52		21 31				22 31				
Pontypridd	a		19 34	20 09			20 55		21 34				22 34				
	d		19 36	20 11			20 57		21 36				22 36				
Abercynon	d			20 19			21 05										
Penrhiwceiber	d			20 25													
Mountain Ash	a			20 28													
	d			20 29													
Fernhill	d			20 32													
Cwmbach	d			20 36													
Aberdare	a			20 44													
Quakers Yard	d						21 09										
Merthyr Vale	a						21 14										
	d						21 16										
Troed Y Rhiw	d						21 20										
Pentre-bach	d						21 23										
Merthyr Tydfil	a						21 32										
Trehafod	d		19 41						21 41				22 41				
Porth	a		19 44						21 44				22 44				
	d		19 45						21 45				22 45				
Dinas Rhondda	d		19 49						21 49				22 49				
Tonypandy	d		19 51						21 51				22 51				
Llwynypia	d		19 53						21 53				22 53				
Ystrad Rhondda	a		19 56						21 56				22 56				
	d		19 59						21 59				22 59				
Ton Pentre	d		20 01						22 01				23 01				
Treorchy	d		20 04						22 04				23 04				
Ynyswen	d		20 07						22 07				23 07				
Treherbert	a		20 14						22 14				23 14				

When events are being held at the Millenium Stadium, services are subject to alteration. Please check times before travelling.

Cardiff - Crewe, Liverpool and Manchester

Route Diagram - see first Page of Table 129

Miles	Miles			AW MX ◇	AW MX ◇	AW MO ◇ A	AW MX ◇	AW ■ B	AW ■ C	AW ■ D	AW ◇ A	AW ◇ E	AW MX F	AW	AW ◇	AW ◇	AW ◇	AW	AW ◇	AW ◇	AW ◇	AW ◇	AW
—	—	Swansea	d								21p52								04 36			07 06	
0	0	**Cardiff Central** 7	d	19p34	20p53	21p04	21p55	22p31	22p31	22p31	23p00	00 30	00 30		04 35	05 10	05 40			06 50	07 21	08 05	
—	—	London Paddington 15 ⊖	d																				
—	—	Reading 7	d																				
11¾	11¾	**Newport (South Wales)**	d	19p48	21p10	21p19	22p11	22p49	22p49	22p49	23p20	00 59	00 59		04 52	05 28	05 57			07 04	07 36	08 19	
18¾	18¾	Cwmbran	d	19p58	21p20	21p30	22p23	23p00	23p00	23p00	23p29	01 10	01 10		05 03	05 38	06 08			07 14	07 46	08 29	
21¾	21¾	Pontypool and New Inn	d	20p03		21p36	22p29	23p08	23p08	23p08	23p35	01 16	01 16		05 09	05 44	06 13				07 52		
31¼	31¼	Abergavenny	d	20p12	21p33	21p46	22p39	23p19	23p19	23p19	23p45	01 27	01 27		05 18	05 53	06 23			07 27	08 01	08 42	
55¼	55¼	**Hereford** 7	a	20p38	21p57	22p12	23p05	23p46	23p46	23p46	00 17	01 54	01 57		05 46	06 17	06 47			07 51	08 25	09 07	
—	—		d	20p39	21p59	22p14	23p07	23p49	23p49	23p49		01 56			05 47	06 25	06 49			07 53	08 27	09 08	
67¾	67¾	Leominster	d	20p52	22p12	22p27	23p20	00 05	00 06	00 06		02 10			06 00	06 38	07 02			08 06		09 21	
78¾	78¾	Ludlow	d	21p03	22p23	22p38	23p31	00 18	00 21	00 21		02 21			06 11	06 49	07 13			08 17	08 48	09 32	
86	86	Craven Arms	d	21p12	22p31	22p48	23p41	00 29	00 32	00 32		02 31			06 20	06 57	07 21		07 54	08 25	08 56		
93¼	93¼	Church Stretton	d	21p21	22p40	22p57	23p50								06 29	07 06	07 30		08 07	08 34	09 05		
106	106	**Shrewsbury**	a	21p37	22p54	23p14	00 05	00 49	01 04	01 03		02 56			06 43	07 20	07 44		08 22	08 48	09 19	09 58	
—	—		d	21p39	23p06	23p19	00 10	00 51	01 06	01 06				05 44	06 44	07 24	07 46	07 57		08 50	09 24	10 00	10 18
113¼	113¼	Yorton	d		23b15	23b28	00x19							05x52				08x06					10x28
116¾	116¾	Wem	d		23p20	23p34	00 24							05 58	06 56		07 57	08 09					10 31
120	120	Prees	d		23b25	23b39	00x29							06x03				08x17					10x39
125	125	Whitchurch (Shrops)	d		23p32	23p46	00 36							06 10	07 04		08 06	08 25		09 06			10 46
129¾	129¾	Wrenbury	d		23b38	23b52	00x42							06x17				08x31					10x53
134¼	134¼	Nantwich	d		23p44	23p59	00 49							06 23	07 13		08 15	08 38		09 16			10 59
138¾	138¾	**Crewe** 10	a		23p53	00 09	01 04	01 31	01 47	01 47				06 35	07 24		08 24	08 47		09 25		10 29	11 09
—	—	Chester	a	22p34	00 27	00 33		01 58	02 14	02 14						08 19					10 19		
—	—	Llandudno Junction	a	23p49				02 41	02 57	02 57						09 11					11 14		
—	—	Bangor (Gwynedd)	a	00 12				02 59	03 15	03 14						09 32					11 37		
—	—	Holyhead	a	00 48				03 33	03 49	03 49						10 14					12 14		
157¾	—	Wilmslow	a												07 44		08 45			09 48		10 49	
163¾	—	Stockport	a												07 54		08 58			09 58		10 58	
169¾	—	**Manchester Piccadilly** 10	a												08 10		09 15			10 15		11 15	

		AW ◇	AW ◇	AW ◇	GW ◇1	AW	AW ◇	AW ◇	AW ◇	AW ◇	GW ◇1	AW	AW ◇	AW ◇	AW ◇	AW	AW ◇	AW ◇	AW ■	AW ■	AW ■ 1	AW G	AW
Swansea	d	07 45		08 55			09 55	09 16		10 55			11 55		12 54		13 55	13 14		14 55			
Cardiff Central 7	d	08 50	09 21	10 05			10 50		11 21	12 05			12 50	13 21	14 05		14 50		15 21	15 50	16 15	16 15	
London Paddington 15 ⊖	d				08 22						10 22												
Reading 7	d				08 52						10 52												
Newport (South Wales)	d	09 04	09 36	10 19			11 04		11 36	12 19			13 04	13 36	14 19		15 04		15 36	16 04	16 29	16 29	
Cwmbran	d	09 14	09 46	10 29			11 14		11 46	12 29			13 14	13 46	14 29		15 14		15 46	16 14	16 40	16 40	
Pontypool and New Inn	d		09 52						11 52					13 52					15 52	16 19			
Abergavenny	d	09 27	10 01	10 42			11 27		12 01	12 42			13 26	14 01	14 43		15 27		16 01	16 29	16 54	16a55	
Hereford 7	a	09 51	10 25	11 06	11 42		11 51		12 25	13 06	13 48		13 53	14 25	15 06		15 51		16 25	16 53			
	d	09 53	10 27	11 08			11 53		12 27	13 08			13 55	14 27	15 08		15 53		16 27	16 54			
Leominster	d	10 06		11 21			12 06			13 21			14 08		15 21		16 06		16 40	17 07			
Ludlow	d	10 17	10 48	11 32			12 17		12 48	13 32			14 19	14 48	15 32		16 17		16 51	17 18			
Craven Arms	d	10 25	10 56				12 25	12 39	12 56				14 27	14 56			16 25	16 40		17 27			
Church Stretton	d	10 39	11 05				12 38	12 52	13 05				14 36	15 05				16 53	17 05	17 36			
Shrewsbury	a	10 52	11 19	11 58			12 52	13 08	13 19	13 58			14 50	15 19	15 58		16 48	17 09	17 19	17 50	18 05		
	d	10 53	11 24	11 59		12 24	12 54		13 24	13 59		14 24	14 52	15 24	15 59	16 24	16 50		17 24	17 51	18 06		18 25
Yorton	d					12x34						14x34				16x34							18 35
Wem	d					12 37						14 37				16 37	17 01						18 38
Prees	d					12x45						14x45				16x45							18 46
Whitchurch (Shrops)	d	11 11				12 52	13 10					14 52	15 08			16 52	17 10			18 09			18 53
Wrenbury	d					12x59						14x59				16x59							19 00
Nantwich	d	11 19				13 05	13 20					15 05	15 18			17 05	17 19			18 19			19 06
Crewe 10	a	11 29		12 29		13 15	13 29			14 29		15 15	15 27		16 29	17 15	17 28			18 28	18 42		19 16
Chester	a		12 19						14 19					16 20					18 20		19 06		
Llandudno Junction	a		13 11						15 11					17 13					19 12		19 52		
Bangor (Gwynedd)	a		13 28						15 28					17 33					19 33		20 09		
Holyhead	a		14 13						16 15					18 19					20 18		20 49		
Wilmslow	a	11 48		12 48			13 48			14 48			15 47		16 48		17 47			18 48			
Stockport	a	11 58		12 58			13 58			14 58			15 58		16 58		17 57			18 58			
Manchester Piccadilly 10	a	12 15		13 15			14 15			15 15			16 15		17 14		18 13			19 15			

A from 21 May
B 2 August
C 27 July
D 26 July
E 26 July, 27 July, 2 August
F not 26 July, 27 July, 2 August
G 4 June, 27 August
b Previous night, stops on request

For connections from Bristol Temple Meads please refer to Table 132. For connections to Runcorn and Liverpool Lime Street please refer to Table 91

When events are being held at the Millenium Stadium, services are subject to alteration. Please check times before travelling.

Table 131

Mondays to Fridays

Cardiff - Crewe, Liverpool and Manchester

Route Diagram - see first Page of Table 129

		AW ■	AW ■	AW ■	AW ■	AW	AW ◇	GW ◇1	AW ◇	AW ◇	AW ◇	GW ◇1 A	AW ◇	GW ◇1	AW ◇	AW ■ B	AW ■ C	AW ■ D	AW ■ E	AW ■ F
Swansea	d	15 55		16 55			17 55			18 21										
Cardiff Central 7	d	16 50	17 21	17 50	18 18		18 50		19 34		20 17		20 53		21 55	22 31	22 31	22 31	22 31	22 31
London Paddington 15 ⊖	d							17 22				18 22		19 22						
Reading 7	d							17 50				18 50		19 52						
Newport (South Wales)	d	17 04	17 36	18 04	18 32		19 05		19 48		20 31		21 10		22 11	22 49	22 49	22 49	22 51	22 51
Cwmbran	d	17 14	17 46	18 14			19 15		19 58		20 41		21 20		22 23	23 00	23 00	23 00	23 03	23 03
Pontypool and New Inn	d		17 52	18 19			19 20		20 03		20 47				22 29	23 08	23 08	23 08	23 11	23 11
Abergavenny	d	17 27	18 01	18 29	18 53		19 30		20 12		20 56		21 33		22 39	23 19	23 19	23 19	23 23	23 23
Hereford 7	a	17 51	18 25	18 53	19 17		19 54	20 27	20 38		21 21	21 33	21 57	22 54	23 05	23 46	23 46	23 46	23 49	23 49
	d	17 53	18 27	18 54	19 18		19 55		20 39		21 22		21 59		23 07	23 49	23 49	23 49	23 51	23 51
Leominster	d	18 06		19 07			20 08		20 52		21 35		22 12		23 20	00 05	00 06	00 06	00 07	00 07
Ludlow	d	18 17	18 48	19 18			20 19		21 03		21 46		22 23		23 31	00 18	00 21	00 21	00 20	00 20
Craven Arms	d	18 25		19 27			20 28		21 12	21 38	21 54		22 31		23 41	00 29	00 32	00 32	00 31	00 31
Church Stretton	d	18 34		19 36			20 37		21 21	21 51	22 03		22 40		23 50					
Shrewsbury	a	18 48	19 14	19 50	20 03		20 51		21 37	22 08	22 17		22 54		00 05	00 49	01 04	01 03	00 50	00 50
	d	18 50	19 24	19 51	20 05	20 32	20 52		21 39		22 19		23 06		00 10	00 51	01 06	01 06	00 52	00 52
Yorton	d					20x39					22x27		23x15		00x19					
Wem	d					20 44					22 31		23 20		00 24					
Prees	d					20x49					22x35		23x25		00x29					
Whitchurch (Shrops)	d	19 06				20 56	21 10				22 42		23 32		00 36					
Wrenbury	d					21x02					22x48		23x38		00x42					
Nantwich	d	19 16				21 08	21 20				22 53		23 44		00 49					
Crewe 10	a	19 25		20 22		21 19	21 29				23 03		23 53		01 04	01 31	01 47	01 47	01 27	01 27
Chester	a		20 20		20 58				22 34				00 27			01 58	02 14	02 14	01 57	01 57
Llandudno Junction	a		21 24		21 46				23 49							02 41	02 57	02 57	02 40	02 40
Bangor (Gwynedd)	a		21 41		22 04				00 12							02 59	03 15	03 14	02 58	02 58
Holyhead	a		22 25		22 36				00 48							03 33	03 49	03 49	03 32	03 37
Wilmslow	a	19 48		20 40			21 48				23 22									
Stockport	a	19 58		20 50			21 58				23 30									
Manchester Piccadilly 10	a	20 15		21 05			22 13				23 48									

Saturdays

		AW ◇	AW ◇	AW ◇	AW ■ G	AW ■ H	AW I	AW ◇ J	AW	AW ◇	AW ◇	AW ◇	AW	AW ◇	AW ◇	AW ◇	AW ◇	AW	AW ◇	AW ◇	AW ◇	GW ◇1	AW
Swansea	d													04 36			06 47		07 45		08 55		
Cardiff Central 7	d	19p34	20p53	21p55	22p31	22p31	00 30	00 30		04 35	05 20	05 40			06 50	07 21	07 50		08 50	09 21	09 55		
London Paddington 15 ⊖	d																					08 21	
Reading 7	d																					08 54	
Newport (South Wales)	d	19p48	21p10	22p11	22p51	22p51	00 46	00 46		04 52	05 35	05 57			07 04	07 36	08 04		09 04	09 36	10 09		
Cwmbran	d	19p58	21p20	22p23	23p03	23p03	00 56	00 56		05 03	05 45	06 08			07 14	07 46	08 14		09 14	09 46	10 19		
Pontypool and New Inn	d	20p03		22p29	23p11	23p11	01 02	01 02		05 09	05 51	06 13				07 51				09 51			
Abergavenny	d	20p12	21p33	22p39	23p23	23p23	01 13	01 13		05 18	06 00	06 23			07 27	08 01	08 27		09 27	10 01	10 32		
Hereford 7	a	20p38	21p57	23p05	23p49	23p49	01 43	01 40		05 46	06 24	06 46			07 51	08 26	08 51		09 51	10 26	10 56	11 41	
	d	20p39	21p59	23p07	23p51	23p51		01 43		05 47	06 26	06 49			07 53	08 27	08 53		09 53	10 28	10 58		
Leominster	d	20p52	22p12	23p20	00 07	00 07		01 56		06 00	06 40	07 02			08 06		09 06		10 06		11 11		
Ludlow	d	21p03	22p23	23p31	00 20	00 20		02 08		06 11	06 51	07 13			08 17	08 48	09 17		10 17	10 49	11 22		
Craven Arms	d	21p12	22p31	23p41	00 31	00 31		02 17		06 20	06 59	07 21		07 54	08 25	08 56			10 25	10 57			
Church Stretton	d	21p21	22p40	23p50						06 29	07 08	07 30		08 07	08 34	09 05			10 34	11 06			
Shrewsbury	a	21p37	22p54	00 05	00 50	00 50		02 43		06 43	07 22	07 44		08 22	08 51	09 19	09 43		10 48	11 20	11 48		
	d	21p39	23p06	00 10	00 52	00 52			05 44	06 44	07 24	07 46	07 57		08 52	09 24	09 44	10 18	10 50	11 24	11 49		12 24
Yorton	d		23b15	00x19					05x52				08x06					10x28					12x34
Wem	d		23p20	00 24					05 58	06 56		07 57	08 09					10 31					12 37
Prees	d		23b25	00x29					06x03				08x17					10x39					12x45
Whitchurch (Shrops)	d		23p32	00 36					06 10	07 04		08 06	08 25		09 09		10 01	10 46	11 06		12 06		12 52
Wrenbury	d		23b38	00x42					06x17				08x31					10x53					12x59
Nantwich	d		23p44	00 49					06 23	07 13		08 15	08 38		09 18		10 10	10 59	11 16		12 15		13 05
Crewe 10	a		23p53	01 04	01 27	01 27			06 35	07 22		08 24	08 47		09 27		10 20	11 09	11 25		12 24		13 15
Chester	a	22p34	00 27		01 57	01 57					08 18					10 19				12 19			
Llandudno Junction	a	23p49			02 40	02 40					09 11					11 11				13 11			
Bangor (Gwynedd)	a	00 12			02 58	02 58					09 32					11 32				13 28			
Holyhead	a	00 48			03 32	03 37					10 14					12 09				14 13			
Wilmslow	a									07 44		08 45			09 47		10 48		11 48		12 48		
Stockport	a									08 01		08 58			09 57		10 58		11 58		12 58		
Manchester Piccadilly 10	a									08 20		09 15			10 14		11 15		12 15		13 15		

A The Cathedrals Express
B 1 August
C 26 July
D 25 July
E 3 August
F 10 August
G 4 August
H 11 August
I not from 4 August until 11 August
J 4 August, 11 August
b Previous night, stops on request

For connections from Bristol Temple Meads please refer to Table 132. For connections to Runcorn and Liverpool Lime Street please refer to Table 91

When events are being held at the Millenium Stadium, services are subject to alteration. Please check times before travelling.

Table 131

Saturdays

Cardiff - Crewe, Liverpool and Manchester

Route Diagram - see first Page of Table 129

Station		AW	AW	AW	AW	GW	AW	AW	AW	AW	AW	AW
		◇	◇	◇	◇	◇1		◇	◇	◇		◇
		⌶	⌶	⌶	⌶	⊡		⌶	⌶	⌶		⌶
Swansea	d	09 55	09 16		10 55			12 00		12 55		14 00
Cardiff Central 7	d	10 55		11 21	11 55			12 55	13 21	13 55		14 55
London Paddington 15 ⊖	d					10 21						
Reading 7	d					10 54						
Newport (South Wales)	d	11 09		11 36	12 09			13 09	13 36	14 09		15 09
Cwmbran	d	11 19		11 46	12 19			13 19	13 46	14 19		15 19
Pontypool and New Inn	d			11 50					13 50			
Abergavenny	d	11 32		12 00	12 32			13 32	14 01	14 32		15 32
Hereford 7	a	11 56		12 26	12 56	13 40		13 56	14 26	14 56		15 56
	d	11 58		12 28	12 58			13 58	14 26	14 58		15 58
Leominster	d	12 11			13 11			14 11		15 11		16 11
Ludlow	d	12 22		12 49	13 22			14 22	14 47	15 22		16 22
Craven Arms	d	12 30	12 37	12 57				14 30	14 55			16 30
Church Stretton	d	12 39	12 51	13 06				14 39	15 04			16 39
Shrewsbury	a	12 53	13 09	13 20	13 48			14 53	15 18	15 48		16 53
	d	12 55		13 24	13 49		14 24	14 55	15 24	15 49	16 24	16 55
Yorton	d						14x34				16x34	
Wem	d						14 37				16 37	
Prees	d						14x45				16x45	
Whitchurch (Shrops)	d				14 06		14 52			16 06	16 52	
Wrenbury	d						14x59				16x59	
Nantwich	d				14 15		15 05			16 15	17 05	
Crewe 10	a	13 26			14 24		15 15	15 25		16 24	17 15	17 26
Chester	a			14 19					16 22			
Llandudno Junction	a			15 11					17 14			
Bangor (Gwynedd)	a			15 28					17 34			
Holyhead	a			16 13					18 20			
Wilmslow	a	13 48			14 48			15 45		16 48		17 45
Stockport	a	13 58			14 58			15 58		16 58		17 58
Manchester Piccadilly 10 ⇌	a	14 15			15 15			16 15		17 15		18 15

Station		AW	AW	AW	AW	AW	AW	AW	AW	GW	AW	AW
			■	■			■	■	■			
		◇								◇1		◇
								A				
			⌶	⌶			⌶	⌶	⌶	⊡		⌶
Swansea	d	13 16		14 55	15 10		15 55		16 55			17 55
Cardiff Central 7	d		15 21	15 55	16 19		16 55	17 21	17 55			18 50
London Paddington 15 ⊖	d									16 21		
Reading 7	d									16 54		
Newport (South Wales)	d		15 36	16 09	16 34		17 09	17 35	18 09			19 04
Cwmbran	d		15 46	16 19	16 44		17 19	17 46	18 19			19 15
Pontypool and New Inn	d		15 52	16 24	16 50			17 52	18 24			19 20
Abergavenny	d		16 01	16 34	17a02		17 32	18 01	18 34			19 29
Hereford 7	a		16 25	16 58			17 56	18 25	18 58	19 45		19 53
	d		16 27	16 59			17 58	18 27	18 59			19 55
Leominster	d		16 40	17 12			18 11		19 12			20 08
Ludlow	d		16 51	17 23			18 22	18 48	19 23			20 19
Craven Arms	d	16 38					18 30	18 56				20 27
Church Stretton	d	16 51	17 05				18 39	19 05				20 36
Shrewsbury	a	17 11	17 19	17 49			18 53	19 19	19 49			20 53
	d		17 24	17 51		18 25	18 55	19 24	19 51		20 32	20 57
Yorton	d					18x35					20x39	
Wem	d					18 38					20 44	
Prees	d					18x46					20x49	
Whitchurch (Shrops)	d			18 07		18 53			20 07		20 56	
Wrenbury	d					19x00					21x02	
Nantwich	d			18 17		19 06			20 17		21 08	
Crewe 10	a			18 28		19 16	19 26		20 26		21 19	21 28
Chester	a		18 19					20 19				
Llandudno Junction	a		19 14					21 24				
Bangor (Gwynedd)	a		19 32					21 41				
Holyhead	a		20 18					22 25				
Wilmslow	a			18 48			19 48		20 45			21 50
Stockport	a			18 58			19 58		20 58			22 00
Manchester Piccadilly 10 ⇌	a			19 15			20 15		21 15			22 15

Station		AW	AW	AW	GW	AW	AW	AW	AW	AW
							■			■
		◇	◇	◇	◇1	◇		◇		
							B			C
					⊡					
Swansea	d		18 21					20 55		
Cardiff Central 7	d	19 34		20 10		20 55	21 20	21 49		22 20
London Paddington 15 ⊖	d				18 21					
Reading 7	d				18 54					
Newport (South Wales)	d	19 48		20 26		21 10	21 35	22 07		22 39
Cwmbran	d	19 58		20 37		21 21	21 45	22 19		22 50
Pontypool and New Inn	d	20 03		20 42			21 53	22 24		22 58
Abergavenny	d	20 12		20 52		21 34	22 04	22 34		23 09
Hereford 7	a	20 38		21 17	21 34	21 58	22 32	22 58		23 36
	d	20 39		21 20		22 00	22 34			23 39
Leominster	d	20 52		21 33		22 14	22 51			23 55
Ludlow	d	21 03		21 44		22 25	23 04			00 08
Craven Arms	d	21 12	21 38	21 53		22 33	23 14			00 19
Church Stretton	d	21 21	21 51	22 03		22 42				
Shrewsbury	a	21 35	22 08	22 17		22 57	23 35			00 39
	d	21 37		22 19		23 06	23 37		23 50	00 42
Yorton	d			22x27		23x14			23x58	
Wem	d			22 32		23 20			00 04	
Prees	d			22x36		23x24			00x07	
Whitchurch (Shrops)	d			22 44		23 31			00 15	
Wrenbury	d			22x49		23x36			00x20	
Nantwich	d			22 55		23 42			00 26	
Crewe 10	a			23 04		23 53	00 13		00 38	01 17
Chester	a	22 31				00 24	00 40			01 44
Llandudno Junction	a	23 38					01 23			02 26
Bangor (Gwynedd)	a						01 40			02 44
Holyhead	a						02 20			03 23
Wilmslow	a			23 24						
Stockport	a			23 32						
Manchester Piccadilly 10 ⇌	a			23 50						

A ⌶ from Shrewsbury

B 28 July

C 4 August

For connections from Bristol Temple Meads please refer to Table 132. For connections to Runcorn and Liverpool Lime Street please refer to Table 91

When events are being held at the Millenium Stadium, services are subject to alteration. Please check times before travelling.

Table 131

Sundays
until 24 June

Cardiff - Crewe, Liverpool and Manchester

Route Diagram - see first Page of Table 129

Station		AW	AW	AW	AW	AW	AW	GW	AW	AW	GW	AW
		◇		◇	◇	◇	◇	◇1	◇	◇	◇1	◇
					⌶	⌶	⌶	⊡	⌶	⌶	⊡	
Swansea	d						09 32			11 32		11 07
Cardiff Central 7	d	20p55			08 30	09 30	10 35		11 35	12 40		
London Paddington 15 ⊖	d							09 35			10 42	
Reading 7	d							10 12			11 21	
Newport (South Wales)	d	21p10			08 49	09 50	10 51		11 50	12 54		
Cwmbran	d	21p21			09 00	10 00	11 02		12 04	13 09		
Pontypool and New Inn	d				09 06	10 06	11 08		12 10	13 15		
Abergavenny	d	21p34			09 15	10 16	11 18		12 20	13 25		
Hereford 7	a	21p58			09 40	10 40	11 44	12 54	12 44	13 49	14 06	
	d	22p00			09 41	10 43	11 50		12 57	13 55		
Leominster	d	22p14			09 55	10 56	12 03		13 10	14 08		
Ludlow	d	22p25			10 06	11 07	12 14		13 21	14 19		
Craven Arms	d	22p33			10 14		12 24			14 28		14 44
Church Stretton	d	22p42			10 23		12 33			14 37		14 57
Shrewsbury	a	22p57			10 37	11 36	12 48		13 47	14 51		15 15
	d	23p06	23p50	09 55	10 39	11 37	12 51		13 50	14 53		
Yorton	d	23b14	23b58			11x45						
Wem	d	23p20	00 04		10 51	11 48						
Prees	d	23b24	00x07			11x55						
Whitchurch (Shrops)	d	23p31	00 15		11 00	12 03						
Wrenbury	d	23b36	00x20			12x08						
Nantwich	d	23p42	00 26		11 09	12 15						
Crewe 10	a	23p53	00 38	10 25	11 22	12 25	13 26		14 22	15 25		
Chester	a	00 24										
Llandudno Junction	a											
Bangor (Gwynedd)	a											
Holyhead	a											
Wilmslow	a			10 46	11 41	12 46	13 49		14 46	15 46		
Stockport	a			10 58		12 58	14 00		14 58	15 58		
Manchester Piccadilly 10 ⇌	a			11 12	12 02	13 15	14 19		15 15	16 15		

Station		AW	AW	AW	GW	AW	AW	AW	GW	AW	AW	AW
		■	■	■		■	■	■			■	■
					◇1	◇			◇1	◇		
						A						
			⌶	⌶	⊡	⌶	⌶	⌶	⊡			⌶
Swansea	d			13 43				15 33		15 26		17 30
Cardiff Central 7	d	13 22	13 40	14 56		15 22	15 56	16 40			17 35	18 40
London Paddington 15 ⊖	d				12 42				14 42			
Reading 7	d				13 21				15 21			
Newport (South Wales)	d	13 36	13 54	15 14		15 36	16 14	16 54			17 49	18 54
Cwmbran	d	13 47	14 09	15 24		15 47	16 24	17 09			18 04	19 09
Pontypool and New Inn	d					15 52		17 15			18 10	
Abergavenny	d	14 00	14 22	15 38		16 02	16 37	17 25			18 20	19 22
Hereford 7	a	14 26	14 47	16 02	16 05	16 27	17 02	17 49	17 58		18 44	19 47
	d	14 26	14 48	16 04		16 28	17 04	17 53			18 49	19 49
Leominster	d		15 01			16 41		18 07			19 03	20 03
Ludlow	d	14 48	15 12	16 25		16 52	17 26	18 18			19 14	20 14
Craven Arms	d					17 00		18 26		19 03		20 22
Church Stretton	d					17 09		18 35		19 16		20 31
Shrewsbury	a	15 21	15 38	16 51		17 23	17 52	18 49		19 31	19 40	20 45
	d	15 22	15 40	16 53		17 30	17 54	18 54			19 41	20 48
Yorton	d		15x48								19x49	
Wem	d		15 51								19 52	
Prees	d		15x58								19x59	
Whitchurch (Shrops)	d		16 06								20 06	
Wrenbury	d		16x11								20x11	
Nantwich	d		16 18								20 18	
Crewe 10	a		16 27	17 25			18 25	19 24			20 27	21 21
Chester	a	16 18				18 25						
Llandudno Junction	a	17 29				19 22						
Bangor (Gwynedd)	a	17 51				19 44						
Holyhead	a	18 37				20 18						
Wilmslow	a		16 46	17 45			18 46	19 46			20 45	21 45
Stockport	a		16 58	17 58			18 58	19 58			20 57	21 58
Manchester Piccadilly 10 ⇌	a		17 15	18 17			19 15	20 17			21 14	22 19

Station		AW	GW	AW	AW	AW
		◇	◇1	◇	◇	◇
			⊡			
Swansea	d					21 52
Cardiff Central 7	d	19 40			21 04	23 00
London Paddington 15 ⊖	d		17 42			
Reading 7	d		18 24			
Newport (South Wales)	d	19 55			21 19	23 20
Cwmbran	d	20 10			21 30	23 29
Pontypool and New Inn	d	20 16			21 36	23 35
Abergavenny	d	20 26			21 46	23 45
Hereford 7	a	20 52	21 03		22 12	00 17
	d	20 54			22 14	
Leominster	d	21 08			22 27	
Ludlow	d	21 19			22 38	
Craven Arms	d	21 29			22 48	
Church Stretton	d	21 38			22 57	
Shrewsbury	a	21 55			23 14	
	d			22 32	23 19	
Yorton	d				23x28	
Wem	d				23 34	
Prees	d				23x39	
Whitchurch (Shrops)	d				23 46	
Wrenbury	d				23x52	
Nantwich	d				23 59	
Crewe 10	a			23 03	00 09	
Chester	a			23 31	00 33	
Llandudno Junction	a					
Bangor (Gwynedd)	a					
Holyhead	a					
Wilmslow	a					
Stockport	a					
Manchester Piccadilly 10 ⇌	a					

A ◇ from Shrewsbury ■ to Shrewsbury

b Previous night, stops on request

For connections from Bristol Temple Meads please refer to Table 132. For connections to Runcorn and Liverpool Lime Street please refer to Table 91

When events are being held at the Millenium Stadium, services are subject to alteration. Please check times before travelling.

Table 131

Sundays

1 July to 9 September

Cardiff - Crewe, Liverpool and Manchester

Route Diagram - see first Page of Table 129

		AW ◇	AW ■ A	AW	AW ■ B	AW ◇ B	AW ◇ A	AW ◇	AW ◇ H	AW ◇ H	AW ◇ H	GW ◇1 ▭
Swansea	d										09 32	
Cardiff Central 7	d	20p55	21p20		22p20	00 30	00 30		08 30	09 30	10 35	
London Paddington 15 ⊖	d											09 42
Reading 7	d											10 11
Newport (South Wales)	d	21p10	21p35		22p39	00 59	00 59		08 49	09 50	10 51	
Cwmbran	d	21p21	21p45		22p50	01 10	01 10		09 00	10 00	11 02	
Pontypool and New Inn	d		21p53		22p58	01 16	01 16		09 06	10 06	11 08	
Abergavenny	d	21p34	22p04		23p09	01 27	01 27		09 15	10 16	11 18	
Hereford 7	a	21p58	22p32		23p36	01 53	01 55		09 40	10 40	11 44	12 54
	d	22p00	22p34		23p39	01 55	01 57		09 41	10 43	11 50	
Leominster	d	22p14	22p51		23p55	02 09	02 11		09 55	10 56	12 03	
Ludlow	d	22p25	23p04		00 08	02 20	02 22		10 06	11 07	12 14	
Craven Arms	d	22p33	23p14		00 19	02 30	02 32		10 14		12 24	
Church Stretton	d	22p42							10 23		12 33	
Shrewsbury	a	22p57	23p35		00 39	02 55	02 57		10 37	11 36	12 48	
	d	23p06	23p37	23p50	00 42			09 55	10 39	11 37	12 51	
Yorton	d	23b14		23b58						11x45		
Wem	d	23p20		00 04					10 51	11 48		
Prees	d	23b24		00x07						11x55		
Whitchurch (Shrops)	d	23p31		00 15					11 00	12 03		
Wrenbury	d	23b36		00x20						12x08		
Nantwich	d	23p42		00 26					11 09	12 15		
Crewe 10	a	23p53	00 13	00 38	01 17			10 25	11 22	12 25	13 26	
Chester	a	00 24	00 40		01 44							
Llandudno Junction	a		01 23		02 26							
Bangor (Gwynedd)	a		01 40		02 44							
Holyhead	a		02 20		03 23							
Wilmslow	a							10 46	11 41	12 46	13 49	
Stockport	a							10 58		12 58	14 00	
Manchester Piccadilly 10	a							11 12	12 02	13 15	14 19	

		AW ◇ H	AW ◇ H	GW ◇1 ▭	AW ◇	AW ■	AW ■ H	AW ■ H	GW ◇1 ▭	AW ■ ◇ C H	AW ■ H	AW ■ H
Swansea	d		11 32		11 07			13 43				15 33
Cardiff Central 7	d	11 35	12 40			13 22	13 40	14 56		15 22	15 56	16 40
London Paddington 15 ⊖	d			10 42					12 42			
Reading 7	d			11 21					13 21			
Newport (South Wales)	d	11 50	12 54			13 36	13 54	15 14		15 36	16 14	16 54
Cwmbran	d	12 04	13 09			13 47	14 09	15 24		15 47	16 24	17 09
Pontypool and New Inn	d	12 10	13 15							15 52		17 15
Abergavenny	d	12 20	13 25			14 00	14 22	15 38		16 02	16 37	17 25
Hereford 7	a	12 44	13 49	14 06		14 26	14 47	16 02	16 05	16 27	17 02	17 49
	d	12 57	13 55			14 26	14 48	16 04		16 28	17 04	17 53
Leominster	d	13 10	14 08				15 01			16 41		18 07
Ludlow	d	13 21	14 19			14 48	15 12	16 25		16 52	17 26	18 18
Craven Arms	d		14 28		14 44					17 00		18 26
Church Stretton	d		14 37		14 57					17 09		18 35
Shrewsbury	a	13 47	14 51		15 15	15 21	15 38	16 51		17 23	17 52	18 49
	d	13 50	14 53			15 22	15 40	16 53		17 30	17 54	18 54
Yorton	d						15x48					
Wem	d						15 51					
Prees	d						15x58					
Whitchurch (Shrops)	d						16 06					
Wrenbury	d						16x11					
Nantwich	d						16 18					
Crewe 10	a	14 22	15 25				16 27	17 25			18 25	19 24
Chester	a					16 18				18 25		
Llandudno Junction	a					17 29				19 22		
Bangor (Gwynedd)	a					17 51				19 44		
Holyhead	a					18 37				20 18		
Wilmslow	a	14 46	15 46				16 46	17 45			18 46	19 46
Stockport	a	14 58	15 58				16 58	17 58			18 58	19 58
Manchester Piccadilly 10	a	15 15	16 15				17 15	18 17			19 15	20 17

		GW ◇1	AW ◇	AW ■	AW ■ H	AW ◇	GW ◇1 ▭	AW ◇	AW ◇	AW ◇
Swansea	d		15 26		17 30					21 52
Cardiff Central 7	d			17 35	18 40	19 40			21 04	23 00
London Paddington 15 ⊖	d	14 42					17 42			
Reading 7	d	15 21					18 21			
Newport (South Wales)	d			17 49	18 54	19 55			21 19	23 20
Cwmbran	d			18 04	19 09	20 10			21 30	23 29
Pontypool and New Inn	d			18 10		20 16			21 36	23 35
Abergavenny	d			18 20	19 22	20 26			21 46	23 45
Hereford 7	a	17 58		18 44	19 47	20 52	21 03		22 12	00 17
	d			18 49	19 49	20 54			22 14	
Leominster	d			19 03	20 03	21 08			22 27	
Ludlow	d			19 14	20 14	21 19			22 38	
Craven Arms	d		19 03		20 22	21 29			22 48	
Church Stretton	d		19 16		20 31	21 38			22 57	
Shrewsbury	a		19 31	19 40	20 45	21 55			23 14	
	d			19 41	20 48			22 32	23 19	
Yorton	d			19x49					23x28	
Wem	d			19 52					23 34	
Prees	d			19x59					23x39	
Whitchurch (Shrops)	d			20 06					23 46	
Wrenbury	d			20x11					23x52	
Nantwich	d			20 18					23 59	
Crewe 10	a			20 27	21 21			23 03	00 09	
Chester	a							23 31	00 33	
Llandudno Junction	a									
Bangor (Gwynedd)	a									
Holyhead	a									
Wilmslow	a			20 45	21 45					
Stockport	a			20 57	21 58					
Manchester Piccadilly 10	a			21 14	22 19					

A 29 July
B 5 August
C ◇ from Shrewsbury ■ to Shrewsbury
b Previous night, stops on request

For connections from Bristol Temple Meads please refer to Table 132. For connections to Runcorn and Liverpool Lime Street please refer to Table 91

When events are being held at the Millenium Stadium, services are subject to alteration. Please check times before travelling.

Table 131

Sundays

16 September to 21 October

Cardiff - Crewe, Liverpool and Manchester

Route Diagram - see first Page of Table 129

		AW ◇	AW	AW ◇	AW ◇ H	AW ◇ H	AW ◇ H	GW ◇1 ▭	AW ◇ H	AW ◇ H
Swansea	d									11 32
Cardiff Central 7	d	20p55			08 30	09 30	10 35		11 35	12 40
London Paddington 15 ⊖	d							09 35		
Reading 7	d							10 12		
Newport (South Wales)	d	21p10			08 49	09 50	10 51		11 50	12 54
Cwmbran	d	21p21			09 00	10 00	11 02		12 04	13 09
Pontypool and New Inn	d				09 06	10 06	11 08		12 10	13 15
Abergavenny	d	21p34			09 15	10 16	11 18		12 20	13 25
Hereford 7	a	21p58			09 40	10 40	11 44	12 54	12 44	13 49
	d	22p00			09 41	10 43	11 50		12 57	13 55
Leominster	d	22p14			09 55	10 56	12 03		13 10	14 08
Ludlow	d	22p25			10 06	11 07	12 14		13 21	14 19
Craven Arms	d	22p33			10 14		12 24			14 28
Church Stretton	d	22p42			10 23		12 33			14 37
Shrewsbury	a	22p57			10 37	11 36	12 48		13 47	14 51
	d	23p06	23p50	09 55	10 39	11 37	12 51		13 50	14 53
Yorton	d	23b14	23b58			11x45				
Wem	d	23p20	00 04		10 51	11 48				
Prees	d	23b24	00x07			11x55				
Whitchurch (Shrops)	d	23p31	00 15		11 00	12 03				
Wrenbury	d	23b36	00x20			12x08				
Nantwich	d	23p42	00 26		11 09	12 15				
Crewe 10	a	23p53	00 38	10 25	11 22	12 25	13 26		14 22	15 25
Chester	a	00 24								
Llandudno Junction	a									
Bangor (Gwynedd)	a									
Holyhead	a									
Wilmslow	a			10 46	11 41	12 47	13 49		14 46	15 46
Stockport	a			10 58		12 58	14 00		14 58	15 58
Manchester Piccadilly 10	a			11 12	12 02	13 12	14 19		15 15	16 15

		GW ◇1 ▭	AW ◇	AW ■	AW ■ H	AW ■ H	GW ◇1 ▭	AW ■ ◇ A H	AW ■ H	AW ■ H	GW ◇1	AW ◇	AW ■	AW ■ H
Swansea	d		11 04			13 43				15 33		15 26		17 30
Cardiff Central 7	d			13 22	13 40	14 56		15 22	15 56	16 40			17 35	18 40
London Paddington 15 ⊖	d	10 42					12 42				14 42			
Reading 7	d	11 21					13 21				15 21			
Newport (South Wales)	d			13 36	13 54	15 14		15 36	16 14	16 54			17 49	18 54
Cwmbran	d			13 47	14 09	15 24		15 47	16 24	17 09			18 04	19 09
Pontypool and New Inn	d							15 52		17 15			18 10	
Abergavenny	d			14 00	14 22	15 38		16 02	16 37	17 25			18 20	19 22
Hereford 7	a	14 06		14 26	14 47	16 02	16 05	16 27	17 02	17 49	17 58		18 44	19 47
	d			14 26	14 48	16 04		16 28	17 04	17 53			18 49	19 49
Leominster	d				15 01			16 41		18 07			19 03	20 03
Ludlow	d			14 48	15 12	16 25		16 52	17 26	18 18			19 14	20 14
Craven Arms	d		14 44					17 00		18 26		19 03		20 22
Church Stretton	d		14 57					17 09		18 35		19 16		20 31
Shrewsbury	a		15 15	15 20	15 38	16 51		17 23	17 52	18 49		19 31	19 40	20 45
	d			15 22	15 40	16 53		17 30	17 54	18 54			19 41	20 48
Yorton	d				15x48								19x49	
Wem	d				15 51								19 52	
Prees	d				15x58								19x59	
Whitchurch (Shrops)	d				16 06								20 06	
Wrenbury	d				16x11								20x11	
Nantwich	d				16 18								20 18	
Crewe 10	a				16 27	17 25			18 25	19 24			20 27	21 21
Chester	a			16 18				18 25						
Llandudno Junction	a			17 29				19 22						
Bangor (Gwynedd)	a			17 52				19 44						
Holyhead	a			18 37				20 18						
Wilmslow	a				16 46	17 45			18 46	19 46			20 45	21 45
Stockport	a				16 58	17 58			18 58	19 58			20 57	21 58
Manchester Piccadilly 10	a				17 15	18 17			19 15	20 17			21 14	22 19

		AW ◇	GW ◇1 ▭	AW ◇	AW ◇	AW ◇
Swansea	d					21 52
Cardiff Central 7	d	19 40			21 04	23 00
London Paddington 15 ⊖	d		17 42			
Reading 7	d		18 24			
Newport (South Wales)	d	19 55			21 19	23 20
Cwmbran	d	20 10			21 30	23 29
Pontypool and New Inn	d	20 16			21 36	23 35
Abergavenny	d	20 26			21 46	23 45
Hereford 7	a	20 52	21 03		22 12	00 17
	d	20 54			22 14	
Leominster	d	21 08			22 27	
Ludlow	d	21 19			22 38	
Craven Arms	d	21 29			22 48	
Church Stretton	d	21 38			22 57	
Shrewsbury	a	21 55			23 14	
	d			22 32	23 19	
Yorton	d				23x28	
Wem	d				23 34	
Prees	d				23x39	
Whitchurch (Shrops)	d				23 46	
Wrenbury	d				23x52	
Nantwich	d				23 59	
Crewe 10	a			23 03	00 09	
Chester	a			23 31	00 33	
Llandudno Junction	a					
Bangor (Gwynedd)	a					
Holyhead	a					
Wilmslow	a					
Stockport	a					
Manchester Piccadilly 10	a					

A ◇ from Shrewsbury ■ to Shrewsbury
b Previous night, stops on request

For connections from Bristol Temple Meads please refer to Table 132. For connections to Runcorn and Liverpool Lime Street please refer to Table 91

When events are being held at the Millenium Stadium, services are subject to alteration. Please check times before travelling.

Sundays
from 28 October

Cardiff - Crewe, Liverpool and Manchester

Route Diagram - see first Page of Table 129

		AW ◇	AW	AW ◇	AW ◇ ⊼	AW ◇ ⊼	AW ◇ ⊼	GW ◇1 ⌂	AW ◇ ⊼	AW ◇ ⊼	GW ◇1 ⌂	AW ◇	AW ■	AW ■ ⊼	AW ■ ⊼	GW ◇1 ⌂	AW ■ ◇ A ⊼	AW ■ ⊼	AW ■ ⊼	GW ◇1 ⌂	AW ◇	AW ■	AW ■ ⊼
Swansea	d									11 32		11 07			13 43				15 33		15 26		17 30
Cardiff Central 7	d	20p55			08 30	09 30	10 35		11 35	12 40			13 22	13 40	14 56		15 22	15 56	16 40			17 35	18 40
London Paddington 15 ⊖	d							09 35			10 42					12 42				14 42			
Reading 7	d							10 12			11 21					13 21				15 21			
Newport (South Wales)	d	21p10			08 49	09 50	10 51		11 50	12 54			13 36	13 54	15 14		15 36	16 14	16 54			17 49	18 54
Cwmbran	d	21p21			09 00	10 00	11 02		12 04	13 09			13 47	14 09	15 24		15 47	16 24	17 09			18 04	19 09
Pontypool and New Inn	d				09 06	10 06	11 08		12 10	13 15							15 52		17 15			18 10	
Abergavenny	d	21p34			09 15	10 16	11 18		12 20	13 25			14 00	14 22	15 38		16 02	16 37	17 25			18 20	19 22
Hereford 7	a	21p58			09 40	10 40	11 44	12 54	12 44	13 49	14 06		14 26	14 47	16 02	16 05	16 27	17 02	17 49	17 58		18 44	19 47
	d	22p00			09 41	10 43	11 50		12 57	13 55			14 26	14 48	16 04		16 28	17 04	17 53			18 49	19 49
Leominster	d	22p14			09 55	10 56	12 03		13 10	14 08				15 01			16 41		18 07			19 03	20 03
Ludlow	d	22p25			10 06	11 07	12 14		13 21	14 19			14 48	15 12	16 25		16 52	17 26	18 18			19 14	20 14
Craven Arms	d	22p33			10 14		12 24			14 28		14 44					17 00		18 26		19 03		20 22
Church Stretton	d	22p42			10 23		12 33			14 37		14 57					17 09		18 35		19 16		20 31
Shrewsbury	a	22p57			10 37	11 36	12 48		13 47	14 51		15 15	15 20	15 38	16 51		17 23	17 52	18 49		19 31	19 40	20 45
	d	23p06	23p50	09 55	10 39	11 37	12 51		13 50	14 53			15 22	15 40	16 53		17 30	17 54	18 54			19 41	20 48
Yorton	d	23b14	23b58			11x45								15x48								19x49	
Wem	d	23p20	00 04		10 51	11 48								15 51								19 52	
Prees	d	23b24	00x07			11x55								15x58								19x59	
Whitchurch (Shrops)	d	23p31	00 15		11 00	12 03								16 06								20 06	
Wrenbury	d	23b36	00x20			12x08								16x11								20x11	
Nantwich	d	23p42	00 26		11 09	12 15								16 18								20 18	
Crewe 10	a	23p53	00 38	10 25	11 22	12 25	13 26		14 22	15 25				16 27	17 25			18 25	19 24			20 27	21 21
Chester	a	00 24											16 18				18 25						
Llandudno Junction	a												17 29				19 22						
Bangor (Gwynedd)	a												17 52				19 44						
Holyhead	a												18 37				20 18						
Wilmslow	a			10 46	11 41	12 47	13 49		14 46	15 46				16 46	17 45			18 46	19 46			20 45	21 45
Stockport	a			10 58		12 58	14 00		14 58	15 58				16 58	17 58			18 58	19 58			20 57	21 58
Manchester Piccadilly 10	a			11 12	12 02	13 12	14 19		15 15	16 15				17 15	18 17			19 15	20 17			21 14	22 19

		AW ◇	GW ◇1 ⌂	AW ◇	AW ◇	AW ◇
Swansea	d					21 52
Cardiff Central 7	d	19 40			21 04	23 00
London Paddington 15 ⊖	d		17 42			
Reading 7	d		18 24			
Newport (South Wales)	d	19 55			21 19	23 20
Cwmbran	d	20 10			21 30	23 29
Pontypool and New Inn	d	20 16			21 36	23 35
Abergavenny	d	20 26			21 46	23 45
Hereford 7	a	20 52	21 03		22 12	00 17
	d	20 54			22 14	
Leominster	d	21 08			22 27	
Ludlow	d	21 19			22 38	
Craven Arms	d	21 29			22 48	
Church Stretton	d	21 38			22 57	
Shrewsbury	a	21 55			23 14	
	d			22 32	23 19	
Yorton	d				23x28	
Wem	d				23 34	
Prees	d				23x39	
Whitchurch (Shrops)	d				23 46	
Wrenbury	d				23x52	
Nantwich	d				23 59	
Crewe 10	a			23 03	00 09	
Chester	a			23 31	00 33	
Llandudno Junction	a					
Bangor (Gwynedd)	a					
Holyhead	a					
Wilmslow	a					
Stockport	a					
Manchester Piccadilly 10	a					

A ◇ from Shrewsbury ■ to Shrewsbury

b Previous night, stops on request

For connections from Bristol Temple Meads please refer to Table 132. For connections to Runcorn and Liverpool Lime Street please refer to Table 91

When events are being held at the Millenium Stadium, services are subject to alteration. Please check times before travelling.

Mondays to Fridays

Manchester, Liverpool and Crewe - Cardiff

Route Diagram - see first Page of Table 129

Miles	Miles			GW MX ◇1	AW MX ◇	AW MO ◇ A	AW MX ◇	AW MX ◇	AW MO A	AW	AW ◇ B	AW ◇	AW C	GW ◇1 D ⌂⊘	AW ◇ ⊼	GW ◇1 E ⌂⊘	AW ◇	AW ◇ ⊼	AW ◇ ⊼	AW ◇ ⊼	AW ◇1 ⊠
0	—	**Manchester Piccadilly** 10	d		20p30	20p30		22p35												06 30	
6	—	Stockport	d		20p39	20p39		22p44												06 39	
12	—	Wilmslow	d		20p46	20p47		22p52												06 46	
—	—	Holyhead	d																04 25		05 32
—	—	Bangor (Gwynedd)	d																04 57		06 02
—	—	Llandudno Junction	d																05 15		06 21
—	—	Chester	d						23p00	04 22							05 13		06 18		07 08
31	35½	**Crewe** 10	d		21p08	21p13		23p14	23p23	04a44					04 54			05 55		07 08	07 33
35½	40	Nantwich	d		21p17	21p21		23p22	23p31						05 02			06 03		07 17	
40	44½	Wrenbury	d		21b23	21b26		23b27	23b37									06x09			
44¾	49¼	Whitchurch (Shrops)	d		21p30	21p35		23p34	23p45						05 13			06 16			
49¾	54¼	Prees	d		21b36	21b40		23b40	23b51									06x22			
53	57½	Wem	d		21p41	21p47		23p45	23p57						05 22			06 27			
56½	61	Yorton	d		21b46	21b51		23b50	00x02									06x32			
63¾	68¼	**Shrewsbury**	a		21p55	22p03		00 04	00 14						05 33		06 08	06 42	07 17	07 42	08 09
—	—		d		21p57	22p04	23p08					05 19			05 40		06 09	06 44	07 19	07 44	08 10
76½	81	Church Stretton	d		22p12	22p20	23p24					05 36			05 55		06 26	06 59		07 59	
83¾	88¼	Craven Arms	d		22p20	22p29	23p32					05 50			06 03		06 34	07 07		08 07	
91	95½	Ludlow	d		22p27	22p37	23p41								06 10		06 43	07 14	07 46	08 15	
102	106½	Leominster	d		22p38	22p49	23p52								06 21		06 54	07 25	07 56	08 26	
114½	119	**Hereford** 7	a		22p56	23p03	00 07								06 36		07 09	07 43	08 12	08 40	
—	—		d	21p51	22p58	23p05	00 09				05 25		05 26	05 35	06 42	06 44	07 10	07 45	08 13	08 42	
138½	143	Abergavenny	d		23p21	23p29	00 33				05 49		05 51		07 05		07 34	08 08	08 36	09 05	
148	152½	Pontypool and New Inn	d		23p30	23p39					05 59		06 02		07 15		07 45	08 17	08 46		
151	155½	Cwmbran	d		23p35	23p44	00 46				06 04		06 07		07 20		07 50	08 22	08 51	09 17	
158	162½	**Newport (South Wales)**	a		23p46	23p54	00 57				06 16		06 19		07 33		08 00	08 37	09 02	09 34	09 40
—	—	Reading 7	a	00 38										08 21		09 14					
—	—	London Paddington 15 ⊖	a	01 17										08 51		09 47					
169¾	174½	**Cardiff Central** 7	a		00 02	00 20	01 18				06 33		06 40		07 51		08 17	08 53	09 23	09 57	09 58
—	—	Swansea	a								07 45	09 08			08 50			09 55		10 55	

		AW	AW ◇ ⊼	AW ◇ ⊼	AW ◇ ⊼	AW ◇ ⊼	AW FO	AW FX	AW ◇ ⊼	AW ◇ ⊼	AW ◇ ⊼	AW ◇ ⊼	AW ◇ ⊼	AW	GW ◇1 ⌂	AW ◇ ⊼	AW ■ ⊼	AW ■ ⊼	AW ◇	AW	GW ◇1 ⌂	AW ■ ⊼	AW ◇ ⊼	AW ■ ⊼
Manchester Piccadilly 10	d		07 30			08 30					09 30		10 30			11 30		12 30				13 30		14 30
Stockport	d		07 39			08 39					09 39		10 39			11 39		12 39				13 39		14 39
Wilmslow	d		07 46			08 46					09 46		10 46			11 46		12 46				13 46		14 46
Holyhead	d				06 28				07 15	07 51		08 05					10 33						12 39	
Bangor (Gwynedd)	d				07 06				08 02	08 21		09 02					11 05						13 07	
Llandudno Junction	d				07 24				08 25	08 39		09 25					11 25						13 25	
Chester	d				08 19				09 19	09 27		10 20					12 19						14 19	
Crewe 10	d	07 40	08 08			09 08	09 20	09 20	09 51		10 08		11 08	11 20		12 08		13 08		13 20		14 08		15 08
Nantwich	d	07 47					09 28	09 28	09 58					11 28						13 28		14 17		
Wrenbury	d	07x53					09x34	09x34						11x35						13x35				
Whitchurch (Shrops)	d	08 00					09 42	09 42	10 09					11 43						13 43		14 28		
Prees	d	08x06					09x48	09x48						11x49						13x49				
Wem	d	08 12					09 54	09 54	10 18					11 55						13 55				
Yorton	d	08x17					10x00	10x00						12x01						14x01				
Shrewsbury	a	08 28	08 37		09 13	09 37	10 11	10 12	10 27	10 22	10 37	11 14	11 37	12 11		12 37	13 14	13 37		14 11		14 45	15 13	15 37
	d		08 40	09 00	09 14	09 40				10 24	10 39	11 16	11 39			12 40	13 15	13 40	14 04			14 50	15 15	15 40
Church Stretton	d			09 18	09 30						10 54		11 54				13 30		14 22			15 05	15 30	
Craven Arms	d			09 28	09 38							11 37					13 38		14 33			15 13	15 38	
Ludlow	d		09 06		09 45	10 06					11 08	11 44	12 08			13 06	13 45	14 06				15 20	15 46	16 06
Leominster	d		09 16			10 16					11 18		12 18			13 16		14 16				15 31		16 16
Hereford 7	a		09 32		10 09	10 32					11 34	12 06	12 34			13 32	14 09	14 32				15 49	16 09	16 32
	d		09 33		10 10	10 33					11 35	12 08	12 35		13 14	13 33	14 11	14 33			15 14	15 51	16 11	16 33
Abergavenny	d		09 56		10 33	10 56					11 58	12 31	12 58			13 56	14 33	14 56				16 14	16 34	16 56
Pontypool and New Inn	d				10 43							12 42					14 44					16 23	16 44	
Cwmbran	d		10 09		10 48	11 09					12 11	12 47	13 11			14 09	14 49	15 09				16 28	16 49	17 09
Newport (South Wales)	a		10 20		11 01	11 20				11 51	12 22	13 00	13 22			14 20	14 58	15 22				16 39	16 59	17 21
Reading 7	a														15 54						17 54			
London Paddington 15 ⊖	a														16 27						18 28			
Cardiff Central 7	a		10 37		11 15	11 37				12 08	12 38	13 22	13 39			14 37	15 19	15 53				16 55	17 15	17 37
Swansea	a		11 34	13 04		12 33					13 33		14 34			15 34		17 01	18 18			18 05		18 37

A from 21 May
B until 20 July, from 3 September
C from 23 July until 31 August
D ⌂ from Reading ⊘ to Reading
E The Cathedrals Express. ⌂ from Reading ⊘ to Reading
b Previous night, stops on request

For connections from Liverpool Lime Street and Runcorn please refer to Table 91. For connections to Bristol Temple Meads please refer to Table 132

When events are being held at the Millenium Stadium, services are subject to alteration. Please check times before travelling.

Manchester, Liverpool and Crewe - Cardiff

Route Diagram - see first Page of Table 129

		AW	AW	AW	AW	AW	AW	AW	AW	AW FX	AW FO	AW FO	AW FX	GW	AW	AW	AW	AW
			■ ✕	◇ ✕	■ ✕	◇		■ ✕	◇ ✕	◇ ✕	◇ ✕	◇	◇	◇■	◇		◇	◇
Manchester Piccadilly [10] ⇌	d		15 30		16 30			17 30		18 30	18 30	19 30	19 30		20 30	21 35		22 35
Stockport	d		15 39		16 39			17 39		18 39	18 39	19 39	19 39		20 39	21 44		22 44
Wilmslow	d		15 46		16 46			17 46		18 46	18 46	19 46	19 46		20 46	21 51		22 52
Holyhead	d			14 34					16 38									
Bangor (Gwynedd)	d			15 04					17 06									
Llandudno Junction	d			15 27					17 25									
Chester	d			16 19					18 18									
Crewe [10]	d	15 20	16 08		17 08		17 20	18 08		19 08	19 08	20 08	20 08		21 08	22 12		23 14
Nantwich	d	15 28	16 17				17 28	18 17		19 17	19 17	20 17	20 17		21 17	22 20		23 22
Wrenbury	d	15x35					17x35			19x23	19x23				21x23	22x26		23x27
Whitchurch (Shrops)	d	15 43	16 28				17 43	18 28		19 29	19 29	20 28	20 28		21 30	22 33		23 34
Prees	d	15x49					17x49			19x35	19x35				21x36	22x39		23x40
Wem	d	15 55	16 36				17 55	18 36		19 40	19 40	20 36	20 36		21 41	22 44		23 45
Yorton	d	16x01					18x01			19x45	19x45				21x46	22x49		23x50
Shrewsbury	a	16 11	16 47	17 14	17 37		18 11	18 47	19 15	19 55	19 55	20 47	20 47		21 55	23 01		00 04
	d		16 50	17 16	17 40	18 05		18 50	19 17	19 56	19 56	20 50	20 50		21 57		23 08	
Church Stretton	d		17 06	17 31		18 22		19 05		20 11	20 11	21 05	21 05		22 12		23 24	
Craven Arms	d		17 14	17 39		18 35		19 13		20 19	20 19	21 13	21 13		22 20		23 32	
Ludlow	d		17 21	17 46	18 06			19 20	19 44	20 27	20 27	21 20	21 20		22 27		23 41	
Leominster	d		17 32	17 57	18 16			19 31		20 37	20 37	21 31	21 31		22 38		23 52	
Hereford [7]	a		17 49	18 12	18 32			19 46	20 08	20 53	20 53	21 46	21 46		22 56		00 07	
	d		17 51	18 14	18 33			19 48	20 09	20 54	20 54	21 50	21 50	21 51	22 58		00 09	
Abergavenny	d		18 14	18 37	18 56			20 11	20 32	21 22	21 22	22 16	22 16		23 21		00 33	
Pontypool and New Inn	d		18 24					20 21		21 32	21 32				23 30			
Cwmbran	d		18 29	18 49	19 09			20 26	20 45	21 37	21 37	22 28	22 28		23 35		00 46	
Newport (South Wales)	a		18 39	19 00	19 22			20 37	20 58	21 50	21 50	22 39	22 41		23 46		00 57	
Reading [7]	a													00 38				
London Paddington [15] ⊖	a													01 17				
Cardiff Central [7]	a		18 55	19 21	19 43			20 58	21 19	22 06	22 06	22 55	23 04		00 02		01 18	
Swansea	a		20 04		20 42	22 08					23 07							

Saturdays

		GW	AW	AW	AW	AW	AW	AW	GW	AW	AW	GW	AW	AW	AW	AW	AW	AW	AW	AW	AW	AW
		◇■	◇	◇	◇		◇		◇■ ⊏	◇ ✕		◇■ A ⊏⊘	◇ ✕	◇ B ✕	◇ C ✕	◇ ✕		◇ ✕	◇ ✕	◇ ✕	◇ ✕	
Manchester Piccadilly [10] ⇌	d		20p30		22p35											06 30		07 30			08 30	
Stockport	d		20p39		22p44											06 39		07 39			08 39	
Wilmslow	d		20p46		22p52											06 46		07 46			08 46	
Holyhead	d													04 25						06 35		
Bangor (Gwynedd)	d													04 57						07 07		
Llandudno Junction	d													05 15						07 25		
Chester	d					04 22								06 12	06 12					08 19		
Crewe [10]	d		21p08		23p14	04a44				04 54			05 55			07 08	07 20	08 08			09 08	09 20
Nantwich	d		21p17		23p22					05 02			06 03			07 17	07 27	08 17				09 28
Wrenbury	d		21b23		23b27								06x09				07x34					09x34
Whitchurch (Shrops)	d		21p30		23p34					05 13			06 16			07 28	07 41	08 27				09 42
Prees	d		21b36		23b40								06x22				07x47					09x48
Wem	d		21p41		23p45					05 22			06 27			07 36	07 53					09 54
Yorton	d		21b46		23b50								06x32				07x58					10x00
Shrewsbury	a		21p55		00 04					05 33			06 42	07 17	07 17	07 47	08 08	08 45		09 13	09 37	10 12
	d		21p57	23p08			05 19			05 40	06 13		06 44	07 19	07 19	07 50		08 46	09 00	09 15	09 40	
Church Stretton	d		22p12	23p24			05 36			05 55	06 28		06 59			08 05		09 01	09 17		09 55	
Craven Arms	d		22p20	23p32			05 47			06 03	06 36		07 07			08 13		09 09	09 30		10 03	
Ludlow	d		22p27	23p41						06 10	06 44		07 14	07 45	07 45	08 20		09 17		09 42	10 10	
Leominster	d		22p38	23p52						06 21	06 55		07 25	07 55	07 55	08 31		09 27			10 21	
Hereford [7]	a		22p56	00 07						06 37	07 09		07 40	08 11	08 11	08 49		09 43		10 05	10 36	
	d	21p51	22p58	00 09				05 42	06 17	06 42	07 11	07 10	07 44	08 12	08 12	08 51		09 44		10 07	10 38	
Abergavenny	d		23p21	00 33				06 07		07 05	07 34		08 07	08 35	08 35	09 14		10 07		10 30	11 01	
Pontypool and New Inn	d		23p30					06 18		07 15	07 44		08 16	08 45	08 45					10 40		
Cwmbran	d		23p35	00 46				06 23		07 20	07 49		08 21	08 50	08 50	09 26		10 20		10 45	11 13	
Newport (South Wales)	a		23p46	00 57				06 34		07 37	08 00		08 31	09 01	09 01	09 37		10 35		10 55	11 27	
Reading [7]	a	00 38							08 54			09 54										
London Paddington [15] ⊖	a	01 17							09 29			10 29										
Cardiff Central [7]	a		00 02	01 18				06 54		07 53	08 19		08 50	09 22	09 22	09 58		10 53		11 15	11 53	
Swansea	a						09 08			08 51			09 57			10 55		11 56	13 06		12 55	

A ⊏ from Reading ⊘ to Reading
B from 15 September
C until 8 September
b Previous night, stops on request

For connections from Liverpool Lime Street and Runcorn please refer to Table 91. For connections to Bristol Temple Meads please refer to Table 132

When events are being held at the Millenium Stadium, services are subject to alteration. Please check times before travelling.

Manchester, Liverpool and Crewe - Cardiff

Route Diagram - see first Page of Table 129

		AW	AW	GW	AW	AW	AW	AW	AW	AW	AW	GW	AW	AW	AW	AW	AW	AW	AW	AW	AW	AW	AW
		◇ ✕	◇ ✕	◇■ ⊏	◇ ✕		◇ ✕	■ ✕	■ ✕	◇		◇■ ⊏	■ ✕	◇ ✕	■ ✕		■ ✕	◇ ✕	■ ✕	◇		■ ✕	◇ ✕
Manchester Piccadilly [10] ⇌	d	09 30			10 30		11 30		12 30				13 30		14 30		15 30		16 30			17 30	
Stockport	d	09 39			10 39		11 39		12 39				13 39		14 39		15 39		16 39			17 39	
Wilmslow	d	09 46			10 46		11 46		12 46				13 46		14 46		15 46		16 46			17 46	
Holyhead	d		08 20					10 33						12 38				14 23					16 38
Bangor (Gwynedd)	d		09 02					11 05						13 07				14 53					17 07
Llandudno Junction	d		09 25					11 25						13 25				15 16					17 25
Chester	d		10 19					12 19						14 19				16 19					18 20
Crewe [10]	d	10 08			11 08	11 20	12 08		13 08		13 20		14 08		15 08	15 20	16 08		17 08		17 20	18 08	
Nantwich	d					11 31	12 17				13 28		14 17			15 28	16 17		17 17		17 28	18 17	
Wrenbury	d					11x42					13x35					15x35					17x35		
Whitchurch (Shrops)	d					11 49	12 27				13 43		14 27			15 43	16 27		17 27		17 43	18 28	
Prees	d					11x56					13x49					15x49					17x49		
Wem	d					12 02					13 55					15 55					17 55		
Yorton	d					12x08					14x01					16x01					18x01		
Shrewsbury	a	10 36	11 14		11 37	12 18	12 45	13 13	13 37		14 11		14 43	15 13	15 37	16 11	16 43	17 14	17 43		18 11	18 45	19 15
	d	10 38	11 15		11 40		12 46	13 15	13 40	14 05			14 45	15 15	15 40		16 45	17 16	17 45	18 05		18 47	19 16
Church Stretton	d	10 54			11 55		13 01		13 55	14 23			15 00		15 55		17 00		18 00	18 23		19 02	
Craven Arms	d	11 02			12 03		13 09		14 03	14 36			15 08		16 03		17 08		18 08	18 36		19 10	
Ludlow	d	11 09	11 41		12 10		13 17	13 40	14 10				15 15	15 41	16 10		17 15	17 42	18 15			19 17	19 41
Leominster	d	11 20			12 21		13 27		14 21				15 26		16 21		17 26		18 26			19 28	
Hereford [7]	a	11 44	12 04		12 36		13 44	14 04	14 36				15 41	16 03	16 36		17 41	18 05	18 41			19 49	20 09
	d	11 46	12 06	12 13	12 38		13 46	14 06	14 38			15 13	15 46	16 06	16 38		17 46	18 07	18 43			19 51	20 11
Abergavenny	d	12 09	12 29		13 01		14 09	14 28	15 01				16 09	16 29	17 01		18 09	18 30	19 06			20 14	20 34
Pontypool and New Inn	d		12 39					14 39						16 39				18 40				20 23	
Cwmbran	d	12 21	12 44		13 13		14 21	14 44	15 13				16 21	16 44	17 13		18 21	18 45	19 18			20 28	20 46
Newport (South Wales)	a	12 35	12 54		13 28		14 33	15 05	15 35				16 33	16 54	17 33		18 33	18 55	19 34			20 39	21 00
Reading [7]	a			14 53								17 55											
London Paddington [15] ⊖	a			15 29								18 29											
Cardiff Central [7]	a	12 53	13 15		13 53		14 53	15 26	15 53				16 53	17 08	17 53		18 53	19 16	19 58			21 00	21 21
Swansea	a	13 55			14 55		15 55		16 58	18 10			18 05		19 02		20 04			22 10			

		GW	GW	AW	AW	AW	AW	AW	AW
		◇■ A	◇■ B	◇ ✕					
Manchester Piccadilly [10] ⇌	d			18 30	19 30	20 30	21 35	22 35	
Stockport	d			18 39	19 39	20 39	21 44	22 44	
Wilmslow	d			18 46	19 46	20 46	21 51	22 52	
Holyhead	d								
Bangor (Gwynedd)	d								
Llandudno Junction	d								
Chester	d								
Crewe [10]	d			19 10	20 08	21 08	22 12	23 14	
Nantwich	d			19 18	20 17	21 17	22 20	23 22	
Wrenbury	d			19x24		21x23	22x26	23x27	
Whitchurch (Shrops)	d			19 31	20 27	21 29	22 33	23 34	
Prees	d			19x37		21x35	22x39	23x40	
Wem	d			19 42	20 36	21 40	22 44	23 45	
Yorton	d			19x47		21x45	22x49	23x50	
Shrewsbury	a			19 56	20 47	21 53	23 01	00 04	
	d			19 58	20 48	21 55			
Church Stretton	d			20 13	21 03	22 10			
Craven Arms	d			20 21	21 11	22 18			
Ludlow	d			20 28	21 19	22 26			
Leominster	d			20 39	21 29	22 37			
Hereford [7]	a			20 54	21 45	22 51			
	d	20 20	20 20	20 56	21 46	22 53			23 15
Abergavenny	d			21 19	22 09	23 16			23 38
Pontypool and New Inn	d			21 28		23 25			
Cwmbran	d			21 33	22 22	23 30			23 50
Newport (South Wales)	a			21 44	22 33	23 45			00 02
Reading [7]	a	23 04	23 08						
London Paddington [15] ⊖	a	23 43	23 46						
Cardiff Central [7]	a			22 04	22 53	00 05			00 26
Swansea	a			23 05					

A from 30 June until 8 September
B until 23 June, from 15 September

For connections from Liverpool Lime Street and Runcorn please refer to Table 91. For connections to Bristol Temple Meads please refer to Table 132

When events are being held at the Millenium Stadium, services are subject to alteration. Please check times before travelling.

Manchester, Liverpool and Crewe - Cardiff

Sundays
until 24 June

Route Diagram - see first Page of Table 129

		AW	AW	AW	AW	AW	AW	AW	AW	GW	AW	AW	GW	AW	AW	GW	AW	AW	AW	GW	AW	AW
					🚌	◇	◇ ⌶	■ ⌶	◇	◇1 ⊏	■ ⌶	◇ ⌶	◇1 ⊏	■ ⌶	■ ⌶	◇1 ⊏	■ ⌶	◇	■ ⌶	◇1	■ ⌶	■ ⌶
Manchester Piccadilly 10 ⇌	d	20p30	22p35				09 30	10 30			11 24			12 30	13 30		14 30		15 30		16 30	17 30
Stockport	d	20p39	22p44				09 39	10 39			11 40			12 40	13 40		14 39		15 39		16 39	17 39
Wilmslow	d	20p46	22p52				09 47	10 48			11 47			12 48	13 47		14 47		15 47		16 47	17 47
Holyhead	d											10 20										
Bangor (Gwynedd)	d											10 59										
Llandudno Junction	d											11 22										
Chester	d											12 21										
Crewe 10	d	21p08	23p14				10 13	11 11			12 13			13 13	14 13		15 10		16 13		17 13	18 13
Nantwich	d	21p17	23p22				10 22							13 21							17 21	
Wrenbury	d	21b23	23b27				10x27							13x26							17x26	
Whitchurch (Shrops)	d	21p29	23p34				10 35							13 34							17 34	
Prees	d	21b35	23b40				10x40							13x39							17x39	
Wem	d	21p40	23p45				10 46							13 45							17 45	
Yorton	d	21b45	23b50				10x50							13x49							17x49	
Shrewsbury	a	21p53	00 04				11 01	11 41			12 43	13 18		13 59	14 43		15 44		16 43		18 00	18 43
	d	21p55			07 50		11 03	11 45	12 07		12 44	13 19		14 01	14 44		15 47	16 18	16 44		18 01	18 44
Church Stretton	d	22p10			08 15		11 19		12 25			13 35			15 00			16 36	17 00			
Craven Arms	d	22p18			08 35		11 27		12 36			13 43			15 08			16 47	17 08			
Ludlow	d	22p26			08 55		11 36	12 13			13 12	13 51		14 28	15 16		16 17		17 16		18 29	19 12
Leominster	d	22p37			09 20		11 47	12 23			13 22	14 02		14 39	15 26		16 28		17 26		18 39	
Hereford 7	a	22p51			09 50		12 02	12 38			13 37	14 17		14 53	15 41		16 43		17 41		18 54	19 34
	d	22p53		23p15		10 09	12 03	12 39		13 32	13 39	14 19	14 32	14 56	15 43	16 35	16 44		17 43	18 30	18 57	19 36
Abergavenny	d	23p16		23p38		10 33	12 27	13 02			14 02	14 42		15 19	16 06		17 08		18 06		19 20	19 59
Pontypool and New Inn	d	23p25				10 43		13 12				14 52			16 16				18 16			
Cwmbran	d	23p30		23p50		10 48	12 40	13 17			14 14	14 57		15 31	16 21		17 21		18 21		19 33	20 11
Newport (South Wales)	a	23p45		00 02		10 59	12 51	13 28			14 28	15 07		15 45	16 31		17 33		18 31		19 49	20 22
Reading 7	a									16 22			17 27			19 27				21 24		
London Paddington 15 ⊖	a									17 04			18 13			20 07				22 07		
Cardiff Central 7	a	00 05		00 26		11 19	13 13	13 44			14 49	15 28		16 02	16 52		17 50		18 50		20 06	20 43
Swansea	a					12 19		15 10	16 04					17 14			19 15	20 16				

		AW	AW	AW	AW	AW	AW
		■ ⌶	◇ ⌶	■ ⌶	◇	◇	
Manchester Piccadilly 10 ⇌	d			18 30	19 30	20 30	
Stockport	d			18 39	19 39	20 39	
Wilmslow	d			18 47	19 47	20 47	
Holyhead	d	16 25	18 25				
Bangor (Gwynedd)	d	17 04	19 04				
Llandudno Junction	d	17 25	19 24				
Chester	d	18 24	20 27				23 00
Crewe 10	d		20a48	19 13	20 13	21 13	23 23
Nantwich	d			19 21		21 21	23 31
Wrenbury	d			19x26		21x26	23x37
Whitchurch (Shrops)	d			19 34		21 35	23 45
Prees	d			19x39		21x40	23x51
Wem	d			19 45		21 47	23 57
Yorton	d			19x49		21x51	00x02
Shrewsbury	a	19 20		20 00	20 42	22 03	00 14
	d	19 21		20 01	20 43	22 04	
Church Stretton	d	19 37			20 59	22 20	
Craven Arms	d	19 45			21 07	22 29	
Ludlow	d	19 53		20 29	21 15	22 37	
Leominster	d	20 04		20 39	21 25	22 49	
Hereford 7	a	20 18		20 54	21 40	23 03	
	d	20 21		20 55	21 42	23 05	
Abergavenny	d	20 46		21 18	22 05	23 29	
Pontypool and New Inn	d	20 56			22 15	23 39	
Cwmbran	d	21 01		21 31	22 20	23 44	
Newport (South Wales)	a	21 14		21 46	22 32	23 54	
Reading 7	a						
London Paddington 15 ⊖	a						
Cardiff Central 7	a	21 36		22 07	22 59	00 20	
Swansea	a						

A ⌶ to Crewe

b Previous night, stops on request

For connections from Liverpool Lime Street and Runcorn please refer to Table 91. For connections to Bristol Temple Meads please refer to Table 132

When events are being held at the Millenium Stadium, services are subject to alteration. Please check times before travelling.

Manchester, Liverpool and Crewe - Cardiff

Sundays
1 July to 9 September

Route Diagram - see first Page of Table 129

		AW	AW	AW	AW	AW	AW	AW	AW	GW	AW	AW	GW	AW	AW	GW	AW	AW	AW	GW	AW	AW
					🚌	◇	◇ ⌶	■ ⌶	◇	◇1 ⊏	■ ⌶	◇ ⌶	◇1 ⊏	■ ⌶	■ ⌶	◇1 ⊏	■ ⌶	◇	■ ⌶	◇1	■ ⌶	■ ⌶
Manchester Piccadilly 10 ⇌	d	20p30	22p35				09 30	10 30			11 24			12 30	13 30		14 30		15 30		16 30	17 30
Stockport	d	20p39	22p44				09 39	10 39			11 40			12 40	13 40		14 39		15 39		16 39	17 39
Wilmslow	d	20p46	22p52				09 47	10 48			11 47			12 48	13 47		14 47		15 47		16 47	17 47
Holyhead	d											10 20										
Bangor (Gwynedd)	d											10 59										
Llandudno Junction	d											11 22										
Chester	d											12 21										
Crewe 10	d	21p08	23p14				10 13	11 11			12 13			13 13	14 13		15 10		16 13		17 13	18 13
Nantwich	d	21p17	23p22				10 22							13 21							17 21	
Wrenbury	d	21b23	23b27				10x27							13x26							17x26	
Whitchurch (Shrops)	d	21p29	23p34				10 35							13 34							17 34	
Prees	d	21b35	23b40				10x40							13x39							17x39	
Wem	d	21p40	23p45				10 46							13 45							17 45	
Yorton	d	21b45	23b50				10x50							13x49							17x49	
Shrewsbury	a	21p53	00 04				11 01	11 41			12 43	13 18		13 59	14 43		15 44		16 43		18 00	18 43
	d	21p55			07 50		11 03	11 45	12 07		12 44	13 19		14 01	14 44		15 47	16 18	16 44		18 01	18 44
Church Stretton	d	22p10			08 15		11 19		12 25			13 35			15 00			16 36	17 00			
Craven Arms	d	22p18			08 35		11 27		12 36			13 43			15 08			16 47	17 08			
Ludlow	d	22p26			08 55		11 36	12 13			13 12	13 51		14 28	15 16		16 17		17 16		18 29	19 12
Leominster	d	22p37			09 20		11 47	12 23			13 22	14 02		14 39	15 26		16 28		17 26		18 39	
Hereford 7	a	22p51			09 50		12 02	12 38			13 37	14 17		14 53	15 41		16 43		17 41		18 54	19 34
	d	22p53		23p15		10 09	12 03	12 39		13 32	13 39	14 19	14 32	14 56	15 43	16 35	16 44		17 43	18 30	18 57	19 36
Abergavenny	d	23p16		23p38		10 33	12 27	13 02			14 02	14 42		15 19	16 06		17 08		18 06		19 20	19 59
Pontypool and New Inn	d	23p25				10 43		13 12				14 52			16 16				18 16			
Cwmbran	d	23p30		23p50		10 48	12 40	13 17			14 14	14 57		15 31	16 21		17 21		18 21		19 33	20 11
Newport (South Wales)	a	23p45		00 02		10 59	12 51	13 28			14 28	15 07		15 45	16 31		17 33		18 31		19 49	20 22
Reading 7	a									16 20			17 21			19 20				21 17		
London Paddington 15 ⊖	a									16 51			17 59			19 56				21 59		
Cardiff Central 7	a	00 05		00 26		11 19	13 13	13 44			14 49	15 28		16 02	16 52		17 50		18 50		20 06	20 43
Swansea	a					12 19		15 10	16 04					17 14			19 15	20 16				

		AW	AW	AW	AW	AW	AW
		■ ⌶	◇ ⌶	■ ⌶	◇	◇	
Manchester Piccadilly 10 ⇌	d			18 30	19 30	20 30	
Stockport	d			18 39	19 39	20 39	
Wilmslow	d			18 47	19 47	20 47	
Holyhead	d	16 25	18 25				
Bangor (Gwynedd)	d	17 04	19 04				
Llandudno Junction	d	17 25	19 24				
Chester	d	18 24	20 27				23 00
Crewe 10	d		20a48	19 13	20 13	21 13	23 23
Nantwich	d			19 21		21 21	23 31
Wrenbury	d			19x26		21x26	23x37
Whitchurch (Shrops)	d			19 34		21 35	23 45
Prees	d			19x39		21x40	23x51
Wem	d			19 45		21 47	23 57
Yorton	d			19x49		21x51	00x02
Shrewsbury	a	19 20		20 00	20 42	22 03	00 14
	d	19 21		20 01	20 43	22 04	
Church Stretton	d	19 37			20 59	22 20	
Craven Arms	d	19 45			21 07	22 29	
Ludlow	d	19 53		20 29	21 15	22 37	
Leominster	d	20 04		20 39	21 25	22 49	
Hereford 7	a	20 18		20 54	21 40	23 03	
	d	20 21		20 55	21 42	23 05	
Abergavenny	d	20 46		21 18	22 05	23 29	
Pontypool and New Inn	d	20 56			22 15	23 39	
Cwmbran	d	21 01		21 31	22 20	23 44	
Newport (South Wales)	a	21 14		21 44	22 32	23 54	
Reading 7	a						
London Paddington 15 ⊖	a						
Cardiff Central 7	a	21 36		22 05	22 59	00 20	
Swansea	a						

b Previous night, stops on request

For connections from Liverpool Lime Street and Runcorn please refer to Table 91. For connections to Bristol Temple Meads please refer to Table 132

When events are being held at the Millenium Stadium, services are subject to alteration. Please check times before travelling.

Table 131

Sundays

16 September to 21 October

Manchester, Liverpool and Crewe - Cardiff

Route Diagram - see first Page of Table 129

		AW	AW	AW	AW		AW	AW	AW	AW		GW	AW	AW	GW	AW	AW	GW	AW	AW		AW	GW	AW	AW
					🚌		◇	◇ ✠	■ ✠	◇		◇1 ⊡	■ ✠	◇ ✠	◇1 ⊡	■ ✠	■ ✠	◇1 ⊡	■ ✠	◇		■ ✠	◇1	■ ✠	■ ✠
Manchester Piccadilly [10] ⇌	d	20p30	22p35					09 30	10 31				11 24			12 30	13 30		14 30			15 30		16 30	17 30
Stockport	d	20p39	22p44					09 39	10 40				11 40			12 40	13 40		14 39			15 39		16 39	17 39
Wilmslow	d	20p46	22p52					09 47	10 48				11 47			12 48	13 47		14 47			15 47		16 47	17 47
Holyhead	d													10 20											
Bangor (Gwynedd)	d													10 59											
Llandudno Junction	d													11 22											
Chester	d													12 21											
Crewe [10]	d	21p08	23p14					10 13	11 11				12 13			13 13	14 13		15 10			16 13		17 13	18 13
Nantwich	d	21p17	23p22					10 22								13 21								17 21	
Wrenbury	d	21b23	23b27					10x27								13x26								17x26	
Whitchurch (Shrops)	d	21p29	23p34					10 35								13 34								17 34	
Prees	d	21b35	23b40					10x40								13x39								17x39	
Wem	d	21p40	23p45					10 46								13 45								17 45	
Yorton	d	21b45	23b50					10x50								13x49								17x49	
Shrewsbury	a	21p53	00 04					11 01	11 41				12 43	13 18		13 59	14 43		15 44			16 43		18 00	18 43
	d	21p55			07 50			11 03	11 45	12 07			12 44	13 19		14 01	14 44		15 47	16 18		16 44		18 01	18 44
Church Stretton	d	22p10			08 15			11 19		12 25				13 35			15 00			16 36		17 00			
Craven Arms	d	22p18			08 35			11 27		12 36				13 43			15 08			16 47		17 08			
Ludlow	d	22p26			08 55			11 36	12 13				13 12	13 51		14 28	15 16		16 17			17 16		18 29	19 12
Leominster	d	22p37			09 20			11 47	12 23				13 22	14 02		14 39	15 26		16 28			17 26		18 39	
Hereford [7]	a	22p51			09 50			12 02	12 38				13 37	14 17		14 53	15 41		16 43			17 41		18 54	19 34
	d	22p53		23p15			10 09	12 03	12 39			13 32	13 39	14 19	14 32	14 56	15 43	16 35	16 44			17 43	18 30	18 57	19 36
Abergavenny	d	23p16		23p38			10 33	12 27	13 02				14 02	14 42		15 19	16 06		17 08			18 06		19 20	19 59
Pontypool and New Inn	d	23p25					10 43		13 12					14 52			16 16					18 16			
Cwmbran	d	23p30		23p50			10 48	12 40	13 17				14 14	14 57		15 31	16 21		17 21			18 21		19 33	20 11
Newport (South Wales)	a	23p45		00 02			10 59	12 51	13 28				14 28	15 07		15 45	16 31		17 33			18 31		19 49	20 22
Reading [7]	a											16 22			17 27			19 27					21 24		
London Paddington [15] ⊖	a											17 07			18 07			20 07					22 07		
Cardiff Central [7]	a	00 05		00 26			11 16	13 13	13 44				14 49	15 28		16 02	16 52		17 50			18 50		20 06	20 43
Swansea	a						12 13		15 10	16 04						17 14			19 15	20 16					

		AW	AW	AW	AW	AW		AW
		■ ✠	◇ ✠	■ ✠	◇	◇		
Manchester Piccadilly [10] ⇌	d			18 30	19 30	20 30		
Stockport	d			18 39	19 39	20 39		
Wilmslow	d			18 47	19 47	20 47		
Holyhead	d	16 25	18 25					
Bangor (Gwynedd)	d	17 04	19 04					
Llandudno Junction	d	17 25	19 24					
Chester	d	18 24	20 27					23 00
Crewe [10]	d		20a48	19 13	20 13	21 13		23 23
Nantwich	d			19 21		21 21		23 31
Wrenbury	d			19x26		21x26		23x37
Whitchurch (Shrops)	d			19 34		21 35		23 45
Prees	d			19x39		21x40		23x51
Wem	d			19 45		21 47		23 57
Yorton	d			19x49		21x51		00x02
Shrewsbury	a	19 19		20 00	20 42	22 03		00 14
	d	19 20		20 01	20 43	22 04		
Church Stretton	d	19 37			20 59	22 20		
Craven Arms	d	19 45			21 07	22 29		
Ludlow	d	19 53		20 29	21 15	22 37		
Leominster	d	20 04		20 39	21 25	22 49		
Hereford [7]	a	20 18		20 54	21 40	23 03		
	d	20 21		20 55	21 42	23 05		
Abergavenny	d	20 46		21 18	22 05	23 29		
Pontypool and New Inn	d	20 56			22 15	23 39		
Cwmbran	d	21 01		21 31	22 20	23 44		
Newport (South Wales)	a	21 14		21 44	22 32	23 54		
Reading [7]	a							
London Paddington [15] ⊖	a							
Cardiff Central [7]	a	21 36		22 05	22 59	00 20		
Swansea	a							

A ✠ to Crewe

b Previous night, stops on request

For connections from Liverpool Lime Street and Runcorn please refer to Table 91. For connections to Bristol Temple Meads please refer to Table 132

When events are being held at the Millenium Stadium, services are subject to alteration. Please check times before travelling.

Table 131

Sundays

from 28 October

Manchester, Liverpool and Crewe - Cardiff

Route Diagram - see first Page of Table 129

		AW	AW	AW	AW		AW	AW	AW			AW		GW	AW	AW		GW	AW	AW			GW	AW	AW
					🚌		◇	◇ ✠	■ ✠			◇		◇1 ⊡	■ ✠	◇ ✠		◇1 ⊡	■ ✠	■ ✠			◇1 ⊡	■ ✠	◇
Manchester Piccadilly [10] ⇌	d	20p30	22p35					09 30	10 31						11 24				12 30	13 30				14 30	
Stockport	d	20p39	22p44					09 39	10 40						11 40				12 40	13 40				14 39	
Wilmslow	d	20p46	22p52					09 47	10 48						11 47				12 48	13 47				14 47	
Holyhead	d															10 20									
Bangor (Gwynedd)	d															10 59									
Llandudno Junction	d															11 22									
Chester	d															12 21									
Crewe [10]	d	21p08	23p14					10 13	11 11						12 13				13 13	14 13				15 10	
Nantwich	d	21p17	23p22					10 22											13 21						
Wrenbury	d	21b23	23b27					10x27											13x26						
Whitchurch (Shrops)	d	21p29	23p34					10 35											13 34						
Prees	d	21b35	23b40					10x40											13x39						
Wem	d	21p40	23p45					10 46											13 45						
Yorton	d	21b45	23b50					10x50											13x49						
Shrewsbury	a	21p53	00 04					11 01	11 41						12 43	13 18			13 59	14 43				15 44	
	d	21p55			07 50			11 03	11 45			12 07			12 44	13 19			14 01	14 44				15 47	16 18
Church Stretton	d	22p10			08 15			11 19				12 25				13 35				15 00					16 36
Craven Arms	d	22p18			08 35			11 27				12 36				13 43				15 08					16 47
Ludlow	d	22p26			08 55			11 36	12 13						13 12	13 51			14 28	15 16				16 17	
Leominster	d	22p37			09 20			11 47	12 23						13 22	14 02			14 39	15 26				16 28	
Hereford [7]	a	22p51			09 50			12 02	12 38						13 37	14 17			14 53	15 41				16 43	
	d	22p53		23p15			10 09	12 03	12 39					13 32	13 39	14 19		14 32	14 56	15 43			16 35	16 44	
Abergavenny	d	23p16		23p38			10 33	12 27	13 02						14 02	14 42			15 19	16 06				17 08	
Pontypool and New Inn	d	23p25					10 43		13 12							14 52				16 16					
Cwmbran	d	23p30		23p50			10 48	12 40	13 17						14 14	14 57			15 31	16 21				17 21	
Newport (South Wales)	a	23p45		00 02			10 59	12 51	13 28						14 28	15 07			15 45	16 31				17 33	
Reading [7]	a													16 22				17 27					19 27		
London Paddington [15] ⊖	a													17 00				18 07					20 07		
Cardiff Central [7]	a	00 05		00 26			11 16	13 13	13 44						14 49	15 28			16 02	16 52				17 50	
Swansea	a						12 13		15 10			16 04							17 14					19 15	20 16

		AW	GW	AW	AW	AW		AW	AW	AW	AW	AW
		■ ✠	◇1	■ ✠	■ ✠	■ ✠		◇ ✠	■ ✠	◇	◇	
Manchester Piccadilly [10] ⇌	d	15 30		16 30	17 30				18 30	19 30	20 30	
Stockport	d	15 39		16 39	17 39				18 39	19 39	20 39	
Wilmslow	d	15 47		16 47	17 47				18 47	19 47	20 47	
Holyhead	d					16 25		18 25				
Bangor (Gwynedd)	d					17 04		19 04				
Llandudno Junction	d					17 25		19 24				
Chester	d					18 24		20 27				23 00
Crewe [10]	d	16 13		17 13	18 13			20a48	19 13	20 13	21 13	23 23
Nantwich	d			17 21					19 21		21 21	23 31
Wrenbury	d			17x26					19x26		21x26	23x37
Whitchurch (Shrops)	d			17 34					19 34		21 35	23 45
Prees	d			17x39					19x39		21x40	23x51
Wem	d			17 45					19 45		21 47	23 57
Yorton	d			17x49					19x49		21x51	00x02
Shrewsbury	a	16 43		18 00	18 43	19 19			20 00	20 42	22 03	00 14
	d	16 44		18 01	18 44	19 20			20 01	20 43	22 04	
Church Stretton	d	17 00				19 37				20 59	22 20	
Craven Arms	d	17 08				19 45				21 07	22 29	
Ludlow	d	17 16		18 29	19 12	19 53			20 29	21 15	22 37	
Leominster	d	17 26		18 39		20 04			20 39	21 25	22 49	
Hereford [7]	a	17 41		18 54	19 34	20 18			20 54	21 40	23 03	
	d	17 43	18 30	18 57	19 36	20 21			20 55	21 42	23 05	
Abergavenny	d	18 06		19 20	19 59	20 46			21 18	22 05	23 29	
Pontypool and New Inn	d	18 16				20 56				22 15	23 39	
Cwmbran	d	18 21		19 33	20 11	21 01			21 31	22 20	23 44	
Newport (South Wales)	a	18 31		19 49	20 22	21 14			21 46	22 32	23 54	
Reading [7]	a		21 24									
London Paddington [15] ⊖	a		22 07									
Cardiff Central [7]	a	18 50		20 06	20 43	21 36			22 07	22 59	00 20	
Swansea	a											

A ✠ to Crewe

b Previous night, stops on request

For connections from Liverpool Lime Street and Runcorn please refer to Table 91. For connections to Bristol Temple Meads please refer to Table 132

When events are being held at the Millenium Stadium, services are subject to alteration. Please check times before travelling.

Network Diagram for Tables 132, 133 ,134

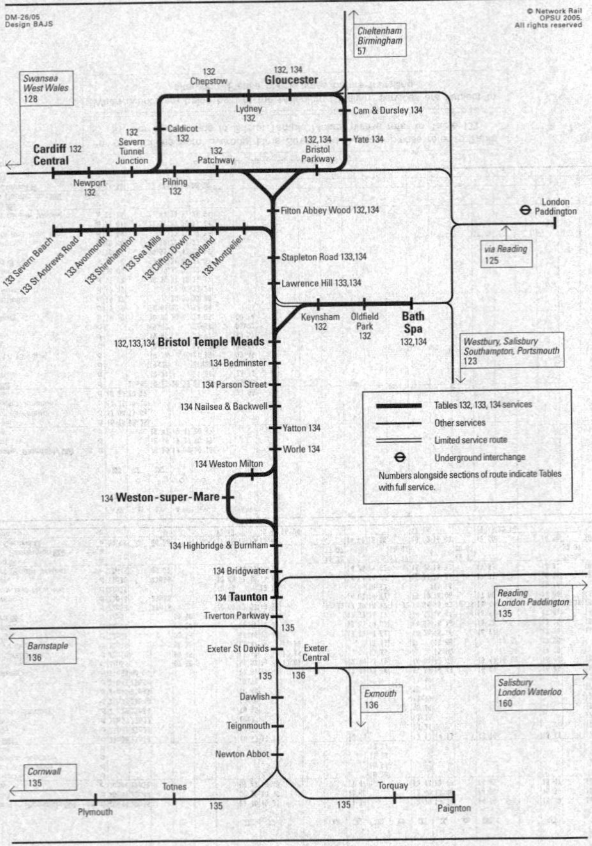

Cardiff - Gloucester, Bristol and Bath Spa

Network Diagram - see first Page of Table 132

Miles	Miles	Miles			AW	GW	AW	AW	AW	GW	GW	AW	GW		GW	GW	AW	GW	GW	GW	GW	GW	GW		XC
					MX	MX	MX																		
								◇	◇	◇1	◇1	◇	◇		◇1	◇1		◇1	◇1	◇1		◇1	◇		◇1
									✠	⊡	⊡	✠			⊡	⊡		⊡	⊡	⊡		⊡	✠		
0	0	0	**Cardiff Central** 7	d	23p19	23p27	00 30	04 35	05 10	05 14	.	05 40	.	.	05 55	.	06 12	06 24	.	.	.	.	06 28	.	06 40
11¾	11¾	11¾	Newport (South Wales)	a	23p39	23p44	00 48	04 50	05 25	05 30	.	05 55	.	.	06 09	.	06 26	06 37	.	.	.	.	06 41	.	06 53
—	—	—		d	23p40	23p45	.	.	.	05 32	.	.	.	.	06 09	.	06 28	06 38	.	.	.	.	06 42	.	06 55
21¾	21¾	21¾	Severn Tunnel Jn	d	23p58	00 03	.	.	.	.	.	.	.	.	.	.	06 38	.	.	.	.	.	06 53	.	07 05
—	—	22½	Caldicot	d	00 01	.	.	.	.	.	.	.	.	.	.	.	06 40	.	.	.	.	.	.	.	07 08
—	—	29¼	Chepstow	d	00 10	.	.	.	.	.	.	.	.	.	.	.	06 49	.	.	.	.	.	.	.	07 16
—	—	37	Lydney	d	00 19	.	.	.	.	.	.	.	.	.	.	.	06 58	.	.	.	.	.	.	.	07 25
—	—	56½	**Gloucester** 7	a	00 39	.	.	.	.	.	.	.	.	.	.	.	07 20	.	.	.	.	.	.	.	07 44
28¾	28¾	—	Pilning	d	.	.	.	.	.	.	.	.	.	.	.	.	.	.	.	.	.	.	.	.	.
32¼	32¼	—	Patchway	d	.	00 16	.	.	.	.	.	.	.	.	.	.	.	.	.	.	.	.	07 06	.	.
—	33½	—	**Bristol Parkway** 7	a	.	.	.	.	.	05 59	.	.	.	.	06 29	.	.	06 58	.	.	.	.	.	.	.
—	—	—		d	.	.	.	.	.	.	.	.	.	.	.	.	.	.	.	.	.	.	.	.	.
33¾	—	—	Filton Abbey Wood	d	.	00 20	.	.	.	.	.	.	.	.	.	.	.	.	.	.	.	.	07 09	.	.
38¼	—	—	**Bristol Temple Meads** 10	a	.	00 33	.	.	.	.	.	.	.	.	.	.	.	.	.	.	.	.	07 17	.	.
—	—	—		d	.	.	.	.	.	.	05 30	.	05 44	.	.	06 00	.	.	06 30	06 40	06 48	07 00	07 22	.	.
42¾	—	—	Keynsham	d	.	.	.	.	.	.	.	.	05 51	.	.	.	.	.	.	.	06 55	.	.	.	.
48¾	—	—	Oldfield Park	d	.	.	.	.	.	.	.	.	05 58	.	.	.	.	.	.	.	07 02	.	.	.	.
49¾	—	—	**Bath Spa** 7	a	.	.	.	.	.	.	05 41	.	06 01	.	.	06 11	.	.	06 41	06 51	07 05	07 11	07 34	.	.

		AW	GW	GW	GW	XC	AW	AW	GW		GW	GW	GW	XC	GW	GW	GW	GW	AW		GW	SW	GW	GW	GW
													■												
		◇	◇1		◇1	◇1		◇	◇1			◇1		◇1	◇1	◇	◇1	◇	◇		◇1	◇1	◇1		◇
			A		B									C											
		✠	⊡		∅			✠	⊡			∅	✠	✠	⊡		∅		✠		∅		⊡		✠
Cardiff Central 7	d	06 50	.	.	06 55	07 00	07 12	07 21	.	.	.	07 25	07 30	07 45	.	.	07 55	08 00	08 05	.	08 25	.	.	.	08 30
Newport (South Wales)	a	07 02	.	.	07 09	07 13	07 26	07 34	.	.	.	07 39	07 44	07 59	.	.	08 09	08 13	08 17	.	08 39	.	.	.	08 42
	d	.	.	.	07 09	07 15	07 27	.	.	.	.	07 39	07 44	08 02	.	.	08 09	08 15	.	.	08 39	.	.	.	08 44
Severn Tunnel Jn	d	.	.	.	.	07 25	07 38	.	.	.	.	.	07 55	.	.	.	.	08 26	.	.	.	.	.	.	08 55
Caldicot	d	.	.	.	.	.	07 40	.	.	.	.	.	.	.	.	.	.	.	.	.	.	.	.	.	.
Chepstow	d	.	.	.	.	.	07 49	.	.	.	.	.	.	.	.	.	.	.	.	.	.	.	.	.	.
Lydney	d	.	.	.	.	.	07 58	.	.	.	.	.	.	08 25	.	.	.	.	.	.	.	.	.	.	.
Gloucester 7	a	.	.	.	.	.	08 20	.	.	.	.	.	.	08 44	.	.	.	.	.	.	.	.	.	.	.
Pilning	d	.	.	.	.	.	.	.	.	.	.	.	.	.	.	.	.	.	.	.	.	.	.	.	.
Patchway	d	.	.	.	.	07 37	.	.	.	.	.	.	.	.	.	.	.	08 39	.	.	.	.	.	.	.
Bristol Parkway 7	a	.	.	.	07 29	.	.	.	.	.	.	07 59	.	.	.	.	08 30	.	.	.	08 59	.	.	.	.
	d	.	.	07 25	.	.	.	.	.	.	07 49	.	.	.	.	08 19	.	.	.	.	.	.	.	.	.
Filton Abbey Wood	d	.	.	07 28	.	07 41	.	.	.	.	07 53	.	08 09	.	.	08 23	.	08 42	.	.	.	.	.	.	09 09
Bristol Temple Meads 10	a	.	.	07 39	.	07 51	.	.	.	.	08 01	.	08 17	.	.	08 36	.	08 50	.	.	.	.	.	.	09 17
	d	.	07 30	07 49	.	.	.	.	08 00	.	08 12	.	08 22	.	08 30	08 41	.	.	.	.	.	08 51	09 00	09 05	09 22
Keynsham	d	.	.	07 56	.	.	.	.	.	.	08 19	.	.	.	.	08 48	.	.	.	.	.	08 58	.	.	.
Oldfield Park	d	.	.	08 03	.	.	.	.	.	.	08 26	.	.	.	.	08 55	.	.	.	.	.	.	.	09 17	.
Bath Spa 7	a	.	07 41	08 05	.	.	.	.	08 11	.	08 28	.	08 34	.	08 41	08 58	.	.	.	.	.	09 05	09 11	09 19	09 34

		XC	AW	GW	GW		GW	GW	AW	AW	GW	GW	GW	XC	GW		GW	GW	GW	AW	AW	GW	GW	GW	XC
		◇1	◇	◇1	◇		◇1	◇		◇	◇1	◇1	◇	◇1	◇1			◇1		◇		◇1	◇1	◇	◇1
		C									D			C											C
		✠	✠	⊡			⊡			✠	⊡	⊡	✠	✠	⊡			⊡		✠		⊡	⊡	✠	✠
Cardiff Central 7	d	08 45	08 50	.	.	.	08 55	09 00	09 12	09 21	09 25	.	09 30	09 45	.	.	.	09 55	10 00	10 05	10 12	10 25	.	10 30	10 45
Newport (South Wales)	a	08 59	09 02	.	.	.	09 09	09 13	09 25	09 34	09 39	.	09 42	09 58	.	.	.	10 08	10 13	10 17	10 25	10 39	.	10 42	10 58
	d	09 02	.	.	.	.	09 09	09 15	09 27	.	09 39	.	09 44	10 00	.	.	.	10 09	10 15	.	10 27	10 39	.	10 44	11 00
Severn Tunnel Jn	d	.	.	.	.	.	.	09 26	09 37	.	.	.	09 55	.	.	.	.	.	10 26	.	10 38	.	.	.	.
Caldicot	d	.	.	.	.	.	.	.	09 39	.	.	.	.	.	.	.	.	.	.	.	10 40	.	.	.	.
Chepstow	d	.	.	.	.	.	.	.	09 48	.	.	.	.	10 18	.	.	.	.	.	.	10 49	.	.	.	.
Lydney	d	.	.	.	.	.	.	.	09 57	.	.	.	.	.	.	.	.	.	.	.	10 58	.	.	.	11 25
Gloucester 7	a	09 44	.	.	.	.	.	.	10 20	.	.	.	.	10 44	.	.	.	.	.	.	11 20	.	.	.	11 44
Pilning	d	.	.	.	.	.	.	.	.	.	.	.	.	.	.	.	.	.	.	.	.	.	.	.	.
Patchway	d	.	.	.	.	.	.	09 39	.	.	.	.	.	.	.	.	.	.	10 39	.	.	.	.	.	.
Bristol Parkway 7	a	.	.	.	.	.	09 30	.	.	.	09 59	.	.	.	.	.	.	10 30	.	.	.	10 59	.	.	.
	d	.	.	.	09 20	.	.	.	.	.	.	.	.	.	.	.	10 22	.	.	.	.	.	.	.	.
Filton Abbey Wood	d	.	.	.	09 23	.	.	09 42	.	.	.	.	10 09	.	.	.	10 25	.	10 42	.	.	.	.	11 09	.
Bristol Temple Meads 10	a	.	.	.	09 34	.	.	09 53	.	.	.	.	10 18	.	.	.	10 37	.	10 51	.	.	.	.	11 18	.
	d	.	.	09 30	09 49	.	.	.	.	.	.	10 00	10 22	.	10 30	.	10 49	.	.	.	.	.	11 00	11 22	.
Keynsham	d	.	.	.	09 56	.	.	.	.	.	.	.	.	.	.	.	10 56	.	.	.	.	.	.	.	.
Oldfield Park	d	.	.	.	10 03	.	.	.	.	.	.	.	.	.	.	.	11 03	.	.	.	.	.	.	.	.
Bath Spa 7	a	.	.	09 41	10 05	.	.	.	.	.	.	10 11	10 34	.	10 41	.	11 06	.	.	.	.	.	11 11	11 34	.

A The Bristolian
B The Capitals United
C ✠ from Newport (South Wales)
D The Red Dragon

When events are being held at the Millenium Stadium, services are subject to alteration. Please check times before travelling.

Cardiff - Gloucester, Bristol and Bath Spa

Network Diagram - see first Page of Table 132

		AW	GW	GW	GW	GW	AW	GW	GW	GW	XC	GW	GW	GW	GW	AW	AW	GW	SW	GW	GW	XC
		◇ ⌶	◇1 ☕	◇	◇1 ☕		◇ ⌶	◇1 ☕	◇1 ☕	◇ ⌶	◇1 A ⌶	◇1 ☕	■ B ⌶	◇1 ☕		◇ ⌶		◇1 C ☕	◇1 ⌶	◇1 ☕	◇ ⌶	◇1 A ⌶
Cardiff Central 7	d	10 50			10 55	11 00	11 21	11 25		11 30	11 45			11 55	12 00	12 05	12 12	12 25			12 30	12 45
Newport (South Wales)	a	11 02			11 08	11 13	11 34	11 39		11 42	11 59			12 08	12 13	12 17	12 25	12 39			12 42	12 59
	d				11 09	11 15		11 39		11 44	12 02			12 09	12 15		12 28	12 39			12 44	13 01
Severn Tunnel Jn	d					11 26									12 26		12 39					
Caldicot	d																12 42					
Chepstow	d										12 18						12 51					13 18
Lydney	d																13 00					
Gloucester 7	a										12 44						13 20					13 44
Pilning	d																					
Patchway	d					11 39									12 39							
Bristol Parkway 7	a				11 30			11 59						12 30				12 59				
	d			11 20									12 22									
Filton Abbey Wood	d			11 23		11 42				12 09			12 25		12 42						13 09	
Bristol Temple Meads 10	a			11 34		11 51				12 18			12 34		12 51						13 18	
	d		11 30	11 49					12 00	12 22		12 30	12 39						12 51	13 00	13 22	
Keynsham	d			11 56									12 46						12 58			
Oldfield Park	d			12 03									12 53									
Bath Spa 7	a		11 41	12 06					12 12	12 34		12 41	12 55						13 05	13 11	13 34	

		AW	GW	GW	GW	GW	AW	AW	GW	GW	GW	XC	GW	GW	GW	GW	AW	GW	GW	GW	XC	AW	GW
		◇ ⌶	◇1 ☕		◇1 ☕	◇	⌶	◇ ⌶	◇1 ∅	◇1 ☕	◇ ⌶	◇1 A ⌶	◇1 ☕	◇	◇1 ☕		◇ ⌶	◇1 ∅	◇1 ☕	◇ ⌶	◇1 A ⌶	◇ ⌶	◇1 ☕
Cardiff Central 7	d	12 50			12 55	13 00	13 12	13 21	13 25		13 30	13 45			13 55	14 00	14 05	14 25		14 30	14 45	14 50	
Newport (South Wales)	a	13 02			13 08	13 13	13 25	13 34	13 39		13 42	13 58			14 08	14 13	14 17	14 39		14 42	14 59	15 02	
	d				13 09	13 15	13 28		13 39		13 44	14 00			14 09	14 15		14 39		14 44	15 01		
Severn Tunnel Jn	d					13 26	13 39									14 26							
Caldicot	d						13 41																
Chepstow	d						13 50					14 25									15 18		
Lydney	d						13 59																
Gloucester 7	a						14 20					14 44									15 44		
Pilning	d																						
Patchway	d					13 39										14 39							
Bristol Parkway 7	a				13 30				13 59						14 30			15 00					
	d			13 20										14 22									
Filton Abbey Wood	d			13 23		13 42					14 09			14 25		14 42				15 09			
Bristol Temple Meads 10	a			13 35		13 51					14 17			14 38		14 51				15 17			
	d		13 30	13 49						14 00	14 22		14 30	14 48					15 00	15 22			15 30
Keynsham	d			13 56										14 55									
Oldfield Park	d			14 03										15 02									
Bath Spa 7	a		13 41	14 06						14 11	14 34		14 41	15 05					15 11	15 34			15 41

		GW	GW	GW	AW	AW	SW	GW	GW	GW	GW	XC	AW	GW	GW	GW	GW	AW	GW	GW	GW
			◇1 ☕			■ ⌶	◇1	◇1 D ☕		◇1 ☕	◇ ⌶	◇1	■ ⌶	◇1 ☕	◇	◇1 ☕		■ ⌶	◇1 ☕		◇1 ☕
Cardiff Central 7	d		14 55	15 00	15 12	15 21				15 25	15 30	15 45	15 50			15 55	16 00	16 05			16 25
Newport (South Wales)	a		15 08	15 13	15 26	15 34				15 39	15 43	15 58	16 02			16 08	16 13	16 18			16 39
	d		15 09	15 15	15 28					15 39	15 44	16 00				16 09	16 15	16 21			16 39
Severn Tunnel Jn	d			15 26	15 37												16 26	16 32			
Caldicot	d				15 40													16 34			
Chepstow	d				15 49							16 18						16 43			
Lydney	d				15 58													16 52			
Gloucester 7	a				16 21							16 44						17 14			
Pilning	d																				
Patchway	d			15 39													16 39				
Bristol Parkway 7	a		15 30							15 59						16 30					16 59
	d	15 20							15 53						16 22					16 46	
Filton Abbey Wood	d	15 23		15 42					15 56		16 09				16 25		16 42			16 49	
Bristol Temple Meads 10	a	15 36		15 51							16 18				16 37		16 51			17 02	
	d	15 44					15 51	16 00			16 22			16 30	16 49				17 00	17 07	
Keynsham	d	15 51					15 58		16 11						16 56					17 14	
Oldfield Park	d	15 58							16 18						17 03					17 21	
Bath Spa 7	a	15 59					16 05	16 11	16 21		16 34			16 41	17 06				17 11	17 24	

A ⌶ from Newport (South Wales)

B ⌶ from Bristol Temple Meads

C The St. David

D The Merchant Venturer

When events are being held at the Millenium Stadium, services are subject to alteration. Please check times before travelling.

Cardiff - Gloucester, Bristol and Bath Spa

Network Diagram - see first Page of Table 132

		GW	GW	XC	AW	GW	GW	GW	GW	AW	AW	GW	GW	GW	GW	XC	AW	GW	GW	GW	GW	AW	AW BHX
			■ ⌶	◇1	■ ⌶	◇1 ☕	◇	◇1 ☕			■ ⌶	◇1 ☕		◇1 ∅	■ ⌶	◇1 A ⌶	■ ⌶	◇1 ☕		◇1 ☕			■ ⌶
Cardiff Central 7	d		16 30	16 45	16 50			16 55	17 00	17 12	17 21			17 25	17 30	17 45	17 50			17 55	18 00	18 12	18 18
Newport (South Wales)	a		16 42	16 58	17 02			17 08	17 13	17 25	17 34			17 39	17 42	17 58	18 02			18 08	18 13	18 25	18 30
	d		16 44	17 00				17 09	17 15	17 28				17 39	17 44	18 00				18 09	18 15	18 27	
Severn Tunnel Jn	d		16 55						17 26	17 39					17 55						18 26	18 38	
Caldicot	d									17 41												18 40	
Chepstow	d									17 50						18 18						18 49	
Lydney	d			17 25						17 59												18 58	
Gloucester 7	a			17 44						18 21						18 44						19 20	
Pilning	d																						
Patchway	d								17 39												18 39		
Bristol Parkway 7	a							17 30						17 59						18 30			
	d						17 20						17 46						18 22				
Filton Abbey Wood	d	16 55	17 09				17 23		17 43				17 49		18 09				18 25		18 42		
Bristol Temple Meads 10	a	17 03	17 18				17 36		17 53				18 01		18 17				18 38		18 53		
	d	17 14	17 22			17 30	17 49					18 00	18 07		18 22			18 30	18 49				
Keynsham	d						17 56						18 14						18 56				
Oldfield Park	d	17 26					18 03						18 21						19 03				
Bath Spa 7	a	17 30	17 35			17 41	18 06					18 11	18 24		18 34			18 41	19 06				

		GW	GW	XC	AW	GW	GW	GW	GW	GW	AW	XC	GW	GW	GW	AW	GW	GW	AW	GW	GW	XC	AW
		◇1 ☕	◇ ⌶	◇1	◇ ⌶	◇1 ☕			◇1 ☕	◇	◇	◇1	◇1 ☕			◇	◇1 ☕	◇	◇	◇1 ☕		◇1	
Cardiff Central 7	d	18 25	18 30	18 45	18 50			19 00	19 25	19 30	19 34	19 50			20 00	20 17	20 25	20 30	20 53		21 00	21 05	21 12
Newport (South Wales)	a	18 39	18 42	18 59	19 03			19 13	19 39	19 42	19 46	20 03			20 13	20 29	20 38	20 44	21 07		21 13	21 18	21 25
	d	18 39	18 44	19 01				19 15	19 39	19 44		20 05			20 15		20 39	20 44			21 15	21 21	21 27
Severn Tunnel Jn	d		18 55					19 26				20 15			20 26						21 25		21 38
Caldicot	d											20 18											21 40
Chepstow	d			19 18								20 26											21 49
Lydney	d											20 35											21 58
Gloucester 7	a			19 45								20 53										22 02	22 21
Pilning	d																						
Patchway	d							19 39							20 39						21 39		
Bristol Parkway 7	a	18 59							19 59								21 01						
	d						19 20																
Filton Abbey Wood	d		19 09				19 23	19 42		20 09					20 42			21 08			21 42		
Bristol Temple Meads 10	a		19 17				19 35	19 51		20 17					20 53			21 19			21 51		
	d		19 22			19 30	19 49			20 22			20 30	20 49				21 23		21 50	22 00		
Keynsham	d						19 56							20 56							22 07		
Oldfield Park	d						20 03							21 03							22 14		
Bath Spa 7	a		19 34			19 41	20 06			20 34			20 41	21 06				21 36		22 01	22 17		

		GW	GW	SW	XC	XC	AW	GW	GW	GW	GW	AW FX	AW FO	GW
		◇1 ☕		1		◇1	◇	◇1 ☕						
Cardiff Central 7	d	21 25	21 30		21 40	21 50	21 55		22 04		22 49	23 19	23 20	23 27
Newport (South Wales)	a	21 38	21 43		21 55	22 03	22 08		22 16		23 06	23 39	23 38	23 44
	d	21 39	21 44		21 56	22 05			22 18		23 06	23 40	23 40	23 45
Severn Tunnel Jn	d		21 55						22 35		23 24	23 58	23 58	00 03
Caldicot	d											00 01	00 01	
Chepstow	d											00 10	00 09	
Lydney	d											00 19	00 18	
Gloucester 7	a					22 46						00 39	00 39	
Pilning	d													
Patchway	d								22 48					00 16
Bristol Parkway 7	a	21 59												
	d													
Filton Abbey Wood	d		22 09						22 52		23 40			00 20
Bristol Temple Meads 10	a		22 22		22 29				23 05		23 49			00 33
	d			22 25				22 35		23 20				
Keynsham	d									23 27				
Oldfield Park	d									23 34				
Bath Spa 7	a			22 37				22 46		23 37				

A ⌶ from Newport (South Wales)

When events are being held at the Millenium Stadium, services are subject to alteration. Please check times before travelling.

2 July to 31 August

Cardiff - Gloucester, Bristol and Bath Spa

Network Diagram - see first Page of Table 132

	AW MX	GW MX	AW MX	AW	AW	AW	GW	GW	AW	GW	GW	GW	AW	GW	GW	GW	GW	GW	XC	AW	GW	GW
			A	◇ B	◇	◇ 🛒	◇■1 ☕	◇■1 ☕	◇ 🛒	◇	◇■1 ☕	◇■1 ☕		◇■1 ☕	◇■1 ☕		◇■1 ☕	◇ 🛒	◇■1	◇ 🛒	◇■1 C ☕	
Cardiff Central d	23p19	23p27	00 30	00 30	04 35	05 10	05 14		05 40		05 55		06 12	06 24				06 28	06 40	06 50		
Newport (South Wales) a	23p39	23p44	00 48	00 49	04 50	05 25	05 30		05 55		06 09		06 26	06 37				06 41	06 53	07 02		
d	23p40	23p45					05 32				06 09		06 28	06 38				06 42	06 55			
Severn Tunnel Jn d	23p58	00 03											06 38					06 53	07 05			
Caldicot d	00 01												06 40						07 08			
Chepstow d	00 10												06 49						07 16			
Lydney d	00 19												06 58						07 25			
Gloucester a	00 39												07 20						07 44			
Pilning d																						
Patchway d		00 16																07 06				
Bristol Parkway a							05 59				06 29			06 58								
d																						07 25
Filton Abbey Wood d		00 20																07 09				07 28
Bristol Temple Meads a		00 33																07 17				07 39
d								05 30		05 44		06 00			06 30	06 48	07 00	07 22			07 30	07 49
Keynsham d										05 51						06 55						07 56
Oldfield Park d										05 58						07 02						08 03
Bath Spa a								05 41		06 01		06 11			06 41	07 05	07 11	07 34			07 41	08 05

	GW	XC	AW	AW	GW	GW	GW	GW	XC	GW	GW	GW	SW	GW	AW	GW	GW	GW	GW	XC	AW	GW
	◇■1 D Ø	◇■1		◇ 🛒	◇■1 ☕		◇■1 Ø	■ 🛒	◇■1 E 🛒	◇■1 ☕	◇	◇■1 Ø	◇■1	◇	◇ 🛒	◇■1 Ø	◇■1 ☕		◇ 🛒	◇■1 E 🛒	◇ 🛒	◇■1 ☕
Cardiff Central d	06 55	07 00	07 12	07 21			07 25	07 30	07 45			07 55		08 00	08 05	08 25			08 30	08 45	08 50	
Newport (South Wales) a	07 09	07 13	07 26	07 34			07 39	07 44	07 59			08 09		08 13	08 17	08 39			08 42	08 59	09 02	
d	07 09	07 15	07 27				07 39	07 44	08 02			08 09		08 15		08 39			08 44	09 02		
Severn Tunnel Jn d		07 25	07 38					07 55						08 26					08 55			
Caldicot d			07 40																			
Chepstow d			07 49																			
Lydney d			07 58						08 25													
Gloucester a			08 20						08 44											09 44		
Pilning d																						
Patchway d		07 37												08 39								
Bristol Parkway a	07 29						07 59					08 30				08 59						
d						07 49					08 19											
Filton Abbey Wood d		07 41				07 53		08 09			08 23			08 42					09 09			
Bristol Temple Meads a		07 51				08 01		08 17			08 36			08 52					09 17			
d					08 00	08 12		08 22		08 30	08 41		08 51				09 00	09 05	09 22			09 30
Keynsham d						08 19					08 48		08 58									
Oldfield Park d						08 26					08 55							09 17				
Bath Spa a					08 11	08 28		08 34		08 41	08 58		09 05				09 11	09 19	09 34			09 41

	GW	GW	GW	AW	AW	GW	GW	GW	XC	GW	GW	GW	GW	AW	AW	GW	GW	GW	XC	AW	GW
	◇	◇■1 ☕	◇		◇ 🛒	◇■1 F ☕	◇■1 ☕	◇ 🛒	◇■1 E 🛒	◇■1 ☕		◇■1 ☕		◇ 🛒		◇■1 ☕	◇■1 ☕	◇ 🛒	◇■1 E 🛒	◇ 🛒	◇■1 ☕
Cardiff Central d		08 55	09 00	09 12	09 21	09 25		09 30	09 45			09 55	10 00	10 05	10 12	10 25		10 30	10 45	10 50	
Newport (South Wales) a		09 09	09 13	09 25	09 34	09 39		09 42	09 58			10 08	10 13	10 17	10 25	10 39		10 42	10 58	11 02	
d		09 09	09 15	09 27		09 39		09 44	10 00			10 09	10 15		10 27	10 39		10 44	11 00		
Severn Tunnel Jn d			09 26	09 37				09 55					10 26		10 38						
Caldicot d				09 39											10 40						
Chepstow d				09 48					10 18						10 49						
Lydney d				09 57											10 58				11 25		
Gloucester a				10 20					10 44						11 20				11 44		
Pilning d																					
Patchway d			09 39										10 39								
Bristol Parkway a		09 30				09 59						10 30				10 59					
d	09 20										10 22										
Filton Abbey Wood d	09 23		09 42					10 09			10 25		10 42					11 09			
Bristol Temple Meads a	09 34		09 53					10 18			10 37		10 51					11 18			
d	09 49						10 00	10 22		10 30	10 49						11 00	11 22			11 30
Keynsham d	09 56										10 56										
Oldfield Park d	10 03										11 03										
Bath Spa a	10 05						10 11	10 34		10 41	11 06						11 11	11 34			11 41

A not 26 July, 27 July, 2 August
B 26 July, 27 July, 2 August
C The Bristolian
D The Capitals United
E 🛒 from Newport (South Wales)
F The Red Dragon

When events are being held at the Millenium Stadium, services are subject to alteration. Please check times before travelling.

2 July to 31 August

Cardiff - Gloucester, Bristol and Bath Spa

Network Diagram - see first Page of Table 132

	GW	GW	GW	AW	GW	GW	GW	XC	GW	GW	GW	GW	AW	AW	GW	SW	GW	GW	XC	AW	GW	GW
	◇	◇■1 ☕		◇ 🛒	◇■1 ☕	◇■1 ☕	◇ 🛒	◇■1 A 🛒	◇■1 ☕	■ B 🛒	◇■1 ☕		◇ 🛒		◇■1 C ☕	◇■1 🛒	◇■1 ☕	◇ 🛒	◇■1 A 🛒	◇ 🛒	◇■1 ☕	
Cardiff Central d		10 55	11 00	11 21	11 25		11 30	11 45			11 55	12 00	12 05	12 12	12 25			12 30	12 45	12 50		
Newport (South Wales) a		11 08	11 13	11 34	11 39		11 42	11 59			12 08	12 13	12 17	12 25	12 39			12 42	12 59	13 02		
d		11 09	11 15		11 39		11 44	12 02			12 09	12 15		12 28	12 39			12 44	13 01			
Severn Tunnel Jn d			11 26									12 26		12 39								
Caldicot d														12 42								
Chepstow d								12 18						12 51					13 18			
Lydney d														13 00								
Gloucester a								12 44						13 20					13 44			
Pilning d																						
Patchway d			11 39									12 39										
Bristol Parkway a		11 30			11 59						12 30				12 59							
d	11 20									12 22												13 20
Filton Abbey Wood d	11 23		11 42				12 09			12 25		12 42						13 09				13 23
Bristol Temple Meads a	11 34		11 51				12 18			12 34		12 51						13 18				13 35
d	11 49					12 00	12 22		12 30	12 39						12 51	13 00	13 22			13 30	13 49
Keynsham d	11 56									12 46						12 58						13 56
Oldfield Park d	12 03									12 53												14 03
Bath Spa a	12 06					12 12	12 34		12 41	12 55						13 05	13 11	13 34			13 41	14 06

	GW	GW	AW	AW	GW	GW	GW	XC	GW	GW	GW	GW	AW	GW	GW	GW	XC	AW	GW	GW	GW
	◇■1 ☕	◇	🛒	◇ 🛒	◇■1 Ø	◇■1 ☕	◇ 🛒	◇■1 A 🛒	◇■1 ☕	◇	◇■1 ☕		◇ 🛒	◇■1 Ø	◇■1 ☕	◇ 🛒	◇■1 A 🛒	◇ 🛒	◇■1 ☕		◇■1 ☕
Cardiff Central d	12 55	13 00	13 12	13 21	13 25		13 30	13 45			13 55	14 00	14 05	14 25		14 30	14 45	14 50			14 55
Newport (South Wales) a	13 08	13 13	13 25	13 34	13 39		13 42	13 58			14 08	14 13	14 17	14 39		14 42	14 59	15 02			15 08
d	13 09	13 15	13 28		13 39		13 44	14 00			14 09	14 15		14 39		14 44	15 01				15 09
Severn Tunnel Jn d		13 26	13 39									14 26									
Caldicot d			13 41																		
Chepstow d			13 50														15 18				
Lydney d			13 59					14 25													
Gloucester a			14 20					14 44									15 44				
Pilning d																					
Patchway d		13 39										14 39									
Bristol Parkway a	13 30				13 59						14 30			15 00							15 30
d										14 22										15 20	
Filton Abbey Wood d		13 42					14 09			14 25		14 42				15 09				15 23	
Bristol Temple Meads a		13 51					14 17			14 38		14 51				15 17				15 36	
d						14 00	14 22		14 30	14 48					15 00	15 22			15 30	15 44	
Keynsham d										14 55										15 51	
Oldfield Park d										15 02										15 58	
Bath Spa a						14 11	14 34		14 41	15 05					15 11	15 34			15 41	15 59	

	GW	AW	AW	SW	GW	GW	GW	GW	XC	AW	GW	GW	GW	GW	AW	AW	AW BHX	GW	GW	GW	GW	GW
			■ 🛒	◇■1	◇■1 D ☕		◇■1 ☕	◇ 🛒	◇■1	■ 🛒	◇■1 ☕	◇	◇■1 ☕		■ 🛒	E	■ ■1 ⊠	◇■1 ☕		◇■1 ☕		■ 🛒
Cardiff Central d	15 00	15 12	15 21				15 25	15 30	15 45	15 50			15 55	16 00	16 05	16 15	16 15			16 25		16 30
Newport (South Wales) a	15 13	15 26	15 34				15 39	15 43	15 58	16 02			16 08	16 13	16 18	16 28	16 28			16 39		16 42
d	15 15	15 28					15 39	15 44	16 00				16 09	16 15	16 21					16 39		16 44
Severn Tunnel Jn d	15 26	15 37												16 26	16 32							16 55
Caldicot d		15 40													16 34							
Chepstow d		15 49							16 18						16 43							
Lydney d		15 58													16 52							
Gloucester a		16 21							16 44						17 14							
Pilning d																						
Patchway d	15 39													16 39								
Bristol Parkway a							15 59						16 30							16 59		
d						15 53						16 22							16 46			
Filton Abbey Wood d	15 42					15 56		16 09				16 25		16 42					16 49		16 55	17 09
Bristol Temple Meads a	15 51							16 18				16 37		16 51					17 02		17 03	17 18
d				15 51	16 00			16 22			16 30	16 49						17 00	17 07		17 14	17 22
Keynsham d				15 58		16 11						16 56							17 14			
Oldfield Park d						16 18						17 03							17 21		17 26	
Bath Spa a				16 05	16 11	16 21		16 34			16 41	17 06						17 11	17 24		17 30	17 35

A 🛒 from Newport (South Wales)
B 🛒 from Bristol Temple Meads
C The St. David
D The Merchant Venturer
E 27 August

When events are being held at the Millenium Stadium, services are subject to alteration. Please check times before travelling.

Cardiff - Gloucester, Bristol and Bath Spa

Mondays to Fridays

2 July to 31 August

Network Diagram - see first Page of Table 132

		XC	AW	GW	GW	GW	GW	AW	AW	GW	GW	GW	GW	XC	AW	GW	GW	GW	GW	AW	AW BHX	GW	GW
		◇1	■ ⊼	◇1 ⊏	◇	◇1 ⊏			■ ⊼	◇1 ⊏		◇1 Ø	■ ⊼	◇1 A ⊼	■ ⊼	◇1 ⊏		◇1 ⊏			■ ⊼	◇1 ⊏	◇ ⊼
Cardiff Central 7	d	16 45	16 50			16 55	17 00	17 12	17 21			17 25	17 30	17 45	17 50			17 55	18 00	18 12	18 18	18 25	18 30
Newport (South Wales)	a	16 58	17 02			17 08	17 13	17 25	17 34			17 39	17 42	17 58	18 02			18 08	18 13	18 25	18 30	18 39	18 42
	d	17 00				17 09	17 15	17 28				17 39	17 44	18 00				18 09	18 15	18 27		18 39	18 44
Severn Tunnel Jn	d						17 26	17 39					17 55						18 26	18 38			18 55
Caldicot	d							17 41												18 40			
Chepstow	d							17 50						18 18						18 49			
Lydney	d	17 25						17 59												18 58			
Gloucester 7	a	17 44						18 21						18 44						19 20			
Pilning	d																						
Patchway	d						17 39												18 39				
Bristol Parkway 7	a					17 30						17 59						18 30				18 59	
	d				17 20						17 46						18 22						
Filton Abbey Wood	d				17 23		17 41				17 49		18 09				18 25		18 42				19 09
Bristol Temple Meads 10	a				17 36		17 53				18 01		18 17				18 38		18 53				19 17
	d			17 30	17 49					18 00	18 07		18 22			18 30	18 49						19 22
Keynsham	d				17 56						18 14						18 56						
Oldfield Park	d				18 03						18 21						19 03						
Bath Spa 7	a			17 41	18 06					18 11	18 24		18 34			18 41	19 06						19 34

		XC	AW	GW	GW	GW	GW	GW	AW	XC	GW	GW	GW	AW	GW	GW	AW	GW	GW	XC	AW	GW
		◇1	◇ ⊼	◇1 ⊏			◇1 ⊏	◇	◇	◇1	◇1 ⊏			◇	◇1 ⊏	◇	◇	◇1 ⊏		◇1		◇1 ⊏
Cardiff Central 7	d	18 45	18 50			19 00	19 25	19 30	19 34	19 50			20 00	20 17	20 25	20 30	20 53		21 00	21 05	21 12	21 25
Newport (South Wales)	a	18 59	19 03			19 13	19 39	19 42	19 46	20 03			20 13	20 29	20 38	20 44	21 07		21 13	21 18	21 25	21 38
	d	19 01				19 15	19 39	19 44		20 05			20 15		20 39	20 44			21 15	21 21	21 27	21 39
Severn Tunnel Jn	d					19 26				20 15			20 26						21 25		21 38	
Caldicot	d									20 18											21 40	
Chepstow	d	19 18								20 26											21 49	
Lydney	d									20 35											21 58	
Gloucester 7	a	19 45								20 53										22 02	22 21	
Pilning	d																					
Patchway	d					19 39							20 39						21 39			
Bristol Parkway 7	a						19 59								21 01							21 59
	d				19 20																	
Filton Abbey Wood	d				19 23	19 42		20 09					20 42			21 08			21 42			
Bristol Temple Meads 10	a				19 35	19 51		20 17					20 53			21 19			21 51			
	d			19 30	19 49			20 22			20 30	20 49				21 23		21 50	22 00			
Keynsham	d				19 56							20 56							22 07			
Oldfield Park	d				20 03							21 03							22 14			
Bath Spa 7	a			19 41	20 06			20 34			20 41	21 06				21 36		22 01	22 17			

		GW	SW	XC	XC	AW	GW	GW	AW	AW	GW	GW	AW FX	AW FO	GW
			1		◇1	◇	◇1 ⊏		■ B	■ C					
Cardiff Central 7	d	21 30		21 40	21 50	21 55		22 04	22 31	22 31		22 49	23 19	23 20	23 27
Newport (South Wales)	a	21 43		21 55	22 03	22 08		22 16	22 43	22 48		23 06	23 39	23 38	23 44
	d	21 44		21 56	22 05			22 18				23 06	23 40	23 40	23 45
Severn Tunnel Jn	d	21 55						22 35				23 24	23 58	23 58	00 03
Caldicot	d												00 01	00 01	
Chepstow	d												00 10	00 09	
Lydney	d												00 19	00 18	
Gloucester 7	a				22 46								00 39	00 39	
Pilning	d														
Patchway	d							22 48							00 16
Bristol Parkway 7	a														
	d														
Filton Abbey Wood	d	22 09						22 52				23 40			00 20
Bristol Temple Meads 10	a	22 22		22 29				23 05				23 49			00 33
	d		22 25				22 35				23 20				
Keynsham	d										23 27				
Oldfield Park	d										23 34				
Bath Spa 7	a		22 37				22 46				23 37				

A ⊼ from Newport (South Wales)

B 3 August, 10 August

C 25 July, 26 July, 1 August

When events are being held at the Millenium Stadium, services are subject to alteration. Please check times before travelling.

Cardiff - Gloucester, Bristol and Bath Spa

Mondays to Fridays

from 3 September

Network Diagram - see first Page of Table 132

		AW MX	GW MX	AW MX	AW	AW	GW	GW	AW	GW	GW	GW	AW	GW	GW	GW	GW	GW	GW	XC	AW	GW	GW
					◇	◇ ⊼	◇1 ⊏	◇1 ⊏	◇ ⊼	◇	◇1 ⊏	◇1 ⊏		◇1 ⊏	◇1 ⊏	◇1 ⊏		◇1 ⊏	◇ ⊼	◇1	◇ ⊼	◇1 A ⊏	
Cardiff Central 7	d	23p19	23p27	00 30	04 35	05 10	05 14		05 40		05 55		06 12	06 24					06 28	06 40	06 50		
Newport (South Wales)	a	23p39	23p44	00 48	04 50	05 25	05 30		05 55		06 09		06 26	06 37					06 41	06 53	07 02		
	d	23p40	23p45				05 32				06 09		06 28	06 38					06 42	06 55			
Severn Tunnel Jn	d	23p58	00 03										06 38						06 53	07 05			
Caldicot	d	00 01											06 40							07 08			
Chepstow	d	00 10											06 49							07 16			
Lydney	d	00 19											06 58							07 25			
Gloucester 7	a	00 39											07 20							07 44			
Pilning	d																						
Patchway	d		00 16																07 06				
Bristol Parkway 7	a						05 59				06 29			06 58									
	d																						07 25
Filton Abbey Wood	d		00 20																07 09				07 28
Bristol Temple Meads 10	a		00 33																07 17				07 39
	d							05 30		05 44		06 00			06 30	06 40	06 48	07 00	07 22			07 30	07 49
Keynsham	d									05 51							06 55						07 56
Oldfield Park	d									05 58							07 02						08 03
Bath Spa 7	a							05 41		06 01		06 11			06 41	06 51	07 05	07 11	07 34			07 41	08 05

		GW	XC	AW	AW	GW	GW	GW	GW	XC	GW	GW	GW	GW	AW	GW	SW	GW	GW	GW	XC	AW	GW
		◇1 B Ø	◇1		◇ ⊼	◇1 ⊏		◇1 Ø	■ ⊼	◇1 C ⊼	◇1 ⊏	◇	◇1 Ø	◇	◇ ⊼	◇1 Ø	◇1	◇1 ⊏		◇ ⊼	◇1 C ⊼	◇ ⊼	◇1 ⊏
Cardiff Central 7	d	06 55	07 00	07 12	07 21			07 25	07 30	07 45			07 55	08 00	08 05	08 25				08 30	08 45	08 50	
Newport (South Wales)	a	07 09	07 13	07 26	07 34			07 39	07 44	07 59			08 09	08 13	08 17	08 39				08 42	08 59	09 02	
	d	07 09	07 15	07 27				07 39	07 44	08 02			08 09	08 15		08 39				08 44	09 02		
Severn Tunnel Jn	d		07 25	07 38					07 55					08 26						08 55			
Caldicot	d			07 40																			
Chepstow	d			07 49																			
Lydney	d			07 58						08 25													
Gloucester 7	a			08 20						08 44											09 44		
Pilning	d																						
Patchway	d		07 37											08 39									
Bristol Parkway 7	a	07 29						07 59					08 30			08 59							
	d						07 49					08 19											
Filton Abbey Wood	d		07 41				07 53		08 09			08 23		08 42						09 09			
Bristol Temple Meads 10	a		07 51				08 01		08 17			08 36		08 50						09 17			
	d					08 00	08 12		08 22		08 30	08 41					08 51	09 00	09 05	09 22			09 30
Keynsham	d						08 19					08 48					08 58						
Oldfield Park	d						08 26					08 55							09 17				
Bath Spa 7	a					08 11	08 28		08 34		08 41	08 58					09 05	09 11	09 19	09 34			09 41

		GW	GW	GW	AW	AW	GW	GW	GW	XC	GW	GW	GW	GW	AW	AW	GW	GW	GW	XC	AW	GW
		◇	◇1 ⊏	◇		◇ ⊼	◇1 D ⊏	◇1 ⊏	◇ ⊼	◇1 C ⊼	◇1 ⊏		◇1 ⊏		◇ ⊼		◇1 ⊏	◇1 ⊏	◇ ⊼	◇1 C ⊼	◇ ⊼	◇1 ⊏
Cardiff Central 7	d		08 55	09 00	09 12	09 21	09 25		09 30	09 45			09 55	10 00	10 05	10 12	10 25		10 30	10 45	10 50	
Newport (South Wales)	a		09 09	09 13	09 25	09 34	09 39		09 42	09 58			10 08	10 13	10 17	10 25	10 39		10 42	10 58	11 02	
	d		09 09	09 15	09 27		09 39		09 44	10 00			10 09	10 15		10 27	10 39		10 44	11 00		
Severn Tunnel Jn	d			09 26	09 37				09 55					10 26		10 38						
Caldicot	d				09 39											10 40						
Chepstow	d				09 48					10 18						10 49						
Lydney	d				09 57											10 58				11 25		
Gloucester 7	a				10 20					10 44						11 20				11 44		
Pilning	d																					
Patchway	d			09 39										10 39								
Bristol Parkway 7	a		09 30				09 59						10 30				10 59					
	d	09 20										10 22										
Filton Abbey Wood	d	09 23		09 42					10 09			10 25		10 42					11 09			
Bristol Temple Meads 10	a	09 34		09 53					10 18			10 37		10 51					11 18			
	d	09 49						10 00	10 22		10 30	10 49						11 00	11 22			11 30
Keynsham	d	09 56										10 56										
Oldfield Park	d	10 03										11 03										
Bath Spa 7	a	10 05						10 11	10 34		10 41	11 06						11 11	11 34			11 41

A The Bristolian

B The Capitals United

C ⊼ from Newport (South Wales)

D The Red Dragon

When events are being held at the Millenium Stadium, services are subject to alteration. Please check times before travelling.

from 3 September

Cardiff - Gloucester, Bristol and Bath Spa

Network Diagram - see first Page of Table 132

		GW	GW	GW	AW	GW	GW	GW	XC	GW	GW	GW	GW	AW	AW	GW	SW	GW	GW	XC	AW	GW	GW
		◇	◇■		◇	◇■	◇■	◇	◇■ A	◇■	■ B	◇■		◇		◇■ C	◇■	◇■	◇	◇■ A	◇	◇■	
Cardiff Central	d		10 55	11 00	11 21	11 25		11 30	11 45			11 55	12 00	12 05	12 12	12 25			12 30	12 45	12 50		
Newport (South Wales)	a		11 08	11 13	11 34	11 39		11 42	11 59			12 08	12 13	12 17	12 25	12 39			12 42	12 59	13 02		
	d		11 09	11 15		11 39		11 44	12 02			12 09	12 15		12 28	12 39			12 44	13 01			
Severn Tunnel Jn	d			11 26									12 26		12 39								
Caldicot	d														12 42								
Chepstow	d								12 18						12 51					13 18			
Lydney	d														13 00								
Gloucester	a								12 44						13 20					13 44			
Pilning	d																						
Patchway	d			11 39									12 39										
Bristol Parkway	a		11 30			11 59						12 30				12 59							
	d	11 20									12 22												13 20
Filton Abbey Wood	d	11 23		11 42				12 09			12 25		12 42						13 09				13 23
Bristol Temple Meads	a	11 34		11 51				12 18			12 34		12 51						13 18				13 35
	d	11 49					12 00	12 22		12 30	12 39						12 51	13 00	13 22			13 30	13 49
Keynsham	d	11 56									12 46						12 58						13 56
Oldfield Park	d	12 03									12 53												14 03
Bath Spa	a	12 06					12 12	12 34		12 41	12 55						13 05	13 11	13 34			13 41	14 06

		GW	GW	AW	AW	GW	GW	GW	XC	GW	GW	GW	GW	AW	GW	GW	GW	XC	AW	GW	GW	GW
		◇■	◇		◇	◇■	◇■	◇	◇■ A	◇■	◇	◇■		◇	◇■	◇■	◇	◇■ A	◇	◇■		◇■
Cardiff Central	d	12 55	13 00	13 12	13 21	13 25		13 30	13 45			13 55	14 00	14 05	14 25		14 30	14 45	14 50			14 55
Newport (South Wales)	a	13 08	13 13	13 25	13 34	13 39		13 42	13 58			14 08	14 13	14 17	14 39		14 42	14 59	15 02			15 08
	d	13 09	13 15	13 28		13 39		13 44	14 00			14 09	14 15		14 39		14 44	15 01				15 09
Severn Tunnel Jn	d		13 26	13 39									14 26									
Caldicot	d			13 41																		
Chepstow	d			13 50														15 18				
Lydney	d			13 59					14 25													
Gloucester	a			14 20					14 44									15 44				
Pilning	d																					
Patchway	d		13 39										14 39									
Bristol Parkway	a	13 30				13 59						14 30			15 00							15 30
	d										14 22										15 20	
Filton Abbey Wood	d		13 42					14 09			14 25		14 42				15 09				15 23	
Bristol Temple Meads	a		13 51					14 17			14 38		14 51				15 17				15 36	
	d						14 00	14 22		14 30	14 48					15 00	15 22			15 30	15 44	
Keynsham	d										14 55										15 51	
Oldfield Park	d										15 02										15 58	
Bath Spa	a						14 11	14 34		14 41	15 05					15 11	15 34			15 41	15 59	

		GW	AW	AW	SW	GW	GW	GW	GW	XC	AW	GW	GW	GW	GW	AW	AW BHX	GW	GW	GW	GW	GW	XC
				■	◇■	◇■ D		◇■	◇	◇■	■	◇■	◇	◇■		■	■ ■	◇■		◇■		■	◇■
Cardiff Central	d	15 00	15 12	15 21				15 25	15 30	15 45	15 50			15 55	16 00	16 05	16 15			16 25		16 30	16 45
Newport (South Wales)	a	15 13	15 26	15 34				15 39	15 43	15 58	16 02			16 08	16 13	16 18	16 28			16 39		16 42	16 58
	d	15 15	15 28					15 39	15 44	16 00				16 09	16 15	16 21				16 39		16 44	17 00
Severn Tunnel Jn	d	15 26	15 37												16 26	16 32						16 55	
Caldicot	d		15 40													16 34							
Chepstow	d		15 49							16 18						16 43							
Lydney	d		15 58													16 52							17 25
Gloucester	a		16 21							16 44						17 14							17 44
Pilning	d																						
Patchway	d	15 39													16 39								
Bristol Parkway	a							15 59						16 30						16 59			
	d						15 53						16 22						16 46				
Filton Abbey Wood	d	15 42					15 56		16 09				16 25		16 42				16 49		16 55	17 09	
Bristol Temple Meads	a	15 51							16 18				16 37		16 51				17 02		17 03	17 18	
	d				15 51	16 00			16 22			16 30	16 49					17 00	17 07		17 14	17 22	
Keynsham	d				15 58		16 11						16 56						17 14				
Oldfield Park	d						16 18						17 03						17 21		17 26		
Bath Spa	a				16 05	16 11	16 21		16 34			16 41	17 06					17 11	17 24		17 30	17 35	

A from Newport (South Wales)

B from Bristol Temple Meads

C The St. David

D The Merchant Venturer

When events are being held at the Millenium Stadium, services are subject to alteration. Please check times before travelling.

Table 132

Mondays to Fridays

from 3 September

Cardiff - Gloucester, Bristol and Bath Spa

Network Diagram - see first Page of Table 132

		AW	GW	GW	GW	GW	AW	AW	GW	GW	GW	GW	XC	AW	GW	GW	GW	GW	AW	AW BHX	GW	GW	XC
		■	◇■	◇	◇■			■	◇■		◇■	■	◇■ A	■	◇■		◇■			■	◇■	◇	◇■
Cardiff Central	d	16 50			16 55	17 00	17 12	17 21			17 25	17 30	17 45	17 50			17 55	18 00	18 12	18 18	18 25	18 30	18 45
Newport (South Wales)	a	17 02			17 08	17 13	17 25	17 34			17 39	17 42	17 58	18 02			18 08	18 13	18 25	18 30	18 39	18 42	18 59
	d				17 09	17 15	17 28				17 39	17 44	18 00				18 09	18 15	18 27		18 39	18 44	19 01
Severn Tunnel Jn	d					17 26	17 39					17 55						18 26	18 38			18 55	
Caldicot	d						17 41												18 40				
Chepstow	d						17 50						18 18						18 49				19 18
Lydney	d						17 59												18 58				
Gloucester	a						18 21						18 44						19 20				19 45
Pilning	d																						
Patchway	d					17 39												18 39					
Bristol Parkway	a				17 30						17 59						18 30				18 59		
	d			17 20						17 46						18 22							
Filton Abbey Wood	d			17 23		17 43				17 49		18 09				18 25		18 42				19 09	
Bristol Temple Meads	a			17 36		17 53				18 01		18 17				18 38		18 53				19 17	
	d		17 30	17 49					18 00	18 07		18 22			18 30	18 49						19 22	
Keynsham	d			17 56						18 14						18 56							
Oldfield Park	d			18 03						18 21						19 03							
Bath Spa	a		17 41	18 06					18 11	18 24		18 34			18 41	19 06						19 34	

		AW	GW	GW	GW	GW	GW	AW	XC	GW	GW	GW	AW	GW	GW	AW	GW	GW	XC	AW	GW	GW
		◇	◇■			◇■	◇	◇	◇■	◇■			◇	◇■	◇	◇	◇■		◇■		◇■	
Cardiff Central	d	18 50			19 00	19 25	19 30	19 34	19 50			20 00	20 17	20 25	20 30	20 53		21 00	21 05	21 12	21 25	21 30
Newport (South Wales)	a	19 03			19 13	19 39	19 42	19 46	20 03			20 13	20 29	20 38	20 44	21 07		21 13	21 18	21 25	21 38	21 43
	d				19 15	19 39	19 44		20 05			20 15		20 39	20 44			21 15	21 21	21 27	21 39	21 44
Severn Tunnel Jn	d				19 26				20 15			20 26						21 25		21 38		21 55
Caldicot	d								20 18											21 40		
Chepstow	d								20 26											21 49		
Lydney	d								20 35											21 58		
Gloucester	a								20 53										22 02	22 21		
Pilning	d																					
Patchway	d				19 39							20 39						21 39				
Bristol Parkway	a					19 59								21 01							21 59	
	d			19 20																		
Filton Abbey Wood	d			19 23	19 42		20 09					20 42			21 08			21 42				22 09
Bristol Temple Meads	a			19 35	19 51		20 17					20 53			21 19			21 51				22 22
	d		19 30	19 49			20 22			20 30	20 49				21 23		21 50	22 00				
Keynsham	d			19 56							20 56							22 07				
Oldfield Park	d			20 03							21 03							22 14				
Bath Spa	a		19 41	20 06			20 34			20 41	21 06				21 36		22 01	22 17				

		SW	XC	XC	AW	GW	GW	GW	GW	AW FX	AW FO	GW
		■		◇■	◇	◇■						
Cardiff Central	d		21 40	21 50	21 55		22 04		22 49	23 19	23 20	23 27
Newport (South Wales)	a		21 55	22 03	22 08		22 16		23 06	23 39	23 38	23 44
	d		21 56	22 05			22 18		23 06	23 40	23 40	23 45
Severn Tunnel Jn	d						22 35		23 24	23 58	23 58	00 03
Caldicot	d									00 01	00 01	
Chepstow	d									00 10	00 09	
Lydney	d									00 19	00 18	
Gloucester	a			22 46						00 39	00 39	
Pilning	d											
Patchway	d						22 48					00 16
Bristol Parkway	a											
	d											
Filton Abbey Wood	d						22 52		23 40			00 20
Bristol Temple Meads	a		22 29				23 05		23 49			00 33
	d	22 25				22 35		23 20				
Keynsham	d							23 27				
Oldfield Park	d							23 34				
Bath Spa	a	22 37				22 46		23 37				

A from Newport (South Wales)

When events are being held at the Millenium Stadium, services are subject to alteration. Please check times before travelling.

Cardiff - Gloucester, Bristol and Bath Spa

Saturdays until 23 June

Network Diagram - see first Page of Table 132

Station		AW	GW	AW	AW	GW	GW	GW	AW	AW	GW	AW	GW	GW	GW	GW	GW	XC	AW	GW	GW	GW	XC
					◇	◇■	◇	◇■	◇	◇	◇■		◇■	◇■		◇■	◇	◇■	◇	◇■	◇■		◇■
Cardiff Central ■	d	23p20	23p27	00 30	04 35			04 55	05 20	05 40	05 55	06 12	06 25				06 30	06 40	06 50	06 55			07 00
Newport (South Wales)	a	23p38	23p44	00 43	04 50			05 09	05 33	05 55	06 09	06 25	06 38				06 43	06 53	07 02	07 08			07 13
	d	23p40	23p45					05 09			06 09	06 28	06 39				06 44	06 55		07 09			07 15
Severn Tunnel Jn	d	23p58	00 03									06 39					06 55	07 05					07 25
Caldicot	d	00 01										06 41						07 08					
Chepstow	d	00 09										06 50						07 16					
Lydney	d	00 18										06 59						07 25					
Gloucester ■	a	00 39										07 20						07 44					
Pilning	d																						
Patchway	d		00 16																				07 37
Bristol Parkway ■	a							05 36			06 29		06 59							07 29			
	d							05 42															
Filton Abbey Wood	d		00 20														07 09						07 41
Bristol Temple Meads ■	a		00 33					05 53									07 18						07 51
	d					05 30	05 49	06 00						06 30	06 49	07 00	07 22				07 30	07 49	
Keynsham	d						05 56								06 56							07 56	
Oldfield Park	d						06 03								07 03							08 03	
Bath Spa ■	a					05 41	06 05	06 11						06 41	07 05	07 11	07 34				07 41	08 05	

Station		AW	AW	GW	GW	GW	XC	AW	GW	GW	GW	SW	GW	GW	GW	GW	GW	XC	AW	GW	GW	GW	AW
			◇	◇■	◇■	◇	◇■ A	◇	◇■	◇	◇■	◇■		◇■	◇■	◇	◇	◇■ A	◇	◇■	◇		
Cardiff Central ■	d	07 12	07 21	07 25		07 30	07 45	07 50			07 55		08 00	08 25			08 30	08 45	08 50			09 00	09 12
Newport (South Wales)	a	07 25	07 34	07 39		07 42	07 59	08 02			08 08		08 13	08 38			08 42	08 58	09 02			09 13	09 24
	d	07 27		07 39		07 44	08 00				08 09		08 15	08 39			08 44	09 00				09 15	09 26
Severn Tunnel Jn	d	07 38				07 55							08 26				08 55					09 26	09 36
Caldicot	d	07 40																					09 38
Chepstow	d	07 49																					09 48
Lydney	d	07 58					08 26																09 56
Gloucester ■	a	08 21					08 45											09 44					10 19
Pilning	d												08 32										
Patchway	d												08 39									09 39	
Bristol Parkway ■	a			07 59							08 30			08 59									
	d									08 19											09 20		
Filton Abbey Wood	d					08 09				08 23			08 42				09 09				09 23	09 42	
Bristol Temple Meads ■	a					08 18				08 34			08 52				09 18				09 34	09 51	
	d				08 00	08 22			08 30	08 39		08 51			09 00	09 09	09 22			09 30	09 49		
Keynsham	d									08 46		08 58				09 16					09 56		
Oldfield Park	d									08 53						09 24					10 03		
Bath Spa ■	a				08 11	08 34			08 41	08 55		09 05			09 11	09 26	09 34			09 41	10 05		

Station		AW	GW	GW	GW	XC	AW	GW	GW	GW	AW	GW	GW	GW	XC	AW	GW	GW	GW	AW	GW	GW
		◇	◇■	◇■	◇ B	◇■ A	◇	◇■				◇■	◇■	◇ B	◇■ A	◇	◇■	◇		◇	◇■	◇■
Cardiff Central ■	d	09 21	09 25		09 30	09 45	09 55			10 00	10 12	10 25		10 30	10 45	10 55			11 00	11 21	11 25	
Newport (South Wales)	a	09 34	09 39		09 42	09 58	10 07			10 13	10 25	10 39		10 42	10 58	11 07			11 13	11 34	11 39	
	d		09 39		09 44	10 00				10 15	10 27	10 39		10 44	11 00				11 15		11 39	
Severn Tunnel Jn	d				09 55					10 26	10 38								11 26			
Caldicot	d										10 40											
Chepstow	d					10 18					10 49											
Lydney	d										10 58				11 25							
Gloucester ■	a					10 44					11 21				11 44							
Pilning	d																					
Patchway	d									10 39									11 39			
Bristol Parkway ■	a		09 59									10 59									11 59	
	d								10 25									11 20				
Filton Abbey Wood	d				10 09				10 28	10 42				11 09				11 23	11 42			
Bristol Temple Meads ■	a				10 18				10 39	10 51				11 18				11 33	11 51			
	d			10 00	10 22			10 30	10 49				11 00	11 22			11 30	11 49				12 00
Keynsham	d								10 56									11 56				
Oldfield Park	d								11 03									12 03				
Bath Spa ■	a			10 11	10 34			10 41	11 05				11 11	11 34			11 41	12 05				12 11

Station		GW	XC	AW	GW	GW	GW	AW	GW	SW	GW	GW	XC	AW	GW	GW	GW	AW	AW	GW	GW	GW	XC
		◇ B	◇■ A	◇	◇■	■ ◇ C			◇■	◇■	◇■	◇	◇■ A	◇	◇■				◇	◇■	◇■	◇	◇■ A
Cardiff Central ■	d	11 30	11 45	11 55			12 00	12 12	12 25			12 30	12 45	12 55			13 00	13 12	13 21	13 25		13 30	13 45
Newport (South Wales)	a	11 42	11 58	12 07			12 13	12 25	12 39			12 42	12 59	13 07			13 13	13 25	13 34	13 38		13 42	13 58
	d	11 44	12 00				12 15	12 27	12 39			12 44	13 00				13 15	13 27		13 39		13 44	14 00
Severn Tunnel Jn	d						12 26	12 38									13 26	13 39					
Caldicot	d							12 40										13 40					
Chepstow	d		12 18					12 49					13 18					13 49					
Lydney	d							12 58										13 58					14 25
Gloucester ■	a		12 44					13 21					13 44					14 21					14 44
Pilning	d																						
Patchway	d						12 39										13 39						
Bristol Parkway ■	a								12 59											13 59			
	d					12 25										13 20							
Filton Abbey Wood	d	12 09				12 28	12 42					13 09				13 23	13 42					14 09	
Bristol Temple Meads ■	a	12 18				12 39	12 51					13 18				13 34	13 53					14 18	
	d	12 22			12 30	12 43				12 51	13 00	13 22			13 30	13 49					14 00	14 22	
Keynsham	d					12 50				12 58						13 56							
Oldfield Park	d					12 57										14 03							
Bath Spa ■	a	12 34			12 41	13 00				13 05	13 11	13 34			13 41	14 05					14 11	14 34	

A ⌶ from Newport (South Wales)
B ⌶ from Bristol Temple Meads
C ◇ from Bristol Temple Meads ■ to Bristol Temple Meads

When events are being held at the Millenium Stadium, services are subject to alteration. Please check times before travelling.

Cardiff - Gloucester, Bristol and Bath Spa

Saturdays until 23 June

Network Diagram - see first Page of Table 132

Station		AW	GW	GW	GW	GW	GW	GW	XC	AW	GW	GW	GW	AW	AW	GW	SW	GW	GW	XC	AW	GW
		◇	◇■	◇		◇■	◇■	◇	◇■ A	◇	◇■				■	◇■	◇■	◇■	◇	◇■	■	◇■
Cardiff Central ■	d	13 55			14 00	14 25		14 30	14 45	14 55			15 00	15 12	15 21	15 25			15 30	15 45	15 55	
Newport (South Wales)	a	14 07			14 13	14 39		14 42	14 59	15 07			15 13	15 25	15 34	15 39			15 42	15 58	16 07	
	d				14 15	14 39		14 44	15 00				15 15	15 27		15 39			15 44	16 00		
Severn Tunnel Jn	d				14 26								15 26	15 37								
Caldicot	d													15 38								
Chepstow	d								15 18					15 47						16 18		
Lydney	d													15 56								
Gloucester ■	a								15 44					16 19						16 44		
Pilning	d																					
Patchway	d				14 39								15 39									
Bristol Parkway ■	a					14 59										15 59						
	d			14 20								15 19										
Filton Abbey Wood	d			14 25	14 42			15 09				15 22	15 42						16 09			
Bristol Temple Meads ■	a			14 36	14 51			15 18				15 33	15 51						16 18			
	d		14 30	14 49			15 00	15 22			15 30	15 38					15 51	16 00	16 22			16 30
Keynsham	d			14 56								15 45					15 58					
Oldfield Park	d			15 03								15 52										
Bath Spa ■	a		14 41	15 05			15 11	15 34			15 41	15 54					16 05	16 11	16 34			16 41

Station		GW	GW	AW	AW	GW	GW	GW	XC	AW	GW	GW	GW	AW	AW	GW	GW	GW	XC	AW	GW	GW	GW
		◇				◇■	◇■	■	◇■	■	◇■	◇			■	◇■	◇■	◇	◇■ A	■	◇■		
Cardiff Central ■	d		16 00	16 12	16 19	16 25		16 30	16 45	16 55			17 00	17 12	17 21	17 25		17 30	17 45	17 55			18 00
Newport (South Wales)	a		16 13	16 23	16 32	16 39		16 42	16 58	17 07			17 13	17 27	17 33	17 39		17 42	17 58	18 07			18 13
	d		16 15	16 26		16 39		16 44	17 00				17 15	17 27		17 39		17 44	18 00				18 15
Severn Tunnel Jn	d		16 26	16 38				16 55					17 26	17 38				17 55					18 26
Caldicot	d			16 40										17 40									
Chepstow	d			16 49										17 49					18 18				
Lydney	d			16 58					17 25					17 58									
Gloucester ■	a			17 19					17 44					18 20					18 44				
Pilning	d																						
Patchway	d		16 39										17 39										18 39
Bristol Parkway ■	a					16 59										17 59							
	d	16 25										17 20										18 25	
Filton Abbey Wood	d	16 28	16 42					17 09				17 23	17 42					18 09				18 28	18 42
Bristol Temple Meads ■	a	16 39	16 51					17 18				17 34	17 51					18 18				18 39	18 51
	d	16 49					17 00	17 22			17 30	17 49					18 00	18 22			18 30	18 49	
Keynsham	d	16 56										17 56										18 56	
Oldfield Park	d	17 03										18 03										19 03	
Bath Spa ■	a	17 06					17 11	17 34			17 41	18 06					18 11	18 34			18 41	19 05	

Station		AW	GW	GW	XC	AW	GW	GW	GW	GW	GW	AW	GW	GW	XC	AW	GW	GW	GW	XC	AW	GW	GW
			◇■	◇	◇■	◇	◇■			◇■	◇	◇	◇■		◇■	◇	◇■		◇	◇■	◇	◇■	
Cardiff Central ■	d	18 12	18 25	18 30	18 45	18 50			19 00	19 25	19 30	19 34		19 55	20 00	20 10	20 25		20 30	20 50	20 55		21 00
Newport (South Wales)	a	18 25	18 39	18 42	18 59	19 03			19 13	19 39	19 42	19 46		20 08	20 13	20 24	20 39		20 43	21 03	21 08		21 13
	d	18 27	18 39	18 44	19 00				19 15	19 39	19 44			20 10	20 15		20 39		20 44	21 05			21 15
Severn Tunnel Jn	d	18 38							19 26					20 21	20 25								21 26
Caldicot	d	18 40													20 28								
Chepstow	d	18 49			19 18										20 36								
Lydney	d	18 58													20 45								
Gloucester ■	a	19 20			19 44										21 04					21 48			
Pilning	d																						
Patchway	d								19 39					20 34									21 38
Bristol Parkway ■	a		18 59							19 59							21 01						
	d							19 21															
Filton Abbey Wood	d			19 09				19 24	19 42		20 09			20 40					21 08				21 42
Bristol Temple Meads ■	a			19 18				19 36	19 51		20 18			20 48					21 18				21 49
	d			19 22			19 30	19 49			20 22		20 33					20 49	21 22			21 47	
Keynsham	d							19 56										20 56					
Oldfield Park	d							20 03										21 03					
Bath Spa ■	a			19 34			19 41	20 05			20 34		20 44					21 06	21 34			22 01	

Station		AW	GW	SW	XC	AW	GW	GW	GW	AW	AW
				■		◇	◇■				🚌
Cardiff Central ■	d	21 12			21 30	21 49		22 00		23 20	
Newport (South Wales)	a	21 25			21 42	22 05		22 13		23 37	
	d	21 27			21 44			22 16			23 50
Severn Tunnel Jn	d	21 38						22 35			00 15
Caldicot	d	21 40									00 25
Chepstow	d	21 49									00 40
Lydney	d	21 58									01 00
Gloucester ■	a	22 22									01 40
Pilning	d										
Patchway	d							22 48			
Bristol Parkway ■	a										
	d										
Filton Abbey Wood	d							22 52			
Bristol Temple Meads ■	a				22 24			23 00			
	d		22 00	22 23			22 30		23 11		
Keynsham	d		22 07						23 18		
Oldfield Park	d		22 14						23 25		
Bath Spa ■	a		22 17	22 34			22 41		23 27		

A ⌶ from Newport (South Wales)

When events are being held at the Millenium Stadium, services are subject to alteration. Please check times before travelling.

Table 132

Saturdays

30 June to 4 August

Cardiff - Gloucester, Bristol and Bath Spa

Network Diagram - see first Page of Table 132

		AW	GW	AW	AW	AW	GW	GW	GW	AW		AW	GW	AW	GW	GW	GW	GW	GW	XC		AW	GW	GW	GW
				A	◇ B	◇	◇1	◇	◇1	◇		◇	◇1		◇1	◇1		◇1	◇	◇1		◇	◇1	◇1	
Cardiff Central	d	23p20	23p27	00 30	00 30	04 35			04 55	05 20		05 40	05 55	06 12	06 25				06 30	06 40		06 50	06 55		
Newport (South Wales)	a	23p38	23p44	00 43	00 44	04 50			05 09	05 33		05 55	06 09	06 25	06 38				06 43	06 53		07 02	07 08		
	d	23p40	23p45						05 09				06 09	06 28	06 39				06 44	06 55			07 09		
Severn Tunnel Jn	d	23p58	00 03											06 39					06 55	07 05					
Caldicot	d	00 01												06 41						07 08					
Chepstow	d	00 09												06 50						07 16					
Lydney	d	00 18												06 59						07 25					
Gloucester	a	00 39												07 20						07 44					
Pilning	d																								
Patchway	d		00 16																						
Bristol Parkway	a								05 36				06 29		06 59								07 29		
	d								05 42																
Filton Abbey Wood	d		00 20																07 09						
Bristol Temple Meads	a		00 33						05 53										07 18						
	d						05 30	05 49	06 00							06 30	06 49	07 00	07 22					07 30	07 49
Keynsham	d							05 56									06 56								07 56
Oldfield Park	d							06 03									07 03								08 03
Bath Spa	a						05 41	06 05	06 11							06 41	07 05	07 11	07 34					07 41	08 05

		XC	AW	AW	GW	GW		GW	XC	AW	GW	GW	GW	SW	GW	GW		GW	GW	GW	XC	AW	GW	GW	GW
		◇1		◇	◇1	◇1		◇	◇1 C	◇	◇1	◇	◇1	◇1		◇1		◇1	◇	◇	◇1 C	◇	◇1	◇	
Cardiff Central	d	07 00	07 12	07 21	07 25			07 30	07 45	07 50			07 55		08 00	08 25				08 30	08 45	08 50			09 00
Newport (South Wales)	a	07 13	07 25	07 34	07 39			07 42	07 59	08 02			08 08		08 13	08 38				08 42	08 58	09 02			09 13
	d	07 15	07 27		07 39			07 44	08 00				08 09		08 15	08 39				08 44	09 00				09 15
Severn Tunnel Jn	d	07 25	07 38					07 55							08 26					08 55					09 26
Caldicot	d		07 40																						
Chepstow	d		07 49																						
Lydney	d		07 58						08 26																
Gloucester	a		08 21						08 45												09 44				
Pilning	d														08 32										
Patchway	d	07 37													08 39										09 39
Bristol Parkway	a				07 59								08 30			08 59									
	d											08 19												09 20	
Filton Abbey Wood	d	07 41						08 09				08 23			08 42					09 09				09 23	09 42
Bristol Temple Meads	a	07 51						08 18				08 34			08 52					09 18				09 34	09 51
	d					08 00		08 22			08 30	08 39		08 51				09 00	09 09	09 22			09 30	09 49	
Keynsham	d											08 46		08 58					09 16					09 56	
Oldfield Park	d											08 53							09 24					10 03	
Bath Spa	a					08 11		08 34			08 41	08 55		09 05				09 11	09 26	09 34			09 41	10 05	

		AW		AW	GW	GW	GW	XC	AW	GW	GW	GW		AW	GW	GW	GW	XC	AW	GW	GW	GW		AW	GW
				◇	◇1	◇1	◇ D	◇1 C	◇	◇1					◇1	◇1	◇ D	◇1 C	◇	◇1	◇			◇	◇1
Cardiff Central	d	09 12		09 21	09 25		09 30	09 45	09 55			10 00		10 12	10 25		10 30	10 45	10 55			11 00		11 21	11 25
Newport (South Wales)	a	09 24		09 34	09 39		09 42	09 58	10 07			10 13		10 25	10 39		10 42	10 58	11 07			11 13		11 34	11 39
	d	09 26			09 39		09 44	10 00				10 15		10 27	10 39		10 44	11 00				11 15			11 39
Severn Tunnel Jn	d	09 36					09 55					10 26		10 38								11 26			
Caldicot	d	09 38												10 40											
Chepstow	d	09 48						10 18						10 49											
Lydney	d	09 56												10 58				11 25							
Gloucester	a	10 19						10 44						11 21				11 44							
Pilning	d																								
Patchway	d											10 39										11 39			
Bristol Parkway	a				09 59										10 59										11 59
	d										10 25										11 20				
Filton Abbey Wood	d						10 09				10 28	10 42					11 09				11 23	11 42			
Bristol Temple Meads	a						10 18				10 39	10 51					11 18				11 33	11 51			
	d					10 00	10 22			10 30	10 49					11 00	11 22			11 30	11 49				
Keynsham	d										10 56										11 56				
Oldfield Park	d										11 03										12 03				
Bath Spa	a					10 11	10 34			10 41	11 05					11 11	11 34			11 41	12 05				

A not 4 August

B 4 August

C from Newport (South Wales)

D from Bristol Temple Meads

When events are being held at the Millenium Stadium, services are subject to alteration. Please check times before travelling.

Table 132

Saturdays

30 June to 4 August

Cardiff - Gloucester, Bristol and Bath Spa

Network Diagram - see first Page of Table 132

		GW	GW	XC	AW	GW	GW	GW		AW	GW	SW	GW	GW	XC	AW	GW	GW		GW	AW	AW	GW	GW	GW
		◇1	◇ A	◇1 B	◇	◇1	■ ◇ C				◇1	◇1	◇1	◇	◇1 B	◇	◇1					◇	◇1	◇1	◇
Cardiff Central	d		11 30	11 45	11 55			12 00		12 12	12 25			12 30	12 45	12 55				13 00	13 12	13 21	13 25		13 30
Newport (South Wales)	a		11 42	11 58	12 07			12 13		12 25	12 39			12 42	12 59	13 07				13 13	13 25	13 34	13 38		13 42
	d		11 44	12 00				12 15		12 27	12 39			12 44	13 00					13 15	13 27		13 39		13 44
Severn Tunnel Jn	d							12 26		12 38										13 26	13 39				
Caldicot	d									12 40											13 40				
Chepstow	d			12 18						12 49					13 18						13 49				
Lydney	d									12 58											13 58				
Gloucester	a			12 44						13 21					13 44						14 21				
Pilning	d																								
Patchway	d							12 39												13 39					
Bristol Parkway	a										12 59												13 59		
	d						12 25											13 20							
Filton Abbey Wood	d		12 09				12 28	12 42						13 09				13 23		13 42					14 09
Bristol Temple Meads	a		12 18				12 39	12 51						13 18				13 34		13 53					14 18
	d	12 00	12 22			12 30	12 43					12 51	13 00	13 22			13 30	13 49						14 00	14 22
Keynsham	d						12 50					12 58						13 56							
Oldfield Park	d						12 57											14 03							
Bath Spa	a	12 11	12 34			12 41	13 00					13 05	13 11	13 34			13 41	14 05						14 11	14 34

		XC	AW	GW		GW	GW	GW	GW	GW	XC	AW	GW	GW		GW	AW	AW	GW	SW	GW	GW	XC	AW	
		◇1 B	◇	◇1		◇		◇1	◇1	◇	◇1 B	◇	◇1					■	◇1	◇1	◇1	◇	◇1	■	
Cardiff Central	d	13 45	13 55				14 00	14 25		14 30	14 45	14 55				15 00	15 12	15 21	15 25			15 30	15 45	15 55	
Newport (South Wales)	a	13 58	14 07				14 13	14 39		14 42	14 59	15 07				15 13	15 25	15 34	15 39			15 42	15 58	16 07	
	d	14 00					14 15	14 39		14 44	15 00					15 15	15 27		15 39			15 44	16 00		
Severn Tunnel Jn	d						14 26									15 26	15 37								
Caldicot	d																15 38								
Chepstow	d										15 18						15 47						16 18		
Lydney	d	14 25															15 56								
Gloucester	a	14 44									15 44						16 19						16 44		
Pilning	d																								
Patchway	d						14 39									15 39									
Bristol Parkway	a							14 59											15 59						
	d					14 20								15 19											
Filton Abbey Wood	d					14 25	14 42			15 09				15 22		15 42						16 09			
Bristol Temple Meads	a					14 36	14 51			15 18				15 33		15 51						16 18			
	d			14 30		14 49			15 00	15 22			15 30	15 38						15 51	16 00	16 22			
Keynsham	d					14 56								15 45						15 58					
Oldfield Park	d					15 03								15 52											
Bath Spa	a			14 41		15 05			15 11	15 34			15 41	15 54						16 05	16 11	16 34			

		GW	GW	GW	AW	AW	GW	GW	GW	XC		AW	GW	GW	GW	AW	AW	GW	GW	GW		XC	AW	GW	GW
		◇1	◇				◇1	◇1	■	◇1		■	◇1	◇			■	◇1	◇1	◇		◇1 B	■	◇1	
Cardiff Central	d			16 00	16 12	16 19	16 25		16 30	16 45		16 55			17 00	17 12	17 21	17 25		17 30		17 45	17 55		
Newport (South Wales)	a			16 13	16 23	16 32	16 39		16 42	16 58		17 07			17 13	17 27	17 33	17 39		17 42		17 58	18 07		
	d			16 15	16 26		16 39		16 44	17 00					17 15	17 27		17 39		17 44		18 00			
Severn Tunnel Jn	d			16 26	16 38				16 55						17 26	17 38				17 55					
Caldicot	d				16 40											17 40									
Chepstow	d				16 49											17 49						18 18			
Lydney	d				16 58					17 25						17 58									
Gloucester	a				17 19					17 44						18 20						18 44			
Pilning	d																								
Patchway	d			16 39											17 39										
Bristol Parkway	a						16 59											17 59							
	d		16 25											17 20											18 25
Filton Abbey Wood	d		16 28	16 42					17 09					17 23	17 42					18 09					18 28
Bristol Temple Meads	a		16 39	16 51					17 18					17 34	17 51					18 18					18 39
	d	16 30	16 49					17 00	17 22				17 30	17 49					18 00	18 22				18 30	18 49
Keynsham	d		16 56											17 56											18 56
Oldfield Park	d		17 03											18 03											19 03
Bath Spa	a	16 41	17 06					17 11	17 34				17 41	18 06					18 11	18 34				18 41	19 05

A from Bristol Temple Meads

B from Newport (South Wales)

C ◇ from Bristol Temple Meads ■ to Bristol Temple Mead

When events are being held at the Millenium Stadium, services are subject to alteration. Please check times before travelling.

Table 132

Cardiff - Gloucester, Bristol and Bath Spa

Saturdays

30 June to 4 August

Network Diagram - see first Page of Table 132

		GW	AW	GW	GW	XC		AW	GW	GW	GW	GW	GW	AW	GW	GW		XC	AW	GW	GW	GW	XC	AW	GW
				◇1 ⊐	◇	◇1		◇ ⌶	◇1 ⊐			◇1 ⊐	◇	◇	◇1 ⊐			◇1	◇	◇1 ⊐		◇	◇1	◇	◇1 ⊐
Cardiff Central 7	d	18 00	18 12	18 25	18 30	18 45		18 50			19 00	19 25	19 30	19 34		19 55		20 00	20 10	20 25		20 30	20 50	20 55	
Newport (South Wales)	a	18 13	18 25	18 39	18 42	18 59		19 03			19 13	19 39	19 42	19 46		20 08		20 13	20 24	20 39		20 43	21 03	21 08	
	d	18 15	18 27	18 39	18 44	19 00					19 15	19 39	19 44			20 10		20 15		20 39		20 44	21 05		
Severn Tunnel Jn	d	18 26	18 38								19 26					20 21		20 25							
Caldicot	d		18 40															20 28							
Chepstow	d		18 49			19 18												20 36							
Lydney	d		18 58															20 45							
Gloucester 7	a		19 20			19 44												21 04					21 48		
Pilning	d																								
Patchway	d	18 39									19 39					20 34									
Bristol Parkway 7	a			18 59								19 59								21 01					
	d									19 21															
Filton Abbey Wood	d	18 42			19 09					19 24	19 42		20 09			20 40						21 08			
Bristol Temple Meads 10	a	18 51			19 18					19 36	19 51		20 18			20 48						21 18			
	d				19 22				19 30	19 49			20 22		20 33						20 49	21 22			21 47
Keynsham	d									19 56											20 56				
Oldfield Park	d									20 03											21 03				
Bath Spa 7	a				19 34				19 41	20 05			20 34		20 44						21 06	21 34			22 01

		GW		AW	AW BHX	GW	SW	XC	AW	GW	GW	AW		GW	AW
					■ A		1		◇	◇1 ⊐		■ B			
Cardiff Central 7	d	21 00		21 12	21 20			21 30	21 49		22 00	22 20			23 20
Newport (South Wales)	a	21 13		21 25	21 32			21 42	22 05		22 13	22 38			23 36
	d	21 15		21 27				21 44			22 16				23 38
Severn Tunnel Jn	d	21 26		21 38							22 35				23 55
Caldicot	d			21 40											23 58
Chepstow	d			21 49											00 07
Lydney	d			21 58											00 16
Gloucester 7	a			22 22											00 40
Pilning	d														
Patchway	d	21 38									22 48				
Bristol Parkway 7	a														
	d														
Filton Abbey Wood	d	21 42									22 52				
Bristol Temple Meads 10	a	21 49						22 24			23 00				
	d					22 00	22 23			22 30				23 11	
Keynsham	d					22 07								23 18	
Oldfield Park	d					22 14								23 25	
Bath Spa 7	a					22 17	22 34			22 41				23 27	

Saturdays

11 August to 8 September

		AW	GW	AW	AW	AW	GW	GW	GW	AW		AW	GW	AW	GW	GW	GW	GW	GW	XC		AW	GW	GW	GW
				C	◇ D	◇	◇1 ⊐	◇	◇1 ⊐	◇ ⌶		◇ ⌶	◇1 ⊐		◇1 ⊐	◇1 ⊐		◇1 ⊐	◇	◇1		◇ ⌶	◇1 ⊐	◇1 ⊐	
Cardiff Central 7	d	23p20	23p27	00 30	00 30	04 35			04 55	05 20		05 40	05 55	06 12	06 25				06 30	06 40		06 50	06 55		
Newport (South Wales)	a	23p38	23p44	00 43	00 44	04 50			05 09	05 33		05 55	06 09	06 25	06 38				06 43	06 53		07 02	07 08		
	d	23p40	23p45						05 09				06 09	06 28	06 39				06 44	06 55			07 09		
Severn Tunnel Jn	d	23p58	00 03											06 39					06 55	07 05					
Caldicot	d	00 01												06 41						07 08					
Chepstow	d	00 09												06 50						07 16					
Lydney	d	00 18												06 59						07 25					
Gloucester 7	a	00 39												07 20						07 44					
Pilning	d																								
Patchway	d		00 16																						
Bristol Parkway 7	a								05 36				06 29		06 59								07 29		
	d								05 42																
Filton Abbey Wood	d		00 20																07 09						
Bristol Temple Meads 10	a		00 33						05 53										07 18						
	d						05 30	05 49	06 00							06 30	06 49	07 00	07 22					07 30	07 49
Keynsham	d							05 56									06 56								07 56
Oldfield Park	d							06 03									07 03								08 03
Bath Spa 7	a						05 41	06 05	06 11							06 41	07 05	07 11	07 34					07 41	08 05

A 28 July
B 4 August
C not 11 August
D 11 August

When events are being held at the Millenium Stadium, services are subject to alteration. Please check times before travelling.

Table 132

Cardiff - Gloucester, Bristol and Bath Spa

Saturdays

11 August to 8 September

Network Diagram - see first Page of Table 132

		XC	AW	AW	GW	GW		GW	XC	AW	GW	GW	GW	SW	GW	GW		GW	GW	GW	XC	AW	GW	GW	GW
		◇1 ⌶		◇ ⌶	◇1 ⊐	◇1 ⊐		◇	◇1 A ⌶	◇ ⌶	◇1 ⊐	◇	◇1 ∅	◇1		◇1 ∅		◇1 ⊐	◇	◇	◇1 A ⌶	◇ ⌶	◇1 ⊐	◇	
Cardiff Central 7	d	07 00	07 12	07 21	07 25			07 30	07 45	07 50			07 55		08 00	08 25				08 30	08 45	08 50			09 00
Newport (South Wales)	a	07 13	07 25	07 34	07 39			07 42	07 59	08 02			08 08		08 13	08 38				08 42	08 58	09 02			09 13
	d	07 15	07 27		07 39			07 44	08 00				08 09		08 15	08 39				08 44	09 00				09 15
Severn Tunnel Jn	d	07 25	07 38					07 55							08 26					08 55					09 26
Caldicot	d		07 40																						
Chepstow	d		07 49																						
Lydney	d		07 58						08 26																
Gloucester 7	a		08 21						08 45												09 44				
Pilning	d														08 32										
Patchway	d	07 37													08 39										09 39
Bristol Parkway 7	a				07 59								08 30			08 59									
	d											08 19												09 20	
Filton Abbey Wood	d	07 41						08 09				08 23			08 42					09 09				09 23	09 42
Bristol Temple Meads 10	a	07 51						08 18				08 34			08 52					09 18				09 34	09 51
	d					08 00		08 22			08 30	08 39		08 51				09 00	09 09	09 22			09 30	09 49	
Keynsham	d											08 46		08 58					09 16					09 56	
Oldfield Park	d											08 53							09 24					10 03	
Bath Spa 7	a					08 11		08 34			08 41	08 55		09 05				09 11	09 26	09 34			09 41	10 05	

		AW		AW	GW	GW	GW	XC	AW	GW	GW	GW		AW	GW	GW	GW	XC	AW	GW	GW	GW		AW	GW
				◇ ⌶	◇1 ⊐	◇1 ⊐	◇ B ⌶	◇1 A ⌶	◇ ⌶	◇1 ⊐					◇1 ⊐	◇1 ⊐	◇ B ⌶	◇1 A ⌶	◇ ⌶	◇1 ⊐	◇			◇ ⌶	◇1 ⊐
Cardiff Central 7	d	09 12		09 21	09 25		09 30	09 45	09 55			10 00		10 12	10 25		10 30	10 45	10 55			11 00		11 21	11 25
Newport (South Wales)	a	09 24		09 34	09 39		09 42	09 58	10 07			10 13		10 25	10 39		10 42	10 58	11 07			11 13		11 34	11 39
	d	09 26			09 39		09 44	10 00				10 15		10 27	10 39		10 44	11 00				11 15			11 39
Severn Tunnel Jn	d	09 36					09 55					10 26		10 38								11 26			
Caldicot	d	09 38												10 40											
Chepstow	d	09 48						10 18						10 49											
Lydney	d	09 56												10 58				11 25							
Gloucester 7	a	10 19						10 44						11 21				11 44							
Pilning	d																								
Patchway	d											10 39										11 39			
Bristol Parkway 7	a				09 59										10 59										11 59
	d										10 25										11 20				
Filton Abbey Wood	d						10 09				10 28	10 42					11 09				11 23	11 42			
Bristol Temple Meads 10	a						10 18				10 39	10 51					11 18				11 33	11 51			
	d					10 00	10 22			10 30	10 49					11 00	11 22			11 30	11 49				
Keynsham	d										10 56										11 56				
Oldfield Park	d										11 03										12 03				
Bath Spa 7	a					10 11	10 34			10 41	11 05					11 11	11 34			11 41	12 05				

		GW	GW	XC	AW	GW	GW	GW		AW	GW	SW	GW	GW	XC	AW	GW	GW		GW	AW	AW	GW	GW	GW
		◇1 ⊐	◇ B ⌶	◇1 A ⌶	◇ ⌶	◇1 ⊐	■ ◇ C				◇1 ⊐	◇1 ⌶	◇1 ⊐	◇	◇1 A ⌶	◇ ⌶	◇1 ⊐				⌶	◇ ⌶	◇1 ⊐	◇1 ⊐	◇
Cardiff Central 7	d		11 30	11 45	11 55			12 00		12 12	12 25			12 30	12 45	12 55				13 00	13 12	13 21	13 25		13 30
Newport (South Wales)	a		11 42	11 58	12 07			12 13		12 25	12 39			12 42	12 59	13 07				13 13	13 25	13 34	13 38		13 42
	d		11 44	12 00				12 15		12 27	12 39			12 44	13 00					13 15	13 27		13 39		13 44
Severn Tunnel Jn	d							12 26		12 38										13 26	13 39				
Caldicot	d									12 40											13 40				
Chepstow	d			12 18						12 49					13 18						13 49				
Lydney	d									12 58											13 58				
Gloucester 7	a			12 44						13 21					13 44						14 21				
Pilning	d																								
Patchway	d							12 39												13 39					
Bristol Parkway 7	a										12 59												13 59		
	d						12 25											13 20							
Filton Abbey Wood	d		12 09				12 28	12 42						13 09				13 23		13 42					14 09
Bristol Temple Meads 10	a		12 18				12 39	12 51						13 18				13 34		13 53					14 18
	d	12 00	12 22			12 30	12 43					12 51	13 00	13 22			13 30	13 49						14 00	14 22
Keynsham	d						12 50					12 58						13 56							
Oldfield Park	d						12 57											14 03							
Bath Spa 7	a	12 11	12 34			12 41	13 00					13 05	13 11	13 34			13 41	14 05						14 11	14 34

A ⌶ from Newport (South Wales)
B ⌶ from Bristol Temple Meads
C ◇ from Bristol Temple Meads ■ to Bristol Temple Meads

When events are being held at the Millenium Stadium, services are subject to alteration. Please check times before travelling.

Saturdays

11 August to 8 September

Cardiff - Gloucester, Bristol and Bath Spa

Network Diagram - see first Page of Table 132

		XC	AW	GW	GW	GW	GW	GW	GW	XC	AW	GW	GW	GW	AW	AW	GW	SW	GW	GW	XC	AW
		◇■ A ⌶	◇ ⌶	◇■ ⊡	◇		◇■ ⊡	◇■ ⊡	◇	◇■ A ⌶	◇ ⌶	◇■ ⊡				■ ⌶	◇■ ⊡	◇■	◇■ ⊡	◇	◇■	■ ⌶
Cardiff Central ■	d	13 45	13 55			14 00	14 25		14 30	14 45	14 55			15 00	15 12	15 21	15 25			15 30	15 45	15 55
Newport (South Wales)	a	13 58	14 07			14 13	14 39		14 42	14 59	15 07			15 13	15 25	15 34	15 39			15 42	15 58	16 07
	d	14 00				14 15	14 39		14 44	15 00				15 15	15 27		15 39			15 44	16 00	
Severn Tunnel Jn	d					14 26								15 26	15 37							
Caldicot	d														15 38							
Chepstow	d									15 18					15 47						16 18	
Lydney	d	14 25													15 56							
Gloucester ■	a	14 44								15 44					16 19						16 44	
Pilning	d																					
Patchway	d					14 39								15 39								
Bristol Parkway ■	a						14 59										15 59					
	d				14 20								15 19									
Filton Abbey Wood	d				14 25	14 42			15 09				15 22	15 42						16 09		
Bristol Temple Meads ■	a				14 36	14 51			15 18				15 33	15 51						16 18		
	d			14 30	14 49			15 00	15 22			15 30	15 38					15 51	16 00	16 22		
Keynsham	d				14 56								15 45					15 58				
Oldfield Park	d				15 03								15 52									
Bath Spa ■	a			14 41	15 05			15 11	15 34			15 41	15 54					16 05	16 11	16 34		

		GW	GW	GW	AW	AW	GW	GW	GW	XC	AW	GW	GW	GW	AW	AW	GW	GW	GW	XC	AW	GW	GW
		◇■ ⊡	◇				◇■ ⊡	◇■ ⊡	■	◇■	■ ⌶	◇■ ⊡	◇			■	◇■ ⊡	◇■ ⊡	◇	◇■ A ⌶	■ ⌶	◇■ ⊡	
Cardiff Central ■	d			16 00	16 12	16 19	16 25		16 30	16 45	16 55			17 00	17 12	17 21	17 25		17 30	17 45	17 55		
Newport (South Wales)	a			16 13	16 23	16 32	16 39		16 42	16 58	17 07			17 13	17 27	17 33	17 39		17 42	17 58	18 07		
	d			16 15	16 26		16 39		16 44	17 00				17 15	17 27		17 39		17 44	18 00			
Severn Tunnel Jn	d			16 26	16 38				16 55					17 26	17 38				17 55				
Caldicot	d				16 40										17 40								
Chepstow	d				16 49										17 49					18 18			
Lydney	d				16 58					17 25					17 58								
Gloucester ■	a				17 19					17 44					18 20					18 44			
Pilning	d																						
Patchway	d			16 39										17 39									
Bristol Parkway ■	a						16 59										17 59						
	d		16 25										17 20										18 25
Filton Abbey Wood	d		16 28	16 42					17 09				17 23	17 42					18 09				18 28
Bristol Temple Meads ■	a		16 39	16 51					17 18				17 34	17 51					18 18				18 39
	d	16 30	16 49					17 00	17 22			17 30	17 49					18 00	18 22			18 30	18 49
Keynsham	d		16 56										17 56										18 56
Oldfield Park	d		17 03										18 03										19 03
Bath Spa ■	a	16 41	17 06					17 11	17 34			17 41	18 06					18 11	18 34			18 41	19 05

		GW	AW	GW	GW	XC	AW	GW	GW	GW	GW	GW	AW	GW	GW	XC	AW	GW	GW	GW	XC	AW	GW
				◇■ ⊡	◇	◇■	◇ ⌶	◇■ ⊡			◇■ ⊡	◇	◇	◇■ ⊡		◇■	◇	◇■ ⊡		◇	◇■	◇	◇■ ⊡
Cardiff Central ■	d	18 00	18 12	18 25	18 30	18 45	18 50			19 00	19 25	19 30	19 34		19 55	20 00	20 10	20 25		20 30	20 50	20 55	
Newport (South Wales)	a	18 13	18 25	18 39	18 42	18 59	19 03			19 13	19 39	19 42	19 46		20 08	20 13	20 24	20 39		20 43	21 03	21 08	
	d	18 15	18 27	18 39	18 44	19 00				19 15	19 39	19 44			20 10	20 15		20 39		20 44	21 05		
Severn Tunnel Jn	d	18 26	18 38							19 26					20 21	20 25							
Caldicot	d		18 40													20 28							
Chepstow	d		18 49			19 18										20 36							
Lydney	d		18 58													20 45							
Gloucester ■	a		19 20			19 44										21 04					21 48		
Pilning	d																						
Patchway	d	18 39								19 39					20 34								
Bristol Parkway ■	a			18 59							19 59							21 01					
	d								19 21														
Filton Abbey Wood	d	18 42			19 09				19 24	19 42		20 09			20 40					21 08			
Bristol Temple Meads ■	a	18 51			19 18				19 36	19 51		20 18			20 48					21 18			
	d				19 22			19 30	19 49			20 22		20 33					20 49	21 22			21 47
Keynsham	d								19 56										20 56				
Oldfield Park	d								20 03										21 03				
Bath Spa ■	a				19 34			19 41	20 05			20 34		20 44					21 06	21 34			22 01

		GW	AW	GW	SW	XC	AW	GW	GW	GW	AW
					■		◇	◇■ ⊡			
Cardiff Central ■	d	21 00	21 12			21 30	21 49		22 00		23 20
Newport (South Wales)	a	21 13	21 25			21 42	22 05		22 13		23 36
	d	21 15	21 27			21 44			22 16		23 38
Severn Tunnel Jn	d	21 26	21 38						22 35		23 55
Caldicot	d		21 40								23 58
Chepstow	d		21 49								00 07
Lydney	d		21 58								00 16
Gloucester ■	a		22 22								00 40
Pilning	d										
Patchway	d	21 38							22 48		
Bristol Parkway ■	a										
	d										
Filton Abbey Wood	d	21 42							22 52		
Bristol Temple Meads ■	a	21 49				22 24			23 00		
	d			22 00	22 23			22 30		23 11	
Keynsham	d			22 07						23 18	
Oldfield Park	d			22 14						23 25	
Bath Spa ■	a			22 17	22 34			22 41		23 27	

A ⌶ from Newport (South Wales)

When events are being held at the Millenium Stadium, services are subject to alteration. Please check times before travelling.

Saturdays

15 September to 20 October

Cardiff - Gloucester, Bristol and Bath Spa

Network Diagram - see first Page of Table 132

		AW	GW	AW	AW	GW	GW	GW	AW	AW	GW	AW	GW	GW	GW	GW	GW	XC	AW	GW	GW	GW	XC
					◇	◇■ ⊡	◇	◇■ ⊡	◇ ⌶	◇ ⌶	◇■ ⊡		◇■ ⊡	◇■ ⊡		◇■ ⊡	◇	◇■	◇ ⌶	◇■ ⊡	◇■ ⊡		◇■ ⌶
Cardiff Central ■	d	23p20	23p27	00 30	04 35			04 55	05 20	05 40	05 55	06 12	06 25				06 30	06 40	06 50	06 55			07 00
Newport (South Wales)	a	23p38	23p44	00 43	04 50			05 09	05 33	05 55	06 09	06 25	06 38				06 43	06 53	07 02	07 08			07 13
	d	23p40	23p45					05 09			06 09	06 28	06 39				06 44	06 55		07 09			07 15
Severn Tunnel Jn	d	23p58	00 03									06 39					06 55	07 05					07 25
Caldicot	d	00 01										06 41						07 08					
Chepstow	d	00 09										06 50						07 16					
Lydney	d	00 18										06 59						07 25					
Gloucester ■	a	00 39										07 20						07 44					
Pilning	d																						
Patchway	d		00 16																				07 37
Bristol Parkway ■	a							05 36			06 29		06 59							07 29			
	d							05 42															
Filton Abbey Wood	d		00 20														07 09						07 41
Bristol Temple Meads ■	a		00 33					05 53									07 18						07 51
	d					05 30	05 49	06 00						06 30	06 49	07 00	07 22				07 30	07 49	
Keynsham	d						05 56								06 56							07 56	
Oldfield Park	d						06 03								07 03							08 03	
Bath Spa ■	a					05 41	06 05	06 11						06 41	07 05	07 11	07 34				07 41	08 05	

		AW	AW	GW	GW	GW	XC	AW	GW	GW	GW	SW	GW	GW	GW	GW	XC	AW	GW	GW	GW	GW	AW
			◇ ⌶	◇■ ⊡	◇■ ⊡	◇	◇■ A ⌶	◇ ⌶	◇■ ⊡	◇	◇■ ⊘	◇■		◇■ ⊘	◇■ ⊡	◇	◇■ A ⌶	◇ ⌶	◇■ ⊡	◇	◇■ ⊡		
Cardiff Central ■	d	07 12	07 21	07 25		07 30	07 45	07 50			07 55		08 00	08 25		08 30	08 45	08 50			08 55	09 00	09 12
Newport (South Wales)	a	07 25	07 34	07 39		07 42	07 59	08 02			08 08		08 13	08 38		08 42	08 58	09 02			09 08	09 13	09 24
	d	07 27		07 39		07 44	08 00				08 09		08 15	08 39		08 44	09 00				09 09	09 15	09 26
Severn Tunnel Jn	d	07 38				07 55							08 26			08 55						09 26	09 36
Caldicot	d	07 40																					09 38
Chepstow	d	07 49																					09 48
Lydney	d	07 58					08 26																09 56
Gloucester ■	a	08 21					08 45										09 44						10 19
Pilning	d												08 32										
Patchway	d												08 39									09 39	
Bristol Parkway ■	a			07 59							08 30			08 59							09 30		
	d									08 19										09 20			
Filton Abbey Wood	d					08 09				08 23			08 42			09 09				09 23		09 42	
Bristol Temple Meads ■	a					08 18				08 34			08 52			09 18				09 34		09 51	
	d				08 00	08 22			08 30	08 39		08 51			09 00	09 22			09 30	09 49			
Keynsham	d									08 46		08 58								09 56			
Oldfield Park	d									08 53										10 03			
Bath Spa ■	a				08 11	08 34			08 41	08 55		09 05			09 11	09 34			09 41	10 05			

		AW	GW	GW	GW	XC	AW	GW	GW	GW	AW	GW	GW	GW	XC	AW	GW	GW	GW	AW	GW	GW
		◇ ⌶	◇■ ⊡	◇■ ⊡	◇ B ⌶	◇■ A ⌶	◇ ⌶	◇■ ⊡				◇■ ⊡	◇■ ⊡	◇ B ⌶	◇■ A ⌶	◇ ⌶	◇■ ⊡	◇		◇ ⌶	◇■ ⊡	◇■ ⊡
Cardiff Central ■	d	09 21	09 25		09 30	09 45	09 55			10 00	10 12	10 25		10 30	10 45	10 55			11 00	11 21	11 25	
Newport (South Wales)	a	09 34	09 39		09 42	09 58	10 07			10 13	10 25	10 39		10 42	10 58	11 07			11 13	11 34	11 39	
	d		09 39		09 44	10 00				10 15	10 27	10 39		10 44	11 00				11 15		11 39	
Severn Tunnel Jn	d				09 55					10 26	10 38								11 26			
Caldicot	d										10 40											
Chepstow	d					10 18					10 49											
Lydney	d										10 58				11 25							
Gloucester ■	a					10 44					11 21				11 44							
Pilning	d																					
Patchway	d									10 39									11 39			
Bristol Parkway ■	a		09 59									10 59									11 59	
	d								10 25									11 20				
Filton Abbey Wood	d				10 09				10 28	10 42				11 09				11 23	11 42			
Bristol Temple Meads ■	a				10 18				10 39	10 51				11 18				11 33	11 51			
	d			10 00	10 22			10 30	10 49				11 00	11 22			11 30	11 49				12 00
Keynsham	d								10 56									11 56				
Oldfield Park	d								11 03									12 03				
Bath Spa ■	a			10 11	10 34			10 41	11 05				11 11	11 34			11 41	12 05				12 11

		GW	XC	AW	GW	GW	GW	AW	GW	SW	GW	GW	XC	AW	GW	GW	GW	AW	AW	GW	GW	GW	XC
		◇ B ⌶	◇■ A ⌶	◇ ⌶	◇■ ⊡	■ ◇ C			◇■ ⊡	◇■ ⌶	◇■ ⊡	◇	◇■ A ⌶	◇ ⌶	◇■ ⊡			⌶	◇ ⌶	◇■ ⊡	◇■ ⊡	◇	◇■ A ⌶
Cardiff Central ■	d	11 30	11 45	11 55			12 00	12 12	12 25			12 30	12 45	12 55			13 00	13 12	13 21	13 25		13 30	13 45
Newport (South Wales)	a	11 42	11 58	12 07			12 13	12 25	12 39			12 42	12 59	13 07			13 13	13 25	13 34	13 38		13 42	13 58
	d	11 44	12 00				12 15	12 27	12 39			12 44	13 00				13 15	13 27		13 39		13 44	14 00
Severn Tunnel Jn	d						12 26	12 38									13 26	13 39					
Caldicot	d							12 40										13 40					
Chepstow	d		12 18					12 49					13 18					13 49					
Lydney	d							12 58										13 58					14 25
Gloucester ■	a		12 44					13 21					13 44					14 21					14 44
Pilning	d																						
Patchway	d						12 39										13 39						
Bristol Parkway ■	a								12 59											13 59			
	d					12 25										13 20							
Filton Abbey Wood	d	12 09				12 28	12 42					13 09				13 23	13 42					14 09	
Bristol Temple Meads ■	a	12 18				12 39	12 51					13 18				13 34	13 53					14 18	
	d	12 22			12 30	12 43				12 51	13 00	13 22			13 30	13 49					14 00	14 22	
Keynsham	d					12 50				12 58						13 56							
Oldfield Park	d					12 57										14 03							
Bath Spa ■	a	12 34			12 41	13 00				13 05	13 11	13 34			13 41	14 05					14 11	14 34	

A ⌶ from Newport (South Wales)
B ⌶ from Bristol Temple Meads
C ◇ from Bristol Temple Meads ■ to Bristol Temple Meads

When events are being held at the Millenium Stadium, services are subject to alteration. Please check times before travelling.

Table 132

Saturdays
15 September to 20 October

Cardiff - Gloucester, Bristol and Bath Spa

Network Diagram - see first Page of Table 132

		AW	GW	GW	GW	GW	GW	GW	XC	AW	GW	GW	GW	AW	AW	GW	SW	GW	GW	XC	AW	GW
		◇ ╤	◇1 ☕	◇		◇1 ☕	◇1 ☕	◇	◇1 A ╤	◇ ╤	◇1 ☕				■ ╤	◇1 ☕	◇1	◇1 ☕	◇	◇1	■ ╤	◇1 ☕
Cardiff Central ■7	d	13 55			14 00	14 25		14 30	14 45	14 55			15 00	15 12	15 21	15 25			15 30	15 45	15 55	
Newport (South Wales)	a	14 07			14 13	14 39		14 42	14 59	15 07			15 13	15 25	15 34	15 39			15 42	15 58	16 07	
	d				14 15	14 39		14 44	15 00				15 15	15 27		15 39			15 44	16 00		
Severn Tunnel Jn	d				14 26								15 26	15 37								
Caldicot	d													15 38								
Chepstow	d								15 18					15 47						16 18		
Lydney	d													15 56								
Gloucester ■7	a								15 44					16 19						16 44		
Pilning	d																					
Patchway	d				14 39								15 39									
Bristol Parkway ■7	a					14 59										15 59						
	d			14 20								15 19										
Filton Abbey Wood	d			14 25	14 42			15 09				15 22	15 42						16 09			
Bristol Temple Meads ■10	a			14 36	14 51			15 18				15 33	15 51						16 18			
	d		14 30	14 49			15 00	15 22			15 30	15 38					15 51	16 00	16 22			16 30
Keynsham	d			14 56								15 45					15 58					
Oldfield Park	d			15 03								15 52										
Bath Spa ■7	a		14 41	15 05			15 11	15 34			15 41	15 54					16 05	16 11	16 34			16 41

		GW	GW	AW	AW	GW	GW	GW	XC	AW	GW	GW	GW	AW	AW	GW	GW	GW	XC	AW	GW	GW	GW
		◇				◇1 ☕	◇1 ☕	■	◇1	■ ╤	◇1 ☕	◇			■	◇1 ☕	◇1 ☕	◇	◇1 A ╤	■ ╤	◇1 ☕		
Cardiff Central ■7	d		16 00	16 12	16 19	16 25		16 30	16 45	16 55			17 00	17 12	17 21	17 25		17 30	17 45	17 55			18 00
Newport (South Wales)	a		16 13	16 23	16 32	16 39		16 42	16 58	17 07			17 13	17 27	17 33	17 39		17 42	17 58	18 07			18 13
	d		16 15	16 26		16 39		16 44	17 00				17 15	17 27		17 39		17 44	18 00				18 15
Severn Tunnel Jn	d		16 26	16 38				16 55					17 26	17 38				17 55					18 26
Caldicot	d			16 40										17 40									
Chepstow	d			16 49										17 49					18 18				
Lydney	d			16 58					17 25					17 58									
Gloucester ■7	a			17 19					17 44					18 20					18 44				
Pilning	d																						
Patchway	d		16 39										17 39										18 39
Bristol Parkway ■7	a					16 59										17 59							
	d	16 25										17 20										18 25	
Filton Abbey Wood	d	16 28	16 42					17 09				17 23	17 42					18 09				18 28	18 42
Bristol Temple Meads ■10	a	16 39	16 51					17 18				17 34	17 51					18 18				18 39	18 51
	d	16 49					17 00	17 22			17 30	17 49					18 00	18 22			18 30	18 49	
Keynsham	d	16 56										17 56										18 56	
Oldfield Park	d	17 03										18 03										19 03	
Bath Spa ■7	a	17 06					17 11	17 34			17 41	18 06					18 11	18 34			18 41	19 05	

		AW	GW	GW	XC	AW	GW	GW	GW	GW	GW	AW	GW	GW	XC	AW	GW	GW	GW	XC	AW	GW	GW
			◇1 ☕	◇	◇1	◇ ╤	◇1 ☕			◇1 ☕	◇	◇	◇1 ☕		◇1	◇	◇1 ☕		◇	◇1	◇	◇1 ☕	
Cardiff Central ■7	d	18 12	18 25	18 30	18 45	18 50			19 00	19 25	19 30	19 34		19 55	20 00	20 10	20 25		20 30	20 50	20 55		21 00
Newport (South Wales)	a	18 25	18 39	18 42	18 59	19 03			19 13	19 39	19 42	19 46		20 08	20 13	20 24	20 39		20 43	21 03	21 08		21 13
	d	18 27	18 39	18 44	19 00				19 15	19 39	19 44			20 10	20 15		20 39		20 44	21 05			21 15
Severn Tunnel Jn	d	18 38							19 26					20 21	20 25								21 26
Caldicot	d	18 40													20 28								
Chepstow	d	18 49			19 18										20 36								
Lydney	d	18 58													20 45								
Gloucester ■7	a	19 20			19 44										21 04					21 48			
Pilning	d																						
Patchway	d								19 39					20 34									21 38
Bristol Parkway ■7	a		18 59							19 59							21 01						
	d							19 21															
Filton Abbey Wood	d			19 09				19 24	19 42		20 09			20 40					21 09				21 42
Bristol Temple Meads ■10	a			19 18				19 36	19 51		20 18			20 48					21 18				21 49
	d			19 22			19 30	19 49			20 22		20 33					20 49	21 22			21 47	
Keynsham	d							19 56										20 56					
Oldfield Park	d							20 03										21 03					
Bath Spa ■7	a			19 34			19 41	20 05			20 34		20 44					21 06	21 34			22 01	

		AW	GW	SW	XC	AW	GW	GW	GW	AW	AW
				■1		◇	◇1 ☕				🚌
Cardiff Central ■7	d	21 12			21 30	21 49		22 00		23 20	
Newport (South Wales)	a	21 25			21 42	22 05		22 13		23 37	
	d	21 27			21 44			22 16			23 50
Severn Tunnel Jn	d	21 38						22 35			00 15
Caldicot	d	21 40									00 25
Chepstow	d	21 49									00 40
Lydney	d	21 58									01 00
Gloucester ■7	a	22 22									01 40
Pilning	d										
Patchway	d							22 48			
Bristol Parkway ■7	a										
	d										
Filton Abbey Wood	d							22 52			
Bristol Temple Meads ■10	a				22 24			23 00			
	d		22 00	22 23			22 30		23 11		
Keynsham	d		22 07						23 18		
Oldfield Park	d		22 14						23 25		
Bath Spa ■7	a		22 17	22 34			22 41		23 27		

A ╤ from Newport (South Wales)

When events are being held at the Millenium Stadium, services are subject to alteration. Please check times before travelling.

Table 132

Saturdays
from 27 October

Cardiff - Gloucester, Bristol and Bath Spa

Network Diagram - see first Page of Table 132

		AW	GW	AW	AW	GW	GW	GW	AW	AW	GW	AW	GW	GW	GW	GW	GW	XC	AW	GW	GW	GW	XC
					◇	◇1 ☕	◇	◇1 ☕	◇ ╤	◇ ╤	◇1 ☕		◇1 ☕	◇1 ☕		◇1 ☕	◇	◇1	◇ ╤	◇1 ☕	◇1 ☕		◇1 ╤
Cardiff Central ■7	d	23p20	23p27	00 30	04 35			04 55	05 20	05 40	05 55	06 12	06 25				06 30	06 40	06 50	06 55			07 00
Newport (South Wales)	a	23p38	23p44	00 43	04 50			05 09	05 33	05 55	06 09	06 25	06 38				06 43	06 53	07 02	07 08			07 13
	d	23p40	23p45					05 09			06 09	06 28	06 39				06 44	06 55		07 09			07 15
Severn Tunnel Jn	d	23p58	00 03									06 39					06 55	07 05					07 25
Caldicot	d	00 01										06 41						07 08					
Chepstow	d	00 09										06 50						07 16					
Lydney	d	00 18										06 59						07 25					
Gloucester ■7	a	00 39										07 20						07 44					
Pilning	d																						
Patchway	d		00 16																				07 37
Bristol Parkway ■7	a							05 36			06 29		06 59							07 29			
	d							05 42															
Filton Abbey Wood	d		00 20														07 09						07 41
Bristol Temple Meads ■10	a		00 33					05 53									07 18						07 51
	d					05 30	05 49	06 00						06 30	06 49	07 00	07 22				07 30	07 49	
Keynsham	d						05 56								06 56							07 56	
Oldfield Park	d						06 03								07 03							08 03	
Bath Spa ■7	a					05 41	06 05	06 11						06 41	07 05	07 11	07 34				07 41	08 05	

		AW	AW	GW	GW	GW	XC	AW	GW	GW	GW	SW	GW	GW	GW	GW	XC	AW	GW	GW	GW	GW	AW
			◇ ╤	◇1 ☕	◇1 ☕	◇	◇1 A ╤	◇ ╤	◇1 ☕	◇	◇1 ⊘	◇1		◇1 ⊘	◇1 ☕	◇	◇1 A ╤	◇ ╤	◇1 ☕	◇	◇1 ☕		
Cardiff Central ■7	d	07 12	07 21	07 25		07 30	07 45	07 50			07 55		08 00	08 25		08 30	08 45	08 50			08 55	09 00	09 12
Newport (South Wales)	a	07 25	07 34	07 39		07 42	07 59	08 02			08 08		08 13	08 38		08 42	08 58	09 02			09 08	09 13	09 24
	d	07 27		07 39		07 44	08 00				08 09		08 15	08 39		08 44	09 00				09 09	09 15	09 26
Severn Tunnel Jn	d	07 38				07 55							08 26			08 55						09 26	09 36
Caldicot	d	07 40																					09 38
Chepstow	d	07 49																					09 48
Lydney	d	07 58					08 26																09 56
Gloucester ■7	a	08 21					08 45										09 44						10 19
Pilning	d												08 32										
Patchway	d												08 39									09 39	
Bristol Parkway ■7	a			07 59							08 30			08 59							09 30		
	d									08 19										09 20			
Filton Abbey Wood	d					08 09				08 23			08 42			09 09				09 23		09 42	
Bristol Temple Meads ■10	a					08 18				08 34			08 52			09 18				09 34		09 51	
	d				08 00	08 22			08 30	08 39		08 51			09 00	09 22			09 30	09 49			
Keynsham	d									08 46		08 58								09 56			
Oldfield Park	d									08 53										10 03			
Bath Spa ■7	a				08 11	08 34			08 41	08 55		09 05			09 11	09 34			09 41	10 05			

		AW	GW	GW	GW	XC	AW	GW	GW	GW	AW	GW	GW	GW	XC	AW	GW	GW	GW	AW	GW	GW
		◇ ╤	◇1 ☕	◇1 ☕	◇ B ╤	◇1 A ╤	◇ ╤	◇1 ☕				◇1 ☕	◇1 ☕	◇ B ╤	◇1 A ╤	◇ ╤	◇1 ☕	◇		◇ ╤	◇1 ☕	◇1 ☕
Cardiff Central ■7	d	09 21	09 25		09 30	09 45	09 55			10 00	10 12	10 25		10 30	10 45	10 55			11 00	11 21	11 25	
Newport (South Wales)	a	09 34	09 39		09 42	09 58	10 07			10 13	10 25	10 39		10 42	10 58	11 07			11 13	11 34	11 39	
	d		09 39		09 44	10 00				10 15	10 27	10 39		10 44	11 00				11 15		11 39	
Severn Tunnel Jn	d				09 55					10 26	10 38								11 26			
Caldicot	d										10 40											
Chepstow	d					10 18					10 49											
Lydney	d										10 58				11 25							
Gloucester ■7	a					10 44					11 21				11 44							
Pilning	d																					
Patchway	d									10 39									11 39			
Bristol Parkway ■7	a		09 59									10 59									11 59	
	d								10 25									11 20				
Filton Abbey Wood	d				10 09				10 28	10 42				11 09				11 23	11 42			
Bristol Temple Meads ■10	a				10 18				10 39	10 51				11 18				11 33	11 51			
	d			10 00	10 22			10 30	10 49				11 00	11 22			11 30	11 49				12 00
Keynsham	d								10 56									11 56				
Oldfield Park	d								11 03									12 03				
Bath Spa ■7	a			10 11	10 34			10 41	11 05				11 11	11 34			11 41	12 05				12 11

		GW	XC	AW	GW	GW	GW	AW	GW	SW	GW	GW	XC	AW	GW	GW	GW	AW	AW	GW	GW	GW	XC
		◇ B ╤	◇1 A ╤	◇ ╤	◇1 ☕	■ ◇ C			◇1 ☕	◇1 ╤	◇1 ☕	◇	◇1 A ╤	◇ ╤	◇1 ☕			╤	◇ ╤	◇1 ☕	◇1 ☕	◇	◇1 A ╤
Cardiff Central ■7	d	11 30	11 45	11 55			12 00	12 12	12 25			12 30	12 45	12 55			13 00	13 12	13 21	13 25		13 30	13 45
Newport (South Wales)	a	11 42	11 58	12 07			12 13	12 25	12 39			12 42	12 59	13 07			13 13	13 25	13 34	13 38		13 42	13 58
	d	11 44	12 00				12 15	12 27	12 39			12 44	13 00				13 15	13 27		13 39		13 44	14 00
Severn Tunnel Jn	d						12 26	12 38									13 26	13 39					
Caldicot	d							12 40										13 40					
Chepstow	d		12 18					12 49					13 18					13 49					
Lydney	d							12 58										13 58					14 25
Gloucester ■7	a		12 44					13 21					13 44					14 21					14 44
Pilning	d																						
Patchway	d						12 39										13 39						
Bristol Parkway ■7	a								12 59											13 59			
	d					12 25										13 20							
Filton Abbey Wood	d	12 09				12 28	12 42					13 09				13 23	13 42					14 09	
Bristol Temple Meads ■10	a	12 18				12 39	12 51					13 18				13 34	13 53					14 18	
	d	12 22			12 30	12 43				12 51	13 00	13 22			13 30	13 49					14 00	14 22	
Keynsham	d					12 50				12 58						13 56							
Oldfield Park	d					12 57										14 03							
Bath Spa ■7	a	12 34			12 41	13 00				13 05	13 11	13 34			13 41	14 05					14 11	14 34	

A ╤ from Newport (South Wales)
B ╤ from Bristol Temple Meads
C ◇ from Bristol Temple Meads ■ to Bristol Temple Meads

When events are being held at the Millenium Stadium, services are subject to alteration. Please check times before travelling.

Table 132

Saturdays from 27 October

Cardiff - Gloucester, Bristol and Bath Spa

Network Diagram - see first Page of Table 132

		AW	GW	GW	GW	GW	GW	GW	XC	AW	GW	GW	GW	AW	AW	GW	SW	GW	GW	XC	AW	GW
		◇ ⌶	◇■ ☕	◇		◇■ ☕	◇■ ☕	◇	◇■ A ⌶	◇ ⌶	◇■ ☕				■ ⌶	◇■ ☕	◇■	◇■ ☕	◇	◇■	■ ⌶	◇■ ☕
Cardiff Central	d	13 55			14 00	14 25		14 30	14 45	14 55			15 00	15 12	15 21	15 25			15 30	15 45	15 55	
Newport (South Wales)	a	14 07			14 13	14 39		14 42	14 59	15 07			15 13	15 25	15 34	15 39			15 42	15 58	16 07	
	d				14 15	14 39		14 44	15 00				15 15	15 27		15 39			15 44	16 00		
Severn Tunnel Jn	d				14 26								15 26	15 37								
Caldicot	d													15 38								
Chepstow	d								15 18					15 47						16 18		
Lydney	d													15 56								
Gloucester	a								15 44					16 19						16 44		
Pilning	d																					
Patchway	d				14 39								15 39									
Bristol Parkway	a					14 59										15 59						
	d			14 20								15 19										
Filton Abbey Wood	d			14 25	14 42			15 09				15 22	15 42						16 09			
Bristol Temple Meads	a			14 36	14 51			15 18				15 33	15 51						16 18			
	d		14 30	14 49			15 00	15 22			15 30	15 38					15 51	16 00	16 22			16 30
Keynsham	d			14 56								15 45					15 58					
Oldfield Park	d			15 03								15 52										
Bath Spa	a		14 41	15 05			15 11	15 34			15 41	15 54					16 05	16 11	16 34			16 41

		GW	GW	AW	AW	GW	GW	GW	XC	AW	GW	GW	GW	AW	AW	GW	GW	GW	XC	AW	GW	GW	GW
		◇				◇■ ☕	◇■ ☕	■	◇■	■ ⌶	◇■ ☕	◇			■	◇■ ☕	◇■ ☕	◇	◇■ A ⌶	■ ⌶	◇■ ☕		
Cardiff Central	d		16 00	16 12	16 19	16 25		16 30	16 45	16 55			17 00	17 12	17 21	17 25		17 30	17 45	17 55			18 00
Newport (South Wales)	a		16 13	16 23	16 32	16 39		16 42	16 58	17 07			17 13	17 27	17 33	17 39		17 42	17 58	18 07			18 13
	d		16 15	16 26		16 39		16 44	17 00				17 15	17 27		17 39		17 44	18 00				18 15
Severn Tunnel Jn	d		16 26	16 38				16 55					17 26	17 38				17 55					18 26
Caldicot	d			16 40										17 40									
Chepstow	d			16 49										17 49					18 18				
Lydney	d			16 58					17 25					17 58									
Gloucester	a			17 19					17 44					18 20					18 44				
Pilning	d																						
Patchway	d		16 39										17 39										18 39
Bristol Parkway	a					16 59										17 59							
	d	16 25										17 20										18 25	
Filton Abbey Wood	d	16 28	16 42					17 09				17 23	17 42					18 09				18 28	18 42
Bristol Temple Meads	a	16 39	16 51					17 18				17 34	17 51					18 18				18 39	18 51
	d	16 49					17 00	17 22			17 30	17 49					18 00	18 22			18 30	18 49	
Keynsham	d	16 56										17 56										18 56	
Oldfield Park	d	17 03										18 03										19 03	
Bath Spa	a	17 06					17 11	17 34			17 41	18 06					18 11	18 34			18 41	19 05	

		AW	GW	GW	XC	AW	GW	GW	GW	GW	GW	AW	GW	GW	XC	AW	GW	GW	GW	XC	AW	GW	GW
			◇■ ☕	◇	◇■	◇ ⌶	◇■ ☕			◇■ ☕	◇	◇	◇■ ☕		◇■	◇	◇■ ☕		◇	◇■	◇	◇■ ☕	
Cardiff Central	d	18 12	18 25	18 30	18 45	18 50			19 00	19 25	19 30	19 34		19 55	20 00	20 10	20 25		20 30	20 50	20 55		21 00
Newport (South Wales)	a	18 25	18 39	18 42	18 59	19 03			19 13	19 39	19 42	19 46		20 08	20 13	20 24	20 39		20 43	21 03	21 08		21 13
	d	18 27	18 39	18 44	19 00				19 15	19 39	19 44			20 10	20 15		20 39		20 44	21 05			21 15
Severn Tunnel Jn	d	18 38							19 26					20 21	20 25								21 26
Caldicot	d	18 40													20 28								
Chepstow	d	18 49			19 18										20 36								
Lydney	d	18 58													20 45								
Gloucester	a	19 20			19 44										21 04					21 48			
Pilning	d																						
Patchway	d								19 39					20 34									21 38
Bristol Parkway	a		18 59							19 59							21 01						
	d							19 21															
Filton Abbey Wood	d			19 09				19 24	19 42		20 09			20 40					21 09				21 42
Bristol Temple Meads	a			19 18				19 36	19 51		20 18			20 48					21 18				21 49
	d			19 22			19 30	19 49			20 22		20 33					20 49	21 22			21 47	
Keynsham	d							19 56										20 56					
Oldfield Park	d							20 03										21 03					
Bath Spa	a			19 34			19 41	20 05			20 34		20 44					21 06	21 34			22 01	

		AW	GW	SW	XC	AW	GW	GW	GW	AW
				■		◇	◇■ ☕			
Cardiff Central	d	21 12			21 30	21 49		22 00		23 20
Newport (South Wales)	a	21 25			21 42	22 05		22 13		23 36
	d	21 27			21 44			22 16		23 38
Severn Tunnel Jn	d	21 38						22 35		23 55
Caldicot	d	21 40								23 58
Chepstow	d	21 49								00 07
Lydney	d	21 58								00 16
Gloucester	a	22 22								00 40
Pilning	d									
Patchway	d							22 48		
Bristol Parkway	a									
	d									
Filton Abbey Wood	d							22 52		
Bristol Temple Meads	a				22 24			23 00		
	d		22 00	22 23			22 30		23 11	
Keynsham	d		22 07						23 18	
Oldfield Park	d		22 14						23 25	
Bath Spa	a		22 17	22 34			22 41		23 27	

A ⌶ from Newport (South Wales)

When events are being held at the Millenium Stadium, services are subject to alteration. Please check times before travelling.

Table 132

Sundays until 24 June

Cardiff - Gloucester, Bristol and Bath Spa

Network Diagram - see first Page of Table 132

		AW	GW	GW	GW	GW	GW	AW	GW	GW	GW	GW	AW	GW	GW	GW	AW	AW	XC	GW	GW	GW	GW
		🚌	◇■ ☕	◇■ ☕	◇■ ☕	◇■ ☕	◇	◇ ⌶	◇■ ☕		◇■ ☕	◇	◇ ⌶	◇■ ☕	◇	◇■ ☕		◇ ⌶	◇■ A ⌶	◇■ ☕	◇■ ☕	■ ◇ B ⌶	◇■ ☕
Cardiff Central	d			07 55			08 05	08 30	09 05			09 15	09 30		10 08	10 15	10 23	10 35	10 45			11 08	11 15
Newport (South Wales)	a			08 11			08 21	08 47	09 18			09 27	09 48		10 20	10 31	10 36	10 48	10 57			11 20	11 31
	d	23p50		08 13			08 23		09 19			09 29			10 22	10 32	10 38		10 59			11 22	11 32
Severn Tunnel Jn	d	00 15					08 40					09 46			10 39		10 56					11 39	
Caldicot	d	00 25															10 58						
Chepstow	d	00 40															11 07						
Lydney	d	01 00															11 16						
Gloucester	a	01 40															11 42		11 49				
Pilning	d																						
Patchway	d											09 59											
Bristol Parkway	a			08 42					09 46							10 59							11 59
	d																						
Filton Abbey Wood	d						08 55					10 03			10 54							11 54	
Bristol Temple Meads	a						09 05					10 13			11 03							12 04	
	d		07 45		08 15	08 45	09 10			09 20	09 48	10 15		10 30	11 10					11 30	12 00	12 15	
Keynsham	d						09 17			09 27					11 17								
Oldfield Park	d						09 24			09 35					11 24								
Bath Spa	a		07 57		08 26	08 57	09 26			09 37	09 58	10 29		10 41	11 26					11 41	12 11	12 27	

		AW	XC	GW	GW	GW	AW	AW	XC	GW	GW	GW	AW	AW	XC	GW	GW	GW	AW	XC	AW	GW	GW
		◇ ⌶	◇■ A ⌶	◇■ ☕	◇	◇■ ☕		◇ ⌶	◇■ A ⌶	◇■ ☕	◇	◇■ ☕	■	■ ⌶	◇■ A ⌶	◇■ ☕	◇	◇■ ☕		◇■ A ⌶	■ ⌶	◇■ ☕	◇■ ☕
Cardiff Central	d	11 35	11 45		12 08	12 15	12 23	12 40	12 45		13 08	13 15	13 22	13 40	13 45		14 08	14 15	14 23	14 45	14 56		
Newport (South Wales)	a	11 49	11 57		12 20	12 31	12 36	12 52	12 57		13 20	13 31	13 35	13 52	13 57		14 20	14 31	14 36	14 57	15 12		
	d		11 59		12 22	12 32	12 38		12 59		13 22	13 32			13 59		14 22	14 32	14 38	14 59			
Severn Tunnel Jn	d				12 39		12 56				13 39						14 39		14 56				
Caldicot	d						12 58												14 58				
Chepstow	d						13 07												15 07				
Lydney	d						13 16												15 16				
Gloucester	a		12 46				13 34		13 47						14 46				15 37	15 46			
Pilning	d																						
Patchway	d				12 52																		
Bristol Parkway	a					12 59						13 59						14 59					
	d																						
Filton Abbey Wood	d				12 57						13 54						14 55						
Bristol Temple Meads	a				13 05						14 04						15 04						
	d			12 30	13 10					13 30	14 15					14 30	15 10					15 30	16 00
Keynsham	d				13 17												15 17						
Oldfield Park	d				13 24												15 24						
Bath Spa	a			12 41	13 26					13 41	14 27					14 41	15 27					15 41	16 11

		SW	GW	GW	AW	XC	AW	GW	GW	GW	GW	AW	GW	GW	AW	XC	GW	GW	GW	AW	GW	AW
		◇■	◇	◇■ ☕	■ ⌶	◇■	■ ⌶	◇■ ☕	◇■ ☕	◇	◇■ ☕		◇■ ☕	◇	■ ⌶	◇■	◇	◇■ ☕	◇		◇■ ☕	■
Cardiff Central	d		15 08	15 15	15 22	15 45	15 56			16 08	16 15	16 23		16 35	16 40	16 45			17 08	17 05	17 15	17 35
Newport (South Wales)	a		15 20	15 31	15 35	15 57	16 12			16 20	16 31	16 36		16 47	16 52	16 57			17 20	17 24	17 29	17 48
	d		15 22	15 32		15 59				16 22	16 32	16 38		16 49		16 59			17 22		17 30	
Severn Tunnel Jn	d		15 39							16 39		16 56							17 39			
Caldicot	d											16 58										
Chepstow	d											17 07										
Lydney	d											17 16										
Gloucester	a					16 46						17 37				17 46						
Pilning	d																					
Patchway	d		15 52																			
Bristol Parkway	a			15 59							16 59										17 59	
	d																					
Filton Abbey Wood	d		15 55							16 55				17 20					17 54			
Bristol Temple Meads	a		16 04							17 06				17 29					18 04			
	d	16 04	16 15					16 30	17 00	17 15			17 30	17 40			17 44	18 00	18 10			
Keynsham	d	16 11								17 22							17 51		18 17			
Oldfield Park	d									17 29							17 58		18 24			
Bath Spa	a	16 18	16 27					16 41	17 11	17 30			17 42	17 52			18 00	18 12	18 26			

A ⌶ from Newport (South Wales)

B ⌶ from Bristol Temple Meads ◇ from Bristol Temple Meads ■ to Bristol Temple Meads

When events are being held at the Millenium Stadium, services are subject to alteration. Please check times before travelling.

Table 132

Cardiff - Gloucester, Bristol and Bath Spa

Sundays until 24 June

Network Diagram - see first Page of Table 132

		GW	GW	XC	GW	GW	GW	AW		AW	XC	GW	GW	GW	AW	XC	GW	GW		GW	GW	AW	XC	GW	AW
		◇■ ☕	■	◇■	◇■ ☕	◇■ ☕	◇			■ ⌶	◇■	◇■ ☕	◇■ ☕	◇	◇	◇■	◇■ ☕			◇■ ☕	◇		◇■	◇■ ☕	◇
Cardiff Central	d		17 40	17 45	17 50		18 08	18 23		18 40	18 45	18 50		19 08	19 40	19 45	19 50				20 18	20 23	20 45	20 55	21 04
Newport (South Wales)	a		17 52	17 57	18 03		18 20	18 36		18 52	18 57	19 03		19 20	19 53	19 58	20 03				20 30	20 36	20 57	21 08	21 17
	d		17 54	17 59	18 04		18 22	18 38			18 59	19 04		19 22		20 00	20 04				20 31	20 38	20 59	21 09	
Severn Tunnel Jn	d						18 39	18 56						19 40							20 48	20 56			
Caldicot	d							18 58														20 58			
Chepstow	d							19 07														21 07			
Lydney	d							19 16														21 16			
Gloucester	a			18 46				19 38			19 47					20 49						21 41	21 47		
Pilning	d																								
Patchway	d						18 52																		
Bristol Parkway	a				18 31							19 31					20 31							21 36	
	d																								
Filton Abbey Wood	d		18 23				18 56							19 55							21 05				
Bristol Temple Meads	a		18 33				19 06							20 05							21 13				
	d	18 30	18 50			19 00	19 10						20 00	20 15				20 50		21 00	21 25				
Keynsham	d						19 17											20 57							
Oldfield Park	d						19 24											21 04							
Bath Spa	a	18 41	19 02			19 11	19 26						20 11	20 27				21 06		21 12	21 37				

		SW	GW	GW		GW	AW	AW
		■	◇■ ☕			⌶		◇
Cardiff Central	d					22 00	22 30	23 00
Newport (South Wales)	a					22 17	22 47	23 18
	d					22 19	22 49	
Severn Tunnel Jn	d					22 36	23 06	
Caldicot	d						23 09	
Chepstow	d						23 18	
Lydney	d						23 27	
Gloucester	a						23 51	
Pilning	d							
Patchway	d					22 49		
Bristol Parkway	a							
	d							
Filton Abbey Wood	d					22 53		
Bristol Temple Meads	a					22 59		
	d	21 35	22 10	22 15		23 10		
Keynsham	d			22 22				
Oldfield Park	d			22 29				
Bath Spa	a	21 47	22 22	22 31		23 22		

Sundays 1 July to 9 September

		AW	AW	AW	GW	GW	GW	GW	GW	AW		GW	GW	GW	GW	AW	GW	GW	GW	AW		AW	XC	GW	GW
			◇ A	◇ B	◇■ ☕	◇■ ☕	◇■ ☕	◇■ ☕	◇	◇ ⌶		◇■ ☕		◇■ ☕	◇	◇ ⌶	◇■ ☕	◇	◇■ ☕			◇ ⌶	◇■ C ⌶	◇■ ☕	◇■ ☕
Cardiff Central	d	23p20	00 30	00 30		07 55			08 05	08 30		09 05			09 15	09 30		10 08	10 15	10 23		10 35	10 45		
Newport (South Wales)	a	23p36	00 47	00 50		08 11			08 21	08 47		09 18			09 27	09 48		10 20	10 31	10 36		10 48	10 57		
	d	23p38				08 13			08 23			09 19			09 29			10 22	10 32	10 38			10 59		
Severn Tunnel Jn	d	23p55							08 40						09 46			10 39		10 56					
Caldicot	d	23p58																		10 58					
Chepstow	d	00 07																		11 07					
Lydney	d	00 16																		11 16					
Gloucester	a	00 40																		11 42			11 49		
Pilning	d																								
Patchway	d														09 59										
Bristol Parkway	a					08 42						09 46							10 59						
	d																								
Filton Abbey Wood	d								08 55						10 03			10 54							
Bristol Temple Meads	a								09 05						10 13			11 03							
	d				07 45		08 15	08 45	09 10				09 20	09 48	10 15		10 30	11 10						11 30	12 00
Keynsham	d								09 17				09 27					11 17							
Oldfield Park	d								09 24				09 35					11 24							
Bath Spa	a				07 57		08 26	08 57	09 26				09 37	09 58	10 29		10 41	11 26						11 41	12 11

A 5 August

B 29 July

C ⌶ from Newport (South Wales)

When events are being held at the Millenium Stadium, services are subject to alteration. Please check times before travelling.

Table 132

Cardiff - Gloucester, Bristol and Bath Spa

Sundays 1 July to 9 September

Network Diagram - see first Page of Table 132

		GW	GW	AW	XC	GW		GW	GW	AW	AW	XC	GW	GW	GW	AW		AW	XC	GW	GW	GW	AW	XC	AW
		■ ◇ A ⌶	◇■ ☕	◇ ⌶	◇■ B ⌶	◇■ ☕		◇	◇■ ☕		◇ ⌶	◇■ B ⌶	◇■ ☕	◇	◇■ ☕	■		■ ⌶	◇■ B ⌶	◇■ ☕	◇	◇■ ☕		◇■ B ⌶	■ ⌶
Cardiff Central	d	11 08	11 15	11 35	11 45			12 08	12 15	12 23	12 40	12 45		13 08	13 15	13 22		13 40	13 45		14 08	14 15	14 23	14 45	14 56
Newport (South Wales)	a	11 20	11 31	11 49	11 57			12 20	12 31	12 36	12 52	12 57		13 20	13 31	13 35		13 52	13 57		14 20	14 31	14 36	14 57	15 12
	d	11 22	11 32		11 59			12 22	12 32	12 38		12 59		13 22	13 32				13 59		14 22	14 32	14 38	14 59	
Severn Tunnel Jn	d	11 39						12 39		12 56				13 39							14 39		14 56		
Caldicot	d									12 58													14 58		
Chepstow	d									13 07													15 07		
Lydney	d									13 16													15 16		
Gloucester	a				12 46					13 34		13 47							14 46				15 37	15 46	
Pilning	d																								
Patchway	d							12 52																	
Bristol Parkway	a		11 59						12 59						13 59							14 59			
	d																								
Filton Abbey Wood	d	11 54						12 57						13 54							14 55				
Bristol Temple Meads	a	12 04						13 05						14 04							15 04				
	d	12 15				12 30		13 10					13 30	14 15						14 30	15 10				
Keynsham	d							13 17													15 17				
Oldfield Park	d							13 24													15 24				
Bath Spa	a	12 27				12 41		13 26					13 41	14 27						14 41	15 27				

		GW		GW	SW	GW	GW	AW	AW	GW	GW	GW		GW	AW	GW	GW	AW	XC	GW	GW	GW		AW	GW
		◇■ ☕		◇■ ☕	◇■	◇	◇■ ☕	■ ⌶	■ ⌶	◇■ ☕	◇■ ☕	◇		◇■ ☕		◇■ ☕	◇	■ ⌶	◇■	◇	◇■ ☕	◇			◇■ ☕
Cardiff Central	d					15 08	15 15	15 22	15 56			16 08		16 15	16 23		16 35	16 40	16 45			17 08		17 05	17 15
Newport (South Wales)	a					15 20	15 31	15 35	16 12			16 20		16 31	16 36		16 47	16 52	16 57			17 20		17 24	17 31
	d					15 22	15 32					16 22		16 32	16 38		16 49		16 59			17 22			17 32
Severn Tunnel Jn	d					15 39						16 39			16 56							17 39			
Caldicot	d														16 58										
Chepstow	d														17 07										
Lydney	d														17 16										
Gloucester	a														17 37				17 46						
Pilning	d																								
Patchway	d					15 52																			
Bristol Parkway	a						15 59							16 59											17 59
	d																								
Filton Abbey Wood	d					15 55						16 55					17 20					17 54			
Bristol Temple Meads	a					16 04						17 06					17 29					18 04			
	d	15 30		16 00	16 04	16 15				16 30	17 00	17 15				17 30	17 40			17 44	18 00	18 10			
Keynsham	d				16 11							17 22								17 51		18 17			
Oldfield Park	d											17 29								17 58		18 24			
Bath Spa	a	15 41		16 11	16 18	16 27				16 41	17 12	17 30				17 42	17 52			18 00	18 12	18 26			

		AW	GW	GW	XC	GW	GW	GW		AW	AW	XC	GW	GW	GW	AW	XC	GW		GW	GW	GW	AW	GW	AW
		■	◇■ ☕	■	◇■	◇■ ☕	◇■ ☕	◇			■ ⌶	◇■	◇■ ☕	◇■ ☕	◇	◇	◇■	◇■ ☕			◇■ ☕	◇		◇■ ☕	◇
Cardiff Central	d	17 35		17 40	17 45	17 50		18 08		18 23	18 40	18 45	18 50		19 08	19 40	19 45	19 50				20 18	20 23	20 55	21 04
Newport (South Wales)	a	17 48		17 52	17 57	18 03		18 20		18 36	18 52	18 57	19 03		19 20	19 53	19 58	20 03				20 30	20 36	21 08	21 17
	d			17 54	17 59	18 04		18 22		18 38		18 59	19 04		19 22		20 00	20 04				20 31	20 38	21 09	
Severn Tunnel Jn	d							18 39		18 56					19 40							20 48	20 56		
Caldicot	d									18 58													20 58		
Chepstow	d									19 07													21 07		
Lydney	d									19 16													21 16		
Gloucester	a				18 46					19 38		19 47					20 49						21 41		
Pilning	d																								
Patchway	d							18 52																	
Bristol Parkway	a					18 31							19 31					20 31						21 36	
	d																								
Filton Abbey Wood	d			18 23				18 56							19 55							21 05			
Bristol Temple Meads	a			18 33				19 06							20 05							21 13			
	d		18 30	18 50			19 00	19 10						20 00	20 15					20 50	21 00	21 25			
Keynsham	d							19 17												20 57					
Oldfield Park	d							19 24												21 04					
Bath Spa	a		18 41	19 02			19 11	19 26						20 11	20 27					21 06	21 13	21 37			

		SW	GW	GW		GW	AW	AW
		■	◇■ ☕			⌶		◇
Cardiff Central	d					22 00	22 30	23 00
Newport (South Wales)	a					22 17	22 47	23 18
	d					22 19	22 49	
Severn Tunnel Jn	d					22 36	23 06	
Caldicot	d						23 09	
Chepstow	d						23 18	
Lydney	d						23 27	
Gloucester	a						23 51	
Pilning	d							
Patchway	d					22 49		
Bristol Parkway	a							
	d							
Filton Abbey Wood	d					22 53		
Bristol Temple Meads	a					22 59		
	d	21 35	22 10	22 15		23 10		
Keynsham	d			22 22				
Oldfield Park	d			22 29				
Bath Spa	a	21 47	22 22	22 31		23 22		

A ⌶ from Bristol Temple Meads ◇ from Bristol Temple Meads ■ to Bristol Temple Meads

B ⌶ from Newport (South Wales)

When events are being held at the Millenium Stadium, services are subject to alteration. Please check times before travelling.

Table 132

Cardiff - Gloucester, Bristol and Bath Spa

Sundays

16 September to 21 October

Network Diagram - see first Page of Table 132

		AW	GW	GW	GW	GW	GW	AW	GW	GW	GW	GW	AW	GW	GW	GW	AW	AW	XC	GW	GW	GW	GW
				◇1			◇	◇			◇	◇1	◇		◇	◇1		◇	◇1 A		◇1	◇ B	◇1
Cardiff Central	d			07 45			07 55	08 30			08 35	09 05	09 30		09 40	10 05	10 23	10 35	10 45			10 55	11 05
Newport (South Wales)	a			08 01			08 11	08 47			08 51	09 18	09 48		09 52	10 18	10 36	10 48	10 57			11 07	11 18
	d	23p50		08 03			08 13				08 54	09 19			09 54	10 19	10 38		10 59			11 09	11 19
Severn Tunnel Jn	d	00 15					08 30				09 10				10 11		10 56					11 26	
Caldicot	d	00 25															10 58						
Chepstow	d	00 40															11 07						
Lydney	d	01 00															11 16						
Gloucester	a	01 40															11 42		11 49				
Pilning	d																						
Patchway	d										09 24												
Bristol Parkway	a			08 31								09 46				10 46							11 46
	d																						
Filton Abbey Wood	d						08 45				09 28				10 26							11 41	
Bristol Temple Meads	a						08 56				09 37				10 36							11 50	
	d		07 35		08 35	08 45			09 05	09 35				09 47						10 46	11 50	12 00	
Keynsham	d				08 50					09 50												12 08	
Oldfield Park	d				09 09					10 09												12 19	
Bath Spa	a		08 10		09 20	09 20			09 40	10 20				10 22						11s21	12 12	12 21	

		AW	XC	GW	GW	GW	AW	AW	XC	GW	GW	GW	AW	AW	XC	GW	GW	GW	AW	XC	AW	GW	GW
		◇	◇1 A	◇1	◇	◇1		◇	◇1 A	◇1	◇	◇1			◇1 A	◇1	◇1	◇		◇1 A		◇1	◇1
Cardiff Central	d	11 35	11 45		11 55	12 05	12 23	12 40	12 45		12 55	13 05	13 22	13 40	13 45	14 05		14 08	14 23	14 45	14 56		
Newport (South Wales)	a	11 49	11 57		12 07	12 18	12 36	12 52	12 57		13 08	13 18	13 35	13 52	13 57	14 18		14 21	14 36	14 57	15 12		
	d		11 59		12 08	12 19	12 38		12 59		13 10	13 19			13 59	14 19		14 23	14 38	14 59			
Severn Tunnel Jn	d				12 25		12 56				13 28							14 40	14 56				
Caldicot	d						12 58												14 58				
Chepstow	d						13 07												15 07				
Lydney	d						13 16												15 16				
Gloucester	a		12 46				13 34		13 47						14 46				15 37	15 46			
Pilning	d																						
Patchway	d				12 38																		
Bristol Parkway	a					12 46						13 46				14 48							
	d																						
Filton Abbey Wood	d				12 42						13 43							14 56					
Bristol Temple Meads	a				12 50						13 50							15 04					
	d			12 52	13 00					13 50	14 00						14 50	15 10				15 30	16 00
Keynsham	d				13 08						14 08							15 18					
Oldfield Park	d				13 19						14 19							15 29					
Bath Spa	a			13 11	13 22					14 12	14 22						15 12	15 32				15 41	16 11

		SW	GW	GW	AW	XC	AW	GW	GW	GW	GW	AW	GW	GW	AW	XC	GW	GW	GW	GW	AW	GW
		◇1	◇	◇1		◇1		◇1	◇1	◇	◇1		◇1	◇		◇1	◇	◇1	◇	◇1		◇1
Cardiff Central	d		15 08	15 15	15 22	15 45	15 56			16 08	16 15	16 23		16 35	16 40	16 45			17 08	17 15	17 35	
Newport (South Wales)	a		15 20	15 31	15 35	15 57	16 12			16 20	16 31	16 36		16 47	16 52	16 57			17 20	17 31	17 48	
	d		15 22	15 32		15 59				16 22	16 32	16 38		16 49		16 59			17 22	17 32		
Severn Tunnel Jn	d		15 39							16 39		16 56							17 39			
Caldicot	d											16 58										
Chepstow	d											17 07										
Lydney	d											17 16										
Gloucester	a					16 46						17 37				17 46						
Pilning	d																					
Patchway	d		15 52																			
Bristol Parkway	a			15 59							16 59									17 59		
	d																					
Filton Abbey Wood	d		15 55							16 55				17 20					17 54			
Bristol Temple Meads	a		16 04							17 06				17 29					18 04			
	d	16 04	16 15					16 30	17 00	17 15			17 30	17 40			17 44	18 00	18 10			18 30
Keynsham	d	16 11								17 22							17 51		18 17			
Oldfield Park	d									17 29							17 58		18 24			
Bath Spa	a	16 18	16 27					16 41	17 11	17 30			17 41	17 52			18 00	18 11	18 26			18 41

A from Newport (South Wales)

B from Bristol Temple Meads ◇ from Bristol Temple Meads ■ to Bristol Temple Meads

When events are being held at the Millenium Stadium, services are subject to alteration. Please check times before travelling.

Table 132

Cardiff - Gloucester, Bristol and Bath Spa

Sundays

16 September to 21 October

Network Diagram - see first Page of Table 132

		GW	XC	GW	GW	GW	AW	AW	XC	GW	GW	GW	AW	XC	GW	GW	GW	GW	AW	GW	AW	SW	GW
			◇1	◇1	◇1	◇			◇1	◇1	◇1	◇	◇	◇1	◇1		◇1	◇		◇1	◇	1	◇1
Cardiff Central	d	17 40	17 45	17 50		18 08	18 23	18 40	18 45	18 50		19 08	19 40	19 45	19 50			20 18	20 23	20 55	21 04		
Newport (South Wales)	a	17 52	17 57	18 03		18 20	18 36	18 52	18 57	19 03		19 20	19 53	19 58	20 03			20 30	20 36	21 08	21 17		
	d	17 54	17 59	18 04		18 22	18 38		18 59	19 04		19 22		20 00	20 04			20 31	20 38	21 09			
Severn Tunnel Jn	d					18 39	18 56					19 40						20 48	20 56				
Caldicot	d						18 58												20 58				
Chepstow	d						19 07												21 07				
Lydney	d						19 16												21 16				
Gloucester	a		18 46				19 38		19 47					20 49					21 41				
Pilning	d																						
Patchway	d					18 52																	
Bristol Parkway	a			18 31						19 31					20 31					21 36			
	d																						
Filton Abbey Wood	d	18 23				18 56						19 55						21 05					
Bristol Temple Meads	a	18 33				19 06						20 05						21 13					
	d	18 50			19 00	19 10					20 00	20 15				20 50	21 00	21 25				21 35	22 10
Keynsham	d					19 17										20 57							
Oldfield Park	d					19 24										21 04							
Bath Spa	a	19 02			19 11	19 26					20 11	20 27				21 06	21 11	21 37				21 47	22 22

		GW	GW	AW	AW
					◇
Cardiff Central	d		22 00	22 30	23 00
Newport (South Wales)	a		22 17	22 47	23 18
	d		22 19	22 49	
Severn Tunnel Jn	d		22 36	23 06	
Caldicot	d			23 09	
Chepstow	d			23 18	
Lydney	d			23 27	
Gloucester	a			23 51	
Pilning	d				
Patchway	d		22 49		
Bristol Parkway	a				
	d				
Filton Abbey Wood	d		22 53		
Bristol Temple Meads	a		22 59		
	d	22 15	23 10		
Keynsham	d	22 22			
Oldfield Park	d	22 29			
Bath Spa	a	22 31	23 30		

Sundays

from 28 October

		AW	GW	GW	GW	GW	GW	AW	GW	GW	GW	AW	GW	GW	GW	AW	AW	GW	GW	GW	AW	GW	GW
			◇1	◇1	1	◇1	◇	◇	◇1	◇1	◇	◇	◇1	◇	◇1		◇	◇1	◇ A	◇1	◇	◇1	◇
Cardiff Central	d	23p20		07 45			08 05	08 30	09 05		09 15	09 30		10 08	10 15	10 23	10 35		11 08	11 15	11 35		12 08
Newport (South Wales)	a	23p36		08 01			08 21	08 47	09 18		09 27	09 48		10 20	10 31	10 36	10 48		11 20	11 31	11 49		12 20
	d	23p38		08 03			08 23		09 19		09 29			10 22	10 32	10 38			11 22	11 32			12 22
Severn Tunnel Jn	d	23p55					08 40				09 46			10 39		10 56			11 39				12 39
Caldicot	d	23p58														10 58							
Chepstow	d	00 07														11 07							
Lydney	d	00 16														11 16							
Gloucester	a	00 40														11 42							
Pilning	d																						
Patchway	d										09 59												12 52
Bristol Parkway	a			08 31					09 46						10 59					11 59			
	d																						
Filton Abbey Wood	d						08 55				10 03			10 54					11 54				12 57
Bristol Temple Meads	a						09 05				10 13			11 03					12 04				13 05
	d		07 45		08 20	08 45	09 10			09 48	10 15		10 30	11 10				11 30	12 15			12 30	13 10
Keynsham	d						09 17							11 17									13 17
Oldfield Park	d						09 24							11 24									13 24
Bath Spa	a		07 57		08 31	08 57	09 26			09 58	10 29		10 41	11 26				11 41	12 27			12 41	13 26

A from Bristol Temple Meads ◇ from Bristol Temple Meads ■ to Bristol Temple Meads

When events are being held at the Millenium Stadium, services are subject to alteration. Please check times before travelling.

Table 132

Sundays from 28 October

Cardiff - Gloucester, Bristol and Bath Spa

Network Diagram - see first Page of Table 132

		GW	AW	AW	GW	GW	GW	GW	AW	AW	GW	GW	GW	AW	XC	AW	GW	GW	SW	GW	GW	AW	XC
		◇■ ⊡		◇ 🍴	◇■ ⊡		◇	◇■ ⊡	▪	▪ 🍴	◇■ ⊡	◇	◇■ ⊡		◇■ A 🍴	▪ 🍴	◇■ ⊡	◇■ ⊡	◇■	◇	◇■ ⊡	▪ 🍴	◇■
Cardiff Central 7	d	12 15	12 23	12 40			13 08	13 15	13 22	13 40		14 08	14 15	14 23	14 45	14 56				15 08	15 15	15 22	15 45
Newport (South Wales)	a	12 31	12 36	12 52			13 20	13 31	13 35	13 52		14 20	14 31	14 36	14 57	15 12				15 20	15 31	15 35	15 57
	d	12 32	12 38				13 22	13 32				14 22	14 32	14 38	14 59					15 22	15 32		15 59
Severn Tunnel Jn	d		12 56				13 39					14 39		14 56						15 39			
Caldicot	d		12 58											14 58									
Chepstow	d		13 07											15 07									
Lydney	d		13 16											15 16									
Gloucester 7	a		13 34											15 37	15 46								16 46
Pilning	d																						
Patchway	d																			15 52			
Bristol Parkway 7	a	12 59						13 59					14 59								15 59		
	d																						
Filton Abbey Wood	d						13 54					14 55								15 55			
Bristol Temple Meads 10	a						14 04					15 04								16 04			
	d				13 30	13 55	14 15				14 30	15 10					15 30	16 00	16 04	16 15			
Keynsham	d					14 02						15 17							16 11				
Oldfield Park	d					14 09						15 24											
Bath Spa 7	a				13 41	14 12	14 27				14 41	15 27					15 41	16 11	16 18	16 27			

		AW	GW	GW	GW	GW	AW	GW	GW	AW	XC	GW	GW	GW	GW	AW	GW	GW	XC	GW	GW	GW
		▪ 🍴	◇■ ⊡	◇■ ⊡	◇	◇■ ⊡		◇■ ⊡	◇	▪ 🍴	◇■	◇	◇■ ⊡	◇	◇■ ⊡	▪	◇■ ⊡	▪	◇■	◇■ ⊡	◇■ ⊡	◇
Cardiff Central 7	d	15 56			16 08	16 15	16 23		16 35	16 40	16 45			17 08	17 15	17 35		17 40	17 45	17 50		18 08
Newport (South Wales)	a	16 12			16 20	16 31	16 36		16 47	16 52	16 57			17 20	17 31	17 48		17 52	17 57	18 03		18 20
	d				16 22	16 32	16 38		16 49		16 59			17 22	17 32			17 54	17 59	18 04		18 22
Severn Tunnel Jn	d				16 39		16 56							17 39								18 39
Caldicot	d						16 58															
Chepstow	d						17 07															
Lydney	d						17 16															
Gloucester 7	a						17 37				17 46								18 46			
Pilning	d																					
Patchway	d																					18 52
Bristol Parkway 7	a					16 59									17 59					18 31		
	d																					
Filton Abbey Wood	d				16 55				17 20					17 54				18 23				18 56
Bristol Temple Meads 10	a				17 06				17 29					18 04				18 33				19 06
	d		16 30	17 00	17 15			17 30	17 40			17 44	18 00	18 10			18 30	18 50			19 00	19 10
Keynsham	d				17 22							17 51		18 17								19 17
Oldfield Park	d				17 29							17 58		18 24								19 24
Bath Spa 7	a		16 41	17 11	17 30			17 41	17 52			18 00	18 11	18 26			18 41	19 02			19 11	19 26

		AW	AW	XC	GW	GW	GW	AW	XC	GW	GW	GW	GW	AW	GW	AW	SW	GW	GW	GW	AW	AW
			▪ 🍴	◇■	◇■ ⊡	◇■ ⊡	◇	◇	◇■	◇■ ⊡		◇■ ⊡	◇		◇■ ⊡	◇	■	◇■ ⊡		🍴		◇
Cardiff Central 7	d	18 23	18 40	18 45	18 50		19 08	19 40	19 45	19 50			20 18	20 23	20 55	21 04				22 00	22 30	23 00
Newport (South Wales)	a	18 36	18 52	18 57	19 03		19 20	19 53	19 58	20 03			20 30	20 36	21 08	21 17				22 17	22 47	23 18
	d	18 38		18 59	19 04		19 22		20 00	20 04			20 31	20 38	21 09					22 19	22 49	
Severn Tunnel Jn	d	18 56					19 40						20 48	20 56						22 36	23 06	
Caldicot	d	18 58												20 58							23 09	
Chepstow	d	19 07												21 07							23 18	
Lydney	d	19 16												21 16							23 27	
Gloucester 7	a	19 38		19 47					20 49					21 41							23 51	
Pilning	d																					
Patchway	d																			22 49		
Bristol Parkway 7	a				19 31					20 31					21 36							
	d																					
Filton Abbey Wood	d						19 55						21 05							22 53		
Bristol Temple Meads 10	a						20 05						21 13							22 59		
	d					20 00	20 15				20 50	21 00	21 25				21 35	22 10	22 15	23 10		
Keynsham	d										20 57								22 22			
Oldfield Park	d										21 04								22 29			
Bath Spa 7	a					20 11	20 27				21 06	21 11	21 37				21 47	22 22	22 31	23 22		

A 🍴 from Newport (South Wales)

When events are being held at the Millenium Stadium, services are subject to alteration. Please check times before travelling.

Table 132

Mondays to Fridays until 1 June

Bath Spa, Bristol and Gloucester - Cardiff

Network Diagram - see first Page of Table 132

Miles	Miles	Miles			GW	AW MX	GW	AW	AW MX	GW MX	GW MX	AW MX	GW	GW MX	GW	XC MX	XC MO	AW	GW	AW	GW	XC	XC
					◇■ A ⊡	◇	◇■ A ⊡	◇ A		◇■ ⊡	◇■ ⊡	◇	◇■ A ⊡	◇■ ⊡	◇■ A ⊡	■	■	◇				◇■ 🍴	◇■
0	—	—	**Bath Spa 7**	d			23p47			23p56				01 15								06 09	
1	—	—	Oldfield Park	d																			
7	—	—	Keynsham	d																			
11½	—	—	**Bristol Temple Meads 10**	a			00 01			00 10			01 03	01 29	01 32							06 20	
—	—	—		d										01 36		05 19	05 19		05 54		06 19	06 27	
16	—	—	Filton Abbey Wood	d															06 01		06 31		
—	0	—	**Bristol Parkway 7**	a												05 28	05 28					06 37	
—	—	—		d	23p12						00 23					05 38	05 38						
17½	—	—	Patchway	d															06 06		06 35		
21	4¾	—	Pilning	d																			
—	—	0	**Gloucester 7**	d					23p13											05 50			06 18
—	—	19½	Lydney	d					23p33											06 09			06 37
—	—	27¼	Chepstow	d					23p42											06 19			06 46
—	—	34	Caldicot	d					23p51											06 26			06 55
28	11¾	34¾	Severn Tunnel Jn	d					23p54										06 17	06 29	06 47		06 58
38	21¾	44¾	Newport (South Wales)	a	23p41				00 06		00 51			02s10		05 58	06 08		06 28	06 41	06 58		07 09
—	—	—		d	23p42	23p47		23p55	00 07		00 52	00 59				06 00	06 10	06 17	06 29	06 44	07 00		07 10
49¾	33½	56½	**Cardiff Central 7**	a	00 01	00 02		00 20	00 35		01 11	01 18		02 31		06 18	06 24	06 33	06 48	07 00	07 20		07 26

		GW	AW	GW	XC	AW	GW	GW	GW	SW	GW	GW	GW	AW	AW	AW	GW	GW	XC	GW	GW	GW	GW
			◇ 🍴	◇■ ⊡	◇■	◇			◇	■	◇■ ⊡	◇	◇■ ⊡	◇ 🍴		◇ 🍴		◇■ ⊡	◇■ B 🍴		▪ 🍴	◇■ ⊡	◇■ C ⊡
Bath Spa 7	d	06 28		06 54				07 08	07 25	07 35		07 48	07 59							08 08	08 22	08 29	
Oldfield Park	d	06 31						07 11	07 28	07 38		07 51								08 11	08 25		
Keynsham	d	06 38						07 18	07 35	07 45		07 58	08 08							08 18	08 34		
Bristol Temple Meads 10	a	06 46		07 07				07 27	07 46	07 52		08 06	08 17							08 29	08 41	08 45	
	d	06 50		07 14			07 19	07 34	07 54			08 10					08 24			08 41	08 54		
Filton Abbey Wood	d	07 02		07 22			07 30	07 43	08 01			08 22					08 33			08 48	09 01		
Bristol Parkway 7	a						07 33	07 47				08 29								08 52			
	d						07 40	07 48			08 07							08 41		08 52			09 07
Patchway	d						07 44		08 06								08 37						
Pilning	d																						
Gloucester 7	d				07 01			08a29							07 58				08 28	09a33			
Lydney	d				07 20										08 17								
Chepstow	d				07 29										08 27				08 54				
Caldicot	d				07 38										08 35								
Severn Tunnel Jn	d	07 14			07 41		07 56								08 38		08 49						
Newport (South Wales)	a	07 25		07 44	07 52		08 07		08 27		08 32				08 50		09 02	09 07	09 12		09 25		09 31
	d	07 27	07 35	07 44	07 53	08 01	08 09		08 27		08 32			08 38	08 52	09 03	09 03	09 08	09 14		09 25		09 32
Cardiff Central 7	a	07 44	07 51	08 00	08 08	08 17	08 24		08 46		08 46			08 53	09 07	09 23	09 24	09 24	09 30		09 43		09 48

		GW	GW	AW	AW BHX	AW	GW	GW	XC	GW	GW	AW	GW	GW	GW	AW	GW	GW	XC	GW	GW	AW	GW
		◇	◇■ D Ø	◇ 🍴	◇■ ⊠			◇■ ⊡	◇■ B 🍴		◇■ ⊡	◇ 🍴	◇ 🍴	◇■ ⊡	◇■ Ø	◇ 🍴		◇■ ⊡	◇■ B 🍴	◇	◇■ ⊡	◇ 🍴	◇ 🍴
Bath Spa 7	d	08 47	08 57							09 15	09 30		09 36	10 00						10 08	10 24		10 36
Oldfield Park	d	08 49								09 18										10 11			
Keynsham	d	08 57								09 25			09 44							10 18			
Bristol Temple Meads 10	a	09 05	09 10							09 35	09 45		09 52	10 15						10 28	10 38		10 48
	d	09 10					09 21			09 41			09 56				10 21			10 41			10 54
Filton Abbey Wood	d	09 22					09 30			09 48			10 03				10 30			10 48			11 01
Bristol Parkway 7	a	09 28								09 52										10 52			
	d							09 41		09 52					10 07			10 41		10 52			
Patchway	d						09 35										10 35						
Pilning	d																						
Gloucester 7	d					08 58			09 24	10a33									10 24	11a34			
Lydney	d					09 17													10 43				
Chepstow	d					09 27			09 50														
Caldicot	d					09 36																	
Severn Tunnel Jn	d					09 38	09 46										10 46						
Newport (South Wales)	a					09 51	09 58	10 04	10 09				10 26		10 31		11 02	11 06	11 11				11 26
	d			09 37	09 41	09 52	10 00	10 05	10 11			10 22	10 26		10 31	11 01	11 02	11 06	11 12			11 22	11 27
Cardiff Central 7	a			09 57	09 58	10 07	10 18	10 21	10 25			10 37	10 43		10 46	11 15	11 23	11 23	11 27			11 37	11 43

A 21 May, 28 May
B 🍴 to Newport (South Wales)
C The St. David
D The Merchant Venturer

When events are being held at the Millenium Stadium, services are subject to alteration. Please check times before travelling.

Table 132

Mondays to Fridays until 1 June

Bath Spa, Bristol and Gloucester - Cardiff

Network Diagram - see first Page of Table 132

		GW	GW	AW	AW	GW	GW	XC	GW	GW	AW	GW	SW	GW	GW	AW	GW	AW	GW	XC	GW	GW
					BHX																	
		◇■	◇■		■	◇	◇■	◇■ A	◇	◇■ B	◇	◇	◇■	◇■	◇■			◇	◇■	◇■ A	◇	◇■
		⊓	⌀		⌶		⊓	⌶		⊓	⌶	⌶		⊓	⌀			⌶	⊓	⌶		⊓
Bath Spa ■	d	11 00							11 08	11 24		11 36	11 47	12 00							12 13	12 24
Oldfield Park	d								11 11												12 15	
Keynsham	d								11 18				11 55								12 23	
Bristol Temple Meads ■	a	11 15							11 28	11 40		11 48	12 05	12 15							12 31	12 39
	d					11 21			11 41			11 54					12 21				12 41	
Filton Abbey Wood	d					11 30			11 48			12 01					12 30				12 48	
Bristol Parkway ■	a								11 52												12 52	
	d		11 07				11 41		11 52						12 07				12 41		12 52	
Patchway	d					11 35											12 35					
Pilning	d																					
Gloucester ■	d			10 58				11 24	12a33							11 58				12 24	13a31	
Lydney	d			11 17												12 17						
Chepstow	d			11 27				11 50								12 27				12 50		
Caldicot	d			11 35												12 35						
Severn Tunnel Jn.	d			11 38		11 46										12 38	12 46					
Newport (South Wales)	a		11 31	11 50		11 58	12 04	12 10				12 25			12 31	12 50	13 00		13 06	13 11		
	d		11 31	11 51	11 53	12 00	12 04	12 11			12 23	12 26			12 32	12 52	13 01	13 00	13 06	13 12		
Cardiff Central ■	a		11 46	12 12	12 08	12 18	12 21	12 28			12 38	12 43			12 46	13 07	13 22	13 22	13 22	13 29		

		AW	GW	GW	GW	GW	GW	GW	GW	XC	AW	GW	GW	GW	AW	AW	GW	GW	XC	GW	GW	GW	SW
		◇	◇	◇■	◇■			◇■	◇■	◇■ A	◇	◇	◇■	◇■		■		◇■	◇■ A	◇	◇■	◇	◇■
		⌶	⌶	⊓	⌀			⊓	⊓	⌶	⌶	⌶	⊓	⌀		⌶		⊓	⌶		⊓	⌶	
Bath Spa ■	d		12 36	13 00			13 22	13 24				13 36	14 00							14 14	14 24	14 36	14 47
Oldfield Park	d						13 25													14 17			
Keynsham	d						13 32													14 24			14 55
Bristol Temple Meads ■	a		12 48	13 15			13 41	13 44				13 48	14 15							14 35	14 39	14 48	15 05
	d		12 54			13 21						13 54					14 21			14 41		14 54	
Filton Abbey Wood	d		13 01			13 30						14 01					14 30			14 48		15 01	
Bristol Parkway ■	a																			14 51			
	d				13 07				13 41					14 07				14 41		14 52			
Patchway	d					13 35											14 35						
Pilning	d																						
Gloucester ■	d									13 24					13 58				14 24	15a32			
Lydney	d									13 43					14 17								
Chepstow	d														14 27				14 50				
Caldicot	d														14 35								
Severn Tunnel Jn.	d					13 46									14 38		14 46						
Newport (South Wales)	a		13 26		13 31	13 58			14 04	14 09		14 26		14 30	14 50		15 02	15 06	15 11			15 25	
	d	13 23	13 26		13 31	14 00			14 05	14 11	14 22	14 27		14 31	14 52	15 00	15 03	15 06	15 12			15 26	
Cardiff Central ■	a	13 39	13 43		13 46	14 18			14 22	14 29	14 37	14 43		14 46	15 07	15 19	15 24	15 22	15 29			15 43	

		GW	GW	AW	AW	GW	GW	GW	XC	GW	GW	GW	GW	GW	AW	AW	GW	GW	XC	GW	GW	AW
		◇■	◇■	■		◇	◇■		◇■ A	◇	◇■	◇	◇■	◇■	■	◇		◇■	◇■ A		◇■	■
		⊓	⊓	⌶	⌶		⊓		⌶		⊓	⌶	⊓	⊓	⌶	⌶		⊓	⌶		⊓	⌶
Bath Spa ■	d	15 00						15 08		15 21	15 24	15 36	16 00							16 08	16 24	
Oldfield Park	d							15 11												16 11		
Keynsham	d							15 18												16 18		
Bristol Temple Meads ■	a	15 15						15 28		15 34	15 40	15 48	16 15							16 29	16 39	
	d					15 21		15 34		15 41		15 54					16 24			16 41		
Filton Abbey Wood	d					15 30				15 48		16 01					16 30			16 48		
Bristol Parkway ■	a							15 48		15 52										16 52		
	d		15 07				15 41			15 52				16 07				16 41		16 52		
Patchway	d					15 35											16 35					
Pilning	d																					
Gloucester ■	d				14 58				15 24	16a33									16 24	17a33		
Lydney	d				15 17														16 43			
Chepstow	d				15 27				15 50										16 52			
Caldicot	d				15 35																	
Severn Tunnel Jn.	d				15 38	15 46											16 46					
Newport (South Wales)	a		15 31		15 50	15 58	16 05		16 10			16 25		16 30			17 00	17 06	17 11			
	d		15 32	15 37	15 52	16 00	16 06		16 12			16 25		16 31	16 40	17 01	17 01	17 06	17 12			17 22
Cardiff Central ■	a		15 46	15 53	16 10	16 18	16 22		16 29			16 43		16 46	16 55	17 15	17 25	17 22	17 28			17 37

A ⌶ to Newport (South Wales)

B The Torbay Express

When events are being held at the Millenium Stadium, services are subject to alteration. Please check times before travelling.

Table 132

Mondays to Fridays until 1 June

Bath Spa, Bristol and Gloucester - Cardiff

Network Diagram - see first Page of Table 132

		GW	GW	GW	AW	GW	GW	GW	XC	GW	GW	GW	GW	GW	AW	AW	AW	GW	GW	XC	GW	GW	AW
		■	◇■			◇■		◇■	◇■	◇	◇■	■	◇■	◇■ A	■		◇		◇■ B	◇■		◇■	■
		⌶	⊓			⊓		⊓			⊓	⌶	⊓	⊓	⌶		⌶		⌀			⊓	⌶
Bath Spa ■	d	16 36		16 43		17 00				17 08	17 27	17 36	18 00								18 08	18 29	
Oldfield Park	d									17 11											18 11		
Keynsham	d			16 51						17 18											18 18		
Bristol Temple Meads ■	a	16 48		16 59		17 15				17 29	17 41	17 48	18 14								18 28	18 44	
	d	16 54		17 10			17 21			17 41		17 54						18 21			18 41		
Filton Abbey Wood	d	17 01		17 22			17 30			17 48		18 01						18 30			18 48		
Bristol Parkway ■	a			17 27						17 52											18 52		
	d		17 07					17 41		17 52				18 07					18 41		18 52		
Patchway	d						17 35											18 35					
Pilning	d																						
Gloucester ■	d				16 58				17 27	18a33						17 59				18 31	19a30		
Lydney	d				17 17											18 18							
Chepstow	d				17 27											18 28							
Caldicot	d				17 35											18 36							
Severn Tunnel Jn.	d	17 14			17 38		17 46					18 14				18 39		18 50					
Newport (South Wales)	a	17 25	17 31		17 50		17 58	18 04	18 10			18 25		18 30		18 51		19 06	19 11	19 16			
	d	17 27	17 31		17 52		18 00	18 04	18 11			18 26		18 31	18 41	18 53	19 01	19 06	19 11	19 17			19 22
Cardiff Central ■	a	17 43	17 46		18 10		18 17	18 19	18 27			18 43		18 48	18 55	19 09	19 21	19 24	19 26	19 33			19 43

		GW	GW	GW	AW	GW	GW	XC	GW	GW	GW	GW	GW	GW	GW	AW	XC	AW	GW	GW	AW	GW	GW
																						FX	FO
		■	◇■	◇■			◇■	◇■		◇■	◇■ C	◇	◇	◇■	◇■	■	◇■		◇	◇■	◇	◇■	◇■
		⌶	⊓	⊓			⊓			⊓	⊓	⌶		⊓	⊓	⌶			⌶	⊓	⌶	⊓	⊓
Bath Spa ■	d	18 36	18 59						19 08	19 24	19 30	19 36	19 49	19 59					20 12	20 30			
Oldfield Park	d								19 11				19 52						20 14				
Keynsham	d								19 18				19 59						20 21				
Bristol Temple Meads ■	a	18 48	19 12						19 29	19 41	19 43	19 48	20 08	20 13					20 30	20 44			
	d	18 54				19 21			19 41			19 54					20 15						
Filton Abbey Wood	d	19 01				19 30			19 48			20 01					20 22						
Bristol Parkway ■	a								19 52														
	d			19 07			19 44		19 52						20 07							20 42	20 43
Patchway	d					19 35											20 25						
Pilning	d																						
Gloucester ■	d				18 58			19 28	20a32									19 58					
Lydney	d				19 17													20 17					
Chepstow	d				19 27													20 27					
Caldicot	d				19 34													20 36					
Severn Tunnel Jn.	d	19 14			19 37	19 46						20 16					20 37	20 39					
Newport (South Wales)	a	19 26		19 31	19 50	20 01	20 07	20 11				20 27			20 31		20 47	20 51				21 04	21 05
	d	19 26		19 31	19 52	20 02	20 08	20 13				20 28			20 33	20 39	20 49	20 52			21 00	21 04	21 07
Cardiff Central ■	a	19 46		19 48	20 09	20 20	20 22	20 27				20 43			20 48	20 58	21 02	21 10			21 19	21 19	21 19

		XC	GW	GW	AW	GW	GW	GW	GW	XC	XC	GW	GW	SW	GW	GW	AW	AW	GW	GW	GW	GW
										FO	FX	FO	FX				FO	FX		FO	FX	
		◇■	◇	◇■	◇			◇■	◇■	◇■	◇■	◇	◇	◇■	◇■		◇	◇	◇■	◇	◇	
			⌶	⊓	⌶			⊓	⌀						⊓				⊓			
Bath Spa ■	d		20 36	21 00			21 08	21 30				21 36	21 36	21 51	22 13	22 25				22 36	22 36	23 02
Oldfield Park	d						21 11									22 28						23 05
Keynsham	d						21 18							21 59		22 35						23 12
Bristol Temple Meads ■	a		20 48	21 15			21 28	21 44				21 48	21 48	22 06	22 30	22 43				22 50	22 48	23 23
	d		20 54			21 19						21 54	21 54							22 54	22 54	
Filton Abbey Wood	d		21 01			21 30						22 01	22 01							23 01	23 01	
Bristol Parkway ■	a																					
	d								21 41										22 45			
Patchway	d					21 34						22 06	22 06							23 06	23 06	
Pilning	d																					
Gloucester ■	d	20 24								21 24	21 24											
Lydney	d									21 43	21 43											
Chepstow	d									21 52	21 52											
Caldicot	d									22 01	22 01											
Severn Tunnel Jn.	d		21 14			21 46				22 04	22 04	22 18	22 18							23 17	23 17	
Newport (South Wales)	a	21 11	21 26			21 58			22 03	22 15	22 15	22 29	22 36						23 19	23 34	23 34	
	d	21 13	21 26		21 52	21 59			22 05	22 16	22 16	22 30	22 37				22 40	22 42	23 19	23 35	23 35	
Cardiff Central ■	a	21 27	21 44		22 06	22 18			22 23	22 31	22 35	22 52	23 00				22 55	23 04	23 40	23 56	23 56	

A The Capitals United

B The Red Dragon

C The Bristolian

When events are being held at the Millenium Stadium, services are subject to alteration. Please check times before travelling.

Bath Spa, Bristol and Gloucester - Cardiff

Mondays to Fridays

until 1 June

Network Diagram - see first Page of Table 132

		GW	AW	AW	AW	GW	GW
				FO	FX	FO	FX
		◇1 ⊏P	◇			◇1 ⊏P	◇1 ⊏P
Bath Spa 7	d	23 19				23 49	23 56
Oldfield Park	d						
Keynsham	d						
Bristol Temple Meads 10	a	23 32				00 03	00 10
	d						
Filton Abbey Wood	d						
Bristol Parkway 7	a						
	d						
Patchway	d						
Pilning	d						
Gloucester 7	d			23 13	23 13		
Lydney	d			23 33	23 33		
Chepstow	d			23 42	23 42		
Caldicot	d			23 51	23 51		
Severn Tunnel Jn.	d			23 54	23 54		
Newport (South Wales)	a			00 06	00 06		
	d		23 47	00 07	00 07		
Cardiff Central 7	a		00 02	00 33	00 35		

Mondays to Fridays

2 July to 31 August

		GW	AW	AW	AW	GW	GW	GW	AW	GW	GW	GW	XC	XC	AW	AW	GW	AW	GW	XC	XC	GW	AW
		MO	MX	MO	MX	MO	MX	MX	MX	MO	MX	MO	MX	MO									
		◇1 ⊏P	◇	◇		◇1 ⊏P	◇1 ⊏P	◇1 ⊏P	◇	◇1 ⊏P	◇1 ⊏P	◇1 ⊏P	1	1	◇ A	B				◇1 ⌶	◇1		◇ ⌶
Bath Spa 7	d					23p55	23p56				01 15									06 09		06 28	
Oldfield Park	d																					06 31	
Keynsham	d																					06 38	
Bristol Temple Meads 10	a					00 09	00 10			01 05	01 29	01 35								06 20		06 46	
	d										01 36		05 19	05 19			05 54		06 19	06 27		06 50	
Filton Abbey Wood	d																06 01		06 31			07 02	
Bristol Parkway 7	a												05 28	05 28						06 37			
	d	23p17						00 23					05 38	05 38									
Patchway	d																06 06		06 35				
Pilning	d																						
Gloucester 7	d				23p13													05 50			06 18		
Lydney	d				23p33													06 09			06 37		
Chepstow	d				23p42													06 19			06 46		
Caldicot	d				23p51													06 26			06 55		
Severn Tunnel Jn.	d				23p54												06 17	06 29	06 47		06 58	07 14	
Newport (South Wales)	a	23p43			00 06			00 51			02s10		05 58	06 08			06 28	06 41	06 58		07 09	07 25	
	d	23p43	23p47	23p55	00 07			00 52	00 59				06 00	06 10	06 17	06 23	06 29	06 44	07 00		07 10	07 27	07 35
Cardiff Central 7	a	00 04	00 02	00 20	00 35			01 11	01 18		02 31		06 18	06 24	06 33	06 40	06 48	07 00	07 20		07 26	07 44	07 51

		GW	XC	AW	GW	GW	GW	SW	GW	GW	GW	AW	AW	AW	GW	GW	XC	GW	GW	GW	GW	GW	GW
		◇1 ⊏P	◇1	◇			◇	1	◇1 ⊏P	◇	◇1 ⊏P	◇ ⌶		◇ ⌶		◇1 ⊏P	◇1 C ⌶		■ ⌶	◇1 ⊏P	◇1 D ⊏P	◇	◇1 E Ø
Bath Spa 7	d	06 54				07 08	07 25	07 35		07 48	07 59							08 08	08 22	08 29		08 47	08 57
Oldfield Park	d					07 11	07 28	07 38		07 51								08 11	08 25			08 49	
Keynsham	d					07 18	07 35	07 45		07 58	08 08							08 18	08 34			08 57	
Bristol Temple Meads 10	a	07 07				07 27	07 46	07 52		08 06	08 17							08 29	08 41	08 45		09 05	09 10
	d	07 14			07 19	07 34	07 54			08 10					08 24			08 41	08 54			09 10	
Filton Abbey Wood	d	07 22			07 30	07 43	08 01			08 22					08 33			08 48	09 01			09 22	
Bristol Parkway 7	a				07 33	07 47				08 29								08 52				09 28	
	d				07 40	07 48			08 07							08 41		08 52			09 07		
Patchway	d				07 44		08 06								08 37								
Pilning	d																						
Gloucester 7	d		07 01			08a29							07 58				08 28	09a33					
Lydney	d		07 20										08 17										
Chepstow	d		07 29										08 27				08 54						
Caldicot	d		07 38										08 35										
Severn Tunnel Jn.	d		07 41		07 56								08 38		08 49								
Newport (South Wales)	a	07 44	07 52		08 07		08 27		08 32				08 50		09 02	09 07	09 12		09 25		09 31		
	d	07 44	07 53	08 01	08 09		08 27		08 32			08 38	08 52	09 03	09 03	09 08	09 14		09 25		09 32		
Cardiff Central 7	a	08 00	08 08	08 17	08 24		08 46		08 46			08 53	09 07	09 23	09 24	09 24	09 30		09 43		09 48		

A from 2 July until 20 July
B from 23 July until 31 August
C ⌶ to Newport (South Wales)
D The St. David
E The Merchant Venturer

When events are being held at the Millenium Stadium, services are subject to alteration. Please check times before travelling.

Bath Spa, Bristol and Gloucester - Cardiff

Mondays to Fridays

2 July to 31 August

Network Diagram - see first Page of Table 132

		AW	AW	AW	GW	GW	XC	GW	GW	AW	GW	GW	GW	AW	GW	GW	XC	GW	GW	AW	GW	GW
			BHX																			
		◇ ⌶	◇1 ⊠			◇1 ⊏P	◇1 A ⌶		◇1 ⊏P	◇ ⌶	◇ ⌶	◇1 ⊏P	◇1 Ø	◇ ⌶		◇1 ⊏P	◇1 A ⌶	◇	◇1 ⊏P	◇ ⌶	◇ ⌶	◇1 ⊏P
Bath Spa 7	d							09 15	09 30		09 36	10 00						10 08	10 24		10 36	11 00
Oldfield Park	d							09 18										10 11				
Keynsham	d							09 25			09 44							10 18				
Bristol Temple Meads 10	a							09 35	09 45		09 52	10 15						10 28	10 38		10 48	11 15
	d				09 21			09 41			09 56				10 21			10 41			10 54	
Filton Abbey Wood	d				09 30			09 48			10 03				10 30			10 48			11 01	
Bristol Parkway 7	a							09 52										10 52				
	d					09 41		09 52					10 07			10 41		10 52				
Patchway	d				09 35										10 35							
Pilning	d																					
Gloucester 7	d			08 58			09 24	10a33									10 24	11a34				
Lydney	d			09 17													10 43					
Chepstow	d			09 27			09 50															
Caldicot	d			09 36																		
Severn Tunnel Jn.	d			09 38	09 46										10 46							
Newport (South Wales)	a			09 51	09 58	10 04	10 09				10 26		10 31		11 02	11 06	11 11				11 26	
	d	09 37	09 41	09 52	10 00	10 05	10 11			10 22	10 26		10 31	11 01	11 02	11 06	11 12			11 22	11 27	
Cardiff Central 7	a	09 57	09 58	10 07	10 18	10 21	10 25			10 37	10 43		10 46	11 15	11 23	11 23	11 27			11 37	11 43	

		GW	AW	AW	GW	GW	XC	GW	GW	AW	GW	SW	GW	GW	AW	GW	AW	GW	XC	GW	GW	AW	GW
				BHX																			
		◇1 Ø		■ ⌶	◇	◇1 ⊏P	◇1 A ⌶	◇	◇1 B ⊏P	◇ ⌶	◇ ⌶	◇1	◇1 ⊏P	◇1 Ø			◇ ⌶	◇1 ⊏P	◇1 A ⌶	◇	◇1 ⊏P	◇ ⌶	◇ ⌶
Bath Spa 7	d							11 08	11 24		11 36	11 47	12 00							12 10	12 24		12 36
Oldfield Park	d							11 11												12 11			
Keynsham	d							11 18				11 55								12 19			
Bristol Temple Meads 10	a							11 28	11 40		11 48	12 05	12 15							12 31	12 39		12 48
	d				11 21			11 41			11 54					12 21				12 41			12 54
Filton Abbey Wood	d				11 30			11 48			12 01					12 30				12 48			13 01
Bristol Parkway 7	a							11 52												12 52			
	d	11 07				11 41		11 52						12 07				12 41		12 52			
Patchway	d				11 35											12 35							
Pilning	d																						
Gloucester 7	d		10 58				11 24	12a33							11 58				12 24	13a31			
Lydney	d		11 17												12 17								
Chepstow	d		11 27				11 50								12 27				12 50				
Caldicot	d		11 35												12 35								
Severn Tunnel Jn.	d		11 38		11 46										12 38	12 46							
Newport (South Wales)	a	11 31	11 50		11 58	12 04	12 10				12 25			12 31	12 50	13 00		13 06	13 11				13 26
	d	11 31	11 51	11 53	12 00	12 04	12 11			12 23	12 26			12 32	12 52	13 01	13 00	13 06	13 12			13 23	13 26
Cardiff Central 7	a	11 46	12 12	12 08	12 18	12 21	12 28			12 38	12 43			12 46	13 07	13 22	13 22	13 22	13 29			13 39	13 43

		GW	GW	GW	GW	GW	GW	XC	AW	GW	GW	GW	AW	AW	GW	GW	XC	GW	GW	GW	SW	GW
		◇1 ⊏P	◇1 Ø			◇1 ⊏P	◇1 ⊏P	◇1 A ⌶	◇ ⌶	◇ ⌶	◇1 ⊏P	◇1 Ø		■ ⌶		◇1 ⊏P	◇1 A ⌶	◇	◇1 ⊏P	◇ ⌶	◇1	◇1 ⊏P
Bath Spa 7	d	13 00			13 22	13 24				13 36	14 00							14 14	14 24	14 36	14 47	15 00
Oldfield Park	d				13 25													14 17				
Keynsham	d				13 32													14 24			14 55	
Bristol Temple Meads 10	a	13 15			13 41	13 44				13 48	14 15							14 35	14 39	14 48	15 05	15 15
	d			13 21						13 54					14 21			14 41		14 54		
Filton Abbey Wood	d			13 30						14 01					14 30			14 48		15 01		
Bristol Parkway 7	a																	14 51				
	d		13 07				13 41					14 07				14 41		14 52				
Patchway	d			13 35											14 35							
Pilning	d																					
Gloucester 7	d							13 24					13 58				14 24	15a32				
Lydney	d							13 43					14 17									
Chepstow	d												14 27				14 50					
Caldicot	d												14 35									
Severn Tunnel Jn.	d			13 46									14 38		14 46							
Newport (South Wales)	a		13 31	13 58			14 04	14 09		14 26		14 30	14 50		15 02	15 06	15 11			15 25		
	d		13 31	14 00			14 05	14 11	14 22	14 27		14 31	14 52	15 00	15 03	15 06	15 12			15 26		
Cardiff Central 7	a		13 46	14 18			14 22	14 29	14 37	14 43		14 46	15 07	15 19	15 24	15 22	15 29			15 43		

A ⌶ to Newport (South Wales)
B The Torbay Express

When events are being held at the Millenium Stadium, services are subject to alteration. Please check times before travelling.

Bath Spa, Bristol and Gloucester - Cardiff

Mondays to Fridays

2 July to 31 August

Network Diagram - see first Page of Table 132

		GW	AW	AW	GW	GW	GW	XC	GW	GW		GW	GW	GW	AW	AW	GW	GW	XC	GW		GW	AW	GW	GW
		◇1 ⊏	■ H	H	◇	◇1 ⊏		◇1 A H	◇	◇1 ⊏		◇ H	◇1 ⊏	◇1 ⊏	■ H	◇ H		◇1 ⊏	◇1 A H			◇1 ⊏	■ H	■ H	◇1 ⊏
Bath Spa 7	d						15 08		15 21	15 24		15 36	16 00							16 08		16 24		16 36	
Oldfield Park	d						15 11													16 11					
Keynsham	d						15 18													16 18					
Bristol Temple Meads 10	a						15 28		15 34	15 40		15 48	16 15							16 29		16 39		16 48	
	d				15 21		15 34		15 41			15 54					16 24			16 41				16 54	
Filton Abbey Wood	d				15 30				15 48			16 01					16 30			16 48				17 01	
Bristol Parkway 7	a						15 48		15 52											16 52					
	d	15 07				15 41			15 52					16 07				16 41		16 52					17 07
Patchway	d				15 35												16 35								
Pilning	d																								
Gloucester 7	d			14 58				15 24	16a33										16 24	17a33					
Lydney	d			15 17															16 43						
Chepstow	d			15 27				15 50											16 52						
Caldicot	d			15 35																					
Severn Tunnel Jn.	d			15 38	15 46												16 46							17 14	
Newport (South Wales)	a	15 31		15 50	15 58	16 05		16 10				16 25		16 30			17 00	17 06	17 11					17 25	17 31
	d	15 32	15 37	15 52	16 00	16 06		16 12				16 25		16 31	16 40	17 01	17 01	17 06	17 12				17 22	17 27	17 31
Cardiff Central 7	a	15 46	15 53	16 10	16 18	16 22		16 29				16 43		16 46	16 55	17 15	17 25	17 22	17 28				17 37	17 43	17 46

		GW	AW	GW	GW	GW		XC	GW	GW	GW	GW	GW	AW	AW	AW		GW	GW	XC	GW	GW	AW	GW	GW
				◇1 ⊏		◇1 ⊏		◇1	◇	◇1 ⊏	■ H	◇1 ⊏	◇1 B ⊏	■ H		◇ H			◇1 C Ø	◇1		◇1 ⊏	■ H	■ H	◇1 ⊏
Bath Spa 7	d	16 43		17 00					17 08	17 27	17 36	18 00									18 08	18 29		18 36	18 59
Oldfield Park	d								17 11												18 11				
Keynsham	d	16 51							17 18												18 18				
Bristol Temple Meads 10	a	16 59		17 15					17 29	17 41	17 48	18 14									18 28	18 44		18 48	19 12
	d	17 10			17 21				17 41		17 54							18 21			18 41			18 54	
Filton Abbey Wood	d	17 22			17 30				17 48		18 01							18 30			18 48			19 01	
Bristol Parkway 7	a	17 27							17 52												18 52				
	d					17 41			17 52				18 07						18 41		18 52				
Patchway	d				17 35													18 35							
Pilning	d																								
Gloucester 7	d		16 58					17 27	18a33						17 59					18 31	19a30				
Lydney	d		17 17												18 18										
Chepstow	d		17 27												18 28										
Caldicot	d		17 35												18 36										
Severn Tunnel Jn.	d		17 38		17 46						18 14				18 39			18 50						19 14	
Newport (South Wales)	a		17 50		17 58	18 04		18 10			18 25		18 30		18 51			19 06	19 11	19 16				19 26	
	d		17 52		18 00	18 04		18 11			18 26		18 31	18 41	18 53	19 01		19 06	19 11	19 17			19 22	19 26	
Cardiff Central 7	a		18 10		18 17	18 19		18 27			18 43		18 48	18 55	19 09	19 21		19 24	19 26	19 33			19 43	19 46	

		GW		AW	GW	GW	XC	GW	GW	GW	GW	GW		GW	GW	AW	XC	AW	GW	GW	AW	GW FX		GW FO	XC
		◇1 ⊏				◇1 ⊏	◇1		◇1 ⊏	◇1 D ⊏	◇ H	◇		◇1 ⊏	◇1 ⊏	■ H	◇1		◇ H	◇1 ⊏	◇ H	◇1 ⊏		◇1 ⊏	◇1
Bath Spa 7	d							19 08	19 24	19 30	19 36	19 49		19 59					20 12	20 30					
Oldfield Park	d							19 11				19 52							20 14						
Keynsham	d							19 18				19 59							20 21						
Bristol Temple Meads 10	a							19 29	19 41	19 43	19 48	20 08		20 13					20 30	20 44					
	d				19 21			19 41			19 54						20 15								
Filton Abbey Wood	d				19 30			19 48			20 01						20 22								
Bristol Parkway 7	a							19 52																	
	d	19 07				19 44		19 52							20 07							20 42		20 43	
Patchway	d				19 35												20 25								
Pilning	d																								
Gloucester 7	d			18 58			19 28	20a32										19 58							20 24
Lydney	d			19 17														20 17							
Chepstow	d			19 27														20 27							
Caldicot	d			19 34														20 36							
Severn Tunnel Jn.	d			19 37	19 46						20 16						20 37	20 39							
Newport (South Wales)	a	19 31		19 50	20 01	20 07	20 11				20 27				20 31		20 47	20 51				21 04		21 05	21 11
	d	19 31		19 52	20 02	20 08	20 13				20 28				20 33	20 39	20 49	20 52			21 00	21 04		21 07	21 13
Cardiff Central 7	a	19 48		20 09	20 20	20 22	20 27				20 43				20 48	20 58	21 02	21 10			21 19	21 19		21 19	21 27

A H to Newport (South Wales)
B The Capitals United
C The Red Dragon
D The Bristolian

When events are being held at the Millenium Stadium, services are subject to alteration. Please check times before travelling.

Bath Spa, Bristol and Gloucester - Cardiff

Mondays to Fridays

2 July to 31 August

Network Diagram - see first Page of Table 132

		GW	GW	AW	GW	GW	GW	GW		XC FO	XC FX	GW FO	GW FX	SW	GW	GW	AW FO	AW FX		GW	GW FO	GW FX	GW	GW	AW
		◇ H	◇1 ⊏	◇ H			◇1 ⊏	◇1 Ø		◇1	◇1	◇	◇	◇1	◇1 ⊏		◇	◇		◇1 ⊏	◇	◇		◇1 ⊏	◇
Bath Spa 7	d	20 36	21 00			21 08	21 30					21 36	21 36	21 51	22 13	22 25					22 36	22 36	23 02	23 19	
Oldfield Park	d					21 11										22 28							23 05		
Keynsham	d					21 18								21 59		22 35							23 12		
Bristol Temple Meads 10	a	20 48	21 15			21 28	21 44					21 48	21 48	22 06	22 30	22 43					22 50	22 48	23 23	23 32	
	d	20 54			21 19							21 54	21 54								22 54	22 54			
Filton Abbey Wood	d	21 01			21 30							22 01	22 01								23 01	23 01			
Bristol Parkway 7	a																								
	d							21 41												22 45					
Patchway	d				21 34							22 06	22 06								23 06	23 06			
Pilning	d																								
Gloucester 7	d									21 24	21 24														
Lydney	d									21 43	21 43														
Chepstow	d									21 52	21 52														
Caldicot	d									22 01	22 01														
Severn Tunnel Jn.	d	21 14			21 46					22 04	22 04	22 18	22 18								23 17	23 17			
Newport (South Wales)	a	21 26			21 58			22 03		22 15	22 15	22 29	22 36							23 19	23 34	23 34			
	d	21 26		21 52	21 59			22 05		22 16	22 16	22 30	22 37				22 40	22 42		23 19	23 35	23 35			23 47
Cardiff Central 7	a	21 44		22 06	22 18			22 23		22 31	22 35	22 52	23 00				22 55	23 04		23 40	23 56	23 56			00 02

		AW FO	AW FX	GW FO		GW FX
				◇1 ⊏		◇1 ⊏
Bath Spa 7	d			23 49		23 56
Oldfield Park	d					
Keynsham	d					
Bristol Temple Meads 10	a			00 03		00 10
	d					
Filton Abbey Wood	d					
Bristol Parkway 7	a					
	d					
Patchway	d					
Pilning	d					
Gloucester 7	d	23 13	23 13			
Lydney	d	23 33	23 33			
Chepstow	d	23 42	23 42			
Caldicot	d	23 51	23 51			
Severn Tunnel Jn.	d	23 54	23 54			
Newport (South Wales)	a	00 06	00 06			
	d	00 07	00 07			
Cardiff Central 7	a	00 33	00 35			

Mondays to Fridays

from 3 September

		GW	GW	AW MX	AW MO	AW MX	GW	GW MX	GW	GW MX		AW MX	GW	GW	GW MX	GW	GW	XC MX	XC MO	AW		GW	AW	GW	XC
		◇1 A ⊏	◇1 B ⊏	◇	◇		◇1 B ⊏	◇1 ⊏	◇1 A ⊏	◇1 ⊏		◇	◇1 B ⊏	◇1 C ⊏	◇1 ⊏	◇1 B ⊏	◇1 C ⊏	1	1	◇					◇1 H
Bath Spa 7	d						23p55	23p56	23p57						01 15										06 09
Oldfield Park	d						↓		↓																
Keynsham	d						↓		↓																
Bristol Temple Meads 10	a						00 09	00 10	00 11				01 05	01 07	01 29	01 35	01 37								06 20
	d												↓	↓	01 36	↓	↓	05 19	05 19			05 54		06 19	06 27
Filton Abbey Wood	d												↓	↓		↓	↓					06 01		06 31	
Bristol Parkway 7	a												↓	↓		↓	↓	05 28	05 28						06 37
	d	23p16	23p17							00 23			↓	↓		↓	↓	05 38	05 38						
Patchway	d	↓	↓										↓	↓		↓	↓					06 06		06 35	
Pilning	d	↓	↓										↓	↓		↓	↓								
Gloucester 7	d	↓	↓			23p13							↓	↓		↓	↓						05 50		
Lydney	d	↓	↓			23p33							↓	↓		↓	↓						06 09		
Chepstow	d	↓	↓			23p42							↓	↓		↓	↓						06 19		
Caldicot	d	↓	↓			23p51							↓	↓		↓	↓						06 26		
Severn Tunnel Jn.	d	↓	↓			23p54							↓	↓		↓	↓					06 17	06 29	06 47	
Newport (South Wales)	a	23p40	23p43			00 06				00 51			↓	↓	02s10	↓	↓	05 58	06 08			06 28	06 41	06 58	
	d	23p43	23p43	23p47	23p55	00 07				00 52		00 59	↓	↓		↓	↓	06 00	06 10	06 17		06 29	06 44	07 00	
Cardiff Central 7	a	00 05	00 04	00 02	00 20	00 35				01 11		01 18			02 31			06 18	06 24	06 33		06 48	07 00	07 20	

A MO from 17 September
B 3 September, 10 September
C MO from 29 October

When events are being held at the Millenium Stadium, services are subject to alteration. Please check times before travelling.

Bath Spa, Bristol and Gloucester - Cardiff

Mondays to Fridays
from 3 September
Network Diagram - see first Page of Table 132

		XC	GW	AW	GW	XC		AW	GW	GW	GW	SW	GW	GW	GW	AW		AW	AW	GW	GW	XC	GW	GW	GW
		◇■		◇ ⊼	◇■ ☕	◇■		◇			◇	■	◇■ ☕	◇	◇■ ☕	◇ ⊼			◇ ⊼		◇■ ☕	◇■ A ⊼		■ ⊼	◇■ ☕
Bath Spa	d		06 28		06 54					07 08	07 25	07 35		07 48	07 59								08 08	08 22	08 29
Oldfield Park	d		06 31							07 11	07 28	07 38		07 51									08 11	08 25	
Keynsham	d		06 38							07 18	07 35	07 45		07 58	08 08								08 18	08 34	
Bristol Temple Meads	a		06 46		07 07					07 27	07 46	07 52		08 06	08 17								08 29	08 41	08 45
	d		06 50		07 14				07 19	07 34	07 54			08 10						08 24			08 41	08 54	
Filton Abbey Wood	d		07 02		07 22				07 30	07 43	08 01			08 22						08 33			08 48	09 01	
Bristol Parkway	a								07 33	07 47				08 29									08 52		
	d								07 40	07 48			08 07								08 41		08 52		
Patchway	d								07 44		08 06									08 37					
Pilning	d																								
Gloucester	d	06 18				07 01				08a29								07 58				08 28	09a33		
Lydney	d	06 37				07 20												08 17							
Chepstow	d	06 46				07 29												08 27				08 54			
Caldicot	d	06 55				07 38												08 35							
Severn Tunnel Jn.	d	06 58	07 14			07 41			07 56									08 38		08 49					
Newport (South Wales)	a	07 09	07 25		07 44	07 52			08 07		08 27		08 32					08 50		09 02	09 07	09 12		09 25	
	d	07 10	07 27	07 35	07 44	07 53		08 01	08 09		08 27		08 32			08 38		08 52	09 03	09 03	09 08	09 14		09 25	
Cardiff Central	a	07 26	07 44	07 51	08 00	08 08		08 17	08 24		08 46		08 46			08 53		09 07	09 23	09 24	09 24	09 30		09 43	

		GW		GW	GW	AW	AW BHX	AW	GW	GW	XC	GW		GW	AW	GW	GW	GW	AW	GW	GW	XC		GW	GW
		◇■ B ☕		◇	◇■ C Ø	◇ ⊼	◇■ ⊠			◇■ ☕	◇■ A ⊼			◇■ ☕	◇ ⊼	◇ ⊼	◇■ ☕	◇■ Ø	◇ ⊼		◇■ ☕	◇■ A ⊼		◇	◇■ ☕
Bath Spa	d			08 47	08 57							09 15		09 30		09 36	10 00							10 08	10 24
Oldfield Park	d			08 49								09 18												10 11	
Keynsham	d			08 57								09 25				09 44								10 18	
Bristol Temple Meads	a			09 05	09 10							09 35		09 45		09 52	10 15							10 28	10 38
	d			09 10					09 21			09 41				09 56				10 21				10 41	
Filton Abbey Wood	d			09 22					09 30			09 48				10 03				10 30				10 48	
Bristol Parkway	a			09 28								09 52												10 52	
	d	09 07								09 41		09 52						10 07			10 41			10 52	
Patchway	d								09 35											10 35					
Pilning	d																								
Gloucester	d							08 58			09 24	10a33										10 24		11a34	
Lydney	d							09 17														10 43			
Chepstow	d							09 27			09 50														
Caldicot	d							09 36																	
Severn Tunnel Jn.	d							09 38	09 46											10 46					
Newport (South Wales)	a	09 31						09 51	09 58	10 04	10 09					10 26		10 31		11 02	11 06	11 11			
	d	09 32				09 37	09 41	09 52	10 00	10 05	10 11				10 22	10 26		10 31	11 01	11 02	11 06	11 12			
Cardiff Central	a	09 48				09 57	09 58	10 07	10 18	10 21	10 25				10 37	10 43		10 46	11 15	11 23	11 23	11 27			

		AW	GW	GW	GW	AW	AW BHX	GW		GW	XC	GW	GW	AW	GW	SW	GW	GW		AW	GW	AW	GW	XC	GW
		◇ ⊼	◇ ⊼	◇■ ☕	◇■ Ø		■ ⊼	◇		◇■ ☕	◇■ A ⊼	◇	◇■ D ☕	◇ ⊼	◇ ⊼	◇■	◇■ ☕	◇■ Ø				◇ ⊼	◇■ ☕	◇■ A ⊼	◇
Bath Spa	d		10 36	11 00								11 08	11 24		11 36	11 47	12 00								12 13
Oldfield Park	d											11 11													12 15
Keynsham	d											11 18				11 55									12 23
Bristol Temple Meads	a		10 48	11 15								11 28	11 40		11 48	12 05	12 15								12 31
	d		10 54					11 21				11 41			11 54						12 21				12 41
Filton Abbey Wood	d		11 01					11 30				11 48			12 01						12 30				12 48
Bristol Parkway	a											11 52													12 52
	d				11 07					11 41		11 52						12 07					12 41		12 52
Patchway	d							11 35													12 35				
Pilning	d																								
Gloucester	d					10 58					11 24	12a33								11 58				12 24	13a31
Lydney	d					11 17														12 17					
Chepstow	d					11 27					11 50									12 27				12 50	
Caldicot	d					11 35														12 35					
Severn Tunnel Jn.	d					11 38		11 46												12 38	12 46				
Newport (South Wales)	a		11 26		11 31	11 50		11 58		12 04	12 10				12 25			12 31		12 50	13 00		13 06	13 11	
	d	11 22	11 27		11 31	11 51	11 53	12 00		12 04	12 11			12 23	12 26			12 32		12 52	13 01	13 00	13 06	13 12	
Cardiff Central	a	11 37	11 43		11 46	12 12	12 08	12 18		12 21	12 28			12 38	12 43			12 46		13 07	13 22	13 22	13 22	13 29	

A ⊼ to Newport (South Wales)
B The St. David
C The Merchant Venturer
D The Torbay Express

When events are being held at the Millenium Stadium, services are subject to alteration. Please check times before travelling.

Bath Spa, Bristol and Gloucester - Cardiff

Mondays to Fridays
from 3 September
Network Diagram - see first Page of Table 132

		GW	AW	GW		GW	GW	GW	GW	GW	GW	XC	AW	GW		GW	GW	AW	AW	GW	GW	XC	GW	GW
		◇■ ☕	◇ ⊼	◇ ⊼		◇■ ☕	◇■ Ø			◇■ ☕	◇■ ☕	◇■ A ⊼	◇ ⊼	◇ ⊼		◇■ ☕	◇■ Ø		■ ⊼		◇■ ☕	◇■ A ⊼	◇	◇■ ☕
Bath Spa	d	12 24		12 36		13 00			13 22	13 24				13 36		14 00							14 14	14 24
Oldfield Park	d								13 25														14 17	
Keynsham	d								13 32														14 24	
Bristol Temple Meads	a	12 39		12 48		13 15			13 41	13 44				13 48		14 15							14 35	14 39
	d			12 54				13 21						13 54						14 21			14 41	
Filton Abbey Wood	d			13 01				13 30						14 01						14 30			14 48	
Bristol Parkway	a																						14 51	
	d						13 07				13 41						14 07				14 41		14 52	
Patchway	d							13 35												14 35				
Pilning	d																							
Gloucester	d											13 24						13 58				14 24	15a32	
Lydney	d											13 43						14 17						
Chepstow	d																	14 27				14 50		
Caldicot	d																	14 35						
Severn Tunnel Jn.	d							13 46										14 38		14 46				
Newport (South Wales)	a			13 26			13 31	13 58			14 04	14 09		14 26			14 30	14 50		15 02	15 06	15 11		
	d		13 23	13 26			13 31	14 00			14 05	14 11	14 22	14 27			14 31	14 52	15 00	15 03	15 06	15 12		
Cardiff Central	a		13 39	13 43			13 46	14 18			14 22	14 29	14 37	14 43			14 46	15 07	15 19	15 24	15 22	15 29		

		GW	SW	GW	GW	AW	AW	GW	GW	GW		XC	GW	GW	GW	GW	GW	AW	AW	GW		GW	XC	GW	GW
		◇ ⊼	◇■	◇■ ☕	◇■ ☕	■ ⊼	⊼	◇	◇■ ☕			◇■ A ⊼	◇	◇■ ☕	◇ ⊼	◇■ ☕	◇■ ☕	■ ⊼	◇ ⊼			◇■ ☕	◇■ A ⊼		◇■ ☕
Bath Spa	d	14 36	14 47	15 00						15 08			15 21	15 24	15 36	16 00								16 08	16 24
Oldfield Park	d									15 11														16 11	
Keynsham	d		14 55							15 18														16 18	
Bristol Temple Meads	a	14 48	15 05	15 15						15 28			15 34	15 40	15 48	16 15								16 29	16 39
	d	14 54						15 21		15 34			15 41		15 54					16 24				16 41	
Filton Abbey Wood	d	15 01						15 30					15 48		16 01					16 30				16 48	
Bristol Parkway	a									15 48			15 52											16 52	
	d				15 07				15 41				15 52				16 07					16 41		16 52	
Patchway	d							15 35												16 35					
Pilning	d																								
Gloucester	d						14 58					15 24	16a33										16 24	17a33	
Lydney	d						15 17																16 43		
Chepstow	d						15 27					15 50											16 52		
Caldicot	d						15 35																		
Severn Tunnel Jn.	d						15 38	15 46												16 46					
Newport (South Wales)	a	15 25			15 31		15 50	15 58	16 05			16 10			16 25		16 30			17 00		17 06	17 11		
	d	15 26			15 32	15 37	15 52	16 00	16 06			16 12			16 25		16 31	16 40	17 01	17 01		17 06	17 12		
Cardiff Central	a	15 43			15 46	15 53	16 10	16 18	16 22			16 29			16 43		16 46	16 55	17 15	17 25		17 22	17 28		

		AW	GW	GW	GW	AW		GW	GW	GW	XC	GW	GW	GW	GW	GW		AW	AW	AW	GW	GW	XC	GW	GW
		■ ⊼	■ ⊼	◇■ ☕				◇■ ☕		◇■ ☕	◇■	◇	◇■ ☕	■ ⊼	◇■ ☕	◇■ B ☕		■ ⊼		◇ ⊼		◇■ C Ø	◇■		◇■ ☕
Bath Spa	d		16 36		16 43			17 00				17 08	17 27	17 36	18 00									18 08	18 29
Oldfield Park	d											17 11												18 11	
Keynsham	d				16 51							17 18												18 18	
Bristol Temple Meads	a		16 48		16 59			17 15				17 29	17 41	17 48	18 14									18 28	18 44
	d		16 54		17 10				17 21			17 41		17 54							18 21			18 41	
Filton Abbey Wood	d		17 01		17 22				17 30			17 48		18 01							18 30			18 48	
Bristol Parkway	a				17 27							17 52												18 52	
	d			17 07						17 41		17 52				18 07						18 41		18 52	
Patchway	d								17 35												18 35				
Pilning	d																								
Gloucester	d					16 58					17 27	18a33							17 59				18 31	19a30	
Lydney	d					17 17													18 18						
Chepstow	d					17 27													18 28						
Caldicot	d					17 35													18 36						
Severn Tunnel Jn.	d		17 14			17 38			17 46					18 14					18 39		18 50				
Newport (South Wales)	a		17 25	17 31		17 50			17 58	18 04	18 10			18 25		18 30			18 51		19 06	19 11	19 16		
	d	17 22	17 27	17 31		17 52			18 00	18 04	18 11			18 26		18 31		18 41	18 53	19 01	19 06	19 11	19 17		
Cardiff Central	a	17 37	17 43	17 46		18 10			18 17	18 19	18 27			18 43		18 48		18 55	19 09	19 21	19 24	19 26	19 33		

A ⊼ to Newport (South Wales)
B The Capitals United
C The Red Dragon

When events are being held at the Millenium Stadium, services are subject to alteration. Please check times before travelling.

Bath Spa, Bristol and Gloucester - Cardiff

Mondays to Fridays
from 3 September

Network Diagram - see first Page of Table 132

		AW ■ 🚌	GW ■ 🚌	GW ◇1 🍴	GW ◇1 🍴	AW	GW	GW ◇1 🍴	XC ◇1	GW	GW ◇1 🍴	GW ◇1 A 🍴	GW ◇ 🚌	GW ◇	GW ◇1 🍴	GW ◇1 🍴	AW ■ 🚌	XC ◇1	AW	GW ◇ 🚌	GW ◇1 🍴	AW ◇ 🚌
Bath Spa 7	d		18 36	18 59						19 08	19 24	19 30	19 36	19 49	19 59					20 12	20 30	
Oldfield Park	d									19 11				19 52						20 14		
Keynsham	d									19 18				19 59						20 21		
Bristol Temple Meads 10	a		18 48	19 12						19 29	19 41	19 43	19 48	20 08	20 13					20 30	20 44	
	d		18 54				19 21			19 41			19 54					20 15				
Filton Abbey Wood	d		19 01				19 30			19 48			20 01					20 22				
Bristol Parkway 7	a									19 52												
	d				19 07			19 44		19 52						20 07						
Patchway	d						19 35											20 25				
Pilning	d																					
Gloucester 7	d					18 58			19 28	20a32									19 58			
Lydney	d					19 17													20 17			
Chepstow	d					19 27													20 27			
Caldicot	d					19 34													20 36			
Severn Tunnel Jn.	d		19 14			19 37	19 46						20 16					20 37	20 39			
Newport (South Wales)	a		19 26		19 31	19 50	20 01	20 07	20 11				20 27			20 31		20 47	20 51			
	d	19 22	19 26		19 31	19 52	20 02	20 08	20 13				20 28			20 33	20 39	20 49	20 52			21 00
Cardiff Central 7	a	19 43	19 46		19 48	20 09	20 20	20 22	20 27				20 43			20 48	20 58	21 02	21 10			21 19

		GW FX ◇1 🍴	GW FO ◇1 🍴	XC ◇1	GW ◇ 🚌	GW ◇1 🍴	AW ◇ 🚌	GW	GW	GW ◇1 🍴	GW ◇1 ⊘	XC FO ◇1	XC FX ◇1	GW FO ◇	GW FX ◇	SW ◇1	GW ◇1 🍴	GW	AW FO ◇	AW FX ◇	GW ◇1 🍴	GW FO ◇	GW FX ◇
Bath Spa 7	d				20 36	21 00			21 08	21 30				21 36	21 36	21 51	22 13	22 25				22 36	22 36
Oldfield Park	d								21 11									22 28					
Keynsham	d								21 18							21 59		22 35					
Bristol Temple Meads 10	a				20 48	21 15			21 28	21 44				21 48	21 48	22 06	22 30	22 43				22 50	22 48
	d				20 54			21 19						21 54	21 54							22 54	22 54
Filton Abbey Wood	d				21 01			21 30						22 01	22 01							23 01	23 01
Bristol Parkway 7	a																						
	d	20 42	20 43								21 41										22 45		
Patchway	d							21 34						22 06	22 06							23 06	23 06
Pilning	d																						
Gloucester 7	d			20 24								21 24	21 24										
Lydney	d											21 43	21 43										
Chepstow	d											21 52	21 52										
Caldicot	d											22 01	22 01										
Severn Tunnel Jn.	d				21 14			21 46				22 04	22 04	22 18	22 18							23 17	23 17
Newport (South Wales)	a	21 04	21 05	21 11	21 26			21 58			22 03	22 15	22 15	22 29	22 36						23 19	23 34	23 34
	d	21 04	21 07	21 13	21 26		21 52	21 59			22 05	22 16	22 16	22 30	22 37				22 40	22 42	23 19	23 35	23 35
Cardiff Central 7	a	21 19	21 19	21 27	21 44		22 06	22 18			22 23	22 31	22 35	22 52	23 00				22 55	23 04	23 40	23 56	23 56

		GW	GW ◇1 🍴	AW ◇	AW FO	AW FX	GW FO ◇1 🍴	GW FX ◇1 🍴
Bath Spa 7	d	23 02	23 19				23 49	23 56
Oldfield Park	d	23 05						
Keynsham	d	23 12						
Bristol Temple Meads 10	a	23 23	23 32				00 03	00 10
	d							
Filton Abbey Wood	d							
Bristol Parkway 7	a							
	d							
Patchway	d							
Pilning	d							
Gloucester 7	d				23 13	23 13		
Lydney	d				23 33	23 33		
Chepstow	d				23 42	23 42		
Caldicot	d				23 51	23 51		
Severn Tunnel Jn.	d				23 54	23 54		
Newport (South Wales)	a				00 06	00 06		
	d			23 47	00 07	00 07		
Cardiff Central 7	a			00 02	00 33	00 35		

A The Bristolian

When events are being held at the Millenium Stadium, services are subject to alteration. Please check times before travelling.

Bath Spa, Bristol and Gloucester - Cardiff

Saturdays
until 23 June

Network Diagram - see first Page of Table 132

		AW ◇	AW	GW ◇1 🍴	GW ◇1 🍴	AW ◇	GW ◇1 🍴	AW	AW	XC ◇1	GW ◇1	GW	AW ◇ 🚌	XC ◇1	GW	GW	SW 1	AW	GW	GW ◇1 🍴	AW ◇ 🚌	AW	GW
Bath Spa 7	d			23p49			01 15									07 08	07 35			08 00			
Oldfield Park	d															07 11	07 38						
Keynsham	d															07 18	07 45						
Bristol Temple Meads 10	a			00 03			01 29									07 29	07 52			08 15			
	d						01 36				06 46	06 50			07 21	07 41			07 54				08 20
Filton Abbey Wood	d										06 54	07 02			07 30	07 48			08 01				08 30
Bristol Parkway 7	a										06 58					07 52							
	d				00 16						07 11					07 52							
Patchway	d														07 34								08 35
Pilning	d																						
Gloucester 7	d		23p13						05 50	06 15				07 00		08a32						07 58	
Lydney	d		23p33						06 09	06 34				07 20								08 17	
Chepstow	d		23p42						06 19	06 43				07 29								08 27	
Caldicot	d		23p51						06 27	06 52				07 38								08 35	
Severn Tunnel Jn.	d		23p54						06 30	06 55		07 14		07 41	07 46							08 38	08 46
Newport (South Wales)	a		00 06		00 38		02s02		06 42	07 06	07 31	07 25		07 52	07 58				08 26			08 50	09 01
	d	23p47	00 07		00 38	00 59		06 38	06 44	07 07	07 31	07 26	07 38	07 53	07 58			08 01	08 27		08 33	08 52	09 01
Cardiff Central 7	a	00 02	00 33		00 53	01 18	02 19	06 54	07 00	07 22	07 47	07 44	07 53	08 08	08 18			08 19	08 43		08 50	09 10	09 21

		AW ◇ 🚌	XC ◇1 A 🚌	GW	GW ◇1 🍴	GW ◇	GW ◇	GW ■ 1 🍴	GW ◇1 🍴	AW ◇ 🚌	AW	GW	XC ◇1 A 🚌	GW	GW ◇1 🍴	GW ◇ B 🚌	GW ◇1 🍴	GW ◇1 🍴	AW ◇ 🚌	AW ◇ 🚌	GW	XC ◇1 A 🚌	GW ◇
Bath Spa 7	d			08 08	08 24	08 30	08 47	09 00						09 08	09 24	09 36	10 00						10 08
Oldfield Park	d			08 11			08 49							09 11									10 11
Keynsham	d			08 18			08 57							09 18									10 18
Bristol Temple Meads 10	a			08 29	08 39	08 44	09 05	09 15						09 27	09 39	09 48	10 15						10 29
	d			08 41		08 54						09 21		09 41		09 54					10 21		10 41
Filton Abbey Wood	d			08 48		09 01						09 30		09 48		10 01					10 30		10 48
Bristol Parkway 7	a			08 52										09 52									10 52
	d			08 52					09 07					09 52				10 07					10 52
Patchway	d											09 35									10 35		
Pilning	d																						
Gloucester 7	d		08 24	09a33							08 58		09 24	10a33								10 24	11a32
Lydney	d										09 17											10 43	
Chepstow	d		08 50								09 27		09 50										
Caldicot	d										09 35												
Severn Tunnel Jn.	d										09 38	09 46									10 46		
Newport (South Wales)	a		09 07			09 25			09 30		09 50	09 58	10 07			10 24		10 31			11 00	11 08	
	d	09 02	09 09			09 25			09 31	09 38	09 52	09 59	10 09			10 24		10 31	10 36	10 57	11 01	11 09	
Cardiff Central 7	a	09 22	09 23			09 43			09 47	09 58	10 07	10 18	10 23			10 43		10 47	10 53	11 15	11 22	11 24	

		GW ◇1 🍴	GW ◇ B 🚌	GW ◇1 🍴	GW ◇1 🍴	AW ◇ 🚌	AW	GW	XC ◇1 A 🚌	GW ◇	GW ◇1 🍴	GW ◇ B 🚌	SW ◇1	GW ◇1 🍴	GW ◇1 ⊘	AW ◇ 🚌	AW	AW ◇ 🚌	GW	XC ◇1 A 🚌	GW ◇	GW ◇1 🍴
Bath Spa 7	d	10 24	10 36	11 00						11 08	11 24	11 36	11 47	12 00							12 17	12 24
Oldfield Park	d									11 11											12 19	
Keynsham	d									11 18			11 55								12 27	
Bristol Temple Meads 10	a	10 39	10 48	11 15						11 29	11 39	11 48	12 05	12 15							12 35	12 39
	d		10 54					11 21		11 41		11 54							12 21		12 41	
Filton Abbey Wood	d		11 01					11 30		11 48		12 01							12 30		12 48	
Bristol Parkway 7	a									11 52											12 52	
	d				11 07					11 52					12 07						12 52	
Patchway	d							11 35											12 35			
Pilning	d																					
Gloucester 7	d						10 58		11 24	12a33							11 58			12 24	13a34	
Lydney	d						11 17										12 17					
Chepstow	d						11 27		11 50								12 27			12 50		
Caldicot	d						11 35										12 35					
Severn Tunnel Jn.	d						11 38	11 46									12 38		12 46			
Newport (South Wales)	a		11 24		11 31		11 50	11 58	12 07			12 24			12 31		12 50		13 00	13 11		
	d		11 24		11 31	11 37	11 52	11 59	12 09			12 24			12 31	12 37	12 52	12 56	13 01	13 12		
Cardiff Central 7	a		11 43		11 46	11 53	12 07	12 18	12 23			12 43			12 46	12 53	13 07	13 15	13 18	13 27		

		GW ◇	GW ◇1 🍴	GW ◇1 ⊘	AW ◇ 🚌	GW	XC ◇1 A 🚌	GW ◇	GW ◇1 🍴	GW ◇	GW ◇1 🍴	GW ◇1 🍴	AW ◇ 🚌	AW	GW	AW ■ 🚌	XC ◇1 A 🚌	GW ◇	GW ◇1 🍴	GW ◇	SW ◇1	GW ◇1 🍴	GW ◇1 🍴
Bath Spa 7	d	12 36	13 00					13 19	13 24	13 36	14 00							14 08	14 24	14 36	14 47	15 00	
Oldfield Park	d							13 22										14 11					
Keynsham	d							13 29										14 18			14 55		
Bristol Temple Meads 10	a	12 48	13 14					13 37	13 42	13 48	14 15							14 28	14 39	14 48	15 05	15 15	
	d	12 54				13 21		13 41		13 54					14 21			14 41		14 54			
Filton Abbey Wood	d	13 01				13 30		13 48		14 01					14 30			14 48		15 01			
Bristol Parkway 7	a							13 52										14 52					
	d			13 07				13 52				14 07						14 52					15 07
Patchway	d					13 35									14 35								
Pilning	d																						
Gloucester 7	d						13 24	14a33						13 58			14 24	15a32					
Lydney	d						13 43							14 17									
Chepstow	d													14 27			14 50						
Caldicot	d													14 35									
Severn Tunnel Jn.	d					13 46								14 38	14 46								
Newport (South Wales)	a	13 25		13 31		13 58	14 08			14 24		14 31		14 50	14 59		15 11			15 25			15 31
	d	13 25		13 31	13 37	13 59	14 09			14 24		14 31	14 37	14 52	15 00	15 06	15 12			15 25			15 31
Cardiff Central 7	a	13 43		13 47	13 53	14 18	14 24			14 43		14 46	14 53	15 09	15 18	15 26	15 27			15 43			15 46

A 🚌 to Newport (South Wales)

B 🚌 to Bristol Temple Meads

When events are being held at the Millenium Stadium, services are subject to alteration. Please check times before travelling.

Table 132

Bath Spa, Bristol and Gloucester - Cardiff

Saturdays until 23 June

Network Diagram - see first Page of Table 132

		AW	AW	GW	XC	GW	GW	GW	GW	GW	AW	AW	GW	XC	GW	GW	GW	GW	GW	AW	AW	GW
		■ ⊼	⊼		◇■ A ⊼	◇	◇■ ☕	◇	◇■ ☕	◇■ ☕	■ ⊼	◇ ⊼		◇■ A ⊼		◇■ ☕	◇	◇■ ☕	◇■ ☕	■ ⊼		
Bath Spa ■	d					15 18	15 24	15 36	16 00						16 08	16 24	16 36	17 00				
Oldfield Park	d					15 21									16 11							
Keynsham	d					15 28									16 18							
Bristol Temple Meads ■	a					15 36	15 41	15 49	16 15						16 29	16 39	16 48	17 15				
	d			15 21		15 41		15 54					16 21		16 41		16 54					17 21
Filton Abbey Wood	d			15 30		15 48		16 01					16 30		16 48		17 01					17 30
Bristol Parkway ■	a					15 52									16 52							
	d					15 52				16 07					16 52				17 07			
Patchway	d			15 35									16 35									17 35
Pilning	d			15 41																		
Gloucester ■	d		14 58		15 24	16a33								16 24	17a33						16 58	
Lydney	d		15 17											16 43							17 17	
Chepstow	d		15 27		15 50									16 52							17 27	
Caldicot	d		15 35																		17 35	
Severn Tunnel Jn.	d		15 38	15 46									16 46				17 14				17 38	17 46
Newport (South Wales)	a		15 50	16 01	16 08			16 24		16 31			17 00	17 10			17 26		17 29		17 50	17 58
	d	15 37	15 52	16 01	16 10			16 24		16 31	16 37	16 56	17 01	17 11			17 26		17 31	17 37	17 52	18 00
Cardiff Central ■	a	15 53	16 07	16 18	16 25			16 43		16 47	16 53	17 08	17 18	17 26			17 43		17 46	17 53	18 10	18 18

		XC	GW	GW	GW	GW	GW	AW	AW	AW	GW	XC	GW	GW	GW	GW	GW	AW	AW	GW	GW	XC	GW
		◇■ ⊼		◇■ ☕	◇	◇■ ☕	◇■ ☕	■ ⊼		◇ ⊼		◇■	◇	◇■ ☕	■	◇■ ☕	◇■ ☕	■ ⊼			◇	◇■	◇■ ☕
Bath Spa ■	d		17 08	17 24	17 36	18 00							18 18	18 24	18 36	19 00					19 08		19 24
Oldfield Park	d		17 11										18 20								19 11		
Keynsham	d		17 18										18 28								19 18		
Bristol Temple Meads ■	a		17 28	17 39	17 48	18 15							18 36	18 39	18 48	19 15					19 26		19 38
	d		17 41		17 54						18 21		18 41		18 54					19 21			
Filton Abbey Wood	d		17 48		18 01						18 30		18 48		19 01					19 28			
Bristol Parkway ■	a		17 52										18 52										
	d		17 52				18 07						18 52				19 07						
Patchway	d										18 35									19 33			
Pilning	d																						
Gloucester ■	d	17 24	18a33						17 58			18 31	19a33						18 58			19 24	
Lydney	d								18 17										19 17				
Chepstow	d								18 27										19 27				
Caldicot	d								18 35										19 34				
Severn Tunnel Jn.	d				18 14				18 38		18 47								19 37	19 46			
Newport (South Wales)	a	18 05			18 25		18 30		18 50		19 05	19 12			19 26		19 30		19 50	19 58		20 05	
	d	18 07			18 25		18 31	18 37	18 52	18 57	19 05	19 14			19 26		19 31	19 41	19 52	19 58		20 07	
Cardiff Central ■	a	18 21			18 43		18 46	18 53	19 10	19 16	19 23	19 29			19 43		19 46	19 58	20 11	20 18		20 21	

		GW	GW	GW	GW	AW	AW	XC	GW	GW	AW	XC	GW	GW	GW	GW	AW	GW	XC	GW	AW	GW	SW
		◇	◇	◇■ ☕	◇■ ☕	■ ⊼		◇■ ⊼	◇	◇■ ☕	◇ ⊼	◇■	◇	◇■ ☕	◇■ ☕		◇ ⊼		◇■	◇■ ☕		◇	◇■
Bath Spa ■	d	19 36	19 47	20 00					20 16	20 24			20 36	21 00		21 08				21 30		21 39	21 51
Oldfield Park	d		19 50						20 18							21 11							
Keynsham	d		19 57						20 25							21 18							21 59
Bristol Temple Meads ■	a	19 48	20 05	20 15					20 33	20 40			20 48	21 16		21 29				21 45		21 51	22 06
	d	19 54						20 21					20 54					21 29				21 54	
Filton Abbey Wood	d	20 01						20 28					21 01					21 36				22 01	
Bristol Parkway ■	a																						
	d				20 07										21 07								
Patchway	d							20 32										21 41				22 06	
Pilning	d																						
Gloucester ■	d						19 58					20 24							21 24				
Lydney	d						20 17												21 43				
Chepstow	d						20 27												21 52				
Caldicot	d						20 35												22 01				
Severn Tunnel Jn.	d						20 38	20 42										21 52	22 04			22 18	
Newport (South Wales)	a	20 25			20 30		20 50	20 55				21 11	21 25		21 30			22 09	22 21			22 38	
	d	20 25			20 31	20 40	20 52	20 57			21 02	21 13	21 25		21 31		21 45	22 11	22 21		22 34	22 38	
Cardiff Central ■	a	20 43			20 44	21 00	21 09	21 11			21 21	21 29	21 43		21 47		22 04	22 30	22 43		22 53	22 58	

A ⊼ to Newport (South Wales)

When events are being held at the Millenium Stadium, services are subject to alteration. Please check times before travelling.

Table 132

Bath Spa, Bristol and Gloucester - Cardiff

Saturdays until 23 June

Network Diagram - see first Page of Table 132

		GW	GW	GW	GW	GW	GW	AW	GW	AW
		◇■ ☕	◇■ ☕		◇	◇■ ☕			◇■ ☕	🚌
Bath Spa ■	d	22 00		22 25	22 36	23 00	23 08			
Oldfield Park	d			22 28			23 11			
Keynsham	d			22 36			23 18			
Bristol Temple Meads ■	a	22 14		22 44	22 50	23 15	23 31			
	d				22 54					
Filton Abbey Wood	d				23 01					
Bristol Parkway ■	a									
	d		22 11						23 28	
Patchway	d				23 06					
Pilning	d									
Gloucester ■	d									23 09
Lydney	d									23 49
Chepstow	d									00 09
Caldicot	d									00 24
Severn Tunnel Jn.	d				23 18					00 34
Newport (South Wales)	a		22 46		23 35				23 57	00 59
	d		22 46		23 36			23 46	23 58	00 59
Cardiff Central ■	a		23 06		23 55			00 05	00 18	01 29

Saturdays 30 June to 4 August

		AW	AW	GW	GW	AW	GW	AW	AW	XC	GW	GW	AW	XC	GW	GW	SW	AW	GW	GW	AW	AW	GW
		◇		◇■ ☕	◇■ ☕	◇	◇■ ☕			◇■	◇■		◇ ⊼	◇■			■			◇■ ☕	◇ ⊼		
Bath Spa ■	d			23p49			01 15									07 08	07 35			08 00			
Oldfield Park	d															07 11	07 38						
Keynsham	d															07 18	07 45						
Bristol Temple Meads ■	a			00 03			01 29									07 29	07 52			08 15			
	d						01 36				06 46	06 50			07 21	07 41			07 54				08 20
Filton Abbey Wood	d										06 54	07 02			07 30	07 48			08 01				08 30
Bristol Parkway ■	a										06 58					07 52							
	d				00 16						07 11					07 52							
Patchway	d														07 34								08 35
Pilning	d																						
Gloucester ■	d		23p13						05 50	06 15				07 00		08a32						07 58	
Lydney	d		23p33						06 09	06 34				07 20								08 17	
Chepstow	d		23p42						06 19	06 43				07 29								08 27	
Caldicot	d		23p51						06 27	06 52				07 38								08 35	
Severn Tunnel Jn.	d		23p54						06 30	06 55		07 14		07 41	07 46							08 38	08 46
Newport (South Wales)	a		00 06		00 38		02s02		06 42	07 06	07 31	07 25		07 52	07 58				08 26			08 50	09 01
	d	23p47	00 07		00 38	00 59		06 38	06 44	07 07	07 31	07 26	07 38	07 53	07 58			08 01	08 27		08 33	08 52	09 01
Cardiff Central ■	a	00 02	00 33		00 53	01 18	02 19	06 54	07 00	07 22	07 47	07 44	07 53	08 08	08 18			08 19	08 43		08 50	09 10	09 21

		AW	XC	GW	GW	GW	GW	GW	GW	AW	AW	GW	XC	GW	GW	GW	GW	GW	AW	AW	GW	XC	GW
		◇ ⊼	◇■ A ⊼		◇■ ☕	◇	◇	■ ■ ☕	◇■ ☕	◇ ⊼			◇■ A ⊼		◇■ ☕	◇ B ⊼	◇■ ☕	◇■ ☕	◇ ⊼	◇ ⊼		◇■ A ⊼	◇
Bath Spa ■	d			08 08	08 24	08 30	08 47	09 00						09 08	09 24	09 36	10 00						10 08
Oldfield Park	d			08 11			08 49							09 11									10 11
Keynsham	d			08 18			08 57							09 18									10 18
Bristol Temple Meads ■	a			08 29	08 39	08 44	09 05	09 15						09 27	09 39	09 48	10 15						10 29
	d			08 41		08 54						09 21		09 41		09 54					10 21		10 41
Filton Abbey Wood	d			08 48		09 01						09 30		09 48		10 01					10 30		10 48
Bristol Parkway ■	a			08 52										09 52									10 52
	d			08 52					09 07					09 52				10 07					10 52
Patchway	d											09 35									10 35		
Pilning	d																						
Gloucester ■	d		08 24	09a33							08 58		09 24	10a33								10 24	11a32
Lydney	d										09 17											10 43	
Chepstow	d		08 50								09 27		09 50										
Caldicot	d										09 35												
Severn Tunnel Jn.	d										09 38	09 46									10 46		
Newport (South Wales)	a		09 07			09 25			09 30		09 50	09 58	10 07			10 24		10 31			11 00	11 08	
	d	09 02	09 09			09 25			09 31	09 38	09 52	09 59	10 09			10 24		10 31	10 36	10 57	11 01	11 09	
Cardiff Central ■	a	09 22	09 23			09 43			09 47	09 58	10 07	10 18	10 23			10 43		10 47	10 53	11 15	11 22	11 24	

A ⊼ to Newport (South Wales)

B ⊼ to Bristol Temple Meads

When events are being held at the Millenium Stadium, services are subject to alteration. Please check times before travelling.

Saturdays
30 June to 4 August

Bath Spa, Bristol and Gloucester - Cardiff

Network Diagram - see first Page of Table 132

		GW	GW	GW	GW	AW	AW	GW	XC	GW	GW	GW	SW	GW	GW	AW	AW	AW	GW	XC	GW	GW
		◇■ ☕	◇ A ✕	◇■ ☕	◇■ ☕	◇ ✕			◇■ B ✕	◇	◇■ ☕	◇ A ✕	◇■	◇■ ☕	◇■ ⊘	◇ ✕		◇ ✕		◇■ B ✕	◇	◇■ ☕
Bath Spa ■	d	10 24	10 36	11 00						11 08	11 24	11 36	11 47	12 00							12 17	12 24
Oldfield Park	d									11 11											12 19	
Keynsham	d									11 18			11 55								12 27	
Bristol Temple Meads ■	a	10 39	10 48	11 15						11 29	11 39	11 48	12 05	12 15							12 35	12 39
	d		10 54					11 21		11 41		11 54							12 21		12 41	
Filton Abbey Wood	d		11 01					11 30		11 48		12 01							12 30		12 48	
Bristol Parkway ■	a									11 52											12 52	
	d				11 07					11 52					12 07						12 52	
Patchway	d							11 35											12 35			
Pilning	d																					
Gloucester ■	d						10 58		11 24	12a33							11 58			12 24	13a34	
Lydney	d						11 17										12 17					
Chepstow	d						11 27		11 50								12 27			12 50		
Caldicot	d						11 35										12 35					
Severn Tunnel Jn.	d						11 38	11 46									12 38		12 46			
Newport (South Wales)	a		11 24		11 31		11 50	11 58	12 07			12 24			12 31		12 50		13 00	13 11		
	d		11 24		11 31	11 37	11 52	11 59	12 09			12 24			12 31	12 37	12 52	12 56	13 01	13 12		
Cardiff Central ■	a		11 43		11 46	11 53	12 07	12 18	12 23			12 43			12 46	12 53	13 07	13 15	13 18	13 27		

		GW	GW	GW	AW	GW	XC	GW	GW	GW	GW	GW	AW	AW	GW	AW	XC	GW	GW	GW	SW	GW	GW
		◇	◇■ ☕	◇■ ⊘	◇ ✕		◇■ B ✕	◇	◇■ ☕	◇	◇■ ☕	◇■ ☕	◇ ✕			■ ✕	◇■ B ✕	◇	◇■ ☕	◇	◇■	◇■ ☕	◇■ ☕
Bath Spa ■	d	12 36	13 00					13 19	13 24	13 36	14 00							14 08	14 24	14 36	14 47	15 00	
Oldfield Park	d							13 22										14 11					
Keynsham	d							13 29										14 18			14 55		
Bristol Temple Meads ■	a	12 48	13 14					13 37	13 42	13 48	14 15							14 28	14 39	14 48	15 05	15 15	
	d	12 54				13 21		13 41		13 54					14 21			14 41		14 54			
Filton Abbey Wood	d	13 01				13 30		13 48		14 01					14 30			14 48		15 01			
Bristol Parkway ■	a							13 52										14 52					
	d			13 07				13 52				14 07						14 52					15 07
Patchway	d					13 35									14 35								
Pilning	d																						
Gloucester ■	d						13 24	14a33						13 58			14 24	15a32					
Lydney	d						13 43							14 17									
Chepstow	d													14 27			14 50						
Caldicot	d													14 35									
Severn Tunnel Jn.	d					13 46								14 38	14 46								
Newport (South Wales)	a	13 25		13 31		13 58	14 08			14 24		14 31		14 50	14 59		15 11			15 25			15 31
	d	13 25		13 31	13 37	13 59	14 09			14 24		14 31	14 37	14 52	15 00	15 06	15 12			15 25			15 31
Cardiff Central ■	a	13 43		13 47	13 53	14 18	14 24			14 43		14 46	14 53	15 09	15 18	15 26	15 27			15 43			15 46

		AW	AW	GW	XC	GW	GW	GW	GW	GW	AW	AW	GW	XC	GW	GW	GW	GW	GW	AW	AW	GW
		■ ✕	✕		◇■ B ✕	◇	◇■ ☕	◇	◇■ ☕	◇■ ☕	■ ✕	◇ ✕		◇■ B ✕		◇■ ☕	◇	◇■ ☕	◇■ ☕	■ ✕		
Bath Spa ■	d					15 18	15 24	15 36	16 00						16 08	16 24	16 36	17 00				
Oldfield Park	d					15 21									16 11							
Keynsham	d					15 28									16 18							
Bristol Temple Meads ■	a					15 36	15 41	15 49	16 15						16 29	16 39	16 48	17 15				
	d			15 21		15 41		15 54					16 21		16 41		16 54					17 21
Filton Abbey Wood	d			15 30		15 48		16 01					16 30		16 48		17 01					17 30
Bristol Parkway ■	a					15 52									16 52							
	d					15 52				16 07					16 52				17 07			
Patchway	d			15 35									16 35									17 35
Pilning	d			15 41																		
Gloucester ■	d		14 58		15 24	16a33								16 24	17a33						16 58	
Lydney	d		15 17											16 43							17 17	
Chepstow	d		15 27		15 50									16 52							17 27	
Caldicot	d		15 35																		17 35	
Severn Tunnel Jn.	d		15 38	15 46									16 46				17 14				17 38	17 46
Newport (South Wales)	a		15 50	16 01	16 08			16 24		16 31			17 00	17 10			17 26		17 29		17 50	17 58
	d	15 37	15 52	16 01	16 10			16 24		16 31	16 37	16 56	17 01	17 11			17 26		17 31	17 37	17 52	18 00
Cardiff Central ■	a	15 53	16 07	16 18	16 25			16 43		16 47	16 53	17 08	17 18	17 26			17 43		17 46	17 53	18 10	18 18

A ✕ to Bristol Temple Meads

B ✕ to Newport (South Wales)

When events are being held at the Millenium Stadium, services are subject to alteration. Please check times before travelling.

Table 132

Saturdays
30 June to 4 August

Bath Spa, Bristol and Gloucester - Cardiff

Network Diagram - see first Page of Table 132

		XC	GW	GW	GW	GW	GW	AW	AW	AW	GW	XC	GW	GW	GW	GW	GW	AW	AW	GW	GW	XC	GW
		◇■ ✕		◇■ ☕	◇	◇■ ☕	◇■ ☕	■ ✕		◇ ✕		◇■	◇	◇■ ☕	■	◇■ ☕	◇■ ☕	■ ✕			◇	◇■	◇■ ☕
Bath Spa ■	d		17 08	17 24	17 36	18 00							18 18	18 24	18 36	19 00					19 08		19 24
Oldfield Park	d		17 11										18 20								19 11		
Keynsham	d		17 18										18 28								19 18		
Bristol Temple Meads ■	a		17 28	17 39	17 48	18 15							18 36	18 39	18 48	19 15					19 26		19 38
	d		17 41		17 54						18 21		18 41		18 54					19 21			
Filton Abbey Wood	d		17 48		18 01						18 30		18 48		19 01					19 28			
Bristol Parkway ■	a		17 52										18 52										
	d		17 52				18 07						18 52				19 07						
Patchway	d										18 35									19 33			
Pilning	d																						
Gloucester ■	d	17 24	18a33						17 58			18 31	19a33						18 58			19 24	
Lydney	d								18 17										19 17				
Chepstow	d								18 27										19 27				
Caldicot	d								18 35										19 34				
Severn Tunnel Jn.	d				18 14				18 38		18 47								19 37	19 46			
Newport (South Wales)	a	18 05			18 25		18 30		18 50		19 05	19 12			19 26		19 30		19 50	19 58		20 05	
	d	18 07			18 25		18 31	18 37	18 52	18 57	19 05	19 14			19 26		19 31	19 41	19 52	19 58		20 07	
Cardiff Central ■	a	18 21			18 43		18 46	18 53	19 10	19 16	19 23	19 29			19 43		19 46	19 58	20 11	20 18		20 21	

		GW	GW	GW	GW	AW	AW	XC	GW	GW	AW	XC	GW	GW	GW	GW	AW	GW	XC	GW	AW	GW	SW
		◇	◇	◇■ ☕	◇■ ☕	■ ✕		◇■ ✕	◇	◇■ ☕	◇ ✕	◇■	◇	◇■ ☕	◇■ ☕		◇ ✕		◇■	◇■ ☕		◇	◇■
Bath Spa ■	d	19 36	19 47	20 00					20 16	20 24			20 36	21 00		21 08				21 30		21 39	21 51
Oldfield Park	d		19 50						20 18							21 11							
Keynsham	d		19 57						20 25							21 18							21 59
Bristol Temple Meads ■	a	19 48	20 05	20 15					20 33	20 40			20 48	21 16		21 29				21 45		21 51	22 06
	d	19 54						20 21					20 54					21 29				21 54	
Filton Abbey Wood	d	20 01						20 28					21 01					21 36				22 01	
Bristol Parkway ■	a																						
	d				20 07										21 07								
Patchway	d							20 32										21 41				22 06	
Pilning	d																						
Gloucester ■	d						19 58					20 24							21 24				
Lydney	d						20 17												21 43				
Chepstow	d						20 27												21 52				
Caldicot	d						20 35												22 01				
Severn Tunnel Jn.	d						20 38	20 42										21 52	22 04			22 18	
Newport (South Wales)	a	20 25			20 30		20 50	20 55				21 11	21 25		21 30			22 09	22 21			22 38	
	d	20 25			20 31	20 40	20 52	20 57			21 02	21 13	21 25		21 31		21 45	22 11	22 21		22 34	22 38	
Cardiff Central ■	a	20 43			20 44	21 00	21 09	21 11			21 21	21 29	21 43		21 47		22 04	22 30	22 43		22 53	22 58	

		GW	GW	GW	GW	GW	GW	AW	GW	AW
		◇■ ☕	◇■ ☕		◇	◇■ ☕			◇■ ☕	
Bath Spa ■	d	22 00		22 25	22 36	23 00	23 08			
Oldfield Park	d			22 28			23 11			
Keynsham	d			22 36			23 18			
Bristol Temple Meads ■	a	22 14		22 44	22 50	23 15	23 31			
	d				22 54					
Filton Abbey Wood	d				23 01					
Bristol Parkway ■	a									
	d		22 11						23 28	
Patchway	d				23 06					
Pilning	d									
Gloucester ■	d									23 09
Lydney	d									23 28
Chepstow	d									23 38
Caldicot	d									23 46
Severn Tunnel Jn.	d				23 18					23 49
Newport (South Wales)	a		22 46		23 35				23 57	00 07
	d		22 46		23 36			23 46	23 58	00 09
Cardiff Central ■	a		23 06		23 55			00 05	00 18	00 35

Saturdays
11 August to 8 September

		AW	AW	GW	GW	AW	GW	AW	AW	XC	GW	GW	AW	XC	GW	GW	SW	AW	GW	GW	AW	AW	GW
		◇		◇■ ☕	◇■ ☕	◇	◇■ ☕			◇■	◇■		◇ ✕	◇■			■			◇■ ☕	◇ ✕		
Bath Spa ■	d			23p49			01 15									07 08	07 35			08 00			
Oldfield Park	d															07 11	07 38						
Keynsham	d															07 18	07 45						
Bristol Temple Meads ■	a			00 03			01 29									07 29	07 52			08 15			
	d						01 36				06 46	06 50			07 21	07 41			07 54				08 20
Filton Abbey Wood	d										06 54	07 02			07 30	07 48			08 01				08 30
Bristol Parkway ■	a										06 58					07 52							
	d				00 16						07 11					07 52							
Patchway	d														07 34								08 35
Pilning	d																						
Gloucester ■	d		23p13						05 50	06 15				07 00		08a32						07 58	
Lydney	d		23p33						06 09	06 34				07 20								08 17	
Chepstow	d		23p42						06 19	06 43				07 29								08 27	
Caldicot	d		23p51						06 27	06 52				07 38								08 35	
Severn Tunnel Jn.	d		23p54						06 30	06 55		07 14		07 41	07 46							08 38	08 46
Newport (South Wales)	a		00 06		00 38		02s02		06 42	07 06	07 31	07 25		07 52	07 58				08 26			08 50	09 01
	d	23p47	00 07		00 38	00 59		06 38	06 44	07 07	07 31	07 26	07 38	07 53	07 58			08 01	08 27		08 33	08 52	09 01
Cardiff Central ■	a	00 02	00 33		00 53	01 18	02 19	06 54	07 00	07 22	07 47	07 44	07 53	08 08	08 18			08 19	08 43		08 50	09 10	09 21

When events are being held at the Millenium Stadium, services are subject to alteration. Please check times before travelling.

Table 132

Saturdays

Bath Spa, Bristol and Gloucester - Cardiff

11 August to 8 September

Network Diagram - see first Page of Table 132

Station		AW	XC	GW	GW	GW	GW	GW	GW	AW	AW	GW	XC	GW	GW	GW	GW	GW	AW	AW	GW	XC	GW
Notes			A										A			B						A	
Bath Spa	d			08 08	08 24	08 30	08 47	09 00						09 08	09 24	09 36	10 00						10 08
Oldfield Park	d			08 11			08 49							09 11									10 11
Keynsham	d			08 18			08 57							09 18									10 18
Bristol Temple Meads	a			08 29	08 39	08 44	09 05	09 15						09 27	09 39	09 48	10 15						10 29
	d			08 41		08 54						09 21		09 41		09 54					10 21		10 41
Filton Abbey Wood	d			08 48		09 01						09 30		09 48		10 01					10 30		10 48
Bristol Parkway	a			08 52										09 52									10 52
	d			08 52					09 07					09 52				10 07					10 52
Patchway	d											09 35									10 35		
Pilning	d																						
Gloucester	d		08 24	09a33							08 58		09 24	10a33								10 24	11a32
Lydney	d										09 17											10 43	
Chepstow	d		08 50								09 27		09 50										
Caldicot	d										09 35												
Severn Tunnel Jn.	d										09 38	09 46									10 46		
Newport (South Wales)	a		09 07			09 25			09 30		09 50	09 58	10 07			10 24		10 31			11 00	11 08	
	d	09 02	09 09			09 25			09 31	09 38	09 52	09 59	10 09			10 24		10 31	10 36	10 57	11 01	11 09	
Cardiff Central	a	09 22	09 23			09 43			09 47	09 58	10 07	10 18	10 23			10 43		10 47	10 53	11 15	11 22	11 24	

Station		GW	GW	GW	GW	AW	AW	GW	XC	GW	GW	GW	SW	GW	GW	AW	AW	AW	GW	XC	GW	GW
Notes			B						A			B								A		
Bath Spa	d	10 24	10 36	11 00						11 08	11 24	11 36	11 47	12 00							12 17	12 24
Oldfield Park	d									11 11											12 19	
Keynsham	d									11 18			11 55								12 27	
Bristol Temple Meads	a	10 39	10 48	11 15						11 29	11 39	11 48	12 05	12 15							12 35	12 39
	d		10 54					11 21		11 41		11 54							12 21		12 41	
Filton Abbey Wood	d		11 01					11 30		11 48		12 01							12 30		12 48	
Bristol Parkway	a									11 52											12 52	
	d				11 07					11 52					12 07						12 52	
Patchway	d							11 35											12 35			
Pilning	d																					
Gloucester	d						10 58		11 24	12a33							11 58			12 24	13a34	
Lydney	d						11 17										12 17					
Chepstow	d						11 27		11 50								12 27			12 50		
Caldicot	d						11 35										12 35					
Severn Tunnel Jn.	d						11 38	11 46									12 38		12 46			
Newport (South Wales)	a		11 24		11 31		11 50	11 58	12 07			12 24			12 31		12 50		13 00	13 11		
	d		11 24		11 31	11 37	11 52	11 59	12 09			12 24			12 31	12 37	12 52	12 56	13 01	13 12		
Cardiff Central	a		11 43		11 46	11 53	12 07	12 18	12 23			12 43			12 46	12 53	13 07	13 15	13 18	13 27		

Station		GW	GW	GW	AW	GW	XC	GW	GW	GW	GW	GW	AW	AW	GW	AW	XC	GW	GW	GW	SW	GW	GW
Notes							A										A						
Bath Spa	d	12 36	13 00					13 19	13 24	13 36	14 00							14 08	14 24	14 36	14 47	15 00	
Oldfield Park	d							13 22										14 11					
Keynsham	d							13 29										14 18			14 55		
Bristol Temple Meads	a	12 48	13 14					13 37	13 42	13 48	14 15							14 28	14 39	14 48	15 05	15 15	
	d	12 54				13 21		13 41		13 54					14 21			14 41		14 54			
Filton Abbey Wood	d	13 01				13 30		13 48		14 01					14 30			14 48		15 01			
Bristol Parkway	a							13 52										14 52					
	d			13 07				13 52				14 07						14 52					15 07
Patchway	d					13 35									14 35								
Pilning	d																						
Gloucester	d						13 24	14a33						13 58			14 24	15a32					
Lydney	d						13 43							14 17									
Chepstow	d													14 27			14 50						
Caldicot	d													14 35									
Severn Tunnel Jn.	d					13 46								14 38	14 46								
Newport (South Wales)	a	13 25		13 31		13 58	14 08			14 24		14 31		14 50	14 59		15 11			15 25			15 31
	d	13 25		13 31	13 37	13 59	14 09			14 24		14 31	14 37	14 52	15 00	15 06	15 12			15 25			15 31
Cardiff Central	a	13 43		13 47	13 53	14 18	14 24			14 43		14 46	14 53	15 09	15 18	15 26	15 27			15 43			15 46

A ⌶ to Newport (South Wales)

B ⌶ to Bristol Temple Meads

When events are being held at the Millenium Stadium, services are subject to alteration. Please check times before travelling.

Table 132

Saturdays

Bath Spa, Bristol and Gloucester - Cardiff

11 August to 8 September

Network Diagram - see first Page of Table 132

Station		AW	AW	GW	XC	GW	GW	GW	GW	GW	AW	AW	GW	XC	GW	GW	GW	GW	GW	AW	AW	GW
Notes					A									A								
Bath Spa	d					15 18	15 24	15 36	16 00						16 08	16 24	16 36	17 00				
Oldfield Park	d					15 21									16 11							
Keynsham	d					15 28									16 18							
Bristol Temple Meads	a					15 36	15 41	15 49	16 15						16 29	16 39	16 48	17 15				
	d			15 21		15 41		15 54					16 21		16 41		16 54					17 21
Filton Abbey Wood	d			15 30		15 48		16 01					16 30		16 48		17 01					17 30
Bristol Parkway	a					15 52									16 52							
	d					15 52				16 07					16 52				17 07			
Patchway	d			15 35									16 35									17 35
Pilning	d			15 41																		
Gloucester	d		14 58		15 24	16a33								16 24	17a33						16 58	
Lydney	d		15 17											16 43							17 17	
Chepstow	d		15 27		15 50									16 52							17 27	
Caldicot	d		15 35																		17 35	
Severn Tunnel Jn.	d		15 38	15 46									16 46				17 14				17 38	17 46
Newport (South Wales)	a		15 50	16 01	16 08			16 24		16 31			17 00	17 10			17 26		17 29		17 50	17 58
	d	15 37	15 52	16 01	16 10			16 24		16 31	16 37	16 56	17 01	17 11			17 26		17 31	17 37	17 52	18 00
Cardiff Central	a	15 53	16 07	16 18	16 25			16 43		16 47	16 53	17 08	17 18	17 26			17 43		17 46	17 53	18 10	18 18

Station		XC	GW	GW	GW	GW	GW	AW	AW	AW	GW	XC	GW	GW	GW	GW	GW	AW	AW	GW	GW	XC	GW
Bath Spa	d		17 08	17 24	17 36	18 00							18 18	18 24	18 36	19 00					19 08		19 24
Oldfield Park	d		17 11										18 20								19 11		
Keynsham	d		17 18										18 28								19 18		
Bristol Temple Meads	a		17 28	17 39	17 48	18 15							18 36	18 39	18 48	19 15					19 26		19 38
	d		17 41		17 54						18 21		18 41		18 54					19 21			
Filton Abbey Wood	d		17 48		18 01						18 30		18 48		19 01					19 28			
Bristol Parkway	a		17 52										18 52										
	d		17 52				18 07						18 52				19 07						
Patchway	d										18 35									19 33			
Pilning	d																						
Gloucester	d	17 24	18a33						17 58			18 31	19a33						18 58			19 24	
Lydney	d								18 17										19 17				
Chepstow	d								18 27										19 27				
Caldicot	d								18 35										19 34				
Severn Tunnel Jn.	d				18 14				18 38		18 47								19 37	19 46			
Newport (South Wales)	a	18 05			18 25		18 30		18 50		19 05	19 12			19 26		19 30		19 50	19 58		20 05	
	d	18 07			18 25		18 31	18 37	18 52	18 57	19 05	19 14			19 26		19 31	19 41	19 52	19 58		20 07	
Cardiff Central	a	18 21			18 43		18 46	18 53	19 10	19 16	19 23	19 29			19 43		19 46	19 58	20 11	20 18		20 21	

Station		GW	GW	GW	GW	AW	AW	XC	GW	GW	AW	XC	GW	GW	GW	GW	AW	GW	XC	GW	AW	GW	SW
Bath Spa	d	19 36	19 47	20 00					20 16	20 24			20 36	21 00		21 08				21 30		21 39	21 51
Oldfield Park	d		19 50						20 18							21 11							
Keynsham	d		19 57						20 25							21 18							21 59
Bristol Temple Meads	a	19 48	20 05	20 15					20 33	20 40			20 48	21 16		21 29				21 45		21 51	22 06
	d	19 54						20 21					20 54					21 29				21 54	
Filton Abbey Wood	d	20 01						20 28					21 01					21 36				22 01	
Bristol Parkway	a																						
	d				20 07										21 07								
Patchway	d							20 32										21 41				22 06	
Pilning	d																						
Gloucester	d						19 58					20 24							21 24				
Lydney	d						20 17												21 43				
Chepstow	d						20 27												21 52				
Caldicot	d						20 35												22 01				
Severn Tunnel Jn.	d						20 38	20 42										21 52	22 04			22 18	
Newport (South Wales)	a	20 25			20 30		20 50	20 55				21 11	21 25		21 30			22 09	22 21			22 38	
	d	20 25			20 31	20 40	20 52	20 57			21 02	21 13	21 25		21 31		21 45	22 11	22 21		22 34	22 38	
Cardiff Central	a	20 43			20 44	21 00	21 09	21 11			21 21	21 29	21 43		21 47		22 04	22 30	22 43		22 53	22 58	

Station		GW	GW	GW	GW	GW	GW	AW	GW	AW
Bath Spa	d	22 00		22 25	22 36	23 00	23 08			
Oldfield Park	d			22 28			23 11			
Keynsham	d			22 36			23 18			
Bristol Temple Meads	a	22 14		22 44	22 50	23 15	23 31			
	d				22 54					
Filton Abbey Wood	d				23 01					
Bristol Parkway	a									
	d		22 11						23 28	
Patchway	d				23 06					
Pilning	d									
Gloucester	d									23 09
Lydney	d									23 28
Chepstow	d									23 38
Caldicot	d									23 46
Severn Tunnel Jn.	d				23 18					23 49
Newport (South Wales)	a		22 46		23 35				23 57	00 07
	d		22 46		23 36			23 46	23 58	00 09
Cardiff Central	a		23 06		23 55			00 05	00 18	00 35

A ⌶ to Newport (South Wales)

When events are being held at the Millenium Stadium, services are subject to alteration. Please check times before travelling.

Table 132

Saturdays

15 September to 20 October

Bath Spa, Bristol and Gloucester - Cardiff

Network Diagram - see first Page of Table 132

		AW	AW	GW	GW	AW	GW	AW	AW	XC		GW	GW	AW	XC	GW	GW	SW	AW	GW		GW	AW	AW	GW
		◇		◇1 ☕	◇1 ☕	◇	◇1 ☕			◇1		◇1		◇ ⊼	◇1			1				◇1 ☕	◇ ⊼		
Bath Spa 7	d			23p49			01 15										07 08	07 35				08 00			
Oldfield Park	d																07 11	07 38							
Keynsham	d																07 18	07 45							
Bristol Temple Meads 10	a			00 03			01 29										07 29	07 52				08 15			
	d						01 36					06 46	06 50			07 21	07 41			07 54					08 20
Filton Abbey Wood	d											06 54	07 02			07 30	07 48			08 01					08 30
Bristol Parkway 7	a											06 58					07 52								
	d				00 16							07 11					07 52								08 35
Patchway	d															07 34									
Pilning	d																								
Gloucester 7	d		23p13						05 50	06 15					07 00		08a32							07 58	
Lydney	d		23p33						06 09	06 34					07 20									08 17	
Chepstow	d		23p42						06 19	06 43					07 29									08 27	
Caldicot	d		23p51						06 27	06 52					07 38									08 35	
Severn Tunnel Jn.	d		23p54						06 30	06 55			07 14		07 41	07 46								08 38	08 46
Newport (South Wales)	a		00 06		00 38		02s02		06 42	07 06		07 31	07 25		07 52	07 58				08 26				08 50	09 01
	d	23p47	00 07		00 38	00 59		06 38	06 44	07 07		07 31	07 26	07 38	07 53	07 58			08 01	08 27			08 33	08 52	09 01
Cardiff Central 7	a	00 02	00 33		00 53	01 18	02 19	06 54	07 00	07 22		07 47	07 44	07 53	08 08	08 18			08 19	08 43			08 50	09 10	09 21

		AW	XC	GW	GW	GW		GW	GW	GW	AW	AW	GW	XC	GW	GW		GW	GW	GW	AW	AW	GW	XC	GW
		◇ ⊼	◇1 A ⊼		◇1 ☕	◇		◇	■ 1 ☕	◇1 ☕	◇ ⊼			◇1 A ⊼		◇1 ☕		◇ B ⊼	◇1 ☕	◇1 ☕	◇ ⊼	◇ ⊼		◇1 A ⊼	◇
Bath Spa 7	d			08 08	08 24	08 30		08 47	09 00						09 08	09 24		09 36	10 00						10 08
Oldfield Park	d			08 11				08 49							09 11										10 11
Keynsham	d			08 18				08 57							09 18										10 18
Bristol Temple Meads 10	a			08 29	08 39	08 44		09 05	09 15						09 27	09 39		09 48	10 15						10 29
	d			08 41		08 54							09 21		09 41			09 54					10 21		10 41
Filton Abbey Wood	d			08 48		09 01							09 30		09 48			10 01					10 30		10 48
Bristol Parkway 7	a			08 52											09 52										10 52
	d			08 52						09 07					09 52					10 07					10 52
Patchway	d												09 35										10 35		
Pilning	d																								
Gloucester 7	d		08 24	09a33								08 58		09 24	10a33									10 24	11a32
Lydney	d											09 17												10 43	
Chepstow	d		08 50									09 27		09 50											
Caldicot	d											09 35													
Severn Tunnel Jn.	d											09 38	09 46										10 46		
Newport (South Wales)	a		09 07			09 25				09 30		09 50	09 58	10 07				10 24		10 31			11 00	11 08	
	d	09 02	09 09			09 25				09 31	09 38	09 52	09 59	10 09				10 24		10 31	10 36	10 57	11 01	11 09	
Cardiff Central 7	a	09 22	09 23			09 43				09 47	09 58	10 07	10 18	10 23				10 43		10 46	10 53	11 15	11 22	11 24	

		GW		GW	GW	GW	AW	AW	GW	XC	GW	GW		GW	SW	GW	GW	AW	AW	AW	GW	XC		GW	GW
		◇1 ☕		◇ B ⊼	◇1 ☕	◇1 ☕	◇ ⊼			◇1 A ⊼	◇	◇1 ☕		◇ B ⊼	◇1	◇1 ☕	◇1 ⊘	◇ ⊼		◇ ⊼		◇1 A ⊼		◇	◇1 ☕
Bath Spa 7	d	10 24		10 36	11 00						11 08	11 24		11 36	11 47	12 00								12 17	12 24
Oldfield Park	d										11 11													12 19	
Keynsham	d										11 18				11 55									12 27	
Bristol Temple Meads 10	a	10 39		10 48	11 15						11 29	11 39		11 48	12 05	12 15								12 35	12 39
	d			10 54					11 21		11 41			11 54							12 21			12 41	
Filton Abbey Wood	d			11 01					11 30		11 48			12 01							12 30			12 48	
Bristol Parkway 7	a										11 52													12 52	
	d					11 07					11 52						12 07							12 52	
Patchway	d								11 35												12 35				
Pilning	d																								
Gloucester 7	d							10 58		11 24	12a33								11 58			12 24		13a34	
Lydney	d							11 17											12 17						
Chepstow	d							11 27		11 50									12 27			12 50			
Caldicot	d							11 35											12 35						
Severn Tunnel Jn.	d							11 38	11 46										12 38		12 46				
Newport (South Wales)	a			11 24		11 31		11 50	11 58	12 07				12 24			12 31		12 50		13 00	13 11			
	d			11 24		11 31	11 37	11 52	11 59	12 09				12 24			12 31	12 37	12 52	12 56	13 01	13 12			
Cardiff Central 7	a			11 43		11 46	11 53	12 07	12 18	12 23				12 43			12 46	12 53	13 07	13 15	13 18	13 27			

		GW	GW	GW	AW	GW	XC	GW		GW	GW	GW	GW	AW	AW	GW	AW	XC		GW	GW	GW	SW	GW	GW
		◇	◇1 ☕	◇1 ⊘	◇ ⊼		◇1 A ⊼	◇		◇1 ☕	◇	◇1 ☕	◇1 ☕	◇ ⊼			■ ⊼	◇1 A ⊼		◇	◇1 ☕	◇	◇1	◇1 ☕	◇1 ☕
Bath Spa 7	d	12 36	13 00					13 19		13 24	13 36	14 00								14 08	14 24	14 36	14 47	15 00	
Oldfield Park	d							13 22												14 11					
Keynsham	d							13 29												14 18			14 55		
Bristol Temple Meads 10	a	12 48	13 14					13 37		13 42	13 48	14 15								14 28	14 39	14 48	15 05	15 15	
	d	12 54				13 21		13 41			13 54					14 21				14 41		14 54			
Filton Abbey Wood	d	13 01				13 30		13 48			14 01					14 30				14 48		15 01			
Bristol Parkway 7	a							13 52												14 52					
	d			13 07				13 52					14 07							14 52					15 07
Patchway	d					13 35										14 35									
Pilning	d																								
Gloucester 7	d						13 24	14a33							13 58			14 24		15a32					
Lydney	d						13 43								14 17										
Chepstow	d														14 27			14 50							
Caldicot	d														14 35										
Severn Tunnel Jn.	d					13 46									14 38	14 46									
Newport (South Wales)	a	13 25		13 31		13 58	14 08				14 24		14 31		14 50	14 59		15 11				15 25			15 31
	d	13 25		13 31	13 37	13 59	14 09				14 24		14 31	14 37	14 52	15 00	15 06	15 12				15 25			15 31
Cardiff Central 7	a	13 43		13 47	13 53	14 18	14 24				14 43		14 46	14 53	15 09	15 18	15 26	15 27				15 43			15 46

A ⊼ to Newport (South Wales)

B ⊼ to Bristol Temple Meads

When events are being held at the Millenium Stadium, services are subject to alteration. Please check times before travelling.

Table 132

Saturdays

15 September to 20 October

Bath Spa, Bristol and Gloucester - Cardiff

Network Diagram - see first Page of Table 132

		AW	AW	GW		XC	GW	GW	GW	GW	GW	AW	AW	GW		XC	GW	GW	GW	GW	GW	AW	AW	GW
		■ ⊼	⊼			◇1 A ⊼	◇	◇1 ☕	◇	◇1 ☕	◇1 ☕	■ ⊼	◇ ⊼			◇1 A ⊼		◇1 ☕	◇	◇1 ☕	◇1 ☕	■ ⊼		
Bath Spa 7	d						15 18	15 24	15 36	16 00							16 08	16 24	16 36	17 00				
Oldfield Park	d						15 21										16 11							
Keynsham	d						15 28										16 18							
Bristol Temple Meads 10	a						15 36	15 41	15 49	16 15							16 29	16 39	16 48	17 15				
	d			15 21			15 41		15 54					16 21			16 41		16 54					17 21
Filton Abbey Wood	d			15 30			15 48		16 01					16 30			16 48		17 01					17 30
Bristol Parkway 7	a						15 52										16 52							
	d						15 52				16 07						16 52				17 07			
Patchway	d			15 35										16 35										17 35
Pilning	d			15 41																				
Gloucester 7	d		14 58			15 24	16a33									16 24	17a33						16 58	
Lydney	d		15 17													16 43							17 17	
Chepstow	d		15 27			15 50										16 52							17 27	
Caldicot	d		15 35																				17 35	
Severn Tunnel Jn.	d		15 38	15 46										16 46					17 14				17 38	17 46
Newport (South Wales)	a		15 50	16 01		16 08			16 24		16 31			17 00		17 10			17 26		17 29		17 50	17 58
	d	15 37	15 52	16 01		16 10			16 24		16 31	16 37	16 56	17 01		17 11			17 26		17 31	17 37	17 52	18 00
Cardiff Central 7	a	15 53	16 07	16 18		16 25			16 43		16 47	16 53	17 08	17 18		17 26			17 43		17 46	17 53	18 10	18 18

		XC	GW	GW	GW	GW	GW	AW	AW	AW		GW	XC	GW	GW	GW	GW	GW	AW	AW		GW	XC	GW	GW
		◇1 ⊼	◇	◇1 ☕	◇	◇1 ☕	◇1 ☕	■ ⊼		◇ ⊼			◇1		◇1 ☕	■	◇1 ☕	◇1 ☕	■ ⊼				◇1		◇1 ☕
Bath Spa 7	d		17 08	17 24	17 36	18 00								18 08	18 24	18 36	19 00							19 08	19 24
Oldfield Park	d		17 11											18 11										19 11	
Keynsham	d		17 18											18 18										19 18	
Bristol Temple Meads 10	a		17 29	17 39	17 48	18 15								18 29	18 39	18 48	19 15							19 29	19 38
	d		17 41		17 54							18 21		18 41		18 54						19 21		19 41	
Filton Abbey Wood	d		17 48		18 01							18 30		18 48		19 01						19 28		19 48	
Bristol Parkway 7	a		17 52											18 52										19 52	
	d		17 52				18 07							18 52				19 07						19 52	
Patchway	d											18 35										19 33			
Pilning	d																								
Gloucester 7	d	17 24	18a33						17 58				18 31	19a33						18 58			19 24	20a33	
Lydney	d								18 17											19 17					
Chepstow	d								18 27											19 27					
Caldicot	d								18 35											19 34					
Severn Tunnel Jn.	d				18 14				18 38			18 47								19 37		19 46			
Newport (South Wales)	a	18 05			18 25		18 30		18 50			19 05	19 12			19 26		19 30		19 50		19 58	20 05		
	d	18 07			18 25		18 31	18 37	18 52	18 57		19 05	19 14			19 26		19 31	19 41	19 52		19 58	20 07		
Cardiff Central 7	a	18 21			18 43		18 46	18 53	19 10	19 16		19 23	19 29			19 43		19 46	19 58	20 11		20 18	20 21		

		GW	GW	GW	GW	AW		AW	XC	GW	GW	AW	GW	XC	GW	GW		GW	GW	AW	GW	XC	GW	AW	GW
		◇	◇	◇1 ☕	◇1 ☕	■ ⊼			◇1 ⊼	◇	◇1 ☕	◇ ⊼	◇1 ☕	◇1	◇	◇1 ☕		◇1 ☕		◇ ⊼		◇1	◇1 ☕		◇
Bath Spa 7	d	19 36	19 47	20 00						20 16	20 24				20 36	21 00			21 08				21 30		21 39
Oldfield Park	d		19 50							20 18									21 11						
Keynsham	d		19 57							20 25									21 18						
Bristol Temple Meads 10	a	19 48	20 05	20 15						20 33	20 40				20 48	21 16			21 29				21 45		21 51
	d	19 54							20 21						20 54						21 29				21 54
Filton Abbey Wood	d	20 01							20 28						21 01						21 36				22 01
Bristol Parkway 7	a																								
	d				20 07								20 40					21 07							
Patchway	d								20 32												21 41				22 06
Pilning	d																								
Gloucester 7	d							19 58						20 24								21 24			
Lydney	d							20 17														21 43			
Chepstow	d							20 27														21 52			
Caldicot	d							20 35														22 01			
Severn Tunnel Jn.	d							20 38	20 42												21 52	22 04			22 18
Newport (South Wales)	a	20 25			20 30			20 50	20 55				21 05	21 11	21 25			21 30			22 09	22 21			22 38
	d	20 25			20 31	20 40		20 52	20 57			21 02	21 07	21 13	21 25			21 31		21 45	22 11	22 21		22 34	22 38
Cardiff Central 7	a	20 43			20 44	21 00		21 09	21 11			21 21	21 23	21 29	21 43			21 47		22 04	22 30	22 43		22 53	22 58

A ⊼ to Newport (South Wales)

When events are being held at the Millenium Stadium, services are subject to alteration. Please check times before travelling.

Bath Spa, Bristol and Gloucester - Cardiff

Saturdays
15 September to 20 October

Network Diagram - see first Page of Table 132

Station		SW		GW	GW	GW	GW	GW	GW	AW	GW	AW
		◇1		◇1 ⊏	◇1 ⊏		◇	◇1 ⊏			◇1 ⊏	⊟
Bath Spa 7	d	21 51		22 00		22 25	22 36	23 01	23 08			
Oldfield Park	d					22 28			23 11			
Keynsham	d	21 59				22 36			23 18			
Bristol Temple Meads 10	a	22 06		22 14		22 44	22 50	23 15	23 31			
	d						22 54					
Filton Abbey Wood	d						23 01					
Bristol Parkway 7	a											
	d				22 11						23 28	
Patchway	d						23 06					
Pilning	d											
Gloucester 7	d											23 09
Lydney	d											23 49
Chepstow	d											00 09
Caldicot	d											00 24
Severn Tunnel Jn.	d						23 18					00 34
Newport (South Wales)	a				22 46		23 35				23 57	00 59
	d				22 46		23 36			23 46	23 58	00 59
Cardiff Central 7	a				23 06		23 55			00 05	00 18	01 29

Saturdays
from 27 October

Station		AW	AW	GW	GW	AW	GW	AW	AW	XC		GW	GW	AW	XC	GW	GW	SW	AW	GW		GW	AW	AW	GW
		◇		◇1 ⊏	◇1 ⊏	◇	◇1 ⊏			◇1		◇1		◇ H	◇1			1				◇1 ⊏	◇ H		
Bath Spa 7	d			23p49			01 15										07 08	07 35				08 00			
Oldfield Park	d																07 11	07 38							
Keynsham	d																07 18	07 45							
Bristol Temple Meads 10	a			00 03			01 29										07 29	07 52				08 15			
	d						01 36					06 46	06 50			07 21	07 41			07 54					08 20
Filton Abbey Wood	d											06 54	07 02			07 30	07 48			08 01					08 30
Bristol Parkway 7	a											06 58					07 52								
	d				00 16							07 11					07 52								
Patchway	d															07 34									08 35
Pilning	d																								
Gloucester 7	d		23p13						05 50	06 15					07 00		08a32							07 58	
Lydney	d		23p33						06 09	06 34					07 20									08 17	
Chepstow	d		23p42						06 19	06 43					07 29									08 27	
Caldicot	d		23p51						06 27	06 52					07 38									08 35	
Severn Tunnel Jn.	d		23p54						06 30	06 55			07 14		07 41	07 46								08 38	08 46
Newport (South Wales)	a		00 06		00 38		02s02		06 42	07 06		07 31	07 25		07 52	07 58				08 26				08 50	09 01
	d	23p47	00 07		00 38	00 59		06 38	06 44	07 07		07 31	07 26	07 38	07 53	07 58			08 01	08 27			08 33	08 52	09 01
Cardiff Central 7	a	00 02	00 33		00 53	01 18	02 19	06 54	07 00	07 22		07 47	07 44	07 53	08 08	08 18			08 19	08 43			08 50	09 10	09 21

Station		AW	XC	GW	GW	GW		GW	GW	GW	AW	AW	GW	XC	GW	GW		GW	GW	GW	AW	AW	GW	XC	GW
		◇ H	◇1 A H		◇1 ⊏	◇		◇	2 1 ⊏	◇1 ⊏	◇ H			◇1 A H		◇1 ⊏		◇ B H	◇1 ⊏	◇1 ⊏	◇ H	◇ H		◇1 A H	◇
Bath Spa 7	d			08 08	08 24	08 30		08 47	09 00						09 08	09 24		09 36	10 00						10 08
Oldfield Park	d			08 11				08 49							09 11										10 11
Keynsham	d			08 18				08 57							09 18										10 18
Bristol Temple Meads 10	a			08 29	08 39	08 44		09 05	09 15						09 27	09 39		09 48	10 15						10 29
	d			08 41		08 54							09 21		09 41			09 54					10 21		10 41
Filton Abbey Wood	d			08 48		09 01							09 30		09 48			10 01					10 30		10 48
Bristol Parkway 7	a			08 52											09 52										10 52
	d			08 52						09 07					09 52					10 07					10 52
Patchway	d												09 35										10 35		
Pilning	d																								
Gloucester 7	d		08 24	09a33								08 58		09 24	10a33									10 24	11a32
Lydney	d											09 17												10 43	
Chepstow	d		08 50									09 27		09 50											
Caldicot	d											09 35													
Severn Tunnel Jn.	d											09 38	09 46										10 46		
Newport (South Wales)	a		09 07			09 25				09 30		09 50	09 58	10 07				10 24		10 31			11 00	11 08	
	d	09 02	09 09			09 25				09 31	09 38	09 52	09 59	10 09				10 24		10 31	10 36	10 57	11 01	11 09	
Cardiff Central 7	a	09 22	09 23			09 43				09 47	09 58	10 07	10 18	10 23				10 43		10 46	10 53	11 15	11 22	11 24	

A H to Newport (South Wales)

B H to Bristol Temple Meads

When events are being held at the Millenium Stadium, services are subject to alteration. Please check times before travelling.

Bath Spa, Bristol and Gloucester - Cardiff

Saturdays
from 27 October

Network Diagram - see first Page of Table 132

Station		GW		GW	GW	GW	AW	AW	GW	XC	GW	GW		GW	SW	GW	GW	AW	AW	AW	GW	XC		GW	GW
		◇1 ⊏		◇ A H	◇1 ⊏	◇1 ⊏	◇ H			◇1 B H	◇	◇1 ⊏		◇ A H	◇1	◇1 ⊏	◇1 Ø	◇ H		◇ H		◇1 B H		◇	◇1 ⊏
Bath Spa 7	d	10 24		10 36	11 00						11 08	11 24		11 36	11 47	12 00								12 17	12 24
Oldfield Park	d										11 11													12 19	
Keynsham	d										11 18				11 55									12 27	
Bristol Temple Meads 10	a	10 39		10 48	11 15						11 29	11 39		11 48	12 05	12 15								12 35	12 39
	d			10 54					11 21		11 41			11 54							12 21			12 41	
Filton Abbey Wood	d			11 01					11 30		11 48			12 01							12 30			12 48	
Bristol Parkway 7	a										11 52													12 52	
	d					11 07					11 52						12 07							12 52	
Patchway	d								11 35												12 35				
Pilning	d																								
Gloucester 7	d							10 58		11 24	12a33								11 58			12 24		13a34	
Lydney	d							11 17											12 17						
Chepstow	d							11 27		11 50									12 27			12 50			
Caldicot	d							11 35											12 35						
Severn Tunnel Jn.	d							11 38	11 46										12 38		12 46				
Newport (South Wales)	a			11 24		11 31		11 50	11 58	12 07				12 24			12 31		12 50		13 00	13 11			
	d			11 24		11 31	11 37	11 52	11 59	12 09				12 24			12 31	12 37	12 52	12 56	13 01	13 12			
Cardiff Central 7	a			11 43		11 46	11 53	12 07	12 18	12 23				12 43			12 46	12 53	13 07	13 15	13 18	13 27			

Station		GW	GW	GW	AW	GW	XC	GW		GW	GW	GW	GW	AW	AW	GW	AW	XC		GW	GW	GW	SW	GW	GW
		◇	◇1 ⊏	◇1 Ø	◇ H		◇1 B H	◇		◇1 ⊏	◇	◇1 ⊏	◇1 ⊏	◇ H			2 H	◇1 B H		◇	◇1 ⊏	◇	◇1	◇1 ⊏	◇1 ⊏
Bath Spa 7	d	12 36	13 00					13 19		13 24	13 36	14 00								14 08	14 24	14 36	14 47	15 00	
Oldfield Park	d							13 22												14 11					
Keynsham	d							13 29												14 18			14 55		
Bristol Temple Meads 10	a	12 48	13 14					13 37		13 42	13 48	14 15								14 28	14 39	14 48	15 05	15 15	
	d	12 54				13 21		13 41			13 54					14 21				14 41		14 54			
Filton Abbey Wood	d	13 01				13 30		13 48			14 01					14 30				14 48		15 01			
Bristol Parkway 7	a							13 52												14 52					
	d			13 07				13 52					14 07							14 52					15 07
Patchway	d					13 35										14 35									
Pilning	d																								
Gloucester 7	d						13 24	14a33							13 58			14 24		15a32					
Lydney	d						13 43								14 17										
Chepstow	d														14 27			14 50							
Caldicot	d														14 35										
Severn Tunnel Jn.	d					13 46									14 38	14 46									
Newport (South Wales)	a	13 25		13 31		13 58	14 08				14 24		14 31		14 50	14 59		15 11				15 25			15 31
	d	13 25		13 31	13 37	13 59	14 09				14 24		14 31	14 37	14 52	15 00	15 06	15 12				15 25			15 31
Cardiff Central 7	a	13 43		13 47	13 53	14 18	14 24				14 43		14 46	14 53	15 09	15 18	15 26	15 27				15 43			15 46

Station		AW	AW	GW		XC	GW	GW	GW	GW	GW	AW	AW	GW		XC	GW	GW	GW	GW	GW	AW	AW	GW
		2 H	H			◇1 B H	◇	◇1 ⊏	◇	◇1 ⊏	◇1 ⊏	2 H	◇ H			◇1 B H		◇1 ⊏	◇	◇1 ⊏	◇1 ⊏	2 H		
Bath Spa 7	d						15 18	15 24	15 36	16 00							16 08	16 24	16 36	17 00				
Oldfield Park	d						15 21										16 11							
Keynsham	d						15 28										16 18							
Bristol Temple Meads 10	a						15 36	15 41	15 49	16 15							16 29	16 39	16 48	17 15				
	d			15 21			15 41		15 54					16 21			16 41		16 54					17 21
Filton Abbey Wood	d			15 30			15 48		16 01					16 30			16 48		17 01					17 30
Bristol Parkway 7	a						15 52										16 52							
	d						15 52				16 07						16 52				17 07			
Patchway	d			15 35										16 35										17 35
Pilning	d			15 41																				
Gloucester 7	d		14 58			15 24	16a33									16 24	17a33						16 58	
Lydney	d		15 17													16 43							17 17	
Chepstow	d		15 27			15 50										16 52							17 27	
Caldicot	d		15 35																				17 35	
Severn Tunnel Jn.	d		15 38	15 46										16 46					17 14				17 38	17 46
Newport (South Wales)	a		15 50	16 01		16 08			16 24		16 31			17 00		17 10			17 26		17 29		17 50	17 58
	d	15 37	15 52	16 01		16 10			16 24		16 31	16 37	16 56	17 01		17 11			17 26		17 31	17 37	17 52	18 00
Cardiff Central 7	a	15 53	16 07	16 18		16 25			16 43		16 47	16 53	17 08	17 18		17 26			17 43		17 46	17 53	18 10	18 18

A H to Bristol Temple Meads

B H to Newport (South Wales)

When events are being held at the Millenium Stadium, services are subject to alteration. Please check times before travelling.

Saturdays
from 27 October

Bath Spa, Bristol and Gloucester - Cardiff

Network Diagram - see first Page of Table 132

		XC	GW	GW	GW	GW	GW	AW	AW	AW		GW	XC	GW	GW	GW	GW	GW	AW	AW		GW	XC	GW	GW
Bath Spa	d		17 08	17 24	17 36	18 00								18 08	18 24	18 36	19 00							19 08	19 24
Oldfield Park	d		17 11											18 11										19 11	
Keynsham	d		17 18											18 18										19 18	
Bristol Temple Meads	a		17 29	17 39	17 48	18 15								18 29	18 39	18 48	19 15							19 29	19 38
	d		17 41		17 54							18 21		18 41		18 54						19 21		19 41	
Filton Abbey Wood	d		17 48		18 01							18 30		18 48		19 01						19 28		19 48	
Bristol Parkway	a		17 52											18 52										19 52	
	d		17 52				18 07							18 52				19 07						19 52	
Patchway	d											18 35										19 33			
Pilning	d																								
Gloucester	d	17 24	18a33						17 58				18 31	19a33						18 58			19 24	20a33	
Lydney	d								18 17											19 17					
Chepstow	d								18 27											19 27					
Caldicot	d								18 35											19 34					
Severn Tunnel Jn.	d				18 14				18 38			18 47								19 37		19 46			
Newport (South Wales)	a	18 05			18 25		18 30		18 50			19 05	19 12			19 26		19 30		19 50		19 58	20 05		
	d	18 07			18 25		18 31	18 37	18 52	18 57		19 05	19 14			19 26		19 31	19 41	19 52		19 58	20 07		
Cardiff Central	a	18 21			18 43		18 46	18 53	19 10	19 16		19 23	19 29			19 43		19 46	19 58	20 11		20 18	20 21		

		GW	GW	GW	GW	AW		AW	XC	GW	GW	AW	GW	XC	GW	GW		GW	GW	AW	GW	XC	GW	AW	GW
Bath Spa	d	19 36	19 47	20 00						20 16	20 24				20 36	21 00			21 08				21 30		21 39
Oldfield Park	d		19 50							20 18									21 11						
Keynsham	d		19 57							20 25									21 18						
Bristol Temple Meads	a	19 48	20 05	20 15						20 33	20 40				20 48	21 16			21 29				21 45		21 51
	d	19 54							20 21						20 54						21 29				21 54
Filton Abbey Wood	d	20 01							20 28						21 01						21 36				22 01
Bristol Parkway	a																								
	d				20 07								20 40					21 07							
Patchway	d								20 32												21 41				22 06
Pilning	d																								
Gloucester	d							19 58						20 24								21 24			
Lydney	d							20 17														21 43			
Chepstow	d							20 27														21 52			
Caldicot	d							20 35														22 01			
Severn Tunnel Jn.	d							20 38	20 42												21 52	22 04			22 18
Newport (South Wales)	a	20 25			20 30			20 50	20 55				21 05	21 11	21 25			21 30			22 09	22 21			22 38
	d	20 25			20 31	20 40		20 52	20 57			21 02	21 07	21 13	21 25			21 31		21 45	22 11	22 21		22 34	22 38
Cardiff Central	a	20 43			20 44	21 00		21 09	21 11			21 21	21 23	21 29	21 43			21 47		22 04	22 30	22 43		22 53	22 58

		SW		GW	GW	GW	GW	GW	GW	AW	GW	AW
Bath Spa	d	21 51		22 00		22 25	22 36	23 01	23 08			
Oldfield Park	d					22 28			23 11			
Keynsham	d	21 59				22 36			23 18			
Bristol Temple Meads	a	22 06		22 14		22 44	22 50	23 15	23 31			
	d						22 54					
Filton Abbey Wood	d						23 01					
Bristol Parkway	a											
	d				22 11						23 28	
Patchway	d						23 06					
Pilning	d											
Gloucester	d											23 09
Lydney	d											23 28
Chepstow	d											23 38
Caldicot	d											23 46
Severn Tunnel Jn.	d						23 18					23 49
Newport (South Wales)	a				22 46		23 35				23 57	00 07
	d				22 46		23 36			23 46	23 58	00 09
Cardiff Central	a				23 06		23 55			00 05	00 18	00 35

When events are being held at the Millenium Stadium, services are subject to alteration. Please check times before travelling.

Sundays
until 24 June

Bath Spa, Bristol and Gloucester - Cardiff

Network Diagram - see first Page of Table 132

		AW	GW	AW	AW	GW	GW	AW	GW	GW		GW	GW	GW	AW	AW	GW	AW	XC	GW		GW	GW	XC	GW
Bath Spa	d					00 13	01 08			09 37			10 16	10 40						11 26		11 40			12 20
Oldfield Park	d												10 19							11 29					12 23
Keynsham	d												10 26							11 36					12 30
Bristol Temple Meads	a					00 25	01 23			09 50			10 33	10 54						11 44		11 54			12 38
	d								09 48											11 48					
Filton Abbey Wood	d								09 55											11 55					
Bristol Parkway	a																								
	d		23p28									10 09					11 18						12 11		
Patchway	d																			12 00					
Pilning	d																								
Gloucester	d				23p09													10 48	11 05					12 05	
Lydney	d				23p49													11 07							
Chepstow	d				00 09													11 17							
Caldicot	d				00 24													11 25							
Severn Tunnel Jn.	d				00 34				10 08									11 28		12 11					
Newport (South Wales)	a		23p57		00 59				10 25			10 33					11 43	11 46	11 48	12 29			12 37	12 52	
	d	23p46	23p58	00 04	00 59			09 27	10 26			10 33			10 55	11 00	11 43	11 48	11 50	12 29			12 37	12 53	
Cardiff Central	a	00 05	00 18	00 26	01 29			09 42	10 41			10 51			11 13	11 19	12 01	12 06	12 08	12 44			12 56	13 12	

		GW	AW	AW	AW	GW		XC A	GW	GW	AW	GW	AW	XC A	GW	AW		GW	SW	GW	AW	XC A	GW	GW	GW
Bath Spa	d	12 40							13 24	13 40					14 28			14 40	14 50				15 28	15 40	16 17
Oldfield Park	d								13 27						14 30										16 19
Keynsham	d								13 34						14 38				14 58						16 27
Bristol Temple Meads	a	12 54							13 42	13 54					14 46			14 53	15 05				15 40	15 54	16 35
	d								13 48						14 50								15 48		
Filton Abbey Wood	d								13 55						14 57								15 55		
Bristol Parkway	a																								
	d					13 11						14 11								15 12					
Patchway	d																								
Pilning	d																								
Gloucester	d				12 30			13 23						14 24		14 33						15 23			
Lydney	d				12 49											14 52									
Chepstow	d				12 59											15 02									
Caldicot	d				13 07											15 10									
Severn Tunnel Jn.	d				13 10				14 08						15 10	15 16							16 08		
Newport (South Wales)	a				13 33	13 37		14 06	14 27			14 37		15 08	15 28	15 34				15 38		16 06	16 26		
	d		12 52	13 29	13 34	13 37		14 08	14 28		14 30	14 37	15 07	15 09	15 28	15 36				15 38	15 46	16 08	16 26		
Cardiff Central	a		13 13	13 44	13 52	13 56		14 26	14 51		14 49	14 56	15 28	15 31	15 43	15 53				15 57	16 02	16 26	16 44		

		AW		GW	XC A	GW	GW	AW	AW	GW	XC	GW		GW	GW	AW	GW	XC A	GW	GW	GW	GW		GW	AW
Bath Spa	d					16 29	16 40					17 26		17 40	18 11				18 28	18 40	19 02	19 07			
Oldfield Park	d											17 29			18 13						19 04				
Keynsham	d											17 36			18 21						19 12				
Bristol Temple Meads	a					16 42	16 53					17 44		17 54	18 33				18 40	18 54	19 20	19 25			
	d					16 48						17 48							18 48						
Filton Abbey Wood	d					16 55						17 55							18 55						
Bristol Parkway	a																								
	d			16 12						17 11							18 12							19 15	
Patchway	d					17 00																			
Pilning	d																								
Gloucester	d				16 23				16 37		17 23							18 23							
Lydney	d								16 56																
Chepstow	d								17 07																
Caldicot	d								17 13																
Severn Tunnel Jn.	d					17 11			17 16			18 08							19 08						
Newport (South Wales)	a			16 38	17 06	17 29			17 37	17 40	18 07	18 26					18 38	19 07	19 26					19 41	
	d	16 31		16 38	17 08	17 29		17 34	17 38	17 41	18 09	18 26				18 33	18 38	19 08	19 26					19 41	19 51
Cardiff Central	a	16 52		16 57	17 27	17 46		17 50	17 57	17 58	18 29	18 44				18 50	18 57	19 27	19 42					19 59	20 06

A to Newport (South Wales)

When events are being held at the Millenium Stadium, services are subject to alteration. Please check times before travelling.

Table 132

Sundays
until 24 June

Bath Spa, Bristol and Gloucester - Cardiff

Network Diagram - see first Page of Table 132

		AW	XC	AW	GW	GW	GW	GW	XC	AW	GW	AW	GW	SW	GW	GW	GW	AW	GW	GW	GW	AW	GW
			A																				
Bath Spa	d				19 27	19 40	20 00				20 27		20 40	20 49	21 05	21 12			21 28	21 40	22 15		
Oldfield Park	d						20 02									21 14					22 17		
Keynsham	d						20 10							20 57		21 22					22 25		
Bristol Temple Meads	a				19 39	19 54	20 18				20 39		20 54	21 04	21 18	21 30			21 40	21 53	22 33		
	d				19 48						20 48								21 48				
Filton Abbey Wood	d				19 55						20 55								21 55				
Bristol Parkway	a																						
	d							20 11									21 12						22 12
Patchway	d				20 00														22 02				
Pilning	d																						
Gloucester	d	18 48	19 28						20 23			20 31											
Lydney	d	19 07										20 50											
Chepstow	d	19 17										21 00											
Caldicot	d	19 25										21 10											
Severn Tunnel Jn.	d	19 32			20 11						21 08	21 13							22 15				
Newport (South Wales)	a	19 54	20 11		20 28			20 37	21 06		21 26	21 31					21 38		22 31				22 37
	d	19 56	20 13	20 23	20 29			20 37	21 08	21 14	21 26	21 33					21 38	21 48	22 31			22 33	22 37
Cardiff Central	a	20 12	20 31	20 43	20 46			20 56	21 26	21 36	21 42	21 49					22 00	22 07	22 53			22 59	23 00

		GW	AW	GW	GW	GW	AW
Bath Spa	d	22 26		22 44		23 47	
Oldfield Park	d						
Keynsham	d						
Bristol Temple Meads	a	22 38		22 57		00 01	
	d	22 48					
Filton Abbey Wood	d	22 55					
Bristol Parkway	a						
	d				23 12		
Patchway	d						
Pilning	d						
Gloucester	d		22 33				
Lydney	d		22 52				
Chepstow	d		23 02				
Caldicot	d		23 10				
Severn Tunnel Jn.	d	23 09	23 14				
Newport (South Wales)	a	23 26	23 33		23 41		
	d	23 27	23 34		23 42		23 55
Cardiff Central	a	23 47	23 54		00 01		00 20

Sundays
1 July to 9 September

		AW	GW	AW	AW	GW	GW	AW	GW	GW	GW	GW	GW	AW	AW	GW	AW	XC	GW	GW	GW	GW	GW
Bath Spa	d					00 13	01 08			09 40		10 27	10 40						11 26	11 40		12 20	12 40
Oldfield Park	d											10 30							11 29			12 23	
Keynsham	d											10 37							11 36			12 30	
Bristol Temple Meads	a					00 25	01 22			09 52		10 45	10 54						11 44	11 55		12 38	12 54
	d								09 48										11 48				
Filton Abbey Wood	d								09 55										11 55				
Bristol Parkway	a																						
	d		23p28								10 08					11 05					12 11		
Patchway	d																		12 00				
Pilning	d																						
Gloucester	d				23p09												10 48	11 05					
Lydney	d				23p28												11 07						
Chepstow	d				23p38												11 17						
Caldicot	d				23p46												11 25						
Severn Tunnel Jn.	d				23p49				10 08								11 28		12 11				
Newport (South Wales)	a		23p57		00 07				10 25		10 33					11 32	11 46	11 48	12 29		12 37		
	d	23p46	23p58	00 04	00 09			09 27	10 26		10 33			10 55	11 00	11 32	11 48	11 50	12 29		12 37		
Cardiff Central	a	00 05	00 18	00 26	00 35			09 42	10 41		10 51			11 13	11 19	11 50	12 06	12 08	12 44		12 56		

A to Newport (South Wales)

When events are being held at the Millenium Stadium, services are subject to alteration. Please check times before travelling.

Table 132

Sundays
1 July to 9 September

Bath Spa, Bristol and Gloucester - Cardiff

Network Diagram - see first Page of Table 132

		AW	XC	AW	AW	GW	XC	GW	GW	AW	GW	AW	XC	GW	AW	GW	SW	GW	AW	XC	GW	GW	GW
							A						A							A			
Bath Spa	d							13 23	13 40					14 26		14 40	14 50				15 28	15 40	16 17
Oldfield Park	d							13 26						14 28									16 19
Keynsham	d							13 33						14 36			14 58						16 27
Bristol Temple Meads	a							13 41	13 54					14 44		14 54	15 05				15 40	15 54	16 35
	d							13 48						14 48							15 48		
Filton Abbey Wood	d							13 55						14 55							15 55		
Bristol Parkway	a																						
	d					13 11					14 11							15 11					
Patchway	d																						
Pilning	d																						
Gloucester	d		12 23		12 30		13 23						14 24		14 33					15 23			
Lydney	d				12 49										14 52								
Chepstow	d				12 59										15 02								
Caldicot	d				13 07										15 10								
Severn Tunnel Jn.	d				13 10			14 08						15 08	15 16						16 08		
Newport (South Wales)	a		13 06		13 33	13 37	14 06	14 27			14 37		15 08	15 26	15 34			15 37		16 06	16 26		
	d	12 52	13 08	13 29	13 34	13 37	14 08	14 28		14 30	14 37	15 07	15 09	15 26	15 36			15 37	15 46	16 08	16 26		
Cardiff Central	a	13 13	13 26	13 44	13 52	13 56	14 26	14 51		14 49	14 56	15 28	15 31	15 41	15 53			15 56	16 02	16 26	16 44		

		AW	GW	XC	GW	GW	AW	AW	GW	XC	GW	GW	GW	AW	GW	XC	GW	GW	GW	GW	GW	AW
				A												A						
Bath Spa	d				16 29	16 40					17 26	17 40	18 11				18 28	18 40	19 02	19 07		
Oldfield Park	d										17 29		18 13						19 04			
Keynsham	d										17 36		18 21						19 12			
Bristol Temple Meads	a				16 42	16 54					17 44	17 54	18 33				18 40	18 54	19 20	19 25		
	d				16 48						17 48						18 48					
Filton Abbey Wood	d				16 55						17 55						18 55					
Bristol Parkway	a																					
	d		16 11						17 11						18 11						19 15	
Patchway	d				17 00																	
Pilning	d																					
Gloucester	d			16 23				16 37		17 23						18 23						
Lydney	d							16 56														
Chepstow	d							17 07														
Caldicot	d							17 13														
Severn Tunnel Jn.	d				17 11			17 16			18 08						19 08					
Newport (South Wales)	a		16 37	17 06	17 29			17 37	17 40	18 07	18 26				18 37	19 07	19 26				19 41	
	d	16 31	16 37	17 08	17 29		17 34	17 38	17 41	18 09	18 26			18 33	18 37	19 08	19 26				19 41	19 51
Cardiff Central	a	16 52	16 56	17 27	17 46		17 50	17 57	17 58	18 29	18 44			18 50	18 56	19 27	19 42				19 59	20 06

		AW	XC	AW	GW	GW	GW	GW	AW	GW	AW	GW	SW	GW	GW	GW	AW	GW	GW	GW	AW	GW	GW
			A																				
Bath Spa	d				19 27	19 40	20 00			20 27		20 40	20 49	21 05	21 11			21 28	21 40	22 15			22 26
Oldfield Park	d						20 02								21 13					22 17			
Keynsham	d						20 10						20 57		21 21					22 25			
Bristol Temple Meads	a				19 39	19 54	20 18			20 39		20 54	21 04	21 18	21 29			21 40	21 54	22 33			22 38
	d				19 48					20 48								21 48					22 48
Filton Abbey Wood	d				19 55					20 55								21 55					22 55
Bristol Parkway	a																						
	d							20 11								21 11						22 05	
Patchway	d				20 00													22 02					
Pilning	d																						
Gloucester	d	18 48	19 28								20 31												
Lydney	d	19 07									20 50												
Chepstow	d	19 17									21 00												
Caldicot	d	19 25									21 10												
Severn Tunnel Jn.	d	19 32			20 11					21 08	21 13							22 15					23 09
Newport (South Wales)	a	19 54	20 11		20 28			20 37		21 26	21 31					21 37		22 31				22 37	23 26
	d	19 56	20 13	20 23	20 29			20 37	21 14	21 26	21 33					21 37	21 46	22 31			22 33	22 38	23 27
Cardiff Central	a	20 12	20 31	20 43	20 46			20 56	21 36	21 42	21 49					21 59	22 05	22 53			22 59	23 00	23 47

A to Newport (South Wales)

When events are being held at the Millenium Stadium, services are subject to alteration. Please check times before travelling.

Table 132

Bath Spa, Bristol and Gloucester - Cardiff

Sundays
1 July to 9 September

Network Diagram - see first Page of Table 132

		AW	GW	GW	AW	GW
			◇1 ⊡	◇1 ⊡	◇	◇1 ⊡
Bath Spa 7	d		22 44			23 55
Oldfield Park	d					
Keynsham	d					
Bristol Temple Meads 10	a		22 57			00 09
	d					
Filton Abbey Wood	d					
Bristol Parkway 7	a					
	d			23 17		
Patchway	d					
Pilning	d					
Gloucester 7	d	22 33				
Lydney	d	22 52				
Chepstow	d	23 02				
Caldicot	d	23 10				
Severn Tunnel Jn.	d	23 14				
Newport (South Wales)	a	23 33		23 43		
	d	23 34		23 43	23 55	
Cardiff Central 7	a	23 54		00 04	00 20	

Sundays
16 September to 21 October

		AW	GW	AW	AW	GW	GW	GW	GW	AW		GW	GW	GW	GW	AW	GW	AW	XC	GW		GW	XC	GW	AW
			◇1 ⊡		🚌	🚌	🚌	🚌	🚌	◇ ⌶		◇	🚌	◇1 ⊡	🚌	◇	◇1 ⊡		◇1 ⌶	■		◇1 ⊡	◇1 ⌶		◇ ⌶
Bath Spa 7	d					00 13	01 00	01 57	09 00				09 50		10 22					11 30				12 22	
Oldfield Park	d														10 30					11 34				12 24	
Keynsham	d														10 54					11 41				12 32	
Bristol Temple Meads 10	a					00 43	01 30	02 27	09 32				10 25		11 14					11 52				12 42	
	d											09 48								11 55					
Filton Abbey Wood	d											09 55								12 03					
Bristol Parkway 7	a																								
	d		23p28											10 11			11 05					12 13			
Patchway	d																			12 08					
Pilning	d																								
Gloucester 7	d				23p09													10 48	11 05				12 05		
Lydney	d				23p49													11 07							
Chepstow	d				00 09													11 17							
Caldicot	d				00 24													11 25							
Severn Tunnel Jn.	d				00 34							10 08						11 28		12 19					
Newport (South Wales)	a		23p57		00 59							10 25		10 36			11 32	11 46	11 48	12 37		12 38	12 52		
	d	23p46	23p58	00 04	00 59					09 27		10 26		10 36		11 00	11 32	11 48	11 50	12 37		12 38	12 53		12 52
Cardiff Central 7	a	00 05	00 18	00 26	01 29					09 42		10 41		10 53		11 16	11 50	12 06	12 08	12 52		12 58	13 12		13 13

		AW	AW	GW	XC	AW		GW	GW	AW	XC	GW	AW	SW	GW	AW		XC	GW	GW	GW	AW	GW	XC	GW
		■ ⌶		◇1 ⊡	◇1 A ⌶	■ ⌶		◇	◇1 ⊡	◇ ⌶	◇1 A ⌶	◇		◇1	◇1 ⊡	■ ⌶		◇1 A ⌶	◇	◇1 ⊡	◇	■ ⌶	◇1 ⊡	◇1 A ⌶	◇
Bath Spa 7	d							13 25				14 25		14 50					15 32	15 40	16 01				16 29
Oldfield Park	d							13 28				14 28									16 03				
Keynsham	d							13 35				14 36		14 58							16 11				
Bristol Temple Meads 10	a							13 45				14 46		15 05					15 43	15 53	16 23				16 42
	d							13 50				14 51							15 48						16 48
Filton Abbey Wood	d							13 58				14 58							15 55						16 55
Bristol Parkway 7	a																								
	d			13 13					14 13						15 13								16 13		
Patchway	d																								17 00
Pilning	d																								
Gloucester 7	d		12 30		13 23						14 24		14 33					15 23						16 23	
Lydney	d		12 49										14 52												
Chepstow	d		12 59										15 02												
Caldicot	d		13 07										15 10												
Severn Tunnel Jn.	d		13 10					14 11				15 11	15 16						16 08						17 11
Newport (South Wales)	a		13 33	13 38	14 06			14 30	14 38		15 08	15 29	15 34		15 38			16 06	16 26				16 38	17 06	17 29
	d	13 29	13 34	13 38	14 08	14 30		14 31	14 38	15 07	15 09	15 29	15 36		15 38	15 46		16 08	16 26			16 31	16 38	17 08	17 29
Cardiff Central 7	a	13 44	13 52	13 58	14 26	14 49		14 54	14 58	15 28	15 31	15 44	15 53		15 58	16 02		16 26	16 44			16 52	16 58	17 27	17 46

A ⌶ to Newport (South Wales)

> When events are being held at the Millenium Stadium, services are subject to alteration. Please check times before travelling.

Table 132

Bath Spa, Bristol and Gloucester - Cardiff

Sundays
16 September to 21 October

Network Diagram - see first Page of Table 132

		GW		AW	AW	GW	XC	GW	GW	AW	GW	XC		GW	GW	GW	GW	GW	AW	AW	AW	GW		GW	GW
		◇1 ⊡		■ ⌶		◇1 ⊡	◇1 ⌶	■	◇1 ⊡	■ ⌶	◇1 ⊡	◇1 A ⌶		◇	◇1 ⊡	◇	◇1 ⊡	◇1 ⊡	■ ⌶		■ ⌶	◇		◇1 ⊡	◇
Bath Spa 7	d	16 40						17 26	17 40					18 28	18 40	19 02	19 07					19 27		19 40	20 00
Oldfield Park	d							17 29								19 04									20 02
Keynsham	d							17 36								19 12									20 10
Bristol Temple Meads 10	a	16 53						17 44	17 53					18 40	18 54	19 20	19 25					19 39		19 53	20 18
	d							17 48						18 48								19 48			
Filton Abbey Wood	d							17 55						18 55								19 55			
Bristol Parkway 7	a																								
	d					17 13					18 13							19 15							
Patchway	d																					20 00			
Pilning	d																								
Gloucester 7	d				16 37		17 23					18 23								18 48					
Lydney	d				16 56															19 07					
Chepstow	d				17 07															19 17					
Caldicot	d				17 13															19 25					
Severn Tunnel Jn.	d				17 16			18 08						19 08						19 32		20 11			
Newport (South Wales)	a				17 37	17 40	18 07	18 26			18 40	19 07		19 26				19 40		19 54		20 28			
	d			17 34	17 38	17 40	18 09	18 26		18 33	18 40	19 08		19 26				19 40	19 51	19 56	20 23	20 29			
Cardiff Central 7	a			17 50	17 57	17 58	18 29	18 44		18 50	19 00	19 27		19 42				20 00	20 06	20 12	20 43	20 46			

		GW	XC	AW	GW	AW	GW	SW		GW	GW	GW	AW	GW	GW	GW	AW	GW		GW	AW	GW	GW	AW	GW
		◇1 ⊡	◇1	■ ⌶	◇		◇1 ⊡	◇1		◇1 ⊡	◇	◇1 ⊡	■ ⌶	◇	◇1 ⊡		◇	◇1 ⊡		◇		◇1 ⊡	◇1 ⊡	◇	◇1 ⊡
Bath Spa 7	d				20 27		20 40	20 49		21 05	21 11			21 28	21 40	22 15				22 26		22 44			23 57
Oldfield Park	d										21 13					22 17									
Keynsham	d							20 57			21 21					22 25									
Bristol Temple Meads 10	a				20 39		20 54	21 04		21 18	21 29			21 40	21 53	22 33				22 38		22 58			00 11
	d				20 48									21 48						22 48					
Filton Abbey Wood	d				20 55									21 55						22 55					
Bristol Parkway 7	a																								
	d	20 13										21 13						22 13					23 16		
Patchway	d													22 02											
Pilning	d																								
Gloucester 7	d		20 23			20 31															22 33				
Lydney	d					20 50															22 52				
Chepstow	d					21 00															23 02				
Caldicot	d					21 10															23 10				
Severn Tunnel Jn.	d				21 08	21 13								22 15						23 09	23 14				
Newport (South Wales)	a	20 38	21 06		21 26	21 31						21 38		22 31				22 38		23 26	23 33		23 40		
	d	20 38	21 08	21 14	21 26	21 33						21 38	21 46	22 31			22 33	22 38		23 27	23 34		23 43	23 55	
Cardiff Central 7	a	20 59	21 26	21 36	21 42	21 49						21 59	22 05	22 53			22 59	23 00		23 47	23 54		00 05	00 20	

Sundays
from 28 October

		AW	GW	AW	AW	GW	GW	AW	GW	GW		GW	GW	GW	AW	GW	AW	GW	GW	GW		GW	GW	AW	AW
			◇1 ⊡			◇1 ⊡	◇1 ⊡	◇ ⌶	◇	◇1 ⊡		◇1 ⊡		◇1 ⊡	◇	◇1 ⊡		■	◇1 ⊡	◇1 ⊡			◇1 ⊡	◇ ⌶	■ ⌶
Bath Spa 7	d					00 16	01 08			09 41			10 27	10 40				11 26	11 40			12 20	12 40		
Oldfield Park	d												10 30					11 29				12 23			
Keynsham	d												10 37					11 36				12 30			
Bristol Temple Meads 10	a					00 28	01 22			09 55			10 45	10 57				11 44	11 54			12 38	12 54		
	d								09 48									11 48							
Filton Abbey Wood	d								09 55									11 55							
Bristol Parkway 7	a																								
	d		23p28									10 10				11 05				12 12					
Patchway	d																	12 00							
Pilning	d																								
Gloucester 7	d				23p09												10 48								
Lydney	d				23p28												11 07								
Chepstow	d				23p38												11 17								
Caldicot	d				23p46												11 25								
Severn Tunnel Jn.	d				23p49				10 08								11 28	12 11							
Newport (South Wales)	a		23p57		00 07				10 25			10 35				11 32	11 46	12 29		12 38					
	d	23p46	23p58	00 04	00 09			09 27	10 26			10 35			11 00	11 32	11 48	12 29		12 38				12 52	13 29
Cardiff Central 7	a	00 05	00 18	00 26	00 35			09 42	10 41			10 53			11 16	11 50	12 06	12 44		12 57				13 13	13 44

A ⌶ to Newport (South Wales)

> When events are being held at the Millenium Stadium, services are subject to alteration. Please check times before travelling.

Table 132

Bath Spa, Bristol and Gloucester - Cardiff

Sundays

from 28 October

Network Diagram - see first Page of Table 132

		AW	GW	GW	GW	AW	GW	AW	GW	AW	GW	SW	GW	AW	XC A	GW	GW	GW	AW	GW	XC A	GW	GW
Bath Spa	d			13 23	13 40				14 26		14 40	14 50				15 28	15 40	16 01				16 29	16 40
Oldfield Park	d			13 26					14 28									16 03					
Keynsham	d			13 33					14 36			14 58						16 11					
Bristol Temple Meads	a			13 41	13 54				14 44		14 54	15 05				15 40	15 53	16 23				16 42	16 53
	d			13 48					14 48							15 48						16 48	
Filton Abbey Wood	d			13 55					14 55							15 55						16 55	
Bristol Parkway	a																						
	d		13 13				14 13						15 13							16 13			
Patchway	d																					17 00	
Pilning	d																						
Gloucester	d	12 30								14 33					15 23						16 23		
Lydney	d	12 49								14 52													
Chepstow	d	12 59								15 02													
Caldicot	d	13 07								15 10													
Severn Tunnel Jn.	d	13 10		14 08					15 08	15 16						16 08						17 11	
Newport (South Wales)	a	13 33	13 38	14 27			14 38		15 26	15 34			15 38		16 06	16 26				16 38	17 06	17 29	
	d	13 34	13 38	14 28		14 30	14 38	15 07	15 26	15 36			15 38	15 46	16 08	16 26			16 31	16 38	17 08	17 29	
Cardiff Central	a	13 52	13 58	14 51		14 49	14 58	15 28	15 41	15 53			15 58	16 02	16 26	16 44			16 52	16 58	17 27	17 46	

		AW	AW	GW	XC	GW	GW	AW	GW	XC A	GW	GW	GW	GW	GW	AW	AW	AW	GW	GW	GW	GW
Bath Spa	d					17 26	17 40				18 28	18 40	19 02	19 07					19 27	19 40	20 00	
Oldfield Park	d					17 29							19 04								20 02	
Keynsham	d					17 36							19 12								20 10	
Bristol Temple Meads	a					17 44	17 53				18 40	18 54	19 20	19 25					19 39	19 53	20 18	
	d					17 48					18 48								19 48			
Filton Abbey Wood	d					17 55					18 55								19 55			
Bristol Parkway	a																					
	d			17 13					18 13						19 15							20 13
Patchway	d																		20 00			
Pilning	d																					
Gloucester	d		16 37		17 23					18 23							18 48					
Lydney	d		16 56														19 07					
Chepstow	d		17 07														19 17					
Caldicot	d		17 13														19 25					
Severn Tunnel Jn.	d		17 16			18 08					19 08						19 32		20 11			
Newport (South Wales)	a		17 37	17 40	18 07	18 26			18 40	19 07	19 26				19 40		19 54		20 28			20 38
	d	17 34	17 38	17 40	18 09	18 26		18 33	18 40	19 08	19 26				19 40	19 51	19 56	20 23	20 29			20 38
Cardiff Central	a	17 50	17 57	17 58	18 29	18 44		18 50	19 00	19 27	19 42				20 00	20 06	20 12	20 43	20 46			20 59

		XC	AW	GW	AW	GW	SW	GW	GW	GW	AW	GW	GW	GW	AW	GW	GW	AW	GW	GW	AW	GW
Bath Spa	d			20 27		20 40	20 49	21 05	21 11			21 28	21 40	22 15			22 26		22 44			23 57
Oldfield Park	d								21 13					22 17								
Keynsham	d						20 57		21 21					22 25								
Bristol Temple Meads	a			20 39		20 54	21 04	21 18	21 29			21 40	21 53	22 33			22 38		22 58			00 11
	d			20 48								21 48					22 48					
Filton Abbey Wood	d			20 55								21 55					22 55					
Bristol Parkway	a																					
	d									21 13						22 13				23 16		
Patchway	d											22 02										
Pilning	d																					
Gloucester	d	20 23			20 31													22 33				
Lydney	d				20 50													22 52				
Chepstow	d				21 00													23 02				
Caldicot	d				21 10													23 10				
Severn Tunnel Jn.	d			21 08	21 13							22 15					23 09	23 14				
Newport (South Wales)	a	21 06		21 26	21 31					21 38		22 31				22 38	23 26	23 33		23 40		
	d	21 08	21 14	21 26	21 33					21 38	21 48	22 31			22 33	22 38	23 27	23 34		23 43	23 55	
Cardiff Central	a	21 26	21 36	21 42	21 49					21 59	22 07	22 53			22 59	23 00	23 47	23 54		00 05	00 20	

A to Newport (South Wales)

When events are being held at the Millenium Stadium, services are subject to alteration. Please check times before travelling.

Table 133

Mondays to Fridays

Bristol - Avonmouth and Severn Beach

Network Diagram - see first Page of Table 132

Miles			GW	GW	GW	GW	GW	GW	GW	GW	GW	GW	GW	GW	GW	GW	GW	GW	GW	GW	GW	GW	GW
0	Bristol Temple Meads	d	05 24	05 48	06 19	06 30	06 50	07 04	07 19	07 47	08 03	08 10	08 36	08 44	09 10	09 16	09 47	10 03	10 34	10 45	11 16	11 44	12 03
1	Lawrence Hill	d	05 27		06 22	06 33	06 53	07 07	07 22	07 50	08 06	08 13	08 39	08 47	09 13	09 19	09 49		10 37	10 49	11 19	11 47	
1½	Stapleton Road	d	05 29	05 51	06a24	06 35	06a55	07 09	07a24	07a52	08 08	08a15	08 41	08a49	09a15	09 21	09a50	10 07	10 39	10a51	11 21	11a49	12 07
2¾	Montpelier	d	05 32	05 55		06 39		07 12			08 11		08 45			09 24		10 10	10 42		11 24		12 10
3¼	Redland	d	05 34	05 57		06 41		07 14			08 13		08 47			09 26		10 12	10 44		11 26		12 12
4	Clifton Down	d	05 37	06 00		06 44		07 17			08 17		08 52			09 29		10 17	10 48		11 29		12 17
6	Sea Mills	d	05 41	06 04		06 48		07 21			08 21		08 56			09 33		10 21	10 52		11 33		12 21
7¼	Shirehampton	d	05 45	06 07		06 52		07 24			08 25		08 59			09 37		10 25	10 56		11 37		12 25
9	Avonmouth	d	05 49	06a14		06 56		07 30			08a31		09a06			09 40		10a31	11a02		11 40		12a31
10	St Andrews Road	d	05x52			06x59		07x33								09x44					11x44		
13½	Severn Beach	a	06 01			07 07		07 41								09 53					11 53		

		GW	GW	GW	GW	GW	GW	GW	GW	GW	GW	GW	GW	GW	GW	GW	GW	GW	GW	GW	GW	GW	GW
Bristol Temple Meads	d	12 34	12 44	13 16	13 46	14 03	14 34	14 45	15 16	15 45	16 03	16 15	16 35	16 44	17 10	17 16	17 46	18 03	18 21	18 48	19 21	19 33	19 45
Lawrence Hill	d	12 37	12 47	13 19	13 47		14 37	14 47	15 19	15 47	16 06	16 18	16 37	16 47	17 13	17 19	17 47	18 06	18 24	18 51	19 24	19 36	19 47
Stapleton Road	d	12 39	12a49	13 21	13a50	14 07	14 39	14a49	15 21	15a50	16 07	16a20	16 39	16a49	17a15	17 21	17a49	18 07	18a26	18 53	19a26	19 38	19a50
Montpelier	d	12 42		13 24		14 10	14 42		15 24		16 10		16 42			17 24		18 10		18 57		19 41	
Redland	d	12 44		13 26		14 12	14 44		15 26		16 12		16 44			17 26		18 12		18 59		19 43	
Clifton Down	d	12 48		13 29		14 17	14 48		15 29		16 17		16 48			17 29		18 17		19 08		19 46	
Sea Mills	d	12 52		13 33		14 21	14 52		15 33		16 21		16 52			17 33		18 21		19 12		19 50	
Shirehampton	d	12 56		13 37		14 25	14 56		15 37		16 25		16 56			17 37		18 25		19 16		19 54	
Avonmouth	d	13a02		13 40		14a31	15a02		15 40		16a31		17a02			17 40		18 29		19a22		20a00	
St Andrews Road	d			13x44					15x44							17x44		18x32					
Severn Beach	a			13 53					15 53							17 53		18 40					

		GW	GW	GW
Bristol Temple Meads	d	20 34	21 19	22 16
Lawrence Hill	d	20 37	21 22	22 19
Stapleton Road	d	20 39	21a24	22 21
Montpelier	d	20 42		22 24
Redland	d	20 44		22 26
Clifton Down	d	20 48		22 29
Sea Mills	d	20 52		22 33
Shirehampton	d	20 56		22 37
Avonmouth	d	20 59		22 40
St Andrews Road	d	21x02		22x44
Severn Beach	a	21 11		22 53

Saturdays

		GW	GW	GW	GW	GW	GW	GW	GW (bus)	GW	GW	GW	GW	GW	GW	GW	GW (bus)	GW	GW	GW	GW	GW	GW
Bristol Temple Meads	d	06 03	06 34	06 50	07 16	07 47	08 03	08 20		08 34	08 45	09 16	09 21	09 45	10 03	10 21		10 34	10 45	11 16	11 21	11 45	12 03
Lawrence Hill	d		06 37	06 53	07 19	07 50	08 06	08 23		08 37	08 48	09 19		09 48				10 37	10 48	11 19		11 48	
Stapleton Road	d	06 07	06 39	06a55	07 21	07a52	08 07	08a25		08 39	08a50	09 21	09a24	09a50	10 07	10a24		10 39	10a50	11 21	11a24	11a50	12 07
Montpelier	d	06 10	06 42		07 24		08 10			08 42		09 24			10 10			10 42		11 24			12 10
Redland	d	06 12	06 44		07 26		08 12			08 44		09 26			10 12			10 44		11 26			12 12
Clifton Down	d	06 17	06 48		07 29		08 17			08 48		09 29			10 17			10 48		11 29			12 17
Sea Mills	d	06 21	06 52		07 33		08 21			08 52		09 33			10 21			10 52		11 33			12 21
Shirehampton	d	06 25	06 56		07 37		08 25			08 56		09 37			10 25			10 56		11 37			12 25
Avonmouth	d	06a31	07a02		07 40		08a31		08 33	09a02		09 40			10a31		10 33	11a02		11 40			12a31
St Andrews Road	d				07x44				08x36			09x44					10x36			11x44			
Severn Beach	a				07 53				08 48			09 53					10 48			11 53			

		GW	GW (bus)	GW	GW	GW	GW	GW	GW	GW	GW (bus)	GW	GW	GW	GW	GW	GW	GW	GW (bus)	GW	GW	GW	GW
Bristol Temple Meads	d	12 21		12 34	12 45	13 16	13 21	13 45	14 03	14 21		14 34	14 45	15 16	15 21	15 45	16 03	16 21		16 34	16 45	17 16	17 21
Lawrence Hill	d			12 37	12 48	13 19		13 48				14 37	14 48	15 19		15 48	16 06			16 37	16 48	17 19	
Stapleton Road	d	12a25		12 39	12a50	13 21	13a24	13a50	14 07	14a25		14 39	14a50	15 21	15a24	15a50	16 07	16a25		16 39	16a50	17 21	17a24
Montpelier	d			12 42		13 24			14 10			14 42		15 24			16 10			16 42		17 24	
Redland	d			12 44		13 26			14 12			14 44		15 26			16 12			16 44		17 26	
Clifton Down	d			12 48		13 29			14 17			14 48		15 29			16 17			16 48		17 29	
Sea Mills	d			12 52		13 33			14 21			14 52		15 33			16 21			16 52		17 33	
Shirehampton	d			12 56		13 37			14 25			14 56		15 37			16 25			16 56		17 37	
Avonmouth	d		12 33	13a02		13 40			14a31		14 33	15a02		15 40			16a31		16 33	17a02		17 40	
St Andrews Road	d		12x36			13x44					14x36			15x44					16x36			17x44	
Severn Beach	a		12 48			13 53					14 48			15 53					16 48			17 53	

		GW	GW	GW	GW	GW	GW	GW	GW
Bristol Temple Meads	d	17 45	18 03	18 21	18 45	19 03	19 45	20 34	22 16
Lawrence Hill	d	17 48	18 06		18 48	19 06	19 48	20 37	22 19
Stapleton Road	d	17a50	18 07	18a24	18a50	19 07	19a50	20 39	22 21
Montpelier	d		18 10			19 10		20 42	22 24
Redland	d		18 12			19 12		20 44	22 26
Clifton Down	d		18 17			19 17		20 48	22 29
Sea Mills	d		18 21			19 21		20 52	22 33
Shirehampton	d		18 25			19 25		20 56	22 37
Avonmouth	d		18 29			19 29		20 59	22 40
St Andrews Road	d		18x32			19x32		21x02	22x44
Severn Beach	a		18 40			19 40		21 11	22 53

Table 133

Sundays until 24 June

Bristol - Avonmouth and Severn Beach

Network Diagram - see first Page of Table 132

		GW	GW	GW ◇	GW	GW	GW	GW	GW	GW	GW	GW
Bristol Temple Meads 10	d	09 08	10 23	11 23	12 23	13 23	14 23	15 23	16 23	16 53	17 53	18 53
Lawrence Hill	d	09 11	10 26	11 26	12 26	13 26	14 26	15 26	16 26	16 56	17 56	18 56
Stapleton Road	d	09 13	10 28	11 28	12 28	13 28	14 28	15 28	16 28	16 58	17 58	18 58
Montpelier	d	09 16	10 31	11 31	12 31	13 31	14 31	15 31	16 31	17 02	18 01	19 01
Redland	d	09 18	10 33	11 33	12 33	13 33	14 33	15 33	16 33	17 04	18 03	19 03
Clifton Down	d	09 21	10 36	11 40	12 36	13 36	14 36	15 36	16 36	17 06	18 06	19 06
Sea Mills	d	09 25	10 40	11 44	12 40	13 40	14 40	15 40	16 40	17 10	18 10	19 10
Shirehampton	d	09 29	10 44	11 47	12 44	13 44	14 44	15 44	16 44	17 14	18 14	19 14
Avonmouth 2	d	09 33	10 47	11 51	12 48	13 48	14 48	15 48	16 48	17 22	18 18	19 18
St Andrews Road	d	09x36	10x51	11x55	12x51	13x51	14x51	15x51	16x51	17x26	18x21	19x21
Severn Beach	a	09 43	10 58	12 02	12 58	13 58	14 58	15 58	16 58	17 33	18 28	19 28

Sundays 1 July to 9 September

		GW	GW	GW ◇	GW	GW	GW	GW	GW	GW	GW	GW
Bristol Temple Meads 10	d	09 08	10 23	11 23	12 23	13 23	14 23	15 23	16 23	16 53	17 53	18 53
Lawrence Hill	d	09 11	10 26	11 26	12 26	13 26	14 26	15 26	16 26	16 56	17 56	18 56
Stapleton Road	d	09 13	10 28	11 28	12 28	13 28	14 28	15 28	16 28	16 58	17 58	18 58
Montpelier	d	09 16	10 31	11 31	12 31	13 31	14 31	15 31	16 31	17 02	18 01	19 01
Redland	d	09 18	10 33	11 33	12 33	13 33	14 33	15 33	16 33	17 04	18 03	19 03
Clifton Down	d	09 21	10 36	11 40	12 36	13 36	14 36	15 36	16 36	17 06	18 06	19 06
Sea Mills	d	09 25	10 40	11 44	12 40	13 40	14 40	15 40	16 40	17 10	18 10	19 10
Shirehampton	d	09 29	10 44	11 47	12 44	13 44	14 44	15 44	16 44	17 14	18 14	19 14
Avonmouth 2	d	09 33	10 47	11 51	12 48	13 48	14 48	15 48	16 48	17 22	18 18	19 18
St Andrews Road	d	09x36	10x51	11x55	12x51	13x51	14x51	15x51	16x51	17x26	18x21	19x21
Severn Beach	a	09 43	10 58	12 02	12 58	13 58	14 58	15 58	16 58	17 33	18 28	19 28

Sundays from 16 September

		GW	GW	GW ◇	GW	GW	GW	GW	GW	GW	GW
Bristol Temple Meads 10	d	09 08	10 23	11 23	12 23	13 23	14 23	15 23	16 23	16 53	17 53
Lawrence Hill	d	09 11	10 26	11 26	12 26	13 26	14 26	15 26	16 26	16 56	17 56
Stapleton Road	d	09 13	10 28	11 28	12 28	13 28	14 28	15 28	16 28	16 58	17 58
Montpelier	d	09 16	10 31	11 31	12 31	13 31	14 31	15 31	16 31	17 02	18 01
Redland	d	09 18	10 33	11 33	12 33	13 33	14 33	15 33	16 33	17 04	18 03
Clifton Down	d	09 21	10 36	11 36	12 36	13 36	14 36	15 36	16 36	17 06	18 06
Sea Mills	d	09 25	10 40	11 40	12 40	13 40	14 40	15 40	16 40	17 10	18 10
Shirehampton	d	09 29	10 44	11 43	12 44	13 44	14 44	15 44	16 44	17 14	18 14
Avonmouth 2	d	09 33	10a49	11a47	12a49	13a49	14a49	15a49	16a47	17 18	18a17
St Andrews Road	d	09x36								17x21	
Severn Beach	a	09 43								17 28	

Table 133

Mondays to Fridays

Severn Beach and Avonmouth - Bristol

Network Diagram - see first Page of Table 132

Miles			GW MX	GW	GW	GW	GW	GW	GW	GW	GW	GW ◇	GW	GW	GW	GW	GW	GW ◇	GW	GW	GW	GW	GW
0	**Severn Beach**	d		06 03				07 18	07 54						09 54					11 54			
3½	St Andrews Road	d		06x09				07x24	08x00						10x00					12x00			
4½	Avonmouth 2	d		06 13	06 31			07 28	08 04		08 38		09 15		10 04		10 35		11 15	12 04	12 35		13 15
6	Shirehampton	d		06 17	06 34			07 32	08 07		08 41		09 18		10 07		10 38		11 18	12 07	12 38		13 18
7½	Sea Mills	d		06 21	06 38			07 36	08 11		08 45		09 22		10 11		10 42		11 22	12 11	12 42		13 22
9½	Clifton Down	d		06 26	06 44			07 40	08 16		08 52		09 30		10 16		10 48		11 31	12 16	12 48		13 31
10¼	Redland	d		06 28	06 46			07 44	08 19		08 54		09 32		10 19		10 51		11 34	12 19	12 51		13 34
10¾	Montpelier	d		06 30	06 48			07 46	08 21		08 56		09 34		10 21		10 53		11 36	12 21	12 53		13 36
12	Stapleton Road	d	00 25	06 36	06 53	07 07	07 33	07 52	08 27	08 53	09 01	09 29	09 39	09 43	10 25	10 30	10 59	11 29	11 40	12 25	12 59	13 29	13 40
12½	Lawrence Hill	d	00 27	06 38	06 56	07 09	07 35	07 55	08 29	08 55	09 03	09 31	09 41			10 32	11 01	11 31	11 42		13 01	13 31	13 42
13½	**Bristol Temple Meads** 10	a	00 33	06 41	07 02	07 12	07 39	07 58	08 32	09 01	09 10	09 34	09 48	09 50	10 32	10 37	11 10	11 34	11 49	12 32	13 10	13 35	13 50

		GW	GW ◇	GW	GW	GW	GW	GW ◇	GW	GW	GW ◇	GW	GW	GW	GW	GW	GW	GW	GW	GW	GW	GW	GW
Severn Beach	d	13 54					15 54								17 54		18 44					21 29	
St Andrews Road	d	14x00					16x00								18x00		18x50					21x35	
Avonmouth 2	d	14 04		14 35		15 15	16 04			16 35		17 15			18 04		18 54		19 32	20 01		21 39	
Shirehampton	d	14 07		14 38		15 18	16 07			16 38		17 18			18 07		18 58		19 35	20 04		21 43	
Sea Mills	d	14 11		14 42		15 22	16 11			16 42		17 22			18 11		19 02		19 39	20 08		21 47	
Clifton Down	d	14 16		14 48		15 31	16 16			16 48		17 31			18 16		19 13		19 46	20 13		21 52	
Redland	d	14 19		14 51		15 34	16 19			16 51		17 34			18 19		19 15		19 49	20 16		21 54	
Montpelier	d	14 21		14 53		15 36	16 21			16 53		17 36			18 21		19 17		19 51	20 18		21 56	
Stapleton Road	d	14 25	14 31	14 59	15 29	15 40	16 24	16 31	16 54	17 00	17 29	17 40	17 54	18 19	18 25	18 31	19 22	19 29	19 56	20 22	20 31	22 02	22 58
Lawrence Hill	d		14 33	15 01	15 31	15 42		16 33	16 56	17 02	17 31	17 42	17 56		18 27	18 32	19 24	19 31	19 58	20 24	20 33	22 04	23 00
Bristol Temple Meads 10	a	14 32	14 38	15 10	15 36	15 50	16 32	16 37	17 02	17 10	17 36	17 50	18 01	18 24	18 34	18 38	19 28	19 35	20 04	20 32	20 38	22 07	23 05

		GW
Severn Beach	d	22 54
St Andrews Road	d	23x00
Avonmouth 2	d	23 04
Shirehampton	d	23 07
Sea Mills	d	23 11
Clifton Down	d	23 16
Redland	d	23 19
Montpelier	d	23 21
Stapleton Road	d	23 25
Lawrence Hill	d	23 27
Bristol Temple Meads 10	a	23 32

Saturdays

		GW	GW	GW	GW	GW	GW 🚌	GW ◇	GW	GW	GW	GW	GW 🚌	GW ◇	GW	GW	GW ■	GW	GW 🚌	GW	GW	GW	GW ◇
Severn Beach	d				07 54		08 55			09 54			10 55			11 54			12 55			13 54	
St Andrews Road	d				08x00		09x07			10x00			11x07			12x00			13x07			14x00	
Avonmouth 2	d		06 35	07 15	08 04	08 35	09a10		09 15	10 04		10 35	11a10		11 15	12 04		12 35	13a10		13 15	14 04	
Shirehampton	d		06 38	07 18	08 07	08 38			09 18	10 07		10 38			11 18	12 07		12 38			13 18	14 07	
Sea Mills	d		06 42	07 22	08 11	08 42			09 22	10 11		10 42			11 22	12 11		12 42			13 22	14 11	
Clifton Down	d		06 48	07 31	08 16	08 47			09 30	10 16		10 48			11 31	12 16		12 47			13 31	14 16	
Redland	d		06 50	07 34	08 19	08 50			09 33	10 19		10 51			11 34	12 19		12 50			13 34	14 19	
Montpelier	d		06 52	07 36	08 21	08 52			09 35	10 21		10 53			11 36	12 21		12 52			13 36	14 21	
Stapleton Road	d	00 25	06 55	07 40	08 24	08 54		09 29	09 39	10 24	10 32	10 59		11 28	11 39	12 24	12 32	12 54		13 27	13 40	14 24	14 31
Lawrence Hill	d	00 27	06 57	07 42	08 26	08 56		09 31	09 41		10 34	11 01		11 30	11 41		12 34	12 56		13 29	13 41		14 33
Bristol Temple Meads 10	a	00 33	07 04	07 49	08 32	09 05		09 34	09 47	10 32	10 39	11 09		11 33	11 48	12 32	12 39	13 07		13 34	13 48	14 32	14 36

		GW	GW 🚌	GW	GW	GW	GW ◇	GW	GW 🚌	GW ◇	GW	GW	GW	GW	GW	GW	GW	GW	GW
Severn Beach	d		14 55			15 54			16 55			17 54			18 54	19 47		21 31	22 54
St Andrews Road	d		15x07			16x00			17x07			18x00			19x00	19x53		21x35	23x00
Avonmouth 2	d	14 35	15a10		15 15	16 04		16 35	17a10		17 15	18 04			19 04	19 57		21 39	23 04
Shirehampton	d	14 38			15 18	16 07		16 38			17 18	18 07			19 07	20 00		21 43	23 07
Sea Mills	d	14 42			15 22	16 11		16 42			17 22	18 11			19 11	20 04		21 47	23 11
Clifton Down	d	14 48			15 31	16 16		16 47			17 31	18 16			19 29	20 09		21 52	23 16
Redland	d	14 51			15 34	16 19		16 50			17 34	18 19			19 31	20 12		21 54	23 19
Montpelier	d	14 53			15 36	16 21		16 52			17 36	18 21			19 33	20 14		21 56	23 21
Stapleton Road	d	14 59		15 27	15 39	16 24	16 34	16 54		17 29	17 39	18 24	18 34	19 29	19 40	20 17	20 34	22 02	23 24
Lawrence Hill	d	15 01		15 29	15 41		16 36	16 56		17 31	17 41	18 26	18 36	19 31	19 42	20 19	20 36	22 04	23 26
Bristol Temple Meads 10	a	15 09		15 33	15 48	16 32	16 39	17 07		17 34	17 48	18 31	18 39	19 36	19 46	20 25	20 39	22 09	23 32

Table 133

Severn Beach and Avonmouth - Bristol

Sundays until 24 June

Network Diagram - see first Page of Table 132

		GW	GW	GW	GW	GW	GW	GW	GW	GW		GW	GW
Severn Beach	d	09 46	11 12	12 12	13 12	14 12	15 12	16 12	17 12	17 42		18 42	19 42
St Andrews Road	d	09x52	11x18	12x18	13x18	14x18	15x18	16x18	17x18	17x48		18x48	19x48
Avonmouth ■	d	09 56	11 22	12 22	13 22	14 22	15 22	16 22	17 22	17 52		18 52	19 52
Shirehampton	d	09 59	11 25	12 25	13 25	14 25	15 25	16 25	17 26	17 56		18 55	19 55
Sea Mills	d	10 03	11 29	12 29	13 29	14 29	15 29	16 29	17 30	18 00		18 59	19 59
Clifton Down	d	10 08	11 41	12 42	13 37	14 37	15 37	16 37	17 35	18 06		19 06	20 04
Redland	d	10 11	11 43	12 44	13 39	14 39	15 39	16 39	17 38	18 09		19 09	20 07
Montpelier	d	10 13	11 45	12 46	13 41	14 41	15 41	16 41	17 40	18 11		19 11	20 09
Stapleton Road	d	10 16	11 50	12 51	13 46	14 48	15 46	16 48	17 44	18 15		19 15	20 15
Lawrence Hill	d	10 18	11 52	12 53	13 48	14 50	15 48	16 50	17 46	18 17		19 17	20 17
Bristol Temple Meads ■	a	10 21	11 56	12 57	13 53	14 56	15 53	16 54	17 50	18 23		19 20	20 20

Sundays 1 July to 9 September

		GW	GW	GW	GW	GW	GW	GW	GW	GW		GW	GW
Severn Beach	d	09 46	11 12	12 12	13 12	14 12	15 12	16 12	17 12	17 42		18 42	19 42
St Andrews Road	d	09x52	11x18	12x18	13x18	14x18	15x18	16x18	17x18	17x48		18x48	19x48
Avonmouth ■	d	09 56	11 22	12 22	13 22	14 22	15 22	16 22	17 22	17 52		18 52	19 52
Shirehampton	d	09 59	11 25	12 25	13 25	14 25	15 25	16 25	17 26	17 56		18 55	19 55
Sea Mills	d	10 03	11 29	12 29	13 29	14 29	15 29	16 29	17 30	18 00		18 59	19 59
Clifton Down	d	10 08	11 41	12 42	13 37	14 37	15 37	16 37	17 35	18 06		19 06	20 04
Redland	d	10 11	11 43	12 44	13 39	14 39	15 39	16 39	17 38	18 09		19 09	20 07
Montpelier	d	10 13	11 45	12 46	13 41	14 41	15 41	16 41	17 40	18 11		19 11	20 09
Stapleton Road	d	10 16	11 50	12 51	13 46	14 48	15 46	16 48	17 44	18 15		19 15	20 15
Lawrence Hill	d	10 18	11 52	12 53	13 48	14 50	15 48	16 50	17 46	18 17		19 17	20 17
Bristol Temple Meads ■	a	10 21	11 56	12 57	13 53	14 54	15 53	16 54	17 50	18 23		19 20	20 20

Sundays from 16 September

		GW	GW	GW	GW	GW	GW	GW	GW	GW		GW
Severn Beach	d	09 46								17 42		
St Andrews Road	d	09x52								17x48		
Avonmouth ■	d	09 56	10 52	11 52	12 52	13 52	14 52	15 52	16 52	17 52		18 22
Shirehampton	d	09 59	10 55	11 55	12 55	13 55	14 55	15 55	16 55	17 56		18 25
Sea Mills	d	10 03	10 59	11 59	12 59	13 59	14 59	15 59	16 59	18 00		18 29
Clifton Down	d	10 08	11 04	12 04	13 04	14 04	15 04	16 04	17 07	18 06		18 34
Redland	d	10 11	11 07	12 07	13 07	14 07	15 07	16 07	17 10	18 09		18 37
Montpelier	d	10 13	11 09	12 09	13 09	14 09	15 09	16 09	17 12	18 11		18 39
Stapleton Road	d	10 16	11 13	12 14	13 13	14 13	15 13	16 13	17 16	18 15		18 43
Lawrence Hill	d	10 18	11 15	12 16	13 15	14 15	15 15	16 15	17 18	18 17		18 45
Bristol Temple Meads ■	a	10 21	11 20	12 20	13 20	14 20	15 20	16 20	17 22	18 23		18 47

Table 134

Gloucester - Taunton

Mondays to Fridays until 29 June

Network Diagram - see first Page of Table 132

Miles			GW	GW	XC	GW	GW	GW	GW	XC	GW		GW	GW	GW	GW	XC	GW	GW	XC	GW		GW	GW	XC
			MX	MX	MX	MX	MO																		
				◇1	◇1		◇1	◇	1	◇1	◇				◇		◇1			◇1	1			◇	◇1
					A		B																		
				⊏⊐			⊏⊐								⊼					⊼	⊼				⊼
0	**Gloucester** ■	d												06 16		06 42			07 10					07 40	
13	Cam & Dursley	d												06 32		06 58			07 25					07 54	
28	Yate	d												06 45		07 12			07 40					08 09	
34	**Bristol Parkway** ■	a												06 54		07 23			07 48					08 19	
—		d			00 03						06 24			06 58		07 25			07 49	07 58			08 12	08 19	08 26
35¼	Filton Abbey Wood	d				00 20					06 27			07 01	07 09	07 28	07 41		07 53		08 09		08 15	08 23	
38¼	Stapleton Road	d				00 25								07 07		07 33									
38¾	Lawrence Hill	d				00 27								07 09		07 35									
39¾	**Bristol Temple Meads** ■	a			00 13	00 33	00 35				06 35			07 12	07 17	07 39	07 51		08 01	08 08	08 17		08 23	08 36	08 40
—		d	23p06	23p35				05 24	06 03	06 34	06 42		06 48	07 18				07 51		08 10			08 25		08 44
40¾	Bedminster	d	23p10										06 50					07 53					08 27		
41½	Parson Street	d	23p12										06 53					07 55					08 29		
47¾	Nailsea & Backwell	d	23p20	23b45					06 14				07 02	07 28				08 04					08 38		
51¾	Yatton	d	23p26	23b52					06 21				07 07	07 33				08 09					08 44		
55¾	Worle	d	23p32	23b58					06 27				07 12	07 39				08 15					08 50		
58½	Weston Milton	d	23p37										07 18					08 20					08 55		
59¾	**Weston-super-Mare**	a	23p40	00s05				05 43	06 36		07 02		07 23	07 47				08 26					08 58		
—		d	23p42					05 45			07 06			07 49									09 00		
67¼	Highbridge & Burnham	d	23p54	00s16				05 55			07 17			08 00									09 10		
73½	Bridgwater	d	00 02	00s24				06 03			07 25			08 08									09 18		
85¼	**Taunton**	a	00s14	00s36				06 16		07 06	07 38			08 24						08 41			09 33		09 15

		GW	GW	GW	XC	GW	GW		GW	XC	GW	GW	XC	GW	GW	GW	XC		GW	XC	GW	GW	GW	XC	GW
		◇		◇1	◇1	◇			◇	◇1		◇	◇1	◇			◇1			◇1	◇		◇	◇1	◇1
				C																					D
				Ø	⊼	⊼				⊼			⊼	⊼			⊼			⊼	⊼			⊼	⊏⊐
Gloucester ■	d								08 41							09 45							10 41		
Cam & Dursley	d								08 56							09 59							10 56		
Yate	d								09 10							10 13							11 10		
Bristol Parkway ■	a								09 19							10 22							11 19		
	d		08 45		08 55		09 12		09 20	09 26	09 34		09 56		10 12	10 22	10 27			10 55		11 12	11 20	11 28	
Filton Abbey Wood	d	08 42	08 48			09 09	09 15		09 23		09 37	09 42		10 09	10 15	10 25			10 42		11 09	11 15	11 23		
Stapleton Road	d		08 53						09 29		09 43					10 30							11 29		
Lawrence Hill	d		08 55						09 31							10 32							11 31		
Bristol Temple Meads ■	a	08 50	09 01		09 14	09 17	09 23		09 34	09 38	09 50	09 53	10 08	10 18	10 23	10 37	10 41		10 51	11 12	11 18	11 23	11 34	11 37	
	d	08 55		09 13			09 26			09 44		09 55			10 25		10 44		10 53	11 15		11 25		11 44	11 47
Bedminster	d						09 28								10 27							11 27			
Parson Street	d						09 31								10 29							11 29			
Nailsea & Backwell	d	09 03					09 40					10 03			10 38				11 03			11 38			
Yatton	d	09 08					09 45					10 08			10 44				11 08			11 44			
Worle	d	09 14					09 51					10 14			10 50				11 14			11 50			
Weston Milton	d						09 56								10 55							11 55			
Weston-super-Mare	a	09 22					10 01					10 22			11 00				11 21	11 32		12 00			12 06
	d	09 29										10 23							11 23	11 37					12 07
Highbridge & Burnham	d	09 40										10 34							11 34						
Bridgwater	d	09 48										10 42							11 42						
Taunton	a	10 01		09 45						10 16		10 58					11 16		11 57	12 00				12 15	12 29

		GW	XC		GW	GW	GW	XC	GW	XC	GW	GW	GW		XC	GW	XC	GW	GW	GW	XC	GW	XC		GW
			◇1		◇			◇1		◇1	◇				◇1	◇	◇1	◇		◇	◇1		◇1		◇
			⊼		⊼			⊼		⊼	⊼				⊼		⊼	⊼			⊼		⊼		⊼
Gloucester ■	d						11 45						12 41							13 45					
Cam & Dursley	d						11 59						12 56							13 59					
Yate	d						12 13						13 10							14 13					
Bristol Parkway ■	a						12 22						13 19							14 22					
	d		11 56			12 12	12 22	12 30		12 56		13 12	13 20		13 27		13 59		14 12	14 22	14 29		14 59		
Filton Abbey Wood	d	11 42			12 09	12 15	12 25		12 42		13 09	13 15	13 23			13 42		14 09	14 15	14 25		14 42			15 09
Stapleton Road	d												13 29							14 31					
Lawrence Hill	d												13 31							14 33					
Bristol Temple Meads ■	a	11 51	12 08		12 18	12 23	12 34	12 40	12 51	13 10	13 18	13 23	13 35		13 38	13 51	14 09	14 17	14 23	14 38	14 41	14 51	15 10		15 17
	d	11 53				12 25		12 44	12 53			13 25			13 44	13 53			14 25		14 44	14 53	15 13		
Bedminster	d					12 27						13 27							14 27						
Parson Street	d					12 29						13 29							14 29						
Nailsea & Backwell	d	12 03				12 38			13 03			13 38				14 03			14 38			15 03			
Yatton	d	12 08				12 44			13 08			13 44				14 08			14 44			15 08			
Worle	d	12 14				12 50			13 14			13 50				14 14			14 50			15 14			
Weston Milton	d					12 55						13 55							14 55						
Weston-super-Mare	a	12 20				13 00			13 21			14 00				14 21			15 00			15 22			
	d	12 22							13 23							14 23						15 28			
Highbridge & Burnham	d	12 33							13 34							14 34						15 38			
Bridgwater	d	12 41							13 42							14 42						15 46			
Taunton	a	12 57						13 16	13 59						14 15	14 55					15 16	16 01	15 44		

A until 22 June
B from 21 May until 25 June
C The Merchant Venturer
D The Torbay Express
b Previous night, stops to set down only

For connections from London Paddington please refer to Table 125

Gloucester - Taunton

until 29 June

Network Diagram - see first Page of Table 132

Station		GW	GW	XC	GW	GW	XC	GW	GW	GW	GW	XC	GW	GW	GW	XC	GW	GW	GW	GW	XC	GW	GW
				◇1			◇1	◇	◇1		◇	◇1				◇1		◇1		◇	◇1		
Gloucester 7	d		14 41								15 45									16 41			
Cam & Dursley	d		14 56								15 59									16 56			
Yate	d		15 10								16 13									17 10			
Bristol Parkway 7	a		15 20								16 22									17 20			
	d	15 12	15 20	15 26		15 53	15 57			16 12	16 22	16 29		16 46		16 58			17 12	17 20	17 27		17 46
Filton Abbey Wood	d	15 15	15 23		15 42	15a56		16 09		16 15	16 25		16 42	16 49	16 55		17 09		17 15	17 23		17 43	17 49
Stapleton Road	d		15 29								16 31			16 54						17 29			17 54
Lawrence Hill	d		15 31								16 33			16 56						17 31			17 56
Bristol Temple Meads 10	a	15 23	15 36	15 39	15 51		16 08	16 18		16 23	16 37	16 40	16 51	17 02	17 03	17 10	17 18		17 23	17 36	17 39	17 53	18 01
	d	15 25		15 44	15 53				16 18	16 25		16 44	16 53			17 13		17 18	17 25		17 44	17 55	
Bedminster	d	15 27			15 55					16 27			16 55						17 27			17 58	
Parson Street	d	15 29			15 57					16 29			16 57						17 29			18 01	
Nailsea & Backwell	d	15 38			16 03				16 29	16 38			17 03					17 28	17 38			18 09	
Yatton	d	15 44			16 08				16 36	16 44			17 08					17 34	17 44			18 15	
Worle	d	15 50			16 14				16 43	16 50			17 14					17 41	17 50			18 21	
Weston Milton	d	15 55			16 21					16 55			17 22						17 55			18 25	
Weston-super-Mare	a	16 00			16 24				16 52	17 00			17 27					17 52	18 00			18 29	
	d				16 24								17 28									18 30	
Highbridge & Burnham	d				16 37								17 38									18 41	
Bridgwater	d				16 45								17 46									18 49	
Taunton	a			16 15	17 00							17 15	18 01			17 44					18 15	19 03	

Station		XC	GW	GW	GW	GW	XC	GW	XC	GW	GW	GW	XC	GW	XC	GW	GW	GW	GW	XC	GW	XC	GW
		◇1		◇1			◇1		◇1	◇1	◇		◇1		◇1	◇	◇1			◇1 A		◇1 A	◇1
Gloucester 7	d					17 45						18 41							19 45				
Cam & Dursley	d					17 58						18 56							19 59				
Yate	d					18 12						19 10							20 13				
Bristol Parkway 7	a					18 22						19 20							20 22				
	d	18 00			18 12	18 22	18 29		18 57			19 20	19 29		19 58			20 11	20 22	20 29		20 56	
Filton Abbey Wood	d		18 09		18 15	18 25		18 42			19 09	19 23		19 42		20 09		20 14	20 25		20 42		
Stapleton Road	d				18 19	18 31						19 29							20 31				
Lawrence Hill	d					18 32						19 31							20 33				
Bristol Temple Meads 10	a	18 10	18 17		18 24	18 38	18 41	18 53	19 06		19 17	19 35	19 38	19 51	20 09	20 17		20 24	20 38	20 40	20 53	21 07	
	d			18 20	18 26		18 44	18 56		19 15			19 44	19 55			20 18			20 44	20 55	21 12	21 18
Bedminster	d				18 27			18 57						19 57							20 57		
Parson Street	d				18 29			18 59						19 59							20 59		
Nailsea & Backwell	d			18 31	18 38			19 08		19 25				20 08			20 29				21 08		21 27
Yatton	d			18 38	18 44			19 13		19 32				20 13			20 36				21 13		21 34
Worle	d			18 45	18 50			19 19		19 38				20 19			20 44				21 19		21 40
Weston Milton	d				18 54			19 23		19 43				20 23			20 49				21 23		
Weston-super-Mare	a			18 51	19 00			19 28		19 48				20 27			20 53				21 27		21 50
	d			18 55				19 29		19 57				20 29							21 33		
Highbridge & Burnham	d			19 08				19 40						20 39							21 44		
Bridgwater	d			19 15				19 48						20 47							21 52		
Taunton	a			19 28			19 15	20 03		20 23			20 16	21 02						21 16	22 07	21 43	

Station		GW	XC	GW	GW	GW	XC	GW	XC	GW	GW	GW	GW	XC	GW
		◇	◇1 A		◇	1	◇1		◇1				◇1	◇1 B	
Gloucester 7	d					21 15			22 05			22 28			
Cam & Dursley	d					21 29									
Yate	d					21 41									
Bristol Parkway 7	a					21 50			22 32			23 04			
	d		21 27			21 51	22 02		22 34			23 05		23 23	
Filton Abbey Wood	d	21 08		21 42		21 56		22 09		22 52					23 40
Stapleton Road	d									22 58					
Lawrence Hill	d									23 00					
Bristol Temple Meads 10	a	21 19	21 36	21 51		22 11	22 13	22 22	22 44	23 05		23 19		23 40	23 49
	d		21 44		21 56						23 06		23 35		
Bedminster	d				21 58						23 10				
Parson Street	d				22 00						23 12				
Nailsea & Backwell	d				22 09						23 20		23s45		
Yatton	d				22 13						23 26		23s52		
Worle	d				22 19						23 32		23s58		
Weston Milton	d				22 23						23 37				
Weston-super-Mare	a				22 28						23 40		00s05		
	d				22 29						23 42				
Highbridge & Burnham	d				22 40						23 54		00s16		
Bridgwater	d				22 48						00 02		00s24		
Taunton	a		22 15		23 01						00s14		00s36		

A to Bristol Temple Meads

B from 25 June until 29 June

For connections from London Paddington please refer to Table 125

Gloucester - Taunton

2 July to 31 August

Network Diagram - see first Page of Table 132

Station		GW MX	GW MX	GW MX	GW	GW	XC	GW	GW	GW	GW	GW	XC	GW	GW	XC	GW	GW	GW	XC	GW	GW	GW
			◇1		◇	1	◇1	◇			◇		◇1			◇1			◇	◇1	◇		◇1 A
Gloucester 7	d									06 16		06 42			07 10				07 40				
Cam & Dursley	d									06 32		06 58			07 25				07 54				
Yate	d									06 45		07 12			07 40				08 09				
Bristol Parkway 7	a									06 54		07 23			07 48				08 19				
	d							06 24		06 58		07 25			07 49	07 58		08 12	08 19	08 26		08 45	
Filton Abbey Wood	d			00 20				06 27		07 01	07 09	07 28	07 41		07 53		08 09	08 15	08 23		08 42	08 48	
Stapleton Road	d			00 25						07 07		07 33										08 53	
Lawrence Hill	d			00 27						07 09		07 35										08 55	
Bristol Temple Meads 10	a			00 33				06 35		07 12	07 17	07 39	07 51		08 01	08 08	08 17	08 23	08 36	08 40	08 52	09 01	
	d	23p06	23p35		05 24	06 03	06 34	06 42	06 48	07 18				07 51		08 10		08 25		08 44	08 55		09 13
Bedminster	d	23p10							06 50					07 53				08 27					
Parson Street	d	23p12							06 53					07 55				08 29					
Nailsea & Backwell	d	23p20	23b45			06 14			07 02	07 28				08 04				08 38			09 03		
Yatton	d	23p26	23b52			06 21			07 07	07 33				08 09				08 44			09 08		
Worle	d	23p32	23b58			06 27			07 12	07 39				08 15				08 50			09 14		
Weston Milton	d	23p37							07 18					08 20				08 55					
Weston-super-Mare	a	23p40	00s05		05 43	06 36		07 02	07 23	07 47				08 26				08 58			09 22		
	d	23p42			05 45			07 06		07 49								09 00			09 29		
Highbridge & Burnham	d	23p54	00s16		05 55			07 17		08 00								09 10			09 40		
Bridgwater	d	00 02	00s24		06 03			07 25		08 08								09 18			09 48		
Taunton	a	00s14	00s36		06 16		07 06	07 38		08 24						08 41		09 33		09 15	10 01		09 45

Station		XC	GW	GW	GW	XC	GW	GW	XC	GW	GW	GW	XC	GW	XC	GW	GW	GW	XC	GW	GW	XC	GW
		◇1	◇		◇	◇1		◇	◇1	◇			◇1		◇1	◇		◇	◇1	◇1 B		◇1	◇
Gloucester 7	d				08 41							09 45						10 41					
Cam & Dursley	d				08 56							09 59						10 56					
Yate	d				09 10							10 13						11 10					
Bristol Parkway 7	a				09 19							10 22						11 19					
	d	08 55		09 12	09 20	09 26	09 34		09 56		10 12	10 22	10 27		10 55		11 12	11 20	11 28			11 56	
Filton Abbey Wood	d		09 09	09 15	09 23		09 37	09 42		10 09	10 15	10 25		10 42		11 09	11 15	11 23			11 42		12 09
Stapleton Road	d				09 29		09 43					10 30						11 29					
Lawrence Hill	d				09 31							10 32						11 31					
Bristol Temple Meads 10	a	09 14	09 17	09 23	09 34	09 38	09 50	09 53	10 08	10 18	10 23	10 37	10 41	10 51	11 12	11 18	11 23	11 34	11 37		11 51	12 08	12 18
	d			09 26		09 44		09 55			10 25		10 44	10 53	11 15		11 25		11 44	11 47	11 53		
Bedminster	d			09 28							10 27						11 27						
Parson Street	d			09 31							10 29						11 29						
Nailsea & Backwell	d			09 40				10 03			10 38			11 03			11 38				12 03		
Yatton	d			09 45				10 08			10 44			11 08			11 44				12 08		
Worle	d			09 51				10 14			10 50			11 14			11 50				12 14		
Weston Milton	d			09 56							10 55						11 55						
Weston-super-Mare	a			10 01				10 22			11 00			11 21	11 32		12 00			12 06	12 20		
	d							10 23						11 23	11 37					12 07	12 22		
Highbridge & Burnham	d							10 34						11 34							12 33		
Bridgwater	d							10 42						11 42							12 41		
Taunton	a					10 16		10 58					11 16	11 57	12 00				12 15	12 29	12 57		

Station		GW	GW	XC	GW	XC	GW	GW	GW	XC	GW	XC	GW	GW	GW	XC	GW	XC	GW	GW	GW	XC
			1	◇1		◇1	◇			◇1	◇	◇1	◇		◇	◇1		◇1	◇			◇1
Gloucester 7	d		11 45						12 41						13 45						14 41	
Cam & Dursley	d		11 59						12 56						13 59						14 56	
Yate	d		12 13						13 10						14 13						15 10	
Bristol Parkway 7	a		12 22						13 19						14 22						15 20	
	d	12 12	12 22	12 30		12 56		13 12	13 20	13 27		13 59		14 12	14 22	14 29		14 59		15 12	15 20	15 26
Filton Abbey Wood	d	12 15	12 25		12 42		13 09	13 15	13 23		13 42		14 09	14 15	14 25		14 42		15 09	15 15	15 23	
Stapleton Road	d								13 29						14 31						15 29	
Lawrence Hill	d								13 31						14 33						15 31	
Bristol Temple Meads 10	a	12 23	12 34	12 40	12 51	13 10	13 18	13 23	13 35	13 38	13 51	14 09	14 17	14 23	14 38	14 41	14 51	15 10	15 17	15 23	15 36	15 39
	d	12 25		12 44	12 53			13 25		13 44	13 53			14 25		14 44	14 53	15 13		15 25		15 44
Bedminster	d	12 27						13 27						14 27						15 27		
Parson Street	d	12 29						13 29						14 29						15 29		
Nailsea & Backwell	d	12 38			13 03			13 38			14 03			14 38			15 03			15 38		
Yatton	d	12 44			13 08			13 44			14 08			14 44			15 08			15 44		
Worle	d	12 50			13 14			13 50			14 14			14 50			15 14			15 50		
Weston Milton	d	12 55						13 55						14 55						15 55		
Weston-super-Mare	a	13 00			13 21			14 00			14 21			15 00			15 22			16 00		
	d				13 23						14 23						15 28					
Highbridge & Burnham	d				13 34						14 34						15 38					
Bridgwater	d				13 42						14 42						15 46					
Taunton	a			13 16	13 59					14 15	14 55					15 16	16 01	15 44				16 15

A The Merchant Venturer

B The Torbay Express

b Previous night, stops to set down only

For connections from London Paddington please refer to Table 125

Gloucester - Taunton

Mondays to Fridays

2 July to 31 August

Network Diagram - see first Page of Table 132

		GW	GW	XC	GW	GW	GW	GW		XC	GW	GW	GW	XC	GW	GW	GW	GW		XC	GW	GW	XC	GW	GW
				◇1 H	◇ H	◇1 ⊡		◇		◇1 H				◇1 H	■ H	◇1 ⊡		◇		◇1 H			◇1 H	■ H	◇1 ⊡
Gloucester 7	d							15 45										16 41							
Cam & Dursley	d							15 59										16 56							
Yate	d							16 13										17 10							
Bristol Parkway 7	a							16 22										17 20							
	d		15 53	15 57			16 12	16 22		16 29		16 46		16 58			17 12	17 20		17 27		17 46	18 00		
Filton Abbey Wood	d	15 42	15a56		16 09		16 15	16 25			16 42	16 49	16 55		17 09		17 15	17 23			17 41	17 49		18 09	
Stapleton Road	d							16 31				16 54						17 29				17 54			
Lawrence Hill	d							16 33				16 56						17 31				17 56			
Bristol Temple Meads 10	a	15 51		16 08	16 18		16 23	16 37		16 40	16 51	17 02	17 03	17 10	17 18		17 23	17 36		17 39	17 53	18 01	18 10	18 17	
	d	15 53				16 18	16 25			16 44	16 53			17 13		17 18	17 25			17 44	17 55				18 20
Bedminster	d	15 55					16 27				16 55						17 27				17 58				
Parson Street	d	15 57					16 29				16 57						17 29				18 01				
Nailsea & Backwell	d	16 03				16 29	16 38				17 03					17 28	17 38				18 09				18 31
Yatton	d	16 08				16 36	16 44				17 08					17 34	17 44				18 15				18 38
Worle	d	16 14				16 43	16 50				17 14					17 41	17 50				18 21				18 45
Weston Milton	d	16 21					16 55				17 22						17 55				18 25				
Weston-super-Mare	a	16 24				16 52	17 00				17 27					17 52	18 00				18 29				18 51
	d	16 24									17 28										18 30				18 55
Highbridge & Burnham	d	16 37									17 38										18 41				19 08
Bridgwater	d	16 45									17 46										18 49				19 15
Taunton	a	17 00								17 15	18 01			17 44						18 15	19 08				19 28

		GW	GW	XC		GW	XC	GW	GW	GW	XC	GW	XC	GW		GW	GW	GW	XC	GW	XC	GW	GW	XC	
				◇1 H			◇1 H	◇1 ⊡	◇ H		◇1 H		◇1 H	◇		◇1 ⊡			◇1 A H		◇1 A H	◇1 ⊡	◇	◇1 A H	
Gloucester 7	d		17 45							18 41								19 45							
Cam & Dursley	d		17 58							18 56								19 59							
Yate	d		18 12							19 10								20 13							
Bristol Parkway 7	a		18 22							19 20								20 22							
	d	18 12	18 22	18 29			18 57			19 20	19 29		19 58				20 11	20 22	20 29		20 56			21 27	
Filton Abbey Wood	d	18 15	18 25			18 42			19 09	19 23		19 42		20 09			20 14	20 25		20 42			21 08		
Stapleton Road	d	18 19	18 31							19 29								20 31							
Lawrence Hill	d		18 32							19 31								20 33							
Bristol Temple Meads 10	a	18 24	18 38	18 41		18 53	19 06		19 17	19 35	19 38	19 51	20 09	20 17			20 24	20 38	20 40	20 53	21 07		21 19	21 36	
	d	18 26		18 44		18 56		19 15			19 44	19 55				20 18			20 44	20 55	21 12	21 18		21 44	
Bedminster	d	18 27				18 57						19 57								20 57					
Parson Street	d	18 29				18 59						19 59								20 59					
Nailsea & Backwell	d	18 38				19 08		19 25				20 08				20 29				21 08		21 27			
Yatton	d	18 44				19 13		19 32				20 13				20 36				21 13		21 34			
Worle	d	18 50				19 19		19 38				20 19				20 44				21 19		21 40			
Weston Milton	d	18 54				19 23		19 43				20 23				20 49				21 23					
Weston-super-Mare	a	19 09				19 28		19 48				20 27				20 53				21 27		21 50			
	d					19 29		19 57				20 29								21 33					
Highbridge & Burnham	d					19 40						20 39								21 44					
Bridgwater	d					19 48						20 47								21 52					
Taunton	a			19 15		20 03		20 23			20 16	21 02							21 16	22 07	21 43			22 15	

		GW	GW	GW	XC	GW	XC	GW	GW	GW		GW	XC	GW
			◇	1	◇1		◇1					◇1 ⊡	◇1	
Gloucester 7	d			21 15			22 05			22 28				
Cam & Dursley	d			21 29										
Yate	d			21 41										
Bristol Parkway 7	a			21 50			22 32			23 04				
	d			21 51	22 02		22 34			23 05			23 23	
Filton Abbey Wood	d	21 42		21 56		22 09		22 52						23 40
Stapleton Road	d							22 58						
Lawrence Hill	d							23 00						
Bristol Temple Meads 10	a	21 51		22 11	22 13	22 22	22 44	23 05		23 19			23 40	23 49
	d		21 56						23 06			23 35		
Bedminster	d		21 58						23 10					
Parson Street	d		22 00						23 12					
Nailsea & Backwell	d		22 09						23 20			23s45		
Yatton	d		22 13						23 26			23s52		
Worle	d		22 19						23 32			23s58		
Weston Milton	d		22 23						23 37					
Weston-super-Mare	a		22 28						23 40			00s05		
	d		22 29						23 42					
Highbridge & Burnham	d		22 40						23 54			00s16		
Bridgwater	d		22 48						00 02			00s24		
Taunton	a		23 01						00s14			00s36		

A H to Bristol Temple Meads

For connections from London Paddington please refer to Table 125

Gloucester - Taunton

Mondays to Fridays

from 3 September

Network Diagram - see first Page of Table 132

		GW MX	GW MX	XC MO	GW MX	GW MO	GW	GW	XC	GW		GW	GW	GW	GW	XC	GW	GW	XC	GW		GW	GW	XC	GW
			◇1 ⊡	◇1 A		◇1 B ⊡	◇	1	◇1	◇				◇ H		◇1			◇1 H	■ H			◇	◇1 H	◇
Gloucester 7	d			23p07									06 16		06 42			07 10					07 40		
Cam & Dursley	d												06 32		06 58			07 25					07 54		
Yate	d												06 45		07 12			07 40					08 09		
Bristol Parkway 7	a			00 01									06 54		07 23			07 48					08 19		
	d			00 04						06 24			06 58		07 25			07 49	07 58			08 12	08 19	08 26	
Filton Abbey Wood	d				00 20					06 27			07 01	07 09	07 28	07 41		07 53		08 09		08 15	08 23		08 42
Stapleton Road	d				00 25								07 07		07 33										
Lawrence Hill	d				00 27								07 09		07 35										
Bristol Temple Meads 10	a			00 14	00 33	00 35				06 35			07 12	07 17	07 39	07 51		08 01	08 08	08 17		08 23	08 36	08 40	08 50
	d	23p06	23p35				05 24	06 03	06 34	06 42		06 48	07 18				07 51		08 10			08 25		08 44	08 55
Bedminster	d	23p10										06 50					07 53					08 27			
Parson Street	d	23p12										06 53					07 55					08 29			
Nailsea & Backwell	d	23p20	23b45					06 14				07 02	07 28				08 04					08 38			09 03
Yatton	d	23p26	23b52					06 21				07 07	07 33				08 09					08 44			09 08
Worle	d	23p32	23b58					06 27				07 12	07 39				08 15					08 50			09 14
Weston Milton	d	23p37										07 18					08 20					08 55			
Weston-super-Mare	a	23p40	00s05				05 43	06 36		07 02		07 23	07 47				08 26					08 58			09 22
	d	23p42					05 45			07 06			07 49									09 00			09 29
Highbridge & Burnham	d	23p54	00s16				05 55			07 17			08 00									09 10			09 40
Bridgwater	d	00 02	00s24				06 03			07 25			08 08									09 18			09 48
Taunton	a	00s14	00s36				06 16		07 06	07 38			08 24						08 41			09 33		09 15	10 01

		GW	GW	XC	GW	GW		GW	XC	GW	GW	XC	GW	GW	GW	XC		GW	XC	GW	GW	GW	XC	GW	GW
			◇1 C ⊘	◇1 H	◇ H			◇	◇1 H		◇	◇1 H	◇ H			◇1 H			◇1 H	◇ H		◇	◇1 H	◇1 D ⊡	
Gloucester 7	d							08 41							09 45							10 41			
Cam & Dursley	d							08 56							09 59							10 56			
Yate	d							09 10							10 13							11 10			
Bristol Parkway 7	a							09 19							10 22							11 19			
	d	08 45		08 55		09 12		09 20	09 26	09 34		09 56		10 12	10 22	10 27			10 55		11 12	11 20	11 28		
Filton Abbey Wood	d	08 48			09 09	09 15		09 23		09 37	09 42		10 09	10 15	10 25			10 42		11 09	11 15	11 23			11 42
Stapleton Road	d	08 53						09 29		09 43					10 30							11 29			
Lawrence Hill	d	08 55						09 31							10 32							11 31			
Bristol Temple Meads 10	a	09 01		09 14	09 17	09 23		09 34	09 38	09 50	09 53	10 08	10 18	10 23	10 37	10 41		10 51	11 12	11 18	11 23	11 34	11 37		11 51
	d		09 13			09 26			09 44		09 55			10 25		10 44		10 53	11 15		11 25		11 44	11 47	11 53
Bedminster	d					09 28								10 27							11 27				
Parson Street	d					09 31								10 29							11 29				
Nailsea & Backwell	d					09 40					10 03			10 38				11 03			11 38				12 03
Yatton	d					09 45					10 08			10 44				11 08			11 44				12 08
Worle	d					09 51					10 14			10 50				11 14			11 50				12 14
Weston Milton	d					09 56								10 55							11 55				
Weston-super-Mare	a					10 01					10 22			11 00				11 21	11 32		12 00			12 06	12 20
	d										10 23							11 23	11 37					12 07	12 22
Highbridge & Burnham	d										10 34							11 34							12 33
Bridgwater	d										10 42							11 42							12 41
Taunton	a		09 45						10 16		10 58					11 16		11 57	12 00				12 15	12 29	12 57

		XC		GW	GW	GW	XC	GW	XC	GW	GW	GW		XC	GW	XC	GW	GW	GW	XC	GW	XC		GW	GW
		◇1 H		◇ H		■	◇1 H		◇1 H	◇ H				◇1 H	◇	◇1 H	◇ H		◇	◇1 H		◇1 H		◇ H	
Gloucester 7	d					11 45						12 41							13 45						
Cam & Dursley	d					11 59						12 56							13 59						
Yate	d					12 13						13 10							14 13						
Bristol Parkway 7	a					12 22						13 19							14 22						
	d	11 56			12 12	12 22	12 30		12 56		13 12	13 20		13 27		13 59		14 12	14 22	14 29		14 59			15 12
Filton Abbey Wood	d			12 09	12 15	12 25		12 42		13 09	13 15	13 23			13 42		14 09	14 15	14 25		14 42			15 09	15 15
Stapleton Road	d											13 29							14 31						
Lawrence Hill	d											13 31							14 33						
Bristol Temple Meads 10	a	12 08		12 18	12 23	12 34	12 40	12 51	13 10	13 18	13 23	13 35		13 38	13 51	14 09	14 17	14 23	14 38	14 41	14 51	15 10		15 17	15 23
	d				12 25		12 44	12 53			13 25			13 44	13 53			14 25		14 44	14 53	15 13			15 25
Bedminster	d				12 27						13 27							14 27							15 27
Parson Street	d				12 29						13 29							14 29							15 29
Nailsea & Backwell	d				12 38			13 03			13 38				14 03			14 38			15 03				15 38
Yatton	d				12 44			13 08			13 44				14 08			14 44			15 08				15 44
Worle	d				12 50			13 14			13 50				14 14			14 50			15 14				15 50
Weston Milton	d				12 55						13 55							14 55							15 55
Weston-super-Mare	a				13 00			13 21			14 00				14 21			15 00			15 22				16 00
	d							13 23							14 23						15 28				
Highbridge & Burnham	d							13 34							14 34						15 38				
Bridgwater	d							13 42							14 42						15 46				
Taunton	a						13 16	13 59						14 15	14 55					15 16	16 01	15 44			

A from 17 September until 22 October
B from 17 September
C The Merchant Venturer
D The Torbay Express
b Previous night, stops to set down only

For connections from London Paddington please refer to Table 125

Table 134

Gloucester - Taunton

Mondays to Fridays

from 3 September

Network Diagram - see first Page of Table 132

		GW	XC	GW	GW	XC	GW	GW	GW	GW	XC	GW	GW	GW	XC	GW	GW	GW	GW	XC	GW	GW	XC
			◇1 ⌶			◇1 ⌶	◇ ⌶	◇1 ⊡		◇	◇1 ⌶				◇1 ⌶	▪ ⌶	◇1 ⊡		◇	◇1 ⌶			◇1 ⌶
Gloucester 7	d	14 41								15 45									16 41				
Cam & Dursley	d	14 56								15 59									16 56				
Yate	d	15 10								16 13									17 10				
Bristol Parkway 7	a	15 20								16 22									17 20				
	d	15 20	15 26		15 53	15 57			16 12	16 22	16 29		16 46		16 58			17 12	17 20	17 27		17 46	18 00
Filton Abbey Wood	d	15 23		15 42	15a56		16 09		16 15	16 25		16 42	16 49	16 55		17 09		17 15	17 23		17 43	17 49	
Stapleton Road	d	15 29								16 31			16 54						17 29			17 54	
Lawrence Hill	d	15 31								16 33			16 56						17 31			17 56	
Bristol Temple Meads 10	a	15 36	15 39	15 51		16 08	16 18		16 23	16 37	16 40	16 51	17 02	17 03	17 10	17 18		17 23	17 36	17 39	17 53	18 01	18 10
	d		15 44	15 53				16 18	16 25		16 44	16 53			17 13		17 18	17 25		17 44	17 55		
Bedminster	d			15 55					16 27			16 55						17 27			17 58		
Parson Street	d			15 57					16 29			16 57						17 29			18 01		
Nailsea & Backwell	d			16 03				16 29	16 38			17 03					17 28	17 38			18 09		
Yatton	d			16 08				16 36	16 44			17 08					17 34	17 44			18 15		
Worle	d			16 14				16 43	16 50			17 14					17 41	17 50			18 21		
Weston Milton	d			16 21					16 55			17 22						17 55			18 25		
Weston-super-Mare	a			16 24				16 52	17 00			17 27					17 52	18 00			18 29		
	d			16 24								17 28									18 30		
Highbridge & Burnham	d			16 37								17 38									18 41		
Bridgwater	d			16 45								17 46									18 49		
Taunton	a		16 15	17 00							17 15	18 01			17 44					18 15	19 03		

		GW	GW	GW	GW	XC	GW	XC	GW	GW	GW	XC	GW	XC	GW	GW	GW	GW	XC	GW	XC	GW
		▪ ⌶	◇1 ⊡			◇1 ⌶		◇1 ⌶	◇1 ⊡	◇ ⌶		◇1 ⌶		◇1 ⌶	◇	◇1 ⊡			◇1 A ⌶		◇1 A ⌶	◇1 ⊡
Gloucester 7	d				17 45						18 41							19 45				
Cam & Dursley	d				17 58						18 56							19 59				
Yate	d				18 12						19 10							20 13				
Bristol Parkway 7	a				18 22						19 20							20 22				
	d			18 12	18 22	18 29		18 57			19 20	19 29		19 58			20 11	20 22	20 29		20 56	
Filton Abbey Wood	d	18 09		18 15	18 25		18 42			19 09	19 23		19 42		20 09		20 14	20 25		20 42		
Stapleton Road	d			18 19	18 31						19 29							20 31				
Lawrence Hill	d				18 32						19 31							20 33				
Bristol Temple Meads 10	a	18 17		18 24	18 38	18 41	18 53	19 06		19 17	19 35	19 38	19 51	20 09	20 17		20 24	20 38	20 40	20 53	21 07	
	d		18 20	18 26		18 44	18 56		19 15			19 44	19 55			20 18			20 44	20 55	21 12	21 18
Bedminster	d			18 27			18 57						19 57							20 57		
Parson Street	d			18 29			18 59						19 59							20 59		
Nailsea & Backwell	d		18 31	18 38			19 08		19 25				20 08			20 29				21 08		21 27
Yatton	d		18 38	18 44			19 13		19 32				20 13			20 36				21 13		21 34
Worle	d		18 45	18 50			19 19		19 38				20 19			20 44				21 19		21 40
Weston Milton	d			18 54			19 23		19 43				20 23			20 49				21 23		
Weston-super-Mare	a		18 51	19 00			19 28		19 48				20 27			20 53				21 27		21 50
	d		18 55				19 29		19 57				20 29							21 33		
Highbridge & Burnham	d		19 08				19 40						20 39							21 44		
Bridgwater	d		19 15				19 48						20 47							21 52		
Taunton	a		19 28			19 15	20 03		20 23			20 16	21 02						21 16	22 07	21 43	

		GW	XC	GW	GW	GW	XC	GW	XC	GW	GW	GW	GW	XC	GW
		◇	◇1 A ⌶		◇	1	◇1		◇1				◇1 ⊡	◇1	
Gloucester 7	d					21 15			22 05			22 28			
Cam & Dursley	d					21 29									
Yate	d					21 41									
Bristol Parkway 7	a					21 50			22 32			23 04			
	d		21 27			21 51	22 02		22 34			23 05		23 23	
Filton Abbey Wood	d	21 08		21 42		21 56		22 09		22 52					23 40
Stapleton Road	d									22 58					
Lawrence Hill	d									23 00					
Bristol Temple Meads 10	a	21 19	21 36	21 51		22 11	22 13	22 22	22 44	23 05		23 19		23 40	23 49
	d		21 44		21 56						23 06		23 35		
Bedminster	d				21 58						23 10				
Parson Street	d				22 00						23 12				
Nailsea & Backwell	d				22 09						23 20		23s45		
Yatton	d				22 13						23 26		23s52		
Worle	d				22 19						23 32		23s58		
Weston Milton	d				22 23						23 37				
Weston-super-Mare	a				22 28						23 40		00s05		
	d				22 29						23 42				
Highbridge & Burnham	d				22 40						23 54		00s16		
Bridgwater	d				22 48						00 02		00s24		
Taunton	a		22 15		23 01						00s14		00s36		

A ⌶ to Bristol Temple Meads

For connections from London Paddington please refer to Table 125

Table 134

Gloucester - Taunton

Saturdays

until 8 September

Network Diagram - see first Page of Table 132

		GW	GW	XC	GW	GW	GW	XC	GW	GW	GW	GW	GW	XC	GW	XC	GW	GW	GW	XC	GW	XC	GW
			◇1 ⊡	◇1 A		◇	◇1 ⊡	◇1		◇			◇	◇1 ⌶		◇1 ⌶	◇		◇	◇1 ⌶		◇1 ⌶	▪ 1 ⊡
Gloucester 7	d											06 19			07 02				07 40				
Cam & Dursley	d											06 35			07 15				07 54				
Yate	d											06 48			07 30				08 09				
Bristol Parkway 7	a											06 58			07 39				08 19				
	d			00 03			05 42					06 58			07 40	07 56		08 12	08 19	08 26		08 56	
Filton Abbey Wood	d				00 20							07 02	07 09	07 41	07 46		08 09	08 15	08 23		08 42		
Stapleton Road	d				00 25																		
Lawrence Hill	d				00 27																		
Bristol Temple Meads 10	a			00 13	00 33		05 53					07 11	07 18	07 51	07 54	08 05	08 18	08 23	08 34	08 38	08 52	09 08	
	d	23p06	23p35			05 24		06 08	06 18	06 36	06 48	07 18			07 56	08 11		08 25		08 44	08 56		09 17
Bedminster	d	23p10									06 50	07 21						08 27					
Parson Street	d	23p12									06 53	07 23						08 29					
Nailsea & Backwell	d	23p20	23b45						06 28		07 01	07 28			08 03			08 38			09 03		
Yatton	d	23p26	23b52						06 34		07 06	07 34			08 08			08 44			09 07		
Worle	d	23p32	23b58						06 40		07 12	07 40			08 14			08 50			09 13		
Weston Milton	d	23p37									07 17	07 46						08 55					
Weston-super-Mare	a	23p40	00s05			05 43			06 45	06 55	07 22	07 47			08 24			09 00			09 23		
	d	23p42				05 45			06 47	06 56		07 50									09 32		
Highbridge & Burnham	d	23p54	00s16			05 55			06 58			08 01									09 44		
Bridgwater	d	00 02	00s24			06 03			07 06			08 09									09 52		
Taunton	a	00s14	00s36			06 16		07 14	07 20	07 24		08 24				08 42				09 14	10 06		09 50

		GW	GW	GW	XC	GW	XC	GW	GW	GW	XC	GW	GW	XC	GW	GW	GW	XC	GW	XC	GW	GW	GW
		◇		◇	◇1 ⌶		◇1 ⌶	◇			◇1 ⌶	◇1 ⊡		◇1 ⌶	◇		◇	◇1 ⌶		◇1 ⌶	◇	◇1 ⊡	
Gloucester 7	d			08 42						09 46							10 42						
Cam & Dursley	d			08 56						10 02							10 56						
Yate	d			09 11						10 16							11 10						
Bristol Parkway 7	a			09 19						10 24							11 19						
	d		09 12	09 20	09 26		09 57		10 12	10 25	10 31			10 59		11 12	11 20	11 26		11 56			12 12
Filton Abbey Wood	d	09 09	09 15	09 23		09 42		10 09	10 15	10 28			10 42		11 09	11 15	11 23		11 42		12 09		12 15
Stapleton Road	d			09 29						10 32							11 28						
Lawrence Hill	d			09 31						10 34							11 30						
Bristol Temple Meads 10	a	09 18	09 23	09 34	09 38	09 51	10 06	10 18	10 23	10 39	10 42		10 51	11 09	11 18	11 23	11 33	11 38	11 51	12 08	12 18		12 23
	d		09 25		09 44	09 55	10 20		10 25		10 44	10 48	10 53	11 12		11 25		11 44	11 53			12 18	12 25
Bedminster	d		09 27						10 27							11 27							12 27
Parson Street	d		09 29						10 29							11 29							12 29
Nailsea & Backwell	d		09 38			10 03			10 38				11 03			11 38			12 03				12 38
Yatton	d		09 44			10 08			10 44				11 08			11 44			12 08				12 44
Worle	d		09 50			10 14			10 50				11 14			11 50			12 14				12 50
Weston Milton	d		09 55						10 55							11 55							12 55
Weston-super-Mare	a		10 00			10 22			11 00			11 06	11 21	11 29		12 00			12 22			12 35	13 00
	d					10 23							11 23	11 39					12 23				
Highbridge & Burnham	d					10 34							11 34						12 34				
Bridgwater	d					10 42							11 42						12 42				
Taunton	a				10 17	10 59	10 59				11 15		11 56	11 59				12 15	12 57				

		GW	XC	GW	XC	GW	GW	GW	XC	GW	XC	GW	GW	GW	GW	XC	GW	XC	GW	GW	GW	XC
		▪	◇1 ⌶		◇1 ⌶	◇			◇1 ⌶		◇1 ⌶	◇	◇1 ⊡		◇	◇1 ⌶		◇1 ⌶	◇			◇1 ⌶
Gloucester 7	d	11 46						12 42							13 42						14 42	
Cam & Dursley	d	12 01						12 56							13 57						14 56	
Yate	d	12 16						13 11							14 11						15 10	
Bristol Parkway 7	a	12 24						13 19							14 20						15 18	
	d	12 25	12 31		12 57		13 12	13 20	13 26		13 58			14 12	14 20	14 28		14 59		15 12	15 19	15 25
Filton Abbey Wood	d	12 28		12 42		13 09	13 15	13 23		13 42		14 09		14 15	14 25		14 42		15 09	15 15	15 22	
Stapleton Road	d	12 32						13 27							14 31						15 27	
Lawrence Hill	d	12 34						13 29							14 33						15 29	
Bristol Temple Meads 10	a	12 39	12 42	12 51	13 07	13 18	13 23	13 34	13 38	13 53	14 08	14 18		14 23	14 36	14 41	14 51	15 09	15 18	15 23	15 33	15 37
	d		12 44	12 53			13 25		13 44	13 55			14 18	14 25		14 44	14 53	15 12		15 25		15 44
Bedminster	d						13 27							14 27						15 27		
Parson Street	d						13 29			13 59				14 29						15 29		
Nailsea & Backwell	d			13 03			13 38			14 07				14 38			15 03			15 38		
Yatton	d			13 08			13 44			14 12				14 44			15 08			15 44		
Worle	d			13 14			13 50			14 18				14 50			15 14			15 50		
Weston Milton	d						13 55							14 55						15 55		
Weston-super-Mare	a			13 22			14 00			14 23			14 35	15 00			15 22			16 00		
	d			13 23						14 23							15 23					
Highbridge & Burnham	d			13 34						14 34							15 34					
Bridgwater	d			13 42						14 42							15 42					
Taunton	a		13 15	13 59					14 15	15 01						15 16	15 59	15 43				16 15

A until 23 June

b Previous night, stops to set down only

For connections from London Paddington please refer to Table 125

Gloucester - Taunton

Saturdays

until 8 September

Network Diagram - see first Page of Table 132

		GW	XC	GW	GW	GW	GW	XC		GW	XC	GW	GW	GW	GW	XC	GW	XC		GW	GW	GW	GW	XC	GW
			◇1 ✠	◇	◇1 ⊡		◇	◇1 ✠			◇1 ✠	■	◇1 ⊡		◇	◇1 ✠		◇1 ✠		◇	◇1 ⊡			◇1 ✠	
Gloucester 7	d						15 45								16 42								17 46		
Cam & Dursley	d						15 59								16 56								18 01		
Yate	d						16 13								17 10								18 16		
Bristol Parkway 7	a						16 24								17 18								18 24		
	d		15 57			16 12	16 25	16 31			16 56			17 12	17 20	17 26		17 56				18 12	18 25	18 31	
Filton Abbey Wood	d	15 42		16 09		16 15	16 28			16 42		17 09		17 15	17 23		17 42			18 09		18 15	18 28		18 42
Stapleton Road	d						16 34								17 29								18 34		
Lawrence Hill	d						16 36								17 31								18 36		
Bristol Temple Meads 10	a	15 51	16 08	16 18		16 23	16 39	16 42		16 51	17 07	17 18		17 23	17 34	17 38	17 51	18 07		18 18		18 23	18 39	18 42	18 51
	d	15 53			16 18	16 25		16 44		16 53			17 18	17 25		17 44	17 53				18 18	18 25		18 44	18 53
Bedminster	d					16 27								17 27								18 27			
Parson Street	d					16 29								17 29								18 29			
Nailsea & Backwell	d	16 03				16 38				17 03				17 38			18 03					18 38			19 03
Yatton	d	16 08				16 44				17 08				17 44			18 08					18 44			19 08
Worle	d	16 14				16 50				17 14				17 50			18 14					18 50			19 14
Weston Milton	d					16 55								17 55								18 55			19 20
Weston-super-Mare	a	16 22			16 35	17 00				17 22			17 35	18 00			18 22				18 36	19 00			19 23
	d	16 23								17 23							18 23				18 40				19 23
Highbridge & Burnham	d	16 34								17 34							18 34								19 34
Bridgwater	d	16 42								17 42							18 42								19 42
Taunton	a	16 57						17 17		17 59						18 15	18 56				19 06			19 15	19 59

		XC	GW	GW		GW	GW	XC	GW	XC	GW	GW	GW	GW		XC	GW	GW	XC	GW	XC	GW	GW	GW	
		◇1 ✠	◇	◇1 ⊡				◇1 ✠		◇1 ✠	◇1 ⊡	◇				◇1 A ✠		◇1 ⊡	◇1 ✠	◇	◇1 A ✠		◇		
Gloucester 7	d						18 42							19 45										21 16	
Cam & Dursley	d						18 56							19 59										21 30	
Yate	d						19 11							20 13										21 44	
Bristol Parkway 7	a						19 20							20 24										21 53	
	d	18 56				19 12	19 21	19 27		19 57			20 17	20 25		20 31			20 56		21 24			21 53	
Filton Abbey Wood	d		19 09			19 15	19 24		19 42			20 09	20 20	20 28			20 40			21 08		21 42		21 57	
Stapleton Road	d						19 29							20 34											
Lawrence Hill	d						19 31							20 36											
Bristol Temple Meads 10	a	19 05	19 18			19 24	19 36	19 39	19 51	20 06		20 18	20 29	20 39		20 42	20 48		21 05	21 18	21 35	21 49		22 05	
	d			19 18				19 44	19 53		20 15					20 44		20 55			21 44		21 59		
Bedminster	d																						22 01		
Parson Street	d																						22 03		
Nailsea & Backwell	d			19 30					20 03									21 04					22 12		
Yatton	d			19 37					20 08									21 11					22 18		
Worle	d			19 43					20 14									21 17					22 24		
Weston Milton	d								20 20									21 22							
Weston-super-Mare	a			19 50					20 23		20 36							21 26					22 29		
	d								20 24		20 38							21 26					22 31		
Highbridge & Burnham	d								20 34									21 39					22 42		
Bridgwater	d								20 42									21 46					22 50		
Taunton	a							20 15	20 59		21 03					21 15		21 58			22 15		23 03		

		XC	GW	XC	GW
		◇1 ✠	◇1 ⊡	◇1	
Gloucester 7	d			22 04	
Cam & Dursley	d				
Yate	d				
Bristol Parkway 7	a			22 30	
	d	21 59		22 31	
Filton Abbey Wood	d				22 52
Stapleton Road	d				
Lawrence Hill	d				
Bristol Temple Meads 10	a	22 12		22 41	23 00
	d		22 17		
Bedminster	d				
Parson Street	d				
Nailsea & Backwell	d		22s27		
Yatton	d		22s34		
Worle	d		22s40		
Weston Milton	d				
Weston-super-Mare	a		22s47		
	d				
Highbridge & Burnham	d		22s58		
Bridgwater	d		23s05		
Taunton	a		23 17		

A ✠ to Bristol Temple Meads

For connections from London Paddington please refer to Table 125

Gloucester - Taunton

Saturdays

15 September to 20 October

Network Diagram - see first Page of Table 132

		GW	GW	GW	GW	GW	XC	GW	GW	GW		GW	GW	XC	GW	XC	GW	GW	GW	XC		GW	XC	GW	GW
			◇1 ⊡		◇	◇1 ⊡	◇1		◇				◇	◇1 ✠		◇1 ✠	◇		◇	◇1 ✠			◇1 ✠	■ 1 ⊡	◇
Gloucester 7	d											06 19			07 02				07 40						
Cam & Dursley	d											06 35			07 15				07 54						
Yate	d											06 48			07 30				08 09						
Bristol Parkway 7	a											06 58			07 39				08 19						
	d					05 42						06 58			07 40	07 56		08 12	08 19	08 26			08 56		
Filton Abbey Wood	d			00 20								07 02	07 09	07 41	07 46		08 09	08 15	08 23			08 42			09 09
Stapleton Road	d			00 25																					
Lawrence Hill	d			00 27																					
Bristol Temple Meads 10	a			00 33		05 53						07 11	07 18	07 51	07 54	08 05	08 18	08 23	08 34	08 38		08 52	09 08		09 18
	d	23p06	23p35		05 24		06 08	06 18	06 36	06 48		07 18			07 56	08 11		08 25		08 44		08 56		09 17	
Bedminster	d	23p10								06 50		07 21						08 27							
Parson Street	d	23p12								06 53		07 23						08 29							
Nailsea & Backwell	d	23p20	23b45					06 28		07 01		07 28			08 03			08 38				09 03			
Yatton	d	23p26	23b52					06 34		07 06		07 34			08 08			08 44				09 07			
Worle	d	23p32	23b58					06 40		07 12		07 40			08 14			08 50				09 13			
Weston Milton	d	23p37								07 17		07 46						08 55							
Weston-super-Mare	a	23p40	00s05		05 43			06 45	06 55	07 22		07 47			08 24			09 00				09 23			
	d	23p42			05 45			06 47	06 56			07 50										09 32			
Highbridge & Burnham	d	23p54	00s16		05 55			06 58				08 01										09 44			
Bridgwater	d	00 02	00s24		06 03			07 06				08 09										09 52			
Taunton	a	00s14	00s36		06 16		07 14	07 20	07 24			08 24				08 42				09 14		10 06		09 50	

		GW	GW	XC	GW	XC		GW	GW	GW	XC	GW	XC	GW	GW	GW		XC	GW	XC	GW	GW	GW	XC	GW
			◇	◇1 ✠		◇1 ✠		◇			◇1 ✠		◇1 ✠	◇		◇		◇1 ✠		◇1 ✠	◇		■	◇1 ✠	
Gloucester 7	d		08 42							09 46						10 42							11 46		
Cam & Dursley	d		08 56							10 02						10 56							12 01		
Yate	d		09 11							10 16						11 10							12 16		
Bristol Parkway 7	a		09 19							10 24						11 19							12 24		
	d	09 12	09 20	09 26		09 57			10 12	10 25	10 31		10 59		11 12	11 20		11 26		11 56		12 12	12 25	12 31	
Filton Abbey Wood	d	09 15	09 23		09 42			10 09	10 15	10 28		10 42		11 09	11 15	11 23			11 42		12 09	12 15	12 28		12 42
Stapleton Road	d		09 29							10 32						11 28							12 32		
Lawrence Hill	d		09 31							10 34						11 30							12 34		
Bristol Temple Meads 10	a	09 23	09 34	09 38	09 51	10 06		10 18	10 23	10 39	10 42	10 51	11 09	11 18	11 23	11 33		11 37	11 51	12 08	12 18	12 23	12 39	12 42	12 51
	d	09 25		09 44	09 55				10 25		10 44	10 53	11 12		11 25			11 44	11 53			12 25		12 44	12 53
Bedminster	d	09 27							10 27						11 27							12 27			
Parson Street	d	09 29							10 29						11 29							12 29			
Nailsea & Backwell	d	09 38			10 03				10 38			11 03			11 38				12 03			12 38			13 03
Yatton	d	09 44			10 08				10 44			11 08			11 44				12 08			12 44			13 08
Worle	d	09 50			10 14				10 50			11 14			11 50				12 14			12 50			13 14
Weston Milton	d	09 55							10 55						11 55							12 55			
Weston-super-Mare	a	10 00			10 22				11 00			11 21	11 29		12 00				12 22			13 00			13 22
	d				10 23							11 23	11 39						12 23						13 23
Highbridge & Burnham	d				10 34							11 34							12 34						13 34
Bridgwater	d				10 42							11 42							12 42						13 42
Taunton	a			10 17	10 59						11 15	11 56	11 59					12 15	12 57					13 15	13 59

		XC		GW	GW	GW	XC	GW	XC	GW	GW	GW		XC	GW	XC	GW	GW	GW	XC	GW	XC		GW	GW
		◇1 ✠		◇			◇1 ✠		◇1 ✠	◇		◇		◇1 ✠		◇1 ✠	◇			◇1 ✠		◇1 ✠		◇	
Gloucester 7	d					12 42						13 42							14 42						
Cam & Dursley	d					12 56						13 57							14 56						
Yate	d					13 11						14 11							15 10						
Bristol Parkway 7	a					13 19						14 20							15 18						
	d	12 57			13 12	13 20	13 26		13 58		14 12	14 20		14 28		14 59		15 12	15 19	15 25		15 57			16 12
Filton Abbey Wood	d			13 09	13 15	13 23		13 42		14 09	14 15	14 25			14 42		15 09	15 15	15 22		15 42			16 09	16 15
Stapleton Road	d					13 27						14 31							15 27						
Lawrence Hill	d					13 29						14 33							15 29						
Bristol Temple Meads 10	a	13 07		13 18	13 23	13 34	13 38	13 53	14 08	14 18	14 23	14 36		14 41	14 51	15 09	15 18	15 23	15 33	15 37	15 51	16 08		16 18	16 23
	d				13 25		13 44	13 55			14 25			14 44	14 53	15 12		15 25		15 44	15 53				16 25
Bedminster	d				13 27						14 27							15 27							16 27
Parson Street	d				13 29			13 59			14 29							15 29							16 29
Nailsea & Backwell	d				13 38			14 07			14 38				15 03			15 38			16 03				16 38
Yatton	d				13 44			14 12			14 44				15 08			15 44			16 08				16 44
Worle	d				13 50			14 18			14 50				15 14			15 50			16 14				16 50
Weston Milton	d				13 55						14 55							15 55							16 55
Weston-super-Mare	a				14 00			14 23			15 00				15 22			16 00			16 22				17 00
	d							14 23							15 23						16 23				
Highbridge & Burnham	d							14 34							15 34						16 34				
Bridgwater	d							14 42							15 42						16 42				
Taunton	a						14 15	15 01						15 16	15 59	15 43				16 15	16 57				

b Previous night, stops to set down only

For connections from London Paddington please refer to Table 125

Table 134

Saturdays
15 September to 20 October

Gloucester - Taunton

Network Diagram - see first Page of Table 132

		GW ◇	XC ◇1	GW	XC ◇1	GW ■	GW	GW ◇	XC ◇1	GW	XC ◇1	GW ◇	GW ◇1	GW	GW	XC ◇1	GW	XC ◇1	GW ◇	GW ◇1	GW	GW	XC ◇1
Gloucester 7	d	15 45						16 42							17 46							18 42	
Cam & Dursley	d	15 59						16 56							18 01							18 56	
Yate	d	16 13						17 10							18 16							19 11	
Bristol Parkway 7	a	16 24						17 18							18 24							19 20	
	d	16 25	16 31		16 56		17 12	17 20	17 26		17 56			18 12	18 25	18 31		18 56			19 12	19 21	19 27
Filton Abbey Wood	d	16 28		16 42		17 09	17 15	17 23		17 42		18 09		18 15	18 28		18 42		19 09		19 15	19 24	
Stapleton Road	d	16 34						17 29							18 34							19 29	
Lawrence Hill	d	16 36						17 31							18 36							19 31	
Bristol Temple Meads 10	a	16 39	16 42	16 51	17 07	17 18	17 23	17 34	17 38	17 51	18 07	18 18		18 23	18 39	18 42	18 51	19 05	19 18		19 24	19 36	19 39
	d		16 44	16 53	17 10		17 25		17 44	17 53			18 18	18 25		18 44	18 53			19 18			19 44
Bedminster	d						17 27							18 27									
Parson Street	d						17 29							18 29									
Nailsea & Backwell	d			17 03			17 38			18 03				18 38			19 03			19 30			
Yatton	d			17 08			17 44			18 08				18 44			19 08			19 37			
Worle	d			17 14			17 50			18 14				18 50			19 14			19 43			
Weston Milton	d						17 55							18 55			19 20						
Weston-super-Mare	a			17 22			18 00			18 22			18 36	19 00			19 23			19 50			
	d			17 23						18 23			18 40				19 23						
Highbridge & Burnham	d			17 34						18 34							19 34						
Bridgwater	d			17 42						18 42							19 42						
Taunton	a		17 17	17 59	17 41				18 15	18 56			19 06			19 15	19 59						20 15

		GW	XC ◇1	GW ◇1	GW ◇	GW	GW	XC ◇1 A	GW	GW ◇1	XC ◇1	GW ◇	XC ◇1 A	GW	GW ◇	GW	XC ◇1	GW ◇1	XC ◇1	GW
Gloucester 7	d						19 45									21 16			22 04	
Cam & Dursley	d						19 59									21 30				
Yate	d						20 13									21 44				
Bristol Parkway 7	a						20 24									21 53			22 30	
	d		19 57			20 17	20 25	20 31			20 56		21 24			21 53	21 59		22 31	
Filton Abbey Wood	d	19 42			20 09	20 20	20 28		20 40			21 09		21 42		21 57				22 52
Stapleton Road	d						20 34													
Lawrence Hill	d						20 36													
Bristol Temple Meads 10	a	19 51	20 06		20 18	20 29	20 39	20 42	20 48		21 05	21 18	21 35	21 49		22 05	22 12		22 41	23 00
	d	19 53		20 15				20 44		20 55			21 44		21 59			22 17		
Bedminster	d														22 01					
Parson Street	d														22 03					
Nailsea & Backwell	d	20 03								21 04					22 12			22s27		
Yatton	d	20 08								21 11					22 18			22s34		
Worle	d	20 14								21 17					22 24			22s40		
Weston Milton	d	20 20								21 22					22 28					
Weston-super-Mare	a	20 23		20 36						21 26					22 31			22s47		
	d	20 24		20 38						21 26					22 33					
Highbridge & Burnham	d	20 34								21 39					22 44			22s58		
Bridgwater	d	20 42								21 46					22 52			23s05		
Taunton	a	20 59		21 03				21 15		21 58			22 15		23 05			23 17		

Saturdays
from 27 October

		GW	GW ◇1	GW	GW ◇	GW ◇1	XC ◇1	GW	GW ◇	GW	GW	GW ◇	XC ◇1	GW	XC ◇1	GW ◇	GW	GW ◇	XC ◇1	GW	XC ◇1	GW ■ 1	GW ◇
Gloucester 7	d										06 19			07 02				07 40					
Cam & Dursley	d										06 35			07 15				07 54					
Yate	d										06 48			07 30				08 09					
Bristol Parkway 7	a										06 58			07 39				08 19					
	d					05 42					06 58			07 40	07 56		08 12	08 19	08 26		08 56		
Filton Abbey Wood	d			00 20							07 02	07 09	07 41	07 46		08 09	08 15	08 23		08 42			09 09
Stapleton Road	d			00 25																			
Lawrence Hill	d			00 27																			
Bristol Temple Meads 10	a			00 33		05 53					07 11	07 18	07 51	07 54	08 05	08 18	08 23	08 34	08 38	08 52	09 08		09 18
	d	23p06	23p35		05 24		06 08	06 18	06 36	06 48	07 18			07 56	08 11		08 25		08 44	08 56		09 17	
Bedminster	d	23p10								06 50	07 21						08 27						
Parson Street	d	23p12								06 53	07 23						08 29						
Nailsea & Backwell	d	23p20	23b45					06 28		07 01	07 28			08 03			08 38			09 03			
Yatton	d	23p26	23b52					06 34		07 06	07 34			08 08			08 44			09 07			
Worle	d	23p32	23b58					06 40		07 12	07 40			08 14			08 50			09 13			
Weston Milton	d	23p37								07 17	07 46						08 55						
Weston-super-Mare	a	23p40	00s05		05 43			06 45	06 55	07 22	07 47			08 24			09 00			09 23			
	d	23p42			05 45			06 47	06 56		07 50									09 32			
Highbridge & Burnham	d	23p54	00s16		05 55			06 58			08 01									09 44			
Bridgwater	d	00 02	00s24		06 03			07 06			08 09									09 52			
Taunton	a	00s14	00s36		06 16		07 14	07 20	07 24		08 24				08 42				09 14	10 06		09 50	

A to Bristol Temple Meads

b Previous night, stops to set down only

For connections from London Paddington please refer to Table 125

Table 134

Saturdays
from 27 October

Gloucester - Taunton

Network Diagram - see first Page of Table 132

		GW	GW ◇	XC ◇1	GW	XC ◇1	GW ◇	GW	GW	XC ◇1	GW	XC ◇1	GW ◇	GW	GW ◇	XC ◇1	GW	XC ◇1	GW ◇	GW	GW ■	XC ◇1	GW
Gloucester 7	d		08 42						09 46						10 42						11 46		
Cam & Dursley	d		08 56						10 02						10 56						12 01		
Yate	d		09 11						10 16						11 10						12 16		
Bristol Parkway 7	a		09 19						10 24						11 19						12 24		
	d	09 12	09 20	09 26		09 57		10 12	10 25	10 31		10 59		11 12	11 20	11 26		11 56		12 12	12 25	12 31	
Filton Abbey Wood	d	09 15	09 23		09 42		10 09	10 15	10 28		10 42		11 09	11 15	11 23		11 42		12 09	12 15	12 28		12 42
Stapleton Road	d		09 29						10 32						11 28						12 32		
Lawrence Hill	d		09 31						10 34						11 30						12 34		
Bristol Temple Meads 10	a	09 23	09 34	09 38	09 51	10 06	10 18	10 23	10 39	10 42	10 51	11 09	11 18	11 23	11 33	11 37	11 51	12 08	12 18	12 23	12 39	12 42	12 51
	d	09 25		09 44	09 55			10 25		10 44	10 53	11 12		11 25		11 44	11 53			12 25		12 44	12 53
Bedminster	d	09 27						10 27						11 27						12 27			
Parson Street	d	09 29						10 29						11 29						12 29			
Nailsea & Backwell	d	09 38			10 03			10 38			11 03			11 38			12 03			12 38			13 03
Yatton	d	09 44			10 08			10 44			11 08			11 44			12 08			12 44			13 08
Worle	d	09 50			10 14			10 50			11 14			11 50			12 14			12 50			13 14
Weston Milton	d	09 55						10 55						11 55						12 55			
Weston-super-Mare	a	10 00			10 22			11 00			11 21	11 29		12 00			12 22			13 00			13 22
	d				10 23						11 23	11 39					12 23						13 23
Highbridge & Burnham	d				10 34						11 34						12 34						13 34
Bridgwater	d				10 42						11 42						12 42						13 42
Taunton	a			10 17	10 59					11 15	11 56	11 59				12 15	12 57					13 15	13 59

		XC ◇1	GW ◇	GW	GW	XC ◇1	GW	XC ◇1	GW ◇	GW	GW ◇	XC ◇1	GW	XC ◇1	GW ◇	GW	GW	XC ◇1	GW	XC ◇1	GW ◇	GW
Gloucester 7	d				12 42						13 42						14 42					
Cam & Dursley	d				12 56						13 57						14 56					
Yate	d				13 11						14 11						15 10					
Bristol Parkway 7	a				13 19						14 20						15 18					
	d	12 57		13 12	13 20	13 26		13 58		14 12	14 20	14 28		14 59		15 12	15 19	15 25		15 57		16 12
Filton Abbey Wood	d		13 09	13 15	13 23		13 42		14 09	14 15	14 25		14 42		15 09	15 15	15 22		15 42		16 09	16 15
Stapleton Road	d				13 27						14 31						15 27					
Lawrence Hill	d				13 29						14 33						15 29					
Bristol Temple Meads 10	a	13 07	13 18	13 23	13 34	13 38	13 53	14 08	14 18	14 23	14 36	14 41	14 51	15 09	15 18	15 23	15 33	15 37	15 51	16 08	16 18	16 23
	d			13 25		13 44	13 55			14 25		14 44	14 53	15 12		15 25		15 44	15 53			16 25
Bedminster	d			13 27						14 27						15 27						16 27
Parson Street	d			13 29			13 59			14 29						15 29						16 29
Nailsea & Backwell	d			13 38			14 07			14 38			15 03			15 38			16 03			16 38
Yatton	d			13 44			14 12			14 44			15 08			15 44			16 08			16 44
Worle	d			13 50			14 18			14 50			15 14			15 50			16 14			16 50
Weston Milton	d			13 55						14 55						15 55						16 55
Weston-super-Mare	a			14 00			14 23			15 00			15 22			16 00			16 22			17 00
	d						14 23						15 23						16 23			
Highbridge & Burnham	d						14 34						15 34						16 34			
Bridgwater	d						14 42						15 42						16 42			
Taunton	a					14 15	15 01					15 16	15 59	15 43				16 15	16 57			

		GW ◇	XC ◇1	GW	XC ◇1	GW ■	GW	GW ◇	XC ◇1	GW	XC ◇1	GW ◇	GW ◇1	GW	GW	XC ◇1	GW	XC ◇1	GW ◇	GW ◇1	GW	GW	XC ◇1
Gloucester 7	d	15 45						16 42							17 46							18 42	
Cam & Dursley	d	15 59						16 56							18 01							18 56	
Yate	d	16 13						17 10							18 16							19 11	
Bristol Parkway 7	a	16 24						17 18							18 24							19 20	
	d	16 25	16 31		16 56		17 12	17 20	17 26		17 56			18 12	18 25	18 31		18 56			19 12	19 21	19 27
Filton Abbey Wood	d	16 28		16 42		17 09	17 15	17 23		17 42		18 09		18 15	18 28		18 42		19 09		19 15	19 24	
Stapleton Road	d	16 34						17 29							18 34							19 29	
Lawrence Hill	d	16 36						17 31							18 36							19 31	
Bristol Temple Meads 10	a	16 39	16 42	16 51	17 07	17 18	17 23	17 34	17 38	17 51	18 07	18 18		18 23	18 39	18 42	18 51	19 05	19 18		19 24	19 36	19 39
	d		16 44	16 53	17 10		17 25		17 44	17 53			18 18	18 25		18 44	18 53			19 18			19 44
Bedminster	d						17 27							18 27									
Parson Street	d						17 29							18 29									
Nailsea & Backwell	d			17 03			17 38			18 03				18 38			19 03			19 30			
Yatton	d			17 08			17 44			18 08				18 44			19 08			19 37			
Worle	d			17 14			17 50			18 14				18 50			19 14			19 43			
Weston Milton	d						17 55							18 55			19 20						
Weston-super-Mare	a			17 22			18 00			18 22			18 36	19 00			19 23			19 50			
	d			17 23						18 23			18 40				19 23						
Highbridge & Burnham	d			17 34						18 34							19 34						
Bridgwater	d			17 42						18 42							19 42						
Taunton	a		17 17	17 59	17 41				18 15	18 56			19 06			19 15	19 59						20 15

For connections from London Paddington please refer to Table 125

Gloucester - Taunton

Saturdays from 27 October

Network Diagram - see first Page of Table 132

		GW	XC	GW	GW	GW	GW	XC	GW	GW	XC	GW	XC	GW	GW	GW	XC	GW	XC	GW
			◇1 ⚲	◇1 ☕	◇			◇1 A ⚲		◇1 ☕	◇1 ⚲	◇	◇1 A ⚲		◇		◇1 ⚲	◇1 ☕	◇1	
Gloucester 7	d						19 45									21 16			22 04	
Cam & Dursley	d						19 59									21 30				
Yate	d						20 13									21 44				
Bristol Parkway 7	a						20 24									21 53			22 30	
	d		19 57			20 17	20 25	20 31			20 56		21 24			21 53	21 59		22 31	
Filton Abbey Wood	d	19 42			20 09	20 20	20 28		20 40			21 09		21 42		21 57				22 52
Stapleton Road	d						20 34													
Lawrence Hill	d						20 36													
Bristol Temple Meads 10	a	19 51	20 06		20 18	20 29	20 39	20 42	20 48		21 05	21 18	21 35	21 49		22 05	22 12		22 41	23 00
	d	19 53		20 15				20 44		20 55			21 44		21 59			22 17		
Bedminster	d														22 01					
Parson Street	d														22 03					
Nailsea & Backwell	d	20 03								21 04					22 12			22s27		
Yatton	d	20 08								21 11					22 18			22s34		
Worle	d	20 14								21 17					22 24			22s40		
Weston Milton	d	20 20								21 22					22 28					
Weston-super-Mare	a	20 23		20 36						21 26					22 31			22s47		
	d	20 24		20 38						21 26					22 33					
Highbridge & Burnham	d	20 34								21 39					22 44			22s58		
Bridgwater	d	20 42								21 46					22 52			23s05		
Taunton	a	20 59		21 03				21 15		21 58			22 15		23 05			23 17		

Sundays until 24 June

		GW	GW	XC	GW	GW	XC	GW	GW	GW	XC	GW	GW	XC	GW	GW	XC	GW	GW	GW	GW	XC	GW
		◇	◇	◇1 ⚲	◇		◇1 ⚲	◇1 ☕	◇		◇1 ⚲	◇		◇1 ⚲	◇1 ☕	■	◇1 ⚲	◇1 ☕	◇			◇1 ⚲	◇1 ☕
Gloucester 7	d												10 18								12 14		
Cam & Dursley	d												10 32								12 28		
Yate	d												10 46								12 42		
Bristol Parkway 7	a												10 52								12 54		
	d										10 23		10 55	11 41			12 41				12 55	13 23	
Filton Abbey Wood	d				08 55				10 03			10 54	10 58			11 54			12 57		13 01		
Stapleton Road	d									10 16													
Lawrence Hill	d									10 18													
Bristol Temple Meads 10	a				09 05				10 13	10 21	10 32	11 03	11 07	11 52		12 04	12 51		13 05		13 10	13 32	
	d	07 30	08 28	08 44		09 05	09 48	09 55		10 23	10 44		11 10	11 54	11 55		12 54	12 55		13 05		13 44	13 56
Bedminster	d									10 26													
Parson Street	d									10 29													
Nailsea & Backwell	d		08 38			09 13				10 37			11 20		12 06					13 15			14 07
Yatton	d	07 43	08 43			09 20				10 42			11 25		12 12					13 20			14 13
Worle	d		08 49			09 26				10 48			11 31		12 19					13 26			14 19
Weston Milton	d																						
Weston-super-Mare	a	07 52	08 55			09 35				10 52			11 37		12 31			13 16		13 31			14 26
	d	07 53	08 59							10 58			11 38					13 18		13 33			
Highbridge & Burnham	d		09 10							11 09			11 48							13 44			
Bridgwater	d	08 09	09 18							11 17			11 56							13 52			
Taunton	a	08 22	09 31	09 15			10 19	10 28		11 31	11 15		12 10	12 26			13 26	13 39		14 06		14 15	

		GW	XC	GW	GW	XC	GW	XC	GW	GW	GW	XC	GW	XC	GW	GW	XC	GW	GW	XC	GW	GW	XC
		◇	◇1 ⚲	◇1 ☕	◇	◇1 ⚲		◇1 ⚲		◇		◇1 ⚲		◇1 ⚲	◇1 ☕	◇	◇1 ⚲		◇	◇1 ⚲	◇		◇1 ⚲
Gloucester 7	d										15 13											17 20	
Cam & Dursley	d										15 27											17 34	
Yate	d										15 41											17 49	
Bristol Parkway 7	a										15 49											17 57	
	d		14 23			14 56		15 26			15 55	16 00		16 23			16 57			17 22		17 58	18 02
Filton Abbey Wood	d	13 54			14 55					15 55	15 57					16 55			17 20		17 54	18 01	
Stapleton Road	d																						
Lawrence Hill	d												←										
Bristol Temple Meads 10	a	14 04	14 32		15 04	15 07		15 36		16 04	16 09	16 11	16 09	16 35		17 06	17 08		17 29	17 35	18 04	18 10	18 13
	d		14 44	14 55			15 10	15 44	15 55		16 25	16 14	16 25	16 44	16 55			17 25		17 44			
Bedminster	d						15 13		15 58		→							17 28					
Parson Street	d								16 00														
Nailsea & Backwell	d						15 22		16 08				16 35		17 06			17 37					
Yatton	d						15 28		16 14				16 40		17 12			17 43					
Worle	d						15 34		16 20				16 46		17 19			17 49					
Weston Milton	d						15 39						16 52					17 58					
Weston-super-Mare	a						15 42		16 25				16 56		17 26			18 01					
	d								16 28						17 31								
Highbridge & Burnham	d								16 40														
Bridgwater	d								16 48														
Taunton	a		15 15	15 29				16 14	17 03			16 45		17 15	17 53					18 18			

A ⚲ to Bristol Temple Meads

For connections from London Paddington please refer to Table 125

Gloucester - Taunton

Sundays until 24 June

Network Diagram - see first Page of Table 132

		GW	GW	XC	GW	GW	XC	GW	XC	GW	GW	XC	GW	XC	GW	XC	GW	XC	GW	GW	XC	XC
		◇	■	◇1 ⚲		◇	◇1 ⚲	◇1 ☕	◇1 ⚲	◇		◇1 ⚲		◇1 A ⚲	◇1 ☕	◇1 ⚲	◇	◇1 A ⚲	◇1 ☕		◇1	◇1
Gloucester 7	d										19 20									21 15		22 07
Cam & Dursley	d										19 35									21 31		
Yate	d										19 49									21 45		
Bristol Parkway 7	a										19 57									21 53		22 34
	d			18 24			18 58		19 23		19 58	20 03		20 23		20 58		21 23		21 55	22 00	22 34
Filton Abbey Wood	d		18 23			18 56				19 55	20 01						21 05			21 58		
Stapleton Road	d												20 15									
Lawrence Hill	d												20 17									
Bristol Temple Meads 10	a		18 33	18 40		19 06	19 08		19 35	20 05	20 11	20 14	20 20	20 35		21 08	21 13	21 32		22 07	22 10	22 45
	d	18 25		18 44	19 05			19 27	19 44			20 19	20 25	20 44	20 55			21 44	21 55			
Bedminster	d				19 08								20 28									
Parson Street	d				19 10																	
Nailsea & Backwell	d	18 35			19 18			19 38					20 36		21 06				22 06			
Yatton	d	18 41			19 24			19 44					20 42		21 12				22 12			
Worle	d	18 47			19 30			19 51					20 48		21 19				22 19			
Weston Milton	d				19 34																	
Weston-super-Mare	a	18 53			19 38			19 58				20 36	20 53		21 26				22 28			
	d	18 58			19 40							20 37	20 58		21 27							
Highbridge & Burnham	d	19 09			19 51								21 09									
Bridgwater	d	19 17			19 59								21 17									
Taunton	a	19 32		19 15	20 13				20 18			20 58	21 33	21 15	21 50			22 15				

		GW	XC	GW	XC
		⚲	◇1		◇1
Gloucester 7	d				
Cam & Dursley	d				
Yate	d				
Bristol Parkway 7	a				
	d		22 54		23 23
Filton Abbey Wood	d	22 53			
Stapleton Road	d				
Lawrence Hill	d				
Bristol Temple Meads 10	a	22 59	23 07		23 33
	d			23 10	
Bedminster	d			23 13	
Parson Street	d			23 15	
Nailsea & Backwell	d			23 23	
Yatton	d			23 29	
Worle	d			23 35	
Weston Milton	d			23 40	
Weston-super-Mare	a			23 43	
	d				
Highbridge & Burnham	d				
Bridgwater	d				
Taunton	a				

Sundays 1 July to 9 September

		GW	GW	XC	GW	GW	XC	GW	GW	GW	XC	GW	GW	XC	GW	GW	XC	GW	GW	GW	XC	GW	GW
		◇	◇	◇1 ⚲	◇		◇1 ⚲	◇1 ☕	◇		◇1 ⚲	◇		◇1 ⚲	◇1 ☕	■	◇1 ⚲	◇			◇1 ⚲	◇1 ☕	◇
Gloucester 7	d												10 18							12 14			
Cam & Dursley	d												10 32							12 28			
Yate	d												10 46							12 42			
Bristol Parkway 7	a												10 52							12 54			
	d										10 23		10 55	11 41			12 23			12 55	13 25		
Filton Abbey Wood	d				08 55				10 03			10 54	10 58			11 54		12 57		13 01			13 54
Stapleton Road	d									10 16													
Lawrence Hill	d									10 18													
Bristol Temple Meads 10	a				09 05				10 13	10 21	10 32	11 03	11 07	11 52		12 04	12 33	13 05		13 10	13 35		14 04
	d	07 30	08 28	08 44		09 05	09 48	09 55		10 23	10 44		11 10	11 54	11 55		12 44		13 05		13 44	13 55	
Bedminster	d									10 26													
Parson Street	d									10 29													
Nailsea & Backwell	d		08 38			09 13				10 37			11 20		12 06				13 15			14 06	
Yatton	d	07 43	08 43			09 20				10 42			11 25		12 12				13 20			14 12	
Worle	d		08 49			09 26				10 48			11 31		12 19				13 26			14 19	
Weston Milton	d																						
Weston-super-Mare	a	07 52	08 55			09 35				10 52			11 37		12 31				13 31			14 26	
	d	07 53	08 59							10 58			11 38						13 33				
Highbridge & Burnham	d		09 10							11 09			11 48						13 44				
Bridgwater	d	08 09	09 18							11 17			11 56						13 52				
Taunton	a	08 22	09 31	09 15			10 19	10 29		11 31	11 15		12 10	12 26			13 16		14 06		14 16		

A ⚲ to Bristol Temple Meads

For connections from London Paddington please refer to Table 125

Table 134

1 July to 9 September

Gloucester - Taunton

Network Diagram - see first Page of Table 132

		XC ◇1 ✠	GW ◇1 ☕	GW ◇	XC ◇1 ✠	GW	XC ◇1 ✠	GW	GW ◇	GW	XC ◇1 ✠	GW
Gloucester 7	d									15 13		
Cam & Dursley	d									15 27		
Yate	d									15 41		
Bristol Parkway 7	a									15 49		
	d	14 23			14 56		15 26			15 55	16 00	
Filton Abbey Wood	d			14 55					15 55	15 57		
Stapleton Road	d											
Lawrence Hill	d											←
Bristol Temple Meads 10	a	14 32		15 04	15 07		15 36		16 04	16 09	16 11	16 09
	d	14 44	14 55			15 10	15 44	15 55		16 25	16 14	16 25
Bedminster	d					15 13		15 58		→		
Parson Street	d							16 00				
Nailsea & Backwell	d					15 22		16 08				16 35
Yatton	d					15 28		16 14				16 40
Worle	d					15 34		16 20				16 46
Weston Milton	d					15 39						16 52
Weston-super-Mare	a					15 42		16 25				16 56
	d							16 28				
Highbridge & Burnham	d							16 40				
Bridgwater	d							16 48				
Taunton	a	15 15	15 29				16 14	17 03			16 45	

		XC ◇1 ✠	GW ◇1 ☕	GW ◇	XC ◇1 ✠	GW	GW ◇	XC ◇1 ✠	GW ◇	GW ◇	GW	XC ◇1 ✠
Gloucester 7	d										17 20	
Cam & Dursley	d										17 34	
Yate	d										17 49	
Bristol Parkway 7	a										17 57	
	d	16 23			16 57			17 22			17 58	18 02
Filton Abbey Wood	d			16 55			17 20		17 54		18 01	
Stapleton Road	d											
Lawrence Hill	d											
Bristol Temple Meads 10	a	16 35		17 06	17 08		17 29	17 35	18 04		18 10	18 13
	d	16 44	16 55			17 25		17 44		18 07		
Bedminster	d					17 28						
Parson Street	d											
Nailsea & Backwell	d		17 07			17 37				18 17		
Yatton	d		17 13			17 43				18 23		
Worle	d		17 19			17 49				18 29		
Weston Milton	d					17 58						
Weston-super-Mare	a		17 26			18 01				18 35		
	d		17 31							18 36		
Highbridge & Burnham	d									18 47		
Bridgwater	d									18 55		
Taunton	a	17 15	17 53					18 18		19 09		

		GW ■	XC ◇1 ✠	GW	GW ◇	XC ◇1 ✠	GW ◇1 ☕	XC ◇1 ✠	GW ◇	GW	XC ◇1 ✠
Gloucester 7	d									19 20	
Cam & Dursley	d									19 35	
Yate	d									19 49	
Bristol Parkway 7	a									19 57	
	d		18 24			18 58		19 23		19 58	20 03
Filton Abbey Wood	d	18 23			18 56				19 55	20 01	
Stapleton Road	d										
Lawrence Hill	d										
Bristol Temple Meads 10	a	18 33	18 40		19 06	19 08		19 35	20 05	20 11	20 14
	d		18 44	19 05			19 27	19 44			20 19
Bedminster	d			19 08							
Parson Street	d			19 10							
Nailsea & Backwell	d			19 18			19 38				
Yatton	d			19 24			19 44				
Worle	d			19 30			19 51				
Weston Milton	d			19 34							
Weston-super-Mare	a			19 38			19 58				20 36
	d			19 40							20 37
Highbridge & Burnham	d			19 51							
Bridgwater	d			19 59							
Taunton	a		19 15	20 13				20 18			20 58

		GW	XC ◇1 A ✠	GW ◇1 ☕	XC ◇1 ✠	GW ◇	XC ◇1 A ✠	GW ◇1 ☕	GW	XC ◇1	XC ◇1	GW ✠
Gloucester 7	d								21 15		22 07	
Cam & Dursley	d								21 31			
Yate	d								21 45			
Bristol Parkway 7	a								21 53		22 34	
	d		20 23		20 58		21 23		21 55	22 00	22 34	
Filton Abbey Wood	d					21 05			21 58			22 53
Stapleton Road	d	20 15										
Lawrence Hill	d	20 17										
Bristol Temple Meads 10	a	20 20	20 35		21 08	21 13	21 32		22 07	22 10	22 45	22 59
	d	20 25	20 44	20 55			21 44	21 55				
Bedminster	d	20 28										
Parson Street	d											
Nailsea & Backwell	d	20 36		21 06				22 06				
Yatton	d	20 42		21 12				22 12				
Worle	d	20 48		21 19				22 19				
Weston Milton	d											
Weston-super-Mare	a	20 53		21 26				22 27				
	d	20 58		21 27								
Highbridge & Burnham	d	21 09										
Bridgwater	d	21 17										
Taunton	a	21 33	21 15	21 50			22 15					

		XC ◇1	GW	XC ◇1
Gloucester 7	d			
Cam & Dursley	d			
Yate	d			
Bristol Parkway 7	a			
	d	22 54		23 23
Filton Abbey Wood	d			
Stapleton Road	d			
Lawrence Hill	d			
Bristol Temple Meads 10	a	23 07		23 33
	d		23 10	
Bedminster	d		23 13	
Parson Street	d		23 15	
Nailsea & Backwell	d		23 23	
Yatton	d		23 29	
Worle	d		23 35	
Weston Milton	d		23 40	
Weston-super-Mare	a		23 43	
	d			
Highbridge & Burnham	d			
Bridgwater	d			
Taunton	a			

A ✠ to Bristol Temple Meads

For connections from London Paddington please refer to Table 125

Table 134

16 September to 21 October

Gloucester - Taunton

Network Diagram - see first Page of Table 132

		GW ◇	GW ◇	GW ◇	GW	GW 🚌	GW ◇	XC ◇1 ✠	GW ◇1 ☕	GW	GW ◇	XC ◇1 ✠
Gloucester 7	d					09 15						
Cam & Dursley	d					09 46						
Yate	d					10 28						
Bristol Parkway 7	a					10 45						
	d											
Filton Abbey Wood	d			08 45			09 28				10 26	
Stapleton Road	d									10 16		
Lawrence Hill	d									10 18		
Bristol Temple Meads 10	a			08 56			09 37			10 21	10 36	
	d	07 30	08 28		09 05			09 48	09 55	10 23		10 44
Bedminster	d											
Parson Street	d											
Nailsea & Backwell	d		08 38		09 13					10 33		
Yatton	d	07 43	08 43		09 20					10 38		
Worle	d		08 49		09 26					10 44		
Weston Milton	d											
Weston-super-Mare	a	07 52	08 55		09 35					10 50		
	d	07 53	08 59							10 55		
Highbridge & Burnham	d		09 10							11 09		
Bridgwater	d	08 09	09 18							11 17		
Taunton	a	08 22	09 31					10 19	10 27	11 31		11 15

		GW	XC ◇1 ✠	GW ■	GW ◇1 ☕	XC ◇1 ✠	GW 🚌	GW ◇	GW	GW	XC ◇1 ✠	GW ◇
Gloucester 7	d		10 12			11 21	11 31				12 21	
Cam & Dursley	d						12 01					
Yate	d						12 41					
Bristol Parkway 7	a		11 11			12 17	13 01				13 17	
	d	10 56	11 25			12 24				13 10	13 24	
Filton Abbey Wood	d	10 59		11 41				12 42		13 13		13 43
Stapleton Road	d											
Lawrence Hill	d											
Bristol Temple Meads 10	a	11 08	11 35	11 50		12 35		12 50		13 23	13 35	13 50
	d	11 10	11 44		11 55	12 54			13 05		13 44	
Bedminster	d											
Parson Street	d											
Nailsea & Backwell	d	11 21			12 06				13 15			
Yatton	d	11 25			12 12				13 20			
Worle	d	11 32			12 19				13 26			
Weston Milton	d											
Weston-super-Mare	a	11 38			12 31				13 31			
	d	11 38							13 33			
Highbridge & Burnham	d	11 49							13 44			
Bridgwater	d	11 57							13 52			
Taunton	a	12 11	12 15			13 26			14 06		14 16	

		GW ◇1 ☕	XC ◇1 ✠	GW 🚌	GW ◇1 ☕	GW ◇	GW	XC ◇1 ✠	GW	GW ◇	GW	XC ◇1 ✠
Gloucester 7	d		13 10	13 15				14 11				15 10
Cam & Dursley	d			13 45								
Yate	d			14 25								
Bristol Parkway 7	a		14 03	14 50				15 08				16 11
	d		14 23				14 58	15 23				16 23
Filton Abbey Wood	d					14 56	15 01			15 55		
Stapleton Road	d											
Lawrence Hill	d											
Bristol Temple Meads 10	a		14 32			15 04	15 09	15 32		16 04		16 32
	d	13 57	14 44		14 55		15 10	15 44	15 55		16 25	16 44
Bedminster	d						15 14		15 58			
Parson Street	d								16 00			
Nailsea & Backwell	d	14 06					15 23		16 08		16 35	
Yatton	d	14 12					15 29		16 14		16 40	
Worle	d	14 19					15 35		16 20		16 46	
Weston Milton	d						15 40				16 52	
Weston-super-Mare	a	14 27					15 43		16 25		16 56	
	d								16 28			
Highbridge & Burnham	d								16 40			
Bridgwater	d								16 48			
Taunton	a		15 15		15 29			16 16	17 03			17 15

		GW 🚌	GW ◇1 ☕	GW ◇	GW	GW ◇	XC ◇1 ✠	GW ◇	GW ◇	GW ■	XC ◇1 ✠	GW 🚌
Gloucester 7	d	15 20					16 10				17 13	17 26
Cam & Dursley	d	15 50										17 56
Yate	d	16 30										18 36
Bristol Parkway 7	a	16 55					17 09				18 07	18 56
	d				17 05		17 22				18 24	
Filton Abbey Wood	d			16 55	17 08	17 20		17 54		18 23		
Stapleton Road	d											
Lawrence Hill	d											
Bristol Temple Meads 10	a			17 06	17 16	17 29	17 35	18 04		18 33	18 40	
	d		16 55		17 25		17 44		18 07		18 44	
Bedminster	d				17 28							
Parson Street	d											
Nailsea & Backwell	d		17 06		17 37				18 17			
Yatton	d		17 12		17 43				18 23			
Worle	d		17 19		17 49				18 29			
Weston Milton	d				17 58							
Weston-super-Mare	a		17 26		18 01				18 35			
	d		17 31						18 36			
Highbridge & Burnham	d								18 47			
Bridgwater	d								18 55			
Taunton	a		17 53				18 18		19 09		19 15	

		GW	GW ◇	GW	GW ◇1 ☕	XC ◇1 ✠	GW ◇	GW	XC ◇1 A ✠	GW 🚌	GW ◇1 ☕
Gloucester 7	d					18 17			19 09	19 30	
Cam & Dursley	d									20 00	
Yate	d									20 40	
Bristol Parkway 7	a					19 13			20 03	21 00	
	d			19 06		19 23			20 23		
Filton Abbey Wood	d		18 56	19 10			19 55				
Stapleton Road	d	18 43									
Lawrence Hill	d	18 45									
Bristol Temple Meads 10	a	18 47	19 06	19 17		19 35	20 05		20 35		
	d	19 05			19 25	19 44		20 25	20 44		20 55
Bedminster	d	19 08						20 28			
Parson Street	d	19 10									
Nailsea & Backwell	d	19 18			19 36			20 36			21 06
Yatton	d	19 24			19 42			20 42			21 12
Worle	d	19 30			19 51			20 48			21 19
Weston Milton	d	19 34									
Weston-super-Mare	a	19 38			19 58			20 53			21 26
	d	19 40						20 58			21 27
Highbridge & Burnham	d	19 51						21 09			
Bridgwater	d	19 59						21 17			
Taunton	a	20 13				20 17		21 33	21 15		21 50

		GW ◇	GW	XC ◇1 A ✠	GW ◇1 ☕	XC ◇1 ✠	GW ✠	GW	XC ◇1	XC ◇1
Gloucester 7	d			20 17		21 13			22 19	23 07
Cam & Dursley	d									
Yate	d									
Bristol Parkway 7	a			21 13		22 06			23 12	00 01
	d		21 10	21 23		22 13			23 21	00 04
Filton Abbey Wood	d	21 05	21 14				22 53			
Stapleton Road	d									
Lawrence Hill	d									
Bristol Temple Meads 10	a	21 13	21 21	21 32		22 22	22 59		23 30	00 14
	d			21 44	21 55			23 10		
Bedminster	d							23 13		
Parson Street	d							23 15		
Nailsea & Backwell	d				22 06			23 23		
Yatton	d				22 12			23 29		
Worle	d				22 19			23 35		
Weston Milton	d							23 40		
Weston-super-Mare	a				22 27			23 43		
	d									
Highbridge & Burnham	d									
Bridgwater	d									
Taunton	a			22 15						

A ✠ to Bristol Temple Meads

For connections from London Paddington please refer to Table 125

Table 134

Sundays

from 28 October

Gloucester - Taunton

Network Diagram - see first Page of Table 132

		GW	GW	XC	GW	GW	XC	GW	GW	GW	XC	GW	GW	XC	GW	GW	XC	GW	GW	GW	XC	GW	GW
		◇	◇	◇1 Ħ	◇		◇1 Ħ	◇1 ☕	◇		◇1 Ħ	◇		◇1 Ħ	◇1 ☕	■	◇1 Ħ	◇			◇1 Ħ	◇1 ☕	◇
Gloucester 7	d												10 18	11 10						12 22			
Cam & Dursley	d												10 32							12 37			
Yate	d												10 46							12 52			
Bristol Parkway 7	a												10 52	11 40						13 00			
	d												10 55	11 41			12 35			13 01			
Filton Abbey Wood	d				08 55				10 03			10 54	10 58			11 54		12 57		13 04			13 54
Stapleton Road	d									10 16													
Lawrence Hill	d									10 18													
Bristol Temple Meads 10	a				09 05				10 13	10 21		11 03	11 07	11 52		12 04	12 46	13 05		13 12			14 04
	d	07 30	08 28	08 44		09 05	09 48	09 55		10 23	10 44		11 10	11 54	11 55		12 54		13 05		13 44	13 55	
Bedminster	d																						
Parson Street	d																						
Nailsea & Backwell	d		08 38			09 13				10 33			11 20		12 06				13 15			14 06	
Yatton	d	07 43	08 43			09 20				10 38			11 25		12 12				13 20			14 12	
Worle	d		08 49			09 26				10 44			11 31		12 19				13 26			14 19	
Weston Milton	d																						
Weston-super-Mare	a	07 52	08 55			09 35				10 50			11 37		12 31				13 31			14 26	
	d	07 53	08 59							10 55			11 38						13 33				
Highbridge & Burnham	d		09 10							11 09			11 48						13 44				
Bridgwater	d	08 09	09 18							11 17			11 56						13 52				
Taunton	a	08 22	09 31	09 15			10 19	10 29		11 31	11 15		12 10	12 26			13 26		14 06		14 15		

		XC	GW	GW	GW	XC	GW	GW	XC	GW	XC	GW	GW	GW	XC	GW	GW	GW	GW	GW	XC	GW	XC
		◇1 Ħ	◇1 ☕	◇		◇1 Ħ		◇	◇1 Ħ		◇1 Ħ	◇1 ☕	◇		◇1 Ħ		◇	◇	◇		◇1 Ħ	■	◇1 Ħ
Gloucester 7	d					14 49								16 13						17 20			
Cam & Dursley	d													16 27						17 34			
Yate	d													16 41						17 49			
Bristol Parkway 7	a					15 18								16 49						17 57			
	d					15 19			16 00		16 23			16 55	17 02					17 58	18 02		18 24
Filton Abbey Wood	d			14 55				15 55					16 55	16 57			17 20	17 54		18 01		18 23	
Stapleton Road	d																						
Lawrence Hill	d																						
Bristol Temple Meads 10	a			15 04		15 29		16 04	16 11		16 35		17 06	17 09	17 11		17 29	18 04		18 10	18 13	18 33	18 40
	d	14 44	14 55		15 10	15 44	15 55		16 14	16 25	16 44	16 55				17 25			18 07				18 44
Bedminster	d				15 13		15 58									17 28							
Parson Street	d						16 00																
Nailsea & Backwell	d				15 22		16 08			16 35		17 06				17 37			18 17				
Yatton	d				15 28		16 14			16 40		17 12				17 43			18 23				
Worle	d				15 34		16 20			16 46		17 19				17 49			18 29				
Weston Milton	d				15 39					16 52						17 58							
Weston-super-Mare	a				15 42		16 25			16 56		17 26				18 01			18 35				
	d						16 28					17 31							18 36				
Highbridge & Burnham	d						16 40												18 47				
Bridgwater	d						16 48												18 55				
Taunton	a	15 15	15 29			16 16	17 03		16 45		17 15	17 53							19 09				19 15

		GW	GW	XC	GW	XC	GW	GW	XC	GW	XC	GW	XC	GW	XC	GW	GW	XC	XC	GW	XC	GW
			◇	◇1 Ħ	◇1 ☕	◇1 Ħ	◇		◇1 Ħ		◇1 A Ħ	◇1 ☕	◇1 Ħ	◇	◇1 A Ħ	◇1 ☕		◇1	◇1	Ħ	◇1	
Gloucester 7	d							19 20									21 15		22 07			
Cam & Dursley	d							19 35									21 31					
Yate	d							19 49									21 45					
Bristol Parkway 7	a							19 57									21 53		22 34			
	d			18 58		19 23		19 58	20 03		20 23		20 58		21 23		21 55	22 00	22 34		22 54	
Filton Abbey Wood	d		18 56				19 55	20 01						21 05			21 58			22 53		
Stapleton Road	d	18 43																				
Lawrence Hill	d	18 45																				
Bristol Temple Meads 10	a	18 47	19 06	19 08		19 35	20 05	20 11	20 14		20 35		21 08	21 13	21 32		22 07	22 10	22 45	22 59	23 07	
	d	19 05			19 25	19 44			20 19	20 25	20 44	20 55			21 44	21 55						23 10
Bedminster	d	19 08								20 28												23 13
Parson Street	d	19 10																				23 15
Nailsea & Backwell	d	19 18			19 36					20 36		21 06				22 06						23 23
Yatton	d	19 24			19 42					20 42		21 12				22 12						23 29
Worle	d	19 30			19 51					20 48		21 19				22 19						23 35
Weston Milton	d	19 34																				23 40
Weston-super-Mare	a	19 38			19 58				20 36	20 53		21 26				22 27						23 43
	d	19 40							20 37	20 58		21 27										
Highbridge & Burnham	d	19 51								21 09												
Bridgwater	d	19 59								21 17												
Taunton	a	20 13				20 17			20 58	21 33	21 15	21 50			22 15							

A Ħ to Bristol Temple Meads

For connections from London Paddington please refer to Table 125

Table 134

Sundays

from 28 October

Gloucester - Taunton

Network Diagram - see first Page of Table 132

		XC
		◇1
Gloucester 7	d	
Cam & Dursley	d	
Yate	d	
Bristol Parkway 7	a	
	d	23 23
Filton Abbey Wood	d	
Stapleton Road	d	
Lawrence Hill	d	
Bristol Temple Meads 10	a	23 33
	d	
Bedminster	d	
Parson Street	d	
Nailsea & Backwell	d	
Yatton	d	
Worle	d	
Weston Milton	d	
Weston-super-Mare	a	
	d	
Highbridge & Burnham	d	
Bridgwater	d	
Taunton	a	

For connections from London Paddington please refer to Table 125

Table 134

Taunton - Gloucester

Mondays to Fridays

until 29 June

Network Diagram - see first Page of Table 132

Miles			GW MO	XC	GW	GW	XC	GW	GW	GW	XC	GW	GW	GW	GW	XC	GW	GW	GW	GW	XC	GW
			A	1			◇1 ⊼			◇1 🍴	◇1 ⊼	◇1 🍴		◇1 B 🍴		◇1 ⊼			◇	◇1 🍴	◇1 ⊼	◇
0	Taunton	d						05 27					06 02		06 34	06 50				06 55		
11¾	Bridgwater	d						05 39					06 14		06 46					07 05		
18	Highbridge & Burnham	d						05 47					06 21		06 54					07 13		
25¾	Weston-super-Mare	a						05 58					06 32		07 04					07 24		
—		d	23p47					06 00		06 20			06 36	06 49	07 08					07 25		
27	Weston Milton	d	23p50							06 25			06 39	06 53	07 11							
29½	Worle	d	23p54					06 05		06 30			06 43	06 59	07 15					07 32		
33½	Yatton	d	23p59					06 12		06 37			06 49	07 06	07 21					07 39		
37½	Nailsea & Backwell	d	00 06					06 18		06 44			06 55	07 13	07 27					07 46		
43¾	Parson Street	d											07 02		07 34							
44½	Bedminster	d	00 15										07 05		07 36			←				
45½	Bristol Temple Meads 10	a	00 19					06 30		06 54			07 09	07 23	07 41	07 24		07 41		07 57		
—		d		05 19	05 54	06 19	06 27		06 50		07 00	07 14	07 19		07 47	07 30	07 34	07 47	07 54		08 00	08 10
46½	Lawrence Hill	d				06 22			06 53				07 22		→			07 50				08 13
47	Stapleton Road	d				06 25			06 56				07 24					07 52				08 16
50	Filton Abbey Wood	d			06a01	06a30			07a01			07a21	07 30				07 43	07 59	08a01			08 22
51¼	Bristol Parkway 7	a		05 28			06 37				07 08		07 33			07 38	07 47	08 05			08 08	08 29
—		d															07 48					
57½	Yate	d															07 57					
72¼	Cam & Dursley	d															08 10					
85¼	Gloucester 7	a															08 29					

		GW	GW	GW	XC	GW	GW	XC	GW	GW	GW	GW	XC	GW	GW	GW	GW	XC	GW	GW	XC	GW	GW
			◇1 🍴		◇1 ⊼			◇1 ⊼	■ ⊼	◇			◇1 ⊼			◇1 🍴	◇ ⊼	◇1 ⊼			◇1 ⊼	◇	
Taunton	d		07 12	07 36	07 51			08 13				08 36	08 51			09 05				09 37	09 51		
Bridgwater	d		07 23	07 48								08 48								09 49			
Highbridge & Burnham	d		07 31	07 56								08 56								09 56			
Weston-super-Mare	a		07 41	08 06				08 32				09 08				09 27				10 07			
	d	07 37	07 49	08 08				08 34			08 41	09 10				09 29			09 45	10 10			
Weston Milton	d	07 40	07 53	08 11							08 44	09 13								10 13			
Worle	d	07 44	07 59	08 15							08 48	09 17							09 50	10 17			
Yatton	d	07 49	08 06	08 21							08 54	09 23				09 40			09 56	10 23			
Nailsea & Backwell	d	07 55	08 13	08 27							09 00	09 29				09 46			10 02	10 29			
Parson Street	d	08 02		08 34							09 07	09 36								10 36			
Bedminster	d	08 04		08 36			←				09 10	09 38			←					10 39			←
Bristol Temple Meads 10	a	08 09	08 24	08 41	08 26		08 41	08 53			09 14	09 42	09 26		09 42	09 56			10 13	10 42	10 25		10 42
	d	08 24		08 44	08 30	08 41	08 44	09 00	08 54	09 10	09 21	09 47	09 30	09 41	09 47		09 56	10 00	10 21	10 45	10 30	10 41	10 45
Lawrence Hill	d			→			08 47			09 13		→			09 49					→			10 49
Stapleton Road	d						08 49			09 15					09 50								10 52
Filton Abbey Wood	d	08a32				08 48	08 55		09a01	09 22	09a30			09 48	09 55		10a03		10a30			10 48	10 57
Bristol Parkway 7	a				08 38	08 52	09 03	09 08		09 28			09 38	09 52	10 03			10 08			10 38	10 52	11 03
	d					08 52								09 52								10 52	
Yate	d					09 01								10 01								11 01	
Cam & Dursley	d					09 14								10 14								11 14	
Gloucester 7	a					09 33								10 33								11 34	

		GW	XC	GW	XC	GW	GW	GW	GW	XC	GW	GW	XC	GW	GW	GW	XC	GW	XC	GW	GW	GW
		◇ ⊼	◇1 ⊼	◇	◇1 ⊼	◇		◇ ⊼		◇1 ⊼	◇1 🍴		◇1 ⊼	◇		◇ ⊼	◇1 ⊼		◇1 ⊼			◇ ⊼
Taunton	d			10 07	10 51				11 04	11 18	11 26		11 51					12 07	12 51			
Bridgwater	d			10 19					11 16									12 19				
Highbridge & Burnham	d			10 27					11 24									12 27				
Weston-super-Mare	a			10 38					11 34									12 38				
	d			10 39			11 10		11 45						12 10			12 39			13 10	
Weston Milton	d						11 13								12 13						13 13	
Worle	d			10 45			11 17		11 50						12 17			12 45			13 17	
Yatton	d			10 51			11 23		11 56						12 23			12 51			13 23	
Nailsea & Backwell	d			10 57			11 29		12 02						12 29			12 57			13 29	
Parson Street	d						11 36								12 36						13 36	
Bedminster	d						11 39					←			12 39						13 39	
Bristol Temple Meads 10	a			11 11	11 23		11 43		12 11	11 52	11 58	12 11	12 23		12 43			13 09	13 24		13 42	
	d	10 54	11 00	11 21	11 30	11 41	11 44	11 54	12 21	12 00		12 21	12 30	12 41	12 44	12 54	13 00	13 21	13 30	13 41	13 46	13 54
Lawrence Hill	d						11 47		→						12 47						13 47	
Stapleton Road	d						11 50								12 50						13 50	
Filton Abbey Wood	d	11a01		11a30		11 48	11 55	12a01				12a30		12 48	12 55	13a01		13a30		13 48	13 55	14a01
Bristol Parkway 7	a		11 08		11 38	11 52	12 03			12 08			12 38	12 52	13 03		13 08		13 38	13 52	14 03	
	d					11 52								12 52						13 52		
Yate	d					12 01								13 01						14 01		
Cam & Dursley	d					12 14								13 14						14 14		
Gloucester 7	a					12 33								13 31						14 33		

A from 21 May until 25 June

B The Bristolian

For connections to London Paddington please refer to Table 125

Table 134

Taunton - Gloucester

Mondays to Fridays

until 29 June

Network Diagram - see first Page of Table 132

		GW	XC	GW	XC	GW	GW	GW	XC	GW	XC	GW	GW	GW	GW	XC	GW	GW	XC	GW	GW	GW	XC
			◇1 ⊼		◇1 ⊼	◇		◇ ⊼	◇1 ⊼	◇	◇1 ⊼		◇		◇ ⊼	◇1 ⊼			◇1 ⊼			■ ⊼	◇1 ⊼
Taunton	d	13 07	13 16		13 54					14 07	14 54					15 12		15 15	15 51				
Bridgwater	d	13 19								14 19								15 27					
Highbridge & Burnham	d	13 27								14 27								15 34					
Weston-super-Mare	a	13 38								14 37						15 37		15 45					
	d	13 39					14 10			14 39				15 10		15 38		15 45			16 10		
Weston Milton	d						14 13							15 13							16 13		
Worle	d	13 45					14 17			14 45				15 17				15 50			16 17		
Yatton	d	13 51					14 23			14 51				15 23				15 56			16 23		
Nailsea & Backwell	d	13 57					14 29			14 57				15 29				16 02			16 29		
Parson Street	d						14 36							15 36							16 36		
Bedminster	d			←			14 39							15 39							16 39		
Bristol Temple Meads 10	a	14 11	13 56	14 11	14 26		14 43			15 08	15 26			15 43		15 55		16 15	16 26		16 43		
	d	14 21	14 00	14 21	14 30	14 41	14 45	14 54	15 00	15 21	15 30	15 34	15 41	15 45	15 54	16 00	16 15	16 24	16 30	16 41	16 44	16 54	17 00
Lawrence Hill	d	→					14 47							15 47			16 18				16 47		
Stapleton Road	d						14 50							15 50			16 20				16 50		
Filton Abbey Wood	d			14a30		14 48	14 55	15a01		15a30			15 48	15 55	16a01		16 26	16a30		16 48	16 55	17a01	
Bristol Parkway 7	a		14 08		14 38	14 51	15 03		15 08		15 38	15 48	15 52	16 03		16 08	16 34		16 38	16 52	17 03		17 08
	d					14 52							15 52							16 52			
Yate	d					15 01							16 01							17 01			
Cam & Dursley	d					15 14							16 14							17 14			
Gloucester 7	a					15 32							16 33							17 33			

		GW	GW	XC	GW	GW	GW	GW	GW	XC	GW	XC	GW	GW	GW	GW	XC	GW	XC	GW	GW	GW	XC
				◇1 ⊼	◇1 🍴	◇		■ ⊼		◇1 ⊼		◇1 ⊼	◇1 🍴			■ ⊼	◇1 ⊼		◇1 ⊼			◇ ⊼	◇1
Taunton	d		16 07	16 54					17 06	17 22		17 51						18 08	18 54				
Bridgwater	d		16 19						17 17									18 19					
Highbridge & Burnham	d		16 27						17 25									18 27					
Weston-super-Mare	a		16 37						17 37									18 38					
	d		16 39		17 10		17 15		17 38				18 08		18 15			18 39			19 10		
Weston Milton	d		16 42						17 41									18 43			19 13		
Worle	d		16 45				17 21		17 45						18 21			18 45			19 17		
Yatton	d		16 51				17 26		17 51						18 27			18 51			19 23		
Nailsea & Backwell	d		16 57				17 32		17 57						18 33			18 57			19 29		
Parson Street	d								18 04									19 07			19 36		
Bedminster	d		17 07						18 06		←							19 09			19 39		
Bristol Temple Meads 10	a		17 11	17 26	17 30		17 44		18 14	17 53	18 14	18 24	18 28		18 44			19 13	19 26		19 43		
	d	17 10	17 21	17 30		17 41	17 46	17 54	18 21	18 00	18 21	18 30		18 41	18 48	18 54	19 00	19 21	19 30	19 41	19 45	19 54	20 00
Lawrence Hill	d	17 13					17 47		→		18 24				18 51			19 24			19 47		
Stapleton Road	d	17 16					17 49				18 26				18a53			19 26			19 50		
Filton Abbey Wood	d	17 22	17a30			17 48	17 55	18a01			18a30			18 48		19a01		19a30		19 48	19 55	20a01	
Bristol Parkway 7	a	17 27		17 38		17 52	18 03			18 08		18 38		18 52			19 08		19 38	19 52	20 03		20 08
	d					17 52								18 52						19 52			20 10
Yate	d					18 01								19 01						20 01			
Cam & Dursley	d					18 14								19 13						20 14			
Gloucester 7	a					18 33								19 30						20 32			20 38

		XC	GW	XC	GW	GW	GW	GW	GW	XC MT WO	XC ThFO	GW	GW	GW	GW	GW	GW	GW
		◇1		◇1 A ⊼		◇ ⊼			◇1 🍴	◇1 B	◇1 C	◇	1		◇1 🍴	◇	◇	
Taunton	d		19 10	19 51				20 30	21 15	21 19	21 19				21 29		22 23	22 45
Bridgwater	d		19 22					20 42							21 39			22 57
Highbridge & Burnham	d		19 31					20 50							21 47			23 05
Weston-super-Mare	a		19 42					21 00							21 57		22 47	23 15
	d		19 49					21 02					21 34		22 01		22 49	23 17
Weston Milton	d							21 05					21 38					23 20
Worle	d		19 55					21 09					21 43		22 08			23 24
Yatton	d		20 01					21 14					21 50		22 15			23 30
Nailsea & Backwell	d		20 07					21 20					21 56		22 21			23 36
Parson Street	d							21 27										23 42
Bedminster	d							21 29										23 45
Bristol Temple Meads 10	a		20 19	20 24				21 35	21 47	21 52	21 51		22 06		22 31		23 12	23 51
	d	20 15		20 30	20 41	20 54	21 19			22 00	22 00	21 54		22 11		22 54		
Lawrence Hill	d						21 22											
Stapleton Road	d						21 24											
Filton Abbey Wood	d	20a21			20 48	21a01	21a30					22a01		22 18		23a01		
Bristol Parkway 7	a			20 38	20 52					22 08	22 08			22 22				
	d				20 52									22 22				
Yate	d				21 01									22 31				
Cam & Dursley	d				21 14									22 44				
Gloucester 7	a				21 31									23 03				

A ⊼ to Bristol Temple Meads

For connections to London Paddington please refer to Table 125

Taunton - Gloucester

2 July to 31 August

Network Diagram - see first Page of Table 132

		GW MO	XC	GW	GW	XC	GW	GW	GW	XC	GW	GW	GW	GW	XC	GW	GW	GW	GW	XC	GW	GW
			1			◇1 🛒			◇1 🍴	◇1 🛒	◇1 🍴		◇1 A 🍴		◇1 🛒			◇	◇1 🍴	◇1 🛒	◇	
Taunton	d						05 27					06 02		06 34	06 50				06 55			
Bridgwater	d						05 39					06 14		06 46					07 05			
Highbridge & Burnham	d						05 47					06 21		06 54					07 13			
Weston-super-Mare	a						05 58					06 32		07 04					07 24			
	d	23p47					06 00		06 20			06 36	06 49	07 08					07 25			07 37
Weston Milton	d	23p50							06 25			06 39	06 53	07 11								07 40
Worle	d	23p54					06 05		06 30			06 43	06 59	07 15					07 32			07 44
Yatton	d	23p59					06 12		06 37			06 49	07 06	07 21					07 39			07 49
Nailsea & Backwell	d	00 06					06 18		06 44			06 55	07 13	07 27					07 46			07 55
Parson Street	d											07 02		07 34								08 02
Bedminster	d	00 15										07 05		07 36			←					08 04
Bristol Temple Meads 10	a	00 19					06 30		06 54			07 09	07 23	07 41	07 24		07 41		07 57			08 09
	d		05 19	05 54	06 19	06 27		06 50		07 00	07 14	07 19		07 47	07 30	07 34	07 47	07 54		08 00	08 10	08 24
Lawrence Hill	d				06 22			06 53				07 22		→			07 50				08 13	
Stapleton Road	d				06 25			06 56				07 24					07 52				08 16	
Filton Abbey Wood	d			06a01	06a30			07a01			07a21	07 30				07 43	07 59	08a01			08 22	08a32
Bristol Parkway 7	a		05 28			06 37				07 08		07 33			07 38	07 47	08 05			08 08	08 29	
	d															07 48						
Yate	d															07 57						
Cam & Dursley	d															08 10						
Gloucester 7	a															08 29						

		GW	GW	XC	GW	GW	XC	GW	GW	GW	GW	XC	GW	GW	GW	GW	XC	GW	GW	XC	GW	GW	GW
		◇1 🍴		◇1 🛒			◇1 🛒	■ 🛒	◇			◇1 🛒			◇1 🍴	◇ 🛒	◇1 🛒			◇1 🛒	◇		◇ 🛒
Taunton	d	07 12	07 36	07 51			08 13				08 36	08 51			09 05				09 37	09 51			
Bridgwater	d	07 23	07 48								08 48								09 49				
Highbridge & Burnham	d	07 31	07 56								08 56								09 56				
Weston-super-Mare	a	07 41	08 06				08 32				09 08				09 27				10 07				
	d	07 49	08 08				08 34			08 41	09 10				09 29			09 45	10 10				
Weston Milton	d	07 53	08 11							08 44	09 13								10 13				
Worle	d	07 59	08 15							08 48	09 17							09 50	10 17				
Yatton	d	08 06	08 21							08 54	09 23				09 40			09 56	10 23				
Nailsea & Backwell	d	08 13	08 27							09 00	09 29				09 46			10 02	10 29				
Parson Street	d		08 34							09 07	09 36								10 36				
Bedminster	d		08 36			←				09 10	09 38			←					10 39			←	
Bristol Temple Meads 10	a	08 24	08 41	08 26		08 41	08 53			09 14	09 42	09 26		09 42	09 56			10 13	10 42	10 25		10 42	
	d		08 44	08 30	08 41	08 44	09 00	08 54	09 10	09 21	09 47	09 30	09 41	09 47		09 56	10 00	10 21	10 45	10 30	10 41	10 45	10 54
Lawrence Hill	d		→			08 47			09 13		→			09 49					→			10 49	
Stapleton Road	d					08 49			09 15					09 50								10 52	
Filton Abbey Wood	d				08 48	08 55		09a01	09 22	09a30			09 48	09 55		10a03		10a30			10 48	10 57	11a01
Bristol Parkway 7	a			08 38	08 52	09 03	09 08		09 28			09 38	09 52	10 03			10 08			10 38	10 52	11 03	
	d				08 52								09 52								10 52		
Yate	d				09 01								10 01								11 01		
Cam & Dursley	d				09 14								10 14								11 14		
Gloucester 7	a				09 33								10 33								11 34		

		XC	GW	XC	GW	GW	GW	GW	XC	GW	GW	XC	GW	GW	GW	XC	GW	XC	GW	GW	GW	GW
		◇1 🛒	◇	◇1 🛒	◇		◇ 🛒		◇1 🛒	◇1 🍴		◇1 🛒	◇		◇ 🛒	◇1 🛒		◇1 🛒			◇ 🛒	
Taunton	d		10 07	10 51				11 04	11 18	11 26		11 51					12 07	12 51				13 07
Bridgwater	d		10 19					11 16									12 19					13 19
Highbridge & Burnham	d		10 27					11 24									12 27					13 27
Weston-super-Mare	a		10 38					11 34									12 38					13 38
	d		10 39			11 10		11 45						12 10			12 39			13 10		13 39
Weston Milton	d					11 13								12 13						13 13		
Worle	d		10 45			11 17		11 50						12 17			12 45			13 17		13 45
Yatton	d		10 51			11 23		11 56						12 23			12 51			13 23		13 51
Nailsea & Backwell	d		10 57			11 29		12 02						12 29			12 57			13 29		13 57
Parson Street	d					11 36								12 36						13 36		
Bedminster	d					11 39					←			12 39						13 39		
Bristol Temple Meads 10	a		11 11	11 23		11 43		12 11	11 52	11 58	12 11	12 23		12 43			13 09	13 24		13 42		14 11
	d	11 00	11 21	11 30	11 41	11 44	11 54	12 21	12 00		12 21	12 30	12 41	12 44	12 54	13 00	13 21	13 30	13 41	13 46	13 54	14 21
Lawrence Hill	d					11 47		→						12 47						13 47		→
Stapleton Road	d					11 50								12 50						13 50		
Filton Abbey Wood	d		11a30		11 48	11 55	12a01				12a30		12 48	12 55	13a01		13a30		13 48	13 55	14a01	
Bristol Parkway 7	a	11 08		11 38	11 52	12 03			12 08			12 38	12 52	13 03		13 08		13 38	13 52	14 03		
	d				11 52								12 52						13 52			
Yate	d				12 01								13 01						14 01			
Cam & Dursley	d				12 14								13 14						14 14			
Gloucester 7	a				12 33								13 31						14 33			

A The Bristolian

For connections to London Paddington please refer to Table 125

Taunton - Gloucester

2 July to 31 August

Network Diagram - see first Page of Table 132

		XC	GW	XC	GW	GW	GW	XC	GW	XC	GW	GW	GW	GW	XC	GW	GW	XC	GW	GW	GW	XC	GW
		◇1 🛒		◇1 🛒	◇		◇ 🛒	◇1 🛒	◇	◇1 🛒		◇		◇ 🛒	◇1 🛒			◇1 🛒			■ 🛒	◇1 🛒	
Taunton	d	13 16		13 54					14 07	14 54					15 12		15 15	15 51					
Bridgwater	d								14 19								15 27						
Highbridge & Burnham	d								14 27								15 34						
Weston-super-Mare	a								14 37						15 37		15 45						
	d					14 10			14 39				15 10		15 38		15 45			16 10			
Weston Milton	d					14 13							15 13							16 13			
Worle	d					14 17			14 45				15 17				15 50			16 17			
Yatton	d					14 23			14 51				15 23				15 56			16 23			
Nailsea & Backwell	d					14 29			14 57				15 29				16 02			16 29			
Parson Street	d					14 36							15 36							16 36			
Bedminster	d		←			14 39							15 39							16 39			
Bristol Temple Meads 10	a	13 56	14 11	14 26		14 43			15 14	15 26			15 43		15 55		16 15	16 26		16 43			
	d	14 00	14 21	14 30	14 41	14 45	14 54	15 00	15 21	15 30	15 34	15 41	15 45	15 54	16 00	16 15	16 24	16 30	16 41	16 44	16 54	17 00	17 10
Lawrence Hill	d					14 47							15 47			16 18				16 47			17 13
Stapleton Road	d					14 50							15 50			16 20				16 50			17 16
Filton Abbey Wood	d		14a30		14 48	14 55	15a01		15a30			15 48	15 55	16a01		16 26	16a30		16 48	16 55	17a01		17 22
Bristol Parkway 7	a	14 08		14 38	14 51	15 03		15 08		15 38	15 48	15 52	16 03		16 08	16 34		16 38	16 52	17 03		17 08	17 27
	d				14 52							15 52							16 52				
Yate	d				15 01							16 01							17 01				
Cam & Dursley	d				15 14							16 14							17 14				
Gloucester 7	a				15 32							16 33							17 33				

		GW	XC	GW	GW	GW	GW	GW	XC	GW	XC	GW	GW	GW	GW	XC	GW	XC	GW	GW	GW	XC
			◇1 🛒	◇1 🍴	◇		■ 🛒		◇1 🛒		◇1 🛒	◇1 🍴			■ 🛒	◇1 🛒		◇1 🛒			◇ 🛒	◇1
Taunton	d	16 07	16 54					17 06	17 22		17 51						18 08	18 54				
Bridgwater	d	16 19						17 17									18 19					
Highbridge & Burnham	d	16 27						17 25									18 27					
Weston-super-Mare	a	16 37						17 37									18 38					
	d	16 39		17 10		17 15		17 38				18 08		18 15			18 39			19 10		
Weston Milton	d	16 42						17 41									18 43			19 13		
Worle	d	16 45				17 21		17 45						18 21			18 45			19 17		
Yatton	d	16 51				17 26		17 51						18 27			18 51			19 23		
Nailsea & Backwell	d	16 57				17 32		17 57						18 33			18 57			19 29		
Parson Street	d							18 04									19 07					
Bedminster	d	17 07						18 06		←							19 09					
Bristol Temple Meads 10	a	17 11	17 26	17 30		17 44		18 14	17 53	18 14	18 24	18 28		18 44			19 17	19 26		19 43		
	d	17 21	17 30		17 41	17 46	17 54	18 21	18 00	18 21	18 30		18 41	18 48	18 54	19 00	19 21	19 30	19 41	19 45	19 54	20 00
Lawrence Hill	d					17 47		→		18 24				18 51			19 24			19 47		
Stapleton Road	d					17 49				18 26				18a53			19 26			19 50		
Filton Abbey Wood	d	17a30			17 48	17 55	18a01			18a30			18 48		19a01		19a30		19 48	19 55	20a01	
Bristol Parkway 7	a		17 38		17 52	18 03			18 08		18 38		18 52			19 08		19 38	19 52	20 03		20 08
	d				17 52								18 52						19 52			20 10
Yate	d				18 01								19 01						20 01			
Cam & Dursley	d				18 14								19 13						20 14			
Gloucester 7	a				18 33								19 30						20 32			20 38

		XC	GW	XC	GW	GW	GW	GW	GW	XC MT WO	XC ThFO	GW	GW	GW	GW	GW	GW	GW
		◇1		◇1 A 🛒		◇ 🛒			◇1 🍴	◇1 B	◇1 C	◇	1		◇1 🍴	◇	◇	
Taunton	d		19 17	19 51				20 30	21 15	21 19	21 19				21 29		22 23	22 45
Bridgwater	d		19 30					20 42							21 39			22 57
Highbridge & Burnham	d		19 38					20 50							21 47			23 05
Weston-super-Mare	a		19 50					21 00							21 57		22 47	23 15
	d		20 08					21 02					21 34		22 01		22 49	23 17
Weston Milton	d							21 05					21 38					23 20
Worle	d		20 14					21 09					21 43		22 08			23 24
Yatton	d		20 21					21 14					21 50		22 15			23 30
Nailsea & Backwell	d		20 27					21 20					21 56		22 21			23 36
Parson Street	d		20 36					21 27										23 42
Bedminster	d		20 39					21 29										23 45
Bristol Temple Meads 10	a		20 45	20 24				21 35	21 47	21 52	21 51		22 06		22 31		23 12	23 51
	d	20 15		20 30	20 41	20 54	21 19			22 00	22 00	21 54		22 11		22 54		
Lawrence Hill	d						21 22											
Stapleton Road	d						21 24											
Filton Abbey Wood	d	20a21			20 48	21a01	21a30					22a01		22 18		23a01		
Bristol Parkway 7	a			20 38	20 52					22 08	22 08			22 22				
	d				20 52									22 22				
Yate	d				21 01									22 31				
Cam & Dursley	d				21 14									22 44				
Gloucester 7	a				21 31									23 03				

A 🛒 to Bristol Temple Meads

For connections to London Paddington please refer to Table 125

Table 134

Mondays to Fridays

from 3 September

Taunton - Gloucester

Network Diagram - see first Page of Table 132

		GW MO	XC	GW	GW	XC	GW	GW	GW	XC	GW	GW	GW	GW	XC	GW	GW	GW	GW	XC	GW	GW
			■1			◇1 ✕			◇1 ⊡	◇1 ✕	◇1 ⊡		◇1 A ⊡		◇1 ✕			◇	◇1 ⊡	◇1 ✕	◇	
Taunton	d						05 27					06 02		06 34	06 50				06 55			
Bridgwater	d						05 39					06 14		06 46					07 05			
Highbridge & Burnham	d						05 47					06 21		06 54					07 13			
Weston-super-Mare	a						05 58					06 32		07 04					07 24			
	d	23p47					06 00		06 20			06 36	06 49	07 08					07 25			07 37
Weston Milton	d	23p50							06 25			06 39	06 53	07 11								07 40
Worle	d	23p54					06 05		06 30			06 43	06 59	07 15					07 32			07 44
Yatton	d	23p59					06 12		06 37			06 49	07 06	07 21					07 39			07 49
Nailsea & Backwell	d	00 06					06 18		06 44			06 55	07 13	07 27					07 46			07 55
Parson Street	d											07 02		07 34								08 02
Bedminster	d	00 15										07 05		07 36			←					08 04
Bristol Temple Meads 10	a	00 19					06 30		06 54			07 09	07 23	07 41	07 24		07 41		07 57			08 09
	d		05 19	05 54	06 19	06 27		06 50		07 00	07 14	07 19		07 47	07 30	07 34	07 47	07 54		08 00	08 10	08 24
Lawrence Hill	d				06 22			06 53				07 22		→			07 50				08 13	
Stapleton Road	d				06 25			06 56				07 24					07 52				08 16	
Filton Abbey Wood	d			06a01	06a30			07a01			07a21	07 30				07 43	07 59	08a01			08 22	08a32
Bristol Parkway 7	a		05 28			06 37				07 08		07 33			07 38	07 47	08 05			08 08	08 29	
	d															07 48						
Yate	d															07 57						
Cam & Dursley	d															08 10						
Gloucester 7	a															08 29						

		GW	GW	XC	GW	GW	XC	GW	GW	GW	GW	XC	GW	GW	GW	GW	XC	GW	GW	XC	GW	GW	GW
		◇1 ⊡		◇1 ✕			◇1 ✕	■ ✕	◇			◇1 ✕			◇1 ⊡	◇ ✕	◇1 ✕			◇1 ✕	◇		◇ ✕
Taunton	d	07 12	07 36	07 51			08 13				08 36	08 51			09 05				09 37	09 51			
Bridgwater	d	07 23	07 48								08 48								09 49				
Highbridge & Burnham	d	07 31	07 56								08 56								09 56				
Weston-super-Mare	a	07 41	08 06				08 32				09 08				09 27				10 07				
	d	07 49	08 08				08 34			08 41	09 10				09 29			09 45	10 10				
Weston Milton	d	07 53	08 11							08 44	09 13								10 13				
Worle	d	07 59	08 15							08 48	09 17							09 50	10 17				
Yatton	d	08 06	08 21							08 54	09 23				09 40			09 56	10 23				
Nailsea & Backwell	d	08 13	08 27							09 00	09 29				09 46			10 02	10 29				
Parson Street	d		08 34							09 07	09 36								10 36				
Bedminster	d		08 36			←				09 10	09 38			←					10 39			←	
Bristol Temple Meads 10	a	08 24	08 41	08 26		08 41	08 53			09 14	09 42	09 26		09 42	09 56			10 13	10 42	10 25		10 42	
	d		08 44	08 30	08 41	08 44	09 00	08 54	09 10	09 21	09 47	09 30	09 41	09 47		09 56	10 00	10 21	10 45	10 30	10 41	10 45	10 54
Lawrence Hill	d		→			08 47			09 13		→			09 49					→			10 49	
Stapleton Road	d					08 49			09 15					09 50								10 52	
Filton Abbey Wood	d				08 48	08 55		09a01	09 22	09a30			09 48	09 55		10a03		10a30			10 48	10 57	11a01
Bristol Parkway 7	a			08 38	08 52	09 03	09 08		09 28			09 38	09 52	10 03			10 08			10 38	10 52	11 03	
	d				08 52								09 52								10 52		
Yate	d				09 01								10 01								11 01		
Cam & Dursley	d				09 14								10 14								11 14		
Gloucester 7	a				09 33								10 33								11 34		

		XC	GW	XC	GW	GW	GW	GW	XC	GW	GW	XC	GW	GW	GW	XC	GW	XC	GW	GW	GW	GW
		◇1 ✕	◇	◇1 ✕	◇		◇ ✕		◇1 ✕	◇1 ⊡		◇1 ✕	◇		◇ ✕	◇1 ✕		◇1 ✕			◇ ✕	
Taunton	d		10 07	10 51				11 04	11 18	11 26		11 51					12 07	12 51				13 07
Bridgwater	d		10 19					11 16									12 19					13 19
Highbridge & Burnham	d		10 27					11 24									12 27					13 27
Weston-super-Mare	a		10 38					11 34									12 38					13 38
	d		10 39			11 10		11 45						12 10			12 39			13 10		13 39
Weston Milton	d					11 13								12 13						13 13		
Worle	d		10 45			11 17		11 50						12 17			12 45			13 17		13 45
Yatton	d		10 51			11 23		11 56						12 23			12 51			13 23		13 51
Nailsea & Backwell	d		10 57			11 29		12 02						12 29			12 57			13 29		13 57
Parson Street	d					11 36								12 36						13 36		
Bedminster	d					11 39					←			12 39						13 39		
Bristol Temple Meads 10	a		11 11	11 23		11 43		12 11	11 52	11 58	12 11	12 23		12 43			13 09	13 24		13 42		14 11
	d	11 00	11 21	11 30	11 41	11 44	11 54	12 21	12 00		12 21	12 30	12 41	12 44	12 54	13 00	13 21	13 30	13 41	13 46	13 54	14 21
Lawrence Hill	d					11 47		→						12 47						13 47		→
Stapleton Road	d					11 50								12 50						13 50		
Filton Abbey Wood	d		11a30		11 48	11 55	12a01				12a30		12 48	12 55	13a01		13a30		13 48	13 55	14a01	
Bristol Parkway 7	a	11 08		11 38	11 52	12 03			12 08			12 38	12 52	13 03		13 08		13 38	13 52	14 03		
	d				11 52								12 52						13 52			
Yate	d				12 01								13 01						14 01			
Cam & Dursley	d				12 14								13 14						14 14			
Gloucester 7	a				12 33								13 31						14 33			

A The Bristolian

For connections to London Paddington please refer to Table 125

Table 134

Mondays to Fridays

from 3 September

Taunton - Gloucester

Network Diagram - see first Page of Table 132

		XC	GW	XC	GW	GW	GW	XC	GW	XC	GW	GW	GW	GW	XC	GW	GW	XC	GW	GW	GW	XC	GW
		◇1 ✕		◇1 ✕	◇		◇ ✕	◇1 ✕	◇	◇1 ✕		◇		◇ ✕	◇1 ✕			◇1 ✕			■ ✕	◇1 ✕	
Taunton	d	13 16		13 54					14 07	14 54					15 12		15 15	15 51					
Bridgwater	d								14 19								15 27						
Highbridge & Burnham	d								14 27								15 34						
Weston-super-Mare	a								14 37						15 37		15 45						
	d					14 10			14 39				15 10		15 38		15 45			16 10			
Weston Milton	d					14 13							15 13							16 13			
Worle	d					14 17			14 45				15 17				15 50			16 17			
Yatton	d					14 23			14 51				15 23				15 56			16 23			
Nailsea & Backwell	d					14 29			14 57				15 29				16 02			16 29			
Parson Street	d					14 36							15 36							16 36			
Bedminster	d		←			14 39							15 39							16 39			
Bristol Temple Meads 10	a	13 56	14 11	14 26		14 43			15 08	15 26			15 43		15 55		16 15	16 26		16 43			
	d	14 00	14 21	14 30	14 41	14 45	14 54	15 00	15 21	15 30	15 34	15 41	15 45	15 54	16 00	16 15	16 24	16 30	16 41	16 44	16 54	17 00	17 10
Lawrence Hill	d					14 47							15 47			16 18				16 47			17 13
Stapleton Road	d					14 50							15 50			16 20				16 50			17 16
Filton Abbey Wood	d		14a30		14 48	14 55	15a01		15a30			15 48	15 55	16a01		16 26	16a30		16 48	16 55	17a01		17 22
Bristol Parkway 7	a	14 08		14 38	14 51	15 03		15 08		15 38	15 48	15 52	16 03		16 08	16 34		16 38	16 52	17 03		17 08	17 27
	d				14 52							15 52							16 52				
Yate	d				15 01							16 01							17 01				
Cam & Dursley	d				15 14							16 14							17 14				
Gloucester 7	a				15 32							16 33							17 33				

		GW	XC	GW	GW	GW	GW	GW	XC	GW	XC	GW	GW	GW	GW	XC	GW	XC	GW	GW	GW	XC
			◇1 ✕	◇1 ⊡	◇		■ ✕		◇1 ✕		◇1 ✕	◇1 ⊡			■ ✕	◇1 ✕		◇1 ✕			◇ ✕	◇1
Taunton	d	16 07	16 54					17 06	17 22		17 51						18 08	18 54				
Bridgwater	d	16 19						17 17									18 19					
Highbridge & Burnham	d	16 27						17 25									18 27					
Weston-super-Mare	a	16 37						17 37									18 38					
	d	16 39		17 10		17 15		17 38				18 08		18 15			18 39			19 10		
Weston Milton	d	16 42						17 41									18 43			19 13		
Worle	d	16 45				17 21		17 45						18 21			18 45			19 17		
Yatton	d	16 51				17 26		17 51						18 27			18 51			19 23		
Nailsea & Backwell	d	16 57				17 32		17 57						18 33			18 57			19 29		
Parson Street	d							18 04									19 07			19 36		
Bedminster	d	17 07						18 06		←							19 09			19 39		
Bristol Temple Meads 10	a	17 11	17 26	17 30		17 44		18 14	17 53	18 14	18 24	18 28		18 44			19 13	19 26		19 43		
	d	17 21	17 30		17 41	17 46	17 54	18 21	18 00	18 21	18 30		18 41	18 48	18 54	19 00	19 21	19 30	19 41	19 45	19 54	20 00
Lawrence Hill	d					17 47		→		18 24				18 51			19 24			19 47		
Stapleton Road	d					17 49				18 26				18a53			19 26			19 50		
Filton Abbey Wood	d	17a30			17 48	17 55	18a01			18a30			18 48		19a01		19a30		19 48	19 55	20a01	
Bristol Parkway 7	a		17 38		17 52	18 03			18 08		18 38		18 52			19 08		19 38	19 52	20 03		20 08
	d				17 52								18 52						19 52			20 10
Yate	d				18 01								19 01						20 01			
Cam & Dursley	d				18 14								19 13						20 14			
Gloucester 7	a				18 33								19 30						20 32			20 38

		XC	GW	XC	GW	GW	GW	GW	GW	XC MT WO	XC ThFO	GW	GW	GW	GW	GW	GW	GW
		◇1		◇1 A ✕		◇ ✕			◇1 ⊡	◇1 B	◇1 C	◇	■1		◇1 ⊡	◇	◇	
Taunton	d		19 10	19 51				20 30	21 15	21 19	21 19				21 29		22 23	22 45
Bridgwater	d		19 22					20 42							21 39			22 57
Highbridge & Burnham	d		19 31					20 50							21 47			23 05
Weston-super-Mare	a		19 42					21 00							21 57		22 47	23 15
	d		19 49					21 02					21 34		22 01		22 49	23 17
Weston Milton	d							21 05					21 38					23 20
Worle	d		19 55					21 09					21 43		22 08			23 24
Yatton	d		20 01					21 14					21 50		22 15			23 30
Nailsea & Backwell	d		20 07					21 20					21 56		22 21			23 36
Parson Street	d							21 27										23 42
Bedminster	d							21 29										23 45
Bristol Temple Meads 10	a		20 19	20 24				21 35	21 47	21 52	21 51		22 06		22 31		23 12	23 51
	d	20 15		20 30	20 41	20 54	21 19			22 00	22 00	21 54		22 11		22 54		
Lawrence Hill	d						21 22											
Stapleton Road	d						21 24											
Filton Abbey Wood	d	20a21			20 48	21a01	21a30					22a01		22 18		23a01		
Bristol Parkway 7	a			20 38	20 52					22 08	22 08			22 22				
	d				20 52									22 22				
Yate	d				21 01									22 31				
Cam & Dursley	d				21 14									22 44				
Gloucester 7	a				21 31									23 03				

A ✕ to Bristol Temple Meads

For connections to London Paddington please refer to Table 125

Taunton - Gloucester

Saturdays
until 23 June

Network Diagram - see first Page of Table 132

		XC	GW	GW	GW	GW	XC	GW	GW	XC		GW	GW	GW	GW	XC	GW	GW	XC	GW		GW	GW	GW	XC
		◇1		◇1		◇1	◇1			◇1					◇1	◇1			◇1				◇	◇1	◇1
Taunton	d		05 28						06 35	06 51					06 54			07 35	07 51					07 59	08 13
Bridgwater	d		05 40						06 48						07 05			07 47						08 10	
Highbridge & Burnham	d		05 48						06 55						07 12			07 55						08 17	
Weston-super-Mare	a		05 59						07 06						07 24			08 06						08 27	
	d		06 01			06 24			07 08						07 24		07 37	08 06						08 30	
Weston Milton	d		06 04						07 11								07 40	08 09							
Worle	d		06 07			06 32			07 16						07 32		07 44	08 15							
Yatton	d		06 12			06 39			07 22						07 39		07 49	08 21						08 41	
Nailsea & Backwell	d		06 18			06 45			07 28						07 46		07 55	08 27						08 47	
Parson Street	d		06 29						07 35								08 02	08 36							
Bedminster	d		06 31						07 38				←				08 04	08 38				←			
Bristol Temple Meads 10	a		06 34			06 56			07 42	07 24			07 42		07 58		08 10	08 41	08 23			08 41		08 57	08 48
	d	06 15		06 46	06 50		07 00	07 21	07 47	07 30		07 41	07 47	07 54		08 00	08 20	08 45	08 30	08 41		08 45	08 54		09 00
Lawrence Hill	d				06 53				→				07 50				08 23	→				08 48			
Stapleton Road	d				06 56								07 52				08 25					08 50			
Filton Abbey Wood	d			06 54	07a01			07a29				07 48	07 59	08a00			08a30			08 48		08 56	09a01		
Bristol Parkway 7	a	06 23		06 58			07 08			07 38		07 52	08 05			08 08			08 38	08 52		09 03			09 08
	d	06 25										07 52								08 52					
Yate	d											08 01								09 01					
Cam & Dursley	d											08 14								09 14					
Gloucester 7	a	06 54										08 32								09 33					

		GW	XC	GW	GW	GW		XC	GW	XC	GW	GW	XC	GW	GW	GW		XC	GW	GW	GW	GW	GW	XC	GW
			◇1			◇		◇1		◇1	◇		◇1	◇		◇1		◇1	◇		◇1	◇		◇1	
Taunton	d		08 51						09 10	09 51			10 09		10 12	10 45		10 54					11 07	11 18	
Bridgwater	d								09 22						10 24								11 19		
Highbridge & Burnham	d								09 30						10 32								11 27		
Weston-super-Mare	a								09 42				10 32		10 40								11 37		
	d	08 39			09 10				09 44			10 10	10 33		10 40					11 10	11 30		11 39		
Weston Milton	d				09 13							10 13								11 13					
Worle	d	08 45			09 18				09 49			10 18			10 46					11 18			11 45		
Yatton	d	08 51			09 23				09 55			10 23			10 52					11 23			11 51		
Nailsea & Backwell	d	08 57			09 29				10 01			10 29			10 58					11 29			11 57		
Parson Street	d				09 36							10 36								11 36					
Bedminster	d				09 38							10 38								11 38					←
Bristol Temple Meads 10	a	09 08	09 25		09 43				10 13	10 25		10 43	10 52		11 13	11 24		11 25		11 43	11 47		12 10	11 54	12 10
	d	09 21	09 30	09 41	09 45	09 54		10 00	10 21	10 30	10 41	10 45	11 00	10 54	11 21			11 30	11 41	11 45		11 54	12 21	12 00	12 21
Lawrence Hill	d				09 48							10 48								11 48			→		
Stapleton Road	d	09 25			09 50				10 25			10 50			11 25					11 50					12 25
Filton Abbey Wood	d	09a30		09 48	09 56	10a01			10a30		10 48	10 56		11a01	11a30				11 48	11 56		12a01			12a29
Bristol Parkway 7	a		09 38	09 52	10 03			10 08		10 38	10 52	11 03	11 08					11 38	11 52	12 03				12 08	
	d			09 52							10 52								11 52						
Yate	d			10 01							11 01								12 01						
Cam & Dursley	d			10 14							11 14								12 14						
Gloucester 7	a			10 33							11 32								12 33						

		XC		GW	GW	GW	XC	GW	GW	XC	GW	GW		GW	XC	GW	XC	GW	GW	GW	XC	GW		GW	XC
		◇1		◇		◇	◇1		◇1	◇1	◇			◇	◇1		◇1	◇		◇	◇1			◇1	◇1
Taunton	d	11 51						12 07		12 51						13 07	13 53					14 07			14 52
Bridgwater	d							12 19								13 19						14 19			
Highbridge & Burnham	d							12 27								13 27						14 27			
Weston-super-Mare	a							12 37								13 37						14 37			
	d				12 10			12 39	13 01			13 10				13 39			14 10			14 39		15 01	
Weston Milton	d				12 13							13 13							14 13						
Worle	d				12 18			12 45				13 18				13 45			14 18			14 45			
Yatton	d				12 23			12 51				13 23				13 51			14 23			14 51			
Nailsea & Backwell	d				12 29			12 57				13 29				13 57			14 29			14 57			
Parson Street	d				12 36							13 36							14 36						
Bedminster	d				12 38							13 38							14 38						
Bristol Temple Meads 10	a	12 24			12 43			13 09	13 19	13 23		13 43				14 11	14 26		14 43			15 10		15 19	15 24
	d	12 30		12 41	12 45	12 54	13 00	13 21		13 30	13 41	13 45		13 54	14 00	14 21	14 30	14 41	14 45	14 54	15 00	15 21			15 30
Lawrence Hill	d				12 48							13 48							14 48						
Stapleton Road	d				12 50			13 25				13 50				14 25			14 50			15 25			
Filton Abbey Wood	d			12 48	12 56	13a01		13a30			13 48	13 56		14a01		14a30		14 48	14 56	15a01		15a30			
Bristol Parkway 7	a	12 38		12 52	13 03		13 08			13 38	13 52	14 03			14 08		14 38	14 52	15 03		15 08				15 38
	d			12 52							13 52							14 52							
Yate	d			13 01							14 01							15 01							
Cam & Dursley	d			13 14							14 14							15 14							
Gloucester 7	a			13 34							14 33							15 32							

For connections to London Paddington please refer to Table 125

Taunton - Gloucester

Saturdays
until 23 June

Network Diagram - see first Page of Table 132

		GW	GW	XC	GW	GW	XC	GW		GW	GW	XC	GW	GW	XC	GW	GW	GW		XC	GW	GW	XC	GW	GW
		◇		◇1	◇		◇1				◇	◇1		◇1	◇1			◇		◇1		◇1	◇1	◇	
Taunton	d			15 04		15 07	15 51						16 07		16 51						17 07		17 54		
Bridgwater	d					15 19							16 19								17 17				
Highbridge & Burnham	d					15 27							16 27								17 25				
Weston-super-Mare	a			15 23		15 37							16 37								17 37				
	d		15 10	15 30		15 39				16 10			16 39	17 01			17 10				17 40	18 01			18 10
Weston Milton	d		15 13							16 13							17 13								18 13
Worle	d		15 18			15 45				16 18			16 45				17 18				17 45				18 18
Yatton	d		15 23			15 51				16 23			16 51				17 23				17 51				18 23
Nailsea & Backwell	d		15 29			15 57				16 29			16 57				17 29				17 57				18 29
Parson Street	d		15 36							16 36			17 04				17 36								18 36
Bedminster	d		15 38							16 38							17 38								18 38
Bristol Temple Meads 10	a		15 43	15 49		16 09	16 24			16 43			17 11	17 19	17 24		17 43				18 11	18 18	18 24		18 43
	d	15 41	15 45	16 00	15 54	16 21	16 30	16 41		16 45	16 54	17 00	17 21		17 30	17 41	17 45	17 54		18 00	18 21		18 30	18 41	18 45
Lawrence Hill	d		15 48							16 48							17 48								18 48
Stapleton Road	d		15 50			16 25				16 50			17 25				17 50				18 25				18 50
Filton Abbey Wood	d	15 48	15 56		16a01	16a30		16 48		16 56	17a01		17a30			17 48	17 56	18a01			18a30			18 48	18 56
Bristol Parkway 7	a	15 52	16 03	16 08			16 38	16 52		17 03		17 08			17 38	17 52	18 03			18 08			18 38	18 52	19 03
	d	15 52						16 52								17 52								18 52	
Yate	d	16 01						17 01								18 01								19 01	
Cam & Dursley	d	16 14						17 14								18 14								19 14	
Gloucester 7	a	16 33						17 33								18 33								19 33	

		GW	XC	GW		XC	GW	GW	GW	GW	XC	XC	XC	GW		GW	GW	GW	GW	GW	GW	GW	GW	GW
		■	◇1			◇1			◇		◇1	◇1	◇1	◇1			◇		◇1	◇		◇1		◇
Taunton	d			18 07		18 51				19 07	19 18		19 54					20 17	21 14			21 30	21 35	
Bridgwater	d			18 19						19 19								20 29					21 47	
Highbridge & Burnham	d			18 27						19 27								20 37					21 55	
Weston-super-Mare	a			18 37						19 37								20 48				21 51	22 05	
	d			18 39				19 10		19 39				20 10				20 50				21 53	22 07	
Weston Milton	d							19 13										20 53					22 10	
Worle	d			18 45				19 18		19 45								20 57					22 14	
Yatton	d			18 51				19 23		19 51								21 03					22 20	
Nailsea & Backwell	d			18 57				19 29		19 57								21 09					22 26	
Parson Street	d							19 36										21 17					22 33	
Bedminster	d							19 38										21 19					22 36	
Bristol Temple Meads 10	a			19 09		19 22		19 43		20 09	19 54		20 26	20 30				21 24	21 47			22 12	22 42	
	d	18 54	19 00	19 21		19 30	19 41	19 45	19 54		20 00	20 21	20 30			20 43	20 54	21 29		21 54	22 06			22 54
Lawrence Hill	d							19 48																
Stapleton Road	d							19 50																
Filton Abbey Wood	d	19a01		19a28			19 48	19 56	20a01			20a27				20 48	21a01	21a36		22a01	22 14			23a01
Bristol Parkway 7	a		19 08			19 38	19 52	20 03			20 08		20 38			20 52					22 17			
	d						19 52									20 52					22 18			
Yate	d						20 01									21 04					22 28			
Cam & Dursley	d						20 14									21 18					22 43			
Gloucester 7	a						20 33									21 34					23 01			

Saturdays
30 June to 8 September

		XC	GW	GW	GW	GW	XC	GW	GW	XC		GW	GW	GW	GW	XC	GW	GW	XC	GW		GW	GW	GW	XC
		◇1		◇1		◇1	◇1			◇1					◇1	◇1			◇1				◇	◇1	◇1
Taunton	d		05 28						06 35	06 51					06 54			07 35	07 51					07 59	08 13
Bridgwater	d		05 40						06 48						07 05			07 47						08 10	
Highbridge & Burnham	d		05 48						06 55						07 12			07 55						08 17	
Weston-super-Mare	a		05 59						07 06						07 24			08 06						08 27	
	d		06 01			06 24			07 08						07 24		07 37	08 06						08 30	
Weston Milton	d		06 04						07 11								07 40	08 09							
Worle	d		06 07			06 32			07 16						07 32		07 44	08 15							
Yatton	d		06 12			06 39			07 22						07 39		07 49	08 21						08 41	
Nailsea & Backwell	d		06 18			06 45			07 28						07 46		07 55	08 27						08 47	
Parson Street	d		06 29						07 35								08 02	08 36							
Bedminster	d		06 31						07 38				←				08 04	08 38				←			
Bristol Temple Meads 10	a		06 34			06 56			07 42	07 24			07 42		07 58		08 10	08 41	08 23			08 41		08 57	08 48
	d	06 15		06 46	06 50		07 00	07 21	07 47	07 30		07 41	07 47	07 54		08 00	08 20	08 45	08 30	08 41		08 45	08 54		09 00
Lawrence Hill	d				06 53				→				07 50				08 23	→				08 48			
Stapleton Road	d				06 56								07 52				08 25					08 50			
Filton Abbey Wood	d			06 54	07a01			07a29				07 48	07 59	08a00			08a30			08 48		08 56	09a01		
Bristol Parkway 7	a	06 23		06 58			07 08			07 38		07 52	08 05			08 08			08 38	08 52		09 03			09 08
	d	06 25										07 52								08 52					
Yate	d											08 01								09 01					
Cam & Dursley	d											08 14								09 14					
Gloucester 7	a	06 54										08 32								09 33					

For connections to London Paddington please refer to Table 125

Table 134

Taunton - Gloucester

Saturdays

30 June to 8 September

Network Diagram - see first Page of Table 132

		GW	XC	GW	GW	GW		XC	GW	XC	GW	GW	XC	GW	GW	GW		XC	GW	GW	GW	GW	GW	XC	GW
			◇1 ⌶			◇		◇1 ⌶		◇1 ⌶	◇		◇1 ⌶	◇		◇1 ⊏		◇1 ⌶	◇		◇1 ⊏	◇		◇1 ⌶	
Taunton	d		08 51						09 10	09 51			10 09		10 12	10 45		10 54					11 07	11 18	
Bridgwater	d								09 22						10 24								11 19		
Highbridge & Burnham	d								09 30						10 32								11 27		
Weston-super-Mare	a								09 42				10 32		10 40								11 37		
	d	08 39			09 10				09 44			10 10	10 33		10 40					11 10	11 30		11 39		
Weston Milton	d				09 13							10 13								11 13					
Worle	d	08 45			09 18				09 49			10 18			10 46					11 18			11 45		
Yatton	d	08 51			09 23				09 55			10 23			10 52					11 23			11 51		
Nailsea & Backwell	d	08 57			09 29				10 01			10 29			10 58					11 29			11 57		
Parson Street	d				09 36							10 36								11 36					
Bedminster	d				09 38							10 38								11 38					←
Bristol Temple Meads 10	a	09 08	09 25		09 43				10 13	10 25		10 43	10 52		11 13	11 24		11 25		11 43	11 47		12 10	11 54	12 10
	d	09 21	09 30	09 41	09 45	09 54		10 00	10 21	10 30	10 41	10 45	11 00	10 54	11 21			11 30	11 41	11 45		11 54	12 21	12 00	12 21
Lawrence Hill	d				09 48							10 48								11 48			→		
Stapleton Road	d	09 25			09 50				10 25			10 50			11 25					11 50					12 25
Filton Abbey Wood	d	09a30		09 48	09 56	10a01			10a30		10 48	10 56		11a01	11a30				11 48	11 56		12a01			12a29
Bristol Parkway 7	a		09 38	09 52	10 03			10 08		10 38	10 52	11 03	11 08					11 38	11 52	12 03				12 08	
	d			09 52							10 52								11 52						
Yate	d			10 01							11 01								12 01						
Cam & Dursley	d			10 14							11 14								12 14						
Gloucester 7	a			10 33							11 32								12 33						

		XC		GW	GW	GW	XC	GW	GW	XC	GW	GW		GW	XC	GW	XC	GW	GW	GW	XC	GW		GW	XC
		◇1 ⌶		◇		◇	◇1 ⌶		◇1 ⊏	◇1 ⌶	◇			◇	◇1 ⌶		◇1 ⌶	◇		◇	◇1 ⌶			◇1 ⊏	◇1 ⌶
Taunton	d	11 51						12 07		12 51						13 07	13 53					14 07			14 52
Bridgwater	d							12 19								13 19						14 19			
Highbridge & Burnham	d							12 27								13 27						14 27			
Weston-super-Mare	a							12 37								13 37						14 37			
	d				12 10			12 39	13 01			13 10				13 39			14 10			14 39		15 01	
Weston Milton	d				12 13							13 13							14 13						
Worle	d				12 18			12 45				13 18				13 45			14 18			14 45			
Yatton	d				12 23			12 51				13 23				13 51			14 23			14 51			
Nailsea & Backwell	d				12 29			12 57				13 29				13 57			14 29			14 57			
Parson Street	d				12 36							13 36							14 36						
Bedminster	d				12 38							13 38							14 38						
Bristol Temple Meads 10	a	12 24			12 43			13 09	13 19	13 23		13 43				14 11	14 26		14 43			15 10		15 19	15 24
	d	12 30		12 41	12 45	12 54	13 00	13 21		13 30	13 41	13 45		13 54	14 00	14 21	14 30	14 41	14 45	14 54	15 00	15 21			15 30
Lawrence Hill	d				12 48							13 48							14 48						
Stapleton Road	d				12 50			13 25				13 50				14 25			14 50			15 25			
Filton Abbey Wood	d			12 48	12 56	13a01		13a30			13 48	13 56		14a01		14a30		14 48	14 56	15a01		15a30			
Bristol Parkway 7	a	12 38		12 52	13 03		13 08			13 38	13 52	14 03			14 08		14 38	14 52	15 03		15 08				15 38
	d			12 52							13 52							14 52							
Yate	d			13 01							14 01							15 01							
Cam & Dursley	d			13 14							14 14							15 14							
Gloucester 7	a			13 34							14 33							15 32							

		GW	GW	XC	GW	GW	XC	GW		GW	GW	XC	GW	GW	XC	GW	GW	GW		XC	GW	GW	XC	GW	GW
		◇		◇1 ⌶	◇		◇1 ⌶				◇	◇1 ⌶		◇1 ⊏	◇1 ⌶			◇		◇1 ⌶		◇1 ⊏	◇1 ⌶	◇	
Taunton	d			15 04		15 07	15 51						16 07		16 51						17 07		17 54		
Bridgwater	d					15 19							16 19								17 17				
Highbridge & Burnham	d					15 27							16 27								17 25				
Weston-super-Mare	a			15 23		15 37							16 37								17 37				
	d		15 10	15 30		15 39				16 10			16 39	17 01			17 10				17 40	18 01			18 10
Weston Milton	d		15 13							16 13							17 13								18 13
Worle	d		15 18			15 45				16 18			16 45				17 18				17 45				18 18
Yatton	d		15 23			15 51				16 23			16 51				17 23				17 51				18 23
Nailsea & Backwell	d		15 29			15 57				16 29			16 57				17 29				17 57				18 29
Parson Street	d		15 36							16 36			17 04				17 36								18 36
Bedminster	d		15 38							16 38							17 38								18 38
Bristol Temple Meads 10	a		15 43	15 49		16 09	16 24			16 43			17 11	17 19	17 25		17 43				18 11	18 18	18 24		18 43
	d	15 41	15 45	16 00	15 54	16 21	16 30	16 41		16 45	16 54	17 00	17 21		17 30	17 41	17 45	17 54		18 00	18 21		18 30	18 41	18 45
Lawrence Hill	d		15 48							16 48							17 48								18 48
Stapleton Road	d		15 50			16 25				16 50			17 25				17 50				18 25				18 50
Filton Abbey Wood	d	15 48	15 56		16a01	16a30		16 48		16 56	17a01		17a30			17 48	17 56	18a01			18a30			18 48	18 56
Bristol Parkway 7	a	15 52	16 03	16 08			16 38	16 52		17 03		17 08			17 38	17 52	18 03			18 08			18 38	18 52	19 03
	d	15 52						16 52								17 52								18 52	
Yate	d	16 01						17 01								18 01								19 01	
Cam & Dursley	d	16 14						17 14								18 14								19 14	
Gloucester 7	a	16 33						17 33								18 33								19 33	

For connections to London Paddington please refer to Table 125

Table 134

Taunton - Gloucester

Saturdays

30 June to 8 September

Network Diagram - see first Page of Table 132

		GW	XC	GW		XC	GW	GW	GW	GW	XC	XC	XC	GW		GW	GW	GW	GW	GW	GW	GW	GW	GW	
		■	◇1 ⌶			◇1 ⌶			◇		◇1	◇1 ⌶	◇1 ⌶	◇1 ⊏			◇		◇1 ⊏	◇		◇1 ⊏		◇	
Taunton	d			18 07		18 51				19 07	19 18		19 54					20 17	21 14			21 30	21 35		
Bridgwater	d			18 19						19 19								20 29					21 47		
Highbridge & Burnham	d			18 27						19 27								20 37					21 55		
Weston-super-Mare	a			18 37						19 37								20 48				21 51	22 05		
	d			18 39				19 10		19 39				20 10				20 50				21 53	22 07		
Weston Milton	d							19 13										20 53					22 10		
Worle	d			18 45				19 18		19 45								20 57					22 14		
Yatton	d			18 51				19 23		19 51								21 03					22 20		
Nailsea & Backwell	d			18 57				19 29		19 57								21 09					22 26		
Parson Street	d							19 36										21 17					22 33		
Bedminster	d							19 38										21 19					22 36		
Bristol Temple Meads 10	a			19 09		19 22		19 43		20 09	19 54		20 26	20 30				21 24	21 47			22 12	22 42		
	d	18 54	19 00	19 21		19 30	19 41	19 45	19 54		20 00	20 21	20 30			20 43	20 54	21 29		21 54	22 06			22 54	
Lawrence Hill	d							19 48																	
Stapleton Road	d							19 50																	
Filton Abbey Wood	d	19a01		19a28			19 48	19 56	20a01			20a27				20 48	21a01	21a36		22a01	22 14			23a01	
Bristol Parkway 7	a		19 08			19 38	19 52	20 03			20 08		20 38			20 52					22 17				
	d						19 52									20 52					22 18				
Yate	d						20 01									21 04					22 28				
Cam & Dursley	d						20 14									21 18					22 43				
Gloucester 7	a						20 33									21 34					23 01				

Saturdays

15 September to 20 October

		XC	GW	GW	GW	GW	XC	GW	GW	XC		GW	GW	GW	GW	XC	GW	GW	XC	GW		GW	GW	GW	XC
		◇1 ⌶		◇1		◇1 ⊏	◇1 ⌶			◇1 ⌶					◇1 ⊏	◇1 ⌶			◇1 ⌶				◇	◇1 ⊏	◇1 ⌶
Taunton	d		05 28						06 35	06 51					06 54			07 35	07 51					07 59	08 13
Bridgwater	d		05 40						06 48						07 05			07 47						08 10	
Highbridge & Burnham	d		05 48						06 55						07 12			07 55						08 17	
Weston-super-Mare	a		05 59						07 06						07 24			08 06						08 27	
	d		06 01			06 24			07 08						07 24		07 37	08 06						08 30	
Weston Milton	d		06 04						07 11								07 40	08 09							
Worle	d		06 07			06 32			07 16						07 32		07 44	08 15							
Yatton	d		06 12			06 39			07 22						07 39		07 49	08 21						08 41	
Nailsea & Backwell	d		06 18			06 45			07 28						07 46		07 55	08 27						08 47	
Parson Street	d		06 29						07 35								08 02	08 36							
Bedminster	d		06 31						07 38				←				08 04	08 38				←			
Bristol Temple Meads 10	a		06 34			06 56			07 42	07 24			07 42		07 58		08 10	08 41	08 23			08 41		08 57	08 48
	d	06 15		06 46	06 50		07 00	07 21	07 47	07 30		07 41	07 47	07 54		08 00	08 20	08 45	08 30	08 41		08 45	08 54		09 00
Lawrence Hill	d				06 53				→				07 50				08 23	→				08 48			
Stapleton Road	d				06 56								07 52				08 25					08 50			
Filton Abbey Wood	d			06 54	07a01			07a29				07 48	07 59	08a00			08a30			08 48		08 56	09a01		
Bristol Parkway 7	a	06 23		06 58			07 08			07 38		07 52	08 05			08 08			08 38	08 52		09 03			09 08
	d	06 25										07 52								08 52					
Yate	d											08 01								09 01					
Cam & Dursley	d											08 14								09 14					
Gloucester 7	a	06 54										08 32								09 33					

		GW	XC	GW	GW	GW		XC	GW	XC	GW	GW	GW	XC	GW	GW		XC	GW	GW	GW	GW	XC	GW	XC
			◇1 ⌶			◇		◇1 ⌶		◇1 ⌶	◇		◇	◇1 ⌶		◇1 ⊏		◇1 ⌶	◇		◇		◇1 ⌶		◇1 ⌶
Taunton	d		08 51						09 10	09 51					10 12	10 45		10 51				11 07	11 18		11 51
Bridgwater	d								09 22						10 24							11 19			
Highbridge & Burnham	d								09 30						10 32							11 27			
Weston-super-Mare	a								09 42						10 40							11 37			
	d	08 39			09 10				09 44			10 10			10 40					11 10		11 39			
Weston Milton	d				09 13							10 13								11 13					
Worle	d	08 45			09 18				09 49			10 18			10 46					11 18		11 45			
Yatton	d	08 51			09 23				09 55			10 23			10 52					11 23		11 51			
Nailsea & Backwell	d	08 57			09 29				10 01			10 29			10 58					11 29		11 57			
Parson Street	d				09 36							10 36								11 36					
Bedminster	d				09 38							10 38								11 38				←	
Bristol Temple Meads 10	a	09 08	09 25		09 43				10 13	10 25		10 43			11 13	11 24		11 25		11 43		12 10	11 54	12 10	12 24
	d	09 21	09 30	09 41	09 45	09 54		10 00	10 21	10 30	10 41	10 45	10 54	11 00	11 21			11 30	11 41	11 45	11 54	12 21	12 00	12 21	12 30
Lawrence Hill	d				09 48							10 48								11 48		→			
Stapleton Road	d	09 25			09 50				10 25			10 50			11 25					11 50				12 25	
Filton Abbey Wood	d	09a30		09 48	09 56	10a01			10a30		10 48	10 56	11a01		11a30				11 48	11 56	12a01			12a29	
Bristol Parkway 7	a		09 38	09 52	10 03			10 08		10 38	10 52	11 03		11 08				11 38	11 52	12 03			12 08		12 38
	d			09 52							10 52								11 52						
Yate	d			10 01							11 01								12 01						
Cam & Dursley	d			10 14							11 14								12 14						
Gloucester 7	a			10 33							11 32								12 33						

For connections to London Paddington please refer to Table 125

Table 134

Taunton - Gloucester

Saturdays

15 September to 20 October

Network Diagram - see first Page of Table 132

		GW ◇	GW	GW ◇	XC ◇1	GW	XC ◇1	GW ◇	GW	GW ◇	GW	XC ◇1	GW	XC ◇1	GW ◇	GW	GW ◇	XC ◇1	GW	XC ◇1	GW ◇	GW
Taunton	d					12 07	12 51				13 07	13 16		13 54					14 07	14 52		
Bridgwater	d					12 19					13 19								14 19			
Highbridge & Burnham	d					12 27					13 27								14 27			
Weston-super-Mare	a					12 37					13 37								14 37			
	d		12 10			12 39			13 10		13 39					14 10			14 39			15 10
Weston Milton	d		12 13						13 13							14 13						15 13
Worle	d		12 18			12 45			13 18		13 45					14 18			14 45			15 18
Yatton	d		12 23			12 51			13 23		13 51					14 23			14 51			15 23
Nailsea & Backwell	d		12 29			12 57			13 29		13 57					14 29			14 57			15 29
Parson Street	d		12 36						13 36							14 36						15 36
Bedminster	d		12 38						13 38				←			14 38						15 38
Bristol Temple Meads 10	a		12 43			13 09	13 23		13 43		14 11	13 55	14 11	14 26		14 43			15 10	15 24		15 43
	d	12 41	12 45	12 54	13 00	13 21	13 30	13 41	13 45	13 54	14 21	14 00	14 21	14 30	14 41	14 45	14 54	15 00	15 21	15 30	15 41	15 45
Lawrence Hill	d		12 48						13 48		→					14 48						15 48
Stapleton Road	d		12 50			13 25			13 50				14 25			14 50			15 25			15 50
Filton Abbey Wood	d	12 48	12 56	13a01		13a30		13 48	13 56	14a01			14a30		14 48	14 56	15a01		15a30		15 48	15 56
Bristol Parkway 7	a	12 52	13 03		13 08		13 38	13 52	14 03			14 08		14 38	14 52	15 03		15 08		15 38	15 52	16 03
	d	12 52						13 52							14 52						15 52	
Yate	d	13 01						14 01							15 01						16 01	
Cam & Dursley	d	13 14						14 14							15 14						16 14	
Gloucester 7	a	13 34						14 33							15 32						16 33	

		XC ◇1	GW ◇	GW	XC ◇1	GW	GW	GW ◇	XC ◇1	GW	XC ◇1	GW ◇	GW	GW ◇	GW	XC ◇1	GW	XC ◇1	GW	GW	GW	XC ◇1	GW
Taunton	d	15 04		15 07	15 51					16 07	16 51				17 07	17 21		17 51					18 07
Bridgwater	d			15 19						16 19					17 17								18 19
Highbridge & Burnham	d			15 27						16 27					17 25								18 27
Weston-super-Mare	a	15 23		15 37						16 37					17 37								18 37
	d	15 30		15 39			16 10			16 39			17 10		17 40					18 10			18 39
Weston Milton	d						16 13						17 13							18 13			
Worle	d			15 45			16 18			16 45			17 18		17 45					18 18			18 45
Yatton	d			15 51			16 23			16 51			17 23		17 51					18 23			18 51
Nailsea & Backwell	d			15 57			16 29			16 57			17 29		17 57					18 29			18 57
Parson Street	d						16 36			17 04			17 36							18 36			
Bedminster	d						16 38						17 38				←			18 38			
Bristol Temple Meads 10	a	15 49		16 09	16 24		16 43			17 11	17 25		17 43		18 11	17 53	18 11	18 25		18 43			19 09
	d	16 00	15 54	16 21	16 30	16 41	16 45	16 54	17 00	17 21	17 30	17 41	17 45	17 54	18 21	18 00	18 21	18 30	18 41	18 45	18 54	19 00	19 21
Lawrence Hill	d						16 48						17 48		→					18 48			
Stapleton Road	d			16 25			16 50			17 25			17 50				18 25			18 50			
Filton Abbey Wood	d		16a01	16a30		16 48	16 56	17a01		17a30		17 48	17 56	18a01			18a30		18 48	18 56	19a01		19a28
Bristol Parkway 7	a	16 08			16 38	16 52	17 03		17 08		17 38	17 52	18 03			18 08		18 38	18 52	19 03		19 08	
	d					16 52						17 52							18 52				
Yate	d					17 01						18 01							19 01				
Cam & Dursley	d					17 14						18 14							19 14				
Gloucester 7	a					17 33						18 33							19 33				

		XC ◇1	GW	GW	GW ◇	XC ◇1	GW	XC ◇1	XC ◇1	GW ◇1	GW	GW ◇	GW	GW ◇1	GW ◇	GW	GW ◇1	GW	GW ◇
Taunton	d	18 54					19 07		19 51				20 17	21 14			21 30	21 35	
Bridgwater	d						19 19						20 29					21 47	
Highbridge & Burnham	d						19 27						20 37					21 55	
Weston-super-Mare	a						19 37						20 48				21 51	22 05	
	d			19 10			19 39			20 10			20 50				21 53	22 07	
Weston Milton	d			19 13									20 53					22 10	
Worle	d			19 18			19 45						20 57					22 14	
Yatton	d			19 23			19 51						21 03					22 20	
Nailsea & Backwell	d			19 29			19 57						21 09					22 26	
Parson Street	d			19 36									21 17					22 33	
Bedminster	d			19 38									21 19					22 36	
Bristol Temple Meads 10	a	19 26		19 43			20 09		20 25	20 30			21 24	21 47			22 12	22 42	
	d	19 30	19 41	19 45	19 54	20 00		20 21	20 30		20 43	20 54	21 29		21 54	22 06			22 54
Lawrence Hill	d			19 48															
Stapleton Road	d			19 50															
Filton Abbey Wood	d		19 48	19 56	20a01			20a27			20 48	21a01	21a36		22a01	22 14			23a01
Bristol Parkway 7	a	19 38	19 52	20 03		20 08			20 38		20 52					22 17			
	d		19 52								20 52					22 18			
Yate	d		20 01								21 04					22 28			
Cam & Dursley	d		20 14								21 18					22 43			
Gloucester 7	a		20 33								21 34					23 01			

For connections to London Paddington please refer to Table 125

Table 134

Taunton - Gloucester

Saturdays

from 27 October

Network Diagram - see first Page of Table 132

		XC ◇1	GW	GW ◇1	GW	GW ◇1	XC ◇1	GW	GW	XC ◇1	GW	GW	GW	GW ◇1	XC ◇1	GW	GW	XC ◇1	GW	GW	GW ◇	GW ◇1	XC ◇1
Taunton	d		05 28						06 35	06 51				06 54			07 35	07 51				07 59	08 13
Bridgwater	d		05 40						06 48					07 05			07 47					08 10	
Highbridge & Burnham	d		05 48						06 55					07 12			07 55					08 17	
Weston-super-Mare	a		05 59						07 06					07 24			08 06					08 27	
	d		06 01			06 24			07 08					07 24		07 37	08 06					08 30	
Weston Milton	d		06 04						07 11							07 40	08 09						
Worle	d		06 07			06 32			07 16					07 32		07 44	08 15						
Yatton	d		06 12			06 39			07 22					07 39		07 49	08 21					08 41	
Nailsea & Backwell	d		06 18			06 45			07 28					07 46		07 55	08 27					08 47	
Parson Street	d		06 29						07 35							08 02	08 36						
Bedminster	d		06 31						07 38			←				08 04	08 38			←			
Bristol Temple Meads 10	a		06 34			06 56			07 42	07 24		07 42		07 58		08 10	08 41	08 23		08 41		08 57	08 48
	d	06 15		06 46	06 50		07 00	07 21	07 47	07 30	07 41	07 47	07 54		08 00	08 20	08 45	08 30	08 41	08 45	08 54		09 00
Lawrence Hill	d				06 53				→			07 50				08 23	→			08 48			
Stapleton Road	d				06 56							07 52				08 25				08 50			
Filton Abbey Wood	d			06 54	07a01			07a29			07 48	07 59	08a00			08a30			08 48	08 56	09a01		
Bristol Parkway 7	a	06 23		06 58			07 08			07 38	07 52	08 05			08 08			08 38	08 52	09 03			09 08
	d	06 25									07 52								08 52				
Yate	d										08 01								09 01				
Cam & Dursley	d										08 14								09 14				
Gloucester 7	a	06 54									08 32								09 33				

		GW	XC ◇1	GW	GW	GW ◇	XC ◇1	GW	XC ◇1	GW ◇	GW	GW ◇	XC ◇1	GW	GW ◇1	XC ◇1	GW ◇	GW	GW ◇	GW	XC ◇1	GW	XC ◇1
Taunton	d		08 51					09 10	09 51					10 12	10 45	10 51				11 07	11 18		11 51
Bridgwater	d							09 22						10 24						11 19			
Highbridge & Burnham	d							09 30						10 32						11 27			
Weston-super-Mare	a							09 42						10 40						11 37			
	d	08 39			09 10			09 44			10 10			10 40				11 10		11 39			
Weston Milton	d				09 13						10 13							11 13					
Worle	d	08 45			09 18			09 49			10 18			10 46				11 18		11 45			
Yatton	d	08 51			09 23			09 55			10 23			10 52				11 23		11 51			
Nailsea & Backwell	d	08 57			09 29			10 01			10 29			10 58				11 29		11 57			
Parson Street	d				09 36						10 36							11 36					
Bedminster	d				09 38						10 38							11 38				←	
Bristol Temple Meads 10	a	09 08	09 25		09 43			10 13	10 25		10 43			11 13	11 24	11 25		11 43		12 10	11 54	12 10	12 24
	d	09 21	09 30	09 41	09 45	09 54	10 00	10 21	10 30	10 41	10 45	10 54	11 00	11 21		11 30	11 41	11 45	11 54	12 21	12 00	12 21	12 30
Lawrence Hill	d				09 48						10 48							11 48		→			
Stapleton Road	d	09 25			09 50			10 25			10 50			11 25				11 50				12 25	
Filton Abbey Wood	d	09a30		09 48	09 56	10a01		10a30		10 48	10 56	11a01		11a30			11 48	11 56	12a01			12a29	
Bristol Parkway 7	a		09 38	09 52	10 03		10 08		10 38	10 52	11 03		11 08			11 38	11 52	12 03			12 08		12 38
	d			09 52						10 52							11 52						
Yate	d			10 01						11 01							12 01						
Cam & Dursley	d			10 14						11 14							12 14						
Gloucester 7	a			10 33						11 32							12 33						

		GW ◇	GW	GW ◇	XC ◇1	GW	XC ◇1	GW ◇	GW	GW ◇	GW	XC ◇1	GW	XC ◇1	GW ◇	GW	GW ◇	XC ◇1	GW	XC ◇1	GW ◇	GW
Taunton	d					12 07	12 51				13 07	13 16		13 54					14 07	14 52		
Bridgwater	d					12 19					13 19								14 19			
Highbridge & Burnham	d					12 27					13 27								14 27			
Weston-super-Mare	a					12 37					13 37								14 37			
	d		12 10			12 39			13 10		13 39					14 10			14 39			15 10
Weston Milton	d		12 13						13 13							14 13						15 13
Worle	d		12 18			12 45			13 18		13 45					14 18			14 45			15 18
Yatton	d		12 23			12 51			13 23		13 51					14 23			14 51			15 23
Nailsea & Backwell	d		12 29			12 57			13 29		13 57					14 29			14 57			15 29
Parson Street	d		12 36						13 36							14 36						15 36
Bedminster	d		12 38						13 38				←			14 38						15 38
Bristol Temple Meads 10	a		12 43			13 09	13 23		13 43		14 11	13 55	14 11	14 26		14 43			15 10	15 24		15 43
	d	12 41	12 45	12 54	13 00	13 21	13 30	13 41	13 45	13 54	14 21	14 00	14 21	14 30	14 41	14 45	14 54	15 00	15 21	15 30	15 41	15 45
Lawrence Hill	d		12 48						13 48		→					14 48						15 48
Stapleton Road	d		12 50			13 25			13 50				14 25			14 50			15 25			15 50
Filton Abbey Wood	d	12 48	12 56	13a01		13a30		13 48	13 56	14a01			14a30		14 48	14 56	15a01		15a30		15 48	15 56
Bristol Parkway 7	a	12 52	13 03		13 08		13 38	13 52	14 03			14 08		14 38	14 52	15 03		15 08		15 38	15 52	16 03
	d	12 52						13 52							14 52						15 52	
Yate	d	13 01						14 01							15 01						16 01	
Cam & Dursley	d	13 14						14 14							15 14						16 14	
Gloucester 7	a	13 34						14 33							15 32						16 33	

For connections to London Paddington please refer to Table 125

Table 134

Taunton - Gloucester

Saturdays from 27 October

Network Diagram - see first Page of Table 132

		XC	GW	GW	XC	GW	GW	GW	XC	GW	XC	GW	GW	GW	GW	XC	GW	XC	GW	GW	GW	XC	GW
		◇1 ⊥	◇		◇1 ⊥			◇	◇1 ⊥		◇1 ⊥	◇		◇		◇1 ⊥		◇1 ⊥			■	◇1 ⊥	
Taunton	d	15 04		15 07	15 51					16 07	16 51				17 07	17 21		17 51					18 07
Bridgwater	d			15 19						16 19					17 17								18 19
Highbridge & Burnham	d			15 27						16 27					17 25								18 27
Weston-super-Mare	a	15 23		15 37						16 37					17 37								18 37
	d	15 30		15 39			16 10			16 39			17 10		17 40					18 10			18 39
Weston Milton	d						16 13						17 13							18 13			
Worle	d			15 45			16 18			16 45			17 18		17 45					18 18			18 45
Yatton	d			15 51			16 23			16 51			17 23		17 51					18 23			18 51
Nailsea & Backwell	d			15 57			16 29			16 57			17 29		17 57					18 29			18 57
Parson Street	d						16 36			17 04			17 36							18 36			
Bedminster	d						16 38						17 38				←			18 38			
Bristol Temple Meads 10	a	15 49		16 09	16 24		16 43			17 11	17 25		17 43		18 11	17 53	18 11	18 25		18 43			19 09
	d	16 00	15 54	16 21	16 30	16 41	16 45	16 54	17 00	17 21	17 30	17 41	17 45	17 54	18 21	18 00	18 21	18 30	18 41	18 45	18 54	19 00	19 21
Lawrence Hill	d						16 48						17 48		→					18 48			
Stapleton Road	d			16 25			16 50			17 25			17 50				18 25			18 50			
Filton Abbey Wood	d		16a01	16a30		16 48	16 56	17a01		17a30		17 48	17 56	18a01			18a30		18 48	18 56	19a01		19a28
Bristol Parkway 7	a	16 08			16 38	16 52	17 03		17 08		17 38	17 52	18 03			18 08		18 38	18 52	19 03		19 08	
	d					16 52						17 52							18 52				
Yate	d					17 01						18 01							19 01				
Cam & Dursley	d					17 14						18 14							19 14				
Gloucester 7	a					17 33						18 33							19 33				

		XC	GW	GW	GW	XC	GW	XC	XC	GW	GW	GW	GW	GW	GW	GW	GW	GW	GW
		◇1 ⊥			◇	◇1		◇1 ⊥	◇1 ⊥	◇1 ⊏		◇		◇1 ⊏	◇		◇1 ⊏		◇
Taunton	d	18 54					19 07		19 51				20 17	21 14			21 30	21 35	
Bridgwater	d						19 19						20 29					21 47	
Highbridge & Burnham	d						19 27						20 37					21 55	
Weston-super-Mare	a						19 37						20 48				21 51	22 05	
	d			19 10			19 39			20 10			20 50				21 53	22 07	
Weston Milton	d			19 13									20 53					22 10	
Worle	d			19 18			19 45						20 57					22 14	
Yatton	d			19 23			19 51						21 03					22 20	
Nailsea & Backwell	d			19 29			19 57						21 09					22 26	
Parson Street	d			19 36									21 17					22 33	
Bedminster	d			19 38									21 19					22 36	
Bristol Temple Meads 10	a	19 26		19 43			20 09		20 25	20 30			21 24	21 47			22 12	22 42	
	d	19 30	19 41	19 45	19 54	20 00		20 21	20 30		20 43	20 54	21 29		21 54	22 06			22 54
Lawrence Hill	d			19 48															
Stapleton Road	d			19 50															
Filton Abbey Wood	d		19 48	19 56	20a01			20a27			20 48	21a01	21a36		22a01	22 14			23a01
Bristol Parkway 7	a	19 38	19 52	20 03		20 08			20 38		20 52					22 17			
	d		19 52								20 52					22 18			
Yate	d		20 01								21 04					22 28			
Cam & Dursley	d		20 14								21 18					22 43			
Gloucester 7	a		20 33								21 34					23 01			

Sundays until 24 June

		GW	XC	GW	GW	GW	XC	GW	XC	GW	GW	GW	XC	GW	XC	GW	XC	GW	GW	XC	XC	GW	GW
		◇1 ⊏	◇1 ⊥		◇	◇1 ⊏	◇1 ⊥	◇	◇1 ⊥	■		◇1 ⊏	◇1 ⊥		◇1 ⊥	◇1 ⊏	◇1 ⊥	◇		◇1 ⊥	◇1 ⊥		◇
Taunton	d				08 35			10 11	10 51		11 36	11 48	11 53		12 00		12 51		13 11	13 25	13 51		
Bridgwater	d				08 47			10 23			11 48								13 23				
Highbridge & Burnham	d				08 55			10 31			11 55								13 30				
Weston-super-Mare	a				09 06			10 41			12 05				12 20				13 41				
	d	08 11			09 08	09 56		10 43			12 07				12 21	12 51			13 43				
Weston Milton	d				09 11						12 10								13 46				
Worle	d	08 18			09 15	10 03		10 49			12 18					12 58			13 50				
Yatton	d	08 25			09 21	10 10		10 55			12 23					13 05			13 56				
Nailsea & Backwell	d	08 31			09 27	10 16		11 01			12 29					13 12			14 02				
Parson Street	d																						
Bedminster	d										12 40												
Bristol Temple Meads 10	a	08 42			09 38	10 27		11 13	11 27		12 43	12 23	12 27		12 45	13 20	13 26		14 14	13 57	14 26		
	d		09 15	09 41	09 48		10 30	11 23	11 30	11 48			12 30	12 41	13 00		13 30	13 48		14 00	14 30	14 41	14 50
Lawrence Hill	d							11 26															
Stapleton Road	d							11a28															
Filton Abbey Wood	d			09 48	09a55					11a55				12 48				13a55				14 48	14a57
Bristol Parkway 7	a		09 23	09 53			10 38		11 38				12 38	12 52	13 08		13 38			14 08	14 38	14 52	
	d		09 25	09 53										12 52								14 53	
Yate	d			10 03										13 02								15 03	
Cam & Dursley	d			10 17										13 16								15 17	
Gloucester 7	a		09 54	10 32										13 31								15 35	

For connections to London Paddington please refer to Table 125

Table 134

Taunton - Gloucester

Sundays until 24 June

Network Diagram - see first Page of Table 132

		XC	GW	XC	GW	XC	GW	XC	GW	GW	GW	XC	GW	XC	GW	GW	GW	XC	GW	GW	XC	GW	GW
		◇1 ⊥	◇1 ⊏	◇1 ⊥	◇	◇1 ⊥		◇1 ⊥		◇		◇1 ⊥	◇1 ⊏	◇1 ⊥	◇	■	◇1 ⊏	◇1 ⊥		◇1 ⊏	◇1 ⊥		◇
Taunton	d			14 54			15 18	15 54				16 01	16 40	16 53			16 59		17 19	17 48	17 53		
Bridgwater	d						15 30										17 10		17 30				
Highbridge & Burnham	d						15 37										17 18		17 37				
Weston-super-Mare	a						15 47					16 20	17 01				17 28		17 48				
	d		14 51				15 49				16 14	16 30	17 02		17 07		17 29		17 50				
Weston Milton	d						15 52				16 17				17 10								
Worle	d		14 58				15 56				16 22				17 17				17 56				
Yatton	d		15 05				16 02				16 28				17 23		17 40		18 02				
Nailsea & Backwell	d		15 11				16 08				16 34				17 29		17 46		18 08				
Parson Street	d										16 41												
Bedminster	d										16 44				17 39								
Bristol Temple Meads 10	a		15 20	15 27			16 20	16 27			16 49	16 54	17 20	17 26	17 42		17 58		18 20	18 25	18 27		
	d	15 00		15 30	15 48	16 00		16 30	16 41	16 48	16 53	17 00		17 30		17 48		18 00			18 30	18 41	18 48
Lawrence Hill	d										16 56												
Stapleton Road	d										16a58												
Filton Abbey Wood	d				15a55				16 48	16a55						17a55						18 48	18a55
Bristol Parkway 7	a	15 08		15 38		16 08		16 38	16 52			17 08		17 38				18 08			18 38	18 52	
	d								16 52													18 52	
Yate	d								17 02													19 02	
Cam & Dursley	d								17 16													19 16	
Gloucester 7	a								17 32													19 33	

		GW	XC	GW	XC	GW	GW	XC	XC	GW	GW	GW	GW	GW	GW	XC	GW	GW	GW
			◇1 ⊥	◇	◇1 ⊥	◇	◇1 ⊏	◇1 ⊥	◇1 ⊥		◇	◇1 ⊏		◇	◇1 ⊏	◇1		◇	
Taunton	d			18 22	18 52		18 57	19 25	19 54				20 20		21 23		21 35		
Bridgwater	d			18 34			19 07						20 32				21 48		
Highbridge & Burnham	d			18 41			19 14						20 40				21 55		
Weston-super-Mare	a			18 52			19 25						20 51				22 05		
	d	18 16		19 12			19 27					20 26	20 55				22 07		23 47
Weston Milton	d	18 19											20 58				22 10		23 50
Worle	d	18 24		19 18								20 33	21 03						23 54
Yatton	d	18 30		19 23			19 36					20 39	21 09				22 18		23 59
Nailsea & Backwell	d	18 36		19 29			19 42					20 46	21 15				22 24		00 06
Parson Street	d	18 43																	
Bedminster	d	18 46											21 26				22 34		00 15
Bristol Temple Meads 10	a	18 50		19 41	19 26		19 54	19 57	20 27			20 57	21 31		22 00		22 38		00 19
	d	18 53	19 00		19 30	19 48		20 00	20 30	20 41	20 48			21 48		22 10		22 48	
Lawrence Hill	d	18 56																	
Stapleton Road	d	18a58																	
Filton Abbey Wood	d					19a55				20 48	20a55			21a55				22a55	
Bristol Parkway 7	a		19 08		19 38			20 08	20 38	20 52						22 18			
	d									20 52									
Yate	d									21 02									
Cam & Dursley	d									21 16									
Gloucester 7	a									21 33									

Sundays 1 July to 9 September

		GW	XC	GW	GW	GW	XC	GW	XC	GW	GW	GW	XC	GW	XC	GW	XC	GW	GW	XC	XC	GW	GW
		◇1 ⊏	◇1 ⊥		◇	◇1 ⊏	◇1 ⊥	◇	◇1 ⊥	■		◇1 ⊏	◇1 ⊥		◇1 ⊥	◇1 ⊏	◇1 ⊥	◇		◇1 ⊥	◇1 ⊥		◇
Taunton	d				08 35			10 11	10 51		11 36	11 48	11 53		12 00		12 51		13 11	13 25	13 51		
Bridgwater	d				08 47			10 23			11 48								13 23				
Highbridge & Burnham	d				08 55			10 31			11 55								13 30				
Weston-super-Mare	a				09 06			10 41			12 05				12 20				13 41				
	d	08 11			09 08	09 56		10 43			12 07				12 21	12 51			13 43				
Weston Milton	d				09 11						12 10								13 46				
Worle	d	08 18			09 15	10 03		10 49			12 18					12 58			13 50				
Yatton	d	08 25			09 21	10 10		10 55			12 23					13 05			13 56				
Nailsea & Backwell	d	08 31			09 27	10 16		11 01			12 29					13 12			14 02				
Parson Street	d																						
Bedminster	d										12 40												
Bristol Temple Meads 10	a	08 42			09 38	10 27		11 13	11 27		12 43	12 23	12 27		12 45	13 20	13 26		14 14	13 57	14 26		
	d		09 15	09 41	09 48		10 30	11 23	11 30	11 48			12 30	12 41	13 00		13 30	13 48		14 00	14 30	14 41	14 48
Lawrence Hill	d							11 26															
Stapleton Road	d							11a28															
Filton Abbey Wood	d			09 48	09a55					11a55				12 48				13a55				14 48	14a55
Bristol Parkway 7	a		09 23	09 53			10 38		11 38				12 38	12 52	13 08		13 38			14 08	14 38	14 52	
	d		09 25	09 53										12 52								14 53	
Yate	d			10 03										13 02								15 03	
Cam & Dursley	d			10 17										13 16								15 17	
Gloucester 7	a		09 54	10 32										13 31								15 35	

For connections to London Paddington please refer to Table 125

Table 134

Taunton - Gloucester

Sundays

1 July to 9 September

Network Diagram - see first Page of Table 132

		XC	GW	XC	GW	GW	XC	GW	GW	GW	XC	GW	XC	GW	GW	GW	XC	GW	GW	XC	GW	GW	GW
		◇1 ⊼	◇1 ⊡	◇1 ⊼	◇		◇1 ⊼		◇		◇1 ⊼	◇1 ⊡	◇1 ⊼	◇	■	◇1 ⊡	◇1 ⊼		◇1 ⊡	◇1 ⊼		◇	
Taunton	d			14 54		15 18	15 54				16 01	16 40	16 53			16 59		17 19	17 48	17 53			
Bridgwater	d					15 30										17 10		17 30					
Highbridge & Burnham	d					15 37										17 18		17 37					
Weston-super-Mare	a					15 47					16 20	17 01				17 28		17 48					
	d		14 51			15 49				16 14	16 30	17 02		17 07		17 29		17 50					18 16
Weston Milton	d					15 52				16 17				17 10									18 19
Worle	d		14 58			15 56				16 22				17 17				17 56					18 24
Yatton	d		15 05			16 02				16 28				17 23		17 40		18 02					18 30
Nailsea & Backwell	d		15 11			16 08				16 34				17 29		17 46		18 08					18 36
Parson Street	d									16 41													18 43
Bedminster	d									16 44				17 39									18 46
Bristol Temple Meads 10	a		15 20	15 27		16 20	16 27			16 49	16 52	17 20	17 26	17 42		17 58		18 20	18 25	18 27			18 50
	d	15 00		15 30	15 48		16 30	16 41	16 48	16 53	17 00		17 30		17 48		18 00			18 30	18 41	18 48	18 53
Lawrence Hill	d									16 56													18 56
Stapleton Road	d									16a58													18a58
Filton Abbey Wood	d				15a55			16 48	16a55						17a55						18 48	18a55	
Bristol Parkway 7	a	15 08		15 38			16 38	16 52			17 08		17 38				18 08			18 38	18 52		
	d							16 52													18 52		
Yate	d							17 02													19 02		
Cam & Dursley	d							17 16													19 16		
Gloucester 7	a							17 32													19 33		

		XC	GW	XC	GW	GW	XC	XC	GW	GW	GW	GW	GW	GW	XC	GW	GW	GW
		◇1 ⊼	◇	◇1 ⊼	◇	◇1 ⊡	◇1 ⊼	◇1 ⊼		◇	◇1 ⊡		◇	◇1 ⊡	◇1		◇	
Taunton	d		18 22	18 52		18 57	19 25	19 54				20 20		21 23		21 35		
Bridgwater	d		18 34			19 07						20 32				21 48		
Highbridge & Burnham	d		18 41			19 14						20 40				21 55		
Weston-super-Mare	a		18 52			19 25						20 51				22 05		
	d		18 53			19 27					20 26	20 55				22 07		23 47
Weston Milton	d											20 58				22 10		23 50
Worle	d		18 59								20 33	21 03						23 54
Yatton	d		19 04			19 36					20 40	21 09				22 18		23 59
Nailsea & Backwell	d		19 10			19 42					20 47	21 15				22 24		00 06
Parson Street	d																	
Bedminster	d											21 26				22 34		00 15
Bristol Temple Meads 10	a		19 23	19 27		19 54	19 57	20 27			20 58	21 31		22 00		22 38		00 19
	d	19 00		19 30	19 48		20 00	20 30	20 41	20 48			21 48		22 10		22 48	
Lawrence Hill	d																	
Stapleton Road	d																	
Filton Abbey Wood	d				19a55				20 48	20a55			21a55				22a55	
Bristol Parkway 7	a	19 08		19 38			20 08	20 38	20 52						22 18			
	d								20 52									
Yate	d								21 02									
Cam & Dursley	d								21 16									
Gloucester 7	a								21 33									

Sundays

16 September to 21 October

		GW	XC	GW	GW	GW	XC	GW	GW	XC	GW	GW	GW	XC	GW	XC	GW	XC	GW	GW	GW	XC	GW
		◇1 ⊡	◇1 ⊼		◇	🚌	◇1 ⊼	◇1 ⊡	◇	◇1 ⊼	◇1 ⊡	■		◇1 ⊼		◇1	🚌	◇1 ⊼	◇1 ⊡	◇		◇1 ⊼	
Taunton	d				08 35				10 19	10 51	11 17		11 36	11 53		12 00		12 51			13 11	13 54	
Bridgwater	d				08 47				10 31				11 48								13 23		
Highbridge & Burnham	d				08 55				10 39				11 55								13 30		
Weston-super-Mare	a				09 06				10 49				12 05			12 20					13 41		
	d	08 20			09 08			10 20	10 51				12 07			12 21			13 15		13 43		
Weston Milton	d				09 11								12 10								13 46		
Worle	d	08 27			09 15			10 27	10 57				12 18						13 22		13 50		
Yatton	d	08 34			09 21			10 34	11 03				12 23						13 29		13 56		
Nailsea & Backwell	d	08 40			09 27			10 40	11 09				12 29						13 36		14 02		
Parson Street	d																						
Bedminster	d												12 40		←								
Bristol Temple Meads 10	a	08 51			09 38			10 51	11 20	11 27	11 50		12 42	12 27	12 42	12 47		13 26	13 47		14 14	14 27	
	d		09 20	09 41	09 48		10 00		11 23	11 30		11 55	12 45	12 30	12 45			13 30		13 50		14 30	14 41
Lawrence Hill	d								11 26				→										
Stapleton Road	d								11a28														
Filton Abbey Wood	d			09 48	09a55							12a03			12 52					13a58			14 48
Bristol Parkway 7	a		09 28	09 52			10 08			11 38				12 39	12 57			13 38				14 38	14 53
	d		09 33			10 02	10 17			11 43				12 49			13 07	13 43				14 45	
Yate	d					10 22											13 27						
Cam & Dursley	d					11 02											14 07						
Gloucester 7	a		10 28			11 29	11 14			12 55				13 52			14 41	14 54				15 56	

For connections to London Paddington please refer to Table 125

Table 134

Taunton - Gloucester

Sundays

16 September to 21 October

Network Diagram - see first Page of Table 132

		GW	GW	GW	XC	GW	GW	XC	GW	GW	GW	XC	GW	GW	XC	GW	GW	GW	GW	GW	XC	GW	GW
		◇	◇1 ⊡	🚌	◇1 ⊼	◇		◇1 ⊼		◇		◇1 ⊼	◇1 ⊡	🚌	◇1 ⊼	◇	■	◇1 ⊡		◇1 ⊡	◇1 ⊼	🚌	◇
Taunton	d				14 54		15 18	15 54				16 01	16 40		16 53			16 59	17 19	17 48	17 53		
Bridgwater	d						15 30											17 10	17 30				
Highbridge & Burnham	d						15 37											17 18	17 37				
Weston-super-Mare	a						15 47					16 20	17 01					17 28	17 48				
	d		14 51				15 49				16 14	16 30	17 02			17 07		17 29	17 50				
Weston Milton	d						15 52				16 17					17 10							
Worle	d		14 58				15 56				16 22					17 17			17 56				
Yatton	d		15 05				16 02				16 28					17 23		17 40	18 02				
Nailsea & Backwell	d		15 11				16 08				16 34					17 29		17 46	18 08				
Parson Street	d										16 41												
Bedminster	d										16 44					17 39							
Bristol Temple Meads 10	a		15 20		15 27		16 20	16 27			16 49	16 52	17 20		17 26	17 42		17 58	18 20	18 25	18 27		
	d	14 51			15 30	15 48		16 30	16 41	16 48	16 53				17 30		17 48		18 25		18 30		18 48
Lawrence Hill	d										16 56												
Stapleton Road	d										16a58												
Filton Abbey Wood	d	14a58				15a55			16 48	16a55							17a55		18 32				18a55
Bristol Parkway 7	a				15 39			16 38	16 53						17 39				18 37		18 42		
	d			15 02	15 47			16 45						17 02	18 02						19 00	18 46	
Yate	d			15 22										17 22								19 06	
Cam & Dursley	d			16 02										18 02								19 46	
Gloucester 7	a			16 37	16 54			17 58						18 37	18 58						19 58	20 16	

		GW	GW	XC	GW	GW	XC	GW	GW	GW	GW	GW	GW	GW	XC	GW	GW	GW
			◇	◇1 ⊼	◇	◇1 ⊡	◇1 ⊼		◇	◇1 ⊡		🚌	◇	◇1 ⊡	◇1		◇	
Taunton	d		18 22	18 52		18 57	19 54				20 20			21 23		21 35		
Bridgwater	d		18 34			19 07					20 32					21 48		
Highbridge & Burnham	d		18 41			19 14					20 40					21 55		
Weston-super-Mare	a		18 52			19 25					20 51					22 05		
	d	18 16	18 53			19 27				20 26	20 55					22 07		23 47
Weston Milton	d	18 19									20 58					22 10		23 50
Worle	d	18 24	18 59							20 33	21 03							23 54
Yatton	d	18 30	19 04			19 36				20 39	21 09					22 18		23 59
Nailsea & Backwell	d	18 36	19 10			19 42				20 46	21 15					22 24		00 06
Parson Street	d	18 43																
Bedminster	d	18 46									21 26					22 34		00 15
Bristol Temple Meads 10	a	18 50	19 23	19 27		19 54	20 26			20 57	21 31			22 00		22 38		00 19
	d			19 30	19 48		20 30	20 41	20 48				21 48		22 10		22 48	
Lawrence Hill	d																	
Stapleton Road	d																	
Filton Abbey Wood	d				19a55			20 48	20a55				21a55				22a55	
Bristol Parkway 7	a			19 38			20 38	20 53							22 19			
	d			19 45			20 43					21 02			22 24			
Yate	d											21 22						
Cam & Dursley	d											22 02						
Gloucester 7	a			20 56			21 55					22 32			23 19			

Sundays

from 28 October

		GW	XC	GW	GW	GW	GW	XC	GW	GW	GW	XC	GW	XC	GW	GW	GW	XC	GW	GW	XC	GW	XC
		◇1 ⊡	◇1 ⊼		◇	◇1 ⊡	◇	◇1 ⊼	■		◇1 ⊡	◇1	◇1 ⊡	◇1 ⊼		◇		◇1 ⊼		◇	◇1 ⊼	◇1 ⊡	◇1
Taunton	d				08 35		10 19	10 51		11 36	11 48	11 53		12 51			13 11	13 51					14 54
Bridgwater	d				08 47		10 31			11 48							13 23						
Highbridge & Burnham	d				08 55		10 39			11 55							13 30						
Weston-super-Mare	a				09 06		10 49			12 05							13 41						
	d	08 11			09 08	09 56	10 51			12 07			12 51				13 43					14 51	
Weston Milton	d				09 11					12 10							13 46						
Worle	d	08 18			09 15	10 03	10 57			12 18			12 58				13 50					14 58	
Yatton	d	08 25			09 21	10 10	11 03			12 23			13 05				13 56					15 05	
Nailsea & Backwell	d	08 31			09 27	10 16	11 09			12 29			13 12				14 02					15 11	
Parson Street	d																						
Bedminster	d									12 40													
Bristol Temple Meads 10	a	08 42			09 38	10 27	11 20	11 27		12 43	12 23	12 27	13 20	13 26			14 14	14 26				15 20	15 27
	d		09 15	09 41	09 48		11 23	11 30	11 48					13 30	13 41	13 48		14 30	14 41	14 48	15 00		15 30
Lawrence Hill	d						11 26																
Stapleton Road	d						11a28																
Filton Abbey Wood	d			09 48	09a55				11a55						13 48	13a55			14 48	14a55			
Bristol Parkway 7	a		09 23	09 53				11 38						13 38	13 52			14 38	14 52		15 08		15 38
	d		09 25	09 53				11 40						13 40	13 52				14 53				
Yate	d			10 03											14 02				15 03				
Cam & Dursley	d			10 17											14 16				15 17				
Gloucester 7	a		09 53	10 32				12 07						14 08	14 31				15 35				

For connections to London Paddington please refer to Table 125

Taunton - Gloucester

Sundays
from 28 October

Network Diagram - see first Page of Table 132

		GW	XC	GW	XC	GW		GW	GW	XC	GW	XC	GW	GW	GW	XC		GW	GW	XC	GW	GW	GW	XC	GW
		◇	◇1 ⌶		◇1 ⌶			◇		◇1 ⌶	◇1 ⊏	◇1 ⌶	◇	■	◇1 ⊏	◇1 ⌶			◇1 ⊏	◇1 ⌶		◇		◇1 ⌶	◇
Taunton	d			15 18	15 54					16 01	16 40	16 53			16 59			17 19	17 48	17 51					18 22
Bridgwater	d			15 30											17 10			17 30							18 34
Highbridge & Burnham	d			15 37											17 18			17 37							18 41
Weston-super-Mare	a			15 47						16 20	17 01				17 28			17 48							18 52
	d			15 49					16 14	16 30	17 02		17 07		17 29			17 50					18 16		18 53
Weston Milton	d			15 52					16 17				17 10										18 19		
Worle	d			15 56					16 22				17 17					17 56					18 24		18 59
Yatton	d			16 02					16 28				17 23		17 40			18 02					18 30		19 04
Nailsea & Backwell	d			16 08					16 34				17 29		17 46			18 08					18 36		19 10
Parson Street	d								16 41														18 43		
Bedminster	d								16 44				17 39										18 46		
Bristol Temple Meads 10	a			16 20	16 27				16 49	16 52	17 22	17 26	17 42		17 58			18 20	18 25	18 27			18 50		19 23
	d	15 48	16 00		16 30	16 41		16 48	16 53	17 00		17 30		17 48		18 00				18 30	18 41	18 48		19 00	
Lawrence Hill	d								16 56																
Stapleton Road	d								16a58																
Filton Abbey Wood	d	15a55				16 48		16a55						17a55							18 48	18a55			
Bristol Parkway 7	a		16 08		16 38	16 52				17 08		17 38				18 08				18 38	18 52			19 08	
	d					16 52															18 52				
Yate	d					17 02															19 02				
Cam & Dursley	d					17 16															19 16				
Gloucester 7	a					17 32															19 33				

		XC		GW	GW	XC	XC	GW	GW	GW	GW	GW		GW	XC	GW	GW	GW
		◇1 ⌶		◇	◇1 ⊏	◇1 ⌶	◇1 ⌶		◇	◇1 ⊏		◇		◇1 ⊏	◇1		◇	
Taunton	d	18 52			18 57	19 25	19 54				20 20			21 23		21 35		
Bridgwater	d				19 07						20 32					21 48		
Highbridge & Burnham	d				19 14						20 40					21 55		
Weston-super-Mare	a				19 25						20 51					22 05		
	d				19 27					20 26	20 55					22 07		23 47
Weston Milton	d										20 58					22 10		23 50
Worle	d									20 33	21 03							23 54
Yatton	d				19 36					20 39	21 09					22 18		23 59
Nailsea & Backwell	d				19 42					20 46	21 15					22 24		00 06
Parson Street	d																	
Bedminster	d										21 26					22 34		00 15
Bristol Temple Meads 10	a	19 27			19 54	19 57	20 27			20 57	21 31			22 00		22 38		00 19
	d	19 30		19 48		20 00	20 30	20 41	20 48			21 48			22 10		22 48	
Lawrence Hill	d																	
Stapleton Road	d																	
Filton Abbey Wood	d			19a55				20 48	20a55			21a55					22a55	
Bristol Parkway 7	a	19 38				20 08	20 38	20 52							22 18			
	d							20 52										
Yate	d							21 02										
Cam & Dursley	d							21 16										
Gloucester 7	a							21 33										

For connections to London Paddington please refer to Table 125

Route Diagram for Tables 135, 136, 139, 140, 142, 143, 144

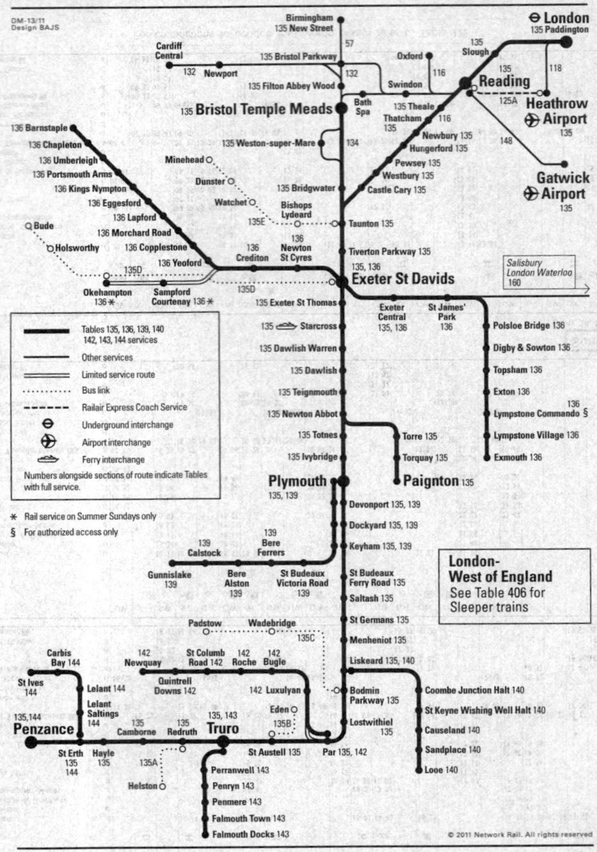

London and Birmingham - Devon and Cornwall

Route Diagram - see first Page of Table 135

Miles	Miles			GW A	GW ◇1 A ✗	GW A	GW ◇1 A ✗	GW ▪ B ✗	GW	GW	XC ◇1 C	GW		XC ◇1 A	GW	GW 1 ✗	GW	GW 1	GW ◇	GW	XC ◇1	GW		GW	GW ◇
0	—	**London Paddington** 15 ⊖	d		20p35		21p45	23p45																	
18½	—	Slough 3	d																						
36	—	**Reading** 7	d		21p02		22p11	00u37																	
41¼	—	Theale	d																						
49½	—	Thatcham	d																						
53	—	Newbury	d		21p18																				
61½	—	Hungerford	d																						
75¼	—	Pewsey	d		21p38																				
95½	—	Westbury	d		21p57			01 45																	
115¼	—	Castle Cary	d		22p15																				
—	0	**Birmingham New Street** 12	d																						
—	—	Cardiff Central 7	d																						
—	—	Newport (South Wales)	d																						
—	—	Swindon	d				22p49																		
—	87	Bristol Parkway 7	d																						
—	88¼	Filton Abbey Wood	d																						06 24
—	—	Bath Spa 7	d				23p19																		06 27
—	92¾	**Bristol Temple Meads** 10	d			23p06	23p35												05 24		06 34				06 42
—	112¾	Weston-super-Mare	d			23p42	00s05												05 45						07 06
—	126½	Bridgwater	d			00 02	00s24												06 03						07 25
143	138¾	Taunton	d		22p37	00s14	00s36	02 35											06 18		07 08				07 39
157¼	—	Tiverton Parkway	d		22p50	00s31	00s49												06 33		07 20				07 54
173¾	—	**Exeter St Davids** 6	a		23p06	00 50	01 07	03 06											06 51		07 34				08 12
—	—	Exmouth	d																	06 45		07 14			
—	—	Exeter Central	d																	07 12		07 43			
—	—	**Exeter St Davids** 6	d		23p08			03 11		05 34		06 11					06 28		06 55	07 18	07 36	07 50			08 14
174¾	—	Exeter St Thomas	d							05 38		06 14							06 58	07 21		07 53			
182¼	—	Starcross	d							05 46		06 22							07 07	07 29		08 01			
184¼	—	Dawlish Warren	d							05 51		06 27							07 12	07 34		08 06			
185¾	—	Dawlish	d							05 55		06 31					06 42		07 16	07 38		08 10			
188¾	—	Teignmouth	d							06 00		06 36					06 47		07 21	07 43		08 15			
193¾	—	Newton Abbot	a		23p28			03 31		06 07		06 44					06 55		07 28	07 50	07 54	08 22			08 35
—	—		d		23p28			03 33	05 42	06 09		06 45					06 55	07 06	07 28	07 52	07 55	08 24			08 35
—	5¼	Torre	d						05 50	06 17		06 53						07 15		08 00		08 33			
—	6	Torquay	d						05 53	06 20		06 56						07 20		08 03		08 36			
—	8¼	Paignton	a						06 00	06 28		07 06						07 29		08 12		08 44			
202½	—	Totnes	d		23p42												07 09		07 42		08 07				08 49
214	—	Ivybridge	d														07 26		07 58						09 05
225¾	—	**Plymouth**	a		00 11			04 12									07 40		08 11		08 34				09 19
—	—		d	22p31				05 43			05 43			06 28		07 02	07 53		08 14						09 21
227	—	Devonport	d													07 07			08 17						09 24
227½	—	Dockyard	d																						
228	—	Keyham	d																						
228¾	—	St Budeaux Ferry Road	d																						
230	—	Saltash	d	22p40												07 15	08 02		08 24						09 31
235	—	St Germans	d	22p47												07 23	08 09		08 31						09 38
240¼	—	Menheniot	d																						
243½	—	Liskeard 6	d	22p59				06 08			06 08			06 51		07 36	08 21		08 43						09 50
252½	—	Bodmin Parkway	d	23p11				06 22			06 22			07 03		07 49	08 33		08 55						10 02
256	—	Lostwithiel	d	23p16				06 28			06 28			07 09		07 55	08 40		09 00						10 07
260½	—	Par	d	23p24				06 37			06 37			07 15		08 04	08a54		09 08					09 17	10 15
—	—	Newquay	a																					10 09	
265	—	St Austell	d	23p31				06 46			06 46			07 22		08 11			09 16						10 22
279½	—	Truro	d	23p50				07 06			07 06			07 39		08 30			09 34						10 40
288½	—	Redruth	d	00 03				07 18			07 18			07 50		08 42			09 47						10 53
292	—	Camborne	d	00 09				07 26			07 26			07 57		08 48			09 53						10 59
298	—	Hayle	d	00 16				07 35			07 35			08 05		08 57			10 00						11 06
299½	—	St Erth	d	00 20				07 41			07 41			08 11	08 28	09 02			10 08						11 10
305¼	—	**Penzance**	a	00 40				07 53			07 53			08 19	08 40	09 12			10 16						11 23

A not 14 May

B not 14 May. The Night Riviera

C 14 May

For connections from Heathrow Airport, Gatwick Airport and Oxford please refer to Tables 125A, 148 and 116

London and Birmingham - Devon and Cornwall

Route Diagram - see first Page of Table 135

		XC ◇1 ⊼	GW	GW ◇1 A ✗	GW ◇	XC ◇1 ⊼	GW	GW ◇1 B ✗		GW ◇	XC ◇1 ⊼	GW	GW ◇1 ✗	GW ◇	GW ◇	GW ◇	XC ◇1 ⊼	GW		GW ◇1 C ✗	XC ◇1 ⊼	XC ◇1 ⊼	GW ◇1 D ✗	GW	GW ◇
London Paddington 15 ⊖	d			07 06				07 30					09 06							10 06			10 00		
Slough 3	d																								
Reading 7	d			07 33				07 57					09 35							10u33			10 27		
Theale	d																								
Thatcham	d																								
Newbury	d			07 48																					
Hungerford	d																								
Pewsey	d			08 07																					
Westbury	d			08 25																					
Castle Cary	d												10 31												
Birmingham New Street 12	d	06 42				07 12					08 12						09 12				09 42	10 12			
Cardiff Central 7	d									08 00						09 00									
Newport (South Wales)	d									08 15						09 15									
Swindon	d							08 27															10 55		
Bristol Parkway 7	d	07 58				08 26					09 26						10 27				10 55	11 28			
Filton Abbey Wood	d									08 42						09 42									
Bath Spa 7	d							08 57															11 24		
Bristol Temple Meads 10	d	08 10				08 44		09 13		08 55	09 44					09 55	10 44				11 15	11 44	11 47		
Weston-super-Mare	d									09 29						10 23					11 37		12 07		
Bridgwater	d									09 48						10 42									
Taunton	d	08 43		09 02		09 17		09 46		10 02	10 17		10 53			10 58	11 18				12 02	12 17	12 29		
Tiverton Parkway	d	08 55		09 15		09 29					10 30		11 06			11 14	11 30				12 14	12 29			
Exeter St Davids 6	a	09 08		09 30		09 42		10 11		10 33	10 45		11 22			11 32	11 45			12 08	12 30	12 42	12 55		
Exmouth	d		08 23				09 23					10 23						11 23						12 23	
Exeter Central	d		08 50				09 50					10 50						11 50						12 50	
Exeter St Davids 6	d	09 10	09 16	09 32	09 35	09 44	09 56	10 13		10 34	10 46	10 56	11 24			11 35	11 47	11 56		12 08	12 32	12 44	12 56	13 03	
Exeter St Thomas	d		09 19				09 59					10 59						11 59						13 06	
Starcross	d		09 27				10 07					11 07						12 07						13 15	
Dawlish Warren	d		09 32				10 12			10 46		11 12						12 22						13 20	
Dawlish	d		09 36				10 16			10 50		11 16						12 27			12 44		13 08	13 24	
Teignmouth	d		09 41				10 21			10 55		11 21						12 32			12 49		13 14	13 29	
Newton Abbot	a	09 29	09 48	09 52	09 56	10 02	10 30	10 34		11 02	11 06	11 29	11 43			11 55	12 06	12 39		12 29	12 55	13 02	13 22	13 36	
	d	09 30	09 50	09 56	09 57	10 03	10 39	10 36		11 03	11 07	11 30	11 44			11 56	12 07	12 40		12 29	12 56	13 03	13 22	13 38	
Torre	d		09 58	10 05			10 47			11 12		11 38						12 49						13 46	
Torquay	d	09 42	10 01	10 09			10 50			11 15		11 41						12 52			13 08		13 34	13 49	
Paignton	a	09 47	10 11	10 19			10 59			11 24		11 51						13 00			13 14		13 43	13 58	
Totnes	d				10 10	10 17		10 49			11 21		11 57			12 09	12 21					13 16			
Ivybridge	d				10 27											12 26									
Plymouth	a				10 41	10 46		11 17			11 48		12 27			12 42	12 49			13 06		13 41			
	d				10 42			11 20							12 39					13 11					
Devonport	d																								
Dockyard	d																								
Keyham	d																								
St Budeaux Ferry Road	d				10 48																				
Saltash	d				10 53										12 48										
St Germans	d				11 00										12 55										
Menheniot	d																								
Liskeard 6	d				11 12			11 44							13 07					13 35					
Bodmin Parkway	d				11 24			11 57							13 19					13 48					
Lostwithiel	d				11 29										13 24										
Par	d				11 37			12 09						12 13	13 32					14 00					14 08
Newquay	a													13 01											14 56
St Austell	d				11 44			12 16							13 39					14 07					
Truro	d				12 02			12 34							13 57					14 25					
Redruth	d				12 15			12 46							14 10					14 37					
Camborne	d				12 21			12 53							14 16					14 45					
Hayle	d				12 28										14 23					14 54					
St Erth	d				12 32			13 05							14 28					14 59					
Penzance	a				12 42			13 17							14 39					15 11					

A The Devon Express

B The Merchant Venturer

C The Cornish Riveira

D The Torbay Express

For connections from Heathrow Airport, Gatwick Airport and Oxford please refer to Tables 125A, 148 and 116

until 18 May

London and Birmingham - Devon and Cornwall

Route Diagram - see first Page of Table 135

		GW	GW	XC	GW	GW	GW	XC	GW	GW	GW	GW	GW	GW	GW	XC	XC	GW	GW	GW	GW	GW
			◇1	◇1		◇1		◇1	◇1		◇		◇1	◇		◇1	◇1				◇1	
			A			B							C								C	
			[buffet] ⊘	[trolley]		[buffet] ⊘		[trolley]	[buffet]				[buffet] ⊘			[trolley]	[trolley]				[buffet] ⊘	
London Paddington 15 ⊖	d		11 06			12 06			12 18				13 06								14 06	
Slough 3	d																					
Reading 7	d		11u33			12 33			12 48				13 33								14 33	
Theale	d								12 56													
Thatcham	d								13 04													
Newbury	d								13 12													
Hungerford	d								13 21													
Pewsey	d		12 03						13 40													
Westbury	d		12 22						13 59													
Castle Cary	d		12 39						14 16													
Birmingham New Street 12	d			11 12				12 12								13 12	13 42					
Cardiff Central 7	d													13 00								
Newport (South Wales)	d													13 15								
Swindon	d																					
Bristol Parkway 7	d			12 30				13 27								14 29	14 59					
Filton Abbey Wood	d													13 42								
Bath Spa 7	d																					
Bristol Temple Meads 10	d			12 44				13 44						13 53		14 44	15 13					
Weston-super-Mare	d													14 23								
Bridgwater	d													14 42								
Taunton	d		13 02	13 18				14 17	14a41				14 48	14 56		15 18	15 46				15 49	
Tiverton Parkway	d		13 15	13 30				14 29					15 01	15 11		15 30	15 58				16 02	
Exeter St Davids 6	a		13 31	13 45		14 08		14 42					15 17	15 31		15 46	16 13				16 18	
Exmouth	d				13 23					14 23								15 23				15 53
Exeter Central	d				13 50					14 50								15 50				16 20
Exeter St Davids 6	d		13 33	13 47	13 56	14 08		14 44		14 56			15 18			15 48		15 56		16 05	16 20	16 26
Exeter St Thomas	d				13 59					14 59								15 59				16 29
Starcross	d				14 07					15 07								16 07				16 37
Dawlish Warren	d				14 23					15 12								16 12		16 18		16 42
Dawlish	d				14 27					15 16								16 16		16 22		16 46
Teignmouth	d				14 32					15 21								16 21		16 27		16 51
Newton Abbot	a		13 52	14 06	14 40	14 28		15 02		15 29			15 39			16 07		16 30		16 35	16 39	16 58
	d		13 53	14 07	14 41	14 29	14 50	15 03		15 30			15 39		15 58	16 08		16 30		16 48	16 40	17 00
Torre	d				14 49					15 38								16 38				17 08
Torquay	d				14 52					15 41								16 41				17 11
Paignton	a				15 00					15 51								16 51				17 20
Totnes	d		14 06	14 21			15 02	15 16					15 53		16 11	16 22				17 02	16 53	
Ivybridge	d						15 19								16 28					17 19		
Plymouth	a		14 36	14 48		15 06	15 37	15 41					16 22		16 44	16 49				17 34	17 21	
	d	13 53				15 12						15 57							17 04		17 23	
Devonport	d											16 00							17 07			
Dockyard	d											16x01							17x08			
Keyham	d											16 03							17 10			
St Budeaux Ferry Road	d											16 06							17 13			
Saltash	d	14 02										16 11							17 17		17 34	
St Germans	d	14 09										16 18							17 24		17 41	
Menheniot	d											16x25							17x32			
Liskeard 6	d	14 21				15 36						16 32							17a40		17 54	
Bodmin Parkway	d	14 33				15 49						16 44									18 07	
Lostwithiel	d	14 38										16 49									18 13	
Par	d	14 46				16 01					16 10	16 57									18 22	
Newquay	a										17 02											
St Austell	d	14 53				16 08						17 06									18 29	
Truro	d	15 11				16 26						17 23									18 47	
Redruth	d	15 24				16 38						17 36									18 59	
Camborne	d	15 30				16 46						17 42									19 07	
Hayle	d	15 37				16 55						17 50									19 16	
St Erth	d	15 42				17 00						17 54									19 21	
Penzance	a	15 53				17 12						18 07									19 33	

A The Mayflower

B The Royal Duchy

C [buffet] from Newton Abbot ⊘ to Newton Abbot

For connections from Heathrow Airport, Gatwick Airport and Oxford please refer to Tables 125A, 148 and 116

Table 135

Mondays to Fridays

until 18 May

London and Birmingham - Devon and Cornwall

Route Diagram - see first Page of Table 135

		XC	GW	GW	GW	GW	GW	GW	GW	GW	XC	GW	XC	GW	GW	GW	XC	GW	GW	GW	GW	XC	GW
		◇1	◇			◇				◇1	◇1		◇1	◇1			◇1	◇1	◇1	◇1		◇1	◇1
			A							B	C						C	D	A			C	E
		[trolley]								[buffet] ⊘	[trolley]		[trolley]	[buffet]			[trolley]	[buffet]	[buffet]	[buffet]		[trolley]	[buffet]
London Paddington 15 ⊖	d									15 06				16 06				16 36	16 36	17 03			17 06
Slough 3	d																						
Reading 7	d									15u33				16 33				17 04	17 04	17 32			17 36
Theale	d																						17 45
Thatcham	d																						17 55
Newbury	d																	17 19	17 19	17 48			18 02
Hungerford	d																	17 29	17 29				18 16
Pewsey	d									16 03								17 44	17 44				18 34
Westbury	d		15 20							16 23								18 04	18 04				
Castle Cary	d		15 49							16 41								18 21	18 21				
Birmingham New Street 12	d	14 12									15 12		15 42				16 12					17 12	
Cardiff Central 7	d																						
Newport (South Wales)	d																						
Swindon	d																						
Bristol Parkway 7	d	15 26									16 29		16 58				17 27					18 29	
Filton Abbey Wood	d																						
Bath Spa 7	d																						19 24
Bristol Temple Meads 10	d	15 44									16 44		17 13				17 44					18 44	19a41
Weston-super-Mare	d																						
Bridgwater	d																						
Taunton	d	16 17	16 24							17 05	17 17		17 45	17 50			18 17	18 43	18 43	18 52		19 17	
Tiverton Parkway	d	16 29	16 41							17 18	17 29		17 57	18 03			18 29	18 56	18 56	19 05		19 29	
Exeter St Davids 6	a	16 42	17 02							17 34	17 42		18 11	18 19			18 42	19 14	19 14	19 21		19 42	
Exmouth	d				16 55										17 58						18 55		
Exeter Central	d			16 46	17 21							17 45			18 25						19 21		
Exeter St Davids 6	d	16 44		16 56	17 26					17 35	17 45	17 50	18 12	18 22	18 30		18 46		19 14	19 22	19 28	19 44	
Exeter St Thomas	d			16 59	17 29							17 54			18 33						19 31		
Starcross	d			17 07	17 37							18 02			18 42						19 39		
Dawlish Warren	d			17 12	17 49							18 07			18 47						19 44		
Dawlish	d			17 16	17 53							18 11	18 24		18 51						19 48		
Teignmouth	d			17 21	17 58							18 16	18 29		18 56						19 53		
Newton Abbot	a	17 02		17 29	18 05					17 56	18 10	18 23	18 35	18 42	19 03		19 07		19 34	19 42	20 00	20 03	
	d	17 04		17 30	18 09					17 57	18 12	18 25	18 37	18 43	19 11		19 08		19 35	19 42	20 09	20 05	
Torre	d			17 38	18 17							18 33			19 19						20 17		
Torquay	d			17 41	18 20							18 36	18 48		19 22						20 20		
Paignton	a			17 51	18 30							18 45	18 55		19 30						20 29		
Totnes	d	17 16								18 10	18 24			18 56			19 21			19 56		20 17	
Ivybridge	d													19 12									
Plymouth	a	17 42								18 38	18 50			19 26			19 46		20 15	20 24		20 43	
	d						17 55	18 17	18 23	18 42	19 01			19 31			19 49			20 26		20 50	
Devonport	d							18 20	18 26														
Dockyard	d							18x21	18x27														
Keyham	d							18 23	18a29														
St Budeaux Ferry Road	d							18 25															
Saltash	d						18 03	18 31						19 40						20 37			
St Germans	d							18 38												20 44			
Menheniot	d							18x45															
Liskeard 6	d						18 20	18a53		19 07	19 24			19 57			20 12			20 56		21 13	
Bodmin Parkway	d						18 32			19 19	19 36			20 10			20 25			21 09		21 26	
Lostwithiel	d						18 37															21 31	
Par	d					18 29	18 45			19 31	19 47			20 22		20 28	20 36			21 21		21 39	
Newquay	a					19 21										21 20							
St Austell	d						18 52			19 39	19 54			20 29			20 43			21 28		21 46	
Truro	d						19 10			20 00	20 11			20 47			21 02			21 46		22 04	
Redruth	d						19 23			20 10	20 26			20 59			21 16			21 58		22 15	
Camborne	d						19 29			20 18	20 32			21 07			21 23					22 22	
Hayle	d						19 36													22 11		22 30	
St Erth	d						19 42			20 28	20 44			21 20			21 34			22 16		22 35	
Penzance	a						19 54			20 42	20 52			21 31			21 42			22 30		22 43	

A 18 May

B The Cornishman

C [trolley] to Plymouth

D not 18 May

E via Trowbridge

For connections from Heathrow Airport, Gatwick Airport and Oxford please refer to Tables 125A, 148 and 116

until 18 May

London and Birmingham - Devon and Cornwall

Route Diagram - see first Page of Table 135

		GW	GW	GW	GW	XC	GW	GW	GW	GW	GW	GW	XC	XC	GW	GW	XC	GW	GW	GW	GW	GW	GW
		◇1 ¤		◇1 A ✕¤	◇1 I ¤	◇1	◇1 B ¤	◇1 C ¤	1 D ✕¤	1 E ✕¤		B	◇1 F	◇1 F	◇1 ¤		◇1 F	◇1 ¤	◇		◇1 ¤	G ¤	H ¤
London Paddington 15 ⊖	d	17 33		18 03	18 06		18 33	18 33	19 03	19 03					19 45			20 35			21 45	23 45	23 45
Slough 3	d																						
Reading 7	d	18 04		18u33	18 37		19 02	19 02	19u33	19 33					20 12			21 02			22 11	00u37	00u37
Theale	d				18 45																		
Thatcham	d				18 55																		
Newbury	d	18 19			19 02		19 17	19 17	19 50	19 50					20 28			21 18					
Hungerford	d				19 16		19 27	19 27															
Pewsey	d	18 41			19 34		19 46	19 46							20 48			21 38					
Westbury	d	19 01			19a52		20 05	20 05							21 06			21 57				01 37	01 45
Castle Cary	d	19 19					20 23	20 23							21 26			22 15					
Birmingham New Street 12	d					18 12							19 12	19 42			20 12						
Cardiff Central 7	d																						
Newport (South Wales)	d																						
Swindon	d																				22 49		
Bristol Parkway 7	d					19 29							20 29	20 56			21 27						
Filton Abbey Wood	d																						
Bath Spa 7	d																				23 19		
Bristol Temple Meads 10	d					19 44							20 44	21 12			21 44		21 56	23 06	23 35		
Weston-super-Mare	d																		22 29	23 42	00s05		
Bridgwater	d																		22 48	00 02	00s24		
Taunton	d	19 41		19 48		20 18	20 46	20 46	20 54	20 54			21 17	21 45	21 48		22 17	22 37	23 03	00s14	00s36	02 35	02 35
Tiverton Parkway	d	19 54				20 30	20 59	20 59	21 07	21 07			21 30	21 57	22 02		22 29	22 50	23 18	00s31	00s49		
Exeter St Davids 6	a	20 09		20 13		20 44	21 15	21 15	21 23	21 23			21 43	22 11	22 18		22 43	23 06	23 36	00 50	01 07	03 06	03 06
Exmouth	d															22 05							
Exeter Central	d										21 21					22 31							
Exeter St Davids 6	d	20 19		20 15		20 46		21 16	21 25	21 25	21 29		21 45	22 12	22 19	22 37	22 44	23 08				03 11	03 11
Exeter St Thomas	d	20 24									21 32					22 40							
Starcross	d	20 33									21 40					22 48							
Dawlish Warren	d	20 38									21 45					22 59							
Dawlish	d	20 43									21 49					23 03							
Teignmouth	d	20 50									21 54					23 08							
Newton Abbot	a	20 57		20 34		21 03		21 36	21 44	21 44	22 01		22 04	22 30	22 39	23 15	23 05	23 28				03 31	03 31
	d	20 58		20 35		21 05		21 36	21 45	21 45	22 03		22 06	22 32	22 40	23 16	23 07	23 28				03 33	03 33
Torre	d	21 08									22 11					23 24							
Torquay	d	21 12									22 14					23 27							
Paignton	a	21 22									22 23					23 37							
Totnes	d			20 48		21 18			21 58	21 58			22 17	22 44	22 53		23 19	23 42					
Ivybridge	d														23 10								
Plymouth	a			21 16		21 48		22 14	22 26	22 26			22 43	23 14	23 25		23 45	00 11				04 14	04 12
	d			21 19					22 29			22 31										05 43	05 43
Devonport	d																						
Dockyard	d																						
Keyham	d																						
St Budeaux Ferry Road	d																						
Saltash	d								22 40			22 40											
St Germans	d								22 47			22 47											
Menheniot	d																						
Liskeard 6	d			21 44					22 59			22 59										06 08	06 08
Bodmin Parkway	d			21 58					23 11			23 11										06 22	06 22
Lostwithiel	d								23 16			23 16										06 28	06 28
Par	d			22 10					23 24			23 24										06 37	06 37
Newquay	a																						
St Austell	d			22 18					23 31			23 31										06 46	06 46
Truro	d			22 36					23 50			23 50										07 06	07 06
Redruth	d			22 48					00 03			00 03										07 18	07 18
Camborne	d								00 09			00 09										07 26	07 26
Hayle	d								00 16			00 16										07 35	07 35
St Erth	d		22 45						00 20			00 20										07 41	07 41
Penzance	a		22 57	23 14					00 40			00 40										07 53	07 53

A The Golden Hind
B not 18 May
C 18 May
D 18 May. The Armada
E not 18 May. The Armada
F to Bristol Temple Meads
G 18 May. The Night Riviera
H not 18 May. The Night Riviera
I to Frome

For connections from Heathrow Airport, Gatwick Airport and Oxford please refer to Tables 125A, 148 and 116

21 May to 29 June

London and Birmingham - Devon and Cornwall

Route Diagram - see first Page of Table 135

		GW MX	GW MO	GW MX	GW MX	GW MX	GW MX	XC MO	XC MX	GW	GW MO	GW	GW	GW	GW	GW	GW	GW	GW	XC	GW	GW	GW
			◇1 ¤	◇1 ¤		◇1 ¤	A ¤	◇1	◇1		¤				1 ¤		1	◇		◇1			◇
London Paddington 15 ⊖	d		19p57	20p35		21p45	23p45				23p50												
Slough 3	d																						
Reading 7	d		20p33	21p02		22p11	00u37				00u37												
Theale	d																						
Thatcham	d																						
Newbury	d			21p18																			
Hungerford	d																						
Pewsey	d			21p38																			
Westbury	d		21p36	21p57			01 45																
Castle Cary	d		21p54	22p15																			
Birmingham New Street 12	d																						
Cardiff Central 7	d																						
Newport (South Wales)	d																						
Swindon	d					22p49																	
Bristol Parkway 7	d																						06 24
Filton Abbey Wood	d																						06 27
Bath Spa 7	d					23p19																	
Bristol Temple Meads 10	d				23p06	23p35					02 55							05 24		06 34			06 42
Weston-super-Mare	d				23p42	00s05												05 45					07 06
Bridgwater	d				00 02	00s24												06 03					07 25
Taunton	d		22p19	22p37	00s14	00s36	02 35											06 18		07 08			07 39
Tiverton Parkway	d		22p33	22p50	00s31	00s49												06 33		07 20			07 54
Exeter St Davids 6	a		22p52	23p06	00 50	01 07	03 06				04 04							06 51		07 34			08 12
Exmouth	d																		06 45		07 14		
Exeter Central	d																		07 12		07 43		
Exeter St Davids 6	d		22p52	23p08			03 11				04 35		05 34	06 11		06 28		06 55	07 18	07 36	07 50		08 14
Exeter St Thomas	d												05 38	06 14				06 58	07 21		07 53		
Starcross	d												05 46	06 22				07 07	07 29		08 01		
Dawlish Warren	d												05 51	06 27				07 12	07 34		08 06		
Dawlish	d		23p06										05 55	06 31		06 42		07 16	07 38		08 10		
Teignmouth	d		23p12										06 00	06 36		06 47		07 21	07 43		08 15		
Newton Abbot	a		23p19	23p28			03 31				04 55		06 07	06 44		06 55		07 28	07 50	07 54	08 22		08 35
	d		23p19	23p28			03 33				04 56	05 42	06 09	06 45		06 55	07 06	07 28	07 52	07 55	08 24		08 35
Torre	d											05 50	06 17	06 53			07 15		08 00		08 33		
Torquay	d											05 53	06 20	06 56			07 20		08 03		08 36		
Paignton	a											06 00	06 28	07 06			07 29		08 12		08 44		
Totnes	d		23p32	23p42												07 09		07 42		08 07			08 49
Ivybridge	d															07 26		07 58					09 05
Plymouth	a		00 01	00 11			04 12				05 35					07 40		08 11		08 34			09 19
	d	22p31					05 43	05 43	06 28		06 28				07 02	07 53		08 14					09 21
Devonport	d														07 07			08 17					09 24
Dockyard	d																						
Keyham	d																						
St Budeaux Ferry Road	d																						
Saltash	d	22p40													07 15	08 02		08 24					09 31
St Germans	d	22p47													07 23	08 09		08 31					09 38
Menheniot	d																						
Liskeard 6	d	22p59					06 08	06 08	06 51		07 09				07 36	08 21		08 43					09 50
Bodmin Parkway	d	23p11					06 22	06 22	07 03		07 23				07 49	08 33		08 55					10 02
Lostwithiel	d	23p16					06 28	06 28	07 09		07 29				07 55	08 40		09 00					10 07
Par	d	23p24					06 37	06 37	07 15		07 38				08 04	08a54		09 08				09 17	10 15
Newquay	a																					10 09	
St Austell	d	23p31					06 46	06 46	07 22		07 46				08 11			09 16					10 22
Truro	d	23p50					07 06	07 06	07 39		08 06				08 30			09 34					10 40
Redruth	d	00 03					07 18	07 18	07 50		08 20				08 42			09 47					10 53
Camborne	d	00 09					07 26	07 26	07 57		08 27				08 48			09 53					10 59
Hayle	d	00 16					07 35	07 35	08 05		08 38				08 57			10 00					11 06
St Erth	d	00 20					07 41	07 41	08 11	08 28	08 45				09 02			10 08					11 10
Penzance	a	00 40					07 53	07 53	08 19	08 40	08 59				09 12			10 16					11 23

A The Night Riviera

For connections from Heathrow Airport, Gatwick Airport and Oxford please refer to Tables 125A, 148 and 116

Table 135

Mondays to Fridays

21 May to 29 June

London and Birmingham - Devon and Cornwall

Route Diagram - see first Page of Table 135

Station		XC ◇■ H	GW	GW ◇■ A ⌐	GW ◇	XC ◇■ H	GW	GW ◇■ B ⌐Ø	GW ◇	XC ◇■ H	GW	GW ◇■ ⌐
London Paddington ⊖	d			07 06				07 30				09 06
Slough	d											
Reading	d			07 33				07 57				09 35
Theale	d											
Thatcham	d											
Newbury	d			07 48								
Hungerford	d											
Pewsey	d			08 07								
Westbury	d			08 25								
Castle Cary	d											10 31
Birmingham New Street	d	06 42				07 12				08 12		
Cardiff Central	d								08 00			
Newport (South Wales)	d								08 15			
Swindon	d							08 27				
Bristol Parkway	d	07 58				08 26				09 26		
Filton Abbey Wood	d								08 42			
Bath Spa	d							08 57				
Bristol Temple Meads	d	08 10				08 44		09 13	08 55	09 44		
Weston-super-Mare	d								09 29			
Bridgwater	d								09 48			
Taunton	d	08 43		09 02		09 17		09 46	10 02	10 17		10 53
Tiverton Parkway	d	08 55		09 15		09 29				10 30		11 06
Exeter St Davids	a	09 08		09 30		09 42		10 11	10 33	10 45		11 22
Exmouth	d		08 23				09 23				10 23	
Exeter Central	d		08 50				09 50				10 50	
Exeter St Davids	d	09 10	09 16	09 32	09 35	09 44	09 56	10 13	10 34	10 46	10 56	11 24
Exeter St Thomas	d		09 19				09 59				10 59	
Starcross	d		09 27				10 07				11 07	
Dawlish Warren	d		09 32				10 12		10 46		11 12	
Dawlish	d		09 36				10 16		10 50		11 16	
Teignmouth	d		09 41				10 21		10 55		11 21	
Newton Abbot	a	09 29	09 48	09 52	09 56	10 02	10 30	10 34	11 02	11 06	11 29	11 43
	d	09 30	09 50	09 56	09 57	10 03	10 39	10 36	11 03	11 07	11 30	11 44
Torre	d		09 58	10 05			10 47		11 12		11 38	
Torquay	d	09 42	10 01	10 09			10 50		11 15		11 41	
Paignton	a	09 47	10 11	10 19			10 59		11 24		11 51	
Totnes	d				10 10	10 17		10 49		11 21		11 57
Ivybridge	d				10 27							
Plymouth	a				10 41	10 46		11 17		11 48		12 27
	d				10 42			11 20				
Devonport	d											
Dockyard	d											
Keyham	d											
St Budeaux Ferry Road	d				10 48							
Saltash	d				10 53							
St Germans	d				11 00							
Menheniot	d											
Liskeard	d				11 12			11 44				
Bodmin Parkway	d				11 24			11 57				
Lostwithiel	d				11 29							
Par	d				11 37			12 09				
Newquay	a											
St Austell	d				11 44			12 16				
Truro	d				12 02			12 34				
Redruth	d				12 15			12 46				
Camborne	d				12 21			12 53				
Hayle	d				12 28							
St Erth	d				12 32			13 05				
Penzance	a				12 42			13 17				

Station		GW ◇	GW ◇	GW ◇	XC ◇■ H	GW	GW ◇■ C ⌐Ø	XC ◇■ H	XC ◇■ H	GW ◇■ D ⌐	GW	GW ◇
London Paddington ⊖	d						10 06			10 00		
Slough	d											
Reading	d						10u33			10 27		
Theale	d											
Thatcham	d											
Newbury	d											
Hungerford	d											
Pewsey	d											
Westbury	d											
Castle Cary	d											
Birmingham New Street	d				09 12			09 42	10 12			
Cardiff Central	d			09 00								
Newport (South Wales)	d			09 15								
Swindon	d									10 55		
Bristol Parkway	d				10 27			10 55	11 28			
Filton Abbey Wood	d			09 42								
Bath Spa	d									11 24		
Bristol Temple Meads	d			09 55	10 44			11 15	11 44	11 47		
Weston-super-Mare	d			10 23				11 37		12 07		
Bridgwater	d			10 42								
Taunton	d			10 58	11 18			12 02	12 17	12 29		
Tiverton Parkway	d			11 14	11 30			12 14	12 29			
Exeter St Davids	a			11 32	11 45		12 08	12 30	12 42	12 55		
Exmouth	d					11 23					12 23	
Exeter Central	d					11 50					12 50	
Exeter St Davids	d			11 35	11 47	11 56	12 08	12 32	12 44	12 56	13 03	
Exeter St Thomas	d					11 59					13 06	
Starcross	d					12 07					13 15	
Dawlish Warren	d					12 22					13 20	
Dawlish	d					12 27		12 44		13 08	13 24	
Teignmouth	d					12 32		12 49		13 14	13 29	
Newton Abbot	a			11 55	12 06	12 39	12 29	12 55	13 02	13 22	13 36	
	d			11 56	12 07	12 40	12 29	12 56	13 03	13 22	13 38	
Torre	d					12 49					13 46	
Torquay	d					12 52		13 08		13 34	13 49	
Paignton	a					13 00		13 14		13 43	13 58	
Totnes	d			12 09	12 21				13 16			
Ivybridge	d			12 26								
Plymouth	a			12 42	12 49		13 06		13 41			
	d		12 39				13 11					
Devonport	d											
Dockyard	d											
Keyham	d											
St Budeaux Ferry Road	d											
Saltash	d		12 48									
St Germans	d		12 55									
Menheniot	d											
Liskeard	d		13 07				13 35					
Bodmin Parkway	d		13 19				13 48					
Lostwithiel	d		13 24									
Par	d	12 13	13 32				14 00					14 08
Newquay	a	13 01										14 56
St Austell	d		13 39				14 07					
Truro	d		13 57				14 25					
Redruth	d		14 10				14 37					
Camborne	d		14 16				14 45					
Hayle	d		14 23				14 54					
St Erth	d		14 28				14 59					
Penzance	a		14 39				15 11					

A The Devon Express
B The Merchant Venturer
C The Cornish Riveira
D The Torbay Express

For connections from Heathrow Airport, Gatwick Airport and Oxford please refer to Tables 125A, 148 and 116

Table 135

Mondays to Fridays

21 May to 29 June

London and Birmingham - Devon and Cornwall

Route Diagram - see first Page of Table 135

Station		GW	GW ◇■ A ⌐Ø	XC ◇■ H	GW	GW ◇■ B ⌐Ø	GW	XC ◇■ H	GW ◇■ ⌐	GW	GW ◇	GW
London Paddington ⊖	d		11 06			12 06			12 18			
Slough	d											
Reading	d		11u33			12 33			12 48			
Theale	d								12 56			
Thatcham	d								13 04			
Newbury	d								13 12			
Hungerford	d								13 21			
Pewsey	d		12 03						13 40			
Westbury	d		12 22						13 59			
Castle Cary	d		12 39						14 16			
Birmingham New Street	d			11 12				12 12				
Cardiff Central	d											
Newport (South Wales)	d											
Swindon	d											
Bristol Parkway	d			12 30				13 27				
Filton Abbey Wood	d											
Bath Spa	d											
Bristol Temple Meads	d			12 44				13 44				
Weston-super-Mare	d											
Bridgwater	d											
Taunton	d		13 02	13 18				14 17	14a41			
Tiverton Parkway	d		13 15	13 30				14 29				
Exeter St Davids	a		13 31	13 45		14 08		14 42				
Exmouth	d				13 23					14 23		
Exeter Central	d				13 50					14 50		
Exeter St Davids	d		13 33	13 47	13 56	14 08		14 44		14 56		
Exeter St Thomas	d				13 59					14 59		
Starcross	d				14 07					15 07		
Dawlish Warren	d				14 23					15 12		
Dawlish	d				14 27					15 16		
Teignmouth	d				14 32					15 21		
Newton Abbot	a		13 52	14 06	14 40	14 28		15 02		15 29		
	d		13 53	14 07	14 41	14 29	14 50	15 03		15 30		
Torre	d				14 49					15 38		
Torquay	d				14 52					15 41		
Paignton	a				15 00					15 51		
Totnes	d		14 06	14 21			15 02	15 16				
Ivybridge	d						15 19					
Plymouth	a		14 36	14 48		15 06	15 37	15 41				
	d	13 53				15 12						15 57
Devonport	d											16 00
Dockyard	d											16x01
Keyham	d											16 03
St Budeaux Ferry Road	d											16 06
Saltash	d	14 02										16 11
St Germans	d	14 09										16 18
Menheniot	d											16x25
Liskeard	d	14 21				15 36						16 32
Bodmin Parkway	d	14 33				15 49						16 44
Lostwithiel	d	14 38										16 49
Par	d	14 46				16 01					16 10	16 57
Newquay	a										17 02	
St Austell	d	14 53				16 08						17 06
Truro	d	15 11				16 26						17 23
Redruth	d	15 24				16 38						17 36
Camborne	d	15 30				16 46						17 42
Hayle	d	15 37				16 55						17 50
St Erth	d	15 42				17 00						17 54
Penzance	a	15 53				17 12						18 07

Station		GW ◇■ C ⌐Ø	GW ◇	GW	XC ◇■ H	XC ◇■ H	GW	GW	GW	GW ◇■ C ⌐Ø	GW
London Paddington ⊖	d	13 06								14 06	
Slough	d										
Reading	d	13 33								14 33	
Theale	d										
Thatcham	d										
Newbury	d										
Hungerford	d										
Pewsey	d										
Westbury	d										
Castle Cary	d										
Birmingham New Street	d				13 12	13 42					
Cardiff Central	d		13 00								
Newport (South Wales)	d		13 15								
Swindon	d										
Bristol Parkway	d				14 29	14 59					
Filton Abbey Wood	d		13 42								
Bath Spa	d										
Bristol Temple Meads	d		13 53		14 44	15 13					
Weston-super-Mare	d		14 23								
Bridgwater	d		14 42								
Taunton	d	14 48	14 56		15 18	15 46				15 49	
Tiverton Parkway	d	15 01	15 11		15 30	15 58				16 02	
Exeter St Davids	a	15 17	15 31		15 46	16 13				16 18	
Exmouth	d						15 23				15 53
Exeter Central	d						15 50				16 20
Exeter St Davids	d	15 18			15 48		15 56		16 05	16 20	16 26
Exeter St Thomas	d						15 59				16 29
Starcross	d						16 07				16 37
Dawlish Warren	d						16 12		16 18		16 42
Dawlish	d						16 16		16 22		16 46
Teignmouth	d						16 21		16 27		16 51
Newton Abbot	a	15 39			16 07		16 30		16 35	16 39	16 58
	d	15 39		15 58	16 08		16 30		16 48	16 40	17 00
Torre	d						16 38				17 08
Torquay	d						16 41				17 11
Paignton	a						16 51				17 20
Totnes	d	15 53		16 11	16 22				17 02	16 53	
Ivybridge	d			16 28					17 19		
Plymouth	a	16 22		16 44	16 49				17 34	17 21	
	d							17 04		17 23	
Devonport	d							17 07			
Dockyard	d							17x08			
Keyham	d							17 10			
St Budeaux Ferry Road	d							17 13			
Saltash	d							17 17		17 34	
St Germans	d							17 24		17 41	
Menheniot	d							17x32			
Liskeard	d							17a40		17 54	
Bodmin Parkway	d									18 07	
Lostwithiel	d									18 13	
Par	d									18 22	
Newquay	a										
St Austell	d									18 29	
Truro	d									18 47	
Redruth	d									18 59	
Camborne	d									19 07	
Hayle	d									19 16	
St Erth	d									19 21	
Penzance	a									19 33	

A The Mayflower
B The Royal Duchy
C ⌐ from Newton Abbot Ø to Newton Abbot

For connections from Heathrow Airport, Gatwick Airport and Oxford please refer to Tables 125A, 148 and 116

21 May to 29 June

London and Birmingham - Devon and Cornwall

Route Diagram - see first Page of Table 135

		XC	GW FO	GW	GW	GW	GW	GW		GW	GW	XC	GW	XC	GW	GW	GW	XC		GW FX	GW FO	GW	GW	XC	GW
		◇1	◇			◇					◇1	◇1		◇1	◇1			◇1		◇1	◇1	◇1		◇1	◇1
											A	B						B						B	C
		⌶									▭⊘	⌶		⌶	▭			⌶		▭	▭	▭		⌶	▭
London Paddington 15 ⊖	d										15 06				16 06					16 36	16 36	17 03			17 06
Slough 3	d																								
Reading 7	d										15u33				16 33					17 04	17 04	17 32			17 36
Theale	d																								17 45
Thatcham	d																								17 55
Newbury	d																			17 19	17 19	17 48			18 02
Hungerford	d																			17 29	17 29				18 16
Pewsey	d										16 03									17 44	17 44				18 34
Westbury	d		15 20								16 23									18 04	18 04				
Castle Cary	d		15 49								16 41									18 21	18 21				
Birmingham New Street 12	d	14 12										15 12		15 42				16 12						17 12	
Cardiff Central 7	d																								
Newport (South Wales)	d																								
Swindon	d																								
Bristol Parkway 7	d	15 26										16 29		16 58				17 27						18 29	
Filton Abbey Wood	d																								
Bath Spa 7	d																								19 24
Bristol Temple Meads 10	d	15 44										16 44		17 13				17 44						18 44	19a41
Weston-super-Mare	d																								
Bridgwater	d																								
Taunton	d	16 17	16 24								17 05	17 17		17 45	17 50			18 17		18 43	18 43	18 52		19 17	
Tiverton Parkway	d	16 29	16 41								17 18	17 29		17 57	18 03			18 29		18 56	18 56	19 05		19 29	
Exeter St Davids 6	a	16 42	17 02								17 34	17 42		18 11	18 19			18 42		19 14	19 14	19 21		19 42	
Exmouth	d				16 55											17 58							18 55		
Exeter Central	d			16 46	17 21								17 45			18 25							19 21		
Exeter St Davids 6	d	16 44		16 56	17 26						17 35	17 45	17 50	18 12	18 22	18 30		18 46			19 14	19 22	19 28	19 44	
Exeter St Thomas	d			16 59	17 29								17 54			18 33							19 31		
Starcross	d			17 07	17 37								18 02			18 42							19 39		
Dawlish Warren	d			17 12	17 49								18 07			18 47							19 44		
Dawlish	d			17 16	17 53								18 11	18 24		18 51							19 48		
Teignmouth	d			17 21	17 58								18 16	18 29		18 56							19 53		
Newton Abbot	a	17 02		17 29	18 05						17 56	18 10	18 23	18 35	18 42	19 03		19 07			19 34	19 42	20 00	20 03	
	d	17 04		17 30	18 09						17 57	18 12	18 25	18 37	18 43	19 11		19 08			19 35	19 42	20 09	20 05	
Torre	d			17 38	18 17								18 33			19 19							20 17		
Torquay	d			17 41	18 20								18 36	18 48		19 22							20 20		
Paignton	a			17 51	18 30								18 45	18 55		19 30							20 29		
Totnes	d	17 16									18 10	18 24			18 56			19 21				19 56		20 17	
Ivybridge	d														19 12										
Plymouth	a	17 42									18 38	18 50			19 26			19 46			20 15	20 24		20 43	
	d						17 55	18 17		18 23	18 42	19 01			19 31			19 49				20 26		20 50	
Devonport	d							18 20		18 26															
Dockyard	d							18x21		18x27															
Keyham	d							18 23		18a29															
St Budeaux Ferry Road	d							18 25																	
Saltash	d						18 03	18 31							19 40							20 37			
St Germans	d							18 38														20 44			
Menheniot	d							18x45																	
Liskeard 6	d						18 20	18a53			19 07	19 24			19 57			20 12				20 56		21 13	
Bodmin Parkway	d						18 32				19 19	19 36			20 10			20 25				21 09		21 26	
Lostwithiel	d						18 37																	21 31	
Par	d					18 29	18 45				19 31	19 47			20 22		20 28	20 36				21 21		21 39	
Newquay	a					19 21											21 20								
St Austell	d						18 52				19 39	19 54			20 29			20 43				21 28		21 46	
Truro	d						19 10				20 00	20 11			20 47			21 02				21 46		22 04	
Redruth	d						19 23				20 10	20 26			20 59			21 16				21 58		22 15	
Camborne	d						19 29				20 18	20 32			21 07			21 23						22 22	
Hayle	d						19 36															22 11		22 30	
St Erth	d						19 42				20 28	20 44			21 20			21 34				22 16		22 35	
Penzance	a						19 54				20 42	20 52			21 31			21 42				22 30		22 43	

A The Cornishman
B ⌶ to Plymouth
C via Trowbridge

For connections from Heathrow Airport, Gatwick Airport and Oxford please refer to Tables 125A, 148 and 116

21 May to 29 June

London and Birmingham - Devon and Cornwall

Route Diagram - see first Page of Table 135

		GW	GW	GW		GW	XC	GW FX	GW FO	GW FO	GW FX	GW	GW FX	XC		XC	GW	GW	XC	GW	GW	GW	GW	GW FO
		◇1		◇1		◇1	◇1	◇1	◇1	■ 1	■ 1			◇1		◇1	◇1		◇1	◇1	◇		◇1	■
				A		E				B	B			C		C			C					D
		▭		✕▭		▭	⌶	▭	▭	✕▭	✕▭			⌶		⌶	▭		⌶	▭			▭	▭
London Paddington 15 ⊖	d	17 33		18 03		18 06		18 33	18 33	19 03	19 03						19 45			20 35			21 45	23 45
Slough 3	d																							
Reading 7	d	18 04		18u33		18 37		19 02	19 02	19u33	19 33						20 12			21 02			22 11	00u37
Theale	d					18 45																		
Thatcham	d					18 55																		
Newbury	d	18 19				19 02		19 17	19 17	19 50	19 50						20 28			21 18				
Hungerford	d					19 16		19 27	19 27															
Pewsey	d	18 41				19 34		19 46	19 46								20 48			21 38				
Westbury	d	19 01				19a52		20 05	20 05								21 06			21 57				01 37
Castle Cary	d	19 19						20 23	20 23								21 26			22 15				
Birmingham New Street 12	d						18 12							19 12		19 42			20 12					
Cardiff Central 7	d																							
Newport (South Wales)	d																							
Swindon	d																						22 49	
Bristol Parkway 7	d						19 29							20 29		20 56			21 27					
Filton Abbey Wood	d																							
Bath Spa 7	d																						23 19	
Bristol Temple Meads 10	d						19 44							20 44		21 12			21 44		21 56	23 06	23 35	
Weston-super-Mare	d																				22 29	23 42	00s05	
Bridgwater	d																				22 48	00 02	00s24	
Taunton	d	19 41		19 48			20 18	20 46	20 46	20 54	20 54			21 17		21 45	21 48		22 17	22 37	23 03	00s14	00s36	02 35
Tiverton Parkway	d	19 54					20 30	20 59	20 59	21 07	21 07			21 30		21 57	22 02		22 29	22 50	23 18	00s31	00s49	
Exeter St Davids 6	a	20 09		20 13			20 44	21 15	21 15	21 23	21 23			21 43		22 11	22 18		22 43	23 06	23 36	00 50	01 07	03 06
Exmouth	d																	22 05						
Exeter Central	d											21 21						22 31						
Exeter St Davids 6	d	20 19		20 15			20 46		21 16	21 25	21 25	21 29		21 45		22 12	22 19	22 37	22 44	23 08				03 11
Exeter St Thomas	d	20 24										21 32						22 40						
Starcross	d	20 33										21 40						22 48						
Dawlish Warren	d	20 38										21 45						22 59						
Dawlish	d	20 43										21 49						23 03						
Teignmouth	d	20 50										21 54						23 08						
Newton Abbot	a	20 57		20 34			21 03		21 36	21 44	21 44	22 01		22 04		22 30	22 39	23 15	23 05	23 28				03 31
	d	20 58		20 35			21 05		21 36	21 45	21 45	22 03		22 06		22 32	22 40	23 16	23 07	23 28				03 33
Torre	d	21 08										22 11						23 24						
Torquay	d	21 12										22 14						23 27						
Paignton	a	21 22										22 23						23 37						
Totnes	d			20 48			21 18			21 58	21 58			22 17		22 44	22 53		23 19	23 42				
Ivybridge	d																23 10							
Plymouth	a			21 16			21 48		22 14	22 26	22 26			22 43		23 14	23 25		23 45	00 11				04 14
	d			21 19						22 29			22 31											05 43
Devonport	d																							
Dockyard	d																							
Keyham	d																							
St Budeaux Ferry Road	d																							
Saltash	d									22 40			22 40											
St Germans	d									22 47			22 47											
Menheniot	d																							
Liskeard 6	d			21 44						22 59			22 59											06 08
Bodmin Parkway	d			21 58						23 11			23 11											06 22
Lostwithiel	d									23 16			23 16											06 28
Par	d			22 10						23 24			23 24											06 37
Newquay	a																							
St Austell	d			22 18						23 31			23 31											06 46
Truro	d			22 36						23 50			23 50											07 06
Redruth	d			22 48						00 03			00 03											07 18
Camborne	d									00 09			00 09											07 26
Hayle	d									00 16			00 16											07 35
St Erth	d		22 45							00 20			00 20											07 41
Penzance	a		22 57	23 14						00 40			00 40											07 53

A The Golden Hind
B The Armada
C ⌶ to Bristol Temple Meads
D The Night Riviera
E to Frome

For connections from Heathrow Airport, Gatwick Airport and Oxford please refer to Tables 125A, 148 and 116

Mondays to Fridays

21 May to 29 June

London and Birmingham - Devon and Cornwall

Route Diagram - see first Page of Table 135

		GW FX
		■
		A
		🛏
		⊡
London Paddington 15 ⊖	d	23 45
Slough 3	d	
Reading 7	d	00u37
Theale	d	
Thatcham	d	
Newbury	d	
Hungerford	d	
Pewsey	d	
Westbury	d	01 45
Castle Cary	d	
Birmingham New Street 12	d	
Cardiff Central 7	d	
Newport (South Wales)	d	
Swindon	d	
Bristol Parkway 7	d	
Filton Abbey Wood	d	
Bath Spa 7	d	
Bristol Temple Meads 10	d	
Weston-super-Mare	d	
Bridgwater	d	
Taunton	d	02 35
Tiverton Parkway	d	
Exeter St Davids 6	a	03 06
Exmouth	d	
Exeter Central	d	
Exeter St Davids 6	d	03 11
Exeter St Thomas	d	
Starcross	d	
Dawlish Warren	d	
Dawlish	d	
Teignmouth	d	
Newton Abbot	a	03 31
	d	03 33
Torre	d	
Torquay	d	
Paignton	a	
Totnes	d	
Ivybridge	d	
Plymouth	a	04 12
	d	05 43
Devonport	d	
Dockyard	d	
Keyham	d	
St Budeaux Ferry Road	d	
Saltash	d	
St Germans	d	
Menheniot	d	
Liskeard 6	d	06 08
Bodmin Parkway	d	06 22
Lostwithiel	d	06 28
Par	d	06 37
Newquay	a	
St Austell	d	06 46
Truro	d	07 06
Redruth	d	07 18
Camborne	d	07 26
Hayle	d	07 35
St Erth	d	07 41
Penzance	a	07 53

A The Night Riviera

For connections from Heathrow Airport, Gatwick Airport and Oxford please refer to Tables 125A, 148 and 116

Mondays to Fridays

2 July to 31 August

London and Birmingham - Devon and Cornwall

Route Diagram - see first Page of Table 135

		GW MX	GW MX	GW MX	GW MX	GW MX	XC MO	XC MX	GW	GW MO		GW	GW	GW	GW	GW	GW	GW	GW	GW		XC	GW	GW	XC
						■				■															
			◇■		◇■		◇■	◇■							■		■	◇		■		◇■		◇	◇■
						A																			
						🛏				🛏															
			⊡		⊡	⊡				⊡					⊡					⊡					H
London Paddington 15 ⊖	d		20p35		21p45	23p45				23p50															
Slough 3	d																								
Reading 7	d		21p02		22p11	00u37				00u37															
Theale	d																								
Thatcham	d																								
Newbury	d		21p18																						
Hungerford	d																								
Pewsey	d		21p38																						
Westbury	d		21p57			01 45																			
Castle Cary	d		22p15																						
Birmingham New Street 12	d																								06 42
Cardiff Central 7	d																								
Newport (South Wales)	d																								
Swindon	d				22p49																				
Bristol Parkway 7	d																							06 24	07 58
Filton Abbey Wood	d																							06 27	
Bath Spa 7	d				23p19																				
Bristol Temple Meads 10	d			23p06	23p35					02 55								05 24				06 34		06 42	08 10
Weston-super-Mare	d			23p42	00s05													05 45						07 06	
Bridgwater	d			00 02	00s24													06 03						07 25	
Taunton	d		22p37	00s14	00s36	02 35												06 18				07 08		07 39	08 43
Tiverton Parkway	d		22p50	00s31	00s49													06 33				07 20		07 54	08 55
Exeter St Davids 6	a		23p06	00 50	01 07	03 06				04 04								06 51				07 34		08 12	09 08
Exmouth	d																		06 45				07 14		
Exeter Central	d																		07 12				07 43		
Exeter St Davids 6	d		23p08			03 11				04 35			05 34	06 11		06 28		06 55	07 18			07 36	07 50	08 14	09 10
Exeter St Thomas	d												05 38	06 14				06 58	07 21				07 53		
Starcross	d												05 46	06 22				07 07	07 29				08 01		
Dawlish Warren	d												05 51	06 27				07 12	07 34				08 06		
Dawlish	d												05 55	06 31		06 42		07 16	07 38				08 10		
Teignmouth	d												06 00	06 36		06 47		07 21	07 43				08 15		
Newton Abbot	a		23p28			03 31				04 55			06 07	06 44		06 55		07 28	07 50			07 54	08 22	08 35	09 29
	d		23p28			03 33				04 56		05 42	06 09	06 45		06 55	07 06	07 28	07 52			07 55	08 24	08 35	09 30
Torre	d											05 50	06 17	06 53			07 15		08 00				08 33		
Torquay	d											05 53	06 20	06 56			07 20		08 03				08 36		09 42
Paignton	a											06 00	06 28	07 06			07 29		08 12				08 44		09 47
Totnes	d		23p42													07 09		07 42				08 07		08 49	
Ivybridge	d															07 26		07 58						09 05	
Plymouth	a		00 11			04 12				05 35						07 40		08 11				08 34		09 19	
	d	22p31				05 43	05 43	06 28		06 28					07 02			08 14		08 20				09 21	
Devonport	d														07 07					08 24				09 24	
Dockyard	d																								
Keyham	d																								
St Budeaux Ferry Road	d																								
Saltash	d	22p40													07 15					08 33				09 31	
St Germans	d	22p47													07 23					08 41				09 38	
Menheniot	d																								
Liskeard 6	d	22p59				06 08	06 08	06 51		07 09					07 36			08 39		08 53				09 50	
Bodmin Parkway	d	23p11				06 22	06 22	07 03		07 23					07 49			08 51						10 02	
Lostwithiel	d	23p16				06 28	06 28	07 09		07 29					07 55			08 56						10 07	
Par	d	23p24				06 37	06 37	07 15		07 38					08 04			09 17		09 14				10 15	
Newquay	a																	10 09							
St Austell	d	23p31				06 46	06 46	07 22		07 46					08 11					09 23				10 22	
Truro	d	23p50				07 06	07 06	07 39		08 06					08 30					09 41				10 40	
Redruth	d	00 03				07 18	07 18	07 50		08 20					08 42					09 55				10 53	
Camborne	d	00 09				07 26	07 26	07 57		08 27					08 48					10 02				10 59	
Hayle	d	00 16				07 35	07 35	08 05		08 38					08 57					10 10				11 06	
St Erth	d	00 20				07 41	07 41	08 11	08 28	08 45					09 02					10 15				11 10	
Penzance	a	00 40				07 53	07 53	08 19	08 40	08 59					09 12					10 27				11 23	

A The Night Riviera

For connections from Heathrow Airport, Gatwick Airport and Oxford please refer to Tables 125A, 148 and 116

London and Birmingham - Devon and Cornwall

Route Diagram - see first Page of Table 135

		GW	GW ◇1 A 🍴	GW ◇	XC ◇1 ⌶	GW		GW ◇	GW ◇1 B 🍴⊘	GW ◇	XC ◇1 ⌶	GW	GW ◇1 C 🍴	GW ◇	XC ◇1 ⌶	GW		GW ◇	GW ◇1 D 🍴⊘	XC ◇1 ⌶	XC ◇1 ⌶	GW ◇1 E 🍴	GW	GW	GW ◇1 F 🍴⊘
London Paddington [15] ⊖	d		07 06						07 30				09 06						10 06			10 00			11 06
Slough [3]	d																								
Reading [7]	d		07 33						07 57				09 35						10u33			10 27			11u33
Theale	d																								
Thatcham	d																								
Newbury	d		07 48																						
Hungerford	d																								
Pewsey	d		08 07																						12 03
Westbury	d		08 25																						12 22
Castle Cary	d												10 31												12 39
Birmingham New Street [12]	d				07 12						08 12				09 12					09 42	10 12				
Cardiff Central [7]	d									08 00				09 00											
Newport (South Wales)	d									08 15				09 15											
Swindon	d								08 27													10 55			
Bristol Parkway [7]	d				08 26						09 26				10 27					10 55	11 28				
Filton Abbey Wood	d									08 42				09 42											
Bath Spa [7]	d								08 57													11 24			
Bristol Temple Meads [10]	d				08 44				09 13	08 55	09 44			09 55	10 44					11 15	11 44	11 47			
Weston-super-Mare	d									09 29				10 23						11 37		12 07			
Bridgwater	d									09 48				10 42											
Taunton	d		09 02		09 17				09 46	10 02	10 17		10 53	10 58	11 18					12 02	12 17	12 29			13 02
Tiverton Parkway	d		09 15		09 29						10 30		11 06	11 14	11 30					12 14	12 29				13 15
Exeter St Davids [6]	a		09 30		09 42				10 11	10 33	10 45		11 22	11 32	11 45				12 08	12 30	12 42	12 55			13 31
Exmouth	d	08 23				09 23						10 23				11 23							12 23		
Exeter Central	d	08 50				09 50						10 50				11 50							12 50		
Exeter St Davids [6]	d	09 16	09 32	09 35	09 44	09 56			10 13	10 34	10 46	10 56	11 24	11 35	11 47	11 56			12 08	12 32	12 44	12 56	13 03		13 33
Exeter St Thomas	d	09 19				09 59						10 59				11 59							13 06		
Starcross	d	09 27				10 07						11 07				12 07							13 15		
Dawlish Warren	d	09 32				10 12				10 46		11 12				12 22							13 20		
Dawlish	d	09 36				10 16				10 50		11 16				12 27				12 44		13 08	13 24		
Teignmouth	d	09 41				10 21				10 55		11 21				12 32				12 49		13 14	13 29		
Newton Abbot	a	09 48	09 52	09 56	10 02	10 30			10 34	11 02	11 06	11 29	11 43	11 55	12 06	12 39			12 29	12 55	13 02	13 22	13 36		13 52
	d	09 50	09 56	09 57	10 03	10 39			10 36	11 03	11 07	11 30	11 44	11 56	12 07	12 40			12 29	12 56	13 03	13 22	13 38		13 53
Torre	d	09 58	10 05			10 47				11 12		11 38				12 49							13 46		
Torquay	d	10 01	10 09			10 50				11 15		11 41				12 52				13 08		13 34	13 49		
Paignton	a	10 11	10 19			10 59				11 24		11 51				13 00				13 14		13 43	13 58		
Totnes	d			10 10	10 17				10 49		11 21		11 57	12 09	12 21						13 16				14 06
Ivybridge	d			10 27										12 26											
Plymouth	a			10 41	10 46				11 17		11 48		12 27	12 42	12 49				13 06		13 41				14 36
	d			10 42					11 20				12 28						13 11					13 53	
Devonport	d																								
Dockyard	d																								
Keyham	d																								
St Budeaux Ferry Road	d			10 48																					
Saltash	d			10 53									12 38											14 02	
St Germans	d			11 00									12 46											14 09	
Menheniot	d																								
Liskeard [6]	d			11 12					11 44				12 58						13 35					14 21	
Bodmin Parkway	d			11 24					11 57				13 13						13 48					14 33	
Lostwithiel	d			11 29									13 19											14 38	
Par	d			11 37				11 42	12 09				13 30					13 37	14 00					14 46	
Newquay	a							12 34					14 30												
St Austell	d			11 44					12 16									13 44	14 07					14 53	
Truro	d			12 02					12 34									14 02	14 25					15 11	
Redruth	d			12 15					12 46									14 15	14 37					15 24	
Camborne	d			12 21					12 53									14 21	14 45					15 30	
Hayle	d			12 28														14 28	14 54					15 37	
St Erth	d			12 32					13 05									14 33	14 59					15 42	
Penzance	a			12 42					13 17									14 44	15 11					15 53	

A The Devon Express
B The Merchant Venturer
C The Atlantic Coast Express
D The Cornish Riveira
E The Torbay Express
F The Mayflower

For connections from Heathrow Airport, Gatwick Airport and Oxford please refer to Tables 125A, 148 and 116

London and Birmingham - Devon and Cornwall

Route Diagram - see first Page of Table 135

		XC ◇1 ⌶		GW	GW ◇1 A 🍴⊘	GW	XC ◇1 ⌶	GW ◇1 🍴	GW	GW	GW ◇	GW ◇1 B 🍴⊘		GW ◇	GW	XC ◇1 ⌶	XC ◇1 ⌶	GW	GW	GW	GW ◇1 B 🍴⊘	GW		XC ◇1 ⌶	GW FO ◇
London Paddington [15] ⊖	d				12 06			12 18				13 06									14 06				
Slough [3]	d																								
Reading [7]	d				12 33			12 48				13 33									14 33				
Theale	d							12 56																	
Thatcham	d							13 04																	
Newbury	d							13 12																	
Hungerford	d							13 21																	
Pewsey	d							13 40																	
Westbury	d							13 59																	15 20
Castle Cary	d							14 16																	15 49
Birmingham New Street [12]	d	11 12					12 12									13 12	13 42							14 12	
Cardiff Central [7]	d													13 00											
Newport (South Wales)	d													13 15											
Swindon	d																								
Bristol Parkway [7]	d	12 30					13 27									14 29	14 59							15 26	
Filton Abbey Wood	d													13 42											
Bath Spa [7]	d																								
Bristol Temple Meads [10]	d	12 44					13 44							13 53		14 44	15 13							15 44	
Weston-super-Mare	d													14 23											
Bridgwater	d													14 42											
Taunton	d	13 18					14 17	14a41				14 48		14 56		15 18	15 46				15 49			16 17	16 24
Tiverton Parkway	d	13 30					14 29					15 01		15 11		15 30	15 58				16 02			16 29	16 41
Exeter St Davids [6]	a	13 45			14 08		14 42					15 17		15 31		15 46	16 13				16 18			16 42	17 02
Exmouth	d			13 23					14 23									15 23				15 53			
Exeter Central	d			13 50					14 50									15 50				16 20			
Exeter St Davids [6]	d	13 47		13 56	14 08		14 44		14 56			15 18				15 48		15 56		16 05	16 20	16 26		16 44	
Exeter St Thomas	d			13 59					14 59									15 59				16 29			
Starcross	d			14 07					15 07									16 07				16 37			
Dawlish Warren	d			14 23					15 12									16 12		16 18		16 42			
Dawlish	d			14 27					15 16									16 16		16 22		16 46			
Teignmouth	d			14 32					15 21									16 21		16 27		16 51			
Newton Abbot	a	14 06		14 40	14 28		15 02		15 29			15 39				16 07		16 30		16 35	16 39	16 58		17 02	
	d	14 07		14 41	14 29	14 50	15 03		15 30			15 39			15 58	16 08		16 30		16 48	16 40	17 00		17 04	
Torre	d			14 49					15 38									16 38				17 08			
Torquay	d			14 52					15 41									16 41				17 11			
Paignton	a			15 00					15 51									16 51				17 20			
Totnes	d	14 21				15 02	15 16					15 53			16 11	16 22				17 02	16 53			17 16	
Ivybridge	d					15 19									16 28					17 19					
Plymouth	a	14 48			15 06	15 37	15 41					16 21			16 44	16 49				17 34	17 21			17 42	
	d				15 12					15 57		16 29							17 04		17 23				
Devonport	d									16 00									17 07						
Dockyard	d									16x01									17x08						
Keyham	d									16 03									17 10						
St Budeaux Ferry Road	d									16 06									17 13						
Saltash	d									16 11									17 17		17 34				
St Germans	d									16 18									17 24		17 41				
Menheniot	d									16x25									17x32						
Liskeard [6]	d				15 36					16a31		16 53							17a40		17 54				
Bodmin Parkway	d				15 49							17 06									18 07				
Lostwithiel	d											17 12									18 13				
Par	d				16 01						16 10	17 21									18 22				
Newquay	a										17 02														
St Austell	d				16 08							17 28									18 29				
Truro	d				16 26							17 46									18 47				
Redruth	d				16 38							17 59									18 59				
Camborne	d				16 46							18 07									19 07				
Hayle	d				16 55							18 15									19 16				
St Erth	d				17 00							18 22									19 21				
Penzance	a				17 12							18 33									19 33				

A The Royal Duchy
B 🍴 from Newton Abbot ⊘ to Newton Abbot

For connections from Heathrow Airport, Gatwick Airport and Oxford please refer to Tables 125A, 148 and 116

2 July to 31 August

London and Birmingham - Devon and Cornwall

Route Diagram - see first Page of Table 135

		GW FO	GW	GW	GW	GW	GW	GW	GW	XC	GW	XC	GW
		◇■			◇				◇■ A	◇■ B		◇■	◇■
		☕							☕⊘	🍴		🍴	☕
London Paddington ■ ⊖	d	14 36							15 06				16 06
Slough ■	d												
Reading ■	d	15u08							15u33				16 33
Theale	d												
Thatcham	d												
Newbury	d												
Hungerford	d												
Pewsey	d								16 03				
Westbury	d	16 15							16 23				
Castle Cary	d	16 32							16 41				
Birmingham New Street ■	d									15 12		15 42	
Cardiff Central ■	d												
Newport (South Wales)	d												
Swindon	d												
Bristol Parkway ■	d									16 29		16 58	
Filton Abbey Wood	d												
Bath Spa ■	d												
Bristol Temple Meads ■	d									16 44		17 13	
Weston-super-Mare	d												
Bridgwater	d												
Taunton	d	16 55							17 05	17 17		17 45	17 50
Tiverton Parkway	d	17 08							17 18	17 29		17 57	18 03
Exeter St Davids ■	a	17 26							17 34	17 42		18 11	18 19
Exmouth	d			16 55									
Exeter Central	d		16 46	17 21							17 45		
Exeter St Davids ■	d		16 56	17 26					17 35	17 45	17 50	18 12	18 22
Exeter St Thomas	d		16 59	17 29							17 54		
Starcross	d		17 07	17 37							18 02		
Dawlish Warren	d		17 12	17 49							18 07		
Dawlish	d		17 16	17 53							18 11	18 24	
Teignmouth	d		17 21	17 58							18 16	18 29	
Newton Abbot	a		17 29	18 05					17 56	18 10	18 23	18 35	18 42
	d		17 30	18 09					17 57	18 12	18 25	18 37	18 43
Torre	d		17 38	18 17							18 33		
Torquay	d		17 41	18 20							18 36	18 48	
Paignton	a		17 51	18 30							18 45	18 55	
Totnes	d								18 10	18 24			18 56
Ivybridge	d												19 12
Plymouth	a								18 38	18 50			19 26
	d					17 55	18 17	18 23	18 42	19 01			19 31
Devonport	d						18 20	18 26					
Dockyard	d						18x21	18x27					
Keyham	d						18 23	18a29					
St Budeaux Ferry Road	d						18 25						
Saltash	d					18 03	18 31						19 40
St Germans	d						18 38						
Menheniot	d						18x45						
Liskeard ■	d					18 20	18a53		19 07	19 24			19 57
Bodmin Parkway	d					18 32			19 19	19 36			20 10
Lostwithiel	d					18 37							
Par	d				18 29	18 45			19 31	19 47			20 22
Newquay	a				19 21								
St Austell	d					18 52			19 39	19 54			20 29
Truro	d					19 10			20 00	20 11			20 47
Redruth	d					19 23			20 10	20 26			20 59
Camborne	d					19 29			20 18	20 32			21 07
Hayle	d					19 36							
St Erth	d					19 42			20 28	20 44			21 20
Penzance	a					19 54			20 42	20 52			21 31

		GW	GW	XC	GW FX	GW FO	GW	GW	XC	GW	GW
				◇■ B	◇■	◇■	◇■		◇■ B	◇■ C	◇■
				🍴	☕	☕	☕		🍴	☕	☕
London Paddington ■ ⊖	d				16 36	16 36	17 03			17 06	17 33
Slough ■	d										
Reading ■	d				17 04	17 04	17 32			17 36	18 04
Theale	d									17 45	
Thatcham	d									17 55	
Newbury	d				17 19	17 19	17 48			18 02	18 19
Hungerford	d				17 29	17 29				18 16	
Pewsey	d				17 44	17 44				18 34	18 41
Westbury	d				18 04	18 04					19 01
Castle Cary	d				18 21	18 21					19 19
Birmingham New Street ■	d			16 12					17 12		
Cardiff Central ■	d										
Newport (South Wales)	d										
Swindon	d										
Bristol Parkway ■	d			17 27					18 29		
Filton Abbey Wood	d										
Bath Spa ■	d									19 24	
Bristol Temple Meads ■	d			17 44					18 44	19a41	
Weston-super-Mare	d										
Bridgwater	d										
Taunton	d			18 17	18 43	18 43	18 52		19 17		19 41
Tiverton Parkway	d			18 29	18 56	18 56	19 05		19 29		19 54
Exeter St Davids ■	a			18 42	19 14	19 14	19 21		19 42		20 09
Exmouth	d	17 58						18 55			
Exeter Central	d	18 25						19 21			
Exeter St Davids ■	d	18 30		18 46		19 14	19 22	19 28	19 44		20 19
Exeter St Thomas	d	18 33						19 31			20 24
Starcross	d	18 42						19 39			20 33
Dawlish Warren	d	18 47						19 44			20 38
Dawlish	d	18 51						19 48			20 43
Teignmouth	d	18 56						19 53			20 50
Newton Abbot	a	19 03		19 07		19 34	19 42	20 00	20 03		20 57
	d	19 11		19 08		19 35	19 42	20 09	20 05		20 58
Torre	d	19 19						20 17			21 08
Torquay	d	19 22						20 20			21 12
Paignton	a	19 30						20 29			21 22
Totnes	d			19 21			19 56		20 17		
Ivybridge	d										
Plymouth	a			19 46		20 15	20 24		20 43		
	d			19 49			20 26		20 50		
Devonport	d										
Dockyard	d										
Keyham	d										
St Budeaux Ferry Road	d										
Saltash	d						20 37				
St Germans	d						20 44				
Menheniot	d										
Liskeard ■	d			20 12			20 56		21 13		
Bodmin Parkway	d			20 25			21 09		21 26		
Lostwithiel	d								21 31		
Par	d		20 28	20 36			21 21		21 39		
Newquay	a		21 20								
St Austell	d			20 43			21 28		21 46		
Truro	d			21 02			21 46		22 04		
Redruth	d			21 16			21 58		22 15		
Camborne	d			21 23					22 22		
Hayle	d						22 11		22 30		
St Erth	d			21 34			22 16		22 35		
Penzance	a			21 42			22 30		22 43		

A The Cornishman
B 🍴 to Plymouth
C via Trowbridge

For connections from Heathrow Airport, Gatwick Airport and Oxford please refer to Tables 125A, 148 and 116

2 July to 31 August

London and Birmingham - Devon and Cornwall

Route Diagram - see first Page of Table 135

		GW	GW	GW	XC	GW FX	GW FO	GW FO	GW FX	GW	GW FX	XC	XC
			◇■ A	◇■ E	◇■	◇■	◇■	■ ■ B	■ ■ B			◇■ C	◇■ C
			✕☕	☕	🍴	☕	☕	✕☕	✕☕			🍴	🍴
London Paddington ■ ⊖	d		18 03	18 06		18 33	18 33	19 03	19 03				
Slough ■	d												
Reading ■	d		18u33	18 37		19 02	19 02	19u33	19 33				
Theale	d			18 45									
Thatcham	d			18 55									
Newbury	d			19 02		19 17	19 17	19 50	19 50				
Hungerford	d			19 16		19 27	19 27						
Pewsey	d			19 34		19 46	19 46						
Westbury	d			19a52		20 05	20 05						
Castle Cary	d					20 23	20 23						
Birmingham New Street ■	d				18 12							19 12	19 42
Cardiff Central ■	d												
Newport (South Wales)	d												
Swindon	d												
Bristol Parkway ■	d				19 29							20 29	20 56
Filton Abbey Wood	d												
Bath Spa ■	d												
Bristol Temple Meads ■	d				19 44							20 44	21 12
Weston-super-Mare	d												
Bridgwater	d												
Taunton	d		19 48		20 18	20 46	20 46	20 54	20 54			21 17	21 45
Tiverton Parkway	d				20 30	20 59	20 59	21 07	21 07			21 30	21 57
Exeter St Davids ■	a		20 13		20 44	21 15	21 15	21 23	21 23			21 43	22 11
Exmouth	d												
Exeter Central	d									21 21			
Exeter St Davids ■	d		20 15		20 46		21 16	21 25	21 25	21 29		21 45	22 12
Exeter St Thomas	d									21 32			
Starcross	d									21 40			
Dawlish Warren	d									21 45			
Dawlish	d									21 49			
Teignmouth	d									21 54			
Newton Abbot	a		20 34		21 03		21 36	21 44	21 44	22 01		22 04	22 30
	d		20 35		21 05		21 36	21 45	21 45	22 03		22 06	22 32
Torre	d									22 11			
Torquay	d									22 14			
Paignton	a									22 23			
Totnes	d		20 48		21 18			21 58	21 58			22 17	22 44
Ivybridge	d												
Plymouth	a		21 16		21 48		22 14	22 26	22 26			22 43	23 14
	d		21 19					22 29			22 31		
Devonport	d												
Dockyard	d												
Keyham	d												
St Budeaux Ferry Road	d												
Saltash	d							22 40			22 40		
St Germans	d							22 47			22 47		
Menheniot	d												
Liskeard ■	d		21 44					22 59			22 59		
Bodmin Parkway	d		21 58					23 11			23 11		
Lostwithiel	d							23 16			23 16		
Par	d		22 10					23 24			23 24		
Newquay	a												
St Austell	d		22 18					23 31			23 31		
Truro	d		22 36					23 50			23 50		
Redruth	d		22 48					00 03			00 03		
Camborne	d							00 09			00 09		
Hayle	d							00 16			00 16		
St Erth	d	22 45						00 20			00 20		
Penzance	a	22 57	23 14					00 40			00 40		

		GW	GW	XC	GW	GW	GW	GW	GW FO	GW FX
		◇■		◇■ C	◇■	◇		◇■	■ D 🛏	■ D 🛏
		☕		🍴	☕			☕	☕	☕
London Paddington ■ ⊖	d	19 45			20 35			21 45	23 45	23 45
Slough ■	d									
Reading ■	d	20 12			21 02			22 11	00u37	00u37
Theale	d									
Thatcham	d									
Newbury	d	20 28			21 18					
Hungerford	d									
Pewsey	d	20 48			21 38					
Westbury	d	21 06			21 57				01 37	01 45
Castle Cary	d	21 26			22 15					
Birmingham New Street ■	d			20 12						
Cardiff Central ■	d									
Newport (South Wales)	d									
Swindon	d							22 49		
Bristol Parkway ■	d			21 27						
Filton Abbey Wood	d									
Bath Spa ■	d							23 19		
Bristol Temple Meads ■	d			21 44		21 56	23 06	23 35		
Weston-super-Mare	d					22 29	23 42	00s05		
Bridgwater	d					22 48	00 02	00s24		
Taunton	d	21 48		22 17	22 37	23 03	00s14	00s36	02 35	02 35
Tiverton Parkway	d	22 02		22 29	22 50	23 18	00s31	00s49		
Exeter St Davids ■	a	22 18		22 43	23 06	23 36	00 50	01 07	03 06	03 06
Exmouth	d		22 05							
Exeter Central	d		22 31							
Exeter St Davids ■	d	22 19	22 37	22 44	23 08				03 11	03 11
Exeter St Thomas	d		22 40							
Starcross	d		22 48							
Dawlish Warren	d		22 59							
Dawlish	d		23 03							
Teignmouth	d		23 08							
Newton Abbot	a	22 39	23 15	23 05	23 28				03 31	03 31
	d	22 40	23 16	23 07	23 28				03 33	03 33
Torre	d		23 24							
Torquay	d		23 27							
Paignton	a		23 37							
Totnes	d	22 53		23 19	23 42					
Ivybridge	d	23 10								
Plymouth	a	23 25		23 45	00 11				04 14	04 12
	d								05 43	05 43
Devonport	d									
Dockyard	d									
Keyham	d									
St Budeaux Ferry Road	d									
Saltash	d									
St Germans	d									
Menheniot	d									
Liskeard ■	d								06 08	06 08
Bodmin Parkway	d								06 22	06 22
Lostwithiel	d								06 28	06 28
Par	d								06 37	06 37
Newquay	a									
St Austell	d								06 46	06 46
Truro	d								07 06	07 06
Redruth	d								07 18	07 18
Camborne	d								07 26	07 26
Hayle	d								07 35	07 35
St Erth	d								07 41	07 41
Penzance	a								07 53	07 53

A The Golden Hind
B The Armada
C 🍴 to Bristol Temple Meads
D The Night Riviera
E to Frome

For connections from Heathrow Airport, Gatwick Airport and Oxford please refer to Tables 125A, 148 and 116

London and Birmingham - Devon and Cornwall

Mondays to Fridays

3 September to 14 September

Route Diagram - see first Page of Table 135

Station		GW A	GW ◇■ A	GW A	GW ◇■ A	GW ■ B	XC MO ◇■	XC ◇■ A	GW	GW MO ■	GW	GW	GW	GW ■	GW	GW ■	GW ◇	GW	XC ◇■	GW	GW	GW ◇	GW
London Paddington ⊖	d		20p35		21p45	23p45				23p50													
Slough	d																						
Reading	d		21p02		22p11	00u37				00u37													
Theale	d																						
Thatcham	d																						
Newbury	d		21p18																				
Hungerford	d																						
Pewsey	d		21p38																				
Westbury	d		21p57			01 45																	
Castle Cary	d		22p15																				
Birmingham New Street	d																						
Cardiff Central	d																						
Newport (South Wales)	d																						
Swindon	d				22p49																		
Bristol Parkway	d																						
Filton Abbey Wood	d																					06 24	
Bath Spa	d				23p19																	06 27	
Bristol Temple Meads	d			23p06	23p35					02 55							05 24		06 34			06 42	
Weston-super-Mare	d			23p42	00s05												05 45					07 06	
Bridgwater	d			00 02	00s24												06 03					07 25	
Taunton	d		22p37	00s14	00s36	02 35											06 18		07 08			07 39	
Tiverton Parkway	d		22p50	00s31	00s49												06 33		07 20			07 54	
Exeter St Davids	a		23p06	00 50	01 07	03 06				04 04							06 51		07 34			08 12	
Exmouth	d																	06 45		07 14			08 23
Exeter Central	d																	07 12		07 43			08 50
Exeter St Davids	d		23p08			03 11				04 35		05 34	06 11		06 28		06 55	07 18	07 36	07 50		08 14	08 58
Exeter St Thomas	d											05 38	06 14				06 58	07 21		07 53			09 01
Starcross	d											05 46	06 22				07 07	07 29		08 01			09 09
Dawlish Warren	d											05 51	06 27				07 12	07 34		08 06			09 21
Dawlish	d											05 55	06 31		06 42		07 16	07 38		08 10			09 25
Teignmouth	d											06 00	06 36		06 47		07 21	07 43		08 15			09 30
Newton Abbot	a		23p28			03 31				04 55		06 07	06 44		06 55		07 28	07 50	07 54	08 22		08 35	09 37
	d		23p28			03 33				04 56	05 42	06 09	06 45		06 55	07 06	07 28	07 52	07 55	08 24		08 35	09 39
Torre	d										05 50	06 17	06 53			07 15		08 00		08 33			09 47
Torquay	d										05 53	06 20	06 56			07 20		08 03		08 36			09 50
Paignton	a										06 00	06 28	07 06			07 29		08 12		08 44			09 57
Totnes	d		23p42												07 09		07 42		08 07			08 49	
Ivybridge	d														07 26		07 58					09 05	
Plymouth	a		00 11			04 12				05 35					07 40		08 11		08 34			09 19	
	d	22p31				05 43	05 43	06 28		06 28				07 02	07 53		08 14					09 21	
Devonport	d													07 07			08 17					09 24	
Dockyard	d																						
Keyham	d																						
St Budeaux Ferry Road	d																						
Saltash	d	22p40												07 15	08 02		08 24					09 31	
St Germans	d	22p47												07 23	08 09		08 31					09 38	
Menheniot	d																						
Liskeard	d	22p59				06 08	06 08	06 51		07 09				07 36	08 21		08 43					09 50	
Bodmin Parkway	d	23p11				06 22	06 22	07 03		07 23				07 49	08 33		08 55					10 02	
Lostwithiel	d	23p16				06 28	06 28	07 09		07 29				07 55	08 40		09 00					10 07	
Par	d	23p24				06 37	06 37	07 15		07 38				08 04	08a54		09 08				09 17	10 15	
Newquay	a																				10 09		
St Austell	d	23p31				06 46	06 46	07 22		07 46				08 11			09 16					10 22	
Truro	d	23p50				07 06	07 06	07 39		08 06				08 30			09 34					10 40	
Redruth	d	00 03				07 18	07 18	07 50		08 20				08 42			09 47					10 53	
Camborne	d	00 09				07 26	07 26	07 57		08 27				08 48			09 53					10 59	
Hayle	d	00 16				07 35	07 35	08 05		08 38				08 57			10 00					11 06	
St Erth	d	00 20				07 41	07 41	08 11	08 28	08 45				09 02			10 08					11 10	
Penzance	a	00 40				07 53	07 53	08 19	08 40	08 59				09 12			10 16					11 23	

A not 3 September, 10 September

B not 3 September, 10 September. The Night Riviera

For connections from Heathrow Airport, Gatwick Airport and Oxford please refer to Tables 125A, 148 and 116

Table 135

London and Birmingham - Devon and Cornwall

Mondays to Fridays

3 September to 14 September

Route Diagram - see first Page of Table 135

Station		XC ◇■	GW ◇■ A	GW ◇	XC ◇■	GW	GW ◇■ B	GW ◇	XC ◇■	GW	GW ◇■	GW ◇	GW ◇	GW ◇	XC ◇■	GW	GW ◇■ C	XC ◇■	XC ◇■	GW ◇■ D	GW	GW ◇	GW
London Paddington ⊖	d		07 06				07 30				09 06						10 06			10 00			
Slough	d																						
Reading	d		07 33				07 57				09 35						10u33			10 27			
Theale	d																						
Thatcham	d																						
Newbury	d		07 48																				
Hungerford	d																						
Pewsey	d		08 07																				
Westbury	d		08 25																				
Castle Cary	d										10 31												
Birmingham New Street	d	06 42			07 12				08 12						09 12			09 42	10 12				
Cardiff Central	d							08 00						09 00									
Newport (South Wales)	d							08 15						09 15									
Swindon	d						08 27													10 55			
Bristol Parkway	d	07 58			08 26				09 26						10 27			10 55	11 28				
Filton Abbey Wood	d							08 42						09 42									
Bath Spa	d						08 57													11 24			
Bristol Temple Meads	d	08 10			08 44		09 13	08 55	09 44					09 55	10 44			11 15	11 44	11 47			
Weston-super-Mare	d							09 29						10 23				11 37		12 07			
Bridgwater	d							09 48						10 42									
Taunton	d	08 43	09 02		09 17		09 46	10 02	10 17		10 53			10 58	11 18			12 02	12 17	12 29			
Tiverton Parkway	d	08 55	09 15		09 29				10 30		11 06			11 14	11 30			12 14	12 29				
Exeter St Davids	a	09 08	09 30		09 42		10 11	10 33	10 45		11 22			11 32	11 45		12 08	12 30	12 42	12 55			
Exmouth	d					09 23				10 23						11 23					12 23		
Exeter Central	d					09 50				10 50						11 50					12 50		
Exeter St Davids	d	09 10	09 32	09 35	09 44	09 56	10 13	10 34	10 46	10 56	11 24			11 35	11 47	11 56	12 08	12 32	12 44	12 56	13 03		
Exeter St Thomas	d					09 59				10 59						11 59					13 06		
Starcross	d					10 07				11 07						12 07					13 15		
Dawlish Warren	d					10 12		10 46		11 12						12 22					13 20		
Dawlish	d					10 16		10 50		11 16						12 27		12 44		13 08	13 24		
Teignmouth	d					10 21		10 55		11 21						12 32		12 49		13 14	13 29		
Newton Abbot	a	09 29	09 52	09 56	10 02	10 30	10 34	11 02	11 06	11 29	11 43			11 55	12 06	12 39	12 29	12 55	13 02	13 22	13 36		
	d	09 30	09 56	09 57	10 03	10 39	10 36	11 03	11 07	11 30	11 44			11 56	12 07	12 40	12 29	12 56	13 03	13 22	13 38		
Torre	d		10 05			10 47		11 12		11 38						12 49					13 46		
Torquay	d	09 42	10 09			10 50		11 15		11 41						12 52		13 08		13 34	13 49		
Paignton	a	09 47	10 19			10 59		11 24		11 51						13 00		13 14		13 43	13 58		
Totnes	d			10 10	10 17		10 49		11 21		11 57			12 09	12 21				13 16				
Ivybridge	d			10 27										12 26									
Plymouth	a			10 41	10 46		11 17		11 48		12 27			12 42	12 49		13 06		13 41				
	d			10 42			11 20						12 39				13 11						13 53
Devonport	d																						
Dockyard	d																						
Keyham	d																						
St Budeaux Ferry Road	d			10 48																			
Saltash	d			10 53									12 48										14 02
St Germans	d			11 00									12 55										14 09
Menheniot	d																						
Liskeard	d			11 12			11 44						13 07				13 35						14 21
Bodmin Parkway	d			11 24			11 57						13 19				13 48						14 33
Lostwithiel	d			11 29									13 24										14 38
Par	d			11 37			12 09					12 13	13 32				14 00					14 08	14 46
Newquay	a											13 01										14 56	
St Austell	d			11 44			12 16						13 39				14 07						14 53
Truro	d			12 02			12 34						13 57				14 25						15 11
Redruth	d			12 15			12 46						14 10				14 37						15 24
Camborne	d			12 21			12 53						14 16				14 45						15 30
Hayle	d			12 28									14 23				14 54						15 37
St Erth	d			12 32			13 05						14 28				14 59						15 42
Penzance	a			12 42			13 17						14 39				15 11						15 53

A The Devon Express

B The Merchant Venturer

C The Cornish Riveira

D The Torbay Express

For connections from Heathrow Airport, Gatwick Airport and Oxford please refer to Tables 125A, 148 and 116

Table 135

Mondays to Fridays

3 September to 14 September

London and Birmingham - Devon and Cornwall

Route Diagram - see first Page of Table 135

		GW ◇1 A 🍴⊘	XC ◇1 ⊼	GW	GW ◇1 B 🍴⊘	GW	XC ◇1 ⊼	GW ◇1 🍴	GW	GW ◇	GW	GW ◇1 C 🍴⊘	GW ◇	GW	XC ◇1 ⊼	XC ◇1 ⊼	GW	GW	GW	GW ◇1 C 🍴⊘	GW	XC ◇1 ⊼
London Paddington 15 ⊖	d	11 06			12 06			12 18				13 06								14 06		
Slough 3	d																					
Reading 7	d	11u33			12 33			12 48				13 33								14 33		
Theale	d							12 56														
Thatcham	d							13 04														
Newbury	d							13 12														
Hungerford	d							13 21														
Pewsey	d	12 03						13 40														
Westbury	d	12 22						13 59														
Castle Cary	d	12 39						14 16														
Birmingham New Street 12	d		11 12				12 12								13 12	13 42						14 12
Cardiff Central 7	d												13 00									
Newport (South Wales)	d												13 15									
Swindon	d																					
Bristol Parkway 7	d		12 30				13 27								14 29	14 59						15 26
Filton Abbey Wood	d												13 42									
Bath Spa 7	d																					
Bristol Temple Meads 10	d		12 44				13 44						13 53		14 44	15 13						15 44
Weston-super-Mare	d												14 23									
Bridgwater	d												14 42									
Taunton	d	13 02	13 18				14 17	14a41				14 48	14 56		15 18	15 46				15 49		16 17
Tiverton Parkway	d	13 15	13 30				14 29					15 01	15 11		15 30	15 58				16 02		16 29
Exeter St Davids 6	a	13 31	13 45		14 08		14 42					15 17	15 31		15 46	16 13				16 18		16 42
Exmouth	d			13 23					14 23								15 23				15 53	
Exeter Central	d			13 50					14 50								15 50				16 20	
Exeter St Davids 6	d	13 33	13 47	13 56	14 08		14 44		14 56			15 18			15 48		15 56		16 05	16 20	16 26	16 44
Exeter St Thomas	d			13 59					14 59								15 59				16 29	
Starcross	d			14 07					15 07								16 07				16 37	
Dawlish Warren	d			14 23					15 12								16 12		16 18		16 42	
Dawlish	d			14 27					15 16								16 16		16 22		16 46	
Teignmouth	d			14 32					15 21								16 21		16 27		16 51	
Newton Abbot	a	13 52	14 06	14 40	14 28		15 02		15 29			15 39			16 07		16 30		16 35	16 39	16 58	17 02
	d	13 53	14 07	14 41	14 29	14 50	15 03		15 30			15 39		15 58	16 08		16 30		16 48	16 40	17 00	17 04
Torre	d			14 49					15 38								16 38				17 08	
Torquay	d			14 52					15 41								16 41				17 11	
Paignton	a			15 00					15 51								16 51				17 20	
Totnes	d	14 06	14 21			15 02	15 16					15 53		16 11	16 22				17 02	16 53		17 16
Ivybridge	d					15 19								16 28					17 19			
Plymouth	a	14 36	14 48		15 06	15 37	15 41					16 22		16 44	16 49				17 34	17 21		17 42
	d				15 12						15 57							17 04		17 23		
Devonport	d										16 00							17 07				
Dockyard	d										16x01							17x08				
Keyham	d										16 03							17 10				
St Budeaux Ferry Road	d										16 06							17 13				
Saltash	d										16 11							17 17		17 34		
St Germans	d										16 18							17 24		17 41		
Menheniot	d										16x25							17x32				
Liskeard 6	d				15 36						16 32							17a40		17 54		
Bodmin Parkway	d				15 49						16 44									18 07		
Lostwithiel	d										16 49									18 13		
Par	d				16 01					16 10	16 57									18 22		
Newquay	a									17 02												
St Austell	d				16 08						17 06									18 29		
Truro	d				16 26						17 23									18 47		
Redruth	d				16 38						17 36									18 59		
Camborne	d				16 46						17 42									19 07		
Hayle	d				16 55						17 50									19 16		
St Erth	d				17 00						17 54									19 21		
Penzance	a				17 12						18 07									19 33		

A The Mayflower

B The Royal Duchy

C 🍴 from Newton Abbot ⊘ to Newton Abbot

For connections from Heathrow Airport, Gatwick Airport and Oxford please refer to Tables 125A, 148 and 116

Table 135

Mondays to Fridays

3 September to 14 September

London and Birmingham - Devon and Cornwall

Route Diagram - see first Page of Table 135

		GW FO ◇	GW	GW	GW ◇	GW	GW	GW	GW ◇1 A 🍴⊘	XC ◇1 B ⊼	GW	XC ◇1 ⊼	GW ◇1 🍴	GW	GW	XC ◇1 B ⊼	GW ◇1 C 🍴	GW FO ◇1 🍴	GW ◇1 🍴	GW	XC ◇1 B ⊼	GW ◇1 C 🍴	GW ◇1 🍴
London Paddington 15 ⊖	d								15 06				16 06				16 36	16 36	17 03			17 06	17 33
Slough 3	d																						
Reading 7	d								15u33				16 33				17 04	17 04	17 32			17 36	18 04
Theale	d																					17 45	
Thatcham	d																					17 55	
Newbury	d																17 19	17 19	17 48			18 02	18 19
Hungerford	d																17 29	17 29				18 16	
Pewsey	d								16 03								17 44	17 44				18 34	18 41
Westbury	d	15 20							16 23								18 04	18 04					19 01
Castle Cary	d	15 49							16 41								18 21	18 21					19 19
Birmingham New Street 12	d									15 12		15 42				16 12					17 12		
Cardiff Central 7	d																						
Newport (South Wales)	d																						
Swindon	d																						
Bristol Parkway 7	d									16 29		16 58				17 27					18 29		
Filton Abbey Wood	d																						
Bath Spa 7	d																					19 24	
Bristol Temple Meads 10	d									16 44		17 13				17 44					18 44	19a41	
Weston-super-Mare	d																						
Bridgwater	d																						
Taunton	d	16 24							17 05	17 17		17 45	17 50			18 17	18 43	18 43	18 52		19 17		19 41
Tiverton Parkway	d	16 41							17 18	17 29		17 57	18 03			18 29	18 56	18 56	19 05		19 29		19 54
Exeter St Davids 6	a	17 02							17 34	17 42		18 11	18 19			18 42	19 14	19 14	19 21		19 42		20 09
Exmouth	d			16 55										17 58						18 55			
Exeter Central	d		16 46	17 21							17 45			18 25						19 21			
Exeter St Davids 6	d		16 56	17 26					17 35	17 45	17 50	18 12	18 22	18 30		18 46		19 14	19 22	19 28	19 44		20 19
Exeter St Thomas	d		16 59	17 29							17 54			18 33						19 31			20 24
Starcross	d		17 07	17 37							18 02			18 42						19 39			20 33
Dawlish Warren	d		17 12	17 49							18 07			18 47						19 44			20 38
Dawlish	d		17 16	17 53							18 11	18 24		18 51						19 48			20 43
Teignmouth	d		17 21	17 58							18 16	18 29		18 56						19 53			20 50
Newton Abbot	a		17 29	18 05					17 56	18 10	18 23	18 35	18 42	19 03		19 07		19 34	19 42	20 00	20 03		20 57
	d		17 30	18 09					17 57	18 12	18 25	18 37	18 43	19 11		19 08		19 35	19 42	20 09	20 05		20 58
Torre	d		17 38	18 17							18 33			19 19						20 17			21 08
Torquay	d		17 41	18 20							18 36	18 48		19 22						20 20			21 12
Paignton	a		17 51	18 30							18 45	18 55		19 30						20 29			21 22
Totnes	d								18 10	18 24			18 56			19 21			19 56		20 17		
Ivybridge	d												19 12										
Plymouth	a								18 38	18 50			19 26			19 46		20 15	20 24		20 43		
	d					17 55	18 17	18 23	18 42	19 01			19 31			19 49			20 26		20 50		
Devonport	d						18 20	18 26															
Dockyard	d						18x21	18x27															
Keyham	d						18 23	18a29															
St Budeaux Ferry Road	d						18 25																
Saltash	d					18 03	18 31						19 40						20 37				
St Germans	d						18 38												20 44				
Menheniot	d						18x45																
Liskeard 6	d					18 20	18a53		19 07	19 24			19 57			20 12			20 56		21 13		
Bodmin Parkway	d					18 32			19 19	19 36			20 10			20 25			21 09		21 26		
Lostwithiel	d					18 37															21 31		
Par	d				18 29	18 45			19 31	19 47			20 22		20 28	20 36			21 21		21 39		
Newquay	a				19 21										21 20								
St Austell	d					18 52			19 39	19 54			20 29			20 43			21 28		21 46		
Truro	d					19 10			20 00	20 11			20 47			21 02			21 46		22 04		
Redruth	d					19 23			20 10	20 26			20 59			21 16			21 58		22 15		
Camborne	d					19 29			20 18	20 32			21 07			21 23					22 22		
Hayle	d					19 36													22 11		22 30		
St Erth	d					19 42			20 28	20 44			21 20			21 34			22 16		22 35		
Penzance	a					19 54			20 42	20 52			21 31			21 42			22 30		22 43		

A The Cornishman

B ⊼ to Plymouth

C not 7 September, 14 September

C via Trowbridge

For connections from Heathrow Airport, Gatwick Airport and Oxford please refer to Tables 125A, 148 and 116

Table 135

Mondays to Fridays

3 September to 14 September

London and Birmingham - Devon and Cornwall

Route Diagram - see first Page of Table 135

		GW	GW	GW	XC	GW	GW FO	GW FO	GW	GW	GW	XC	XC	GW	GW	XC	GW	GW	GW	GW	GW FO	GW
			A	H		B		C	D		B	E	E			E					F	G
London Paddington ⊖	d		18 03	18 06		18 33	18 33	19 03	19 03					19 45			20 35			21 45	23 45	23 45
Slough	d																					
Reading	d		18u33	18 37		19 02	19 02	19u33	19 33					20 12			21 02			22 11	00u37	00u37
Theale	d			18 45																		
Thatcham	d			18 55																		
Newbury	d			19 02		19 17	19 17	19 50	19 50					20 28			21 18					
Hungerford	d			19 16		19 27	19 27															
Pewsey	d			19 34		19 46	19 46							20 48			21 38					
Westbury	d			19a52		20 05	20 05							21 06			21 57				01 37	01 45
Castle Cary	d					20 23	20 23							21 26			22 15					
Birmingham New Street	d				18 12							19 12	19 42			20 12						
Cardiff Central	d																					
Newport (South Wales)	d																					
Swindon	d																			22 49		
Bristol Parkway	d				19 29							20 29	20 56			21 27						
Filton Abbey Wood	d																					
Bath Spa	d																			23 19		
Bristol Temple Meads	d				19 44							20 44	21 12			21 44		21 56	23 06	23 35		
Weston-super-Mare	d																	22 29	23 42	00s05		
Bridgwater	d																	22 48	00 02	00s24		
Taunton	d		19 48		20 18	20 46	20 46	20 54	20 54			21 17	21 45	21 48		22 17	22 37	23 03	00s14	00s36	02 35	02 35
Tiverton Parkway	d				20 30	20 59	20 59	21 07	21 07			21 30	21 57	22 02		22 29	22 50	23 18	00s31	00s49		
Exeter St Davids	a		20 13		20 44	21 15	21 15	21 23	21 23			21 43	22 11	22 18		22 43	23 06	23 36	00 50	01 07	03 06	03 06
Exmouth	d														22 05							
Exeter Central	d									21 21					22 31							
Exeter St Davids	d		20 15		20 46		21 16	21 25	21 25	21 29		21 45	22 12	22 19	22 37	22 44	23 08				03 11	03 11
Exeter St Thomas	d									21 32					22 40							
Starcross	d									21 40					22 48							
Dawlish Warren	d									21 45					22 59							
Dawlish	d									21 49					23 03							
Teignmouth	d									21 54					23 08							
Newton Abbot	a		20 34		21 03		21 36	21 44	21 44	22 01		22 04	22 30	22 39	23 15	23 05	23 28				03 31	03 31
	d		20 35		21 05		21 36	21 45	21 45	22 03		22 06	22 32	22 40	23 16	23 07	23 28				03 33	03 33
Torre	d									22 11					23 24							
Torquay	d									22 14					23 27							
Paignton	a									22 23					23 37							
Totnes	d		20 48		21 18			21 58	21 58			22 17	22 44	22 53		23 19	23 42					
Ivybridge	d													23 10								
Plymouth	a		21 16		21 48		22 14	22 26	22 26			22 43	23 14	23 25		23 45	00 11				04 14	04 12
	d		21 19					22 29			22 31										05 43	05 43
Devonport	d																					
Dockyard	d																					
Keyham	d																					
St Budeaux Ferry Road	d																					
Saltash	d							22 40			22 40											
St Germans	d							22 47			22 47											
Menheniot	d																					
Liskeard	d		21 44					22 59			22 59										06 08	06 08
Bodmin Parkway	d		21 58					23 11			23 11										06 22	06 22
Lostwithiel	d							23 16			23 16										06 28	06 28
Par	d		22 10					23 24			23 24										06 37	06 37
Newquay	a																					
St Austell	d		22 18					23 31			23 31										06 46	06 46
Truro	d		22 36					23 50			23 50										07 06	07 06
Redruth	d		22 48					00 03			00 03										07 18	07 18
Camborne	d							00 09			00 09										07 26	07 26
Hayle	d							00 16			00 16										07 35	07 35
St Erth	d	22 45						00 20			00 20										07 41	07 41
Penzance	a	22 57	23 14					00 40			00 40										07 53	07 53

A The Golden Hind
B not 7 September, 14 September
C The Armada
D not 7 September, 14 September. The Armada
E to Bristol Temple Meads
F The Night Riviera
G not 7 September, 14 September. The Night Riviera
H to Frome

For connections from Heathrow Airport, Gatwick Airport and Oxford please refer to Tables 125A, 148 and 116

Table 135

Mondays to Fridays

from 17 September

London and Birmingham - Devon and Cornwall

Route Diagram - see first Page of Table 135

		GW MX	GW MX	GW MX	GW MX	GW MX	XC MO	XC MX	GW	GW MO	GW MO	GW	GW	GW	GW	GW	GW	GW	GW	XC	GW	GW	GW
						A				B	C												
London Paddington ⊖	d		20p35		21p45	23p45				23p50	23p50												
Slough	d																						
Reading	d		21p02		22p11	00u37				00u37	00u38												
Theale	d																						
Thatcham	d																						
Newbury	d		21p18																				
Hungerford	d																						
Pewsey	d		21p38																				
Westbury	d		21p57			01 45																	
Castle Cary	d		22p15																				
Birmingham New Street	d																						
Cardiff Central	d																						
Newport (South Wales)	d																						
Swindon	d				22p49																		
Bristol Parkway	d																						06 24
Filton Abbey Wood	d																						06 27
Bath Spa	d				23p19																		
Bristol Temple Meads	d			23p06	23p35					02 55	02 55							05 24		06 34			06 42
Weston-super-Mare	d			23p42	00s05													05 45					07 06
Bridgwater	d			00 02	00s24													06 03					07 25
Taunton	d		22p37	00s14	00s36	02 35												06 18		07 08			07 39
Tiverton Parkway	d		22p50	00s31	00s49													06 33		07 20			07 54
Exeter St Davids	a		23p06	00 50	01 07	03 06				04 04	04 04							06 51		07 34			08 12
Exmouth	d																		06 45		07 14		
Exeter Central	d																		07 12		07 43		
Exeter St Davids	d		23p08			03 11				04 35	04 35		05 34	06 11		06 28		06 55	07 18	07 36	07 50		08 14
Exeter St Thomas	d												05 38	06 14				06 58	07 21		07 53		
Starcross	d												05 46	06 22				07 07	07 29		08 01		
Dawlish Warren	d												05 51	06 27				07 12	07 34		08 06		
Dawlish	d												05 55	06 31		06 42		07 16	07 38		08 10		
Teignmouth	d												06 00	06 36		06 47		07 21	07 43		08 15		
Newton Abbot	a		23p28			03 31				04 55	04 55		06 07	06 44		06 55		07 28	07 50	07 54	08 22		08 35
	d		23p28			03 33				04 56	04 56	05 42	06 09	06 45		06 55	07 06	07 28	07 52	07 55	08 24		08 35
Torre	d											05 50	06 17	06 53			07 15		08 00		08 33		
Torquay	d											05 53	06 20	06 56			07 20		08 03		08 36		
Paignton	a											06 00	06 28	07 06			07 29		08 12		08 44		
Totnes	d		23p42													07 09		07 42		08 07			08 49
Ivybridge	d															07 26		07 58					09 05
Plymouth	a		00 11			04 12				05 35	05 35					07 40		08 11		08 34			09 19
	d	22p35				05 43	05 43	06 28		06 28	06 28				07 02	07 53		08 14					09 21
Devonport	d														07 07			08 17					09 24
Dockyard	d																						
Keyham	d																						
St Budeaux Ferry Road	d																						
Saltash	d	22p44													07 15	08 02		08 24					09 31
St Germans	d	22p51													07 23	08 09		08 31					09 38
Menheniot	d																						
Liskeard	d	23p03				06 08	06 08	06 51		07 09	07 09				07 36	08 21		08 43					09 50
Bodmin Parkway	d	23p15				06 22	06 22	07 03		07 23	07 23				07 49	08 33		08 55					10 02
Lostwithiel	d	23p20				06 28	06 28	07 09		07 29	07 29				07 55	08 40		09 00					10 07
Par	d	23p28				06 37	06 37	07 15		07 38	07 38				08 04	08a54		09 08				09 17	10 15
Newquay	a																					10 09	
St Austell	d	23p35				06 46	06 46	07 22		07 46	07 46				08 11			09 16					10 22
Truro	d	23p54				07 06	07 06	07 39		08 06	08 06				08 30			09 34					10 40
Redruth	d	00 07				07 18	07 18	07 50		08 20	08 20				08 42			09 47					10 53
Camborne	d	00 13				07 26	07 26	07 57		08 27	08 27				08 48			09 53					10 59
Hayle	d	00 20				07 35	07 35	08 05		08 38	08 38				08 57			10 00					11 06
St Erth	d	00 24				07 41	07 41	08 11	08 28	08 45	08 45				09 02			10 08					11 10
Penzance	a	00 40				07 53	07 53	08 19	08 40	08 59	08 59				09 12			10 16					11 23

A The Night Riviera
B from 29 October
C from 17 September until 22 October

For connections from Heathrow Airport, Gatwick Airport and Oxford please refer to Tables 125A, 148 and 116

London and Birmingham - Devon and Cornwall

Route Diagram - see first Page of Table 135

		GW	XC	GW	GW	XC	GW	GW	GW	XC	GW	GW	GW	GW	GW	XC	GW	GW	XC	XC	GW	GW	GW
			◇1 🛒	◇1 A ☕	◇	◇1 🛒		◇1 B ☕⊘	◇	◇1 🛒		◇1 ☕	◇	◇	◇	◇1 🛒		◇1 C ☕⊘	◇1 🛒	◇1 🛒	◇1 D ☕		◇
London Paddington 15 ⊖	d			07 06				07 30				09 06						10 06			10 00		
Slough 3	d																						
Reading 7	d			07 33				07 57				09 35						10u33			10 27		
Theale	d																						
Thatcham	d																						
Newbury	d			07 48																			
Hungerford	d																						
Pewsey	d			08 07																			
Westbury	d			08 25																			
Castle Cary	d											10 31											
Birmingham New Street 12	d		06 42			07 12				08 12						09 12			09 42	10 12			
Cardiff Central 7	d								08 00						09 00								
Newport (South Wales)	d								08 15						09 15								
Swindon	d							08 27													10 55		
Bristol Parkway 7	d		07 58			08 26				09 26						10 27			10 55	11 28			
Filton Abbey Wood	d								08 42						09 42								
Bath Spa 7	d							08 57													11 24		
Bristol Temple Meads 10	d		08 10			08 44		09 13	08 55	09 44					09 55	10 44			11 15	11 44	11 47		
Weston-super-Mare	d								09 29						10 23				11 37		12 07		
Bridgwater	d								09 48						10 42								
Taunton	d		08 43	09 02		09 17		09 46	10 02	10 17		10 53			10 58	11 18			12 02	12 17	12 29		
Tiverton Parkway	d		08 55	09 15		09 29				10 30		11 06			11 14	11 30			12 14	12 29			
Exeter St Davids 6	a		09 08	09 30		09 42		10 11	10 33	10 45		11 22			11 32	11 45		12 08	12 30	12 42	12 55		
Exmouth	d	08 23					09 23				10 23						11 23					12 23	
Exeter Central	d	08 50					09 50				10 50						11 50					12 50	
Exeter St Davids 6	d	08 58	09 10	09 32	09 35	09 44	09 56	10 13	10 34	10 46	10 56	11 24			11 35	11 47	11 56	12 08	12 32	12 44	12 56	13 03	
Exeter St Thomas	d	09 01					09 59				10 59						11 59					13 06	
Starcross	d	09 09					10 07				11 07						12 07					13 15	
Dawlish Warren	d	09 21					10 12		10 46		11 12						12 22					13 20	
Dawlish	d	09 25					10 16		10 50		11 16						12 27		12 44		13 08	13 24	
Teignmouth	d	09 30					10 21		10 55		11 21						12 32		12 49		13 14	13 29	
Newton Abbot	a	09 37	09 29	09 52	09 56	10 02	10 30	10 34	11 02	11 06	11 29	11 43			11 55	12 06	12 39	12 29	12 55	13 02	13 22	13 36	
	d	09 39	09 30	09 56	09 57	10 03	10 39	10 36	11 03	11 07	11 30	11 44			11 56	12 07	12 40	12 29	12 56	13 03	13 22	13 38	
Torre	d	09 47		10 05			10 47		11 12		11 38						12 49					13 46	
Torquay	d	09 50	09 42	10 09			10 50		11 15		11 41						12 52		13 08		13 34	13 49	
Paignton	a	09 57	09 47	10 19			10 59		11 24		11 51						13 00		13 14		13 43	13 58	
Totnes	d				10 10	10 17		10 49		11 21		11 57			12 09	12 21				13 16			
Ivybridge	d				10 27										12 26								
Plymouth	a				10 41	10 46		11 17		11 48		12 27			12 42	12 49		13 06		13 41			
	d				10 42			11 20						12 39				13 11					
Devonport	d																						
Dockyard	d																						
Keyham	d																						
St Budeaux Ferry Road	d				10 48																		
Saltash	d				10 53									12 48									
St Germans	d				11 00									12 55									
Menheniot	d																						
Liskeard 8	d				11 12			11 44						13 07				13 35					
Bodmin Parkway	d				11 24			11 57						13 19				13 48					
Lostwithiel	d				11 29									13 24									
Par	d				11 37			12 09					12 13	13 32				14 00					14 07
Newquay	a												13 01										14 59
St Austell	d				11 44			12 16						13 39				14 07					
Truro	d				12 02			12 34						13 57				14 25					
Redruth	d				12 15			12 46						14 10				14 37					
Camborne	d				12 21			12 53						14 16				14 45					
Hayle	d				12 28									14 23				14 54					
St Erth	d				12 32			13 05						14 28				14 59					
Penzance	a				12 42			13 17						14 39				15 11					

A The Devon Express
B The Merchant Venturer
C The Cornish Riveira
D The Torbay Express

For connections from Heathrow Airport, Gatwick Airport and Oxford please refer to Tables 125A, 148 and 116

London and Birmingham - Devon and Cornwall

Route Diagram - see first Page of Table 135

		GW	GW	XC	GW	GW	GW	XC	GW	GW	GW	GW	GW	GW	GW	XC	XC	GW	GW	GW	GW	GW
			◇1 A ☕⊘	◇1 🛒		◇1 B ☕⊘		◇1 🛒	◇1 ☕		◇		◇1 C ☕⊘	◇		◇1 🛒	◇1 🛒				◇1 C ☕⊘	
London Paddington 15 ⊖	d		11 06			12 06			12 18				13 06								14 06	
Slough 3	d																					
Reading 7	d		11u33			12 33			12 48				13 33								14 33	
Theale	d								12 56													
Thatcham	d								13 04													
Newbury	d								13 12													
Hungerford	d								13 21													
Pewsey	d		12 03						13 40													
Westbury	d		12 22						13 59													
Castle Cary	d		12 39						14 16													
Birmingham New Street 12	d			11 12				12 12								13 12	13 42					
Cardiff Central 7	d													13 00								
Newport (South Wales)	d													13 15								
Swindon	d																					
Bristol Parkway 7	d			12 30				13 27								14 29	14 59					
Filton Abbey Wood	d													13 42								
Bath Spa 7	d																					
Bristol Temple Meads 10	d			12 44				13 44						13 53		14 44	15 13					
Weston-super-Mare	d													14 23								
Bridgwater	d													14 42								
Taunton	d		13 02	13 18				14 17	14a41				14 48	14 56		15 18	15 46				15 49	
Tiverton Parkway	d		13 15	13 30				14 29					15 01	15 11		15 30	15 58				16 02	
Exeter St Davids 6	a		13 31	13 45		14 08		14 42					15 17	15 31		15 46	16 13				16 18	
Exmouth	d				13 23					14 23								15 23				15 53
Exeter Central	d				13 50					14 50								15 50				16 20
Exeter St Davids 6	d		13 33	13 47	13 56	14 08		14 44		14 56			15 18			15 48		15 56		16 05	16 20	16 26
Exeter St Thomas	d				13 59					14 59								15 59				16 29
Starcross	d				14 07					15 07								16 07				16 37
Dawlish Warren	d				14 23					15 12								16 12		16 18		16 42
Dawlish	d				14 27					15 16								16 16		16 22		16 46
Teignmouth	d				14 32					15 21								16 21		16 27		16 51
Newton Abbot	a		13 52	14 06	14 40	14 28		15 02		15 29			15 39			16 07		16 30		16 35	16 39	16 58
	d		13 53	14 07	14 41	14 29	14 50	15 03		15 30			15 39		15 58	16 08		16 30		16 48	16 40	17 00
Torre	d				14 49					15 38								16 38				17 08
Torquay	d				14 52					15 41								16 41				17 11
Paignton	a				15 00					15 51								16 51				17 20
Totnes	d		14 06	14 21			15 02	15 16					15 53		16 11	16 22				17 02	16 53	
Ivybridge	d						15 19								16 28					17 19		
Plymouth	a		14 36	14 48		15 06	15 37	15 41					16 22		16 44	16 49				17 34	17 21	
	d	13 53				15 12						15 57							17 04		17 23	
Devonport	d											16 00							17 07			
Dockyard	d											16x01							17x08			
Keyham	d											16 03							17 10			
St Budeaux Ferry Road	d											16 06							17 13			
Saltash	d	14 02										16 11							17 17		17 34	
St Germans	d	14 09										16 18							17 24		17 41	
Menheniot	d											16x25							17x32			
Liskeard 8	d	14 21				15 36						16 32							17a40		17 54	
Bodmin Parkway	d	14 33				15 49						16 44									18 07	
Lostwithiel	d	14 38										16 49									18 13	
Par	d	14 46				16 01					16 10	16 57									18 22	
Newquay	a										17 02											
St Austell	d	14 53				16 08						17 06									18 29	
Truro	d	15 11				16 26						17 23									18 47	
Redruth	d	15 24				16 38						17 36									18 59	
Camborne	d	15 30				16 46						17 42									19 07	
Hayle	d	15 37				16 55						17 50									19 16	
St Erth	d	15 42				17 00						17 54									19 21	
Penzance	a	15 53				17 12						18 07									19 33	

A The Mayflower
B The Royal Duchy
C ☕ from Newton Abbot ⊘ to Newton Abbot

For connections from Heathrow Airport, Gatwick Airport and Oxford please refer to Tables 125A, 148 and 116

Table 135

Mondays to Fridays

from 17 September

London and Birmingham - Devon and Cornwall

Route Diagram - see first Page of Table 135

		XC	GW FO	GW	GW	GW	GW	GW		GW	GW	XC	GW	XC	GW	GW	GW	XC		GW FX	GW FO	GW	GW	XC	GW
		◇1	◇			◇					◇1	◇1		◇1	◇1			◇1		◇1	◇1	◇1		◇1	◇1
											A	B						B						B	C
		🛒									☕	🛒		🛒	☕			🛒		☕	☕	☕		🛒	☕
London Paddington 15 ⊖	d										15 06				16 06					16 33	16 33	17 03			17 06
Slough 3	d																								
Reading 7	d										15u33				16 33					17 04	17 04	17 32			17 36
Theale	d																								17 45
Thatcham	d																								17 55
Newbury	d																			17 19	17 19	17 48			18 02
Hungerford	d																			17 29	17 29				18 16
Pewsey	d										16 03									17 44	17 44				18 34
Westbury	d		15 20								16 23									18 04	18 04				
Castle Cary	d		15 49								16 41									18 21	18 21				
Birmingham New Street 12	d	14 12										15 12		15 42				16 12						17 12	
Cardiff Central 7	d																								
Newport (South Wales)	d																								
Swindon	d																								
Bristol Parkway 7	d	15 26										16 29		16 58				17 27						18 29	
Filton Abbey Wood	d																								
Bath Spa 7	d																								19 24
Bristol Temple Meads 10	d	15 44										16 44		17 13				17 44						18 44	19a41
Weston-super-Mare	d																								
Bridgwater	d																								
Taunton	d	16 17	16 24								17 05	17 17		17 45	17 50			18 17		18 43	18 43	18 52		19 17	
Tiverton Parkway	d	16 29	16 41								17 18	17 29		17 57	18 03			18 29		18 56	18 56	19 05		19 29	
Exeter St Davids 6	a	16 42	17 02								17 34	17 42		18 11	18 19			18 42		19 14	19 14	19 21		19 42	
Exmouth	d				16 55											17 58							18 55		
Exeter Central	d			16 46	17 21								17 45			18 25							19 21		
Exeter St Davids 6	d	16 44		16 56	17 26						17 35	17 45	17 50	18 12	18 22	18 30		18 46			19 14	19 22	19 28	19 44	
Exeter St Thomas	d			16 59	17 29								17 54			18 33							19 31		
Starcross	d			17 07	17 37								18 02			18 42							19 39		
Dawlish Warren	d			17 12	17 49								18 07			18 47							19 44		
Dawlish	d			17 16	17 53								18 11	18 24		18 51							19 48		
Teignmouth	d			17 21	17 58								18 16	18 29		18 56							19 53		
Newton Abbot	a	17 02		17 29	18 05						17 56	18 10	18 23	18 35	18 42	19 03		19 07			19 34	19 42	20 00	20 03	
	d	17 04		17 30	18 09						17 57	18 12	18 25	18 37	18 43	19 11		19 08			19 35	19 42	20 09	20 05	
Torre	d			17 38	18 17								18 33			19 19							20 17		
Torquay	d			17 41	18 20								18 36	18 48		19 22							20 20		
Paignton	a			17 51	18 30								18 45	18 55		19 30							20 29		
Totnes	d	17 16									18 10	18 24			18 56			19 21				19 56		20 17	
Ivybridge	d														19 12										
Plymouth	a	17 42									18 38	18 50			19 26			19 46			20 15	20 24		20 43	
	d						17 55	18 17		18 23	18 42	19 01			19 31			19 49				20 26		20 50	
Devonport	d							18 20		18 26															
Dockyard	d							18x21		18x27															
Keyham	d							18 23		18a29															
St Budeaux Ferry Road	d							18 25																	
Saltash	d						18 03	18 31							19 40							20 37			
St Germans	d							18 38														20 44			
Menheniot	d							18x45																	
Liskeard 6	d						18 20	18a53			19 07	19 24			19 57			20 12				20 56		21 13	
Bodmin Parkway	d						18 32				19 19	19 36			20 10			20 25				21 09		21 26	
Lostwithiel	d						18 37																	21 31	
Par	d					18 29	18 45				19 31	19 47			20 22		20 28	20 36				21 21		21 39	
Newquay	a					19 21											21 20								
St Austell	d						18 52				19 39	19 54			20 29			20 43				21 28		21 46	
Truro	d						19 10				20 00	20 11			20 47			21 02				21 46		22 04	
Redruth	d						19 23				20 10	20 26			20 59			21 16				21 58		22 15	
Camborne	d						19 29				20 18	20 32			21 07			21 23						22 22	
Hayle	d						19 36															22 11		22 30	
St Erth	d						19 42				20 28	20 44			21 20			21 34				22 16		22 35	
Penzance	a						19 54				20 42	20 52			21 31			21 42				22 30		22 43	

A The Cornishman

B 🛒 to Plymouth

C via Trowbridge

For connections from Heathrow Airport, Gatwick Airport and Oxford please refer to Tables 125A, 148 and 116

Table 135

Mondays to Fridays

from 17 September

London and Birmingham - Devon and Cornwall

Route Diagram - see first Page of Table 135

		GW	GW	GW		GW	XC	GW FX	GW FO	GW FO	GW FX	GW	GW FX	XC		XC	GW	GW	XC	GW	GW	GW	GW	GW FO	GW FX
		◇1		◇1		◇1	◇1	◇1	◇1	1	1			◇1		◇1	◇1		◇1	◇1	◇		◇1		
				A		E				B	B			C		C			C					D	D
		☕		🍴☕		☕	🛒	☕	☕	🍴☕	🍴☕			🛒		🛒	☕		🛒	☕			☕	🛏 ☕	🛏 ☕
London Paddington 15 ⊖	d	17 33		18 03		18 06		18 33	18 33	19 03	19 03						19 45			20 35			21 45	23 45	23 45
Slough 3	d																								
Reading 7	d	18 04		18u33		18 37		19 02	19 02	19u33	19 33						20 12			21 02			22 11	00u37	00u37
Theale	d					18 45																			
Thatcham	d					18 55																			
Newbury	d	18 19				19 02		19 17	19 17	19 50	19 50						20 28			21 18					
Hungerford	d					19 16		19 27	19 27																
Pewsey	d	18 41				19 34		19 46	19 46								20 48			21 38					
Westbury	d	19 01				19a52		20 05	20 05								21 06			21 57				01 37	01 45
Castle Cary	d	19 19						20 23	20 23								21 26			22 15					
Birmingham New Street 12	d						18 12							19 12		19 42			20 12						
Cardiff Central 7	d																								
Newport (South Wales)	d																								
Swindon	d																						22 49		
Bristol Parkway 7	d						19 29							20 29		20 56			21 27						
Filton Abbey Wood	d																								
Bath Spa 7	d																						23 19		
Bristol Temple Meads 10	d						19 44							20 44		21 12			21 44		21 56	23 06	23 35		
Weston-super-Mare	d																				22 29	23 42	00s05		
Bridgwater	d																				22 48	00 02	00s24		
Taunton	d	19 41		19 48			20 18	20 46	20 46	20 54	20 54			21 17		21 45	21 48		22 17	22 37	23 03	00s14	00s36	02 35	02 35
Tiverton Parkway	d	19 54					20 30	20 59	20 59	21 07	21 07			21 30		21 57	22 02		22 29	22 50	23 18	00s31	00s49		
Exeter St Davids 6	a	20 09		20 13			20 44	21 15	21 15	21 23	21 23			21 43		22 11	22 18		22 43	23 06	23 36	00 50	01 07	03 06	03 06
Exmouth	d																	22 05							
Exeter Central	d											21 21						22 31							
Exeter St Davids 6	d	20 19		20 15			20 46		21 16	21 25	21 25	21 29		21 45		22 12	22 19	22 37	22 44	23 08				03 11	03 11
Exeter St Thomas	d	20 24										21 32						22 40							
Starcross	d	20 33										21 40						22 48							
Dawlish Warren	d	20 38										21 45						22 59							
Dawlish	d	20 43										21 49						23 03							
Teignmouth	d	20 50										21 54						23 08							
Newton Abbot	a	20 57		20 34			21 03		21 36	21 44	21 44	22 01		22 04		22 30	22 39	23 15	23 05	23 28				03 31	03 31
	d	20 58		20 35			21 05		21 36	21 45	21 45	22 03		22 06		22 32	22 40	23 16	23 07	23 28				03 33	03 33
Torre	d	21 08										22 11						23 24							
Torquay	d	21 12										22 14						23 27							
Paignton	a	21 22										22 23						23 37							
Totnes	d			20 48			21 18			21 58	21 58			22 17		22 44	22 53		23 19	23 42					
Ivybridge	d																23 10								
Plymouth	a			21 16			21 48		22 14	22 26	22 26			22 43		23 14	23 25		23 45	00 11				04 14	04 12
	d			21 19						22 29			22 35											05 43	05 43
Devonport	d																								
Dockyard	d																								
Keyham	d																								
St Budeaux Ferry Road	d																								
Saltash	d									22 39			22 44												
St Germans	d									22 46			22 51												
Menheniot	d																								
Liskeard 6	d			21 44						22 59			23 03											06 08	06 08
Bodmin Parkway	d			21 58						23 13			23 15											06 22	06 22
Lostwithiel	d									23 20			23 20											06 28	06 28
Par	d			22 10						23 28			23 28											06 37	06 37
Newquay	a																								
St Austell	d			22 18						23 35			23 35											06 46	06 46
Truro	d			22 36						23 54			23 54											07 06	07 06
Redruth	d			22 48						00 07			00 07											07 18	07 18
Camborne	d									00 13			00 13											07 26	07 26
Hayle	d									00 20			00 20											07 35	07 35
St Erth	d		22 45							00 24			00 24											07 41	07 41
Penzance	a		22 57	23 14						00 40			00 40											07 53	07 53

A The Golden Hind

B The Armada

C 🛒 to Bristol Temple Meads

D The Night Riviera

E to Frome

For connections from Heathrow Airport, Gatwick Airport and Oxford please refer to Tables 125A, 148 and 116

Saturdays until 23 June

London and Birmingham - Devon and Cornwall

Route Diagram - see first Page of Table 135

		GW	GW	GW	GW	GW	GW	GW	GW	XC		GW	GW	GW	XC	GW	GW	GW	GW	GW		XC	GW	GW	GW
		■ 1 A ✕▭	◇1 ▭		◇1 ▭	■ B ▭				◇1			◇		◇1		◇1 ▭	◇				◇1 ☕	■ 1 ⊘		
London Paddington ⊖	d	19p03	20p35		21p45	23p45																			
Slough	d																								
Reading	d	19b33	21p02		22p11	00u37																			
Theale	d																								
Thatcham	d																								
Newbury	d	19p50	21p18																						
Hungerford	d																								
Pewsey	d		21p38																						
Westbury	d		21p57			01 37																			
Castle Cary	d		22p15																						
Birmingham New Street	d																					06 42			
Cardiff Central	d																								
Newport (South Wales)	d																								
Swindon	d				22p49																				
Bristol Parkway	d																					07 56			
Filton Abbey Wood	d																								
Bath Spa	d				23p19																				
Bristol Temple Meads	d			23p06	23p35								05 24		06 08			06 36				08 11			
Weston-super-Mare	d			23p42	00s05								05 45					06 56							
Bridgwater	d			00 02	00s24								06 03												
Taunton	d	20p54	22p37	00s14	00s36	02 35							06 18		07 17			07 25				08 43			
Tiverton Parkway	d	21p07	22p50	00s31	00s49								06 33		07 29			07 41				08 55			
Exeter St Davids	a	21p23	23p06	00 50	01 07	03 06							06 52		07 42			08 00				09 09			
Exmouth	d															07 15				08 23					
Exeter Central	d															07 43				08 50					
Exeter St Davids	d	21p25	23p08			03 11	05 18	05 36	06 11				06 56		07 44	07 50		08 04	08 37	08 57		09 10			09 28
Exeter St Thomas	d						05 22	05 40	06 14				06 59			07 53		08 07		08 59					
Starcross	d						05 30	05 48	06 22				07 05			08 01				09 07					
Dawlish Warren	d						05 35	05 53	06 27				07 10			08 06				09 24					
Dawlish	d						05 39	05 57	06 31				07 14			08 10		08 20	08 51	09 28					
Teignmouth	d						05 44	06 02	06 36				07 19			08 15		08 25	08 56	09 33					
Newton Abbot	a	21p44	23p28			03 31	05 51	06 09	06 45				07 26		08 02	08 22		08 32	09 03	09 40		09 28			09 48
	d	21p45	23p28			03 33	05 52	06 11	06 45				07 26	07 40	08 03	08 24		08 32	09 06	09 41		09 30			09 49
Torre	d						06 00	06 19	06 53					07 48		08 32				09 50					
Torquay	d						06 03	06 22	06 56					07 51		08 35			09 16	09 53		09 41			
Paignton	a						06 11	06 30	07 06					07 59		08 44			09 25	10 01		09 47			
Totnes	d	21p58	23p42										07 40		08 16			08 46							10 02
Ivybridge	d												07 56					09 02							10 19
Plymouth	a	22p26	00 11			04 14							08 13		08 41			09 16							10 32
	d	22p29				05 43				06 35			08 18				08 57						09 24	09 58	10 33
Devonport	d												08 21											10 01	
Dockyard	d																								
Keyham	d																								
St Budeaux Ferry Road	d																								10 39
Saltash	d	22p40											08 28										09 34	10 08	10 44
St Germans	d	22p47											08 35											10 15	10 51
Menheniot	d																							10x22	
Liskeard	d	22p59				06 08				06 59			08 47				09 23						09 51	10 29	11 03
Bodmin Parkway	d	23p11				06 22				07 12			08 59				09 36						10 04	10 41	11 15
Lostwithiel	d	23p16				06 28				07 18			09 04										10 10	10 46	11 20
Par	d	23p24				06 37				07 28			09 12				09 46						10 17	10a53	11 28
Newquay	a									08 27							10 55								
St Austell	d	23p31				06 46							09 20										10 25		11 37
Truro	d	23p50				07 06							09 37										10 43		11 55
Redruth	d	00 03				07 18							09 50										10 55		12 08
Camborne	d	00 09				07 26							09 56										11 02		12 14
Hayle	d	00 16				07 35							10 03										11 11		12 21
St Erth	d	00 20				07 41						08 28	10 08										11 18		12 25
Penzance	a	00 40				07 53						08 40	10 18										11 28		12 36

A The Armada

B The Night Riviera

b Previous night, stops to pick up only

For connections from Heathrow Airport, Gatwick Airport and Oxford please refer to Tables 125A, 148 and 116

Saturdays until 23 June

London and Birmingham - Devon and Cornwall

Route Diagram - see first Page of Table 135

		XC	GW	GW	GW	GW		GW	XC	GW	GW	GW	XC	XC	GW	GW		XC	XC	GW	GW	GW	GW	XC	GW
		◇1 ☕	■ ◇1 ▭		■ ◇1 ▭				◇1 ☕		■ ◇1 B ▭	■ ◇1 ▭⊘	◇1 ☕	◇1 ☕		■ ◇1 ▭⊘		◇1 ☕	◇1 D ☕			■ ◇1 ▭	■ ◇1 ▭⊘	◇1 ☕	■ 1 ▭
London Paddington ⊖	d		07 36		07 30						08 35	09 06				10 06						10 35	11 06		11 35
Slough	d																								
Reading	d		08u06		07 57						09u04	09u34				10u33						11u04	11u34		12u06
Theale	d																								
Thatcham	d																								
Newbury	d										09 21														
Hungerford	d																								
Pewsey	d										09 40											11 36			
Westbury	d										09 58											11 54			
Castle Cary	d										10 15											12 12			
Birmingham New Street	d	07 12							08 12				08 42	09 12				09 42	10 12					11 12	
Cardiff Central	d																								
Newport (South Wales)	d																								
Swindon	d				08 30																				
Bristol Parkway	d	08 26							09 26				09 57	10 31				10 59	11 26					12 31	
Filton Abbey Wood	d																								
Bath Spa	d				09 00																				
Bristol Temple Meads	d	08 44			09 17				09 44				10 20	10 44				11 12	11 44					12 44	
Weston-super-Mare	d																	11 39							
Bridgwater	d																								
Taunton	d	09 17			09 51				10 18		10 37	10 50	11 01	11 17				12 01	12 17			12 35	12 50	13 17	
Tiverton Parkway	d	09 29							10 30		10 50	11 03	11 13	11 29				12 13	12 29			12 49		13 29	
Exeter St Davids	a	09 41	09 51		10 16				10 46		11 06	11 19	11 26	11 42		12 09		12 26	12 42			13 04	13 15	13 42	13 52
Exmouth	d			09 23						10 23					11 23						12 23				
Exeter Central	d			09 52				10 30		10 50					11 50						12 50				
Exeter St Davids	d	09 44	09 54	09 58	10 19	10 25		10 35	10 48	10 56	11 08	11 22	11 29	11 45	11 56	12 11		12 29	12 45	12 52	12 56	13 08	13 18	13 44	13 55
Exeter St Thomas	d			09 59						10 59					11 59						12 59				
Starcross	d			10 08						11 07					12 07						13 07				
Dawlish Warren	d			10 13				10 47		11 13	11 19				12 13					13 04	13 12				
Dawlish	d			10 18				10 51	11 01	11 17	11 24				12 17			12 41		13 08	13 16	13 22			
Teignmouth	d			10 23				10 56	11 07	11 23	11 31				12 23			12 46		13 13	13 21	13 28			
Newton Abbot	a	10 02		10 32	10 38	10 46		11 03	11 14	11 31	11 38	11 42	11 47	12 03	12 31	12 31		12 52	13 08	13 20	13 29	13 35	13 38	14 02	
	d	10 03		10 33	10 39	10 48		11 04	11 15	11 32	11 39	11 42	11 49	12 05	12 38	12 32		12 53	13 09	13 21	13 30	13 37	13 39	14 04	
Torre	d			10 41		10 56				11 40					12 45						13 38				
Torquay	d			10 44		10 59		11 14	11 28	11 43	11 51				12 48			13 05			13 41	13 50			
Paignton	a			10 52		11 07		11 23	11 35	11 51	12 01				12 56			13 11			13 49	14 00			
Totnes	d	10 16			10 52							11 56	12 05	12 17					13 22	13 34			13 52	14 16	
Ivybridge	d																			13 50					
Plymouth	a	10 41	10 51		11 20							12 24	12 31	12 43		13 13			13 48	14 05			14 21	14 42	14 51
	d		10 53		11 23							12 28	12 39			13 15			13 50				14 24		14 54
Devonport	d																								
Dockyard	d																								
Keyham	d																								
St Budeaux Ferry Road	d																								
Saltash	d											12 38													
St Germans	d																								
Menheniot	d																								
Liskeard	d				11 47							12 55	13 04			13 40			14 13				14 49		
Bodmin Parkway	d				12 01							13 08	13 18			13 54			14 26				15 02		
Lostwithiel	d																		14 32						15 32
Par	d		11 41		12 12								13 31			14 06			14 40						15 43
Newquay	a		12 44										14 41												16 52
St Austell	d				12 20							13 23				14 14			14 48				15 17		
Truro	d				12 38							13 41				14 30			15 07				15 35		
Redruth	d				12 50							13 55				14 44			15 19				15 48		
Camborne	d				12 57							14 02				14 50			15 26				15 55		
Hayle	d											14 11				15 00			15 34				16 04		
St Erth	d				13 10							14 19				15 06			15 40				16 10		
Penzance	a				13 22							14 28				15 18			15 49				16 21		

B The Torbay Express

D ☕ to Plymouth

For connections from Heathrow Airport, Gatwick Airport and Oxford please refer to Tables 125A, 148 and 116

Table 135

Saturdays
until 23 June

London and Birmingham - Devon and Cornwall

Route Diagram - see first Page of Table 135

		GW		GW	GW	XC	GW	GW	GW	GW	XC	GW		GW	XC	GW	GW	XC	GW	GW	GW	GW		XC	GW
		■ ◇1 A ⊡⊘				◇1 ╤		■ ◇1 B ⊡		■ 1 ⊡	◇1 ╤				◇1 ╤		◇1 ⊡	◇1 C ╤				◇1 ⊡		◇1 C ╤	1 D
London Paddington 15 ⊖	d	12 06						12 35		13 06							14 06					15 06			
Slough 3	d																								
Reading 7	d	12u32						13u06		13u32							14u32					15u32			
Theale	d																								
Thatcham	d																								
Newbury	d							13 22																	
Hungerford	d																								
Pewsey	d							13 40														16 04			
Westbury	d							13 59														16 23			
Castle Cary	d							14 16														16 40			
Birmingham New Street 12	d					12 12					13 12				13 42			14 12						15 12	
Cardiff Central 7	d																								
Newport (South Wales)	d																								
Swindon	d																								
Bristol Parkway 7	d					13 26					14 28				14 59			15 25						16 31	
Filton Abbey Wood	d																								
Bath Spa 7	d																								
Bristol Temple Meads 10	d					13 44					14 44				15 12			15 44						16 44	
Weston-super-Mare	d																								
Bridgwater	d																								
Taunton	d					14 17		14 39		14 48	15 18				15 44		15 48	16 17				17 03		17 18	
Tiverton Parkway	d					14 29				15 01	15 30				15 56		16 01	16 29				17 16		17 31	
Exeter St Davids 6	a	14 09				14 45		15 03		15 17	15 45				16 10		16 17	16 42				17 31		17 46	
Exmouth	d			13 23			14 23							15 23						16 55					
Exeter Central	d			13 50			14 50							15 50					16 48	17 21					
Exeter St Davids 6	d	14 11		14 16	14 30	14 48	14 56	15 06		15 19	15 47			15 57	16 11		16 18	16 44	16 56	17 27		17 34		17 48	17 53
Exeter St Thomas	d			14 18			14 59							15 59					16 59	17 30					
Starcross	d			14 26			15 07							16 07					17 07	17 35					
Dawlish Warren	d			14 32	14 42	15 02	15 12	15 18						16 12	16 31				17 12	17 49					18 05
Dawlish	d			14 36	14 46	15 07	15 16	15 24						16 16	16 36				17 16	17 53					18 09
Teignmouth	d			14 41	14 51	15 14	15 21	15 30						16 21	16 41				17 21	17 58					18 14
Newton Abbot	a	14 30		14 49	14 58	15 20	15 29	15 37		15 42	16 06			16 29	16 47		16 38		17 29	18 05		17 53		18 10	18 21
	d	14 32		14 50	15 00	15 22	15 30	15 38		15 42	16 07	16 18		16 30	16 49		16 39		17 30	18 09		17 55		18 12	18 22
Torre	d			14 58	15 08		15 38							16 38					17 38	18 17					
Torquay	d			15 01	15 11	15 34	15 41	15 51						16 41	17 01				17 41	18 20					
Paignton	a			15 09	15 19	15 42	15 51	15 58						16 51	17 08				17 51	18 27					
Totnes	d									15 56	16 21	16 31					16 52	17 13				18 08		18 25	18 35
Ivybridge	d											16 47					17 08								18 51
Plymouth	a	15 09								16 23	16 48	17 05					17 23	17 39				18 37		18 52	19 05
	d	15 11							16 03	16 26	16 52						17 26	17 42			17 52			18 56	19 08
Devonport	d																				17 55				
Dockyard	d																				17x57				
Keyham	d																				17 59				
St Budeaux Ferry Road	d																				18 01				
Saltash	d								16 12												18 06				19 17
St Germans	d								16 19												18 12				19 24
Menheniot	d								16x27												18x19				
Liskeard 6	d	15 36							16 33	16 50	17 15						17 51	18 05			18 26			19 19	19 36
Bodmin Parkway	d	15 49							16 45	17 03	17 29						18 03	18 17			18 38			19 34	19 48
Lostwithiel	d								16 50												18 44				19 53
Par	d	16 01							16a56		17 42						18 16	18 28			18 52			19 45	20 01
Newquay	a										18 45														
St Austell	d	16 08								17 20							18 23	18 35			18 59			19 53	20 08
Truro	d	16 26								17 37							18 41	18 52			19 17			20 12	20 26
Redruth	d	16 38								17 50							18 53	19 09			19 30			20 27	20 43
Camborne	d	16 46								17 57							19 01	19 16			19 36			20 35	20 49
Hayle	d									18 06											19 43				
St Erth	d	16 58								18 13						18 32	19 12	19 27			19 48			20 46	20 58
Penzance	a	17 10								18 25						18 44	19 24	19 35			19 57			20 56	21 08

A ⊡ from Newton Abbot ⊘ to Newton Abbot ◇ from Newton Abbot ■ to Newton Abbot
B ◇ from Castle Cary ■ to Castle Cary
C ╤ to Plymouth
D 1 from Plymouth

For connections from Heathrow Airport, Gatwick Airport and Oxford please refer to Tables 125A, 148 and 116

Table 135

Saturdays
until 23 June

London and Birmingham - Devon and Cornwall

Route Diagram - see first Page of Table 135

		GW	GW	GW	XC	GW	GW	GW		GW	GW	GW	XC	GW	GW	XC	GW	GW		XC	GW	XC	GW	GW
		◇1 ⊡			◇1 A ╤			◇1 ⊡		◇1 ⊡			◇1 ╤		◇1 ⊡	◇1 ╤		◇1 ⊡		◇1 B ╤	◇1 ⊡	◇1 B ╤	◇	◇1 ⊡
London Paddington 15 ⊖	d	16 06						17 06		16 30					18 06			19 06			20 06			20 30
Slough 3	d																							
Reading 7	d	16u32						17u32		16 57					18u32			19 32			20 33			20 57
Theale	d																							
Thatcham	d																							
Newbury	d																	19 49			20 47			
Hungerford	d																							
Pewsey	d							18 03										20 09			21 07			
Westbury	d							18 22										20 27			21 26			
Castle Cary	d							18 41										20 44			21 43			
Birmingham New Street 12	d				16 12								17 12			18 12				19 12		20 12		
Cardiff Central 7	d																							
Newport (South Wales)	d																							
Swindon	d									17 30														21 30
Bristol Parkway 7	d				17 26								18 31			19 27				20 31		21 24		
Filton Abbey Wood	d																							
Bath Spa 7	d									18 00														22 00
Bristol Temple Meads 10	d				17 44					18 18			18 44			19 44				20 44		21 44	21 59	22 17
Weston-super-Mare	d									18 40													22 31	22s47
Bridgwater	d																						22 50	23s05
Taunton	d	17 49			18 17			19 02		19 06			19 17		19 47	20 17		21 07		21 17	22 06	22 17	23 03	23 18
Tiverton Parkway	d	18 02			18 29			19 15		19 21			19 29			20 29		21 20		21 29	22 19	22 29	23 18	23 31
Exeter St Davids 6	a	18 18			18 42			19 31		19 36			19 43		20 13	20 42		21 36		21 42	22 35	22 43	23 36	23 47
Exmouth	d		17 55											19 38			20 08							
Exeter Central	d		18 21											20 01			20 35							
Exeter St Davids 6	d	18 19	18 27		18 46	18 56	19 16	19 34		19 39			19 45	20 07	20 16	20 45	20 56	21 38		21 45	22 38	22 46		
Exeter St Thomas	d		18 29				19 19							20 10			20 59							
Starcross	d		18 37				19 27							20 18			21 07							
Dawlish Warren	d		18 42				19 32							20 32			21 12							
Dawlish	d		18 46			19 09	19 36							20 36			21 16				22 48			
Teignmouth	d		18 51			19 14	19 41							20 41			21 21				22 54			
Newton Abbot	a	18 40	18 59		19 04	19 21	19 49	19 53		19 58			20 03	20 48	20 37	21 03	21 28	21 58		22 04	23 02	23 10		
	d	18 41	19 01		19 05	19 22	19 50	19 54		19 59			20 05	20 49	20 37	21 05	21 30	21 58		22 08	23 03	23 11		
Torre	d		19 09				19 58			20 09				20 57			21 38							
Torquay	d		19 12			19 32	20 01			20 13				21 00			21 41							
Paignton	a		19 21			19 40	20 09			20 22				21 07			21 48							
Totnes	d	18 54			19 18			20 07					20 17		20 51	21 17		22 12		22 21	23 16	23 27		
Ivybridge	d	19 11																						
Plymouth	a	19 24			19 43			20 35					20 43		21 19	21 43		22 40		22 47	23 46	23 53		
	d	19 29			19 48							20 42			21 20									
Devonport	d																							
Dockyard	d																							
Keyham	d																							
St Budeaux Ferry Road	d																							
Saltash	d											20 51												
St Germans	d											20 58												
Menheniot	d																							
Liskeard 6	d	19 54			20 11							21 10			21 45									
Bodmin Parkway	d	20 07			20 23							21 22			21 59									
Lostwithiel	d				20 29							21 27												
Par	d	20 18		20 22	20 36							21 35			22 11									
Newquay	a			21 11																				
St Austell	d	20 26			20 43							21 44			22 18									
Truro	d	20 44			21 02							22 03			22 36									
Redruth	d	20 58			21 13							22 16			22 48									
Camborne	d	21 05			21 19							22 22			22 56									
Hayle	d				21 27							22 29			23 03									
St Erth	d	21 17			21 32						22 20	22 33			23 09									
Penzance	a	21 27			21 43						22 32	22 42			23 22									

A ╤ to Plymouth
B ╤ to Bristol Temple Meads

For connections from Heathrow Airport, Gatwick Airport and Oxford please refer to Tables 125A, 148 and 116

Table 135

Saturdays

30 June to 8 September

London and Birmingham - Devon and Cornwall

Route Diagram - see first Page of Table 135

		GW	GW	GW	GW	GW	GW	GW	GW	XC		GW	GW	GW	XC	GW	GW	GW	GW	GW		XC	GW	GW	GW
		■				■																	■		
		1	◇1		◇1					◇1			◇		◇1		◇1	◇				◇1	1		
		A				B																			
		✕⊡	⊡		⊡	🛏 ⊡											⊡					⌶	⊘		
London Paddington 15 ⊖	d	19p03	20p35		21p45	23p45																			
Slough 3	d																								
Reading 7	d	19b33	21p02		22p11	00u37																			
Theale	d																								
Thatcham	d																								
Newbury	d	19p50	21p18																						
Hungerford	d																								
Pewsey	d		21p38																						
Westbury	d		21p57			01 37																			
Castle Cary	d		22p15																						
Birmingham New Street 12	d																					06 42			
Cardiff Central 7	d																								
Newport (South Wales)	d																								
Swindon	d				22p49																				
Bristol Parkway 7	d																					07 56			
Filton Abbey Wood	d																								
Bath Spa 7	d				23p19																				
Bristol Temple Meads 10	d			23p06	23p35								05 24		06 08			06 36				08 11			
Weston-super-Mare	d			23p42	00s05								05 45					06 56							
Bridgwater	d			00 02	00s24								06 03												
Taunton	d	20p54	22p37	00s14	00s36	02 35							06 18		07 17			07 25				08 43			
Tiverton Parkway	d	21p07	22p50	00s31	00s49								06 33		07 29			07 41				08 55			
Exeter St Davids 6	a	21p23	23p06	00 50	01 07	03 06							06 52		07 42			08 00				09 09			
Exmouth	d															07 15				08 23					
Exeter Central	d															07 43				08 50					
Exeter St Davids 6	d	21p25	23p08			03 11	05 18	05 36	06 11				06 56		07 44	07 50		08 04	08 37	08 57		09 10			09 28
Exeter St Thomas	d						05 22	05 40	06 14				06 59			07 53		08 07		08 59					
Starcross	d						05 30	05 48	06 22				07 05			08 01				09 07					
Dawlish Warren	d						05 35	05 53	06 27				07 10			08 06				09 24					
Dawlish	d						05 39	05 57	06 31				07 14			08 10		08 20	08 51	09 28					
Teignmouth	d						05 44	06 02	06 36				07 19			08 15		08 25	08 56	09 33					
Newton Abbot	a	21p44	23p28			03 31	05 51	06 09	06 45				07 26		08 02	08 22		08 32	09 03	09 40		09 28			09 48
	d	21p45	23p28			03 33	05 52	06 11	06 45				07 26	07 40	08 03	08 24		08 32	09 06	09 41		09 30			09 49
Torre	d						06 00	06 19	06 53					07 48		08 32				09 50					
Torquay	d						06 03	06 22	06 56					07 51		08 35			09 16	09 53		09 41			
Paignton	a						06 11	06 30	07 06					07 59		08 44			09 25	10 01		09 47			
Totnes	d	21p58	23p42										07 40		08 16			08 46							10 02
Ivybridge	d												07 56					09 02							10 19
Plymouth	a	22p26	00 11			04 14							08 13		08 41			09 16							10 32
	d	22p29				05 43				06 35			08 18				08 57						09 24	09 58	10 33
Devonport	d												08 21											10 01	
Dockyard	d																								
Keyham	d																								
St Budeaux Ferry Road	d																								10 39
Saltash	d	22p40											08 28										09 34	10 08	10 44
St Germans	d	22p47											08 35											10 15	10 51
Menheniot	d																							10x22	
Liskeard 6	d	22p59				06 08				06 59			08 47				09 23						09 51	10 29	11 03
Bodmin Parkway	d	23p11				06 22				07 12			08 59				09 36						10 04	10 41	11 15
Lostwithiel	d	23p16				06 28				07 18			09 04										10 10	10 46	11 20
Par	d	23p24				06 37				07 28			09 12				09 46						10 17	10a53	11 28
Newquay	a									08 27							10 55								
St Austell	d	23p31				06 46							09 20										10 25		11 37
Truro	d	23p50				07 06							09 37										10 43		11 55
Redruth	d	00 03				07 18							09 50										10 55		12 08
Camborne	d	00 09				07 26							09 56										11 02		12 14
Hayle	d	00 16				07 35							10 03										11 11		12 21
St Erth	d	00 20				07 41						08 28	10 08										11 18		12 25
Penzance	a	00 40				07 53						08 40	10 18										11 28		12 36

A The Armada

B The Night Riviera

b Previous night, stops to pick up only

For connections from Heathrow Airport, Gatwick Airport and Oxford please refer to Tables 125A, 148 and 116

Table 135

Saturdays

30 June to 8 September

London and Birmingham - Devon and Cornwall

Route Diagram - see first Page of Table 135

		XC	GW	GW	GW	GW		GW	XC	GW	GW	GW	XC	XC	GW	GW		XC	XC	GW	GW	GW	GW	XC	GW
			■		■						■	■				■						■	■		■
		◇1	◇1		◇1				◇1		◇1	◇1	◇1	◇1		◇1		◇1	◇1			◇1	◇1	◇1	1
											B	C				C			D				C		
		⌶	⊡		⊡				⌶		⊡	⊡⊘	⌶	⌶		⊡⊘		⌶	⌶			⊡	⊡⊘	⌶	⊡
London Paddington 15 ⊖	d		07 36		07 30						08 35	09 06				10 06						10 35	11 06		11 35
Slough 3	d																								
Reading 7	d		08u06		07 57						09u04	09u34				10u33						11u04	11u34		12u06
Theale	d																								
Thatcham	d																								
Newbury	d										09 21														
Hungerford	d																								
Pewsey	d										09 40											11 36			
Westbury	d										09 58											11 54			
Castle Cary	d										10 15											12 12			
Birmingham New Street 12	d	07 12							08 12				08 42	09 12				09 42	10 12					11 12	
Cardiff Central 7	d																								
Newport (South Wales)	d																								
Swindon	d				08 30																				
Bristol Parkway 7	d	08 26							09 26				09 57	10 31				10 59	11 26					12 31	
Filton Abbey Wood	d																								
Bath Spa 7	d				09 00																				
Bristol Temple Meads 10	d	08 44			09 17				09 44				10 20	10 44				11 12	11 44					12 44	
Weston-super-Mare	d																	11 39							
Bridgwater	d																								
Taunton	d	09 17			09 51				10 18		10 37	10 50	11 01	11 17				12 01	12 17			12 35	12 50	13 17	
Tiverton Parkway	d	09 29							10 30		10 50	11 03	11 13	11 29				12 13	12 29			12 49		13 29	
Exeter St Davids 6	a	09 41	09 51		10 16				10 46		11 06	11 19	11 26	11 42		12 09		12 26	12 42			13 04	13 15	13 42	13 52
Exmouth	d			09 23						10 23					11 23						12 23				
Exeter Central	d			09 52				10 30		10 50					11 50						12 50				
Exeter St Davids 6	d	09 44	09 54	09 58	10 19	10 25		10 35	10 48	10 56	11 08	11 22	11 29	11 45	11 56	12 11		12 29	12 45	12 52	12 56	13 08	13 18	13 44	13 55
Exeter St Thomas	d			09 59						10 59					11 59						12 59				
Starcross	d			10 08						11 07					12 07						13 07				
Dawlish Warren	d			10 13				10 47		11 13	11 19				12 13					13 04	13 12				
Dawlish	d			10 18				10 51	11 01	11 17	11 24				12 17			12 41		13 08	13 16	13 22			
Teignmouth	d			10 23				10 56	11 07	11 23	11 31				12 23			12 46		13 13	13 21	13 28			
Newton Abbot	a	10 02		10 32	10 38	10 46		11 03	11 14	11 31	11 38	11 42	11 47	12 03	12 31	12 31		12 52	13 08	13 20	13 29	13 35	13 38	14 02	
	d	10 03		10 33	10 39	10 48		11 04	11 15	11 32	11 39	11 42	11 49	12 05	12 38	12 32		12 53	13 09	13 21	13 30	13 37	13 39	14 04	
Torre	d			10 41		10 56				11 40					12 45						13 38				
Torquay	d			10 44		10 59		11 14	11 28	11 43	11 51				12 48			13 05			13 41	13 50			
Paignton	a			10 52		11 07		11 23	11 35	11 51	12 01				12 56			13 11			13 49	14 00			
Totnes	d	10 16			10 52							11 56	12 05	12 17					13 22	13 34			13 52	14 16	
Ivybridge	d																			13 50					
Plymouth	a	10 41	10 51		11 20							12 24	12 31	12 43		13 13			13 48	14 05			14 21	14 42	14 51
	d		10 53		11 23							12 28	12 39			13 15			13 50				14 24		14 54
Devonport	d																								
Dockyard	d																								
Keyham	d																								
St Budeaux Ferry Road	d																								
Saltash	d											12 38													
St Germans	d																								
Menheniot	d																								
Liskeard 6	d				11 47							12 55	13 04			13 40			14 13				14 49		
Bodmin Parkway	d				12 01							13 08	13 18			13 54			14 26				15 02		
Lostwithiel	d																		14 32						15 32
Par	d		11 41		12 12								13 31			14 06			14 40						15 43
Newquay	a		12 44										14 41												16 52
St Austell	d				12 20							13 23				14 14			14 48				15 17		
Truro	d				12 38							13 41				14 30			15 07				15 35		
Redruth	d				12 50							13 55				14 44			15 19				15 48		
Camborne	d				12 57							14 02				14 50			15 26				15 55		
Hayle	d											14 11				15 00			15 34				16 04		
St Erth	d				13 10							14 19				15 06			15 40				16 10		
Penzance	a				13 22							14 28				15 18			15 49				16 21		

B The Torbay Express

C ⊡ from Newton Abbot ⊘ to Newton Abbot ◇ from Newton Abbot ■ to Newton Abbot

D ⌶ to Plymouth

For connections from Heathrow Airport, Gatwick Airport and Oxford please refer to Tables 125A, 148 and 116

London and Birmingham - Devon and Cornwall

Route Diagram - see first Page of Table 135

		GW ■ ◇■ A 🍴⊘		GW	GW	XC ◇■ 🛒	GW	GW ■ ◇■ B 🍴	GW	GW ■ ■ 🍴	XC ◇■ 🛒	GW		GW	XC ◇■ 🛒	GW	GW ◇■ 🍴	XC ◇■ C 🛒	GW	GW	GW	GW ◇■ 🍴		XC ◇■ C 🛒	GW ■ D
London Paddington 15 ⊖	d	12 06						12 35		13 06							14 06					15 06			
Slough 3	d																								
Reading 7	d	12u32						13u06		13u32							14u32					15u32			
Theale	d																								
Thatcham	d																								
Newbury	d							13 22																	
Hungerford	d																								
Pewsey	d							13 40														16 04			
Westbury	d							13 59														16 23			
Castle Cary	d							14 16														16 40			
Birmingham New Street 12	d					12 12					13 12				13 42			14 12						15 12	
Cardiff Central 7	d																								
Newport (South Wales)	d																								
Swindon	d																								
Bristol Parkway 7	d					13 26					14 28				14 59			15 25						16 31	
Filton Abbey Wood	d																								
Bath Spa 7	d																								
Bristol Temple Meads 10	d					13 44					14 44				15 12			15 44						16 44	
Weston-super-Mare	d																								
Bridgwater	d																								
Taunton	d					14 17		14 39		14 48	15 18				15 44		15 48	16 17				17 03		17 18	
Tiverton Parkway	d					14 29				15 01	15 30				15 56		16 01	16 29				17 16		17 31	
Exeter St Davids 6	a	14 09				14 45		15 03		15 17	15 45				16 10		16 17	16 42				17 31		17 46	
Exmouth	d			13 23			14 23							15 23						16 55					
Exeter Central	d			13 50			14 50							15 50					16 48	17 21					
Exeter St Davids 6	d	14 11		14 16	14 30	14 48	14 56	15 06		15 19	15 47			15 57	16 11		16 18	16 44	16 56	17 27		17 34		17 48	17 53
Exeter St Thomas	d			14 18			14 59							15 59					16 59	17 30					
Starcross	d			14 26			15 07							16 07					17 07	17 35					
Dawlish Warren	d			14 32	14 42	15 02	15 12	15 18						16 12	16 31				17 12	17 49					18 05
Dawlish	d			14 36	14 46	15 07	15 16	15 24						16 16	16 36				17 16	17 53					18 09
Teignmouth	d			14 41	14 51	15 14	15 21	15 30						16 21	16 41				17 21	17 58					18 14
Newton Abbot	a	14 30		14 49	14 58	15 20	15 29	15 37		15 42	16 06			16 29	16 47		16 38		17 29	18 05		17 53		18 10	18 21
	d	14 32		14 50	15 00	15 22	15 30	15 38		15 42	16 07	16 18		16 30	16 49		16 39		17 30	18 09		17 55		18 12	18 22
Torre	d			14 58	15 08		15 38							16 38					17 38	18 17					
Torquay	d			15 01	15 11	15 34	15 41	15 51						16 41	17 01				17 41	18 20					
Paignton	a			15 09	15 19	15 42	15 51	15 58						16 51	17 08				17 51	18 27					
Totnes	d									15 56	16 21	16 31					16 52	17 13				18 08		18 25	18 35
Ivybridge	d											16 47					17 08								18 51
Plymouth	a	15 09								16 23	16 48	17 05					17 23	17 39				18 37		18 52	19 05
	d	15 11							16 03	16 26	16 52						17 26	17 42			17 52			18 56	19 08
Devonport	d																				17 55				
Dockyard	d																				17x57				
Keyham	d																				17 59				
St Budeaux Ferry Road	d																				18 01				
Saltash	d								16 12												18 06				19 17
St Germans	d								16 19												18 12				19 24
Menheniot	d								16x27												18x19				
Liskeard 6	d	15 36							16 33	16 50	17 15						17 51	18 05			18 26			19 19	19 36
Bodmin Parkway	d	15 49							16 45	17 03	17 29						18 03	18 17			18 38			19 34	19 48
Lostwithiel	d								16 50												18 44				19 53
Par	d	16 01							16a56		17 42						18 16	18 28			18 52			19 45	20 01
Newquay	a										18 45														
St Austell	d	16 08								17 20							18 23	18 35			18 59			19 53	20 08
Truro	d	16 26								17 37							18 41	18 52			19 17			20 12	20 26
Redruth	d	16 38								17 50							18 53	19 09			19 30			20 27	20 43
Camborne	d	16 46								17 57							19 01	19 16			19 36			20 35	20 49
Hayle	d									18 06											19 43				
St Erth	d	16 58								18 13					18 32	19 12	19 27				19 48			20 46	20 58
Penzance	a	17 10								18 25					18 44	19 24	19 35				19 57			20 56	21 08

A 🍴 from Newton Abbot ⊘ to Newton Abbot ◇ from Newton Abbot ■ to Newton Abbot

B ◇ from Castle Cary ■ to Castle Cary

C 🛒 to Plymouth

D ■ from Plymouth

For connections from Heathrow Airport, Gatwick Airport and Oxford please refer to Tables 125A, 148 and 116

London and Birmingham - Devon and Cornwall

Route Diagram - see first Page of Table 135

		GW ◇■ 🍴	GW	GW	XC ◇■ A 🛒	GW	GW	GW ◇■ 🍴		GW ◇■ 🍴	GW	GW	XC ◇■ 🛒	GW	GW ◇■ 🍴	XC ◇■ 🛒	GW	GW ◇■ 🍴		XC ◇■ B 🛒	GW ◇■ 🍴	XC ◇■ B 🛒	GW ◇	GW ◇■ 🍴
London Paddington 15 ⊖	d	16 06						17 06		16 30					18 06			19 06			20 06			20 30
Slough 3	d																							
Reading 7	d	16u32						17u32		16 57					18u32			19 32			20 33			20 57
Theale	d																							
Thatcham	d																							
Newbury	d																	19 49			20 47			
Hungerford	d																							
Pewsey	d							18 03										20 09			21 07			
Westbury	d							18 22										20 27			21 26			
Castle Cary	d							18 41										20 44			21 43			
Birmingham New Street 12	d				16 12								17 12			18 12				19 12		20 12		
Cardiff Central 7	d																							
Newport (South Wales)	d																							
Swindon	d									17 30														21 30
Bristol Parkway 7	d				17 26								18 31			19 27				20 31		21 24		
Filton Abbey Wood	d																							
Bath Spa 7	d									18 00														22 00
Bristol Temple Meads 10	d				17 44					18 18			18 44			19 44				20 44		21 44	21 59	22 17
Weston-super-Mare	d									18 40													22 31	22s47
Bridgwater	d																						22 50	23s05
Taunton	d	17 49			18 17			19 02		19 06			19 17		19 47	20 17		21 07		21 17	22 06	22 17	23 03	23 18
Tiverton Parkway	d	18 02			18 29			19 15		19 21			19 29			20 29		21 20		21 29	22 19	22 29	23 18	23 31
Exeter St Davids 6	a	18 18			18 42			19 31		19 36			19 43		20 13	20 42		21 36		21 42	22 35	22 43	23 36	23 47
Exmouth	d		17 55											19 38			20 08							
Exeter Central	d		18 21											20 01			20 35							
Exeter St Davids 6	d	18 19	18 27		18 46	18 56	19 16	19 34		19 39			19 45	20 07	20 16	20 45	20 56	21 38		21 45	22 38	22 46		
Exeter St Thomas	d		18 29				19 19							20 10			20 59							
Starcross	d		18 37				19 27							20 18			21 07							
Dawlish Warren	d		18 42				19 32							20 32			21 12							
Dawlish	d		18 46			19 09	19 36							20 36			21 16				22 48			
Teignmouth	d		18 51			19 14	19 41							20 41			21 21				22 54			
Newton Abbot	a	18 40	18 59		19 04	19 21	19 49	19 53		19 58			20 03	20 48	20 37	21 03	21 28	21 58		22 04	23 02	23 10		
	d	18 41	19 01		19 05	19 22	19 50	19 54		19 59			20 05	20 49	20 37	21 05	21 30	21 58		22 08	23 03	23 11		
Torre	d		19 09				19 58			20 09				20 57			21 38							
Torquay	d		19 12			19 32	20 01			20 13				21 00			21 41							
Paignton	a		19 21			19 40	20 09			20 22				21 07			21 48							
Totnes	d	18 54			19 18			20 07					20 17		20 51	21 17		22 12		22 21	23 16	23 27		
Ivybridge	d	19 11																						
Plymouth	a	19 24			19 43			20 35					20 43		21 19	21 43		22 40		22 47	23 46	23 53		
	d	19 29			19 48							20 42			21 20									
Devonport	d																							
Dockyard	d																							
Keyham	d																							
St Budeaux Ferry Road	d																							
Saltash	d											20 51												
St Germans	d											20 58												
Menheniot	d																							
Liskeard 6	d	19 54			20 11							21 10			21 45									
Bodmin Parkway	d	20 07			20 23							21 22			21 59									
Lostwithiel	d				20 29							21 27												
Par	d	20 18		20 22	20 36							21 35			22 11									
Newquay	a			21 11																				
St Austell	d	20 26			20 43							21 44			22 18									
Truro	d	20 44			21 02							22 03			22 36									
Redruth	d	20 58			21 13							22 16			22 48									
Camborne	d	21 05			21 19							22 22			22 56									
Hayle	d				21 27							22 29			23 03									
St Erth	d	21 17			21 32						22 20	22 33			23 09									
Penzance	a	21 27			21 43						22 32	22 42			23 22									

A 🛒 to Plymouth

B 🛒 to Bristol Temple Meads

For connections from Heathrow Airport, Gatwick Airport and Oxford please refer to Tables 125A, 148 and 116

Table 135

Saturdays

15 September to 20 October

London and Birmingham - Devon and Cornwall

Route Diagram - see first Page of Table 135

		GW	GW	GW	GW	GW	GW	GW	GW	GW		GW	GW	XC	GW	GW	GW	XC	GW	GW		GW	GW	GW	XC
		■ 1 A ✕	■ 1 B ✕	◇1		◇1		■ C						◇1		◇		◇1				◇			◇1
London Paddington 15 ⊖	d	19p03	19p03	20p35		21p45		23p45																	
Slough 3	d																								
Reading 7	d	19b33	19b33	21p02		22p11		00u37																	
Theale	d																								
Thatcham	d																								
Newbury	d	19p50	19p50	21p18																					
Hungerford	d																								
Pewsey	d			21p38																					
Westbury	d			21p57				01 37																	
Castle Cary	d			22p15																					
Birmingham New Street 12	d																								06 42
Cardiff Central 7	d																								
Newport (South Wales)	d																								
Swindon	d					22p49																			
Bristol Parkway 7	d																								07 56
Filton Abbey Wood	d																								
Bath Spa 7	d					23p19																			
Bristol Temple Meads 10	d				23p06	23p35										05 24		06 08				06 36			08 11
Weston-super-Mare	d				23p42	00s05										05 45						06 56			
Bridgwater	d				00 02	00s24										06 03									
Taunton	d	20p54	20p54	22p37	00s14	00s36		02 35								06 18		07 17				07 25			08 43
Tiverton Parkway	d	21p07	21p07	22p50	00s31	00s49										06 33		07 29				07 41			08 55
Exeter St Davids 6	a	21p23	21p23	23p06	00 50	01 07		03 06								06 52		07 42				07 59			09 09
Exmouth	d																		07 15					08 23	
Exeter Central	d																		07 43					08 50	
Exeter St Davids 6	d	21p25	21p25	23p08				03 11	05 18	05 36		06 11				06 56		07 44	07 50			08 00	08 37	08 56	09 10
Exeter St Thomas	d								05 22	05 40		06 14				06 59			07 53			08 04		08 59	
Starcross	d								05 30	05 48		06 22				07 05			08 01					09 07	
Dawlish Warren	d								05 35	05 53		06 27				07 10			08 06					09 24	
Dawlish	d								05 39	05 57		06 31				07 14			08 10			08 17	08 51	09 28	
Teignmouth	d								05 44	06 02		06 36				07 19			08 15			08 22	08 56	09 33	
Newton Abbot	a	21p44	21p44	23p28				03 31	05 51	06 09		06 45				07 26		08 02	08 22			08 29	09 03	09 40	09 28
	d	21p45	21p45	23p28				03 33	05 52	06 11		06 45				07 26	07 40	08 03	08 24			08 31	09 06	09 41	09 30
Torre	d								06 00	06 19		06 53					07 48		08 32					09 50	
Torquay	d								06 03	06 22		06 56					07 51		08 35				09 16	09 53	09 41
Paignton	a								06 11	06 30		07 06					07 59		08 44				09 25	10 01	09 47
Totnes	d	21p58	21p58	23p42												07 40		08 16				08 45			
Ivybridge	d															07 56						09 02			
Plymouth	a	22p26	22p26	00 11				04 14								08 13		08 41				09 16			
	d	22p29	22p29					05 43						06 28		08 18						09 19			
Devonport	d															08 21									
Dockyard	d																								
Keyham	d																								
St Budeaux Ferry Road	d																								
Saltash	d	22p40	22p39													08 28						09 28			
St Germans	d	22p47	22p46													08 35						09 36			
Menheniot	d																								
Liskeard 6	d	22p59	22p59					06 08						06 51		08 47						09 49			
Bodmin Parkway	d	23p11	23p13					06 22						07 03		08 59						10 02			
Lostwithiel	d	23p16	23p20					06 28						07 08		09 04									
Par	d	23p24	23p28				06 09	06 37					06 52	07 15		09 12				09 18		10 14			
Newquay	a												07 44							10 10					
St Austell	d	23p31	23p35				06 16	06 46						07 21		09 20						10 22			
Truro	d	23p50	23p54				06 35	07 06						07 38		09 37						10 40			
Redruth	d	00 03	00 07				06 48	07 18						07 50		09 50						10 55			
Camborne	d	00 09	00 13				06 54	07 26						07 56		09 56						11 02			
Hayle	d	00 16	00 20				07 01	07 35						08 04		10 03						11 10			
St Erth	d	00 20	00 24				07 04	07 41						08 10	08 28	10 08						11 18			
Penzance	a	00 40	00 40				07 16	07 53						08 19	08 40	10 18						11 26			

A 15 September. The Armada
B not 15 September The Armada
C The Night Riviera
b Previous night, stops to pick up only

For connections from Heathrow Airport, Gatwick Airport and Oxford please refer to Tables 125A, 148 and 116

Table 135

Saturdays

15 September to 20 October

London and Birmingham - Devon and Cornwall

Route Diagram - see first Page of Table 135

		GW	GW	XC	GW	GW		GW	GW	XC	GW	GW	GW	XC	GW	GW		GW	GW	XC	XC	GW	GW	GW	GW
				◇1		■ ◇1 A				◇1	◇1		◇1 B	◇1		◇		◇	◇1 B	◇1	◇1			◇	
London Paddington 15 ⊖	d					07 30					08 18		09 06						10 06						
Slough 3	d																								
Reading 7	d					07 57					08 48		09 32						10 33						
Theale	d										08 58														
Thatcham	d										09 07														
Newbury	d										09 14														
Hungerford	d										09 23														
Pewsey	d										09 41														
Westbury	d										10 00														
Castle Cary	d										10 18														
Birmingham New Street 12	d			07 12						08 12				09 12						09 42	10 12				
Cardiff Central 7	d																								
Newport (South Wales)	d																								
Swindon	d					08 30																			
Bristol Parkway 7	d			08 26						09 26				10 31						10 59	11 26				
Filton Abbey Wood	d																								
Bath Spa 7	d					09 00																			
Bristol Temple Meads 10	d			08 44		09 17				09 44				10 44						11 12	11 44				
Weston-super-Mare	d																			11 39					
Bridgwater	d																								
Taunton	d			09 17		09 51				10 18	10 40		10 48	11 17						12 01	12 17				
Tiverton Parkway	d			09 29						10 30	10 53		11 01	11 29						12 13	12 29				
Exeter St Davids 6	a			09 41		10 16				10 46	11 09		11 17	11 42					12 09	12 26	12 42				
Exmouth	d				09 23							10 23			11 23								12 23		
Exeter Central	d				09 52				10 30			10 50			11 50								12 50		
Exeter St Davids 6	d		09 28	09 44	09 58	10 19		10 25	10 35	10 48		10 56	11 19	11 45	11 56				12 11	12 29	12 45	12 52	12 56		
Exeter St Thomas	d				09 59							10 59			11 59								12 59		
Starcross	d				10 07							11 07			12 07								13 07		
Dawlish Warren	d				10 12				10 47			11 12			12 12							13 04	13 12		
Dawlish	d				10 16				10 51			11 16			12 16					12 41		13 08	13 16		
Teignmouth	d				10 21				10 56			11 21			12 21					12 46		13 13	13 21		
Newton Abbot	a		09 48	10 02	10 30	10 38		10 46	11 03	11 09		11 29	11 38	12 03	12 29				12 31	12 52	13 03	13 20	13 29		
	d		09 49	10 03	10 31	10 39		10 48	11 04	11 10		11 30	11 38	12 05	12 36				12 32	12 53	13 05	13 21	13 30		
Torre	d				10 39			10 56				11 38			12 43								13 38		
Torquay	d				10 42			10 59	11 14			11 41			12 46					13 05			13 41		
Paignton	a				10 50			11 07	11 23			11 51			12 54					13 11			13 49		
Totnes	d		10 02	10 16		10 52				11 24			11 52	12 17							13 17	13 34			
Ivybridge	d		10 19										12 07									13 50			
Plymouth	a		10 32	10 41		11 20				11 51			12 24	12 43					13 13		13 43	14 05			
	d	09 51	10 33			11 23												12 44	13 15						14 15
Devonport	d	09 54																							
Dockyard	d																								
Keyham	d																								
St Budeaux Ferry Road	d		10 39																						
Saltash	d	10 01	10 44															12 53							14 24
St Germans	d	10 08	10 51															13 00							14 32
Menheniot	d	10x15																							
Liskeard 6	d	10 22	11 03			11 47												13 12	13 40						14 45
Bodmin Parkway	d	10 34	11 15			12 00												13 24	13 54						14 58
Lostwithiel	d	10 39	11 20															13 29							15 04
Par	d	10 46	11 28			12 11										12 15		13 37	14 06					14 08	15 12
Newquay	a															13 07								14 55	
St Austell	d	10 54	11 37			12 19												13 45	14 14						15 21
Truro	d	11 10	11 55			12 37												14 02	14 30						15 39
Redruth	d	11 24	12 08			12 49												14 15	14 44						15 53
Camborne	d	11 30	12 14			12 56												14 21	14 50						16 00
Hayle	d	11 38	12 21															14 28	15 00						
St Erth	d	11 42	12 25			13 08												14 33	15 05						16 12
Penzance	a	11 55	12 36			13 20												14 42	15 17						16 21

A ◇ from Exeter St Davids ■ to Exeter St Davids
B from Newton Abbot; to Newton Abbot

For connections from Heathrow Airport, Gatwick Airport and Oxford please refer to Tables 125A, 148 and 116

Table 135

London and Birmingham - Devon and Cornwall

Saturdays

15 September to 20 October

Route Diagram - see first Page of Table 135

		GW		XC	GW	GW	GW	XC	GW	GW	GW	GW		GW	XC	XC	GW	GW	GW	GW	XC	GW		GW	GW
		◇1		◇1		◇1		◇1	◇1		◇			1	◇1	◇1				◇1	◇1				◇
		A				A																			
		🍴⊘		🛒		🍴⊘		🛒	🍴					🍴	🛒	🛒				🍴	🛒				
London Paddington 15 ⊖	d	11 06				12 06			12 18					13 06						14 06					
Slough 3	d																								
Reading 7	d	11 32				12 32			12 48					13 32						14 32					
Theale	d								12 57																
Thatcham	d								13 05																
Newbury	d								13 13																
Hungerford	d								13 21																
Pewsey	d	12 03							13 39																
Westbury	d	12 22							13 58																
Castle Cary	d	12 40							14 14																
Birmingham New Street 12	d			11 12				12 12							13 12	13 42					14 12				
Cardiff Central 7	d																								
Newport (South Wales)	d																								
Swindon	d																								
Bristol Parkway 7	d			12 31				13 26							14 28	14 59					15 25				
Filton Abbey Wood	d																								
Bath Spa 7	d																								
Bristol Temple Meads 10	d			12 44				13 44							14 44	15 12					15 44				
Weston-super-Mare	d																								
Bridgwater	d																								
Taunton	d	13 02		13 17				14 17	14a37					14 48	15 18	15 44				15 48	16 17				
Tiverton Parkway	d	13 15		13 29				14 29						15 01	15 30	15 56				16 01	16 29				
Exeter St Davids 6	a	13 31		13 42		14 09		14 42						15 17	15 45	16 10				16 17	16 42				
Exmouth	d				13 23					14 23								15 23						16 55	
Exeter Central	d				13 50					14 50								15 50				16 48		17 21	
Exeter St Davids 6	d	13 33		13 44	13 57	14 11	14 30	14 44		14 56				15 18	15 47			15 57		16 18	16 44	16 56		17 27	
Exeter St Thomas	d				13 59					14 59								15 59				16 59		17 30	
Starcross	d				14 07					15 07								16 07				17 07		17 35	
Dawlish Warren	d				14 24		14 42			15 12								16 12				17 12		17 49	
Dawlish	d				14 28		14 46			15 16								16 16				17 16		17 53	
Teignmouth	d				14 33		14 51			15 21								16 21				17 21		17 58	
Newton Abbot	a	13 51		14 02	14 41	14 30	14 58	15 02		15 29				15 39	16 06			16 29		16 38	17 02	17 29		18 05	
	d	13 53		14 04	14 42	14 32	15 00	15 04		15 30				15 39	16 07		16 18	16 30		16 39	17 04	17 30		18 09	
Torre	d				14 50		15 08			15 38								16 38				17 38		18 17	
Torquay	d				14 53		15 11			15 41								16 41				17 41		18 20	
Paignton	a				15 01		15 19			15 51								16 51				17 51		18 27	
Totnes	d	14 05		14 16				15 16						15 53	16 21		16 31			16 52	17 16				
Ivybridge	d																16 47			17 08					
Plymouth	a	14 34		14 42		15 09		15 42						16 20	16 48		17 05			17 23	17 42				
	d					15 11						16 03		16 26						17 26					
Devonport	d																								
Dockyard	d																								
Keyham	d																								
St Budeaux Ferry Road	d																								
Saltash	d											16 12													
St Germans	d											16 19													
Menheniot	d											16x27													
Liskeard 6	d					15 36						16 33		16 50						17 51					
Bodmin Parkway	d					15 49						16 45		17 03						18 03					
Lostwithiel	d											16 50													
Par	d					16 01					16 15	16 57								18 16					18 21
Newquay	a										17 07														19 13
St Austell	d					16 08						17 05		17 20						18 23					
Truro	d					16 26						17 23		17 37						18 41					
Redruth	d					16 38						17 36		17 50						18 53					
Camborne	d					16 46						17 42		17 57						19 01					
Hayle	d											17 49		18 06											
St Erth	d					16 57						17 54		18 12					18 32	19 12					
Penzance	a					17 09						18 03		18 24					18 44	19 24					

A 🍴 from Newton Abbot ⊘ to Newton Abbot

For connections from Heathrow Airport, Gatwick Airport and Oxford please refer to Tables 125A, 148 and 116

Table 135

London and Birmingham - Devon and Cornwall

Saturdays

15 September to 20 October

Route Diagram - see first Page of Table 135

		GW	GW	XC	GW	XC	GW	GW		GW	XC	GW	GW	GW	GW	GW	XC	GW		GW	XC	GW	GW	XC	GW
			◇1	◇1	1	◇1	◇1				◇1				◇1	◇1	◇1			◇1	◇1		◇1	◇1	◇1
				A	B						A						A							C	
			🍴	🛒		🛒	🍴				🛒				🍴	🍴	🛒			🍴	🛒		🍴	🛒	🍴
London Paddington 15 ⊖	d		15 06				16 06								17 06	16 30				18 06			19 06		20 06
Slough 3	d																								
Reading 7	d		15 32				16 32								17 32	16 57				18 32			19 32		20 33
Theale	d																								
Thatcham	d																								
Newbury	d																						19 49		20 47
Hungerford	d																								
Pewsey	d		16 04												18 03								20 09		21 07
Westbury	d		16 23												18 22								20 27		21 26
Castle Cary	d		16 40												18 41								20 44		21 43
Birmingham New Street 12	d			15 12		15 42					16 12						17 12				18 12			19 12	
Cardiff Central 7	d																								
Newport (South Wales)	d																								
Swindon	d															17 30									
Bristol Parkway 7	d			16 31		16 56					17 26						18 31				19 27			20 31	
Filton Abbey Wood	d																								
Bath Spa 7	d															18 00									
Bristol Temple Meads 10	d			16 44		17 10					17 44					18 18	18 44				19 44			20 44	
Weston-super-Mare	d															18 40									
Bridgwater	d																								
Taunton	d		17 03	17 18		17 42	17 49				18 17				19 02	19 06	19 17			19 47	20 17		21 07	21 17	22 06
Tiverton Parkway	d		17 16	17 31		17 54	18 02				18 29				19 15	19 21	19 29				20 29		21 20	21 29	22 19
Exeter St Davids 6	a		17 31	17 46		18 08	18 18				18 42				19 31	19 36	19 43			20 13	20 42		21 36	21 42	22 35
Exmouth	d							17 55										19 38				20 08			
Exeter Central	d							18 21										20 01				20 35			
Exeter St Davids 6	d		17 34	17 48	17 53	18 10	18 20	18 27			18 46	18 56	19 16		19 34	19 39	19 45	20 07		20 16	20 45	20 56	21 38	21 45	22 38
Exeter St Thomas	d							18 29					19 19					20 10				20 59			
Starcross	d							18 37					19 27					20 18				21 07			
Dawlish Warren	d				18 05			18 42					19 32					20 32				21 12			
Dawlish	d				18 09	18 22		18 46				19 09	19 36					20 36				21 16			22 48
Teignmouth	d				18 14	18 27		18 51				19 14	19 41					20 41				21 21			22 54
Newton Abbot	a		17 53	18 10	18 21	18 33	18 40	18 59			19 04	19 21	19 49		19 53	19 58	20 03	20 48		20 37	21 03	21 28	21 58	22 04	23 02
	d		17 55	18 12	18 22	18 35	18 41	19 01			19 05	19 22	19 50		19 54	19 59	20 05	20 49		20 37	21 05	21 30	21 58	22 08	23 03
Torre	d							19 09					19 58			20 09		20 57				21 38			
Torquay	d					18 46		19 12				19 32	20 01			20 12		21 00				21 41			
Paignton	a					18 53		19 21				19 40	20 09			20 21		21 07				21 48			
Totnes	d		18 08	18 25	18 35		18 54				19 18				20 07		20 17			20 51	21 17		22 12	22 21	23 16
Ivybridge	d				18 51		19 11																		
Plymouth	a		18 36	18 52	19 05		19 26				19 43				20 35		20 43			21 19	21 43		22 40	22 47	23 46
	d	17 52	18 41	18 56	19 08						19 48				20 38		20 58			21 20					
Devonport	d	17 55																							
Dockyard	d	17x57																							
Keyham	d	17 59																							
St Budeaux Ferry Road	d	18 01																							
Saltash	d	18 06			19 17										20 49										
St Germans	d	18 12			19 24										20 56										
Menheniot	d	18x19																							
Liskeard 6	d	18 26	19 06	19 19	19 36						20 11				21 08		21 25			21 45					
Bodmin Parkway	d	18 38	19 19	19 34	19 48						20 23				21 21		21 38			21 59					
Lostwithiel	d	18 44			19 53						20 29														
Par	d	18 52	19 31	19 45	20 01					20 15	20 36				21 33		21 49			22 11					
Newquay	a									21 07															
St Austell	d	18 59	19 39	19 53	20 08						20 43				21 43		21 56			22 18					
Truro	d	19 17	20 00	20 12	20 26						21 02				22 03		22 13			22 36					
Redruth	d	19 30	20 10	20 27	20 43						21 13				22 13		22 28			22 48					
Camborne	d	19 36	20 18	20 35	20 49						21 19						22 35			22 56					
Hayle	d	19 43									21 27									23 03					
St Erth	d	19 48	20 29	20 46	20 58						21 32			22 20	22 30		22 46			23 09					
Penzance	a	19 57	20 40	20 56	21 08						21 43			22 32	22 42		22 54			23 22					

A 🛒 to Plymouth B 1 from Plymouth C 🛒 to Bristol Temple Meads

For connections from Heathrow Airport, Gatwick Airport and Oxford please refer to Tables 125A, 148 and 116

Saturdays
15 September to 20 October

London and Birmingham - Devon and Cornwall

Route Diagram - see first Page of Table 135

		XC	GW	GW
		◇1	◇	◇1
		A		
		⊼		⊐
London Paddington 15 ⊖	d			20 30
Slough 3	d			
Reading 7	d			20 57
Theale	d			
Thatcham	d			
Newbury	d			
Hungerford	d			
Pewsey	d			
Westbury	d			
Castle Cary	d			
Birmingham New Street 12	d	20 12		
Cardiff Central 7	d			
Newport (South Wales)	d			
Swindon	d			21 30
Bristol Parkway 7	d	21 24		
Filton Abbey Wood	d			
Bath Spa 7	d			22 00
Bristol Temple Meads 10	d	21 44	21 59	22 17
Weston-super-Mare	d		22 33	22s47
Bridgwater	d		22 52	23s05
Taunton	d	22 17	23 05	23 18
Tiverton Parkway	d	22 29	23 20	23 31
Exeter St Davids 6	a	22 43	23 38	23 47
Exmouth	d			
Exeter Central	d			
Exeter St Davids 6	d	22 46		
Exeter St Thomas	d			
Starcross	d			
Dawlish Warren	d			
Dawlish	d			
Teignmouth	d			
Newton Abbot	a	23 10		
	d	23 11		
Torre	d			
Torquay	d			
Paignton	a			
Totnes	d	23 27		
Ivybridge	d			
Plymouth	a	23 53		
	d			
Devonport	d			
Dockyard	d			
Keyham	d			
St Budeaux Ferry Road	d			
Saltash	d			
St Germans	d			
Menheniot	d			
Liskeard 8	d			
Bodmin Parkway	d			
Lostwithiel	d			
Par	d			
Newquay	a			
St Austell	d			
Truro	d			
Redruth	d			
Camborne	d			
Hayle	d			
St Erth	d			
Penzance	a			

A ⊼ to Bristol Temple Meads

For connections from Heathrow Airport, Gatwick Airport and Oxford please refer to Tables 125A, 148 and 116

Saturdays
from 27 October

London and Birmingham - Devon and Cornwall

Route Diagram - see first Page of Table 135

		GW	GW	GW	GW	GW	GW	GW	GW	GW		GW	XC	GW	GW	GW	XC	GW	GW	GW		GW	GW	XC	GW
		■ 1	◇1		◇1		■						◇1		◇		◇1			◇				◇1	
		A					B																		
		✕ ⊐	⊐		⊐		⊨ ⊐																	⊼	
London Paddington 15 ⊖	d	19p03	20p35		21p45		23p45																		
Slough 3	d																								
Reading 7	d	19b33	21p02		22p11		00u37																		
Theale	d																								
Thatcham	d																								
Newbury	d	19p50	21p18																						
Hungerford	d																								
Pewsey	d		21p38																						
Westbury	d		21p57				01 37																		
Castle Cary	d		22p15																						
Birmingham New Street 12	d																							06 42	
Cardiff Central 7	d																								
Newport (South Wales)	d																								
Swindon	d				22p49																				
Bristol Parkway 7	d																							07 56	
Filton Abbey Wood	d																								
Bath Spa 7	d				23p19																				
Bristol Temple Meads 10	d			23p06	23p35										05 24		06 08			06 36				08 11	
Weston-super-Mare	d			23p42	00s05										05 45					06 56					
Bridgwater	d			00 02	00s24										06 03										
Taunton	d	20p54	22p37	00s14	00s36		02 35								06 18		07 17			07 25				08 43	
Tiverton Parkway	d	21p07	22p50	00s31	00s49										06 33		07 29			07 41				08 55	
Exeter St Davids 6	a	21p23	23p06	00 50	01 07		03 06								06 52		07 42			07 59				09 09	
Exmouth	d																	07 15					08 23		
Exeter Central	d																	07 43					08 50		
Exeter St Davids 6	d	21p25	23p08				03 11	05 18	05 36	06 11					06 56		07 44	07 50		08 00		08 37	08 56	09 10	
Exeter St Thomas	d							05 22	05 40	06 14					06 59			07 53		08 04			08 59		
Starcross	d							05 30	05 48	06 22					07 05			08 01					09 07		
Dawlish Warren	d							05 35	05 53	06 27					07 10			08 06					09 24		
Dawlish	d							05 39	05 57	06 31					07 14			08 10		08 17		08 51	09 28		
Teignmouth	d							05 44	06 02	06 36					07 19			08 15		08 22		08 56	09 33		
Newton Abbot	a	21p44	23p28				03 31	05 51	06 09	06 45					07 26		08 02	08 22		08 29		09 03	09 40	09 28	
	d	21p45	23p28				03 33	05 52	06 11	06 45					07 26	07 40	08 03	08 24		08 31		09 06	09 41	09 30	
Torre	d							06 00	06 19	06 53						07 48		08 32					09 50		
Torquay	d							06 03	06 22	06 56						07 51		08 35				09 16	09 53	09 41	
Paignton	a							06 11	06 30	07 06						07 59		08 44				09 25	10 01	09 47	
Totnes	d	21p58	23p42												07 40		08 16			08 45					
Ivybridge	d														07 56					09 02					
Plymouth	a	22p26	00 11				04 14								08 13		08 41			09 16					
	d	22p29					05 43						06 28		08 18					09 19					09 51
Devonport	d														08 21										09 54
Dockyard	d																								
Keyham	d																								
St Budeaux Ferry Road	d																								
Saltash	d	22p39													08 28					09 28					10 01
St Germans	d	22p46													08 35					09 36					10 08
Menheniot	d																								10x15
Liskeard 8	d	22p59					06 08						06 51		08 47					09 49					10 22
Bodmin Parkway	d	23p13					06 22						07 03		08 59					10 02					10 34
Lostwithiel	d	23p20					06 28						07 08		09 04										10 39
Par	d	23p28				06 09	06 37					06 52	07 15		09 12				09 18	10 14					10 46
Newquay	a											07 44							10 10						
St Austell	d	23p35				06 16	06 46						07 21		09 20					10 22					10 54
Truro	d	23p54				06 35	07 06						07 38		09 37					10 40					11 10
Redruth	d	00 07				06 48	07 18						07 50		09 50					10 55					11 24
Camborne	d	00 13				06 54	07 26						07 56		09 56					11 02					11 30
Hayle	d	00 20				07 01	07 35						08 04		10 03					11 10					11 38
St Erth	d	00 24				07 04	07 41						08 10	08 28	10 08					11 18					11 42
Penzance	a	00 40				07 16	07 53						08 19	08 40	10 18					11 26					11 55

A The Armada
B The Night Riviera
b Previous night, stops to pick up only

For connections from Heathrow Airport, Gatwick Airport and Oxford please refer to Tables 125A, 148 and 116

London and Birmingham - Devon and Cornwall

Saturdays from 27 October

Route Diagram - see first Page of Table 135

		GW	XC	GW	GW	GW	GW	XC	GW	GW	GW	XC	GW	GW	GW	GW	XC	XC	GW	GW	GW	GW	GW
			◇1		■ ◇1 A			◇1	◇1		◇1 B	◇1		◇	◇	◇1 B	◇1	◇1			◇		◇1 B
London Paddington 15 ⊖	d				07 30				08 18		09 06					10 06							11 06
Slough 3	d																						
Reading 7	d				07 57				08 48		09 32					10 33							11 32
Theale	d								08 58														
Thatcham	d								09 07														
Newbury	d								09 14														
Hungerford	d								09 23														
Pewsey	d								09 41														12 03
Westbury	d								10 00														12 22
Castle Cary	d								10 18														12 40
Birmingham New Street 12	d		07 12					08 12				09 12					09 42	10 12					
Cardiff Central 7	d																						
Newport (South Wales)	d																						
Swindon	d				08 30																		
Bristol Parkway 7	d		08 26					09 26				10 31					10 59	11 26					
Filton Abbey Wood	d																						
Bath Spa 7	d				09 00																		
Bristol Temple Meads 10	d		08 44		09 17			09 44				10 44					11 12	11 44					
Weston-super-Mare	d																11 39						
Bridgwater	d																						
Taunton	d		09 17		09 51			10 18	10 40		10 48	11 17					12 01	12 17					13 02
Tiverton Parkway	d		09 29					10 30	10 53		11 01	11 29					12 13	12 29					13 15
Exeter St Davids 6	a		09 41		10 16			10 46	11 09		11 17	11 42				12 09	12 26	12 42					13 31
Exmouth	d			09 23						10 23			11 23							12 23			
Exeter Central	d			09 52			10 30			10 50			11 50							12 50			
Exeter St Davids 6	d	09 28	09 44	09 58	10 19	10 25	10 35	10 48		10 56	11 19	11 45	11 56			12 11	12 29	12 45	12 52	12 56			13 33
Exeter St Thomas	d			09 59						10 59			11 59							12 59			
Starcross	d			10 07						11 07			12 07							13 07			
Dawlish Warren	d			10 12			10 47			11 12			12 12						13 04	13 12			
Dawlish	d			10 16			10 51			11 16			12 16				12 41		13 08	13 16			
Teignmouth	d			10 21			10 56			11 21			12 21				12 46		13 13	13 21			
Newton Abbot	a	09 48	10 02	10 30	10 38	10 46	11 03	11 09		11 29	11 38	12 03	12 29			12 31	12 52	13 03	13 20	13 29			13 51
	d	09 49	10 03	10 31	10 39	10 48	11 04	11 10		11 30	11 38	12 05	12 36			12 32	12 53	13 05	13 21	13 30			13 53
Torre	d			10 39		10 56				11 38			12 43							13 38			
Torquay	d			10 42		10 59	11 14			11 41			12 46				13 05			13 41			
Paignton	a			10 50		11 07	11 23			11 51			12 54				13 11			13 49			
Totnes	d	10 02	10 16		10 52			11 24			11 52	12 17						13 17	13 34				14 05
Ivybridge	d	10 19									12 07								13 50				
Plymouth	a	10 32	10 41		11 20			11 51			12 24	12 43				13 13		13 43	14 05				14 34
	d	10 33			11 23										12 44	13 15						14 15	
Devonport	d																						
Dockyard	d																						
Keyham	d																						
St Budeaux Ferry Road	d	10 39																					
Saltash	d	10 44													12 53							14 24	
St Germans	d	10 51													13 00							14 32	
Menheniot	d																						
Liskeard 6	d	11 03			11 47										13 12	13 40						14 45	
Bodmin Parkway	d	11 15			12 00										13 24	13 54						14 58	
Lostwithiel	d	11 20													13 29							15 04	
Par	d	11 28			12 11									12 15	13 37	14 06					14 08	15 12	
Newquay	a													13 07							14 55		
St Austell	d	11 37			12 19										13 45	14 14						15 21	
Truro	d	11 55			12 37										14 02	14 30						15 39	
Redruth	d	12 08			12 49										14 15	14 44						15 53	
Camborne	d	12 14			12 56										14 21	14 50						16 00	
Hayle	d	12 21													14 28	15 00							
St Erth	d	12 25			13 08										14 33	15 05						16 12	
Penzance	a	12 36			13 20										14 42	15 17						16 21	

A ◇ from Exeter St Davids ■ to Exeter St Davids **B** 🍴 from Newton Abbot ⊘ to Newton Abbot

For connections from Heathrow Airport, Gatwick Airport and Oxford please refer to Tables 125A, 148 and 116

London and Birmingham - Devon and Cornwall

Saturdays from 27 October

Route Diagram - see first Page of Table 135

		XC	GW	GW	GW	XC	GW	GW	GW	GW	GW	XC	XC	GW	GW	GW	GW	XC	GW	GW	GW	GW
		◇1		◇1 A		◇1	◇1		◇		■ 1	◇1	◇1				◇1	◇1			◇	
London Paddington 15 ⊖	d			12 06			12 18				13 06						14 06					
Slough 3	d																					
Reading 7	d			12 32			12 48				13 32						14 32					
Theale	d						12 57															
Thatcham	d						13 05															
Newbury	d						13 13															
Hungerford	d						13 21															
Pewsey	d						13 39															
Westbury	d						13 58															
Castle Cary	d						14 14															
Birmingham New Street 12	d	11 12				12 12						13 12	13 42					14 12				
Cardiff Central 7	d																					
Newport (South Wales)	d																					
Swindon	d																					
Bristol Parkway 7	d	12 31				13 26						14 28	14 59					15 25				
Filton Abbey Wood	d																					
Bath Spa 7	d																					
Bristol Temple Meads 10	d	12 44				13 44						14 44	15 12					15 44				
Weston-super-Mare	d																					
Bridgwater	d																					
Taunton	d	13 17				14 17	14a37				14 48	15 18	15 44				15 48	16 17				
Tiverton Parkway	d	13 29				14 29					15 01	15 30	15 56				16 01	16 29				
Exeter St Davids 6	a	13 42		14 09		14 42					15 17	15 45	16 10				16 17	16 42				
Exmouth	d		13 23					14 23							15 23					16 55		
Exeter Central	d		13 50					14 50							15 50				16 48	17 21		
Exeter St Davids 6	d	13 44	13 57	14 11	14 30	14 44		14 56			15 18	15 47			15 57		16 18	16 44	16 56	17 27		
Exeter St Thomas	d		13 59					14 59							15 59				16 59	17 30		
Starcross	d		14 07					15 07							16 07				17 07	17 35		
Dawlish Warren	d		14 24		14 42			15 12							16 12				17 12	17 49		
Dawlish	d		14 28		14 46			15 16							16 16				17 16	17 53		
Teignmouth	d		14 33		14 51			15 21							16 21				17 21	17 58		
Newton Abbot	a	14 02	14 41	14 30	14 58	15 02		15 29			15 39	16 06			16 29		16 38	17 02	17 29	18 05		
	d	14 04	14 42	14 32	15 00	15 04		15 30			15 39	16 07		16 18	16 30		16 39	17 04	17 30	18 09		
Torre	d		14 50		15 08			15 38							16 38				17 38	18 17		
Torquay	d		14 53		15 11			15 41							16 41				17 41	18 20		
Paignton	a		15 01		15 19			15 51							16 51				17 51	18 27		
Totnes	d	14 16				15 16					15 53	16 21		16 31			16 52	17 16				
Ivybridge	d													16 47			17 08					
Plymouth	a	14 42		15 09		15 42					16 20	16 48		17 05			17 23	17 42				
	d			15 11						16 03	16 26						17 26					17 52
Devonport	d																					17 55
Dockyard	d																					17x57
Keyham	d																					17 59
St Budeaux Ferry Road	d																					18 01
Saltash	d									16 12												18 06
St Germans	d									16 19												18 12
Menheniot	d									16x27												18x19
Liskeard 6	d			15 36						16 33	16 50						17 51					18 26
Bodmin Parkway	d			15 49						16 45	17 03						18 03					18 38
Lostwithiel	d									16 50												18 44
Par	d			16 01					16 15	16 57							18 16				18 21	18 52
Newquay	a								17 07												19 13	
St Austell	d			16 08						17 05	17 20						18 23					18 59
Truro	d			16 26						17 23	17 37						18 41					19 17
Redruth	d			16 38						17 36	17 50						18 53					19 30
Camborne	d			16 46						17 42	17 57						19 01					19 36
Hayle	d									17 49	18 06											19 43
St Erth	d			16 57						17 54	18 12					18 32	19 12					19 48
Penzance	a			17 09						18 03	18 24					18 44	19 24					19 57

A 🍴 from Newton Abbot ⊘ to Newton Abbot

For connections from Heathrow Airport, Gatwick Airport and Oxford please refer to Tables 125A, 148 and 116

Table 135

Saturdays
from 27 October

London and Birmingham - Devon and Cornwall

Route Diagram - see first Page of Table 135

		GW	XC	GW	XC	GW	GW	GW		XC	GW	GW	GW	GW	GW	XC	GW	GW		XC	GW	GW	XC	GW	XC
		◇1	◇1	1	◇1	◇1				◇1				◇1	◇1	◇1		◇1		◇1		◇1	◇1	◇1	◇1
			A	B						A						A							C		C
		🍽	🛒		🛒	🍽				🛒				🍽	🍽	🛒		🍽		🛒		🍽	🛒	🍽	🛒
London Paddington 15 ⊖	d	15 06				16 06								17 06	16 30			18 06				19 06		20 06	
Slough 3	d																								
Reading 7	d	15 32				16 32								17 32	16 57			18 32				19 32		20 33	
Theale	d																								
Thatcham	d																								
Newbury	d																					19 49		20 47	
Hungerford	d																								
Pewsey	d	16 04												18 03								20 09		21 07	
Westbury	d	16 23												18 22								20 27		21 26	
Castle Cary	d	16 40												18 41								20 44		21 43	
Birmingham New Street 12	d		15 12		15 42					16 12						17 12				18 12			19 12		20 12
Cardiff Central 7	d																								
Newport (South Wales)	d																								
Swindon	d														17 30										
Bristol Parkway 7	d		16 31		16 56					17 26						18 31				19 27			20 31		21 24
Filton Abbey Wood	d																								
Bath Spa 7	d														18 00										
Bristol Temple Meads 10	d		16 44		17 10					17 44					18 18	18 44				19 44			20 44		21 44
Weston-super-Mare	d														18 40										
Bridgwater	d																								
Taunton	d	17 03	17 18		17 42	17 49				18 17				19 02	19 06	19 17		19 47		20 17		21 07	21 17	22 06	22 17
Tiverton Parkway	d	17 16	17 31		17 54	18 02				18 29				19 15	19 21	19 29				20 29		21 20	21 29	22 19	22 29
Exeter St Davids 6	a	17 31	17 46		18 08	18 18				18 42				19 31	19 36	19 43		20 13		20 42		21 36	21 42	22 35	22 43
Exmouth	d						17 55										19 38				20 08				
Exeter Central	d						18 21										20 01				20 35				
Exeter St Davids 6	d	17 34	17 48	17 53	18 10	18 20	18 27			18 46	18 56	19 16		19 34	19 39	19 45	20 07	20 16		20 45	20 56	21 38	21 45	22 38	22 46
Exeter St Thomas	d						18 29					19 19					20 10				20 59				
Starcross	d						18 37					19 27					20 18				21 07				
Dawlish Warren	d			18 05			18 42					19 32					20 32				21 12				
Dawlish	d			18 09	18 22		18 46				19 09	19 36					20 36				21 16			22 48	
Teignmouth	d			18 14	18 27		18 51				19 14	19 41					20 41				21 21			22 54	
Newton Abbot	a	17 53	18 10	18 21	18 33	18 40	18 59			19 04	19 21	19 49		19 53	19 58	20 03	20 48	20 37		21 03	21 28	21 58	22 04	23 02	23 10
	d	17 55	18 12	18 22	18 35	18 41	19 01			19 05	19 22	19 50		19 54	19 59	20 05	20 49	20 37		21 05	21 30	21 58	22 08	23 03	23 11
Torre	d						19 09					19 58			20 09		20 57				21 38				
Torquay	d				18 46		19 12				19 32	20 01			20 12		21 00				21 41				
Paignton	a				18 53		19 21				19 40	20 09			20 21		21 07				21 48				
Totnes	d	18 08	18 25	18 35		18 54				19 18				20 07		20 17		20 51		21 17		22 12	22 21	23 16	23 27
Ivybridge	d			18 51		19 11																			
Plymouth	a	18 36	18 52	19 05		19 26				19 43				20 35		20 43		21 19		21 43		22 40	22 47	23 46	23 53
	d	18 41	18 56	19 08						19 48				20 38		20 58		21 20							
Devonport	d																								
Dockyard	d																								
Keyham	d																								
St Budeaux Ferry Road	d																								
Saltash	d			19 17										20 49											
St Germans	d			19 24										20 56											
Menheniot	d																								
Liskeard 6	d	19 06	19 19	19 36						20 11				21 08		21 25		21 45							
Bodmin Parkway	d	19 19	19 34	19 48						20 23				21 21		21 38		21 59							
Lostwithiel	d			19 53						20 29															
Par	d	19 31	19 45	20 01				20 15		20 36				21 33		21 49		22 11							
Newquay	a							21 07																	
St Austell	d	19 39	19 53	20 08						20 43				21 43		21 56		22 18							
Truro	d	20 00	20 12	20 26						21 02				22 03		22 13		22 36							
Redruth	d	20 10	20 27	20 43						21 13				22 13		22 28		22 48							
Camborne	d	20 18	20 35	20 49						21 19						22 35		22 56							
Hayle	d									21 27								23 03							
St Erth	d	20 29	20 46	20 58						21 32			22 20	22 30		22 46		23 09							
Penzance	a	20 40	20 56	21 08						21 43			22 32	22 42		22 54		23 22							

A 🛒 to Plymouth

B 1 from Plymouth

C 🛒 to Bristol Temple Meads

For connections from Heathrow Airport, Gatwick Airport and Oxford please refer to Tables 125A, 148 and 116

Table 135

Saturdays
from 27 October

London and Birmingham - Devon and Cornwall

Route Diagram - see first Page of Table 135

		GW	GW
		◇	◇1
			🍽
London Paddington 15 ⊖	d		20 30
Slough 3	d		
Reading 7	d		20 57
Theale	d		
Thatcham	d		
Newbury	d		
Hungerford	d		
Pewsey	d		
Westbury	d		
Castle Cary	d		
Birmingham New Street 12	d		
Cardiff Central 7	d		
Newport (South Wales)	d		
Swindon	d		21 30
Bristol Parkway 7	d		
Filton Abbey Wood	d		
Bath Spa 7	d		22 00
Bristol Temple Meads 10	d	21 59	22 17
Weston-super-Mare	d	22 33	22s47
Bridgwater	d	22 52	23s05
Taunton	d	23 05	23 18
Tiverton Parkway	d	23 20	23 31
Exeter St Davids 6	a	23 38	23 47
Exmouth	d		
Exeter Central	d		
Exeter St Davids 6	d		
Exeter St Thomas	d		
Starcross	d		
Dawlish Warren	d		
Dawlish	d		
Teignmouth	d		
Newton Abbot	a		
	d		
Torre	d		
Torquay	d		
Paignton	a		
Totnes	d		
Ivybridge	d		
Plymouth	a		
	d		
Devonport	d		
Dockyard	d		
Keyham	d		
St Budeaux Ferry Road	d		
Saltash	d		
St Germans	d		
Menheniot	d		
Liskeard 6	d		
Bodmin Parkway	d		
Lostwithiel	d		
Par	d		
Newquay	a		
St Austell	d		
Truro	d		
Redruth	d		
Camborne	d		
Hayle	d		
St Erth	d		
Penzance	a		

For connections from Heathrow Airport, Gatwick Airport and Oxford please refer to Tables 125A, 148 and 116

Table 135

London and Birmingham - Devon and Cornwall

Sundays until 24 June

Route Diagram - see first Page of Table 135

		GW	GW	XC	GW	GW	XC	GW	GW	GW		XC	GW	GW	GW	XC	GW	GW	GW	GW		XC	GW	GW	GW
				■ ◇ A	🛒	◇	◇■ 🛒			◇		◇■ 🛒		◇■ ⊏	◇■ ⊏	◇■ B 🛒	🚌			◇■ ⊏		◇■ 🛒		◇■ ⊏	
London Paddington ■ ⊖	d													08 00	08 37					09 30				10 30	
Slough ■	d																								
Reading ■	d													08 35	09 15					10 05				11 05	
Theale	d																								
Thatcham	d																								
Newbury	d																								
Hungerford	d																								
Pewsey	d																09 30								
Westbury	d																			11 18					
Castle Cary	d																			11 35					
Birmingham New Street ■	d															09 12						10 30			
Cardiff Central ■	d																								
Newport (South Wales)	d																								
Swindon	d													09 08	09 48		10a15								
Bristol Parkway ■	d															10 23						11 41			
Filton Abbey Wood	d																								
Bath Spa ■	d													09 37											
Bristol Temple Meads ■	d					07 30	08 44			08 28		09 48		09 55		10 44						11 54			
Weston-super-Mare	d					07 53				08 59															
Bridgwater	d					08 09				09 18															
Taunton	d					08 24	09 16			09 32		10 21		10 28	11 00	11 16				11 57		12 27		12 45	
Tiverton Parkway	d					08 39	09 28			09 48		10 33		10 42	11 13	11 29						12 39		12 58	
Exeter St Davids ■	a					08 56	09 42			10 05		10 46		10 58	11 29	11 42				12 21		12 56		13 14	
Exmouth	d							09 10					10 21					11 24					12 29		
Exeter Central	d							09 36					10 48					11 52					12 55		13 20
Exeter St Davids ■	d	08 52				09 05	09 44	09 54		10 06		10 48	10 53	11 01	11 29	11 44		11 57	12 15	12 24		12 58	13 01	13 15	13 25
Exeter St Thomas	d	08 55						09 57					10 56					12 00							
Starcross	d	09 03						10 05					11 04					12 08							
Dawlish Warren	d	09 08						10 10					11 09					12 13					13 12		
Dawlish	d	09 12				09 18		10 14		10 21			11 13	11 19				12 17					13 16		13 38
Teignmouth	d	09 17				09 23		10 19		10 26			11 18	11 25				12 22					13 21		13 43
Newton Abbot	a	09 24				09 30	10 03	10 26		10 31		11 07	11 25	11 31	11 49	12 02		12 29	12 35	12 43		13 17	13 28	13 36	13 50
	d	09 26				09 30	10 04	10 37		10 33		11 09	11 27	11 32	11 50	12 03		12 31	12 36	12 45		13 18	13 29	13 37	13 52
Torre	d	09 34						10 45					11 35					12 39					13 37		14 00
Torquay	d	09 37						10 48					11 38					12 42					13 40		14 03
Paignton	a	09 44						10 54					11 45					12 49					13 47		14 10
Totnes	d					09 43	10 17			10 46		11 21		11 45	12 04	12 16			12 48	12 57		13 32			
Ivybridge	d					10 00													13 04						
Plymouth	a					10 14	10 43			11 15		11 48		12 14	12 31	12 42			13 17	13 26		13 59		14 14	
	d			09 01	09 10	10 15				11 15				12 15	12 35	12 55				13 30				14 20	
Devonport	d				09 13	10 19																			
Dockyard	d																								
Keyham	d																								
St Budeaux Ferry Road	d																								
Saltash	d				09 21	10 26				11 26															
St Germans	d				09 27	10 33				11 33															
Menheniot	d					10x41																			
Liskeard ■	d			09 26	09 43	10 47				11 45				12 40	12 59	13 18				13 55				14 44	
Bodmin Parkway	d			09 39	09 55	10 59				11 57				12 56	13 14	13 30				14 07				14 58	
Lostwithiel	d				10 01	11 04				12 02															
Par	d		09 00	09 56	10 09	11 12			11 53	12 10				13 08	13 25	13 41				14 20					
Newquay	a		09 52	11 10					12 50											15 26					
St Austell	d				10 16	11 21				12 18				13 15	13 31	13 48								15 14	
Truro	d				10 35	11 40				12 35				13 34	13 51	14 05								15 32	
Redruth	d				10 48	11 53				12 48				13 46	14 02	14 19								15 43	
Camborne	d				10 54	11 59				12 54				13 54	14 10	14 25								15 51	
Hayle	d				11 01	12 06				13 01															
St Erth	d				11 06	12 10				13 06				14 07	14 23	14 37								16 03	
Penzance	a				11 18	12 21				13 16				14 17	14 33	14 49								16 15	

A ◇ to Par ■ from Par

B 🛒 to Plymouth

For connections from Heathrow Airport, Gatwick Airport and Oxford please refer to Tables 125A, 148 and 116

Table 135

London and Birmingham - Devon and Cornwall

Sundays until 24 June

Route Diagram - see first Page of Table 135

		XC	GW	GW	GW	GW		GW	XC	GW	GW	GW	GW	XC	GW	GW		GW	GW	GW	XC	GW	GW	GW	GW
		◇■ 🛒		◇■ ⊏	🚌	🛒		◇■ ⊏	◇■ 🛒		◇	◇■ ⊏		◇■ 🛒	◇■ ⊏			🚌	◇	◇■ ⊏	◇■ 🛒		◇		◇■ ⊏
London Paddington ■ ⊖	d			11 03				11 30				12 30			13 03					13 30					14 30
Slough ■	d																								
Reading ■	d			11 38				12 05				13 05			13 38					14 05					15 05
Theale	d																								
Thatcham	d																								
Newbury	d																								
Hungerford	d																								
Pewsey	d				11 34													15 30							
Westbury	d																								
Castle Cary	d																			15 26					
Birmingham New Street ■	d	11 30							12 12					13 12							14 12				
Cardiff Central ■	d																								
Newport (South Wales)	d																								
Swindon	d			12 11	12a19			12 35				13 35			14 11			16a15							
Bristol Parkway ■	d	12 41							13 23					14 23							15 26				
Filton Abbey Wood	d																								
Bath Spa ■	d			12 40											14 40										
Bristol Temple Meads ■	d	12 54		12 55					13 44					14 44	14 55						15 44				
Weston-super-Mare	d			13 18																					
Bridgwater	d																								
Taunton	d	13 26		13 41				13 54	14 17			14 56		15 17	15 30					15 46	16 15				16 38
Tiverton Parkway	d	13 39							14 29			15 09		15 29							16 27				16 51
Exeter St Davids ■	a	13 55		14 05				14 18	14 44			15 24		15 43	15 54					16 12	16 44				17 06
Exmouth	d		13 24							14 31						15 24						16 24			
Exeter Central	d		13 50							14 57			15 20			15 50						16 50			
Exeter St Davids ■	d	13 57	14 00	14 07				14 18	14 46	15 03		15 25	15 31	15 44	15 56	16 00			16 10	16 23	16 45	16 56			17 08
Exeter St Thomas	d		14 03													16 03			16 12						
Starcross	d		14 11													16 11									
Dawlish Warren	d		14 16	14 22												16 16									
Dawlish	d		14 20	14 26						15 15			15 43			16 20			16 25			17 09			
Teignmouth	d		14 25	14 32						15 20			15 48			16 25			16 30			17 14			
Newton Abbot	a	14 16	14 32	14 38				14 43	15 04	15 27		15 46	15 55	16 02	16 16	16 32			16 36	16 42	17 04	17 21			17 26
	d	14 17	14 34	14 41				14 44	15 04	15 28		15 46	15 56	16 03	16 17	16 33			16 36	16 43	17 06	17 22			17 27
Torre	d		14 42							15 37			16 04			16 41						17 31			
Torquay	d		14 45	14 53						15 40			16 07			16 44						17 34			
Paignton	a		14 53	15 00						15 50			16 15			16 51						17 41			
Totnes	d	14 31						14 57	15 18			16 00		16 16					16 52	17 01	17 19				17 42
Ivybridge	d																		17 08						
Plymouth	a	14 57						15 25	15 43			16 29		16 42	16 55				17 22	17 30	17 46				18 09
	d					14 58		15 35				16 35							17 35						18 25
Devonport	d																								
Dockyard	d																								
Keyham	d																								
St Budeaux Ferry Road	d																								
Saltash	d					15 07													17 44						
St Germans	d					15 14													17 51						
Menheniot	d																		17x59						
Liskeard ■	d					15 26		15 57				16 58							18 05						18 51
Bodmin Parkway	d					15 39		16 12				17 11							18 17						19 05
Lostwithiel	d					15 45													18 22						
Par	d					15 53		16 24			16 36	17 24							18 30				18 45		19 16
Newquay	a										17 30												19 37		
St Austell	d					16 00		16 32				17 30							18 37						19 24
Truro	d					16 19		16 50				17 48							18 55						19 40
Redruth	d					16 32		17 02				18 01							19 08						19 54
Camborne	d					16 38		17 10				18 09							19 14						20 06
Hayle	d					16 45													19 21						
St Erth	d					16 50		17 22				18 22							19 25					20 05	20 16
Penzance	a					17 00		17 35				18 32							19 37					20 14	20 27

For connections from Heathrow Airport, Gatwick Airport and Oxford please refer to Tables 125A, 148 and 116

Sundays
until 24 June

London and Birmingham - Devon and Cornwall

Route Diagram - see first Page of Table 135

		XC	XC	GW	GW	GW	XC	GW	GW	XC	GW	GW	GW	GW	XC	GW	XC	XC	GW	GW	GW	GW
		◇1	◇1		◇1		◇1		◇1	◇1		◇		◇1	◇1		◇1	◇1	◇1	◇1		
			A							A								B				
London Paddington	d				15 30				16 30					17 57					18 57	19 03		
Slough	d																					
Reading	d				16 05				17 05					18 32					19 32	19 38		
Theale	d																					
Thatcham	d																					
Newbury	d																					
Hungerford	d																					
Pewsey	d										17 55										20 05	
Westbury	d				17 04														20 41			
Castle Cary	d				17 22														20 59			
Birmingham New Street	d	14 42	15 12				16 12			17 12					18 12		18 42	19 12				
Cardiff Central	d																					
Newport (South Wales)	d																					
Swindon	d								17 35		18a40			19 01						20 11	20a50	
Bristol Parkway	d	16 00	16 23				17 22			18 24					19 23		20 03	20 23				
Filton Abbey Wood	d																					
Bath Spa	d																			20 40		
Bristol Temple Meads	d	16 14	16 44				17 44			18 44		18 25			19 44		20 19	20 44		20 55		
Weston-super-Mare	d											18 58					20 37			21 27		
Bridgwater	d											19 17										
Taunton	d	16 46	17 17		17 44		18 20		18 42	19 17		19 32		20 07	20 20		20 59	21 17	21 21	21 51		
Tiverton Parkway	d	16 58	17 29		17 57		18 32		18 54	19 29		19 48		20 21	20 32		21 12	21 29	21 34	22 04		
Exeter St Davids	a	17 12	17 43		18 12		18 46		19 10	19 47		20 06		20 36	20 46		21 25	21 43	21 50	22 19		
Exmouth	d			17 24				18 24					19 24			20 24						21 24
Exeter Central	d			17 50				18 49					19 50			20 50						21 50
Exeter St Davids	d	17 14	17 44	17 56	18 13		18 47	18 56	19 11	19 49			19 56	20 36	20 47	20 56	21 27	21 46	21 50			21 56
Exeter St Thomas	d			17 59				18 59					19 59									21 59
Starcross	d			18 07				19 07					20 07									22 07
Dawlish Warren	d			18 12				19 12					20 12									22 12
Dawlish	d	17 26		18 16				19 16					20 16			21 09	21 39					22 16
Teignmouth	d	17 31		18 21				19 21					20 21			21 14	21 44					22 21
Newton Abbot	a	17 37	18 02	18 28	18 33		19 05	19 28	19 33	20 07			20 28	20 58	21 05	21 21	21 50	22 07	22 13			22 29
	d	17 38	18 03	18 29	18 35		19 07	19 30	19 33	20 08			20 30	20 58	21 07	21 22	21 51	22 09	22 14			22 30
Torre	d			18 37				19 38					20 38			21 31						22 38
Torquay	d	17 50		18 40				19 41					20 41			21 34	22 03					22 41
Paignton	a	17 56		18 47				19 48					20 48			21 41	22 09					22 49
Totnes	d		18 16				19 19		19 47	20 21				21 12	21 19			22 25	22 33			
Ivybridge	d																					
Plymouth	a		18 42		19 12		19 45		20 15	20 46				21 39	21 45			22 50	23 00			
	d		18 55			19 43			20 25	20 50				21 40								
Devonport	d																					
Dockyard	d																					
Keyham	d																					
St Budeaux Ferry Road	d																					
Saltash	d					19 52																
St Germans	d					19 59																
Menheniot	d																					
Liskeard	d		19 18			20 11			20 49	21 13				22 05								
Bodmin Parkway	d		19 30			20 23			21 02	21 25				22 19								
Lostwithiel	d					20 28																
Par	d		19 41			20 36			21 13	21 36				22 30								
Newquay	a																					
St Austell	d		19 52			20 43			21 20	21 43				22 38								
Truro	d		20 09			21 00			21 37	22 01				22 55								
Redruth	d		20 20			21 14			21 51	22 12				23 09								
Camborne	d		20 28			21 20			21 57	22 19				23 17								
Hayle	d					21 27																
St Erth	d		20 39			21 32			22 10	22 30				23 28								
Penzance	a		20 47			21 42			22 22	22 38				23 41								

A to Plymouth

B to Bristol Temple Meads

For connections from Heathrow Airport, Gatwick Airport and Oxford please refer to Tables 125A, 148 and 116

Sundays
until 24 June

London and Birmingham - Devon and Cornwall

Route Diagram - see first Page of Table 135

		XC	GW	GW	GW	GW
		◇1	◇1	◇1		
		A				
London Paddington	d		19 57	20 57		23 50
Slough	d					
Reading	d		20 33	21 33		00u37
Theale	d					
Thatcham	d					
Newbury	d					
Hungerford	d					
Pewsey	d				22 00	
Westbury	d		21 36			
Castle Cary	d		21 54			
Birmingham New Street	d	20 12				
Cardiff Central	d					
Newport (South Wales)	d					
Swindon	d				22a45	
Bristol Parkway	d	21 23				
Filton Abbey Wood	d					
Bath Spa	d					
Bristol Temple Meads	d	21 44				02 55
Weston-super-Mare	d					
Bridgwater	d					
Taunton	d	22 17	22 19	23s00		
Tiverton Parkway	d	22 29	22 33	23s13		
Exeter St Davids	a	22 46	22 52	23 29		04 04
Exmouth	d					
Exeter Central	d					
Exeter St Davids	d	22 47	22 52			04 35
Exeter St Thomas	d					
Starcross	d					
Dawlish Warren	d					
Dawlish	d		23 06			
Teignmouth	d		23 12			
Newton Abbot	a	23 05	23 19			04 55
	d	23 07	23 19			04 56
Torre	d					
Torquay	d					
Paignton	a					
Totnes	d	23 21	23 32			
Ivybridge	d					
Plymouth	a	23 47	00 01			05 35
	d					06 28
Devonport	d					
Dockyard	d					
Keyham	d					
St Budeaux Ferry Road	d					
Saltash	d					
St Germans	d					
Menheniot	d					
Liskeard	d					07 09
Bodmin Parkway	d					07 23
Lostwithiel	d					07 29
Par	d					07 38
Newquay	a					
St Austell	d					07 46
Truro	d					08 06
Redruth	d					08 20
Camborne	d					08 27
Hayle	d					08 38
St Erth	d					08 45
Penzance	a					08 59

A to Bristol Temple Meads

For connections from Heathrow Airport, Gatwick Airport and Oxford please refer to Tables 125A, 148 and 116

Table 135

Sundays

1 July to 9 September

London and Birmingham - Devon and Cornwall

Route Diagram - see first Page of Table 135

		GW	GW	XC	GW	GW	XC	GW	GW	GW		XC	GW	GW	GW	XC	GW	GW	GW	XC		GW	GW	GW	XC
				■ ◇ A	⊼	◇	◇1 ⊼			◇		◇1 ⊼		◇1 ☕	◇1 ☕	◇1 B ⊼			◇1 ☕	◇1 ⊼			◇1 ☕		◇1 ⊼
London Paddington 15 ⊖	d													08 00	08 57				09 57				10 57		
Slough 3	d																								
Reading 7	d													08 34	09 33				10 33				11 33		
Theale	d																								
Thatcham	d																								
Newbury	d														09 49										
Hungerford	d																								
Pewsey	d																		11 05						
Westbury	d														10 25										
Castle Cary	d																		11 35						
Birmingham New Street 12	d															09 12				10 30					11 12
Cardiff Central 7	d																								
Newport (South Wales)	d																								
Swindon	d													09 09											
Bristol Parkway 7	d															10 23				11 41					12 23
Filton Abbey Wood	d																								
Bath Spa 7	d													09 40											
Bristol Temple Meads 10	d					07 30	08 44			08 28		09 48		09 55		10 44				11 54					12 44
Weston-super-Mare	d					07 53				08 59															
Bridgwater	d					08 09				09 18															
Taunton	d					08 24	09 16			09 32		10 21		10 29	11 00	11 16			11 57	12 28			12 47		13 16
Tiverton Parkway	d					08 39	09 28			09 48		10 33		10 42	11 13	11 29				12 41					13 29
Exeter St Davids 6	a					08 56	09 42			10 05		10 46		10 58	11 29	11 42			12 21	12 56			13 14		13 45
Exmouth	d							09 10					10 21				11 24					12 29			
Exeter Central	d							09 36					10 48				11 52					12 55		13 20	
Exeter St Davids 6	d	08 52				09 05	09 44	09 54		10 06		10 48	10 53	11 01	11 29	11 44	11 57	12 15	12 24	12 57		13 01	13 15	13 25	13 47
Exeter St Thomas	d	08 55						09 57					10 56				12 00								
Starcross	d	09 03						10 05					11 04				12 08								
Dawlish Warren	d	09 08						10 10					11 09				12 13					13 12			
Dawlish	d	09 12				09 18		10 14		10 21			11 13	11 19			12 17					13 16		13 38	
Teignmouth	d	09 17				09 23		10 19		10 26			11 18	11 25			12 22					13 21		13 43	
Newton Abbot	a	09 24				09 30	10 03	10 26		10 31		11 07	11 25	11 31	11 51	12 02	12 29	12 35	12 43	13 16		13 28	13 35	13 50	14 06
	d	09 26				09 30	10 04	10 37		10 33		11 09	11 27	11 32	11 53	12 03	12 31	12 36	12 45	13 18		13 29	13 37	13 52	14 08
Torre	d	09 34						10 45					11 35				12 39					13 37		14 00	
Torquay	d	09 37						10 48					11 38				12 42					13 40		14 03	
Paignton	a	09 44						10 54					11 45				12 49					13 47		14 10	
Totnes	d					09 43	10 17			10 46		11 21		11 45	12 04	12 16		12 48	12 57	13 32					14 21
Ivybridge	d					10 00												13 04							
Plymouth	a					10 14	10 43			11 15		11 48		12 14	12 35	12 42		13 17	13 25	13 59			14 14		14 48
	d			09 01	09 10	10 15				11 15				12 15	12 35	12 55			13 30				14 20		
Devonport	d				09 13	10 19																			
Dockyard	d																								
Keyham	d																								
St Budeaux Ferry Road	d																								
Saltash	d				09 21	10 26				11 26															
St Germans	d				09 27	10 33				11 33															
Menheniot	d					10x41																			
Liskeard 6	d			09 26	09 43	10 47				11 45				12 40	12 59	13 18			13 55				14 44		
Bodmin Parkway	d			09 39	09 55	10 59				11 57				12 56	13 14	13 30			14 07				14 58		
Lostwithiel	d				10 01	11 04				12 02															
Par	d		09 00	09 56	10 09	11 12			11 53	12 10				13 08	13 25	13 41			14 20						
Newquay	a		09 52	11 10					12 50										15 26						
St Austell	d				10 16	11 21				12 18				13 15	13 31	13 48							15 13		
Truro	d				10 35	11 40				12 35				13 34	13 51	14 05							15 32		
Redruth	d				10 48	11 53				12 48				13 46	14 02	14 19							15 42		
Camborne	d				10 54	11 59				12 54				13 54	14 10	14 25							15 50		
Hayle	d				11 01	12 06				13 01															
St Erth	d				11 06	12 10				13 06				14 07	14 23	14 37							16 03		
Penzance	a				11 18	12 21				13 16				14 17	14 33	14 49							16 15		

A ◇ to Par ■ from Par

B ⊼ to Plymouth

For connections from Heathrow Airport, Gatwick Airport and Oxford please refer to Tables 125A, 148 and 116

Table 135

Sundays

1 July to 9 September

London and Birmingham - Devon and Cornwall

Route Diagram - see first Page of Table 135

		GW	GW	GW	GW	XC		GW	GW	GW	GW	XC	GW	GW	GW	GW		XC	GW	XC	GW	GW	GW	XC	GW
			◇1 ☕	⊼	◇1 ☕	◇1 ⊼			◇	◇1 ☕		◇1 ⊼	◇1 ☕		◇	◇1 ☕		◇1 ⊼		◇1 ⊼	◇		◇1 ☕	◇1 A ⊼	
London Paddington 15 ⊖	d		11 35		11 57					12 57			13 03			13 57							14 57		
Slough 3	d																								
Reading 7	d		12 03		12 33					13 33			13 38			14 33							15 33		
Theale	d																								
Thatcham	d																								
Newbury	d				12 49											14 49									
Hungerford	d																								
Pewsey	d		12 41																						
Westbury	d		13 06							14 20															
Castle Cary	d		13 24													15 36									
Birmingham New Street 12	d					12 12						13 12						14 12		14 42				15 12	
Cardiff Central 7	d																								
Newport (South Wales)	d																								
Swindon	d												14 11												
Bristol Parkway 7	d					13 25						14 23						15 26		16 00				16 23	
Filton Abbey Wood	d																								
Bath Spa 7	d												14 40												
Bristol Temple Meads 10	d					13 44						14 44	14 55					15 44		16 14				16 44	
Weston-super-Mare	d																								
Bridgwater	d																								
Taunton	d		13 45		13 54	14 17				14 56		15 17	15 30			15 56		16 15		16 46			16 52	17 17	
Tiverton Parkway	d					14 30				15 09		15 29						16 27		16 58			17 05	17 29	
Exeter St Davids 6	a		14 11		14 20	14 45				15 24		15 43	15 54			16 22		16 44		17 12			17 20	17 43	
Exmouth	d	13 24						14 31						15 24					16 24						17 24
Exeter Central	d	13 50						14 57			15 20			15 50					16 50						17 50
Exeter St Davids 6	d	14 00	14 12		14 22	14 47		15 03		15 25	15 31	15 44	15 56	16 00	16 10	16 23		16 45	16 56	17 14			17 22	17 44	17 56
Exeter St Thomas	d	14 03												16 03	16 12										17 59
Starcross	d	14 11												16 11											18 07
Dawlish Warren	d	14 16	14 25											16 16											18 12
Dawlish	d	14 20	14 30					15 15			15 43			16 20	16 25				17 09	17 26					18 16
Teignmouth	d	14 25	14 36					15 20			15 48			16 25	16 30				17 14	17 31					18 21
Newton Abbot	a	14 32	14 43		14 47	15 06		15 27		15 46	15 55	16 02	16 16	16 32	16 36	16 42		17 04	17 21	17 37			17 40	18 02	18 28
	d	14 34	14 43		14 48	15 08		15 28		15 46	15 56	16 03	16 17	16 33	16 36	16 43		17 06	17 22	17 38			17 41	18 03	18 29
Torre	d	14 42						15 37			16 04			16 41					17 31						18 37
Torquay	d	14 45	14 56					15 40			16 07			16 44					17 34	17 50					18 40
Paignton	a	14 53	15 03					15 50			16 15			16 51					17 41	17 56					18 47
Totnes	d				15 01	15 21				16 00		16 16			16 52	17 01		17 19					17 56	18 16	
Ivybridge	d														17 08										
Plymouth	a				15 30	15 48				16 28		16 42	16 55		17 22	17 30		17 46					18 22	18 42	
	d			14 58	15 35					16 35					17 35								18 25	18 55	
Devonport	d																								
Dockyard	d																								
Keyham	d																								
St Budeaux Ferry Road	d																								
Saltash	d			15 07											17 45										
St Germans	d			15 14											17 52										
Menheniot	d														18x00										
Liskeard 6	d			15 26	16 00					16 58					18 06								18 51	19 18	
Bodmin Parkway	d			15 39	16 13					17 11					18 18								19 05	19 30	
Lostwithiel	d			15 45											18 23										
Par	d			15 53	16 25				16 36	17 24					18 31						18 45		19 16	19 41	
Newquay	a								17 30												19 37				
St Austell	d			16 00	16 32					17 30					18 38								19 24	19 52	
Truro	d			16 19	16 51					17 48					18 56								19 41	20 09	
Redruth	d			16 32	17 03					18 01					19 09								19 54	20 20	
Camborne	d			16 38	17 11					18 09					19 15								20 05	20 28	
Hayle	d			16 45											19 22										
St Erth	d			16 50	17 22					18 22					19 26							20 05	20 17	20 39	
Penzance	a			17 00	17 35					18 32					19 38							20 14	20 27	20 47	

A ⊼ to Plymouth

For connections from Heathrow Airport, Gatwick Airport and Oxford please refer to Tables 125A, 148 and 116

Sundays

1 July to 9 September

London and Birmingham - Devon and Cornwall

Route Diagram - see first Page of Table 135

		GW	GW	XC	GW	GW	GW	XC	GW	GW	XC	GW	GW	XC	XC	GW	GW	GW	XC	GW	GW
		◇■ ☕		◇■ 🛒		◇■ ☕	◇	◇■ A 🛒		◇■ ☕	◇■ 🛒		◇■ ☕	◇■ 🛒	◇■ B 🛒	◇■ ☕		◇■ ☕	◇■ B 🛒	◇■ ☕	■ ☕
London Paddington 15 ⊖	d	15 57				16 57				17 57			18 57			19 03		19 57		20 57	23 50
Slough 3	d																				
Reading 7	d	16 33				17 33				18 32			19 33			19 38		20 33		21 33	00u37
Theale	d																				
Thatcham	d																				
Newbury	d	16 48								18 49								20 50			
Hungerford	d																				
Pewsey	d									19 09								21 10			
Westbury	d	17 25								19 28								21 29			
Castle Cary	d	17 42											20 30					21 47			
Birmingham New Street 12	d			16 12				17 12			18 12			18 42	19 12				20 12		
Cardiff Central 7	d																				
Newport (South Wales)	d																				
Swindon	d															20 11					
Bristol Parkway 7	d			17 22				18 24			19 23			20 03	20 23				21 23		
Filton Abbey Wood	d																				
Bath Spa 7	d															20 40					
Bristol Temple Meads 10	d			17 44			18 07	18 44			19 44			20 19	20 44	20 55			21 44		02 55
Weston-super-Mare	d						18 36							20 37		21 27					
Bridgwater	d						18 55														
Taunton	d	18 05		18 20		18 50	19 10	19 17		20 03	20 20		20 52	20 59	21 17	21 51		22 07	22 17	22s49	
Tiverton Parkway	d	18 18		18 32		19 03	19 25	19 29		20 17	20 32		21 05	21 12	21 29	22 04		22 20	22 29	23s03	
Exeter St Davids 6	a	18 36		18 46		19 18	19 43	19 47		20 33	20 46		21 21	21 27	21 43	22 19		22 36	22 46	23 19	04 04
Exmouth	d				18 24				19 24			20 24					21 24				
Exeter Central	d				18 49				19 50			20 50					21 50				
Exeter St Davids 6	d	18 37		18 47	18 56	19 20		19 49	19 56	20 34	20 47	20 56	21 22	21 29	21 44		21 56	22 37	22 47		04 35
Exeter St Thomas	d				18 59				19 59								21 59				
Starcross	d				19 07				20 07								22 07				
Dawlish Warren	d				19 12				20 12								22 12				
Dawlish	d				19 16				20 16			21 09	21 36	21 41			22 16				
Teignmouth	d				19 21				20 21			21 14	21 42	21 47			22 21				
Newton Abbot	a	18 57		19 05	19 28	19 39		20 07	20 28	20 54	21 05	21 21	21 48	21 53	22 02		22 29	22 57	23 05		04 55
	d	18 59		19 07	19 30	19 39		20 08	20 30	20 54	21 07	21 22	21 49	21 55	22 04		22 30	22 58	23 07		04 56
Torre	d				19 38				20 38			21 31					22 38				
Torquay	d				19 41				20 41			21 34		22 07			22 41				
Paignton	a				19 48				20 48			21 41		22 13			22 49				
Totnes	d			19 19		19 55		20 21		21 08	21 19		22 03		22 20			23 11	23 21		
Ivybridge	d																				
Plymouth	a	19 36		19 45		20 21		20 46		21 35	21 45		22 30		22 45			23 40	23 47		05 35
	d		19 43			20 25		20 50		21 40											06 28
Devonport	d																				
Dockyard	d																				
Keyham	d																				
St Budeaux Ferry Road	d																				
Saltash	d		19 52																		
St Germans	d		19 59																		
Menheniot	d																				
Liskeard 6	d		20 11			20 48		21 13		22 05											07 09
Bodmin Parkway	d		20 23			21 02		21 25		22 19											07 23
Lostwithiel	d		20 28																		07 29
Par	d		20 36			21 13		21 36		22 30											07 38
Newquay	a																				
St Austell	d		20 43			21 21		21 43		22 38											07 46
Truro	d		21 00			21 38		22 01		22 55											08 06
Redruth	d		21 14			21 51		22 12		23 09											08 20
Camborne	d		21 20			21 59		22 19		23 17											08 27
Hayle	d		21 27																		08 38
St Erth	d		21 32			22 10		22 30		23 28											08 45
Penzance	a		21 42			22 22		22 38		23 41											08 59

A 🛒 to Plymouth

B 🛒 to Bristol Temple Meads

For connections from Heathrow Airport, Gatwick Airport and Oxford please refer to Tables 125A, 148 and 116

Sundays

16 September to 21 October

London and Birmingham - Devon and Cornwall

Route Diagram - see first Page of Table 135

		GW	GW	GW	GW	GW	GW	XC	GW	GW	GW	GW	XC	GW	GW	GW	XC	GW	GW	GW	XC	GW	GW
			🛒		◇		◇	◇■ 🛒		◇■ ☕	◇■ ☕		◇■ A 🛒			◇■ ☕	◇■ 🛒		◇■ ☕		◇■ 🛒		◇■ ☕
London Paddington 15 ⊖	d									07 57	08 57					09 57			10 57				11 27
Slough 3	d																						
Reading 7	d									08 32	09 32					10 32			11 32				12 02
Theale	d																						
Thatcham	d																						
Newbury	d										09 49												
Hungerford	d																						
Pewsey	d															11 05							12 41
Westbury	d										10 24												13 06
Castle Cary	d															11 35							13 24
Birmingham New Street 12	d																09 12				10 30		
Cardiff Central 7	d																						
Newport (South Wales)	d																						
Swindon	d									09 15													
Bristol Parkway 7	d																11 25				12 24		
Filton Abbey Wood	d																						
Bath Spa 7	d																						
Bristol Temple Meads 10	d				07 30		08 28	09 48		09 55			10 44				11 44				12 54		
Weston-super-Mare	d				07 53		08 59																
Bridgwater	d				08 09		09 18																
Taunton	d				08 24		09 32	10 21		10 28	11 00		11 16			11 57	12 16		12 47		13 27		13 45
Tiverton Parkway	d				08 39		09 48	10 33		10 42	11 13		11 29				12 29				13 40		13 58
Exeter St Davids 6	a				08 56		10 05	10 46		10 58	11 28		11 42			12 21	12 42		13 14		13 55		14 14
Exmouth	d					09 10			10 21					11 24				12 29				13 24	
Exeter Central	d					09 36			10 48					11 52				12 55		13 20		13 50	
Exeter St Davids 6	d	08 52			09 05	09 54	10 06	10 48	10 53	11 00	11 29		11 44	11 57	12 15	12 24	12 44	13 01	13 15	13 25	13 57	14 00	14 15
Exeter St Thomas	d	08 55				09 57			10 56					12 00								14 03	
Starcross	d	09 03				10 05			11 04					12 08								14 11	
Dawlish Warren	d	09 08				10 10			11 09					12 13				13 12				14 16	
Dawlish	d	09 12			09 18	10 14	10 21		11 13	11 19				12 17				13 16		13 38		14 20	14 29
Teignmouth	d	09 17			09 23	10 19	10 26		11 18	11 25				12 22				13 21		13 43		14 25	14 35
Newton Abbot	a	09 24			09 30	10 26	10 31	11 07	11 25	11 31	11 49		12 02	12 29	12 35	12 43	13 02	13 28	13 35	13 50	14 16	14 33	14 42
	d	09 26			09 30	10 37	10 33	11 09	11 27	11 32	11 50		12 03	12 31	12 36	12 45	13 04	13 29	13 37	13 52	14 18	14 36	14 42
Torre	d	09 34				10 45			11 35					12 39				13 37		14 00		14 44	
Torquay	d	09 37				10 48			11 38					12 42				13 40		14 03		14 47	14 54
Paignton	a	09 44				10 54			11 45					12 49				13 47		14 10		14 53	15 03
Totnes	d				09 43		10 46	11 21		11 45	12 04		12 16		12 48	12 57	13 16				14 31		
Ivybridge	d				10 00										13 04								
Plymouth	a				10 14		11 15	11 48		12 13	12 33		12 42		13 17	13 26	13 42		14 14		14 58		
	d		09 10		10 15		11 15				12 35		12 55						14 20				
Devonport	d				10 19																		
Dockyard	d																						
Keyham	d																						
St Budeaux Ferry Road	d		09 16																				
Saltash	d		09 20		10 26		11 26																
St Germans	d		09 26		10 33		11 33																
Menheniot	d				10x41																		
Liskeard 6	d		09 43		10 47		11 45				12 59		13 18						14 44				
Bodmin Parkway	d		09 55		10 59		11 57				13 13		13 30						14 58				
Lostwithiel	d		10 01		11 04		12 02																
Par	d		10 09	10 18	11 12		12 10				13 24	13 31	13 41										
Newquay	a			11 10								14 23											
St Austell	d		10 16		11 21		12 18				13 31		13 48						15 14				
Truro	d		10 35		11 40		12 35				13 50		14 05						15 32				
Redruth	d		10 48		11 53		12 48				14 02		14 19						15 43				
Camborne	d		10 54		11 59		12 54				14 10		14 25						15 51				
Hayle	d		11 01		12 06		13 01																
St Erth	d		11 06		12 10		13 06				14 23		14 37						16 03				
Penzance	a		11 18		12 21		13 16				14 33		14 49						16 21				

A 🛒 to Plymouth

For connections from Heathrow Airport, Gatwick Airport and Oxford please refer to Tables 125A, 148 and 116

Table 135

Sundays

16 September to 21 October

London and Birmingham - Devon and Cornwall

Route Diagram - see first Page of Table 135

		GW	GW	XC	GW	GW	GW	GW	XC	GW	GW	GW	GW	XC	GW	GW	GW	XC	GW	GW	GW	XC	GW
		⌶	◇1 ⊐	◇1 ⌶		◇	◇1 ⊐		◇1 ⌶	◇1 ⊐		◇	◇1 ⊐	◇1 ⌶			◇1 ⊐	◇1 A ⌶		◇1 ⊐		◇1 ⌶	
London Paddington 15 ⊖	d		11 57				12 57			13 03			13 57				14 57			15 57			
Slough 3	d																						
Reading 7	d		12 32				13 32			13 38			14 32				15 32			16 32			
Theale	d																						
Thatcham	d																						
Newbury	d		12 49										14 49							16 49			
Hungerford	d																						
Pewsey	d																						
Westbury	d						14 20													17 25			
Castle Cary	d												15 36							17 42			
Birmingham New Street 12	d			11 30					12 12					13 12				14 12				15 12	
Cardiff Central 7	d																						
Newport (South Wales)	d																						
Swindon	d									14 11													
Bristol Parkway 7	d			13 24					14 23					15 23				16 23				17 22	
Filton Abbey Wood	d																						
Bath Spa 7	d																						
Bristol Temple Meads 10	d			13 44					14 44	14 55				15 44				16 44				17 44	
Weston-super-Mare	d																						
Bridgwater	d																						
Taunton	d		13 54	14 17			14 56		15 17	15 30			15 56	16 18			16 51	17 17		18 05		18 20	
Tiverton Parkway	d			14 30			15 09		15 29					16 31			17 04	17 29		18 18		18 32	
Exeter St Davids 6	a		14 21	14 45			15 24		15 43	15 54			16 22	16 46			17 19	17 43		18 36		18 46	
Exmouth	d				14 31						15 24				16 24				17 24				18 24
Exeter Central	d				14 59			15 20			15 50				16 50				17 50				18 49
Exeter St Davids 6	d		14 22	14 47	15 05		15 25	15 31	15 44	15 56	16 00	16 10	16 23	16 47	16 56		17 21	17 44	17 56	18 37		18 47	18 56
Exeter St Thomas	d										16 03	16 12							17 59				18 59
Starcross	d										16 11								18 07				19 07
Dawlish Warren	d										16 16								18 12				19 12
Dawlish	d				15 17			15 43			16 20	16 25			17 09				18 16				19 16
Teignmouth	d				15 22			15 48			16 25	16 30			17 14				18 21				19 21
Newton Abbot	a		14 45	15 06	15 29		15 46	15 55	16 02	16 16	16 32	16 36	16 42	17 06	17 21		17 39	18 02	18 28	18 57		19 05	19 28
	d		14 47	15 08	15 30		15 46	15 56	16 03	16 17	16 33	16 36	16 43	17 07	17 22		17 40	18 03	18 29	18 59		19 07	19 30
Torre	d				15 39			16 04			16 41				17 31				18 37				19 38
Torquay	d				15 42			16 07			16 44				17 34				18 40				19 41
Paignton	a				15 50			16 15			16 51				17 41				18 47				19 48
Totnes	d		14 59	15 21			16 00		16 16			16 52	17 01	17 21			17 55	18 16				19 19	
Ivybridge	d											17 08											
Plymouth	a		15 28	15 48			16 29		16 42	16 55		17 22	17 30	17 48			18 21	18 42		19 36		19 45	
	d	14 58	15 35				16 35					17 35					18 25	18 55			19 43		
Devonport	d																						
Dockyard	d																						
Keyham	d																						
St Budeaux Ferry Road	d																						
Saltash	d	15 07										17 44									19 52		
St Germans	d	15 14										17 51									19 59		
Menheniot	d											17x59											
Liskeard 6	d	15 26	15 57				16 59					18 05					18 50	19 18			20 11		
Bodmin Parkway	d	15 39	16 12				17 12					18 17					19 04	19 30			20 23		
Lostwithiel	d	15 45										18 22									20 28		
Par	d	15 53	16 24			16 30	17 23					18 30					19 16	19 41			20 36		
Newquay	a					17 22																	
St Austell	d	16 00	16 32				17 31					18 37					19 23	19 52			20 43		
Truro	d	16 19	16 50				17 49					18 55					19 41	20 09			21 00		
Redruth	d	16 32	17 02				18 02					19 08					19 53	20 20			21 14		
Camborne	d	16 38	17 10				18 10					19 14					20 02	20 28			21 20		
Hayle	d	16 45										19 21									21 27		
St Erth	d	16 50	17 22				18 22					19 25				20 05	20 15	20 39			21 32		
Penzance	a	17 00	17 35				18 33					19 37				20 14	20 27	20 47			21 42		

A ⌶ to Plymouth

For connections from Heathrow Airport, Gatwick Airport and Oxford please refer to Tables 125A, 148 and 116

Table 135

Sundays

16 September to 21 October

London and Birmingham - Devon and Cornwall

Route Diagram - see first Page of Table 135

		GW	GW	XC	GW	GW	XC	GW	GW	XC	GW	GW	GW	XC	GW	GW
		◇1 ⊐	◇	◇1 A ⌶		◇1 ⊐	◇1 ⌶		◇1 ⊐	◇1 B ⌶	◇1 ⊐		◇1 ⊐	◇1 B ⌶	◇1 ⊐	🛏 ⊐
London Paddington 15 ⊖	d	16 57				17 57			18 57		19 03		19 57		20 57	23 50
Slough 3	d															
Reading 7	d	17 32				18 32			19 32		19 38		20 32		21 33	00u38
Theale	d															
Thatcham	d															
Newbury	d					18 49							20 50			
Hungerford	d															
Pewsey	d					19 10							21 10			
Westbury	d					19 29							21 29			
Castle Cary	d								20 30				21 47			
Birmingham New Street 12	d			16 12			17 12			18 12				19 12		
Cardiff Central 7	d															
Newport (South Wales)	d															
Swindon	d										20 11					
Bristol Parkway 7	d			18 24			19 23			20 23				21 23		
Filton Abbey Wood	d															
Bath Spa 7	d										20 40					
Bristol Temple Meads 10	d		18 07	18 44			19 44			20 44	20 55			21 44		02 55
Weston-super-Mare	d		18 36								21 27					
Bridgwater	d		18 55													
Taunton	d	18 50	19 10	19 17		20 03	20 19		20 52	21 17	21 51		22 07	22 17	22s49	
Tiverton Parkway	d	19 03	19 25	19 29		20 17	20 31		21 05	21 29	22 04		22 20	22 29	23s03	
Exeter St Davids 6	a	19 18	19 43	19 47		20 32	20 45		21 21	21 43	22 19		22 36	22 46	23 19	04 04
Exmouth	d				19 24			20 24				21 24				
Exeter Central	d				19 50			20 50				21 50				
Exeter St Davids 6	d	19 20		19 49	19 56	20 32	20 46	20 56	21 22	21 44		21 56	22 37	22 47		04 35
Exeter St Thomas	d				19 59							21 59				
Starcross	d				20 07							22 07				
Dawlish Warren	d				20 12							22 12				
Dawlish	d				20 16			21 09	21 36			22 16				
Teignmouth	d				20 21			21 14	21 42			22 21				
Newton Abbot	a	19 39		20 07	20 28	20 54	21 04	21 21	21 48	22 02		22 29	22 57	23 05		04 55
	d	19 39		20 08	20 30	20 54	21 06	21 22	21 49	22 04		22 30	22 58	23 07		04 56
Torre	d				20 38			21 31				22 38				
Torquay	d				20 41			21 34				22 41				
Paignton	a				20 48			21 41				22 49				
Totnes	d	19 55		20 21		21 08	21 18		22 03	22 20			23 11	23 21		
Ivybridge	d															
Plymouth	a	20 21		20 46		21 35	21 44		22 30	22 45			23 40	23 47		05 35
	d	20 25		20 50		21 40										06 28
Devonport	d															
Dockyard	d															
Keyham	d															
St Budeaux Ferry Road	d															
Saltash	d															
St Germans	d															
Menheniot	d															
Liskeard 6	d	20 49		21 13		22 04										07 09
Bodmin Parkway	d	21 02		21 25		22 17										07 23
Lostwithiel	d															07 29
Par	d	21 13		21 36		22 30										07 38
Newquay	a															
St Austell	d	21 20		21 43		22 38										07 46
Truro	d	21 37		22 01		22 53										08 06
Redruth	d	21 51		22 12		23 08										08 20
Camborne	d	21 57		22 19		23 15										08 27
Hayle	d															08 38
St Erth	d	22 10		22 30		23 27										08 45
Penzance	a	22 22		22 38		23 38										08 59

A ⌶ to Plymouth

B ⌶ to Bristol Temple Meads

For connections from Heathrow Airport, Gatwick Airport and Oxford please refer to Tables 125A, 148 and 116

Sundays
from 28 October

London and Birmingham - Devon and Cornwall

Route Diagram - see first Page of Table 135

		GW	GW	GW	GW	XC	GW	GW	XC	GW	GW	GW	GW	XC	GW	GW	GW	XC	GW	GW	GW	XC	GW
					◇	◇1		◇	◇1		◇1	◇1		◇1			◇1	◇1		◇1		◇1	
														A									
			⌶			⌶			⌶		🍽	🍽		⌶			🍽	⌶		🍽		⌶	
London Paddington 15 ⊖	d										08 00	08 57					09 57			10 57			
Slough 3	d																						
Reading 7	d										08 34	09 32					10 32			11 32			
Theale	d																						
Thatcham	d																						
Newbury	d											09 49											
Hungerford	d																						
Pewsey	d																11 05						
Westbury	d											10 24											
Castle Cary	d																11 35						
Birmingham New Street 12	d																					11 03	
Cardiff Central 7	d																						
Newport (South Wales)	d																						
Swindon	d										09 11												
Bristol Parkway 7	d																	11 41				12 35	
Filton Abbey Wood	d																						
Bath Spa 7	d										09 41												
Bristol Temple Meads 10	d				07 30	08 44		08 28	09 48		09 55			10 44				11 54				12 54	
Weston-super-Mare	d				07 53			08 59															
Bridgwater	d				08 09			09 18															
Taunton	d				08 24	09 16		09 32	10 21		10 30	11 00		11 16			11 57	12 28		12 47		13 27	
Tiverton Parkway	d				08 39	09 28		09 48	10 33		10 44	11 13		11 29				12 41				13 40	
Exeter St Davids 6	a				08 56	09 42		10 05	10 46		11 00	11 29		11 42			12 21	12 56		13 14		13 55	
Exmouth	d						09 10			10 21					11 24				12 29				13 24
Exeter Central	d						09 36			10 48					11 52				12 55		13 20		13 50
Exeter St Davids 6	d	08 52			09 05	09 44	09 54	10 06	10 48	10 53	11 02	11 29		11 44	11 57	12 15	12 24	12 57	13 01	13 15	13 25	13 57	14 00
Exeter St Thomas	d	08 55					09 57			10 56					12 00								14 03
Starcross	d	09 03					10 05			11 04					12 08								14 11
Dawlish Warren	d	09 08					10 10			11 09					12 13				13 12				14 16
Dawlish	d	09 12			09 18		10 14	10 21		11 13	11 19				12 17				13 16		13 38		14 20
Teignmouth	d	09 17			09 23		10 19	10 26		11 18	11 25				12 22				13 21		13 43		14 25
Newton Abbot	a	09 24			09 30	10 03	10 26	10 31	11 07	11 25	11 31	11 49		12 02	12 29	12 35	12 43	13 17	13 28	13 35	13 50	14 16	14 33
	d	09 26			09 30	10 04	10 37	10 33	11 09	11 27	11 32	11 50		12 03	12 31	12 36	12 45	13 18	13 29	13 37	13 52	14 17	14 36
Torre	d	09 34					10 45			11 35					12 39				13 37		14 00		14 44
Torquay	d	09 37					10 48			11 38					12 42				13 40		14 03		14 47
Paignton	a	09 44					10 54			11 45					12 49				13 47		14 10		14 53
Totnes	d				09 43	10 17		10 46	11 21		11 45	12 04		12 16		12 48	12 57	13 31				14 31	
Ivybridge	d				10 00											13 04							
Plymouth	a				10 14	10 43		11 15	11 48		12 13	12 33		12 42		13 17	13 26	13 58		14 14		14 57	
	d		09 15		10 15			11 15				12 35		12 55						14 20			
Devonport	d				10 19																		
Dockyard	d																						
Keyham	d																						
St Budeaux Ferry Road	d		09 21																				
Saltash	d		09 25		10 26			11 26															
St Germans	d		09 31		10 33			11 33															
Menheniot	d				10x41																		
Liskeard 6	d		09 43		10 47			11 45				12 59		13 18						14 44			
Bodmin Parkway	d		09 55		10 59			11 57				13 13		13 30						14 58			
Lostwithiel	d		10 01		11 04			12 02															
Par	d		10 09	10 18	11 12			12 10				13 24	13 31	13 41									
Newquay	a			11 10									14 23										
St Austell	d		10 16		11 21			12 18				13 31		13 48						15 14			
Truro	d		10 35		11 40			12 35				13 50		14 05						15 32			
Redruth	d		10 48		11 53			12 48				14 02		14 19						15 43			
Camborne	d		10 54		11 59			12 54				14 10		14 25						15 51			
Hayle	d		11 01		12 06			13 01															
St Erth	d		11 06		12 10			13 06				14 23		14 37						16 03			
Penzance	a		11 18		12 21			13 16				14 33		14 49						16 21			

A ⌶ to Plymouth

For connections from Heathrow Airport, Gatwick Airport and Oxford please refer to Tables 125A, 148 and 116

Sundays
from 28 October

London and Birmingham - Devon and Cornwall

Route Diagram - see first Page of Table 135

		GW	GW	GW	XC	GW	GW	GW	GW	XC	GW	GW	GW	GW	XC	GW	XC	GW	GW	XC	GW	GW	GW
		◇1		◇1	◇1		◇	◇1		◇1	◇1		◇	◇1	◇1		◇1		◇1	◇1		◇1	
																				A			
		🍽	⌶	🍽	⌶			🍽		⌶	🍽			🍽	⌶		⌶		🍽	⌶		🍽	
London Paddington 15 ⊖	d	11 27		11 57				12 57			13 03			13 57					14 57			15 57	
Slough 3	d																						
Reading 7	d	12 02		12 32				13 32			13 38			14 32					15 32			16 32	
Theale	d																						
Thatcham	d																						
Newbury	d			12 49										14 49								16 47	
Hungerford	d																						
Pewsey	d	12 41																					
Westbury	d	13 06						14 20														17 25	
Castle Cary	d	13 24												15 36								17 42	
Birmingham New Street 12	d														13 29		14 42			15 12			
Cardiff Central 7	d																						
Newport (South Wales)	d																						
Swindon	d										14 11												
Bristol Parkway 7	d														15 19		16 00			16 23			
Filton Abbey Wood	d																						
Bath Spa 7	d										14 40												
Bristol Temple Meads 10	d				13 44					14 44	14 55				15 44		16 14			16 44			
Weston-super-Mare	d																						
Bridgwater	d																						
Taunton	d	13 45		13 54	14 17			14 56		15 17	15 30			15 56	16 18		16 46		16 51	17 17		18 05	
Tiverton Parkway	d	13 58			14 29			15 09		15 29					16 31		16 58		17 04	17 29		18 18	
Exeter St Davids 6	a	14 14		14 21	14 44			15 24		15 43	15 54			16 22	16 46		17 12		17 19	17 43		18 36	
Exmouth	d					14 31						15 24				16 24					17 24		18 24
Exeter Central	d					14 59			15 20			15 50				16 50					17 50		18 49
Exeter St Davids 6	d	14 15		14 22	14 46	15 05		15 25	15 31	15 44	15 56	16 00	16 10	16 23	16 47	16 56	17 14		17 21	17 44	17 56	18 37	18 56
Exeter St Thomas	d											16 03	16 12								17 59		18 59
Starcross	d											16 11									18 07		19 07
Dawlish Warren	d											16 16									18 12		19 12
Dawlish	d	14 29				15 17			15 43			16 20	16 25			17 09	17 26				18 16		19 16
Teignmouth	d	14 35				15 22			15 48			16 25	16 30			17 14	17 31				18 21		19 21
Newton Abbot	a	14 42		14 45	15 04	15 29		15 46	15 55	16 02	16 16	16 32	16 36	16 42	17 06	17 21	17 37		17 40	18 02	18 28	18 57	19 28
	d	14 42		14 47	15 04	15 30		15 46	15 56	16 03	16 17	16 33	16 36	16 43	17 07	17 22	17 38		17 40	18 03	18 29	18 59	19 30
Torre	d					15 39			16 04			16 41				17 31					18 37		19 38
Torquay	d	14 54				15 42			16 07			16 44				17 34	17 50				18 40		19 41
Paignton	a	15 03				15 50			16 15			16 51				17 41	17 56				18 47		19 48
Totnes	d			14 59	15 18			16 00		16 16			16 52	17 01	17 21				17 56	18 16			
Ivybridge	d												17 08										
Plymouth	a			15 28	15 43			16 29		16 42	16 55		17 22	17 30	17 48				18 22	18 42		19 36	
	d		14 58	15 35				16 35					17 35						18 25	18 55			
Devonport	d																						
Dockyard	d																						
Keyham	d																						
St Budeaux Ferry Road	d																						
Saltash	d		15 07										17 44										
St Germans	d		15 14										17 51										
Menheniot	d												17x59										
Liskeard 6	d		15 26	15 57				16 59					18 05						18 50	19 18			
Bodmin Parkway	d		15 39	16 12				17 12					18 17						19 04	19 30			
Lostwithiel	d		15 45										18 22										
Par	d		15 53	16 24			16 30	17 23					18 30						19 16	19 41			
Newquay	a						17 22																
St Austell	d		16 00	16 32				17 31					18 37						19 23	19 52			
Truro	d		16 19	16 50				17 49					18 55						19 41	20 09			
Redruth	d		16 32	17 02				18 02					19 08						19 53	20 20			
Camborne	d		16 38	17 10				18 10					19 14						20 02	20 28			
Hayle	d		16 45										19 21										
St Erth	d		16 50	17 22				18 22					19 25					20 05	20 15	20 39			
Penzance	a		17 00	17 35				18 33					19 37					20 14	20 27	20 47			

A ⌶ to Plymouth

For connections from Heathrow Airport, Gatwick Airport and Oxford please refer to Tables 125A, 148 and 116

Table 135

Sundays

from 28 October

London and Birmingham - Devon and Cornwall

Route Diagram - see first Page of Table 135

		GW	GW	GW	XC	GW	GW	XC	GW	GW	XC	XC	GW	GW	GW	XC	GW	GW
			◇1	◇	◇1		◇1	◇1		◇1	◇1	◇1	◇1		◇1	◇1	◇1	■
					A							B				B		
			☕		🛒		☕	🛒		☕	🛒	🛒	☕		☕	🛒	☕	🛏 ☕
London Paddington 15 ⊖	d		16 57				17 57			18 57			19 03		19 57		20 57	23 50
Slough 3	d																	
Reading 7	d		17 32				18 32			19 32			19 38		20 32		21 33	00u37
Theale	d																	
Thatcham	d																	
Newbury	d						18 49								20 50			
Hungerford	d																	
Pewsey	d						19 10								21 10			
Westbury	d						19 29								21 29			
Castle Cary	d									20 30					21 47			
Birmingham New Street 12	d				17 12			18 12			18 42	19 12				20 12		
Cardiff Central 7	d																	
Newport (South Wales)	d																	
Swindon	d												20 11					
Bristol Parkway 7	d				18 24			19 23			20 03	20 23				21 23		
Filton Abbey Wood	d																	
Bath Spa 7	d												20 40					
Bristol Temple Meads 10	d			18 07	18 44			19 44			20 19	20 44	20 55			21 44		02 55
Weston-super-Mare	d			18 36							20 37		21 27					
Bridgwater	d			18 55														
Taunton	d		18 50	19 10	19 17		20 03	20 19		20 52	20 59	21 17	21 51		22 07	22 17	22s49	
Tiverton Parkway	d		19 03	19 25	19 29		20 17	20 31		21 05	21 12	21 29	22 04		22 20	22 29	23s03	
Exeter St Davids 6	a		19 18	19 43	19 47		20 32	20 45		21 21	21 27	21 43	22 19		22 36	22 46	23 19	04 04
Exmouth	d					19 24			20 24					21 24				
Exeter Central	d					19 50			20 50					21 50				
Exeter St Davids 6	d		19 20		19 49	19 56	20 32	20 46	20 56	21 22	21 30	21 44		21 56	22 37	22 47		04 35
Exeter St Thomas	d					19 59								21 59				
Starcross	d					20 07								22 07				
Dawlish Warren	d					20 12								22 12				
Dawlish	d					20 16			21 09	21 36	21 42			22 16				
Teignmouth	d					20 21			21 14	21 42	21 47			22 21				
Newton Abbot	a		19 39		20 07	20 28	20 54	21 04	21 21	21 48	21 54	22 02		22 29	22 57	23 05		04 55
	d		19 39		20 08	20 30	20 54	21 06	21 22	21 49	21 56	22 04		22 30	22 58	23 07		04 56
Torre	d					20 38			21 31					22 38				
Torquay	d					20 41			21 34					22 41				
Paignton	a					20 48			21 41					22 49				
Totnes	d		19 55		20 21		21 08	21 18		22 03		22 20			23 11	23 21		
Ivybridge	d																	
Plymouth	a		20 21		20 46		21 35	21 44		22 30	22 37	22 45			23 40	23 47		05 35
	d	19 43	20 25		20 50		21 40											06 28
Devonport	d																	
Dockyard	d																	
Keyham	d																	
St Budeaux Ferry Road	d																	
Saltash	d	19 52																
St Germans	d	19 59																
Menheniot	d																	
Liskeard 6	d	20 11	20 49		21 13		22 04											07 09
Bodmin Parkway	d	20 23	21 02		21 25		22 17											07 23
Lostwithiel	d	20 28																07 29
Par	d	20 36	21 13		21 36		22 30											07 38
Newquay	a																	
St Austell	d	20 43	21 20		21 43		22 38											07 46
Truro	d	21 00	21 37		22 01		22 53											08 06
Redruth	d	21 14	21 51		22 12		23 08											08 20
Camborne	d	21 20	21 57		22 19		23 15											08 27
Hayle	d	21 27																08 38
St Erth	d	21 32	22 10		22 30		23 27											08 45
Penzance	a	21 42	22 22		22 38		23 38											08 59

A 🛒 to Plymouth

B 🛒 to Bristol Temple Meads

For connections from Heathrow Airport, Gatwick Airport and Oxford please refer to Tables 125A, 148 and 116

Table 135

Mondays to Fridays

until 29 June

Cornwall and Devon - Birmingham and London

Route Diagram - see first Page of Table 135

Miles	Miles			GW MO	GW MX	GW MO	GW MX	XC MX	GW	GW	GW	GW	GW	XC	GW	GW	GW	GW	XC	XC	GW	GW	GW
						■	■																
				◇1				◇1	◇1	◇1	◇1		◇1	◇1	◇1	◇1			◇1	◇1	◇1		
				A		A	B				C					D					E		
				☕		🛏 ☕	🛏 ☕		☕	☕	☕⊘		☕	🛒	☕	☕⊘			🛒	🛒	☕⊘		
0	—	**Penzance**	d			21p15	21p45	22p08													05 05	05 21	
5¾	—	St Erth	d			21p25	21p55	22p16															
7¼	—	Hayle	d					22p20														05 31	
13¼	—	Camborne	d			21p38	22p07	22p30														05 40	
16¾	—	Redruth	d			21p45	22p14	22p36													05 25		
25¾	—	Truro	d			22p00	22p27	22p48													05 38	05a55	
40¼	—	St Austell	d			22p18	22p45	23p04													05 55		
—	—	Newquay	d																				
44¾	—	Par	d				22p54	23p12															
49¼	—	Lostwithiel	d					23p19															
52¾	—	Bodmin Parkway	d			22p35	23p06	23p26													06 11		
61¾	—	Liskeard 6	d			22p50	23p21	23p39													06 26		
65	—	Menheniot	d																				
70¼	—	St Germans	d																				
75¼	—	Saltash	d																				
76½	—	St Budeaux Ferry Road	d																				
77¼	—	Keyham	d																				
77¾	—	Dockyard	d																				
78¼	—	Devonport	d																				
79½	—	**Plymouth**	a			23p15	23p45	00 04													06 51		
—	—		d	19p55		23p20	23p51						05 09	05 20	05 30	05 53			06 25		06 55		
90¼	—	Ivybridge	d																				
102¼	—	Totnes	d			23p48	00 20							05 45	05 58				06 50				
—	0	Paignton	d		23p41												06 10	06 34		07 02			07 12
—	2¼	Torquay	d		23p46												06 15	06 39		07 08			07 17
—	3	Torre	d		23p49												06 18	06 42					07 20
111½	8¼	Newton Abbot	a	20p31	23p57	23p59	00 32						05 45	05 56	06 09	06 28	06 26	06 50	07 01	07 18	07 30		07 27
—	—		d	20p32	23p59	00 01	00 33						05 47	06 02	06 11	06 31	06 34	06 52	07 03	07 19	07 32		07 37
116½	—	Teignmouth	d		00 06								05 54				06 41	06 59		07 26			07 45
119¼	—	Dawlish	d		00 11										06 21		06 46	07 04		07 31			07 50
121	—	Dawlish Warren	d		00 16												06 51	07 15					07 55
123	—	Starcross	d		00 20												06 55	07 19					07 59
130½	—	Exeter St Thomas	d		00 29												07 04	07 28					08 09
131½	—	**Exeter St Davids** 6	a	20p53	00 34	00 23	00 55						06 10	06 19	06 33	06 51	07 09	07 33	07 21	07 43	07 52		08 14
—	—	Exeter Central	a														07 14	07 39					08 19
—	—	Exmouth	a														07 43	08 18					08 48
—	—	**Exeter St Davids** 6	d	20p55		01 06	01 06				05 46	06 00	06 12	06 22	06 35	06 52			07 23	07 45	07 53		
148	—	Tiverton Parkway	d	21p10							06 02	06 17	06 27	06 36	06 51				07 37	07 58			
162¼	—	Taunton	d	21p23			01 36				06 17	06 34	06 55	06 50	07 06	07 18			07 51	08 13	08 19		
—	11¾	Bridgwater	a									06 46	07 05										
—	25¾	Weston-super-Mare	a									07 04	07 24							08 32			
—	45½	**Bristol Temple Meads** 10	a	22p00								07 41	07 57	07 24					08 26	08 53			
—	—	Bath Spa 7	a	22p22									08 11										
—	—	Filton Abbey Wood	a									07 58											
—	51¼	Bristol Parkway 7	a									08 05		07 38					08 38	09 08			
—	—	Swindon	a	22p50									08 40										
—	—	Newport (South Wales)	a																				
—	—	Cardiff Central 7	a																				
—	138¼	**Birmingham New Street** 12	a											08 56					09 56	10 26			
190	—	Castle Cary	d								06 38				07 27								
209¾	—	Westbury	d						06 06	06 18	07 01				07 51								
230	—	Pewsey	d						06 24	06 36	07 19				08 09								
243¾	—	Hungerford	a						06 36	06 54	07 32												
252¼	—	Newbury	a						06 49	07 08	07 46				08 29								
255¾	—	Thatcham	a						06 56	07 15													
264½	—	Theale	a						07 06	07 25													
269¼	—	**Reading** 7	a	23p28		04s02	04s00		07 19	07 37	08 06		09 14		08 50	08 32					09 32		
286¾	—	Slough 3	a																				
305¼	—	**London Paddington** 15 ⊖	a	00 13		05 05	05 25		07 53	08 09	08 38		09 44		09 21	09 00					10 02		

A from 21 May until 25 June

B The Night Riviera

C ☕ from Reading ⊘ to Reading

D The Armada

E The Golden Hind

For connections to Oxford, Gatwick Airport and Heathrow Airport please refer to Tables 116, 148 and 125A

Table 135

Mondays to Fridays

until 29 June

Cornwall and Devon - Birmingham and London

Route Diagram - see first Page of Table 135

		XC	GW	GW	GW	GW	XC	GW	GW	GW	XC	XC	GW	GW	XC	GW	GW	GW	GW	XC	XC	GW	GW
		◇1 ⊼	◇1 ⊏	◇1 A ⊏Ø		◇	◇1 B ⊼	◇1 ⊏Ø			◇1 ⊼	◇1 ⊼	◇1 ⊏		◇1 B ⊼	1 C ⊏		◇1 ⊏		◇1 ⊼	◇1 B ⊼	◇	
Penzance	d			05 41		06 00	06 28	06 45	06 55				07 41		08 28	08 44	08 57				09 40		
St Erth	d					06 09	06 36	06 55	07a03				07 51		08 36	08 54	09a05				09 48		
Hayle	d					06 12							07 55								09 52		
Camborne	d			05 58		06 21	06 46	07 06					08 05		08 46	09 06					10 01		
Redruth	d			06 05		06 27	06 52	07 13					08 12		08 52	09 13					10 08		
Truro	d			06 18		06 39	07 04	07 26					08 25		09 04	09 26					10 19		
St Austell	d			06 35		06 56	07 20	07 44					08 43		09 20	09 43					10 35		
Newquay	d																					10 13	
Par	d			06 43		07 03	07 28	07 52					08 51		09 28	09 51					10 43	11a02	
Lostwithiel	d			06 51		07 10		08 00													10 50		
Bodmin Parkway	d			06 57		07 16	07 39	08 06					09 03		09 39	10 03					10 57		
Liskeard 6	d			07 11		07 29	07 53	08 20					09 16		09 51	10 16					11 09		
Menheniot	d					07x33																	
St Germans	d			07 22		07 41		08 31					09 27										
Saltash	d			07 30		07 48		08 39					09 35										
St Budeaux Ferry Road	d					07 52																	
Keyham	d					07 54																	
Dockyard	d					07x56																	
Devonport	d					07 58																	
Plymouth	a			07 41		08 04	08 20	08 49					09 46		10 18	10 41					11 39		
	d	07 25		07 48		08 06	08 25	08 53			09 25		09 48		10 25	10 44				11 25	11 50		
Ivybridge	d					08 21		09 08					10 03										
Totnes	d	07 50		08 16		08 36	08 50	09 23			09 50		10 19		10 50					11 50	12 15		
Paignton	d		07 40		08 23					09 13		10 07		10 15				11 06	11 23				12 13
Torquay	d		07 46		08 28					09 18		10 13		10 23				11 12	11 28				12 18
Torre	d		07 50		08 31					09 21				10 26				11 16	11 31				12 21
Newton Abbot	a	08 01	07 58	08 27	08 39	08 48	09 01	09 34		09 29	10 01	10 23	10 31	10 35	11 01			11 24	11 39	12 01	12 26		12 30
	d	08 03	08 06	08 29	08 41	08 49	09 03	09 36		09 39	10 03	10 24	10 32	10 36	11 03			11 26	11 41	12 03	12 28		12 31
Teignmouth	d		08 13		08 48	08 56				09 46		10 31		10 44				11 33	11 48				12 38
Dawlish	d		08 19		08 53	09 01				09 51		10 36		10 49				11 39	11 53				12 43
Dawlish Warren	d				08 58					09 55				10 53					11 58				12 54
Starcross	d		08 25		09 02					09 59				10 57					12 02				12 58
Exeter St Thomas	d		08 34		09 11					10 09				11 07					12 11				13 07
Exeter St Davids 6	a	08 21	08 39	08 49	09 15	09 18	09 22	09 56		10 14	10 21	10 48	10 54	11 10	11 21	11 38		11 52	12 16	12 21	12 46		13 13
Exeter Central	a				09 21					10 21				11 21					12 21				13 21
Exmouth	a				09 50					10 50				11 50					12 50				13 50
Exeter St Davids 6	d	08 23	08 41	08 51		09 33	09 23	09 58			10 23	10 50	10 56		11 23	11 40		11 55		12 23	12 48		
Tiverton Parkway	d	08 37		09 06		09 50	09 37	10 13			10 37	11 03	11 11		11 37			12 09		12 37	13 02		
Taunton	d	08 51	09 05	09 21		10 07	09 51	10 28			10 51	11 18	11 26		11 51			12 24		12 51	13 16		
Bridgwater	a					10 19																	
Weston-super-Mare	a		09 27			10 38																	
Bristol Temple Meads 10	a	09 26	09 56			11 11	10 25				11 23	11 52	11 58		12 23					13 24	13 56		
Bath Spa 7	a		10 11										12 12										
Filton Abbey Wood	a					11 30																	
Bristol Parkway 7	a	09 38					10 38				11 38	12 08			12 38					13 38	14 08		
Swindon	a		10 40										12 40										
Newport (South Wales)	a					11 58																	
Cardiff Central 7	a					12 18																	
Birmingham New Street 12	a	10 56					11 58				12 56	13 26			13 56					14 56	15 26		
Castle Cary	d			09 42														12 45					
Westbury	d			10 01				11 05										13 05					
Pewsey	d			10 18														13 21					
Hungerford	a																	13 39					
Newbury	a																	13 48					
Thatcham	a																	13 55					
Theale	a																	14 04					
Reading 7	a		11 09	10 50				11 50					13 09			13 15		14 15					
Slough 3	a																						
London Paddington 15 ⊖	a		11 38	11 24				12 23					13 38			13 44		14 44					

B ⊼ from Plymouth

C The Cornish Riviera

For connections to Oxford, Gatwick Airport and Heathrow Airport please refer to Tables 116, 148 and 125A

Table 135

Mondays to Fridays

until 29 June

Cornwall and Devon - Birmingham and London

Route Diagram - see first Page of Table 135

		GW	XC	GW	GW	GW	GW	XC	XC	GW	GW	GW	GW	GW	XC	GW	GW	GW	XC	GW	XC	GW
		1 A ✕⊏	◇1 ⊼	◇	◇	◇1 ✕⊏		◇1 ⊼	◇1 ⊼	◇	◇	◇1 ⊏	◇1 C ⊏		◇1 ⊼		◇1 D ⊏	◇	◇1 ⊼		◇1 ⊼	◇1 E ⊏
Penzance	d	10 00		10 46						11 41								12 51				14 00
St Erth	d	10 10		10 55						11 50								13 03				14 10
Hayle	d			10 58						11 53								13 06				
Camborne	d	10 21		11 07						12 02								13 15				14 21
Redruth	d	10 28		11 13						12 08								13 21				14 28
Truro	d	10 41		11 25						12 19								13 32				14 41
St Austell	d	10 58		11 42						12 36								13 49				14 58
Newquay	d										13 03											
Par	d	11 07		11 50						12 44	13a52							13 57				15 06
Lostwithiel	d			11 56						12 50								14 04				
Bodmin Parkway	d	11 19		12 02						12 56								14 10				15 18
Liskeard 6	d	11 33		12 16						13 09								14 23				15 31
Menheniot	d									13x13												
St Germans	d			12 27						13 22								14 34				
Saltash	d			12 34						13 29								14 42				
St Budeaux Ferry Road	d																					
Keyham	d																					
Dockyard	d																					
Devonport	d																					
Plymouth	a	11 58		12 45						13 39								14 51				15 56
	d	12 01	12 23			12 55		13 23		13 41					14 25		15 00	15 08	15 23			16 00
Ivybridge	d									13 56								15 23				
Totnes	d	12 29	12 49			13 23		13 49		14 11					14 50		15 28	15 38	15 49			16 28
Paignton	d				12 48		13 13		14 01				14 15	14 23		15 13				16 12		
Torquay	d				12 53		13 18		14 07				14 21	14 28		15 18				16 17		
Torre	d				12 56		13 21							14 31		15 21				16 21		
Newton Abbot	a	12 41	13 01		13 04	13 34	13 30	14 01	14 17	14 24			14 31	14 39	15 01	15 29	15 39	15 52	16 01	16 29		16 39
	d	12 42	13 03		13 06	13 36	13 41	14 03	14 18				14 33	14 41	15 03	15 31	15 41		16 03	16 31		16 41
Teignmouth	d				13 13		13 48		14 25				14 40	14 48		15 38				16 38		
Dawlish	d				13 18		13 53		14 30				14 46	14 53		15 43				16 43		
Dawlish Warren	d						13 58							14 58		15 54				16 54		
Starcross	d						14 02							15 02		15 58				16 58		
Exeter St Thomas	d						14 11							15 11		16 07				17 07		
Exeter St Davids 6	a	13 02	13 23		13 31	13 56	14 16	14 23	14 42				14 59	15 16	15 21	16 13	16 01		16 23	17 13		17 01
Exeter Central	a						14 21							15 21		16 21				17 21		
Exmouth	a						14 50							15 50		16 50				17 51		
Exeter St Davids 6	d	13 04	13 25		13 33	13 58		14 25	14 44				15 01		15 23		16 03		16 25		16 54	17 03
Tiverton Parkway	d	13 19	13 39		13 50			14 39	14 57				15 15		15 37		16 17		16 39		17 08	17 18
Taunton	d	13 34	13 54		14 07	14 23		14 54	15 12			15 23	15 30		15 51		16 31		16 54		17 22	17 32
Bridgwater	a				14 18																	
Weston-super-Mare	a				14 37				15 37													
Bristol Temple Meads 10	a		14 26		15 08			15 26	15 55						16 26				17 26		17 53	
Bath Spa 7	a																					
Filton Abbey Wood	a				15 30																	
Bristol Parkway 7	a		14 38					15 38	16 08						16 38				17 38		18 08	
Swindon	a																					
Newport (South Wales)	a				15 58																	
Cardiff Central 7	a				16 18																	
Birmingham New Street 12	a		15 56					16 56	17 26						17 56				18 55		19 26	
Castle Cary	d					14 44							15 51									
Westbury	d					15 03						16 08										
Pewsey	d											16 25										
Hungerford	a											16 39										
Newbury	a											16 48										
Thatcham	a											16 55										
Theale	a											17 04										
Reading 7	a	14 50				15 50						17 15	16 49				17 49					18 49
Slough 3	a																					
London Paddington 15 ⊖	a	15 24				16 22						17 54	17 24				18 21					19 24

A The Cornishman

C The Torbay Express

D The Mayflower

E The Royal Duchy

For connections to Oxford, Gatwick Airport and Heathrow Airport please refer to Tables 116, 148 and 125A

Cornwall and Devon - Birmingham and London

Route Diagram - see first Page of Table 135

		GW	XC	GW	GW	GW	GW	XC	GW	GW		GW	GW	GW	XC	GW	GW	GW	GW	GW		GW	GW	GW	GW
																	FX	FO				FX	FO		
		◇	◇■	◇		◇■		◇■				◇■			◇■		◇	◇	◇			◇■	◇■	◇■	
												A			B										
			⌶			🍽		⌶				🍽⊘			⌶							🍽	🍽	🍽	
Penzance	d			14 49								16 00					16 44	16 44						17 39	
St Erth	d			14 58								16 10					16 53	16 53						17 49	
Hayle	d			15 01													16 56	16 56						17 53	
Camborne	d			15 10								16 20					17 05	17 05						18 03	
Redruth	d			15 16								16 28					17 11	17 11						18 11	
Truro	d			15 27								16 41					17 24	17 24						18 23	
St Austell	d			15 44								16 58					17 41	17 41						18 40	
Newquay	d	14 58																	17 22						19 25
Par	d	15a47		15 52								17 07					17 48	17 48	18a13					18 49	20a13
Lostwithiel	d			15 58								17 14					17 55	17 55							
Bodmin Parkway	d			16 04								17 21					18 01	18 01						19 01	
Liskeard ■	d			16 17								17 34	17 49				18 14	18 14						19 14	
Menheniot	d			16x21																					
St Germans	d			16 30									18 00				18 25	18 25							
Saltash	d			16 37									18 07				18 32	18 32							
St Budeaux Ferry Road	d			16 41									18 12												
Keyham	d			16 43																					
Dockyard	d			16x45																					
Devonport	d			16 47																					
Plymouth	a			16 52								18 00	18 19				18 42	18 42						19 39	
	d		16 25			16 57		17 23		17 45		18 03			18 25		18 44	18 44						19 42	
Ivybridge	d					17 12				18 02							18 59	18 59							
Totnes	d		16 50			17 28		17 49		18 17		18 31			18 50		19 14	19 14						20 10	
Paignton	d				16 55		17 26		17 52					18 35		18 52				19 33					
Torquay	d				17 00		17 31		17 57					18 40		18 57				19 38					
Torre	d				17 03		17 34		18 00					18 43						19 41					
Newton Abbot	a		17 01		17 11	17 38	17 42	18 01	18 08	18 29		18 43		18 50	19 01	19 07	19 26	19 26		19 49				20 21	
	d		17 03		17 13	17 41	17 44	18 03	18 10	18 30		18 44		18 53	19 03	19 09	19 27	19 27		19 50				20 23	
Teignmouth	d				17 20		17 51		18 17	18 37				19 00		19 16				19 58					
Dawlish	d				17 25		17 56		18 22	18 43				19 05		19 21				20 03					
Dawlish Warren	d				17 30		18 01		18 27	18 47				19 16		19 26				20 07					
Starcross	d				17 34		18 05		18 31					19 20						20 11					
Exeter St Thomas	d				17 43		18 14		18 40					19 29						20 21					
Exeter St Davids ■	a		17 21		17 50	18 01	18 18	18 23	18 46	19 00		19 03		19 33	19 21	19 40	19 49	19 49		20 26				20 43	
Exeter Central	a				17 55		18 23		18 53											20 33					
Exmouth	a				18 25		18 52		19 23											21 01					
Exeter St Davids ■	d		17 23			18 03		18 25				19 06			19 23			19 49				19 55		20 45	
Tiverton Parkway	d		17 37			18 17		18 39				19 21			19 37			20 06				20 10		21 00	
Taunton	d		17 51			18 31		18 54				19 36			19 51			20a22				20 25	20 27	21 15	
Bridgwater	a																								
Weston-super-Mare	a																								
Bristol Temple Meads ■	a		18 24					19 26							20 24									21 47	
Bath Spa ■	a																							22 01	
Filton Abbey Wood	a																								
Bristol Parkway ■	a		18 38					19 38							20 38										
Swindon	a																								
Newport (South Wales)	a																							22 33	
Cardiff Central ■	a																								
Birmingham New Street ■	a		19 56					20 52							22 06										
Castle Cary	d					18 54																20 46	20 46		
Westbury	d					19 12																21 05	21 05		
Pewsey	d					19 29																21 22	21 22		
Hungerford	a																								
Newbury	a					19 49																21 42	21 42		
Thatcham	a																								
Theale	a																								
Reading ■	a					20 06						20 50										21 59	21 59	23 06	
Slough ■	a																								
London Paddington ■ ⊖	a					20 39						21 21										22 30	22 30	23 41	

A 🍽 to Plymouth 🍽 from Reading ⊘ from Plymouth to Reading

B ⌶ to Bristol Temple Meads

For connections to Oxford, Gatwick Airport and Heathrow Airport please refer to Tables 116, 148 and 125A

Cornwall and Devon - Birmingham and London

Route Diagram - see first Page of Table 135

		GW	XC	XC	GW	GW		GW	GW	GW	GW	GW	GW	GW	GW	GW		XC
			ThFO	MT WO					FX	FO					FO	FX		
															■	■		
			◇■	◇■		■				■		◇						◇■
			A	B											C	C		
															🛏 🍽	🛏 🍽		
Penzance	d	19 16							20 18	20 18					21 45	21 45		22 08
St Erth	d	19 25							20 27	20 27					21 55	21 55		22 16
Hayle	d	19 28							20 32	20 32								22 20
Camborne	d	19 37							20 41	20 41					22 07	22 07		22 30
Redruth	d	19 43							20 49	20 49					22 14	22 14		22 36
Truro	d	19 55							21 02	21 02					22 27	22 27		22 48
St Austell	d	20 12							21 19	21 19					22 45	22 45		23 04
Newquay	d										21 26							
Par	d	20 19							21 27	21 27	22a16				22 54	22 54		23 12
Lostwithiel	d	20 26							21 34	21 34								23 19
Bodmin Parkway	d	20 32							21 40	21 40					23 06	23 06		23 26
Liskeard ■	d	20 45							21 53	21 53					23 21	23 21		23 39
Menheniot	d	20x49																
St Germans	d	20 58							22 04	22 04								
Saltash	d	21 05							22 12	22 12								
St Budeaux Ferry Road	d	21 09																
Keyham	d	21 11																
Dockyard	d	21x13																
Devonport	d	21 15																
Plymouth	a	21 20							22 25	22 25					23 45	23 45		00 04
	d							21 25							23 51	23 51		
Ivybridge	d							21 40										
Totnes	d							21 55							00 20	00 20		
Paignton	d		20 14	20 14	20 34	21 31							22 30	23 41				
Torquay	d		20 20	20 20	20 39	21 37							22 35	23 46				
Torre	d				20 42	21 41							22 38	23 49				
Newton Abbot	a		20 30	20 30	20 50	21 52		22 01					22 46	23 57	00 32	00 32		
	d		20 31	20 31	20 52			22 02					22 48	23 59	00 33	00 33		
Teignmouth	d				20 59			22 14					22 55	00 06				
Dawlish	d				21 04			22 19					23 00	00 11				
Dawlish Warren	d				21 09			22 23					23 05	00 16				
Starcross	d				21 13			22 27					23 09	00 20				
Exeter St Thomas	d				21 22			22 36					23 18	00 29				
Exeter St Davids ■	a		20 50	20 50	21 28			22 40					23 22	00 34	00 55	00 55		
Exeter Central	a				21 35													
Exmouth	a				22 02													
Exeter St Davids ■	d		20 52	20 52								21 49			01 06	01 06		
Tiverton Parkway	d		21 04	21 04								22 06						
Taunton	d		21 19	21 19								22 23			01 36	01 36		
Bridgwater	a																	
Weston-super-Mare	a											22 47						
Bristol Temple Meads ■	a		21 51	21 52								23 12						
Bath Spa ■	a																	
Filton Abbey Wood	a																	
Bristol Parkway ■	a		22 08	22 08														
Swindon	a																	
Newport (South Wales)	a																	
Cardiff Central ■	a																	
Birmingham New Street ■	a		23 44	23 44														
Castle Cary	d																	
Westbury	d																	
Pewsey	d																	
Hungerford	a																	
Newbury	a																	
Thatcham	a																	
Theale	a																	
Reading ■	a														04s00	04s00		
Slough ■	a																	
London Paddington ■ ⊖	a														05 13	05 25		

C The Night Riviera

For connections to Oxford, Gatwick Airport and Heathrow Airport please refer to Tables 116, 148 and 125A

2 July to 31 August

Cornwall and Devon - Birmingham and London

Route Diagram - see first Page of Table 135

		GW	GW	GW	GW	XC	GW	GW	GW	GW		GW	XC	GW	GW	GW	GW	XC	XC	GW		GW	GW	XC	GW
		MO	MX	MO	MX	MX																			
		◇1 ⊐		▪ ⊐	▪ A ⊐	◇1	◇1 ⊐	◇1 ⊐	◇1 B ⊐⊘			◇1 ⊐	◇1 ⌶	◇1 ⊐	◇1 C ⊐⊘			◇1 ⌶	◇1 ⌶	◇1 D ⊐⊘				◇1 ⌶	◇1 ⊐
Penzance	d			21p15	21p45	22p08														05 05		05 21			
St Erth	d			21p25	21p55	22p16																			
Hayle	d					22p20																05 31			
Camborne	d			21p38	22p07	22p30																05 40			
Redruth	d			21p45	22p14	22p36														05 25					
Truro	d			22p00	22p27	22p48														05 38		05a55			
St Austell	d			22p18	22p45	23p04														05 55					
Newquay	d																								
Par	d				22p54	23p12																			
Lostwithiel	d					23p19																			
Bodmin Parkway	d			22p35	23p06	23p26														06 11					
Liskeard 6	d			22p50	23p21	23p39														06 26					
Menheniot	d																								
St Germans	d																								
Saltash	d																								
St Budeaux Ferry Road	d																								
Keyham	d																								
Dockyard	d																								
Devonport	d																								
Plymouth	a			23p15	23p45	00 04														06 51					
	d	19p55		23p20	23p51							05 09	05 20	05 30	05 53			06 25		06 55				07 25	
Ivybridge	d																								
Totnes	d			23p48	00 20								05 45	05 58				06 50						07 50	
Paignton	d		23p41													06 10	06 34		07 02				07 12		07 40
Torquay	d		23p46													06 15	06 39		07 08				07 17		07 46
Torre	d		23p49													06 18	06 42						07 20		07 50
Newton Abbot	a	20p31	23p57	23p59	00 32							05 45	05 56	06 09	06 28	06 26	06 50	07 01	07 18	07 30			07 27	08 01	07 58
	d	20p32	23p59	00 01	00 33							05 47	06 02	06 11	06 31	06 34	06 52	07 03	07 19	07 32			07 37	08 03	08 06
Teignmouth	d		00 06									05 54				06 41	06 59		07 26				07 45		08 13
Dawlish	d		00 11											06 21		06 46	07 04		07 31				07 50		08 19
Dawlish Warren	d		00 16													06 51	07 15						07 55		
Starcross	d		00 20													06 55	07 19						07 59		08 25
Exeter St Thomas	d		00 29													07 04	07 28						08 09		08 34
Exeter St Davids 6	a	20p53	00 34	00 23	00 55							06 10	06 19	06 33	06 51	07 09	07 33	07 21	07 43	07 52			08 14	08 21	08 39
Exeter Central	a															07 14	07 39						08 19		
Exmouth	a															07 43	08 18						08 48		
Exeter St Davids 6	d	20p55		01 06	01 06				05 46	06 00		06 12	06 22	06 35	06 52			07 23	07 45	07 53				08 23	08 41
Tiverton Parkway	d	21p10							06 02	06 17		06 27	06 36	06 51				07 37	07 58					08 37	
Taunton	d	21p23			01 36				06 17	06 34		06 55	06 50	07 06	07 18			07 51	08 13	08 19				08 51	09 05
Bridgwater	a									06 46		07 05													
Weston-super-Mare	a									07 04		07 24							08 32						09 27
Bristol Temple Meads 10	a	22p00								07 41		07 57	07 24					08 26	08 53					09 26	09 56
Bath Spa 7	a	22p22										08 11													10 11
Filton Abbey Wood	a									07 58															
Bristol Parkway 7	a									08 05			07 38					08 38	09 08					09 38	
Swindon	a	22p50										08 40													10 40
Newport (South Wales)	a																								
Cardiff Central 7	a																								
Birmingham New Street 12	a												08 56					09 56	10 26					10 56	
Castle Cary	d								06 38					07 27											
Westbury	d						06 06	06 18	07 01					07 51											
Pewsey	d						06 24	06 36	07 19					08 09											
Hungerford	a						06 36	06 54	07 32																
Newbury	a						06 49	07 08	07 46					08 29											
Thatcham	a						06 56	07 15																	
Theale	a						07 06	07 25																	
Reading 7	a	23p28		04s02	04s00		07 19	07 37	08 06			09 14		08 50	08 32					09 32					11 09
Slough 3	a																								
London Paddington 15 ⊖	a	00 05		05 05	05 25		07 53	08 09	08 38			09 44		09 21	09 00					10 02					11 38

A The Night Riviera
B ⊐ from Reading ⊘ to Reading
C The Armada
D The Golden Hind

For connections to Oxford, Gatwick Airport and Heathrow Airport please refer to Tables 116, 148 and 125A

2 July to 31 August

Cornwall and Devon - Birmingham and London

Route Diagram - see first Page of Table 135

		GW	GW	GW	XC	GW		GW	GW	XC	XC	GW	GW	XC	GW	GW		GW	GW	XC	XC	GW	GW	GW	XC
		◇1 ⊐⊘		◇	◇1 B ⌶	◇1 ⊐⊘				◇1 ⌶	◇1 ⌶	◇1 ⊐		◇1 B ⌶	▪ 1 C ⊐			◇1 ⊐		◇1 ⌶	◇1 B ⌶	◇		▪ 1 D ✕⊐	◇1 ⌶
Penzance	d	05 41		06 00	06 28	06 45		06 55				07 41		08 28	08 44	08 57					09 40			10 00	
St Erth	d			06 09	06 36	06 55		07a03				07 51		08 36	08 54	09a05					09 48			10 10	
Hayle	d			06 12								07 55									09 52				
Camborne	d	05 58		06 21	06 46	07 06						08 05		08 46	09 06						10 01			10 21	
Redruth	d	06 05		06 27	06 52	07 13						08 12		08 52	09 13						10 08			10 28	
Truro	d	06 18		06 39	07 04	07 26						08 25		09 04	09 26						10 19			10 41	
St Austell	d	06 35		06 56	07 20	07 44						08 43		09 20	09 43						10 35			10 58	
Newquay	d																					10 13			
Par	d	06 43		07 03	07 28	07 52						08 51		09 28	09 51						10 43	11a02		11 07	
Lostwithiel	d	06 51		07 10		08 00															10 50				
Bodmin Parkway	d	06 57		07 16	07 39	08 06						09 03		09 39	10 03						10 57			11 19	
Liskeard 6	d	07 11		07 29	07 53	08 20						09 16		09 51	10 16						11 09			11 33	
Menheniot	d			07x33																					
St Germans	d	07 22		07 41		08 31						09 27													
Saltash	d	07 30		07 48		08 39						09 35													
St Budeaux Ferry Road	d			07 52																					
Keyham	d			07 54																					
Dockyard	d			07x56																					
Devonport	d			07 58																					
Plymouth	a	07 41		08 04	08 20	08 49						09 46		10 18	10 41						11 39			11 58	
	d	07 48		08 06	08 25	08 53				09 25		09 48		10 25	10 44					11 25	11 50			12 01	12 23
Ivybridge	d			08 21		09 08						10 03													
Totnes	d	08 16		08 36	08 50	09 23				09 50		10 19		10 50						11 50	12 15			12 29	12 49
Paignton	d		08 23						09 13		10 07		10 15					11 06	11 23				12 13		
Torquay	d		08 28						09 18		10 13		10 23					11 12	11 28				12 18		
Torre	d		08 31						09 21				10 26					11 16	11 31				12 21		
Newton Abbot	a	08 27	08 39	08 48	09 01	09 34			09 29	10 01	10 23	10 31	10 35	11 01				11 24	11 39	12 01	12 26		12 30	12 41	13 01
	d	08 29	08 41	08 49	09 03	09 36			09 39	10 03	10 24	10 32	10 36	11 03				11 26	11 41	12 03	12 28		12 31	12 42	13 03
Teignmouth	d		08 48	08 56					09 46		10 31		10 44					11 33	11 48				12 38		
Dawlish	d		08 53	09 01					09 51		10 36		10 49					11 39	11 53				12 43		
Dawlish Warren	d		08 58						09 55				10 53						11 58				12 54		
Starcross	d		09 02						09 59				10 57						12 02				12 58		
Exeter St Thomas	d		09 11						10 09				11 07						12 11				13 07		
Exeter St Davids 6	a	08 49	09 15	09 18	09 22	09 56			10 14	10 21	10 48	10 54	11 10	11 21	11 38			11 52	12 16	12 21	12 46		13 13	13 02	13 23
Exeter Central	a		09 21						10 21				11 21						12 21				13 21		
Exmouth	a		09 50						10 50				11 50						12 50				13 50		
Exeter St Davids 6	d	08 51		09 33	09 23	09 58				10 23	10 50	10 56		11 23	11 40			11 55		12 23	12 48			13 04	13 25
Tiverton Parkway	d	09 06		09 50	09 37	10 13				10 37	11 03	11 11		11 37				12 09		12 37	13 02			13 19	13 39
Taunton	d	09 21		10 07	09 51	10 28				10 51	11 18	11 26		11 51				12 24		12 51	13 16			13 34	13 54
Bridgwater	a			10 19																					
Weston-super-Mare	a			10 38																					
Bristol Temple Meads 10	a			11 11	10 25					11 23	11 52	11 58		12 23						13 24	13 56				14 26
Bath Spa 7	a											12 12													
Filton Abbey Wood	a			11 30																					
Bristol Parkway 7	a				10 38					11 38	12 08			12 38						13 38	14 08				14 38
Swindon	a											12 40													
Newport (South Wales)	a			11 58																					
Cardiff Central 7	a			12 18																					
Birmingham New Street 12	a				11 58					12 56	13 26			13 56						14 56	15 26				15 56
Castle Cary	d	09 42																12 45							
Westbury	d	10 01				11 05												13 05							
Pewsey	d	10 18																13 21							
Hungerford	a																	13 39							
Newbury	a																	13 48							
Thatcham	a																	13 55							
Theale	a																	14 04							
Reading 7	a	10 50				11 50						13 09			13 15			14 15						14 50	
Slough 3	a																								
London Paddington 15 ⊖	a	11 24				12 23						13 38			13 44			14 44						15 24	

B ⌶ from Plymouth
C The Cornish Riviera
D The Cornishman

For connections to Oxford, Gatwick Airport and Heathrow Airport please refer to Tables 116, 148 and 125A

Table 135

Mondays to Fridays

2 July to 31 August

Cornwall and Devon - Birmingham and London

Route Diagram - see first Page of Table 135

		GW		GW	GW	XC	XC	GW	GW	GW	GW	GW		XC	GW	GW	GW	XC	GW	XC	GW	GW		XC	GW
		◇		◇1		◇1	◇1	◇	◇	◇1	◇1			◇1		◇1	◇	◇1		◇1	◇1	◇		◇1	
				A							B					C					D				
				✕☕		🛒	🛒			☕	☕			🛒		☕		🛒		🛒	☕			🛒	
Penzance	d			10 47				11 41									12 51				14 00	14 52			
St Erth	d			10 57				11 50									13 03				14 10	15 01			
Hayle	d			11 01				11 53									13 06					15 04			
Camborne	d			11 11				12 02									13 15				14 21	15 13			
Redruth	d			11 18				12 08									13 21				14 28	15 19			
Truro	d			11 31				12 19									13 32				14 41	15 30			
St Austell	d			11 49				12 36									13 49				14 58	15 47			
Newquay	d								12 40																
Par	d			11 57				12 44	13a34								13 57				15 06	15a54			
Lostwithiel	d							12 50									14 04								
Bodmin Parkway	d			12 08				12 56									14 10				15 18				
Liskeard 6	d			12 21				13 09									14 23				15 31				
Menheniot	d							13x13																	
St Germans	d			12 33				13 22									14 34								
Saltash	d			12 41				13 29									14 42								
St Budeaux Ferry Road	d																								
Keyham	d																								
Dockyard	d																								
Devonport	d																								
Plymouth	a			12 51				13 39									14 51				15 56				
	d			12 55		13 23		13 41						14 25		15 00	15 08	15 23			16 00			16 25	
Ivybridge	d							13 56									15 23								
Totnes	d			13 23		13 49		14 11						14 50		15 28	15 38	15 49			16 28			16 50	
Paignton	d	12 48			13 13		14 01				14 15	14 23			15 13				16 12						16 55
Torquay	d	12 53			13 18		14 07				14 21	14 28			15 18				16 17						17 00
Torre	d	12 56			13 21							14 31			15 21				16 21						17 03
Newton Abbot	a	13 04		13 34	13 30	14 01	14 17	14 24			14 31	14 39		15 01	15 29	15 39	15 52	16 01	16 29		16 39			17 01	17 11
	d	13 06		13 36	13 41	14 03	14 18				14 33	14 41		15 03	15 31	15 41		16 03	16 31		16 41			17 03	17 13
Teignmouth	d	13 13			13 48		14 25				14 40	14 48			15 38				16 38						17 20
Dawlish	d	13 18			13 53		14 30				14 46	14 53			15 43				16 43						17 25
Dawlish Warren	d				13 58							14 58			15 54				16 54						17 30
Starcross	d				14 02							15 02			15 58				16 58						17 34
Exeter St Thomas	d				14 11							15 11			16 07				17 07						17 43
Exeter St Davids 6	a	13 31		13 56	14 16	14 23	14 42				14 59	15 16		15 21	16 13	16 01		16 23	17 13		17 01			17 21	17 50
Exeter Central	a				14 21							15 21			16 21				17 21						17 55
Exmouth	a				14 50							15 50			16 50				17 51						18 25
Exeter St Davids 6	d	13 33		13 58		14 25	14 44				15 01			15 23		16 03		16 25		16 54	17 03			17 23	
Tiverton Parkway	d	13 50				14 39	14 57				15 15			15 37		16 17		16 39		17 08	17 18			17 37	
Taunton	d	14 07		14 23		14 54	15 12			15 23	15 30			15 51		16 31		16 54		17 22	17 32			17 51	
Bridgwater	a	14 18																							
Weston-super-Mare	a	14 37					15 37																		
Bristol Temple Meads 10	a	15 14				15 26	15 55							16 26				17 26		17 53				18 24	
Bath Spa 7	a																								
Filton Abbey Wood	a	15 30																							
Bristol Parkway 7	a					15 38	16 08							16 38				17 38		18 08				18 38	
Swindon	a																								
Newport (South Wales)	a	15 58																							
Cardiff Central 7	a	16 18																							
Birmingham New Street 12	a					16 56	17 26							17 56				18 55		19 26				19 56	
Castle Cary	d			14 44							15 51														
Westbury	d			15 03						16 08															
Pewsey	d									16 25															
Hungerford	a									16 39															
Newbury	a									16 48															
Thatcham	a									16 55															
Theale	a									17 04															
Reading 7	a			15 50						17 15	16 49					17 49					18 49				
Slough 3	a																								
London Paddington 15 ⊖	a			16 22						17 54	17 24					18 21					19 24				

A ☕ to Plymouth ☕ from Westbury ✕ from Plymouth to Westbury

B The Torbay Express

C The Mayflower

D The Royal Duchy

For connections to Oxford, Gatwick Airport and Heathrow Airport please refer to Tables 116, 148 and 125A

Table 135

Mondays to Fridays

2 July to 31 August

Cornwall and Devon - Birmingham and London

Route Diagram - see first Page of Table 135

		GW	GW	GW	GW FO	XC	GW	GW		GW	GW	GW	XC	GW	GW FX	GW FO	GW	GW		GW FX	GW FO	GW	GW	GW	XC ThFO
		◇1			◇1	◇1				◇1			◇1		◇	◇	◇			◇1	◇1	◇1		1	◇1
		A								B			C												D
		☕			☕	🛒				☕⊘			🛒							☕	☕	☕			
Penzance	d									16 00					16 44	16 44						17 39		19 13	
St Erth	d									16 10					16 53	16 53						17 49		19 23	
Hayle	d														16 56	16 56						17 53		19 27	
Camborne	d									16 20					17 05	17 05						18 03		19 38	
Redruth	d									16 28					17 11	17 11						18 11		19 45	
Truro	d									16 41					17 24	17 24						18 23		19 58	
St Austell	d									16 58					17 41	17 41						18 40		20 15	
Newquay	d	15 00															17 22						19 25		
Par	d	16 00								17 07					17 48	17 48	18a13					18 49	20a13	20 24	
Lostwithiel	d	16 09								17 14					17 55	17 55								20 31	
Bodmin Parkway	d	16 16								17 21					18 01	18 01						19 01		20 38	
Liskeard 6	d	16 29	16 43							17 34	17 49				18 14	18 14						19 14		20 51	
Menheniot	d		16x47																						
St Germans	d		16 55								18 00				18 25	18 25									
Saltash	d		17 02								18 07				18 32	18 32									
St Budeaux Ferry Road	d		17 06								18 12														
Keyham	d		17 08																						
Dockyard	d		17x10																						
Devonport	d		17 12																						
Plymouth	a	16 54	17 18							18 00	18 19				18 42	18 42						19 39		21 16	
	d	16 57				17 23		17 45		18 03			18 25		18 44	18 44						19 42			
Ivybridge	d	17 12						18 02							18 59	18 59									
Totnes	d	17 28				17 49		18 17		18 31			18 50		19 14	19 14						20 10			
Paignton	d			17 26			17 52					18 35		18 52				19 33							20 14
Torquay	d			17 31			17 57					18 40		18 57				19 38							20 20
Torre	d			17 34			18 00					18 43						19 41							
Newton Abbot	a	17 38		17 42		18 01	18 08	18 29		18 43		18 50	19 01	19 07	19 26	19 26		19 49				20 21			20 30
	d	17 41		17 44		18 03	18 10	18 30		18 44		18 53	19 03	19 09	19 27	19 27		19 50				20 23			20 31
Teignmouth	d			17 51			18 17	18 37				19 00		19 16				19 58							
Dawlish	d			17 56			18 22	18 43				19 05		19 21				20 03							
Dawlish Warren	d			18 01			18 27	18 47				19 16		19 26				20 07							
Starcross	d			18 05			18 31					19 20						20 11							
Exeter St Thomas	d			18 14			18 40					19 29						20 21							
Exeter St Davids 6	a	18 01		18 18		18 23	18 46	19 00		19 03		19 33	19 21	19 40	19 49	19 49		20 26				20 43			20 50
Exeter Central	a			18 23			18 53											20 33							
Exmouth	a			18 52			19 23											21 01							
Exeter St Davids 6	d	18 03			18 20	18 25				19 06			19 23			19 49				19 55		20 45			20 52
Tiverton Parkway	d	18 17				18 39				19 21			19 37			20 06				20 10		21 00			21 04
Taunton	d	18 31			18 48	18 54				19 36			19 51			20a22				20 25	20 27	21 15			21 19
Bridgwater	a																								
Weston-super-Mare	a																								
Bristol Temple Meads 10	a					19 26							20 24									21 47			21 51
Bath Spa 7	a																					22 01			
Filton Abbey Wood	a																								
Bristol Parkway 7	a					19 38							20 38												22 08
Swindon	a																					22 33			
Newport (South Wales)	a																								
Cardiff Central 7	a																								
Birmingham New Street 12	a					20 52							22 06												23 44
Castle Cary	d	18 54																		20 46	20 46				
Westbury	d	19 12																		21 05	21 05				
Pewsey	d	19 29																		21 22	21 22				
Hungerford	a																								
Newbury	a	19 49																		21 42	21 42				
Thatcham	a																								
Theale	a																								
Reading 7	a	20 06			20 20					20 50										21 59	21 59	23 06			
Slough 3	a																								
London Paddington 15 ⊖	a	20 39			20 52					21 21										22 30	22 30	23 41			

A The Atlantic Coast Express

B ☕ to Plymouth ☕ from Reading ⊘ from Plymouth to Reading

C 🛒 to Bristol Temple Meads

For connections to Oxford, Gatwick Airport and Heathrow Airport please refer to Tables 116, 148 and 125A

2 July to 31 August

Cornwall and Devon - Birmingham and London

Route Diagram - see first Page of Table 135

		XC MT WO ◇■ A	GW	GW ■		GW	GW	GW FX	GW FO ■	GW	GW ◇	GW	GW	GW FO ■ B 🛏 ⊡		GW FX ■ B 🛏 ⊡	XC ◇■
Penzance	d							20 18	20 18					21 45		21 45	22 08
St Erth	d							20 27	20 27					21 55		21 55	22 16
Hayle	d							20 32	20 32								22 20
Camborne	d							20 41	20 41					22 07		22 07	22 30
Redruth	d							20 49	20 49					22 14		22 14	22 36
Truro	d							21 02	21 02					22 27		22 27	22 48
St Austell	d							21 19	21 19					22 45		22 45	23 04
Newquay	d									21 26							
Par	d							21 27	21 27	22a16				22 54		22 54	23 12
Lostwithiel	d							21 34	21 34								23 19
Bodmin Parkway	d							21 40	21 40					23 06		23 06	23 26
Liskeard ■	d						21 03	21 53	21 53					23 21		23 21	23 39
Menheniot	d						21x07										
St Germans	d						21 15	22 04	22 04								
Saltash	d						21 30	22 12	22 12								
St Budeaux Ferry Road	d						21 34										
Keyham	d						21 36										
Dockyard	d						21x38										
Devonport	d						21 40										
Plymouth	a						21 46	22 25	22 25					23 45		23 45	00 04
	d					21 25								23 51		23 51	
Ivybridge	d					21 40											
Totnes	d					21 55								00 20		00 20	
Paignton	d	20 14	20 34	21 31								22 30	23 41				
Torquay	d	20 20	20 39	21 37								22 35	23 46				
Torre	d		20 42	21 41								22 38	23 49				
Newton Abbot	a	20 30	20 50	21 52		22 01						22 46	23 57	00 32		00 32	
	d	20 31	20 52			22 02						22 48	23 59	00 33		00 33	
Teignmouth	d		20 59			22 14						22 55	00 06				
Dawlish	d		21 04			22 19						23 00	00 11				
Dawlish Warren	d		21 09			22 23						23 05	00 16				
Starcross	d		21 13			22 27						23 09	00 20				
Exeter St Thomas	d		21 22			22 36						23 18	00 29				
Exeter St Davids ■	a	20 50	21 28			22 40						23 22	00 34	00 55		00 55	
Exeter Central	a		21 35														
Exmouth	a		22 02														
Exeter St Davids ■	d	20 52									21 49			01 06		01 06	
Tiverton Parkway	d	21 04									22 06						
Taunton	d	21 19									22 23			01 36		01 36	
Bridgwater	a																
Weston-super-Mare	a										22 47						
Bristol Temple Meads ■	a	21 52									23 12						
Bath Spa ■	a																
Filton Abbey Wood	a																
Bristol Parkway ■	a	22 08															
Swindon	a																
Newport (South Wales)	a																
Cardiff Central ■	a																
Birmingham New Street ■	a	23 44															
Castle Cary	d																
Westbury	d																
Pewsey	d																
Hungerford	a																
Newbury	a																
Thatcham	a																
Theale	a																
Reading ■	a													04s00		04s00	
Slough ■	a																
London Paddington ■ ⊖	a													05 13		05 25	

B The Night Riviera

For connections to Oxford, Gatwick Airport and Heathrow Airport please refer to Tables 116, 148 and 125A

from 3 September

Cornwall and Devon - Birmingham and London

Route Diagram - see first Page of Table 135

		GW ◇■ A ⊡	GW MO ◇■ B ⊡	GW MO ◇■ C ⊡	GW MX	GW ■ A 🛏 ⊡	GW MO ■ B 🛏 ⊡	GW MO ■ C 🛏 ⊡	GW MX ■ D 🛏 ⊡	XC MX ◇■		GW ◇■ ⊡	GW ◇■ ⊡	GW ◇■ E ⊡⊘	GW	GW ◇■ ⊡	XC ◇■ 🛒	GW ◇■ ⊡	GW ◇■ F ⊡⊘	GW		GW	XC ◇■ 🛒	XC ◇■ 🛒	GW ◇■ G ⊡⊘
Penzance	d					21p15	21p15	21p15	21p45	22p08															05 05
St Erth	d					21p25	21p25	21p25	21p55	22p16															
Hayle	d									22p20															
Camborne	d					21p38	21p38	21p38	22p07	22p30															
Redruth	d					21p45	21p45	21p45	22p14	22p36															05 25
Truro	d					22p00	22p00	22p00	22p27	22p48															05 38
St Austell	d					22p18	22p18	22p18	22p45	23p04															05 55
Newquay	d																								
Par	d								22p54	23p12															
Lostwithiel	d									23p19															
Bodmin Parkway	d					22p35	22p35	22p35	23p06	23p26															06 11
Liskeard ■	d					22p50	22p50	22p50	23p21	23p39															06 26
Menheniot	d																								
St Germans	d																								
Saltash	d																								
St Budeaux Ferry Road	d																								
Keyham	d																								
Dockyard	d																								
Devonport	d																								
Plymouth	a					23p15	23p15	23p15	23p45	00 04															06 51
	d	19p55	19p55	19p55		23p20	23p20	23p20	23p51							05 09	05 20	05 30	05 53				06 25		06 55
Ivybridge	d																								
Totnes	d					23p48	23p48	23p48	00 20								05 45	05 58					06 50		
Paignton	d				23p41															06 10		06 34		07 02	
Torquay	d				23p46															06 15		06 39		07 08	
Torre	d				23p49															06 18		06 42			
Newton Abbot	a	20p31	20p31	20p31	23p57	23p59	23p59	23p59	00 32							05 45	05 56	06 09	06 28	06 26		06 50	07 01	07 18	07 30
	d	20p32	20p32	20p32	23p59	00 01	00 01	00 01	00 33							05 47	06 02	06 11	06 31	06 34		06 52	07 03	07 19	07 32
Teignmouth	d				00 06											05 54				06 41		06 59		07 26	
Dawlish	d				00 11													06 21		06 46		07 04		07 31	
Dawlish Warren	d				00 16															06 51		07 15			
Starcross	d				00 20															06 55		07 19			
Exeter St Thomas	d				00 29															07 04		07 28			
Exeter St Davids ■	a	20p53	20p53	20p53	00 34	00 23	00 23	00 23	00 55							06 10	06 19	06 33	06 51	07 09		07 33	07 21	07 43	07 52
Exeter Central	a																			07 14		07 39			
Exmouth	a																			07 43		08 18			
Exeter St Davids ■	d	20p55	20p55	20p55		01 06	01 06	01 06	01 06					05 46	06 00	06 12	06 22	06 35	06 52				07 23	07 45	07 53
Tiverton Parkway	d	21p10	21p10	21p10										06 02	06 17	06 27	06 36	06 51					07 37	07 58	
Taunton	d	21p23	21p23	21p23					01 36					06 17	06 34	06 55	06 50	07 06	07 18				07 51	08 13	08 19
Bridgwater	a														06 46	07 05									
Weston-super-Mare	a														07 04	07 24								08 32	
Bristol Temple Meads ■	a	22p00	22p00	22p00											07 41	07 57	07 24						08 26	08 53	
Bath Spa ■	a	22p22	22p22	22p22												08 11									
Filton Abbey Wood	a														07 58										
Bristol Parkway ■	a														08 05		07 38						08 38	09 08	
Swindon	a	22p50	22p50	22p50												08 40									
Newport (South Wales)	a																								
Cardiff Central ■	a																								
Birmingham New Street ■	a																08 56						09 56	10 26	
Castle Cary	d													06 38				07 27							
Westbury	d											06 06	06 18	07 01				07 51							
Pewsey	d											06 24	06 36	07 19				08 09							
Hungerford	a											06 36	06 54	07 32											
Newbury	a											06 49	07 08	07 46				08 29							
Thatcham	a											06 56	07 15												
Theale	a											07 06	07 25												
Reading ■	a	23p28	23p28	23p28		04s02	04s03	04s07	04s00			07 19	07 37	08 06		09 14		08 50	08 32						09 32
Slough ■	a																								
London Paddington ■ ⊖	a	00 05	00 12	00 13		05 05	05 05	05 05	05 25			07 53	08 09	08 38		09 44		09 21	09 00						10 02

A 3 September, 10 September
B from 17 September until 22 October
C from 29 October
D The Night Riviera
E ⊡ from Reading ⊘ to Reading
F The Armada
G The Golden Hind

For connections to Oxford, Gatwick Airport and Heathrow Airport please refer to Tables 116, 148 and 125A

Cornwall and Devon - Birmingham and London

Route Diagram - see first Page of Table 135

		GW	GW	XC	GW	GW	GW	GW	XC	GW	GW	GW	XC	XC	GW	GW	XC	GW	GW	GW	GW	XC	XC
				◇1	◇1	◇1		◇	◇1	◇1			◇1	◇1	◇1		◇1	■1		◇1		◇1	◇1
									B								B	C					B
				⌶	▭	▭Ø			⌶	▭Ø			⌶	⌶	▭		⌶	▭		▭		⌶	⌶
Penzance	d	05 21				05 41		06 00	06 28	06 45	06 55				07 41		08 28	08 44	08 57				09 40
St Erth	d							06 09	06 36	06 55	07a03				07 51		08 36	08 54	09a05				09 48
Hayle	d	05 31						06 12							07 55								09 52
Camborne	d	05 40				05 58		06 21	06 46	07 06					08 05		08 46	09 06					10 01
Redruth	d					06 05		06 27	06 52	07 13					08 12		08 52	09 13					10 08
Truro	d	05a55				06 18		06 39	07 04	07 26					08 25		09 04	09 26					10 19
St Austell	d					06 35		06 56	07 20	07 44					08 43		09 20	09 43					10 35
Newquay	d																						
Par	d					06 43		07 03	07 28	07 52					08 51		09 28	09 51					10 43
Lostwithiel	d					06 51		07 10		08 00													10 50
Bodmin Parkway	d					06 57		07 16	07 39	08 06					09 03		09 39	10 03					10 57
Liskeard ■	d					07 11		07 29	07 53	08 20					09 16		09 51	10 16					11 09
Menheniot	d							07x33															
St Germans	d					07 22		07 41		08 31					09 27								
Saltash	d					07 30		07 48		08 39					09 35								
St Budeaux Ferry Road	d							07 52															
Keyham	d							07 54															
Dockyard	d							07x56															
Devonport	d							07 58															
Plymouth	a					07 41		08 04	08 20	08 49					09 46		10 18	10 41					11 39
	d			07 25		07 48		08 06	08 25	08 53			09 25		09 48		10 25	10 44				11 25	11 50
Ivybridge	d							08 21		09 08					10 03								
Totnes	d			07 50		08 16		08 36	08 50	09 23			09 50		10 19		10 50					11 50	12 15
Paignton	d		07 12		07 40		08 23					09 13		10 07		10 15				11 06	11 23		
Torquay	d		07 17		07 46		08 28					09 18		10 13		10 23				11 12	11 28		
Torre	d		07 20		07 50		08 31					09 21				10 26				11 16	11 31		
Newton Abbot	a		07 27	08 01	07 58	08 27	08 39	08 48	09 01	09 34		09 29	10 01	10 23	10 31	10 35	11 01			11 24	11 39	12 01	12 26
	d		07 37	08 03	08 06	08 29	08 41	08 49	09 03	09 36		09 39	10 03	10 24	10 32	10 36	11 03			11 26	11 41	12 03	12 28
Teignmouth	d		07 45		08 13		08 48	08 56				09 46		10 31		10 44				11 33	11 48		
Dawlish	d		07 50		08 19		08 53	09 01				09 51		10 36		10 49				11 39	11 53		
Dawlish Warren	d		07 55				08 58					09 55				10 53					11 58		
Starcross	d		07 59		08 25		09 02					09 59				10 57					12 02		
Exeter St Thomas	d		08 09		08 34		09 11					10 09				11 07					12 11		
Exeter St Davids ■	a		08 14	08 21	08 39	08 49	09 15	09 18	09 22	09 56		10 14	10 21	10 48	10 54	11 10	11 21	11 38		11 52	12 16	12 21	12 46
Exeter Central	a		08 19				09 21					10 21				11 21					12 21		
Exmouth	a		08 48				09 50					10 50				11 50					12 50		
Exeter St Davids ■	d			08 23	08 41	08 51		09 33	09 23	09 58			10 23	10 50	10 56		11 23	11 40		11 55		12 23	12 48
Tiverton Parkway	d			08 37		09 06		09 50	09 37	10 13			10 37	11 03	11 11		11 37			12 09		12 37	13 02
Taunton	d			08 51	09 05	09 21		10 07	09 51	10 28			10 51	11 18	11 26		11 51			12 24		12 51	13 16
Bridgwater	a							10 19															
Weston-super-Mare	a				09 27			10 38															
Bristol Temple Meads ■	a			09 26	09 56			11 11	10 25				11 23	11 52	11 58		12 23					13 24	13 56
Bath Spa ■	a				10 11										12 12								
Filton Abbey Wood	a							11 30															
Bristol Parkway ■	a			09 38					10 38				11 38	12 08			12 38					13 38	14 08
Swindon	a				10 40										12 40								
Newport (South Wales)	a							11 58															
Cardiff Central ■	a							12 18															
Birmingham New Street ■	a			10 56					11 58				12 56	13 26			13 56					14 56	15 26
Castle Cary	d					09 42														12 45			
Westbury	d					10 01				11 05										13 05			
Pewsey	d					10 18														13 21			
Hungerford	a																			13 39			
Newbury	a																			13 48			
Thatcham	a																			13 55			
Theale	a																			14 04			
Reading ■	a				11 09	10 50				11 50					13 09			13 15		14 15			
Slough ■	a																						
London Paddington ■ ⊖	a				11 38	11 24				12 23					13 38			13 44		14 44			

B ⌶ from Plymouth

C The Cornish Riviera

For connections to Oxford, Gatwick Airport and Heathrow Airport please refer to Tables 116, 148 and 125A

Cornwall and Devon - Birmingham and London

Route Diagram - see first Page of Table 135

		GW	GW	GW	XC	GW	GW	GW	GW	GW	XC	XC	GW	GW	GW	GW	GW	XC	GW	GW	GW	XC
		◇		■1	◇1	◇	◇	◇1	◇1		◇1	◇1	◇	◇	◇1	◇1		◇1		◇1	◇	◇1
				A				B	C							D				E		
				✕▭	⌶			✕▭	✕▭		⌶	⌶			▭	▭		⌶		▭		⌶
Penzance	d			10 00		10 46							11 41								12 51	
St Erth	d			10 10		10 55							11 50								13 03	
Hayle	d					10 58							11 53								13 06	
Camborne	d			10 21		11 07							12 02								13 15	
Redruth	d			10 28		11 13							12 08								13 21	
Truro	d			10 41		11 25							12 19								13 32	
St Austell	d			10 58		11 42							12 36								13 49	
Newquay	d	10 13												13 03								
Par	d	11a02		11 07		11 50							12 44	13a52							13 57	
Lostwithiel	d					11 56							12 50								14 04	
Bodmin Parkway	d			11 19		12 02							12 56								14 10	
Liskeard ■	d			11 33		12 16							13 09								14 23	
Menheniot	d												13x13									
St Germans	d					12 27							13 22								14 34	
Saltash	d					12 34							13 29								14 42	
St Budeaux Ferry Road	d																					
Keyham	d																					
Dockyard	d																					
Devonport	d																					
Plymouth	a			11 58		12 45							13 39								14 51	
	d			12 01	12 23			12 55	12 55		13 23		13 41					14 25		15 00	15 08	15 23
Ivybridge	d												13 56								15 23	
Totnes	d			12 29	12 49			13 23	13 23		13 49		14 11					14 50		15 28	15 38	15 49
Paignton	d		12 13				12 48			13 13		14 01				14 15	14 23		15 13			
Torquay	d		12 18				12 53			13 18		14 07				14 21	14 28		15 18			
Torre	d		12 21				12 56			13 21							14 31		15 21			
Newton Abbot	a		12 30	12 41	13 01		13 04	13 34	13 34	13 30	14 01	14 17	14 24			14 31	14 39	15 01	15 29	15 39	15 52	16 01
	d		12 31	12 42	13 03		13 06	13 36	13 36	13 41	14 03	14 18				14 33	14 41	15 03	15 31	15 41		16 03
Teignmouth	d		12 38				13 13			13 48		14 25				14 40	14 48		15 38			
Dawlish	d		12 43				13 18			13 53		14 30				14 46	14 53		15 43			
Dawlish Warren	d		12 54							13 58							14 58		15 54			
Starcross	d		12 58							14 02							15 02		15 58			
Exeter St Thomas	d		13 07							14 11							15 11		16 07			
Exeter St Davids ■	a		13 13	13 02	13 23		13 31	13 56	13 56	14 16	14 23	14 42				14 59	15 16	15 21	16 13	16 01		16 23
Exeter Central	a		13 21							14 21							15 21		16 21			
Exmouth	a		13 50							14 50							15 50		16 50			
Exeter St Davids ■	d			13 04	13 25		13 33	13 58	13 58		14 25	14 44				15 01		15 23		16 03		16 25
Tiverton Parkway	d			13 19	13 39		13 50				14 39	14 57				15 15		15 37		16 17		16 39
Taunton	d			13 34	13 54		14 07	14 23	14 23		14 54	15 12			15 23	15 30		15 51		16 31		16 54
Bridgwater	a						14 18															
Weston-super-Mare	a						14 37					15 37										
Bristol Temple Meads ■	a				14 26		15 08				15 26	15 55						16 26				17 26
Bath Spa ■	a																					
Filton Abbey Wood	a						15 30															
Bristol Parkway ■	a				14 38						15 38	16 08						16 38				17 38
Swindon	a																					
Newport (South Wales)	a						15 58															
Cardiff Central ■	a						16 18															
Birmingham New Street ■	a				15 56						16 56	17 26						17 56				18 55
Castle Cary	d							14 44	14 44							15 51						
Westbury	d							15 03	15 03						16 08							
Pewsey	d														16 25							
Hungerford	a														16 39							
Newbury	a														16 48							
Thatcham	a														16 55							
Theale	a														17 04							
Reading ■	a			14 50				15 50	15 50						17 15	16 49				17 49		
Slough ■	a																					
London Paddington ■ ⊖	a			15 24				16 22	16 24						17 54	17 24				18 21		

A The Cornishman

B from 3 September until 14 September

C from 17 September

D The Torbay Express

E The Mayflower

For connections to Oxford, Gatwick Airport and Heathrow Airport please refer to Tables 116, 148 and 125A

Table 135

Mondays to Fridays

from 3 September

Cornwall and Devon - Birmingham and London

Route Diagram - see first Page of Table 135

		GW	XC	GW	GW	GW	XC	GW	GW	GW	GW	XC	GW	GW	GW	GW	GW	XC	GW	GW FX	GW FO	GW	GW
			◇1 ⌶	◇1 A ⊐	◇ B	◇ C	◇1 ⌶	◇		◇1 ⊐		◇1 ⌶			◇1 D ⊐Ø			◇1 E ⌶		◇	◇	◇	
Penzance	d			14 00				14 49							16 00					16 44	16 44		
St Erth	d			14 10				14 58							16 10					16 53	16 53		
Hayle	d							15 01												16 56	16 56		
Camborne	d			14 21				15 10							16 20					17 05	17 05		
Redruth	d			14 28				15 16							16 28					17 11	17 11		
Truro	d			14 41				15 27							16 41					17 24	17 24		
St Austell	d			14 58				15 44							16 58					17 41	17 41		
Newquay	d				14 58	15 01																17 22	
Par	d			15 06	15a47	15a47		15 52							17 07					17 48	17 48	18a13	
Lostwithiel	d							15 58							17 14					17 55	17 55		
Bodmin Parkway	d			15 18				16 04							17 21					18 01	18 01		
Liskeard 6	d			15 31				16 17							17 34	17 49				18 14	18 14		
Menheniot	d							16x21															
St Germans	d							16 30								18 00				18 25	18 25		
Saltash	d							16 37								18 07				18 32	18 32		
St Budeaux Ferry Road	d							16 41								18 12							
Keyham	d							16 43															
Dockyard	d							16x45															
Devonport	d							16 47															
Plymouth	a			15 56				16 52							18 00	18 19				18 42	18 42		
	d			16 00			16 25			16 57		17 23		17 45	18 03			18 25		18 44	18 44		
Ivybridge	d									17 12				18 02						18 59	18 59		
Totnes	d			16 28			16 50			17 28		17 49		18 17	18 31			18 50		19 14	19 14		
Paignton	d	16 12							16 55		17 26		17 52				18 35		18 52				19 33
Torquay	d	16 17							17 00		17 31		17 57				18 40		18 57				19 38
Torre	d	16 21							17 03		17 34		18 00				18 43						19 41
Newton Abbot	a	16 29		16 39			17 01		17 11	17 38	17 42	18 01	18 08	18 29	18 43		18 50	19 01	19 07	19 26	19 26		19 49
	d	16 31		16 41			17 03		17 13	17 41	17 44	18 03	18 10	18 30	18 44		18 53	19 03	19 09	19 27	19 27		19 50
Teignmouth	d	16 38							17 20		17 51		18 17	18 37			19 00		19 16				19 58
Dawlish	d	16 43							17 25		17 56		18 22	18 43			19 05		19 21				20 03
Dawlish Warren	d	16 54							17 30		18 01		18 27	18 47			19 16		19 26				20 07
Starcross	d	16 58							17 34		18 05		18 31				19 20						20 11
Exeter St Thomas	d	17 07							17 43		18 14		18 40				19 29						20 21
Exeter St Davids 6	a	17 13		17 01			17 21		17 50	18 01	18 18	18 23	18 46	19 00	19 03		19 33	19 21	19 40	19 49	19 49		20 26
Exeter Central	a	17 21							17 55		18 23		18 53										20 33
Exmouth	a	17 51							18 25		18 52		19 23										21 01
Exeter St Davids 6	d		16 54	17 03			17 23			18 03		18 25			19 06			19 23			19 49		
Tiverton Parkway	d		17 08	17 18			17 37			18 17		18 39			19 21			19 37			20 06		
Taunton	d		17 22	17 32			17 51			18 31		18 54			19 36			19 51			20a22		
Bridgwater	a																						
Weston-super-Mare	a																						
Bristol Temple Meads 10	a		17 53				18 24					19 26						20 24					
Bath Spa 7	a																						
Filton Abbey Wood	a																						
Bristol Parkway 7	a		18 08				18 38					19 38						20 38					
Swindon	a																						
Newport (South Wales)	a																						
Cardiff Central 7	a																						
Birmingham New Street 12	a		19 26				19 56					20 52						22 06					
Castle Cary	d									18 54													
Westbury	d									19 12													
Pewsey	d									19 29													
Hungerford	a																						
Newbury	a									19 49													
Thatcham	a																						
Theale	a																						
Reading 7	a			18 49						20 06					20 50								
Slough 3	a																						
London Paddington 15 ⊖	a			19 24						20 39					21 21								

A The Royal Duchy
B from 3 September until 14 September
C from 17 September
D ⊐ to Plymouth ⊐ from Reading Ø from Plymouth to Reading
E ⌶ to Bristol Temple Meads

For connections to Oxford, Gatwick Airport and Heathrow Airport please refer to Tables 116, 148 and 125A

Table 135

Mondays to Fridays

from 3 September

Cornwall and Devon - Birmingham and London

Route Diagram - see first Page of Table 135

		GW FX	GW FO	GW	GW	GW	XC ThFO	XC MTWO	GW	GW	GW	GW FX	GW FO	GW	GW	GW	GW	GW FO	GW FX	XC
		◇1 ⊐	◇1 ⊐	◇1 ⊐			◇1 A	◇1 B		1			1		◇			Sleeper C ⊐	Sleeper C ⊐	◇1
Penzance	d			17 39		19 16						20 18	20 18					21 45	21 45	22 08
St Erth	d			17 49		19 25						20 27	20 27					21 55	21 55	22 16
Hayle	d			17 53		19 28						20 32	20 32							22 20
Camborne	d			18 03		19 37						20 41	20 41					22 07	22 07	22 30
Redruth	d			18 11		19 43						20 49	20 49					22 14	22 14	22 36
Truro	d			18 23		19 55						21 02	21 02					22 27	22 27	22 48
St Austell	d			18 40		20 12						21 19	21 19					22 45	22 45	23 04
Newquay	d				19 25									21 26						
Par	d			18 49	20a13	20 19						21 27	21 27	22a16				22 54	22 54	23 12
Lostwithiel	d					20 26						21 34	21 34							23 19
Bodmin Parkway	d			19 01		20 32						21 40	21 40					23 06	23 06	23 26
Liskeard 6	d			19 14		20 45						21 53	21 53					23 21	23 21	23 39
Menheniot	d					20x49														
St Germans	d					20 58						22 04	22 04							
Saltash	d					21 05						22 12	22 12							
St Budeaux Ferry Road	d					21 09														
Keyham	d					21 11														
Dockyard	d					21x13														
Devonport	d					21 15														
Plymouth	a			19 39		21 20						22 25	22 25					23 45	23 45	00 04
	d			19 42							21 25							23 51	23 51	
Ivybridge	d										21 40									
Totnes	d			20 10							21 55							00 20	00 20	
Paignton	d						20 14	20 14	20 34	21 31						22 30	23 41			
Torquay	d						20 20	20 20	20 39	21 37						22 35	23 46			
Torre	d								20 42	21 41						22 38	23 49			
Newton Abbot	a			20 21			20 30	20 30	20 50	21 52	22 01					22 46	23 57	00 32	00 32	
	d			20 23			20 31	20 31	20 52		22 02					22 48	23 59	00 33	00 33	
Teignmouth	d								20 59		22 14					22 55	00 06			
Dawlish	d								21 04		22 19					23 00	00 11			
Dawlish Warren	d								21 09		22 23					23 05	00 16			
Starcross	d								21 13		22 27					23 09	00 20			
Exeter St Thomas	d								21 22		22 36					23 18	00 29			
Exeter St Davids 6	a			20 43			20 50	20 50	21 28		22 40					23 22	00 34	00 55	00 55	
Exeter Central	a								21 35											
Exmouth	a								22 02											
Exeter St Davids 6	d	19 55		20 45			20 52	20 52							21 49			01 06	01 06	
Tiverton Parkway	d	20 10		21 00			21 04	21 04							22 06					
Taunton	d	20 25	20 27	21 15			21 19	21 19							22 23			01 36	01 36	
Bridgwater	a																			
Weston-super-Mare	a														22 47					
Bristol Temple Meads 10	a			21 47			21 51	21 52							23 12					
Bath Spa 7	a			22 01																
Filton Abbey Wood	a																			
Bristol Parkway 7	a						22 08	22 08												
Swindon	a			22 33																
Newport (South Wales)	a																			
Cardiff Central 7	a																			
Birmingham New Street 12	a						23 44	23 44												
Castle Cary	d	20 46	20 46																	
Westbury	d	21 05	21 05																	
Pewsey	d	21 22	21 22																	
Hungerford	a																			
Newbury	a	21 42	21 42																	
Thatcham	a																			
Theale	a																			
Reading 7	a	21 59	21 59	23 06														04s00	04s00	
Slough 3	a																			
London Paddington 15 ⊖	a	22 30	22 30	23 41														05 13	05 25	

C The Night Riviera

For connections to Oxford, Gatwick Airport and Heathrow Airport please refer to Tables 116, 148 and 125A

Saturdays until 23 June

Cornwall and Devon - Birmingham and London

Route Diagram - see first Page of Table 135

		GW	GW	XC	GW	GW	XC	GW	GW	GW	XC	GW	XC	GW	GW	XC	GW	GW	GW	GW	XC	GW	XC
			■ A 🛏 ⊡	◇■			◇■ ⌶	◇■ ⊡			◇■ ⌶	◇■ ⊡	◇■ ⌶		◇■ B ⊡⊘	◇■ ⌶		◇■ C ⊡⊘			◇■ D ⌶		◇■ ⌶
Penzance	d		21p45	22p08	05 20												05 37				06 30	06 41	
St Erth	d		21p55	22p16													05 45				06 38	06a49	
Hayle	d			22p20													05 48				06 41		
Camborne	d		22p07	22p30	05 37												05 58				06 51		
Redruth	d		22p14	22p36	05 43												06 04				06 57		
Truro	d		22p27	22p48	05a55												06 15				07 09		
St Austell	d		22p45	23p04													06 32				07 25		
Newquay	d																						
Par	d		22p54	23p12													06 39				07 32		
Lostwithiel	d			23p19													06 46				07 39		
Bodmin Parkway	d		23p06	23p26													06 52				07 46		
Liskeard ■	d		23p21	23p39													07 07				07 58		
Menheniot	d																07x11						
St Germans	d																07 19						
Saltash	d																07 26						
St Budeaux Ferry Road	d																07 30						
Keyham	d																07 32						
Dockyard	d																07x34						
Devonport	d																07 36						
Plymouth	a		23p45	00 04													07 42				08 22		
	d		23p51				05 25	05 40			06 25				06 55	07 25		07 47		08 06	08 25		08 38
Ivybridge	d																			08 21			
Totnes	d		00 20				05 50	06 07			06 50					07 50		08 14		08 35	08 50		09 03
Paignton	d	23p41							06 13	06 34			07 02	07 11					08 06				
Torquay	d	23p46							06 18	06 39			07 08	07 16					08 11				
Torre	d	23p49							06 21	06 42				07 19					08 14				
Newton Abbot	a	23p57	00 32				06 01	06 18	06 29	06 50	07 01		07 18	07 27	07 30	08 01		08 26	08 22	08 47	09 01		09 14
	d	23p59	00 33				06 03	06 20	06 31	06 52	07 03		07 19		07 32	08 03		08 27	08 34	08 48	09 03		09 16
Teignmouth	d	00 06							06 38	06 59			07 26						08 41	08 55			
Dawlish	d	00 11							06 43	07 04			07 31						08 46	09 00			
Dawlish Warren	d	00 16							06 48	07 15									08 51				09 28
Starcross	d	00 20							06 52	07 19									08 55				
Exeter St Thomas	d	00 29							07 01	07 28									09 04				
Exeter St Davids ■	a	00 34	00 55				06 21	06 40	07 06	07 33	07 21		07 43		07 52	08 21		08 47	09 09	09 16	09 21		09 39
Exeter Central	a								07 14	07 39									09 21				
Exmouth	a								07 43	08 18									09 50				
Exeter St Davids ■	d		01 06			06 00	06 23	06 41			07 23	07 29	07 45		07 54	08 23		08 49			09 23		09 41
Tiverton Parkway	d					06 18	06 37	06 56			07 37	07 44	07 58		08 09	08 37		09 04			09 37		09 54
Taunton	d		01 36			06 35	06 51	07 11			07 51	07 59	08 13		08 24	08 51		09 19			09 51		10 09
Bridgwater	a					06 47						08 09											
Weston-super-Mare	a					07 06						08 27											10 32
Bristol Temple Meads ■	a					07 42	07 24				08 23	08 57	08 48			09 25					10 25		10 52
Bath Spa ■	a											09 11											
Filton Abbey Wood	a					07 58																	
Bristol Parkway ■	a					08 05	07 38				08 38		09 08			09 38					10 38		11 08
Swindon	a											09 40											
Newport (South Wales)	a																						
Cardiff Central ■	a																						
Birmingham New Street ■	a						08 56				09 56		10 26			10 56					11 56		12 26
Castle Cary	d							07 33										09 40					
Westbury	d							07 56										09 59					
Pewsey	d							08 13										10 16					
Hungerford	a																						
Newbury	a							08 33															
Thatcham	a																						
Theale	a																						
Reading ■	a		04s00					08 52				10 11			09 39			10 51					
Slough ■	a																						
London Paddington ■ ⊖	a		05 13					09 21				10 39			10 11			11 24					

A The Night Riviera
B ⊡ from Reading ⊘ to Reading
C ⊡ from Castle Cary ⊘ to Castle Cary
D ⌶ from Plymouth

For connections to Oxford, Gatwick Airport and Heathrow Airport please refer to Tables 116, 148 and 125A

Saturdays until 23 June

Cornwall and Devon - Birmingham and London

Route Diagram - see first Page of Table 135

		GW	GW	GW	GW	XC	GW	XC	GW	XC	GW	GW	GW	GW	XC	GW	GW	XC	GW	GW	GW	GW	GW
		■ ⊡		◇■ ⊡		◇■ ⌶	■ ⊡	◇■ ⌶		◇■ A ⌶	■ ⊡				◇■ A ⌶		■ ⊡	◇■ ⌶				■ ◇■ B ⊡	■ C ⊡⊘
Penzance	d	06 50					07 18			08 28	08 39	08 54					09 54						11 00
St Erth	d	07 00					07 29			08 36	08 50	09a02					10 05						11 11
Hayle	d						07 34				08 55						10 10						11 16
Camborne	d	07 11					07 44			08 46	09 06						10 20						11 26
Redruth	d	07 18					07 51			08 52	09 13						10 27						11 33
Truro	d	07 31					08 05			09 04	09 26						10 40						11 46
St Austell	d	07 48					08 22			09 20	09 44						10 58						12 04
Newquay	d														09 27								
Par	d	07 56					08 30			09 28	09 51				10 26		11 06			11 31			
Lostwithiel	d	08 04					08 38													11 38			
Bodmin Parkway	d	08 10					08 44			09 39	10 02				10 43		11 18			11 44			12 21
Liskeard ■	d	08 23					08 57			09 51	10 15				10 55		11 31			11 58			12 34
Menheniot	d																			12x02			
St Germans	d						09 09													12 09			
Saltash	d						09 17													12 15			
St Budeaux Ferry Road	d																						
Keyham	d																						
Dockyard	d																						
Devonport	d																						
Plymouth	a	08 49					09 26			10 18	10 40				11 19		11 56			12 27			12 58
	d	08 52				09 18	09 33			10 25	10 43				11 25		12 00			12 35			13 00
Ivybridge	d						09 48										12 15			12 50			
Totnes	d	09 19				09 43	10 02			10 50					11 50		12 29			13 04			13 28
Paignton	d		09 04	09 18	09 30			10 07	10 23				10 56	11 13		12 13		12 34	12 49		13 00	13 07	
Torquay	d		09 09	09 25	09 35			10 13	10 28				11 01	11 18		12 18		12 41	12 54		13 05	13 15	
Torre	d		09 12	09 29	09 38				10 31				11 04	11 21		12 21					13 08		
Newton Abbot	a	09 30	09 20	09 38	09 47	09 54	10 14	10 23	10 38	11 01			11 12	11 29	12 01	12 30	12 41	12 51	13 04	13 16	13 16	13 25	13 40
	d	09 32	09 35	09 39	09 48	09 56	10 15	10 24	10 41	11 03			11 23	11 41	12 03	12 32	12 42	12 53	13 06	13 16	13 21	13 26	13 42
Teignmouth	d		09 42	09 49	09 56	10 03		10 31	10 48				11 30	11 48		12 39		13 02	13 13		13 28	13 35	
Dawlish	d		09 47	09 57	10 02	10 09		10 36	10 53				11 35	11 53		12 44		13 09	13 18		13 33	13 43	
Dawlish Warren	d		09 52	10 02	10 07	10 14			10 58				11 40	11 58		12 55			13 23		13 38	13 55	
Starcross	d		09 56						11 02				11 44	12 02		12 59					13 42		
Exeter St Thomas	d		10 05						11 11				11 53	12 11		13 08					13 51		
Exeter St Davids ■	a	09 52	10 10	10 13	10 18	10 24	10 35	10 48	11 15	11 21	11 37		11 58	12 16	12 21	13 13	13 02	13 22	13 35	13 38	13 59	14 08	14 02
Exeter Central	a		10 21						11 21					12 21		13 21					14 21		
Exmouth	a		10 50						11 50					12 50		13 50					14 50		
Exeter St Davids ■	d	09 54		10 15		10 26	10 38	10 50		11 23	11 40				12 23		13 05	13 24				14 11	14 05
Tiverton Parkway	d	10 09		10 30		10 40		11 03		11 37					12 37		13 20	13 39					
Taunton	d	10 24		10 45		10 54	11 03	11 18		11 51					12 51		13 35	13 53				14 44	14 30
Bridgwater	a																						
Weston-super-Mare	a																						
Bristol Temple Meads ■	a			11 24		11 25		11 54		12 24					13 23			14 26					
Bath Spa ■	a			11 41																			
Filton Abbey Wood	a																						
Bristol Parkway ■	a					11 38		12 08		12 38					13 38			14 38					
Swindon	a			12 09																			
Newport (South Wales)	a																						
Cardiff Central ■	a																						
Birmingham New Street ■	a					12 56		13 26		13 56					14 56			15 55					
Castle Cary	d						11 24															15 08	
Westbury	d	11 02					11 45															15 28	
Pewsey	d						12 01															15 45	
Hungerford	a																						
Newbury	a																					16 05	
Thatcham	a																						
Theale	a																						
Reading ■	a	11 51		12 45			12 40				13 17						14 52					16 25	15 51
Slough ■	a																						
London Paddington ■ ⊖	a	12 23		13 13			13 09				13 46						15 23					17 02	16 23

A ⌶ from Plymouth
B ◇ from Exeter St Davids ■ to Exeter St Davids
C ⊡ to Plymouth ⊡ from Reading ⊘ from Plymouth to Reading

For connections to Oxford, Gatwick Airport and Heathrow Airport please refer to Tables 116, 148 and 125A

Table 135

Saturdays until 23 June

Cornwall and Devon - Birmingham and London

Route Diagram - see first Page of Table 135

		GW		XC	XC	GW	GW	GW	XC	GW	GW	GW		XC	GW	GW	GW	GW	GW	XC	GW	GW		XC	GW
		■1		◇1	◇1	■1 A		■◇1 B	◇1		■1	◇		◇1				◇1	◇	◇1	◇1			◇1	
Penzance	d					11 58						13 00						14 01	14 52						
St Erth	d					12 09						13 09						14 11	15 01						
Hayle	d					12 14						13 12							15 04						
Camborne	d					12 24						13 21						14 22	15 14						
Redruth	d					12 31						13 27						14 29	15 20						
Truro	d					12 44						13 38						14 42	15 31						
St Austell	d					13 02						13 55						14 59	15 48						
Newquay	d	11 21									13 14													15 25	
Par	d	12 26									14 16	14 25						15 07	15 55						
Lostwithiel	d											14 31							16 02						
Bodmin Parkway	d					13 19						14 37						15 19	16 08					16 37	
Liskeard 6	d					13 32						14 50						15 33	16 21					16 51	
Menheniot	d																		16x25						
St Germans	d											15 01							16 33						
Saltash	d											15 09							16 39						
St Budeaux Ferry Road	d																								
Keyham	d																								
Dockyard	d																								
Devonport	d											15 15													
Plymouth	a	13 10				13 56					15 00	15 20						15 58	16 51					17 15	
	d	13 14		13 25		14 00			14 25		15 07			15 25		15 32		16 01						17 25	
Ivybridge	d															15 47									
Totnes	d			13 50					14 50					15 50		16 01		16 28						17 50	
Paignton	d				13 53		14 13	14 31		15 13					15 43		16 13			16 36	17 03	17 13			17 52
Torquay	d				13 59		14 18	14 38		15 18					15 48		16 18			16 43	17 10	17 19			17 57
Torre	d						14 21			15 21							16 21					17 22			18 00
Newton Abbot	a			14 01	14 09	14 35	14 29	14 48	15 01	15 29	15 42			16 01	15 58	16 13	16 29	16 41		16 54	17 21	17 30		18 01	18 08
	d			14 03	14 10	14 36	14 40	14 50	15 03	15 34	15 44			16 03	16 09		16 31	16 41		16 55	17 22	17 41		18 03	18 10
Teignmouth	d				14 17		14 48	14 58		15 42					16 16		16 39			17 03	17 30	17 49			18 18
Dawlish	d				14 22		14 53	15 04		15 48					16 21		16 44			17 10	17 37	17 54			18 23
Dawlish Warren	d						14 57	15 17		15 58							16 55				17 42	17 59			18 28
Starcross	d						15 01			16 02							16 59					18 04			18 33
Exeter St Thomas	d						15 11			16 12							17 09					18 13			18 42
Exeter St Davids 6	a	14 15		14 21	14 34	14 56	15 15	15 28	15 21	16 15	16 04			16 21	16 34		17 15	17 01		17 23	17 56	18 18		18 21	18 47
Exeter Central	a						15 21			16 21					16 44		17 21					18 23			18 53
Exmouth	a						15 50			16 50							17 50					18 52			19 22
Exeter St Davids 6	d	14 18		14 23	14 36	14 59		15 32	15 23		16 06			16 23				17 03		17 25	18 02			18 23	
Tiverton Parkway	d			14 37	14 49	15 14			15 37		16 21			16 37				17 17		17 39	18 17			18 37	
Taunton	d			14 52	15 04	15 29		15 57	15 51		16 36			16 51				17 32		17 54	18 32			18 51	
Bridgwater	a																								
Weston-super-Mare	a				15 23																				
Bristol Temple Meads 10	a			15 24	15 49				16 24					17 24						18 24				19 22	
Bath Spa 7	a																								
Filton Abbey Wood	a																								
Bristol Parkway 7	a			15 38	16 08				16 38					17 38						18 38				19 38	
Swindon	a																								
Newport (South Wales)	a																								
Cardiff Central 7	a																								
Birmingham New Street 12	a			16 56	17 26				17 56					18 56						19 58				20 54	
Castle Cary	d					15 50		16 19													18 53				
Westbury	d							16 38													19 12				
Pewsey	d							16 54																	
Hungerford	a																								
Newbury	a																				19 45				
Thatcham	a																								
Theale	a																								
Reading 7	a	15 59				16 50		17 34			17 53							18 49			20 07				
Slough 3	a																								
London Paddington 15 ⊖	a	16 32				17 21		18 08			18 23							19 22			20 37				

A from Reading ⊘ to Reading

B ◇ from Exeter St Davids ■ to Exeter St Davids

For connections to Oxford, Gatwick Airport and Heathrow Airport please refer to Tables 116, 148 and 125A

Table 135

Saturdays until 23 June

Cornwall and Devon - Birmingham and London

Route Diagram - see first Page of Table 135

		GW	XC	GW	XC	GW	GW	GW		GW	GW	GW	GW	GW	GW	GW	GW	GW		XC	GW	GW	XC	GW
			◇1	◇1	◇1						■1		◇1							◇1			◇1	
Penzance	d			15 52	16 25	16 44							17 40	18 50				19 06					21 32	
St Erth	d			16 02	16 35	16 54							17 50	18a58				19 15					21 42	
Hayle	d					16 58							17 54					19 18						
Camborne	d			16 13	16 46	17 09							18 04					19 27					21 53	
Redruth	d			16 20	16 53	17 16							18 11					19 33					22 00	
Truro	d			16 33	17 06	17 29							18 24					19 44					22 13	
St Austell	d			16 51	17 23	17 46							18 41					20 01					22 30	
Newquay	d										17 20									19 55		21 21		
Par	d			16 59		17 54					18 22		18 49		19 00			20 09				22 09	22 38	
Lostwithiel	d			17 06		18 02									19 07			20 15				22 18		
Bodmin Parkway	d			17 13	17 40	18 08					18 34		19 01		19 13			20 21		21 07		22 24	22 49	
Liskeard 6	d			17 26	17 53	18 21					18 47		19 14		19 26			20 34		21 20	21 53	22 37	23 02	
Menheniot	d																	20x39				22x41		
St Germans	d					18 33									19 37			20 47				22 49		
Saltash	d					18 40									19 44			20 54				22 55		
St Budeaux Ferry Road	d																	20 58				22 59		
Keyham	d																	21 00				23 01		
Dockyard	d																	21x02				23x03		
Devonport	d																	21 04				23 05		
Plymouth	a			17 51	18 19	18 50					19 14		19 39		19 55			21 10		21 47	22 18	23 12	23 27	
	d	17 38		17 54	18 23			18 56			19 18		19 42					21 15						
Ivybridge	d	17 53						19 13										21 30						
Totnes	d	18 07		18 21	18 49			19 27					20 09					21 44						
Paignton	d		18 05				18 53			19 21		19 50				20 13	21 13							21 53
Torquay	d		18 12				18 58			19 26		19 55				20 18	21 18							21 58
Torre	d						19 01			19 29						20 21	21 21							22 01
Newton Abbot	a	18 19	18 22	18 32	19 01		19 10	19 39		19 38	19 53	20 05	20 20			20 29	21 29	21 56						22 09
	d	18 19	18 23	18 34	19 03		19 12	19 40		19 44	19 55	20 07	20 22			20 31	21 31	21 56						22 11
Teignmouth	d	18 26					19 19	19 47		19 51		20 14				20 38	21 38	22 03						22 18
Dawlish	d	18 31					19 24	19 53		19 56		20 19				20 43	21 43	22 08						22 23
Dawlish Warren	d	18 47					19 29			20 06		20 24				20 48	21 48							22 28
Starcross	d						19 33			20 10						20 52	21 52							22 32
Exeter St Thomas	d						19 42			20 20						21 01	22 01							22 41
Exeter St Davids 6	a	18 59	18 48	18 54	19 23		19 45	20 06		20 25	20 14	20 36	20 42			21 05	22 05	22 22						22 45
Exeter Central	a									20 33														
Exmouth	a									21 01														
Exeter St Davids 6	d		18 50	18 56	19 25						20 16		20 44											
Tiverton Parkway	d		19 04	19 11	19 39								20 59											
Taunton	d		19 18	19 26	19 54						20 42		21 14											
Bridgwater	a																							
Weston-super-Mare	a																							
Bristol Temple Meads 10	a		19 54		20 26								21 47											
Bath Spa 7	a												22 01											
Filton Abbey Wood	a																							
Bristol Parkway 7	a		20 08		20 38																			
Swindon	a												22 29											
Newport (South Wales)	a																							
Cardiff Central 7	a																							
Birmingham New Street 12	a		21 38		21 52																			
Castle Cary	d			19 47																				
Westbury	d			20 06																				
Pewsey	d			20 23																				
Hungerford	a																							
Newbury	a																							
Thatcham	a																							
Theale	a																							
Reading 7	a			20 58							21 59		23 04											
Slough 3	a																							
London Paddington 15 ⊖	a			21 32							22 26		23 36											

For connections to Oxford, Gatwick Airport and Heathrow Airport please refer to Tables 116, 148 and 125A

Table 135

Saturdays

30 June to 8 September

Cornwall and Devon - Birmingham and London

Route Diagram - see first Page of Table 135

Station		GW	GW	XC	GW	GW	XC	GW	GW	GW	XC	GW	XC	GW	GW	XC	GW	GW	GW	GW	XC	GW	XC
			■ A	◇■			◇■	◇■			◇■	◇■	◇■		◇■ B	◇■		◇■ C			◇■ D		◇■
Penzance	d		21p45	22p08	05 20											05 37				06 30	06 41	
St Erth	d		21p55	22p16												05 45				06 38	06a49	
Hayle	d			22p20												05 48				06 41		
Camborne	d		22p07	22p30	05 37											05 58				06 51		
Redruth	d		22p14	22p36	05 43											06 04				06 57		
Truro	d		22p27	22p48	05a55											06 15				07 09		
St Austell	d		22p45	23p04												06 32				07 25		
Newquay	d																						
Par	d		22p54	23p12												06 39				07 32		
Lostwithiel	d			23p19												06 46				07 39		
Bodmin Parkway	d		23p06	23p26												06 52				07 46		
Liskeard	d		23p21	23p39												07 07				07 58		
Menheniot	d																07x11						
St Germans	d																07 19						
Saltash	d																07 26						
St Budeaux Ferry Road	d																07 30						
Keyham	d																07 32						
Dockyard	d																07x34						
Devonport	d																07 36						
Plymouth	a		23p45	00 04												07 42				08 22		
	d		23p51				05 25	05 40			06 25				06 55	07 25		07 47		08 06	08 25		08 38
Ivybridge	d																			08 21			
Totnes	d		00 20				05 50	06 07			06 50					07 50		08 14		08 35	08 50		09 03
Paignton	d	23p41							06 13	06 34			07 02	07 11					08 06				
Torquay	d	23p46							06 18	06 39			07 08	07 16					08 11				
Torre	d	23p49							06 21	06 42				07 19					08 14				
Newton Abbot	a	23p57	00 32				06 01	06 18	06 29	06 50	07 01		07 18	07 27	07 30	08 01		08 26	08 22	08 47	09 01		09 14
	d	23p59	00 33				06 03	06 20	06 31	06 52	07 03		07 19		07 32	08 03		08 27	08 34	08 48	09 03		09 16
Teignmouth	d	00 06							06 38	06 59			07 26						08 41	08 55			
Dawlish	d	00 11							06 43	07 04			07 31						08 46	09 00			
Dawlish Warren	d	00 16							06 48	07 15									08 51				09 28
Starcross	d	00 20							06 52	07 19									08 55				
Exeter St Thomas	d	00 29							07 01	07 28									09 04				
Exeter St Davids	a	00 34	00 55				06 21	06 40	07 06	07 33	07 21		07 43		07 52	08 21		08 47	09 09	09 16	09 21		09 39
Exeter Central	a								07 14	07 39									09 21				
Exmouth	a								07 43	08 18									09 50				
Exeter St Davids	d		01 06			06 00	06 23	06 41			07 23	07 29	07 45		07 54	08 23		08 49			09 23		09 41
Tiverton Parkway	d					06 18	06 37	06 56			07 37	07 44	07 58		08 09	08 37		09 04			09 37		09 54
Taunton	d		01 36			06 35	06 51	07 11			07 51	07 59	08 13		08 24	08 51		09 19			09 51		10 09
Bridgwater	a					06 47						08 09										
Weston-super-Mare	a					07 06						08 27										10 32
Bristol Temple Meads	a					07 42	07 24				08 23	08 57	08 48			09 25					10 25		10 52
Bath Spa	a											09 11										
Filton Abbey Wood	a					07 58																
Bristol Parkway	a					08 05	07 38				08 38		09 08			09 38					10 38		11 08
Swindon	a											09 40										
Newport (South Wales)	a																						
Cardiff Central	a																						
Birmingham New Street	a						08 56				09 56		10 26			10 56					11 56		12 26
Castle Cary	d							07 33										09 40				
Westbury	d							07 56										09 59				
Pewsey	d							08 13										10 16				
Hungerford	a																						
Newbury	a							08 33														
Thatcham	a																						
Theale	a																						
Reading	a		04s00					08 52				10 11			09 39			10 51					
Slough	a																						
London Paddington ⊖	a		05 13					09 21				10 39			10 11			11 24					

A The Night Riviera
B ⊏⊐ from Reading ⊘ to Reading
C ⊏⊐ from Castle Cary ⊘ to Castle Cary
D ⊤ from Plymouth

For connections to Oxford, Gatwick Airport and Heathrow Airport please refer to Tables 116, 148 and 125A

Table 135

Saturdays

30 June to 8 September

Cornwall and Devon - Birmingham and London

Route Diagram - see first Page of Table 135

Station		GW	GW	GW	GW	XC	GW	XC	GW	XC	GW	GW	GW	GW	XC	GW	GW	XC	GW	GW	GW	GW	GW
		■		◇■		◇■	■	◇■		◇■ A	■				◇■ A		■	◇■				◇■ B	■ C
Penzance	d	06 50					07 18			08 28	08 39	08 54					09 54						11 00
St Erth	d	07 00					07 29			08 36	08 50	09a02					10 05						11 11
Hayle	d						07 34				08 55						10 10						11 16
Camborne	d	07 11					07 44			08 46	09 06						10 20						11 26
Redruth	d	07 18					07 51			08 52	09 13						10 27						11 33
Truro	d	07 31					08 05			09 04	09 26						10 40						11 46
St Austell	d	07 48					08 22			09 20	09 44						10 58						12 04
Newquay	d														09 27								
Par	d	07 56					08 30			09 28	09 51				10 26		11 06			11 31			
Lostwithiel	d	08 04					08 38													11 38			
Bodmin Parkway	d	08 10					08 44			09 39	10 02				10 43		11 18			11 44			12 21
Liskeard	d	08 23					08 57			09 51	10 15				10 55		11 31			11 58			12 34
Menheniot	d																			12x02			
St Germans	d						09 09													12 09			
Saltash	d						09 17													12 15			
St Budeaux Ferry Road	d																						
Keyham	d																						
Dockyard	d																						
Devonport	d																						
Plymouth	a	08 49					09 26			10 18	10 40				11 19		11 56			12 27			12 58
	d	08 52				09 18	09 33			10 25	10 43				11 25		12 00			12 35			13 00
Ivybridge	d						09 48										12 15			12 50			
Totnes	d	09 19				09 43	10 02			10 50					11 50		12 29			13 04			13 28
Paignton	d		09 04	09 18	09 30			10 07	10 23				10 56	11 13		12 13		12 34	12 49		13 00	13 07	
Torquay	d		09 09	09 25	09 35			10 13	10 28				11 01	11 18		12 18		12 41	12 54		13 05	13 15	
Torre	d		09 12	09 29	09 38				10 31				11 04	11 21		12 21					13 08		
Newton Abbot	a	09 30	09 20	09 38	09 47	09 54	10 14	10 23	10 38	11 01			11 12	11 29	12 01	12 30	12 41	12 51	13 04	13 16	13 16	13 25	13 40
	d	09 32	09 35	09 39	09 48	09 56	10 15	10 24	10 41	11 03			11 23	11 41	12 03	12 32	12 42	12 53	13 06	13 16	13 21	13 26	13 42
Teignmouth	d		09 42	09 49	09 56	10 03		10 31	10 48				11 30	11 48		12 39		13 02	13 13		13 28	13 35	
Dawlish	d		09 47	09 57	10 02	10 09		10 36	10 53				11 35	11 53		12 44		13 09	13 18		13 33	13 43	
Dawlish Warren	d		09 52	10 02	10 07	10 14			10 58				11 40	11 58		12 55			13 23		13 38	13 55	
Starcross	d		09 56						11 02				11 44	12 02		12 59					13 42		
Exeter St Thomas	d		10 05						11 11				11 53	12 11		13 08					13 51		
Exeter St Davids	a	09 52	10 10	10 13	10 18	10 24	10 35	10 48	11 15	11 21	11 37		11 58	12 16	12 21	13 13	13 02	13 22	13 35	13 38	13 59	14 08	14 02
Exeter Central	a		10 21						11 21					12 21		13 21					14 21		
Exmouth	a		10 50						11 50					12 50		13 50					14 50		
Exeter St Davids	d	09 54		10 15		10 26	10 38	10 50		11 23	11 40				12 23		13 05	13 24				14 11	14 05
Tiverton Parkway	d	10 09		10 30		10 40		11 03		11 37					12 37		13 20	13 39					
Taunton	d	10 24		10 45		10 54	11 03	11 18		11 51					12 51		13 35	13 53				14 44	14 30
Bridgwater	a																						
Weston-super-Mare	a																						
Bristol Temple Meads	a			11 24		11 25		11 54		12 24					13 23			14 26					
Bath Spa	a			11 41																		
Filton Abbey Wood	a																						
Bristol Parkway	a					11 38		12 08		12 38					13 38			14 38					
Swindon	a			12 09																		
Newport (South Wales)	a																						
Cardiff Central	a																						
Birmingham New Street	a					12 56		13 26		13 56					14 56			15 55					
Castle Cary	d						11 24															15 08	
Westbury	d	11 02					11 45															15 28	
Pewsey	d						12 01															15 45	
Hungerford	a																						
Newbury	a																						16 05	
Thatcham	a																						
Theale	a																						
Reading	a	11 51		12 45			12 40				13 17						14 52					16 25	15 51
Slough	a																						
London Paddington ⊖	a	12 23		13 13			13 09				13 46						15 23					17 02	16 23

A ⊤ from Plymouth
B ◇ from Exeter St Davids ■ to Exeter St Davids
C ⊏⊐ to Plymouth ⊏⊐ from Reading ⊘ from Plymouth to Reading

For connections to Oxford, Gatwick Airport and Heathrow Airport please refer to Tables 116, 148 and 125A

Table 135

Saturdays

30 June to 8 September

Cornwall and Devon - Birmingham and London

Route Diagram - see first Page of Table 135

		GW		XC	XC	GW	GW	GW	XC	GW	GW	GW		XC	GW	GW	GW	GW	GW	XC	GW	GW		XC	GW
		■ 1 ⌐		◇1 ⌶	◇1 ⌶	■ 1 A ⌐⊘		◇1 B ⌐	◇1 ⌶		■ 1 ⌐	◇		◇1 ⌶				◇1 ⌐	◇	◇1 ⌶	◇1 ⌐			◇1 ⌶	
Penzance	d					11 58						13 00						14 01	14 52						
St Erth	d					12 09						13 09						14 11	15 01						
Hayle	d					12 14						13 12							15 04						
Camborne	d					12 24						13 21						14 22	15 14						
Redruth	d					12 31						13 27						14 29	15 20						
Truro	d					12 44						13 38						14 42	15 31						
St Austell	d					13 02						13 55						14 59	15 48						
Newquay	d	11 21									13 14													15 25	
Par	d	12 26									14 16	14 25						15 07	15 55						
Lostwithiel	d											14 31							16 02						
Bodmin Parkway	d					13 19						14 37						15 19	16 08					16 37	
Liskeard 6	d					13 32						14 50						15 33	16 21					16 51	
Menheniot	d																		16x25						
St Germans	d											15 01							16 33						
Saltash	d											15 09							16 39						
St Budeaux Ferry Road	d																								
Keyham	d																								
Dockyard	d																								
Devonport	d											15 15													
Plymouth	a	13 10				13 56					15 00	15 20						15 58	16 51					17 15	
	d	13 14		13 25		14 00			14 25		15 07			15 25		15 32		16 01						17 25	
Ivybridge	d															15 47									
Totnes	d			13 50					14 50					15 50		16 01		16 28						17 50	
Paignton	d				13 53		14 13	14 31		15 13					15 43		16 13			16 36	17 03	17 13			17 52
Torquay	d				13 59		14 18	14 38		15 18					15 48		16 18			16 43	17 10	17 19			17 57
Torre	d						14 21			15 21							16 21					17 22			18 00
Newton Abbot	a			14 01	14 09	14 35	14 29	14 48	15 01	15 29	15 42			16 01	15 58	16 13	16 29	16 41		16 54	17 21	17 30		18 01	18 08
	d			14 03	14 10	14 36	14 40	14 50	15 03	15 34	15 44			16 03	16 09		16 31	16 41		16 55	17 22	17 41		18 03	18 10
Teignmouth	d				14 17		14 48	14 58		15 42					16 16		16 39			17 03	17 30	17 49			18 18
Dawlish	d				14 22		14 53	15 04		15 48					16 21		16 44			17 10	17 37	17 54			18 23
Dawlish Warren	d						14 57	15 17		15 58							16 55				17 42	17 59			18 28
Starcross	d						15 01			16 02							16 59					18 04			18 33
Exeter St Thomas	d						15 11			16 12							17 09					18 13			18 42
Exeter St Davids 6	a	14 15		14 21	14 34	14 56	15 15	15 28	15 21	16 15	16 04			16 21	16 34		17 15	17 01		17 23	17 56	18 18		18 21	18 47
Exeter Central	a						15 21			16 21					16 44		17 21					18 23			18 53
Exmouth	a						15 50			16 50							17 50					18 52			19 22
Exeter St Davids 6	d	14 18		14 23	14 36	14 59		15 32	15 23		16 06			16 23				17 03		17 25	18 02			18 23	
Tiverton Parkway	d			14 37	14 49	15 14			15 37		16 21			16 37				17 17		17 39	18 17			18 37	
Taunton	d			14 52	15 04	15 29		15 57	15 51		16 36			16 51				17 32		17 54	18 32			18 51	
Bridgwater	a																								
Weston-super-Mare	a				15 23																				
Bristol Temple Meads 10	a			15 24	15 49				16 24					17 25						18 24				19 22	
Bath Spa 7	a																								
Filton Abbey Wood	a																								
Bristol Parkway 7	a			15 38	16 08				16 38					17 38						18 38				19 38	
Swindon	a																								
Newport (South Wales)	a																								
Cardiff Central 7	a																								
Birmingham New Street 12	a			16 56	17 26				17 56					18 56						19 58				20 54	
Castle Cary	d					15 50		16 19													18 53				
Westbury	d							16 38													19 12				
Pewsey	d							16 54																	
Hungerford	a																								
Newbury	a																				19 45				
Thatcham	a																								
Theale	a																								
Reading 7	a	15 59				16 50		17 34			17 53							18 49			20 07				
Slough 3	a																								
London Paddington 15 ⊖	a	16 32				17 21		18 08			18 23							19 22			20 37				

A ⌐ from Reading ⊘ to Reading

B ◇ from Exeter St Davids ■ to Exeter St Davids

For connections to Oxford, Gatwick Airport and Heathrow Airport please refer to Tables 116, 148 and 125A

Table 135

Saturdays

30 June to 8 September

Cornwall and Devon - Birmingham and London

Route Diagram - see first Page of Table 135

		GW	XC	GW	XC	GW	GW	GW		GW	GW	GW	GW	GW	GW	GW	GW	GW		XC	GW	GW	XC	GW
			◇1	◇1 ⌐	◇1 ⌶						■ 1 ⌐		◇1 ⌐							◇1			◇1	
Penzance	d			15 52	16 25	16 44							17 40	18 50				19 06					21 32	
St Erth	d			16 02	16 35	16 54							17 50	18a58				19 15					21 42	
Hayle	d					16 58							17 54					19 18						
Camborne	d			16 13	16 46	17 09							18 04					19 27					21 53	
Redruth	d			16 20	16 53	17 16							18 11					19 33					22 00	
Truro	d			16 33	17 06	17 29							18 24					19 44					22 13	
St Austell	d			16 51	17 23	17 46							18 41					20 01					22 30	
Newquay	d										17 20									19 55		21 21		
Par	d			16 59		17 54					18 22		18 49		19 00			20 09				22 09	22 38	
Lostwithiel	d			17 06		18 02									19 07			20 15				22 18		
Bodmin Parkway	d			17 13	17 40	18 08					18 34		19 01		19 13			20 21		21 07		22 24	22 49	
Liskeard 6	d			17 26	17 53	18 21					18 47		19 14		19 26			20 34		21 20	21 53	22 37	23 02	
Menheniot	d																	20x39				22x41		
St Germans	d					18 33									19 37			20 47				22 49		
Saltash	d					18 40									19 44			20 54				22 55		
St Budeaux Ferry Road	d																	20 58				22 59		
Keyham	d																	21 00				23 01		
Dockyard	d																	21x02				23x03		
Devonport	d																	21 04				23 05		
Plymouth	a			17 51	18 19	18 50					19 14		19 39		19 55			21 10		21 47	22 18	23 12	23 27	
	d	17 38		17 54	18 23			18 56			19 18		19 42					21 15						
Ivybridge	d	17 53						19 13										21 30						
Totnes	d	18 07		18 21	18 49			19 27					20 09					21 44						
Paignton	d		18 05				18 53			19 21		19 50				20 13	21 13							21 53
Torquay	d		18 12				18 58			19 26		19 55				20 18	21 18							21 58
Torre	d						19 01			19 29						20 21	21 21							22 01
Newton Abbot	a	18 19	18 22	18 32	19 01		19 10	19 39		19 38	19 53	20 05	20 20			20 29	21 29	21 56						22 09
	d	18 19	18 23	18 34	19 03		19 12	19 40		19 44	19 55	20 07	20 22			20 31	21 31	21 56						22 11
Teignmouth	d	18 26					19 19	19 47		19 51		20 14				20 38	21 38	22 03						22 18
Dawlish	d	18 31					19 24	19 53		19 56		20 19				20 43	21 43	22 08						22 23
Dawlish Warren	d	18 47					19 29			20 06		20 24				20 48	21 48							22 28
Starcross	d						19 33			20 10						20 52	21 52							22 32
Exeter St Thomas	d						19 42			20 20						21 01	22 01							22 41
Exeter St Davids 6	a	18 59	18 48	18 54	19 23		19 45	20 06		20 25	20 14	20 36	20 42			21 05	22 05	22 22						22 45
Exeter Central	a									20 33														
Exmouth	a									21 01														
Exeter St Davids 6	d		18 50	18 56	19 25						20 16		20 44											
Tiverton Parkway	d		19 04	19 11	19 39								20 59											
Taunton	d		19 18	19 26	19 54						20 42		21 14											
Bridgwater	a																							
Weston-super-Mare	a																							
Bristol Temple Meads 10	a		19 54		20 26								21 47											
Bath Spa 7	a												22 01											
Filton Abbey Wood	a																							
Bristol Parkway 7	a		20 08		20 38																			
Swindon	a												22 29											
Newport (South Wales)	a																							
Cardiff Central 7	a																							
Birmingham New Street 12	a		21 38		21 52																			
Castle Cary	d			19 47																				
Westbury	d			20 06																				
Pewsey	d			20 23																				
Hungerford	a																							
Newbury	a																							
Thatcham	a																							
Theale	a																							
Reading 7	a			20 58							21 59		23 04											
Slough 3	a																							
London Paddington 15 ⊖	a			21 32							22 26		23 36											

For connections to Oxford, Gatwick Airport and Heathrow Airport please refer to Tables 116, 148 and 125A

Cornwall and Devon - Birmingham and London

15 September to 20 October

Route Diagram - see first Page of Table 135

		GW	GW	XC	GW	GW	XC	GW	GW	GW	XC	GW	XC	GW	GW	XC	GW	GW	GW	GW	XC	GW	GW
			■ A 🛏 ⊏	◇■			◇■ ⌶	◇■ ⊏			◇■ ⌶	◇■ ⊏	◇■ ⌶		◇■ B ⊏⊘	◇■ ⌶		◇■ C ⊏⊘			◇■ D ⌶		■ ■ ⊏
Penzance	d		21p45	22p08	05 20												05 37				06 30	06 41	06 50
St Erth	d		21p55	22p16													05 45				06 38	06a49	07 00
Hayle	d			22p20													05 48				06 41		
Camborne	d		22p07	22p30	05 37												05 58				06 51		07 11
Redruth	d		22p14	22p36	05 43												06 04				06 57		07 18
Truro	d		22p27	22p48	05a55												06 15				07 09		07 31
St Austell	d		22p45	23p04													06 32				07 25		07 48
Newquay	d																						
Par	d		22p54	23p12													06 39				07 32		07 56
Lostwithiel	d			23p19													06 46				07 39		08 04
Bodmin Parkway	d		23p06	23p26													06 52				07 46		08 10
Liskeard ■	d		23p21	23p39													07 07				07 58		08 23
Menheniot	d																07x11						
St Germans	d																07 19						
Saltash	d																07 26						
St Budeaux Ferry Road	d																07 30						
Keyham	d																07 32						
Dockyard	d																07x34						
Devonport	d																07 36						
Plymouth	a		23p45	00 04													07 42				08 22		08 49
	d		23p51				05 25	05 40			06 25				06 55	07 25		07 47		08 06	08 25		08 52
Ivybridge	d																			08 21			
Totnes	d		00 20				05 50	06 07			06 50					07 50		08 14		08 35	08 50		09 19
Paignton	d	23p41							06 13	06 34			07 02	07 11					08 06				
Torquay	d	23p46							06 18	06 39			07 08	07 16					08 11				
Torre	d	23p49							06 21	06 42				07 19					08 14				
Newton Abbot	a	23p57	00 32				06 01	06 18	06 29	06 50	07 01		07 18	07 27	07 30	08 01		08 26	08 22	08 47	09 01		09 30
	d	23p59	00 33				06 03	06 20	06 31	06 52	07 03		07 19		07 32	08 03		08 27	08 34	08 48	09 03		09 32
Teignmouth	d	00 06							06 38	06 59			07 26						08 41	08 55			
Dawlish	d	00 11							06 43	07 04			07 31						08 46	09 00			
Dawlish Warren	d	00 16							06 48	07 15									08 51				
Starcross	d	00 20							06 52	07 19									08 55				
Exeter St Thomas	d	00 29							07 01	07 28									09 04				
Exeter St Davids ■	a	00 34	00 55				06 21	06 40	07 06	07 33	07 21		07 43		07 52	08 21		08 47	09 09	09 16	09 21		09 52
Exeter Central	a								07 14	07 39									09 21				
Exmouth	a								07 43	08 18									09 50				
Exeter St Davids ■	d		01 06			06 00	06 23	06 41			07 23	07 29	07 45		07 54	08 23		08 49			09 23		09 54
Tiverton Parkway	d					06 18	06 37	06 56			07 37	07 44	07 58		08 09	08 37		09 04			09 37		10 09
Taunton	d		01 36			06 35	06 51	07 11			07 51	07 59	08 13		08 24	08 51		09 19			09 51		10 24
Bridgwater	a					06 47						08 09											
Weston-super-Mare	a					07 06						08 27											
Bristol Temple Meads ■	a					07 42	07 24				08 23	08 57	08 48			09 25					10 25		
Bath Spa ■	a											09 11											
Filton Abbey Wood	a					07 58																	
Bristol Parkway ■	a					08 05	07 38				08 38		09 08			09 38					10 38		
Swindon	a											09 40											
Newport (South Wales)	a																						
Cardiff Central ■	a																						
Birmingham New Street ■	a						08 56				09 56		10 26			10 56					11 56		
Castle Cary	d							07 33										09 40					
Westbury	d							07 56										09 59					11 02
Pewsey	d							08 13										10 16					
Hungerford	a																						
Newbury	a							08 33															
Thatcham	a																						
Theale	a																						
Reading ■	a		04s00					08 52				10 11			09 39			10 51					11 51
Slough ■	a																						
London Paddington ■ ⊖	a		05 13					09 21				10 39			10 11			11 24					12 23

A The Night Riviera
B ⊏ from Reading ⊘ to Reading
C ⊏ from Castle Cary ⊘ to Castle Cary
D ⌶ from Plymouth

For connections to Oxford, Gatwick Airport and Heathrow Airport please refer to Tables 116, 148 and 125A

Cornwall and Devon - Birmingham and London

15 September to 20 October

Route Diagram - see first Page of Table 135

		GW	GW	GW	GW	XC	GW	XC	GW	GW	XC	GW	GW	GW	GW	GW	XC	XC	GW	GW	GW	XC	GW
		◇		◇■ ⊏		◇■ ⌶		◇■ ⌶	◇■ ⊏		◇■ A ⌶	◇■ ⊏				◇■ ⊏	◇■ ⌶	◇■ ⌶	◇		◇■ ⊏	◇■ ⌶	
Penzance	d						07 35		07 59		08 28	08 45	08 54					09 43			10 00		10 36
St Erth	d						07 48		08 09		08 36	08 55	09a02					09 51			10 10		10 45
Hayle	d						07 52		08 13														10 48
Camborne	d						08 02		08 23		08 46	09 06						10 01			10 21		10 58
Redruth	d						08 09		08 30		08 52	09 13						10 07			10 28		11 04
Truro	d						08 20		08 43		09 04	09 26						10 19			10 41		11 15
St Austell	d						08 36		09 01		09 20	09 43						10 35			10 58		11 32
Newquay	d	07 48																	10 12				
Par	d	08a39					08 44		09 09		09 28	09 51						10 42	11a01		11 07		11 39
Lostwithiel	d						08 51											10 49					11 46
Bodmin Parkway	d						08 57		09 20		09 39	10 03						10 56			11 18		11 52
Liskeard ■	d						09 10		09 33		09 51	10 16						11 09			11 31		12 06
Menheniot	d																						12x10
St Germans	d						09 22																12 17
Saltash	d						09 29																12 23
St Budeaux Ferry Road	d																						
Keyham	d																						
Dockyard	d																						
Devonport	d																						
Plymouth	a						09 40		09 59		10 18	10 40						11 33			11 59		12 36
	d					09 25			10 02		10 25	10 44					11 25	11 48			12 00	12 23	
Ivybridge	d								10 17												12 15		
Totnes	d					09 50			10 31		10 50						11 50	12 13			12 29	12 49	
Paignton	d		09 04	09 18	09 30			10 07		10 23				10 56	11 13					12 13			
Torquay	d		09 09	09 25	09 35			10 13		10 28				11 01	11 18					12 18			
Torre	d		09 12	09 29	09 38					10 31				11 04	11 21					12 21			
Newton Abbot	a		09 20	09 38	09 47	10 01		10 23	10 43	10 38	11 01			11 12	11 29		12 01	12 24		12 30	12 41	13 01	
	d		09 35	09 39	09 48	10 03		10 24	10 44	10 47	11 03			11 23	11 41		12 03	12 25		12 32	12 42	13 03	
Teignmouth	d		09 42	09 49	09 56			10 31		10 55				11 30	11 48					12 39			
Dawlish	d		09 47	09 57	10 02			10 36		11 00				11 35	11 53					12 44			
Dawlish Warren	d		09 52	10 02	10 07					11 04				11 40	11 58					12 55			
Starcross	d		09 56											11 44	12 02					12 59			
Exeter St Thomas	d		10 05											11 53	12 11					13 08			
Exeter St Davids ■	a		10 10	10 13	10 18	10 21		10 48	11 04	11 16	11 21	11 38		11 58	12 16		12 21	12 44		13 13	13 02	13 23	
Exeter Central	a		10 21							11 21					12 21					13 21			
Exmouth	a		10 50							11 50					12 50					13 50			
Exeter St Davids ■	d			10 15		10 23		10 50	11 06		11 23	11 40				11 54	12 23	12 48			13 04	13 25	
Tiverton Parkway	d			10 30		10 37		11 03	11 21		11 37					12 09	12 37	13 02			13 19	13 39	
Taunton	d			10 45		10 51		11 18	11 36		11 51					12 24	12 51	13 16			13 34	13 54	
Bridgwater	a																						
Weston-super-Mare	a																						
Bristol Temple Meads ■	a			11 24		11 25		11 54			12 24						13 23	13 55				14 26	
Bath Spa ■	a			11 41																			
Filton Abbey Wood	a																						
Bristol Parkway ■	a					11 38		12 08			12 38						13 38	14 08				14 38	
Swindon	a			12 09																			
Newport (South Wales)	a																						
Cardiff Central ■	a																						
Birmingham New Street ■	a					12 56		13 26			13 56						14 56	15 26				15 55	
Castle Cary	d															12 45							
Westbury	d															13 05							
Pewsey	d															13 22							
Hungerford	a															13 39							
Newbury	a															13 49							
Thatcham	a															13 56							
Theale	a															14 05							
Reading ■	a			12 44					12 52			13 17				14 19					14 51		
Slough ■	a																						
London Paddington ■ ⊖	a			13 12					13 21			13 46				14 45					15 22		

A ⌶ from Plymouth

For connections to Oxford, Gatwick Airport and Heathrow Airport please refer to Tables 116, 148 and 125A

Table 135

Saturdays

15 September to 20 October

Cornwall and Devon - Birmingham and London

Route Diagram - see first Page of Table 135

		GW		GW ◇1 A ▭⊘	GW	XC ◇1 ⌶	GW ◇	GW ◇	XC ◇1 ⌶	GW ◇1 ▭	GW ◇1 B ▭⊘	GW		XC ◇1 ⌶	GW ◇	GW	GW ◇1 ▭	XC ◇1 ⌶	GW	GW	GW	XC ◇1 ⌶		GW ◇1 ▭	GW ◇
Penzance	d			10 58			11 46								13 00									14 01	
St Erth	d			11 08			11 56								13 09									14 11	
Hayle	d						12 00								13 12										
Camborne	d			11 19			12 10								13 21									14 22	
Redruth	d			11 26			12 16								13 27									14 29	
Truro	d			11 39			12 29								13 38									14 42	
St Austell	d			11 56			12 47								13 55									14 59	
Newquay	d							13 09																	14 59
Par	d						12 55	13a59							14 03									15 07	15a48
Lostwithiel	d						13 02								14 09										
Bodmin Parkway	d			12 13			13 09								14 15									15 19	
Liskeard 6	d			12 26			13 23								14 28									15 33	
Menheniot	d						13x28																		
St Germans	d						13 36								14 39										
Saltash	d						13 45								14 47										
St Budeaux Ferry Road	d																								
Keyham	d																								
Dockyard	d																								
Devonport	d														14 52										
Plymouth	a			12 52			13 55								14 58									15 58	
	d			12 54		13 25					14 00			14 25			15 04	15 25		15 32				16 01	
Ivybridge	d																			15 47					
Totnes	d			13 21		13 50								14 50			15 31	15 50		16 01				16 28	
Paignton	d	12 43			13 13				13 53			14 13				15 13			15 43		16 13				
Torquay	d	12 48			13 18				13 59			14 18				15 18			15 48		16 18				
Torre	d				13 21							14 21				15 21					16 21				
Newton Abbot	a	12 58		13 34	13 29	14 01			14 09		14 35	14 29		15 01		15 29	15 42	16 01	15 58	16 13	16 29			16 41	
	d	13 06		13 35	13 41	14 03			14 10		14 36	14 40		15 03		15 34	15 44	16 03	16 09		16 31			16 41	
Teignmouth	d	13 13			13 48				14 17			14 48				15 42			16 16		16 38				
Dawlish	d	13 18			13 53				14 22			14 53				15 47			16 21		16 43				
Dawlish Warren	d	13 23			13 58							14 57				15 58					16 55				
Starcross	d				14 02							15 01				16 02					16 59				
Exeter St Thomas	d				14 11							15 11				16 12					17 08				
Exeter St Davids 6	a	13 35		13 55	14 16	14 21			14 34		14 56	15 15		15 21		16 15	16 04	16 21	16 34		17 15			17 01	
Exeter Central	a				14 21							15 21				16 21			16 44		17 21				
Exmouth	a				14 50							15 50				16 50					17 50				
Exeter St Davids 6	d			13 57		14 24			14 36		14 58			15 23			16 06	16 23				16 53		17 03	
Tiverton Parkway	d					14 37			14 49		15 13			15 37			16 21	16 37				17 07		17 17	
Taunton	d			14 23		14 52			15 04	15 19	15 28			15 51			16 36	16 51				17 21		17 32	
Bridgwater	a																								
Weston-super-Mare	a								15 23																
Bristol Temple Meads 10	a					15 24			15 49					16 24				17 25				17 53			
Bath Spa 7	a																								
Filton Abbey Wood	a																								
Bristol Parkway 7	a					15 38			16 08					16 38				17 38				18 08			
Swindon	a																								
Newport (South Wales)	a																								
Cardiff Central 7	a																								
Birmingham New Street 12	a					16 56			17 26					17 56				18 56				19 26			
Castle Cary	d			14 44							15 49														
Westbury	d			15 03						16 07															
Pewsey	d									16 25															
Hungerford	a									16 41															
Newbury	a									16 52															
Thatcham	a									16 58															
Theale	a									17 07															
Reading 7	a			15 51						17 17	16 50						17 53							18 49	
Slough 3	a																								
London Paddington 15 ⊖	a			16 23						17 51	17 21						18 21							19 22	

A ▭ to Plymouth ▭ from Reading ⊘ from Plymouth to Reading

B ▭ from Reading ⊘ to Reading

For connections to Oxford, Gatwick Airport and Heathrow Airport please refer to Tables 116, 148 and 125A

Table 135

Saturdays

15 September to 20 October

Cornwall and Devon - Birmingham and London

Route Diagram - see first Page of Table 135

		XC ◇1 ⌶	GW ◇	GW ◇1 ▭	GW	XC ◇1 ⌶	GW	GW		GW ◇1 ▭	XC ◇1 ⌶	GW	GW	GW ◇	GW	GW	GW ◇1 ▭	GW		GW	GW	GW 1	GW	GW	GW
Penzance	d		14 52							15 52			16 41				17 40	18 50						19 06	
St Erth	d		15 01							16 02			16 51				17 50	18a58						19 15	
Hayle	d		15 04										16 55				17 54							19 18	
Camborne	d		15 14							16 13			17 05				18 04							19 27	
Redruth	d		15 20							16 20			17 12				18 11							19 33	
Truro	d		15 31							16 33			17 25				18 24							19 44	
St Austell	d		15 48							16 51			17 43				18 41							20 01	
Newquay	d													17 21						19 17					21 18
Par	d		15 55							16 59			17 51	18a10			18 49			20a03				20 09	22 09
Lostwithiel	d		16 02							17 06			17 58											20 15	22 18
Bodmin Parkway	d		16 08							17 13			18 05				19 01							20 21	22 24
Liskeard 6	d		16 21							17 26			18 19				19 14							20 34	22 37
Menheniot	d		16x25																					20x39	22x41
St Germans	d		16 33										18 31											20 47	22 49
Saltash	d		16 39										18 38											20 54	22 55
St Budeaux Ferry Road	d																							20 58	22 59
Keyham	d																							21 00	23 01
Dockyard	d																							21x02	23x03
Devonport	d																							21 04	23 05
Plymouth	a		16 51							17 51			18 49				19 39							21 10	23 12
	d	16 25		16 57		17 23		17 38		17 54	18 25		18 51				19 42							21 15	
Ivybridge	d			17 12				17 53					19 07											21 30	
Totnes	d	16 50		17 27		17 49		18 07		18 21	18 50		19 22				20 09							21 44	
Paignton	d				17 13		17 52					18 53			19 21	19 50					20 13	20 46	21 13		
Torquay	d				17 18		17 57					18 58			19 26	19 55					20 18	20 52	21 18		
Torre	d				17 21		18 00					19 01			19 29						20 21		21 21		
Newton Abbot	a	17 01		17 38	17 29	18 01	18 08	18 19		18 32	19 01	19 10	19 34		19 38	20 05	20 20				20 29	21 02	21 29	21 56	
	d	17 03		17 40	17 43	18 03	18 10	18 19		18 34	19 03	19 12	19 35		19 40	20 07	20 22				20 31	21 04	21 31	21 56	
Teignmouth	d				17 50		18 17	18 26				19 19	19 43		19 47	20 14					20 38		21 38	22 03	
Dawlish	d				17 55		18 22	18 31				19 24	19 48		19 52	20 19					20 43		21 43	22 08	
Dawlish Warren	d				18 00		18 27	18 47				19 29			20 06	20 24					20 48		21 48		
Starcross	d				18 04		18 31					19 33			20 10						20 52		21 52		
Exeter St Thomas	d				18 13		18 40					19 42			20 20						21 01		22 01		
Exeter St Davids 6	a	17 21		18 00	18 18	18 23	18 46	18 59		18 54	19 21	19 45	20 01		20 25	20 36	20 42				21 05	21 24	22 05	22 22	
Exeter Central	a				18 23		18 53								20 33										
Exmouth	a				18 52		19 22								21 01										
Exeter St Davids 6	d	17 23		18 02		18 25				18 56	19 23						20 44								
Tiverton Parkway	d	17 37		18 17		18 39				19 11	19 37						20 59								
Taunton	d	17 51		18 32		18 54				19 26	19 51						21 14								
Bridgwater	a																								
Weston-super-Mare	a																								
Bristol Temple Meads 10	a	18 25				19 26					20 25						21 47								
Bath Spa 7	a																22 01								
Filton Abbey Wood	a																								
Bristol Parkway 7	a	18 38				19 38					20 38														
Swindon	a																22 29								
Newport (South Wales)	a																								
Cardiff Central 7	a																								
Birmingham New Street 12	a	19 58				20 53					21 53														
Castle Cary	d			18 53						19 47															
Westbury	d			19 12						20 06															
Pewsey	d									20 23															
Hungerford	a																								
Newbury	a			19 45																					
Thatcham	a																								
Theale	a																								
Reading 7	a			20 07						20 58							23 04								
Slough 3	a																								
London Paddington 15 ⊖	a			20 37						21 32							23 36								

For connections to Oxford, Gatwick Airport and Heathrow Airport please refer to Tables 116, 148 and 125A

Table 135

Saturdays

15 September to 20 October

Cornwall and Devon - Birmingham and London

Route Diagram - see first Page of Table 135

		XC	GW
		◇1	
Penzance	d	21 32	
St Erth	d	21 42	
Hayle	d		
Camborne	d	21 53	
Redruth	d	22 00	
Truro	d	22 13	
St Austell	d	22 30	
Newquay	d		
Par	d	22 38	
Lostwithiel	d		
Bodmin Parkway	d	22 49	
Liskeard 6	d	23 02	
Menheniot	d		
St Germans	d		
Saltash	d		
St Budeaux Ferry Road	d		
Keyham	d		
Dockyard	d		
Devonport	d		
Plymouth	a	23 27	
	d		
Ivybridge	d		
Totnes	d		
Paignton	d		21 53
Torquay	d		21 58
Torre	d		22 01
Newton Abbot	a		22 09
	d		22 11
Teignmouth	d		22 18
Dawlish	d		22 23
Dawlish Warren	d		22 28
Starcross	d		22 32
Exeter St Thomas	d		22 41
Exeter St Davids 6	a		22 45
Exeter Central	a		
Exmouth	a		
Exeter St Davids 6	d		
Tiverton Parkway	d		
Taunton	d		
Bridgwater	a		
Weston-super-Mare	a		
Bristol Temple Meads 10	a		
Bath Spa 7	a		
Filton Abbey Wood	a		
Bristol Parkway 7	a		
Swindon	a		
Newport (South Wales)	a		
Cardiff Central 7	a		
Birmingham New Street 12	a		
Castle Cary	d		
Westbury	d		
Pewsey	d		
Hungerford	a		
Newbury	a		
Thatcham	a		
Theale	a		
Reading 7	a		
Slough 3	a		
London Paddington 15 ⊖	a		

For connections to Oxford, Gatwick Airport and Heathrow Airport please refer to Tables 116, 148 and 125A

Table 135

Saturdays

from 27 October

Cornwall and Devon - Birmingham and London

Route Diagram - see first Page of Table 135

		GW	GW	XC	GW	GW	XC	GW	GW	GW		XC	GW	XC	GW	GW	XC	GW	GW	GW		GW	XC	GW	GW
			A	◇1			◇1	◇1				◇1	◇1	◇1		◇1 B	◇1		◇1 C				◇1 D		1
			🛏 ☕				🛒	☕				🛒	☕	🛒		☕⊘	🛒		☕⊘				🛒		☕
Penzance	d		21p45	22p08	05 20													05 37					06 30	06 41	06 50
St Erth	d		21p55	22p16														05 45					06 38	06a49	07 00
Hayle	d			22p20														05 48					06 41		
Camborne	d		22p07	22p30	05 37													05 58					06 51		07 11
Redruth	d		22p14	22p36	05 43													06 04					06 57		07 18
Truro	d		22p27	22p48	05a55													06 15					07 09		07 31
St Austell	d		22p45	23p04														06 32					07 25		07 48
Newquay	d																								
Par	d		22p54	23p12														06 39					07 32		07 56
Lostwithiel	d			23p19														06 46					07 39		08 04
Bodmin Parkway	d		23p06	23p26														06 52					07 46		08 10
Liskeard 6	d		23p21	23p39														07 07					07 58		08 23
Menheniot	d																	07x11							
St Germans	d																	07 19							
Saltash	d																	07 26							
St Budeaux Ferry Road	d																	07 30							
Keyham	d																	07 32							
Dockyard	d																	07x34							
Devonport	d																	07 36							
Plymouth	a		23p45	00 04														07 42					08 22		08 49
	d		23p51				05 25	05 40				06 25				06 55	07 25		07 47			08 06	08 25		08 52
Ivybridge	d																					08 21			
Totnes	d		00 20				05 50	06 07				06 50					07 50		08 14			08 35	08 50		09 19
Paignton	d	23p41							06 13	06 34				07 02	07 11					08 06					
Torquay	d	23p46							06 18	06 39				07 08	07 16					08 11					
Torre	d	23p49							06 21	06 42					07 19					08 14					
Newton Abbot	a	23p57	00 32				06 01	06 18	06 29	06 50		07 01		07 18	07 27	07 30	08 01		08 26	08 22		08 47	09 01		09 30
	d	23p59	00 33				06 03	06 20	06 31	06 52		07 03		07 19		07 32	08 03		08 27	08 34		08 48	09 03		09 32
Teignmouth	d	00 06							06 38	06 59				07 26						08 41		08 55			
Dawlish	d	00 11							06 43	07 04				07 31						08 46		09 00			
Dawlish Warren	d	00 16							06 48	07 15										08 51					
Starcross	d	00 20							06 52	07 19										08 55					
Exeter St Thomas	d	00 29							07 01	07 28										09 04					
Exeter St Davids 6	a	00 34	00 55				06 21	06 40	07 06	07 33		07 21		07 43		07 52	08 21		08 47	09 09		09 16	09 21		09 52
Exeter Central	a								07 14	07 39										09 21					
Exmouth	a								07 43	08 18										09 50					
Exeter St Davids 6	d		01 06			06 00	06 23	06 41				07 23	07 29	07 45		07 54	08 23		08 49				09 23		09 54
Tiverton Parkway	d					06 18	06 37	06 56				07 37	07 44	07 58		08 09	08 37		09 04				09 37		10 09
Taunton	d		01 36			06 35	06 51	07 11				07 51	07 59	08 13		08 24	08 51		09 19				09 51		10 24
Bridgwater	a					06 47							08 09												
Weston-super-Mare	a					07 06							08 27												
Bristol Temple Meads 10	a					07 42	07 24					08 23	08 57	08 48			09 25						10 25		
Bath Spa 7	a												09 11												
Filton Abbey Wood	a					07 58																			
Bristol Parkway 7	a					08 05	07 38					08 38		09 08			09 38						10 38		
Swindon	a												09 40												
Newport (South Wales)	a																								
Cardiff Central 7	a																								
Birmingham New Street 12	a						08 56					09 56		10 26			10 56						11 56		
Castle Cary	d							07 33											09 40						
Westbury	d							07 56											09 59						11 02
Pewsey	d							08 13											10 16						
Hungerford	a																								
Newbury	a							08 33																	
Thatcham	a																								
Theale	a																								
Reading 7	a		04s00					08 52					10 11			09 39			10 51						11 51
Slough 3	a																								
London Paddington 15 ⊖	a		05 13					09 21					10 39			10 11			11 24						12 23

A The Night Riviera

B ☕ from Reading ⊘ to Reading

C ☕ from Castle Cary ⊘ to Castle Cary

D 🛒 from Plymouth

For connections to Oxford, Gatwick Airport and Heathrow Airport please refer to Tables 116, 148 and 125A

Table 135

Saturdays
from 27 October

Cornwall and Devon - Birmingham and London

Route Diagram - see first Page of Table 135

		GW	GW	GW	GW	XC	GW	XC	GW	GW	XC	GW	GW	GW	GW	GW	XC	XC	GW	GW	GW	XC	GW
		◇		◇■ ☕		◇■ ✕		◇■ ✕	◇■ ☕		◇■ A ✕	◇■ ☕				◇■ ☕	◇■ ✕	◇■ ✕	◇		◇■ ☕	◇■ ✕	
Penzance	d						07 35		07 59		08 28	08 45	08 54					09 43			10 00		10 36
St Erth	d						07 48		08 09		08 36	08 55	09a02					09 51			10 10		10 45
Hayle	d						07 52		08 13														10 48
Camborne	d						08 02		08 23		08 46	09 06						10 01			10 21		10 58
Redruth	d						08 09		08 30		08 52	09 13						10 07			10 28		11 04
Truro	d						08 20		08 43		09 04	09 26						10 19			10 41		11 15
St Austell	d						08 36		09 01		09 20	09 43						10 35			10 58		11 32
Newquay	d	07 48																	10 12				
Par	d	08a39					08 44		09 09		09 28	09 51						10 42	11a01		11 07		11 39
Lostwithiel	d						08 51											10 49					11 46
Bodmin Parkway	d						08 57		09 20		09 39	10 03						10 56			11 18		11 52
Liskeard ■	d						09 10		09 33		09 51	10 16						11 09			11 31		12 06
Menheniot	d																						12x10
St Germans	d						09 22																12 17
Saltash	d						09 29																12 23
St Budeaux Ferry Road	d																						
Keyham	d																						
Dockyard	d																						
Devonport	d																						
Plymouth	a						09 40		09 59		10 18	10 40						11 33			11 59		12 36
	d					09 25			10 02		10 25	10 44					11 25	11 48			12 00	12 23	
Ivybridge	d								10 17												12 15		
Totnes	d					09 50			10 31		10 50						11 50	12 13			12 29	12 49	
Paignton	d		09 04	09 18	09 30			10 07		10 23				10 56	11 13					12 13			
Torquay	d		09 09	09 25	09 35			10 13		10 28				11 01	11 18					12 18			
Torre	d		09 12	09 29	09 38					10 31				11 04	11 21					12 21			
Newton Abbot	a		09 20	09 38	09 47	10 01		10 23	10 43	10 38	11 01			11 12	11 29		12 01	12 24		12 30	12 41	13 01	
	d		09 35	09 39	09 48	10 03		10 24	10 44	10 47	11 03			11 23	11 41		12 03	12 25		12 32	12 42	13 03	
Teignmouth	d		09 42	09 49	09 56			10 31		10 55				11 30	11 48					12 39			
Dawlish	d		09 47	09 57	10 02			10 36		11 00				11 35	11 53					12 44			
Dawlish Warren	d		09 52	10 02	10 07					11 04				11 40	11 58					12 55			
Starcross	d		09 56											11 44	12 02					12 59			
Exeter St Thomas	d		10 05											11 53	12 11					13 08			
Exeter St Davids ■	a		10 10	10 13	10 18	10 21		10 48	11 04	11 16	11 21	11 38		11 58	12 16		12 21	12 44		13 13	13 02	13 23	
Exeter Central	a		10 21							11 21					12 21					13 21			
Exmouth	a		10 50							11 50					12 50					13 50			
Exeter St Davids ■	d			10 15		10 23		10 50	11 06		11 23	11 40				11 54	12 23	12 48			13 04	13 25	
Tiverton Parkway	d			10 30		10 37		11 03	11 21		11 37					12 09	12 37	13 02			13 19	13 39	
Taunton	d			10 45		10 51		11 18	11 36		11 51					12 24	12 51	13 16			13 34	13 54	
Bridgwater	a																						
Weston-super-Mare	a																						
Bristol Temple Meads ■	a			11 24		11 25		11 54			12 24						13 23	13 55				14 26	
Bath Spa ■	a			11 41																			
Filton Abbey Wood	a																						
Bristol Parkway ■	a					11 38		12 08			12 38						13 38	14 08				14 38	
Swindon	a			12 09																			
Newport (South Wales)	a																						
Cardiff Central ■	a																						
Birmingham New Street ■	a					12 56		13 26			13 56						14 56	15 26				15 55	
Castle Cary	d															12 45							
Westbury	d															13 05							
Pewsey	d															13 22							
Hungerford	a															13 39							
Newbury	a															13 49							
Thatcham	a															13 56							
Theale	a															14 05							
Reading ■	a			12 44					12 52			13 17				14 19					14 51		
Slough ■	a																						
London Paddington ■ ⊖	a			13 12					13 21			13 46				14 45					15 22		

A ✕ from Plymouth

For connections to Oxford, Gatwick Airport and Heathrow Airport please refer to Tables 116, 148 and 125A

Table 135

Saturdays
from 27 October

Cornwall and Devon - Birmingham and London

Route Diagram - see first Page of Table 135

		GW	GW	GW	XC	GW	GW	XC	GW	GW	GW	XC	GW	GW	GW	XC	GW	GW	GW	XC	GW	GW
			◇■ A ☕⊘		◇■ ✕	◇	◇	◇■ ✕	◇■ ☕	◇■ B ☕⊘		◇■ ✕	◇		◇■ ☕	◇■ ✕				◇■ ✕	◇■ ☕	◇
Penzance	d		10 58			11 46							13 00								14 01	
St Erth	d		11 08			11 56							13 09								14 11	
Hayle	d					12 00							13 12									
Camborne	d		11 19			12 10							13 21								14 22	
Redruth	d		11 26			12 16							13 27								14 29	
Truro	d		11 39			12 29							13 38								14 42	
St Austell	d		11 56			12 47							13 55								14 59	
Newquay	d						13 09															14 59
Par	d					12 55	13a59						14 03								15 07	15a48
Lostwithiel	d					13 02							14 09									
Bodmin Parkway	d		12 13			13 09							14 15								15 19	
Liskeard ■	d		12 26			13 23							14 28								15 33	
Menheniot	d					13x28																
St Germans	d					13 36							14 39									
Saltash	d					13 45							14 47									
St Budeaux Ferry Road	d																					
Keyham	d																					
Dockyard	d																					
Devonport	d												14 52									
Plymouth	a		12 52			13 55							14 58								15 58	
	d		12 54		13 25					14 00		14 25			15 04	15 25		15 32			16 01	
Ivybridge	d																	15 47				
Totnes	d		13 21		13 50							14 50			15 31	15 50		16 01			16 28	
Paignton	d	12 43		13 13				13 53			14 13			15 13			15 43		16 13			
Torquay	d	12 48		13 18				13 59			14 18			15 18			15 48		16 18			
Torre	d			13 21							14 21			15 21					16 21			
Newton Abbot	a	12 58	13 34	13 29	14 01			14 09		14 35	14 29	15 01		15 29	15 42	16 01	15 58	16 13	16 29		16 41	
	d	13 06	13 35	13 41	14 03			14 10		14 36	14 40	15 03		15 34	15 44	16 03	16 09		16 31		16 41	
Teignmouth	d	13 13		13 48				14 17			14 48			15 42			16 16		16 38			
Dawlish	d	13 18		13 53				14 22			14 53			15 47			16 21		16 43			
Dawlish Warren	d	13 23		13 58							14 57			15 58					16 55			
Starcross	d			14 02							15 01			16 02					16 59			
Exeter St Thomas	d			14 11							15 11			16 12					17 08			
Exeter St Davids ■	a	13 35	13 55	14 16	14 21			14 34		14 56	15 15	15 21		16 15	16 04	16 21	16 34		17 15		17 01	
Exeter Central	a			14 21							15 21			16 21			16 44		17 21			
Exmouth	a			14 50							15 50			16 50					17 50			
Exeter St Davids ■	d		13 57		14 23			14 36		14 58		15 23			16 06	16 23				16 53	17 03	
Tiverton Parkway	d				14 37			14 49		15 13		15 37			16 21	16 37				17 07	17 17	
Taunton	d		14 23		14 52			15 04	15 19	15 28		15 51			16 36	16 51				17 21	17 32	
Bridgwater	a																					
Weston-super-Mare	a							15 23														
Bristol Temple Meads ■	a				15 24			15 49				16 24				17 25				17 53		
Bath Spa ■	a																					
Filton Abbey Wood	a																					
Bristol Parkway ■	a				15 38			16 08				16 38				17 38				18 08		
Swindon	a																					
Newport (South Wales)	a																					
Cardiff Central ■	a																					
Birmingham New Street ■	a				16 56			17 26				17 56				18 56				19 26		
Castle Cary	d		14 44							15 49												
Westbury	d		15 03						16 07													
Pewsey	d								16 25													
Hungerford	a								16 41													
Newbury	a								16 52													
Thatcham	a								16 58													
Theale	a								17 07													
Reading ■	a		15 51						17 17	16 50					17 53						18 49	
Slough ■	a																					
London Paddington ■ ⊖	a		16 23						17 51	17 21					18 21						19 22	

A ☕ to Plymouth ☕ from Reading ⊘ from Plymouth to Reading

B ☕ from Reading ⊘ to Reading

For connections to Oxford, Gatwick Airport and Heathrow Airport please refer to Tables 116, 148 and 125A

Saturdays
from 27 October

Cornwall and Devon - Birmingham and London

Route Diagram - see first Page of Table 135

		XC	GW	GW	GW	XC	GW	GW	GW	XC	GW	GW	GW	GW	GW	GW	GW	GW	GW	GW	GW	GW	GW
		◇1	◇	◇1		◇1			◇1	◇1			◇			◇1				1			
Penzance	d		14 52						15 52			16 41				17 40	18 50					19 06	
St Erth	d		15 01						16 02			16 51				17 50	18a58					19 15	
Hayle	d		15 04									16 55				17 54						19 18	
Camborne	d		15 14						16 13			17 05				18 04						19 27	
Redruth	d		15 20						16 20			17 12				18 11						19 33	
Truro	d		15 31						16 33			17 25				18 24						19 44	
St Austell	d		15 48						16 51			17 43				18 41						20 01	
Newquay	d												17 21					19 17					21 18
Par	d		15 55						16 59			17 51	18a10			18 49		20a03				20 09	22 09
Lostwithiel	d		16 02						17 06			17 58										20 15	22 18
Bodmin Parkway	d		16 08						17 13			18 05				19 01						20 21	22 24
Liskeard 8	d		16 21						17 26			18 19				19 14						20 34	22 37
Menheniot	d		16x25																			20x39	22x41
St Germans	d		16 33									18 31										20 47	22 49
Saltash	d		16 39									18 38										20 54	22 55
St Budeaux Ferry Road	d																					20 58	22 59
Keyham	d																					21 00	23 01
Dockyard	d																					21x02	23x03
Devonport	d																					21 04	23 05
Plymouth	a		16 51						17 51			18 49				19 39						21 10	23 12
	d	16 25		16 57		17 23		17 38	17 54	18 25		18 51				19 42						21 15	
Ivybridge	d			17 12				17 53				19 07										21 30	
Totnes	d	16 50		17 27		17 49		18 07	18 21	18 50		19 22				20 09						21 44	
Paignton	d				17 13		17 52				18 53			19 21	19 50				20 13	20 46	21 13		
Torquay	d				17 18		17 57				18 58			19 26	19 55				20 18	20 52	21 18		
Torre	d				17 21		18 00				19 01			19 29					20 21		21 21		
Newton Abbot	a	17 01		17 38	17 29	18 01	18 08	18 19	18 32	19 01	19 10	19 34		19 38	20 05	20 20			20 29	21 02	21 29	21 56	
	d	17 03		17 40	17 43	18 03	18 10	18 19	18 34	19 03	19 12	19 35		19 40	20 07	20 22			20 31	21 04	21 31	21 56	
Teignmouth	d				17 50		18 17	18 26			19 19	19 43		19 47	20 14				20 38		21 38	22 03	
Dawlish	d				17 55		18 22	18 31			19 24	19 48		19 52	20 19				20 43		21 43	22 08	
Dawlish Warren	d				18 00		18 27	18 47			19 29			20 06	20 24				20 48		21 48		
Starcross	d				18 04		18 31				19 33			20 10					20 52		21 52		
Exeter St Thomas	d				18 13		18 40				19 42			20 20					21 01		22 01		
Exeter St Davids 6	a	17 21		18 00	18 18	18 23	18 46	18 59	18 54	19 21	19 45	20 01		20 25	20 36	20 42			21 05	21 24	22 05	22 22	
Exeter Central	a				18 23		18 53							20 33									
Exmouth	a				18 52		19 22							21 01									
Exeter St Davids 6	d	17 23		18 02		18 25			18 56	19 23						20 44							
Tiverton Parkway	d	17 37		18 17		18 39			19 11	19 37						20 59							
Taunton	d	17 51		18 32		18 54			19 26	19 51						21 14							
Bridgwater	a																						
Weston-super-Mare	a																						
Bristol Temple Meads 10	a	18 25				19 26				20 25						21 47							
Bath Spa 7	a															22 01							
Filton Abbey Wood	a																						
Bristol Parkway 7	a	18 38				19 38				20 38													
Swindon	a															22 29							
Newport (South Wales)	a																						
Cardiff Central 7	a																						
Birmingham New Street 12	a	19 58				20 53				21 53													
Castle Cary	d			18 53					19 47														
Westbury	d			19 12					20 06														
Pewsey	d								20 23														
Hungerford	a																						
Newbury	a			19 45																			
Thatcham	a																						
Theale	a																						
Reading 7	a			20 07					20 58							23 04							
Slough 3	a																						
London Paddington 15 ⊖	a			20 37					21 32							23 36							

For connections to Oxford, Gatwick Airport and Heathrow Airport please refer to Tables 116, 148 and 125A

Saturdays
from 27 October

Cornwall and Devon - Birmingham and London

Route Diagram - see first Page of Table 135

		XC	GW
		◇1	
Penzance	d	21 32	
St Erth	d	21 42	
Hayle	d		
Camborne	d	21 53	
Redruth	d	22 00	
Truro	d	22 13	
St Austell	d	22 30	
Newquay	d		
Par	d	22 38	
Lostwithiel	d		
Bodmin Parkway	d	22 49	
Liskeard 8	d	23 02	
Menheniot	d		
St Germans	d		
Saltash	d		
St Budeaux Ferry Road	d		
Keyham	d		
Dockyard	d		
Devonport	d		
Plymouth	a	23 27	
	d		
Ivybridge	d		
Totnes	d		
Paignton	d		21 53
Torquay	d		21 58
Torre	d		22 01
Newton Abbot	a		22 09
	d		22 11
Teignmouth	d		22 18
Dawlish	d		22 23
Dawlish Warren	d		22 28
Starcross	d		22 32
Exeter St Thomas	d		22 41
Exeter St Davids 6	a		22 45
Exeter Central	a		
Exmouth	a		
Exeter St Davids 6	d		
Tiverton Parkway	d		
Taunton	d		
Bridgwater	a		
Weston-super-Mare	a		
Bristol Temple Meads 10	a		
Bath Spa 7	a		
Filton Abbey Wood	a		
Bristol Parkway 7	a		
Swindon	a		
Newport (South Wales)	a		
Cardiff Central 7	a		
Birmingham New Street 12	a		
Castle Cary	d		
Westbury	d		
Pewsey	d		
Hungerford	a		
Newbury	a		
Thatcham	a		
Theale	a		
Reading 7	a		
Slough 3	a		
London Paddington 15 ⊖	a		

For connections to Oxford, Gatwick Airport and Heathrow Airport please refer to Tables 116, 148 and 125A

Table 135

Sundays until 24 June

Cornwall and Devon - Birmingham and London

Route Diagram - see first Page of Table 135

		GW	GW	GW	GW	XC	GW	GW	XC	XC		GW	GW	GW	XC	GW	GW	GW	XC	XC		GW	XC	GW	XC
		◇	◇1	◇	◇1	◇1		◇1	◇1	◇1		◇1			◇1 A	◇		◇1	◇1	◇1			◇1	◇1	◇1 A
			⊡		⊡	⊼		⊡	⊼	⊼		⊡			⊼			⊡	⊼	⊼			⊼	⊡	⊼
Penzance	d											08 35	08 45		09 30			09 47						11 05	
St Erth	d											08 44	08a53		09 38			09 57						11 14	
Hayle	d											08 49													
Camborne	d											09 00			09 48			10 08						11 27	
Redruth	d											09 06			09 54			10 14						11 33	
Truro	d											09 20			10 06			10 27						11 47	
St Austell	d											09 36			10 22			10 44						12 03	
Newquay	d															09 54									11 30
Par	d											09 45			10 30	10a47		10 53						12 11	12 29
Lostwithiel	d																								
Bodmin Parkway	d											09 57			10 41			11 06						12 24	12 41
Liskeard [6]	d											10 10			10 53			11 19						12 37	12 54
Menheniot	d																								
St Germans	d																	11 30							
Saltash	d											10 28													
St Budeaux Ferry Road	d																								
Keyham	d																								
Dockyard	d																								
Devonport	d																								
Plymouth	a											10 35			11 17			11 44						13 05	13 19
	d				08 40	09 25		10 10	10 25			10 40			11 25			11 45	12 00	12 25			12 52	13 05	13 23
Ivybridge	d																								
Totnes	d				09 07	09 50		10 40	10 50			11 07			11 50			12 15		12 50				13 34	13 49
Paignton	d						09 49			10 50				11 00			11 49					12 57			
Torquay	d						09 54			10 56				11 05			11 54					13 02			
Torre	d						09 57							11 08			11 57					13 05			
Newton Abbot	a				09 19	10 01	10 05	10 52	11 01	11 06		11 19		11 16	12 01		12 05	12 28	12 34	13 01		13 13	13 26	13 46	14 01
	d				09 20	10 03	10 07	10 54	11 03	11 08		11 21		11 25	12 03		12 07	12 29	12 36	13 03		13 15	13 27	13 47	14 03
Teignmouth	d				09 27		10 14			11 15				11 32			12 14					13 22			
Dawlish	d				09 33		10 19			11 20				11 37			12 19					13 27			
Dawlish Warren	d						10 24										12 24								
Starcross	d						10 28										12 28								
Exeter St Thomas	d						10 37										12 37								
Exeter St Davids [6]	a				09 47	10 21	10 41	11 14	11 21	11 30		11 41		11 52	12 21		12 42	12 49	12 55	13 21		13 41	13 46	14 07	14 23
Exeter Central	a						10 49							11 58			12 51					13 51			
Exmouth	a						11 18							12 25			13 20					14 18			
Exeter St Davids [6]	d	08 01	08 30	09 35	09 48	10 23		11 18	11 23	11 32		11 43			12 23			12 50	12 57	13 23			13 48	14 09	14 25
Tiverton Parkway	d	08 18	08 45	09 53		10 37		11 33	11 37	11 46		11 58			12 37				13 10	13 37				14 23	14 39
Taunton	d	08 35	08 59	10 11	10 14	10 51		11 48	11 53	12 00		12 13			12 51			13 16	13 25	13 51				14 38	14 54
Bridgwater	a	08 46		10 23																					
Weston-super-Mare	a	09 06		10 41						12 20															
Bristol Temple Meads [10]	a	09 38		11 13		11 27		12 23	12 27	12 45					13 26				13 57	14 26			14 40		15 27
Bath Spa [7]	a							12 41																	
Filton Abbey Wood	a	09 55																							
Bristol Parkway [7]	a					11 38			12 38	13 08					13 38				14 08	14 38			15 08		15 38
Swindon	a							13 10																	
Newport (South Wales)	a	10 25																							
Cardiff Central [7]	a	10 41																							
Birmingham New Street [12]	a					12 50			13 50	14 26					14 50				15 27	15 50			16 26		16 50
Castle Cary	d		09 21									12 34													
Westbury	d		09 41		10 51							12 53						13 54							
Pewsey	d																								
Hungerford	a																								
Newbury	a																								
Thatcham	a																								
Theale	a																								
Reading [7]	a		10 53		11 51			13 45				13 56						14 52						16 17	
Slough [3]	a																								
London Paddington [15] ⊖	a		11 29		12 29			14 22				14 33						15 29						17 01	

A ⊼ from Plymouth

For connections to Oxford, Gatwick Airport and Heathrow Airport please refer to Tables 116, 148 and 125A

Table 135

Sundays until 24 June

Cornwall and Devon - Birmingham and London

Route Diagram - see first Page of Table 135

		GW	GW	GW	GW	XC		XC	GW	GW	GW	GW	XC	GW	GW	GW		GW	GW	GW	XC	GW	GW	GW	XC
			◇1			◇1		◇1 A	◇		◇1	◇1	◇1	◇1	◇1			◇		◇1	◇1		◇	◇1	◇1 A
			⊡			⊼		⊼			⊡	⊡	⊼	⊡	⊡					⊡	⊼			⊡	⊼
Penzance	d		11 40		12 05			12 25			12 43							13 41					14 40	15 10	15 30
St Erth	d		11 50		12 14			12 33			12 52							13 51					14 49	15 20	15 38
Hayle	d							12 37										13 54					14 52		
Camborne	d		12 02		12 25			12 46			13 06							14 04					15 01	15 32	15 51
Redruth	d		12 08		12 31			12 53			13 12							14 10					15 07	15 39	15 57
Truro	d		12 21		12 43			13 04			13 25							14 21					15 18	15 51	16 09
St Austell	d		12 38		12 59			13 21			13 43							14 38					15 35	16 09	16 25
Newquay	d								12 55																
Par	d		12 46		13 06			13 28	13a44		13 50							14 45					15 43	16 17	16 33
Lostwithiel	d				13 13			13 35										14 52					15 49		
Bodmin Parkway	d		12 59		13 19			13 42			14 03							14 58					15 55	16 28	16 44
Liskeard [6]	d		13 12		13 33			13 55			14 16							15 11					16 09	16 41	16 56
Menheniot	d				13 38																				
St Germans	d				13 46													15 21					16 19		
Saltash	d				13 54													15 29					16 27		
St Budeaux Ferry Road	d																								
Keyham	d																								
Dockyard	d																								
Devonport	d																								
Plymouth	a		13 35		14 03			14 19			14 42							15 38					16 37	17 07	17 20
	d		13 44		14 06	14 23		14 35			14 45	15 05	15 23		15 33			15 49		16 10	16 25		16 38	17 10	17 26
Ivybridge	d				14 21													16 07					16 53		
Totnes	d		14 11		14 35	14 49		15 00			15 12	15 35	15 49		16 01			16 21		16 42	16 49		17 07	17 38	17 52
Paignton	d	13 51		14 19						14 57				15 45		16 00			16 21			16 55			
Torquay	d	13 56		14 24						15 02				15 51		16 05			16 26			17 00			
Torre	d	13 59		14 27						15 05				15 56		16 08			16 29			17 03			
Newton Abbot	a	14 07	14 23	14 35	14 47	15 01		15 11		15 13	15 24	15 47	16 01	16 04	16 12	16 16		16 33	16 37	16 53	17 01	17 11	17 19	17 49	18 02
	d	14 08	14 25	14 37	14 48	15 03		15 12		15 15	15 25	15 48	16 03	16 05	16 14	16 17		16 34	16 38	16 55	17 02	17 12	17 20	17 51	18 04
Teignmouth	d	14 15		14 44	14 55					15 22				16 13		16 24			16 45			17 19	17 27		
Dawlish	d	14 20		14 49	15 00					15 27				16 18		16 29			16 50			17 24	17 32		
Dawlish Warren	d	14 25		14 54												16 34			16 55			17 29			
Starcross	d	14 29		14 58															16 59						
Exeter St Thomas	d	14 38		15 07															17 08						
Exeter St Davids [6]	a	14 41	14 46	15 12	15 16	15 23		15 31		15 41	15 45	16 08	16 23	16 32	16 38	16 46		16 55	17 13	17 17	17 22	17 41	17 46	18 11	18 21
Exeter Central	a	14 51		15 17						15 51						16 52			17 18			17 51			
Exmouth	a	15 18								16 18						17 19						18 18			
Exeter St Davids [6]	d		14 47			15 25		15 33			15 47	16 10	16 24	16 34	16 39					17 19	17 24		17 51	18 13	18 23
Tiverton Parkway	d					15 38		15 46			16 02	16 25	16 37		16 55					17 34	17 38			18 28	18 38
Taunton	d		15 12			15 54		16 01			16 17	16 40	16 53	16 59	17 09					17 48	17 53		18 22	18 43	18 52
Bridgwater	a													17 09									18 33		
Weston-super-Mare	a							16 20				17 01		17 28									18 52		
Bristol Temple Meads [10]	a					16 27		16 54				17 20	17 26	17 58						18 25	18 27		19 41		19 26
Bath Spa [7]	a											17 42		18 12						18 41					
Filton Abbey Wood	a																								
Bristol Parkway [7]	a					16 38		17 08					17 38								18 38				19 38
Swindon	a											18 10		18 39						19 11					
Newport (South Wales)	a																								
Cardiff Central [7]	a																								
Birmingham New Street [12]	a					17 49		18 27					18 51								19 56				20 50
Castle Cary	d		15 34												17 31										
Westbury	d		15 52												17 51										
Pewsey	d																								
Hungerford	a																								
Newbury	a																								
Thatcham	a																								
Theale	a																								
Reading [7]	a		16 53								17 48	18 46		19 12	18 55					19 47				20 21	
Slough [3]	a																								
London Paddington [15] ⊖	a		17 32								18 27	19 22		19 59	19 31					20 27				21 01	

A ⊼ from Plymouth

For connections to Oxford, Gatwick Airport and Heathrow Airport please refer to Tables 116, 148 and 125A

Table 135

Sundays until 24 June

Cornwall and Devon - Birmingham and London

Route Diagram - see first Page of Table 135

		GW	GW	XC	GW	GW	XC	GW	GW	GW	GW	GW	GW	GW	GW	GW	GW	GW	GW
			◇■ ☕	◇■ 🛒	◇■ ☕	◇	◇■ 🛒		◇■ ☕	🛒		◇■ ☕				🛒			■ 🛏 ☕
Penzance	d		15 50						17 25	17 50				19 00		20 05			21 15
St Erth	d		16 00						17 34	17 59				19 09		20 14			21 25
Hayle	d									18 02						20 17			
Camborne	d		16 11						17 47	18 12				19 20		20 26			21 38
Redruth	d		16 18						17 54	18 18				19 26		20 32			21 45
Truro	d		16 31						18 06	18 30				19 38		20 44			22 00
St Austell	d		16 48						18 24	18 47				19 55		21 01			22 18
Newquay	d				16 15	17 32									19 40				
Par	d				17 15	18a21			18 32	18 54				20 03	20a29	21 09			
Lostwithiel	d				17 25					19 01				20 09					
Bodmin Parkway	d		17 05		17 30				18 44	19 08				20 15		21 21			22 35
Liskeard ■	d		17 18		17 43				18 57	19 22				20 28		21 35			22 50
Menheniot	d													20x33					
St Germans	d													20 41					
Saltash	d									19 40				20 48					
St Budeaux Ferry Road	d																		
Keyham	d																		
Dockyard	d																		
Devonport	d									19 47				20 56					
Plymouth	a		17 42		18 10				19 21	19 50				21 00		22 01			23 15
	d		17 45		18 10		18 23		19 25			19 55		21 15					23 20
Ivybridge	d																		
Totnes	d		18 14		18 40		18 49		19 52					21 42					23 48
Paignton	d	17 49		18 20				18 55			19 55		20 55				21 52	23 00	
Torquay	d	17 54		18 26				19 00			20 00		21 00				21 57	23 05	
Torre	d	17 57						19 03			20 03		21 03				22 00	23 08	
Newton Abbot	a	18 05	18 25	18 36	18 51		19 01	19 11	20 04		20 11	20 31	21 11	21 54			22 08	23 16	23 59
	d	18 07	18 26	18 37	18 52		19 03	19 13	20 05		20 13	20 32	21 13	21 55			22 10	23 18	00 01
Teignmouth	d	18 14						19 20			20 20		21 20	22 02			22 17	23 25	
Dawlish	d	18 19						19 25			20 25		21 25	22 07			22 22	23 30	
Dawlish Warren	d	18 24						19 30			20 30						22 27	23 35	
Starcross	d	18 28						19 34			20 34						22 31	23 39	
Exeter St Thomas	d	18 37						19 43			20 43						22 40	23 48	
Exeter St Davids ■	a	18 40	18 47	18 56	19 14		19 23	19 48	20 25		20 48	20 53	21 40	22 21			22 43	23 52	00 23
Exeter Central	a	18 51						19 54			20 54		21 51				22 51		
Exmouth	a	19 18						20 21			21 21		22 18				23 18		
Exeter St Davids ■	d		18 49	18 58	19 15		19 25		20 26			20 55							
Tiverton Parkway	d			19 11	19 30		19 38		20 42			21 10							01 06
Taunton	d		19 14	19 25	19 44		19 54		20 57			21 23							
Bridgwater	a																		
Weston-super-Mare	a																		
Bristol Temple Meads ■	a			19 57			20 27					22 00							
Bath Spa ■	a											22 22							
Filton Abbey Wood	a																		
Bristol Parkway ■	a			20 08			20 38												
Swindon	a											22 50							
Newport (South Wales)	a																		
Cardiff Central ■	a																		
Birmingham New Street ■	a			21 20			21 51												
Castle Cary	d		19 35						21 19										
Westbury	d		19 54						21 40										
Pewsey	d																		
Hungerford	a																		
Newbury	a																		
Thatcham	a																		
Theale	a																		
Reading ■	a		20 59		21 18				22 44			23 28							04s02
Slough ■	a																		
London Paddington ■ ⊖	a		21 43		22 01				23 28			00 13							05 05

For connections to Oxford, Gatwick Airport and Heathrow Airport please refer to Tables 116, 148 and 125A

Table 135

Sundays 1 July to 9 September

Cornwall and Devon - Birmingham and London

Route Diagram - see first Page of Table 135

		GW	GW	GW	GW	XC	GW	GW	XC	XC	GW	GW	GW	XC	GW	GW	GW	XC	XC	GW	XC	GW	XC
		◇	◇■ ☕	◇	◇■ ☕	◇■ 🛒		◇■ ☕	◇■ 🛒	◇■ 🛒	◇■ ☕			◇■ A 🛒	◇		◇■ ☕	◇■ 🛒	◇■ 🛒		◇■ 🛒	◇■ ☕	◇■ A 🛒
Penzance	d										08 35	08 45		09 30			09 47					11 00	
St Erth	d										08 44	08a53		09 38			09 57					11 10	
Hayle	d										08 49												
Camborne	d										09 00			09 48			10 08					11 22	
Redruth	d										09 06			09 54			10 14					11 28	
Truro	d										09 20			10 06			10 27					11 42	
St Austell	d										09 36			10 22			10 45					11 59	
Newquay	d														09 54								11 30
Par	d										09 45			10 30	10a47		10 53					12 07	12 29
Lostwithiel	d																						
Bodmin Parkway	d										09 57			10 41			11 05					12 19	12 41
Liskeard ■	d										10 10			10 53			11 19					12 32	12 54
Menheniot	d																						
St Germans	d																11 30						
Saltash	d										10 27												
St Budeaux Ferry Road	d																						
Keyham	d																						
Dockyard	d																						
Devonport	d																						
Plymouth	a										10 35			11 17			11 45					12 58	13 19
	d				08 40	09 25		10 10	10 25		10 40			11 25			11 45	12 00	12 25		12 52	13 00	13 23
Ivybridge	d																						
Totnes	d				09 07	09 50		10 40	10 50		11 07			11 50			12 16		12 50			13 29	13 49
Paignton	d						09 49			10 50			11 00			11 49				12 57			
Torquay	d						09 54			10 56			11 05			11 54				13 02			
Torre	d						09 57						11 08			11 57				13 05			
Newton Abbot	a				09 19	10 01	10 05	10 52	11 01	11 06	11 19		11 16	12 01		12 05	12 28	12 34	13 01	13 13	13 26	13 40	14 01
	d				09 20	10 03	10 07	10 54	11 03	11 08	11 21		11 25	12 03		12 07	12 30	12 36	13 03	13 15	13 27	13 42	14 03
Teignmouth	d				09 27		10 14			11 15			11 32			12 14				13 22			
Dawlish	d				09 33		10 19			11 20			11 37			12 19				13 27			
Dawlish Warren	d						10 24									12 24							
Starcross	d						10 28									12 28							
Exeter St Thomas	d						10 37									12 37							
Exeter St Davids ■	a				09 47	10 21	10 41	11 14	11 21	11 30	11 41		11 52	12 21		12 42	12 49	12 55	13 21	13 41	13 46	14 02	14 23
Exeter Central	a						10 49						11 58			12 51				13 51			
Exmouth	a						11 18						12 25			13 20				14 18			
Exeter St Davids ■	d	08 01	08 43	09 35	09 48	10 23		11 18	11 23	11 32	11 43			12 23			12 50	12 57	13 23		13 48	14 04	14 25
Tiverton Parkway	d	08 18	08 58	09 53		10 37		11 33	11 37	11 46	11 58			12 37				13 10	13 37			14 18	14 39
Taunton	d	08 35	09 12	10 11	10 14	10 51		11 48	11 53	12 00	12 13			12 51			13 16	13 25	13 51			14 33	14 54
Bridgwater	a	08 46		10 23																			
Weston-super-Mare	a	09 06		10 41						12 20													
Bristol Temple Meads ■	a	09 38		11 13		11 27		12 23	12 27	12 45				13 26				13 57	14 26		14 40		15 27
Bath Spa ■	a							12 41															
Filton Abbey Wood	a	09 55																					
Bristol Parkway ■	a					11 38			12 38	13 08				13 38				14 08	14 38		15 08		15 38
Swindon	a							13 10															
Newport (South Wales)	a	10 25																					
Cardiff Central ■	a	10 41																					
Birmingham New Street ■	a					12 50			13 50	14 26				14 50				15 27	15 50		16 26		16 50
Castle Cary	d		09 34								12 34												
Westbury	d		09 54		10 51						12 53						13 59						
Pewsey	d		10 11								13 10												
Hungerford	a																						
Newbury	a		10 31		11 26						13 30												
Thatcham	a																						
Theale	a																						
Reading ■	a		10 48		11 46			13 45			13 48						14 48					15 49	
Slough ■	a																						
London Paddington ■ ⊖	a		11 21		12 17			14 14			14 21						15 21					16 21	

A 🛒 from Plymouth

For connections to Oxford, Gatwick Airport and Heathrow Airport please refer to Tables 116, 148 and 125A

Table 135

1 July to 9 September

Cornwall and Devon - Birmingham and London

Route Diagram - see first Page of Table 135

		GW	GW ◇1 ⊏	GW	GW	XC ◇1 ⚒	XC ◇1 A ⚒	GW ◇	GW	GW ◇1 ⊏	GW ◇1 ⊏	XC ◇1 ⚒	GW ◇1 ⊏	GW	GW ◇1 ⊏	GW ◇	GW	GW ◇1 ⊏	XC ◇1 ⚒	GW	GW ◇	GW ◇1 ⊏	XC ◇1 A ⚒
Penzance	d		11 40		12 05		12 30			12 56						13 41					14 40	15 00	15 30
St Erth	d		11 50		12 14		12 40			13 04						13 51					14 49	15 11	15 38
Hayle	d						12 44									13 54					14 52		
Camborne	d		12 02		12 25		12 56			13 17						14 04					15 01	15 23	15 51
Redruth	d		12 08		12 31		13 02			13 23						14 10					15 07	15 30	15 57
Truro	d		12 21		12 43		13 14			13 36						14 21					15 18	15 42	16 09
St Austell	d		12 38		12 59		13 30			13 55						14 38					15 35	16 00	16 25
Newquay	d							13 05															
Par	d		12 46		13 06		13 38	13a54		14 02						14 45					15 43	16 08	16 33
Lostwithiel	d				13 13		13 45									14 52					15 49		
Bodmin Parkway	d		12 59		13 19		13 52			14 15						14 58					15 55	16 19	16 44
Liskeard ■	d		13 12		13 33		14 04			14 28						15 11					16 09	16 32	16 56
Menheniot	d				13 38																		
St Germans	d				13 46											15 21					16 19		
Saltash	d				13 54											15 29					16 27		
St Budeaux Ferry Road	d																						
Keyham	d																						
Dockyard	d																						
Devonport	d																						
Plymouth	a		13 35		14 03		14 28			14 54						15 38					16 37	16 58	17 20
	d		13 44		14 06	14 23	14 35			14 58	15 08	15 23			15 43	15 49		16 12	16 25		16 38	17 00	17 26
Ivybridge	d				14 21											16 07					16 53		
Totnes	d		14 11		14 35	14 49	15 00			15 25	15 35	15 49			16 11	16 21		16 41	16 49		17 07	17 28	17 52
Paignton	d	13 51		14 19					14 57				15 45	15 54			16 21			16 55			
Torquay	d	13 56		14 24					15 02				15 51	15 59			16 26			17 00			
Torre	d	13 59		14 27					15 05				15 56	16 02			16 29			17 03			
Newton Abbot	a	14 07	14 23	14 35	14 47	15 01	15 11		15 13	15 37	15 47	16 01	16 04	16 10	16 22	16 33	16 37	16 53	17 01	17 11	17 19	17 39	18 02
	d	14 08	14 25	14 37	14 48	15 03	15 12		15 15	15 38	15 48	16 03	16 05	16 11	16 24	16 34	16 38	16 54	17 02	17 12	17 20	17 41	18 04
Teignmouth	d	14 15		14 44	14 55				15 22				16 13	16 18			16 45			17 19	17 27		
Dawlish	d	14 20		14 49	15 00				15 27				16 18	16 23			16 50			17 24	17 32		
Dawlish Warren	d	14 25		14 54										16 28			16 55			17 29			
Starcross	d	14 29		14 58													16 59						
Exeter St Thomas	d	14 38		15 07													17 08						
Exeter St Davids ■	a	14 41	14 46	15 12	15 16	15 23	15 31		15 41	15 58	16 08	16 23	16 32	16 39	16 44	16 55	17 13	17 16	17 22	17 41	17 46	18 01	18 21
Exeter Central	a	14 51		15 17					15 51					16 51			17 18			17 51			
Exmouth	a	15 18							16 18					17 18						18 18			
Exeter St Davids ■	d		14 47			15 25	15 33			16 01	16 10	16 24	16 34		16 45			17 19	17 24		17 51	18 05	18 23
Tiverton Parkway	d					15 38	15 46			16 16	16 25	16 37			17 01			17 34	17 38			18 20	18 38
Taunton	d		15 12			15 54	16 01			16 31	16 40	16 53	16 59		17 15			17 48	17 53		18 22	18 35	18 52
Bridgwater	a												17 09								18 33		
Weston-super-Mare	a						16 20				17 01		17 28								18 52		
Bristol Temple Meads ■	a					16 27	16 52				17 20	17 26	17 58					18 25	18 27		19 23		19 27
Bath Spa ■	a										17 42		18 12					18 41					
Filton Abbey Wood	a																						
Bristol Parkway ■	a					16 38	17 08					17 38							18 38				19 38
Swindon	a										18 10		18 39					19 11					
Newport (South Wales)	a																						
Cardiff Central ■	a																						
Birmingham New Street ■	a					17 49	18 27					18 51							19 56				20 50
Castle Cary	d		15 34												17 37								
Westbury	d		15 52												17 56							19 11	
Pewsey	d		16 10												18 13								
Hungerford	a																						
Newbury	a		16 31												18 33								
Thatcham	a																						
Theale	a																						
Reading ■	a		16 49							17 47	18 42		19 12		18 52			19 43				19 57	
Slough ■	a																						
London Paddington ■ ⊖	a		17 21							18 21	19 13		19 42		19 21			20 14				20 25	

A ⚒ from Plymouth

For connections to Oxford, Gatwick Airport and Heathrow Airport please refer to Tables 116, 148 and 125A

Table 135

1 July to 9 September

Cornwall and Devon - Birmingham and London

Route Diagram - see first Page of Table 135

		GW	GW ◇1 ⊏	XC ◇1 ⚒	GW ◇1 ⊏	GW ◇	XC ◇1 ⚒	GW	GW ◇1 ⊏	GW ⚒	GW	GW ◇1 ⊏	GW	GW	GW	GW ⚒	GW	GW	GW ■ 🛏 ⊏
Penzance	d		15 50						17 25	17 50				19 00		20 05			21 15
St Erth	d		16 00						17 34	17 59				19 09		20 14			21 25
Hayle	d									18 02						20 17			
Camborne	d		16 11						17 46	18 12				19 20		20 26			21 38
Redruth	d		16 18						17 53	18 18				19 26		20 32			21 45
Truro	d		16 31						18 05	18 30				19 38		20 44			22 00
St Austell	d		16 48						18 24	18 47				19 55		21 01			22 18
Newquay	d				16 15	17 32									19 40				
Par	d				17 15	18a21			18 32	18 54				20 03	20a29	21 09			
Lostwithiel	d				17 25					19 01				20 09					
Bodmin Parkway	d		17 05		17 30				18 44	19 08				20 15		21 21			22 35
Liskeard ■	d		17 18		17 43				18 57	19 22				20 28		21 35			22 50
Menheniot	d													20x33					
St Germans	d													20 41					
Saltash	d									19 40				20 48					
St Budeaux Ferry Road	d																		
Keyham	d																		
Dockyard	d																		
Devonport	d									19 47				20 56					
Plymouth	a		17 42		18 10				19 21	19 50				21 00		22 00			23 15
	d		17 45		18 10		18 23		19 25			19 55		21 15					23 20
Ivybridge	d																		
Totnes	d		18 14		18 40		18 49		19 52					21 42					23 48
Paignton	d	17 49		18 20				18 55			19 55		20 55				21 52	23 00	
Torquay	d	17 54		18 26				19 00			20 00		21 00				21 57	23 05	
Torre	d	17 57						19 03			20 03		21 03				22 00	23 08	
Newton Abbot	a	18 05	18 25	18 36	18 51		19 01	19 11	20 04		20 11	20 31	21 11	21 54			22 08	23 16	23 59
	d	18 07	18 26	18 37	18 52		19 03	19 13	20 05		20 13	20 32	21 13	21 55			22 10	23 18	00 01
Teignmouth	d	18 14						19 20			20 20		21 20	22 02			22 17	23 25	
Dawlish	d	18 19						19 25			20 25		21 25	22 07			22 22	23 30	
Dawlish Warren	d	18 24						19 30			20 30						22 27	23 35	
Starcross	d	18 28						19 34			20 34						22 31	23 39	
Exeter St Thomas	d	18 37						19 43			20 43						22 40	23 48	
Exeter St Davids ■	a	18 40	18 47	18 56	19 14		19 23	19 48	20 25		20 48	20 53	21 40	22 21			22 43	23 52	00 23
Exeter Central	a	18 51						19 54			20 54		21 51				22 51		
Exmouth	a	19 18						20 21			21 21		22 18				23 18		
Exeter St Davids ■	d		18 49	18 58	19 15		19 25		20 26			20 55							01 06
Tiverton Parkway	d			19 11	19 30		19 38		20 42			21 10							
Taunton	d		19 14	19 25	19 44		19 54		20 55			21 23							
Bridgwater	a																		
Weston-super-Mare	a																		
Bristol Temple Meads ■	a			19 57			20 27					22 00							
Bath Spa ■	a											22 22							
Filton Abbey Wood	a																		
Bristol Parkway ■	a			20 08			20 38												
Swindon	a											22 50							
Newport (South Wales)	a																		
Cardiff Central ■	a																		
Birmingham New Street ■	a			21 20			21 51												
Castle Cary	d				20 06				21 19										
Westbury	d				20 26				21 40										
Pewsey	d								21 58										
Hungerford	a																		
Newbury	a		20 23						22 18										
Thatcham	a																		
Theale	a																		
Reading ■	a		20 42		21 11				22 36			23 28							04s02
Slough ■	a																		
London Paddington ■ ⊖	a		21 14		21 40				23 06			00 05							05 05

For connections to Oxford, Gatwick Airport and Heathrow Airport please refer to Tables 116, 148 and 125A

Table 135

Sundays

16 September to 21 October

Cornwall and Devon - Birmingham and London

Route Diagram - see first Page of Table 135

		GW	GW	GW	GW	XC	GW	GW	XC	XC	GW	GW	XC	GW	GW	GW	XC	GW	GW	GW	XC	GW	GW
		◇	◇1 ☕	◇	◇1 ☕	◇1 🛒		◇1 ☕	◇1 🛒	◇1	◇1 ☕		◇1 A 🛒		◇1 ☕	◇	◇1 🛒		◇1 ☕		◇1 🛒		◇1 ☕
Penzance	d										08 35		09 30		09 47				11 00	11 45			
St Erth	d										08 44		09 38		09 57				11 10	11a53			
Hayle	d										08 49												
Camborne	d										09 00		09 48		10 08				11 23				
Redruth	d										09 06		09 54		10 14				11 29				
Truro	d										09 20		10 06		10 27				11 42				
St Austell	d										09 36		10 22		10 44				11 59				
Newquay	d															11 12							
Par	d										09 45		10 30		10 53	12a01			12 07				
Lostwithiel	d																						
Bodmin Parkway	d										09 57		10 41		11 06				12 19				
Liskeard [6]	d										10 10		10 53		11 19				12 33				
Menheniot	d																						
St Germans	d														11 30								
Saltash	d										10 28												
St Budeaux Ferry Road	d																						
Keyham	d																						
Dockyard	d																						
Devonport	d																						
Plymouth	a										10 35		11 17		11 44				12 58				
	d				08 40	09 25		09 45	10 25		10 40		11 25		11 45		12 23		13 00		13 23		13 44
Ivybridge	d																						
Totnes	d				09 07	09 50		10 13	10 50		11 07		11 50		12 15		12 49		13 28		13 49		14 11
Paignton	d						09 49			10 50		11 00		11 49				12 57				13 51	
Torquay	d						09 54			10 56		11 05		11 54				13 02				13 56	
Torre	d						09 57					11 08		11 57				13 05				13 59	
Newton Abbot	a				09 19	10 01	10 05	10 24	11 01	11 06	11 19	11 16	12 01	12 05	12 28		13 01	13 13	13 40		14 01	14 07	14 23
	d				09 21	10 03	10 07	10 26	11 03	11 08	11 21	11 25	12 03	12 07	12 29		13 03	13 15	13 41		14 03	14 08	14 25
Teignmouth	d				09 28		10 14			11 15		11 32		12 14				13 22				14 15	
Dawlish	d				09 34		10 19			11 20		11 37		12 19				13 27				14 20	
Dawlish Warren	d						10 24							12 24								14 25	
Starcross	d						10 28							12 28								14 29	
Exeter St Thomas	d						10 37							12 37								14 38	
Exeter St Davids [6]	a				09 47	10 21	10 41	10 46	11 21	11 30	11 41	11 52	12 21	12 42	12 49		13 23	13 41	14 01		14 23	14 41	14 44
Exeter Central	a						10 49					11 58		12 51				13 51				14 53	
Exmouth	a						11 18					12 25		13 20				14 18				15 20	
Exeter St Davids [6]	d	08 01	08 43	09 35	09 49	10 23		10 48	11 23	11 32	11 43		12 23		12 50		13 25		14 03		14 25		14 46
Tiverton Parkway	d	08 18	08 58	09 53		10 37		11 02	11 37	11 46	11 58		12 37				13 39		14 17		14 38		
Taunton	d	08 35	09 12	10 19	10 14	10 51		11 17	11 53	12 00	12 12		12 51		13 16		13 54		14 32		14 54		15 12
Bridgwater	a	08 46		10 31																			
Weston-super-Mare	a	09 06		10 49						12 20													
Bristol Temple Meads [10]	a	09 38		11 20		11 27		11 50	12 27	12 47			13 26				14 27				15 27		
Bath Spa [7]	a							12 12															
Filton Abbey Wood	a	09 55																					
Bristol Parkway [7]	a					11 38			12 39				13 38				14 38				15 39		
Swindon	a							12 40															
Newport (South Wales)	a	10 25																					
Cardiff Central [7]	a	10 41																					
Birmingham New Street [12]	a					13 50			14 50				15 50				16 50				17 49		
Castle Cary	d		09 34								12 33												15 34
Westbury	d		09 54		10 51						12 53				13 59								15 52
Pewsey	d		10 11								13 10												16 10
Hungerford	a																						
Newbury	a		10 31		11 26						13 30												16 31
Thatcham	a																						
Theale	a																						
Reading [7]	a		10 48		11 49			13 19			13 49				14 49				15 49				16 49
Slough [3]	a																						
London Paddington [15] ⊖	a		11 29		12 29			13 59			14 29				15 29				16 30				17 30

A 🛒 from Plymouth

For connections to Oxford, Gatwick Airport and Heathrow Airport please refer to Tables 116, 148 and 125A

Table 135

Sundays

16 September to 21 October

Cornwall and Devon - Birmingham and London

Route Diagram - see first Page of Table 135

		GW	GW	XC	XC	GW	GW	GW	XC	GW	GW	GW	GW	GW	GW	XC	GW	GW	GW	GW	XC	GW	GW
				◇1 🛒	◇1 A 🛒		◇1 ☕	◇1 ☕	◇1 🛒	◇1 ☕		◇1 ☕	◇		◇1 ☕	◇1 🛒		◇	◇	◇1 ☕	◇1 A 🛒		◇1 ☕
Penzance	d		12 05		12 30		12 56						13 41					14 40		15 00	15 30		
St Erth	d		12 14		12 40		13 06						13 51					14 50		15 10	15 38		
Hayle	d				12 44								13 54					14 53					
Camborne	d		12 25		12 56		13 19						14 04					15 02		15 22	15 51		
Redruth	d		12 31		13 02		13 25						14 10					15 08		15 29	15 57		
Truro	d		12 43		13 14		13 38						14 21					15 19		15 41	16 09		
St Austell	d		12 59		13 30		13 56						14 38					15 36		15 59	16 25		
Newquay	d																		15 10				
Par	d		13 06		13 38		14 03						14 45					15 43	15a59	16 07	16 33		
Lostwithiel	d		13 13		13 45								14 52					15 50					
Bodmin Parkway	d		13 19		13 52		14 16						14 58					15 56		16 18	16 44		
Liskeard [6]	d		13 33		14 04		14 29						15 11					16 09		16 31	16 56		
Menheniot	d		13 38																				
St Germans	d		13 46										15 21					16 19					
Saltash	d		13 54										15 29					16 27					
St Budeaux Ferry Road	d																						
Keyham	d																						
Dockyard	d																						
Devonport	d																						
Plymouth	a		14 03		14 28		14 54						15 38					16 37		16 57	17 20		
	d		14 06	14 23	14 35		14 55	15 05	15 23			15 43	15 49		16 10	16 23		16 38		17 00	17 26		17 45
Ivybridge	d		14 21										16 07					16 53					
Totnes	d		14 35	14 49	15 00		15 25	15 35	15 49			16 11	16 21		16 39	16 49		17 07		17 28	17 52		18 13
Paignton	d	14 19				14 57				15 45	15 54			16 21			16 55					17 49	
Torquay	d	14 24				15 02				15 51	15 59			16 26			17 00					17 54	
Torre	d	14 27				15 05				15 56	16 02			16 29			17 03					17 57	
Newton Abbot	a	14 35	14 47	15 01	15 11	15 13	15 37	15 47	16 01	16 04	16 10	16 22	16 33	16 37	16 51	17 01	17 11	17 19		17 39	18 02	18 05	18 25
	d	14 37	14 48	15 03	15 12	15 15	15 38	15 48	16 03	16 05	16 11	16 24	16 34	16 38	16 52	17 02	17 12	17 20		17 40	18 04	18 07	18 26
Teignmouth	d	14 44	14 55			15 22				16 13	16 18			16 45			17 19	17 27				18 14	
Dawlish	d	14 49	15 00			15 27				16 18	16 23			16 50			17 24	17 32				18 19	
Dawlish Warren	d	14 54									16 28			16 55			17 29					18 24	
Starcross	d	14 58												16 59								18 28	
Exeter St Thomas	d	15 07												17 08								18 37	
Exeter St Davids [6]	a	15 12	15 16	15 23	15 31	15 41	15 58	16 08	16 23	16 32	16 39	16 44	16 55	17 13	17 17	17 22	17 41	17 46		18 01	18 21	18 40	18 47
Exeter Central	a	15 17				15 53					16 53			17 18			17 51					18 53	
Exmouth	a					16 20					17 20						18 18					19 20	
Exeter St Davids [6]	d			15 25	15 33		16 01	16 10	16 24	16 34		16 45			17 19	17 24		17 51		18 02	18 23		18 49
Tiverton Parkway	d			15 38	15 46		16 16	16 25	16 37			17 01			17 34	17 39				18 18	18 38		
Taunton	d			15 54	16 01		16 31	16 40	16 53	16 59		17 15			17 48	17 53		18 22		18 33	18 52		19 11
Bridgwater	a									17 09								18 33					
Weston-super-Mare	a				16 20			17 01		17 28								18 52					
Bristol Temple Meads [10]	a			16 27	16 52			17 20	17 26	17 58					18 25	18 27		19 23			19 27		
Bath Spa [7]	a							17 41		18 11					18 41								
Filton Abbey Wood	a																						
Bristol Parkway [7]	a			16 38					17 39							18 42					19 38		
Swindon	a							18 10		18 40					19 10								
Newport (South Wales)	a																						
Cardiff Central [7]	a																						
Birmingham New Street [12]	a			18 51					19 51							20 51					21 51		
Castle Cary	d											17 37											
Westbury	d											17 56											19 51
Pewsey	d											18 13											
Hungerford	a																						
Newbury	a											18 33											20 24
Thatcham	a																						
Theale	a																						
Reading [7]	a						17 49	18 46		19 19		18 49			19 46					19 49			20 50
Slough [3]	a																						
London Paddington [15] ⊖	a						18 29	19 23		19 59		19 29			20 23					20 29			21 29

A 🛒 from Plymouth

For connections to Oxford, Gatwick Airport and Heathrow Airport please refer to Tables 116, 148 and 125A

Table 135

Sundays

16 September to 21 October

Cornwall and Devon - Birmingham and London

Route Diagram - see first Page of Table 135

		GW	GW	XC	GW	GW	GW	GW	GW	GW	GW	GW	GW	GW
		◇1 ☐		◇1 ⊼		◇1 ☐		◇1 ☐			⊼			■ ☐
Penzance	d	16 10				17 25				19 00	20 05			21 15
St Erth	d	16 21				17 34				19 09	20 14			21 25
Hayle	d										20 17			
Camborne	d	16 33				17 46				19 20	20 26			21 38
Redruth	d	16 40				17 53				19 26	20 32			21 45
Truro	d	16 53				18 05				19 38	20 44			22 00
St Austell	d	17 10				18 24				19 55	21 01			22 18
Newquay	d		17 30											
Par	d	17 17	18a19			18 32				20 03	21 09			
Lostwithiel	d									20 09				
Bodmin Parkway	d	17 29				18 44				20 15	21 21			22 35
Liskeard ■	d	17 42				18 57				20 28	21 35			22 50
Menheniot	d									20x33				
St Germans	d									20 41				
Saltash	d	18 00								20 48				
St Budeaux Ferry Road	d													
Keyham	d													
Dockyard	d													
Devonport	d									20 56				
Plymouth	a	18 10				19 21				21 00	22 00			23 15
	d	18 10		18 23		19 25		19 55		21 15				23 20
Ivybridge	d													
Totnes	d	18 40		18 49		19 52				21 42				23 48
Paignton	d				18 55		19 55		20 55			21 52	23 00	
Torquay	d				19 00		20 00		21 00			21 57	23 05	
Torre	d				19 03		20 03		21 03			22 00	23 08	
Newton Abbot	a	18 52		19 01	19 11	20 04	20 11	20 31	21 11	21 54		22 08	23 16	23 59
	d	18 52		19 03	19 13	20 05	20 13	20 32	21 13	21 55		22 10	23 18	00 01
Teignmouth	d				19 20		20 20		21 20	22 02		22 17	23 25	
Dawlish	d				19 25		20 25		21 25	22 07		22 22	23 30	
Dawlish Warren	d				19 30		20 30					22 27	23 35	
Starcross	d				19 34		20 34					22 31	23 39	
Exeter St Thomas	d				19 43		20 43					22 40	23 48	
Exeter St Davids ■	a	19 14		19 23	19 48	20 25	20 49	20 53	21 40	22 21		22 43	23 52	00 23
Exeter Central	a				19 54		20 55		21 51			22 51		
Exmouth	a				20 21		21 22		22 18			23 18		
Exeter St Davids ■	d	19 16		19 25		20 26		20 55						01 06
Tiverton Parkway	d	19 31		19 39		20 42		21 10						
Taunton	d	19 45		19 54		20 55		21 23						
Bridgwater	a													
Weston-super-Mare	a													
Bristol Temple Meads ■	a			20 26				22 00						
Bath Spa ■	a							22 22						
Filton Abbey Wood	a													
Bristol Parkway ■	a			20 38										
Swindon	a							22 50						
Newport (South Wales)	a													
Cardiff Central ■	a													
Birmingham New Street ■	a			22 50										
Castle Cary	d	20 07				21 19								
Westbury	d	20 27				21 40								
Pewsey	d					21 58								
Hungerford	a													
Newbury	a					22 18								
Thatcham	a													
Theale	a													
Reading ■	a	21 19				22 36		23 28						04s03
Slough ■	a													
London Paddington ■ ⊖	a	21 59				23 16		00 12						05 05

For connections to Oxford, Gatwick Airport and Heathrow Airport please refer to Tables 116, 148 and 125A

Table 135

Sundays

from 28 October

Cornwall and Devon - Birmingham and London

Route Diagram - see first Page of Table 135

		GW	GW	GW	GW	XC	GW	GW	XC	GW	GW	XC	GW	GW	GW	XC	GW	XC	GW	GW	XC	GW	GW
		◇	◇1 ☐	◇	◇1 ☐	◇1 ⊼		◇1 ☐	◇1	◇1 ☐		◇1 A ⊼		◇1 ☐	◇	◇1 ⊼		◇1 ⊼	◇1 ☐		◇1		◇1 ☐
Penzance	d									08 35		09 30		09 47					11 00	11 45			
St Erth	d									08 44		09 38		09 57					11 10	11a53			
Hayle	d									08 49													
Camborne	d									09 00		09 48		10 08					11 23				
Redruth	d									09 06		09 54		10 14					11 29				
Truro	d									09 20		10 06		10 27					11 42				
St Austell	d									09 36		10 22		10 44					11 59				
Newquay	d														11 12								
Par	d									09 45		10 30		10 53	12a01				12 07				
Lostwithiel	d																						
Bodmin Parkway	d									09 57		10 41		11 06					12 19				
Liskeard ■	d									10 10		10 53		11 19					12 33				
Menheniot	d																						
St Germans	d													11 30									
Saltash	d									10 28													
St Budeaux Ferry Road	d																						
Keyham	d																						
Dockyard	d																						
Devonport	d																						
Plymouth	a									10 35		11 17		11 44					12 58				
	d				08 40	09 25		10 10	10 25	10 40		11 25		11 45		12 25		12 52	13 00		13 23		13 44
Ivybridge	d																						
Totnes	d				09 07	09 50		10 40	10 50	11 07		11 50		12 15		12 50			13 28		13 49		14 11
Paignton	d						09 49				11 00		11 49				12 57					13 51	
Torquay	d						09 54				11 05		11 54				13 02					13 56	
Torre	d						09 57				11 08		11 57				13 05					13 59	
Newton Abbot	a				09 19	10 01	10 05	10 52	11 01	11 19	11 16	12 01	12 05	12 28		13 01	13 13	13 26	13 40		14 01	14 07	14 23
	d				09 21	10 03	10 07	10 54	11 03	11 21	11 25	12 03	12 07	12 29		13 03	13 15	13 27	13 41		14 03	14 08	14 25
Teignmouth	d				09 28		10 14				11 32		12 14				13 22					14 15	
Dawlish	d				09 34		10 19				11 37		12 19				13 27					14 20	
Dawlish Warren	d						10 24						12 24									14 25	
Starcross	d						10 28						12 28									14 29	
Exeter St Thomas	d						10 37						12 37									14 38	
Exeter St Davids ■	a				09 47	10 21	10 41	11 14	11 21	11 41	11 52	12 21	12 42	12 49		13 21	13 41	13 46	14 01		14 23	14 41	14 44
Exeter Central	a						10 49				11 58		12 51				13 51					14 53	
Exmouth	a						11 18				12 25		13 20				14 18					15 20	
Exeter St Davids ■	d	08 01	08 43	09 35	09 49	10 23		11 18	11 23	11 43		12 23		12 50		13 23		13 48	14 03		14 25		14 46
Tiverton Parkway	d	08 18	08 58	09 53		10 37		11 33	11 37	11 58		12 37				13 37			14 17		14 39		
Taunton	d	08 35	09 12	10 19	10 14	10 51		11 48	11 53	12 12		12 51		13 16		13 51			14 32		14 54		15 12
Bridgwater	a	08 46		10 31																			
Weston-super-Mare	a	09 06		10 49																			
Bristol Temple Meads ■	a	09 38		11 20		11 27		12 23	12 27			13 26				14 26		14 40			15 27		
Bath Spa ■	a							12 41															
Filton Abbey Wood	a	09 55																					
Bristol Parkway ■	a					11 38						13 38				14 38		15 08			15 38		
Swindon	a							13 10															
Newport (South Wales)	a	10 25																					
Cardiff Central ■	a	10 41																					
Birmingham New Street ■	a					13 38						15 23				15 50		16 26			16 50		
Castle Cary	d		09 34							12 33													15 34
Westbury	d		09 54		10 51					12 53				13 59									15 52
Pewsey	d		10 11							13 10													16 10
Hungerford	a																						
Newbury	a		10 31		11 26					13 30													16 31
Thatcham	a																						
Theale	a																						
Reading ■	a		10 48		11 49			13 47		13 49				14 49					15 49				16 49
Slough ■	a																						
London Paddington ■ ⊖	a		11 29		12 29			14 22		14 29				15 29					16 30				17 30

A ⊼ from Plymouth

For connections to Oxford, Gatwick Airport and Heathrow Airport please refer to Tables 116, 148 and 125A

Table 135

Sundays from 28 October

Cornwall and Devon - Birmingham and London

Route Diagram - see first Page of Table 135

		GW	GW	XC	XC	GW	GW	GW	XC	GW	GW	GW	GW	GW	GW	XC	GW	GW	GW	GW	XC	GW	GW
				◇1	◇1		◇1	◇1	◇1	◇1		◇1	◇		◇1	◇1		◇	◇	◇1	◇1		◇1
					A																A		
				✠	✠		⊡	⊡	✠	⊡		⊡			⊡	✠				⊡	✠		⊡
Penzance	d		12 05		12 30		12 56						13 41					14 40		15 00	15 30		
St Erth	d		12 14		12 40		13 06						13 51					14 50		15 10	15 38		
Hayle	d				12 44								13 54					14 53					
Camborne	d		12 25		12 56		13 19						14 04					15 02		15 22	15 51		
Redruth	d		12 31		13 02		13 25						14 10					15 08		15 29	15 57		
Truro	d		12 43		13 14		13 38						14 21					15 19		15 41	16 09		
St Austell	d		12 59		13 30		13 56						14 38					15 36		15 59	16 25		
Newquay	d																		15 10				
Par	d		13 06		13 38		14 03						14 45					15 43	15a59	16 07	16 33		
Lostwithiel	d		13 13		13 45								14 52					15 50					
Bodmin Parkway	d		13 19		13 52		14 16						14 58					15 56		16 18	16 44		
Liskeard [6]	d		13 33		14 04		14 29						15 11					16 09		16 31	16 56		
Menheniot	d		13 38																				
St Germans	d		13 46										15 21					16 19					
Saltash	d		13 54										15 29					16 27					
St Budeaux Ferry Road	d																						
Keyham	d																						
Dockyard	d																						
Devonport	d																						
Plymouth	a		14 03		14 28		14 54						15 38					16 37		16 57	17 20		
	d		14 06	14 23	14 35		14 55	15 05	15 23			15 43	15 49		16 10	16 25		16 38		17 00	17 26		17 45
Ivybridge	d		14 21										16 07					16 53					
Totnes	d		14 35	14 49	15 00		15 25	15 35	15 49			16 11	16 21		16 42	16 49		17 07		17 28	17 52		18 13
Paignton	d	14 19				14 57				15 45	15 54			16 21			16 55					17 49	
Torquay	d	14 24				15 02				15 51	15 59			16 26			17 00					17 54	
Torre	d	14 27				15 05				15 56	16 02			16 29			17 03					17 57	
Newton Abbot	a	14 35	14 47	15 01	15 11	15 13	15 37	15 47	16 01	16 04	16 10	16 22	16 33	16 37	16 53	17 01	17 11	17 19		17 39	18 02	18 05	18 25
	d	14 37	14 48	15 03	15 12	15 15	15 38	15 48	16 03	16 05	16 11	16 24	16 34	16 38	16 55	17 02	17 12	17 20		17 40	18 04	18 07	18 26
Teignmouth	d	14 44	14 55			15 22				16 13	16 18			16 45			17 19	17 27				18 14	
Dawlish	d	14 49	15 00			15 27				16 18	16 23			16 50			17 24	17 32				18 19	
Dawlish Warren	d	14 54									16 28			16 55			17 29					18 24	
Starcross	d	14 58												16 59								18 28	
Exeter St Thomas	d	15 07												17 08								18 37	
Exeter St Davids [6]	a	15 12	15 16	15 23	15 31	15 41	15 58	16 08	16 23	16 32	16 39	16 44	16 55	17 13	17 17	17 21	17 41	17 46		18 01	18 21	18 40	18 47
Exeter Central	a	15 17				15 53					16 53			17 18			17 51					18 53	
Exmouth	a					16 20					17 20						18 18					19 20	
Exeter St Davids [6]	d			15 25	15 33		16 01	16 10	16 24	16 34		16 45			17 19	17 24		17 51		18 02	18 23		18 49
Tiverton Parkway	d			15 38	15 46		16 16	16 25	16 37			17 01			17 34	17 38				18 18	18 38		
Taunton	d			15 54	16 01		16 31	16 40	16 53	16 59		17 15			17 48	17 51		18 22		18 33	18 52		19 11
Bridgwater	a									17 09								18 33					
Weston-super-Mare	a				16 20			17 01		17 28								18 52					
Bristol Temple Meads [10]	a			16 27	16 52			17 22	17 26	17 58					18 25	18 27		19 23			19 27		
Bath Spa [7]	a							17 41		18 11					18 41								
Filton Abbey Wood	a																						
Bristol Parkway [7]	a			16 38	17 08				17 38							18 38					19 38		
Swindon	a							18 10		18 40					19 10								
Newport (South Wales)	a																						
Cardiff Central [7]	a																						
Birmingham New Street [12]	a			17 49	18 27				18 51							19 50					20 50		
Castle Cary	d											17 37											
Westbury	d											17 56											19 51
Pewsey	d											18 13											
Hungerford	a																						
Newbury	a											18 33											20 24
Thatcham	a																						
Theale	a																						
Reading [7]	a						17 49	18 46		19 19		18 49			19 46					19 49			20 47
Slough [3]	a																						
London Paddington [15] ⊖	a						18 29	19 22		19 59		19 29			20 22					20 29			21 29

A ✠ from Plymouth

For connections to Oxford, Gatwick Airport and Heathrow Airport please refer to Tables 116, 148 and 125A

Table 135

Sundays from 28 October

Cornwall and Devon - Birmingham and London

Route Diagram - see first Page of Table 135

		XC	GW	GW	XC	GW	GW	GW	GW	GW	GW	GW	GW	GW	GW
		◇1	◇1		◇1		◇1		◇1						■
		✠	⊡		✠		⊡		⊡			✠			⊡
Penzance	d		16 10				17 25				19 00	20 05			21 15
St Erth	d		16 21				17 34				19 09	20 14			21 25
Hayle	d											20 17			
Camborne	d		16 33				17 46				19 20	20 26			21 38
Redruth	d		16 40				17 53				19 26	20 32			21 45
Truro	d		16 53				18 05				19 38	20 44			22 00
St Austell	d		17 10				18 24				19 55	21 01			22 18
Newquay	d			17 30											
Par	d		17 17	18a19			18 32				20 03	21 09			
Lostwithiel	d										20 09				
Bodmin Parkway	d		17 29				18 44				20 15	21 21			22 35
Liskeard [6]	d		17 42				18 57				20 28	21 35			22 50
Menheniot	d										20x33				
St Germans	d										20 41				
Saltash	d		18 00								20 48				
St Budeaux Ferry Road	d														
Keyham	d														
Dockyard	d														
Devonport	d										20 56				
Plymouth	a		18 10				19 21				21 00	22 00			23 15
	d		18 10		18 23		19 25		19 55		21 15				23 20
Ivybridge	d														
Totnes	d		18 40		18 49		19 52				21 42				23 48
Paignton	d	18 20				18 55		19 55		20 55			21 52	23 00	
Torquay	d	18 26				19 00		20 00		21 00			21 57	23 05	
Torre	d					19 03		20 03		21 03			22 00	23 08	
Newton Abbot	a	18 36	18 52		19 01	19 11	20 04	20 11	20 31	21 11	21 54		22 08	23 16	23 59
	d	18 37	18 52		19 03	19 13	20 05	20 13	20 32	21 13	21 55		22 10	23 18	00 01
Teignmouth	d					19 20		20 20		21 20	22 02		22 17	23 25	
Dawlish	d					19 25		20 25		21 25	22 07		22 22	23 30	
Dawlish Warren	d					19 30		20 30					22 27	23 35	
Starcross	d					19 34		20 34					22 31	23 39	
Exeter St Thomas	d					19 43		20 43					22 40	23 48	
Exeter St Davids [6]	a	18 56	19 14		19 23	19 48	20 25	20 49	20 53	21 40	22 21		22 43	23 52	00 23
Exeter Central	a					19 54		20 55		21 51			22 51		
Exmouth	a					20 21		21 22		22 18			23 18		
Exeter St Davids [6]	d	18 58	19 16		19 25		20 26		20 55						01 06
Tiverton Parkway	d	19 11	19 31		19 38		20 42		21 10						
Taunton	d	19 25	19 45		19 54		20 55		21 23						
Bridgwater	a														
Weston-super-Mare	a														
Bristol Temple Meads [10]	a	19 57			20 27				22 00						
Bath Spa [7]	a								22 22						
Filton Abbey Wood	a														
Bristol Parkway [7]	a	20 08			20 38										
Swindon	a								22 50						
Newport (South Wales)	a														
Cardiff Central [7]	a														
Birmingham New Street [12]	a	21 20			21 51										
Castle Cary	d		20 07				21 19								
Westbury	d		20 27				21 40								
Pewsey	d						21 58								
Hungerford	a														
Newbury	a						22 18								
Thatcham	a														
Theale	a														
Reading [7]	a		21 19				22 36		23 28						04s07
Slough [3]	a														
London Paddington [15] ⊖	a		21 59				23 16		00 13						05 05

For connections to Oxford, Gatwick Airport and Heathrow Airport please refer to Tables 116, 148 and 125A

Table 135A

Mondays to Fridays

Redruth - Helston

Bus Service

		GW BHX	GW BHX	GW BHX	GW BHX	GW	GW BHX	GW BHX	GW	GW BHX	GW BHX	GW BHX	GW	GW BHX	GW BHX	GW	GW BHX	GW BHX	GW BHX
Redruth	d	08 00	08 00	09 05	09 15	10 10	10 15	11 15	12 10	12 15	13 15	14 05	14 10	14 15	15 15	16 10	16 15	17 00	17 00
Helston Coinagehall St	a	08 34	08 38	09 37	09 47	10 42	10 47	11 47	12 42	12 47	13 47	14 37	14 42	14 47	15 47	16 42	16 47	17 32	17 42

		GW BHX	GW	GW BHX	GW BHX
Redruth	d	17 15	18 10	18 15	19 15
Helston Coinagehall St	a	17 47	18 42	18 47	19 47

Saturdays

		GW A	GW A	GW	GW	GW	GW	GW	GW	GW	GW	GW
Redruth	d	08 00	09 15	10 15	11 15	12 15	13 15	14 15	15 15	16 15	17 15	18 15
Helston Coinagehall St	a	08 29	09 47	10 47	11 47	12 47	13 47	14 47	15 47	16 47	17 47	18 47

Sundays

		GW	GW	GW	GW	GW
Redruth	d	10 10	12 10	14 10	16 10	18 10
Helston Coinagehall St	a	10 42	12 42	14 42	16 42	18 42

A Operates on School Holidays only

Table 135A

Mondays to Fridays

Helston - Redruth

Bus Service

		GW BHX	GW BHX B	GW BHX	GW BHX B	GW	GW BHX B	GW BHX	GW BHX B	GW	GW BHX B	GW BHX	GW BHX B	GW	GW BHX B	GW BHX A	GW	GW BHX A	GW BHX A
Helston Coinagehall St	d	07 05	07 10	08 06	08 10	09 12	09 35	10 27	10 35	10 42	11 35	12 27	12 35	12 42	13 35	14 35	14 42	15 15	15 35
Redruth	a	07 39	07 44	08 55	08 55	09 44	10 09	11 01	11 09	11 14	12 09	13 01	13 09	13 14	14 09	15 09	15 14	15 54	16 09

		GW BHX A	GW BHX A	GW	GW BHX	GW BHX B	GW BHX A	GW A
Helston Coinagehall St	d	16 30	16 35	16 42	17 30	17 35	18 30	18 42
Redruth	a	17 04	17 09	17 14	18 04	18 09	19 02	19 14

Saturdays

		GW	GW	GW	GW	GW	GW	GW	GW	GW	GW	GW
Helston Coinagehall St	d	07 10	08 10	09 35	10 35	11 35	12 35	13 35	14 35	15 35	16 35	17 35
Redruth	a	07 44	08 44	10 09	11 09	12 09	13 09	14 09	15 09	16 09	17 09	18 09

Sundays

		GW	GW	GW	GW	GW	GW
Helston Coinagehall St	d	09 12	10 42	12 42	14 42	16 42	18 42
Redruth	a	09 44	11 14	13 14	15 14	17 14	19 14

A Runs during school holidays only.

B Runs during College Holidays only.

Table 135B

Mondays to Fridays

St. Austell - Eden Project

Bus Service

		GW BHX	GW BHX	GW	GW BHX	GW	GW	GW BHX	GW	GW	GW BHX	GW BHX	GW BHX	GW	GW BHX	GW	GW	GW BHX	GW BHX	GW BHX	GW	GW	GW BHX
St Austell	d	08 35	08 45	08 50	09 30	09 35	10 35	10 40	11 35	11 40	11 50	12 30	12 35	13 35	13 55	14 35	14 45	15 02	15 35	16 10	16 25	16 35	17 05
Eden Project	a	08 57	09 04	09 09	09 49	09 57	10 57	10 59	11 57	11 59	12 09	12 49	12 57	13 57	14 14	14 57	15 04	15 21	15 57	16 29	16 44	16 57	17 24

		GW	GW BHX
St Austell	d	17 10	17 35
Eden Project	a	17 29	17 57

Saturdays

		GW	GW	GW	GW	GW	GW	GW	GW	GW	GW	GW	GW	GW	GW	GW	GW	GW	GW
St Austell	d	08 35	08 45	09 30	09 35	10 35	10 40	11 35	12 05	12 35	13 35	13 55	14 35	15 02	15 35	15 50	16 35	17 00	17 35
Eden Project	a	08 57	09 04	09 49	09 57	10 57	10 59	11 57	12 24	12 57	13 57	14 14	14 57	15 21	15 57	16 09	16 57	17 19	17 57

Sundays

		GW	GW	GW	GW	GW	GW	GW	GW	GW	GW	GW	GW	GW	GW	GW
St Austell	d	08 50	09 35	10 35	11 35	11 40	12 30	12 35	13 35	14 35	14 45	15 35	16 25	16 35	17 10	17 35
Eden Project	a	09 09	09 57	10 57	11 57	11 59	12 49	12 57	13 57	14 57	15 04	15 57	16 44	16 57	17 29	17 57

Table 135B

Mondays to Fridays

Eden Project - St. Austell

Bus Service

		GW BHX	GW BHX	GW	GW BHX	GW	GW BHX	GW	GW BHX	GW BHX	GW	GW BHX	GW BHX	GW	GW BHX	GW	GW	GW BHX	GW	GW	GW BHX	GW	GW BHX
Eden Project	d	09 00	09 10	09 50	09 55	10 00	10 00	11 00	11 00	11 15	12 00	12 00	12 10	13 00	13 00	13 05	14 00	14 00	14 25	15 00	15 00	15 15	15 22
St Austell	a	09 24	09 29	10 09	10 14	10 22	10 24	11 22	11 24	11 34	12 22	12 24	12 29	13 22	13 24	13 24	14 22	14 24	14 44	15 22	15 24	15 34	15 41

		GW	GW	GW	GW BHX	GW	GW	GW BHX	GW
Eden Project	d	16 00	16 00	16 05	16 30	16 50	17 00	17 00	18 00
St Austell	a	16 22	16 24	16 24	16 49	17 09	17 22	17 24	18 24

Saturdays

		GW	GW	GW	GW	GW	GW	GW	GW	GW	GW	GW	GW	GW	GW	GW	GW	GW	GW
Eden Project	d	09 00	09 10	09 55	10 00	11 00	11 15	12 00	13 00	13 15	14 00	14 25	15 00	15 22	16 00	16 25	17 00	17 55	18 00
St Austell	a	09 24	09 29	10 14	10 24	11 24	11 34	12 24	13 24	13 34	14 24	14 44	15 24	15 41	16 24	16 44	17 24	18 14	18 24

Sundays

		GW	GW	GW	GW	GW	GW	GW	GW	GW	GW	GW	GW	GW	GW	GW
Eden Project	d	09 50	10 00	11 00	12 00	13 00	13 05	14 00	14 25	15 00	15 15	16 00	16 05	16 50	17 00	18 00
St Austell	a	10 09	10 22	11 22	12 22	13 22	13 24	14 22	14 44	15 22	15 34	16 22	16 24	17 09	17 22	18 24

Table 135C

Mondays to Saturdays

Bodmin - Wadebridge and Padstow

Bus Service

		GW BHX	GW BHX	GW	GW BHX	GW	GW BHX	GW	GW BHX	GW BHX	GW BHX	GW	GW	GW	GW
Bodmin Parkway	d	07 25	08 30	09 30	10 30	11 30	12 30	13 30	14 30	15 30	16 30	17 30	18 30	19 30	22 00
Bodmin Mount Folly	a	07 35	08 40	09 40	10 40	11 40	12 40	13 40	14 40	15 40	16 40	17 40	18 40	19 40	22 10
Wadebridge Bus Station	a	07 55	09 00	10 00	11 00	12 00	13 00	14 00	15 00	16 00	17 00	18 00	19 00	20 00	22 30
Padstow Old Rly Station	a	08 27	09 27	10 27	11 27	12 27	13 27	14 27	15 27	16 27	17 27	18 27	19 27	20 27	22 57

Sundays

		GW	GW	GW	GW	GW	GW
Bodmin Parkway	d	09 30	11 30	13 30	15 30	17 30	19 30
Bodmin Mount Folly	a	09 40	11 40	13 40	15 40	17 40	19 40
Wadebridge Bus Station	a	10 00	12 00	14 00	16 00	18 00	20 00
Padstow Old Rly Station	a	10 27	12 27	14 27	16 27	18 27	20 27

Table 135C

Mondays to Saturdays

Padstow and Wadebridge - Bodmin

Bus Service

		GW BHX	GW BHX	GW	GW	GW	GW BHX	GW BHX	GW BHX	GW BHX	GW BHX	GW BHX	GW BHX	GW	GW BHX
Padstow Old Rly Station	d	06 30	07 30	08 30	09 30	10 30	11 30	12 30	13 30	14 30	15 30	16 30	17 30	18 30	20 30
Wadebridge Bus Station	d	06 55	07 55	08 55	09 55	10 55	11 55	12 55	13 55	14 55	15 55	16 55	17 55	18 55	20 55
Bodmin Mount Folly	d	07 15	08 15	09 15	10 15	11 15	12 15	13 15	14 15	15 15	16 15	17 15	18 15	19 15	21 15
Bodmin Parkway	a	07 25	08 25	09 25	10 25	11 25	12 25	13 25	14 25	15 25	16 25	17 25	18 25	19 25	21 25

Sundays

		GW	GW	GW	GW	GW	GW
Padstow Old Rly Station	d	08 30	10 30	12 30	14 30	16 30	18 30
Wadebridge Bus Station	d	08 55	10 55	12 55	14 55	16 55	18 55
Bodmin Mount Folly	d	09 15	11 15	13 15	15 15	17 15	19 15
Bodmin Parkway	a	09 25	11 25	13 25	15 25	17 25	19 25

Table 135D

Mondays to Saturdays

Exeter - Okehampton, Holsworthy and Bude

Bus Service

		GW BHX	GW BHX	GW BHX	GW	GW BHX	GW BHX	GW BHX	GW	GW BHX	GW BHX	GW	GW	GW BHX	GW	GW BHX	GW BHX
Exeter St Davids	d	08 00	08 50	09 45	10 20	10 45	11 20	11 45	11 50	12 20	13 20	13 20	13 45	14 20	15 20	15 20	15 45
Okehampton West Street	a	08 45	09 40	10 25	11 05	11 25	12 10	12 25	12 35	13 05	14 00	14 05	14 25	15 10	16 05	16 10	16 25
Holsworthy Library	a			11 03				13 03	13 15		14 40		15 03				17 03
Holsworthy Cattle Market	a																
Bude Strand	a			11 25				13 25	13 35		15 00		15 25				17 25

		GW BHX	GW	GW	GW BHX	GW BHX
Exeter St Davids	d	16 20	16 50	17 50	17 55	18 35
Okehampton West Street	a	17 00	17 30	18 35	18 35	19 20
Holsworthy Library	a			19 15	19 13	19 55
Holsworthy Cattle Market	a					
Bude Strand	a			19 35	19 35	20 15

Sundays

		GW	GW	GW	GW	GW	GW
Exeter St Davids	d	10 20	11 50	13 20	15 20	16 50	17 50
Okehampton West Street	a	11 05	12 35	14 05	16 05	17 30	18 35
Holsworthy Library	a		13 15				19 15
Holsworthy Cattle Market	a						
Bude Strand	a		13 35				19 35

Table 135D

Mondays to Saturdays

Bude, Holsworthy and Okehampton - Exeter

Bus Service

		GW BHX	GW BHX	GW BHX	GW BHX	GW BHX	GW BHX	GW BHX	GW	GW BHX	GW BHX	GW	GW BHX	GW BHX	GW BHX	GW	GW BHX
Bude Strand	d	06 40				08 40		09 00	09 45				11 30				13 30
Holsworthy Church	d	07 02				09 05		09 22	10 05				11 52				13 52
Holsworthy Cattle Market	d																
Okehampton West Street	d	07 45	09 10	09 25	09 35	09 45	09 55	10 05	10 40	11 10	11 40	11 45	12 35	13 10	14 10	14 15	14 35
Exeter St Davids	a	08 25	09 55	10 00	10 15	10 20	10 40	10 45	11 30	11 45	12 25	12 30	13 15	13 55	14 50	15 00	15 15

		GW A	GW BHX	GW BHX	GW SX BHX	GW BHX	GW SO	GW A
Bude Strand	d				15 27	15 30	15 30	15 45
Holsworthy Church	d				15 57	15 55	15 57	16 05
Holsworthy Cattle Market	d							
Okehampton West Street	d	14 45	15 10	15 40	16 40	16 40	16 40	16 40
Exeter St Davids	a	15 30	15 45	16 25	17 25	17x25	17 25	17 30

Sundays

		GW	GW	GW	GW	GW
Bude Strand	d	09 45				15 45
Holsworthy Church	d	10 05				16 05
Holsworthy Cattle Market	d					
Okehampton West Street	d	10 40	11 45	14 15	14 45	16 40
Exeter St Davids	a	11 30	12 30	15 00	15 30	17 30

Table 135E

Mondays to Saturdays
until 2 June

Taunton - Watchet, Dunster and Minehead

Bus Service

		GW SX BHX	GW	GW BHX	GW BHX	GW BHX	GW BHX A	GW BHX B	GW C	GW D	GW BHX E	GW BHX F	GW BHX G	GW BHX H	GW BHX I	GW BHX J	GW K	GW BHX L	GW BHX M	GW BHX N	GW O
Taunton	d	05 41	06 21	07 17	07 47	08 17	08 47	09 17	09 47	10 17	10 47	11 17	11 47	12 17	12 47	13 17	13 47	14 17	14 47	15 17	15 47
Bishops Lydeard Hithermead	a	05 56	06 36	07 32	08 02	08 32	09 02	09 32	10 02	10 32	11 02	11 32	12 02	12 32	13 02	13 32	14 02	14 32	15 02	15 32	16 02
Watchet (West Somerset Ry)	a	06 25	07 05	08 01	08 31	09 01	09 35	10 05	10 35	11 05	11 35	12 05	12 35	13 05	13 35	14 05	14 35	15 05	15 35	16 05	16 35
Dunster Steep	a	06 39	07 19	08 19	08 49	09 19	09 53	10 23	10 53	11 23	11 53	12 23	12 53	13 23	13 53	14 23	14 53	15 23	15 53	16 23	16 53
Minehead Parade	a	06 47	07 27	08 27	08 57	09 27	10 01	10 31	11 01	11 31	12 01	12 31	13 01	13 31	14 01	14 31	15 01	15 31	16 01	16 31	17 01
Minehead Butlins	a	06 52	07 32	08 32	09 02	09 32	10 06	10 36	11 06	11 36	12 06	12 36	13 06	13 36	14 06	14 36	15 06	15 36	16 06	16 36	17 06

		GW BHX P	GW BHX	GW SX BHX	GW SO	GW BHX	GW	GW BHX	GW BHX	GW BHX
Taunton	d	16 17	16 47	17 12	17 12	17 37	18 07	18 37	20 16	22 16
Bishops Lydeard Hithermead	a	16 32	17 02	.	17 27	17 52	18 22	18 52	20 31	22 31
Watchet (West Somerset Ry)	a	17 05	17 31	17 54	17 56	18 21	18 51	19 21	21 00	23 00
Dunster Steep	a	17 23	17 49	18 12	18 14	18 39	19 09	19 39	21 14	23 14
Minehead Parade	a	17 31	17 57	18 20	18 22	18 47	19 17	19 47	21 22	23 22
Minehead Butlins	a	17 36	18 02	18 25	18 27	18 52	19 22	19 52	21 27	23 27

Mondays to Saturdays
4 June to 25 August

		GW SX BHX Q	GW	GW BHX	GW BHX	GW BHX	GW BHX T	GW BHX U	GW W	GW X	GW BHX Y	GW BHX Z	GW BHX AA	GW BHX BB	GW BHX CC	GW BHX DD
Taunton	d	05 41	06 21	07 17	07 47	08 17	08 47	09 17	09 47	10 17	10 47	11 17	11 47	12 17	12 47	13 17
Bishops Lydeard Hithermead	a	05 56	06 36	07 32	08 02	08 32	09 02	09 32	10 02	10 32	11 02	11 32	12 02	12 32	13 02	13 32
Watchet (West Somerset Ry)	a	06 25	07 05	08 01	08 31	09 01	09 35	10 05	10 35	11 05	11 35	12 05	12 35	13 05	13 35	14 05
Dunster Steep	a	06 39	07 19	08 19	08 49	09 19	09 53	10 23	10 53	11 23	11 53	12 23	12 53	13 23	13 53	14 23
Minehead Parade	a	06 47	07 27	08 27	08 57	09 27	10 01	10 31	11 01	11 31	12 01	12 31	13 01	13 31	14 01	14 31
Minehead Butlins	a	06 52	07 32	08 32	09 02	09 32	10 06	10 36	11 06	11 36	12 06	12 36	13 06	13 36	14 06	14 36

		GW FF	GW BHX GG	GW BHX HH	GW BHX II	GW KK	GW BHX LL	GW BHX	GW BHX Q	GW SO	GW BHX	GW R	GW BHX R	GW BHX R	GW BHX R
Taunton	d	13 47	14 17	14 47	15 17	15 47	16 17	16 47	17 12	17 12	17 37	18 07	18 37	20 16	22 16
Bishops Lydeard Hithermead	a	14 02	14 32	15 02	15 32	16 02	16 32	17 02		17 27	17 52	18 22	18 52	20 31	22 31
Watchet (West Somerset Ry)	a	14 35	15 05	15 35	16 05	16 35	17 05	17 31	17 54	17 56	18 21	18 51	19 21	21 00	23 00
Dunster Steep	a	14 53	15 23	15 53	16 23	16 53	17 23	17 49	18 12	18 14	18 39	19 09	19 39	21 14	23 14
Minehead Parade	a	15 01	15 31	16 01	16 31	17 01	17 31	17 57	18 20	18 22	18 47	19 17	19 47	21 22	23 22
Minehead Butlins	a	15 06	15 36	16 06	16 36	17 06	17 36	18 02	18 25	18 27	18 52	19 22	19 52	21 27	23 27

Also Stops at West Somerset Railway(WSR) station at

- **A** 0906 on railway operating days
- **B** 0936 on railway operating days
- **C** 1006 on railway operating days
- **D** 1036 on railway operating days
- **E** 1106 on railway operating days
- **F** 1136 on railway operating days
- **G** 1206 on railway operating days
- **H** 1236 on railway operating days
- **I** 1306 on railway operating days
- **J** 1336 on railway operating days
- **K** 1406 on railway operating days
- **L** 1436 on railway operating days
- **M** 1506 on railway operating days
- **N** 1536 on railway operating days
- **O** 1606 on railway operating days
- **P** 1636 on railway operating days
- **Q** from 6 June until 24 August
- **T** 0906 on railway operating days
- **U** 0936 on railway operating days
- **W** 1006 on railway operating days
- **X** 1036 on railway operating days
- **Y** 1106 on railway operating days
- **Z** 1136 on railway operating days
- **AA** 1206 on railway operating days
- **BB** 1236 on railway operating days
- **CC** 1306 on railway operating days
- **DD** 1336 on railway operating days
- **FF** 1406 on railway operating days
- **GG** 1436 on railway operating days
- **HH** 1506 on railway operating days
- **II** 1536 on railway operating days
- **KK** 1606 on railway operating days
- **LL** 1636 on railway operating days

WSR is an abbreviation for West Somerset Railway

Table 135E

Mondays to Saturdays
from 27 August

Taunton - Watchet, Dunster and Minehead

Bus Service

		GW SX BHX A	GW	GW BHX	GW BHX	GW BHX	GW BHX D	GW BHX E	GW G	GW H	GW BHX I	GW BHX J	GW BHX L	GW BHX M	GW BHX N	GW BHX O
Taunton	d	05 41	06 21	07 17	07 47	08 17	08 47	09 17	09 47	10 17	10 47	11 17	11 47	12 17	12 47	13 17
Bishops Lydeard Hithermead	a	05 56	06 36	07 32	08 02	08 32	09 02	09 32	10 02	10 32	11 02	11 32	12 02	12 32	13 02	13 32
Watchet (West Somerset Ry)	a	06 25	07 05	08 01	08 31	09 01	09 35	10 05	10 35	11 05	11 35	12 05	12 35	13 05	13 35	14 05
Dunster Steep	a	06 39	07 19	08 19	08 49	09 19	09 53	10 23	10 53	11 23	11 53	12 23	12 53	13 23	13 53	14 23
Minehead Parade	a	06 47	07 27	08 27	08 57	09 27	10 01	10 31	11 01	11 31	12 01	12 31	13 01	13 31	14 01	14 31
Minehead Butlins	a	06 52	07 32	08 32	09 02	09 32	10 06	10 36	11 06	11 36	12 06	12 36	13 06	13 36	14 06	14 36

		GW Q	GW BHX R	GW BHX S	GW BHX T	GW V	GW BHX W	GW BHX	GW BHX A	GW SO	GW BHX	GW	GW BHX	GW BHX	GW BHX
Taunton	d	13 47	14 17	14 47	15 17	15 47	16 17	16 47	17 12	17 12	17 37	18 07	18 37	20 16	22 16
Bishops Lydeard Hithermead	a	14 02	14 32	15 02	15 32	16 02	16 32	17 02		17 27	17 52	18 22	18 52	20 31	22 31
Watchet (West Somerset Ry)	a	14 35	15 05	15 35	16 05	16 35	17 05	17 31	17 54	17 56	18 21	18 51	19 21	21 00	23 00
Dunster Steep	a	14 53	15 23	15 53	16 23	16 53	17 23	17 49	18 12	18 14	18 39	19 09	19 39	21 14	23 14
Minehead Parade	a	15 01	15 31	16 01	16 31	17 01	17 31	17 57	18 20	18 22	18 47	19 17	19 47	21 22	23 22
Minehead Butlins	a	15 06	15 36	16 06	16 36	17 06	17 36	18 02	18 25	18 27	18 52	19 22	19 52	21 27	23 27

Sundays

		GW BHX	GW X	GW Y	GW	GW Z	GW	GW [	GW	GW	GW
Taunton	d	08 22	09 22	11 28	12 38	13 38	14 38	15 38	16 38	17 38	19 38
Bishops Lydeard Hithermead	a	08 37	09 37	11 43	12 53	13 53	14 53	15 53	16 53	17 53	19 53
Watchet (West Somerset Ry)	a	09 10	10 10	12 13	13 22	14 23	15 22	16 23	17 22	18 22	20 22
Dunster Steep	a	09 28	10 28	12 30	13 39	14 40	15 39	16 40	17 39	18 39	20 39
Minehead Parade	a	09 36	10 36	12 38	13 47	14 48	15 47	16 48	17 47	18 47	20 47
Minehead Butlins	a	09 41	10 41	12 43	13 52	14 53	15 52	16 53	17 52	18 52	20 52

Also Stops at West Somerset Railway(WSR) station at

- **A** from 28 August
- **D** 0906 on railway operating days
- **E** 0936 on railway operating days
- **G** 1006 on railway operating days
- **H** 1036 on railway operating days
- **I** 1106 on railway operating days
- **J** 1136 on railway operating days
- **L** 1206 on railway operating days
- **M** 1236 on railway operating days
- **N** 1306 on railway operating days
- **O** 1336 on railway operating days
- **Q** 1406 on railway operating days
- **R** 1436 on railway operating days
- **S** 1506 on railway operating days
- **T** 1536 on railway operating days
- **V** 1606 on railway operating days
- **W** 1636 on railway operating days
- **X** 0941 on railway operating days
- **Y** 1146 on railway operating days
- **Z** 1356 on railway operating days
- **[** 1556 on railway operating days

WSR is an abbreviation for West Somerset Railway

Table 135E

Minehead, Dunster and Watchet - Taunton

Bus Service

Mondays to Saturdays until 2 June

		GW	GW	GW SX BHX	GW SX BHX	GW SO	GW BHX	GW	GW	GW	GW SX BHX	GW SO	GW	GW A	GW B	GW C	GW D	GW E	GW F	GW G	GW H
Minehead Butlins	d	05 45	06 30	06 50	07 00	07 00	07 50	08 20	08 50	09 20	09 50	09 50	10 20	10 50	11 20	11 50	12 20	12 50	13 20	13 50	14 20
Minehead Bancks Street	d	05 50	06 35	06 58	07 08	07 10	08 00	08 30	09 00	09 30	10 00	10 00	10 30	11 00	11 30	12 00	12 30	13 00	13 30	14 00	14 30
Dunster Steep	d	05 58	06 43	07 06	07 16	07 18	08 08	08 38	09 08	09 38	10 08	10 08	10 38	11 08	11 38	12 08	12 38	13 08	13 38	14 08	14 38
Watchet (West Somerset Ry)	d	06 13	06 58	07 25	07 35	07 37	08 27	08 57	09 27	09 57	10 27	10 27	10 57	11 27	11 57	12 27	12 57	13 27	13 57	14 27	14 57
Bishops Lydeard Hithermead	d	06 41	07 26	07 54		08 06	08 56	09 26	09 56	10 26	10 56	10 57	11 26	12 00	12 30	13 00	13 30	14 00	14 30	15 00	15 30
Taunton	a	06 55	07 40	08 14	08 23	08 20	09 10	09 40	10 10	10 40	11 10	11 10	11 40	12 14	12 44	13 14	13 44	14 14	14 44	15 14	15 44

		GW I	GW J	GW K	GW L	GW M	GW N	GW O	GW	GW
Minehead Butlins	d	14 50	15 20	15 50	16 20	16 50	17 20	17 50	19 40	21 30
Minehead Bancks Street	d	15 00	15 30	16 00	16 30	17 00	17 30	18 00	19 45	21 35
Dunster Steep	d	15 08	15 38	16 08	16 38	17 08	17 38	18 08	19 53	21 43
Watchet (West Somerset Ry)	d	15 27	15 57	16 27	16 57	17 27	17 57	18 27	20 08	21 58
Bishops Lydeard Hithermead	d	16 00	16 30	17 00	17 30	18 00	18 30	19 00	20 36	22 26
Taunton	a	16 14	16 44	17 14	17 44	18 14	18 44	19 14	20 50	22 40

Mondays to Saturdays 4 June to 25 August

		GW	GW	GW SX BHX Q	GW SX BHX Q	GW SO	GW BHX	GW	GW	GW	GW SX BHX	GW SO	GW	GW A	GW	GW S	GW T	GW U	GW W	GW X
Minehead Butlins	d	05 45	06 30	06 50	07 00	07 00	07 50	08 20	08 50	09 20	09 50	09 50	10 20	10 50	11 20	11 50	12 20	12 50	13 20	13 50
Minehead Bancks Street	d	05 50	06 35	06 58	07 08	07 10	08 00	08 30	09 00	09 30	10 00	10 00	10 30	11 00	11 30	12 00	12 30	13 00	13 30	14 00
Dunster Steep	d	05 58	06 43	07 06	07 16	07 18	08 08	08 38	09 08	09 38	10 08	10 08	10 38	11 08	11 38	12 08	12 38	13 08	13 38	14 08
Watchet (West Somerset Ry)	d	06 13	06 58	07 25	07 35	07 37	08 27	08 57	09 27	09 57	10 27	10 27	10 57	11 27	11 57	12 27	12 57	13 27	13 57	14 27
Bishops Lydeard Hithermead	d	06 41	07 26	07 54		08 06	08 56	09 26	09 56	10 26	10 56	10 57	11 26	12 00	12 30	13 00	13 30	14 00	14 30	15 00
Taunton	a	06 55	07 40	08 14	08 23	08 20	09 10	09 40	10 10	10 40	11 10	11 10	11 40	12 14	12 44	13 14	13 44	14 14	14 44	15 14

		GW Z	GW [	GW BB	GW CC	GW DD	GW EE	GW GG	GW HH	GW	GW
Minehead Butlins	d	14 20	14 50	15 20	15 50	16 20	16 50	17 20	17 50	19 40	21 30
Minehead Bancks Street	d	14 30	15 00	15 30	16 00	16 30	17 00	17 30	18 00	19 45	21 35
Dunster Steep	d	14 38	15 08	15 38	16 08	16 38	17 08	17 38	18 08	19 53	21 43
Watchet (West Somerset Ry)	d	14 57	15 27	15 57	16 27	16 57	17 27	17 57	18 27	20 08	21 58
Bishops Lydeard Hithermead	d	15 30	16 00	16 30	17 00	17 30	18 00	18 30	19 00	20 36	22 26
Taunton	a	15 44	16 14	16 44	17 14	17 44	18 14	18 44	19 14	20 50	22 40

Mondays to Saturdays from 27 August

		GW	GW	GW SX BHX JJ	GW SX BHX JJ	GW SO	GW BHX	GW	GW	GW	GW SX BHX	GW SO	GW	GW A	GW KK	GW LL	GW MM	GW NN	GW PP	GW QQ
Minehead Butlins	d	05 45	06 30	06 50	07 00	07 00	07 50	08 20	08 50	09 20	09 50	09 50	1020	10 50	11 20	11 50	12 20	12 50	13 20	13 50
Minehead Bancks Street	d	05 50	06 35	06 58	07 08	07 10	08 00	08 30	09 00	09 30	10 00	10 00	1030	11 00	11 30	12 00	12 30	13 00	13 30	14 00
Dunster Steep	d	05 58	06 43	07 06	07 16	07 18	08 08	08 38	09 08	09 38	10 08	10 08	1038	11 08	11 38	12 08	12 38	13 08	13 38	14 08
Watchet (West Somerset Ry)	d	06 13	06 58	07 25	07 35	07 37	08 27	08 57	09 27	09 57	10 27	10 27	1057	11 27	11 57	12 27	12 57	13 27	13 57	14 27
Bishops Lydeard Hithermead	d	06 41	07 26	07 54		08 06	08 56	09 26	09 56	10 26	10 56	10 57	1126	12 00	12 30	13 00	13 30	14 00	14 30	15 00
Taunton	a	06 55	07 40	08 14	08 23	08 20	09 10	09 40	10 10	10 40	11 10	11 10	1140	12 14	12 44	13 14	13 44	14 14	14 44	15 14

Also Stops at West Somerset Railway(WSR) station at

- **A** 1156 on railway operating days
- **B** 1226 on railway operating days
- **C** 1256 on railway operating days
- **D** 1326 on railway operating days
- **E** 1356 on railway operating days
- **F** 1426 on railway operating days
- **G** 1456 on railway operating days
- **H** 1526 on railway operating days
- **I** 1556 on railway operating days
- **J** 1626 on railway operating days
- **K** 1656 on railway operating days
- **L** 1726 on railway operating days
- **M** 1756 on railway operating days
- **N** 1826 on railway operating days
- **O** 1856 on railway operating days
- **Q** from 6 June until 24 August
- **R** 1226 on railway operating days
- **S** 1256 on railway operating days
- **T** 1326 on railway operating days
- **U** 1356 on railway operating days
- **W** 1426 on railway operating days
- **X** 1456 on railway operating days
- **Z** 1526 on railway operating days
- **[** 1556 on railway operating days
- **BB** 1626 on railway operating days
- **CC** 1656 on railway operating days
- **DD** 1726 on railway operating days
- **EE** 1756 on railway operating days
- **GG** 1826 on railway operating days
- **HH** 1856 on railway operating days
- **JJ** from 28 August
- **KK** 1226 on railway operating days
- **LL** 1256 on railway operating days
- **MM** 1326 on railway operating days
- **NN** 1356 on railway operating days
- **PP** 1426 on railway operating days
- **QQ** 1456 on railway operating days

WSR is an abbreviation for West Somerset Railway

Table 135E

Minehead, Dunster and Watchet - Taunton

Bus Service

Mondays to Saturdays from 27 August

		GW B	GW C	GW E	GW F	GW G	GW H	GW J	GW K	GW	GW
Minehead Butlins	d	14 20	14 50	15 20	15 50	16 20	16 50	17 20	17 50	19 40	21 30
Minehead Bancks Street	d	14 30	15 00	15 30	16 00	16 30	17 00	17 30	18 00	19 45	21 35
Dunster Steep	d	14 38	15 08	15 38	16 08	16 38	17 08	17 38	18 08	19 53	21 43
Watchet (West Somerset Ry)	d	14 57	15 27	15 57	16 27	16 57	17 27	17 57	18 27	20 08	21 58
Bishops Lydeard Hithermead	d	15 30	16 00	16 30	17 00	17 30	18 00	18 30	19 00	20 36	22 26
Taunton	a	15 44	16 14	16 44	17 14	17 44	18 14	18 44	19 14	20 50	22 40

Sundays

		GW	GW	GW M	GW N	GW	GW O	GW	GW P	GW	GW
Minehead Butlins	d	08 50	09 50	10 50	12 58	13 58	14 58	15 58	16 58	17 58	18 58
Minehead Bancks Street	d	09 00	10 00	11 00	13 06	14 06	15 06	16 06	17 06	18 06	19 06
Dunster Steep	d	09 08	10 08	11 08	13 14	14 14	15 14	16 14	17 14	18 14	19 14
Watchet (West Somerset Ry)	d	09 27	10 27	11 27	13 32	14 32	15 32	16 32	17 32	18 32	19 32
Bishops Lydeard Hithermead	d	09 56	10 56	12 00	14 03	15 00	16 03	17 00	18 03	19 00	20 00
Taunton	a	10 10	11 10	12 14	14 16	15 13	16 16	17 13	18 16	19 13	20 13

Also Stops at West Somerset Railway(WSR) station at

- **B** 1526 on railway operating days
- **C** 1556 on railway operating days
- **E** 1626 on railway operating days
- **F** 1656 on railway operating days
- **G** 1726 on railway operating days
- **H** 1756 on railway operating days
- **J** 1826 on railway operating days
- **K** 1856 on railway operating days
- **M** 1156 on railway operating days
- **N** 1359 on railway operating days
- **O** 1559 on railway operating days
- **P** 1759 on railway operating days

WSR is an abbreviation for West Somerset Railway

Table 136

Mondays to Fridays

Exmouth - Exeter - Barnstaple

Route Diagram - see first Page of Table 135

Miles	Miles			SW MX ◇1 H	GW MO A	GW MX	GW B	GW C	SW 1	GW	GW	SW 1	GW	SW 1	GW	GW	GW	GW	GW	SW ◇1	GW	GW	SW ◇1 H
0	—	**Exmouth**	d		23p59	00 02				06 12	06 45		07 14		07 53		08 23		08 53		09 23	09 53	
2	—	Lympstone Village	d		00 03	00 06				06 16	06 49		07 18		07 57		08 27		08 57		09 27	09 57	
3	—	Lympstone Commando	d		00x04	00x07				06x17	06x52		07x20		07x58		08x29		08x58		09x28		
3½	—	Exton	d		00x06	00x09				06x19	06x53		07x21		08x00		08x30		09x00		09x30		
5	—	Topsham	d		00 11	00 14				06 24	06 58		07 29		08 05		08 35		09 05		09 35	10 05	
7	—	Digby & Sowton	d		00 15	00 19				06 29	07 03		07 33		08 10		08 40		09 10		09 40	10 10	
9	—	Polsloe Bridge	d		00 19	00 22				06 32	07 06		07 37		08 14		08 44		09 14		09 44		
10	—	St James' Park	d		00 21	00 25				06 35	07 09		07 40		08 17	08 34	08 47		09 17		09 47		
10½	—	**Exeter Central**	a		00 24	00s27				06 37	07 11		07 42		08 20	08 36	08 49		09 19		09 50	10 16	
—	—		d	23p57	00 25				06 32	06 38	07 12	07 39	07 43	08 15	08 24	08 37	08 50	09 06	09 20	09 39	09 50	10 17	10 39
11¼	—	**Exeter St Davids** 6	a	00 01	00 28	00 31			06 35	06 41	07 15	07 42	07 46	08 18	08 26	08 42	08 54	09 11	09 24	09 42	09 54	10 21	10 42
—	—		d				05 50	05 54		06 48					08 31				09 27			10 27	
15½	—	Newton St Cyres	d																				
18¼	0	Crediton	d				06 01	06 05		06 59					08 42				09 38			10 38	
21¾	3½	Yeoford	d				06x07	06x11		07x05					08x48				09x44			10x44	
—	14¾	Sampford Courtenay	d																				
—	18	Okehampton	a																				
24½	—	Copplestone	d				06x12	06x16		07x10					08x53				09x49			10x49	
26¼	—	Morchard Road	d							07x13					08x56				09x52			10x52	
28¾	—	Lapford	d							07x17													
32½	—	Eggesford	d				06 27	06 31		07 33					09 11				10 08			11 08	
36½	—	Kings Nympton	d							07x38					09x17								
39¼	—	Portsmouth Arms	d							07x43													
43½	—	Umberleigh	d				06x41	06x45		07x49					09x27				10x23			11x23	
45¾	—	Chapelton	d							07x53													
50¼	—	**Barnstaple**	a				06 55	06 59		08 01					09 39				10 35			11 35	

		GW	GW	SW ◇1 H	GW	GW	SW ◇1 H	GW	GW	SW ◇1 H	GW	GW	SW ◇1 H	GW	GW	SW ◇1 H	GW	GW	SW ◇1 H	GW	GW	GW	SW ◇1 H
Exmouth	d	10 23	10 53		11 23	11 53		12 23	12 53		13 23	13 53		14 23	14 53		15 23	15 53			16 25	16 55	
Lympstone Village	d	10 27	10 57		11 27	11 57		12 27	12 57		13 27	13 57		14 27	14 57		15 27	15 57			16 29	16 59	
Lympstone Commando	d	10x28			11x28			12x28			13x28			14x28			15x28	15x58			16x30	17x00	
Exton	d	10x30			11x30			12x30			13x30			14x30			15x30	16x00			16x32	17x02	
Topsham	d	10 35	11 05		11 35	12 05		12 35	13 05		13 35	14 05		14 35	15 05		15 35	16 05			16 37	17 07	
Digby & Sowton	d	10 40	11 10		11 40	12 10		12 40	13 10		13 40	14 10		14 40	15 10		15 40	16 10			16 42	17 12	
Polsloe Bridge	d	10 44			11 44			12 44			13 44			14 44			15 44	16 14			16 46	17 15	
St James' Park	d	10 47			11 47			12 47			13 47			14 47			15 47	16 17		16 43	16 48	17 18	
Exeter Central	a	10 49	11 16		11 49	12 16		12 49	13 16		13 49	14 16		14 49	15 16		15 49	16 19		16 45	16 51	17 20	
	d	10 50	11 17	11 39	11 50	12 17	12 39	12 50	13 17	13 39	13 50	14 17	14 39	14 50	15 17	15 39	15 50	16 20	16 37	16 46	16 53	17 21	17 36
Exeter St Davids 6	a	10 54	11 21	11 42	11 54	12 21	12 42	12 54	13 21	13 42	13 54	14 21	14 42	14 54	15 21	15 42	15 54	16 25	16 42	16 49	16 56	17 24	17 42
	d		11 27			12 27			13 27			14 27			15 27						16 57		
Newton St Cyres	d																						
Crediton	d		11 38			12 38			13 38			14 38			15 38						17 08		
Yeoford	d		11x44			12x44			13x44			14x44			15x44						17x15		
Sampford Courtenay	d																						
Okehampton	a																						
Copplestone	d		11x49			12x49			13x49			14x49			15x49						17x19		
Morchard Road	d		11x52			12x52			13x52			14x52			15x52						17x22		
Lapford	d																				17x27		
Eggesford	d		12 08			13 08			14 08			15 08			16 08						17 37		
Kings Nympton	d								14x15												17x44		
Portsmouth Arms	d																						
Umberleigh	d		12x23			13x23			14x23			15x23			16x23						17x54		
Chapelton	d																						
Barnstaple	a		12 35			13 37			14 37			15 35			16 35						18 07		

		GW	GW	GW	SW ◇1 H	GW	GW	GW	SW ◇1 H	GW	GW	SW ◇1 H	GW	GW	GW	SW ◇1 H	GW	GW	SW ◇1 H	GW FO	GW	SW ◇1 H
Exmouth	d		17 25	17 58		18 27		18 55		19 35	20 08				21 04			22 05			23 10	
Lympstone Village	d		17 29	18 02		18 31		18 59		19 42	20 12				21 08			22 09			23 14	
Lympstone Commando	d		17x30	18x04				19x00			20x13				21x09			22x10			23x15	
Exton	d		17x32	18x06				19x02			20x15				21x11			22x12			23x17	
Topsham	d		17 37	18 11		18 37		19 07		19 49	20 20				21 16			22 17			23 22	
Digby & Sowton	d		17 42	18 15		18 42		19 12		19 54	20 25				21 21			22 22			23 27	
Polsloe Bridge	d		17 45	18 19				19 15			20 28				21 24			22 25			23 30	
St James' Park	d	17 40	17 48	18 21				19 18			20 31				21 27			22 28			23 33	
Exeter Central	a	17 42	17 50	18 24		18 49		19 20		20 00	20 34				21 29			22 30			23 36	
	d	17 45	17 51	18 25	18 39	18 49	19 02	19 21	19 40	20 01	20 35	20 40	20 55	21 21	21 30	21 39	21 55	22 31	22 42	22 48	23 37	23 57
Exeter St Davids 6	a	17 48	17 55	18 28	18 42	18 53	19 06	19 25	19 45	20 05	20 38	20 44	20 58	21 25	21 34	21 44	22 00	22 34	22 45	22 51	23 41	00 01
	d		17 57			18 57							21 00							22 52		
Newton St Cyres	d		18x04			19x04							21x07									
Crediton	d		18 11			19 11							21 14							23 05		
Yeoford	d		18x17			19x17							21x20							23x11		
Sampford Courtenay	d																					
Okehampton	a																					
Copplestone	d		18x22			19x22							21x26							23x16		
Morchard Road	d		18x25			19x25							21x29							23x19		
Lapford	d		18x29										21x33							23x23		
Eggesford	d		18 41			19 42							21 43							23 33		
Kings Nympton	d		18x48										21x48							23x39		
Portsmouth Arms	d		18x52										21x53									
Umberleigh	d		18x59			19x56							21x59							23x49		
Chapelton	d		19x03										22x03									
Barnstaple	a		19 13			20 08							22 13							23 59		

A from 21 May **B** from 17 September **C** until 14 September

For connections at Exeter St Davids please refer to Table 135

Table 136

Saturdays

until 8 September

Exmouth - Exeter - Barnstaple

Route Diagram - see first Page of Table 135

		SW ◇1 H	GW	GW	SW 1	GW	SW 1	GW	SW 1	GW	GW	GW	SW ◇1	GW	GW	GW	SW ◇1 H	GW	GW	SW ◇1 H	GW	GW	SW ◇1 H
Exmouth	d		00 02			06 12		07 15		07 53	08 23	08 53		09 23	09 53			10 23	10 53		11 23	11 53	
Lympstone Village	d		00 06			06 16		07 19		07 57	08 27	08 57		09 27	09 57			10 27	10 57		11 27	11 57	
Lympstone Commando	d		00x07			06x17		07x21		07x58	08x29	08x58		09x28	09x58			10x28	10x58		11x28	11x58	
Exton	d		00x09			06x19		07x22		08x00	08x30	09x00		09x30				10x30			11x30		
Topsham	d		00 14			06 24		07 29		08 05	08 35	09 05		09 35	10 05			10 35	11 05		11 35	12 05	
Digby & Sowton	d		00 19			06 29		07 33		08 10	08 40	09 10		09 40	10 10			10 40	11 10		11 40	12 10	
Polsloe Bridge	d		00 22			06 32		07 37		08 14	08 44	09 14		09 44				10 44			11 44		
St James' Park	d		00 25			06 35		07 40		08 17	08 47	09 17		09 47				10 47			11 47		
Exeter Central	a		00s27			06 37		07 42		08 20	08 49	09 19		09 50	10 16			10 49	11 17		11 49	12 16	
	d	23p57			06 32	06 38	07 39	07 43	08 15	08 24	08 50	09 20	09 39	09 52	10 17	10 30	10 39	10 50	11 17	11 39	11 50	12 17	12 39
Exeter St Davids 6	a	00 01	00 31		06 35	06 41	07 42	07 46	08 18	08 26	08 54	09 24	09 42	09 54	10 21	10 33	10 42	10 54	11 21	11 42	11 54	12 21	12 42
	d			05 54		06 55				08 31		09 27			10 30				11 27			12 27	
Newton St Cyres	d																						
Crediton	d			06 05		07 06				08 42		09 38			10 41				11 38			12 38	
Yeoford	d			06x11		07x12				08x48		09x44			10x47				11x44			12x44	
Sampford Courtenay	d																						
Okehampton	a																						
Copplestone	d			06x16		07x18				08x53		09x49			10x53				11x49			12x49	
Morchard Road	d					07x21				08x56		09x52			10x56				11x52			12x52	
Lapford	d					07x25																	
Eggesford	d			06 31		07 38				09 11		10 08			11 08				12 08			13 08	
Kings Nympton	d					07x43				09x17													
Portsmouth Arms	d					07x48																	
Umberleigh	d			06x45		07x54				09x27		10x23			11x23				12x23			13x23	
Chapelton	d					07x58																	
Barnstaple	a			06 59		08 07				09 39		10 35			11 35				12 35			13 37	

		GW	GW	SW ◇1 H	GW	GW	SW ◇1 H	GW	GW	SW ◇1 H	GW	GW	SW ◇1 H	GW	GW	GW	GW	SW ◇1 H	GW	GW	SW ◇1 H	GW	GW
Exmouth	d	12 23	12 53		13 23	13 53		14 23	14 53		15 23	15 53			16 25		16 55		17 25	17 55		18 27	18 55
Lympstone Village	d	12 27	12 57		13 27	13 57		14 27	14 57		15 27	15 57			16 29		16 59		17 29	17 59		18 31	18 59
Lympstone Commando	d	12x28	12x58		13x28	13x58		14x28	14x58		15x28	15x58			16x30		17x00		17x30	18x01			19x00
Exton	d	12x30			13x30			14x30			15x30	16x00			16x32		17x02		17x32	18x03			19x02
Topsham	d	12 35	13 05		13 35	14 05		14 35	15 05		15 35	16 05			16 37		17 07		17 37	18 07		18 37	19 07
Digby & Sowton	d	12 40	13 10		13 40	14 10		14 40	15 10		15 40	16 10			16 42		17 12		17 42	18 12		18 42	19 12
Polsloe Bridge	d	12 44			13 44			14 44			15 44	16 14			16 46		17 15		17 45	18 15			19 15
St James' Park	d	12 47			13 47			14 47			15 47	16 17			16 48	17 05	17 18		17 48	18 18			19 18
Exeter Central	a	12 49	13 16		13 49	14 16		14 49	15 16		15 49	16 19			16 51	17 07	17 20		17 50	18 20		18 49	19 20
	d	12 50	13 17	13 39	13 50	14 17	14 39	14 50	15 17	15 39	15 50	16 20	16 37	16 48	16 53	17 08	17 21	17 39	17 51	18 21	18 37	18 49	19 21
Exeter St Davids 6	a	12 54	13 21	13 42	13 54	14 22	14 42	14 54	15 21	15 42	15 54	16 25	16 42	16 51	16 56	17 11	17 24	17 42	17 55	18 26	18 42	18 53	19 25
	d		13 27			14 27			15 27						16 57				17 57			18 57	
Newton St Cyres	d																		18x04			19x04	
Crediton	d		13 38			14 38			15 38						17 08				18 11			19 11	
Yeoford	d		13x44			14x44			15x44						17x15				18x17			19x18	
Sampford Courtenay	d																						
Okehampton	a																						
Copplestone	d		13x49			14x49			15x49						17x19				18x22			19x22	
Morchard Road	d		13x52			14x52			15x52						17x22				18x25			19x25	
Lapford	d														17x27				18x29				
Eggesford	d		14 08			15 08			16 08						17 37				18 41			19 42	
Kings Nympton	d		14x15												17x44				18x48				
Portsmouth Arms	d																		18x52				
Umberleigh	d		14x23			15x23			16x23						17x54				18x59			19x56	
Chapelton	d																		19x03				
Barnstaple	a		14 37			15 35			16 35						18 07				19 13			20 08	

		SW ◇1 H	GW	GW	SW ◇1 H	GW	GW	SW ◇1 H	GW	SW ◇1 H	GW	GW
Exmouth	d		19 38	20 08			21 04		22 11		23 10	23 43
Lympstone Village	d		19 42	20 12			21 08		22 15		23 14	23 47
Lympstone Commando	d			20x13			21x09		22x16		23x15	23x48
Exton	d			20x15			21x11		22x18		23x17	23x50
Topsham	d		19 49	20 20			21 16		22 23		23 22	23 55
Digby & Sowton	d		19 54	20 25			21 21		22 28		23 27	23 59
Polsloe Bridge	d			20 28			21 24		22 31		23 30	00 03
St James' Park	d			20 31			21 27		22 34		23 33	00 06
Exeter Central	a		20 00	20 34			21 29		22 36		23 36	00 08
	d	19 39	20 01	20 35	20 40	20 52	21 30	21 39	22 37	22 42	23 37	00 09
Exeter St Davids 6	a	19 42	20 05	20 38	20 43	20 55	21 34	21 42	22 40	22 45	23 41	00 14
	d					21 00						
Newton St Cyres	d					21x07						
Crediton	d					21 14						
Yeoford	d					21x20						
Sampford Courtenay	d											
Okehampton	a											
Copplestone	d					21x26						
Morchard Road	d					21x29						
Lapford	d					21x33						
Eggesford	d					21 43						
Kings Nympton	d					21x48						
Portsmouth Arms	d					21x53						
Umberleigh	d					21x59						
Chapelton	d					22x03						
Barnstaple	a					22 13						

For connections at Exeter St Davids please refer to Table 135

Table 136

from 15 September

Exmouth - Exeter - Barnstaple

Route Diagram - see first Page of Table 135

		SW	GW	GW	SW	GW	SW	GW	SW	GW	GW	GW	SW	GW	GW	GW	SW	GW	GW	SW	GW	GW	SW
		◇1 ⌶			1		1		1				◇1				◇1 ⌶			◇1 ⌶			◇1 ⌶
Exmouth	d		00 02			06 12		07 15		07 53	08 23	08 53		09 23	09 53			10 23	10 53		11 23	11 53	
Lympstone Village	d		00 06			06 16		07 19		07 57	08 27	08 57		09 27	09 57			10 27	10 57		11 27	11 57	
Lympstone Commando	d		00x07			06x17		07x21		07x58	08x29	08x58		09x28	09x58			10x28	10x58		11x28	11x58	
Exton	d		00x09			06x19		07x22		08x00	08x30	09x00		09x30				10x30			11x30		
Topsham	d		00 14			06 24		07 29		08 05	08 35	09 05		09 35	10 05			10 35	11 05		11 35	12 05	
Digby & Sowton	d		00 19			06 29		07 33		08 10	08 40	09 10		09 40	10 10			10 40	11 10		11 40	12 10	
Polsloe Bridge	d		00 22			06 32		07 37		08 14	08 44	09 14		09 44				10 44			11 44		
St James' Park	d		00 25			06 35		07 40		08 17	08 47	09 17		09 47				10 47			11 47		
Exeter Central	a		00s27			06 37		07 42		08 20	08 49	09 19		09 50	10 16			10 49	11 16		11 49	12 16	
	d	23p57			06 32	06 38	07 39	07 43	08 15	08 24	08 50	09 20	09 39	09 52	10 17	10 30	10 39	10 50	11 17	11 39	11 50	12 17	12 39
Exeter St Davids 6	a	00 01	00 31		06 35	06 41	07 42	07 46	08 18	08 26	08 54	09 24	09 42	09 54	10 21	10 33	10 42	10 54	11 21	11 42	11 54	12 21	12 42
	d			05 54		06 55				08 31		09 27			10 27				11 27			12 27	
Newton St Cyres	d																						
Crediton	d			06 05		07 06				08 42		09 38			10 38				11 38			12 38	
Yeoford	d			06x11		07x12				08x48		09x44			10x44				11x44			12x44	
Sampford Courtenay	d																						
Okehampton	a																						
Copplestone	d			06x16		07x18				08x53		09x49			10x49				11x49			12x49	
Morchard Road	d					07x21				08x56		09x52			10x52				11x52			12x52	
Lapford	d					07x25																	
Eggesford	d			06 31		07 38				09 11		10 08			11 08				12 08			13 08	
Kings Nympton	d					07x43				09x17													
Portsmouth Arms	d					07x48																	
Umberleigh	d			06x45		07x54				09x27		10x23			11x23				12x23			13x23	
Chapelton	d					07x58																	
Barnstaple	a			06 59		08 07				09 39		10 35			11 35				12 35			13 37	

		GW	GW	SW	GW	GW	SW	GW	GW	SW	GW	GW	SW	GW	GW	GW	GW	SW	GW	GW	SW	GW	GW
				◇1 ⌶			◇1 ⌶			◇1 ⌶			◇1 ⌶					◇1 ⌶			◇1 ⌶		
Exmouth	d	12 23	12 53		13 23	13 53		14 23	14 53		15 23	15 53			16 25		16 55		17 25	17 55		18 27	18 55
Lympstone Village	d	12 27	12 57		13 27	13 57		14 27	14 57		15 27	15 57			16 29		16 59		17 29	17 59		18 31	18 59
Lympstone Commando	d	12x28	12x58		13x28	13x58		14x28	14x58		15x28	15x58			16x30		17x00		17x30	18x01			19x00
Exton	d	12x30			13x30			14x30			15x30	16x00			16x32		17x02		17x32	18x03			19x02
Topsham	d	12 35	13 05		13 35	14 05		14 35	15 05		15 35	16 05			16 37		17 07		17 37	18 07		18 37	19 07
Digby & Sowton	d	12 40	13 10		13 40	14 10		14 40	15 10		15 40	16 10			16 42		17 12		17 42	18 12		18 42	19 12
Polsloe Bridge	d	12 44			13 44			14 44			15 44	16 14			16 46		17 15		17 45	18 15			19 15
St James' Park	d	12 47			13 47			14 47			15 47	16 17			16 48	17 05	17 18		17 48	18 18			19 18
Exeter Central	a	12 49	13 16		13 49	14 16		14 49	15 16		15 49	16 19			16 51	17 07	17 20		17 50	18 20		18 49	19 20
	d	12 50	13 17	13 39	13 50	14 17	14 39	14 50	15 17	15 39	15 50	16 20	16 37	16 48	16 53	17 08	17 21	17 39	17 51	18 21	18 37	18 49	19 21
Exeter St Davids 6	a	12 54	13 21	13 42	13 54	14 22	14 42	14 54	15 21	15 42	15 54	16 25	16 42	16 51	16 56	17 11	17 24	17 42	17 55	18 26	18 42	18 53	19 25
	d		13 27			14 27			15 27						16 57				17 57			18 57	
Newton St Cyres	d																		18x04			19x04	
Crediton	d		13 38			14 38			15 38						17 08				18 11			19 11	
Yeoford	d		13x44			14x44			15x44						17x15				18x17			19x18	
Sampford Courtenay	d																						
Okehampton	a																						
Copplestone	d		13x49			14x49			15x49						17x19				18x22			19x22	
Morchard Road	d		13x52			14x52			15x52						17x22				18x25			19x25	
Lapford	d														17x27				18x29				
Eggesford	d		14 08			15 08			16 08						17 37				18 41			19 42	
Kings Nympton	d		14x15												17x44				18x48				
Portsmouth Arms	d																		18x52				
Umberleigh	d		14x23			15x23			16x23						17x54				18x59			19x56	
Chapelton	d																		19x03				
Barnstaple	a		14 37			15 35			16 35						18 07				19 13			20 08	

		SW	GW	GW	SW	GW	GW	SW	GW	SW	GW	GW
		◇1 ⌶			◇1 ⌶			◇1 ⌶		◇1 ⌶		
Exmouth	d		19 38	20 08			21 04		22 11		23 10	23 43
Lympstone Village	d		19 42	20 12			21 08		22 15		23 14	23 47
Lympstone Commando	d			20x13			21x09		22x16		23x15	23x48
Exton	d			20x15			21x11		22x18		23x17	23x50
Topsham	d		19 49	20 20			21 16		22 23		23 22	23 55
Digby & Sowton	d		19 54	20 25			21 21		22 28		23 27	23 59
Polsloe Bridge	d			20 28			21 24		22 31		23 30	00 03
St James' Park	d			20 31			21 27		22 34		23 33	00 06
Exeter Central	a		20 00	20 34			21 29		22 36		23 36	00 08
	d	19 39	20 01	20 35	20 40	20 52	21 30	21 39	22 37	22 42	23 37	00 09
Exeter St Davids 6	a	19 42	20 05	20 38	20 43	20 55	21 34	21 42	22 40	22 45	23 41	00 14
	d					21 00						
Newton St Cyres	d					21x07						
Crediton	d					21 14						
Yeoford	d					21x20						
Sampford Courtenay	d											
Okehampton	a											
Copplestone	d					21x26						
Morchard Road	d					21x29						
Lapford	d					21x33						
Eggesford	d					21 43						
Kings Nympton	d					21x48						
Portsmouth Arms	d					21x53						
Umberleigh	d					21x59						
Chapelton	d					22x03						
Barnstaple	a					22 13						

For connections at Exeter St Davids please refer to Table 135

Table 136

until 9 September

Exmouth - Exeter - Barnstaple

Route Diagram - see first Page of Table 135

		GW	GW	SW	GW	GW	GW	SW	GW	GW	SW	GW	GW	SW	GW	GW	GW	SW	GW	GW	SW	GW	GW
				1	A			◇1		A	◇1 ⌶			◇1 ⌶		A		◇1 ⌶			◇1 ⌶		A
Exmouth	d	23p43				09 10			10 21			11 24			12 29				13 24			14 31	
Lympstone Village	d	23p47				09 14			10 25			11 28			12 33				13 28			14 35	
Lympstone Commando	d	23b48				09x15			10x26			11x29			12x34				13x29			14x36	
Exton	d	23b50				09x17			10x28			11x31			12x36				13x31			14x38	
Topsham	d	23p55				09 22			10 33			11 36			12 41				13 36			14 43	
Digby & Sowton	d	23p59				09 27			10 38			11 41			12 46				13 41			14 48	
Polsloe Bridge	d	00 03				09 30			10 41			11 44			12 49				13 44			14 51	
St James' Park	d	00 06			09 01	09 33			10 44	11 00		11 47			12 52	13 03			13 47			14 54	15 03
Exeter Central	a	00 08			09 03	09 36			10 46	11 02		11 49			12 54	13 05			13 49			14 56	15 05
	d	00 09		08 58	09 04	09 36		10 42	10 48	11 03	11 42	11 52	11 59	12 42	12 55	13 06	13 20	13 42	13 50	13 55	14 42	14 57	15 06
Exeter St Davids 6	a	00 14		09 01	09 07	09 40		10 45	10 51	11 06	11 45	11 55	12 02	12 45	12 58	13 10	13 23	13 45	13 53	13 58	14 45	15 01	15 09
	d		08 39		09 08		09 53			11 07			12 03			13 10				13 59			15 09
Newton St Cyres	d		08x47										12x11										
Crediton	d		08 53		09 18		10 04			11 17			12 17			13 21				14 20			15 20
Yeoford	d		09x00				10x11						12x24							14x27			
Sampford Courtenay	d				09 43					11 41						13 45							15 44
Okehampton	a				09 51					11 49						13 53							15 51
Copplestone	d		09x05				10x16						12x30							14x33			
Morchard Road	d		09x08				10x19						12x33							14x36			
Lapford	d		09x12										12x37										
Eggesford	d		09 22				10 31						12 46							14 48			
Kings Nympton	d		09x29										12x52							14x54			
Portsmouth Arms	d		09x33										12x57							14x59			
Umberleigh	d		09x40				10x46						13x03							15x05			
Chapelton	d		09x44										13x07										
Barnstaple	a		09 52				10 57						13 14							15 15			

		GW	SW	GW	GW	SW	GW	GW	SW	GW	GW	SW	GW	SW	GW	GW	SW	GW	SW	GW	SW	GW	GW
			◇1 ⌶			◇1 ⌶		A	◇1 ⌶			◇1 ⌶		◇1 ⌶			◇1 ⌶		◇1 ⌶		◇1 ⌶		
Exmouth	d			15 24			16 24			17 24			18 24		19 24			20 24		21 24		22 29	23 29
Lympstone Village	d			15 28			16 28			17 28			18 28		19 28			20 28		21 28		22 33	23 33
Lympstone Commando	d			15x29			16x29			17x29			18x29		19x29			20x29		21x29		22x34	23x34
Exton	d			15x31			16x31			17x31			18x31		19x31			20x31		21x31		22x36	23x36
Topsham	d			15 36			16 36			17 36			18 35		19 36			20 36		21 36		22 42	23 42
Digby & Sowton	d			15 41			16 41			17 41			18 40		19 41			20 41		21 41		22 46	23 47
Polsloe Bridge	d			15 44			16 44			17 44			18 43		19 44			20 44		21 44		22 50	23 50
St James' Park	d			15 47			16 47	17 02		17 47			18 46		19 47			20 47		21 47		22 53	23 53
Exeter Central	a			15 49			16 49	17 04		17 49			18 48		19 49			20 49		21 49		22 55	23 55
	d	15 20	15 42	15 50	15 59	16 42	16 50	17 05	17 42	17 50	17 56	18 42	18 49	19 42	19 50	19 56	20 42	20 50	21 42	21 50	22 42	22 56	23 56
Exeter St Davids 6	a	15 23	15 45	15 53	16 02	16 45	16 53	17 08	17 45	17 53	17 59	18 45	18 53	19 45	19 53	19 59	20 45	20 53	21 45	21 53	22 45	22 59	23 59
	d				16 04			17 08			17 59					20 01							
Newton St Cyres	d				16x12											20x08							
Crediton	d				16 19			17 19			18 16					20 18							
Yeoford	d				16x26						18x23					20x24							
Sampford Courtenay	d							17 43															
Okehampton	a							17 50															
Copplestone	d				16x31						18x28					20x30							
Morchard Road	d				16x34						18x31					20x33							
Lapford	d				16x38											20x37							
Eggesford	d				16 45						18 44					20x47							
Kings Nympton	d				16x53											20x52							
Portsmouth Arms	d				16x56											20x57							
Umberleigh	d				17x04						18x58					21x03							
Chapelton	d				17x08											21x07							
Barnstaple	a				17 17						19 08					21 15							

		GW
Exmouth	d	23 59
Lympstone Village	d	00 03
Lympstone Commando	d	00x04
Exton	d	00x06
Topsham	d	00 11
Digby & Sowton	d	00 15
Polsloe Bridge	d	00 19
St James' Park	d	00 21
Exeter Central	a	00 24
	d	00 25
Exeter St Davids 6	a	00 28
	d	
Newton St Cyres	d	
Crediton	d	
Yeoford	d	
Sampford Courtenay	d	
Okehampton	a	
Copplestone	d	
Morchard Road	d	
Lapford	d	
Eggesford	d	
Kings Nympton	d	
Portsmouth Arms	d	
Umberleigh	d	
Chapelton	d	
Barnstaple	a	

A not from 20 May until 27 May

b Previous night, stops on request

For connections at Exeter St Davids please refer to Table 135

Table 136

Sundays
16 September to 23 September

Exmouth - Exeter - Barnstaple

Route Diagram - see first Page of Table 135

		GW	GW	SW 1	GW	GW	GW	SW ◇1	GW	GW	SW ◇1	GW	GW	SW ◇1	GW	GW	GW	SW ◇1	GW	GW	SW ◇1	GW	GW
Exmouth	d	23p43				09 10			10 21			11 24			12 29				13 24			14 31	
Lympstone Village	d	23p47				09 14			10 25			11 28			12 33				13 28			14 35	
Lympstone Commando	d	23b48				09x15			10x26			11x29			12x34				13x29			14x36	
Exton	d	23b50				09x17			10x28			11x31			12x36				13x31			14x38	
Topsham	d	23p55				09 22			10 33			11 36			12 41				13 36			14 43	
Digby & Sowton	d	23p59				09 27			10 38			11 41			12 46				13 41			14 48	
Polsloe Bridge	d	00 03				09 30			10 41			11 44			12 49				13 44			14 51	
St James' Park	d	00 06			09 01	09 33			10 44	11 00		11 47			12 52	13 03			13 47			14 54	15 03
Exeter Central	a	00 08			09 03	09 36			10 46	11 02		11 49			12 54	13 05			13 49			14 58	15 05
	d	00 09		08 58	09 04	09 36		10 42	10 48	11 03	11 42	11 52	11 59	12 42	12 55	13 06	13 20	13 42	13 50	13 55	14 42	14 59	15 06
Exeter St Davids 6	a	00 14		09 01	09 07	09 40		10 45	10 51	11 06	11 45	11 55	12 02	12 45	12 58	13 10	13 23	13 45	13 53	13 58	14 45	15 03	15 09
	d		08 39		09 08		09 53			11 07			12 03			13 10				13 59			15 09
Newton St Cyres	d		08x47										12x11										
Crediton	d		08 53		09 18		10 04			11 17			12 17			13 21				14 20			15 20
Yeoford	d		09x00				10x11						12x24							14x27			
Sampford Courtenay	d				09 43					11 41						13 45							15 44
Okehampton	a				09 51					11 49						13 53							15 51
Copplestone	d		09x05				10x16						12x30							14x33			
Morchard Road	d		09x08				10x19						12x33							14x36			
Lapford	d		09x12										12x37										
Eggesford	d		09 22				10 31						12 46							14 48			
Kings Nympton	d		09x29										12x52							14x54			
Portsmouth Arms	d		09x33										12x57							14x59			
Umberleigh	d		09x40				10x46						13x03							15x05			
Chapelton	d		09x44										13x07										
Barnstaple	a		09 52				10 57						13 14							15 15			

		GW	SW ◇1	GW	GW	SW ◇1	GW	GW	SW ◇1	GW	GW	SW ◇1	GW	SW ◇1	GW	GW	SW ◇1	GW	SW ◇1	GW	SW ◇1	GW	GW
Exmouth	d			15 24			16 24			17 24			18 24		19 24			20 24		21 24		22 29	23 29
Lympstone Village	d			15 28			16 28			17 28			18 28		19 28			20 28		21 28		22 33	23 33
Lympstone Commando	d			15x29			16x29			17x29			18x29		19x29			20x29		21x29		22x34	23x34
Exton	d			15x31			16x31			17x31			18x31		19x31			20x31		21x31		22x36	23x36
Topsham	d			15 36			16 36			17 36			18 35		19 36			20 36		21 36		22 42	23 42
Digby & Sowton	d			15 41			16 41			17 41			18 40		19 41			20 41		21 41		22 46	23 47
Polsloe Bridge	d			15 44			16 44			17 44			18 43		19 44			20 44		21 44		22 50	23 50
St James' Park	d			15 47			16 47	17 02		17 47			18 46		19 47			20 47		21 47		22 53	23 53
Exeter Central	a			15 49			16 49	17 04		17 49			18 48		19 49			20 49		21 49		22 55	23 55
	d	15 20	15 42	15 50	15 59	16 42	16 50	17 05	17 42	17 50	17 56	18 42	18 49	19 42	19 50	19 56	20 42	20 50	21 42	21 50	22 42	22 56	23 56
Exeter St Davids 6	a	15 23	15 45	15 53	16 02	16 45	16 53	17 08	17 45	17 53	17 59	18 45	18 53	19 45	19 53	19 59	20 45	20 53	21 45	21 53	22 45	22 59	23 59
	d				16 04			17 08			17 59					20 01							
Newton St Cyres	d				16x12											20x08							
Crediton	d				16 19			17 19			18 16					20 18							
Yeoford	d				16x26						18x23					20x24							
Sampford Courtenay	d							17 43															
Okehampton	a							17 50															
Copplestone	d				16x31						18x28					20x30							
Morchard Road	d				16x34						18x31					20x33							
Lapford	d				16x38											20x37							
Eggesford	d				16 45						18 44					20x47							
Kings Nympton	d				16x53											20x52							
Portsmouth Arms	d				16x56											20x57							
Umberleigh	d				17x04						18x58					21x03							
Chapelton	d				17x08											21x07							
Barnstaple	a				17 17						19 08					21 15							

		GW
Exmouth	d	23 59
Lympstone Village	d	00 03
Lympstone Commando	d	00x04
Exton	d	00x06
Topsham	d	00 11
Digby & Sowton	d	00 15
Polsloe Bridge	d	00 19
St James' Park	d	00 21
Exeter Central	a	00 24
	d	00 25
Exeter St Davids 6	a	00 28
	d	
Newton St Cyres	d	
Crediton	d	
Yeoford	d	
Sampford Courtenay	d	
Okehampton	a	
Copplestone	d	
Morchard Road	d	
Lapford	d	
Eggesford	d	
Kings Nympton	d	
Portsmouth Arms	d	
Umberleigh	d	
Chapelton	d	
Barnstaple	a	

b Previous night, stops on request

For connections at Exeter St Davids please refer to Table 135

Table 136

Sundays
from 30 September

Exmouth - Exeter - Barnstaple

Route Diagram - see first Page of Table 135

		GW	GW	SW 1	GW	GW	SW ◇1	GW	SW ◇1	GW	GW	SW ◇1	GW	GW	SW ◇1	GW	GW	SW ◇1	GW	GW	SW ◇1	GW	GW
Exmouth	d	23p43			09 10			10 21		11 24			12 29			13 24			14 31			15 24	
Lympstone Village	d	23p47			09 14			10 25		11 28			12 33			13 28			14 35			15 28	
Lympstone Commando	d	23b48			09x15			10x26		11x29			12x34			13x29			14x36			15x29	
Exton	d	23b50			09x17			10x28		11x31			12x36			13x31			14x38			15x31	
Topsham	d	23p55			09 22			10 33		11 36			12 41			13 36			14 43			15 36	
Digby & Sowton	d	23p59			09 27			10 38		11 41			12 46			13 41			14 48			15 41	
Polsloe Bridge	d	00 03			09 30			10 41		11 44			12 49			13 44			14 51			15 44	
St James' Park	d	00 06			09 33			10 44		11 47			12 52			13 47			14 54			15 47	
Exeter Central	a	00 08			09 36			10 46		11 49			12 54			13 49			14 58			15 49	
	d	00 09		08 58	09 36		10 42	10 48	11 42	11 52	11 59	12 42	12 55	13 20	13 42	13 50	13 55	14 42	14 59	15 20	15 42	15 50	15 59
Exeter St Davids 6	a	00 14		09 01	09 40		10 45	10 51	11 45	11 55	12 02	12 45	12 58	13 23	13 45	13 53	13 58	14 45	15 03	15 23	15 45	15 53	16 02
	d		08 39			09 53					12 03						13 59						16 04
Newton St Cyres	d		08x47								12x11												16x12
Crediton	d		08 53			10 04					12 17						14 20						16 19
Yeoford	d		09x00			10x11					12x24						14x27						16x26
Sampford Courtenay	d																						
Okehampton	a																						
Copplestone	d		09x05			10x16					12x30						14x33						16x31
Morchard Road	d		09x08			10x19					12x33						14x36						16x34
Lapford	d		09x12								12x37												16x38
Eggesford	d		09 22			10 31					12 46						14 48						16 45
Kings Nympton	d		09x29								12x52						14x54						16x53
Portsmouth Arms	d		09x33								12x57						14x59						16x56
Umberleigh	d		09x40			10x46					13x03						15x05						17x04
Chapelton	d		09x44								13x07												17x08
Barnstaple	a		09 52			10 57					13 14						15 15						17 17

		SW ◇1	GW	SW ◇1	GW	GW	SW ◇1	GW	SW ◇1	GW	GW	SW ◇1	GW	SW ◇1	GW	SW ◇1	GW	GW	GW
Exmouth	d		16 24		17 24			18 24		19 24			20 24		21 24		22 29	23 29	23 59
Lympstone Village	d		16 28		17 28			18 28		19 28			20 28		21 28		22 33	23 33	00 03
Lympstone Commando	d		16x29		17x29			18x29		19x29			20x29		21x29		22x34	23x34	00x04
Exton	d		16x31		17x31			18x31		19x31			20x31		21x31		22x36	23x36	00x06
Topsham	d		16 36		17 36			18 35		19 36			20 36		21 36		22 42	23 42	00 11
Digby & Sowton	d		16 41		17 41			18 40		19 41			20 41		21 41		22 46	23 47	00 15
Polsloe Bridge	d		16 44		17 44			18 43		19 44			20 44		21 44		22 50	23 50	00 19
St James' Park	d		16 47		17 47			18 46		19 47			20 47		21 47		22 53	23 53	00 21
Exeter Central	a		16 49		17 49			18 48		19 49			20 49		21 49		22 55	23 55	00 24
	d	16 42	16 50	17 42	17 50	17 56	18 42	18 49	19 42	19 50	19 56	20 42	20 50	21 42	21 50	22 42	22 56	23 56	00 25
Exeter St Davids 6	a	16 45	16 53	17 45	17 53	17 59	18 45	18 53	19 45	19 53	19 59	20 45	20 53	21 45	21 53	22 45	22 59	23 59	00 28
	d					17 59					20 01								
Newton St Cyres	d										20x08								
Crediton	d					18 16					20 18								
Yeoford	d					18x23					20x24								
Sampford Courtenay	d																		
Okehampton	a																		
Copplestone	d					18x28					20x30								
Morchard Road	d					18x31					20x33								
Lapford	d										20x37								
Eggesford	d					18 44					20x47								
Kings Nympton	d										20x52								
Portsmouth Arms	d										20x57								
Umberleigh	d					18x58					21x03								
Chapelton	d										21x07								
Barnstaple	a					19 08					21 15								

b Previous night, stops on request

For connections at Exeter St Davids please refer to Table 135

Barnstaple - Exeter - Exmouth

Mondays to Fridays

Route Diagram - see first Page of Table 135

Miles	Miles			SW ◇■ 🛒	GW	GW	GW	SW ◇■ 🛒	GW	SW ◇■ 🛒	GW	GW		GW	SW ◇■ 🛒	GW	GW	GW	SW ◇■ 🛒	GW	GW	SW ◇■ 🛒		GW	GW
0	—	**Barnstaple**	d									07 00								08 43				09 43	
4¼	—	Chapelton	d									07x05													
6¾	—	Umberleigh	d									07x09								08x51				09x51	
10¾	—	Portsmouth Arms	d									07x16													
13¾	—	Kings Nympton	d									07x21								09x03					
17½	—	Eggesford	d									07 30								09 07				10 07	
21½	—	Lapford	d									07x35								09x14					
23¾	—	Morchard Road	d									07x40								09x17				10x16	
25½	—	Copplestone	d									07x43								09x22				10x20	
—	0	Okehampton	d																						
—	3¾	Sampford Courtenay	d																						
28½	14½	Yeoford	d									07x48								09x25				10x24	
32	18	Crediton	d									07 55								09 37				10 37	
34¾	—	Newton St Cyres	d									07x58													
39	—	**Exeter St Davids ■**	a									08 07								09 48				10 48	
—	—		d	05 10	05 44	06 06	06 29	06 41	07 11	07 26	07 36	08 09		08 16	08 26	08 48	08 59	09 18	09 26	09 50	10 18	10 26		10 50	11 18
39¾	—	**Exeter Central**	a	05 13	05 47	06 09	06 32	06 44	07 14	07 29	07 39	08 12		08 19	08 29	08 51	09 04	09 21	09 29	09 53	10 21	10 29		10 53	11 21
—	—		d		05 48	06 10	06 39		07 15		07 52	08 13		08 20		08 52		09 22		09 54	10 22			10 54	11 22
40¼	—	St James' Park	d			06 12	06 41		07 17		07 54	08a17		08 22		08 54		09 24			10 24				11 24
41¼	—	Polsloe Bridge	d			06 15	06 44		07 20		07 57			08 25		08 57		09 27			10 27				11 27
43¼	—	Digby & Sowton	d		05 54	06 19	06 48		07 24		08 01			08 29		09 01		09 31		10 01	10 31			11 01	11 31
45¼	—	Topsham	d		05 58	06 25	06 57		07 28		08 05			08 35		09 05		09 35		10 05	10 35			11 05	11 35
46¾	—	Exton	d			06x27	07x00		07x31		08x08			08x38		09x08		09x38			10x38				11x38
47¼	—	Lympstone Commando	d			06x29	07x02		07x33		08x10			08x40		09x10		09x40			10x40				11x40
48¼	—	Lympstone Village	d		06 03	06 31	07 05		07 36		08 13			08 43		09 13		09 43		10 11	10 43			11 11	11 43
50¼	—	**Exmouth**	a		06 10	06 38	07 10		07 43		08 18			08 48		09 20		09 50		10 19	10 50			11 19	11 50

		SW ◇■ 🛒	GW	GW	SW ◇■ 🛒	GW	GW	SW ◇■ 🛒		GW	GW	SW ◇■ 🛒	GW	GW	SW ◇■ 🛒	GW	GW	GW		SW ◇■ 🛒	GW	GW	GW	SW ◇■ 🛒	SW ■
Barnstaple	d		10 43			11 43				12 43			13 43			14 43					15 43				
Chapelton	d																								
Umberleigh	d		10x51			11x51				12x51			13x51			14x51					15x51				
Portsmouth Arms	d																								
Kings Nympton	d									13x02															
Eggesford	d		11 07			12 07				13 07			14 07			15 07					16 07				
Lapford	d																								
Morchard Road	d		11x16			12x16				13x16			14x16			15x16					16x16				
Copplestone	d		11x20			12x20				13x20			14x20			15x20					16x20				
Okehampton	d																								
Sampford Courtenay	d																								
Yeoford	d		11x24			12x24				13x24			14x24			15x24					16x24				
Crediton	d		11 37			12 37				13 37			14 37			15 37					16 37				
Newton St Cyres	d																								
Exeter St Davids ■	a		11 48			12 48				13 48			14 48			15 48					16 48				
	d	11 26	11 50	12 18	12 26	12 50	13 18	13 26		13 50	14 18	14 26	14 51	15 18	15 26	15 50	16 08	16 18		16 26	16 50	17 10	17 18	17 26	17 46
Exeter Central	a	11 29	11 53	12 21	12 29	12 53	13 21	13 29		13 53	14 21	14 29	14 54	15 21	15 29	15 53	16 11	16 21		16 29	16 53	17 13	17 21	17 29	17 49
	d		11 54	12 22		12 54	13 22			13 54	14 22		14 55	15 22		15 54	16 12	16 22			16 54	17 14	17 22		
St James' Park	d			12 24			13 24				14 24			15 24			16a16	16 24			16 56	17a18	17 24		
Polsloe Bridge	d			12 27			13 27				14 27			15 27				16 27			16 59		17 27		
Digby & Sowton	d		12 01	12 31		13 01	13 31			14 01	14 31		15 01	15 31		16 01		16 31			17 03		17 31		
Topsham	d		12 05	12 35		13 05	13 35			14 05	14 35		15 05	15 35		16 05		16 37			17 07		17 37		
Exton	d			12x38			13x38				14x38			15x38				16x38			17x10		17x38		
Lympstone Commando	d			12x40			13x40				14x40			15x40				16x40			17x12		17x40		
Lympstone Village	d		12 11	12 43		13 11	13 43			14 11	14 43		15 11	15 43		16 11		16 43			17 15		17 43		
Exmouth	a		12 19	12 50		13 19	13 50			14 19	14 50		15 19	15 50		16 19		16 50			17 22		17 51		

		GW	GW	SW ◇■ 🛒		GW	GW	SW ◇■	GW	GW	SW ◇■ 🛒	GW	GW	SW ■		GW	GW	GW	SW ■	GW
Barnstaple	d					17 08			18 13	19 16							20 24			22 16
Chapelton	d					17x14														
Umberleigh	d					17x18			18x21	19x24							20x32			22x24
Portsmouth Arms	d								18x28											
Kings Nympton	d					17 29			18x33											
Eggesford	d					17 37			18 40	19 40							20 49			22 40
Lapford	d					17 43			18x47											
Morchard Road	d					17x46			18x51	19x49							20x58			22x48
Copplestone	d					17x50			18x55	19x53							21x01			22x52
Okehampton	d																			
Sampford Courtenay	d																			
Yeoford	d					17x54			18x59	19x57							21x05			22x56
Crediton	d					18 12			19 12	20 06							21 16			23 05
Newton St Cyres	d					18x15				20x09							21x19			23x08
Exeter St Davids ■	a					18 29			19 25	20 17							21 34			23 16
	d	17 52	18 20	18 26		18 33	18 50	19 26	19 32	20 19	20 26	20 30	21 14	21 23		21 32	21 38	22 36	22 57	23 28
Exeter Central	a	17 55	18 23	18 29		18 38	18 53	19 29	19 35	20 24	20 29	20 33	21 19	21 26		21 35	21 41	22 39	23 00	23 31
	d	17 56	18 24				18 54		19 36			20 34				21 35		22 40		23 32
St James' Park	d	17 58	18 26				18 56		19 38			20 36				21 37		22 42		23 34
Polsloe Bridge	d	18 01	18 29				18 59		19 41			20 39				21 40		22 45		23 37
Digby & Sowton	d	18 05	18 33				19 03		19 45			20 43				21 44		22 49		23 41
Topsham	d	18 09	18 37				19 07		19 49			20 47				21 49		22 53		23 45
Exton	d	18x12	18x38				19x10		19x52			20x49				21x51		22x56		23x47
Lympstone Commando	d	18x14	18x40				19x12		19x54			20x51				21x53		22x58		23x49
Lympstone Village	d	18 17	18 43				19 15		19 57			20 54				21 56		23 01		23 52
Exmouth	a	18 25	18 52				19 23		20 03			21 01				22 02		23 08		23 59

For connections at Exeter St Davids please refer to Table 135

Barnstaple - Exeter - Exmouth

Saturdays

until 8 September

Route Diagram - see first Page of Table 135

		GW	SW ◇■ 🛒	GW	GW	SW ◇■ 🛒	GW	SW ◇■ 🛒	GW	GW		SW ◇■ 🛒	GW	GW	SW ◇■ 🛒	GW	GW	SW ◇■ 🛒	GW	GW		SW ◇■ 🛒	GW	GW	SW ◇■ 🛒
Barnstaple	d	00 05								07 08						08 43			09 43				10 43		
Chapelton	d									07x13															
Umberleigh	d									07x17						08x51			09x51				10x51		
Portsmouth Arms	d									07x24															
Kings Nympton	d									07x29						09x02									
Eggesford	d									07 38						09 07			10 07				11 07		
Lapford	d									07x43						09x14									
Morchard Road	d									07x48						09x17			10x16				11x16		
Copplestone	d									07x51						09x22			10x20				11x20		
Okehampton	d																								
Sampford Courtenay	d																								
Yeoford	d									07x57						09x25			10x24				11x24		
Crediton	d									08 04						09 37			10 39				11 37		
Newton St Cyres	d									08x07															
Exeter St Davids ■	a	01 00								08 16						09 48			10 50				11 48		
	d		05 10	05 44	06 29	06 41	07 11	07 26	07 36	08 16		08 26	08 48	09 18	09 26	09 50	10 18	10 26	10 52	11 18		11 26	11 50	12 18	12 26
Exeter Central	a		05 13	05 47	06 32	06 44	07 14	07 29	07 39	08 19		08 29	08 51	09 21	09 29	09 51	10 21	10 29	10 53	11 21		11 29	11 51	12 21	12 29
	d			05 48	06 39		07 15		07 52	08 20			08 52	09 22		09 52	10 22		10 54	11 22			11 52	12 22	
St James' Park	d				06 41		07 17		07 54	08 23			08 54	09 24		09 54	10 24			11 24				12 24	
Polsloe Bridge	d				06 44		07 20		07 57	08 27			08 57	09 27		09 57	10 27			11 27				12 27	
Digby & Sowton	d			05 54	06 48		07 24		08 01	08 31			09 01	09 31		10 01	10 31		11 01	11 31			12 01	12 31	
Topsham	d			05 58	06 52		07 28		08 05	08 35			09 05	09 35		10 05	10 35		11 05	11 35			12 05	12 35	
Exton	d				06x54		07x31		08x08	08x38			09x08	09x38		10x08	10x38			11x38				12x38	
Lympstone Commando	d				06x56		07x33		08x10	08x40			09x10	09x40		10x10	10x40		11x09	11x40			12x09	12x40	
Lympstone Village	d			06 03	06 59		07 36		08 13	08 43			09 13	09 43		10 11	10 43		11 11	11 43			12 11	12 43	
Exmouth	a			06 10	07 04		07 43		08 18	08 48			09 20	09 50		10 19	10 50		11 19	11 50			12 19	12 50	

		GW	GW	SW ◇■ 🛒	GW	GW		SW ◇■ 🛒	GW	GW	SW ◇■ 🛒	GW	GW	SW ◇■ 🛒	GW	GW		GW	GW	SW ◇■ 🛒	GW	GW	SW ◇■ 🛒	GW	SW ◇■
Barnstaple	d	11 43			12 43				13 43			14 43				15 43		17 08							
Chapelton	d																	17x14							
Umberleigh	d	11x51			12x51				13x51			14x51				15x51		17x18							
Portsmouth Arms	d																								
Kings Nympton	d				13x02													17x29							
Eggesford	d	12 07			13 07				14 07			15 07				16 07		17 37							
Lapford	d																	17x43							
Morchard Road	d	12x16			13x16				14x16			15x16				16x16		17x46							
Copplestone	d	12x20			13x20				14x20			15x20				16x20		17x50							
Okehampton	d																								
Sampford Courtenay	d																								
Yeoford	d	12x24			13x24				14x24			15x24				16x24		17x54							
Crediton	d	12 37			13 37				14 37			15 37				16 37		18 10							
Newton St Cyres	d																	18x13							
Exeter St Davids ■	a	12 48			13 48				14 48			15 48				16 48		18 22							
	d	12 50	13 18	13 26	13 50	14 18		14 26	14 50	15 18	15 26	15 50	16 18	16 26	16 41	16 50			17 18	17 26	17 50	18 20	18 26	18 50	19 26
Exeter Central	a	12 51	13 21	13 29	13 51	14 21		14 29	14 51	15 21	15 29	15 51	16 21	16 29	16 44	16 53			17 21	17 29	17 53	18 23	18 29	18 53	19 29
	d	12 52	13 22		13 52	14 22			14 52	15 22		15 52	16 22			16 54			17 22		17 54	18 24		18 54	
St James' Park	d		13 24		13 54	14 24				15 24		15 57	16 24			16 56			17 24		17 56	18 26		18 56	
Polsloe Bridge	d		13 27			14 27				15 27			16 27			16 59			17 27		17 59	18 29		18 59	
Digby & Sowton	d	13 01	13 31		14 01	14 31			15 01	15 31		16 01	16 31			17 03			17 31		18 03	18 33		19 03	
Topsham	d	13 05	13 35		14 05	14 35			15 05	15 35		16 05	16 37			17 07			17 37		18 07	18 37		19 07	
Exton	d		13x38			14x38				15x38			16x38			17x10			17x38		18x10	18x38		19x10	
Lympstone Commando	d	13x09	13x40		14x09	14x40			15x09	15x40		16x09	16x40			17x12			17x40		18x12	18x40		19x12	
Lympstone Village	d	13 11	13 43		14 11	14 43			15 11	15 43		16 11	16 43			17 15			17 43		18 15	18 43		19 15	
Exmouth	a	13 19	13 50		14 19	14 50			15 19	15 50		16 19	16 50			17 22			17 50		18 22	18 52		19 22	

		GW		GW	SW ◇■ 🛒	GW	SW ■	GW	GW	GW	GW	SW ■		GW
Barnstaple	d	18 13		19 16				20 24		22 18				
Chapelton	d									22x23				
Umberleigh	d	18x21		19x24				20x32		22x27				
Portsmouth Arms	d	18x28								22x34				
Kings Nympton	d	18x33								22x39				
Eggesford	d	18 40		19 40				20 49		22 47				
Lapford	d	18x47								22x52				
Morchard Road	d	18x51		19x49				20x58		22x57				
Copplestone	d	18x55		19x53				21x01		23x00				
Okehampton	d													
Sampford Courtenay	d													
Yeoford	d	18x59		19x58				21x06		23x05				
Crediton	d	19 11		20 06				21 16		23 13				
Newton St Cyres	d			20x09				21x19		23x16				
Exeter St Davids ■	a	19 24		20 18				21 30		23 26				
	d	19 32		20 20	20 26	20 30	21 26	21 32	21 38		22 36	22 57		23 06
Exeter Central	a	19 35		20 25	20 29	20 33	21 29	21 37	21 41		22 39	23 00		23 09
	d	19 36				20 34			21 42		22 40			23 10
St James' Park	d	19 38				20 36			21 44		22 42			23 12
Polsloe Bridge	d	19 41				20 39			21 47		22 45			23 15
Digby & Sowton	d	19 45				20 43			21 51		22 49			23 19
Topsham	d	19 49				20 47			21 55		22 53			23 23
Exton	d	19x52				20x49			21x57		22x56			23x25
Lympstone Commando	d	19x54				20x51			21x59		22x58			23x27
Lympstone Village	d	19 57				20 54			22 03		23 01			23 31
Exmouth	a	20 03				21 01			22 09		23 08			23 36

For connections at Exeter St Davids please refer to Table 135

Table 136

Barnstaple - Exeter - Exmouth

Saturdays from 15 September

Route Diagram - see first Page of Table 135

		GW	SW	GW	GW	SW	GW	SW	GW	GW		SW	GW	GW	SW	GW	GW	SW	GW	GW		SW	GW	GW	SW
			◇1 ⊼			◇1 ⊼		◇1 ⊼				◇1 ⊼			◇1 ⊼			◇1 ⊼				◇1 ⊼			◇1 ⊼
Barnstaple	d	00 05								07 08						08 43			09 43				10 43		
Chapelton	d									07x13															
Umberleigh	d									07x17						08x51			09x51				10x51		
Portsmouth Arms	d									07x24															
Kings Nympton	d									07x29						09x02									
Eggesford	d	00s27								07 38						09 07			10 07				11 07		
Lapford	d									07x43						09x14									
Morchard Road	d									07x48						09x17			10x16				11x16		
Copplestone	d									07x51						09x22			10x20				11x20		
Okehampton	d																								
Sampford Courtenay	d																								
Yeoford	d									07x57						09x25			10x24				11x24		
Crediton	d	00s47								08 04						09 37			10 37				11 37		
Newton St Cyres	d									08x07															
Exeter St Davids 6	a	01 00								08 16						09 48			10 48				11 48		
	d		05 10	05 44	06 29	06 41	07 11	07 26	07 36	08 16		08 26	08 48	09 18	09 26	09 50	10 18	10 26	10 50	11 18		11 26	11 50	12 18	12 26
Exeter Central	a		05 13	05 47	06 32	06 44	07 14	07 29	07 39	08 19		08 29	08 51	09 21	09 29	09 51	10 21	10 29	10 51	11 21		11 29	11 51	12 21	12 29
	d			05 48	06 39		07 15		07 52	08 20			08 52	09 22		09 52	10 22		10 52	11 22			11 52	12 22	
St James' Park	d				06 41		07 17		07 54	08 23			08 54	09 24		09 54	10 24			11 24				12 24	
Polsloe Bridge	d				06 44		07 20		07 57	08 27			08 57	09 27		09 57	10 27			11 27				12 27	
Digby & Sowton	d			05 54	06 48		07 24		08 01	08 31			09 01	09 31		10 01	10 31		11 01	11 31			12 01	12 31	
Topsham	d			05 58	06 52		07 28		08 05	08 35			09 05	09 35		10 05	10 35		11 05	11 35			12 05	12 35	
Exton	d				06x54		07x31		08x08	08x38			09x08	09x38		10x08	10x38			11x38				12x38	
Lympstone Commando	d				06x56		07x33		08x10	08x40			09x10	09x40		10x10	10x40		11x09	11x40			12x09	12x40	
Lympstone Village	d			06 03	06 59		07 36		08 13	08 43			09 13	09 43		10 11	10 43		11 11	11 43			12 11	12 43	
Exmouth	a			06 10	07 04		07 43		08 18	08 48			09 20	09 50		10 19	10 50		11 19	11 50			12 19	12 50	

		GW	GW	SW	GW	GW		SW	GW	GW	SW	GW	GW	SW	GW	GW		GW	GW	SW	GW	GW	SW	GW	SW
				◇1 ⊼				◇1 ⊼			◇1 ⊼			◇1 ⊼						◇1 ⊼			◇1 ⊼		◇1
Barnstaple	d	11 43			12 43				13 43			14 43				15 43		17 08							
Chapelton	d																	17x14							
Umberleigh	d	11x51			12x51				13x51			14x51				15x51		17x18							
Portsmouth Arms	d																								
Kings Nympton	d				13x02													17x29							
Eggesford	d	12 07			13 07				14 07			15 07				16 07		17 37							
Lapford	d																	17x43							
Morchard Road	d	12x16			13x16				14x16			15x16				16x16		17x46							
Copplestone	d	12x20			13x20				14x20			15x20				16x20		17x50							
Okehampton	d																								
Sampford Courtenay	d																								
Yeoford	d	12x24			13x24				14x24			15x24				16x24		17x54							
Crediton	d	12 37			13 37				14 37			15 37				16 37		18 10							
Newton St Cyres	d																	18x13							
Exeter St Davids 6	a	12 48			13 48				14 48			15 48				16 48		18 22							
	d	12 50	13 18	13 26	13 50	14 18		14 26	14 50	15 18	15 26	15 50	16 18	16 26	16 41	16 50			17 18	17 26	17 50	18 20	18 26	18 50	19 26
Exeter Central	a	12 51	13 21	13 29	13 51	14 21		14 29	14 51	15 21	15 29	15 51	16 21	16 29	16 44	16 53			17 21	17 29	17 53	18 23	18 29	18 53	19 29
	d	12 52	13 22		13 52	14 22			14 52	15 22		15 52	16 22			16 54			17 22		17 54	18 24		18 54	
St James' Park	d		13 24		13 54	14 24				15 24		15 57	16 24			16 56			17 24		17 56	18 26		18 56	
Polsloe Bridge	d		13 27			14 27				15 27			16 27			16 59			17 27		17 59	18 29		18 59	
Digby & Sowton	d	13 01	13 31		14 01	14 31			15 01	15 31		16 01	16 31			17 03			17 31		18 03	18 33		19 03	
Topsham	d	13 05	13 35		14 05	14 35			15 05	15 35		16 05	16 37			17 07			17 37		18 07	18 37		19 07	
Exton	d		13x38			14x38				15x38			16x38			17x10			17x38		18x10	18x38		19x10	
Lympstone Commando	d	13x09	13x40		14x09	14x40			15x09	15x40		16x09	16x40			17x12			17x40		18x12	18x40		19x12	
Lympstone Village	d	13 11	13 43		14 11	14 43			15 11	15 43		16 11	16 43			17 15			17 43		18 15	18 43		19 15	
Exmouth	a	13 19	13 50		14 19	14 50			15 19	15 50		16 19	16 50			17 22			17 50		18 22	18 52		19 22	

		GW		GW	SW	GW	SW	GW	GW	GW	GW	SW		GW
					◇1 ⊼		1					1		
Barnstaple	d	18 13		19 16				20 24		22 18				
Chapelton	d									22x23				
Umberleigh	d	18x21		19x24				20x32		22x27				
Portsmouth Arms	d	18x28								22x34				
Kings Nympton	d	18x33								22x39				
Eggesford	d	18 40		19 40				20 49		22 47				
Lapford	d	18x47								22x52				
Morchard Road	d	18x51		19x49				20x58		22x57				
Copplestone	d	18x55		19x53				21x01		23x00				
Okehampton	d													
Sampford Courtenay	d													
Yeoford	d	18x59		19x58				21x06		23x05				
Crediton	d	19 11		20 06				21 16		23 13				
Newton St Cyres	d			20x09				21x19		23x16				
Exeter St Davids 6	a	19 24		20 18				21 30		23 26				
	d	19 32		20 20	20 26	20 30	21 26	21 32	21 38		22 36	22 57		23 06
Exeter Central	a	19 35		20 25	20 29	20 33	21 29	21 37	21 41		22 39	23 00		23 09
	d	19 36				20 34			21 42		22 40			23 10
St James' Park	d	19 38				20 36			21 44		22 42			23 12
Polsloe Bridge	d	19 41				20 39			21 47		22 45			23 15
Digby & Sowton	d	19 45				20 43			21 51		22 49			23 19
Topsham	d	19 49				20 47			21 55		22 53			23 23
Exton	d	19x52				20x49			21x57		22x56			23x25
Lympstone Commando	d	19x54				20x51			21x59		22x58			23x27
Lympstone Village	d	19 57				20 54			22 03		23 01			23 31
Exmouth	a	20 03				21 01			22 09		23 08			23 36

For connections at Exeter St Davids please refer to Table 135

Table 136

Barnstaple - Exeter - Exmouth

Sundays until 24 June

Route Diagram - see first Page of Table 135

		GW	SW	GW	SW	GW	GW	GW	SW	GW		SW	GW	GW	GW	SW	GW	SW	GW	GW		GW	GW	SW	GW
			◇1 ⊼		◇1 ⊼	A			◇1 ⊼			◇1 ⊼		A		◇1 ⊼		◇1 ⊼		A				◇1 ⊼	
Barnstaple	d							10 00					11 26						13 24						
Chapelton	d							10x06											13x30						
Umberleigh	d							10x10					11x34						13x33						
Portsmouth Arms	d							10x17											13x41						
Kings Nympton	d							10x22											13x46						
Eggesford	d							10 32					11 52						13 54						
Lapford	d							10x37											14x00						
Morchard Road	d							10x41					12x00						14x04						
Copplestone	d							10x45					12x04						14x07						
Okehampton	d					09 55								11 58						14 00					
Sampford Courtenay	d					10 02								12 05						14 07					
Yeoford	d							10x50					12x09						14x13						
Crediton	d					10 25		10 58					12 18	12 28					14 21	14 31					
Newton St Cyres	d							11x01					12x21						14x25						
Exeter St Davids 6	a					10 35		11 11					12 32	12 38					14 33	14 41					
	d	08 30	09 26	09 45	10 26	10 36	10 46	11 13	11 26	11 55		12 26	12 33	12 39	12 48	13 26	13 48	14 26	14 35	14 41		14 48	15 14	15 26	15 48
Exeter Central	a	08 33	09 29	09 48	10 29	10 39	10 49	11 16	11 29	11 58		12 29	12 36	12 42	12 51	13 29	13 51	14 29	14 38	14 44		14 51	15 17	15 29	15 51
	d	08 34		09 49		10 39	10 52			11 59				12 42	12 53		13 52			14 45		14 52			15 51
St James' Park	d	08 36		09 51		10a41	10 54			12 01				12a44	12 55		13 54			14a47		14 54			15 53
Polsloe Bridge	d	08 39		09 54			10 57			12 04					12 58		13 57					14 57			15 56
Digby & Sowton	d	08 43		09 58			11 01			12 08					13 02		14 01					15 01			16 00
Topsham	d	08 47		10 03			11 05			12 12					13 07		14 06					15 06			16 05
Exton	d	08x49		10x05			11x07			12x14					13x09		14x08					15x08			16x07
Lympstone Commando	d	08x51		10x07			11x09			12x16					13x11		14x10					15x10			16x09
Lympstone Village	d	08 55		10 10			11 13			12 20					13 14		14 13					15 13			16 13
Exmouth	a	09 00		10 15			11 18			12 25					13 20		14 18					15 18			16 18

		SW	GW	GW	GW	GW		SW	GW	SW	GW	GW	GW	GW	SW	GW		SW	GW	SW	GW	GW	GW	SW	GW
		◇1 ⊼		A				◇1 ⊼		◇1 ⊼		A			◇1			◇1		1				1	
Barnstaple	d		15 23								17 20			19 20							21 30				
Chapelton	d										17x25										21x36				
Umberleigh	d		15x31								17x29			19x28							21x39				
Portsmouth Arms	d		15x38								17x36										21x47				
Kings Nympton	d		15x43								17x41										21x52				
Eggesford	d		15 52								17 50			19 45							22 00				
Lapford	d										17x55										22x06				
Morchard Road	d		16x00								18x00			19x53							22x10				
Copplestone	d		16x03								18x03			19x57							22x13				
Okehampton	d			15 56								17 59													
Sampford Courtenay	d			16 03								18 07													
Yeoford	d		16x09								18x09			20x02							22x19				
Crediton	d		16 17	16 27							18 18	18 30		20 15							22 28				
Newton St Cyres	d		16x21								18x22			20x18							22x31				
Exeter St Davids 6	a		16 28	16 37							18 32	18 41		20 27							22 42				
	d	16 26	16 30	16 37	16 49	17 15		17 26	17 48	18 26	18 33		18 48		19 26	19 51		20 26	20 51	21 26		21 48	22 48	23 15	23 25
Exeter Central	a	16 29	16 33	16 40	16 52	17 18		17 29	17 51	18 29	18 36		18 51		19 29	19 54		20 29	20 54	21 29		21 51	22 51	23 18	23 28
	d			16 41	16 52				17 51				18 52			19 55			20 55			21 51	22 52		23 29
St James' Park	d			16a43	16 54				17 53				18 54			19 57			20 57			21 53	22 54		23 31
Polsloe Bridge	d				16 57				17 56				18 57			20 00			21 00			21 56	22 57		23 34
Digby & Sowton	d				17 01				18 00				19 01			20 04			21 04			22 00	23 01		23 38
Topsham	d				17 06				18 05				19 06			20 08			21 08			22 05	23 06		23 42
Exton	d				17x08				18x07				19x08			20x10			21x10			22x07	23x08		23x44
Lympstone Commando	d				17x10				18x09				19x11			20x12			21x12			22x09	23x11		23x46
Lympstone Village	d				17 14				18 13				19 13			20 16			21 16			22 13	23 13		23 50
Exmouth	a				17 19				18 18				19 18			20 21			21 21			22 18	23 18		23 54

A not from 20 May until 27 May

For connections at Exeter St Davids please refer to Table 135

Table 136

Barnstaple - Exeter - Exmouth

Sundays
1 July to 9 September

Route Diagram - see first Page of Table 135

		GW	SW ◇1 ⊼	GW	SW ◇1 ⊼	GW	GW	GW	SW ◇1 ⊼	GW	SW ◇1 ⊼	GW	GW	GW	SW ◇1 ⊼	GW	SW ◇1 ⊼	GW	GW	GW	GW	SW ◇1 ⊼	GW
Barnstaple	d							10 00				11 26						13 24					
Chapelton	d							10 06										13x30					
Umberleigh	d							10x10				11x34						13x33					
Portsmouth Arms	d							10 17										13x41					
Kings Nympton	d							10 22										13x46					
Eggesford	d							10 32				11 52						13 54					
Lapford	d							10x37										14x00					
Morchard Road	d							10x41				12x00						14x04					
Copplestone	d							10x45				12x04						14x07					
Okehampton	d					09 55							11 58						14 00				
Sampford Courtenay	d					10 02							12 05						14 07				
Yeoford	d							10x50				12x09						14x13					
Crediton	d					10 25		10 58				12 18	12 28					14 21	14 31				
Newton St Cyres	d							11x01				12x21						14x25					
Exeter St Davids ■	a					10 35		11 11				12 32	12 38					14 33	14 41				
	d	08 30	09 26	09 45	10 26	10 36	10 46	11 13	11 26	11 55	12 26	12 33	12 39	12 48	13 26	13 48	14 26	14 35	14 41	14 48	15 14	15 26	15 48
Exeter Central	a	08 33	09 29	09 48	10 29	10 39	10 49	11 16	11 29	11 58	12 29	12 36	12 42	12 51	13 29	13 51	14 29	14 38	14 44	14 51	15 17	15 29	15 51
	d	08 34		09 49		10 39	10 52			11 59			12 42	12 53		13 52			14 45	14 52			15 51
St James' Park	d	08 36		09 51		10a41	10 54			12 01			12a44	12 55		13 54			14a47	14 54			15 53
Polsloe Bridge	d	08 39		09 54			10 57			12 04				12 58		13 57				14 57			15 56
Digby & Sowton	d	08 43		09 58			11 01			12 08				13 02		14 01				15 01			16 00
Topsham	d	08 47		10 03			11 05			12 12				13 07		14 06				15 06			16 05
Exton	d	08x49		10x05			11x07			12x14				13x09		14x08				15x08			16x07
Lympstone Commando	d	08x51		10x07			11x09			12x16				13x11		14x10				15x10			16x09
Lympstone Village	d	08 55		10 10			11 13			12 20				13 14		14 13				15 13			16 13
Exmouth	a	09 00		10 15			11 18			12 25				13 20		14 18				15 18			16 18

		SW ◇1 ⊼	GW	GW	GW	GW	SW ◇1 ⊼	GW	SW ◇1 ⊼	GW	GW	GW	GW	SW ◇1	GW	SW ◇1	GW	SW 1	GW	GW	GW	SW 1	GW
Barnstaple	d		15 23							17 20			19 20						21 30				
Chapelton	d									17x25									21x36				
Umberleigh	d		15x31							17x29			19x28						21x39				
Portsmouth Arms	d		15x38							17x36									21x47				
Kings Nympton	d		15x43							17x41									21x52				
Eggesford	d		15 52							17 50			19 45						22 00				
Lapford	d									17x55									22x06				
Morchard Road	d		16x00							18x00			19x53						22x10				
Copplestone	d		16x03							18x03			19x57						22x13				
Okehampton	d			15 56							17 59												
Sampford Courtenay	d			16 03							18 07												
Yeoford	d		16x09							18x09			20x02						22x19				
Crediton	d		16 17	16 27						18 18	18 30		20 15						22 28				
Newton St Cyres	d		16x21							18x22			20x18						22x31				
Exeter St Davids ■	a		16 28	16 37						18 32	18 41		20 27						22 42				
	d	16 26	16 30	16 37	16 48	17 15	17 26	17 48	18 26	18 33		18 48		19 26	19 51	20 26	20 51	21 26		21 48	22 48	23 15	23 25
Exeter Central	a	16 29	16 33	16 40	16 51	17 18	17 29	17 51	18 29	18 36		18 51		19 29	19 54	20 29	20 54	21 29		21 51	22 51	23 18	23 28
	d			16 41	16 51			17 51				18 52			19 55		20 55			21 51	22 52		23 29
St James' Park	d			16a43	16 53			17 53				18 54			19 57		20 57			21 53	22 54		23 31
Polsloe Bridge	d				16 56			17 56				18 57			20 00		21 00			21 56	22 57		23 34
Digby & Sowton	d				17 00			18 00				19 01			20 04		21 04			22 00	23 01		23 38
Topsham	d				17 05			18 05				19 06			20 08		21 08			22 05	23 06		23 42
Exton	d				17x07			18x07				19x08			20x10		21x10			22x07	23x08		23x44
Lympstone Commando	d				17x09			18x09				19x11			20x12		21x12			22x09	23x11		23x46
Lympstone Village	d				17 13			18 13				19 13			20 16		21 16			22 13	23 13		23 50
Exmouth	a				17 18			18 18				19 18			20 21		21 21			22 18	23 18		23 54

Sundays
16 September to 23 September

		GW	SW ◇1 ⊼	GW	SW ◇1 ⊼	GW	GW	GW	SW ◇1 ⊼	GW	SW ◇1 ⊼	GW	GW	GW	SW ◇1 ⊼	GW	SW ◇1 ⊼	GW	GW	GW	GW	SW ◇1 ⊼	GW
Barnstaple	d							10 00				11 26						13 24					
Chapelton	d							10x06										13x30					
Umberleigh	d							10x10				11x34						13x33					
Portsmouth Arms	d							10x17										13x41					
Kings Nympton	d							10x22										13x46					
Eggesford	d							10 32				11 52						13 54					
Lapford	d							10x37										14x00					
Morchard Road	d							10x41				12x00						14x04					
Copplestone	d							10x45				12x04						14x07					
Okehampton	d					09 55							11 58						14 00				
Sampford Courtenay	d					10 02							12 05						14 07				
Yeoford	d							10x50				12x09						14x13					
Crediton	d					10 25		10 58				12 18	12 28					14 21	14 31				
Newton St Cyres	d							11x01				12x21						14x25					
Exeter St Davids ■	a					10 35		11 11				12 32	12 38					14 33	14 41				
	d	08 30	09 26	09 45	10 26	10 36	10 46	11 13	11 26	11 55	12 26	12 33	12 39	12 48	13 26	13 48	14 26	14 35	14 41	14 50	15 14	15 26	15 50
Exeter Central	a	08 33	09 29	09 48	10 29	10 39	10 49	11 16	11 29	11 58	12 29	12 36	12 42	12 51	13 29	13 51	14 29	14 38	14 44	14 53	15 17	15 29	15 53
	d	08 34		09 49		10 39	10 52			11 59			12 42	12 53		13 52			14 45	14 54			15 53
St James' Park	d	08 36		09 51		10a41	10 54			12 01			12a44	12 55		13 54			14a47	14 56			15 55
Polsloe Bridge	d	08 39		09 54			10 57			12 04				12 58		13 57				14 59			15 58
Digby & Sowton	d	08 43		09 58			11 01			12 08				13 02		14 01				15 03			16 02
Topsham	d	08 47		10 03			11 05			12 12				13 07		14 06				15 08			16 07
Exton	d	08x49		10x05			11x07			12x14				13x09		14x08				15x10			16x09
Lympstone Commando	d	08x51		10x07			11x09			12x16				13x11		14x10				15x12			16x11
Lympstone Village	d	08 55		10 10			11 13			12 20				13 14		14 13				15 15			16 15
Exmouth	a	09 00		10 15			11 18			12 25				13 20		14 18				15 20			16 20

For connections at Exeter St Davids please refer to Table 135

Table 136

Barnstaple - Exeter - Exmouth

Sundays
16 September to 23 September

Route Diagram - see first Page of Table 135

		SW ◇1 ⊼	GW	GW	GW	GW	SW ◇1 ⊼	GW	SW ◇1 ⊼	GW	GW	GW	GW	SW ◇1	GW	SW ◇1	GW	SW 1	GW	GW	GW	SW 1	GW
Barnstaple	d		15 23							17 20			19 20						21 30				
Chapelton	d									17x25									21x36				
Umberleigh	d		15x31							17x29			19x28						21x39				
Portsmouth Arms	d		15x38							17x36									21x47				
Kings Nympton	d		15x43							17x41									21x52				
Eggesford	d		15 52							17 50			19 45						22 00				
Lapford	d									17x55									22x06				
Morchard Road	d		16x00							18x00			19x53						22x10				
Copplestone	d		16x03							18x03			19x57						22x13				
Okehampton	d			15 56							17 59												
Sampford Courtenay	d			16 03							18 07												
Yeoford	d		16x09							18x09			20x02						22x19				
Crediton	d		16 17	16 27						18 18	18 30		20 15						22 28				
Newton St Cyres	d		16x21							18x22			20x18						22x31				
Exeter St Davids ■	a		16 28	16 37						18 32	18 41		20 27						22 42				
	d	16 26	16 30	16 37	16 50	17 15	17 26	17 48	18 26	18 33		18 50		19 26	19 51	20 26	20 52	21 26		21 48	22 48	23 15	23 25
Exeter Central	a	16 29	16 33	16 40	16 53	17 18	17 29	17 51	18 29	18 36		18 53		19 29	19 54	20 29	20 55	21 29		21 51	22 51	23 18	23 28
	d			16 41	16 53			17 51				18 54			19 55		20 56			21 51	22 52		23 29
St James' Park	d			16a43	16 55			17 53				18 56			19 57		20 58			21 53	22 54		23 31
Polsloe Bridge	d				16 58			17 56				18 59			20 00		21 01			21 56	22 57		23 34
Digby & Sowton	d				17 02			18 00				19 03			20 04		21 05			22 00	23 01		23 38
Topsham	d				17 07			18 05				19 08			20 08		21 09			22 05	23 06		23 42
Exton	d				17x09			18x07				19x10			20x10		21x11			22x07	23x08		23x44
Lympstone Commando	d				17x11			18x09				19x13			20x12		21x13			22x09	23x11		23x46
Lympstone Village	d				17 15			18 13				19 15			20 16		21 17			22 13	23 13		23 50
Exmouth	a				17 20			18 18				19 20			20 21		21 22			22 18	23 18		23 54

Sundays
from 30 September

		GW	SW ◇1 ⊼	GW	SW ◇1 ⊼	GW	GW	SW ◇1 ⊼	GW	SW ◇1 ⊼	GW	GW	SW ◇1 ⊼	GW	SW ◇1 ⊼	GW	GW	GW	SW ◇1 ⊼	GW	SW ◇1 ⊼	GW	GW
Barnstaple	d						10 00				11 26					13 24						15 23	
Chapelton	d						10x06									13x30							
Umberleigh	d						10x10				11x34					13x33						15x31	
Portsmouth Arms	d						10x17									13x41						15x38	
Kings Nympton	d						10x22									13x46						15x43	
Eggesford	d						10 32				11 52					13 54						15 52	
Lapford	d						10x37									14x00							
Morchard Road	d						10x41				12x00					14x04						16x00	
Copplestone	d						10x45				12x04					14x07						16x03	
Okehampton	d																						
Sampford Courtenay	d																						
Yeoford	d						10x50				12x09					14x13						16x09	
Crediton	d						10 58				12 18					14 21						16 17	
Newton St Cyres	d						11x01				12x21					14x25						16x21	
Exeter St Davids ■	a						11 11				12 32					14 33						16 28	
	d	08 30	09 26	09 45	10 26	10 46	11 13	11 26	11 55	12 26	12 33	12 48	13 26	13 48	14 26	14 35	14 50	15 14	15 26	15 50	16 26	16 30	16 50
Exeter Central	a	08 33	09 29	09 48	10 29	10 49	11 16	11 29	11 58	12 29	12 36	12 51	13 29	13 51	14 29	14 38	14 53	15 17	15 29	15 53	16 29	16 33	16 53
	d	08 34		09 49		10 52			11 59			12 53		13 52			14 54			15 53			16 53
St James' Park	d	08 36		09 51		10 54			12 01			12 55		13 54			14 56			15 55			16 55
Polsloe Bridge	d	08 39		09 54		10 57			12 04			12 58		13 57			14 59			15 58			16 58
Digby & Sowton	d	08 43		09 58		11 01			12 08			13 02		14 01			15 03			16 02			17 02
Topsham	d	08 47		10 03		11 05			12 12			13 07		14 06			15 08			16 07			17 07
Exton	d	08x49		10x05		11x07			12x14			13x09		14x08			15x10			16x09			17x09
Lympstone Commando	d	08x51		10x07		11x09			12x16			13x11		14x10			15x12			16x11			17x11
Lympstone Village	d	08 55		10 10		11 13			12 20			13 14		14 13			15 15			16 15			17 15
Exmouth	a	09 00		10 15		11 18			12 25			13 20		14 18			15 20			16 20			17 20

		GW	SW ◇1 ⊼	GW	SW ◇1 ⊼	GW	GW	GW	SW ◇1	GW	SW ◇1	GW	SW 1	GW	GW	GW	SW 1	GW
Barnstaple	d					17 20		19 20						21 30				
Chapelton	d					17x25								21x36				
Umberleigh	d					17x29		19x28						21x39				
Portsmouth Arms	d					17x36								21x47				
Kings Nympton	d					17x41								21x52				
Eggesford	d					17 50		19 45						22 00				
Lapford	d					17x55								22x06				
Morchard Road	d					18x00		19x53						22x10				
Copplestone	d					18x03		19x57						22x13				
Okehampton	d																	
Sampford Courtenay	d																	
Yeoford	d					18x09		20x02						22x19				
Crediton	d					18 18		20 15						22 28				
Newton St Cyres	d					18x22		20x18						22x31				
Exeter St Davids ■	a					18 32		20 27						22 42				
	d	17 15	17 26	17 48	18 26	18 33	18 50		19 26	19 51	20 26	20 52	21 26		21 48	22 48	23 15	23 25
Exeter Central	a	17 18	17 29	17 51	18 29	18 36	18 53		19 29	19 54	20 29	20 55	21 29		21 51	22 51	23 18	23 28
	d			17 51			18 54			19 55		20 56			21 51	22 52		23 29
St James' Park	d			17 53			18 56			19 57		20 58			21 53	22 54		23 31
Polsloe Bridge	d			17 56			18 59			20 00		21 01			21 56	22 57		23 34
Digby & Sowton	d			18 00			19 03			20 04		21 05			22 00	23 01		23 38
Topsham	d			18 05			19 08			20 08		21 09			22 05	23 06		23 42
Exton	d			18x07			19x10			20x10		21x11			22x07	23x08		23x44
Lympstone Commando	d			18x09			19x13			20x12		21x13			22x09	23x11		23x46
Lympstone Village	d			18 13			19 15			20 16		21 17			22 13	23 13		23 50
Exmouth	a			18 18			19 20			20 21		21 22			22 18	23 18		23 54

For connections at Exeter St Davids please refer to Table 135

Table 139

Plymouth - Gunnislake

Route Diagram - see first Page of Table 135

Mondays to Fridays
until 29 June

Miles			GW	GW	GW	GW	GW	GW	GW	GW	GW	GW	GW	GW	GW	GW	GW	GW
					1 ⊏⊐	◇		◇	◇									
0	**Plymouth**	d	05 06	06 41	07 02	08 14	08 40	09 21	10 42	10 54	12 54	14 54	15 57	16 38	17 04	18 17	18 23	21 31
1¼	Devonport	d		06 44	07a06	08a17	08 43	09a24		10 57	12 57	14 57	16 00	16 41	17 07	18 20	18 26	21 34
1½	Dockyard	d		06x45			08x44			10x58	12x58	14x58	16x01	16x42	17x08	18x21	18x27	21x35
2¼	Keyham	d		06 47			08 46			11 00	13 00	15 00	16 03	16 44	17 10	18 23	18 29	21 37
—	St Budeaux Ferry Road	a							10 48				16 06		17 13	18 25		
3	St Budeaux Victoria Road	d	05 12	06 51			08 50			11 04	13 04	15 04		16 48			18 33	21 41
7¼	Bere Ferrers	d		06 58			08 57			11 11	13 11	15 11		16 55			18 40	21 48
10	Bere Alston	a	05 25	07 05			09 04			11 18	13 19	15 18		17 02			18 47	21 55
—		d	05 27	07 07			09 06			11 20	13 20	15 20		17 04			18 49	21 57
11¾	Calstock	d	05 34	07 14			09 13			11 27	13 27	15 27		17 11			18 56	22 04
14½	**Gunnislake**	a	05 50	07 27			09 26			11 40	13 41	15 40		17 24			19 09	22 17

Mondays to Fridays
2 July to 31 August

		GW	GW	GW	GW	GW	GW	GW	GW	GW	GW	GW	GW	GW	GW	GW	GW
				1 ⊏⊐	1 ⊏⊐		◇	◇									
Plymouth	d	05 06	06 41	07 02	08 20	08 40	09 21	10 42	10 54	12 54	14 54	15 57	16 38	17 04	18 17	18 23	21 31
Devonport	d		06 44	07a06	08a24	08 43	09a24		10 57	12 57	14 57	16 00	16 41	17 07	18 20	18 26	21 34
Dockyard	d		06x45			08x44			10x58	12x58	14x58	16x01	16x42	17x08	18x21	18x27	21x35
Keyham	d		06 47			08 46			11 00	13 00	15 00	16 03	16 44	17 10	18 23	18 29	21 37
St Budeaux Ferry Road	a							10 48				16 06		17 13	18 25		
St Budeaux Victoria Road	d	05 12	06 51			08 50			11 04	13 04	15 04		16 48			18 33	21 41
Bere Ferrers	d		06 58			08 57			11 11	13 11	15 11		16 55			18 40	21 48
Bere Alston	a	05 25	07 05			09 04			11 18	13 19	15 18		17 02			18 47	21 55
	d	05 27	07 07			09 06			11 20	13 20	15 20		17 04			18 49	21 57
Calstock	d	05 34	07 14			09 13			11 27	13 27	15 27		17 11			18 56	22 04
Gunnislake	a	05 50	07 27			09 26			11 40	13 41	15 40		17 24			19 09	22 17

Mondays to Fridays
from 3 September

		GW	GW	GW	GW	GW	GW	GW	GW	GW	GW	GW	GW	GW	GW	GW	GW
				1 ⊏⊐	◇		◇	◇									
Plymouth	d	05 06	06 41	07 02	08 14	08 40	09 21	10 42	10 54	12 54	14 54	15 57	16 38	17 04	18 17	18 23	21 31
Devonport	d		06 44	07a06	08a17	08 43	09a24		10 57	12 57	14 57	16 00	16 41	17 07	18 20	18 26	21 34
Dockyard	d		06x45			08x44			10x58	12x58	14x58	16x01	16x42	17x08	18x21	18x27	21x35
Keyham	d		06 47			08 46			11 00	13 00	15 00	16 03	16 44	17 10	18 23	18 29	21 37
St Budeaux Ferry Road	a							10 48				16 06		17 13	18 25		
St Budeaux Victoria Road	d	05 12	06 51			08 50			11 04	13 04	15 04		16 48			18 33	21 41
Bere Ferrers	d		06 58			08 57			11 11	13 11	15 11		16 55			18 40	21 48
Bere Alston	a	05 25	07 05			09 04			11 18	13 19	15 18		17 02			18 47	21 55
	d	05 27	07 07			09 06			11 20	13 20	15 20		17 04			18 49	21 57
Calstock	d	05 34	07 14			09 13			11 27	13 27	15 27		17 11			18 56	22 04
Gunnislake	a	05 50	07 27			09 26			11 40	13 41	15 40		17 24			19 09	22 17

Saturdays
until 8 September

		GW	GW	GW	GW	GW	GW	GW	GW	GW	GW	GW	GW
			◇										
Plymouth	d	06 40	08 18	08 40	09 58	10 33	10 59	12 54	14 47	16 38	17 52	18 23	21 31
Devonport	d	06 43	08a21	08 43	10a01		11 02	12 57	14 50	16 41	17 55	18 26	21 34
Dockyard	d	06x44		08x44			11x03	12x58	14x51	16x42	17x57	18x27	21x35
Keyham	d	06 46		08 46			11 05	13 00	14 53	16 44	17 59	18 29	21 37
St Budeaux Ferry Road	a					10 39					18 00		
St Budeaux Victoria Road	d	06 50		08 50			11 09	13 04	14 57	16 48		18 33	21 41
Bere Ferrers	d	06 57		08 57			11 16	13 11	15 04	16 55		18 40	21 48
Bere Alston	a	07 04		09 04			11 23	13 18	15 11	17 02		18 47	21 55
	d	07 06		09 06			11 25	13 20	15 13	17 04		18 49	21 57
Calstock	d	07 13		09 13			11 32	13 27	15 20	17 11		18 56	22 04
Gunnislake	a	07 26		09 26			11 45	13 40	15 33	17 25		19 09	22 17

Saturdays
from 15 September

		GW	GW	GW	GW	GW	GW	GW	GW	GW	GW	GW	GW
			◇										
Plymouth	d	06 40	08 18	08 40	09 51	10 33	10 54	12 54	14 47	16 38	17 52	18 23	21 31
Devonport	d	06 43	08a21	08 43	09a54		10 57	12 57	14 50	16 41	17 55	18 26	21 34
Dockyard	d	06x44		08x44			10x58	12x58	14x51	16x42	17x57	18x27	21x35
Keyham	d	06 46		08 46			11 00	13 00	14 53	16 44	17 59	18 29	21 37
St Budeaux Ferry Road	a					10 39					18 00		
St Budeaux Victoria Road	d	06 50		08 50			11 04	13 04	14 57	16 48		18 33	21 41
Bere Ferrers	d	06 57		08 57			11 11	13 11	15 04	16 55		18 40	21 48
Bere Alston	a	07 04		09 04			11 18	13 18	15 11	17 02		18 47	21 55
	d	07 06		09 06			11 20	13 20	15 13	17 04		18 49	21 57
Calstock	d	07 13		09 13			11 27	13 27	15 20	17 11		18 56	22 04
Gunnislake	a	07 26		09 26			11 40	13 40	15 33	17 25		19 09	22 17

Table 139

Plymouth - Gunnislake

Route Diagram - see first Page of Table 135

Sundays
until 9 September

		GW	GW	GW	GW	GW	GW	GW
			🚌	◇				
Plymouth	d	09 04	09 10	10 15	11 06	13 13	15 17	17 41
Devonport	d	09 07	09a13	10a19	11 09	13 16	15 20	17 44
Dockyard	d	09x08			11x10	13x17	15x21	17x45
Keyham	d	09 10			11 12	13 19	15 23	17 47
St Budeaux Ferry Road	a							
St Budeaux Victoria Road	d	09 14			11 16	13 23	15 27	17 51
Bere Ferrers	d	09 21			11 23	13 30	15 34	17 58
Bere Alston	a	09 28			11 30	13 37	15 41	18 05
	d	09 30			11 32	13 39	15 43	18 07
Calstock	d	09 37			11 39	13 46	15 50	18 14
Gunnislake	a	09 50			11 52	13 59	16 03	18 27

Sundays
16 September to 28 October

		GW	GW	GW	GW	GW	GW	GW	GW
		A 🚌	B 🚌		◇				
Plymouth	d	09 10	09 15	09 30	10 15	11 40	13 45	15 40	17 45
Devonport	d			09 33	10a19	11 43	13 48	15 43	17 48
Dockyard	d			09x34		11x44	13x49	15x44	17x49
Keyham	d			09 36		11 46	13 51	15 46	17 51
St Budeaux Ferry Road	a	09 16	09 21						
St Budeaux Victoria Road	d			09 40		11 50	13 55	15 50	17 55
Bere Ferrers	d			09 47		11 57	14 02	15 57	18 02
Bere Alston	a			09 54		12 04	14 09	16 04	18 09
	d			09 56		12 06	14 11	16 06	18 11
Calstock	d			10 03		12 13	14 18	16 13	18 18
Gunnislake	a			10 16		12 26	14 31	16 26	18 31

Sundays
from 4 November

		GW	GW	GW	GW	GW	GW	GW
		🚌		◇				
Plymouth	d	09 15	09 30	10 15	11 40	13 45	15 40	17 45
Devonport	d		09 33	10a19	11 43	13 48	15 43	17 48
Dockyard	d		09x34		11x44	13x49	15x44	17x49
Keyham	d		09 36		11 46	13 51	15 46	17 51
St Budeaux Ferry Road	a	09 21						
St Budeaux Victoria Road	d		09 40		11 50	13 55	15 50	17 55
Bere Ferrers	d		09 47		11 57	14 02	15 57	18 02
Bere Alston	a		09 54		12 04	14 09	16 04	18 09
	d		09 56		12 06	14 11	16 06	18 11
Calstock	d		10 03		12 13	14 18	16 13	18 18
Gunnislake	a		10 16		12 26	14 31	16 26	18 31

A not 28 October

B 28 October

Table 139

Gunnislake - Plymouth

Mondays to Fridays
until 29 June

Route Diagram - see first Page of Table 135

Miles			GW	GW	GW	GW	GW	GW	GW	GW	GW	GW	GW	GW	GW
				◇						◇					
0	**Gunnislake**	d	05 50		07 31	09 29	11 45	13 45	15 45		17 29		19 13		22 21
3	Calstock	d	06 01		07 42	09 40	11 56	13 56	15 56		17 40		19 24		22 32
4½	Bere Alston	a	06 08		07 49	09 47	12 03	14 03	16 03		17 47		19 31		22 39
—		d	06 10		07 51	09 49	12 05	14 05	16 05		17 49		19 33		22 41
7½	Bere Ferrers	d	06 15		07 56	09 54	12 10	14 10	16 10		17 54		19 38		22 46
11½	St Budeaux Victoria Road	d	06 24		08 05	10 03	12 19	14 19	16 19		18 03		19 47		22 55
—	St Budeaux Ferry Road	d		07 52						16 41		18 12		21 09	
12½	Keyham	d	06 26	07 54	08 07	10 05	12 21	14 21	16 21	16 43	18 05		19 49	21 11	22 57
13	Dockyard	d	06x28	07x56	08x09	10x07	12x23	14x23	16x23	16x45	18x07		19x51	21x13	22x59
13½	Devonport	d	06 31	07 58	08 11	10 09	12 25	14 25	16 25	16 47	18 09		19 53	21 15	23 01
14½	**Plymouth**	a	06 36	08 04	08 17	10 14	12 30	14 30	16 30	16 52	18 14	18 19	19 58	21 20	23 06

Mondays to Fridays
2 July to 31 August

		GW	GW	GW	GW	GW	GW	GW	GW	GW	GW	GW	GW	GW
			◇											
Gunnislake	d	05 50		07 31	09 29	11 45	13 45	15 45		17 29		19 13		22 21
Calstock	d	06 01		07 42	09 40	11 56	13 56	15 56		17 40		19 24		22 32
Bere Alston	a	06 08		07 49	09 47	12 03	14 03	16 03		17 47		19 31		22 39
	d	06 10		07 51	09 49	12 05	14 05	16 05		17 49		19 33		22 41
Bere Ferrers	d	06 15		07 56	09 54	12 10	14 10	16 10		17 54		19 38		22 46
St Budeaux Victoria Road	d	06 24		08 05	10 03	12 19	14 19	16 19		18 03		19 47		22 55
St Budeaux Ferry Road	d		07 52						17 06		18 12		21 34	
Keyham	d	06 26	07 54	08 07	10 05	12 21	14 21	16 21	17 08	18 05		19 49	21 36	22 57
Dockyard	d	06x28	07x56	08x09	10x07	12x23	14x23	16x23	17x10	18x07		19x51	21x38	22x59
Devonport	d	06 31	07 58	08 11	10 09	12 25	14 25	16 25	17 12	18 09		19 53	21 40	23 01
Plymouth	a	06 36	08 04	08 17	10 14	12 30	14 30	16 30	17 18	18 14	18 19	19 58	21 46	23 06

Mondays to Fridays
from 3 September

		GW	GW	GW	GW	GW	GW	GW	GW	GW	GW	GW	GW	GW
			◇						◇					
Gunnislake	d	05 50		07 31	09 29	11 45	13 45	15 45		17 29		19 13		22 21
Calstock	d	06 01		07 42	09 40	11 56	13 56	15 56		17 40		19 24		22 32
Bere Alston	a	06 08		07 49	09 47	12 03	14 03	16 03		17 47		19 31		22 39
	d	06 10		07 51	09 49	12 05	14 05	16 05		17 49		19 33		22 41
Bere Ferrers	d	06 15		07 56	09 54	12 10	14 10	16 10		17 54		19 38		22 46
St Budeaux Victoria Road	d	06 24		08 05	10 03	12 19	14 19	16 19		18 03		19 47		22 55
St Budeaux Ferry Road	d		07 52						16 41		18 12		21 09	
Keyham	d	06 26	07 54	08 07	10 05	12 21	14 21	16 21	16 43	18 05		19 49	21 11	22 57
Dockyard	d	06x28	07x56	08x09	10x07	12x23	14x23	16x23	16x45	18x07		19x51	21x13	22x59
Devonport	d	06 31	07 58	08 11	10 09	12 25	14 25	16 25	16 47	18 09		19 53	21 15	23 01
Plymouth	a	06 36	08 04	08 17	10 14	12 30	14 30	16 30	16 52	18 14	18 19	19 58	21 20	23 06

Saturdays
until 8 September

		GW	GW	GW	GW	GW	GW	GW	GW	GW	GW	GW	GW
							◇						
Gunnislake	d		07 31	09 29	11 52	13 45		15 45	17 29	19 17		22 21	
Calstock	d		07 42	09 40	12 03	13 56		15 56	17 40	19 28		22 32	
Bere Alston	a		07 49	09 47	12 10	14 03		16 03	17 47	19 35		22 39	
	d		07 51	09 49	12 12	14 05		16 05	17 49	19 37		22 41	
Bere Ferrers	d		07 56	09 54	12 17	14 10		16 10	17 54	19 42		22 46	
St Budeaux Victoria Road	d		08 05	10 03	12 26	14 19		16 19	18 03	19 51		22 55	
St Budeaux Ferry Road	d	07 30									20 58		22 59
Keyham	d	07 32	08 07	10 05	12 28	14 21		16 21	18 05	19 53	21 00	22 57	23 01
Dockyard	d	07x34	08x09	10x07	12x30	14x23		16x23	18x07	19x55	21x02	22x59	23x03
Devonport	d	07 36	08 11	10 09	12 32	14 25	15 15	16 25	18 09	19 57	21 04	23 01	23 05
Plymouth	a	07 42	08 17	10 14	12 37	14 30	15 20	16 30	18 14	20 02	21 10	23 06	23 12

Saturdays
from 15 September

		GW	GW	GW	GW	GW	GW	GW	GW	GW	GW	GW	GW
							◇						
Gunnislake	d		07 31	09 29	11 45	13 45		15 45	17 29	19 17		22 21	
Calstock	d		07 42	09 40	11 56	13 56		15 56	17 40	19 28		22 32	
Bere Alston	a		07 49	09 47	12 03	14 03		16 03	17 47	19 35		22 39	
	d		07 51	09 49	12 05	14 05		16 05	17 49	19 37		22 41	
Bere Ferrers	d		07 56	09 54	12 10	14 10		16 10	17 54	19 42		22 46	
St Budeaux Victoria Road	d		08 05	10 03	12 19	14 19		16 19	18 03	19 51		22 55	
St Budeaux Ferry Road	d	07 30									20 58		22 59
Keyham	d	07 32	08 07	10 05	12 21	14 21		16 21	18 05	19 53	21 00	22 57	23 01
Dockyard	d	07x34	08x09	10x07	12x23	14x23		16x23	18x07	19x55	21x02	22x59	23x03
Devonport	d	07 36	08 11	10 09	12 25	14 25	14 52	16 25	18 09	19 57	21 04	23 01	23 05
Plymouth	a	07 42	08 17	10 14	12 30	14 30	14 58	16 30	18 14	20 02	21 10	23 06	23 12

Table 139

Gunnislake - Plymouth

Sundays
until 9 September

Route Diagram - see first Page of Table 135

		GW	GW	GW	GW	GW	GW	GW
							🚌	
Gunnislake	d	10 18	12 07	14 05	16 07	18 44		
Calstock	d	10 29	12 18	14 16	16 18	18 55		
Bere Alston	a	10 36	12 25	14 23	16 25	19 02		
	d	10 38	12 27	14 25	16 27	19 04		
Bere Ferrers	d	10 43	12 32	14 30	16 32	19 09		
St Budeaux Victoria Road	d	10 52	12 41	14 39	16 41	19 18		
St Budeaux Ferry Road	d							
Keyham	d	10 54	12 43	14 41	16 43	19 20		
Dockyard	d	10x56	12x45	14x43	16x45	19x22		
Devonport	d	10 58	12 47	14 45	16 47	19 24	19 47	20 56
Plymouth	a	11 03	12 52	14 50	16 52	19 29	19 50	21 00

Sundays
16 September to 28 October

		GW	GW	GW	GW	GW	GW
Gunnislake	d	10 25	12 45	14 45	16 54	18 44	
Calstock	d	10 36	12 56	14 56	17 05	18 55	
Bere Alston	a	10 43	13 03	15 03	17 12	19 02	
	d	10 45	13 05	15 05	17 14	19 04	
Bere Ferrers	d	10 50	13 10	15 10	17 19	19 09	
St Budeaux Victoria Road	d	10 59	13 19	15 19	17 28	19 18	
St Budeaux Ferry Road	d						
Keyham	d	11 01	13 21	15 21	17 30	19 20	
Dockyard	d	11x03	13x23	15x23	17x32	19x22	
Devonport	d	11 05	13 25	15 25	17 34	19 24	20 56
Plymouth	a	11 10	13 30	15 30	17 39	19 29	21 00

Sundays
from 4 November

		GW	GW	GW	GW	GW	GW
Gunnislake	d	10 25	12 45	14 45	16 54	18 44	
Calstock	d	10 36	12 56	14 56	17 05	18 55	
Bere Alston	a	10 43	13 03	15 03	17 12	19 02	
	d	10 45	13 05	15 05	17 14	19 04	
Bere Ferrers	d	10 50	13 10	15 10	17 19	19 09	
St Budeaux Victoria Road	d	10 59	13 19	15 19	17 28	19 18	
St Budeaux Ferry Road	d						
Keyham	d	11 01	13 21	15 21	17 30	19 20	
Dockyard	d	11x03	13x23	15x23	17x32	19x22	
Devonport	d	11 05	13 25	15 25	17 34	19 24	20 56
Plymouth	a	11 10	13 30	15 30	17 39	19 29	21 00

Table 140

Mondays to Fridays

Liskeard - Looe

Route Diagram - see first Page of Table 135

Miles			GW	GW	GW	GW	GW	GW	GW	GW	GW	GW	GW	GW
0	**Liskeard** ■	d	06 05	07 14	08 33	09 58	11 18	12 15	13 19	14 28	15 41	16 41	18 01	19 18
2	Coombe Junction Halt	a			08 39	10 04								
—		d			08 42	10 07								
3¾	St Keyne Wishing Well Halt	d	06x17	07x26	08x48	10x13		12x27	13x31		15x53	16x53	18x13	19x31
5	Causeland	d	06x21	07x30	08x52	10x17		12x31	13x35		15x57	16x57	18x17	19x33
6½	Sandplace	d	06x24	07x33	08x56	10x20		12x34	13x38		16x00	17x00	18x20	19x38
8¾	**Looe**	a	06 36	07 45	09 04	10 29	11 46	12 46	13 50	14 56	16 12	17 12	18 32	19 49

Saturdays
until 8 September

		GW	GW	GW	GW	GW	GW	GW	GW	GW	GW	GW	GW	GW
Liskeard ■	d	06 01	07 12	08 35	09 58	11 08	12 12	13 24	14 28	15 42	16 56	18 01	19 28	20 40
Coombe Junction Halt	a			08 41	10 04									
	d			08 44	10 06									
St Keyne Wishing Well Halt	d	06x13	07x24	08x50	10x13		12x24	13x37		15x54	17x09	18x13	19x41	20x53
Causeland	d	06x17	07x28	08x54	10x17		12x28	13x40		15x58	17x12	18x17	19x43	20x55
Sandplace	d	06x20	07x31	08x58	10x20		12x31	13x44		16x01	17x16	18x20	19x48	21x00
Looe	a	06 32	07 43	09 06	10 29	11 36	12 43	13 55	14 56	16 13	17 27	18 32	19 59	21 11

Saturdays
from 15 September

		GW	GW	GW	GW	GW	GW	GW	GW	GW	GW	GW	GW
Liskeard ■	d	06 01	07 12	08 35	09 58	11 08	12 12	13 24	14 28	15 42	16 56	18 01	19 28
Coombe Junction Halt	a			08 41	10 04								
	d			08 44	10 06								
St Keyne Wishing Well Halt	d	06x13	07x24	08x50	10x13		12x24	13x37		15x54	17x09	18x13	19x41
Causeland	d	06x17	07x28	08x54	10x17		12x28	13x40		15x58	17x12	18x17	19x43
Sandplace	d	06x20	07x31	08x58	10x20		12x31	13x44		16x01	17x16	18x20	19x48
Looe	a	06 32	07 43	09 06	10 29	11 36	12 43	13 55	14 56	16 13	17 27	18 32	19 59

Sundays
until 9 September

		GW	GW	GW	GW	GW	GW	GW	GW
Liskeard ■	d	10 12	11 26	12 50	14 00	15 03	16 10	17 35	20 15
Coombe Junction Halt	a								
	d								
St Keyne Wishing Well Halt	d	10x25	11x39	13x03	14x13	15x16	16x23	17x48	20x28
Causeland	d	10x28	11x42	13x06	14x16	15x19	16x26	17x51	20x31
Sandplace	d	10x32	11x46	13x10	14x20	15x23	16x30	17x55	20x35
Looe	a	10 41	11 55	13 19	14 29	15 32	16 39	18 04	20 44

Sundays
16 September to 28 October

		GW	GW	GW	GW	GW	GW	GW	GW
Liskeard ■	d	10 12	11 26	13 04	14 07	15 20	16 36	17 40	20 15
Coombe Junction Halt	a								
	d								
St Keyne Wishing Well Halt	d	10x25	11x39	13x17	14x20	15x33	16x49	17x53	20x28
Causeland	d	10x28	11x42	13x20	14x23	15x36	16x52	17x56	20x31
Sandplace	d	10x32	11x46	13x24	14x27	15x40	16x56	18x00	20x35
Looe	a	10 41	11 55	13 33	14 36	15 49	17 05	18 09	20 44

For connections at Liskeard please refer to Table 135

Table 140

Mondays to Fridays

Looe - Liskeard

Route Diagram - see first Page of Table 135

Miles			GW	GW	GW	GW	GW	GW	GW	GW	GW	GW	GW	GW
0	**Looe**	d	06 37	07 46	09 09	10 32	11 47	12 47	13 51	14 57	16 13	17 15	18 33	19 52
2¼	Sandplace	d	06x42	07x51	09x14	10x37		12x52		15x02		17x20	18x38	19x57
3¾	Causeland	d	06x46	07x55	09x18	10x41		12x56		15x06		17x24	18x42	20x01
5	St Keyne Wishing Well Halt	d	06x49	07x58	09x21	10x44		12x59		15x09		17x27	18x45	20x04
6¾	Coombe Junction Halt	a			09 27	10 50								
—		d			09 29	10 52								
8¾	**Liskeard** ■	a	07 05	08 14	09 40	11 03	12 11	13 17	14 15	15 25	16 39	17 43	19 01	20 22

Saturdays
until 8 September

		GW	GW	GW	GW	GW	GW	GW	GW	GW	GW	GW	GW	GW
Looe	d	06 33	07 47	09 09	10 32	11 37	12 44	13 56	14 56	16 14	17 28	18 33	20 00	21 12
Sandplace	d	06x38	07x52	09x14	10x37		12x49		15x01	16x19	17x33	18x38	20x05	21x17
Causeland	d	06x42	07x56	09x18	10x41		12x53		15x05	16x23	17x37	18x42	20x09	21x21
St Keyne Wishing Well Halt	d	06x45	07x59	09x21	10x45		12x56		15x08	16x27	17x41	18x45	20x13	21x25
Coombe Junction Halt	a			09 27	10 50									
	d			09 29	10 52									
Liskeard ■	a	07 01	08 15	09 40	11 03	12 01	13 12	14 20	15 25	16 44	17 58	19 01	20 28	21 40

Saturdays
from 15 September

		GW	GW	GW	GW	GW	GW	GW	GW	GW	GW	GW	GW
Looe	d	06 33	07 47	09 09	10 32	11 37	12 44	13 56	14 56	16 14	17 28	18 33	20 00
Sandplace	d	06x38	07x52	09x14	10x37		12x49		15x01	16x19	17x33	18x38	20x05
Causeland	d	06x42	07x56	09x18	10x41		12x53		15x05	16x23	17x37	18x42	20x09
St Keyne Wishing Well Halt	d	06x45	07x59	09x21	10x45		12x56		15x08	16x27	17x41	18x45	20x13
Coombe Junction Halt	a			09 27	10 50								
	d			09 29	10 52								
Liskeard ■	a	07 01	08 15	09 40	11 03	12 01	13 12	14 20	15 25	16 44	17 58	19 01	20 28

Sundays
until 9 September

		GW	GW	GW	GW	GW	GW	GW	GW
Looe	d	10 45	11 58	13 22	14 32	15 35	16 42	18 20	20 50
Sandplace	d	10x50	12x03	13x27	14x37	15x40	16x47	18x25	20x55
Causeland	d	10x54	12x07	13x31	14x41	15x44	16x51	18x29	20x59
St Keyne Wishing Well Halt	d	10x58	12x11	13x35	14x45	15x48	16x55	18x33	21x03
Coombe Junction Halt	a								
	d								
Liskeard ■	a	11 13	12 26	13 50	15 00	16 03	17 10	18 48	21 18

Sundays
16 September to 28 October

		GW	GW	GW	GW	GW	GW	GW	GW
Looe	d	10 45	11 58	13 36	14 39	15 55	17 08	18 15	20 50
Sandplace	d	10x50	12x03	13x41	14x44	16x00	17x13	18x20	20x55
Causeland	d	10x54	12x07	13x45	14x48	16x04	17x17	18x24	20x59
St Keyne Wishing Well Halt	d	10x58	12x11	13x49	14x52	16x08	17x21	18x28	21x03
Coombe Junction Halt	a								
	d								
Liskeard ■	a	11 13	12 26	14 04	15 07	16 23	17 36	18 43	21 18

For connections at Liskeard please refer to Table 135

Table 142

Par - Newquay

Mondays to Fridays until 29 June

Route Diagram - see first Page of Table 135

Miles			GW	GW	GW	GW	GW	GW
				◇	◇	◇	◇	
0	Par	d	09 17	12 13	14 08	16 10	18 29	20 28
4¼	Luxulyan	d	09x28			16x21	18x40	20x39
6¼	Bugle	d	09x34	12x30	14x25	16x26	18x46	20x45
8¾	Roche	d	09x38			16x32	18x50	20x49
14½	St Columb Road	d	09x50			16x43	19x02	21x01
18¼	Quintrell Downs	d	09 58			16 51	19 10	21 09
20¾	Newquay	a	10 09	13 01	14 56	17 02	19 21	21 20

Mondays to Fridays 2 July to 31 August

		GW	GW	GW	GW	GW	GW
		◇	◇	◇1 A ☕	◇	◇	
Par	d	09 17	11 42	13 30	16 10	18 29	20 28
Luxulyan	d	09x28	11x53		16x21	18x40	20x39
Bugle	d	09x34	11x59		16x26	18x46	20x45
Roche	d	09x38	12x03		16x32	18x50	20x49
St Columb Road	d	09x50	12x15		16x43	19x02	21x01
Quintrell Downs	d	09 58	12 23		16 51	19 10	21 09
Newquay	a	10 09	12 34	14 30	17 02	19 21	21 20

Mondays to Fridays 3 September to 14 September

		GW	GW	GW	GW	GW	GW
			◇	◇	◇	◇	
Par	d	09 17	12 13	14 08	16 10	18 29	20 28
Luxulyan	d	09x28			16x21	18x40	20x39
Bugle	d	09x34	12x30	14x25	16x26	18x46	20x45
Roche	d	09x38			16x32	18x50	20x49
St Columb Road	d	09x50			16x43	19x02	21x01
Quintrell Downs	d	09 58			16 51	19 10	21 09
Newquay	a	10 09	13 01	14 56	17 02	19 21	21 20

Mondays to Fridays from 17 September

		GW	GW	GW	GW	GW	GW
			◇	◇	◇	◇	
Par	d	09 17	12 13	14 07	16 10	18 29	20 28
Luxulyan	d	09x28		14x18	16x21	18x40	20x39
Bugle	d	09x34	12x30	14x24	16x26	18x46	20x45
Roche	d	09x38		14x29	16x32	18x50	20x49
St Columb Road	d	09x50		14x40	16x43	19x02	21x01
Quintrell Downs	d	09 58		14 48	16 51	19 10	21 09
Newquay	a	10 09	13 01	14 59	17 02	19 21	21 20

Saturdays until 8 September

		XC	GW	GW	XC	GW	XC	GW
		◇1	◇1 ☕	◇1 ☕	◇1 🛒	■ 1 ☕	◇1 🛒	
Par	d	07 28	09 46	11 41	13 31	15 43	17 42	20 22
Luxulyan	d							
Bugle	d							
Roche	d							
St Columb Road	d							
Quintrell Downs	d							
Newquay	a	08 27	10 55	12 44	14 41	16 52	18 45	21 11

Saturdays from 15 September

		GW	GW	GW	GW	GW	GW	GW
				◇	◇	◇	◇	
Par	d	06 52	09 18	12 15	14 08	16 15	18 21	20 15
Luxulyan	d	07x03	09x29	12x26		16x26	18x32	20x26
Bugle	d	07x09	09x35	12x32	14x25	16x32	18x38	20x32
Roche	d	07x14	09x39	12x37		16x37	18x43	20x37
St Columb Road	d	07x25	09x51	12x48		16x48	18x54	20x48
Quintrell Downs	d	07 33	09 59	12 56		16 56	19 02	20 56
Newquay	a	07 44	10 10	13 07	14 55	17 07	19 13	21 07

A The Atlantic Coast Express

For connections at Par please refer to Table 135

Table 142

Par - Newquay

Sundays until 24 June

Route Diagram - see first Page of Table 135

		GW	XC	GW	GW	GW	GW
			■		◇1 ☕	◇	◇
Par	d	09 00	09 56	11 53	14 20	16 36	18 45
Luxulyan	d	09x11		12x04			18x56
Bugle	d	09x17		12x16		16 58	19x02
Roche	d	09x22		12x20			19x07
St Columb Road	d	09x33		12x32			19x18
Quintrell Downs	d	09 41		12 39			19 26
Newquay	a	09 52	11 10	12 50	15 26	17 30	19 37

Sundays 1 July to 9 September

		GW	XC	GW	GW	GW	GW
			■		◇1 ☕	◇	◇
Par	d	09 00	09 56	11 53	14 20	16 36	18 45
Luxulyan	d	09x11		12x04			18x56
Bugle	d	09x17		12x16		16 58	19x02
Roche	d	09x22		12x20			19x07
St Columb Road	d	09x33		12x32			19x18
Quintrell Downs	d	09 41		12 39			19 26
Newquay	a	09 52	11 10	12 50	15 26	17 30	19 37

Sundays from 16 September

		GW	GW	GW
				◇
Par	d	10 18	13 31	16 30
Luxulyan	d	10x29	13x42	16x41
Bugle	d	10x35	13x48	16x47
Roche	d	10x40	13x53	16x52
St Columb Road	d	10x51	14x04	17x03
Quintrell Downs	d	10 59	14 12	17 11
Newquay	a	11 10	14 23	17 22

For connections at Par please refer to Table 135

Table 142

Newquay - Par

Route Diagram - see first Page of Table 135

Mondays to Fridays
until 29 June

Miles			GW ◇	GW ◇	GW ◇	GW ◇	GW	GW
0	**Newquay**	d	10 13	13 03	14 58	17 22	19 25	21 26
2½	Quintrell Downs	d	10 19	13 09	15 04	17 28	19 31	21 32
6½	St Columb Road	d	10x26	13x16	15x11	17x35		21x39
12	Roche	d	10x38	13x28	15x23	17x47		21x51
14½	Bugle	d	10x42	13x32	15x27	17x51	19x54	21x55
16½	Luxulyan	d	10x48	13x38	15x33	17x57		22x01
20¾	**Par**	a	11 02	13 52	15 47	18 13	20 13	22 16

Mondays to Fridays
2 July to 31 August

		GW ◇	GW ◇	GW ◇ 1 A ⊡	GW ◇	GW	GW
Newquay	d	10 13	12 40	15 00	17 22	19 25	21 26
Quintrell Downs	d	10 19	12 46		17 28	19 31	21 32
St Columb Road	d	10x26	12x53		17x35		21x39
Roche	d	10x38	13x05		17x47		21x51
Bugle	d	10x42	13x09		17x51	19x54	21x55
Luxulyan	d	10x48	13x18		17x57		22x01
Par	a	11 02	13 34	15 59	18 13	20 13	22 16

Mondays to Fridays
3 September to 14 September

		GW ◇	GW ◇	GW ◇	GW ◇	GW	GW
Newquay	d	10 13	13 03	14 58	17 22	19 25	21 26
Quintrell Downs	d	10 19	13 09	15 04	17 28	19 31	21 32
St Columb Road	d	10x26	13x16	15x11	17x35		21x39
Roche	d	10x38	13x28	15x23	17x47		21x51
Bugle	d	10x42	13x32	15x27	17x51	19x54	21x55
Luxulyan	d	10x48	13x38	15x33	17x57		22x01
Par	a	11 02	13 52	15 47	18 13	20 13	22 16

Mondays to Fridays
from 17 September

		GW ◇	GW ◇	GW ◇	GW ◇	GW	GW
Newquay	d	10 13	13 03	15 01	17 22	19 25	21 26
Quintrell Downs	d	10 19	13 09	15 07	17 28	19 31	21 32
St Columb Road	d	10x26	13x16		17x35		21x39
Roche	d	10x38	13x28		17x47		21x51
Bugle	d	10x42	13x32	15x28	17x51	19x54	21x55
Luxulyan	d	10x48	13x38		17x57		22x01
Par	a	11 02	13 52	15 47	18 13	20 13	22 16

Saturdays
until 8 September

		XC ◇ 1	GW ■ 1 ⊡	GW ■ 1 ⊡	GW ■ 1 ⊡	GW
Newquay	d	09 27	11 21	13 14	17 20	21 21
Quintrell Downs	d					
St Columb Road	d					
Roche	d					
Bugle	d					
Luxulyan	d					
Par	a	10 24	12 24	14 15	18 20	22 07

Saturdays
from 15 September

		GW ◇	GW ◇	GW ◇	GW ◇	GW ◇	GW	GW
Newquay	d	07 48	10 12	13 09	14 59	17 21	19 17	21 18
Quintrell Downs	d	07 54	10 18	13 15	15 05	17 27	19 23	21 24
St Columb Road	d	08x02	10x26	13x23	15x13	17x35		21x32
Roche	d	08x13	10x37	13x34	15x24	17x46		21x43
Bugle	d	08x18	10x42	13x39	15x29	17x51	19x46	21x48
Luxulyan	d	08x23	10x47	13x44	15x34	17x56		21x53
Par	a	08 39	11 01	13 59	15 48	18 10	20 03	22 07

A The Atlantic Coast Express

For connections at Par please refer to Table 135

Table 142

Newquay - Par

Route Diagram - see first Page of Table 135

Sundays
until 9 September

		GW ◇	XC ◇ 1	GW ◇ A	GW ◇ B	GW ◇ 1 ⊡	GW ◇	GW
Newquay	d	09 54	11 30	12 55	13 05	16 15	17 32	19 40
Quintrell Downs	d	10 00		13 01	13 11		17 38	19 46
St Columb Road	d	10x08		13x09	13x19		17x46	19x54
Roche	d	10x19		13x20	13x30		17x57	20x05
Bugle	d	10x24		13x25	13x35		18x02	20x10
Luxulyan	d	10x33		13x30	13x40		18x07	20x15
Par	a	10 47	12 28	13 44	13 54	17 14	18 21	20 29

Sundays
from 16 September

		GW ◇	GW ◇	GW
Newquay	d	11 12	15 10	17 30
Quintrell Downs	d	11 18	15 16	17 36
St Columb Road	d	11x26	15x24	17x44
Roche	d	11x37	15x35	17x55
Bugle	d	11x42	15x40	18x00
Luxulyan	d	11x47	15x45	18x05
Par	a	12 01	15 59	18 19

A until 24 June

B from 1 July until 9 September

For connections at Par please refer to Table 135

Table 143

Mondays to Fridays

Truro - Falmouth

Route Diagram - see first Page of Table 135

Miles			GW	GW	GW	GW	GW	GW	GW	GW	GW		GW	GW	GW	GW	GW	GW	GW	GW	GW		GW	GW	GW
0	**Truro**	d	06 04	06 31	07 14	07 47	08 20	08 51	09 20	09 51	10 20		10 51	11 20	11 51	12 20	12 51	13 20	13 51	14 20	14 51		15 20	15 51	16 20
4¼	Perranwell	d	06x10	06x37	07x20	07x53	08x26		09x26		10x26			11x26		12x26		13x26		14x26			15x26		16x26
8¼	Penryn	d	06 18	06 45	07 28	08 01	08 34	09 04	09 34	10 04	10 34		11 04	11 34	12 04	12 34	13 04	13 34	14 04	14 34	15 04		15 34	16 04	16 34
10¼	Penmere	d	06 23	06 50	07 33	08 06	08 39	09 09	09 39	10 09	10 39		11 09	11 39	12 09	12 39	13 09	13 39	14 09	14 39	15 09		15 39	16 09	16 39
11¾	Falmouth Town	d	06 26	06 53	07 36	08 09	08 42	09 12	09 42	10 12	10 42		11 12	11 42	12 12	12 42	13 12	13 42	14 12	14 42	15 12		15 42	16 12	16 42
12¼	**Falmouth Docks**	a	06 28	06 55	07 38	08 11	08 44	09 14	09 44	10 14	10 44		11 14	11 44	12 14	12 44	13 14	13 44	14 14	14 44	15 14		15 44	16 14	16 44

		GW	GW	GW	GW	GW	GW		GW	GW
Truro	d	16 51	17 27	17 59	18 31	19 02	20 04		21 05	22 08
Perranwell	d	16x57	17x33	18x05	18x37	19x08	20x10		21x11	22x14
Penryn	d	17 05	17 41	18 13	18 45	19 16	20 18		21 19	22 22
Penmere	d	17 10	17 46	18 18	18 50	19 21	20 23		21 24	22 27
Falmouth Town	d	17 13	17 49	18 21	18 53	19 24	20 26		21 27	22 30
Falmouth Docks	a	17 15	17 51	18 23	18 55	19 26	20 28		21 29	22 32

Saturdays

		GW	GW	GW	GW	GW	GW	GW	GW	GW		GW	GW	GW	GW	GW	GW	GW	GW	GW		GW	GW	GW	GW
Truro	d	06 04	06 31	07 14	07 47	08 20	08 51	09 20	09 51	10 20		10 51	11 20	11 51	12 20	12 51	13 20	13 51	14 20	14 51		15 20	15 51	16 20	16 51
Perranwell	d	06x10	06x37	07x19	07x53	08x26		09x26		10x26			11x26		12x26		13x26		14x26			15x26		16x26	16x57
Penryn	d	06 18	06 45	07 27	08 01	08 34	09 04	09 34	10 04	10 34		11 04	11 34	12 04	12 34	13 04	13 34	14 04	14 34	15 04		15 34	16 04	16 34	17 05
Penmere	d	06 23	06 50	07 32	08 06	08 39	09 09	09 39	10 09	10 39		11 09	11 39	12 09	12 39	13 09	13 39	14 09	14 39	15 09		15 39	16 09	16 39	17 10
Falmouth Town	d	06 26	06 53	07 35	08 09	08 42	09 12	09 42	10 12	10 42		11 12	11 42	12 12	12 42	13 12	13 42	14 12	14 42	15 12		15 42	16 12	16 42	17 13
Falmouth Docks	a	06 28	06 55	07 38	08 11	08 44	09 14	09 44	10 14	10 44		11 14	11 44	12 14	12 44	13 14	13 44	14 14	14 44	15 14		15 44	16 14	16 44	17 15

		GW	GW	GW	GW	GW		GW	GW
Truro	d	17 27	17 59	18 31	19 02	20 04		21 05	22 06
Perranwell	d	17x33	18x05	18x37	19x08	20x10		21x11	22x12
Penryn	d	17 41	18 13	18 45	19 16	20 18		21 19	22 20
Penmere	d	17 46	18 18	18 50	19 21	20 23		21 24	22 25
Falmouth Town	d	17 49	18 21	18 53	19 24	20 26		21 27	22 28
Falmouth Docks	a	17 51	18 23	18 55	19 26	20 28		21 29	22 30

Sundays

		GW	GW	GW	GW	GW	GW	GW	GW	GW		GW
Truro	d	10 38	12 09	13 07	14 10	15 35	17 00	18 10	19 46	21 03		22 04
Perranwell	d	10x45	12x16	13x14	14x17	15x42	17x07	18x17	19x53	21x10		22x11
Penryn	d	10 52	12 23	13 21	14 24	15 49	17 14	18 24	20 00	21 17		22 18
Penmere	d	10 57	12 28	13 26	14 29	15 53	17 19	18 29	20 05	21 22		22 23
Falmouth Town	d	11 00	12 31	13 29	14 32	15 56	17 22	18 32	20 08	21 25		22 26
Falmouth Docks	a	11 02	12 33	13 31	14 34	16 00	17 24	18 34	20 10	21 27		22 28

For connections at Truro please refer to Table 135

Table 143

Mondays to Fridays

Falmouth - Truro

Route Diagram - see first Page of Table 135

Miles			GW	GW	GW	GW	GW	GW	GW	GW	GW		GW	GW	GW	GW	GW	GW	GW	GW	GW		GW	GW	GW
0	**Falmouth Docks**	d	06 31	07 15	07 47	08 20	08 50	09 20	09 50	10 20	10 50		11 20	11 50	12 20	12 50	13 20	13 50	14 20	14 50	15 20		15 50	16 20	16 50
0½	Falmouth Town	d	06 34	07 18	07 50	08 23	08 53	09 23	09 53	10 23	10 53		11 23	11 53	12 23	12 53	13 23	13 53	14 23	14 53	15 23		15 53	16 23	16 53
2	Penmere	d	06 37	07 21	07 53	08 26	08 56	09 26	09 56	10 26	10 56		11 26	11 56	12 26	12 56	13 26	13 56	14 26	14 56	15 26		15 56	16 26	16 56
4	Penryn	d	06 45	07 29	08 01	08 34	09 04	09 34	10 04	10 34	11 04		11 34	12 04	12 34	13 04	13 34	14 04	14 34	15 04	15 34		16 04	16 34	17 04
8	Perranwell	d	06x51	07x35	08x07	08x40		09x40		10x40			11x40		12x40		13x40		14x40		15x40			16x40	17x11
12¼	**Truro**	a	06 59	07 43	08 15	08 48	09 18	09 48	10 18	10 48	11 18		11 48	12 17	12 48	13 18	13 48	14 18	14 48	15 18	15 48		16 18	16 48	17 19

		GW	GW	GW	GW	GW	GW		GW	GW
Falmouth Docks	d	17 27	17 59	18 31	19 02	19 29	20 31		21 32	22 35
Falmouth Town	d	17 30	18 02	18 34	19 05	19 32	20 34		21 35	22 38
Penmere	d	17 33	18 05	18 37	19 08	19 35	20 37		21 38	22 41
Penryn	d	17 40	18 13	18 45	19 16	19 40	20 42		21 43	22 46
Perranwell	d	17x48	18x19	18x51	19x22	19x46	20x48		21x49	22x52
Truro	a	17 55	18 27	18 59	19 30	19 55	20 57		21 59	23 02

Mondays to Fridays

		GW	GW	GW	GW	GW	GW	GW	GW	GW		GW	GW	GW	GW	GW	GW	GW	GW	GW		GW	GW	GW	GW
Falmouth Docks	d	06 31	07 15	07 47	08 20	08 50	09 20	09 50	10 20	10 50		11 20	11 50	12 20	12 50	13 20	13 50	14 20	14 50	15 20		15 50	16 20	16 50	17 27
Falmouth Town	d	06 34	07 18	07 50	08 23	08 53	09 23	09 53	10 23	10 53		11 23	11 53	12 23	12 53	13 23	13 53	14 23	14 53	15 23		15 53	16 23	16 53	17 30
Penmere	d	06 37	07 21	07 53	08 26	08 56	09 26	09 56	10 26	10 56		11 26	11 56	12 26	12 56	13 26	13 56	14 26	14 56	15 26		15 56	16 26	16 56	17 33
Penryn	d	06 45	07 29	08 01	08 34	09 04	09 34	10 04	10 34	11 04		11 34	12 04	12 34	13 04	13 34	14 04	14 34	15 04	15 34		16 04	16 34	17 04	17 40
Perranwell	d	06x51	07x35	08x07	08x40		09x40		10x40			11x40		12x40		13x40		14x40		15x40			16x40	17x11	17x48
Truro	a	06 59	07 43	08 15	08 48	09 18	09 48	10 18	10 48	11 18		11 48	12 17	12 48	13 18	13 48	14 18	14 48	15 18	15 48		16 18	16 48	17 19	17 55

		GW	GW	GW	GW	GW		GW	GW
Falmouth Docks	d	17 59	18 31	19 02	19 29	20 31		21 32	22 35
Falmouth Town	d	18 02	18 34	19 05	19 32	20 34		21 35	22 38
Penmere	d	18 05	18 37	19 08	19 35	20 37		21 38	22 41
Penryn	d	18 13	18 45	19 16	19 40	20 42		21 43	22 46
Perranwell	d	18x19	18x51	19x22	19x46	20x48		21x49	22x52
Truro	a	18 27	18 59	19 30	19 55	20 57		21 59	23 02

Sundays
until 24 June

		GW	GW	GW	GW	GW	GW	GW	GW	GW		GW
Falmouth Docks	d	11 09	12 35	13 34	14 44	16 02	17 30	18 37	20 13	21 30		22 39
Falmouth Town	d	11 12	12 39	13 37	14 47	16 05	17 33	18 40	20 16	21 33		22 42
Penmere	d	11 15	12 42	13 40	14 50	16 07	17 36	18 43	20 19	21 36		22 45
Penryn	d	11 20	12 47	13 45	14 55	16 12	17 41	18 48	20 24	21 40		22 50
Perranwell	d	11x27	12x54	13x52	15x02	16x19	17x48	18x55	20x31	21x47		22x57
Truro	a	11 35	13 02	14 00	15 10	16 26	17 56	19 03	20 39	21 55		23 05

Sundays
1 July to 9 September

		GW	GW	GW	GW	GW	GW	GW	GW	GW		GW
Falmouth Docks	d	11 09	12 35	13 34	14 44	16 02	17 30	18 37	20 13	21 30		22 32
Falmouth Town	d	11 12	12 39	13 37	14 47	16 05	17 33	18 40	20 16	21 33		22 35
Penmere	d	11 15	12 42	13 40	14 50	16 07	17 36	18 43	20 19	21 36		22 38
Penryn	d	11 20	12 47	13 45	14 55	16 12	17 41	18 48	20 24	21 40		22 43
Perranwell	d	11x27	12x54	13x52	15x02	16x19	17x48	18x55	20x31	21x47		22x50
Truro	a	11 35	13 02	14 00	15 10	16 26	17 56	19 03	20 39	21 55		23 01

Sundays
from 16 September

		GW	GW	GW	GW	GW	GW	GW	GW	GW		GW
Falmouth Docks	d	11 09	12 35	13 34	14 44	16 14	17 30	18 37	20 13	21 30		22 32
Falmouth Town	d	11 12	12 39	13 37	14 47	16 17	17 33	18 40	20 16	21 33		22 35
Penmere	d	11 15	12 42	13 40	14 50	16 20	17 36	18 43	20 19	21 36		22 38
Penryn	d	11 20	12 47	13 45	14 55	16 25	17 41	18 48	20 24	21 40		22 43
Perranwell	d	11x27	12x54	13x52	15x02	16x32	17x48	18x55	20x31	21x47		22x50
Truro	a	11 35	13 02	14 00	15 10	16 39	17 56	19 03	20 39	21 55		23 01

For connections at Truro please refer to Table 135

Table 144 — Mondays to Fridays

St Erth - St Ives

Route Diagram - see first Page of Table 135

Miles			GW	GW	GW	GW	GW	GW	GW	GW	GW	GW	GW	GW	GW	GW	GW	GW	GW	GW	GW	GW	GW
—	Penzance	d	06 55		08 57																		
0	**St Erth**	d	07 03	08 01	09 05	09 38	10 18	10 48	11 18	11 48	12 18	12 48	13 18	13 48	14 18	14 48	15 18	15 48	16 18	16 48	17 17	17 48	18 18
0¾	Lelant Saltings	d			09 09	09 41	10 21	10 51	11 21	11 51	12 21	12 51	13 21	13 51	14 21	14 51	15 21	15 51	16 21		17 20		18 21
1	Lelant	d	07x07	08x03	09x10															16x50		17x50	18x22
3	Carbis Bay	d	07 12	08 09	09 16	09 47		10 57		11 57		12 57		13 57		14 57		15 57		16 56		17 56	18 27
4¼	**St Ives**	a	07 15	08 14	09 19	09 52	10 31	11 02	11 31	12 02	12 31	13 02	13 31	14 02	14 31	15 02	15 31	16 02	16 31	17 01	17 30	18 01	18 33

		GW	GW	GW	GW	GW	GW	GW
Penzance	d							
St Erth	d	18 48	19 18	19 48	20 18	20 48	21 23	21 58
Lelant Saltings	d		19 21		20 21			22 01
Lelant	d	18x51		19x51		20x51	21x25	22x02
Carbis Bay	d	18 56		19 56		20 56	21 31	22 08
St Ives	a	19 03	19 31	20 01	20 31	21 02	21 36	22 13

Saturdays
until 8 September

		GW	GW	GW	GW	GW	GW	GW	GW	GW	GW	GW	GW	GW	GW	GW	GW	GW	GW	GW	GW	GW	GW
Penzance	d	06 41		08 54																		18 50	
St Erth	d	06 50	08 00	09 03	09 35	10 13	10 48	11 18	11 48	12 18	12 48	13 18	13 48	14 20	14 48	15 18	15 48	16 18	16 48	17 17	17 59	18 59	19 53
Lelant Saltings	d			09 06	09 38	10 16	10 51	11 21	11 51	12 21	12 51	13 21	13 51	14 23	14 51	15 21	15 51	16 21		17 20	18 02	19 02	19 56
Lelant	d	06x53	08x03	09x08															16x51		18x04	19x04	19x58
Carbis Bay	d	06 58	08 08	09 13	09 44		10 57		11 57		12 57		13 57		14 57		15 57		16 56	17 26	18 09	19 09	20 03
St Ives	a	07 03	08 13	09 18	09 49	10 26	11 02	11 31	12 02	12 31	13 02	13 31	14 02	14 33	15 02	15 31	16 02	16 31	17 01	17 31	18 13	19 14	20 07

		GW	GW	GW
Penzance	d			
St Erth	d	20 33	21 06	21 47
Lelant Saltings	d	20 36	21 07	21 48
Lelant	d	20x38	21x09	21x50
Carbis Bay	d	20 43	21 14	21 55
St Ives	a	20 47	21 19	22 01

Saturdays
from 15 September

		GW	GW	GW	GW	GW	GW	GW	GW	GW	GW	GW	GW	GW	GW	GW	GW	GW	GW	GW	GW	GW	GW
Penzance	d	06 41		08 54																		18 50	
St Erth	d	06 50	08 00	09 03	09 35	10 13	10 48	11 18	11 48	12 18	12 48	13 18	13 48	14 18	14 48	15 18	15 48	16 18	16 48	17 17	17 59	18 59	19 53
Lelant Saltings	d			09 06	09 38	10 16	10 51	11 21	11 51	12 21	12 51	13 21	13 51	14 21	14 51	15 21	15 51	16 21		17 20	18 02	19 02	19 56
Lelant	d	06x53	08x03	09x08															16x51		18x04	19x04	19x58
Carbis Bay	d	06 58	08 08	09 13	09 44		10 57		11 57		12 57		13 57		14 57		15 57		16 56	17 26	18 09	19 09	20 03
St Ives	a	07 03	08 13	09 18	09 49	10 26	11 02	11 31	12 02	12 31	13 02	13 31	14 02	14 31	15 02	15 31	16 02	16 31	17 01	17 31	18 13	19 14	20 07

		GW	GW	GW
Penzance	d			
St Erth	d	20 33	21 06	21 47
Lelant Saltings	d	20 36	21 07	21 48
Lelant	d	20x38	21x09	21x50
Carbis Bay	d	20 43	21 14	21 55
St Ives	a	20 47	21 19	22 01

Sundays
until 9 September

		GW	GW	GW	GW	GW	GW	GW	GW	GW	GW	GW	GW	GW	GW	GW	GW	GW	GW	GW
Penzance	d	08 45																		
St Erth	d	08 53	09 26	10 00	10 30	11 13	11 43	12 12	12 42	13 11	13 41	14 11	14 41	15 11	15 41	16 11	16 41	17 25	18 25	19 30
Lelant Saltings	d	08 56	09 30	10 04	10 33	11 16	11 46	12 15	12 45	13 14	13 44	14 14	14 44	15 14	15 44	16 14	16 44	17 28	18 28	19 33
Lelant	d	08x58																17x30	18x30	19 35
Carbis Bay	d	09 03			10 39		11 52		12 51		13 50		14 50		15 50		16 50	17 35	18 35	19 40
St Ives	a	09 09	09 40	10 14	10 44	11 26	11 57	12 25	12 56	13 24	13 55	14 24	14 55	15 24	15 55	16 24	16 55	17 40	18 39	19 45

Sundays
from 16 September

		GW	GW	GW	GW	GW	GW	GW	GW	GW	GW	GW	GW	GW	GW
Penzance	d	11 45													
St Erth	d	11 56	12 30	13 18	13 48	14 18	14 48	15 18	15 48	16 18	16 48	17 18	17 48	18 30	19 30
Lelant Saltings	d	11 59	12 33	13 21	13 51	14 21	14 51	15 21	15 51	16 21	16 51	17 21	17 51	18 33	19 33
Lelant	d	12x01											17x53	18x35	19x35
Carbis Bay	d	12 06	12 39		13 57		14 57		15 57		16 57		17 58	18 40	19 40
St Ives	a	12 12	12 44	13 31	14 02	14 31	15 02	15 31	16 02	16 31	17 02	17 31	18 02	18 45	19 45

For connections at St Erth please refer to Table 135

Table 144 — Mondays to Fridays

St Ives - St Erth

Route Diagram - see first Page of Table 135

Miles			GW	GW	GW	GW	GW	GW	GW	GW	GW	GW	GW	GW	GW	GW	GW	GW	GW	GW	GW	GW	GW
0	**St Ives**	d	07 25	08 15	09 22	09 53	10 33	11 03	11 33	12 03	12 33	13 03	13 33	14 03	14 33	15 03	15 33	16 03	16 33	17 03	17 31	18 03	18 33
1¼	Carbis Bay	d	07 28	08 18	09 25		10 36		11 36		12 36		13 36		14 36		15 36		16 36		17 34		18 36
3¼	Lelant	d	07x33	08x23	09x30																17x39		18x41
3½	Lelant Saltings	d			09 33		10 43		11 43		12 43		13 43	14 13	14 43	15 13	15 43	16 13	16 43	17 12	17 42	18 13	18 44
4¼	**St Erth**	a	07 37	08 28	09 37	10 05	10 47	11 16	11 47	12 16	12 47	13 16	13 47	14 17	14 47	15 17	15 47	16 17	16 47	17 16	17 45	18 17	18 48
—	Penzance	a		08 40																			

		GW	GW	GW	GW	GW	GW	GW
St Ives	d	19 03	19 32	20 03	20 33	21 03	21 37	22 31
Carbis Bay	d		19 35		20 36	21 06	21 40	22 34
Lelant	d		19x40		20x41	21x11	21x45	22x39
Lelant Saltings	d		19 43	20 12	20 44	21 14		22 41
St Erth	a	19 16	19 47	20 16	20 47	21 18	21 51	22 45
Penzance	a							22 57

Saturdays
until 8 September

		GW	GW	GW	GW	GW	GW	GW	GW	GW	GW	GW	GW	GW	GW	GW	GW	GW	GW	GW	GW	GW	GW
St Ives	d	07 12	08 15	09 20	09 50	10 27	11 03	11 33	12 03	12 33	13 03	13 33	14 03	14 33	15 03	15 33	16 03	16 33	17 03	17 32	18 17	19 26	20 10
Carbis Bay	d	07 15	08 18	09 23		10 30		11 36		12 36		13 36		14 36		15 36		16 36		17 35	18 20	19 29	20 13
Lelant	d	07x20	08x23			10x35														17x40	18x25	19x34	20x18
Lelant Saltings	d			09 30		10 38		11 43		12 43		13 43	14 12	14 43	15 12	15 43	16 12	16 43	17 12	17 43	18 28	19 37	20 21
St Erth	a	07 24	08 27	09 33	10 00	10 40	11 13	11 47	12 15	12 47	13 15	13 47	14 14	14 47	15 16	15 47	16 16	16 46	17 16	17 45	18 31	19 41	20 23
Penzance	a		08 40																		18 44		

		GW	GW	GW
St Ives	d	20 49	21 24	22 05
Carbis Bay	d	20 52	21 27	22 08
Lelant	d	20x57	21x32	22x13
Lelant Saltings	d	21 00	21 35	22 16
St Erth	a	21 02	21 37	22 19
Penzance	a			22 32

Saturdays
from 15 September

		GW	GW	GW	GW	GW	GW	GW	GW	GW	GW	GW	GW	GW	GW	GW	GW	GW	GW	GW	GW	GW	GW
St Ives	d	07 12	08 15	09 20	09 50	10 27	11 03	11 33	12 03	12 33	13 03	13 33	14 03	14 33	15 03	15 33	16 03	16 33	17 03	17 32	18 17	19 26	20 10
Carbis Bay	d	07 15	08 18	09 23		10 30		11 36		12 36		13 36		14 36		15 36		16 36		17 35	18 20	19 29	20 13
Lelant	d	07x20	08x23			10x35														17x40	18x25	19x34	20x18
Lelant Saltings	d			09 30		10 38		11 43		12 43		13 43	14 12	14 43	15 12	15 43	16 12	16 43	17 12	17 43	18 28	19 37	20 21
St Erth	a	07 24	08 27	09 33	10 00	10 40	11 13	11 47	12 15	12 47	13 15	13 47	14 14	14 47	15 16	15 47	16 16	16 46	17 16	17 45	18 31	19 41	20 23
Penzance	a		08 40																		18 44		

		GW	GW	GW
St Ives	d	20 49	21 24	22 05
Carbis Bay	d	20 52	21 27	22 08
Lelant	d	20x57	21x32	22x13
Lelant Saltings	d	21 00	21 35	22 16
St Erth	a	21 02	21 37	22 19
Penzance	a			22 32

Sundays
until 9 September

		GW	GW	GW	GW	GW	GW	GW	GW	GW	GW	GW	GW	GW	GW	GW	GW	GW	GW	GW
St Ives	d	09 10	09 41	10 15	10 50	11 28	11 56	12 27	12 57	13 26	13 56	14 25	14 56	15 25	15 56	16 25	17 05	17 41	18 41	19 50
Carbis Bay	d	09 13				11 31		12 30		13 29		14 28		15 28		16 28		17 44	18 44	19 53
Lelant	d	09x18																17x49	18x49	19x58
Lelant Saltings	d	09 21	09 50	10 24	10 59	11 38	12 07	12 37	13 06	13 36	14 05	14 35	15 05	15 35	16 05	16 35	17 14	17 52	18 52	20 01
St Erth	a	09 24	09 52	10 28	11 01	11 42	12 09	12 41	13 10	13 40	14 09	14 39	15 07	15 37	16 07	16 37	17 16	17 54	18 56	20 04
Penzance	a																			20 14

Sundays
from 16 September

		GW	GW	GW	GW	GW	GW	GW	GW	GW	GW	GW	GW	GW	GW
St Ives	d	12 13	12 48	13 33	14 03	14 33	15 03	15 33	16 03	16 33	17 03	17 33	18 03	18 50	19 50
Carbis Bay	d	12 16	12 51	13 36		14 36		15 36		16 36		17 36		18 51	19 53
Lelant	d	12x21											18x10	18x58	19x58
Lelant Saltings	d	12 24	12 58	13 43	14 12	14 43	15 12	15 43	16 12	16 43	17 12	17 43	18 13	19 01	20 01
St Erth	a	12 26	13 00	13 45	14 16	14 45	15 14	15 45	16 16	16 47	17 16	17 47	18 17	19 03	20 04
Penzance	a														20 14

For connections at St Erth please refer to Table 135

Network Diagram for Tables 148, 149

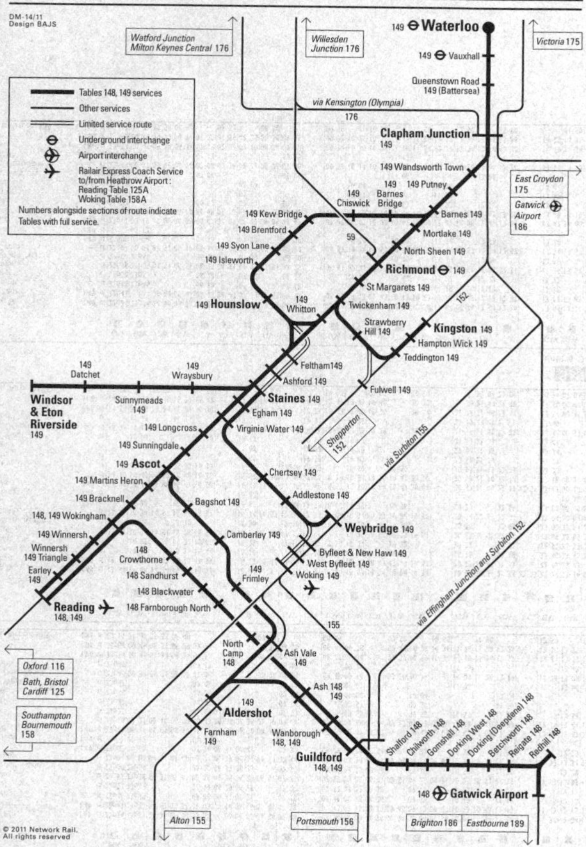

Reading - Guildford, Redhill and Gatwick Airport

Network Diagram - see first Page of Table 148

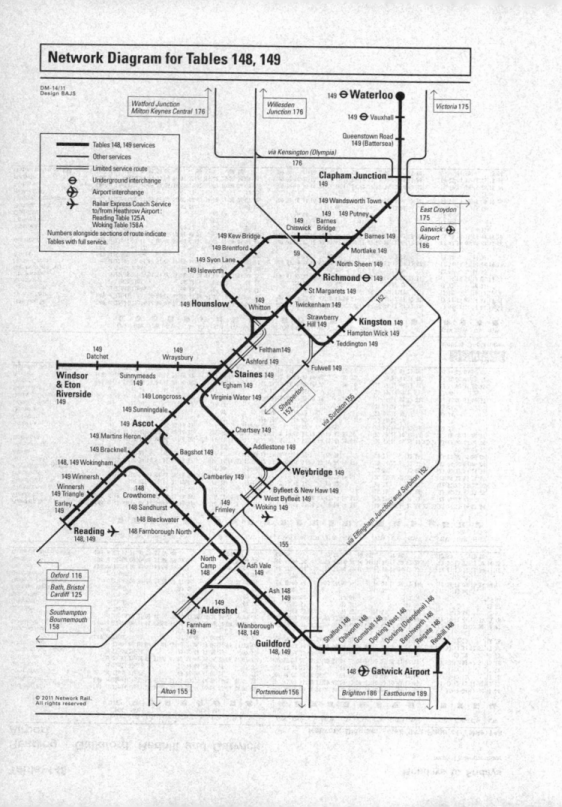

Miles				GW	GW	GW	GW	GW	GW	GW	GW	GW	GW	GW	GW	GW	GW	GW	GW	GW	GW	GW	GW
				MX	MO A	MX																	
0	Reading	149	d	22p34	23p15	23p34	04 34	05 24	05 54	06 06	06 34	07 04	07 34	08 04	08 20	08 34	09 04	09 34	10 04	10 34	11 04	11 34	12 04
6¾	Wokingham	149	d	22p43	23p24	23p43	04 43	05 33	06 03	06 16	06 43	07 13	07 43	08 13	08 29	08 43	09 13	09 43	10 13	10 43	11 13	11 43	12 13
10	Crowthorne		d	22p48	23p29	23p48			06 08	06 21		07 18	07 48	08 18	08 34		09 18		10 18		11 18		12 18
11½	Sandhurst		d	22p52	23p33	23p52			06 12	06 25		07 22	07 52	08 22	08 38		09 22		10 22		11 22		12 22
13½	Blackwater		d	22p55	23p36	23p55	04 51	05 41	06 15	06 28	06 51	07 25	07 55	08 25	08 41	08 51	09 25	09 51	10 25	10 51	11 25	11 51	12 25
15½	Farnborough North		d	23p00	23p41	23p59			06 20	06 33		07 30	08 00	08 30	08 46		09 30		10 30		11 30		12 30
17½	North Camp		d	23p04	23p45	00 04	04 57	05 48	06 24	06 37	06 57	07 34	08 04	08 34	08 50	09 01	09 34	09 57	10 34	10 57	11 34	11 57	12 34
19½	Ash	149	d	23p08	23p49	00 08			06 28	06 41		07 38	08 08	08 38	08 54		09 38		10 38		11 38		12 38
21½	Wanborough	149	d			00 12			06 32														
25¾	Guildford	149	a	23p17	23p58	00 19	05 09	05 59	06 39	06 50	07 08	07 47	08 17	08 47	09 03	09 13	09 47	10 09	10 47	11 08	11 47	12 08	12 47
—			d	23p18	23p59	00 21	05 10	06 00	06 43	06 58	07 10	07 48	08 18	08 48	09 04	09 13	09 48	10 10	10 48	11 10	11 48	12 10	12 48
27¾	Shalford		d	23p23					06 48	07a04		07 53		08 53	09a11		09 53		10 53		11 53		12 53
29¾	Chilworth		d	23p27					06 52			07 57		08 57			09 57				11 57		
33½	Gomshall		d	23p34					06 58			08 04		09 04			10 04				12 04		
38¼	Dorking West		d	23p41					07 06			08 11		09 11					11 06				13 06
39	Dorking Deepdene		d	23p44	00 19	00 37	05 26	06 17	07 08		07 26	08 14	08 35	09 14		09 30	10 11	10 26	11 08	11 26	12 11	12 26	13 08
41¾	Betchworth		d	23p49					07 13			08 19		09 19					11 13				13 13
44½	Reigate	186	d	23p54	00 26	00 45	05 34	06 24	07 18		07 34	08 24	08 42	09 24		09 37	10 19	10 34	11 19	11 34	12 19	12 34	13 19
46½	Redhill	186	a	23p58	00 30	00 49	05 39	06 29	07 24		07 38	08 30	08 46	09 30		09 42	10 25	10 38	11 25	11 38	12 25	12 38	13 25
52¼	Gatwick Airport	186	a	00 11	00 41	01 03	05 54	06 40			07 50		08 59			09 59		10 50		11 50		12 50	

			GW	GW	GW	GW	GW	GW	GW	GW	GW	GW	GW	GW	GW	GW	GW	GW	GW	GW	GW	XC	GW	GW
																						◇		FX
Reading	149	d	12 34	13 04	13 34	14 04	14 34	15 04	15 28	16 04	16 34	16 51	17 04	17 34	18 04	18 34	19 04	19 34	20 04	20 34	21 34	22 23	22 34	23 34
Wokingham	149	d	12 43	13 13	13 43	14 13	14 43	15 13	15 39	16 13	16 43	17 00	17 13	17 43	18 13	18 43	19 13	19 43	20 13	20 43	21 43		22 43	23 43
Crowthorne		d		13 18		14 18		15 18	15 44	16 18		17 06	17 18	17 48	18 18		19 18		20 18		21 48		22 48	23 48
Sandhurst		d		13 22		14 22		15 22	15 48	16 22		17 10	17 22	17 52	18 22		19 22		20 22		21 52		22 52	23 52
Blackwater		d	12 51	13 25	13 51	14 25	14 51	15 25	15 51	16 25	16 51	17 13	17 25	17 55	18 25	18 51	19 25	19 51	20 25	20 51	21 55		22 55	23 55
Farnborough North		d		13 30		14 30		15 30		16 30		17 18	17 30	18 00	18 30		19 30		20 30		22 00		23 00	23 59
North Camp		d	12 57	13 34	13 57	14 34	14 57	15 34	15 57	16 34	16 57	17 22	17 34	18 04	18 34	18 57	19 34	19 57	20 34	20 57	22 04		23 04	00 04
Ash	149	d		13 38		14 38		15 38		16 38		17 26	17 38	18 08	18 38		19 38		20 38		22 08		23 08	00 08
Wanborough	149	d								16 42			17 42		18 42									00 12
Guildford	149	a	13 08	13 47	14 08	14 47	15 08	15 47	16 08	16 49	17 08	17 35	17 49	18 17	18 50	19 08	19 47	20 08	20 47	21 08	22 17	22 59	23 17	00 19
		d	13 10	13 48	14 10	14 48	15 10	15 48	16 10	16 50	17 10	17 40	17 50	18 18	18 54	19 10	19 48	20 10	20 48	21 10	22 18		23 18	00 21
Shalford		d		13 53		14 53		15 53	16 15	16 55		17a48	17 55		18 59		19a55		20 53	21 15	22 23		23 23	
Chilworth		d		13 57				15 57		16 59			17 59		19 03				20 58	21 19			23 27	
Gomshall		d		14 04				16 04		17 06			18 06		19 10				21 04	21 25			23 34	
Dorking West		d				15 06			16 28	17 13			18 13		19 17				21 12	21 33			23 41	
Dorking Deepdene		d	13 26	14 11	14 26	15 08	15 26	16 11	16 30	17 16	17 26		18 16	18 35	19 20	19 27		20 26	21 14	21 35	22 37		23 44	00 37
Betchworth		d				15 13		16 16		17 21			18 21		19 25				21 19	21 40			23 49	
Reigate	186	d	13 34	14 19	14 34	15 19	15 34	16 21	16 38	17 26	17 34		18 26	18 42	19 30	19 36		20 34	21 24	21 45	22 44		23 54	00 45
Redhill	186	a	13 38	14 25	14 38	15 25	15 38	16 27	16 42	17 32	17 38		18 32	18 47	19 35	19 40		20 38	21 30	21 49	22 48		23 58	00 49
Gatwick Airport	186	a	13 50		14 50		15 50		16 59		17 54			19 00		19 55		20 50		22 06	23 06		00 11	01 03

			GW
			FO
Reading	149	d	23 34
Wokingham	149	d	
Crowthorne		d	23 48
Sandhurst		d	23 52
Blackwater		d	23 55
Farnborough North		d	23 59
North Camp		d	00 04
Ash	149	d	00 08
Wanborough	149	d	00 12
Guildford	149	a	00 19
		d	00 21
Shalford		d	
Chilworth		d	
Gomshall		d	
Dorking West		d	
Dorking Deepdene		d	00 37
Betchworth		d	
Reigate	186	d	00 45
Redhill	186	a	00 49
Gatwick Airport	186	a	01 03

A from 21 May until 10 September

Mondays to Fridays
from 17 September

Reading - Guildford, Redhill and Gatwick Airport

Network Diagram - see first Page of Table 148

			GW MX 1	GW MX 1	GW 1	GW 1	GW 1	GW MO 1	GW MX 1	GW 1	GW 1	GW 1	GW 1	GW 1	GW 1	GW 1	GW 1	GW 1	GW 1	GW 1	GW 1	GW 1	GW 1	GW 1
Reading 7	149	d	22p34	23p34	04 34	05 24	05 54	06 06	06 06	06 34	07 04	07 34	08 04	08 20	08 34	09 04	09 34	10 04	10 34	11 04	11 34	12 04	12 34	13 04
Wokingham	149	d	22p43	23p43	04 43	05 33	06 03	06 16	06 16	06 43	07 13	07 43	08 13	08 29	08 43	09 13	09 43	10 13	10 43	11 13	11 43	12 13	12 43	13 13
Crowthorne		d	22p48	23p48			06 08	06 21	06 21		07 18	07 48	08 18	08 34		09 18		10 18		11 18		12 18		13 18
Sandhurst		d	22p52	23p52			06 12	06 25	06 25		07 22	07 52	08 22	08 38		09 22		10 22		11 22		12 22		13 22
Blackwater		d	22p55	23p55	04 51	05 41	06 15	06 28	06 28	06 51	07 25	07 55	08 25	08 41	08 51	09 25	09 51	10 25	10 51	11 25	11 51	12 25	12 51	13 25
Farnborough North		d	23p00	23p59			06 20	06 33	06 33		07 30	08 00	08 30	08 46		09 30		10 30		11 30		12 30		13 30
North Camp		d	23p04	00 04	04 57	05 48	06 24	06 37	06 37	06 57	07 34	08 04	08 34	08 50	09 01	09 34	09 57	10 34	10 57	11 34	11 57	12 34	12 57	13 34
Ash 5	149	d	23p08	00 08			06 28	06 41	06 41		07 38	08 08	08 38	08 54		09 38		10 38		11 38		12 38		13 38
Wanborough	149	d		00 12			06 32																	
Guildford	149	a	23p17	00 19	05 09	05 59	06 39	06 50	06 50	07 08	07 47	08 17	08 47	09 03	09 13	09 47	10 09	10 47	11 08	11 47	12 08	12 47	13 08	13 47
		d	23p18	00 21	05 10	06 00	06 43	06 58	06 58	07 10	07 48	08 18	08 48	09 04	09 13	09 48	10 10	10 48	11 10	11 48	12 10	12 48	13 10	13 48
Shalford		d	23p23				06 48	07a04	07a04		07 53		08 53	09a11		09 53		10 53		11 53		12 53		13 53
Chilworth		d	23p27				06 52				07 57		08 57			09 57				11 57				13 57
Gomshall		d	23p34				06 58				08 04		09 04			10 04				12 04				14 04
Dorking West		d	23p41				07 06				08 11		09 11					11 06				13 06		
Dorking Deepdene		d	23p44	00 37	05 26	06 17	07 08			07 26	08 14	08 35	09 14		09 30	10 11	10 26	11 08	11 26	12 11	12 26	13 08	13 26	14 11
Betchworth		d	23p49				07 13				08 19		09 19					11 13				13 13		
Reigate	186	d	23p54	00 45	05 34	06 24	07 18			07 34	08 24	08 42	09 24		09 37	10 19	10 34	11 19	11 34	12 19	12 34	13 19	13 34	14 19
Redhill	186	a	23p58	00 49	05 39	06 29	07 24			07 38	08 30	08 46	09 30		09 42	10 25	10 38	11 25	11 38	12 25	12 38	13 25	13 38	14 25
Gatwick Airport 10	186	a	00 11	01 03	05 54	06 40				07 50		08 59			09 59		10 50		11 50		12 50		13 50	

			GW 1	GW 1	GW 1	GW 1	GW 1	GW 1	GW 1	GW 1	GW 1	GW 1	GW 1	GW 1	GW 1	GW 1	GW 1	GW 1	GW 1	XC ◇1	GW 1	GW FX 1	GW FO 1
Reading 7	149	d	13 34	14 04	14 34	15 04	15 28	16 04	16 34	16 51	17 04	17 34	18 04	18 34	19 04	19 34	20 04	20 34	21 34	22 23	22 34	23 34	23 34
Wokingham	149	d	13 43	14 13	14 43	15 13	15 39	16 13	16 43	17 00	17 13	17 43	18 13	18 43	19 13	19 43	20 13	20 43	21 43		22 43	23 43	
Crowthorne		d		14 18		15 18	15 44	16 18		17 06	17 18	17 48	18 18		19 18		20 18		21 48		22 48	23 48	23 48
Sandhurst		d		14 22		15 22	15 48	16 22		17 10	17 22	17 52	18 22		19 22		20 22		21 52		22 52	23 52	23 52
Blackwater		d	13 51	14 25	14 51	15 25	15 51	16 25	16 51	17 13	17 25	17 55	18 25	18 51	19 25	19 51	20 25	20 51	21 55		22 55	23 55	23 55
Farnborough North		d		14 30		15 30		16 30		17 18	17 30	18 00	18 30		19 30		20 30		22 00		23 00	23 59	23 59
North Camp		d	13 57	14 34	14 57	15 34	15 57	16 34	16 57	17 22	17 34	18 04	18 34	18 57	19 34	19 57	20 34	20 57	22 04		23 04	00 04	00 04
Ash 5	149	d		14 38		15 38		16 38		17 26	17 38	18 08	18 38		19 38		20 38		22 08		23 08	00 08	00 08
Wanborough	149	d						16 42			17 42											00 12	00 12
Guildford	149	a	14 08	14 47	15 08	15 47	16 08	16 49	17 08	17 35	17 49	18 17	18 50	19 08	19 47	20 08	20 47	21 08	22 17	22 59	23 17	00 19	00 19
		d	14 10	14 48	15 10	15 48	16 10	16 50	17 10	17 40	17 50	18 18	18 54	19 10	19 48	20 10	20 48	21 10	22 18		23 18	00 21	00 21
Shalford		d		14 53		15 53	16 15	16 55		17a48	17 55		18 59		19a55		20 53	21 15	22 23		23 23		
Chilworth		d				15 57		16 59			17 59		19 03				20 58	21 19			23 27		
Gomshall		d				16 04		17 06			18 06		19 10	19 21			21 04	21 25			23 34		
Dorking West		d		15 06			16 28	17 13			18 13		19 17				21 12	21 33			23 41		
Dorking Deepdene		d	14 26	15 08	15 26	16 11	16 30	17 16	17 26		18 16	18 35	19 20	19 29		20 26	21 14	21 35	22 37		23 44	00 37	00 37
Betchworth		d		15 13		16 16		17 21			18 21		19 25				21 19	21 40			23 49		
Reigate	186	d	14 34	15 19	15 34	16 21	16 38	17 26	17 34		18 26	18 42	19 30	19 36		20 34	21 24	21 45	22 44		23 54	00 45	00 45
Redhill	186	a	14 38	15 25	15 38	16 27	16 42	17 32	17 38		18 32	18 47	19 35	19 40		20 38	21 30	21 49	22 48		23 58	00 49	00 49
Gatwick Airport 10	186	a	14 50		15 50		16 59		17 54			19 00		19 55		20 50		22 06	23 06		00 11	01 03	01 03

Saturdays
until 8 September

			GW 1	GW 1	GW 1	GW 1	GW 1	GW 1	GW 1	GW 1	GW 1	GW 1	GW 1	GW 1	GW 1	GW 1	GW 1	GW 1	GW 1	GW 1	GW 1	GW 1	GW 1	GW 1
Reading 7	149	d	22p34	23p34	04 34	05 34	06 04	06 34	07 04	07 34	08 04	08 34	09 04	09 34	10 04	10 34	11 04	11 34	12 04	12 34	13 04	13 34	14 04	14 34
Wokingham	149	d	22p43		04 43	05 43	06 13	06 43	07 13	07 43	08 13	08 43	09 13	09 43	10 13	10 43	11 13	11 43	12 13	12 43	13 13	13 43	14 13	14 43
Crowthorne		d	22p48	23p48			06 18		07 18		08 18		09 18		10 18		11 18		12 18		13 18		14 18	
Sandhurst		d	22p52	23p52			06 22		07 22		08 22		09 22		10 22		11 22		12 22		13 22		14 22	
Blackwater		d	22p55	23p55	04 51	05 51	06 25	06 51	07 25	07 51	08 25	08 51	09 25	09 51	10 25	10 51	11 25	11 51	12 25	12 51	13 25	13 51	14 25	14 51
Farnborough North		d	23p00	23p59			06 30		07 30		08 30		09 30		10 30		11 30		12 30		13 30		14 30	
North Camp		d	23p04	00 04	04 57	05 57	06 34	06 57	07 34	07 57	08 34	08 57	09 34	09 57	10 34	10 57	11 34	11 57	12 34	12 57	13 34	13 57	14 34	14 57
Ash 5	149	d	23p08	00 08			06 38		07 38		08 38		09 38		10 38		11 38		12 38		13 38		14 38	
Wanborough	149	d		00 12																				
Guildford	149	a	23p17	00 19	05 08	06 08	06 47	07 09	07 47	08 08	08 47	09 08	09 47	10 08	10 47	11 08	11 47	12 08	12 47	13 08	13 47	14 08	14 47	15 08
		d	23p18	00 21	05 10	06 10	06 48	07 10	07 48	08 10	08 48	09 10	09 48	10 10	10 48	11 10	11 48	12 10	12 48	13 10	13 48	14 10	14 48	15 10
Shalford		d	23p23				06 53		07 53		08 53		09 53		10 53		11 53		12 53		13 53		14 53	
Chilworth		d	23p27						07 57				09 57				11 57				13 57			
Gomshall		d	23p34						08 04				10 04				12 04				14 04			
Dorking West		d	23p41				07 06				09 06				11 06				13 06				15 06	
Dorking Deepdene		d	23p44	00 37	05 26	06 26	07 08	07 26	08 11	08 26	09 08	09 26	10 11	10 26	11 08	11 26	12 11	12 26	13 08	13 26	14 11	14 26	15 08	15 26
Betchworth		d	23p49				07 13				09 13				11 13				13 13				15 13	
Reigate	186	d	23p54	00 45	05 34	06 34	07 18	07 34	08 19	08 34	09 18	09 34	10 19	10 34	11 18	11 34	12 19	12 34	13 18	13 34	14 19	14 34	15 18	15 34
Redhill	186	a	23p58	00 49	05 39	06 39	07 25	07 39	08 25	08 38	09 25	09 38	10 25	10 38	11 25	11 38	12 25	12 38	13 25	13 38	14 25	14 38	15 25	15 38
Gatwick Airport 10	186	a	00 11	01 03	05 58	06 50		07 50		08 50		09 50		10 50		11 50		12 50		13 50		14 50		15 50

Saturdays
until 8 September

Reading - Guildford, Redhill and Gatwick Airport

Network Diagram - see first Page of Table 148

			GW 1	GW 1	GW 1	GW 1	GW 1	GW 1	GW 1	GW 1	GW 1	GW 1	GW 1	GW 1	GW 1	XC ◇1	GW 1	GW 1
Reading 7	149	d	15 04	15 34	16 04	16 34	17 04	17 34	18 04	18 34	19 04	19 34	20 04	20 34	21 34	22 15	22 34	23 34
Wokingham	149	d	15 13	15 43	16 13	16 43	17 13	17 43	18 13	18 43	19 13	19 43	20 13	20 43	21 43		22 43	
Crowthorne		d	15 18		16 18		17 18		18 18		19 18		20 18		21 48		22 48	23 48
Sandhurst		d	15 22		16 22		17 22		18 22		19 22		20 22		21 52		22 52	23 52
Blackwater		d	15 25	15 51	16 25	16 51	17 25	17 51	18 25	18 51	19 25	19 51	20 25	20 51	21 55		22 55	23 55
Farnborough North		d	15 30		16 30		17 30		18 30		19 30		20 30		22 00		23 00	23 59
North Camp		d	15 34	15 57	16 34	16 57	17 34	17 57	18 34	18 57	19 34	19 57	20 34	20 57	22 04		23 04	00 04
Ash 5	149	d	15 38		16 38		17 38		18 38		19 38		20 38		22 08		23 08	00 08
Wanborough	149	d																00 12
Guildford	149	a	15 47	16 08	16 47	17 08	17 47	18 08	18 47	19 08	19 47	20 08	20 47	21 08	22 17	22 59	23 17	00 19
		d	15 48	16 10	16 48	17 10	17 48	18 10	18 48	19 10	19 48	20 10	20 48	21 10	22 18		23 18	00 21
Shalford		d	15 53		16 53		17 53		18 53		19 53		20 53	21 15	22 23		23 23	
Chilworth		d	15 57				17 57				19 57			21 19			23 27	
Gomshall		d	16 04				18 04				20 04			21 25			23 34	
Dorking West		d			17 06				19 06				21 06		22 36		23 41	
Dorking Deepdene		d	16 11	16 26	17 08	17 26	18 11	18 26	19 08	19 26	20 11	20 26	21 08	21 33	22 38		23 44	00 37
Betchworth		d			17 13				19 13				21 13		22 43		23 49	
Reigate	186	d	16 19	16 34	17 18	17 34	18 19	18 34	19 18	19 34	20 19	20 34	21 18	21 40	22 48		23 54	00 45
Redhill	186	a	16 25	16 38	17 25	17 38	18 25	18 38	19 25	19 38	20 25	20 38	21 25	21 44	22 52		23 58	00 49
Gatwick Airport 10	186	a		16 50		17 50		18 50		19 50		20 50		21 59	23 05		00 10	01 02

Saturdays
15 September to 20 October

			GW 1	GW 1	GW 1	GW 1	GW 1	GW 1	GW 1	GW 1	GW 1	GW 1	GW 1	GW 1	GW 1	GW 1	GW 1	GW 1	GW 1	GW 1	GW 1	GW 1	GW 1	GW 1
Reading 7	149	d	22p34	23p34	04 34	05 34	06 04	06 34	07 04	07 34	08 04	08 34	09 04	09 34	10 04	10 34	11 04	11 34	12 04	12 34	13 04	13 34	14 04	14 34
Wokingham	149	d	22p43		04 43	05 43	06 13	06 43	07 13	07 43	08 13	08 43	09 13	09 43	10 13	10 43	11 13	11 43	12 13	12 43	13 13	13 43	14 13	14 43
Crowthorne		d	22p48	23p48			06 18		07 18		08 18		09 18		10 18		11 18		12 18		13 18		14 18	
Sandhurst		d	22p52	23p52			06 22		07 22		08 22		09 22		10 22		11 22		12 22		13 22		14 22	
Blackwater		d	22p55	23p55	04 51	05 51	06 25	06 51	07 25	07 51	08 25	08 51	09 25	09 51	10 25	10 51	11 25	11 51	12 25	12 51	13 25	13 51	14 25	14 51
Farnborough North		d	23p00	23p59			06 30		07 30		08 30		09 30		10 30		11 30		12 30		13 30		14 30	
North Camp		d	23p04	00 04	04 57	05 57	06 34	06 57	07 34	07 57	08 34	08 57	09 34	09 57	10 34	10 57	11 34	11 57	12 34	12 57	13 34	13 57	14 34	14 57
Ash 5	149	d	23p08	00 08			06 38		07 38		08 38		09 38		10 38		11 38		12 38		13 38		14 38	
Wanborough	149	d		00 12																				
Guildford	149	a	23p17	00 19	05 08	06 08	06 47	07 09	07 47	08 08	08 47	09 08	09 47	10 08	10 47	11 08	11 47	12 08	12 47	13 08	13 47	14 08	14 47	15 08
		d	23p18	00 21	05 10	06 10	06 48	07 10	07 48	08 10	08 48	09 10	09 48	10 10	10 48	11 10	11 48	12 10	12 48	13 10	13 48	14 10	14 48	15 10
Shalford		d	23p23				06 53		07 53		08 53		09 53		10 53		11 53		12 53		13 53		14 53	
Chilworth		d	23p27						07 57				09 57				11 57				13 57			
Gomshall		d	23p34						08 04				10 04				12 04				14 04			
Dorking West		d	23p41				07 06				09 06				11 06				13 06				15 06	
Dorking Deepdene		d	23p44	00 37	05 26	06 26	07 08	07 26	08 11	08 26	09 08	09 26	10 11	10 26	11 08	11 26	12 11	12 26	13 08	13 26	14 11	14 26	15 08	15 26
Betchworth		d	23p49				07 13				09 13				11 13				13 13				15 13	
Reigate	186	d	23p54	00 45	05 34	06 34	07 18	07 34	08 19	08 34	09 18	09 34	10 19	10 34	11 18	11 34	12 19	12 34	13 18	13 34	14 19	14 34	15 18	15 34
Redhill	186	a	23p58	00 49	05 39	06 39	07 25	07 39	08 25	08 38	09 25	09 38	10 25	10 38	11 25	11 38	12 25	12 38	13 25	13 38	14 25	14 38	15 25	15 38
Gatwick Airport 10	186	a	00 11	01 03	05 58	06 50		07 50		08 50		09 50		10 50		11 50		12 50		13 50		14 50		15 50

			GW 1	GW 1	GW 1	GW 1	GW 1	GW 1	GW 1	GW 1	GW 1	GW 1	GW 1	GW 1	GW 1	XC ◇1	GW 1	GW 1
Reading 7	149	d	15 04	15 34	16 04	16 34	17 04	17 34	18 04	18 34	19 04	19 34	20 04	20 34	21 34	22 15	22 34	23 34
Wokingham	149	d	15 13	15 43	16 13	16 43	17 13	17 43	18 13	18 43	19 13	19 43	20 13	20 43	21 43		22 43	
Crowthorne		d	15 18		16 18		17 18		18 18		19 18		20 18		21 48		22 48	23 48
Sandhurst		d	15 22		16 22		17 22		18 22		19 22		20 22		21 52		22 52	23 52
Blackwater		d	15 25	15 51	16 25	16 51	17 25	17 51	18 25	18 51	19 25	19 51	20 25	20 51	21 55		22 55	23 55
Farnborough North		d	15 30		16 30		17 30		18 30		19 30		20 30		22 00		23 00	23 59
North Camp		d	15 34	15 57	16 34	16 57	17 34	17 57	18 34	18 57	19 34	19 57	20 34	20 57	22 04		23 04	00 04
Ash 5	149	d	15 38		16 38		17 38		18 38		19 38		20 38		22 08		23 08	00 08
Wanborough	149	d																00 12
Guildford	149	a	15 47	16 08	16 47	17 08	17 47	18 08	18 47	19 08	19 47	20 08	20 47	21 08	22 17	22 59	23 17	00 19
		d	15 48	16 10	16 48	17 10	17 48	18 10	18 48	19 10	19 48	20 10	20 48	21 10	22 18		23 18	00 21
Shalford		d	15 53		16 53		17 53		18 53		19 53		20 53	21 15	22 23		23 23	
Chilworth		d	15 57				17 57				19 57			21 19			23 27	
Gomshall		d	16 04				18 04				20 04			21 25			23 34	
Dorking West		d			17 06				19 06				21 06		22 36		23 41	
Dorking Deepdene		d	16 11	16 26	17 08	17 26	18 11	18 26	19 08	19 26	20 11	20 26	21 08	21 33	22 38		23 44	00 37
Betchworth		d			17 13				19 13				21 13		22 43		23 49	
Reigate	186	d	16 19	16 34	17 18	17 34	18 19	18 34	19 18	19 34	20 19	20 34	21 18	21 40	22 48		23 54	00 45
Redhill	186	a	16 25	16 38	17 25	17 38	18 25	18 38	19 25	19 38	20 25	20 38	21 25	21 44	22 52		23 58	00 49
Gatwick Airport 10	186	a		16 50		17 50		18 50		19 50		20 50		21 59	23 05		00 10	01 02

Reading - Guildford, Redhill and Gatwick Airport

Saturdays from 27 October

Network Diagram - see first Page of Table 148

Station	Table		GW	GW	GW	GW	GW	GW	GW	GW	GW	GW	GW	GW	GW	GW	GW	GW	GW	GW	GW	GW	GW	GW
Reading	149	d	22p34	23p34	04 34	05 34	06 04	06 34	07 04	07 34	08 04	08 34	09 04	09 34	10 04	10 34	11 04	11 34	12 04	12 34	13 04	13 34	14 04	14 34
Wokingham	149	d	22p43		04 43	05 43	06 13	06 43	07 13	07 43	08 13	08 43	09 13	09 43	10 13	10 43	11 13	11 43	12 13	12 43	13 13	13 43	14 13	14 43
Crowthorne		d	22p48	23p48			06 18		07 18		08 18		09 18		10 18		11 18		12 18		13 18		14 18	
Sandhurst		d	22p52	23p52			06 22		07 22		08 22		09 22		10 22		11 22		12 22		13 22		14 22	
Blackwater		d	22p55	23p55	04 51	05 51	06 25	06 51	07 25	07 51	08 25	08 51	09 25	09 51	10 25	10 51	11 25	11 51	12 25	12 51	13 25	13 51	14 25	14 51
Farnborough North		d	23p00	23p59			06 30		07 30		08 30		09 30		10 30		11 30		12 30		13 30		14 30	
North Camp		d	23p04	00 04	04 57	05 57	06 34	06 57	07 34	07 57	08 34	08 57	09 34	09 57	10 34	10 57	11 34	11 57	12 34	12 57	13 34	13 57	14 34	14 57
Ash	149	d	23p08	00 08			06 38		07 38		08 38		09 38		10 38		11 38		12 38		13 38		14 38	
Wanborough	149	d		00 12																				
Guildford	149	a	23p17	00 19	05 08	06 08	06 47	07 09	07 47	08 08	08 47	09 08	09 47	10 08	10 47	11 08	11 47	12 08	12 47	13 08	13 47	14 08	14 47	15 08
		d	23p18	00 21	05 10	06 10	06 48	07 10	07 48	08 10	08 48	09 10	09 48	10 10	10 48	11 10	11 48	12 10	12 48	13 10	13 48	14 10	14 48	15 10
Shalford		d	23p23				06 53		07 53		08 53		09 53		10 53		11 53		12 53		13 53		14 53	
Chilworth		d	23p27						07 57				09 57				11 57				13 57			
Gomshall		d	23p34						08 04				10 04				12 04				14 04			
Dorking West		d	23p41				07 06				09 06				11 06				13 06				15 06	
Dorking Deepdene		d	23p44	00 37	05 26	06 26	07 08	07 26	08 11	08 26	09 08	09 26	10 11	10 26	11 08	11 26	12 11	12 26	13 08	13 26	14 11	14 26	15 08	15 26
Betchworth		d	23p49				07 13				09 13				11 13				13 13				15 13	
Reigate	186	d	23p54	00 45	05 34	06 34	07 18	07 34	08 19	08 34	09 18	09 34	10 19	10 34	11 18	11 34	12 19	12 34	13 18	13 34	14 19	14 34	15 18	15 34
Redhill	186	a	23p58	00 49	05 39	06 39	07 25	07 39	08 25	08 38	09 25	09 38	10 25	10 38	11 25	11 38	12 25	12 38	13 25	13 38	14 25	14 38	15 25	15 38
Gatwick Airport	186	a	00 11	01 03	05 58	06 50		07 50		08 50		09 50		10 50		11 50		12 50		13 50		14 50		15 50

Station	Table		GW	GW	GW	GW	GW	GW	GW	GW	GW	GW	GW	GW	GW	XC	GW	GW
Reading	149	d	15 04	15 34	16 04	16 34	17 04	17 34	18 04	18 34	19 04	19 34	20 04	20 34	21 34	22 15	22 34	23 34
Wokingham	149	d	15 13	15 43	16 13	16 43	17 13	17 43	18 13	18 43	19 13	19 43	20 13	20 43	21 43		22 43	
Crowthorne		d	15 18		16 18		17 18		18 18		19 18		20 18		21 48		22 48	23 48
Sandhurst		d	15 22		16 22		17 22		18 22		19 22		20 22		21 52		22 52	23 52
Blackwater		d	15 25	15 51	16 25	16 51	17 25	17 51	18 25	18 51	19 25	19 51	20 25	20 51	21 55		22 55	23 55
Farnborough North		d	15 30		16 30		17 30		18 30		19 30		20 30		22 00		23 00	23 59
North Camp		d	15 34	15 57	16 34	16 57	17 34	17 57	18 34	18 57	19 34	19 57	20 34	20 57	22 04		23 04	00 04
Ash	149	d	15 38		16 38		17 38		18 38		19 38		20 38		22 08		23 08	00 08
Wanborough	149	d																00 12
Guildford	149	a	15 47	16 08	16 47	17 08	17 47	18 08	18 47	19 08	19 47	20 08	20 47	21 08	22 17	22 59	23 17	00 19
		d	15 48	16 10	16 48	17 10	17 48	18 10	18 48	19 10	19 48	20 10	20 48	21 10	22 18		23 18	00 21
Shalford		d	15 53		16 53		17 53		18 53		19 53		20 53	21 15	22 23		23 23	
Chilworth		d	15 57				17 57				19 57			21 19			23 27	
Gomshall		d	16 04				18 04				20 04			21 25			23 34	
Dorking West		d			17 06				19 06				21 06		22 36		23 41	
Dorking Deepdene		d	16 11	16 26	17 08	17 26	18 11	18 26	19 08	19 26	20 11	20 26	21 08	21 33	22 38		23 44	00 37
Betchworth		d			17 13				19 13				21 13		22 43		23 49	
Reigate	186	d	16 19	16 34	17 18	17 34	18 19	18 34	19 18	19 34	20 19	20 34	21 18	21 40	22 48		23 54	00 45
Redhill	186	a	16 25	16 38	17 25	17 38	18 25	18 38	19 25	19 38	20 25	20 38	21 25	21 44	22 52		23 58	00 49
Gatwick Airport	186	a		16 50		17 50		18 50		19 50		20 50		21 59	23 05		00 10	01 02

Sundays until 9 September

Station	Table		GW	GW	GW	GW	GW	GW	GW	GW	GW	GW	GW	GW	GW	GW	GW	GW	GW	GW	GW	XC	GW
Reading	149	d	22p34	23p34	06 03	07 03	08 03	09 03	10 03	11 03	12 03	13 03	14 03	15 03	16 03	17 03	18 03	19 03	20 03	21 03	22 03	22 14	23 15
Wokingham	149	d	22p43		06 11	07 11	08 11	09 11	10 11	11 11	12 11	13 11	14 11	15 11	16 11	17 11	18 11	19 11	20 11	21 11	22 11		23 24
Crowthorne		d	22p48	23p48		07 17		09 17		11 17		13 17		15 17		17 17		19 17		21 17			23 29
Sandhurst		d	22p52	23p52		07 21		09 21		11 21		13 21		15 21		17 21		19 21		21 21			23 33
Blackwater		d	22p55	23p55	06 20	07 24	08 19	09 24	10 19	11 24	12 19	13 24	14 19	15 24	16 19	17 24	18 19	19 24	20 19	21 24	22 19		23 36
Farnborough North		d	23p00	23p59		07 29		09 29		11 29		13 29		15 29		17 29		19 29		21 29			23 41
North Camp		d	23p04	00 04	06 27	07 33	08 26	09 33	10 26	11 33	12 26	13 33	14 26	15 33	16 26	17 33	18 26	19 33	20 26	21 33	22 26		23 45
Ash	149	d	23p08	00 08		07 37		09 37		11 37		13 37		15 37		17 37		19 37		21 37			23 49
Wanborough	149	d		00 12																			
Guildford	149	a	23p17	00 19	06 38	07 46	08 37	09 46	10 37	11 46	12 37	13 46	14 37	15 46	16 37	17 46	18 37	19 46	20 37	21 46	22 37	22 42	23 58
		d	23p18	00 21	06 40	07 47	08 39	09 47	10 39	11 47	12 39	13 47	14 39	15 47	16 39	17 47	18 39	19 47	20 39	21 47	22 39		23 59
Shalford		d	23p23				08 44		10 44		12 44		14 44		16 44		18 44		20 44		22 44		
Chilworth		d	23p27				08 48		10 48		12 48		14 48		16 48		18 48		20 48		22 48		
Gomshall		d	23p34				08 54		10 54		12 54		14 54		16 54		18 54		20 54		22 54		
Dorking West		d	23p41				09 02		11 02		13 02		15 02		17 02		19 02		21 02		23 02		
Dorking Deepdene		d	23p44	00 37	06 57	08 04	09 04	10 04	11 04	12 04	13 04	14 04	15 04	16 04	17 04	18 04	19 04	20 04	21 04	22 04	23 04		00 19
Betchworth		d	23p49				09 09		11 09		13 09		15 09		17 09		19 09		21 09		23 09		
Reigate	186	d	23p54	00 45	07 05	08 13	09 13	10 13	11 13	12 13	13 13	14 13	15 13	16 13	17 13	18 13	19 13	20 13	21 13	22 13	23 13		00 26
Redhill	186	a	23p58	00 49	07 09	08 18	09 18	10 18	11 18	12 18	13 18	14 18	15 18	16 18	17 18	18 18	19 18	20 18	21 18	22 18	23 18		00 30
Gatwick Airport	186	a	00 10	01 02	07 27	08 33	09 33	10 33	11 33	12 33	13 33	14 33	15 33	16 33	17 33	18 34	19 34	20 34	21 34	22 33	23 34		00 41

Reading - Guildford, Redhill and Gatwick Airport

Sundays 16 September to 21 October

Network Diagram - see first Page of Table 148

Station	Table		GW	GW	GW	GW	GW	GW	GW	GW	GW	GW	GW	GW	GW	GW	GW	GW	GW	GW	GW	XC
Reading	149	d	22p34	23p34	06 03	07 03	08 03	09 03	10 03	11 03	12 03	13 03	14 03	15 03	16 03	17 03	18 03	19 03	20 03	21 03	22 03	22 13
Wokingham	149	d	22p43		06 11	07 11	08 11	09 11	10 11	11 11	12 11	13 11	14 11	15 11	16 11	17 11	18 11	19 11	20 11	21 11	22 11	
Crowthorne		d	22p48	23p48		07 17		09 17		11 17		13 17		15 17		17 17		19 17		21 17		
Sandhurst		d	22p52	23p52		07 21		09 21		11 21		13 21		15 21		17 21		19 21		21 21		
Blackwater		d	22p55	23p55	06 20	07 24	08 19	09 24	10 19	11 24	12 19	13 24	14 19	15 24	16 19	17 24	18 19	19 24	20 19	21 24	22 19	
Farnborough North		d	23p00	23p59		07 29		09 29		11 29		13 29		15 29		17 29		19 29		21 29		
North Camp		d	23p04	00 04	06 27	07 33	08 26	09 33	10 26	11 33	12 26	13 33	14 26	15 33	16 26	17 33	18 26	19 33	20 26	21 33	22 26	
Ash	149	d	23p08	00 08		07 37		09 37		11 37		13 37		15 37		17 37		19 37		21 37		
Wanborough	149	d		00 12																		
Guildford	149	a	23p17	00 19	06 38	07 46	08 37	09 46	10 37	11 46	12 37	13 46	14 37	15 46	16 37	17 46	18 37	19 46	20 37	21 46	22 37	22 42
		d	23p18	00 21	06 40	07 47	08 39	09 47	10 39	11 47	12 39	13 47	14 39	15 47	16 39	17 47	18 39	19 47	20 39	21 47	22 39	
Shalford		d	23p23				08 44		10 44		12 44		14 44		16 44		18 44		20 44		22 44	
Chilworth		d	23p27				08 48		10 48		12 48		14 48		16 48		18 48		20 48		22 48	
Gomshall		d	23p34				08 54		10 54		12 54		14 54		16 54		18 54		20 54		22 54	
Dorking West		d	23p41				09 02		11 02		13 02		15 02		17 02		19 02		21 02		23 02	
Dorking Deepdene		d	23p44	00 37	06 57	08 04	09 04	10 04	11 04	12 04	13 04	14 04	15 04	16 04	17 04	18 04	19 04	20 04	21 04	22 04	23 04	
Betchworth		d	23p49				09 09		11 09		13 09		15 09		17 09		19 09		21 09		23 09	
Reigate	186	d	23p54	00 45	07 05	08 13	09 13	10 13	11 13	12 13	13 13	14 13	15 13	16 13	17 13	18 13	19 13	20 13	21 13	22 13	23 13	
Redhill	186	a	23p58	00 49	07 09	08 18	09 18	10 18	11 18	12 18	13 18	14 18	15 18	16 18	17 18	18 18	19 18	20 18	21 18	22 18	23 18	
Gatwick Airport	186	a	00 10	01 02	07 27	08 31	09 33	10 30	11 30	12 30	13 30	14 30	15 30	16 30	17 30	18 30	19 30	20 30	21 30	22 30	23 31	

Sundays from 28 October

Station	Table		GW	GW	GW	GW	GW	GW	GW	GW	GW	GW	GW	GW	GW	GW	GW	GW	GW	GW	GW	XC
Reading	149	d	22p34	23p34	06 03	07 03	08 03	09 03	10 03	11 03	12 03	13 03	14 03	15 03	16 03	17 03	18 03	19 03	20 03	21 03	22 03	22 14
Wokingham	149	d	22p43		06 11	07 11	08 11	09 11	10 11	11 11	12 11	13 11	14 11	15 11	16 11	17 11	18 11	19 11	20 11	21 11	22 11	
Crowthorne		d	22p48	23p48		07 17		09 17		11 17		13 17		15 17		17 17		19 17		21 17		
Sandhurst		d	22p52	23p52		07 21		09 21		11 21		13 21		15 21		17 21		19 21		21 21		
Blackwater		d	22p55	23p55	06 20	07 24	08 19	09 24	10 19	11 24	12 19	13 24	14 19	15 24	16 19	17 24	18 19	19 24	20 19	21 24	22 19	
Farnborough North		d	23p00	23p59		07 29		09 29		11 29		13 29		15 29		17 29		19 29		21 29		
North Camp		d	23p04	00 04	06 27	07 33	08 26	09 33	10 26	11 33	12 26	13 33	14 26	15 33	16 26	17 33	18 26	19 33	20 26	21 33	22 26	
Ash	149	d	23p08	00 08		07 37		09 37		11 37		13 37		15 37		17 37		19 37		21 37		
Wanborough	149	d		00 12																		
Guildford	149	a	23p17	00 19	06 38	07 46	08 37	09 46	10 37	11 46	12 37	13 46	14 37	15 46	16 37	17 46	18 37	19 46	20 37	21 46	22 37	22 42
		d	23p18	00 21	06 40	07 47	08 39	09 47	10 39	11 47	12 39	13 47	14 39	15 47	16 39	17 47	18 39	19 47	20 39	21 47	22 39	
Shalford		d	23p23				08 44		10 44		12 44		14 44		16 44		18 44		20 44		22 44	
Chilworth		d	23p27				08 48		10 48		12 48		14 48		16 48		18 48		20 48		22 48	
Gomshall		d	23p34				08 54		10 54		12 54		14 54		16 54		18 54		20 54		22 54	
Dorking West		d	23p41				09 02		11 02		13 02		15 02		17 02		19 02		21 02		23 02	
Dorking Deepdene		d	23p44	00 37	06 57	08 04	09 04	10 04	11 04	12 04	13 04	14 04	15 04	16 04	17 04	18 04	19 04	20 04	21 04	22 04	23 04	
Betchworth		d	23p49				09 09		11 09		13 09		15 09		17 09		19 09		21 09		23 09	
Reigate	186	d	23p54	00 45	07 05	08 13	09 13	10 13	11 13	12 13	13 13	14 13	15 13	16 13	17 13	18 13	19 13	20 13	21 13	22 13	23 13	
Redhill	186	a	23p58	00 49	07 09	08 18	09 18	10 18	11 18	12 18	13 18	14 18	15 18	16 18	17 18	18 18	19 18	20 18	21 18	22 18	23 18	
Gatwick Airport	186	a	00 10	01 02	07 27	08 31	09 33	10 30	11 30	12 30	13 30	14 30	15 30	16 30	17 30	18 30	19 30	20 30	21 30	22 30	23 31	

Gatwick Airport, Redhill and Guildford - Reading

Mondays to Fridays
until 14 September

Network Diagram - see first Page of Table 148

Miles	Station		GW MX	GW MO A	GW MX	XC	GW	GW	GW	GW	GW	GW	GW	GW	GW	GW	GW	GW	GW	GW	GW	GW	GW
0	Gatwick Airport 10	186 d	22p22	23p08	23p18		05 31	05 56			06 58		07 58			09 07		10 03		11 03		12 03	
5¾	Redhill	186 d	22p33	23p20	23p28		05 43	06 13	06 24		07 10	07 28	08 08	08 33		09 23	09 34	10 13	10 34	11 13	11 34	12 13	12 34
—	Reigate	186 d	22p38	23p24	23p33		05 49	06 18	06 28		07 15	07 32	08 13	08 37		09 28	09 38	10 18	10 38	11 18	11 38	12 18	12 38
10½	Betchworth	d	22p43						06 33			07 37		08 42			09 43		10 43				12 43
13¼	Dorking Deepdene	d	22p47	23p32	23p40		05 56	06 25	06 37		07 22	07 41	08 20	08 46		09 35	09 47	10 25	10 47	11 25	11 45	12 25	12 47
14	Dorking West	d	22p50						06 40			07 44		08 49			09 50		10 50				12 50
18¾	Gomshall	d	22p58						06 48		07 30	07 52		08 57			09 58				11 53		
22½	Chilworth	d	23p04						06 54			07 58		09 03			10 04				11 59		
24½	Shalford	d	23p08						06 58	07 21		08 02		09 07	09 31		10 08		11 03		12 03		13 03
26½	Guildford	a	23p12	23p49	00 01		06 12	06 41	07 03	07 25	07 41	08 06	08 36	09 11	09 36	09 53	10 12	10 42	11 08	11 42	12 08	12 42	13 08
—		d	23p14	23p52	00 02	06 02	06 13	06 43	07 04	07 27	07 43	08 13	08 38	09 13	09 38	09 54	10 14	10 44	11 09	11 44	12 09	12 44	13 09
30¾	Wanborough	149 d	23p21				06 20		07 12			08 20		09 20									
32¾	Ash 5	149 d	23p26	00 01			06 25	06 52	07 16	07 36	07 52	08 25		09 25	09 47		10 23		11 19		12 19		13 19
34¾	North Camp	d	23p30	00 05	00 14		06 29	06 56	07 20	07 41	07 56	08 29	08 50	09 29	09 51		10 27	10 56	11 23	11 56	12 23	12 56	13 23
36¾	Farnborough North	d	23p34	00 09			06 33	07 00	07 24	07 45	08 00	08 33		09 33			10 31		11 27		12 27		13 27
38¾	Blackwater	d	23p38	00 14	00 20		06 37	07 05	07 29	07 49	08 05	08 37	08 56	09 37	09 58		10 36	11 02	11 31	12 02	12 31	13 02	13 31
40¾	Sandhurst	d	23p42	00 16			06 41	07 08	07 32	07 53	08 08	08 41		09 41			10 39		11 35		12 35		13 35
42¼	Crowthorne	d	23p46	00 20			06 45	07 12	07 36	07 57	08 12	08 45		09 45			10 43		11 39		12 39		13 39
45½	Wokingham	149 d	23p51	00 25	00 29		06 50	07 17	07 41	08 02	08 17	08 50	09 04	09 51	10 06		10 48	11 10	11 44	12 10	12 44	13 10	13 44
52¼	Reading 7	149 a	00 01	00 37	00 39	06 31	06 58	07 29	07 52	08 17	08 28	09 00	09 17	10 01	10 17	10 23	10 59	11 19	11 54	12 19	12 54	13 19	13 54

Station		GW	GW	GW	GW	GW	GW	GW	GW	GW	GW	GW	GW	GW	GW	GW	GW	GW	GW	GW	GW	GW
Gatwick Airport 10	186 d	13 03		14 03		15 03		16 03		17 03			18 03		19 16		20 03		21 03		22 22	23 18
Redhill	186 d	13 13	13 34	14 13	14 34	15 13	15 29	16 13	16 32	17 13		17 43	18 13	18 43	19 26		20 13	20 34	21 13	21 35	22 33	23 28
Reigate	186 d	13 18	13 38	14 18	14 38	15 18	15 34	16 18	16 36	17 18		17 48	18 18	18 47	19 30		20 18	20 40	21 18	21 39	22 38	23 33
Betchworth	d				14 43		15 38		16 41			17 52		18 52				20 45		21 44	22 43	
Dorking Deepdene	d	13 25	13 45	14 25	14 47	15 25	15 43	16 25	16 45	17 25		17 57	18 25	18 56	19 37		20 25	20 49	21 25	21 48	22 47	23 40
Dorking West	d				14 50		15 45					17 59		18 59				20 52		21 51	22 50	
Gomshall	d		13 53				15 53		16 53			18 07		19 07				21 00		21 59	22 58	
Chilworth	d		13 59				15 59		16 59			18 13		19 13				21 06		22 05	23 04	
Shalford	d		14 03		15 03		16 03		17 03		17 58	18 17		19 17		20 02		21 10		22 09	23 08	
Guildford	a	13 42	14 08	14 42	15 08	15 42	16 08	16 42	17 08	17 43	18 02	18 22	18 41	19 22	19 54	20 06	20 42	21 14	21 42	22 13	23 12	00 01
	d	13 44	14 09	14 44	15 09	15 44	16 14	16 44	17 09	17 44	18 04	18 26	18 47	19 36	19 55	20 10	20 44	21 16	21 44	22 15	23 14	00 02
Wanborough	149 d																				23 21	
Ash 5	149 d		14 19		15 19		16 24		17 19	17 54	18 14	18 35		19 46		20 19		21 25		22 23	23 26	
North Camp	d	13 56	14 23	14 56	15 23	15 56	16 28	16 56	17 23	17 58	18 18	18 39	19 01	19 50	20 07	20 23	20 56	21 29	21 56	22 27	23 30	00 14
Farnborough North	d		14 27		15 27		16 32		17 27	18 02	18 22	18 42		19 54		20 27		21 33		22 31	23 34	
Blackwater	d	14 02	14 31	15 02	15 31	16 02	16 36	17 02	17 31	18 07	18 27	18 47	19 07	19 58	20 14	20 31	21 02	21 38	22 02	22 36	23 38	00 20
Sandhurst	d		14 35		15 35		16 40		17 35		18 30	18 51		20 02		20 35		21 41		22 39	23 42	
Crowthorne	d		14 39		15 39		16 44		17 39		18 34	18 59		20 06		20 39		21 45		22 43	23 46	
Wokingham	149 d	14 10	14 44	15 10	15 43	16 10	16 48	17 10	17 44	18 15	18 39	19 04	19 15	20 11	20 22	20 43	21 10	21 50	22 10	22 48	23 51	00 29
Reading 7	149 a	14 19	14 54	15 19	15 54	16 24	17 00	17 19	17 54	18 24	18 50	19 17	19 25	20 21	20 32	20 55	21 19	22 01	22 19	23 01	00 01	00 39

Mondays to Fridays
from 17 September

Station		GW MX	GW MO	GW MX	XC	GW	GW	GW	GW	GW	GW	GW	GW	GW	GW	GW	GW	GW	GW	GW	GW	GW	GW
Gatwick Airport 10	186 d	22p22	23p08	23p18		05 31	05 56			06 58		07 58			09 07		10 03		11 03		12 03		13 03
Redhill	186 d	22p33	23p20	23p28		05 43	06 13	06 24		07 10	07 28	08 08	08 33		09 23	09 34	10 13	10 34	11 13	11 34	12 13	12 34	13 13
Reigate	186 d	22p38	23p24	23p33		05 49	06 18	06 28		07 15	07 32	08 13	08 37		09 28	09 38	10 18	10 38	11 18	11 38	12 18	12 38	13 18
Betchworth	d	22p43						06 33			07 37		08 42			09 43		10 43				12 43	
Dorking Deepdene	d	22p47	23p32	23p40		05 56	06 25	06 37		07 22	07 41	08 20	08 46		09 35	09 47	10 25	10 47	11 25	11 45	12 25	12 47	13 25
Dorking West	d	22p50						06 40			07 44		08 49			09 50		10 50				12 50	
Gomshall	d	22p58						06 48		07 30	07 52		08 57			09 58				11 53			
Chilworth	d	23p04						06 54			07 58		09 03			10 04				11 59			
Shalford	d	23p08						06 58	07 21		08 02		09 07	09 31		10 08		11 03		12 03		13 03	
Guildford	a	23p12	23p49	00 01		06 12	06 41	07 03	07 25	07 41	08 06	08 36	09 11	09 36	09 53	10 12	10 42	11 08	11 42	12 08	12 42	13 08	13 42
	d	23p14	23p52	00 02	06 02	06 13	06 43	07 04	07 27	07 43	08 13	08 38	09 13	09 38	09 54	10 14	10 44	11 09	11 44	12 09	12 44	13 09	13 44
Wanborough	149 d	23p21				06 20		07 12			08 20		09 20										
Ash 5	149 d	23p26	00 01			06 25	06 52	07 16	07 36	07 52	08 25		09 25	09 47		10 23		11 19		12 19		13 19	
North Camp	d	23p30	00 05	00 14		06 29	06 56	07 20	07 41	07 56	08 29	08 50	09 29	09 51		10 27	10 56	11 23	11 56	12 23	12 56	13 23	13 56
Farnborough North	d	23p34	00 09			06 33	07 00	07 24	07 45	08 00	08 33		09 33			10 31		11 27		12 27		13 27	
Blackwater	d	23p38	00 14	00 20		06 37	07 05	07 29	07 49	08 05	08 37	08 56	09 37	09 58		10 36	11 02	11 31	12 02	12 31	13 02	13 31	14 02
Sandhurst	d	23p42	00 16			06 41	07 08	07 32	07 53	08 08	08 41		09 41			10 39		11 35		12 35		13 35	
Crowthorne	d	23p46	00 20			06 45	07 12	07 36	07 57	08 12	08 45		09 45			10 43		11 39		12 39		13 39	
Wokingham	149 d	23p51	00 25	00 29		06 50	07 17	07 41	08 02	08 17	08 50	09 04	09 51	10 06		10 48	11 10	11 44	12 10	12 44	13 10	13 44	14 10
Reading 7	149 a	00 01	00 37	00 39	06 31	06 58	07 29	07 52	08 17	08 28	09 00	09 17	10 01	10 17	10 23	10 59	11 19	11 54	12 19	12 54	13 19	13 54	14 19

A from 21 May until 10 September

Gatwick Airport, Redhill and Guildford - Reading

Mondays to Fridays
from 17 September

Network Diagram - see first Page of Table 148

Station		GW	GW	GW	GW	GW	GW	GW	GW	GW	GW	GW	GW	GW	GW	GW	GW	GW	GW	GW	GW
Gatwick Airport 10	186 d		14 03		15 03		16 03		17 03			18 03		19 16		20 03		21 03		22 22	23 18
Redhill	186 d	13 34	14 13	14 34	15 13	15 29	16 13	16 32	17 13		17 43	18 13	18 43	19 26		20 13	20 34	21 13	21 35	22 33	23 28
Reigate	186 d	13 38	14 18	14 38	15 18	15 34	16 18	16 36	17 18		17 48	18 18	18 47	19 30		20 18	20 40	21 18	21 39	22 38	23 33
Betchworth	d			14 43		15 38		16 41			17 52		18 52				20 45		21 44	22 43	
Dorking Deepdene	d	13 45	14 25	14 47	15 25	15 43	16 25	16 45	17 25		17 57	18 25	18 56	19 37		20 25	20 49	21 25	21 48	22 47	23 40
Dorking West	d			14 50		15 45					17 59		18 59				20 52		21 51	22 50	
Gomshall	d	13 53				15 53		16 53			18 07		19 07				21 00		21 59	22 58	
Chilworth	d	13 59				15 59		16 59			18 13		19 13				21 06		22 05	23 04	
Shalford	d	14 03		15 03		16 03		17 03		17 58	18 17		19 17		20 02		21 10		22 09	23 08	
Guildford	a	14 08	14 42	15 08	15 42	16 08	16 42	17 08	17 43	18 02	18 22	18 41	19 22	19 54	20 06	20 42	21 14	21 42	22 13	23 12	00 01
	d	14 09	14 44	15 09	15 44	16 14	16 44	17 09	17 44	18 04	18 26	18 47	19 36	19 55	20 10	20 44	21 16	21 44	22 15	23 14	00 02
Wanborough	149 d																			23 21	
Ash 5	149 d	14 19		15 19		16 24		17 19	17 54	18 14	18 35		19 46		20 19		21 25		22 23	23 26	
North Camp	d	14 23	14 56	15 23	15 56	16 28	16 56	17 23	17 58	18 18	18 39	19 01	19 50	20 07	20 23	20 56	21 29	21 56	22 27	23 30	00 14
Farnborough North	d	14 27		15 27		16 32		17 27	18 02	18 22	18 42		19 54		20 27		21 33		22 31	23 34	
Blackwater	d	14 31	15 02	15 31	16 02	16 36	17 02	17 31	18 07	18 27	18 47	19 07	19 58	20 14	20 31	21 02	21 38	22 02	22 36	23 38	00 20
Sandhurst	d	14 35		15 35		16 40		17 35		18 30	18 51		20 02		20 35		21 41		22 39	23 42	
Crowthorne	d	14 39		15 39		16 44		17 39		18 34	18 59		20 06		20 39		21 45		22 43	23 46	
Wokingham	149 d	14 44	15 10	15 43	16 10	16 48	17 10	17 44	18 15	18 39	19 04	19 15	20 11	20 22	20 43	21 10	21 50	22 10	22 48	23 51	00 29
Reading 7	149 a	14 54	15 19	15 54	16 24	17 00	17 19	17 54	18 24	18 50	19 17	19 25	20 21	20 32	20 55	21 19	22 01	22 19	23 01	00 01	00 39

Saturdays
until 8 September

Station		GW	GW	XC	GW	GW	GW	GW	GW	GW	GW	GW	GW	GW	GW	GW	GW	GW	GW	GW	GW	GW	GW
Gatwick Airport 10	186 d	22p22	23p18		05 31	06 03		07 03		08 03		09 03		10 03		11 03		12 03		13 03		14 03	
Redhill	186 d	22p33	23p28		05 41	06 13	06 34	07 13	07 34	08 13	08 34	09 13	09 34	10 13	10 34	11 13	11 34	12 13	12 34	13 13	13 34	14 13	14 34
Reigate	186 d	22p38	23p33		05 47	06 18	06 38	07 18	07 38	08 18	08 38	09 18	09 38	10 18	10 38	11 18	11 38	12 18	12 38	13 18	13 38	14 18	14 38
Betchworth	d	22p43					06 43				08 43				10 43				12 43				14 43
Dorking Deepdene	d	22p47	23p40		05 54	06 25	06 47	07 25	07 45	08 25	08 47	09 25	09 45	10 25	10 47	11 25	11 45	12 25	12 47	13 25	13 45	14 25	14 47
Dorking West	d	22p50					06 50				08 50				10 50				12 50				14 50
Gomshall	d	22p58							07 53				09 53				11 53				13 53		
Chilworth	d	23p04							07 59				09 59				11 59				13 59		
Shalford	d	23p08					07 03		08 03		09 03		10 03		11 03		12 03		13 03		14 03		15 03
Guildford	a	23p12	00 01		06 12	06 43	07 08	07 41	08 08	08 42	09 08	09 42	10 08	10 42	11 08	11 42	12 08	12 42	13 08	13 42	14 08	14 42	15 08
	d	23p14	00 02	06 09	06 12	06 44	07 09	07 44	08 09	08 44	09 09	09 44	10 09	10 44	11 09	11 44	12 09	12 44	13 09	13 44	14 09	14 44	15 09
Wanborough	149 d	23p21			06 21																		
Ash 5	149 d	23p26			06 24		07 19		08 19		09 19		10 19		11 19		12 19		13 19		14 19		15 19
North Camp	d	23p30	00 14		06 28	06 56	07 23	07 56	08 23	08 56	09 23	09 56	10 23	10 56	11 23	11 56	12 23	12 56	13 23	13 56	14 23	14 56	15 23
Farnborough North	d	23p34			06 32		07 27		08 27		09 27		10 27		11 27		12 27		13 27		14 27		15 27
Blackwater	d	23p38	00 20		06 38	07 02	07 31	08 02	08 31	09 02	09 31	10 02	10 31	11 02	11 31	12 02	12 31	13 02	13 31	14 02	14 31	15 02	15 31
Sandhurst	d	23p42			06 40		07 35		08 35		09 35		10 35		11 35		12 35		13 35		14 35		15 35
Crowthorne	d	23p46			06 44		07 39		08 39		09 39		10 39		11 39		12 39		13 39		14 39		15 39
Wokingham	149 d	23p51	00 29		06 49	07 10	07 44	08 10	08 44	09 10	09 44	10 10	10 44	11 10	11 44	12 10	12 44	13 10	13 44	14 10	14 44	15 10	15 44
Reading 7	149 a	00 01	00 39	06 44	07 03	07 19	07 54	08 19	08 54	09 19	09 54	10 19	10 54	11 19	11 54	12 19	12 54	13 19	13 54	14 19	14 54	15 19	15 54

Station		GW	GW	GW	GW	GW	GW	GW	GW	GW	GW	GW	GW	GW	GW	GW	GW
Gatwick Airport 10	186 d	15 03		16 03		17 03		18 03		19 03		20 03		21 03		22 22	23 18
Redhill	186 d	15 13	15 34	16 13	16 34	17 13	17 34	18 13	18 34	19 13	19 34	20 13	20 34	21 13	21 36	22 33	23 28
Reigate	186 d	15 18	15 38	16 18	16 38	17 18	17 38	18 18	18 38	19 18	19 38	20 18	20 38	21 18	21 40	22 38	23 33
Betchworth	d				16 43				18 43				20 43			22 43	
Dorking Deepdene	d	15 25	15 45	16 25	16 47	17 25	17 45	18 25	18 47	19 25	19 45	20 25	20 47	21 25	21 47	22 47	23 40
Dorking West	d				16 50				18 50				20 50			22 50	
Gomshall	d		15 53				17 53				19 53				21 55	22 58	
Chilworth	d		15 59				17 59				19 59				22 01	23 04	
Shalford	d		16 03		17 03		18 03		19 03		20 03		21 03		22 05	23 08	
Guildford	a	15 42	16 08	16 42	17 08	17 42	18 08	18 42	19 08	19 42	20 08	20 42	21 08	21 42	22 13	23 13	00 01
	d	15 44	16 09	16 44	17 09	17 44	18 09	18 44	19 09	19 44	20 09	20 44	21 09	21 44	22 14	23 14	00 02
Wanborough	149 d															23 22	
Ash 5	149 d		16 19		17 19		18 19		19 19		20 19		21 19		22 24	23 26	
North Camp	d	15 56	16 23	16 56	17 23	17 56	18 23	18 56	19 23	19 56	20 23	20 56	21 23	21 56	22 28	23 30	00 14
Farnborough North	d		16 27		17 27		18 27		19 27		20 27		21 27		22 32	23 34	
Blackwater	d	16 02	16 31	17 02	17 31	18 02	18 31	19 02	19 31	20 02	20 31	21 02	21 31	22 02	22 36	23 39	00 20
Sandhurst	d		16 35		17 35		18 35		19 35		20 35		21 35		22 40	23 42	
Crowthorne	d		16 39		17 39		18 39		19 39		20 39		21 39		22 44	23 46	
Wokingham	149 d	16 10	16 44	17 10	17 44	18 10	18 44	19 10	19 44	20 10	20 44	21 10	21 44	22 10	22 49	23 51	00 29
Reading 7	149 a	16 19	16 54	17 19	17 54	18 19	18 54	19 19	19 52	20 19	20 54	21 19	21 54	22 19	22 57	00 01	00 38

Gatwick Airport, Redhill and Guildford - Reading

Saturdays
15 September to 20 October

Network Diagram - see first Page of Table 148

			GW	GW	XC	GW	GW	GW	GW	GW	GW	GW	GW	GW	GW	GW	GW	GW	GW	GW	GW	GW
Gatwick Airport 10	186	d	22p22	23p18		05 31	06 03		07 03		08 03		09 03		10 03		11 03		12 03		13 03		14 03	
Redhill	186	d	22p33	23p28		05 41	06 13	06 34	07 13	07 34	08 13	08 34	09 13	09 34	10 13	10 34	11 13	11 34	12 13	12 34	13 13	13 34	14 13	14 34
Reigate	186	d	22p38	23p33		05 47	06 18	06 38	07 18	07 38	08 18	08 38	09 18	09 38	10 18	10 38	11 18	11 38	12 18	12 38	13 18	13 38	14 18	14 38
Betchworth		d	22p43					06 43				08 43				10 43				12 43				14 43
Dorking Deepdene		d	22p47	23p40		05 54	06 25	06 47	07 25	07 45	08 25	08 47	09 25	09 45	10 25	10 47	11 25	11 45	12 25	12 47	13 25	13 45	14 25	14 47
Dorking West		d	22p50					06 50				08 50				10 50				12 50				14 50
Gomshall		d	22p58							07 53				09 53				11 53				13 53		
Chilworth		d	23p04							07 59				09 59				11 59				13 59		
Shalford		d	23p08					07 03		08 03		09 03		10 03		11 03		12 03		13 03		14 03		15 03
Guildford		a	23p12	00 01		06 12	06 43	07 08	07 41	08 08	08 42	09 08	09 42	10 08	10 42	11 08	11 42	12 08	12 42	13 08	13 42	14 08	14 42	15 08
		d	23p14	00 02	06 09	06 12	06 44	07 09	07 44	08 09	08 44	09 09	09 44	10 09	10 44	11 09	11 44	12 09	12 44	13 09	13 44	14 09	14 44	15 09
Wanborough	149	d	23p21			06 21																		
Ash 5	149	d	23p26			06 24		07 19		08 19		09 19		10 19		11 19		12 19		13 19		14 19		15 19
North Camp		d	23p30	00 14		06 28	06 56	07 23	07 56	08 23	08 56	09 23	09 56	10 23	10 56	11 23	11 56	12 23	12 56	13 23	13 56	14 23	14 56	15 23
Farnborough North		d	23p34			06 32		07 27		08 27		09 27		10 27		11 27		12 27		13 27		14 27		15 27
Blackwater		d	23p38	00 20		06 38	07 02	07 31	08 02	08 31	09 02	09 31	10 02	10 31	11 02	11 31	12 02	12 31	13 02	13 31	14 02	14 31	15 02	15 31
Sandhurst		d	23p42			06 40		07 35		08 35		09 35		10 35		11 35		12 35		13 35		14 35		15 35
Crowthorne		d	23p46			06 44		07 39		08 39		09 39		10 39		11 39		12 39		13 39		14 39		15 39
Wokingham	149	d	23p51	00 29		06 49	07 10	07 44	08 10	08 44	09 10	09 44	10 10	10 44	11 10	11 44	12 10	12 44	13 10	13 44	14 10	14 44	15 10	15 44
Reading 7	149	a	00 01	00 39	06 44	07 03	07 19	07 54	08 19	08 54	09 19	09 54	10 19	10 54	11 19	11 54	12 19	12 54	13 19	13 54	14 19	14 54	15 19	15 54

			GW	GW	GW	GW	GW	GW	GW	GW	GW	GW	GW	GW	GW	GW	GW	GW
Gatwick Airport 10	186	d	15 03		16 03		17 03		18 03		19 03		20 03		21 03		22 22	23 18
Redhill	186	d	15 13	15 34	16 13	16 34	17 13	17 34	18 13	18 34	19 13	19 34	20 13	20 34	21 13	21 36	22 33	23 28
Reigate	186	d	15 18	15 38	16 18	16 38	17 18	17 38	18 18	18 38	19 18	19 38	20 18	20 38	21 18	21 40	22 38	23 33
Betchworth		d				16 43				18 43				20 43			22 43	
Dorking Deepdene		d	15 25	15 45	16 25	16 47	17 25	17 45	18 25	18 47	19 25	19 45	20 25	20 47	21 25	21 47	22 47	23 40
Dorking West		d				16 50				18 50				20 50			22 50	
Gomshall		d		15 53				17 53				19 53				21 55	22 58	
Chilworth		d		15 59				17 59				19 59				22 01	23 04	
Shalford		d		16 03		17 03		18 03		19 03		20 03		21 03		22 05	23 08	
Guildford		a	15 42	16 08	16 42	17 08	17 42	18 08	18 42	19 08	19 42	20 08	20 42	21 08	21 42	22 13	23 13	00 01
		d	15 44	16 09	16 44	17 09	17 44	18 09	18 44	19 09	19 44	20 09	20 44	21 09	21 44	22 14	23 14	00 02
Wanborough	149	d															23 22	
Ash 5	149	d		16 19		17 19		18 19		19 19		20 19		21 19		22 24	23 26	
North Camp		d	15 56	16 23	16 56	17 23	17 56	18 23	18 56	19 23	19 56	20 23	20 56	21 23	21 56	22 28	23 30	00 14
Farnborough North		d		16 27		17 27		18 27		19 27		20 27		21 27		22 32	23 34	
Blackwater		d	16 02	16 31	17 02	17 31	18 02	18 31	19 02	19 31	20 02	20 31	21 02	21 31	22 02	22 36	23 39	00 20
Sandhurst		d		16 35		17 35		18 35		19 35		20 35		21 35		22 40	23 42	
Crowthorne		d		16 39		17 39		18 39		19 39		20 39		21 39		22 44	23 46	
Wokingham	149	d	16 10	16 44	17 10	17 44	18 10	18 44	19 10	19 44	20 10	20 44	21 10	21 44	22 10	22 49	23 51	00 29
Reading 7	149	a	16 19	16 54	17 19	17 54	18 19	18 54	19 19	19 54	20 19	20 54	21 19	21 54	22 19	22 57	00 01	00 37

Saturdays
from 27 October

			GW	GW	XC	GW	GW	GW	GW	GW	GW	GW	GW	GW	GW	GW	GW	GW	GW	GW	GW	GW
Gatwick Airport 10	186	d	22p22	23p18		05 31	06 03		07 03		08 03		09 03		10 03		11 03		12 03		13 03		14 03	
Redhill	186	d	22p33	23p28		05 41	06 13	06 34	07 13	07 34	08 13	08 34	09 13	09 34	10 13	10 34	11 13	11 34	12 13	12 34	13 13	13 34	14 13	14 34
Reigate	186	d	22p38	23p33		05 47	06 18	06 38	07 18	07 38	08 18	08 38	09 18	09 38	10 18	10 38	11 18	11 38	12 18	12 38	13 18	13 38	14 18	14 38
Betchworth		d	22p43					06 43				08 43				10 43				12 43				14 43
Dorking Deepdene		d	22p47	23p40		05 54	06 25	06 47	07 25	07 45	08 25	08 47	09 25	09 45	10 25	10 47	11 25	11 45	12 25	12 47	13 25	13 45	14 25	14 47
Dorking West		d	22p50					06 50				08 50				10 50				12 50				14 50
Gomshall		d	22p58							07 53				09 53				11 53				13 53		
Chilworth		d	23p04							07 59				09 59				11 59				13 59		
Shalford		d	23p08					07 03		08 03		09 03		10 03		11 03		12 03		13 03		14 03		15 03
Guildford		a	23p12	00 01		06 12	06 43	07 08	07 41	08 08	08 42	09 08	09 42	10 08	10 42	11 08	11 42	12 08	12 42	13 08	13 42	14 08	14 42	15 08
		d	23p14	00 02	06 09	06 12	06 44	07 09	07 44	08 09	08 44	09 09	09 44	10 09	10 44	11 09	11 44	12 09	12 44	13 09	13 44	14 09	14 44	15 09
Wanborough	149	d	23p21			06 21																		
Ash 5	149	d	23p26			06 24		07 19		08 19		09 19		10 19		11 19		12 19		13 19		14 19		15 19
North Camp		d	23p30	00 14		06 28	06 56	07 23	07 56	08 23	08 56	09 23	09 56	10 23	10 56	11 23	11 56	12 23	12 56	13 23	13 56	14 23	14 56	15 23
Farnborough North		d	23p34			06 32		07 27		08 27		09 27		10 27		11 27		12 27		13 27		14 27		15 27
Blackwater		d	23p38	00 20		06 38	07 02	07 31	08 02	08 31	09 02	09 31	10 02	10 31	11 02	11 31	12 02	12 31	13 02	13 31	14 02	14 31	15 02	15 31
Sandhurst		d	23p42			06 40		07 35		08 35		09 35		10 35		11 35		12 35		13 35		14 35		15 35
Crowthorne		d	23p46			06 44		07 39		08 39		09 39		10 39		11 39		12 39		13 39		14 39		15 39
Wokingham	149	d	23p51	00 29		06 49	07 10	07 44	08 10	08 44	09 10	09 44	10 10	10 44	11 10	11 44	12 10	12 44	13 10	13 44	14 10	14 44	15 10	15 44
Reading 7	149	a	00 01	00 39	06 44	07 03	07 19	07 54	08 19	08 54	09 19	09 54	10 19	10 54	11 19	11 54	12 19	12 54	13 19	13 54	14 19	14 54	15 19	15 54

Gatwick Airport, Redhill and Guildford - Reading

Saturdays
from 27 October

Network Diagram - see first Page of Table 148

			GW	GW	GW	GW	GW	GW	GW	GW	GW	GW	GW	GW	GW	GW	GW	GW
Gatwick Airport 10	186	d	15 03		16 03		17 03		18 03		19 03		20 03		21 03		22 22	23 18
Redhill	186	d	15 13	15 34	16 13	16 34	17 13	17 34	18 13	18 34	19 13	19 34	20 13	20 34	21 13	21 36	22 33	23 28
Reigate	186	d	15 18	15 38	16 18	16 38	17 18	17 38	18 18	18 38	19 18	19 38	20 18	20 38	21 18	21 40	22 38	23 33
Betchworth		d				16 43				18 43				20 43			22 43	
Dorking Deepdene		d	15 25	15 45	16 25	16 47	17 25	17 45	18 25	18 47	19 25	19 45	20 25	20 47	21 25	21 47	22 47	23 40
Dorking West		d				16 50				18 50				20 50			22 50	
Gomshall		d		15 53				17 53				19 53				21 55	22 58	
Chilworth		d		15 59				17 59				19 59				22 01	23 04	
Shalford		d		16 03		17 03		18 03		19 03		20 03		21 03		22 05	23 08	
Guildford		a	15 42	16 08	16 42	17 08	17 42	18 08	18 42	19 08	19 42	20 08	20 42	21 08	21 42	22 13	23 13	00 01
		d	15 44	16 09	16 44	17 09	17 44	18 09	18 44	19 09	19 44	20 09	20 44	21 09	21 44	22 14	23 14	00 02
Wanborough	149	d															23 22	
Ash 5	149	d		16 19		17 19		18 19		19 19		20 19		21 19		22 24	23 26	
North Camp		d	15 56	16 23	16 56	17 23	17 56	18 23	18 56	19 23	19 56	20 23	20 56	21 23	21 56	22 28	23 30	00 14
Farnborough North		d		16 27		17 27		18 27		19 27		20 27		21 27		22 32	23 34	
Blackwater		d	16 02	16 31	17 02	17 31	18 02	18 31	19 02	19 31	20 02	20 31	21 02	21 31	22 02	22 36	23 39	00 20
Sandhurst		d		16 35		17 35		18 35		19 35		20 35		21 35		22 40	23 42	
Crowthorne		d		16 39		17 39		18 39		19 39		20 39		21 39		22 44	23 46	
Wokingham	149	d	16 10	16 44	17 10	17 44	18 10	18 44	19 10	19 44	20 10	20 44	21 10	21 44	22 10	22 49	23 51	00 29
Reading 7	149	a	16 19	16 54	17 19	17 54	18 19	18 54	19 19	19 54	20 19	20 54	21 19	21 54	22 19	22 57	00 01	00 38

Sundays
until 9 September

			GW	GW	GW	GW	GW	GW	GW	GW	XC	GW	GW	GW	GW	GW	GW	GW	GW	GW	GW	GW	GW
Gatwick Airport 10	186	d	22p22	23p18	06 08	07 08	08 08	09 08	10 08	11 08		12 08	13 08	14 08	15 08	16 08	17 08	18 08	19 08	20 08	21 08	22 08	23 08
Redhill	186	d	22p33	23p28	06 20	07 20	08 19	09 20	10 19	11 20		12 19	13 20	14 19	15 20	16 19	17 20	18 19	19 20	20 19	21 20	22 19	23 20
Reigate	186	d	22p38	23p33	06 24	07 24	08 23	09 24	10 23	11 24		12 23	13 24	14 23	15 24	16 23	17 24	18 23	19 24	20 23	21 24	22 23	23 24
Betchworth		d	22p43				08 28		10 28			12 28		14 28		16 28		18 28		20 28		22 28	
Dorking Deepdene		d	22p47	23p40	06 32	07 32	08 32	09 32	10 32	11 32		12 32	13 32	14 31	15 32	16 31	17 32	18 31	19 32	20 31	21 32	22 31	23 32
Dorking West		d	22p50				08 35		10 35			12 35		14 35		16 35		18 35		20 35		22 35	
Gomshall		d	22p58				08 43		10 43			12 43		14 43		16 43		18 43		20 43		22 43	
Chilworth		d	23p04				08 49		10 49			12 49		14 49		16 49		18 49		20 49		22 49	
Shalford		d	23p08				08 53		10 53			12 53		14 53		16 53		18 53		20 53		22 53	
Guildford		a	23p13	00 01	06 49	07 50	08 57	09 50	10 57	11 52		12 57	13 50	14 57	15 50	16 57	17 50	18 57	19 50	20 57	21 50	22 57	23 49
		d	23p14	00 02	06 50	07 52	08 59	09 52	10 59	11 52	12 14	12 59	13 52	14 59	15 52	16 59	17 52	18 59	19 52	20 58	21 52	22 59	23 52
Wanborough	149	d	23p22																				
Ash 5	149	d	23p26			08 02		10 02		12 02			14 02		16 02		18 02		20 02		22 02		00 01
North Camp		d	23p30	00 14	07 02	08 06	09 11	10 06	11 11	12 06		13 11	14 06	15 11	16 06	17 11	18 06	19 11	20 06	21 10	22 06	23 11	00 05
Farnborough North		d	23p34			08 10		10 10		12 10			14 10		16 10		18 10		20 10		22 10		00 09
Blackwater		d	23p39	00 20	07 09	08 14	09 17	10 14	11 17	12 14		13 17	14 14	15 17	16 14	17 17	18 14	19 17	20 14	21 17	22 14	23 17	00 14
Sandhurst		d	23p42			08 18		10 18		12 18			14 18		16 18		18 18		20 18		22 18		00 16
Crowthorne		d	23p46			08 22		10 22		12 22			14 22		16 22		18 22		20 22		22 22		00 20
Wokingham	149	d	23p51	00 29	07 17	08 26	09 26	10 26	11 26	12 26		13 26	14 26	15 26	16 26	17 26	18 26	19 26	20 26	21 26	22 26	23 26	00 25
Reading 7	149	a	00 01	00 38	07 25	08 35	09 35	10 35	11 35	12 35	12 50	13 35	14 35	15 35	16 35	17 35	18 35	19 35	20 35	21 35	22 38	23 37	00 37

Sundays
16 September to 21 October

			GW	GW	GW	GW	GW	GW	GW	GW	XC	GW	GW	GW	GW	GW	GW	GW	GW	GW	GW	GW	GW
Gatwick Airport 10	186	d	22p22	23p18	06 08	07 08	08 08	09 08	10 08	11 08		12 08	13 08	14 08	15 08	16 08	17 08	18 08	19 08	20 08	21 08	22 08	23 08
Redhill	186	d	22p33	23p28	06 20	07 20	08 19	09 20	10 19	11 20		12 19	13 20	14 19	15 20	16 19	17 20	18 19	19 20	20 19	21 20	22 19	23 20
Reigate	186	d	22p38	23p33	06 24	07 24	08 23	09 24	10 23	11 24		12 23	13 24	14 23	15 24	16 23	17 24	18 23	19 24	20 23	21 24	22 23	23 24
Betchworth		d	22p43				08 28		10 28			12 28		14 28		16 28		18 28		20 28		22 28	
Dorking Deepdene		d	22p47	23p40	06 32	07 32	08 32	09 32	10 32	11 32		12 32	13 32	14 31	15 32	16 31	17 32	18 31	19 32	20 31	21 32	22 31	23 32
Dorking West		d	22p50				08 35		10 35			12 35		14 35		16 35		18 35		20 35		22 35	
Gomshall		d	22p58				08 43		10 43			12 43		14 43		16 43		18 43		20 43		22 43	
Chilworth		d	23p04				08 49		10 49			12 49		14 49		16 49		18 49		20 49		22 49	
Shalford		d	23p08				08 53		10 53			12 53		14 53		16 53		18 53		20 53		22 53	
Guildford		a	23p13	00 01	06 49	07 50	08 57	09 50	10 57	11 52		12 57	13 50	14 57	15 50	16 57	17 50	18 57	19 50	20 57	21 50	22 57	23 49
		d	23p14	00 02	06 50	07 52	08 59	09 52	10 59	11 52	12 14	12 59	13 52	14 59	15 52	16 59	17 52	18 59	19 52	20 58	21 52	22 59	23 52
Wanborough	149	d	23p22																				
Ash 5	149	d	23p26			08 02		10 02		12 02			14 02		16 02		18 02		20 02		22 02		00 01
North Camp		d	23p30	00 14	07 02	08 06	09 11	10 06	11 11	12 06		13 11	14 06	15 11	16 06	17 11	18 06	19 11	20 06	21 10	22 06	23 11	00 05
Farnborough North		d	23p34			08 10		10 10		12 10			14 10		16 10		18 10		20 10		22 10		00 09
Blackwater		d	23p39	00 20	07 09	08 14	09 17	10 14	11 17	12 14		13 17	14 14	15 17	16 14	17 17	18 14	19 17	20 14	21 17	22 14	23 17	00 14
Sandhurst		d	23p42			08 18		10 18		12 18			14 18		16 18		18 18		20 18		22 18		00 16
Crowthorne		d	23p46			08 22		10 22		12 22			14 22		16 22		18 22		20 22		22 22		00 20
Wokingham	149	d	23p51	00 29	07 17	08 26	09 26	10 26	11 26	12 26		13 26	14 26	15 26	16 26	17 26	18 26	19 26	20 26	21 26	22 26	23 26	00 25
Reading 7	149	a	00 01	00 37	07 25	08 35	09 35	10 35	11 35	12 35	12 50	13 35	14 35	15 35	16 35	17 35	18 35	19 35	20 35	21 35	22 38	23 37	00 37

Table 148

Sundays from 28 October

Gatwick Airport, Redhill and Guildford - Reading

Network Diagram - see first Page of Table 148

			GW ■	GW ■	GW ■	GW ■	GW ■	GW ■	GW ■	GW ■	XC ◇■ ✠	GW ■	GW ■	GW ■	GW ■	GW ■	GW ■	GW ■	GW ■	GW ■	GW ■	GW ■	GW ■
Gatwick Airport ■	186	d	22p22	23p18	06 08	07 08	08 08	09 08	10 08	11 08		12 08	13 08	14 08	15 08	16 08	17 08	18 08	19 08	20 08	21 08	22 08	23 08
Redhill	186	d	22p33	23p28	06 20	07 20	08 19	09 20	10 19	11 20		12 19	13 20	14 19	15 20	16 19	17 20	18 19	19 20	20 19	21 20	22 19	23 20
Reigate	186	d	22p38	23p33	06 24	07 24	08 23	09 24	10 23	11 24		12 23	13 24	14 23	15 24	16 23	17 24	18 23	19 24	20 23	21 24	22 23	23 24
Betchworth		d	22p43				08 28		10 28			12 28		14 28		16 28		18 28		20 28		22 28	
Dorking Deepdene		d	22p47	23p40	06 32	07 32	08 32	09 32	10 32	11 32		12 32	13 32	14 31	15 32	16 31	17 32	18 31	19 32	20 31	21 32	22 31	23 32
Dorking West		d	22p50				08 35		10 35			12 35		14 35		16 35		18 35		20 35		22 35	
Gomshall		d	22p58				08 43		10 43			12 43		14 43		16 43		18 43		20 43		22 43	
Chilworth		d	23p04				08 49		10 49			12 49		14 49		16 49		18 49		20 49		22 49	
Shalford		d	23p08				08 53		10 53			12 53		14 53		16 53		18 53		20 53		22 53	
Guildford		a	23p13	00 01	06 49	07 50	08 57	09 50	10 57	11 52		12 57	13 50	14 57	15 50	16 57	17 50	18 57	19 50	20 57	21 50	22 57	23 49
		d	23p14	00 02	06 50	07 52	08 59	09 52	10 59	11 52	12 14	12 59	13 52	14 59	15 52	16 59	17 52	18 59	19 52	20 58	21 52	22 59	23 52
Wanborough	149	d	23p22																				
Ash ■	149	d	23p26			08 02		10 02		12 02			14 02		16 02		18 02		20 02		22 02		00 01
North Camp		d	23p30	00 14	07 02	08 06	09 11	10 06	11 11	12 06		13 11	14 06	15 11	16 06	17 11	18 06	19 11	20 06	21 10	22 06	23 11	00 05
Farnborough North		d	23p34			08 10		10 10		12 10			14 10		16 10		18 10		20 10		22 10		00 09
Blackwater		d	23p39	00 20	07 09	08 14	09 17	10 14	11 17	12 14		13 17	14 14	15 17	16 14	17 17	18 14	19 17	20 14	21 17	22 14	23 17	00 14
Sandhurst		d	23p42			08 18		10 18		12 18			14 18		16 18		18 18		20 18		22 18		00 16
Crowthorne		d	23p46			08 22		10 22		12 22			14 22		16 22		18 22		20 22		22 22		00 20
Wokingham	149	d	23p51	00 29	07 17	08 26	09 26	10 26	11 26	12 26		13 26	14 26	15 26	16 26	17 26	18 26	19 26	20 26	21 26	22 26	23 26	00 25
Reading ■	149	a	00 01	00 38	07 25	08 35	09 35	10 35	11 35	12 35	12 50	13 35	14 35	15 35	16 35	17 35	18 35	19 35	20 35	21 35	22 38	23 37	00 37

Table 149

Mondays to Fridays until 5 October

London - Hounslow, Richmond, Kingston, Windsor, Weybridge, Ascot, Guildford and Reading

Network Diagram - see first Page of Table 148

Miles	Miles	Miles			SW MO ■ A	SW MX ■	SW MO A	SW MX	SW MO ■ A	SW MX	SW MX ■	SW MX	SW MX	SW MX B	SW MX	SW MX ■ B	SW MO ■ C	SW MX	SW MO D	SW MO C	SW MX E	SW ■ F	SW MO C
0	—	0	**London Waterloo** ■ ⊖	d	22p39	22p50	22p50	22p52	23p09	23p13	23p20	23p22	23p33	23p38			23p39			23p44	23p50	23p50	
1¼	—	1¼	Vauxhall ⊖	d	22p43		22p54	22p56	23p13	23p17		23p26	23p37				23p43			23p48		23p54	
2¾	—	2¾	Queenstown Rd.(Battersea)	d			22p57	22p59				23p29	23p40							23p51			
4	—	4	**Clapham Junction** ■	d	22p49	22p58	23p00	23p02	23p19	23p23	23p28	23p32	23p43	23p46			23p49			23p54	23p58	00 01	
4¾	—	4¾	Wandsworth Town	d			23p03	23p05				23p35	23p46							23p57			
5¾	—	5¾	Putney	d	22p53		23p06	23p08	23p23	23p27		23p38	23p49				23p53			23p59		00 04	
7	0	7	Barnes	d			23p09	23p12				23p42	23p52							00 03			
—	0½	—	Barnes Bridge	d			23p11	23p14				23p44											
—	1½	—	Chiswick	d			23p13	23p17				23p47											
—	2½	—	Kew Bridge	d			23p16	23p20				23p50											
—	3½	—	Brentford	d			23p19	23p23				23p53											
—	4¼	—	Syon Lane	d			23p21	23p25				23p55											
—	5	—	Isleworth	d			23p23	23p27				23p57											
—	6½	—	**Hounslow**	d			23p26	23p31				00 01											
8¼	—	8¼	Mortlake	d									23p54							00 05			
9	—	9	North Sheen	d									23p56					←		00 07			←
9¾	—	9¾	**Richmond** ⊖	d	22p59	23p06			23p29	23p33	23p37		23p59	23p54			23p59	23p59		00 10	00 06	00 10	00 10
10¾	—	10¾	St Margarets	d									→					00 01		→			00 12
11¼	—	11¼	Twickenham	a	23p02	23p10			23p32	23p36	23p41			23p58			00 02	00 03			00 10	00 13	00 14
—	—	—		d	23p03	23p10			23p33	23p37	23p41			23p58			00 03	00 04			00 10	00 14	00 15
12¼	—	—	Strawberry Hill	d														00 07					
12½	—	—	Fulwell	a																			
13½	—	—	Teddington	a														00 11					
14¾	—	—	Hampton Wick	a														00 14					
15¼	—	—	**Kingston**	a														00 16					
—	—	12½	Whitton	d						23p40					←								00 18
—	—	14¾	Feltham	d	23p09	23p16	23p32	23p36	23p39	23p44	23p48	00 06		00 04	00 06		00 09				00 16	00 20	00 22
—	—	17½	Ashford (Surrey)	d			23p36	23p40		23p48		→			00 10								00 26
0	—	19	**Staines**	d	23p15	23p23	23p40	23p44	23p45	23p52	23p56			00 11	00 14		00 15		00 21		00 23	00 26	00a30
2½	—	—	Wraysbury	d						23p56													
3¾	—	—	Sunnymeads	d						23p59													
4¾	—	—	Datchet	d						00 02													
6¾	—	—	**Windsor & Eton Riverside**	a						00 06													
—	—	21	Egham	d	23p20	23p27	23p45	23p49	23p50		00 01			00 15	00 19		00 20		00s25		00 27	00 31	
0	—	23¾	Virginia Water	a	23p24	23p31	23p49	23p53	23p54		00 05			00 19	00 23		00 24		00s30		00 31	00 35	
—	—	—		d	23p24	23p31	23p49	23p53	23p54		00 05			00 19	00 23		00 24				00 31	00 35	
2½	—	—	Chertsey	d			23p55	23p59							00 29				00s35				
4	—	—	Addlestone	d			23p58	00 02							00a32				00s38				
5	—	—	**Weybridge**	a											00 38								
7¼	—	—	Byfleet & New Haw	d			00 02	00 06											00s42				
8½	—	—	West Byfleet	d			00 05	00 09											00s45				
11	—	—	Woking	a			00 11	00 15											00 51				
—	—	25¼	Longcross	d																			
—	—	27	Sunningdale	d	23p29	23p37			23p59		00 11			00 25			00 29				00 37	00 40	
—	0	29	**Ascot** ■	d	23p34	23p43			00 04		00 15			00 30		00 32	00 34				00 42	00 45	
—	3¼	—	Bagshot	d												00 38							
—	6½	—	Camberley	a												00 44							
—	8¾	—	Frimley	d												00 48							
—	12	—	Ash Vale	d												00 57							
—	14½	—	**Aldershot**	a												01s02							
—	—	—		d																			
—	17¼	—	Ash ■	d																			
—	19¼	—	Wanborough	d																			
—	23½	—	**Guildford**	a																			
—	—	31¼	Martins Heron	d	23p38	23p47			00 08		00 19			00 34			00 38				00 46	00 49	
—	—	32¼	Bracknell	d	23p41	23p50			00 11		00 23			00 37			00 41				00 49	00 52	
—	—	36¾	**Wokingham**	d	23p48	23p57			00 18		00 32			00 44			00 48				00 56	00 59	
—	—	38¾	Winnersh	d	23p51	23p59			00 21		00 36						00 51					01 02	
—	—	39¼	Winnersh Triangle	d	23p53	00 02			00 23		00 38						00 53					01 04	
—	—	40½	Earley	d	23p56	00 05			00 26		00 40						00 56					01 07	
—	—	43½	**Reading** ■	a	00 01	00 10			00 31		00 45			00 52			01 01				01 04	01 12	

A from 21 May until 1 October
B not from 31 July until 10 August, from 30 August until 7 September
C from 21 May until 23 July, 20 August, 27 August, 17 September, 24 September, 1 October
D until 23 July, 20 August, 27 August, 17 September, 24 September, 1 October
E from 31 July until 7 September, not from 14 August until 29 August
F 30 July, 6 August, 13 August, 3 September, 10 September

Table 149

Mondays to Fridays
until 5 October

London - Hounslow, Richmond, Kingston, Windsor, Weybridge, Ascot, Guildford and Reading

Network Diagram - see first Page of Table 148

		SW A	SW MX ■ B	SW ■	SW ■	SW MX	SW A	SW MX	SW A	SW MX	SW	SW C	SW	SW ■	SW	SW ■	SW	SW	SW	SW ■	SW ■	SW	SW
London Waterloo 15 ⊖	d					23p52	23p54	23p58			00 18	00 38				05 05		05 33			05 50		05 58
Vauxhall ⊖	d					23p56	23p58	00 02			00 22	00 42				05 09		05 37					06 02
Queenstown Rd.(Battersea)	d					23p59	00 01				00 25					05 12		05 40					
Clapham Junction 10	d					00 02	00 04	00 08			00 29	00 48				05 15		05 43			05 58		06 08
Wandsworth Town	d					00 05	00 07				00 32					05 18		05 46					
Putney	d					00 08	00 09	00 12			00 35	00 52				05 21		05 49					06 12
Barnes	d					00 12	00 13				00 38	00 55				05 24		05 52					
Barnes Bridge	d					00 14																	
Chiswick	d					00 17																	
Kew Bridge	d					00 20																	
Brentford	d					00 23																	
Syon Lane	d					00 25																	
Isleworth	d					00 27																	
Hounslow	d					00 31																	
Mortlake	d						00 15				00 40					05 26		05 54					
North Sheen	d						00 17		←		00 42					05 28		05 56					
Richmond ⊖	d						00 20	00 18	00 20		00 45	01 00				05 31		05 59			06 06		06 18
St Margarets	d						→		00 22		00 47					05 33		06 01					
Twickenham	a							00 21	00 24		00 49	01 03				05 35		06 03			06 10		06 21
	d							00 22	00 25		00 50	01 04	04 52			05 36	05 53	06 05			06 10	06 17	06 22
Strawberry Hill	d										00s53		04 55					06 08					
Fulwell	a																						
Teddington	a										00s56		04 58					06 11					
Hampton Wick	a										00s59		05 01					06 14					
Kingston	a										01 01		05 03					06 16					
Whitton	d							00 25	00 28	←		01 07				05 39	05 56					06a20	06 25
Feltham	d					00 37		00 29	00 32	00 37		01 11				05 43	06 00				06 16		06 29
Ashford (Surrey)	d					→		00 33	00 36	00 41		01 15				05 47	06 04						06 33
Staines	d	00 33						00a37	00a40	00a46		01a19		05 23	05 44	05 53	06 08		06 14		06 23		06 37
Wraysbury	d																06 12						06 41
Sunnymeads	d																06 15						06 44
Datchet	d																06 18						06 47
Windsor & Eton Riverside	a																06 22						06 51
Egham	d	00s37												05 27	05 49	05 57			06 19		06 27		
Virginia Water	a	00s42												05 31	05 53	06 01			06 23		06 31		
	d													05 31	05 53	06 01			06 23		06 31		
Chertsey	d	00s47													05 59				06 29				
Addlestone	d	00s50													06 02				06 32				
Weybridge	a														06 07				06 37				
Byfleet & New Haw	d	00s54																					
West Byfleet	d	00s57																					
Woking	a	01 03																					
Longcross	d																				06 35		
Sunningdale	d													05 37		06 07					06 37		
Ascot 8	d		00 44											05 43		06 13				06 23	06 43		
Bagshot	d		00 50																	06 29			
Camberley	a		00 56																	06 35			
Frimley	d		01 00																	06 43			
Ash Vale	d		01 09																	06 49			
Aldershot	a		01s13																	06 56			
	d			06 08	06 38															07 08			
Ash 5	d			06 15	06 45															07 15			
Wanborough	d			06 18	06 48															07 18			
Guildford	a			06 25	06 55															07 25			
Martins Heron	d													05 47		06 17					06 47		
Bracknell	d													05 50		06 20					06 50		
Wokingham	d													05 57		06 27					06 57		
Winnersh	d													06 00		06 30					07 00		
Winnersh Triangle	d													06 02		06 32					07 02		
Earley	d													06 05		06 35					07 05		
Reading 7	a													06 10		06 40					07 10		

A 30 July, 6 August, 13 August, 3 September, 10 September

B from 31 July until 7 September, not from 14 August until 29 August

C from 30 July until 10 September, not from 14 August until 29 August

Table 149

Mondays to Fridays
until 5 October

London - Hounslow, Richmond, Kingston, Windsor, Weybridge, Ascot, Guildford and Reading

Network Diagram - see first Page of Table 148

		SW	SW	SW ■	SW	SW ■	SW	SW ■	SW	SW	SW	SW	SW	SW	SW ■	SW	SW ■	SW	SW	SW	SW	SW	SW
London Waterloo 15 ⊖	d	06 03			06 15	06 20				06 22	06 28		06 33	06 45	06 50			06 52	06 58		07 03		07 15
Vauxhall ⊖	d	06 07			06 19					06 26	06 32		06 37	06 49				06 56	07 02		07 07		07 19
Queenstown Rd.(Battersea)	d	06 10			06 22					06 29			06 40	06 52				06 59			07 10		07 22
Clapham Junction 10	d	06 13			06 25	06 28				06 32	06 38		06 43	06 55	06 58			07 02	07 08		07 13		07 25
Wandsworth Town	d	06 16			06 28					06 35			06 46	06 58				07 05			07 16		07 28
Putney	d	06 19			06 31					06 38	06 42		06 49	07 01				07 08	07 12		07 19		07 31
Barnes	d	06 22			06 35					06 42			06 52	07 05				07 12			07 22		07 35
Barnes Bridge	d									06 44								07 14					
Chiswick	d									06 47								07 17					
Kew Bridge	d									06 50								07 20					
Brentford	d									06 53								07 23					
Syon Lane	d									06 55								07 25					
Isleworth	d									06 57								07 27					
Hounslow	d								06 48	07 01								07 31					
Mortlake	d	06 24			06 37								06 54	07 07							07 24		07 37
North Sheen	d	06 26			06 39		←						06 56	07 09		←					07 26		07 39
Richmond ⊖	d	06 29			06 42	06 36	06 42				06 48		06 59	07 12	07 06	07 12			07 18		07 29		07 42
St Margarets	d	06 31			→		06 44						07 01	→		07 14					07 31		→
Twickenham	a	06 33				06 40	06 46		06 56		06 51		07 03		07 10	07 16			07 21		07 33		
	d	06 34				06 40	06 47				06 52		07 04		07 10	07 17			07 22		07 34	07 37	
Strawberry Hill	d	06 37											07 07								07 37	07 47	
Fulwell	a																						
Teddington	a	06 40											07 10								07 40	07 50	
Hampton Wick	a	06 44											07 14								07 44	07 52	
Kingston	a	06 46											07 16								07 46	07 54	
Whitton	d						06a50				06 55	←				07a20			07 25	←			
Feltham	d					06 46				07 06	06 59	07 06			07 16			07 36	07 29	07 36			
Ashford (Surrey)	d									→	07 03	07 10						→	07 33	07 40			
Staines	d		06 44			06 53					07 07	07 14			07 23				07 37	07 44			
Wraysbury	d										07 11								07 41				
Sunnymeads	d										07 14								07 44				
Datchet	d										07 17								07 47				
Windsor & Eton Riverside	a										07 21								07 51				
Egham	d		06 49			06 57						07 19			07 27					07 49			
Virginia Water	a		06 53			07 01						07 23			07 31					07 53			
	d		06 53			07 01						07 23			07 31					07 53			
Chertsey	d		06 59									07 29								07 59			
Addlestone	d		07 02									07 32								08 02			
Weybridge	a		07 07									07 37								08 07			
Byfleet & New Haw	d																						
West Byfleet	d																						
Woking	a																						
Longcross	d					07 05									07 35								
Sunningdale	d					07 07									07 37								
Ascot 8	d			06 53		07 13		07 23							07 43		07 53						
Bagshot	d			06 59				07 29									07 59						
Camberley	a			07 05				07 35									08 05						
Frimley	d			07 13				07 43									08 13						
Ash Vale	d			07 19				07 49									08 19						
Aldershot	a			07 26				07 54									08 24						
	d			07 38				08 08									08 38						
Ash 5	d			07 45				08 15									08 45						
Wanborough	d			07 48				08 18									08 48						
Guildford	a			07 55				08 25									08 55						
Martins Heron	d					07 17									07 47								
Bracknell	d					07 20									07 50								
Wokingham	d					07 27									07 57								
Winnersh	d					07 30									08 00								
Winnersh Triangle	d					07 32									08 02								
Earley	d					07 35									08 05								
Reading 7	a					07 40									08 10								

Table 149

Mondays to Fridays
until 5 October

London - Hounslow, Richmond, Kingston, Windsor, Weybridge, Ascot, Guildford and Reading

Network Diagram - see first Page of Table 148

		SW ■	SW	SW	SW	SW ■	SW	SW	SW	SW	SW	SW ■	SW	SW ■	SW	SW	SW	SW ■	SW	SW	SW	SW
London Waterloo ■ ⊖	d	07 20		07 22	07 28			07 33	07 37		07 45	07 50			07 52	07 58	08 03	08 07			08 10	08 15
Vauxhall ⊖	d			07 26	07 32			07 37	07 41		07 49				07 56	08 02	08 07				08 14	08 19
Queenstown Rd.(Battersea)	d			07 29				07 40	07 44		07 52				07 59		08 10				08 17	08 22
Clapham Junction ■	d	07 28		07 32	07 38			07 43	07 47		07 55	07 58			08 02	08 08	08 13	08 16			08 20	08 25
Wandsworth Town	d			07 35				07 46	07 50		07 58				08 05		08 16				08 23	08 28
Putney	d			07 38	07 42			07 49	07 53		08 01				08 08	08 12	08 19				08 26	08 31
Barnes	d			07 42				07 52	07 57		08 05				08 12		08 23				08 29	08 35
Barnes Bridge	d			07 44					07 59						08 14						08 31	
Chiswick	d			07 47					08 02						08 17						08 34	
Kew Bridge	d			07 50					08 05						08 20						08 36	
Brentford	d			07 53					08 08						08 23						08 39	
Syon Lane	d			07 55					08 10						08 25						08 41	
Isleworth	d			07 57					08 12						08 27						08 43	
Hounslow	d			08 01					08a18						08 31						08 48	
Mortlake	d							07 54			08 07						08 25					08 37
North Sheen	d		←					07 56			08 09		←				08 27			←		08 39
Richmond ⊖	d	07 36	07 42		07 48	07 54		07 59			08 12	08 06	08 12			08 18	08 30	08 24		08 30		08 42
St Margarets	d		07 44					08 01			→		08 14				→			08 32		→
Twickenham	a	07 40	07 46		07 51	07 57		08 03				08 10	08 16			08 21		08 28		08 34		
	d	07 40	07 47		07 52	07 58		08 04		08 07		08 10	08 17			08 22		08 28		08 35		
Strawberry Hill	d							08 07		08 17										08 38		
Fulwell	a																					
Teddington	a							08 10		08 20										08 41		
Hampton Wick	a							08 14		08 22										08 44		
Kingston	a							08 16		08 24										08 46		
Whitton	d		07a50		07 55		←						08a20			08 25			←		08a53	
Feltham	d	07 46		08 06	07 59	08 04	08 06					08 16			08 36	08 29		08 34	08 36			
Ashford (Surrey)	d			→	08 03	08 08	08 10								→	08 33		08 38	08 40			
Staines	d	07 53			08 07	08 12	08 14					08 23				08 37		08 42	08 44			
Wraysbury	d				08 11											08 41						
Sunnymeads	d				08 14											08 44						
Datchet	d				08 17											08 47						
Windsor & Eton Riverside	a				08 21											08 51						
Egham	d	07 57				08 16	08 19					08 27						08 47	08 49			
Virginia Water	a	08 01					08 23					08 31						08 51	08 53			
	d	08 01					08 23					08 31						08 51	08 53			
Chertsey	d						08 29												08 59			
Addlestone	d						08 32												09 02			
Weybridge	a						08 38												09 08			
Byfleet & New Haw	d																					
West Byfleet	d																					
Woking	a																					
Longcross	d	08 05										08 35						08 54				
Sunningdale	d	08 07										08 37						08 58				
Ascot ■	d	08 13				08 26						08 43		08 53				09 02				
Bagshot	d					08 32								08 59								
Camberley	a					08 38								09 05								
Frimley	d					08 43								09 13								
Ash Vale	d					08 49								09 19								
Aldershot	a					08 54								09 25								
	d					09 08								09 38								
Ash ■	d					09 15								09 45								
Wanborough	d					09 18								09 48								
Guildford	a					09 25								09 55								
Martins Heron	d	08 17										08 47						09 06				
Bracknell	d	08 20										08 50						09 10				
Wokingham	d	08 27										08 57						09 17				
Winnersh	d	08 30										09 00						09 20				
Winnersh Triangle	d	08 32										09 02						09 22				
Earley	d	08 35										09 05						09 25				
Reading ■	a	08 40										09 10						09 30				

Table 149

Mondays to Fridays
until 5 October

London - Hounslow, Richmond, Kingston, Windsor, Weybridge, Ascot, Guildford and Reading

Network Diagram - see first Page of Table 148

		SW ■	SW	SW ■	SW	SW	SW	SW ■	SW	SW	SW	SW	SW ■	SW	SW ■	SW	SW	SW	SW	SW	SW	SW ■	SW
London Waterloo ■ ⊖	d	08 20			08 22	08 28	08 33	08 37			08 40	08 43	08 50			08 52	08 58		09 03	09 07	09 15	09 20	
Vauxhall ⊖	d				08 26	08 32	08 37				08 44	08 47				08 56	09 02		09 07	09 11	09 19		
Queenstown Rd.(Battersea)	d				08 29		08 40				08 47	08 50				08 59			09 10	09 14	09 22		
Clapham Junction ■	d	08 28			08 32	08 38	08 43	08 45			08 50	08 55	08 58			09 02	09 08		09 13	09 17	09 25	09 28	
Wandsworth Town	d				08 35		08 46				08 53	08 58				09 05			09 16	09 20	09 28		
Putney	d				08 38	08 42	08 49				08 56	09 01				09 08	09 12		09 19	09 23	09 31		
Barnes	d				08 42		08 52				08 59	09 05				09 12			09 22	09 27	09 35		
Barnes Bridge	d				08 44						09 01					09 14				09 29			
Chiswick	d				08 47						09 03					09 17				09 32			
Kew Bridge	d				08 50						09 06					09 20				09 35			
Brentford	d				08 53						09 09					09 23				09 38			
Syon Lane	d				08 55						09 11					09 25				09 40			
Isleworth	d				08 57						09 13					09 27				09 42			
Hounslow	d				09 01						09 18					09 31				09 48			
Mortlake	d						08 54					09 07							09 24		09 37		
North Sheen	d		←				08 56			←		09 09		←					09 26		09 39		←
Richmond ⊖	d	08 36	08 42			08 48	08 59	08 54		08 59		09 12	09 06	09 12			09 18		09 29		09 42	09 36	09 42
St Margarets	d		08 44				→			09 01		→		09 14					09 31		→		09 44
Twickenham	a	08 40	08 46			08 51		08 57		09 03			09 10	09 16			09 21		09 33			09 40	09 46
	d	08 40	08 47			08 52		08 58		09 04			09 10	09 17			09 22		09 34			09 40	09 47
Strawberry Hill	d									09 07									09 37				
Fulwell	a																						
Teddington	a									09 10									09 40				
Hampton Wick	a									09 14									09 44				
Kingston	a									09 16									09 46				
Whitton	d		08a50			08 55			←		09a23			09a20			09 25	←		09a53			09a50
Feltham	d	08 46			09 06	08 59		09 04	09 06				09 16			09 36	09 29	09 36				09 46	
Ashford (Surrey)	d				→	09 03		09 08	09 10							→	09 33	09 40					
Staines	d	08 53				09 07		09 12	09 14				09 23				09 37	09 44				09 53	
Wraysbury	d					09 11											09 41						
Sunnymeads	d					09 14											09 44						
Datchet	d					09 17											09 47						
Windsor & Eton Riverside	a					09 21											09 51						
Egham	d	08 57						09 16	09 19				09 27					09 49				09 57	
Virginia Water	a	09 01						09 20	09 23				09 31					09 53				10 01	
	d	09 01						09 20	09 23				09 31					09 53				10 01	
Chertsey	d								09 29									09 59					
Addlestone	d								09 32									10 02					
Weybridge	a								09 37									10 07					
Byfleet & New Haw	d																						
West Byfleet	d																						
Woking	a																						
Longcross	d																						
Sunningdale	d	09 07						09 26					09 37									10 07	
Ascot ■	d	09 13		09 23				09 30					09 43		09 53							10 13	
Bagshot	d			09 29											09 59								
Camberley	a			09 35											10 05								
Frimley	d			09 43											10 13								
Ash Vale	d			09 49											10 19								
Aldershot	a			09 54											10 24								
	d			10 08											10 38								
Ash ■	d			10 15											10 45								
Wanborough	d			10 18											10 48								
Guildford	a			10 25											10 55								
Martins Heron	d	09 17						09 34					09 47									10 17	
Bracknell	d	09 20						09 38					09 50									10 20	
Wokingham	d	09 27						09 47					09 57									10 27	
Winnersh	d	09 30											10 00									10 30	
Winnersh Triangle	d	09 32											10 02									10 32	
Earley	d	09 35											10 05									10 35	
Reading ■	a	09 40						09 55					10 10									10 40	

Table 149

Mondays to Fridays

until 5 October

London - Hounslow, Richmond, Kingston, Windsor, Weybridge, Ascot, Guildford and Reading

Network Diagram - see first Page of Table 148

		SW ■	SW	SW	SW	SW	SW	SW	SW ■	SW	SW ■	SW	SW	SW	SW	SW	SW	SW ■	SW	SW ■	SW	SW
London Waterloo 15 ⊖	d		09 22	09 28		09 33	09 37	09 45	09 50			09 52	09 58		10 03	10 07	10 15	10 20			10 22	10 28
Vauxhall ⊖	d		09 26	09 32		09 37	09 41	09 49				09 56	10 02		10 07	10 11	10 19				10 26	10 32
Queenstown Rd.(Battersea)	d		09 29			09 40	09 44	09 52				09 59			10 10	10 14	10 22				10 29	
Clapham Junction 10	d		09 32	09 38		09 43	09 47	09 55	09 58			10 02	10 08		10 13	10 17	10 25	10 28			10 32	10 38
Wandsworth Town	d		09 35			09 46	09 50	09 58				10 05			10 16	10 20	10 28				10 35	
Putney	d		09 38	09 42		09 49	09 53	10 01				10 08	10 12		10 19	10 23	10 31				10 38	10 42
Barnes	d		09 42			09 52	09 57	10 05				10 12			10 22	10 27	10 35				10 42	
Barnes Bridge	d		09 44				09 59					10 14				10 29					10 44	
Chiswick	d		09 47				10 02					10 17				10 32					10 47	
Kew Bridge	d		09 50				10 05					10 20				10 35					10 50	
Brentford	d		09 53				10 08					10 23				10 38					10 53	
Syon Lane	d		09 55				10 10					10 25				10 40					10 55	
Isleworth	d		09 57				10 12					10 27				10 42					10 57	
Hounslow	d		10 01				10 18					10 31				10 48					11 01	
Mortlake	d					09 54		10 07							10 24		10 37					
North Sheen	d					09 56		10 09		←					10 26		10 39		←			
Richmond ⊖	d			09 48		09 59		10 12	10 06	10 12			10 18		10 29		10 42	10 36	10 42			10 48
St Margarets	d					10 01		→		10 14					10 31		→		10 44			
Twickenham	a			09 51		10 03			10 10	10 16			10 21		10 33			10 40	10 46			10 51
	d			09 52		10 04			10 10	10 17			10 22		10 34			10 40	10 47			10 52
Strawberry Hill	d					10 07									10 37							
Fulwell	a																					
Teddington	a					10 10									10 40							
Hampton Wick	a					10 14									10 44							
Kingston	a					10 16									10 46							
Whitton	d			09 55	←		10a26			10a20			10 25	←		10a56			10a50			10 55
Feltham	d		10 06	09 59	10 06				10 16			10 36	10 29	10 36				10 46			11 06	10 59
Ashford (Surrey)	d		→	10 03	10 10							→	10 33	10 40							→	11 03
Staines	d			10 07	10 14				10 23				10 37	10 44				10 53				11 07
Wraysbury	d			10 11									10 41									11 11
Sunnymeads	d			10 14									10 44									11 14
Datchet	d			10 17									10 47									11 17
Windsor & Eton Riverside	a			10 21									10 51									11 21
Egham	d				10 19				10 27					10 49				10 57				
Virginia Water	a				10 23				10 31					10 53				11 01				
	d				10 23				10 31					10 53				11 01				
Chertsey	d				10 29									10 59								
Addlestone	d				10 32									11 02								
Weybridge	a				10 37									11 07								
Byfleet & New Haw	d																					
West Byfleet	d																					
Woking	a																					
Longcross	d																					
Sunningdale	d								10 37									11 07				
Ascot 5	d	10 23							10 43		10 53							11 13		11 23		
Bagshot	d	10 29									10 59									11 29		
Camberley	a	10 35									11 05									11 35		
Frimley	d	10 43									11 13									11 43		
Ash Vale	d	10 49									11 19									11 49		
Aldershot	a	10 54									11 24									11 54		
	d	11 08									11 38									12 08		
Ash 5	d	11 15									11 45									12 15		
Wanborough	d	11 18									11 48									12 18		
Guildford	a	11 25									11 55									12 25		
Martins Heron	d								10 47									11 17				
Bracknell	d								10 50									11 20				
Wokingham	d								10 57									11 27				
Winnersh	d								11 00									11 30				
Winnersh Triangle	d								11 02									11 32				
Earley	d								11 05									11 35				
Reading 7	a								11 10									11 40				

Table 149

Mondays to Fridays

until 5 October

London - Hounslow, Richmond, Kingston, Windsor, Weybridge, Ascot, Guildford and Reading

Network Diagram - see first Page of Table 148

		SW	SW	SW	SW	SW ■	SW	SW ■	SW	SW	SW	SW	SW	SW	SW ■	SW	SW ■	SW	SW	SW	SW	SW	SW
London Waterloo 15 ⊖	d		10 33	10 37	10 45	10 50			10 52	10 58		11 03	11 07	11 15	11 20			11 22	11 28		11 33	11 37	11 45
Vauxhall ⊖	d		10 37	10 41	10 49				10 56	11 02		11 07	11 11	11 19				11 26	11 32		11 37	11 41	11 49
Queenstown Rd.(Battersea)	d		10 40	10 44	10 52				10 59			11 10	11 14	11 22				11 29			11 40	11 44	11 52
Clapham Junction 10	d		10 43	10 47	10 55	10 58			11 02	11 08		11 13	11 17	11 25	11 28			11 32	11 38		11 43	11 47	11 55
Wandsworth Town	d		10 46	10 50	10 58				11 05			11 16	11 20	11 28				11 35			11 46	11 50	11 58
Putney	d		10 49	10 53	11 01				11 08	11 12		11 19	11 23	11 31				11 38	11 42		11 49	11 53	12 01
Barnes	d		10 52	10 57	11 05				11 12			11 22	11 27	11 35				11 42			11 52	11 57	12 05
Barnes Bridge	d			10 59					11 14				11 29					11 44				11 59	
Chiswick	d			11 02					11 17				11 32					11 47				12 02	
Kew Bridge	d			11 05					11 20				11 35					11 50				12 05	
Brentford	d			11 08					11 23				11 38					11 53				12 08	
Syon Lane	d			11 10					11 25				11 40					11 55				12 10	
Isleworth	d			11 12					11 27				11 42					11 57				12 12	
Hounslow	d			11 18					11 31				11 48					12 01				12 18	
Mortlake	d		10 54		11 07							11 24		11 37							11 54		12 07
North Sheen	d		10 56		11 09		←					11 26		11 39		←					11 56		12 09
Richmond ⊖	d		10 59		11 12	11 06	11 12			11 18		11 29		11 42	11 36	11 42			11 48		11 59		12 12
St Margarets	d		11 01		→		11 14					11 31		→		11 44					12 01		→
Twickenham	a		11 03			11 10	11 16			11 21		11 33			11 40	11 46			11 51		12 03		
	d		11 04			11 10	11 17			11 22		11 34			11 40	11 47			11 52		12 04		
Strawberry Hill	d		11 07									11 37									12 07		
Fulwell	a																						
Teddington	a		11 10									11 40									12 10		
Hampton Wick	a		11 14									11 44									12 14		
Kingston	a		11 16									11 46									12 16		
Whitton	d	←		11a23			11a20			11 25	←		11a53			11a50			11 55	←		12a23	
Feltham	d	11 06				11 16			11 36	11 29	11 36				11 46			12 06	11 59	12 06			
Ashford (Surrey)	d	11 10							→	11 33	11 40							→	12 03	12 10			
Staines	d	11 14				11 23				11 37	11 44				11 53				12 07	12 14			
Wraysbury	d									11 41									12 11				
Sunnymeads	d									11 44									12 14				
Datchet	d									11 47									12 17				
Windsor & Eton Riverside	a									11 51									12 21				
Egham	d	11 19				11 27					11 49				11 57					12 19			
Virginia Water	a	11 23				11 31					11 53				12 01					12 23			
	d	11 23				11 31					11 53				12 01					12 23			
Chertsey	d	11 29									11 59									12 29			
Addlestone	d	11 32									12 02									12 32			
Weybridge	a	11 37									12 07									12 37			
Byfleet & New Haw	d																						
West Byfleet	d																						
Woking	a																						
Longcross	d																						
Sunningdale	d					11 37									12 07								
Ascot 5	d					11 43		11 53							12 13		12 23						
Bagshot	d							11 59									12 29						
Camberley	a							12 05									12 35						
Frimley	d							12 13									12 43						
Ash Vale	d							12 19									12 49						
Aldershot	a							12 24									12 54						
	d							12 38									13 08						
Ash 5	d							12 45									13 15						
Wanborough	d							12 48									13 18						
Guildford	a							12 55									13 25						
Martins Heron	d					11 47									12 17								
Bracknell	d					11 50									12 20								
Wokingham	d					11 57									12 27								
Winnersh	d					12 00									12 30								
Winnersh Triangle	d					12 02									12 32								
Earley	d					12 05									12 35								
Reading 7	a					12 10									12 40								

Table 149

Mondays to Fridays
until 5 October

London - Hounslow, Richmond, Kingston, Windsor, Weybridge, Ascot, Guildford and Reading

Network Diagram - see first Page of Table 148

		SW ■	SW	SW ■	SW	SW	SW	SW	SW	SW	SW ■	SW	SW ■	SW	SW	SW	SW	SW	SW	SW ■	SW	SW ■	SW
London Waterloo ⊖	d	11 50			11 52	11 58		12 03	12 07	12 15	12 20			12 22	12 28		12 33	12 37	12 45	12 50			12 52
Vauxhall ⊖	d				11 56	12 02		12 07	12 11	12 19				12 26	12 32		12 37	12 41	12 49				12 56
Queenstown Rd.(Battersea)	d				11 59			12 10	12 14	12 22				12 29			12 40	12 44	12 52				12 59
Clapham Junction	d	11 58			12 02	12 08		12 13	12 17	12 25	12 28			12 32	12 38		12 43	12 47	12 55	12 58			13 02
Wandsworth Town	d				12 05			12 16	12 20	12 28				12 35			12 46	12 50	12 58				13 05
Putney	d				12 08	12 12		12 19	12 23	12 31				12 38	12 42		12 49	12 53	13 01				13 08
Barnes	d				12 12			12 22	12 27	12 35				12 42			12 52	12 57	13 05				13 12
Barnes Bridge	d				12 14				12 29					12 44				12 59					13 14
Chiswick	d				12 17				12 32					12 47				13 02					13 17
Kew Bridge	d				12 20				12 35					12 50				13 05					13 20
Brentford	d				12 23				12 38					12 53				13 08					13 23
Syon Lane	d				12 25				12 40					12 55				13 10					13 25
Isleworth	d				12 27				12 42					12 57				13 12					13 27
Hounslow	d				12 31				12 48					13 01				13 18					13 31
Mortlake	d							12 24		12 37							12 54		13 07				
North Sheen	d		←					12 26		12 39		←					12 56		13 09		←		
Richmond ⊖	d	12 06	12 12			12 18		12 29		12 42	12 36	12 42			12 48		12 59		13 12	13 06	13 12		
St Margarets	d		12 14					12 31		→		12 44					13 01		→		13 14		
Twickenham	a	12 10	12 16			12 21		12 33			12 40	12 46			12 51		13 03			13 10	13 16		
	d	12 10	12 17			12 22		12 34			12 40	12 47			12 52		13 04			13 10	13 17		
Strawberry Hill	d							12 37									13 07						
Fulwell	a																						
Teddington	a							12 40									13 10						
Hampton Wick	a							12 44									13 14						
Kingston	a							12 46									13 16						
Whitton	d		12a20			12 25	←		12a53			12a50			12 55	←		13a23			13a20		
Feltham	d	12 16			12 36	12 29	12 36				12 46			13 06	12 59	13 06				13 16			13 36
Ashford (Surrey)	d				→	12 33	12 40							→	13 03	13 10							→
Staines	d	12 23				12 37	12 44				12 53				13 07	13 14				13 23			
Wraysbury	d					12 41									13 11								
Sunnymeads	d					12 44									13 14								
Datchet	d					12 47									13 17								
Windsor & Eton Riverside	a					12 51									13 21								
Egham	d	12 27					12 49				12 57					13 19				13 27			
Virginia Water	a	12 31					12 53				13 01					13 23				13 31			
	d	12 31					12 53				13 01					13 23				13 31			
Chertsey	d						12 59									13 29							
Addlestone	d						13 02									13 32							
Weybridge	a						13 07									13 37							
Byfleet & New Haw	d																						
West Byfleet	d																						
Woking	a																						
Longcross	d																			13 35			
Sunningdale	d	12 37									13 07									13 37			
Ascot ■	d	12 43		12 53							13 13		13 23							13 43		13 53	
Bagshot	d			12 59									13 29									13 59	
Camberley	a			13 05									13 35									14 05	
Frimley	d			13 13									13 43									14 13	
Ash Vale	d			13 19									13 49									14 19	
Aldershot	a			13 24									13 54									14 24	
	d			13 38									14 08									14 38	
Ash ■	d			13 45									14 15									14 45	
Wanborough	d			13 48									14 18									14 48	
Guildford	a			13 55									14 25									14 55	
Martins Heron	d	12 47									13 17									13 47			
Bracknell	d	12 50									13 20									13 50			
Wokingham	d	12 57									13 27									13 57			
Winnersh	d	13 00									13 30									14 00			
Winnersh Triangle	d	13 02									13 32									14 02			
Earley	d	13 05									13 35									14 05			
Reading ■	a	13 10									13 40									14 10			

Table 149

Mondays to Fridays
until 5 October

London - Hounslow, Richmond, Kingston, Windsor, Weybridge, Ascot, Guildford and Reading

Network Diagram - see first Page of Table 148

		SW	SW	SW	SW	SW	SW ■	SW	SW ■	SW	SW	SW	SW	SW	SW	SW ■	SW	SW ■	SW	SW	SW	SW
London Waterloo ⊖	d	12 58		13 03	13 07	13 15	13 20			13 22	13 28		13 33	13 37	13 45	13 50			13 52	13 58		14 03
Vauxhall ⊖	d	13 02		13 07	13 11	13 19				13 26	13 32		13 37	13 41	13 49				13 56	14 02		14 07
Queenstown Rd.(Battersea)	d			13 10	13 14	13 22				13 29			13 40	13 44	13 52				13 59			14 10
Clapham Junction	d	13 08		13 13	13 17	13 25	13 28			13 32	13 38		13 43	13 47	13 55	13 58			14 02	14 08		14 13
Wandsworth Town	d			13 16	13 20	13 28				13 35			13 46	13 50	13 58				14 05			14 16
Putney	d	13 12		13 19	13 23	13 31				13 38	13 42		13 49	13 53	14 01				14 08	14 12		14 19
Barnes	d			13 22	13 27	13 35				13 42			13 52	13 57	14 05				14 12			14 22
Barnes Bridge	d				13 29					13 44				13 59					14 14			
Chiswick	d				13 32					13 47				14 02					14 17			
Kew Bridge	d				13 35					13 50				14 05					14 20			
Brentford	d				13 38					13 53				14 08					14 23			
Syon Lane	d				13 40					13 55				14 10					14 25			
Isleworth	d				13 42					13 57				14 12					14 27			
Hounslow	d				13 48					14 01				14 18					14 31			
Mortlake	d			13 24		13 37							13 54		14 07							14 24
North Sheen	d			13 26		13 39		←					13 56		14 09		←					14 26
Richmond ⊖	d	13 18		13 29		13 42	13 36	13 42			13 48		13 59		14 12	14 06	14 12			14 18		14 29
St Margarets	d			13 31		→		13 44					14 01		→		14 14					14 31
Twickenham	a	13 21		13 33			13 40	13 46			13 51		14 03			14 10	14 16			14 21		14 33
	d	13 22		13 34			13 40	13 47			13 52		14 04			14 10	14 17			14 22		14 34
Strawberry Hill	d			13 37									14 07									14 37
Fulwell	a																					
Teddington	a			13 40									14 10									14 40
Hampton Wick	a			13 44									14 14									14 44
Kingston	a			13 46									14 16									14 46
Whitton	d	13 25	←		13a53			13a50			13 55	←		14a23			14a20			14 25	←	
Feltham	d	13 29	13 36				13 46			14 06	13 59	14 06				14 16			14 36	14 29	14 36	
Ashford (Surrey)	d	13 33	13 40							→	14 03	14 10							→	14 33	14 40	
Staines	d	13 37	13 44				13 53				14 07	14 14				14 23				14 37	14 44	
Wraysbury	d	13 41									14 11									14 41		
Sunnymeads	d	13 44									14 14									14 44		
Datchet	d	13 47									14 17									14 47		
Windsor & Eton Riverside	a	13 51									14 21									14 51		
Egham	d		13 49				13 57					14 19				14 27					14 49	
Virginia Water	a		13 53				14 01					14 23				14 31					14 53	
	d		13 53				14 01					14 23				14 31					14 53	
Chertsey	d		13 59									14 29									14 59	
Addlestone	d		14 02									14 32									15 02	
Weybridge	a		14 07									14 37									15 07	
Byfleet & New Haw	d																					
West Byfleet	d																					
Woking	a																					
Longcross	d																					
Sunningdale	d						14 07									14 37						
Ascot ■	d						14 13		14 23							14 43		14 53				
Bagshot	d								14 29									14 59				
Camberley	a								14 35									15 05				
Frimley	d								14 43									15 13				
Ash Vale	d								14 49									15 19				
Aldershot	a								14 54									15 24				
	d								15 08									15 38				
Ash ■	d								15 15									15 45				
Wanborough	d								15 18									15 48				
Guildford	a								15 25									15 55				
Martins Heron	d						14 17									14 47						
Bracknell	d						14 20									14 50						
Wokingham	d						14 27									14 57						
Winnersh	d						14 30									15 00						
Winnersh Triangle	d						14 32									15 02						
Earley	d						14 35									15 05						
Reading ■	a						14 40									15 10						

Table 149

Mondays to Fridays
until 5 October

London - Hounslow, Richmond, Kingston, Windsor, Weybridge, Ascot, Guildford and Reading

Network Diagram - see first Page of Table 148

		SW	SW	SW ■	SW	SW ■	SW	SW	SW	SW	SW	SW	SW ■	SW	SW ■	SW	SW	SW	SW	SW	SW	SW ■	SW
London Waterloo 15 ⊖	d	14 07	14 15	14 20			14 22	14 28		14 33	14 37	14 45	14 50			14 52	14 58		15 03	15 07	15 15	15 20	
Vauxhall ⊖	d	14 11	14 19				14 26	14 32		14 37	14 41	14 49				14 56	15 02		15 07	15 11	15 19		
Queenstown Rd.(Battersea)	d	14 14	14 22				14 29			14 40	14 44	14 52				14 59			15 10	15 14	15 22		
Clapham Junction 10	d	14 17	14 25	14 28			14 32	14 38		14 43	14 47	14 55	14 58			15 02	15 08		15 13	15 17	15 25	15 28	
Wandsworth Town	d	14 20	14 28				14 35			14 46	14 50	14 58				15 05			15 16	15 20	15 28		
Putney	d	14 23	14 31				14 38	14 42		14 49	14 53	15 01				15 08	15 12		15 19	15 23	15 31		
Barnes	d	14 27	14 35				14 42			14 52	14 57	15 05				15 12			15 22	15 27	15 35		
Barnes Bridge	d	14 29					14 44				14 59					15 14				15 29			
Chiswick	d	14 32					14 47				15 02					15 17				15 32			
Kew Bridge	d	14 35					14 50				15 05					15 20				15 35			
Brentford	d	14 38					14 53				15 08					15 23				15 38			
Syon Lane	d	14 40					14 55				15 10					15 25				15 40			
Isleworth	d	14 42					14 57				15 12					15 27				15 42			
Hounslow	d	14 48					15 01				15 18					15 31				15 48			
Mortlake	d		14 37							14 54		15 07							15 24		15 37		
North Sheen	d		14 39		←					14 56		15 09		←					15 26		15 39		←
Richmond ⊖	d		14 42	14 36	14 42			14 48		14 59		15 12	15 06	15 12			15 18		15 29		15 42	15 36	15 42
St Margarets	d		→		14 44					15 01		→		15 14					15 31		→		15 44
Twickenham	a			14 40	14 46			14 51		15 03			15 10	15 16			15 21		15 33			15 40	15 46
	d			14 40	14 47			14 52		15 04			15 10	15 17			15 22		15 34			15 40	15 47
Strawberry Hill	d									15 07									15 37				
Fulwell	a																						
Teddington	a									15 10									15 40				
Hampton Wick	a									15 14									15 44				
Kingston	a									15 16									15 46				
Whitton	d	14a53			14a50			14 55	←		15a23			15a20			15 25	←		15a53			15a50
Feltham	d			14 46			15 06	14 59	15 06				15 16			15 36	15 29	15 36				15 46	
Ashford (Surrey)	d						→	15 03	15 10							→	15 33	15 40					
Staines	d			14 53				15 07	15 14				15 23				15 37	15 44				15 53	
Wraysbury	d							15 11									15 41						
Sunnymeads	d							15 14									15 44						
Datchet	d							15 17									15 47						
Windsor & Eton Riverside	a							15 21									15 51						
Egham	d			14 57					15 19				15 27					15 49				15 57	
Virginia Water	a			15 01					15 23				15 31					15 53				16 01	
	d			15 01					15 23				15 31					15 53				16 01	
Chertsey	d								15 29									15 59					
Addlestone	d								15 32									16 02					
Weybridge	a								15 37									16 07					
Byfleet & New Haw	d																						
West Byfleet	d																						
Woking	a																						
Longcross	d																						
Sunningdale	d			15 07									15 37									16 07	
Ascot 3	d			15 13		15 23							15 43		15 53							16 13	
Bagshot	d					15 29									15 59								
Camberley	a					15 35									16 05								
Frimley	d					15 43									16 13								
Ash Vale	d					15 49									16 19								
Aldershot	a					15 54									16 24								
	d					16 08									16 38								
Ash 5	d					16 15									16 45								
Wanborough	d					16 18									16 48								
Guildford	a					16 25									16 55								
Martins Heron	d			15 17									15 47									16 17	
Bracknell	d			15 20									15 50									16 20	
Wokingham	d			15 27									15 57									16 27	
Winnersh	d			15 30									16 00									16 30	
Winnersh Triangle	d			15 32									16 02									16 32	
Earley	d			15 35									16 05									16 35	
Reading 7	a			15 40									16 10									16 40	

Table 149

Mondays to Fridays
until 5 October

London - Hounslow, Richmond, Kingston, Windsor, Weybridge, Ascot, Guildford and Reading

Network Diagram - see first Page of Table 148

		SW ■	SW	SW	SW	SW	SW	SW	SW ■	SW	SW ■	SW	SW	SW	SW ◇■	SW	SW	SW	SW	SW ◇■	SW	SW ■
London Waterloo 15 ⊖	d		15 22	15 28		15 33	15 37	15 45	15 50			15 52	15 58	16 01	16 05			16 07	16 15	16 20		
Vauxhall ⊖	d		15 26	15 32		15 37	15 41	15 49				15 56	16 02	16 05	16 09			16 11	16 19			
Queenstown Rd.(Battersea)	d		15 29			15 40	15 44	15 52				15 59		16 08				16 14	16 22			
Clapham Junction 10	d		15 32	15 38		15 43	15 47	15 55	15 58			16 02	16 08	16 11	16 15			16 17	16 25	16 28		
Wandsworth Town	d		15 35			15 46	15 50	15 58				16 05		16 14				16 20	16 28			
Putney	d		15 38	15 42		15 49	15 53	16 01				16 08	16 12	16 17				16 23	16 31			
Barnes	d		15 42			15 52	15 57	16 05				16 12		16 22				16 27	16 35			
Barnes Bridge	d		15 44				15 59					16 14						16 29				
Chiswick	d		15 47				16 02					16 17						16 32				
Kew Bridge	d		15 50				16 05					16 20						16 35				
Brentford	d		15 53				16 08					16 23						16 38				
Syon Lane	d		15 55				16 10					16 25						16 40				
Isleworth	d		15 57				16 12					16 27						16 42				
Hounslow	d		16 01				16 18					16 31						16 48				
Mortlake	d					15 54		16 07						16 24					16 37			
North Sheen	d					15 56		16 09		←				16 26			←		16 39		←	
Richmond ⊖	d			15 48		15 59		16 12	16 06	16 12			16 18	16 29	16 23		16 29		16 42	16 36	16 42	
St Margarets	d					16 01		→		16 14				→			16 31		→		16 44	
Twickenham	a			15 51		16 03			16 10	16 16			16 21		16 27		16 33			16 40	16 46	
	d			15 52		16 04			16 10	16 17			16 22		16 27		16 34			16 40	16 47	
Strawberry Hill	d					16 07											16 37					
Fulwell	a																					
Teddington	a					16 10											16 42					
Hampton Wick	a					16 14											16 46					
Kingston	a					16 16											16 48					
Whitton	d			15 55	←		16a23			16a20			16 25			←		16a53			16a50	
Feltham	d		16 06	15 59	16 06				16 16			16 36	16 29		16 33	16 36				16 46		
Ashford (Surrey)	d		→	16 03	16 10							→	16 33		16 37	16 40						
Staines	d			16 07	16 14				16 23				16 37		16 41	16 44				16 53		
Wraysbury	d			16 11									16 41									
Sunnymeads	d			16 14									16 44									
Datchet	d			16 17									16 47									
Windsor & Eton Riverside	a			16 21									16 51									
Egham	d				16 19				16 27						16 46	16 49				16 57		
Virginia Water	a				16 23				16 31						16 50	16 53				17 01		
	d				16 23				16 31						16 50	16 53				17 01		
Chertsey	d				16 29											16 59						
Addlestone	d				16 32											17 02						
Weybridge	a				16 37											17 07						
Byfleet & New Haw	d																					
West Byfleet	d																					
Woking	a																					
Longcross	d																					
Sunningdale	d								16 37						16 55					17 07		
Ascot 3	d	16 23							16 43		16 53				17 00					17 13		17 23
Bagshot	d	16 29									16 59											17 29
Camberley	a	16 35									17 05											17 35
Frimley	d	16 43									17 13											17 43
Ash Vale	d	16 49									17 19											17 49
Aldershot	a	16 54									17 24											17 54
	d	17 08									17 38											18 08
Ash 5	d	17 15									17 45											18 15
Wanborough	d	17 18									17 48											18 18
Guildford	a	17 25									17 55											18 25
Martins Heron	d								16 47						17 04					17 17		
Bracknell	d								16 50						17 07					17 20		
Wokingham	d								16 57						17 17					17 27		
Winnersh	d								17 00											17 30		
Winnersh Triangle	d								17 02											17 32		
Earley	d								17 05											17 35		
Reading 7	a								17 10						17 27					17 42		

Table 149

Mondays to Fridays
until 5 October

London - Hounslow, Richmond, Kingston, Windsor, Weybridge, Ascot, Guildford and Reading

Network Diagram - see first Page of Table 148

		SW	SW	SW	SW	SW	SW	SW	SW	SW	SW	SW	SW	SW	SW	SW	SW	SW	SW	SW	SW	SW	SW
		◇	◇		◇ 1	◇				◇ 1		◇	◇		◇ 1	◇					◇ 1		◇
London Waterloo [15] ⊖	d	16 22	16 28	16 31	16 35			16 37	16 45	16 50		16 52	16 58	17 01	17 05			17 07	17 13	17 15	17 20		17 22
Vauxhall ⊖	d	16 26	16 32	16 35	16 39			16 41	16 49			16 56	17 02	17 05	17 09			17 11	17 17	17 19			17 26
Queenstown Rd.(Battersea)	d	16 29		16 38				16 44	16 52			16 59		17 08				17 14		17 22			17 29
Clapham Junction [10]	d	16 32	16 38	16 41	16 45			16 47	16 55	16 58		17 02	17 08	17 11	17 15			17 17	17 23	17 25	17 28		17 32
Wandsworth Town	d	16 35		16 44				16 50	16 58			17 05		17 14				17 20		17 28			17 35
Putney	d	16 38	16 42	16 47				16 53	17 01			17 08	17 12	17 17				17 23	17 27	17 31			17 38
Barnes	d	16 42		16 52				16 57	17 05			17 12		17 22				17 27		17 35			17 42
Barnes Bridge	d	16 44						16 59				17 14						17 29					17 44
Chiswick	d	16 47						17 02				17 17						17 32					17 47
Kew Bridge	d	16 50						17 05				17 20						17 35					17 50
Brentford	d	16 53						17 08				17 23						17 38					17 53
Syon Lane	d	16 55						17 10				17 25						17 40					17 55
Isleworth	d	16 57						17 12				17 27						17 42					17 57
Hounslow	d	17 01						17 18				17 31						17 48					18 01
Mortlake	d			16 54					17 07					17 24						17 37			
North Sheen	d			16 56			←		17 09		←			17 26			←			17 39		←	
Richmond ⊖	d		16 48	16 59	16 53		16 59		17 12	17 06	17 12		17 18	17 29	17 23		17 29		17 33	17 42	17 36	17 42	
St Margarets	d			→			17 01		→		17 14			→			17 31			→		17 44	
Twickenham	a		16 51		16 57		17 03			17 10	17 16		17 21		17 27		17 33		17 37		17 40	17 46	
	d		16 52		16 57		17 04			17 10	17 17		17 22		17 27		17 34		17 37		17 40	17 47	
Strawberry Hill	d						17 07										17 37		17 41				
Fulwell	a																						
Teddington	a						17 12										17 42		17 46				
Hampton Wick	a						17 16										17 46		17 54				
Kingston	a						17 18										17 48		17 56				
Whitton	d		16 55			←		17a23			17a20		17 25			←		17a53				17a50	
Feltham	d	17 06	16 59		17 03	17 06				17 16		17 36	17 29		17 33	17 36					17 46		18 06
Ashford (Surrey)	d	→	17 03		17 07	17 10						→	17 33		17 37	17 40							→
Staines	d		17 07		17 11	17 14				17 23			17 37		17 41	17 44					17 53		
Wraysbury	d		17 11										17 41										
Sunnymeads	d		17 14										17 44										
Datchet	d		17 17										17 47										
Windsor & Eton Riverside	a		17 23										17 53										
Egham	d				17 16	17 19				17 27					17 46	17 49					17 57		
Virginia Water	a				17 20	17 23				17 31					17 50	17 53					18 01		
	d				17 20	17 23				17 31					17 50	17 53					18 01		
Chertsey	d					17 29										17 59							
Addlestone	d					17 32										18 02							
Weybridge	a					17 40										18 10							
Byfleet & New Haw	d																						
West Byfleet	d																						
Woking	a																						
Longcross	d				17 23																		
Sunningdale	d				17 27					17 37					17 55						18 07		
Ascot [3]	d				17 31					17 43					18 01						18 13		
Bagshot	d														18 07								
Camberley	a														18 13								
Frimley	d														18 17								
Ash Vale	d														18 24								
Aldershot	a														18 31								
	d																						
Ash [5]	d																						
Wanborough	d																						
Guildford	a																						
Martins Heron	d				17 35					17 47											18 17		
Bracknell	d				17 39					17 50											18 20		
Wokingham	d				17 47					17 57											18 27		
Winnersh	d									18 00											18 30		
Winnersh Triangle	d									18 02											18 32		
Earley	d									18 05											18 35		
Reading [7]	a				17 58					18 12											18 42		

Table 149

Mondays to Fridays
until 5 October

London - Hounslow, Richmond, Kingston, Windsor, Weybridge, Ascot, Guildford and Reading

Network Diagram - see first Page of Table 148

		SW	SW	SW	SW	SW	SW	SW	SW	SW	SW	SW	SW	SW	SW	SW	SW	SW	SW	SW	SW	SW	SW
		1	◇	1	1		◇ 1	◇					◇ 1		◇	◇		◇ 1	◇				
London Waterloo [15] ⊖	d	17 25	17 28			17 31	17 35			17 37	17 43	17 45	17 50		17 52	17 58	18 01	18 05			18 07	18 13	18 15
Vauxhall ⊖	d		17 32			17 35	17 39			17 41	17 47	17 49			17 56	18 02	18 05	18 09			18 11	18 17	18 19
Queenstown Rd.(Battersea)	d					17 38				17 44		17 52			17 59		18 08				18 14		18 22
Clapham Junction [10]	d		17 38			17 41	17 45			17 47	17 53	17 55	17 58		18 02	18 08	18 11	18 15			18 17	18 23	18 25
Wandsworth Town	d					17 44				17 50		17 58			18 05		18 14				18 20		18 28
Putney	d		17 42			17 47				17 53	17 57	18 01			18 08	18 12	18 17				18 23	18 27	18 31
Barnes	d					17 52				17 57		18 05			18 12		18 22				18 27		18 35
Barnes Bridge	d									17 59					18 14						18 29		
Chiswick	d									18 02					18 17						18 32		
Kew Bridge	d									18 05					18 20						18 35		
Brentford	d									18 08					18 23						18 38		
Syon Lane	d									18 10					18 25						18 40		
Isleworth	d									18 12					18 27						18 42		
Hounslow	d									18 18					18 31						18 48		
Mortlake	d					17 54						18 07					18 24						18 37
North Sheen	d					17 56			←			18 09		←			18 26			←			18 39
Richmond ⊖	d		17 48			17 59	17 53		17 59		18 03	18 12	18 06	18 12		18 18	18 29	18 23		18 29		18 33	18 42
St Margarets	d					→			18 01			→		18 14			→			18 31			→
Twickenham	a		17 51				17 57		18 03		18 07		18 10	18 16		18 21		18 27		18 33		18 37	
	d		17 52				17 57		18 04		18 07		18 10	18 17		18 22		18 27		18 34		18 37	
Strawberry Hill	d								18 07		18 11									18 37		18 41	
Fulwell	a										18 13											18 43	
Teddington	a								18 12											18 42			
Hampton Wick	a								18 16											18 46			
Kingston	a								18 18											18 48			
Whitton	d		17 55					←		18a23				18a20		18 25			←		18a53		
Feltham	d		17 59				18 03	18 06					18 16		18 36	18 29		18 33	18 36				
Ashford (Surrey)	d		18 03				18 07	18 10							→	18 33		18 37	18 40				
Staines	d		18 07				18 11	18 14					18 23			18 37		18 41	18 44				
Wraysbury	d		18 11													18 41							
Sunnymeads	d		18 14													18 44							
Datchet	d		18 17													18 47							
Windsor & Eton Riverside	a		18 23													18 53							
Egham	d						18 16	18 19					18 27					18 46	18 49				
Virginia Water	a						18 20	18 23					18 31					18 50	18 53				
	d						18 20	18 23					18 31					18 50	18 53				
Chertsey	d							18 29											18 59				
Addlestone	d							18 32											19 02				
Weybridge	a							18 40											19 10				
Byfleet & New Haw	d																						
West Byfleet	d																						
Woking	a	17 50																					
Longcross	d												18 35										
Sunningdale	d						18 25						18 37					18 55					
Ascot [3]	d				18 23		18 30						18 43					19 02					
Bagshot	d				18 29													19 08					
Camberley	a				18 35													19 14					
Frimley	d				18 43													19 19					
Ash Vale	d	18 03			18 49													19 26					
Aldershot	a	18 08			18 54													19 34					
	d			18 38	19 08																		
Ash [5]	d			18 45	19 15																		
Wanborough	d			18 48	19 18																		
Guildford	a			18 55	19 25																		
Martins Heron	d						18 34						18 47										
Bracknell	d						18 37						18 50										
Wokingham	d						18 47						18 57										
Winnersh	d												19 00										
Winnersh Triangle	d												19 02										
Earley	d												19 05										
Reading [7]	a						18 57						19 12										

Table 149

Mondays to Fridays

until 5 October

London - Hounslow, Richmond, Kingston, Windsor, Weybridge, Ascot, Guildford and Reading

Network Diagram - see first Page of Table 148

		SW ◇1	SW	SW ◇	SW 1	SW ◇	SW 1	SW 1	SW	SW ◇1	SW ◇	SW	SW	SW	SW	SW ◇1	SW	SW 1	SW ◇	SW ◇	SW	SW 1
London Waterloo 15 ⊖	d	18 20		18 22	18 25	18 28			18 31	18 35			18 37	18 43	18 45	18 50			18 52	18 58	19 01	19 05
Vauxhall ⊖	d			18 26		18 32			18 35	18 39			18 41	18 47	18 49				18 56	19 02	19 05	19 09
Queenstown Rd.(Battersea)	d			18 29					18 38				18 44		18 52				18 59		19 08	
Clapham Junction 10	d	18 28		18 32		18 38			18 41	18 45			18 47	18 53	18 55	18 58			19 02	19 08	19 11	19 15
Wandsworth Town	d			18 35					18 44				18 50		18 58				19 05		19 14	
Putney	d			18 38		18 42			18 47				18 53	18 57	19 01				19 08	19 12	19 17	
Barnes	d			18 42					18 52				18 57		19 05				19 12		19 22	
Barnes Bridge	d			18 44									18 59						19 14			
Chiswick	d			18 47									19 02						19 17			
Kew Bridge	d			18 50									19 05						19 20			
Brentford	d			18 53									19 08						19 23			
Syon Lane	d			18 55									19 10						19 25			
Isleworth	d			18 57									19 12						19 27			
Hounslow	d			19 01									19 18						19 31			
Mortlake	d								18 54						19 07						19 24	
North Sheen	d		←						18 56			←			19 09		←				19 26	
Richmond ⊖	d	18 36	18 42			18 48			18 59	18 53		18 59		19 03	19 12	19 06	19 12			19 18	19 29	19 23
St Margarets	d		18 44						→			19 01			→		19 14				→	
Twickenham	a	18 40	18 46			18 51				18 57		19 03		19 07		19 10	19 16			19 21		19 27
	d	18 40	18 47			18 52				18 57		19 04		19 07		19 10	19 17			19 22		19 27
Strawberry Hill	d											19 07		19 11								
Fulwell	a													19 13								
Teddington	a											19 12										
Hampton Wick	a											19 16										
Kingston	a											19 18										
Whitton	d		18a50			18 55					←		19a23				19a20			19 25		
Feltham	d	18 46		19 06		18 59				19 03	19 06					19 16			19 36	19 29		19 33
Ashford (Surrey)	d			→		19 03				19 07	19 10								→	19 33		19 37
Staines	d	18 53				19 07				19 11	19 14					19 23				19 37		19 41
Wraysbury	d					19 11														19 41		
Sunnymeads	d					19 14														19 44		
Datchet	d					19 17														19 47		
Windsor & Eton Riverside	a					19 23														19 53		
Egham	d	18 57								19 16	19 19					19 27						19 46
Virginia Water	a	19 01								19 20	19 23					19 31						19 50
	d	19 01								19 20	19 23					19 31						19 50
Chertsey	d										19 29											
Addlestone	d										19 32											
Weybridge	a										19 40											
Byfleet & New Haw	d																					
West Byfleet	d																					
Woking	a				18 52																	
Longcross	d																					
Sunningdale	d	19 07								19 25						19 37						19 55
Ascot 3	d	19 13						19 23		19 30						19 43		19 53				20 00
Bagshot	d							19 29										19 59				
Camberley	a							19 35										20 05				
Frimley	d							19 43										20 13				
Ash Vale	d				19 05			19 49										20 19				
Aldershot	a				19 10			19 54										20 24				
	d						19 38	20 08										20 38				
Ash 5	d						19 45	20 15										20 45				
Wanborough	d						19 48	20 18										20 48				
Guildford	a						19 55	20 25										20 55				
Martins Heron	d	19 17								19 34						19 47						20 04
Bracknell	d	19 20								19 37						19 50						20 07
Wokingham	d	19 27								19 47						19 57						20 17
Winnersh	d	19 30														20 00						
Winnersh Triangle	d	19 32														20 02						
Earley	d	19 35														20 05						
Reading 7	a	19 42								19 57						20 12						20 25

Table 149

Mondays to Fridays

until 5 October

London - Hounslow, Richmond, Kingston, Windsor, Weybridge, Ascot, Guildford and Reading

Network Diagram - see first Page of Table 148

		SW ◇	SW	SW	SW	SW 1	SW	SW 1	SW	SW	SW	SW	SW	SW	SW 1	SW	SW 1	SW	SW	SW	SW	SW	SW
London Waterloo 15 ⊖	d			19 07	19 15	19 20			19 22	19 28		19 33	19 37	19 45	19 50			19 52	19 58		20 03	20 07	20 15
Vauxhall ⊖	d			19 11	19 19				19 26	19 32		19 37	19 41	19 49				19 56	20 02		20 07	20 11	20 19
Queenstown Rd.(Battersea)	d			19 14	19 22				19 29			19 40	19 44	19 52				19 59			20 10	20 14	20 22
Clapham Junction 10	d			19 17	19 25	19 28			19 32	19 38		19 43	19 47	19 55	19 58			20 02	20 08		20 13	20 17	20 25
Wandsworth Town	d			19 20	19 28				19 35			19 46	19 50	19 58				20 05			20 16	20 20	20 28
Putney	d			19 23	19 31				19 38	19 42		19 49	19 53	20 01				20 08	20 12		20 19	20 23	20 31
Barnes	d			19 27	19 35				19 42			19 52	19 57	20 05				20 12			20 22	20 27	20 35
Barnes Bridge	d			19 29					19 44				19 59					20 14				20 29	
Chiswick	d			19 32					19 47				20 02					20 17				20 32	
Kew Bridge	d			19 35					19 50				20 05					20 20				20 35	
Brentford	d			19 38					19 53				20 08					20 23				20 38	
Syon Lane	d			19 40					19 55				20 10					20 25				20 40	
Isleworth	d			19 42					19 57				20 12					20 27				20 42	
Hounslow	d			19 48					20 01				20 18					20 31				20 48	
Mortlake	d				19 37							19 54		20 07							20 24		20 37
North Sheen	d		←		19 39		←					19 56		20 09		←					20 26		20 39
Richmond ⊖	d		19 29		19 42	19 36	19 42			19 48		19 59		20 12	20 06	20 12			20 18		20 29		20 42
St Margarets	d		19 31		→		19 44					20 01		→		20 14					20 31		→
Twickenham	a		19 33			19 40	19 46			19 51		20 03			20 10	20 16			20 21		20 33		
	d		19 34			19 40	19 47			19 52		20 04			20 10	20 17			20 22		20 34		
Strawberry Hill	d		19 37									20 07									20 37		
Fulwell	a																						
Teddington	a		19 42									20 10									20 40		
Hampton Wick	a		19 46									20 14									20 44		
Kingston	a		19 48									20 16									20 46		
Whitton	d	←		19a53			19a50			19 55	←		20a23			20a20			20 25	←		20a53	
Feltham	d	19 36				19 46			20 06	19 59	20 06				20 16			20 36	20 29	20 36			
Ashford (Surrey)	d	19 40							→	20 03	20 10							→	20 33	20 40			
Staines	d	19 44				19 53				20 07	20 14				20 23				20 37	20 44			
Wraysbury	d									20 11									20 41				
Sunnymeads	d									20 14									20 44				
Datchet	d									20 17									20 47				
Windsor & Eton Riverside	a									20 21									20 51				
Egham	d	19 49				19 57					20 19				20 27					20 49			
Virginia Water	a	19 53				20 01					20 23				20 31					20 53			
	d	19 53				20 01					20 23				20 31					20 53			
Chertsey	d	19 59									20 29									20 59			
Addlestone	d	20 02									20 32									21 02			
Weybridge	a	20 10									20 37									21 07			
Byfleet & New Haw	d																						
West Byfleet	d																						
Woking	a																						
Longcross	d																						
Sunningdale	d					20 07									20 37								
Ascot 3	d					20 13		20 23							20 43		20 53						
Bagshot	d							20 29									20 59						
Camberley	a							20 35									21 05						
Frimley	d							20 43									21 13						
Ash Vale	d							20 49									21 19						
Aldershot	a							20 54									21 24						
	d							21 08									21 38						
Ash 5	d							21 15									21 45						
Wanborough	d							21 18									21 48						
Guildford	a							21 25									21 55						
Martins Heron	d					20 17									20 47								
Bracknell	d					20 20									20 50								
Wokingham	d					20 27									20 57								
Winnersh	d					20 30									21 00								
Winnersh Triangle	d					20 32									21 02								
Earley	d					20 35									21 05								
Reading 7	a					20 40									21 10								

Table 149

Mondays to Fridays
until 5 October

London - Hounslow, Richmond, Kingston, Windsor, Weybridge, Ascot, Guildford and Reading

Network Diagram - see first Page of Table 148

		SW [1]	SW	SW [1]	SW [1]	SW	SW	SW	SW	SW	SW	SW [1]	SW	SW	SW	SW	SW	SW	SW	SW [1]	SW	SW [1]
London Waterloo [15] ⊖	d	20 20				20 22	20 28		20 33	20 37	20 45	20 50		20 52	20 58		21 03	21 07	21 15	21 20		
Vauxhall ⊖	d					20 26	20 32		20 37	20 41	20 49			20 56	21 02		21 07	21 11	21 19			
Queenstown Rd.(Battersea)	d					20 29			20 40	20 44	20 52			20 59			21 10	21 14	21 22			
Clapham Junction [10]	d	20 28				20 32	20 38		20 43	20 47	20 55	20 58		21 02	21 08		21 13	21 17	21 25	21 28		
Wandsworth Town	d					20 35			20 46	20 50	20 58			21 05			21 16	21 20	21 28			
Putney	d					20 38	20 42		20 49	20 53	21 01			21 08	21 12		21 19	21 23	21 31			
Barnes	d					20 42			20 52	20 57	21 05			21 12			21 22	21 27	21 35			
Barnes Bridge	d					20 44				20 59				21 14				21 29				
Chiswick	d					20 47				21 02				21 17				21 32				
Kew Bridge	d					20 50				21 05				21 20				21 35				
Brentford	d					20 53				21 08				21 23				21 38				
Syon Lane	d					20 55				21 10				21 25				21 40				
Isleworth	d					20 57				21 12				21 27				21 42				
Hounslow	d					21 01				21 18				21 31				21 48				
Mortlake	d								20 54		21 07						21 24		21 37			
North Sheen	d		←						20 56		21 09		←				21 26		21 39		←	
Richmond ⊖	d	20 36	20 42				20 48		20 59		21 12	21 06	21 12		21 18		21 29		21 42	21 36	21 42	
St Margarets	d		20 44						21 01		→		21 14				21 31		→		21 44	
Twickenham	a	20 40	20 46				20 51		21 03			21 10	21 16		21 21		21 33			21 40	21 46	
	d	20 40	20 47				20 52		21 04			21 10	21 17		21 22		21 34			21 40	21 47	
Strawberry Hill	d								21 07								21 37					
Fulwell	a																					
Teddington	a								21 10								21 40					
Hampton Wick	a								21 14								21 44					
Kingston	a								21 16								21 46					
Whitton	d		20a50				20 55	←		21a23			21a20		21 25	←		21a53			21a50	
Feltham	d	20 46				21 06	20 59	21 06				21 16		21 36	21 29	21 36				21 46		
Ashford (Surrey)	d					→	21 03	21 10						→	21 33	21 40						
Staines	d	20 53					21 07	21 14				21 23			21 37	21 44				21 53		
Wraysbury	d						21 11								21 41							
Sunnymeads	d						21 14								21 44							
Datchet	d						21 17								21 47							
Windsor & Eton Riverside	a						21 21								21 51							
Egham	d	20 57						21 19				21 27				21 49				21 57		
Virginia Water	a	21 01						21 23				21 31				21 53				22 01		
	d	21 01						21 23				21 31				21 53				22 01		
Chertsey	d							21 29								21 59						
Addlestone	d							21 32								22 02						
Weybridge	a							21 37								22 07						
Byfleet & New Haw	d																					
West Byfleet	d																					
Woking	a																					
Longcross	d																					
Sunningdale	d	21 07										21 37								22 07		
Ascot [3]	d	21 13		21 23								21 43								22 13		22 23
Bagshot	d			21 29																		22 29
Camberley	a			21 35																		22 35
Frimley	d			21 43																		22 43
Ash Vale	d			21 49																		22 49
Aldershot	a			21 54																		22 54
	d			22 08	22 38																	23 08
Ash [5]	d			22 15	22 45																	23 15
Wanborough	d			22 18	22 48																	23 18
Guildford	a			22 25	22 55																	23 25
Martins Heron	d	21 17										21 47								22 17		
Bracknell	d	21 20										21 50								22 20		
Wokingham	d	21 27										21 57								22 27		
Winnersh	d	21 30										22 00								22 30		
Winnersh Triangle	d	21 32										22 02								22 32		
Earley	d	21 35										22 05								22 35		
Reading [7]	a	21 40										22 10								22 40		

Table 149

Mondays to Fridays
until 5 October

London - Hounslow, Richmond, Kingston, Windsor, Weybridge, Ascot, Guildford and Reading

Network Diagram - see first Page of Table 148

		SW	SW	SW	SW	SW	SW	SW [1]	SW	SW	SW	SW	SW	SW [1]	SW [1]	SW	SW	SW	SW	SW [1]	SW	SW	SW
London Waterloo [15] ⊖	d	21 22	21 28		21 33	21 37	21 45	21 50		21 52	21 58		22 03	22 20		22 22	22 28		22 33	22 50	22 52	22 58	
Vauxhall ⊖	d	21 26	21 32		21 37	21 41	21 49			21 56	22 02		22 07			22 26	22 32		22 37		22 56	23 02	
Queenstown Rd.(Battersea)	d	21 29			21 40	21 44	21 52			21 59			22 10			22 29			22 40		22 59		
Clapham Junction [10]	d	21 32	21 38		21 43	21 47	21 55	21 58		22 02	22 08		22 13	22 28		22 32	22 38		22 43	22 58	23 02	23 08	
Wandsworth Town	d	21 35			21 46	21 50	21 58			22 05			22 16			22 35			22 46		23 05		
Putney	d	21 38	21 42		21 49	21 53	22 01			22 08	22 12		22 19			22 38	22 42		22 49		23 08	23 12	
Barnes	d	21 42			21 52	21 57	22 05			22 12			22 22			22 42			22 52		23 12		
Barnes Bridge	d	21 44				21 59				22 14						22 44					23 14		
Chiswick	d	21 47				22 02				22 17						22 47					23 17		
Kew Bridge	d	21 50				22 05				22 20						22 50					23 20		
Brentford	d	21 53				22 08				22 23						22 53					23 23		
Syon Lane	d	21 55				22 10				22 25						22 55					23 25		
Isleworth	d	21 57				22 12				22 27						22 57					23 27		
Hounslow	d	22 01				22 18				22 31						23 01					23 31		
Mortlake	d				21 54		22 07						22 24						22 54				
North Sheen	d				21 56		22 09		←				22 26						22 56				
Richmond ⊖	d		21 48		21 59		22 12	22 06	22 12		22 18		22 29	22 36			22 48		22 59	23 06		23 18	
St Margarets	d				22 01		→		22 14				22 31						23 01				
Twickenham	a		21 51		22 03			22 10	22 16		22 21		22 33	22 40			22 51		23 03	23 10		23 21	
	d		21 52		22 04			22 10			22 22		22 34	22 40			22 52		23 04	23 10		23 22	
Strawberry Hill	d				22 07								22 37						23 07				
Fulwell	a																						
Teddington	a				22 10								22 40						23 10				
Hampton Wick	a				22 14								22 44						23 14				
Kingston	a				22 16								22 46						23 16				
Whitton	d		21 55	←		22a23					22 25	←					22 55	←				23 25	←
Feltham	d	22 06	21 59	22 06				22 16		22 36	22 29	22 36		22 46		23 06	22 59	23 06		23 16	23 36	23 29	23 36
Ashford (Surrey)	d	→	22 03	22 10						→	22 33	22 40				→	23 03	23 10			→	23 33	23 40
Staines	d		22 07	22 14				22 23			22 37	22 44		22 53			23 07	23 14		23 23		23 37	23 44
Wraysbury	d		22 11								22 41						23 11					23 41	
Sunnymeads	d		22 14								22 44						23 14					23 44	
Datchet	d		22 17								22 47						23 17					23 47	
Windsor & Eton Riverside	a		22 21								22 51						23 21					23 51	
Egham	d			22 19				22 27				22 49		22 57				23 19		23 27			23 49
Virginia Water	a			22 23				22 31				22 53		23 01				23 23		23 31			23 53
	d			22 23				22 31				22 53		23 01				23 23		23 31			23 53
Chertsey	d			22 29								22 59						23 29					23 59
Addlestone	d			22 32								23 02						23a32					00 02
Weybridge	a			22 37								23 07						23 37					
Byfleet & New Haw	d																						00 06
West Byfleet	d																						00 09
Woking	a																						00 15
Longcross	d																						
Sunningdale	d							22 37						23 07						23 37			
Ascot [3]	d							22 43						23 13	23 23					23 43			
Bagshot	d														23 29								
Camberley	a														23 35								
Frimley	d														23 43								
Ash Vale	d														23 49								
Aldershot	a														23 54								
	d																						
Ash [5]	d																						
Wanborough	d																						
Guildford	a																						
Martins Heron	d							22 47						23 17						23 47			
Bracknell	d							22 50						23 20						23 50			
Wokingham	d							22 57						23 27						23 57			
Winnersh	d							23 00						23 30						23 59			
Winnersh Triangle	d							23 02						23 32						00 02			
Earley	d							23 05						23 35						00 05			
Reading [7]	a							23 10						23 40						00 10			

Table 149

Mondays to Fridays
until 5 October

London - Hounslow, Richmond, Kingston, Windsor, Weybridge, Ascot, Guildford and Reading

Network Diagram - see first Page of Table 148

		SW	SW	SW	SW	SW	SW	SW	SW	SW	SW	SW	SW
				[1]			A			B			
London Waterloo [15] ⊖	d	23 03	23 13	23 20	23 22	23 33	23 38			23 50	23 52	23 58	
Vauxhall ⊖	d	23 07	23 17		23 26	23 37					23 56	00 02	
Queenstown Rd.(Battersea)	d	23 10			23 29	23 40					23 59		
Clapham Junction [10]	d	23 13	23 23	23 28	23 32	23 43	23 46			23 58	00 02	00 08	
Wandsworth Town	d	23 16			23 35	23 46					00 05		
Putney	d	23 19	23 27		23 38	23 49					00 08	00 12	
Barnes	d	23 22			23 42	23 52					00 12		
Barnes Bridge	d				23 44						00 14		
Chiswick	d				23 47						00 17		
Kew Bridge	d				23 50						00 20		
Brentford	d				23 53						00 23		
Syon Lane	d				23 55						00 25		
Isleworth	d				23 57						00 27		
Hounslow	d				00 01						00 31		
Mortlake	d	23 24				23 54							
North Sheen	d	23 26				23 56			←				
Richmond ⊖	d	23 29	23 33	23 37		23 59	23 54		23 59	00 06		00 18	
St Margarets	d	23 31				→			00 01				
Twickenham	a	23 33	23 36	23 41			23 58		00 03	00 10		00 21	
	d	23 34	23 37	23 41			23 58		00 04	00 10		00 22	
Strawberry Hill	d	23 37							00 07				
Fulwell	a												
Teddington	a	23 40							00 11				
Hampton Wick	a	23 44							00 14				
Kingston	a	23 46							00 16				
Whitton	d		23 40					←				00 25	←
Feltham	d		23 44	23 48	00 06		00 04	00 06		00 16	00 37	00 29	00 37
Ashford (Surrey)	d		23 48		→			00 10			→	00 33	00 41
Staines	d		23 52	23 56			00 11	00 14		00 23		00a37	00a46
Wraysbury	d		23 56										
Sunnymeads	d		23 59										
Datchet	d		00 02										
Windsor & Eton Riverside	a		00 06										
Egham	d			00 01			00 15	00 19		00 27			
Virginia Water	a			00 05			00 19	00 23		00 31			
	d			00 05			00 19	00 23		00 31			
Chertsey	d							00 29					
Addlestone	d							00a32					
Weybridge	a							00 38					
Byfleet & New Haw	d												
West Byfleet	d												
Woking	a												
Longcross	d												
Sunningdale	d			00 11			00 25			00 37			
Ascot [3]	d			00 15			00 30			00 42			
Bagshot	d												
Camberley	a												
Frimley	d												
Ash Vale	d												
Aldershot	a												
	d												
Ash [5]	d												
Wanborough	d												
Guildford	a												
Martins Heron	d			00 19			00 34			00 46			
Bracknell	d			00 23			00 37			00 49			
Wokingham	d			00 32			00 44			00 56			
Winnersh	d			00 36									
Winnersh Triangle	d			00 38									
Earley	d			00 40									
Reading [7]	a			00 45			00 52			01 04			

A not from 27 July until 10 August, from 29 August until 7 September

B from 27 July until 7 September, not from 13 August until 28 August

Table 149

Mondays to Fridays
from 8 October

London - Hounslow, Richmond, Kingston, Windsor, Weybridge, Ascot, Guildford and Reading

Network Diagram - see first Page of Table 148

		SW	SW	SW	SW	SW	SW	SW	SW	SW	SW	SW	SW	SW	SW	SW	SW	SW	SW	SW	SW	SW	SW
		MO	MX	MO	MX	MO	MX	MX	MX	MX	MX	MX	MX	MO	MX	MO	MO			MX	MX	MX	
		[1]	[1]			[1]		[1]					[1]	[1]				[1]	[1]				
London Waterloo [15] ⊖	d	22p39	22p50	22p50	22p52	23p09	23p13	23p20	23p22	23p33	23p38			23p39			23p44			23p52	23p58		00 18
Vauxhall ⊖	d	22p43		22p54	22p56	23p13	23p17		23p26	23p37				23p43			23p48			23p56	00 02		00 22
Queenstown Rd.(Battersea)	d			22p57	22p59				23p29	23p40							23p51			23p59			00 25
Clapham Junction [10]	d	22p49	22p58	23p00	23p02	23p19	23p23	23p28	23p32	23p43	23p46			23p49			23p54			00 02	00 08		00 29
Wandsworth Town	d			23p03	23p05				23p35	23p46							23p57			00 05			00 32
Putney	d	22p53		23p06	23p08	23p23	23p27		23p38	23p49				23p53			23p59			00 08	00 12		00 35
Barnes	d			23p09	23p12				23p42	23p52							00 03			00 12			00 38
Barnes Bridge	d			23p11	23p14				23p44											00 14			
Chiswick	d			23p13	23p17				23p47											00 17			
Kew Bridge	d			23p16	23p20				23p50											00 20			
Brentford	d			23p19	23p23				23p53											00 23			
Syon Lane	d			23p21	23p25				23p55											00 25			
Isleworth	d			23p23	23p27				23p57											00 27			
Hounslow	d			23p26	23p31				00 01											00 31			
Mortlake	d									23p54							00 05						00 40
North Sheen	d									23p56					←		00 07						00 42
Richmond ⊖	d	22p59	23p06			23p29	23p33	23p37		23p59	23p54			23p59	23p59		00 10				00 18		00 45
St Margarets	d									→					00 01		00 12						00 47
Twickenham	a	23p02	23p10			23p32	23p36	23p41			23p58			00 02	00 03		00 14				00 21		00 49
	d	23p03	23p10			23p33	23p37	23p41			23p58			00 03	00 04		00 15				00 22		00 50
Strawberry Hill	d														00 07								00s53
Fulwell	a																						
Teddington	a														00 11								00s56
Hampton Wick	a														00 14								00s59
Kingston	a														00 16								01 01
Whitton	d						23p40					←					00 18				00 25	←	
Feltham	d	23p09	23p16	23p32	23p36	23p39	23p44	23p48	00 06		00 04	00 06		00 09			00 22			00 37	00 29	00 37	
Ashford (Surrey)	d			23p36	23p40		23p48		→			00 10					00 26			→	00 33	00 41	
Staines	d	23p15	23p23	23p40	23p44	23p45	23p52	23p56			00 11	00 14		00 15		00 21	00a30				00a37	00a46	
Wraysbury	d						23p56																
Sunnymeads	d						23p59																
Datchet	d						00 04																
Windsor & Eton Riverside	a						00 09																
Egham	d	23p20	23p27	23p45	23p49	23p50		00 01			00 15	00 19		00 20		00s25							
Virginia Water	a	23p24	23p31	23p49	23p53	23p54		00 05			00 19	00 23		00 24		00s30							
	d	23p24	23p31	23p49	23p53	23p54		00 05			00 19	00 23		00 24									
Chertsey	d			23p55	23p59							00 29				00s35							
Addlestone	d			23p58	00 02							00a32				00s38							
Weybridge	a											00 38											
Byfleet & New Haw	d			00 02	00 06											00s42							
West Byfleet	d			00 05	00 09											00s45							
Woking	a			00 11	00 15											00 51							
Longcross	d																						
Sunningdale	d	23p29	23p37			23p59		00 11			00 25			00 29									
Ascot [3]	d	23p34	23p43			00 04		00 15			00 30		00 32	00 34									
Bagshot	d												00 38										
Camberley	a												00 44										
Frimley	d												00 48										
Ash Vale	d												00 57										
Aldershot	a												01s02										
	d																	06 08	06 38				
Ash [5]	d																	06 15	06 45				
Wanborough	d																	06 18	06 48				
Guildford	a																	06 25	06 55				
Martins Heron	d	23p38	23p47			00 08		00 19			00 34			00 38									
Bracknell	d	23p41	23p50			00 11		00 23			00 37			00 41									
Wokingham	d	23p48	23p57			00 18		00 32			00 44			00 48									
Winnersh	d	23p51	23p59			00 21		00 36						00 51									
Winnersh Triangle	d	23p53	00 02			00 23		00 38						00 53									
Earley	d	23p56	00 05			00 26		00 40						00 56									
Reading [7]	a	00 04	00 13			00 34		00 48			00 55			01 04									

Table 149

Mondays to Fridays

from 8 October

London - Hounslow, Richmond, Kingston, Windsor, Weybridge, Ascot, Guildford and Reading

Network Diagram - see first Page of Table 148

		SW	SW 1	SW	SW 1	SW		SW	SW	SW 1	SW 1	SW	SW	SW	SW	SW 1		SW	SW 1	SW	SW 1	SW	SW	SW	SW
London Waterloo 15 ⊖	d				05 05			05 33			05 50		05 58	06 03				06 15	06 20				06 22	06 28	
Vauxhall ⊖	d				05 09			05 37					06 02	06 07				06 19					06 26	06 32	
Queenstown Rd.(Battersea)	d				05 12			05 40						06 10				06 22					06 29		
Clapham Junction 10	d				05 15			05 43			05 58		06 08	06 13				06 25	06 28				06 32	06 38	
Wandsworth Town	d				05 18			05 46						06 16				06 28					06 35		
Putney	d				05 21			05 49					06 12	06 19				06 31					06 38	06 42	
Barnes	d				05 24			05 52						06 22				06 35					06 42		
Barnes Bridge	d																						06 44		
Chiswick	d																						06 47		
Kew Bridge	d																						06 50		
Brentford	d																						06 53		
Syon Lane	d																						06 55		
Isleworth	d																						06 57		
Hounslow	d																					06 48	07 01		
Mortlake	d				05 26			05 54						06 24				06 37							
North Sheen	d				05 28			05 56						06 26				06 39		←					
Richmond ⊖	d				05 31			05 59			06 06		06 18	06 29				06 42	06 36	06 42				06 48	
St Margarets	d				05 33			06 01						06 31				→		06 44					
Twickenham	a				05 35			06 03			06 10		06 21	06 33					06 40	06 46		06 56		06 51	
	d	04 52			05 36	05 53		06 05			06 10	06 17	06 22	06 34					06 40	06 47				06 52	
Strawberry Hill	d	04 55						06 08						06 37											
Fulwell	a																								
Teddington	a	04 58						06 11						06 40											
Hampton Wick	a	05 01						06 14						06 44											
Kingston	a	05 03						06 16						06 46											
Whitton	d				05 39	05 56						06a20	06 25							06a50				06 55	←
Feltham	d				05 43	06 00					06 16		06 29						06 46				07 06	06 59	07 06
Ashford (Surrey)	d				05 47	06 04							06 33										→	07 03	07 10
Staines	d		05 23	05 44	05 53	06 08			06 14		06 23		06 37		06 44				06 53					07 07	07 14
Wraysbury	d					06 13							06 42											07 12	
Sunnymeads	d					06 16							06 45											07 15	
Datchet	d					06 20							06 49											07 19	
Windsor & Eton Riverside	a					06 24							06 54											07 24	
Egham	d		05 27	05 49	05 57				06 19		06 27				06 49				06 57						07 19
Virginia Water	a		05 31	05 53	06 01				06 23		06 31				06 53				07 01						07 23
	d		05 31	05 53	06 01				06 23		06 31				06 53				07 01						07 23
Chertsey	d			05 59					06 29						06 59										07 29
Addlestone	d			06 02					06 32						07 02										07 32
Weybridge	a			06 07					06 37						07 07										07 37
Byfleet & New Haw	d																								
West Byfleet	d																								
Woking	a																								
Longcross	d										06 35								07 05						
Sunningdale	d		05 37		06 07						06 37								07 07						
Ascot 3	d		05 43		06 13					06 23	06 43					06 53			07 13		07 23				
Bagshot	d									06 29						06 59					07 29				
Camberley	a									06 35						07 05					07 35				
Frimley	d									06 43						07 13					07 43				
Ash Vale	d									06 49						07 19					07 49				
Aldershot	a									06 56						07 26					07 54				
	d									07 08						07 38					08 08				
Ash 5	d									07 15						07 45					08 15				
Wanborough	d									07 18						07 48					08 18				
Guildford	a									07 25						07 55					08 25				
Martins Heron	d		05 47		06 17						06 47								07 17						
Bracknell	d		05 50		06 20						06 50								07 20						
Wokingham	d		05 57		06 27						06 57								07 27						
Winnersh	d		06 00		06 30						07 00								07 30						
Winnersh Triangle	d		06 02		06 32						07 02								07 32						
Earley	d		06 05		06 37						07 07								07 37						
Reading 7	a		06 13		06 43						07 13								07 43						

Table 149

Mondays to Fridays

from 8 October

London - Hounslow, Richmond, Kingston, Windsor, Weybridge, Ascot, Guildford and Reading

Network Diagram - see first Page of Table 148

		SW		SW	SW 1	SW	SW 1	SW	SW	SW	SW	SW		SW	SW 1	SW	SW	SW	SW 1	SW	SW	SW		SW	SW
London Waterloo 15 ⊖	d	06 33		06 45	06 50			06 52	06 58		07 03			07 15	07 20		07 22	07 28			07 33	07 37			07 45
Vauxhall ⊖	d	06 37		06 49				06 56	07 02		07 07			07 19			07 26	07 32			07 37	07 41			07 49
Queenstown Rd.(Battersea)	d	06 40		06 52				06 59			07 10			07 22			07 29				07 40	07 44			07 52
Clapham Junction 10	d	06 43		06 55	06 58			07 02	07 08		07 13			07 25	07 28		07 32	07 38			07 43	07 47			07 55
Wandsworth Town	d	06 46		06 58				07 05			07 16			07 28			07 35				07 46	07 50			07 58
Putney	d	06 49		07 01				07 08	07 12		07 19			07 31			07 38	07 42			07 49	07 53			08 01
Barnes	d	06 52		07 05				07 12			07 22			07 35			07 42				07 52	07 57			08 05
Barnes Bridge	d							07 14									07 44					07 59			
Chiswick	d							07 17									07 47					08 02			
Kew Bridge	d							07 20									07 50					08 05			
Brentford	d							07 23									07 53					08 08			
Syon Lane	d							07 25									07 55					08 10			
Isleworth	d							07 27									07 57					08 12			
Hounslow	d							07 31									08 01					08a18			
Mortlake	d	06 54		07 07							07 24			07 37							07 54				08 07
North Sheen	d	06 56		07 09		←					07 26			07 39		←					07 56				08 09
Richmond ⊖	d	06 59		07 12	07 06	07 12			07 18		07 29			07 42	07 36	07 42		07 48	07 54		07 59				08 12
St Margarets	d	07 01		→		07 14					07 31			→		07 44					08 01				→
Twickenham	a	07 03			07 10	07 16			07 21		07 33				07 40	07 46		07 51	07 57		08 03				
	d	07 04			07 10	07 17			07 22		07 34	07 37			07 40	07 47		07 52	07 58		08 04			08 07	
Strawberry Hill	d	07 07									07 37	07 47									08 07			08 17	
Fulwell	a																								
Teddington	a	07 10									07 40	07 50									08 10			08 20	
Hampton Wick	a	07 14									07 44	07 52									08 14			08 22	
Kingston	a	07 16									07 46	07 54									08 16			08 24	
Whitton	d					07a20			07 25	←						07a50		07 55		←					
Feltham	d				07 16			07 36	07 29	07 36					07 46		08 06	07 59	08 04	08 06					
Ashford (Surrey)	d							→	07 33	07 40							→	08 03	08 08	08 10					
Staines	d				07 23				07 37	07 44					07 53			08 07	08 12	08 14					
Wraysbury	d								07 42									08 12							
Sunnymeads	d								07 45									08 15							
Datchet	d								07 49									08 19							
Windsor & Eton Riverside	a								07 54									08 24							
Egham	d				07 27					07 49					07 57				08 16	08 19					
Virginia Water	a				07 31					07 53					08 01					08 23					
	d				07 31					07 53					08 01					08 23					
Chertsey	d									07 59										08 29					
Addlestone	d									08 02										08 32					
Weybridge	a									08 07										08 38					
Byfleet & New Haw	d																								
West Byfleet	d																								
Woking	a																								
Longcross	d				07 35										08 05										
Sunningdale	d				07 37										08 07										
Ascot 3	d				07 43		07 53								08 13				08 26						
Bagshot	d						07 59												08 32						
Camberley	a						08 05												08 38						
Frimley	d						08 13												08 43						
Ash Vale	d						08 19												08 49						
Aldershot	a						08 24												08 54						
	d						08 38												09 08						
Ash 5	d						08 45												09 15						
Wanborough	d						08 48												09 18						
Guildford	a						08 55												09 25						
Martins Heron	d				07 47										08 17										
Bracknell	d				07 50										08 20										
Wokingham	d				07 57										08 27										
Winnersh	d				08 00										08 30										
Winnersh Triangle	d				08 02										08 32										
Earley	d				08 07										08 37										
Reading 7	a				08 13										08 43										

London - Hounslow, Richmond, Kingston, Windsor, Weybridge, Ascot, Guildford and Reading

Network Diagram - see first Page of Table 148

		SW ■	SW	SW ■	SW	SW	SW	SW ■	SW	SW	SW	SW	SW ■	SW	SW ■	SW	SW	SW	SW ■	SW	SW	SW	SW
London Waterloo ⊖	d	07 50			07 52	07 58	08 03	08 07			08 10	08 15	08 20			08 22	08 28	08 33	08 37			08 40	08 43
Vauxhall ⊖	d				07 56	08 02	08 07				08 14	08 19				08 26	08 32	08 37				08 44	08 47
Queenstown Rd.(Battersea)	d				07 59		08 10				08 17	08 22				08 29		08 40				08 47	08 50
Clapham Junction	d	07 58			08 02	08 08	08 13	08 16			08 20	08 25	08 28			08 32	08 38	08 43	08 45			08 50	08 55
Wandsworth Town	d				08 05		08 16				08 23	08 28				08 35		08 46				08 53	08 58
Putney	d				08 08	08 12	08 19				08 26	08 31				08 38	08 42	08 49				08 56	09 01
Barnes	d				08 12		08 23				08 29	08 35				08 42		08 52				08 59	09 05
Barnes Bridge	d				08 14						08 31					08 44						09 01	
Chiswick	d				08 17						08 34					08 47						09 03	
Kew Bridge	d				08 20						08 36					08 50						09 06	
Brentford	d				08 23						08 39					08 53						09 09	
Syon Lane	d				08 25						08 41					08 55						09 11	
Isleworth	d				08 27						08 43					08 57						09 13	
Hounslow	d				08 31						08 48					09 01						09 18	
Mortlake	d						08 25					08 37						08 54					09 07
North Sheen	d		←				08 27			←		08 39		←				08 56			←		09 09
Richmond ⊖	d	08 06	08 12			08 18	08 30	08 24		08 30		08 42	08 36	08 42			08 48	08 59	08 54		08 59		09 12
St Margarets	d		08 14				→			08 32		→		08 44				→			09 01		→
Twickenham	a	08 10	08 16			08 21		08 28		08 34			08 40	08 46			08 51		08 57		09 03		
	d	08 10	08 17			08 22		08 28		08 35			08 40	08 47			08 52		08 58		09 04		
Strawberry Hill	d									08 38											09 07		
Fulwell	a																						
Teddington	a									08 41											09 10		
Hampton Wick	a									08 44											09 14		
Kingston	a									08 46											09 16		
Whitton	d		08a20			08 25			←		08a53			08a50			08 55			←		09a23	
Feltham	d	08 16			08 36	08 29		08 34	08 36				08 46			09 06	08 59		09 04	09 06			
Ashford (Surrey)	d				→	08 33		08 38	08 40							→	09 03		09 08	09 10			
Staines	d	08 23				08 37		08 42	08 44				08 53				09 07		09 12	09 14			
Wraysbury	d					08 42											09 12						
Sunnymeads	d					08 45											09 15						
Datchet	d					08 49											09 19						
Windsor & Eton Riverside	a					08 54											09 24						
Egham	d	08 27						08 47	08 49				08 57						09 16	09 19			
Virginia Water	a	08 31						08 51	08 53				09 01						09 20	09 23			
	d	08 31						08 51	08 53				09 01						09 20	09 23			
Chertsey	d								08 59											09 29			
Addlestone	d								09 02											09 32			
Weybridge	a								09 08											09 37			
Byfleet & New Haw	d																						
West Byfleet	d																						
Woking	a																						
Longcross	d	08 35						08 54															
Sunningdale	d	08 37						08 58					09 07						09 26				
Ascot ■	d	08 43		08 53				09 02					09 13		09 23				09 30				
Bagshot	d			08 59											09 29								
Camberley	a			09 05											09 35								
Frimley	d			09 13											09 43								
Ash Vale	d			09 19											09 49								
Aldershot	a			09 25											09 54								
	d			09 38											10 08								
Ash ■	d			09 45											10 15								
Wanborough	d			09 48											10 18								
Guildford	a			09 55											10 25								
Martins Heron	d	08 47						09 06					09 17						09 34				
Bracknell	d	08 50						09 10					09 20						09 38				
Wokingham	d	08 57						09 17					09 27						09 47				
Winnersh	d	09 00						09 20					09 30										
Winnersh Triangle	d	09 02						09 22					09 32										
Earley	d	09 07						09 27					09 37										
Reading ■	a	09 13						09 33					09 43						09 58				

London - Hounslow, Richmond, Kingston, Windsor, Weybridge, Ascot, Guildford and Reading

Network Diagram - see first Page of Table 148

		SW ■	SW	SW ■	SW	SW	SW	SW	SW	SW	SW ■	SW	SW ■	SW	SW	SW	SW	SW	SW	SW ■	SW	SW ■
London Waterloo ⊖	d	08 50			08 52	08 58		09 03	09 07	09 15	09 20			09 22	09 28		09 33	09 37	09 45	09 50		
Vauxhall ⊖	d				08 56	09 02		09 07	09 11	09 19				09 26	09 32		09 37	09 41	09 49			
Queenstown Rd.(Battersea)	d				08 59			09 10	09 14	09 22				09 29			09 40	09 44	09 52			
Clapham Junction	d	08 58			09 02	09 08		09 13	09 17	09 25	09 28			09 32	09 38		09 43	09 47	09 55	09 58		
Wandsworth Town	d				09 05			09 16	09 20	09 28				09 35			09 46	09 50	09 58			
Putney	d				09 08	09 12		09 19	09 23	09 31				09 38	09 42		09 49	09 53	10 01			
Barnes	d				09 12			09 22	09 27	09 35				09 42			09 52	09 57	10 05			
Barnes Bridge	d				09 14				09 29					09 44				09 59				
Chiswick	d				09 17				09 32					09 47				10 02				
Kew Bridge	d				09 20				09 35					09 50				10 05				
Brentford	d				09 23				09 38					09 53				10 08				
Syon Lane	d				09 25				09 40					09 55				10 10				
Isleworth	d				09 27				09 42					09 57				10 12				
Hounslow	d				09 31				09 48					10 01				10 18				
Mortlake	d							09 24		09 37							09 54		10 07			
North Sheen	d		←					09 26		09 39		←					09 56		10 09		←	
Richmond ⊖	d	09 06	09 12			09 18		09 29		09 42	09 36	09 42			09 48		09 59		10 12	10 06	10 12	
St Margarets	d		09 14					09 31		→		09 44					10 01		→		10 14	
Twickenham	a	09 10	09 16			09 21		09 33			09 40	09 46			09 51		10 03			10 10	10 16	
	d	09 10	09 17			09 22		09 34			09 40	09 47			09 52		10 04			10 10	10 17	
Strawberry Hill	d							09 37									10 07					
Fulwell	a																					
Teddington	a							09 40									10 10					
Hampton Wick	a							09 44									10 14					
Kingston	a							09 46									10 16					
Whitton	d		09a20			09 25	←		09a53			09a50			09 55	←		10a26			10a20	
Feltham	d	09 16			09 36	09 29	09 36				09 46			10 06	09 59	10 06				10 16		
Ashford (Surrey)	d				→	09 33	09 40							→	10 03	10 10						
Staines	d	09 23				09 37	09 44				09 53				10 07	10 14				10 23		
Wraysbury	d					09 42									10 12							
Sunnymeads	d					09 45									10 15							
Datchet	d					09 49									10 19							
Windsor & Eton Riverside	a					09 54									10 24							
Egham	d	09 27					09 49				09 57					10 19				10 27		
Virginia Water	a	09 31					09 53				10 01					10 23				10 31		
	d	09 31					09 53				10 01					10 23				10 31		
Chertsey	d						09 59									10 29						
Addlestone	d						10 02									10 32						
Weybridge	a						10 07									10 37						
Byfleet & New Haw	d																					
West Byfleet	d																					
Woking	a																					
Longcross	d																					
Sunningdale	d	09 37									10 07									10 37		
Ascot ■	d	09 43		09 53							10 13		10 23							10 43		10 53
Bagshot	d			09 59									10 29									10 59
Camberley	a			10 05									10 35									11 05
Frimley	d			10 13									10 43									11 13
Ash Vale	d			10 19									10 49									11 19
Aldershot	a			10 24									10 54									11 24
	d			10 38									11 08									11 38
Ash ■	d			10 45									11 15									11 45
Wanborough	d			10 48									11 18									11 48
Guildford	a			10 55									11 25									11 55
Martins Heron	d	09 47									10 17									10 47		
Bracknell	d	09 50									10 20									10 50		
Wokingham	d	09 57									10 27									10 57		
Winnersh	d	10 00									10 30									11 00		
Winnersh Triangle	d	10 02									10 32									11 02		
Earley	d	10 07									10 37									11 07		
Reading ■	a	10 13									10 43									11 13		

Table 149

Mondays to Fridays
from 8 October

London - Hounslow, Richmond, Kingston, Windsor, Weybridge, Ascot, Guildford and Reading

Network Diagram - see first Page of Table 148

		SW	SW	SW	SW	SW	SW	SW ■	SW	SW ■	SW	SW	SW	SW	SW	SW	SW ■	SW	SW ■	SW	SW	SW	SW
London Waterloo 15 ⊖	d	09 52	09 58		10 03	10 07	10 15	10 20			10 22	10 28		10 33	10 37	10 45	10 50			10 52	10 58		11 03
Vauxhall ⊖	d	09 56	10 02		10 07	10 11	10 19				10 26	10 32		10 37	10 41	10 49				10 56	11 02		11 07
Queenstown Rd.(Battersea)	d	09 59			10 10	10 14	10 22				10 29			10 40	10 44	10 52				10 59			11 10
Clapham Junction 10	d	10 02	10 08		10 13	10 17	10 25	10 28			10 32	10 38		10 43	10 47	10 55	10 58			11 02	11 08		11 13
Wandsworth Town	d	10 05			10 16	10 20	10 28				10 35			10 46	10 50	10 58				11 05			11 16
Putney	d	10 08	10 12		10 19	10 23	10 31				10 38	10 42		10 49	10 53	11 01				11 08	11 12		11 19
Barnes	d	10 12			10 22	10 27	10 35				10 42			10 52	10 57	11 05				11 12			11 22
Barnes Bridge	d	10 14				10 29					10 44				10 59					11 14			
Chiswick	d	10 17				10 32					10 47				11 02					11 17			
Kew Bridge	d	10 20				10 35					10 50				11 05					11 20			
Brentford	d	10 23				10 38					10 53				11 08					11 23			
Syon Lane	d	10 25				10 40					10 55				11 10					11 25			
Isleworth	d	10 27				10 42					10 57				11 12					11 27			
Hounslow	d	10 31				10 48					11 01				11 18					11 31			
Mortlake	d				10 24		10 37							10 54		11 07							11 24
North Sheen	d				10 26		10 39		←					10 56		11 09		←					11 26
Richmond ⊖	d		10 18		10 29		10 42	10 36	10 42			10 48		10 59		11 12	11 06	11 12			11 18		11 29
St Margarets	d				10 31		→		10 44					11 01		→		11 14					11 31
Twickenham	a		10 21		10 33			10 40	10 46			10 51		11 03			11 10	11 16			11 21		11 33
	d		10 22		10 34			10 40	10 47			10 52		11 04			11 10	11 17			11 22		11 34
Strawberry Hill	d				10 37									11 07									11 37
Fulwell	a																						
Teddington	a				10 40									11 10									11 40
Hampton Wick	a				10 44									11 14									11 44
Kingston	a				10 46									11 16									11 46
Whitton	d		10 25	←		10a56			10a50			10 55	←		11a23			11a20			11 25	←	
Feltham	d	10 36	10 29	10 36				10 46			11 06	10 59	11 06				11 16			11 36	11 29	11 36	
Ashford (Surrey)	d	→	10 33	10 40							→	11 03	11 10							→	11 33	11 40	
Staines	d		10 37	10 44				10 53				11 07	11 14				11 23				11 37	11 44	
Wraysbury	d		10 42									11 12									11 42		
Sunnymeads	d		10 45									11 15									11 45		
Datchet	d		10 49									11 19									11 49		
Windsor & Eton Riverside	a		10 54									11 24									11 54		
Egham	d			10 49				10 57					11 19				11 27					11 49	
Virginia Water	a			10 53				11 01					11 23				11 31					11 53	
	d			10 53				11 01					11 23				11 31					11 53	
Chertsey	d			10 59									11 29									11 59	
Addlestone	d			11 02									11 32									12 02	
Weybridge	a			11 07									11 37									12 07	
Byfleet & New Haw	d																						
West Byfleet	d																						
Woking	a																						
Longcross	d																						
Sunningdale	d							11 07									11 37						
Ascot 3	d							11 13		11 23							11 43		11 53				
Bagshot	d									11 29									11 59				
Camberley	a									11 35									12 05				
Frimley	d									11 43									12 13				
Ash Vale	d									11 49									12 19				
Aldershot	a									11 54									12 24				
	d									12 08									12 38				
Ash 5	d									12 15									12 45				
Wanborough	d									12 18									12 48				
Guildford	a									12 25									12 55				
Martins Heron	d							11 17									11 47						
Bracknell	d							11 20									11 50						
Wokingham	d							11 27									11 57						
Winnersh	d							11 30									12 00						
Winnersh Triangle	d							11 32									12 02						
Earley	d							11 37									12 07						
Reading 7	a							11 43									12 13						

Table 149

Mondays to Fridays
from 8 October

London - Hounslow, Richmond, Kingston, Windsor, Weybridge, Ascot, Guildford and Reading

Network Diagram - see first Page of Table 148

		SW	SW	SW ■	SW	SW ■	SW	SW	SW	SW	SW	SW	SW ■	SW	SW ■	SW	SW	SW	SW	SW	SW	SW ■	SW
London Waterloo 15 ⊖	d	11 07	11 15	11 20			11 22	11 28		11 33	11 37	11 45	11 50			11 52	11 58		12 03	12 07	12 15	12 20	
Vauxhall ⊖	d	11 11	11 19				11 26	11 32		11 37	11 41	11 49				11 56	12 02		12 07	12 11	12 19		
Queenstown Rd.(Battersea)	d	11 14	11 22				11 29			11 40	11 44	11 52				11 59			12 10	12 14	12 22		
Clapham Junction 10	d	11 17	11 25	11 28			11 32	11 38		11 43	11 47	11 55	11 58			12 02	12 08		12 13	12 17	12 25	12 28	
Wandsworth Town	d	11 20	11 28				11 35			11 46	11 50	11 58				12 05			12 16	12 20	12 28		
Putney	d	11 23	11 31				11 38	11 42		11 49	11 53	12 01				12 08	12 12		12 19	12 23	12 31		
Barnes	d	11 27	11 35				11 42			11 52	11 57	12 05				12 12			12 22	12 27	12 35		
Barnes Bridge	d	11 29					11 44				11 59					12 14				12 29			
Chiswick	d	11 32					11 47				12 02					12 17				12 32			
Kew Bridge	d	11 35					11 50				12 05					12 20				12 35			
Brentford	d	11 38					11 53				12 08					12 23				12 38			
Syon Lane	d	11 40					11 55				12 10					12 25				12 40			
Isleworth	d	11 42					11 57				12 12					12 27				12 42			
Hounslow	d	11 48					12 01				12 18					12 31				12 48			
Mortlake	d		11 37							11 54		12 07							12 24		12 37		
North Sheen	d		11 39		←					11 56		12 09		←					12 26		12 39		←
Richmond ⊖	d		11 42	11 36	11 42			11 48		11 59		12 12	12 06	12 12			12 18		12 29		12 42	12 36	12 42
St Margarets	d		→		11 44					12 01		→		12 14					12 31		→		12 44
Twickenham	a			11 40	11 46			11 51		12 03			12 10	12 16			12 21		12 33			12 40	12 46
	d			11 40	11 47			11 52		12 04			12 10	12 17			12 22		12 34			12 40	12 47
Strawberry Hill	d									12 07									12 37				
Fulwell	a																						
Teddington	a									12 10									12 40				
Hampton Wick	a									12 14									12 44				
Kingston	a									12 16									12 46				
Whitton	d	11a53			11a50			11 55	←		12a23			12a20			12 25	←		12a53			12a50
Feltham	d			11 46			12 06	11 59	12 06				12 16			12 36	12 29	12 36				12 46	
Ashford (Surrey)	d						→	12 03	12 10							→	12 33	12 40					
Staines	d			11 53				12 07	12 14				12 23				12 37	12 44				12 53	
Wraysbury	d							12 12									12 42						
Sunnymeads	d							12 15									12 45						
Datchet	d							12 19									12 49						
Windsor & Eton Riverside	a							12 24									12 54						
Egham	d			11 57					12 19				12 27					12 49				12 57	
Virginia Water	a			12 01					12 23				12 31					12 53				13 01	
	d			12 01					12 23				12 31					12 53				13 01	
Chertsey	d								12 29									12 59					
Addlestone	d								12 32									13 02					
Weybridge	a								12 37									13 07					
Byfleet & New Haw	d																						
West Byfleet	d																						
Woking	a																						
Longcross	d																						
Sunningdale	d			12 07									12 37									13 07	
Ascot 3	d			12 13		12 23							12 43		12 53							13 13	
Bagshot	d					12 29									12 59								
Camberley	a					12 35									13 05								
Frimley	d					12 43									13 13								
Ash Vale	d					12 49									13 19								
Aldershot	a					12 54									13 24								
	d					13 08									13 38								
Ash 5	d					13 15									13 45								
Wanborough	d					13 18									13 48								
Guildford	a					13 25									13 55								
Martins Heron	d			12 17									12 47									13 17	
Bracknell	d			12 20									12 50									13 20	
Wokingham	d			12 27									12 57									13 27	
Winnersh	d			12 30									13 00									13 30	
Winnersh Triangle	d			12 32									13 02									13 32	
Earley	d			12 37									13 07									13 37	
Reading 7	a			12 43									13 13									13 43	

from 8 October

London - Hounslow, Richmond, Kingston, Windsor, Weybridge, Ascot, Guildford and Reading

Network Diagram - see first Page of Table 148

		SW [1]		SW	SW	SW	SW	SW	SW	SW [1]	SW	SW [1]		SW	SW	SW	SW	SW	SW	SW [1]	SW	SW [1]		SW	SW
London Waterloo [15] ⊖	d			12 22	12 28		12 33	12 37	12 45	12 50				12 52	12 58		13 03	13 07	13 15	13 20				13 22	13 28
Vauxhall ⊖	d			12 26	12 32		12 37	12 41	12 49					12 56	13 02		13 07	13 11	13 19					13 26	13 32
Queenstown Rd.(Battersea)	d			12 29			12 40	12 44	12 52					12 59			13 10	13 14	13 22					13 29	
Clapham Junction [10]	d			12 32	12 38		12 43	12 47	12 55	12 58				13 02	13 08		13 13	13 17	13 25	13 28				13 32	13 38
Wandsworth Town	d			12 35			12 46	12 50	12 58					13 05			13 16	13 20	13 28					13 35	
Putney	d			12 38	12 42		12 49	12 53	13 01					13 08	13 12		13 19	13 23	13 31					13 38	13 42
Barnes	d			12 42			12 52	12 57	13 05					13 12			13 22	13 27	13 35					13 42	
Barnes Bridge	d			12 44				12 59						13 14				13 29						13 44	
Chiswick	d			12 47				13 02						13 17				13 32						13 47	
Kew Bridge	d			12 50				13 05						13 20				13 35						13 50	
Brentford	d			12 53				13 08						13 23				13 38						13 53	
Syon Lane	d			12 55				13 10						13 25				13 40						13 55	
Isleworth	d			12 57				13 12						13 27				13 42						13 57	
Hounslow	d			13 01				13 18						13 31				13 48						14 01	
Mortlake	d						12 54		13 07								13 24		13 37						
North Sheen	d						12 56		13 09		←						13 26		13 39		←				
Richmond ⊖	d				12 48		12 59		13 12	13 06	13 12				13 18		13 29		13 42	13 36	13 42				13 48
St Margarets	d						13 01		→		13 14						13 31		→		13 44				
Twickenham	a				12 51		13 03			13 10	13 16				13 21		13 33			13 40	13 46				13 51
	d				12 52		13 04			13 10	13 17				13 22		13 34			13 40	13 47				13 52
Strawberry Hill	d						13 07										13 37								
Fulwell	a																								
Teddington	a						13 10										13 40								
Hampton Wick	a						13 14										13 44								
Kingston	a						13 16										13 46								
Whitton	d				12 55	←		13a23			13a20				13 25	←		13a53			13a50				13 55
Feltham	d			13 06	12 59	13 06				13 16				13 36	13 29	13 36				13 46				14 06	13 59
Ashford (Surrey)	d			→	13 03	13 10								→	13 33	13 40								→	14 03
Staines	d				13 07	13 14				13 23					13 37	13 44				13 53					14 07
Wraysbury	d				13 12										13 42										14 12
Sunnymeads	d				13 15										13 45										14 15
Datchet	d				13 19										13 49										14 19
Windsor & Eton Riverside	a				13 24										13 54										14 24
Egham	d					13 19				13 27						13 49				13 57					
Virginia Water	a					13 23				13 31						13 53				14 01					
	d					13 23				13 31						13 53				14 01					
Chertsey	d					13 29										13 59									
Addlestone	d					13 32										14 02									
Weybridge	a					13 37										14 07									
Byfleet & New Haw	d																								
West Byfleet	d																								
Woking	a																								
Longcross	d									13 35															
Sunningdale	d									13 37										14 07					
Ascot [3]	d	13 23								13 43		13 53								14 13		14 23			
Bagshot	d	13 29										13 59										14 29			
Camberley	a	13 35										14 05										14 35			
Frimley	d	13 43										14 13										14 43			
Ash Vale	d	13 49										14 19										14 49			
Aldershot	a	13 54										14 24										14 54			
	d	14 08										14 38										15 08			
Ash [5]	d	14 15										14 45										15 15			
Wanborough	d	14 18										14 48										15 18			
Guildford	a	14 25										14 55										15 25			
Martins Heron	d									13 47										14 17					
Bracknell	d									13 50										14 20					
Wokingham	d									13 57										14 27					
Winnersh	d									14 00										14 30					
Winnersh Triangle	d									14 02										14 32					
Earley	d									14 07										14 37					
Reading [7]	a									14 13										14 43					

from 8 October

London - Hounslow, Richmond, Kingston, Windsor, Weybridge, Ascot, Guildford and Reading

Network Diagram - see first Page of Table 148

		SW	SW	SW	SW	SW [1]	SW	SW [1]		SW	SW	SW	SW	SW	SW	SW [1]	SW	SW [1]		SW	SW	SW	SW	SW	SW
London Waterloo [15] ⊖	d		13 33	13 37	13 45	13 50				13 52	13 58		14 03	14 07	14 15	14 20				14 22	14 28		14 33	14 37	14 45
Vauxhall ⊖	d		13 37	13 41	13 49					13 56	14 02		14 07	14 11	14 19					14 26	14 32		14 37	14 41	14 49
Queenstown Rd.(Battersea)	d		13 40	13 44	13 52					13 59			14 10	14 14	14 22					14 29			14 40	14 44	14 52
Clapham Junction [10]	d		13 43	13 47	13 55	13 58				14 02	14 08		14 13	14 17	14 25	14 28				14 32	14 38		14 43	14 47	14 55
Wandsworth Town	d		13 46	13 50	13 58					14 05			14 16	14 20	14 28					14 35			14 46	14 50	14 58
Putney	d		13 49	13 53	14 01					14 08	14 12		14 19	14 23	14 31					14 38	14 42		14 49	14 53	15 01
Barnes	d		13 52	13 57	14 05					14 12			14 22	14 27	14 35					14 42			14 52	14 57	15 05
Barnes Bridge	d			13 59						14 14				14 29						14 44				14 59	
Chiswick	d			14 02						14 17				14 32						14 47				15 02	
Kew Bridge	d			14 05						14 20				14 35						14 50				15 05	
Brentford	d			14 08						14 23				14 38						14 53				15 08	
Syon Lane	d			14 10						14 25				14 40						14 55				15 10	
Isleworth	d			14 12						14 27				14 42						14 57				15 12	
Hounslow	d			14 18						14 31				14 48						15 01				15 18	
Mortlake	d		13 54		14 07								14 24		14 37								14 54		15 07
North Sheen	d		13 56		14 09		←						14 26		14 39		←						14 56		15 09
Richmond ⊖	d		13 59		14 12	14 06	14 12				14 18		14 29		14 42	14 36	14 42				14 48		14 59		15 12
St Margarets	d		14 01		→		14 14						14 31		→		14 44						15 01		→
Twickenham	a		14 03			14 10	14 16				14 21		14 33			14 40	14 46				14 51		15 03		
	d		14 04			14 10	14 17				14 22		14 34			14 40	14 47				14 52		15 04		
Strawberry Hill	d		14 07										14 37										15 07		
Fulwell	a																								
Teddington	a		14 10										14 40										15 10		
Hampton Wick	a		14 14										14 44										15 14		
Kingston	a		14 16										14 46										15 16		
Whitton	d	←		14a23			14a20				14 25	←		14a53			14a50				14 55	←		15a23	
Feltham	d	14 06				14 16				14 36	14 29	14 36				14 46				15 06	14 59	15 06			
Ashford (Surrey)	d	14 10								→	14 33	14 40								→	15 03	15 10			
Staines	d	14 14				14 23					14 37	14 44				14 53					15 07	15 14			
Wraysbury	d										14 42										15 12				
Sunnymeads	d										14 45										15 15				
Datchet	d										14 49										15 19				
Windsor & Eton Riverside	a										14 54										15 24				
Egham	d	14 19				14 27						14 49				14 57						15 19			
Virginia Water	a	14 23				14 31						14 53				15 01						15 23			
	d	14 23				14 31						14 53				15 01						15 23			
Chertsey	d	14 29										14 59										15 29			
Addlestone	d	14 32										15 02										15 32			
Weybridge	a	14 37										15 07										15 37			
Byfleet & New Haw	d																								
West Byfleet	d																								
Woking	a																								
Longcross	d																								
Sunningdale	d					14 37										15 07									
Ascot [3]	d					14 43		14 53								15 13		15 23							
Bagshot	d							14 59										15 29							
Camberley	a							15 05										15 35							
Frimley	d							15 13										15 43							
Ash Vale	d							15 19										15 49							
Aldershot	a							15 24										15 54							
	d							15 38										16 08							
Ash [5]	d							15 45										16 15							
Wanborough	d							15 48										16 18							
Guildford	a							15 55										16 25							
Martins Heron	d					14 47										15 17									
Bracknell	d					14 50										15 20									
Wokingham	d					14 57										15 27									
Winnersh	d					15 00										15 30									
Winnersh Triangle	d					15 02										15 32									
Earley	d					15 07										15 37									
Reading [7]	a					15 13										15 43									

London - Hounslow, Richmond, Kingston, Windsor, Weybridge, Ascot, Guildford and Reading

Network Diagram - see first Page of Table 148

		SW ■	SW	SW ■	SW	SW	SW	SW	SW	SW	SW ■	SW	SW ■	SW	SW	SW	SW	SW	SW	SW ■	SW	SW ■
London Waterloo ■ ⊖	d	14 50			14 52	14 58		15 03	15 07	15 15	15 20			15 22	15 28		15 33	15 37	15 45	15 50		
Vauxhall ⊖	d				14 56	15 02		15 07	15 11	15 19				15 26	15 32		15 37	15 41	15 49			
Queenstown Rd.(Battersea)	d				14 59			15 10	15 14	15 22				15 29			15 40	15 44	15 52			
Clapham Junction ■	d	14 58			15 02	15 08		15 13	15 17	15 25	15 28			15 32	15 38		15 43	15 47	15 55	15 58		
Wandsworth Town	d				15 05			15 16	15 20	15 28				15 35			15 46	15 50	15 58			
Putney	d				15 08	15 12		15 19	15 23	15 31				15 38	15 42		15 49	15 53	16 01			
Barnes	d				15 12			15 22	15 27	15 35				15 42			15 52	15 57	16 05			
Barnes Bridge	d				15 14				15 29					15 44				15 59				
Chiswick	d				15 17				15 32					15 47				16 02				
Kew Bridge	d				15 20				15 35					15 50				16 05				
Brentford	d				15 23				15 38					15 53				16 08				
Syon Lane	d				15 25				15 40					15 55				16 10				
Isleworth	d				15 27				15 42					15 57				16 12				
Hounslow	d				15 31				15 48					16 01				16 18				
Mortlake	d							15 24		15 37							15 54		16 07			
North Sheen	d		←					15 26		15 39		←					15 56		16 09		←	
Richmond ⊖	d	15 06	15 12			15 18		15 29		15 42	15 36	15 42			15 48		15 59		16 12	16 06	16 12	
St Margarets	d		15 14					15 31		→		15 44					16 01		→		16 14	
Twickenham	a	15 10	15 16			15 21		15 33			15 40	15 46			15 51		16 03			16 10	16 16	
	d	15 10	15 17			15 22		15 34			15 40	15 47			15 52		16 04			16 10	16 17	
Strawberry Hill	d							15 37									16 07					
Fulwell	a																					
Teddington	a							15 40									16 10					
Hampton Wick	a							15 44									16 14					
Kingston	a							15 46									16 16					
Whitton	d		15a20			15 25	←		15a53			15a50			15 55	←		16a23			16a20	
Feltham	d	15 16			15 36	15 29	15 36				15 46			16 06	15 59	16 06				16 16		
Ashford (Surrey)	d				→	15 33	15 40							→	16 03	16 10						
Staines	d	15 23				15 37	15 44				15 53				16 07	16 14				16 23		
Wraysbury	d					15 42									16 12							
Sunnymeads	d					15 45									16 15							
Datchet	d					15 49									16 19							
Windsor & Eton Riverside	a					15 54									16 24							
Egham	d	15 27					15 49				15 57					16 19				16 27		
Virginia Water	a	15 31					15 53				16 01					16 23				16 31		
	d	15 31					15 53				16 01					16 23				16 31		
Chertsey	d						15 59									16 29						
Addlestone	d						16 02									16 32						
Weybridge	a						16 07									16 37						
Byfleet & New Haw	d																					
West Byfleet	d																					
Woking	a																					
Longcross	d																					
Sunningdale	d	15 37									16 07									16 37		
Ascot ■	d	15 43		15 53							16 13		16 23							16 43		16 53
Bagshot	d			15 59									16 29									16 59
Camberley	a			16 05									16 35									17 05
Frimley	d			16 13									16 43									17 13
Ash Vale	d			16 19									16 49									17 19
Aldershot	a			16 24									16 54									17 24
	d			16 38									17 08									17 38
Ash ■	d			16 45									17 15									17 45
Wanborough	d			16 48									17 18									17 48
Guildford	a			16 55									17 25									17 55
Martins Heron	d	15 47									16 17									16 47		
Bracknell	d	15 50									16 20									16 50		
Wokingham	d	15 57									16 27									16 57		
Winnersh	d	16 00									16 30									17 00		
Winnersh Triangle	d	16 02									16 32									17 02		
Earley	d	16 07									16 35									17 07		
Reading ■	a	16 13									16 43									17 13		

London - Hounslow, Richmond, Kingston, Windsor, Weybridge, Ascot, Guildford and Reading

Network Diagram - see first Page of Table 148

		SW	SW	SW	SW ◇■	SW	SW	SW	SW	SW ◇■	SW	SW ■	SW ◇	SW ◇	SW	SW ◇■	SW ◇	SW	SW	SW	SW ◇■	SW	SW ◇
London Waterloo ■ ⊖	d	15 52	15 58	16 01	16 05			16 07	16 15	16 20			16 22	16 28	16 31	16 35			16 37	16 45	16 50		16 52
Vauxhall ⊖	d	15 56	16 02	16 05	16 09			16 11	16 19				16 26	16 32	16 35	16 39			16 41	16 49			16 56
Queenstown Rd.(Battersea)	d	15 59		16 08				16 14	16 22				16 29		16 38				16 44	16 52			16 59
Clapham Junction ■	d	16 02	16 08	16 11	16 15			16 17	16 25	16 28			16 32	16 38	16 41	16 45			16 47	16 55	16 58		17 02
Wandsworth Town	d	16 05		16 14				16 20	16 28				16 35		16 44				16 50	16 58			17 05
Putney	d	16 08	16 12	16 17				16 23	16 31				16 38	16 42	16 47				16 53	17 01			17 08
Barnes	d	16 12		16 22				16 27	16 35				16 42		16 52				16 57	17 05			17 12
Barnes Bridge	d	16 14						16 29					16 44						16 59				17 14
Chiswick	d	16 17						16 32					16 47						17 02				17 17
Kew Bridge	d	16 20						16 35					16 50						17 05				17 20
Brentford	d	16 23						16 38					16 53						17 08				17 23
Syon Lane	d	16 25						16 40					16 55						17 10				17 25
Isleworth	d	16 27						16 42					16 57						17 12				17 27
Hounslow	d	16 31						16 48					17 01						17 18				17 31
Mortlake	d			16 24					16 37						16 54					17 07			
North Sheen	d			16 26			←		16 39		←				16 56			←		17 09		←	
Richmond ⊖	d		16 18	16 29	16 23		16 29		16 42	16 36	16 42			16 48	16 59	16 53		16 59		17 12	17 06	17 12	
St Margarets	d			→			16 31		→		16 44				→			17 01		→		17 14	
Twickenham	a		16 21		16 27		16 33			16 40	16 46			16 51		16 57		17 03			17 10	17 16	
	d		16 22		16 27		16 34			16 40	16 47			16 52		16 57		17 04			17 10	17 17	
Strawberry Hill	d						16 37											17 07					
Fulwell	a																						
Teddington	a						16 42											17 12					
Hampton Wick	a						16 46											17 16					
Kingston	a						16 48											17 18					
Whitton	d		16 25			←		16a53			16a50			16 55			←		17a23			17a20	
Feltham	d	16 36	16 29		16 33	16 36				16 46			17 06	16 59		17 03	17 06				17 16		17 36
Ashford (Surrey)	d	→	16 33		16 37	16 40							→	17 03		17 07	17 10						→
Staines	d		16 37		16 41	16 44				16 53				17 07		17 11	17 14				17 23		
Wraysbury	d		16 42											17 12									
Sunnymeads	d		16 45											17 15									
Datchet	d		16 49											17 19									
Windsor & Eton Riverside	a		16 54											17 26									
Egham	d				16 46	16 49				16 57						17 16	17 19				17 27		
Virginia Water	a				16 50	16 53				17 01						17 20	17 23				17 31		
	d				16 50	16 53				17 01						17 20	17 23				17 31		
Chertsey	d					16 59											17 29						
Addlestone	d					17 02											17 32						
Weybridge	a					17 07											17 40						
Byfleet & New Haw	d																						
West Byfleet	d																						
Woking	a																						
Longcross	d															17 23							
Sunningdale	d				16 55					17 07						17 27					17 37		
Ascot ■	d				17 00					17 13		17 23				17 31					17 43		
Bagshot	d											17 29											
Camberley	a											17 35											
Frimley	d											17 43											
Ash Vale	d											17 49											
Aldershot	a											17 54											
	d											18 08											
Ash ■	d											18 15											
Wanborough	d											18 18											
Guildford	a											18 25											
Martins Heron	d				17 04					17 17						17 35					17 47		
Bracknell	d				17 07					17 20						17 39					17 50		
Wokingham	d				17 17					17 27						17 47					17 57		
Winnersh	d									17 30											18 00		
Winnersh Triangle	d									17 32											18 02		
Earley	d									17 37											18 07		
Reading ■	a				17 30					17 45						18 01					18 15		

Table 149

Mondays to Fridays

from 8 October

London - Hounslow, Richmond, Kingston, Windsor, Weybridge, Ascot, Guildford and Reading

Network Diagram - see first Page of Table 148

		SW ◇	SW	SW ◇1	SW ◇	SW		SW	SW	SW	SW ◇1	SW	SW ◇	SW 1	SW ◇	SW 1		SW 1	SW	SW ◇1	SW ◇	SW	SW	SW	SW
London Waterloo 15 ⊖	d	16 58	17 01	17 05				17 07	17 13	17 15	17 20		17 22	17 25	17 28				17 31	17 35			17 37	17 43	17 45
Vauxhall ⊖	d	17 02	17 05	17 09				17 11	17 17	17 19			17 26		17 32				17 35	17 39			17 41	17 47	17 49
Queenstown Rd.(Battersea)	d		17 08					17 14		17 22			17 29						17 38				17 44		17 52
Clapham Junction 10	d	17 08	17 11	17 15				17 17	17 23	17 25	17 28		17 32		17 38				17 41	17 45			17 47	17 53	17 55
Wandsworth Town	d		17 14					17 20		17 28			17 35						17 44				17 50		17 58
Putney	d	17 12	17 17					17 23	17 27	17 31			17 38		17 42				17 47				17 53	17 57	18 01
Barnes	d		17 22					17 27		17 35			17 42						17 52				17 57		18 05
Barnes Bridge	d							17 29					17 44										17 59		
Chiswick	d							17 32					17 47										18 02		
Kew Bridge	d							17 35					17 50										18 05		
Brentford	d							17 38					17 53										18 08		
Syon Lane	d							17 40					17 55										18 10		
Isleworth	d							17 42					17 57										18 12		
Hounslow	d							17 48					18 01										18 18		
Mortlake	d		17 24							17 37									17 54						18 07
North Sheen	d		17 26			←				17 39		←							17 56			←			18 09
Richmond ⊖	d	17 18	17 29	17 23		17 29			17 33	17 42	17 36	17 42			17 48				17 59	17 53		17 59		18 03	18 12
St Margarets	d		→			17 31				→		17 44							→			18 01			→
Twickenham	a	17 21		17 27		17 33			17 37		17 40	17 46			17 51					17 57		18 03		18 07	
	d	17 22		17 27		17 34			17 37		17 40	17 47			17 52					17 57		18 04		18 07	
Strawberry Hill	d					17 37			17 41													18 07		18 11	
Fulwell	a																							18 13	
Teddington	a					17 42			17 46													18 12			
Hampton Wick	a					17 46			17 54													18 16			
Kingston	a					17 48			17 56													18 18			
Whitton	d	17 25			←			17a53				17a50			17 55						←		18a23		
Feltham	d	17 29		17 33	17 36						17 46		18 06		17 59					18 03	18 06				
Ashford (Surrey)	d	17 33		17 37	17 40								→		18 03					18 07	18 10				
Staines	d	17 37		17 41	17 44						17 53				18 07					18 11	18 14				
Wraysbury	d	17 42													18 12										
Sunnymeads	d	17 45													18 15										
Datchet	d	17 49													18 19										
Windsor & Eton Riverside	a	17 56													18 26										
Egham	d			17 46	17 49						17 57									18 16	18 19				
Virginia Water	a			17 50	17 53						18 01									18 20	18 23				
	d			17 50	17 53						18 01									18 20	18 23				
Chertsey	d				17 59																18 29				
Addlestone	d				18 02																18 32				
Weybridge	a				18 10																18 40				
Byfleet & New Haw	d																								
West Byfleet	d																								
Woking	a													17 50											
Longcross	d																								
Sunningdale	d			17 55							18 07									18 25					
Ascot 3	d			18 01							18 13							18 23		18 30					
Bagshot	d			18 07														18 29							
Camberley	a			18 13														18 35							
Frimley	d			18 17														18 43							
Ash Vale	d			18 24										18 03				18 49							
Aldershot	a			18 34										18 08				18 54							
	d															18 38		19 08							
Ash 5	d															18 45		19 15							
Wanborough	d															18 48		19 18							
Guildford	a															18 55		19 25							
Martins Heron	d										18 17									18 34					
Bracknell	d										18 20									18 37					
Wokingham	d										18 27									18 47					
Winnersh	d										18 30														
Winnersh Triangle	d										18 32														
Earley	d										18 37														
Reading 7	a										18 45									19 00					

Table 149

Mondays to Fridays

from 8 October

London - Hounslow, Richmond, Kingston, Windsor, Weybridge, Ascot, Guildford and Reading

Network Diagram - see first Page of Table 148

		SW ◇1		SW	SW ◇	SW ◇	SW	SW ◇1	SW ◇	SW	SW	SW		SW	SW ◇1	SW	SW ◇	SW 1	SW ◇	SW 1	SW 1	SW		SW ◇1	SW ◇
London Waterloo 15 ⊖	d	17 50			17 52	17 58	18 01	18 05			18 07	18 13		18 15	18 20		18 22	18 25	18 28			18 31		18 35	
Vauxhall ⊖	d				17 56	18 02	18 05	18 09			18 11	18 17		18 19			18 26		18 32			18 35		18 39	
Queenstown Rd.(Battersea)	d				17 59		18 08				18 14			18 22			18 29					18 38			
Clapham Junction 10	d	17 58			18 02	18 08	18 11	18 15			18 17	18 23		18 25	18 28		18 32		18 38			18 41		18 45	
Wandsworth Town	d				18 05		18 14				18 20			18 28			18 35					18 44			
Putney	d				18 08	18 12	18 17				18 23	18 27		18 31			18 38		18 42			18 47			
Barnes	d				18 12		18 22				18 27			18 35			18 42					18 52			
Barnes Bridge	d				18 14						18 29						18 44								
Chiswick	d				18 17						18 32						18 47								
Kew Bridge	d				18 20						18 35						18 50								
Brentford	d				18 23						18 38						18 53								
Syon Lane	d				18 25						18 40						18 55								
Isleworth	d				18 27						18 42						18 57								
Hounslow	d				18 31						18 48						19 01								
Mortlake	d						18 24							18 37								18 54			
North Sheen	d			←			18 26			←				18 39		←						18 56			
Richmond ⊖	d	18 06		18 12		18 18	18 29	18 23		18 29		18 33		18 42	18 36	18 42			18 48			18 59		18 53	
St Margarets	d			18 14			→			18 31				→		18 44						→			
Twickenham	a	18 10		18 16		18 21		18 27		18 33		18 37			18 40	18 46			18 51					18 57	
	d	18 10		18 17		18 22		18 27		18 34		18 37			18 40	18 47			18 52					18 57	
Strawberry Hill	d									18 37		18 41													
Fulwell	a											18 43													
Teddington	a									18 42															
Hampton Wick	a									18 46															
Kingston	a									18 48															
Whitton	d			18a20		18 25			←		18a53					18a50			18 55						←
Feltham	d	18 16			18 36	18 29		18 33	18 36						18 46		19 06		18 59					19 03	19 06
Ashford (Surrey)	d				→	18 33		18 37	18 40								→		19 03					19 07	19 10
Staines	d	18 23				18 37		18 41	18 44						18 53				19 07					19 11	19 14
Wraysbury	d					18 42													19 12						
Sunnymeads	d					18 45													19 15						
Datchet	d					18 49													19 19						
Windsor & Eton Riverside	a					18 56													19 26						
Egham	d	18 27						18 46	18 49						18 57									19 16	19 19
Virginia Water	a	18 31						18 50	18 53						19 01									19 20	19 23
	d	18 31						18 50	18 53						19 01									19 20	19 23
Chertsey	d								18 59																19 29
Addlestone	d								19 02																19 32
Weybridge	a								19 10																19 40
Byfleet & New Haw	d																								
West Byfleet	d																								
Woking	a																	18 52							
Longcross	d	18 35																							
Sunningdale	d	18 37						18 55							19 07									19 25	
Ascot 3	d	18 43						19 02							19 13						19 23			19 30	
Bagshot	d							19 08													19 29				
Camberley	a							19 14													19 35				
Frimley	d							19 19													19 43				
Ash Vale	d							19 26										19 05			19 49				
Aldershot	a							19 34										19 10			19 54				
	d																			19 38	20 08				
Ash 5	d																			19 45	20 15				
Wanborough	d																			19 48	20 18				
Guildford	a																			19 55	20 25				
Martins Heron	d	18 47													19 17									19 34	
Bracknell	d	18 50													19 20									19 37	
Wokingham	d	18 57													19 27									19 47	
Winnersh	d	19 00													19 30										
Winnersh Triangle	d	19 02													19 32										
Earley	d	19 07													19 37										
Reading 7	a	19 15													19 45									20 00	

Table 149

Mondays to Fridays

from 8 October

London - Hounslow, Richmond, Kingston, Windsor, Weybridge, Ascot, Guildford and Reading

Network Diagram - see first Page of Table 148

		SW	SW	SW	SW	SW	SW	SW	SW	SW	SW	SW	SW	SW	SW	SW	SW	SW	SW	SW	SW	SW	SW
						◇ 1		1	◇	◇		1	◇				1		1				
London Waterloo 15 ⊖	d		18 37	18 43	18 45	18 50			18 52	18 58	19 01	19 05			19 07	19 15	19 20			19 22	19 28		19 33
Vauxhall ⊖	d		18 41	18 47	18 49				18 56	19 02	19 05	19 09			19 11	19 19				19 26	19 32		19 37
Queenstown Rd.(Battersea)	d		18 44		18 52				18 59		19 08				19 14	19 22				19 29			19 40
Clapham Junction 10	d		18 47	18 53	18 55	18 58			19 02	19 08	19 11	19 15			19 17	19 25	19 28			19 32	19 38		19 43
Wandsworth Town	d		18 50		18 58				19 05		19 14				19 20	19 28				19 35			19 46
Putney	d		18 53	18 57	19 01				19 08	19 12	19 17				19 23	19 31				19 38	19 42		19 49
Barnes	d		18 57		19 05				19 12		19 22				19 27	19 35				19 42			19 52
Barnes Bridge	d		18 59						19 14						19 29					19 44			
Chiswick	d		19 02						19 17						19 32					19 47			
Kew Bridge	d		19 05						19 20						19 35					19 50			
Brentford	d		19 08						19 23						19 38					19 53			
Syon Lane	d		19 10						19 25						19 40					19 55			
Isleworth	d		19 12						19 27						19 42					19 57			
Hounslow	d		19 18						19 31						19 48					20 01			
Mortlake	d				19 07						19 24					19 37							19 54
North Sheen	d	←			19 09		←				19 26			←		19 39		←					19 56
Richmond ⊖	d	18 59		19 03	19 12	19 06	19 12			19 18	19 29	19 23		19 29		19 42	19 36	19 42			19 48		19 59
St Margarets	d	19 01			→		19 14				→			19 31		→		19 44					20 01
Twickenham	a	19 03		19 07		19 10	19 16			19 21		19 27		19 33			19 40	19 46			19 51		20 03
	d	19 04		19 07		19 10	19 17			19 22		19 27		19 34			19 40	19 47			19 52		20 04
Strawberry Hill	d	19 07		19 11										19 37									20 07
Fulwell	a			19 13																			
Teddington	a	19 12												19 42									20 10
Hampton Wick	a	19 16												19 46									20 14
Kingston	a	19 18												19 48									20 16
Whitton	d		19a23				19a20			19 25			←		19a53			19a50			19 55	←	
Feltham	d					19 16			19 36	19 29		19 33	19 36				19 46			20 06	19 59	20 06	
Ashford (Surrey)	d								→	19 33		19 37	19 40							→	20 03	20 10	
Staines	d					19 23				19 37		19 41	19 44				19 53				20 07	20 14	
Wraysbury	d									19 42											20 12		
Sunnymeads	d									19 45											20 15		
Datchet	d									19 49											20 19		
Windsor & Eton Riverside	a									19 56											20 24		
Egham	d					19 27						19 46	19 49				19 57					20 19	
Virginia Water	a					19 31						19 50	19 53				20 01					20 23	
	d					19 31						19 50	19 53				20 01					20 23	
Chertsey	d												19 59									20 29	
Addlestone	d												20 02									20 32	
Weybridge	a												20 10									20 37	
Byfleet & New Haw	d																						
West Byfleet	d																						
Woking	a																						
Longcross	d																						
Sunningdale	d					19 37						19 55					20 07						
Ascot 3	d					19 43		19 53				20 00					20 13		20 23				
Bagshot	d							19 59											20 29				
Camberley	a							20 05											20 35				
Frimley	d							20 13											20 43				
Ash Vale	d							20 19											20 49				
Aldershot	a							20 24											20 54				
	d							20 38											21 08				
Ash 5	d							20 45											21 15				
Wanborough	d							20 48											21 18				
Guildford	a							20 55											21 25				
Martins Heron	d					19 47						20 04					20 17						
Bracknell	d					19 50						20 07					20 20						
Wokingham	d					19 57						20 17					20 27						
Winnersh	d					20 00											20 30						
Winnersh Triangle	d					20 02											20 32						
Earley	d					20 07											20 37						
Reading 7	a					20 15						20 28					20 43						

Table 149

Mondays to Fridays

from 8 October

London - Hounslow, Richmond, Kingston, Windsor, Weybridge, Ascot, Guildford and Reading

Network Diagram - see first Page of Table 148

		SW	SW	SW	SW	SW	SW	SW	SW	SW	SW	SW	SW	SW	SW	SW	SW	SW	SW	SW	SW	SW
				1		1							1		1	1						
London Waterloo 15 ⊖	d	19 37	19 45	19 50			19 52	19 58		20 03	20 07	20 15	20 20				20 22	20 28		20 33	20 37	20 45
Vauxhall ⊖	d	19 41	19 49				19 56	20 02		20 07	20 11	20 19					20 26	20 32		20 37	20 41	20 49
Queenstown Rd.(Battersea)	d	19 44	19 52				19 59			20 10	20 14	20 22					20 29			20 40	20 44	20 52
Clapham Junction 10	d	19 47	19 55	19 58			20 02	20 08		20 13	20 17	20 25	20 28				20 32	20 38		20 43	20 47	20 55
Wandsworth Town	d	19 50	19 58				20 05			20 16	20 20	20 28					20 35			20 46	20 50	20 58
Putney	d	19 53	20 01				20 08	20 12		20 19	20 23	20 31					20 38	20 42		20 49	20 53	21 01
Barnes	d	19 57	20 05				20 12			20 22	20 27	20 35					20 42			20 52	20 57	21 05
Barnes Bridge	d	19 59					20 14				20 29						20 44				20 59	
Chiswick	d	20 02					20 17				20 32						20 47				21 02	
Kew Bridge	d	20 05					20 20				20 35						20 50				21 05	
Brentford	d	20 08					20 23				20 38						20 53				21 08	
Syon Lane	d	20 10					20 25				20 40						20 55				21 10	
Isleworth	d	20 12					20 27				20 42						20 57				21 12	
Hounslow	d	20 18					20 31				20 48						21 01				21 18	
Mortlake	d		20 07							20 24		20 37								20 54		21 07
North Sheen	d		20 09		←					20 26		20 39		←						20 56		21 09
Richmond ⊖	d		20 12	20 06	20 12			20 18		20 29		20 42	20 36	20 42				20 48		20 59		21 12
St Margarets	d		→		20 14					20 31		→		20 44						21 01		→
Twickenham	a			20 10	20 16			20 21		20 33			20 40	20 46				20 51		21 03		
	d			20 10	20 17			20 22		20 34			20 40	20 47				20 52		21 04		
Strawberry Hill	d									20 37										21 07		
Fulwell	a																					
Teddington	a									20 40										21 10		
Hampton Wick	a									20 44										21 14		
Kingston	a									20 46										21 16		
Whitton	d	20a23			20a20			20 25	←		20a53			20a50				20 55	←		21a23	
Feltham	d			20 16			20 36	20 29	20 36				20 46				21 06	20 59	21 06			
Ashford (Surrey)	d						→	20 33	20 40								→	21 03	21 10			
Staines	d			20 23				20 37	20 44				20 53					21 07	21 14			
Wraysbury	d							20 42										21 12				
Sunnymeads	d							20 45										21 15				
Datchet	d							20 49										21 19				
Windsor & Eton Riverside	a							20 54										21 24				
Egham	d			20 27					20 49				20 57						21 19			
Virginia Water	a			20 31					20 53				21 01						21 23			
	d			20 31					20 53				21 01						21 23			
Chertsey	d								20 59										21 29			
Addlestone	d								21 02										21 32			
Weybridge	a								21 07										21 37			
Byfleet & New Haw	d																					
West Byfleet	d																					
Woking	a																					
Longcross	d																					
Sunningdale	d			20 37									21 07									
Ascot 3	d			20 43		20 53							21 13		21 23							
Bagshot	d					20 59									21 29							
Camberley	a					21 05									21 35							
Frimley	d					21 13									21 43							
Ash Vale	d					21 19									21 49							
Aldershot	a					21 24									21 54							
	d					21 38									22 08	22 38						
Ash 5	d					21 45									22 15	22 45						
Wanborough	d					21 48									22 18	22 48						
Guildford	a					21 55									22 25	22 55						
Martins Heron	d			20 47									21 17									
Bracknell	d			20 50									21 20									
Wokingham	d			20 57									21 27									
Winnersh	d			21 00									21 30									
Winnersh Triangle	d			21 02									21 32									
Earley	d			21 07									21 37									
Reading 7	a			21 13									21 43									

Table 149

Mondays to Fridays
from 8 October

London - Hounslow, Richmond, Kingston, Windsor, Weybridge, Ascot, Guildford and Reading

Network Diagram - see first Page of Table 148

		SW 1	SW	SW	SW	SW	SW	SW	SW	SW 1	SW	SW 1	SW	SW	SW	SW	SW	SW	SW 1	SW	SW	SW	SW
London Waterloo 15 ⊖	d	20 50		20 52	20 58		21 03	21 07	21 15	21 20			21 22	21 28		21 33	21 37	21 45	21 50		21 52	21 58	
Vauxhall ⊖	d			20 56	21 02		21 07	21 11	21 19				21 26	21 32		21 37	21 41	21 49			21 56	22 02	
Queenstown Rd.(Battersea)	d			20 59			21 10	21 14	21 22				21 29			21 40	21 44	21 52			21 59		
Clapham Junction 10	d	20 58		21 02	21 08		21 13	21 17	21 25	21 28			21 32	21 38		21 43	21 47	21 55	21 58		22 02	22 08	
Wandsworth Town	d			21 05			21 16	21 20	21 28				21 35			21 46	21 50	21 58			22 05		
Putney	d			21 08	21 12		21 19	21 23	21 31				21 38	21 42		21 49	21 53	22 01			22 08	22 12	
Barnes	d			21 12			21 22	21 27	21 35				21 42			21 52	21 57	22 05			22 12		
Barnes Bridge	d			21 14				21 29					21 44				21 59				22 14		
Chiswick	d			21 17				21 32					21 47				22 02				22 17		
Kew Bridge	d			21 20				21 35					21 50				22 05				22 20		
Brentford	d			21 23				21 38					21 53				22 08				22 23		
Syon Lane	d			21 25				21 40					21 55				22 10				22 25		
Isleworth	d			21 27				21 42					21 57				22 12				22 27		
Hounslow	d			21 31				21 48					22 01				22 18				22 31		
Mortlake	d						21 24		21 37							21 54		22 07					
North Sheen	d		←				21 26		21 39		←					21 56		22 09		←			
Richmond ⊖	d	21 06	21 12		21 18		21 29		21 42	21 36	21 42			21 48		21 59		22 12	22 06	22 12		22 18	
St Margarets	d		21 14				21 31		→		21 44					22 01		→		22 14			
Twickenham	a	21 10	21 16		21 21		21 33			21 40	21 46			21 51		22 03			22 10	22 16		22 21	
	d	21 10	21 17		21 22		21 34			21 40	21 47			21 52		22 04			22 10			22 22	
Strawberry Hill	d						21 37									22 07							
Fulwell	a																						
Teddington	a						21 40									22 10							
Hampton Wick	a						21 44									22 14							
Kingston	a						21 46									22 16							
Whitton	d		21a20		21 25	←		21a53			21a50			21 55	←		22a23					22 25	←
Feltham	d	21 16		21 36	21 29	21 36				21 46			22 06	21 59	22 06				22 16		22 36	22 29	22 36
Ashford (Surrey)	d			→	21 33	21 40							→	22 03	22 10						→	22 33	22 40
Staines	d	21 23			21 37	21 44				21 53				22 07	22 14				22 23			22 37	22 44
Wraysbury	d				21 42									22 12								22 42	
Sunnymeads	d				21 45									22 15								22 45	
Datchet	d				21 49									22 19								22 49	
Windsor & Eton Riverside	a				21 54									22 24								22 56	
Egham	d	21 27				21 49				21 57					22 19				22 27				22 49
Virginia Water	a	21 31				21 53				22 01					22 23				22 31				22 53
	d	21 31				21 53				22 01					22 23				22 31				22 53
Chertsey	d					21 59									22 29								22 59
Addlestone	d					22 02									22 32								23 02
Weybridge	a					22 07									22 37								23 07
Byfleet & New Haw	d																						
West Byfleet	d																						
Woking	a																						
Longcross	d																						
Sunningdale	d	21 37								22 07									22 37				
Ascot 3	d	21 43								22 13		22 23							22 43				
Bagshot	d											22 29											
Camberley	a											22 35											
Frimley	d											22 43											
Ash Vale	d											22 49											
Aldershot	a											22 54											
	d											23 08											
Ash 5	d											23 15											
Wanborough	d											23 18											
Guildford	a											23 25											
Martins Heron	d	21 47								22 17									22 47				
Bracknell	d	21 50								22 20									22 50				
Wokingham	d	21 57								22 27									22 57				
Winnersh	d	22 00								22 30									23 00				
Winnersh Triangle	d	22 02								22 32									23 02				
Earley	d	22 07								22 37									23 06				
Reading 7	a	22 13								22 43									23 13				

Table 149

Mondays to Fridays
from 8 October

London - Hounslow, Richmond, Kingston, Windsor, Weybridge, Ascot, Guildford and Reading

Network Diagram - see first Page of Table 148

		SW	SW 1	SW 1	SW	SW	SW	SW	SW 1	SW	SW	SW	SW	SW	SW 1	SW	SW	SW	SW	SW	SW	SW	SW
London Waterloo 15 ⊖	d	22 03	22 20		22 22	22 28		22 33	22 50	22 52	22 58		23 03	23 13	23 20	23 22	23 33	23 38			23 52	23 58	
Vauxhall ⊖	d	22 07			22 26	22 32		22 37		22 56	23 02		23 07	23 17		23 26	23 37				23 56	00 02	
Queenstown Rd.(Battersea)	d	22 10			22 29			22 40		22 59			23 10			23 29	23 40				23 59		
Clapham Junction 10	d	22 13	22 28		22 32	22 38		22 43	22 58	23 02	23 08		23 13	23 23	23 28	23 32	23 43	23 46			00 02	00 08	
Wandsworth Town	d	22 16			22 35			22 46		23 05			23 16			23 35	23 46				00 05		
Putney	d	22 19			22 38	22 42		22 49		23 08	23 12		23 19	23 27		23 38	23 49				00 08	00 12	
Barnes	d	22 22			22 42			22 52		23 12			23 22			23 42	23 52				00 12		
Barnes Bridge	d				22 44					23 14						23 44					00 14		
Chiswick	d				22 47					23 17						23 47					00 17		
Kew Bridge	d				22 50					23 20						23 50					00 20		
Brentford	d				22 53					23 23						23 53					00 23		
Syon Lane	d				22 55					23 25						23 55					00 25		
Isleworth	d				22 57					23 27						23 57					00 27		
Hounslow	d				23 01					23 31						00 01					00 31		
Mortlake	d	22 24						22 54					23 24				23 54						
North Sheen	d	22 26						22 56					23 26				23 56			←			
Richmond ⊖	d	22 29	22 36			22 48		22 59	23 06		23 18		23 29	23 33	23 37		23 59	23 54		23 59		00 18	
St Margarets	d	22 31						23 01					23 31				→			00 01			
Twickenham	a	22 33	22 40			22 51		23 03	23 10		23 21		23 33	23 36	23 41			23 58		00 03		00 21	
	d	22 34	22 40			22 52		23 04	23 10		23 22		23 34	23 37	23 41			23 58		00 04		00 22	
Strawberry Hill	d	22 37						23 07					23 37							00 07			
Fulwell	a																						
Teddington	a	22 40						23 10					23 40							00 11			
Hampton Wick	a	22 44						23 14					23 44							00 14			
Kingston	a	22 46						23 16					23 46							00 16			
Whitton	d					22 55	←				23 25	←		23 40					←			00 25	←
Feltham	d		22 46		23 06	22 59	23 06		23 16	23 36	23 29	23 36		23 44	23 48	00 06		00 04	00 06		00 37	00 29	00 37
Ashford (Surrey)	d				→	23 03	23 10			→	23 33	23 40		23 48		→			00 10		→	00 33	00 41
Staines	d		22 53			23 07	23 14		23 23		23 37	23 44		23 52	23 56			00 11	00 14			00a37	00a46
Wraysbury	d					23 11					23 42			23 56									
Sunnymeads	d					23 14					23 45			23 59									
Datchet	d					23 17					23 49			00 04									
Windsor & Eton Riverside	a					23 24					23 54			00 09									
Egham	d		22 57				23 19		23 27			23 49			00 01			00 15	00 19				
Virginia Water	a		23 01				23 23		23 31			23 53			00 05			00 19	00 23				
	d		23 01				23 23		23 31			23 53			00 05			00 19	00 23				
Chertsey	d						23 29					23 59							00 29				
Addlestone	d						23a32					00 02							00a32				
Weybridge	a						23 37												00 38				
Byfleet & New Haw	d											00 06											
West Byfleet	d											00 09											
Woking	a											00 15											
Longcross	d																						
Sunningdale	d		23 07						23 37						00 11			00 25					
Ascot 3	d		23 13	23 23					23 43						00 15			00 30					
Bagshot	d			23 29																			
Camberley	a			23 35																			
Frimley	d			23 43																			
Ash Vale	d			23 49																			
Aldershot	a			23 54																			
	d																						
Ash 5	d																						
Wanborough	d																						
Guildford	a																						
Martins Heron	d		23 17						23 47						00 19			00 34					
Bracknell	d		23 20						23 50						00 23			00 37					
Wokingham	d		23 27						23 57						00 32			00 44					
Winnersh	d		23 30						23 59						00 36								
Winnersh Triangle	d		23 32						00 02						00 38								
Earley	d		23 37						00 05						00 40								
Reading 7	a		23 43						00 13						00 48			00 55					

Table 149

Saturdays
until 6 October

London - Hounslow, Richmond, Kingston, Windsor, Weybridge, Ascot, Guildford and Reading

Network Diagram - see first Page of Table 148

		SW ■	SW	SW	SW ■	SW	SW	SW A	SW	SW	SW ■ A	SW B	SW ■ B	SW ■	SW ■	SW ■	SW	SW	SW	SW	SW B	SW	SW ■
London Waterloo ■ ⊖	d	22p50	22p52	23p13	23p20	23p22	23p33	23p38				23p50					23p52	23p58		00 18	00 38		
Vauxhall ⊖	d		22p56	23p17		23p26	23p37										23p56	00 02		00 22	00 42		
Queenstown Rd.(Battersea)	d		22p59			23p29	23p40										23p59			00 25			
Clapham Junction ■	d	22p58	23p02	23p23	23p28	23p32	23p43	23p46				23p58					00 02	00 08		00 29	00 48		
Wandsworth Town	d		23p05			23p35	23p46										00 05			00 32			
Putney	d		23p08	23p27		23p38	23p49										00 08	00 12		00 35	00 52		
Barnes	d		23p12			23p42	23p52										00 12			00 38	00 55		
Barnes Bridge	d		23p14			23p44											00 14						
Chiswick	d		23p17			23p47											00 17						
Kew Bridge	d		23p20			23p50											00 20						
Brentford	d		23p23			23p53											00 23						
Syon Lane	d		23p25			23p55											00 25						
Isleworth	d		23p27			23p57											00 27						
Hounslow	d		23p31			00 01											00 31						
Mortlake	d						23p54													00 40			
North Sheen	d						23p56			←										00 42			
Richmond ⊖	d	23p06		23p33	23p37		23p59	23p54		23p59		00 06						00 18		00 45	01 00		
St Margarets	d						→			00 01										00 47			
Twickenham	a	23p10		23p36	23p41			23p58		00 03		00 10						00 21		00 49	01 03		
	d	23p10		23p37	23p41			23p58		00 04		00 10						00 22		00 50	01 04	04 52	
Strawberry Hill	d									00 07										00s53		04 55	
Fulwell	a																						
Teddington	a									00 11										00s56		04 58	
Hampton Wick	a									00 14										00s59		05 01	
Kingston	a									00 16										01 01		05 03	
Whitton	d			23p40					←									00 25	←		01 07		
Feltham	d	23p16	23p36	23p44	23p48	00 06		00 04	00 06			00 16					00 37	00 29	00 37		01 11		
Ashford (Surrey)	d		23p40	23p48		→			00 10								→	00 33	00 41		01 15		
Staines	d	23p23	23p44	23p52	23p56			00 11	00 14			00 23						00a37	00a46		01a19		05 23
Wraysbury	d			23p56																			
Sunnymeads	d			23p59																			
Datchet	d			00 02																			
Windsor & Eton Riverside	a			00 06																			
Egham	d	23p27	23p49		00 01			00 15	00 19			00 27											05 27
Virginia Water	a	23p31	23p53		00 05			00 19	00 23			00 31											05 31
	d	23p31	23p53		00 05			00 19	00 23			00 31											05 31
Chertsey	d		23p59						00 29														
Addlestone	d		00 02						00a32														
Weybridge	a								00 38														
Byfleet & New Haw	d		00 06																				
West Byfleet	d		00 09																				
Woking	a		00 15																				
Longcross	d																						
Sunningdale	d	23p37			00 11			00 25				00 37											05 37
Ascot ■	d	23p43			00 15			00 30			00 32	00 42	00 44										05 43
Bagshot	d										00 38		00 50										
Camberley	a										00 44		00 56										
Frimley	d										00 48		01 00										
Ash Vale	d										00 57		01 09										
Aldershot	a										01s02		01s13										
	d													06 08	06 38	07 08							
Ash ■	d													06 15	06 45	07 15							
Wanborough	d													06 18	06 48	07 18							
Guildford	a													06 25	06 55	07 25							
Martins Heron	d	23p47			00 19			00 34				00 46											05 47
Bracknell	d	23p50			00 23			00 37				00 49											05 50
Wokingham	d	23p57			00 32			00 44				00 56											05 57
Winnersh	d	23p59			00 36																		06 00
Winnersh Triangle	d	00 02			00 38																		06 02
Earley	d	00 05			00 40																		06 05
Reading ■	a	00 10			00 45			00 52				01 04											06 10

A until 21 July, 18 August, 25 August, 15 September, 22 September, 29 September, 6 October

B 28 July, 4 August, 11 August, 1 September, 8 September

Table 149

Saturdays
until 6 October

London - Hounslow, Richmond, Kingston, Windsor, Weybridge, Ascot, Guildford and Reading

Network Diagram - see first Page of Table 148

		SW	SW ■	SW	SW	SW	SW	SW ■	SW	SW	SW	SW ■	SW ■ A	SW ■	SW ■	SW	SW	SW	SW	SW B	SW ■ C	SW ■ B	SW ■
London Waterloo ■ ⊖	d		05 05			05 33		05 50	05 58	06 03				06 20		06 22	06 28		06 33	06 43	06 50	06 50	
Vauxhall ⊖	d		05 09			05 37			06 02	06 07						06 26	06 32		06 37	06 47			
Queenstown Rd.(Battersea)	d		05 12			05 40				06 10						06 29			06 40				
Clapham Junction ■	d		05 15			05 43		05 58	06 08	06 13				06 28		06 32	06 38		06 43	06 53	06 58	06 58	
Wandsworth Town	d		05 18			05 46				06 16						06 35			06 46				
Putney	d		05 21			05 49			06 12	06 19						06 38	06 42		06 49	06 57			
Barnes	d		05 24			05 52				06 22						06 42			06 52				
Barnes Bridge	d															06 44							
Chiswick	d															06 47							
Kew Bridge	d															06 50							
Brentford	d															06 53							
Syon Lane	d															06 55							
Isleworth	d															06 57							
Hounslow	d															07 01							
Mortlake	d		05 26			05 54				06 24									06 54				
North Sheen	d		05 28			05 56				06 26									06 56				
Richmond ⊖	d		05 31			05 59		06 06	06 18	06 29				06 36			06 48		06 59	07 03	07 06	07 07	
St Margarets	d		05 33			06 01				06 31									07 01				
Twickenham	a		05 35			06 03		06 10	06 21	06 33				06 40			06 51		07 03	07 07	07 10	07 11	
	d		05 36	05 38	05 53	06 04		06 10	06 22	06 34				06 40			06 52		07 04	07 07	07 10	07 11	
Strawberry Hill	d					06 07				06 37									07 07				
Fulwell	a																						
Teddington	a					06 10				06 40									07 10				
Hampton Wick	a					06 14				06 44									07 14				
Kingston	a					06 16				06 46									07 16				
Whitton	d		05 39	05a41	05 56				06 25								06 55	←					
Feltham	d		05 43		06 00			06 16	06 29					06 46		07 06	06 59	07 06		07 13	07 16	07 17	
Ashford (Surrey)	d		05 47		06 04				06 33							→	07 03	07 10					
Staines	d	05 44	05 53		06 08		06 16	06 23	06 37		06 44			06 53			07 07	07 14		07 19	07 23	07 24	
Wraysbury	d				06 12				06 41								07 11			07 23			
Sunnymeads	d				06 15				06 44								07 14			07 26			
Datchet	d				06 18				06 47								07 17			07 29			
Windsor & Eton Riverside	a				06 22				06 51								07 21			07 33			
Egham	d	05 49	05 57				06 20	06 27			06 49			06 57				07 19			07 27	07 28	
Virginia Water	a	05 53	06 01				06 25	06 31			06 53			07 01				07 23			07 31	07 32	
	d	05 53	06 01				06 25	06 31			06 53			07 01				07 23			07 31	07 32	
Chertsey	d	05 59					06 30				06 59							07 29					
Addlestone	d	06 02					06 33				07 02							07 32					
Weybridge	a	06 07					06 38				07 07							07 37					
Byfleet & New Haw	d																						
West Byfleet	d																						
Woking	a																						
Longcross	d																						
Sunningdale	d		06 07					06 37						07 07							07 37	07 37	
Ascot ■	d		06 13					06 43				06 53	06 53	07 13							07 43	07 43	07 53
Bagshot	d											06 59	06 59										07 59
Camberley	a											07 05	07 05										08 05
Frimley	d											07 13	07 13										08 13
Ash Vale	d											07 19	07 19										08 19
Aldershot	a											07 24	07 26										08 24
	d											07 38	07 38		08 08								08 38
Ash ■	d											07 45	07 45		08 15								08 45
Wanborough	d											07 48	07 48		08 18								08 48
Guildford	a											07 55	07 55		08 25								08 55
Martins Heron	d		06 17					06 47						07 17							07 47	07 47	
Bracknell	d		06 20					06 50						07 20							07 50	07 50	
Wokingham	d		06 27					06 57						07 27							07 57	07 57	
Winnersh	d		06 30					07 00						07 30							08 00	08 00	
Winnersh Triangle	d		06 32					07 02						07 32							08 02	08 02	
Earley	d		06 35					07 05						07 35							08 05	08 05	
Reading ■	a		06 40					07 10						07 40							08 10	08 10	

A 21 July

B 28 July, 4 August, 11 August, 1 September

C until 21 July, from 18 August until 6 October, not 1 September

Table 149

Saturdays until 6 October

London - Hounslow, Richmond, Kingston, Windsor, Weybridge, Ascot, Guildford and Reading

Network Diagram - see first Page of Table 148

		SW		SW	SW	SW	SW	SW ■	SW	SW ■	SW	SW		SW	SW	SW	SW	SW ■	SW	SW ■	SW	SW		SW	SW
London Waterloo 15 ⊖	d	06 52		06 58		07 03	07 15	07 20			07 22	07 28			07 33	07 37	07 45	07 50			07 52	07 58			08 03
Vauxhall ⊖	d	06 56		07 02		07 07	07 19				07 26	07 32			07 37	07 41	07 49				07 56	08 02			08 07
Queenstown Rd.(Battersea)	d	06 59				07 10	07 22				07 29				07 40	07 44	07 52				07 59				08 10
Clapham Junction 10	d	07 02		07 08		07 13	07 25	07 28			07 32	07 38			07 43	07 47	07 55	07 58			08 02	08 08			08 13
Wandsworth Town	d	07 05				07 16	07 28				07 35				07 46	07 50	07 58				08 05				08 16
Putney	d	07 08		07 12		07 19	07 31				07 38	07 42			07 49	07 53	08 01				08 08	08 12			08 19
Barnes	d	07 12				07 22	07 35				07 42				07 52	07 57	08 05				08 12				08 22
Barnes Bridge	d	07 14									07 44					07 59					08 14				
Chiswick	d	07 17									07 47					08 02					08 17				
Kew Bridge	d	07 20									07 50					08 05					08 20				
Brentford	d	07 23									07 53					08 08					08 23				
Syon Lane	d	07 25									07 55					08 10					08 25				
Isleworth	d	07 27									07 57					08 12					08 27				
Hounslow	d	07 31									08 01					08 18					08 31				
Mortlake	d					07 24	07 37								07 54		08 07								08 24
North Sheen	d					07 26	07 39		←						07 56		08 09		←						08 26
Richmond ⊖	d			07 18		07 29	07 42	07 36	07 42			07 48			07 59		08 12	08 06	08 12			08 18			08 29
St Margarets	d					07 31	→		07 44						08 01		→		08 14						08 31
Twickenham	a			07 21		07 33		07 40	07 46			07 51			08 03			08 10	08 16			08 21			08 33
	d			07 22		07 34		07 40	07 47			07 52			08 04			08 10	08 17			08 22			08 34
Strawberry Hill	d					07 37									08 07										08 37
Fulwell	a																								
Teddington	a					07 40									08 10										08 40
Hampton Wick	a					07 44									08 14										08 44
Kingston	a					07 46									08 16										08 46
Whitton	d			07 25	←				07a50			07 55		←		08a23			08a20			08 25		←	
Feltham	d	07 36		07 29	07 36			07 46			08 06	07 59		08 06				08 16			08 36	08 29		08 36	
Ashford (Surrey)	d	→		07 33	07 40						→	08 03		08 10							→	08 33		08 40	
Staines	d			07 37	07 44			07 53				08 07		08 14				08 23				08 37		08 44	
Wraysbury	d			07 41								08 11										08 41			
Sunnymeads	d			07 44								08 14										08 44			
Datchet	d			07 47								08 17										08 47			
Windsor & Eton Riverside	a			07 51								08 21										08 51			
Egham	d				07 49			07 57						08 19				08 27						08 49	
Virginia Water	a				07 53			08 01						08 23				08 31						08 53	
	d				07 53			08 01						08 23				08 31						08 53	
Chertsey	d				07 59									08 29										08 59	
Addlestone	d				08 02									08 32										09 02	
Weybridge	a				08 07									08 37										09 07	
Byfleet & New Haw	d																								
West Byfleet	d																								
Woking	a																								
Longcross	d																								
Sunningdale	d							08 07										08 37							
Ascot 3	d							08 13		08 23								08 43		08 53					
Bagshot	d									08 29										08 59					
Camberley	a									08 35										09 05					
Frimley	d									08 43										09 13					
Ash Vale	d									08 49										09 19					
Aldershot	a									08 54										09 24					
	d									09 08										09 38					
Ash 5	d									09 15										09 45					
Wanborough	d									09 18										09 48					
Guildford	a									09 25										09 55					
Martins Heron	d							08 17										08 47							
Bracknell	d							08 20										08 50							
Wokingham	d							08 27										08 57							
Winnersh	d							08 30										09 00							
Winnersh Triangle	d							08 32										09 02							
Earley	d							08 35										09 05							
Reading 7	a							08 40										09 10							

Table 149

Saturdays until 6 October

London - Hounslow, Richmond, Kingston, Windsor, Weybridge, Ascot, Guildford and Reading

Network Diagram - see first Page of Table 148

		SW	SW	SW ■	SW	SW ■	SW	SW		SW	SW	SW	SW	SW ■	SW	SW ■	SW	SW		SW	SW	SW	SW	SW ■	SW
London Waterloo 15 ⊖	d	08 07	08 15	08 20			08 22	08 28			08 33	08 37	08 45	08 50			08 52	08 58			09 03	09 07	09 15	09 20	
Vauxhall ⊖	d	08 11	08 19				08 26	08 32			08 37	08 41	08 49				08 56	09 02			09 07	09 11	09 19		
Queenstown Rd.(Battersea)	d	08 14	08 22				08 29				08 40	08 44	08 52				08 59				09 10	09 14	09 22		
Clapham Junction 10	d	08 17	08 25	08 28			08 32	08 38			08 43	08 47	08 55	08 58			09 02	09 08			09 13	09 17	09 25	09 28	
Wandsworth Town	d	08 20	08 28				08 35				08 46	08 50	08 58				09 05				09 16	09 20	09 28		
Putney	d	08 23	08 31				08 38	08 42			08 49	08 53	09 01				09 08	09 12			09 19	09 23	09 31		
Barnes	d	08 27	08 35				08 42				08 52	08 57	09 05				09 12				09 22	09 27	09 35		
Barnes Bridge	d	08 29					08 44					08 59					09 14					09 29			
Chiswick	d	08 32					08 47					09 02					09 17					09 32			
Kew Bridge	d	08 35					08 50					09 05					09 20					09 35			
Brentford	d	08 38					08 53					09 08					09 23					09 38			
Syon Lane	d	08 40					08 55					09 10					09 25					09 40			
Isleworth	d	08 42					08 57					09 12					09 27					09 42			
Hounslow	d	08 48					09 01					09 18					09 31					09 48			
Mortlake	d		08 37								08 54		09 07								09 24		09 37		
North Sheen	d		08 39		←						08 56		09 09		←						09 26		09 39		←
Richmond ⊖	d		08 42	08 36	08 42			08 48			08 59		09 12	09 06	09 12			09 18			09 29		09 42	09 36	09 42
St Margarets	d		→		08 44						09 01		→		09 14						09 31		→		09 44
Twickenham	a			08 40	08 46			08 51			09 03			09 10	09 16			09 21			09 33			09 40	09 46
	d			08 40	08 47			08 52			09 04			09 10	09 17			09 22			09 34			09 40	09 47
Strawberry Hill	d										09 07										09 37				
Fulwell	a																								
Teddington	a										09 10										09 40				
Hampton Wick	a										09 14										09 44				
Kingston	a										09 16										09 46				
Whitton	d	08a53			08a50			08 55		←		09a23			09a20			09 25		←		09a53			09a50
Feltham	d			08 46			09 06	08 59		09 06				09 16			09 36	09 29		09 36				09 46	
Ashford (Surrey)	d						→	09 03		09 10							→	09 33		09 40					
Staines	d			08 53				09 07		09 14				09 23				09 37		09 44				09 53	
Wraysbury	d							09 11										09 41							
Sunnymeads	d							09 14										09 44							
Datchet	d							09 17										09 47							
Windsor & Eton Riverside	a							09 21										09 51							
Egham	d			08 57						09 19				09 27						09 49				09 57	
Virginia Water	a			09 01						09 23				09 31						09 53				10 01	
	d			09 01						09 23				09 31						09 53				10 01	
Chertsey	d									09 29										09 59					
Addlestone	d									09 32										10 02					
Weybridge	a									09 37										10 07					
Byfleet & New Haw	d																								
West Byfleet	d																								
Woking	a																								
Longcross	d																								
Sunningdale	d			09 07										09 37										10 07	
Ascot 3	d			09 13		09 23								09 43		09 53								10 13	
Bagshot	d					09 29										09 59									
Camberley	a					09 35										10 05									
Frimley	d					09 43										10 13									
Ash Vale	d					09 49										10 19									
Aldershot	a					09 54										10 24									
	d					10 08										10 38									
Ash 5	d					10 15										10 45									
Wanborough	d					10 18										10 48									
Guildford	a					10 25										10 55									
Martins Heron	d			09 17										09 47										10 17	
Bracknell	d			09 20										09 50										10 20	
Wokingham	d			09 27										09 57										10 27	
Winnersh	d			09 30										10 00										10 30	
Winnersh Triangle	d			09 32										10 02										10 32	
Earley	d			09 35										10 05										10 35	
Reading 7	a			09 40										10 10										10 40	

London - Hounslow, Richmond, Kingston, Windsor, Weybridge, Ascot, Guildford and Reading

Network Diagram - see first Page of Table 148

		SW 1	SW	SW		SW	SW	SW	SW	SW 1	SW	SW 1	SW	SW		SW	SW	SW	SW	SW 1	SW	SW 1	SW	SW	
London Waterloo 15 ⊖	d		09 22	09 28			09 33	09 37	09 45	09 50			09 52	09 58			10 03	10 07	10 15	10 20			10 22	10 28	
Vauxhall ⊖	d		09 26	09 32			09 37	09 41	09 49				09 56	10 02			10 07	10 11	10 19				10 26	10 32	
Queenstown Rd.(Battersea)	d		09 29				09 40	09 44	09 52				09 59				10 10	10 14	10 22				10 29		
Clapham Junction 10	d		09 32	09 38			09 43	09 47	09 55	09 58			10 02	10 08			10 13	10 17	10 25	10 28			10 32	10 38	
Wandsworth Town	d		09 35				09 46	09 50	09 58				10 05				10 16	10 20	10 28				10 35		
Putney	d		09 38	09 42			09 49	09 53	10 01				10 08	10 12			10 19	10 23	10 31				10 38	10 42	
Barnes	d		09 42				09 52	09 57	10 05				10 12				10 22	10 27	10 35				10 42		
Barnes Bridge	d		09 44					09 59					10 14					10 29					10 44		
Chiswick	d		09 47					10 02					10 17					10 32					10 47		
Kew Bridge	d		09 50					10 05					10 20					10 35					10 50		
Brentford	d		09 53					10 08					10 23					10 38					10 53		
Syon Lane	d		09 55					10 10					10 25					10 40					10 55		
Isleworth	d		09 57					10 12					10 27					10 42					10 57		
Hounslow	d		10 01					10 18					10 31					10 48					11 01		
Mortlake	d						09 54		10 07								10 24		10 37						
North Sheen	d						09 56		10 09		←						10 26		10 39		←				
Richmond ⊖	d			09 48			09 59		10 12	10 06	10 12			10 18			10 29		10 42	10 36	10 42			10 48	
St Margarets	d						10 01		→		10 14						10 31		→		10 44				
Twickenham	a			09 51			10 03			10 10	10 16			10 21			10 33			10 40	10 46			10 51	
	d			09 52			10 04			10 10	10 17			10 22			10 34			10 40	10 47			10 52	
Strawberry Hill	d						10 07										10 37								
Fulwell	a																								
Teddington	a						10 10										10 40								
Hampton Wick	a						10 14										10 44								
Kingston	a						10 16										10 46								
Whitton	d			09 55		←		10a23			10a20			10 25		←		10a53			10a50			10 55	
Feltham	d		10 06	09 59		10 06				10 16			10 36	10 29		10 36				10 46			11 06	10 59	
Ashford (Surrey)	d		→	10 03		10 10							→	10 33		10 40							→	11 03	
Staines	d			10 07		10 14				10 23				10 37		10 44				10 53				11 07	
Wraysbury	d			10 11										10 41										11 11	
Sunnymeads	d			10 14										10 44										11 14	
Datchet	d			10 17										10 47										11 17	
Windsor & Eton Riverside	a			10 21										10 51										11 21	
Egham	d					10 19				10 27						10 49				10 57					
Virginia Water	a					10 23				10 31						10 53				11 01					
	d					10 23				10 31						10 53				11 01					
Chertsey	d					10 29										10 59									
Addlestone	d					10 32										11 02									
Weybridge	a					10 37										11 07									
Byfleet & New Haw	d																								
West Byfleet	d																								
Woking	a																								
Longcross	d																								
Sunningdale	d									10 37										11 07					
Ascot 3	d	10 23								10 43		10 53								11 13		11 23			
Bagshot	d	10 29										10 59										11 29			
Camberley	a	10 35										11 05										11 35			
Frimley	d	10 43										11 13										11 43			
Ash Vale	d	10 49										11 19										11 49			
Aldershot	a	10 54										11 24										11 54			
	d	11 08										11 38										12 08			
Ash 5	d	11 15										11 45										12 15			
Wanborough	d	11 18										11 48										12 18			
Guildford	a	11 25										11 55										12 25			
Martins Heron	d									10 47										11 17					
Bracknell	d									10 50										11 20					
Wokingham	d									10 57										11 27					
Winnersh	d									11 00										11 30					
Winnersh Triangle	d									11 02										11 32					
Earley	d									11 05										11 35					
Reading 7	a									11 10										11 40					

London - Hounslow, Richmond, Kingston, Windsor, Weybridge, Ascot, Guildford and Reading

Network Diagram - see first Page of Table 148

		SW	SW	SW	SW	SW 1	SW	SW 1	SW	SW		SW	SW	SW	SW	SW 1	SW	SW 1	SW	SW		SW	SW	SW	SW
London Waterloo 15 ⊖	d		10 33	10 37	10 45	10 50			10 52	10 58			11 03	11 07	11 15	11 20			11 22	11 28			11 33	11 37	11 45
Vauxhall ⊖	d		10 37	10 41	10 49				10 56	11 02			11 07	11 11	11 19				11 26	11 32			11 37	11 41	11 49
Queenstown Rd.(Battersea)	d		10 40	10 44	10 52				10 59				11 10	11 14	11 22				11 29				11 40	11 44	11 52
Clapham Junction 10	d		10 43	10 47	10 55	10 58			11 02	11 08			11 13	11 17	11 25	11 28			11 32	11 38			11 43	11 47	11 55
Wandsworth Town	d		10 46	10 50	10 58				11 05				11 16	11 20	11 28				11 35				11 46	11 50	11 58
Putney	d		10 49	10 53	11 01				11 08	11 12			11 19	11 23	11 31				11 38	11 42			11 49	11 53	12 01
Barnes	d		10 52	10 57	11 05				11 12				11 22	11 27	11 35				11 42				11 52	11 57	12 05
Barnes Bridge	d			10 59					11 14					11 29					11 44					11 59	
Chiswick	d			11 02					11 17					11 32					11 47					12 02	
Kew Bridge	d			11 05					11 20					11 35					11 50					12 05	
Brentford	d			11 08					11 23					11 38					11 53					12 08	
Syon Lane	d			11 10					11 25					11 40					11 55					12 10	
Isleworth	d			11 12					11 27					11 42					11 57					12 12	
Hounslow	d			11 18					11 31					11 48					12 01					12 18	
Mortlake	d		10 54		11 07								11 24		11 37								11 54		12 07
North Sheen	d		10 56		11 09		←						11 26		11 39		←						11 56		12 09
Richmond ⊖	d		10 59		11 12	11 06	11 12			11 18			11 29		11 42	11 36	11 42			11 48			11 59		12 12
St Margarets	d		11 01		→		11 14						11 31		→		11 44						12 01		→
Twickenham	a		11 03			11 10	11 16			11 21			11 33			11 40	11 46			11 51			12 03		
	d		11 04			11 10	11 17			11 22			11 34			11 40	11 47			11 52			12 04		
Strawberry Hill	d		11 07										11 37										12 07		
Fulwell	a																								
Teddington	a		11 10										11 40										12 10		
Hampton Wick	a		11 14										11 44										12 14		
Kingston	a		11 16										11 46										12 16		
Whitton	d	←		11a23			11a20			11 25		←		11a53			11a50			11 55		←		12a23	
Feltham	d	11 06				11 16			11 36	11 29		11 36				11 46			12 06	11 59		12 06			
Ashford (Surrey)	d	11 10							→	11 33		11 40							→	12 03		12 10			
Staines	d	11 14				11 23				11 37		11 44				11 53				12 07		12 14			
Wraysbury	d									11 41										12 11					
Sunnymeads	d									11 44										12 14					
Datchet	d									11 47										12 17					
Windsor & Eton Riverside	a									11 51										12 21					
Egham	d	11 19				11 27						11 49				11 57						12 19			
Virginia Water	a	11 23				11 31						11 53				12 01						12 23			
	d	11 23				11 31						11 53				12 01						12 23			
Chertsey	d	11 29										11 59										12 29			
Addlestone	d	11 32										12 02										12 32			
Weybridge	a	11 37										12 07										12 37			
Byfleet & New Haw	d																								
West Byfleet	d																								
Woking	a																								
Longcross	d																								
Sunningdale	d					11 37										12 07									
Ascot 3	d					11 43		11 53								12 13		12 23							
Bagshot	d							11 59										12 29							
Camberley	a							12 05										12 35							
Frimley	d							12 13										12 43							
Ash Vale	d							12 19										12 49							
Aldershot	a							12 24										12 54							
	d							12 38										13 08							
Ash 5	d							12 45										13 15							
Wanborough	d							12 48										13 18							
Guildford	a							12 55										13 25							
Martins Heron	d					11 47										12 17									
Bracknell	d					11 50										12 20									
Wokingham	d					11 57										12 27									
Winnersh	d					12 00										12 30									
Winnersh Triangle	d					12 02										12 32									
Earley	d					12 05										12 35									
Reading 7	a					12 10										12 40									

Table 149

Saturdays
until 6 October

London - Hounslow, Richmond, Kingston, Windsor, Weybridge, Ascot, Guildford and Reading

Network Diagram - see first Page of Table 148

		SW 1	SW	SW 1	SW	SW		SW	SW	SW	SW	SW 1	SW	SW 1	SW	SW		SW	SW	SW	SW	SW 1	SW	SW 1	SW
London Waterloo 15 ⊖	d	11 50			11 52	11 58			12 03	12 07	12 15	12 20			12 22	12 28			12 33	12 37	12 45	12 50			12 52
Vauxhall ⊖	d				11 56	12 02			12 07	12 11	12 19				12 26	12 32			12 37	12 41	12 49				12 56
Queenstown Rd.(Battersea)	d				11 59				12 10	12 14	12 22				12 29				12 40	12 44	12 52				12 59
Clapham Junction 10	d	11 58			12 02	12 08			12 13	12 17	12 25	12 28			12 32	12 38			12 43	12 47	12 55	12 58			13 02
Wandsworth Town	d				12 05				12 16	12 20	12 28				12 35				12 46	12 50	12 58				13 05
Putney	d				12 08	12 12			12 19	12 23	12 31				12 38	12 42			12 49	12 53	13 01				13 08
Barnes	d				12 12				12 22	12 27	12 35				12 42				12 52	12 57	13 05				13 12
Barnes Bridge	d				12 14					12 29					12 44					12 59					13 14
Chiswick	d				12 17					12 32					12 47					13 02					13 17
Kew Bridge	d				12 20					12 35					12 50					13 05					13 20
Brentford	d				12 23					12 38					12 53					13 08					13 23
Syon Lane	d				12 25					12 40					12 55					13 10					13 25
Isleworth	d				12 27					12 42					12 57					13 12					13 27
Hounslow	d				12 31					12 48					13 01					13 18					13 31
Mortlake	d								12 24		12 37								12 54		13 07				
North Sheen	d		←						12 26		12 39		←						12 56		13 09		←		
Richmond ⊖	d	12 06	12 12			12 18			12 29		12 42	12 36	12 42			12 48			12 59		13 12	13 06	13 12		
St Margarets	d		12 14						12 31		→		12 44						13 01		→		13 14		
Twickenham	a	12 10	12 16			12 21			12 33			12 40	12 46			12 51			13 03			13 10	13 16		
	d	12 10	12 17			12 22			12 34			12 40	12 47			12 52			13 04			13 10	13 17		
Strawberry Hill	d								12 37										13 07						
Fulwell	a																								
Teddington	a								12 40										13 10						
Hampton Wick	a								12 44										13 14						
Kingston	a								12 46										13 16						
Whitton	d		12a20			12 25		←		12a53			12a50			12 55		←		13a23			13a20		
Feltham	d	12 16			12 36	12 29		12 36				12 46			13 06	12 59		13 06				13 16			13 36
Ashford (Surrey)	d				→	12 33		12 40							→	13 03		13 10							→
Staines	d	12 23				12 37		12 44				12 53				13 07		13 14				13 23			
Wraysbury	d					12 41										13 11									
Sunnymeads	d					12 44										13 14									
Datchet	d					12 47										13 17									
Windsor & Eton Riverside	a					12 51										13 21									
Egham	d	12 27						12 49				12 57						13 19				13 27			
Virginia Water	a	12 31						12 53				13 01						13 23				13 31			
	d	12 31						12 53				13 01						13 23				13 31			
Chertsey	d							12 59										13 29							
Addlestone	d							13 02										13 32							
Weybridge	a							13 07										13 37							
Byfleet & New Haw	d																								
West Byfleet	d																								
Woking	a																								
Longcross	d																								
Sunningdale	d	12 37										13 07										13 37			
Ascot 3	d	12 43		12 53								13 13		13 23								13 43		13 53	
Bagshot	d			12 59										13 29										13 59	
Camberley	a			13 05										13 35										14 05	
Frimley	d			13 13										13 43										14 13	
Ash Vale	d			13 19										13 49										14 19	
Aldershot	a			13 24										13 54										14 24	
	d			13 38										14 08										14 38	
Ash 5	d			13 45										14 15										14 45	
Wanborough	d			13 48										14 18										14 48	
Guildford	a			13 55										14 25										14 55	
Martins Heron	d	12 47										13 17										13 47			
Bracknell	d	12 50										13 20										13 50			
Wokingham	d	12 57										13 27										13 57			
Winnersh	d	13 00										13 30										14 00			
Winnersh Triangle	d	13 02										13 32										14 02			
Earley	d	13 05										13 35										14 05			
Reading 7	a	13 10										13 40										14 10			

Table 149

Saturdays
until 6 October

London - Hounslow, Richmond, Kingston, Windsor, Weybridge, Ascot, Guildford and Reading

Network Diagram - see first Page of Table 148

		SW		SW	SW	SW	SW	SW 1	SW	SW 1	SW	SW		SW	SW	SW	SW	SW 1	SW	SW 1	SW	SW		SW	SW
London Waterloo 15 ⊖	d	12 58			13 03	13 07	13 15	13 20			13 22	13 28			13 33	13 37	13 45	13 50			13 52	13 58			14 03
Vauxhall ⊖	d	13 02			13 07	13 11	13 19				13 26	13 32			13 37	13 41	13 49				13 56	14 02			14 07
Queenstown Rd.(Battersea)	d				13 10	13 14	13 22				13 29				13 40	13 44	13 52				13 59				14 10
Clapham Junction 10	d	13 08			13 13	13 17	13 25	13 28			13 32	13 38			13 43	13 47	13 55	13 58			14 02	14 08			14 13
Wandsworth Town	d				13 16	13 20	13 28				13 35				13 46	13 50	13 58				14 05				14 16
Putney	d	13 12			13 19	13 23	13 31				13 38	13 42			13 49	13 53	14 01				14 08	14 12			14 19
Barnes	d				13 22	13 27	13 35				13 42				13 52	13 57	14 05				14 12				14 22
Barnes Bridge	d					13 29					13 44					13 59					14 14				
Chiswick	d					13 32					13 47					14 02					14 17				
Kew Bridge	d					13 35					13 50					14 05					14 20				
Brentford	d					13 38					13 53					14 08					14 23				
Syon Lane	d					13 40					13 55					14 10					14 25				
Isleworth	d					13 42					13 57					14 12					14 27				
Hounslow	d					13 48					14 01					14 18					14 31				
Mortlake	d				13 24		13 37								13 54		14 07								14 24
North Sheen	d				13 26		13 39		←						13 56		14 09		←						14 26
Richmond ⊖	d	13 18			13 29		13 42	13 36	13 42			13 48			13 59		14 12	14 06	14 12			14 18			14 29
St Margarets	d				13 31		→		13 44						14 01		→		14 14						14 31
Twickenham	a	13 21			13 33			13 40	13 46			13 51			14 03			14 10	14 16			14 21			14 33
	d	13 22			13 34			13 40	13 47			13 52			14 04			14 10	14 17			14 22			14 34
Strawberry Hill	d				13 37										14 07										14 37
Fulwell	a																								
Teddington	a				13 40										14 10										14 40
Hampton Wick	a				13 44										14 14										14 44
Kingston	a				13 46										14 16										14 46
Whitton	d	13 25		←		13a53			13a50			13 55		←		14a23			14a20			14 25		←	
Feltham	d	13 29		13 36				13 46			14 06	13 59		14 06				14 16			14 36	14 29		14 36	
Ashford (Surrey)	d	13 33		13 40							→	14 03		14 10							→	14 33		14 40	
Staines	d	13 37		13 44				13 53				14 07		14 14				14 23				14 37		14 44	
Wraysbury	d	13 41										14 11										14 41			
Sunnymeads	d	13 44										14 14										14 44			
Datchet	d	13 47										14 17										14 47			
Windsor & Eton Riverside	a	13 51										14 21										14 51			
Egham	d			13 49				13 57						14 19				14 27						14 49	
Virginia Water	a			13 53				14 01						14 23				14 31						14 53	
	d			13 53				14 01						14 23				14 31						14 53	
Chertsey	d			13 59										14 29										14 59	
Addlestone	d			14 02										14 32										15 02	
Weybridge	a			14 07										14 37										15 07	
Byfleet & New Haw	d																								
West Byfleet	d																								
Woking	a																								
Longcross	d																								
Sunningdale	d							14 07										14 37							
Ascot 3	d							14 13		14 23								14 43		14 53					
Bagshot	d									14 29										14 59					
Camberley	a									14 35										15 05					
Frimley	d									14 43										15 13					
Ash Vale	d									14 49										15 19					
Aldershot	a									14 54										15 24					
	d									15 08										15 38					
Ash 5	d									15 15										15 45					
Wanborough	d									15 18										15 48					
Guildford	a									15 25										15 55					
Martins Heron	d							14 17										14 47							
Bracknell	d							14 20										14 50							
Wokingham	d							14 27										14 57							
Winnersh	d							14 30										15 00							
Winnersh Triangle	d							14 32										15 02							
Earley	d							14 35										15 05							
Reading 7	a							14 40										15 10							

Table 149

Saturdays
until 6 October

London - Hounslow, Richmond, Kingston, Windsor, Weybridge, Ascot, Guildford and Reading

Network Diagram - see first Page of Table 148

		SW	SW	SW 1	SW	SW 1	SW	SW		SW	SW	SW	SW	SW 1	SW	SW 1	SW	SW		SW	SW	SW	SW	SW 1	SW
London Waterloo 15 ⊖	d	14 07	14 15	14 20			14 22	14 28			14 33	14 37	14 45	14 50			14 52	14 58			15 03	15 07	15 15	15 20	
Vauxhall ⊖	d	14 11	14 19				14 26	14 32			14 37	14 41	14 49				14 56	15 02			15 07	15 11	15 19		
Queenstown Rd.(Battersea)	d	14 14	14 22				14 29				14 40	14 44	14 52				14 59				15 10	15 14	15 22		
Clapham Junction 10	d	14 17	14 25	14 28			14 32	14 38			14 43	14 47	14 55	14 58			15 02	15 08			15 13	15 17	15 25	15 28	
Wandsworth Town	d	14 20	14 28				14 35				14 46	14 50	14 58				15 05				15 16	15 20	15 28		
Putney	d	14 23	14 31				14 38	14 42			14 49	14 53	15 01				15 08	15 12			15 19	15 23	15 31		
Barnes	d	14 27	14 35				14 42				14 52	14 57	15 05				15 12				15 22	15 27	15 35		
Barnes Bridge	d	14 29					14 44					14 59					15 14					15 29			
Chiswick	d	14 32					14 47					15 02					15 17					15 32			
Kew Bridge	d	14 35					14 50					15 05					15 20					15 35			
Brentford	d	14 38					14 53					15 08					15 23					15 38			
Syon Lane	d	14 40					14 55					15 10					15 25					15 40			
Isleworth	d	14 42					14 57					15 12					15 27					15 42			
Hounslow	d	14 48					15 01					15 18					15 31					15 48			
Mortlake	d		14 37								14 54		15 07								15 24		15 37		
North Sheen	d		14 39		←						14 56		15 09		←						15 26		15 39		←
Richmond ⊖	d		14 42	14 36	14 42			14 48			14 59		15 12	15 06	15 12			15 18			15 29		15 42	15 36	15 42
St Margarets	d		→		14 44						15 01		→		15 14						15 31		→		15 44
Twickenham	a			14 40	14 46			14 51			15 03			15 10	15 16			15 21			15 33			15 40	15 46
	d			14 40	14 47			14 52			15 04			15 10	15 17			15 22			15 34			15 40	15 47
Strawberry Hill	d										15 07										15 37				
Fulwell	a																								
Teddington	a										15 10										15 40				
Hampton Wick	a										15 14										15 44				
Kingston	a										15 16										15 46				
Whitton	d	14a53			14a50			14 55		←		15a23			15a20			15 25		←		15a53			15a50
Feltham	d			14 46			15 06	14 59		15 06				15 16			15 36	15 29		15 36				15 46	
Ashford (Surrey)	d						→	15 03		15 10							→	15 33		15 40					
Staines	d			14 53				15 07		15 14				15 23				15 37		15 44				15 53	
Wraysbury	d							15 11										15 41							
Sunnymeads	d							15 14										15 44							
Datchet	d							15 17										15 47							
Windsor & Eton Riverside	a							15 22										15 51							
Egham	d			14 57						15 19				15 27						15 49				15 57	
Virginia Water	a			15 01						15 23				15 31						15 53				16 01	
	d			15 01						15 23				15 31						15 53				16 01	
Chertsey	d									15 29										15 59					
Addlestone	d									15 32										16 02					
Weybridge	a									15 37										16 07					
Byfleet & New Haw	d																								
West Byfleet	d																								
Woking	a																								
Longcross	d																								
Sunningdale	d			15 07										15 37										16 07	
Ascot 3	d			15 13		15 23								15 43		15 53								16 13	
Bagshot	d					15 29										15 59									
Camberley	a					15 35										16 05									
Frimley	d					15 43										16 13									
Ash Vale	d					15 49										16 19									
Aldershot	a					15 54										16 24									
	d					16 08										16 38									
Ash 5	d					16 15										16 45									
Wanborough	d					16 18										16 48									
Guildford	a					16 25										16 55									
Martins Heron	d			15 17										15 47										16 17	
Bracknell	d			15 20										15 50										16 20	
Wokingham	d			15 27										15 57										16 27	
Winnersh	d			15 30										16 00										16 30	
Winnersh Triangle	d			15 32										16 02										16 32	
Earley	d			15 35										16 05										16 35	
Reading 7	a			15 40										16 10										16 40	

Table 149

Saturdays
until 6 October

London - Hounslow, Richmond, Kingston, Windsor, Weybridge, Ascot, Guildford and Reading

Network Diagram - see first Page of Table 148

		SW 1	SW	SW		SW	SW	SW	SW	SW 1	SW	SW 1	SW	SW		SW	SW	SW	SW	SW 1	SW	SW 1	SW	SW
London Waterloo 15 ⊖	d		15 22	15 28			15 33	15 37	15 45	15 50			15 52	15 58			16 03	16 07	16 15	16 20			16 22	16 28
Vauxhall ⊖	d		15 26	15 32			15 37	15 41	15 49				15 56	16 02			16 07	16 11	16 19				16 26	16 32
Queenstown Rd.(Battersea)	d		15 29				15 40	15 44	15 52				15 59				16 10	16 14	16 22				16 29	
Clapham Junction 10	d		15 32	15 38			15 43	15 47	15 55	15 58			16 02	16 08			16 13	16 17	16 25	16 28			16 32	16 38
Wandsworth Town	d		15 35				15 46	15 50	15 58				16 05				16 16	16 20	16 28				16 35	
Putney	d		15 38	15 42			15 49	15 53	16 01				16 08	16 12			16 19	16 23	16 31				16 38	16 42
Barnes	d		15 42				15 52	15 57	16 05				16 12				16 22	16 27	16 35				16 42	
Barnes Bridge	d		15 44					15 59					16 14					16 29					16 44	
Chiswick	d		15 47					16 02					16 17					16 32					16 47	
Kew Bridge	d		15 50					16 05					16 20					16 35					16 50	
Brentford	d		15 53					16 08					16 23					16 38					16 53	
Syon Lane	d		15 55					16 10					16 25					16 40					16 55	
Isleworth	d		15 57					16 12					16 27					16 42					16 57	
Hounslow	d		16 01					16 18					16 31					16 48					17 01	
Mortlake	d						15 54		16 07								16 24		16 37					
North Sheen	d						15 56		16 09		←						16 26		16 39		←			
Richmond ⊖	d			15 48			15 59		16 12	16 06	16 12			16 18			16 29		16 42	16 36	16 42			16 48
St Margarets	d						16 01		→		16 14						16 31		→		16 44			
Twickenham	a			15 51			16 03			16 10	16 16			16 21			16 33			16 40	16 46			16 51
	d			15 52			16 04			16 10	16 17			16 22			16 34			16 40	16 47			16 52
Strawberry Hill	d						16 07										16 37							
Fulwell	a																							
Teddington	a						16 10										16 40							
Hampton Wick	a						16 14										16 44							
Kingston	a						16 16										16 46							
Whitton	d			15 55		←		16a23			16a20			16 25		←		16a53			16a50			16 55
Feltham	d		16 06	15 59		16 06				16 16			16 36	16 29		16 36				16 46			17 06	16 59
Ashford (Surrey)	d		→	16 03		16 10							→	16 33		16 40							→	17 03
Staines	d			16 07		16 14				16 23				16 37		16 44				16 53				17 07
Wraysbury	d			16 11										16 41										17 11
Sunnymeads	d			16 14										16 44										17 14
Datchet	d			16 17										16 47										17 17
Windsor & Eton Riverside	a			16 21										16 51										17 21
Egham	d					16 19				16 27						16 49				16 57				
Virginia Water	a					16 23				16 31						16 53				17 01				
	d					16 23				16 31						16 53				17 01				
Chertsey	d					16 29										16 59								
Addlestone	d					16 32										17 02								
Weybridge	a					16 42										17 07								
Byfleet & New Haw	d																							
West Byfleet	d																							
Woking	a																							
Longcross	d																							
Sunningdale	d									16 37										17 07				
Ascot 3	d	16 23								16 43		16 53								17 13		17 23		
Bagshot	d	16 29										16 59										17 29		
Camberley	a	16 35										17 05										17 35		
Frimley	d	16 43										17 13										17 43		
Ash Vale	d	16 49										17 19										17 49		
Aldershot	a	16 54										17 24										17 54		
	d	17 08										17 38										18 08		
Ash 5	d	17 15										17 45										18 15		
Wanborough	d	17 18										17 48										18 18		
Guildford	a	17 25										17 55										18 25		
Martins Heron	d									16 47										17 17				
Bracknell	d									16 50										17 20				
Wokingham	d									16 57										17 27				
Winnersh	d									17 00										17 30				
Winnersh Triangle	d									17 02										17 32				
Earley	d									17 05										17 35				
Reading 7	a									17 10										17 40				

Table 149

Saturdays until 6 October

London - Hounslow, Richmond, Kingston, Windsor, Weybridge, Ascot, Guildford and Reading

Network Diagram - see first Page of Table 148

		SW	SW	SW	SW	SW 1	SW	SW 1	SW	SW	SW	SW	SW	SW	SW 1	SW	SW 1	SW	SW	SW	SW	SW	SW
London Waterloo 15 ⊖	d		16 33	16 37	16 45	16 50			16 52	16 58		17 03	17 07	17 15	17 20			17 22	17 28		17 33	17 37	17 45
Vauxhall ⊖	d		16 37	16 41	16 49				16 56	17 02		17 07	17 11	17 19				17 26	17 32		17 37	17 41	17 49
Queenstown Rd.(Battersea)	d		16 40	16 44	16 52				16 59			17 10	17 14	17 22				17 29			17 40	17 44	17 52
Clapham Junction 10	d		16 43	16 47	16 55	16 58			17 02	17 08		17 13	17 17	17 25	17 28			17 32	17 38		17 43	17 47	17 55
Wandsworth Town	d		16 46	16 50	16 58				17 05			17 16	17 20	17 28				17 35			17 46	17 50	17 58
Putney	d		16 49	16 53	17 01				17 08	17 12		17 19	17 23	17 31				17 38	17 42		17 49	17 53	18 01
Barnes	d		16 52	16 57	17 05				17 12			17 22	17 27	17 35				17 42			17 52	17 57	18 05
Barnes Bridge	d			16 59					17 14				17 29					17 44				17 59	
Chiswick	d			17 02					17 17				17 32					17 47				18 02	
Kew Bridge	d			17 05					17 20				17 35					17 50				18 05	
Brentford	d			17 08					17 23				17 38					17 53				18 08	
Syon Lane	d			17 10					17 25				17 40					17 55				18 10	
Isleworth	d			17 12					17 27				17 42					17 57				18 12	
Hounslow	d			17 18					17 31				17 48					18 01				18 18	
Mortlake	d		16 54		17 07							17 24		17 37							17 54		18 07
North Sheen	d		16 56		17 09		←					17 26		17 39		←					17 56		18 09
Richmond ⊖	d		16 59		17 12	17 06	17 12			17 18		17 29		17 42	17 36	17 42			17 48		17 59		18 12
St Margarets	d		17 01		→		17 14					17 31		→		17 44					18 01		→
Twickenham	a		17 03			17 10	17 16			17 21		17 33			17 40	17 46			17 51		18 03		
	d		17 04			17 10	17 17			17 22		17 34			17 40	17 47			17 52		18 04		
Strawberry Hill	d		17 07									17 37									18 07		
Fulwell	a																						
Teddington	a		17 10									17 40									18 10		
Hampton Wick	a		17 14									17 44									18 14		
Kingston	a		17 16									17 46									18 16		
Whitton	d	←		17a23			17a20			17 25	←		17a53			17a50			17 55	←		18a23	
Feltham	d	17 06				17 16			17 36	17 29	17 36				17 46			18 06	17 59	18 06			
Ashford (Surrey)	d	17 10							→	17 33	17 40							→	18 03	18 10			
Staines	d	17 14				17 23				17 37	17 44				17 53				18 07	18 14			
Wraysbury	d									17 41									18 11				
Sunnymeads	d									17 44									18 14				
Datchet	d									17 47									18 17				
Windsor & Eton Riverside	a									17 51									18 21				
Egham	d	17 19				17 27					17 49				17 57					18 19			
Virginia Water	a	17 23				17 31					17 53				18 01					18 23			
	d	17 23				17 31					17 53				18 01					18 23			
Chertsey	d	17 29									17 59									18 29			
Addlestone	d	17 32									18 02									18 32			
Weybridge	a	17 37									18 07									18 37			
Byfleet & New Haw	d																						
West Byfleet	d																						
Woking	a																						
Longcross	d																						
Sunningdale	d					17 37									18 07								
Ascot 3	d					17 43		17 53							18 13		18 23						
Bagshot	d							17 59									18 29						
Camberley	a							18 05									18 35						
Frimley	d							18 13									18 43						
Ash Vale	d							18 19									18 49						
Aldershot	a							18 24									18 54						
	d							18 38									19 08						
Ash 5	d							18 45									19 15						
Wanborough	d							18 48									19 18						
Guildford	a							18 55									19 25						
Martins Heron	d					17 47									18 17								
Bracknell	d					17 50									18 20								
Wokingham	d					17 57									18 27								
Winnersh	d					18 00									18 30								
Winnersh Triangle	d					18 02									18 32								
Earley	d					18 05									18 35								
Reading 7	a					18 10									18 40								

Table 149

Saturdays until 6 October

London - Hounslow, Richmond, Kingston, Windsor, Weybridge, Ascot, Guildford and Reading

Network Diagram - see first Page of Table 148

		SW 1	SW	SW 1	SW	SW	SW	SW	SW	SW	SW 1	SW	SW 1	SW	SW	SW	SW	SW	SW	SW 1	SW	SW 1	SW
London Waterloo 15 ⊖	d	17 50			17 52	17 58		18 03	18 07	18 15	18 20			18 22	18 28		18 33	18 37	18 45	18 50			18 52
Vauxhall ⊖	d				17 56	18 02		18 07	18 11	18 19				18 26	18 32		18 37	18 41	18 49				18 56
Queenstown Rd.(Battersea)	d				17 59			18 10	18 14	18 22				18 29			18 40	18 44	18 52				18 59
Clapham Junction 10	d	17 58			18 02	18 08		18 13	18 17	18 25	18 28			18 32	18 38		18 43	18 47	18 55	18 58			19 02
Wandsworth Town	d				18 05			18 16	18 20	18 28				18 35			18 46	18 50	18 58				19 05
Putney	d				18 08	18 12		18 19	18 23	18 31				18 38	18 42		18 49	18 53	19 01				19 08
Barnes	d				18 12			18 22	18 27	18 35				18 42			18 52	18 57	19 05				19 12
Barnes Bridge	d				18 14				18 29					18 44				18 59					19 14
Chiswick	d				18 17				18 32					18 47				19 02					19 17
Kew Bridge	d				18 20				18 35					18 50				19 05					19 20
Brentford	d				18 23				18 38					18 53				19 08					19 23
Syon Lane	d				18 25				18 40					18 55				19 10					19 25
Isleworth	d				18 27				18 42					18 57				19 12					19 27
Hounslow	d				18 31				18 48					19 01				19 18					19 31
Mortlake	d							18 24		18 37							18 54		19 07				
North Sheen	d		←					18 26		18 39		←					18 56		19 09		←		
Richmond ⊖	d	18 06	18 12			18 18		18 29		18 42	18 36	18 42			18 48		18 59		19 12	19 06	19 12		
St Margarets	d		18 14					18 31		→		18 44					19 01		→		19 14		
Twickenham	a	18 10	18 16			18 21		18 33			18 40	18 46			18 51		19 03			19 10	19 16		
	d	18 10	18 17			18 22		18 34			18 40	18 47			18 52		19 04			19 10	19 17		
Strawberry Hill	d							18 37									19 07						
Fulwell	a																						
Teddington	a							18 40									19 10						
Hampton Wick	a							18 44									19 14						
Kingston	a							18 46									19 16						
Whitton	d		18a20			18 25	←		18a53			18a50			18 55	←		19a23			19a20		
Feltham	d	18 16			18 36	18 29	18 36				18 46			19 06	18 59	19 06				19 16			19 36
Ashford (Surrey)	d				→	18 33	18 40							→	19 03	19 10							→
Staines	d	18 23				18 37	18 44				18 53				19 07	19 14				19 23			
Wraysbury	d					18 41									19 11								
Sunnymeads	d					18 44									19 14								
Datchet	d					18 47									19 17								
Windsor & Eton Riverside	a					18 51									19 21								
Egham	d	18 27					18 49				18 57					19 19				19 27			
Virginia Water	a	18 31					18 53				19 01					19 23				19 31			
	d	18 31					18 53				19 01					19 23				19 31			
Chertsey	d						18 59									19 29							
Addlestone	d						19 02									19 32							
Weybridge	a						19 07									19 37							
Byfleet & New Haw	d																						
West Byfleet	d																						
Woking	a																						
Longcross	d																						
Sunningdale	d	18 37									19 07									19 37			
Ascot 3	d	18 43		18 53							19 13		19 23							19 43		19 53	
Bagshot	d			18 59									19 29									19 59	
Camberley	a			19 05									19 35									20 05	
Frimley	d			19 13									19 43									20 13	
Ash Vale	d			19 19									19 49									20 19	
Aldershot	a			19 24									19 54									20 24	
	d			19 38									20 08									20 38	
Ash 5	d			19 45									20 15									20 45	
Wanborough	d			19 48									20 18									20 48	
Guildford	a			19 55									20 25									20 55	
Martins Heron	d	18 47									19 17									19 47			
Bracknell	d	18 50									19 20									19 50			
Wokingham	d	18 57									19 27									19 57			
Winnersh	d	19 00									19 30									20 00			
Winnersh Triangle	d	19 02									19 32									20 02			
Earley	d	19 05									19 35									20 05			
Reading 7	a	19 10									19 40									20 10			

Saturdays until 6 October

London - Hounslow, Richmond, Kingston, Windsor, Weybridge, Ascot, Guildford and Reading

Network Diagram - see first Page of Table 148

		SW		SW	SW	SW	SW	SW ■	SW	SW ■	SW	SW		SW	SW	SW	SW	SW ■	SW	SW ■	SW	SW		SW	SW
London Waterloo 15 ⊖	d	18 58			19 03	19 07	19 15	19 20			19 22	19 28			19 33	19 37	19 45	19 50			19 52	19 58			20 03
Vauxhall ⊖	d	19 02			19 07	19 11	19 19				19 26	19 32			19 37	19 41	19 49				19 56	20 02			20 07
Queenstown Rd.(Battersea)	d				19 10	19 14	19 22				19 29				19 40	19 44	19 52				19 59				20 10
Clapham Junction 10	d	19 08			19 13	19 17	19 25	19 28			19 32	19 38			19 43	19 47	19 55	19 58			20 02	20 08			20 13
Wandsworth Town	d				19 16	19 20	19 28				19 35				19 46	19 50	19 58				20 05				20 16
Putney	d	19 12			19 19	19 23	19 31				19 38	19 42			19 49	19 53	20 01				20 08	20 12			20 19
Barnes	d				19 22	19 27	19 35				19 42				19 52	19 57	20 05				20 12				20 22
Barnes Bridge	d					19 29					19 44					19 59					20 14				
Chiswick	d					19 32					19 47					20 02					20 17				
Kew Bridge	d					19 35					19 50					20 05					20 20				
Brentford	d					19 38					19 53					20 08					20 23				
Syon Lane	d					19 40					19 55					20 10					20 25				
Isleworth	d					19 42					19 57					20 12					20 27				
Hounslow	d					19 48					20 01					20 18					20 31				
Mortlake	d				19 24		19 37								19 54		20 07								20 24
North Sheen	d				19 26		19 39		←						19 56		20 09		←						20 26
Richmond ⊖	d	19 18			19 29		19 42	19 36	19 42			19 48			19 59		20 12	20 06	20 12			20 18			20 29
St Margarets	d				19 31		→		19 44						20 01		→		20 14						20 31
Twickenham	a	19 21			19 33			19 40	19 46			19 51			20 03			20 10	20 16			20 21			20 33
	d	19 22			19 34			19 40	19 47			19 52			20 04			20 10	20 17			20 22			20 34
Strawberry Hill	d				19 37										20 07										20 37
Fulwell	a																								
Teddington	a				19 40										20 10										20 40
Hampton Wick	a				19 44										20 14										20 44
Kingston	a				19 46										20 16										20 46
Whitton	d	19 25		←		19a53			19a50			19 55		←		20a23			20a20			20 25		←	
Feltham	d	19 29		19 36				19 46			20 06	19 59		20 06				20 16			20 36	20 29		20 36	
Ashford (Surrey)	d	19 33		19 40							→	20 03		20 10							→	20 33		20 40	
Staines	d	19 37		19 44				19 53				20 07		20 14				20 23				20 37		20 44	
Wraysbury	d	19 41										20 11										20 41			
Sunnymeads	d	19 44										20 14										20 44			
Datchet	d	19 47										20 17										20 47			
Windsor & Eton Riverside	a	19 51										20 21										20 51			
Egham	d			19 49				19 57						20 19				20 27						20 49	
Virginia Water	a			19 53				20 01						20 23				20 31						20 53	
	d			19 53				20 01						20 23				20 31						20 53	
Chertsey	d			19 59										20 29										20 59	
Addlestone	d			20 02										20 32										21 02	
Weybridge	a			20 07										20 37										21 07	
Byfleet & New Haw	d																								
West Byfleet	d																								
Woking	a																								
Longcross	d																								
Sunningdale	d							20 07										20 37							
Ascot 3	d							20 13		20 23								20 43		20 53					
Bagshot	d									20 29										20 59					
Camberley	a									20 35										21 05					
Frimley	d									20 43										21 13					
Ash Vale	d									20 49										21 19					
Aldershot	a									20 54										21 24					
	d									21 08										21 38					
Ash 5	d									21 15										21 45					
Wanborough	d									21 18										21 48					
Guildford	a									21 25										21 55					
Martins Heron	d							20 17										20 47							
Bracknell	d							20 20										20 50							
Wokingham	d							20 27										20 57							
Winnersh	d							20 30										21 00							
Winnersh Triangle	d							20 32										21 02							
Earley	d							20 35										21 05							
Reading 7	a							20 40										21 10							

Saturdays until 6 October

London - Hounslow, Richmond, Kingston, Windsor, Weybridge, Ascot, Guildford and Reading

Network Diagram - see first Page of Table 148

		SW	SW	SW ■	SW	SW ■	SW ■	SW		SW	SW	SW	SW	SW	SW ■	SW	SW	SW		SW	SW	SW	SW	SW ■	SW
London Waterloo 15 ⊖	d	20 07	20 15	20 20				20 22		20 28		20 33	20 37	20 45	20 50		20 52	20 58			21 03	21 07	21 15	21 20	
Vauxhall ⊖	d	20 11	20 19					20 26		20 32		20 37	20 41	20 49			20 56	21 02			21 07	21 11	21 19		
Queenstown Rd.(Battersea)	d	20 14	20 22					20 29				20 40	20 44	20 52			20 59				21 10	21 14	21 22		
Clapham Junction 10	d	20 17	20 25	20 28				20 32		20 38		20 43	20 47	20 55	20 58		21 02	21 08			21 13	21 17	21 25	21 28	
Wandsworth Town	d	20 20	20 28					20 35				20 46	20 50	20 58			21 05				21 16	21 20	21 28		
Putney	d	20 23	20 31					20 38		20 42		20 49	20 53	21 01			21 08	21 12			21 19	21 23	21 31		
Barnes	d	20 27	20 35					20 42				20 52	20 57	21 05			21 12				21 22	21 27	21 35		
Barnes Bridge	d	20 29						20 44					20 59				21 14					21 29			
Chiswick	d	20 32						20 47					21 02				21 17					21 32			
Kew Bridge	d	20 35						20 50					21 05				21 20					21 35			
Brentford	d	20 38						20 53					21 08				21 23					21 38			
Syon Lane	d	20 40						20 55					21 10				21 25					21 40			
Isleworth	d	20 42						20 57					21 12				21 27					21 42			
Hounslow	d	20 48						21 01					21 18				21 31					21 48			
Mortlake	d		20 37									20 54		21 07							21 24		21 37		
North Sheen	d		20 39		←							20 56		21 09		←					21 26		21 39		←
Richmond ⊖	d		20 42	20 36	20 42					20 48		20 59		21 12	21 06	21 12		21 18			21 29		21 42	21 36	21 42
St Margarets	d		→		20 44							21 01		→		21 14					21 31		→		21 44
Twickenham	a			20 40	20 46					20 51		21 03			21 10	21 16		21 21			21 33			21 40	21 46
	d			20 40	20 47					20 52		21 04			21 10	21 17		21 22			21 34			21 40	21 47
Strawberry Hill	d											21 07									21 37				
Fulwell	a																								
Teddington	a											21 10									21 40				
Hampton Wick	a											21 14									21 44				
Kingston	a											21 16									21 46				
Whitton	d	20a53			20a50					20 55	←		21a23			21a20		21 25		←		21a53			21a50
Feltham	d			20 46				21 06		20 59	21 06				21 16		21 36	21 29		21 36				21 46	
Ashford (Surrey)	d							→		21 03	21 10						→	21 33		21 40					
Staines	d			20 53						21 07	21 14				21 23			21 37		21 44				21 53	
Wraysbury	d									21 11								21 41							
Sunnymeads	d									21 14								21 44							
Datchet	d									21 17								21 47							
Windsor & Eton Riverside	a									21 21								21 51							
Egham	d			20 57							21 19				21 27					21 49				21 57	
Virginia Water	a			21 01							21 23				21 31					21 53				22 01	
	d			21 01							21 23				21 31					21 53				22 01	
Chertsey	d										21 29									21 59					
Addlestone	d										21 32									22 02					
Weybridge	a										21 37									22 07					
Byfleet & New Haw	d																								
West Byfleet	d																								
Woking	a																								
Longcross	d																								
Sunningdale	d			21 07											21 37									22 07	
Ascot 3	d			21 13		21 23									21 43									22 13	
Bagshot	d					21 29																			
Camberley	a					21 35																			
Frimley	d					21 43																			
Ash Vale	d					21 49																			
Aldershot	a					21 54																			
	d					22 08	22 38																		
Ash 5	d					22 15	22 45																		
Wanborough	d					22 18	22 48																		
Guildford	a					22 25	22 55																		
Martins Heron	d			21 17											21 47									22 17	
Bracknell	d			21 20											21 50									22 20	
Wokingham	d			21 27											21 57									22 27	
Winnersh	d			21 30											22 00									22 30	
Winnersh Triangle	d			21 32											22 02									22 32	
Earley	d			21 35											22 05									22 35	
Reading 7	a			21 40											22 10									22 40	

Table 149

Saturdays until 6 October

London - Hounslow, Richmond, Kingston, Windsor, Weybridge, Ascot, Guildford and Reading

Network Diagram - see first Page of Table 148

		SW ■	SW	SW		SW	SW	SW	SW	SW ■	SW	SW	SW	SW		SW	SW ■	SW ■	SW	SW	SW	SW	SW ■	SW
London Waterloo ■ ⊖	d		21 22	21 28			21 33	21 37	21 45	21 50		21 52	21 58			22 03	22 20		22 22	22 28		22 33	22 50	22 52
Vauxhall ⊖	d		21 26	21 32			21 37	21 41	21 49			21 56	22 02			22 07			22 26	22 32		22 37		22 56
Queenstown Rd.(Battersea)	d		21 29				21 40	21 44	21 52			21 59				22 10			22 29			22 40		22 59
Clapham Junction ■	d		21 32	21 38			21 43	21 47	21 55	21 58		22 02	22 08			22 13	22 28		22 32	22 38		22 43	22 58	23 02
Wandsworth Town	d		21 35				21 46	21 50	21 58			22 05				22 16			22 35			22 46		23 05
Putney	d		21 38	21 42			21 49	21 53	22 01			22 08	22 12			22 19			22 38	22 42		22 49		23 08
Barnes	d		21 42				21 52	21 57	22 05			22 12				22 22			22 42			22 52		23 12
Barnes Bridge	d		21 44					21 59				22 14							22 44					23 14
Chiswick	d		21 47					22 02				22 17							22 47					23 17
Kew Bridge	d		21 50					22 05				22 20							22 50					23 20
Brentford	d		21 53					22 08				22 23							22 53					23 23
Syon Lane	d		21 55					22 10				22 25							22 55					23 25
Isleworth	d		21 57					22 12				22 27							22 57					23 27
Hounslow	d		22 01					22 18				22 31							23 01					23 31
Mortlake	d						21 54		22 07							22 24						22 54		
North Sheen	d						21 56		22 09		←					22 26						22 56		
Richmond ⊖	d			21 48			21 59		22 12	22 06	22 12		22 18			22 29	22 36			22 48		22 59	23 06	
St Margarets	d						22 01		→		22 14					22 31						23 01		
Twickenham	a			21 51			22 03			22 10	22 16		22 21			22 33	22 40			22 51		23 03	23 10	
	d			21 52			22 04			22 10			22 22			22 34	22 40			22 52		23 04	23 10	
Strawberry Hill	d						22 07									22 37						23 07		
Fulwell	a																							
Teddington	a						22 10									22 40						23 10		
Hampton Wick	a						22 14									22 44						23 14		
Kingston	a						22 16									22 46						23 16		
Whitton	d			21 55		←		22a23					22 25	←						22 55	←			
Feltham	d		22 06	21 59		22 06				22 16		22 36	22 29	22 36			22 46		23 06	22 59	23 06		23 16	23 36
Ashford (Surrey)	d		→	22 03		22 10						→	22 33	22 40					→	23 03	23 10			→
Staines	d			22 07		22 14				22 23			22 37	22 44			22 53			23 07	23 14		23 23	
Wraysbury	d			22 11									22 41							23 11				
Sunnymeads	d			22 14									22 44							23 14				
Datchet	d			22 17									22 47							23 17				
Windsor & Eton Riverside	a			22 21									22 51							23 21				
Egham	d					22 19				22 27				22 49			22 57				23 19		23 27	
Virginia Water	a					22 23				22 31				22 53			23 01				23 23		23 31	
	d					22 23				22 31				22 53			23 01				23 23		23 31	
Chertsey	d					22 29								22 59							23 29			
Addlestone	d					22 32								23 02							23a32			
Weybridge	a					22 37								23 07							23 37			
Byfleet & New Haw	d																							
West Byfleet	d																							
Woking	a																							
Longcross	d																							
Sunningdale	d									22 37							23 07						23 37	
Ascot ■	d	22 23								22 43							23 13	23 23					23 43	
Bagshot	d	22 29																23 29						
Camberley	a	22 35																23 35						
Frimley	d	22 43																23 43						
Ash Vale	d	22 49																23 49						
Aldershot	a	22 54																23 54						
	d	23 08																						
Ash ■	d	23 15																						
Wanborough	d	23 18																						
Guildford	a	23 25																						
Martins Heron	d									22 47							23 17						23 47	
Bracknell	d									22 50							23 20						23 50	
Wokingham	d									22 57							23 27						23 57	
Winnersh	d									23 00							23 30						23 59	
Winnersh Triangle	d									23 02							23 32						00 02	
Earley	d									23 05							23 35						00 05	
Reading ■	a									23 10							23 40						00 10	

Table 149

Saturdays until 6 October

London - Hounslow, Richmond, Kingston, Windsor, Weybridge, Ascot, Guildford and Reading

Network Diagram - see first Page of Table 148

		SW	SW	SW	SW	SW ■	SW	SW	SW	SW		SW	SW	SW	SW	SW
									A				B			
London Waterloo ■ ⊖	d	22 58		23 03	23 13	23 20	23 22	23 33	23 38				23 50	23 52	23 58	
Vauxhall ⊖	d	23 02		23 07	23 17		23 26	23 37						23 56	00 02	
Queenstown Rd.(Battersea)	d			23 10			23 29	23 40						23 59		
Clapham Junction ■	d	23 08		23 13	23 23	23 28	23 32	23 43	23 46				23 58	00 02	00 08	
Wandsworth Town	d			23 16			23 35	23 46						00 05		
Putney	d	23 12		23 19	23 27		23 38	23 49						00 08	00 12	
Barnes	d			23 22			23 42	23 52						00 12		
Barnes Bridge	d						23 44							00 14		
Chiswick	d						23 47							00 17		
Kew Bridge	d						23 50							00 20		
Brentford	d						23 53							00 23		
Syon Lane	d						23 55							00 25		
Isleworth	d						23 57							00 27		
Hounslow	d						00 01							00 31		
Mortlake	d			23 24				23 54								
North Sheen	d			23 26				23 56				←				
Richmond ⊖	d	23 18		23 29	23 33	23 37		23 59	23 54			23 59	00 06		00 18	
St Margarets	d			23 31				→				00 01				
Twickenham	a	23 21		23 33	23 37	23 41			23 58			00 04	00 10		00 21	
	d	23 22		23 34	23 37	23 41			23 58			00 04	00 10		00 22	
Strawberry Hill	d			23 37								00 07				
Fulwell	a															
Teddington	a			23 40								00 11				
Hampton Wick	a			23 44								00 14				
Kingston	a			23 46								00 16				
Whitton	d	23 25	←		23 40					←					00 25	←
Feltham	d	23 29	23 36		23 44	23 48	00 06		00 04	00 06			00 16	00 36	00 29	00 36
Ashford (Surrey)	d	23 33	23 40		23 48		→			00 10				→	00 33	00 40
Staines	d	23 37	23 44		23 52	23 56			00 11	00 14			00 23		00a37	00a46
Wraysbury	d	23 41			23 56											
Sunnymeads	d	23 44			23 59											
Datchet	d	23 47			00 02											
Windsor & Eton Riverside	a	23 51			00 06											
Egham	d		23 49			00 01			00 15	00 19			00 27			
Virginia Water	a		23 53			00 05			00 19	00 23			00 31			
	d		23 53			00 05			00 19	00 23			00 31			
Chertsey	d		23 59							00 29						
Addlestone	d		00 02							00a32						
Weybridge	a									00 38						
Byfleet & New Haw	d		00 06													
West Byfleet	d		00 09													
Woking	a		00 15													
Longcross	d															
Sunningdale	d					00 11			00 25				00 37			
Ascot ■	d					00 15			00 30				00 42			
Bagshot	d															
Camberley	a															
Frimley	d															
Ash Vale	d															
Aldershot	a															
	d															
Ash ■	d															
Wanborough	d															
Guildford	a															
Martins Heron	d					00 19			00 34				00 46			
Bracknell	d					00 23			00 37				00 49			
Wokingham	d					00 32			00 44				00 56			
Winnersh	d					00 36										
Winnersh Triangle	d					00 38										
Earley	d					00 40										
Reading ■	a					00 45			00 52				01 04			

A until 21 July, 18 August, 25 August, 15 September, 22 September, 29 September, 6 October

B 28 July, 4 August, 11 August, 1 September, 8 September

Table 149

Saturdays from 13 October

London - Hounslow, Richmond, Kingston, Windsor, Weybridge, Ascot, Guildford and Reading

Network Diagram - see first Page of Table 148

		SW 1	SW	SW	SW 1	SW	SW	SW	SW	SW	SW 1	SW 1	SW 1	SW 1	SW	SW	SW	SW	SW	SW 1	SW	SW 1	SW
London Waterloo 15 ⊖	d	22p50	22p52	23p13	23p20	23p22	23p33	23p38							23p52	23p58		00 18				05 05	
Vauxhall ⊖	d		22p56	23p17		23p26	23p37								23p56	00 02		00 22				05 09	
Queenstown Rd.(Battersea)	d		22p59			23p29	23p40								23p59			00 25				05 12	
Clapham Junction 10	d	22p58	23p02	23p23	23p28	23p32	23p43	23p46							00 02	00 08		00 29				05 15	
Wandsworth Town	d		23p05			23p35	23p46								00 05			00 32				05 18	
Putney	d		23p08	23p27		23p38	23p49								00 08	00 12		00 35				05 21	
Barnes	d		23p12			23p42	23p52								00 12			00 38				05 24	
Barnes Bridge	d		23p14			23p44									00 14								
Chiswick	d		23p17			23p47									00 17								
Kew Bridge	d		23p20			23p50									00 20								
Brentford	d		23p23			23p53									00 23								
Syon Lane	d		23p25			23p55									00 25								
Isleworth	d		23p27			23p57									00 27								
Hounslow	d		23p31			00 01									00 31								
Mortlake	d						23p54											00 40				05 26	
North Sheen	d						23p56			←								00 42				05 28	
Richmond ⊖	d	23p06		23p33	23p37		23p59	23p54		23p59						00 18		00 45				05 31	
St Margarets	d						→			00 01								00 47				05 33	
Twickenham	a	23p10		23p36	23p41			23p58		00 03						00 21		00 49				05 35	
	d	23p10		23p37	23p41			23p58		00 04						00 22		00 50	04 52			05 36	05 38
Strawberry Hill	d									00 07								00s53	04 55				
Fulwell	a																						
Teddington	a									00 11								00s56	04 58				
Hampton Wick	a									00 14								00s59	05 01				
Kingston	a									00 16								01 01	05 03				
Whitton	d			23p40					←							00 25	←					05 39	05a41
Feltham	d	23p16	23p36	23p44	23p48	00 06		00 04	00 06						00 37	00 29	00 37					05 43	
Ashford (Surrey)	d		23p40	23p48		→			00 10						→	00 33	00 41					05 47	
Staines	d	23p23	23p44	23p52	23p56			00 11	00 14							00a37	00a46			05 23	05 44	05 53	
Wraysbury	d			23p56																			
Sunnymeads	d			23p59																			
Datchet	d			00 04																			
Windsor & Eton Riverside	a			00 09																			
Egham	d	23p27	23p49		00 01			00 15	00 19											05 27	05 49	05 57	
Virginia Water	a	23p31	23p53		00 05			00 19	00 23											05 31	05 53	06 01	
	d	23p31	23p53		00 05			00 19	00 23											05 31	05 53	06 01	
Chertsey	d		23p59						00 29												05 59		
Addlestone	d		00 02						00a32												06 02		
Weybridge	a								00 38												06 07		
Byfleet & New Haw	d		00 06																				
West Byfleet	d		00 09																				
Woking	a		00 15																				
Longcross	d																						
Sunningdale	d	23p37			00 11			00 25												05 37		06 07	
Ascot 3	d	23p43			00 15			00 30			00 32									05 43		06 13	
Bagshot	d										00 38												
Camberley	a										00 44												
Frimley	d										00 48												
Ash Vale	d										00 57												
Aldershot	a										01s02												
	d											06 08	06 38	07 08									
Ash 5	d											06 15	06 45	07 15									
Wanborough	d											06 18	06 48	07 18									
Guildford	a											06 25	06 55	07 25									
Martins Heron	d	23p47			00 19			00 34												05 47		06 17	
Bracknell	d	23p50			00 23			00 37												05 50		06 20	
Wokingham	d	23p57			00 32			00 44												05 57		06 27	
Winnersh	d	23p59			00 36															06 00		06 30	
Winnersh Triangle	d	00 02			00 38															06 02		06 32	
Earley	d	00 05			00 40															06 07		06 35	
Reading 7	a	00 13			00 48			00 55												06 13		06 43	

Table 149

Saturdays from 13 October

London - Hounslow, Richmond, Kingston, Windsor, Weybridge, Ascot, Guildford and Reading

Network Diagram - see first Page of Table 148

		SW	SW	SW	SW 1	SW	SW	SW	SW 1	SW 1	SW 1	SW	SW	SW	SW	SW 1	SW 1	SW	SW	SW	SW	SW	SW 1
London Waterloo 15 ⊖	d		05 33		05 50	05 58	06 03			06 20		06 22	06 28		06 33	06 50		06 52	06 58		07 03	07 15	07 20
Vauxhall ⊖	d		05 37			06 02	06 07					06 26	06 32		06 37			06 56	07 02		07 07	07 19	
Queenstown Rd.(Battersea)	d		05 40				06 10					06 29			06 40			06 59			07 10	07 22	
Clapham Junction 10	d		05 43		05 58	06 08	06 13			06 28		06 32	06 38		06 43	06 58		07 02	07 08		07 13	07 25	07 28
Wandsworth Town	d		05 46				06 16					06 35			06 46			07 05			07 16	07 28	
Putney	d		05 49			06 12	06 19					06 38	06 42		06 49			07 08	07 12		07 19	07 31	
Barnes	d		05 52				06 22					06 42			06 52			07 12			07 22	07 35	
Barnes Bridge	d											06 44						07 14					
Chiswick	d											06 47						07 17					
Kew Bridge	d											06 50						07 20					
Brentford	d											06 53						07 23					
Syon Lane	d											06 55						07 25					
Isleworth	d											06 57						07 27					
Hounslow	d											07 01						07 31					
Mortlake	d		05 54				06 24								06 54						07 24	07 37	
North Sheen	d		05 56				06 26								06 56						07 26	07 39	
Richmond ⊖	d		05 59		06 06	06 18	06 29			06 36			06 48		06 59	07 06			07 18		07 29	07 42	07 36
St Margarets	d		06 01				06 31								07 01						07 31	→	
Twickenham	a		06 03		06 10	06 21	06 33			06 40			06 51		07 03	07 10			07 21		07 33		07 40
	d	05 53	06 04		06 10	06 22	06 34			06 40			06 52		07 04	07 10			07 22		07 34		07 40
Strawberry Hill	d		06 07				06 37								07 07						07 37		
Fulwell	a																						
Teddington	a		06 10				06 40								07 10						07 40		
Hampton Wick	a		06 14				06 44								07 14						07 44		
Kingston	a		06 16				06 46								07 16						07 46		
Whitton	d	05 56				06 25							06 55	←					07 25	←			
Feltham	d	06 00			06 16	06 29				06 46		07 06	06 59	07 06		07 16		07 36	07 29	07 36			07 46
Ashford (Surrey)	d	06 04				06 33						→	07 03	07 10				→	07 33	07 40			
Staines	d	06 08		06 16	06 23	06 37		06 44		06 53			07 07	07 14		07 23			07 37	07 44			07 53
Wraysbury	d	06 13				06 42							07 12						07 42				
Sunnymeads	d	06 16				06 45							07 15						07 45				
Datchet	d	06 20				06 49							07 19						07 49				
Windsor & Eton Riverside	a	06 24				06 54							07 24						07 54				
Egham	d			06 20	06 27			06 49		06 57				07 19		07 27				07 49			07 57
Virginia Water	a			06 25	06 31			06 53		07 01				07 23		07 31				07 53			08 01
	d			06 25	06 31			06 53		07 01				07 23		07 31				07 53			08 01
Chertsey	d			06 30				06 59						07 29						07 59			
Addlestone	d			06 33				07 02						07 32						08 02			
Weybridge	a			06 38				07 07						07 37						08 07			
Byfleet & New Haw	d																						
West Byfleet	d																						
Woking	a																						
Longcross	d																						
Sunningdale	d				06 37					07 07						07 37							08 07
Ascot 3	d				06 43				06 53	07 13						07 43	07 53						08 13
Bagshot	d								06 59								07 59						
Camberley	a								07 05								08 05						
Frimley	d								07 13								08 13						
Ash Vale	d								07 19								08 19						
Aldershot	a								07 24								08 24						
	d								07 38		08 08						08 38						
Ash 5	d								07 45		08 15						08 45						
Wanborough	d								07 48		08 18						08 48						
Guildford	a								07 55		08 25						08 55						
Martins Heron	d				06 47					07 17						07 47							08 17
Bracknell	d				06 50					07 20						07 50							08 20
Wokingham	d				06 57					07 27						07 57							08 27
Winnersh	d				07 00					07 30						08 00							08 30
Winnersh Triangle	d				07 02					07 32						08 02							08 32
Earley	d				07 07					07 37						08 07							08 37
Reading 7	a				07 13					07 43						08 13							08 43

Table 149

Saturdays from 13 October

London - Hounslow, Richmond, Kingston, Windsor, Weybridge, Ascot, Guildford and Reading

Network Diagram - see first Page of Table 148

		SW		SW 1	SW	SW	SW	SW	SW	SW	SW 1	SW		SW 1	SW	SW	SW	SW	SW	SW	SW 1	SW		SW 1	SW
London Waterloo 15	⊖ d				07 22	07 28		07 33	07 37	07 45	07 50				07 52	07 58		08 03	08 07	08 15	08 20				08 22
Vauxhall	⊖ d				07 26	07 32		07 37	07 41	07 49					07 56	08 02		08 07	08 11	08 19					08 26
Queenstown Rd.(Battersea)	d				07 29			07 40	07 44	07 52					07 59			08 10	08 14	08 22					08 29
Clapham Junction 10	d				07 32	07 38		07 43	07 47	07 55	07 58				08 02	08 08		08 13	08 17	08 25	08 28				08 32
Wandsworth Town	d				07 35			07 46	07 50	07 58					08 05			08 16	08 20	08 28					08 35
Putney	d				07 38	07 42		07 49	07 53	08 01					08 08	08 12		08 19	08 23	08 31					08 38
Barnes	d				07 42			07 52	07 57	08 05					08 12			08 22	08 27	08 35					08 42
Barnes Bridge	d				07 44				07 59						08 14				08 29						08 44
Chiswick	d				07 47				08 02						08 17				08 32						08 47
Kew Bridge	d				07 50				08 05						08 20				08 35						08 50
Brentford	d				07 53				08 08						08 23				08 38						08 53
Syon Lane	d				07 55				08 10						08 25				08 40						08 55
Isleworth	d				07 57				08 12						08 27				08 42						08 57
Hounslow	d				08 01				08 18						08 31				08 48						09 01
Mortlake	d							07 54		08 07								08 24		08 37					
North Sheen	d	←						07 56		08 09		←						08 26		08 39		←			
Richmond	⊖ d	07 42				07 48		07 59		08 12	08 06	08 12				08 18		08 29		08 42	08 36	08 42			
St Margarets	d	07 44						08 01		→		08 14						08 31		→		08 44			
Twickenham	a	07 46				07 51		08 03			08 10	08 16				08 21		08 33			08 40	08 46			
	d	07 47				07 52		08 04			08 10	08 17				08 22		08 34			08 40	08 47			
Strawberry Hill	d							08 07										08 37							
Fulwell	a																								
Teddington	a							08 10										08 40							
Hampton Wick	a							08 14										08 44							
Kingston	a							08 16										08 46							
Whitton	d	07a50				07 55	←		08a23			08a20				08 25	←		08a53			08a50			
Feltham	d				08 06	07 59	08 06				08 16				08 36	08 29	08 36				08 46				09 06
Ashford (Surrey)	d				→	08 03	08 10								→	08 33	08 40								→
Staines	d					08 07	08 14				08 23					08 37	08 44				08 53				
Wraysbury	d					08 12										08 42									
Sunnymeads	d					08 15										08 45									
Datchet	d					08 19										08 49									
Windsor & Eton Riverside	a					08 24										08 54									
Egham	d						08 19				08 27						08 49				08 57				
Virginia Water	a						08 23				08 31						08 53				09 01				
	d						08 23				08 31						08 53				09 01				
Chertsey	d						08 29										08 59								
Addlestone	d						08 32										09 02								
Weybridge	a						08 37										09 07								
Byfleet & New Haw	d																								
West Byfleet	d																								
Woking	a																								
Longcross	d																								
Sunningdale	d										08 37										09 07				
Ascot 3	d			08 23							08 43			08 53							09 13			09 23	
Bagshot	d			08 29										08 59										09 29	
Camberley	a			08 35										09 05										09 35	
Frimley	d			08 43										09 13										09 43	
Ash Vale	d			08 49										09 19										09 49	
Aldershot	a			08 54										09 24										09 54	
	d			09 08										09 38										10 08	
Ash 5	d			09 15										09 45										10 15	
Wanborough	d			09 18										09 48										10 18	
Guildford	a			09 25										09 55										10 25	
Martins Heron	d										08 47										09 17				
Bracknell	d										08 50										09 20				
Wokingham	d										08 57										09 27				
Winnersh	d										09 00										09 30				
Winnersh Triangle	d										09 02										09 32				
Earley	d										09 07										09 37				
Reading 7	a										09 13										09 43				

Table 149

Saturdays from 13 October

London - Hounslow, Richmond, Kingston, Windsor, Weybridge, Ascot, Guildford and Reading

Network Diagram - see first Page of Table 148

		SW	SW	SW	SW	SW	SW 1	SW		SW 1	SW	SW	SW	SW	SW	SW	SW 1	SW		SW 1	SW	SW	SW	SW	SW
London Waterloo 15	⊖ d	08 28		08 33	08 37	08 45	08 50				08 52	08 58		09 03	09 07	09 15	09 20				09 22	09 28		09 33	09 37
Vauxhall	⊖ d	08 32		08 37	08 41	08 49					08 56	09 02		09 07	09 11	09 19					09 26	09 32		09 37	09 41
Queenstown Rd.(Battersea)	d			08 40	08 44	08 52					08 59			09 10	09 14	09 22					09 29			09 40	09 44
Clapham Junction 10	d	08 38		08 43	08 47	08 55	08 58				09 02	09 08		09 13	09 17	09 25	09 28				09 32	09 38		09 43	09 47
Wandsworth Town	d			08 46	08 50	08 58					09 05			09 16	09 20	09 28					09 35			09 46	09 50
Putney	d	08 42		08 49	08 53	09 01					09 08	09 12		09 19	09 23	09 31					09 38	09 42		09 49	09 53
Barnes	d			08 52	08 57	09 05					09 12			09 22	09 27	09 35					09 42			09 52	09 57
Barnes Bridge	d				08 59						09 14				09 29						09 44				09 59
Chiswick	d				09 02						09 17				09 32						09 47				10 02
Kew Bridge	d				09 05						09 20				09 35						09 50				10 05
Brentford	d				09 08						09 23				09 38						09 53				10 08
Syon Lane	d				09 10						09 25				09 40						09 55				10 10
Isleworth	d				09 12						09 27				09 42						09 57				10 12
Hounslow	d				09 18						09 31				09 48						10 01				10 18
Mortlake	d			08 54		09 07								09 24		09 37								09 54	
North Sheen	d			08 56		09 09		←						09 26		09 39		←						09 56	
Richmond	⊖ d	08 48		08 59		09 12	09 06	09 12				09 18		09 29		09 42	09 36	09 42				09 48		09 59	
St Margarets	d			09 01		→		09 14						09 31		→		09 44						10 01	
Twickenham	a	08 51		09 03			09 10	09 16				09 21		09 33			09 40	09 46				09 51		10 03	
	d	08 52		09 04			09 10	09 17				09 22		09 34			09 40	09 47				09 52		10 04	
Strawberry Hill	d			09 07										09 37										10 07	
Fulwell	a																								
Teddington	a			09 10										09 40										10 10	
Hampton Wick	a			09 14										09 44										10 14	
Kingston	a			09 16										09 46										10 16	
Whitton	d	08 55	←		09a23			09a20				09 25	←		09a53			09a50				09 55	←		10a23
Feltham	d	08 59	09 06				09 16				09 36	09 29	09 36				09 46				10 06	09 59	10 06		
Ashford (Surrey)	d	09 03	09 10								→	09 33	09 40								→	10 03	10 10		
Staines	d	09 07	09 14				09 23					09 37	09 44				09 53					10 07	10 14		
Wraysbury	d	09 12										09 42										10 12			
Sunnymeads	d	09 15										09 45										10 15			
Datchet	d	09 19										09 49										10 19			
Windsor & Eton Riverside	a	09 24										09 54										10 24			
Egham	d		09 19				09 27						09 49				09 57						10 19		
Virginia Water	a		09 23				09 31						09 53				10 01						10 23		
	d		09 23				09 31						09 53				10 01						10 23		
Chertsey	d		09 29										09 59										10 29		
Addlestone	d		09 32										10 02										10 32		
Weybridge	a		09 37										10 07										10 37		
Byfleet & New Haw	d																								
West Byfleet	d																								
Woking	a																								
Longcross	d																								
Sunningdale	d						09 37										10 07								
Ascot 3	d						09 43			09 53							10 13			10 23					
Bagshot	d									09 59										10 29					
Camberley	a									10 05										10 35					
Frimley	d									10 13										10 43					
Ash Vale	d									10 19										10 49					
Aldershot	a									10 24										10 54					
	d									10 38										11 08					
Ash 5	d									10 45										11 15					
Wanborough	d									10 48										11 18					
Guildford	a									10 55										11 25					
Martins Heron	d						09 47										10 17								
Bracknell	d						09 50										10 20								
Wokingham	d						09 57										10 27								
Winnersh	d						10 00										10 30								
Winnersh Triangle	d						10 02										10 32								
Earley	d						10 07										10 37								
Reading 7	a						10 13										10 43								

Table 149

Saturdays
from 13 October

London - Hounslow, Richmond, Kingston, Windsor, Weybridge, Ascot, Guildford and Reading

Network Diagram - see first Page of Table 148

Station		SW	SW ■	SW	SW ■	SW	SW	SW	SW	SW	SW	SW ■	SW	SW ■	SW	SW	SW	SW	SW	SW	SW ■	SW
London Waterloo 15 ⊖	d	09 45	09 50			09 52	09 58		10 03	10 07	10 15	10 20			10 22	10 28		10 33	10 37	10 45	10 50	
Vauxhall ⊖	d	09 49				09 56	10 02		10 07	10 11	10 19				10 26	10 32		10 37	10 41	10 49		
Queenstown Rd.(Battersea)	d	09 52				09 59			10 10	10 14	10 22				10 29			10 40	10 44	10 52		
Clapham Junction 10	d	09 55	09 58			10 02	10 08		10 13	10 17	10 25	10 28			10 32	10 38		10 43	10 47	10 55	10 58	
Wandsworth Town	d	09 58				10 05			10 16	10 20	10 28				10 35			10 46	10 50	10 58		
Putney	d	10 01				10 08	10 12		10 19	10 23	10 31				10 38	10 42		10 49	10 53	11 01		
Barnes	d	10 05				10 12			10 22	10 27	10 35				10 42			10 52	10 57	11 05		
Barnes Bridge	d					10 14				10 29					10 44				10 59			
Chiswick	d					10 17				10 32					10 47				11 02			
Kew Bridge	d					10 20				10 35					10 50				11 05			
Brentford	d					10 23				10 38					10 53				11 08			
Syon Lane	d					10 25				10 40					10 55				11 10			
Isleworth	d					10 27				10 42					10 57				11 12			
Hounslow	d					10 31				10 48					11 01				11 18			
Mortlake	d	10 07							10 24		10 37							10 54		11 07		
North Sheen	d	10 09		←					10 26		10 39		←					10 56		11 09		←
Richmond ⊖	d	10 12	10 06	10 12			10 18		10 29		10 42	10 36	10 42			10 48		10 59		11 12	11 06	11 12
St Margarets	d	→		10 14					10 31		→		10 44					11 01		→		11 14
Twickenham	a		10 10	10 16			10 21		10 33			10 40	10 46			10 51		11 03			11 10	11 16
	d		10 10	10 17			10 22		10 34			10 40	10 47			10 52		11 04			11 10	11 17
Strawberry Hill	d								10 37									11 07				
Fulwell	a																					
Teddington	a								10 40									11 10				
Hampton Wick	a								10 44									11 14				
Kingston	a								10 46									11 16				
Whitton	d			10a20			10 25	←		10a53			10a50			10 55	←		11a23			11a20
Feltham	d		10 16			10 36	10 29	10 36				10 46			11 06	10 59	11 06				11 16	
Ashford (Surrey)	d					→	10 33	10 40							→	11 03	11 10					
Staines	d		10 23				10 37	10 44				10 53				11 07	11 14				11 23	
Wraysbury	d						10 42									11 12						
Sunnymeads	d						10 45									11 15						
Datchet	d						10 49									11 19						
Windsor & Eton Riverside	a						10 54									11 24						
Egham	d		10 27					10 49				10 57					11 19				11 27	
Virginia Water	a		10 31					10 53				11 01					11 23				11 31	
	d		10 31					10 53				11 01					11 23				11 31	
Chertsey	d							10 59									11 29					
Addlestone	d							11 02									11 32					
Weybridge	a							11 07									11 37					
Byfleet & New Haw	d																					
West Byfleet	d																					
Woking	a																					
Longcross	d																					
Sunningdale	d		10 37									11 07									11 37	
Ascot 3	d		10 43		10 53							11 13		11 23							11 43	
Bagshot	d				10 59									11 29								
Camberley	a				11 05									11 35								
Frimley	d				11 13									11 43								
Ash Vale	d				11 19									11 49								
Aldershot	a				11 24									11 54								
	d				11 38									12 08								
Ash 5	d				11 45									12 15								
Wanborough	d				11 48									12 18								
Guildford	a				11 55									12 25								
Martins Heron	d		10 47									11 17									11 47	
Bracknell	d		10 50									11 20									11 50	
Wokingham	d		10 57									11 27									11 57	
Winnersh	d		11 00									11 30									12 00	
Winnersh Triangle	d		11 02									11 32									12 02	
Earley	d		11 07									11 37									12 07	
Reading 7	a		11 13									11 43									12 13	

Table 149

Saturdays
from 13 October

London - Hounslow, Richmond, Kingston, Windsor, Weybridge, Ascot, Guildford and Reading

Network Diagram - see first Page of Table 148

Station		SW ■	SW	SW	SW	SW	SW	SW	SW ■	SW	SW ■	SW	SW	SW	SW	SW	SW	SW ■	SW	SW ■	SW	SW	SW
London Waterloo 15 ⊖	d		10 52	10 58		11 03	11 07	11 15	11 20			11 22	11 28		11 33	11 37	11 45	11 50			11 52	11 58	
Vauxhall ⊖	d		10 56	11 02		11 07	11 11	11 19				11 26	11 32		11 37	11 41	11 49				11 56	12 02	
Queenstown Rd.(Battersea)	d		10 59			11 10	11 14	11 22				11 29			11 40	11 44	11 52				11 59		
Clapham Junction 10	d		11 02	11 08		11 13	11 17	11 25	11 28			11 32	11 38		11 43	11 47	11 55	11 58			12 02	12 08	
Wandsworth Town	d		11 05			11 16	11 20	11 28				11 35			11 46	11 50	11 58				12 05		
Putney	d		11 08	11 12		11 19	11 23	11 31				11 38	11 42		11 49	11 53	12 01				12 08	12 12	
Barnes	d		11 12			11 22	11 27	11 35				11 42			11 52	11 57	12 05				12 12		
Barnes Bridge	d		11 14				11 29					11 44				11 59					12 14		
Chiswick	d		11 17				11 32					11 47				12 02					12 17		
Kew Bridge	d		11 20				11 35					11 50				12 05					12 20		
Brentford	d		11 23				11 38					11 53				12 08					12 23		
Syon Lane	d		11 25				11 40					11 55				12 10					12 25		
Isleworth	d		11 27				11 42					11 57				12 12					12 27		
Hounslow	d		11 31				11 48					12 01				12 18					12 31		
Mortlake	d					11 24		11 37							11 54		12 07						
North Sheen	d					11 26		11 39		←					11 56		12 09		←				
Richmond ⊖	d			11 18		11 29		11 42	11 36	11 42			11 48		11 59		12 12	12 06	12 12			12 18	
St Margarets	d					11 31		→		11 44					12 01		→		12 14				
Twickenham	a			11 21		11 33			11 40	11 46			11 51		12 03			12 10	12 16			12 21	
	d			11 22		11 34			11 40	11 47			11 52		12 04			12 10	12 17			12 22	
Strawberry Hill	d					11 37									12 07								
Fulwell	a																						
Teddington	a					11 40									12 10								
Hampton Wick	a					11 44									12 14								
Kingston	a					11 46									12 16								
Whitton	d			11 25	←		11a53			11a50			11 55	←		12a23			12a20			12 25	←
Feltham	d		11 36	11 29	11 36				11 46			12 06	11 59	12 06				12 16			12 36	12 29	12 36
Ashford (Surrey)	d		→	11 33	11 40							→	12 03	12 10							→	12 33	12 40
Staines	d			11 37	11 44				11 53				12 07	12 14				12 23				12 37	12 44
Wraysbury	d			11 42									12 12									12 42	
Sunnymeads	d			11 45									12 15									12 45	
Datchet	d			11 49									12 19									12 49	
Windsor & Eton Riverside	a			11 54									12 24									12 54	
Egham	d				11 49				11 57					12 19				12 27					12 49
Virginia Water	a				11 53				12 01					12 23				12 31					12 53
	d				11 53				12 01					12 23				12 31					12 53
Chertsey	d				11 59									12 29									12 59
Addlestone	d				12 02									12 32									13 02
Weybridge	a				12 07									12 37									13 07
Byfleet & New Haw	d																						
West Byfleet	d																						
Woking	a																						
Longcross	d																						
Sunningdale	d								12 07									12 37					
Ascot 3	d	11 53							12 13		12 23							12 43		12 53			
Bagshot	d	11 59									12 29									12 59			
Camberley	a	12 05									12 35									13 05			
Frimley	d	12 13									12 43									13 13			
Ash Vale	d	12 19									12 49									13 19			
Aldershot	a	12 24									12 54									13 24			
	d	12 38									13 08									13 38			
Ash 5	d	12 45									13 15									13 45			
Wanborough	d	12 48									13 18									13 48			
Guildford	a	12 55									13 25									13 55			
Martins Heron	d								12 17									12 47					
Bracknell	d								12 20									12 50					
Wokingham	d								12 27									12 57					
Winnersh	d								12 30									13 00					
Winnersh Triangle	d								12 32									13 02					
Earley	d								12 37									13 07					
Reading 7	a								12 43									13 13					

Table 149

Saturdays from 13 October

London - Hounslow, Richmond, Kingston, Windsor, Weybridge, Ascot, Guildford and Reading

Network Diagram - see first Page of Table 148

		SW	SW	SW	SW 1	SW		SW 1	SW	SW	SW	SW	SW	SW	SW 1	SW		SW 1	SW	SW	SW	SW	SW	SW	SW 1
London Waterloo 15 ⊖	d	12 03	12 07	12 15	12 20				12 22	12 28		12 33	12 37	12 45	12 50				12 52	12 58		13 03	13 07	13 15	13 20
Vauxhall ⊖	d	12 07	12 11	12 19					12 26	12 32		12 37	12 41	12 49					12 56	13 02		13 07	13 11	13 19	
Queenstown Rd.(Battersea)	d	12 10	12 14	12 22					12 29			12 40	12 44	12 52					12 59			13 10	13 14	13 22	
Clapham Junction 10	d	12 13	12 17	12 25	12 28				12 32	12 38		12 43	12 47	12 55	12 58				13 02	13 08		13 13	13 17	13 25	13 28
Wandsworth Town	d	12 16	12 20	12 28					12 35			12 46	12 50	12 58					13 05			13 16	13 20	13 28	
Putney	d	12 19	12 23	12 31					12 38	12 42		12 49	12 53	13 01					13 08	13 12		13 19	13 23	13 31	
Barnes	d	12 22	12 27	12 35					12 42			12 52	12 57	13 05					13 12			13 22	13 27	13 35	
Barnes Bridge	d		12 29						12 44				12 59						13 14				13 29		
Chiswick	d		12 32						12 47				13 02						13 17				13 32		
Kew Bridge	d		12 35						12 50				13 05						13 20				13 35		
Brentford	d		12 38						12 53				13 08						13 23				13 38		
Syon Lane	d		12 40						12 55				13 10						13 25				13 40		
Isleworth	d		12 42						12 57				13 12						13 27				13 42		
Hounslow	d		12 48						13 01				13 18						13 31				13 48		
Mortlake	d	12 24		12 37								12 54		13 07								13 24		13 37	
North Sheen	d	12 26		12 39		←						12 56		13 09		←						13 26		13 39	
Richmond ⊖	d	12 29		12 42	12 36	12 42				12 48		12 59		13 12	13 06	13 12				13 18		13 29		13 42	13 36
St Margarets	d	12 31		→		12 44						13 01		→		13 14						13 31		→	
Twickenham	a	12 33			12 40	12 46				12 51		13 03			13 10	13 16				13 21		13 33			13 40
	d	12 34			12 40	12 47				12 52		13 04			13 10	13 17				13 22		13 34			13 40
Strawberry Hill	d	12 37										13 07										13 37			
Fulwell	a																								
Teddington	a	12 40										13 10										13 40			
Hampton Wick	a	12 44										13 14										13 44			
Kingston	a	12 46										13 16										13 46			
Whitton	d		12a53			12a50				12 55	←		13a23			13a20			13 25	←			13a53		
Feltham	d				12 46				13 06	12 59	13 06				13 16			13 36	13 29	13 36					13 46
Ashford (Surrey)	d								→	13 03	13 10							→	13 33	13 40					
Staines	d				12 53					13 07	13 14				13 23				13 37	13 44					13 53
Wraysbury	d									13 12									13 42						
Sunnymeads	d									13 15									13 45						
Datchet	d									13 19									13 49						
Windsor & Eton Riverside	a									13 24									13 54						
Egham	d				12 57						13 19				13 27					13 49					13 57
Virginia Water	a				13 01						13 23				13 31					13 53					14 01
	d				13 01						13 23				13 31					13 53					14 01
Chertsey	d										13 29									13 59					
Addlestone	d										13 32									14 02					
Weybridge	a										13 37									14 07					
Byfleet & New Haw	d																								
West Byfleet	d																								
Woking	a																								
Longcross	d																								
Sunningdale	d				13 07										13 37										14 07
Ascot 3	d				13 13			13 23							13 43			13 53							14 13
Bagshot	d							13 29										13 59							
Camberley	a							13 35										14 05							
Frimley	d							13 43										14 13							
Ash Vale	d							13 49										14 19							
Aldershot	a							13 54										14 24							
	d							14 08										14 38							
Ash 5	d							14 15										14 45							
Wanborough	d							14 18										14 48							
Guildford	a							14 25										14 55							
Martins Heron	d				13 17										13 47										14 17
Bracknell	d				13 20										13 50										14 20
Wokingham	d				13 27										13 57										14 27
Winnersh	d				13 30										14 00										14 30
Winnersh Triangle	d				13 32										14 02										14 32
Earley	d				13 37										14 07										14 37
Reading 7	a				13 43										14 13										14 43

Table 149

Saturdays from 13 October

London - Hounslow, Richmond, Kingston, Windsor, Weybridge, Ascot, Guildford and Reading

Network Diagram - see first Page of Table 148

		SW		SW 1	SW	SW	SW	SW	SW	SW	SW 1	SW		SW 1	SW	SW	SW	SW	SW	SW	SW 1	SW		SW 1	SW
London Waterloo 15 ⊖	d				13 22	13 28		13 33	13 37	13 45	13 50				13 52	13 58		14 03	14 07	14 15	14 20				14 22
Vauxhall ⊖	d				13 26	13 32		13 37	13 41	13 49					13 56	14 02		14 07	14 11	14 19					14 26
Queenstown Rd.(Battersea)	d				13 29			13 40	13 44	13 52					13 59			14 10	14 14	14 22					14 29
Clapham Junction 10	d				13 32	13 38		13 43	13 47	13 55	13 58				14 02	14 08		14 13	14 17	14 25	14 28				14 32
Wandsworth Town	d				13 35			13 46	13 50	13 58					14 05			14 16	14 20	14 28					14 35
Putney	d				13 38	13 42		13 49	13 53	14 01					14 08	14 12		14 19	14 23	14 31					14 38
Barnes	d				13 42			13 52	13 57	14 05					14 12			14 22	14 27	14 35					14 42
Barnes Bridge	d				13 44				13 59						14 14				14 29						14 44
Chiswick	d				13 47				14 02						14 17				14 32						14 47
Kew Bridge	d				13 50				14 05						14 20				14 35						14 50
Brentford	d				13 53				14 08						14 23				14 38						14 53
Syon Lane	d				13 55				14 10						14 25				14 40						14 55
Isleworth	d				13 57				14 12						14 27				14 42						14 57
Hounslow	d				14 01				14 18						14 31				14 48						15 01
Mortlake	d							13 54		14 07								14 24		14 37					
North Sheen	d	←						13 56		14 09		←						14 26		14 39		←			
Richmond ⊖	d	13 42				13 48		13 59		14 12	14 06	14 12				14 18		14 29		14 42	14 36	14 42			
St Margarets	d	13 44						14 01		→		14 14						14 31		→		14 44			
Twickenham	a	13 46				13 51		14 03			14 10	14 16				14 21		14 33			14 40	14 46			
	d	13 47				13 52		14 04			14 10	14 17				14 22		14 34			14 40	14 47			
Strawberry Hill	d							14 07										14 37							
Fulwell	a																								
Teddington	a							14 10										14 40							
Hampton Wick	a							14 14										14 44							
Kingston	a							14 16										14 46							
Whitton	d	13a50				13 55	←		14a23			14a20				14 25	←		14a53			14a50			
Feltham	d				14 06	13 59	14 06				14 16				14 36	14 29	14 36				14 46				15 06
Ashford (Surrey)	d				→	14 03	14 10								→	14 33	14 40								→
Staines	d					14 07	14 14				14 23					14 37	14 44				14 53				
Wraysbury	d					14 12										14 42									
Sunnymeads	d					14 15										14 45									
Datchet	d					14 19										14 49									
Windsor & Eton Riverside	a					14 24										14 54									
Egham	d						14 19				14 27						14 49				14 57				
Virginia Water	a						14 23				14 31						14 53				15 01				
	d						14 23				14 31						14 53				15 01				
Chertsey	d						14 29										14 59								
Addlestone	d						14 32										15 02								
Weybridge	a						14 37										15 07								
Byfleet & New Haw	d																								
West Byfleet	d																								
Woking	a																								
Longcross	d																								
Sunningdale	d										14 37										15 07				
Ascot 3	d			14 23							14 43			14 53							15 13			15 23	
Bagshot	d			14 29										14 59										15 29	
Camberley	a			14 35										15 05										15 35	
Frimley	d			14 43										15 13										15 43	
Ash Vale	d			14 49										15 19										15 49	
Aldershot	a			14 54										15 24										15 54	
	d			15 08										15 38										16 08	
Ash 5	d			15 15										15 45										16 15	
Wanborough	d			15 18										15 48										16 18	
Guildford	a			15 25										15 55										16 25	
Martins Heron	d										14 47										15 17				
Bracknell	d										14 50										15 20				
Wokingham	d										14 57										15 27				
Winnersh	d										15 00										15 30				
Winnersh Triangle	d										15 02										15 32				
Earley	d										15 07										15 37				
Reading 7	a										15 13										15 43				

Table 149

Saturdays
from 13 October

London - Hounslow, Richmond, Kingston, Windsor, Weybridge, Ascot, Guildford and Reading

Network Diagram - see first Page of Table 148

		SW	SW	SW	SW	SW	SW ■	SW		SW ■	SW	SW	SW	SW	SW	SW	SW ■	SW		SW ■	SW	SW	SW	SW	SW
London Waterloo 15 ⊖	d	14 28		14 33	14 37	14 45	14 50				14 52	14 58		15 03	15 07	15 15	15 20				15 22	15 28		15 33	15 37
Vauxhall ⊖	d	14 32		14 37	14 41	14 49					14 56	15 02		15 07	15 11	15 19					15 26	15 32		15 37	15 41
Queenstown Rd.(Battersea)	d			14 40	14 44	14 52					14 59			15 10	15 14	15 22					15 29			15 40	15 44
Clapham Junction 10	d	14 38		14 43	14 47	14 55	14 58				15 02	15 08		15 13	15 17	15 25	15 28				15 32	15 38		15 43	15 47
Wandsworth Town	d			14 46	14 50	14 58					15 05			15 16	15 20	15 28					15 35			15 46	15 50
Putney	d	14 42		14 49	14 53	15 01					15 08	15 12		15 19	15 23	15 31					15 38	15 42		15 49	15 53
Barnes	d			14 52	14 57	15 05					15 12			15 22	15 27	15 35					15 42			15 52	15 57
Barnes Bridge	d				14 59						15 14				15 29						15 44				15 59
Chiswick	d				15 02						15 17				15 32						15 47				16 02
Kew Bridge	d				15 05						15 20				15 35						15 50				16 05
Brentford	d				15 08						15 23				15 38						15 53				16 08
Syon Lane	d				15 10						15 25				15 40						15 55				16 10
Isleworth	d				15 12						15 27				15 42						15 57				16 12
Hounslow	d				15 18						15 31				15 48						16 01				16 18
Mortlake	d			14 54		15 07								15 24		15 37								15 54	
North Sheen	d			14 56		15 09		←						15 26		15 39		←						15 56	
Richmond ⊖	d	14 48		14 59		15 12	15 06	15 12				15 18		15 29		15 42	15 36	15 42				15 48		15 59	
St Margarets	d			15 01		→		15 14						15 31		→		15 44						16 01	
Twickenham	a	14 51		15 03			15 10	15 16				15 21		15 33			15 40	15 46				15 51		16 03	
	d	14 52		15 04			15 10	15 17				15 22		15 34			15 40	15 47				15 52		16 04	
Strawberry Hill	d			15 07										15 37										16 07	
Fulwell	a																								
Teddington	a			15 10										15 40										16 10	
Hampton Wick	a			15 14										15 44										16 14	
Kingston	a			15 16										15 46										16 16	
Whitton	d	14 55	←		15a23			15a20				15 25	←		15a53			15a50				15 55	←		16a23
Feltham	d	14 59	15 06				15 16				15 36	15 29	15 36				15 46				16 06	15 59	16 06		
Ashford (Surrey)	d	15 03	15 10								→	15 33	15 40								→	16 03	16 10		
Staines	d	15 07	15 14				15 23					15 37	15 44				15 53					16 07	16 14		
Wraysbury	d	15 12										15 42										16 12			
Sunnymeads	d	15 15										15 45										16 15			
Datchet	d	15 19										15 49										16 19			
Windsor & Eton Riverside	a	15 24										15 54										16 24			
Egham	d		15 19				15 27						15 49				15 57						16 19		
Virginia Water	a		15 23				15 31						15 53				16 01						16 23		
	d		15 23				15 31						15 53				16 01						16 23		
Chertsey	d		15 29										15 59										16 29		
Addlestone	d		15 32										16 02										16 32		
Weybridge	a		15 37										16 07										16 42		
Byfleet & New Haw	d																								
West Byfleet	d																								
Woking	a																								
Longcross	d																								
Sunningdale	d						15 37										16 07								
Ascot 3	d						15 43			15 53							16 13			16 23					
Bagshot	d									15 59										16 29					
Camberley	a									16 05										16 35					
Frimley	d									16 13										16 43					
Ash Vale	d									16 19										16 49					
Aldershot	a									16 24										16 54					
	d									16 38										17 08					
Ash 5	d									16 45										17 15					
Wanborough	d									16 48										17 18					
Guildford	a									16 55										17 25					
Martins Heron	d						15 47										16 17								
Bracknell	d						15 50										16 20								
Wokingham	d						15 57										16 27								
Winnersh	d						16 00										16 30								
Winnersh Triangle	d						16 02										16 32								
Earley	d						16 07										16 37								
Reading 7	a						16 13										16 43								

Table 149

Saturdays
from 13 October

London - Hounslow, Richmond, Kingston, Windsor, Weybridge, Ascot, Guildford and Reading

Network Diagram - see first Page of Table 148

		SW	SW ■	SW		SW ■	SW	SW	SW	SW	SW	SW	SW ■	SW		SW ■	SW	SW	SW	SW	SW	SW	SW ■	SW	
London Waterloo 15 ⊖	d	15 45	15 50				15 52	15 58		16 03	16 07	16 15	16 20				16 22	16 28		16 33	16 37	16 45	16 50		
Vauxhall ⊖	d	15 49					15 56	16 02		16 07	16 11	16 19					16 26	16 32		16 37	16 41	16 49			
Queenstown Rd.(Battersea)	d	15 52					15 59			16 10	16 14	16 22					16 29			16 40	16 44	16 52			
Clapham Junction 10	d	15 55	15 58				16 02	16 08		16 13	16 17	16 25	16 28				16 32	16 38		16 43	16 47	16 55	16 58		
Wandsworth Town	d	15 58					16 05			16 16	16 20	16 28					16 35			16 46	16 50	16 58			
Putney	d	16 01					16 08	16 12		16 19	16 23	16 31					16 38	16 42		16 49	16 53	17 01			
Barnes	d	16 05					16 12			16 22	16 27	16 35					16 42			16 52	16 57	17 05			
Barnes Bridge	d						16 14				16 29						16 44				16 59				
Chiswick	d						16 17				16 32						16 47				17 02				
Kew Bridge	d						16 20				16 35						16 50				17 05				
Brentford	d						16 23				16 38						16 53				17 08				
Syon Lane	d						16 25				16 40						16 55				17 10				
Isleworth	d						16 27				16 42						16 57				17 12				
Hounslow	d						16 31				16 48						17 01				17 18				
Mortlake	d	16 07								16 24		16 37								16 54		17 07			
North Sheen	d	16 09		←						16 26		16 39		←						16 56		17 09		←	
Richmond ⊖	d	16 12	16 06	16 12				16 18		16 29		16 42	16 36	16 42				16 48		16 59		17 12	17 06	17 12	
St Margarets	d	→		16 14						16 31		→		16 44						17 01		→		17 14	
Twickenham	a		16 10	16 16				16 21		16 33			16 40	16 46				16 51		17 03			17 10	17 16	
	d		16 10	16 17				16 22		16 34			16 40	16 47				16 52		17 04			17 10	17 17	
Strawberry Hill	d									16 37										17 07					
Fulwell	a																								
Teddington	a									16 40										17 10					
Hampton Wick	a									16 44										17 14					
Kingston	a									16 46										17 16					
Whitton	d			16a20				16 25	←		16a53			16a50				16 55	←		17a23			17a20	
Feltham	d		16 16				16 36	16 29	16 36				16 46				17 06	16 59	17 06				17 16		
Ashford (Surrey)	d						→	16 33	16 40								→	17 03	17 10						
Staines	d		16 23					16 37	16 44				16 53					17 07	17 14				17 23		
Wraysbury	d							16 42										17 12							
Sunnymeads	d							16 45										17 15							
Datchet	d							16 49										17 19							
Windsor & Eton Riverside	a							16 54										17 24							
Egham	d		16 27						16 49				16 57						17 19				17 27		
Virginia Water	a		16 31						16 53				17 01						17 23				17 31		
	d		16 31						16 53				17 01						17 23				17 31		
Chertsey	d								16 59										17 29						
Addlestone	d								17 02										17 32						
Weybridge	a								17 07										17 37						
Byfleet & New Haw	d																								
West Byfleet	d																								
Woking	a																								
Longcross	d																								
Sunningdale	d		16 37										17 07										17 37		
Ascot 3	d		16 43			16 53							17 13			17 23							17 43		
Bagshot	d					16 59										17 29									
Camberley	a					17 05										17 35									
Frimley	d					17 13										17 43									
Ash Vale	d					17 19										17 49									
Aldershot	a					17 24										17 54									
	d					17 38										18 08									
Ash 5	d					17 45										18 15									
Wanborough	d					17 48										18 18									
Guildford	a					17 55										18 25									
Martins Heron	d		16 47										17 17										17 47		
Bracknell	d		16 50										17 20										17 50		
Wokingham	d		16 57										17 27										17 57		
Winnersh	d		17 00										17 30										18 00		
Winnersh Triangle	d		17 02										17 32										18 02		
Earley	d		17 07										17 37										18 07		
Reading 7	a		17 13										17 43										18 13		

London - Hounslow, Richmond, Kingston, Windsor, Weybridge, Ascot, Guildford and Reading

Saturdays
from 13 October

Network Diagram - see first Page of Table 148

		SW ■	SW	SW	SW	SW	SW	SW	SW ■	SW		SW ■	SW	SW	SW	SW	SW	SW	SW ■	SW		SW ■	SW	SW	SW
London Waterloo 15 ⊖	d		16 52	16 58		17 03	17 07	17 15	17 20				17 22	17 28		17 33	17 37	17 45	17 50				17 52	17 58	
Vauxhall ⊖	d		16 56	17 02		17 07	17 11	17 19					17 26	17 32		17 37	17 41	17 49					17 56	18 02	
Queenstown Rd.(Battersea)	d		16 59			17 10	17 14	17 22					17 29			17 40	17 44	17 52					17 59		
Clapham Junction 10	d		17 02	17 08		17 13	17 17	17 25	17 28				17 32	17 38		17 43	17 47	17 55	17 58				18 02	18 08	
Wandsworth Town	d		17 05			17 16	17 20	17 28					17 35			17 46	17 50	17 58					18 05		
Putney	d		17 08	17 12		17 19	17 23	17 31					17 38	17 42		17 49	17 53	18 01					18 08	18 12	
Barnes	d		17 12			17 22	17 27	17 35					17 42			17 52	17 57	18 05					18 12		
Barnes Bridge	d		17 14				17 29						17 44				17 59						18 14		
Chiswick	d		17 17				17 32						17 47				18 02						18 17		
Kew Bridge	d		17 20				17 35						17 50				18 05						18 20		
Brentford	d		17 23				17 38						17 53				18 08						18 23		
Syon Lane	d		17 25				17 40						17 55				18 10						18 25		
Isleworth	d		17 27				17 42						17 57				18 12						18 27		
Hounslow	d		17 31				17 48						18 01				18 18						18 31		
Mortlake	d					17 24		17 37								17 54		18 07							
North Sheen	d					17 26		17 39		←						17 56		18 09		←					
Richmond ⊖	d			17 18		17 29		17 42	17 36	17 42				17 48		17 59		18 12	18 06	18 12				18 18	
St Margarets	d					17 31		→		17 44						18 01		→		18 14					
Twickenham	a			17 21		17 33			17 40	17 46				17 51		18 03			18 10	18 16				18 21	
	d			17 22		17 34			17 40	17 47				17 52		18 04			18 10	18 17				18 22	
Strawberry Hill	d					17 37										18 07									
Fulwell	a																								
Teddington	a					17 40										18 10									
Hampton Wick	a					17 44										18 14									
Kingston	a					17 46										18 16									
Whitton	d			17 25	←		17a53			17a50				17 55	←		18a23			18a20				18 25	←
Feltham	d		17 36	17 29	17 36				17 46				18 06	17 59	18 06				18 16				18 36	18 29	18 36
Ashford (Surrey)	d		→	17 33	17 40								→	18 03	18 10								→	18 33	18 40
Staines	d			17 37	17 44				17 53					18 07	18 14				18 23					18 37	18 44
Wraysbury	d			17 42										18 12										18 42	
Sunnymeads	d			17 45										18 15										18 45	
Datchet	d			17 49										18 19										18 49	
Windsor & Eton Riverside	a			17 54										18 24										18 54	
Egham	d				17 49				17 57						18 19				18 27						18 49
Virginia Water	a				17 53				18 01						18 23				18 31						18 53
	d				17 53				18 01						18 23				18 31						18 53
Chertsey	d				17 59										18 29										18 59
Addlestone	d				18 02										18 32										19 02
Weybridge	a				18 07										18 37										19 07
Byfleet & New Haw	d																								
West Byfleet	d																								
Woking	a																								
Longcross	d																								
Sunningdale	d								18 07										18 37						
Ascot 3	d	17 53							18 13			18 23							18 43			18 53			
Bagshot	d	17 59										18 29										18 59			
Camberley	a	18 05										18 35										19 05			
Frimley	d	18 13										18 43										19 13			
Ash Vale	d	18 19										18 49										19 19			
Aldershot	a	18 24										18 54										19 24			
	d	18 38										19 08										19 38			
Ash 5	d	18 45										19 15										19 45			
Wanborough	d	18 48										19 18										19 48			
Guildford	a	18 55										19 25										19 55			
Martins Heron	d								18 17										18 47						
Bracknell	d								18 20										18 50						
Wokingham	d								18 27										18 57						
Winnersh	d								18 30										19 00						
Winnersh Triangle	d								18 32										19 02						
Earley	d								18 37										19 07						
Reading 7	a								18 43										19 13						

Table 149

London - Hounslow, Richmond, Kingston, Windsor, Weybridge, Ascot, Guildford and Reading

Saturdays
from 13 October

Network Diagram - see first Page of Table 148

		SW	SW	SW	SW ■	SW		SW ■	SW	SW	SW	SW	SW	SW	SW ■	SW		SW ■	SW	SW	SW	SW	SW	SW	SW ■
London Waterloo 15 ⊖	d	18 03	18 07	18 15	18 20				18 22	18 28		18 33	18 37	18 45	18 50				18 52	18 58		19 03	19 07	19 15	19 20
Vauxhall ⊖	d	18 07	18 11	18 19					18 26	18 32		18 37	18 41	18 49					18 56	19 02		19 07	19 11	19 19	
Queenstown Rd.(Battersea)	d	18 10	18 14	18 22					18 29			18 40	18 44	18 52					18 59			19 10	19 14	19 22	
Clapham Junction 10	d	18 13	18 17	18 25	18 28				18 32	18 38		18 43	18 47	18 55	18 58				19 02	19 08		19 13	19 17	19 25	19 28
Wandsworth Town	d	18 16	18 20	18 28					18 35			18 46	18 50	18 58					19 05			19 16	19 20	19 28	
Putney	d	18 19	18 23	18 31					18 38	18 42		18 49	18 53	19 01					19 08	19 12		19 19	19 23	19 31	
Barnes	d	18 22	18 27	18 35					18 42			18 52	18 57	19 05					19 12			19 22	19 27	19 35	
Barnes Bridge	d		18 29						18 44				18 59						19 14				19 29		
Chiswick	d		18 32						18 47				19 02						19 17				19 32		
Kew Bridge	d		18 35						18 50				19 05						19 20				19 35		
Brentford	d		18 38						18 53				19 08						19 23				19 38		
Syon Lane	d		18 40						18 55				19 10						19 25				19 40		
Isleworth	d		18 42						18 57				19 12						19 27				19 42		
Hounslow	d		18 48						19 01				19 18						19 31				19 48		
Mortlake	d	18 24		18 37								18 54		19 07								19 24		19 37	
North Sheen	d	18 26		18 39		←						18 56		19 09		←						19 26		19 39	
Richmond ⊖	d	18 29		18 42	18 36	18 42				18 48		18 59		19 12	19 06	19 12				19 18		19 29		19 42	19 36
St Margarets	d	18 31		→		18 44						19 01		→		19 14						19 31		→	
Twickenham	a	18 33			18 40	18 46				18 51		19 03			19 10	19 16				19 21		19 33			19 40
	d	18 34			18 40	18 47				18 52		19 04			19 10	19 17				19 22		19 34			19 40
Strawberry Hill	d	18 37										19 07										19 37			
Fulwell	a																								
Teddington	a	18 40										19 10										19 40			
Hampton Wick	a	18 44										19 14										19 44			
Kingston	a	18 46										19 16										19 46			
Whitton	d		18a53			18a50				18 55	←		19a23			19a20				19 25	←		19a53		
Feltham	d				18 46				19 06	18 59	19 06				19 16				19 36	19 29	19 36				19 46
Ashford (Surrey)	d								→	19 03	19 10								→	19 33	19 40				
Staines	d				18 53					19 07	19 14				19 23					19 37	19 44				19 53
Wraysbury	d									19 12										19 42					
Sunnymeads	d									19 15										19 45					
Datchet	d									19 19										19 49					
Windsor & Eton Riverside	a									19 24										19 54					
Egham	d				18 57						19 19				19 27						19 49				19 57
Virginia Water	a				19 01						19 23				19 31						19 53				20 01
	d				19 01						19 23				19 31						19 53				20 01
Chertsey	d										19 29										19 59				
Addlestone	d										19 32										20 02				
Weybridge	a										19 37										20 07				
Byfleet & New Haw	d																								
West Byfleet	d																								
Woking	a																								
Longcross	d																								
Sunningdale	d				19 07										19 37										20 07
Ascot 3	d				19 13			19 23							19 43			19 53							20 13
Bagshot	d							19 29										19 59							
Camberley	a							19 35										20 05							
Frimley	d							19 43										20 13							
Ash Vale	d							19 49										20 19							
Aldershot	a							19 54										20 24							
	d							20 08										20 38							
Ash 5	d							20 15										20 45							
Wanborough	d							20 18										20 48							
Guildford	a							20 25										20 55							
Martins Heron	d				19 17										19 47										20 17
Bracknell	d				19 20										19 50										20 20
Wokingham	d				19 27										19 57										20 27
Winnersh	d				19 30										20 00										20 30
Winnersh Triangle	d				19 32										20 02										20 32
Earley	d				19 37										20 07										20 37
Reading 7	a				19 43										20 13										20 43

Table 149

Saturdays from 13 October

London - Hounslow, Richmond, Kingston, Windsor, Weybridge, Ascot, Guildford and Reading

Network Diagram - see first Page of Table 148

		SW		SW 1	SW	SW	SW	SW	SW	SW	SW 1	SW		SW 1	SW	SW	SW	SW	SW	SW	SW 1	SW		SW 1	SW 1
London Waterloo 15 ⊖	d				19 22	19 28		19 33	19 37	19 45	19 50				19 52	19 58		20 03	20 07	20 15	20 20				
Vauxhall ⊖	d				19 26	19 32		19 37	19 41	19 49					19 56	20 02		20 07	20 11	20 19					
Queenstown Rd.(Battersea)	d				19 29			19 40	19 44	19 52					19 59			20 10	20 14	20 22					
Clapham Junction 10	d				19 32	19 38		19 43	19 47	19 55	19 58				20 02	20 08		20 13	20 17	20 25	20 28				
Wandsworth Town	d				19 35			19 46	19 50	19 58					20 05			20 16	20 20	20 28					
Putney	d				19 38	19 42		19 49	19 53	20 01					20 08	20 12		20 19	20 23	20 31					
Barnes	d				19 42			19 52	19 57	20 05					20 12			20 22	20 27	20 35					
Barnes Bridge	d				19 44				19 59						20 14				20 29						
Chiswick	d				19 47				20 02						20 17				20 32						
Kew Bridge	d				19 50				20 05						20 20				20 35						
Brentford	d				19 53				20 08						20 23				20 38						
Syon Lane	d				19 55				20 10						20 25				20 40						
Isleworth	d				19 57				20 12						20 27				20 42						
Hounslow	d				20 01				20 18						20 31				20 48						
Mortlake	d							19 54		20 07								20 24		20 37					
North Sheen	d	←						19 56		20 09		←						20 26		20 39		←			
Richmond ⊖	d	19 42				19 48		19 59		20 12	20 06	20 12				20 18		20 29		20 42	20 36	20 42			
St Margarets	d	19 44						20 01		→		20 14						20 31		→		20 44			
Twickenham	a	19 46				19 51		20 03			20 10	20 16				20 21		20 33			20 40	20 46			
	d	19 47				19 52		20 04			20 10	20 17				20 22		20 34			20 40	20 47			
Strawberry Hill	d							20 07										20 37							
Fulwell	a																								
Teddington	a							20 10										20 40							
Hampton Wick	a							20 14										20 44							
Kingston	a							20 16										20 46							
Whitton	d	19a50				19 55	←		20a23			20a20				20 25	←		20a53			20a50			
Feltham	d				20 06	19 59	20 06				20 16				20 36	20 29	20 36				20 46				
Ashford (Surrey)	d				→	20 03	20 10								→	20 33	20 40								
Staines	d					20 07	20 14				20 23					20 37	20 44				20 53				
Wraysbury	d					20 12										20 42									
Sunnymeads	d					20 15										20 45									
Datchet	d					20 19										20 49									
Windsor & Eton Riverside	a					20 24										20 54									
Egham	d						20 19				20 27						20 49				20 57				
Virginia Water	a						20 23				20 31						20 53				21 01				
	d						20 23				20 31						20 53				21 01				
Chertsey	d						20 29										20 59								
Addlestone	d						20 32										21 02								
Weybridge	a						20 37										21 07								
Byfleet & New Haw	d																								
West Byfleet	d																								
Woking	a																								
Longcross	d																								
Sunningdale	d										20 37										21 07				
Ascot 3	d			20 23							20 43			20 53							21 13			21 23	
Bagshot	d			20 29										20 59										21 29	
Camberley	a			20 35										21 05										21 35	
Frimley	d			20 43										21 13										21 43	
Ash Vale	d			20 49										21 19										21 49	
Aldershot	a			20 54										21 24										21 54	
	d			21 08										21 38										22 08	22 38
Ash 5	d			21 15										21 45										22 15	22 45
Wanborough	d			21 18										21 48										22 18	22 48
Guildford	a			21 25										21 55										22 25	22 55
Martins Heron	d										20 47										21 17				
Bracknell	d										20 50										21 20				
Wokingham	d										20 57										21 27				
Winnersh	d										21 00										21 30				
Winnersh Triangle	d										21 02										21 32				
Earley	d										21 07										21 37				
Reading 7	a										21 13										21 43				

Table 149

Saturdays from 13 October

London - Hounslow, Richmond, Kingston, Windsor, Weybridge, Ascot, Guildford and Reading

Network Diagram - see first Page of Table 148

		SW	SW	SW	SW	SW	SW	SW 1		SW	SW	SW	SW	SW	SW	SW	SW 1	SW		SW 1	SW	SW	SW	SW	SW
London Waterloo 15 ⊖	d	20 22	20 28		20 33	20 37	20 45	20 50			20 52	20 58		21 03	21 07	21 15	21 20				21 22	21 28		21 33	21 37
Vauxhall ⊖	d	20 26	20 32		20 37	20 41	20 49				20 56	21 02		21 07	21 11	21 19					21 26	21 32		21 37	21 41
Queenstown Rd.(Battersea)	d	20 29			20 40	20 44	20 52				20 59			21 10	21 14	21 22					21 29			21 40	21 44
Clapham Junction 10	d	20 32	20 38		20 43	20 47	20 55	20 58			21 02	21 08		21 13	21 17	21 25	21 28				21 32	21 38		21 43	21 47
Wandsworth Town	d	20 35			20 46	20 50	20 58				21 05			21 16	21 20	21 28					21 35			21 46	21 50
Putney	d	20 38	20 42		20 49	20 53	21 01				21 08	21 12		21 19	21 23	21 31					21 38	21 42		21 49	21 53
Barnes	d	20 42			20 52	20 57	21 05				21 12			21 22	21 27	21 35					21 42			21 52	21 57
Barnes Bridge	d	20 44				20 59					21 14				21 29						21 44				21 59
Chiswick	d	20 47				21 02					21 17				21 32						21 47				22 02
Kew Bridge	d	20 50				21 05					21 20				21 35						21 50				22 05
Brentford	d	20 53				21 08					21 23				21 38						21 53				22 08
Syon Lane	d	20 55				21 10					21 25				21 40						21 55				22 10
Isleworth	d	20 57				21 12					21 27				21 42						21 57				22 12
Hounslow	d	21 01				21 18					21 31				21 48						22 01				22 18
Mortlake	d				20 54		21 07							21 24		21 37								21 54	
North Sheen	d				20 56		21 09			←				21 26		21 39		←						21 56	
Richmond ⊖	d		20 48		20 59		21 12	21 06		21 12		21 18		21 29		21 42	21 36	21 42				21 48		21 59	
St Margarets	d				21 01		→			21 14				21 31		→		21 44						22 01	
Twickenham	a		20 51		21 03			21 10		21 16		21 21		21 33			21 40	21 46				21 51		22 03	
	d		20 52		21 04			21 10		21 17		21 22		21 34			21 40	21 47				21 52		22 04	
Strawberry Hill	d				21 07									21 37										22 07	
Fulwell	a																								
Teddington	a				21 10									21 40										22 10	
Hampton Wick	a				21 14									21 44										22 14	
Kingston	a				21 16									21 46										22 16	
Whitton	d		20 55	←		21a23				21a20		21 25	←		21a53			21a50				21 55	←		22a23
Feltham	d	21 06	20 59	21 06				21 16			21 36	21 29	21 36				21 46				22 06	21 59	22 06		
Ashford (Surrey)	d	→	21 03	21 10							→	21 33	21 40								→	22 03	22 10		
Staines	d		21 07	21 14				21 23				21 37	21 44				21 53					22 07	22 14		
Wraysbury	d		21 12									21 42										22 12			
Sunnymeads	d		21 15									21 45										22 15			
Datchet	d		21 19									21 49										22 19			
Windsor & Eton Riverside	a		21 24									21 54										22 24			
Egham	d			21 19				21 27					21 49				21 57						22 19		
Virginia Water	a			21 23				21 31					21 53				22 01						22 23		
	d			21 23				21 31					21 53				22 01						22 23		
Chertsey	d			21 29									21 59										22 29		
Addlestone	d			21 32									22 02										22 32		
Weybridge	a			21 37									22 07										22 37		
Byfleet & New Haw	d																								
West Byfleet	d																								
Woking	a																								
Longcross	d																								
Sunningdale	d							21 37									22 07								
Ascot 3	d							21 43									22 13			22 23					
Bagshot	d																			22 29					
Camberley	a																			22 35					
Frimley	d																			22 43					
Ash Vale	d																			22 49					
Aldershot	a																			22 54					
	d																			23 08					
Ash 5	d																			23 15					
Wanborough	d																			23 18					
Guildford	a																			23 25					
Martins Heron	d							21 47									22 17								
Bracknell	d							21 50									22 20								
Wokingham	d							21 57									22 27								
Winnersh	d							22 00									22 30								
Winnersh Triangle	d							22 02									22 32								
Earley	d							22 07									22 37								
Reading 7	a							22 13									22 42								

Table 149

London - Hounslow, Richmond, Kingston, Windsor, Weybridge, Ascot, Guildford and Reading

Network Diagram - see first Page of Table 148

			SW	SW 1	SW	SW	SW	SW	SW	SW 1	SW 1	SW	SW	SW	SW	SW 1	SW	SW	SW	SW	SW	SW 1	SW
London Waterloo 15	⊖	d	21 45	21 50		21 52	21 58		22 03	22 20		22 22	22 28		22 33	22 50	22 52	22 58		23 03	23 13	23 20	23 22
Vauxhall	⊖	d	21 49			21 56	22 02		22 07			22 26	22 32		22 37		22 56	23 02		23 07	23 17		23 26
Queenstown Rd.(Battersea)		d	21 52			21 59			22 10			22 29			22 40		22 59			23 10			23 29
Clapham Junction 10		d	21 55	21 58		22 02	22 08		22 13	22 28		22 32	22 38		22 43	22 58	23 02	23 08		23 13	23 23	23 28	23 32
Wandsworth Town		d	21 58			22 05			22 16			22 35			22 46		23 05			23 16			23 35
Putney		d	22 01			22 08	22 12		22 19			22 38	22 42		22 49		23 08	23 12		23 19	23 27		23 38
Barnes		d	22 05			22 12			22 22			22 42			22 52		23 12			23 22			23 42
Barnes Bridge		d				22 14						22 44					23 14						23 44
Chiswick		d				22 17						22 47					23 17						23 47
Kew Bridge		d				22 20						22 50					23 20						23 50
Brentford		d				22 23						22 53					23 23						23 53
Syon Lane		d				22 25						22 55					23 25						23 55
Isleworth		d				22 27						22 57					23 27						23 57
Hounslow		d				22 31						23 01					23 31						00 01
Mortlake		d	22 07						22 24						22 54					23 24			
North Sheen		d	22 09		←				22 26						22 56					23 26			
Richmond	⊖	d	22 12	22 06	22 12		22 18		22 29	22 36			22 48		22 59	23 06		23 18		23 29	23 33	23 37	
St Margarets		d	→		22 14				22 31						23 01					23 31			
Twickenham		a		22 10	22 16		22 21		22 33	22 40			22 51		23 03	23 10		23 21		23 33	23 37	23 41	
		d		22 10			22 22		22 34	22 40			22 52		23 04	23 10		23 22		23 34	23 37	23 41	
Strawberry Hill		d							22 37						23 07					23 37			
Fulwell		a																					
Teddington		a							22 40						23 10					23 40			
Hampton Wick		a							22 44						23 14					23 44			
Kingston		a							22 46						23 16					23 46			
Whitton		d					22 25	←					22 55	←				23 25	←		23 40		
Feltham		d		22 16		22 36	22 29	22 36		22 46		23 06	22 59	23 06		23 16	23 36	23 29	23 36		23 44	23 48	00 06
Ashford (Surrey)		d				→	22 33	22 40				→	23 03	23 10			→	23 33	23 40		23 48		→
Staines		d		22 23			22 37	22 44		22 53			23 07	23 14		23 23		23 37	23 44		23 52	23 56	
Wraysbury		d					22 42						23 11					23 42			23 57		
Sunnymeads		d					22 45						23 14					23 45			23 59		
Datchet		d					22 49						23 17					23 49			00 04		
Windsor & Eton Riverside		a					22 56						23 24					23 54			00 09		
Egham		d		22 27				22 49		22 57				23 19		23 27			23 49			00 01	
Virginia Water		a		22 31				22 53		23 01				23 23		23 31			23 53			00 05	
		d		22 31				22 53		23 01				23 23		23 31			23 53			00 05	
Chertsey		d						22 59						23 29					23 59				
Addlestone		d						23 02						23a32					00 02				
Weybridge		a						23 07						23 37									
Byfleet & New Haw		d																	00 06				
West Byfleet		d																	00 09				
Woking		a																	00 15				
Longcross		d																					
Sunningdale		d		22 37						23 07						23 37						00 11	
Ascot 3		d		22 43						23 13	23 23					23 43						00 15	
Bagshot		d									23 29												
Camberley		a									23 35												
Frimley		d									23 43												
Ash Vale		d									23 49												
Aldershot		a									23 54												
		d																					
Ash 5		d																					
Wanborough		d																					
Guildford		a																					
Martins Heron		d		22 47						23 17						23 47						00 19	
Bracknell		d		22 50						23 20						23 50						00 23	
Wokingham		d		22 57						23 27						23 57						00 32	
Winnersh		d		23 00						23 30						23 59						00 36	
Winnersh Triangle		d		23 02						23 32						00 02						00 38	
Earley		d		23 05						23 37						00 05						00 40	
Reading 7		a		23 13						23 43						00 13						00 48	

Table 149

London - Hounslow, Richmond, Kingston, Windsor, Weybridge, Ascot, Guildford and Reading

Network Diagram - see first Page of Table 148

			SW	SW	SW	SW	SW	SW	SW
London Waterloo 15	⊖	d	23 33	23 38			23 52	23 58	
Vauxhall	⊖	d	23 37				23 56	00 02	
Queenstown Rd.(Battersea)		d	23 40				23 59		
Clapham Junction 10		d	23 43	23 46			00 02	00 08	
Wandsworth Town		d	23 46				00 05		
Putney		d	23 49				00 08	00 12	
Barnes		d	23 52				00 12		
Barnes Bridge		d					00 14		
Chiswick		d					00 17		
Kew Bridge		d					00 20		
Brentford		d					00 23		
Syon Lane		d					00 25		
Isleworth		d					00 27		
Hounslow		d					00 31		
Mortlake		d	23 54						
North Sheen		d	23 56			←			
Richmond	⊖	d	23 59	23 54		23 59		00 18	
St Margarets		d	→			00 01			
Twickenham		a		23 58		00 04		00 21	
		d		23 58		00 04		00 22	
Strawberry Hill		d				00 07			
Fulwell		a							
Teddington		a				00 11			
Hampton Wick		a				00 14			
Kingston		a				00 16			
Whitton		d			←			00 25	←
Feltham		d		00 04	00 06		00 36	00 29	00 36
Ashford (Surrey)		d			00 10		→	00 33	00 40
Staines		d		00 11	00 14			00a37	00a46
Wraysbury		d							
Sunnymeads		d							
Datchet		d							
Windsor & Eton Riverside		a							
Egham		d		00 15	00 19				
Virginia Water		a		00 19	00 23				
		d		00 19	00 23				
Chertsey		d			00 29				
Addlestone		d			00a32				
Weybridge		a			00 38				
Byfleet & New Haw		d							
West Byfleet		d							
Woking		a							
Longcross		d							
Sunningdale		d		00 25					
Ascot 3		d		00 30					
Bagshot		d							
Camberley		a							
Frimley		d							
Ash Vale		d							
Aldershot		a							
		d							
Ash 5		d							
Wanborough		d							
Guildford		a							
Martins Heron		d		00 34					
Bracknell		d		00 37					
Wokingham		d		00 44					
Winnersh		d							
Winnersh Triangle		d							
Earley		d							
Reading 7		a		00 55					

Table 149

Sundays until 30 September

London - Hounslow, Richmond, Kingston, Windsor, Weybridge, Ascot, Guildford and Reading

Network Diagram - see first Page of Table 148

		SW ■	SW	SW	SW ■	SW	SW	SW A	SW	SW		SW ■ A	SW B	SW ■ B	SW ■	SW	SW	SW	SW	SW B			SW		SW
London Waterloo ■ ⊖	d	22p50	22p52	23p13	23p20	23p22	23p33	23p38					23p50			23p52	23p58		00 18	00 38			06 14		
Vauxhall ⊖	d		22p56	23p17		23p26	23p37									23p56	00 02		00 22	00 42			06 18		
Queenstown Rd.(Battersea)	d		22p59			23p29	23p40									23p59			00 26				06 21		
Clapham Junction ■	d	22p58	23p02	23p23	23p28	23p32	23p43	23p46					23p58			00 02	00 08		00 29	00 48			06 24		
Wandsworth Town	d		23p05			23p35	23p46									00 05			00 32				06 27		
Putney	d		23p08	23p27		23p38	23p49									00 08	00 12		00 35	00 52			06 30		
Barnes	d		23p12			23p42	23p52									00 12			00 38	00 55			06 33		
Barnes Bridge	d		23p14			23p44										00 14									
Chiswick	d		23p17			23p47										00 17									
Kew Bridge	d		23p20			23p50										00 20									
Brentford	d		23p23			23p53										00 23									
Syon Lane	d		23p25			23p55										00 25									
Isleworth	d		23p27			23p57										00 27									
Hounslow	d		23p31			00 01										00 31									
Mortlake	d						23p54												00 40				06 35		
North Sheen	d						23p56			←									00 42				06 37		
Richmond ⊖	d	23p06		23p33	23p37		23p59	23p54		23p59			00 06				00 18		00 45	01 00			06 40		
St Margarets	d						→			00 01									00 47				06 42		
Twickenham	a	23p10		23p37	23p41			23p58		00 04			00 10				00 21		00 49	01 03			06 44		
	d	23p10		23p37	23p41			23p58		00 04			00 10				00 22		00 50	01 04			06 45		
Strawberry Hill	d									00 07									00s53				06 49		
Fulwell	a																								
Teddington	a									00 11									00s56				06 52		
Hampton Wick	a									00 14									00s59				06 57		
Kingston	a									00 16									01 01				06 59		
Whitton	d			23p40					←								00 25	←		01 07					
Feltham	d	23p16	23p36	23p44	23p48	00 06		00 04	00 06				00 16			00 36	00 29	00 36		01 11					
Ashford (Surrey)	d		23p40	23p48		→			00 10							→	00 33	00 40		01 15					
Staines	d	23p23	23p44	23p52	23p56			00 11	00 14				00 23				00a37	00a46		01a19					06 32
Wraysbury	d			23p56																					
Sunnymeads	d			23p59																					
Datchet	d			00 02																					
Windsor & Eton Riverside	a			00 06																					
Egham	d	23p27	23p49		00 01			00 15	00 19				00 27												06 36
Virginia Water	a	23p31	23p53		00 05			00 19	00 23				00 31												06 41
	d	23p31	23p53		00 05			00 19	00 23				00 31												06 41
Chertsey	d		23p59						00 29																06 46
Addlestone	d		00 02						00a32																06 49
Weybridge	a								00 38																06 53
Byfleet & New Haw	d		00 06																						
West Byfleet	d		00 09																						
Woking	a		00 15																						
Longcross	d																								
Sunningdale	d	23p37			00 11			00 25					00 37												
Ascot ■	d	23p43			00 15			00 30				00 32	00 42	00 44											
Bagshot	d											00 38		00 50											
Camberley	a											00 44		00 56											
Frimley	d											00 48		01 00											
Ash Vale	d											00 57		01 09											
Aldershot	a											01s02		01s13											
	d														07 48										
Ash ■	d														07 55										
Wanborough	d														07 58										
Guildford	a														08 05										
Martins Heron	d	23p47			00 19			00 34					00 46												
Bracknell	d	23p50			00 23			00 37					00 49												
Wokingham	d	23p57			00 32			00 44					00 56												
Winnersh	d	23p59			00 36																				
Winnersh Triangle	d	00 02			00 38																				
Earley	d	00 05			00 40																				
Reading ■	a	00 10			00 45			00 52					01 04												

A until 22 July, 19 August, 26 August, 16 September, 23 September, 30 September

B 29 July, 5 August, 12 August, 2 September, 9 September

Table 149

Sundays until 30 September

London - Hounslow, Richmond, Kingston, Windsor, Weybridge, Ascot, Guildford and Reading

Network Diagram - see first Page of Table 148

		SW	SW	SW ■	SW A	SW B		SW C	SW ■	SW ■	SW	SW	SW ■	SW	SW ■	SW ■		SW	SW	SW ■	SW	SW	SW ■	SW ■	SW
London Waterloo ■ ⊖	d	06 44		07 09	07 12	07 14		07 14			07 44	07 50	08 09	08 14		08 39		08 44	08 50	09 09	09 14	09 25		09 39	09 44
Vauxhall ⊖	d	06 48		07 13	07 16	07 18		07 19			07 48	07 54	08 13	08 18		08 43		08 48	08 54	09 13	09 18	09 29		09 43	09 48
Queenstown Rd.(Battersea)	d	06 51				07 21		07 22			07 51	07 57		08 21				08 51	08 57		09 21				09 51
Clapham Junction ■	d	06 54		07 19	07 22	07 24		07 25			07 54	08 00	08 19	08 24		08 49		08 54	09 00	09 19	09 24	09 35		09 49	09 54
Wandsworth Town	d	06 57				07 27		07 28			07 57	08 03		08 27				08 57	09 03		09 27				09 57
Putney	d	07 00		07 23	07 27	07 30		07 31			08 00	08 06	08 23	08 30		08 53		09 00	09 06	09 23	09 30	09 39		09 53	10 00
Barnes	d	07 03				07 33		07 34			08 03	08 09		08 33				09 03	09 09		09 33				10 03
Barnes Bridge	d											08 11							09 11						
Chiswick	d											08 13							09 13						
Kew Bridge	d											08 16							09 16						
Brentford	d											08 19							09 19						
Syon Lane	d											08 21							09 21						
Isleworth	d											08 23							09 23						
Hounslow	d											08 26							09 26						
Mortlake	d	07 05				07 35		07 36			08 05			08 35				09 05			09 35				10 05
North Sheen	d	07 07				07 37		07 38			08 07			08 37				09 07			09 37				10 07
Richmond ⊖	d	07 10		07 29	07 33	07 40		07 41			08 10		08 29	08 40		08 59		09 10		09 29	09 40	09 45		09 59	10 10
St Margarets	d	07 12				07 42		07 43			08 12			08 42				09 12			09 42				10 12
Twickenham	a	07 14		07 32	07 36	07 44		07 45			08 14		08 32	08 44		09 02		09 14		09 32	09 44	09 48		10 02	10 14
	d	07 15		07 33	07 37	07 45		07 46			08 15		08 33	08 45		09 03		09 15		09 33	09 45	09 49		10 03	10 15
Strawberry Hill	d					07 49		07 50						08 49							09 49				
Fulwell	a																								
Teddington	a					07 52		07 53						08 52							09 52				
Hampton Wick	a					07 57		07 57						08 57							09 57				
Kingston	a					07 59		07 59						08 59							09 59				
Whitton	d	07 18			07 40						08 18							09 18				09 52			10 18
Feltham	d	07 22		07 39	07 44						08 22	08 32	08 39			09 09		09 22	09 32	09 39		09 56		10 09	10 22
Ashford (Surrey)	d	07 26			07 48						08 26	08 36						09 26	09 36			10 00			10 26
Staines	d	07 30	07 40	07 45	07 52					08 15	08 30	08 40	08 45			09 15		09 30	09 40	09 45		10 04		10 15	10 30
Wraysbury	d	07 34									08 34							09 34							10 34
Sunnymeads	d	07 37									08 37							09 37							10 37
Datchet	d	07 40			08 01						08 40							09 40				10 12			10 40
Windsor & Eton Riverside	a	07 44			08 06						08 44							09 44				10 16			10 44
Egham	d		07 45	07 50						08 20		08 45	08 50			09 20			09 45	09 50				10 20	
Virginia Water	a		07 49	07 54						08 24		08 49	08 54			09 24			09 49	09 54				10 24	
	d		07 49	07 54						08 24		08 49	08 54			09 24			09 49	09 54				10 24	
Chertsey	d		07 55									08 55							09 55						
Addlestone	d		07 58									08 58							09 58						
Weybridge	a																								
Byfleet & New Haw	d		08 02									09 02							10 02						
West Byfleet	d		08 05									09 05							10 05						
Woking	a		08 11									09 11							10 11						
Longcross	d																								
Sunningdale	d			07 59						08 29			08 59			09 29				09 59				10 29	
Ascot ■	d			08 04					08 13	08 34			09 04		09 13	09 34				10 04			10 13	10 34	
Bagshot	d								08 19						09 19								10 19		
Camberley	a								08 25						09 25								10 25		
Frimley	d								08 29						09 29								10 29		
Ash Vale	d								08 36						09 36								10 36		
Aldershot	a								08 41						09 41								10 41		
	d								08 48						09 48								10 48		
Ash ■	d								08 55						09 55								10 55		
Wanborough	d								08 58						09 58								10 58		
Guildford	a								09 05						10 05								11 05		
Martins Heron	d			08 08						08 38			09 08			09 38				10 08				10 38	
Bracknell	d			08 11						08 41			09 11			09 41				10 11				10 41	
Wokingham	d			08 18						08 48			09 18			09 48				10 18				10 48	
Winnersh	d			08 21						08 51			09 21			09 51				10 21				10 51	
Winnersh Triangle	d			08 23						08 53			09 23			09 53				10 23				10 53	
Earley	d			08 26						08 56			09 26			09 56				10 26				10 56	
Reading ■	a			08 31						09 01			09 31			10 01				10 31				11 01	

A 29 July, 2 September

B until 22 July, 19 August, 26 August, 16 September, 23 September, 30 September

C 29 July, 5 August, 12 August, 2 September, 9 September

Table 149

until 30 September

London - Hounslow, Richmond, Kingston, Windsor, Weybridge, Ascot, Guildford and Reading

Network Diagram - see first Page of Table 148

		SW	SW ■	SW	SW	SW ■	SW ■	SW	SW	SW ■	SW	SW	SW ■	SW ■	SW	SW	SW ■	SW	SW	SW ■	SW ■	SW
London Waterloo ■ ⊖	d	09 50	10 09	10 14	10 25		10 39	10 44	10 50	11 09	11 14	11 25		11 39	11 44	11 50	12 09	12 14	12 25		12 39	12 44
Vauxhall ⊖	d	09 54	10 13	10 18	10 29		10 43	10 48	10 54	11 13	11 19	11 29		11 43	11 48	11 54	12 13	12 19	12 29		12 43	12 48
Queenstown Rd.(Battersea)	d	09 57		10 21				10 51	10 57		11 22				11 51	11 57		12 22				12 51
Clapham Junction ■	d	10 00	10 19	10 24	10 35		10 49	10 54	11 00	11 19	11 25	11 35		11 49	11 54	12 00	12 19	12 25	12 35		12 49	12 54
Wandsworth Town	d	10 03		10 27				10 57	11 03		11 28				11 57	12 03		12 28				12 57
Putney	d	10 06	10 23	10 30	10 39		10 53	11 00	11 06	11 23	11 31	11 39		11 53	12 00	12 06	12 23	12 31	12 39		12 53	13 00
Barnes	d	10 09		10 33				11 03	11 09		11 34				12 03	12 09		12 34				13 03
Barnes Bridge	d	10 11							11 11							12 11						
Chiswick	d	10 13							11 13							12 13						
Kew Bridge	d	10 16							11 16							12 16						
Brentford	d	10 19							11 19							12 19						
Syon Lane	d	10 21							11 21							12 21						
Isleworth	d	10 23							11 23							12 23						
Hounslow	d	10 26							11 26							12 26						
Mortlake	d			10 35				11 05			11 36				12 05			12 36				13 05
North Sheen	d			10 37				11 07			11 38				12 07			12 38				13 07
Richmond ⊖	d		10 29	10 40	10 45		10 59	11 10		11 29	11 41	11 45		11 59	12 10		12 29	12 41	12 45		12 59	13 10
St Margarets	d			10 42				11 12			11 43				12 12			12 43				13 12
Twickenham	a		10 32	10 44	10 48		11 02	11 14		11 32	11 45	11 48		12 02	12 14		12 32	12 45	12 48		13 02	13 14
	d		10 33	10 45	10 49		11 03	11 15		11 33	11 46	11 49		12 03	12 15		12 33	12 46	12 49		13 03	13 15
Strawberry Hill	d			10 49							11 50							12 50				
Fulwell	a																					
Teddington	a			10 52							11 53							12 53				
Hampton Wick	a			10 57							11 57							12 57				
Kingston	a			10 59							11 59							12 59				
Whitton	d				10 52			11 18				11 52			12 18				12 52			13 18
Feltham	d	10 32	10 39		10 56		11 09	11 22	11 32	11 39		11 56		12 09	12 22	12 32	12 39		12 56		13 09	13 22
Ashford (Surrey)	d	10 36			11 00			11 26	11 36			12 00			12 26	12 36			13 00			13 26
Staines	d	10 40	10 45		11 04		11 15	11 30	11 40	11 45		12 04		12 15	12 30	12 40	12 45		13 04		13 15	13 30
Wraysbury	d							11 34							12 34							13 34
Sunnymeads	d							11 37							12 37							13 37
Datchet	d				11 12			11 40				12 12			12 40				13 12			13 40
Windsor & Eton Riverside	a				11 16			11 44				12 16			12 44				13 16			13 44
Egham	d	10 45	10 50				11 20		11 45	11 50				12 20		12 45	12 50				13 20	
Virginia Water	a	10 49	10 54				11 24		11 49	11 54				12 24		12 49	12 54				13 24	
	d	10 49	10 54				11 24		11 49	11 54				12 24		12 49	12 54				13 24	
Chertsey	d	10 55							11 55							12 55						
Addlestone	d	10 58							11 58							12 58						
Weybridge	a																					
Byfleet & New Haw	d	11 02							12 02							13 02						
West Byfleet	d	11 05							12 05							13 05						
Woking	a	11 11							12 11							13 11						
Longcross	d																					
Sunningdale	d		10 59				11 29			11 59				12 29			12 59				13 29	
Ascot ■	d		11 04			11 13	11 34			12 04			12 13	12 34			13 04			13 13	13 34	
Bagshot	d					11 19							12 19							13 19		
Camberley	a					11 25							12 25							13 25		
Frimley	d					11 29							12 29							13 29		
Ash Vale	d					11 36							12 36							13 36		
Aldershot	a					11 41							12 41							13 41		
	d					11 48							12 48							13 48		
Ash ■	d					11 55							12 55							13 55		
Wanborough	d					11 58							12 58							13 58		
Guildford	a					12 05							13 05							14 05		
Martins Heron	d		11 08				11 38			12 08				12 38			13 08				13 38	
Bracknell	d		11 11				11 41			12 11				12 41			13 11				13 41	
Wokingham	d		11 18				11 48			12 18				12 48			13 18				13 48	
Winnersh	d		11 21				11 51			12 21				12 51			13 21				13 51	
Winnersh Triangle	d		11 23				11 53			12 23				12 53			13 23				13 53	
Earley	d		11 26				11 56			12 26				12 56			13 26				13 56	
Reading ■	a		11 31				12 01			12 31				13 01			13 31				14 01	

Table 149

until 30 September

London - Hounslow, Richmond, Kingston, Windsor, Weybridge, Ascot, Guildford and Reading

Network Diagram - see first Page of Table 148

		SW	SW ■	SW	SW	SW ■	SW ■	SW	SW	SW		SW	SW ■	SW	SW ■	SW ■	SW	SW	SW	SW ■	SW	SW ■
London Waterloo ■ ⊖	d	12 50	13 09	13 14	13 25		13 39	13 44	13 50	13 56		19 56	20 09	20 14		20 39	20 44	20 50	20 56	21 09	21 14	
Vauxhall ⊖	d	12 54	13 13	13 18	13 29		13 43	13 48	13 54	14 00		20 00	20 13	20 18		20 43	20 48	20 54	21 00	21 13	21 18	
Queenstown Rd.(Battersea)	d	12 57		13 21				13 51	13 57	14 03		20 03		20 21			20 51	20 57	21 03		21 21	
Clapham Junction ■	d	13 00	13 19	13 24	13 35		13 49	13 54	14 00	14 06		20 06	20 19	20 24		20 49	20 54	21 00	21 06	21 19	21 24	
Wandsworth Town	d	13 03		13 27				13 57	14 03	14 09		20 09		20 27			20 57	21 03	21 09		21 27	
Putney	d	13 06	13 23	13 30	13 39		13 53	14 00	14 06	14 12		20 12	20 23	20 30		20 53	21 00	21 06	21 12	21 23	21 30	
Barnes	d	13 09		13 33				14 03	14 09	14 15		20 15		20 33			21 03	21 09	21 15		21 33	
Barnes Bridge	d	13 11							14 11									21 11				
Chiswick	d	13 13							14 13									21 13				
Kew Bridge	d	13 16							14 16									21 16				
Brentford	d	13 19							14 19									21 19				
Syon Lane	d	13 21							14 21									21 21				
Isleworth	d	13 23							14 23									21 23				
Hounslow	d	13 26							14 26									21 26				
Mortlake	d			13 35				14 05		14 17		20 17		20 35			21 05		21 17		21 35	
North Sheen	d			13 37				14 07		14 19		20 19		20 37			21 07		21 19		21 37	
Richmond ⊖	d		13 29	13 40	13 45		13 59	14 10		14 22		20 22	20 29	20 40		20 59	21 10		21 22	21 29	21 40	
St Margarets	d			13 42				14 12		14 24		20 24		20 42			21 12		21 24		21 42	
Twickenham	a		13 32	13 44	13 48		14 02	14 14		14 26		20 26	20 32	20 44		21 02	21 14		21 26	21 32	21 44	
	d		13 33	13 45	13 49		14 03	14 15		14 27		20 27	20 33	20 45		21 03	21 15		21 27	21 33	21 45	
Strawberry Hill	d			13 49						14 30		20 30		20 49					21 30		21 49	
Fulwell	a																					
Teddington	a			13 52						14 33		20 33		20 52					21 33		21 52	
Hampton Wick	a			13 57						14 36		20 36		20 57					21 36		21 57	
Kingston	a			13 59						14 38		20 38		20 59					21 38		21 59	
Whitton	d				13 52			14 18									21 18					
Feltham	d	13 32	13 39		13 56		14 09	14 22	14 32		and at the same minutes past each hour until		20 39			21 09	21 22	21 32		21 39		
Ashford (Surrey)	d	13 36			14 00			14 26	14 36								21 26	21 36				
Staines	d	13 40	13 45		14 04		14 15	14 30	14 40				20 45			21 15	21 30	21 40		21 45		
Wraysbury	d							14 34									21 34					
Sunnymeads	d							14 37									21 37					
Datchet	d				14 12			14 40									21 40					
Windsor & Eton Riverside	a				14 16			14 44									21 44					
Egham	d	13 45	13 50				14 20		14 45				20 50			21 20		21 45		21 50		
Virginia Water	a	13 49	13 54				14 24		14 49				20 54			21 24		21 49		21 54		
	d	13 49	13 54				14 24		14 49				20 54			21 24		21 49		21 54		
Chertsey	d	13 55							14 55									21 55				
Addlestone	d	13 58							14 58									21 58				
Weybridge	a																					
Byfleet & New Haw	d	14 02							15 02									22 02				
West Byfleet	d	14 05							15 05									22 05				
Woking	a	14 11							15 11									22 11				
Longcross	d																					
Sunningdale	d		13 59				14 29						20 59			21 29				21 59		
Ascot ■	d		14 04			14 13	14 34						21 04		21 13	21 34				22 04		22 13
Bagshot	d					14 19									21 19							22 19
Camberley	a					14 25									21 25							22 25
Frimley	d					14 29									21 29							22 29
Ash Vale	d					14 36									21 36							22 36
Aldershot	a					14 41									21 41							22 41
	d					14 48									21 48							22 48
Ash ■	d					14 55									21 55							22 55
Wanborough	d					14 58									21 58							22 58
Guildford	a					15 05									22 05							23 05
Martins Heron	d		14 08				14 38						21 08			21 38				22 08		
Bracknell	d		14 11				14 41						21 11			21 41				22 11		
Wokingham	d		14 18				14 48						21 18			21 48				22 18		
Winnersh	d		14 21				14 51						21 21			21 51				22 21		
Winnersh Triangle	d		14 23				14 53						21 23			21 53				22 23		
Earley	d		14 26				14 56						21 26			21 56				22 26		
Reading ■	a		14 31				15 01						21 31			22 01				22 31		

Sundays until 30 September

London - Hounslow, Richmond, Kingston, Windsor, Weybridge, Ascot, Guildford and Reading

Network Diagram - see first Page of Table 148

		SW ■	SW	SW	SW	SW ■	SW	SW ■	SW ■	SW	SW	SW	SW ■	SW	SW ■ A	SW A	SW ■ B	SW A	SW B
London Waterloo ■ ⊖	d	21 39	21 44	21 50	21 56	22 09	22 14		22 39	22 44	22 50	22 56	23 09	23 14	23 39	23 44	23 50		23 54
Vauxhall ⊖	d	21 43	21 48	21 54	22 00	22 13	22 18		22 43	22 48	22 54	23 00	23 13	23 18	23 43	23 48	23 54		23 58
Queenstown Rd.(Battersea)	d		21 51	21 57	22 03		22 21			22 51	22 57	23 03		23 21		23 51			00 01
Clapham Junction ■	d	21 49	21 54	22 00	22 06	22 19	22 24		22 49	22 54	23 00	23 06	23 19	23 24	23 49	23 54	00 01		00 04
Wandsworth Town	d		21 57	22 03	22 09		22 27			22 57	23 03	23 09		23 27		23 57			00 07
Putney	d	21 53	22 00	22 06	22 12	22 23	22 30		22 53	23 00	23 06	23 12	23 23	23 30	23 53	23 59	00 04		00 09
Barnes	d		22 03	22 09	22 15		22 33			23 03	23 09	23 15		23 33		00 03			00 13
Barnes Bridge	d			22 11							23 11								
Chiswick	d			22 13							23 13								
Kew Bridge	d			22 16							23 16								
Brentford	d			22 19							23 19								
Syon Lane	d			22 21							23 21								
Isleworth	d			22 23							23 23								
Hounslow	d			22 26							23 26								
Mortlake	d		22 05		22 17		22 35			23 05		23 17		23 35		00 05			00 15
North Sheen	d		22 07		22 19		22 37			23 07		23 19		23 37		00 07			00 17
Richmond ⊖	d	21 59	22 10		22 22	22 29	22 40		22 59	23 10		23 22	23 29	23 40	23 59	00 10	00 10		00 20
St Margarets	d		22 12		22 24		22 42			23 12		23 24		23 42		00 12			00 22
Twickenham	a	22 02	22 14		22 26	22 32	22 44		23 02	23 14		23 26	23 32	23 44	00 02	00 14	00 13		00 24
	d	22 03	22 15		22 27	22 33	22 45		23 03	23 15		23 27	23 33	23 45	00 03	00 15	00 14		00 25
Strawberry Hill	d				22 30		22 49					23 30		23 48					
Fulwell	a																		
Teddington	a				22 33		22 52					23 33		23 51					
Hampton Wick	a				22 36		22 57					23 36		23 54					
Kingston	a				22 38		22 59					23 38		23 56					
Whitton	d		22 18							23 18						00 18		←	00 28
Feltham	d	22 09	22 22	22 32		22 39			23 09	23 22	23 32		23 39		00 09	00 22	00 20	00 22	00 32
Ashford (Surrey)	d		22 26	22 36						23 26	23 36					→		00 26	00 36
Staines	d	22 15	22 30	22 40		22 45			23 15	23 30	23 40		23 45		00 15		00 26	00a30	00a40
Wraysbury	d		22 34							23 34									
Sunnymeads	d		22 37							23 37									
Datchet	d		22 40							23 40									
Windsor & Eton Riverside	a		22 44							23 44									
Egham	d	22 20		22 45		22 50			23 20		23 45		23 50		00 20		00 31		
Virginia Water	a	22 24		22 49		22 54			23 24		23 49		23 54		00 24		00 35		
	d	22 24		22 49		22 54			23 24		23 49		23 54		00 24		00 35		
Chertsey	d			22 55							23 55								
Addlestone	d			22 58							23 58								
Weybridge	a																		
Byfleet & New Haw	d			23 02							00 02								
West Byfleet	d			23 05							00 05								
Woking	a			23 11							00 11								
Longcross	d																		
Sunningdale	d	22 29				22 59			23 29				23 59		00 29		00 40		
Ascot ■	d	22 34				23 04		23 13	23 34				00 04		00 34		00 45		
Bagshot	d							23 19											
Camberley	a							23 25											
Frimley	d							23 29											
Ash Vale	d							23 36											
Aldershot	a							23 41											
	d																		
Ash ■	d																		
Wanborough	d																		
Guildford	a																		
Martins Heron	d	22 38				23 08			23 38				00 08		00 38		00 49		
Bracknell	d	22 41				23 11			23 41				00 11		00 41		00 52		
Wokingham	d	22 48				23 18			23 48				00 18		00 48		00 59		
Winnersh	d	22 51				23 21			23 51				00 21		00 51		01 02		
Winnersh Triangle	d	22 53				23 23			23 53				00 23		00 53		01 04		
Earley	d	22 56				23 26			23 56				00 26		00 56		01 07		
Reading ■	a	23 01				23 31			00 01				00 31		01 01		01 12		

A until 22 July, 19 August, 26 August, 16 September, 23 September, 30 September

B 29 July, 5 August, 12 August, 2 September, 9 September

Table 149

Sundays from 7 October

London - Hounslow, Richmond, Kingston, Windsor, Weybridge, Ascot, Guildford and Reading

Network Diagram - see first Page of Table 148

		SW ■ A	SW ■ B	SW	SW A	SW B	SW ■ A	SW ■ B	SW	SW	SW A	SW B	SW	SW	SW ■	SW ■	SW	SW	SW	SW	SW
London Waterloo ■ ⊖	d	22p50	22p50	22p52	23p13	23p13	23p20	23p20	23p22	23p33	23p38	23p38					23p52	23p58		00 18	06 14
Vauxhall ⊖	d			22p56	23p17	23p17			23p26	23p37							23p56	00 02		00 22	06 18
Queenstown Rd.(Battersea)	d			22p59					23p29	23p40							23p59			00 26	06 21
Clapham Junction ■	d	22p58	22p58	23p02	23p23	23p23	23p28	23p28	23p32	23p43	23p46	23p46					00 02	00 08		00 29	06 24
Wandsworth Town	d			23p05					23p35	23p46							00 05			00 32	06 27
Putney	d			23p08	23p27	23p27			23p38	23p49							00 08	00 12		00 35	06 30
Barnes	d			23p12					23p42	23p52							00 12			00 38	06 33
Barnes Bridge	d			23p14					23p44								00 14				
Chiswick	d			23p17					23p47								00 17				
Kew Bridge	d			23p20					23p50								00 20				
Brentford	d			23p23					23p53								00 23				
Syon Lane	d			23p25					23p55								00 25				
Isleworth	d			23p27					23p57								00 27				
Hounslow	d			23p31					00 01								00 31				
Mortlake	d									23p54										00 40	06 35
North Sheen	d									23p56				←						00 42	06 37
Richmond ⊖	d	23p06	23p06		23p33	23p33	23p37	23p37		23p59	23p54	23p54		23p59				00 18		00 45	06 40
St Margarets	d									→				00 01						00 47	06 42
Twickenham	a	23p10	23p10		23p37	23p37	23p41	23p41			23p58	23p58		00 04				00 21		00 49	06 44
	d	23p10	23p10		23p37	23p37	23p41	23p41			23p58	23p58		00 04				00 22		00 50	06 45
Strawberry Hill	d													00 07						00s53	06 49
Fulwell	a																				
Teddington	a													00 11						00s56	06 52
Hampton Wick	a													00 14						00s59	06 57
Kingston	a													00 16						01 01	06 59
Whitton	d				23p40	23p40							←					00 25	←		
Feltham	d	23p16	23p16	23p36	23p44	23p44	23p48	23p48	00 06		00 04	00 04	00 06				00 36	00 29	00 36		
Ashford (Surrey)	d			23p40	23p48	23p48			→				00 10				→	00 33	00 40		
Staines	d	23p23	23p23	23p44	23p52	23p52	23p56	23p56			00 11	00 11	00 14					00a37	00a46		
Wraysbury	d				23p56	23p57															
Sunnymeads	d				23p59	23p59															
Datchet	d				00 02	00 04															
Windsor & Eton Riverside	a				00 06	00 09															
Egham	d	23p27	23p27	23p49			00 01	00 01			00 15	00 15	00 19								
Virginia Water	a	23p31	23p31	23p53			00 05	00 05			00 19	00 19	00 23								
	d	23p31	23p31	23p53			00 05	00 05			00 19	00 19	00 23								
Chertsey	d			23p59									00 29								
Addlestone	d			00 02									00a32								
Weybridge	a																				
Byfleet & New Haw	d			00 06																	
West Byfleet	d			00 09																	
Woking	a			00 15																	
Longcross	d																				
Sunningdale	d	23p37	23p37				00 11	00 11			00 25	00 25									
Ascot ■	d	23p43	23p43				00 15	00 15			00 30	00 30			00 32						
Bagshot	d														00 38						
Camberley	a														00 44						
Frimley	d														00 48						
Ash Vale	d														00 57						
Aldershot	a														01s02						
	d															07 48					
Ash ■	d															07 55					
Wanborough	d															07 58					
Guildford	a															08 05					
Martins Heron	d	23p47	23p47				00 19	00 19			00 34	00 34									
Bracknell	d	23p50	23p50				00 23	00 23			00 37	00 37									
Wokingham	d	23p57	23p57				00 32	00 32			00 44	00 44									
Winnersh	d	23p59	23p59				00 36	00 36													
Winnersh Triangle	d	00 02	00 02				00 38	00 38													
Earley	d	00 05	00 05				00 40	00 40													
Reading ■	a	00 10	00 13				00 45	00 48			00 52	00 55									

A 7 October

B not 7 October

Table 149

London - Hounslow, Richmond, Kingston, Windsor, Weybridge, Ascot, Guildford and Reading

Sundays
from 7 October

Network Diagram - see first Page of Table 148

		SW	SW	SW	SW	SW		SW	SW	SW	SW	SW	SW	SW	SW	SW		SW	SW	SW	SW	SW	SW	SW	SW
					■			■	■			■		■	■				■			■	■		
London Waterloo 15 ⊖	d		06 44		07 09	07 14				07 44	07 50	08 09	08 14		08 39	08 44		08 50	09 09	09 14	09 25		09 39	09 44	09 50
Vauxhall ⊖	d		06 48		07 13	07 18				07 48	07 54	08 13	08 18		08 43	08 48		08 54	09 13	09 18	09 29		09 43	09 48	09 54
Queenstown Rd.(Battersea)	d		06 51			07 21				07 51	07 57		08 21			08 51		08 57		09 21				09 51	09 57
Clapham Junction 10	d		06 54		07 19	07 24				07 54	08 00	08 19	08 24		08 49	08 54		09 00	09 19	09 24	09 35		09 49	09 54	10 00
Wandsworth Town	d		06 57			07 27				07 57	08 03		08 27			08 57		09 03		09 27				09 57	10 03
Putney	d		07 00		07 23	07 30				08 00	08 06	08 23	08 30		08 53	09 00		09 06	09 23	09 30	09 39		09 53	10 00	10 06
Barnes	d		07 03			07 33				08 03	08 09		08 33			09 03		09 09		09 33				10 03	10 09
Barnes Bridge	d										08 11							09 11							10 11
Chiswick	d										08 13							09 13							10 13
Kew Bridge	d										08 16							09 16							10 16
Brentford	d										08 19							09 19							10 19
Syon Lane	d										08 21							09 21							10 21
Isleworth	d										08 23							09 23							10 23
Hounslow	d										08 26							09 26							10 26
Mortlake	d		07 05			07 35				08 05			08 35			09 05				09 35				10 05	
North Sheen	d		07 07			07 37				08 07			08 37			09 07				09 37				10 07	
Richmond ⊖	d		07 10		07 29	07 40				08 10		08 29	08 40		08 59	09 10			09 29	09 40	09 45		09 59	10 10	
St Margarets	d		07 12			07 42				08 12			08 42			09 12				09 42				10 12	
Twickenham	a		07 14		07 32	07 44				08 14		08 32	08 44		09 02	09 14			09 32	09 44	09 48		10 02	10 14	
	d		07 15		07 33	07 45				08 15		08 33	08 45		09 03	09 15			09 33	09 45	09 49		10 03	10 15	
Strawberry Hill	d					07 49							08 49							09 49					
Fulwell	a																								
Teddington	a					07 52							08 52							09 52					
Hampton Wick	a					07 57							08 57							09 57					
Kingston	a					07 59							08 59							09 59					
Whitton	d		07 18							08 18						09 18					09 52			10 18	
Feltham	d		07 22		07 39					08 22	08 32	08 39			09 09	09 22		09 32	09 39		09 56		10 09	10 22	10 32
Ashford (Surrey)	d		07 26							08 26	08 36					09 26		09 36			10 00			10 26	10 36
Staines	d	06 32	07 30	07 40	07 45				08 15	08 30	08 40	08 45			09 15	09 30		09 40	09 45		10 04		10 15	10 30	10 40
Wraysbury	d		07 35							08 35						09 35								10 35	
Sunnymeads	d		07 38							08 38						09 38								10 38	
Datchet	d		07 42							08 42						09 42					10 13			10 42	
Windsor & Eton Riverside	a		07 46							08 46						09 46					10 18			10 46	
Egham	d	06 36		07 45	07 50				08 20		08 45	08 50			09 20			09 45	09 50				10 20		10 45
Virginia Water	a	06 41		07 49	07 54				08 24		08 49	08 54			09 24			09 49	09 54				10 24		10 49
	d	06 41		07 49	07 54				08 24		08 49	08 54			09 24			09 49	09 54				10 24		10 49
Chertsey	d	06 46		07 55							08 55							09 55							10 55
Addlestone	d	06 49		07 58							08 58							09 58							10 58
Weybridge	a	06 53																							
Byfleet & New Haw	d			08 02							09 02							10 02							11 02
West Byfleet	d			08 05							09 05							10 05							11 05
Woking	a			08 11							09 11							10 11							11 11
Longcross	d																								
Sunningdale	d				07 59				08 29			08 59			09 29				09 59				10 29		
Ascot 3	d				08 04			08 13	08 34			09 04		09 13	09 34				10 04			10 13	10 34		
Bagshot	d							08 19						09 19								10 19			
Camberley	a							08 25						09 25								10 25			
Frimley	d							08 29						09 29								10 29			
Ash Vale	d							08 36						09 36								10 36			
Aldershot	a							08 41						09 41								10 41			
	d							08 48						09 48								10 48			
Ash 5	d							08 55						09 55								10 55			
Wanborough	d							08 58						09 58								10 58			
Guildford	a							09 05						10 05								11 05			
Martins Heron	d				08 08				08 38			09 08			09 38				10 08				10 38		
Bracknell	d				08 11				08 41			09 11			09 41				10 11				10 41		
Wokingham	d				08 18				08 48			09 18			09 48				10 18				10 48		
Winnersh	d				08 21				08 51			09 21			09 51				10 21				10 51		
Winnersh Triangle	d				08 23				08 53			09 23			09 53				10 23				10 53		
Earley	d				08 26				08 56			09 26			09 56				10 26				10 56		
Reading 7	a				08 34				09 04			09 34			10 04				10 34				11 04		

Table 149

London - Hounslow, Richmond, Kingston, Windsor, Weybridge, Ascot, Guildford and Reading

Sundays
from 7 October

Network Diagram - see first Page of Table 148

		SW		SW	SW	SW	SW	SW	SW	SW	SW	SW		SW	SW	SW	SW	SW	SW	SW	SW	SW		SW	SW
		■				■	■			■				■	■			■			■	■			
London Waterloo 15 ⊖	d	10 09		10 14	10 25		10 39	10 44	10 50	11 09	11 14	11 25			11 39	11 44	11 50	12 09	12 14	12 25		12 39		12 44	12 50
Vauxhall ⊖	d	10 13		10 18	10 29		10 43	10 48	10 54	11 13	11 19	11 29			11 43	11 48	11 54	12 13	12 19	12 29		12 43		12 48	12 54
Queenstown Rd.(Battersea)	d			10 21				10 51	10 57		11 22					11 51	11 57		12 22					12 51	12 57
Clapham Junction 10	d	10 19		10 24	10 35		10 49	10 54	11 00	11 19	11 25	11 35			11 49	11 54	12 00	12 19	12 25	12 35		12 49		12 54	13 00
Wandsworth Town	d			10 27				10 57	11 03		11 28					11 57	12 03		12 28					12 57	13 03
Putney	d	10 23		10 30	10 39		10 53	11 00	11 06	11 23	11 31	11 39			11 53	12 00	12 06	12 23	12 31	12 39		12 53		13 00	13 06
Barnes	d			10 33				11 03	11 09		11 34					12 03	12 09		12 34					13 03	13 09
Barnes Bridge	d								11 11								12 11								13 11
Chiswick	d								11 13								12 13								13 13
Kew Bridge	d								11 16								12 16								13 16
Brentford	d								11 19								12 19								13 19
Syon Lane	d								11 21								12 21								13 21
Isleworth	d								11 23								12 23								13 23
Hounslow	d								11 26								12 26								13 26
Mortlake	d			10 35				11 05			11 36					12 05			12 36					13 05	
North Sheen	d			10 37				11 07			11 38					12 07			12 38					13 07	
Richmond ⊖	d	10 29		10 40	10 45		10 59	11 10		11 29	11 41	11 45			11 59	12 10		12 29	12 41	12 45		12 59		13 10	
St Margarets	d			10 42				11 12			11 43					12 12			12 43					13 12	
Twickenham	a	10 32		10 44	10 48		11 02	11 14		11 32	11 45	11 48			12 02	12 14		12 32	12 45	12 48		13 02		13 14	
	d	10 33		10 45	10 49		11 03	11 15		11 33	11 46	11 49			12 03	12 15		12 33	12 46	12 49		13 03		13 15	
Strawberry Hill	d			10 49							11 50								12 50						
Fulwell	a																								
Teddington	a			10 52							11 53								12 53						
Hampton Wick	a			10 57							11 57								12 57						
Kingston	a			10 59							11 59								12 59						
Whitton	d				10 52			11 18				11 52				12 18				12 52				13 18	
Feltham	d	10 39			10 56		11 09	11 22	11 32	11 39		11 56			12 09	12 22	12 32	12 39		12 56		13 09		13 22	13 32
Ashford (Surrey)	d				11 00			11 26	11 36			12 00				12 26	12 36			13 00				13 26	13 36
Staines	d	10 45			11 04		11 15	11 30	11 40	11 45		12 04			12 15	12 30	12 40	12 45		13 04		13 15		13 30	13 40
Wraysbury	d							11 35								12 35								13 35	
Sunnymeads	d							11 38								12 38								13 38	
Datchet	d				11 13			11 42				12 13				12 42				13 13				13 42	
Windsor & Eton Riverside	a				11 18			11 46				12 18				12 46				13 18				13 46	
Egham	d	10 50					11 20		11 45	11 50					12 20		12 45	12 50				13 20			13 45
Virginia Water	a	10 54					11 24		11 49	11 54					12 24		12 49	12 54				13 24			13 49
	d	10 54					11 24		11 49	11 54					12 24		12 49	12 54				13 24			13 49
Chertsey	d								11 55								12 55								13 55
Addlestone	d								11 58								12 58								13 58
Weybridge	a																								
Byfleet & New Haw	d								12 02								13 02								14 02
West Byfleet	d								12 05								13 05								14 05
Woking	a								12 11								13 11								14 11
Longcross	d																								
Sunningdale	d	10 59					11 29			11 59					12 29			12 59				13 29			
Ascot 3	d	11 04				11 13	11 34			12 04				12 13	12 34			13 04			13 13	13 34			
Bagshot	d					11 19								12 19							13 19				
Camberley	a					11 25								12 25							13 25				
Frimley	d					11 29								12 29							13 29				
Ash Vale	d					11 36								12 36							13 36				
Aldershot	a					11 41								12 41							13 41				
	d					11 48								12 48							13 48				
Ash 5	d					11 55								12 55							13 55				
Wanborough	d					11 58								12 58							13 58				
Guildford	a					12 05								13 05							14 05				
Martins Heron	d	11 08					11 38			12 08					12 38			13 08				13 38			
Bracknell	d	11 11					11 41			12 11					12 41			13 11				13 41			
Wokingham	d	11 18					11 48			12 18					12 48			13 18				13 48			
Winnersh	d	11 21					11 51			12 21					12 51			13 21				13 51			
Winnersh Triangle	d	11 23					11 53			12 23					12 53			13 23				13 53			
Earley	d	11 26					11 56			12 26					12 56			13 26				13 56			
Reading 7	a	11 34					12 04			12 34					13 04			13 34				14 04			

Table 149

Sundays
from 7 October

London - Hounslow, Richmond, Kingston, Windsor, Weybridge, Ascot, Guildford and Reading

Network Diagram - see first Page of Table 148

		SW 1	SW	SW	SW 1	SW 1	SW	SW		SW	and at the same minutes past each hour until	SW	SW 1	SW	SW 1	SW 1	SW		SW	SW	SW 1	SW	SW 1	SW 1
London Waterloo 15 ⊖	d	13 09	13 14	13 25		13 39	13 44	13 50		13 56		19 56	20 09	20 14		20 39	20 44		20 50	20 56	21 09	21 14		21 39
Vauxhall ⊖	d	13 13	13 18	13 29		13 43	13 48	13 54		14 00		20 00	20 13	20 18		20 43	20 48		20 54	21 00	21 13	21 18		21 43
Queenstown Rd.(Battersea)	d		13 21				13 51	13 57		14 03		20 03		20 21			20 51		20 57	21 03		21 21		
Clapham Junction 10	d	13 19	13 24	13 35		13 49	13 54	14 00		14 06		20 06	20 19	20 24		20 49	20 54		21 00	21 06	21 19	21 24		21 49
Wandsworth Town	d		13 27				13 57	14 03		14 09		20 09		20 27			20 57		21 03	21 09		21 27		
Putney	d	13 23	13 30	13 39		13 53	14 00	14 06		14 12		20 12	20 23	20 30		20 53	21 00		21 06	21 12	21 23	21 30		21 53
Barnes	d		13 33				14 03	14 09		14 15		20 15		20 33			21 03		21 09	21 15		21 33		
Barnes Bridge	d							14 11											21 11					
Chiswick	d							14 13											21 13					
Kew Bridge	d							14 16											21 16					
Brentford	d							14 19											21 19					
Syon Lane	d							14 21											21 21					
Isleworth	d							14 23											21 23					
Hounslow	d							14 26											21 26					
Mortlake	d		13 35				14 05			14 17		20 17		20 35			21 05			21 17		21 35		
North Sheen	d		13 37				14 07			14 19		20 19		20 37			21 07			21 19		21 37		
Richmond ⊖	d	13 29	13 40	13 45		13 59	14 10			14 22		20 22	20 29	20 40		20 59	21 10			21 22	21 29	21 40		21 59
St Margarets	d		13 42				14 12			14 24		20 24		20 42			21 12			21 24		21 42		
Twickenham	a	13 32	13 44	13 48		14 02	14 14			14 26		20 26	20 32	20 44		21 02	21 14			21 26	21 32	21 44		22 02
	d	13 33	13 45	13 49		14 03	14 15			14 27		20 27	20 33	20 45		21 03	21 15			21 27	21 33	21 45		22 03
Strawberry Hill	d		13 49							14 30		20 30		20 49						21 30		21 49		
Fulwell	a																							
Teddington	a		13 52							14 33		20 33		20 52						21 33		21 52		
Hampton Wick	a		13 57							14 36		20 36		20 57						21 36		21 57		
Kingston	a		13 59							14 38		20 38		20 59						21 38		21 59		
Whitton	d			13 52			14 18										21 18							
Feltham	d	13 39		13 56		14 09	14 22	14 32					20 39			21 09	21 22		21 32		21 39			22 09
Ashford (Surrey)	d			14 00			14 26	14 36									21 26		21 36					
Staines	d	13 45		14 04		14 15	14 30	14 40					20 45			21 15	21 30		21 40		21 45			22 15
Wraysbury	d						14 35										21 35							
Sunnymeads	d						14 38										21 38							
Datchet	d			14 13			14 42										21 42							
Windsor & Eton Riverside	a			14 18			14 46										21 46							
Egham	d	13 50				14 20		14 45					20 50			21 20			21 45		21 50			22 20
Virginia Water	a	13 54				14 24		14 49					20 54			21 24			21 49		21 54			22 24
	d	13 54				14 24		14 49					20 54			21 24			21 49		21 54			22 24
Chertsey	d							14 55											21 55					
Addlestone	d							14 58											21 58					
Weybridge	a																							
Byfleet & New Haw	d							15 02											22 02					
West Byfleet	d							15 05											22 05					
Woking	a							15 11											22 11					
Longcross	d																							
Sunningdale	d	13 59				14 29							20 59			21 29					21 59			22 29
Ascot 3	d	14 04			14 13	14 34							21 04		21 13	21 34					22 04		22 13	22 34
Bagshot	d				14 19										21 19								22 19	
Camberley	a				14 25										21 25								22 25	
Frimley	d				14 29										21 29								22 29	
Ash Vale	d				14 36										21 36								22 36	
Aldershot	a				14 41										21 41								22 41	
	d				14 48										21 48								22 48	
Ash 5	d				14 55										21 55								22 55	
Wanborough	d				14 58										21 58								22 58	
Guildford	a				15 05										22 05								23 05	
Martins Heron	d	14 08				14 38							21 08			21 38					22 08			22 38
Bracknell	d	14 11				14 41							21 11			21 41					22 11			22 41
Wokingham	d	14 18				14 48							21 18			21 48					22 18			22 48
Winnersh	d	14 21				14 51							21 21			21 51					22 21			22 51
Winnersh Triangle	d	14 23				14 53							21 23			21 53					22 23			22 53
Earley	d	14 26				14 56							21 26			21 56					22 26			22 56
Reading 7	a	14 34				15 04							21 34			22 04					22 34			23 04

Table 149

Sundays
from 7 October

London - Hounslow, Richmond, Kingston, Windsor, Weybridge, Ascot, Guildford and Reading

Network Diagram - see first Page of Table 148

		SW	SW	SW		SW 1	SW	SW 1	SW 1	SW	SW	SW	SW 1	SW		SW 1	SW
London Waterloo 15 ⊖	d	21 44	21 50	21 56		22 09	22 14		22 39	22 44	22 50	22 56	23 09	23 14		23 39	23 44
Vauxhall ⊖	d	21 48	21 54	22 00		22 13	22 18		22 43	22 48	22 54	23 00	23 13	23 18		23 43	23 48
Queenstown Rd.(Battersea)	d	21 51	21 57	22 03			22 21			22 51	22 57	23 03		23 21			23 51
Clapham Junction 10	d	21 54	22 00	22 06		22 19	22 24		22 49	22 54	23 00	23 06	23 19	23 24		23 49	23 54
Wandsworth Town	d	21 57	22 03	22 09			22 27			22 57	23 03	23 09		23 27			23 57
Putney	d	22 00	22 06	22 12		22 23	22 30		22 53	23 00	23 06	23 12	23 23	23 30		23 53	23 59
Barnes	d	22 03	22 09	22 15			22 33			23 03	23 09	23 15		23 33			00 03
Barnes Bridge	d		22 11								23 11						
Chiswick	d		22 13								23 13						
Kew Bridge	d		22 16								23 16						
Brentford	d		22 19								23 19						
Syon Lane	d		22 21								23 21						
Isleworth	d		22 23								23 23						
Hounslow	d		22 26								23 26						
Mortlake	d	22 05		22 17			22 35			23 05		23 17		23 35			00 05
North Sheen	d	22 07		22 19			22 37			23 07		23 19		23 37			00 07
Richmond ⊖	d	22 10		22 22		22 29	22 40		22 59	23 10		23 22	23 29	23 40		23 59	00 10
St Margarets	d	22 12		22 24			22 42			23 12		23 24		23 42			00 12
Twickenham	a	22 14		22 26		22 32	22 44		23 02	23 14		23 26	23 32	23 44		00 02	00 14
	d	22 15		22 27		22 33	22 45		23 03	23 15		23 27	23 33	23 45		00 03	00 15
Strawberry Hill	d			22 30			22 49					23 30		23 48			
Fulwell	a																
Teddington	a			22 33			22 52					23 33		23 51			
Hampton Wick	a			22 36			22 57					23 36		23 54			
Kingston	a			22 38			22 59					23 38		23 56			
Whitton	d	22 18								23 18							00 18
Feltham	d	22 22	22 32			22 39			23 09	23 22	23 32		23 39			00 09	00 22
Ashford (Surrey)	d	22 26	22 36							23 26	23 36						00 26
Staines	d	22 30	22 40			22 45			23 15	23 30	23 40		23 45			00 15	00a30
Wraysbury	d	22 35								23 35							
Sunnymeads	d	22 38								23 38							
Datchet	d	22 42								23 42							
Windsor & Eton Riverside	a	22 46								23 46							
Egham	d		22 45			22 50			23 20		23 45		23 50			00 20	
Virginia Water	a		22 49			22 54			23 24		23 49		23 54			00 24	
	d		22 49			22 54			23 24		23 49		23 54			00 24	
Chertsey	d		22 55								23 55						
Addlestone	d		22 58								23 58						
Weybridge	a																
Byfleet & New Haw	d		23 02								00 02						
West Byfleet	d		23 05								00 05						
Woking	a		23 11								00 11						
Longcross	d																
Sunningdale	d					22 59			23 29				23 59			00 29	
Ascot 3	d					23 04		23 13	23 34				00 04			00 34	
Bagshot	d							23 19									
Camberley	a							23 25									
Frimley	d							23 29									
Ash Vale	d							23 36									
Aldershot	a							23 41									
	d																
Ash 5	d																
Wanborough	d																
Guildford	a																
Martins Heron	d					23 08			23 38				00 08			00 38	
Bracknell	d					23 11			23 41				00 11			00 41	
Wokingham	d					23 18			23 48				00 18			00 48	
Winnersh	d					23 21			23 51				00 21			00 51	
Winnersh Triangle	d					23 23			23 53				00 23			00 53	
Earley	d					23 26			23 56				00 26			00 56	
Reading 7	a					23 34			00 04				00 34			01 04	

Table 149

Mondays to Fridays

until 5 October

Reading, Guildford, Ascot, Weybridge, Windsor, Kingston, Richmond and Hounslow - London

Network Diagram - see first Page of Table 148

Miles	Miles	Miles	Miles			SW MO A	SW MO A	SW MX [1]	SW MX	SW MO [1] A	SW MX	SW MX [1]	SW	SW	SW		SW	SW	SW	SW	SW ◇	SW ◇	SW ◇	SW ◇[1]	SW [1]
—	—	0	—	**Reading** [7]	d			22p42		22p54		23p12												05 42	
—	—	3	—	Earley	d			22p47		22p59		23p17												05 47	
—	—	4¼	—	Winnersh Triangle	d			22p49		23p01		23p19												05 49	
—	—	4¾	—	Winnersh	d			22p51		23p03		23p21												05 51	
—	—	6¾	—	**Wokingham**	d			22p56		23p08		23p26												05 56	
—	—	11¼	—	Bracknell	d			23p02		23p14		23p32												06 02	
—	—	12¼	—	Martins Heron	d			23p05		23p17		23p35												06 05	
—	0	—	—	**Guildford**	d																				
—	4¼	—	—	Wanborough	d																				
—	6¼	—	—	Ash [5]	d																				
—	9	—	—	**Aldershot**	a																				
—	—	—	—		d																				05 58
—	11½	—	—	Ash Vale	d																				06 02
—	14¾	—	—	Frimley	d																				06 10
—	17	—	—	Camberley	a																				06 14
—	—	—	—		d																				06 18
—	20¼	—	—	Bagshot	d																				06 23
—	23½	14½	—	**Ascot** [3]	d			23p10		23p22		23p40												06 10	06a30
—	—	16½	—	Sunningdale	d			23p13		23p25		23p43												06 13	
—	—	18¼	—	Longcross	d																				
0	—	—	—	Woking	d		22p52														05 27				
2½	—	—	—	West Byfleet	d		22p56														05 32				
3¾	—	—	—	Byfleet & New Haw	d		23p00														05 35				
5¼	—	—	—	**Weybridge**	d																				
7	—	—	—	Addlestone	d		23p04														05 39				
8½	—	—	—	Chertsey	d		23p07														05 42				
11	—	20¼	—	Virginia Water	a		23p12	23p19		23p30		23p49									05 47			06 19	
—	—	—	—		d		23p12	23p19		23p30		23p49									05 54			06 19	
—	—	22½	—	Egham	d		23p16	23p23		23p34		23p53									05 57			06 23	
—	—	—	0	**Windsor & Eton Riverside**	d	23p01																05 53			
—	—	—	2	Datchet	d	23p04																05 56			
—	—	—	3	Sunnymeads	d	23p07																05 59			
—	—	—	4¼	Wraysbury	d	23p10																06 02			
—	—	24½	6¾	**Staines**	d	23p16	23p21	23p29		23p39		23p59		04 58				05 37			06 03	06 08		06 29	
—	—	26	—	Ashford (Surrey)	d	23p19	23p24							05 01				05 40			06 06	06 11			
—	—	28¾	—	Feltham	d	23p24	23p29	23p35		23p46		00 05		05 06				05 45			06 11	06 16		06 35	
—	—	31	—	Whitton	d	23p28								05 10				05 49				06 20			
0	—	—	—	**Kingston**	d				23p29		23p55		01 17							05 59					
0½	—	—	—	Hampton Wick	d				23p31		23p57		01s22							06 01					
1¾	—	—	—	Teddington	d				23p35		23p59		01 25							06 05					
2¾	—	—	—	Fulwell	d												05 36								
3	—	—	—	Strawberry Hill	d				23p38		00 03		01 28				05 38			06 08					
4	—	32¼	—	Twickenham	a	23p31		23p40	23p42	23p51	00 07	00 10		05 13			05 42	05 52		06 12		06 23		06 40	
—	—	—	—		d	23p32		23p41	23p43	23p51		00 11		05 13			05 43	05 53		06 13		06 23		06 41	
4½	—	32¾	—	St Margarets	d	23p34			23p45					05 15			05 45			06 15					
5½	—	33¾	—	**Richmond** ⊖	d	23p37		23p45	23p49	23p56		00 15		05 19			05 49	05 58		06 19		06 28		06 45	
6¼	—	34½	—	North Sheen	d	23p39			23p51					05 21			05 51			06 21					
7	—	35¼	—	Mortlake	d	23p42			23p53					05 23			05 53			06 23					
—	0	—	—	**Hounslow**	d		23p35								05 31				06 01		06 16				
—	—	—	—	Isleworth	d		23p38								05 34				06 04		06 19				
—	2¼	—	—	Syon Lane	d		23p40								05 36				06 06		06 21				
—	3	—	—	Brentford	d		23p42								05 39				06 09		06 24				
—	4	—	—	Kew Bridge	d		23p45								05 41				06 11		06 26				
—	5	—	—	Chiswick	d		23p47								05 44				06 14		06 29				
—	6	—	—	Barnes Bridge	d		23p50								05 46				06 16		06 31				
8¼	6½	36½	—	Barnes	d	23p45	23p53		23p56					05 26	05 49		05 56		06 19	06 26	06 34		←		
9½	—	37¾	—	Putney	d	23p48	23p56		23p59	00 02				05 29	05 52		05 59	06 04	06 22	06 29	06 37	06 34	06 37	06 52	
10½	—	38¾	—	Wandsworth Town	d	23p51	23p59		00 02					05 32	05 55		06 02		06 25	06 32	→		06 40		
11¼	—	39½	—	Clapham Junction [10]	d	23p54	00 02	23p54	00 05	00 07		00 24		05 35	05 58		06 05	06 09	06 28	06 35		06 39	06 43	06 56	
12½	—	41¾	—	Queenstown Rd.(Battersea)	d	23p57	00 05		00 08					05 38	06 01		06 08		06 31	06 38			06 46		
14	—	42¼	—	Vauxhall ⊖	d	23p59	00 08		00 12	00 12				05 42	06 05		06 12	06 15	06 35	06 42		06 45	06 50		
15¼	—	43½	—	**London Waterloo** [15] ⊖	a	00 05	00 13	00 04	00 16	00 17		00 37		05 46	06 09		06 16	06 19	06 39	06 46		06 49	06 56	07 07	

A from 21 May until 1 October

Table 149

Mondays to Fridays

until 5 October

Reading, Guildford, Ascot, Weybridge, Windsor, Kingston, Richmond and Hounslow - London

Network Diagram - see first Page of Table 148

		SW	SW	SW	SW ◇	SW	SW	SW	SW ◇[1]	SW		SW	SW ◇	SW ◇	SW ◇	SW	SW	SW ◇[1]	SW [1]	SW ◇[1]		SW	SW ◇	SW ◇	SW ◇
Reading [7]	d								06 12											06 42					
Earley	d								06 17											06 47					
Winnersh Triangle	d								06 19											06 49					
Winnersh	d								06 21											06 51					
Wokingham	d								06 26											06 56					
Bracknell	d								06 32											07 02					
Martins Heron	d								06 35											07 05					
Guildford	d																		06 30						
Wanborough	d																		06 36						
Ash [5]	d																		06 40						
Aldershot	a																		06 47						
	d																	06 28							
Ash Vale	d																	06 32							
Frimley	d																	06 40							
Camberley	a																	06 44							
	d																	06 47							
Bagshot	d																	06 52							
Ascot [3]	d								06 40									06 59		07 10					
Sunningdale	d								06 43									07 02		07 13					
Longcross	d																								
Woking	d																								
West Byfleet	d																								
Byfleet & New Haw	d																								
Weybridge	d												06 33										07 03		
Addlestone	d												06 37										07 07		
Chertsey	d												06 40										07 10		
Virginia Water	a								06 49				06 45					07 08		07 19			07 15		
	d								06 49				06 54					07 08		07 19			07 24		
Egham	d								06 53				06 57					07 12		07 23			07 27		
Windsor & Eton Riverside	d				06 23									06 53										07 23	
Datchet	d				06 26									06 56										07 26	
Sunnymeads	d				06 29									06 59										07 29	
Wraysbury	d				06 32									07 02										07 32	
Staines	d			06 33	06 38				06 59				07 03	07 08				07 18		07 29			07 33	07 38	
Ashford (Surrey)	d			06 36	06 41								07 06	07 11				07 21					07 36	07 41	
Feltham	d			06 41	06 46				07 05				07 11	07 16				07 26		07 35			07 41	07 46	
Whitton	d	06 20			06 50		06 50	06 53						07 20			07 20	07 30						07 50	
Kingston	d		06 29									06 59										07 29			
Hampton Wick	d		06 31									07 01										07 31			
Teddington	d		06 35									07 05										07 35			
Fulwell	d															07 12									
Strawberry Hill	d		06 38									07 08				07 14						07 38			
Twickenham	a		06 42		06 53			06 56	07 10			07 12		07 23		07 18		07 33		07 40		07 42		07 53	
	d		06 43		06 53			06 58	07 11			07 13		07 23		07 27		07 33		07 41		07 43		07 53	
St Margarets	d		06 45					07 00				07 15				07 29						07 45			
Richmond ⊖	d		06 49		06 58			07 04	07 15			07 19		07 28		07 32		07 38		07 45		07 49		07 58	
North Sheen	d		06 51					07 06				07 21				07 34						07 51			
Mortlake	d		06 53					07 08				07 23				07 37						07 53			
Hounslow	d	06 31		06 46			07 01						07 16				07 31						07 46		
Isleworth	d	06 34		06 49			07 04						07 19				07 34						07 49		
Syon Lane	d	06 36		06 51			07 06						07 21				07 36						07 51		
Brentford	d	06 39		06 54			07 09						07 24				07 39						07 54		
Kew Bridge	d	06 41		06 56			07 11						07 26				07 41						07 56		
Chiswick	d	06 44		06 59			07 14						07 29				07 44						07 59		
Barnes Bridge	d	06 46		07 01			07 16			←			07 31				07 46						08 01		
Barnes	d	06 49	06 56	07 04		←	07 19	07 11		07 19		07 26	07 34		←	07 40	07 49					07 56	08 04		←
Putney	d	06 52	06 59	07 07	07 04	07 07	→	07 14	07 22	07 22		07 29	07 37	07 34	07 37	07 43	07 52					07 59	08 07	08 04	08 07
Wandsworth Town	d	06 55	07 02	→		07 10		07 17		07 25		07 32	→		07 40	07 46	07 55					08 02	→		08 10
Clapham Junction [10]	d	06 58	07 05		07 09	07 13		07 20	07 26	07 28		07 35		07 39	07 43	07 49	07 58	07 47		07 54		08 05		08 09	08 13
Queenstown Rd.(Battersea)	d	07 01	07 08			07 16		07 23		07 31		07 38			07 46	07 52	08 01					08 08			08 16
Vauxhall ⊖	d	07 05	07 12		07 15	07 20		07 27		07 35		07 42		07 45	07 50	07 56	08 05	07 53				08 12		08 15	08 20
London Waterloo [15] ⊖	a	07 11	07 18		07 21	07 28		07 34	07 37	07 43		07 48		07 51	07 58	08 04	08 11	07 59		08 06		08 18		08 21	08 28

Table 149

Mondays to Fridays
until 5 October

Reading, Guildford, Ascot, Weybridge, Windsor, Kingston, Richmond and Hounslow - London

Network Diagram - see first Page of Table 148

		SW	SW	SW	SW	SW		SW	SW	SW	SW	SW	SW	SW	SW	SW		SW	SW	SW	SW	SW	SW	SW	SW
				◇1	1	◇1			◇	◇1	◇	◇			◇1	◇1		1		◇	◇	◇			◇1
Reading	d					07 12				07 24						07 42									08 12
Earley	d					07 17										07 47									08 17
Winnersh Triangle	d					07 19										07 49									08 19
Winnersh	d					07 21										07 51									08 21
Wokingham	d					07 26				07 33						07 56									08 26
Bracknell	d					07 32				07 39						08 02									08 32
Martins Heron	d					07 35				07 42						08 05									08 35
Guildford	d				07 00													07 30							
Wanborough	d				07 06													07 36							
Ash	d				07 10													07 40							
Aldershot	a				07 17													07 47							
	d			07 00											07 30			08 00							
Ash Vale	d			07 04											07 34			08 04							
Frimley	d			07 10											07 40			08 10							
Camberley	a			07 14											07 44			08 14							
	d			07 17											07 47			08 18							
Bagshot	d			07 22											07 52			08 23							
Ascot	d			07 29		07 40				07 47					07 59	08 10		08a30							08 40
Sunningdale	d			07 32		07 43				07 50					08 02	08 13									08 43
Longcross	d															08 16									08 46
Woking	d																								
West Byfleet	d																								
Byfleet & New Haw	d																								
Weybridge	d								07 33											08 03					
Addlestone	d								07 37											08 07					
Chertsey	d								07 40											08 10					
Virginia Water	a			07 38					07 45	07 55					08 08	08 19				08 15					08 49
	d			07 38					07 51	07 55					08 08	08 19				08 24					08 49
Egham	d			07 42		07 50			07 54	07 58					08 12	08 23				08 27					08 53
Windsor & Eton Riverside	d										07 53										08 23				
Datchet	d										07 56										08 26				
Sunnymeads	d										07 59										08 29				
Wraysbury	d										08 02										08 32				
Staines	d			07 48		07 56			08 00	08 04	08 08				08 18	08 29				08 33	08 38				08 59
Ashford (Surrey)	d			07 51					08 03		08 11				08 21					08 36	08 41				
Feltham	d			07 56		08 02			08 08	08 12	08 16				08 26	08 35				08 41	08 46				09 05
Whitton	d		07 50	08 00							08 20			08 20	08 30						08 50		08 50	08 53	
Kingston	d							07 59											08 29						
Hampton Wick	d							08 01											08 31						
Teddington	d							08 05											08 35						
Fulwell	d	07 42											08 12												
Strawberry Hill	d	07 44						08 08					08 14						08 38						
Twickenham	a	07 48		08 03		08 09		08 12		08 17	08 23		08 18		08 33	08 40			08 42		08 53			08 56	09 10
	d	07 57		08 03		08 09		08 13		08 18	08 23		08 27		08 33	08 41			08 43		08 53			08 58	09 11
St Margarets	d	07 59						08 15					08 29						08 45					09 00	
Richmond ⊖	d	08 02		08 08		08 14		08 19		08 24	08 28		08 32		08 38	08 45			08 49		08 58			09 04	09 15
North Sheen	d	08 04						08 21					08 34						08 51					09 06	
Mortlake	d	08 07						08 23					08 37						08 53					09 08	
Hounslow	d		08 01						08 16					08 31						08 46			09 01		
Isleworth	d		08 04						08 19					08 34						08 49			09 04		
Syon Lane	d		08 06						08 21					08 36						08 51			09 06		
Brentford	d		08 09						08 24					08 39						08 54			09 09		
Kew Bridge	d		08 11						08 26					08 41						08 56			09 11		
Chiswick	d		08 14						08 29					08 44						08 59			09 14		
Barnes Bridge	d		08 16						08 31					08 46						09 01			09 16		
Barnes	d	08 10	08 19					08 26	08 34			←	08 40	08 49					08 56	09 04		←	09 19	09 11	
Putney	d	08 13	08 22					08 29	08 37		08 34	08 37	08 43	08 52					08 59	09 07	09 04	09 07	→	09 14	
Wandsworth Town	d	08 16	08 25					08 32	→			08 40	08 46	08 55					09 02	→		09 10		09 17	
Clapham Junction	d	08 19	08 28	08 17		08 22		08 35		08 33	08 39	08 43	08 49	08 58	08 47	08 54			09 05		09 09	09 13		09 20	09 24
Queenstown Rd.(Battersea)	d	08 22	08 31					08 38				08 46	08 52	09 01					09 08			09 16		09 23	
Vauxhall ⊖	d	08 26	08 35	08 23				08 42		08 38	08 45	08 50	08 56	09 05	08 53				09 12		09 15	09 20		09 27	
London Waterloo ⊖	a	08 34	08 43	08 29		08 38		08 49		08 46	08 51	08 58	09 04	09 13	09 00	09 06			09 18		09 21	09 28		09 34	09 34

Table 149

Mondays to Fridays
until 5 October

Reading, Guildford, Ascot, Weybridge, Windsor, Kingston, Richmond and Hounslow - London

Network Diagram - see first Page of Table 148

		SW		SW	SW	SW	SW	SW	SW	SW	SW	SW		SW	SW	SW	SW	SW	SW	SW	SW	SW		SW	SW
				1		◇	◇	◇			1			1							1				
Reading	d										08 42										09 12				
Earley	d										08 47										09 17				
Winnersh Triangle	d										08 49										09 19				
Winnersh	d										08 51										09 21				
Wokingham	d										08 56										09 26				
Bracknell	d										09 02										09 32				
Martins Heron	d										09 05										09 35				
Guildford	d			08 00										08 30											
Wanborough	d			08 06										08 36											
Ash	d			08 10										08 40											
Aldershot	a			08 17										08 47											
	d			08 30										09 00											
Ash Vale	d			08 34										09 04											
Frimley	d			08 40										09 10											
Camberley	a			08 44										09 14											
	d			08 48										09 18											
Bagshot	d			08 53										09 23											
Ascot	d			09a00							09 10			09a30							09 40				
Sunningdale	d										09 13										09 43				
Longcross	d										09 16														
Woking	d																								
West Byfleet	d																								
Byfleet & New Haw	d																								
Weybridge	d					08 33										09 03									09 33
Addlestone	d					08 37										09 07									09 37
Chertsey	d					08 40										09 10									09 40
Virginia Water	a					08 45					09 19					09 15					09 49				09 45
	d					08 54					09 19					09 24					09 49				09 54
Egham	d					08 57					09 23					09 27					09 53				09 57
Windsor & Eton Riverside	d						08 53										09 23								
Datchet	d						08 56										09 26								
Sunnymeads	d						08 59										09 29								
Wraysbury	d						09 02										09 32								
Staines	d					09 03	09 08				09 29					09 33	09 38				09 59				10 03
Ashford (Surrey)	d					09 06	09 11									09 36	09 41								10 06
Feltham	d					09 11	09 16				09 35					09 41	09 46				10 05				10 11
Whitton	d						09 20		09 20	09 23							09 50		09 50	09 53					
Kingston	d				08 59										09 29									09 59	
Hampton Wick	d				09 01										09 31									10 01	
Teddington	d				09 05										09 35									10 05	
Fulwell	d																								
Strawberry Hill	d				09 08										09 38									10 08	
Twickenham	a				09 12		09 23			09 26	09 40				09 42		09 53			09 56	10 10			10 12	
	d				09 13		09 23			09 28	09 41				09 43		09 53			09 58	10 11			10 13	
St Margarets	d				09 15					09 30					09 45					10 00				10 15	
Richmond ⊖	d				09 19		09 28			09 34	09 45				09 49		09 58			10 04	10 15			10 19	
North Sheen	d				09 21					09 36					09 51					10 06				10 21	
Mortlake	d				09 23					09 38					09 53					10 08				10 23	
Hounslow	d					09 16			09 31							09 46			10 01						10 16
Isleworth	d					09 19			09 34							09 49			10 04						10 19
Syon Lane	d					09 21			09 36							09 51			10 06						10 21
Brentford	d					09 24			09 39							09 54			10 09						10 24
Kew Bridge	d					09 26			09 41							09 56			10 11						10 26
Chiswick	d					09 29			09 44							09 59			10 14						10 29
Barnes Bridge	d	←				09 31			09 46			←				10 01			10 16			←			10 31
Barnes	d	09 19			09 26	09 34		←	09 49	09 41		09 49			09 56	10 04		←	10 19	10 11		10 19		10 26	10 34
Putney	d	09 22			09 29	09 37	09 34	09 37	→	09 44		09 52			09 59	10 07	10 04	10 07	→	10 14		10 22		10 29	10 37
Wandsworth Town	d	09 25			09 32	→		09 40		09 47		09 55			10 02	→		10 10		10 17		10 25		10 32	→
Clapham Junction	d	09 28			09 35		09 39	09 43		09 50	09 54	09 58			10 05		10 09	10 13		10 20	10 24	10 28		10 35	
Queenstown Rd.(Battersea)	d	09 31			09 38			09 46		09 53		10 01			10 08			10 16		10 23		10 31		10 38	
Vauxhall ⊖	d	09 35			09 42		09 45	09 50		09 57		10 05			10 12		10 15	10 20		10 27		10 35		10 42	
London Waterloo ⊖	a	09 43			09 48		09 51	09 58		10 02	10 04	10 11			10 16		10 19	10 26		10 32	10 34	10 41		10 46	

Table 149

Mondays to Fridays
until 5 October

Reading, Guildford, Ascot, Weybridge, Windsor, Kingston, Richmond and Hounslow - London

Network Diagram - see first Page of Table 148

		SW	SW 1	SW	SW 1	SW	SW	SW 1	SW	SW	SW	SW	SW 1	SW	SW 1	SW	SW	SW 1	SW	SW 1	SW	SW	SW
Reading 7	d		09 25					09 42					09 56					10 12					
Earley	d		09 30					09 47					10 01					10 17					
Winnersh Triangle	d		09 32					09 49					10 03					10 19					
Winnersh	d		09 34					09 51					10 05					10 21					
Wokingham	d		09 39					09 56					10 10					10 26					
Bracknell	d		09 46					10 02					10 16					10 32					
Martins Heron	d		09 49					10 05					10 19					10 35					
Guildford	d				09 00										09 30					10 00			
Wanborough	d				09 06										09 36					10 06			
Ash 5	d				09 10										09 40					10 10			
Aldershot	a				09 17										09 47					10 17			
	d				09 30										10 00					10 30			
Ash Vale	d				09 34										10 04					10 34			
Frimley	d				09 40										10 10					10 40			
Camberley	a				09 44										10 14					10 44			
	d				09 48										10 18					10 48			
Bagshot	d				09 53										10 23					10 53			
Ascot 3	d		09 55		10a00			10 10					10 25		10a30			10 40		11a00			
Sunningdale	d		09 58					10 13					10 28					10 43					
Longcross	d																						
Woking	d																						
West Byfleet	d																						
Byfleet & New Haw	d																						
Weybridge	d										10 03											10 33	
Addlestone	d										10 07											10 37	
Chertsey	d										10 10											10 40	
Virginia Water	a		10 03					10 19			10 15		10 33					10 49				10 45	
	d		10 03					10 19			10 24		10 33					10 49				10 54	
Egham	d		10 06					10 23			10 27		10 36					10 53				10 57	
Windsor & Eton Riverside	d	09 53										10 23											10 53
Datchet	d	09 56										10 26											10 56
Sunnymeads	d	09 59										10 29											10 59
Wraysbury	d	10 02										10 32											11 02
Staines	d	10 08	10 14					10 29			10 33	10 38	10 44					10 59				11 03	11 08
Ashford (Surrey)	d	10 11									10 36	10 41										11 06	11 11
Feltham	d	10 16	10 20					10 35			10 41	10 46	10 50					11 05				11 11	11 16
Whitton	d	10 20				10 20	10 26					10 50				10 50	10 56						11 20
Kingston	d									10 29											10 59		
Hampton Wick	d									10 31											11 01		
Teddington	d									10 35											11 05		
Fulwell	d																						
Strawberry Hill	d									10 38											11 08		
Twickenham	a	10 23	10 27				10 28	10 40		10 42		10 53	10 57				10 58	11 10			11 12		11 23
	d	10 23	10 27				10 28	10 41		10 43		10 53	10 57				10 58	11 11			11 13		11 23
St Margarets	d						10 30			10 45							11 00				11 15		
Richmond ⊖	d	10 28	10 32				10 34	10 45		10 49		10 58	11 02				11 04	11 15			11 19		11 28
North Sheen	d						10 36			10 51							11 06				11 21		
Mortlake	d						10 38			10 53							11 08				11 23		
Hounslow	d					10 31					10 46					11 01						11 16	
Isleworth	d					10 34					10 49					11 04						11 19	
Syon Lane	d					10 36					10 51					11 06						11 21	
Brentford	d					10 39					10 54					11 09						11 24	
Kew Bridge	d					10 41					10 56					11 11						11 26	
Chiswick	d					10 44					10 59					11 14						11 29	
Barnes Bridge	d					10 46			←		11 01					11 16			←			11 31	
Barnes	d			←		10 49	10 41		10 49	10 56	11 04			←		11 19	11 11		11 19		11 26	11 34	
Putney	d	10 34		10 37		→	10 44		10 52	10 59	11 07	11 04		11 07		→	11 14		11 22		11 29	11 37	11 34
Wandsworth Town	d			10 40			10 47		10 55	11 02	→			11 10			11 17		11 25		11 32	→	
Clapham Junction 10	d	10 39	10 42	10 43			10 50	10 54	10 58	11 05		11 09	11 12	11 13			11 20	11 24	11 28		11 35		11 39
Queenstown Rd.(Battersea)	d			10 47			10 53		11 01	11 08				11 17			11 23		11 31		11 38		
Vauxhall ⊖	d	10 45		10 50			10 57		11 05	11 12		11 15		11 20			11 27		11 35		11 42		11 45
London Waterloo 15 ⊖	a	10 49	10 53	10 56			11 02	11 04	11 11	11 16		11 19	11 25	11 27			11 32	11 34	11 41		11 46		11 49

Table 149

Mondays to Fridays
until 5 October

Reading, Guildford, Ascot, Weybridge, Windsor, Kingston, Richmond and Hounslow - London

Network Diagram - see first Page of Table 148

		SW	SW	SW	SW 1	SW	SW 1	SW	SW	SW	SW	SW	SW	SW 1	SW	SW 1	SW	SW	SW	SW	SW	SW
Reading 7	d				10 42									11 12								
Earley	d				10 47									11 17								
Winnersh Triangle	d				10 49									11 19								
Winnersh	d				10 51									11 21								
Wokingham	d				10 56									11 26								
Bracknell	d				11 02									11 32								
Martins Heron	d				11 05									11 35								
Guildford	d						10 30									11 00						
Wanborough	d						10 36									11 06						
Ash 5	d						10 40									11 10						
Aldershot	a						10 47									11 17						
	d						11 00									11 30						
Ash Vale	d						11 04									11 34						
Frimley	d						11 10									11 40						
Camberley	a						11 14									11 44						
	d						11 18									11 48						
Bagshot	d						11 23									11 53						
Ascot 3	d				11 10		11a30							11 40		12a00						
Sunningdale	d				11 13									11 43								
Longcross	d																					
Woking	d																					
West Byfleet	d																					
Byfleet & New Haw	d																					
Weybridge	d								11 03									11 33				
Addlestone	d								11 07									11 37				
Chertsey	d								11 10									11 40				
Virginia Water	a				11 19				11 15					11 49				11 45				
	d				11 19				11 24					11 49				11 54				
Egham	d				11 23				11 27					11 53				11 57				
Windsor & Eton Riverside	d									11 23									11 53			
Datchet	d									11 26									11 56			
Sunnymeads	d									11 29									11 59			
Wraysbury	d									11 32									12 02			
Staines	d				11 29				11 33	11 38				11 59				12 03	12 08			
Ashford (Surrey)	d								11 36	11 41								12 06	12 11			
Feltham	d				11 35				11 41	11 46				12 05				12 11	12 16			
Whitton	d		11 20	11 23						11 50		11 50	11 53						12 20		12 20	12 23
Kingston	d							11 29									11 59					
Hampton Wick	d							11 31									12 01					
Teddington	d							11 35									12 05					
Fulwell	d																					
Strawberry Hill	d							11 38									12 08					
Twickenham	a			11 26	11 40			11 42		11 53			11 56	12 10			12 12		12 23			12 26
	d			11 28	11 41			11 43		11 53			11 58	12 11			12 13		12 23			12 28
St Margarets	d			11 30				11 45					12 00				12 15					12 30
Richmond ⊖	d			11 34	11 45			11 49		11 58			12 04	12 15			12 19		12 28			12 34
North Sheen	d			11 36				11 51					12 06				12 21					12 36
Mortlake	d			11 38				11 53					12 08				12 23					12 38
Hounslow	d		11 31						11 46			12 01						12 16			12 31	
Isleworth	d		11 34						11 49			12 04						12 19			12 34	
Syon Lane	d		11 36						11 51			12 06						12 21			12 36	
Brentford	d		11 39						11 54			12 09						12 24			12 39	
Kew Bridge	d		11 41						11 56			12 11						12 26			12 41	
Chiswick	d		11 44						11 59			12 14						12 29			12 44	
Barnes Bridge	d		11 46			←			12 01			12 16			←			12 31			12 46	
Barnes	d	←	11 49	11 41		11 49		11 56	12 04		←	12 19	12 11		12 19		12 26	12 34		←	12 49	12 41
Putney	d	11 37	→	11 44		11 52		11 59	12 07	12 04	12 07	→	12 14		12 22		12 29	12 37	12 34	12 37	→	12 44
Wandsworth Town	d	11 40		11 47		11 55		12 02	→		12 10		12 17		12 25		12 32	→		12 40		12 47
Clapham Junction 10	d	11 43		11 50	11 54	11 58		12 05		12 09	12 13		12 20	12 25	12 28		12 35		12 39	12 43		12 50
Queenstown Rd.(Battersea)	d	11 46		11 53		12 01		12 08			12 16		12 23		12 31		12 38			12 46		12 53
Vauxhall ⊖	d	11 50		11 57		12 05		12 12		12 15	12 20		12 27		12 35		12 42		12 45	12 50		12 57
London Waterloo 15 ⊖	a	11 56		12 02	12 04	12 11		12 16		12 19	12 26		12 32	12 34	12 41		12 46		12 49	12 56		13 02

Table 149

Mondays to Fridays
until 5 October

Reading, Guildford, Ascot, Weybridge, Windsor, Kingston, Richmond and Hounslow - London

Network Diagram - see first Page of Table 148

		SW ■	SW	SW ■	SW	SW	SW	SW	SW	SW		SW ■	SW	SW ■	SW	SW	SW	SW	SW	SW		SW ■	SW	SW ■	SW
Reading ■	d	11 42										12 12										12 42			
Earley	d	11 47										12 17										12 47			
Winnersh Triangle	d	11 49										12 19										12 49			
Winnersh	d	11 51										12 21										12 51			
Wokingham	d	11 56										12 26										12 56			
Bracknell	d	12 02										12 32										13 02			
Martins Heron	d	12 05										12 35										13 05			
Guildford	d			11 30										12 00										12 30	
Wanborough	d			11 36										12 06										12 36	
Ash ■	d			11 40										12 10										12 40	
Aldershot	a			11 47										12 17										12 47	
	d			12 00										12 30										13 00	
Ash Vale	d			12 04										12 34										13 04	
Frimley	d			12 10										12 40										13 10	
Camberley	a			12 14										12 44										13 14	
	d			12 18										12 48										13 18	
Bagshot	d			12 23										12 53										13 23	
Ascot ■	d	12 10		12a30								12 40		13a00								13 10		13a30	
Sunningdale	d	12 13										12 43										13 13			
Longcross	d																					13 16			
Woking	d																								
West Byfleet	d																								
Byfleet & New Haw	d																								
Weybridge	d					12 03										12 33									
Addlestone	d					12 07										12 37									
Chertsey	d					12 10										12 40									
Virginia Water	a	12 19				12 15						12 49				12 45						13 19			
	d	12 19				12 24						12 49				12 54						13 19			
Egham	d	12 23				12 27						12 53				12 57						13 23			
Windsor & Eton Riverside	d						12 23										12 53								
Datchet	d						12 26										12 56								
Sunnymeads	d						12 29										12 59								
Wraysbury	d						12 32										13 02								
Staines	d	12 29				12 33	12 38					12 59				13 03	13 08					13 29			
Ashford (Surrey)	d					12 36	12 41									13 06	13 11								
Feltham	d	12 35				12 41	12 46					13 05				13 11	13 16					13 35			
Whitton	d						12 50		12 50	12 53							13 20		13 20	13 23					
Kingston	d				12 29										12 59										13 29
Hampton Wick	d				12 31										13 01										13 31
Teddington	d				12 35										13 05										13 35
Fulwell	d																								
Strawberry Hill	d				12 38										13 08										13 38
Twickenham	a	12 40			12 42		12 53			12 56		13 10			13 12		13 23			13 26		13 40			13 42
	d	12 41			12 43		12 53			12 58		13 11			13 13		13 23			13 28		13 41			13 43
St Margarets	d				12 45					13 00					13 15					13 30					13 45
Richmond ⊖	d	12 45			12 49		12 58			13 04		13 15			13 19		13 28			13 34		13 45			13 49
North Sheen	d				12 51					13 06					13 21					13 36					13 51
Mortlake	d				12 53					13 08					13 23					13 38					13 53
Hounslow	d					12 46			13 01							13 16			13 31						
Isleworth	d					12 49			13 04							13 19			13 34						
Syon Lane	d					12 51			13 06							13 21			13 36						
Brentford	d					12 54			13 09							13 24			13 39						
Kew Bridge	d					12 56			13 11							13 26			13 41						
Chiswick	d					12 59			13 14							13 29			13 44						
Barnes Bridge	d		←			13 01			13 16				←			13 31			13 46				←		
Barnes	d		12 49		12 56	13 04		←	13 19	13 11			13 19		13 26	13 34		←	13 49	13 41			13 49		13 56
Putney	d		12 52		12 59	13 07	13 04	13 07	→	13 14			13 22		13 29	13 37	13 34	13 37	→	13 44			13 52		13 59
Wandsworth Town	d		12 55		13 02	→		13 10		13 17			13 25		13 32	→		13 40		13 47			13 55		14 02
Clapham Junction ■	d	12 54	12 58		13 05		13 09	13 13		13 20		13 24	13 28		13 35		13 39	13 43		13 50		13 54	13 58		14 05
Queenstown Rd.(Battersea)	d		13 01		13 08			13 16		13 23			13 31		13 38			13 46		13 53			14 01		14 08
Vauxhall ⊖	d		13 05		13 12		13 15	13 20		13 27			13 35		13 42		13 45	13 50		13 57			14 05		14 12
London Waterloo ■ ⊖	a	13 04	13 11		13 16		13 19	13 26		13 32		13 34	13 41		13 46		13 49	13 56		14 02		14 04	14 11		14 16

Table 149

Mondays to Fridays
until 5 October

Reading, Guildford, Ascot, Weybridge, Windsor, Kingston, Richmond and Hounslow - London

Network Diagram - see first Page of Table 148

		SW	SW	SW	SW	SW		SW ■	SW	SW ■	SW	SW	SW	SW	SW	SW		SW ■	SW	SW ■	SW	SW	SW	SW	SW
Reading ■	d							13 12										13 42							
Earley	d							13 17										13 47							
Winnersh Triangle	d							13 19										13 49							
Winnersh	d							13 21										13 51							
Wokingham	d							13 26										13 56							
Bracknell	d							13 32										14 02							
Martins Heron	d							13 35										14 05							
Guildford	d									13 00										13 30					
Wanborough	d									13 06										13 36					
Ash ■	d									13 10										13 40					
Aldershot	a									13 17										13 47					
	d									13 30										14 00					
Ash Vale	d									13 34										14 04					
Frimley	d									13 40										14 10					
Camberley	a									13 44										14 14					
	d									13 48										14 18					
Bagshot	d									13 53										14 23					
Ascot ■	d							13 40		14a00								14 10		14a30					
Sunningdale	d							13 43										14 13							
Longcross	d																								
Woking	d																								
West Byfleet	d																								
Byfleet & New Haw	d																								
Weybridge	d	13 03										13 33										14 03			
Addlestone	d	13 07										13 37										14 07			
Chertsey	d	13 10										13 40										14 10			
Virginia Water	a	13 15						13 49				13 45						14 19				14 15			
	d	13 24						13 49				13 54						14 19				14 24			
Egham	d	13 27						13 53				13 57						14 23				14 27			
Windsor & Eton Riverside	d		13 23										13 53										14 23		
Datchet	d		13 26										13 56										14 26		
Sunnymeads	d		13 29										13 59										14 29		
Wraysbury	d		13 32										14 02										14 32		
Staines	d	13 33	13 38					13 59				14 03	14 08					14 29				14 33	14 38		
Ashford (Surrey)	d	13 36	13 41									14 06	14 11									14 36	14 41		
Feltham	d	13 41	13 46					14 05				14 11	14 16					14 35				14 41	14 46		
Whitton	d		13 50		13 50	13 53							14 20		14 20	14 23							14 50		14 50
Kingston	d										13 59										14 29				
Hampton Wick	d										14 01										14 31				
Teddington	d										14 05										14 35				
Fulwell	d																								
Strawberry Hill	d										14 08										14 38				
Twickenham	a		13 53			13 56		14 10			14 12		14 23			14 26		14 40			14 42		14 53		
	d		13 53			13 58		14 11			14 13		14 23			14 28		14 41			14 43		14 53		
St Margarets	d					14 00					14 15					14 30					14 45				
Richmond ⊖	d		13 58			14 04		14 15			14 19		14 28			14 34		14 45			14 49		14 58		
North Sheen	d					14 06					14 21					14 36					14 51				
Mortlake	d					14 08					14 23					14 38					14 53				
Hounslow	d	13 46			14 01							14 16			14 31							14 46			15 01
Isleworth	d	13 49			14 04							14 19			14 34							14 49			15 04
Syon Lane	d	13 51			14 06							14 21			14 36							14 51			15 06
Brentford	d	13 54			14 09							14 24			14 39							14 54			15 09
Kew Bridge	d	13 56			14 11							14 26			14 41							14 56			15 11
Chiswick	d	13 59			14 14							14 29			14 44							14 59			15 14
Barnes Bridge	d	14 01			14 16				←			14 31			14 46				←			15 01			15 16
Barnes	d	14 04		←	14 19	14 11			14 19		14 26	14 34		←	14 49	14 41			14 49		14 56	15 04		←	15 19
Putney	d	14 07	14 04	14 07	→	14 14			14 22		14 29	14 37	14 34	14 37	→	14 44			14 52		14 59	15 07	15 04	15 07	→
Wandsworth Town	d	→		14 10		14 17			14 25		14 32	→		14 40		14 47			14 55		15 02	→		15 10	
Clapham Junction ■	d		14 09	14 13		14 20		14 24	14 28		14 35		14 39	14 43		14 50		14 54	14 58		15 05		15 09	15 13	
Queenstown Rd.(Battersea)	d			14 16		14 23			14 31		14 38			14 46		14 53			15 01		15 08			15 16	
Vauxhall ⊖	d		14 15	14 20		14 27			14 35		14 42		14 45	14 50		14 57			15 05		15 12		15 15	15 20	
London Waterloo ■ ⊖	a		14 19	14 26		14 32		14 34	14 41		14 46		14 49	14 56		15 02		15 04	15 11		15 16		15 19	15 26	

Table 149

Mondays to Fridays
until 5 October

Reading, Guildford, Ascot, Weybridge, Windsor, Kingston, Richmond and Hounslow - London

Network Diagram - see first Page of Table 148

		SW		SW 1	SW	SW 1	SW	SW	SW	SW	SW	SW		SW 1	SW	SW 1	SW	SW	SW	SW	SW	SW		SW 1	SW
Reading 7	d			14 12										14 42										15 12	
Earley	d			14 17										14 47										15 17	
Winnersh Triangle	d			14 19										14 49										15 19	
Winnersh	d			14 21										14 51										15 21	
Wokingham	d			14 26										14 56										15 26	
Bracknell	d			14 32										15 02										15 32	
Martins Heron	d			14 35										15 05										15 35	
Guildford	d					14 00										14 30									
Wanborough	d					14 06										14 36									
Ash 5	d					14 10										14 40									
Aldershot	a					14 17										14 47									
	d					14 30										15 00									
Ash Vale	d					14 34										15 04									
Frimley	d					14 40										15 10									
Camberley	a					14 44										15 14									
	d					14 48										15 18									
Bagshot	d					14 53										15 23									
Ascot 3	d			14 40		15a00								15 10		15a30								15 40	
Sunningdale	d			14 43										15 13										15 43	
Longcross	d																								
Woking	d																								
West Byfleet	d																								
Byfleet & New Haw	d																								
Weybridge	d							14 33										15 03							
Addlestone	d							14 37										15 07							
Chertsey	d							14 40										15 10							
Virginia Water	a			14 49				14 45						15 19				15 15						15 49	
	d			14 49				14 54						15 19				15 24						15 49	
Egham	d			14 53				14 57						15 23				15 27						15 53	
Windsor & Eton Riverside	d								14 53										15 23						
Datchet	d								14 56										15 26						
Sunnymeads	d								14 59										15 29						
Wraysbury	d								15 02										15 32						
Staines	d			14 59				15 03	15 08					15 29				15 33	15 38					15 59	
Ashford (Surrey)	d							15 06	15 11									15 36	15 41						
Feltham	d			15 05				15 11	15 16					15 35				15 41	15 46						
Whitton	d	14 53							15 20		15 20	15 23							15 50		15 50	15 53		16 05	
Kingston	d						14 59										15 29								
Hampton Wick	d						15 01										15 31								
Teddington	d						15 05										15 35								
Fulwell	d																								
Strawberry Hill	d						15 08										15 38								
Twickenham	a	14 56		15 10			15 12		15 23			15 26		15 40			15 42		15 53			15 56		16 10	
	d	14 58		15 11			15 13		15 23			15 28		15 41			15 43		15 53			15 58		16 11	
St Margarets	d	15 00					15 15					15 30					15 45					16 00			
Richmond ⊖	d	15 04		15 15			15 19		15 28			15 34		15 45			15 49		15 58			16 04		16 15	
North Sheen	d	15 06					15 21					15 36					15 51					16 06			
Mortlake	d	15 08					15 23					15 38					15 53					16 08			
Hounslow	d							15 16			15 31							15 46			16 01				
Isleworth	d							15 19			15 34							15 49			16 04				
Syon Lane	d							15 21			15 36							15 51			16 06				
Brentford	d							15 24			15 39							15 54			16 09				
Kew Bridge	d							15 26			15 41							15 56			16 11				
Chiswick	d							15 29			15 44							15 59			16 14				
Barnes Bridge	d				←			15 31			15 46				←			16 01			16 16				←
Barnes	d	15 11			15 19		15 26	15 34		←	15 49	15 41			15 49		15 56	16 04		←	16 19	16 11			16 19
Putney	d	15 14			15 22		15 29	15 37	15 34	15 37	→	15 44			15 52		15 59	16 07	16 04	16 07	→	16 14			16 22
Wandsworth Town	d	15 17			15 25		15 32	→		15 40		15 47			15 55		16 02	→		16 10		16 17			16 25
Clapham Junction 10	d	15 20		15 24	15 28		15 35		15 39	15 43		15 50		15 54	15 58		16 05		16 09	16 13		16 20		16 24	16 28
Queenstown Rd.(Battersea)	d	15 23			15 31		15 38			15 46		15 53			16 01		16 08			16 16		16 23			16 31
Vauxhall ⊖	d	15 27			15 35		15 42		15 45	15 50		15 57			16 05		16 12		16 15	16 20		16 27			16 35
London Waterloo 15 ⊖	a	15 32		15 34	15 41		15 46		15 49	15 56		16 02		16 05	16 11		16 19		16 19	16 26		16 32		16 34	16 41

Table 149

Mondays to Fridays
until 5 October

Reading, Guildford, Ascot, Weybridge, Windsor, Kingston, Richmond and Hounslow - London

Network Diagram - see first Page of Table 148

		SW 1	SW	SW	SW	SW	SW	SW		SW 1	SW	SW 1	SW	SW	SW	SW	SW	SW		SW 1	SW	SW 1	SW	SW	SW
Reading 7	d									15 42										16 12					
Earley	d									15 47										16 17					
Winnersh Triangle	d									15 49										16 19					
Winnersh	d									15 51										16 21					
Wokingham	d									15 56										16 26					
Bracknell	d									16 02										16 32					
Martins Heron	d									16 05										16 35					
Guildford	d	15 00										15 30										16 00			
Wanborough	d	15 06										15 36										16 06			
Ash 5	d	15 10										15 40										16 10			
Aldershot	a	15 17										15 47										16 17			
	d	15 30										16 00										16 30			
Ash Vale	d	15 34										16 04										16 34			
Frimley	d	15 40										16 10										16 40			
Camberley	a	15 44										16 14										16 44			
	d	15 48										16 18										16 48			
Bagshot	d	15 53										16 23										16 53			
Ascot 3	d	16a00								16 10		16a30								16 40		17a00			
Sunningdale	d									16 13										16 43					
Longcross	d																								
Woking	d																								
West Byfleet	d																								
Byfleet & New Haw	d																								
Weybridge	d			15 33										16 03										16 33	
Addlestone	d			15 37										16 07										16 37	
Chertsey	d			15 40										16 10										16 40	
Virginia Water	a			15 45						16 19				16 15						16 49				16 45	
	d			15 54						16 19				16 24						16 49				16 54	
Egham	d			15 57						16 23				16 27						16 53				16 57	
Windsor & Eton Riverside	d				15 53										16 23										16 53
Datchet	d				15 56										16 26										16 56
Sunnymeads	d				15 59										16 29										16 59
Wraysbury	d				16 02										16 32										17 02
Staines	d			16 03	16 08					16 29				16 33	16 38					16 59				17 03	17 08
Ashford (Surrey)	d			16 06	16 11									16 36	16 41									17 06	17 11
Feltham	d			16 11	16 16					16 35				16 41	16 46					17 05				17 11	17 16
Whitton	d				16 20		16 20	16 23							16 50		16 50	16 53							17 20
Kingston	d		15 59										16 29										16 59		
Hampton Wick	d		16 01										16 31										17 01		
Teddington	d		16 05										16 35										17 05		
Fulwell	d																								
Strawberry Hill	d		16 08										16 38										17 08		
Twickenham	a		16 12		16 23			16 26		16 40			16 42		16 53			16 56		17 10			17 12		17 23
	d		16 13		16 23			16 28		16 41			16 43		16 53			16 58		17 11			17 13		17 23
St Margarets	d		16 15					16 30					16 45					17 00					17 15		
Richmond ⊖	d		16 19		16 28			16 34		16 45			16 49		16 58			17 04		17 15			17 19		17 28
North Sheen	d		16 21					16 36					16 51					17 06					17 21		
Mortlake	d		16 23					16 38					16 53					17 08					17 23		
Hounslow	d			16 16			16 31							16 46			17 01							17 16	
Isleworth	d			16 19			16 34							16 49			17 04							17 19	
Syon Lane	d			16 21			16 36							16 51			17 06							17 21	
Brentford	d			16 24			16 39							16 54			17 09							17 24	
Kew Bridge	d			16 26			16 41							16 56			17 11							17 26	
Chiswick	d			16 29			16 44							16 59			17 14							17 29	
Barnes Bridge	d			16 31			16 46				←			17 01			17 16				←			17 31	
Barnes	d		16 26	16 34		←	16 49	16 41			16 49		16 56	17 04		←	17 19	17 11			17 19		17 26	17 34	
Putney	d		16 29	16 37	16 34	16 37	→	16 44			16 52		16 59	17 07	17 05	17 07	→	17 14			17 22		17 29	17 37	17 34
Wandsworth Town	d		16 32	→		16 40		16 47			16 55		17 02	→		17 10		17 17			17 25		17 32	→	
Clapham Junction 10	d		16 35		16 39	16 43		16 50		16 54	16 58		17 05		17 09	17 13		17 20		17 24	17 28		17 35		17 39
Queenstown Rd.(Battersea)	d		16 38			16 46		16 53			17 01		17 08			17 16		17 23			17 31		17 38		
Vauxhall ⊖	d		16 42		16 45	16 50		16 57			17 05		17 12		17 15	17 20		17 27			17 35		17 42		17 45
London Waterloo 15 ⊖	a		16 49		16 49	16 56		17 02		17 04	17 11		17 19		17 19	17 26		17 32		17 33	17 41		17 49		17 49

Table 149

Mondays to Fridays
until 5 October

Reading, Guildford, Ascot, Weybridge, Windsor, Kingston, Richmond and Hounslow - London

Network Diagram - see first Page of Table 148

		SW	SW	SW	SW 1	SW	SW 1	SW	SW	SW	SW	SW	SW	SW 1	SW	SW	SW	SW	SW	SW 1	SW 1	SW
Reading 7	d				16 42									17 12						17 22		
Earley	d				16 47									17 17						17 27		
Winnersh Triangle	d				16 49									17 19						17 29		
Winnersh	d				16 51									17 21						17 31		
Wokingham	d				16 56									17 26						17 36		
Bracknell	d				17 02									17 32						17 42		
Martins Heron	d				17 05									17 35						17 45		
Guildford	d						16 30														17 00	
Wanborough	d						16 36														17 06	
Ash 5	d						16 40														17 10	
Aldershot	a						16 47														17 17	
	d						17 00														17 30	
Ash Vale	d						17 04														17 34	
Frimley	d						17 10														17 40	
Camberley	a						17 14														17 44	
	d						17 18														17 48	
Bagshot	d						17 23														17 53	
Ascot 3	d				17 10		17a30							17 40						17 55	18a00	
Sunningdale	d				17 13									17 43						17 58		
Longcross	d				17 16																	
Woking	d																					
West Byfleet	d																					
Byfleet & New Haw	d																					
Weybridge	d								17 03								17 37					
Addlestone	d								17 07								17 41					
Chertsey	d								17 10								17 44					
Virginia Water	a				17 19				17 15					17 49			17 49			18 03		
	d				17 19				17 24					17 49			17 54			18 03		
Egham	d				17 23				17 27					17 53			17 57			18 06		
Windsor & Eton Riverside	d									17 23								17 53				
Datchet	d									17 26								17 56				
Sunnymeads	d									17 29								17 59				
Wraysbury	d									17 32								18 02				
Staines	d				17 29				17 33	17 38				17 59			18 03	18 08		18 14		
Ashford (Surrey)	d								17 36	17 41							18 06	18 11				
Feltham	d				17 35				17 41	17 46				18 05			18 11	18 16		18 20		
Whitton	d		17 20	17 23						17 50		17 50	17 53					18 20				18 20
Kingston	d							17 29								17 59						
Hampton Wick	d							17 31								18 01						
Teddington	d							17 35								18 05						
Fulwell	d																					
Strawberry Hill	d							17 38								18 08						
Twickenham	a			17 26	17 40			17 42		17 53			17 56	18 10		18 12		18 23				
	d			17 28	17 41			17 43		17 53			17 58	18 11		18 13		18 23				
St Margarets	d			17 30				17 45					18 00			18 15						
Richmond ⊖	d			17 34	17 45			17 49		17 58			18 04	18 15		18 19		18 28				
North Sheen	d			17 36				17 51					18 06			18 21						
Mortlake	d			17 38				17 53					18 08			18 23						
Hounslow	d		17 31						17 46			18 01					18 16			18 26		18 31
Isleworth	d		17 34						17 49			18 04					18 19					18 34
Syon Lane	d		17 36						17 51			18 06					18 21					18 36
Brentford	d		17 39						17 54			18 09					18 24			18 31		18 39
Kew Bridge	d		17 41						17 56			18 11					18 26					18 41
Chiswick	d		17 44						17 59			18 14					18 29					18 44
Barnes Bridge	d		17 46			←			18 01			18 16			←		18 31					18 46
Barnes	d	←	17 49	17 41		17 49		17 56	18 04		←	18 19	18 11		18 19	18 26	18 34		←			18 49
Putney	d	17 37	→	17 44		17 52		17 59	18 07	18 04	18 07	→	18 14		18 22	18 29	18 37	18 34	18 37	18 39		→
Wandsworth Town	d	17 40		17 47		17 55		18 02	→		18 10		18 17		18 25	18 32	→		18 40			
Clapham Junction 10	d	17 43		17 50	17 54	17 58		18 05		18 09	18 13		18 20	18 24	18 28	18 35		18 39	18 43	18 44		
Queenstown Rd.(Battersea)	d	17 46		17 53		18 01		18 08			18 16		18 23		18 31	18 38			18 46			
Vauxhall ⊖	d	17 50		17 57		18 05		18 12		18 15	18 20		18 27		18 35	18 42		18 45	18 50			
London Waterloo 15 ⊖	a	17 56		18 02	18 04	18 11		18 19		18 19	18 26		18 32	18 34	18 41	18 49		18 49	18 56	18 56		

Table 149

Mondays to Fridays
until 5 October

Reading, Guildford, Ascot, Weybridge, Windsor, Kingston, Richmond and Hounslow - London

Network Diagram - see first Page of Table 148

		SW	SW 1	SW	SW	SW	SW	SW	SW 1	SW 1	SW	SW	SW 1	SW	SW 1	SW	SW	SW	SW	SW	SW	SW 1	SW
Reading 7	d		17 42						17 53				18 12									18 42	
Earley	d		17 47						17 58				18 17									18 47	
Winnersh Triangle	d		17 49						18 00				18 19									18 49	
Winnersh	d		17 51						18 02				18 21									18 51	
Wokingham	d		17 56						18 07				18 26									18 56	
Bracknell	d		18 02						18 13				18 32									19 02	
Martins Heron	d		18 05						18 16				18 35									19 05	
Guildford	d									17 30					18 00								
Wanborough	d									17 36					18 06								
Ash 5	d									17 40					18 10								
Aldershot	a									17 47					18 17								
	d									18 00					18 30								
Ash Vale	d									18 04					18 34								
Frimley	d									18 10					18 40								
Camberley	a									18 14					18 44								
	d									18 18					18 48								
Bagshot	d									18 23					18 53								
Ascot 3	d		18 10						18 25	18a30			18 40		19a00							19 10	
Sunningdale	d		18 13						18 28				18 43									19 13	
Longcross	d		18 16										18 46									19 16	
Woking	d																						
West Byfleet	d																						
Byfleet & New Haw	d																						
Weybridge	d					18 07											18 37						
Addlestone	d					18 11											18 41						
Chertsey	d					18 14											18 44						
Virginia Water	a		18 19			18 19			18 33				18 49				18 49					19 19	
	d		18 19			18 24			18 33				18 49				18 54					19 19	
Egham	d		18 23			18 27			18 37				18 53				18 57					19 23	
Windsor & Eton Riverside	d						18 23											18 53					
Datchet	d						18 26											18 56					
Sunnymeads	d						18 29											18 59					
Wraysbury	d						18 32											19 02					
Staines	d		18 29			18 33	18 38		18 44				18 59				19 03	19 08				19 29	
Ashford (Surrey)	d					18 36	18 41										19 06	19 11					
Feltham	d		18 35			18 41	18 46		18 50				19 05				19 11	19 16				19 35	
Whitton	d	18 23					18 50				18 50	18 53						19 20		19 20	19 23		
Kingston	d				18 29											18 59							
Hampton Wick	d				18 31											19 01							
Teddington	d				18 35											19 05							
Fulwell	d																						
Strawberry Hill	d				18 38											19 08							
Twickenham	a	18 26	18 40		18 42		18 53					18 56	19 10			19 12		19 23			19 26	19 40	
	d	18 28	18 41		18 43		18 53					18 58	19 11			19 13		19 23			19 28	19 41	
St Margarets	d	18 30			18 45							19 00				19 15					19 30		
Richmond ⊖	d	18 34	18 45		18 49		18 58					19 04	19 15			19 19		19 28			19 34	19 45	
North Sheen	d	18 36			18 51							19 06				19 21					19 36		
Mortlake	d	18 38			18 53							19 08				19 23					19 38		
Hounslow	d					18 46			18 56		19 01						19 16			19 31			
Isleworth	d					18 49					19 04						19 19			19 34			
Syon Lane	d					18 51					19 06						19 21			19 36			
Brentford	d					18 54			19 01		19 09						19 24			19 39			
Kew Bridge	d					18 56					19 11						19 26			19 41			
Chiswick	d					18 59					19 14						19 29			19 44			
Barnes Bridge	d			←		19 01					19 16			←			19 31			19 46			←
Barnes	d	18 41		18 49	18 56	19 04		←			19 19	19 11		19 19		19 26	19 34		←	19 49	19 41		19 49
Putney	d	18 44		18 52	18 59	19 07	19 04	19 07	19 09		→	19 14		19 22		19 29	19 37	19 34	19 37	→	19 44		19 52
Wandsworth Town	d	18 47		18 55	19 02	→		19 10				19 17		19 25		19 32	→		19 40		19 47		19 55
Clapham Junction 10	d	18 50	18 54	18 58	19 05		19 09	19 13	19 14			19 20	19 24	19 28		19 35		19 39	19 43		19 50	19 54	19 58
Queenstown Rd.(Battersea)	d	18 53		19 01	19 08			19 16				19 23		19 31		19 38			19 46		19 53		20 01
Vauxhall ⊖	d	18 57		19 05	19 12		19 15	19 20				19 27		19 35		19 42		19 45	19 50		19 57		20 05
London Waterloo 15 ⊖	a	19 02	19 04	19 11	19 16		19 19	19 26	19 28			19 32	19 34	19 41		19 46		19 49	19 56		20 02	20 04	20 09

Mondays to Fridays

until 5 October

Reading, Guildford, Ascot, Weybridge, Windsor, Kingston, Richmond and Hounslow - London

Network Diagram - see first Page of Table 148

		SW ■	SW ■	SW	SW	SW		SW	SW	SW	SW ■	SW	SW ■	SW	SW	SW		SW	SW	SW	SW ■	SW	SW ■	SW	SW
Reading 7	d	18 52									19 12										19 42				
Earley	d	18 57									19 17										19 47				
Winnersh Triangle	d	18 59									19 19										19 49				
Winnersh	d	19 01									19 21										19 51				
Wokingham	d	19 06									19 26										19 56				
Bracknell	d	19 12									19 32										20 02				
Martins Heron	d	19 15									19 35										20 05				
Guildford	d		18 30										19 00										19 30		
Wanborough	d		18 36										19 06										19 36		
Ash 5	d		18 40										19 10										19 40		
Aldershot	a		18 47										19 17										19 47		
	d		19 00										19 30										20 00		
Ash Vale	d		19 04										19 34										20 04		
Frimley	d		19 10										19 40										20 10		
Camberley	a		19 14										19 44										20 14		
	d		19 18										19 48										20 18		
Bagshot	d		19 23										19 53										20 23		
Ascot 3	d	19a19	19a30								19 40		20a00								20 10		20a30		
Sunningdale	d										19 43										20 13				
Longcross	d										19 46										20 16				
Woking	d																								
West Byfleet	d																								
Byfleet & New Haw	d																								
Weybridge	d				19 07										19 37										20 03
Addlestone	d				19 11										19 41										20 07
Chertsey	d				19 14										19 44										20 10
Virginia Water	a				19 19						19 49				19 49						20 19				20 15
	d				19 24						19 49				19 54						20 19				20 24
Egham	d				19 27						19 53				19 57						20 23				20 27
Windsor & Eton Riverside	d					19 23										19 53									
Datchet	d					19 26										19 56									
Sunnymeads	d					19 29										19 59									
Wraysbury	d					19 32										20 02									
Staines	d				19 33	19 38					19 59				20 03	20 08					20 29				20 33
Ashford (Surrey)	d				19 36	19 41									20 06	20 11									20 36
Feltham	d				19 41	19 46					20 05				20 11	20 16					20 35				20 41
Whitton	d					19 50			19 50	19 53						20 20			20 20	20 23					
Kingston	d			19 29										19 59										20 29	
Hampton Wick	d			19 31										20 01										20 31	
Teddington	d			19 35										20 05										20 35	
Fulwell	d																								
Strawberry Hill	d			19 38										20 08										20 38	
Twickenham	a			19 42		19 53				19 56	20 10			20 12		20 23				20 26	20 40			20 42	
	d			19 43		19 53				19 58	20 11			20 13		20 23				20 28	20 41			20 43	
St Margarets	d			19 45						20 00				20 15						20 30				20 45	
Richmond ⊖	d			19 49		19 58				20 04	20 15			20 19		20 28				20 34	20 45			20 49	
North Sheen	d			19 51						20 06				20 21						20 36				20 51	
Mortlake	d			19 53						20 08				20 23						20 38				20 53	
Hounslow	d				19 46				20 01						20 16				20 31						20 46
Isleworth	d				19 49				20 04						20 19				20 34						20 49
Syon Lane	d				19 51				20 06						20 21				20 36						20 51
Brentford	d				19 54				20 09						20 24				20 39						20 54
Kew Bridge	d				19 56				20 11						20 26				20 41						20 56
Chiswick	d				19 59				20 14						20 29				20 44						20 59
Barnes Bridge	d				20 01				20 16			←			20 31				20 46			←			21 01
Barnes	d			19 56	20 04			←	20 19	20 11		20 19		20 26	20 34			←	20 49	20 41		20 49		20 56	21 04
Putney	d			19 59	20 07	20 04		20 07	→	20 14		20 22		20 29	20 37	20 34		20 37	→	20 44		20 52		20 59	21 07
Wandsworth Town	d			20 02	→			20 10		20 17		20 25		20 32	→			20 40		20 47		20 55		21 02	→
Clapham Junction 10	d			20 05		20 09		20 13		20 20	20 24	20 28		20 35		20 39		20 43		20 50	20 54	20 58		21 05	
Queenstown Rd.(Battersea)	d			20 08				20 16		20 23		20 31		20 38				20 46		20 53		21 01		21 08	
Vauxhall ⊖	d			20 12		20 15		20 20		20 27		20 35		20 42		20 45		20 50		20 57		21 05		21 12	
London Waterloo 15 ⊖	a			20 16		20 19		20 26		20 32	20 34	20 41		20 46		20 49		20 56		21 02	21 04	21 11		21 16	

Mondays to Fridays

until 5 October

Reading, Guildford, Ascot, Weybridge, Windsor, Kingston, Richmond and Hounslow - London

Network Diagram - see first Page of Table 148

		SW		SW	SW	SW	SW ■	SW	SW ■	SW ■	SW	SW		SW	SW	SW	SW	SW ■	SW	SW	SW	SW		SW	SW
Reading 7	d						20 12											20 42							
Earley	d						20 17											20 47							
Winnersh Triangle	d						20 19											20 49							
Winnersh	d						20 21											20 51							
Wokingham	d						20 26											20 56							
Bracknell	d						20 32											21 02							
Martins Heron	d						20 35											21 05							
Guildford	d								20 00	20 30															
Wanborough	d								20 06	20 36															
Ash 5	d								20 10	20 40															
Aldershot	a								20 17	20 47															
	d								20 30																
Ash Vale	d								20 34																
Frimley	d								20 40																
Camberley	a								20 44																
	d								20 48																
Bagshot	d								20 53																
Ascot 3	d						20 40		21a00									21 10							
Sunningdale	d						20 43											21 13							
Longcross	d						20 46																		
Woking	d																								
West Byfleet	d																								
Byfleet & New Haw	d																								
Weybridge	d											20 33									21 03				
Addlestone	d											20 37									21 07				
Chertsey	d											20 40									21 10				
Virginia Water	a						20 49					20 45						21 19			21 15				
	d						20 49					20 54						21 19			21 24				
Egham	d						20 53					20 57						21 23			21 27				
Windsor & Eton Riverside	d	20 23												20 53								21 23			
Datchet	d	20 26												20 56								21 26			
Sunnymeads	d	20 29												20 59								21 29			
Wraysbury	d	20 32												21 02								21 32			
Staines	d	20 38					20 59					21 03		21 08				21 29			21 33	21 38			
Ashford (Surrey)	d	20 41										21 06		21 11							21 36	21 41			
Feltham	d	20 46					21 05					21 11		21 16				21 35			21 41	21 46			
Whitton	d	20 50			20 50	20 53								21 20		21 20	21 23					21 50			21 50
Kingston	d										20 59									21 29					
Hampton Wick	d										21 01									21 31					
Teddington	d										21 05									21 35					
Fulwell	d																								
Strawberry Hill	d										21 08									21 38					
Twickenham	a	20 53				20 56	21 10				21 12			21 23			21 26	21 40		21 42		21 53			
	d	20 53				20 58	21 11				21 13			21 23			21 28	21 41		21 43		21 53			
St Margarets	d					21 00					21 15						21 30			21 45					
Richmond ⊖	d	20 58				21 04	21 15				21 19			21 28			21 34	21 45		21 49		21 58			
North Sheen	d					21 06					21 21						21 36			21 51					
Mortlake	d					21 08					21 23						21 38			21 53					
Hounslow	d				21 01							21 16				21 31					21 46				22 01
Isleworth	d				21 04							21 19				21 34					21 49				22 04
Syon Lane	d				21 06							21 21				21 36					21 51				22 06
Brentford	d				21 09							21 24				21 39					21 54				22 09
Kew Bridge	d				21 11							21 26				21 41					21 56				22 11
Chiswick	d				21 14							21 29				21 44					21 59				22 14
Barnes Bridge	d				21 16			←				21 31				21 46			←		22 01				22 16
Barnes	d			←	21 19	21 11		21 19			21 26	21 34			←	21 49	21 41		21 49	21 56	22 04			←	22 19
Putney	d	21 04		21 07	→	21 14		21 22			21 29	21 37		21 34	21 37	→	21 44		21 52	21 59	22 07	22 04		22 07	→
Wandsworth Town	d			21 10		21 17		21 25			21 32	→			21 40		21 47		21 55	22 02	→			22 10	
Clapham Junction 10	d	21 09		21 13		21 20	21 24	21 28			21 35			21 39	21 43		21 50	21 54	21 58	22 05		22 09		22 13	
Queenstown Rd.(Battersea)	d			21 16		21 23		21 31			21 38				21 46		21 53		22 01	22 08				22 16	
Vauxhall ⊖	d	21 15		21 20		21 27		21 35			21 42			21 45	21 50		21 57		22 05	22 12		22 15		22 20	
London Waterloo 15 ⊖	a	21 19		21 26		21 32	21 34	21 41			21 46			21 49	21 56		22 02	22 04	22 11	22 16		22 19		22 26	

Table 149

Mondays to Fridays
until 5 October

Reading, Guildford, Ascot, Weybridge, Windsor, Kingston, Richmond and Hounslow - London

Network Diagram - see first Page of Table 148

		SW	SW ■	SW	SW ■	SW ■	SW	SW		SW	SW	SW	SW ■
Reading ■	d		21 12										21 42
Earley	d		21 17										21 47
Winnersh Triangle	d		21 19										21 49
Winnersh	d		21 21										21 51
Wokingham	d		21 26										21 56
Bracknell	d		21 32										22 02
Martins Heron	d		21 35										22 05
Guildford	d				21 00	21 30							
Wanborough	d				21 06	21 36							
Ash ■	d				21 10	21 40							
Aldershot	a				21 17	21 47							
	d				21 30								
Ash Vale	d				21 34								
Frimley	d				21 40								
Camberley	a				21 44								
	d				21 48								
Bagshot	d				21 53								
Ascot ■	d		21 40		22a00								22 10
Sunningdale	d		21 43										22 13
Longcross	d												
Woking	d												
West Byfleet	d												
Byfleet & New Haw	d												
Weybridge	d							21 33					
Addlestone	d							21 37					
Chertsey	d							21 40					
Virginia Water	a		21 49					21 45					22 19
	d		21 49					21 54					22 19
Egham	d		21 53					21 57					22 23
Windsor & Eton Riverside	d									21 53			
Datchet	d									21 56			
Sunnymeads	d									21 59			
Wraysbury	d									22 02			
Staines	d		21 59					22 03		22 08			22 29
Ashford (Surrey)	d							22 06		22 11			
Feltham	d		22 05					22 11		22 16			22 35
Whitton	d	21 53								22 20		22 23	
Kingston	d						21 59						
Hampton Wick	d						22 01						
Teddington	d						22 05						
Fulwell	d												
Strawberry Hill	d						22 08						
Twickenham	a	21 56	22 10				22 12			22 23		22 26	22 40
	d	21 58	22 11				22 13			22 23		22 28	22 41
St Margarets	d	22 00					22 15					22 30	
Richmond ⊖	d	22 04	22 15				22 19			22 28		22 34	22 45
North Sheen	d	22 06					22 21					22 36	
Mortlake	d	22 08					22 23					22 38	
Hounslow	d							22 16					
Isleworth	d							22 19					
Syon Lane	d							22 21					
Brentford	d							22 24					
Kew Bridge	d							22 26					
Chiswick	d							22 29					
Barnes Bridge	d			←				22 31					
Barnes	d	22 11		22 19			22 26	22 34			←	22 41	
Putney	d	22 14		22 22			22 29	22 37		22 34	22 37	22 44	
Wandsworth Town	d	22 17		22 25			22 32	→			22 40	22 47	
Clapham Junction ■	d	22 20	22 24	22 28			22 35			22 39	22 43	22 50	22 54
Queenstown Rd.(Battersea)	d	22 23		22 31			22 38				22 46	22 53	
Vauxhall ⊖	d	22 27		22 35			22 42			22 45	22 50	22 57	
London Waterloo ■ ⊖	a	22 32	22 34	22 41			22 46			22 49	22 56	23 02	23 04

		SW	SW	SW	SW	SW ■		SW ■	SW ■	SW	SW	SW A	SW B
Reading ■	d					22 12							
Earley	d					22 17							
Winnersh Triangle	d					22 19							
Winnersh	d					22 21							
Wokingham	d					22 26							
Bracknell	d					22 32							
Martins Heron	d					22 35							
Guildford	d							22 00	22 30				
Wanborough	d							22 06	22 36				
Ash ■	d							22 10	22 40				
Aldershot	a							22 17	22 47				
	d							22 30					
Ash Vale	d							22 34					
Frimley	d							22 40					
Camberley	a							22 44					
	d							22 48					
Bagshot	d							22 53					
Ascot ■	d					22 40		23a00					
Sunningdale	d					22 43							
Longcross	d												
Woking	d												
West Byfleet	d												
Byfleet & New Haw	d												
Weybridge	d		22 03								22 33		
Addlestone	d		22 07								22 37		
Chertsey	d		22 10								22 40		
Virginia Water	a		22 15			22 49					22 45		
	d		22 24			22 49					22 54		
Egham	d		22 27			22 53					22 57		
Windsor & Eton Riverside	d			22 23								22 53	22 53
Datchet	d			22 26								22 56	22 56
Sunnymeads	d			22 29								22 59	22 59
Wraysbury	d			22 32								23 02	23 02
Staines	d		22 33	22 38		22 59					23 03	23 08	23 08
Ashford (Surrey)	d		22 36	22 41							23 06	23 11	23 11
Feltham	d		22 41	22 46		23 05					23 11	23 16	23 16
Whitton	d			22 50								23 20	23 20
Kingston	d	22 29								22 59			
Hampton Wick	d	22 31								23 01			
Teddington	d	22 35								23 05			
Fulwell	d												
Strawberry Hill	d	22 38								23 08			
Twickenham	a	22 42		22 53		23 10				23 12		23 23	23 23
	d	22 43		22 53		23 11				23 13		23 23	23 23
St Margarets	d	22 45								23 15			
Richmond ⊖	d	22 49		22 58		23 15				23 19		23 28	23 28
North Sheen	d	22 51								23 21			
Mortlake	d	22 53								23 23			
Hounslow	d		22 46								23 16		
Isleworth	d		22 49								23 19		
Syon Lane	d		22 51								23 21		
Brentford	d		22 54								23 24		
Kew Bridge	d		22 56								23 26		
Chiswick	d		22 59								23 29		
Barnes Bridge	d		23 01								23 31		
Barnes	d	22 56	23 04		←					23 26	23 34		
Putney	d	22 59	23 07	23 04	23 07					23 29	23 37	23 34	23 34
Wandsworth Town	d	23 02	→		23 10					23 32	→		
Clapham Junction ■	d	23 05		23 09	23 13	23 24				23 35		23 39	23 39
Queenstown Rd.(Battersea)	d	23 08			23 16					23 38			
Vauxhall ⊖	d	23 12		23 15	23 20					23 42		23 45	23 45
London Waterloo ■ ⊖	a	23 16		23 19	23 26	23 34				23 46		23 49	23 51

A until 26 July, FX from 30 July until 6 September, also from 17 August until 24 August, from 10 September until 5 October

B 27 July, 3 August, 10 August, 31 August, 7 September

Table 149

Mondays to Fridays
until 5 October

Reading, Guildford, Ascot, Weybridge, Windsor, Kingston, Richmond and Hounslow - London

Network Diagram - see first Page of Table 148

		SW	SW ■	SW		SW	SW	SW	SW ■	SW ■	SW ■	SW
Reading ■	d		22 42						23 12			
Earley	d		22 47						23 17			
Winnersh Triangle	d		22 49						23 19			
Winnersh	d		22 51						23 21			
Wokingham	d		22 56						23 26			
Bracknell	d		23 02						23 32			
Martins Heron	d		23 05						23 35			
Guildford	d									23 00	23 30	
Wanborough	d									23 06	23 36	
Ash ■	d									23 10	23 40	
Aldershot	a									23 17	23 47	
	d									23 30		
Ash Vale	d									23 34		
Frimley	d									23 40		
Camberley	a									23 44		
	d									23 48		
Bagshot	d									23 53		
Ascot ■	d		23 10						23 40	00a01		
Sunningdale	d		23 13						23 43			
Longcross	d											
Woking	d											
West Byfleet	d											
Byfleet & New Haw	d											
Weybridge	d			23 03								23 33
Addlestone	d			23 07								23 37
Chertsey	d			23 10								23 40
Virginia Water	a		23 19	23 15					23 49			23 45
	d		23 19	23 24					23 49			23 54
Egham	d		23 23	23 27					23 53			23 57
Windsor & Eton Riverside	d					23 28						
Datchet	d					23 31						
Sunnymeads	d					23 34						
Wraysbury	d					23 37						
Staines	d		23 29	23a32		23a42			23 59			00a02
Ashford (Surrey)	d											
Feltham	d		23 35						00 05			
Whitton	d											
Kingston	d						23 29	23 55				
Hampton Wick	d						23 31	23 57				
Teddington	d						23 35	23 59				
Fulwell	d											
Strawberry Hill	d						23 38	00 03				
Twickenham	a		23 40				23 42	00 07	00 10			
	d		23 41				23 43		00 11			
St Margarets	d						23 45					
Richmond ⊖	d		23 45				23 49		00 15			
North Sheen	d						23 51					
Mortlake	d						23 53					
Hounslow	d											
Isleworth	d											
Syon Lane	d											
Brentford	d											
Kew Bridge	d											
Chiswick	d											
Barnes Bridge	d											
Barnes	d	←					23 56					
Putney	d	23 37					23 59					
Wandsworth Town	d	23 40					00 02					
Clapham Junction ■	d	23 43	23 54				00 05		00 24			
Queenstown Rd.(Battersea)	d	23 46					00 08					
Vauxhall ⊖	d	23 50					00 12					
London Waterloo ■ ⊖	a	23 56	00 04				00 16		00 37			

Table 149

Mondays to Fridays

from 8 October

Reading, Guildford, Ascot, Weybridge, Windsor, Kingston, Richmond and Hounslow - London

Network Diagram - see first Page of Table 148

		SW MO	SW MO	SW MX [1]	SW MX	SW MO [1]	SW MX	SW MX [1]	SW	SW	SW	SW	SW	SW	SW	SW ◇	SW ◇	SW ◇	SW ◇[1]	SW [1]	SW	SW	SW	SW ◇
Reading [7]	d			22p39		22p54		23p12											05 39					
Earley	d			22p44		22p59		23p17											05 44					
Winnersh Triangle	d			22p46		23p01		23p19											05 46					
Winnersh	d			22p48		23p03		23p21											05 48					
Wokingham	d			22p53		23p08		23p26											05 53					
Bracknell	d			22p59		23p14		23p32											05 59					
Martins Heron	d			23p02		23p17		23p35											06 02					
Guildford	d																							
Wanborough	d																							
Ash [5]	d																							
Aldershot	a																							
	d																			05 58				
Ash Vale	d																			06 02				
Frimley	d																			06 10				
Camberley	a																			06 14				
	d																			06 18				
Bagshot	d																			06 23				
Ascot [3]	d			23p07		23p22		23p40											06 07	06a30				
Sunningdale	d			23p10		23p25		23p43											06 10					
Longcross	d																							
Woking	d		22p52													05 27								
West Byfleet	d		22p56													05 32								
Byfleet & New Haw	d		23p00													05 35								
Weybridge	d																							
Addlestone	d		23p04													05 39								
Chertsey	d		23p07													05 42								
Virginia Water	a		23p12	23p19		23p30		23p49								05 47			06 19					
	d		23p12	23p19		23p30		23p49								05 54			06 19					
Egham	d		23p16	23p23		23p34		23p53								05 57			06 23					
Windsor & Eton Riverside	d	23p01															05 51							06 21
Datchet	d	23p04															05 55							06 25
Sunnymeads	d	23p07															05 58							06 28
Wraysbury	d	23p10															06 02							06 32
Staines	d	23p16	23p21	23p29		23p39		23p59		04 58			05 37			06 03	06 08		06 29				06 33	06 38
Ashford (Surrey)	d	23p19	23p24							05 01			05 40			06 06	06 11						06 36	06 41
Feltham	d	23p24	23p29	23p35		23p46		00 05		05 06			05 45			06 11	06 16		06 35				06 41	06 46
Whitton	d	23p28								05 10			05 49				06 20				06 20			06 50
Kingston	d				23p29		23p55		01 17						05 59							06 29		
Hampton Wick	d				23p31		23p57		01s22						06 01							06 31		
Teddington	d				23p35		23p59		01 25						06 05							06 35		
Fulwell	d											05 36												
Strawberry Hill	d				23p38		00 03		01 28			05 38			06 08							06 38		
Twickenham	a	23p31		23p40	23p42	23p51	00 07	00 10		05 13		05 42	05 52		06 12		06 23		06 40			06 42		06 53
	d	23p32		23p41	23p43	23p51		00 11		05 13		05 43	05 53		06 13		06 23		06 41			06 43		06 53
St Margarets	d	23p34			23p45					05 15		05 45			06 15							06 45		
Richmond ⊖	d	23p37		23p45	23p49	23p56		00 15		05 19		05 49	05 58		06 19		06 28		06 45			06 49		06 58
North Sheen	d	23p39			23p51					05 21		05 51			06 21							06 51		
Mortlake	d	23p42			23p53					05 23		05 53			06 23							06 53		
Hounslow	d		23p35								05 31			06 01		06 16					06 31		06 46	
Isleworth	d		23p38								05 34			06 04		06 19					06 34		06 49	
Syon Lane	d		23p40								05 36			06 06		06 21					06 36		06 51	
Brentford	d		23p42								05 39			06 09		06 24					06 39		06 54	
Kew Bridge	d		23p45								05 41			06 11		06 26					06 41		06 56	
Chiswick	d		23p47								05 44			06 14		06 29					06 44		06 59	
Barnes Bridge	d		23p50								05 46			06 16		06 31					06 46		07 01	
Barnes	d	23p45	23p53		23p56					05 26	05 49	05 56		06 19	06 26	06 34		←			06 49	06 56	07 04	
Putney	d	23p48	23p56		23p59	00 02				05 29	05 52	05 59	06 04	06 22	06 29	06 37	06 34	06 37	06 52		06 52	06 59	07 07	07 04
Wandsworth Town	d	23p51	23p59		00 02					05 32	05 55	06 02		06 25	06 32	→		06 40			06 55	07 02	→	
Clapham Junction [10]	d	23p54	00 02	23p54	00 05	00 07		00 24		05 35	05 58	06 05	06 09	06 28	06 35		06 39	06 43	06 56		06 58	07 05		07 09
Queenstown Rd.(Battersea)	d	23p57	00 05		00 08					05 38	06 01	06 08		06 31	06 38			06 46			07 01	07 08		
Vauxhall ⊖	d	23p59	00 08		00 12	00 12				05 42	06 05	06 12	06 15	06 35	06 42		06 45	06 50			07 05	07 12		07 15
London Waterloo [15] ⊖	a	00 05	00 13	00 04	00 16	00 17		00 37		05 46	06 09	06 16	06 19	06 39	06 46		06 49	06 56	07 07		07 11	07 18		07 21

Table 149

Mondays to Fridays

from 8 October

Reading, Guildford, Ascot, Weybridge, Windsor, Kingston, Richmond and Hounslow - London

Network Diagram - see first Page of Table 148

		SW	SW	SW	SW ◇[1]	SW	SW	SW ◇	SW ◇	SW ◇	SW	SW	SW ◇[1]	SW [1]	SW ◇[1]	SW	SW ◇	SW ◇	SW ◇	SW	SW	SW ◇[1]	SW [1]
Reading [7]	d				06 12										06 39								
Earley	d				06 17										06 44								
Winnersh Triangle	d				06 19										06 46								
Winnersh	d				06 21										06 48								
Wokingham	d				06 26										06 53								
Bracknell	d				06 32										06 59								
Martins Heron	d				06 35										07 02								
Guildford	d													06 30									07 00
Wanborough	d													06 36									07 06
Ash [5]	d													06 40									07 10
Aldershot	a													06 47									07 17
	d												06 28									06 59	
Ash Vale	d												06 32									07 03	
Frimley	d												06 39									07 09	
Camberley	a												06 43									07 13	
	d												06 44									07 14	
Bagshot	d												06 49									07 19	
Ascot [3]	d				06 40								06 56		07 07							07 26	
Sunningdale	d				06 43								06 59		07 10							07 29	
Longcross	d																						
Woking	d																						
West Byfleet	d																						
Byfleet & New Haw	d																						
Weybridge	d							06 33									07 03						
Addlestone	d							06 37									07 07						
Chertsey	d							06 40									07 10						
Virginia Water	a				06 49			06 45					07 08		07 19		07 15					07 38	
	d				06 49			06 54					07 08		07 19		07 24					07 38	
Egham	d				06 53			06 57					07 12		07 23		07 27					07 42	
Windsor & Eton Riverside	d								06 51									07 21					
Datchet	d								06 55									07 25					
Sunnymeads	d								06 58									07 28					
Wraysbury	d								07 02									07 32					
Staines	d				06 59			07 03	07 08				07 18		07 29		07 33	07 38				07 48	
Ashford (Surrey)	d							07 06	07 11				07 21				07 36	07 41				07 51	
Feltham	d				07 05			07 11	07 16				07 26		07 35		07 41	07 46				07 56	
Whitton	d		06 50	06 53					07 20			07 20	07 30					07 50			07 50	08 00	
Kingston	d						06 59									07 29							
Hampton Wick	d						07 01									07 31							
Teddington	d						07 05									07 35							
Fulwell	d										07 12									07 42			
Strawberry Hill	d						07 08				07 14					07 38				07 44			
Twickenham	a			06 56	07 10		07 12		07 23		07 18		07 33		07 40	07 42		07 53		07 48		08 03	
	d			06 58	07 11		07 13		07 23		07 27		07 33		07 41	07 43		07 53		07 57		08 03	
St Margarets	d			07 00			07 15				07 29					07 45				07 59			
Richmond ⊖	d			07 04	07 15		07 19		07 28		07 32		07 38		07 45	07 49		07 58		08 02		08 08	
North Sheen	d			07 06			07 21				07 34					07 51				08 04			
Mortlake	d			07 08			07 23				07 37					07 53				08 07			
Hounslow	d		07 01					07 16				07 31					07 46				08 01		
Isleworth	d		07 04					07 19				07 34					07 49				08 04		
Syon Lane	d		07 06					07 21				07 36					07 51				08 06		
Brentford	d		07 09					07 24				07 39					07 54				08 09		
Kew Bridge	d		07 11					07 26				07 41					07 56				08 11		
Chiswick	d		07 14					07 29				07 44					07 59				08 14		
Barnes Bridge	d		07 16			←		07 31				07 46					08 01				08 16		
Barnes	d	←	07 19	07 11		07 19	07 26	07 34		←	07 40	07 49				07 56	08 04		←	08 10	08 19		
Putney	d	07 07	→	07 14	07 22	07 22	07 29	07 37	07 34	07 37	07 43	07 52				07 59	08 07	08 04	08 07	08 13	08 22		
Wandsworth Town	d	07 10		07 17		07 25	07 32	→		07 40	07 46	07 55				08 02	→		08 10	08 16	08 25		
Clapham Junction [10]	d	07 13		07 20	07 26	07 28	07 35		07 39	07 43	07 49	07 58	07 47		07 54	08 05		08 09	08 13	08 19	08 28	08 17	
Queenstown Rd.(Battersea)	d	07 16		07 23		07 31	07 38			07 46	07 52	08 01				08 08			08 16	08 22	08 31		
Vauxhall ⊖	d	07 20		07 27		07 35	07 42		07 45	07 50	07 56	08 05	07 53			08 12		08 15	08 20	08 26	08 35	08 23	
London Waterloo [15] ⊖	a	07 28		07 34	07 37	07 43	07 48		07 51	07 58	08 04	08 11	07 59		08 06	08 18		08 21	08 28	08 34	08 43	08 29	

Table 149

Mondays to Fridays

from 8 October

Reading, Guildford, Ascot, Weybridge, Windsor, Kingston, Richmond and Hounslow - London

Network Diagram - see first Page of Table 148

		SW ◇[1]		SW	SW ◇	SW ◇[1]	SW ◇	SW ◇	SW	SW	SW ◇[1]	SW ◇[1]		SW [1]	SW	SW ◇	SW ◇	SW ◇	SW	SW	SW ◇[1]	SW		SW [1]	SW
Reading [7]	d	07 09				07 24						07 39									08 09				
Earley	d	07 14										07 44									08 14				
Winnersh Triangle	d	07 16										07 46									08 16				
Winnersh	d	07 18										07 48									08 18				
Wokingham	d	07 23				07 33						07 53									08 23				
Bracknell	d	07 29				07 39						07 59									08 29				
Martins Heron	d	07 32				07 42						08 02									08 32				
Guildford	d													07 30										08 00	
Wanborough	d													07 36										08 06	
Ash [5]	d													07 40										08 10	
Aldershot	a													07 47										08 17	
	d										07 29			08 00										08 30	
Ash Vale	d										07 33			08 04										08 34	
Frimley	d										07 39			08 10										08 40	
Camberley	a										07 43			08 14										08 44	
	d										07 44			08 18										08 48	
Bagshot	d										07 49			08 23										08 53	
Ascot [3]	d	07 37				07 47					07 56	08 07		08a30							08 37			09a00	
Sunningdale	d	07 40				07 50					07 59	08 10									08 40				
Longcross	d											08 13									08 43				
Woking	d																								
West Byfleet	d																								
Byfleet & New Haw	d																								
Weybridge	d				07 33											08 03									
Addlestone	d				07 37											08 07									
Chertsey	d				07 40											08 10									
Virginia Water	a				07 45	07 55					08 08	08 19				08 15					08 49				
	d				07 51	07 55					08 08	08 19				08 24					08 49				
Egham	d	07 50			07 54	07 58					08 12	08 23				08 27					08 53				
Windsor & Eton Riverside	d						07 51										08 21								
Datchet	d						07 55										08 25								
Sunnymeads	d						07 58										08 28								
Wraysbury	d						08 02										08 32								
Staines	d	07 56			08 00	08 04	08 08				08 18	08 29				08 33	08 38				08 59				
Ashford (Surrey)	d				08 03		08 11				08 21					08 36	08 41								
Feltham	d	08 02			08 08	08 12	08 16				08 26	08 35				08 41	08 46				09 05				
Whitton	d						08 20			08 20	08 30						08 50		08 50	08 53					
Kingston	d			07 59											08 29										08 59
Hampton Wick	d			08 01											08 31										09 01
Teddington	d			08 05											08 35										09 05
Fulwell	d								08 12																
Strawberry Hill	d			08 08					08 14						08 38										09 08
Twickenham	a	08 09		08 12		08 17	08 23		08 18		08 33	08 40			08 42		08 53			08 56	09 10				09 12
	d	08 09		08 13		08 18	08 23		08 27		08 33	08 41			08 43		08 53			08 58	09 11				09 13
St Margarets	d			08 15					08 29						08 45					09 00					09 15
Richmond ⊖	d	08 14		08 19		08 24	08 28		08 32		08 38	08 45			08 49		08 58			09 04	09 15				09 19
North Sheen	d			08 21					08 34						08 51					09 06					09 21
Mortlake	d			08 23					08 37						08 53					09 08					09 23
Hounslow	d				08 16					08 31						08 46			09 01						
Isleworth	d				08 19					08 34						08 49			09 04						
Syon Lane	d				08 21					08 36						08 51			09 06						
Brentford	d				08 24					08 39						08 54			09 09						
Kew Bridge	d				08 26					08 41						08 56			09 11						
Chiswick	d				08 29					08 44						08 59			09 14						
Barnes Bridge	d				08 31					08 46						09 01			09 16			←			
Barnes	d			08 26	08 34			←	08 40	08 49					08 56	09 04		←	09 19	09 11		09 19			09 26
Putney	d			08 29	08 37		08 34	08 37	08 43	08 52					08 59	09 07	09 04	09 07	→	09 14		09 22			09 29
Wandsworth Town	d			08 32	→			08 40	08 46	08 55					09 02	→		09 10		09 17		09 25			09 32
Clapham Junction [10]	d	08 22		08 35		08 33	08 39	08 43	08 49	08 58	08 47	08 54			09 05		09 09	09 13		09 20	09 24	09 28			09 35
Queenstown Rd.(Battersea)	d			08 38				08 46	08 52	09 01					09 08			09 16		09 23		09 31			09 38
Vauxhall ⊖	d			08 42		08 38	08 45	08 50	08 56	09 05	08 53				09 12		09 15	09 20		09 27		09 35			09 42
London Waterloo [15] ⊖	a	08 38		08 49		08 46	08 51	08 58	09 04	09 13	09 00	09 06			09 18		09 21	09 28		09 34	09 34	09 43			09 48

Table 149

Mondays to Fridays

from 8 October

Reading, Guildford, Ascot, Weybridge, Windsor, Kingston, Richmond and Hounslow - London

Network Diagram - see first Page of Table 148

		SW ◇	SW ◇	SW ◇	SW	SW	SW [1]	SW		SW [1]	SW	SW	SW	SW	SW	SW	SW [1]	SW		SW	SW	SW	SW [1]	SW	SW [1]
Reading [7]	d						08 39										09 09						09 22		
Earley	d						08 44										09 14						09 27		
Winnersh Triangle	d						08 46										09 16						09 29		
Winnersh	d						08 48										09 18						09 31		
Wokingham	d						08 53										09 23						09 36		
Bracknell	d						08 59										09 29						09 43		
Martins Heron	d						09 02										09 32						09 46		
Guildford	d									08 30															09 00
Wanborough	d									08 36															09 06
Ash [5]	d									08 40															09 10
Aldershot	a									08 47															09 17
	d									09 00															09 30
Ash Vale	d									09 04															09 34
Frimley	d									09 10															09 40
Camberley	a									09 14															09 44
	d									09 18															09 48
Bagshot	d									09 23															09 53
Ascot [3]	d						09 07			09a30							09 37						09 52		10a00
Sunningdale	d						09 10										09 40						09 55		
Longcross	d						09 13																		
Woking	d																								
West Byfleet	d																								
Byfleet & New Haw	d																								
Weybridge	d	08 33										09 03									09 33				
Addlestone	d	08 37										09 07									09 37				
Chertsey	d	08 40										09 10									09 40				
Virginia Water	a	08 45					09 19					09 15					09 49				09 45		10 03		
	d	08 54					09 19					09 24					09 49				09 54		10 03		
Egham	d	08 57					09 23					09 27					09 53				09 57		10 06		
Windsor & Eton Riverside	d		08 51										09 21									09 51			
Datchet	d		08 55										09 25									09 55			
Sunnymeads	d		08 58										09 28									09 58			
Wraysbury	d		09 02										09 32									10 02			
Staines	d	09 03	09 08				09 29					09 33	09 38				09 59				10 03	10 08	10 14		
Ashford (Surrey)	d	09 06	09 11									09 36	09 41								10 06	10 11			
Feltham	d	09 11	09 16				09 35					09 41	09 46				10 05				10 11	10 16	10 20		
Whitton	d		09 20		09 20	09 23							09 50		09 50	09 53						10 20			
Kingston	d										09 29									09 59					
Hampton Wick	d										09 31									10 01					
Teddington	d										09 35									10 05					
Fulwell	d																								
Strawberry Hill	d										09 38									10 08					
Twickenham	a		09 23			09 26	09 40				09 42		09 53			09 56	10 10			10 12		10 23	10 27		
	d		09 23			09 28	09 41				09 43		09 53			09 58	10 11			10 13		10 23	10 27		
St Margarets	d					09 30					09 45					10 00				10 15					
Richmond ⊖	d		09 28			09 34	09 45				09 49		09 58			10 04	10 15			10 19		10 28	10 32		
North Sheen	d					09 36					09 51					10 06				10 21					
Mortlake	d					09 38					09 53					10 08				10 23					
Hounslow	d	09 16			09 31							09 46			10 01						10 16				
Isleworth	d	09 19			09 34							09 49			10 04						10 19				
Syon Lane	d	09 21			09 36							09 51			10 06						10 21				
Brentford	d	09 24			09 39							09 54			10 09						10 24				
Kew Bridge	d	09 26			09 41							09 56			10 11						10 26				
Chiswick	d	09 29			09 44							09 59			10 14						10 29				
Barnes Bridge	d	09 31			09 46			←				10 01			10 16			←			10 31				
Barnes	d	09 34		←	09 49	09 41		09 49			09 56	10 04		←	10 19	10 11		10 19		10 26	10 34			←	
Putney	d	09 37	09 34	09 37	→	09 44		09 52			09 59	10 07	10 04	10 07	→	10 14		10 22		10 29	10 37	10 34		10 37	
Wandsworth Town	d	→		09 40		09 47		09 55			10 02	→		10 10		10 17		10 25		10 32	→			10 40	
Clapham Junction [10]	d		09 39	09 43		09 50	09 54	09 58			10 05		10 09	10 13		10 20	10 24	10 28		10 35		10 39	10 42	10 43	
Queenstown Rd.(Battersea)	d			09 46		09 53		10 01			10 08			10 16		10 23		10 31		10 38				10 47	
Vauxhall ⊖	d		09 45	09 50		09 57		10 05			10 12		10 15	10 20		10 27		10 35		10 42		10 45		10 50	
London Waterloo [15] ⊖	a		09 51	09 58		10 02	10 04	10 11			10 16		10 19	10 26		10 32	10 34	10 41		10 46		10 49	10 53	10 56	

Table 149

Mondays to Fridays
from 8 October

Reading, Guildford, Ascot, Weybridge, Windsor, Kingston, Richmond and Hounslow - London

Network Diagram - see first Page of Table 148

		SW	SW	SW ■	SW	SW	SW	SW	SW ■	SW	SW ■	SW	SW	SW ■	SW	SW ■	SW	SW	SW	SW	SW	SW
Reading ■	d			09 39					09 53					10 09								
Earley	d			09 44					09 58					10 14								
Winnersh Triangle	d			09 46					10 00					10 16								
Winnersh	d			09 48					10 02					10 18								
Wokingham	d			09 53					10 07					10 23								
Bracknell	d			09 59					10 13					10 29								
Martins Heron	d			10 02					10 16					10 32								
Guildford	d										09 30					10 00						
Wanborough	d										09 36					10 06						
Ash ■	d										09 40					10 10						
Aldershot	a										09 47					10 17						
	d										10 00					10 30						
Ash Vale	d										10 04					10 34						
Frimley	d										10 10					10 40						
Camberley	a										10 14					10 44						
	d										10 18					10 48						
Bagshot	d										10 23					10 53						
Ascot ■	d			10 07					10 22		10a30			10 37		11a00						
Sunningdale	d			10 10					10 25					10 40								
Longcross	d																					
Woking	d																					
West Byfleet	d																					
Byfleet & New Haw	d																					
Weybridge	d						10 03											10 33				
Addlestone	d						10 07											10 37				
Chertsey	d						10 10											10 40				
Virginia Water	a			10 19			10 15		10 33					10 49				10 45				
	d			10 19			10 24		10 33					10 49				10 54				
Egham	d			10 23			10 27		10 36					10 53				10 57				
Windsor & Eton Riverside	d							10 21											10 51			
Datchet	d							10 25											10 55			
Sunnymeads	d							10 28											10 58			
Wraysbury	d							10 32											11 02			
Staines	d			10 29			10 33	10 38	10 44					10 59				11 03	11 08			
Ashford (Surrey)	d						10 36	10 41										11 06	11 11			
Feltham	d			10 35			10 41	10 46	10 50					11 05				11 11	11 16			
Whitton	d	10 20	10 26					10 50				10 50	10 56						11 20		11 20	11 23
Kingston	d					10 29											10 59					
Hampton Wick	d					10 31											11 01					
Teddington	d					10 35											11 05					
Fulwell	d																					
Strawberry Hill	d					10 38											11 08					
Twickenham	a		10 28	10 40		10 42		10 53	10 57				10 58	11 10			11 12		11 23			11 26
	d		10 28	10 41		10 43		10 53	10 57				10 58	11 11			11 13		11 23			11 28
St Margarets	d		10 30			10 45							11 00				11 15					11 30
Richmond ⊖	d		10 34	10 45		10 49		10 58	11 02				11 04	11 15			11 19		11 28			11 34
North Sheen	d		10 36			10 51							11 06				11 21					11 36
Mortlake	d		10 38			10 53							11 08				11 23					11 38
Hounslow	d	10 31					10 46					11 01						11 16			11 31	
Isleworth	d	10 34					10 49					11 04						11 19			11 34	
Syon Lane	d	10 36					10 51					11 06						11 21			11 36	
Brentford	d	10 39					10 54					11 09						11 24			11 39	
Kew Bridge	d	10 41					10 56					11 11						11 26			11 41	
Chiswick	d	10 44					10 59					11 14						11 29			11 44	
Barnes Bridge	d	10 46			←		11 01					11 16			←			11 31			11 46	
Barnes	d	10 49	10 41		10 49	10 56	11 04			←		11 19	11 11		11 19		11 26	11 34		←	11 49	11 41
Putney	d	→	10 44		10 52	10 59	11 07	11 04		11 07		→	11 14		11 22		11 29	11 37	11 34	11 37	→	11 44
Wandsworth Town	d		10 47		10 55	11 02	→			11 10			11 17		11 25		11 32	→		11 40		11 47
Clapham Junction ■	d		10 50	10 54	10 58	11 05		11 09	11 12	11 13			11 20	11 24	11 28		11 35		11 39	11 43		11 50
Queenstown Rd.(Battersea)	d		10 53		11 01	11 08				11 17			11 23		11 31		11 38			11 46		11 53
Vauxhall ⊖	d		10 57		11 05	11 12		11 15		11 20			11 27		11 35		11 42		11 45	11 50		11 57
London Waterloo ■ ⊖	a		11 02	11 04	11 11	11 16		11 19	11 25	11 27			11 32	11 34	11 41		11 46		11 49	11 56		12 02

Table 149

Mondays to Fridays
from 8 October

Reading, Guildford, Ascot, Weybridge, Windsor, Kingston, Richmond and Hounslow - London

Network Diagram - see first Page of Table 148

		SW ■	SW	SW ■	SW	SW	SW	SW	SW	SW	SW ■	SW	SW ■	SW	SW	SW	SW	SW	SW	SW ■	SW	SW ■	SW
Reading ■	d	10 39									11 09									11 39			
Earley	d	10 44									11 14									11 44			
Winnersh Triangle	d	10 46									11 16									11 46			
Winnersh	d	10 48									11 18									11 48			
Wokingham	d	10 53									11 23									11 53			
Bracknell	d	10 59									11 29									11 59			
Martins Heron	d	11 02									11 32									12 02			
Guildford	d			10 30									11 00									11 30	
Wanborough	d			10 36									11 06									11 36	
Ash ■	d			10 40									11 10									11 40	
Aldershot	a			10 47									11 17									11 47	
	d			11 00									11 30									12 00	
Ash Vale	d			11 04									11 34									12 04	
Frimley	d			11 10									11 40									12 10	
Camberley	a			11 14									11 44									12 14	
	d			11 18									11 48									12 18	
Bagshot	d			11 23									11 53									12 23	
Ascot ■	d	11 07		11a30							11 37		12a00							12 07		12a30	
Sunningdale	d	11 10									11 40									12 10			
Longcross	d																						
Woking	d																						
West Byfleet	d																						
Byfleet & New Haw	d																						
Weybridge	d					11 03									11 33								
Addlestone	d					11 07									11 37								
Chertsey	d					11 10									11 40								
Virginia Water	a	11 19				11 15					11 49				11 45					12 19			
	d	11 19				11 24					11 49				11 54					12 19			
Egham	d	11 23				11 27					11 53				11 57					12 23			
Windsor & Eton Riverside	d						11 21									11 51							
Datchet	d						11 25									11 55							
Sunnymeads	d						11 28									11 58							
Wraysbury	d						11 32									12 02							
Staines	d	11 29				11 33	11 38				11 59				12 03	12 08				12 29			
Ashford (Surrey)	d					11 36	11 41								12 06	12 11							
Feltham	d	11 35				11 41	11 46				12 05				12 11	12 16				12 35			
Whitton	d						11 50		11 50	11 53						12 20		12 20	12 23				
Kingston	d				11 29									11 59									12 29
Hampton Wick	d				11 31									12 01									12 31
Teddington	d				11 35									12 05									12 35
Fulwell	d																						
Strawberry Hill	d				11 38									12 08									12 38
Twickenham	a	11 40			11 42		11 53			11 56	12 10			12 12		12 23			12 26	12 40			12 42
	d	11 41			11 43		11 53			11 58	12 11			12 13		12 23			12 28	12 41			12 43
St Margarets	d				11 45					12 00				12 15					12 30				12 45
Richmond ⊖	d	11 45			11 49		11 58			12 04	12 15			12 19		12 28			12 34	12 45			12 49
North Sheen	d				11 51					12 06				12 21					12 36				12 51
Mortlake	d				11 53					12 08				12 23					12 38				12 53
Hounslow	d					11 46			12 01						12 16			12 31					
Isleworth	d					11 49			12 04						12 19			12 34					
Syon Lane	d					11 51			12 06						12 21			12 36					
Brentford	d					11 54			12 09						12 24			12 39					
Kew Bridge	d					11 56			12 11						12 26			12 41					
Chiswick	d					11 59			12 14						12 29			12 44					
Barnes Bridge	d		←			12 01			12 16			←			12 31			12 46			←		
Barnes	d		11 49		11 56	12 04		←	12 19	12 11		12 19		12 26	12 34		←	12 49	12 41		12 49		12 56
Putney	d		11 52		11 59	12 07	12 04	12 07	→	12 14		12 22		12 29	12 37	12 34	12 37	→	12 44		12 52		12 59
Wandsworth Town	d		11 55		12 02	→		12 10		12 17		12 25		12 32	→		12 40		12 47		12 55		13 02
Clapham Junction ■	d	11 54	11 58		12 05		12 09	12 13		12 20	12 25	12 28		12 35		12 39	12 43		12 50	12 54	12 58		13 05
Queenstown Rd.(Battersea)	d		12 01		12 08			12 16		12 23		12 31		12 38			12 46		12 53		13 01		13 08
Vauxhall ⊖	d		12 05		12 12		12 15	12 20		12 27		12 35		12 42		12 45	12 50		12 57		13 05		13 12
London Waterloo ■ ⊖	a	12 04	12 11		12 16		12 19	12 26		12 32	12 34	12 41		12 46		12 49	12 56		13 02	13 04	13 11		13 16

Table 149

Mondays to Fridays
from 8 October

Reading, Guildford, Ascot, Weybridge, Windsor, Kingston, Richmond and Hounslow - London

Network Diagram - see first Page of Table 148

		SW	SW	SW	SW	SW		SW [1]	SW	SW [1]	SW	SW	SW	SW	SW	SW		SW [1]	SW	SW [1]	SW	SW	SW	SW	SW
Reading [7]	d							12 09										12 39							
Earley	d							12 14										12 44							
Winnersh Triangle	d							12 16										12 46							
Winnersh	d							12 18										12 48							
Wokingham	d							12 23										12 53							
Bracknell	d							12 29										12 59							
Martins Heron	d							12 32										13 02							
Guildford	d									12 00										12 30					
Wanborough	d									12 06										12 36					
Ash [5]	d									12 10										12 40					
Aldershot	a									12 17										12 47					
	d									12 30										13 00					
Ash Vale	d									12 34										13 04					
Frimley	d									12 40										13 10					
Camberley	a									12 44										13 14					
	d									12 48										13 18					
Bagshot	d									12 53										13 23					
Ascot [3]	d							12 37		13a00								13 07		13a30					
Sunningdale	d							12 40										13 10							
Longcross	d																	13 13							
Woking	d																								
West Byfleet	d																								
Byfleet & New Haw	d																								
Weybridge	d	12 03										12 33										13 03			
Addlestone	d	12 07										12 37										13 07			
Chertsey	d	12 10										12 40										13 10			
Virginia Water	a	12 15						12 49				12 45						13 19				13 15			
	d	12 24						12 49				12 54						13 19				13 24			
Egham	d	12 27						12 53				12 57						13 23				13 27			
Windsor & Eton Riverside	d		12 21										12 51										13 21		
Datchet	d		12 25										12 55										13 25		
Sunnymeads	d		12 28										12 58										13 28		
Wraysbury	d		12 32										13 02										13 32		
Staines	d	12 33	12 38					12 59				13 03	13 08					13 29				13 33	13 38		
Ashford (Surrey)	d	12 36	12 41									13 06	13 11									13 36	13 41		
Feltham	d	12 41	12 46					13 05				13 11	13 16					13 35				13 41	13 46		
Whitton	d		12 50		12 50	12 53							13 20		13 20	13 23							13 50		13 50
Kingston	d										12 59										13 29				
Hampton Wick	d										13 01										13 31				
Teddington	d										13 05										13 35				
Fulwell	d																								
Strawberry Hill	d										13 08										13 38				
Twickenham	a		12 53			12 56		13 10			13 12		13 23			13 26		13 40			13 42		13 53		
	d		12 53			12 58		13 11			13 13		13 23			13 28		13 41			13 43		13 53		
St Margarets	d					13 00					13 15					13 30					13 45				
Richmond ⊖	d		12 58			13 04		13 15			13 19		13 28			13 34		13 45			13 49		13 58		
North Sheen	d					13 06					13 21					13 36					13 51				
Mortlake	d					13 08					13 23					13 38					13 53				
Hounslow	d	12 46			13 01							13 16			13 31							13 46			14 01
Isleworth	d	12 49			13 04							13 19			13 34							13 49			14 04
Syon Lane	d	12 51			13 06							13 21			13 36							13 51			14 06
Brentford	d	12 54			13 09							13 24			13 39							13 54			14 09
Kew Bridge	d	12 56			13 11							13 26			13 41							13 56			14 11
Chiswick	d	12 59			13 14							13 29			13 44							13 59			14 14
Barnes Bridge	d	13 01			13 16				←			13 31			13 46				←			14 01			14 16
Barnes	d	13 04		←	13 19	13 11			13 19		13 26	13 34		←	13 49	13 41			13 49		13 56	14 04		←	14 19
Putney	d	13 07	13 04	13 07	→	13 14			13 22		13 29	13 37	13 34	13 37	→	13 44			13 52		13 59	14 07	14 04	14 07	→
Wandsworth Town	d	→		13 10		13 17			13 25		13 32	→		13 40		13 47			13 55		14 02	→		14 10	
Clapham Junction [10]	d		13 09	13 13		13 20		13 24	13 28		13 35		13 39	13 43		13 50		13 54	13 58		14 05		14 09	14 13	
Queenstown Rd.(Battersea)	d			13 16		13 23			13 31		13 38			13 46		13 53			14 01		14 08			14 16	
Vauxhall ⊖	d		13 15	13 20		13 27			13 35		13 42		13 45	13 50		13 57			14 05		14 12		14 15	14 20	
London Waterloo [15] ⊖	a		13 19	13 26		13 32		13 34	13 41		13 46		13 49	13 56		14 02		14 04	14 11		14 16		14 19	14 26	

Table 149

Mondays to Fridays
from 8 October

Reading, Guildford, Ascot, Weybridge, Windsor, Kingston, Richmond and Hounslow - London

Network Diagram - see first Page of Table 148

		SW		SW [1]	SW	SW [1]	SW	SW	SW	SW	SW	SW		SW [1]	SW	SW [1]	SW	SW	SW	SW	SW	SW		SW [1]	SW
Reading [7]	d			13 09										13 39										14 09	
Earley	d			13 14										13 44										14 14	
Winnersh Triangle	d			13 16										13 46										14 16	
Winnersh	d			13 18										13 48										14 18	
Wokingham	d			13 23										13 53										14 23	
Bracknell	d			13 29										13 59										14 29	
Martins Heron	d			13 32										14 02										14 32	
Guildford	d					13 00										13 30									
Wanborough	d					13 06										13 36									
Ash [5]	d					13 10										13 40									
Aldershot	a					13 17										13 47									
	d					13 30										14 00									
Ash Vale	d					13 34										14 04									
Frimley	d					13 40										14 10									
Camberley	a					13 44										14 14									
	d					13 48										14 18									
Bagshot	d					13 53										14 23									
Ascot [3]	d			13 37		14a00								14 07		14a30								14 37	
Sunningdale	d			13 40										14 10										14 40	
Longcross	d																								
Woking	d																								
West Byfleet	d																								
Byfleet & New Haw	d																								
Weybridge	d							13 33										14 03							
Addlestone	d							13 37										14 07							
Chertsey	d							13 40										14 10							
Virginia Water	a			13 49				13 45						14 19				14 15						14 49	
	d			13 49				13 54						14 19				14 24						14 49	
Egham	d			13 53				13 57						14 23				14 27						14 53	
Windsor & Eton Riverside	d								13 51										14 21						
Datchet	d								13 55										14 25						
Sunnymeads	d								13 58										14 28						
Wraysbury	d								14 02										14 32						
Staines	d			13 59				14 03	14 08					14 29				14 33	14 38					14 59	
Ashford (Surrey)	d							14 06	14 11									14 36	14 41						
Feltham	d			14 05				14 11	14 16					14 35				14 41	14 46					15 05	
Whitton	d	13 53							14 20		14 20	14 23							14 50		14 50	14 53			
Kingston	d						13 59										14 29								
Hampton Wick	d						14 01										14 31								
Teddington	d						14 05										14 35								
Fulwell	d																								
Strawberry Hill	d						14 08										14 38								
Twickenham	a	13 56		14 10			14 12		14 23			14 26		14 40			14 42		14 53			14 56		15 10	
	d	13 58		14 11			14 13		14 23			14 28		14 41			14 43		14 53			14 58		15 11	
St Margarets	d	14 00					14 15					14 30					14 45					15 00			
Richmond ⊖	d	14 04		14 15			14 19		14 28			14 34		14 45			14 49		14 58			15 04		15 15	
North Sheen	d	14 06					14 21					14 36					14 51					15 06			
Mortlake	d	14 08					14 23					14 38					14 53					15 08			
Hounslow	d							14 16			14 31							14 46			15 01				
Isleworth	d							14 19			14 34							14 49			15 04				
Syon Lane	d							14 21			14 36							14 51			15 06				
Brentford	d							14 24			14 39							14 54			15 09				
Kew Bridge	d							14 26			14 41							14 56			15 11				
Chiswick	d							14 29			14 44							14 59			15 14				
Barnes Bridge	d				←			14 31			14 46				←			15 01			15 16				←
Barnes	d	14 11			14 19		14 26	14 34		←	14 49	14 41			14 49		14 56	15 04		←	15 19	15 11			15 19
Putney	d	14 14			14 22		14 29	14 37	14 34	14 37	→	14 44			14 52		14 59	15 07	15 04	15 07	→	15 14			15 22
Wandsworth Town	d	14 17			14 25		14 32	→		14 40		14 47			14 55		15 02	→		15 10		15 17			15 25
Clapham Junction [10]	d	14 20		14 24	14 28		14 35		14 39	14 43		14 50		14 54	14 58		15 05		15 09	15 13		15 20		15 24	15 28
Queenstown Rd.(Battersea)	d	14 23			14 31		14 38			14 46		14 53			15 01		15 08			15 16		15 23			15 31
Vauxhall ⊖	d	14 27			14 35		14 42		14 45	14 50		14 57			15 05		15 12		15 15	15 20		15 27			15 35
London Waterloo [15] ⊖	a	14 32		14 34	14 41		14 46		14 49	14 56		15 02		15 04	15 11		15 16		15 19	15 26		15 32		15 34	15 41

Table 149

Mondays to Fridays
from 8 October

Reading, Guildford, Ascot, Weybridge, Windsor, Kingston, Richmond and Hounslow - London

Network Diagram - see first Page of Table 148

		SW [1]	SW	SW	SW	SW	SW	SW		SW [1]	SW	SW [1]	SW	SW	SW	SW	SW	SW		SW [1]	SW	SW [1]	SW	SW	SW
Reading [7]	d									14 39										15 09					
Earley	d									14 44										15 14					
Winnersh Triangle	d									14 46										15 16					
Winnersh	d									14 48										15 18					
Wokingham	d									14 53										15 23					
Bracknell	d									14 59										15 29					
Martins Heron	d									15 02										15 32					
Guildford	d	14 00										14 30										15 00			
Wanborough	d	14 06										14 36										15 06			
Ash [6]	d	14 10										14 40										15 10			
Aldershot	a	14 17										14 47										15 17			
	d	14 30										15 00										15 30			
Ash Vale	d	14 34										15 04										15 34			
Frimley	d	14 40										15 10										15 40			
Camberley	a	14 44										15 14										15 44			
	d	14 48										15 18										15 48			
Bagshot	d	14 53										15 23										15 53			
Ascot [3]	d	15a00								15 07		15a30								15 37		16a00			
Sunningdale	d									15 10										15 40					
Longcross	d																								
Woking	d																								
West Byfleet	d																								
Byfleet & New Haw	d																								
Weybridge	d			14 33										15 03										15 33	
Addlestone	d			14 37										15 07										15 37	
Chertsey	d			14 40										15 10										15 40	
Virginia Water	a			14 45						15 19				15 15						15 49				15 45	
	d			14 54						15 19				15 24						15 49				15 54	
Egham	d			14 57						15 23				15 27						15 53				15 57	
Windsor & Eton Riverside	d				14 51										15 21										15 51
Datchet	d				14 55										15 25										15 55
Sunnymeads	d				14 58										15 28										15 58
Wraysbury	d				15 02										15 32										16 02
Staines	d			15 03	15 08					15 29				15 33	15 38					15 59				16 03	16 08
Ashford (Surrey)	d			15 06	15 11									15 36	15 41									16 06	16 11
Feltham	d			15 11	15 16					15 35				15 41	15 46					16 05				16 11	16 16
Whitton	d				15 20		15 20	15 23							15 50		15 50	15 53							16 20
Kingston	d		14 59										15 29										15 59		
Hampton Wick	d		15 01										15 31										16 01		
Teddington	d		15 05										15 35										16 05		
Fulwell	d																								
Strawberry Hill	d		15 08										15 38										16 08		
Twickenham	a		15 12		15 23			15 26		15 40			15 42		15 53			15 56		16 10			16 12		16 23
	d		15 13		15 23			15 28		15 41			15 43		15 53			15 58		16 11			16 13		16 23
St Margarets	d		15 15					15 30					15 45					16 00					16 15		
Richmond ⊖	d		15 19		15 28			15 34		15 45			15 49		15 58			16 04		16 15			16 19		16 28
North Sheen	d		15 21					15 36					15 51					16 06					16 21		
Mortlake	d		15 23					15 38					15 53					16 08					16 23		
Hounslow	d			15 16			15 31							15 46			16 01							16 16	
Isleworth	d			15 19			15 34							15 49			16 04							16 19	
Syon Lane	d			15 21			15 36							15 51			16 06							16 21	
Brentford	d			15 24			15 39							15 54			16 09							16 24	
Kew Bridge	d			15 26			15 41							15 56			16 11							16 26	
Chiswick	d			15 29			15 44							15 59			16 14							16 29	
Barnes Bridge	d			15 31			15 46				←			16 01			16 16				←			16 31	
Barnes	d		15 26	15 34		←	15 49	15 41			15 49		15 56	16 04		←	16 19	16 11			16 19		16 26	16 34	
Putney	d		15 29	15 37	15 34	15 37	→	15 44			15 52		15 59	16 07	16 04	16 07	→	16 14			16 22		16 29	16 37	16 34
Wandsworth Town	d		15 32	→		15 40		15 47			15 55		16 02	→		16 10		16 17			16 25		16 32	→	
Clapham Junction [10]	d		15 35		15 39	15 43		15 50		15 54	15 58		16 05		16 09	16 13		16 20		16 24	16 28		16 35		16 39
Queenstown Rd.(Battersea)	d		15 38			15 46		15 53			16 01		16 08			16 16		16 23			16 31		16 38		
Vauxhall ⊖	d		15 42		15 45	15 50		15 57			16 05		16 12		16 15	16 20		16 27			16 35		16 42		16 45
London Waterloo [15] ⊖	a		15 46		15 49	15 56		16 02		16 05	16 11		16 19		16 19	16 26		16 32		16 34	16 41		16 49		16 49

Table 149

Mondays to Fridays
from 8 October

Reading, Guildford, Ascot, Weybridge, Windsor, Kingston, Richmond and Hounslow - London

Network Diagram - see first Page of Table 148

		SW	SW	SW		SW [1]	SW	SW [1]	SW	SW	SW	SW	SW	SW		SW [1]	SW	SW [1]	SW	SW	SW	SW	SW	SW
Reading [7]	d					15 39										16 09								
Earley	d					15 44										16 14								
Winnersh Triangle	d					15 46										16 16								
Winnersh	d					15 48										16 18								
Wokingham	d					15 53										16 23								
Bracknell	d					15 59										16 29								
Martins Heron	d					16 02										16 32								
Guildford	d							15 30										16 00						
Wanborough	d							15 36										16 06						
Ash [6]	d							15 40										16 10						
Aldershot	a							15 47										16 17						
	d							16 00										16 30						
Ash Vale	d							16 04										16 34						
Frimley	d							16 10										16 40						
Camberley	a							16 14										16 44						
	d							16 18										16 48						
Bagshot	d							16 23										16 53						
Ascot [3]	d					16 07		16a30								16 37		17a00						
Sunningdale	d					16 10										16 40								
Longcross	d																							
Woking	d																							
West Byfleet	d																							
Byfleet & New Haw	d																							
Weybridge	d									16 03										16 33				
Addlestone	d									16 07										16 37				
Chertsey	d									16 10										16 40				
Virginia Water	a					16 19				16 15						16 49				16 45				
	d					16 19				16 24						16 49				16 54				
Egham	d					16 23				16 27						16 53				16 57				
Windsor & Eton Riverside	d										16 21										16 51			
Datchet	d										16 25										16 55			
Sunnymeads	d										16 28										16 58			
Wraysbury	d										16 32										17 02			
Staines	d					16 29				16 33	16 38					16 59				17 03	17 08			
Ashford (Surrey)	d									16 36	16 41									17 06	17 11			
Feltham	d					16 35				16 41	16 46					17 05				17 11	17 16			
Whitton	d		16 20	16 23							16 50		16 50	16 53							17 20		17 20	17 23
Kingston	d								16 29										16 59					
Hampton Wick	d								16 31										17 01					
Teddington	d								16 35										17 05					
Fulwell	d																							
Strawberry Hill	d								16 38										17 08					
Twickenham	a			16 26		16 40			16 42		16 53			16 56		17 10			17 12		17 23			17 26
	d			16 28		16 41			16 43		16 53			16 58		17 11			17 13		17 23			17 28
St Margarets	d			16 30					16 45					17 00					17 15					17 30
Richmond ⊖	d			16 34		16 45			16 49		16 58			17 04		17 15			17 19		17 28			17 34
North Sheen	d			16 36					16 51					17 06					17 21					17 36
Mortlake	d			16 38					16 53					17 08					17 23					17 38
Hounslow	d		16 31							16 46			17 01							17 16			17 31	
Isleworth	d		16 34							16 49			17 04							17 19			17 34	
Syon Lane	d		16 36							16 51			17 06							17 21			17 36	
Brentford	d		16 39							16 54			17 09							17 24			17 39	
Kew Bridge	d		16 41							16 56			17 11							17 26			17 41	
Chiswick	d		16 44							16 59			17 14							17 29			17 44	
Barnes Bridge	d		16 46				←			17 01			17 16				←			17 31			17 46	
Barnes	d	←	16 49	16 41			16 49		16 56	17 04		←	17 19	17 11			17 19		17 26	17 34		←	17 49	17 41
Putney	d	16 37	→	16 44			16 52		16 59	17 07	17 05	17 07	→	17 14			17 22		17 29	17 37	17 34	17 37	→	17 44
Wandsworth Town	d	16 40		16 47			16 55		17 02	→		17 10		17 17			17 25		17 32	→		17 40		17 47
Clapham Junction [10]	d	16 43		16 50		16 54	16 58		17 05		17 09	17 13		17 20		17 24	17 28		17 35		17 39	17 43		17 50
Queenstown Rd.(Battersea)	d	16 46		16 53			17 01		17 08			17 16		17 23			17 31		17 38			17 46		17 53
Vauxhall ⊖	d	16 50		16 57			17 05		17 12		17 15	17 20		17 27			17 35		17 42		17 45	17 50		17 57
London Waterloo [15] ⊖	a	16 56		17 02		17 04	17 11		17 19		17 19	17 26		17 32		17 33	17 41		17 49		17 49	17 56		18 02

Table 149

Mondays to Fridays
from 8 October

Reading, Guildford, Ascot, Weybridge, Windsor, Kingston, Richmond and Hounslow - London

Network Diagram - see first Page of Table 148

Station		SW ■	SW	SW ■	SW	SW	SW	SW	SW	SW		SW ■	SW	SW	SW	SW	SW	SW ■	SW ■	SW		SW	SW ■	SW	SW
Reading ■	d	16 41										17 09						17 22					17 39		
Earley	d	16 46										17 14						17 27					17 44		
Winnersh Triangle	d	16 48										17 16						17 29					17 46		
Winnersh	d	16 50										17 18						17 31					17 48		
Wokingham	d	16 55										17 23						17 36					17 53		
Bracknell	d	17 01										17 29						17 42					17 59		
Martins Heron	d	17 04										17 32						17 45					18 02		
Guildford	d			16 30															17 00						
Wanborough	d			16 36															17 06						
Ash ■	d			16 40															17 10						
Aldershot	a			16 47															17 17						
	d			17 00															17 30						
Ash Vale	d			17 04															17 34						
Frimley	d			17 10															17 40						
Camberley	a			17 14															17 44						
	d			17 18															17 48						
Bagshot	d			17 23															17 53						
Ascot ■	d	17 09		17a30								17 37						17 55	18a00				18 07		
Sunningdale	d	17 12										17 40						17 58					18 10		
Longcross	d	17 15																					18 13		
Woking	d																								
West Byfleet	d																								
Byfleet & New Haw	d																								
Weybridge	d					17 03									17 37										
Addlestone	d					17 07									17 41										
Chertsey	d					17 10									17 44										
Virginia Water	a	17 19				17 15						17 49			17 49			18 03					18 19		
	d	17 19				17 24						17 49			17 54			18 03					18 19		
Egham	d	17 23				17 27						17 53			17 57			18 06					18 23		
Windsor & Eton Riverside	d						17 21									17 51									
Datchet	d						17 25									17 55									
Sunnymeads	d						17 28									17 58									
Wraysbury	d						17 32									18 02									
Staines	d	17 29				17 33	17 38					17 59			18 03	18 08		18 14					18 29		
Ashford (Surrey)	d					17 36	17 41								18 06	18 11									
Feltham	d	17 35				17 41	17 46					18 05			18 11	18 16		18 20					18 35		
Whitton	d						17 50		17 50	17 53						18 20				18 20		18 23			
Kingston	d				17 29									17 59											18 29
Hampton Wick	d				17 31									18 01											18 31
Teddington	d				17 35									18 05											18 35
Fulwell	d																								
Strawberry Hill	d				17 38									18 08											18 38
Twickenham	a	17 40			17 42		17 53			17 56		18 10		18 12		18 23						18 26	18 40		18 42
	d	17 41			17 43		17 53			17 58		18 11		18 13		18 23						18 28	18 41		18 43
St Margarets	d				17 45					18 00				18 15								18 30			18 45
Richmond ⊖	d	17 45			17 49		17 58			18 04		18 15		18 19		18 28						18 34	18 45		18 49
North Sheen	d				17 51					18 06				18 21								18 36			18 51
Mortlake	d				17 53					18 08				18 23								18 38			18 53
Hounslow	d					17 46			18 01						18 16			18 26		18 31					
Isleworth	d					17 49			18 04						18 19					18 34					
Syon Lane	d					17 51			18 06						18 21					18 36					
Brentford	d					17 54			18 09						18 24			18 31		18 39					
Kew Bridge	d					17 56			18 11						18 26					18 41					
Chiswick	d					17 59			18 14						18 29					18 44					
Barnes Bridge	d		←			18 01			18 16				←		18 31					18 46				←	
Barnes	d		17 49		17 56	18 04		←	18 19	18 11			18 19	18 26	18 34		←			18 49		18 41		18 49	18 56
Putney	d		17 52		17 59	18 07	18 04	18 07	→	18 14			18 22	18 29	18 37	18 34	18 37	18 39		→		18 44		18 52	18 59
Wandsworth Town	d		17 55		18 02	→		18 10		18 17			18 25	18 32	→		18 40					18 47		18 55	19 02
Clapham Junction ■	d	17 54	17 58		18 05		18 09	18 13		18 20		18 24	18 28	18 35		18 39	18 43	18 44				18 50	18 54	18 58	19 05
Queenstown Rd.(Battersea)	d		18 01		18 08			18 16		18 23			18 31	18 38			18 46					18 53		19 01	19 08
Vauxhall ⊖	d		18 05		18 12		18 15	18 20		18 27			18 35	18 42		18 45	18 50					18 57		19 05	19 12
London Waterloo ■ ⊖	a	18 04	18 11		18 19		18 19	18 26		18 32		18 34	18 41	18 49		18 49	18 56	18 56				19 02	19 04	19 11	19 16

Table 149

Mondays to Fridays
from 8 October

Reading, Guildford, Ascot, Weybridge, Windsor, Kingston, Richmond and Hounslow - London

Network Diagram - see first Page of Table 148

Station		SW	SW	SW	SW ■	SW ■		SW	SW	SW ■	SW	SW ■	SW	SW	SW	SW		SW	SW	SW ■	SW	SW ■	SW ■	SW	SW
Reading ■	d				17 53					18 09										18 39		18 52			
Earley	d				17 58					18 14										18 44		18 57			
Winnersh Triangle	d				18 00					18 16										18 46		18 59			
Winnersh	d				18 02					18 18										18 48		19 01			
Wokingham	d				18 07					18 23										18 53		19 06			
Bracknell	d				18 13					18 29										18 59		19 12			
Martins Heron	d				18 16					18 32										19 02		19 15			
Guildford	d					17 30						18 00											18 30		
Wanborough	d					17 36						18 06											18 36		
Ash ■	d					17 40						18 10											18 40		
Aldershot	a					17 47						18 17											18 47		
	d					18 00						18 30											19 00		
Ash Vale	d					18 04						18 34											19 04		
Frimley	d					18 10						18 40											19 10		
Camberley	a					18 14						18 44											19 14		
	d					18 18						18 48											19 18		
Bagshot	d					18 23						18 53											19 23		
Ascot ■	d				18 25	18a30				18 37		19a00								19 07		19a19	19a30		
Sunningdale	d				18 28					18 40										19 10					
Longcross	d									18 43										19 13					
Woking	d																								
West Byfleet	d																								
Byfleet & New Haw	d																								
Weybridge	d	18 07												18 37											19 07
Addlestone	d	18 11												18 41											19 11
Chertsey	d	18 14												18 44											19 14
Virginia Water	a	18 19			18 33					18 49				18 49						19 19					19 19
	d	18 24			18 33					18 49				18 54						19 19					19 24
Egham	d	18 27			18 37					18 53				18 57						19 23					19 27
Windsor & Eton Riverside	d		18 21												18 51										
Datchet	d		18 25												18 55										
Sunnymeads	d		18 28												18 58										
Wraysbury	d		18 32												19 02										
Staines	d	18 33	18 38		18 44					18 59				19 03	19 08					19 29					19 33
Ashford (Surrey)	d	18 36	18 41											19 06	19 11										19 36
Feltham	d	18 41	18 46		18 50					19 05				19 11	19 16					19 35					19 41
Whitton	d		18 50					18 50	18 53						19 20			19 20	19 23						
Kingston	d												18 59											19 29	
Hampton Wick	d												19 01											19 31	
Teddington	d												19 05											19 35	
Fulwell	d																								
Strawberry Hill	d												19 08											19 38	
Twickenham	a		18 53						18 56	19 10			19 12		19 23				19 26	19 40				19 42	
	d		18 53						18 58	19 11			19 13		19 23				19 28	19 41				19 43	
St Margarets	d								19 00				19 15						19 30					19 45	
Richmond ⊖	d		18 58						19 04	19 15			19 19		19 28				19 34	19 45				19 49	
North Sheen	d								19 06				19 21						19 36					19 51	
Mortlake	d								19 08				19 23						19 38					19 53	
Hounslow	d	18 46			18 56			19 01						19 16				19 31							19 46
Isleworth	d	18 49						19 04						19 19				19 34							19 49
Syon Lane	d	18 51						19 06						19 21				19 36							19 51
Brentford	d	18 54			19 01			19 09						19 24				19 39							19 54
Kew Bridge	d	18 56						19 11						19 26				19 41							19 56
Chiswick	d	18 59						19 14						19 29				19 44							19 59
Barnes Bridge	d	19 01						19 16			←			19 31				19 46			←				20 01
Barnes	d	19 04		←				19 19	19 11		19 19		19 26	19 34		←		19 49	19 41		19 49			19 56	20 04
Putney	d	19 07	19 04	19 07	19 09			→	19 14		19 22		19 29	19 37	19 34	19 37		→	19 44		19 52			19 59	20 07
Wandsworth Town	d	→		19 10					19 17		19 25		19 32	→		19 40			19 47		19 55			20 02	→
Clapham Junction ■	d		19 09	19 13	19 14				19 20	19 24	19 28		19 35		19 39	19 43			19 50	19 54	19 58			20 05	
Queenstown Rd.(Battersea)	d			19 16					19 23		19 31		19 38			19 46			19 53		20 01			20 08	
Vauxhall ⊖	d		19 15	19 20					19 27		19 35		19 42		19 45	19 50			19 57		20 05			20 12	
London Waterloo ■ ⊖	a		19 19	19 26	19 28				19 32	19 34	19 41		19 46		19 49	19 56			20 02	20 04	20 09			20 16	

from 8 October

Reading, Guildford, Ascot, Weybridge, Windsor, Kingston, Richmond and Hounslow - London

Network Diagram - see first Page of Table 148

		SW		SW	SW	SW	SW 1	SW	SW 1	SW	SW	SW		SW	SW	SW	SW 1	SW	SW 1	SW	SW	SW		SW	SW
Reading 7	d						19 09										19 39								
Earley	d						19 14										19 44								
Winnersh Triangle	d						19 16										19 46								
Winnersh	d						19 18										19 48								
Wokingham	d						19 23										19 53								
Bracknell	d						19 29										19 59								
Martins Heron	d						19 32										20 02								
Guildford	d								19 00										19 30						
Wanborough	d								19 06										19 36						
Ash 5	d								19 10										19 40						
Aldershot	a								19 17										19 47						
	d								19 30										20 00						
Ash Vale	d								19 34										20 04						
Frimley	d								19 40										20 10						
Camberley	a								19 44										20 14						
	d								19 48										20 18						
Bagshot	d								19 53										20 23						
Ascot 3	d						19 37		20a00								20 07		20a30						
Sunningdale	d						19 40										20 10								
Longcross	d						19 43										20 13								
Woking	d																								
West Byfleet	d																								
Byfleet & New Haw	d																								
Weybridge	d										19 37										20 03				
Addlestone	d										19 41										20 07				
Chertsey	d										19 44										20 10				
Virginia Water	a						19 49				19 49						20 19				20 15				
	d						19 49				19 54						20 19				20 24				
Egham	d						19 53				19 57						20 23				20 27				
Windsor & Eton Riverside	d	19 21										19 51										20 21			
Datchet	d	19 25										19 55										20 25			
Sunnymeads	d	19 28										19 58										20 28			
Wraysbury	d	19 32										20 02										20 32			
Staines	d	19 38					19 59				20 03	20 08					20 29				20 33	20 38			
Ashford (Surrey)	d	19 41									20 06	20 11									20 36	20 41			
Feltham	d	19 46					20 05				20 11	20 16					20 35				20 41	20 46			
Whitton	d	19 50			19 50	19 53						20 20			20 20	20 23						20 50			20 50
Kingston	d									19 59										20 29					
Hampton Wick	d									20 01										20 31					
Teddington	d									20 05										20 35					
Fulwell	d																								
Strawberry Hill	d									20 08										20 38					
Twickenham	a	19 53				19 56	20 10			20 12		20 23				20 26	20 40			20 42		20 53			
	d	19 53				19 58	20 11			20 13		20 23				20 28	20 41			20 43		20 53			
St Margarets	d					20 00				20 15						20 30				20 45					
Richmond ⊖	d	19 58				20 04	20 15			20 19		20 28				20 34	20 45			20 49		20 58			
North Sheen	d					20 06				20 21						20 36				20 51					
Mortlake	d					20 08				20 23						20 38				20 53					
Hounslow	d				20 01						20 16				20 31						20 46				21 01
Isleworth	d				20 04						20 19				20 34						20 49				21 04
Syon Lane	d				20 06						20 21				20 36						20 51				21 06
Brentford	d				20 09						20 24				20 39						20 54				21 09
Kew Bridge	d				20 11						20 26				20 41						20 56				21 11
Chiswick	d				20 14						20 29				20 44						20 59				21 14
Barnes Bridge	d				20 16			←			20 31				20 46			←			21 01				21 16
Barnes	d			←	20 19	20 11		20 19		20 26	20 34			←	20 49	20 41		20 49		20 56	21 04			←	21 19
Putney	d	20 04		20 07	→	20 14		20 22		20 29	20 37	20 34		20 37	→	20 44		20 52		20 59	21 07	21 04		21 07	→
Wandsworth Town	d			20 10		20 17		20 25		20 32	→			20 40		20 47		20 55		21 02	→			21 10	
Clapham Junction 10	d	20 09		20 13		20 20	20 24	20 28		20 35		20 39		20 43		20 50	20 54	20 58		21 05		21 09		21 13	
Queenstown Rd.(Battersea)	d			20 16		20 23		20 31		20 38				20 46		20 53		21 01		21 08				21 16	
Vauxhall ⊖	d	20 15		20 20		20 27		20 35		20 42		20 45		20 50		20 57		21 05		21 12		21 15		21 20	
London Waterloo 15 ⊖	a	20 19		20 26		20 32	20 34	20 41		20 46		20 49		20 56		21 02	21 04	21 11		21 16		21 19		21 26	

from 8 October

Reading, Guildford, Ascot, Weybridge, Windsor, Kingston, Richmond and Hounslow - London

Network Diagram - see first Page of Table 148

		SW	SW 1	SW	SW 1	SW 1	SW	SW		SW	SW	SW	SW	SW 1	SW	SW	SW	SW		SW	SW	SW	SW 1	SW	SW 1
Reading 7	d		20 09											20 39									21 09		
Earley	d		20 14											20 44									21 14		
Winnersh Triangle	d		20 16											20 46									21 16		
Winnersh	d		20 18											20 48									21 18		
Wokingham	d		20 23											20 53									21 23		
Bracknell	d		20 29											20 59									21 29		
Martins Heron	d		20 32											21 02									21 32		
Guildford	d				20 00	20 30																			21 00
Wanborough	d				20 06	20 36																			21 06
Ash 5	d				20 10	20 40																			21 10
Aldershot	a				20 17	20 47																			21 17
	d				20 30																				21 30
Ash Vale	d				20 34																				21 34
Frimley	d				20 40																				21 40
Camberley	a				20 44																				21 44
	d				20 48																				21 48
Bagshot	d				20 53																				21 53
Ascot 3	d		20 37		21a00									21 07									21 37		22a00
Sunningdale	d		20 40											21 10									21 40		
Longcross	d		20 43																						
Woking	d																								
West Byfleet	d																								
Byfleet & New Haw	d																								
Weybridge	d							20 33									21 03								
Addlestone	d							20 37									21 07								
Chertsey	d							20 40									21 10								
Virginia Water	a		20 49					20 45						21 19			21 15						21 49		
	d		20 49					20 54						21 19			21 24						21 49		
Egham	d		20 53					20 57						21 23			21 27						21 53		
Windsor & Eton Riverside	d									20 51								21 21							
Datchet	d									20 55								21 25							
Sunnymeads	d									20 58								21 28							
Wraysbury	d									21 02								21 32							
Staines	d		20 59					21 03		21 08				21 29			21 33	21 38					21 59		
Ashford (Surrey)	d							21 06		21 11							21 36	21 41							
Feltham	d		21 05					21 11		21 16				21 35			21 41	21 46					22 05		
Whitton	d	20 53								21 20		21 20	21 23					21 50			21 50	21 53			
Kingston	d						20 59									21 29									
Hampton Wick	d						21 01									21 31									
Teddington	d						21 05									21 35									
Fulwell	d																								
Strawberry Hill	d						21 08									21 38									
Twickenham	a	20 56	21 10				21 12			21 23			21 26	21 40		21 42		21 53				21 56	22 10		
	d	20 58	21 11				21 13			21 23			21 28	21 41		21 43		21 53				21 58	22 11		
St Margarets	d	21 00					21 15						21 30			21 45						22 00			
Richmond ⊖	d	21 04	21 15				21 19			21 28			21 34	21 45		21 49		21 58				22 04	22 15		
North Sheen	d	21 06					21 21						21 36			21 51						22 06			
Mortlake	d	21 08					21 23						21 38			21 53						22 08			
Hounslow	d							21 16				21 31					21 46				22 01				
Isleworth	d							21 19				21 34					21 49				22 04				
Syon Lane	d							21 21				21 36					21 51				22 06				
Brentford	d							21 24				21 39					21 54				22 09				
Kew Bridge	d							21 26				21 41					21 56				22 11				
Chiswick	d							21 29				21 44					21 59				22 14				
Barnes Bridge	d			←				21 31				21 46			←		22 01				22 16			←	
Barnes	d	21 11		21 19			21 26	21 34			←	21 49	21 41		21 49	21 56	22 04			←	22 19	22 11		22 19	
Putney	d	21 14		21 22			21 29	21 37		21 34	21 37	→	21 44		21 52	21 59	22 07	22 04		22 07	→	22 14		22 22	
Wandsworth Town	d	21 17		21 25			21 32	→			21 40		21 47		21 55	22 02	→			22 10		22 17		22 25	
Clapham Junction 10	d	21 20	21 24	21 28			21 35			21 39	21 43		21 50	21 54	21 58	22 05		22 09		22 13		22 20	22 24	22 28	
Queenstown Rd.(Battersea)	d	21 23		21 31			21 38				21 46		21 53		22 01	22 08				22 16		22 23		22 31	
Vauxhall ⊖	d	21 27		21 35			21 42			21 45	21 50		21 57		22 05	22 12		22 15		22 20		22 27		22 35	
London Waterloo 15 ⊖	a	21 32	21 34	21 41			21 46			21 49	21 56		22 02	22 04	22 11	22 16		22 19		22 26		22 32	22 34	22 41	

Table 149

Mondays to Fridays
from 8 October

Reading, Guildford, Ascot, Weybridge, Windsor, Kingston, Richmond and Hounslow - London

Network Diagram - see first Page of Table 148

		SW ■	SW	SW		SW	SW	SW	SW ■	SW	SW	SW	SW	SW ■		SW ■	SW ■	SW	SW	SW	SW	SW ■	SW	SW
Reading 7	d								21 39					22 09								22 39		
Earley	d								21 44					22 14								22 44		
Winnersh Triangle	d								21 46					22 16								22 46		
Winnersh	d								21 48					22 18								22 48		
Wokingham	d								21 53					22 23								22 53		
Bracknell	d								21 59					22 29								22 59		
Martins Heron	d								22 02					22 32								23 02		
Guildford	d	21 30														22 00	22 30							
Wanborough	d	21 36														22 06	22 36							
Ash 5	d	21 40														22 10	22 40							
Aldershot	a	21 47														22 17	22 47							
	d															22 30								
Ash Vale	d															22 34								
Frimley	d															22 40								
Camberley	a															22 44								
	d															22 48								
Bagshot	d															22 53								
Ascot 3	d								22 07					22 37		23a00						23 07		
Sunningdale	d								22 10					22 40								23 10		
Longcross	d																							
Woking	d																							
West Byfleet	d																							
Byfleet & New Haw	d																							
Weybridge	d			21 33							22 03								22 33				23 03	
Addlestone	d			21 37							22 07								22 37				23 07	
Chertsey	d			21 40							22 10								22 40				23 10	
Virginia Water	a			21 45					22 19		22 15			22 49					22 45			23 19	23 15	
	d			21 54					22 19		22 24			22 49					22 54			23 19	23 24	
Egham	d			21 57					22 23		22 27			22 53					22 57			23 23	23 27	
Windsor & Eton Riverside	d					21 51						22 21								22 53				23 28
Datchet	d					21 55						22 25								22 56				23 31
Sunnymeads	d					21 58						22 28								22 59				23 34
Wraysbury	d					22 02						22 32								23 02				23 37
Staines	d			22 03		22 08			22 29		22 33	22 38		22 59					23 03	23 08		23 29	23a32	23a42
Ashford (Surrey)	d			22 06		22 11					22 36	22 41							23 06	23 11				
Feltham	d			22 11		22 16			22 35		22 41	22 46		23 05					23 11	23 16		23 35		
Whitton	d					22 20		22 23				22 50								23 20				
Kingston	d		21 59							22 29								22 59						
Hampton Wick	d		22 01							22 31								23 01						
Teddington	d		22 05							22 35								23 05						
Fulwell	d																							
Strawberry Hill	d		22 08							22 38								23 08						
Twickenham	a		22 12			22 23		22 26	22 40	22 42		22 53		23 10				23 12		23 23		23 40		
	d		22 13			22 23		22 28	22 41	22 43		22 53		23 11				23 13		23 23		23 41		
St Margarets	d		22 15					22 30		22 45								23 15						
Richmond ⊖	d		22 19			22 28		22 34	22 45	22 49		22 58		23 15				23 19		23 28		23 45		
North Sheen	d		22 21					22 36		22 51								23 21						
Mortlake	d		22 23					22 38		22 53								23 23						
Hounslow	d			22 16							22 46								23 16					
Isleworth	d			22 19							22 49								23 19					
Syon Lane	d			22 21							22 51								23 21					
Brentford	d			22 24							22 54								23 24					
Kew Bridge	d			22 26							22 56								23 26					
Chiswick	d			22 29							22 59								23 29					
Barnes Bridge	d			22 31							23 01								23 31					
Barnes	d		22 26	22 34			←	22 41		22 56	23 04		←					23 26	23 34		←			
Putney	d		22 29	22 37		22 34	22 37	22 44		22 59	23 07	23 04	23 07					23 29	23 37	23 34	23 37			
Wandsworth Town	d		22 32	→			22 40	22 47		23 02	→		23 10					23 32	→		23 40			
Clapham Junction 10	d		22 35			22 39	22 43	22 50	22 54	23 05		23 09	23 13	23 24				23 35		23 39	23 43	23 54		
Queenstown Rd.(Battersea)	d		22 38				22 46	22 53		23 08			23 16					23 38			23 46			
Vauxhall ⊖	d		22 42			22 45	22 50	22 57		23 12		23 15	23 20					23 42		23 45	23 50			
London Waterloo 15 ⊖	a		22 46			22 49	22 56	23 02	23 04	23 16		23 19	23 26	23 34				23 46		23 49	23 56	00 04		

Table 149

Mondays to Fridays
from 8 October

Reading, Guildford, Ascot, Weybridge, Windsor, Kingston, Richmond and Hounslow - London

Network Diagram - see first Page of Table 148

		SW	SW	SW ■	SW ■	SW ■	SW
Reading 7	d			23 12			
Earley	d			23 17			
Winnersh Triangle	d			23 19			
Winnersh	d			23 21			
Wokingham	d			23 26			
Bracknell	d			23 32			
Martins Heron	d			23 35			
Guildford	d				23 00	23 30	
Wanborough	d				23 06	23 36	
Ash 5	d				23 10	23 40	
Aldershot	a				23 17	23 47	
	d				23 30		
Ash Vale	d				23 34		
Frimley	d				23 40		
Camberley	a				23 44		
	d				23 48		
Bagshot	d				23 53		
Ascot 3	d			23 40	00a01		
Sunningdale	d			23 43			
Longcross	d						
Woking	d						
West Byfleet	d						
Byfleet & New Haw	d						
Weybridge	d						23 33
Addlestone	d						23 37
Chertsey	d						23 40
Virginia Water	a			23 49			23 45
	d			23 49			23 54
Egham	d			23 53			23 57
Windsor & Eton Riverside	d						
Datchet	d						
Sunnymeads	d						
Wraysbury	d						
Staines	d			23 59			00a02
Ashford (Surrey)	d						
Feltham	d			00 05			
Whitton	d						
Kingston	d	23 29	23 55				
Hampton Wick	d	23 31	23 57				
Teddington	d	23 35	23 59				
Fulwell	d						
Strawberry Hill	d	23 38	00 03				
Twickenham	a	23 42	00 07	00 10			
	d	23 43		00 11			
St Margarets	d	23 45					
Richmond ⊖	d	23 49		00 15			
North Sheen	d	23 51					
Mortlake	d	23 53					
Hounslow	d						
Isleworth	d						
Syon Lane	d						
Brentford	d						
Kew Bridge	d						
Chiswick	d						
Barnes Bridge	d						
Barnes	d	23 56					
Putney	d	23 59					
Wandsworth Town	d	00 02					
Clapham Junction 10	d	00 05		00 24			
Queenstown Rd.(Battersea)	d	00 08					
Vauxhall ⊖	d	00 12					
London Waterloo 15 ⊖	a	00 16		00 37			

Reading, Guildford, Ascot, Weybridge, Windsor, Kingston, Richmond and Hounslow - London

Network Diagram - see first Page of Table 148

		SW ■	SW	SW	SW ■	SW	SW	SW	SW	SW	SW	SW	SW	SW	SW	SW ■	SW ■	SW	SW	SW	SW	SW ■	SW	SW
Reading 7	d	22p42			23p12											05 42						06 12		
Earley	d	22p47			23p17											05 47						06 17		
Winnersh Triangle	d	22p49			23p19											05 49						06 19		
Winnersh	d	22p51			23p21											05 51						06 21		
Wokingham	d	22p56			23p26											05 56						06 26		
Bracknell	d	23p02			23p32											06 02						06 32		
Martins Heron	d	23p05			23p35											06 05						06 35		
Guildford	d																							
Wanborough	d																							
Ash 5	d																							
Aldershot	a																							
	d																06 00							
Ash Vale	d																06 04							
Frimley	d																06 10							
Camberley	a																06 14							
	d																06 18							
Bagshot	d																06 23							
Ascot 3	d	23p10			23p40											06 10	06a30					06 40		
Sunningdale	d	23p13			23p43											06 13						06 43		
Longcross	d																							
Woking	d											05 27												
West Byfleet	d											05 32												
Byfleet & New Haw	d											05 35												
Weybridge	d																							06 33
Addlestone	d											05 39												06 37
Chertsey	d											05 42												06 40
Virginia Water	a	23p19			23p49								05 47			06 19						06 49		06 45
	d	23p19			23p49								05 54			06 19						06 49		06 54
Egham	d	23p23			23p53								05 57			06 23						06 53		06 57
Windsor & Eton Riverside	d													05 53						06 23				
Datchet	d													05 56						06 26				
Sunnymeads	d													05 59						06 29				
Wraysbury	d													06 02						06 32				
Staines	d	23p29			23p59		04 58			05 37			06 03	06 08		06 29			06 33	06 38		06 59		07 03
Ashford (Surrey)	d						05 01			05 40			06 06	06 11					06 36	06 41				07 06
Feltham	d	23p35			00 05		05 06			05 45			06 11	06 16		06 35			06 41	06 46		07 05		07 11
Whitton	d						05 10		05 41	05 49				06 20						06 50				
Kingston	d		23p29	23p55		01 17	01 17					05 59						06 29					06 59	
Hampton Wick	d		23p31	23p57		01s22	01s22					06 01						06 31					07 01	
Teddington	d		23p35	23p59		01 25	01 25					06 05						06 35					07 05	
Fulwell	d																							
Strawberry Hill	d		23p38	00 03		01 28	01 28	05 38				06 08						06 38					07 08	
Twickenham	a	23p40	23p42	00 07	00 10		05 13	05 41		05 52		06 12		06 23		06 40		06 42		06 53		07 10	07 12	
	d	23p41	23p43		00 11		05 13	05 43		05 53		06 13		06 23		06 41		06 43		06 53		07 11	07 13	
St Margarets	d		23p45				05 15	05 45				06 15						06 45					07 15	
Richmond ⊖	d	23p45	23p49		00 15		05 19	05 49		05 58		06 19		06 28		06 45		06 49		06 58		07 15	07 19	
North Sheen	d		23p51				05 21	05 51				06 21						06 51					07 21	
Mortlake	d		23p53				05 23	05 53				06 23						06 53					07 23	
Hounslow	d								05 46				06 16						06 46					07 16
Isleworth	d								05 49				06 19						06 49					07 19
Syon Lane	d								05 51				06 21						06 51					07 21
Brentford	d								05 54				06 24						06 54					07 24
Kew Bridge	d								05 56				06 26						06 56					07 26
Chiswick	d								05 59				06 29						06 59					07 29
Barnes Bridge	d								06 01				06 31						07 01					07 31
Barnes	d		23p56				05 26	05 56	06 04		←	06 26	06 34		←			06 56	07 04		←		07 26	07 34
Putney	d		23p59				05 29	05 59	06 07	06 04	06 07	06 29	06 37	06 34	06 37			06 59	07 07	07 04	07 07		07 29	07 37
Wandsworth Town	d		00 02				05 32	06 02	→		06 10	06 32	→		06 40			07 02	→		07 10		07 32	→
Clapham Junction 10	d	23p54	00 05		00 24		05 35	06 05		06 09	06 13	06 35		06 39	06 43	06 54		07 05		07 09	07 13	07 24	07 35	
Queenstown Rd.(Battersea)	d		00 08				05 38	06 08			06 16	06 38			06 46			07 08			07 16		07 38	
Vauxhall ⊖	d		00 12				05 42	06 12		06 15	06 20	06 42		06 45	06 50			07 12		07 15	07 20		07 42	
London Waterloo 15 ⊖	a	00 04	00 16		00 37		05 46	06 16		06 19	06 26	06 46		06 49	06 56	07 04		07 16		07 19	07 26	07 34	07 46	

Reading, Guildford, Ascot, Weybridge, Windsor, Kingston, Richmond and Hounslow - London

Network Diagram - see first Page of Table 148

		SW	SW	SW ■	SW ■	SW	SW	SW	SW	SW	SW	SW ■	SW ■	SW	SW	SW	SW	SW	SW	SW	SW ■	SW	SW ■
Reading 7	d			06 42								07 12									07 42		
Earley	d			06 47								07 17									07 47		
Winnersh Triangle	d			06 49								07 19									07 49		
Winnersh	d			06 51								07 21									07 51		
Wokingham	d			06 56								07 26									07 56		
Bracknell	d			07 02								07 32									08 02		
Martins Heron	d			07 05								07 35									08 05		
Guildford	d				06 30								07 00										07 30
Wanborough	d				06 36								07 06										07 36
Ash 5	d				06 40								07 10										07 40
Aldershot	a				06 47								07 17										07 47
	d				07 00								07 30										08 00
Ash Vale	d				07 04								07 34										08 04
Frimley	d				07 10								07 40										08 10
Camberley	a				07 14								07 44										08 14
	d				07 18								07 48										08 18
Bagshot	d				07 23								07 53										08 23
Ascot 3	d			07 10	07a30							07 40	08a00								08 10		08a30
Sunningdale	d			07 13								07 43									08 13		
Longcross	d																						
Woking	d																						
West Byfleet	d																						
Byfleet & New Haw	d																						
Weybridge	d							07 03								07 33							
Addlestone	d							07 07								07 37							
Chertsey	d							07 10								07 40							
Virginia Water	a			07 19				07 15				07 49				07 45					08 19		
	d			07 19				07 24				07 49				07 54					08 19		
Egham	d			07 23				07 27				07 53				07 57					08 23		
Windsor & Eton Riverside	d	06 53							07 23								07 53						
Datchet	d	06 56							07 26								07 56						
Sunnymeads	d	06 59							07 29								07 59						
Wraysbury	d	07 02							07 32								08 02						
Staines	d	07 08		07 29				07 33	07 38			07 59				08 03	08 08				08 29		
Ashford (Surrey)	d	07 11						07 36	07 41							08 06	08 11						
Feltham	d	07 16		07 35				07 41	07 46			08 05				08 11	08 16				08 35		
Whitton	d	07 20							07 50					07 50			08 20		08 20	08 23			
Kingston	d						07 29								07 59								
Hampton Wick	d						07 31								08 01								
Teddington	d						07 35								08 05								
Fulwell	d																						
Strawberry Hill	d						07 38								08 08								
Twickenham	a	07 23		07 40			07 42		07 53			08 10			08 12		08 23			08 26	08 40		
	d	07 23		07 41			07 43		07 53		07 58	08 11			08 13		08 23			08 28	08 41		
St Margarets	d						07 45				08 00				08 15					08 30			
Richmond ⊖	d	07 28		07 45			07 49		07 58		08 04	08 15			08 19		08 28			08 34	08 45		
North Sheen	d						07 51				08 06				08 21					08 36			
Mortlake	d						07 53				08 08				08 23					08 38			
Hounslow	d					07 31		07 46						08 01		08 16			08 31				
Isleworth	d					07 34		07 49						08 04		08 19			08 34				
Syon Lane	d					07 36		07 51						08 06		08 21			08 36				
Brentford	d					07 39		07 54						08 09		08 24			08 39				
Kew Bridge	d					07 41		07 56						08 11		08 26			08 41				
Chiswick	d					07 44		07 59						08 14		08 29			08 44				
Barnes Bridge	d					07 46		08 01						08 16		08 31			08 46			←	
Barnes	d		←			07 49	07 56	08 04		←	08 11			08 19	08 26	08 34		←	08 49	08 41		08 49	
Putney	d	07 34	07 37			07 52	07 59	08 07	08 04	08 07	08 14			08 22	08 29	08 37	08 34	08 37	→	08 44		08 52	
Wandsworth Town	d		07 40			07 55	08 02	→		08 10	08 17			08 25	08 32	→		08 40		08 47		08 55	
Clapham Junction 10	d	07 39	07 43	07 54		07 58	08 05		08 09	08 13	08 20	08 24		08 28	08 35		08 39	08 43		08 50	08 54	08 58	
Queenstown Rd.(Battersea)	d		07 46			08 01	08 08			08 16	08 23			08 31	08 38			08 46		08 53		09 01	
Vauxhall ⊖	d	07 45	07 50			08 05	08 12		08 15	08 20	08 27			08 35	08 42		08 45	08 50		08 57		09 05	
London Waterloo 15 ⊖	a	07 49	07 56	08 04		08 11	08 16		08 19	08 26	08 32	08 34		08 41	08 46		08 49	08 56		09 02	09 04	09 11	

Table 149

Saturdays
until 6 October

Reading, Guildford, Ascot, Weybridge, Windsor, Kingston, Richmond and Hounslow - London

Network Diagram - see first Page of Table 148

		SW		SW	SW	SW	SW	SW	SW ■	SW	SW ■	SW		SW	SW	SW	SW	SW	SW ■	SW	SW ■	SW		SW	SW
Reading [7]	d								08 12										08 42						
Earley	d								08 17										08 47						
Winnersh Triangle	d								08 19										08 49						
Winnersh	d								08 21										08 51						
Wokingham	d								08 26										08 56						
Bracknell	d								08 32										09 02						
Martins Heron	d								08 35										09 05						
Guildford	d										08 00										08 30				
Wanborough	d										08 06										08 36				
Ash [5]	d										08 10										08 40				
Aldershot	a										08 17										08 47				
	d										08 30										09 00				
Ash Vale	d										08 34										09 04				
Frimley	d										08 40										09 10				
Camberley	a										08 44										09 14				
	d										08 48										09 18				
Bagshot	d										08 53										09 23				
Ascot [3]	d								08 40		09a00								09 10		09a30				
Sunningdale	d								08 43										09 13						
Longcross	d																								
Woking	d																								
West Byfleet	d																								
Byfleet & New Haw	d																								
Weybridge	d			08 03										08 33										09 03	
Addlestone	d			08 07										08 37										09 07	
Chertsey	d			08 10										08 40										09 10	
Virginia Water	a			08 15					08 49					08 45					09 19					09 15	
	d			08 24					08 49					08 54					09 19					09 24	
Egham	d			08 27					08 53					08 57					09 23					09 27	
Windsor & Eton Riverside	d				08 23										08 53										09 23
Datchet	d				08 26										08 56										09 26
Sunnymeads	d				08 29										08 59										09 29
Wraysbury	d				08 32										09 02										09 32
Staines	d			08 33	08 38				08 59					09 03	09 08				09 29					09 33	09 38
Ashford (Surrey)	d			08 36	08 41									09 06	09 11									09 36	09 41
Feltham	d			08 41	08 46				09 05					09 11	09 16				09 35					09 41	09 46
Whitton	d				08 50		08 50	08 53							09 20		09 20	09 23							09 50
Kingston	d	08 29										08 59										09 29			
Hampton Wick	d	08 31										09 01										09 31			
Teddington	d	08 35										09 05										09 35			
Fulwell	d																								
Strawberry Hill	d	08 38										09 08										09 38			
Twickenham	a	08 42			08 53			08 56	09 10			09 12			09 23			09 26	09 40			09 42			09 53
	d	08 43			08 53			08 58	09 11			09 13			09 23			09 28	09 41			09 43			09 53
St Margarets	d	08 45						09 00				09 15						09 30				09 45			
Richmond ⊖	d	08 49			08 58			09 04	09 15			09 19			09 28			09 34	09 45			09 49			09 58
North Sheen	d	08 51						09 06				09 21						09 36				09 51			
Mortlake	d	08 53						09 08				09 23						09 38				09 53			
Hounslow	d			08 46			09 01							09 16			09 31							09 46	
Isleworth	d			08 49			09 04							09 19			09 34							09 49	
Syon Lane	d			08 51			09 06							09 21			09 36							09 51	
Brentford	d			08 54			09 09							09 24			09 39							09 54	
Kew Bridge	d			08 56			09 11							09 26			09 41							09 56	
Chiswick	d			08 59			09 14							09 29			09 44							09 59	
Barnes Bridge	d			09 01			09 16			←				09 31			09 46			←				10 01	
Barnes	d	08 56		09 04		←	09 19	09 11		09 19		09 26		09 34		←	09 49	09 41		09 49		09 56		10 04	
Putney	d	08 59		09 07	09 04	09 07	→	09 14		09 22		09 29		09 37	09 34	09 37	→	09 44		09 52		09 59		10 07	10 04
Wandsworth Town	d	09 02		→		09 10		09 17		09 25		09 32		→		09 40		09 47		09 55		10 02		→	
Clapham Junction [10]	d	09 05			09 09	09 13		09 20	09 24	09 28		09 35			09 39	09 43		09 50	09 54	09 58		10 05			10 09
Queenstown Rd.(Battersea)	d	09 08				09 16		09 23		09 31		09 38				09 46		09 53		10 01		10 08			
Vauxhall ⊖	d	09 12			09 15	09 20		09 27		09 35		09 42			09 45	09 50		09 57		10 05		10 12			10 15
London Waterloo [15] ⊖	a	09 16			09 19	09 26		09 32	09 34	09 41		09 46			09 49	09 56		10 02	10 04	10 11		10 16			10 19

Table 149

Saturdays
until 6 October

Reading, Guildford, Ascot, Weybridge, Windsor, Kingston, Richmond and Hounslow - London

Network Diagram - see first Page of Table 148

		SW	SW	SW	SW ■	SW	SW ■	SW		SW	SW	SW	SW	SW	SW ■	SW	SW ■	SW		SW	SW	SW	SW	SW	SW ■
Reading [7]	d				09 12										09 42										10 12
Earley	d				09 17										09 47										10 17
Winnersh Triangle	d				09 19										09 49										10 19
Winnersh	d				09 21										09 51										10 21
Wokingham	d				09 26										09 56										10 26
Bracknell	d				09 32										10 02										10 32
Martins Heron	d				09 35										10 05										10 35
Guildford	d						09 00										09 30								
Wanborough	d						09 06										09 36								
Ash [5]	d						09 10										09 40								
Aldershot	a						09 17										09 47								
	d						09 30										10 00								
Ash Vale	d						09 34										10 04								
Frimley	d						09 40										10 10								
Camberley	a						09 44										10 14								
	d						09 48										10 18								
Bagshot	d						09 53										10 23								
Ascot [3]	d				09 40		10a00								10 10		10a30								10 40
Sunningdale	d				09 43										10 13										10 43
Longcross	d																								
Woking	d																								
West Byfleet	d																								
Byfleet & New Haw	d																								
Weybridge	d									09 33										10 03					
Addlestone	d									09 37										10 07					
Chertsey	d									09 40										10 10					
Virginia Water	a				09 49					09 45					10 19					10 15					10 49
	d				09 49					09 54					10 19					10 24					10 49
Egham	d				09 53					09 57					10 23					10 27					10 53
Windsor & Eton Riverside	d										09 53										10 23				
Datchet	d										09 56										10 26				
Sunnymeads	d										09 59										10 29				
Wraysbury	d										10 02										10 32				
Staines	d				09 59					10 03	10 08				10 29					10 33	10 38				10 59
Ashford (Surrey)	d									10 06	10 11									10 36	10 41				
Feltham	d				10 05					10 11	10 16				10 35					10 41	10 46				11 05
Whitton	d		09 50	09 53							10 20		10 20	10 23							10 50		10 50	10 53	
Kingston	d							09 59										10 29							
Hampton Wick	d							10 01										10 31							
Teddington	d							10 05										10 35							
Fulwell	d																								
Strawberry Hill	d							10 08										10 38							
Twickenham	a			09 56	10 10			10 12			10 23			10 26	10 40			10 42			10 53			10 56	11 10
	d			09 58	10 11			10 13			10 23			10 28	10 41			10 43			10 53			10 58	11 11
St Margarets	d			10 00				10 15						10 30				10 45						11 00	
Richmond ⊖	d			10 04	10 15			10 19			10 28			10 34	10 45			10 49			10 58			11 04	11 15
North Sheen	d			10 06				10 21						10 36				10 51						11 06	
Mortlake	d			10 08				10 23						10 38				10 53						11 08	
Hounslow	d		10 01							10 16			10 31							10 46			11 01		
Isleworth	d		10 04							10 19			10 34							10 49			11 04		
Syon Lane	d		10 06							10 21			10 36							10 51			11 06		
Brentford	d		10 09							10 24			10 39							10 54			11 09		
Kew Bridge	d		10 11							10 26			10 41							10 56			11 11		
Chiswick	d		10 14							10 29			10 44							10 59			11 14		
Barnes Bridge	d		10 16			←				10 31			10 46			←				11 01			11 16		
Barnes	d	←	10 19	10 11		10 19		10 26		10 34		←	10 49	10 41		10 49		10 56		11 04		←	11 19	11 11	
Putney	d	10 07	→	10 14		10 22		10 29		10 37	10 34	10 37	→	10 44		10 52		10 59		11 07	11 04	11 07	→	11 14	
Wandsworth Town	d	10 10		10 17		10 25		10 32		→		10 40		10 47		10 55		11 02		→		11 10		11 17	
Clapham Junction [10]	d	10 13		10 20	10 24	10 28		10 35			10 39	10 43		10 50	10 54	10 58		11 05			11 09	11 13		11 20	11 24
Queenstown Rd.(Battersea)	d	10 16		10 23		10 31		10 38				10 46		10 53		11 01		11 08				11 16		11 23	
Vauxhall ⊖	d	10 20		10 27		10 35		10 42			10 45	10 50		10 57		11 05		11 12			11 15	11 20		11 27	
London Waterloo [15] ⊖	a	10 26		10 32	10 34	10 41		10 46			10 49	10 56		11 02	11 04	11 11		11 16			11 19	11 26		11 32	11 34

Table 149

Saturdays
until 6 October

Reading, Guildford, Ascot, Weybridge, Windsor, Kingston, Richmond and Hounslow - London

Network Diagram - see first Page of Table 148

		SW	SW 1	SW		SW	SW	SW	SW	SW	SW 1	SW	SW 1	SW		SW	SW	SW	SW	SW	SW 1	SW	SW 1	SW	
Reading 7	d										10 42										11 12				
Earley	d										10 47										11 17				
Winnersh Triangle	d										10 49										11 19				
Winnersh	d										10 51										11 21				
Wokingham	d										10 56										11 26				
Bracknell	d										11 02										11 32				
Martins Heron	d										11 05										11 35				
Guildford	d		10 00										10 30										11 00		
Wanborough	d		10 06										10 36										11 06		
Ash 5	d		10 10										10 40										11 10		
Aldershot	a		10 17										10 47										11 17		
	d		10 30										11 00										11 30		
Ash Vale	d		10 34										11 04										11 34		
Frimley	d		10 40										11 10										11 40		
Camberley	a		10 44										11 14										11 44		
	d		10 48										11 18										11 48		
Bagshot	d		10 53										11 23										11 53		
Ascot 3	d		11a00								11 10		11a30								11 40		12a00		
Sunningdale	d										11 13										11 43				
Longcross	d																								
Woking	d																								
West Byfleet	d																								
Byfleet & New Haw	d																								
Weybridge	d					10 33										11 03									
Addlestone	d					10 37										11 07									
Chertsey	d					10 40										11 10									
Virginia Water	a					10 45					11 19					11 15					11 49				
	d					10 54					11 19					11 24					11 49				
Egham	d					10 57					11 23					11 27					11 53				
Windsor & Eton Riverside	d						10 53										11 23								
Datchet	d						10 56										11 26								
Sunnymeads	d						10 59										11 29								
Wraysbury	d						11 02										11 32								
Staines	d					11 03	11 08				11 29					11 33	11 38				11 59				
Ashford (Surrey)	d					11 06	11 11									11 36	11 41								
Feltham	d					11 11	11 16				11 35					11 41	11 46				12 05				
Whitton	d						11 20		11 20	11 23							11 50		11 50	11 53					
Kingston	d			10 59										11 29										11 59	
Hampton Wick	d			11 01										11 31										12 01	
Teddington	d			11 05										11 35										12 05	
Fulwell	d																								
Strawberry Hill	d			11 08										11 38										12 08	
Twickenham	a			11 12			11 23			11 26	11 40			11 42			11 53			11 56	12 10			12 12	
	d			11 13			11 23			11 28	11 41			11 43			11 53			11 58	12 11			12 13	
St Margarets	d			11 15						11 30				11 45						12 00				12 15	
Richmond ⊖	d			11 19			11 28			11 34	11 45			11 49			11 58			12 04	12 15			12 19	
North Sheen	d			11 21						11 36				11 51						12 06				12 21	
Mortlake	d			11 23						11 38				11 53						12 08				12 23	
Hounslow	d					11 16			11 31							11 46			12 01						
Isleworth	d					11 19			11 34							11 49			12 04						
Syon Lane	d					11 21			11 36							11 51			12 06						
Brentford	d					11 24			11 39							11 54			12 09						
Kew Bridge	d					11 26			11 41							11 56			12 11						
Chiswick	d					11 29			11 44							11 59			12 14						
Barnes Bridge	d	←				11 31			11 46			←				12 01			12 16			←			
Barnes	d	11 19		11 26		11 34		←	11 49	11 41		11 49		11 56		12 04		←	12 19	12 11		12 19		12 26	
Putney	d	11 22		11 29		11 37	11 34	11 37	→	11 44		11 52		11 59		12 07	12 04	12 07	→	12 14		12 22		12 29	
Wandsworth Town	d	11 25		11 32		→		11 40		11 47		11 55		12 02		→		12 10		12 17		12 25		12 32	
Clapham Junction 10	d	11 28		11 35			11 39	11 43		11 50	11 54	11 58		12 05			12 09	12 13		12 20	12 24	12 28		12 35	
Queenstown Rd.(Battersea)	d	11 31		11 38				11 46		11 53		12 01		12 08				12 16		12 23		12 31		12 38	
Vauxhall ⊖	d	11 35		11 42			11 45	11 50		11 57		12 05		12 12			12 15	12 20		12 27		12 35		12 42	
London Waterloo 15 ⊖	a	11 41		11 46			11 49	11 56		12 02	12 04	12 11		12 16			12 19	12 26		12 32	12 34	12 41		12 46	

Table 149

Saturdays
until 6 October

Reading, Guildford, Ascot, Weybridge, Windsor, Kingston, Richmond and Hounslow - London

Network Diagram - see first Page of Table 148

		SW	SW	SW	SW	SW	SW 1	SW	SW 1	SW		SW	SW	SW	SW	SW	SW 1	SW	SW 1	SW		SW	SW	SW	SW
Reading 7	d						11 42										12 12								
Earley	d						11 47										12 17								
Winnersh Triangle	d						11 49										12 19								
Winnersh	d						11 51										12 21								
Wokingham	d						11 56										12 26								
Bracknell	d						12 02										12 32								
Martins Heron	d						12 05										12 35								
Guildford	d								11 30										12 00						
Wanborough	d								11 36										12 06						
Ash 5	d								11 40										12 10						
Aldershot	a								11 47										12 17						
	d								12 00										12 30						
Ash Vale	d								12 04										12 34						
Frimley	d								12 10										12 40						
Camberley	a								12 14										12 44						
	d								12 18										12 48						
Bagshot	d								12 23										12 53						
Ascot 3	d						12 10		12a30								12 40		13a00						
Sunningdale	d						12 13										12 43								
Longcross	d																								
Woking	d																								
West Byfleet	d																								
Byfleet & New Haw	d																								
Weybridge	d	11 33										12 03										12 33			
Addlestone	d	11 37										12 07										12 37			
Chertsey	d	11 40										12 10										12 40			
Virginia Water	a	11 45					12 19					12 15					12 49					12 45			
	d	11 54					12 19					12 24					12 49					12 54			
Egham	d	11 57					12 23					12 27					12 53					12 57			
Windsor & Eton Riverside	d		11 53										12 23										12 53		
Datchet	d		11 56										12 26										12 56		
Sunnymeads	d		11 59										12 29										12 59		
Wraysbury	d		12 02										12 32										13 02		
Staines	d	12 03	12 08				12 29					12 33	12 38				12 59					13 03	13 08		
Ashford (Surrey)	d	12 06	12 11									12 36	12 41									13 06	13 11		
Feltham	d	12 11	12 16				12 35					12 41	12 46				13 05					13 11	13 16		
Whitton	d		12 20		12 20	12 23							12 50		12 50	12 53							13 20		13 20
Kingston	d									12 29										12 59					
Hampton Wick	d									12 31										13 01					
Teddington	d									12 35										13 05					
Fulwell	d																								
Strawberry Hill	d									12 38										13 08					
Twickenham	a		12 23			12 27	12 40			12 42			12 53			12 56	13 10			13 12			13 23		
	d		12 23			12 28	12 41			12 43			12 53			12 58	13 11			13 13			13 23		
St Margarets	d					12 30				12 45						13 00				13 15					
Richmond ⊖	d		12 28			12 34	12 45			12 49			12 58			13 04	13 15			13 19			13 28		
North Sheen	d					12 36				12 51						13 06				13 21					
Mortlake	d					12 38				12 53						13 08				13 23					
Hounslow	d	12 16			12 31							12 46			13 01							13 16			13 31
Isleworth	d	12 19			12 34							12 49			13 04							13 19			13 34
Syon Lane	d	12 21			12 36							12 51			13 06							13 21			13 36
Brentford	d	12 24			12 39							12 54			13 09							13 24			13 39
Kew Bridge	d	12 26			12 41							12 56			13 11							13 26			13 41
Chiswick	d	12 29			12 44							12 59			13 14							13 29			13 44
Barnes Bridge	d	12 31			12 46			←				13 01			13 16			←				13 31			13 46
Barnes	d	12 34		←	12 49	12 41		12 49		12 56		13 04		←	13 19	13 11		13 19		13 26		13 34		←	13 49
Putney	d	12 37	12 34	12 37	→	12 44		12 52		12 59		13 07	13 04	13 07	→	13 14		13 22		13 29		13 37	13 34	13 37	→
Wandsworth Town	d	→		12 40		12 47		12 55		13 02		→		13 10		13 17		13 25		13 32		→		13 40	
Clapham Junction 10	d		12 39	12 43		12 50	12 54	12 58		13 05			13 09	13 13		13 20	13 24	13 28		13 35			13 39	13 43	
Queenstown Rd.(Battersea)	d			12 46		12 53		13 01		13 08				13 16		13 23		13 31		13 38				13 46	
Vauxhall ⊖	d		12 45	12 50		12 57		13 05		13 12			13 15	13 20		13 27		13 35		13 42			13 45	13 50	
London Waterloo 15 ⊖	a		12 49	12 56		13 02	13 04	13 11		13 16			13 19	13 26		13 32	13 34	13 41		13 46			13 49	13 56	

Saturdays until 6 October

Reading, Guildford, Ascot, Weybridge, Windsor, Kingston, Richmond and Hounslow - London

Network Diagram - see first Page of Table 148

		SW	SW ■	SW	SW ■	SW		SW	SW	SW	SW	SW	SW ■	SW	SW ■	SW		SW	SW	SW	SW	SW	SW ■	SW	SW ■
Reading ■	d		12 42										13 12										13 42		
Earley	d		12 47										13 17										13 47		
Winnersh Triangle	d		12 49										13 19										13 49		
Winnersh	d		12 51										13 21										13 51		
Wokingham	d		12 56										13 26										13 56		
Bracknell	d		13 02										13 32										14 02		
Martins Heron	d		13 05										13 35										14 05		
Guildford	d				12 30										13 00										13 30
Wanborough	d				12 36										13 06										13 36
Ash ■	d				12 40										13 10										13 40
Aldershot	a				12 47										13 17										13 47
	d				13 00										13 30										14 00
Ash Vale	d				13 04										13 34										14 04
Frimley	d				13 10										13 40										14 10
Camberley	a				13 14										13 44										14 14
	d				13 18										13 48										14 18
Bagshot	d				13 23										13 53										14 23
Ascot ■	d		13 10		13a30								13 40		14a00								14 10		14a30
Sunningdale	d		13 13										13 43										14 13		
Longcross	d																								
Woking	d																								
West Byfleet	d																								
Byfleet & New Haw	d																								
Weybridge	d							13 03										13 33							
Addlestone	d							13 07										13 37							
Chertsey	d							13 10										13 40							
Virginia Water	a		13 19					13 15					13 49					13 45					14 19		
	d		13 19					13 24					13 49					13 54					14 19		
Egham	d		13 23					13 27					13 53					13 57					14 23		
Windsor & Eton Riverside	d								13 23										13 53						
Datchet	d								13 26										13 56						
Sunnymeads	d								13 29										13 59						
Wraysbury	d								13 32										14 02						
Staines	d		13 29					13 33	13 38				13 59					14 03	14 08				14 29		
Ashford (Surrey)	d							13 36	13 41									14 06	14 11						
Feltham	d		13 35					13 41	13 46				14 05					14 11	14 16				14 35		
Whitton	d	13 23							13 50		13 50	13 53							14 20		14 20	14 23			
Kingston	d					13 29										13 59									
Hampton Wick	d					13 31										14 01									
Teddington	d					13 35										14 05									
Fulwell	d																								
Strawberry Hill	d					13 38										14 08									
Twickenham	a	13 26	13 40			13 42			13 53			13 56	14 10			14 12			14 23			14 26	14 40		
	d	13 28	13 41			13 43			13 53			13 58	14 11			14 13			14 23			14 28	14 41		
St Margarets	d	13 30				13 45						14 00				14 15						14 30			
Richmond ⊖	d	13 34	13 45			13 49			13 58			14 04	14 15			14 19			14 28			14 34	14 45		
North Sheen	d	13 36				13 51						14 06				14 21						14 36			
Mortlake	d	13 38				13 53						14 08				14 23						14 38			
Hounslow	d							13 46			14 01							14 16			14 31				
Isleworth	d							13 49			14 04							14 19			14 34				
Syon Lane	d							13 51			14 06							14 21			14 36				
Brentford	d							13 54			14 09							14 24			14 39				
Kew Bridge	d							13 56			14 11							14 26			14 41				
Chiswick	d							13 59			14 14							14 29			14 44				
Barnes Bridge	d			←				14 01			14 16			←				14 31			14 46			←	
Barnes	d	13 41		13 49		13 56		14 04		←	14 19	14 11		14 19		14 26		14 34		←	14 49	14 41		14 49	
Putney	d	13 44		13 52		13 59		14 07	14 04	14 07	→	14 14		14 22		14 29		14 37	14 34	14 37	→	14 44		14 52	
Wandsworth Town	d	13 47		13 55		14 02		→		14 10		14 17		14 25		14 32		→		14 40		14 47		14 55	
Clapham Junction ■	d	13 50	13 54	13 58		14 05			14 09	14 13		14 20	14 24	14 28		14 35			14 39	14 43		14 50	14 54	14 58	
Queenstown Rd.(Battersea)	d	13 53		14 01		14 08				14 16		14 23		14 31		14 38				14 46		14 53		15 01	
Vauxhall ⊖	d	13 57		14 05		14 12			14 15	14 20		14 27		14 35		14 42			14 45	14 50		14 57		15 05	
London Waterloo ■ ⊖	a	14 02	14 04	14 11		14 16			14 19	14 26		14 32	14 34	14 41		14 46			14 49	14 56		15 02	15 04	15 11	

Saturdays until 6 October

Reading, Guildford, Ascot, Weybridge, Windsor, Kingston, Richmond and Hounslow - London

Network Diagram - see first Page of Table 148

		SW		SW	SW	SW	SW	SW	SW ■	SW	SW ■	SW		SW	SW	SW	SW	SW	SW ■	SW	SW ■	SW		SW	SW
Reading ■	d								14 12										14 42						
Earley	d								14 17										14 47						
Winnersh Triangle	d								14 19										14 49						
Winnersh	d								14 21										14 51						
Wokingham	d								14 26										14 56						
Bracknell	d								14 32										15 02						
Martins Heron	d								14 35										15 05						
Guildford	d										14 00										14 30				
Wanborough	d										14 06										14 36				
Ash ■	d										14 10										14 40				
Aldershot	a										14 17										14 47				
	d										14 30										15 00				
Ash Vale	d										14 34										15 04				
Frimley	d										14 40										15 10				
Camberley	a										14 44										15 14				
	d										14 48										15 18				
Bagshot	d										14 53										15 23				
Ascot ■	d								14 40		15a00								15 10		15a30				
Sunningdale	d								14 43										15 13						
Longcross	d																								
Woking	d																								
West Byfleet	d																								
Byfleet & New Haw	d																								
Weybridge	d			14 03										14 33										15 03	
Addlestone	d			14 07										14 37										15 07	
Chertsey	d			14 10										14 40										15 10	
Virginia Water	a			14 15					14 49					14 45					15 19					15 15	
	d			14 24					14 49					14 54					15 19					15 24	
Egham	d			14 27					14 53					14 57					15 23					15 27	
Windsor & Eton Riverside	d				14 23										14 53										15 23
Datchet	d				14 26										14 56										15 26
Sunnymeads	d				14 29										14 59										15 29
Wraysbury	d				14 32										15 02										15 32
Staines	d			14 33	14 38				14 59					15 03	15 08				15 29					15 33	15 38
Ashford (Surrey)	d			14 36	14 41									15 06	15 11									15 36	15 41
Feltham	d			14 41	14 46				15 05					15 11	15 16				15 35					15 41	15 46
Whitton	d				14 50		14 50	14 53							15 20		15 20	15 23							15 50
Kingston	d	14 29										14 59										15 29			
Hampton Wick	d	14 31										15 01										15 31			
Teddington	d	14 35										15 05										15 35			
Fulwell	d																								
Strawberry Hill	d	14 38										15 08										15 38			
Twickenham	a	14 42			14 53			14 56	15 10			15 12			15 23			15 26	15 40			15 42			15 53
	d	14 43			14 53			14 58	15 11			15 13			15 23			15 28	15 41			15 43			15 53
St Margarets	d	14 45						15 00				15 15						15 30				15 45			
Richmond ⊖	d	14 49			14 58			15 04	15 15			15 19			15 28			15 34	15 45			15 49			15 58
North Sheen	d	14 51						15 06				15 21						15 36				15 51			
Mortlake	d	14 53						15 08				15 23						15 38				15 53			
Hounslow	d			14 46			15 01							15 16			15 31							15 46	
Isleworth	d			14 49			15 04							15 19			15 34							15 49	
Syon Lane	d			14 51			15 06							15 21			15 36							15 51	
Brentford	d			14 54			15 09							15 24			15 39							15 54	
Kew Bridge	d			14 56			15 11							15 26			15 41							15 56	
Chiswick	d			14 59			15 14							15 29			15 44							15 59	
Barnes Bridge	d			15 01			15 16			←				15 31			15 46			←				16 01	
Barnes	d	14 56		15 04		←	15 19	15 11		15 19		15 26		15 34		←	15 49	15 41		15 49		15 56		16 04	
Putney	d	14 59		15 07	15 04	15 07	→	15 14		15 22		15 29		15 37	15 34	15 37	→	15 44		15 52		15 59		16 07	16 04
Wandsworth Town	d	15 02		→		15 10		15 17		15 25		15 32		→		15 40		15 47		15 55		16 02		→	
Clapham Junction ■	d	15 05			15 09	15 13		15 20	15 24	15 28		15 35			15 39	15 43		15 50	15 54	15 58		16 05			16 09
Queenstown Rd.(Battersea)	d	15 08				15 16		15 23		15 31		15 38				15 46		15 53		16 01		16 08			
Vauxhall ⊖	d	15 12			15 15	15 20		15 27		15 35		15 42			15 45	15 50		15 57		16 05		16 12			16 15
London Waterloo ■ ⊖	a	15 16			15 19	15 26		15 32	15 34	15 41		15 46			15 49	15 56		16 02	16 04	16 11		16 16			16 19

Saturdays until 6 October

Reading, Guildford, Ascot, Weybridge, Windsor, Kingston, Richmond and Hounslow - London

Network Diagram - see first Page of Table 148

		SW	SW	SW	SW 1	SW	SW 1	SW		SW	SW	SW	SW	SW	SW 1	SW	SW 1	SW		SW	SW	SW	SW	SW	SW 1
Reading 7	d				15 12										15 42										16 12
Earley	d				15 17										15 47										16 17
Winnersh Triangle	d				15 19										15 49										16 19
Winnersh	d				15 21										15 51										16 21
Wokingham	d				15 26										15 56										16 26
Bracknell	d				15 32										16 02										16 32
Martins Heron	d				15 35										16 05										16 35
Guildford	d						15 00										15 30								
Wanborough	d						15 06										15 36								
Ash 5	d						15 10										15 40								
Aldershot	a						15 17										15 47								
	d						15 30										16 00								
Ash Vale	d						15 34										16 04								
Frimley	d						15 40										16 10								
Camberley	a						15 44										16 14								
	d						15 48										16 18								
Bagshot	d						15 53										16 23								
Ascot 3	d				15 40		16a00								16 10		16a30								16 40
Sunningdale	d				15 43										16 13										16 43
Longcross	d																								
Woking	d																								
West Byfleet	d																								
Byfleet & New Haw	d																								
Weybridge	d									15 33										16 03					
Addlestone	d									15 37										16 07					
Chertsey	d									15 40										16 10					
Virginia Water	a				15 49					15 45					16 19					16 15					16 49
	d				15 49					15 54					16 19					16 24					16 49
Egham	d				15 53					15 57					16 23					16 27					16 53
Windsor & Eton Riverside	d										15 53										16 23				
Datchet	d										15 56										16 26				
Sunnymeads	d										15 59										16 29				
Wraysbury	d										16 02										16 32				
Staines	d				15 59					16 03	16 08				16 29					16 33	16 38				16 59
Ashford (Surrey)	d									16 06	16 11									16 36	16 41				
Feltham	d				16 05					16 11	16 16				16 35					16 41	16 46				17 05
Whitton	d		15 50	15 53							16 20		16 20	16 23							16 50		16 50	16 53	
Kingston	d							15 59										16 29							
Hampton Wick	d							16 01										16 31							
Teddington	d							16 05										16 35							
Fulwell	d																								
Strawberry Hill	d							16 08										16 38							
Twickenham	a			15 56	16 10			16 12			16 23			16 26	16 40			16 42			16 53			16 56	17 10
	d			15 58	16 11			16 13			16 23			16 28	16 41			16 43			16 53			16 58	17 11
St Margarets	d			16 00				16 15						16 30				16 45						17 00	
Richmond ⊖	d			16 04	16 15			16 19			16 28			16 34	16 45			16 49			16 58			17 04	17 15
North Sheen	d			16 06				16 21						16 36				16 51						17 06	
Mortlake	d			16 08				16 23						16 38				16 53						17 08	
Hounslow	d		16 01							16 16			16 31							16 46			17 01		
Isleworth	d		16 04							16 19			16 34							16 49			17 04		
Syon Lane	d		16 06							16 21			16 36							16 51			17 06		
Brentford	d		16 09							16 24			16 39							16 54			17 09		
Kew Bridge	d		16 11							16 26			16 41							16 56			17 11		
Chiswick	d		16 14							16 29			16 44							16 59			17 14		
Barnes Bridge	d		16 16			←				16 31			16 46			←				17 01			17 16		
Barnes	d	←	16 19	16 11		16 19		16 26		16 34		←	16 49	16 41		16 49		16 56		17 04		←	17 19	17 11	
Putney	d	16 07	→	16 14		16 22		16 29		16 37	16 34	16 37	→	16 44		16 52		16 59		17 07	17 04	17 07	→	17 14	
Wandsworth Town	d	16 10		16 17		16 25		16 32		→		16 40		16 47		16 55		17 02		→		17 10		17 17	
Clapham Junction 10	d	16 13		16 20	16 24	16 28		16 35			16 39	16 43		16 50	16 54	16 58		17 05			17 09	17 13		17 20	17 24
Queenstown Rd.(Battersea)	d	16 16		16 23		16 31		16 38				16 46		16 53		17 01		17 08				17 16		17 23	
Vauxhall ⊖	d	16 20		16 27		16 35		16 42			16 45	16 50		16 57		17 05		17 12			17 15	17 20		17 27	
London Waterloo 15 ⊖	a	16 26		16 32	16 34	16 41		16 46			16 49	16 56		17 02	17 04	17 11		17 16			17 19	17 26		17 32	17 34

Table 149

Saturdays until 6 October

Reading, Guildford, Ascot, Weybridge, Windsor, Kingston, Richmond and Hounslow - London

Network Diagram - see first Page of Table 148

		SW	SW 1	SW		SW	SW	SW	SW	SW	SW 1	SW	SW 1	SW		SW	SW	SW	SW	SW	SW 1	SW	SW 1	SW	
Reading 7	d										16 42										17 12				
Earley	d										16 47										17 17				
Winnersh Triangle	d										16 49										17 19				
Winnersh	d										16 51										17 21				
Wokingham	d										16 56										17 26				
Bracknell	d										17 02										17 32				
Martins Heron	d										17 05										17 35				
Guildford	d		16 00										16 30										17 00		
Wanborough	d		16 06										16 36										17 06		
Ash 5	d		16 10										16 40										17 10		
Aldershot	a		16 17										16 47										17 17		
	d		16 30										17 00										17 30		
Ash Vale	d		16 34										17 04										17 34		
Frimley	d		16 40										17 10										17 40		
Camberley	a		16 44										17 14										17 44		
	d		16 48										17 18										17 48		
Bagshot	d		16 53										17 23										17 53		
Ascot 3	d		17a00								17 10		17a30								17 40		18a00		
Sunningdale	d										17 13										17 43				
Longcross	d																								
Woking	d																								
West Byfleet	d																								
Byfleet & New Haw	d																								
Weybridge	d					16 33										17 03									
Addlestone	d					16 37										17 07									
Chertsey	d					16 40										17 10									
Virginia Water	a					16 45					17 19					17 15					17 49				
	d					16 54					17 19					17 24					17 49				
Egham	d					16 57					17 23					17 27					17 53				
Windsor & Eton Riverside	d						16 53										17 23								
Datchet	d						16 56										17 26								
Sunnymeads	d						16 59										17 29								
Wraysbury	d						17 02										17 32								
Staines	d					17 03	17 08				17 29					17 33	17 38				17 59				
Ashford (Surrey)	d					17 06	17 11									17 36	17 41								
Feltham	d					17 11	17 16				17 35					17 41	17 46				18 05				
Whitton	d						17 20		17 20	17 23							17 50		17 50	17 53					
Kingston	d			16 59										17 29										17 59	
Hampton Wick	d			17 01										17 31										18 01	
Teddington	d			17 05										17 35										18 05	
Fulwell	d																								
Strawberry Hill	d			17 08										17 38										18 08	
Twickenham	a			17 12			17 23			17 26	17 40			17 42			17 53			17 56	18 10			18 12	
	d			17 13			17 23			17 28	17 41			17 43			17 53			17 58	18 11			18 13	
St Margarets	d			17 15						17 30				17 45						18 00				18 15	
Richmond ⊖	d			17 19			17 28			17 34	17 45			17 49			17 58			18 04	18 15			18 19	
North Sheen	d			17 21						17 36				17 51						18 06				18 21	
Mortlake	d			17 23						17 38				17 53						18 08				18 23	
Hounslow	d					17 16			17 31							17 46			18 01						
Isleworth	d					17 19			17 34							17 49			18 04						
Syon Lane	d					17 21			17 36							17 51			18 06						
Brentford	d					17 24			17 39							17 54			18 09						
Kew Bridge	d					17 26			17 41							17 56			18 11						
Chiswick	d					17 29			17 44							17 59			18 14						
Barnes Bridge	d	←				17 31			17 46			←				18 01			18 16			←			
Barnes	d	17 19		17 26		17 34		←	17 49	17 41		17 49		17 56		18 04		←	18 19	18 11		18 19		18 26	
Putney	d	17 22		17 29		17 37	17 34	17 37	→	17 44		17 52		17 59		18 07	18 04	18 07	→	18 14		18 22		18 29	
Wandsworth Town	d	17 25		17 32		→		17 40		17 47		17 55		18 02		→		18 10		18 17		18 25		18 32	
Clapham Junction 10	d	17 28		17 35			17 39	17 43		17 50	17 54	17 58		18 05			18 09	18 13		18 20	18 24	18 28		18 35	
Queenstown Rd.(Battersea)	d	17 31		17 38				17 46		17 53		18 01		18 08				18 16		18 23		18 31		18 38	
Vauxhall ⊖	d	17 35		17 42			17 45	17 50		17 57		18 05		18 12			18 15	18 20		18 27		18 35		18 42	
London Waterloo 15 ⊖	a	17 41		17 46			17 49	17 56		18 02	18 04	18 11		18 16			18 19	18 26		18 32	18 34	18 41		18 46	

Table 149

Saturdays
until 6 October

Reading, Guildford, Ascot, Weybridge, Windsor, Kingston, Richmond and Hounslow - London

Network Diagram - see first Page of Table 148

		SW	SW	SW	SW	SW	SW ■	SW	SW ■	SW	SW	SW	SW	SW	SW	SW ■	SW	SW ■	SW	SW	SW	SW	SW
Reading ■	d						17 42									18 12							
Earley	d						17 47									18 17							
Winnersh Triangle	d						17 49									18 19							
Winnersh	d						17 51									18 21							
Wokingham	d						17 56									18 26							
Bracknell	d						18 02									18 32							
Martins Heron	d						18 05									18 35							
Guildford	d								17 30									18 00					
Wanborough	d								17 36									18 06					
Ash ■	d								17 40									18 10					
Aldershot	a								17 47									18 17					
	d								18 00									18 30					
Ash Vale	d								18 04									18 34					
Frimley	d								18 10									18 40					
Camberley	a								18 14									18 44					
	d								18 18									18 48					
Bagshot	d								18 23									18 53					
Ascot ■	d						18 10		18a30							18 40		19a00					
Sunningdale	d						18 13									18 43							
Longcross	d																						
Woking	d																						
West Byfleet	d																						
Byfleet & New Haw	d																						
Weybridge	d	17 33									18 03									18 33			
Addlestone	d	17 37									18 07									18 37			
Chertsey	d	17 40									18 10									18 40			
Virginia Water	a	17 45					18 19				18 15					18 49				18 45			
	d	17 54					18 19				18 24					18 49				18 54			
Egham	d	17 57					18 23				18 27					18 53				18 57			
Windsor & Eton Riverside	d		17 53									18 23									18 53		
Datchet	d		17 56									18 26									18 56		
Sunnymeads	d		17 59									18 29									18 59		
Wraysbury	d		18 02									18 32									19 02		
Staines	d	18 03	18 08				18 29				18 33	18 38				18 59				19 03	19 08		
Ashford (Surrey)	d	18 06	18 11								18 36	18 41								19 06	19 11		
Feltham	d	18 11	18 16				18 35				18 41	18 46				19 05				19 11	19 16		
Whitton	d		18 20		18 20	18 23						18 50		18 50	18 53						19 20		19 20
Kingston	d									18 29									18 59				
Hampton Wick	d									18 31									19 01				
Teddington	d									18 35									19 05				
Fulwell	d																						
Strawberry Hill	d									18 38									19 08				
Twickenham	a		18 23			18 26	18 40			18 42		18 53			18 56	19 10			19 12		19 23		
	d		18 23			18 28	18 41			18 43		18 53			18 58	19 11			19 13		19 23		
St Margarets	d					18 30				18 45					19 00				19 15				
Richmond ⊖	d		18 28			18 34	18 45			18 49		18 58			19 04	19 15			19 19		19 28		
North Sheen	d					18 36				18 51					19 06				19 21				
Mortlake	d					18 38				18 53					19 08				19 23				
Hounslow	d	18 16			18 31						18 46			19 01						19 16			19 31
Isleworth	d	18 19			18 34						18 49			19 04						19 19			19 34
Syon Lane	d	18 21			18 36						18 51			19 06						19 21			19 36
Brentford	d	18 24			18 39						18 54			19 09						19 24			19 39
Kew Bridge	d	18 26			18 41						18 56			19 11						19 26			19 41
Chiswick	d	18 29			18 44						18 59			19 14						19 29			19 44
Barnes Bridge	d	18 31			18 46			←			19 01			19 16			←			19 31			19 46
Barnes	d	18 34		←	18 49	18 41		18 49		18 56	19 04		←	19 19	19 11		19 19		19 26	19 34		←	19 49
Putney	d	18 37	18 34	18 37	→	18 44		18 52		18 59	19 07	19 04	19 07	→	19 14		19 22		19 29	19 37	19 34	19 37	→
Wandsworth Town	d	→		18 40		18 47		18 55		19 02	→		19 10		19 17		19 25		19 32	→		19 40	
Clapham Junction ■	d		18 39	18 43		18 50	18 54	18 58		19 05		19 09	19 13		19 20	19 24	19 28		19 35		19 39	19 43	
Queenstown Rd.(Battersea)	d			18 46		18 53		19 01		19 08			19 16		19 23		19 31		19 38			19 46	
Vauxhall ⊖	d		18 45	18 50		18 57		19 05		19 12		19 15	19 20		19 27		19 35		19 42		19 45	19 50	
London Waterloo ■ ⊖	a		18 49	18 56		19 02	19 04	19 11		19 16		19 19	19 26		19 32	19 34	19 41		19 46		19 49	19 56	

Table 149

Saturdays
until 6 October

Reading, Guildford, Ascot, Weybridge, Windsor, Kingston, Richmond and Hounslow - London

Network Diagram - see first Page of Table 148

		SW	SW ■	SW	SW ■	SW	SW	SW	SW	SW	SW	SW ■	SW	SW ■	SW	SW	SW	SW	SW	SW	SW ■	SW	SW ■
Reading ■	d		18 42									19 12									19 42		
Earley	d		18 47									19 17									19 47		
Winnersh Triangle	d		18 49									19 19									19 49		
Winnersh	d		18 51									19 21									19 51		
Wokingham	d		18 56									19 26									19 56		
Bracknell	d		19 02									19 32									20 02		
Martins Heron	d		19 05									19 35									20 05		
Guildford	d				18 30									19 00									19 30
Wanborough	d				18 36									19 06									19 36
Ash ■	d				18 40									19 10									19 40
Aldershot	a				18 47									19 17									19 47
	d				19 00									19 30									20 00
Ash Vale	d				19 04									19 34									20 04
Frimley	d				19 10									19 40									20 10
Camberley	a				19 14									19 44									20 14
	d				19 18									19 48									20 18
Bagshot	d				19 23									19 53									20 23
Ascot ■	d		19 10		19a30							19 40		20a00							20 10		20a30
Sunningdale	d		19 13									19 43									20 13		
Longcross	d																						
Woking	d																						
West Byfleet	d																						
Byfleet & New Haw	d																						
Weybridge	d						19 03									19 33							
Addlestone	d						19 07									19 37							
Chertsey	d						19 10									19 40							
Virginia Water	a		19 19				19 15					19 49				19 45					20 19		
	d		19 19				19 24					19 49				19 54					20 19		
Egham	d		19 23				19 27					19 53				19 57					20 23		
Windsor & Eton Riverside	d							19 23									19 53						
Datchet	d							19 26									19 56						
Sunnymeads	d							19 29									19 59						
Wraysbury	d							19 32									20 02						
Staines	d		19 29				19 33	19 38				19 59				20 03	20 08				20 29		
Ashford (Surrey)	d						19 36	19 41								20 06	20 11						
Feltham	d		19 35				19 41	19 46				20 05				20 11	20 16				20 35		
Whitton	d	19 23						19 50		19 50	19 53						20 20		20 20	20 23			
Kingston	d					19 29									19 59								
Hampton Wick	d					19 31									20 01								
Teddington	d					19 35									20 05								
Fulwell	d																						
Strawberry Hill	d					19 38									20 08								
Twickenham	a	19 26	19 40			19 42		19 53			19 56	20 10			20 12		20 23			20 26	20 40		
	d	19 28	19 41			19 43		19 53			19 58	20 11			20 13		20 23			20 28	20 41		
St Margarets	d	19 30				19 45					20 00				20 15					20 30			
Richmond ⊖	d	19 34	19 45			19 49		19 58			20 04	20 15			20 19		20 28			20 34	20 45		
North Sheen	d	19 36				19 51					20 06				20 21					20 36			
Mortlake	d	19 38				19 53					20 08				20 23					20 38			
Hounslow	d						19 46			20 01						20 16			20 31				
Isleworth	d						19 49			20 04						20 19			20 34				
Syon Lane	d						19 51			20 06						20 21			20 36				
Brentford	d						19 54			20 09						20 24			20 39				
Kew Bridge	d						19 56			20 11						20 26			20 41				
Chiswick	d						19 59			20 14						20 29			20 44				
Barnes Bridge	d			←			20 01			20 16			←			20 31			20 46			←	
Barnes	d	19 41		19 49		19 56	20 04		←	20 19	20 11		20 19		20 26	20 34		←	20 49	20 41		20 49	
Putney	d	19 44		19 52		19 59	20 07	20 04	20 07	→	20 14		20 22		20 29	20 37	20 34	20 37	→	20 44		20 52	
Wandsworth Town	d	19 47		19 55		20 02	→		20 10		20 17		20 25		20 32	→		20 40		20 47		20 55	
Clapham Junction ■	d	19 50	19 54	19 58		20 05		20 09	20 13		20 20	20 24	20 28		20 35		20 39	20 43		20 50	20 54	20 58	
Queenstown Rd.(Battersea)	d	19 53		20 01		20 08			20 16		20 23		20 31		20 38			20 46		20 53		21 01	
Vauxhall ⊖	d	19 57		20 05		20 12		20 15	20 20		20 27		20 35		20 42		20 45	20 50		20 57		21 05	
London Waterloo ■ ⊖	a	20 02	20 04	20 11		20 16		20 19	20 26		20 32	20 34	20 41		20 46		20 49	20 56		21 02	21 04	21 11	

Saturdays
until 6 October

Reading, Guildford, Ascot, Weybridge, Windsor, Kingston, Richmond and Hounslow - London

Network Diagram - see first Page of Table 148

		SW	SW	SW	SW	SW	SW	SW ■	SW	SW ■	SW ■	SW	SW	SW	SW	SW	SW	SW ■	SW	SW	SW	SW
Reading 7	d							20 12										20 42				
Earley	d							20 17										20 47				
Winnersh Triangle	d							20 19										20 49				
Winnersh	d							20 21										20 51				
Wokingham	d							20 26										20 56				
Bracknell	d							20 32										21 02				
Martins Heron	d							20 35										21 05				
Guildford	d									20 00	20 30											
Wanborough	d									20 06	20 36											
Ash 5	d									20 10	20 40											
Aldershot	a									20 17	20 47											
	d									20 30												
Ash Vale	d									20 34												
Frimley	d									20 40												
Camberley	a									20 44												
	d									20 48												
Bagshot	d									20 53												
Ascot 3	d							20 40		21a00								21 10				
Sunningdale	d							20 43										21 13				
Longcross	d																					
Woking	d																					
West Byfleet	d																					
Byfleet & New Haw	d																					
Weybridge	d		20 03										20 33								21 03	
Addlestone	d		20 07										20 37								21 07	
Chertsey	d		20 10										20 40								21 10	
Virginia Water	a		20 15					20 49					20 45					21 19			21 15	
	d		20 24					20 49					20 54					21 19			21 24	
Egham	d		20 27					20 53					20 57					21 23			21 27	
Windsor & Eton Riverside	d			20 23										20 53								21 23
Datchet	d			20 26										20 56								21 26
Sunnymeads	d			20 29										20 59								21 29
Wraysbury	d			20 32										21 02								21 32
Staines	d		20 33	20 38				20 59					21 03	21 08				21 29			21 33	21 38
Ashford (Surrey)	d		20 36	20 41									21 06	21 11							21 36	21 41
Feltham	d		20 41	20 46				21 05					21 11	21 16				21 35			21 41	21 46
Whitton	d			20 50		20 50	20 53							21 20		21 20	21 23					21 50
Kingston	d	20 29										20 59								21 29		
Hampton Wick	d	20 31										21 01								21 31		
Teddington	d	20 35										21 05								21 35		
Fulwell	d																					
Strawberry Hill	d	20 38										21 08								21 38		
Twickenham	a	20 42		20 53			20 56	21 10				21 12		21 23			21 26	21 40		21 42		21 53
	d	20 43		20 53			20 58	21 11				21 13		21 23			21 28	21 41		21 43		21 53
St Margarets	d	20 45					21 00					21 15					21 30			21 45		
Richmond ⊖	d	20 49		20 58			21 04	21 15				21 19		21 28			21 34	21 45		21 49		21 58
North Sheen	d	20 51					21 06					21 21					21 36			21 51		
Mortlake	d	20 53					21 08					21 23					21 38			21 53		
Hounslow	d		20 46			21 01							21 16			21 31					21 46	
Isleworth	d		20 49			21 04							21 19			21 34					21 49	
Syon Lane	d		20 51			21 06							21 21			21 36					21 51	
Brentford	d		20 54			21 09							21 24			21 39					21 54	
Kew Bridge	d		20 56			21 11							21 26			21 41					21 56	
Chiswick	d		20 59			21 14							21 29			21 44					21 59	
Barnes Bridge	d		21 01			21 16			←				21 31			21 46			←		22 01	
Barnes	d	20 56	21 04		←	21 19	21 11		21 19			21 26	21 34		←	21 49	21 41		21 49	21 56	22 04	
Putney	d	20 59	21 07	21 04	21 07	→	21 14		21 22			21 29	21 37	21 34	21 37	→	21 44		21 52	21 59	22 07	22 04
Wandsworth Town	d	21 02	→		21 10		21 17		21 25			21 32	→		21 40		21 47		21 55	22 02	→	
Clapham Junction 10	d	21 05		21 09	21 13		21 20	21 24	21 28			21 35		21 39	21 43		21 50	21 54	21 58	22 05		22 09
Queenstown Rd.(Battersea)	d	21 08			21 16		21 23		21 31			21 38			21 46		21 53		22 01	22 08		
Vauxhall ⊖	d	21 12		21 15	21 20		21 27		21 35			21 42		21 45	21 50		21 57		22 05	22 12		22 15
London Waterloo 15 ⊖	a	21 16		21 19	21 26		21 32	21 34	21 41			21 46		21 49	21 56		22 02	22 04	22 11	22 16		22 19

Table 149

Saturdays
until 6 October

Reading, Guildford, Ascot, Weybridge, Windsor, Kingston, Richmond and Hounslow - London

Network Diagram - see first Page of Table 148

		SW	SW	SW	SW ■	SW	SW ■	SW ■	SW	SW	SW	SW	SW	SW ■	SW	SW	SW	SW	SW ■	SW ■	SW ■	SW	SW
Reading 7	d				21 12									21 42					22 12				
Earley	d				21 17									21 47					22 17				
Winnersh Triangle	d				21 19									21 49					22 19				
Winnersh	d				21 21									21 51					22 21				
Wokingham	d				21 26									21 56					22 26				
Bracknell	d				21 32									22 02					22 32				
Martins Heron	d				21 35									22 05					22 35				
Guildford	d						21 00	21 30												22 00	22 30		
Wanborough	d						21 06	21 36												22 06	22 36		
Ash 5	d						21 10	21 40												22 10	22 40		
Aldershot	a						21 17	21 47												22 17	22 47		
	d						21 30													22 30			
Ash Vale	d						21 34													22 34			
Frimley	d						21 40													22 40			
Camberley	a						21 44													22 44			
	d						21 48													22 48			
Bagshot	d						21 53													22 53			
Ascot 3	d				21 40		22a00							22 10					22 40	23a00			
Sunningdale	d				21 43									22 13					22 43				
Longcross	d																						
Woking	d																						
West Byfleet	d																						
Byfleet & New Haw	d																						
Weybridge	d									21 33						22 03							22 33
Addlestone	d									21 37						22 07							22 37
Chertsey	d									21 40						22 10							22 40
Virginia Water	a				21 49					21 45				22 19		22 15			22 49				22 45
	d				21 49					21 54				22 19		22 24			22 49				22 54
Egham	d				21 53					21 57				22 23		22 27			22 53				22 57
Windsor & Eton Riverside	d										21 53						22 23						
Datchet	d										21 56						22 26						
Sunnymeads	d										21 59						22 29						
Wraysbury	d										22 02						22 32						
Staines	d				21 59					22 03	22 08			22 29		22 33	22 38		22 59				23 03
Ashford (Surrey)	d									22 06	22 11					22 36	22 41						23 06
Feltham	d				22 05					22 11	22 16			22 35		22 41	22 46		23 05				23 11
Whitton	d		21 50	21 53							22 20		22 23				22 50						
Kingston	d								21 59						22 29							22 59	
Hampton Wick	d								22 01						22 31							23 01	
Teddington	d								22 05						22 35							23 05	
Fulwell	d																						
Strawberry Hill	d								22 08						22 38							23 08	
Twickenham	a			21 56	22 10				22 12		22 23		22 26	22 40	22 42		22 53		23 10			23 12	
	d			21 58	22 11				22 13		22 23		22 28	22 41	22 43		22 53		23 11			23 13	
St Margarets	d			22 00					22 15				22 30		22 45							23 15	
Richmond ⊖	d			22 04	22 15				22 19		22 28		22 34	22 45	22 49		22 58		23 15			23 19	
North Sheen	d			22 06					22 21				22 36		22 51							23 21	
Mortlake	d			22 08					22 23				22 38		22 53							23 23	
Hounslow	d		22 01							22 16						22 46							23 16
Isleworth	d		22 04							22 19						22 49							23 19
Syon Lane	d		22 06							22 21						22 51							23 21
Brentford	d		22 09							22 24						22 54							23 24
Kew Bridge	d		22 11							22 26						22 56							23 26
Chiswick	d		22 14							22 29						22 59							23 29
Barnes Bridge	d		22 16			←				22 31						23 01							23 31
Barnes	d	←	22 19	22 11		22 19			22 26	22 34		←	22 41		22 56	23 04		←				23 26	23 34
Putney	d	22 07	→	22 14		22 22			22 29	22 37	22 34	22 37	22 44		22 59	23 07	23 04	23 07				23 29	23 37
Wandsworth Town	d	22 10		22 17		22 25			22 32	→		22 40	22 47		23 02	→		23 10				23 32	→
Clapham Junction 10	d	22 13		22 20	22 24	22 28			22 35		22 39	22 43	22 50	22 54	23 05		23 09	23 13	23 24			23 35	
Queenstown Rd.(Battersea)	d	22 16		22 23		22 31			22 38			22 46	22 53		23 08			23 16				23 38	
Vauxhall ⊖	d	22 20		22 27		22 35			22 42		22 45	22 50	22 57		23 12		23 15	23 20				23 42	
London Waterloo 15 ⊖	a	22 26		22 32	22 34	22 41			22 46		22 49	22 56	23 02	23 04	23 17		23 19	23 26	23 34			23 46	

Table 149

Saturdays until 6 October

Reading, Guildford, Ascot, Weybridge, Windsor, Kingston, Richmond and Hounslow - London

Network Diagram - see first Page of Table 148

		SW	SW	SW ■		SW	SW	SW	SW	SW ■	SW ■	SW ■	SW
Reading ■	d			22 42						23 12			
Earley	d			22 47						23 17			
Winnersh Triangle	d			22 49						23 19			
Winnersh	d			22 51						23 21			
Wokingham	d			22 56						23 26			
Bracknell	d			23 02						23 32			
Martins Heron	d			23 05						23 35			
Guildford	d										23 00	23 30	
Wanborough	d										23 06	23 36	
Ash ■	d										23 10	23 40	
Aldershot	a										23 17	23 47	
	d										23 30		
Ash Vale	d										23 34		
Frimley	d										23 40		
Camberley	a										23 44		
	d										23 48		
Bagshot	d										23 53		
Ascot ■	d			23 10						23 40	00a01		
Sunningdale	d			23 13						23 43			
Longcross	d												
Woking	d												
West Byfleet	d												
Byfleet & New Haw	d												
Weybridge	d					23 03							23 33
Addlestone	d					23 07							23 37
Chertsey	d					23 10							23 40
Virginia Water	a			23 19		23 15				23 49			23 45
	d			23 19		23 24				23 49			23 54
Egham	d			23 23		23 27				23 53			23 57
Windsor & Eton Riverside	d	22 53					23 28						
Datchet	d	22 56					23 31						
Sunnymeads	d	22 59					23 34						
Wraysbury	d	23 02					23 37						
Staines	d	23 08		23 29		23a32	23a42			23 59			00a02
Ashford (Surrey)	d	23 11											
Feltham	d	23 16		23 35						00 05			
Whitton	d	23 20											
Kingston	d							23 29	23 55				
Hampton Wick	d							23 31	23 57				
Teddington	d							23 35	23 59				
Fulwell	d												
Strawberry Hill	d							23 38	00 03				
Twickenham	a	23 23		23 40				23 42	00 07	00 10			
	d	23 23		23 41				23 43		00 11			
St Margarets	d							23 45					
Richmond ⊖	d	23 28		23 45				23 49		00 15			
North Sheen	d							23 51					
Mortlake	d							23 53					
Hounslow	d												
Isleworth	d												
Syon Lane	d												
Brentford	d												
Kew Bridge	d												
Chiswick	d												
Barnes Bridge	d												
Barnes	d		←					23 56					
Putney	d	23 34	23 37					23 59					
Wandsworth Town	d		23 40					00 02					
Clapham Junction ■	d	23 39	23 43	23 54				00 05		00 24			
Queenstown Rd.(Battersea)	d		23 46					00 08					
Vauxhall ⊖	d	23 45	23 50					00 12					
London Waterloo ■ ⊖	a	23 49	23 56	00 02				00 16		00 37			

Table 149

Saturdays from 13 October

Reading, Guildford, Ascot, Weybridge, Windsor, Kingston, Richmond and Hounslow - London

Network Diagram - see first Page of Table 148

		SW ■	SW	SW	SW ■	SW	SW	SW	SW	SW	SW	SW	SW		SW	SW	SW ■	SW ■	SW	SW	SW	SW	SW ■	SW	SW
Reading ■	d	22p39			23p12												05 39						06 09		
Earley	d	22p44			23p17												05 44						06 14		
Winnersh Triangle	d	22p46			23p19												05 46						06 16		
Winnersh	d	22p48			23p21												05 48						06 18		
Wokingham	d	22p53			23p26												05 53						06 23		
Bracknell	d	22p59			23p32												05 59						06 29		
Martins Heron	d	23p02			23p35												06 02						06 32		
Guildford	d																								
Wanborough	d																								
Ash ■	d																								
Aldershot	a																								
	d																	06 00							
Ash Vale	d																	06 04							
Frimley	d																	06 10							
Camberley	a																	06 14							
	d																	06 18							
Bagshot	d																	06 23							
Ascot ■	d	23p07			23p40												06 07	06a30					06 37		
Sunningdale	d	23p10			23p43												06 10						06 40		
Longcross	d																								
Woking	d												05 27												
West Byfleet	d												05 32												
Byfleet & New Haw	d												05 35												
Weybridge	d																								06 33
Addlestone	d												05 39												06 37
Chertsey	d												05 42												06 40
Virginia Water	a	23p19			23p49								05 47				06 19						06 49		06 45
	d	23p19			23p49								05 54				06 19						06 49		06 54
Egham	d	23p23			23p53								05 57				06 23						06 53		06 57
Windsor & Eton Riverside	d														05 51						06 21				
Datchet	d														05 55						06 25				
Sunnymeads	d														05 58						06 28				
Wraysbury	d														06 02						06 32				
Staines	d	23p29			23p59		04 58			05 37			06 03		06 08		06 29			06 33	06 38		06 59		07 03
Ashford (Surrey)	d						05 01			05 40			06 06		06 11					06 36	06 41				07 06
Feltham	d	23p35			00 05		05 06			05 45			06 11		06 16		06 35			06 41	06 46		07 05		07 11
Whitton	d						05 10		05 41	05 49					06 20						06 50				
Kingston	d		23p29	23p55		01 17	01 17					05 59							06 29					06 59	
Hampton Wick	d		23p31	23p57		01s22	01s22					06 01							06 31					07 01	
Teddington	d		23p35	23p59		01 25	01 25					06 05							06 35					07 05	
Fulwell	d																								
Strawberry Hill	d		23p38	00 03		01 28	01 28	05 38				06 08							06 38					07 08	
Twickenham	a	23p40	23p42	00 07	00 10		05 13	05 41		05 52		06 12			06 23		06 40		06 42		06 53		07 10	07 12	
	d	23p41	23p43		00 11		05 13	05 43		05 53		06 13			06 23		06 41		06 43		06 53		07 11	07 13	
St Margarets	d		23p45				05 15	05 45				06 15							06 45					07 15	
Richmond ⊖	d	23p45	23p49		00 15		05 19	05 49		05 58		06 19			06 28		06 45		06 49		06 58		07 15	07 19	
North Sheen	d		23p51				05 21	05 51				06 21							06 51					07 21	
Mortlake	d		23p53				05 23	05 53				06 23							06 53					07 23	
Hounslow	d								05 46				06 16							06 46					07 16
Isleworth	d								05 49				06 19							06 49					07 19
Syon Lane	d								05 51				06 21							06 51					07 21
Brentford	d								05 54				06 24							06 54					07 24
Kew Bridge	d								05 56				06 26							06 56					07 26
Chiswick	d								05 59				06 29							06 59					07 29
Barnes Bridge	d								06 01				06 31							07 01					07 31
Barnes	d		23p56				05 26	05 56	06 04		←	06 26	06 34			←			06 56	07 04		←		07 26	07 34
Putney	d		23p59				05 29	05 59	06 07	06 04	06 07	06 29	06 37		06 34	06 37			06 59	07 07	07 04	07 07		07 29	07 37
Wandsworth Town	d		00 02				05 32	06 02	→		06 10	06 32	→			06 40			07 02	→		07 10		07 32	→
Clapham Junction ■	d	23p54	00 05		00 24		05 35	06 05		06 09	06 13	06 35			06 39	06 43	06 54		07 05		07 09	07 13	07 24	07 35	
Queenstown Rd.(Battersea)	d		00 08				05 38	06 08			06 16	06 38				06 46			07 08			07 16		07 38	
Vauxhall ⊖	d		00 12				05 42	06 12		06 15	06 20	06 42			06 45	06 50			07 12		07 15	07 20		07 42	
London Waterloo ■ ⊖	a	00 04	00 16		00 37		05 46	06 16		06 19	06 26	06 46			06 49	06 56	07 04		07 16		07 19	07 26	07 34	07 46	

Table 149

Saturdays
from 13 October

Reading, Guildford, Ascot, Weybridge, Windsor, Kingston, Richmond and Hounslow - London

Network Diagram - see first Page of Table 148

		SW	SW	SW ■	SW ■	SW		SW	SW	SW	SW	SW	SW ■	SW ■	SW	SW		SW	SW	SW	SW	SW	SW ■	SW	SW ■
Reading ■	d			06 39									07 09										07 39		
Earley	d			06 44									07 14										07 44		
Winnersh Triangle	d			06 46									07 16										07 46		
Winnersh	d			06 48									07 18										07 48		
Wokingham	d			06 53									07 23										07 53		
Bracknell	d			06 59									07 29										07 59		
Martins Heron	d			07 02									07 32										08 02		
Guildford	d				06 30									07 00											07 30
Wanborough	d				06 36									07 06											07 36
Ash ■	d				06 40									07 10											07 40
Aldershot	a				06 47									07 17											07 47
	d				07 00									07 30											08 00
Ash Vale	d				07 04									07 34											08 04
Frimley	d				07 10									07 40											08 10
Camberley	a				07 14									07 44											08 14
	d				07 18									07 48											08 18
Bagshot	d				07 23									07 53											08 23
Ascot ■	d			07 07	07a30								07 37	08a00									08 07		08a30
Sunningdale	d			07 10									07 40										08 10		
Longcross	d																								
Woking	d																								
West Byfleet	d																								
Byfleet & New Haw	d																								
Weybridge	d								07 03									07 33							
Addlestone	d								07 07									07 37							
Chertsey	d								07 10									07 40							
Virginia Water	a			07 19					07 15				07 49					07 45					08 19		
	d			07 19					07 24				07 49					07 54					08 19		
Egham	d			07 23					07 27				07 53					07 57					08 23		
Windsor & Eton Riverside	d	06 51								07 21									07 51						
Datchet	d	06 55								07 25									07 55						
Sunnymeads	d	06 58								07 28									07 58						
Wraysbury	d	07 02								07 32									08 02						
Staines	d	07 08		07 29					07 33	07 38			07 59					08 03	08 08				08 29		
Ashford (Surrey)	d	07 11							07 36	07 41								08 06	08 11						
Feltham	d	07 16		07 35					07 41	07 46			08 05					08 11	08 16				08 35		
Whitton	d	07 20								07 50					07 50				08 20		08 20	08 23			
Kingston	d							07 29								07 59									
Hampton Wick	d							07 31								08 01									
Teddington	d							07 35								08 05									
Fulwell	d																								
Strawberry Hill	d							07 38								08 08									
Twickenham	a	07 23		07 40				07 42		07 53			08 10			08 12			08 23			08 26	08 40		
	d	07 23		07 41				07 43		07 53		07 58	08 11			08 13			08 23			08 28	08 41		
St Margarets	d							07 45				08 00				08 15						08 30			
Richmond ⊖	d	07 28		07 45				07 49		07 58		08 04	08 15			08 19			08 28			08 34	08 45		
North Sheen	d							07 51				08 06				08 21						08 36			
Mortlake	d							07 53				08 08				08 23						08 38			
Hounslow	d					07 31			07 46						08 01			08 16			08 31				
Isleworth	d					07 34			07 49						08 04			08 19			08 34				
Syon Lane	d					07 36			07 51						08 06			08 21			08 36				
Brentford	d					07 39			07 54						08 09			08 24			08 39				
Kew Bridge	d					07 41			07 56						08 11			08 26			08 41				
Chiswick	d					07 44			07 59						08 14			08 29			08 44				
Barnes Bridge	d					07 46			08 01						08 16			08 31			08 46			←	
Barnes	d		←			07 49		07 56	08 04		←	08 11			08 19	08 26		08 34		←	08 49	08 41		08 49	
Putney	d	07 34	07 37			07 52		07 59	08 07	08 04	08 07	08 14			08 22	08 29		08 37	08 34	08 37	→	08 44		08 52	
Wandsworth Town	d		07 40			07 55		08 02	→		08 10	08 17			08 25	08 32		→		08 40		08 47		08 55	
Clapham Junction ■	d	07 39	07 43	07 54		07 58		08 05		08 09	08 13	08 20	08 24		08 28	08 35			08 39	08 43		08 50	08 54	08 58	
Queenstown Rd.(Battersea)	d		07 46			08 01		08 08			08 16	08 23			08 31	08 38				08 46		08 53		09 01	
Vauxhall ⊖	d	07 45	07 50			08 05		08 12		08 15	08 20	08 27			08 35	08 42			08 45	08 50		08 57		09 05	
London Waterloo ■ ⊖	a	07 49	07 56	08 04		08 11		08 16		08 19	08 26	08 32	08 34		08 41	08 46			08 49	08 56		09 02	09 04	09 11	

Table 149

Saturdays
from 13 October

Reading, Guildford, Ascot, Weybridge, Windsor, Kingston, Richmond and Hounslow - London

Network Diagram - see first Page of Table 148

		SW		SW	SW	SW	SW	SW	SW ■	SW	SW ■	SW		SW	SW	SW	SW	SW	SW ■	SW	SW ■	SW		SW	SW
Reading ■	d								08 09										08 39						
Earley	d								08 14										08 44						
Winnersh Triangle	d								08 16										08 46						
Winnersh	d								08 18										08 48						
Wokingham	d								08 23										08 53						
Bracknell	d								08 29										08 59						
Martins Heron	d								08 32										09 02						
Guildford	d										08 00										08 30				
Wanborough	d										08 06										08 36				
Ash ■	d										08 10										08 40				
Aldershot	a										08 17										08 47				
	d										08 30										09 00				
Ash Vale	d										08 34										09 04				
Frimley	d										08 40										09 10				
Camberley	a										08 44										09 14				
	d										08 48										09 18				
Bagshot	d										08 53										09 23				
Ascot ■	d								08 37		09a00								09 07		09a30				
Sunningdale	d								08 40										09 10						
Longcross	d																								
Woking	d																								
West Byfleet	d																								
Byfleet & New Haw	d																								
Weybridge	d			08 03										08 33										09 03	
Addlestone	d			08 07										08 37										09 07	
Chertsey	d			08 10										08 40										09 10	
Virginia Water	a			08 15					08 49					08 45					09 19					09 15	
	d			08 24					08 49					08 54					09 19					09 24	
Egham	d			08 27					08 53					08 57					09 23					09 27	
Windsor & Eton Riverside	d				08 21										08 51										09 21
Datchet	d				08 25										08 55										09 25
Sunnymeads	d				08 28										08 58										09 28
Wraysbury	d				08 32										09 02										09 32
Staines	d			08 33	08 38				08 59					09 03	09 08				09 29					09 33	09 38
Ashford (Surrey)	d			08 36	08 41									09 06	09 11									09 36	09 41
Feltham	d			08 41	08 46				09 05					09 11	09 16				09 35					09 41	09 46
Whitton	d				08 50		08 50	08 53							09 20		09 20	09 23							09 50
Kingston	d	08 29										08 59										09 29			
Hampton Wick	d	08 31										09 01										09 31			
Teddington	d	08 35										09 05										09 35			
Fulwell	d																								
Strawberry Hill	d	08 38										09 08										09 38			
Twickenham	a	08 42			08 53			08 56	09 10			09 12			09 23			09 26	09 40			09 42			09 53
	d	08 43			08 53			08 58	09 11			09 13			09 23			09 28	09 41			09 43			09 53
St Margarets	d	08 45						09 00				09 15						09 30				09 45			
Richmond ⊖	d	08 49			08 58			09 04	09 15			09 19			09 28			09 34	09 45			09 49			09 58
North Sheen	d	08 51						09 06				09 21						09 36				09 51			
Mortlake	d	08 53						09 08				09 23						09 38				09 53			
Hounslow	d			08 46			09 01							09 16			09 31							09 46	
Isleworth	d			08 49			09 04							09 19			09 34							09 49	
Syon Lane	d			08 51			09 06							09 21			09 36							09 51	
Brentford	d			08 54			09 09							09 24			09 39							09 54	
Kew Bridge	d			08 56			09 11							09 26			09 41							09 56	
Chiswick	d			08 59			09 14							09 29			09 44							09 59	
Barnes Bridge	d			09 01			09 16			←				09 31			09 46			←				10 01	
Barnes	d	08 56		09 04		←	09 19	09 11		09 19		09 26		09 34		←	09 49	09 41		09 49		09 56		10 04	
Putney	d	08 59		09 07	09 04	09 07	→	09 14		09 22		09 29		09 37	09 34	09 37	→	09 44		09 52		09 59		10 07	10 04
Wandsworth Town	d	09 02		→		09 10		09 17		09 25		09 32		→		09 40		09 47		09 55		10 02		→	
Clapham Junction ■	d	09 05			09 09	09 13		09 20	09 24	09 28		09 35			09 39	09 43		09 50	09 54	09 58		10 05			10 09
Queenstown Rd.(Battersea)	d	09 08				09 16		09 23		09 31		09 38				09 46		09 53		10 01		10 08			
Vauxhall ⊖	d	09 12			09 15	09 20		09 27		09 35		09 42			09 45	09 50		09 57		10 05		10 12			10 15
London Waterloo ■ ⊖	a	09 16			09 19	09 26		09 32	09 34	09 41		09 46			09 49	09 56		10 02	10 04	10 11		10 16			10 19

Table 149

Saturdays from 13 October

Reading, Guildford, Ascot, Weybridge, Windsor, Kingston, Richmond and Hounslow - London

Network Diagram - see first Page of Table 148

		SW	SW	SW	SW ■	SW	SW ■	SW		SW	SW	SW	SW
Reading ■	d				09 09								
Earley	d				09 14								
Winnersh Triangle	d				09 16								
Winnersh	d				09 18								
Wokingham	d				09 23								
Bracknell	d				09 29								
Martins Heron	d				09 32								
Guildford	d						09 00						
Wanborough	d						09 06						
Ash ■	d						09 10						
Aldershot	a						09 17						
	d						09 30						
Ash Vale	d						09 34						
Frimley	d						09 40						
Camberley	a						09 44						
	d						09 48						
Bagshot	d						09 53						
Ascot ■	d				09 37		10a00						
Sunningdale	d				09 40								
Longcross	d												
Woking	d												
West Byfleet	d												
Byfleet & New Haw	d												
Weybridge	d									09 33			
Addlestone	d									09 37			
Chertsey	d									09 40			
Virginia Water	a				09 49					09 45			
	d				09 49					09 54			
Egham	d				09 53					09 57			
Windsor & Eton Riverside	d										09 51		
Datchet	d										09 55		
Sunnymeads	d										09 58		
Wraysbury	d										10 02		
Staines	d				09 59					10 03	10 08		
Ashford (Surrey)	d									10 06	10 11		
Feltham	d				10 05					10 11	10 16		
Whitton	d		09 50	09 53							10 20		10 20
Kingston	d							09 59					
Hampton Wick	d							10 01					
Teddington	d							10 05					
Fulwell	d												
Strawberry Hill	d							10 08					
Twickenham	a			09 56	10 10			10 12			10 23		
	d			09 58	10 11			10 13			10 23		
St Margarets	d			10 00				10 15					
Richmond ⊖	d			10 04	10 15			10 19			10 28		
North Sheen	d			10 06				10 21					
Mortlake	d			10 08				10 23					
Hounslow	d		10 01							10 16			10 31
Isleworth	d		10 04							10 19			10 34
Syon Lane	d		10 06							10 21			10 36
Brentford	d		10 09							10 24			10 39
Kew Bridge	d		10 11							10 26			10 41
Chiswick	d		10 14							10 29			10 44
Barnes Bridge	d		10 16			←				10 31			10 46
Barnes	d	←	10 19	10 11		10 19		10 26		10 34		←	10 49
Putney	d	10 07	→	10 14		10 22		10 29		10 37	10 34	10 37	→
Wandsworth Town	d	10 10		10 17		10 25		10 32		→		10 40	
Clapham Junction ■	d	10 13		10 20	10 24	10 28		10 35			10 39	10 43	
Queenstown Rd.(Battersea)	d	10 16		10 23		10 31		10 38				10 46	
Vauxhall ⊖	d	10 20		10 27		10 35		10 42			10 45	10 50	
London Waterloo ■ ⊖	a	10 26		10 32	10 34	10 41		10 46			10 49	10 56	

		SW	SW ■	SW	SW ■	SW		SW	SW	SW	SW	SW	SW ■
Reading ■	d		09 39										10 09
Earley	d		09 44										10 14
Winnersh Triangle	d		09 46										10 16
Winnersh	d		09 48										10 18
Wokingham	d		09 53										10 23
Bracknell	d		09 59										10 29
Martins Heron	d		10 02										10 32
Guildford	d				09 30								
Wanborough	d				09 36								
Ash ■	d				09 40								
Aldershot	a				09 47								
	d				10 00								
Ash Vale	d				10 04								
Frimley	d				10 10								
Camberley	a				10 14								
	d				10 18								
Bagshot	d				10 23								
Ascot ■	d		10 07		10a30								10 37
Sunningdale	d		10 10										10 40
Longcross	d												
Woking	d												
West Byfleet	d												
Byfleet & New Haw	d												
Weybridge	d							10 03					
Addlestone	d							10 07					
Chertsey	d							10 10					
Virginia Water	a		10 19					10 15					10 49
	d		10 19					10 24					10 49
Egham	d		10 23					10 27					10 53
Windsor & Eton Riverside	d								10 21				
Datchet	d								10 25				
Sunnymeads	d								10 28				
Wraysbury	d								10 32				
Staines	d		10 29					10 33	10 38				10 59
Ashford (Surrey)	d							10 36	10 41				
Feltham	d		10 35					10 41	10 46				11 05
Whitton	d	10 23							10 50		10 50	10 53	
Kingston	d					10 29							
Hampton Wick	d					10 31							
Teddington	d					10 35							
Fulwell	d												
Strawberry Hill	d					10 38							
Twickenham	a	10 26	10 40			10 42			10 53			10 56	11 10
	d	10 28	10 41			10 43			10 53			10 58	11 11
St Margarets	d	10 30				10 45						11 00	
Richmond ⊖	d	10 34	10 45			10 49			10 58			11 04	11 15
North Sheen	d	10 36				10 51						11 06	
Mortlake	d	10 38				10 53						11 08	
Hounslow	d							10 46			11 01		
Isleworth	d							10 49			11 04		
Syon Lane	d							10 51			11 06		
Brentford	d							10 54			11 09		
Kew Bridge	d							10 56			11 11		
Chiswick	d							10 59			11 14		
Barnes Bridge	d			←				11 01			11 16		
Barnes	d	10 41		10 49		10 56		11 04		←	11 19	11 11	
Putney	d	10 44		10 52		10 59		11 07	11 04	11 07	→	11 14	
Wandsworth Town	d	10 47		10 55		11 02		→		11 10		11 17	
Clapham Junction ■	d	10 50	10 54	10 58		11 05			11 09	11 13		11 20	11 24
Queenstown Rd.(Battersea)	d	10 53		11 01		11 08				11 16		11 23	
Vauxhall ⊖	d	10 57		11 05		11 12			11 15	11 20		11 27	
London Waterloo ■ ⊖	a	11 02	11 04	11 11		11 16			11 19	11 26		11 32	11 34

Table 149

Saturdays from 13 October

Reading, Guildford, Ascot, Weybridge, Windsor, Kingston, Richmond and Hounslow - London

Network Diagram - see first Page of Table 148

		SW	SW ■	SW		SW	SW	SW	SW	SW	SW ■	SW	SW ■
Reading ■	d										10 39		
Earley	d										10 44		
Winnersh Triangle	d										10 46		
Winnersh	d										10 48		
Wokingham	d										10 53		
Bracknell	d										10 59		
Martins Heron	d										11 02		
Guildford	d		10 00										10 30
Wanborough	d		10 06										10 36
Ash ■	d		10 10										10 40
Aldershot	a		10 17										10 47
	d		10 30										11 00
Ash Vale	d		10 34										11 04
Frimley	d		10 40										11 10
Camberley	a		10 44										11 14
	d		10 48										11 18
Bagshot	d		10 53										11 23
Ascot ■	d		11a00								11 07		11a30
Sunningdale	d										11 10		
Longcross	d												
Woking	d												
West Byfleet	d												
Byfleet & New Haw	d												
Weybridge	d					10 33							
Addlestone	d					10 37							
Chertsey	d					10 40							
Virginia Water	a					10 45					11 19		
	d					10 54					11 19		
Egham	d					10 57					11 23		
Windsor & Eton Riverside	d						10 51						
Datchet	d						10 55						
Sunnymeads	d						10 58						
Wraysbury	d						11 02						
Staines	d					11 03	11 08				11 29		
Ashford (Surrey)	d					11 06	11 11						
Feltham	d					11 11	11 16				11 35		
Whitton	d						11 20		11 20	11 23			
Kingston	d			10 59									
Hampton Wick	d			11 01									
Teddington	d			11 05									
Fulwell	d												
Strawberry Hill	d			11 08									
Twickenham	a			11 12			11 23			11 26	11 40		
	d			11 13			11 23			11 28	11 41		
St Margarets	d			11 15						11 30			
Richmond ⊖	d			11 19			11 28			11 34	11 45		
North Sheen	d			11 21						11 36			
Mortlake	d			11 23						11 38			
Hounslow	d					11 16			11 31				
Isleworth	d					11 19			11 34				
Syon Lane	d					11 21			11 36				
Brentford	d					11 24			11 39				
Kew Bridge	d					11 26			11 41				
Chiswick	d					11 29			11 44				
Barnes Bridge	d	←				11 31			11 46			←	
Barnes	d	11 19		11 26		11 34		←	11 49	11 41		11 49	
Putney	d	11 22		11 29		11 37	11 34	11 37	→	11 44		11 52	
Wandsworth Town	d	11 25		11 32		→		11 40		11 47		11 55	
Clapham Junction ■	d	11 28		11 35			11 39	11 43		11 50	11 54	11 58	
Queenstown Rd.(Battersea)	d	11 31		11 38				11 46		11 53		12 01	
Vauxhall ⊖	d	11 35		11 42			11 45	11 50		11 57		12 05	
London Waterloo ■ ⊖	a	11 41		11 46			11 49	11 56		12 02	12 04	12 11	

		SW		SW	SW	SW	SW	SW	SW ■	SW	SW ■	SW
Reading ■	d								11 09			
Earley	d								11 14			
Winnersh Triangle	d								11 16			
Winnersh	d								11 18			
Wokingham	d								11 23			
Bracknell	d								11 29			
Martins Heron	d								11 32			
Guildford	d										11 00	
Wanborough	d										11 06	
Ash ■	d										11 10	
Aldershot	a										11 17	
	d										11 30	
Ash Vale	d										11 34	
Frimley	d										11 40	
Camberley	a										11 44	
	d										11 48	
Bagshot	d										11 53	
Ascot ■	d								11 37		12a00	
Sunningdale	d								11 40			
Longcross	d											
Woking	d											
West Byfleet	d											
Byfleet & New Haw	d											
Weybridge	d			11 03								
Addlestone	d			11 07								
Chertsey	d			11 10								
Virginia Water	a			11 15					11 49			
	d			11 24					11 49			
Egham	d			11 27					11 53			
Windsor & Eton Riverside	d				11 21							
Datchet	d				11 25							
Sunnymeads	d				11 28							
Wraysbury	d				11 32							
Staines	d			11 33	11 38				11 59			
Ashford (Surrey)	d			11 36	11 41							
Feltham	d			11 41	11 46				12 05			
Whitton	d				11 50		11 50	11 53				
Kingston	d	11 29										11 59
Hampton Wick	d	11 31										12 01
Teddington	d	11 35										12 05
Fulwell	d											
Strawberry Hill	d	11 38										12 08
Twickenham	a	11 42			11 53			11 56	12 10			12 12
	d	11 43			11 53			11 58	12 11			12 13
St Margarets	d	11 45						12 00				12 15
Richmond ⊖	d	11 49			11 58			12 04	12 15			12 19
North Sheen	d	11 51						12 06				12 21
Mortlake	d	11 53						12 08				12 23
Hounslow	d			11 46			12 01					
Isleworth	d			11 49			12 04					
Syon Lane	d			11 51			12 06					
Brentford	d			11 54			12 09					
Kew Bridge	d			11 56			12 11					
Chiswick	d			11 59			12 14					
Barnes Bridge	d			12 01			12 16			←		
Barnes	d	11 56		12 04		←	12 19	12 11		12 19		12 26
Putney	d	11 59		12 07	12 04	12 07	→	12 14		12 22		12 29
Wandsworth Town	d	12 02		→		12 10		12 17		12 25		12 32
Clapham Junction ■	d	12 05			12 09	12 13		12 20	12 24	12 28		12 35
Queenstown Rd.(Battersea)	d	12 08				12 16		12 23		12 31		12 38
Vauxhall ⊖	d	12 12			12 15	12 20		12 27		12 35		12 42
London Waterloo ■ ⊖	a	12 16			12 19	12 26		12 32	12 34	12 41		12 46

Table 149

Saturdays from 13 October

Reading, Guildford, Ascot, Weybridge, Windsor, Kingston, Richmond and Hounslow - London

Network Diagram - see first Page of Table 148

		SW	SW	SW	SW	SW	SW 1	SW	SW 1	SW	SW	SW	SW	SW	SW	SW 1	SW	SW 1	SW	SW	SW	SW	SW
Reading	d						11 39									12 09							
Earley	d						11 44									12 14							
Winnersh Triangle	d						11 46									12 16							
Winnersh	d						11 48									12 18							
Wokingham	d						11 53									12 23							
Bracknell	d						11 59									12 29							
Martins Heron	d						12 02									12 32							
Guildford	d								11 30									12 00					
Wanborough	d								11 36									12 06					
Ash	d								11 40									12 10					
Aldershot	a								11 47									12 17					
	d								12 00									12 30					
Ash Vale	d								12 04									12 34					
Frimley	d								12 10									12 40					
Camberley	a								12 14									12 44					
	d								12 18									12 48					
Bagshot	d								12 23									12 53					
Ascot	d						12 07		12a30							12 37		13a00					
Sunningdale	d						12 10									12 40							
Longcross	d																						
Woking	d																						
West Byfleet	d																						
Byfleet & New Haw	d																						
Weybridge	d	11 33									12 03									12 33			
Addlestone	d	11 37									12 07									12 37			
Chertsey	d	11 40									12 10									12 40			
Virginia Water	a	11 45					12 19				12 15					12 49				12 45			
	d	11 54					12 19				12 24					12 49				12 54			
Egham	d	11 57					12 23				12 27					12 53				12 57			
Windsor & Eton Riverside	d		11 51									12 21									12 51		
Datchet	d		11 55									12 25									12 55		
Sunnymeads	d		11 58									12 28									12 58		
Wraysbury	d		12 02									12 32									13 02		
Staines	d	12 03	12 08				12 29				12 33	12 38				12 59				13 03	13 08		
Ashford (Surrey)	d	12 06	12 11								12 36	12 41								13 06	13 11		
Feltham	d	12 11	12 16				12 35				12 41	12 46				13 05				13 11	13 16		
Whitton	d		12 20		12 20	12 23						12 50		12 50	12 53						13 20		13 20
Kingston	d									12 29									12 59				
Hampton Wick	d									12 31									13 01				
Teddington	d									12 35									13 05				
Fulwell	d																						
Strawberry Hill	d									12 38									13 08				
Twickenham	a		12 23			12 27	12 40			12 42		12 53			12 56	13 10			13 12		13 23		
	d		12 23			12 28	12 41			12 43		12 53			12 58	13 11			13 13		13 23		
St Margarets	d					12 30				12 45					13 00				13 15				
Richmond ⊖	d		12 28			12 34	12 45			12 49		12 58			13 04	13 15			13 19		13 28		
North Sheen	d					12 36				12 51					13 06				13 21				
Mortlake	d					12 38				12 53					13 08				13 23				
Hounslow	d	12 16			12 31						12 46			13 01						13 16			13 31
Isleworth	d	12 19			12 34						12 49			13 04						13 19			13 34
Syon Lane	d	12 21			12 36						12 51			13 06						13 21			13 36
Brentford	d	12 24			12 39						12 54			13 09						13 24			13 39
Kew Bridge	d	12 26			12 41						12 56			13 11						13 26			13 41
Chiswick	d	12 29			12 44						12 59			13 14						13 29			13 44
Barnes Bridge	d	12 31			12 46			←			13 01			13 16			←			13 31			13 46
Barnes	d	12 34		←	12 49	12 41		12 49		12 56	13 04		←	13 19	13 11		13 19		13 26	13 34		←	13 49
Putney	d	12 37	12 34	12 37	→	12 44		12 52		12 59	13 07	13 04	13 07	→	13 14		13 22		13 29	13 37	13 34	13 37	→
Wandsworth Town	d	→		12 40		12 47		12 55		13 02	→		13 10		13 17		13 25		13 32	→		13 40	
Clapham Junction 10	d		12 39	12 43		12 50	12 54	12 58		13 05		13 09	13 13		13 20	13 24	13 28		13 35		13 39	13 43	
Queenstown Rd.(Battersea)	d			12 46		12 53		13 01		13 08			13 16		13 23		13 31		13 38			13 46	
Vauxhall ⊖	d		12 45	12 50		12 57		13 05		13 12		13 15	13 20		13 27		13 35		13 42		13 45	13 50	
London Waterloo 15 ⊖	a		12 49	12 56		13 02	13 04	13 11		13 16		13 19	13 26		13 32	13 34	13 41		13 46		13 49	13 56	

Table 149

Saturdays from 13 October

Reading, Guildford, Ascot, Weybridge, Windsor, Kingston, Richmond and Hounslow - London

Network Diagram - see first Page of Table 148

		SW	SW 1	SW	SW 1	SW	SW	SW	SW	SW	SW	SW 1	SW	SW 1	SW	SW	SW	SW	SW	SW	SW 1	SW	SW 1
Reading	d		12 39									13 09									13 39		
Earley	d		12 44									13 14									13 44		
Winnersh Triangle	d		12 46									13 16									13 46		
Winnersh	d		12 48									13 18									13 48		
Wokingham	d		12 53									13 23									13 53		
Bracknell	d		12 59									13 29									13 59		
Martins Heron	d		13 02									13 32									14 02		
Guildford	d				12 30									13 00									13 30
Wanborough	d				12 36									13 06									13 36
Ash	d				12 40									13 10									13 40
Aldershot	a				12 47									13 17									13 47
	d				13 00									13 30									14 00
Ash Vale	d				13 04									13 34									14 04
Frimley	d				13 10									13 40									14 10
Camberley	a				13 14									13 44									14 14
	d				13 18									13 48									14 18
Bagshot	d				13 23									13 53									14 23
Ascot	d		13 07		13a30							13 37		14a00							14 07		14a30
Sunningdale	d		13 10									13 40									14 10		
Longcross	d																						
Woking	d																						
West Byfleet	d																						
Byfleet & New Haw	d																						
Weybridge	d						13 03									13 33							
Addlestone	d						13 07									13 37							
Chertsey	d						13 10									13 40							
Virginia Water	a		13 19				13 15					13 49				13 45					14 19		
	d		13 19				13 24					13 49				13 54					14 19		
Egham	d		13 23				13 27					13 53				13 57					14 23		
Windsor & Eton Riverside	d							13 21									13 51						
Datchet	d							13 25									13 55						
Sunnymeads	d							13 28									13 58						
Wraysbury	d							13 32									14 02						
Staines	d		13 29				13 33	13 38				13 59				14 03	14 08				14 29		
Ashford (Surrey)	d						13 36	13 41								14 06	14 11						
Feltham	d		13 35				13 41	13 46				14 05				14 11	14 16				14 35		
Whitton	d	13 23						13 50		13 50	13 53						14 20		14 20	14 23			
Kingston	d					13 29									13 59								
Hampton Wick	d					13 31									14 01								
Teddington	d					13 35									14 05								
Fulwell	d																						
Strawberry Hill	d					13 38									14 08								
Twickenham	a	13 26	13 40			13 42		13 53			13 56	14 10			14 12		14 23			14 26	14 40		
	d	13 28	13 41			13 43		13 53			13 58	14 11			14 13		14 23			14 28	14 41		
St Margarets	d	13 30				13 45					14 00				14 15					14 30			
Richmond ⊖	d	13 34	13 45			13 49		13 58			14 04	14 15			14 19		14 28			14 34	14 45		
North Sheen	d	13 36				13 51					14 06				14 21					14 36			
Mortlake	d	13 38				13 53					14 08				14 23					14 38			
Hounslow	d						13 46			14 01						14 16			14 31				
Isleworth	d						13 49			14 04						14 19			14 34				
Syon Lane	d						13 51			14 06						14 21			14 36				
Brentford	d						13 54			14 09						14 24			14 39				
Kew Bridge	d						13 56			14 11						14 26			14 41				
Chiswick	d						13 59			14 14						14 29			14 44				
Barnes Bridge	d			←			14 01			14 16			←			14 31			14 46			←	
Barnes	d	13 41		13 49		13 56	14 04		←	14 19	14 11		14 19		14 26	14 34		←	14 49	14 41		14 49	
Putney	d	13 44		13 52		13 59	14 07	14 04	14 07	→	14 14		14 22		14 29	14 37	14 34	14 37	→	14 44		14 52	
Wandsworth Town	d	13 47		13 55		14 02	→		14 10		14 17		14 25		14 32	→		14 40		14 47		14 55	
Clapham Junction 10	d	13 50	13 54	13 58		14 05		14 09	14 13		14 20	14 24	14 28		14 35		14 39	14 43		14 50	14 54	14 58	
Queenstown Rd.(Battersea)	d	13 53		14 01		14 08			14 16		14 23		14 31		14 38			14 46		14 53		15 01	
Vauxhall ⊖	d	13 57		14 05		14 12		14 15	14 20		14 27		14 35		14 42		14 45	14 50		14 57		15 05	
London Waterloo 15 ⊖	a	14 02	14 04	14 11		14 16		14 19	14 26		14 32	14 34	14 41		14 46		14 49	14 56		15 02	15 04	15 11	

Table 149

Saturdays
from 13 October

Reading, Guildford, Ascot, Weybridge, Windsor, Kingston, Richmond and Hounslow - London

Network Diagram - see first Page of Table 148

		SW		SW	SW	SW	SW	SW	SW	SW	SW	SW		SW	SW	SW	SW	SW	SW	SW	SW	SW		SW	SW
									■		■								■		■				
Reading ■	d								14 09										14 39						
Earley	d								14 14										14 44						
Winnersh Triangle	d								14 16										14 46						
Winnersh	d								14 18										14 48						
Wokingham	d								14 23										14 53						
Bracknell	d								14 29										14 59						
Martins Heron	d								14 32										15 02						
Guildford	d										14 00										14 30				
Wanborough	d										14 06										14 36				
Ash ■	d										14 10										14 40				
Aldershot	a										14 17										14 47				
	d										14 30										15 00				
Ash Vale	d										14 34										15 04				
Frimley	d										14 40										15 10				
Camberley	a										14 44										15 14				
	d										14 48										15 18				
Bagshot	d										14 53										15 23				
Ascot ■	d								14 37		15a00								15 07		15a30				
Sunningdale	d								14 40										15 10						
Longcross	d																								
Woking	d																								
West Byfleet	d																								
Byfleet & New Haw	d																								
Weybridge	d			14 03										14 33										15 03	
Addlestone	d			14 07										14 37										15 07	
Chertsey	d			14 10										14 40										15 10	
Virginia Water	a			14 15					14 49					14 45					15 19					15 15	
	d			14 24					14 49					14 54					15 19					15 24	
Egham	d			14 27					14 53					14 57					15 23					15 27	
Windsor & Eton Riverside	d				14 21										14 51										15 21
Datchet	d				14 25										14 55										15 25
Sunnymeads	d				14 28										14 58										15 28
Wraysbury	d				14 32										15 02										15 32
Staines	d			14 33	14 38				14 59					15 03	15 08				15 29					15 33	15 38
Ashford (Surrey)	d			14 36	14 41									15 06	15 11									15 36	15 41
Feltham	d			14 41	14 46				15 05					15 11	15 16				15 35					15 41	15 46
Whitton	d				14 50		14 50	14 53							15 20		15 20	15 23							15 50
Kingston	d	14 29										14 59										15 29			
Hampton Wick	d	14 31										15 01										15 31			
Teddington	d	14 35										15 05										15 35			
Fulwell	d																								
Strawberry Hill	d	14 38										15 08										15 38			
Twickenham	a	14 42			14 53			14 56	15 10			15 12			15 23			15 26	15 40			15 42			15 53
	d	14 43			14 53			14 58	15 11			15 13			15 23			15 28	15 41			15 43			15 53
St Margarets	d	14 45						15 00				15 15						15 30				15 45			
Richmond ⊖	d	14 49			14 58			15 04	15 15			15 19			15 28			15 34	15 45			15 49			15 58
North Sheen	d	14 51						15 06				15 21						15 36				15 51			
Mortlake	d	14 53						15 08				15 23						15 38				15 53			
Hounslow	d			14 46			15 01							15 16			15 31							15 46	
Isleworth	d			14 49			15 04							15 19			15 34							15 49	
Syon Lane	d			14 51			15 06							15 21			15 36							15 51	
Brentford	d			14 54			15 09							15 24			15 39							15 54	
Kew Bridge	d			14 56			15 11							15 26			15 41							15 56	
Chiswick	d			14 59			15 14							15 29			15 44							15 59	
Barnes Bridge	d			15 01			15 16			←				15 31			15 46			←				16 01	
Barnes	d	14 56		15 04		←	15 19	15 11		15 19		15 26		15 34		←	15 49	15 41		15 49		15 56		16 04	
Putney	d	14 59		15 07	15 04	15 07	→	15 14		15 22		15 29		15 37	15 34	15 37	→	15 44		15 52		15 59		16 07	16 04
Wandsworth Town	d	15 02		→		15 10		15 17		15 25		15 32		→		15 40		15 47		15 55		16 02		→	
Clapham Junction ■	d	15 05			15 09	15 13		15 20	15 24	15 28		15 35			15 39	15 43		15 50	15 54	15 58		16 05			16 09
Queenstown Rd.(Battersea)	d	15 08				15 16		15 23		15 31		15 38				15 46		15 53		16 01		16 08			
Vauxhall ⊖	d	15 12			15 15	15 20		15 27		15 35		15 42			15 45	15 50		15 57		16 05		16 12			16 15
London Waterloo ■ ⊖	a	15 16			15 19	15 26		15 32	15 34	15 41		15 46			15 49	15 56		16 02	16 04	16 11		16 16			16 19

Table 149

Saturdays
from 13 October

Reading, Guildford, Ascot, Weybridge, Windsor, Kingston, Richmond and Hounslow - London

Network Diagram - see first Page of Table 148

		SW	SW	SW	SW	SW	SW	SW		SW	SW	SW	SW	SW	SW	SW	SW	SW		SW	SW	SW	SW	SW	SW
					■		■								■		■								■
Reading ■	d				15 09										15 39										16 09
Earley	d				15 14										15 44										16 14
Winnersh Triangle	d				15 16										15 46										16 16
Winnersh	d				15 18										15 48										16 18
Wokingham	d				15 23										15 53										16 23
Bracknell	d				15 29										15 59										16 29
Martins Heron	d				15 32										16 02										16 32
Guildford	d						15 00										15 30								
Wanborough	d						15 06										15 36								
Ash ■	d						15 10										15 40								
Aldershot	a						15 17										15 47								
	d						15 30										16 00								
Ash Vale	d						15 34										16 04								
Frimley	d						15 40										16 10								
Camberley	a						15 44										16 14								
	d						15 48										16 18								
Bagshot	d						15 53										16 23								
Ascot ■	d				15 37		16a00								16 07		16a30								16 37
Sunningdale	d				15 40										16 10										16 40
Longcross	d																								
Woking	d																								
West Byfleet	d																								
Byfleet & New Haw	d																								
Weybridge	d									15 33										16 03					
Addlestone	d									15 37										16 07					
Chertsey	d									15 40										16 10					
Virginia Water	a				15 49					15 45					16 19					16 15					16 49
	d				15 49					15 54					16 19					16 24					16 49
Egham	d				15 53					15 57					16 23					16 27					16 53
Windsor & Eton Riverside	d										15 51										16 21				
Datchet	d										15 55										16 25				
Sunnymeads	d										15 58										16 28				
Wraysbury	d										16 02										16 32				
Staines	d				15 59					16 03	16 08				16 29					16 33	16 38				16 59
Ashford (Surrey)	d									16 06	16 11									16 36	16 41				
Feltham	d				16 05					16 11	16 16				16 35					16 41	16 46				17 05
Whitton	d		15 50	15 53							16 20		16 20	16 23							16 50		16 50	16 53	
Kingston	d							15 59										16 29							
Hampton Wick	d							16 01										16 31							
Teddington	d							16 05										16 35							
Fulwell	d																								
Strawberry Hill	d							16 08										16 38							
Twickenham	a			15 56	16 10			16 12			16 23			16 26	16 40			16 42			16 53			16 56	17 10
	d			15 58	16 11			16 13			16 23			16 28	16 41			16 43			16 53			16 58	17 11
St Margarets	d			16 00				16 15						16 30				16 45						17 00	
Richmond ⊖	d			16 04	16 15			16 19			16 28			16 34	16 45			16 49			16 58			17 04	17 15
North Sheen	d			16 06				16 21						16 36				16 51						17 06	
Mortlake	d			16 08				16 23						16 38				16 53						17 08	
Hounslow	d		16 01							16 16			16 31							16 46			17 01		
Isleworth	d		16 04							16 19			16 34							16 49			17 04		
Syon Lane	d		16 06							16 21			16 36							16 51			17 06		
Brentford	d		16 09							16 24			16 39							16 54			17 09		
Kew Bridge	d		16 11							16 26			16 41							16 56			17 11		
Chiswick	d		16 14							16 29			16 44							16 59			17 14		
Barnes Bridge	d		16 16			←				16 31			16 46			←				17 01			17 16		
Barnes	d	←	16 19	16 11		16 19		16 26		16 34		←	16 49	16 41		16 49		16 56		17 04		←	17 19	17 11	
Putney	d	16 07	→	16 14		16 22		16 29		16 37	16 34	16 37	→	16 44		16 52		16 59		17 07	17 04	17 07	→	17 14	
Wandsworth Town	d	16 10		16 17		16 25		16 32		→		16 40		16 47		16 55		17 02		→		17 10		17 17	
Clapham Junction ■	d	16 13		16 20	16 24	16 28		16 35			16 39	16 43		16 50	16 54	16 58		17 05			17 09	17 13		17 20	17 24
Queenstown Rd.(Battersea)	d	16 16		16 23		16 31		16 38				16 46		16 53		17 01		17 08				17 16		17 23	
Vauxhall ⊖	d	16 20		16 27		16 35		16 42			16 45	16 50		16 57		17 05		17 12			17 15	17 20		17 27	
London Waterloo ■ ⊖	a	16 26		16 32	16 34	16 41		16 46			16 49	16 56		17 02	17 04	17 11		17 16			17 19	17 26		17 32	17 34

Table 149

Saturdays
from 13 October

Reading, Guildford, Ascot, Weybridge, Windsor, Kingston, Richmond and Hounslow - London

Network Diagram - see first Page of Table 148

		SW	SW 1	SW	SW	SW	SW	SW	SW	SW 1	SW	SW 1	SW	SW	SW	SW	SW	SW	SW 1	SW	SW 1	SW
Reading 7	d									16 39									17 09			
Earley	d									16 44									17 14			
Winnersh Triangle	d									16 46									17 16			
Winnersh	d									16 48									17 18			
Wokingham	d									16 53									17 23			
Bracknell	d									16 59									17 29			
Martins Heron	d									17 02									17 32			
Guildford	d		16 00									16 30									17 00	
Wanborough	d		16 06									16 36									17 06	
Ash 5	d		16 10									16 40									17 10	
Aldershot	a		16 17									16 47									17 17	
	d		16 30									17 00									17 30	
Ash Vale	d		16 34									17 04									17 34	
Frimley	d		16 40									17 10									17 40	
Camberley	a		16 44									17 14									17 44	
	d		16 48									17 18									17 48	
Bagshot	d		16 53									17 23									17 53	
Ascot 3	d		17a00							17 07		17a30							17 37		18a00	
Sunningdale	d									17 10									17 40			
Longcross	d																					
Woking	d																					
West Byfleet	d																					
Byfleet & New Haw	d																					
Weybridge	d				16 33									17 03								
Addlestone	d				16 37									17 07								
Chertsey	d				16 40									17 10								
Virginia Water	a				16 45					17 19				17 15					17 49			
	d				16 54					17 19				17 24					17 49			
Egham	d				16 57					17 23				17 27					17 53			
Windsor & Eton Riverside	d					16 51									17 21							
Datchet	d					16 55									17 25							
Sunnymeads	d					16 58									17 28							
Wraysbury	d					17 02									17 32							
Staines	d				17 03	17 08				17 29				17 33	17 38				17 59			
Ashford (Surrey)	d				17 06	17 11								17 36	17 41							
Feltham	d				17 11	17 16				17 35				17 41	17 46				18 05			
Whitton	d					17 20		17 20	17 23						17 50		17 50	17 53				
Kingston	d			16 59									17 29									17 59
Hampton Wick	d			17 01									17 31									18 01
Teddington	d			17 05									17 35									18 05
Fulwell	d																					
Strawberry Hill	d			17 08									17 38									18 08
Twickenham	a			17 12		17 23			17 26	17 40			17 42		17 53			17 56	18 10			18 12
	d			17 13		17 23			17 28	17 41			17 43		17 53			17 58	18 11			18 13
St Margarets	d			17 15					17 30				17 45					18 00				18 15
Richmond ⊖	d			17 19		17 28			17 34	17 45			17 49		17 58			18 04	18 15			18 19
North Sheen	d			17 21					17 36				17 51					18 06				18 21
Mortlake	d			17 23					17 38				17 53					18 08				18 23
Hounslow	d				17 16			17 31						17 46			18 01					
Isleworth	d				17 19			17 34						17 49			18 04					
Syon Lane	d				17 21			17 36						17 51			18 06					
Brentford	d				17 24			17 39						17 54			18 09					
Kew Bridge	d				17 26			17 41						17 56			18 11					
Chiswick	d				17 29			17 44						17 59			18 14					
Barnes Bridge	d	←			17 31			17 46			←			18 01			18 16			←		
Barnes	d	17 19		17 26	17 34		←	17 49	17 41		17 49		17 56	18 04		←	18 19	18 11		18 19		18 26
Putney	d	17 22		17 29	17 37	17 34	17 37	→	17 44		17 52		17 59	18 07	18 04	18 07	→	18 14		18 22		18 29
Wandsworth Town	d	17 25		17 32	→		17 40		17 47		17 55		18 02	→		18 10		18 17		18 25		18 32
Clapham Junction 10	d	17 28		17 35		17 39	17 43		17 50	17 54	17 58		18 05		18 09	18 13		18 20	18 24	18 28		18 35
Queenstown Rd.(Battersea)	d	17 31		17 38			17 46		17 53		18 01		18 08			18 16		18 23		18 31		18 38
Vauxhall ⊖	d	17 35		17 42		17 45	17 50		17 57		18 05		18 12		18 15	18 20		18 27		18 35		18 42
London Waterloo 15 ⊖	a	17 41		17 46		17 49	17 56		18 02	18 04	18 11		18 16		18 19	18 26		18 32	18 34	18 41		18 46

Table 149

Saturdays
from 13 October

Reading, Guildford, Ascot, Weybridge, Windsor, Kingston, Richmond and Hounslow - London

Network Diagram - see first Page of Table 148

		SW	SW	SW	SW	SW	SW 1	SW	SW 1	SW	SW	SW	SW	SW	SW	SW 1	SW	SW 1	SW	SW	SW	SW	SW
Reading 7	d						17 39									18 09							
Earley	d						17 44									18 14							
Winnersh Triangle	d						17 46									18 16							
Winnersh	d						17 48									18 18							
Wokingham	d						17 53									18 23							
Bracknell	d						17 59									18 29							
Martins Heron	d						18 02									18 32							
Guildford	d								17 30									18 00					
Wanborough	d								17 36									18 06					
Ash 5	d								17 40									18 10					
Aldershot	a								17 47									18 17					
	d								18 00									18 30					
Ash Vale	d								18 04									18 34					
Frimley	d								18 10									18 40					
Camberley	a								18 14									18 44					
	d								18 18									18 48					
Bagshot	d								18 23									18 53					
Ascot 3	d						18 07		18a30							18 37		19a00					
Sunningdale	d						18 10									18 40							
Longcross	d																						
Woking	d																						
West Byfleet	d																						
Byfleet & New Haw	d																						
Weybridge	d	17 33									18 03									18 33			
Addlestone	d	17 37									18 07									18 37			
Chertsey	d	17 40									18 10									18 40			
Virginia Water	a	17 45					18 19				18 15					18 49				18 45			
	d	17 54					18 19				18 24					18 49				18 54			
Egham	d	17 57					18 23				18 27					18 53				18 57			
Windsor & Eton Riverside	d		17 51									18 21									18 51		
Datchet	d		17 55									18 25									18 55		
Sunnymeads	d		17 58									18 28									18 58		
Wraysbury	d		18 02									18 32									19 02		
Staines	d	18 03	18 08				18 29				18 33	18 38				18 59				19 03	19 08		
Ashford (Surrey)	d	18 06	18 11								18 36	18 41								19 06	19 11		
Feltham	d	18 11	18 16				18 35				18 41	18 46				19 05				19 11	19 16		
Whitton	d		18 20		18 20	18 23						18 50		18 50	18 53						19 20		19 20
Kingston	d									18 29									18 59				
Hampton Wick	d									18 31									19 01				
Teddington	d									18 35									19 05				
Fulwell	d																						
Strawberry Hill	d									18 38									19 08				
Twickenham	a		18 23			18 26	18 40			18 42		18 53			18 56	19 10			19 12		19 23		
	d		18 23			18 28	18 41			18 43		18 53			18 58	19 11			19 13		19 23		
St Margarets	d					18 30				18 45					19 00				19 15				
Richmond ⊖	d		18 28			18 34	18 45			18 49		18 58			19 04	19 15			19 19		19 28		
North Sheen	d					18 36				18 51					19 06				19 21				
Mortlake	d					18 38				18 53					19 08				19 23				
Hounslow	d	18 16			18 31						18 46			19 01						19 16			19 31
Isleworth	d	18 19			18 34						18 49			19 04						19 19			19 34
Syon Lane	d	18 21			18 36						18 51			19 06						19 21			19 36
Brentford	d	18 24			18 39						18 54			19 09						19 24			19 39
Kew Bridge	d	18 26			18 41						18 56			19 11						19 26			19 41
Chiswick	d	18 29			18 44						18 59			19 14						19 29			19 44
Barnes Bridge	d	18 31			18 46			←			19 01			19 16			←			19 31			19 46
Barnes	d	18 34		←	18 49	18 41		18 49		18 56	19 04		←	19 19	19 11		19 19		19 26	19 34		←	19 49
Putney	d	18 37	18 34	18 37	→	18 44		18 52		18 59	19 07	19 04	19 07	→	19 14		19 22		19 29	19 37	19 34	19 37	→
Wandsworth Town	d	→		18 40		18 47		18 55		19 02	→		19 10		19 17		19 25		19 32	→		19 40	
Clapham Junction 10	d		18 39	18 43		18 50	18 54	18 58		19 05		19 09	19 13		19 20	19 24	19 28		19 35		19 39	19 43	
Queenstown Rd.(Battersea)	d			18 46		18 53		19 01		19 08			19 16		19 23		19 31		19 38			19 46	
Vauxhall ⊖	d		18 45	18 50		18 57		19 05		19 12		19 15	19 20		19 27		19 35		19 42		19 45	19 50	
London Waterloo 15 ⊖	a		18 49	18 56		19 02	19 04	19 11		19 16		19 19	19 26		19 32	19 34	19 41		19 46		19 49	19 56	

Table 149

Saturdays from 13 October

Reading, Guildford, Ascot, Weybridge, Windsor, Kingston, Richmond and Hounslow - London

Network Diagram - see first Page of Table 148

		SW	SW [1]	SW	SW [1]	SW		SW	SW	SW	SW	SW	SW [1]	SW	SW [1]	SW		SW	SW	SW	SW	SW	SW [1]	SW	SW [1]
Reading [7]	d		18 39										19 09										19 39		
Earley	d		18 44										19 14										19 44		
Winnersh Triangle	d		18 46										19 16										19 46		
Winnersh	d		18 48										19 18										19 48		
Wokingham	d		18 53										19 23										19 53		
Bracknell	d		18 59										19 29										19 59		
Martins Heron	d		19 02										19 32										20 02		
Guildford	d				18 30										19 00										19 30
Wanborough	d				18 36										19 06										19 36
Ash [5]	d				18 40										19 10										19 40
Aldershot	a				18 47										19 17										19 47
	d				19 00										19 30										20 00
Ash Vale	d				19 04										19 34										20 04
Frimley	d				19 10										19 40										20 10
Camberley	a				19 14										19 44										20 14
	d				19 18										19 48										20 18
Bagshot	d				19 23										19 53										20 23
Ascot [5]	d		19 07		19a30								19 37		20a00								20 07		20a30
Sunningdale	d		19 10										19 40										20 10		
Longcross	d																								
Woking	d																								
West Byfleet	d																								
Byfleet & New Haw	d																								
Weybridge	d							19 03										19 33							
Addlestone	d							19 07										19 37							
Chertsey	d							19 10										19 40							
Virginia Water	a		19 19					19 15					19 49					19 45					20 19		
	d		19 19					19 24					19 49					19 54					20 19		
Egham	d		19 23					19 27					19 53					19 57					20 23		
Windsor & Eton Riverside	d								19 21										19 51						
Datchet	d								19 25										19 55						
Sunnymeads	d								19 28										19 58						
Wraysbury	d								19 32										20 02						
Staines	d		19 29					19 33	19 38				19 59					20 03	20 08				20 29		
Ashford (Surrey)	d							19 36	19 41									20 06	20 11						
Feltham	d		19 35					19 41	19 46				20 05					20 11	20 16				20 35		
Whitton	d	19 23							19 50		19 50	19 53							20 20		20 20	20 23			
Kingston	d					19 29										19 59									
Hampton Wick	d					19 31										20 01									
Teddington	d					19 35										20 05									
Fulwell	d																								
Strawberry Hill	d					19 38										20 08									
Twickenham	a	19 26	19 40			19 42			19 53			19 56	20 10			20 12			20 23			20 26	20 40		
	d	19 28	19 41			19 43			19 53			19 58	20 11			20 13			20 23			20 28	20 41		
St Margarets	d	19 30				19 45						20 00				20 15						20 30			
Richmond ⊖	d	19 34	19 45			19 49			19 58			20 04	20 15			20 19			20 28			20 34	20 45		
North Sheen	d	19 36				19 51						20 06				20 21						20 36			
Mortlake	d	19 38				19 53						20 08				20 23						20 38			
Hounslow	d							19 46			20 01							20 16			20 31				
Isleworth	d							19 49			20 04							20 19			20 34				
Syon Lane	d							19 51			20 06							20 21			20 36				
Brentford	d							19 54			20 09							20 24			20 39				
Kew Bridge	d							19 56			20 11							20 26			20 41				
Chiswick	d							19 59			20 14							20 29			20 44				
Barnes Bridge	d			←				20 01			20 16			←				20 31			20 46			←	
Barnes	d	19 41		19 49		19 56		20 04		←	20 19	20 11		20 19		20 26		20 34		←	20 49	20 41		20 49	
Putney	d	19 44		19 52		19 59		20 07	20 04	20 07	→	20 14		20 22		20 29		20 37	20 34	20 37	→	20 44		20 52	
Wandsworth Town	d	19 47		19 55		20 02		→		20 10		20 17		20 25		20 32		→		20 40		20 47		20 55	
Clapham Junction [10]	d	19 50	19 54	19 58		20 05			20 09	20 13		20 20	20 24	20 28		20 35			20 39	20 43		20 50	20 54	20 58	
Queenstown Rd.(Battersea)	d	19 53		20 01		20 08				20 16		20 23		20 31		20 38				20 46		20 53		21 01	
Vauxhall ⊖	d	19 57		20 05		20 12			20 15	20 20		20 27		20 35		20 42			20 45	20 50		20 57		21 05	
London Waterloo [15] ⊖	a	20 02	20 04	20 11		20 16			20 19	20 26		20 32	20 34	20 41		20 46			20 49	20 56		21 02	21 04	21 11	

Table 149

Saturdays from 13 October

Reading, Guildford, Ascot, Weybridge, Windsor, Kingston, Richmond and Hounslow - London

Network Diagram - see first Page of Table 148

		SW		SW	SW	SW	SW	SW	SW [1]	SW	SW [1]	SW [1]		SW	SW	SW	SW	SW	SW	SW [1]	SW	SW		SW	SW
Reading [7]	d								20 09											20 39					
Earley	d								20 14											20 44					
Winnersh Triangle	d								20 16											20 46					
Winnersh	d								20 18											20 48					
Wokingham	d								20 23											20 53					
Bracknell	d								20 29											20 59					
Martins Heron	d								20 32											21 02					
Guildford	d										20 00	20 30													
Wanborough	d										20 06	20 36													
Ash [5]	d										20 10	20 40													
Aldershot	a										20 17	20 47													
	d										20 30														
Ash Vale	d										20 34														
Frimley	d										20 40														
Camberley	a										20 44														
	d										20 48														
Bagshot	d										20 53														
Ascot [5]	d								20 37		21a00									21 07					
Sunningdale	d								20 40											21 10					
Longcross	d																								
Woking	d																								
West Byfleet	d																								
Byfleet & New Haw	d																								
Weybridge	d			20 03											20 33									21 03	
Addlestone	d			20 07											20 37									21 07	
Chertsey	d			20 10											20 40									21 10	
Virginia Water	a			20 15					20 49						20 45					21 19				21 15	
	d			20 24					20 49						20 54					21 19				21 24	
Egham	d			20 27					20 53						20 57					21 23				21 27	
Windsor & Eton Riverside	d				20 21											20 51									21 21
Datchet	d				20 25											20 55									21 25
Sunnymeads	d				20 28											20 58									21 28
Wraysbury	d				20 32											21 02									21 32
Staines	d			20 33	20 38				20 59						21 03	21 08				21 29				21 33	21 38
Ashford (Surrey)	d			20 36	20 41										21 06	21 11								21 36	21 41
Feltham	d			20 41	20 46				21 05						21 11	21 16				21 35				21 41	21 46
Whitton	d				20 50		20 50	20 53								21 20		21 20	21 23						21 50
Kingston	d	20 29												20 59								21 29			
Hampton Wick	d	20 31												21 01								21 31			
Teddington	d	20 35												21 05								21 35			
Fulwell	d																								
Strawberry Hill	d	20 38												21 08								21 38			
Twickenham	a	20 42			20 53			20 56	21 10					21 12		21 23			21 26	21 40		21 42			21 53
	d	20 43			20 53			20 58	21 11					21 13		21 23			21 28	21 41		21 43			21 53
St Margarets	d	20 45						21 00						21 15					21 30			21 45			
Richmond ⊖	d	20 49			20 58			21 04	21 15					21 19		21 28			21 34	21 45		21 49			21 58
North Sheen	d	20 51						21 06						21 21					21 36			21 51			
Mortlake	d	20 53						21 08						21 23					21 38			21 53			
Hounslow	d			20 46			21 01								21 16			21 31						21 46	
Isleworth	d			20 49			21 04								21 19			21 34						21 49	
Syon Lane	d			20 51			21 06								21 21			21 36						21 51	
Brentford	d			20 54			21 09								21 24			21 39						21 54	
Kew Bridge	d			20 56			21 11								21 26			21 41						21 56	
Chiswick	d			20 59			21 14								21 29			21 44						21 59	
Barnes Bridge	d			21 01			21 16			←					21 31			21 46			←			22 01	
Barnes	d	20 56		21 04		←	21 19	21 11		21 19				21 26	21 34		←	21 49	21 41		21 49	21 56		22 04	
Putney	d	20 59		21 07	21 04	21 07	→	21 14		21 22				21 29	21 37	21 34	21 37	→	21 44		21 52	21 59		22 07	22 04
Wandsworth Town	d	21 02		→		21 10		21 17		21 25				21 32	→		21 40		21 47		21 55	22 02		→	
Clapham Junction [10]	d	21 05			21 09	21 13		21 20	21 24	21 28				21 35		21 39	21 43		21 50	21 54	21 58	22 05			22 09
Queenstown Rd.(Battersea)	d	21 08				21 16		21 23		21 31				21 38			21 46		21 53		22 01	22 08			
Vauxhall ⊖	d	21 12			21 15	21 20		21 27		21 35				21 42		21 45	21 50		21 57		22 05	22 12			22 15
London Waterloo [15] ⊖	a	21 16			21 19	21 26		21 32	21 34	21 41				21 46		21 49	21 56		22 02	22 04	22 11	22 16			22 19

Saturdays
from 13 October

Reading, Guildford, Ascot, Weybridge, Windsor, Kingston, Richmond and Hounslow - London

Network Diagram - see first Page of Table 148

		SW	SW	SW	SW [1]	SW	SW [1]	SW [1]		SW	SW	SW	SW	SW	SW [1]	SW	SW	SW		SW	SW [1]	SW [1]	SW [1]	SW	SW
Reading [7]	d				21 09										21 39						22 09				
Earley	d				21 14										21 44						22 14				
Winnersh Triangle	d				21 16										21 46						22 16				
Winnersh	d				21 18										21 48						22 18				
Wokingham	d				21 23										21 53						22 23				
Bracknell	d				21 29										21 59						22 29				
Martins Heron	d				21 32										22 02						22 32				
Guildford	d						21 00	21 30														22 00	22 30		
Wanborough	d						21 06	21 36														22 06	22 36		
Ash [5]	d						21 10	21 40														22 10	22 40		
Aldershot	a						21 17	21 47														22 17	22 47		
	d						21 30															22 30			
Ash Vale	d						21 34															22 34			
Frimley	d						21 40															22 40			
Camberley	a						21 44															22 44			
	d						21 48															22 48			
Bagshot	d						21 53															22 53			
Ascot [3]	d				21 37		22a00								22 07						22 37	23a00			
Sunningdale	d				21 40										22 10						22 40				
Longcross	d																								
Woking	d																								
West Byfleet	d																								
Byfleet & New Haw	d																								
Weybridge	d										21 33						22 03								22 33
Addlestone	d										21 37						22 07								22 37
Chertsey	d										21 40						22 10								22 40
Virginia Water	a				21 49						21 45				22 19		22 15				22 49				22 45
	d				21 49						21 54				22 19		22 24				22 49				22 54
Egham	d				21 53						21 57				22 23		22 27				22 53				22 57
Windsor & Eton Riverside	d											21 51						22 21							
Datchet	d											21 55						22 25							
Sunnymeads	d											21 58						22 28							
Wraysbury	d											22 02						22 32							
Staines	d				21 59						22 03	22 08			22 29		22 33	22 38			22 59				23 03
Ashford (Surrey)	d										22 06	22 11					22 36	22 41							23 06
Feltham	d				22 05						22 11	22 16			22 35		22 41	22 46			23 05				23 11
Whitton	d		21 50	21 53								22 20		22 23				22 50							
Kingston	d									21 59						22 29								22 59	
Hampton Wick	d									22 01						22 31								23 01	
Teddington	d									22 05						22 35								23 05	
Fulwell	d																								
Strawberry Hill	d									22 08						22 38								23 08	
Twickenham	a			21 56	22 10					22 12		22 23		22 26	22 40	22 42		22 53			23 10			23 12	
	d			21 58	22 11					22 13		22 23		22 28	22 41	22 43		22 53			23 11			23 13	
St Margarets	d			22 00						22 15				22 30		22 45								23 15	
Richmond ⊖	d			22 04	22 15					22 19		22 28		22 34	22 45	22 49		22 58			23 15			23 19	
North Sheen	d			22 06						22 21				22 36		22 51								23 21	
Mortlake	d			22 08						22 23				22 38		22 53								23 23	
Hounslow	d		22 01								22 16						22 46								23 16
Isleworth	d		22 04								22 19						22 49								23 19
Syon Lane	d		22 06								22 21						22 51								23 21
Brentford	d		22 09								22 24						22 54								23 24
Kew Bridge	d		22 11								22 26						22 56								23 26
Chiswick	d		22 14								22 29						22 59								23 29
Barnes Bridge	d		22 16			←					22 31						23 01								23 31
Barnes	d	←	22 19	22 11		22 19				22 26	22 34		←	22 41		22 56	23 04			←				23 26	23 34
Putney	d	22 07	→	22 14		22 22				22 29	22 37	22 34	22 37	22 44		22 59	23 07	23 04		23 07				23 29	23 37
Wandsworth Town	d	22 10		22 17		22 25				22 32	→		22 40	22 47		23 02	→			23 10				23 32	→
Clapham Junction [10]	d	22 13		22 20	22 24	22 28				22 35		22 39	22 43	22 50	22 54	23 05		23 09		23 13	23 24			23 35	
Queenstown Rd.(Battersea)	d	22 16		22 23		22 31				22 38			22 46	22 53		23 08				23 16				23 38	
Vauxhall ⊖	d	22 20		22 27		22 35				22 42		22 45	22 50	22 57		23 12		23 15		23 20				23 42	
London Waterloo [15] ⊖	a	22 26		22 32	22 34	22 41				22 46		22 49	22 56	23 02	23 04	23 17		23 19		23 26	23 34			23 46	

Saturdays
from 13 October

Reading, Guildford, Ascot, Weybridge, Windsor, Kingston, Richmond and Hounslow - London

Network Diagram - see first Page of Table 148

		SW	SW	SW [1]		SW	SW	SW	SW	SW [1]	SW [1]	SW [1]	SW
Reading [7]	d			22 39						23 12			
Earley	d			22 44						23 17			
Winnersh Triangle	d			22 46						23 19			
Winnersh	d			22 48						23 21			
Wokingham	d			22 53						23 26			
Bracknell	d			22 59						23 32			
Martins Heron	d			23 02						23 35			
Guildford	d										23 00	23 30	
Wanborough	d										23 06	23 36	
Ash [5]	d										23 10	23 40	
Aldershot	a										23 17	23 47	
	d										23 30		
Ash Vale	d										23 34		
Frimley	d										23 40		
Camberley	a										23 44		
	d										23 48		
Bagshot	d										23 53		
Ascot [3]	d			23 07						23 40	00a01		
Sunningdale	d			23 10						23 43			
Longcross	d												
Woking	d												
West Byfleet	d												
Byfleet & New Haw	d												
Weybridge	d					23 03							23 33
Addlestone	d					23 07							23 37
Chertsey	d					23 10							23 40
Virginia Water	a			23 19		23 15				23 49			23 45
	d			23 19		23 24				23 49			23 54
Egham	d			23 23		23 27				23 53			23 57
Windsor & Eton Riverside	d	22 53					23 28						
Datchet	d	22 56					23 31						
Sunnymeads	d	22 59					23 34						
Wraysbury	d	23 02					23 37						
Staines	d	23 08		23 29		23a32	23a42			23 59			00a02
Ashford (Surrey)	d	23 11											
Feltham	d	23 16		23 35						00 05			
Whitton	d	23 20											
Kingston	d							23 29	23 55				
Hampton Wick	d							23 31	23 57				
Teddington	d							23 35	23 59				
Fulwell	d												
Strawberry Hill	d							23 38	00 03				
Twickenham	a	23 23		23 40				23 42	00 07	00 10			
	d	23 23		23 41				23 43		00 11			
St Margarets	d							23 45					
Richmond ⊖	d	23 28		23 45				23 49		00 15			
North Sheen	d							23 51					
Mortlake	d							23 53					
Hounslow	d												
Isleworth	d												
Syon Lane	d												
Brentford	d												
Kew Bridge	d												
Chiswick	d												
Barnes Bridge	d												
Barnes	d		←					23 56					
Putney	d	23 34	23 37					23 59					
Wandsworth Town	d		23 40					00 02					
Clapham Junction [10]	d	23 39	23 43	23 54				00 05		00 24			
Queenstown Rd.(Battersea)	d		23 46					00 08					
Vauxhall ⊖	d	23 45	23 50					00 12					
London Waterloo [15] ⊖	a	23 49	23 56	00 02				00 16		00 37			

Reading, Guildford, Ascot, Weybridge, Windsor, Kingston, Richmond and Hounslow - London

Network Diagram - see first Page of Table 148

		SW 1	SW	SW	SW 1	SW	SW	SW	SW	SW 1	SW	SW	SW	SW 1	SW	SW 1	SW 1	SW	SW	SW 1	SW	SW 1	SW 1
Reading 7	d	22p42			23p12									07 54		08 24				08 54		09 24	
Earley	d	22p47			23p17									07 59		08 29				08 59		09 29	
Winnersh Triangle	d	22p49			23p19									08 01		08 31				09 01		09 31	
Winnersh	d	22p51			23p21									08 03		08 33				09 03		09 33	
Wokingham	d	22p56			23p26									08 08		08 38				09 08		09 38	
Bracknell	d	23p02			23p32									08 14		08 44				09 14		09 44	
Martins Heron	d	23p05			23p35									08 17		08 47				09 17		09 47	
Guildford	d									07 17							08 17						09 17
Wanborough	d									07 23							08 23						09 23
Ash 5	d									07 27							08 27						09 27
Aldershot	a									07 34							08 34						09 34
	d									07 40							08 40						09 40
Ash Vale	d									07 45							08 45						09 45
Frimley	d									07 51							08 51						09 51
Camberley	a									07 55							08 55						09 55
	d									07 55							08 55						09 55
Bagshot	d									08 01							09 01						10 01
Ascot	d	23p10			23p40					08a07				08 22		08 52	09a07			09 22		09 52	10a07
Sunningdale	d	23p13			23p43									08 25		08 55				09 25		09 55	
Longcross	d																						
Woking	d												07 52						08 52				
West Byfleet	d												07 56						08 56				
Byfleet & New Haw	d												08 00						09 00				
Weybridge	d								07 00														
Addlestone	d								07 04				08 04						09 04				
Chertsey	d								07 07				08 07						09 07				
Virginia Water	a	23p19			23p49				07 12				08 12	08 30		09 00			09 12	09 30		10 00	
	d	23p19			23p49				07 12				08 12	08 30		09 00			09 12	09 30		10 00	
Egham	d	23p23			23p53				07 16				08 16	08 34		09 04			09 16	09 34		10 04	
Windsor & Eton Riverside	d							07 01				08 01						09 01					
Datchet	d							07 04				08 04						09 04					
Sunnymeads	d							07 07				08 07						09 07					
Wraysbury	d							07 10				08 10						09 10					
Staines	d	23p29			23p59			07 16	07 21			08 16	08 21	08 39		09 09		09 16	09 21	09 39		10 09	
Ashford (Surrey)	d							07 19	07 24			08 19	08 24					09 19	09 24				
Feltham	d	23p35			00 05			07 24	07 29			08 24	08 29	08 46		09 16		09 24	09 29	09 46		10 16	
Whitton	d							07 28				08 28						09 28					
Kingston	d		23p29	23p55		02 11	06 49				07 49				08 49						09 49		
Hampton Wick	d		23p31	23p57		02s13	06 51				07 51				08 51						09 51		
Teddington	d		23p35	23p59		02s15	06 56				07 56				08 56						09 56		
Fulwell	d																						
Strawberry Hill	d		23p38	00 03		02s18	06 59				07 59				08 59						09 59		
Twickenham	a	23p40	23p42	00 07	00 10	02 22	07 02	07 31			08 02	08 31		08 51	09 02	09 21		09 31		09 51	10 02	10 21	
	d	23p41	23p43		00 11		07 03	07 32			08 03	08 32		08 51	09 03	09 21		09 32		09 51	10 03	10 21	
St Margarets	d		23p45				07 05	07 34			08 05	08 34			09 05			09 34			10 05		
Richmond ⊖	d	23p45	23p49		00 15		07 09	07 37			08 09	08 37		08 56	09 09	09 26		09 37		09 56	10 09	10 26	
North Sheen	d		23p51				07 11	07 39			08 11	08 39			09 11			09 39			10 11		
Mortlake	d		23p53				07 13	07 42			08 13	08 42			09 13			09 42			10 13		
Hounslow	d								07 35				08 35						09 35				
Isleworth	d								07 38				08 38						09 38				
Syon Lane	d								07 40				08 40						09 40				
Brentford	d								07 42				08 42						09 42				
Kew Bridge	d								07 45				08 45						09 45				
Chiswick	d								07 47				08 47						09 47				
Barnes Bridge	d								07 50				08 50						09 50				
Barnes	d		23p56				07 16	07 45	07 53		08 16	08 45	08 53		09 16			09 45	09 53		10 16		
Putney	d		23p59				07 19	07 48	07 56		08 19	08 48	08 56	09 02	09 19	09 32		09 48	09 56	10 02	10 19	10 32	
Wandsworth Town	d		00 02				07 22	07 51	07 59		08 22	08 51	08 59		09 22			09 51	09 59		10 22		
Clapham Junction 10	d	23p54	00 05		00 24		07 25	07 54	08 02		08 25	08 54	09 02	09 07	09 25	09 37		09 54	10 02	10 07	10 25	10 37	
Queenstown Rd.(Battersea)	d		00 08				07 28	07 57	08 05		08 28	08 57	09 05		09 28			09 57	10 05		10 28		
Vauxhall ⊖	d		00 12				07 32	08 00	08 08		08 32	09 00	09 08	09 12	09 32	09 42		10 00	10 08	10 12	10 32	10 42	
London Waterloo 15 ⊖	a	00 02	00 16		00 37		07 41	08 10	08 13		08 41	09 10	09 13	09 23	09 41	09 53		10 10	10 13	10 23	10 41	10 53	

Reading, Guildford, Ascot, Weybridge, Windsor, Kingston, Richmond and Hounslow - London

Network Diagram - see first Page of Table 148

		SW	SW	SW 1	SW	SW	SW 1	SW 1	SW	SW	SW 1	SW	SW	SW 1	SW 1	SW	SW	SW 1	SW	SW	SW 1	SW 1	SW
Reading 7	d			09 54			10 24				10 54			11 24				11 54			12 24		
Earley	d			09 59			10 29				10 59			11 29				11 59			12 29		
Winnersh Triangle	d			10 01			10 31				11 01			11 31				12 01			12 31		
Winnersh	d			10 03			10 33				11 03			11 33				12 03			12 33		
Wokingham	d			10 08			10 38				11 08			11 38				12 08			12 38		
Bracknell	d			10 14			10 44				11 14			11 44				12 14			12 44		
Martins Heron	d			10 17			10 47				11 17			11 47				12 17			12 47		
Guildford	d							10 17							11 17							12 17	
Wanborough	d							10 23							11 23							12 23	
Ash 5	d							10 27							11 27							12 27	
Aldershot	a							10 34							11 34							12 34	
	d							10 40							11 40							12 40	
Ash Vale	d							10 45							11 45							12 45	
Frimley	d							10 51							11 51							12 51	
Camberley	a							10 55							11 55							12 55	
	d							10 55							11 55							12 55	
Bagshot	d							11 01							12 01							13 01	
Ascot	d			10 22			10 52	11a07			11 22			11 52	12a07			12 22			12 52	13a07	
Sunningdale	d			10 25			10 55				11 25			11 55				12 25			12 55		
Longcross	d																						
Woking	d		09 52							10 52							11 52						
West Byfleet	d		09 56							10 56							11 56						
Byfleet & New Haw	d		10 00							11 00							12 00						
Weybridge	d																						
Addlestone	d		10 04							11 04							12 04						
Chertsey	d		10 07							11 07							12 07						
Virginia Water	a		10 12	10 30			11 00			11 12	11 30			12 00			12 12	12 30			13 00		
	d		10 12	10 30			11 00			11 12	11 30			12 00			12 12	12 30			13 00		
Egham	d		10 16	10 34			11 04			11 16	11 34			12 04			12 16	12 34			13 04		
Windsor & Eton Riverside	d	10 01			10 34				11 01			11 34				12 01			12 34				
Datchet	d	10 04			10 37				11 04			11 37				12 04			12 37				
Sunnymeads	d	10 07							11 07							12 07							
Wraysbury	d	10 10							11 10							12 10							
Staines	d	10 16	10 21	10 39	10 45		11 09		11 16	11 21	11 39	11 45		12 09		12 16	12 21	12 39	12 45		13 09		
Ashford (Surrey)	d	10 19	10 24		10 48				11 19	11 24		11 48				12 19	12 24		12 48				
Feltham	d	10 24	10 29	10 46	10 53		11 16		11 24	11 29	11 46	11 53		12 16		12 24	12 29	12 46	12 53		13 16		
Whitton	d	10 28			10 57				11 28			11 57				12 28			12 57				
Kingston	d					10 49							11 49							12 49			13 11
Hampton Wick	d					10 51							11 51							12 51			13 13
Teddington	d					10 56							11 56							12 56			13 16
Fulwell	d																						
Strawberry Hill	d					10 59							11 59							12 59			13 19
Twickenham	a	10 31		10 51	11 00	11 02	11 21		11 31		11 51	12 00	12 02	12 21		12 31		12 51	13 00	13 02	13 21		13 22
	d	10 32		10 51	11 01	11 03	11 21		11 32		11 51	12 01	12 03	12 21		12 32		12 51	13 01	13 03	13 21		13 23
St Margarets	d	10 34				11 05			11 34				12 05			12 34				13 05			13 25
Richmond ⊖	d	10 37		10 56	11 05	11 09	11 26		11 37		11 56	12 05	12 09	12 26		12 37		12 56	13 05	13 09	13 26		13 29
North Sheen	d	10 39				11 11			11 39				12 11			12 39				13 11			13 31
Mortlake	d	10 42				11 13			11 42				12 13			12 42				13 13			13 33
Hounslow	d		10 35							11 35							12 35						
Isleworth	d		10 38							11 38							12 38						
Syon Lane	d		10 40							11 40							12 40						
Brentford	d		10 42							11 42							12 42						
Kew Bridge	d		10 45							11 45							12 45						
Chiswick	d		10 47							11 47							12 47						
Barnes Bridge	d		10 50							11 50							12 50						
Barnes	d	10 45	10 53			11 16			11 45	11 53			12 16			12 45	12 53			13 16			13 36
Putney	d	10 48	10 56	11 02	11 14	11 19	11 32		11 48	11 56	12 02	12 14	12 19	12 32		12 48	12 56	13 02	13 14	13 19	13 32		13 39
Wandsworth Town	d	10 51	10 59			11 22			11 51	11 59			12 22			12 51	12 59			13 22			13 42
Clapham Junction 10	d	10 53	11 02	11 07	11 18	11 25	11 37		11 53	12 02	12 07	12 18	12 25	12 37		12 53	13 02	13 07	13 18	13 25	13 37		13 45
Queenstown Rd.(Battersea)	d	10 57	11 05			11 28			11 57	12 05			12 28			12 57	13 05			13 28			13 48
Vauxhall ⊖	d	11 00	11 08	11 12	11 24	11 32	11 42		12 00	12 08	12 12	12 24	12 32	12 42		13 00	13 08	13 12	13 24	13 32	13 42		13 52
London Waterloo 15 ⊖	a	11 10	11 13	11 23	11 34	11 41	11 53		12 10	12 13	12 23	12 34	12 41	12 53		13 10	13 13	13 23	13 34	13 41	13 53		14 00

Table 149

Sundays until 30 September

Reading, Guildford, Ascot, Weybridge, Windsor, Kingston, Richmond and Hounslow - London

Network Diagram - see first Page of Table 148

		SW		SW	SW [1]	SW	SW	SW [1]	SW [1]	SW	SW	SW		SW [1]	SW	SW	SW [1]		SW [1]	SW [1]	SW		SW	SW
Reading [7]	d				12 54			13 24						13 54			14 24		20 24					
Earley	d				12 59			13 29						13 59			14 29		20 29					
Winnersh Triangle	d				13 01			13 31						14 01			14 31		20 31					
Winnersh	d				13 03			13 33						14 03			14 33		20 33					
Wokingham	d				13 08			13 38						14 08			14 38		20 38					
Bracknell	d				13 14			13 44						14 14			14 44		20 44					
Martins Heron	d				13 17			13 47						14 17			14 47		20 47					
Guildford	d								13 17											20 17				
Wanborough	d								13 23											20 23				
Ash [5]	d								13 27											20 27				
Aldershot	a								13 34											20 34				
	d								13 40											20 40				
Ash Vale	d								13 45											20 45				
Frimley	d								13 51											20 51				
Camberley	a								13 55											20 55				
	d								13 55											20 55				
Bagshot	d								14 01											21 01				
Ascot [3]	d				13 22			13 52	14a07					14 22			14 52		20 52	21a07				
Sunningdale	d				13 25			13 55						14 25			14 55		20 55					
Longcross	d																							
Woking	d			12 52								13 52												20 52
West Byfleet	d			12 56								13 56												20 56
Byfleet & New Haw	d			13 00								14 00												21 00
Weybridge	d																							
Addlestone	d			13 04								14 04												21 04
Chertsey	d			13 07								14 07												21 07
Virginia Water	a			13 12	13 30			14 00				14 12		14 30			15 00	and at	21 00					21 12
	d			13 12	13 30			14 00				14 12		14 30			15 00	the same	21 00					21 12
Egham	d			13 16	13 34			14 04				14 16		14 34			15 04	minutes	21 04					21 16
Windsor & Eton Riverside	d	13 01				13 34					14 01				14 34			past					21 01	
Datchet	d	13 04				13 37					14 04				14 37			each					21 04	
Sunnymeads	d	13 07									14 07							hour until					21 07	
Wraysbury	d	13 10									14 10												21 10	
Staines	d	13 16		13 21	13 39	13 45		14 09			14 16	14 21		14 39	14 45		15 09		21 09				21 16	21 21
Ashford (Surrey)	d	13 19		13 24		13 48					14 19	14 24			14 48								21 19	21 24
Feltham	d	13 24		13 29	13 46	13 53		14 16			14 24	14 29		14 46	14 53		15 16		21 16				21 24	21 29
Whitton	d	13 28				13 57					14 28				14 57								21 28	
Kingston	d						13 49			14 11						14 49					21 11			
Hampton Wick	d						13 51			14 13						14 51					21 13			
Teddington	d						13 56			14 16						14 56					21 16			
Fulwell	d																							
Strawberry Hill	d						13 59			14 19						14 59					21 19			
Twickenham	a	13 31			13 51	14 00	14 02	14 21		14 22	14 31			14 51	15 00	15 02	15 21		21 21		21 22		21 31	
	d	13 32			13 51	14 01	14 03	14 21		14 23	14 32			14 51	15 01	15 03	15 21		21 21		21 23		21 32	
St Margarets	d	13 34					14 05			14 25	14 34					15 05					21 25		21 34	
Richmond ⊖	d	13 37			13 56	14 05	14 09	14 26		14 29	14 37			14 56	15 05	15 09	15 26		21 26		21 29		21 37	
North Sheen	d	13 39					14 11			14 31	14 39					15 11					21 31		21 39	
Mortlake	d	13 42					14 13			14 33	14 42					15 13					21 33		21 42	
Hounslow	d			13 35								14 35												21 35
Isleworth	d			13 38								14 38												21 38
Syon Lane	d			13 40								14 40												21 40
Brentford	d			13 42								14 42												21 42
Kew Bridge	d			13 45								14 45												21 45
Chiswick	d			13 47								14 47												21 47
Barnes Bridge	d			13 50								14 50												21 50
Barnes	d	13 45		13 53			14 16			14 36	14 45	14 53				15 16					21 36		21 45	21 53
Putney	d	13 48		13 56	14 02	14 14	14 19	14 32		14 39	14 48	14 56		15 02	15 14	15 19	15 32		21 32		21 39		21 48	21 56
Wandsworth Town	d	13 51		13 59			14 22			14 42	14 51	14 59				15 22					21 42		21 51	21 59
Clapham Junction [10]	d	13 54		14 02	14 07	14 18	14 25	14 37		14 45	14 54	15 02		15 07	15 18	15 25	15 37		21 37		21 45		21 54	22 02
Queenstown Rd.(Battersea)	d	13 57		14 05			14 28			14 48	14 57	15 05				15 28					21 48		21 57	22 05
Vauxhall ⊖	d	14 00		14 08	14 12	14 24	14 32	14 42		14 52	15 00	15 08		15 12	15 24	15 32	15 42		21 42		21 52		22 00	22 08
London Waterloo [15] ⊖	a	14 10		14 13	14 23	14 34	14 41	14 53		15 00	15 05	15 13		15 18	15 29	15 36	15 48		21 48		22 00		22 05	22 13

Table 149

Sundays until 30 September

Reading, Guildford, Ascot, Weybridge, Windsor, Kingston, Richmond and Hounslow - London

Network Diagram - see first Page of Table 148

		SW [1]	SW	SW [1]	SW [1]	SW	SW	SW		SW [1]	SW	SW [1]	SW [1]	SW	SW	SW	SW [1]	SW	SW [1]
Reading [7]	d	20 54		21 24						21 54		22 24					22 54		
Earley	d	20 59		21 29						21 59		22 29					22 59		
Winnersh Triangle	d	21 01		21 31						22 01		22 31					23 01		
Winnersh	d	21 03		21 33						22 03		22 33					23 03		
Wokingham	d	21 08		21 38						22 08		22 38					23 08		
Bracknell	d	21 14		21 44						22 14		22 44					23 14		
Martins Heron	d	21 17		21 47						22 17		22 47					23 17		
Guildford	d				21 17								22 17						23 17
Wanborough	d				21 23								22 23						23 23
Ash [5]	d				21 27								22 27						23 27
Aldershot	a				21 34								22 34						23 34
	d				21 40								22 40						
Ash Vale	d				21 45								22 45						
Frimley	d				21 51								22 51						
Camberley	a				21 55								22 55						
	d				21 55								22 55						
Bagshot	d				22 01								23 01						
Ascot [3]	d	21 22		21 52	22a07					22 22		22 52	23a07				23 22		
Sunningdale	d	21 25		21 55						22 25		22 55					23 25		
Longcross	d																		
Woking	d							21 52								22 52			
West Byfleet	d							21 56								22 56			
Byfleet & New Haw	d							22 00								23 00			
Weybridge	d																		
Addlestone	d							22 04								23 04			
Chertsey	d							22 07								23 07			
Virginia Water	a	21 30		22 00				22 12		22 30		23 00				23 12	23 30		
	d	21 30		22 00				22 12		22 30		23 00				23 12	23 30		
Egham	d	21 34		22 04				22 16		22 34		23 04				23 16	23 34		
Windsor & Eton Riverside	d						22 01								23 01				
Datchet	d						22 04								23 04				
Sunnymeads	d						22 07								23 07				
Wraysbury	d						22 10								23 10				
Staines	d	21 39		22 09			22 16	22 21		22 39		23 09			23 16	23 21	23 39		
Ashford (Surrey)	d						22 19	22 24							23 19	23 24			
Feltham	d	21 46		22 16			22 24	22 29		22 46		23 16			23 24	23 29	23 46		
Whitton	d						22 28								23 28				
Kingston	d		21 49			22 11					22 49			23 11				23 47	
Hampton Wick	d		21 51			22 13					22 51			23 13				23 49	
Teddington	d		21 56			22 16					22 56			23 16				23 51	
Fulwell	d																		
Strawberry Hill	d		21 59			22 19					22 59			23 19				23 54	
Twickenham	a	21 51	22 02	22 21		22 22	22 31			22 51	23 02	23 21		23 22	23 31		23 51		
	d	21 51	22 03	22 21		22 23	22 32			22 51	23 03	23 21		23 23	23 32		23 51		
St Margarets	d		22 05			22 25	22 34				23 05			23 25	23 34				
Richmond ⊖	d	21 56	22 09	22 26		22 29	22 37			22 56	23 09	23 26		23 29	23 37		23 56		
North Sheen	d		22 11			22 31	22 39				23 11			23 31	23 39				
Mortlake	d		22 13			22 33	22 42				23 13			23 33	23 42				
Hounslow	d							22 35								23 35			
Isleworth	d							22 38								23 38			
Syon Lane	d							22 40								23 40			
Brentford	d							22 42								23 42			
Kew Bridge	d							22 45								23 45			
Chiswick	d							22 47								23 47			
Barnes Bridge	d							22 50								23 50			
Barnes	d		22 16			22 36	22 45	22 53			23 16			23 36	23 45	23 53			
Putney	d	22 02	22 19	22 32		22 39	22 48	22 56		23 02	23 19	23 32		23 39	23 48	23 56	00 02		
Wandsworth Town	d		22 22			22 42	22 51	22 59			23 22			23 42	23 51	23 59			
Clapham Junction [10]	d	22 07	22 25	22 37		22 45	22 54	23 02		23 07	23 25	23 37		23 45	23 54	00 02	00 07		
Queenstown Rd.(Battersea)	d		22 28			22 48	22 57	23 05			23 28			23 48	23 57	00 05			
Vauxhall ⊖	d	22 12	22 32	22 42		22 52	23 00	23 08		23 12	23 32	23 42		23 52	23 59	00 08	00 12		
London Waterloo [15] ⊖	a	22 18	22 36	22 48		23 00	23 05	23 13		23 18	23 36	23 48		23 59	00 05	00 13	00 17		

Table 149

Sundays from 7 October

Reading, Guildford, Ascot, Weybridge, Windsor, Kingston, Richmond and Hounslow - London

Network Diagram - see first Page of Table 148

		SW ■ A	SW ■ B	SW	SW	SW ■	SW	SW	SW	SW		SW ■	SW	SW	SW	SW ■	SW	SW ■	SW ■	SW		SW	SW ■	SW	SW ■
Reading ■	d	22p39	22p42			23p12										07 51		08 21					08 51		09 21
Earley	d	22p44	22p47			23p17										07 56		08 26					08 56		09 26
Winnersh Triangle	d	22p46	22p49			23p19										07 58		08 28					08 58		09 28
Winnersh	d	22p48	22p51			23p21										08 00		08 30					09 00		09 30
Wokingham	d	22p53	22p56			23p26										08 05		08 35					09 05		09 35
Bracknell	d	22p59	23p02			23p32										08 11		08 41					09 11		09 41
Martins Heron	d	23p02	23p05			23p35										08 14		08 44					09 14		09 44
Guildford	d											07 17							08 17						
Wanborough	d											07 23							08 23						
Ash ■	d											07 27							08 27						
Aldershot	a											07 34							08 34						
	d											07 40							08 40						
Ash Vale	d											07 45							08 45						
Frimley	d											07 51							08 51						
Camberley	a											07 55							08 55						
	d											07 55							08 55						
Bagshot	d											08 01							09 01						
Ascot ■	d	23p07	23p10			23p40						08a07				08 19		08 49	09a07				09 19		09 49
Sunningdale	d	23p10	23p13			23p43										08 22		08 52					09 22		09 52
Longcross	d																								
Woking	d														07 52							08 52			
West Byfleet	d														07 56							08 56			
Byfleet & New Haw	d														08 00							09 00			
Weybridge	d									07 00															
Addlestone	d									07 04					08 04							09 04			
Chertsey	d									07 07					08 07							09 07			
Virginia Water	a	23p19	23p19			23p49				07 12					08 12	08 30		09 00				09 12	09 30		10 00
	d	23p19	23p19			23p49				07 12					08 12	08 30		09 00				09 12	09 30		10 00
Egham	d	23p23	23p23			23p53				07 16					08 16	08 34		09 04				09 16	09 34		10 04
Windsor & Eton Riverside	d								06 59					07 59						08 59					
Datchet	d								07 03					08 03						09 03					
Sunnymeads	d								07 06					08 06						09 06					
Wraysbury	d								07 10					08 10						09 10					
Staines	d	23p29	23p29			23p59			07 16	07 21				08 16	08 21	08 39		09 09		09 16		09 21	09 39		10 09
Ashford (Surrey)	d								07 19	07 24				08 19	08 24					09 19		09 24			
Feltham	d	23p35	23p35			00 05			07 24	07 29				08 24	08 29	08 46		09 16		09 24		09 29	09 46		10 16
Whitton	d								07 28					08 28						09 28					
Kingston	d			23p29	23p55		02 11	06 49					07 49				08 49							09 49	
Hampton Wick	d			23p31	23p57		02s13	06 51					07 51				08 51							09 51	
Teddington	d			23p35	23p59		02s15	06 56					07 56				08 56							09 56	
Fulwell	d																								
Strawberry Hill	d			23p38	00 03		02s18	06 59					07 59				08 59							09 59	
Twickenham	a	23p40	23p40	23p42	00 07	00 10	02 22	07 02	07 31				08 02	08 31		08 51	09 02	09 21		09 31			09 51	10 02	10 21
	d	23p41	23p41	23p43		00 11		07 03	07 32				08 03	08 32		08 51	09 03	09 21		09 32			09 51	10 03	10 21
St Margarets	d			23p45				07 05	07 34				08 05	08 34			09 05			09 34				10 05	
Richmond ⊖	d	23p45	23p45	23p49		00 15		07 09	07 37				08 09	08 37		08 56	09 09	09 26		09 37			09 56	10 09	10 26
North Sheen	d			23p51				07 11	07 39				08 11	08 39			09 11			09 39				10 11	
Mortlake	d			23p53				07 13	07 42				08 13	08 42			09 13			09 42				10 13	
Hounslow	d									07 35					08 35							09 35			
Isleworth	d									07 38					08 38							09 38			
Syon Lane	d									07 40					08 40							09 40			
Brentford	d									07 42					08 42							09 42			
Kew Bridge	d									07 45					08 45							09 45			
Chiswick	d									07 47					08 47							09 47			
Barnes Bridge	d									07 50					08 50							09 50			
Barnes	d			23p56				07 16	07 45	07 53			08 16	08 45	08 53		09 16			09 45		09 53		10 16	
Putney	d			23p59				07 19	07 48	07 56			08 19	08 48	08 56	09 02	09 19	09 32		09 48		09 56	10 02	10 19	10 32
Wandsworth Town	d			00 02				07 22	07 51	07 59			08 22	08 51	08 59		09 22			09 51		09 59		10 22	
Clapham Junction ■	d	23p54	23p54	00 05		00 24		07 25	07 54	08 02			08 25	08 54	09 02	09 07	09 25	09 37		09 54		10 02	10 07	10 25	10 37
Queenstown Rd.(Battersea)	d			00 08				07 28	07 57	08 05			08 28	08 57	09 05		09 28			09 57		10 05		10 28	
Vauxhall ⊖	d			00 12				07 32	08 00	08 08			08 32	09 00	09 08	09 12	09 32	09 42		10 00		10 08	10 12	10 32	10 42
London Waterloo ■ ⊖	a	00 02	00 02	00 16		00 37		07 41	08 10	08 13			08 41	09 10	09 13	09 23	09 41	09 53		10 10		10 13	10 23	10 41	10 53

A not 7 October

B 7 October

Table 149

Sundays from 7 October

Reading, Guildford, Ascot, Weybridge, Windsor, Kingston, Richmond and Hounslow - London

Network Diagram - see first Page of Table 148

		SW ■	SW	SW	SW ■	SW		SW	SW ■	SW ■	SW	SW	SW ■	SW	SW	SW ■		SW ■	SW	SW	SW ■	SW	SW	SW ■	SW ■
Reading ■	d				09 51				10 21				10 51			11 21					11 51			12 21	
Earley	d				09 56				10 26				10 56			11 26					11 56			12 26	
Winnersh Triangle	d				09 58				10 28				10 58			11 28					11 58			12 28	
Winnersh	d				10 00				10 30				11 00			11 30					12 00			12 30	
Wokingham	d				10 05				10 35				11 05			11 35					12 05			12 35	
Bracknell	d				10 11				10 41				11 11			11 41					12 11			12 41	
Martins Heron	d				10 14				10 44				11 14			11 44					12 14			12 44	
Guildford	d	09 17								10 17								11 17							12 17
Wanborough	d	09 23								10 23								11 23							12 23
Ash ■	d	09 27								10 27								11 27							12 27
Aldershot	a	09 34								10 34								11 34							12 34
	d	09 40								10 40								11 40							12 40
Ash Vale	d	09 45								10 45								11 45							12 45
Frimley	d	09 51								10 51								11 51							12 51
Camberley	a	09 55								10 55								11 55							12 55
	d	09 55								10 55								11 55							12 55
Bagshot	d	10 01								11 01								12 01							13 01
Ascot ■	d	10a07			10 19				10 49	11a07			11 19			11 49		12a07			12 19			12 49	13a07
Sunningdale	d				10 22				10 52				11 22			11 52					12 22			12 52	
Longcross	d																								
Woking	d			09 52								10 52								11 52					
West Byfleet	d			09 56								10 56								11 56					
Byfleet & New Haw	d			10 00								11 00								12 00					
Weybridge	d																								
Addlestone	d			10 04								11 04								12 04					
Chertsey	d			10 07								11 07								12 07					
Virginia Water	a			10 12	10 30				11 00			11 12	11 30			12 00				12 12	12 30			13 00	
	d			10 12	10 30				11 00			11 12	11 30			12 00				12 12	12 30			13 00	
Egham	d			10 16	10 34				11 04			11 16	11 34			12 04				12 16	12 34			13 04	
Windsor & Eton Riverside	d		09 59			10 32					10 59			11 32					11 59			12 32			
Datchet	d		10 03			10 36					11 03			11 36					12 03			12 36			
Sunnymeads	d		10 06								11 06								12 06						
Wraysbury	d		10 10								11 10								12 10						
Staines	d		10 16	10 21	10 39	10 45			11 09		11 16	11 21	11 39	11 45		12 09			12 16	12 21	12 39	12 45		13 09	
Ashford (Surrey)	d		10 19	10 24		10 48					11 19	11 24		11 48					12 19	12 24		12 48			
Feltham	d		10 24	10 29	10 46	10 53			11 16		11 24	11 29	11 46	11 53		12 16			12 24	12 29	12 46	12 53		13 16	
Whitton	d		10 28			10 57					11 28			11 57					12 28			12 57			
Kingston	d							10 49							11 49								12 49		
Hampton Wick	d							10 51							11 51								12 51		
Teddington	d							10 56							11 56								12 56		
Fulwell	d																								
Strawberry Hill	d							10 59							11 59								12 59		
Twickenham	a		10 31		10 51	11 00		11 02	11 21		11 31		11 51	12 00	12 02	12 21			12 31		12 51	13 00	13 02	13 21	
	d		10 32		10 51	11 01		11 03	11 21		11 32		11 51	12 01	12 03	12 21			12 32		12 51	13 01	13 03	13 21	
St Margarets	d		10 34					11 05			11 34				12 05				12 34				13 05		
Richmond ⊖	d		10 37		10 56	11 05		11 09	11 26		11 37		11 56	12 05	12 09	12 26			12 37		12 56	13 05	13 09	13 26	
North Sheen	d		10 39					11 11			11 39				12 11				12 39				13 11		
Mortlake	d		10 42					11 13			11 42				12 13				12 42				13 13		
Hounslow	d			10 35								11 35								12 35					
Isleworth	d			10 38								11 38								12 38					
Syon Lane	d			10 40								11 40								12 40					
Brentford	d			10 42								11 42								12 42					
Kew Bridge	d			10 45								11 45								12 45					
Chiswick	d			10 47								11 47								12 47					
Barnes Bridge	d			10 50								11 50								12 50					
Barnes	d		10 45	10 53				11 16			11 45	11 53			12 16				12 45	12 53			13 16		
Putney	d		10 48	10 56	11 02	11 14		11 19	11 32		11 48	11 56	12 02	12 14	12 19	12 32			12 48	12 56	13 02	13 14	13 19	13 32	
Wandsworth Town	d		10 51	10 59				11 22			11 51	11 59			12 22				12 51	12 59			13 22		
Clapham Junction ■	d		10 53	11 02	11 07	11 18		11 25	11 37		11 53	12 02	12 07	12 18	12 25	12 37			12 53	13 02	13 07	13 18	13 25	13 37	
Queenstown Rd.(Battersea)	d		10 57	11 05				11 28			11 57	12 05			12 28				12 57	13 05			13 28		
Vauxhall ⊖	d		11 00	11 08	11 12	11 24		11 32	11 42		12 00	12 08	12 12	12 24	12 32	12 42			13 00	13 08	13 12	13 24	13 32	13 42	
London Waterloo ■ ⊖	a		11 10	11 13	11 23	11 34		11 41	11 53		12 10	12 13	12 23	12 34	12 41	12 53			13 10	13 13	13 23	13 34	13 41	13 53	

Sundays
from 7 October

Reading, Guildford, Ascot, Weybridge, Windsor, Kingston, Richmond and Hounslow - London

Network Diagram - see first Page of Table 148

		SW		SW	SW	SW ■	SW	SW	SW ■	SW ■	SW	SW		SW	SW ■	SW	SW	SW ■		SW ■	SW ■		SW	SW
Reading ■7	d					12 51			13 21						13 51			14 21		20 21				
Earley	d					12 56			13 26						13 56			14 26		20 26				
Winnersh Triangle	d					12 58			13 28						13 58			14 28		20 28				
Winnersh	d					13 00			13 30						14 00			14 30		20 30				
Wokingham	d					13 05			13 35						14 05			14 35		20 35				
Bracknell	d					13 11			13 41						14 11			14 41		20 41				
Martins Heron	d					13 14			13 44						14 14			14 44		20 44				
Guildford	d									13 17											20 17			
Wanborough	d									13 23											20 23			
Ash ■5	d									13 27											20 27			
Aldershot	a									13 34											20 34			
	d									13 40											20 40			
Ash Vale	d									13 45											20 45			
Frimley	d									13 51											20 51			
Camberley	a									13 55											20 55			
	d									13 55											20 55			
Bagshot	d									14 01											21 01			
Ascot ■3	d					13 19			13 49	14a07					14 19			14 49		20 49	21a07			
Sunningdale	d					13 22			13 52						14 22			14 52		20 52				
Longcross	d																							
Woking	d				12 52									13 52										
West Byfleet	d				12 56									13 56										
Byfleet & New Haw	d				13 00									14 00										
Weybridge	d																							
Addlestone	d				13 04									14 04										
Chertsey	d				13 07									14 07										
Virginia Water	a				13 12	13 30			14 00					14 12	14 30			15 00	and at the same minutes past each hour until	21 00				
	d				13 12	13 30			14 00					14 12	14 30			15 00		21 00				
Egham	d				13 16	13 34			14 04					14 16	14 34			15 04		21 04				
Windsor & Eton Riverside	d			12 59			13 32					13 59				14 32								20 59
Datchet	d			13 03			13 36					14 03				14 36								21 03
Sunnymeads	d			13 06								14 06												21 06
Wraysbury	d			13 10								14 10												21 10
Staines	d			13 16	13 21	13 39	13 45		14 09			14 16		14 21	14 39	14 45		15 09		21 09				21 16
Ashford (Surrey)	d			13 19	13 24		13 48					14 19		14 24		14 48								21 19
Feltham	d			13 24	13 29	13 46	13 53		14 16			14 24		14 29	14 46	14 53		15 16		21 16				21 24
Whitton	d			13 28			13 57					14 28				14 57								21 28
Kingston	d	13 11						13 49			14 11						14 49						21 11	
Hampton Wick	d	13 13						13 51			14 13						14 51						21 13	
Teddington	d	13 16						13 56			14 16						14 56						21 16	
Fulwell	d																							
Strawberry Hill	d	13 19						13 59			14 19						14 59						21 19	
Twickenham	a	13 22		13 31		13 51	14 00	14 02	14 21		14 22	14 31			14 51	15 00	15 02	15 21		21 21			21 22	21 31
	d	13 23		13 32		13 51	14 01	14 03	14 21		14 23	14 32			14 51	15 01	15 03	15 21		21 21			21 23	21 32
St Margarets	d	13 25		13 34				14 05			14 25	14 34					15 05						21 25	21 34
Richmond ⊖	d	13 29		13 37		13 56	14 05	14 09	14 26		14 29	14 37			14 56	15 05	15 09	15 26		21 26			21 29	21 37
North Sheen	d	13 31		13 39				14 11			14 31	14 39					15 11						21 31	21 39
Mortlake	d	13 33		13 42				14 13			14 33	14 42					15 13						21 33	21 42
Hounslow	d				13 35									14 35										
Isleworth	d				13 38									14 38										
Syon Lane	d				13 40									14 40										
Brentford	d				13 42									14 42										
Kew Bridge	d				13 45									14 45										
Chiswick	d				13 47									14 47										
Barnes Bridge	d				13 50									14 50										
Barnes	d	13 36		13 45	13 53			14 16			14 36	14 45		14 53			15 16						21 36	21 45
Putney	d	13 39		13 48	13 56	14 02	14 14	14 19	14 32		14 39	14 48		14 56	15 02	15 14	15 19	15 32		21 32			21 39	21 48
Wandsworth Town	d	13 42		13 51	13 59			14 22			14 42	14 51		14 59			15 22						21 42	21 51
Clapham Junction ■10	d	13 45		13 54	14 02	14 07	14 18	14 25	14 37		14 45	14 54		15 02	15 07	15 18	15 25	15 37		21 37			21 45	21 54
Queenstown Rd.(Battersea)	d	13 48		13 57	14 05			14 28			14 48	14 57		15 05			15 28						21 48	21 57
Vauxhall ⊖	d	13 52		14 00	14 08	14 12	14 24	14 32	14 42		14 52	15 00		15 08	15 12	15 24	15 32	15 42		21 42			21 52	22 00
London Waterloo ■15 ⊖	a	14 00		14 10	14 13	14 23	14 34	14 41	14 53		15 00	15 05		15 13	15 18	15 29	15 36	15 48		21 48			22 00	22 05

Table 149

Sundays
from 7 October

Reading, Guildford, Ascot, Weybridge, Windsor, Kingston, Richmond and Hounslow - London

Network Diagram - see first Page of Table 148

		SW	SW ■	SW	SW ■	SW ■	SW	SW		SW	SW ■	SW	SW ■	SW ■	SW	SW	SW	SW ■	SW	SW ■
Reading ■7	d		20 51		21 21						21 51		22 21					22 54		
Earley	d		20 56		21 26						21 56		22 26					22 59		
Winnersh Triangle	d		20 58		21 28						21 58		22 28					23 01		
Winnersh	d		21 00		21 30						22 00		22 30					23 03		
Wokingham	d		21 05		21 35						22 05		22 35					23 08		
Bracknell	d		21 11		21 41						22 11		22 41					23 14		
Martins Heron	d		21 14		21 44						22 14		22 44					23 17		
Guildford	d					21 17								22 17						23 17
Wanborough	d					21 23								22 23						23 23
Ash ■5	d					21 27								22 27						23 27
Aldershot	a					21 34								22 34						23 34
	d					21 40								22 40						
Ash Vale	d					21 45								22 45						
Frimley	d					21 51								22 51						
Camberley	a					21 55								22 55						
	d					21 55								22 55						
Bagshot	d					22 01								23 01						
Ascot ■3	d		21 19		21 49	22a07					22 19		22 49	23a07				23 22		
Sunningdale	d		21 22		21 52						22 22		22 52					23 25		
Longcross	d																			
Woking	d	20 52								21 52							22 52			
West Byfleet	d	20 56								21 56							22 56			
Byfleet & New Haw	d	21 00								22 00							23 00			
Weybridge	d																			
Addlestone	d	21 04								22 04							23 04			
Chertsey	d	21 07								22 07							23 07			
Virginia Water	a	21 12	21 30		22 00					22 12	22 30		23 00				23 12	23 30		
	d	21 12	21 30		22 00					22 12	22 30		23 00				23 12	23 30		
Egham	d	21 16	21 34		22 04					22 16	22 34		23 04				23 16	23 34		
Windsor & Eton Riverside	d							21 59								23 01				
Datchet	d							22 03								23 04				
Sunnymeads	d							22 06								23 07				
Wraysbury	d							22 10								23 10				
Staines	d	21 21	21 39		22 09			22 16		22 21	22 39		23 09			23 16	23 21	23 39		
Ashford (Surrey)	d	21 24						22 19		22 24						23 19	23 24			
Feltham	d	21 29	21 46		22 16			22 24		22 29	22 46		23 16			23 24	23 29	23 46		
Whitton	d							22 28								23 28				
Kingston	d			21 49			22 11					22 49			23 11				23 47	
Hampton Wick	d			21 51			22 13					22 51			23 13				23 49	
Teddington	d			21 56			22 16					22 56			23 16				23 51	
Fulwell	d																			
Strawberry Hill	d			21 59			22 19					22 59			23 19				23 54	
Twickenham	a		21 51	22 02	22 21		22 22	22 31			22 51	23 02	23 21		23 22	23 31		23 51		
	d		21 51	22 03	22 21		22 23	22 32			22 51	23 03	23 21		23 23	23 32		23 51		
St Margarets	d			22 05			22 25	22 34				23 05			23 25	23 34				
Richmond ⊖	d		21 56	22 09	22 26		22 29	22 37			22 56	23 09	23 26		23 29	23 37		23 56		
North Sheen	d			22 11			22 31	22 39				23 11			23 31	23 39				
Mortlake	d			22 13			22 33	22 42				23 13			23 33	23 42				
Hounslow	d	21 35								22 35							23 35			
Isleworth	d	21 38								22 38							23 38			
Syon Lane	d	21 40								22 40							23 40			
Brentford	d	21 42								22 42							23 42			
Kew Bridge	d	21 45								22 45							23 45			
Chiswick	d	21 47								22 47							23 47			
Barnes Bridge	d	21 50								22 50							23 50			
Barnes	d	21 53		22 16			22 36	22 45		22 53		23 16			23 36	23 45	23 53			
Putney	d	21 56	22 02	22 19	22 32		22 39	22 48		22 56	23 02	23 19	23 32		23 39	23 48	23 56	00 02		
Wandsworth Town	d	21 59		22 22			22 42	22 51		22 59		23 22			23 42	23 51	23 59			
Clapham Junction ■10	d	22 02	22 07	22 25	22 37		22 45	22 54		23 02	23 07	23 25	23 37		23 45	23 54	00 02	00 07		
Queenstown Rd.(Battersea)	d	22 05		22 28			22 48	22 57		23 05		23 28			23 48	23 57	00 05			
Vauxhall ⊖	d	22 08	22 12	22 32	22 42		22 52	23 00		23 08	23 12	23 32	23 42		23 52	23 59	00 08	00 12		
London Waterloo ■15 ⊖	a	22 13	22 18	22 36	22 48		23 00	23 05		23 13	23 18	23 36	23 48		23 59	00 05	00 13	00 17		

Network Diagram for Table 152

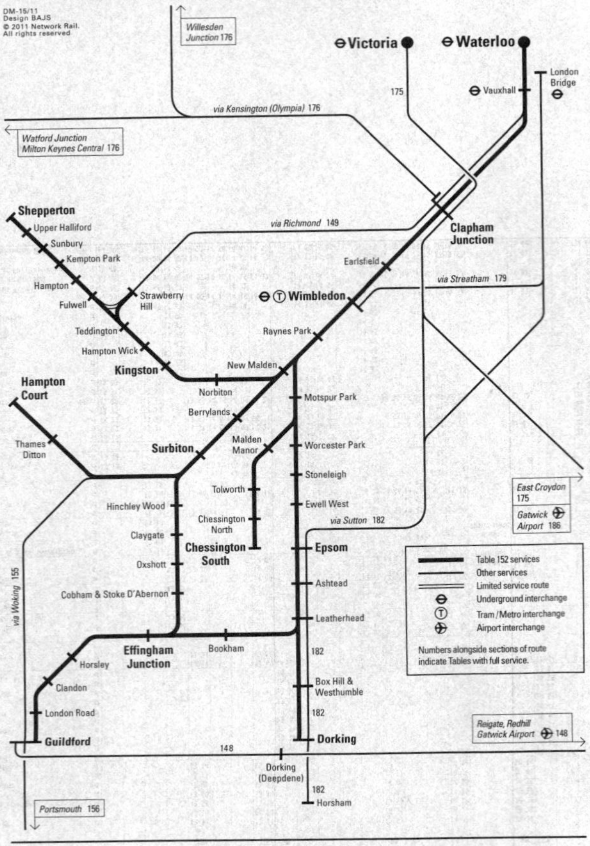

Table 152

Mondays to Fridays
until 5 October

London - Chessington South, Dorking, Guildford, Shepperton and Hampton Court

Network Diagram - see first Page of Table 152

Miles	Miles	Miles	Miles	Miles			SW MX	SW MO A	SW MO A	SW MX	SW MX	SW MO A	SW MX	SW MX	SW MX	SW MX	SW MO	SW MX	SW MX B	SW MX C	SW MX B	SW MX C
0	—	—	—	0	**London Waterloo** ⊖	d	23p03	23p00	23p10	23p12	23p27	23p32	23p36	23p42	23p50	23p57	00 01	00 09	00 15	00 15	00 27	00 27
1¼	—	—	—	1¼	Vauxhall ⊖	d	23p07	23p04	23p14	23p16	23p31	23p36	23p40	23p46	23p54	00 01	00 04	00 13	00 19	00 19	00 31	00 31
4	—	—	—	4	**Clapham Junction**	d	23p12	23p09	23p19	23p21	23p36	23p41	23p45	23p51	23p59	00 06	00 09	00 20	00 25	00 25	00 37	00 37
5½	—	—	—	5½	Earlsfield	d	23p15	23p12	23p22	23p24	23p39	23p44	23p48	23p54	00 02	00 09	00 12	00 23	00 29	00 29	00s41	00s41
7¼	—	—	—	7¼	**Wimbledon** ⊖	d	23p19	23p16	23p26	23p28	23p43	23p48	23p52	23p58	00 06	00 13	00 16	00 27	00 33	00 33	00 45	00 45
8¾	—	0	0	8¾	Raynes Park	d				23p31	23p46	23p52	23p55	00 01		00 16	00 19		00 36	00 36	00 48	00 48
—	—	1	1	—	Motspur Park	d						23p55		00 04					00 38	00 38		
—	—	—	2½	—	Malden Manor	d																
—	—	—	3½	—	Tolworth	d																
—	—	—	4½	—	Chessington North	d																
—	—	—	5¼	—	**Chessington South**	a																
—	—	2	—	—	Worcester Park	d						23p57		00 06					00 41	00 41		
—	—	3¼	—	—	Stoneleigh	d						23p59		00 09					00 44	00 44		
—	—	4¼	—	—	Ewell West	d						00 03		00 12					00 46	00 46		
—	—	5½	—	—	**Epsom**	a						00 06		00 15					00 50	00 50		
—	—	—	—	—		d								00 19						00 51		
—	—	7½	—	—	Ashtead	d								00 23						00s55		
—	0	9¼	—	—	Leatherhead	d								00 26						00s58		
—	—	12½	—	—	Box Hill & Westhumble	d																
—	—	13¼	—	—	**Dorking**	a																
9¾	—	—	—	9¾	New Malden	d				23p34	23p49		23p58			00 19	00 22				00 50	00 50
—	—	—	—	11¼	Norbiton	d				23p37	23p52					00 22						
—	—	—	—	12	Kingston	a				23p40	23p55					00 25						
—	—	—	—	—		d				23p40	23p55					00 25						
—	—	—	—	12½	Hampton Wick	d				23p42	23p57					00 27						
—	—	—	—	13¾	Teddington	d				23p45	23p59					00 30						
—	—	—	—	—	Strawberry Hill	a					00 03											
—	—	—	—	14¾	Fulwell	d				23p49						00 34						
—	—	—	—	16½	Hampton	d				23p53						00 38						
—	—	—	—	18¼	Kempton Park	d				23p56						00 41						
—	—	—	—	18¾	Sunbury	d				23p58						00 43						
—	—	—	—	19¾	Upper Halliford	d				23p59						00 45						
—	—	—	—	20¾	**Shepperton**	a				00 03						00 48						
11	—	—	—	—	Berrylands	d							23p59				00 25				00s53	00s53
12	—	—	0	—	**Surbiton**	d	23p27	23p32	23p35				00 05		00 14		00 31	00 35			00a56	00 57
—	—	—	2	—	Thames Ditton	d							00 09									
—	—	—	3	—	**Hampton Court**	a							00 12									
14	—	—	—	—	Hinchley Wood	d	23p31	23p36							00 18		00 35					
15¼	—	—	—	—	Claygate	d	23p34	23p39							00 20		00 38					
17	—	—	—	—	Oxshott	d	23p37	23p42							00 24		00 41					
19	—	—	—	—	Cobham & Stoke D'abernon	d	23p41	23p46							00 27		00 45					
—	2¼	—	—	—	Bookham	d								00 31						01s03		
21¼	4¼	—	—	—	Effingham Junction	d	23p45	23p50						00 36	00 32		00 49			01s07		
22¼	—	—	—	—	Horsley	d	23p48	23p53						00 39	00 34		00 52			01s10		
25½	—	—	—	—	Clandon	d	23p53	23p58						00 44	00 39		00 57			01s15		
28¾	—	—	—	—	London Road (Guildford)	d	23p58	00 03						00 49	00 44		01 02			01s20		
30	—	—	—	—	**Guildford**	a	00 02	00 07	00 13					00 53	00 48		01 06	01 07		01 24		01 33

A from 21 May until 1 October

B not from 31 July until 10 August, from 30 August until 7 September

C from 31 July until 7 September, not from 14 August until 29 August

Table 152

Mondays to Fridays

until 5 October

London - Chessington South, Dorking, Guildford, Shepperton and Hampton Court

Network Diagram - see first Page of Table 152

		SW	SW 1	SW	SW 1	SW	SW	SW	SW	SW	SW	SW	SW	SW	SW	SW	SW	SW	SW
London Waterloo [15] ⊖	d	00 42	05 00	05 12	05 20		05 47	05 50				06 03	06 06	06 12	06 16	06 20	06 24	06 27	06 33
Vauxhall ⊖	d	00 46	05 04	05 16	05 24		05 51	05 54				06 07	06 10	06 16	06 20	06 24	06 28	06 31	06 37
Clapham Junction [10]	d	00 51	05 11	05 21	05 29		05 56	05 59				06 12	06 15	06 21	06 25	06 29	06 33	06 36	06 42
Earlsfield	d		05 14	05 24	05 32		05 59	06 02				06 15	06 18	06 24	06 28	06 32	06 36	06 39	06 45
Wimbledon [6] ⊖	d	01 05	05 18	05 28	05 36	05 49	06 03	06 06		06 13	06 16	06 19	06 22	06 28	06 32	06 36	06 40	06 43	06 49
Raynes Park [6]	d	01 08		05 31			06 06			06 16	06 19		06 25	06 31	06 35		06 43	06 46	
Motspur Park	d						06 09				06 21				06 38		06 46		
Malden Manor	d										06 25				06 41				
Tolworth	d										06 27				06 44				
Chessington North	d										06 30				06 47				
Chessington South	a										06 32				06 49				
Worcester Park	d						06 11										06 48		
Stoneleigh	d						06 14										06 51		
Ewell West	d						06 17										06 54		
Epsom [3]	a						06 20										06 57		
	d						06 21										06 58		
Ashtead	d						06 25										07 02		
Leatherhead	d						06 28										07 05		
Box Hill & Westhumble	d																		
Dorking [4]	a																07 11		
New Malden [6]	d	01 11		05 34						06 19			06 28	06 34				06 49	
Norbiton	d	01 14		05 37						06 22				06 37				06 52	
Kingston	a	01 17		05 40						06 25				06 40				06 55	
	d	01 17		05 40					05 59	06 29				06 40				06 59	
Hampton Wick	d	01s22		05 42					06 01	06 31				06 42				07 01	
Teddington	d	01s25		05 45					06 05	06 35				06 45				07 05	
Strawberry Hill	a	01 28							06 08	06 38								07 08	
Fulwell	d			05 49										06 49					
Hampton	d			05 53										06 53					
Kempton Park	d			05 56										06 56					
Sunbury	d			05 58										06 58					
Upper Halliford	d			06 00										07 00					
Shepperton	a			06 03										07 03					
Berrylands	d												06 30						
Surbiton [6]	d		05 26		05 44	05 57		06a13				06 27	06 35			06 44			06 57
Thames Ditton	d												06 39						
Hampton Court	a												06 42						
Hinchley Wood	d					06 01						06 31							07 01
Claygate	d					06 04						06 34							07 04
Oxshott	d					06 07						06 37							07 07
Cobham & Stoke D'abernon	d					06 11						06 41							07 11
Bookham	d						06 33												
Effingham Junction [6]	d					06 15	06 37					06 45							07 15
Horsley	d					06 18						06 48							07 18
Clandon	d					06 23						06 53							07 23
London Road (Guildford)	d					06 28	06 46					06 58							07 28
Guildford	a		06 00		06 21	06 32	06 50					07 02				07 20			07 32

Table 152

Mondays to Fridays

until 5 October

London - Chessington South, Dorking, Guildford, Shepperton and Hampton Court

Network Diagram - see first Page of Table 152

		SW	SW	SW	SW	SW	SW	SW	SW	SW	SW	SW	SW	SW	SW	SW	SW	SW	SW	SW	SW
London Waterloo [15] ⊖	d	06 36	06 39	06 42	06 46	06 50	06 54	06 57	07 03	07 06	07 09	07 12	07 16	07 20	07 24	07 27	07 33	07 36	07 39	07 42	07 46
Vauxhall ⊖	d	06 40	06 43	06 46	06 50	06 54	06 58	07 01	07 07	07 10	07 13	07 16	07 20	07 24	07 28	07 31	07 37	07 40	07 43	07 46	07 50
Clapham Junction [10]	d	06 45	06 48	06 51	06 55	06 59	07 03	07 06	07 12	07 15	07 18	07 21	07 25	07 29	07 33	07 36	07 42	07 45	07 48	07 51	07 55
Earlsfield	d	06 48	06 51	06 54	06 58	07 02	07 06	07 09	07 15	07 18	07 21	07 24	07 28	07 32	07 36	07 39	07 45	07 48	07 51	07 54	07 58
Wimbledon [6] ⊖	d	06 52	06 55	06 58	07 02	07 06	07 10	07 13	07 19	07 22	07 25	07 28	07 32	07 36	07 40	07 43	07 49	07 52	07 55	07 58	08 02
Raynes Park [6]	d	06 55	06 58	07 01	07 05		07 13	07 16		07 25	07 28	07 31	07 35		07 43	07 46		07 55	07 58	08 01	08 05
Motspur Park	d				07 08		07 16				07 31		07 38		07 46				08 01		08 08
Malden Manor	d				07 11								07 41								08 11
Tolworth	d				07 14								07 44								08 14
Chessington North	d				07 17								07 47								08 17
Chessington South	a				07 19								07 49								08 19
Worcester Park	d		07 02				07 18				07 33				07 48				08 03		
Stoneleigh	d		07 05				07 21				07 36				07 51				08 06		
Ewell West	d		07 08				07 24				07 39				07 54				08 09		
Epsom [3]	a		07 11				07 27				07 42				07 58				08 13		
	d		07 12				07 28								07 58				08 17		
Ashtead	d		07 16				07 32								08 02				08 21		
Leatherhead	d		07 19				07 35								08 05				08 24		
Box Hill & Westhumble	d																				
Dorking [4]	a						07 41								08 12						
New Malden [6]	d	06 58		07 04				07 19		07 28		07 34				07 49		07 58		08 04	
Norbiton	d			07 07				07 22				07 37				07 52				08 07	
Kingston	a			07 10				07 25				07 40				07 55				08 10	
	d			07 10				07 29				07 40				07 59				08 10	
Hampton Wick	d			07 12				07 31				07 42				08 01				08 12	
Teddington	d			07 15				07 35				07 45				08 05				08 15	
Strawberry Hill	a							07 38								08 08					
Fulwell	d			07 19								07 49								08 19	
Hampton	d			07 23								07 53								08 23	
Kempton Park	d			07 26								07 56								08 26	
Sunbury	d			07 28								07 58								08 28	
Upper Halliford	d			07 30								08 00								08 30	
Shepperton	a			07 33								08 03								08 33	
Berrylands	d	07 00								07 30								08 00			
Surbiton [6]	d	07 05				07 14			07 27	07 35				07a43			07 57	08 05			
Thames Ditton	d	07 09								07 39								08 09			
Hampton Court	a	07 12								07 42								08 12			
Hinchley Wood	d								07 31								08 01				
Claygate	d								07 34								08 04				
Oxshott	d								07 37								08 07				
Cobham & Stoke D'abernon	d								07 41								08 11				
Bookham	d		07 24																08 29		
Effingham Junction [6]	d		07a28						07 45								08 15		08 33		
Horsley	d								07 48								08 18		08 36		
Clandon	d								07 53								08 23		08 41		
London Road (Guildford)	d								07 58								08 28		08 46		
Guildford	a					07 47			08 02								08 32		08 50		

		SW	SW	SW	SW	SW	SW	SW	SW	SW	SW	SW	SW	SW	SW	SW	SW	SW	SW	SW
London Waterloo [15] ⊖	d	07 50	07 54	07 57	08 03	08 06	08 09	08 12	08 16	08 20	08 24	08 27	08 33	08 36	08 39	08 42	08 46	08 50	08 54	08 57
Vauxhall ⊖	d	07 54	07 58	08 01	08 07	08 10	08 13	08 16	08 20	08 24	08 28	08 31	08 37	08 40	08 43	08 46	08 50	08 54	08 58	09 01
Clapham Junction [10]	d	07 59	08 03	08 06	08 12	08 15	08 18	08 21	08 25	08 29	08 33	08 36	08 42	08 45	08 48	08 51	08 55	08 59	09 03	09 06
Earlsfield	d	08 02	08 06	08 09	08 15	08 18	08 21	08 24	08 28	08 32	08 36	08 39	08 45	08 48	08 51	08 54	08 58	09 02	09 06	09 09
Wimbledon [6] ⊖	d	08 06	08 10	08 13	08 19	08 22	08 25	08 28	08 32	08 36	08 40	08 43	08 49	08 52	08 55	08 58	09 02	09 06	09 10	09 13
Raynes Park [6]	d		08 13	08 16		08 25	08 28	08 31	08 35		08 43	08 46		08 55	08 58	09 01	09 05		09 13	09 16
Motspur Park	d		08 16				08 31		08 38		08 46				09 01		09 08		09 16	
Malden Manor	d								08 41								09 11			
Tolworth	d								08 44								09 14			
Chessington North	d								08 47								09 17			
Chessington South	a								08 49								09 19			
Worcester Park	d		08 18				08 33				08 48				09 03				09 18	
Stoneleigh	d		08 21				08 36				08 51				09 06				09 21	
Ewell West	d		08 24				08 39				08 54				09 09				09 24	
Epsom [3]	a		08 27				08 42				08 57				09 16				09 27	
	d		08 28				08 47				08 58				09 17				09 28	
Ashtead	d		08 32				08 51				09 02				09 21				09 32	
Leatherhead	d		08 35				08 54				09 05				09 24				09 35	
Box Hill & Westhumble	d																			
Dorking [4]	a		08 41								09 11								09 41	
New Malden [6]	d			08 19		08 28		08 34				08 49		08 58		09 04				09 19
Norbiton	d			08 22				08 37				08 52				09 07				09 22
Kingston	a			08 25				08 39				08 55				09 10				09 25
	d			08 29				08 40				08 59				09 10				09 29
Hampton Wick	d			08 31				08 42				09 01				09 12				09 31
Teddington	d			08 35				08 45				09 05				09 15				09 35
Strawberry Hill	a			08 38								09 08								09 38
Fulwell	d							08 49								09 19				
Hampton	d							08 53								09 23				
Kempton Park	d							08 56								09 26				
Sunbury	d							08 58								09 28				
Upper Halliford	d							09 00								09 30				
Shepperton	a							09 04								09 33				
Berrylands	d					08 30								09 00						
Surbiton [6]	d	08 14			08 27	08 35				08a43			08 57	09 05				09a13		
Thames Ditton	d					08 39								09 09						
Hampton Court	a					08 42								09 12						
Hinchley Wood	d				08 31								09 01							
Claygate	d				08 34								09 04							
Oxshott	d				08 37								09 07							
Cobham & Stoke D'abernon	d				08 41								09 11							
Bookham	d						08 59								09 29					
Effingham Junction [6]	d				08 45		09 03						09 15		09 33					
Horsley	d				08 48		09 06						09 18		09 36					
Clandon	d				08 53		09 11						09 23		09 41					
London Road (Guildford)	d				08 58		09 16						09 28		09 46					
Guildford	a	08 50			09 04		09 20						09 32		09 50					

Table 152

Mondays to Fridays
until 5 October

London - Chessington South, Dorking, Guildford, Shepperton and Hampton Court

Network Diagram - see first Page of Table 152

		SW		SW	SW	SW	SW	SW	SW		SW	SW		SW	SW	SW	SW	SW	SW		SW	SW		SW	SW
London Waterloo 15 ⊖	d	09 03		09 06	09 09	09 12	09 16	09 20	09 24		09 27	09 33		09 36	09 39	09 42	09 46	09 50	09 54		09 57	10 03		10 06	10 09
Vauxhall ⊖	d	09 07		09 10	09 13	09 16	09 20	09 24	09 28		09 31	09 37		09 40	09 43	09 46	09 50	09 54	09 58		10 01	10 07		10 10	10 13
Clapham Junction 10	d	09 12		09 15	09 18	09 21	09 25	09 29	09 33		09 36	09 42		09 45	09 48	09 51	09 55	09 59	10 03		10 06	10 12		10 15	10 18
Earlsfield	d	09 15		09 18	09 21	09 24	09 28	09 32	09 36		09 39	09 45		09 48	09 51	09 54	09 58	10 02	10 06		10 09	10 15		10 18	10 21
Wimbledon 6 ⊖ ⇌	d	09 19		09 22	09 25	09 28	09 32	09 36	09 40		09 43	09 49		09 52	09 55	09 58	10 02	10 06	10 10		10 13	10 19		10 22	10 25
Raynes Park 6	d			09 25	09 28	09 31	09 35		09 43		09 46			09 55	09 58	10 01	10 05		10 13		10 16			10 25	10 28
Motspur Park	d				09 31		09 38		09 46						10 01		10 08		10 16						10 31
Malden Manor	d						09 41										10 11								
Tolworth	d						09 44										10 14								
Chessington North	d						09 47										10 17								
Chessington South	a						09 49										10 19								
Worcester Park	d				09 33				09 48						10 03				10 18						10 33
Stoneleigh	d				09 36				09 51						10 06				10 21						10 36
Ewell West	d				09 39				09 54						10 09				10 24						10 39
Epsom 3	a				09 42				09 57						10 16				10 27						10 46
	d				09 47				09 58						10 17				10 28						10 47
Ashtead	d				09 51				10 02						10 21				10 32						10 51
Leatherhead	d				09 54				10 05						10 24				10 35						10 54
Box Hill & Westhumble	d																								
Dorking 4	a								10 11										10 41						
New Malden 6	d			09 28		09 34					09 49			09 58		10 04					10 19			10 28	
Norbiton	d					09 37					09 52					10 07					10 22				
Kingston	a					09 40					09 55					10 10					10 25				
	d					09 40					09 59					10 10					10 29				
Hampton Wick	d					09 42					10 01					10 12					10 31				
Teddington	d					09 45					10 05					10 15					10 35				
Strawberry Hill	a										10 08										10 38				
Fulwell	d					09 49										10 19									
Hampton	d					09 53										10 23									
Kempton Park	d					09 56										10 26									
Sunbury	d					09 58										10 28									
Upper Halliford	d					10 00										10 30									
Shepperton	a					10 03										10 33									
Berrylands	d			09 30										10 00										10 30	
Surbiton 6	d	09 27		09 35				09a43				09 57		10 05				10a13				10 27		10 35	
Thames Ditton	d			09 39										10 09										10 39	
Hampton Court	a			09 42										10 12										10 42	
Hinchley Wood	d	09 31										10 01										10 31			
Claygate	d	09 34										10 04										10 34			
Oxshott	d	09 37										10 07										10 37			
Cobham & Stoke D'abernon	d	09 41										10 11										10 41			
Bookham	d				09 59										10 29										10 59
Effingham Junction 6	d	09 45			10 03							10 15			10 33							10 45			11 03
Horsley	d	09 48			10 06							10 18			10 36							10 48			11 06
Clandon	d	09 53			10 11							10 23			10 41							10 53			11 11
London Road (Guildford)	d	09 58			10 16							10 28			10 46							10 58			11 16
Guildford	a	10 02			10 20							10 32			10 50							11 02			11 20

Table 152

Mondays to Fridays
until 5 October

London - Chessington South, Dorking, Guildford, Shepperton and Hampton Court

Network Diagram - see first Page of Table 152

		SW	SW	SW			SW	SW	SW		SW	SW	SW	SW	SW		SW	SW	SW		SW	SW	SW	SW	SW
London Waterloo 15 ⊖	d	10 12	10 16	10 20			10 24	10 27	10 33		10 36	10 39	10 42	10 46	10 50		10 54	10 57	11 03		11 06	11 09	11 12	11 16	11 20
Vauxhall ⊖	d	10 16	10 20	10 24			10 28	10 31	10 37		10 40	10 43	10 46	10 50	10 54		10 58	11 01	11 07		11 10	11 13	11 16	11 20	11 24
Clapham Junction 10	d	10 21	10 25	10 29			10 33	10 36	10 42		10 45	10 48	10 51	10 55	10 59		11 03	11 06	11 12		11 15	11 18	11 21	11 25	11 29
Earlsfield	d	10 24	10 28	10 32			10 36	10 39	10 45		10 48	10 51	10 54	10 58	11 02		11 06	11 09	11 15		11 18	11 21	11 24	11 28	11 32
Wimbledon 6 ⊖ ⇌	d	10 28	10 32	10 36			10 40	10 43	10 49		10 52	10 55	10 58	11 02	11 06		11 10	11 13	11 19		11 22	11 25	11 28	11 32	11 36
Raynes Park 6	d	10 31	10 35				10 43	10 46			10 55	10 58	11 01	11 05			11 13	11 16			11 25	11 28	11 31	11 35	
Motspur Park	d		10 38				10 46					11 01		11 08			11 16					11 31		11 38	
Malden Manor	d		10 41											11 11										11 41	
Tolworth	d		10 44											11 14										11 44	
Chessington North	d		10 47											11 17										11 47	
Chessington South	a		10 49											11 19										11 49	
Worcester Park	d						10 48					11 03					11 18					11 33			
Stoneleigh	d						10 51					11 06					11 21					11 36			
Ewell West	d						10 54					11 09					11 24					11 39			
Epsom 3	a						10 57					11 16					11 27					11 46			
	d						10 58					11 17					11 28					11 47			
Ashtead	d						11 02					11 21					11 32					11 51			
Leatherhead	d						11 05					11 24					11 35					11 54			
Box Hill & Westhumble	d																								
Dorking 4	a						11 11										11 41								
New Malden 6	d	10 34						10 49			10 58		11 04					11 19			11 28		11 34		
Norbiton	d	10 37						10 52					11 07					11 22					11 37		
Kingston	a	10 40						10 55					11 10					11 25					11 40		
	d	10 40						10 59					11 10					11 29					11 40		
Hampton Wick	d	10 42						11 01					11 12					11 31					11 42		
Teddington	d	10 45						11 05					11 15					11 35					11 45		
Strawberry Hill	a							11 08										11 38							
Fulwell	d	10 49											11 19										11 49		
Hampton	d	10 53											11 23										11 53		
Kempton Park	d	10 56											11 26										11 56		
Sunbury	d	10 58											11 28										11 58		
Upper Halliford	d	11 00											11 30										12 00		
Shepperton	a	11 03											11 33										12 03		
Berrylands	d										11 00										11 30				
Surbiton 6	d			10a43					10 57		11 05				11a13				11 27		11 35				11a43
Thames Ditton	d										11 09										11 39				
Hampton Court	a										11 12										11 42				
Hinchley Wood	d								11 01										11 31						
Claygate	d								11 04										11 34						
Oxshott	d								11 07										11 37						
Cobham & Stoke D'abernon	d								11 11										11 41						
Bookham	d											11 29										11 59			
Effingham Junction 6	d								11 15			11 33							11 45			12 03			
Horsley	d								11 18			11 36							11 48			12 06			
Clandon	d								11 23			11 41							11 53			12 11			
London Road (Guildford)	d								11 28			11 46							11 58			12 16			
Guildford	a								11 32			11 50							12 02			12 20			

London - Chessington South, Dorking, Guildford, Shepperton and Hampton Court

Network Diagram - see first Page of Table 152

		SW	SW	SW	SW	SW	SW	SW	SW	SW	SW	SW	SW	SW	SW	SW	SW	SW	SW	SW
London Waterloo ⊖	d	11 24	11 27	11 33	11 36	11 39	11 42	11 46	11 50	11 54	11 57	12 03	12 06	12 09	12 12	12 16	12 20	12 24	12 27	12 33
Vauxhall ⊖	d	11 28	11 31	11 37	11 40	11 43	11 46	11 50	11 54	11 58	12 01	12 07	12 10	12 13	12 16	12 20	12 24	12 28	12 31	12 37
Clapham Junction	d	11 33	11 36	11 42	11 45	11 48	11 51	11 55	11 59	12 03	12 06	12 12	12 15	12 18	12 21	12 25	12 29	12 33	12 36	12 42
Earlsfield	d	11 36	11 39	11 45	11 48	11 51	11 54	11 58	12 02	12 06	12 09	12 15	12 18	12 21	12 24	12 28	12 32	12 36	12 39	12 45
Wimbledon ⊖	d	11 40	11 43	11 49	11 52	11 55	11 58	12 02	12 06	12 10	12 13	12 19	12 22	12 25	12 28	12 32	12 36	12 40	12 43	12 49
Raynes Park	d	11 43	11 46		11 55	11 58	12 01	12 05		12 13	12 16		12 25	12 28	12 31	12 35		12 43	12 46	
Motspur Park	d	11 46				12 01		12 08		12 16				12 31		12 38		12 46		
Malden Manor	d							12 11								12 41				
Tolworth	d							12 14								12 44				
Chessington North	d							12 17								12 47				
Chessington South	a							12 19								12 49				
Worcester Park	d	11 48				12 03				12 18				12 33				12 48		
Stoneleigh	d	11 51				12 06				12 21				12 36				12 51		
Ewell West	d	11 54				12 09				12 24				12 39				12 54		
Epsom	a	11 57				12 16				12 27				12 46				12 57		
	d	11 58				12 17				12 28				12 47				12 58		
Ashtead	d	12 02				12 21				12 32				12 51				13 02		
Leatherhead	d	12 05				12 24				12 35				12 54				13 05		
Box Hill & Westhumble	d																			
Dorking	a	12 11								12 41								13 11		
New Malden	d		11 49		11 58		12 04				12 19		12 28		12 34				12 49	
Norbiton	d		11 52				12 07				12 22				12 37				12 52	
Kingston	a		11 55				12 10				12 25				12 40				12 55	
	d		11 59				12 10				12 29				12 40				12 59	
Hampton Wick	d		12 01				12 12				12 31				12 42				13 01	
Teddington	d		12 05				12 15				12 35				12 45				13 05	
Strawberry Hill	a		12 08								12 38								13 08	
Fulwell	d						12 19								12 49					
Hampton	d						12 23								12 53					
Kempton Park	d						12 26								12 56					
Sunbury	d						12 28								12 58					
Upper Halliford	d						12 30								13 00					
Shepperton	a						12 33								13 03					
Berrylands	d				12 00								12 30							
Surbiton	d			11 57	12 05				12a13			12 27	12 35				12a43			12 57
Thames Ditton	d				12 09								12 39							
Hampton Court	a				12 12								12 42							
Hinchley Wood	d			12 01								12 31								13 01
Claygate	d			12 04								12 34								13 04
Oxshott	d			12 07								12 37								13 07
Cobham & Stoke D'abernon	d			12 11								12 41								13 11
Bookham	d					12 29								12 59						
Effingham Junction	d			12 15		12 33						12 45		13 03						13 15
Horsley	d			12 18		12 36						12 48		13 06						13 18
Clandon	d			12 23		12 41						12 53		13 11						13 23
London Road (Guildford)	d			12 28		12 46						12 58		13 16						13 28
Guildford	a			12 32		12 50						13 02		13 20						13 32

		SW	SW	SW	SW	SW	SW	SW	SW	SW	SW	SW	SW	SW	SW	SW	SW	SW	SW	SW
London Waterloo ⊖	d	12 36	12 39	12 42	12 46	12 50	12 54	12 57	13 03	13 06	13 09	13 12	13 16	13 20	13 24	13 27	13 33	13 36	13 39	13 42
Vauxhall ⊖	d	12 40	12 43	12 46	12 50	12 54	12 58	13 01	13 07	13 10	13 13	13 16	13 20	13 24	13 28	13 31	13 37	13 40	13 43	13 46
Clapham Junction	d	12 45	12 48	12 51	12 55	12 59	13 03	13 06	13 12	13 15	13 18	13 21	13 25	13 29	13 33	13 36	13 42	13 45	13 48	13 51
Earlsfield	d	12 48	12 51	12 54	12 58	13 02	13 06	13 09	13 15	13 18	13 21	13 24	13 28	13 32	13 36	13 39	13 45	13 48	13 51	13 54
Wimbledon ⊖	d	12 52	12 55	12 58	13 02	13 06	13 10	13 13	13 19	13 22	13 25	13 28	13 32	13 36	13 40	13 43	13 49	13 52	13 55	13 58
Raynes Park	d	12 55	12 58	13 01	13 05		13 13	13 16		13 25	13 28	13 31	13 35		13 43	13 46		13 55	13 58	14 01
Motspur Park	d		13 01		13 08		13 16				13 31		13 38		13 46				14 01	
Malden Manor	d				13 11								13 41							
Tolworth	d				13 14								13 44							
Chessington North	d				13 17								13 47							
Chessington South	a				13 19								13 49							
Worcester Park	d		13 03				13 18				13 33				13 48				14 03	
Stoneleigh	d		13 06				13 21				13 36				13 51				14 06	
Ewell West	d		13 09				13 24				13 39				13 54				14 09	
Epsom	a		13 16				13 27				13 46				13 57				14 16	
	d		13 17				13 28				13 47				13 58				14 17	
Ashtead	d		13 21				13 32				13 51				14 02				14 21	
Leatherhead	d		13 24				13 35				13 54				14 05				14 24	
Box Hill & Westhumble	d																			
Dorking	a						13 41								14 11					
New Malden	d	12 58		13 04				13 19		13 28		13 34				13 49		13 58		14 04
Norbiton	d			13 07				13 22				13 37				13 52				14 07
Kingston	a			13 10				13 25				13 40				13 55				14 10
	d			13 10				13 29				13 40				13 59				14 10
Hampton Wick	d			13 12				13 31				13 42				14 01				14 12
Teddington	d			13 15				13 35				13 45				14 05				14 15
Strawberry Hill	a							13 38								14 08				
Fulwell	d			13 19								13 49								14 19
Hampton	d			13 23								13 53								14 23
Kempton Park	d			13 26								13 56								14 26
Sunbury	d			13 28								13 58								14 28
Upper Halliford	d			13 30								14 00								14 30
Shepperton	a			13 33								14 03								14 33
Berrylands	d	13 00								13 30								14 00		
Surbiton	d	13 05				13a13			13 27	13 35				13a43			13 57	14 05		
Thames Ditton	d	13 09								13 39								14 09		
Hampton Court	a	13 12								13 42								14 12		
Hinchley Wood	d								13 31								14 01			
Claygate	d								13 34								14 04			
Oxshott	d								13 37								14 07			
Cobham & Stoke D'abernon	d								13 41								14 11			
Bookham	d		13 29								13 59								14 29	
Effingham Junction	d		13 33						13 45		14 03						14 15		14 33	
Horsley	d		13 36						13 48		14 06						14 18		14 36	
Clandon	d		13 41						13 53		14 11						14 23		14 41	
London Road (Guildford)	d		13 46						13 58		14 16						14 28		14 46	
Guildford	a		13 50						14 02		14 20						14 32		14 50	

London - Chessington South, Dorking, Guildford, Shepperton and Hampton Court

Network Diagram - see first Page of Table 152

		SW	SW	SW	SW	SW	SW	SW	SW	SW	SW	SW	SW	SW	SW	SW	SW	SW	SW	SW
London Waterloo ⊖	d	13 46	13 50	13 54	13 57	14 03	14 06	14 09	14 12	14 16	14 20	14 24	14 27	14 33	14 36	14 39	14 42	14 46	14 50	14 54
Vauxhall ⊖	d	13 50	13 54	13 58	14 01	14 07	14 10	14 13	14 16	14 20	14 24	14 28	14 31	14 37	14 40	14 43	14 46	14 50	14 54	14 58
Clapham Junction	d	13 55	13 59	14 03	14 06	14 12	14 15	14 18	14 21	14 25	14 29	14 33	14 36	14 42	14 45	14 48	14 51	14 55	14 59	15 03
Earlsfield	d	13 58	14 02	14 06	14 09	14 15	14 18	14 21	14 24	14 28	14 32	14 36	14 39	14 45	14 48	14 51	14 54	14 58	15 02	15 06
Wimbledon ⊖	d	14 02	14 06	14 10	14 13	14 19	14 22	14 25	14 28	14 32	14 36	14 40	14 43	14 49	14 52	14 55	14 58	15 02	15 06	15 10
Raynes Park	d	14 05		14 13	14 16		14 25	14 28	14 31	14 35		14 43	14 46		14 55	14 58	15 01	15 05		15 13
Motspur Park	d	14 08		14 16				14 31		14 38		14 46				15 01		15 08		15 16
Malden Manor	d	14 11								14 41								15 11		
Tolworth	d	14 14								14 44								15 14		
Chessington North	d	14 17								14 47								15 17		
Chessington South	a	14 19								14 49								15 19		
Worcester Park	d			14 18				14 33				14 48				15 03				15 18
Stoneleigh	d			14 21				14 36				14 51				15 06				15 21
Ewell West	d			14 24				14 39				14 54				15 09				15 24
Epsom	a			14 27				14 46				14 57				15 16				15 27
	d			14 28				14 47				14 58				15 17				15 28
Ashtead	d			14 32				14 51				15 02				15 21				15 32
Leatherhead	d			14 35				14 54				15 05				15 24				15 35
Box Hill & Westhumble	d																			
Dorking	a			14 41								15 11								15 41
New Malden	d				14 19		14 28		14 34				14 49		14 58		15 04			
Norbiton	d				14 22				14 37				14 52				15 07			
Kingston	a				14 25				14 40				14 55				15 10			
	d				14 29				14 40				14 59				15 10			
Hampton Wick	d				14 31				14 42				15 01				15 12			
Teddington	d				14 35				14 45				15 05				15 15			
Strawberry Hill	a				14 38								15 08							
Fulwell	d								14 49								15 19			
Hampton	d								14 53								15 23			
Kempton Park	d								14 56								15 26			
Sunbury	d								14 58								15 28			
Upper Halliford	d								15 00								15 30			
Shepperton	a								15 03								15 33			
Berrylands	d						14 30								15 00					
Surbiton	d		14a13			14 27	14 35				14a43			14 57	15 05				15a13	
Thames Ditton	d						14 39								15 09					
Hampton Court	a						14 42								15 12					
Hinchley Wood	d					14 31								15 01						
Claygate	d					14 34								15 04						
Oxshott	d					14 37								15 07						
Cobham & Stoke D'abernon	d					14 41								15 11						
Bookham	d							14 59								15 29				
Effingham Junction	d					14 45		15 03						15 15		15 33				
Horsley	d					14 48		15 06						15 18		15 36				
Clandon	d					14 53		15 11						15 23		15 41				
London Road (Guildford)	d					14 58		15 16						15 28		15 46				
Guildford	a					15 02		15 20						15 32		15 50				

		SW	SW	SW	SW	SW	SW	SW	SW	SW	SW	SW	SW	SW	SW	SW	SW	SW	SW	SW
London Waterloo ⊖	d	14 57	15 03	15 06	15 09	15 12	15 16	15 20	15 24	15 27	15 33	15 36	15 39	15 42	15 46	15 50	15 54	15 57	16 03	16 06
Vauxhall ⊖	d	15 01	15 07	15 10	15 13	15 16	15 20	15 24	15 28	15 31	15 37	15 40	15 43	15 46	15 50	15 54	15 58	16 01	16 07	16 10
Clapham Junction	d	15 06	15 12	15 15	15 18	15 21	15 25	15 29	15 33	15 36	15 42	15 45	15 48	15 51	15 55	15 59	16 03	16 06	16 12	16 15
Earlsfield	d	15 09	15 15	15 18	15 21	15 24	15 28	15 32	15 36	15 39	15 45	15 48	15 51	15 54	15 58	16 02	16 06	16 09	16 15	16 18
Wimbledon ⊖	d	15 13	15 19	15 22	15 25	15 28	15 32	15 36	15 40	15 43	15 49	15 52	15 55	15 58	16 02	16 06	16 10	16 13	16 19	16 22
Raynes Park	d	15 16		15 25	15 28	15 31	15 35		15 43	15 46		15 55	15 58	16 01	16 05		16 13	16 16		16 25
Motspur Park	d				15 31		15 38		15 46				16 01		16 08		16 16			
Malden Manor	d						15 41								16 11					
Tolworth	d						15 44								16 14					
Chessington North	d						15 47								16 17					
Chessington South	a						15 49								16 19					
Worcester Park	d				15 33				15 48				16 03				16 18			
Stoneleigh	d				15 36				15 51				16 06				16 21			
Ewell West	d				15 39				15 54				16 09				16 24			
Epsom	a				15 46				15 57				16 15				16 27			
	d				15 47				15 58				16 17				16 28			
Ashtead	d				15 51				16 02				16 21				16 32			
Leatherhead	d				15 54				16 05				16 24				16 35			
Box Hill & Westhumble	d																			
Dorking	a								16 11								16 41			
New Malden	d	15 19		15 28		15 34				15 49		15 58		16 04				16 19		16 28
Norbiton	d	15 22				15 37				15 52				16 07				16 22		
Kingston	a	15 25				15 40				15 55				16 10				16 25		
	d	15 29				15 40				15 59				16 10				16 29		
Hampton Wick	d	15 31				15 42				16 01				16 12				16 31		
Teddington	d	15 35				15 45				16 05				16 15				16 35		
Strawberry Hill	a	15 38								16 08								16 38		
Fulwell	d					15 49								16 19						
Hampton	d					15 53								16 23						
Kempton Park	d					15 56								16 26						
Sunbury	d					15 58								16 28						
Upper Halliford	d					16 00								16 30						
Shepperton	a					16 03								16 33						
Berrylands	d			15 30								16 00								16 30
Surbiton	d		15 27	15 35				15a43			15 57	16 05				16a13			16 27	16 35
Thames Ditton	d			15 39								16 09								16 39
Hampton Court	a			15 42								16 12								16 44
Hinchley Wood	d		15 31								16 01								16 31	
Claygate	d		15 34								16 04								16 34	
Oxshott	d		15 37								16 07								16 37	
Cobham & Stoke D'abernon	d		15 41								16 11								16 41	
Bookham	d				15 59								16 29							
Effingham Junction	d		15 45		16 03						16 15		16 33						16 45	
Horsley	d		15 48		16 06						16 18		16 36						16 48	
Clandon	d		15 53		16 11						16 23		16 41						16 53	
London Road (Guildford)	d		15 58		16 16						16 28		16 46						16 58	
Guildford	a		16 02		16 20						16 32		16 50						17 04	

Table 152

Mondays to Fridays

until 5 October

London - Chessington South, Dorking, Guildford, Shepperton and Hampton Court

Network Diagram - see first Page of Table 152

		SW	SW	SW	SW	SW	SW	SW	SW	SW	SW	SW	SW	SW	SW	SW	SW	SW	SW
London Waterloo ⊖	d	16 09	16 12	16 16	16 20	16 24	16 27	16 33	16 36	16 39	16 42	16 46	16 50	16 54	16 57	17 02	17 06	17 09	17 12
Vauxhall ⊖	d	16 13	16 16	16 20	16 24	16 28	16 31	16 37	16 40	16 43	16 46	16 50	16 54	16 58	17 01	17 07	17 10	17 13	17 16
Clapham Junction	d	16 18	16 21	16 25	16 29	16 33	16 36	16 42	16 45	16 48	16 51	16 55	16 59	17 03	17 06	17 12	17 15	17 18	17 21
Earlsfield	d	16 21	16 24	16 28	16 32	16 36	16 39	16 45	16 48	16 51	16 54	16 58	17 02	17 06	17 09	17 15	17 18	17 21	17 24
Wimbledon ⊖	d	16 25	16 28	16 32	16 36	16 40	16 43	16 49	16 52	16 55	16 58	17 02	17 06	17 10	17 13	17 19	17 22	17 25	17 28
Raynes Park	d	16 28	16 31	16 35		16 43	16 46		16 55	16 58	17 01	17 05		17 13	17 16		17 25	17 28	17 31
Motspur Park	d	16 31		16 38		16 46				17 01		17 08		17 16				17 31	
Malden Manor	d			16 41								17 11							
Tolworth	d			16 44								17 14							
Chessington North	d			16 47								17 17							
Chessington South	a			16 51								17 21							
Worcester Park	d	16 33				16 48				17 03				17 18				17 33	
Stoneleigh	d	16 36				16 51				17 06				17 21				17 36	
Ewell West	d	16 39				16 54				17 09				17 24				17 39	
Epsom	a	16 46				16 57				17 12				17 27				17 42	
	d	16 47				16 58				17 17				17 28				17 47	
Ashtead	d	16 51				17 02				17 21				17 32				17 51	
Leatherhead	d	16 54				17 05				17 24				17 35				17 54	
Box Hill & Westhumble	d					17 10								17 40					
Dorking	a					17 14								17 44					
New Malden	d		16 34				16 49		16 58		17 04				17 19		17 28		17 34
Norbiton	d		16 37				16 52				17 07				17 22				17 37
Kingston	a		16 40				16 55				17 10				17 25				17 40
	d		16 40				16 59				17 10				17 29				17 40
Hampton Wick	d		16 42				17 01				17 12				17 31				17 42
Teddington	d		16 45				17 05				17 15				17 35				17 45
Strawberry Hill	a						17 08								17 38				
Fulwell	d		16 49								17 19								17 49
Hampton	d		16 53								17 23								17 53
Kempton Park	d		16 56								17 26								17 56
Sunbury	d		16 58								17 28								17 58
Upper Halliford	d		17 00								17 30								18 00
Shepperton	a		17 05								17 35								18 06
Berrylands	d								17 00								17 30		
Surbiton	d				16a43			16 57	17 05				17a13			17 27	17 35		
Thames Ditton	d								17 09								17 39		
Hampton Court	a								17 14								17 44		
Hinchley Wood	d							17 01								17 31			
Claygate	d							17 04								17 34			
Oxshott	d							17 07								17 37			
Cobham & Stoke D'abernon	d							17 11								17 41			
Bookham	d	16 59								17 29								17 59	
Effingham Junction	d	17 03						17 15		17 33						17 45		18a05	
Horsley	d	17 06						17 18		17 36						17 48			
Clandon	d	17 11						17 23		17 41						17 53			
London Road (Guildford)	d	17 16						17 28		17 46						17 58			
Guildford	a	17 22						17 34		17 52						18 04			

Table 152

Mondays to Fridays

until 5 October

London - Chessington South, Dorking, Guildford, Shepperton and Hampton Court

Network Diagram - see first Page of Table 152

		SW	SW	SW	SW	SW	SW	SW	SW	SW	SW	SW	SW	SW	SW	SW	SW	SW
London Waterloo ⊖	d	17 16	17 20	17 24	17 27	17 30	17 32	17 36	17 39	17 43	17 42	17 46	17 50	17 54	17 57	18 00	18 02	18 06
Vauxhall ⊖	d	17 20	17 24	17 28	17 31	17 34	17 37	17 40	17 43	17 47	17 46	17 50	17 54	17 58	18 01	18 04	18 07	18 10
Clapham Junction	d	17 25	17 29	17 33	17 36	17 39	17 42	17 45	17 48		17 51	17 55	17 59	18 03	18 06	18 09	18 12	18 15
Earlsfield	d	17 28	17 32	17 36	17 39	17 42	17 45	17 48	17 51		17 54	17 58	18 02	18 06	18 09	18 12	18 15	18 18
Wimbledon ⊖	d	17 32	17 36	17 40	17 43	17 46	17 49	17 52	17 55		17 58	18 02	18 06	18 10	18 13	18 16	18 19	18 22
Raynes Park	d	17 35		17 43	17 46	17 49		17 55	17 58		18 01	18 05		18 13	18 16	18 19		18 25
Motspur Park	d	17 38				17 52			18 01			18 08				18 22		
Malden Manor	d	17 41										18 11						
Tolworth	d	17 44										18 14						
Chessington North	d	17 47										18 17						
Chessington South	a	17 51										18 21						
Worcester Park	d			17 47		17 54			18 03					18 17		18 24		
Stoneleigh	d					17 57			18 06							18 27		
Ewell West	d					18 00			18 09							18 30		
Epsom	a			17 54		18 07			18 15					18 24		18 35		
	d			17 54					18 17					18 24				
Ashtead	d			17 58					18 21					18 28				
Leatherhead	d			18 01					18 24					18 31				
Box Hill & Westhumble	d			18 06										18 36				
Dorking	a			18 11										18 41				
New Malden	d				17 49			17 58			18 04				18 19			18 28
Norbiton	d				17 52						18 07				18 22			
Kingston	a				17 55						18 10				18 25			
	d				17 59						18 10				18 29			
Hampton Wick	d				18 01						18 12				18 31			
Teddington	d				18 05						18 15				18 35			
Strawberry Hill	a				18 08					18 11					18 38			
Fulwell	d									18 13	18 19							
Hampton	d									18 17	18 23							
Kempton Park	d										18 26							
Sunbury	d									18 21	18 28							
Upper Halliford	d									18 23	18 30							
Shepperton	a									18 28	18 40							
Berrylands	d							18 00										18 30
Surbiton	d		17a43				17 57	18 05					18a13				18 27	18 35
Thames Ditton	d							18 09										18 39
Hampton Court	a							18 14										18 44
Hinchley Wood	d						18 05										18 35	
Claygate	d						18 08										18 38	
Oxshott	d						18 11										18 41	
Cobham & Stoke D'abernon	d						18 15										18 45	
Bookham	d								18 29									
Effingham Junction	d						18 20		18a42								18 50	
Horsley	d						18 22										18 52	
Clandon	d						18 27										18 57	
London Road (Guildford)	d						18 32										19 02	
Guildford	a						18 38										19 09	

London - Chessington South, Dorking, Guildford, Shepperton and Hampton Court

Network Diagram - see first Page of Table 152

		SW	SW	SW	SW	SW	SW	SW	SW	SW	SW	SW	SW	SW	SW	SW	SW	SW	SW	SW
London Waterloo 15 ⊖	d	18 09	18 13	18 12	18 16	18 20	18 24	18 27	18 30	18 32	18 36	18 39	18 43	18 42	18 46	18 48	18 50	18 54	18 57	19 00
Vauxhall ⊖	d	18 13	18 17	18 16	18 20	18 24	18 28	18 31	18 34	18 37	18 40	18 43	18 47	18 46	18 50		18 54	18 58	19 01	19 04
Clapham Junction 10	d	18 18		18 21	18 25	18 29	18 33	18 36	18 39	18 42	18 45	18 48		18 51	18 55		18 59	19 03	19 06	19 09
Earlsfield	d	18 21		18 24	18 28	18 32	18 36	18 39	18 42	18 45	18 48	18 51		18 54	18 58		19 02	19 06	19 09	19 12
Wimbledon 6 ⊖	d	18 25		18 28	18 32	18 36	18 40	18 43	18 46	18 49	18 52	18 55		18 58	19 02		19 06	19 10	19 13	19 16
Raynes Park 6	d	18 28		18 31	18 35		18 43	18 46	18 49		18 55	18 58		19 01	19 05			19 13	19 16	19 19
Motspur Park	d	18 31			18 38				18 52			19 01			19 08					19 22
Malden Manor	d				18 41										19 11					
Tolworth	d				18 44										19 14					
Chessington North	d				18 47										19 17					
Chessington South	a				18 51										19 21					
Worcester Park	d	18 33					18 47		18 54			19 03						19 17		19 24
Stoneleigh	d	18 36							18 57			19 06								19 27
Ewell West	d	18 39							19 00			19 09								19 30
Epsom 3	a	18 46					18 54		19 07			19 16						19 24		19 35
	d	18 47					18 54					19 17						19 24		
Ashtead	d	18 51					18 58					19 21						19 28		
Leatherhead	d	18 54					19 01					19 24						19 31		
Box Hill & Westhumble	d						19 06											19 36		
Dorking 4	a						19 11											19 41		
New Malden 6	d			18 34				18 49			18 58			19 04					19 19	
Norbiton	d			18 37				18 52						19 07					19 22	
Kingston	a			18 40				18 55						19 10					19 25	
	d			18 40				18 59						19 10					19 29	
Hampton Wick	d			18 42				19 01						19 12					19 31	
Teddington	d			18 45				19 05						19 15					19 35	
Strawberry Hill	a		18 41					19 08					19 11						19 38	
Fulwell	d		18 43	18 49									19 13	19 19						
Hampton	d		18 47	18 53									19 17	19 23						
Kempton Park	d			18 56										19 26						
Sunbury	d		18 51	18 58									19 21	19 28						
Upper Halliford	d		18 53	19 00									19 23	19 30						
Shepperton	a		18 58	19 10									19 28	19 36						
Berrylands	d										19 00									
Surbiton 6	d					18a43				18 57	19 05					19 06	19a13			
Thames Ditton	d										19 09									
Hampton Court	a										19 14									
Hinchley Wood	d									19 01						19 10				
Claygate	d									19 04						19 13				
Oxshott	d									19 07						19 16				
Cobham & Stoke D'abernon	d									19 11						19 20				
Bookham	d	18 59										19 29								
Effingham Junction 6	d	19 03								19 15		19 33				19 24				
Horsley	d	19 06								19 18		19 36				19 27				
Clandon	d	19 11								19 23		19 41				19 32				
London Road (Guildford)	d	19 16								19 28		19 46				19 37				
Guildford	a	19 22								19 34		19 52				19 43				

London - Chessington South, Dorking, Guildford, Shepperton and Hampton Court

Network Diagram - see first Page of Table 152

		SW	SW	SW	SW	SW	SW	SW	SW	SW	SW	SW	SW	SW	SW	SW	SW	SW	SW	SW
London Waterloo 15 ⊖	d	19 02	19 06	19 09	19 12	19 16	19 20	19 23	19 24	19 27	19 33	19 36	19 39	19 42	19 46	19 50	19 54	19 57	20 03	20 06
Vauxhall ⊖	d	19 07	19 10	19 13	19 16	19 20	19 24		19 28	19 31	19 37	19 40	19 43	19 46	19 50	19 54	19 58	20 01	20 07	20 10
Clapham Junction 10	d	19 12	19 15	19 18	19 21	19 25	19 29		19 33	19 36	19 42	19 45	19 48	19 51	19 55	19 59	20 03	20 06	20 12	20 15
Earlsfield	d	19 15	19 18	19 21	19 24	19 28	19 32		19 36	19 39	19 45	19 48	19 51	19 54	19 58	20 02	20 06	20 09	20 15	20 18
Wimbledon 6 ⊖	d	19 19	19 22	19 25	19 28	19 32	19 36		19 40	19 43	19 49	19 52	19 55	19 58	20 02	20 06	20 10	20 13	20 19	20 22
Raynes Park 6	d		19 25	19 28	19 31	19 35			19 43	19 46		19 55	19 58	20 01	20 05		20 13	20 16		20 25
Motspur Park	d			19 31		19 38			19 46				20 01		20 08		20 16			
Malden Manor	d					19 41									20 11					
Tolworth	d					19 44									20 14					
Chessington North	d					19 47									20 17					
Chessington South	a					19 49									20 19					
Worcester Park	d			19 33					19 48				20 03				20 18			
Stoneleigh	d			19 36					19 51				20 06				20 21			
Ewell West	d			19 39					19 54				20 09				20 24			
Epsom 3	a			19 44					19 57				20 16				20 27			
	d			19 47					19 58				20 17							
Ashtead	d			19 51					20 02				20 21							
Leatherhead	d			19 54					20 05				20 24							
Box Hill & Westhumble	d								20 10											
Dorking 4	a								20 14											
New Malden 6	d		19 28		19 34					19 49		19 58		20 04				20 19		20 28
Norbiton	d				19 37					19 52				20 07				20 22		
Kingston	a				19 40					19 55				20 10				20 25		
	d				19 40					19 59				20 10				20 29		
Hampton Wick	d				19 42					20 01				20 12				20 31		
Teddington	d				19 45					20 05				20 15				20 35		
Strawberry Hill	a									20 08								20 38		
Fulwell	d				19 49									20 19						
Hampton	d				19 53									20 23						
Kempton Park	d				19 56									20 26						
Sunbury	d				19 58									20 28						
Upper Halliford	d				20 00									20 30						
Shepperton	a				20 03									20 33						
Berrylands	d		19 30									20 00								20 30
Surbiton 6	d	19 27	19 35				19a43	19a39			19 57	20 05				20a13			20 27	20 35
Thames Ditton	d		19 39									20 09								20 39
Hampton Court	a		19 42									20 12								20 42
Hinchley Wood	d	19 31									20 01								20 31	
Claygate	d	19 34									20 04								20 34	
Oxshott	d	19 37									20 07								20 37	
Cobham & Stoke D'abernon	d	19 41									20 11								20 41	
Bookham	d			19 59									20 29							
Effingham Junction 6	d	19 45		20 03							20 15		20 33						20 45	
Horsley	d	19 48		20 06							20 18		20 36						20 48	
Clandon	d	19 53		20 11							20 23		20 41						20 53	
London Road (Guildford)	d	19 58		20 16							20 28		20 46						20 58	
Guildford	a	20 02		20 20							20 32		20 50						21 02	

		SW	SW	SW	SW	SW	SW	SW	SW	SW	SW	SW	SW	SW	SW	SW	SW	SW	SW	SW	SW
London Waterloo 15 ⊖	d	20 09	20 12	20 16	20 20	20 24	20 27	20 33	20 36	20 39	20 42	20 46	20 50	20 54	20 57	21 03	21 09	21 12	21 20	21 24	21 27
Vauxhall ⊖	d	20 13	20 16	20 20	20 24	20 28	20 31	20 37	20 40	20 43	20 46	20 50	20 54	20 58	21 01	21 07	21 13	21 16	21 24	21 28	21 31
Clapham Junction 10	d	20 18	20 21	20 25	20 29	20 33	20 36	20 42	20 45	20 48	20 51	20 55	20 59	21 03	21 06	21 12	21 18	21 21	21 29	21 33	21 36
Earlsfield	d	20 21	20 24	20 28	20 32	20 36	20 39	20 45	20 48	20 51	20 54	20 58	21 02	21 06	21 09	21 15	21 21	21 24	21 32	21 36	21 39
Wimbledon 6 ⊖	d	20 25	20 28	20 32	20 36	20 40	20 43	20 49	20 52	20 55	20 58	21 02	21 06	21 10	21 13	21 19	21 25	21 28	21 36	21 40	21 43
Raynes Park 6	d	20 28	20 31	20 35		20 43	20 46		20 55	20 58	21 01	21 05		21 13	21 16		21 28	21 31		21 43	21 46
Motspur Park	d	20 31		20 38		20 46				21 01		21 08		21 16			21 31			21 46	
Malden Manor	d			20 41								21 11									
Tolworth	d			20 44								21 14									
Chessington North	d			20 47								21 17									
Chessington South	a			20 49								21 19									
Worcester Park	d	20 33				20 48				21 03				21 18			21 33			21 48	
Stoneleigh	d	20 36				20 51				21 06				21 21			21 36			21 51	
Ewell West	d	20 39				20 54				21 09				21 24			21 39			21 54	
Epsom 3	a	20 42				20 57				21 12				21 27			21 42			21 57	
	d	20 43								21 13							21 43				
Ashtead	d	20 47								21 17							21 47				
Leatherhead	d	20 50								21 20							21 50				
Box Hill & Westhumble	d	20 55															21 55				
Dorking 4	a	20 57															21 57				
New Malden 6	d		20 34				20 49		20 58		21 04				21 19			21 34			21 49
Norbiton	d		20 37				20 52				21 07				21 22			21 37			21 52
Kingston	a		20 40				20 55				21 10				21 25			21 40			21 55
	d		20 40				20 59				21 10				21 29			21 40			21 59
Hampton Wick	d		20 42				21 01				21 12				21 31			21 42			22 01
Teddington	d		20 45				21 05				21 15				21 35			21 45			22 05
Strawberry Hill	a						21 08								21 38						22 08
Fulwell	d		20 49								21 19							21 49			
Hampton	d		20 53								21 23							21 53			
Kempton Park	d		20 56								21 26							21 56			
Sunbury	d		20 58								21 28							21 58			
Upper Halliford	d		21 00								21 30							22 00			
Shepperton	a		21 03								21 33							22 03			
Berrylands	d								21 00												
Surbiton 6	d				20a43			20 57	21 05				21a13			21 27			21a43		
Thames Ditton	d								21 09												
Hampton Court	a								21 12												
Hinchley Wood	d							21 01								21 31					
Claygate	d							21 04								21 34					
Oxshott	d							21 07								21 37					
Cobham & Stoke D'abernon	d							21 11								21 41					
Bookham	d									21 25											
Effingham Junction 6	d							21 15		21 29						21 45					
Horsley	d							21 18		21 32						21 48					
Clandon	d							21 23		21 37						21 53					
London Road (Guildford)	d							21 28		21 42						21 58					
Guildford	a							21 32		21 46						22 02					

London - Chessington South, Dorking, Guildford, Shepperton and Hampton Court

Network Diagram - see first Page of Table 152

Station		SW	SW	SW	SW	SW	SW	SW	SW	SW	SW	SW	SW	SW	SW	SW	SW	SW	SW	SW
London Waterloo 15 ⊖	d	21 33	21 36	21 39	21 42	21 46	21 50	21 54	21 57	22 03	22 09	22 12	22 20	22 27	22 33	22 36	22 39	22 42	22 50	22 57
Vauxhall ⊖	d	21 37	21 40	21 43	21 46	21 50	21 54	21 58	22 01	22 07	22 13	22 16	22 24	22 31	22 37	22 40	22 43	22 46	22 54	23 01
Clapham Junction 10	d	21 42	21 45	21 48	21 51	21 55	21 59	22 03	22 06	22 12	22 18	22 21	22 29	22 36	22 42	22 45	22 48	22 51	22 59	23 06
Earlsfield	d	21 45	21 48	21 51	21 54	21 58	22 02	22 06	22 09	22 15	22 21	22 24	22 32	22 39	22 45	22 48	22 51	22 54	23 02	23 09
Wimbledon 6 ⊖ ⇌	d	21 49	21 52	21 55	21 58	22 02	22 06	22 10	22 13	22 19	22 25	22 28	22 36	22 43	22 49	22 52	22 55	22 58	23 06	23 13
Raynes Park 6	d		21 55	21 58	22 01	22 05		22 13	22 16		22 28	22 31		22 46		22 55	22 58	23 01		23 16
Motspur Park	d			22 01		22 08		22 16			22 31						23 01			
Malden Manor	d					22 11														
Tolworth	d					22 14														
Chessington North	d					22 17														
Chessington South	a					22 19														
Worcester Park	d			22 03				22 18			22 33						23 03			
Stoneleigh	d			22 06				22 21			22 36						23 06			
Ewell West	d			22 09				22 24			22 39						23 09			
Epsom 3	a			22 12				22 27			22 42						23 12			
	d			22 13							22 43						23 13			
Ashtead	d			22 17							22 47						23 17			
Leatherhead	d			22 20							22 50						23 20			
Box Hill & Westhumble	d										22 55									
Dorking 4	a										22 57									
New Malden 6	d		21 58		22 04				22 19			22 34		22 49		22 58		23 04		23 19
Norbiton	d				22 07				22 22			22 37		22 52				23 07		23 22
Kingston	a				22 10				22 25			22 40		22 55				23 10		23 25
	d				22 10				22 29			22 40		22 59				23 10		23 29
Hampton Wick	d				22 12				22 31			22 42		23 01				23 12		23 31
Teddington	d				22 15				22 35			22 45		23 05				23 15		23 35
Strawberry Hill	a								22 38					23 08						23 38
Fulwell	d				22 19							22 49						23 19		
Hampton	d				22 23							22 53						23 23		
Kempton Park	d				22 26							22 56						23 26		
Sunbury	d				22 28							22 58						23 28		
Upper Halliford	d				22 30							23 00						23 30		
Shepperton	a				22 33							23 03						23 33		
Berrylands	d		22 00													23 00				
Surbiton 6	d	21 57	22 05				22 14			22 27			22a43		22 57	23 05			23a13	
Thames Ditton	d		22 09													23 09				
Hampton Court	a		22 12													23 12				
Hinchley Wood	d	22 01								22 31					23 01					
Claygate	d	22 04								22 34					23 04					
Oxshott	d	22 07								22 37					23 07					
Cobham & Stoke D'abernon	d	22 11								22 41					23 11					
Bookham	d			22 25													23 25			
Effingham Junction 6	d	22 15		22 29						22 45					23 15		23 29			
Horsley	d	22 18		22 32						22 48					23 18		23 32			
Clandon	d	22 23		22 37						22 53					23 23		23 37			
London Road (Guildford)	d	22 28		22 42						22 58					23 28		23 42			
Guildford	a	22 32		22 46			22 47			23 02					23 32		23 46			

Station		SW	SW	SW	SW	SW	SW	SW	SW	SW	SW
London Waterloo 15 ⊖	d	23 00	23 03	23 09	23 12	23 20	23 27	23 36	23 42	23 50	23 57
Vauxhall ⊖	d	23 04	23 07	23 13	23 16	23 24	23 31	23 40	23 46	23 54	00 01
Clapham Junction 10	d	23 09	23 12	23 18	23 21	23 29	23 36	23 45	23 51	23 59	00 06
Earlsfield	d	23 12	23 15	23 21	23 24	23 32	23 39	23 48	23 54	00 02	00 09
Wimbledon 6 ⊖ ⇌	d	23 16	23 19	23 25	23 28	23 36	23 43	23 52	23 58	00 06	00 13
Raynes Park 6	d	23 19		23 28	23 31		23 46	23 55	00 01		00 16
Motspur Park	d	23 22		23 31					00 04		
Malden Manor	d	23 25									
Tolworth	d	23 28									
Chessington North	d	23 31									
Chessington South	a	23 33									
Worcester Park	d			23 33					00 06		
Stoneleigh	d			23 36					00 09		
Ewell West	d			23 39					00 12		
Epsom 3	a			23 42					00 15		
	d			23 43					00 19		
Ashtead	d			23 47					00 23		
Leatherhead	d			23 50					00 26		
Box Hill & Westhumble	d			23 55							
Dorking 4	a			23 57							
New Malden 6	d				23 34		23 49	23 58			00 19
Norbiton	d				23 37		23 52				00 22
Kingston	a				23 40		23 55				00 25
	d				23 40		23 55				00 25
Hampton Wick	d				23 42		23 57				00 27
Teddington	d				23 45		23 59				00 30
Strawberry Hill	a						00 03				
Fulwell	d				23 49						00 34
Hampton	d				23 53						00 38
Kempton Park	d				23 56						00 41
Sunbury	d				23 58						00 43
Upper Halliford	d				23 59						00 45
Shepperton	a				00 03						00 48
Berrylands	d							23 59			
Surbiton 6	d		23 27			23a43		00 05		00 14	
Thames Ditton	d							00 09			
Hampton Court	a							00 12			
Hinchley Wood	d		23 31							00 18	
Claygate	d		23 34							00 20	
Oxshott	d		23 37							00 24	
Cobham & Stoke D'abernon	d		23 41							00 27	
Bookham	d								00 31		
Effingham Junction 6	d		23 45						00 36	00 32	
Horsley	d		23 48						00 39	00 34	
Clandon	d		23 53						00 44	00 39	
London Road (Guildford)	d		23 58						00 49	00 44	
Guildford	a		00 02						00 53	00 48	

London - Chessington South, Dorking, Guildford, Shepperton and Hampton Court

Network Diagram - see first Page of Table 152

Station		SW MX	SW MO	SW MO	SW MX	SW MX	SW MO	SW MX	SW MX	SW MX	SW MX	SW MO	SW MX	SW MX	SW	SW MX	SW	SW [1]	SW	SW [1]	SW
London Waterloo 15 ⊖	d	23p03	23p00	23p10	23p12	23p27	23p32	23p36	23p42	23p50	23p57	00 01	00 09	00 15	00 18	00 27	00 42	05 00	05 12	05 20	
Vauxhall ⊖	d	23p07	23p04	23p14	23p16	23p31	23p36	23p40	23p46	23p54	00 01	00 04	00 13	00 19	00 22	00 31	00 46	05 04	05 16	05 24	
Clapham Junction 10	d	23p12	23p09	23p19	23p21	23p36	23p41	23p45	23p51	23p59	00 06	00 09	00 20	00 25		00 37	00 51	05 11	05 21	05 29	
Earlsfield	d	23p15	23p12	23p22	23p24	23p39	23p44	23p48	23p54	00 02	00 09	00 12	00 23	00 29		00s41		05 14	05 24	05 32	
Wimbledon 6 ⊖ ⇌	d	23p19	23p16	23p26	23p28	23p43	23p48	23p52	23p58	00 06	00 13	00 16	00 27	00 33		00 45	01 05	05 18	05 28	05 36	05 49
Raynes Park 6	d				23p31	23p46	23p52	23p55	00 01		00 16	00 19		00 36		00 48	01 08		05 31		
Motspur Park	d						23p55		00 04					00 38							
Malden Manor	d																				
Tolworth	d																				
Chessington North	d																				
Chessington South	a																				
Worcester Park	d						23p57		00 06					00 41							
Stoneleigh	d						23p59		00 09					00 44							
Ewell West	d						00 03		00 12					00 46							
Epsom 3	a						00 06		00 15					00 50							
	d								00 19												
Ashtead	d								00 23												
Leatherhead	d								00 26												
Box Hill & Westhumble	d																				
Dorking 4	a																				
New Malden 6	d				23p34	23p49		23p58			00 19	00 22				00 50	01 11		05 34		
Norbiton	d				23p37	23p52					00 22						01 14		05 37		
Kingston	a				23p40	23p55					00 25				01 01		01 17		05 40		
	d				23p40	23p55					00 25						01 17		05 40		
Hampton Wick	d				23p42	23p57					00 27						01s22		05 42		
Teddington	d				23p45	23p59					00 30						01s25		05 45		
Strawberry Hill	a					00 03											01 28				
Fulwell	d				23p49						00 34								05 49		
Hampton	d				23p53						00 38								05 53		
Kempton Park	d				23p56						00 41								05 56		
Sunbury	d				23p58						00 43								05 58		
Upper Halliford	d				23p59						00 45								06 00		
Shepperton	a				00 05						00 50								06 05		
Berrylands	d							23p59				00 25				00s53					
Surbiton 6	d	23p27	23p32	23p35				00 05		00 14		00 31	00 35			00a56		05 26		05 44	05 57
Thames Ditton	d							00 09													
Hampton Court	a							00 12													
Hinchley Wood	d	23p31	23p36							00 18		00 35									06 01
Claygate	d	23p34	23p39							00 20		00 38									06 04
Oxshott	d	23p37	23p42							00 24		00 41									06 07
Cobham & Stoke D'abernon	d	23p41	23p46							00 27		00 45									06 11
Bookham	d								00 31												
Effingham Junction 6	d	23p45	23p50						00 36	00 32		00 49									06 15
Horsley	d	23p48	23p53						00 39	00 34		00 52									06 18
Clandon	d	23p53	23p58						00 44	00 39		00 57									06 23
London Road (Guildford)	d	23p58	00 03						00 49	00 44		01 02									06 28
Guildford	a	00 05	00 10	00 13					00 56	00 51		01 09	01 07					06 00		06 21	06 35

Table 152

Mondays to Fridays
from 8 October

London - Chessington South, Dorking, Guildford, Shepperton and Hampton Court

Network Diagram - see first Page of Table 152

		SW	SW	SW	SW	SW	SW	SW	SW	SW	SW	SW	SW	SW	SW	SW	SW	SW	SW	SW	SW
London Waterloo 15 ⊖	d	05 47	05 50				06 03	06 06	06 12	06 16	06 20	06 24	06 27	06 33	06 36	06 39	06 42	06 46	06 50	06 54	06 57
Vauxhall ⊖	d	05 51	05 54				06 07	06 10	06 16	06 20	06 24	06 28	06 31	06 37	06 40	06 43	06 46	06 50	06 54	06 58	07 01
Clapham Junction 10	d	05 56	05 59				06 12	06 15	06 21	06 25	06 29	06 33	06 36	06 42	06 45	06 48	06 51	06 55	06 59	07 03	07 06
Earlsfield	d	05 59	06 02				06 15	06 18	06 24	06 28	06 32	06 36	06 39	06 45	06 48	06 51	06 54	06 58	07 02	07 06	07 09
Wimbledon 6 ⊖	d	06 03	06 06		06 13	06 16	06 19	06 22	06 28	06 32	06 36	06 40	06 43	06 49	06 52	06 55	06 58	07 02	07 06	07 10	07 13
Raynes Park 6	d	06 06			06 16	06 19		06 25	06 31	06 35		06 43	06 46		06 55	06 58	07 01	07 05		07 13	07 16
Motspur Park	d	06 09				06 21				06 38		06 46						07 08		07 16	
Malden Manor	d					06 25				06 41								07 11			
Tolworth	d					06 27				06 44								07 14			
Chessington North	d					06 30				06 47								07 17			
Chessington South	a					06 32				06 49								07 19			
Worcester Park	d	06 11										06 48				07 02				07 18	
Stoneleigh	d	06 14										06 51				07 05				07 21	
Ewell West	d	06 17										06 54				07 08				07 24	
Epsom 3	a	06 20										06 57				07 11				07 27	
	d	06 21										06 58				07 12				07 28	
Ashtead	d	06 25										07 02				07 16				07 32	
Leatherhead	d	06 28										07 05				07 19				07 35	
Box Hill & Westhumble	d																				
Dorking 4	a											07 13								07 43	
New Malden 6	d				06 19			06 28	06 34				06 49		06 58		07 04				07 19
Norbiton	d				06 22				06 37				06 52				07 07				07 22
Kingston	a				06 25				06 40				06 55				07 10				07 25
	d			05 59	06 29				06 40				06 59				07 10				07 29
Hampton Wick	d			06 01	06 31				06 42				07 01				07 12				07 31
Teddington	d			06 05	06 35				06 45				07 05				07 15				07 35
Strawberry Hill	a			06 08	06 38								07 08								07 38
Fulwell	d								06 49								07 19				
Hampton	d								06 53								07 23				
Kempton Park	d								06 56								07 26				
Sunbury	d								06 58								07 28				
Upper Halliford	d								07 00								07 30				
Shepperton	a								07 05								07 35				
Berrylands	d							06 30							07 00						
Surbiton 6	d		06a13				06 27	06 35			06 44			06 57	07 05				07 14		
Thames Ditton	d							06 39							07 09						
Hampton Court	a							06 42							07 12						
Hinchley Wood	d						06 31							07 01							
Claygate	d						06 34							07 04							
Oxshott	d						06 37							07 07							
Cobham & Stoke D'abernon	d						06 41							07 11							
Bookham	d	06 33														07 24					
Effingham Junction 6	d	06 37					06 45							07 15		07a28					
Horsley	d						06 48							07 18							
Clandon	d						06 53							07 23							
London Road (Guildford)	d	06 46					06 58							07 28							
Guildford	a	06 53					07 05				07 20			07 35					07 47		

		SW	SW	SW	SW	SW	SW	SW	SW	SW	SW	SW	SW	SW	SW	SW	SW	SW	SW
London Waterloo 15 ⊖	d	07 03	07 06	07 09	07 12	07 16	07 20	07 24	07 27	07 33	07 36	07 39	07 42	07 46	07 50	07 54	07 57	08 03	08 06
Vauxhall ⊖	d	07 07	07 10	07 13	07 16	07 20	07 24	07 28	07 31	07 37	07 40	07 43	07 46	07 50	07 54	07 58	08 01	08 07	08 10
Clapham Junction 10	d	07 12	07 15	07 18	07 21	07 25	07 29	07 33	07 36	07 42	07 45	07 48	07 51	07 55	07 59	08 03	08 06	08 12	08 15
Earlsfield	d	07 15	07 18	07 21	07 24	07 28	07 32	07 36	07 39	07 45	07 48	07 51	07 54	07 58	08 02	08 06	08 09	08 15	08 18
Wimbledon 6 ⊖	d	07 19	07 22	07 25	07 28	07 32	07 36	07 40	07 43	07 49	07 52	07 55	07 58	08 02	08 06	08 10	08 13	08 19	08 22
Raynes Park 6	d		07 25	07 28	07 31	07 35		07 43	07 46		07 55	07 58	08 01	08 05		08 13	08 16		08 25
Motspur Park	d			07 31		07 38		07 46				08 01		08 08		08 16			
Malden Manor	d					07 41								08 11					
Tolworth	d					07 44								08 14					
Chessington North	d					07 47								08 17					
Chessington South	a					07 49								08 19					
Worcester Park	d			07 33				07 48				08 03				08 18			
Stoneleigh	d			07 36				07 51				08 06				08 21			
Ewell West	d			07 39				07 54				08 09				08 24			
Epsom 3	a			07 42				07 58				08 13				08 27			
	d							07 58				08 17				08 28			
Ashtead	d							08 02				08 21				08 32			
Leatherhead	d							08 05				08 24				08 35			
Box Hill & Westhumble	d																		
Dorking 4	a							08 14								08 43			
New Malden 6	d		07 28		07 34				07 49		07 58		08 04				08 19		08 28
Norbiton	d				07 37				07 52				08 07				08 22		
Kingston	a				07 40				07 55				08 10				08 25		
	d				07 40				07 59				08 10				08 29		
Hampton Wick	d				07 42				08 01				08 12				08 31		
Teddington	d				07 45				08 05				08 15				08 35		
Strawberry Hill	a								08 08								08 38		
Fulwell	d				07 49								08 19						
Hampton	d				07 53								08 23						
Kempton Park	d				07 56								08 26						
Sunbury	d				07 58								08 28						
Upper Halliford	d				08 00								08 30						
Shepperton	a				08 05								08 35						
Berrylands	d		07 30								08 00								08 30
Surbiton 6	d	07 27	07 35				07a43			07 57	08 05				08 14			08 27	08 35
Thames Ditton	d		07 39								08 09								08 39
Hampton Court	a		07 42								08 12								08 42
Hinchley Wood	d	07 31								08 01								08 31	
Claygate	d	07 34								08 04								08 34	
Oxshott	d	07 37								08 07								08 37	
Cobham & Stoke D'abernon	d	07 41								08 11								08 41	
Bookham	d											08 29							
Effingham Junction 6	d	07 45								08 15		08 33						08 45	
Horsley	d	07 48								08 18		08 36						08 48	
Clandon	d	07 53								08 23		08 41						08 53	
London Road (Guildford)	d	07 58								08 28		08 46						08 58	
Guildford	a	08 05								08 35		08 53			08 50			09 07	

Table 152

Mondays to Fridays
from 8 October

London - Chessington South, Dorking, Guildford, Shepperton and Hampton Court

Network Diagram - see first Page of Table 152

		SW	SW	SW	SW	SW	SW	SW	SW	SW	SW	SW	SW	SW	SW	SW	SW	SW	SW	SW	SW
London Waterloo 15 ⊖	d	08 09	08 12	08 16	08 20	08 24	08 27	08 33	08 36	08 39	08 42	08 46	08 50	08 54	08 57	09 03	09 06	09 09	09 12	09 16	09 20
Vauxhall ⊖	d	08 13	08 16	08 20	08 24	08 28	08 31	08 37	08 40	08 43	08 46	08 50	08 54	08 58	09 01	09 07	09 10	09 13	09 16	09 20	09 24
Clapham Junction 10	d	08 18	08 21	08 25	08 29	08 33	08 36	08 42	08 45	08 48	08 51	08 55	08 59	09 03	09 06	09 12	09 15	09 18	09 21	09 25	09 29
Earlsfield	d	08 21	08 24	08 28	08 32	08 36	08 39	08 45	08 48	08 51	08 54	08 58	09 02	09 06	09 09	09 15	09 18	09 21	09 24	09 28	09 32
Wimbledon 6 ⊖	d	08 25	08 28	08 32	08 36	08 40	08 43	08 49	08 52	08 55	08 58	09 02	09 06	09 10	09 13	09 19	09 22	09 25	09 28	09 32	09 36
Raynes Park 6	d	08 28	08 31	08 35		08 43	08 46		08 55	08 58	09 01	09 05		09 13	09 16		09 25	09 28	09 31	09 35	
Motspur Park	d	08 31		08 38		08 46				09 01		09 08		09 16				09 31		09 38	
Malden Manor	d			08 41								09 11								09 41	
Tolworth	d			08 44								09 14								09 44	
Chessington North	d			08 47								09 17								09 47	
Chessington South	a			08 49								09 19								09 49	
Worcester Park	d	08 33				08 48				09 03				09 18				09 33			
Stoneleigh	d	08 36				08 51				09 06				09 21				09 36			
Ewell West	d	08 39				08 54				09 09				09 24				09 39			
Epsom 3	a	08 42				08 57				09 16				09 27				09 42			
	d	08 47				08 58				09 17				09 28				09 47			
Ashtead	d	08 51				09 02				09 21				09 32				09 51			
Leatherhead	d	08 54				09 05				09 24				09 35				09 54			
Box Hill & Westhumble	d																				
Dorking 4	a					09 13								09 43							
New Malden 6	d		08 34				08 49		08 58		09 04				09 19		09 28		09 34		
Norbiton	d		08 37				08 52				09 07				09 22				09 37		
Kingston	a		08 39				08 55				09 10				09 25				09 40		
	d		08 40				08 59				09 10				09 29				09 40		
Hampton Wick	d		08 42				09 01				09 12				09 31				09 42		
Teddington	d		08 45				09 05				09 15				09 35				09 45		
Strawberry Hill	a						09 08								09 38						
Fulwell	d		08 49								09 19								09 49		
Hampton	d		08 53								09 23								09 53		
Kempton Park	d		08 56								09 26								09 56		
Sunbury	d		08 58								09 28								09 58		
Upper Halliford	d		09 00								09 30								10 00		
Shepperton	a		09 06								09 35								10 05		
Berrylands	d								09 00								09 30				
Surbiton 6	d				08a43			08 57	09 05				09a13			09 27	09 35				09a43
Thames Ditton	d								09 09								09 39				
Hampton Court	a								09 12								09 42				
Hinchley Wood	d							09 01								09 31					
Claygate	d							09 04								09 34					
Oxshott	d							09 07								09 37					
Cobham & Stoke D'abernon	d							09 11								09 41					
Bookham	d	08 59								09 29								09 59			
Effingham Junction 6	d	09 03						09 15		09 33						09 45		10 03			
Horsley	d	09 06						09 18		09 36						09 48		10 06			
Clandon	d	09 11						09 23		09 41						09 53		10 11			
London Road (Guildford)	d	09 16						09 28		09 46						09 58		10 16			
Guildford	a	09 23						09 35		09 53						10 05		10 23			

London - Chessington South, Dorking, Guildford, Shepperton and Hampton Court

Network Diagram - see first Page of Table 152

		SW	SW	SW	SW	SW	SW	SW	SW	SW	SW	SW	SW	SW	SW	SW	SW	SW	SW
London Waterloo ⊖	d	09 24	09 27	09 33	09 36	09 39	09 42	09 46	09 50	09 54	09 57	10 03	10 06	10 09	10 12	10 16	10 20	10 24	10 27
Vauxhall ⊖	d	09 28	09 31	09 37	09 40	09 43	09 46	09 50	09 54	09 58	10 01	10 07	10 10	10 13	10 16	10 20	10 24	10 28	10 31
Clapham Junction	d	09 33	09 36	09 42	09 45	09 48	09 51	09 55	09 59	10 03	10 06	10 12	10 15	10 18	10 21	10 25	10 29	10 33	10 36
Earlsfield	d	09 36	09 39	09 45	09 48	09 51	09 54	09 58	10 02	10 06	10 09	10 15	10 18	10 21	10 24	10 28	10 32	10 36	10 39
Wimbledon ⊖	d	09 40	09 43	09 49	09 52	09 55	09 58	10 02	10 06	10 10	10 13	10 19	10 22	10 25	10 28	10 32	10 36	10 40	10 43
Raynes Park	d	09 43	09 46		09 55	09 58	10 01	10 05		10 13	10 16		10 25	10 28	10 31	10 35		10 43	10 46
Motspur Park	d	09 46				10 01		10 08		10 16				10 31		10 38		10 46	
Malden Manor	d							10 11								10 41			
Tolworth	d							10 14								10 44			
Chessington North	d							10 17								10 47			
Chessington South	a							10 19								10 49			
Worcester Park	d	09 48				10 03				10 18				10 33				10 48	
Stoneleigh	d	09 51				10 06				10 21				10 36				10 51	
Ewell West	d	09 54				10 09				10 24				10 39				10 54	
Epsom	a	09 57				10 16				10 27				10 46				10 57	
	d	09 58				10 17				10 28				10 47				10 58	
Ashtead	d	10 02				10 21				10 32				10 51				11 02	
Leatherhead	d	10 05				10 24				10 35				10 54				11 05	
Box Hill & Westhumble	d																		
Dorking	a	10 13								10 43								11 13	
New Malden	d		09 49		09 58		10 04				10 19		10 28		10 34				10 49
Norbiton	d		09 52				10 07				10 22				10 37				10 52
Kingston	a		09 55				10 10				10 25				10 40				10 55
	d		09 59				10 10				10 29				10 40				10 59
Hampton Wick	d		10 01				10 12				10 31				10 42				11 01
Teddington	d		10 05				10 15				10 35				10 45				11 05
Strawberry Hill	a		10 08								10 38								11 08
Fulwell	d						10 19								10 49				
Hampton	d						10 23								10 53				
Kempton Park	d						10 26								10 56				
Sunbury	d						10 28								10 58				
Upper Halliford	d						10 30								11 00				
Shepperton	a						10 35								11 05				
Berrylands	d				10 00								10 30						
Surbiton	d			09 57	10 05				10a13			10 27	10 35				10a43		
Thames Ditton	d				10 09								10 39						
Hampton Court	a				10 12								10 42						
Hinchley Wood	d			10 01								10 31							
Claygate	d			10 04								10 34							
Oxshott	d			10 07								10 37							
Cobham & Stoke D'abernon	d			10 11								10 41							
Bookham	d					10 29								10 59					
Effingham Junction	d			10 15		10 33						10 45		11 03					
Horsley	d			10 18		10 36						10 48		11 06					
Clandon	d			10 23		10 41						10 53		11 11					
London Road (Guildford)	d			10 28		10 46						10 58		11 16					
Guildford	a			10 35		10 53						11 05		11 23					

London - Chessington South, Dorking, Guildford, Shepperton and Hampton Court

Network Diagram - see first Page of Table 152

		SW	SW	SW	SW	SW	SW	SW	SW	SW	SW	SW	SW	SW	SW	SW	SW	SW	SW	SW
London Waterloo ⊖	d	10 33	10 36	10 39	10 42	10 46	10 50	10 54	10 57	11 03	11 06	11 09	11 12	11 16	11 20	11 24	11 27	11 33	11 36	11 39
Vauxhall ⊖	d	10 37	10 40	10 43	10 46	10 50	10 54	10 58	11 01	11 07	11 10	11 13	11 16	11 20	11 24	11 28	11 31	11 37	11 40	11 43
Clapham Junction	d	10 42	10 45	10 48	10 51	10 55	10 59	11 03	11 06	11 12	11 15	11 18	11 21	11 25	11 29	11 33	11 36	11 42	11 45	11 48
Earlsfield	d	10 45	10 48	10 51	10 54	10 58	11 02	11 06	11 09	11 15	11 18	11 21	11 24	11 28	11 32	11 36	11 39	11 45	11 48	11 51
Wimbledon ⊖	d	10 49	10 52	10 55	10 58	11 02	11 06	11 10	11 13	11 19	11 22	11 25	11 28	11 32	11 36	11 40	11 43	11 49	11 52	11 55
Raynes Park	d		10 55	10 58	11 01	11 05		11 13	11 16		11 25	11 28	11 31	11 35		11 43	11 46		11 55	11 58
Motspur Park	d			11 01		11 08		11 16				11 31		11 38		11 46				12 01
Malden Manor	d					11 11								11 41						
Tolworth	d					11 14								11 44						
Chessington North	d					11 17								11 47						
Chessington South	a					11 19								11 49						
Worcester Park	d			11 03				11 18				11 33				11 48				12 03
Stoneleigh	d			11 06				11 21				11 36				11 51				12 06
Ewell West	d			11 09				11 24				11 39				11 54				12 09
Epsom	a			11 16				11 27				11 46				11 57				12 16
	d			11 17				11 28				11 47				11 58				12 17
Ashtead	d			11 21				11 32				11 51				12 02				12 21
Leatherhead	d			11 24				11 35				11 54				12 05				12 24
Box Hill & Westhumble	d																			
Dorking	a							11 43								12 13				
New Malden	d		10 58		11 04				11 19		11 28		11 34				11 49		11 58	
Norbiton	d				11 07				11 22				11 37				11 52			
Kingston	a				11 10				11 25				11 40				11 55			
	d				11 10				11 29				11 40				11 59			
Hampton Wick	d				11 12				11 31				11 42				12 01			
Teddington	d				11 15				11 35				11 45				12 05			
Strawberry Hill	a								11 38								12 08			
Fulwell	d				11 19								11 49							
Hampton	d				11 23								11 53							
Kempton Park	d				11 26								11 56							
Sunbury	d				11 28								11 58							
Upper Halliford	d				11 30								12 00							
Shepperton	a				11 35								12 05							
Berrylands	d		11 00								11 30								12 00	
Surbiton	d	10 57	11 05				11a13			11 27	11 35				11a43			11 57	12 05	
Thames Ditton	d		11 09								11 39								12 09	
Hampton Court	a		11 12								11 42								12 12	
Hinchley Wood	d	11 01								11 31								12 01		
Claygate	d	11 04								11 34								12 04		
Oxshott	d	11 07								11 37								12 07		
Cobham & Stoke D'abernon	d	11 11								11 41								12 11		
Bookham	d			11 29								11 59								12 29
Effingham Junction	d	11 15		11 33						11 45		12 03						12 15		12 33
Horsley	d	11 18		11 36						11 48		12 06						12 18		12 36
Clandon	d	11 23		11 41						11 53		12 11						12 23		12 41
London Road (Guildford)	d	11 28		11 46						11 58		12 16						12 28		12 46
Guildford	a	11 35		11 53						12 05		12 23						12 35		12 53

		SW	SW	SW	SW	SW	SW	SW	SW	SW	SW	SW	SW	SW	SW	SW	SW	SW	SW	SW	SW
London Waterloo ⊖	d	11 42	11 46	11 50	11 54	11 57	12 03	12 06	12 09	12 12	12 16	12 20	12 24	12 27	12 33	12 36	12 39	12 42	12 46	12 50	12 54
Vauxhall ⊖	d	11 46	11 50	11 54	11 58	12 01	12 07	12 10	12 13	12 16	12 20	12 24	12 28	12 31	12 37	12 40	12 43	12 46	12 50	12 54	12 58
Clapham Junction	d	11 51	11 55	11 59	12 03	12 06	12 12	12 15	12 18	12 21	12 25	12 29	12 33	12 36	12 42	12 45	12 48	12 51	12 55	12 59	13 03
Earlsfield	d	11 54	11 58	12 02	12 06	12 09	12 15	12 18	12 21	12 24	12 28	12 32	12 36	12 39	12 45	12 48	12 51	12 54	12 58	13 02	13 06
Wimbledon ⊖	d	11 58	12 02	12 06	12 10	12 13	12 19	12 22	12 25	12 28	12 32	12 36	12 40	12 43	12 49	12 52	12 55	12 58	13 02	13 06	13 10
Raynes Park	d	12 01	12 05		12 13	12 16		12 25	12 28	12 31	12 35		12 43	12 46		12 55	12 58	13 01	13 05		13 13
Motspur Park	d		12 08		12 16				12 31		12 38		12 46				13 01		13 08		13 16
Malden Manor	d		12 11								12 41								13 11		
Tolworth	d		12 14								12 44								13 14		
Chessington North	d		12 17								12 47								13 17		
Chessington South	a		12 19								12 49								13 19		
Worcester Park	d				12 18				12 33				12 48				13 03				13 18
Stoneleigh	d				12 21				12 36				12 51				13 06				13 21
Ewell West	d				12 24				12 39				12 54				13 09				13 24
Epsom	a				12 27				12 46				12 57				13 16				13 27
	d				12 28				12 47				12 58				13 17				13 28
Ashtead	d				12 32				12 51				13 02				13 21				13 32
Leatherhead	d				12 35				12 54				13 05				13 24				13 35
Box Hill & Westhumble	d																				
Dorking	a				12 43								13 13								13 43
New Malden	d	12 04				12 19		12 28		12 34				12 49		12 58		13 04			
Norbiton	d	12 07				12 22				12 37				12 52				13 07			
Kingston	a	12 10				12 25				12 40				12 55				13 10			
	d	12 10				12 29				12 40				12 59				13 10			
Hampton Wick	d	12 12				12 31				12 42				13 01				13 12			
Teddington	d	12 15				12 35				12 45				13 05				13 15			
Strawberry Hill	a					12 38								13 08							
Fulwell	d	12 19								12 49								13 19			
Hampton	d	12 23								12 53								13 23			
Kempton Park	d	12 26								12 56								13 26			
Sunbury	d	12 28								12 58								13 28			
Upper Halliford	d	12 30								13 00								13 30			
Shepperton	a	12 35								13 05								13 35			
Berrylands	d							12 30								13 00					
Surbiton	d			12a13			12 27	12 35				12a43			12 57	13 05				13a13	
Thames Ditton	d							12 39								13 09					
Hampton Court	a							12 42								13 12					
Hinchley Wood	d						12 31								13 01						
Claygate	d						12 34								13 04						
Oxshott	d						12 37								13 07						
Cobham & Stoke D'abernon	d						12 41								13 11						
Bookham	d								12 59								13 29				
Effingham Junction	d						12 45		13 03						13 15		13 33				
Horsley	d						12 48		13 06						13 18		13 36				
Clandon	d						12 53		13 11						13 23		13 41				
London Road (Guildford)	d						12 58		13 16						13 28		13 46				
Guildford	a						13 05		13 23						13 35		13 53				

London - Chessington South, Dorking, Guildford, Shepperton and Hampton Court

Network Diagram - see first Page of Table 152

		SW	SW	SW	SW	SW	SW	SW	SW	SW	SW	SW	SW	SW	SW	SW	SW	SW	SW
London Waterloo 15 ⊖	d	12 57	13 03	13 06	13 09	13 12	13 16	13 20	13 24	13 27	13 33	13 36	13 39	13 42	13 46	13 50	13 54	13 57	14 03
Vauxhall ⊖	d	13 01	13 07	13 10	13 13	13 16	13 20	13 24	13 28	13 31	13 37	13 40	13 43	13 46	13 50	13 54	13 58	14 01	14 07
Clapham Junction 10	d	13 06	13 12	13 15	13 18	13 21	13 25	13 29	13 33	13 36	13 42	13 45	13 48	13 51	13 55	13 59	14 03	14 06	14 12
Earlsfield	d	13 09	13 15	13 18	13 21	13 24	13 28	13 32	13 36	13 39	13 45	13 48	13 51	13 54	13 58	14 02	14 06	14 09	14 15
Wimbledon 6 ⊖ ⇌	d	13 13	13 19	13 22	13 25	13 28	13 32	13 36	13 40	13 43	13 49	13 52	13 55	13 58	14 02	14 06	14 10	14 13	14 19
Raynes Park 6	d	13 16		13 25	13 28	13 31	13 35		13 43	13 46		13 55	13 58	14 01	14 05		14 13	14 16	
Motspur Park	d				13 31		13 38		13 46				14 01		14 08		14 16		
Malden Manor	d						13 41								14 11				
Tolworth	d						13 44								14 14				
Chessington North	d						13 47								14 17				
Chessington South	a						13 49								14 19				
Worcester Park	d				13 33				13 48				14 03				14 18		
Stoneleigh	d				13 36				13 51				14 06				14 21		
Ewell West	d				13 39				13 54				14 09				14 24		
Epsom 3	a				13 46				13 57				14 16				14 27		
	d				13 47				13 58				14 17				14 28		
Ashtead	d				13 51				14 02				14 21				14 32		
Leatherhead	d				13 54				14 05				14 24				14 35		
Box Hill & Westhumble	d																		
Dorking 4	a								14 13								14 43		
New Malden 6	d	13 19		13 28		13 34				13 49		13 58		14 04				14 19	
Norbiton	d	13 22				13 37				13 52				14 07				14 22	
Kingston	a	13 25				13 40				13 55				14 10				14 25	
	d	13 29				13 40				13 59				14 10				14 29	
Hampton Wick	d	13 31				13 42				14 01				14 12				14 31	
Teddington	d	13 35				13 45				14 05				14 15				14 35	
Strawberry Hill	a	13 38								14 08								14 38	
Fulwell	d					13 49								14 19					
Hampton	d					13 53								14 23					
Kempton Park	d					13 56								14 26					
Sunbury	d					13 58								14 28					
Upper Halliford	d					14 00								14 30					
Shepperton	a					14 05								14 35					
Berrylands	d			13 30								14 00							
Surbiton 6	d		13 27	13 35				13a43			13 57	14 05				14a13			14 27
Thames Ditton	d			13 39								14 09							
Hampton Court	a			13 42								14 12							
Hinchley Wood	d		13 31								14 01								14 31
Claygate	d		13 34								14 04								14 34
Oxshott	d		13 37								14 07								14 37
Cobham & Stoke D'abernon	d		13 41								14 11								14 41
Bookham	d				13 59								14 29						
Effingham Junction 6	d		13 45		14 03						14 15		14 33						14 45
Horsley	d		13 48		14 06						14 18		14 36						14 48
Clandon	d		13 53		14 11						14 23		14 41						14 53
London Road (Guildford)	d		13 58		14 16						14 28		14 46						14 58
Guildford	a		14 05		14 23						14 35		14 53						15 05

		SW	SW	SW	SW	SW	SW	SW	SW	SW	SW	SW	SW	SW	SW	SW	SW	SW	SW	SW	SW
London Waterloo 15 ⊖	d	14 06	14 09	14 12	14 16	14 20	14 24	14 27	14 33	14 36	14 39	14 42	14 46	14 50	14 54	14 57	15 03	15 06	15 09	15 12	15 16
Vauxhall ⊖	d	14 10	14 13	14 16	14 20	14 24	14 28	14 31	14 37	14 40	14 43	14 46	14 50	14 54	14 58	15 01	15 07	15 10	15 13	15 16	15 20
Clapham Junction 10	d	14 15	14 18	14 21	14 25	14 29	14 33	14 36	14 42	14 45	14 48	14 51	14 55	14 59	15 03	15 06	15 12	15 15	15 18	15 21	15 25
Earlsfield	d	14 18	14 21	14 24	14 28	14 32	14 36	14 39	14 45	14 48	14 51	14 54	14 58	15 02	15 06	15 09	15 15	15 18	15 21	15 24	15 28
Wimbledon 6 ⊖ ⇌	d	14 22	14 25	14 28	14 32	14 36	14 40	14 43	14 49	14 52	14 55	14 58	15 02	15 06	15 10	15 13	15 19	15 22	15 25	15 28	15 32
Raynes Park 6	d	14 25	14 28	14 31	14 35		14 43	14 46		14 55	14 58	15 01	15 05		15 13	15 16		15 25	15 28	15 31	15 35
Motspur Park	d		14 31		14 38		14 46				15 01		15 08		15 16				15 31		15 38
Malden Manor	d				14 41								15 11								15 41
Tolworth	d				14 44								15 14								15 44
Chessington North	d				14 47								15 17								15 47
Chessington South	a				14 49								15 19								15 49
Worcester Park	d		14 33				14 48				15 03				15 18				15 33		
Stoneleigh	d		14 36				14 51				15 06				15 21				15 36		
Ewell West	d		14 39				14 54				15 09				15 24				15 39		
Epsom 3	a		14 46				14 57				15 16				15 27				15 46		
	d		14 47				14 58				15 17				15 28				15 47		
Ashtead	d		14 51				15 02				15 21				15 32				15 51		
Leatherhead	d		14 54				15 05				15 24				15 35				15 54		
Box Hill & Westhumble	d																				
Dorking 4	a						15 13								15 43						
New Malden 6	d	14 28		14 34				14 49		14 58		15 04				15 19		15 28		15 34	
Norbiton	d			14 37				14 52				15 07				15 22				15 37	
Kingston	a			14 40				14 55				15 10				15 25				15 40	
	d			14 40				14 59				15 10				15 29				15 40	
Hampton Wick	d			14 42				15 01				15 12				15 31				15 42	
Teddington	d			14 45				15 05				15 15				15 35				15 45	
Strawberry Hill	a							15 08								15 38					
Fulwell	d			14 49								15 19								15 49	
Hampton	d			14 53								15 23								15 53	
Kempton Park	d			14 56								15 26								15 56	
Sunbury	d			14 58								15 28								15 58	
Upper Halliford	d			15 00								15 30								16 00	
Shepperton	a			15 05								15 35								16 05	
Berrylands	d	14 30								15 00								15 30			
Surbiton 6	d	14 35				14a43			14 57	15 05				15a13			15 27	15 35			
Thames Ditton	d	14 39								15 09								15 39			
Hampton Court	a	14 42								15 12								15 42			
Hinchley Wood	d								15 01								15 31				
Claygate	d								15 04								15 34				
Oxshott	d								15 07								15 37				
Cobham & Stoke D'abernon	d								15 11								15 41				
Bookham	d		14 59								15 29								15 59		
Effingham Junction 6	d		15 03						15 15		15 33						15 45		16 03		
Horsley	d		15 06						15 18		15 36						15 48		16 06		
Clandon	d		15 11						15 23		15 41						15 53		16 11		
London Road (Guildford)	d		15 16						15 28		15 46						15 58		16 16		
Guildford	a		15 23						15 35		15 53						16 05		16 23		

London - Chessington South, Dorking, Guildford, Shepperton and Hampton Court

Network Diagram - see first Page of Table 152

		SW	SW	SW	SW	SW	SW	SW	SW	SW	SW	SW	SW	SW	SW	SW	SW	SW	SW	SW
London Waterloo 15 ⊖	d	15 20	15 24	15 27	15 33	15 36	15 39	15 42	15 46	15 50	15 54	15 57	16 03	16 06	16 09	16 12	16 16	16 20	16 24	16 27
Vauxhall ⊖	d	15 24	15 28	15 31	15 37	15 40	15 43	15 46	15 50	15 54	15 58	16 01	16 07	16 10	16 13	16 16	16 20	16 24	16 28	16 31
Clapham Junction 10	d	15 29	15 33	15 36	15 42	15 45	15 48	15 51	15 55	15 59	16 03	16 06	16 12	16 15	16 18	16 21	16 25	16 29	16 33	16 36
Earlsfield	d	15 32	15 36	15 39	15 45	15 48	15 51	15 54	15 58	16 02	16 06	16 09	16 15	16 18	16 21	16 24	16 28	16 32	16 36	16 39
Wimbledon 6 ⊖ ⇌	d	15 36	15 40	15 43	15 49	15 52	15 55	15 58	16 02	16 06	16 10	16 13	16 19	16 22	16 25	16 28	16 32	16 36	16 40	16 43
Raynes Park 6	d		15 43	15 46		15 55	15 58	16 01	16 05		16 13	16 16		16 25	16 28	16 31	16 35		16 43	16 46
Motspur Park	d		15 46				16 01		16 08		16 16				16 31		16 38		16 46	
Malden Manor	d								16 11								16 41			
Tolworth	d								16 14								16 44			
Chessington North	d								16 17								16 47			
Chessington South	a								16 19								16 51			
Worcester Park	d		15 48				16 03				16 18				16 33				16 48	
Stoneleigh	d		15 51				16 06				16 21				16 36				16 51	
Ewell West	d		15 54				16 09				16 24				16 39				16 54	
Epsom 3	a		15 57				16 15				16 27				16 46				16 57	
	d		15 58				16 17				16 28				16 47				16 58	
Ashtead	d		16 02				16 21				16 32				16 51				17 02	
Leatherhead	d		16 05				16 24				16 35				16 54				17 05	
Box Hill & Westhumble	d																		17 10	
Dorking 4	a		16 13								16 43								17 16	
New Malden 6	d			15 49		15 58		16 04				16 19		16 28		16 34				16 49
Norbiton	d			15 52				16 07				16 22				16 37				16 52
Kingston	a			15 55				16 10				16 25				16 40				16 55
	d			15 59				16 10				16 29				16 40				16 59
Hampton Wick	d			16 01				16 12				16 31				16 42				17 01
Teddington	d			16 05				16 15				16 35				16 45				17 05
Strawberry Hill	a			16 08								16 38								17 08
Fulwell	d							16 19								16 49				
Hampton	d							16 23								16 53				
Kempton Park	d							16 26								16 56				
Sunbury	d							16 28								16 58				
Upper Halliford	d							16 30								17 00				
Shepperton	a							16 35								17 07				
Berrylands	d					16 00								16 30						
Surbiton 6	d	15a43			15 57	16 05				16a13			16 27	16 35				16a43		
Thames Ditton	d					16 09								16 39						
Hampton Court	a					16 12								16 44						
Hinchley Wood	d				16 01								16 31							
Claygate	d				16 04								16 34							
Oxshott	d				16 07								16 37							
Cobham & Stoke D'abernon	d				16 11								16 41							
Bookham	d						16 29								16 59					
Effingham Junction 6	d				16 15		16 33						16 45		17 03					
Horsley	d				16 18		16 36						16 48		17 06					
Clandon	d				16 23		16 41						16 53		17 11					
London Road (Guildford)	d				16 28		16 46						16 58		17 16					
Guildford	a				16 35		16 53						17 07		17 25					

Table 152

Mondays to Fridays
from 8 October

London - Chessington South, Dorking, Guildford, Shepperton and Hampton Court

Network Diagram - see first Page of Table 152

		SW	SW	SW	SW	SW	SW	SW	SW	SW	SW	SW	SW	SW	SW	SW	SW	SW	SW
London Waterloo 15 ⊖	d	16 33	16 36	16 39	16 42	16 46	16 50	16 54	16 57	17 02	17 06	17 09	17 12	17 16	17 20	17 24	17 27	17 30	17 32
Vauxhall ⊖	d	16 37	16 40	16 43	16 46	16 50	16 54	16 58	17 01	17 07	17 10	17 13	17 16	17 20	17 24	17 28	17 31	17 34	17 37
Clapham Junction 10	d	16 42	16 45	16 48	16 51	16 55	16 59	17 03	17 06	17 12	17 15	17 18	17 21	17 25	17 29	17 33	17 36	17 39	17 42
Earlsfield	d	16 45	16 48	16 51	16 54	16 58	17 02	17 06	17 09	17 15	17 18	17 21	17 24	17 28	17 32	17 36	17 39	17 42	17 45
Wimbledon 6 ⊖	d	16 49	16 52	16 55	16 58	17 02	17 06	17 10	17 13	17 19	17 22	17 25	17 28	17 32	17 36	17 40	17 43	17 46	17 49
Raynes Park 6	d		16 55	16 58	17 01	17 05		17 13	17 16		17 25	17 28	17 31	17 35		17 43	17 46	17 49	
Motspur Park	d			17 01		17 08		17 16				17 31		17 38				17 52	
Malden Manor	d					17 11								17 41					
Tolworth	d					17 14								17 44					
Chessington North	d					17 17								17 47					
Chessington South	a					17 21								17 51					
Worcester Park	d			17 03				17 18				17 33				17 47		17 54	
Stoneleigh	d			17 06				17 21				17 36						17 57	
Ewell West	d			17 09				17 24				17 39						18 00	
Epsom 3	a			17 12				17 27				17 42				17 54		18 07	
	d			17 17				17 28				17 47				17 54			
Ashtead	d			17 21				17 32				17 51				17 58			
Leatherhead	d			17 24				17 35				17 54				18 01			
Box Hill & Westhumble	d							17 40								18 06			
Dorking 4	a							17 46								18 13			
New Malden 6	d		16 58		17 04				17 19		17 28		17 34				17 49		
Norbiton	d				17 07				17 22				17 37				17 52		
Kingston	a				17 10				17 25				17 40				17 55		
	d				17 10				17 29				17 40				17 59		
Hampton Wick	d				17 12				17 31				17 42				18 01		
Teddington	d				17 15				17 35				17 45				18 05		
Strawberry Hill	a								17 38								18 08		
Fulwell	d				17 19								17 49						
Hampton	d				17 23								17 53						
Kempton Park	d				17 26								17 56						
Sunbury	d				17 28								17 58						
Upper Halliford	d				17 30								18 00						
Shepperton	a				17 37								18 08						
Berrylands	d		17 00								17 30								
Surbiton 6	d	16 57	17 05				17a13			17 27	17 35				17a43				17 57
Thames Ditton	d		17 09								17 39								
Hampton Court	a		17 14								17 44								
Hinchley Wood	d	17 01								17 31									18 05
Claygate	d	17 04								17 34									18 08
Oxshott	d	17 07								17 37									18 11
Cobham & Stoke D'abernon	d	17 11								17 41									18 15
Bookham	d			17 29								17 59							
Effingham Junction 6	d	17 15		17 33						17 45		18a05							18 20
Horsley	d	17 18		17 36						17 48									18 22
Clandon	d	17 23		17 41						17 53									18 27
London Road (Guildford)	d	17 28		17 46						17 58									18 32
Guildford	a	17 37		17 55						18 04									18 38

Table 152

Mondays to Fridays
from 8 October

London - Chessington South, Dorking, Guildford, Shepperton and Hampton Court

Network Diagram - see first Page of Table 152

		SW	SW	SW	SW	SW	SW	SW	SW	SW	SW	SW	SW	SW	SW	SW	SW	SW	SW
London Waterloo 15 ⊖	d	17 36	17 39	17 43	17 42	17 46	17 50	17 54	17 57	18 00	18 02	18 06	18 09	18 13	18 12	18 16	18 20	18 24	18 27
Vauxhall ⊖	d	17 40	17 43	17 47	17 46	17 50	17 54	17 58	18 01	18 04	18 07	18 10	18 13	18 17	18 16	18 20	18 24	18 28	18 31
Clapham Junction 10	d	17 45	17 48		17 51	17 55	17 59	18 03	18 06	18 09	18 12	18 15	18 18		18 21	18 25	18 29	18 33	18 36
Earlsfield	d	17 48	17 51		17 54	17 58	18 02	18 06	18 09	18 12	18 15	18 18	18 21		18 24	18 28	18 32	18 36	18 39
Wimbledon 6 ⊖	d	17 52	17 55		17 58	18 02	18 06	18 10	18 13	18 16	18 19	18 22	18 25		18 28	18 32	18 36	18 40	18 43
Raynes Park 6	d	17 55	17 58		18 01	18 05		18 13	18 16	18 19		18 25	18 28		18 31	18 35		18 43	18 46
Motspur Park	d		18 01			18 08				18 22			18 31			18 38			
Malden Manor	d					18 11										18 41			
Tolworth	d					18 14										18 44			
Chessington North	d					18 17										18 47			
Chessington South	a					18 21										18 51			
Worcester Park	d		18 03					18 17		18 24			18 33					18 47	
Stoneleigh	d		18 06							18 27			18 36						
Ewell West	d		18 09							18 30			18 39						
Epsom 3	a		18 15					18 24		18 35			18 46					18 54	
	d		18 17					18 24					18 47					18 54	
Ashtead	d		18 21					18 28					18 51					18 58	
Leatherhead	d		18 24					18 31					18 54					19 01	
Box Hill & Westhumble	d							18 36										19 06	
Dorking 4	a							18 43										19 13	
New Malden 6	d	17 58			18 04				18 19			18 28			18 34				18 49
Norbiton	d				18 07				18 22						18 37				18 52
Kingston	a				18 10				18 25						18 40				18 55
	d				18 10				18 29						18 40				18 59
Hampton Wick	d				18 12				18 31						18 42				19 01
Teddington	d				18 15				18 35						18 45				19 05
Strawberry Hill	a			18 11					18 38					18 41					19 08
Fulwell	d			18 13	18 19									18 43	18 49				
Hampton	d			18 17	18 23									18 47	18 53				
Kempton Park	d				18 26										18 56				
Sunbury	d			18 21	18 28									18 51	18 58				
Upper Halliford	d			18 23	18 30									18 53	19 00				
Shepperton	a			18 30	18 40									19 00	19 10				
Berrylands	d	18 00										18 30							
Surbiton 6	d	18 05					18a13				18 27	18 35					18a43		
Thames Ditton	d	18 09										18 39							
Hampton Court	a	18 14										18 44							
Hinchley Wood	d										18 35								
Claygate	d										18 38								
Oxshott	d										18 41								
Cobham & Stoke D'abernon	d										18 45								
Bookham	d		18 29										18 59						
Effingham Junction 6	d		18a42								18 50		19 03						
Horsley	d										18 52		19 06						
Clandon	d										18 57		19 11						
London Road (Guildford)	d										19 02		19 16						
Guildford	a										19 09		19 25						

Table 152

Mondays to Fridays

from 8 October

London - Chessington South, Dorking, Guildford, Shepperton and Hampton Court

Network Diagram - see first Page of Table 152

		SW			SW	SW	SW	SW	SW	SW	SW	SW		SW	SW	SW			SW	SW	SW	SW		SW	SW
London Waterloo 15 ⊖	d	18 30			18 32	18 36	18 39	18 43	18 42	18 46	18 48	18 50		18 54	18 57	19 00			19 02	19 06	19 09	19 12		19 16	19 20
Vauxhall ⊖	d	18 34			18 37	18 40	18 43	18 47	18 46	18 50		18 54		18 58	19 01	19 04			19 07	19 10	19 13	19 16		19 20	19 24
Clapham Junction 10	d	18 39			18 42	18 45	18 48		18 51	18 55		18 59		19 03	19 06	19 09			19 12	19 15	19 18	19 21		19 25	19 29
Earlsfield	d	18 42			18 45	18 48	18 51		18 54	18 58		19 02		19 06	19 09	19 12			19 15	19 18	19 21	19 24		19 28	19 32
Wimbledon 6 ⊖ 🚊	d	18 46			18 49	18 52	18 55		18 58	19 02		19 06		19 10	19 13	19 16			19 19	19 22	19 25	19 28		19 32	19 36
Raynes Park 6	d	18 49				18 55	18 58		19 01	19 05				19 13	19 16	19 19				19 25	19 28	19 31		19 35	
Motspur Park	d	18 52					19 01			19 08						19 22					19 31			19 38	
Malden Manor	d									19 11														19 41	
Tolworth	d									19 14														19 44	
Chessington North	d									19 17														19 47	
Chessington South	a									19 21														19 49	
Worcester Park	d	18 54					19 03							19 17		19 24					19 33				
Stoneleigh	d	18 57					19 06									19 27					19 36				
Ewell West	d	19 00					19 09									19 30					19 39				
Epsom 3	a	19 07					19 16							19 24		19 35					19 44				
	d						19 17							19 24							19 47				
Ashtead	d						19 21							19 28							19 51				
Leatherhead	d						19 24							19 31							19 54				
Box Hill & Westhumble	d													19 36											
Dorking 4	a													19 43											
New Malden 6	d					18 58			19 04						19 19					19 28		19 34			
Norbiton	d								19 07						19 22							19 37			
Kingston	a								19 10						19 25							19 40			
	d								19 10						19 29							19 40			
Hampton Wick	d								19 12						19 31							19 42			
Teddington	d								19 15						19 35							19 45			
Strawberry Hill	a							19 11							19 38										
Fulwell	d							19 13	19 19													19 49			
Hampton	d							19 17	19 23													19 53			
Kempton Park	d								19 26													19 56			
Sunbury	d							19 21	19 28													19 58			
Upper Halliford	d							19 23	19 30													20 00			
Shepperton	a							19 30	19 39													20 06			
Berrylands	d					19 00														19 30					
Surbiton 6	d				18 57	19 05					19 06	19a13							19 27	19 35					19a43
Thames Ditton	d					19 09														19 39					
Hampton Court	a					19 14														19 42					
Hinchley Wood	d				19 01						19 10								19 31						
Claygate	d				19 04						19 13								19 34						
Oxshott	d				19 07						19 16								19 37						
Cobham & Stoke D'abernon	d				19 11						19 20								19 41						
Bookham	d						19 29														19 59				
Effingham Junction 6	d				19 15		19 33				19 24								19 45		20 03				
Horsley	d				19 18		19 36				19 27								19 48		20 06				
Clandon	d				19 23		19 41				19 32								19 53		20 11				
London Road (Guildford)	d				19 28		19 46				19 37								19 58		20 16				
Guildford	a				19 37		19 55				19 46								20 02		20 23				

Table 152

Mondays to Fridays

from 8 October

London - Chessington South, Dorking, Guildford, Shepperton and Hampton Court

Network Diagram - see first Page of Table 152

		SW	SW	SW	SW		SW	SW		SW	SW	SW	SW	SW	SW		SW	SW		SW	SW	SW	SW	SW	SW
London Waterloo 15 ⊖	d	19 23	19 24	19 27	19 33		19 36	19 39		19 42	19 46	19 50	19 54	19 57	20 03		20 06	20 09		20 12	20 16	20 20	20 24	20 27	20 33
Vauxhall ⊖	d		19 28	19 31	19 37		19 40	19 43		19 46	19 50	19 54	19 58	20 01	20 07		20 10	20 13		20 16	20 20	20 24	20 28	20 31	20 37
Clapham Junction 10	d		19 33	19 36	19 42		19 45	19 48		19 51	19 55	19 59	20 03	20 06	20 12		20 15	20 18		20 21	20 25	20 29	20 33	20 36	20 42
Earlsfield	d		19 36	19 39	19 45		19 48	19 51		19 54	19 58	20 02	20 06	20 09	20 15		20 18	20 21		20 24	20 28	20 32	20 36	20 39	20 45
Wimbledon 6 ⊖ 🚊	d		19 40	19 43	19 49		19 52	19 55		19 58	20 02	20 06	20 10	20 13	20 19		20 22	20 25		20 28	20 32	20 36	20 40	20 43	20 49
Raynes Park 6	d		19 43	19 46			19 55	19 58		20 01	20 05		20 13	20 16			20 25	20 28		20 31	20 35		20 43	20 46	
Motspur Park	d		19 46					20 01			20 08		20 16					20 31			20 38		20 46		
Malden Manor	d										20 11										20 41				
Tolworth	d										20 14										20 44				
Chessington North	d										20 17										20 47				
Chessington South	a										20 19										20 49				
Worcester Park	d		19 48					20 03					20 18					20 33					20 48		
Stoneleigh	d		19 51					20 06					20 21					20 36					20 51		
Ewell West	d		19 54					20 09					20 24					20 39					20 54		
Epsom 3	a		19 57					20 16					20 27					20 42					20 57		
	d		19 58					20 17										20 43							
Ashtead	d		20 02					20 21										20 47							
Leatherhead	d		20 05					20 24										20 50							
Box Hill & Westhumble	d		20 10															20 55							
Dorking 4	a		20 14															20 59							
New Malden 6	d			19 49			19 58			20 04				20 19			20 28			20 34				20 49	
Norbiton	d			19 52						20 07				20 22						20 37				20 52	
Kingston	a			19 55						20 10				20 25						20 40				20 55	
	d			19 59						20 10				20 29						20 40				20 59	
Hampton Wick	d			20 01						20 12				20 31						20 42				21 01	
Teddington	d			20 05						20 15				20 35						20 45				21 05	
Strawberry Hill	a			20 08										20 38										21 08	
Fulwell	d									20 19										20 49					
Hampton	d									20 23										20 53					
Kempton Park	d									20 26										20 56					
Sunbury	d									20 28										20 58					
Upper Halliford	d									20 30										21 00					
Shepperton	a									20 35										21 05					
Berrylands	d						20 00										20 30								
Surbiton 6	d	19a39			19 57		20 05					20a13			20 27		20 35					20a43			20 57
Thames Ditton	d						20 09										20 39								
Hampton Court	a						20 12										20 42								
Hinchley Wood	d				20 01										20 31										21 01
Claygate	d				20 04										20 34										21 04
Oxshott	d				20 07										20 37										21 07
Cobham & Stoke D'abernon	d				20 11										20 41										21 11
Bookham	d							20 29																	
Effingham Junction 6	d				20 15			20 33							20 45										21 15
Horsley	d				20 18			20 36							20 48										21 18
Clandon	d				20 23			20 41							20 53										21 23
London Road (Guildford)	d				20 28			20 46							20 58										21 28
Guildford	a				20 35			20 53							21 05										21 35

			SW	SW		SW	SW	SW	SW	SW	SW		SW	SW		SW	SW	SW	SW		SW	SW	SW	SW	
London Waterloo 15 ⊖	d		20 36	20 39		20 42	20 46	20 50	20 54	20 57	21 03		21 09	21 12		21 20	21 24	21 27	21 33		21 36	21 39	21 42	21 46	
Vauxhall ⊖	d		20 40	20 43		20 46	20 50	20 54	20 58	21 01	21 07		21 13	21 16		21 24	21 28	21 31	21 37		21 40	21 43	21 46	21 50	
Clapham Junction 10	d		20 45	20 48		20 51	20 55	20 59	21 03	21 06	21 12		21 18	21 21		21 29	21 33	21 36	21 42		21 45	21 48	21 51	21 55	
Earlsfield	d		20 48	20 51		20 54	20 58	21 02	21 06	21 09	21 15		21 21	21 24		21 32	21 36	21 39	21 45		21 48	21 51	21 54	21 58	
Wimbledon 6 ⊖ 🚊	d		20 52	20 55		20 58	21 02	21 06	21 10	21 13	21 19		21 25	21 28		21 36	21 40	21 43	21 49		21 52	21 55	21 58	22 02	
Raynes Park 6	d		20 55	20 58		21 01	21 05		21 13	21 16			21 28	21 31			21 43	21 46			21 55	21 58	22 01	22 05	
Motspur Park	d			21 01			21 08		21 16				21 31				21 46					22 01		22 08	
Malden Manor	d						21 11																	22 11	
Tolworth	d						21 14																	22 14	
Chessington North	d						21 17																	22 17	
Chessington South	a						21 19																	22 19	
Worcester Park	d			21 03					21 18				21 33				21 48					22 03			
Stoneleigh	d			21 06					21 21				21 36				21 51					22 06			
Ewell West	d			21 09					21 24				21 39				21 54					22 09			
Epsom 3	a			21 12					21 27				21 42				21 57					22 12			
	d			21 13									21 43									22 13			
Ashtead	d			21 17									21 47									22 17			
Leatherhead	d			21 20									21 50									22 20			
Box Hill & Westhumble	d												21 55												
Dorking 4	a												21 59												
New Malden 6	d		20 58			21 04				21 19				21 34				21 49			21 58		22 04		
Norbiton	d					21 07				21 22				21 37				21 52					22 07		
Kingston	a					21 10				21 25				21 40				21 55					22 10		
	d					21 10				21 29				21 40				21 59					22 10		
Hampton Wick	d					21 12				21 31				21 42				22 01					22 12		
Teddington	d					21 15				21 35				21 45				22 05					22 15		
Strawberry Hill	a									21 38								22 08							
Fulwell	d					21 19								21 49									22 19		
Hampton	d					21 23								21 53									22 23		
Kempton Park	d					21 26								21 56									22 26		
Sunbury	d					21 28								21 58									22 28		
Upper Halliford	d					21 30								22 00									22 30		
Shepperton	a					21 35								22 05									22 35		
Berrylands	d		21 00																		22 00				
Surbiton 6	d		21 05					21a13			21 27					21a43			21 57		22 05				
Thames Ditton	d		21 09																		22 09				
Hampton Court	a		21 12																		22 12				
Hinchley Wood	d										21 31								22 01						
Claygate	d										21 34								22 04						
Oxshott	d										21 37								22 07						
Cobham & Stoke D'abernon	d										21 41								22 11						
Bookham	d			21 25																		22 25			
Effingham Junction 6	d			21 29							21 45								22 15			22 29			
Horsley	d			21 32							21 48								22 18			22 32			
Clandon	d			21 37							21 53								22 23			22 37			
London Road (Guildford)	d			21 42							21 58								22 28			22 42			
Guildford	a			21 49							22 05								22 35			22 49			

Mondays to Fridays from 8 October

London - Chessington South, Dorking, Guildford, Shepperton and Hampton Court

Network Diagram - see first Page of Table 152

		SW	SW	SW	SW	SW	SW	SW	SW	SW	SW	SW	SW	SW	SW	SW	SW	SW	SW	SW
London Waterloo 15 ⊖	d	21 50	21 54	21 57	22 03	22 09	22 12	22 20	22 27	22 33	22 36	22 39	22 42	22 50	22 57	23 00	23 03	23 09	23 12	23 20
Vauxhall ⊖	d	21 54	21 58	22 01	22 07	22 13	22 16	22 24	22 31	22 37	22 40	22 43	22 46	22 54	23 01	23 04	23 07	23 13	23 16	23 24
Clapham Junction 10	d	21 59	22 03	22 06	22 12	22 18	22 21	22 29	22 36	22 42	22 45	22 48	22 51	22 59	23 06	23 09	23 12	23 18	23 21	23 29
Earlsfield	d	22 02	22 06	22 09	22 15	22 21	22 24	22 32	22 39	22 45	22 48	22 51	22 54	23 02	23 09	23 12	23 15	23 21	23 24	23 32
Wimbledon 6 ⊖	d	22 06	22 10	22 13	22 19	22 25	22 28	22 36	22 43	22 49	22 52	22 55	22 58	23 06	23 13	23 16	23 19	23 25	23 28	23 36
Raynes Park 6	d		22 13	22 16		22 28	22 31		22 46		22 55	22 58	23 01		23 16	23 19		23 28	23 31	
Motspur Park	d		22 16			22 31						23 01				23 22		23 31		
Malden Manor	d															23 25				
Tolworth	d															23 28				
Chessington North	d															23 31				
Chessington South	a															23 33				
Worcester Park	d		22 18			22 33						23 03						23 33		
Stoneleigh	d		22 21			22 36						23 06						23 36		
Ewell West	d		22 24			22 39						23 09						23 39		
Epsom 3	a		22 27			22 42						23 12						23 42		
	d					22 43						23 13						23 43		
Ashtead	d					22 47						23 17						23 47		
Leatherhead	d					22 50						23 20						23 50		
Box Hill & Westhumble	d					22 55												23 55		
Dorking 4	a					22 59												23 59		
New Malden 6	d			22 19			22 34		22 49		22 58		23 04		23 19				23 34	
Norbiton	d			22 22			22 37		22 52				23 07		23 22				23 37	
Kingston	a			22 25			22 40		22 55				23 10		23 25				23 40	
	d			22 29			22 40		22 59				23 10		23 29				23 40	
Hampton Wick	d			22 31			22 42		23 01				23 12		23 31				23 42	
Teddington	d			22 35			22 45		23 05				23 15		23 35				23 45	
Strawberry Hill	a			22 38					23 08						23 38					
Fulwell	d						22 49						23 19						23 49	
Hampton	d						22 53						23 23						23 53	
Kempton Park	d						22 56						23 26						23 56	
Sunbury	d						22 58						23 28						23 58	
Upper Halliford	d						23 00						23 30						23 59	
Shepperton	a						23 05						23 35						00 05	
Berrylands	d										23 00									
Surbiton 6	d	22 14			22 27			22a43		22 57	23 05			23a13			23 27			23a43
Thames Ditton	d										23 09									
Hampton Court	a										23 12									
Hinchley Wood	d				22 31					23 01							23 31			
Claygate	d				22 34					23 04							23 34			
Oxshott	d				22 37					23 07							23 37			
Cobham & Stoke D'abernon	d				22 41					23 11							23 41			
Bookham	d											23 25								
Effingham Junction 6	d				22 45					23 15		23 29					23 45			
Horsley	d				22 48					23 18		23 32					23 48			
Clandon	d				22 53					23 23		23 37					23 53			
London Road (Guildford)	d				22 58					23 28		23 42					23 58			
Guildford	a	22 47			23 05					23 35		23 49					00 05			

		SW	SW	SW	SW	SW
London Waterloo 15 ⊖	d	23 27	23 36	23 42	23 50	23 57
Vauxhall ⊖	d	23 31	23 40	23 46	23 54	00 01
Clapham Junction 10	d	23 36	23 45	23 51	23 59	00 06
Earlsfield	d	23 39	23 48	23 54	00 02	00 09
Wimbledon 6 ⊖	d	23 43	23 52	23 58	00 06	00 13
Raynes Park 6	d	23 46	23 55	00 01		00 16
Motspur Park	d			00 04		
Malden Manor	d					
Tolworth	d					
Chessington North	d					
Chessington South	a					
Worcester Park	d			00 06		
Stoneleigh	d			00 09		
Ewell West	d			00 12		
Epsom 3	a			00 15		
	d			00 19		
Ashtead	d			00 23		
Leatherhead	d			00 26		
Box Hill & Westhumble	d					
Dorking 4	a					
New Malden 6	d	23 49	23 58			00 19
Norbiton	d	23 52				00 22
Kingston	a	23 55				00 25
	d	23 55				00 25
Hampton Wick	d	23 57				00 27
Teddington	d	23 59				00 30
Strawberry Hill	a	00 03				
Fulwell	d					00 34
Hampton	d					00 38
Kempton Park	d					00 41
Sunbury	d					00 43
Upper Halliford	d					00 45
Shepperton	a					00 50
Berrylands	d		23 59			
Surbiton 6	d		00 05		00 14	
Thames Ditton	d		00 09			
Hampton Court	a		00 12			
Hinchley Wood	d				00 18	
Claygate	d				00 20	
Oxshott	d				00 24	
Cobham & Stoke D'abernon	d				00 27	
Bookham	d			00 31		
Effingham Junction 6	d			00 36	00 32	
Horsley	d			00 39	00 34	
Clandon	d			00 44	00 39	
London Road (Guildford)	d			00 49	00 44	
Guildford	a			00 56	00 51	

Saturdays until 6 October

London - Chessington South, Dorking, Guildford, Shepperton and Hampton Court

Network Diagram - see first Page of Table 152

		SW	SW	SW	SW	SW	SW	SW	SW	SW	SW	SW	SW	SW	SW	SW	SW	SW	SW	SW
										A	B	A	B		■		■			
London Waterloo 15 ⊖	d	23p03	23p12	23p27	23p36	23p42	23p50	23p57	00 09	00 15	00 15	00 27	00 27	00 42	05 00	05 12	05 20	05 50		
Vauxhall ⊖	d	23p07	23p16	23p31	23p40	23p46	23p54	00 01	00 13	00 19	00 19	00 31	00 31	00 46	05 04	05 16	05 24	05 54		
Clapham Junction 10	d	23p12	23p21	23p36	23p45	23p51	23p59	00 06	00 20	00 25	00 25	00 37	00 37	00 51	05 11	05 21	05 29	05 59		
Earlsfield	d	23p15	23p24	23p39	23p48	23p54	00 02	00 09	00 23	00 29	00 29	00s41	00s41		05 14	05 24	05 32	06 02		
Wimbledon 6 ⊖	d	23p19	23p28	23p43	23p52	23p58	00 06	00 13	00 27	00 33	00 33	00 45	00 45	01 05	05 18	05 28	05 36	06 06		06 13
Raynes Park 6	d		23p31	23p46	23p55	00 01		00 16		00 36	00 36	00 48	00 48	01 08		05 31				06 16
Motspur Park	d					00 04				00 38	00 38									
Malden Manor	d																			
Tolworth	d																			
Chessington North	d																			
Chessington South	a																			
Worcester Park	d					00 06				00 41	00 41									
Stoneleigh	d					00 09				00 44	00 44									
Ewell West	d					00 12				00 46	00 46									
Epsom 3	a					00 15				00 50	00 50									
	d					00 19					00 51									
Ashtead	d					00 23					00s55									
Leatherhead	d					00 26					00s58									
Box Hill & Westhumble	d																			
Dorking 4	a																			
New Malden 6	d		23p34	23p49	23p58			00 19				00 50	00 50	01 11		05 34				06 19
Norbiton	d		23p37	23p52				00 22						01 14		05 37				06 22
Kingston	a		23p40	23p55				00 25						01 17		05 40				06 25
	d		23p40	23p55				00 25						01 17		05 40			05 59	06 29
Hampton Wick	d		23p42	23p57				00 27						01s19		05 42			06 01	06 31
Teddington	d		23p45	23p59				00 30						01s22		05 45			06 05	06 35
Strawberry Hill	a			00 03										01 28					06 08	06 38
Fulwell	d		23p49					00 34								05 49				
Hampton	d		23p53					00 38								05 53				
Kempton Park	d		23p56					00 41								05 56				
Sunbury	d		23p58					00 43								05 58				
Upper Halliford	d		23p59					00 45								06 00				
Shepperton	a		00 03					00 48								06 03				
Berrylands	d				23p59							00s53	00s53							
Surbiton 6	d	23p27			00 05		00 14		00 35			00a56	00 57		05 26		05 44	06a13		
Thames Ditton	d				00 09															
Hampton Court	a				00 12															
Hinchley Wood	d	23p31					00 18													
Claygate	d	23p34					00 20													
Oxshott	d	23p37					00 24													
Cobham & Stoke D'abernon	d	23p41					00 27													
Bookham	d					00 31					01s03									
Effingham Junction 6	d	23p45				00 36	00 32				01s07									
Horsley	d	23p48				00 39	00 34				01s10									
Clandon	d	23p53				00 44	00 39				01s15									
London Road (Guildford)	d	23p58				00 49	00 44				01s20									
Guildford	a	00 02				00 53	00 48		01 07		01 24		01 33		06 00		06 23			

A until 21 July, 18 August, 25 August, 15 September, 22 September, 29 September, 6 October

B 28 July, 4 August, 11 August, 1 September, 8 September

Table 152

Saturdays
until 6 October

London - Chessington South, Dorking, Guildford, Shepperton and Hampton Court

Network Diagram - see first Page of Table 152

			SW	SW	SW	SW		SW	SW		SW	SW	SW	SW	SW	SW		SW		SW	SW	SW	SW	SW	SW
London Waterloo 15 ⊖	d		06 06	06 12	06 16	06 20		06 27	06 33		06 36	06 39	06 42	06 46	06 50	06 57		07 03		07 06	07 09	07 12	07 16	07 20	07 24
Vauxhall ⊖	d		06 10	06 16	06 20	06 24		06 31	06 37		06 40	06 43	06 46	06 50	06 54	07 01		07 07		07 10	07 13	07 16	07 20	07 24	07 28
Clapham Junction 10	d		06 15	06 21	06 25	06 29		06 36	06 42		06 45	06 48	06 51	06 55	06 59	07 06		07 12		07 15	07 18	07 21	07 25	07 29	07 33
Earlsfield	d		06 18	06 24	06 28	06 32		06 39	06 45		06 48	06 51	06 54	06 58	07 02	07 09		07 15		07 18	07 21	07 24	07 28	07 32	07 36
Wimbledon 6 ⊖	d		06 22	06 28	06 32	06 36		06 43	06 49		06 52	06 55	06 58	07 02	07 06	07 13		07 19		07 22	07 25	07 28	07 32	07 36	07 40
Raynes Park 6	d		06 25	06 31	06 35			06 46			06 55	06 58	07 01	07 05		07 16				07 25	07 28	07 31	07 35		07 43
Motspur Park	d				06 38							07 01		07 08							07 31		07 38		07 46
Malden Manor	d				06 41									07 11									07 41		
Tolworth	d				06 44									07 14									07 44		
Chessington North	d				06 47									07 17									07 47		
Chessington South	a				06 49									07 19									07 49		
Worcester Park	d											07 03									07 33				07 48
Stoneleigh	d											07 06									07 36				07 51
Ewell West	d											07 09									07 39				07 54
Epsom 3	a											07 16									07 46				07 57
	d											07 17									07 47				07 58
Ashtead	d											07 21									07 51				08 02
Leatherhead	d											07 24									07 54				08 05
Box Hill & Westhumble	d																								
Dorking 4	a																								08 11
New Malden 6	d		06 28	06 34				06 49			06 58		07 04			07 19				07 28		07 34			
Norbiton	d			06 37				06 52					07 07			07 22						07 37			
Kingston	a			06 40				06 55					07 10			07 25						07 40			
	d			06 40				06 59					07 10			07 29						07 40			
Hampton Wick	d			06 42				07 01					07 12			07 31						07 42			
Teddington	d			06 45				07 05					07 15			07 35						07 45			
Strawberry Hill	a							07 08								07 38									
Fulwell	d			06 49									07 19									07 49			
Hampton	d			06 53									07 23									07 53			
Kempton Park	d			06 56									07 26									07 56			
Sunbury	d			06 58									07 28									07 58			
Upper Halliford	d			07 00									07 30									08 00			
Shepperton	a			07 03									07 33									08 03			
Berrylands	d		06 30								07 00									07 30					
Surbiton 6	d		06 35			06a43			06 57		07 05				07a13			07 27		07 35				07a43	
Thames Ditton	d		06 39								07 09									07 39					
Hampton Court	a		06 42								07 12									07 42					
Hinchley Wood	d								07 01									07 31							
Claygate	d								07 04									07 34							
Oxshott	d								07 07									07 37							
Cobham & Stoke D'abernon	d								07 11									07 41							
Bookham	d											07 29									07 59				
Effingham Junction 6	d								07 15			07 33						07 45			08 03				
Horsley	d								07 18			07 36						07 48			08 06				
Clandon	d								07 23			07 41						07 53			08 11				
London Road (Guildford)	d								07 28			07 46						07 58			08 16				
Guildford	a								07 32			07 50						08 02			08 20				

		SW		SW		SW	SW	SW	SW	SW	SW	SW		SW		SW	SW	SW	SW	SW	SW	SW		SW	
London Waterloo 15 ⊖	d	07 27		07 33		07 36	07 39	07 42	07 46	07 50	07 54	07 57		08 03		08 06	08 09	08 12	08 16	08 20	08 24	08 27		08 33	
Vauxhall ⊖	d	07 31		07 37		07 40	07 43	07 46	07 50	07 54	07 58	08 01		08 07		08 10	08 13	08 16	08 20	08 24	08 28	08 31		08 37	
Clapham Junction 10	d	07 36		07 42		07 45	07 48	07 51	07 55	07 59	08 03	08 06		08 12		08 15	08 18	08 21	08 25	08 29	08 33	08 36		08 42	
Earlsfield	d	07 39		07 45		07 48	07 51	07 54	07 58	08 02	08 06	08 09		08 15		08 18	08 21	08 24	08 28	08 32	08 36	08 39		08 45	
Wimbledon 6 ⊖	d	07 43		07 49		07 52	07 55	07 58	08 02	08 06	08 10	08 13		08 19		08 22	08 25	08 28	08 32	08 36	08 40	08 43		08 49	
Raynes Park 6	d	07 46				07 55	07 58	08 01	08 05		08 13	08 16				08 25	08 28	08 31	08 35		08 43	08 46			
Motspur Park	d						08 01		08 08		08 16						08 31		08 38		08 46				
Malden Manor	d								08 11										08 41						
Tolworth	d								08 14										08 44						
Chessington North	d								08 17										08 47						
Chessington South	a								08 19										08 49						
Worcester Park	d						08 03				08 18						08 33				08 48				
Stoneleigh	d						08 06				08 21						08 36				08 51				
Ewell West	d						08 09				08 24						08 39				08 54				
Epsom 3	a						08 16				08 27						08 46				08 57				
	d						08 17				08 28						08 47				08 58				
Ashtead	d						08 21				08 32						08 51				09 02				
Leatherhead	d						08 24				08 35						08 54				09 05				
Box Hill & Westhumble	d																								
Dorking 4	a										08 41										09 11				
New Malden 6	d	07 49				07 58		08 04				08 19				08 28		08 34				08 49			
Norbiton	d	07 52						08 07				08 22						08 37				08 52			
Kingston	a	07 55						08 10				08 25						08 40				08 55			
	d	07 59						08 10				08 29						08 40				08 59			
Hampton Wick	d	08 01						08 12				08 31						08 42				09 01			
Teddington	d	08 05						08 15				08 35						08 45				09 05			
Strawberry Hill	a	08 08										08 38										09 08			
Fulwell	d							08 19										08 49							
Hampton	d							08 23										08 53							
Kempton Park	d							08 26										08 56							
Sunbury	d							08 28										08 58							
Upper Halliford	d							08 30										09 00							
Shepperton	a							08 33										09 03							
Berrylands	d					08 00										08 30									
Surbiton 6	d			07 57		08 05				08a13				08 27		08 35				08a43				08 57	
Thames Ditton	d					08 09										08 39									
Hampton Court	a					08 12										08 42									
Hinchley Wood	d			08 01										08 31										09 01	
Claygate	d			08 04										08 34										09 04	
Oxshott	d			08 07										08 37										09 07	
Cobham & Stoke D'abernon	d			08 11										08 41										09 11	
Bookham	d						08 29										08 59								
Effingham Junction 6	d			08 15			08 33							08 45			09 03							09 15	
Horsley	d			08 18			08 36							08 48			09 06							09 18	
Clandon	d			08 23			08 41							08 53			09 11							09 23	
London Road (Guildford)	d			08 28			08 46							08 58			09 16							09 28	
Guildford	a			08 32			08 50							09 02			09 20							09 32	

Table 152

Saturdays
until 6 October

London - Chessington South, Dorking, Guildford, Shepperton and Hampton Court

Network Diagram - see first Page of Table 152

		SW	SW	SW	SW	SW	SW	SW		SW		SW	SW	SW	SW	SW	SW	SW		SW		SW	SW	SW	SW
London Waterloo 15 ⊖	d	08 36	08 39	08 42	08 46	08 50	08 54	08 57		09 03		09 06	09 09	09 12	09 16	09 20	09 24	09 27		09 33		09 36	09 39	09 42	09 46
Vauxhall ⊖	d	08 40	08 43	08 46	08 50	08 54	08 58	09 01		09 07		09 10	09 13	09 16	09 20	09 24	09 28	09 31		09 37		09 40	09 43	09 46	09 50
Clapham Junction 10	d	08 45	08 48	08 51	08 55	08 59	09 03	09 06		09 12		09 15	09 18	09 21	09 25	09 29	09 33	09 36		09 42		09 45	09 48	09 51	09 55
Earlsfield	d	08 48	08 51	08 54	08 58	09 02	09 06	09 09		09 15		09 18	09 21	09 24	09 28	09 32	09 36	09 39		09 45		09 48	09 51	09 54	09 58
Wimbledon 6 ⊖	d	08 52	08 55	08 58	09 02	09 06	09 10	09 13		09 19		09 22	09 25	09 28	09 32	09 36	09 40	09 43		09 49		09 52	09 55	09 58	10 02
Raynes Park 6	d	08 55	08 58	09 01	09 05		09 13	09 16				09 25	09 28	09 31	09 35		09 43	09 46				09 55	09 58	10 01	10 05
Motspur Park	d		09 01		09 08		09 16						09 31		09 38		09 46						10 01		10 08
Malden Manor	d				09 11										09 41										10 11
Tolworth	d				09 14										09 44										10 14
Chessington North	d				09 17										09 47										10 17
Chessington South	a				09 19										09 49										10 19
Worcester Park	d		09 03				09 18						09 33				09 48						10 03		
Stoneleigh	d		09 06				09 21						09 36				09 51						10 06		
Ewell West	d		09 09				09 24						09 39				09 54						10 09		
Epsom 3	a		09 16				09 27						09 46				09 57						10 16		
	d		09 17				09 28						09 47				09 58						10 17		
Ashtead	d		09 21				09 32						09 51				10 02						10 21		
Leatherhead	d		09 24				09 35						09 54				10 05						10 24		
Box Hill & Westhumble	d																								
Dorking 4	a						09 41										10 11								
New Malden 6	d	08 58		09 04				09 19				09 28		09 34				09 49				09 58		10 04	
Norbiton	d			09 07				09 22						09 37				09 52						10 07	
Kingston	a			09 10				09 25						09 40				09 55						10 10	
	d			09 10				09 29						09 40				09 59						10 10	
Hampton Wick	d			09 12				09 31						09 42				10 01						10 12	
Teddington	d			09 15				09 35						09 45				10 05						10 15	
Strawberry Hill	a							09 38										10 08							
Fulwell	d			09 19										09 49										10 19	
Hampton	d			09 23										09 53										10 23	
Kempton Park	d			09 26										09 56										10 26	
Sunbury	d			09 28										09 58										10 28	
Upper Halliford	d			09 30										10 00										10 30	
Shepperton	a			09 33										10 03										10 33	
Berrylands	d	09 00										09 30										10 00			
Surbiton 6	d	09 05				09a13				09 27		09 35				09a43				09 57		10 05			
Thames Ditton	d	09 09										09 39										10 09			
Hampton Court	a	09 12										09 42										10 12			
Hinchley Wood	d									09 31										10 01					
Claygate	d									09 34										10 04					
Oxshott	d									09 37										10 07					
Cobham & Stoke D'abernon	d									09 41										10 11					
Bookham	d		09 29										09 59										10 29		
Effingham Junction 6	d		09 33							09 45			10 03							10 15			10 33		
Horsley	d		09 36							09 48			10 06							10 18			10 36		
Clandon	d		09 41							09 53			10 11							10 23			10 41		
London Road (Guildford)	d		09 46							09 58			10 16							10 28			10 46		
Guildford	a		09 50							10 02			10 20							10 32			10 50		

		SW	SW	SW		SW		SW	SW	SW	SW	SW	SW	SW		SW		SW	SW	SW	SW	SW	SW	SW	
London Waterloo 15 ⊖	d	09 50	09 54	09 57		10 03		10 06	10 09	10 12	10 16	10 20	10 24	10 27		10 33		10 36	10 39	10 42	10 46	10 50	10 54	10 57	
Vauxhall ⊖	d	09 54	09 58	10 01		10 07		10 10	10 13	10 16	10 20	10 24	10 28	10 31		10 37		10 40	10 43	10 46	10 50	10 54	10 58	11 01	
Clapham Junction 10	d	09 59	10 03	10 06		10 12		10 15	10 18	10 21	10 25	10 29	10 33	10 36		10 42		10 45	10 48	10 51	10 55	10 59	11 03	11 06	
Earlsfield	d	10 02	10 06	10 09		10 15		10 18	10 21	10 24	10 28	10 32	10 36	10 39		10 45		10 48	10 51	10 54	10 58	11 02	11 06	11 09	
Wimbledon 6 ⊖	d	10 06	10 10	10 13		10 19		10 22	10 25	10 28	10 32	10 36	10 40	10 43		10 49		10 52	10 55	10 58	11 02	11 06	11 10	11 13	
Raynes Park 6	d		10 13	10 16				10 25	10 28	10 31	10 35		10 43	10 46				10 55	10 58	11 01	11 05		11 13	11 16	
Motspur Park	d		10 16						10 31		10 38		10 46						11 01		11 08		11 16		
Malden Manor	d										10 41										11 11				
Tolworth	d										10 44										11 14				
Chessington North	d										10 47										11 17				
Chessington South	a										10 49										11 19				
Worcester Park	d		10 18						10 33				10 48						11 03				11 18		
Stoneleigh	d		10 21						10 36				10 51						11 06				11 21		
Ewell West	d		10 24						10 39				10 54						11 09				11 24		
Epsom 3	a		10 27						10 46				10 57						11 16				11 27		
	d		10 28						10 47				10 58						11 17				11 28		
Ashtead	d		10 32						10 51				11 02						11 21				11 32		
Leatherhead	d		10 35						10 54				11 05						11 24				11 35		
Box Hill & Westhumble	d																								
Dorking 4	a		10 41										11 11										11 41		
New Malden 6	d			10 19				10 28		10 34				10 49				10 58		11 04				11 19	
Norbiton	d			10 22						10 37				10 52						11 07				11 22	
Kingston	a			10 25						10 40				10 55						11 10				11 25	
	d			10 29						10 40				10 59						11 10				11 29	
Hampton Wick	d			10 31						10 42				11 01						11 12				11 31	
Teddington	d			10 35						10 45				11 05						11 15				11 35	
Strawberry Hill	a			10 38										11 08										11 38	
Fulwell	d									10 49										11 19					
Hampton	d									10 53										11 23					
Kempton Park	d									10 56										11 26					
Sunbury	d									10 58										11 28					
Upper Halliford	d									11 00										11 30					
Shepperton	a									11 03										11 33					
Berrylands	d							10 30										11 00							
Surbiton 6	d	10a13				10 27		10 35				10a43				10 57		11 05				11a13			
Thames Ditton	d							10 39										11 09							
Hampton Court	a							10 42										11 12							
Hinchley Wood	d					10 31										11 01									
Claygate	d					10 34										11 04									
Oxshott	d					10 37										11 07									
Cobham & Stoke D'abernon	d					10 41										11 11									
Bookham	d								10 59										11 29						
Effingham Junction 6	d					10 45			11 03							11 15			11 33						
Horsley	d					10 48			11 06							11 18			11 36						
Clandon	d					10 53			11 11							11 23			11 41						
London Road (Guildford)	d					10 58			11 16							11 28			11 46						
Guildford	a					11 02			11 20							11 32			11 50						

Table 152

Saturdays until 6 October

London - Chessington South, Dorking, Guildford, Shepperton and Hampton Court

Network Diagram - see first Page of Table 152

		SW		SW	SW	SW	SW	SW	SW	SW		SW		SW	SW	SW	SW	SW	SW	SW		SW		SW	SW
London Waterloo ⊖	d	11 03		11 06	11 09	11 12	11 16	11 20	11 24	11 27		11 33		11 36	11 39	11 42	11 46	11 50	11 54	11 57		12 03		12 06	12 09
Vauxhall ⊖	d	11 07		11 10	11 13	11 16	11 20	11 24	11 28	11 31		11 37		11 40	11 43	11 46	11 50	11 54	11 58	12 01		12 07		12 10	12 13
Clapham Junction	d	11 12		11 15	11 18	11 21	11 25	11 29	11 33	11 36		11 42		11 45	11 48	11 51	11 55	11 59	12 03	12 06		12 12		12 15	12 18
Earlsfield	d	11 15		11 18	11 21	11 24	11 28	11 32	11 36	11 39		11 45		11 48	11 51	11 54	11 58	12 02	12 06	12 09		12 15		12 18	12 21
Wimbledon ⊖	d	11 19		11 22	11 25	11 28	11 32	11 36	11 40	11 43		11 49		11 52	11 55	11 58	12 02	12 06	12 10	12 13		12 19		12 22	12 25
Raynes Park	d			11 25	11 28	11 31	11 35		11 43	11 46				11 55	11 58	12 01	12 05		12 13	12 16				12 25	12 28
Motspur Park	d				11 31		11 38		11 46						12 01		12 08		12 16						12 31
Malden Manor	d						11 41										12 11								
Tolworth	d						11 44										12 14								
Chessington North	d						11 47										12 17								
Chessington South	a						11 49										12 19								
Worcester Park	d				11 33				11 48						12 03				12 18						12 33
Stoneleigh	d				11 36				11 51						12 06				12 21						12 36
Ewell West	d				11 39				11 54						12 09				12 24						12 39
Epsom	a				11 46				11 57						12 16				12 27						12 46
	d				11 47				11 58						12 17				12 28						12 47
Ashtead	d				11 51				12 02						12 21				12 32						12 51
Leatherhead	d				11 54				12 05						12 24				12 35						12 54
Box Hill & Westhumble	d																								
Dorking	a								12 11										12 41						
New Malden	d			11 28		11 34				11 49				11 58		12 04				12 19				12 28	
Norbiton	d					11 37				11 52						12 07				12 22					
Kingston	a					11 40				11 55						12 10				12 25					
	d					11 40				11 59						12 10				12 29					
Hampton Wick	d					11 42				12 01						12 12				12 31					
Teddington	d					11 45				12 05						12 15				12 35					
Strawberry Hill	a									12 08										12 38					
Fulwell	d					11 49										12 19									
Hampton	d					11 53										12 23									
Kempton Park	d					11 56										12 26									
Sunbury	d					11 58										12 28									
Upper Halliford	d					12 00										12 30									
Shepperton	a					12 03										12 33									
Berrylands	d			11 30										12 00										12 30	
Surbiton	d	11 27		11 35				11a43				11 57		12 05				12a13				12 27		12 35	
Thames Ditton	d			11 39										12 09										12 39	
Hampton Court	a			11 42										12 12										12 42	
Hinchley Wood	d	11 31										12 01										12 31			
Claygate	d	11 34										12 04										12 34			
Oxshott	d	11 37										12 07										12 37			
Cobham & Stoke D'abernon	d	11 41										12 11										12 41			
Bookham	d				11 59										12 29										12 59
Effingham Junction	d	11 45			12 03							12 15			12 33							12 45			13 03
Horsley	d	11 48			12 06							12 18			12 36							12 48			13 06
Clandon	d	11 53			12 11							12 23			12 41							12 53			13 11
London Road (Guildford)	d	11 58			12 16							12 28			12 46							12 58			13 16
Guildford	a	12 02			12 20							12 32			12 50							13 02			13 20

		SW	SW	SW	SW	SW		SW		SW	SW	SW	SW	SW	SW	SW		SW		SW	SW	SW	SW	SW	SW
London Waterloo ⊖	d	12 12	12 16	12 20	12 24	12 27		12 33		12 36	12 39	12 42	12 46	12 50	12 54	12 57		13 03		13 06	13 09	13 12	13 16	13 20	13 24
Vauxhall ⊖	d	12 16	12 20	12 24	12 28	12 31		12 37		12 40	12 43	12 46	12 50	12 54	12 58	13 01		13 07		13 10	13 13	13 16	13 20	13 24	13 28
Clapham Junction	d	12 21	12 25	12 29	12 33	12 36		12 42		12 45	12 48	12 51	12 55	12 59	13 03	13 06		13 12		13 15	13 18	13 21	13 25	13 29	13 33
Earlsfield	d	12 24	12 28	12 32	12 36	12 39		12 45		12 48	12 51	12 54	12 58	13 02	13 06	13 09		13 15		13 18	13 21	13 24	13 28	13 32	13 36
Wimbledon ⊖	d	12 28	12 32	12 36	12 40	12 43		12 49		12 52	12 55	12 58	13 02	13 06	13 10	13 13		13 19		13 22	13 25	13 28	13 32	13 36	13 40
Raynes Park	d	12 31	12 35		12 43	12 46				12 55	12 58	13 01	13 05		13 13	13 16				13 25	13 28	13 31	13 35		13 43
Motspur Park	d		12 38		12 46						13 01		13 08		13 16						13 31		13 38		13 46
Malden Manor	d		12 41										13 11										13 41		
Tolworth	d		12 44										13 14										13 44		
Chessington North	d		12 47										13 17										13 47		
Chessington South	a		12 49										13 19										13 49		
Worcester Park	d				12 48						13 03				13 18						13 33				13 48
Stoneleigh	d				12 51						13 06				13 21						13 36				13 51
Ewell West	d				12 54						13 09				13 24						13 39				13 54
Epsom	a				12 57						13 16				13 27						13 46				13 57
	d				12 58						13 17				13 28						13 47				13 58
Ashtead	d				13 02						13 21				13 32						13 51				14 02
Leatherhead	d				13 05						13 24				13 35						13 54				14 05
Box Hill & Westhumble	d																								
Dorking	a				13 11										13 41										14 11
New Malden	d	12 34				12 49				12 58		13 04				13 19				13 28		13 34			
Norbiton	d	12 37				12 52						13 07				13 22						13 37			
Kingston	a	12 40				12 55						13 10				13 25						13 40			
	d	12 40				12 59						13 10				13 29						13 40			
Hampton Wick	d	12 42				13 01						13 12				13 31						13 42			
Teddington	d	12 45				13 05						13 15				13 35						13 45			
Strawberry Hill	a					13 08										13 38									
Fulwell	d	12 49										13 19										13 49			
Hampton	d	12 53										13 23										13 53			
Kempton Park	d	12 56										13 26										13 56			
Sunbury	d	12 58										13 28										13 58			
Upper Halliford	d	13 00										13 30										14 00			
Shepperton	a	13 03										13 33										14 03			
Berrylands	d									13 00										13 30					
Surbiton	d			12a43				12 57		13 05				13a13				13 27		13 35				13a43	
Thames Ditton	d									13 09										13 39					
Hampton Court	a									13 12										13 42					
Hinchley Wood	d							13 01										13 31							
Claygate	d							13 04										13 34							
Oxshott	d							13 07										13 37							
Cobham & Stoke D'abernon	d							13 11										13 41							
Bookham	d										13 29										13 59				
Effingham Junction	d							13 15			13 33							13 45			14 03				
Horsley	d							13 18			13 36							13 48			14 06				
Clandon	d							13 23			13 41							13 53			14 11				
London Road (Guildford)	d							13 28			13 46							13 58			14 16				
Guildford	a							13 32			13 50							14 02			14 20				

Table 152

Saturdays until 6 October

London - Chessington South, Dorking, Guildford, Shepperton and Hampton Court

Network Diagram - see first Page of Table 152

		SW		SW		SW	SW	SW	SW	SW	SW	SW		SW		SW	SW	SW	SW	SW	SW	SW		SW	
London Waterloo ⊖	d	13 27		13 33		13 36	13 39	13 42	13 46	13 50	13 54	13 57		14 03		14 06	14 09	14 12	14 16	14 20	14 24	14 27		14 33	
Vauxhall ⊖	d	13 31		13 37		13 40	13 43	13 46	13 50	13 54	13 58	14 01		14 07		14 10	14 13	14 16	14 20	14 24	14 28	14 31		14 37	
Clapham Junction	d	13 36		13 42		13 45	13 48	13 51	13 55	13 59	14 03	14 06		14 12		14 15	14 18	14 21	14 25	14 29	14 33	14 36		14 42	
Earlsfield	d	13 39		13 45		13 48	13 51	13 54	13 58	14 02	14 06	14 09		14 15		14 18	14 21	14 24	14 28	14 32	14 36	14 39		14 45	
Wimbledon ⊖	d	13 43		13 49		13 52	13 55	13 58	14 02	14 06	14 10	14 13		14 19		14 22	14 25	14 28	14 32	14 36	14 40	14 43		14 49	
Raynes Park	d	13 46				13 55	13 58	14 01	14 05		14 13	14 16				14 25	14 28	14 31	14 35		14 43	14 46			
Motspur Park	d						14 01		14 08		14 16						14 31		14 38		14 46				
Malden Manor	d								14 11										14 41						
Tolworth	d								14 14										14 44						
Chessington North	d								14 17										14 47						
Chessington South	a								14 19										14 49						
Worcester Park	d						14 03				14 18						14 33				14 48				
Stoneleigh	d						14 06				14 21						14 36				14 51				
Ewell West	d						14 09				14 24						14 39				14 54				
Epsom	a						14 16				14 27						14 46				14 57				
	d						14 17				14 28						14 47				14 58				
Ashtead	d						14 21				14 32						14 51				15 02				
Leatherhead	d						14 24				14 35						14 54				15 05				
Box Hill & Westhumble	d																								
Dorking	a										14 41										15 11				
New Malden	d	13 49				13 58		14 04				14 19				14 28		14 34				14 49			
Norbiton	d	13 52						14 07				14 22						14 37				14 52			
Kingston	a	13 55						14 10				14 25						14 40				14 55			
	d	13 59						14 10				14 29						14 40				14 59			
Hampton Wick	d	14 01						14 12				14 31						14 42				15 01			
Teddington	d	14 05						14 15				14 35						14 45				15 05			
Strawberry Hill	a	14 08										14 38										15 08			
Fulwell	d							14 19										14 49							
Hampton	d							14 23										14 53							
Kempton Park	d							14 26										14 56							
Sunbury	d							14 28										14 58							
Upper Halliford	d							14 30										15 00							
Shepperton	a							14 33										15 03							
Berrylands	d					14 00										14 30									
Surbiton	d			13 57		14 05				14a13				14 27		14 35				14a43				14 57	
Thames Ditton	d					14 09										14 39									
Hampton Court	a					14 12										14 42									
Hinchley Wood	d			14 01										14 31										15 01	
Claygate	d			14 04										14 34										15 04	
Oxshott	d			14 07										14 37										15 07	
Cobham & Stoke D'abernon	d			14 11										14 41										15 11	
Bookham	d						14 29										14 59								
Effingham Junction	d			14 15			14 33							14 45			15 03							15 15	
Horsley	d			14 18			14 36							14 48			15 06							15 18	
Clandon	d			14 23			14 41							14 53			15 11							15 23	
London Road (Guildford)	d			14 28			14 46							14 58			15 16							15 28	
Guildford	a			14 32			14 50							15 02			15 20							15 32	

		SW	SW	SW	SW	SW	SW	SW		SW		SW	SW	SW	SW	SW	SW	SW		SW		SW	SW	SW	SW
London Waterloo ⊖	d	14 36	14 39	14 42	14 46	14 50	14 54	14 57		15 03		15 06	15 09	15 12	15 16	15 20	15 24	15 27		15 33		15 36	15 39	15 42	15 46
Vauxhall ⊖	d	14 40	14 43	14 46	14 50	14 54	14 58	15 01		15 07		15 10	15 13	15 16	15 20	15 24	15 28	15 31		15 37		15 40	15 43	15 46	15 50
Clapham Junction	d	14 45	14 48	14 51	14 55	14 59	15 03	15 06		15 12		15 15	15 18	15 21	15 25	15 29	15 33	15 36		15 42		15 45	15 48	15 51	15 55
Earlsfield	d	14 48	14 51	14 54	14 58	15 02	15 06	15 09		15 15		15 18	15 21	15 24	15 28	15 32	15 36	15 39		15 45		15 48	15 51	15 54	15 58
Wimbledon ⊖	d	14 52	14 55	14 58	15 02	15 06	15 10	15 13		15 19		15 22	15 25	15 28	15 32	15 36	15 40	15 43		15 49		15 52	15 55	15 58	16 02
Raynes Park	d	14 55	14 58	15 01	15 05		15 13	15 16				15 25	15 28	15 31	15 35		15 43	15 46				15 55	15 58	16 01	16 05
Motspur Park	d		15 01		15 08		15 16						15 31		15 38		15 46						16 01		16 08
Malden Manor	d				15 11										15 41										16 11
Tolworth	d				15 14										15 44										16 14
Chessington North	d				15 17										15 47										16 17
Chessington South	a				15 19										15 49										16 19
Worcester Park	d		15 03				15 18						15 33				15 48						16 03		
Stoneleigh	d		15 06				15 21						15 36				15 51						16 06		
Ewell West	d		15 09				15 24						15 39				15 54						16 09		
Epsom	a		15 16				15 27						15 46				15 57						16 16		
	d		15 17				15 28						15 47				15 58						16 17		
Ashtead	d		15 21				15 32						15 51				16 02						16 21		
Leatherhead	d		15 24				15 35						15 54				16 05						16 24		
Box Hill & Westhumble	d																								
Dorking	a						15 41										16 11								
New Malden	d	14 58		15 04				15 19				15 28		15 34				15 49				15 58		16 04	
Norbiton	d			15 07				15 22						15 37				15 52						16 07	
Kingston	a			15 10				15 25						15 40				15 55						16 10	
	d			15 10				15 29						15 40				15 59						16 10	
Hampton Wick	d			15 12				15 31						15 42				16 01						16 12	
Teddington	d			15 15				15 35						15 45				16 05						16 15	
Strawberry Hill	a							15 38										16 08							
Fulwell	d			15 19										15 49										16 19	
Hampton	d			15 23										15 53										16 23	
Kempton Park	d			15 26										15 56										16 26	
Sunbury	d			15 28										15 58										16 28	
Upper Halliford	d			15 30										16 00										16 30	
Shepperton	a			15 33										16 03										16 33	
Berrylands	d	15 00										15 30										16 00			
Surbiton	d	15 05				15a13				15 27		15 35				15a43				15 57		16 05			
Thames Ditton	d	15 09										15 39										16 09			
Hampton Court	a	15 12										15 42										16 12			
Hinchley Wood	d									15 31										16 01					
Claygate	d									15 34										16 04					
Oxshott	d									15 37										16 07					
Cobham & Stoke D'abernon	d									15 41										16 11					
Bookham	d		15 29										15 59										16 29		
Effingham Junction	d		15 33							15 45			16 03							16 15			16 33		
Horsley	d		15 36							15 48			16 06							16 18			16 36		
Clandon	d		15 41							15 53			16 11							16 23			16 41		
London Road (Guildford)	d		15 46							15 58			16 16							16 28			16 46		
Guildford	a		15 50							16 02			16 20							16 32			16 50		

London - Chessington South, Dorking, Guildford, Shepperton and Hampton Court

Network Diagram - see first Page of Table 152

Station		SW	SW	SW		SW		SW	SW	SW	SW	SW	SW	SW		SW		SW	SW	SW	SW	SW	SW	SW
London Waterloo 15 ⊖	d	15 50	15 54	15 57		16 03		16 06	16 09	16 12	16 16	16 20	16 24	16 27		16 33		16 36	16 39	16 42	16 46	16 50	16 54	16 57
Vauxhall ⊖	d	15 54	15 58	16 01		16 07		16 10	16 13	16 16	16 20	16 24	16 28	16 31		16 37		16 40	16 43	16 46	16 50	16 54	16 58	17 01
Clapham Junction 10	d	15 59	16 03	16 06		16 12		16 15	16 18	16 21	16 25	16 29	16 33	16 36		16 42		16 45	16 48	16 51	16 55	16 59	17 03	17 06
Earlsfield	d	16 02	16 06	16 09		16 15		16 18	16 21	16 24	16 28	16 32	16 36	16 39		16 45		16 48	16 51	16 54	16 58	17 02	17 06	17 09
Wimbledon 6 ⊖ ⇌	d	16 06	16 10	16 13		16 19		16 22	16 25	16 28	16 32	16 36	16 40	16 43		16 49		16 52	16 55	16 58	17 02	17 06	17 10	17 13
Raynes Park 6	d		16 13	16 16				16 25	16 28	16 31	16 35		16 43	16 46				16 55	16 58	17 01	17 05		17 13	17 16
Motspur Park	d		16 16						16 31		16 38		16 46						17 01		17 08		17 16	
Malden Manor	d										16 41										17 11			
Tolworth	d										16 44										17 14			
Chessington North	d										16 47										17 17			
Chessington South	a										16 49										17 19			
Worcester Park	d		16 18						16 33				16 48						17 03				17 18	
Stoneleigh	d		16 21						16 36				16 51						17 06				17 21	
Ewell West	d		16 24						16 39				16 54						17 09				17 24	
Epsom 3	a		16 27						16 46				16 57						17 16				17 27	
	d		16 28						16 47				16 58						17 17				17 28	
Ashtead	d		16 32						16 51				17 02						17 21				17 32	
Leatherhead	d		16 35						16 54				17 05						17 24				17 35	
Box Hill & Westhumble	d																							
Dorking 4	a		16 41										17 11										17 41	
New Malden 6	d			16 19				16 28		16 34				16 49				16 58		17 04				17 19
Norbiton	d			16 22						16 37				16 52						17 07				17 22
Kingston	a			16 25						16 40				16 55						17 10				17 25
	d			16 29						16 40				16 59						17 10				17 29
Hampton Wick	d			16 31						16 42				17 01						17 12				17 31
Teddington	d			16 35						16 45				17 05						17 15				17 35
Strawberry Hill	a			16 38										17 08										17 38
Fulwell	d									16 49										17 19				
Hampton	d									16 53										17 23				
Kempton Park	d									16 56										17 26				
Sunbury	d									16 58										17 28				
Upper Halliford	d									17 00										17 30				
Shepperton	a									17 03										17 33				
Berrylands	d							16 30										17 00						
Surbiton 6	d	16a13				16 27		16 35				16a43				16 57		17 05				17a13		
Thames Ditton	d							16 39										17 09						
Hampton Court	a							16 42										17 12						
Hinchley Wood	d					16 31										17 01								
Claygate	d					16 34										17 04								
Oxshott	d					16 37										17 07								
Cobham & Stoke D'abernon	d					16 41										17 11								
Bookham	d								16 59										17 29					
Effingham Junction 6	d					16 45			17 03							17 15			17 33					
Horsley	d					16 48			17 06							17 18			17 36					
Clandon	d					16 53			17 11							17 23			17 41					
London Road (Guildford)	d					16 58			17 16							17 28			17 46					
Guildford	a					17 02			17 20							17 32			17 50					

Station		SW		SW	SW	SW	SW	SW	SW	SW		SW		SW	SW	SW	SW	SW	SW	SW		SW		SW	SW
London Waterloo 15 ⊖	d	17 03		17 06	17 09	17 12	17 16	17 20	17 24	17 27		17 33		17 36	17 39	17 42	17 46	17 50	17 54	17 57		18 03		18 06	18 09
Vauxhall ⊖	d	17 07		17 10	17 13	17 16	17 20	17 24	17 28	17 31		17 37		17 40	17 43	17 46	17 50	17 54	17 58	18 01		18 07		18 10	18 13
Clapham Junction 10	d	17 12		17 15	17 18	17 21	17 25	17 29	17 33	17 36		17 42		17 45	17 48	17 51	17 55	17 59	18 03	18 06		18 12		18 15	18 18
Earlsfield	d	17 15		17 18	17 21	17 24	17 28	17 32	17 36	17 39		17 45		17 48	17 51	17 54	17 58	18 02	18 06	18 09		18 15		18 18	18 21
Wimbledon 6 ⊖ ⇌	d	17 19		17 22	17 25	17 28	17 32	17 36	17 40	17 43		17 49		17 52	17 55	17 58	18 02	18 06	18 10	18 13		18 19		18 22	18 25
Raynes Park 6	d			17 25	17 28	17 31	17 35		17 43	17 46				17 55	17 58	18 01	18 05		18 13	18 16				18 25	18 28
Motspur Park	d				17 31		17 38		17 46						18 01		18 08		18 16						18 31
Malden Manor	d						17 41										18 11								
Tolworth	d						17 44										18 14								
Chessington North	d						17 47										18 17								
Chessington South	a						17 49										18 19								
Worcester Park	d				17 33				17 48						18 03				18 18						18 33
Stoneleigh	d				17 36				17 51						18 06				18 21						18 36
Ewell West	d				17 39				17 54						18 09				18 24						18 39
Epsom 3	a				17 46				17 57						18 16				18 27						18 46
	d				17 47				17 58						18 17				18 28						18 47
Ashtead	d				17 51				18 02						18 21				18 32						18 51
Leatherhead	d				17 54				18 05						18 24				18 35						18 54
Box Hill & Westhumble	d																								
Dorking 4	a								18 11										18 41						
New Malden 6	d			17 28		17 34				17 49				17 58		18 04				18 19				18 28	
Norbiton	d					17 37				17 52						18 07				18 22					
Kingston	a					17 40				17 55						18 10				18 25					
	d					17 40				17 59						18 10				18 29					
Hampton Wick	d					17 42				18 01						18 12				18 31					
Teddington	d					17 45				18 05						18 15				18 35					
Strawberry Hill	a									18 08										18 38					
Fulwell	d					17 49										18 19									
Hampton	d					17 53										18 23									
Kempton Park	d					17 56										18 26									
Sunbury	d					17 58										18 28									
Upper Halliford	d					18 00										18 30									
Shepperton	a					18 03										18 33									
Berrylands	d			17 30										18 00										18 30	
Surbiton 6	d	17 27		17 35				17a43				17 57		18 05				18a13				18 27		18 35	
Thames Ditton	d			17 39										18 09										18 39	
Hampton Court	a			17 42										18 12										18 42	
Hinchley Wood	d	17 31										18 01										18 31			
Claygate	d	17 34										18 04										18 34			
Oxshott	d	17 37										18 07										18 37			
Cobham & Stoke D'abernon	d	17 41										18 11										18 41			
Bookham	d				17 59										18 29										18 59
Effingham Junction 6	d	17 45			18 03							18 15			18 33							18 45			19 03
Horsley	d	17 48			18 06							18 18			18 36							18 48			19 06
Clandon	d	17 53			18 11							18 23			18 41							18 53			19 11
London Road (Guildford)	d	17 58			18 16							18 28			18 46							18 58			19 16
Guildford	a	18 02			18 20							18 32			18 50							19 02			19 20

London - Chessington South, Dorking, Guildford, Shepperton and Hampton Court

Network Diagram - see first Page of Table 152

Station		SW	SW	SW	SW	SW		SW		SW	SW	SW	SW	SW	SW	SW		SW		SW	SW	SW	SW	SW	SW
London Waterloo 15 ⊖	d	18 12	18 16	18 20	18 24	18 27		18 33		18 36	18 39	18 42	18 46	18 50	18 54	18 57		19 03		19 06	19 09	19 12	19 16	19 20	19 24
Vauxhall ⊖	d	18 16	18 20	18 24	18 28	18 31		18 37		18 40	18 43	18 46	18 50	18 54	18 58	19 01		19 07		19 10	19 13	19 16	19 20	19 24	19 28
Clapham Junction 10	d	18 21	18 25	18 29	18 33	18 36		18 42		18 45	18 48	18 51	18 55	18 59	19 03	19 06		19 12		19 15	19 18	19 21	19 25	19 29	19 33
Earlsfield	d	18 24	18 28	18 32	18 36	18 39		18 45		18 48	18 51	18 54	18 58	19 02	19 06	19 09		19 15		19 18	19 21	19 24	19 28	19 32	19 36
Wimbledon 6 ⊖ ⇌	d	18 28	18 32	18 36	18 40	18 43		18 49		18 52	18 55	18 58	19 02	19 06	19 10	19 13		19 19		19 22	19 25	19 28	19 32	19 36	19 40
Raynes Park 6	d	18 31	18 35		18 43	18 46				18 55	18 58	19 01	19 05		19 13	19 16				19 25	19 28	19 31	19 35		19 43
Motspur Park	d		18 38		18 46						19 01		19 08		19 16						19 31		19 38		19 46
Malden Manor	d		18 41										19 11										19 41		
Tolworth	d		18 44										19 14										19 44		
Chessington North	d		18 47										19 17										19 47		
Chessington South	a		18 49										19 19										19 49		
Worcester Park	d				18 48						19 03				19 18						19 33				19 48
Stoneleigh	d				18 51						19 06				19 21						19 36				19 51
Ewell West	d				18 54						19 09				19 24						19 39				19 54
Epsom 3	a				18 57						19 16				19 27						19 46				19 57
	d				18 58						19 17				19 28						19 47				19 58
Ashtead	d				19 02						19 21				19 32						19 51				20 02
Leatherhead	d				19 05						19 24				19 35						19 54				20 05
Box Hill & Westhumble	d																								
Dorking 4	a				19 11										19 41										20 11
New Malden 6	d	18 34				18 49				18 58		19 04				19 19				19 28		19 34			
Norbiton	d	18 37				18 52						19 07				19 22						19 37			
Kingston	a	18 40				18 55						19 10				19 25						19 40			
	d	18 40				18 59						19 10				19 29						19 40			
Hampton Wick	d	18 42				19 01						19 12				19 31						19 42			
Teddington	d	18 45				19 05						19 15				19 35						19 45			
Strawberry Hill	a					19 08										19 38									
Fulwell	d	18 49										19 19										19 49			
Hampton	d	18 53										19 23										19 53			
Kempton Park	d	18 56										19 26										19 56			
Sunbury	d	18 58										19 28										19 58			
Upper Halliford	d	19 00										19 30										20 00			
Shepperton	a	19 03										19 33										20 03			
Berrylands	d									19 00										19 30					
Surbiton 6	d			18a43				18 57		19 05				19a13				19 27		19 35				19a43	
Thames Ditton	d									19 09										19 39					
Hampton Court	a									19 12										19 42					
Hinchley Wood	d							19 01										19 31							
Claygate	d							19 04										19 34							
Oxshott	d							19 07										19 37							
Cobham & Stoke D'abernon	d							19 11										19 41							
Bookham	d										19 29										19 59				
Effingham Junction 6	d							19 15			19 33							19 45			20 03				
Horsley	d							19 18			19 36							19 48			20 06				
Clandon	d							19 23			19 41							19 53			20 11				
London Road (Guildford)	d							19 28			19 46							19 58			20 16				
Guildford	a							19 32			19 50							20 02			20 20				

Station		SW		SW		SW	SW	SW	SW	SW	SW	SW		SW		SW	SW	SW	SW	SW	SW	SW		SW
London Waterloo 15 ⊖	d	19 27		19 33		19 36	19 39	19 42	19 46	19 50	19 54	19 57		20 03		20 06	20 09	20 12	20 16	20 20	20 24	20 27		20 33
Vauxhall ⊖	d	19 31		19 37		19 40	19 43	19 46	19 50	19 54	19 58	20 01		20 07		20 10	20 13	20 16	20 20	20 24	20 28	20 31		20 37
Clapham Junction 10	d	19 36		19 42		19 45	19 48	19 51	19 55	19 59	20 03	20 06		20 12		20 15	20 18	20 21	20 25	20 29	20 33	20 36		20 42
Earlsfield	d	19 39		19 45		19 48	19 51	19 54	19 58	20 02	20 06	20 09		20 15		20 18	20 21	20 24	20 28	20 32	20 36	20 39		20 45
Wimbledon 6 ⊖ ⇌	d	19 43		19 49		19 52	19 55	19 58	20 02	20 06	20 10	20 13		20 19		20 22	20 25	20 28	20 32	20 36	20 40	20 43		20 49
Raynes Park 6	d	19 46				19 55	19 58	20 01	20 05		20 13	20 16				20 25	20 28	20 31	20 35		20 43	20 46		
Motspur Park	d						20 01		20 08		20 16						20 31		20 38		20 46			
Malden Manor	d								20 11										20 41					
Tolworth	d								20 14										20 44					
Chessington North	d								20 17										20 47					
Chessington South	a								20 19										20 49					
Worcester Park	d						20 03				20 18						20 33				20 48			
Stoneleigh	d						20 06				20 21						20 36				20 51			
Ewell West	d						20 09				20 24						20 39				20 54			
Epsom 3	a						20 16				20 27						20 46				20 57			
	d						20 17										20 47							
Ashtead	d						20 21										20 51							
Leatherhead	d						20 24										20 54							
Box Hill & Westhumble	d																							
Dorking 4	a																21 00							
New Malden 6	d	19 49				19 58		20 04				20 19				20 28		20 34				20 49		
Norbiton	d	19 52						20 07				20 22						20 37				20 52		
Kingston	a	19 55						20 10				20 25						20 40				20 55		
	d	19 59						20 10				20 29						20 40				20 59		
Hampton Wick	d	20 01						20 12				20 31						20 42				21 01		
Teddington	d	20 05						20 15				20 35						20 45				21 05		
Strawberry Hill	a	20 08										20 38										21 08		
Fulwell	d							20 19										20 49						
Hampton	d							20 23										20 53						
Kempton Park	d							20 26										20 56						
Sunbury	d							20 28										20 58						
Upper Halliford	d							20 30										21 00						
Shepperton	a							20 33										21 03						
Berrylands	d					20 00										20 30								
Surbiton 6	d			19 57		20 05				20a13				20 27		20 35				20a43				20 57
Thames Ditton	d					20 09										20 39								
Hampton Court	a					20 12										20 42								
Hinchley Wood	d			20 01										20 31										21 01
Claygate	d			20 04										20 34										21 04
Oxshott	d			20 07										20 37										21 07
Cobham & Stoke D'abernon	d			20 11										20 41										21 11
Bookham	d						20 29																	
Effingham Junction 6	d			20 15			20 33							20 45										21 15
Horsley	d			20 18			20 36							20 48										21 18
Clandon	d			20 23			20 41							20 53										21 23
London Road (Guildford)	d			20 28			20 46							20 58										21 28
Guildford	a			20 32			20 50							21 02										21 32

London - Chessington South, Dorking, Guildford, Shepperton and Hampton Court

Network Diagram - see first Page of Table 152

		SW	SW	SW	SW	SW	SW	SW		SW		SW	SW	SW	SW	SW	SW			SW	SW	SW	SW	SW	SW
London Waterloo 15 ⊖	d	20 36	20 39	20 42	20 46	20 50	20 54	20 57		21 03		21 09	21 12	21 20	21 24	21 27	21 33			21 36	21 39	21 42	21 46	21 50	21 54
Vauxhall ⊖	d	20 40	20 43	20 46	20 50	20 54	20 58	21 01		21 07		21 13	21 16	21 24	21 28	21 31	21 37			21 40	21 43	21 46	21 50	21 54	21 58
Clapham Junction 10	d	20 45	20 48	20 51	20 55	20 59	21 03	21 06		21 12		21 18	21 21	21 29	21 33	21 36	21 42			21 45	21 48	21 51	21 55	21 59	22 03
Earlsfield	d	20 48	20 51	20 54	20 58	21 02	21 06	21 09		21 15		21 21	21 24	21 32	21 36	21 39	21 45			21 48	21 51	21 54	21 58	22 02	22 06
Wimbledon 6 ⊖	d	20 52	20 55	20 58	21 02	21 06	21 10	21 13		21 19		21 25	21 28	21 36	21 40	21 43	21 49			21 52	21 55	21 58	22 02	22 06	22 10
Raynes Park 6	d	20 55	20 58	21 01	21 05		21 13	21 16				21 28	21 31		21 43	21 46				21 55	21 58	22 01	22 05		22 13
Motspur Park	d		21 01		21 08		21 16					21 31			21 46						22 01		22 08		22 16
Malden Manor	d				21 11																		22 11		
Tolworth	d				21 14																		22 14		
Chessington North	d				21 17																		22 17		
Chessington South	a				21 19																		22 19		
Worcester Park	d		21 03				21 18					21 33			21 48						22 03				22 18
Stoneleigh	d		21 06				21 21					21 36			21 51						22 06				22 21
Ewell West	d		21 09				21 24					21 39			21 54						22 09				22 24
Epsom 3	a		21 16				21 27					21 46			21 57						22 16				22 27
	d		21 17									21 47									22 17				
Ashtead	d		21 21									21 51									22 21				
Leatherhead	d		21 24									21 54									22 24				
Box Hill & Westhumble	d																								
Dorking 4	a											22 00													
New Malden 6	d	20 58		21 04				21 19					21 34			21 49				21 58		22 04			
Norbiton	d			21 07				21 22					21 37			21 52						22 07			
Kingston	a			21 10				21 25					21 40			21 55						22 10			
	d			21 10				21 29					21 40			21 59						22 10			
Hampton Wick	d			21 12				21 31					21 42			22 01						22 12			
Teddington	d			21 15				21 35					21 45			22 05						22 15			
Strawberry Hill	a							21 38								22 08									
Fulwell	d			21 19									21 49									22 19			
Hampton	d			21 23									21 53									22 23			
Kempton Park	d			21 26									21 56									22 26			
Sunbury	d			21 28									21 58									22 28			
Upper Halliford	d			21 30									22 00									22 30			
Shepperton	a			21 33									22 03									22 33			
Berrylands	d	21 00																		22 00					
Surbiton 6	d	21 05				21a13				21 27				21a43			21 57			22 05				22 14	
Thames Ditton	d	21 09																		22 09					
Hampton Court	a	21 12																		22 12					
Hinchley Wood	d									21 31							22 01								
Claygate	d									21 34							22 04								
Oxshott	d									21 37							22 07								
Cobham & Stoke D'abernon	d									21 41							22 11								
Bookham	d		21 29																		22 29				
Effingham Junction 6	d		21 33							21 45							22 15				22 33				
Horsley	d		21 36							21 48							22 18				22 36				
Clandon	d		21 41							21 53							22 23				22 41				
London Road (Guildford)	d		21 46							21 58							22 28				22 46				
Guildford	a		21 50							22 02							22 32				22 50			22 47	

		SW	SW			SW	SW	SW	SW	SW		SW	SW	SW		SW	SW	SW	SW		SW	SW	SW	SW	
London Waterloo 15 ⊖	d	21 57	22 03			22 09	22 12	22 20	22 27	22 33		22 36	22 39	22 42		22 50	22 57	23 00	23 03		23 09	23 12	23 20	23 27	
Vauxhall ⊖	d	22 01	22 07			22 13	22 16	22 24	22 31	22 37		22 40	22 43	22 46		22 54	23 01	23 04	23 07		23 13	23 16	23 24	23 31	
Clapham Junction 10	d	22 06	22 12			22 18	22 21	22 29	22 36	22 42		22 45	22 48	22 51		22 59	23 06	23 09	23 12		23 18	23 21	23 29	23 36	
Earlsfield	d	22 09	22 15			22 21	22 24	22 32	22 39	22 45		22 48	22 51	22 54		23 02	23 09	23 12	23 15		23 21	23 24	23 32	23 39	
Wimbledon 6 ⊖	d	22 13	22 19			22 25	22 28	22 36	22 43	22 49		22 52	22 55	22 58		23 06	23 13	23 16	23 19		23 25	23 28	23 36	23 43	
Raynes Park 6	d	22 16				22 28	22 31		22 46			22 55	22 58	23 01			23 16	23 19			23 28	23 31		23 46	
Motspur Park	d					22 31							23 01					23 22			23 31				
Malden Manor	d																	23 25							
Tolworth	d																	23 28							
Chessington North	d																	23 31							
Chessington South	a																	23 33							
Worcester Park	d					22 33							23 03								23 33				
Stoneleigh	d					22 36							23 06								23 36				
Ewell West	d					22 39							23 09								23 39				
Epsom 3	a					22 46							23 12								23 42				
	d					22 47							23 17								23 47				
Ashtead	d					22 51							23 21								23 51				
Leatherhead	d					22 54							23 24								23 54				
Box Hill & Westhumble	d																								
Dorking 4	a					23 00															00 01				
New Malden 6	d	22 19					22 34		22 49			22 58		23 04			23 19					23 34		23 49	
Norbiton	d	22 22					22 37		22 52					23 07			23 22					23 37		23 52	
Kingston	a	22 25					22 40		22 55					23 10			23 25					23 40		23 55	
	d	22 29					22 40		22 59					23 10			23 29					23 40		23 55	
Hampton Wick	d	22 31					22 42		23 01					23 12			23 31					23 42		23 57	
Teddington	d	22 35					22 45		23 05					23 15			23 35					23 45		23 59	
Strawberry Hill	a	22 38							23 08								23 38							00 03	
Fulwell	d						22 49							23 19								23 49			
Hampton	d						22 53							23 23								23 53			
Kempton Park	d						22 56							23 26								23 56			
Sunbury	d						22 58							23 28								23 58			
Upper Halliford	d						23 00							23 30								23 59			
Shepperton	a						23 03							23 33								00 03			
Berrylands	d											23 00													
Surbiton 6	d		22 27					22a43		22 57		23 05				23a13			23 27				23a43		
Thames Ditton	d											23 09													
Hampton Court	a											23 12													
Hinchley Wood	d		22 31							23 01									23 31						
Claygate	d		22 34							23 04									23 34						
Oxshott	d		22 37							23 07									23 37						
Cobham & Stoke D'abernon	d		22 41							23 11									23 41						
Bookham	d												23 29												
Effingham Junction 6	d		22 45							23 15			23 33						23 45						
Horsley	d		22 48							23 18			23 36						23 48						
Clandon	d		22 53							23 23			23 41						23 53						
London Road (Guildford)	d		22 58							23 28			23 46						23 58						
Guildford	a		23 02							23 32			23 50						00 02						

Table 152

Saturdays
until 6 October

London - Chessington South, Dorking, Guildford, Shepperton and Hampton Court

Network Diagram - see first Page of Table 152

			SW	SW	SW	SW
London Waterloo 15 ⊖	d		23 36	23 42	23 50	23 57
Vauxhall ⊖	d		23 40	23 46	23 54	00 01
Clapham Junction 10	d		23 45	23 51	23 59	00 06
Earlsfield	d		23 48	23 54	00 02	00 09
Wimbledon 6 ⊖	d		23 52	23 58	00 06	00 13
Raynes Park 6	d		23 55	00 01		00 16
Motspur Park	d			00 04		
Malden Manor	d					
Tolworth	d					
Chessington North	d					
Chessington South	a					
Worcester Park	d			00 06		
Stoneleigh	d			00 09		
Ewell West	d			00 12		
Epsom 3	a			00 15		
	d			00 19		
Ashtead	d			00 23		
Leatherhead	d			00 26		
Box Hill & Westhumble	d					
Dorking 4	a					
New Malden 6	d		23 58			00 19
Norbiton	d					00 22
Kingston	a					00 25
	d					00 25
Hampton Wick	d					00 27
Teddington	d					00 30
Strawberry Hill	a					
Fulwell	d					00 34
Hampton	d					00 38
Kempton Park	d					00 41
Sunbury	d					00 43
Upper Halliford	d					00 45
Shepperton	a					00 48
Berrylands	d		23 59			
Surbiton 6	d		00 05		00 14	
Thames Ditton	d		00 09			
Hampton Court	a		00 12			
Hinchley Wood	d				00 18	
Claygate	d				00 20	
Oxshott	d				00 24	
Cobham & Stoke D'abernon	d				00 27	
Bookham	d			00 31		
Effingham Junction 6	d			00 36	00 32	
Horsley	d			00 39	00 34	
Clandon	d			00 44	00 39	
London Road (Guildford)	d			00 49	00 44	
Guildford	a			00 53	00 48	

Table 152

Saturdays from 13 October

London - Chessington South, Dorking, Guildford, Shepperton and Hampton Court

Network Diagram - see first Page of Table 152

		SW	SW	SW		SW	SW	SW	SW	SW		SW		SW	SW	SW [1]	SW	SW [1]		SW		SW	SW		SW
London Waterloo 15 ⊖	d	23p03	23p12	23p27		23p36	23p42	23p50	23p57	00 09		00 15		00 27	00 42	05 00	05 12	05 20		05 50					06 06
Vauxhall ⊖	d	23p07	23p16	23p31		23p40	23p46	23p54	00 01	00 13		00 19		00 31	00 46	05 04	05 16	05 24		05 54					06 10
Clapham Junction 10	d	23p12	23p21	23p36		23p45	23p51	23p59	00 06	00 20		00 25		00 37	00 51	05 11	05 21	05 29		05 59					06 15
Earlsfield	d	23p15	23p24	23p39		23p48	23p54	00 02	00 09	00 23		00 29		00s41		05 14	05 24	05 32		06 02					06 18
Wimbledon 6 ⊖	d	23p19	23p28	23p43		23p52	23p58	00 06	00 13	00 27		00 33		00 45	01 05	05 18	05 28	05 36		06 06			06 13		06 22
Raynes Park 6	d		23p31	23p46		23p55	00 01		00 16			00 36		00 48	01 08		05 31						06 16		06 25
Motspur Park	d						00 04					00 38													
Malden Manor	d																								
Tolworth	d																								
Chessington North	d																								
Chessington South	a																								
Worcester Park	d						00 06					00 41													
Stoneleigh	d						00 09					00 44													
Ewell West	d						00 12					00 46													
Epsom 3	a						00 15					00 50													
	d						00 19																		
Ashtead	d						00 23																		
Leatherhead	d						00 26																		
Box Hill & Westhumble	d																								
Dorking 4	a																								
New Malden 6	d		23p34	23p49		23p58			00 19					00 50	01 11		05 34						06 19		06 28
Norbiton	d		23p37	23p52					00 22						01 14		05 37						06 22		
Kingston	a		23p40	23p55					00 25						01 17		05 40						06 25		
	d		23p40	23p55					00 25						01 17		05 40					05 59	06 29		
Hampton Wick	d		23p42	23p57					00 27						01s19		05 42					06 01	06 31		
Teddington	d		23p45	23p59					00 30						01s22		05 45					06 05	06 35		
Strawberry Hill	a			00 03											01 28							06 08	06 38		
Fulwell	d		23p49						00 34								05 49								
Hampton	d		23p53						00 38								05 53								
Kempton Park	d		23p56						00 41								05 56								
Sunbury	d		23p58						00 43								05 58								
Upper Halliford	d		23p59						00 45								06 00								
Shepperton	a		00 05						00 50								06 05								
Berrylands	d					23p59								00s53											06 30
Surbiton 6	d	23p27				00 05		00 14		00 35				00a56		05 26		05 44		06a13					06 35
Thames Ditton	d					00 09																			06 39
Hampton Court	a					00 12																			06 42
Hinchley Wood	d	23p31						00 18																	
Claygate	d	23p34						00 20																	
Oxshott	d	23p37						00 24																	
Cobham & Stoke D'abernon	d	23p41						00 27																	
Bookham	d						00 31																		
Effingham Junction 6	d	23p45					00 36	00 32																	
Horsley	d	23p48					00 39	00 34																	
Clandon	d	23p53					00 44	00 39																	
London Road (Guildford)	d	23p58					00 49	00 44																	
Guildford	a	00 05					00 56	00 51		01 07						06 00		06 23							

Table 152

Saturdays from 13 October

London - Chessington South, Dorking, Guildford, Shepperton and Hampton Court

Network Diagram - see first Page of Table 152

		SW	SW	SW	SW	SW			SW	SW	SW	SW	SW	SW	SW			SW	SW	SW	SW	SW	SW	SW	SW
London Waterloo 15 ⊖	d	06 12	06 16	06 20	06 27	06 33			06 36	06 39	06 42	06 46	06 50	06 57	07 03			07 06	07 09	07 12	07 16	07 20	07 24	07 27	07 33
Vauxhall ⊖	d	06 16	06 20	06 24	06 31	06 37			06 40	06 43	06 46	06 50	06 54	07 01	07 07			07 10	07 13	07 16	07 20	07 24	07 28	07 31	07 37
Clapham Junction 10	d	06 21	06 25	06 29	06 36	06 42			06 45	06 48	06 51	06 55	06 59	07 06	07 12			07 15	07 18	07 21	07 25	07 29	07 33	07 36	07 42
Earlsfield	d	06 24	06 28	06 32	06 39	06 45			06 48	06 51	06 54	06 58	07 02	07 09	07 15			07 18	07 21	07 24	07 28	07 32	07 36	07 39	07 45
Wimbledon 6 ⊖	d	06 28	06 32	06 36	06 43	06 49			06 52	06 55	06 58	07 02	07 06	07 13	07 19			07 22	07 25	07 28	07 32	07 36	07 40	07 43	07 49
Raynes Park 6	d	06 31	06 35		06 46				06 55	06 58	07 01	07 05		07 16				07 25	07 28	07 31	07 35		07 43	07 46	
Motspur Park	d		06 38							07 01		07 08							07 31		07 38		07 46		
Malden Manor	d		06 41									07 11									07 41				
Tolworth	d		06 44									07 14									07 44				
Chessington North	d		06 47									07 17									07 47				
Chessington South	a		06 49									07 19									07 49				
Worcester Park	d									07 03									07 33				07 48		
Stoneleigh	d									07 06									07 36				07 51		
Ewell West	d									07 09									07 39				07 54		
Epsom 3	a									07 16									07 46				07 57		
	d									07 17									07 47				07 58		
Ashtead	d									07 21									07 51				08 02		
Leatherhead	d									07 24									07 54				08 05		
Box Hill & Westhumble	d																								
Dorking 4	a																						08 13		
New Malden 6	d	06 34			06 49				06 58		07 04			07 19				07 28		07 34				07 49	
Norbiton	d	06 37			06 52						07 07			07 22						07 37				07 52	
Kingston	a	06 40			06 55						07 10			07 25						07 40				07 55	
	d	06 40			06 59						07 10			07 29						07 40				07 59	
Hampton Wick	d	06 42			07 01						07 12			07 31						07 42				08 01	
Teddington	d	06 45			07 05						07 15			07 35						07 45				08 05	
Strawberry Hill	a				07 08									07 38										08 08	
Fulwell	d	06 49									07 19									07 49					
Hampton	d	06 53									07 23									07 53					
Kempton Park	d	06 56									07 26									07 56					
Sunbury	d	06 58									07 28									07 58					
Upper Halliford	d	07 00									07 30									08 00					
Shepperton	a	07 05									07 35									08 05					
Berrylands	d								07 00									07 30							
Surbiton 6	d			06a43		06 57			07 05				07a13		07 27			07 35				07a43			07 57
Thames Ditton	d								07 09									07 39							
Hampton Court	a								07 12									07 42							
Hinchley Wood	d					07 01									07 31										08 01
Claygate	d					07 04									07 34										08 04
Oxshott	d					07 07									07 37										08 07
Cobham & Stoke D'abernon	d					07 11									07 41										08 11
Bookham	d									07 29									07 59						
Effingham Junction 6	d					07 15				07 33					07 45				08 03						08 15
Horsley	d					07 18				07 36					07 48				08 06						08 18
Clandon	d					07 23				07 41					07 53				08 11						08 23
London Road (Guildford)	d					07 28				07 46					07 58				08 16						08 28
Guildford	a					07 35				07 53					08 05				08 23						08 35

				SW	SW	SW	SW	SW	SW	SW	SW			SW	SW	SW	SW	SW	SW	SW	SW			SW	SW
London Waterloo 15 ⊖	d			07 36	07 39	07 42	07 46	07 50	07 54	07 57	08 03			08 06	08 09	08 12	08 16	08 20	08 24	08 27	08 33			08 36	08 39
Vauxhall ⊖	d			07 40	07 43	07 46	07 50	07 54	07 58	08 01	08 07			08 10	08 13	08 16	08 20	08 24	08 28	08 31	08 37			08 40	08 43
Clapham Junction 10	d			07 45	07 48	07 51	07 55	07 59	08 03	08 06	08 12			08 15	08 18	08 21	08 25	08 29	08 33	08 36	08 42			08 45	08 48
Earlsfield	d			07 48	07 51	07 54	07 58	08 02	08 06	08 09	08 15			08 18	08 21	08 24	08 28	08 32	08 36	08 39	08 45			08 48	08 51
Wimbledon 6 ⊖	d			07 52	07 55	07 58	08 02	08 06	08 10	08 13	08 19			08 22	08 25	08 28	08 32	08 36	08 40	08 43	08 49			08 52	08 55
Raynes Park 6	d			07 55	07 58	08 01	08 05		08 13	08 16				08 25	08 28	08 31	08 35		08 43	08 46				08 55	08 58
Motspur Park	d				08 01		08 08		08 16						08 31		08 38		08 46						09 01
Malden Manor	d						08 11										08 41								
Tolworth	d						08 14										08 44								
Chessington North	d						08 17										08 47								
Chessington South	a						08 19										08 49								
Worcester Park	d				08 03				08 18						08 33				08 48						09 03
Stoneleigh	d				08 06				08 21						08 36				08 51						09 06
Ewell West	d				08 09				08 24						08 39				08 54						09 09
Epsom 3	a				08 16				08 27						08 46				08 57						09 16
	d				08 17				08 28						08 47				08 58						09 17
Ashtead	d				08 21				08 32						08 51				09 02						09 21
Leatherhead	d				08 24				08 35						08 54				09 05						09 24
Box Hill & Westhumble	d																								
Dorking 4	a								08 43										09 13						
New Malden 6	d			07 58		08 04				08 19				08 28		08 34				08 49				08 58	
Norbiton	d					08 07				08 22						08 37				08 52					
Kingston	a					08 10				08 25						08 40				08 55					
	d					08 10				08 29						08 40				08 59					
Hampton Wick	d					08 12				08 31						08 42				09 01					
Teddington	d					08 15				08 35						08 45				09 05					
Strawberry Hill	a									08 38										09 08					
Fulwell	d					08 19										08 49									
Hampton	d					08 23										08 53									
Kempton Park	d					08 26										08 56									
Sunbury	d					08 28										08 58									
Upper Halliford	d					08 30										09 00									
Shepperton	a					08 35										09 05									
Berrylands	d			08 00										08 30										09 00	
Surbiton 6	d			08 05				08a13			08 27			08 35				08a43			08 57			09 05	
Thames Ditton	d			08 09										08 39										09 09	
Hampton Court	a			08 12										08 42										09 12	
Hinchley Wood	d										08 31										09 01				
Claygate	d										08 34										09 04				
Oxshott	d										08 37										09 07				
Cobham & Stoke D'abernon	d										08 41										09 11				
Bookham	d				08 29										08 59										09 29
Effingham Junction 6	d				08 33						08 45				09 03						09 15				09 33
Horsley	d				08 36						08 48				09 06						09 18				09 36
Clandon	d				08 41						08 53				09 11						09 23				09 41
London Road (Guildford)	d				08 46						08 58				09 16						09 28				09 46
Guildford	a				08 53						09 05				09 23						09 35				09 53

Saturdays
from 13 October

London - Chessington South, Dorking, Guildford, Shepperton and Hampton Court

Network Diagram - see first Page of Table 152

		SW	SW	SW	SW	SW	SW	SW	SW	SW	SW	SW	SW	SW	SW	SW	SW	SW	SW	SW	SW
London Waterloo 15 ⊖	d	08 42	08 46	08 50	08 54	08 57	09 03	09 06	09 09	09 12	09 16	09 20	09 24	09 27	09 33	09 36	09 39	09 42	09 46	09 50	09 54
Vauxhall ⊖	d	08 46	08 50	08 54	08 58	09 01	09 07	09 10	09 13	09 16	09 20	09 24	09 28	09 31	09 37	09 40	09 43	09 46	09 50	09 54	09 58
Clapham Junction 10	d	08 51	08 55	08 59	09 03	09 06	09 12	09 15	09 18	09 21	09 25	09 29	09 33	09 36	09 42	09 45	09 48	09 51	09 55	09 59	10 03
Earlsfield	d	08 54	08 58	09 02	09 06	09 09	09 15	09 18	09 21	09 24	09 28	09 32	09 36	09 39	09 45	09 48	09 51	09 54	09 58	10 02	10 06
Wimbledon 6 ⊖	d	08 58	09 02	09 06	09 10	09 13	09 19	09 22	09 25	09 28	09 32	09 36	09 40	09 43	09 49	09 52	09 55	09 58	10 02	10 06	10 10
Raynes Park 6	d	09 01	09 05		09 13	09 16		09 25	09 28	09 31	09 35		09 43	09 46		09 55	09 58	10 01	10 05		10 13
Motspur Park	d		09 08		09 16				09 31		09 38		09 46				10 01		10 08		10 16
Malden Manor	d		09 11								09 41								10 11		
Tolworth	d		09 14								09 44								10 14		
Chessington North	d		09 17								09 47								10 17		
Chessington South	a		09 19								09 49								10 19		
Worcester Park	d				09 18				09 33				09 48				10 03				10 18
Stoneleigh	d				09 21				09 36				09 51				10 06				10 21
Ewell West	d				09 24				09 39				09 54				10 09				10 24
Epsom 3	a				09 27				09 46				09 57				10 16				10 27
	d				09 28				09 47				09 58				10 17				10 28
Ashtead	d				09 32				09 51				10 02				10 21				10 32
Leatherhead	d				09 35				09 54				10 05				10 24				10 35
Box Hill & Westhumble	d																				
Dorking 4	a				09 43								10 13								10 43
New Malden 6	d	09 04				09 19		09 28		09 34				09 49		09 58		10 04			
Norbiton	d	09 07				09 22				09 37				09 52				10 07			
Kingston	a	09 10				09 25				09 40				09 55				10 10			
	d	09 10				09 29				09 40				09 59				10 10			
Hampton Wick	d	09 12				09 31				09 42				10 01				10 12			
Teddington	d	09 15				09 35				09 45				10 05				10 15			
Strawberry Hill	a					09 38								10 08							
Fulwell	d	09 19								09 49								10 19			
Hampton	d	09 23								09 53								10 23			
Kempton Park	d	09 26								09 56								10 26			
Sunbury	d	09 28								09 58								10 28			
Upper Halliford	d	09 30								10 00								10 30			
Shepperton	a	09 35								10 05								10 35			
Berrylands	d							09 30								10 00					
Surbiton 6	d			09a13			09 27	09 35				09a43			09 57	10 05				10a13	
Thames Ditton	d							09 39								10 09					
Hampton Court	a							09 42								10 12					
Hinchley Wood	d						09 31								10 01						
Claygate	d						09 34								10 04						
Oxshott	d						09 37								10 07						
Cobham & Stoke D'abernon	d						09 41								10 11						
Bookham	d								09 59								10 29				
Effingham Junction 6	d						09 45		10 03						10 15		10 33				
Horsley	d						09 48		10 06						10 18		10 36				
Clandon	d						09 53		10 11						10 23		10 41				
London Road (Guildford)	d						09 58		10 16						10 28		10 46				
Guildford	a						10 05		10 23						10 35		10 53				

		SW	SW	SW	SW	SW	SW	SW	SW	SW	SW	SW	SW	SW	SW	SW	SW	SW	SW
London Waterloo 15 ⊖	d	09 57	10 03	10 06	10 09	10 12	10 16	10 20	10 24	10 27	10 33	10 36	10 39	10 42	10 46	10 50	10 54	10 57	11 03
Vauxhall ⊖	d	10 01	10 07	10 10	10 13	10 16	10 20	10 24	10 28	10 31	10 37	10 40	10 43	10 46	10 50	10 54	10 58	11 01	11 07
Clapham Junction 10	d	10 06	10 12	10 15	10 18	10 21	10 25	10 29	10 33	10 36	10 42	10 45	10 48	10 51	10 55	10 59	11 03	11 06	11 12
Earlsfield	d	10 09	10 15	10 18	10 21	10 24	10 28	10 32	10 36	10 39	10 45	10 48	10 51	10 54	10 58	11 02	11 06	11 09	11 15
Wimbledon 6 ⊖	d	10 13	10 19	10 22	10 25	10 28	10 32	10 36	10 40	10 43	10 49	10 52	10 55	10 58	11 02	11 06	11 10	11 13	11 19
Raynes Park 6	d	10 16		10 25	10 28	10 31	10 35		10 43	10 46		10 55	10 58	11 01	11 05		11 13	11 16	
Motspur Park	d				10 31		10 38		10 46				11 01		11 08		11 16		
Malden Manor	d						10 41								11 11				
Tolworth	d						10 44								11 14				
Chessington North	d						10 47								11 17				
Chessington South	a						10 49								11 19				
Worcester Park	d				10 33				10 48				11 03				11 18		
Stoneleigh	d				10 36				10 51				11 06				11 21		
Ewell West	d				10 39				10 54				11 09				11 24		
Epsom 3	a				10 46				10 57				11 16				11 27		
	d				10 47				10 58				11 17				11 28		
Ashtead	d				10 51				11 02				11 21				11 32		
Leatherhead	d				10 54				11 05				11 24				11 35		
Box Hill & Westhumble	d																		
Dorking 4	a								11 13								11 43		
New Malden 6	d	10 19		10 28		10 34				10 49		10 58		11 04				11 19	
Norbiton	d	10 22				10 37				10 52				11 07				11 22	
Kingston	a	10 25				10 40				10 55				11 10				11 25	
	d	10 29				10 40				10 59				11 10				11 29	
Hampton Wick	d	10 31				10 42				11 01				11 12				11 31	
Teddington	d	10 35				10 45				11 05				11 15				11 35	
Strawberry Hill	a	10 38								11 08								11 38	
Fulwell	d					10 49								11 19					
Hampton	d					10 53								11 23					
Kempton Park	d					10 56								11 26					
Sunbury	d					10 58								11 28					
Upper Halliford	d					11 00								11 30					
Shepperton	a					11 05								11 35					
Berrylands	d			10 30								11 00							
Surbiton 6	d		10 27	10 35				10a43			10 57	11 05				11a13			11 27
Thames Ditton	d			10 39								11 09							
Hampton Court	a			10 42								11 12							
Hinchley Wood	d		10 31								11 01								11 31
Claygate	d		10 34								11 04								11 34
Oxshott	d		10 37								11 07								11 37
Cobham & Stoke D'abernon	d		10 41								11 11								11 41
Bookham	d				10 59								11 29						
Effingham Junction 6	d		10 45		11 03						11 15		11 33						11 45
Horsley	d		10 48		11 06						11 18		11 36						11 48
Clandon	d		10 53		11 11						11 23		11 41						11 53
London Road (Guildford)	d		10 58		11 16						11 28		11 46						11 58
Guildford	a		11 05		11 23						11 35		11 53						12 05

Saturdays
from 13 October

London - Chessington South, Dorking, Guildford, Shepperton and Hampton Court

Network Diagram - see first Page of Table 152

		SW	SW	SW	SW	SW	SW	SW	SW	SW	SW	SW	SW	SW	SW	SW	SW	SW	SW	SW	SW
London Waterloo 15 ⊖	d	11 06	11 09	11 12	11 16	11 20	11 24	11 27	11 33	11 36	11 39	11 42	11 46	11 50	11 54	11 57	12 03	12 06	12 09	12 12	12 16
Vauxhall ⊖	d	11 10	11 13	11 16	11 20	11 24	11 28	11 31	11 37	11 40	11 43	11 46	11 50	11 54	11 58	12 01	12 07	12 10	12 13	12 16	12 20
Clapham Junction 10	d	11 15	11 18	11 21	11 25	11 29	11 33	11 36	11 42	11 45	11 48	11 51	11 55	11 59	12 03	12 06	12 12	12 15	12 18	12 21	12 25
Earlsfield	d	11 18	11 21	11 24	11 28	11 32	11 36	11 39	11 45	11 48	11 51	11 54	11 58	12 02	12 06	12 09	12 15	12 18	12 21	12 24	12 28
Wimbledon 6 ⊖	d	11 22	11 25	11 28	11 32	11 36	11 40	11 43	11 49	11 52	11 55	11 58	12 02	12 06	12 10	12 13	12 19	12 22	12 25	12 28	12 32
Raynes Park 6	d	11 25	11 28	11 31	11 35		11 43	11 46		11 55	11 58	12 01	12 05		12 13	12 16		12 25	12 28	12 31	12 35
Motspur Park	d		11 31		11 38		11 46				12 01		12 08		12 16				12 31		12 38
Malden Manor	d				11 41								12 11								12 41
Tolworth	d				11 44								12 14								12 44
Chessington North	d				11 47								12 17								12 47
Chessington South	a				11 49								12 19								12 49
Worcester Park	d		11 33				11 48				12 03				12 18				12 33		
Stoneleigh	d		11 36				11 51				12 06				12 21				12 36		
Ewell West	d		11 39				11 54				12 09				12 24				12 39		
Epsom 3	a		11 46				11 57				12 16				12 27				12 46		
	d		11 47				11 58				12 17				12 28				12 47		
Ashtead	d		11 51				12 02				12 21				12 32				12 51		
Leatherhead	d		11 54				12 05				12 24				12 35				12 54		
Box Hill & Westhumble	d																				
Dorking 4	a						12 13								12 43						
New Malden 6	d	11 28		11 34				11 49		11 58		12 04				12 19		12 28		12 34	
Norbiton	d			11 37				11 52				12 07				12 22				12 37	
Kingston	a			11 40				11 55				12 10				12 25				12 40	
	d			11 40				11 59				12 10				12 29				12 40	
Hampton Wick	d			11 42				12 01				12 12				12 31				12 42	
Teddington	d			11 45				12 05				12 15				12 35				12 45	
Strawberry Hill	a							12 08								12 38					
Fulwell	d			11 49								12 19								12 49	
Hampton	d			11 53								12 23								12 53	
Kempton Park	d			11 56								12 26								12 56	
Sunbury	d			11 58								12 28								12 58	
Upper Halliford	d			12 00								12 30								13 00	
Shepperton	a			12 05								12 35								13 05	
Berrylands	d	11 30								12 00								12 30			
Surbiton 6	d	11 35				11a43			11 57	12 05				12a13			12 27	12 35			
Thames Ditton	d	11 39								12 09								12 39			
Hampton Court	a	11 42								12 12								12 42			
Hinchley Wood	d								12 01								12 31				
Claygate	d								12 04								12 34				
Oxshott	d								12 07								12 37				
Cobham & Stoke D'abernon	d								12 11								12 41				
Bookham	d		11 59								12 29								12 59		
Effingham Junction 6	d		12 03						12 15		12 33						12 45		13 03		
Horsley	d		12 06						12 18		12 36						12 48		13 06		
Clandon	d		12 11						12 23		12 41						12 53		13 11		
London Road (Guildford)	d		12 16						12 28		12 46						12 58		13 16		
Guildford	a		12 23						12 35		12 53						13 05		13 23		

		SW	SW	SW	SW	SW	SW	SW	SW	SW	SW	SW	SW	SW	SW	SW	SW	SW	SW	SW	SW
London Waterloo 15 ⊖	d	12 20	12 24	12 27	12 33	12 36	12 39	12 42	12 46	12 50	12 54	12 57	13 03	13 06	13 09	13 12	13 16	13 20	13 24	13 27	13 33
Vauxhall ⊖	d	12 24	12 28	12 31	12 37	12 40	12 43	12 46	12 50	12 54	12 58	13 01	13 07	13 10	13 13	13 16	13 20	13 24	13 28	13 31	13 37
Clapham Junction 10	d	12 29	12 33	12 36	12 42	12 45	12 48	12 51	12 55	12 59	13 03	13 06	13 12	13 15	13 18	13 21	13 25	13 29	13 33	13 36	13 42
Earlsfield	d	12 32	12 36	12 39	12 45	12 48	12 51	12 54	12 58	13 02	13 06	13 09	13 15	13 18	13 21	13 24	13 28	13 32	13 36	13 39	13 45
Wimbledon 6 ⊖	d	12 36	12 40	12 43	12 49	12 52	12 55	12 58	13 02	13 06	13 10	13 13	13 19	13 22	13 25	13 28	13 32	13 36	13 40	13 43	13 49
Raynes Park 6	d		12 43	12 46		12 55	12 58	13 01	13 05		13 13	13 16		13 25	13 28	13 31	13 35		13 43	13 46	
Motspur Park	d		12 46				13 01		13 08		13 16				13 31		13 38		13 46		
Malden Manor	d								13 11								13 41				
Tolworth	d								13 14								13 44				
Chessington North	d								13 17								13 47				
Chessington South	a								13 19								13 49				
Worcester Park	d		12 48				13 03				13 18				13 33				13 48		
Stoneleigh	d		12 51				13 06				13 21				13 36				13 51		
Ewell West	d		12 54				13 09				13 24				13 39				13 54		
Epsom 3	a		12 57				13 16				13 27				13 46				13 57		
	d		12 58				13 17				13 28				13 47				13 58		
Ashtead	d		13 02				13 21				13 32				13 51				14 02		
Leatherhead	d		13 05				13 24				13 35				13 54				14 05		
Box Hill & Westhumble	d																				
Dorking 4	a		13 13								13 43								14 13		
New Malden 6	d			12 49		12 58		13 04				13 19		13 28		13 34				13 49	
Norbiton	d			12 52				13 07				13 22				13 37				13 52	
Kingston	a			12 55				13 10				13 25				13 40				13 55	
	d			12 59				13 10				13 29				13 40				13 59	
Hampton Wick	d			13 01				13 12				13 31				13 42				14 01	
Teddington	d			13 05				13 15				13 35				13 45				14 05	
Strawberry Hill	a			13 08								13 38								14 08	
Fulwell	d							13 19								13 49					
Hampton	d							13 23								13 53					
Kempton Park	d							13 26								13 56					
Sunbury	d							13 28								13 58					
Upper Halliford	d							13 30								14 00					
Shepperton	a							13 35								14 05					
Berrylands	d					13 00								13 30							
Surbiton 6	d	12a43			12 57	13 05				13a13			13 27	13 35				13a43			13 57
Thames Ditton	d					13 09								13 39							
Hampton Court	a					13 12								13 42							
Hinchley Wood	d				13 01								13 31								14 01
Claygate	d				13 04								13 34								14 04
Oxshott	d				13 07								13 37								14 07
Cobham & Stoke D'abernon	d				13 11								13 41								14 11
Bookham	d						13 29								13 59						
Effingham Junction 6	d				13 15		13 33						13 45		14 03						14 15
Horsley	d				13 18		13 36						13 48		14 06						14 18
Clandon	d				13 23		13 41						13 53		14 11						14 23
London Road (Guildford)	d				13 28		13 46						13 58		14 16						14 28
Guildford	a				13 35		13 53						14 05		14 23						14 35

Table 152

Saturdays from 13 October

London - Chessington South, Dorking, Guildford, Shepperton and Hampton Court

Network Diagram - see first Page of Table 152

		SW	SW	SW	SW	SW	SW	SW	SW	SW	SW	SW	SW	SW	SW	SW	SW	SW	SW
London Waterloo 15 ⊖	d	13 36	13 39	13 42	13 46	13 50	13 54	13 57	14 03	14 06	14 09	14 12	14 16	14 20	14 24	14 27	14 33	14 36	14 39
Vauxhall ⊖	d	13 40	13 43	13 46	13 50	13 54	13 58	14 01	14 07	14 10	14 13	14 16	14 20	14 24	14 28	14 31	14 37	14 40	14 43
Clapham Junction 10	d	13 45	13 48	13 51	13 55	13 59	14 03	14 06	14 12	14 15	14 18	14 21	14 25	14 29	14 33	14 36	14 42	14 45	14 48
Earlsfield	d	13 48	13 51	13 54	13 58	14 02	14 06	14 09	14 15	14 18	14 21	14 24	14 28	14 32	14 36	14 39	14 45	14 48	14 51
Wimbledon 6 ⊖	d	13 52	13 55	13 58	14 02	14 06	14 10	14 13	14 19	14 22	14 25	14 28	14 32	14 36	14 40	14 43	14 49	14 52	14 55
Raynes Park 6	d	13 55	13 58	14 01	14 05		14 13	14 16		14 25	14 28	14 31	14 35		14 43	14 46		14 55	14 58
Motspur Park	d		14 01		14 08		14 16				14 31		14 38		14 46				15 01
Malden Manor	d				14 11								14 41						
Tolworth	d				14 14								14 44						
Chessington North	d				14 17								14 47						
Chessington South	a				14 19								14 49						
Worcester Park	d		14 03				14 18				14 33				14 48				15 03
Stoneleigh	d		14 06				14 21				14 36				14 51				15 06
Ewell West	d		14 09				14 24				14 39				14 54				15 09
Epsom 3	a		14 16				14 27				14 46				14 57				15 16
	d		14 17				14 28				14 47				14 58				15 17
Ashtead	d		14 21				14 32				14 51				15 02				15 21
Leatherhead	d		14 24				14 35				14 54				15 05				15 24
Box Hill & Westhumble	d																		
Dorking 4	a						14 43								15 13				
New Malden 6	d	13 58		14 04				14 19		14 28		14 34				14 49		14 58	
Norbiton	d			14 07				14 22				14 37				14 52			
Kingston	a			14 10				14 25				14 40				14 55			
	d			14 10				14 29				14 40				14 59			
Hampton Wick	d			14 12				14 31				14 42				15 01			
Teddington	d			14 15				14 35				14 45				15 05			
Strawberry Hill	a							14 38								15 08			
Fulwell	d			14 19								14 49							
Hampton	d			14 23								14 53							
Kempton Park	d			14 26								14 56							
Sunbury	d			14 28								14 58							
Upper Halliford	d			14 30								15 00							
Shepperton	a			14 35								15 05							
Berrylands	d	14 00								14 30								15 00	
Surbiton 6	d	14 05				14a13			14 27	14 35				14a43			14 57	15 05	
Thames Ditton	d	14 09								14 39								15 09	
Hampton Court	a	14 12								14 42								15 12	
Hinchley Wood	d								14 31								15 01		
Claygate	d								14 34								15 04		
Oxshott	d								14 37								15 07		
Cobham & Stoke D'abernon	d								14 41								15 11		
Bookham	d		14 29								14 59								15 29
Effingham Junction 6	d		14 33						14 45		15 03						15 15		15 33
Horsley	d		14 36						14 48		15 06						15 18		15 36
Clandon	d		14 41						14 53		15 11						15 23		15 41
London Road (Guildford)	d		14 46						14 58		15 16						15 28		15 46
Guildford	a		14 53						15 05		15 23						15 35		15 53

		SW	SW	SW	SW	SW	SW	SW	SW	SW	SW	SW	SW	SW	SW	SW	SW	SW	SW	SW	SW
London Waterloo 15 ⊖	d	14 42	14 46	14 50	14 54	14 57	15 03	15 06	15 09	15 12	15 16	15 20	15 24	15 27	15 33	15 36	15 39	15 42	15 46	15 50	15 54
Vauxhall ⊖	d	14 46	14 50	14 54	14 58	15 01	15 07	15 10	15 13	15 16	15 20	15 24	15 28	15 31	15 37	15 40	15 43	15 46	15 50	15 54	15 58
Clapham Junction 10	d	14 51	14 55	14 59	15 03	15 06	15 12	15 15	15 18	15 21	15 25	15 29	15 33	15 36	15 42	15 45	15 48	15 51	15 55	15 59	16 03
Earlsfield	d	14 54	14 58	15 02	15 06	15 09	15 15	15 18	15 21	15 24	15 28	15 32	15 36	15 39	15 45	15 48	15 51	15 54	15 58	16 02	16 06
Wimbledon 6 ⊖	d	14 58	15 02	15 06	15 10	15 13	15 19	15 22	15 25	15 28	15 32	15 36	15 40	15 43	15 49	15 52	15 55	15 58	16 02	16 06	16 10
Raynes Park 6	d	15 01	15 05		15 13	15 16		15 25	15 28	15 31	15 35		15 43	15 46		15 55	15 58	16 01	16 05		16 13
Motspur Park	d		15 08		15 16				15 31		15 38		15 46				16 01		16 08		16 16
Malden Manor	d		15 11								15 41								16 11		
Tolworth	d		15 14								15 44								16 14		
Chessington North	d		15 17								15 47								16 17		
Chessington South	a		15 19								15 49								16 19		
Worcester Park	d				15 18				15 33				15 48				16 03				16 18
Stoneleigh	d				15 21				15 36				15 51				16 06				16 21
Ewell West	d				15 24				15 39				15 54				16 09				16 24
Epsom 3	a				15 27				15 46				15 57				16 16				16 27
	d				15 28				15 47				15 58				16 17				16 28
Ashtead	d				15 32				15 51				16 02				16 21				16 32
Leatherhead	d				15 35				15 54				16 05				16 24				16 35
Box Hill & Westhumble	d																				
Dorking 4	a				15 43								16 13								16 43
New Malden 6	d	15 04				15 19		15 28		15 34				15 49		15 58		16 04			
Norbiton	d	15 07				15 22				15 37				15 52				16 07			
Kingston	a	15 10				15 25				15 40				15 55				16 10			
	d	15 10				15 29				15 40				15 59				16 10			
Hampton Wick	d	15 12				15 31				15 42				16 01				16 12			
Teddington	d	15 15				15 35				15 45				16 05				16 15			
Strawberry Hill	a					15 38								16 08							
Fulwell	d	15 19								15 49								16 19			
Hampton	d	15 23								15 53								16 23			
Kempton Park	d	15 26								15 56								16 26			
Sunbury	d	15 28								15 58								16 28			
Upper Halliford	d	15 30								16 00								16 30			
Shepperton	a	15 35								16 05								16 35			
Berrylands	d							15 30								16 00					
Surbiton 6	d			15a13			15 27	15 35				15a43			15 57	16 05				16a13	
Thames Ditton	d							15 39								16 09					
Hampton Court	a							15 42								16 12					
Hinchley Wood	d						15 31								16 01						
Claygate	d						15 34								16 04						
Oxshott	d						15 37								16 07						
Cobham & Stoke D'abernon	d						15 41								16 11						
Bookham	d								15 59								16 29				
Effingham Junction 6	d						15 45		16 03						16 15		16 33				
Horsley	d						15 48		16 06						16 18		16 36				
Clandon	d						15 53		16 11						16 23		16 41				
London Road (Guildford)	d						15 58		16 16						16 28		16 46				
Guildford	a						16 05		16 23						16 35		16 53				

Table 152

Saturdays from 13 October

London - Chessington South, Dorking, Guildford, Shepperton and Hampton Court

Network Diagram - see first Page of Table 152

		SW	SW	SW	SW	SW	SW	SW	SW	SW	SW	SW	SW	SW	SW	SW	SW	SW	SW
London Waterloo 15 ⊖	d	15 57	16 03	16 06	16 09	16 12	16 16	16 20	16 24	16 27	16 33	16 36	16 39	16 42	16 46	16 50	16 54	16 57	17 03
Vauxhall ⊖	d	16 01	16 07	16 10	16 13	16 16	16 20	16 24	16 28	16 31	16 37	16 40	16 43	16 46	16 50	16 54	16 58	17 01	17 07
Clapham Junction 10	d	16 06	16 12	16 15	16 18	16 21	16 25	16 29	16 33	16 36	16 42	16 45	16 48	16 51	16 55	16 59	17 03	17 06	17 12
Earlsfield	d	16 09	16 15	16 18	16 21	16 24	16 28	16 32	16 36	16 39	16 45	16 48	16 51	16 54	16 58	17 02	17 06	17 09	17 15
Wimbledon 6 ⊖	d	16 13	16 19	16 22	16 25	16 28	16 32	16 36	16 40	16 43	16 49	16 52	16 55	16 58	17 02	17 06	17 10	17 13	17 19
Raynes Park 6	d	16 16		16 25	16 28	16 31	16 35		16 43	16 46		16 55	16 58	17 01	17 05		17 13	17 16	
Motspur Park	d				16 31		16 38		16 46				17 01		17 08		17 16		
Malden Manor	d						16 41								17 11				
Tolworth	d						16 44								17 14				
Chessington North	d						16 47								17 17				
Chessington South	a						16 49								17 19				
Worcester Park	d				16 33				16 48				17 03				17 18		
Stoneleigh	d				16 36				16 51				17 06				17 21		
Ewell West	d				16 39				16 54				17 09				17 24		
Epsom 3	a				16 46				16 57				17 16				17 27		
	d				16 47				16 58				17 17				17 28		
Ashtead	d				16 51				17 02				17 21				17 32		
Leatherhead	d				16 54				17 05				17 24				17 35		
Box Hill & Westhumble	d																		
Dorking 4	a								17 13								17 43		
New Malden 6	d	16 19		16 28		16 34				16 49		16 58		17 04				17 19	
Norbiton	d	16 22				16 37				16 52				17 07				17 22	
Kingston	a	16 25				16 40				16 55				17 10				17 25	
	d	16 29				16 40				16 59				17 10				17 29	
Hampton Wick	d	16 31				16 42				17 01				17 12				17 31	
Teddington	d	16 35				16 45				17 05				17 15				17 35	
Strawberry Hill	a	16 38								17 08								17 38	
Fulwell	d					16 49								17 19					
Hampton	d					16 53								17 23					
Kempton Park	d					16 56								17 26					
Sunbury	d					16 58								17 28					
Upper Halliford	d					17 00								17 30					
Shepperton	a					17 05								17 35					
Berrylands	d			16 30								17 00							
Surbiton 6	d		16 27	16 35				16a43			16 57	17 05				17a13			17 27
Thames Ditton	d			16 39								17 09							
Hampton Court	a			16 42								17 12							
Hinchley Wood	d		16 31								17 01								17 31
Claygate	d		16 34								17 04								17 34
Oxshott	d		16 37								17 07								17 37
Cobham & Stoke D'abernon	d		16 41								17 11								17 41
Bookham	d				16 59								17 29						
Effingham Junction 6	d		16 45		17 03						17 15		17 33						17 45
Horsley	d		16 48		17 06						17 18		17 36						17 48
Clandon	d		16 53		17 11						17 23		17 41						17 53
London Road (Guildford)	d		16 58		17 16						17 28		17 46						17 58
Guildford	a		17 05		17 23						17 35		17 53						18 05

		SW	SW	SW	SW	SW	SW	SW	SW	SW	SW	SW	SW	SW	SW	SW	SW	SW	SW	SW	SW
London Waterloo 15 ⊖	d	17 06	17 09	17 12	17 16	17 20	17 24	17 27	17 33	17 36	17 39	17 42	17 46	17 50	17 54	17 57	18 03	18 06	18 09	18 12	18 16
Vauxhall ⊖	d	17 10	17 13	17 16	17 20	17 24	17 28	17 31	17 37	17 40	17 43	17 46	17 50	17 54	17 58	18 01	18 07	18 10	18 13	18 16	18 20
Clapham Junction 10	d	17 15	17 18	17 21	17 25	17 29	17 33	17 36	17 42	17 45	17 48	17 51	17 55	17 59	18 03	18 06	18 12	18 15	18 18	18 21	18 25
Earlsfield	d	17 18	17 21	17 24	17 28	17 32	17 36	17 39	17 45	17 48	17 51	17 54	17 58	18 02	18 06	18 09	18 15	18 18	18 21	18 24	18 28
Wimbledon 6 ⊖	d	17 22	17 25	17 28	17 32	17 36	17 40	17 43	17 49	17 52	17 55	17 58	18 02	18 06	18 10	18 13	18 19	18 22	18 25	18 28	18 32
Raynes Park 6	d	17 25	17 28	17 31	17 35		17 43	17 46		17 55	17 58	18 01	18 05		18 13	18 16		18 25	18 28	18 31	18 35
Motspur Park	d		17 31		17 38		17 46				18 01		18 08		18 16				18 31		18 38
Malden Manor	d				17 41								18 11								18 41
Tolworth	d				17 44								18 14								18 44
Chessington North	d				17 47								18 17								18 47
Chessington South	a				17 49								18 19								18 49
Worcester Park	d		17 33				17 48				18 03				18 18				18 33		
Stoneleigh	d		17 36				17 51				18 06				18 21				18 36		
Ewell West	d		17 39				17 54				18 09				18 24				18 39		
Epsom 3	a		17 46				17 57				18 16				18 27				18 46		
	d		17 47				17 58				18 17				18 28				18 47		
Ashtead	d		17 51				18 02				18 21				18 32				18 51		
Leatherhead	d		17 54				18 05				18 24				18 35				18 54		
Box Hill & Westhumble	d																				
Dorking 4	a						18 13								18 43						
New Malden 6	d	17 28		17 34				17 49		17 58		18 04				18 19		18 28		18 34	
Norbiton	d			17 37				17 52				18 07				18 22				18 37	
Kingston	a			17 40				17 55				18 10				18 25				18 40	
	d			17 40				17 59				18 10				18 29				18 40	
Hampton Wick	d			17 42				18 01				18 12				18 31				18 42	
Teddington	d			17 45				18 05				18 15				18 35				18 45	
Strawberry Hill	a							18 08								18 38					
Fulwell	d			17 49								18 19								18 49	
Hampton	d			17 53								18 23								18 53	
Kempton Park	d			17 56								18 26								18 56	
Sunbury	d			17 58								18 28								18 58	
Upper Halliford	d			18 00								18 30								19 00	
Shepperton	a			18 05								18 35								19 05	
Berrylands	d	17 30								18 00								18 30			
Surbiton 6	d	17 35				17a43			17 57	18 05				18a13			18 27	18 35			
Thames Ditton	d	17 39								18 09								18 39			
Hampton Court	a	17 42								18 12								18 42			
Hinchley Wood	d								18 01								18 31				
Claygate	d								18 04								18 34				
Oxshott	d								18 07								18 37				
Cobham & Stoke D'abernon	d								18 11								18 41				
Bookham	d		17 59								18 29								18 59		
Effingham Junction 6	d		18 03						18 15		18 33						18 45		19 03		
Horsley	d		18 06						18 18		18 36						18 48		19 06		
Clandon	d		18 11						18 23		18 41						18 53		19 11		
London Road (Guildford)	d		18 16						18 28		18 46						18 58		19 16		
Guildford	a		18 23						18 35		18 53						19 05		19 23		

London - Chessington South, Dorking, Guildford, Shepperton and Hampton Court

Network Diagram - see first Page of Table 152

		SW	SW	SW	SW	SW	SW	SW	SW	SW	SW	SW	SW	SW	SW	SW	SW	SW	SW	SW	SW
London Waterloo 15 ⊖	d	18 20	18 24	18 27	18 33	18 36	18 39	18 42	18 46	18 50	18 54	18 57	19 03	19 06	19 09	19 12	19 16	19 20	19 24	19 27	19 33
Vauxhall ⊖	d	18 24	18 28	18 31	18 37	18 40	18 43	18 46	18 50	18 54	18 58	19 01	19 07	19 10	19 13	19 16	19 20	19 24	19 28	19 31	19 37
Clapham Junction 10	d	18 29	18 33	18 36	18 42	18 45	18 48	18 51	18 55	18 59	19 03	19 06	19 12	19 15	19 18	19 21	19 25	19 29	19 33	19 36	19 42
Earlsfield	d	18 32	18 36	18 39	18 45	18 48	18 51	18 54	18 58	19 02	19 06	19 09	19 15	19 18	19 21	19 24	19 28	19 32	19 36	19 39	19 45
Wimbledon 6 ⊖ ⇌	d	18 36	18 40	18 43	18 49	18 52	18 55	18 58	19 02	19 06	19 10	19 13	19 19	19 22	19 25	19 28	19 32	19 36	19 40	19 43	19 49
Raynes Park 6	d		18 43	18 46		18 55	18 58	19 01	19 05		19 13	19 16		19 25	19 28	19 31	19 35		19 43	19 46	
Motspur Park	d		18 46				19 01		19 08		19 16				19 31		19 38		19 46		
Malden Manor	d								19 11								19 41				
Tolworth	d								19 14								19 44				
Chessington North	d								19 17								19 47				
Chessington South	a								19 19								19 49				
Worcester Park	d		18 48				19 03				19 18				19 33				19 48		
Stoneleigh	d		18 51				19 06				19 21				19 36				19 51		
Ewell West	d		18 54				19 09				19 24				19 39				19 54		
Epsom 3	a		18 57				19 16				19 27				19 46				19 57		
	d		18 58				19 17				19 28				19 47				19 58		
Ashtead	d		19 02				19 21				19 32				19 51				20 02		
Leatherhead	d		19 05				19 24				19 35				19 54				20 05		
Box Hill & Westhumble	d																				
Dorking 4	a		19 13								19 43								20 13		
New Malden 6	d			18 49		18 58		19 04				19 19		19 28		19 34				19 49	
Norbiton	d			18 52				19 07				19 22				19 37				19 52	
Kingston	a			18 55				19 10				19 25				19 40				19 55	
	d			18 59				19 10				19 29				19 40				19 59	
Hampton Wick	d			19 01				19 12				19 31				19 42				20 01	
Teddington	d			19 05				19 15				19 35				19 45				20 05	
Strawberry Hill	a			19 08								19 38								20 08	
Fulwell	d							19 19								19 49					
Hampton	d							19 23								19 53					
Kempton Park	d							19 26								19 56					
Sunbury	d							19 28								19 58					
Upper Halliford	d							19 30								20 00					
Shepperton	a							19 35								20 05					
Berrylands	d					19 00								19 30							
Surbiton 6	d	18a43			18 57	19 05				19a13			19 27	19 35				19a43			19 57
Thames Ditton	d					19 09								19 39							
Hampton Court	a					19 12								19 42							
Hinchley Wood	d				19 01								19 31								20 01
Claygate	d				19 04								19 34								20 04
Oxshott	d				19 07								19 37								20 07
Cobham & Stoke D'abernon	d				19 11								19 41								20 11
Bookham	d						19 29								19 59						
Effingham Junction 6	d				19 15		19 33						19 45		20 03						20 15
Horsley	d				19 18		19 36						19 48		20 06						20 18
Clandon	d				19 23		19 41						19 53		20 11						20 23
London Road (Guildford)	d				19 28		19 46						19 58		20 16						20 28
Guildford	a				19 35		19 53						20 05		20 23						20 35

		SW	SW	SW	SW	SW	SW	SW	SW	SW	SW	SW	SW	SW	SW	SW	SW	SW	SW
London Waterloo 15 ⊖	d	19 36	19 39	19 42	19 46	19 50	19 54	19 57	20 03	20 06	20 09	20 12	20 16	20 20	20 24	20 27	20 33	20 36	20 39
Vauxhall ⊖	d	19 40	19 43	19 46	19 50	19 54	19 58	20 01	20 07	20 10	20 13	20 16	20 20	20 24	20 28	20 31	20 37	20 40	20 43
Clapham Junction 10	d	19 45	19 48	19 51	19 55	19 59	20 03	20 06	20 12	20 15	20 18	20 21	20 25	20 29	20 33	20 36	20 42	20 45	20 48
Earlsfield	d	19 48	19 51	19 54	19 58	20 02	20 06	20 09	20 15	20 18	20 21	20 24	20 28	20 32	20 36	20 39	20 45	20 48	20 51
Wimbledon 6 ⊖ ⇌	d	19 52	19 55	19 58	20 02	20 06	20 10	20 13	20 19	20 22	20 25	20 28	20 32	20 36	20 40	20 43	20 49	20 52	20 55
Raynes Park 6	d	19 55	19 58	20 01	20 05		20 13	20 16		20 25	20 28	20 31	20 35		20 43	20 46		20 55	20 58
Motspur Park	d		20 01		20 08		20 16				20 31		20 38		20 46				21 01
Malden Manor	d				20 11								20 41						
Tolworth	d				20 14								20 44						
Chessington North	d				20 17								20 47						
Chessington South	a				20 19								20 49						
Worcester Park	d		20 03				20 18				20 33				20 48				21 03
Stoneleigh	d		20 06				20 21				20 36				20 51				21 06
Ewell West	d		20 09				20 24				20 39				20 54				21 09
Epsom 3	a		20 16				20 27				20 46				20 57				21 16
	d		20 17								20 47								21 17
Ashtead	d		20 21								20 51								21 21
Leatherhead	d		20 24								20 54								21 24
Box Hill & Westhumble	d																		
Dorking 4	a										21 02								
New Malden 6	d	19 58		20 04				20 19		20 28		20 34				20 49		20 58	
Norbiton	d			20 07				20 22				20 37				20 52			
Kingston	a			20 10				20 25				20 40				20 55			
	d			20 10				20 29				20 40				20 59			
Hampton Wick	d			20 12				20 31				20 42				21 01			
Teddington	d			20 15				20 35				20 45				21 05			
Strawberry Hill	a							20 38								21 08			
Fulwell	d			20 19								20 49							
Hampton	d			20 23								20 53							
Kempton Park	d			20 26								20 56							
Sunbury	d			20 28								20 58							
Upper Halliford	d			20 30								21 00							
Shepperton	a			20 35								21 05							
Berrylands	d	20 00								20 30								21 00	
Surbiton 6	d	20 05				20a13			20 27	20 35				20a43			20 57	21 05	
Thames Ditton	d	20 09								20 39								21 09	
Hampton Court	a	20 12								20 42								21 12	
Hinchley Wood	d								20 31								21 01		
Claygate	d								20 34								21 04		
Oxshott	d								20 37								21 07		
Cobham & Stoke D'abernon	d								20 41								21 11		
Bookham	d		20 29																21 29
Effingham Junction 6	d		20 33						20 45								21 15		21 33
Horsley	d		20 36						20 48								21 18		21 36
Clandon	d		20 41						20 53								21 23		21 41
London Road (Guildford)	d		20 46						20 58								21 28		21 46
Guildford	a		20 53						21 05								21 35		21 53

Table 152

Saturdays
from 13 October

London - Chessington South, Dorking, Guildford, Shepperton and Hampton Court

Network Diagram - see first Page of Table 152

		SW	SW	SW	SW	SW	SW	SW	SW	SW	SW	SW	SW	SW	SW	SW	SW	SW	SW	SW	SW
London Waterloo 15 ⊖	d	20 42	20 46	20 50	20 54	20 57	21 03	21 09	21 12	21 20	21 24	21 27	21 33	21 36	21 39	21 42	21 46	21 50	21 54	21 57	22 03
Vauxhall ⊖	d	20 46	20 50	20 54	20 58	21 01	21 07	21 13	21 16	21 24	21 28	21 31	21 37	21 40	21 43	21 46	21 50	21 54	21 58	22 01	22 07
Clapham Junction 10	d	20 51	20 55	20 59	21 03	21 06	21 12	21 18	21 21	21 29	21 33	21 36	21 42	21 45	21 48	21 51	21 55	21 59	22 03	22 06	22 12
Earlsfield	d	20 54	20 58	21 02	21 06	21 09	21 15	21 21	21 24	21 32	21 36	21 39	21 45	21 48	21 51	21 54	21 58	22 02	22 06	22 09	22 15
Wimbledon 6 ⊖ ⇌	d	20 58	21 02	21 06	21 10	21 13	21 19	21 25	21 28	21 36	21 40	21 43	21 49	21 52	21 55	21 58	22 02	22 06	22 10	22 13	22 19
Raynes Park 6	d	21 01	21 05		21 13	21 16		21 28	21 31		21 43	21 46		21 55	21 58	22 01	22 05		22 13	22 16	
Motspur Park	d		21 08		21 16			21 31			21 46				22 01		22 08		22 16		
Malden Manor	d		21 11														22 11				
Tolworth	d		21 14														22 14				
Chessington North	d		21 17														22 17				
Chessington South	a		21 19														22 19				
Worcester Park	d				21 18			21 33			21 48				22 03				22 18		
Stoneleigh	d				21 21			21 36			21 51				22 06				22 21		
Ewell West	d				21 24			21 39			21 54				22 09				22 24		
Epsom 3	a				21 27			21 46			21 57				22 16				22 27		
	d							21 47							22 17						
Ashtead	d							21 51							22 21						
Leatherhead	d							21 54							22 24						
Box Hill & Westhumble	d																				
Dorking 4	a							22 02													
New Malden 6	d	21 04				21 19			21 34			21 49		21 58		22 04				22 19	
Norbiton	d	21 07				21 22			21 37			21 52				22 07				22 22	
Kingston	a	21 10				21 25			21 40			21 55				22 10				22 25	
	d	21 10				21 29			21 40			21 59				22 10				22 29	
Hampton Wick	d	21 12				21 31			21 42			22 01				22 12				22 31	
Teddington	d	21 15				21 35			21 45			22 05				22 15				22 35	
Strawberry Hill	a					21 38						22 08								22 38	
Fulwell	d	21 19							21 49							22 19					
Hampton	d	21 23							21 53							22 23					
Kempton Park	d	21 26							21 56							22 26					
Sunbury	d	21 28							21 58							22 28					
Upper Halliford	d	21 30							22 00							22 30					
Shepperton	a	21 35							22 05							22 35					
Berrylands	d													22 00							
Surbiton 6	d			21a13			21 27			21a43			21 57	22 05				22 14			22 27
Thames Ditton	d													22 09							
Hampton Court	a													22 12							
Hinchley Wood	d						21 31						22 01								22 31
Claygate	d						21 34						22 04								22 34
Oxshott	d						21 37						22 07								22 37
Cobham & Stoke D'abernon	d						21 41						22 11								22 41
Bookham	d														22 29						
Effingham Junction 6	d						21 45						22 15		22 33						22 45
Horsley	d						21 48						22 18		22 36						22 48
Clandon	d						21 53						22 23		22 41						22 53
London Road (Guildford)	d						21 58						22 28		22 46						22 58
Guildford	a						22 05						22 35		22 53			22 47			23 05

		SW	SW	SW	SW	SW	SW	SW	SW	SW	SW	SW	SW	SW	SW	SW	SW	SW
London Waterloo 15 ⊖	d	22 09	22 12	22 20	22 27	22 33	22 36	22 39	22 42	22 50	22 57	23 00	23 03	23 09	23 12	23 20	23 27	23 36
Vauxhall ⊖	d	22 13	22 16	22 24	22 31	22 37	22 40	22 43	22 46	22 54	23 01	23 04	23 07	23 13	23 16	23 24	23 31	23 40
Clapham Junction 10	d	22 18	22 21	22 29	22 36	22 42	22 45	22 48	22 51	22 59	23 06	23 09	23 12	23 18	23 21	23 29	23 36	23 45
Earlsfield	d	22 21	22 24	22 32	22 39	22 45	22 48	22 51	22 54	23 02	23 09	23 12	23 15	23 21	23 24	23 32	23 39	23 48
Wimbledon 6 ⊖ ⇌	d	22 25	22 28	22 36	22 43	22 49	22 52	22 55	22 58	23 06	23 13	23 16	23 19	23 25	23 28	23 36	23 43	23 52
Raynes Park 6	d	22 28	22 31		22 46		22 55	22 58	23 01		23 16	23 19		23 28	23 31		23 46	23 55
Motspur Park	d	22 31						23 01				23 22		23 31				
Malden Manor	d											23 25						
Tolworth	d											23 28						
Chessington North	d											23 31						
Chessington South	a											23 33						
Worcester Park	d	22 33						23 03						23 33				
Stoneleigh	d	22 36						23 06						23 36				
Ewell West	d	22 39						23 09						23 39				
Epsom 3	a	22 46						23 12						23 42				
	d	22 47						23 17						23 47				
Ashtead	d	22 51						23 21						23 51				
Leatherhead	d	22 54						23 24						23 54				
Box Hill & Westhumble	d																	
Dorking 4	a	23 02												00 03				
New Malden 6	d		22 34		22 49		22 58		23 04		23 19				23 34		23 49	23 58
Norbiton	d		22 37		22 52				23 07		23 22				23 37		23 52	
Kingston	a		22 40		22 55				23 10		23 25				23 40		23 55	
	d		22 40		22 59				23 10		23 29				23 40		23 55	
Hampton Wick	d		22 42		23 01				23 12		23 31				23 42		23 57	
Teddington	d		22 45		23 05				23 15		23 35				23 45		23 59	
Strawberry Hill	a				23 08						23 38						00 03	
Fulwell	d		22 49						23 19						23 49			
Hampton	d		22 53						23 23						23 53			
Kempton Park	d		22 56						23 26						23 56			
Sunbury	d		22 58						23 28						23 58			
Upper Halliford	d		23 00						23 30						23 59			
Shepperton	a		23 05						23 35						00 05			
Berrylands	d						23 00											23 59
Surbiton 6	d			22a43		22 57	23 05			23a13			23 27			23a43		00 05
Thames Ditton	d						23 09											00 09
Hampton Court	a						23 12											00 12
Hinchley Wood	d					23 01							23 31					
Claygate	d					23 04							23 34					
Oxshott	d					23 07							23 37					
Cobham & Stoke D'abernon	d					23 11							23 41					
Bookham	d							23 29										
Effingham Junction 6	d					23 15		23 33					23 45					
Horsley	d					23 18		23 36					23 48					
Clandon	d					23 23		23 41					23 53					
London Road (Guildford)	d					23 28		23 46					23 58					
Guildford	a					23 35		23 53					00 05					

Table 152

London - Chessington South, Dorking, Guildford, Shepperton and Hampton Court

Saturdays
from 13 October

Network Diagram - see first Page of Table 152

Station		SW	SW	SW
London Waterloo 15 ⊖	d	23 42	23 50	23 57
Vauxhall ⊖	d	23 46	23 54	00 01
Clapham Junction 10	d	23 51	23 59	00 06
Earlsfield	d	23 54	00 02	00 09
Wimbledon 6 ⊖ ⇌	d	23 58	00 06	00 13
Raynes Park 6	d	00 01		00 16
Motspur Park	d	00 04		
Malden Manor	d			
Tolworth	d			
Chessington North	d			
Chessington South	a			
Worcester Park	d	00 06		
Stoneleigh	d	00 09		
Ewell West	d	00 12		
Epsom 3	a	00 15		
	d	00 19		
Ashtead	d	00 23		
Leatherhead	d	00 26		
Box Hill & Westhumble	d			
Dorking 4	a			
New Malden 6	d			00 19
Norbiton	d			00 22
Kingston	a			00 25
	d			00 25
Hampton Wick	d			00 27
Teddington	d			00 30
Strawberry Hill	a			
Fulwell	d			00 34
Hampton	d			00 38
Kempton Park	d			00 41
Sunbury	d			00 43
Upper Halliford	d			00 45
Shepperton	a			00 50
Berrylands	d			
Surbiton 6	d		00 14	
Thames Ditton	d			
Hampton Court	a			
Hinchley Wood	d		00 18	
Claygate	d		00 20	
Oxshott	d		00 24	
Cobham & Stoke D'abernon	d		00 27	
Bookham	d	00 31		
Effingham Junction 6	d	00 36	00 32	
Horsley	d	00 39	00 34	
Clandon	d	00 44	00 39	
London Road (Guildford)	d	00 49	00 44	
Guildford	a	00 56	00 51	

Table 152

London - Chessington South, Dorking, Guildford, Shepperton and Hampton Court

Sundays
until 30 September

Network Diagram - see first Page of Table 152

Station		SW	SW	SW	SW	SW	SW	SW	SW
London Waterloo 15 ⊖	d	23p03	23p09	23p12	23p27	23p36	23p42	23p50	23p57
Vauxhall ⊖	d	23p07	23p13	23p16	23p31	23p40	23p46	23p54	00 01
Clapham Junction 10	d	23p12	23p18	23p21	23p36	23p45	23p51	23p59	00 06
Earlsfield	d	23p15	23p21	23p24	23p39	23p48	23p54	00 02	00 09
Wimbledon 6 ⊖ ⇌	d	23p19	23p25	23p28	23p43	23p52	23p58	00 06	00 13
Raynes Park 6	d		23p28	23p31	23p46	23p55	00 01		00 16
Motspur Park	d		23p31				00 04		
Malden Manor	d								
Tolworth	d								
Chessington North	d								
Chessington South	a								
Worcester Park	d		23p33				00 06		
Stoneleigh	d		23p36				00 09		
Ewell West	d		23p39				00 12		
Epsom 3	a		23p42				00 15		
	d		23p47				00 19		
Ashtead	d		23p51				00 23		
Leatherhead	d		23p54				00 26		
Box Hill & Westhumble	d								
Dorking 4	a		00 01						
New Malden 6	d			23p34	23p49	23p58			00 19
Norbiton	d			23p37	23p52				00 22
Kingston	a			23p40	23p55				00 25
	d			23p40	23p55				00 25
Hampton Wick	d			23p42	23p57				00 27
Teddington	d			23p45	23p59				00 30
Strawberry Hill	a				00 03				
Fulwell	d			23p49					00 34
Hampton	d			23p53					00 38
Kempton Park	d			23p56					00 41
Sunbury	d			23p58					00 43
Upper Halliford	d			23p59					00 45
Shepperton	a			00 03					00 48
Berrylands	d					23p59			
Surbiton 6	d	23p27				00 05		00 14	
Thames Ditton	d					00 09			
Hampton Court	a					00 12			
Hinchley Wood	d	23p31						00 18	
Claygate	d	23p34						00 20	
Oxshott	d	23p37						00 24	
Cobham & Stoke D'abernon	d	23p41						00 27	
Bookham	d						00 31		
Effingham Junction 6	d	23p45					00 36	00 32	
Horsley	d	23p48					00 39	00 34	
Clandon	d	23p53					00 44	00 39	
London Road (Guildford)	d	23p58					00 49	00 44	
Guildford	a	00 02					00 53	00 48	

Station		SW	SW A	SW B	SW A	SW B	SW	SW	SW	SW	SW	SW
London Waterloo 15 ⊖	d	00 09	00 15	00 15	00 27	00 27	00 42	01 42	06 18		06 57	
Vauxhall ⊖	d	00 13	00 19	00 19	00 31	00 31	00 46	01 46	06 22		07 01	
Clapham Junction 10	d	00 20	00 25	00 25	00 37	00 37	00 51	01 53	06 27		07 06	
Earlsfield	d	00 23	00 29	00 29	00s41	00s41					07 09	
Wimbledon 6 ⊖ ⇌	d	00 27	00 33	00 33	00 45	00 45	01 05	01 59	06 34	06 48	07 13	07 16
Raynes Park 6	d		00 36	00 36	00 48	00 48	01 08	02 02	06 37	06 52	07 16	
Motspur Park	d		00 38	00 38						06 55		
Malden Manor	d											
Tolworth	d											
Chessington North	d											
Chessington South	a											
Worcester Park	d		00 41	00 41						06 57		
Stoneleigh	d		00 44	00 44						07 00		
Ewell West	d		00 46	00 46						07 03		
Epsom 3	a		00 50	00 50						07 06		
	d			00 51								
Ashtead	d			00 55								
Leatherhead	d			00 58								
Box Hill & Westhumble	d											
Dorking 4	a											
New Malden 6	d				00 50	00 50	01 11	02 04	06 40		07 19	
Norbiton	d						01 14	02 08	06 43			
Kingston	a						01 17	02 10	06 46			
	d						01 17	02 11	06 49			
Hampton Wick	d						01s22	02s13	06 51			
Teddington	d						01s25	02s15	06 56			
Strawberry Hill	a						01 28	02s18	06 59			
Fulwell	d											
Hampton	d											
Kempton Park	d											
Sunbury	d											
Upper Halliford	d											
Shepperton	a											
Berrylands	d				00s53	00s53					07 21	
Surbiton 6	d	00 35			00a56	00 57					07 25	07 32
Thames Ditton	d										07 30	
Hampton Court	a										07 33	
Hinchley Wood	d											07 36
Claygate	d											07 39
Oxshott	d											07 42
Cobham & Stoke D'abernon	d											07 46
Bookham	d			01 03								
Effingham Junction 6	d			01 07								07 50
Horsley	d			01 10								07 53
Clandon	d			01 15								07 58
London Road (Guildford)	d			01 20								08 03
Guildford	a	01 07		01 24		01 33						08 07

A until 22 July, 19 August, 26 August, 16 September, 23 September, 30 September

B 29 July, 5 August, 12 August, 2 September, 9 September

Table 152

Sundays
until 30 September

London - Chessington South, Dorking, Guildford, Shepperton and Hampton Court

Network Diagram - see first Page of Table 152

		SW	SW			SW		SW	SW	SW	SW	SW	SW	SW	SW	SW		SW		SW	SW	SW	SW	SW	SW
London Waterloo 15 ⊖	d		07 10			07 18			07 27		07 40	07 48		07 57		08 02		08 10		08 18	08 21	08 27	08 32	08 40	08 48
Vauxhall ⊖	d		07 14			07 22			07 31		07 44	07 52		08 01		08 06		08 14		08 22	08 25	08 31	08 36	08 44	08 52
Clapham Junction 10	d		07 19			07 27			07 36		07 49	07 57		08 06		08 11		08 19		08 27	08 30	08 36	08 41	08 49	08 57
Earlsfield	d		07 22			07 30			07 39		07 52	08 00		08 09		08 14		08 22		08 30	08 33	08 39	08 44	08 52	09 00
Wimbledon 6 ⊖	d	07 20	07 26			07 34		07 37	07 43	07 48	07 56	08 04	08 07	08 13	08 17	08 18		08 26		08 34	08 37	08 43	08 48	08 56	09 04
Raynes Park 6	d	07 23				07 37		07 40	07 46	07 52		08 07	08 10	08 16		08 22				08 37	08 40	08 46	08 52		09 07
Motspur Park	d	07 26						07 43		07 55			08 13			08 25					08 43		08 55		
Malden Manor	d							07 46					08 16								08 46				
Tolworth	d							07 49					08 19								08 49				
Chessington North	d							07 52					08 22								08 52				
Chessington South	a							07 54					08 24								08 54				
Worcester Park	d	07 28								07 57						08 27							08 57		
Stoneleigh	d	07 31								08 00						08 30							09 00		
Ewell West	d	07 34								08 03						08 33							09 03		
Epsom 3	a	07 37								08 06						08 36							09 06		
	d									08 08						08 38							09 08		
Ashtead	d									08 12						08 42							09 12		
Leatherhead	d									08 15						08 45							09 15		
Box Hill & Westhumble	d																								
Dorking 4	a															08 51									
New Malden 6	d					07 40			07 49			08 10		08 19						08 40		08 49			09 10
Norbiton	d					07 43						08 13								08 43					09 13
Kingston	a					07 46						08 16								08 46					09 16
	d					07 49						08 16								08 49					09 16
Hampton Wick	d					07 51						08 18								08 51					09 18
Teddington	d					07 56						08 21								08 56					09 21
Strawberry Hill	a					07 59														08 59					
Fulwell	d											08 25													09 25
Hampton	d											08 29													09 29
Kempton Park	d											08 32													09 32
Sunbury	d											08 34													09 34
Upper Halliford	d											08 36													09 36
Shepperton	a											08 39													09 39
Berrylands	d								07 51					08 21								08 51			
Surbiton 6	d		07 35						07 55		08 05			08 25	08 32			08 35				08 55		09 05	
Thames Ditton	d								08 00					08 30								09 00			
Hampton Court	a								08 03					08 33								09 03			
Hinchley Wood	d														08 36										
Claygate	d														08 39										
Oxshott	d														08 42										
Cobham & Stoke D'abernon	d														08 46										
Bookham	d									08 21													09 21		
Effingham Junction 6	d									08 25					08 50								09 25		
Horsley	d									08 27					08 53								09 27		
Clandon	d									08 32					08 58								09 32		
London Road (Guildford)	d									08 37					09 03								09 37		
Guildford	a		08 14							08 41	08 40				09 07			09 10					09 41	09 40	

A until 22 July, 19 August, 26 August, 16 September, 23 September, 30 September

B 29 July, 5 August, 12 August, 2 September, 9 September

Table 152

Sundays
until 30 September

London - Chessington South, Dorking, Guildford, Shepperton and Hampton Court

Network Diagram - see first Page of Table 152

		SW		SW	SW	SW	SW		SW	SW	SW	SW		SW	SW	SW	SW	SW	SW	SW		SW		SW	SW
London Waterloo 15 ⊖	d	08 51		08 57		09 02	09 10		09 18	09 21	09 27	09 32		09 40	09 48	09 51	09 57		10 02	10 10		10 18		10 21	10 27
Vauxhall ⊖	d	08 55		09 01		09 06	09 14		09 22	09 25	09 31	09 36		09 44	09 52	09 55	10 01		10 06	10 14		10 22		10 25	10 31
Clapham Junction 10	d	09 00		09 06		09 11	09 19		09 27	09 30	09 36	09 41		09 49	09 57	10 00	10 06		10 11	10 19		10 27		10 30	10 36
Earlsfield	d	09 03		09 09		09 14	09 22		09 30	09 33	09 39	09 44		09 52	10 00	10 03	10 09		10 14	10 22		10 30		10 33	10 39
Wimbledon 6 ⊖	d	09 07		09 13	09 17	09 18	09 26		09 34	09 37	09 43	09 48		09 56	10 04	10 07	10 13	10 17	10 18	10 26		10 34		10 37	10 43
Raynes Park 6	d	09 10		09 16		09 22			09 37	09 40	09 46	09 52			10 07	10 10	10 16		10 22			10 37		10 40	10 46
Motspur Park	d	09 13				09 25				09 43		09 55				10 13			10 25					10 43	
Malden Manor	d	09 16								09 46						10 16								10 46	
Tolworth	d	09 19								09 49						10 19								10 49	
Chessington North	d	09 22								09 52						10 22								10 52	
Chessington South	a	09 24								09 54						10 24								10 54	
Worcester Park	d					09 27						09 57							10 27						
Stoneleigh	d					09 30						10 00							10 30						
Ewell West	d					09 33						10 03							10 33						
Epsom 3	a					09 36						10 06							10 36						
	d					09 38						10 08							10 38						
Ashtead	d					09 42						10 12							10 42						
Leatherhead	d					09 45						10 15							10 45						
Box Hill & Westhumble	d																								
Dorking 4	a					09 51													10 51						
New Malden 6	d			09 19					09 40		09 49				10 10		10 19					10 40			10 49
Norbiton	d								09 43						10 13							10 43			
Kingston	a								09 46						10 16							10 46			
	d								09 49						10 16							10 49			
Hampton Wick	d								09 51						10 18							10 51			
Teddington	d								09 56						10 21							10 56			
Strawberry Hill	a								09 59													10 59			
Fulwell	d														10 25										
Hampton	d														10 29										
Kempton Park	d														10 32										
Sunbury	d														10 34										
Upper Halliford	d														10 36										
Shepperton	a														10 39										
Berrylands	d			09 21							09 51						10 21								10 51
Surbiton 6	d			09 25	09 32		09 35				09 55			10 05			10 25	10 32		10 35					10 55
Thames Ditton	d			09 30							10 00						10 30								11 00
Hampton Court	a			09 33							10 03						10 33								11 03
Hinchley Wood	d				09 36													10 36							
Claygate	d				09 39													10 39							
Oxshott	d				09 42													10 42							
Cobham & Stoke D'abernon	d				09 46													10 46							
Bookham	d											10 21													
Effingham Junction 6	d				09 50							10 25						10 50							
Horsley	d				09 53							10 27						10 53							
Clandon	d				09 58							10 32						10 58							
London Road (Guildford)	d				10 03							10 37						11 03							
Guildford	a				10 07		10 10					10 41		10 44				11 07		11 14					

		SW	SW	SW	SW	SW	SW	SW		SW		SW	SW	SW	SW	SW	SW	SW		SW	SW	SW	SW		SW
London Waterloo 15 ⊖	d	10 32	10 40	10 48	10 51	10 57		11 02		11 10		11 18	11 21	11 27	11 32	11 40	11 48	11 51		11 57		12 02	12 10		12 18
Vauxhall ⊖	d	10 36	10 44	10 52	10 55	11 01		11 06		11 14		11 22	11 25	11 31	11 36	11 44	11 52	11 55		12 01		12 06	12 14		12 22
Clapham Junction 10	d	10 41	10 49	10 57	11 00	11 06		11 11		11 19		11 27	11 30	11 36	11 41	11 49	11 57	12 00		12 06		12 11	12 19		12 27
Earlsfield	d	10 44	10 52	11 00	11 03	11 09		11 14		11 22		11 30	11 33	11 39	11 44	11 52	12 00	12 03		12 09		12 14	12 22		12 30
Wimbledon 6 ⊖	d	10 48	10 56	11 04	11 07	11 13	11 17	11 18		11 26		11 34	11 37	11 43	11 48	11 56	12 04	12 07		12 13	12 17	12 18	12 26		12 34
Raynes Park 6	d	10 52		11 07	11 10	11 16		11 22				11 37	11 40	11 46	11 52		12 07	12 10		12 16		12 22			12 37
Motspur Park	d	10 55			11 13			11 25					11 43		11 55			12 13				12 25			
Malden Manor	d				11 16								11 46					12 16							
Tolworth	d				11 19								11 49					12 19							
Chessington North	d				11 22								11 52					12 22							
Chessington South	a				11 24								11 54					12 24							
Worcester Park	d	10 57						11 27							11 57							12 27			
Stoneleigh	d	11 00						11 30							12 00							12 30			
Ewell West	d	11 03						11 33							12 03							12 33			
Epsom 3	a	11 06						11 36							12 06							12 36			
	d	11 08						11 38							12 08							12 38			
Ashtead	d	11 12						11 42							12 12							12 42			
Leatherhead	d	11 15						11 45							12 15							12 45			
Box Hill & Westhumble	d																								
Dorking 4	a							11 51														12 51			
New Malden 6	d			11 10		11 19						11 40		11 49			12 10			12 19					12 40
Norbiton	d			11 13								11 43					12 13								12 43
Kingston	a			11 16								11 46					12 16								12 46
	d			11 16								11 49					12 16								12 49
Hampton Wick	d			11 18								11 51					12 18								12 51
Teddington	d			11 21								11 56					12 21								12 56
Strawberry Hill	a											11 59													12 59
Fulwell	d			11 25													12 25								
Hampton	d			11 29													12 29								
Kempton Park	d			11 32													12 32								
Sunbury	d			11 34													12 34								
Upper Halliford	d			11 36													12 36								
Shepperton	a			11 39													12 39								
Berrylands	d					11 21								11 51						12 21					
Surbiton 6	d		11 05			11 25	11 32			11 35				11 55		12 05				12 25	12 32		12 35		
Thames Ditton	d					11 30								12 00						12 30					
Hampton Court	a					11 33								12 03						12 33					
Hinchley Wood	d						11 36														12 36				
Claygate	d						11 39														12 39				
Oxshott	d						11 42														12 42				
Cobham & Stoke D'abernon	d						11 46														12 46				
Bookham	d	11 21													12 21										
Effingham Junction 6	d	11 25					11 50								12 25						12 50				
Horsley	d	11 27					11 53								12 27						12 53				
Clandon	d	11 32					11 58								12 32						12 58				
London Road (Guildford)	d	11 37					12 03								12 37						13 03				
Guildford	a	11 41	11 44				12 07			12 14					12 41	12 44					13 07		13 14		

Table 152

Sundays until 30 September

London - Chessington South, Dorking, Guildford, Shepperton and Hampton Court

Network Diagram - see first Page of Table 152

		SW	SW	SW	SW	SW	SW	SW	SW	SW	SW	SW	SW	SW	SW	SW	SW	SW	SW	SW
London Waterloo ⊖	d	12 21	12 27	12 32	12 40		12 48	12 51	12 57	13 00	13 02	13 10	13 18	13 21	13 27	13 32	13 40		13 48	13 51
Vauxhall ⊖	d	12 25	12 31	12 36	12 44		12 52	12 55	13 01	13 04	13 06	13 14	13 22	13 25	13 31	13 36	13 44		13 52	13 55
Clapham Junction	d	12 30	12 36	12 41	12 49		12 57	13 00	13 06	13 09	13 11	13 19	13 27	13 30	13 36	13 41	13 49		13 57	14 00
Earlsfield	d	12 33	12 39	12 44	12 52		13 00	13 03	13 09	13 12	13 14	13 22	13 30	13 33	13 39	13 44	13 52		14 00	14 03
Wimbledon ⊖	d	12 37	12 43	12 48	12 56		13 04	13 07	13 13	13 16	13 18	13 26	13 34	13 37	13 43	13 48	13 56		14 04	14 07
Raynes Park	d	12 40	12 46	12 52			13 07	13 10	13 16		13 22		13 37	13 40	13 46	13 52			14 07	14 10
Motspur Park	d	12 43		12 55				13 13			13 25			13 43		13 55				14 13
Malden Manor	d	12 46						13 16						13 46						14 16
Tolworth	d	12 49						13 19						13 49						14 19
Chessington North	d	12 52						13 22						13 52						14 22
Chessington South	a	12 54						13 24						13 54						14 24
Worcester Park	d			12 57							13 27					13 57				
Stoneleigh	d			13 00							13 30					14 00				
Ewell West	d			13 03							13 33					14 03				
Epsom	a			13 06							13 36					14 06				
	d			13 08							13 38					14 08				
Ashtead	d			13 12							13 42					14 12				
Leatherhead	d			13 15							13 45					14 15				
Box Hill & Westhumble	d																			
Dorking	a										13 51									
New Malden	d		12 49				13 10		13 19				13 40		13 49				14 10	
Norbiton	d						13 13						13 43						14 13	
Kingston	a						13 16						13 46						14 16	
	d					13 11	13 16						13 49					14 11	14 16	
Hampton Wick	d					13 13	13 18						13 51					14 13	14 18	
Teddington	d					13 16	13 21						13 56					14 16	14 21	
Strawberry Hill	a					13 19							13 59					14 19		
Fulwell	d						13 25												14 25	
Hampton	d						13 29												14 29	
Kempton Park	d						13 32												14 32	
Sunbury	d						13 34												14 34	
Upper Halliford	d						13 36												14 36	
Shepperton	a						13 39												14 39	
Berrylands	d		12 51						13 21						13 51					
Surbiton	d		12 55		13 05				13 25	13 32		13 35			13 55		14 05			
Thames Ditton	d		13 00						13 30						14 00					
Hampton Court	a		13 03						13 33						14 03					
Hinchley Wood	d									13 36										
Claygate	d									13 39										
Oxshott	d									13 42										
Cobham & Stoke D'abernon	d									13 46										
Bookham	d			13 21												14 21				
Effingham Junction	d			13 25						13 50						14 25				
Horsley	d			13 27						13 53						14 27				
Clandon	d			13 32						13 58						14 32				
London Road (Guildford)	d			13 37						14 03						14 37				
Guildford	a			13 41	13 44					14 07		14 14				14 41	14 44			

		SW	SW	SW	SW	SW	SW	SW	SW	SW	SW	SW	SW	SW	SW	SW	SW	SW	SW	SW
London Waterloo ⊖	d	13 57	14 00	14 02	14 10	14 18	14 21	14 27	14 32	14 40		14 48	14 51	14 57	15 00	15 02	15 10	15 18	15 21	15 27
Vauxhall ⊖	d	14 01	14 04	14 06	14 14	14 22	14 25	14 31	14 36	14 44		14 52	14 55	15 01	15 04	15 06	15 14	15 22	15 25	15 31
Clapham Junction	d	14 06	14 09	14 11	14 19	14 27	14 30	14 36	14 41	14 49		14 57	15 00	15 06	15 09	15 11	15 19	15 27	15 30	15 36
Earlsfield	d	14 09	14 12	14 14	14 22	14 30	14 33	14 39	14 44	14 52		15 00	15 03	15 09	15 12	15 14	15 22	15 30	15 33	15 39
Wimbledon ⊖	d	14 13	14 16	14 18	14 26	14 34	14 37	14 43	14 48	14 56		15 04	15 07	15 13	15 16	15 18	15 26	15 34	15 37	15 43
Raynes Park	d	14 16		14 22		14 37	14 40	14 46	14 52			15 07	15 10	15 16		15 22		15 37	15 40	15 46
Motspur Park	d			14 25			14 43		14 55				15 13			15 25			15 43	
Malden Manor	d						14 46						15 16						15 46	
Tolworth	d						14 49						15 19						15 49	
Chessington North	d						14 52						15 22						15 52	
Chessington South	a						14 54						15 24						15 54	
Worcester Park	d			14 27					14 57							15 27				
Stoneleigh	d			14 30					15 00							15 30				
Ewell West	d			14 33					15 03							15 33				
Epsom	a			14 36					15 06							15 36				
	d			14 38					15 08							15 38				
Ashtead	d			14 42					15 12							15 42				
Leatherhead	d			14 45					15 15							15 45				
Box Hill & Westhumble	d																			
Dorking	a			14 51												15 51				
New Malden	d	14 19				14 40		14 49				15 10		15 19				15 40		15 49
Norbiton	d					14 43						15 13						15 43		
Kingston	a					14 46						15 16						15 46		
	d					14 49					15 11	15 16						15 49		
Hampton Wick	d					14 51					15 13	15 18						15 51		
Teddington	d					14 56					15 16	15 21						15 56		
Strawberry Hill	a					14 59					15 19							15 59		
Fulwell	d											15 25								
Hampton	d											15 29								
Kempton Park	d											15 32								
Sunbury	d											15 34								
Upper Halliford	d											15 36								
Shepperton	a											15 39								
Berrylands	d	14 21						14 51						15 21						15 51
Surbiton	d	14 25	14 32		14 35			14 55		15 05				15 25	15 32		15 35			15 55
Thames Ditton	d	14 30						15 00						15 30						16 00
Hampton Court	a	14 33						15 03						15 33						16 03
Hinchley Wood	d		14 36												15 36					
Claygate	d		14 39												15 39					
Oxshott	d		14 42												15 42					
Cobham & Stoke D'abernon	d		14 46												15 46					
Bookham	d								15 21											
Effingham Junction	d		14 50						15 25						15 50					
Horsley	d		14 53						15 27						15 53					
Clandon	d		14 58						15 32						15 58					
London Road (Guildford)	d		15 03						15 37						16 03					
Guildford	a		15 07		15 14				15 41	15 44					16 07		16 14			

Table 152

Sundays until 30 September

London - Chessington South, Dorking, Guildford, Shepperton and Hampton Court

Network Diagram - see first Page of Table 152

		SW	SW	SW	SW	SW	SW	SW	SW	SW	SW	SW	SW	SW	SW	SW	SW	SW	SW	SW
London Waterloo ⊖	d	15 32	15 40		15 48	15 51	15 57	16 00	16 02	16 10	16 18	16 21	16 27	16 32	16 40		16 48	16 51	16 57	17 00
Vauxhall ⊖	d	15 36	15 44		15 52	15 55	16 01	16 04	16 06	16 14	16 22	16 25	16 31	16 36	16 44		16 52	16 55	17 01	17 04
Clapham Junction	d	15 41	15 49		15 57	16 00	16 06	16 09	16 11	16 19	16 27	16 30	16 36	16 41	16 49		16 57	17 00	17 06	17 09
Earlsfield	d	15 44	15 52		16 00	16 03	16 09	16 12	16 14	16 22	16 30	16 33	16 39	16 44	16 52		17 00	17 03	17 09	17 12
Wimbledon ⊖	d	15 48	15 56		16 04	16 07	16 13	16 16	16 18	16 26	16 34	16 37	16 43	16 48	16 56		17 04	17 07	17 13	17 16
Raynes Park	d	15 52			16 07	16 10	16 16		16 22		16 37	16 40	16 46	16 52			17 07	17 10	17 16	
Motspur Park	d	15 55				16 13			16 25			16 43		16 55				17 13		
Malden Manor	d					16 16						16 46						17 16		
Tolworth	d					16 19						16 49						17 19		
Chessington North	d					16 22						16 52						17 22		
Chessington South	a					16 24						16 54						17 24		
Worcester Park	d	15 57							16 27					16 57						
Stoneleigh	d	16 00							16 30					17 00						
Ewell West	d	16 03							16 33					17 03						
Epsom	a	16 06							16 36					17 06						
	d	16 08							16 38					17 08						
Ashtead	d	16 12							16 42					17 12						
Leatherhead	d	16 15							16 45					17 15						
Box Hill & Westhumble	d																			
Dorking	a								16 51											
New Malden	d				16 10		16 19				16 40		16 49				17 10		17 19	
Norbiton	d				16 13						16 43						17 13			
Kingston	a				16 16						16 46						17 16			
	d			16 11	16 16						16 49					17 11	17 16			
Hampton Wick	d			16 13	16 18						16 51					17 13	17 18			
Teddington	d			16 16	16 21						16 56					17 16	17 21			
Strawberry Hill	a			16 19							16 59					17 19				
Fulwell	d				16 25												17 25			
Hampton	d				16 29												17 29			
Kempton Park	d				16 32												17 32			
Sunbury	d				16 34												17 34			
Upper Halliford	d				16 36												17 36			
Shepperton	a				16 39												17 39			
Berrylands	d						16 21						16 51						17 21	
Surbiton	d		16 05				16 25	16 32		16 35			16 55		17 05				17 25	17 32
Thames Ditton	d						16 30						17 00						17 30	
Hampton Court	a						16 33						17 03						17 33	
Hinchley Wood	d							16 36												17 36
Claygate	d							16 39												17 39
Oxshott	d							16 42												17 42
Cobham & Stoke D'abernon	d							16 46												17 46
Bookham	d	16 21												17 21						
Effingham Junction	d	16 25						16 50						17 25						17 50
Horsley	d	16 27						16 53						17 27						17 53
Clandon	d	16 32						16 58						17 32						17 58
London Road (Guildford)	d	16 37						17 03						17 37						18 03
Guildford	a	16 41	16 44					17 07		17 14				17 41	17 44					18 07

		SW	SW	SW	SW	SW	SW	SW	SW	SW	SW	SW	SW	SW	SW	SW	SW	SW	SW
London Waterloo ⊖	d	17 02	17 10	17 18	17 21	17 27	17 32	17 40		17 48	17 51	17 57	18 00	18 02	18 10	18 18	18 21	18 27	18 32
Vauxhall ⊖	d	17 06	17 14	17 22	17 25	17 31	17 36	17 44		17 52	17 55	18 01	18 04	18 06	18 14	18 22	18 25	18 31	18 36
Clapham Junction	d	17 11	17 19	17 27	17 30	17 36	17 41	17 49		17 57	18 00	18 06	18 09	18 11	18 19	18 27	18 30	18 36	18 41
Earlsfield	d	17 14	17 22	17 30	17 33	17 39	17 44	17 52		18 00	18 03	18 09	18 12	18 14	18 22	18 30	18 33	18 39	18 44
Wimbledon ⊖	d	17 18	17 26	17 34	17 37	17 43	17 48	17 56		18 04	18 07	18 13	18 16	18 18	18 26	18 34	18 37	18 43	18 48
Raynes Park	d	17 22		17 37	17 40	17 46	17 52			18 07	18 10	18 16		18 22		18 37	18 40	18 46	18 52
Motspur Park	d	17 25			17 43		17 55				18 13			18 25			18 43		18 55
Malden Manor	d				17 46						18 16						18 46		
Tolworth	d				17 49						18 19						18 49		
Chessington North	d				17 52						18 22						18 52		
Chessington South	a				17 54						18 24						18 54		
Worcester Park	d	17 27					17 57							18 27					18 57
Stoneleigh	d	17 30					18 00							18 30					19 00
Ewell West	d	17 33					18 03							18 33					19 03
Epsom	a	17 36					18 06							18 36					19 06
	d	17 38					18 08							18 38					19 08
Ashtead	d	17 42					18 12							18 42					19 12
Leatherhead	d	17 45					18 15							18 45					19 15
Box Hill & Westhumble	d																		
Dorking	a	17 51												18 51					
New Malden	d			17 40		17 49				18 10		18 19				18 40		18 49	
Norbiton	d			17 43						18 13						18 43			
Kingston	a			17 46						18 16						18 46			
	d			17 49					18 11	18 16						18 49			
Hampton Wick	d			17 51					18 13	18 18						18 51			
Teddington	d			17 56					18 16	18 21						18 56			
Strawberry Hill	a			17 59					18 19							18 59			
Fulwell	d									18 25									
Hampton	d									18 29									
Kempton Park	d									18 32									
Sunbury	d									18 34									
Upper Halliford	d									18 36									
Shepperton	a									18 39									
Berrylands	d					17 51						18 21						18 51	
Surbiton	d		17 35			17 55		18 05				18 25	18 32		18 35			18 55	
Thames Ditton	d					18 00						18 30						19 00	
Hampton Court	a					18 03						18 33						19 03	
Hinchley Wood	d												18 36						
Claygate	d												18 39						
Oxshott	d												18 42						
Cobham & Stoke D'abernon	d												18 46						
Bookham	d						18 21												19 21
Effingham Junction	d						18 25						18 50						19 25
Horsley	d						18 27						18 53						19 27
Clandon	d						18 32						18 58						19 32
London Road (Guildford)	d						18 37						19 03						19 37
Guildford	a		18 14				18 41	18 44					19 07		19 14				19 41

Sundays
until 30 September

London - Chessington South, Dorking, Guildford, Shepperton and Hampton Court

Network Diagram - see first Page of Table 152

		SW	SW	SW	SW	SW	SW	SW	SW	SW	SW	SW	SW	SW	SW	SW	SW	SW	SW	SW
London Waterloo 15 ⊖	d	18 40		18 48	18 51	18 57	19 00	19 02	19 10	19 18	19 21	19 27	19 32	19 40		19 48	19 57	20 00	20 02	20 10
Vauxhall ⊖	d	18 44		18 52	18 55	19 01	19 04	19 06	19 14	19 22	19 25	19 31	19 36	19 44		19 52	20 01	20 04	20 06	20 14
Clapham Junction 10	d	18 49		18 57	19 00	19 06	19 09	19 11	19 19	19 27	19 30	19 36	19 41	19 49		19 57	20 06	20 09	20 11	20 19
Earlsfield	d	18 52		19 00	19 03	19 09	19 12	19 14	19 22	19 30	19 33	19 39	19 44	19 52		20 00	20 09	20 12	20 14	20 22
Wimbledon 6 ⊖	d	18 56		19 04	19 07	19 13	19 16	19 18	19 26	19 34	19 37	19 43	19 48	19 56		20 04	20 13	20 16	20 18	20 26
Raynes Park 6	d			19 07	19 10	19 16		19 22		19 37	19 40	19 46	19 52			20 07	20 16		20 22	
Motspur Park	d				19 13			19 25			19 43		19 55						20 25	
Malden Manor	d				19 16						19 46									
Tolworth	d				19 19						19 49									
Chessington North	d				19 22						19 52									
Chessington South	a				19 24						19 54									
Worcester Park	d							19 27					19 57						20 27	
Stoneleigh	d							19 30					20 00						20 30	
Ewell West	d							19 33					20 03						20 33	
Epsom 3	a							19 36					20 06						20 36	
	d							19 38					20 08						20 38	
Ashtead	d							19 42					20 12						20 42	
Leatherhead	d							19 45					20 15						20 45	
Box Hill & Westhumble	d																			
Dorking 4	a							19 51											20 51	
New Malden 6	d			19 10		19 19				19 40		19 49				20 10	20 19			
Norbiton	d			19 13						19 43						20 13				
Kingston	a			19 16						19 46						20 16				
	d		19 11	19 16						19 49					20 11	20 16				
Hampton Wick	d		19 13	19 18						19 51					20 13	20 18				
Teddington	d		19 16	19 21						19 56					20 16	20 21				
Strawberry Hill	a		19 19							19 59					20 19					
Fulwell	d			19 25												20 25				
Hampton	d			19 29												20 29				
Kempton Park	d			19 32												20 32				
Sunbury	d			19 34												20 34				
Upper Halliford	d			19 36												20 36				
Shepperton	a			19 39												20 39				
Berrylands	d					19 21						19 51					20 21			
Surbiton 6	d	19 05				19 25	19 32		19 35			19 55		20 05			20 25	20 32		20 35
Thames Ditton	d					19 30						20 00					20 30			
Hampton Court	a					19 33						20 03					20 33			
Hinchley Wood	d						19 36											20 36		
Claygate	d						19 39											20 39		
Oxshott	d						19 42											20 42		
Cobham & Stoke D'abernon	d						19 46											20 46		
Bookham	d												20 21							
Effingham Junction 6	d						19 50						20 25					20 50		
Horsley	d						19 53						20 27					20 53		
Clandon	d						19 58						20 32					20 58		
London Road (Guildford)	d						20 03						20 37					21 03		
Guildford	a	19 44					20 07		20 14				20 41	20 44				21 07		21 14

		SW	SW	SW	SW	SW	SW	SW	SW	SW	SW	SW	SW	SW	SW	SW	SW
London Waterloo 15 ⊖	d	20 18	20 21	20 27	20 32	20 40		20 48	20 57	21 00	21 02	21 10	21 18	21 21	21 32	21 40		21 48
Vauxhall ⊖	d	20 22	20 25	20 31	20 36	20 44		20 52	21 01	21 04	21 06	21 14	21 22	21 25	21 36	21 44		21 52
Clapham Junction 10	d	20 27	20 30	20 36	20 41	20 49		20 57	21 06	21 09	21 11	21 19	21 27	21 30	21 41	21 49		21 57
Earlsfield	d	20 30	20 33	20 39	20 44	20 52		21 00	21 09	21 12	21 14	21 22	21 30	21 33	21 44	21 52		22 00
Wimbledon 6 ⊖	d	20 34	20 37	20 43	20 48	20 56		21 04	21 13	21 16	21 18	21 26	21 34	21 37	21 48	21 56		22 04
Raynes Park 6	d	20 37	20 40	20 46	20 52			21 07	21 16		21 22		21 37	21 40	21 52			22 07
Motspur Park	d		20 43		20 55						21 25			21 43	21 55			
Malden Manor	d		20 46											21 46				
Tolworth	d		20 49											21 49				
Chessington North	d		20 52											21 52				
Chessington South	a		20 54											21 54				
Worcester Park	d				20 57						21 27				21 57			
Stoneleigh	d				21 00						21 30				22 00			
Ewell West	d				21 03						21 33				22 03			
Epsom 3	a				21 06						21 36				22 06			
	d				21 08						21 38				22 08			
Ashtead	d				21 12						21 42				22 12			
Leatherhead	d				21 15						21 45				22 15			
Box Hill & Westhumble	d																	
Dorking 4	a										21 51							
New Malden 6	d	20 40		20 49				21 10	21 19				21 40					22 10
Norbiton	d	20 43						21 13					21 43					22 13
Kingston	a	20 46						21 16					21 46					22 16
	d	20 49					21 11	21 16					21 49				22 11	22 16
Hampton Wick	d	20 51					21 13	21 18					21 51				22 13	22 18
Teddington	d	20 56					21 16	21 21					21 56				22 16	22 21
Strawberry Hill	a	20 59					21 19						21 59				22 19	
Fulwell	d							21 25										22 25
Hampton	d							21 29										22 29
Kempton Park	d							21 32										22 32
Sunbury	d							21 34										22 34
Upper Halliford	d							21 36										22 36
Shepperton	a							21 39										22 39
Berrylands	d			20 51					21 21									
Surbiton 6	d			20 55		21 05			21 25	21 32		21 35				22 05		
Thames Ditton	d			21 00					21 30									
Hampton Court	a			21 03					21 33									
Hinchley Wood	d									21 36								
Claygate	d									21 39								
Oxshott	d									21 42								
Cobham & Stoke D'abernon	d									21 46								
Bookham	d				21 21										22 21			
Effingham Junction 6	d				21 25					21 50					22 25			
Horsley	d				21 27					21 53					22 27			
Clandon	d				21 32					21 58					22 32			
London Road (Guildford)	d				21 37					22 03					22 37			
Guildford	a				21 41	21 44				22 07		22 14			22 41	22 44		

Sundays
until 30 September

London - Chessington South, Dorking, Guildford, Shepperton and Hampton Court

Network Diagram - see first Page of Table 152

		SW	SW	SW	SW	SW	SW	SW	SW	SW	SW	SW	SW	SW	SW	SW	SW	SW 1
London Waterloo 15 ⊖	d	21 57	22 00	22 02	22 10	22 18	22 21	22 32	22 40		22 48	22 51	22 57	23 00	23 02	23 10	23 18	23 32	23 40
Vauxhall ⊖	d	22 01	22 04	22 06	22 14	22 22	22 25	22 36	22 44		22 52	22 55	23 01	23 04	23 06	23 14	23 22	23 36	23 44
Clapham Junction 10	d	22 06	22 09	22 11	22 19	22 27	22 30	22 41	22 49		22 57	23 00	23 06	23 09	23 11	23 19	23 27	23 41	23 49
Earlsfield	d	22 09	22 12	22 14	22 22	22 30	22 33	22 44	22 52		23 00	23 03	23 09	23 12	23 14	23 22	23 30	23 44	23 52
Wimbledon 6 ⊖	d	22 13	22 16	22 18	22 26	22 34	22 37	22 48	22 56		23 04	23 07	23 13	23 16	23 18	23 26	23 34	23 48	23 56
Raynes Park 6	d	22 16		22 22		22 37	22 40	22 52			23 07	23 10	23 16		23 22		23 37	23 52	
Motspur Park	d			22 25			22 43	22 55				23 13			23 25			23 55	
Malden Manor	d						22 46					23 16							
Tolworth	d						22 49					23 19							
Chessington North	d						22 52					23 22							
Chessington South	a						22 54					23 24							
Worcester Park	d			22 27				22 57							23 27			23 57	
Stoneleigh	d			22 30				23 00							23 30			23 59	
Ewell West	d			22 33				23 03							23 33			00 03	
Epsom 3	a			22 36				23 06							23 36			00 06	
	d			22 38				23 08											
Ashtead	d			22 42				23 12											
Leatherhead	d			22 45				23 15											
Box Hill & Westhumble	d																		
Dorking 4	a			22 51															
New Malden 6	d	22 19				22 40					23 10		23 19				23 40		
Norbiton	d					22 43					23 13						23 43		
Kingston	a					22 46					23 16						23 46		
	d					22 49				23 11	23 16						23 47		
Hampton Wick	d					22 51				23 13	23 18						23 49		
Teddington	d					22 56				23 16	23 21						23 51		
Strawberry Hill	a					22 59				23 19							23 54		
Fulwell	d										23 25								
Hampton	d										23 29								
Kempton Park	d										23 32								
Sunbury	d										23 34								
Upper Halliford	d										23 36								
Shepperton	a										23 39								
Berrylands	d	22 21											23 21						
Surbiton 6	d	22 25	22 32		22 35				23 05				23 25	23 32		23 35			00a04
Thames Ditton	d	22 30											23 30						
Hampton Court	a	22 33											23 33						
Hinchley Wood	d		22 36											23 36					
Claygate	d		22 39											23 39					
Oxshott	d		22 42											23 42					
Cobham & Stoke D'abernon	d		22 46											23 46					
Bookham	d							23 21											
Effingham Junction 6	d		22 50					23 25						23 50					
Horsley	d		22 53					23 27						23 53					
Clandon	d		22 58					23 32						23 58					
London Road (Guildford)	d		23 03					23 37						00 03					
Guildford	a		23 07		23 13			23 41	23 45					00 07		00 13			

Sundays from 7 October

London - Chessington South, Dorking, Guildford, Shepperton and Hampton Court

Network Diagram - see first Page of Table 152

Station		SW A	SW B	SW A	SW B	SW A	SW B	SW	SW	SW A	SW B	SW A	SW B	SW A	SW B	SW	SW	SW	SW	SW
London Waterloo ⊖	d	23p03	23p03	23p09	23p09	23p12	23p12	23p27	23p36	23p42	23p42	23p50	23p50	23p57	23p57	00 09	00 15	00 27	00 42	01 42
Vauxhall ⊖	d	23p07	23p07	23p13	23p13	23p16	23p16	23p31	23p40	23p46	23p46	23p54	23p54	00 01	00 01	00 13	00 19	00 31	00 46	01 46
Clapham Junction	d	23p12	23p12	23p18	23p18	23p21	23p21	23p36	23p45	23p51	23p51	23p59	23p59	00 06	00 06	00 20	00 25	00 37	00 51	01 53
Earlsfield	d	23p15	23p15	23p21	23p21	23p24	23p24	23p39	23p48	23p54	23p54	00 02	00 02	00 09	00 09	00 23	00 29	00s41		
Wimbledon ⊖	d	23p19	23p19	23p25	23p25	23p28	23p28	23p43	23p52	23p58	23p58	00 06	00 06	00 13	00 13	00 27	00 33	00 45	01 05	01 59
Raynes Park	d			23p28	23p28	23p31	23p31	23p46	23p55	00 01	00 01			00 16	00 16		00 36	00 48	01 08	02 02
Motspur Park	d			23p31	23p31					00 04	00 04						00 38			
Malden Manor	d																			
Tolworth	d																			
Chessington North	d																			
Chessington South	a																			
Worcester Park	d			23p33	23p33					00 06	00 06						00 41			
Stoneleigh	d			23p36	23p36					00 09	00 09						00 44			
Ewell West	d			23p39	23p39					00 12	00 12						00 46			
Epsom	a			23p42	23p42					00 15	00 15						00 50			
	d			23p47	23p47					00 19	00 19									
Ashtead	d			23p51	23p51					00 23	00 23									
Leatherhead	d			23p54	23p54					00 26	00 26									
Box Hill & Westhumble	d																			
Dorking	a			00 01	00 03															
New Malden	d					23p34	23p34	23p49	23p58					00 19	00 19			00 50	01 11	02 04
Norbiton	d					23p37	23p37	23p52						00 22	00 22				01 14	02 08
Kingston	a					23p40	23p40	23p55						00 25	00 25				01 17	02 10
	d					23p40	23p40	23p55						00 25	00 25				01 17	02 11
Hampton Wick	d					23p42	23p42	23p57						00 27	00 27				01s22	02s13
Teddington	d					23p45	23p45	23p59						00 30	00 30				01s25	02s15
Strawberry Hill	a							00 03											01 28	02s18
Fulwell	d					23p49	23p49							00 34	00 34					
Hampton	d					23p53	23p53							00 38	00 38					
Kempton Park	d					23p56	23p56							00 41	00 41					
Sunbury	d					23p58	23p58							00 43	00 43					
Upper Halliford	d					23p59	23p59							00 45	00 45					
Shepperton	a					00 03	00 05							00 48	00 50					
Berrylands	d								23p59									00s53		
Surbiton	d	23p27	23p27						00 05			00 14	00 14			00 35		00a56		
Thames Ditton	d								00 09											
Hampton Court	a								00 12											
Hinchley Wood	d	23p31	23p31									00 18	00 18							
Claygate	d	23p34	23p34									00 20	00 20							
Oxshott	d	23p37	23p37									00 24	00 24							
Cobham & Stoke D'abernon	d	23p41	23p41									00 27	00 27							
Bookham	d									00 31	00 31									
Effingham Junction	d	23p45	23p45							00 36	00 36	00 32	00 32							
Horsley	d	23p48	23p48							00 39	00 39	00 34	00 34							
Clandon	d	23p53	23p53							00 44	00 44	00 39	00 39							
London Road (Guildford)	d	23p58	23p58							00 49	00 49	00 44	00 44							
Guildford	a	00 02	00 05							00 53	00 56	00 48	00 51			01 07				

A 7 October

B not 7 October

Table 152

Sundays from 7 October

London - Chessington South, Dorking, Guildford, Shepperton and Hampton Court

Network Diagram - see first Page of Table 152

Station		SW	SW	SW	SW	SW	SW	SW	SW	SW	SW	SW	SW	SW	SW	SW	SW	SW	SW	SW	SW
London Waterloo ⊖	d	06 18		06 57			07 10	07 18		07 27		07 40	07 48		07 57		08 02	08 10	08 18	08 21	08 27
Vauxhall ⊖	d	06 22		07 01			07 14	07 22		07 31		07 44	07 52		08 01		08 06	08 14	08 22	08 25	08 31
Clapham Junction	d	06 27		07 06			07 19	07 27		07 36		07 49	07 57		08 06		08 11	08 19	08 27	08 30	08 36
Earlsfield	d			07 09			07 22	07 30		07 39		07 52	08 00		08 09		08 14	08 22	08 30	08 33	08 39
Wimbledon ⊖	d	06 34	06 48	07 13	07 16	07 20	07 26	07 34	07 37	07 43	07 48	07 56	08 04	08 07	08 13	08 17	08 18	08 26	08 34	08 37	08 43
Raynes Park	d	06 37	06 52	07 16		07 23		07 37	07 40	07 46	07 52		08 07	08 10	08 16		08 22		08 37	08 40	08 46
Motspur Park	d		06 55			07 26			07 43		07 55			08 13			08 25			08 43	
Malden Manor	d								07 46					08 16						08 46	
Tolworth	d								07 49					08 19						08 49	
Chessington North	d								07 52					08 22						08 52	
Chessington South	a								07 54					08 24						08 54	
Worcester Park	d		06 57			07 28					07 57						08 27				
Stoneleigh	d		07 00			07 31					08 00						08 30				
Ewell West	d		07 03			07 34					08 03						08 33				
Epsom	a		07 06			07 37					08 06						08 36				
	d										08 08						08 38				
Ashtead	d										08 12						08 42				
Leatherhead	d										08 15						08 45				
Box Hill & Westhumble	d																				
Dorking	a																08 53				
New Malden	d	06 40		07 19				07 40		07 49			08 10		08 19				08 40		08 49
Norbiton	d	06 43						07 43					08 13						08 43		
Kingston	a	06 46						07 46					08 16						08 46		
	d	06 49						07 49					08 16						08 49		
Hampton Wick	d	06 51						07 51					08 18						08 51		
Teddington	d	06 56						07 56					08 21						08 56		
Strawberry Hill	a	06 59						07 59											08 59		
Fulwell	d												08 25								
Hampton	d												08 29								
Kempton Park	d												08 32								
Sunbury	d												08 34								
Upper Halliford	d												08 36								
Shepperton	a												08 41								
Berrylands	d			07 21						07 51					08 21						08 51
Surbiton	d			07 25	07 32		07 35			07 55		08 05			08 25	08 32		08 35			08 55
Thames Ditton	d			07 30						08 00					08 30						09 00
Hampton Court	a			07 33						08 03					08 33						09 03
Hinchley Wood	d				07 36											08 36					
Claygate	d				07 39											08 39					
Oxshott	d				07 42											08 42					
Cobham & Stoke D'abernon	d				07 46											08 46					
Bookham	d										08 21										
Effingham Junction	d				07 50						08 25					08 50					
Horsley	d				07 53						08 27					08 53					
Clandon	d				07 58						08 32					08 58					
London Road (Guildford)	d				08 03						08 37					09 03					
Guildford	a				08 10		08 14				08 44	08 40				09 10		09 10			

Station		SW	SW	SW	SW	SW	SW	SW	SW	SW	SW	SW	SW	SW	SW	SW	SW	SW	SW	SW
London Waterloo ⊖	d	08 32	08 40	08 48	08 51	08 57		09 02	09 10	09 18	09 21	09 27	09 32	09 40	09 48	09 51	09 57		10 02	10 10
Vauxhall ⊖	d	08 36	08 44	08 52	08 55	09 01		09 06	09 14	09 22	09 25	09 31	09 36	09 44	09 52	09 55	10 01		10 06	10 14
Clapham Junction	d	08 41	08 49	08 57	09 00	09 06		09 11	09 19	09 27	09 30	09 36	09 41	09 49	09 57	10 00	10 06		10 11	10 19
Earlsfield	d	08 44	08 52	09 00	09 03	09 09		09 14	09 22	09 30	09 33	09 39	09 44	09 52	10 00	10 03	10 09		10 14	10 22
Wimbledon ⊖	d	08 48	08 56	09 04	09 07	09 13	09 17	09 18	09 26	09 34	09 37	09 43	09 48	09 56	10 04	10 07	10 13	10 17	10 18	10 26
Raynes Park	d	08 52		09 07	09 10	09 16		09 22		09 37	09 40	09 46	09 52		10 07	10 10	10 16		10 22	
Motspur Park	d	08 55			09 13			09 25			09 43		09 55			10 13			10 25	
Malden Manor	d				09 16						09 46					10 16				
Tolworth	d				09 19						09 49					10 19				
Chessington North	d				09 22						09 52					10 22				
Chessington South	a				09 24						09 54					10 24				
Worcester Park	d	08 57						09 27					09 57						10 27	
Stoneleigh	d	09 00						09 30					10 00						10 30	
Ewell West	d	09 03						09 33					10 03						10 33	
Epsom	a	09 06						09 36					10 06						10 36	
	d	09 08						09 38					10 08						10 38	
Ashtead	d	09 12						09 42					10 12						10 42	
Leatherhead	d	09 15						09 45					10 15						10 45	
Box Hill & Westhumble	d																			
Dorking	a							09 53											10 53	
New Malden	d			09 10		09 19				09 40		09 49			10 10		10 19			
Norbiton	d			09 13						09 43					10 13					
Kingston	a			09 16						09 46					10 16					
	d			09 16						09 49					10 16					
Hampton Wick	d			09 18						09 51					10 18					
Teddington	d			09 21						09 56					10 21					
Strawberry Hill	a									09 59										
Fulwell	d			09 25											10 25					
Hampton	d			09 29											10 29					
Kempton Park	d			09 32											10 32					
Sunbury	d			09 34											10 34					
Upper Halliford	d			09 36											10 36					
Shepperton	a			09 41											10 41					
Berrylands	d					09 21						09 51					10 21			
Surbiton	d		09 05			09 25	09 32		09 35			09 55		10 05			10 25	10 32		10 35
Thames Ditton	d					09 30						10 00					10 30			
Hampton Court	a					09 33						10 03					10 33			
Hinchley Wood	d						09 36											10 36		
Claygate	d						09 39											10 39		
Oxshott	d						09 42											10 42		
Cobham & Stoke D'abernon	d						09 46											10 46		
Bookham	d	09 21											10 21							
Effingham Junction	d	09 25					09 50						10 25					10 50		
Horsley	d	09 27					09 53						10 27					10 53		
Clandon	d	09 32					09 58						10 32					10 58		
London Road (Guildford)	d	09 37					10 03						10 37					11 03		
Guildford	a	09 44	09 40				10 10		10 10				10 44	10 44				11 10		11 14

Table 152

Sundays
from 7 October

London - Chessington South, Dorking, Guildford, Shepperton and Hampton Court

Network Diagram - see first Page of Table 152

		SW	SW	SW	SW	SW	SW	SW	SW	SW	SW	SW	SW	SW	SW	SW	SW	SW	SW	SW	SW	SW
London Waterloo [15] ⊖	d	10 18	10 21	10 27	10 32	10 40	10 48	10 51	10 57		11 02	11 10	11 18	11 21	11 27	11 32	11 40	11 48	11 51	11 57		12 02
Vauxhall ⊖	d	10 22	10 25	10 31	10 36	10 44	10 52	10 55	11 01		11 06	11 14	11 22	11 25	11 31	11 36	11 44	11 52	11 55	12 01		12 06
Clapham Junction [10]	d	10 27	10 30	10 36	10 41	10 49	10 57	11 00	11 06		11 11	11 19	11 27	11 30	11 36	11 41	11 49	11 57	12 00	12 06		12 11
Earlsfield	d	10 30	10 33	10 39	10 44	10 52	11 00	11 03	11 09		11 14	11 22	11 30	11 33	11 39	11 44	11 52	12 00	12 03	12 09		12 14
Wimbledon [6] ⊖ ⇌	d	10 34	10 37	10 43	10 48	10 56	11 04	11 07	11 13	11 17	11 18	11 26	11 34	11 37	11 43	11 48	11 56	12 04	12 07	12 13	12 17	12 18
Raynes Park [6]	d	10 37	10 40	10 46	10 52		11 07	11 10	11 16		11 22		11 37	11 40	11 46	11 52		12 07	12 10	12 16		12 22
Motspur Park	d		10 43		10 55			11 13			11 25			11 43		11 55			12 13			12 25
Malden Manor	d		10 46					11 16						11 46					12 16			
Tolworth	d		10 49					11 19						11 49					12 19			
Chessington North	d		10 52					11 22						11 52					12 22			
Chessington South	a		10 54					11 24						11 54					12 24			
Worcester Park	d				10 57						11 27					11 57						12 27
Stoneleigh	d				11 00						11 30					12 00						12 30
Ewell West	d				11 03						11 33					12 03						12 33
Epsom [3]	a				11 06						11 36					12 06						12 36
	d				11 08						11 38					12 08						12 38
Ashtead	d				11 12						11 42					12 12						12 42
Leatherhead	d				11 15						11 45					12 15						12 45
Box Hill & Westhumble	d																					
Dorking [4]	a										11 53											12 53
New Malden [6]	d	10 40		10 49			11 10		11 19				11 40		11 49			12 10		12 19		
Norbiton	d	10 43					11 13						11 43					12 13				
Kingston	a	10 46					11 16						11 46					12 16				
	d	10 49					11 16						11 49					12 16				
Hampton Wick	d	10 51					11 18						11 51					12 18				
Teddington	d	10 56					11 21						11 56					12 21				
Strawberry Hill	a	10 59											11 59									
Fulwell	d						11 25											12 25				
Hampton	d						11 29											12 29				
Kempton Park	d						11 32											12 32				
Sunbury	d						11 34											12 34				
Upper Halliford	d						11 36											12 36				
Shepperton	a						11 41											12 41				
Berrylands	d			10 51					11 21						11 51					12 21		
Surbiton [6]	d			10 55		11 05			11 25	11 32		11 35			11 55		12 05			12 25	12 32	
Thames Ditton	d			11 00					11 30						12 00					12 30		
Hampton Court	a			11 03					11 33						12 03					12 33		
Hinchley Wood	d									11 36											12 36	
Claygate	d									11 39											12 39	
Oxshott	d									11 42											12 42	
Cobham & Stoke D'abernon	d									11 46											12 46	
Bookham	d				11 21											12 21						
Effingham Junction [6]	d				11 25					11 50						12 25					12 50	
Horsley	d				11 27					11 53						12 27					12 53	
Clandon	d				11 32					11 58						12 32					12 58	
London Road (Guildford)	d				11 37					12 03						12 37					13 03	
Guildford	a				11 44	11 44				12 10		12 14				12 44	12 44				13 10	

		SW	SW	SW	SW	SW	SW	SW	SW	SW	SW	SW	SW	SW	SW	SW	SW	SW	SW	SW
London Waterloo [15] ⊖	d	12 10	12 18	12 21	12 27	12 32	12 40		12 48	12 51	12 57	13 00	13 02	13 10	13 18	13 21	13 27	13 32	13 40	
Vauxhall ⊖	d	12 14	12 22	12 25	12 31	12 36	12 44		12 52	12 55	13 01	13 04	13 06	13 14	13 22	13 25	13 31	13 36	13 44	
Clapham Junction [10]	d	12 19	12 27	12 30	12 36	12 41	12 49		12 57	13 00	13 06	13 09	13 11	13 19	13 27	13 30	13 36	13 41	13 49	
Earlsfield	d	12 22	12 30	12 33	12 39	12 44	12 52		13 00	13 03	13 09	13 12	13 14	13 22	13 30	13 33	13 39	13 44	13 52	
Wimbledon [6] ⊖ ⇌	d	12 26	12 34	12 37	12 43	12 48	12 56		13 04	13 07	13 13	13 16	13 18	13 26	13 34	13 37	13 43	13 48	13 56	
Raynes Park [6]	d		12 37	12 40	12 46	12 52			13 07	13 10	13 16		13 22		13 37	13 40	13 46	13 52		
Motspur Park	d			12 43		12 55				13 13			13 25			13 43		13 55		
Malden Manor	d			12 46						13 16						13 46				
Tolworth	d			12 49						13 19						13 49				
Chessington North	d			12 52						13 22						13 52				
Chessington South	a			12 54						13 24						13 54				
Worcester Park	d					12 57							13 27					13 57		
Stoneleigh	d					13 00							13 30					14 00		
Ewell West	d					13 03							13 33					14 03		
Epsom [3]	a					13 06							13 36					14 06		
	d					13 08							13 38					14 08		
Ashtead	d					13 12							13 42					14 12		
Leatherhead	d					13 15							13 45					14 15		
Box Hill & Westhumble	d																			
Dorking [4]	a												13 53							
New Malden [6]	d		12 40		12 49				13 10		13 19				13 40		13 49			
Norbiton	d		12 43						13 13						13 43					
Kingston	a		12 46						13 16						13 46					
	d		12 49					13 11	13 16						13 49					14 11
Hampton Wick	d		12 51					13 13	13 18						13 51					14 13
Teddington	d		12 56					13 16	13 21						13 56					14 16
Strawberry Hill	a		12 59					13 19							13 59					14 19
Fulwell	d								13 25											
Hampton	d								13 29											
Kempton Park	d								13 32											
Sunbury	d								13 34											
Upper Halliford	d								13 36											
Shepperton	a								13 41											
Berrylands	d				12 51						13 21						13 51			
Surbiton [6]	d	12 35			12 55		13 05				13 25	13 32		13 35			13 55		14 05	
Thames Ditton	d				13 00						13 30						14 00			
Hampton Court	a				13 03						13 33						14 03			
Hinchley Wood	d											13 36								
Claygate	d											13 39								
Oxshott	d											13 42								
Cobham & Stoke D'abernon	d											13 46								
Bookham	d					13 21												14 21		
Effingham Junction [6]	d					13 25						13 50						14 25		
Horsley	d					13 27						13 53						14 27		
Clandon	d					13 32						13 58						14 32		
London Road (Guildford)	d					13 37						14 03						14 37		
Guildford	a	13 14				13 44	13 44					14 10		14 14				14 44	14 44	

Table 152

Sundays
from 7 October

London - Chessington South, Dorking, Guildford, Shepperton and Hampton Court

Network Diagram - see first Page of Table 152

		SW	SW	SW	SW	SW	SW	SW	SW	SW	SW	SW	SW	SW	SW	SW	SW	SW	SW
London Waterloo [15] ⊖	d	13 48	13 51	13 57	14 00	14 02	14 10	14 18	14 21	14 27	14 32	14 40		14 48	14 51	14 57	15 00	15 02	15 10
Vauxhall ⊖	d	13 52	13 55	14 01	14 04	14 06	14 14	14 22	14 25	14 31	14 36	14 44		14 52	14 55	15 01	15 04	15 06	15 14
Clapham Junction [10]	d	13 57	14 00	14 06	14 09	14 11	14 19	14 27	14 30	14 36	14 41	14 49		14 57	15 00	15 06	15 09	15 11	15 19
Earlsfield	d	14 00	14 03	14 09	14 12	14 14	14 22	14 30	14 33	14 39	14 44	14 52		15 00	15 03	15 09	15 12	15 14	15 22
Wimbledon [6] ⊖ ⇌	d	14 04	14 07	14 13	14 16	14 18	14 26	14 34	14 37	14 43	14 48	14 56		15 04	15 07	15 13	15 16	15 18	15 26
Raynes Park [6]	d	14 07	14 10	14 16		14 22		14 37	14 40	14 46	14 52			15 07	15 10	15 16		15 22	
Motspur Park	d		14 13			14 25			14 43		14 55				15 13			15 25	
Malden Manor	d		14 16						14 46						15 16				
Tolworth	d		14 19						14 49						15 19				
Chessington North	d		14 22						14 52						15 22				
Chessington South	a		14 24						14 54						15 24				
Worcester Park	d					14 27					14 57							15 27	
Stoneleigh	d					14 30					15 00							15 30	
Ewell West	d					14 33					15 03							15 33	
Epsom [3]	a					14 36					15 06							15 36	
	d					14 38					15 08							15 38	
Ashtead	d					14 42					15 12							15 42	
Leatherhead	d					14 45					15 15							15 45	
Box Hill & Westhumble	d																		
Dorking [4]	a					14 53												15 53	
New Malden [6]	d	14 10		14 19				14 40		14 49				15 10		15 19			
Norbiton	d	14 13						14 43						15 13					
Kingston	a	14 16						14 46						15 16					
	d	14 16						14 49					15 11	15 16					
Hampton Wick	d	14 18						14 51					15 13	15 18					
Teddington	d	14 21						14 56					15 16	15 21					
Strawberry Hill	a							14 59					15 19						
Fulwell	d	14 25												15 25					
Hampton	d	14 29												15 29					
Kempton Park	d	14 32												15 32					
Sunbury	d	14 34												15 34					
Upper Halliford	d	14 36												15 36					
Shepperton	a	14 41												15 41					
Berrylands	d			14 21						14 51						15 21			
Surbiton [6]	d			14 25	14 32		14 35			14 55		15 05				15 25	15 32		15 35
Thames Ditton	d			14 30						15 00						15 30			
Hampton Court	a			14 33						15 03						15 33			
Hinchley Wood	d				14 36												15 36		
Claygate	d				14 39												15 39		
Oxshott	d				14 42												15 42		
Cobham & Stoke D'abernon	d				14 46												15 46		
Bookham	d										15 21								
Effingham Junction [6]	d				14 50						15 25						15 50		
Horsley	d				14 53						15 27						15 53		
Clandon	d				14 58						15 32						15 58		
London Road (Guildford)	d				15 03						15 37						16 03		
Guildford	a				15 10		15 14				15 44	15 44					16 10		16 14

		SW	SW	SW	SW	SW	SW	SW	SW	SW	SW	SW	SW	SW	SW	SW	SW	SW	SW	SW	SW
London Waterloo [15] ⊖	d	15 18	15 21	15 27	15 32	15 40		15 48	15 51	15 57	16 00	16 02	16 10	16 18	16 21	16 27	16 32	16 40		16 48	16 51
Vauxhall ⊖	d	15 22	15 25	15 31	15 36	15 44		15 52	15 55	16 01	16 04	16 06	16 14	16 22	16 25	16 31	16 36	16 44		16 52	16 55
Clapham Junction [10]	d	15 27	15 30	15 36	15 41	15 49		15 57	16 00	16 06	16 09	16 11	16 19	16 27	16 30	16 36	16 41	16 49		16 57	17 00
Earlsfield	d	15 30	15 33	15 39	15 44	15 52		16 00	16 03	16 09	16 12	16 14	16 22	16 30	16 33	16 39	16 44	16 52		17 00	17 03
Wimbledon [6] ⊖ ⇌	d	15 34	15 37	15 43	15 48	15 56		16 04	16 07	16 13	16 16	16 18	16 26	16 34	16 37	16 43	16 48	16 56		17 04	17 07
Raynes Park [6]	d	15 37	15 40	15 46	15 52			16 07	16 10	16 16		16 22		16 37	16 40	16 46	16 52			17 07	17 10
Motspur Park	d		15 43		15 55				16 13			16 25			16 43		16 55				17 13
Malden Manor	d		15 46						16 16						16 46						17 16
Tolworth	d		15 49						16 19						16 49						17 19
Chessington North	d		15 52						16 22						16 52						17 22
Chessington South	a		15 54						16 24						16 54						17 24
Worcester Park	d				15 57							16 27					16 57				
Stoneleigh	d				16 00							16 30					17 00				
Ewell West	d				16 03							16 33					17 03				
Epsom [3]	a				16 06							16 36					17 06				
	d				16 08							16 38					17 08				
Ashtead	d				16 12							16 42					17 12				
Leatherhead	d				16 15							16 45					17 15				
Box Hill & Westhumble	d																				
Dorking [4]	a											16 53									
New Malden [6]	d	15 40		15 49				16 10		16 19				16 40		16 49				17 10	
Norbiton	d	15 43						16 13						16 43						17 13	
Kingston	a	15 46						16 16						16 46						17 16	
	d	15 49					16 11	16 16						16 49					17 11	17 16	
Hampton Wick	d	15 51					16 13	16 18						16 51					17 13	17 18	
Teddington	d	15 56					16 16	16 21						16 56					17 16	17 21	
Strawberry Hill	a	15 59					16 19							16 59					17 19		
Fulwell	d							16 25												17 25	
Hampton	d							16 29												17 29	
Kempton Park	d							16 32												17 32	
Sunbury	d							16 34												17 34	
Upper Halliford	d							16 36												17 36	
Shepperton	a							16 41												17 41	
Berrylands	d			15 51						16 21						16 51					
Surbiton [6]	d			15 55		16 05				16 25	16 32		16 35			16 55		17 05			
Thames Ditton	d			16 00						16 30						17 00					
Hampton Court	a			16 03						16 33						17 03					
Hinchley Wood	d										16 36										
Claygate	d										16 39										
Oxshott	d										16 42										
Cobham & Stoke D'abernon	d										16 46										
Bookham	d				16 21												17 21				
Effingham Junction [6]	d				16 25						16 50						17 25				
Horsley	d				16 27						16 53						17 27				
Clandon	d				16 32						16 58						17 32				
London Road (Guildford)	d				16 37						17 03						17 37				
Guildford	a				16 44	16 44					17 10		17 14				17 44	17 44			

Table 152

Sundays from 7 October

London - Chessington South, Dorking, Guildford, Shepperton and Hampton Court

Network Diagram - see first Page of Table 152

				SW	SW	SW	SW		SW	SW	SW	SW		SW	SW	SW	SW		SW	SW	SW	SW			SW
London Waterloo 15 ⊖	d			16 57	17 00	17 02	17 10		17 18	17 21	17 27	17 32		17 40		17 48	17 51		17 57	18 00	18 02	18 10			18 18
Vauxhall ⊖	d			17 01	17 04	17 06	17 14		17 22	17 25	17 31	17 36		17 44		17 52	17 55		18 01	18 04	18 06	18 14			18 22
Clapham Junction 10	d			17 06	17 09	17 11	17 19		17 27	17 30	17 36	17 41		17 49		17 57	18 00		18 06	18 09	18 11	18 19			18 27
Earlsfield	d			17 09	17 12	17 14	17 22		17 30	17 33	17 39	17 44		17 52		18 00	18 03		18 09	18 12	18 14	18 22			18 30
Wimbledon 6 ⊖ ⇌	d			17 13	17 16	17 18	17 26		17 34	17 37	17 43	17 48		17 56		18 04	18 07		18 13	18 16	18 18	18 26			18 34
Raynes Park 6	d			17 16		17 22			17 37	17 40	17 46	17 52				18 07	18 10		18 16		18 22				18 37
Motspur Park	d					17 25				17 43		17 55					18 13				18 25				
Malden Manor	d									17 46							18 16								
Tolworth	d									17 49							18 19								
Chessington North	d									17 52							18 22								
Chessington South	a									17 54							18 24								
Worcester Park	d					17 27						17 57									18 27				
Stoneleigh	d					17 30						18 00									18 30				
Ewell West	d					17 33						18 03									18 33				
Epsom 3	a					17 36						18 06									18 36				
	d					17 38						18 08									18 38				
Ashtead	d					17 42						18 12									18 42				
Leatherhead	d					17 45						18 15									18 45				
Box Hill & Westhumble	d																								
Dorking 4	a					17 53															18 53				
New Malden 6	d			17 19					17 40		17 49					18 10			18 19						18 40
Norbiton	d								17 43							18 13									18 43
Kingston	a								17 46							18 16									18 46
	d								17 49						18 11	18 16									18 49
Hampton Wick	d								17 51						18 13	18 18									18 51
Teddington	d								17 56						18 16	18 21									18 56
Strawberry Hill	a								17 59						18 19										18 59
Fulwell	d															18 25									
Hampton	d															18 29									
Kempton Park	d															18 32									
Sunbury	d															18 34									
Upper Halliford	d															18 36									
Shepperton	a															18 41									
Berrylands	d			17 21							17 51								18 21						
Surbiton 6	d			17 25	17 32		17 35				17 55			18 05					18 25	18 32		18 35			
Thames Ditton	d			17 30							18 00								18 30						
Hampton Court	a			17 33							18 03								18 33						
Hinchley Wood	d				17 36															18 36					
Claygate	d				17 39															18 39					
Oxshott	d				17 42															18 42					
Cobham & Stoke D'abernon	d				17 46															18 46					
Bookham	d											18 21													
Effingham Junction 6	d				17 50							18 25								18 50					
Horsley	d				17 53							18 27								18 53					
Clandon	d				17 58							18 32								18 58					
London Road (Guildford)	d				18 03							18 37								19 03					
Guildford	a				18 10		18 14					18 44		18 44						19 10		19 14			

		SW	SW	SW	SW	SW	SW	SW			SW	SW	SW	SW		SW	SW	SW		SW	SW	SW	SW		SW
London Waterloo 15 ⊖	d	18 21	18 27	18 32	18 40		18 48	18 51			18 57	19 00	19 02	19 10		19 18	19 21	19 27		19 32	19 40		19 48		19 57
Vauxhall ⊖	d	18 25	18 31	18 36	18 44		18 52	18 55			19 01	19 04	19 06	19 14		19 22	19 25	19 31		19 36	19 44		19 52		20 01
Clapham Junction 10	d	18 30	18 36	18 41	18 49		18 57	19 00			19 06	19 09	19 11	19 19		19 27	19 30	19 36		19 41	19 49		19 57		20 06
Earlsfield	d	18 33	18 39	18 44	18 52		19 00	19 03			19 09	19 12	19 14	19 22		19 30	19 33	19 39		19 44	19 52		20 00		20 09
Wimbledon 6 ⊖ ⇌	d	18 37	18 43	18 48	18 56		19 04	19 07			19 13	19 16	19 18	19 26		19 34	19 37	19 43		19 48	19 56		20 04		20 13
Raynes Park 6	d	18 40	18 46	18 52			19 07	19 10			19 16		19 22			19 37	19 40	19 46		19 52			20 07		20 16
Motspur Park	d	18 43		18 55				19 13					19 25				19 43			19 55					
Malden Manor	d	18 46						19 16									19 46								
Tolworth	d	18 49						19 19									19 49								
Chessington North	d	18 52						19 22									19 52								
Chessington South	a	18 54						19 24									19 54								
Worcester Park	d			18 57									19 27							19 57					
Stoneleigh	d			19 00									19 30							20 00					
Ewell West	d			19 03									19 33							20 03					
Epsom 3	a			19 06									19 36							20 06					
	d			19 08									19 38							20 08					
Ashtead	d			19 12									19 42							20 12					
Leatherhead	d			19 15									19 45							20 15					
Box Hill & Westhumble	d																								
Dorking 4	a												19 53												
New Malden 6	d		18 49				19 10				19 19					19 40		19 49					20 10		20 19
Norbiton	d						19 13									19 43							20 13		
Kingston	a						19 16									19 46							20 16		
	d					19 11	19 16									19 49						20 11	20 16		
Hampton Wick	d					19 13	19 18									19 51						20 13	20 18		
Teddington	d					19 16	19 21									19 56						20 16	20 21		
Strawberry Hill	a					19 19										19 59						20 19			
Fulwell	d						19 25																20 25		
Hampton	d						19 29																20 29		
Kempton Park	d						19 32																20 32		
Sunbury	d						19 34																20 34		
Upper Halliford	d						19 36																20 36		
Shepperton	a						19 41																20 41		
Berrylands	d		18 51								19 21							19 51							20 21
Surbiton 6	d		18 55		19 05						19 25	19 32		19 35				19 55			20 05				20 25
Thames Ditton	d		19 00								19 30							20 00							20 30
Hampton Court	a		19 03								19 33							20 03							20 33
Hinchley Wood	d											19 36													
Claygate	d											19 39													
Oxshott	d											19 42													
Cobham & Stoke D'abernon	d											19 46													
Bookham	d			19 21																20 21					
Effingham Junction 6	d			19 25								19 50								20 25					
Horsley	d			19 27								19 53								20 27					
Clandon	d			19 32								19 58								20 32					
London Road (Guildford)	d			19 37								20 03								20 37					
Guildford	a			19 44	19 44							20 10		20 14						20 44	20 44				

Table 152

Sundays from 7 October

London - Chessington South, Dorking, Guildford, Shepperton and Hampton Court

Network Diagram - see first Page of Table 152

		SW	SW	SW			SW	SW	SW	SW	SW	SW	SW			SW	SW	SW	SW		SW	SW	SW	SW	
London Waterloo 15 ⊖	d	20 00	20 02	20 10			20 18	20 21	20 27	20 32	20 40		20 48			20 57	21 00	21 02	21 10		21 18	21 21	21 32	21 40	
Vauxhall ⊖	d	20 04	20 06	20 14			20 22	20 25	20 31	20 36	20 44		20 52			21 01	21 04	21 06	21 14		21 22	21 25	21 36	21 44	
Clapham Junction 10	d	20 09	20 11	20 19			20 27	20 30	20 36	20 41	20 49		20 57			21 06	21 09	21 11	21 19		21 27	21 30	21 41	21 49	
Earlsfield	d	20 12	20 14	20 22			20 30	20 33	20 39	20 44	20 52		21 00			21 09	21 12	21 14	21 22		21 30	21 33	21 44	21 52	
Wimbledon 6 ⊖ ⇌	d	20 16	20 18	20 26			20 34	20 37	20 43	20 48	20 56		21 04			21 13	21 16	21 18	21 26		21 34	21 37	21 48	21 56	
Raynes Park 6	d		20 22				20 37	20 40	20 46	20 52			21 07			21 16		21 22			21 37	21 40	21 52		
Motspur Park	d		20 25					20 43		20 55								21 25				21 43	21 55		
Malden Manor	d							20 46														21 46			
Tolworth	d							20 49														21 49			
Chessington North	d							20 52														21 52			
Chessington South	a							20 54														21 54			
Worcester Park	d		20 27							20 57								21 27					21 57		
Stoneleigh	d		20 30							21 00								21 30					22 00		
Ewell West	d		20 33							21 03								21 33					22 03		
Epsom 3	a		20 36							21 06								21 36					22 06		
	d		20 38							21 08								21 38					22 08		
Ashtead	d		20 42							21 12								21 42					22 12		
Leatherhead	d		20 45							21 15								21 45					22 15		
Box Hill & Westhumble	d																								
Dorking 4	a		20 53															21 53							
New Malden 6	d						20 40		20 49				21 10			21 19					21 40				
Norbiton	d						20 43						21 13								21 43				
Kingston	a						20 46						21 16								21 46				
	d						20 49					21 11	21 16								21 49				
Hampton Wick	d						20 51					21 13	21 18								21 51				
Teddington	d						20 56					21 16	21 21								21 56				
Strawberry Hill	a						20 59					21 19									21 59				
Fulwell	d												21 25												
Hampton	d												21 29												
Kempton Park	d												21 32												
Sunbury	d												21 34												
Upper Halliford	d												21 36												
Shepperton	a												21 41												
Berrylands	d								20 51							21 21									
Surbiton 6	d	20 32		20 35					20 55		21 05					21 25	21 32		21 35					22 05	
Thames Ditton	d								21 00							21 30									
Hampton Court	a								21 03							21 33									
Hinchley Wood	d	20 36															21 36								
Claygate	d	20 39															21 39								
Oxshott	d	20 42															21 42								
Cobham & Stoke D'abernon	d	20 46															21 46								
Bookham	d									21 21													22 21		
Effingham Junction 6	d	20 50								21 25							21 50						22 25		
Horsley	d	20 53								21 27							21 53						22 27		
Clandon	d	20 58								21 32							21 58						22 32		
London Road (Guildford)	d	21 03								21 37							22 03						22 37		
Guildford	a	21 10		21 14						21 44	21 44						22 10		22 14				22 44	22 44	

		SW	SW		SW	SW	SW	SW		SW		SW	SW	SW	SW	SW	SW		SW	SW		SW	SW		SW
London Waterloo 15 ⊖	d		21 48		21 57	22 00	22 02	22 10		22 18		22 21	22 32	22 40		22 48	22 51		22 57	23 00		23 02	23 10		23 18
Vauxhall ⊖	d		21 52		22 01	22 04	22 06	22 14		22 22		22 25	22 36	22 44		22 52	22 55		23 01	23 04		23 06	23 14		23 22
Clapham Junction 10	d		21 57		22 06	22 09	22 11	22 19		22 27		22 30	22 41	22 49		22 57	23 00		23 06	23 09		23 11	23 19		23 27
Earlsfield	d		22 00		22 09	22 12	22 14	22 22		22 30		22 33	22 44	22 52		23 00	23 03		23 09	23 12		23 14	23 22		23 30
Wimbledon 6 ⊖ ⇌	d		22 04		22 13	22 16	22 18	22 26		22 34		22 37	22 48	22 56		23 04	23 07		23 13	23 16		23 18	23 26		23 34
Raynes Park 6	d		22 07		22 16		22 22			22 37		22 40	22 52			23 07	23 10		23 16			23 22			23 37
Motspur Park	d						22 25					22 43	22 55				23 13					23 25			
Malden Manor	d											22 46					23 16								
Tolworth	d											22 49					23 19								
Chessington North	d											22 52					23 22								
Chessington South	a											22 54					23 24								
Worcester Park	d						22 27						22 57									23 27			
Stoneleigh	d						22 30						23 00									23 30			
Ewell West	d						22 33						23 03									23 33			
Epsom 3	a						22 36						23 06									23 36			
	d						22 38						23 08												
Ashtead	d						22 42						23 12												
Leatherhead	d						22 45						23 15												
Box Hill & Westhumble	d																								
Dorking 4	a						22 53																		
New Malden 6	d		22 10		22 19					22 40						23 10			23 19						23 40
Norbiton	d		22 13							22 43						23 13									23 43
Kingston	a		22 16							22 46						23 16									23 46
	d	22 11	22 16							22 49					23 11	23 16									23 47
Hampton Wick	d	22 13	22 18							22 51					23 13	23 18									23 49
Teddington	d	22 16	22 21							22 56					23 16	23 21									23 51
Strawberry Hill	a	22 19								22 59					23 19										23 54
Fulwell	d		22 25													23 25									
Hampton	d		22 29													23 29									
Kempton Park	d		22 32													23 32									
Sunbury	d		22 34													23 34									
Upper Halliford	d		22 36													23 36									
Shepperton	a		22 41													23 41									
Berrylands	d				22 21														23 21						
Surbiton 6	d				22 25	22 32		22 35						23 05					23 25	23 32			23 35		
Thames Ditton	d				22 30														23 30						
Hampton Court	a				22 33														23 33						
Hinchley Wood	d					22 36														23 36					
Claygate	d					22 39														23 39					
Oxshott	d					22 42														23 42					
Cobham & Stoke D'abernon	d					22 46														23 46					
Bookham	d												23 21												
Effingham Junction 6	d					22 50							23 25							23 50					
Horsley	d					22 53							23 27							23 53					
Clandon	d					22 58							23 32							23 58					
London Road (Guildford)	d					23 03							23 37							00 03					
Guildford	a					23 10		23 13					23 44	23 45						00 10			00 13		

Table 152

Sundays
from 7 October

London - Chessington South, Dorking, Guildford, Shepperton and Hampton Court

Network Diagram - see first Page of Table 152

		SW	SW 1
London Waterloo 15 ⊖	d	23 32	23 40
Vauxhall ⊖	d	23 36	23 44
Clapham Junction 10	d	23 41	23 49
Earlsfield	d	23 44	23 52
Wimbledon 6 ⊖ ⇌	d	23 48	23 56
Raynes Park 6	d	23 52	
Motspur Park	d	23 55	
Malden Manor	d		
Tolworth	d		
Chessington North	d		
Chessington South	a		
Worcester Park	d	23 57	
Stoneleigh	d	23 59	
Ewell West	d	00 03	
Epsom 3	a	00 06	
	d		
Ashtead	d		
Leatherhead	d		
Box Hill & Westhumble	d		
Dorking 4	a		
New Malden 6	d		
Norbiton	d		
Kingston	a		
	d		
Hampton Wick	d		
Teddington	d		
Strawberry Hill	a		
Fulwell	d		
Hampton	d		
Kempton Park	d		
Sunbury	d		
Upper Halliford	d		
Shepperton	a		
Berrylands	d		
Surbiton 6	d		00a04
Thames Ditton	d		
Hampton Court	a		
Hinchley Wood	d		
Claygate	d		
Oxshott	d		
Cobham & Stoke D'abernon	d		
Bookham	d		
Effingham Junction 6	d		
Horsley	d		
Clandon	d		
London Road (Guildford)	d		
Guildford	a		

Table 152

Mondays to Fridays
until 5 October

Hampton Court, Shepperton, Guildford, Dorking and Chessington South - London

Network Diagram - see first Page of Table 152

Miles	Miles	Miles	Miles	Miles			SW MO A	SW MX	SW MX	SW MX B	SW MX C	SW MO A	SW MX	SW D	SW E	SW F	SW G	SW H	SW MO I	SW J	SW MX	SW K	SW
0	—	—	—	—	**Guildford**	d			23p08														04 00
1¼	—	—	—	—	London Road (Guildford)	d			23p12														
4½	—	—	—	—	Clandon	d			23p17														
7¾	—	—	—	—	Horsley	d			23p21														
8¾	0	—	—	—	Effingham Junction 6	d			23p24														
—	1¾	—	—	—	Bookham	d																	
11	—	—	—	—	Cobham & Stoke d'Abernon	d			23p28														
13	—	—	—	—	Oxshott	d			23p31														
14¾	—	—	—	—	Claygate	d			23p34														
16	—	—	—	—	Hinchley Wood	d			23p37														
—	—	—	0	—	**Hampton Court**	d						23p45											
—	—	—	1	—	Thames Ditton	d						23p47											
18	—	—	3	—	**Surbiton** 6	d			23p42			23p53											04 24
19	—	—	—	—	Berrylands	d						23p55											
—	—	—	—	0	**Shepperton**	d	23p11	23p11															
—	—	—	—	1½	Upper Halliford	d	23p14	23p14															
—	—	—	—	2	Sunbury	d	23p16	23p16															
—	—	—	—	2½	Kempton Park	d	23p18	23p18															
—	—	—	—	4¼	Hampton	d	23p21	23p21															
—	—	—	—	6	Fulwell	d	23p24	23p24															
—	—	—	0	—	Strawberry Hill	d				23p37	23p37		00 07										
—	—	—	1¼	7	Teddington	d	23p29	23p29		23p41	23p41		00 11	00s56	00s56	00s56	00s56	00s56	00s56	00s56	00s56	00s56	
—	—	—	—	8¼	Hampton Wick	d	23p31	23p31		23p44	23p44		00 14	00s59	00s59	00s59	00s59	00s59	00s59	00s59	00s59	00s59	
—	—	—	—	8¾	Kingston	a	23p33	23p33		23p46	23p46		00 16	01s01	01s01	01s01	01s01	01s01	01s01	01s01	01 01	01s01	
—	—	—	—	—		d	23p34	23p34		23p49	23p49												
—	—	—	—	9½	Norbiton	d	23p36	23p36		23p51	23p51												
20	—	—	—	11	New Malden 6	d	23p40	23p41		23p55	23p55	23p58											
—	—	0	—	—	**Dorking** 4	d																	
—	—	0¾	—	—	Box Hill & Westhumble	d																	
—	4½	4	—	—	Leatherhead	d																	
—	—	5¾	—	—	Ashtead	d																	
—	—	7¾	—	—	**Epsom** 3	a																	
—	—	—	—	—		d																	
—	—	9	—	—	Ewell West	d																	
—	—	10	—	—	Stoneleigh	d																	
—	—	11¼	—	—	Worcester Park	d																	
—	0	—	—	—	**Chessington South**	d																	
—	0¾	—	—	—	Chessington North	d																	
—	1¾	—	—	—	Tolworth	d																	
—	2¾	—	—	—	Malden Manor	d																	
—	3¾	12¾	—	—	Motspur Park	d																	
21¼	5¼	13¾	—	12	Raynes Park 6	d	23p43	23p43		23p58	23p58	00 01											
22¾	6¾	14¾	—	13½	**Wimbledon** 6 ⊖ ⇌	d	23p47	23p50	23p53	00 02	00 02	00a04											04 32
24½	8½	16½	—	15¼	Earlsfield	d	23p50	23p53	23p56	00 05	00 05												
26	10	18	—	16¾	**Clapham Junction** 10	d	23p54	23p57	23p59	00 09	00 09												04 44
28¾	12¾	20¾	—	19½	Vauxhall ⊖	d	23p59	00 02	00 05	00 14	00 14												
30	14	22	—	20¾	**London Waterloo** 15 ⊖	a	00 04	00 10	00 14	00 22	00 24												04 53

A from 21 May until 1 October
B not from 31 July until 10 August, from 30 August until 7 September
C from 31 July until 7 September, not from 14 August until 29 August
D 3 September
E 13 August
F 6 August
G 10 September
H 20 August, 27 August
I until 23 July
J 30 July
K 17 September, 24 September, 1 October

until 5 October

Hampton Court, Shepperton, Guildford, Dorking and Chessington South - London

Network Diagram - see first Page of Table 152

			SW	SW	SW	SW		SW	SW		SW		SW		SW	SW	SW	SW		SW	SW		SW	SW	SW
Guildford	d			04 58				05 14			05 38										05 58		06 07		
London Road (Guildford)	d			05 02							05 42										06 02		06 11		
Clandon	d			05 07							05 47										06 07		06 16		
Horsley	d			05 11							05 51										06 11		06 20		
Effingham Junction 6	d			05 16							05 54										06 16		06 24		
Bookham	d			05 19																	06 19				
Cobham & Stoke d'Abernon	d										05 58												06 27		
Oxshott	d										06 01												06 31		
Claygate	d										06 04												06 34		
Hinchley Wood	d										06 07												06 37		
Hampton Court	d								05 54									06 24							
Thames Ditton	d								05 56									06 26							
Surbiton 6	d							05 57	06 02		06 12					06 28		06 32					06 42		
Berrylands	d								06 04									06 34							
Shepperton	d				05 23															06 11					
Upper Halliford	d				05 26															06 14					
Sunbury	d				05 28															06 16					
Kempton Park	d																								
Hampton	d				05 33															06 21					
Fulwell	d				05 36															06 24					
Strawberry Hill	d		04 55		05 38										06 08										06 37
Teddington	d		04 59			05 44									06 11					06 29					06 41
Hampton Wick	d		05 01			05 46									06 14					06 31					06 44
Kingston	a		05 03			05 48									06 16					06 33					06 46
	d		05 04			05 49									06 19					06 34					06 49
Norbiton	d		05 06			05 51									06 21					06 36					06 51
New Malden 6	d		05 10			05 55			06 07						06 25			06 37		06 40					06 55
Dorking 4	d												05 48												
Box Hill & Westhumble	d												05 50												
Leatherhead	d			05 24									05 56								06 24				
Ashtead	d			05 28									05 59								06 28				
Epsom 3	a			05 32									06 04								06 32				
	d			05 34									06 04				06 18				06 34				
Ewell West	d			05 37									06 07				06 21				06 37				
Stoneleigh	d			05 40									06 10				06 24				06 40				
Worcester Park	d			05 42									06 12				06 27				06 42				
Chessington South	d																							06 40	
Chessington North	d																							06 42	
Tolworth	d																							06 44	
Malden Manor	d																							06 47	
Motspur Park	d			05 46									06 16				06 30				06 46			06 50	
Raynes Park 6	d		05 13	05 49		05 58			06 10				06 19		06 28		06 34	06 40		06 43	06 49			06 54	06 58
Wimbledon 6 ⊖ ⇌	d		05 17	05 53		06 02		06 05	06 14		06 20		06 23		06 32	06 35	06 38	06 44		06 47	06 53		06 50	06 58	07 02
Earlsfield	d		05 21	05 57		06 05		06 08	06 17		06 24		06 27		06 35	06 39	06 42	06 47		06 50	06 57		06 54	07 01	07 05
Clapham Junction 10	d		05 25	06 01		06 09		06 12	06 21		06 28		06 31		06 39	06 43	06 46	06 51		06 54	07 01		06 58	07 05	07 09
Vauxhall ⊖	d		05 30	06 06	06 12	06 14		06 17	06 26		06 33		06 36		06 44	06 48	06 51	06 56		06 59	07 06		07 03	07 10	07 14
London Waterloo 15 ⊖	a		05 35	06 11	06 16	06 19		06 22	06 31		06 37		06 40		06 49	06 52	06 55	07 03		07 06	07 12		07 09	07 17	07 21

until 5 October

Hampton Court, Shepperton, Guildford, Dorking and Chessington South - London

Network Diagram - see first Page of Table 152

		SW	SW	SW			SW		SW	SW	SW		SW	SW	SW	SW	SW			SW		SW	SW	SW	SW
Guildford	d								06 28	06 37													06 58	07 07	07 17
London Road (Guildford)	d								06 32	06 41													07 02	07 11	07 21
Clandon	d								06 37	06 46													07 07	07 16	07 26
Horsley	d								06 41	06 50													07 11	07 20	07 30
Effingham Junction 6	d								06 48	06 54													07 16	07 24	07 34
Bookham	d								06 51														07 19		
Cobham & Stoke d'Abernon	d									06 57														07 27	07 37
Oxshott	d									07 01														07 31	07 41
Claygate	d									07 04														07 34	07 44
Hinchley Wood	d									07 07														07 37	07 47
Hampton Court	d			06 54																07 24					
Thames Ditton	d			06 56																07 26					
Surbiton 6	d	06 57		07 02						07 12										07 32				07 42	07 53
Berrylands	d			07 04																07 34					
Shepperton	d						06 41										07 00					07 11			
Upper Halliford	d						06 44										07 03					07 14			
Sunbury	d						06 46										07 05					07 16			
Kempton Park	d																								
Hampton	d						06 51										07 09					07 21			
Fulwell	d						06 54										07 12					07 24			
Strawberry Hill	d												07 07				07 14								
Teddington	d						06 59						07 11		07 20							07 29			
Hampton Wick	d						07 01						07 14		07 22							07 31			
Kingston	a						07 03						07 16		07 24							07 33			
	d						07 04						07 19		07 26							07 34			
Norbiton	d						07 06						07 21		07 28							07 36			
New Malden 6	d			07 07			07 10						07 25		07 32					07 37		07 40		07 46	
Dorking 4	d		06 32											07 02											
Box Hill & Westhumble	d		06 34											07 04											
Leatherhead	d		06 39						06 56					07 09									07 26		
Ashtead	d		06 43						06 59					07 13									07 29		
Epsom 3	a		06 47						07 04					07 17									07 34		
	d		06 48						07 04					07 18		07 22							07 34		
Ewell West	d		06 51						07 07							07 25							07 37		
Stoneleigh	d		06 53						07 10							07 27							07 40		
Worcester Park	d		06 56						07 12					07 25		07 30							07 43		
Chessington South	d										07 10														
Chessington North	d										07 12														
Tolworth	d										07 14														
Malden Manor	d										07 17														
Motspur Park	d		07 00						07 16		07 20					07 34							07 46		
Raynes Park 6	d		07 04	07 10			07 13		07 19		07 24		07 28	07 31	07 34	07 37				07 40		07 43	07 50		
Wimbledon 6 ⊖ ⇌	d	07 05	07 08	07 14			07 17		07 23	07 20	07 28		07 32	07 35	07 38	07 41				07 44		07 47	07 54	07 51	
Earlsfield	d	07 08	07 11	07 17			07 20		07 27	07 24	07 31		07 35	07 38	07 42	07 45				07 48		07 51	07 58	07 54	
Clapham Junction 10	d	07 12	07 15	07 21			07 24		07 31	07 28	07 35		07 39	07 42	07 46	07 49				07 52		07 55	08 02	07 58	
Vauxhall ⊖	d	07 17	07 20	07 26			07 29		07 36	07 33	07 40		07 44	07 47	07 51	07 54	07 56			07 57		08 00	08 07	08 03	
London Waterloo 15 ⊖	a	07 24	07 27	07 33			07 36		07 42	07 39	07 47		07 51	07 54	07 57	08 00	08 04			08 04		08 06	08 13	08 11	08 13

Table 152

Mondays to Fridays
until 5 October

Hampton Court, Shepperton, Guildford, Dorking and Chessington South - London

Network Diagram - see first Page of Table 152

		SW			SW	SW	SW	SW	SW		SW		SW		SW	SW			SW	SW	SW	SW	SW		SW
Guildford	d															07 37									
London Road (Guildford)	d															07 41									
Clandon	d															07 46									
Horsley	d															07 50									
Effingham Junction 6	d														07 46	07 54									
Bookham	d														07 49										
Cobham & Stoke d'Abernon	d															07 57									
Oxshott	d															08 01									
Claygate	d															08 04									
Hinchley Wood	d															08 07									
Hampton Court	d										07 54														
Thames Ditton	d										07 56														
Surbiton 6	d										08 02					08 12									
Berrylands	d										08 04														
Shepperton	d						07 30						07 41									08 00			
Upper Halliford	d						07 33						07 44									08 03			
Sunbury	d						07 35						07 46									08 05			
Kempton Park	d																								
Hampton	d						07 39						07 51									08 09			
Fulwell	d						07 42						07 54									08 12			
Strawberry Hill	d				07 37		07 44	07 47												08 07		08 14	08 17		
Teddington	d				07 41			07 50					07 59							08 11			08 20		
Hampton Wick	d				07 44			07 52					08 01							08 14			08 22		
Kingston	a				07 46			07 54					08 03							08 16			08 24		
	d				07 49			07 56					08 04							08 19			08 26		
Norbiton	d				07 51			07 58					08 06							08 21			08 28		
New Malden 6	d				07 55			08 02			08 07		08 10			08 16				08 25			08 32		
Dorking 4	d					07 32															08 02				
Box Hill & Westhumble	d					07 34															08 04				
Leatherhead	d					07 39									07 56						08 09				
Ashtead	d					07 43									07 59						08 13				
Epsom 3	a					07 47									08 04						08 17				
	d					07 48			07 52						08 04						08 18				08 22
Ewell West	d								07 55						08 07										08 25
Stoneleigh	d								07 57						08 10										08 27
Worcester Park	d					07 55			08 00						08 13						08 25				08 30
Chessington South	d	07 40																	08 10						
Chessington North	d	07 42																	08 12						
Tolworth	d	07 44																	08 14						
Malden Manor	d	07 47																	08 17						
Motspur Park	d	07 50							08 04						08 16				08 20						08 34
Raynes Park 6	d	07 54			07 58	08 01		08 04	08 07		08 10		08 13		08 20				08 24	08 28	08 31		08 34		08 37
Wimbledon 6 ⊖ ⛴	d	07 58			08 02	08 05		08 08	08 11		08 14		08 17		08 24	08 21			08 28	08 32	08 35		08 38		08 41
Earlsfield	d	08 01			08 05	08 08		08 12	08 15		08 18		08 21		08 28	08 24			08 31	08 35	08 38		08 42		08 45
Clapham Junction 10	d	08 05			08 09	08 12		08 16	08 19		08 22		08 25		08 32	08 28			08 35	08 39	08 42		08 46		08 49
Vauxhall ⊖	d	08 10			08 14	08 17	08 26	08 21	08 24		08 27		08 30		08 37	08 33			08 40	08 44	08 47	08 56	08 51		08 54
London Waterloo 15 ⊖	a	08 17			08 21	08 24	08 34	08 27	08 30		08 33		08 36		08 43	08 40			08 47	08 51	08 54	09 04	08 57		09 00

Table 152

Mondays to Fridays
until 5 October

Hampton Court, Shepperton, Guildford, Dorking and Chessington South - London

Network Diagram - see first Page of Table 152

			SW		SW	SW	SW		SW		SW	SW	SW	SW		SW	SW	SW			SW	SW	SW	SW	SW
Guildford	d					07 58	08 07					08 20						08 37					08 46		
London Road (Guildford)	d					08 02	08 11											08 41							
Clandon	d					08 07	08 16											08 46							
Horsley	d					08 11	08 20											08 50							
Effingham Junction 6	d					08 16	08 24										08 48	08 54							
Bookham	d					08 19											08 51								
Cobham & Stoke d'Abernon	d						08 27											08 57							
Oxshott	d						08 31											09 01							
Claygate	d						08 34											09 04							
Hinchley Wood	d						08 37											09 07							
Hampton Court	d		08 24											08 54											09 24
Thames Ditton	d		08 26											08 56											09 26
Surbiton 6	d		08 32				08 42					08 57		09 02				09 12					09 27		09 32
Berrylands	d		08 34											09 04											09 34
Shepperton	d				08 11											08 41									
Upper Halliford	d				08 14											08 44									
Sunbury	d				08 16											08 46									
Kempton Park	d																								
Hampton	d				08 21											08 51									
Fulwell	d				08 24											08 54									
Strawberry Hill	d										08 38											09 07			
Teddington	d				08 29						08 41					08 59						09 11			
Hampton Wick	d				08 31						08 44					09 01						09 14			
Kingston	a				08 33						08 46					09 03						09 16			
	d				08 34						08 49					09 04						09 19			
Norbiton	d				08 36						08 51					09 06						09 21			
New Malden 6	d		08 37		08 40						08 55			09 07		09 10						09 25			09 37
Dorking 4	d												08 31											09 02	
Box Hill & Westhumble	d												08 33											09 04	
Leatherhead	d					08 25							08 38				08 56							09 09	
Ashtead	d					08 28							08 42				08 59							09 13	
Epsom 3	a					08 33							08 46				09 04							09 17	
	d					08 34							08 48				09 04							09 18	
Ewell West	d					08 37							08 51				09 07							09 21	
Stoneleigh	d					08 40							08 54				09 10							09 24	
Worcester Park	d					08 42							08 57				09 12							09 27	
Chessington South	d								08 40												09 10				
Chessington North	d								08 42												09 12				
Tolworth	d								08 44												09 14				
Malden Manor	d								08 47												09 17				
Motspur Park	d					08 46			08 50				09 00				09 16				09 20			09 30	
Raynes Park 6	d		08 40		08 43	08 49			08 54		08 58		09 04	09 10		09 13	09 19				09 24	09 28		09 34	09 40
Wimbledon 6 ⊖ ⛴	d		08 44		08 47	08 53			08 58		09 02	09 05	09 08	09 14		09 17	09 23	09 20			09 28	09 32	09 35	09 38	09 44
Earlsfield	d		08 48		08 51	08 57			09 01		09 05	09 08	09 12	09 17		09 20	09 27	09 24			09 31	09 35	09 38	09 42	09 47
Clapham Junction 10	d		08 52		08 55	09 01			09 05		09 09	09 12	09 16	09 21		09 24	09 31	09 28			09 35	09 39	09 42	09 46	09 51
Vauxhall ⊖	d		08 57		09 00	09 06			09 10		09 14	09 17	09 21	09 26		09 29	09 36	09 33			09 40	09 44	09 47	09 51	09 56
London Waterloo 15 ⊖	a		09 03		09 06	09 12	09 01		09 17		09 21	09 24	09 27	09 33		09 36	09 42	09 39			09 47	09 51	09 54	09 57	10 01

Hampton Court, Shepperton, Guildford, Dorking and Chessington South - London

Mondays to Fridays

until 5 October

Network Diagram - see first Page of Table 152

		SW	SW	SW	SW	SW	SW	SW	SW	SW	SW	SW	SW	SW	SW	SW	SW	SW	SW	SW
Guildford	d		08 58	09 08							09 28	09 38							09 58	10 08
London Road (Guildford)	d		09 02	09 12							09 32	09 42							10 02	10 12
Clandon	d		09 07	09 17							09 37	09 47							10 07	10 17
Horsley	d		09 11	09 21							09 41	09 51							10 11	10 21
Effingham Junction [6]	d		09 16	09 24							09 46	09 54							10 16	10 24
Bookham	d		09 19								09 49								10 19	
Cobham & Stoke d'Abernon	d			09 28								09 58								10 28
Oxshott	d			09 31								10 01								10 31
Claygate	d			09 34								10 04								10 34
Hinchley Wood	d			09 37								10 07								10 37
Hampton Court	d								09 54								10 24			
Thames Ditton	d								09 56								10 26			
Surbiton [6]	d			09 42			09 57		10 02			10 12			10 27		10 32			10 42
Berrylands	d								10 04								10 34			
Shepperton	d	09 11								09 41								10 11		
Upper Halliford	d	09 14								09 44								10 14		
Sunbury	d	09 16								09 46								10 16		
Kempton Park	d	09 18								09 48								10 18		
Hampton	d	09 21								09 51								10 21		
Fulwell	d	09 24								09 54								10 24		
Strawberry Hill	d					09 37								10 07						
Teddington	d	09 29				09 41				09 59				10 11				10 29		
Hampton Wick	d	09 31				09 44				10 01				10 14				10 31		
Kingston	a	09 33				09 46				10 03				10 16				10 33		
	d	09 34				09 49				10 04				10 19				10 34		
Norbiton	d	09 36				09 51				10 06				10 21				10 36		
New Malden [6]	d	09 40				09 55			10 07	10 10				10 25			10 37	10 40		
Dorking [4]	d							09 35								10 05				
Box Hill & Westhumble	d																			
Leatherhead	d		09 24					09 41			09 54					10 11			10 24	
Ashtead	d		09 28					09 45			09 58					10 14			10 28	
Epsom [3]	a		09 32					09 49			10 02					10 19			10 32	
	d		09 35					09 50			10 05					10 20			10 35	
Ewell West	d		09 38					09 53			10 08					10 23			10 38	
Stoneleigh	d		09 40					09 55			10 10					10 25			10 40	
Worcester Park	d		09 43					09 58			10 13					10 28			10 43	
Chessington South	d				09 40								10 10							
Chessington North	d				09 42								10 12							
Tolworth	d				09 44								10 14							
Malden Manor	d				09 47								10 17							
Motspur Park	d		09 46		09 50			10 01			10 16		10 20			10 31			10 46	
Raynes Park [6]	d	09 43	09 49		09 53	09 58		10 04	10 10	10 13	10 19		10 23	10 28		10 34	10 40	10 43	10 49	
Wimbledon [6] ⊖	d	09 47	09 53	09 50	09 57	10 02	10 05	10 08	10 14	10 17	10 23	10 20	10 27	10 32	10 35	10 38	10 44	10 47	10 53	10 50
Earlsfield	d	09 50	09 57	09 54	10 01	10 05	10 08	10 12	10 17	10 20	10 27	10 24	10 31	10 35	10 38	10 42	10 47	10 50	10 57	10 54
Clapham Junction [10]	d	09 54	10 01	09 58	10 05	10 09	10 12	10 16	10 21	10 24	10 31	10 28	10 35	10 39	10 42	10 46	10 51	10 54	11 01	10 58
Vauxhall ⊖	d	09 59	10 06	10 03	10 10	10 14	10 17	10 21	10 26	10 29	10 36	10 33	10 40	10 44	10 47	10 51	10 56	10 59	11 06	11 03
London Waterloo [15] ⊖	a	10 04	10 10	10 07	10 15	10 19	10 22	10 25	10 31	10 34	10 40	10 37	10 45	10 49	10 52	10 55	11 01	11 04	11 10	11 07

		SW	SW	SW	SW	SW	SW	SW	SW	SW	SW	SW	SW	SW	SW	SW	SW	SW	SW	SW
Guildford	d							10 28	10 38							10 58	11 08			
London Road (Guildford)	d							10 32	10 42							11 02	11 12			
Clandon	d							10 37	10 47							11 07	11 17			
Horsley	d							10 41	10 51							11 11	11 21			
Effingham Junction [6]	d							10 46	10 54							11 16	11 24			
Bookham	d							10 49								11 19				
Cobham & Stoke d'Abernon	d								10 58								11 28			
Oxshott	d								11 01								11 31			
Claygate	d								11 04								11 34			
Hinchley Wood	d								11 07								11 37			
Hampton Court	d					10 54								11 24						
Thames Ditton	d					10 56								11 26						
Surbiton [6]	d			10 57		11 02			11 12			11 27		11 32			11 42			11 57
Berrylands	d					11 04								11 34						
Shepperton	d						10 41								11 11					
Upper Halliford	d						10 44								11 14					
Sunbury	d						10 46								11 16					
Kempton Park	d						10 48								11 18					
Hampton	d						10 51								11 21					
Fulwell	d						10 54								11 24					
Strawberry Hill	d		10 37								11 07								11 37	
Teddington	d		10 41				10 59				11 11				11 29				11 41	
Hampton Wick	d		10 44				11 01				11 14				11 31				11 44	
Kingston	a		10 46				11 03				11 16				11 33				11 46	
	d		10 49				11 04				11 19				11 34				11 49	
Norbiton	d		10 51				11 06				11 21				11 36				11 51	
New Malden [6]	d		10 55			11 07	11 10				11 25			11 37	11 40				11 55	
Dorking [4]	d				10 35								11 05							
Box Hill & Westhumble	d																			
Leatherhead	d				10 41			10 54					11 11			11 24				
Ashtead	d				10 44			10 58					11 14			11 28				
Epsom [3]	a				10 49			11 02					11 19			11 32				
	d				10 50			11 05					11 20			11 35				
Ewell West	d				10 53			11 08					11 23			11 38				
Stoneleigh	d				10 55			11 10					11 25			11 40				
Worcester Park	d				10 58			11 13					11 28			11 43				
Chessington South	d	10 40								11 10								11 40		
Chessington North	d	10 42								11 12								11 42		
Tolworth	d	10 44								11 14								11 44		
Malden Manor	d	10 47								11 17								11 47		
Motspur Park	d	10 50			11 01			11 16		11 20			11 31			11 46		11 50		
Raynes Park [6]	d	10 53	10 58		11 04	11 10	11 13	11 19		11 23	11 28		11 34	11 40	11 43	11 49		11 53	11 58	
Wimbledon [6] ⊖	d	10 57	11 02	11 05	11 08	11 14	11 17	11 23	11 20	11 27	11 32	11 35	11 38	11 44	11 47	11 53	11 50	11 57	12 02	12 05
Earlsfield	d	11 01	11 05	11 08	11 12	11 17	11 20	11 27	11 24	11 31	11 35	11 38	11 42	11 47	11 50	11 57	11 54	12 01	12 05	12 08
Clapham Junction [10]	d	11 05	11 09	11 12	11 16	11 21	11 24	11 31	11 28	11 35	11 39	11 42	11 46	11 51	11 54	12 01	11 58	12 05	12 09	12 12
Vauxhall ⊖	d	11 10	11 14	11 17	11 21	11 26	11 29	11 36	11 33	11 40	11 44	11 47	11 51	11 56	11 59	12 06	12 03	12 10	12 14	12 17
London Waterloo [15] ⊖	a	11 15	11 19	11 22	11 25	11 31	11 34	11 40	11 37	11 45	11 49	11 52	11 55	12 01	12 04	12 10	12 07	12 15	12 19	12 22

Hampton Court, Shepperton, Guildford, Dorking and Chessington South - London

Mondays to Fridays

until 5 October

Network Diagram - see first Page of Table 152

		SW	SW	SW	SW	SW	SW	SW	SW	SW	SW	SW	SW	SW	SW	SW	SW	SW	SW	SW [1]
Guildford	d				11 28	11 38							11 58	12 08						
London Road (Guildford)	d				11 32	11 42							12 02	12 12						
Clandon	d				11 37	11 47							12 07	12 17						
Horsley	d				11 41	11 51							12 11	12 21						
Effingham Junction [6]	d				11 46	11 54							12 16	12 24						
Bookham	d				11 49								12 19							
Cobham & Stoke d'Abernon	d					11 58								12 28						
Oxshott	d					12 01								12 31						
Claygate	d					12 04								12 34						
Hinchley Wood	d					12 07								12 37						
Hampton Court	d		11 54								12 24								12 54	
Thames Ditton	d		11 56								12 26								12 56	
Surbiton [6]	d		12 02			12 12			12 27		12 32			12 42			12 57		13 02	13 08
Berrylands	d		12 04								12 34								13 04	
Shepperton	d			11 41								12 11								
Upper Halliford	d			11 44								12 14								
Sunbury	d			11 46								12 16								
Kempton Park	d			11 48								12 18								
Hampton	d			11 51								12 21								
Fulwell	d			11 54								12 24								
Strawberry Hill	d							12 07								12 37				
Teddington	d			11 59				12 11				12 29				12 41				
Hampton Wick	d			12 01				12 14				12 31				12 44				
Kingston	a			12 03				12 16				12 33				12 46				
	d			12 04				12 19				12 34				12 49				
Norbiton	d			12 06				12 21				12 36				12 51				
New Malden [6]	d		12 07	12 10				12 25			12 37	12 40				12 55			13 07	
Dorking [4]	d	11 35								12 05								12 35		
Box Hill & Westhumble	d																			
Leatherhead	d	11 41			11 54					12 11			12 24					12 41		
Ashtead	d	11 44			11 58					12 14			12 28					12 44		
Epsom [3]	a	11 49			12 02					12 19			12 32					12 49		
	d	11 50			12 05					12 20			12 35					12 50		
Ewell West	d	11 53			12 08					12 23			12 38					12 53		
Stoneleigh	d	11 55			12 10					12 25			12 40					12 55		
Worcester Park	d	11 58			12 13					12 28			12 43					12 58		
Chessington South	d						12 10								12 40					
Chessington North	d						12 12								12 42					
Tolworth	d						12 14								12 44					
Malden Manor	d						12 17								12 47					
Motspur Park	d	12 01			12 16		12 20			12 31			12 46		12 50			13 01		
Raynes Park [6]	d	12 04	12 10	12 13	12 19		12 23	12 28		12 34	12 40	12 43	12 49		12 53	12 58		13 04	13 10	
Wimbledon [6] ⊖	d	12 08	12 14	12 17	12 23	12 20	12 27	12 32	12 35	12 38	12 44	12 47	12 53	12 50	12 57	13 02	13 05	13 08	13 14	
Earlsfield	d	12 12	12 17	12 20	12 27	12 24	12 31	12 35	12 38	12 42	12 47	12 50	12 57	12 54	13 01	13 05	13 08	13 12	13 17	
Clapham Junction [10]	d	12 16	12 21	12 24	12 31	12 28	12 35	12 39	12 42	12 46	12 51	12 54	13 01	12 58	13 05	13 09	13 12	13 16	13 21	
Vauxhall ⊖	d	12 21	12 26	12 29	12 36	12 33	12 40	12 44	12 47	12 51	12 56	12 59	13 06	13 03	13 10	13 14	13 17	13 21	13 26	
London Waterloo [15] ⊖	a	12 25	12 31	12 34	12 40	12 37	12 45	12 49	12 52	12 55	13 01	13 04	13 10	13 07	13 15	13 19	13 22	13 25	13 31	13 25

Hampton Court, Shepperton, Guildford, Dorking and Chessington South - London

Network Diagram - see first Page of Table 152

		SW	SW		SW	SW	SW	SW	SW	SW		SW	SW		SW	SW	SW	SW	SW	SW		SW	SW		SW
Guildford	d		12 28		12 38								12 58		13 08								13 28		13 38
London Road (Guildford)	d		12 32		12 42								13 02		13 12								13 32		13 42
Clandon	d		12 37		12 47								13 07		13 17								13 37		13 47
Horsley	d		12 41		12 51								13 11		13 21								13 41		13 51
Effingham Junction ■	d		12 46		12 54								13 16		13 24								13 46		13 54
Bookham	d		12 49										13 19										13 49		
Cobham & Stoke d'Abernon	d				12 58										13 28										13 58
Oxshott	d				13 01										13 31										14 01
Claygate	d				13 04										13 34										14 04
Hinchley Wood	d				13 07										13 37										14 07
Hampton Court	d									13 24										13 54					
Thames Ditton	d									13 26										13 56					
Surbiton ■	d				13 12			13 27		13 32					13 42			13 57		14 02					14 12
Berrylands	d									13 34										14 04					
Shepperton	d	12 41										13 11										13 41			
Upper Halliford	d	12 44										13 14										13 44			
Sunbury	d	12 46										13 16										13 46			
Kempton Park	d	12 48										13 18										13 48			
Hampton	d	12 51										13 21										13 51			
Fulwell	d	12 54										13 24										13 54			
Strawberry Hill	d						13 07										13 37								
Teddington	d	12 59					13 11					13 29					13 41					13 59			
Hampton Wick	d	13 01					13 14					13 31					13 44					14 01			
Kingston	a	13 03					13 16					13 33					13 46					14 03			
	d	13 04					13 19					13 34					13 49					14 04			
Norbiton	d	13 06					13 21					13 36					13 51					14 06			
New Malden ■	d	13 10					13 25			13 37		13 40					13 55			14 07		14 10			
Dorking ■	d								13 05										13 35						
Box Hill & Westhumble	d																								
Leatherhead	d		12 54						13 11				13 24						13 41				13 54		
Ashtead	d		12 58						13 14				13 28						13 44				13 58		
Epsom ■	a		13 02						13 19				13 32						13 49				14 02		
	d		13 05						13 20				13 35						13 50				14 05		
Ewell West	d		13 08						13 23				13 38						13 53				14 08		
Stoneleigh	d		13 10						13 25				13 40						13 55				14 10		
Worcester Park	d		13 13						13 28				13 43						13 58				14 13		
Chessington South	d					13 10										13 40									
Chessington North	d					13 12										13 42									
Tolworth	d					13 14										13 44									
Malden Manor	d					13 17										13 47									
Motspur Park	d		13 16			13 20			13 31				13 46			13 50			14 01				14 16		
Raynes Park ■	d	13 13	13 19			13 23	13 28		13 34	13 40		13 43	13 49			13 53	13 58		14 04	14 10		14 13	14 19		
Wimbledon ■ ⊖	d	13 17	13 23		13 20	13 27	13 32	13 35	13 38	13 44		13 47	13 53		13 50	13 57	14 02	14 05	14 08	14 14		14 17	14 23		14 20
Earlsfield	d	13 20	13 27		13 24	13 31	13 35	13 38	13 42	13 47		13 50	13 57		13 54	14 01	14 05	14 08	14 12	14 17		14 20	14 27		14 24
Clapham Junction ■	d	13 24	13 31		13 28	13 35	13 39	13 42	13 46	13 51		13 54	14 01		13 58	14 05	14 09	14 12	14 16	14 21		14 24	14 31		14 28
Vauxhall ⊖	d	13 29	13 36		13 33	13 40	13 44	13 47	13 51	13 56		13 59	14 06		14 03	14 10	14 14	14 17	14 21	14 26		14 29	14 36		14 33
London Waterloo ■ ⊖	a	13 34	13 40		13 37	13 45	13 49	13 52	13 55	14 01		14 04	14 10		14 07	14 15	14 19	14 22	14 25	14 31		14 34	14 40		14 37

		SW	SW	SW	SW	SW		SW	SW		SW	SW	SW	SW	SW	SW		SW	SW		SW	SW	SW	SW	SW
Guildford	d								13 58		14 08								14 28		14 38				
London Road (Guildford)	d								14 02		14 12								14 32		14 42				
Clandon	d								14 07		14 17								14 37		14 47				
Horsley	d								14 11		14 21								14 41		14 51				
Effingham Junction ■	d								14 16		14 24								14 46		14 54				
Bookham	d								14 19										14 49						
Cobham & Stoke d'Abernon	d										14 28										14 58				
Oxshott	d										14 31										15 01				
Claygate	d										14 34										15 04				
Hinchley Wood	d										14 37										15 07				
Hampton Court	d					14 24										14 54									
Thames Ditton	d					14 26										14 56									
Surbiton ■	d			14 27		14 32					14 42			14 57		15 02					15 12			15 27	
Berrylands	d					14 34										15 04									
Shepperton	d							14 11										14 41							
Upper Halliford	d							14 14										14 44							
Sunbury	d							14 16										14 46							
Kempton Park	d							14 18										14 48							
Hampton	d							14 21										14 51							
Fulwell	d							14 24										14 54							
Strawberry Hill	d		14 07										14 37										15 07		
Teddington	d		14 11					14 29					14 41					14 59					15 11		
Hampton Wick	d		14 14					14 31					14 44					15 01					15 14		
Kingston	a		14 16					14 33					14 46					15 03					15 16		
	d		14 19					14 34					14 49					15 04					15 19		
Norbiton	d		14 21					14 36					14 51					15 06					15 21		
New Malden ■	d		14 25			14 37		14 40					14 55			15 07		15 10					15 25		
Dorking ■	d				14 05										14 35										15 05
Box Hill & Westhumble	d																								
Leatherhead	d				14 11				14 24						14 41				14 54						15 11
Ashtead	d				14 14				14 28						14 44				14 58						15 14
Epsom ■	a				14 19				14 32						14 49				15 02						15 19
	d				14 20				14 35						14 50				15 05						15 20
Ewell West	d				14 23				14 38						14 53				15 08						15 23
Stoneleigh	d				14 25				14 40						14 55				15 10						15 25
Worcester Park	d				14 28				14 43						14 58				15 13						15 28
Chessington South	d	14 10										14 40										15 10			
Chessington North	d	14 12										14 42										15 12			
Tolworth	d	14 14										14 44										15 14			
Malden Manor	d	14 17										14 47										15 17			
Motspur Park	d	14 20			14 31				14 46			14 50			15 01				15 16			15 20			15 31
Raynes Park ■	d	14 23	14 28		14 34	14 40		14 43	14 49			14 53	14 58		15 04	15 10		15 13	15 19			15 23	15 28		15 34
Wimbledon ■ ⊖	d	14 27	14 32	14 35	14 38	14 44		14 47	14 53		14 50	14 57	15 02	15 05	15 08	15 14		15 17	15 23		15 20	15 27	15 32	15 35	15 38
Earlsfield	d	14 31	14 35	14 38	14 42	14 47		14 50	14 57		14 54	15 01	15 05	15 08	15 12	15 17		15 20	15 27		15 24	15 31	15 35	15 38	15 42
Clapham Junction ■	d	14 35	14 39	14 42	14 46	14 51		14 54	15 01		14 58	15 05	15 09	15 12	15 16	15 21		15 24	15 31		15 28	15 35	15 39	15 42	15 46
Vauxhall ⊖	d	14 40	14 44	14 47	14 51	14 56		14 59	15 06		15 03	15 10	15 14	15 17	15 21	15 26		15 29	15 36		15 33	15 40	15 44	15 47	15 51
London Waterloo ■ ⊖	a	14 45	14 49	14 52	14 55	15 01		15 04	15 10		15 07	15 15	15 19	15 22	15 25	15 31		15 34	15 40		15 37	15 45	15 49	15 52	15 55

Table 152 — Mondays to Fridays until 5 October

Hampton Court, Shepperton, Guildford, Dorking and Chessington South - London

Network Diagram - see first Page of Table 152

		SW		SW	SW		SW	SW	SW	SW	SW	SW		SW	SW		SW	SW	SW	SW	SW	SW		SW	SW
Guildford	d				14 58		15 08								15 28		15 38								15 58
London Road (Guildford)	d				15 02		15 12								15 32		15 42								16 02
Clandon	d				15 07		15 17								15 37		15 47								16 07
Horsley	d				15 11		15 21								15 41		15 51								16 11
Effingham Junction ■	d				15 16		15 24								15 46		15 54								16 16
Bookham	d				15 19										15 49										16 19
Cobham & Stoke d'Abernon	d						15 28										15 58								
Oxshott	d						15 31										16 01								
Claygate	d						15 34										16 04								
Hinchley Wood	d						15 37										16 07								
Hampton Court	d	15 24										15 54										16 24			
Thames Ditton	d	15 26										15 56										16 26			
Surbiton ■	d	15 32					15 42			15 57		16 02					16 12			16 27		16 32			
Berrylands	d	15 34										16 04										16 34			
Shepperton	d			15 11										15 41										16 11	
Upper Halliford	d			15 14										15 44										16 14	
Sunbury	d			15 16										15 46										16 16	
Kempton Park	d			15 18										15 48										16 18	
Hampton	d			15 21										15 51										16 21	
Fulwell	d			15 24										15 54										16 24	
Strawberry Hill	d								15 37										16 07						
Teddington	d			15 29					15 41					15 59					16 11					16 29	
Hampton Wick	d			15 31					15 44					16 01					16 14					16 31	
Kingston	a			15 33					15 46					16 03					16 16					16 33	
	d			15 34					15 49					16 04					16 19					16 34	
Norbiton	d			15 36					15 51					16 06					16 21					16 36	
New Malden ■	d	15 37		15 40					15 55			16 07		16 10					16 25			16 37		16 40	
Dorking ■	d										15 35										16 05				
Box Hill & Westhumble	d																								
Leatherhead	d				15 24						15 41				15 54						16 11				16 24
Ashtead	d				15 28						15 44				15 58						16 14				16 28
Epsom ■	a				15 32						15 49				16 02						16 19				16 32
	d				15 35						15 50				16 05						16 20				16 35
Ewell West	d				15 38						15 53				16 08						16 23				16 38
Stoneleigh	d				15 40						15 55				16 10						16 25				16 40
Worcester Park	d				15 43						15 58				16 13						16 28				16 43
Chessington South	d							15 40										16 10							
Chessington North	d							15 42										16 12							
Tolworth	d							15 44										16 14							
Malden Manor	d							15 47										16 17							
Motspur Park	d				15 46			15 50			16 01				16 16			16 20			16 31				16 46
Raynes Park ■	d	15 40		15 43	15 49			15 53	15 58		16 04	16 10		16 13	16 19			16 23	16 28		16 34	16 40		16 43	16 49
Wimbledon ■ ⊖	d	15 44		15 47	15 53		15 50	15 57	16 02	16 05	16 08	16 14		16 17	16 23		16 20	16 27	16 32	16 35	16 38	16 44		16 47	16 53
Earlsfield	d	15 47		15 50	15 57		15 54	16 01	16 05	16 08	16 12	16 17		16 20	16 27		16 24	16 31	16 35	16 38	16 42	16 47		16 50	16 57
Clapham Junction ■	d	15 51		15 54	16 01		15 58	16 05	16 09	16 12	16 16	16 21		16 24	16 31		16 28	16 35	16 39	16 42	16 46	16 51		16 54	17 01
Vauxhall ⊖	d	15 56		15 59	16 06		16 03	16 10	16 14	16 17	16 21	16 26		16 29	16 36		16 33	16 40	16 44	16 47	16 51	16 56		16 59	17 06
London Waterloo ■ ⊖	a	16 01		16 04	16 10		16 07	16 15	16 19	16 22	16 25	16 31		16 34	16 40		16 37	16 45	16 49	16 52	16 55	17 01		17 05	17 10

			SW	SW	SW	SW	SW	SW		SW	SW		SW	SW	SW	SW	SW	SW		SW	SW		SW	SW	SW
Guildford	d		16 08								16 28		16 38								16 58		17 08		
London Road (Guildford)	d		16 12								16 32		16 42								17 02		17 12		
Clandon	d		16 17								16 37		16 47								17 07		17 17		
Horsley	d		16 21								16 41		16 51								17 11		17 21		
Effingham Junction ■	d		16 24								16 46		16 54								17 16		17 24		
Bookham	d										16 49										17 19				
Cobham & Stoke d'Abernon	d		16 28										16 58										17 28		
Oxshott	d		16 31										17 01										17 31		
Claygate	d		16 34										17 04										17 34		
Hinchley Wood	d		16 37										17 07										17 37		
Hampton Court	d							16 54										17 24							
Thames Ditton	d							16 56										17 26							
Surbiton ■	d		16 42			16 57		17 02					17 12			17 27		17 32					17 42		
Berrylands	d							17 04										17 34							
Shepperton	d									16 41										17 11					
Upper Halliford	d									16 44										17 14					
Sunbury	d									16 46										17 16					
Kempton Park	d									16 48										17 18					
Hampton	d									16 51										17 21					
Fulwell	d									16 54										17 24					
Strawberry Hill	d				16 37										17 07										17 37
Teddington	d				16 43					16 59					17 13					17 29					17 43
Hampton Wick	d				16 46					17 01					17 16					17 31					17 46
Kingston	a				16 48					17 03					17 18					17 33					17 48
	d				16 49					17 04					17 19					17 34					17 49
Norbiton	d				16 51					17 06					17 21					17 36					17 51
New Malden ■	d				16 55			17 07		17 10					17 25			17 37		17 40					17 55
Dorking ■	d						16 35										17 05								
Box Hill & Westhumble	d																								
Leatherhead	d						16 41				16 54						17 11				17 24				
Ashtead	d						16 44				16 58						17 14				17 28				
Epsom ■	a						16 49				17 02						17 19				17 32				
	d						16 50				17 05						17 20				17 35				
Ewell West	d						16 53				17 08						17 23				17 38				
Stoneleigh	d						16 55				17 10						17 25				17 40				
Worcester Park	d						16 58				17 13						17 28				17 43				
Chessington South	d			16 40										17 10										17 40	
Chessington North	d			16 42										17 12										17 42	
Tolworth	d			16 44										17 14										17 44	
Malden Manor	d			16 47										17 17										17 47	
Motspur Park	d			16 50			17 01				17 16			17 20			17 31				17 46			17 50	
Raynes Park ■	d			16 53	16 58		17 04	17 10		17 13	17 19			17 23	17 28		17 34	17 40		17 43	17 49			17 53	17 58
Wimbledon ■ ⊖	d		16 50	16 57	17 02	17 05	17 08	17 14		17 17	17 23		17 20	17 27	17 32	17 35	17 38	17 44		17 47	17 53		17 50	17 57	18 02
Earlsfield	d		16 54	17 01	17 05	17 08	17 12	17 17		17 20	17 27		17 24	17 31	17 35	17 38	17 42	17 47		17 50	17 57		17 54	18 01	18 05
Clapham Junction ■	d		16 58	17 05	17 09	17 12	17 16	17 21		17 24	17 31		17 28	17 35	17 39	17 42	17 46	17 51		17 54	18 01		17 58	18 05	18 09
Vauxhall ⊖	d		17 03	17 10	17 14	17 17	17 21	17 26		17 29	17 36		17 33	17 40	17 44	17 47	17 51	17 56		17 59	18 06		18 03	18 10	18 14
London Waterloo ■ ⊖	a		17 07	17 16	17 19	17 22	17 25	17 31		17 35	17 40		17 37	17 45	17 49	17 52	17 55	18 01		18 05	18 10		18 07	18 15	18 19

Hampton Court, Shepperton, Guildford, Dorking and Chessington South - London

Network Diagram - see first Page of Table 152

		SW	SW	SW		SW	SW		SW	SW	SW	SW	SW	SW	SW		SW		SW	SW	SW	SW	SW	SW	SW
Guildford	d								17 28	17 38									17 58	18 08					
London Road (Guildford)	d								17 32	17 42									18 02	18 12					
Clandon	d								17 37	17 47									18 07	18 17					
Horsley	d								17 41	17 51									18 11	18 21					
Effingham Junction	d								17 46	17 54									18 16	18 24					
Bookham	d								17 49										18 19						
Cobham & Stoke d'Abernon	d									17 58										18 28					
Oxshott	d									18 01										18 31					
Claygate	d									18 04										18 34					
Hinchley Wood	d									18 07										18 37					
Hampton Court	d					17 54									18 24										18 54
Thames Ditton	d					17 56									18 26										18 56
Surbiton	d	17 57				18 02				18 12			18 27		18 32					18 42			18 57		19 02
Berrylands	d					18 04									18 34										19 04
Shepperton	d						17 41										18 11								
Upper Halliford	d						17 44										18 14								
Sunbury	d						17 46										18 16								
Kempton Park	d						17 48										18 18								
Hampton	d						17 51										18 21								
Fulwell	d						17 54										18 24								
Strawberry Hill	d			17 41								18 07										18 37			
Teddington	d			17 52			17 59					18 13					18 29					18 43			
Hampton Wick	d			17 54			18 01					18 16					18 31					18 46			
Kingston	a			17 56			18 03					18 18					18 33					18 48			
	d			17 58			18 04					18 19					18 34					18 49			
Norbiton	d			18 00			18 06					18 21					18 36					18 51			
New Malden	d			18 04		18 07	18 10					18 25			18 37		18 40					18 55			19 07
Dorking	d		17 35											18 05										18 35	
Box Hill & Westhumble	d																								
Leatherhead	d		17 41						17 54					18 11					18 24					18 41	
Ashtead	d		17 45						17 58					18 14					18 28					18 45	
Epsom	a		17 49						18 02					18 19					18 32					18 49	
	d		17 50						18 05					18 20					18 35					18 50	
Ewell West	d		17 53						18 08					18 23					18 38					18 53	
Stoneleigh	d		17 55						18 10					18 25					18 40					18 55	
Worcester Park	d		17 58						18 13					18 28					18 43					18 58	
Chessington South	d										18 10										18 40				
Chessington North	d										18 12										18 42				
Tolworth	d										18 14										18 44				
Malden Manor	d										18 17										18 47				
Motspur Park	d		18 01						18 16		18 20			18 31					18 46		18 50			19 01	
Raynes Park	d		18 04	18 07		18 10	18 13		18 19		18 23	18 28		18 34	18 40		18 43		18 49		18 53	18 58		19 04	19 10
Wimbledon ⊖	d	18 05	18 08	18 11		18 14	18 17		18 23	18 20	18 27	18 32	18 35	18 38	18 44		18 47		18 53	18 50	18 57	19 02	19 05	19 08	19 14
Earlsfield	d	18 08	18 12	18 15		18 17	18 20		18 27	18 24	18 31	18 35	18 38	18 42	18 47		18 50		18 57	18 54	19 01	19 05	19 08	19 12	19 17
Clapham Junction	d	18 12	18 16	18 19		18 21	18 24		18 31	18 28	18 35	18 39	18 42	18 46	18 51		18 54		19 01	18 58	19 05	19 09	19 12	19 16	19 21
Vauxhall ⊖	d	18 17	18 21	18 24		18 26	18 29		18 36	18 33	18 40	18 44	18 47	18 51	18 56		18 59		19 06	19 03	19 10	19 14	19 17	19 21	19 26
London Waterloo ⊖	a	18 23	18 25	18 29		18 31	18 35		18 40	18 37	18 47	18 49	18 52	18 55	19 01		19 05		19 10	19 07	19 14	19 19	19 23	19 27	19 31

			SW		SW	SW	SW	SW	SW	SW	SW		SW		SW	SW	SW	SW	SW	SW	SW		SW		SW
Guildford	d				18 38										19 08										19 28
London Road (Guildford)	d				18 42										19 12										19 32
Clandon	d				18 47										19 17										19 37
Horsley	d				18 51										19 21										19 41
Effingham Junction	d				18 54					18 59					19 25										19 46
Bookham	d									19 02															19 49
Cobham & Stoke d'Abernon	d				18 58										19 28										
Oxshott	d				19 01										19 32										
Claygate	d				19 04										19 35										
Hinchley Wood	d				19 07										19 37										
Hampton Court	d										19 24										19 54				
Thames Ditton	d										19 26										19 56				
Surbiton	d				19 12				19 27		19 32				19 42				19 57		20 02				
Berrylands	d										19 34										20 04				
Shepperton	d		18 36										19 06										19 41		
Upper Halliford	d		18 39										19 09										19 44		
Sunbury	d		18 41										19 11										19 46		
Kempton Park	d		18 43										19 13										19 48		
Hampton	d		18 51										19 21										19 51		
Fulwell	d		18 54										19 24										19 54		
Strawberry Hill	d							19 07										19 37							
Teddington	d		18 59					19 13					19 29					19 43					19 59		
Hampton Wick	d		19 01					19 16					19 31					19 46					20 01		
Kingston	a		19 03					19 18					19 33					19 48					20 04		
	d		19 04					19 19					19 34					19 49					20 04		
Norbiton	d		19 06					19 21					19 36					19 51					20 06		
New Malden	d		19 10					19 25			19 37		19 40					19 55			20 07		20 10		
Dorking	d					18 50														19 33					
Box Hill & Westhumble	d																								
Leatherhead	d					18 56				19 08										19 39					19 54
Ashtead	d					18 59				19 12										19 42					19 58
Epsom	a					19 04				19 16										19 47					20 02
	d					19 05				19 20						19 35				19 50					20 05
Ewell West	d					19 08				19 23						19 38				19 53					20 08
Stoneleigh	d					19 10				19 25						19 40				19 55					20 10
Worcester Park	d					19 13				19 28						19 43				19 58					20 13
Chessington South	d						19 10										19 40								
Chessington North	d						19 12										19 42								
Tolworth	d						19 14										19 44								
Malden Manor	d						19 17										19 47								
Motspur Park	d					19 16	19 20			19 31						19 46	19 50			20 01					20 16
Raynes Park	d		19 13			19 19	19 23	19 28		19 34	19 40		19 43			19 49	19 53	19 58		20 04	20 10		20 13		20 19
Wimbledon ⊖	d		19 17		19 20	19 23	19 27	19 32	19 35	19 38	19 44		19 47		19 50	19 53	19 57	20 02	20 05	20 08	20 14		20 17		20 23
Earlsfield	d		19 20		19 24	19 27	19 31	19 35	19 38	19 42	19 47		19 50		19 54	19 57	20 01	20 05	20 08	20 12	20 17		20 20		20 27
Clapham Junction	d		19 24		19 28	19 31	19 35	19 39	19 42	19 46	19 51		19 54		19 58	20 01	20 05	20 09	20 12	20 16	20 21		20 24		20 31
Vauxhall ⊖	d		19 29		19 33	19 36	19 40	19 44	19 47	19 51	19 56		19 59		20 03	20 06	20 10	20 14	20 17	20 21	20 26		20 29		20 36
London Waterloo ⊖	a		19 34		19 37	19 41	19 45	19 49	19 52	19 55	20 01		20 04		20 07	20 10	20 15	20 19	20 22	20 25	20 31		20 35		20 41

Table 152

Mondays to Fridays
until 5 October

Hampton Court, Shepperton, Guildford, Dorking and Chessington South - London

Network Diagram - see first Page of Table 152

		SW	SW	SW	SW	SW	SW		SW		SW	SW	SW	SW	SW	SW	SW		SW		SW	SW	SW	SW	SW
Guildford	d	19 38									19 58	20 08									20 38				
London Road (Guildford)	d	19 42									20 02	20 12									20 42				
Clandon	d	19 47									20 07	20 17									20 47				
Horsley	d	19 51									20 11	20 21									20 51				
Effingham Junction	d	19 54									20 16	20 24									20 54				
Bookham	d										20 19														
Cobham & Stoke d'Abernon	d	19 58										20 28									20 58				
Oxshott	d	20 01										20 31									21 01				
Claygate	d	20 04										20 34									21 04				
Hinchley Wood	d	20 07										20 37									21 07				
Hampton Court	d						20 24										20 54								
Thames Ditton	d						20 26										20 56								
Surbiton	d	20 12			20 27		20 32					20 42			20 57		21 02				21 12				21 27
Berrylands	d						20 34										21 04								
Shepperton	d								20 11										20 41						
Upper Halliford	d								20 14										20 44						
Sunbury	d								20 16										20 46						
Kempton Park	d								20 18										20 48						
Hampton	d								20 21										20 51						
Fulwell	d								20 24										20 54						
Strawberry Hill	d			20 07										20 37										21 07	
Teddington	d			20 11					20 29					20 41					20 59					21 11	
Hampton Wick	d			20 14					20 31					20 44					21 01					21 14	
Kingston	a			20 16					20 33					20 46					21 03					21 16	
	d			20 19					20 34					20 49					21 04					21 19	
Norbiton	d			20 21					20 36					20 51					21 06					21 21	
New Malden	d			20 25			20 37		20 40					20 55			21 07		21 10					21 25	
Dorking	d					20 05										20 35									
Box Hill & Westhumble	d																								
Leatherhead	d					20 11					20 24					20 41									
Ashtead	d					20 14					20 28					20 44									
Epsom	a					20 19					20 32					20 49									
	d					20 20					20 35					20 50						21 05			
Ewell West	d					20 23					20 38					20 53						21 08			
Stoneleigh	d					20 25					20 40					20 55						21 10			
Worcester Park	d					20 28					20 43					20 58						21 13			
Chessington South	d		20 10										20 40										21 10		
Chessington North	d		20 12										20 42										21 12		
Tolworth	d		20 14										20 44										21 14		
Malden Manor	d		20 17										20 47										21 17		
Motspur Park	d		20 20			20 31					20 46		20 50			21 01						21 16	21 20		
Raynes Park	d		20 23	20 28		20 34	20 40		20 43		20 49		20 53	20 58		21 04	21 10		21 13			21 19	21 23	21 28	
Wimbledon ⊖	d	20 20	20 27	20 32	20 35	20 38	20 44		20 47		20 53	20 50	20 57	21 02	21 05	21 08	21 14		21 17		21 20	21 23	21 27	21 32	21 35
Earlsfield	d	20 24	20 31	20 35	20 38	20 42	20 47		20 50		20 57	20 54	21 01	21 05	21 08	21 12	21 17		21 20		21 24	21 27	21 31	21 35	21 38
Clapham Junction	d	20 28	20 35	20 39	20 42	20 46	20 51		20 54		21 01	20 58	21 05	21 09	21 12	21 16	21 21		21 24		21 28	21 31	21 35	21 39	21 42
Vauxhall ⊖	d	20 33	20 40	20 44	20 47	20 51	20 56		20 59		21 06	21 03	21 10	21 14	21 17	21 21	21 26		21 29		21 33	21 36	21 40	21 44	21 47
London Waterloo ⊖	a	20 38	20 46	20 49	20 52	20 55	21 01		21 04		21 10	21 07	21 15	21 19	21 22	21 25	21 31		21 34		21 37	21 40	21 45	21 49	21 52

		SW	SW		SW		SW	SW	SW	SW	SW	SW		SW	SW		SW	SW	SW	SW		SW	SW	SW	SW
Guildford	d	20 46					21 08								21 38				21 46				22 08		
London Road (Guildford)	d	20 50					21 12								21 42				21 50				22 12		
Clandon	d	20 55					21 17								21 47				21 55				22 17		
Horsley	d	20 59					21 21								21 51				21 59				22 21		
Effingham Junction	d	21 03					21 24								21 54				22 03				22 24		
Bookham	d	21 06																	22 06						
Cobham & Stoke d'Abernon	d						21 28								21 58								22 28		
Oxshott	d						21 31								22 01								22 31		
Claygate	d						21 34								22 04								22 34		
Hinchley Wood	d						21 37								22 07								22 37		
Hampton Court	d		21 24																	22 24					
Thames Ditton	d		21 26																	22 26					
Surbiton	d		21 32				21 42				21 57				22 12			22 27		22 32			22 42		
Berrylands	d		21 34																	22 34					
Shepperton	d				21 11									21 41								22 11			
Upper Halliford	d				21 14									21 44								22 14			
Sunbury	d				21 16									21 46								22 16			
Kempton Park	d				21 18									21 48								22 18			
Hampton	d				21 21									21 51								22 21			
Fulwell	d				21 24									21 54								22 24			
Strawberry Hill	d									21 37							22 07								22 37
Teddington	d				21 29					21 41				21 59			22 11					22 29			22 41
Hampton Wick	d				21 31					21 44				22 01			22 14					22 31			22 44
Kingston	a				21 33					21 46				22 03			22 16					22 33			22 46
	d				21 34					21 49				22 04			22 19					22 34			22 49
Norbiton	d				21 36					21 51				22 06			22 21					22 36			22 51
New Malden	d		21 37		21 40					21 55				22 10			22 25			22 37		22 40			22 55
Dorking	d											21 35													
Box Hill & Westhumble	d																								
Leatherhead	d	21 11										21 41							22 11						
Ashtead	d	21 14										21 44							22 14						
Epsom	a	21 19										21 49							22 19						
	d	21 20						21 35				21 50							22 20						
Ewell West	d	21 23						21 38				21 53							22 23						
Stoneleigh	d	21 25						21 40				21 55							22 25						
Worcester Park	d	21 28						21 43				21 58							22 28						
Chessington South	d								21 40															22 40	
Chessington North	d								21 42															22 42	
Tolworth	d								21 44															22 44	
Malden Manor	d								21 47															22 47	
Motspur Park	d	21 31						21 46	21 50			22 01							22 31					22 50	
Raynes Park	d	21 34	21 40		21 43			21 49	21 53	21 58		22 04		22 13			22 28		22 34	22 40		22 43		22 53	22 58
Wimbledon ⊖	d	21 38	21 44		21 47		21 50	21 53	21 57	22 02	22 05	22 08		22 17	22 20		22 32	22 35	22 38	22 44		22 47	22 50	22 57	23 02
Earlsfield	d	21 42	21 47		21 50		21 54	21 57	22 01	22 05	22 08	22 12		22 20	22 24		22 35	22 38	22 42	22 47		22 50	22 54	23 01	23 05
Clapham Junction	d	21 46	21 51		21 54		21 58	22 01	22 05	22 09	22 12	22 16		22 24	22 28		22 39	22 42	22 46	22 51		22 54	22 58	23 05	23 09
Vauxhall ⊖	d	21 51	21 56		21 59		22 03	22 06	22 10	22 14	22 17	22 21		22 29	22 33		22 44	22 47	22 51	22 56		22 59	23 03	23 10	23 14
London Waterloo ⊖	a	21 55	22 01		22 04		22 07	22 10	22 16	22 19	22 22	22 25		22 34	22 39		22 49	22 52	22 55	23 01		23 04	23 07	23 15	23 19

Table 152

Mondays to Fridays
until 5 October

Hampton Court, Shepperton, Guildford, Dorking and Chessington South - London

Network Diagram - see first Page of Table 152

		SW	SW	SW	SW	SW	SW	SW	SW	SW	SW	SN	SW	SW A	SW FX B
Guildford	d	22 20			22 38		22 46	22 55			23 08				
London Road (Guildford)	d				22 42		22 50				23 12				
Clandon	d				22 47		22 55				23 17				
Horsley	d				22 51		22 59				23 21				
Effingham Junction ■	d				22 54		23 03				23 24				
Bookham	d						23 06								
Cobham & Stoke d'Abernon	d				22 58						23 28				
Oxshott	d				23 01						23 31				
Claygate	d				23 04						23 34				
Hinchley Wood	d				23 07						23 37				
Hampton Court	d								23 24						
Thames Ditton	d								23 26						
Surbiton ■	d	22 57			23 12			23 30	23 33		23 42				
Berrylands	d								23 35						
Shepperton	d			22 41						23 11					
Upper Halliford	d			22 44						23 14					
Sunbury	d			22 46						23 16					
Kempton Park	d			22 48						23 18					
Hampton	d			22 51						23 21					
Fulwell	d			22 54						23 24					
Strawberry Hill	d					23 07								23 37	23 37
Teddington	d			22 59		23 11				23 29				23 41	23 41
Hampton Wick	d			23 01		23 14				23 31				23 44	23 44
Kingston	a			23 03		23 16				23 33				23 46	23 46
	d			23 04		23 19				23 34				23 49	23 49
Norbiton	d			23 06		23 21				23 36				23 51	23 51
New Malden ■	d			23 10		23 25			23 38	23 41				23 55	23 55
Dorking ■	d		22 35									23 30			
Box Hill & Westhumble	d														
Leatherhead	d		22 41				23 11					23 36			
Ashtead	d		22 44				23 14					23 39			
Epsom ■	a		22 49				23 19					23 45			
	d		22 50				23 20								
Ewell West	d		22 53				23 23								
Stoneleigh	d		22 55				23 25								
Worcester Park	d		22 58				23 28								
Chessington South	d												23 40		
Chessington North	d												23 42		
Tolworth	d												23 44		
Malden Manor	d												23 47		
Motspur Park	d		23 01				23 31						23 50		
Raynes Park ■	d		23 04	23 13		23 28	23 37		23 41	23 43			23 54	23 58	23 58
Wimbledon ■ ⊖ ⇌	d	23 05	23 08	23 17	23 20	23 32	23 41	23 37	23a45	23 50	23 53		23a57	00 02	00 02
Earlsfield	d	23 08	23 12	23 20	23 24	23 36	23 44	23 41		23 53	23 56			00 05	00 05
Clapham Junction ■	d	23 12	23 16	23 24	23 28	23 40	23 48	23 45		23 57	23 59			00 09	00 09
Vauxhall ⊖	d	23 17	23 21	23 29	23 33	23 45	23 53	23 50		00 02	00 05			00 14	00 14
London Waterloo ■ ⊖	a	23 23	23 27	23 34	23 37	23 49	23 58	23 54		00 10	00 14			00 22	00 24

A not from 30 July until 2 August, from 6 August until 9 August, 29 August, 30 August, from 3 September until 6 September

B from 30 July until 6 September, not from 13 August until 28 August

Table 152

Mondays to Fridays
from 8 October

Hampton Court, Shepperton, Guildford, Dorking and Chessington South - London

Network Diagram - see first Page of Table 152

		SW MO	SW MX	SW MX	SW MX	SW MO	SW MX	SW MX	SW MO	SW	SW	SW	SW	SW	SW	SW	SW	SW	SW
Guildford	d			23p08						04 00		04 58			05 14		05 35		
London Road (Guildford)	d			23p12								05 02					05 39		
Clandon	d			23p17								05 07					05 44		
Horsley	d			23p21								05 11					05 48		
Effingham Junction ■	d			23p24								05 16					05 51		
Bookham	d											05 19							
Cobham & Stoke d'Abernon	d			23p28													05 55		
Oxshott	d			23p31													05 58		
Claygate	d			23p34													06 01		
Hinchley Wood	d			23p37													06 04		
Hampton Court	d					23p45										05 54			
Thames Ditton	d					23p47										05 56			
Surbiton ■	d			23p42		23p53				04 24					05 57	06 02	06 12		
Berrylands	d					23p55										06 04			
Shepperton	d	23p11	23p11										05 23						
Upper Halliford	d	23p14	23p14										05 26						
Sunbury	d	23p16	23p16										05 28						
Kempton Park	d	23p18	23p18																
Hampton	d	23p21	23p21										05 33						
Fulwell	d	23p24	23p24										05 36						
Strawberry Hill	d				23p37		00 07				04 55		05 38						06 08
Teddington	d	23p29	23p29		23p41		00 11	00s56	00s56		04 59			05 44					06 11
Hampton Wick	d	23p31	23p31		23p44		00 14	00s59	00s59		05 01			05 46					06 14
Kingston	a	23p33	23p33		23p46		00 16	01 01	01 01		05 03			05 48					06 16
	d	23p34	23p34		23p49						05 04			05 49					06 19
Norbiton	d	23p36	23p36		23p51						05 06			05 51					06 21
New Malden ■	d	23p40	23p41		23p55	23p58					05 10			05 55		06 07			06 25
Dorking ■	d																	05 48	
Box Hill & Westhumble	d																	05 50	
Leatherhead	d											05 24						05 56	
Ashtead	d											05 28						05 59	
Epsom ■	a											05 32						06 04	
	d											05 34						06 04	
Ewell West	d											05 37						06 07	
Stoneleigh	d											05 40						06 10	
Worcester Park	d											05 42						06 12	
Chessington South	d																		
Chessington North	d																		
Tolworth	d																		
Malden Manor	d																		
Motspur Park	d											05 46						06 16	
Raynes Park ■	d	23p43	23p43		23p58	00 01					05 13	05 49		05 58		06 10		06 19	06 28
Wimbledon ■ ⊖ ⇌	d	23p47	23p50	23p53	00 02	00a04				04 32	05 17	05 53		06 02	06 05	06 14	06 20	06 23	06 32
Earlsfield	d	23p50	23p53	23p56	00 05						05 21	05 57		06 05	06 08	06 17	06 24	06 27	06 35
Clapham Junction ■	d	23p54	23p57	23p59	00 09					04 44	05 25	06 01		06 09	06 12	06 21	06 28	06 31	06 39
Vauxhall ⊖	d	23p59	00 02	00 05	00 14						05 30	06 06	06 12	06 14	06 17	06 26	06 33	06 36	06 44
London Waterloo ■ ⊖	a	00 04	00 10	00 14	00 22					04 53	05 35	06 11	06 16	06 19	06 22	06 31	06 37	06 40	06 49

Mondays to Fridays

from 8 October

Hampton Court, Shepperton, Guildford, Dorking and Chessington South - London

Network Diagram - see first Page of Table 152

		SW	SW	SW		SW		SW	SW	SW	SW	SW	SW	SW				SW	SW	SW	SW		SW	SW	SW
Guildford	d							05 58	06 04										06 28	06 34					
London Road (Guildford)	d							06 02	06 08										06 32	06 38					
Clandon	d							06 07	06 13										06 37	06 43					
Horsley	d							06 11	06 17										06 41	06 47					
Effingham Junction 6	d							06 16	06 21										06 48	06 53					
Bookham	d							06 19											06 51						
Cobham & Stoke d'Abernon	d								06 24											06 56					
Oxshott	d								06 28											07 00					
Claygate	d								06 31											07 03					
Hinchley Wood	d								06 34											07 06					
Hampton Court	d			06 24										06 54											
Thames Ditton	d			06 26										06 56											
Surbiton 6	d	06 28		06 32					06 42			06 57		07 02						07 12					
Berrylands	d			06 34										07 04											
Shepperton	d					06 11												06 41							
Upper Halliford	d					06 14												06 44							
Sunbury	d					06 16												06 46							
Kempton Park	d																								
Hampton	d					06 21												06 51							
Fulwell	d					06 24												06 54							
Strawberry Hill	d										06 37												07 07		
Teddington	d					06 29					06 41							06 59					07 11		07 20
Hampton Wick	d					06 31					06 44							07 01					07 14		07 22
Kingston	a					06 33					06 46							07 03					07 16		07 24
	d					06 34					06 49							07 04					07 19		07 26
Norbiton	d					06 36					06 51							07 06					07 21		07 28
New Malden 6	d			06 37		06 40					06 55			07 07				07 10					07 25		07 32
Dorking 4	d												06 32											07 02	
Box Hill & Westhumble	d												06 34											07 04	
Leatherhead	d							06 24					06 39						06 56					07 09	
Ashtead	d							06 28					06 43						06 59					07 13	
Epsom 3	a							06 32					06 47						07 04					07 17	
	d		06 18					06 34					06 48						07 04					07 18	
Ewell West	d		06 21					06 37					06 51						07 07						
Stoneleigh	d		06 24					06 40					06 53						07 10						
Worcester Park	d		06 27					06 42					06 56						07 12					07 25	
Chessington South	d									06 40											07 10				
Chessington North	d									06 42											07 12				
Tolworth	d									06 44											07 14				
Malden Manor	d									06 47											07 17				
Motspur Park	d		06 30					06 46		06 50			07 00						07 16		07 20				
Raynes Park 6	d		06 34	06 40		06 43		06 49		06 54	06 58		07 04	07 10				07 13	07 19		07 24		07 28	07 31	07 34
Wimbledon 6 ⊖	d	06 35	06 38	06 44		06 47		06 53	06 50	06 58	07 02	07 05	07 08	07 14				07 17	07 23	07 20	07 28		07 32	07 35	07 38
Earlsfield	d	06 39	06 42	06 47		06 50		06 57	06 54	07 01	07 05	07 08	07 11	07 17				07 20	07 27	07 24	07 31		07 35	07 38	07 42
Clapham Junction 10	d	06 43	06 46	06 51		06 54		07 01	06 58	07 05	07 09	07 12	07 15	07 21				07 24	07 31	07 28	07 35		07 39	07 42	07 46
Vauxhall ⊖	d	06 48	06 51	06 56		06 59		07 06	07 03	07 10	07 14	07 17	07 20	07 26				07 29	07 36	07 33	07 40		07 44	07 47	07 51
London Waterloo 15 ⊖	a	06 52	06 55	07 03		07 06		07 12	07 09	07 17	07 21	07 24	07 27	07 33				07 36	07 42	07 39	07 47		07 51	07 54	07 57

Table 152

Mondays to Fridays

from 8 October

Hampton Court, Shepperton, Guildford, Dorking and Chessington South - London

Network Diagram - see first Page of Table 152

		SW		SW		SW		SW	SW	SW	SW	SW			SW	SW	SW	SW	SW		SW			SW	SW
Guildford	d								06 58	07 04	07 14														
London Road (Guildford)	d								07 02	07 08	07 18														
Clandon	d								07 07	07 13	07 23														
Horsley	d								07 11	07 17	07 27														
Effingham Junction 6	d								07 16	07 21	07 31														07 46
Bookham	d								07 19																07 49
Cobham & Stoke d'Abernon	d									07 24	07 34														
Oxshott	d									07 28	07 38														
Claygate	d									07 31	07 41														
Hinchley Wood	d									07 34	07 44														
Hampton Court	d					07 24															07 54				
Thames Ditton	d					07 26															07 56				
Surbiton 6	d					07 32				07 42	07 53										08 02				
Berrylands	d					07 34															08 04				
Shepperton	d			07 00				07 11									07 30							07 41	
Upper Halliford	d			07 03				07 14									07 33							07 44	
Sunbury	d			07 05				07 16									07 35							07 46	
Kempton Park	d																								
Hampton	d			07 09				07 21									07 39							07 51	
Fulwell	d			07 12				07 24									07 42							07 54	
Strawberry Hill	d			07 14											07 37		07 44	07 47							
Teddington	d							07 29							07 41			07 50						07 59	
Hampton Wick	d							07 31							07 44			07 52						08 01	
Kingston	a							07 33							07 46			07 54						08 03	
	d							07 34							07 49			07 56						08 04	
Norbiton	d							07 36							07 51			07 58						08 06	
New Malden 6	d					07 37		07 40		07 46					07 55			08 02			08 07			08 10	
Dorking 4	d															07 32									
Box Hill & Westhumble	d															07 34									
Leatherhead	d								07 26							07 39									07 56
Ashtead	d								07 29							07 43									07 59
Epsom 3	a								07 34							07 47									08 04
	d	07 22							07 34							07 48			07 52						08 04
Ewell West	d	07 25							07 37										07 55						08 07
Stoneleigh	d	07 27							07 40										07 57						08 10
Worcester Park	d	07 30							07 43							07 55			08 00						08 13
Chessington South	d											07 40													
Chessington North	d											07 42													
Tolworth	d											07 44													
Malden Manor	d											07 47													
Motspur Park	d	07 34							07 46			07 50							08 04						08 16
Raynes Park 6	d	07 37				07 40		07 43	07 50			07 54			07 58	08 01		08 04	08 07		08 10			08 13	08 20
Wimbledon 6 ⊖	d	07 41				07 44		07 47	07 54	07 51		07 58			08 02	08 05		08 08	08 11		08 14			08 17	08 24
Earlsfield	d	07 45				07 48		07 51	07 58	07 54		08 01			08 05	08 08		08 12	08 15		08 18			08 21	08 28
Clapham Junction 10	d	07 49				07 52		07 55	08 02	07 58		08 05			08 09	08 12		08 16	08 19		08 22			08 25	08 32
Vauxhall ⊖	d	07 54		07 56		07 57		08 00	08 07	08 03		08 10			08 14	08 17	08 26	08 21	08 24		08 27			08 30	08 37
London Waterloo 15 ⊖	a	08 00		08 04		08 04		08 06	08 13	08 11	08 13	08 17			08 21	08 24	08 34	08 27	08 30		08 33			08 36	08 43

Table 152

Mondays to Fridays
from 8 October

Hampton Court, Shepperton, Guildford, Dorking and Chessington South - London

Network Diagram - see first Page of Table 152

		SW	SW	SW	SW	SW	SW	SW	SW	SW	SW	SW	SW	SW	SW	SW	SW
Guildford	d	07 34									07 58	08 04			08 20		
London Road (Guildford)	d	07 38									08 02	08 08					
Clandon	d	07 43									08 07	08 13					
Horsley	d	07 47									08 11	08 17					
Effingham Junction	d	07 51									08 16	08 21					
Bookham	d										08 19						
Cobham & Stoke d'Abernon	d	07 54										08 24					
Oxshott	d	07 58										08 28					
Claygate	d	08 01										08 31					
Hinchley Wood	d	08 04										08 34					
Hampton Court	d								08 24								08 54
Thames Ditton	d								08 26								08 56
Surbiton	d	08 12							08 32			08 42			08 57		09 02
Berrylands	d								08 34								09 04
Shepperton	d					08 00				08 11							
Upper Halliford	d					08 03				08 14							
Sunbury	d					08 05				08 16							
Kempton Park	d																
Hampton	d					08 09				08 21							
Fulwell	d					08 12				08 24							
Strawberry Hill	d			08 07		08 14	08 17							08 38			
Teddington	d			08 11			08 20			08 29				08 41			
Hampton Wick	d			08 14			08 22			08 31				08 44			
Kingston	a			08 16			08 24			08 33				08 46			
	d			08 19			08 26			08 34				08 49			
Norbiton	d			08 21			08 28			08 36				08 51			
New Malden	d	08 16		08 25			08 32		08 37	08 40				08 55			09 07
Dorking	d				08 02											08 31	
Box Hill & Westhumble	d				08 04											08 33	
Leatherhead	d				08 09						08 25					08 38	
Ashtead	d				08 13						08 28					08 42	
Epsom	a				08 17						08 33					08 46	
	d				08 18			08 22			08 34					08 48	
Ewell West	d							08 25			08 37					08 51	
Stoneleigh	d							08 27			08 40					08 54	
Worcester Park	d				08 25			08 30			08 42					08 57	
Chessington South	d		08 10										08 40				
Chessington North	d		08 12										08 42				
Tolworth	d		08 14										08 44				
Malden Manor	d		08 17										08 47				
Motspur Park	d		08 20					08 34			08 46		08 50			09 00	
Raynes Park	d		08 24	08 28	08 31		08 34	08 37	08 40	08 43	08 49		08 54	08 58		09 04	09 10
Wimbledon ⊖	d	08 21	08 28	08 32	08 35		08 38	08 41	08 44	08 47	08 53		08 58	09 02	09 05	09 08	09 14
Earlsfield	d	08 24	08 31	08 35	08 38		08 42	08 45	08 48	08 51	08 57		09 01	09 05	09 08	09 12	09 17
Clapham Junction	d	08 28	08 35	08 39	08 42		08 46	08 49	08 52	08 55	09 01		09 05	09 09	09 12	09 16	09 21
Vauxhall ⊖	d	08 33	08 40	08 44	08 47	08 56	08 51	08 54	08 57	09 00	09 06		09 10	09 14	09 17	09 21	09 26
London Waterloo ⊖	a	08 40	08 47	08 51	08 54	09 04	08 57	09 00	09 03	09 06	09 12	09 01	09 17	09 21	09 24	09 27	09 33

Table 152

Mondays to Fridays
from 8 October

Hampton Court, Shepperton, Guildford, Dorking and Chessington South - London

Network Diagram - see first Page of Table 152

		SW	SW	SW	SW	SW	SW	SW	SW	SW	SW	SW	SW	SW	SW	SW	SW	SW	SW
Guildford	d			08 34			08 46				08 58	09 05							09 28
London Road (Guildford)	d			08 38							09 02	09 09							09 32
Clandon	d			08 43							09 07	09 14							09 37
Horsley	d			08 47							09 11	09 18							09 41
Effingham Junction	d		08 48	08 53							09 16	09 21							09 46
Bookham	d		08 51								09 19								09 49
Cobham & Stoke d'Abernon	d			08 56								09 25							
Oxshott	d			09 00								09 28							
Claygate	d			09 03								09 31							
Hinchley Wood	d			09 06								09 34							
Hampton Court	d								09 24								09 54		
Thames Ditton	d								09 26								09 56		
Surbiton	d			09 12			09 27		09 32			09 42			09 57		10 02		
Berrylands	d								09 34								10 04		
Shepperton	d	08 41								09 11								09 41	
Upper Halliford	d	08 44								09 14								09 44	
Sunbury	d	08 46								09 16								09 46	
Kempton Park	d									09 18								09 48	
Hampton	d	08 51								09 21								09 51	
Fulwell	d	08 54								09 24								09 54	
Strawberry Hill	d					09 07								09 37					
Teddington	d	08 59				09 11				09 29				09 41				09 59	
Hampton Wick	d	09 01				09 14				09 31				09 44				10 01	
Kingston	a	09 03				09 16				09 33				09 46				10 03	
	d	09 04				09 19				09 34				09 49				10 04	
Norbiton	d	09 06				09 21				09 36				09 51				10 06	
New Malden	d	09 10				09 25			09 37	09 40				09 55			10 07	10 10	
Dorking	d							09 02								09 35			
Box Hill & Westhumble	d							09 04											
Leatherhead	d		08 56					09 09			09 24					09 41			09 54
Ashtead	d		08 59					09 13			09 28					09 45			09 58
Epsom	a		09 04					09 17			09 32					09 49			10 02
	d		09 04					09 18			09 35					09 50			10 05
Ewell West	d		09 07					09 21			09 38					09 53			10 08
Stoneleigh	d		09 10					09 24			09 40					09 55			10 10
Worcester Park	d		09 12					09 27			09 43					09 58			10 13
Chessington South	d				09 10								09 40						
Chessington North	d				09 12								09 42						
Tolworth	d				09 14								09 44						
Malden Manor	d				09 17								09 47						
Motspur Park	d		09 16		09 20			09 30			09 46		09 50			10 01			10 16
Raynes Park	d	09 13	09 19		09 24	09 28		09 34	09 40	09 43	09 49		09 53	09 58		10 04	10 10	10 13	10 19
Wimbledon ⊖	d	09 17	09 23	09 20	09 28	09 32	09 35	09 38	09 44	09 47	09 53	09 50	09 57	10 02	10 05	10 08	10 14	10 17	10 23
Earlsfield	d	09 20	09 27	09 24	09 31	09 35	09 38	09 42	09 47	09 50	09 57	09 54	10 01	10 05	10 08	10 12	10 17	10 20	10 27
Clapham Junction	d	09 24	09 31	09 28	09 35	09 39	09 42	09 46	09 51	09 54	10 01	09 58	10 05	10 09	10 12	10 16	10 21	10 24	10 31
Vauxhall ⊖	d	09 29	09 36	09 33	09 40	09 44	09 47	09 51	09 56	09 59	10 06	10 03	10 10	10 14	10 17	10 21	10 26	10 29	10 36
London Waterloo ⊖	a	09 36	09 42	09 39	09 47	09 51	09 54	09 57	10 01	10 04	10 10	10 07	10 15	10 19	10 22	10 25	10 31	10 34	10 40

from 8 October

Hampton Court, Shepperton, Guildford, Dorking and Chessington South - London

Network Diagram - see first Page of Table 152

		SW	SW	SW	SW	SW	SW		SW	SW		SW	SW	SW	SW	SW	SW		SW	SW		SW	SW	SW	SW
Guildford	d	09 35								09 58		10 05								10 28		10 35			
London Road (Guildford)	d	09 39								10 02		10 09								10 32		10 39			
Clandon	d	09 44								10 07		10 14								10 37		10 44			
Horsley	d	09 48								10 11		10 18								10 41		10 48			
Effingham Junction [6]	d	09 51								10 16		10 21								10 46		10 51			
Bookham	d									10 19										10 49					
Cobham & Stoke d'Abernon	d	09 55										10 25										10 55			
Oxshott	d	09 58										10 28										10 58			
Claygate	d	10 01										10 31										11 01			
Hinchley Wood	d	10 04										10 34										11 04			
Hampton Court	d						10 24										10 54								
Thames Ditton	d						10 26										10 56								
Surbiton [6]	d	10 12			10 27		10 32					10 42			10 57		11 02					11 12			11 27
Berrylands	d						10 34										11 04								
Shepperton	d								10 11										10 41						
Upper Halliford	d								10 14										10 44						
Sunbury	d								10 16										10 46						
Kempton Park	d								10 18										10 48						
Hampton	d								10 21										10 51						
Fulwell	d								10 24										10 54						
Strawberry Hill	d			10 07										10 37										11 07	
Teddington	d			10 11					10 29					10 41					10 59					11 11	
Hampton Wick	d			10 14					10 31					10 44					11 01					11 14	
Kingston	a			10 16					10 33					10 46					11 03					11 16	
	d			10 19					10 34					10 49					11 04					11 19	
Norbiton	d			10 21					10 36					10 51					11 06					11 21	
New Malden [6]	d			10 25			10 37		10 40					10 55			11 07		11 10					11 25	
Dorking [4]	d					10 05										10 35									
Box Hill & Westhumble	d																								
Leatherhead	d					10 11				10 24						10 41				10 54					
Ashtead	d					10 14				10 28						10 44				10 58					
Epsom [3]	a					10 19				10 32						10 49				11 02					
	d					10 20				10 35						10 50				11 05					
Ewell West	d					10 23				10 38						10 53				11 08					
Stoneleigh	d					10 25				10 40						10 55				11 10					
Worcester Park	d					10 28				10 43						10 58				11 13					
Chessington South	d		10 10										10 40										11 10		
Chessington North	d		10 12										10 42										11 12		
Tolworth	d		10 14										10 44										11 14		
Malden Manor	d		10 17										10 47										11 17		
Motspur Park	d		10 20			10 31				10 46			10 50			11 01				11 16			11 20		
Raynes Park [6]	d		10 23	10 28		10 34	10 40		10 43	10 49			10 53	10 58		11 04	11 10		11 13	11 19			11 23	11 28	
Wimbledon [6] ⊖ ⛴	d	10 20	10 27	10 32	10 35	10 38	10 44		10 47	10 53		10 50	10 57	11 02	11 05	11 08	11 14		11 17	11 23		11 20	11 27	11 32	11 35
Earlsfield	d	10 24	10 31	10 35	10 38	10 42	10 47		10 50	10 57		10 54	11 01	11 05	11 08	11 12	11 17		11 20	11 27		11 24	11 31	11 35	11 38
Clapham Junction [10]	d	10 28	10 35	10 39	10 42	10 46	10 51		10 54	11 01		10 58	11 05	11 09	11 12	11 16	11 21		11 24	11 31		11 28	11 35	11 39	11 42
Vauxhall ⊖	d	10 33	10 40	10 44	10 47	10 51	10 56		10 59	11 06		11 03	11 10	11 14	11 17	11 21	11 26		11 29	11 36		11 33	11 40	11 44	11 47
London Waterloo [15] ⊖	a	10 37	10 45	10 49	10 52	10 55	11 01		11 04	11 10		11 07	11 15	11 19	11 22	11 25	11 31		11 34	11 40		11 37	11 45	11 49	11 52

		SW	SW		SW	SW		SW	SW	SW	SW	SW	SW		SW	SW		SW	SW	SW	SW	SW	SW		SW
Guildford	d					10 58		11 05								11 28		11 35							
London Road (Guildford)	d					11 02		11 09								11 32		11 39							
Clandon	d					11 07		11 14								11 37		11 44							
Horsley	d					11 11		11 18								11 41		11 48							
Effingham Junction [6]	d					11 16		11 21								11 46		11 51							
Bookham	d					11 19										11 49									
Cobham & Stoke d'Abernon	d							11 25										11 55							
Oxshott	d							11 28										11 58							
Claygate	d							11 31										12 01							
Hinchley Wood	d							11 34										12 04							
Hampton Court	d		11 24										11 54										12 24		
Thames Ditton	d		11 26										11 56										12 26		
Surbiton [6]	d		11 32					11 42			11 57		12 02					12 12			12 27		12 32		
Berrylands	d		11 34										12 04										12 34		
Shepperton	d				11 11										11 41										12 11
Upper Halliford	d				11 14										11 44										12 14
Sunbury	d				11 16										11 46										12 16
Kempton Park	d				11 18										11 48										12 18
Hampton	d				11 21										11 51										12 21
Fulwell	d				11 24										11 54										12 24
Strawberry Hill	d									11 37										12 07					
Teddington	d				11 29					11 41					11 59					12 11					12 29
Hampton Wick	d				11 31					11 44					12 01					12 14					12 31
Kingston	a				11 33					11 46					12 03					12 16					12 33
	d				11 34					11 49					12 04					12 19					12 34
Norbiton	d				11 36					11 51					12 06					12 21					12 36
New Malden [6]	d		11 37		11 40					11 55			12 07		12 10					12 25			12 37		12 40
Dorking [4]	d	11 05										11 35										12 05			
Box Hill & Westhumble	d																								
Leatherhead	d	11 11				11 24						11 41				11 54						12 11			
Ashtead	d	11 14				11 28						11 44				11 58						12 14			
Epsom [3]	a	11 19				11 32						11 49				12 02						12 19			
	d	11 20				11 35						11 50				12 05						12 20			
Ewell West	d	11 23				11 38						11 53				12 08						12 23			
Stoneleigh	d	11 25				11 40						11 55				12 10						12 25			
Worcester Park	d	11 28				11 43						11 58				12 13						12 28			
Chessington South	d								11 40										12 10						
Chessington North	d								11 42										12 12						
Tolworth	d								11 44										12 14						
Malden Manor	d								11 47										12 17						
Motspur Park	d	11 31				11 46			11 50			12 01				12 16			12 20			12 31			
Raynes Park [6]	d	11 34	11 40		11 43	11 49			11 53	11 58		12 04	12 10		12 13	12 19			12 23	12 28		12 34	12 40		12 43
Wimbledon [6] ⊖ ⛴	d	11 38	11 44		11 47	11 53		11 50	11 57	12 02	12 05	12 08	12 14		12 17	12 23		12 20	12 27	12 32	12 35	12 38	12 44		12 47
Earlsfield	d	11 42	11 47		11 50	11 57		11 54	12 01	12 05	12 08	12 12	12 17		12 20	12 27		12 24	12 31	12 35	12 38	12 42	12 47		12 50
Clapham Junction [10]	d	11 46	11 51		11 54	12 01		11 58	12 05	12 09	12 12	12 16	12 21		12 24	12 31		12 28	12 35	12 39	12 42	12 46	12 51		12 54
Vauxhall ⊖	d	11 51	11 56		11 59	12 06		12 03	12 10	12 14	12 17	12 21	12 26		12 29	12 36		12 33	12 40	12 44	12 47	12 51	12 56		12 59
London Waterloo [15] ⊖	a	11 55	12 01		12 04	12 10		12 07	12 15	12 19	12 22	12 25	12 31		12 34	12 40		12 37	12 45	12 49	12 52	12 55	13 01		13 04

Table 152

Mondays to Fridays

from 8 October

Hampton Court, Shepperton, Guildford, Dorking and Chessington South - London

Network Diagram - see first Page of Table 152

		SW		SW	SW	SW	SW	SW	SW	SW [1]		SW		SW	SW	SW	SW	SW	SW	SW		SW		SW	SW
Guildford	d	11 58		12 05										12 28	12 35									12 58	13 05
London Road (Guildford)	d	12 02		12 09										12 32	12 39									13 02	13 09
Clandon	d	12 07		12 14										12 37	12 44									13 07	13 14
Horsley	d	12 11		12 18										12 41	12 48									13 11	13 18
Effingham Junction [6]	d	12 16		12 21										12 46	12 51									13 16	13 21
Bookham	d	12 19												12 49										13 19	
Cobham & Stoke d'Abernon	d			12 25											12 55										13 25
Oxshott	d			12 28											12 58										13 28
Claygate	d			12 31											13 01										13 31
Hinchley Wood	d			12 34											13 04										13 34
Hampton Court	d								12 54											13 24					
Thames Ditton	d								12 56											13 26					
Surbiton [6]	d			12 42			12 57		13 02	13 08					13 12			13 27		13 32					13 42
Berrylands	d								13 04											13 34					
Shepperton	d											12 41										13 11			
Upper Halliford	d											12 44										13 14			
Sunbury	d											12 46										13 16			
Kempton Park	d											12 48										13 18			
Hampton	d											12 51										13 21			
Fulwell	d											12 54										13 24			
Strawberry Hill	d					12 37											13 07								
Teddington	d					12 41						12 59					13 11					13 29			
Hampton Wick	d					12 44						13 01					13 14					13 31			
Kingston	a					12 46						13 03					13 16					13 33			
	d					12 49						13 04					13 19					13 34			
Norbiton	d					12 51						13 06					13 21					13 36			
New Malden [6]	d					12 55			13 07			13 10					13 25			13 37		13 40			
Dorking [4]	d							12 35											13 05						
Box Hill & Westhumble	d																								
Leatherhead	d	12 24						12 41						12 54					13 11					13 24	
Ashtead	d	12 28						12 44						12 58					13 14					13 28	
Epsom [3]	a	12 32						12 49						13 02					13 19					13 32	
	d	12 35						12 50						13 05					13 20					13 35	
Ewell West	d	12 38						12 53						13 08					13 23					13 38	
Stoneleigh	d	12 40						12 55						13 10					13 25					13 40	
Worcester Park	d	12 43						12 58						13 13					13 28					13 43	
Chessington South	d				12 40											13 10									
Chessington North	d				12 42											13 12									
Tolworth	d				12 44											13 14									
Malden Manor	d				12 47											13 17									
Motspur Park	d	12 46			12 50			13 01						13 16		13 20			13 31					13 46	
Raynes Park [6]	d	12 49			12 53	12 58		13 04	13 10			13 13		13 19		13 23	13 28		13 34	13 40		13 43		13 49	
Wimbledon [6] ⊖ ⛴	d	12 53		12 50	12 57	13 02	13 05	13 08	13 14			13 17		13 23	13 20	13 27	13 32	13 35	13 38	13 44		13 47		13 53	13 50
Earlsfield	d	12 57		12 54	13 01	13 05	13 08	13 12	13 17			13 20		13 27	13 24	13 31	13 35	13 38	13 42	13 47		13 50		13 57	13 54
Clapham Junction [10]	d	13 01		12 58	13 05	13 09	13 12	13 16	13 21			13 24		13 31	13 28	13 35	13 39	13 42	13 46	13 51		13 54		14 01	13 58
Vauxhall ⊖	d	13 06		13 03	13 10	13 14	13 17	13 21	13 26			13 29		13 36	13 33	13 40	13 44	13 47	13 51	13 56		13 59		14 06	14 03
London Waterloo [15] ⊖	a	13 10		13 07	13 15	13 19	13 22	13 25	13 31	13 25		13 34		13 40	13 37	13 45	13 49	13 52	13 55	14 01		14 04		14 10	14 07

from 8 October

Hampton Court, Shepperton, Guildford, Dorking and Chessington South - London

Network Diagram - see first Page of Table 152

		SW	SW	SW	SW	SW		SW		SW	SW	SW	SW	SW	SW	SW		SW		SW	SW	SW	SW	SW	SW
Guildford	d									13 28	13 35									13 58	14 05				
London Road (Guildford)	d									13 32	13 39									14 02	14 09				
Clandon	d									13 37	13 44									14 07	14 14				
Horsley	d									13 41	13 48									14 11	14 18				
Effingham Junction 6	d									13 46	13 51									14 16	14 21				
Bookham	d									13 49										14 19					
Cobham & Stoke d'Abernon	d										13 55										14 25				
Oxshott	d										13 58										14 28				
Claygate	d										14 01										14 31				
Hinchley Wood	d										14 04										14 34				
Hampton Court	d					13 54										14 24									
Thames Ditton	d					13 56										14 26									
Surbiton 6	d			13 57		14 02					14 12			14 27		14 32					14 42			14 57	
Berrylands	d					14 04										14 34									
Shepperton	d							13 41										14 11							
Upper Halliford	d							13 44										14 14							
Sunbury	d							13 46										14 16							
Kempton Park	d							13 48										14 18							
Hampton	d							13 51										14 21							
Fulwell	d							13 54										14 24							
Strawberry Hill	d		13 37										14 07										14 37		
Teddington	d		13 41					13 59					14 11					14 29					14 41		
Hampton Wick	d		13 44					14 01					14 14					14 31					14 44		
Kingston	a		13 46					14 03					14 16					14 33					14 46		
	d		13 49					14 04					14 19					14 34					14 49		
Norbiton	d		13 51					14 06					14 21					14 36					14 51		
New Malden 6	d		13 55			14 07		14 10					14 25			14 37		14 40					14 55		
Dorking 4	d				13 35										14 05										14 35
Box Hill & Westhumble	d																								
Leatherhead	d				13 41					13 54					14 11					14 24					14 41
Ashtead	d				13 44					13 58					14 14					14 28					14 44
Epsom 3	a				13 49					14 02					14 19					14 32					14 49
	d				13 50					14 05					14 20					14 35					14 50
Ewell West	d				13 53					14 08					14 23					14 38					14 53
Stoneleigh	d				13 55					14 10					14 25					14 40					14 55
Worcester Park	d				13 58					14 13					14 28					14 43					14 58
Chessington South	d	13 40										14 10										14 40			
Chessington North	d	13 42										14 12										14 42			
Tolworth	d	13 44										14 14										14 44			
Malden Manor	d	13 47										14 17										14 47			
Motspur Park	d	13 50			14 01					14 16		14 20			14 31					14 46		14 50			15 01
Raynes Park 6	d	13 53	13 58		14 04	14 10		14 13		14 19		14 23	14 28		14 34	14 40		14 43		14 49		14 53	14 58		15 04
Wimbledon 6 ⊖ ⇌	d	13 57	14 02	14 05	14 08	14 14		14 17		14 23	14 20	14 27	14 32	14 35	14 38	14 44		14 47		14 53	14 50	14 57	15 02	15 05	15 08
Earlsfield	d	14 01	14 05	14 08	14 12	14 17		14 20		14 27	14 24	14 31	14 35	14 38	14 42	14 47		14 50		14 57	14 54	15 01	15 05	15 08	15 12
Clapham Junction 10	d	14 05	14 09	14 12	14 16	14 21		14 24		14 31	14 28	14 35	14 39	14 42	14 46	14 51		14 54		15 01	14 58	15 05	15 09	15 12	15 16
Vauxhall ⊖	d	14 10	14 14	14 17	14 21	14 26		14 29		14 36	14 33	14 40	14 44	14 47	14 51	14 56		14 59		15 06	15 03	15 10	15 14	15 17	15 21
London Waterloo 15 ⊖	a	14 15	14 19	14 22	14 25	14 31		14 34		14 40	14 37	14 45	14 49	14 52	14 55	15 01		15 04		15 10	15 07	15 15	15 19	15 22	15 25

		SW		SW		SW	SW	SW	SW	SW	SW	SW		SW		SW	SW	SW	SW	SW	SW	SW		SW	
Guildford	d					14 28	14 35									14 58	15 05								
London Road (Guildford)	d					14 32	14 39									15 02	15 09								
Clandon	d					14 37	14 44									15 07	15 14								
Horsley	d					14 41	14 48									15 11	15 18								
Effingham Junction 6	d					14 46	14 51									15 16	15 21								
Bookham	d					14 49										15 19									
Cobham & Stoke d'Abernon	d						14 55										15 25								
Oxshott	d						14 58										15 28								
Claygate	d						15 01										15 31								
Hinchley Wood	d						15 04										15 34								
Hampton Court	d	14 54										15 24										15 54			
Thames Ditton	d	14 56										15 26										15 56			
Surbiton 6	d	15 02					15 12			15 27		15 32					15 42			15 57		16 02			
Berrylands	d	15 04										15 34										16 04			
Shepperton	d			14 41										15 11										15 41	
Upper Halliford	d			14 44										15 14										15 44	
Sunbury	d			14 46										15 16										15 46	
Kempton Park	d			14 48										15 18										15 48	
Hampton	d			14 51										15 21										15 51	
Fulwell	d			14 54										15 24										15 54	
Strawberry Hill	d								15 07										15 37						
Teddington	d			14 59					15 11					15 29					15 41					15 59	
Hampton Wick	d			15 01					15 14					15 31					15 44					16 01	
Kingston	a			15 03					15 16					15 33					15 46					16 03	
	d			15 04					15 19					15 34					15 49					16 04	
Norbiton	d			15 06					15 21					15 36					15 51					16 06	
New Malden 6	d	15 07		15 10					15 25			15 37		15 40					15 55			16 07		16 10	
Dorking 4	d										15 05										15 35				
Box Hill & Westhumble	d																								
Leatherhead	d					14 54					15 11					15 24					15 41				
Ashtead	d					14 58					15 14					15 28					15 44				
Epsom 3	a					15 02					15 19					15 32					15 49				
	d					15 05					15 20					15 35					15 50				
Ewell West	d					15 08					15 23					15 38					15 53				
Stoneleigh	d					15 10					15 25					15 40					15 55				
Worcester Park	d					15 13					15 28					15 43					15 58				
Chessington South	d							15 10										15 40							
Chessington North	d							15 12										15 42							
Tolworth	d							15 14										15 44							
Malden Manor	d							15 17										15 47							
Motspur Park	d					15 16		15 20			15 31					15 46		15 50			16 01				
Raynes Park 6	d	15 10		15 13		15 19		15 23	15 28		15 34	15 40		15 43		15 49		15 53	15 58		16 04	16 10		16 13	
Wimbledon 6 ⊖ ⇌	d	15 14		15 17		15 23	15 20	15 27	15 32	15 35	15 38	15 44		15 47		15 53	15 50	15 57	16 02	16 05	16 08	16 14		16 17	
Earlsfield	d	15 17		15 20		15 27	15 24	15 31	15 35	15 38	15 42	15 47		15 50		15 57	15 54	16 01	16 05	16 08	16 12	16 17		16 20	
Clapham Junction 10	d	15 21		15 24		15 31	15 28	15 35	15 39	15 42	15 46	15 51		15 54		16 01	15 58	16 05	16 09	16 12	16 16	16 21		16 24	
Vauxhall ⊖	d	15 26		15 29		15 36	15 33	15 40	15 44	15 47	15 51	15 56		15 59		16 06	16 03	16 10	16 14	16 17	16 21	16 26		16 29	
London Waterloo 15 ⊖	a	15 31		15 34		15 40	15 37	15 45	15 49	15 52	15 55	16 01		16 04		16 10	16 07	16 15	16 19	16 22	16 25	16 31		16 34	

from 8 October

Hampton Court, Shepperton, Guildford, Dorking and Chessington South - London

Network Diagram - see first Page of Table 152

		SW	SW	SW	SW	SW	SW	SW		SW		SW	SW	SW	SW	SW	SW	SW		SW		SW	SW	SW	SW
Guildford	d	15 28	15 35									15 58	16 05									16 28	16 35		
London Road (Guildford)	d	15 32	15 39									16 02	16 09									16 32	16 39		
Clandon	d	15 37	15 44									16 07	16 14									16 37	16 44		
Horsley	d	15 41	15 48									16 11	16 18									16 41	16 48		
Effingham Junction 6	d	15 46	15 51									16 16	16 21									16 46	16 51		
Bookham	d	15 49										16 19										16 49			
Cobham & Stoke d'Abernon	d		15 55										16 25										16 55		
Oxshott	d		15 58										16 28										16 58		
Claygate	d		16 01										16 31										17 01		
Hinchley Wood	d		16 04										16 34										17 04		
Hampton Court	d							16 24										16 54							
Thames Ditton	d							16 26										16 56							
Surbiton 6	d		16 12			16 27		16 32					16 42			16 57		17 02					17 12		
Berrylands	d							16 34										17 04							
Shepperton	d									16 11										16 41					
Upper Halliford	d									16 14										16 44					
Sunbury	d									16 16										16 46					
Kempton Park	d									16 18										16 48					
Hampton	d									16 21										16 51					
Fulwell	d									16 24										16 54					
Strawberry Hill	d				16 07										16 37										17 07
Teddington	d				16 11					16 29					16 43					16 59					17 13
Hampton Wick	d				16 14					16 31					16 46					17 01					17 16
Kingston	a				16 16					16 33					16 48					17 03					17 18
	d				16 19					16 34					16 49					17 04					17 19
Norbiton	d				16 21					16 36					16 51					17 06					17 21
New Malden 6	d				16 25			16 37		16 40					16 55			17 07		17 10					17 25
Dorking 4	d						16 05										16 35								
Box Hill & Westhumble	d																								
Leatherhead	d	15 54					16 11					16 24					16 41					16 54			
Ashtead	d	15 58					16 14					16 28					16 44					16 58			
Epsom 3	a	16 02					16 19					16 32					16 49					17 02			
	d	16 05					16 20					16 35					16 50					17 05			
Ewell West	d	16 08					16 23					16 38					16 53					17 08			
Stoneleigh	d	16 10					16 25					16 40					16 55					17 10			
Worcester Park	d	16 13					16 28					16 43					16 58					17 13			
Chessington South	d			16 10										16 40										17 10	
Chessington North	d			16 12										16 42										17 12	
Tolworth	d			16 14										16 44										17 14	
Malden Manor	d			16 17										16 47										17 17	
Motspur Park	d	16 16		16 20			16 31					16 46		16 50			17 01					17 16		17 20	
Raynes Park 6	d	16 19		16 23	16 28		16 34	16 40		16 43		16 49		16 53	16 58		17 04	17 10		17 13		17 19		17 23	17 28
Wimbledon 6 ⊖ ⇌	d	16 23	16 20	16 27	16 32	16 35	16 38	16 44		16 47		16 53	16 50	16 57	17 02	17 05	17 08	17 14		17 17		17 23	17 20	17 27	17 32
Earlsfield	d	16 27	16 24	16 31	16 35	16 38	16 42	16 47		16 50		16 57	16 54	17 01	17 05	17 08	17 12	17 17		17 20		17 27	17 24	17 31	17 35
Clapham Junction 10	d	16 31	16 28	16 35	16 39	16 42	16 46	16 51		16 54		17 01	16 58	17 05	17 09	17 12	17 16	17 21		17 24		17 31	17 28	17 35	17 39
Vauxhall ⊖	d	16 36	16 33	16 40	16 44	16 47	16 51	16 56		16 59		17 06	17 03	17 10	17 14	17 17	17 21	17 26		17 29		17 36	17 33	17 40	17 44
London Waterloo 15 ⊖	a	16 40	16 37	16 45	16 49	16 52	16 55	17 01		17 05		17 10	17 07	17 16	17 19	17 22	17 25	17 31		17 35		17 40	17 37	17 45	17 49

		SW	SW	SW		SW		SW	SW	SW	SW	SW	SW	SW		SW		SW	SW	SW	SW	SW	SW	SW	SW
Guildford	d							16 58	17 05										17 28	17 35					
London Road (Guildford)	d							17 02	17 09										17 32	17 39					
Clandon	d							17 07	17 14										17 37	17 44					
Horsley	d							17 11	17 18										17 41	17 48					
Effingham Junction 6	d							17 16	17 21										17 46	17 51					
Bookham	d							17 19											17 49						
Cobham & Stoke d'Abernon	d								17 25											17 55					
Oxshott	d								17 28											17 58					
Claygate	d								17 31											18 01					
Hinchley Wood	d								17 34											18 04					
Hampton Court	d			17 24												17 54									18 24
Thames Ditton	d			17 26												17 56									18 26
Surbiton 6	d	17 27		17 32					17 42			17 57				18 02				18 12			18 27		18 32
Berrylands	d			17 34												18 04									18 34
Shepperton	d					17 11												17 41							
Upper Halliford	d					17 14												17 44							
Sunbury	d					17 16												17 46							
Kempton Park	d					17 18												17 48							
Hampton	d					17 21												17 51							
Fulwell	d					17 24												17 54							
Strawberry Hill	d										17 37			17 41								18 07			
Teddington	d					17 29					17 43			17 52				17 59				18 13			
Hampton Wick	d					17 31					17 46			17 54				18 01				18 16			
Kingston	a					17 33					17 48			17 56				18 03				18 18			
	d					17 34					17 49			17 58				18 04				18 19			
Norbiton	d					17 36					17 51			18 00				18 06				18 21			
New Malden 6	d			17 37		17 40					17 55			18 04		18 07		18 10				18 25			18 37
Dorking 4	d		17 05										17 35											18 05	
Box Hill & Westhumble	d																								
Leatherhead	d		17 11					17 24					17 41						17 54					18 11	
Ashtead	d		17 14					17 28					17 45						17 58					18 14	
Epsom 3	a		17 19					17 32					17 49						18 02					18 19	
	d		17 20					17 35					17 50						18 05					18 20	
Ewell West	d		17 23					17 38					17 53						18 08					18 23	
Stoneleigh	d		17 25					17 40					17 55						18 10					18 25	
Worcester Park	d		17 28					17 43					17 58						18 13					18 28	
Chessington South	d									17 40											18 10				
Chessington North	d									17 42											18 12				
Tolworth	d									17 44											18 14				
Malden Manor	d									17 47											18 17				
Motspur Park	d		17 31					17 46		17 50			18 01						18 16		18 20			18 31	
Raynes Park 6	d		17 34	17 40		17 43		17 49		17 53	17 58		18 04	18 07		18 10		18 13	18 19		18 23	18 28		18 34	18 40
Wimbledon 6 ⊖ ⇌	d	17 35	17 38	17 44		17 47		17 53	17 50	17 57	18 02	18 05	18 08	18 11		18 14		18 17	18 23	18 20	18 27	18 32	18 35	18 38	18 44
Earlsfield	d	17 38	17 42	17 47		17 50		17 57	17 54	18 01	18 05	18 08	18 12	18 15		18 17		18 20	18 27	18 24	18 31	18 35	18 38	18 42	18 47
Clapham Junction 10	d	17 42	17 46	17 51		17 54		18 01	17 58	18 05	18 09	18 12	18 16	18 19		18 21		18 24	18 31	18 28	18 35	18 39	18 42	18 46	18 51
Vauxhall ⊖	d	17 47	17 51	17 56		17 59		18 06	18 03	18 10	18 14	18 17	18 21	18 24		18 26		18 29	18 36	18 33	18 40	18 44	18 47	18 51	18 56
London Waterloo 15 ⊖	a	17 52	17 55	18 01		18 05		18 10	18 07	18 15	18 19	18 23	18 25	18 29		18 31		18 35	18 40	18 37	18 47	18 49	18 52	18 55	19 01

from 8 October

Hampton Court, Shepperton, Guildford, Dorking and Chessington South - London

Network Diagram - see first Page of Table 152

		SW	SW	SW	SW	SW	SW	SW	SW	SW	SW	SW	SW	SW	SW	SW	SW	SW	SW
Guildford	d		17 58	18 05							18 35								19 08
London Road (Guildford)	d		18 02	18 09							18 39								19 12
Clandon	d		18 07	18 14							18 44								19 17
Horsley	d		18 11	18 20							18 48								19 21
Effingham Junction ■	d		18 16	18 23							18 51					18 59			19 25
Bookham	d		18 19													19 02			
Cobham & Stoke d'Abernon	d			18 27							18 55								19 28
Oxshott	d			18 30							18 58								19 32
Claygate	d			18 33							19 01								19 35
Hinchley Wood	d			18 36							19 04								19 37
Hampton Court	d								18 54								19 24		
Thames Ditton	d								18 56								19 26		
Surbiton ■	d			18 42			18 57		19 02		19 12				19 27		19 32		19 42
Berrylands	d								19 04								19 34		
Shepperton	d	18 11								18 36								19 06	
Upper Halliford	d	18 14								18 39								19 09	
Sunbury	d	18 16								18 41								19 11	
Kempton Park	d	18 18								18 43								19 13	
Hampton	d	18 21								18 51								19 21	
Fulwell	d	18 24								18 54								19 24	
Strawberry Hill	d					18 37								19 07					
Teddington	d	18 29				18 43				18 59				19 13				19 29	
Hampton Wick	d	18 31				18 46				19 01				19 16				19 31	
Kingston	a	18 33				18 48				19 03				19 18				19 33	
	d	18 34				18 49				19 04				19 19				19 34	
Norbiton	d	18 36				18 51				19 06				19 21				19 36	
New Malden ■	d	18 40				18 55			19 07	19 10				19 25			19 37	19 40	
Dorking ■	d							18 35				18 50							
Box Hill & Westhumble	d																		
Leatherhead	d		18 24					18 41				18 56				19 08			
Ashtead	d		18 28					18 45				18 59				19 12			
Epsom ■	a		18 32					18 49				19 04				19 16			
	d		18 35					18 50				19 05				19 20			
Ewell West	d		18 38					18 53				19 08				19 23			
Stoneleigh	d		18 40					18 55				19 10				19 25			
Worcester Park	d		18 43					18 58				19 13				19 28			
Chessington South	d				18 40								19 10						
Chessington North	d				18 42								19 12						
Tolworth	d				18 44								19 14						
Malden Manor	d				18 47								19 17						
Motspur Park	d		18 46		18 50			19 01				19 16	19 20			19 31			
Raynes Park ■	d	18 43	18 49		18 53	18 58		19 04	19 10	19 13		19 19	19 23	19 28		19 34	19 40	19 43	
Wimbledon ■ ⊖ ⇌	d	18 47	18 53	18 50	18 57	19 02	19 05	19 08	19 14	19 17	19 20	19 23	19 27	19 32	19 35	19 38	19 44	19 47	19 50
Earlsfield	d	18 50	18 57	18 54	19 01	19 05	19 08	19 12	19 17	19 20	19 24	19 27	19 31	19 35	19 38	19 42	19 47	19 50	19 54
Clapham Junction ■	d	18 54	19 01	18 58	19 05	19 09	19 12	19 16	19 21	19 24	19 28	19 31	19 35	19 39	19 42	19 46	19 51	19 54	19 58
Vauxhall ⊖	d	18 59	19 06	19 03	19 10	19 14	19 17	19 21	19 26	19 29	19 33	19 36	19 40	19 44	19 47	19 51	19 56	19 59	20 03
London Waterloo ■ ⊖	a	19 05	19 10	19 07	19 14	19 19	19 23	19 27	19 31	19 34	19 37	19 41	19 45	19 49	19 52	19 55	20 01	20 04	20 07

		SW	SW	SW	SW	SW	SW	SW	SW	SW	SW	SW	SW	SW	SW	SW	SW	SW	SW	SW	SW
Guildford	d								19 28	19 35							19 58	20 05			
London Road (Guildford)	d								19 32	19 39							20 02	20 09			
Clandon	d								19 37	19 44							20 07	20 14			
Horsley	d								19 41	19 48							20 11	20 18			
Effingham Junction ■	d								19 46	19 51							20 16	20 21			
Bookham	d								19 49								20 19				
Cobham & Stoke d'Abernon	d									19 55								20 25			
Oxshott	d									19 58								20 28			
Claygate	d									20 01								20 31			
Hinchley Wood	d									20 04								20 34			
Hampton Court	d						19 54								20 24						
Thames Ditton	d						19 56								20 26						
Surbiton ■	d				19 57		20 02			20 12			20 27		20 32			20 42			20 57
Berrylands	d						20 04								20 34						
Shepperton	d							19 41								20 11					
Upper Halliford	d							19 44								20 14					
Sunbury	d							19 46								20 16					
Kempton Park	d							19 48								20 18					
Hampton	d							19 51								20 21					
Fulwell	d							19 54								20 24					
Strawberry Hill	d			19 37								20 07								20 37	
Teddington	d			19 43				19 59				20 11				20 29				20 41	
Hampton Wick	d			19 46				20 01				20 14				20 31				20 44	
Kingston	a			19 48				20 04				20 16				20 33				20 46	
	d			19 49				20 04				20 19				20 34				20 49	
Norbiton	d			19 51				20 06				20 21				20 36				20 51	
New Malden ■	d			19 55			20 07	20 10				20 25			20 37	20 40				20 55	
Dorking ■	d					19 33								20 05							
Box Hill & Westhumble	d																				
Leatherhead	d					19 39			19 54					20 11			20 24				
Ashtead	d					19 42			19 58					20 14			20 28				
Epsom ■	a					19 47			20 02					20 19			20 32				
	d	19 35				19 50			20 05					20 20			20 35				
Ewell West	d	19 38				19 53			20 08					20 23			20 38				
Stoneleigh	d	19 40				19 55			20 10					20 25			20 40				
Worcester Park	d	19 43				19 58			20 13					20 28			20 43				
Chessington South	d		19 40								20 10								20 40		
Chessington North	d		19 42								20 12								20 42		
Tolworth	d		19 44								20 14								20 44		
Malden Manor	d		19 47								20 17								20 47		
Motspur Park	d	19 46	19 50			20 01			20 16		20 20			20 31			20 46		20 50		
Raynes Park ■	d	19 49	19 53	19 58		20 04	20 10	20 13	20 19		20 23	20 28		20 34	20 40	20 43	20 49		20 53	20 58	
Wimbledon ■ ⊖ ⇌	d	19 53	19 57	20 02	20 05	20 08	20 14	20 17	20 23	20 20	20 27	20 32	20 35	20 38	20 44	20 47	20 53	20 50	20 57	21 02	21 05
Earlsfield	d	19 57	20 01	20 05	20 08	20 12	20 17	20 20	20 27	20 24	20 31	20 35	20 38	20 42	20 47	20 50	20 57	20 54	21 01	21 05	21 08
Clapham Junction ■	d	20 01	20 05	20 09	20 12	20 16	20 21	20 24	20 31	20 28	20 35	20 39	20 42	20 46	20 51	20 54	21 01	20 58	21 05	21 09	21 12
Vauxhall ⊖	d	20 06	20 10	20 14	20 17	20 21	20 26	20 29	20 36	20 33	20 40	20 44	20 47	20 51	20 56	20 59	21 06	21 03	21 10	21 14	21 17
London Waterloo ■ ⊖	a	20 10	20 15	20 19	20 22	20 25	20 31	20 35	20 41	20 38	20 46	20 49	20 52	20 55	21 01	21 04	21 10	21 07	21 15	21 19	21 22

from 8 October

Hampton Court, Shepperton, Guildford, Dorking and Chessington South - London

Network Diagram - see first Page of Table 152

		SW	SW	SW	SW	SW	SW	SW	SW	SW	SW	SW	SW	SW	SW	SW	SW	SW	SW
Guildford	d				20 35					20 46			21 05						
London Road (Guildford)	d				20 39					20 50			21 09						
Clandon	d				20 44					20 55			21 14						
Horsley	d				20 48					20 59			21 18						
Effingham Junction ■	d				20 51					21 03			21 21						
Bookham	d									21 06									
Cobham & Stoke d'Abernon	d				20 55								21 25						
Oxshott	d				20 58								21 28						
Claygate	d				21 01								21 31						
Hinchley Wood	d				21 04								21 34						
Hampton Court	d		20 54								21 24								
Thames Ditton	d		20 56								21 26								
Surbiton ■	d		21 02		21 12				21 27		21 32		21 42				21 57		
Berrylands	d		21 04								21 34								
Shepperton	d			20 41								21 11							21 41
Upper Halliford	d			20 44								21 14							21 44
Sunbury	d			20 46								21 16							21 46
Kempton Park	d			20 48								21 18							21 48
Hampton	d			20 51								21 21							21 51
Fulwell	d			20 54								21 24							21 54
Strawberry Hill	d							21 07								21 37			
Teddington	d			20 59				21 11				21 29				21 41			21 59
Hampton Wick	d			21 01				21 14				21 31				21 44			22 01
Kingston	a			21 03				21 16				21 33				21 46			22 03
	d			21 04				21 19				21 34				21 49			22 04
Norbiton	d			21 06				21 21				21 36				21 51			22 06
New Malden ■	d		21 07	21 10				21 25			21 37	21 40				21 55			22 10
Dorking ■	d	20 35																21 35	
Box Hill & Westhumble	d																		
Leatherhead	d	20 41								21 11								21 41	
Ashtead	d	20 44								21 14								21 44	
Epsom ■	a	20 49								21 19								21 49	
	d	20 50				21 05				21 20				21 35				21 50	
Ewell West	d	20 53				21 08				21 23				21 38				21 53	
Stoneleigh	d	20 55				21 10				21 25				21 40				21 55	
Worcester Park	d	20 58				21 13				21 28				21 43				21 58	
Chessington South	d						21 10								21 40				
Chessington North	d						21 12								21 42				
Tolworth	d						21 14								21 44				
Malden Manor	d						21 17								21 47				
Motspur Park	d	21 01				21 16	21 20			21 31				21 46	21 50			22 01	
Raynes Park ■	d	21 04	21 10	21 13		21 19	21 23	21 28		21 34	21 40	21 43		21 49	21 53	21 58		22 04	22 13
Wimbledon ■ ⊖ ⇌	d	21 08	21 14	21 17	21 20	21 23	21 27	21 32	21 35	21 38	21 44	21 47	21 50	21 53	21 57	22 02	22 05	22 08	22 17
Earlsfield	d	21 12	21 17	21 20	21 24	21 27	21 31	21 35	21 38	21 42	21 47	21 50	21 54	21 57	22 01	22 05	22 08	22 12	22 20
Clapham Junction ■	d	21 16	21 21	21 24	21 28	21 31	21 35	21 39	21 42	21 46	21 51	21 54	21 58	22 01	22 05	22 09	22 12	22 16	22 24
Vauxhall ⊖	d	21 21	21 26	21 29	21 33	21 36	21 40	21 44	21 47	21 51	21 56	21 59	22 03	22 06	22 10	22 14	22 17	22 21	22 29
London Waterloo ■ ⊖	a	21 25	21 31	21 34	21 37	21 40	21 45	21 49	21 52	21 55	22 01	22 04	22 07	22 10	22 16	22 19	22 22	22 25	22 34

		SW	SW	SW	SW	SW	SW	SW	SW	SW	SW	SW	SW	SW	SW	SW	SW	SW	SW	SW	SN
Guildford	d	21 35			21 46			22 05			22 20			22 35		22 46	22 55			23 08	
London Road (Guildford)	d	21 39			21 50			22 09						22 39		22 50				23 12	
Clandon	d	21 44			21 55			22 14						22 44		22 55				23 17	
Horsley	d	21 48			21 59			22 18						22 48		22 59				23 21	
Effingham Junction ■	d	21 51			22 03			22 21						22 51		23 03				23 24	
Bookham	d				22 06											23 06					
Cobham & Stoke d'Abernon	d	21 55						22 25						22 55						23 28	
Oxshott	d	21 58						22 28						22 58						23 31	
Claygate	d	22 01						22 31						23 01						23 34	
Hinchley Wood	d	22 04						22 34						23 04						23 37	
Hampton Court	d					22 24												23 24			
Thames Ditton	d					22 26												23 26			
Surbiton ■	d	22 12		22 27		22 32		22 42			22 57			23 12			23 30	23 33		23 42	
Berrylands	d					22 34												23 35			
Shepperton	d						22 11						22 41						23 11		
Upper Halliford	d						22 14						22 44						23 14		
Sunbury	d						22 16						22 46						23 16		
Kempton Park	d						22 18						22 48						23 18		
Hampton	d						22 21						22 51						23 21		
Fulwell	d						22 24						22 54						23 24		
Strawberry Hill	d		22 07							22 37					23 07						
Teddington	d		22 11				22 29			22 41			22 59		23 11				23 29		
Hampton Wick	d		22 14				22 31			22 44			23 01		23 14				23 31		
Kingston	a		22 16				22 33			22 46			23 03		23 16				23 33		
	d		22 19				22 34			22 49			23 04		23 19				23 34		
Norbiton	d		22 21				22 36			22 51			23 06		23 21				23 36		
New Malden ■	d		22 25			22 37	22 40			22 55			23 10		23 25			23 38	23 41		
Dorking ■	d											22 35									23 30
Box Hill & Westhumble	d																				
Leatherhead	d				22 11							22 41				23 11					23 36
Ashtead	d				22 14							22 44				23 14					23 39
Epsom ■	a				22 19							22 49				23 19					23 45
	d				22 20							22 50				23 20					
Ewell West	d				22 23							22 53				23 23					
Stoneleigh	d				22 25							22 55				23 25					
Worcester Park	d				22 28							22 58				23 28					
Chessington South	d								22 40												
Chessington North	d								22 42												
Tolworth	d								22 44												
Malden Manor	d								22 47												
Motspur Park	d				22 31				22 50			23 01				23 31					
Raynes Park ■	d		22 28		22 34	22 40	22 43		22 53	22 58		23 04	23 13		23 28	23 37		23 41	23 43		
Wimbledon ■ ⊖ ⇌	d	22 20	22 32	22 35	22 38	22 44	22 47	22 50	22 57	23 02	23 05	23 08	23 17	23 20	23 32	23 41	23 37	23a45	23 50	23 53	
Earlsfield	d	22 24	22 35	22 38	22 42	22 47	22 50	22 54	23 01	23 05	23 08	23 12	23 20	23 24	23 36	23 44	23 41		23 53	23 56	
Clapham Junction ■	d	22 28	22 39	22 42	22 46	22 51	22 54	22 58	23 05	23 09	23 12	23 16	23 24	23 28	23 40	23 48	23 45		23 57	23 59	
Vauxhall ⊖	d	22 33	22 44	22 47	22 51	22 56	22 59	23 03	23 10	23 14	23 17	23 21	23 29	23 33	23 45	23 53	23 50		00 02	00 05	
London Waterloo ■ ⊖	a	22 39	22 49	22 52	22 55	23 01	23 04	23 07	23 15	23 19	23 23	23 27	23 34	23 37	23 49	23 58	23 54		00 10	00 14	

Mondays to Fridays
from 8 October

Hampton Court, Shepperton, Guildford, Dorking and Chessington South - London

Network Diagram - see first Page of Table 152

Station		SW	SW
Guildford	d		
London Road (Guildford)	d		
Clandon	d		
Horsley	d		
Effingham Junction 6	d		
Bookham	d		
Cobham & Stoke d'Abernon	d		
Oxshott	d		
Claygate	d		
Hinchley Wood	d		
Hampton Court	d		
Thames Ditton	d		
Surbiton 6	d		
Berrylands	d		
Shepperton	d		
Upper Halliford	d		
Sunbury	d		
Kempton Park	d		
Hampton	d		
Fulwell	d		
Strawberry Hill	d		23 37
Teddington	d		23 41
Hampton Wick	d		23 44
Kingston	a		23 46
	d		23 49
Norbiton	d		23 51
New Malden 6	d		23 55
Dorking 4	d		
Box Hill & Westhumble	d		
Leatherhead	d		
Ashtead	d		
Epsom 3	a		
	d		
Ewell West	d		
Stoneleigh	d		
Worcester Park	d		
Chessington South	d	23 40	
Chessington North	d	23 42	
Tolworth	d	23 44	
Malden Manor	d	23 47	
Motspur Park	d	23 50	
Raynes Park 6	d	23 54	23 58
Wimbledon 6 ⊖ ⇌	d	23a57	00 02
Earlsfield	d		00 05
Clapham Junction 10	d		00 09
Vauxhall ⊖	d		00 14
London Waterloo 15 ⊖	a		00 22

Saturdays
until 6 October

Hampton Court, Shepperton, Guildford, Dorking and Chessington South - London

Network Diagram - see first Page of Table 152

Station		SW	SW	SW	SW	SW	SW	SW	SW	SW	SW	SW	SW	SW	SW	SW	SW	SW	SW	SW
Guildford	d		23p08				04 00					05 14								
London Road (Guildford)	d		23p12																	
Clandon	d		23p17																	
Horsley	d		23p21																	
Effingham Junction 6	d		23p24																	
Bookham	d																			
Cobham & Stoke d'Abernon	d		23p28																	
Oxshott	d		23p31																	
Claygate	d		23p34																	
Hinchley Wood	d		23p37																	
Hampton Court	d												05 54					06 24		
Thames Ditton	d												05 56					06 26		
Surbiton 6	d		23p42				04 24					05 57	06 02				06 27	06 32		
Berrylands	d												06 04					06 34		
Shepperton	d	23p11																	06 11	
Upper Halliford	d	23p14																	06 14	
Sunbury	d	23p16																	06 16	
Kempton Park	d	23p18																	06 18	
Hampton	d	23p21																	06 21	
Fulwell	d	23p24																	06 24	
Strawberry Hill	d			23p37	00 07			04 55		05 38					06 07	06 08				
Teddington	d	23p29		23p41	00 11	00s56		04 59			05 44				06 11				06 29	
Hampton Wick	d	23p31		23p44	00 14	00s59		05 01			05 46				06 14				06 31	
Kingston	a	23p33		23p46	00 16	01 01		05 03			05 48				06 16				06 33	
	d	23p34		23p49				05 04			05 49				06 19				06 34	
Norbiton	d	23p36		23p51				05 06			05 51				06 21				06 36	
New Malden 6	d	23p41		23p55				05 10			05 55		06 07		06 25			06 37	06 40	
Dorking 4	d																			
Box Hill & Westhumble	d																			
Leatherhead	d																			
Ashtead	d																			
Epsom 3	a																			
	d								05 35					06 05						06 35
Ewell West	d								05 38					06 08						06 38
Stoneleigh	d								05 40					06 10						06 40
Worcester Park	d								05 43					06 13						06 43
Chessington South	d																			
Chessington North	d																			
Tolworth	d																			
Malden Manor	d																			
Motspur Park	d								05 46					06 16						06 46
Raynes Park 6	d	23p43		23p58				05 13	05 49		05 58		06 10	06 19	06 28			06 40	06 43	06 49
Wimbledon 6 ⊖ ⇌	d	23p50	23p53	00 02			04 32	05 17	05 53		06 02	06 05	06 14	06 23	06 32		06 35	06 44	06 47	06 53
Earlsfield	d	23p53	23p56	00 05				05 21	05 57		06 05	06 08	06 17	06 27	06 35		06 38	06 47	06 50	06 57
Clapham Junction 10	d	23p57	23p59	00 09			04 44	05 25	06 01		06 09	06 12	06 21	06 31	06 39		06 42	06 51	06 54	07 01
Vauxhall ⊖	d	00 02	00 05	00 14				05 30	06 06	06 12	06 14	06 17	06 26	06 36	06 44	06 42	06 47	06 56	06 59	07 06
London Waterloo 15 ⊖	a	00 10	00 14	00 22			04 53	05 35	06 11	06 16	06 19	06 22	06 31	06 40	06 49	06 46	06 52	07 01	07 04	07 10

Station		SW	SW	SW	SW	SW	SW	SW	SW	SW	SW	SW	SW	SW	SW	SW	SW	SW	SW	SW
Guildford	d						06 28	06 38						06 58	07 08					
London Road (Guildford)	d						06 32	06 42						07 02	07 12					
Clandon	d						06 37	06 47						07 07	07 17					
Horsley	d						06 41	06 51						07 11	07 21					
Effingham Junction 6	d						06 46	06 54						07 16	07 24					
Bookham	d						06 49							07 19						
Cobham & Stoke d'Abernon	d							06 58							07 28					
Oxshott	d							07 01							07 31					
Claygate	d							07 04							07 34					
Hinchley Wood	d							07 07							07 37					
Hampton Court	d				06 54							07 24							07 54	
Thames Ditton	d				06 56							07 26							07 56	
Surbiton 6	d			06 57	07 02			07 12			07 27	07 32			07 42			07 57	08 02	
Berrylands	d				07 04							07 34							08 04	
Shepperton	d					06 41							07 11							07 41
Upper Halliford	d					06 44							07 14							07 44
Sunbury	d					06 46							07 16							07 46
Kempton Park	d					06 48							07 18							07 48
Hampton	d					06 51							07 21							07 51
Fulwell	d					06 54							07 24							07 54
Strawberry Hill	d		06 37							07 07							07 37			
Teddington	d		06 41			06 59				07 11			07 29				07 41			07 59
Hampton Wick	d		06 44			07 01				07 14			07 31				07 44			08 01
Kingston	a		06 46			07 03				07 16			07 33				07 46			08 03
	d		06 49			07 04				07 19			07 34				07 49			08 04
Norbiton	d		06 51			07 06				07 21			07 36				07 51			08 06
New Malden 6	d		06 55		07 07	07 10				07 25		07 37	07 40				07 55		08 07	08 10
Dorking 4	d																			
Box Hill & Westhumble	d																			
Leatherhead	d						06 54							07 24						
Ashtead	d						06 58							07 28						
Epsom 3	a						07 02							07 32						
	d						07 05							07 35						
Ewell West	d						07 08							07 38						
Stoneleigh	d						07 10							07 40						
Worcester Park	d						07 13							07 43						
Chessington South	d	06 40							07 10							07 40				
Chessington North	d	06 42							07 12							07 42				
Tolworth	d	06 44							07 14							07 44				
Malden Manor	d	06 47							07 17							07 47				
Motspur Park	d	06 50					07 16		07 20					07 46		07 50				
Raynes Park 6	d	06 53	06 58		07 10	07 13	07 19		07 23	07 28		07 40	07 43	07 49		07 53	07 58		08 10	08 13
Wimbledon 6 ⊖ ⇌	d	06 57	07 02	07 05	07 14	07 17	07 23	07 20	07 27	07 32	07 35	07 44	07 47	07 53	07 50	07 57	08 02	08 05	08 14	08 17
Earlsfield	d	07 01	07 05	07 08	07 17	07 20	07 27	07 24	07 31	07 35	07 38	07 47	07 50	07 57	07 54	08 01	08 05	08 08	08 17	08 20
Clapham Junction 10	d	07 05	07 09	07 12	07 21	07 24	07 31	07 28	07 35	07 39	07 42	07 51	07 54	08 01	07 58	08 05	08 09	08 12	08 21	08 24
Vauxhall ⊖	d	07 10	07 14	07 17	07 26	07 29	07 36	07 33	07 40	07 44	07 47	07 56	07 59	08 06	08 03	08 10	08 14	08 17	08 26	08 29
London Waterloo 15 ⊖	a	07 15	07 19	07 22	07 31	07 34	07 40	07 37	07 45	07 49	07 52	08 01	08 04	08 10	08 07	08 15	08 19	08 22	08 31	08 34

Saturdays
until 6 October

Hampton Court, Shepperton, Guildford, Dorking and Chessington South - London

Network Diagram - see first Page of Table 152

		SW	SW	SW	SW	SW	SW	SW	SW	SW	SW	SW	SW	SW	SW	SW	SW	SW	SW	SW
Guildford	d	07 28	07 38							07 58	08 08							08 28	08 38	
London Road (Guildford)	d	07 32	07 42							08 02	08 12							08 32	08 42	
Clandon	d	07 37	07 47							08 07	08 17							08 37	08 47	
Horsley	d	07 41	07 51							08 11	08 21							08 41	08 51	
Effingham Junction ■	d	07 46	07 54							08 16	08 24							08 46	08 54	
Bookham	d	07 49								08 19								08 49		
Cobham & Stoke d'Abernon	d		07 58								08 28								08 58	
Oxshott	d		08 01								08 31								09 01	
Claygate	d		08 04								08 34								09 04	
Hinchley Wood	d		08 07								08 37								09 07	
Hampton Court	d							08 24								08 54				
Thames Ditton	d							08 26								08 56				
Surbiton ■	d		08 12			08 27		08 32			08 42			08 57		09 02			09 12	
Berrylands	d							08 34								09 04				
Shepperton	d								08 11								08 41			
Upper Halliford	d								08 14								08 44			
Sunbury	d								08 16								08 46			
Kempton Park	d								08 18								08 48			
Hampton	d								08 21								08 51			
Fulwell	d								08 24								08 54			
Strawberry Hill	d				08 07								08 37							
Teddington	d				08 11				08 29				08 41				08 59			
Hampton Wick	d				08 14				08 31				08 44				09 01			
Kingston	a				08 16				08 33				08 46				09 03			
	d				08 19				08 34				08 49				09 04			
Norbiton	d				08 21				08 36				08 51				09 06			
New Malden ■	d				08 25			08 37	08 40				08 55			09 07	09 10			
Dorking ■	d						08 05								08 35					
Box Hill & Westhumble	d																			
Leatherhead	d	07 54					08 11			08 24					08 41			08 54		
Ashtead	d	07 58					08 14			08 28					08 44			08 58		
Epsom ■	a	08 02					08 19			08 32					08 49			09 02		
	d	08 05					08 20			08 35					08 50			09 05		
Ewell West	d	08 08					08 23			08 38					08 53			09 08		
Stoneleigh	d	08 10					08 25			08 40					08 55			09 10		
Worcester Park	d	08 13					08 28			08 43					08 58			09 13		
Chessington South	d			08 10								08 40								09 10
Chessington North	d			08 12								08 42								09 12
Tolworth	d			08 14								08 44								09 14
Malden Manor	d			08 17								08 47								09 17
Motspur Park	d	08 16		08 20			08 31			08 46		08 50			09 01			09 16		09 20
Raynes Park ■	d	08 19		08 23	08 28		08 34	08 40	08 43	08 49		08 53	08 58		09 04	09 10	09 13	09 19		09 23
Wimbledon ■ ⊖ ⛴	d	08 23	08 20	08 27	08 32	08 35	08 38	08 44	08 47	08 53	08 50	08 57	09 02	09 05	09 08	09 14	09 17	09 23	09 20	09 27
Earlsfield	d	08 27	08 24	08 31	08 35	08 38	08 42	08 47	08 50	08 57	08 54	09 01	09 05	09 08	09 12	09 17	09 20	09 27	09 24	09 31
Clapham Junction ■	d	08 31	08 28	08 35	08 39	08 42	08 46	08 51	08 54	09 01	08 58	09 05	09 09	09 12	09 16	09 21	09 24	09 31	09 28	09 35
Vauxhall ⊖	d	08 36	08 33	08 40	08 44	08 47	08 51	08 56	08 59	09 06	09 03	09 10	09 14	09 17	09 21	09 26	09 29	09 36	09 33	09 40
London Waterloo ■ ⊖	a	08 40	08 37	08 45	08 49	08 52	08 55	09 01	09 04	09 10	09 07	09 15	09 19	09 22	09 25	09 31	09 34	09 40	09 37	09 45

		SW	SW	SW	SW	SW	SW	SW	SW	SW	SW	SW	SW	SW	SW	SW	SW	SW	SW	SW	SW
Guildford	d						08 58	09 08							09 28	09 38					
London Road (Guildford)	d						09 02	09 12							09 32	09 42					
Clandon	d						09 07	09 17							09 37	09 47					
Horsley	d						09 11	09 21							09 41	09 51					
Effingham Junction ■	d						09 16	09 24							09 46	09 54					
Bookham	d						09 19								09 49						
Cobham & Stoke d'Abernon	d							09 28								09 58					
Oxshott	d							09 31								10 01					
Claygate	d							09 34								10 04					
Hinchley Wood	d							09 37								10 07					
Hampton Court	d				09 24								09 54								10 24
Thames Ditton	d				09 26								09 56								10 26
Surbiton ■	d		09 27		09 32			09 42			09 57		10 02			10 12			10 27		10 32
Berrylands	d				09 34								10 04								10 34
Shepperton	d					09 11								09 41							
Upper Halliford	d					09 14								09 44							
Sunbury	d					09 16								09 46							
Kempton Park	d					09 18								09 48							
Hampton	d					09 21								09 51							
Fulwell	d					09 24								09 54							
Strawberry Hill	d	09 07								09 37								10 07			
Teddington	d	09 11				09 29				09 41				09 59				10 11			
Hampton Wick	d	09 14				09 31				09 44				10 01				10 14			
Kingston	a	09 16				09 33				09 46				10 03				10 16			
	d	09 19				09 34				09 49				10 04				10 19			
Norbiton	d	09 21				09 36				09 51				10 06				10 21			
New Malden ■	d	09 25			09 37	09 40				09 55			10 07	10 10				10 25			10 37
Dorking ■	d			09 05								09 35								10 05	
Box Hill & Westhumble	d																				
Leatherhead	d			09 11			09 24					09 41			09 54					10 11	
Ashtead	d			09 14			09 28					09 44			09 58					10 14	
Epsom ■	a			09 19			09 32					09 49			10 02					10 19	
	d			09 20			09 35					09 50			10 05					10 20	
Ewell West	d			09 23			09 38					09 53			10 08					10 23	
Stoneleigh	d			09 25			09 40					09 55			10 10					10 25	
Worcester Park	d			09 28			09 43					09 58			10 13					10 28	
Chessington South	d								09 40								10 10				
Chessington North	d								09 42								10 12				
Tolworth	d								09 44								10 14				
Malden Manor	d								09 47								10 17				
Motspur Park	d			09 31			09 46		09 50			10 01			10 16		10 20			10 31	
Raynes Park ■	d	09 28		09 34	09 40	09 43	09 49		09 53	09 58		10 04	10 10	10 13	10 19		10 23	10 28		10 34	10 40
Wimbledon ■ ⊖ ⛴	d	09 32	09 35	09 38	09 44	09 47	09 53	09 50	09 57	10 02	10 05	10 08	10 14	10 17	10 23	10 20	10 27	10 32	10 35	10 38	10 44
Earlsfield	d	09 35	09 38	09 42	09 47	09 50	09 57	09 54	10 01	10 05	10 08	10 12	10 17	10 20	10 27	10 24	10 31	10 35	10 38	10 42	10 47
Clapham Junction ■	d	09 39	09 42	09 46	09 51	09 54	10 01	09 58	10 05	10 09	10 12	10 16	10 21	10 24	10 31	10 28	10 35	10 39	10 42	10 46	10 51
Vauxhall ⊖	d	09 44	09 47	09 51	09 56	09 59	10 06	10 03	10 10	10 14	10 17	10 21	10 26	10 29	10 36	10 33	10 40	10 44	10 47	10 51	10 56
London Waterloo ■ ⊖	a	09 49	09 52	09 55	10 01	10 04	10 10	10 07	10 15	10 19	10 22	10 25	10 31	10 34	10 40	10 37	10 45	10 49	10 52	10 55	11 01

Table 152

Saturdays
until 6 October

Hampton Court, Shepperton, Guildford, Dorking and Chessington South - London

Network Diagram - see first Page of Table 152

		SW	SW	SW	SW	SW	SW	SW	SW	SW	SW	SW	SW	SW	SW	SW	SW	SW	SW
Guildford	d		09 58	10 08							10 28	10 38							10 58
London Road (Guildford)	d		10 02	10 12							10 32	10 42							11 02
Clandon	d		10 07	10 17							10 37	10 47							11 07
Horsley	d		10 11	10 21							10 41	10 51							11 11
Effingham Junction ■	d		10 16	10 24							10 46	10 54							11 16
Bookham	d		10 19								10 49								11 19
Cobham & Stoke d'Abernon	d			10 28								10 58							
Oxshott	d			10 31								11 01							
Claygate	d			10 34								11 04							
Hinchley Wood	d			10 37								11 07							
Hampton Court	d								10 54								11 24		
Thames Ditton	d								10 56								11 26		
Surbiton ■	d			10 42			10 57		11 02			11 12			11 27		11 32		
Berrylands	d								11 04								11 34		
Shepperton	d	10 11								10 41								11 11	
Upper Halliford	d	10 14								10 44								11 14	
Sunbury	d	10 16								10 46								11 16	
Kempton Park	d	10 18								10 48								11 18	
Hampton	d	10 21								10 51								11 21	
Fulwell	d	10 24								10 54								11 24	
Strawberry Hill	d					10 37								11 07					
Teddington	d	10 29				10 41				10 59				11 11				11 29	
Hampton Wick	d	10 31				10 44				11 01				11 14				11 31	
Kingston	a	10 33				10 46				11 03				11 16				11 33	
	d	10 34				10 49				11 04				11 19				11 34	
Norbiton	d	10 36				10 51				11 06				11 21				11 36	
New Malden ■	d	10 40				10 55			11 07	11 10				11 25			11 37	11 40	
Dorking ■	d							10 35								11 05			
Box Hill & Westhumble	d																		
Leatherhead	d		10 24					10 41			10 54					11 11			11 24
Ashtead	d		10 28					10 44			10 58					11 14			11 28
Epsom ■	a		10 32					10 49			11 02					11 19			11 32
	d		10 35					10 50			11 05					11 20			11 35
Ewell West	d		10 38					10 53			11 08					11 23			11 38
Stoneleigh	d		10 40					10 55			11 10					11 25			11 40
Worcester Park	d		10 43					10 58			11 13					11 28			11 43
Chessington South	d				10 40								11 10						
Chessington North	d				10 42								11 12						
Tolworth	d				10 44								11 14						
Malden Manor	d				10 47								11 17						
Motspur Park	d		10 46		10 50			11 01			11 16		11 20			11 31			11 46
Raynes Park ■	d	10 43	10 49		10 53	10 58		11 04	11 10	11 13	11 19		11 23	11 28		11 34	11 40	11 43	11 49
Wimbledon ■ ⊖ ⛴	d	10 47	10 53	10 50	10 57	11 02	11 05	11 08	11 14	11 17	11 23	11 20	11 27	11 32	11 35	11 38	11 44	11 47	11 53
Earlsfield	d	10 50	10 57	10 54	11 01	11 05	11 08	11 12	11 17	11 20	11 27	11 24	11 31	11 35	11 38	11 42	11 47	11 50	11 57
Clapham Junction ■	d	10 54	11 01	10 58	11 05	11 09	11 12	11 16	11 21	11 24	11 31	11 28	11 35	11 39	11 42	11 46	11 51	11 54	12 01
Vauxhall ⊖	d	10 59	11 06	11 03	11 10	11 14	11 17	11 21	11 26	11 29	11 36	11 33	11 40	11 44	11 47	11 51	11 56	11 59	12 06
London Waterloo ■ ⊖	a	11 04	11 10	11 07	11 15	11 19	11 22	11 25	11 31	11 34	11 40	11 37	11 45	11 49	11 52	11 55	12 01	12 04	12 10

		SW	SW	SW	SW	SW	SW	SW	SW	SW	SW	SW	SW	SW	SW	SW	SW	SW	SW	SW	SW
Guildford	d	11 08							11 28	11 38							11 58	12 08			
London Road (Guildford)	d	11 12							11 32	11 42							12 02	12 12			
Clandon	d	11 17							11 37	11 47							12 07	12 17			
Horsley	d	11 21							11 41	11 51							12 11	12 21			
Effingham Junction ■	d	11 24							11 46	11 54							12 16	12 24			
Bookham	d								11 49								12 19				
Cobham & Stoke d'Abernon	d	11 28								11 58								12 28			
Oxshott	d	11 31								12 01								12 31			
Claygate	d	11 34								12 04								12 34			
Hinchley Wood	d	11 37								12 07								12 37			
Hampton Court	d						11 54								12 24						
Thames Ditton	d						11 56								12 26						
Surbiton ■	d	11 42			11 57		12 02			12 12			12 27		12 32			12 42			12 57
Berrylands	d						12 04								12 34						
Shepperton	d							11 41								12 11					
Upper Halliford	d							11 44								12 14					
Sunbury	d							11 46								12 16					
Kempton Park	d							11 48								12 18					
Hampton	d							11 51								12 21					
Fulwell	d							11 54								12 24					
Strawberry Hill	d			11 37								12 07								12 37	
Teddington	d			11 41				11 59				12 11				12 29				12 41	
Hampton Wick	d			11 44				12 01				12 14				12 31				12 44	
Kingston	a			11 46				12 03				12 16				12 33				12 46	
	d			11 49				12 04				12 19				12 34				12 49	
Norbiton	d			11 51				12 06				12 21				12 36				12 51	
New Malden ■	d			11 55			12 07	12 10				12 25			12 37	12 40				12 55	
Dorking ■	d					11 35								12 05							
Box Hill & Westhumble	d																				
Leatherhead	d					11 41			11 54					12 11			12 24				
Ashtead	d					11 44			11 58					12 14			12 28				
Epsom ■	a					11 49			12 02					12 19			12 32				
	d					11 50			12 05					12 20			12 35				
Ewell West	d					11 53			12 08					12 23			12 38				
Stoneleigh	d					11 55			12 10					12 25			12 40				
Worcester Park	d					11 58			12 13					12 28			12 43				
Chessington South	d		11 40								12 10								12 40		
Chessington North	d		11 42								12 12								12 42		
Tolworth	d		11 44								12 14								12 44		
Malden Manor	d		11 47								12 17								12 47		
Motspur Park	d		11 50			12 01			12 16		12 20			12 31			12 46		12 50		
Raynes Park ■	d		11 53	11 58		12 04	12 10	12 13	12 19		12 23	12 28		12 34	12 40	12 43	12 49		12 53	12 58	
Wimbledon ■ ⊖ ⛴	d	11 50	11 57	12 02	12 05	12 08	12 14	12 17	12 23	12 20	12 27	12 32	12 35	12 38	12 44	12 47	12 53	12 50	12 57	13 02	13 05
Earlsfield	d	11 54	12 01	12 05	12 08	12 12	12 17	12 20	12 27	12 24	12 31	12 35	12 38	12 42	12 47	12 50	12 57	12 54	13 01	13 05	13 08
Clapham Junction ■	d	11 58	12 05	12 09	12 12	12 16	12 21	12 24	12 31	12 28	12 35	12 39	12 42	12 46	12 51	12 54	13 01	12 58	13 05	13 09	13 12
Vauxhall ⊖	d	12 03	12 10	12 14	12 17	12 21	12 26	12 29	12 36	12 33	12 40	12 44	12 47	12 51	12 56	12 59	13 06	13 03	13 10	13 14	13 17
London Waterloo ■ ⊖	a	12 07	12 15	12 19	12 22	12 25	12 31	12 34	12 40	12 37	12 45	12 49	12 52	12 55	13 01	13 04	13 10	13 07	13 15	13 19	13 22

Table 152

Saturdays until 6 October

Hampton Court, Shepperton, Guildford, Dorking and Chessington South - London

Network Diagram - see first Page of Table 152

		SW	SW	SW	SW	SW	SW	SW	SW	SW	SW	SW	SW	SW	SW	SW	SW	SW	SW	SW
Guildford	d				12 28	12 38							12 58	13 08						
London Road (Guildford)	d				12 32	12 42							13 02	13 12						
Clandon	d				12 37	12 47							13 07	13 17						
Horsley	d				12 41	12 51							13 11	13 21						
Effingham Junction	d				12 46	12 54							13 16	13 24						
Bookham	d				12 49								13 19							
Cobham & Stoke d'Abernon	d					12 58								13 28						
Oxshott	d					13 01								13 31						
Claygate	d					13 04								13 34						
Hinchley Wood	d					13 07								13 37						
Hampton Court	d		12 54								13 24								13 54	
Thames Ditton	d		12 56								13 26								13 56	
Surbiton	d		13 02			13 12			13 27		13 32			13 42			13 57		14 02	
Berrylands	d		13 04								13 34								14 04	
Shepperton	d			12 41								13 11								13 41
Upper Halliford	d			12 44								13 14								13 44
Sunbury	d			12 46								13 16								13 46
Kempton Park	d			12 48								13 18								13 48
Hampton	d			12 51								13 21								13 51
Fulwell	d			12 54								13 24								13 54
Strawberry Hill	d							13 07								13 37				
Teddington	d			12 59				13 11				13 29				13 41				13 59
Hampton Wick	d			13 01				13 14				13 31				13 44				14 01
Kingston	a			13 03				13 16				13 33				13 46				14 03
	d			13 04				13 19				13 34				13 49				14 04
Norbiton	d			13 06				13 21				13 36				13 51				14 06
New Malden	d		13 07	13 10				13 25			13 37	13 40				13 55			14 07	14 10
Dorking	d	12 35								13 05								13 35		
Box Hill & Westhumble	d																			
Leatherhead	d	12 41			12 54					13 11			13 24					13 41		
Ashtead	d	12 44			12 58					13 14			13 28					13 44		
Epsom	a	12 49			13 02					13 19			13 32					13 49		
	d	12 50			13 05					13 20			13 35					13 50		
Ewell West	d	12 53			13 08					13 23			13 38					13 53		
Stoneleigh	d	12 55			13 10					13 25			13 40					13 55		
Worcester Park	d	12 58			13 13					13 28			13 43					13 58		
Chessington South	d						13 10								13 40					
Chessington North	d						13 12								13 42					
Tolworth	d						13 14								13 44					
Malden Manor	d						13 17								13 47					
Motspur Park	d	13 01			13 16		13 20			13 31			13 46		13 50			14 01		
Raynes Park	d	13 04	13 10	13 13	13 19		13 23	13 28		13 34	13 40	13 43	13 49		13 53	13 58		14 04	14 10	14 13
Wimbledon	d	13 08	13 14	13 17	13 23	13 20	13 27	13 32	13 35	13 38	13 44	13 47	13 53	13 50	13 57	14 02	14 05	14 08	14 14	14 17
Earlsfield	d	13 12	13 17	13 20	13 27	13 24	13 31	13 35	13 38	13 42	13 47	13 50	13 57	13 54	14 01	14 05	14 08	14 12	14 17	14 20
Clapham Junction	d	13 16	13 21	13 24	13 31	13 28	13 35	13 39	13 42	13 46	13 51	13 54	14 01	13 58	14 05	14 09	14 12	14 16	14 21	14 24
Vauxhall	d	13 21	13 26	13 29	13 36	13 33	13 40	13 44	13 47	13 51	13 56	13 59	14 06	14 03	14 10	14 14	14 17	14 21	14 26	14 29
London Waterloo	a	13 25	13 31	13 34	13 40	13 37	13 45	13 49	13 52	13 55	14 01	14 04	14 10	14 07	14 15	14 19	14 22	14 25	14 31	14 34

		SW	SW	SW	SW	SW	SW	SW	SW	SW	SW	SW	SW	SW	SW	SW	SW	SW	SW	SW
Guildford	d	13 28	13 38							13 58	14 08							14 28	14 38	
London Road (Guildford)	d	13 32	13 42							14 02	14 12							14 32	14 42	
Clandon	d	13 37	13 47							14 07	14 17							14 37	14 47	
Horsley	d	13 41	13 51							14 11	14 21							14 41	14 51	
Effingham Junction	d	13 46	13 54							14 16	14 24							14 46	14 54	
Bookham	d	13 49								14 19								14 49		
Cobham & Stoke d'Abernon	d		13 58								14 28								14 58	
Oxshott	d		14 01								14 31								15 01	
Claygate	d		14 04								14 34								15 04	
Hinchley Wood	d		14 07								14 37								15 07	
Hampton Court	d							14 24								14 54				
Thames Ditton	d							14 26								14 56				
Surbiton	d		14 12			14 27		14 32			14 42			14 57		15 02			15 12	
Berrylands	d							14 34								15 04				
Shepperton	d								14 11								14 41			
Upper Halliford	d								14 14								14 44			
Sunbury	d								14 16								14 46			
Kempton Park	d								14 18								14 48			
Hampton	d								14 21								14 51			
Fulwell	d								14 24								14 54			
Strawberry Hill	d				14 07								14 37							
Teddington	d				14 11				14 29				14 41				14 59			
Hampton Wick	d				14 14				14 31				14 44				15 01			
Kingston	a				14 16				14 33				14 46				15 03			
	d				14 19				14 34				14 49				15 04			
Norbiton	d				14 21				14 36				14 51				15 06			
New Malden	d				14 25			14 37	14 40				14 55			15 07	15 10			
Dorking	d						14 05								14 35					
Box Hill & Westhumble	d																			
Leatherhead	d	13 54					14 11			14 24					14 41			14 54		
Ashtead	d	13 58					14 14			14 28					14 44			14 58		
Epsom	a	14 02					14 19			14 32					14 49			15 02		
	d	14 05					14 20			14 35					14 50			15 05		
Ewell West	d	14 08					14 23			14 38					14 53			15 08		
Stoneleigh	d	14 10					14 25			14 40					14 55			15 10		
Worcester Park	d	14 13					14 28			14 43					14 58			15 13		
Chessington South	d			14 10								14 40								15 10
Chessington North	d			14 12								14 42								15 12
Tolworth	d			14 14								14 44								15 14
Malden Manor	d			14 17								14 47								15 17
Motspur Park	d	14 16		14 20			14 31			14 46		14 50			15 01			15 16		15 20
Raynes Park	d	14 19		14 23	14 28		14 34	14 40	14 43	14 49		14 53	14 58		15 04	15 10	15 13	15 19		15 23
Wimbledon	d	14 23	14 20	14 27	14 32	14 35	14 38	14 44	14 47	14 53	14 50	14 57	15 02	15 05	15 08	15 14	15 17	15 23	15 20	15 27
Earlsfield	d	14 27	14 24	14 31	14 35	14 38	14 42	14 47	14 50	14 57	14 54	15 01	15 05	15 08	15 12	15 17	15 20	15 27	15 24	15 31
Clapham Junction	d	14 31	14 28	14 35	14 39	14 42	14 46	14 51	14 54	15 01	14 58	15 05	15 09	15 12	15 16	15 21	15 24	15 31	15 28	15 35
Vauxhall	d	14 36	14 33	14 40	14 44	14 47	14 51	14 56	14 59	15 06	15 03	15 10	15 14	15 17	15 21	15 26	15 29	15 36	15 33	15 40
London Waterloo	a	14 40	14 37	14 45	14 49	14 52	14 55	15 01	15 04	15 10	15 07	15 15	15 19	15 22	15 25	15 31	15 34	15 40	15 37	15 45

Table 152

Saturdays until 6 October

Hampton Court, Shepperton, Guildford, Dorking and Chessington South - London

Network Diagram - see first Page of Table 152

		SW	SW	SW	SW	SW	SW	SW	SW	SW	SW	SW	SW	SW	SW	SW	SW	SW	SW	SW	SW
Guildford	d						14 58	15 08							15 28	15 38					
London Road (Guildford)	d						15 02	15 12							15 32	15 42					
Clandon	d						15 07	15 17							15 37	15 47					
Horsley	d						15 11	15 21							15 41	15 51					
Effingham Junction	d						15 16	15 24							15 46	15 54					
Bookham	d						15 19								15 49						
Cobham & Stoke d'Abernon	d							15 28								15 58					
Oxshott	d							15 31								16 01					
Claygate	d							15 34								16 04					
Hinchley Wood	d							15 37								16 07					
Hampton Court	d				15 24								15 54								16 24
Thames Ditton	d				15 26								15 56								16 26
Surbiton	d		15 27		15 32			15 42			15 57		16 02			16 12			16 27		16 32
Berrylands	d				15 34								16 04								16 34
Shepperton	d					15 11								15 41							
Upper Halliford	d					15 14								15 44							
Sunbury	d					15 16								15 46							
Kempton Park	d					15 18								15 48							
Hampton	d					15 21								15 51							
Fulwell	d					15 24								15 54							
Strawberry Hill	d	15 07								15 37								16 07			
Teddington	d	15 11				15 29				15 41				15 59				16 11			
Hampton Wick	d	15 14				15 31				15 44				16 01				16 14			
Kingston	a	15 16				15 33				15 46				16 03				16 16			
	d	15 19				15 34				15 49				16 04				16 19			
Norbiton	d	15 21				15 36				15 51				16 06				16 21			
New Malden	d	15 25			15 37	15 40				15 55			16 07	16 10				16 25			16 37
Dorking	d			15 05								15 35								16 05	
Box Hill & Westhumble	d																				
Leatherhead	d			15 11			15 24					15 41			15 54					16 11	
Ashtead	d			15 14			15 28					15 44			15 58					16 14	
Epsom	a			15 19			15 32					15 49			16 02					16 19	
	d			15 20			15 35					15 50			16 05					16 20	
Ewell West	d			15 23			15 38					15 53			16 08					16 23	
Stoneleigh	d			15 25			15 40					15 55			16 10					16 25	
Worcester Park	d			15 28			15 43					15 58			16 13					16 28	
Chessington South	d								15 40								16 10				
Chessington North	d								15 42								16 12				
Tolworth	d								15 44								16 14				
Malden Manor	d								15 47								16 17				
Motspur Park	d			15 31			15 46		15 50			16 01			16 16		16 20			16 31	
Raynes Park	d	15 28		15 34	15 40	15 43	15 49		15 53	15 58		16 04	16 10	16 13	16 19		16 23	16 28		16 34	16 40
Wimbledon	d	15 32	15 35	15 38	15 44	15 47	15 53	15 50	15 57	16 02	16 05	16 08	16 14	16 17	16 23	16 20	16 27	16 32	16 35	16 38	16 44
Earlsfield	d	15 35	15 38	15 42	15 47	15 50	15 57	15 54	16 01	16 05	16 08	16 12	16 17	16 20	16 27	16 24	16 31	16 35	16 38	16 42	16 47
Clapham Junction	d	15 39	15 42	15 46	15 51	15 54	16 01	15 58	16 05	16 09	16 12	16 16	16 21	16 24	16 31	16 28	16 35	16 39	16 42	16 46	16 51
Vauxhall	d	15 44	15 47	15 51	15 56	15 59	16 06	16 03	16 10	16 14	16 17	16 21	16 26	16 29	16 36	16 33	16 40	16 44	16 47	16 51	16 56
London Waterloo	a	15 49	15 52	15 55	16 01	16 04	16 10	16 07	16 15	16 19	16 22	16 25	16 31	16 34	16 40	16 37	16 45	16 49	16 52	16 55	17 01

		SW	SW	SW	SW	SW	SW	SW	SW	SW	SW	SW	SW	SW	SW	SW	SW	SW	SW
Guildford	d		15 58	16 08							16 28	16 38							16 58
London Road (Guildford)	d		16 02	16 12							16 32	16 42							17 02
Clandon	d		16 07	16 17							16 37	16 47							17 07
Horsley	d		16 11	16 21							16 41	16 51							17 11
Effingham Junction	d		16 16	16 24							16 46	16 54							17 16
Bookham	d		16 19								16 49								17 19
Cobham & Stoke d'Abernon	d			16 28								16 58							
Oxshott	d			16 31								17 01							
Claygate	d			16 34								17 04							
Hinchley Wood	d			16 37								17 07							
Hampton Court	d								16 54								17 24		
Thames Ditton	d								16 56								17 26		
Surbiton	d			16 42			16 57		17 02			17 12			17 27		17 32		
Berrylands	d								17 04								17 34		
Shepperton	d	16 11								16 41								17 11	
Upper Halliford	d	16 14								16 44								17 14	
Sunbury	d	16 16								16 46								17 16	
Kempton Park	d	16 18								16 48								17 18	
Hampton	d	16 21								16 51								17 21	
Fulwell	d	16 24								16 54								17 24	
Strawberry Hill	d					16 37								17 07					
Teddington	d	16 29				16 41				16 59				17 11				17 29	
Hampton Wick	d	16 31				16 44				17 01				17 14				17 31	
Kingston	a	16 33				16 46				17 03				17 16				17 33	
	d	16 34				16 49				17 04				17 19				17 34	
Norbiton	d	16 36				16 51				17 06				17 21				17 36	
New Malden	d	16 40				16 55			17 07	17 10				17 25			17 37	17 40	
Dorking	d							16 35								17 05			
Box Hill & Westhumble	d																		
Leatherhead	d		16 24					16 41			16 54					17 11			17 24
Ashtead	d		16 28					16 44			16 58					17 14			17 28
Epsom	a		16 32					16 49			17 02					17 19			17 32
	d		16 35					16 50			17 05					17 20			17 35
Ewell West	d		16 38					16 53			17 08					17 23			17 38
Stoneleigh	d		16 40					16 55			17 10					17 25			17 40
Worcester Park	d		16 43					16 58			17 13					17 28			17 43
Chessington South	d				16 40								17 10						
Chessington North	d				16 42								17 12						
Tolworth	d				16 44								17 14						
Malden Manor	d				16 47								17 17						
Motspur Park	d		16 46		16 50			17 01			17 16		17 20			17 31			17 46
Raynes Park	d	16 43	16 49		16 53	16 58		17 04	17 10	17 13	17 19		17 23	17 28		17 34	17 40	17 43	17 49
Wimbledon	d	16 47	16 53	16 50	16 57	17 02	17 05	17 08	17 14	17 17	17 23	17 20	17 27	17 32	17 35	17 38	17 44	17 47	17 53
Earlsfield	d	16 50	16 57	16 54	17 01	17 05	17 08	17 12	17 17	17 20	17 27	17 24	17 31	17 35	17 38	17 42	17 47	17 50	17 57
Clapham Junction	d	16 54	17 01	16 58	17 05	17 09	17 12	17 16	17 21	17 24	17 31	17 28	17 35	17 39	17 42	17 46	17 51	17 54	18 01
Vauxhall	d	16 59	17 06	17 03	17 10	17 14	17 17	17 21	17 26	17 29	17 36	17 33	17 40	17 44	17 47	17 51	17 56	17 59	18 06
London Waterloo	a	17 04	17 10	17 07	17 15	17 19	17 22	17 25	17 31	17 34	17 40	17 37	17 45	17 49	17 52	17 55	18 01	18 04	18 10

Table 152

Saturdays until 6 October

Hampton Court, Shepperton, Guildford, Dorking and Chessington South - London

Network Diagram - see first Page of Table 152

		SW	SW	SW	SW	SW	SW	SW	SW	SW	SW	SW	SW	SW	SW	SW	SW	SW	SW	SW	SW
Guildford	d	17 08							17 28	17 38							17 58	18 08			
London Road (Guildford)	d	17 12							17 32	17 42							18 02	18 12			
Clandon	d	17 17							17 37	17 47							18 07	18 17			
Horsley	d	17 21							17 41	17 51							18 11	18 21			
Effingham Junction	d	17 24							17 46	17 54							18 16	18 24			
Bookham	d								17 49								18 19				
Cobham & Stoke d'Abernon	d	17 28								17 58								18 28			
Oxshott	d	17 31								18 01								18 31			
Claygate	d	17 34								18 04								18 34			
Hinchley Wood	d	17 37								18 07								18 37			
Hampton Court	d						17 54								18 24						
Thames Ditton	d						17 56								18 26						
Surbiton	d	17 42			17 57		18 02			18 12			18 27		18 32			18 42			18 57
Berrylands	d						18 04								18 34						
Shepperton	d							17 41								18 11					
Upper Halliford	d							17 44								18 14					
Sunbury	d							17 46								18 16					
Kempton Park	d							17 48								18 18					
Hampton	d							17 51								18 21					
Fulwell	d							17 54								18 24					
Strawberry Hill	d			17 37								18 07								18 37	
Teddington	d			17 41				17 59				18 11				18 29				18 41	
Hampton Wick	d			17 44				18 01				18 14				18 31				18 44	
Kingston	a			17 46				18 03				18 16				18 33				18 46	
	d			17 49				18 04				18 19				18 34				18 49	
Norbiton	d			17 51				18 06				18 21				18 36				18 51	
New Malden	d			17 55			18 07	18 10				18 25			18 37	18 40				18 55	
Dorking	d					17 35								18 05							
Box Hill & Westhumble	d																				
Leatherhead	d					17 41			17 54					18 11			18 24				
Ashtead	d					17 44			17 58					18 14			18 28				
Epsom	a					17 49			18 02					18 19			18 32				
	d					17 50			18 05					18 20			18 35				
Ewell West	d					17 53			18 08					18 23			18 38				
Stoneleigh	d					17 55			18 10					18 25			18 40				
Worcester Park	d					17 58			18 13					18 28			18 43				
Chessington South	d		17 40								18 10								18 40		
Chessington North	d		17 42								18 12								18 42		
Tolworth	d		17 44								18 14								18 44		
Malden Manor	d		17 47								18 17								18 47		
Motspur Park	d		17 50			18 01			18 16		18 20			18 31			18 46		18 50		
Raynes Park	d		17 53	17 58		18 04	18 10	18 13	18 19		18 23	18 28		18 34	18 40	18 43	18 49		18 53	18 58	
Wimbledon ⊖	d	17 50	17 57	18 02	18 05	18 08	18 14	18 17	18 23	18 20	18 27	18 32	18 35	18 38	18 44	18 47	18 53	18 50	18 57	19 02	19 05
Earlsfield	d	17 54	18 01	18 05	18 08	18 12	18 17	18 20	18 27	18 24	18 31	18 35	18 38	18 42	18 47	18 50	18 57	18 54	19 01	19 05	19 08
Clapham Junction	d	17 58	18 05	18 09	18 12	18 16	18 21	18 24	18 31	18 28	18 35	18 39	18 42	18 46	18 51	18 54	19 01	18 58	19 05	19 09	19 12
Vauxhall ⊖	d	18 03	18 10	18 14	18 17	18 21	18 26	18 29	18 36	18 33	18 40	18 44	18 47	18 51	18 56	18 59	19 06	19 03	19 10	19 14	19 17
London Waterloo ⊖	a	18 07	18 15	18 19	18 22	18 25	18 31	18 34	18 40	18 37	18 45	18 49	18 52	18 55	19 01	19 04	19 10	19 07	19 15	19 19	19 22

		SW	SW	SW	SW	SW	SW	SW	SW	SW	SW	SW	SW	SW	SW	SW	SW	SW	SW	SW
Guildford	d				18 28	18 38							18 58	19 08						
London Road (Guildford)	d				18 32	18 42							19 02	19 12						
Clandon	d				18 37	18 47							19 07	19 17						
Horsley	d				18 41	18 51							19 11	19 21						
Effingham Junction	d				18 46	18 54							19 16	19 24						
Bookham	d				18 49								19 19							
Cobham & Stoke d'Abernon	d					18 58								19 28						
Oxshott	d					19 01								19 31						
Claygate	d					19 04								19 34						
Hinchley Wood	d					19 07								19 37						
Hampton Court	d		18 54								19 24								19 54	
Thames Ditton	d		18 56								19 26								19 56	
Surbiton	d		19 02			19 12			19 27		19 32			19 42			19 57		20 02	
Berrylands	d		19 04								19 34								20 04	
Shepperton	d			18 41								19 11								19 41
Upper Halliford	d			18 44								19 14								19 44
Sunbury	d			18 46								19 16								19 46
Kempton Park	d			18 48								19 18								19 48
Hampton	d			18 51								19 21								19 51
Fulwell	d			18 54								19 24								19 54
Strawberry Hill	d							19 07								19 37				
Teddington	d			18 59				19 11				19 29				19 41				19 59
Hampton Wick	d			19 01				19 14				19 31				19 44				20 01
Kingston	a			19 03				19 16				19 33				19 46				20 03
	d			19 04				19 19				19 34				19 49				20 04
Norbiton	d			19 06				19 21				19 36				19 51				20 06
New Malden	d		19 07	19 10				19 25			19 37	19 40				19 55			20 07	20 10
Dorking	d	18 35								19 05								19 35		
Box Hill & Westhumble	d																			
Leatherhead	d	18 41			18 54					19 11			19 24					19 41		
Ashtead	d	18 44			18 58					19 14			19 28					19 44		
Epsom	a	18 49			19 02					19 19			19 32					19 49		
	d	18 50			19 05					19 20			19 35					19 50		
Ewell West	d	18 53			19 08					19 23			19 38					19 53		
Stoneleigh	d	18 55			19 10					19 25			19 40					19 55		
Worcester Park	d	18 58			19 13					19 28			19 43					19 58		
Chessington South	d						19 10								19 40					
Chessington North	d						19 12								19 42					
Tolworth	d						19 14								19 44					
Malden Manor	d						19 17								19 47					
Motspur Park	d	19 01			19 16		19 20			19 31			19 46		19 50			20 01		
Raynes Park	d	19 04	19 10	19 13	19 19		19 23	19 28		19 34	19 40	19 43	19 49		19 53	19 58		20 04	20 10	20 13
Wimbledon ⊖	d	19 08	19 14	19 17	19 23	19 20	19 27	19 32	19 35	19 38	19 44	19 47	19 53	19 50	19 57	20 02	20 05	20 08	20 14	20 17
Earlsfield	d	19 12	19 17	19 20	19 27	19 24	19 31	19 35	19 38	19 42	19 47	19 50	19 57	19 54	20 01	20 05	20 08	20 12	20 17	20 20
Clapham Junction	d	19 16	19 21	19 24	19 31	19 28	19 35	19 39	19 42	19 46	19 51	19 54	20 01	19 58	20 05	20 09	20 12	20 16	20 21	20 24
Vauxhall ⊖	d	19 21	19 26	19 29	19 36	19 33	19 40	19 44	19 47	19 51	19 56	19 59	20 06	20 03	20 10	20 14	20 17	20 21	20 26	20 29
London Waterloo ⊖	a	19 25	19 31	19 34	19 40	19 37	19 45	19 49	19 52	19 55	20 01	20 04	20 10	20 07	20 15	20 19	20 22	20 25	20 31	20 34

Table 152

Saturdays until 6 October

Hampton Court, Shepperton, Guildford, Dorking and Chessington South - London

Network Diagram - see first Page of Table 152

		SW	SW	SW	SW	SW	SW	SW	SW	SW	SW	SW	SW	SW	SW	SW	SW	SW	SW	SW
Guildford	d	19 28	19 38							19 58	20 08							20 38		
London Road (Guildford)	d	19 32	19 42							20 02	20 12							20 42		
Clandon	d	19 37	19 47							20 07	20 17							20 47		
Horsley	d	19 41	19 51							20 11	20 21							20 51		
Effingham Junction	d	19 46	19 54							20 16	20 24							20 54		
Bookham	d	19 49								20 19										
Cobham & Stoke d'Abernon	d		19 58								20 28							20 58		
Oxshott	d		20 01								20 31							21 01		
Claygate	d		20 04								20 34							21 04		
Hinchley Wood	d		20 07								20 37							21 07		
Hampton Court	d							20 24								20 54				
Thames Ditton	d							20 26								20 56				
Surbiton	d		20 12			20 27		20 32			20 42			20 57		21 02		21 12		
Berrylands	d							20 34								21 04				
Shepperton	d								20 11								20 41			
Upper Halliford	d								20 14								20 44			
Sunbury	d								20 16								20 46			
Kempton Park	d								20 18								20 48			
Hampton	d								20 21								20 51			
Fulwell	d								20 24								20 54			
Strawberry Hill	d				20 07								20 37							
Teddington	d				20 11				20 29				20 41				20 59			
Hampton Wick	d				20 14				20 31				20 44				21 01			
Kingston	a				20 16				20 33				20 46				21 03			
	d				20 19				20 34				20 49				21 04			
Norbiton	d				20 21				20 36				20 51				21 06			
New Malden	d				20 25			20 37	20 40				20 55			21 07	21 10			
Dorking	d						20 05								20 35					
Box Hill & Westhumble	d																			
Leatherhead	d	19 54					20 11			20 24					20 41					
Ashtead	d	19 58					20 14			20 28					20 44					
Epsom	a	20 02					20 19			20 32					20 49					
	d	20 05					20 20			20 35					20 50				21 05	
Ewell West	d	20 08					20 23			20 38					20 53				21 08	
Stoneleigh	d	20 10					20 25			20 40					20 55				21 10	
Worcester Park	d	20 13					20 28			20 43					20 58				21 13	
Chessington South	d			20 10								20 40								21 10
Chessington North	d			20 12								20 42								21 12
Tolworth	d			20 14								20 44								21 14
Malden Manor	d			20 17								20 47								21 17
Motspur Park	d	20 16		20 20			20 31			20 46		20 50			21 01				21 16	21 20
Raynes Park	d	20 19		20 23	20 28		20 34	20 40	20 43	20 49		20 53	20 58		21 04	21 10	21 13		21 19	21 23
Wimbledon ⊖	d	20 23	20 20	20 27	20 32	20 35	20 38	20 44	20 47	20 53	20 50	20 57	21 02	21 05	21 08	21 14	21 17	21 20	21 23	21 27
Earlsfield	d	20 27	20 24	20 31	20 35	20 38	20 42	20 47	20 50	20 57	20 54	21 01	21 05	21 08	21 12	21 17	21 20	21 24	21 27	21 31
Clapham Junction	d	20 31	20 28	20 35	20 39	20 42	20 46	20 51	20 54	21 01	20 58	21 05	21 09	21 12	21 16	21 21	21 24	21 28	21 31	21 35
Vauxhall ⊖	d	20 36	20 33	20 40	20 44	20 47	20 51	20 56	20 59	21 06	21 03	21 10	21 14	21 17	21 21	21 26	21 29	21 33	21 36	21 40
London Waterloo ⊖	a	20 40	20 37	20 45	20 49	20 52	20 55	21 01	21 04	21 10	21 07	21 15	21 19	21 23	21 25	21 31	21 34	21 37	21 40	21 45

		SW	SW	SW	SW	SW	SW	SW	SW	SW	SW	SW	SW	SW	SW	SW	SW	SW	SW	SW
Guildford	d			20 46			21 08							21 38			21 46			22 08
London Road (Guildford)	d			20 50			21 12							21 42			21 50			22 12
Clandon	d			20 55			21 17							21 47			21 55			22 17
Horsley	d			20 59			21 21							21 51			21 59			22 21
Effingham Junction	d			21 03			21 24							21 54			22 03			22 24
Bookham	d			21 06													22 06			
Cobham & Stoke d'Abernon	d						21 28							21 58						22 28
Oxshott	d						21 31							22 01						22 31
Claygate	d						21 34							22 04						22 34
Hinchley Wood	d						21 37							22 07						22 37
Hampton Court	d				21 24													22 24		
Thames Ditton	d				21 26													22 26		
Surbiton	d		21 27		21 32		21 42				21 57			22 12		22 27		22 32		22 42
Berrylands	d				21 34													22 34		
Shepperton	d					21 11							21 41						22 11	
Upper Halliford	d					21 14							21 44						22 14	
Sunbury	d					21 16							21 46						22 16	
Kempton Park	d					21 18							21 48						22 18	
Hampton	d					21 21							21 51						22 21	
Fulwell	d					21 24							21 54						22 24	
Strawberry Hill	d	21 07								21 37					22 07					
Teddington	d	21 11				21 29				21 41			21 59		22 11				22 29	
Hampton Wick	d	21 14				21 31				21 44			22 01		22 14				22 31	
Kingston	a	21 16				21 33				21 46			22 03		22 16				22 33	
	d	21 19				21 34				21 49			22 04		22 19				22 34	
Norbiton	d	21 21				21 36				21 51			22 06		22 21				22 36	
New Malden	d	21 25			21 37	21 40				21 55			22 10		22 25			22 37	22 40	
Dorking	d											21 35								
Box Hill & Westhumble	d																			
Leatherhead	d			21 11								21 41					22 11			
Ashtead	d			21 14								21 44					22 14			
Epsom	a			21 19								21 49					22 19			
	d			21 20				21 35				21 50					22 20			
Ewell West	d			21 23				21 38				21 53					22 23			
Stoneleigh	d			21 25				21 40				21 55					22 25			
Worcester Park	d			21 28				21 43				21 58					22 28			
Chessington South	d								21 40											
Chessington North	d								21 42											
Tolworth	d								21 44											
Malden Manor	d								21 47											
Motspur Park	d			21 31				21 46	21 50			22 01					22 31			
Raynes Park	d	21 28		21 34	21 40	21 43		21 49	21 53	21 58		22 04	22 13		22 28		22 34	22 40	22 43	
Wimbledon ⊖	d	21 32	21 35	21 38	21 44	21 47	21 50	21 53	21 57	22 02	22 05	22 08	22 17	22 20	22 32	22 35	22 38	22 44	22 47	22 50
Earlsfield	d	21 35	21 38	21 42	21 47	21 50	21 54	21 57	22 01	22 05	22 08	22 12	22 20	22 24	22 35	22 38	22 42	22 47	22 50	22 54
Clapham Junction	d	21 39	21 42	21 46	21 51	21 54	21 58	22 01	22 05	22 09	22 12	22 16	22 24	22 28	22 39	22 42	22 46	22 51	22 54	22 58
Vauxhall ⊖	d	21 44	21 47	21 51	21 56	21 59	22 03	22 06	22 10	22 14	22 17	22 21	22 29	22 33	22 44	22 47	22 51	22 56	22 59	23 03
London Waterloo ⊖	a	21 49	21 52	21 55	22 01	22 04	22 07	22 10	22 15	22 19	22 22	22 25	22 34	22 39	22 49	22 52	22 55	23 01	23 04	23 07

Table 152

Saturdays
until 6 October

Hampton Court, Shepperton, Guildford, Dorking and Chessington South - London

Network Diagram - see first Page of Table 152

		SW	SW	SW		SW		SW	SW	SW	SW	SW	SW	SW		SW	SN	SW	SW
Guildford	d			22 20					22 38		22 46	22 55				23 08			
London Road (Guildford)	d								22 42		22 50					23 12			
Clandon	d								22 47		22 55					23 17			
Horsley	d								22 51		22 59					23 21			
Effingham Junction 6	d								22 54		23 03					23 24			
Bookham	d										23 06								
Cobham & Stoke d'Abernon	d								22 58							23 28			
Oxshott	d								23 01							23 31			
Claygate	d								23 04							23 34			
Hinchley Wood	d								23 07							23 37			
Hampton Court	d												23 24						
Thames Ditton	d												23 26						
Surbiton 6	d			22 57					23 12			23 30	23 33			23 42			
Berrylands	d												23 35						
Shepperton	d							22 41						23 11					
Upper Halliford	d							22 44						23 14					
Sunbury	d							22 46						23 16					
Kempton Park	d							22 48						23 18					
Hampton	d							22 51						23 21					
Fulwell	d							22 54						23 24					
Strawberry Hill	d		22 37							23 07									23 37
Teddington	d		22 41					22 59		23 11				23 29					23 41
Hampton Wick	d		22 44					23 01		23 14				23 31					23 44
Kingston	a		22 46					23 03		23 16				23 33					23 46
	d		22 49					23 04		23 19				23 34					23 49
Norbiton	d		22 51					23 06		23 21				23 36					23 51
New Malden 6	d		22 55					23 10		23 25			23 38	23 41					23 55
Dorking 4	d					22 35											23 30		
Box Hill & Westhumble	d																		
Leatherhead	d					22 41					23 11						23 36		
Ashtead	d					22 44					23 14						23 39		
Epsom 3	a					22 49					23 19						23 45		
	d					22 50					23 20								
Ewell West	d					22 53					23 23								
Stoneleigh	d					22 55					23 25								
Worcester Park	d					22 58					23 28								
Chessington South	d	22 40																23 40	
Chessington North	d	22 42																23 42	
Tolworth	d	22 44																23 44	
Malden Manor	d	22 47																23 47	
Motspur Park	d	22 50				23 01					23 31							23 50	
Raynes Park 6	d	22 53	22 58			23 04		23 13		23 28	23 37		23 41	23 43				23 54	23 58
Wimbledon 6 ⊖	d	22 57	23 02	23 05		23 08		23 17	23 20	23 32	23 41	23 37	23 46	23 49		23 52		23a57	00 02
Earlsfield	d	23 01	23 05	23 08		23 12		23 20	23 24	23 35	23 44	23 41	23 50	23 53		23 56			00 05
Clapham Junction 10	d	23 05	23 09	23 12		23 16		23 24	23 28	23 39	23 48	23 45	23 53	23 56		23 58			00 09
Vauxhall ⊖	d	23 10	23 14	23 17		23 21		23 29	23 33	23 44	23 53	23 50	23 58	00 01		00 04			00 15
London Waterloo 15 ⊖	a	23 15	23 19	23 22		23 25		23 34	23 37	23 49	23 58	23 54	00 03	00 06		00 14			00 22

Table 152

Saturdays
from 13 October

Hampton Court, Shepperton, Guildford, Dorking and Chessington South - London

Network Diagram - see first Page of Table 152

			SW	SW	SW	SW	SW	SW	SW	SW		SW	SW	SW	SW		SW	SW	SW	SW		SW		SW	SW
Guildford	d			23p08				04 00						05 14											
London Road (Guildford)	d			23p12																					
Clandon	d			23p17																					
Horsley	d			23p21																					
Effingham Junction 6	d			23p24																					
Bookham	d																								
Cobham & Stoke d'Abernon	d			23p28																					
Oxshott	d			23p31																					
Claygate	d			23p34																					
Hinchley Wood	d			23p37																					
Hampton Court	d														05 54							06 24			
Thames Ditton	d														05 56							06 26			
Surbiton 6	d			23p42				04 24						05 57	06 02					06 27		06 32			
Berrylands	d														06 04							06 34			
Shepperton	d		23p11																					06 11	
Upper Halliford	d		23p14																					06 14	
Sunbury	d		23p16																					06 16	
Kempton Park	d		23p18																					06 18	
Hampton	d		23p21																					06 21	
Fulwell	d		23p24																					06 24	
Strawberry Hill	d				23p37	00 07			04 55			05 38						06 07	06 08						
Teddington	d		23p29		23p41	00 11	00s56		04 59				05 44					06 11						06 29	
Hampton Wick	d		23p31		23p44	00 14	00s59		05 01				05 46					06 14						06 31	
Kingston	a		23p33		23p46	00 16	01 01		05 03				05 48					06 16						06 33	
	d		23p34		23p49				05 04				05 49					06 19						06 34	
Norbiton	d		23p36		23p51				05 06				05 51					06 21						06 36	
New Malden 6	d		23p41		23p55				05 10				05 55		06 07			06 25				06 37		06 40	
Dorking 4	d																								
Box Hill & Westhumble	d																								
Leatherhead	d																								
Ashtead	d																								
Epsom 3	a																								
	d									05 35							06 05								06 35
Ewell West	d									05 38							06 08								06 38
Stoneleigh	d									05 40							06 10								06 40
Worcester Park	d									05 43							06 13								06 43
Chessington South	d																								
Chessington North	d																								
Tolworth	d																								
Malden Manor	d																								
Motspur Park	d									05 46							06 16								06 46
Raynes Park 6	d		23p43		23p58				05 13	05 49			05 58		06 10		06 19	06 28				06 40		06 43	06 49
Wimbledon 6 ⊖	d		23p50	23p53	00 02			04 32	05 17	05 53			06 02	06 05	06 14		06 23	06 32		06 35		06 44		06 47	06 53
Earlsfield	d		23p53	23p56	00 05				05 21	05 57			06 05	06 08	06 17		06 27	06 35		06 38		06 47		06 50	06 57
Clapham Junction 10	d		23p57	23p59	00 09			04 44	05 25	06 01			06 09	06 12	06 21		06 31	06 39		06 42		06 51		06 54	07 01
Vauxhall ⊖	d		00 02	00 05	00 14				05 30	06 06		06 12	06 14	06 17	06 26		06 36	06 44	06 42	06 47		06 56		06 59	07 06
London Waterloo 15 ⊖	a		00 10	00 14	00 22			04 53	05 35	06 11		06 16	06 19	06 22	06 31		06 40	06 49	06 46	06 52		07 01		07 04	07 10

		SW	SW	SW	SW			SW	SW	SW	SW	SW	SW	SW		SW		SW	SW	SW	SW	SW	SW		SW
Guildford	d								06 28	06 35								06 58	07 05						
London Road (Guildford)	d								06 32	06 39								07 02	07 09						
Clandon	d								06 37	06 44								07 07	07 14						
Horsley	d								06 41	06 48								07 11	07 18						
Effingham Junction 6	d								06 46	06 51								07 16	07 21						
Bookham	d								06 49									07 19							
Cobham & Stoke d'Abernon	d									06 55									07 25						
Oxshott	d									06 58									07 28						
Claygate	d									07 01									07 31						
Hinchley Wood	d									07 04									07 34						
Hampton Court	d				06 54									07 24									07 54		
Thames Ditton	d				06 56									07 26									07 56		
Surbiton 6	d			06 57	07 02					07 12			07 27	07 32					07 42			07 57	08 02		
Berrylands	d				07 04									07 34									08 04		
Shepperton	d							06 41								07 11									07 41
Upper Halliford	d							06 44								07 14									07 44
Sunbury	d							06 46								07 16									07 46
Kempton Park	d							06 48								07 18									07 48
Hampton	d							06 51								07 21									07 51
Fulwell	d							06 54								07 24									07 54
Strawberry Hill	d		06 37									07 07									07 37				
Teddington	d		06 41					06 59				07 11				07 29					07 41				07 59
Hampton Wick	d		06 44					07 01				07 14				07 31					07 44				08 01
Kingston	a		06 46					07 03				07 16				07 33					07 46				08 03
	d		06 49					07 04				07 19				07 34					07 49				08 04
Norbiton	d		06 51					07 06				07 21				07 36					07 51				08 06
New Malden 6	d		06 55		07 07			07 10				07 25		07 37		07 40					07 55		08 07		08 10
Dorking 4	d																								
Box Hill & Westhumble	d																								
Leatherhead	d								06 54									07 24							
Ashtead	d								06 58									07 28							
Epsom 3	a								07 02									07 32							
	d								07 05									07 35							
Ewell West	d								07 08									07 38							
Stoneleigh	d								07 10									07 40							
Worcester Park	d								07 13									07 43							
Chessington South	d	06 40									07 10									07 40					
Chessington North	d	06 42									07 12									07 42					
Tolworth	d	06 44									07 14									07 44					
Malden Manor	d	06 47									07 17									07 47					
Motspur Park	d	06 50							07 16		07 20							07 46		07 50					
Raynes Park 6	d	06 53	06 58		07 10			07 13	07 19		07 23	07 28		07 40		07 43		07 49		07 53	07 58		08 10		08 13
Wimbledon 6 ⊖	d	06 57	07 02	07 05	07 14			07 17	07 23	07 20	07 27	07 32	07 35	07 44		07 47		07 53	07 50	07 57	08 02	08 05	08 14		08 17
Earlsfield	d	07 01	07 05	07 08	07 17			07 20	07 27	07 24	07 31	07 35	07 38	07 47		07 50		07 57	07 54	08 01	08 05	08 08	08 17		08 20
Clapham Junction 10	d	07 05	07 09	07 12	07 21			07 24	07 31	07 28	07 35	07 39	07 42	07 51		07 54		08 01	07 58	08 05	08 09	08 12	08 21		08 24
Vauxhall ⊖	d	07 10	07 14	07 17	07 26			07 29	07 36	07 33	07 40	07 44	07 47	07 56		07 59		08 06	08 03	08 10	08 14	08 17	08 26		08 29
London Waterloo 15 ⊖	a	07 15	07 19	07 22	07 31			07 34	07 40	07 37	07 45	07 49	07 52	08 01		08 04		08 10	08 07	08 15	08 19	08 22	08 31		08 34

Saturdays from 13 October

Hampton Court, Shepperton, Guildford, Dorking and Chessington South - London

Network Diagram - see first Page of Table 152

		SW	SW	SW	SW	SW	SW	SW	SW	SW	SW	SW	SW	SW	SW	SW	SW	SW	SW	SW
Guildford	d	07 28	07 35							07 58	08 05							08 28	08 35	
London Road (Guildford)	d	07 32	07 39							08 02	08 09							08 32	08 39	
Clandon	d	07 37	07 44							08 07	08 14							08 37	08 44	
Horsley	d	07 41	07 48							08 11	08 18							08 41	08 48	
Effingham Junction	d	07 46	07 51							08 16	08 21							08 46	08 51	
Bookham	d	07 49								08 19								08 49		
Cobham & Stoke d'Abernon	d		07 55								08 25								08 55	
Oxshott	d		07 58								08 28								08 58	
Claygate	d		08 01								08 31								09 01	
Hinchley Wood	d		08 04								08 34								09 04	
Hampton Court	d							08 24								08 54				
Thames Ditton	d							08 26								08 56				
Surbiton	d		08 12			08 27		08 32			08 42			08 57		09 02			09 12	
Berrylands	d							08 34								09 04				
Shepperton	d								08 11								08 41			
Upper Halliford	d								08 14								08 44			
Sunbury	d								08 16								08 46			
Kempton Park	d								08 18								08 48			
Hampton	d								08 21								08 51			
Fulwell	d								08 24								08 54			
Strawberry Hill	d				08 07								08 37							
Teddington	d				08 11				08 29				08 41				08 59			
Hampton Wick	d				08 14				08 31				08 44				09 01			
Kingston	a				08 16				08 33				08 46				09 03			
	d				08 19				08 34				08 49				09 04			
Norbiton	d				08 21				08 36				08 51				09 06			
New Malden	d				08 25			08 37	08 40				08 55			09 07	09 10			
Dorking	d						08 05								08 35					
Box Hill & Westhumble	d																			
Leatherhead	d	07 54					08 11			08 24					08 41			08 54		
Ashtead	d	07 58					08 14			08 28					08 44			08 58		
Epsom	a	08 02					08 19			08 32					08 49			09 02		
	d	08 05					08 20			08 35					08 50			09 05		
Ewell West	d	08 08					08 23			08 38					08 53			09 08		
Stoneleigh	d	08 10					08 25			08 40					08 55			09 10		
Worcester Park	d	08 13					08 28			08 43					08 58			09 13		
Chessington South	d			08 10								08 40								09 10
Chessington North	d			08 12								08 42								09 12
Tolworth	d			08 14								08 44								09 14
Malden Manor	d			08 17								08 47								09 17
Motspur Park	d	08 16		08 20			08 31			08 46		08 50			09 01			09 16		09 20
Raynes Park	d	08 19		08 23	08 28		08 34	08 40	08 43	08 49		08 53	08 58		09 04	09 10	09 13	09 19		09 23
Wimbledon ⊖	d	08 23	08 20	08 27	08 32	08 35	08 38	08 44	08 47	08 53	08 50	08 57	09 02	09 05	09 08	09 14	09 17	09 23	09 20	09 27
Earlsfield	d	08 27	08 24	08 31	08 35	08 38	08 42	08 47	08 50	08 57	08 54	09 01	09 05	09 08	09 12	09 17	09 20	09 27	09 24	09 31
Clapham Junction	d	08 31	08 28	08 35	08 39	08 42	08 46	08 51	08 54	09 01	08 58	09 05	09 09	09 12	09 16	09 21	09 24	09 31	09 28	09 35
Vauxhall ⊖	d	08 36	08 33	08 40	08 44	08 47	08 51	08 56	08 59	09 06	09 03	09 10	09 14	09 17	09 21	09 26	09 29	09 36	09 33	09 40
London Waterloo ⊖	a	08 40	08 37	08 45	08 49	08 52	08 55	09 01	09 04	09 10	09 07	09 15	09 19	09 22	09 25	09 31	09 34	09 40	09 37	09 45

		SW	SW	SW	SW	SW	SW	SW	SW	SW	SW	SW	SW	SW	SW	SW	SW	SW	SW	SW	SW
Guildford	d						08 58	09 05							09 28	09 35					
London Road (Guildford)	d						09 02	09 09							09 32	09 39					
Clandon	d						09 07	09 14							09 37	09 44					
Horsley	d						09 11	09 18							09 41	09 48					
Effingham Junction	d						09 16	09 21							09 46	09 51					
Bookham	d						09 19								09 49						
Cobham & Stoke d'Abernon	d							09 25								09 55					
Oxshott	d							09 28								09 58					
Claygate	d							09 31								10 01					
Hinchley Wood	d							09 34								10 04					
Hampton Court	d				09 24								09 54								10 24
Thames Ditton	d				09 26								09 56								10 26
Surbiton	d		09 27		09 32			09 42			09 57		10 02			10 12			10 27		10 32
Berrylands	d				09 34								10 04								10 34
Shepperton	d					09 11								09 41							
Upper Halliford	d					09 14								09 44							
Sunbury	d					09 16								09 46							
Kempton Park	d					09 18								09 48							
Hampton	d					09 21								09 51							
Fulwell	d					09 24								09 54							
Strawberry Hill	d	09 07								09 37								10 07			
Teddington	d	09 11				09 29				09 41				09 59				10 11			
Hampton Wick	d	09 14				09 31				09 44				10 01				10 14			
Kingston	a	09 16				09 33				09 46				10 03				10 16			
	d	09 19				09 34				09 49				10 04				10 19			
Norbiton	d	09 21				09 36				09 51				10 06				10 21			
New Malden	d	09 25			09 37	09 40				09 55			10 07	10 10				10 25			10 37
Dorking	d			09 05								09 35								10 05	
Box Hill & Westhumble	d																				
Leatherhead	d			09 11			09 24					09 41			09 54					10 11	
Ashtead	d			09 14			09 28					09 44			09 58					10 14	
Epsom	a			09 19			09 32					09 49			10 02					10 19	
	d			09 20			09 35					09 50			10 05					10 20	
Ewell West	d			09 23			09 38					09 53			10 08					10 23	
Stoneleigh	d			09 25			09 40					09 55			10 10					10 25	
Worcester Park	d			09 28			09 43					09 58			10 13					10 28	
Chessington South	d								09 40								10 10				
Chessington North	d								09 42								10 12				
Tolworth	d								09 44								10 14				
Malden Manor	d								09 47								10 17				
Motspur Park	d			09 31			09 46		09 50			10 01			10 16		10 20			10 31	
Raynes Park	d	09 28		09 34	09 40	09 43	09 49		09 53	09 58		10 04	10 10	10 13	10 19		10 23	10 28		10 34	10 40
Wimbledon ⊖	d	09 32	09 35	09 38	09 44	09 47	09 53	09 50	09 57	10 02	10 05	10 08	10 14	10 17	10 23	10 20	10 27	10 32	10 35	10 38	10 44
Earlsfield	d	09 35	09 38	09 42	09 47	09 50	09 57	09 54	10 01	10 05	10 08	10 12	10 17	10 20	10 27	10 24	10 31	10 35	10 38	10 42	10 47
Clapham Junction	d	09 39	09 42	09 46	09 51	09 54	10 01	09 58	10 05	10 09	10 12	10 16	10 21	10 24	10 31	10 28	10 35	10 39	10 42	10 46	10 51
Vauxhall ⊖	d	09 44	09 47	09 51	09 56	09 59	10 06	10 03	10 10	10 14	10 17	10 21	10 26	10 29	10 36	10 33	10 40	10 44	10 47	10 51	10 56
London Waterloo ⊖	a	09 49	09 52	09 55	10 01	10 04	10 10	10 07	10 15	10 19	10 22	10 25	10 31	10 34	10 40	10 37	10 45	10 49	10 52	10 55	11 01

Table 152

Saturdays from 13 October

Hampton Court, Shepperton, Guildford, Dorking and Chessington South - London

Network Diagram - see first Page of Table 152

		SW	SW	SW	SW	SW	SW	SW	SW	SW	SW	SW	SW	SW	SW	SW	SW	SW	SW
Guildford	d		09 58	10 05							10 28	10 35							10 58
London Road (Guildford)	d		10 02	10 09							10 32	10 39							11 02
Clandon	d		10 07	10 14							10 37	10 44							11 07
Horsley	d		10 11	10 18							10 41	10 48							11 11
Effingham Junction	d		10 16	10 21							10 46	10 51							11 16
Bookham	d		10 19								10 49								11 19
Cobham & Stoke d'Abernon	d			10 25								10 55							
Oxshott	d			10 28								10 58							
Claygate	d			10 31								11 01							
Hinchley Wood	d			10 34								11 04							
Hampton Court	d								10 54								11 24		
Thames Ditton	d								10 56								11 26		
Surbiton	d			10 42			10 57		11 02			11 12			11 27		11 32		
Berrylands	d								11 04								11 34		
Shepperton	d	10 11								10 41								11 11	
Upper Halliford	d	10 14								10 44								11 14	
Sunbury	d	10 16								10 46								11 16	
Kempton Park	d	10 18								10 48								11 18	
Hampton	d	10 21								10 51								11 21	
Fulwell	d	10 24								10 54								11 24	
Strawberry Hill	d					10 37								11 07					
Teddington	d	10 29				10 41				10 59				11 11				11 29	
Hampton Wick	d	10 31				10 44				11 01				11 14				11 31	
Kingston	a	10 33				10 46				11 03				11 16				11 33	
	d	10 34				10 49				11 04				11 19				11 34	
Norbiton	d	10 36				10 51				11 06				11 21				11 36	
New Malden	d	10 40				10 55			11 07	11 10				11 25			11 37	11 40	
Dorking	d							10 35								11 05			
Box Hill & Westhumble	d																		
Leatherhead	d		10 24					10 41			10 54					11 11			11 24
Ashtead	d		10 28					10 44			10 58					11 14			11 28
Epsom	a		10 32					10 49			11 02					11 19			11 32
	d		10 35					10 50			11 05					11 20			11 35
Ewell West	d		10 38					10 53			11 08					11 23			11 38
Stoneleigh	d		10 40					10 55			11 10					11 25			11 40
Worcester Park	d		10 43					10 58			11 13					11 28			11 43
Chessington South	d				10 40								11 10						
Chessington North	d				10 42								11 12						
Tolworth	d				10 44								11 14						
Malden Manor	d				10 47								11 17						
Motspur Park	d		10 46		10 50			11 01			11 16		11 20			11 31			11 46
Raynes Park	d	10 43	10 49		10 53	10 58		11 04	11 10	11 13	11 19		11 23	11 28		11 34	11 40	11 43	11 49
Wimbledon ⊖	d	10 47	10 53	10 50	10 57	11 02	11 05	11 08	11 14	11 17	11 23	11 20	11 27	11 32	11 35	11 38	11 44	11 47	11 53
Earlsfield	d	10 50	10 57	10 54	11 01	11 05	11 08	11 12	11 17	11 20	11 27	11 24	11 31	11 35	11 38	11 42	11 47	11 50	11 57
Clapham Junction	d	10 54	11 01	10 58	11 05	11 09	11 12	11 16	11 21	11 24	11 31	11 28	11 35	11 39	11 42	11 46	11 51	11 54	12 01
Vauxhall ⊖	d	10 59	11 06	11 03	11 10	11 14	11 17	11 21	11 26	11 29	11 36	11 33	11 40	11 44	11 47	11 51	11 56	11 59	12 06
London Waterloo ⊖	a	11 04	11 10	11 07	11 15	11 19	11 22	11 25	11 31	11 34	11 40	11 37	11 45	11 49	11 52	11 55	12 01	12 04	12 10

		SW	SW	SW	SW	SW	SW	SW	SW	SW	SW	SW	SW	SW	SW	SW	SW	SW	SW	SW	SW
Guildford	d	11 05							11 28	11 35							11 58	12 05			
London Road (Guildford)	d	11 09							11 32	11 39							12 02	12 09			
Clandon	d	11 14							11 37	11 44							12 07	12 14			
Horsley	d	11 18							11 41	11 48							12 11	12 18			
Effingham Junction	d	11 21							11 46	11 51							12 16	12 21			
Bookham	d								11 49								12 19				
Cobham & Stoke d'Abernon	d	11 25								11 55								12 25			
Oxshott	d	11 28								11 58								12 28			
Claygate	d	11 31								12 01								12 31			
Hinchley Wood	d	11 34								12 04								12 34			
Hampton Court	d						11 54								12 24						
Thames Ditton	d						11 56								12 26						
Surbiton	d	11 42			11 57		12 02			12 12			12 27		12 32			12 42			12 57
Berrylands	d						12 04								12 34						
Shepperton	d							11 41								12 11					
Upper Halliford	d							11 44								12 14					
Sunbury	d							11 46								12 16					
Kempton Park	d							11 48								12 18					
Hampton	d							11 51								12 21					
Fulwell	d							11 54								12 24					
Strawberry Hill	d			11 37								12 07								12 37	
Teddington	d			11 41				11 59				12 11				12 29				12 41	
Hampton Wick	d			11 44				12 01				12 14				12 31				12 44	
Kingston	a			11 46				12 03				12 16				12 33				12 46	
	d			11 49				12 04				12 19				12 34				12 49	
Norbiton	d			11 51				12 06				12 21				12 36				12 51	
New Malden	d			11 55			12 07	12 10				12 25			12 37	12 40				12 55	
Dorking	d					11 35								12 05							
Box Hill & Westhumble	d																				
Leatherhead	d					11 41			11 54					12 11			12 24				
Ashtead	d					11 44			11 58					12 14			12 28				
Epsom	a					11 49			12 02					12 19			12 32				
	d					11 50			12 05					12 20			12 35				
Ewell West	d					11 53			12 08					12 23			12 38				
Stoneleigh	d					11 55			12 10					12 25			12 40				
Worcester Park	d					11 58			12 13					12 28			12 43				
Chessington South	d		11 40								12 10								12 40		
Chessington North	d		11 42								12 12								12 42		
Tolworth	d		11 44								12 14								12 44		
Malden Manor	d		11 47								12 17								12 47		
Motspur Park	d		11 50			12 01			12 16		12 20			12 31			12 46		12 50		
Raynes Park	d		11 53	11 58		12 04	12 10	12 13	12 19		12 23	12 28		12 34	12 40	12 43	12 49		12 53	12 58	
Wimbledon ⊖	d	11 50	11 57	12 02	12 05	12 08	12 14	12 17	12 23	12 20	12 27	12 32	12 35	12 38	12 44	12 47	12 53	12 50	12 57	13 02	13 05
Earlsfield	d	11 54	12 01	12 05	12 08	12 12	12 17	12 20	12 27	12 24	12 31	12 35	12 38	12 42	12 47	12 50	12 57	12 54	13 01	13 05	13 08
Clapham Junction	d	11 58	12 05	12 09	12 12	12 16	12 21	12 24	12 31	12 28	12 35	12 39	12 42	12 46	12 51	12 54	13 01	12 58	13 05	13 09	13 12
Vauxhall ⊖	d	12 03	12 10	12 14	12 17	12 21	12 26	12 29	12 36	12 33	12 40	12 44	12 47	12 51	12 56	12 59	13 06	13 03	13 10	13 14	13 17
London Waterloo ⊖	a	12 07	12 15	12 19	12 22	12 25	12 31	12 34	12 40	12 37	12 45	12 49	12 52	12 55	13 01	13 04	13 10	13 07	13 15	13 19	13 22

Saturdays
from 13 October

Hampton Court, Shepperton, Guildford, Dorking and Chessington South - London

Network Diagram - see first Page of Table 152

		SW	SW		SW	SW		SW	SW	SW	SW	SW	SW		SW	SW		SW	SW	SW	SW	SW	SW		SW
Guildford	d					12 28		12 35								12 58		13 05							
London Road (Guildford)	d					12 32		12 39								13 02		13 09							
Clandon	d					12 37		12 44								13 07		13 14							
Horsley	d					12 41		12 48								13 11		13 18							
Effingham Junction	d					12 46		12 51								13 16		13 21							
Bookham	d					12 49										13 19									
Cobham & Stoke d'Abernon	d							12 55										13 25							
Oxshott	d							12 58										13 28							
Claygate	d							13 01										13 31							
Hinchley Wood	d							13 04										13 34							
Hampton Court	d		12 54										13 24										13 54		
Thames Ditton	d		12 56										13 26										13 56		
Surbiton	d		13 02					13 12			13 27		13 32					13 42			13 57		14 02		
Berrylands	d		13 04										13 34										14 04		
Shepperton	d				12 41										13 11										13 41
Upper Halliford	d				12 44										13 14										13 44
Sunbury	d				12 46										13 16										13 46
Kempton Park	d				12 48										13 18										13 48
Hampton	d				12 51										13 21										13 51
Fulwell	d				12 54										13 24										13 54
Strawberry Hill	d									13 07										13 37					
Teddington	d				12 59					13 11					13 29					13 41					13 59
Hampton Wick	d				13 01					13 14					13 31					13 44					14 01
Kingston	a				13 03					13 16					13 33					13 46					14 03
	d				13 04					13 19					13 34					13 49					14 04
Norbiton	d				13 06					13 21					13 36					13 51					14 06
New Malden	d		13 07		13 10					13 25			13 37		13 40					13 55			14 07		14 10
Dorking	d	12 35										13 05										13 35			
Box Hill & Westhumble	d																								
Leatherhead	d	12 41				12 54						13 11				13 24						13 41			
Ashtead	d	12 44				12 58						13 14				13 28						13 44			
Epsom	a	12 49				13 02						13 19				13 32						13 49			
	d	12 50				13 05						13 20				13 35						13 50			
Ewell West	d	12 53				13 08						13 23				13 38						13 53			
Stoneleigh	d	12 55				13 10						13 25				13 40						13 55			
Worcester Park	d	12 58				13 13						13 28				13 43						13 58			
Chessington South	d								13 10										13 40						
Chessington North	d								13 12										13 42						
Tolworth	d								13 14										13 44						
Malden Manor	d								13 17										13 47						
Motspur Park	d	13 01				13 16			13 20			13 31				13 46			13 50			14 01			
Raynes Park	d	13 04	13 10		13 13	13 19			13 23	13 28		13 34	13 40		13 43	13 49			13 53	13 58		14 04	14 10		14 13
Wimbledon	d	13 08	13 14		13 17	13 23		13 20	13 27	13 32	13 35	13 38	13 44		13 47	13 53		13 50	13 57	14 02	14 05	14 08	14 14		14 17
Earlsfield	d	13 12	13 17		13 20	13 27		13 24	13 31	13 35	13 38	13 42	13 47		13 50	13 57		13 54	14 01	14 05	14 08	14 12	14 17		14 20
Clapham Junction	d	13 16	13 21		13 24	13 31		13 28	13 35	13 39	13 42	13 46	13 51		13 54	14 01		13 58	14 05	14 09	14 12	14 16	14 21		14 24
Vauxhall	d	13 21	13 26		13 29	13 36		13 33	13 40	13 44	13 47	13 51	13 56		13 59	14 06		14 03	14 10	14 14	14 17	14 21	14 26		14 29
London Waterloo	a	13 25	13 31		13 34	13 40		13 37	13 45	13 49	13 52	13 55	14 01		14 04	14 10		14 07	14 15	14 19	14 22	14 25	14 31		14 34

		SW		SW	SW	SW	SW	SW	SW		SW	SW		SW	SW	SW	SW	SW	SW		SW	SW		SW	SW
Guildford	d	13 28		13 35								13 58		14 05								14 28		14 35	
London Road (Guildford)	d	13 32		13 39								14 02		14 09								14 32		14 39	
Clandon	d	13 37		13 44								14 07		14 14								14 37		14 44	
Horsley	d	13 41		13 48								14 11		14 18								14 41		14 48	
Effingham Junction	d	13 46		13 51								14 16		14 21								14 46		14 51	
Bookham	d	13 49										14 19										14 49			
Cobham & Stoke d'Abernon	d			13 55										14 25										14 55	
Oxshott	d			13 58										14 28										14 58	
Claygate	d			14 01										14 31										15 01	
Hinchley Wood	d			14 04										14 34										15 04	
Hampton Court	d								14 24										14 54						
Thames Ditton	d								14 26										14 56						
Surbiton	d			14 12			14 27		14 32					14 42			14 57		15 02					15 12	
Berrylands	d								14 34										15 04						
Shepperton	d										14 11										14 41				
Upper Halliford	d										14 14										14 44				
Sunbury	d										14 16										14 46				
Kempton Park	d										14 18										14 48				
Hampton	d										14 21										14 51				
Fulwell	d										14 24										14 54				
Strawberry Hill	d					14 07										14 37									
Teddington	d					14 11					14 29					14 41					14 59				
Hampton Wick	d					14 14					14 31					14 44					15 01				
Kingston	a					14 16					14 33					14 46					15 03				
	d					14 19					14 34					14 49					15 04				
Norbiton	d					14 21					14 36					14 51					15 06				
New Malden	d					14 25			14 37		14 40					14 55			15 07		15 10				
Dorking	d							14 05										14 35							
Box Hill & Westhumble	d																								
Leatherhead	d	13 54						14 11				14 24						14 41				14 54			
Ashtead	d	13 58						14 14				14 28						14 44				14 58			
Epsom	a	14 02						14 19				14 32						14 49				15 02			
	d	14 05						14 20				14 35						14 50				15 05			
Ewell West	d	14 08						14 23				14 38						14 53				15 08			
Stoneleigh	d	14 10						14 25				14 40						14 55				15 10			
Worcester Park	d	14 13						14 28				14 43						14 58				15 13			
Chessington South	d				14 10										14 40										15 10
Chessington North	d				14 12										14 42										15 12
Tolworth	d				14 14										14 44										15 14
Malden Manor	d				14 17										14 47										15 17
Motspur Park	d	14 16			14 20			14 31				14 46			14 50			15 01				15 16			15 20
Raynes Park	d	14 19			14 23	14 28		14 34	14 40		14 43	14 49			14 53	14 58		15 04	15 10		15 13	15 19			15 23
Wimbledon	d	14 23		14 20	14 27	14 32	14 35	14 38	14 44		14 47	14 53		14 50	14 57	15 02	15 05	15 08	15 14		15 17	15 23		15 20	15 27
Earlsfield	d	14 27		14 24	14 31	14 35	14 38	14 42	14 47		14 50	14 57		14 54	15 01	15 05	15 08	15 12	15 17		15 20	15 27		15 24	15 31
Clapham Junction	d	14 31		14 28	14 35	14 39	14 42	14 46	14 51		14 54	15 01		14 58	15 05	15 09	15 12	15 16	15 21		15 24	15 31		15 28	15 35
Vauxhall	d	14 36		14 33	14 40	14 44	14 47	14 51	14 56		14 59	15 06		15 03	15 10	15 14	15 17	15 21	15 26		15 29	15 36		15 33	15 40
London Waterloo	a	14 40		14 37	14 45	14 49	14 52	14 55	15 01		15 04	15 10		15 07	15 15	15 19	15 22	15 25	15 31		15 34	15 40		15 37	15 45

Saturdays
from 13 October

Hampton Court, Shepperton, Guildford, Dorking and Chessington South - London

Network Diagram - see first Page of Table 152

		SW	SW	SW	SW		SW	SW		SW	SW	SW	SW	SW	SW		SW	SW		SW	SW	SW	SW	SW	SW
Guildford	d							14 58		15 05								15 28		15 35					
London Road (Guildford)	d							15 02		15 09								15 32		15 39					
Clandon	d							15 07		15 14								15 37		15 44					
Horsley	d							15 11		15 18								15 41		15 48					
Effingham Junction	d							15 16		15 21								15 46		15 51					
Bookham	d							15 19										15 49							
Cobham & Stoke d'Abernon	d									15 25										15 55					
Oxshott	d									15 28										15 58					
Claygate	d									15 31										16 01					
Hinchley Wood	d									15 34										16 04					
Hampton Court	d				15 24										15 54										16 24
Thames Ditton	d				15 26										15 56										16 26
Surbiton	d		15 27		15 32					15 42			15 57		16 02					16 12			16 27		16 32
Berrylands	d				15 34										16 04										16 34
Shepperton	d						15 11										15 41								
Upper Halliford	d						15 14										15 44								
Sunbury	d						15 16										15 46								
Kempton Park	d						15 18										15 48								
Hampton	d						15 21										15 51								
Fulwell	d						15 24										15 54								
Strawberry Hill	d	15 07										15 37										16 07			
Teddington	d	15 11					15 29					15 41					15 59					16 11			
Hampton Wick	d	15 14					15 31					15 44					16 01					16 14			
Kingston	a	15 16					15 33					15 46					16 03					16 16			
	d	15 19					15 34					15 49					16 04					16 19			
Norbiton	d	15 21					15 36					15 51					16 06					16 21			
New Malden	d	15 25			15 37		15 40					15 55			16 07		16 10					16 25			16 37
Dorking	d			15 05										15 35										16 05	
Box Hill & Westhumble	d																								
Leatherhead	d			15 11				15 24						15 41				15 54						16 11	
Ashtead	d			15 14				15 28						15 44				15 58						16 14	
Epsom	a			15 19				15 32						15 49				16 02						16 19	
	d			15 20				15 35						15 50				16 05						16 20	
Ewell West	d			15 23				15 38						15 53				16 08						16 23	
Stoneleigh	d			15 25				15 40						15 55				16 10						16 25	
Worcester Park	d			15 28				15 43						15 58				16 13						16 28	
Chessington South	d										15 40										16 10				
Chessington North	d										15 42										16 12				
Tolworth	d										15 44										16 14				
Malden Manor	d										15 47										16 17				
Motspur Park	d			15 31				15 46			15 50			16 01				16 16			16 20			16 31	
Raynes Park	d	15 28		15 34	15 40		15 43	15 49			15 53	15 58		16 04	16 10		16 13	16 19			16 23	16 28		16 34	16 40
Wimbledon	d	15 32	15 35	15 38	15 44		15 47	15 53		15 50	15 57	16 02	16 05	16 08	16 14		16 17	16 23		16 20	16 27	16 32	16 35	16 38	16 44
Earlsfield	d	15 35	15 38	15 42	15 47		15 50	15 57		15 54	16 01	16 05	16 08	16 12	16 17		16 20	16 27		16 24	16 31	16 35	16 38	16 42	16 47
Clapham Junction	d	15 39	15 42	15 46	15 51		15 54	16 01		15 58	16 05	16 09	16 12	16 16	16 21		16 24	16 31		16 28	16 35	16 39	16 42	16 46	16 51
Vauxhall	d	15 44	15 47	15 51	15 56		15 59	16 06		16 03	16 10	16 14	16 17	16 21	16 26		16 29	16 36		16 33	16 40	16 44	16 47	16 51	16 56
London Waterloo	a	15 49	15 52	15 55	16 01		16 04	16 10		16 07	16 15	16 19	16 22	16 25	16 31		16 34	16 40		16 37	16 45	16 49	16 52	16 55	17 01

			SW	SW		SW	SW	SW	SW	SW	SW		SW	SW		SW	SW	SW	SW	SW	SW		SW	SW	
Guildford	d			15 58		16 05								16 28		16 35								16 58	
London Road (Guildford)	d			16 02		16 09								16 32		16 39								17 02	
Clandon	d			16 07		16 14								16 37		16 44								17 07	
Horsley	d			16 11		16 18								16 41		16 48								17 11	
Effingham Junction	d			16 16		16 21								16 46		16 51								17 16	
Bookham	d			16 19										16 49										17 19	
Cobham & Stoke d'Abernon	d					16 25										16 55									
Oxshott	d					16 28										16 58									
Claygate	d					16 31										17 01									
Hinchley Wood	d					16 34										17 04									
Hampton Court	d										16 54										17 24				
Thames Ditton	d										16 56										17 26				
Surbiton	d					16 42			16 57		17 02					17 12			17 27		17 32				
Berrylands	d										17 04										17 34				
Shepperton	d		16 11										16 41										17 11		
Upper Halliford	d		16 14										16 44										17 14		
Sunbury	d		16 16										16 46										17 16		
Kempton Park	d		16 18										16 48										17 18		
Hampton	d		16 21										16 51										17 21		
Fulwell	d		16 24										16 54										17 24		
Strawberry Hill	d							16 37										17 07							
Teddington	d		16 29					16 41					16 59					17 11					17 29		
Hampton Wick	d		16 31					16 44					17 01					17 14					17 31		
Kingston	a		16 33					16 46					17 03					17 16					17 33		
	d		16 34					16 49					17 04					17 19					17 34		
Norbiton	d		16 36					16 51					17 06					17 21					17 36		
New Malden	d		16 40					16 55			17 07		17 10					17 25			17 37		17 40		
Dorking	d									16 35										17 05					
Box Hill & Westhumble	d																								
Leatherhead	d			16 24						16 41				16 54						17 11				17 24	
Ashtead	d			16 28						16 44				16 58						17 14				17 28	
Epsom	a			16 32						16 49				17 02						17 19				17 32	
	d			16 35						16 50				17 05						17 20				17 35	
Ewell West	d			16 38						16 53				17 08						17 23				17 38	
Stoneleigh	d			16 40						16 55				17 10						17 25				17 40	
Worcester Park	d			16 43						16 58				17 13						17 28				17 43	
Chessington South	d						16 40										17 10								
Chessington North	d						16 42										17 12								
Tolworth	d						16 44										17 14								
Malden Manor	d						16 47										17 17								
Motspur Park	d			16 46			16 50			17 01				17 16			17 20			17 31				17 46	
Raynes Park	d		16 43	16 49			16 53	16 58		17 04	17 10		17 13	17 19			17 23	17 28		17 34	17 40		17 43	17 49	
Wimbledon	d		16 47	16 53		16 50	16 57	17 02	17 05	17 08	17 14		17 17	17 23		17 20	17 27	17 32	17 35	17 38	17 44		17 47	17 53	
Earlsfield	d		16 50	16 57		16 54	17 01	17 05	17 08	17 12	17 17		17 20	17 27		17 24	17 31	17 35	17 38	17 42	17 47		17 50	17 57	
Clapham Junction	d		16 54	17 01		16 58	17 05	17 09	17 12	17 16	17 21		17 24	17 31		17 28	17 35	17 39	17 42	17 46	17 51		17 54	18 01	
Vauxhall	d		16 59	17 06		17 03	17 10	17 14	17 17	17 21	17 26		17 29	17 36		17 33	17 40	17 44	17 47	17 51	17 56		17 59	18 06	
London Waterloo	a		17 04	17 10		17 07	17 15	17 19	17 22	17 25	17 31		17 34	17 40		17 37	17 45	17 49	17 52	17 55	18 01		18 04	18 10	

Hampton Court, Shepperton, Guildford, Dorking and Chessington South - London

Network Diagram - see first Page of Table 152

		SW	SW	SW	SW	SW	SW	SW	SW	SW	SW	SW	SW	SW	SW	SW	SW	SW	SW	SW	SW
Guildford	d	17 05							17 28	17 35							17 58	18 05			
London Road (Guildford)	d	17 09							17 32	17 39							18 02	18 09			
Clandon	d	17 14							17 37	17 44							18 07	18 14			
Horsley	d	17 18							17 41	17 48							18 11	18 18			
Effingham Junction 6	d	17 21							17 46	17 51							18 16	18 21			
Bookham	d								17 49								18 19				
Cobham & Stoke d'Abernon	d	17 25								17 55								18 25			
Oxshott	d	17 28								17 58								18 28			
Claygate	d	17 31								18 01								18 31			
Hinchley Wood	d	17 34								18 04								18 34			
Hampton Court	d						17 54								18 24						
Thames Ditton	d						17 56								18 26						
Surbiton 6	d	17 42			17 57		18 02			18 12			18 27		18 32			18 42			18 57
Berrylands	d						18 04								18 34						
Shepperton	d							17 41								18 11					
Upper Halliford	d							17 44								18 14					
Sunbury	d							17 46								18 16					
Kempton Park	d							17 48								18 18					
Hampton	d							17 51								18 21					
Fulwell	d							17 54								18 24					
Strawberry Hill	d			17 37								18 07								18 37	
Teddington	d			17 41				17 59				18 11				18 29				18 41	
Hampton Wick	d			17 44				18 01				18 14				18 31				18 44	
Kingston	a			17 46				18 03				18 16				18 33				18 46	
	d			17 49				18 04				18 19				18 34				18 49	
Norbiton	d			17 51				18 06				18 21				18 36				18 51	
New Malden 6	d			17 55			18 07	18 10				18 25			18 37	18 40				18 55	
Dorking 4	d					17 35								18 05							
Box Hill & Westhumble	d																				
Leatherhead	d					17 41			17 54					18 11			18 24				
Ashtead	d					17 44			17 58					18 14			18 28				
Epsom 3	a					17 49			18 02					18 19			18 32				
	d					17 50			18 05					18 20			18 35				
Ewell West	d					17 53			18 08					18 23			18 38				
Stoneleigh	d					17 55			18 10					18 25			18 40				
Worcester Park	d					17 58			18 13					18 28			18 43				
Chessington South	d		17 40								18 10								18 40		
Chessington North	d		17 42								18 12								18 42		
Tolworth	d		17 44								18 14								18 44		
Malden Manor	d		17 47								18 17								18 47		
Motspur Park	d		17 50			18 01			18 16		18 20			18 31			18 46		18 50		
Raynes Park 6	d		17 53	17 58		18 04	18 10	18 13	18 19		18 23	18 28		18 34	18 40	18 43	18 49		18 53	18 58	
Wimbledon 6 ⊖	d	17 50	17 57	18 02	18 05	18 08	18 14	18 17	18 23	18 20	18 27	18 32	18 35	18 38	18 44	18 47	18 53	18 50	18 57	19 02	19 05
Earlsfield	d	17 54	18 01	18 05	18 08	18 12	18 17	18 20	18 27	18 24	18 31	18 35	18 38	18 42	18 47	18 50	18 57	18 54	19 01	19 05	19 08
Clapham Junction 10	d	17 58	18 05	18 09	18 12	18 16	18 21	18 24	18 31	18 28	18 35	18 39	18 42	18 46	18 51	18 54	19 01	18 58	19 05	19 09	19 12
Vauxhall ⊖	d	18 03	18 10	18 14	18 17	18 21	18 26	18 29	18 36	18 33	18 40	18 44	18 47	18 51	18 56	18 59	19 06	19 03	19 10	19 14	19 17
London Waterloo 15 ⊖	a	18 07	18 15	18 19	18 22	18 25	18 31	18 34	18 40	18 37	18 45	18 49	18 52	18 55	19 01	19 04	19 10	19 07	19 15	19 19	19 22

		SW	SW	SW	SW	SW	SW	SW	SW	SW	SW	SW	SW	SW	SW	SW	SW	SW	SW	SW
Guildford	d				18 28	18 35							18 58	19 05						
London Road (Guildford)	d				18 32	18 39							19 02	19 09						
Clandon	d				18 37	18 44							19 07	19 14						
Horsley	d				18 41	18 48							19 11	19 18						
Effingham Junction 6	d				18 46	18 51							19 16	19 21						
Bookham	d				18 49								19 19							
Cobham & Stoke d'Abernon	d					18 55								19 25						
Oxshott	d					18 58								19 28						
Claygate	d					19 01								19 31						
Hinchley Wood	d					19 04								19 34						
Hampton Court	d		18 54								19 24								19 54	
Thames Ditton	d		18 56								19 26								19 56	
Surbiton 6	d		19 02			19 12			19 27		19 32			19 42			19 57		20 02	
Berrylands	d		19 04								19 34								20 04	
Shepperton	d			18 41								19 11								19 41
Upper Halliford	d			18 44								19 14								19 44
Sunbury	d			18 46								19 16								19 46
Kempton Park	d			18 48								19 18								19 48
Hampton	d			18 51								19 21								19 51
Fulwell	d			18 54								19 24								19 54
Strawberry Hill	d							19 07								19 37				
Teddington	d			18 59				19 11				19 29				19 41				19 59
Hampton Wick	d			19 01				19 14				19 31				19 44				20 01
Kingston	a			19 03				19 16				19 33				19 46				20 03
	d			19 04				19 19				19 34				19 49				20 04
Norbiton	d			19 06				19 21				19 36				19 51				20 06
New Malden 6	d		19 07	19 10				19 25			19 37	19 40				19 55			20 07	20 10
Dorking 4	d	18 35								19 05								19 35		
Box Hill & Westhumble	d																			
Leatherhead	d	18 41			18 54					19 11			19 24					19 41		
Ashtead	d	18 44			18 58					19 14			19 28					19 44		
Epsom 3	a	18 49			19 02					19 19			19 32					19 49		
	d	18 50			19 05					19 20			19 35					19 50		
Ewell West	d	18 53			19 08					19 23			19 38					19 53		
Stoneleigh	d	18 55			19 10					19 25			19 40					19 55		
Worcester Park	d	18 58			19 13					19 28			19 43					19 58		
Chessington South	d						19 10								19 40					
Chessington North	d						19 12								19 42					
Tolworth	d						19 14								19 44					
Malden Manor	d						19 17								19 47					
Motspur Park	d	19 01			19 16		19 20			19 31			19 46		19 50			20 01		
Raynes Park 6	d	19 04	19 10	19 13	19 19		19 23	19 28		19 34	19 40	19 43	19 49		19 53	19 58		20 04	20 10	20 13
Wimbledon 6 ⊖	d	19 08	19 14	19 17	19 23	19 20	19 27	19 32	19 35	19 38	19 44	19 47	19 53	19 50	19 57	20 02	20 05	20 08	20 14	20 17
Earlsfield	d	19 12	19 17	19 20	19 27	19 24	19 31	19 35	19 38	19 42	19 47	19 50	19 57	19 54	20 01	20 05	20 08	20 12	20 17	20 20
Clapham Junction 10	d	19 16	19 21	19 24	19 31	19 28	19 35	19 39	19 42	19 46	19 51	19 54	20 01	19 58	20 05	20 09	20 12	20 16	20 21	20 24
Vauxhall ⊖	d	19 21	19 26	19 29	19 36	19 33	19 40	19 44	19 47	19 51	19 56	19 59	20 06	20 03	20 10	20 14	20 17	20 21	20 26	20 29
London Waterloo 15 ⊖	a	19 25	19 31	19 34	19 40	19 37	19 45	19 49	19 52	19 55	20 01	20 04	20 10	20 07	20 15	20 19	20 22	20 25	20 31	20 34

Table 152

Saturdays
from 13 October

Hampton Court, Shepperton, Guildford, Dorking and Chessington South - London

Network Diagram - see first Page of Table 152

		SW	SW	SW	SW	SW	SW	SW	SW	SW	SW	SW	SW	SW	SW	SW	SW	SW	SW	SW
Guildford	d	19 28	19 35							19 58	20 05							20 35		
London Road (Guildford)	d	19 32	19 39							20 02	20 09							20 39		
Clandon	d	19 37	19 44							20 07	20 14							20 44		
Horsley	d	19 41	19 48							20 11	20 18							20 48		
Effingham Junction 6	d	19 46	19 51							20 16	20 21							20 51		
Bookham	d	19 49								20 19										
Cobham & Stoke d'Abernon	d		19 55								20 25							20 55		
Oxshott	d		19 58								20 28							20 58		
Claygate	d		20 01								20 31							21 01		
Hinchley Wood	d		20 04								20 34							21 04		
Hampton Court	d							20 24								20 54				
Thames Ditton	d							20 26								20 56				
Surbiton 6	d		20 12			20 27		20 32			20 42			20 57		21 02		21 12		
Berrylands	d							20 34								21 04				
Shepperton	d								20 11								20 41			
Upper Halliford	d								20 14								20 44			
Sunbury	d								20 16								20 46			
Kempton Park	d								20 18								20 48			
Hampton	d								20 21								20 51			
Fulwell	d								20 24								20 54			
Strawberry Hill	d				20 07								20 37							
Teddington	d				20 11				20 29				20 41				20 59			
Hampton Wick	d				20 14				20 31				20 44				21 01			
Kingston	a				20 16				20 33				20 46				21 03			
	d				20 19				20 34				20 49				21 04			
Norbiton	d				20 21				20 36				20 51				21 06			
New Malden 6	d				20 25			20 37	20 40				20 55			21 07	21 10			
Dorking 4	d						20 05								20 35					
Box Hill & Westhumble	d																			
Leatherhead	d	19 54					20 11			20 24					20 41					
Ashtead	d	19 58					20 14			20 28					20 44					
Epsom 3	a	20 02					20 19			20 32					20 49					
	d	20 05					20 20			20 35					20 50				21 05	
Ewell West	d	20 08					20 23			20 38					20 53				21 08	
Stoneleigh	d	20 10					20 25			20 40					20 55				21 10	
Worcester Park	d	20 13					20 28			20 43					20 58				21 13	
Chessington South	d			20 10								20 40								21 10
Chessington North	d			20 12								20 42								21 12
Tolworth	d			20 14								20 44								21 14
Malden Manor	d			20 17								20 47								21 17
Motspur Park	d	20 16		20 20			20 31			20 46		20 50			21 01				21 16	21 20
Raynes Park 6	d	20 19		20 23	20 28		20 34	20 40	20 43	20 49		20 53	20 58		21 04	21 10	21 13		21 19	21 23
Wimbledon 6 ⊖	d	20 23	20 20	20 27	20 32	20 35	20 38	20 44	20 47	20 53	20 50	20 57	21 02	21 05	21 08	21 14	21 17	21 20	21 23	21 27
Earlsfield	d	20 27	20 24	20 31	20 35	20 38	20 42	20 47	20 50	20 57	20 54	21 01	21 05	21 08	21 12	21 17	21 20	21 24	21 27	21 31
Clapham Junction 10	d	20 31	20 28	20 35	20 39	20 42	20 46	20 51	20 54	21 01	20 58	21 05	21 09	21 12	21 16	21 21	21 24	21 28	21 31	21 35
Vauxhall ⊖	d	20 36	20 33	20 40	20 44	20 47	20 51	20 56	20 59	21 06	21 03	21 10	21 14	21 17	21 21	21 26	21 29	21 33	21 36	21 40
London Waterloo 15 ⊖	a	20 40	20 37	20 45	20 49	20 52	20 55	21 01	21 04	21 10	21 07	21 15	21 19	21 23	21 25	21 31	21 34	21 37	21 40	21 45

		SW	SW	SW	SW	SW	SW	SW	SW	SW	SW	SW	SW	SW	SW	SW	SW	SW	SW	SW
Guildford	d			20 46			21 05							21 35			21 46			22 05
London Road (Guildford)	d			20 50			21 09							21 39			21 50			22 09
Clandon	d			20 55			21 14							21 44			21 55			22 14
Horsley	d			20 59			21 18							21 48			21 59			22 18
Effingham Junction 6	d			21 03			21 21							21 51			22 03			22 21
Bookham	d			21 06													22 06			
Cobham & Stoke d'Abernon	d						21 25							21 55						22 25
Oxshott	d						21 28							21 58						22 28
Claygate	d						21 31							22 01						22 31
Hinchley Wood	d						21 34							22 04						22 34
Hampton Court	d				21 24													22 24		
Thames Ditton	d				21 26													22 26		
Surbiton 6	d		21 27		21 32		21 42				21 57			22 12		22 27		22 32		22 42
Berrylands	d				21 34													22 34		
Shepperton	d					21 11							21 41						22 11	
Upper Halliford	d					21 14							21 44						22 14	
Sunbury	d					21 16							21 46						22 16	
Kempton Park	d					21 18							21 48						22 18	
Hampton	d					21 21							21 51						22 21	
Fulwell	d					21 24							21 54						22 24	
Strawberry Hill	d	21 07								21 37					22 07					
Teddington	d	21 11				21 29				21 41			21 59		22 11				22 29	
Hampton Wick	d	21 14				21 31				21 44			22 01		22 14				22 31	
Kingston	a	21 16				21 33				21 46			22 03		22 16				22 33	
	d	21 19				21 34				21 49			22 04		22 19				22 34	
Norbiton	d	21 21				21 36				21 51			22 06		22 21				22 36	
New Malden 6	d	21 25			21 37	21 40				21 55			22 10		22 25			22 37	22 40	
Dorking 4	d											21 35								
Box Hill & Westhumble	d																			
Leatherhead	d			21 11								21 41					22 11			
Ashtead	d			21 14								21 44					22 14			
Epsom 3	a			21 19								21 49					22 19			
	d			21 20				21 35				21 50					22 20			
Ewell West	d			21 23				21 38				21 53					22 23			
Stoneleigh	d			21 25				21 40				21 55					22 25			
Worcester Park	d			21 28				21 43				21 58					22 28			
Chessington South	d								21 40											
Chessington North	d								21 42											
Tolworth	d								21 44											
Malden Manor	d								21 47											
Motspur Park	d			21 31				21 46	21 50			22 01					22 31			
Raynes Park 6	d	21 28		21 34	21 40	21 43		21 49	21 53	21 58		22 04	22 13		22 28		22 34	22 40	22 43	
Wimbledon 6 ⊖	d	21 32	21 35	21 38	21 44	21 47	21 50	21 53	21 57	22 02	22 05	22 08	22 17	22 20	22 32	22 35	22 38	22 44	22 47	22 50
Earlsfield	d	21 35	21 38	21 42	21 47	21 50	21 54	21 57	22 01	22 05	22 08	22 12	22 20	22 24	22 35	22 38	22 42	22 47	22 50	22 54
Clapham Junction 10	d	21 39	21 42	21 46	21 51	21 54	21 58	22 01	22 05	22 09	22 12	22 16	22 24	22 28	22 39	22 42	22 46	22 51	22 54	22 58
Vauxhall ⊖	d	21 44	21 47	21 51	21 56	21 59	22 03	22 06	22 10	22 14	22 17	22 21	22 29	22 33	22 44	22 47	22 51	22 56	22 59	23 03
London Waterloo 15 ⊖	a	21 49	21 52	21 55	22 01	22 04	22 07	22 10	22 15	22 19	22 22	22 25	22 34	22 39	22 49	22 52	22 55	23 01	23 04	23 07

Table 152

Saturdays
from 13 October

Hampton Court, Shepperton, Guildford, Dorking and Chessington South - London

Network Diagram - see first Page of Table 152

		SW	SW	SW	SW	SW	SW	SW	SW	SW	SW	SW	SW	SN	SW	SW
Guildford	d			22 20			22 35		22 46	22 55			23 08			
London Road (Guildford)	d						22 39		22 50				23 12			
Clandon	d						22 44		22 55				23 17			
Horsley	d						22 48		22 59				23 21			
Effingham Junction	d						22 51		23 03				23 24			
Bookham	d								23 06							
Cobham & Stoke d'Abernon	d						22 55						23 28			
Oxshott	d						22 58						23 31			
Claygate	d						23 01						23 34			
Hinchley Wood	d						23 04						23 37			
Hampton Court	d										23 24					
Thames Ditton	d										23 26					
Surbiton	d			22 57			23 12			23 30	23 33		23 42			
Berrylands	d										23 35					
Shepperton	d					22 41						23 11				
Upper Halliford	d					22 44						23 14				
Sunbury	d					22 46						23 16				
Kempton Park	d					22 48						23 18				
Hampton	d					22 51						23 21				
Fulwell	d					22 54						23 24				
Strawberry Hill	d		22 37					23 07								23 37
Teddington	d		22 41			22 59		23 11				23 29				23 41
Hampton Wick	d		22 44			23 01		23 14				23 31				23 44
Kingston	a		22 46			23 03		23 16				23 33				23 46
	d		22 49			23 04		23 19				23 34				23 49
Norbiton	d		22 51			23 06		23 21				23 36				23 51
New Malden	d		22 55			23 10		23 25			23 38	23 41				23 55
Dorking	d				22 35									23 30		
Box Hill & Westhumble	d															
Leatherhead	d				22 41				23 11					23 36		
Ashtead	d				22 44				23 14					23 39		
Epsom	a				22 49				23 19					23 45		
	d				22 50				23 20							
Ewell West	d				22 53				23 23							
Stoneleigh	d				22 55				23 25							
Worcester Park	d				22 58				23 28							
Chessington South	d	22 40													23 40	
Chessington North	d	22 42													23 42	
Tolworth	d	22 44													23 44	
Malden Manor	d	22 47													23 47	
Motspur Park	d	22 50			23 01				23 31						23 50	
Raynes Park	d	22 53	22 58		23 04	23 13		23 28	23 37		23 41	23 43			23 54	23 58
Wimbledon ⊖	d	22 57	23 02	23 05	23 08	23 17	23 20	23 32	23 41	23 37	23 46	23 49	23 52		23a57	00 02
Earlsfield	d	23 01	23 05	23 08	23 12	23 20	23 24	23 35	23 44	23 41	23 50	23 53	23 56			00 05
Clapham Junction	d	23 05	23 09	23 12	23 16	23 24	23 28	23 39	23 48	23 45	23 53	23 56	23 58			00 09
Vauxhall ⊖	d	23 10	23 14	23 17	23 21	23 29	23 33	23 44	23 53	23 50	23 58	00 01	00 04			00 15
London Waterloo ⊖	a	23 15	23 19	23 22	23 25	23 34	23 37	23 49	23 58	23 54	00 03	00 06	00 14			00 22

Table 152

Sundays
until 30 September

Hampton Court, Shepperton, Guildford, Dorking and Chessington South - London

Network Diagram - see first Page of Table 152

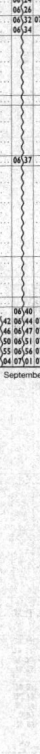

		SW	SW	SW	SW	SW	SW	SW	SW	SW A	SW B	SW	SW	SW	SW	SW	SW	SW	SW	SW
Guildford	d			23p08											06 57				07 27	
London Road (Guildford)	d			23p12																
Clandon	d			23p17																
Horsley	d			23p21																
Effingham Junction	d			23p24																
Bookham	d																			
Cobham & Stoke d'Abernon	d			23p28																
Oxshott	d			23p31																
Claygate	d			23p34																
Hinchley Wood	d			23p37																
Hampton Court	d	23p24									06 24							07 35		
Thames Ditton	d	23p26									06 26							07 37		
Surbiton	d	23p33		23p42							06 32	07 00			07 30			07 43	08 00	
Berrylands	d	23p35									06 34							07 45		
Shepperton	d		23p11														07 11			
Upper Halliford	d		23p14														07 14			
Sunbury	d		23p16														07 16			
Kempton Park	d		23p18														07 18			
Hampton	d		23p21														07 21			
Fulwell	d		23p24														07 24			
Strawberry Hill	d				23p37	00 07							06 49							
Teddington	d		23p29		23p41	00 11	00s56						06 55				07 29			
Hampton Wick	d		23p31		23p44	00 14	00s59						06 57				07 31			
Kingston	a		23p33		23p46	00 16	01 01						06 59				07 33			
	d		23p34		23p49								07 04				07 34			
Norbiton	d		23p36		23p51								07 06				07 36			
New Malden	d	23p38	23p41		23p55						06 37		07 10				07 40	07 48		
Dorking	d																			
Box Hill & Westhumble	d																			
Leatherhead	d																			
Ashtead	d																			
Epsom	a																			
	d															07 24				07 54
Ewell West	d															07 27				07 57
Stoneleigh	d															07 29				07 59
Worcester Park	d															07 32				08 02
Chessington South	d																			
Chessington North	d																			
Tolworth	d																			
Malden Manor	d																			
Motspur Park	d															07 35				08 05
Raynes Park	d	23p41	23p43		23p58						06 40		07 13			07 38	07 43	07 51		08 08
Wimbledon ⊖	d	23p46	23p49	23p52	00 02			05 31	06 12	06 42	06 44	07 08	07 19	07 31	07 38	07 42	07 47	07 55	08 08	08 12
Earlsfield	d	23p50	23p53	23p56	00 05					06 46	06 47	07 11	07 22	07 34	07 41	07 46	07 50	07 58	08 11	08 16
Clapham Junction	d	23p53	23p56	23p58	00 09			05 38	06 20	06 50	06 51	07 15	07 26	07 38	07 45	07 50	07 54	08 02	08 15	08 20
Vauxhall ⊖	d	23p58	00 01	00 04	00 15			05 43	06 25	06 55	06 56	07 20	07 31	07 43	07 50	07 55	07 59	08 07	08 20	08 25
London Waterloo ⊖	a	00 03	00 06	00 14	00 22			05 54	06 34	07 04	07 01	07 30	07 41	07 53	08 00	08 04	08 07	08 17	08 30	08 34

A until 22 July, 19 August, 26 August, 16 September, 23 September, 30 September

B 29 July, 5 August, 12 August, 2 September, 9 September

Hampton Court, Shepperton, Guildford, Dorking and Chessington South - London

Sundays until 30 September

Network Diagram - see first Page of Table 152

		SW	SW	SW	SW	SW	SW	SW	SW	SW	SW	SW	SW	SW	SW	SW	SW	SW	SW	SW	SW
		A	B	1																	
Guildford	d						07 50	07 57					08 20	08 27				08 50	08 57		
London Road (Guildford)	d						07 54						08 24					08 54			
Clandon	d						07 59						08 29					08 59			
Horsley	d						08 03						08 33					09 03			
Effingham Junction	d						08 06						08 36					09 06			
Bookham	d												08 39								
Cobham & Stoke d'Abernon	d						08 10											09 10			
Oxshott	d						08 13											09 13			
Claygate	d						08 16											09 16			
Hinchley Wood	d						08 19											09 19			
Hampton Court	d				08 05						08 35					09 05					
Thames Ditton	d				08 07						08 37					09 07					
Surbiton	d			08 10	08 13		08 24	08 30			08 43			09 00		09 13		09 24	09 30		
Berrylands	d				08 15						08 45					09 15					
Shepperton	d									08 11											09 11
Upper Halliford	d									08 14											09 14
Sunbury	d									08 16											09 16
Kempton Park	d									08 18											09 18
Hampton	d									08 21											09 21
Fulwell	d									08 24											09 24
Strawberry Hill	d	07 49	07 50												08 49						
Teddington	d	07 55	07 55							08 29					08 55						09 29
Hampton Wick	d	07 57	07 57							08 31					08 57						09 31
Kingston	a	07 59	07 59							08 33					08 59						09 33
	d	08 04	08 04							08 34					09 04						09 34
Norbiton	d	08 06	08 06							08 36					09 06						09 36
New Malden	d	08 10	08 10		08 18					08 40	08 48				09 10	09 18					09 40
Dorking	d																			09 08	
Box Hill & Westhumble	d																				
Leatherhead	d												08 45							09 15	
Ashtead	d												08 48							09 18	
Epsom	a												08 53							09 23	
	d								08 24				08 54							09 24	
Ewell West	d								08 27				08 57							09 27	
Stoneleigh	d								08 29				08 59							09 29	
Worcester Park	d								08 32				09 02							09 32	
Chessington South	d					08 10						08 40					09 10				
Chessington North	d					08 12						08 42					09 12				
Tolworth	d					08 14						08 44					09 14				
Malden Manor	d					08 17						08 47					09 17				
Motspur Park	d					08 20			08 35			08 50	09 05				09 20			09 35	
Raynes Park	d	08 13	08 13		08 21	08 24			08 38	08 43	08 51	08 54	09 08		09 13	09 21	09 24			09 38	09 43
Wimbledon	d	08 17	08 17	08 20	08 25	08 28	08a33	08 38	08 42	08 47	08 55	08 58	09 12	09 08	09 17	09 25	09 28	09a33	09 38	09 42	09 47
Earlsfield	d	08 20	08 20		08 28	08 31		08 41	08 46	08 50	08 58	09 01	09 16	09 11	09 20	09 28	09 31		09 41	09 46	09 50
Clapham Junction	d	08 24	08 24	08 28	08 34	08 37		08 45	08 50	08 54	09 02	09 09	09 20	09 15	09 24	09 33	09 36		09 45	09 50	09 54
Vauxhall	d	08 29	08 29		08 39	08 42		08 50	08 55	08 59	09 07	09 14	09 25	09 20	09 29	09 38	09 41		09 50	09 55	09 59
London Waterloo	a	08 39	08 39	08 41	08 47	08 50		09 00	09 04	09 07	09 17	09 20	09 34	09 30	09 39	09 47	09 50		10 00	10 04	10 07

A until 22 July, 19 August, 26 August, 16 September, 23 September, 30 September

B 29 July, 5 August, 12 August, 2 September, 9 September

Hampton Court, Shepperton, Guildford, Dorking and Chessington South - London

Sundays until 30 September

Network Diagram - see first Page of Table 152

		SW	SW	SW	SW	SW	SW	SW	SW	SW	SW	SW	SW	SW	SW	SW	SW	SW	SW	SW
Guildford	d			09 20	09 27				09 50	09 57					10 20	10 27				10 50
London Road (Guildford)	d			09 24					09 54						10 24					10 54
Clandon	d			09 29					09 59						10 29					10 59
Horsley	d			09 33					10 03						10 33					11 03
Effingham Junction	d			09 36					10 06						10 36					11 06
Bookham	d			09 39											10 39					
Cobham & Stoke d'Abernon	d								10 10											11 10
Oxshott	d								10 13											11 13
Claygate	d								10 16											11 16
Hinchley Wood	d								10 19											11 19
Hampton Court	d	09 35					10 05						10 35					11 05		
Thames Ditton	d	09 37					10 07						10 37					11 07		
Surbiton	d	09 43			10 00		10 13		10 24	10 30			10 43			11 00		11 13		11 24
Berrylands	d	09 45					10 15						10 45					11 15		
Shepperton	d											10 11								
Upper Halliford	d											10 14								
Sunbury	d											10 16								
Kempton Park	d											10 18								
Hampton	d											10 21								
Fulwell	d											10 24								
Strawberry Hill	d					09 49											10 49			
Teddington	d					09 55						10 29					10 55			
Hampton Wick	d					09 57						10 31					10 57			
Kingston	a					09 59						10 33					10 59			
	d					10 04						10 34					11 04			
Norbiton	d					10 06						10 36					11 06			
New Malden	d	09 48				10 10	10 18					10 40	10 48				11 10	11 18		
Dorking	d										10 08									
Box Hill & Westhumble	d																			
Leatherhead	d			09 45							10 15				10 45					
Ashtead	d			09 48							10 18				10 48					
Epsom	a			09 53							10 23				10 53					
	d			09 54							10 24				10 54					
Ewell West	d			09 57							10 27				10 57					
Stoneleigh	d			09 59							10 29				10 59					
Worcester Park	d			10 02							10 32				11 02					
Chessington South	d		09 40					10 10						10 40					11 10	
Chessington North	d		09 42					10 12						10 42					11 12	
Tolworth	d		09 44					10 14						10 44					11 14	
Malden Manor	d		09 47					10 17						10 47					11 17	
Motspur Park	d		09 50	10 05				10 20			10 35			10 50	11 05				11 20	
Raynes Park	d	09 51	09 54	10 08		10 13	10 21	10 24			10 38	10 43	10 51	10 54	11 08		11 13	11 21	11 24	
Wimbledon	d	09 55	09 58	10 12	10 08	10 17	10 25	10 28	10a33	10 38	10 42	10 47	10 55	10 58	11 12	11 08	11 17	11 25	11 28	11a33
Earlsfield	d	09 58	10 01	10 16	10 11	10 20	10 28	10 31		10 41	10 46	10 50	10 58	11 01	11 16	11 11	11 20	11 28	11 31	
Clapham Junction	d	10 06	10 09	10 20	10 15	10 24	10 32	10 36		10 45	10 50	10 54	11 02	11 05	11 20	11 15	11 24	11 32	11 35	
Vauxhall	d	10 11	10 14	10 25	10 20	10 32	10 37	10 41		10 50	10 55	10 59	11 07	11 13	11 25	11 20	11 32	11 37	11 40	
London Waterloo	a	10 17	10 20	10 34	10 30	10 39	10 45	10 50		11 00	11 04	11 07	11 17	11 20	11 34	11 30	11 39	11 47	11 50	

		SW	SW	SW	SW	SW	SW	SW	SW	SW	SW	SW	SW	SW	SW	SW	SW	SW	SW	SW	SW	SW
Guildford	d	10 57					11 20	11 27				11 50	11 57					12 20	12 27			
London Road (Guildford)	d						11 24					11 54						12 24				
Clandon	d						11 29					11 59						12 29				
Horsley	d						11 33					12 03						12 33				
Effingham Junction	d						11 36					12 06						12 36				
Bookham	d						11 39											12 39				
Cobham & Stoke d'Abernon	d											12 10										
Oxshott	d											12 13										
Claygate	d											12 16										
Hinchley Wood	d											12 19										
Hampton Court	d				11 35					12 05						12 35					13 05	
Thames Ditton	d				11 37					12 07						12 37					13 07	
Surbiton	d	11 30			11 43			12 00		12 13		12 24	12 30			12 43			13 00		13 13	
Berrylands	d				11 45					12 15						12 45					13 15	
Shepperton	d			11 11											12 11							
Upper Halliford	d			11 14											12 14							
Sunbury	d			11 16											12 16							
Kempton Park	d			11 18											12 18							
Hampton	d			11 21											12 21							
Fulwell	d			11 24											12 24							
Strawberry Hill	d								11 50											12 50		
Teddington	d			11 29					11 55						12 29					12 55		
Hampton Wick	d			11 31					11 57						12 31					12 57		
Kingston	a			11 33					11 59						12 33					12 59		
	d			11 34					12 04						12 34					13 04		
Norbiton	d			11 36					12 06						12 36					13 06		
New Malden	d			11 40	11 48				12 10	12 18					12 40	12 48				13 10	13 18	
Dorking	d		11 08											12 08								
Box Hill & Westhumble	d																					
Leatherhead	d		11 15				11 45							12 15				12 45				
Ashtead	d		11 18				11 48							12 18				12 48				
Epsom	a		11 23				11 53							12 23				12 53				
	d		11 24				11 54							12 24				12 54				
Ewell West	d		11 27				11 57							12 27				12 57				
Stoneleigh	d		11 29				11 59							12 29				12 59				
Worcester Park	d		11 32				12 02							12 32				13 02				
Chessington South	d					11 40					12 10						12 40					13 10
Chessington North	d					11 42					12 12						12 42					13 12
Tolworth	d					11 44					12 14						12 44					13 14
Malden Manor	d					11 47					12 17						12 47					13 17
Motspur Park	d		11 35			11 50	12 05				12 20			12 35			12 50	13 05				13 20
Raynes Park	d		11 38	11 43	11 51	11 54	12 08		12 13	12 21	12 24			12 38	12 43	12 51	12 54	13 08		13 13	13 21	13 24
Wimbledon	d	11 38	11 42	11 47	11 55	11 58	12 12	12 08	12 17	12 25	12 28	12 31	12 38	12 42	12 47	12 55	12 58	13 12	13 08	13 17	13 25	13 28
Earlsfield	d	11 41	11 46	11 50	11 58	12 01	12 16	12 11	12 20	12 28	12 31	12 35	12 41	12 46	12 50	12 58	13 01	13 16	13 11	13 20	13 28	13 31
Clapham Junction	d	11 45	11 50	11 54	12 02	12 05	12 20	12 15	12 24	12 32	12 35	12 39	12 45	12 50	12 54	13 02	13 05	13 20	13 15	13 24	13 32	13 35
Vauxhall	d	11 50	11 55	11 59	12 07	12 13	12 25	12 20	12 29	12 37	12 40	12 44	12 50	12 55	12 59	13 07	13 10	13 25	13 20	13 29	13 37	13 40
London Waterloo	a	12 00	12 04	12 07	12 17	12 22	12 34	12 30	12 39	12 47	12 50	12 53	13 00	13 04	13 07	13 17	13 20	13 34	13 30	13 39	13 47	13 50

Table 152

Sundays
until 30 September

Hampton Court, Shepperton, Guildford, Dorking and Chessington South - London

Network Diagram - see first Page of Table 152

		SW		SW		SW	SW	SW	SW	SW	SW	SW	SW	SW		SW	SW		SW	SW	SW	SW	SW	SW
Guildford	d	12 50		12 57							13 20	13 27					13 50		13 57					
London Road (Guildford)	d	12 54									13 24						13 54							
Clandon	d	12 59									13 29						13 59							
Horsley	d	13 03									13 33						14 03							
Effingham Junction 6	d	13 06									13 36						14 06							
Bookham	d										13 39													
Cobham & Stoke d'Abernon	d	13 10															14 10							
Oxshott	d	13 13															14 13							
Claygate	d	13 16															14 16							
Hinchley Wood	d	13 19															14 19							
Hampton Court	d								13 35					14 05										14 35
Thames Ditton	d								13 37					14 07										14 37
Surbiton 6	d	13 24		13 30					13 43			14 00		14 13			14 24		14 30					14 43
Berrylands	d								13 45					14 15										14 45
Shepperton	d							13 11														14 11		
Upper Halliford	d							13 14														14 14		
Sunbury	d							13 16														14 16		
Kempton Park	d							13 18														14 18		
Hampton	d							13 21														14 21		
Fulwell	d							13 24														14 24		
Strawberry Hill	d					13 19							13 49							14 19			14 30	
Teddington	d							13 29					13 55									14 29	14 33	
Hampton Wick	d							13 31					13 57									14 31	14 36	
Kingston	a							13 33					13 59									14 33	14 38	
	d							13 34					14 04									14 34		
Norbiton	d							13 36					14 06									14 36		
New Malden 6	d							13 40	13 48				14 10	14 18								14 40		14 48
Dorking 4	d						13 08														14 08			
Box Hill & Westhumble	d																							
Leatherhead	d						13 15				13 45										14 15			
Ashtead	d						13 18				13 48										14 18			
Epsom 3	a						13 23				13 53										14 23			
	d						13 24				13 54										14 24			
Ewell West	d						13 27				13 57										14 27			
Stoneleigh	d						13 29				13 59										14 29			
Worcester Park	d						13 32				14 02										14 32			
Chessington South	d									13 40						14 10								
Chessington North	d									13 42						14 12								
Tolworth	d									13 44						14 14								
Malden Manor	d									13 47						14 17								
Motspur Park	d						13 35			13 50	14 05					14 20					14 35			
Raynes Park 6	d						13 38	13 43	13 51	13 54	14 08		14 13	14 21		14 24					14 38	14 43		14 51
Wimbledon 6 ⊖ ⇌	d	13 31		13 38			13 42	13 47	13 55	13 58	14 12	14 08	14 17	14 25		14 28	14 31		14 38		14 42	14 47		14 55
Earlsfield	d	13 35		13 41			13 46	13 50	13 58	14 01	14 16	14 11	14 20	14 28		14 31	14 35		14 41		14 46	14 50		14 58
Clapham Junction 10	d	13 39		13 45			13 50	13 54	14 02	14 05	14 20	14 15	14 24	14 32		14 35	14 39		14 45		14 50	14 54		15 02
Vauxhall ⊖	d	13 44		13 50		13 52	13 55	13 59	14 07	14 10	14 25	14 20	14 29	14 37		14 40	14 44		14 50	14 52	14 55	14 59		15 07
London Waterloo 15 ⊖	a	13 53		14 00		14 00	14 04	14 07	14 17	14 20	14 34	14 30	14 34	14 42		14 45	14 48		14 55	15 00	14 59	15 04		15 12

		SW	SW	SW	SW	SW	SW	SW		SW		SW	SW	SW	SW	SW	SW	SW	SW	SW		SW	SW	SW
Guildford	d		14 20	14 27				14 50		14 57								15 20	15 27					15 50
London Road (Guildford)	d		14 24					14 54										15 24						15 54
Clandon	d		14 29					14 59										15 29						15 59
Horsley	d		14 33					15 03										15 33						16 03
Effingham Junction 6	d		14 36					15 06										15 36						16 06
Bookham	d		14 39															15 39						
Cobham & Stoke d'Abernon	d							15 10																16 10
Oxshott	d							15 13																16 13
Claygate	d							15 16																16 16
Hinchley Wood	d							15 19																16 19
Hampton Court	d					15 05										15 35						16 05		
Thames Ditton	d					15 07										15 37						16 07		
Surbiton 6	d			15 00		15 13		15 24		15 30						15 43			16 00			16 13		16 24
Berrylands	d					15 15										15 45						16 15		
Shepperton	d													15 11										
Upper Halliford	d													15 14										
Sunbury	d													15 16										
Kempton Park	d													15 18										
Hampton	d													15 21										
Fulwell	d													15 24										
Strawberry Hill	d				14 49							15 19			15 30					15 49				
Teddington	d				14 55									15 29	15 33					15 55				
Hampton Wick	d				14 57									15 31	15 36					15 57				
Kingston	a				14 59									15 33	15 38					15 59				
	d				15 04									15 34						16 04				
Norbiton	d				15 06									15 36						16 06				
New Malden 6	d				15 10	15 18								15 40		15 48				16 10		16 18		
Dorking 4	d												15 08											
Box Hill & Westhumble	d																							
Leatherhead	d		14 45										15 15					15 45						
Ashtead	d		14 48										15 18					15 48						
Epsom 3	a		14 53										15 23					15 53						
	d		14 54										15 24					15 54						
Ewell West	d		14 57										15 27					15 57						
Stoneleigh	d		14 59										15 29					15 59						
Worcester Park	d		15 02										15 32					16 02						
Chessington South	d	14 40					15 10										15 40						16 10	
Chessington North	d	14 42					15 12										15 42						16 12	
Tolworth	d	14 44					15 14										15 44						16 14	
Malden Manor	d	14 47					15 17										15 47						16 17	
Motspur Park	d	14 50	15 05				15 20						15 35				15 50	16 05					16 20	
Raynes Park 6	d	14 54	15 08		15 13	15 21	15 24						15 38	15 43		15 51	15 54	16 08		16 13		16 21	16 24	
Wimbledon 6 ⊖ ⇌	d	14 58	15 12	15 08	15 17	15 25	15 28	15 31		15 38			15 42	15 47		15 55	15 58	16 12	16 08	16 17		16 25	16 28	16 31
Earlsfield	d	15 01	15 16	15 11	15 20	15 28	15 31	15 35		15 41			15 46	15 50		15 58	16 01	16 16	16 11	16 20		16 28	16 31	16 35
Clapham Junction 10	d	15 05	15 20	15 15	15 24	15 32	15 35	15 39		15 45			15 50	15 54		16 02	16 05	16 20	16 15	16 24		16 32	16 35	16 39
Vauxhall ⊖	d	15 10	15 25	15 20	15 29	15 37	15 40	15 44		15 50		15 52	15 55	15 59		16 07	16 10	16 25	16 20	16 29		16 37	16 40	16 44
London Waterloo 15 ⊖	a	15 15	15 29	15 25	15 34	15 42	15 45	15 48		15 55		16 00	15 59	16 04		16 12	16 15	16 29	16 25	16 34		16 42	16 45	16 48

Table 152

Sundays
until 30 September

Hampton Court, Shepperton, Guildford, Dorking and Chessington South - London

Network Diagram - see first Page of Table 152

		SW	SW	SW	SW	SW		SW	SW	SW	SW	SW	SW	SW	SW			SW	SW	SW	SW	SW	SW	SW	SW
Guildford	d	15 57								16 20	16 27				16 50			16 57							17 20
London Road (Guildford)	d									16 24					16 54										17 24
Clandon	d									16 29					16 59										17 29
Horsley	d									16 33					17 03										17 33
Effingham Junction 6	d									16 36					17 06										17 36
Bookham	d									16 39															17 39
Cobham & Stoke d'Abernon	d														17 10										
Oxshott	d														17 13										
Claygate	d														17 16										
Hinchley Wood	d														17 19										
Hampton Court	d							16 35					17 05										17 35		
Thames Ditton	d							16 37					17 07										17 37		
Surbiton 6	d	16 30						16 43			17 00		17 13		17 24			17 30					17 43		
Berrylands	d							16 45					17 15										17 45		
Shepperton	d				16 11																17 11				
Upper Halliford	d				16 14																17 14				
Sunbury	d				16 16																17 16				
Kempton Park	d				16 18																17 18				
Hampton	d				16 21																17 21				
Fulwell	d				16 24																17 24				
Strawberry Hill	d		16 19			16 30						16 49							17 19			17 30			
Teddington	d				16 29	16 33						16 55									17 29	17 33			
Hampton Wick	d				16 31	16 36						16 57									17 31	17 36			
Kingston	a				16 33	16 38						16 59									17 33	17 38			
	d				16 34							17 04									17 34				
Norbiton	d				16 36							17 06									17 36				
New Malden 6	d				16 40			16 48				17 10	17 18								17 40		17 48		
Dorking 4	d			16 08																17 08					
Box Hill & Westhumble	d																								
Leatherhead	d			16 15						16 45										17 15					17 45
Ashtead	d			16 18						16 48										17 18					17 48
Epsom 3	a			16 23						16 53										17 23					17 53
	d			16 24						16 54										17 24					17 54
Ewell West	d			16 27						16 57										17 27					17 57
Stoneleigh	d			16 29						16 59										17 29					17 59
Worcester Park	d			16 32						17 02										17 32					18 02
Chessington South	d								16 40					17 10										17 40	
Chessington North	d								16 42					17 12										17 42	
Tolworth	d								16 44					17 14										17 44	
Malden Manor	d								16 47					17 17										17 47	
Motspur Park	d			16 35					16 50	17 05				17 20						17 35				17 50	18 05
Raynes Park 6	d			16 38	16 43			16 51	16 54	17 08		17 13	17 21	17 24						17 38	17 43		17 51	17 54	18 08
Wimbledon 6 ⊖ ⇌	d	16 38		16 42	16 47			16 55	16 58	17 12	17 08	17 17	17 25	17 28	17 31			17 38		17 42	17 47		17 55	17 58	18 12
Earlsfield	d	16 41		16 46	16 50			16 58	17 01	17 16	17 11	17 20	17 28	17 31	17 35			17 41		17 46	17 50		17 58	18 01	18 16
Clapham Junction 10	d	16 45		16 50	16 54			17 02	17 05	17 20	17 15	17 24	17 32	17 35	17 39			17 45		17 50	17 54		18 02	18 05	18 20
Vauxhall ⊖	d	16 50	16 52	16 55	16 59			17 07	17 10	17 25	17 20	17 29	17 37	17 40	17 44			17 50	17 52	17 55	17 59		18 07	18 10	18 25
London Waterloo 15 ⊖	a	16 55	17 00	16 59	17 04			17 12	17 15	17 29	17 25	17 34	17 42	17 45	17 48			17 55	18 00	17 59	18 04		18 12	18 15	18 29

		SW		SW	SW	SW	SW		SW	SW	SW	SW		SW	SW	SW	SW	SW	SW	SW	SW	SW			SW
Guildford	d	17 27					17 50		17 57								18 20	18 27				18 50			18 57
London Road (Guildford)	d						17 54										18 24					18 54			
Clandon	d						17 59										18 29					18 59			
Horsley	d						18 03										18 33					19 03			
Effingham Junction 6	d						18 06										18 36					19 06			
Bookham	d																18 39								
Cobham & Stoke d'Abernon	d						18 10															19 10			
Oxshott	d						18 13															19 13			
Claygate	d						18 16															19 16			
Hinchley Wood	d						18 19															19 19			
Hampton Court	d				18 05										18 35					19 05					
Thames Ditton	d				18 07										18 37					19 07					
Surbiton 6	d	18 00			18 13		18 24		18 30						18 43			19 00		19 13		19 24			19 30
Berrylands	d				18 15										18 45					19 15					
Shepperton	d											18 11													
Upper Halliford	d											18 14													
Sunbury	d											18 16													
Kempton Park	d											18 18													
Hampton	d											18 21													
Fulwell	d											18 24													
Strawberry Hill	d			17 49						18 19				18 30					18 49						
Teddington	d			17 55								18 29		18 33					18 55						
Hampton Wick	d			17 57								18 31		18 36					18 57						
Kingston	a			17 59								18 33		18 38					18 59						
	d			18 04								18 34							19 04						
Norbiton	d			18 06								18 36							19 06						
New Malden 6	d			18 10	18 18							18 40			18 48				19 10	19 18					
Dorking 4	d										18 08														
Box Hill & Westhumble	d																								
Leatherhead	d										18 15						18 45								
Ashtead	d										18 18						18 48								
Epsom 3	a										18 23						18 53								
	d										18 24						18 54								
Ewell West	d										18 27						18 57								
Stoneleigh	d										18 29						18 59								
Worcester Park	d										18 32						19 02								
Chessington South	d					18 10										18 40					19 10				
Chessington North	d					18 12										18 42					19 12				
Tolworth	d					18 14										18 44					19 14				
Malden Manor	d					18 17										18 47					19 17				
Motspur Park	d					18 20					18 35					18 50	19 05				19 20				
Raynes Park 6	d			18 13	18 21	18 24					18 38	18 43			18 51	18 54	19 08		19 13	19 21	19 24				
Wimbledon 6 ⊖ ⇌	d	18 08		18 17	18 25	18 28	18 31		18 38		18 42	18 47			18 55	18 58	19 12	19 08	19 17	19 25	19 28	19 31			19 38
Earlsfield	d	18 11		18 20	18 28	18 31	18 35		18 41		18 46	18 50			18 58	19 01	19 16	19 11	19 20	19 28	19 31	19 35			19 41
Clapham Junction 10	d	18 15		18 24	18 32	18 35	18 39		18 45		18 50	18 54			19 02	19 05	19 20	19 15	19 24	19 32	19 35	19 39			19 45
Vauxhall ⊖	d	18 20		18 29	18 37	18 40	18 44		18 50	18 52	18 55	18 59			19 07	19 10	19 25	19 20	19 29	19 37	19 40	19 44			19 50
London Waterloo 15 ⊖	a	18 25		18 34	18 42	18 45	18 48		18 55	19 00	18 59	19 04			19 12	19 15	19 29	19 25	19 34	19 42	19 45	19 48			19 55

Table 152

Sundays
until 30 September

Hampton Court, Shepperton, Guildford, Dorking and Chessington South - London

Network Diagram - see first Page of Table 152

		SW	SW	SW	SW	SW	SW	SW		SW	SW	SW	SW	SW		SW	SW	SW		SW	SW	SW	SW	SW	SW
Guildford	d							19 20		19 27				19 50		19 57							20 20	20 27	
London Road (Guildford)	d							19 24						19 54									20 24		
Clandon	d							19 29						19 59									20 29		
Horsley	d							19 33						20 03									20 33		
Effingham Junction 6	d							19 36						20 06									20 36		
Bookham	d							19 39															20 39		
Cobham & Stoke d'Abernon	d													20 10											
Oxshott	d													20 13											
Claygate	d													20 16											
Hinchley Wood	d													20 19											
Hampton Court	d					19 35						20 05										20 35			
Thames Ditton	d					19 37						20 07										20 37			
Surbiton 6	d					19 43				20 00		20 13		20 24		20 30						20 43		21 00	
Berrylands	d					19 45						20 15										20 45			
Shepperton	d			19 11																20 11					
Upper Halliford	d			19 14																20 14					
Sunbury	d			19 16																20 16					
Kempton Park	d			19 18																20 18					
Hampton	d			19 21																20 21					
Fulwell	d			19 24																20 24					
Strawberry Hill	d	19 19			19 30						19 49						20 19				20 30				20 49
Teddington	d			19 29	19 33						19 55									20 29	20 33				20 55
Hampton Wick	d			19 31	19 36						19 57									20 31	20 36				20 57
Kingston	a			19 33	19 38						19 59									20 33	20 38				20 59
	d			19 34							20 04									20 34					21 04
Norbiton	d			19 36							20 06									20 36					21 06
New Malden 6	d			19 40		19 48					20 10	20 18								20 40		20 48			21 10
Dorking 4	d		19 08															20 08							
Box Hill & Westhumble	d																								
Leatherhead	d		19 15					19 45										20 15					20 45		
Ashtead	d		19 18					19 48										20 18					20 48		
Epsom 3	a		19 23					19 53										20 23					20 53		
	d		19 24					19 54										20 24					20 54		
Ewell West	d		19 27					19 57										20 27					20 57		
Stoneleigh	d		19 29					19 59										20 29					20 59		
Worcester Park	d		19 32					20 02										20 32					21 02		
Chessington South	d						19 40						20 10												
Chessington North	d						19 42						20 12												
Tolworth	d						19 44						20 14												
Malden Manor	d						19 47						20 17												
Motspur Park	d		19 35				19 50	20 05					20 20					20 35					21 05		
Raynes Park 6	d		19 38	19 43		19 51	19 54	20 08			20 13	20 21	20 24					20 38		20 43		20 51	21 08		21 13
Wimbledon 6 ⊖	d		19 42	19 47		19 55	19 58	20 12		20 08	20 17	20 25	20 28	20 31		20 38		20 42		20 47		20 55	21 12	21 08	21 17
Earlsfield	d		19 46	19 50		19 58	20 01	20 16		20 11	20 20	20 28	20 31	20 35		20 41		20 46		20 50		20 58	21 16	21 11	21 20
Clapham Junction 10	d		19 50	19 54		20 02	20 05	20 20		20 15	20 24	20 32	20 35	20 39		20 45		20 50		20 54		21 02	21 20	21 15	21 24
Vauxhall ⊖	d	19 52	19 55	19 59		20 07	20 10	20 25		20 20	20 29	20 37	20 40	20 44		20 50	20 52	20 55		20 59		21 07	21 25	21 20	21 29
London Waterloo 15 ⊖	a	20 00	19 59	20 04		20 12	20 15	20 29		20 25	20 34	20 42	20 45	20 48		20 55	21 00	21 00		21 04		21 13	21 29	21 25	21 35

		SW	SW	SW			SW	SW	SW	SW	SW	SW	SW	SW		SW	SW	SW	SW		SW	SW	SW	SW	
Guildford	d			20 50			20 57						21 20	21 27					21 50		21 57				
London Road (Guildford)	d			20 54									21 24						21 54						
Clandon	d			20 59									21 29						21 59						
Horsley	d			21 03									21 33						22 03						
Effingham Junction 6	d			21 06									21 36						22 06						
Bookham	d												21 39												
Cobham & Stoke d'Abernon	d			21 10															22 10						
Oxshott	d			21 13															22 13						
Claygate	d			21 16															22 16						
Hinchley Wood	d			21 19															22 19						
Hampton Court	d	21 05										21 35					22 05								
Thames Ditton	d	21 07										21 37					22 07								
Surbiton 6	d	21 13		21 24			21 30					21 43		22 00			22 13		22 24		22 30				
Berrylands	d	21 15										21 45					22 15								
Shepperton	d									21 11														22 11	
Upper Halliford	d									21 14														22 14	
Sunbury	d									21 16														22 16	
Kempton Park	d									21 18														22 18	
Hampton	d									21 21														22 21	
Fulwell	d									21 24														22 24	
Strawberry Hill	d							21 19			21 30					21 49						22 19			
Teddington	d									21 29	21 33					21 55								22 29	
Hampton Wick	d									21 31	21 36					21 57								22 31	
Kingston	a									21 33	21 38					21 59								22 33	
	d									21 34						22 04								22 34	
Norbiton	d									21 36						22 06								22 36	
New Malden 6	d	21 18								21 40		21 48				22 10	22 18							22 40	
Dorking 4	d								21 08														22 08		
Box Hill & Westhumble	d																								
Leatherhead	d								21 15				21 45										22 15		
Ashtead	d								21 18				21 48										22 18		
Epsom 3	a								21 23				21 53										22 23		
	d								21 24				21 54										22 24		
Ewell West	d								21 27				21 57										22 27		
Stoneleigh	d								21 29				21 59										22 29		
Worcester Park	d								21 32				22 02										22 32		
Chessington South	d		21 10															22 10							
Chessington North	d		21 12															22 12							
Tolworth	d		21 14															22 14							
Malden Manor	d		21 17															22 17							
Motspur Park	d		21 20						21 35				22 05					22 20					22 35		
Raynes Park 6	d	21 21	21 24						21 38	21 43		21 51	22 08			22 13	22 21	22 24					22 38	22 43	
Wimbledon 6 ⊖	d	21 25	21 28	21 31			21 38		21 42	21 47		21 55	22 12	22 08		22 17	22 25	22 28	22 31		22 38		22 42	22 47	
Earlsfield	d	21 28	21 31	21 35			21 41		21 46	21 50		21 58	22 16	22 11		22 20	22 28	22 31	22 35		22 41		22 46	22 50	
Clapham Junction 10	d	21 32	21 35	21 39			21 45		21 50	21 54		22 02	22 20	22 15		22 24	22 32	22 35	22 39		22 45		22 50	22 54	
Vauxhall ⊖	d	21 37	21 40	21 44			21 50	21 52	21 55	21 59		22 07	22 25	22 20		22 29	22 37	22 40	22 44		22 50	22 52	22 55	22 59	
London Waterloo 15 ⊖	a	21 42	21 45	21 48			21 55	22 00	22 00	22 04		22 12	22 29	22 25		22 35	22 42	22 45	22 48		22 55	23 00	23 00	23 04	

Table 152

Sundays
until 30 September

Hampton Court, Shepperton, Guildford, Dorking and Chessington South - London

Network Diagram - see first Page of Table 152

		SW	SW	SW	SW	SW	SW	SW	SW	SW		SW	SW	SW	SW	SW	SW
Guildford	d	22 20	22 27					22 50	22 57								
London Road (Guildford)	d	22 24						22 54									
Clandon	d	22 29						22 59									
Horsley	d	22 33						23 03									
Effingham Junction 6	d	22 36						23 06									
Bookham	d	22 39															
Cobham & Stoke d'Abernon	d							23 10									
Oxshott	d							23 13									
Claygate	d							23 16									
Hinchley Wood	d							23 19									
Hampton Court	d					23 05										23 45	
Thames Ditton	d					23 07										23 47	
Surbiton 6	d		23 00			23 13		23 24	23 30							23 53	
Berrylands	d					23 15										23 55	
Shepperton	d												23 11				
Upper Halliford	d												23 14				
Sunbury	d												23 16				
Kempton Park	d												23 18				
Hampton	d												23 21				
Fulwell	d												23 24				
Strawberry Hill	d			22 30	22 49					23 19				23 30			23 48
Teddington	d			22 33	22 55								23 29	23 33			23 51
Hampton Wick	d			22 36	22 57								23 31	23 36			23 54
Kingston	a			22 38	22 59								23 33	23 38			23 56
	d				23 04								23 34				
Norbiton	d				23 06								23 36				
New Malden 6	d				23 10	23 18							23 40			23 58	
Dorking 4	d											23 08					
Box Hill & Westhumble	d																
Leatherhead	d	22 45										23 15					
Ashtead	d	22 48										23 18					
Epsom 3	a	22 53										23 23					
	d	22 54										23 24					
Ewell West	d	22 57										23 27					
Stoneleigh	d	22 59										23 29					
Worcester Park	d	23 02										23 32					
Chessington South	d						23 10								23 40		
Chessington North	d						23 12								23 42		
Tolworth	d						23 14								23 44		
Malden Manor	d						23 17								23 47		
Motspur Park	d	23 05					23 20					23 35			23 50		
Raynes Park 6	d	23 08			23 13	23 21	23 24					23 38	23 43		23 54	00 01	
Wimbledon 6 ⊖	d	23 12	23 08		23 17	23 25	23 28	23 31	23 38			23 42	23 47		23a59	00a04	
Earlsfield	d	23 16	23 11		23 20	23 28	23 31	23 35	23 41			23 46	23 50				
Clapham Junction 10	d	23 20	23 15		23 24	23 32	23 35	23 39	23 45			23 50	23 54				
Vauxhall ⊖	d	23 25	23 20		23 29	23 37	23 40	23 44	23 50	23 52		23 55	23 59				
London Waterloo 15 ⊖	a	23 29	23 25		23 35	23 42	23 45	23 48	23 55	23 59		23 59	00 04				

Table 152

Sundays from 7 October

Hampton Court, Shepperton, Guildford, Dorking and Chessington South - London

Network Diagram - see first Page of Table 152

		SW	SW	SW	SW	SW	SW	SW	SW	SW	SW	SW	SW	SW	SW	SW	SW	SW	SW	SW
Guildford	d			23p08										06 57				07 27		
London Road (Guildford)	d			23p12																
Clandon	d			23p17																
Horsley	d			23p21																
Effingham Junction	d			23p24																
Bookham	d																			
Cobham & Stoke d'Abernon	d			23p28																
Oxshott	d			23p31																
Claygate	d			23p34																
Hinchley Wood	d			23p37																
Hampton Court	d	23p24															07 35			
Thames Ditton	d	23p26															07 37			
Surbiton	d	23p33		23p42							07 00			07 30			07 43	08 00		
Berrylands	d	23p35															07 45			
Shepperton	d		23p11													07 11				
Upper Halliford	d		23p14													07 14				
Sunbury	d		23p16													07 16				
Kempton Park	d		23p18													07 18				
Hampton	d		23p21													07 21				
Fulwell	d		23p24													07 24				
Strawberry Hill	d				23p37	00 07						06 49								07 49
Teddington	d		23p29		23p41	00 11	00s56					06 55				07 29				07 55
Hampton Wick	d		23p31		23p44	00 14	00s59					06 57				07 31				07 57
Kingston	a		23p33		23p46	00 16	01 01					06 59				07 33				07 59
	d		23p34		23p49							07 04				07 34				08 04
Norbiton	d		23p36		23p51							07 06				07 36				08 06
New Malden	d	23p38	23p41		23p55							07 10				07 40	07 48			08 10
Dorking	d																			
Box Hill & Westhumble	d																			
Leatherhead	d																			
Ashtead	d																			
Epsom	a																			
	d														07 24				07 54	
Ewell West	d														07 27				07 57	
Stoneleigh	d														07 29				07 59	
Worcester Park	d														07 32				08 02	
Chessington South	d																			
Chessington North	d																			
Tolworth	d																			
Malden Manor	d																			
Motspur Park	d														07 35				08 05	
Raynes Park	d	23p41	23p43		23p58							07 13			07 38	07 43	07 51		08 08	08 13
Wimbledon	d	23p46	23p49	23p52	00 02			05 31	06 12	06 42	07 08	07 19	07 31	07 38	07 42	07 47	07 55	08 08	08 12	08 17
Earlsfield	d	23p50	23p53	23p56	00 05					06 46	07 11	07 22	07 34	07 41	07 46	07 50	07 58	08 11	08 16	08 20
Clapham Junction	d	23p53	23p56	23p58	00 09			05 38	06 20	06 50	07 15	07 26	07 38	07 45	07 50	07 54	08 02	08 15	08 20	08 24
Vauxhall	d	23p58	00 01	00 04	00 15			05 43	06 25	06 55	07 20	07 31	07 43	07 50	07 55	07 59	08 07	08 20	08 25	08 29
London Waterloo	a	00 03	00 06	00 14	00 22			05 54	06 34	07 04	07 30	07 41	07 53	08 00	08 04	08 07	08 17	08 30	08 34	08 39

		SW	SW	SW	SW	SW	SW	SW	SW	SW	SW	SW	SW	SW	SW	SW	SW	SW	SW	SW	SW
Guildford	d			07 48	07 57					08 18	08 27				08 48	08 57					09 18
London Road (Guildford)	d			07 52						08 22					08 52						09 22
Clandon	d			07 57						08 27					08 57						09 27
Horsley	d			08 01						08 31					09 01						09 31
Effingham Junction	d			08 04						08 34					09 04						09 34
Bookham	d									08 37											09 37
Cobham & Stoke d'Abernon	d			08 08											09 08						
Oxshott	d			08 11											09 11						
Claygate	d			08 14											09 14						
Hinchley Wood	d			08 17											09 17						
Hampton Court	d	08 05						08 35					09 05						09 35		
Thames Ditton	d	08 07						08 37					09 07						09 37		
Surbiton	d	08 13		08 24	08 30			08 43			09 00		09 13		09 24	09 30			09 43		
Berrylands	d	08 15						08 45					09 15						09 45		
Shepperton	d						08 11											09 11			
Upper Halliford	d						08 14											09 14			
Sunbury	d						08 16											09 16			
Kempton Park	d						08 18											09 18			
Hampton	d						08 21											09 21			
Fulwell	d						08 24											09 24			
Strawberry Hill	d											08 49									
Teddington	d						08 29					08 55						09 29			
Hampton Wick	d						08 31					08 57						09 31			
Kingston	a						08 33					08 59						09 33			
	d						08 34					09 04						09 34			
Norbiton	d						08 36					09 06						09 36			
New Malden	d	08 18					08 40	08 48				09 10	09 18					09 40	09 48		
Dorking	d																09 08				
Box Hill & Westhumble	d																				
Leatherhead	d									08 45							09 15				09 45
Ashtead	d									08 48							09 18				09 48
Epsom	a									08 53							09 23				09 53
	d					08 24				08 54							09 24				09 54
Ewell West	d					08 27				08 57							09 27				09 57
Stoneleigh	d					08 29				08 59							09 29				09 59
Worcester Park	d					08 32				09 02							09 32				10 02
Chessington South	d		08 10						08 40					09 10						09 40	
Chessington North	d		08 12						08 42					09 12						09 42	
Tolworth	d		08 14						08 44					09 14						09 44	
Malden Manor	d		08 17						08 47					09 17						09 47	
Motspur Park	d		08 20			08 35			08 50	09 05				09 20			09 35			09 50	10 05
Raynes Park	d	08 21	08 24			08 38	08 43	08 51	08 54	09 08		09 13	09 21	09 24			09 38	09 43	09 51	09 54	10 08
Wimbledon	d	08 25	08 28	08a33	08 38	08 42	08 47	08 55	08 58	09 12	09 08	09 17	09 25	09 28	09a33	09 38	09 42	09 47	09 55	09 58	10 12
Earlsfield	d	08 28	08 31		08 41	08 46	08 50	08 58	09 01	09 16	09 11	09 20	09 28	09 31		09 41	09 46	09 50	09 58	10 01	10 16
Clapham Junction	d	08 34	08 37		08 45	08 50	08 54	09 02	09 09	09 20	09 15	09 24	09 33	09 36		09 45	09 50	09 54	10 06	10 09	10 20
Vauxhall	d	08 39	08 42		08 50	08 55	08 59	09 07	09 14	09 25	09 20	09 29	09 38	09 41		09 50	09 55	09 59	10 11	10 14	10 25
London Waterloo	a	08 47	08 50		09 00	09 04	09 07	09 17	09 20	09 34	09 30	09 39	09 47	09 50		10 00	10 04	10 07	10 17	10 20	10 34

Table 152

Sundays from 7 October

Hampton Court, Shepperton, Guildford, Dorking and Chessington South - London

Network Diagram - see first Page of Table 152

		SW	SW	SW	SW	SW	SW	SW	SW	SW	SW	SW	SW	SW	SW	SW	SW	SW	SW	SW
Guildford	d	09 27				09 48	09 57					10 18	10 27				10 48	10 57		
London Road (Guildford)	d					09 52						10 22					10 52			
Clandon	d					09 57						10 27					10 57			
Horsley	d					10 01						10 31					11 01			
Effingham Junction	d					10 04						10 34					11 04			
Bookham	d											10 37								
Cobham & Stoke d'Abernon	d					10 08											11 08			
Oxshott	d					10 11											11 11			
Claygate	d					10 14											11 14			
Hinchley Wood	d					10 17											11 17			
Hampton Court	d			10 05						10 35					11 05					
Thames Ditton	d			10 07						10 37					11 07					
Surbiton	d	10 00		10 13		10 24	10 30			10 43			11 00		11 13		11 24	11 30		
Berrylands	d			10 15						10 45					11 15					
Shepperton	d								10 11											11 11
Upper Halliford	d								10 14											11 14
Sunbury	d								10 16											11 16
Kempton Park	d								10 18											11 18
Hampton	d								10 21											11 21
Fulwell	d								10 24											11 24
Strawberry Hill	d		09 49											10 49						
Teddington	d		09 55						10 29					10 55						11 29
Hampton Wick	d		09 57						10 31					10 57						11 31
Kingston	a		09 59						10 33					10 59						11 33
	d		10 04						10 34					11 04						11 34
Norbiton	d		10 06						10 36					11 06						11 36
New Malden	d		10 10	10 18					10 40	10 48				11 10	11 18					11 40
Dorking	d							10 08											11 08	
Box Hill & Westhumble	d																			
Leatherhead	d							10 15				10 45							11 15	
Ashtead	d							10 18				10 48							11 18	
Epsom	a							10 23				10 53							11 23	
	d							10 24				10 54							11 24	
Ewell West	d							10 27				10 57							11 27	
Stoneleigh	d							10 29				10 59							11 29	
Worcester Park	d							10 32				11 02							11 32	
Chessington South	d				10 10						10 40					11 10				
Chessington North	d				10 12						10 42					11 12				
Tolworth	d				10 14						10 44					11 14				
Malden Manor	d				10 17						10 47					11 17				
Motspur Park	d				10 20			10 35			10 50	11 05				11 20			11 35	
Raynes Park	d		10 13	10 21	10 24			10 38	10 43	10 51	10 54	11 08		11 13	11 21	11 24			11 38	11 43
Wimbledon	d	10 08	10 17	10 25	10 28	10a33	10 38	10 42	10 47	10 55	10 58	11 12	11 08	11 17	11 25	11 28	11a33	11 38	11 42	11 47
Earlsfield	d	10 11	10 20	10 28	10 31		10 41	10 46	10 50	10 58	11 01	11 16	11 11	11 20	11 28	11 31		11 41	11 46	11 50
Clapham Junction	d	10 15	10 24	10 32	10 36		10 45	10 50	10 54	11 02	11 05	11 20	11 15	11 24	11 32	11 35		11 45	11 50	11 54
Vauxhall	d	10 20	10 32	10 37	10 41		10 50	10 55	10 59	11 07	11 13	11 25	11 20	11 32	11 37	11 40		11 50	11 55	11 59
London Waterloo	a	10 30	10 39	10 45	10 50		11 00	11 04	11 07	11 17	11 20	11 34	11 30	11 39	11 47	11 50		12 00	12 04	12 07

		SW	SW	SW	SW	SW	SW	SW	SW	SW	SW	SW	SW	SW	SW	SW	SW	SW	SW	SW	SW
Guildford	d			11 18	11 27				11 48	11 57					12 18	12 27				12 48	12 57
London Road (Guildford)	d			11 22					11 52						12 22					12 52	
Clandon	d			11 27					11 57						12 27					12 57	
Horsley	d			11 31					12 01						12 31					13 01	
Effingham Junction	d			11 34					12 04						12 34					13 04	
Bookham	d			11 37											12 37						
Cobham & Stoke d'Abernon	d								12 08											13 08	
Oxshott	d								12 11											13 11	
Claygate	d								12 14											13 14	
Hinchley Wood	d								12 17											13 17	
Hampton Court	d	11 35					12 05						12 35					13 05			
Thames Ditton	d	11 37					12 07						12 37					13 07			
Surbiton	d	11 43			12 00		12 13		12 24	12 30			12 43			13 00		13 13		13 24	13 30
Berrylands	d	11 45					12 15						12 45					13 15			
Shepperton	d											12 11									
Upper Halliford	d											12 14									
Sunbury	d											12 16									
Kempton Park	d											12 18									
Hampton	d											12 21									
Fulwell	d											12 24									
Strawberry Hill	d					11 50											12 50				
Teddington	d					11 55						12 29					12 55				
Hampton Wick	d					11 57						12 31					12 57				
Kingston	a					11 59						12 33					12 59				
	d					12 04						12 34					13 04				
Norbiton	d					12 06						12 36					13 06				
New Malden	d	11 48				12 10	12 18					12 40	12 48				13 10	13 18			
Dorking	d										12 08										
Box Hill & Westhumble	d																				
Leatherhead	d			11 45							12 15				12 45						
Ashtead	d			11 48							12 18				12 48						
Epsom	a			11 53							12 23				12 53						
	d			11 54							12 24				12 54						
Ewell West	d			11 57							12 27				12 57						
Stoneleigh	d			11 59							12 29				12 59						
Worcester Park	d			12 02							12 32				13 02						
Chessington South	d		11 40					12 10						12 40					13 10		
Chessington North	d		11 42					12 12						12 42					13 12		
Tolworth	d		11 44					12 14						12 44					13 14		
Malden Manor	d		11 47					12 17						12 47					13 17		
Motspur Park	d		11 50	12 05				12 20			12 35			12 50	13 05				13 20		
Raynes Park	d	11 51	11 54	12 08		12 13	12 21	12 24			12 38	12 43	12 51	12 54	13 08		13 13	13 21	13 24		
Wimbledon	d	11 55	11 58	12 12	12 08	12 17	12 25	12 28	12 31	12 38	12 42	12 47	12 55	12 58	13 12	13 08	13 17	13 25	13 28	13 31	13 38
Earlsfield	d	11 58	12 01	12 16	12 11	12 20	12 28	12 31	12 35	12 41	12 46	12 50	12 58	13 01	13 16	13 11	13 20	13 28	13 31	13 35	13 41
Clapham Junction	d	12 02	12 05	12 20	12 15	12 24	12 32	12 35	12 39	12 45	12 50	12 54	13 02	13 05	13 20	13 15	13 24	13 32	13 35	13 39	13 45
Vauxhall	d	12 07	12 13	12 25	12 20	12 29	12 37	12 40	12 44	12 50	12 55	12 59	13 07	13 10	13 25	13 20	13 29	13 37	13 40	13 44	13 50
London Waterloo	a	12 17	12 22	12 34	12 30	12 39	12 47	12 50	12 53	13 00	13 04	13 07	13 17	13 20	13 34	13 30	13 39	13 47	13 50	13 53	14 00

Table 152

Sundays from 7 October

Hampton Court, Shepperton, Guildford, Dorking and Chessington South - London

Network Diagram - see first Page of Table 152

Station		SW	SW	SW	SW	SW	SW	SW	SW	SW	SW	SW	SW	SW	SW	SW	SW	SW	SW	SW	SW
Guildford	d						13 18	13 27				13 48	13 57							14 18	14 27
London Road (Guildford)	d						13 22					13 52								14 22	
Clandon	d						13 27					13 57								14 27	
Horsley	d						13 31					14 01								14 31	
Effingham Junction 6	d						13 34					14 04								14 34	
Bookham	d						13 37													14 37	
Cobham & Stoke d'Abernon	d											14 08									
Oxshott	d											14 11									
Claygate	d											14 14									
Hinchley Wood	d											14 17									
Hampton Court	d				13 35					14 05								14 35			
Thames Ditton	d				13 37					14 07								14 37			
Surbiton 6	d				13 43			14 00		14 13		14 24	14 30					14 43			15 00
Berrylands	d				13 45					14 15								14 45			
Shepperton	d			13 11												14 11					
Upper Halliford	d			13 14												14 14					
Sunbury	d			13 16												14 16					
Kempton Park	d			13 18												14 18					
Hampton	d			13 21												14 21					
Fulwell	d			13 24												14 24					
Strawberry Hill	d	13 19							13 49					14 19			14 30				
Teddington	d			13 29					13 55							14 29	14 33				
Hampton Wick	d			13 31					13 57							14 31	14 36				
Kingston	a			13 33					13 59							14 33	14 38				
	d			13 34					14 04							14 34					
Norbiton	d			13 36					14 06							14 36					
New Malden 6	d			13 40	13 48				14 10	14 18						14 40		14 48			
Dorking 4	d		13 08												14 08						
Box Hill & Westhumble	d																				
Leatherhead	d		13 15				13 45								14 15					14 45	
Ashtead	d		13 18				13 48								14 18					14 48	
Epsom 3	a		13 23				13 53								14 23					14 53	
	d		13 24				13 54								14 24					14 54	
Ewell West	d		13 27				13 57								14 27					14 57	
Stoneleigh	d		13 29				13 59								14 29					14 59	
Worcester Park	d		13 32				14 02								14 32					15 02	
Chessington South	d					13 40					14 10								14 40		
Chessington North	d					13 42					14 12								14 42		
Tolworth	d					13 44					14 14								14 44		
Malden Manor	d					13 47					14 17								14 47		
Motspur Park	d		13 35			13 50	14 05				14 20				14 35				14 50	15 05	
Raynes Park 6	d		13 38	13 43	13 51	13 54	14 08		14 13	14 21	14 24				14 38	14 43		14 51	14 54	15 08	
Wimbledon 6 ⊖	d		13 42	13 47	13 55	13 58	14 12	14 08	14 17	14 25	14 28	14 31	14 38		14 42	14 47		14 55	14 58	15 12	15 08
Earlsfield	d		13 46	13 50	13 58	14 01	14 16	14 11	14 20	14 28	14 31	14 35	14 41		14 46	14 50		14 58	15 01	15 16	15 11
Clapham Junction 10	d		13 50	13 54	14 02	14 05	14 20	14 15	14 24	14 32	14 35	14 39	14 45		14 50	14 54		15 02	15 05	15 20	15 15
Vauxhall ⊖	d	13 52	13 55	13 59	14 07	14 10	14 25	14 20	14 29	14 37	14 40	14 44	14 50	14 52	14 55	14 59		15 07	15 10	15 25	15 20
London Waterloo 15 ⊖	a	14 00	14 04	14 07	14 17	14 20	14 34	14 30	14 34	14 42	14 45	14 48	14 55	15 00	14 59	15 04		15 12	15 15	15 29	15 25

Station		SW	SW	SW	SW	SW	SW	SW	SW	SW	SW	SW	SW	SW	SW	SW	SW	SW	SW	SW	SW
Guildford	d				14 48	14 57							15 18	15 27				15 48	15 57		
London Road (Guildford)	d				14 52								15 22					15 52			
Clandon	d				14 57								15 27					15 57			
Horsley	d				15 01								15 31					16 01			
Effingham Junction 6	d				15 04								15 34					16 04			
Bookham	d												15 37								
Cobham & Stoke d'Abernon	d				15 08													16 08			
Oxshott	d				15 11													16 11			
Claygate	d				15 14													16 14			
Hinchley Wood	d				15 17													16 17			
Hampton Court	d		15 05								15 35					16 05					
Thames Ditton	d		15 07								15 37					16 07					
Surbiton 6	d		15 13		15 24	15 30					15 43			16 00		16 13		16 24	16 30		
Berrylands	d		15 15								15 45					16 15					
Shepperton	d								15 11												
Upper Halliford	d								15 14												
Sunbury	d								15 16												
Kempton Park	d								15 18												
Hampton	d								15 21												
Fulwell	d								15 24												
Strawberry Hill	d	14 49					15 19			15 30					15 49					16 19	
Teddington	d	14 55							15 29	15 33					15 55						
Hampton Wick	d	14 57							15 31	15 36					15 57						
Kingston	a	14 59							15 33	15 38					15 59						
	d	15 04							15 34						16 04						
Norbiton	d	15 06							15 36						16 06						
New Malden 6	d	15 10	15 18						15 40		15 48				16 10	16 18					
Dorking 4	d							15 08													16 08
Box Hill & Westhumble	d																				
Leatherhead	d							15 15					15 45								16 15
Ashtead	d							15 18					15 48								16 18
Epsom 3	a							15 23					15 53								16 23
	d							15 24					15 54								16 24
Ewell West	d							15 27					15 57								16 27
Stoneleigh	d							15 29					15 59								16 29
Worcester Park	d							15 32					16 02								16 32
Chessington South	d			15 10								15 40					16 10				
Chessington North	d			15 12								15 42					16 12				
Tolworth	d			15 14								15 44					16 14				
Malden Manor	d			15 17								15 47					16 17				
Motspur Park	d			15 20				15 35				15 50	16 05				16 20				16 35
Raynes Park 6	d	15 13	15 21	15 24				15 38	15 43		15 51	15 54	16 08		16 13	16 21	16 24				16 38
Wimbledon 6 ⊖	d	15 17	15 25	15 28	15 31	15 38		15 42	15 47		15 55	15 58	16 12	16 08	16 17	16 25	16 28	16 31	16 38		16 42
Earlsfield	d	15 20	15 28	15 31	15 35	15 41		15 46	15 50		15 58	16 01	16 16	16 11	16 20	16 28	16 31	16 35	16 41		16 46
Clapham Junction 10	d	15 24	15 32	15 35	15 39	15 45		15 50	15 54		16 02	16 05	16 20	16 15	16 24	16 32	16 35	16 39	16 45		16 50
Vauxhall ⊖	d	15 29	15 37	15 40	15 44	15 50	15 52	15 55	15 59		16 07	16 10	16 25	16 20	16 29	16 37	16 40	16 44	16 50	16 52	16 55
London Waterloo 15 ⊖	a	15 34	15 42	15 45	15 48	15 55	16 00	15 59	16 04		16 12	16 15	16 29	16 25	16 34	16 42	16 45	16 48	16 55	17 00	16 59

Table 152

Sundays from 7 October

Hampton Court, Shepperton, Guildford, Dorking and Chessington South - London

Network Diagram - see first Page of Table 152

Station		SW	SW	SW	SW	SW	SW	SW	SW	SW	SW	SW	SW	SW	SW	SW	SW	SW	SW	SW	SW	SW
Guildford	d					16 18	16 27				16 48	16 57							17 18	17 27		
London Road (Guildford)	d					16 22					16 52								17 22			
Clandon	d					16 27					16 57								17 27			
Horsley	d					16 31					17 01								17 31			
Effingham Junction 6	d					16 34					17 04								17 34			
Bookham	d					16 37													17 37			
Cobham & Stoke d'Abernon	d										17 08											
Oxshott	d										17 11											
Claygate	d										17 14											
Hinchley Wood	d										17 17											
Hampton Court	d			16 35					17 05								17 35					18 05
Thames Ditton	d			16 37					17 07								17 37					18 07
Surbiton 6	d			16 43			17 00		17 13		17 24	17 30					17 43			18 00		18 13
Berrylands	d			16 45					17 15								17 45					18 15
Shepperton	d	16 11													17 11							
Upper Halliford	d	16 14													17 14							
Sunbury	d	16 16													17 16							
Kempton Park	d	16 18													17 18							
Hampton	d	16 21													17 21							
Fulwell	d	16 24													17 24							
Strawberry Hill	d		16 30					16 49					17 19			17 30					17 49	
Teddington	d	16 29	16 33					16 55							17 29	17 33					17 55	
Hampton Wick	d	16 31	16 36					16 57							17 31	17 36					17 57	
Kingston	a	16 33	16 38					16 59							17 33	17 38					17 59	
	d	16 34						17 04							17 34						18 04	
Norbiton	d	16 36						17 06							17 36						18 06	
New Malden 6	d	16 40		16 48				17 10	17 18						17 40		17 48				18 10	18 18
Dorking 4	d													17 08								
Box Hill & Westhumble	d																					
Leatherhead	d					16 45								17 15					17 45			
Ashtead	d					16 48								17 18					17 48			
Epsom 3	a					16 53								17 23					17 53			
	d					16 54								17 24					17 54			
Ewell West	d					16 57								17 27					17 57			
Stoneleigh	d					16 59								17 29					17 59			
Worcester Park	d					17 02								17 32					18 02			
Chessington South	d				16 40					17 10								17 40				
Chessington North	d				16 42					17 12								17 42				
Tolworth	d				16 44					17 14								17 44				
Malden Manor	d				16 47					17 17								17 47				
Motspur Park	d				16 50	17 05				17 20				17 35				17 50	18 05			
Raynes Park 6	d	16 43		16 51	16 54	17 08		17 13	17 21	17 24				17 38	17 43		17 51	17 54	18 08		18 13	18 21
Wimbledon 6 ⊖	d	16 47		16 55	16 58	17 12	17 08	17 17	17 25	17 28	17 31	17 38		17 42	17 47		17 55	17 58	18 12	18 08	18 17	18 25
Earlsfield	d	16 50		16 58	17 01	17 16	17 11	17 20	17 28	17 31	17 35	17 41		17 46	17 50		17 58	18 01	18 16	18 11	18 20	18 28
Clapham Junction 10	d	16 54		17 02	17 05	17 20	17 15	17 24	17 32	17 35	17 39	17 45		17 50	17 54		18 02	18 05	18 20	18 15	18 24	18 32
Vauxhall ⊖	d	16 59		17 07	17 10	17 25	17 20	17 29	17 37	17 40	17 44	17 50	17 52	17 55	17 59		18 07	18 10	18 25	18 20	18 29	18 37
London Waterloo 15 ⊖	a	17 04		17 12	17 15	17 29	17 25	17 34	17 42	17 45	17 48	17 55	18 00	17 59	18 04		18 12	18 15	18 29	18 25	18 34	18 42

Station		SW	SW	SW	SW	SW	SW	SW	SW	SW	SW	SW	SW	SW	SW	SW	SW	SW	SW	SW
Guildford	d		17 48	17 57							18 18	18 27				18 48	18 57			
London Road (Guildford)	d		17 52								18 22					18 52				
Clandon	d		17 57								18 27					18 57				
Horsley	d		18 01								18 31					19 01				
Effingham Junction 6	d		18 04								18 34					19 04				
Bookham	d										18 37									
Cobham & Stoke d'Abernon	d		18 08													19 08				
Oxshott	d		18 11													19 11				
Claygate	d		18 14													19 14				
Hinchley Wood	d		18 17													19 17				
Hampton Court	d								18 35					19 05						
Thames Ditton	d								18 37					19 07						
Surbiton 6	d		18 24	18 30					18 43			19 00		19 13		19 24	19 30			
Berrylands	d								18 45					19 15						
Shepperton	d						18 11													19 11
Upper Halliford	d						18 14													19 14
Sunbury	d						18 16													19 16
Kempton Park	d						18 18													19 18
Hampton	d						18 21													19 21
Fulwell	d						18 24													19 24
Strawberry Hill	d				18 19			18 30					18 49					19 19		
Teddington	d						18 29	18 33					18 55							19 29
Hampton Wick	d						18 31	18 36					18 57							19 31
Kingston	a						18 33	18 38					18 59							19 33
	d						18 34						19 04							19 34
Norbiton	d						18 36						19 06							19 36
New Malden 6	d						18 40		18 48				19 10	19 18						19 40
Dorking 4	d					18 08													19 08	
Box Hill & Westhumble	d																			
Leatherhead	d					18 15					18 45								19 15	
Ashtead	d					18 18					18 48								19 18	
Epsom 3	a					18 23					18 53								19 23	
	d					18 24					18 54								19 24	
Ewell West	d					18 27					18 57								19 27	
Stoneleigh	d					18 29					18 59								19 29	
Worcester Park	d					18 32					19 02								19 32	
Chessington South	d	18 10								18 40					19 10					
Chessington North	d	18 12								18 42					19 12					
Tolworth	d	18 14								18 44					19 14					
Malden Manor	d	18 17								18 47					19 17					
Motspur Park	d	18 20				18 35				18 50	19 05				19 20				19 35	
Raynes Park 6	d	18 24				18 38	18 43		18 51	18 54	19 08		19 13	19 21	19 24				19 38	19 43
Wimbledon 6 ⊖	d	18 28	18 31	18 38		18 42	18 47		18 55	18 58	19 12	19 08	19 17	19 25	19 28	19 31	19 38		19 42	19 47
Earlsfield	d	18 31	18 35	18 41		18 46	18 50		18 58	19 01	19 16	19 11	19 20	19 28	19 31	19 35	19 41		19 46	19 50
Clapham Junction 10	d	18 35	18 39	18 45		18 50	18 54		19 02	19 05	19 20	19 15	19 24	19 32	19 35	19 39	19 45		19 50	19 54
Vauxhall ⊖	d	18 40	18 44	18 50	18 52	18 55	18 59		19 07	19 10	19 25	19 20	19 29	19 37	19 40	19 44	19 50	19 52	19 55	19 59
London Waterloo 15 ⊖	a	18 45	18 48	18 55	19 00	18 59	19 04		19 12	19 15	19 29	19 25	19 34	19 42	19 45	19 48	19 55	20 00	19 59	20 04

Table 152

Sundays
from 7 October

Hampton Court, Shepperton, Guildford, Dorking and Chessington South - London

Network Diagram - see first Page of Table 152

		SW	SW	SW	SW	SW	SW	SW		SW	SW		SW	SW	SW	SW	SW	SW		SW	SW	SW	SW	SW	SW
Guildford	d				19 18	19 27					19 48		19 57							20 18	20 27				20 48
London Road (Guildford)	d				19 22						19 52									20 22					20 52
Clandon	d				19 27						19 57									20 27					20 57
Horsley	d				19 31						20 01									20 31					21 01
Effingham Junction 6	d				19 34						20 04									20 34					21 04
Bookham	d				19 37															20 37					
Cobham & Stoke d'Abernon	d										20 08														21 08
Oxshott	d										20 11														21 11
Claygate	d										20 14														21 14
Hinchley Wood	d										20 17														21 17
Hampton Court	d		19 35					20 05										20 35					21 05		
Thames Ditton	d		19 37					20 07										20 37					21 07		
Surbiton 6	d		19 43			20 00		20 13			20 24		20 30					20 43			21 00		21 13		21 24
Berrylands	d		19 45					20 15										20 45					21 15		
Shepperton	d															20 11									
Upper Halliford	d															20 14									
Sunbury	d															20 16									
Kempton Park	d															20 18									
Hampton	d															20 21									
Fulwell	d															20 24									
Strawberry Hill	d	19 30					19 49							20 19			20 30					20 49			
Teddington	d	19 33					19 55									20 29	20 33					20 55			
Hampton Wick	d	19 36					19 57									20 31	20 36					20 57			
Kingston	a	19 38					19 59									20 33	20 38					20 59			
	d						20 04									20 34						21 04			
Norbiton	d						20 06									20 36						21 06			
New Malden 6	d		19 48				20 10	20 18								20 40		20 48				21 10	21 18		
Dorking 4	d														20 08										
Box Hill & Westhumble	d																								
Leatherhead	d				19 45										20 15					20 45					
Ashtead	d				19 48										20 18					20 48					
Epsom 3	a				19 53										20 23					20 53					
	d				19 54										20 24					20 54					
Ewell West	d				19 57										20 27					20 57					
Stoneleigh	d				19 59										20 29					20 59					
Worcester Park	d				20 02										20 32					21 02					
Chessington South	d			19 40						20 10														21 10	
Chessington North	d			19 42						20 12														21 12	
Tolworth	d			19 44						20 14														21 14	
Malden Manor	d			19 47						20 17														21 17	
Motspur Park	d			19 50	20 05					20 20					20 35					21 05				21 20	
Raynes Park 6	d		19 51	19 54	20 08		20 13	20 21		20 24					20 38	20 43		20 51		21 08		21 13	21 21	21 24	
Wimbledon 8 ⊖	d		19 55	19 58	20 12	20 08	20 17	20 25		20 28	20 31		20 38		20 42	20 47		20 55		21 12	21 08	21 17	21 25	21 28	21 31
Earlsfield	d		19 58	20 01	20 16	20 11	20 20	20 28		20 31	20 35		20 41		20 46	20 50		20 58		21 16	21 11	21 20	21 28	21 31	21 35
Clapham Junction 10	d		20 02	20 05	20 20	20 15	20 24	20 32		20 35	20 39		20 45		20 50	20 54		21 02		21 20	21 15	21 24	21 32	21 35	21 39
Vauxhall ⊖	d		20 07	20 10	20 25	20 20	20 29	20 37		20 40	20 44		20 50	20 52	20 55	20 59		21 07		21 25	21 20	21 29	21 37	21 40	21 44
London Waterloo 15 ⊖	a		20 12	20 15	20 29	20 25	20 34	20 42		20 45	20 48		20 55	21 00	21 00	21 04		21 13		21 29	21 25	21 35	21 42	21 45	21 48

			SW	SW		SW	SW	SW	SW	SW	SW	SW	SW	SW		SW		SW	SW	SW	SW	SW	SW	SW	
Guildford	d		20 57							21 18	21 27					21 48		21 57					22 20	22 27	
London Road (Guildford)	d									21 22						21 52							22 24		
Clandon	d									21 27						21 57							22 29		
Horsley	d									21 31						22 01							22 33		
Effingham Junction 6	d									21 34						22 04							22 36		
Bookham	d									21 37													22 39		
Cobham & Stoke d'Abernon	d															22 08									
Oxshott	d															22 11									
Claygate	d															22 14									
Hinchley Wood	d															22 17									
Hampton Court	d								21 35				22 05												
Thames Ditton	d								21 37				22 07												
Surbiton 6	d		21 30						21 43		22 00		22 13			22 24		22 30						23 00	
Berrylands	d								21 45				22 15												
Shepperton	d						21 11														22 11				
Upper Halliford	d						21 14														22 14				
Sunbury	d						21 16														22 16				
Kempton Park	d						21 18														22 18				
Hampton	d						21 21														22 21				
Fulwell	d						21 24														22 24				
Strawberry Hill	d			21 19				21 30				21 49							22 19					22 30	
Teddington	d						21 29	21 33				21 55									22 29			22 33	
Hampton Wick	d						21 31	21 36				21 57									22 31			22 36	
Kingston	a						21 33	21 38				21 59									22 33			22 38	
	d						21 34					22 04									22 34				
Norbiton	d						21 36					22 06									22 36				
New Malden 6	d						21 40		21 48			22 10	22 18								22 40				
Dorking 4	d					21 08														22 08					
Box Hill & Westhumble	d																								
Leatherhead	d					21 15				21 45										22 15		22 45			
Ashtead	d					21 18				21 48										22 18		22 48			
Epsom 3	a					21 23				21 53										22 23		22 53			
	d					21 24				21 54										22 24		22 54			
Ewell West	d					21 27				21 57										22 27		22 57			
Stoneleigh	d					21 29				21 59										22 29		22 59			
Worcester Park	d					21 32				22 02										22 32		23 02			
Chessington South	d													22 10											
Chessington North	d													22 12											
Tolworth	d													22 14											
Malden Manor	d													22 17											
Motspur Park	d					21 35				22 05				22 20						22 35		23 05			
Raynes Park 6	d					21 38	21 43		21 51	22 08		22 13	22 21	22 24						22 38	22 43	23 08			
Wimbledon 8 ⊖	d		21 38			21 42	21 47		21 55	22 12	22 08	22 17	22 25	22 28		22 31		22 38		22 42	22 47	23 12	23 08		
Earlsfield	d		21 41			21 46	21 50		21 58	22 16	22 11	22 20	22 28	22 31		22 35		22 41		22 46	22 50	23 16	23 11		
Clapham Junction 10	d		21 45			21 50	21 54		22 02	22 20	22 15	22 24	22 32	22 35		22 39		22 45		22 50	22 54	23 20	23 15		
Vauxhall ⊖	d		21 50	21 52		21 55	21 59		22 07	22 25	22 20	22 29	22 37	22 40		22 44		22 50	22 52	22 55	22 59	23 25	23 20		
London Waterloo 15 ⊖	a		21 55	22 00		22 00	22 04		22 12	22 29	22 25	22 35	22 42	22 45		22 48		22 55	23 00	23 00	23 04	23 29	23 25		

Table 152

Sundays
from 7 October

Hampton Court, Shepperton, Guildford, Dorking and Chessington South - London

Network Diagram - see first Page of Table 152

		SW	SW	SW	SW	SW	SW	SW	SW	SW		SW	SW	SW
Guildford	d				22 50	22 57								
London Road (Guildford)	d				22 54									
Clandon	d				22 59									
Horsley	d				23 03									
Effingham Junction 6	d				23 06									
Bookham	d													
Cobham & Stoke d'Abernon	d				23 10									
Oxshott	d				23 13									
Claygate	d				23 16									
Hinchley Wood	d				23 19									
Hampton Court	d		23 05										23 45	
Thames Ditton	d		23 07										23 47	
Surbiton 6	d		23 13		23 24	23 30							23 53	
Berrylands	d		23 15										23 55	
Shepperton	d								23 11					
Upper Halliford	d								23 14					
Sunbury	d								23 16					
Kempton Park	d								23 18					
Hampton	d								23 21					
Fulwell	d								23 24					
Strawberry Hill	d	22 49					23 19			23 30				23 48
Teddington	d	22 55							23 29	23 33				23 51
Hampton Wick	d	22 57							23 31	23 36				23 54
Kingston	a	22 59							23 33	23 38				23 56
	d	23 04							23 34					
Norbiton	d	23 06							23 36					
New Malden 6	d	23 10	23 18						23 40				23 58	
Dorking 4	d							23 08						
Box Hill & Westhumble	d													
Leatherhead	d							23 15						
Ashtead	d							23 18						
Epsom 3	a							23 23						
	d							23 24						
Ewell West	d							23 27						
Stoneleigh	d							23 29						
Worcester Park	d							23 32						
Chessington South	d			23 10								23 40		
Chessington North	d			23 12								23 42		
Tolworth	d			23 14								23 44		
Malden Manor	d			23 17								23 47		
Motspur Park	d			23 20				23 35				23 50		
Raynes Park 6	d	23 13	23 21	23 24				23 38	23 43			23 54	00 01	
Wimbledon 8 ⊖	d	23 17	23 25	23 28	23 31	23 38		23 42	23 47			23a59	00a04	
Earlsfield	d	23 20	23 28	23 31	23 35	23 41		23 46	23 50					
Clapham Junction 10	d	23 24	23 32	23 35	23 39	23 45		23 50	23 54					
Vauxhall ⊖	d	23 29	23 37	23 40	23 44	23 50	23 52	23 55	23 59					
London Waterloo 15 ⊖	a	23 35	23 42	23 45	23 48	23 55	23 59	23 59	00 04					

Network Diagram for Tables 155, 156, 157

DM-16/11
Design BAJS

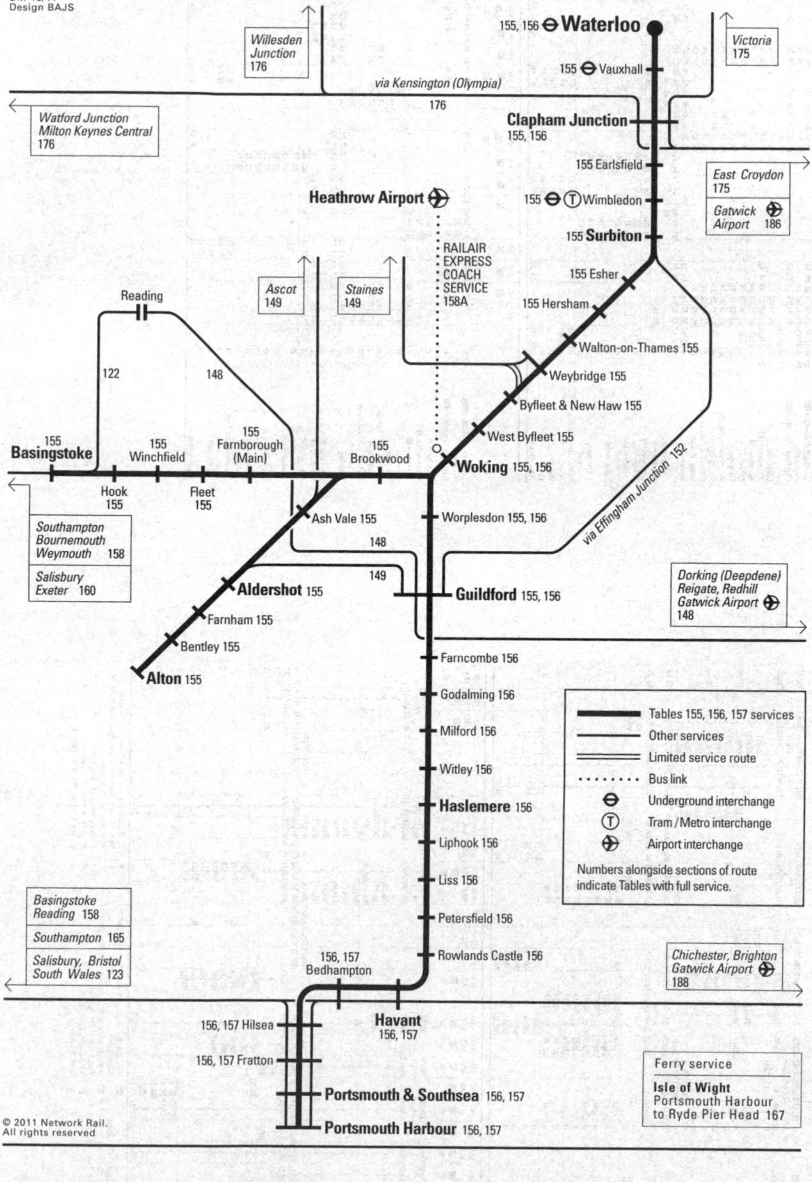

Table 155

Mondays to Fridays

until 5 October

London - Woking, Guildford, Alton and Basingstoke

Network Diagram - see first Page of Table 155

Miles	Miles	Miles			SW MO ■ A	SW MO A	SW MX	SW MX ■	SW MO ■ A		SW MO A	SW MX ■	SW MX		SW MX ■	SW MO ■ B	SW MX ■	SW MO A	SW MX	SW MO ■ B	SW MX ■ C	SW MO ■ A	SW MX ■ C		SW MX ■
0	—	—	**London Waterloo** 15 ⊖	d	22p37	22p50	22p52	22p53	23p07		23p10	23p12	23p20		23p23	23p30	23p35			23p35	23p40	23p40	23p45		23p48
1¼	—	—	Vauxhall ⊖	d		22p54	22p56				23p14		23p24									23p44			
4	—	—	Clapham Junction 10	d	22p46			23b00	23p15		23p19		23p29		23b30	23b39	23b42			23b44	23b47	23p49	23b52		23b55
—	—	—		d		23p00	23p02					23b19													
5½	—	—	Earlsfield	d							23p22		23p32									23p52			
7¼	—	—	Wimbledon 6 ⊖	d	22p53				23p22		23p26		23p36						←			23p56			
12	—	—	**Surbiton** 6	d	23p02			23p11	23p30		23p35	23p38	23p44		23p41				23p44			00 05			00 09
14½	—	—	Esher	d							23p39		→						23p48			00 09			
16	—	—	Hersham	d							23p42								23p51			00 12			
17	—	—	Walton-on-Thames	d	23p09						23p45	23p45							23p54			00 15			00 16
19	—	—	Weybridge	d	23p13						23p49	23p49							23p57			00 19			00 20
20½	—	—	Byfleet & New Haw	d		00 02	00 06				23p51								00 01			00 21			
21¾	—	—	West Byfleet	d		00 05	00 09	23p21			23p54				23p55			←	00 03			00 24			
24½	0	—	**Woking**	a	23p19	00 11	00 15	23p29	23p42		23p59	23p55			23p59	00 01	00 01	23p59	00 08	00 07	00 06	00 30	00 11		00 26
—	—	—		d	23p26			23p30	23p46	23p49	00 05	23p57			00 01	00 03	00 03	00 05		00 08	00 08	00 35	00 13		00 28
—	2½	—	Worplesdon	d							→											→	00 18		→
—	6	—	**Guildford**	a												00 10		00 13					00 24		
28	—	0	Brookwood	d	23p32			23p36	23p51	23p55		00 03			00 07										
—	—	4½	Ash Vale	d	23p40			23p44		00 03					00 15										
—	—	7	**Aldershot**	a	23p45			23p49		00 07					00 19										
—	—	—		d	23p48			23p50		00 08					00 20										
—	—	10	Farnham	a	23p54			23p55		00 13					00 25										
—	—	—		d	23p55			23p58		00 14					00 26										
—	—	14	Bentley	d				00 04		00 24					00 33										
—	—	18¾	**Alton**	a	00 07			00 11		00 31					00 40										
33¼	—	—	Farnborough (Main)	d					23p59			00 10					00 14			00 18					
36½	—	—	Fleet	d					00 04			00 16					00 20			00 24					
40	—	—	Winchfield	d					00 10			00 21													
42¼	—	—	Hook	d					00 14			00 26													
47¾	—	—	**Basingstoke**	a					00 21			00 33					00 33			00 39	00 27				

		SW ■ D	SW MX ■ E	SW ■ D	SW ■ D	SW MX ■	SW MX ■ E	SW MO ■ A	SW MX ■ C		SW MX ■ C	SW F	SW MO G	SW H	SW MX	SW MX ■ E	SW MX	SW MX E	SW ■ I		SW J	SW K	SW MO ■	SW MX ■ E	SW MX E
London Waterloo 15 ⊖	d	23p50	23p55		23p55		00 05		00 05						00 09	00 20		00 27	00 30				00 50	00 50	
Vauxhall ⊖	d														00 13			00 31							
Clapham Junction 10	d	23b59	00u02		00u04		00u12		00u12						00 20	00u27		00 37	00u37				00 57	00u57	
	d																								
Earlsfield	d														00 23			00s41							
Wimbledon 6 ⊖	d								00u18						00 27			00 45	00u43						
Surbiton 6	d														00 35	00 38		00 57							
Esher	d														00s39			01s01							
Hersham	d														00s42			01s04							
Walton-on-Thames	d														00s44			01s06							
Weybridge	d														00s48			01s10							
Byfleet & New Haw	d														00s51			01s12							
West Byfleet	d			←		←		←				00s45	00s45	00s45	00s54		←	01s15			00s57	00s57			←
Woking	a	00 21	00 20	00 21	00 27	00 26	00 31	00 30	00 35			00 51	00 51	00 51	00 58	00 50	00 58	01 20	00 59		01 03	01 03	01 16	01 19	01 20
	d	00 23	00 21	00 23	00 28	00 28	00 32	00 35	00 37		00 40				01 00	00 51	01 00	01 21	01 00				01 18	01 20	01 21
Worplesdon	d	→					00 37								→			→							01s27
Guildford	a			00 30			00 43										01 07						01s26	01s28	01 33
Brookwood	d					00 34		00 41			00 45					00 57									
Ash Vale	d							00 48			00 53					01 05									
Aldershot	a							00 53			00 58					01 09									
	d							00 54			00 59					01 10									
Farnham	a							00 59			01 04					01 15									
	d										01 05					01 16									
Bentley	d										01s11					01s22									
Alton	a										01 18					01 29									
Farnborough (Main)	d				00 38	00 41																			
Fleet	d				00 44	00 47																			
Winchfield	d					00s52																			
Hook	d					00s57																			
Basingstoke	a		00 43		00 59	01 06			00 55										01 18						

A from 21 May until 1 October
B from 21 May until 23 July, 20 August, 27 August, 17 September, 24 September, 1 October
C not from 31 July until 10 August, from 30 August until 7 September
D 30 July, 6 August, 13 August, 3 September, 10 September
E from 31 July until 7 September, not from 14 August until 29 August
F 20 August, 27 August
G until 23 July
H 17 September, 24 September, 1 October
I from 30 July until 10 September, not from 14 August until 29 August
J 3 September, 10 September
K 30 July, 6 August, 13 August
b Previous night, stops to pick up only

Table 155

Mondays to Fridays

until 5 October

London - Woking, Guildford, Alton and Basingstoke

Network Diagram - see first Page of Table 155

		SW ■	SW ■	SW ■	SW ◇■		SW ■	SW ■	SW ■	SW ■	SW	SW ■	SW ■	SW ■	SW		SW ◇■	SW ■	SW	SW ■	SW ■	SW ■	SW	SW ■	SW ◇■
London Waterloo 15 ⊖	d	01 05	05 00	05 20	05 30						05 50	06 12	06 15		06 20		06 30			06 42	06 45		06 50	06 53	07 10
Vauxhall ⊖	d	01 09	05 04	05 24							05 54				06 24								06 54		
Clapham Junction 10	d		05 11	05 29	05u37						05 59	06u19	06u22		06 29		06u37			06u49	06u52		06 59	07u00	07u17
	d	01 15																							
Earlsfield	d		05 14	05 32							06 02				06 32								07 02		
Wimbledon 6 ⊖	d	01s27	05 18	05 36	05 43						06 06				06 36								07 06		
Surbiton 6	d	01s35	05 26	05 44							06 14	06 30			06 44					07 00			07 14	07 11	
Esher	d		05 30	05 48							06 18				06 48								→		
Hersham	d		05 33	05 51							06 21				06 51										
Walton-on-Thames	d		05 37	05 54							06 24	06 37			06 54					07 07					
Weybridge	d		05 41	05 57							06 27	06 41			06 57					07 11					
Byfleet & New Haw	d		05 44	06 00							06 30				07 00										
West Byfleet	d		05 47	06 03				←			06 33			←	07 03				←			←		07 21	
Woking	a	01 48	05 51	06 08	05 59			06 08			06 38	06 48	06 41	06 48	07 07		06 56		07 07	07 18	07 11	07 18		07 26	07 35
	d	01 49	05 53	06 11	06 01		06 02	06 11	06 19	06 30		06 50	06 43	06 50	07 10		06 57	06 58	07 10	07 19	07 13	07 19		07 30	07 36
Worplesdon	d			→				06 16				→	06 48		→					→	07 18				
Guildford	a		06 00					06 21					06 53						07 20		07 23				
Brookwood	d						06 08		06 25	06 36				06 56				07 06				07 25		07 36	
Ash Vale	d						06 16			06 44								07 14						07 44	
Aldershot	a						06 21			06 49								07 19						07 49	
	d						06 21			06 50								07 20						07 50	
Farnham	a						06 27			06 55								07 25						07 55	
	d						06 27			06 56								07 26						07 56	
Bentley	d						06 34			07 02								07 32						08 02	
Alton	a						06 41			07 10								07 40						08 10	
Farnborough (Main)	d	01s58							06 33					07 04								07 33			
Fleet	d	02s04							06 38					07 09								07 38			
Winchfield	d								06 44					07 15								07 44			
Hook	d								06 48					07 19								07 48			
Basingstoke	a	02s16			06 20				06 58					07 28			07 16					07 56			07 55

			SW	SW ■	SW ■	SW ■	SW	SW ■	SW ■	SW ■	SW ◇■		SW	SW ■	SW ■	SW ■	SW ◇■	SW ■	SW	SW ■	SW ■		SW ■	SW ◇■	SW ■
London Waterloo 15 ⊖	d			07 12	07 15		07 20	07 23	07 30		07 35			07 39	07 42	07 45	07 50		07 50	07 53	08 00			08 05	08 09
Vauxhall ⊖	d						07 24												07 54						
Clapham Junction 10	d			07u20	07u23		07 29	07u30						07u46		07u52	07u57		07 59	08u00				08u12	
	d																								
Earlsfield	d						07 32												08 02						
Wimbledon 6 ⊖	d		←				07 36						←						08 06						
Surbiton 6	d		07 14	07 31			07 44	07 41					07 44		08 00				08 14	08 11					
Esher	d		07 18				→						07 48						→						
Hersham	d		07 21										07 51												
Walton-on-Thames	d		07 24	07 38									07 54		08 07										
Weybridge	d		07 27	07 42									07 57		08 11										
Byfleet & New Haw	d		07 30										08 00												
West Byfleet	d		07 33			←		07 51		←			08 03					←		08 21			←		
Woking	a		07 37	07 48	07 42	07 48		07 59	07 54	07 59	07 58		08 08		08 18	08 12	08 15	08 18		08 29	08 24		08 29		08 33
	d		07 39	07 50	07 44	07 50		08 00	07 55	08 00	08 00				08 19	08 14	08 16	08 19		08 30	08 25		08 30		08 35
Worplesdon	d			→	07 49			→							→	08 19				→					
Guildford	a		07 47		07 54				08 03							08 24					08 35				
Brookwood	d					07 56				08 06								08 25					08 36		
Ash Vale	d									08 14													08 44		
Aldershot	a									08 19													08 49		
	d									08 20													08 50		
Farnham	a									08 25													08 55		
	d									08 26													08 56		
Bentley	d									08 32													09 02		
Alton	a									08 39													09 10		
Farnborough (Main)	d					08 03								08 13				08 33							08 45
Fleet	d					08 09								08 19				08 38							
Winchfield	d					08 14												08 44							
Hook	d					08 19												08 48							
Basingstoke	a					08 26					08 19			08 32			08 37	08 58						08 47	08 58

London - Woking, Guildford, Alton and Basingstoke

Network Diagram - see first Page of Table 155

	SW	SW ■	SW ■	SW ◇■ ⊼	SW ■	SW		SW ■	SW ■ ⊼	SW ◇■ ⊼	SW ■	SW	SW ■	SW ■	SW ■	SW ◇■ ⊼		SW ■	SW	SW ■	SW ■ ⊼	SW ■	SW ◇■ ⊼	SW ■
London Waterloo [15] ⊖ d		08 12	08 15	08 20		08 20		08 23	08 30	08 35			08 39	08 42	08 45	08 50			08 50	08 53	09 00		09 05	09 09
Vauxhall ⊖ d						08 24													08 54					
Clapham Junction [10] d		08u19	08u22	08u27		08 29							08u46		08u52				08 59	09u00			09u12	
d																								
Earlsfield d						08 32													09 02					
Wimbledon [6] ⊖ d	←					08 36						←							09 06					
Surbiton [6] d	08 14	08 30				08 44		08 41				08 44		09 00					09 14	09 11				
Esher d	08 18					→						08 48							→					
Hersham d	08 21											08 51												
Walton-on-Thames d	08 24	08 37										08 54		09 07										
Weybridge d	08 27	08 41										08 57		09 11										
Byfleet & New Haw d	08 30											09 00												
West Byfleet d	08 33				←			08 51			←	09 03						←		09 21		←		
Woking a	08 37	08 49	08 42	08 46	08 49			09 00	08 55	08 58	09 00	09 08		09 18	09 11	09 15		09 18		09 29	09 24	09 29		09 33
d	08 39	08 49	08 44	08 46	08 49			09 00	08 55		09 00			09 19	09 13	09 16		09 19		09 30	09 25	09 30		09 35
Worplesdon d		→	08 49					→						→	09 18					→				
Guildford a	08 50		08 54						09 05						09 23						09 33			
Brookwood d					08 55						09 06							09 25				09 36		
Ash Vale d											09 14											09 44		
Aldershot a											09 20											09 49		
d											09 20											09 50		
Farnham a											09 26											09 55		
d											09 26											09 56		
Bentley d																						10 02		
Alton a											09 39											10 10		
Farnborough (Main) d					09 03								09 13					09 33						09 45
Fleet d					09 08								09 19					09 38						
Winchfield d					09 14													09 44						
Hook d					09 18													09 48						
Basingstoke a				09 05	09 28								09 31			09 36		09 58					09 47	09 58

	SW	SW ■		SW ■	SW ◇■ ⊼	SW ■	SW	SW ■	SW ■ ⊼	SW ◇■ ⊼	SW ■	SW		SW ■	SW ■	SW ■	SW ◇■ ⊼	SW ■	SW	SW ■	SW ■ ⊼	SW ■		SW ◇■ ⊼
London Waterloo [15] ⊖ d		09 12		09 15	09 20		09 20	09 23	09 30	09 35				09 39	09 42	09 45	09 50		09 50	09 53	10 00			10 05
Vauxhall ⊖ d							09 24												09 54					
Clapham Junction [10] d		09u19		09u22	09u27		09 29							09u46		09u52			09 59	10u00				10u12
d																								
Earlsfield d							09 32												10 02					
Wimbledon [6] ⊖ d	←						09 36					←							10 06					
Surbiton [6] d	09 14	09 30					09 44	09 41				09 44			10 00				10 14	10 11				
Esher d	09 18						→					09 48							→					
Hersham d	09 21											09 51												
Walton-on-Thames d	09 24	09 37										09 54			10 07									
Weybridge d	09 27	09 41										09 57			10 11									
Byfleet & New Haw d	09 30											10 00												
West Byfleet d	09 33					←		09 51			←	10 03						←		10 21		←		
Woking a	09 38	09 48		09 42	09 45	09 48		09 59	09 54	09 58	09 59	10 08			10 18	10 11	10 14	10 18		10 29	10 24	10 29		
d		09 49		09 43	09 46	09 49		10 00	09 55		10 00				10 19	10 13	10 16	10 19		10 30	10 25	10 30		
Worplesdon d		→						→							→	10 18				→				
Guildford a				09 52					10 03							10 23					10 33			
Brookwood d						09 55					10 06							10 25				10 36		
Ash Vale d											10 14											10 44		
Aldershot a											10 19											10 49		
d											10 20											10 50		
Farnham a											10 25											10 55		
d											10 26											10 56		
Bentley d																						11 02		
Alton a											10 37											11 10		
Farnborough (Main) d						10 03								10 13				10 33						
Fleet d						10 08								10 19				10 38						
Winchfield d						10 14												10 44						
Hook d						10 18												10 48						
Basingstoke a					10 05	10 28								10 31			10 36	10 58						10 47

London - Woking, Guildford, Alton and Basingstoke

Network Diagram - see first Page of Table 155

	SW ■	SW	SW ■	SW ■	SW ◇■ ⊼	SW ■	SW	SW ■		SW ■ ⊼	SW ◇■ ⊼	SW ■	SW	SW ■	SW ■	SW ■	SW ◇■ ⊼	SW ■		SW	SW ■	SW ■ ⊼	SW ■	SW ◇■ ⊼
London Waterloo [15] ⊖ d	10 09		10 12	10 15	10 20		10 20	10 23		10 30	10 35			10 39	10 42	10 45	10 50			10 50	10 53	11 00		11 05
Vauxhall ⊖ d							10 24													10 54				
Clapham Junction [10] d			10u19	10u22	10u27		10 29							10u46		10u52				10 59	11u00			11u12
d																								
Earlsfield d							10 32													11 02				
Wimbledon [6] ⊖ d		←					10 36						←							11 06				
Surbiton [6] d		10 14	10 30				10 44	10 41					10 44		11 00					11 14	11 11			
Esher d		10 18					→						10 48							→				
Hersham d		10 21											10 51											
Walton-on-Thames d		10 24	10 37										10 54		11 07									
Weybridge d		10 27	10 41										10 57		11 11									
Byfleet & New Haw d		10 30											11 00											
West Byfleet d		10 33				←		10 51				←	11 03					←			11 21		←	
Woking a	10 33	10 38	10 48	10 41	10 45	10 48		10 59		10 54	10 58	10 59	11 08		11 18	11 11	11 14	11 18			11 29	11 24	11 29	
d	10 35		10 49	10 43	10 46	10 49		11 00		10 55		11 00			11 19	11 13	11 16	11 19			11 30	11 25	11 30	
Worplesdon d			→					→							→	11 18					→			
Guildford a				10 50						11 03						11 23						11 33		
Brookwood d						10 55						11 06						11 25					11 36	
Ash Vale d												11 14											11 44	
Aldershot a												11 19											11 49	
d												11 20											11 50	
Farnham a												11 25											11 55	
d																							11 56	
Bentley d																							12 02	
Alton a																							12 10	
Farnborough (Main) d	10 45					11 03								11 13				11 33						
Fleet d						11 08								11 19				11 38						
Winchfield d						11 14												11 44						
Hook d						11 18												11 48						
Basingstoke a	10 58				11 05	11 28								11 31			11 36	11 58						11 47

	SW ■	SW	SW ■	SW ■		SW ◇■ ⊼	SW ■	SW	SW ■	SW ■ ⊼	SW ◇■ ⊼	SW ■	SW	SW ■		SW ■	SW ■	SW ◇■ ⊼	SW ■	SW	SW ■	SW ■ ⊼	SW ■	SW ◇■ ⊼
London Waterloo [15] ⊖ d	11 09		11 12	11 15		11 20		11 20	11 23	11 30	11 35			11 39		11 42	11 45	11 50		11 50	11 53	12 00		12 05
Vauxhall ⊖ d								11 24												11 54				
Clapham Junction [10] d			11u19	11u22		11u27		11 29						11u46			11u52			11 59	12u00			12u12
d																								
Earlsfield d								11 32												12 02				
Wimbledon [6] ⊖ d		←						11 36					←							12 06				
Surbiton [6] d		11 14	11 30					11 44	11 41				11 44			12 00				12 14	12 11			
Esher d		11 18						→					11 48							→				
Hersham d		11 21											11 51											
Walton-on-Thames d		11 24	11 37										11 54			12 07								
Weybridge d		11 27	11 41										11 57			12 11								
Byfleet & New Haw d		11 30											12 00											
West Byfleet d		11 33					←		11 51			←	12 03						←		12 21		←	
Woking a	11 33	11 38	11 48	11 41		11 45	11 48		11 59	11 54	11 58	11 59	12 08			12 18	12 11	12 14	12 18		12 29	12 24	12 29	
d	11 35		11 49	11 43		11 46	11 49		12 00	11 55		12 00				12 19	12 13	12 16	12 19		12 30	12 25	12 30	
Worplesdon d			→						→							→	12 18				→			
Guildford a				11 50						12 03							12 23					12 33		
Brookwood d							11 55					12 06							12 25				12 36	
Ash Vale d												12 14											12 44	
Aldershot a												12 19											12 49	
d												12 20											12 50	
Farnham a												12 25											12 55	
d												12 26											12 56	
Bentley d																							13 02	
Alton a												12 37											13 10	
Farnborough (Main) d	11 45						12 03							12 13					12 33					
Fleet d							12 08							12 19					12 38					
Winchfield d							12 14												12 44					
Hook d							12 18												12 48					
Basingstoke a	11 58					12 05	12 28							12 31				12 36	12 58					12 47

Table 155

Mondays to Fridays
until 5 October

London - Woking, Guildford, Alton and Basingstoke

Network Diagram - see first Page of Table 155

Station		SW ■	SW	SW ■	SW ■	SW ◇■ ⌶	SW ■	SW	SW ■	SW ■ ⌶	SW ◇■ ⌶	SW ■	SW	SW ■	SW ■	SW ■	SW ◇■ ⌶	SW ■	SW	SW ■	SW ■ ⌶	SW ■
London Waterloo ■ ⊖	d	12 09		12 12	12 15	12 20		12 20	12 23	12 30	12 35			12 39	12 42	12 45	12 50		12 50	12 53	13 00	
Vauxhall ⊖	d							12 24											12 54			
Clapham Junction ■	d			12u19	12u22	12u27		12 29						12u46		12u52			12 59	13u00		
	d																					
Earlsfield	d							12 32											13 02			
Wimbledon ■ ⊖	d		←					12 36					←						13 06			
Surbiton ■	d		12 14	12 30				12 44	12 41				12 44		13 00				13 14	13 11		
Esher	d		12 18					→					12 48						→			
Hersham	d		12 21										12 51									
Walton-on-Thames	d		12 24	12 37									12 54		13 07							
Weybridge	d		12 27	12 41									12 57		13 11							
Byfleet & New Haw	d		12 30										13 00									
West Byfleet	d		12 33				←		12 51			←	13 03					←		13 21		←
Woking	a	12 33	12 38	12 48	12 41	12 45	12 48		12 59	12 54	12 58	12 59	13 08		13 18	13 11	13 14	13 18		13 29	13 24	13 29
	d	12 35		12 49	12 43	12 46	12 49		13 00	12 55		13 00			13 19	13 13	13 16	13 19		13 30	13 25	13 30
Worplesdon	d			→					→						→	13 18				→		
Guildford	a				12 50					13 03						13 23					13 33	
Brookwood	d						12 55					13 06						13 25				13 36
Ash Vale	d											13 14										13 44
Aldershot	a											13 19										13 49
	d											13 20										13 50
Farnham	a											13 25										13 55
	d											13 26										13 56
Bentley	d																					14 02
Alton	a											13 37										14 11
Farnborough (Main)	d	12 45					13 03							13 13				13 33				
Fleet	d						13 08							13 19				13 38				
Winchfield	d						13 14											13 44				
Hook	d						13 18											13 48				
Basingstoke	a	12 58				13 05	13 28							13 31			13 36	13 58				

Station		SW ◇■ ⌶	SW ■	SW	SW ■	SW ■	SW ◇■ ⌶	SW ■	SW	SW ■	SW ■ ⌶	SW ◇■ ⌶	SW ■	SW	SW ■	SW ■	SW ■	SW ◇■ ⌶	SW ■	SW	SW ■	SW ■ ⌶	SW ■
London Waterloo ■ ⊖	d	13 05	13 09		13 12	13 15	13 20		13 20	13 23	13 30	13 35			13 39	13 42	13 45	13 50		13 50	13 53	14 00	
Vauxhall ⊖	d								13 24											13 54			
Clapham Junction ■	d	13u12			13u19	13u22	13u27		13 29						13u46		13u52			13 59	14u00		
	d																						
Earlsfield	d								13 32											14 02			
Wimbledon ■ ⊖	d			←					13 36					←						14 06			
Surbiton ■	d			13 14	13 30				13 44	13 41				13 44		14 00				14 14	14 11		
Esher	d			13 18					→					13 48						→			
Hersham	d			13 21										13 51									
Walton-on-Thames	d			13 24	13 37									13 54		14 07							
Weybridge	d			13 27	13 41									13 57		14 11							
Byfleet & New Haw	d			13 30										14 00									
West Byfleet	d			13 33				←		13 51			←	14 03					←		14 21		←
Woking	a		13 33	13 38	13 48	13 41	13 45	13 48		13 59	13 54	13 58	13 59	14 08		14 18	14 11	14 14	14 18		14 29	14 24	14 29
	d		13 35		13 49	13 43	13 46	13 49		14 00	13 55		14 00			14 19	14 13	14 16	14 19		14 30	14 25	14 30
Worplesdon	d				→					→						→	14 18				→		
Guildford	a					13 50					14 03						14 23					14 33	
Brookwood	d							13 55					14 06						14 25				14 36
Ash Vale	d												14 14										14 44
Aldershot	a												14 19										14 49
	d												14 20										14 50
Farnham	a												14 25										14 55
	d												14 26										14 56
Bentley	d																						15 02
Alton	a												14 37										15 10
Farnborough (Main)	d		13 45					14 03							14 13				14 33				
Fleet	d							14 08							14 19				14 38				
Winchfield	d							14 14											14 44				
Hook	d							14 18											14 48				
Basingstoke	a	13 47	13 58				14 05	14 28							14 31			14 36	14 58				

Table 155

Mondays to Fridays
until 5 October

London - Woking, Guildford, Alton and Basingstoke

Network Diagram - see first Page of Table 155

Station		SW ◇■ ⌶	SW ■	SW	SW ■	SW ■	SW ◇■ ⌶	SW ■	SW	SW ■	SW ■ ⌶	SW ◇■ ⌶	SW ■	SW	SW ■	SW ■	SW ■	SW ◇■ ⌶	SW ■	SW	SW ■	SW ■ ⌶
London Waterloo ■ ⊖	d	14 05	14 09		14 12	14 15	14 20		14 20	14 23	14 30	14 35			14 39	14 42	14 45	14 50		14 50	14 53	15 00
Vauxhall ⊖	d								14 24											14 54		
Clapham Junction ■	d	14u12			14u19	14u22	14u27		14 29						14u46		14u52			14 59	15u00	
	d																					
Earlsfield	d								14 32											15 02		
Wimbledon ■ ⊖	d			←					14 36					←						15 06		
Surbiton ■	d			14 14	14 30				14 44	14 41				14 44		15 00				15 14	15 11	
Esher	d			14 18					→					14 48						→		
Hersham	d			14 21										14 51								
Walton-on-Thames	d			14 24	14 37									14 54		15 07						
Weybridge	d			14 27	14 41									14 57		15 11						
Byfleet & New Haw	d			14 30										15 00								
West Byfleet	d			14 33				←		14 51			←	15 03					←		15 21	
Woking	a		14 33	14 38	14 48	14 41	14 45	14 48		14 59	14 54	14 58	14 59	15 08		15 18	15 11	15 14	15 18		15 29	15 24
	d		14 35		14 49	14 43	14 46	14 49		15 00	14 55		15 00			15 19	15 13	15 16	15 19		15 30	15 25
Worplesdon	d				→					→						→	15 18				→	
Guildford	a					14 50					15 03						15 23					15 33
Brookwood	d							14 55					15 06						15 25			
Ash Vale	d												15 14									
Aldershot	a												15 19									
	d												15 20									
Farnham	a												15 25									
	d												15 26									
Bentley	d																					
Alton	a												15 37									
Farnborough (Main)	d		14 45					15 03							15 13				15 33			
Fleet	d							15 08							15 19				15 38			
Winchfield	d							15 14											15 44			
Hook	d							15 18											15 48			
Basingstoke	a	14 47	14 58				15 05	15 28							15 31			15 36	15 58			

Station		SW ■	SW ◇■ ⌶	SW ■	SW	SW ■	SW ■	SW ◇■ ⌶	SW ■	SW	SW ■	SW ■ ⌶	SW ◇■ ⌶	SW ■	SW	SW ■	SW ■	SW ■	SW ◇■ ⌶	SW ■	SW	SW ■	SW ■ ⌶
London Waterloo ■ ⊖	d		15 05	15 09		15 12	15 15	15 20		15 20	15 23	15 30	15 35			15 39	15 42	15 45	15 50		15 50	15 53	16 00
Vauxhall ⊖	d									15 24											15 54		
Clapham Junction ■	d		15u12			15u19	15u22	15u27		15 29						15u46		15u52	15u57		15 59	16u00	
	d																						
Earlsfield	d									15 32											16 02		
Wimbledon ■ ⊖	d				←					15 36					←						16 06		
Surbiton ■	d				15 14	15 30				15 44	15 41				15 44		16 00				16 14	16 11	
Esher	d				15 18					→					15 48						→		
Hersham	d				15 21										15 51								
Walton-on-Thames	d				15 24	15 37									15 54		16 07						
Weybridge	d				15 27	15 41									15 57		16 11						
Byfleet & New Haw	d				15 30										16 00								
West Byfleet	d	←			15 33				←		15 51			←	16 03					←		16 21	
Woking	a	15 29		15 33	15 38	15 48	15 41	15 45	15 48		15 59	15 54	15 58	15 59	16 08		16 18	16 11	16 15	16 18		16 29	16 24
	d	15 30		15 35		15 49	15 43	15 46	15 49		16 00	15 55		16 00			16 19	16 13	16 16	16 19		16 30	16 25
Worplesdon	d					→	15 48				→						→					→	
Guildford	a						15 53					16 03						16 20					16 33
Brookwood	d	15 36							15 55					16 06						16 25			
Ash Vale	d	15 44												16 14									
Aldershot	a	15 49												16 19									
	d	15 50												16 20									
Farnham	a	15 55												16 25									
	d	15 56												16 26									
Bentley	d	16 02																					
Alton	a	16 10												16 37									
Farnborough (Main)	d			15 45					16 03							16 13				16 33			
Fleet	d								16 08							16 19				16 38			
Winchfield	d								16 14											16 44			
Hook	d								16 18											16 48			
Basingstoke	a		15 47	15 58				16 05	16 28							16 31			16 36	16 58			

Table 155

Mondays to Fridays
until 5 October

London - Woking, Guildford, Alton and Basingstoke

Network Diagram - see first Page of Table 155

	SW ■	SW ◇■ 🍴	SW ■	SW		SW ■	SW ■	SW ◇■ 🍴	SW ■	SW	SW ■	SW ■ 🍴	SW ■	SW		SW ◇■ 🍴	SW ■	SW ■	SW ■	SW ◇■ 🍴	SW ■	SW	SW ■	SW ■ 🍴
London Waterloo 15 ⊖ d		16 05	16 09			16 12	16 15	16 20		16 20	16 25	16 30				16 35	16 39	16 42	16 45	16 50		16 50	16 55	17 00
Vauxhall ⊖ d										16 24												16 54		
Clapham Junction 10 d		16u12				16u19	16u22	16u27		16 29							16u46		16u52	16u57		16 59	17u02	
d																								
Earlsfield d										16 32												17 02		
Wimbledon 6 ⊖ d				←						16 36				←								17 06		
Surbiton 6 d				16 14		16 30				16 44	16 41			16 44				17 00				17 14		
Esher d				16 18						→				16 48								17 18		
Hersham d				16 21										16 51								17 21		
Walton-on-Thames d				16 24		16 37								16 54				17 07				17 24		
Weybridge d				16 27		16 41								16 57				17 11				17 27		
Byfleet & New Haw d				16 30										17 00								17 30		
West Byfleet d	←			16 33					←		16 51		←	17 03							←	17 33	17 21	
Woking a	16 29		16 33	16 38		16 48	16 41	16 45	16 48		16 59	16 54	16 59	17 10				17 18	17 11		17 18	17 43	17 29	17 24
d	16 30		16 35			16 49	16 43	16 46	16 49		17 00	16 55	17 00					17 19	17 13	17u16	17 19		17 30	17 25
Worplesdon d						→	16 48				→							→					→	17 30
Guildford a							16 53					17 03							17 20					17 36
Brookwood d	16 36								16 55				17 06								17 25			
Ash Vale d	16 44												17 14											
Aldershot a	16 49												17 19											
d	16 50												17 20											
Farnham a	16 55												17 25											
d	16 56												17 26											
Bentley d	17 02												17 32											
Alton a	17 10												17 41											
Farnborough (Main) d			16 45						17 03								17 13				17 33			
Fleet d									17 08								17 19				17 38			
Winchfield d									17 14												17 44			
Hook d									17 18												17 48			
Basingstoke a		16 47	16 58					17 05	17 30								17 31			17 36	18 00			

		SW ■	SW ■	SW ■	SW ■	SW ■	SW ■	SW ◇■ 🍴	SW	SW ■		SW ■	SW ■	SW ■ 🍴	SW	SW ■	SW ■	SW ■	SW ■	SW ■		SW ■	SW ◇■ 🍴	SW
London Waterloo 15 ⊖ d			17 02	17 09	17 12	17 15		17 20	17 20	17 23		17 25		17 30		17 32	17 39	17 41	17 45	17 48			17 50	17 50
Vauxhall ⊖ d									17 24															17 54
Clapham Junction 10 d									17 29															17 59
d																								
Earlsfield d									17 32															18 02
Wimbledon 6 ⊖ d									17 36						←									18 06
Surbiton 6 d			17 18						17 44	17 39					17 44	17 48								18 14
Esher d			17 22						→						17 48	17 52								→
Hersham d			17 25												17 51	17 55								
Walton-on-Thames d			17 29												17 54	17 59								
Weybridge d			17 33												17 57	18 03								
Byfleet & New Haw d			17 36												18 00	18 06								
West Byfleet d		←	17 39				←						←		18 03	18 09						←		
Woking a		17 29	17 44	17 32	17 36	17 38	17 44			17 51		17 50	17 51	17 54	18 10	18 14	18 02			18 11		18 14		
d		17 30	17 46	17 34	17 37	17 40	17 46	17u46		17 52		17 51	17 52	17 56		18 16	18 04			18 13		18 16		
Worplesdon d			→			17 45				→				18 00		→						18 21		
Guildford a						17 51	17 56							18 06					18 21			18 29		
Brookwood d		17 36			17 43								18 00					18 11						
Ash Vale d		17 44										18 03												
Aldershot a		17 49										18 08												
d		17 50										18 09												
Farnham a		17 55										18 14												
d		17 56										18 15												
Bentley d		18 02										18 24												
Alton a		18 11										18 32												
Farnborough (Main) d					17 51								18 08					18 19						
Fleet d					17 56								18 13					18 24						
Winchfield d					18 02								18 19					18 30						
Hook d					18 06								18 23					18 34						
Basingstoke a				17 52	18 16			18 05					18 32				18 22	18 45		18 31			18 37	

Table 155

Mondays to Fridays
until 5 October

London - Woking, Guildford, Alton and Basingstoke

Network Diagram - see first Page of Table 155

	SW ■	SW ■	SW ■	SW	SW ■ 🍴	SW ■		SW ■	SW ■	SW ■	SW ■	SW ◇■ 🍴	SW	SW ■	SW ■	SW ■ 🍴		SW	SW ■	SW ■	SW ■	SW ■	SW ◇■ 🍴	SW ■
London Waterloo 15 ⊖ d	17 53	17 55			18 00	18 02		18 09	18 12	18 15	18 18	18 20	18 20	18 23	18 25	18 30			18 32	18 39	18 41	18 45	18 50	
Vauxhall ⊖ d													18 24											
Clapham Junction 10 d												18u27	18 29		18u33					18u46				
d																								
Earlsfield d													18 32											
Wimbledon 6 ⊖ d				←									18 36					←						
Surbiton 6 d	18 09			18 14		18 18							18 44	18 40				18 44	18 48					
Esher d				18 18		18 22							→					18 48	18 52					
Hersham d				18 21		18 25												18 51	18 55					
Walton-on-Thames d				18 24		18 29												18 54	18 59					
Weybridge d				18 27		18 33												18 57	19 03					
Byfleet & New Haw d				18 30		18 36												19 00	19 06					
West Byfleet d	18 19		←	18 33		18 39												19 03	19 09			19 08		←
Woking a	18 23	18 20	18 23	18 41		18 48		18 33			18 42	18 45		18 52	18 52	18 57		19 12	19 18	19 05		19 13	19 17	19 18
d	18 25	18 21	18 25					18 35			18 43	18 46		18 54	18 53	18 58			19 20	19 06		19 14	19 18	19 20
Worplesdon d	→										18 48								→					
Guildford a					18 32					18 50	18 54					19 06						19 23		
Brookwood d		18 27							18 41					19 02							19 13			
Ash Vale d		18 35													19 05									
Aldershot a		18 40													19 10									
d		18 41													19 11									
Farnham a		18 46													19 16									
d		18 48													19 18									
Bentley d		18 54													19 24									
Alton a		19 03													19 33									
Farnborough (Main) d			18 39						18 48					19 10							19 20			19 31
Fleet d			18 44						18 54					19 15							19 26			19 37
Winchfield d			18 50						18 59					19 21							19 31			19 42
Hook d			18 54						19 04					19 25							19 36			19 47
Basingstoke a			19 03					18 53	19 16			19 05		19 34						19 28	19 47		19 37	19 59

	SW	SW ■		SW ■ 🍴	SW ■	SW ◇■ 🍴	SW ■	SW ■	SW ■	SW ◇■ 🍴	SW	SW ■		SW ■ 🍴	SW ◇■ 🍴	SW ■	SW ■	SW ■	SW ■	SW ◇■ 🍴	SW ■	SW		SW ■
London Waterloo 15 ⊖ d	18 50	18 55		19 00	19 02	19 05	19 09	19 12	19 15	19 20	19 20	19 25		19 30	19 35		19 39	19 42	19 45	19 50		19 50		19 53
Vauxhall ⊖ d	18 54										19 24											19 54		
Clapham Junction 10 d	18 59	19u02				19u12		19u19	19u22	19u27	19 29	19u32					19u46		19u52			19 59		20u00
d																								
Earlsfield d	19 02										19 32											20 02		
Wimbledon 6 ⊖ d	19 06										19 36											20 06		
Surbiton 6 d	19 14				19 18						19 44							20 00				20 14		20 11
Esher d	19 18				19 22						19 48											→		
Hersham d	19 21				19 25						19 51													
Walton-on-Thames d	19 24				19 29						19 54							20 07						
Weybridge d	19 27				19 33						19 57							20 11						
Byfleet & New Haw d	19 30				19 36						20 00													
West Byfleet d	19 33				19 39						20 03	19 51				←					←			20 21
Woking a	19 42	19 21		19 24	19 48		19 33	19 38	19 43	19 45	20 08	19 59		19 54	19 58	19 59		20 18	20 11	20 14	20 18			20 29
d		19 23		19 25			19 35	19 39	19 45	19 46		20 00		19 55		20 00		20 19	20 13	20 16	20 19			20 30
Worplesdon d				19 30								→						→	20 18					→
Guildford a				19 36					19 52					20 03					20 23					
Brookwood d		19 30						19 45								20 06					20 25			
Ash Vale d		19 37														20 14								
Aldershot a		19 42														20 19								
d		19 43														20 20								
Farnham a		19 48														20 25								
d		19 49														20 26								
Bentley d		19 55														20 32								
Alton a		20 04														20 39								
Farnborough (Main) d							19 45	19 53									20 13				20 33			
Fleet d								19 58									20 19				20 38			
Winchfield d								20 04													20 44			
Hook d								20 09													20 48			
Basingstoke a						19 47	19 58	20 16		20 06							20 31			20 36	20 58			

Table 155

Mondays to Fridays

until 5 October

London - Woking, Guildford, Alton and Basingstoke

Network Diagram - see first Page of Table 155

		SW 1 ✠	SW 1	SW ◇1 ✠	SW 1	SW	SW 1	SW 1	SW ◇1 ✠	SW 1	SW	SW 1	SW 1 ✠	SW ◇1 ✠	SW 1	SW	SW 1	SW 1	SW 1	SW 1	SW	SW 1	SW 1 ✠
London Waterloo ⊖	d	20 00		20 05	20 09		20 12	20 15	20 20		20 20	20 23	20 30	20 35			20 39	20 42	20 45		20 50	20 53	21 00
Vauxhall ⊖	d										20 24										20 54		
Clapham Junction	d			20u12			20u19	20u22	20u27		20 29						20u46		20u52		20 59	21u00	
	d																						
Earlsfield	d										20 32										21 02		
Wimbledon ⊖	d					←					20 36					←					21 06		
Surbiton	d					20 14	20 30				20 44	20 41				20 44		21 00			21 14	21 11	
Esher	d					20 18					→					20 48					→		
Hersham	d					20 21										20 51							
Walton-on-Thames	d					20 24	20 37									20 54		21 07					
Weybridge	d					20 27	20 41									20 57		21 11					
Byfleet & New Haw	d					20 30										21 00							
West Byfleet	d		←			20 33				←		20 51			←	21 03				←		21 21	
Woking	a	20 24	20 29		20 33	20 38	20 48	20 41	20 45	20 48		20 59	20 54	20 58	20 59	21 08		21 18	21 11	21 18		21 29	21 24
	d	20 25	20 30		20 35		20 49	20 43	20 46	20 49		21 00	20 55		21 00			21 19	21 13	21 19		21 30	21 25
Worplesdon	d						→					→						→	21 18			→	
Guildford	a	20 33						20 50					21 03						21 23				21 33
Brookwood	d		20 36							20 55					21 06					21 25			
Ash Vale	d		20 44												21 14								
Aldershot	a		20 49												21 19								
	d		20 50												21 20								
Farnham	a		20 55												21 25								
	d		20 56												21 26								
Bentley	d		21 02												21 32								
Alton	a		21 10												21 39								
Farnborough (Main)	d				20 45					21 03							21 13			21 33			
Fleet	d									21 08							21 19			21 38			
Winchfield	d									21 14										21 44			
Hook	d									21 18										21 48			
Basingstoke	a			20 47	20 58				21 05	21 28							21 31			21 58			

		SW 1	SW ◇1 ✠	SW	SW 1	SW ◇1 ✠	SW	SW 1	SW 1 ✠	SW ◇1 ✠	SW 1	SW	SW 1	SW 1	SW 1	SW 1	SW	SW 1	SW 1	SW 1	SW ◇1 ✠	SW	SW 1
London Waterloo ⊖	d		21 05		21 12	21 20	21 20	21 23	21 30	21 35			21 39	21 42	21 45		21 50	21 53	22 00		22 05		22 12
Vauxhall ⊖	d						21 24										21 54						
Clapham Junction	d		21u12		21u19	21u27	21 29						21u46		21u52		21 59	22u00			22u12		22u19
	d																						
Earlsfield	d						21 32										22 02						
Wimbledon ⊖	d			←			21 36					←					22 06					←	
Surbiton	d			21 14	21 30		21 44	21 41				21 44		22 00			22 14	22 11				22 14	22 30
Esher	d			21 18			→					21 48					→					22 18	
Hersham	d			21 21								21 51										22 21	
Walton-on-Thames	d			21 24	21 37							21 54		22 07								22 24	22 37
Weybridge	d			21 27	21 41							21 57		22 11								22 27	22 41
Byfleet & New Haw	d			21 30								22 00										22 30	
West Byfleet	d	←		21 33				21 51			←	22 03				←		22 21		←		22 33	
Woking	a	21 29	21 31	21 38	21 48	21 45		21 59	21 54	21 58	21 59	22 08		22 18	22 11	22 18		22 29	22 24	22 29	22 31	22 37	22 48
	d	21 30	21 32		21 49	21 49		22 00	21 55		22 00			22 19	22 13	22 19		22 30	22 25	22 30	22 32	22 39	22 49
Worplesdon	d							→						→	22 18			→					
Guildford	a								22 03						22 23				22 33			22 47	
Brookwood	d	21 36			21 55						22 06					22 25				22 36			22 55
Ash Vale	d	21 44									22 14									22 44			
Aldershot	a	21 49									22 19									22 49			
	d	21 50									22 20									22 50			
Farnham	a	21 55									22 25									22 55			
	d	21 56									22 26									22 56			
Bentley	d	22 02									22 32									23 02			
Alton	a	22 10									22 39									23 10			
Farnborough (Main)	d				22 03								22 13			22 33							23 03
Fleet	d				22 08								22 19			22 38							23 08
Winchfield	d				22 14											22 44							23 14
Hook	d				22 18											22 48							23 18
Basingstoke	a		21 51		22 28	22 12							22 31			22 58					22 51		23 27

Table 155

Mondays to Fridays

until 5 October

London - Woking, Guildford, Alton and Basingstoke

Network Diagram - see first Page of Table 155

		SW 1 ✠	SW	SW 1	SW 1	SW ◇1 ✠	SW 1	SW	SW 1	SW 1	SW 1	SW 1	SW	SW	SW 1	SW ◇1	SW	SW 1	SW 1	SW 1	SW	SW 1
London Waterloo ⊖	d	22 20	22 20	22 23	22 30	22 35			22 39	22 42	22 45		22 50	22 52	22 53	23 05		23 12	23 15		23 20	23 23
Vauxhall ⊖	d		22 24										22 54	22 56							23 24	
Clapham Junction	d	22u27	22 29	22u30					22u46	22u49	22u52		22 59		23u00	23u12			23u22		23 29	23u30
	d													23 02				23u19				
Earlsfield	d		22 32										23 02								23 32	
Wimbledon ⊖	d		22 36					←					23 06				←				23 36	
Surbiton	d		22 44	22 41				22 44		23 00			23 14		23 11		23 14	23 38			23 44	23 41
Esher	d		→					22 48					→				23 18				→	
Hersham	d							22 51									23 21					
Walton-on-Thames	d							22 54		23 07							23 24	23 45				
Weybridge	d							22 57		23 11							23 27	23 49				
Byfleet & New Haw	d							23 00						00 06			23 30					
West Byfleet	d			22 51			←	23 03				←		00 09	23 21		23 33			←		23 55
Woking	a	22 45		22 59	22 54	22 58	22 59	23 08		23 18	23 11	23 18		00 15	23 29	23 31	23 38	23 55	23 41	23 55		23 59
	d	22 49		23 00	22 55		23 00			23 19	23 13	23 19			23 30	23 32		23 57	23 43	23 57		00 01
Worplesdon	d			→						→	23 18							→				
Guildford	a				23 03						23 23								23 51			
Brookwood	d						23 06					23 25			23 36					00 03		00 07
Ash Vale	d						23 14								23 44							00 15
Aldershot	a						23 19								23 49							00 19
	d						23 20								23 50							00 20
Farnham	a						23 25								23 55							00 25
	d						23 26								23 58							00 26
Bentley	d						23 33								00 04							00 33
Alton	a						23 40								00 11							00 40
Farnborough (Main)	d								23 16			23 33								00 10		
Fleet	d								23 21			23 38								00 16		
Winchfield	d											23 44								00 21		
Hook	d											23 48								00 26		
Basingstoke	a	23 09							23 33			23 57				23 53				00 33		

		SW 1	SW	SW 1 A	SW 1 A	SW 1	SW 1 B	SW 1
London Waterloo ⊖	d	23 35		23 40	23 45	23 48	23 55	
Vauxhall ⊖	d							
Clapham Junction	d	23u42		23u47	23u52	23u55	00u02	
	d							
Earlsfield	d							
Wimbledon ⊖	d		←					
Surbiton	d		23 44			00 09		
Esher	d		23 48					
Hersham	d		23 51					
Walton-on-Thames	d		23 54			00 16		
Weybridge	d		23 57			00 20		
Byfleet & New Haw	d		00 01					
West Byfleet	d		00 03					←
Woking	a	00 01	00 08	00 06	00 11	00 26	00 20	00 26
	d	00 03		00 08	00 13	00 28	00 21	00 28
Worplesdon	d				00 18	→		
Guildford	a				00 24			
Brookwood	d							00 34
Ash Vale	d							
Aldershot	a							
	d							
Farnham	a							
	d							
Bentley	d							
Alton	a							
Farnborough (Main)	d	00 14						00 41
Fleet	d	00 20						00 47
Winchfield	d							00s52
Hook	d							00s57
Basingstoke	a	00 33		00 27			00 43	01 06

A not from 27 July until 10 August, from 29 August until 7 September

B from 27 July until 7 September, not from 13 August until 28 August

Table 155

Mondays to Fridays
from 8 October

London - Woking, Guildford, Alton and Basingstoke

Network Diagram - see first Page of Table 155

		SW MO ■	SW MO	SW MX	SW MX ■	SW MO ■		SW MO	SW MX ■	SW MX		SW MX ■	SW MO ■	SW MX ■	SW MO	SW MX	SW MO ■	SW MX ■	SW MO ■	SW MX ■		SW MX ■	SW MO ■	SW MX ■	SW MX ■
London Waterloo 15 ⊖	d	22p37	22p50	22p52	22p53	23p07		23p10	23p12	23p20		23p23	23p30	23p35			23p35	23p40	23p40	23p45		23p48		00 05	
Vauxhall ⊖	d		22p54	22p56				23p14		23p24									23p44						
Clapham Junction 10	d	22p46			23b00	23p15		23p19		23p29		23b30	23b39	23b42			23b44	23b47	23p49	23b52		23b55		00u12	
	d		23p00	23p02					23b19																
Earlsfield	d							23p22		23p32									23p52						
Wimbledon 6 ⊖	d	22p53				23p22		23p26		23p36						←			23p56					00u18	
Surbiton 6	d	23p02			23p11	23p30		23p35	23p38	23p44		23p41				23p44			00 05			00 09			
Esher	d							23p39		→						23p48			00 09						
Hersham	d							23p42								23p51			00 12						
Walton-on-Thames	d	23p09						23p45	23p45							23p54			00 15			00 16			
Weybridge	d	23p13						23p49	23p49							23p57			00 19			00 20			
Byfleet & New Haw	d		00 02	00 06				23p51								00 01			00 21						
West Byfleet	d		00 05	00 09	23p21			23p54				23p55			←	00 03			00 24				←		
Woking	a	23p19	00 11	00 15	23p29	23p42		23p59	23p55			23p59	00 01	00 01	23p59	00 08	00 07	00 06	00 30	00 11		00 26	00 30	00 35	
	d	23p26			23p30	23p46	23p49	00 05	23p57			00 01	00 03	00 03	00 05		00 08	00 08	00 35	00 13		00 28	00 35	00 37	00 40
Worplesdon	d							→											→	00 18					
Guildford	a												00 10		00 13					00 24					
Brookwood	d	23p32			23p36	23p51	23p55		00 03			00 07										00 34	00 41		00 45
Ash Vale	d	23p40			23p44		00 03					00 15											00 48		00 53
Aldershot	a	23p45			23p49		00 07					00 19											00 53		00 58
	d	23p48			23p50		00 08					00 20											00 54		00 59
Farnham	a	23p54			23p55		00 13					00 25											00 59		01 04
	d	23p55			23p58		00 14					00 26													01 05
Bentley	d				00 04		00 24					00 33													01s11
Alton	a	00 07			00 11		00 31					00 40													01 18
Farnborough (Main)	d					23p59			00 10					00 14			00 18					00 41			
Fleet	d					00 04			00 16					00 20			00 24					00 47			
Winchfield	d					00 10			00 21													00s52			
Hook	d					00 14			00 26													00s57			
Basingstoke	a					00 21			00 33					00 33			00 39	00 27				01 06		00 55	

		SW MO	SW MX	SW MO ■	SW ■	SW ■		SW ■	SW ◇■	SW ■	SW ■	SW ■	SW ■	SW	SW ■	SW ■		SW ■	SW	SW ◇■	SW ■	SW	SW ■	SW ■	SW ■
London Waterloo 15 ⊖	d		00 09	00 50	01 05	05 00		05 20	05 30					05 50	06 12	06 15			06 20	06 30			06 42	06 45	
Vauxhall ⊖	d		00 13		01 09	05 04		05 24						05 54					06 24						
Clapham Junction 10	d		00 20	00 57		05 11		05 29	05u37					05 59	06u19	06u22			06 29	06u37			06u49	06u52	
	d				01 15																				
Earlsfield	d		00 23			05 14		05 32						06 02					06 32						
Wimbledon 6 ⊖	d		00 27		01s27	05 18		05 36	05 43					06 06					06 36						
Surbiton 6	d		00 35		01s35	05 26		05 44						06 14	06 30				06 44				07 00		
Esher	d		00s39			05 30		05 48						06 18					06 48						
Hersham	d		00s42			05 33		05 51						06 21					06 51						
Walton-on-Thames	d		00s44			05 37		05 54						06 24	06 37				06 54				07 07		
Weybridge	d		00s48			05 41		05 57						06 27	06 41				06 57				07 11		
Byfleet & New Haw	d		00s51			05 44		06 00						06 30					07 00						
West Byfleet	d	00s45	00s54			05 47		06 03			←			06 33				←	07 03			←			←
Woking	a	00 51	00 58	01 16	01 48	05 51		06 08	05 59		06 08			06 38	06 48	06 41		06 48	07 07	06 56		07 07	07 18	07 11	07 18
	d		01 00	01 18	01 49	05 53		06 11	06 01	06 02	06 11	06 19	06 30		06 50	06 43		06 50	07 10	06 57	06 58	07 10	07 19	07 13	07 19
Worplesdon	d							→			06 16				→	06 48			→				→	07 18	
Guildford	a		01 07	01s26		06 00					06 21					06 53						07 20		07 23	
Brookwood	d									06 08		06 25	06 36					06 56			07 06				07 25
Ash Vale	d									06 16			06 44								07 14				
Aldershot	a									06 21			06 49								07 19				
	d									06 21			06 50								07 20				
Farnham	a									06 27			06 55								07 25				
	d									06 27			06 56								07 26				
Bentley	d									06 34			07 02								07 32				
Alton	a									06 41			07 10								07 40				
Farnborough (Main)	d				01s58							06 33						07 04							07 33
Fleet	d				02s04							06 38						07 09							07 38
Winchfield	d											06 44						07 15							07 44
Hook	d											06 48						07 19							07 48
Basingstoke	a				02s16				06 20			06 58						07 28		07 16					07 56

b Previous night, stops to pick up only

Table 155

Mondays to Fridays
from 8 October

London - Woking, Guildford, Alton and Basingstoke

Network Diagram - see first Page of Table 155

		SW		SW ■	SW ◇■ 🍴	SW	SW ■	SW ■	SW ■	SW	SW ■	SW ■ 🍴		SW ■	SW ◇■ 🍴	SW	SW ■ 🍴	SW ■	SW ■	SW ◇■ 🍴	SW ■	SW		SW ■	SW ■ 🍴
London Waterloo 15 ⊖	d	06 50		06 53	07 10		07 12	07 15		07 20	07 23	07 30			07 35		07 39	07 42	07 45	07 50		07 50		07 53	08 00
Vauxhall ⊖	d	06 54								07 24												07 54			
Clapham Junction 10	d	06 59		07u00	07u17		07u20	07u23		07 29	07u30						07u46		07u52	07u57		07 59		08u00	
	d																								
Earlsfield	d	07 02								07 32												08 02			
Wimbledon 6 ⊖	d	07 06				←				07 36						←						08 06			
Surbiton 6	d	07 14		07 11		07 14	07 31			07 44	07 41					07 44		08 00				08 14		08 11	
Esher	d	→				07 18				→						07 48						→			
Hersham	d					07 21										07 51									
Walton-on-Thames	d					07 24	07 38									07 54		08 07							
Weybridge	d					07 27	07 42									07 57		08 11							
Byfleet & New Haw	d					07 30										08 00									
West Byfleet	d			07 21		07 33			←		07 51			←		08 03					←			08 21	
Woking	a			07 26	07 35	07 37	07 48	07 42	07 48		07 59	07 54		07 59	07 58	08 08		08 18	08 12	08 15	08 18			08 29	08 24
	d			07 30	07 36	07 39	07 50	07 44	07 50		08 00	07 55		08 00	08 00			08 19	08 14	08 16	08 19			08 30	08 25
Worplesdon	d						→	07 49			→							→	08 19					→	
Guildford	a					07 47		07 54				08 03							08 24						08 35
Brookwood	d			07 36					07 56					08 06							08 25				
Ash Vale	d			07 44										08 14											
Aldershot	a			07 49										08 19											
	d			07 50										08 20											
Farnham	a			07 55										08 25											
	d			07 56										08 26											
Bentley	d			08 02										08 32											
Alton	a			08 10										08 39											
Farnborough (Main)	d								08 03								08 13				08 33				
Fleet	d								08 09								08 19				08 38				
Winchfield	d								08 14												08 44				
Hook	d								08 19												08 48				
Basingstoke	a				07 55				08 26						08 19		08 32			08 37	08 58				

		SW ■	SW ◇■ 🍴	SW ■	SW	SW ■	SW ■	SW ◇■ 🍴		SW ■	SW	SW ■	SW ■ 🍴	SW ◇■ 🍴	SW ■	SW	SW ■	SW ■		SW ■	SW ◇■ 🍴	SW ■	SW	SW ■	SW ■ 🍴
London Waterloo 15 ⊖	d		08 05	08 09		08 12	08 15	08 20			08 20	08 23	08 30	08 35			08 39	08 42		08 45	08 50		08 50	08 53	09 00
Vauxhall ⊖	d										08 24												08 54		
Clapham Junction 10	d		08u12			08u19	08u22	08u27			08 29						08u46			08u52			08 59	09u00	
	d																								
Earlsfield	d										08 32												09 02		
Wimbledon 6 ⊖	d				←						08 36					←							09 06		
Surbiton 6	d				08 14	08 30					08 44	08 41				08 44		09 00					09 14	09 11	
Esher	d				08 18						→					08 48							→		
Hersham	d				08 21											08 51									
Walton-on-Thames	d				08 24	08 37										08 54		09 07							
Weybridge	d				08 27	08 41										08 57		09 11							
Byfleet & New Haw	d				08 30											09 00									
West Byfleet	d	←			08 33					←		08 51			←	09 03						←		09 21	
Woking	a	08 29		08 33	08 37	08 49	08 42	08 46		08 49		09 00	08 55	08 58	09 00	09 08		09 18		09 11	09 15	09 18		09 29	09 24
	d	08 30		08 35	08 39	08 49	08 44	08 46		08 49		09 00	08 55		09 00			09 19		09 13	09 16	09 19		09 30	09 25
Worplesdon	d					→	08 49					→						→		09 18				→	
Guildford	a				08 50		08 54						09 05							09 23					09 33
Brookwood	d	08 36								08 55					09 06							09 25			
Ash Vale	d	08 44													09 14										
Aldershot	a	08 49													09 20										
	d	08 50													09 20										
Farnham	a	08 55													09 26										
	d	08 56													09 26										
Bentley	d	09 02																							
Alton	a	09 10													09 39										
Farnborough (Main)	d			08 45						09 03							09 13					09 33			
Fleet	d									09 08							09 19					09 38			
Winchfield	d									09 14												09 44			
Hook	d									09 18												09 48			
Basingstoke	a		08 47	08 58				09 05		09 28							09 31				09 36	09 58			

London - Woking, Guildford, Alton and Basingstoke

Network Diagram - see first Page of Table 155

Station		SW 1	SW ◇1 H	SW 1		SW	SW 1	SW 1	SW ◇1 H	SW 1	SW	SW 1	SW 1 H	SW ◇1 H		SW 1	SW	SW 1	SW 1	SW 1	SW ◇1 H	SW 1	SW	SW 1	
London Waterloo 15 ⊖	d		09 05	09 09			09 12	09 15	09 20		09 20	09 23	09 30	09 35				09 39	09 42	09 45	09 50		09 50	09 53	
Vauxhall ⊖	d										09 24												09 54		
Clapham Junction 10	d		09u12				09u19	09u22	09u27		09 29							09u46		09u52			09 59	10u00	
	d																								
Earlsfield	d										09 32												10 02		
Wimbledon 5 ⊖	d					←					09 36						←						10 06		
Surbiton 5	d					09 14	09 30				09 44	09 41					09 44		10 00				10 14	10 11	
Esher	d					09 18					→						09 48						→		
Hersham	d					09 21											09 51								
Walton-on-Thames	d					09 24	09 37										09 54		10 07						
Weybridge	d					09 27	09 41										09 57		10 11						
Byfleet & New Haw	d					09 30											10 00								
West Byfleet	d	←				09 33				←		09 51				←	10 03					←		10 21	
Woking	a	09 29		09 33		09 38	09 48	09 42	09 45	09 48		09 59	09 54	09 58		09 59	10 08		10 18	10 11	10 14	10 18		10 29	
	d	09 30		09 35			09 49	09 43	09 46	09 49		10 00	09 55			10 00			10 19	10 13	10 16	10 19		10 30	
Worplesdon	d						→					→							→	10 18				→	
Guildford	a							09 52					10 03							10 23					
Brookwood	d	09 36								09 55						10 06						10 25			
Ash Vale	d	09 44														10 14									
Aldershot	a	09 49														10 19									
	d	09 50														10 20									
Farnham	a	09 55														10 25									
	d	09 56														10 26									
Bentley	d	10 02														10 52									
Alton	a	10 10														10 59									
Farnborough (Main)	d			09 45						10 03								10 13				10 33			
Fleet	d									10 08								10 19				10 38			
Winchfield	d									10 14												10 44			
Hook	d									10 18												10 48			
Basingstoke	a		09 47	09 58					10 05	10 28								10 31			10 36	10 58			

Station		SW 1 H	SW 1	SW ◇1 H	SW 1	SW	SW 1	SW 1	SW ◇1 H	SW 1		SW	SW 1	SW 1 H	SW ◇1 H	SW 1	SW	SW 1	SW 1	SW 1		SW ◇1 H	SW 1	SW	SW 1
London Waterloo 15 ⊖	d	10 00		10 05	10 09		10 12	10 15	10 20			10 20	10 23	10 30	10 35			10 39	10 42	10 45		10 50		10 50	10 53
Vauxhall ⊖	d											10 24												10 54	
Clapham Junction 10	d			10u12			10u19	10u22	10u27			10 29						10u46		10u52				10 59	11u00
	d																								
Earlsfield	d											10 32												11 02	
Wimbledon 5 ⊖	d					←						10 36					←							11 06	
Surbiton 5	d					10 14	10 30					10 44	10 41				10 44		11 00					11 14	11 11
Esher	d					10 18						→					10 48							→	
Hersham	d					10 21											10 51								
Walton-on-Thames	d					10 24	10 37										10 54		11 07						
Weybridge	d					10 27	10 41										10 57		11 11						
Byfleet & New Haw	d					10 30											11 00								
West Byfleet	d		←			10 33				←			10 51			←	11 03						←		11 21
Woking	a	10 24	10 29		10 33	10 38	10 48	10 41	10 45	10 48			10 59	10 54	10 58	10 59	11 08		11 18	11 11		11 14	11 18		11 29
	d	10 25	10 30		10 35		10 49	10 43	10 46	10 49			11 00	10 55		11 00			11 19	11 13		11 16	11 19		11 30
Worplesdon	d						→						→						→	11 18					→
Guildford	a	10 33						10 50						11 03						11 23					
Brookwood	d		10 36							10 55						11 06							11 25		
Ash Vale	d		10 44													11 14									
Aldershot	a		10 49													11 19									
	d		10 50													11 20									
Farnham	a		10 55													11 25									
	d		10 56																						
Bentley	d		11 02																						
Alton	a		11 10																						
Farnborough (Main)	d				10 45					11 03								11 13					11 33		
Fleet	d									11 08								11 19					11 38		
Winchfield	d									11 14													11 44		
Hook	d									11 18													11 48		
Basingstoke	a			10 47	10 58				11 05	11 28								11 31				11 36	11 58		

London - Woking, Guildford, Alton and Basingstoke

Network Diagram - see first Page of Table 155

Station		SW 1 H	SW 1	SW ◇1 H	SW 1	SW		SW 1	SW 1	SW ◇1 H	SW 1	SW	SW 1	SW 1 H	SW ◇1 H	SW 1		SW	SW 1	SW 1	SW 1	SW ◇1 H	SW 1	SW	SW 1
London Waterloo 15 ⊖	d	11 00		11 05	11 09			11 12	11 15	11 20		11 20	11 23	11 30	11 35				11 39	11 42	11 45	11 50		11 50	11 53
Vauxhall ⊖	d											11 24												11 54	
Clapham Junction 10	d			11u12				11u19	11u22	11u27		11 29							11u46		11u52			11 59	12u00
	d																								
Earlsfield	d											11 32												12 02	
Wimbledon 5 ⊖	d					←						11 36						←						12 06	
Surbiton 5	d					11 14		11 30				11 44	11 41					11 44		12 00				12 14	12 11
Esher	d					11 18						→						11 48						→	
Hersham	d					11 21												11 51							
Walton-on-Thames	d					11 24		11 37										11 54		12 07					
Weybridge	d					11 27		11 41										11 57		12 11					
Byfleet & New Haw	d					11 30												12 00							
West Byfleet	d		←			11 33					←		11 51			←		12 03					←		12 21
Woking	a	11 24	11 29		11 33	11 38		11 48	11 41	11 45	11 48		11 59	11 54	11 58	11 59		12 08		12 18	12 11	12 14	12 18		12 29
	d	11 25	11 30		11 35			11 49	11 43	11 46	11 49		12 00	11 55		12 00				12 19	12 13	12 16	12 19		12 30
Worplesdon	d							→					→							→	12 18				→
Guildford	a	11 33							11 50					12 03							12 23				
Brookwood	d		11 36								11 55					12 06							12 25		
Ash Vale	d		11 44													12 14									
Aldershot	a		11 49													12 19									
	d		11 50													12 20									
Farnham	a		11 55													12 25									
	d		11 56													12 26									
Bentley	d		12 02																						
Alton	a		12 10													12 37									
Farnborough (Main)	d				11 45						12 03								12 13				12 33		
Fleet	d										12 08								12 19				12 38		
Winchfield	d										12 14												12 44		
Hook	d										12 18												12 48		
Basingstoke	a			11 47	11 58					12 05	12 28								12 31			12 36	12 58		

Station		SW 1 H		SW 1	SW ◇1 H	SW 1	SW	SW 1	SW 1	SW ◇1 H	SW 1	SW		SW 1	SW 1 H	SW ◇1 H	SW 1	SW	SW 1	SW 1	SW 1	SW ◇1 H		SW 1	SW
London Waterloo 15 ⊖	d	12 00			12 05	12 09		12 12	12 15	12 20		12 20		12 23	12 30	12 35			12 39	12 42	12 45	12 50			12 50
Vauxhall ⊖	d											12 24													12 54
Clapham Junction 10	d				12u12			12u19	12u22	12u27		12 29							12u46		12u52				12 59
	d																								
Earlsfield	d											12 32													13 02
Wimbledon 5 ⊖	d						←					12 36						←							13 06
Surbiton 5	d						12 14	12 30				12 44		12 41				12 44		13 00					13 14
Esher	d						12 18					→						12 48							→
Hersham	d						12 21											12 51							
Walton-on-Thames	d						12 24	12 37										12 54		13 07					
Weybridge	d						12 27	12 41										12 57		13 11					
Byfleet & New Haw	d						12 30											13 00							
West Byfleet	d			←			12 33				←			12 51			←	13 03						←	
Woking	a	12 24		12 29		12 33	12 38	12 48	12 41	12 45	12 48			12 59	12 54	12 58	12 59	13 08		13 18	13 11	13 14		13 18	
	d	12 25		12 30		12 35		12 49	12 43	12 46	12 49			13 00	12 55		13 00			13 19	13 13	13 16		13 19	
Worplesdon	d							→						→						→	13 18				
Guildford	a	12 33							12 50						13 03						13 23				
Brookwood	d			12 36							12 55						13 06							13 25	
Ash Vale	d			12 44													13 14								
Aldershot	a			12 49													13 19								
	d			12 50													13 20								
Farnham	a			12 55													13 25								
	d			12 56													13 26								
Bentley	d			13 02																					
Alton	a			13 10													13 37								
Farnborough (Main)	d					12 45					13 03								13 13					13 33	
Fleet	d										13 08								13 19					13 38	
Winchfield	d										13 14													13 44	
Hook	d										13 18													13 48	
Basingstoke	a				12 47	12 58				13 05	13 28								13 31			13 36		13 58	

Table 155

London - Woking, Guildford, Alton and Basingstoke

Mondays to Fridays
from 8 October

Network Diagram - see first Page of Table 155

		SW 1	SW 1 ⊼	SW 1	SW ◇1 ⊼	SW 1	SW	SW 1		SW 1	SW ◇1 ⊼	SW 1	SW	SW 1	SW 1 ⊼	SW ◇1 ⊼	SW 1	SW		SW 1	SW 1	SW 1	SW ◇1 ⊼	SW 1	SW
London Waterloo 15 ⊖	d	12 53	13 00		13 05	13 09		13 12		13 15	13 20		13 20	13 23	13 30	13 35				13 39	13 42	13 45	13 50		13 50
Vauxhall ⊖	d												13 24												13 54
Clapham Junction 10	d	13u00			13u12			13u19		13u22	13u27		13 29							13u46		13u52			13 59
	d																								
Earlsfield	d												13 32												14 02
Wimbledon 6 ⊖	d						←						13 36					←							14 06
Surbiton 6	d	13 11					13 14	13 30					13 44	13 41				13 44			14 00				14 14
Esher	d						13 18						→					13 48							→
Hersham	d						13 21											13 51							
Walton-on-Thames	d						13 24	13 37										13 54			14 07				
Weybridge	d						13 27	13 41										13 57			14 11				
Byfleet & New Haw	d						13 30											14 00							
West Byfleet	d	13 21		←			13 33					←		13 51			←	14 03						←	
Woking	a	13 29	13 24	13 29		13 33	13 38	13 48		13 41	13 45	13 48		13 59	13 54	13 58	13 59	14 08			14 18	14 11	14 14	14 18	
	d	13 30	13 25	13 30		13 35		13 49		13 43	13 46	13 49		14 00	13 55		14 00				14 19	14 13	14 16	14 19	
Worplesdon	d	→						→						→							→	14 18			
Guildford	a		13 33							13 50					14 03							14 23			
Brookwood	d			13 36								13 55					14 06							14 25	
Ash Vale	d			13 44													14 14								
Aldershot	a			13 49													14 19								
	d			13 50													14 20								
Farnham	a			13 55													14 25								
	d			13 56													14 26								
Bentley	d			14 02																					
Alton	a			14 11													14 37								
Farnborough (Main)	d					13 45						14 03								14 13				14 33	
Fleet	d											14 08								14 19				14 38	
Winchfield	d											14 14												14 44	
Hook	d											14 18												14 48	
Basingstoke	a				13 47	13 58					14 05	14 28								14 31			14 36	14 58	

		SW 1	SW 1 ⊼	SW 1		SW ◇1 ⊼	SW 1	SW	SW 1	SW 1	SW ◇1 ⊼	SW 1	SW	SW 1		SW 1 ⊼	SW ◇1 ⊼	SW 1	SW	SW 1	SW 1	SW 1	SW ◇1 ⊼	SW 1
London Waterloo 15 ⊖	d	13 53	14 00			14 05	14 09		14 12	14 15	14 20		14 20	14 23		14 30	14 35			14 39	14 42	14 45	14 50	
Vauxhall ⊖	d												14 24											
Clapham Junction 10	d	14u00				14u12			14u19	14u22	14u27		14 29							14u46		14u52		
	d																							
Earlsfield	d												14 32											
Wimbledon 6 ⊖	d							←					14 36						←					
Surbiton 6	d	14 11						14 14	14 30				14 44	14 41					14 44		15 00			
Esher	d							14 18					→						14 48					
Hersham	d							14 21											14 51					
Walton-on-Thames	d							14 24	14 37										14 54		15 07			
Weybridge	d							14 27	14 41										14 57		15 11			
Byfleet & New Haw	d							14 30											15 00					
West Byfleet	d	14 21		←				14 33				←		14 51				←	15 03					←
Woking	a	14 29	14 24	14 29			14 33	14 38	14 48	14 41	14 45	14 48		14 59		14 54	14 58	14 59	15 08		15 18	15 11	15 14	15 18
	d	14 30	14 25	14 30			14 35		14 49	14 43	14 46	14 49		15 00		14 55		15 00			15 19	15 13	15 16	15 19
Worplesdon	d	→							→					→							→	15 18		
Guildford	a		14 33							14 50						15 03						15 23		
Brookwood	d			14 36								14 55						15 06						15 25
Ash Vale	d			14 44														15 14						
Aldershot	a			14 49														15 19						
	d			14 50														15 20						
Farnham	a			14 55														15 25						
	d			14 56														15 26						
Bentley	d			15 02																				
Alton	a			15 10														15 37						
Farnborough (Main)	d						14 45					15 03								15 13				15 33
Fleet	d											15 08								15 19				15 38
Winchfield	d											15 14												15 44
Hook	d											15 18												15 48
Basingstoke	a					14 47	14 58				15 05	15 28								15 31			15 36	15 58

Table 155

London - Woking, Guildford, Alton and Basingstoke

Mondays to Fridays
from 8 October

Network Diagram - see first Page of Table 155

		SW	SW 1	SW 1 ⊼	SW 1	SW ◇1 ⊼	SW 1	SW	SW 1	SW 1		SW ◇1 ⊼	SW 1	SW	SW 1	SW 1 ⊼	SW ◇1 ⊼	SW 1	SW	SW 1		SW 1	SW 1	SW ◇1 ⊼	SW 1
London Waterloo 15 ⊖	d	14 50	14 53	15 00		15 05	15 09		15 12	15 15		15 20		15 20	15 23	15 30	15 35			15 39		15 42	15 45	15 50	
Vauxhall ⊖	d	14 54												15 24											
Clapham Junction 10	d	14 59	15u00			15u12			15u19	15u22		15u27		15 29						15u46			15u52	15u57	
	d																								
Earlsfield	d	15 02												15 32											
Wimbledon 6 ⊖	d	15 06						←						15 36					←						
Surbiton 6	d	15 14	15 11					15 14	15 30					15 44	15 41				15 44			16 00			
Esher	d	→						15 18						→					15 48						
Hersham	d							15 21											15 51						
Walton-on-Thames	d							15 24	15 37										15 54			16 07			
Weybridge	d							15 27	15 41										15 57			16 11			
Byfleet & New Haw	d							15 30											16 00						
West Byfleet	d		15 21		←			15 33					←		15 51			←	16 03						←
Woking	a		15 29	15 24	15 29		15 33	15 38	15 48	15 41		15 45	15 48		15 59	15 54	15 58	15 59	16 08			16 18	16 11	16 15	16 18
	d		15 30	15 25	15 30		15 35		15 49	15 43		15 46	15 49		16 00	15 55		16 00				16 19	16 13	16 16	16 19
Worplesdon	d		→						→	15 48					→							→			
Guildford	a			15 33						15 53						16 03							16 20		
Brookwood	d				15 36								15 55					16 06							16 25
Ash Vale	d				15 44													16 14							
Aldershot	a				15 49													16 19							
	d				15 50													16 20							
Farnham	a				15 55													16 25							
	d				15 56													16 26							
Bentley	d				16 02																				
Alton	a				16 10													16 37							
Farnborough (Main)	d						15 45						16 03							16 13					16 33
Fleet	d												16 08							16 19					16 38
Winchfield	d												16 14												16 44
Hook	d												16 18												16 48
Basingstoke	a					15 47	15 58					16 05	16 28							16 31				16 36	16 58

		SW	SW 1	SW 1 ⊼	SW 1	SW ◇1 ⊼		SW 1	SW	SW 1	SW 1	SW ◇1 ⊼	SW 1	SW	SW 1	SW 1 ⊼		SW 1	SW	SW ◇1 ⊼	SW 1	SW 1	SW 1	SW ◇1 ⊼	SW 1
London Waterloo 15 ⊖	d	15 50	15 53	16 00		16 05		16 09		16 12	16 15	16 20		16 20	16 25	16 30				16 35	16 39	16 42	16 45	16 50	
Vauxhall ⊖	d	15 54												16 24											
Clapham Junction 10	d	15 59	16u00			16u12				16u19	16u22	16u27		16 29							16u46		16u52	16u57	
	d																								
Earlsfield	d	16 02												16 32											
Wimbledon 6 ⊖	d	16 06							←					16 36					←						
Surbiton 6	d	16 14	16 11						16 14	16 30				16 44	16 41				16 44			17 00			
Esher	d	→							16 18					→					16 48						
Hersham	d								16 21										16 51						
Walton-on-Thames	d								16 24	16 37									16 54			17 07			
Weybridge	d								16 27	16 41									16 57			17 11			
Byfleet & New Haw	d								16 30										17 00						
West Byfleet	d		16 21		←				16 33				←		16 51			←	17 03						←
Woking	a		16 29	16 24	16 29			16 33	16 38	16 48	16 41	16 45	16 48		16 59	16 54		16 59	17 10			17 18	17 11		17 18
	d		16 30	16 25	16 30			16 35		16 49	16 43	16 46	16 49		17 00	16 55		17 00				17 19	17 13	17u16	17 19
Worplesdon	d		→							→	16 48				→							→			
Guildford	a			16 33							16 53					17 03							17 20		
Brookwood	d				16 36								16 55					17 06							17 25
Ash Vale	d				16 44													17 14							
Aldershot	a				16 49													17 19							
	d				16 50													17 20							
Farnham	a				16 55													17 25							
	d				16 56													17 26							
Bentley	d				17 02													17 32							
Alton	a				17 10													17 41							
Farnborough (Main)	d							16 45					17 03								17 13				17 33
Fleet	d												17 08								17 19				17 38
Winchfield	d												17 14												17 44
Hook	d												17 18												17 48
Basingstoke	a					16 47		16 58				17 05	17 30								17 31			17 36	18 00

London - Woking, Guildford, Alton and Basingstoke

Network Diagram - see first Page of Table 155

		SW		SW ■	SW ■ 🚲	SW ■	SW ■	SW ■	SW ■	SW ■	SW ■	SW ◇■ 🚲		SW	SW ■	SW ■	SW ■	SW ■ 🚲	SW	SW ■	SW ■	SW ■		SW ■	SW ■
London Waterloo 15 ⊖	d	16 50		16 55	17 00		17 02	17 09	17 12	17 15		17 20		17 20	17 23	17 25		17 30		17 32	17 39	17 41		17 45	17 48
Vauxhall ⊖	d	16 54												17 24											
Clapham Junction 10	d	16 59		17u02										17 29											
	d																								
Earlsfield	d	17 02												17 32											
Wimbledon 6 ⊖	d	17 06												17 36					←						
Surbiton 6	d	17 14					17 18							17 44	17 39				17 44	17 48					
Esher	d	17 18					17 22							→					17 48	17 52					
Hersham	d	17 21					17 25												17 51	17 55					
Walton-on-Thames	d	17 24					17 29												17 54	17 59					
Weybridge	d	17 27					17 33												17 57	18 03					
Byfleet & New Haw	d	17 30					17 36												18 00	18 06					
West Byfleet	d	17 33		17 21		←	17 39				←						←		18 03	18 09					
Woking	a	17 43		17 29	17 24	17 29	17 44	17 32	17 36	17 38	17 44				17 51	17 50	17 51	17 54	18 10	18 14	18 02				18 11
	d			17 30	17 25	17 30	17 46	17 34	17 37	17 40	17 46	17u46			17 52	17 51	17 52	17 56		18 16	18 04				18 13
Worplesdon	d			→	17 30		→			17 45					→			18 00		→					
Guildford	a				17 36					17 51	17 56							18 06						18 21	
Brookwood	d					17 36			17 43								18 00					18 11			
Ash Vale	d					17 44										18 03									
Aldershot	a					17 49										18 08									
	d					17 50										18 09									
Farnham	a					17 55										18 14									
	d					17 56										18 15									
Bentley	d					18 02										18 24									
Alton	a					18 11										18 32									
Farnborough (Main)	d								17 51								18 08					18 19			
Fleet	d								17 56								18 13					18 24			
Winchfield	d								18 02								18 19					18 30			
Hook	d								18 06								18 23					18 34			
Basingstoke	a							17 52	18 16			18 05					18 32				18 22	18 45			18 31

		SW ■	SW ◇■ 🚲	SW	SW ■	SW ■	SW ■	SW		SW ■ 🚲	SW ■	SW ■	SW ■	SW ■	SW ■	SW ◇■ 🚲	SW	SW ■		SW ■	SW ■ 🚲	SW	SW ■	SW ■	SW ■
London Waterloo 15 ⊖	d		17 50	17 50	17 53	17 55				18 00	18 02	18 09	18 12	18 15	18 18	18 20	18 20	18 23		18 25	18 30		18 32	18 39	18 41
Vauxhall ⊖	d			17 54													18 24								
Clapham Junction 10	d			17 59												18u27	18 29			18u33				18u46	
	d																								
Earlsfield	d			18 02													18 32								
Wimbledon 6 ⊖	d			18 06				←									18 36					←			
Surbiton 6	d			18 14	18 09			18 14			18 18						18 44	18 40				18 44	18 48		
Esher	d			→				18 18			18 22						→					18 48	18 52		
Hersham	d							18 21			18 25											18 51	18 55		
Walton-on-Thames	d							18 24			18 29											18 54	18 59		
Weybridge	d							18 27			18 33											18 57	19 03		
Byfleet & New Haw	d							18 30			18 36											19 00	19 06		
West Byfleet	d	←			18 19		←	18 33			18 39											19 03	19 09		
Woking	a	18 14			18 23	18 20	18 23	18 41			18 48	18 33			18 42	18 45		18 52		18 52	18 57	19 12	19 18	19 05	
	d	18 16			18 25	18 21	18 25					18 35			18 43	18 46		18 54		18 53	18 58		19 20	19 06	
Worplesdon	d	18 21			→										18 48								→		
Guildford	a	18 29								18 32				18 50	18 54						19 06				
Brookwood	d					18 27							18 41					19 02							19 13
Ash Vale	d					18 35														19 05					
Aldershot	a					18 40														19 10					
	d					18 41														19 11					
Farnham	a					18 46														19 16					
	d					18 48														19 18					
Bentley	d					18 54														19 24					
Alton	a					19 03														19 33					
Farnborough (Main)	d						18 39						18 48					19 10							19 20
Fleet	d						18 44						18 54					19 15							19 26
Winchfield	d						18 50						18 59					19 21							19 31
Hook	d						18 54						19 04					19 25							19 36
Basingstoke	a		18 37				19 03					18 53	19 16			19 05		19 34						19 28	19 47

London - Woking, Guildford, Alton and Basingstoke

Network Diagram - see first Page of Table 155

		SW ■	SW ◇■ 🚲	SW ■		SW	SW ■	SW ■ 🚲	SW ■	SW ◇■ 🚲	SW ■	SW ■	SW ■	SW ◇■ 🚲		SW	SW ■	SW ■ 🚲	SW ◇■ 🚲	SW ■	SW ■	SW ■	SW ■	SW ◇■ 🚲
London Waterloo 15 ⊖	d	18 45	18 50			18 50	18 55	19 00	19 02	19 05	19 09	19 12	19 15	19 20		19 20	19 25	19 30	19 35		19 39	19 42	19 45	19 50
Vauxhall ⊖	d					18 54										19 24								
Clapham Junction 10	d					18 59	19u02			19u12		19u19	19u22	19u27		19 29	19u32				19u46		19u52	
	d																							
Earlsfield	d					19 02										19 32								
Wimbledon 6 ⊖	d					19 06										19 36								
Surbiton 6	d					19 14			19 18							19 44						20 00		
Esher	d					19 18			19 22							19 48								
Hersham	d					19 21			19 25							19 51								
Walton-on-Thames	d					19 24			19 29							19 54						20 07		
Weybridge	d					19 27			19 33							19 57						20 11		
Byfleet & New Haw	d					19 30			19 36							20 00								
West Byfleet	d	19 08		←		19 33			19 39							20 03	19 51			←				
Woking	a	19 13	19 17	19 18		19 42	19 21	19 24	19 48		19 33	19 38	19 43	19 45		20 08	19 59	19 54	19 58	19 59		20 18	20 11	20 14
	d	19 14	19 18	19 20			19 23	19 25			19 35	19 39	19 45	19 46			20 00	19 55		20 00		20 19	20 13	20 16
Worplesdon	d							19 30									→					→	20 18	
Guildford	a	19 23						19 36					19 52					20 03					20 23	
Brookwood	d						19 30					19 45								20 06				
Ash Vale	d						19 37													20 14				
Aldershot	a						19 42													20 19				
	d						19 43													20 20				
Farnham	a						19 48													20 25				
	d						19 49													20 26				
Bentley	d						19 55													20 32				
Alton	a						20 04													20 39				
Farnborough (Main)	d			19 31							19 45	19 53									20 13			
Fleet	d			19 37								19 58									20 19			
Winchfield	d			19 42								20 04												
Hook	d			19 47								20 09												
Basingstoke	a		19 37	19 59						19 47	19 58	20 16		20 06							20 31			20 36

		SW ■	SW	SW ■	SW ■ 🚲	SW ■	SW ◇■ 🚲	SW ■	SW	SW ■		SW ■	SW ◇■ 🚲	SW ■	SW	SW ■	SW ■ 🚲	SW ◇■ 🚲	SW ■	SW		SW ■	SW ■	SW ■	SW ■
London Waterloo 15 ⊖	d		19 50	19 53	20 00		20 05	20 09		20 12		20 15	20 20		20 20	20 23	20 30	20 35				20 39	20 42	20 45	
Vauxhall ⊖	d		19 54												20 24										
Clapham Junction 10	d		19 59	20u00			20u12			20u19		20u22	20u27		20 29							20u46		20u52	
	d																								
Earlsfield	d		20 02												20 32										
Wimbledon 6 ⊖	d		20 06						←						20 36					←					
Surbiton 6	d		20 14	20 11					20 14	20 30					20 44	20 41				20 44			21 00		
Esher	d		→						20 18						→					20 48					
Hersham	d								20 21											20 51					
Walton-on-Thames	d								20 24	20 37										20 54			21 07		
Weybridge	d								20 27	20 41										20 57			21 11		
Byfleet & New Haw	d								20 30											21 00					
West Byfleet	d	←		20 21		←			20 33					←		20 51			←	21 03					←
Woking	a	20 18		20 29	20 24	20 29		20 33	20 38	20 48		20 41	20 45	20 48		20 59	20 54	20 58	20 59	21 08			21 18	21 11	21 18
	d	20 19		20 30	20 25	20 30		20 35		20 49		20 43	20 46	20 49		21 00	20 55		21 00				21 19	21 13	21 19
Worplesdon	d			→						→						→							→	21 18	
Guildford	a				20 33							20 50					21 03							21 23	
Brookwood	d	20 25				20 36								20 55					21 06						21 25
Ash Vale	d					20 44													21 14						
Aldershot	a					20 49													21 19						
	d					20 50													21 20						
Farnham	a					20 55													21 25						
	d					20 56													21 26						
Bentley	d					21 02													21 32						
Alton	a					21 10													21 39						
Farnborough (Main)	d	20 33						20 45						21 03								21 13			21 33
Fleet	d	20 38												21 08								21 19			21 38
Winchfield	d	20 44												21 14											21 44
Hook	d	20 48												21 18											21 48
Basingstoke	a	20 58					20 47	20 58					21 05	21 28								21 31			21 58

London - Woking, Guildford, Alton and Basingstoke

Network Diagram - see first Page of Table 155

		SW	SW ■	SW ■ ⊥	SW ■	SW ◇■ ⊥		SW	SW ■	SW ◇■ ⊥	SW	SW ■	SW ■ ⊥	SW ◇■ ⊥	SW ■	SW		SW ■	SW ■	SW ■	SW ■	SW	SW ■	SW ■	SW ■
London Waterloo ■15 ⊖	d	20 50	20 53	21 00		21 05			21 12	21 20	21 20	21 23	21 30	21 35				21 39	21 42	21 45		21 50	21 53	22 00	
Vauxhall ⊖	d	20 54									21 24											21 54			
Clapham Junction ■10	d	20 59	21u00			21u12			21u19	21u27	21 29							21u46		21u52		21 59	22u00		
	d																								
Earlsfield	d	21 02									21 32											22 02			
Wimbledon ■ ⊖	d	21 06						←			21 36					←						22 06			
Surbiton ■	d	21 14	21 11					21 14	21 30		21 44	21 41				21 44			22 00			22 14	22 11		
Esher	d	→						21 18			→					21 48						→			
Hersham	d							21 21								21 51									
Walton-on-Thames	d							21 24	21 37							21 54			22 07						
Weybridge	d							21 27	21 41							21 57			22 11						
Byfleet & New Haw	d							21 30								22 00									
West Byfleet	d		21 21		←			21 33				21 51			←	22 03					←		22 21		←
Woking	a		21 29	21 24	21 29	21 31		21 38	21 48	21 45		21 59	21 54	21 58	21 59	22 08			22 18	22 11	22 18		22 29	22 24	22 29
	d		21 30	21 25	21 30	21 32			21 49	21 49		22 00	21 55		22 00				22 19	22 13	22 19		22 30	22 25	22 30
Worplesdon	d		→									→							→	22 18			→		
Guildford	a			21 33									22 03							22 23				22 33	
Brookwood	d				21 36				21 55						22 06						22 25				22 36
Ash Vale	d				21 44										22 14										22 44
Aldershot	a				21 49										22 19										22 49
	d				21 50										22 20										22 50
Farnham	a				21 55										22 25										22 55
	d				21 56										22 26										22 56
Bentley	d				22 02										22 32										23 02
Alton	a				22 10										22 39										23 10
Farnborough (Main)	d								22 03									22 13			22 33				
Fleet	d								22 08									22 19			22 38				
Winchfield	d								22 14												22 44				
Hook	d								22 18												22 48				
Basingstoke	a					21 51			22 28	22 12								22 31			22 58				

		SW ◇■ ⊥		SW	SW ■	SW ■ ⊥	SW	SW ■	SW ■	SW ◇■ ⊥	SW ■	SW		SW ■	SW ■	SW ■	SW ■	SW	SW	SW ■	SW ◇■	SW		SW ■	SW ■
London Waterloo ■15 ⊖	d	22 05			22 12	22 20	22 20	22 23	22 30	22 35				22 39	22 42	22 45		22 50	22 52	22 53	23 05			23 12	23 15
Vauxhall ⊖	d						22 24											22 54	22 56						
Clapham Junction ■10	d	22u12			22u19	22u27	22 29	22u30						22u46	22u49	22u52		22 59		23u00	23u12				23u22
	d																		23 02					23u19	
Earlsfield	d						22 32											23 02							
Wimbledon ■ ⊖	d			←			22 36					←						23 06				←			
Surbiton ■	d			22 14	22 30		22 44	22 41				22 44			23 00			23 14		23 11		23 14		23 38	
Esher	d			22 18			→					22 48						→				23 18			
Hersham	d			22 21								22 51										23 21			
Walton-on-Thames	d			22 24	22 37							22 54			23 07							23 24		23 45	
Weybridge	d			22 27	22 41							22 57			23 11							23 27		23 49	
Byfleet & New Haw	d			22 30								23 00							00 06			23 30			
West Byfleet	d			22 33				22 51			←	23 03					←		00 09	23 21		23 33			
Woking	a	22 31		22 37	22 48	22 45		22 59	22 54	22 58	22 59	23 08			23 18	23 11	23 18		00 15	23 29	23 31	23 38		23 55	23 41
	d	22 32		22 39	22 49	22 49		23 00	22 55		23 00				23 19	23 13	23 19			23 30	23 32			23 57	23 43
Worplesdon	d							→							→	23 18								→	
Guildford	a			22 47					23 03							23 23									23 51
Brookwood	d				22 55						23 06						23 25			23 36					
Ash Vale	d										23 14									23 44					
Aldershot	a										23 19									23 49					
	d										23 20									23 50					
Farnham	a										23 25									23 55					
	d										23 26									23 58					
Bentley	d										23 33									00 04					
Alton	a										23 40									00 11					
Farnborough (Main)	d				23 03									23 16			23 33								
Fleet	d				23 08									23 21			23 38								
Winchfield	d				23 14												23 44								
Hook	d				23 18												23 48								
Basingstoke	a	22 51			23 27	23 09								23 33			23 57				23 53				

London - Woking, Guildford, Alton and Basingstoke

Network Diagram - see first Page of Table 155

		SW ■	SW	SW ■	SW ■	SW	SW ■	SW ■		SW ■
London Waterloo ■15 ⊖	d		23 20	23 23	23 35		23 40	23 45		23 48
Vauxhall ⊖	d		23 24							
Clapham Junction ■10	d		23 29	23u30	23u42		23u47	23u52		23u55
	d									
Earlsfield	d		23 32							
Wimbledon ■ ⊖	d		23 36			←				
Surbiton ■	d		23 44	23 41		23 44				00 09
Esher	d		→			23 48				
Hersham	d					23 51				
Walton-on-Thames	d					23 54				00 16
Weybridge	d					23 57				00 20
Byfleet & New Haw	d					00 01				
West Byfleet	d	←		23 55		00 03				
Woking	a	23 55		23 59	00 01	00 08	00 06	00 11		00 26
	d	23 57		00 01	00 03		00 08	00 13		00 28
Worplesdon	d							00 18		
Guildford	a							00 24		
Brookwood	d	00 03		00 07						00 34
Ash Vale	d			00 15						
Aldershot	a			00 19						
	d			00 20						
Farnham	a			00 25						
	d			00 26						
Bentley	d			00 33						
Alton	a			00 40						
Farnborough (Main)	d	00 10			00 14					00 41
Fleet	d	00 16			00 20					00 47
Winchfield	d	00 21								00s52
Hook	d	00 26								00s57
Basingstoke	a	00 33			00 33		00 27			01 06

Saturdays
until 6 October

		SW	SW ■	SW ■	SW	SW ■	SW ■	SW	SW ■ A	SW ■ A		SW ■	SW ■ B	SW ■	SW ■ B	SW ■ A	SW ■ A	SW	SW ■ B	SW		SW B	SW ■ B	SW ■ B	SW B
London Waterloo ■15 ⊖	d	22p52	22p53	23p12	23p20	23p23	23p35		23p40	23p45		23p48	23p55		00 05	00 05		00 09	00 20			00 27	00 30	00 50	
Vauxhall ⊖	d	22p56			23p24													00 13				00 31			
Clapham Junction ■10	d		23b00		23p29	23b30	23b42		23b47	23b52		23b55	00u02		00u12	00u12		00 20	00u27			00 37	00u37	00u57	
	d	23p02		23b19																					
Earlsfield	d				23p32													00 23				00s41			
Wimbledon ■ ⊖	d				23p36			←								00u18		00 27				00 45	00u43		
Surbiton ■	d		23p11	23p38	23p44	23p41		23p44				00 09						00 35	00 38			00 57			
Esher	d				→			23p48										00s39				01s01			
Hersham	d							23p51										00s42				01s04			
Walton-on-Thames	d			23p45				23p54				00 16						00s44				01s06			
Weybridge	d			23p49				23p57				00 20						00s48				01s10			
Byfleet & New Haw	d	00 06						00 01										00s51				01s12			
West Byfleet	d	00 09	23p21			23p55		00 03						←				00s54		←		01s15			←
Woking	a	00 15	23p29	23p55		23p59	00 01	00 08	00 06	00 11		00 26	00 20	00 26	00 31	00 35		00 58	00 50	00 58		01 20	00 59	01 19	01 20
	d		23p30	23p57		00 01	00 03		00 08	00 13		00 28	00 21	00 28	00 32	00 37	00 40	01 00	00 51	01 00		01 21	01 00	01 20	01 21
Worplesdon	d									00 18		→			00 37			→				→			01s27
Guildford	a									00 24					00 43					01 07				01s28	01 33
Brookwood	d		23p36	00 03		00 07								00 34			00 45		00 57						
Ash Vale	d		23p44			00 15											00 53		01 05						
Aldershot	a		23p49			00 19											00 58		01 09						
	d		23p50			00 20											00 59		01 10						
Farnham	a		23p55			00 25											01 04		01 15						
	d		23p58			00 26											01 05		01 16						
Bentley	d		00 04			00 33											01s11		01s22						
Alton	a		00 11			00 40											01 18		01 29						
Farnborough (Main)	d			00 10			00 14							00 41											
Fleet	d			00 16			00 20							00 47											
Winchfield	d			00 21										00s52											
Hook	d			00 26										00s57											
Basingstoke	a			00 33			00 33		00 27				00 43	01 06		00 55							01 18		

A until 21 July, 18 August, 25 August, 15 September, 22 September, 29 September, 6 October

B 28 July, 4 August, 11 August, 1 September, 8 September

b Previous night, stops to pick up only

Table 155

Saturdays until 6 October

London - Woking, Guildford, Alton and Basingstoke

Network Diagram - see first Page of Table 155

		SW ■	SW ■	SW ■	SW ◇■	SW ■	SW ■	SW ■	SW ■	SW	SW ■	SW ■	SW ■	SW	SW ◇■	SW ■	SW ■	SW ■	SW ■	SW	SW ■	SW ◇■ 🍴	SW
London Waterloo ⊖	d	01 05	05 00	05 20	05 30					05 50	06 12	06 15		06 20	06 30		06 42	06 45		06 50	06 53	07 10	
Vauxhall ⊖	d	01 09	05 04	05 24						05 54				06 24						06 54			
Clapham Junction	d	01 15	05 11	05 29	05u37					05 59	06u19	06u22		06 29	06u37		06u49	06u52		06 59	07u00	07u17	
Earlsfield	d		05 14	05 32						06 02				06 32						07 02			
Wimbledon ⊖	d	01s20	05 18	05 36	05 43					06 06				06 36						07 06			←
Surbiton	d	01s28	05 26	05 44						06 14	06 30			06 44			07 00			07 14	07 11		07 14
Esher	d		05 30	05 48						06 18				06 48						→			07 18
Hersham	d		05 33	05 51						06 21				06 51									07 21
Walton-on-Thames	d		05 37	05 54						06 24	06 37			06 54			07 07						07 24
Weybridge	d		05 41	05 57						06 27	06 41			06 57			07 11						07 27
Byfleet & New Haw	d		05 44	06 00						06 30				07 00									07 30
West Byfleet	d		05 47	06 03			←			06 33			←	07 03					←		07 21		07 33
Woking	a	01 41	05 51	06 08	05 59		06 08			06 38	06 48	06 41	06 48	07 08	06 56		07 18	07 11	07 18		07 26	07 35	07 38
	d	01 42	05 53	06 13	06 01	06 02	06 13	06 19	06 30		06 49	06 43	06 49		06 57	07 00	07 19	07 13	07 19		07 30	07 36	
Worplesdon	d			→			06 18				→						→	07 18					
Guildford	a		06 00				06 23					06 51						07 23					
Brookwood	d					06 08		06 25	06 36				06 55			07 06			07 25		07 36		
Ash Vale	d					06 16			06 44							07 14					07 44		
Aldershot	a					06 21			06 49							07 19					07 49		
	d					06 21			06 50							07 20					07 50		
Farnham	a					06 27			06 55							07 25					07 55		
	d					06 27			06 56							07 26					07 56		
Bentley	d					06 34			07 02							07 32					08 02		
Alton	a					06 41			07 10							07 40					08 10		
Farnborough (Main)	d	01s51						06 33					07 03						07 33				
Fleet	d	01s57						06 38					07 08						07 38				
Winchfield	d							06 43					07 14						07 44				
Hook	d							06 48					07 18						07 48				
Basingstoke	a	02s09			06 20			06 58					07 28		07 16				07 58			07 57	

		SW ■	SW ■	SW ■	SW	SW ■	SW ■	SW ■	SW ◇■	SW	SW ■	SW ■	SW ■	SW ◇■ 🍴	SW ■	SW	SW ■	SW ■	SW ■	SW ◇■	SW ■	SW
London Waterloo ⊖	d	07 12	07 15		07 20	07 23	07 30		07 35		07 39	07 42	07 45	07 50		07 50	07 53	08 00		08 05	08 09	
Vauxhall ⊖	d				07 24											07 54						
Clapham Junction	d	07u20	07u23		07 29	07u30					07u46		07u52	07u57		07 59	08u00			08u12		
Earlsfield	d				07 32											08 02						
Wimbledon ⊖	d				07 36					←						08 06						←
Surbiton	d	07 31			07 44	07 41				07 44		08 00				08 14	08 11					08 14
Esher	d				→					07 48						→						08 18
Hersham	d									07 51												08 21
Walton-on-Thames	d	07 38								07 54		08 07										08 24
Weybridge	d	07 42								07 57		08 11										08 27
Byfleet & New Haw	d									08 00												08 30
West Byfleet	d			←		07 51		←		08 03					←		08 21		←			08 33
Woking	a	07 48	07 42	07 48		07 59	07 54	07 59	07 58	08 08		08 18	08 11	08 15	08 18		08 29	08 24	08 29		08 33	08 38
	d	07 50	07 44	07 50		08 00	07 55	08 00	08 00			08 19	08 13	08 16	08 19		08 30	08 25	08 30		08 35	
Worplesdon	d	→				→						→	08 18				→					
Guildford	a		07 51				08 03						08 23					08 33				
Brookwood	d			07 56				08 06							08 25				08 36			
Ash Vale	d							08 14											08 44			
Aldershot	a							08 19											08 49			
	d							08 20											08 50			
Farnham	a							08 25											08 55			
	d							08 26											08 56			
Bentley	d							08 32											09 02			
Alton	a							08 39											09 10			
Farnborough (Main)	d			08 03							08 13				08 33						08 45	
Fleet	d			08 09							08 19				08 38							
Winchfield	d			08 14											08 44							
Hook	d			08 19											08 48							
Basingstoke	a			08 28					08 20		08 31			08 36	08 58					08 47	08 58	

Table 155

Saturdays until 6 October

London - Woking, Guildford, Alton and Basingstoke

Network Diagram - see first Page of Table 155

		SW ■	SW ■	SW ◇■ 🍴	SW ■	SW	SW ■	SW ■	SW ◇■ 🍴	SW ■	SW	SW ■	SW ■	SW ■	SW ◇■ 🍴	SW ■	SW	SW ■	SW ■ 🍴	SW ■	SW ◇■ 🍴	SW ■	SW
London Waterloo ⊖	d	08 12	08 15	08 20		08 20	08 23	08 30	08 35			08 39	08 42	08 45	08 50		08 50	08 53	09 00		09 05	09 09	
Vauxhall ⊖	d					08 24											08 54						
Clapham Junction	d	08u19	08u22	08u27		08 29						08u46		08u52			08 59	09u00			09u12		
Earlsfield	d					08 32											09 02						
Wimbledon ⊖	d					08 36					←						09 06						←
Surbiton	d	08 30				08 44	08 41				08 44		09 00				09 14	09 11					09 14
Esher	d					→					08 48						→						09 18
Hersham	d										08 51												09 21
Walton-on-Thames	d	08 37									08 54		09 07										09 24
Weybridge	d	08 41									08 57		09 11										09 27
Byfleet & New Haw	d										09 00												09 30
West Byfleet	d				←		08 51			←	09 03					←		09 21		←			09 33
Woking	a	08 48	08 41	08 45	08 48		08 59	08 54	08 58	08 59	09 08		09 18	09 11	09 14	09 18		09 29	09 24	09 29		09 33	09 38
	d	08 49	08 43	08 46	08 49		09 00	08 55		09 00			09 19	09 13	09 16	09 19		09 30	09 25	09 30		09 35	
Worplesdon	d	→					→						→	09 18				→					
Guildford	a		08 50					09 03						09 23					09 33				
Brookwood	d				08 55					09 06						09 25				09 36			
Ash Vale	d									09 14										09 44			
Aldershot	a									09 19										09 49			
	d									09 20										09 50			
Farnham	a									09 25										09 55			
	d									09 26										09 56			
Bentley	d																			10 02			
Alton	a									09 37										10 10			
Farnborough (Main)	d				09 03							09 13				09 33						09 45	
Fleet	d				09 08							09 19				09 38							
Winchfield	d				09 14											09 44							
Hook	d				09 18											09 48							
Basingstoke	a			09 05	09 28							09 31			09 36	09 58					09 47	09 58	

		SW ■	SW ■	SW ◇■ 🍴	SW ■	SW	SW ■	SW ■ 🍴	SW ◇■ 🍴	SW ■	SW	SW ■	SW ■	SW ■	SW ◇■ 🍴	SW ■	SW	SW ■	SW ■ 🍴	SW ■	SW ◇■ 🍴	SW ■
London Waterloo ⊖	d	09 12	09 15	09 20		09 20	09 23	09 30	09 35			09 39	09 42	09 45	09 50		09 50	09 53	10 00		10 05	10 09
Vauxhall ⊖	d					09 24											09 54					
Clapham Junction	d	09u19	09u22	09u27		09 29						09u46		09u52			09 59	10u00			10u12	
Earlsfield	d					09 32											10 02					
Wimbledon ⊖	d					09 36					←						10 06					
Surbiton	d	09 30				09 44	09 41				09 44		10 00				10 14	10 11				
Esher	d					→					09 48						→					
Hersham	d										09 51											
Walton-on-Thames	d	09 37									09 54		10 07									
Weybridge	d	09 41									09 57		10 11									
Byfleet & New Haw	d										10 00											
West Byfleet	d				←		09 51			←	10 03					←		10 21		←		
Woking	a	09 48	09 41	09 45	09 48		09 59	09 54	09 58	09 59	10 08		10 18	10 11	10 14	10 18		10 29	10 24	10 29		10 33
	d	09 49	09 43	09 46	09 49		10 00	09 55		10 00			10 19	10 13	10 16	10 19		10 30	10 25	10 30		10 35
Worplesdon	d	→					→						→	10 18				→				
Guildford	a		09 50					10 03						10 23					10 33			
Brookwood	d				09 55					10 06						10 25				10 36		
Ash Vale	d									10 14										10 44		
Aldershot	a									10 19										10 49		
	d									10 20										10 50		
Farnham	a									10 25										10 55		
	d									10 26										10 56		
Bentley	d																			11 02		
Alton	a									10 37										11 10		
Farnborough (Main)	d				10 03							10 13				10 33						10 45
Fleet	d				10 08							10 19				10 38						
Winchfield	d				10 14											10 44						
Hook	d				10 18											10 48						
Basingstoke	a			10 05	10 28							10 31			10 36	10 58					10 47	10 58

Table 155

Saturdays until 6 October

London - Woking, Guildford, Alton and Basingstoke

Network Diagram - see first Page of Table 155

		SW 1	SW	SW 1	SW 1	SW ◇1 ⫟	SW 1	SW	SW 1	SW 1 ⫟	SW ◇1 ⫟	SW 1	SW	SW 1	SW 1	SW 1	SW ◇1 ⫟	SW 1	SW	SW 1	SW 1 ⫟	SW 1
London Waterloo 15 ⊖	d	14 09		14 12	14 15	14 20		14 20	14 23	14 30	14 35			14 39	14 42	14 45	14 50		14 50	14 53	15 00	
Vauxhall ⊖	d							14 24											14 54			
Clapham Junction 10	d			14u19	14u22	14u27		14 29						14u46		14u52			14 59	15u00		
Earlsfield	d							14 32											15 02			
Wimbledon 6 ⊖	d		←					14 36					←						15 06			
Surbiton 6	d		14 14	14 30				14 44	14 41				14 44		15 00				15 14	15 11		
Esher	d		14 18					→					14 48						→			
Hersham	d		14 21										14 51									
Walton-on-Thames	d		14 24	14 37									14 54		15 07							
Weybridge	d		14 27	14 41									14 57		15 11							
Byfleet & New Haw	d		14 30										15 00									
West Byfleet	d		14 33				←		14 51			←	15 03					←		15 21		←
Woking	a	14 33	14 38	14 48	14 41	14 45	14 48		14 59	14 54	14 58	14 59	15 08		15 18	15 11	15 14	15 18		15 29	15 24	15 29
	d	14 35		14 49	14 43	14 46	14 49		15 00	14 55		15 00			15 19	15 13	15 16	15 19		15 30	15 25	15 30
Worplesdon	d			→					→						→	15 18				→		
Guildford	a				14 50					15 03						15 23					15 33	
Brookwood	d						14 55					15 06						15 25				15 36
Ash Vale	d											15 14										15 44
Aldershot	a											15 19										15 49
	d											15 20										15 50
Farnham	a											15 25										15 55
	d											15 26										15 56
Bentley	d																					16 02
Alton	a											15 37										16 10
Farnborough (Main)	d	14 45					15 03							15 13				15 33				
Fleet	d						15 08							15 19				15 38				
Winchfield	d						15 14											15 44				
Hook	d						15 18											15 48				
Basingstoke	a	14 58				15 05	15 28							15 31			15 36	15 58				

		SW ◇1 ⫟	SW 1	SW	SW 1	SW 1	SW ◇1 ⫟	SW 1	SW	SW 1	SW 1 ⫟	SW ◇1 ⫟	SW 1	SW	SW 1	SW 1	SW 1	SW ◇1 ⫟	SW 1	SW	SW 1	SW 1 ⫟	SW 1
London Waterloo 15 ⊖	d	15 05	15 09		15 12	15 15	15 20		15 20	15 23	15 30	15 35			15 39	15 42	15 45	15 50		15 50	15 53	16 00	
Vauxhall ⊖	d								15 24											15 54			
Clapham Junction 10	d	15u12			15u19	15u22	15u27		15 29						15u46		15u52			15 59	16u00		
Earlsfield	d								15 32											16 02			
Wimbledon 6 ⊖	d			←					15 36					←						16 06			
Surbiton 6	d			15 14	15 30				15 44	15 41				15 44		16 00				16 14	16 11		
Esher	d			15 18					→					15 48						→			
Hersham	d			15 21										15 51									
Walton-on-Thames	d			15 24	15 37									15 54		16 07							
Weybridge	d			15 27	15 41									15 57		16 11							
Byfleet & New Haw	d			15 30										16 00									
West Byfleet	d			15 33				←		15 51			←	16 03					←		16 21		←
Woking	a		15 33	15 38	15 48	15 41	15 45	15 48		15 59	15 54	15 58	15 59	16 08		16 18	16 11	16 14	16 18		16 29	16 24	16 29
	d		15 35		15 49	15 43	15 46	15 49		16 00	15 55		16 00			16 19	16 13	16 16	16 19		16 30	16 25	16 30
Worplesdon	d				→					→						→	16 18				→		
Guildford	a					15 50					16 03						16 23					16 33	
Brookwood	d							15 55					16 06						16 25				16 36
Ash Vale	d												16 14										16 44
Aldershot	a												16 19										16 49
	d												16 20										16 50
Farnham	a												16 25										16 55
	d												16 26										16 56
Bentley	d																						17 02
Alton	a												16 37										17 10
Farnborough (Main)	d		15 45					16 03							16 13				16 33				
Fleet	d							16 08							16 19				16 38				
Winchfield	d							16 14											16 44				
Hook	d							16 18											16 48				
Basingstoke	a	15 47	15 58				16 05	16 28							16 31			16 36	16 58				

Table 155

Saturdays until 6 October

London - Woking, Guildford, Alton and Basingstoke

Network Diagram - see first Page of Table 155

		SW ◇1 ⫟	SW 1	SW	SW 1	SW 1	SW ◇1 ⫟	SW 1	SW	SW 1	SW 1 ⫟	SW ◇1 ⫟	SW 1	SW	SW 1	SW 1	SW 1	SW ◇1 ⫟	SW 1	SW	SW 1	SW 1 ⫟	SW 1
London Waterloo 15 ⊖	d	16 05	16 09		16 12	16 15	16 20		16 20	16 23	16 30	16 35			16 39	16 42	16 45	16 50		16 50	16 53	17 00	
Vauxhall ⊖	d								16 24											16 54			
Clapham Junction 10	d	16u12			16u19	16u22	16u27		16 29						16u46		16u52			16 59	17u00		
Earlsfield	d								16 32											17 02			
Wimbledon 6 ⊖	d			←					16 36					←						17 06			
Surbiton 6	d			16 14	16 30				16 44	16 41				16 44		17 00				17 14	17 11		
Esher	d			16 18					→					16 48						→			
Hersham	d			16 21										16 51									
Walton-on-Thames	d			16 24	16 37									16 54		17 07							
Weybridge	d			16 27	16 41									16 57		17 11							
Byfleet & New Haw	d			16 30										17 00									
West Byfleet	d			16 33				←		16 51			←	17 03					←		17 21		←
Woking	a		16 33	16 38	16 48	16 41	16 45	16 48		16 59	16 54	16 58	16 59	17 08		17 18	17 11	17 14	17 18		17 29	17 24	17 29
	d		16 35		16 49	16 43	16 46	16 49		17 00	16 55		17 00			17 19	17 13	17 16	17 19		17 30	17 25	17 30
Worplesdon	d				→					→						→	17 18				→		
Guildford	a					16 50					17 03						17 23					17 33	
Brookwood	d							16 55					17 06						17 25				17 36
Ash Vale	d												17 14										17 44
Aldershot	a												17 19										17 49
	d												17 20										17 50
Farnham	a												17 25										17 55
	d												17 26										17 56
Bentley	d												17 32										18 02
Alton	a												17 39										18 10
Farnborough (Main)	d		16 45					17 03							17 13				17 33				
Fleet	d							17 08							17 19				17 38				
Winchfield	d							17 14											17 44				
Hook	d							17 18											17 48				
Basingstoke	a	16 47	16 58				17 05	17 28							17 31			17 36	17 58				

		SW ◇1 ⊐	SW 1	SW	SW 1	SW 1	SW ◇1 ⫟	SW 1	SW	SW 1	SW 1 ⫟	SW ◇1 ⫟	SW 1	SW	SW 1	SW 1	SW 1	SW ◇1 ⫟	SW 1	SW	SW 1	SW 1 ⫟
London Waterloo 15 ⊖	d	17 05	17 09		17 12	17 15	17 20		17 20	17 23	17 30	17 35			17 39	17 42	17 45	17 50		17 50	17 53	18 00
Vauxhall ⊖	d								17 24											17 54		
Clapham Junction 10	d	17u12			17u19	17u22	17u27		17 29						17u46		17u52			17 59	18u00	
Earlsfield	d								17 32											18 02		
Wimbledon 6 ⊖	d			←					17 36					←						18 06		
Surbiton 6	d			17 14	17 30				17 44	17 41				17 44		18 00				18 14	18 11	
Esher	d			17 18					→					17 48						→		
Hersham	d			17 21										17 51								
Walton-on-Thames	d			17 24	17 37									17 54		18 07						
Weybridge	d			17 27	17 41									17 57		18 11						
Byfleet & New Haw	d			17 30										18 00								
West Byfleet	d			17 33				←		17 51			←	18 03					←		18 21	
Woking	a		17 33	17 38	17 48	17 41	17 45	17 48		17 59	17 54	17 58	17 59	18 08		18 18	18 11	18 14	18 18		18 29	18 24
	d		17 35		17 49	17 43	17 46	17 49		18 00	17 55		18 00			18 19	18 13	18 16	18 19		18 30	18 25
Worplesdon	d				→					→						→	18 18				→	
Guildford	a					17 50					18 03						18 23					18 33
Brookwood	d							17 55					18 06						18 25			
Ash Vale	d												18 14									
Aldershot	a												18 19									
	d												18 20									
Farnham	a												18 25									
	d												18 26									
Bentley	d												18 32									
Alton	a												18 39									
Farnborough (Main)	d		17 45					18 03							18 13				18 33			
Fleet	d							18 08							18 19				18 38			
Winchfield	d							18 14											18 44			
Hook	d							18 18											18 48			
Basingstoke	a	17 47	17 58				18 05	18 28							18 31			18 36	18 58			

Table 155

Saturdays
until 6 October

London - Woking, Guildford, Alton and Basingstoke

Network Diagram - see first Page of Table 155

		SW	SW ■	SW ■	SW ◇■ ⫤	SW ■	SW	SW ■	SW ■ ⫤	SW ◇■ ⫤		SW ■	SW	SW ■	SW ■	SW ■	SW ◇■ ⫤	SW ■	SW	SW ■		SW ■ ⫤	SW ■	SW ◇■ ⫤	SW ■
London Waterloo 15 ⊖	d		10 12	10 15	10 20		10 20	10 23	10 30	10 35				10 39	10 42	10 45	10 50		10 50	10 53		11 00		11 05	11 09
Vauxhall ⊖	d						10 24												10 54						
Clapham Junction 10	d		10u19	10u22	10u27		10 29							10u46		10u52			10 59	11u00				11u12	
	d																								
Earlsfield	d						10 32												11 02						
Wimbledon ■ ⊖	d	←					10 36						←						11 06						
Surbiton ■	d	10 14	10 30				10 44	10 41					10 44		11 00				11 14	11 11					
Esher	d	10 18					→						10 48						→						
Hersham	d	10 21											10 51												
Walton-on-Thames	d	10 24	10 37										10 54		11 07										
Weybridge	d	10 27	10 41										10 57		11 11										
Byfleet & New Haw	d	10 30											11 00												
West Byfleet	d	10 33				←		10 51				←	11 03					←		11 21			←		
Woking	a	10 38	10 48	10 41	10 45	10 48		10 59	10 54	10 58		10 59	11 08		11 18	11 11	11 14	11 18		11 29		11 24	11 29		11 33
	d		10 49	10 43	10 46	10 49		11 00	10 55			11 00			11 19	11 13	11 16	11 19		11 30		11 25	11 30		11 35
Worplesdon	d		→					→							→	11 18				→					
Guildford	a			10 50					11 03							11 23						11 33			
Brookwood	d					10 55						11 06						11 25					11 36		
Ash Vale	d											11 14											11 44		
Aldershot	a											11 19											11 49		
	d											11 20											11 50		
Farnham	a											11 25											11 55		
	d											11 26											11 56		
Bentley	d																						12 02		
Alton	a											11 37											12 10		
Farnborough (Main)	d					11 03								11 13				11 33							11 45
Fleet	d					11 08								11 19				11 38							
Winchfield	d					11 14												11 44							
Hook	d					11 18												11 48							
Basingstoke	a				11 05	11 28								11 31			11 36	11 58						11 47	11 58

		SW	SW ■	SW ■	SW ◇■ ⫤	SW ■		SW	SW ■	SW ■ ⫤	SW ◇■ ⫤	SW ■	SW	SW ■	SW ■	SW ■		SW ◇■ ⫤	SW ■	SW	SW ■	SW ■ ⫤	SW ■	SW ◇■ ⫤	SW ■
London Waterloo 15 ⊖	d		11 12	11 15	11 20			11 20	11 23	11 30	11 35			11 39	11 42	11 45		11 50		11 50	11 53	12 00		12 05	12 09
Vauxhall ⊖	d							11 24												11 54					
Clapham Junction 10	d		11u19	11u22	11u27			11 29						11u46		11u52				11 59	12u00			12u12	
	d																								
Earlsfield	d							11 32												12 02					
Wimbledon ■ ⊖	d	←						11 36					←							12 06					
Surbiton ■	d	11 14	11 30					11 44	11 41				11 44		12 00					12 14	12 11				
Esher	d	11 18						→					11 48							→					
Hersham	d	11 21											11 51												
Walton-on-Thames	d	11 24	11 37										11 54		12 07										
Weybridge	d	11 27	11 41										11 57		12 11										
Byfleet & New Haw	d	11 30											12 00												
West Byfleet	d	11 33				←			11 51			←	12 03						←		12 21		←		
Woking	a	11 38	11 48	11 41	11 45	11 48			11 59	11 54	11 58	11 59	12 08		12 18	12 11		12 14	12 18		12 29	12 24	12 29		12 33
	d		11 49	11 43	11 46	11 49			12 00	11 55		12 00			12 19	12 13		12 16	12 19		12 30	12 25	12 30		12 35
Worplesdon	d		→						→						→	12 18					→				
Guildford	a			11 50						12 03						12 23						12 33			
Brookwood	d					11 55						12 06							12 25				12 36		
Ash Vale	d											12 14											12 44		
Aldershot	a											12 19											12 49		
	d											12 20											12 50		
Farnham	a											12 25											12 55		
	d											12 26											12 56		
Bentley	d																						13 02		
Alton	a											12 37											13 10		
Farnborough (Main)	d					12 03								12 13					12 33						12 45
Fleet	d					12 08								12 19					12 38						
Winchfield	d					12 14													12 44						
Hook	d					12 18													12 48						
Basingstoke	a				12 05	12 28								12 31				12 36	12 58					12 47	12 58

Table 155

Saturdays
until 6 October

London - Woking, Guildford, Alton and Basingstoke

Network Diagram - see first Page of Table 155

		SW		SW ■	SW ■	SW ◇■ ⫤	SW ■	SW	SW ■	SW ■ ⫤	SW ◇■ ⫤	SW ■		SW	SW ■	SW ■	SW ■	SW ◇■ ⫤	SW ■	SW	SW ■	SW ■ ⫤		SW ■	SW ◇■ ⫤
London Waterloo 15 ⊖	d			12 12	12 15	12 20		12 20	12 23	12 30	12 35				12 39	12 42	12 45	12 50		12 50	12 53	13 00			13 05
Vauxhall ⊖	d							12 24												12 54					
Clapham Junction 10	d			12u19	12u22	12u27		12 29							12u46		12u52			12 59	13u00				13u12
	d																								
Earlsfield	d							12 32												13 02					
Wimbledon ■ ⊖	d	←						12 36						←						13 06					
Surbiton ■	d	12 14		12 30				12 44	12 41					12 44		13 00				13 14	13 11				
Esher	d	12 18						→						12 48						→					
Hersham	d	12 21												12 51											
Walton-on-Thames	d	12 24		12 37										12 54		13 07									
Weybridge	d	12 27		12 41										12 57		13 11									
Byfleet & New Haw	d	12 30												13 00											
West Byfleet	d	12 33					←		12 51			←		13 03					←		13 21			←	
Woking	a	12 38		12 48	12 41	12 45	12 48		12 59	12 54	12 58	12 59		13 08		13 18	13 11	13 14	13 18		13 29	13 24		13 29	
	d			12 49	12 43	12 46	12 49		13 00	12 55		13 00				13 19	13 13	13 16	13 19		13 30	13 25		13 30	
Worplesdon	d			→					→							→	13 18				→				
Guildford	a				12 50					13 03							13 23					13 33			
Brookwood	d						12 55					13 06							13 25					13 36	
Ash Vale	d											13 14												13 44	
Aldershot	a											13 19												13 49	
	d											13 20												13 50	
Farnham	a											13 25												13 55	
	d											13 26												13 56	
Bentley	d																							14 02	
Alton	a											13 37												14 10	
Farnborough (Main)	d						13 03								13 13				13 33						
Fleet	d						13 08								13 19				13 38						
Winchfield	d						13 14												13 44						
Hook	d						13 18												13 48						
Basingstoke	a					13 05	13 28								13 31			13 36	13 58						13 47

		SW ■	SW	SW ■	SW ■	SW ◇■ ⫤	SW ■	SW		SW ■	SW ■ ⫤	SW ◇■ ⫤	SW ■	SW	SW ■	SW ■	SW ■	SW ◇■ ⫤		SW ■	SW	SW ■	SW ■ ⫤	SW ■	SW ◇■ ⫤
London Waterloo 15 ⊖	d	13 09		13 12	13 15	13 20		13 20		13 23	13 30	13 35			13 39	13 42	13 45	13 50			13 50	13 53	14 00		14 05
Vauxhall ⊖	d							13 24													13 54				
Clapham Junction 10	d			13u19	13u22	13u27		13 29							13u46		13u52				13 59	14u00			14u12
	d																								
Earlsfield	d							13 32													14 02				
Wimbledon ■ ⊖	d		←					13 36						←							14 06				
Surbiton ■	d		13 14	13 30				13 44		13 41				13 44		14 00					14 14	14 11			
Esher	d		13 18					→						13 48							→				
Hersham	d		13 21											13 51											
Walton-on-Thames	d		13 24	13 37										13 54		14 07									
Weybridge	d		13 27	13 41										13 57		14 11									
Byfleet & New Haw	d		13 30											14 00											
West Byfleet	d		13 33				←			13 51			←	14 03						←		14 21		←	
Woking	a	13 33	13 38	13 48	13 41	13 45	13 48			13 59	13 54	13 58	13 59	14 08		14 18	14 11	14 14		14 18		14 29	14 24	14 29	
	d	13 35		13 49	13 43	13 46	13 49			14 00	13 55		14 00			14 19	14 13	14 16		14 19		14 30	14 25	14 30	
Worplesdon	d			→						→						→	14 18					→			
Guildford	a				13 50						14 03						14 23						14 33		
Brookwood	d						13 55						14 06							14 25				14 36	
Ash Vale	d												14 14											14 44	
Aldershot	a												14 19											14 49	
	d												14 20											14 50	
Farnham	a												14 25											14 55	
	d												14 26											14 56	
Bentley	d																							15 02	
Alton	a												14 37											15 10	
Farnborough (Main)	d	13 45					14 03								14 13					14 33					
Fleet	d						14 08								14 19					14 38					
Winchfield	d						14 14													14 44					
Hook	d						14 18													14 48					
Basingstoke	a	13 58				14 05	14 28								14 31			14 36		14 58					14 47

London - Woking, Guildford, Alton and Basingstoke

Network Diagram - see first Page of Table 155

		SW 1	SW ◇1 ✠	SW 1	SW	SW 1	SW 1	SW ◇1 ✠	SW 1	SW	SW 1	SW 1 ✠	SW ◇1 ✠	SW 1	SW	SW 1	SW 1	SW 1	SW ◇1 ✠	SW 1	SW	SW 1	SW 1 ✠
London Waterloo 15 ⊖	d		18 05	18 09		18 12	18 15	18 20		18 20	18 23	18 30	18 35			18 39	18 42	18 45	18 50		18 50	18 53	19 00
Vauxhall ⊖	d									18 24											18 54		
Clapham Junction 10	d		18u12			18u19	18u22	18u27		18 29						18u46		18u52			18 59	19u00	
Earlsfield	d									18 32											19 02		
Wimbledon 6 ⊖	d				←					18 36					←						19 06		
Surbiton 6	d				18 14	18 30				18 44	18 41				18 44		19 00				19 14	19 11	
Esher	d				18 18					→					18 48						→		
Hersham	d				18 21										18 51								
Walton-on-Thames	d				18 24	18 37									18 54		19 07						
Weybridge	d				18 27	18 41									18 57		19 11						
Byfleet & New Haw	d				18 30										19 00								
West Byfleet	d	←			18 33				←		18 51			←	19 03					←		19 21	
Woking	a	18 29		18 33	18 38	18 48	18 41	18 45	18 48		18 59	18 54	18 58	18 59	19 08		19 18	19 11	19 15	19 18		19 29	19 24
	d	18 30		18 35		18 49	18 43	18 46	18 49		19 00	18 55		19 00			19 19	19 13	19 16	19 19		19 30	19 25
Worplesdon	d					→					→						→	19 18				→	
Guildford	a						18 50					19 03						19 23					19 33
Brookwood	d	18 36							18 55					19 06						19 25			
Ash Vale	d	18 44												19 14									
Aldershot	a	18 49												19 19									
	d	18 50												19 20									
Farnham	a	18 55												19 25									
	d	18 56												19 26									
Bentley	d	19 02												19 32									
Alton	a	19 10												19 39									
Farnborough (Main)	d			18 45					19 03							19 13				19 33			
Fleet	d								19 08							19 19				19 38			
Winchfield	d								19 14											19 44			
Hook	d								19 18											19 48			
Basingstoke	a		18 47	18 58				19 05	19 28							19 31			19 36	19 58			

		SW 1	SW ◇1 ✠	SW 1	SW	SW 1	SW 1	SW ◇1 ✠	SW 1	SW	SW 1	SW 1 ✠	SW ◇1 ✠	SW 1	SW	SW 1	SW 1	SW 1	SW ◇1 ✠	SW 1	SW	SW 1
London Waterloo 15 ⊖	d		19 05	19 09		19 12	19 15	19 20		19 20	19 23	19 30	19 35			19 39	19 42	19 45	19 50		19 50	19 53
Vauxhall ⊖	d									19 24											19 54	
Clapham Junction 10	d		19u12			19u19	19u22	19u27		19 29						19u46		19u52			19 59	20u00
Earlsfield	d									19 32											20 02	
Wimbledon 6 ⊖	d				←					19 36					←						20 06	
Surbiton 6	d				19 14	19 30				19 44	19 41				19 44		20 00				20 14	20 11
Esher	d				19 18					→					19 48						→	
Hersham	d				19 21										19 51							
Walton-on-Thames	d				19 24	19 37									19 54		20 07					
Weybridge	d				19 27	19 41									19 57		20 11					
Byfleet & New Haw	d				19 30										20 00							
West Byfleet	d	←			19 33				←		19 51			←	20 03					←		20 21
Woking	a	19 29		19 33	19 38	19 48	19 41	19 45	19 48		19 59	19 54	19 58	19 59	20 08		20 18	20 11	20 14	20 18		20 29
	d	19 30		19 35		19 49	19 43	19 46	19 49		20 00	19 55		20 00			20 19	20 13	20 16	20 19		20 30
Worplesdon	d					→					→						→	20 18				→
Guildford	a						19 50					20 03						20 23				
Brookwood	d	19 36							19 55					20 06						20 25		
Ash Vale	d	19 44												20 14								
Aldershot	a	19 49												20 19								
	d	19 50												20 20								
Farnham	a	19 55												20 25								
	d	19 56												20 26								
Bentley	d	20 02												20 32								
Alton	a	20 10												20 39								
Farnborough (Main)	d			19 45					20 03							20 13				20 33		
Fleet	d								20 08							20 19				20 38		
Winchfield	d								20 14											20 44		
Hook	d								20 18											20 48		
Basingstoke	a		19 47	19 58				20 05	20 28							20 31			20 36	20 58		

Table 155

Saturdays until 6 October

London - Woking, Guildford, Alton and Basingstoke

Network Diagram - see first Page of Table 155

		SW 1	SW 1	SW ◇1 ✠	SW 1	SW	SW 1	SW 1	SW ◇1 ✠	SW 1	SW	SW 1	SW 1	SW ◇1 ✠	SW 1	SW	SW 1	SW 1	SW 1	SW 1	SW	SW 1	SW 1
London Waterloo 15 ⊖	d	20 00		20 05	20 09		20 12	20 15	20 20		20 20	20 23	20 30	20 35			20 39	20 42	20 45		20 50	20 53	21 00
Vauxhall ⊖	d										20 24										20 54		
Clapham Junction 10	d			20u12			20u19	20u22	20u27		20 29						20u46		20u52		20 59	21u00	
Earlsfield	d										20 32										21 02		
Wimbledon 6 ⊖	d					←					20 36					←					21 06		
Surbiton 6	d					20 14	20 30				20 44	20 41				20 44		21 00			21 14	21 11	
Esher	d					20 18					→					20 48					→		
Hersham	d					20 21										20 51							
Walton-on-Thames	d					20 24	20 37									20 54		21 07					
Weybridge	d					20 27	20 41									20 57		21 11					
Byfleet & New Haw	d					20 30										21 00							
West Byfleet	d		←			20 33				←		20 51			←	21 03				←		21 21	
Woking	a	20 24	20 29		20 33	20 38	20 48	20 41	20 45	20 48		20 59	20 54	20 58	20 59	21 08		21 18	21 11	21 18		21 29	21 24
	d	20 25	20 30		20 35		20 49	20 43	20 46	20 49		21 00	20 55		21 00			21 19	21 13	21 19		21 30	21 25
Worplesdon	d						→					→						→	21 18			→	
Guildford	a	20 33						20 50					21 03						21 23				21 33
Brookwood	d		20 36							20 55					21 06					21 25			
Ash Vale	d		20 44												21 14								
Aldershot	a		20 49												21 19								
	d		20 50												21 20								
Farnham	a		20 55												21 25								
	d		20 56												21 26								
Bentley	d		21 02												21 32								
Alton	a		21 10												21 39								
Farnborough (Main)	d				20 45					21 03							21 13			21 33			
Fleet	d									21 08							21 19			21 38			
Winchfield	d									21 14										21 44			
Hook	d									21 18										21 48			
Basingstoke	a			20 47	20 58				21 05	21 28							21 31			21 58			

		SW 1	SW ◇1 ✠	SW	SW 1	SW ◇1 ✠	SW	SW 1	SW 1	SW ◇1 ✠	SW 1	SW	SW 1	SW 1	SW 1	SW 1	SW	SW 1	SW 1	SW 1	SW ◇1 ✠	SW	SW 1
London Waterloo 15 ⊖	d		21 05		21 12	21 20	21 20	21 23	21 30	21 35			21 39	21 42	21 45		21 50	21 53	22 00		22 05		22 12
Vauxhall ⊖	d						21 24										21 54						
Clapham Junction 10	d		21u12		21u19	21u27	21 29						21u46		21u52		21 59	22u00			22u12		22u19
Earlsfield	d						21 32										22 02						
Wimbledon 6 ⊖	d			←			21 36					←					22 06					←	
Surbiton 6	d			21 14	21 30		21 44	21 41				21 44		22 00			22 14	22 11				22 14	22 30
Esher	d			21 18			→					21 48					→					22 18	
Hersham	d			21 21								21 51										22 21	
Walton-on-Thames	d			21 24	21 37							21 54		22 07								22 24	22 37
Weybridge	d			21 27	21 41							21 57		22 11								22 27	22 41
Byfleet & New Haw	d			21 30								22 00										22 30	
West Byfleet	d	←		21 33				21 51			←	22 03				←		22 21		←		22 33	
Woking	a	21 29	21 31	21 38	21 48	21 45		21 59	21 54	21 58	21 59	22 08		22 18	22 11	22 18		22 29	22 24	22 29	22 31	22 37	22 48
	d	21 30	21 32		21 49	21 49		22 00	21 55		22 00			22 19	22 13	22 19		22 30	22 25	22 30	22 32	22 39	22 49
Worplesdon	d							→						→	22 18			→					
Guildford	a								22 03						22 23				22 33			22 47	
Brookwood	d	21 36			21 55						22 06					22 25				22 36			22 55
Ash Vale	d	21 44									22 14									22 44			
Aldershot	a	21 49									22 19									22 49			
	d	21 50									22 20									22 50			
Farnham	a	21 55									22 25									22 55			
	d	21 56									22 26									22 56			
Bentley	d	22 02									22 32									23 02			
Alton	a	22 10									22 39									23 10			
Farnborough (Main)	d				22 03								22 13			22 33							23 03
Fleet	d				22 08								22 19			22 38							23 08
Winchfield	d				22 14											22 44							23 14
Hook	d				22 18											22 48							23 18
Basingstoke	a		21 51		22 25	22 12							22 31			22 58					22 51		23 25

Saturdays
until 6 October

London - Woking, Guildford, Alton and Basingstoke

Network Diagram - see first Page of Table 155

		SW 1 🛒		SW	SW 1	SW 1	SW ◇1 🛒	SW 1	SW	SW 1	SW 1	SW 1		SW 1	SW	SW	SW 1	SW ◇1	SW	SW 1	SW 1	SW 1		SW	SW 1
London Waterloo 15 ⊖	d	22 20		22 20	22 23	22 30	22 35			22 39	22 42	22 45			22 50	22 52	22 53	23 05		23 12	23 15			23 20	23 23
Vauxhall ⊖	d			22 24											22 54	22 56								23 24	
Clapham Junction 10	d	22u27		22 29	22u30					22u46	22u49	22u52			22 59		23u00	23u12			23u22			23 29	23u30
	d															23 02				23u19					
Earlsfield	d			22 32											23 02									23 32	
Wimbledon 6 ⊖	d			22 36					←						23 06				←					23 36	
Surbiton 6	d			22 44	22 41				22 44		23 00				23 14		23 11		23 14	23 38				23 44	23 41
Esher	d			→					22 48						→				23 18					→	
Hersham	d								22 51										23 21						
Walton-on-Thames	d								22 54		23 07								23 24	23 45					
Weybridge	d								22 57		23 11								23 27	23 49					
Byfleet & New Haw	d								23 00							00 06			23 30						
West Byfleet	d				22 51			←	23 03					←		00 09	23 21		23 33			←			23 55
Woking	a	22 45			22 59	22 54	22 58	22 59	23 08		23 18	23 11		23 18		00 15	23 29	23 31	23 38	23 55	23 41	23 55			23 59
	d	22 49			23 00	22 55		23 00			23 19	23 13		23 19			23 30	23 32		23 57	23 43	23 57			00 01
Worplesdon	d				→						→	23 18								→					
Guildford	a					23 03						23 23									23 51				
Brookwood	d							23 06						23 25			23 36					00 03			00 07
Ash Vale	d							23 14									23 44								00 15
Aldershot	a							23 19									23 49								00 19
	d							23 20									23 50								00 20
Farnham	a							23 25									23 55								00 25
	d							23 26									23 58								00 26
Bentley	d							23 33									00 04								00 33
Alton	a							23 40									00 11								00 40
Farnborough (Main)	d									23 16				23 33								00 10			
Fleet	d									23 21				23 38								00 16			
Winchfield	d													23 44								00 21			
Hook	d													23 48								00 26			
Basingstoke	a	23 10								23 34				23 55				23 51				00 33			

		SW 1	SW	SW 1 A	SW 1 A	SW 1	SW 1 B	SW 1
London Waterloo 15 ⊖	d	23 35		23 40	23 45	23 48	23 55	
Vauxhall ⊖	d							
Clapham Junction 10	d	23u42		23u47	23u52	23u54	00u02	
	d							
Earlsfield	d							
Wimbledon 6 ⊖	d		←					
Surbiton 6	d		23 44			00 09		
Esher	d		23 48					
Hersham	d		23 51					
Walton-on-Thames	d		23 54			00 16		
Weybridge	d		23 57			00 20		
Byfleet & New Haw	d		23 59					
West Byfleet	d		00 03					←
Woking	a	00 01	00 08	00 06	00 11	00 26	00 20	00 26
	d	00 03		00 08	00 13	00 28	00 21	00 28
Worplesdon	d				00 18	→		
Guildford	a				00 24			
Brookwood	d							00 34
Ash Vale	d							
Aldershot	a							
	d							
Farnham	a							
	d							
Bentley	d							
Alton	a							
Farnborough (Main)	d	00 14						00 41
Fleet	d	00 20						00 47
Winchfield	d							00s52
Hook	d							00s57
Basingstoke	a	00 33		00 27			00 43	01 06

A until 21 July, 18 August, 25 August, 15 September, 22 September, 29 September, 6 October

B 28 July, 4 August, 11 August, 1 September, 8 September

Saturdays
from 13 October

London - Woking, Guildford, Alton and Basingstoke

Network Diagram - see first Page of Table 155

		SW	SW 1	SW 1	SW	SW 1	SW 1	SW	SW 1	SW 1		SW 1	SW 1	SW 1	SW	SW 1	SW 1	SW 1	SW ◇1	SW 1		SW 1	SW 1	SW 1	SW
London Waterloo 15 ⊖	d	22p52	22p53	23p12	23p20	23p23	23p35		23p40	23p45		23p48	00 05		00 09	01 05	05 00	05 20	05 30						05 50
Vauxhall ⊖	d	22p56			23p24										00 13	01 09	05 04	05 24							05 54
Clapham Junction 10	d		23b00		23p29	23b30	23b42		23b47	23b52		23b55	00u12		00 20	01 15	05 11	05 29	05u37						05 59
	d	23p02		23b19																					
Earlsfield	d				23p32										00 23		05 14	05 32							06 02
Wimbledon 6 ⊖	d				23p36			←					00u18		00 27	01s20	05 18	05 36	05 43						06 06
Surbiton 6	d		23p11	23p38	23p44	23p41		23p44				00 09			00 35	01s28	05 26	05 44							06 14
Esher	d				→			23p48							00s39		05 30	05 48							06 18
Hersham	d							23p51							00s42		05 33	05 51							06 21
Walton-on-Thames	d			23p45				23p54				00 16			00s44		05 37	05 54							06 24
Weybridge	d			23p49				23p57				00 20			00s48		05 41	05 57							06 27
Byfleet & New Haw	d	00 06						00 01							00s51		05 44	06 00							06 30
West Byfleet	d	00 09	23p21			23p55		00 03							00s54		05 47	06 03				←			06 33
Woking	a	00 15	23p29	23p55		23p59	00 01	00 08	00 06	00 11		00 26	00 35		00 58	01 41	05 51	06 08	05 59			06 08			06 38
	d		23p30	23p57		00 01	00 03		00 08	00 13		00 28	00 37	00 40	01 00	01 42	05 53	06 13	06 01	06 02		06 13	06 19	06 30	
Worplesdon	d									00 18								→				06 18			
Guildford	a									00 24					01 07		06 00					06 23			
Brookwood	d		23p36	00 03		00 07						00 34		00 45						06 08			06 25	06 36	
Ash Vale	d		23p44			00 15								00 53						06 16				06 44	
Aldershot	a		23p49			00 19								00 58						06 21				06 49	
	d		23p50			00 20								00 59						06 21				06 50	
Farnham	a		23p55			00 25								01 04						06 27				06 55	
	d		23p58			00 26								01 05						06 27				06 56	
Bentley	d		00 04			00 33								01s11						06 34				07 02	
Alton	a		00 11			00 40								01 18						06 41				07 10	
Farnborough (Main)	d			00 10			00 14					00 41				01s51							06 33		
Fleet	d			00 16			00 20					00 47				01s57							06 38		
Winchfield	d			00 21								00s52											06 43		
Hook	d			00 26								00s57											06 48		
Basingstoke	a			00 33			00 33		00 27			01 06	00 55			02s09			06 20				06 58		

		SW 1	SW 1	SW 1	SW	SW ◇1		SW 1	SW 1	SW 1	SW 1	SW	SW 1	SW ◇1 🛒	SW	SW 1		SW 1	SW 1	SW	SW 1	SW 1	SW 1	SW ◇1	SW
London Waterloo 15 ⊖	d	06 12	06 15		06 20	06 30			06 42	06 45		06 50	06 53	07 10		07 12		07 15		07 20	07 23	07 30		07 35	
Vauxhall ⊖	d				06 24							06 54								07 24					
Clapham Junction 10	d	06u19	06u22		06 29	06u37			06u49	06u52		06 59	07u00	07u17		07u20		07u23		07 29	07u30				
	d																								
Earlsfield	d				06 32							07 02								07 32					
Wimbledon 6 ⊖	d				06 36							07 06			←					07 36					←
Surbiton 6	d	06 30			06 44				07 00			07 14	07 11		07 14	07 31				07 44	07 41				07 44
Esher	d				06 48							→			07 18					→					07 48
Hersham	d				06 51										07 21										07 51
Walton-on-Thames	d	06 37			06 54				07 07						07 24	07 38									07 54
Weybridge	d	06 41			06 57				07 11						07 27	07 42									07 57
Byfleet & New Haw	d				07 00										07 30										08 00
West Byfleet	d			←	07 03						←		07 21		07 33				←		07 51		←		08 03
Woking	a	06 48	06 41	06 48	07 08	06 56			07 18	07 11	07 18		07 26	07 35	07 38	07 48		07 42	07 48		07 59	07 54	07 59	07 58	08 08
	d	06 49	06 43	06 49		06 57		07 00	07 19	07 13	07 19		07 30	07 36		07 50		07 44	07 50		08 00	07 55	08 00	08 00	
Worplesdon	d	→							→	07 18						→					→				
Guildford	a		06 51							07 23								07 51				08 03			
Brookwood	d			06 55				07 06			07 25		07 36						07 56				08 06		
Ash Vale	d							07 14					07 44										08 14		
Aldershot	a							07 19					07 49										08 19		
	d							07 20					07 50										08 20		
Farnham	a							07 25					07 55										08 25		
	d							07 26					07 56										08 26		
Bentley	d							07 32					08 02										08 32		
Alton	a							07 40					08 10										08 39		
Farnborough (Main)	d			07 03							07 33								08 03						
Fleet	d			07 08							07 38								08 09						
Winchfield	d			07 14							07 44								08 14						
Hook	d			07 18							07 48								08 19						
Basingstoke	a			07 28		07 16					07 58			07 57					08 28					08 20	

b Previous night, stops to pick up only

Table 155

Saturdays
from 13 October

London - Woking, Guildford, Alton and Basingstoke

Network Diagram - see first Page of Table 155

		SW ■		SW ■	SW ■	SW ◇■ ✠	SW ■	SW	SW ■	SW ■	SW ■	SW ◇■		SW ■	SW	SW ■	SW ■	SW ◇■ ✠	SW ■	SW	SW ■	SW ■		SW ◇■ ✠	SW ■
London Waterloo 15 ⊖	d	07 39		07 42	07 45	07 50		07 50	07 53	08 00		08 05		08 09		08 12	08 15	08 20		08 20	08 23	08 30		08 35	
Vauxhall ⊖	d							07 54												08 24					
Clapham Junction 10	d	07u46			07u52	07u57		07 59	08u00			08u12				08u19	08u22	08u27		08 29					
	d																								
Earlsfield	d							08 02												08 32					
Wimbledon 6 ⊖	d							08 06							←					08 36					
Surbiton 6	d			08 00				08 14	08 11						08 14	08 30				08 44	08 41				
Esher	d							→							08 18					→					
Hersham	d														08 21										
Walton-on-Thames	d			08 07											08 24	08 37									
Weybridge	d			08 11											08 27	08 41									
Byfleet & New Haw	d														08 30										
West Byfleet	d						←		08 21		←				08 33				←		08 51				←
Woking	a			08 18	08 11	08 15	08 18		08 29	08 24	08 29			08 33	08 38	08 48	08 41	08 45	08 48		08 59	08 54		08 58	08 59
	d			08 19	08 13	08 16	08 19		08 30	08 25	08 30			08 35		08 49	08 43	08 46	08 49		09 00	08 55			09 00
Worplesdon	d			→	08 18				→							→					→				
Guildford	a				08 23					08 33							08 50					09 03			
Brookwood	d						08 25				08 36								08 55						09 06
Ash Vale	d										08 44														09 14
Aldershot	a										08 49														09 19
	d										08 50														09 20
Farnham	a										08 55														09 25
	d										08 56														09 26
Bentley	d										09 02														
Alton	a										09 10														09 37
Farnborough (Main)	d	08 13					08 33							08 45					09 03						
Fleet	d	08 19					08 38												09 08						
Winchfield	d						08 44												09 14						
Hook	d						08 48												09 18						
Basingstoke	a	08 31				08 36	08 58					08 47		08 58				09 05	09 28						

		SW	SW ■	SW ■	SW ■	SW ◇■ ✠	SW ■	SW		SW ■	SW ■ ✠	SW ■	SW ◇■ ✠	SW ■	SW	SW ■	SW ■	SW ◇■ ✠		SW ■	SW	SW ■	SW ■ ✠	SW ◇■ ✠	SW ■
London Waterloo 15 ⊖	d		08 39	08 42	08 45	08 50		08 50		08 53	09 00		09 05	09 09		09 12	09 15	09 20			09 20	09 23	09 30	09 35	
Vauxhall ⊖	d							08 54													09 24				
Clapham Junction 10	d		08u46		08u52			08 59		09u00			09u12			09u19	09u22	09u27			09 29				
	d																								
Earlsfield	d							09 02													09 32				
Wimbledon 6 ⊖	d	←						09 06							←						09 36				
Surbiton 6	d	08 44		09 00				09 14		09 11					09 14	09 30					09 44	09 41			
Esher	d	08 48						→							09 18						→				
Hersham	d	08 51													09 21										
Walton-on-Thames	d	08 54		09 07											09 24	09 37									
Weybridge	d	08 57		09 11											09 27	09 41									
Byfleet & New Haw	d	09 00													09 30										
West Byfleet	d	09 03					←			09 21		←			09 33					←		09 51			←
Woking	a	09 08		09 18	09 11	09 14	09 18			09 29	09 24	09 29		09 33	09 38	09 48	09 41	09 45		09 48		09 59	09 54	09 58	09 59
	d			09 19	09 13	09 16	09 19			09 30	09 25	09 30		09 35		09 49	09 43	09 46		09 49		10 00	09 55		10 00
Worplesdon	d			→	09 18					→						→						→			
Guildford	a				09 23						09 33						09 50						10 03		
Brookwood	d						09 25					09 36								09 55					10 06
Ash Vale	d											09 44													10 14
Aldershot	a											09 49													10 19
	d											09 50													10 20
Farnham	a											09 55													10 25
	d											09 56													10 26
Bentley	d											10 02													
Alton	a											10 29													10 37
Farnborough (Main)	d		09 13				09 33							09 45						10 03					
Fleet	d		09 19				09 38													10 08					
Winchfield	d						09 44													10 14					
Hook	d						09 48													10 18					
Basingstoke	a		09 31			09 36	09 58						09 47	09 58				10 05		10 28					

Table 155

Saturdays
from 13 October

London - Woking, Guildford, Alton and Basingstoke

Network Diagram - see first Page of Table 155

		SW	SW ■	SW ■		SW ■	SW ◇■ ✠	SW ■	SW	SW ■	SW ■ ✠	SW ■	SW ◇■ ✠	SW ■		SW	SW ■	SW ■	SW ◇■ ✠	SW ■	SW	SW ■	SW ■ ✠	SW ◇■ ✠	
London Waterloo 15 ⊖	d		09 39	09 42		09 45	09 50		09 50	09 53	10 00		10 05	10 09			10 12	10 15	10 20		10 20	10 23	10 30	10 35	
Vauxhall ⊖	d								09 54												10 24				
Clapham Junction 10	d		09u46			09u52			09 59	10u00			10u12				10u19	10u22	10u27		10 29				
	d																								
Earlsfield	d								10 02												10 32				
Wimbledon 6 ⊖	d	←							10 06							←					10 36				
Surbiton 6	d	09 44		10 00					10 14	10 11						10 14	10 30				10 44	10 41			
Esher	d	09 48							→							10 18					→				
Hersham	d	09 51														10 21									
Walton-on-Thames	d	09 54		10 07												10 24	10 37								
Weybridge	d	09 57		10 11												10 27	10 41								
Byfleet & New Haw	d	10 00														10 30									
West Byfleet	d	10 03						←		10 21		←				10 33				←		10 51			
Woking	a	10 08		10 18		10 11	10 14	10 18		10 29	10 24	10 29		10 33		10 38	10 48	10 41	10 45	10 48		10 59	10 54	10 58	
	d			10 19		10 13	10 16	10 19		10 30	10 25	10 30		10 35			10 49	10 43	10 46	10 49		11 00	10 55		
Worplesdon	d			→		10 18				→							→					→			
Guildford	a					10 23					10 33							10 50					11 03		
Brookwood	d							10 25				10 36								10 55					
Ash Vale	d											10 44													
Aldershot	a											10 49													
	d											10 50													
Farnham	a											10 55													
	d											10 56													
Bentley	d											11 02													
Alton	a											11 10													
Farnborough (Main)	d		10 13					10 33						10 45						11 03					
Fleet	d		10 19					10 38												11 08					
Winchfield	d							10 44												11 14					
Hook	d							10 48												11 18					
Basingstoke	a		10 31				10 36	10 58					10 47	10 58					11 05	11 28					

		SW ■	SW	SW ■	SW ■	SW ■	SW ◇■ ✠	SW ■	SW	SW ■		SW ■ ✠	SW ■	SW ◇■ ✠	SW ■	SW	SW ■	SW ■	SW ◇■ ✠	SW ■		SW	SW ■	SW ■ ✠	SW ◇■ ✠
London Waterloo 15 ⊖	d			10 39	10 42	10 45	10 50		10 50	10 53		11 00		11 05	11 09		11 12	11 15	11 20			11 20	11 23	11 30	11 35
Vauxhall ⊖	d								10 54													11 24			
Clapham Junction 10	d			10u46		10u52			10 59	11u00				11u12			11u19	11u22	11u27			11 29			
	d																								
Earlsfield	d								11 02													11 32			
Wimbledon 6 ⊖	d		←						11 06							←						11 36			
Surbiton 6	d		10 44		11 00				11 14	11 11						11 14	11 30					11 44	11 41		
Esher	d		10 48						→							11 18						→			
Hersham	d		10 51													11 21									
Walton-on-Thames	d		10 54		11 07											11 24	11 37								
Weybridge	d		10 57		11 11											11 27	11 41								
Byfleet & New Haw	d		11 00													11 30									
West Byfleet	d	←	11 03					←		11 21			←			11 33				←			11 51		
Woking	a	10 59	11 08		11 18	11 11	11 14	11 18		11 29		11 24	11 29		11 33	11 38	11 48	11 41	11 45	11 48			11 59	11 54	11 58
	d	11 00			11 19	11 13	11 16	11 19		11 30		11 25	11 30		11 35		11 49	11 43	11 46	11 49			12 00	11 55	
Worplesdon	d				→	11 18				→							→						→		
Guildford	a					11 23						11 33						11 50						12 03	
Brookwood	d	11 06						11 25					11 36							11 55					
Ash Vale	d	11 14											11 44												
Aldershot	a	11 19											11 49												
	d	11 20											11 50												
Farnham	a	11 25											11 55												
	d	11 26											11 56												
Bentley	d												12 02												
Alton	a	11 37											12 10												
Farnborough (Main)	d			11 13				11 33							11 45					12 03					
Fleet	d			11 19				11 38												12 08					
Winchfield	d							11 44												12 14					
Hook	d							11 48												12 18					
Basingstoke	a			11 31			11 36	11 58						11 47	11 58				12 05	12 28					

Table 155

Saturdays
from 13 October

London - Woking, Guildford, Alton and Basingstoke

Network Diagram - see first Page of Table 155

		SW ■	SW	SW ■	SW ■	SW ■		SW ◇■ ✠	SW ■	SW	SW ■	SW ■ ✠	SW ■	SW ◇■ ✠	SW ■	SW		SW ■	SW ■	SW ◇■ ✠	SW ■	SW	SW ■	SW ■ ✠	SW ◇■ ✠
London Waterloo ⊖	d			11 39	11 42	11 45		11 50		11 50	11 53	12 00		12 05	12 09			12 12	12 15	12 20		12 20	12 23	12 30	12 35
Vauxhall ⊖	d									11 54												12 24			
Clapham Junction	d			11u46		11u52				11 59	12u00			12u12				12u19	12u22	12u27		12 29			
	d																								
Earlsfield	d									12 02												12 32			
Wimbledon ⊖	d		←							12 06						←						12 36			
Surbiton	d		11 44		12 00					12 14	12 11					12 14		12 30				12 44	12 41		
Esher	d		11 48							→						12 18						→			
Hersham	d		11 51													12 21									
Walton-on-Thames	d		11 54		12 07											12 24		12 37							
Weybridge	d		11 57		12 11											12 27		12 41							
Byfleet & New Haw	d		12 00													12 30									
West Byfleet	d	←	12 03						←		12 21		←			12 33					←		12 51		
Woking	a	11 59	12 08		12 18	12 11		12 14	12 18		12 29	12 24	12 29		12 33	12 38		12 48	12 41	12 45	12 48		12 59	12 54	12 58
	d	12 00			12 19	12 13		12 16	12 19		12 30	12 25	12 30		12 35			12 49	12 43	12 46	12 49		13 00	12 55	
Worplesdon	d				→	12 18					→							→					→		
Guildford	a					12 23						12 33							12 50					13 03	
Brookwood	d	12 06							12 25				12 36								12 55				
Ash Vale	d	12 14											12 44												
Aldershot	a	12 19											12 49												
	d	12 20											12 50												
Farnham	a	12 25											12 55												
	d	12 26											12 56												
Bentley	d												13 02												
Alton	a	12 37											13 10												
Farnborough (Main)	d			12 13					12 33						12 45						13 03				
Fleet	d			12 19					12 38												13 08				
Winchfield	d								12 44												13 14				
Hook	d								12 48												13 18				
Basingstoke	a			12 31				12 36	12 58					12 47	12 58					13 05	13 28				

		SW ■		SW	SW ■	SW ■	SW ■	SW ◇■ ✠	SW ■	SW	SW ■	SW ■ ✠		SW ■	SW ◇■ ✠	SW ■	SW	SW ■	SW ■	SW ◇■ ✠	SW ■	SW		SW ■	SW ■ ✠
London Waterloo ⊖	d				12 39	12 42	12 45	12 50		12 50	12 53	13 00			13 05	13 09		13 12	13 15	13 20		13 20		13 23	13 30
Vauxhall ⊖	d									12 54												13 24			
Clapham Junction	d				12u46		12u52			12 59	13u00				13u12			13u19	13u22	13u27		13 29			
	d																								
Earlsfield	d									13 02												13 32			
Wimbledon ⊖	d			←						13 06							←					13 36			
Surbiton	d			12 44		13 00				13 14	13 11						13 14	13 30				13 44		13 41	
Esher	d			12 48						→							13 18					→			
Hersham	d			12 51													13 21								
Walton-on-Thames	d			12 54		13 07											13 24	13 37							
Weybridge	d			12 57		13 11											13 27	13 41							
Byfleet & New Haw	d			13 00													13 30								
West Byfleet	d	←		13 03					←		13 21			←			13 33				←			13 51	
Woking	a	12 59		13 08		13 18	13 11	13 14	13 18		13 29	13 24		13 29		13 33	13 38	13 48	13 41	13 45	13 48			13 59	13 54
	d	13 00				13 19	13 13	13 16	13 19		13 30	13 25		13 30		13 35		13 49	13 43	13 46	13 49			14 00	13 55
Worplesdon	d					→	13 18				→							→						→	
Guildford	a						13 23					13 33							13 50						14 03
Brookwood	d	13 06							13 25					13 36							13 55				
Ash Vale	d	13 14												13 44											
Aldershot	a	13 19												13 49											
	d	13 20												13 50											
Farnham	a	13 25												13 55											
	d	13 26												13 56											
Bentley	d													14 02											
Alton	a	13 37												14 10											
Farnborough (Main)	d				13 13				13 33							13 45					14 03				
Fleet	d				13 19				13 38												14 08				
Winchfield	d								13 44												14 14				
Hook	d								13 48												14 18				
Basingstoke	a				13 31			13 36	13 58						13 47	13 58				14 05	14 28				

Table 155

Saturdays
from 13 October

London - Woking, Guildford, Alton and Basingstoke

Network Diagram - see first Page of Table 155

		SW ◇■ ✠	SW ■	SW	SW ■	SW ■	SW ■	SW ◇■ ✠		SW ■	SW	SW ■	SW ■ ✠	SW ■	SW ◇■ ✠	SW ■	SW	SW ■		SW ■	SW ◇■ ✠	SW ■	SW	SW ■	SW ■ ✠
London Waterloo ⊖	d	13 35			13 39	13 42	13 45	13 50			13 50	13 53	14 00		14 05	14 09		14 12		14 15	14 20		14 20	14 23	14 30
Vauxhall ⊖	d										13 54												14 24		
Clapham Junction	d				13u46		13u52				13 59	14u00			14u12			14u19		14u22	14u27		14 29		
	d																								
Earlsfield	d										14 02												14 32		
Wimbledon ⊖	d			←							14 06						←						14 36		
Surbiton	d			13 44		14 00					14 14	14 11					14 14	14 30					14 44	14 41	
Esher	d			13 48							→						14 18						→		
Hersham	d			13 51													14 21								
Walton-on-Thames	d			13 54		14 07											14 24	14 37							
Weybridge	d			13 57		14 11											14 27	14 41							
Byfleet & New Haw	d			14 00													14 30								
West Byfleet	d		←	14 03						←		14 21		←			14 33					←		14 51	
Woking	a	13 58	13 59	14 08		14 18	14 11	14 14		14 18		14 29	14 24	14 29		14 33	14 38	14 48		14 41	14 45	14 48		14 59	14 54
	d		14 00			14 19	14 13	14 16		14 19		14 30	14 25	14 30		14 35		14 49		14 43	14 46	14 49		15 00	14 55
Worplesdon	d					→	14 18					→						→						→	
Guildford	a						14 23						14 33							14 50					15 03
Brookwood	d		14 06							14 25				14 36								14 55			
Ash Vale	d		14 14											14 44											
Aldershot	a		14 19											14 49											
	d		14 20											14 50											
Farnham	a		14 25											14 55											
	d		14 26											14 56											
Bentley	d													15 02											
Alton	a		14 37											15 10											
Farnborough (Main)	d				14 13					14 33						14 45						15 03			
Fleet	d				14 19					14 38												15 08			
Winchfield	d									14 44												15 14			
Hook	d									14 48												15 18			
Basingstoke	a				14 31			14 36		14 58					14 47	14 58					15 05	15 28			

		SW ◇■ ✠	SW ■	SW		SW ■	SW ■	SW ■	SW ◇■ ✠	SW ■	SW	SW ■	SW ■ ✠	SW ■		SW ◇■ ✠	SW ■	SW	SW ■	SW ■	SW ◇■ ✠	SW ■	SW	SW ■	
London Waterloo ⊖	d	14 35				14 39	14 42	14 45	14 50		14 50	14 53	15 00			15 05	15 09		15 12	15 15	15 20		15 20	15 23	
Vauxhall ⊖	d										14 54												15 24		
Clapham Junction	d					14u46		14u52			14 59	15u00				15u12			15u19	15u22	15u27		15 29		
	d																								
Earlsfield	d										15 02												15 32		
Wimbledon ⊖	d			←							15 06							←					15 36		
Surbiton	d			14 44			15 00				15 14	15 11						15 14	15 30				15 44	15 41	
Esher	d			14 48							→							15 18					→		
Hersham	d			14 51														15 21							
Walton-on-Thames	d			14 54			15 07											15 24	15 37						
Weybridge	d			14 57			15 11											15 27	15 41						
Byfleet & New Haw	d			15 00														15 30							
West Byfleet	d		←	15 03						←		15 21		←				15 33				←		15 51	
Woking	a	14 58	14 59	15 08			15 18	15 11	15 14	15 18		15 29	15 24	15 29			15 33	15 38	15 48	15 41	15 45	15 48		15 59	
	d		15 00				15 19	15 13	15 16	15 19		15 30	15 25	15 30			15 35		15 49	15 43	15 46	15 49		16 00	
Worplesdon	d						→	15 18				→							→					→	
Guildford	a							15 23					15 33							15 50					
Brookwood	d		15 06							15 25				15 36								15 55			
Ash Vale	d		15 14											15 44											
Aldershot	a		15 19											15 49											
	d		15 20											15 50											
Farnham	a		15 25											15 55											
	d		15 26											15 56											
Bentley	d													16 02											
Alton	a		15 37											16 10											
Farnborough (Main)	d					15 13				15 33							15 45					16 03			
Fleet	d					15 19				15 38												16 08			
Winchfield	d									15 44												16 14			
Hook	d									15 48												16 18			
Basingstoke	a					15 31			15 36	15 58						15 47	15 58				16 05	16 28			

Saturdays from 13 October

London - Woking, Guildford, Alton and Basingstoke

Network Diagram - see first Page of Table 155

		SW ■ ✠	SW ◇■ ✠	SW ■	SW	SW ■	SW ■	SW ■	SW ◇■ ✠	SW ■		SW	SW ■	SW ■ ✠	SW ■	SW ◇■ ✠	SW ■	SW	SW ■	SW ■		SW ◇■ ✠	SW ■	SW	SW ■
London Waterloo [15] ⊖	d	15 30	15 35			15 39	15 42	15 45	15 50			15 50	15 53	16 00		16 05	16 09		16 12	16 15		16 20		16 20	16 23
Vauxhall ⊖	d											15 54												16 24	
Clapham Junction [10]	d					15u46		15u52				15 59	16u00			16u12			16u19	16u22		16u27		16 29	
	d																								
Earlsfield	d											16 02												16 32	
Wimbledon [6] ⊖	d				←							16 06						←						16 36	
Surbiton [6]	d				15 44		16 00					16 14	16 11					16 14	16 30					16 44	16 41
Esher	d				15 48							→						16 18						→	
Hersham	d				15 51													16 21							
Walton-on-Thames	d				15 54		16 07											16 24	16 37						
Weybridge	d				15 57		16 11											16 27	16 41						
Byfleet & New Haw	d				16 00													16 30							
West Byfleet	d			←	16 03					←			16 21		←			16 33					←		16 51
Woking	a	15 54	15 58	15 59	16 08		16 18	16 11	16 14	16 18			16 29	16 24	16 29		16 33	16 38	16 48	16 41		16 45	16 48		16 59
	d	15 55		16 00			16 19	16 13	16 16	16 19			16 30	16 25	16 30		16 35		16 49	16 43		16 46	16 49		17 00
Worplesdon	d						→	16 18					→						→						→
Guildford	a	16 03						16 23						16 33						16 50					
Brookwood	d			16 06						16 25					16 36								16 55		
Ash Vale	d			16 14											16 44										
Aldershot	a			16 19											16 49										
	d			16 20											16 50										
Farnham	a			16 25											16 55										
	d			16 26											16 56										
Bentley	d														17 02										
Alton	a			16 37											17 10										
Farnborough (Main)	d					16 13				16 33							16 45						17 03		
Fleet	d					16 19				16 38													17 08		
Winchfield	d									16 44													17 14		
Hook	d									16 48													17 18		
Basingstoke	a					16 31			16 36	16 58						16 47	16 58					17 05	17 28		

		SW ■ ✠	SW ◇■ ✠	SW ■	SW	SW ■		SW ■	SW ■	SW ◇■ ✠	SW ■	SW	SW ■	SW ■ ✠	SW ■	SW ◇■ ⊡		SW ■	SW	SW ■	SW ■	SW ◇■ ✠	SW ■	SW	SW ■
London Waterloo [15] ⊖	d	16 30	16 35			16 39		16 42	16 45	16 50		16 50	16 53	17 00		17 05		17 09		17 12	17 15	17 20		17 20	17 23
Vauxhall ⊖	d											16 54												17 24	
Clapham Junction [10]	d					16u46			16u52			16 59	17u00			17u12				17u19	17u22	17u27		17 29	
	d																								
Earlsfield	d											17 02												17 32	
Wimbledon [6] ⊖	d				←							17 06							←					17 36	
Surbiton [6]	d				16 44			17 00				17 14	17 11						17 14	17 30				17 44	17 41
Esher	d				16 48							→							17 18					→	
Hersham	d				16 51														17 21						
Walton-on-Thames	d				16 54			17 07											17 24	17 37					
Weybridge	d				16 57			17 11											17 27	17 41					
Byfleet & New Haw	d				17 00														17 30						
West Byfleet	d			←	17 03						←		17 21		←				17 33				←		17 51
Woking	a	16 54	16 58	16 59	17 08			17 18	17 11	17 14	17 18		17 29	17 24	17 29			17 33	17 38	17 48	17 41	17 45	17 48		17 59
	d	16 55		17 00				17 19	17 13	17 16	17 19		17 30	17 25	17 30			17 35		17 49	17 43	17 46	17 49		18 00
Worplesdon	d							→	17 18				→							→					→
Guildford	a	17 03							17 23					17 33							17 50				
Brookwood	d			17 06							17 25				17 36								17 55		
Ash Vale	d			17 14											17 44										
Aldershot	a			17 19											17 49										
	d			17 20											17 50										
Farnham	a			17 25											17 55										
	d			17 26											17 56										
Bentley	d			17 32											18 02										
Alton	a			17 39											18 10										
Farnborough (Main)	d					17 13					17 33							17 45					18 03		
Fleet	d					17 19					17 38												18 08		
Winchfield	d										17 44												18 14		
Hook	d										17 48												18 18		
Basingstoke	a					17 31				17 36	17 58					17 47		17 58				18 05	18 28		

Table 155

Saturdays from 13 October

London - Woking, Guildford, Alton and Basingstoke

Network Diagram - see first Page of Table 155

		SW ■ ✠		SW ◇■ ✠	SW ■	SW	SW ■	SW ■	SW ■	SW ◇■ ✠	SW ■	SW		SW ■	SW ■ ✠	SW ■	SW ◇■ ✠	SW ■	SW	SW ■	SW ■	SW ◇■ ✠		SW ■	SW
London Waterloo [15] ⊖	d	17 30		17 35			17 39	17 42	17 45	17 50		17 50		17 53	18 00		18 05	18 09		18 12	18 15	18 20			18 20
Vauxhall ⊖	d											17 54													18 24
Clapham Junction [10]	d						17u46		17u52			17 59		18u00			18u12			18u19	18u22	18u27			18 29
	d																								
Earlsfield	d											18 02													18 32
Wimbledon [6] ⊖	d					←						18 06							←						18 36
Surbiton [6]	d					17 44		18 00				18 14		18 11					18 14	18 30					18 44
Esher	d					17 48						→							18 18						→
Hersham	d					17 51													18 21						
Walton-on-Thames	d					17 54		18 07											18 24	18 37					
Weybridge	d					17 57		18 11											18 27	18 41					
Byfleet & New Haw	d					18 00													18 30						
West Byfleet	d				←	18 03					←			18 21		←			18 33					←	
Woking	a	17 54		17 58	17 59	18 08		18 18	18 11	18 14	18 18			18 29	18 24	18 29		18 33	18 38	18 48	18 41	18 45		18 48	
	d	17 55			18 00			18 19	18 13	18 16	18 19			18 30	18 25	18 30		18 35		18 49	18 43	18 46		18 49	
Worplesdon	d							→	18 18					→						→					
Guildford	a	18 03							18 23						18 33						18 50				
Brookwood	d				18 06						18 25					18 36								18 55	
Ash Vale	d				18 14											18 44									
Aldershot	a				18 19											18 49									
	d				18 20											18 50									
Farnham	a				18 25											18 55									
	d				18 26											18 56									
Bentley	d				18 32											19 02									
Alton	a				18 39											19 10									
Farnborough (Main)	d						18 13				18 33							18 45						19 03	
Fleet	d						18 19				18 38													19 08	
Winchfield	d										18 44													19 14	
Hook	d										18 48													19 18	
Basingstoke	a						18 31			18 36	18 58						18 47	18 58				19 05		19 28	

		SW ■	SW ■ ✠	SW ◇■ ✠	SW ■	SW	SW ■	SW ■		SW ■	SW ◇■ ✠	SW ■	SW	SW ■	SW ■ ✠	SW ■	SW ◇■ ✠	SW ■		SW	SW ■	SW ■	SW ◇■ ✠	SW ■	SW
London Waterloo [15] ⊖	d	18 23	18 30	18 35			18 39	18 42		18 45	18 50		18 50	18 53	19 00		19 05	19 09			19 12	19 15	19 20		19 20
Vauxhall ⊖	d												18 54												19 24
Clapham Junction [10]	d						18u46			18u52			18 59	19u00			19u12				19u19	19u22	19u27		19 29
	d																								
Earlsfield	d												19 02												19 32
Wimbledon [6] ⊖	d					←							19 06							←					19 36
Surbiton [6]	d	18 41				18 44		19 00					19 14	19 11						19 14	19 30				19 44
Esher	d					18 48							→							19 18					→
Hersham	d					18 51														19 21					
Walton-on-Thames	d					18 54		19 07												19 24	19 37				
Weybridge	d					18 57		19 11												19 27	19 41				
Byfleet & New Haw	d					19 00														19 30					
West Byfleet	d	18 51			←	19 03						←		19 21		←				19 33				←	
Woking	a	18 59	18 54	18 58	18 59	19 08		19 18		19 11	19 15	19 18		19 29	19 24	19 29		19 33		19 38	19 48	19 41	19 45	19 48	
	d	19 00	18 55		19 00			19 19		19 13	19 16	19 19		19 30	19 25	19 30		19 35			19 49	19 43	19 46	19 49	
Worplesdon	d	→						→		19 18				→							→				
Guildford	a		19 03							19 23					19 33							19 50			
Brookwood	d				19 06							19 25				19 36								19 55	
Ash Vale	d				19 14											19 44									
Aldershot	a				19 19											19 49									
	d				19 20											19 50									
Farnham	a				19 25											19 55									
	d				19 26											19 56									
Bentley	d				19 32											20 02									
Alton	a				19 39											20 10									
Farnborough (Main)	d						19 13					19 33						19 45						20 03	
Fleet	d						19 19					19 38												20 08	
Winchfield	d											19 44												20 14	
Hook	d											19 48												20 18	
Basingstoke	a						19 31				19 36	19 58					19 47	19 58					20 05	20 28	

London - Woking, Guildford, Alton and Basingstoke

Network Diagram - see first Page of Table 155

		SW ■	SW ■ ⊼	SW ◇■ ⊼	SW ■	SW	SW ■	SW ■	SW ■	SW ◇■ ⊼	SW ■	SW	SW ■	SW ■	SW ■	SW ◇■ ⊼	SW ■	SW	SW ■	SW ■	SW ◇■ ⊼	SW ■
London Waterloo [15] ⊖	d	19 23	19 30	19 35			19 39	19 42	19 45	19 50		19 50	19 53	20 00		20 05	20 09		20 12	20 15	20 20	
Vauxhall ⊖	d											19 54										
Clapham Junction [10]	d						19u46		19u52			19 59	20u00			20u12			20u19	20u22	20u27	
	d																					
Earlsfield	d											20 02										
Wimbledon [6] ⊖	d					←						20 06						←				
Surbiton [6]	d	19 41				19 44		20 00				20 14	20 11					20 14	20 30			
Esher	d					19 48						→						20 18				
Hersham	d					19 51												20 21				
Walton-on-Thames	d					19 54		20 07										20 24	20 37			
Weybridge	d					19 57		20 11										20 27	20 41			
Byfleet & New Haw	d					20 00												20 30				
West Byfleet	d	19 51			←	20 03					←		20 21		←			20 33				←
Woking	a	19 59	19 54	19 58	19 59	20 08		20 18	20 11	20 14	20 18		20 29	20 24	20 29		20 33	20 38	20 48	20 41	20 45	20 48
	d	20 00	19 55		20 00			20 19	20 13	20 16	20 19		20 30	20 25	20 30		20 35		20 49	20 43	20 46	20 49
Worplesdon	d	→						→	20 18				→						→			
Guildford	a		20 03						20 23					20 33						20 50		
Brookwood	d				20 06						20 25				20 36							20 55
Ash Vale	d				20 14										20 44							
Aldershot	a				20 19										20 49							
	d				20 20										20 50							
Farnham	a				20 25										20 55							
	d				20 26										20 56							
Bentley	d				20 32										21 02							
Alton	a				20 39										21 10							
Farnborough (Main)	d						20 13				20 33						20 45					21 03
Fleet	d						20 19				20 38											21 08
Winchfield	d										20 44											21 14
Hook	d										20 48											21 18
Basingstoke	a						20 31			20 36	20 58					20 47	20 58				21 05	21 28

		SW	SW ■	SW ■	SW ◇■ ⊼	SW ■	SW	SW ■	SW ■	SW ■	SW ■	SW	SW ■	SW ■	SW ■	SW ◇■ ⊼	SW	SW ■	SW ◇■ ⊼	SW	SW ■	SW ■	SW ◇■ ⊼
London Waterloo [15] ⊖	d	20 20	20 23	20 30	20 35			20 39	20 42	20 45		20 50	20 53	21 00		21 05		21 12	21 20	21 20	21 23	21 30	21 35
Vauxhall ⊖	d	20 24										20 54								21 24			
Clapham Junction [10]	d	20 29						20u46		20u52		20 59	21u00			21u12		21u19	21u27	21 29			
	d																						
Earlsfield	d	20 32										21 02								21 32			
Wimbledon [6] ⊖	d	20 36					←					21 06					←			21 36			
Surbiton [6]	d	20 44	20 41				20 44		21 00			21 14	21 11				21 14	21 30		21 44	21 41		
Esher	d	→					20 48					→					21 18			→			
Hersham	d						20 51										21 21						
Walton-on-Thames	d						20 54		21 07								21 24	21 37					
Weybridge	d						20 57		21 11								21 27	21 41					
Byfleet & New Haw	d						21 00										21 30						
West Byfleet	d		20 51			←	21 03				←		21 21		←		21 33				21 51		
Woking	a		20 59	20 54	20 58	20 59	21 08		21 18	21 11	21 18		21 29	21 24	21 29	21 31	21 38	21 48	21 45		21 59	21 54	21 58
	d		21 00	20 55		21 00			21 19	21 13	21 19		21 30	21 25	21 30	21 32		21 49	21 49		22 00	21 55	
Worplesdon	d		→						→	21 18			→								→		
Guildford	a			21 03						21 23				21 33								22 03	
Brookwood	d					21 06					21 25				21 36			21 55					
Ash Vale	d					21 14									21 44								
Aldershot	a					21 19									21 49								
	d					21 20									21 50								
Farnham	a					21 25									21 55								
	d					21 26									21 56								
Bentley	d					21 32									22 02								
Alton	a					21 39									22 10								
Farnborough (Main)	d							21 13			21 33							22 03					
Fleet	d							21 19			21 38							22 08					
Winchfield	d										21 44							22 14					
Hook	d										21 48							22 18					
Basingstoke	a							21 31			21 58					21 51		22 25	22 12				

Table 155

Saturdays
from 13 October

London - Woking, Guildford, Alton and Basingstoke

Network Diagram - see first Page of Table 155

		SW ■	SW	SW ■	SW ■	SW ■	SW ■	SW	SW ■	SW ■	SW ■	SW ◇■ ⊼	SW	SW ■	SW ■ ⊼	SW	SW ■	SW ■	SW ◇■ ⊼	SW ■	SW	SW ■	SW ■
London Waterloo [15] ⊖	d			21 39	21 42	21 45		21 50	21 53	22 00		22 05		22 12	22 20	22 20	22 23	22 30	22 35			22 39	22 42
Vauxhall ⊖	d							21 54								22 24							
Clapham Junction [10]	d			21u46		21u52		21 59	22u00			22u12		22u19	22u27	22 29	22u30					22u46	22u49
	d																						
Earlsfield	d							22 02								22 32							
Wimbledon [6] ⊖	d		←					22 06					←			22 36					←		
Surbiton [6]	d		21 44		22 00			22 14	22 11				22 14	22 30		22 44	22 41				22 44		23 00
Esher	d		21 48					→					22 18			→					22 48		
Hersham	d		21 51										22 21								22 51		
Walton-on-Thames	d		21 54		22 07								22 24	22 37							22 54		23 07
Weybridge	d		21 57		22 11								22 27	22 41							22 57		23 11
Byfleet & New Haw	d		22 00										22 30								23 00		
West Byfleet	d	←	22 03				←		22 21		←		22 33				22 51			←	23 03		
Woking	a	21 59	22 08		22 18	22 11	22 18		22 29	22 24	22 29	22 31	22 37	22 48	22 45		22 59	22 54	22 58	22 59	23 08		23 18
	d	22 00			22 19	22 13	22 19		22 30	22 25	22 30	22 32	22 39	22 49	22 49		23 00	22 55		23 00			23 19
Worplesdon	d				→	22 18			→								→						→
Guildford	a					22 23				22 33			22 47					23 03					
Brookwood	d	22 06					22 25				22 36			22 55						23 06			
Ash Vale	d	22 14									22 44									23 14			
Aldershot	a	22 19									22 49									23 19			
	d	22 20									22 50									23 20			
Farnham	a	22 25									22 55									23 25			
	d	22 26									22 56									23 26			
Bentley	d	22 32									23 02									23 33			
Alton	a	22 39									23 10									23 40			
Farnborough (Main)	d			22 13			22 33							23 03								23 16	
Fleet	d			22 19			22 38							23 08								23 21	
Winchfield	d						22 44							23 14									
Hook	d						22 48							23 18									
Basingstoke	a			22 31			22 58					22 51		23 25	23 10							23 34	

		SW ■	SW ■	SW	SW	SW ■	SW ◇■	SW	SW ■	SW ■	SW ■	SW	SW ■	SW ■	SW	SW ■	SW ■	SW ■
London Waterloo [15] ⊖	d	22 45		22 50	22 52	22 53	23 05		23 12	23 15		23 20	23 23	23 35		23 40	23 45	23 48
Vauxhall ⊖	d			22 54	22 56							23 24						
Clapham Junction [10]	d	22u52		22 59		23u00	23u12			23u22		23 29	23u30	23u42		23u47	23u52	23u54
	d				23 02				23u19									
Earlsfield	d			23 02								23 32						
Wimbledon [6] ⊖	d			23 06				←				23 36			←			
Surbiton [6]	d			23 14		23 11		23 14	23 38			23 44	23 41		23 44			00 09
Esher	d			→				23 18				→			23 48			
Hersham	d							23 21							23 51			
Walton-on-Thames	d							23 24	23 45						23 54			00 16
Weybridge	d							23 27	23 49						23 57			00 20
Byfleet & New Haw	d				00 06			23 30							23 59			
West Byfleet	d		←		00 09	23 21		23 33			←		23 55		00 03			
Woking	a	23 11	23 18		00 15	23 29	23 31	23 38	23 55	23 41	23 55		23 59	00 01	00 08	00 06	00 11	00 26
	d	23 13	23 19			23 30	23 32		23 57	23 43	23 57		00 01	00 03		00 08	00 13	00 28
Worplesdon	d	23 18							→								00 18	
Guildford	a	23 23								23 51							00 24	
Brookwood	d		23 25			23 36					00 03		00 07					00 34
Ash Vale	d					23 44							00 15					
Aldershot	a					23 49							00 19					
	d					23 50							00 20					
Farnham	a					23 55							00 25					
	d					23 58							00 26					
Bentley	d					00 04							00 33					
Alton	a					00 11							00 40					
Farnborough (Main)	d		23 33								00 10			00 14				00 41
Fleet	d		23 38								00 16			00 20				00 47
Winchfield	d		23 44								00 21							00s52
Hook	d		23 48								00 26							00s57
Basingstoke	a		23 55				23 51				00 33			00 33		00 27		01 06

London - Woking, Guildford, Alton and Basingstoke

Network Diagram - see first Page of Table 155

	SW	SW ■	SW ■	SW	SW ■	SW ■	SW	SW ■ A	SW ■ A	SW ■	SW ■ B	SW ■	SW ■ B	SW ■ A	SW ■ A	SW	SW ■ B	SW	SW B	SW ■ B	SW ■ B	SW B
London Waterloo ⊖ d	22p52	22p53	23p12	23p20	23p23	23p35		23p40	23p45	23p48	23p55		00 05	00 05		00 09	00 20		00 27	00 30	00 50	
Vauxhall ⊖ d	22p56			23p24												00 13			00 31			
Clapham Junction d		23b00		23p29	23b30	23b42		23b47	23b52	23b54	00u02		00u12	00u12		00 20	00u27		00 37	00u37	00u57	
d	23p02		23b19																			
Earlsfield d				23p32												00 23			00s41			
Wimbledon ⊖ d				23p36			←							00u18		00 27			00 45	00u43		
Surbiton d		23p11	23p38	23p44	23p41		23p44			00 09						00 35	00 38		00 57			
Esher d				→			23p48									00s39			01s01			
Hersham d							23p51									00s42			01s04			
Walton-on-Thames d			23p45				23p54			00 16						00s44			01s06			
Weybridge d			23p49				23p57			00 20						00s48			01s10			
Byfleet & New Haw d	00 06						23p59									00s51			01s12			
West Byfleet d	00 09	23p21			23p55		00 03					←				00s54		←	01s15			←
Woking a	00 15	23p29	23p55		23p59	00 01	00 08	00 06	00 11	00 26	00 20	00 26	00 31	00 35		00 58	00 50	00 58	01 20	00 59	01 19	01 20
d		23p30	23p57		00 01	00 03		00 08	00 13	00 28	00 21	00 28	00 32	00 37	00 40	01 00	00 51	01 00	01 21	01 00	01 20	01 21
Worplesdon d									00 18	→			00 37			→			→			01s27
Guildford a									00 24				00 43					01 07			01s28	01 33
Brookwood d		23p36	00 03		00 07							00 34			00 45		00 57					
Ash Vale d		23p44			00 15										00 53		01 05					
Aldershot a		23p49			00 19										00 58		01 09					
d		23p50			00 20										00 59		01 10					
Farnham a		23p55			00 25										01 04		01 15					
d		23p58			00 26										01 05		01 16					
Bentley d		00 04			00 33										01s11		01s22					
Alton a		00 11			00 40										01 18		01 29					
Farnborough (Main) d			00 10			00 14						00 41										
Fleet d			00 16			00 20						00 47										
Winchfield d			00 21									00s52										
Hook d			00 26									00s57										
Basingstoke a			00 33			00 33		00 27			00 43	01 06		00 55						01 18		

	SW ■	SW ■	SW ■	SW ■	SW	SW ■ C	SW	SW	SW ◇■	SW	SW ■	SW ■	SW	SW ◇■ H	SW ■	SW	SW ■	SW ◇■	SW	SW	SW ◇■
London Waterloo ⊖ d	01 05				07 10	07 35		07 40	07 54		08 00	08 07	08 10	08 15			08 30	08 35		08 40	08 54
Vauxhall ⊖ d	01 09				07 14			07 44					08 14							08 44	
Clapham Junction d					07 19	07u45		07 49	08u03		08u09	08 15	08 19	08u22			08u39	08u45		08 49	09u03
d	01 15																				
Earlsfield d					07 22			07 52					08 22							08 52	
Wimbledon ⊖ d	01s27				07 26			07 56				08 22	08 26							08 56	
Surbiton d	01s35				07 35			08 05				08 30	08 35							09 05	
Esher d					07 39			08 09					08 39							09 09	
Hersham d					07 42			08 12					08 42							09 12	
Walton-on-Thames d					07 45			08 15					08 45							09 15	
Weybridge d					07 49			08 19					08 49							09 19	
Byfleet & New Haw d					07 51		08 02	08 21					08 51						09 02	09 21	
West Byfleet d					07 54		08 05	08 24		←			08 54		←	←			09 05	09 24	
Woking a	01 48				07 59	08 08	08 11	08 29	08 27	08 29	08 34	08 42	08 59	08 46	08 42	08 59	09 03	09 08	09 11	09 29	09 27
d	01 49	07 32	07 46	07 49	08 05	08 09		08 32	08 28	08 32	08 35	08 46 / 08 49	09 02	08 47	08 49	09 02	09 04	09 09		09 32	09 28
Worplesdon d								→				→	→							→	
Guildford a		07 39			08 14					08 40	08 43					09 10	09 12				
Brookwood d			07 51	07 55								08 51			08 55						
Ash Vale d				08 03											09 03						
Aldershot a				08 07											09 07						
d				08 08											09 08						
Farnham a				08 13											09 13						
d				08 14											09 14						
Bentley d				08 24											09 24						
Alton a				08 31											09 31						
Farnborough (Main) d	01s58		07 59									08 59									
Fleet d	02s04		08 04									09 04									
Winchfield d			08 10									09 10									
Hook d			08 14									09 14									
Basingstoke a	02s16		08 21			08 27			08 46			09 21		09 06				09 28			09 46

A until 22 July, 19 August, 26 August, 16 September, 23 September, 30 September

B 29 July, 5 August, 12 August, 2 September, 9 September

C 29 July, 5 August, 2 September

b Previous night, stops to pick up only

London - Woking, Guildford, Alton and Basingstoke

Network Diagram - see first Page of Table 155

	SW	SW ■	SW ■	SW	SW ◇■ H	SW ■	SW	SW ■	SW ◇■	SW	SW	SW ◇■	SW ■	SW	SW ■	SW	SW ◇■ H	SW ■	SW ■
London Waterloo ⊖ d		09 00	09 07	09 10	09 15			09 30	09 35		09 40	09 54	10 00		10 07	10 10	10 15		10 30
Vauxhall ⊖ d				09 14							09 44					10 14			
Clapham Junction d		09u09	09 15	09 19	09u22			09u39	09u45		09 49	10u03	10u09		10 15	10 19	10u22		10u39
d																			
Earlsfield d				09 22							09 52					10 22			
Wimbledon ⊖ d			09 22	09 26							09 56				10 22	10 26			
Surbiton d			09 30	09 35							10 05				10 30	10 35			
Esher d				09 39							10 09					10 39			
Hersham d				09 42							10 12					10 42			
Walton-on-Thames d				09 45							10 15					10 45			
Weybridge d				09 49							10 19					10 49			
Byfleet & New Haw d				09 51						10 02	10 21					10 51			
West Byfleet d	←			09 54		←	←			10 05	10 24			←		10 54		←	
Woking a	09 29	09 34	09 42	09 59	09 46	09 42	09 59	10 03	10 08	10 11	10 29	10 26	10 31	10 29	10 42	10 59	10 45	10 42	11 01
d	09 32	09 35	09 46 / 09 49	10 02	09 47	09 49	10 02	10 04	10 09		10 35	10 28	10 32	10 35	10 46 / 10 49	11 05	10 46	10 49	11 02
Worplesdon d			→	→							→				→	→			
Guildford a	09 40	09 43					10 10	10 12					10 40	10 44					11 10
Brookwood d			09 51			09 55									10 51			10 55	
Ash Vale d						10 03												11 03	
Aldershot a						10 07												11 07	
d						10 08												11 08	
Farnham a						10 13												11 13	
d						10 14												11 14	
Bentley d						10 24												11 24	
Alton a						10 31												11 31	
Farnborough (Main) d			09 59												10 59				
Fleet d			10 04												11 04				
Winchfield d			10 10												11 10				
Hook d			10 14												11 14				
Basingstoke a			10 21		10 06				10 28			10 46			11 21		11 05		

	SW	SW ◇■ H	SW	SW	SW ◇■	SW ■	SW	SW ■	SW	SW ◇■ H	SW ■	SW ■ H	SW	SW ◇■ H	SW	SW	SW ◇■ H	SW ■	SW
London Waterloo ⊖ d		10 35		10 40	10 54	11 00		11 07	11 10	11 15		11 30		11 35		11 40	11 54	12 00	
Vauxhall ⊖ d				10 44					11 14							11 44			
Clapham Junction d		10u45		10 49	11u04	11u09		11 15	11 19	11u22		11u39		11u45		11 49	12u04	12u09	
d																			
Earlsfield d				10 52					11 22							11 52			
Wimbledon ⊖ d				10 56				11 22	11 26							11 56			
Surbiton d				11 05				11 30	11 35							12 05			
Esher d				11 09					11 39							12 09			
Hersham d				11 12					11 42							12 12			
Walton-on-Thames d				11 15					11 45							12 15			
Weybridge d				11 19					11 49							12 19			
Byfleet & New Haw d			11 02	11 21					11 51						12 02	12 21			
West Byfleet d	←		11 05	11 24			←		11 54		←		←		12 05	12 24			←
Woking a	10 59	11 06	11 11	11 29	11 26	11 31	11 29	11 42	11 59	11 45	11 42	12 01	11 59	12 06	12 11	12 29	12 26	12 31	12 29
d	11 05	11 07		11 35	11 28	11 32	11 35	11 46 / 11 49	12 05	11 46	11 49	12 02	12 05	12 07		12 35	12 28	12 32	12 35
Worplesdon d				→				→	→							→			
Guildford a	11 14					11 40	11 44					12 10	12 14					12 40	12 44
Brookwood d								11 51			11 55								
Ash Vale d											12 03								
Aldershot a											12 07								
d											12 08								
Farnham a											12 13								
d											12 14								
Bentley d											12 24								
Alton a											12 31								
Farnborough (Main) d								11 59											
Fleet d								12 04											
Winchfield d								12 10											
Hook d								12 14											
Basingstoke a		11 26			11 46			12 21		12 05				12 26			12 46		

Table 155

London - Woking, Guildford, Alton and Basingstoke

Sundays
until 30 September

Network Diagram - see first Page of Table 155

		SW 1		SW	SW ◇1 ✠	SW 1	SW 1 ✠	SW	SW ◇1 ✠	SW	SW	SW ◇1 ✠	SW 1	SW	SW 1		SW	SW ◇1 ✠	SW 1	SW 1 ✠	SW	SW ◇1 ✠	SW	SW
London Waterloo 15 ⊖	d	12 07		12 10	12 15		12 30		12 35		12 40	12 54	13 00		13 07		13 10	13 15		13 30		13 35		13 40
Vauxhall ⊖	d			12 14							12 44						13 14							13 44
Clapham Junction 10	d	12 15		12 19	12u22		12u39		12u42		12 49	13u03	13u09		13 15		13 19	13u22		13u39		13u42		13 49
	d																							
Earlsfield	d			12 22							12 52						13 22							13 52
Wimbledon 5 ⊖	d	12 22		12 26							12 56				13 22		13 26							13 56
Surbiton 5	d	12 30		12 35							13 05				13 30		13 35							14 05
Esher	d			12 39							13 09						13 39							14 09
Hersham	d			12 42							13 12						13 42							14 12
Walton-on-Thames	d			12 45							13 15						13 45							14 15
Weybridge	d			12 49							13 19						13 49							14 19
Byfleet & New Haw	d			12 51						13 02	13 21						13 51						14 02	14 21
West Byfleet	d			12 54		←		←		13 05	13 24			←			13 54		←		←		14 05	14 24
Woking	a	12 42		12 59	12 45	12 42	13 01	12 59	13 06	13 11	13 29	13 26	13 31	13 29	13 42		13 59	13 45	13 42	14 01	13 59	14 06	14 11	14 29
	d	12 46	12 49	13 05	12 46	12 49	13 02	13 05	13 07		13 35	13 28	13 32	13 35	13 46	13 49	14 05	13 46	13 49	14 02	14 05	14 07		14 35
Worplesdon	d		→	→							→					→	→							→
Guildford	a						13 10	13 14					13 40	13 44						14 10	14 14			
Brookwood	d	12 51				12 55									13 51				13 55					
Ash Vale	d					13 03													14 03					
Aldershot	a					13 07													14 07					
	d					13 08													14 08					
Farnham	a					13 13													14 13					
	d					13 14													14 14					
Bentley	d					13 24													14 24					
Alton	a					13 31													14 31					
Farnborough (Main)	d	12 59													13 59									
Fleet	d	13 04													14 04									
Winchfield	d	13 10													14 10									
Hook	d	13 14													14 14									
Basingstoke	a	13 21			13 05				13 26			13 46			14 21			14 05				14 26		

		SW ◇1 ✠	SW 1	SW	SW 1		SW	SW ◇1 ✠	SW 1	SW 1 ✠	SW	SW ◇1 ✠	SW	SW	SW ◇1 ✠	SW 1	SW	SW 1		SW	SW ◇1 ✠	SW 1
London Waterloo 15 ⊖	d	13 54	14 00		14 07		14 10	14 15		14 30		14 35		14 40	14 54	15 00		15 07		15 10	15 15	
Vauxhall ⊖	d						14 14							14 44						15 14		
Clapham Junction 10	d	14u03	14u09		14 15		14 19	14u22		14u39		14u42		14 49	15u03	15u09		15 15		15 19	15u22	
	d																					
Earlsfield	d						14 22							14 52						15 22		
Wimbledon 5 ⊖	d				14 22		14 26							14 56				15 22		15 26		
Surbiton 5	d				14 30		14 35							15 05				15 30		15 35		
Esher	d						14 39							15 09						15 39		
Hersham	d						14 42							15 12						15 42		
Walton-on-Thames	d						14 45							15 15						15 45		
Weybridge	d						14 49							15 19						15 49		
Byfleet & New Haw	d						14 51						15 02	15 21						15 51		
West Byfleet	d			←			14 54		←		←		15 05	15 24			←			15 54		←
Woking	a	14 26	14 31	14 29	14 42		14 59	14 45	14 42	15 01	14 59	15 06	15 11	15 29	15 26	15 31	15 29	15 42		15 59	15 45	15 42
	d	14 28	14 32	14 35	14 46	14 49	15 05	14 46	14 49	15 02	15 05	15 07		15 35	15 28	15 32	15 35	15 46	15 49	16 05	15 46	15 49
Worplesdon	d					→	→							→					→	→		
Guildford	a		14 40	14 44						15 10	15 14					15 40	15 44					
Brookwood	d				14 51				14 55									15 51				15 55
Ash Vale	d								15 03													16 03
Aldershot	a								15 07													16 07
	d								15 08													16 08
Farnham	a								15 13													16 13
	d								15 14													16 14
Bentley	d								15 24													16 24
Alton	a								15 31													16 31
Farnborough (Main)	d				14 59													15 59				
Fleet	d				15 04													16 04				
Winchfield	d				15 10													16 10				
Hook	d				15 14													16 14				
Basingstoke	a	14 46			15 21			15 05				15 26			15 46			16 21			16 05	

Table 155

London - Woking, Guildford, Alton and Basingstoke

Sundays
until 30 September

Network Diagram - see first Page of Table 155

		SW 1 ✠	SW	SW ◇1 ✠	SW	SW 1		SW	SW ◇1 ✠	SW 1	SW	SW 1		SW	SW ◇1 ✠	SW 1	SW 1 ✠	SW	SW ◇1 ✠	SW	SW 1		SW
London Waterloo 15 ⊖	d	15 30		15 35		15 37		15 40	15 54	16 00		16 07		16 10	16 15		16 30		16 35		16 37		16 40
Vauxhall ⊖	d							15 44						16 14									16 44
Clapham Junction 10	d	15u39		15u42		15 46		15 49	16u03	16u09		16 15		16 19	16u22		16u39		16u42		16 46		16 49
	d																						
Earlsfield	d							15 52						16 22									16 52
Wimbledon 5 ⊖	d					15 53		15 56				16 22		16 26							16 53		16 56
Surbiton 5	d					16 02		16 05				16 30		16 35							17 02		17 05
Esher	d							16 09						16 39									17 09
Hersham	d							16 12						16 42									17 12
Walton-on-Thames	d					16 09		16 15						16 45							17 09		17 15
Weybridge	d					16 13		16 19						16 49							17 13		17 19
Byfleet & New Haw	d				16 02			16 21						16 51						17 02			17 21
West Byfleet	d		←		16 05			16 24			←			16 54		←		←		17 05			17 24
Woking	a	16 01	15 59	16 06	16 11	16 19		16 29	16 26	16 31	16 29	16 42		16 59	16 45	16 42	17 01	16 59	17 06	17 11	17 19		17 29
	d	16 02	16 05	16 07		16 23	16 26	16 35	16 28	16 32	16 35	16 46	16 49	17 05	16 46	16 49	17 02	17 05	17 07		17 23	17 26	17 35
Worplesdon	d							→					→	→									→
Guildford	a	16 10	16 14							16 40	16 44						17 10	17 14					
Brookwood	d					16 28	16 32					16 51				16 55					17 28	17 32	
Ash Vale	d						16 40									17 03						17 40	
Aldershot	a						16 45									17 07						17 45	
	d						16 46									17 08						17 46	
Farnham	a						16 51									17 13						17 51	
	d						16 55									17 14						17 55	
Bentley	d															17 24							
Alton	a						17 07									17 31						18 07	
Farnborough (Main)	d					16 36						16 59									17 36		
Fleet	d					16 41						17 04									17 41		
Winchfield	d											17 10											
Hook	d											17 14											
Basingstoke	a			16 26		16 54			16 46			17 21			17 05				17 26		17 54		

		SW ◇1 ✠	SW 1	SW	SW 1		SW	SW ◇1 ✠	SW 1	SW 1 ✠	SW	SW ◇1 ✠	SW	SW 1		SW	SW ◇1 ✠	SW 1	SW	SW 1		SW
London Waterloo 15 ⊖	d	16 54	17 00		17 07		17 10	17 15		17 30		17 35		17 37		17 40	17 54	18 00		18 07		18 10
Vauxhall ⊖	d						17 14									17 44						18 14
Clapham Junction 10	d	17u03	17u09		17 15		17 19	17u22		17u39		17u42		17 46		17 49	18u03	18u09		18 15		18 19
	d																					
Earlsfield	d						17 22									17 52						18 22
Wimbledon 5 ⊖	d				17 22		17 26							17 53		17 56				18 22		18 26
Surbiton 5	d				17 30		17 35							18 02		18 05				18 30		18 35
Esher	d						17 39									18 09						18 39
Hersham	d						17 42									18 12						18 42
Walton-on-Thames	d						17 45							18 09		18 15						18 45
Weybridge	d						17 49							18 13		18 19						18 49
Byfleet & New Haw	d						17 51						18 02			18 21						18 51
West Byfleet	d			←			17 54		←		←		18 05			18 24			←			18 54
Woking	a	17 26	17 31	17 29	17 42		17 59	17 45	17 42	18 01	17 59	18 06	18 11	18 19		18 29	18 26	18 31	18 29	18 42		18 59
	d	17 28	17 32	17 35	17 46	17 49	18 05	17 46	17 49	18 02	18 05	18 07		18 23	18 26	18 35	18 28	18 32	18 35	18 46	18 49	19 05
Worplesdon	d					→	→									→					→	→
Guildford	a		17 40	17 44						18 10	18 14							18 40	18 44			
Brookwood	d				17 51				17 55					18 28	18 32					18 51		
Ash Vale	d								18 03						18 40							
Aldershot	a								18 07						18 45							
	d								18 08						18 46							
Farnham	a								18 13						18 51							
	d								18 14						18 55							
Bentley	d								18 24													
Alton	a								18 31						19 07							
Farnborough (Main)	d				17 59									18 36						18 59		
Fleet	d				18 04									18 41						19 04		
Winchfield	d				18 10															19 10		
Hook	d				18 14															19 14		
Basingstoke	a	17 46			18 21			18 05				18 26		18 54			18 46			19 21		

Table 155

Sundays until 30 September

London - Woking, Guildford, Alton and Basingstoke

Network Diagram - see first Page of Table 155

		SW ◇1 ⊼	SW 1	SW 1 ⊼	SW	SW ◇1 ⊼	SW	SW 1		SW	SW ◇1 ⊼	SW 1	SW	SW 1		SW	SW ◇1 ⊼	SW 1	SW 1 ⊼	SW	SW ◇1 ⊼	SW
London Waterloo 15 ⊖	d	18 15		18 30		18 35		18 37		18 40	18 54	19 00		19 07		19 10	19 15		19 30		19 35	
Vauxhall ⊖	d									18 44						19 14						
Clapham Junction 10	d	18u22		18u39		18u42		18 46		18 49	19u03	19u09		19 15		19 19	19u22		19u39		19u42	
Earlsfield	d									18 52						19 22						
Wimbledon 6 ⊖	d							18 53		18 56				19 22		19 26						
Surbiton 6	d							19 02		19 05				19 30		19 35						
Esher	d									19 09						19 39						
Hersham	d									19 12						19 42						
Walton-on-Thames	d							19 09		19 15						19 45						
Weybridge	d							19 13		19 19						19 49						
Byfleet & New Haw	d						19 02			19 21						19 51						20 02
West Byfleet	d		←		←		19 05			19 24			←			19 54		←		←		20 05
Woking	a	18 45	18 42	19 01	18 59	19 06	19 11	19 19		19 29	19 26	19 31	19 29	19 42		19 59	19 45	19 42	20 01	19 59	20 06	20 11
	d	18 46	18 49	19 02	19 05	19 07		19 23	19 26	19 35	19 28	19 32	19 35	19 46	19 49	20 05	19 46	19 49	20 02	20 05	20 07	
Worplesdon	d									→					→	→						
Guildford	a			19 10	19 14							19 40	19 44						20 10	20 14		
Brookwood	d		18 55					19 28	19 32					19 51				19 55				
Ash Vale	d		19 03						19 40									20 03				
Aldershot	a		19 07						19 45									20 07				
	d		19 08						19 46									20 08				
Farnham	a		19 13						19 51									20 13				
	d		19 14						19 55									20 14				
Bentley	d		19 24															20 24				
Alton	a		19 31						20 07									20 31				
Farnborough (Main)	d							19 36						19 59								
Fleet	d							19 41						20 04								
Winchfield	d													20 10								
Hook	d													20 14								
Basingstoke	a	19 05				19 26		19 54			19 46			20 21			20 05				20 26	

		SW 1		SW	SW ◇1	SW 1	SW	SW 1		SW	SW ◇1 ⊼	SW 1	SW 1 ⊼	SW	SW ◇1 ⊼	SW	SW 1		SW	SW ◇1	SW 1	SW
London Waterloo 15 ⊖	d	19 37		19 40	19 54	20 00		20 07		20 10	20 15		20 30		20 35		20 37		20 40	20 54	21 00	
Vauxhall ⊖	d			19 44						20 14									20 44			
Clapham Junction 10	d	19 46		19 49	20u03	20u09		20 15		20 19	20u22		20u39		20u42		20 46		20 49	21u03	21u09	
Earlsfield	d			19 52						20 22									20 52			
Wimbledon 6 ⊖	d	19 53		19 56				20 22		20 26							20 53		20 56			
Surbiton 6	d	20 02		20 05				20 30		20 35							21 02		21 05			
Esher	d			20 09						20 39									21 09			
Hersham	d			20 12						20 42									21 12			
Walton-on-Thames	d	20 09		20 15						20 45							21 09		21 15			
Weybridge	d	20 13		20 19						20 49							21 13		21 19			
Byfleet & New Haw	d			20 21						20 51						21 02			21 21			
West Byfleet	d			20 24			←			20 54		←		←		21 05			21 24			←
Woking	a	20 19		20 29	20 26	20 31	20 29	20 42		20 59	20 45	20 42	21 01	20 59	21 06	21 11	21 19		21 29	21 26	21 31	21 29
	d	20 23	20 26	20 35	20 28	20 32	20 35	20 46	20 49	21 05	20 46	20 49	21 02	21 05	21 07		21 23	21 26	21 35	21 28	21 32	21 35
Worplesdon	d			→					→	→									→			
Guildford	a					20 40	20 44						21 10	21 14							21 40	21 44
Brookwood	d	20 28	20 32					20 51				20 55					21 28	21 32				
Ash Vale	d		20 40									21 03						21 40				
Aldershot	a		20 45									21 07						21 45				
	d		20 46									21 08						21 46				
Farnham	a		20 51									21 13						21 51				
	d		20 55									21 14						21 55				
Bentley	d											21 24										
Alton	a		21 07									21 31						22 07				
Farnborough (Main)	d	20 36						20 59									21 36					
Fleet	d	20 41						21 04									21 41					
Winchfield	d							21 10														
Hook	d							21 14														
Basingstoke	a	20 54			20 46			21 21			21 05				21 26		21 54			21 46		

Table 155

Sundays until 30 September

London - Woking, Guildford, Alton and Basingstoke

Network Diagram - see first Page of Table 155

		SW 1		SW	SW ◇1 ⊼	SW 1	SW 1	SW	SW ◇1 ⊼	SW	SW 1		SW	SW ◇1	SW 1	SW	SW 1		SW	SW 1 ⊼	SW 1	SW 1
London Waterloo 15 ⊖	d	21 07		21 10	21 15		21 30		21 35		21 37		21 40	21 54	22 00		22 07		22 10	22 15		22 30
Vauxhall ⊖	d			21 14									21 44						22 14			
Clapham Junction 10	d	21 15		21 19	21u22		21u39		21u42		21 46		21 49	22u03	22u09		22 15		22 19	22u22		22u39
Earlsfield	d			21 22									21 52						22 22			
Wimbledon 6 ⊖	d	21 22		21 26							21 53		21 56				22 22		22 26			
Surbiton 6	d	21 30		21 35							22 02		22 05				22 30		22 35			
Esher	d			21 39									22 09						22 39			
Hersham	d			21 42									22 12						22 42			
Walton-on-Thames	d			21 45							22 09		22 15						22 45			
Weybridge	d			21 49							22 13		22 19						22 49			
Byfleet & New Haw	d			21 51						22 02			22 21						22 51			
West Byfleet	d			21 54		←		←		22 05			22 24			←			22 54		←	
Woking	a	21 42		21 59	21 45	21 42	22 01	21 59	22 06	22 11	22 19		22 29	22 26	22 31	22 29	22 42		22 59	22 45	22 42	23 01
	d	21 46	21 49	22 05	21 46	21 49	22 02	22 05	22 07		22 23	22 26	22 35	22 28	22 32	22 35	22 46	22 49	23 05	22 46	22 49	23 02
Worplesdon	d		→	→									→					→	→			
Guildford	a						22 10	22 14							22 40	22 44						23 10
Brookwood	d	21 51				21 55					22 28	22 32					22 51				22 55	
Ash Vale	d					22 03						22 40									23 03	
Aldershot	a					22 07						22 45									23 07	
	d					22 08						22 46									23 08	
Farnham	a					22 13						22 51									23 13	
	d					22 14						22 55									23 14	
Bentley	d					22 24															23 24	
Alton	a					22 31						23 07									23 31	
Farnborough (Main)	d	21 59									22 36						22 59					
Fleet	d	22 04									22 41						23 04					
Winchfield	d	22 10															23 10					
Hook	d	22 14															23 14					
Basingstoke	a	22 21			22 05				22 26		22 54			22 46			23 21			23 05		

		SW	SW	SW 1		SW	SW ◇1 ⊼	SW 1	SW	SW 1		SW	SW 1 A	SW	SW 1 A	SW	SW 1	SW 1 B	SW 1 B	SW 1
London Waterloo 15 ⊖	d			22 37		22 40	22 54	23 00		23 07		23 10	23 30		23 35		23 40	23 50	23 55	
Vauxhall ⊖	d					22 44						23 14					23 44			
Clapham Junction 10	d			22 46		22 49	23u03	23u09		23 15		23 19	23u39		23u44		23 49	23u59	00u04	
Earlsfield	d					22 52						23 22					23 52			
Wimbledon 6 ⊖	d			22 53		22 56				23 22		23 26					23 56			
Surbiton 6	d			23 02		23 05				23 30		23 35					00 05			
Esher	d					23 09						23 39					00 09			
Hersham	d					23 12						23 42					00 12			
Walton-on-Thames	d			23 09		23 15						23 45					00 15			
Weybridge	d			23 13		23 19						23 49					00 19			
Byfleet & New Haw	d		23 02			23 21						23 51				00 02	00 21			
West Byfleet	d	←	23 05			23 24			←			23 54		←		00 05	00 24			←
Woking	a	22 59	23 11	23 19		23 29	23 26	23 31	23 29	23 42		23 59	00 01	23 59	00 07	00 11	00 30	00 21	00 27	00 30
	d	23 05		23 23	23 26	23 35	23 28	23 32	23 35	23 46	23 49	00 05	00 03	00 05	00 08		00 35	00 23	00 28	00 35
Worplesdon	d					→						→					→			
Guildford	a	23 13						23 40	23 45				00 10	00 13				00 30		
Brookwood	d			23 28	23 32					23 51	23 55									00 41
Ash Vale	d				23 40						00 03									00 48
Aldershot	a				23 45						00 07									00 53
	d				23 48						00 08									00 54
Farnham	a				23 54						00 13									00 59
	d				23 55						00 14									
Bentley	d										00 24									
Alton	a				00 07						00 31									
Farnborough (Main)	d			23 36						23 59					00 18				00 38	
Fleet	d			23 41						00 04					00 24				00 44	
Winchfield	d									00 10										
Hook	d									00 14										
Basingstoke	a			23 54			23 46			00 21					00 39				00 59	

A until 22 July, 19 August, 26 August, 16 September, 23 September, 30 September

B 29 July, 5 August, 12 August, 2 September, 9 September

Table 155

Sundays
from 7 October

London - Woking, Guildford, Alton and Basingstoke

Network Diagram - see first Page of Table 155

		SW	SW ■	SW ■	SW	SW ■	SW ■	SW	SW ■	SW ■		SW ■	SW ■	SW ■	SW	SW ■	SW ■	SW ■	SW ■	SW		SW	SW	SW ◇■	SW
London Waterloo ■ ⊖	d	22p52	22p53	23p12	23p20	23p23	23p35		23p40	23p45		23p48	00 05		00 09	01 05				07 10			07 40	07 54	
Vauxhall ⊖	d	22p56			23p24										00 13	01 09				07 14			07 44		
Clapham Junction ■	d		23b00		23p29	23b30	23b42		23b47	23b52		23b54	00u12		00 20					07 19			07 49	08u03	
	d	23p02		23b19												01 15									
Earlsfield	d				23p32										00 23					07 22			07 52		
Wimbledon ■ ⊖	d				23p36			←					00u18		00 27	01s27				07 26			07 56		
Surbiton ■	d		23p11	23p38	23p44	23p41		23p44				00 09			00 35	01s35				07 35			08 05		
Esher	d				→			23p48							00s39					07 39			08 09		
Hersham	d							23p51							00s42					07 42			08 12		
Walton-on-Thames	d			23p45				23p54				00 16			00s44					07 45			08 15		
Weybridge	d			23p49				23p57				00 20			00s48					07 49			08 19		
Byfleet & New Haw	d	00 06						23p59							00s51					07 51		08 02	08 21		
West Byfleet	d	00 09	23p21			23p55		00 03							00s54					07 54		08 05	08 24		←
Woking	a	00 15	23p29	23p55		23p59	00 01	00 08	00 06	00 11		00 26	00 35		00 58	01 48				07 59		08 11	08 29	08 27	08 29
	d		23p30	23p57		00 01	00 03		00 08	00 13		00 28	00 37	00 40	01 00	01 49	07 32	07 46	07 49	08 05			08 32	08 28	08 32
Worplesdon	d									00 18													→		
Guildford	a									00 24					01 07		07 39			08 14					08 40
Brookwood	d		23p36	00 03		00 07						00 34		00 45				07 51	07 55						
Ash Vale	d		23p44			00 15								00 53					08 03						
Aldershot	a		23p49			00 19								00 58					08 07						
	d		23p50			00 20								00 59					08 08						
Farnham	a		23p55			00 25								01 04					08 13						
	d		23p58			00 26								01 05					08 14						
Bentley	d		00 04			00 33								01s11					08 24						
Alton	a		00 11			00 40								01 18					08 31						
Farnborough (Main)	d			00 10			00 14					00 41				01s58		07 59							
Fleet	d			00 16			00 20					00 47				02s04		08 04							
Winchfield	d			00 21								00s52						08 10							
Hook	d			00 26								00s57						08 14							
Basingstoke	a			00 33			00 33		00 27			01 06	00 55			02s16		08 21						08 46	

		SW ■	SW ■		SW		SW ◇■ ⌶	SW ■	SW	SW ■	SW ◇■	SW	SW		SW ◇■	SW		SW ■	SW ■		SW	SW ◇■ ⌶	SW ■	SW	SW ■
London Waterloo ■ ⊖	d	08 00	08 07		08 10		08 15			08 30	08 35		08 40		08 54			09 00	09 07		09 10	09 15			09 30
Vauxhall ⊖	d				08 14								08 44								09 14				
Clapham Junction ■	d	08u09	08 15		08 19		08u22			08u39	08u45		08 49		09u03			09u09	09 15		09 19	09u22			09u39
	d																								
Earlsfield	d				08 22								08 52								09 22				
Wimbledon ■ ⊖	d		08 22		08 26								08 56						09 22		09 26				
Surbiton ■	d		08 30		08 35								09 05						09 30		09 35				
Esher	d				08 39								09 09								09 39				
Hersham	d				08 42								09 12								09 42				
Walton-on-Thames	d				08 45								09 15								09 45				
Weybridge	d				08 49								09 19								09 49				
Byfleet & New Haw	d				08 51							09 02	09 21								09 51				
West Byfleet	d				08 54			←	←			09 05	09 24			←					09 54		←	←	
Woking	a	08 34	08 42		08 59		08 46	08 42	08 59	09 03	09 08	09 11	09 29		09 27	09 29		09 34	09 42		09 59	09 46	09 42	09 59	10 03
	d	08 35	08 46	08 49	09 02		08 47	08 49	09 02	09 04	09 09		09 32		09 28	09 32		09 35	09 46	09 49	10 02	09 47	09 49	10 02	10 04
Worplesdon	d			→	→								→							→	→				
Guildford	a	08 43							09 10	09 12						09 40		09 43						10 10	10 12
Brookwood	d		08 51					08 55											09 51				09 55		
Ash Vale	d							09 03															10 03		
Aldershot	a							09 07															10 07		
	d							09 08															10 08		
Farnham	a							09 13															10 13		
	d							09 14															10 14		
Bentley	d							09 24															10 24		
Alton	a							09 31															10 31		
Farnborough (Main)	d		08 59																09 59						
Fleet	d		09 04																10 04						
Winchfield	d		09 10																10 10						
Hook	d		09 14																10 14						
Basingstoke	a		09 21				09 06				09 28				09 46				10 21			10 06			

b Previous night, stops to pick up only

Table 155

Sundays
from 7 October

London - Woking, Guildford, Alton and Basingstoke

Network Diagram - see first Page of Table 155

		SW ◇■		SW	SW	SW ◇■	SW ■	SW	SW ■		SW	SW ◇■ ⌶		SW ■	SW ■	SW	SW ◇■ ⌶	SW	SW	SW ◇■	SW ■	SW		SW ■	
London Waterloo ■ ⊖	d	09 35			09 40	09 54	10 00		10 07		10 10	10 15			10 30		10 35		10 40	10 54	11 00			11 07	
Vauxhall ⊖	d				09 44						10 14								10 44						
Clapham Junction ■	d	09u45			09 49	10u03	10u09		10 15		10 19	10u22			10u39		10u45		10 49	11u04	11u09			11 15	
	d																								
Earlsfield	d				09 52						10 22								10 52						
Wimbledon ■ ⊖	d				09 56				10 22		10 26								10 56					11 22	
Surbiton ■	d				10 05				10 30		10 35								11 05					11 30	
Esher	d				10 09						10 39								11 09						
Hersham	d				10 12						10 42								11 12						
Walton-on-Thames	d				10 15						10 45								11 15						
Weybridge	d				10 19						10 49								11 19						
Byfleet & New Haw	d			10 02	10 21						10 51							11 02	11 21						
West Byfleet	d			10 05	10 24			←			10 54			←		←		11 05	11 24			←			
Woking	a	10 08		10 11	10 29	10 26	10 31	10 29	10 42		10 59	10 45		10 42	11 01	10 59	11 06	11 11	11 29	11 26	11 31	11 29		11 42	
	d	10 09			10 35	10 28	10 32	10 35	10 46	10 49	11 05	10 46		10 49	11 02	11 05	11 07		11 35	11 28	11 32	11 35		11 46	11 49
Worplesdon	d				→					→	→								→						→
Guildford	a						10 40	10 44							11 10	11 14					11 40	11 44			
Brookwood	d								10 51					10 55										11 51	
Ash Vale	d													11 03											
Aldershot	a													11 07											
	d													11 08											
Farnham	a													11 13											
	d													11 14											
Bentley	d													11 24											
Alton	a													11 31											
Farnborough (Main)	d								10 59															11 59	
Fleet	d								11 04															12 04	
Winchfield	d								11 10															12 10	
Hook	d								11 14															12 14	
Basingstoke	a	10 28				10 46			11 21			11 05					11 26			11 46				12 21	

		SW	SW ◇■ ⌶	SW ■	SW ■ ⌶	SW	SW ◇■ ⌶	SW	SW		SW ◇■ ⌶	SW ■	SW	SW ■		SW	SW ◇■ ⌶	SW ■		SW ■ ⌶	SW	SW ◇■ ⌶	SW	SW	SW ◇■ ⌶
London Waterloo ■ ⊖	d	11 10	11 15		11 30		11 35		11 40		11 54	12 00		12 07		12 10	12 15			12 30		12 35		12 40	12 54
Vauxhall ⊖	d	11 14							11 44							12 14								12 44	
Clapham Junction ■	d	11 19	11u22		11u39		11u45		11 49		12u04	12u09		12 15		12 19	12u22			12u39		12u42		12 49	13u03
	d																								
Earlsfield	d	11 22							11 52							12 22								12 52	
Wimbledon ■ ⊖	d	11 26							11 56					12 22		12 26								12 56	
Surbiton ■	d	11 35							12 05					12 30		12 35								13 05	
Esher	d	11 39							12 09							12 39								13 09	
Hersham	d	11 42							12 12							12 42								13 12	
Walton-on-Thames	d	11 45							12 15							12 45								13 15	
Weybridge	d	11 49							12 19							12 49								13 19	
Byfleet & New Haw	d	11 51						12 02	12 21							12 51							13 02	13 21	
West Byfleet	d	11 54		←		←		12 05	12 24				←			12 54		←			←		13 05	13 24	
Woking	a	11 59	11 45	11 42	12 01	11 59	12 06	12 11	12 29		12 26	12 31	12 29	12 42		12 59	12 45	12 42		13 01	12 59	13 06	13 11	13 29	13 26
	d	12 05	11 46	11 49	12 02	12 05	12 07		12 35		12 28	12 32	12 35	12 46	12 49	13 05	12 46	12 49		13 02	13 05	13 07		13 35	13 28
Worplesdon	d	→							→						→	→								→	
Guildford	a				12 10	12 14						12 40	12 44							13 10	13 14				
Brookwood	d			11 55										12 51				12 55							
Ash Vale	d			12 03														13 03							
Aldershot	a			12 07														13 07							
	d			12 08														13 08							
Farnham	a			12 13														13 13							
	d			12 14														13 14							
Bentley	d			12 24														13 24							
Alton	a			12 31														13 31							
Farnborough (Main)	d													12 59											
Fleet	d													13 04											
Winchfield	d													13 10											
Hook	d													13 14											
Basingstoke	a		12 05				12 26				12 46			13 21			13 05					13 26			13 46

Table 155

Sundays from 7 October

London - Woking, Guildford, Alton and Basingstoke

Network Diagram - see first Page of Table 155

	SW 1	SW	SW 1		SW	SW ◇1 ⚲	SW 1	SW 1 ⚲	SW	SW ◇1 ⚲	SW	SW	SW ◇1 ⚲	SW 1	SW	SW 1		SW	SW ◇1 ⚲	SW 1	SW 1 ⚲	SW
London Waterloo ⊖ d	13 00		13 07		13 10	13 15		13 30		13 35		13 40	13 54	14 00		14 07		14 10	14 15		14 30	
Vauxhall ⊖ d					13 14							13 44						14 14				
Clapham Junction d	13u09		13 15		13 19	13u22		13u39		13u42		13 49	14u03	14u09		14 15		14 19	14u22		14u39	
Earlsfield d					13 22							13 52						14 22				
Wimbledon ⊖ d			13 22		13 26							13 56				14 22		14 26				
Surbiton d			13 30		13 35							14 05				14 30		14 35				
Esher d					13 39							14 09						14 39				
Hersham d					13 42							14 12						14 42				
Walton-on-Thames d					13 45							14 15						14 45				
Weybridge d					13 49							14 19						14 49				
Byfleet & New Haw d					13 51						14 02	14 21						14 51				
West Byfleet d		←			13 54		←		←		14 05	14 24			←			14 54		←		←
Woking a	13 31	13 29	13 42		13 59	13 45	13 42	14 01	13 59	14 06	14 11	14 29	14 26	14 31	14 29	14 42		14 59	14 45	14 42	15 01	14 59
d	13 32	13 35	13 46	13 49	14 05	13 46	13 49	14 02	14 05	14 07		14 35	14 28	14 32	14 35	14 46	14 49	15 05	14 46	14 49	15 02	15 05
Worplesdon d				→	→							→					→	→				
Guildford a	13 40	13 44						14 10	14 14					14 40	14 44						15 10	15 14
Brookwood d			13 51				13 55									14 51				14 55		
Ash Vale d							14 03													15 03		
Aldershot a							14 07													15 07		
d							14 08													15 08		
Farnham a							14 13													15 13		
d							14 14													15 14		
Bentley d							14 24													15 24		
Alton a							14 31													15 31		
Farnborough (Main) d			13 59													14 59						
Fleet d			14 04													15 04						
Winchfield d			14 10													15 10						
Hook d			14 14													15 14						
Basingstoke a			14 21			14 05				14 26			14 46			15 21			15 05			

	SW ◇1 ⚲	SW	SW	SW ◇1 ⚲	SW 1	SW	SW 1		SW	SW ◇1 ⚲	SW 1	SW 1 ⚲	SW	SW ◇1 ⚲	SW	SW 1		SW	SW ◇1 ⚲	SW 1	SW
London Waterloo ⊖ d	14 35		14 40	14 54	15 00		15 07		15 10	15 15		15 30		15 35		15 37		15 40	15 54	16 00	
Vauxhall ⊖ d			14 44						15 14									15 44			
Clapham Junction d	14u42		14 49	15u03	15u09		15 15		15 19	15u22		15u39		15u42		15 46		15 49	16u03	16u09	
Earlsfield d			14 52						15 22									15 52			
Wimbledon ⊖ d			14 56				15 22		15 26							15 53		15 56			
Surbiton d			15 05				15 30		15 35							16 02		16 05			
Esher d			15 09						15 39									16 09			
Hersham d			15 12						15 42									16 12			
Walton-on-Thames d			15 15						15 45							16 09		16 15			
Weybridge d			15 19						15 49							16 13		16 19			
Byfleet & New Haw d		15 02	15 21						15 51						16 02			16 21			
West Byfleet d		15 05	15 24			←			15 54		←		←		16 05			16 24			←
Woking a	15 06	15 11	15 29	15 26	15 31	15 29	15 42		15 59	15 45	15 42	16 01	15 59	16 06	16 11	16 19		16 29	16 26	16 31	16 29
d	15 07		15 35	15 28	15 32	15 35	15 46	15 49	16 05	15 46	15 49	16 02	16 05	16 07		16 23	16 26	16 35	16 28	16 32	16 35
Worplesdon d			→					→	→									→			
Guildford a					15 40	15 44						16 10	16 14							16 40	16 44
Brookwood d							15 51				15 55					16 28	16 32				
Ash Vale d											16 03						16 40				
Aldershot a											16 07						16 45				
d											16 08						16 46				
Farnham a											16 13						16 51				
d											16 14						16 55				
Bentley d											16 24										
Alton a											16 31						17 07				
Farnborough (Main) d							15 59									16 36					
Fleet d							16 04									16 41					
Winchfield d							16 10														
Hook d							16 14														
Basingstoke a	15 26			15 46			16 21			16 05				16 26		16 54			16 46		

Table 155

Sundays from 7 October

London - Woking, Guildford, Alton and Basingstoke

Network Diagram - see first Page of Table 155

	SW 1		SW	SW ◇1 ⚲	SW 1	SW 1 ⚲	SW	SW ◇1 ⚲	SW	SW 1		SW	SW ◇1 ⚲	SW 1	SW	SW 1		SW	SW ◇1 ⚲	SW 1	SW 1 ⚲	SW
London Waterloo ⊖ d	16 07		16 10	16 15		16 30		16 35		16 37		16 40	16 54	17 00		17 07		17 10	17 15		17 30	
Vauxhall ⊖ d			16 14									16 44						17 14				
Clapham Junction d	16 15		16 19	16u22		16u39		16u42		16 46		16 49	17u03	17u09		17 15		17 19	17u22		17u39	
Earlsfield d			16 22									16 52						17 22				
Wimbledon ⊖ d	16 22		16 26							16 53		16 56				17 22		17 26				
Surbiton d	16 30		16 35							17 02		17 05				17 30		17 35				
Esher d			16 39									17 09						17 39				
Hersham d			16 42									17 12						17 42				
Walton-on-Thames d			16 45							17 09		17 15						17 45				
Weybridge d			16 49							17 13		17 19						17 49				
Byfleet & New Haw d			16 51						17 02			17 21						17 51				
West Byfleet d			16 54		←		←		17 05			17 24			←			17 54		←		←
Woking a	16 42		16 59	16 45	16 42	17 01	16 59	17 06	17 11	17 19		17 29	17 26	17 31	17 29	17 42		17 59	17 45	17 42	18 01	17 59
d	16 46	16 49	17 05	16 46	16 49	17 02	17 05	17 07		17 23	17 26	17 35	17 28	17 32	17 35	17 46	17 49	18 05	17 46	17 49	18 02	18 05
Worplesdon d		→	→									→					→	→				
Guildford a						17 10	17 14							17 40	17 44						18 10	18 14
Brookwood d	16 51				16 55					17 28	17 32					17 51				17 55		
Ash Vale d					17 03						17 40									18 03		
Aldershot a					17 07						17 45									18 07		
d					17 08						17 46									18 08		
Farnham a					17 13						17 51									18 13		
d					17 14						17 55									18 14		
Bentley d					17 24															18 24		
Alton a					17 31						18 07									18 31		
Farnborough (Main) d	16 59									17 36						17 59						
Fleet d	17 04									17 41						18 04						
Winchfield d	17 10															18 10						
Hook d	17 14															18 14						
Basingstoke a	17 21			17 05				17 26		17 54			17 46			18 21			18 05			

	SW ◇1 ⚲	SW	SW 1		SW	SW ◇1 ⚲	SW 1	SW	SW 1		SW	SW ◇1 ⚲	SW 1	SW 1 ⚲	SW	SW ◇1 ⚲	SW	SW 1		SW	SW ◇1 ⚲
London Waterloo ⊖ d	17 35		17 37		17 40	17 54	18 00		18 07		18 10	18 15		18 30		18 35		18 37		18 40	18 54
Vauxhall ⊖ d					17 44						18 14									18 44	
Clapham Junction d	17u42		17 46		17 49	18u03	18u09		18 15		18 19	18u22		18u39		18u42		18 46		18 49	19u03
Earlsfield d					17 52						18 22									18 52	
Wimbledon ⊖ d			17 53		17 56				18 22		18 26							18 53		18 56	
Surbiton d			18 02		18 05				18 30		18 35							19 02		19 05	
Esher d					18 09						18 39									19 09	
Hersham d					18 12						18 42									19 12	
Walton-on-Thames d			18 09		18 15						18 45							19 09		19 15	
Weybridge d			18 13		18 19						18 49							19 13		19 19	
Byfleet & New Haw d		18 02			18 21						18 51						19 02			19 21	
West Byfleet d		18 05			18 24			←			18 54		←		←		19 05			19 24	
Woking a	18 06	18 11	18 19		18 29	18 26	18 31	18 29	18 42		18 59	18 45	18 42	19 01	18 59	19 06	19 11	19 19		19 29	19 26
d	18 07		18 23	18 26	18 35	18 28	18 32	18 35	18 46	18 49	19 05	18 46	18 49	19 02	19 05	19 07		19 23	19 26	19 35	19 28
Worplesdon d					→					→	→									→	
Guildford a							18 40	18 44						19 10	19 14						
Brookwood d			18 28	18 32					18 51				18 55					19 28	19 32		
Ash Vale d				18 40									19 03						19 40		
Aldershot a				18 45									19 07						19 45		
d				18 46									19 08						19 46		
Farnham a				18 51									19 13						19 51		
d				18 55									19 14						19 55		
Bentley d													19 24								
Alton a				19 07									19 31						20 07		
Farnborough (Main) d			18 36						18 59									19 36			
Fleet d			18 41						19 04									19 41			
Winchfield d									19 10												
Hook d									19 14												
Basingstoke a	18 26		18 54			18 46			19 21			19 05				19 26		19 54			19 46

Table 155

Sundays
from 7 October

London - Woking, Guildford, Alton and Basingstoke

Network Diagram - see first Page of Table 155

		SW 1	SW	SW 1		SW	SW ◇1 ⌶	SW 1	SW 1 ⌶	SW		SW ◇1 ⌶	SW	SW 1		SW	SW ◇1	SW 1	SW	SW 1			SW	SW ◇1 ⌶	SW 1
London Waterloo 15 ⊖	d	19 00		19 07		19 10	19 15		19 30			19 35		19 37		19 40	19 54	20 00		20 07			20 10	20 15	
Vauxhall ⊖	d					19 14										19 44							20 14		
Clapham Junction 10	d	19u09		19 15		19 19	19u22		19u39			19u42		19 46		19 49	20u03	20u09		20 15			20 19	20u22	
	d																								
Earlsfield	d					19 22										19 52							20 22		
Wimbledon 6 ⊖	d			19 22		19 26								19 53		19 56				20 22			20 26		
Surbiton 6	d			19 30		19 35								20 02		20 05				20 30			20 35		
Esher	d					19 39										20 09							20 39		
Hersham	d					19 42										20 12							20 42		
Walton-on-Thames	d					19 45								20 09		20 15							20 45		
Weybridge	d					19 49								20 13		20 19							20 49		
Byfleet & New Haw	d					19 51							20 02			20 21							20 51		
West Byfleet	d		←			19 54		←		←			20 05			20 24			←				20 54		←
Woking	a	19 31	19 29	19 42		19 59	19 45	19 42	20 01	19 59		20 06	20 11	20 19		20 29	20 26	20 31	20 29	20 42			20 59	20 45	20 42
	d	19 32	19 35	19 46	19 49	20 05	19 46	19 49	20 02	20 05		20 07		20 23	20 26	20 35	20 28	20 32	20 35	20 46	20 49		21 05	20 46	20 49
Worplesdon	d				→	→										→					→		→		
Guildford	a	19 40	19 44						20 10	20 14								20 40	20 44						
Brookwood	d			19 51				19 55						20 28	20 32					20 51					20 55
Ash Vale	d							20 03							20 40										21 03
Aldershot	a							20 07							20 45										21 07
	d							20 08							20 46										21 08
Farnham	a							20 13							20 51										21 13
	d							20 14							20 55										21 14
Bentley	d							20 24																	21 24
Alton	a							20 31							21 07										21 31
Farnborough (Main)	d			19 59										20 36						20 59					
Fleet	d			20 04										20 41						21 04					
Winchfield	d			20 10																21 10					
Hook	d			20 14																21 14					
Basingstoke	a			20 21			20 05					20 26		20 54			20 46			21 21				21 05	

		SW 1 ⌶	SW	SW ◇1 ⌶	SW	SW 1		SW		SW ◇1	SW 1	SW	SW 1		SW	SW ◇1 ⌶	SW 1		SW 1	SW	SW ◇1 ⌶	SW	SW 1		SW
London Waterloo 15 ⊖	d	20 30		20 35		20 37		20 40		20 54	21 00		21 07		21 10	21 15			21 30		21 35		21 37		21 40
Vauxhall ⊖	d							20 44							21 14										21 44
Clapham Junction 10	d	20u39		20u42		20 46		20 49		21u03	21u09		21 15		21 19	21u22			21u39		21u42		21 46		21 49
	d																								
Earlsfield	d							20 52							21 22										21 52
Wimbledon 6 ⊖	d					20 53		20 56					21 22		21 26								21 53		21 56
Surbiton 6	d					21 02		21 05					21 30		21 35								22 02		22 05
Esher	d							21 09							21 39										22 09
Hersham	d							21 12							21 42										22 12
Walton-on-Thames	d					21 09		21 15							21 45								22 09		22 15
Weybridge	d					21 13		21 19							21 49								22 13		22 19
Byfleet & New Haw	d				21 02			21 21							21 51							22 02			22 21
West Byfleet	d		←		21 05			21 24				←			21 54		←			←		22 05			22 24
Woking	a	21 01	20 59	21 06	21 11	21 19		21 29		21 26	21 31	21 29	21 42		21 59	21 45	21 42		22 01	21 59	22 06	22 11	22 19		22 29
	d	21 02	21 05	21 07		21 23	21 26	21 35		21 28	21 32	21 35	21 46	21 49	22 05	21 46	21 49		22 02	22 05	22 07		22 23	22 26	22 35
Worplesdon	d							→						→	→										→
Guildford	a	21 10	21 14								21 40	21 44							22 10	22 14					
Brookwood	d					21 28	21 32						21 51				21 55						22 28	22 32	
Ash Vale	d						21 40										22 03							22 40	
Aldershot	a						21 45										22 07							22 45	
	d						21 46										22 08							22 46	
Farnham	a						21 51										22 13							22 51	
	d						21 55										22 14							22 55	
Bentley	d																22 24								
Alton	a						22 07										22 31							23 07	
Farnborough (Main)	d					21 36							21 59										22 36		
Fleet	d					21 41							22 04										22 41		
Winchfield	d												22 10												
Hook	d												22 14												
Basingstoke	a			21 26		21 54				21 46			22 21			22 05					22 26		22 54		

Table 155

Sundays
from 7 October

London - Woking, Guildford, Alton and Basingstoke

Network Diagram - see first Page of Table 155

		SW ◇1	SW 1		SW	SW 1		SW	SW 1 ⌶	SW 1	SW 1	SW	SW	SW 1			SW	SW ◇1 ⌶	SW 1	SW	SW 1		SW	SW 1
London Waterloo 15 ⊖	d	21 54	22 00			22 07		22 10	22 15		22 30			22 37			22 40	22 54	23 00		23 07		23 10	23 30
Vauxhall ⊖	d							22 14									22 44						23 14	
Clapham Junction 10	d	22u03	22u09			22 15		22 19	22u22		22u39			22 46			22 49	23u03	23u09		23 15		23 19	23u39
	d																							
Earlsfield	d							22 22									22 52						23 22	
Wimbledon 6 ⊖	d					22 22		22 26						22 53			22 56				23 22		23 26	
Surbiton 6	d					22 30		22 35						23 02			23 05				23 30		23 35	
Esher	d							22 39									23 09						23 39	
Hersham	d							22 42									23 12						23 42	
Walton-on-Thames	d							22 45						23 09			23 15						23 45	
Weybridge	d							22 49						23 13			23 19						23 49	
Byfleet & New Haw	d							22 51					23 02				23 21						23 51	
West Byfleet	d				←			22 54		←		←	23 05				23 24			←			23 54	
Woking	a	22 26	22 31		22 29	22 42		22 59	22 45	22 42	23 01	22 59	23 11	23 19			23 29	23 26	23 31	23 29	23 42		23 59	00 01
	d	22 28	22 32		22 35	22 46	22 49	23 05	22 46	22 49	23 02	23 05		23 23	23 26		23 35	23 28	23 32	23 35	23 46	23 49	00 05	00 03
Worplesdon	d						→	→									→						→	
Guildford	a		22 40		22 44						23 10	23 13							23 40	23 45				00 10
Brookwood	d					22 51				22 55				23 28	23 32						23 51	23 55		
Ash Vale	d									23 03					23 40							00 03		
Aldershot	a									23 07					23 45							00 07		
	d									23 08					23 48							00 08		
Farnham	a									23 13					23 54							00 13		
	d									23 14					23 55							00 14		
Bentley	d									23 24												00 24		
Alton	a									23 31					00 07							00 31		
Farnborough (Main)	d					22 59								23 36							23 59			
Fleet	d					23 04								23 41							00 04			
Winchfield	d					23 10															00 10			
Hook	d					23 14															00 14			
Basingstoke	a	22 46				23 21			23 05					23 54				23 46			00 21			

		SW	SW 1	SW	SW 1
London Waterloo 15 ⊖	d		23 35		23 40
Vauxhall ⊖	d				23 44
Clapham Junction 10	d		23u44		23 49
	d				
Earlsfield	d				23 52
Wimbledon 6 ⊖	d				23 56
Surbiton 6	d				00 05
Esher	d				00 09
Hersham	d				00 12
Walton-on-Thames	d				00 15
Weybridge	d				00 19
Byfleet & New Haw	d			00 02	00 21
West Byfleet	d	←		00 05	00 24
Woking	a	23 59	00 07	00 11	00 30
	d	00 05	00 08		00 35
Worplesdon	d				
Guildford	a	00 13			
Brookwood	d				00 41
Ash Vale	d				00 48
Aldershot	a				00 53
	d				00 54
Farnham	a				00 59
	d				
Bentley	d				
Alton	a				
Farnborough (Main)	d		00 18		
Fleet	d		00 24		
Winchfield	d				
Hook	d				
Basingstoke	a		00 39		

Basingstoke, Alton, Guildford and Woking - Waterloo

Network Diagram - see first Page of Table 155

Miles	Miles	Miles			SW MO A	SW MX 1	SW MO 1 A	SW MX 1	SW MX 1	SW MO 1 A	SW MX 1	SW MO 1 A	SW MX 1	SW MO ◇1 A	SW MO 1 A	SW MX 1 B	SW MX 1 C	SW	SW ◇	SW 1	SW	SW	SW 1
0	—	—	**Basingstoke**	d				22p54	23p13					23p44		23p44	23p44			04 54			
5½	—	—	Hook	d				23p01								23p51	23p51			05 01			
7¾	—	—	Winchfield	d				23p05								23p55	23p55			05 05			
11¼	—	—	Fleet	d				23p10								00 01	00 02			05 10			
14½	—	—	Farnborough (Main)	d				23p16								00 06	00 06			05 16			
—	0	—	**Alton**	d		22p44	22p45																
—	4¾	—	Bentley	d		22p51																	
—	8¾	—	Farnham	a		22p56	22p55																
—	—	—		d		22p58	23p00																
—	11¾	—	**Aldershot**	d		23p04	23p06																
—	14¾	—	Ash Vale	d		23p09	23p11																
19¾	18¾	—	Brookwood	d		23p16	23p18	23p23								00 13	00 13			05 23			
—	—	0	**Guildford**	d								23p35	23p39		00 05			04 00			05 14		05 50
—	—	3½	Worplesdon	d							←		23p44								05 19		05 55
23½	—	6	**Woking**	a		23p21	23p24	23p28	23p31		23p28	23p42	23p49	00 02	00 13	00 18	00 18	04 08		05 28	05 24		06 00
—	—	—		d	22p52	23p22	23p28	23p33	23p32		23p33	23p45	23p56	00 04		00 20	00 20	04 10	05 27	05 29	05 33	05 43	06 01
26	—	—	West Byfleet	d	22p56	23p27		→			23p37					00 25	00 25		05 32		05 37	05 47	
27¼	—	—	Byfleet & New Haw	d	23p00						23p40								05 35		05 40		
28¾	—	—	Weybridge	d			23p34				23p43					00 29	00 29				05 43	05 51	
30¾	—	—	Walton-on-Thames	d			23p38				23p47					00 33	00 33				05 47	05 55	
31¾	—	—	Hersham	d							23p49										05 49		
33¼	—	—	Esher	d							23p52										05 52		
35¾	—	—	**Surbiton** 6	a		23p37	23p45				23p57					00 39	00 39	04 24		05 40	05 56	06 01	
40½	—	—	Wimbledon 6 ⊖	a			23p53				00 06					00 47	00 47	04 31		05 48	06 04		
42¼	—	—	Earlsfield	a						←											06 08		
43¾	—	—	Clapham Junction 10	a		23p51	23p59		23p55	23p59		00 04	00 19	00 23		00 53	00 53	04 43			06 12		06 20
—	—	—		a	00 01		→				00 21									06 00			
46½	—	—	Vauxhall ⊖	a	00 08						00 30									06 07	06 17		
47¾	—	—	**London Waterloo** 15 ⊖	a	00 13	00 02			00 09	00 10	00 35	00 14	00 33	00 33		01 04	01 04	04 53		06 12	06 22	06 20	06 29

		SW	SW 1	SW 1	SW ◇1 🛒	SW	SW 1	SW 1	SW 1	SW	SW 1	SW 1 🛒	SW 1	SW ◇1 🛒	SW 1	SW	SW ◇1 🛒	SW 1	SW 1	SW 1	SW 1	SW 1	SW ◇1 🛒
Basingstoke	d		05 39	05 54	05 59				06 23					06 27			06 35					06 42	06 51
Hook	d			06 01					06 31														
Winchfield	d			06 05					06 35														
Fleet	d		05 50	06 10					06 40													06 54	
Farnborough (Main)	d		05 56	06 16					06 46													07 00	
Alton	d						05 42								06 12								
Bentley	d						05 49								06 19								
Farnham	a						05 54								06 24								
	d						05 56								06 26								
Aldershot	d						06 02								06 32								
Ash Vale	d						06 07								06 37								
Brookwood	d			06 23			06 14		06 53						06 44								
Guildford	d										06 24	06 31								06 53			
Worplesdon	d							←			06 30							←		06 59			
Woking	a		06 05	06 28	06 18		06 19	06 28	06 58		06 35	06 39		06 46	06 49		06 53	06 58		07 03		07 10	
	d	06 04	06 06	06 29	06 19		06 20	06 29	06 59	06 32	06 37	06 41	06 41	06 47	06 50		06 55	06 59	07 02	07 05	07 07	07 11	
West Byfleet	d	06 08		→			06 25		→	06 36			06 46						07 07		07 16		
Byfleet & New Haw	d	06 11								06 39			06 49								07 19		
Weybridge	d	06 14								06 43			06 52						07 11		07 22		
Walton-on-Thames	d	06 18								06 47			06 57						07 16		07 27		
Hersham	d	06 20								06 49			07 00						07 19		07 30		
Esher	d	06 23								06 52			07 03						07 22		07 33		
Surbiton 6	a	06 27					06 35	06 40		06 56			07 07						07 26		07 37		
Wimbledon 6 ⊖	a	06 35						06 47		07 04													
Earlsfield	a	06 39				←				07 08						←							
Clapham Junction 10	a	06 42	06 25		06 38	06 42	06 46	06 54		07 12	06 58	07 02			07 10	07 12	07 14	07 20		07 24			07 28
	a	→								→													
Vauxhall ⊖	a					06 47										07 17							
London Waterloo 15 ⊖	a		06 34		06 49	06 52	06 54	07 04			07 08	07 12	07 26	07 14	07 20	07 24	07 24	07 31	07 49	07 36	07 56	07 41	07 39

A from 21 May until 1 October **B** not from 30 August until 7 September **C** from 30 August until 7 September

Table 155

Mondays to Fridays
until 5 October

Basingstoke, Alton, Guildford and Woking - Waterloo

Network Diagram - see first Page of Table 155

		SW 1	SW 1	SW 1 🛒	SW 1	SW 1	SW 1	SW 1	SW ◇1	SW 1	SW 1	SW 1	SW 1	SW 1	SW 1	SW ◇1 🛒	SW 1 🛒	SW 1	SW 1	SW 1	SW 1	SW 1	SW 1
Basingstoke	d				06 54	07 06	07 17								07 24	07 29				07 36	07 47		
Hook	d				07 01	07 13									07 31					07 43			
Winchfield	d				07 05	07 17									07 35					07 47			
Fleet	d				07 10	07 22									07 40					07 52			
Farnborough (Main)	d				07 16	07 28									07 46					07 58			
Alton	d		06 44										07 14										
Bentley	d		06 51										07 21										
Farnham	a		06 56										07 26										
	d		06 58										07 28						07 39				
Aldershot	d		07 04										07 34						07 46				
Ash Vale	d		07 09										07 39						07 50				
Brookwood	d		07 16		07 23								07 46		07 53				07 57				
Guildford	d	07 07		07 17						07 34				07 45			07 54						08 03
Worplesdon	d									07 40				07 50								←	
Woking	a	07 15	07 21	07 25	07 28								07 51	07 54	07 58				08 03	08 08	08 05	08 08	08 11
	d	07 17	07 22	07 26	07 29			07 32	07 40			07 47	07 52	07 56	07 59			08 02	08 05	08 09	08 06	08 09	08 12
West Byfleet	d							07 37			07 46	07 54						08 06	08 16	→			
Byfleet & New Haw	d										07 49	07 57							08 19				
Weybridge	d							07 41			07 52	08 01						08 11	08 22				
Walton-on-Thames	d							07 46			07 57	08 06						08 15	08 27				
Hersham	d							07 49			08 00	08 09						08 17	08 30				
Esher	d							07 52			08 03	08 13						08 20	08 33				
Surbiton 6	a							07 56			08 07	08 18						08 24	08 37				
Wimbledon 6 ⊖	a																						
Earlsfield	a																						
Clapham Junction 10	a																						
	a																						
Vauxhall ⊖	a																						
London Waterloo 15 ⊖	a	07 45	07 51	07 54	07 59	08 06	08 01	08 19	08 08	08 11	08 26	08 36	08 22	08 24	08 29	08 14	08 32	08 46	08 59		08 34	08 39	08 41

		SW	SW 1	SW ◇1 🛒	SW 1	SW 1 🛒	SW 1	SW 1	SW	SW 1	SW 1	SW 1	SW 1	SW 1	SW ◇1 🛒	SW 1	SW	SW ◇1 🛒	SW 1	SW 1 🛒	SW 1	SW 1
Basingstoke	d		07 52	07 59				08 05		08 16			08 24		08 29			08 35			08 43	
Hook	d		07 59					08 12					08 31									
Winchfield	d		08 04					08 16					08 35									
Fleet	d		08 09					08 22					08 40								08 54	
Farnborough (Main)	d		08 16					08 28					08 46								09 00	
Alton	d				07 44											08 14						
Bentley	d				07 51											08 21						
Farnham	a				07 56											08 26						
	d				07 58											08 28						
Aldershot	d				08 04											08 34						
Ash Vale	d				08 09											08 39						
Brookwood	d		08 23		08 16								08 53			08 46						
Guildford	d					08 15			08 20			08 31								08 54		
Worplesdon	d					08 20	←				←	08 37							←			
Woking	a		08 28	08 18	08 21	08 26	08 28	08 38	08 30	08 34	08 38	08 41	08 58		08 48	08 51		08 53	08 58			
	d	08 17	08 29	08 19	08 23	08 27	08 29	08 39	08 32	08 36	08 39	08 43	08 59	08 47	08 49	08 52		08 55	08 59			
West Byfleet	d	08 26	→					→	08 36				→	08 54								
Byfleet & New Haw	d	08 29							08 39					08 57								
Weybridge	d	08 32							08 43					09 02								
Walton-on-Thames	d	08 36							08 47					09 07								
Hersham	d	08 39							08 49					09 10								
Esher	d	08 43							08 52					09 13								←
Surbiton 6	a	08 47							08 56					09 18					09 10			09 18
Wimbledon 6 ⊖	a								09 04					→								
Earlsfield	a								09 08								←					
Clapham Junction 10	a								09 12			09 03					09 12	09 14			09 26	
	a								→													
Vauxhall ⊖	a																09 17					
London Waterloo 15 ⊖	a	09 06		08 46	08 52	08 55	09 00			09 03	09 10	09 13			09 17	09 21	09 24	09 25	09 29	09 31	09 38	09 40

until 5 October

Basingstoke, Alton, Guildford and Woking - Waterloo

Network Diagram - see first Page of Table 155

		SW	SW 1	SW 1	SW ◇1 ⊼	SW	SW 1	SW ◇1 ⊼	SW 1 ⊼	SW 1	SW 1	SW	SW 1	SW 1	SW 1	SW ◇1 ⊼	SW	SW 1	SW ◇1 ⊼	SW 1 ⊼	SW 1 ⊼	SW 1	SW 1
Basingstoke	d			08 54	08 59								09 17		09 24	09 30			09 36		09 43		09 54
Hook	d			09 01											09 31								10 01
Winchfield	d			09 05											09 35								10 05
Fleet	d			09 10											09 40						09 54		10 10
Farnborough (Main)	d			09 16									09 30		09 46						10 00		10 16
Alton	d						08 44											09 14					
Bentley	d						08 51											09 21					
Farnham	a						08 56											09 26					
	d						08 58											09 28					
Aldershot	d						09 04											09 34					
Ash Vale	d						09 09											09 39					
Brookwood	d			09 23			09 16								09 53			09 46					10 23
Guildford	d	08 46	09 03						09 17					09 34						09 47			
Worplesdon	d	08 51									←			09 40								←	
Woking	a	08 59	09 11	09 28	09 18		09 21		09 27		09 28		09 39	09 44	09 58	09 49		09 51	09 54	09 59		09 58	10 28
	d	09 02	09 13	09 29	09 19		09 22	09 24	09 28		09 29	09 33	09 41	09 46	09 59	09 50		09 52	09 56	09 59		09 59	10 29
West Byfleet	d	09 06		→			09 27					09 37			→			09 57					→
Byfleet & New Haw	d	09 09										09 40											
Weybridge	d	09 13									09 36	09 43										10 06	
Walton-on-Thames	d	09 17									09 40	09 47										10 10	
Hersham	d	09 19										09 49											
Esher	d	09 22										09 52											
Surbiton 6	a	09 26					09 37				09 46	09 56						10 07				10 16	
Wimbledon 6 ⊖	a	09 34										10 04											
Earlsfield	a	09 38				←				←		10 08					←						
Clapham Junction 10	a	09 42	09 32		09 38	09 42	09 50	09 43		09 50	09 57	10 12		10 05		10 09	10 12		10 15		10 25		
	a	→					→					→											
Vauxhall ⊖	a					09 47											10 17						
London Waterloo 15 ⊖	a		09 43		09 51	09 54		09 53	09 55	09 59	10 05		10 08	10 13		10 19	10 22	10 25	10 23	10 27	10 34	10 36	

		SW	SW 1	SW ◇1 ⊼	SW ◇1 ⊼	SW	SW 1	SW 1 ⊼	SW 1	SW	SW 1	SW 1	SW 1	SW ◇1 ⊼	SW ◇1 ⊼	SW	SW 1	SW 1 ⊼	SW 1	SW 1	SW 1	SW
Basingstoke	d			09 57							10 17		10 24	10 30	10 35				10 43		10 54	
Hook	d												10 31								11 01	
Winchfield	d												10 35								11 05	
Fleet	d												10 40						10 54		11 10	
Farnborough (Main)	d										10 30		10 46						11 00		11 16	
Alton	d						09 44										10 14					
Bentley	d						09 51										10 21					
Farnham	a						09 56										10 26					
	d						09 58										10 28					
Aldershot	d						10 04										10 34					
Ash Vale	d						10 09										10 39					
Brookwood	d						10 16						10 53				10 46				11 23	
Guildford	d		10 02					10 17				10 34						10 47				
Worplesdon	d								←			10 40								←		
Woking	a		10 11	10 15			10 21	10 25	10 28		10 39	10 44	10 58	10 49			10 51	10 57		10 58	11 28	
	d	10 03	10 12	10 17	10 21		10 22	10 26	10 29	10 33	10 41	10 46	10 59	10 50			10 52	10 59		10 59	11 29	11 03
West Byfleet	d	10 07					10 27			10 37			→				10 57				→	11 07
Byfleet & New Haw	d	10 10								10 40												11 10
Weybridge	d	10 13							10 36	10 43										11 06		11 13
Walton-on-Thames	d	10 17							10 40	10 47										11 10		11 17
Hersham	d	10 19								10 49												11 19
Esher	d	10 22								10 52												11 22
Surbiton 6	a	10 26					10 37		10 46	10 56							11 07			11 16		11 26
Wimbledon 6 ⊖	a	10 34								11 04												11 34
Earlsfield	a	10 38				←				11 08						←						11 38
Clapham Junction 10	a	10 42	10 31	10 36		10 42	10 48		10 57	11 12		11 05			11 12	11 12			11 25			11 42
	a	→								→												→
Vauxhall ⊖	a					10 47										11 17						
London Waterloo 15 ⊖	a		10 40	10 49	10 49	10 52	10 57	10 51	11 05		11 08	11 13		11 19	11 20	11 22	11 27	11 24	11 34	11 36		

Table 155 Mondays to Fridays

until 5 October

Basingstoke, Alton, Guildford and Woking - Waterloo

Network Diagram - see first Page of Table 155

		SW 1	SW ◇1 ⊼	SW ◇1 ⊼	SW	SW 1	SW 1 ⊼	SW 1	SW	SW 1	SW 1	SW 1	SW ◇1 ⊼	SW ◇1 ⊼	SW	SW 1	SW 1 ⊼	SW 1	SW 1	SW 1	SW	SW 1	SW ◇1 ⊼
Basingstoke	d		10 57							11 17		11 24	11 30	11 35				11 43		11 54			11 57
Hook	d											11 31								12 01			
Winchfield	d											11 35								12 05			
Fleet	d											11 40						11 54		12 10			
Farnborough (Main)	d									11 30		11 46						12 00		12 16			
Alton	d					10 44										11 15							
Bentley	d					10 51																	
Farnham	a					10 56										11 25							
	d					10 58										11 28							
Aldershot	d					11 04										11 34							
Ash Vale	d					11 09										11 39							
Brookwood	d					11 16						11 53				11 46				12 23			
Guildford	d	11 02					11 17				11 34						11 47					12 02	
Worplesdon	d							←			11 40								←				
Woking	a	11 11	11 15			11 21	11 25	11 28		11 39	11 44	11 58	11 49			11 51	11 57		11 58	12 28		12 11	12 15
	d	11 12	11 17	11 21		11 22	11 26	11 29	11 33	11 41	11 46	11 59	11 50			11 52	11 59		11 59	12 29	12 03	12 12	12 17
West Byfleet	d					11 27			11 37			→				11 57				→	12 07		
Byfleet & New Haw	d								11 40												12 10		
Weybridge	d							11 36	11 43										12 06		12 13		
Walton-on-Thames	d							11 40	11 47										12 10		12 17		
Hersham	d								11 49												12 19		
Esher	d								11 52												12 22		
Surbiton 6	a					11 37		11 46	11 56							12 07			12 16		12 26		
Wimbledon 6 ⊖	a								12 04												12 34		
Earlsfield	a				←				12 08						←						12 38		
Clapham Junction 10	a	11 31	11 36		11 42	11 48		11 57	12 12		12 05			12 12	12 12			12 25			12 42	12 31	12 36
	a								→												→		
Vauxhall ⊖	a				11 47										12 17								
London Waterloo 15 ⊖	a	11 40	11 49	11 49	11 52	11 57	11 51	12 06		12 08	12 13		12 19	12 20	12 22	12 27	12 23	12 34	12 36			12 40	12 49

		SW ◇1 ⊼	SW	SW 1	SW 1 ⊼	SW 1	SW	SW 1	SW 1	SW 1	SW ◇1 ⊼	SW ◇1 ⊼	SW	SW 1	SW 1 ⊼	SW 1	SW 1	SW 1	SW	SW 1	SW ◇1 ⊼	SW ◇1 ⊼	SW
Basingstoke	d							12 17		12 24	12 30	12 35				12 43		12 54			12 57		
Hook	d									12 31								13 01					
Winchfield	d									12 35								13 05					
Fleet	d									12 40						12 54		13 10					
Farnborough (Main)	d							12 30		12 46						13 00		13 16					
Alton	d			11 44																			
Bentley	d			11 51																			
Farnham	a			11 56																			
	d			11 58										12 28									
Aldershot	d			12 04										12 34									
Ash Vale	d			12 09										12 39									
Brookwood	d			12 16						12 53				12 46				13 23					
Guildford	d				12 17				12 34						12 47					13 02			
Worplesdon	d					←			12 40								←						
Woking	a			12 21	12 25	12 28		12 39	12 44	12 58	12 49			12 51	12 57		12 58	13 28		13 11	13 15		
	d	12 21		12 22	12 26	12 29	12 33	12 41	12 46	12 59	12 50			12 52	12 59		12 59	13 29	13 03	13 12	13 17	13 21	
West Byfleet	d			12 27			12 37			→				12 57				→	13 07				
Byfleet & New Haw	d						12 40												13 10				
Weybridge	d					12 36	12 43										13 06		13 13				
Walton-on-Thames	d					12 40	12 47										13 10		13 17				
Hersham	d						12 49												13 19				
Esher	d						12 52												13 22				
Surbiton 6	a			12 37		12 46	12 56							13 07			13 16		13 26				
Wimbledon 6 ⊖	a						13 04												13 34				
Earlsfield	a		←				13 08						←						13 38				←
Clapham Junction 10	a		12 42	12 48		12 57	13 12		13 05			13 12	13 12			13 25			13 42	13 31	13 36		13 42
	a						→												→				
Vauxhall ⊖	a		12 47										13 17										13 47
London Waterloo 15 ⊖	a	12 49	12 52	12 57	12 51	13 05		13 07	13 13		13 19	13 20	13 22	13 25	13 23	13 34	13 36			13 40	13 49	13 49	13 52

Basingstoke, Alton, Guildford and Woking - Waterloo

Network Diagram - see first Page of Table 155

		SW 1	SW 1 ⊼	SW 1	SW	SW 1	SW 1	SW 1	SW ◇1 ⊼	SW ◇1 ⊼	SW	SW 1	SW 1 ⊼	SW 1	SW 1	SW 1	SW	SW 1	SW ◇1 ⊼	SW ◇1 ⊼	SW	SW 1
Basingstoke	d					13 17		13 24	13 30	13 35				13 43		13 54			13 57			
Hook	d							13 31								14 01						
Winchfield	d							13 35								14 05						
Fleet	d							13 40						13 54		14 10						
Farnborough (Main)	d					13 30		13 46						14 00		14 16						
Alton	d	12 44										13 15										13 44
Bentley	d	12 51																				13 51
Farnham	a	12 56										13 25										13 56
	d	12 58										13 28										13 58
Aldershot	d	13 04										13 34										14 04
Ash Vale	d	13 09										13 39										14 09
Brookwood	d	13 16						13 53				13 46				14 23						14 16
Guildford	d		13 17				13 34						13 47					14 02				
Worplesdon	d			←			13 40								←							
Woking	a	13 21	13 25	13 28		13 39	13 44	13 58	13 49			13 51	13 57		13 58	14 28		14 11	14 15			14 21
	d	13 22	13 26	13 29	13 33	13 41	13 46	13 59	13 50			13 52	13 59		13 59	14 29	14 03	14 12	14 17	14 21		14 22
West Byfleet	d	13 27			13 37			→				13 57				→	14 07					14 27
Byfleet & New Haw	d				13 40												14 10					
Weybridge	d			13 36	13 43										14 06		14 13					
Walton-on-Thames	d			13 40	13 47										14 10		14 17					
Hersham	d				13 49												14 19					
Esher	d				13 52												14 22					
Surbiton 6	a	13 37		13 46	13 56							14 07			14 16		14 26					14 37
Wimbledon 6 ⊖	a				14 04												14 34					
Earlsfield	a				14 08						←						14 38				←	
Clapham Junction 10	a	13 48		13 57	14 12		14 05			14 12	14 12			14 25			14 42	14 31	14 36		14 42	14 48
	a				→												→					
Vauxhall ⊖	a										14 17										14 47	
London Waterloo 15 ⊖	a	13 57	13 51	14 05		14 07	14 13		14 19	14 20	14 22	14 25	14 23	14 34	14 36			14 40	14 49	14 49	14 52	14 57

		SW 1 ⊼	SW 1	SW	SW 1	SW 1	SW 1	SW ◇1 ⊼	SW ◇1 ⊼	SW	SW 1	SW 1 ⊼	SW 1	SW 1	SW 1	SW	SW 1	SW ◇1 ⊼	SW ◇1 ⊼	SW	SW 1	SW 1 ⊼	SW 1
Basingstoke	d				14 17		14 24	14 30	14 35				14 43		14 54			14 57					
Hook	d						14 31								15 01								
Winchfield	d						14 35								15 05								
Fleet	d						14 40						14 54		15 10								
Farnborough (Main)	d				14 30		14 46						15 00		15 16								
Alton	d										14 15										14 44		
Bentley	d																				14 51		
Farnham	a										14 25										14 56		
	d										14 28										14 58		
Aldershot	d										14 34										15 04		
Ash Vale	d										14 39										15 09		
Brookwood	d						14 53				14 46				15 23						15 16		
Guildford	d	14 17				14 34						14 47					15 02					15 17	
Worplesdon	d		←			14 40								←									←
Woking	a	14 25	14 28		14 39	14 44	14 58	14 49			14 51	14 57		14 58	15 28		15 11	15 15			15 21	15 25	15 28
	d	14 26	14 29	14 33	14 41	14 46	14 59	14 50			14 52	14 59		14 59	15 29	15 03	15 12	15 17	15 21		15 22	15 26	15 29
West Byfleet	d			14 37			→				14 57				→	15 07					15 27		
Byfleet & New Haw	d			14 40												15 10							
Weybridge	d		14 36	14 43										15 06		15 13							15 36
Walton-on-Thames	d		14 40	14 47										15 10		15 17							15 40
Hersham	d			14 49												15 19							
Esher	d			14 52												15 22							
Surbiton 6	a		14 46	14 56							15 07			15 16		15 26					15 37		15 46
Wimbledon 6 ⊖	a			15 04												15 34							
Earlsfield	a			15 08						←						15 38				←			
Clapham Junction 10	a		14 57	15 12		15 05			15 12	15 12			15 25			15 42	15 31	15 36		15 42	15 48		15 57
	a			→												→							
Vauxhall ⊖	a									15 17										15 47			
London Waterloo 15 ⊖	a	14 51	15 05		15 08	15 13		15 19	15 20	15 22	15 25	15 23	15 34	15 37			15 43	15 49	15 49	15 52	15 57	15 51	16 05

Basingstoke, Alton, Guildford and Woking - Waterloo

Network Diagram - see first Page of Table 155

		SW	SW 1	SW 1	SW 1	SW ◇1 ⊼	SW ◇1 ⊼	SW	SW 1	SW 1 ⊼	SW 1	SW 1	SW 1	SW	SW 1	SW ◇1 ⊼	SW ◇1 ⊼	SW	SW 1	SW 1 ⊼	SW 1	SW
Basingstoke	d		15 17		15 24	15 30	15 35				15 43		15 54			15 57						
Hook	d				15 31								16 01									
Winchfield	d				15 35								16 05									
Fleet	d				15 40						15 54		16 10									
Farnborough (Main)	d		15 30		15 46						16 00		16 16									
Alton	d								15 15										15 44			
Bentley	d																		15 51			
Farnham	a								15 25										15 56			
	d								15 28										15 58			
Aldershot	d								15 34										16 04			
Ash Vale	d								15 39										16 09			
Brookwood	d				15 53				15 46				16 23						16 16			
Guildford	d			15 34						15 47					16 00					16 17		
Worplesdon	d			15 40								←			16 06						←	
Woking	a		15 39	15 44	15 58	15 49			15 51	15 57		15 58	16 28		16 11	16 15			16 21	16 25	16 28	
	d	15 33	15 41	15 46	15 59	15 50			15 52	15 59		15 59	16 29	16 03	16 12	16 17	16 21		16 22	16 26	16 29	16 33
West Byfleet	d	15 37			→				15 57				→	16 07					16 27			16 37
Byfleet & New Haw	d	15 40												16 10								16 40
Weybridge	d	15 43										16 06		16 13							16 36	16 43
Walton-on-Thames	d	15 47										16 10		16 17							16 40	16 47
Hersham	d	15 49												16 19								16 49
Esher	d	15 52												16 22								16 52
Surbiton 6	a	15 56							16 07			16 16		16 26					16 37		16 46	16 56
Wimbledon 6 ⊖	a	16 04												16 34								17 04
Earlsfield	a	16 08						←						16 38				←				17 08
Clapham Junction 10	a	16 12		16 05			16 12	16 12			16 25			16 42	16 31	16 36		16 42	16 48		16 57	17 12
	a	→												→								→
Vauxhall ⊖	a							16 17										16 47				
London Waterloo 15 ⊖	a		16 07	16 13		16 19	16 20	16 22	16 29	16 24	16 34	16 36			16 40	16 49	16 49	16 52	16 59	16 51	17 08	

		SW 1	SW 1	SW 1	SW ◇1 ⊼	SW ◇1 ⊼	SW	SW 1	SW 1	SW 1	SW 1	SW 1	SW	SW 1 ⊼	SW ◇1 ⊼	SW ◇1 ⊼	SW	SW 1	SW 1 ⊼	SW 1	SW	SW 1	SW 1
Basingstoke	d	16 17		16 24	16 30	16 35					16 43	16 54			16 57							17 17	
Hook	d			16 31								17 01											
Winchfield	d			16 35								17 05											
Fleet	d			16 40							16 54	17 10											
Farnborough (Main)	d	16 30		16 46							17 00	17 16										17 30	
Alton	d							16 15										16 44					
Bentley	d																	16 51					
Farnham	a							16 25										16 56					
	d							16 28										16 58					
Aldershot	d							16 34										17 04					
Ash Vale	d							16 39										17 09					
Brookwood	d			16 53				16 46				17 23						17 16					
Guildford	d		16 34						16 47					17 00					17 17				17 34
Worplesdon	d		16 40							←				17 06						←			17 40
Woking	a	16 39	16 44	16 58	16 49			16 51	16 57	16 58		17 28		17 11	17 15			17 21	17 25	17 28		17 39	17 44
	d	16 41	16 46	16 59	16 50			16 52	16 59	16 59		17 29	17 03	17 12	17 17	17 21		17 22	17 26	17 29	17 33	17 41	17 46
West Byfleet	d			→				16 57				→	17 07					17 27			17 37		
Byfleet & New Haw	d												17 10								17 40		
Weybridge	d									17 06			17 13							17 36	17 43		
Walton-on-Thames	d									17 10			17 17							17 40	17 47		
Hersham	d												17 19								17 49		
Esher	d												17 22								17 52		
Surbiton 6	a							17 07		17 16			17 26					17 37		17 46	17 56		
Wimbledon 6 ⊖	a												17 34								18 04		
Earlsfield	a						←						17 38				←				18 08		
Clapham Junction 10	a		17 05			17 12	17 12				17 25		17 42	17 31	17 36		17 42	17 48		17 57	18 12		18 05
	a												→								→		
Vauxhall ⊖	a						17 17										17 47						
London Waterloo 15 ⊖	a	17 08	17 14		17 19	17 20	17 22	17 29	17 27	17 35	17 36			17 43	17 44	17 50	17 52	17 59	17 54	18 09		18 08	18 14

Basingstoke, Alton, Guildford and Woking - Waterloo

Network Diagram - see first Page of Table 155

		SW [1]	SW ◇[1] 🛒	SW	SW ◇[1] 🛒		SW [1]	SW [1]	SW [1]	SW [1]	SW [1]	SW	SW [1] 🛒	SW ◇[1] 🛒	SW ◇[1] 🛒		SW	SW [1]	SW [1] 🛒	SW [1]	SW	SW [1]	SW [1]	SW [1]	SW ◇[1] 🛒
Basingstoke	d	17 24	17 30		17 36				17 43		17 54			17 57								18 17		18 24	18 30
Hook	d	17 31									18 01													18 31	
Winchfield	d	17 35									18 05													18 35	
Fleet	d	17 40							17 54		18 10													18 40	
Farnborough (Main)	d	17 46							18 00		18 16											18 30		18 46	
Alton	d						17 14											17 44							
Bentley	d						17 21											17 51							
Farnham	a						17 26											17 56							
	d						17 28											17 58							
Aldershot	d						17 34											18 04							
Ash Vale	d						17 39											18 09							
Brookwood	d	17 53					17 46				18 23							18 16						18 53	
Guildford	d							17 47					18 00						18 17				18 34		
Worplesdon	d									←			18 06							←			18 40		
Woking	a	17 58	17 49				17 51	17 58		17 58	18 28		18 11	18 15				18 21		18 28		18 39	18 44	18 58	18 49
	d	17 59	17 51				17 52	17 59		17 59	18 29	18 03	18 12	18 17	18 21			18 22		18 29	18 33	18 41	18 46	18 59	18 50
West Byfleet	d	→					17 57				→	18 07						18 27			18 37			→	
Byfleet & New Haw	d											18 10									18 40				
Weybridge	d									18 06		18 13								18 36	18 43				
Walton-on-Thames	d									18 10		18 17								18 40	18 47				
Hersham	d											18 19									18 49				
Esher	d											18 22									18 52				
Surbiton [6]	a						18 07			18 16		18 26						18 37		18 47	18 56				
Wimbledon [6] ⊖	a											18 34									19 04				
Earlsfield	a			←								18 38					←				19 08				
Clapham Junction [10]	a			18 12	18 12				18 25			18 42	18 31	18 36			18 42	18 48		18 58	19 11		19 05		
	a											→									→				
Vauxhall ⊖	a			18 17													18 47								
London Waterloo [15] ⊖	a		18 21	18 23	18 23		18 29	18 27	18 34	18 38			18 43	18 45	18 47		18 52	18 57	18 59	19 06		19 08	19 13		19 19

			SW	SW ◇[1] 🛒	SW [1]	SW [1]	SW [1] 🛒	SW [1]	SW	SW [1]	SW ◇[1] 🛒		SW [1]	SW ◇[1] 🛒	SW [1] 🛒	SW [1]	SW	SW [1]	SW [1]	SW [1]	SW ◇[1] 🛒		SW	SW ◇[1] 🛒	SW [1]
Basingstoke	d			18 35				18 43		18 54	19 02							19 17		19 24	19 30			19 35	
Hook	d									19 01										19 31					
Winchfield	d									19 05										19 35					
Fleet	d							18 54		19 10										19 40					
Farnborough (Main)	d							19 00		19 16								19 30		19 46					
Alton	d				18 14								18 35												19 07
Bentley	d				18 23								18 42												
Farnham	a				18 27								18 47												19 17
	d				18 28								18 58												19 28
Aldershot	d				18 34								19 04												19 34
Ash Vale	d				18 39								19 09												19 39
Brookwood	d				18 46					19 23			19 16							19 53					19 46
Guildford	d						18 55								19 21				19 34						
Worplesdon	d					←										←			19 40						
Woking	a				18 52	18 58	19 03			19 28	19 20		19 21		19 28	19 28		19 39	19 45	19 58	19 49				19 51
	d				18 52	18 59	19 05		19 03	19 29	19 22		19 22	19 25	19 30	19 29	19 33	19 41	19 46	19 59	19 50				19 52
West Byfleet	d				18 57				19 07	→			19 27				19 37			→					19 57
Byfleet & New Haw	d								19 10								19 40								
Weybridge	d					19 06			19 13							19 36	19 43								
Walton-on-Thames	d					19 10			19 17							19 40	19 47								
Hersham	d								19 19								19 49								
Esher	d								19 22								19 52								
Surbiton [6]	a				19 07	19 16			19 26				19 37			19 46	19 56								20 07
Wimbledon [6] ⊖	a								19 34								20 04								
Earlsfield	a		←						19 38								20 08						←		
Clapham Junction [10]	a		19 11	19 12				19 26	19 41		19 41		19 48			19 57	20 11		20 05				20 11	20 12	
	a																→								
Vauxhall ⊖	a		19 16						19 46														20 16		
London Waterloo [15] ⊖	a		19 23	19 20	19 25	19 39	19 29	19 34	19 52		19 49		19 57	19 51	19 59	20 05		20 08	20 14		20 19		20 22	20 20	20 26

Basingstoke, Alton, Guildford and Woking - Waterloo

Network Diagram - see first Page of Table 155

		SW [1] 🛒	SW [1]	SW [1]	SW	SW [1]	SW ◇[1] 🛒		SW	SW [1]	SW [1]	SW [1]	SW ◇[1] 🛒	SW [1]	SW	SW [1]	SW [1]		SW [1]	SW [1]	SW ◇[1] 🛒	SW [1]	SW	SW [1]	SW ◇[1] 🛒
Basingstoke	d		19 43									19 54	20 09			20 17				20 24	20 36			20 43	
Hook	d											20 01								20 31					
Winchfield	d											20 05								20 35					
Fleet	d		19 54									20 10								20 40				20 54	
Farnborough (Main)	d		20 00									20 16				20 30				20 46				21 00	
Alton	d									19 35							20 15								
Bentley	d									19 42															
Farnham	a									19 47							20 25								
	d									19 58							20 28								
Aldershot	d									20 04							20 34								
Ash Vale	d									20 09							20 39								
Brookwood	d									20 16		20 23					20 46			20 53					
Guildford	d	19 47				20 02					20 17								20 39			20 47			
Worplesdon	d			←															20 44						
Woking	a	19 57		19 58		20 11				20 21	20 25	20 28	20 29			20 39	20 51		20 52	20 58		20 56		21 09	
	d	19 59		19 59	20 03	20 12	20 21			20 22	20 26	20 29	20 30		20 33	20 41	20 52		20 53	20 59		20 59	21 03	21 10	21 21
West Byfleet	d				20 07					20 27					20 37		20 57						21 07		
Byfleet & New Haw	d				20 10										20 40								21 10		
Weybridge	d			20 06	20 13							20 36			20 43					21 06			21 13		
Walton-on-Thames	d			20 10	20 17							20 40			20 47					21 10			21 17		
Hersham	d				20 19										20 49								21 19		
Esher	d				20 22										20 52								21 22		
Surbiton [6]	a			20 16	20 26					20 37		20 46			20 56		21 07			21 16			21 26		
Wimbledon [6] ⊖	a				20 35										21 05								21 34		
Earlsfield	a				20 38				←					←	21 08								21 38		
Clapham Junction [10]	a		20 25		20 41	20 31			20 41	20 48		20 57	20 52	20 57	21 11				21 12		21 16		21 42	21 29	
	a				→							→											→		
Vauxhall ⊖	a								20 46						21 16										
London Waterloo [15] ⊖	a	20 24	20 34	20 36		20 40	20 49		20 52	20 57	20 50		21 00	21 05	21 22	21 07	21 29		21 21	21 34	21 24	21 27		21 38	21 49

		SW	SW [1]		SW [1]	SW [1]	SW ◇[1] 🛒	SW [1]	SW	SW [1]	SW	SW [1]	SW [1]		SW ◇[1]	SW [1]	SW	SW [1]	SW [1]	SW	SW [1]	SW [1]	SW ◇[1]		SW [1]
Basingstoke	d					20 54	21 09						21 24		21 35			21 43				21 54	22 09		
Hook	d					21 01							21 31									22 01			
Winchfield	d					21 05							21 35									22 05			
Fleet	d					21 10							21 40					21 54				22 10			
Farnborough (Main)	d					21 16							21 46					22 00				22 16			
Alton	d		20 44									21 15									21 44				
Bentley	d		20 51																		21 51				
Farnham	a		20 56									21 25									21 56				
	d		20 58									21 28									21 58				
Aldershot	d		21 04									21 34									22 04				
Ash Vale	d		21 09									21 39									22 09				
Brookwood	d		21 16			21 23						21 46	21 53								22 16	22 23			
Guildford	d				21 17					21 39						21 47									
Worplesdon	d									21 44															
Woking	a		21 21		21 25	21 28	21 29			21 49		21 51	21 58			21 57		22 09			22 21	22 28	22 28		
	d		21 22		21 26	21 29	21 30		21 33	21 50		21 52	21 59			21 59	22 03	22 10	22 21		22 22	22 29	22 29		
West Byfleet	d		21 27						21 37			21 57					22 07				22 27				
Byfleet & New Haw	d								21 40								22 10								
Weybridge	d					21 36			21 43				22 06				22 13					22 36			
Walton-on-Thames	d					21 40			21 47				22 10				22 17					22 40			
Hersham	d								21 49								22 19								
Esher	d								21 52								22 22								
Surbiton [6]	a		21 37			21 46			21 56			22 07	22 16				22 26				22 37	22 46			
Wimbledon [6] ⊖	a								22 04								22 34								
Earlsfield	a	←						←	22 08		←						22 38			←					←
Clapham Junction [10]	a	21 42	21 48			21 57	21 52	21 57	22 12	22 09	22 12				22 14		22 42	22 29		22 42	22 52	22 57	22 48		22 52
	a					→			→								→				→	→			
Vauxhall ⊖	a	21 47									22 17									22 47					
London Waterloo [15] ⊖	a	21 52	21 57		21 50		22 04	22 06		22 18	22 22	22 27	22 34		22 22	22 27		22 38	22 49	22 52			22 58		23 01

until 5 October

Basingstoke, Alton, Guildford and Woking - Waterloo

Network Diagram - see first Page of Table 155

	SW ■	SW	SW ■	SW	SW ■	SW ■	SW ◇■	SW ■	SW	SW ■	SW	SW ■	SW ■	SW ■	SW ■	SW ■	SW FO ■ A	SW FX ■ B	SW ■ C	SW FX ■ D	SW ■
Basingstoke d						22 24	22 36			22 43			22 54	23 13					23 44	23 44	
Hook d						22 31							23 01						23 51	23 51	
Winchfield d						22 35							23 05						23 55	23 55	
Fleet d						22 40				22 54			23 10						00 01	00 02	
Farnborough (Main) d						22 46				23 00			23 16						00 06	00 06	
Alton d					22 15							22 44				23 15					23 46
Bentley d												22 51									23 53
Farnham a					22 25							22 56				23 25					23 58
d					22 28							22 58				23 28					
Aldershot d					22 34							23 04				23 34					
Ash Vale d					22 39							23 09				23 39					
Brookwood d					22 46	22 53						23 16	23 23			23 46			00 13	00 13	
Guildford d		22 20	22 39						22 55								23 39	23 39			
Worplesdon d			22 44					←							←		23 44	23 44			
Woking a		22 32	22 49		22 51	22 58	22 54	22 58	23 05	23 09		23 21	23 28	23 31	23 28	23 51	23 49	23 49	00 18	00 18	
d		22 33	22 50		22 52	22 59	22 55	22 59	23 06	23 10		23 22	23 33	23 32	23 33		23 56	23 56	00 20	00 20	
West Byfleet d		22 37			22 57	→			23 10			23 27	→		23 37				00 25	00 25	
Byfleet & New Haw d		22 40							23 13						23 40						
Weybridge d		22 43						23 06	23 16						23 43				00 29	00 29	
Walton-on-Thames d		22 47						23 10	23 20						23 47				00 33	00 33	
Hersham d		22 49							23 22						23 49						
Esher d		22 52							23 25						23 52						
Surbiton ■ a		22 56			23 07			23 16	23 29			23 37			23 57				00 39	00 39	
Wimbledon ■ ⊖ a		23 04							23 37						00 06				00 47	00 47	
Earlsfield a	←	23 08		←					23 41		←										
Clapham Junction ■ a	22 57	23 12	23 09	23 12			23 14		23 44	23 29	23 44	23 51		23 55			00 19	00 19	00 53	00 53	
a		→							→						00 21						
Vauxhall ⊖ a				23 17							23 49				00 30						
London Waterloo ■ ⊖ a	23 08		23 19	23 23	23 27		23 23	23 32		23 42	23 54	00 02		00 09	00 35		00 32	00 33	01 04	01 04	

Mondays to Fridays

from 8 October

	SW MO	SW MX ■	SW MO ■	SW MX ■	SW MX ■	SW MO ■	SW MX ■	SW MO ■	SW MX ■	SW MO ◇■	SW MO ■	SW MX ■	SW	SW ◇	SW ■	SW	SW	SW ■	SW	SW ■	SW ■	SW ◇■ 🍴
Basingstoke d				22p54	23p13					23p44		23p44			04 54					05 39	05 54	05 59
Hook d				23p01								23p51			05 01						06 01	
Winchfield d				23p05								23p55			05 05						06 05	
Fleet d				23p10								00 01			05 10					05 50	06 10	
Farnborough (Main) d				23p16								00 06			05 16					05 56	06 16	
Alton d		22p44	22p45																			
Bentley d		22p51																				
Farnham a		22p56	22p55																			
d		22p58	23p00																			
Aldershot d		23p04	23p06																			
Ash Vale d		23p09	23p11																			
Brookwood d		23p16	23p18	23p23								00 13			05 23						06 23	
Guildford d								23p35	23p39		00 05		04 00			05 14		05 50				
Worplesdon d							←		23p44							05 19		05 55				
Woking a		23p21	23p24	23p28	23p31		23p28	23p42	23p49	00 02	00 13	00 18	04 08		05 28	05 24		06 00		06 05	06 28	06 18
d	22p52	23p22	23p28	23p33	23p32		23p33	23p45	23p56	00 04		00 20	04 10	05 27	05 29	05 33	05 43	06 01	06 04	06 06	06 29	06 19
West Byfleet d	22p56	23p27		→			23p37					00 25		05 32		05 37	05 47		06 08		→	
Byfleet & New Haw d	23p00						23p40							05 35		05 40			06 11			
Weybridge d			23p34				23p43					00 29				05 43	05 51		06 14			
Walton-on-Thames d			23p38				23p47					00 33				05 47	05 55		06 18			
Hersham d							23p49									05 49			06 20			
Esher d							23p52									05 52			06 23			
Surbiton ■ a		23p37	23p45				23p57					00 39	04 24		05 40	05 56	06 01		06 27			
Wimbledon ■ ⊖ a			23p53				00 06					00 47	04 31		05 48	06 04			06 35			
Earlsfield a						←										06 08			06 39			
Clapham Junction ■ a		23p51	23p59		23p55	23p59		00 04	00 19	00 23		00 53	04 43			06 12		06 20	06 42	06 25		06 38
a	00 01		→				00 21								06 00				→			
Vauxhall ⊖ a	00 08						00 30								06 07	06 17						
London Waterloo ■ ⊖ a	00 13	00 02			00 09	00 10	00 35	00 14	00 33	00 33		01 04	04 53		06 15	06 22	06 20	06 29		06 34		06 49

A until 20 July, 17 August, 24 August, 14 September, 21 September, 28 September, 5 October

B until 19 July, from 23 July until 13 September, not 17 August, 24 August, also FX from 17 September until 4 October

C not 29 August, 30 August, from 3 September until 6 September

D from 29 August until 6 September

from 8 October

Basingstoke, Alton, Guildford and Woking - Waterloo

Network Diagram - see first Page of Table 155

	SW	SW ■	SW ■	SW ■	SW	SW ■	SW ■ 🍴	SW ■	SW ◇■ 🍴	SW ■	SW	SW ◇■ 🍴	SW ■	SW ■	SW ■	SW ■	SW ■	SW ◇■ 🍴	SW ■	SW ■	SW ■ 🍴	SW ■
Basingstoke d				06 23					06 27			06 35					06 42	06 51				06 54
Hook d				06 31																		07 01
Winchfield d				06 35																		07 05
Fleet d				06 40													06 54					07 10
Farnborough (Main) d				06 46													07 00					07 16
Alton d		05 42								06 12										06 44		
Bentley d		05 49								06 19										06 51		
Farnham a		05 54								06 24										06 56		
d		05 56								06 26										06 58		
Aldershot d		06 02								06 32										07 04		
Ash Vale d		06 07								06 37										07 09		
Brookwood d		06 14		06 53						06 44										07 16		07 23
Guildford d						06 24	06 31								06 53				07 07		07 17	
Worplesdon d			←			06 30							←		06 59							
Woking a		06 19	06 28	06 58		06 35	06 39		06 46	06 49		06 53	06 58		07 03		07 10		07 15	07 21	07 25	07 28
d		06 20	06 29	06 59	06 32	06 37	06 41	06 41	06 47	06 50		06 55	06 59	07 02	07 05	07 07	07 11		07 17	07 22	07 26	07 29
West Byfleet d		06 25		→	06 36			06 46						07 07		07 16						
Byfleet & New Haw d					06 39			06 49								07 19						
Weybridge d					06 43			06 52						07 11		07 22						
Walton-on-Thames d					06 47			06 57						07 16		07 27						
Hersham d					06 49			07 00						07 19		07 30						
Esher d					06 52			07 03						07 22		07 33						
Surbiton ■ a		06 35	06 40		06 56			07 07						07 26		07 37						
Wimbledon ■ ⊖ a			06 47		07 04																	
Earlsfield a	←				07 08						←											
Clapham Junction ■ a	06 42	06 46	06 54		07 12	06 58	07 02			07 10	07 12	07 14	07 20		07 24			07 28				
a					→																	
Vauxhall ⊖ a	06 47										07 17											
London Waterloo ■ ⊖ a	06 52	06 56	07 04			07 08	07 12	07 26	07 14	07 20	07 24	07 24	07 31	07 49	07 36	07 56	07 41	07 39	07 45	07 51	07 54	07 59

	SW ■	SW ■	SW ■	SW ◇■	SW ■	SW ■	SW ■	SW ■	SW ■	SW ■	SW ◇■ 🍴	SW ■ 🍴	SW ■	SW ■	SW ■	SW ■	SW ■	SW ■	SW	SW ■	SW ◇■ 🍴
Basingstoke d	07 06	07 17								07 24	07 29				07 36	07 47				07 52	07 59
Hook d	07 13									07 31					07 43					07 59	
Winchfield d	07 17									07 35					07 47					08 04	
Fleet d	07 22									07 40					07 52					08 09	
Farnborough (Main) d	07 28									07 46					07 58					08 16	
Alton d								07 14													
Bentley d								07 21													
Farnham a								07 26													
d								07 28						07 39							
Aldershot d								07 34						07 46							
Ash Vale d								07 39						07 50							
Brookwood d								07 46		07 53				07 57						08 23	
Guildford d					07 34				07 45			07 54						08 03			
Worplesdon d					07 40				07 50								←				
Woking a								07 51	07 54	07 58				08 03	08 08	08 05	08 08	08 11		08 28	08 18
d			07 32	07 40			07 47	07 52	07 56	07 59			08 02	08 05	08 09	08 06	08 09	08 12	08 17	08 29	08 19
West Byfleet d			07 37			07 46	07 54						08 06	08 16	→				08 26	→	
Byfleet & New Haw d						07 49	07 57							08 19					08 29		
Weybridge d			07 41			07 52	08 01						08 11	08 22					08 32		
Walton-on-Thames d			07 46			07 57	08 06						08 15	08 27					08 36		
Hersham d			07 49			08 00	08 09						08 17	08 30					08 39		
Esher d			07 52			08 03	08 13						08 20	08 33					08 43		
Surbiton ■ a			07 56			08 07	08 18						08 24	08 37					08 47		
Wimbledon ■ ⊖ a																					
Earlsfield a																					
Clapham Junction ■ a																					
a																					
Vauxhall ⊖ a																					
London Waterloo ■ ⊖ a	08 06	08 01	08 19	08 08	08 11	08 26	08 36	08 22	08 24	08 29	08 14	08 32	08 46	08 59		08 34	08 39	08 41	09 06		08 46

Basingstoke, Alton, Guildford and Woking - Waterloo

Network Diagram - see first Page of Table 155

		SW ■	SW ■ ⇄	SW ■	SW ■	SW	SW ■	SW ■		SW ■	SW ■	SW ■	SW ◇■ ⇄	SW ■	SW	SW ◇■ ⇄	SW ■	SW ■ ⇄		SW ■	SW ■	SW	SW ■	SW ■	SW ◇■ ⇄
Basingstoke	d				08 05		08 16				08 24		08 29			08 35				08 43				08 54	08 59
Hook	d				08 12						08 31													09 01	
Winchfield	d				08 16						08 35													09 05	
Fleet	d				08 22						08 40									08 54				09 10	
Farnborough (Main)	d				08 28						08 46									09 00				09 16	
Alton	d	07 44												08 14											
Bentley	d	07 51												08 21											
Farnham	a	07 56												08 26											
	d	07 58												08 28											
Aldershot	d	08 04												08 34											
Ash Vale	d	08 09												08 39											
Brookwood	d	08 16									08 53			08 46										09 23	
Guildford	d		08 15			08 20				08 31								08 54				08 46	09 03		
Worplesdon	d		08 20	←				←		08 37							←					08 51			
Woking	a	08 21	08 26	08 28	08 38	08 30	08 34	08 38		08 41	08 58		08 48	08 51		08 53	08 58					08 59	09 11	09 28	09 18
	d	08 23	08 27	08 29	08 39	08 32	08 36	08 39		08 43	08 59	08 47	08 49	08 52		08 55	08 59					09 02	09 13	09 29	09 19
West Byfleet	d				→	08 36					→	08 54										09 06		→	
Byfleet & New Haw	d					08 39						08 57										09 09			
Weybridge	d					08 43						09 02										09 13			
Walton-on-Thames	d					08 47						09 07										09 17			
Hersham	d					08 49						09 10										09 19			
Esher	d					08 52						09 13									←	09 22			
Surbiton ■	a					08 56						09 18					09 10				09 18	09 26			
Wimbledon ■ ⊖	a					09 04						→										09 34			
Earlsfield	a					09 08									←							09 38			
Clapham Junction ■	a					09 12				09 03					09 12	09 14				09 26		09 42	09 32		09 38
	a					→																→			
Vauxhall ⊖	a														09 17										
London Waterloo ■ ⊖	a	08 52	08 55	09 00			09 03	09 10		09 13			09 17	09 21	09 24	09 25	09 29	09 31		09 38	09 40		09 43		09 51

		SW	SW ■	SW ◇■ ⇄		SW ■ ⇄	SW ■	SW ■	SW	SW ■	SW ■	SW ■	SW ◇■ ⇄	SW		SW ■	SW ◇■ ⇄	SW ■ ⇄	SW ■ ⇄	SW ■	SW ■	SW	SW ■	SW ◇■ ⇄
Basingstoke	d									09 17		09 24	09 30				09 36		09 43		09 54			09 57
Hook	d											09 31									10 01			
Winchfield	d											09 35									10 05			
Fleet	d											09 40							09 54		10 10			
Farnborough (Main)	d									09 30		09 46							10 00		10 16			
Alton	d		08 44													09 14								
Bentley	d		08 51													09 21								
Farnham	a		08 56													09 26								
	d		08 58													09 28								
Aldershot	d		09 04													09 34								
Ash Vale	d		09 09													09 39								
Brookwood	d		09 16									09 53				09 46					10 23			
Guildford	d					09 17					09 34							09 47					10 02	
Worplesdon	d							←			09 40									←				
Woking	a		09 21			09 27		09 28		09 39	09 44	09 58	09 49			09 51	09 54	09 59		09 58	10 28		10 11	10 15
	d		09 22	09 24		09 28		09 29	09 33	09 41	09 46	09 59	09 50			09 52	09 56	09 59		09 59	10 29	10 03	10 12	10 17
West Byfleet	d		09 27						09 37			→				09 57					→	10 07		
Byfleet & New Haw	d								09 40													10 10		
Weybridge	d							09 36	09 43											10 06		10 13		
Walton-on-Thames	d							09 40	09 47											10 10		10 17		
Hersham	d								09 49													10 19		
Esher	d								09 52													10 22		
Surbiton ■	a		09 37					09 46	09 56							10 07				10 16		10 26		
Wimbledon ■ ⊖	a								10 04													10 34		
Earlsfield	a	←					←		10 08					←								10 38		
Clapham Junction ■	a	09 42	09 50	09 43			09 50	09 57	10 12		10 05		10 09	10 12			10 15		10 25			10 42	10 31	10 36
	a		→						→													→		
Vauxhall ⊖	a	09 47												10 17										
London Waterloo ■ ⊖	a	09 54		09 53		09 55	09 59	10 05		10 08	10 13		10 19	10 22		10 25	10 23	10 27	10 34	10 36			10 40	10 49

Basingstoke, Alton, Guildford and Woking - Waterloo

Network Diagram - see first Page of Table 155

		SW ◇■ ⇄	SW	SW ■	SW ■ ⇄	SW ■	SW	SW ■	SW ■	SW ■		SW ◇■ ⇄	SW ◇■ ⇄	SW	SW ■	SW ■ ⇄	SW ■	SW ■	SW ■	SW		SW ■	SW ◇■ ⇄	SW ◇■ ⇄	SW
Basingstoke	d							10 17		10 24		10 30	10 35				10 43		10 54				10 57		
Hook	d									10 31									11 01						
Winchfield	d									10 35									11 05						
Fleet	d									10 40							10 54		11 10						
Farnborough (Main)	d							10 30		10 46							11 00		11 16						
Alton	d			09 44											10 14										
Bentley	d			09 51											10 21										
Farnham	a			09 56											10 26										
	d			09 58											10 28										
Aldershot	d			10 04											10 34										
Ash Vale	d			10 09											10 39										
Brookwood	d			10 16						10 53					10 46				11 23						
Guildford	d				10 17				10 34							10 47						11 02			
Worplesdon	d					←			10 40									←							
Woking	a			10 21	10 25	10 28		10 39	10 44	10 58		10 49			10 51	10 57		10 58	11 28			11 11	11 15		
	d	10 21		10 22	10 26	10 29	10 33	10 41	10 46	10 59		10 50			10 52	10 59		10 59	11 29	11 03		11 12	11 17	11 21	
West Byfleet	d			10 27			10 37			→					10 57				→	11 07					
Byfleet & New Haw	d						10 40													11 10					
Weybridge	d					10 36	10 43											11 06		11 13					
Walton-on-Thames	d					10 40	10 47											11 10		11 17					
Hersham	d						10 49													11 19					
Esher	d						10 52													11 22					
Surbiton ■	a			10 37		10 46	10 56								11 07			11 16		11 26					
Wimbledon ■ ⊖	a						11 04													11 34					
Earlsfield	a		←				11 08							←						11 38					←
Clapham Junction ■	a		10 42	10 48		10 57	11 12		11 05				11 12	11 12			11 25			11 42		11 31	11 36		11 42
	a						→													→					
Vauxhall ⊖	a		10 47											11 17											11 47
London Waterloo ■ ⊖	a	10 49	10 52	10 57	10 51	11 05		11 08	11 13			11 19	11 20	11 22	11 27	11 24	11 34	11 36				11 40	11 49	11 49	11 52

		SW ■	SW ■ ⇄	SW ■	SW	SW ■		SW ■	SW ■	SW ◇■ ⇄	SW ◇■ ⇄	SW	SW ■	SW ■ ⇄	SW ■	SW ■		SW ■	SW	SW ■	SW ◇■ ⇄	SW ◇■ ⇄	SW	SW ■	SW ■ ⇄
Basingstoke	d					11 17			11 24	11 30	11 35				11 43			11 54			11 57				
Hook	d								11 31									12 01							
Winchfield	d								11 35									12 05							
Fleet	d								11 40						11 54			12 10							
Farnborough (Main)	d					11 30			11 46						12 00			12 16							
Alton	d	10 44											11 15											11 44	
Bentley	d	10 51																						11 51	
Farnham	a	10 56											11 25											11 56	
	d	10 58											11 28											11 58	
Aldershot	d	11 04											11 34											12 04	
Ash Vale	d	11 09											11 39											12 09	
Brookwood	d	11 16							11 53				11 46					12 23						12 16	
Guildford	d		11 17					11 34						11 47						12 02					12 17
Worplesdon	d			←				11 40								←									
Woking	a	11 21	11 25	11 28		11 39		11 44	11 58	11 49			11 51	11 57		11 58		12 28		12 11	12 15			12 21	12 25
	d	11 22	11 26	11 29	11 33	11 41		11 46	11 59	11 50			11 52	11 59		11 59		12 29	12 03	12 12	12 17	12 21		12 22	12 26
West Byfleet	d	11 27			11 37				→				11 57					→	12 07					12 27	
Byfleet & New Haw	d				11 40														12 10						
Weybridge	d			11 36	11 43											12 06			12 13						
Walton-on-Thames	d			11 40	11 47											12 10			12 17						
Hersham	d				11 49														12 19						
Esher	d				11 52														12 22						
Surbiton ■	a	11 37		11 46	11 56								12 07			12 16			12 26					12 37	
Wimbledon ■ ⊖	a				12 04														12 34						
Earlsfield	a				12 08							←							12 38				←		
Clapham Junction ■	a	11 48		11 57	12 12			12 05			12 12	12 12			12 25				12 42	12 31	12 36		12 42	12 48	
	a				→														→						
Vauxhall ⊖	a											12 17											12 47		
London Waterloo ■ ⊖	a	11 57	11 51	12 06		12 08		12 13		12 19	12 20	12 22	12 27	12 23	12 34	12 36				12 40	12 49	12 49	12 52	12 57	12 51

Table 155

Mondays to Fridays

from 8 October

Basingstoke, Alton, Guildford and Woking - Waterloo

Network Diagram - see first Page of Table 155

		SW 1		SW	SW 1	SW 1	SW 1	SW ◇1 🍴	SW ◇1 🍴	SW	SW 1	SW 1 🍴		SW 1	SW 1	SW 1	SW	SW 1	SW ◇1 🍴	SW ◇1 🍴	SW	SW 1		SW 1 🍴	SW 1
Basingstoke	d				12 17		12 24	12 30	12 35					12 43		12 54			12 57						
Hook	d						12 31									13 01									
Winchfield	d						12 35									13 05									
Fleet	d						12 40							12 54		13 10									
Farnborough (Main)	d				12 30		12 46							13 00		13 16									
Alton	d																					12 44			
Bentley	d																					12 51			
Farnham	a																					12 56			
	d										12 28											12 58			
Aldershot	d										12 34											13 04			
Ash Vale	d										12 39											13 09			
Brookwood	d						12 53				12 46					13 23						13 16			
Guildford	d					12 34						12 47						13 02						13 17	
Worplesdon	d	←				12 40									←										←
Woking	a	12 28			12 39	12 44	12 58	12 49			12 51	12 57			12 58	13 28		13 11	13 15			13 21		13 25	13 28
	d	12 29		12 33	12 41	12 46	12 59	12 50			12 52	12 59			12 59	13 29	13 03	13 12	13 17	13 21		13 22		13 26	13 29
West Byfleet	d			12 37			→				12 57					→	13 07					13 27			
Byfleet & New Haw	d			12 40													13 10								
Weybridge	d	12 36		12 43											13 06		13 13								13 36
Walton-on-Thames	d	12 40		12 47											13 10		13 17								13 40
Hersham	d			12 49													13 19								
Esher	d			12 52													13 22								
Surbiton 6	a	12 46		12 56							13 07				13 16		13 26					13 37			13 46
Wimbledon 6 ⊖	a			13 04													13 34								
Earlsfield	a			13 08						←							13 38				←				
Clapham Junction 10	a	12 57		13 12		13 05			13 12	13 12				13 25			13 42	13 31	13 36		13 42	13 48			13 57
	a			→													→								
Vauxhall ⊖	a									13 17											13 47				
London Waterloo 15 ⊖	a	13 05			13 07	13 13		13 19	13 20	13 22	13 25	13 23		13 34	13 36			13 40	13 49	13 49	13 52	13 57		13 51	14 05

		SW	SW 1	SW 1	SW 1	SW ◇1 🍴	SW ◇1 🍴	SW		SW 1	SW 1 🍴	SW 1	SW 1	SW 1	SW	SW 1	SW ◇1 🍴	SW ◇1 🍴		SW	SW 1	SW 1 🍴	SW 1	SW	SW 1
Basingstoke	d		13 17		13 24	13 30	13 35					13 43		13 54			13 57								14 17
Hook	d				13 31									14 01											
Winchfield	d				13 35									14 05											
Fleet	d				13 40							13 54		14 10											
Farnborough (Main)	d		13 30		13 46							14 00		14 16											14 30
Alton	d									13 15											13 44				
Bentley	d																				13 51				
Farnham	a									13 25											13 56				
	d									13 28											13 58				
Aldershot	d									13 34											14 04				
Ash Vale	d									13 39											14 09				
Brookwood	d				13 53					13 46				14 23							14 16				
Guildford	d			13 34							13 47					14 02						14 17			
Worplesdon	d			13 40									←										←		
Woking	a		13 39	13 44	13 58	13 49				13 51	13 57		13 58	14 28		14 11	14 15				14 21	14 25	14 28		14 39
	d	13 33	13 41	13 46	13 59	13 50				13 52	13 59		13 59	14 29	14 03	14 12	14 17	14 21			14 22	14 26	14 29	14 33	14 41
West Byfleet	d	13 37			→					13 57				→	14 07						14 27			14 37	
Byfleet & New Haw	d	13 40													14 10									14 40	
Weybridge	d	13 43											14 06		14 13								14 36	14 43	
Walton-on-Thames	d	13 47											14 10		14 17								14 40	14 47	
Hersham	d	13 49													14 19									14 49	
Esher	d	13 52													14 22									14 52	
Surbiton 6	a	13 56								14 07			14 16		14 26						14 37		14 46	14 56	
Wimbledon 6 ⊖	a	14 04													14 34									15 04	
Earlsfield	a	14 08						←							14 38					←				15 08	
Clapham Junction 10	a	14 12		14 05			14 12	14 12				14 25			14 42	14 31	14 36			14 42	14 48		14 57	15 12	
	a	→													→									→	
Vauxhall ⊖	a							14 17												14 47					
London Waterloo 15 ⊖	a		14 07	14 13		14 19	14 20	14 22		14 25	14 23	14 34	14 36			14 40	14 49	14 49		14 52	14 57	14 51	15 05		15 08

Table 155

Mondays to Fridays

from 8 October

Basingstoke, Alton, Guildford and Woking - Waterloo

Network Diagram - see first Page of Table 155

		SW 1	SW 1	SW ◇1 🍴		SW ◇1 🍴	SW	SW 1	SW 1 🍴	SW 1	SW 1	SW 1	SW	SW 1		SW ◇1 🍴	SW ◇1 🍴	SW	SW 1	SW 1 🍴	SW 1	SW	SW 1	SW 1	
Basingstoke	d		14 24	14 30		14 35				14 43		14 54				14 57							15 17		
Hook	d		14 31									15 01													
Winchfield	d		14 35									15 05													
Fleet	d		14 40							14 54		15 10													
Farnborough (Main)	d		14 46							15 00		15 16											15 30		
Alton	d							14 15											14 44						
Bentley	d																		14 51						
Farnham	a							14 25											14 56						
	d							14 28											14 58						
Aldershot	d							14 34											15 04						
Ash Vale	d							14 39											15 09						
Brookwood	d		14 53					14 46				15 23							15 16						
Guildford	d	14 34							14 47					15 02						15 17				15 34	
Worplesdon	d	14 40									←										←			15 40	
Woking	a	14 44	14 58	14 49				14 51	14 57		14 58	15 28		15 11		15 15			15 21	15 25	15 28		15 39	15 44	
	d	14 46	14 59	14 50				14 52	14 59		14 59	15 29	15 03	15 12		15 17	15 21		15 22	15 26	15 29	15 33	15 41	15 46	
West Byfleet	d		→					14 57				→	15 07						15 27			15 37			
Byfleet & New Haw	d												15 10									15 40			
Weybridge	d										15 06		15 13								15 36	15 43			
Walton-on-Thames	d										15 10		15 17								15 40	15 47			
Hersham	d												15 19									15 49			
Esher	d												15 22									15 52			
Surbiton 6	a							15 07			15 16		15 26						15 37		15 46	15 56			
Wimbledon 6 ⊖	a												15 34									16 04			
Earlsfield	a						←						15 38					←				16 08			
Clapham Junction 10	a	15 05				15 12	15 12			15 25			15 42	15 31		15 36		15 42	15 48		15 57	16 12		16 05	
	a												→									→			
Vauxhall ⊖	a						15 17											15 47							
London Waterloo 15 ⊖	a	15 13		15 19		15 20	15 22	15 25	15 23	15 34	15 37			15 43		15 49	15 49	15 52	15 57	15 51	16 05		16 07	16 13	

		SW 1	SW ◇1 🍴	SW ◇1 🍴	SW	SW 1	SW 1 🍴	SW 1	SW 1	SW 1		SW	SW 1	SW ◇1 🍴	SW ◇1 🍴	SW	SW 1	SW 1 🍴	SW 1	SW		SW 1	SW 1	SW 1	SW ◇1 🍴
Basingstoke	d	15 24	15 30	15 35				15 43		15 54				15 57								16 17		16 24	16 30
Hook	d	15 31								16 01														16 31	
Winchfield	d	15 35								16 05														16 35	
Fleet	d	15 40						15 54		16 10														16 40	
Farnborough (Main)	d	15 46						16 00		16 16												16 30		16 46	
Alton	d					15 15											15 44								
Bentley	d																15 51								
Farnham	a					15 25											15 56								
	d					15 28											15 58								
Aldershot	d					15 34											16 04								
Ash Vale	d					15 39											16 09								
Brookwood	d	15 53				15 46				16 23							16 16							16 53	
Guildford	d						15 47						16 00					16 17					16 34		
Worplesdon	d								←				16 06						←				16 40		
Woking	a	15 58	15 49			15 51	15 57		15 58	16 28			16 11	16 15			16 21	16 25	16 28			16 39	16 44	16 58	16 49
	d	15 59	15 50			15 52	15 59		15 59	16 29		16 03	16 12	16 17	16 21		16 22	16 26	16 29	16 33		16 41	16 46	16 59	16 50
West Byfleet	d	→				15 57				→		16 07					16 27			16 37				→	
Byfleet & New Haw	d											16 10								16 40					
Weybridge	d								16 06			16 13							16 36	16 43					
Walton-on-Thames	d								16 10			16 17							16 40	16 47					
Hersham	d											16 19								16 49					
Esher	d											16 22								16 52					
Surbiton 6	a					16 07			16 16			16 26					16 37		16 46	16 56					
Wimbledon 6 ⊖	a											16 34								17 04					
Earlsfield	a				←							16 38				←				17 08					
Clapham Junction 10	a			16 12	16 12			16 25				16 42	16 31	16 36		16 42	16 48		16 57	17 12			17 05		
	a											→								→					
Vauxhall ⊖	a				16 17											16 47									
London Waterloo 15 ⊖	a		16 19	16 20	16 22	16 29	16 24	16 34	16 36				16 40	16 49	16 49	16 52	16 59	16 51	17 08			17 08	17 14		17 19

Basingstoke, Alton, Guildford and Woking - Waterloo

Network Diagram - see first Page of Table 155

		SW ◇1 ✠	SW	SW 1	SW 1	SW 1		SW 1	SW 1	SW	SW 1 ✠	SW ◇1 ✠	SW ◇1 ✠	SW	SW 1	SW 1 ✠		SW 1	SW	SW 1	SW 1	SW 1	SW ◇1 ✠	SW	SW ◇1 ✠
Basingstoke	d	16 35						16 43	16 54			16 57								17 17		17 24	17 30		17 36
Hook	d								17 01													17 31			
Winchfield	d								17 05													17 35			
Fleet	d							16 54	17 10													17 40			
Farnborough (Main)	d							17 00	17 16											17 30		17 46			
Alton	d			16 15											16 44										
Bentley	d														16 51										
Farnham	a			16 25											16 56										
	d			16 28											16 58										
Aldershot	d			16 34											17 04										
Ash Vale	d			16 39											17 09										
Brookwood	d			16 46					17 23						17 16							17 53			
Guildford	d				16 47						17 00					17 17					17 34				
Worplesdon	d					←					17 06							←			17 40				
Woking	a			16 51	16 57	16 58			17 28		17 11	17 15			17 21	17 25		17 28		17 39	17 44	17 58	17 49		
	d			16 52	16 59	16 59			17 29	17 03	17 12	17 17	17 21		17 22	17 26		17 29	17 33	17 41	17 46	17 59	17 51		
West Byfleet	d			16 57					→	17 07					17 27				17 37			→			
Byfleet & New Haw	d									17 10									17 40						
Weybridge	d					17 06				17 13								17 36	17 43						
Walton-on-Thames	d					17 10				17 17								17 40	17 47						
Hersham	d									17 19									17 49						
Esher	d									17 22									17 52						
Surbiton 6	a			17 07		17 16				17 26					17 37			17 46	17 56						
Wimbledon 6 ⊖	a									17 34									18 04						
Earlsfield	a		←							17 38				←					18 08					←	
Clapham Junction 10	a	17 12	17 12					17 25		17 42	17 31	17 36		17 42	17 48			17 57	18 12		18 05			18 12	18 12
	a									→									→						
Vauxhall ⊖	a		17 17											17 47										18 17	
London Waterloo 15 ⊖	a	17 20	17 22	17 29	17 27	17 35		17 36			17 43	17 44	17 50	17 52	17 59	17 54		18 09		18 08	18 14		18 21	18 23	18 23

		SW 1		SW 1	SW 1	SW 1	SW 1	SW	SW 1 ✠	SW ◇1 ✠	SW ◇1 ✠	SW		SW 1	SW 1 ✠	SW 1	SW	SW 1	SW 1	SW 1	SW ◇1 ✠	SW		SW ◇1 ✠	SW 1
Basingstoke	d				17 43		17 54			17 57								18 17		18 24	18 30			18 35	
Hook	d						18 01													18 31					
Winchfield	d						18 05													18 35					
Fleet	d				17 54		18 10													18 40					
Farnborough (Main)	d				18 00		18 16											18 30		18 46					
Alton	d	17 14												17 44											18 14
Bentley	d	17 21												17 51											18 23
Farnham	a	17 26												17 56											18 27
	d	17 28												17 58											18 28
Aldershot	d	17 34												18 04											18 34
Ash Vale	d	17 39												18 09											18 39
Brookwood	d	17 46					18 23							18 16						18 53					18 46
Guildford	d			17 47					18 00						18 17				18 34						
Worplesdon	d					←			18 06							←			18 40						
Woking	a	17 51		17 58		17 58	18 28		18 11	18 15				18 21		18 28		18 39	18 44	18 58	18 49				18 52
	d	17 52		17 59		17 59	18 29	18 03	18 12	18 17	18 21			18 22		18 29	18 33	18 41	18 46	18 59	18 50				18 52
West Byfleet	d	17 57					→	18 07						18 27			18 37			→					18 57
Byfleet & New Haw	d							18 10									18 40								
Weybridge	d					18 06		18 13								18 36	18 43								
Walton-on-Thames	d					18 10		18 17								18 40	18 47								
Hersham	d							18 19									18 49								
Esher	d							18 22									18 52								
Surbiton 6	a	18 07				18 16		18 26						18 37		18 47	18 56								19 07
Wimbledon 6 ⊖	a							18 34									19 04								
Earlsfield	a							18 38				←					19 08					←			
Clapham Junction 10	a				18 25			18 42	18 31	18 36		18 42		18 48		18 58	19 11		19 05			19 11		19 12	
	a							→									→								
Vauxhall ⊖	a											18 47										19 16			
London Waterloo 15 ⊖	a	18 29		18 27	18 34	18 38			18 43	18 45	18 47	18 52		18 57	18 59	19 06		19 08	19 13		19 19	19 23		19 20	19 25

Basingstoke, Alton, Guildford and Woking - Waterloo

Network Diagram - see first Page of Table 155

		SW 1	SW 1 ✠	SW 1	SW	SW 1	SW ◇1 ✠	SW 1		SW ◇1 ✠	SW 1 ✠	SW 1	SW	SW 1	SW 1	SW 1	SW ◇1 ✠	SW		SW ◇1 ✠	SW 1	SW 1 ✠	SW 1	SW 1	SW
Basingstoke	d			18 43		18 54	19 02							19 17		19 24	19 30			19 35			19 43		
Hook	d					19 01										19 31									
Winchfield	d					19 05										19 35									
Fleet	d			18 54		19 10										19 40							19 54		
Farnborough (Main)	d			19 00		19 16								19 30		19 46							20 00		
Alton	d							18 35													19 07				
Bentley	d							18 42																	
Farnham	a							18 47													19 17				
	d							18 58													19 28				
Aldershot	d							19 04													19 34				
Ash Vale	d							19 09													19 39				
Brookwood	d					19 23		19 16								19 53					19 46				
Guildford	d		18 55								19 21				19 34							19 47			
Worplesdon	d	←										←			19 40									←	
Woking	a	18 58	19 03			19 28	19 20	19 21			19 28	19 28		19 39	19 45	19 58	19 49				19 51	19 57		19 58	
	d	18 59	19 05		19 03	19 29	19 22	19 22		19 25	19 30	19 29	19 33	19 41	19 46	19 59	19 50				19 52	19 59		19 59	20 03
West Byfleet	d				19 07	→		19 27					19 37			→					19 57				20 07
Byfleet & New Haw	d				19 10								19 40												20 10
Weybridge	d	19 06			19 13							19 36	19 43											20 06	20 13
Walton-on-Thames	d	19 10			19 17							19 40	19 47											20 10	20 17
Hersham	d				19 19								19 49												20 19
Esher	d				19 22								19 52												20 22
Surbiton 6	a	19 16			19 26			19 37				19 46	19 56								20 07			20 16	20 26
Wimbledon 6 ⊖	a				19 34								20 04												20 35
Earlsfield	a				19 38								20 08					←							20 38
Clapham Junction 10	a			19 26	19 41		19 41	19 48				19 57	20 11		20 05			20 11		20 12			20 25		20 41
	a												→												→
Vauxhall ⊖	a				19 46													20 16							
London Waterloo 15 ⊖	a	19 39	19 29	19 34	19 52		19 49	19 57		19 51	19 59	20 05		20 08	20 14		20 19	20 22		20 20	20 26	20 24	20 34	20 36	

		SW 1	SW ◇1 ✠	SW		SW 1	SW 1	SW 1	SW ◇1 ✠	SW 1	SW	SW 1	SW 1	SW 1		SW 1	SW ◇1 ✠	SW 1	SW	SW 1	SW ◇1 ✠	SW	SW 1	SW 1	
Basingstoke	d							19 54	20 09			20 17				20 24	20 36			20 43					
Hook	d							20 01								20 31									
Winchfield	d							20 05								20 35									
Fleet	d							20 10								20 40				20 54					
Farnborough (Main)	d							20 16				20 30				20 46				21 00					
Alton	d					19 35							20 15										20 44		
Bentley	d					19 42																	20 51		
Farnham	a					19 47							20 25										20 56		
	d					19 58							20 28										20 58		
Aldershot	d					20 04							20 34										21 04		
Ash Vale	d					20 09							20 39										21 09		
Brookwood	d					20 16		20 23					20 46			20 53							21 16		
Guildford	d	20 02					20 17							20 39				20 47						21 17	
Worplesdon	d													20 44											
Woking	a	20 11				20 21	20 25	20 28	20 29			20 39	20 51	20 52		20 58		20 56		21 09			21 21	21 25	
	d	20 12	20 21			20 22	20 26	20 29	20 30		20 33	20 41	20 52	20 53		20 59		20 59	21 03	21 10	21 21		21 22	21 26	
West Byfleet	d					20 27					20 37		20 57						21 07				21 27		
Byfleet & New Haw	d										20 40								21 10						
Weybridge	d							20 36			20 43					21 06			21 13						
Walton-on-Thames	d							20 40			20 47					21 10			21 17						
Hersham	d										20 49								21 19						
Esher	d										20 52								21 22						
Surbiton 6	a					20 37		20 46			20 56		21 07			21 16			21 26				21 37		
Wimbledon 6 ⊖	a										21 05								21 34						
Earlsfield	a			←						←	21 08								21 38			←			
Clapham Junction 10	a	20 31		20 41		20 48		20 57	20 52	20 57	21 11			21 12			21 16		21 42	21 29		21 42	21 48		
	a							→											→						
Vauxhall ⊖	a			20 46							21 16											21 47			
London Waterloo 15 ⊖	a	20 40	20 49	20 52		20 57	20 50		21 00	21 05	21 22	21 07	21 29	21 21		21 34	21 24	21 27		21 38	21 49	21 52	21 57	21 50	

Table 155

Basingstoke, Alton, Guildford and Woking - Waterloo

Mondays to Fridays
from 8 October

Network Diagram - see first Page of Table 155

		SW	SW	SW	SW	SW	SW	SW	SW	SW		SW	SW	SW	SW	SW	SW	SW	SW	SW		SW	SW	SW	SW
		■	◇■ H	■		■		■	■	◇■		■		■	■		■	■	◇■	■		■		■	
Basingstoke	d	20 54	21 09						21 24	21 35				21 43				21 54	22 09						
Hook	d	21 01							21 31									22 01							
Winchfield	d	21 05							21 35									22 05							
Fleet	d	21 10							21 40					21 54				22 10							
Farnborough (Main)	d	21 16							21 46					22 00				22 16							
Alton	d							21 15									21 44								
Bentley	d																21 51								
Farnham	a							21 25									21 56								
	d							21 28									21 58								
Aldershot	d							21 34									22 04								
Ash Vale	d							21 39									22 09								
Brookwood	d	21 23						21 46	21 53								22 16	22 23							
Guildford	d					21 39						21 47											22 20	22 39	
Worplesdon	d					21 44																		22 44	
Woking	a	21 28	21 29			21 49		21 51	21 58			21 57		22 09			22 21	22 28	22 28				22 32	22 49	
	d	21 29	21 30		21 33	21 50		21 52	21 59			21 59	22 03	22 10	22 21		22 22	22 29	22 29				22 33	22 50	
West Byfleet	d				21 37			21 57					22 07				22 27						22 37		
Byfleet & New Haw	d				21 40								22 10										22 40		
Weybridge	d	21 36			21 43				22 06				22 13					22 36					22 43		
Walton-on-Thames	d	21 40			21 47				22 10				22 17					22 40					22 47		
Hersham	d				21 49								22 19										22 49		
Esher	d				21 52								22 22										22 52		
Surbiton ■	a	21 46			21 56			22 07	22 16				22 26				22 37	22 46					22 56		
Wimbledon ■ ⊖	a				22 04								22 34										23 04		
Earlsfield	a			←	22 08		←						22 38			←				←		←	23 08		←
Clapham Junction ■	a	21 57	21 52	21 57	22 12	22 09	22 12			22 14			22 42	22 29		22 42	22 52	22 57	22 48	22 52		22 57	23 12	23 09	23 12
	a	→			→								→				→	→					→		
Vauxhall ⊖	a						22 17									22 47									23 17
London Waterloo ■ ⊖	a		22 04	22 06		22 18	22 22	22 27	22 34	22 22		22 27		22 38	22 49	22 52			22 58	23 01		23 08		23 19	23 23

		SW	SW	SW	SW	SW		SW	SW	SW	SW	SW	SW	SW	SW FO	SW FX		SW	SW						
		■	■	◇■	■			■		■	■	■	■	■	■	■		■	■						
Basingstoke	d		22 24	22 36				22 43			22 54	23 13						23 44							
Hook	d		22 31								23 01							23 51							
Winchfield	d		22 35								23 05							23 55							
Fleet	d		22 40					22 54			23 10							00 01							
Farnborough (Main)	d		22 46					23 00			23 16							00 06							
Alton	d	22 15								22 44				23 15					23 46						
Bentley	d									22 51									23 53						
Farnham	a	22 25								22 56				23 25					23 58						
	d	22 28								22 58				23 28											
Aldershot	d	22 34								23 04				23 34											
Ash Vale	d	22 39								23 09				23 39											
Brookwood	d	22 46	22 53							23 16	23 23			23 46				00 13							
Guildford	d					22 55									23 39	23 39									
Worplesdon	d				←								←		23 44	23 44									
Woking	a	22 51	22 58	22 54	22 58	23 05		23 09		23 21	23 28	23 31	23 28	23 51	23 49	23 49		00 18							
	d	22 52	22 59	22 55	22 59	23 06		23 10		23 22	23 33	23 32	23 33		23 56	23 56		00 20							
West Byfleet	d	22 57	→			23 10				23 27	→		23 37					00 25							
Byfleet & New Haw	d					23 13							23 40												
Weybridge	d				23 06	23 16							23 43					00 29							
Walton-on-Thames	d				23 10	23 20							23 47					00 33							
Hersham	d					23 22							23 49												
Esher	d					23 25							23 52												
Surbiton ■	a	23 07			23 16	23 29				23 37			23 57					00 39							
Wimbledon ■ ⊖	a					23 37							00 06					00 47							
Earlsfield	a					23 41			←																
Clapham Junction ■	a			23 14		23 44		23 29	23 44	23 51		23 55			00 19	00 19		00 53							
	a					→							00 21												
Vauxhall ⊖	a								23 49				00 30												
London Waterloo ■ ⊖	a	23 27		23 23	23 32			23 42	23 54	00 02		00 09	00 35		00 32	00 33		01 04							

Table 155

Basingstoke, Alton, Guildford and Woking - Waterloo

Saturdays
until 6 October

Network Diagram - see first Page of Table 155

		SW	SW	SW	SW	SW	SW	SW	SW	SW		SW	SW	SW	SW	SW	SW	SW	SW	SW		SW	SW	SW	SW
		■	■	■	■	■ A	■ B	■				■		■		■	◇■ H		■	■			■	◇■ H	
Basingstoke	d		22p54	23p13				23p44				04 54		05 54			05 59			06 24				06 30	
Hook	d		23p01					23p51				05 01		06 01						06 31					
Winchfield	d		23p05					23p55				05 05		06 05						06 35					
Fleet	d		23p10					00 01				05 10		06 10						06 40					
Farnborough (Main)	d		23p16					00 06				05 16		06 16						06 46					
Alton	d	22p44																							
Bentley	d	22p51																							
Farnham	a	22p56																							
	d	22p58																							
Aldershot	d	23p04																							
Ash Vale	d	23p09																							
Brookwood	d	23p16	23p23					00 13				05 23		06 23						06 53					
Guildford	d					23p39	23p39		04 00				05 14			06 02							06 34		
Worplesdon	d				←	23p44	23p44						05 19						←				06 40		
Woking	a	23p21	23p28	23p31	23p28	23p49	23p49	00 18	04 08			05 28	05 24	06 28		06 11	06 18		06 28	06 58			06 44	06 49	
	d	23p22	23p33	23p32	23p33	23p56	23p56	00 20	04 10	05 27		05 29	05 33	06 29	06 03	06 13	06 19		06 29	06 59		06 33	06 46	06 50	
West Byfleet	d	23p27	→		23p37			00 25		05 32			05 37	→	06 07					→		06 37			
Byfleet & New Haw	d				23p40					05 35			05 40		06 10							06 40			
Weybridge	d				23p43			00 29					05 43		06 13				06 36			06 43			
Walton-on-Thames	d				23p47			00 33					05 47		06 17				06 40			06 47			
Hersham	d				23p49								05 49		06 19							06 49			
Esher	d				23p52								05 52		06 22							06 52			
Surbiton ■	a	23p37			23p57			00 39	04 24			05 40	05 56		06 26				06 46			06 56			
Wimbledon ■ ⊖	a				00 06			00 47	04 31			05 48	06 04		06 34							07 04			
Earlsfield	a												06 08		06 38			←				07 08			←
Clapham Junction ■	a	23p51		23p55		00 19	00 19	00 53	04 43				06 12		06 42	06 32	06 38	06 42	06 57			07 12	07 05		07 12
	a				00 21					06 43		06 00			→							→			
Vauxhall ⊖	a				00 30					06 49		06 07	06 17					06 47							07 17
London Waterloo ■ ⊖	a	00 02		00 09	00 35	00 32	00 33	01 04	04 53	06 56		06 12	06 22			06 40	06 49	06 52	07 05				07 13	07 19	07 22

		SW	SW	SW	SW	SW		SW	SW	SW	SW	SW	SW	SW	SW	SW		SW	SW	SW	SW	SW	SW	SW	SW
		■	■	■	■			■	◇■ H		■	◇■ H	■	■		■		◇■ H		■	■ H	■		■	■
Basingstoke	d		06 40		06 54				06 57			07 09		07 24				07 30						07 43	
Hook	d				07 01									07 31											
Winchfield	d				07 05									07 35											
Fleet	d				07 10									07 40										07 54	
Farnborough (Main)	d				07 16									07 46										08 00	
Alton	d	06 14									06 44									07 14					
Bentley	d	06 21									06 51									07 21					
Farnham	a	06 26									06 56									07 26					
	d	06 28									06 58									07 28					
Aldershot	d	06 34									07 04									07 34					
Ash Vale	d	06 39									07 09									07 39					
Brookwood	d	06 46			07 23						07 16			07 53						07 46					
Guildford	d							07 02								07 34					07 47				08 02
Worplesdon	d			←									←			07 40						←			
Woking	a	06 51	06 58	06 58	07 28			07 11	07 15		07 21	07 27	07 28	07 58		07 44		07 49		07 51	07 57	07 58		08 09	08 10
	d	06 52	07 00	06 59	07 29	07 03		07 12	07 17		07 22	07 29	07 29	07 59	07 33	07 46		07 50		07 52	07 59	07 59	08 03	08 11	08 13
West Byfleet	d	06 57			→	07 07					07 27			→	07 37					07 57			08 07		
Byfleet & New Haw	d					07 10									07 40								08 10		
Weybridge	d			07 06		07 13							07 36		07 43							08 06	08 13		
Walton-on-Thames	d			07 10		07 17							07 40		07 47							08 10	08 17		
Hersham	d					07 19									07 49								08 19		
Esher	d					07 22									07 52								08 22		
Surbiton ■	a	07 07		07 16		07 26					07 37		07 46		07 56					08 07		08 16	08 26		
Wimbledon ■ ⊖	a					07 34									08 04								08 34		
Earlsfield	a					07 38				←					08 08				←				08 38		
Clapham Junction ■	a	07 18	07 23			07 42		07 31	07 36	07 42	07 50		07 57		08 12	08 05			08 12				08 42	08 30	08 33
	a					→									→								→		
Vauxhall ⊖	a									07 47									08 17						
London Waterloo ■ ⊖	a	07 27	07 31	07 33				07 40	07 49	07 52	07 58	07 53	08 05			08 13		08 19	08 22	08 25	08 23	08 34		08 39	08 42

A until 21 July, 18 August, 25 August, 15 September, 22 September, 29 September, 6 October

B 28 July, 4 August, 11 August, 1 September, 8 September

Table 155

Basingstoke, Alton, Guildford and Woking - Waterloo

Network Diagram - see first Page of Table 155

		SW ■		SW ◇■ ⇆	SW	SW ■	SW ◇■ ⇆	SW ■ ⇆	SW ■	SW	SW ■	SW ■		SW ■	SW ◇■ ⇆	SW ◇■ ⇆	SW	SW ■	SW ■ ⇆	SW ■	SW ■	SW ■		SW	SW ■
Basingstoke	d	07 54		07 57							08 17			08 24	08 30	08 35				08 43		08 54			
Hook	d	08 01												08 31								09 01			
Winchfield	d	08 05												08 35								09 05			
Fleet	d	08 10												08 40						08 54		09 10			
Farnborough (Main)	d	08 16									08 30			08 46						09 00		09 16			
Alton	d					07 44												08 14							
Bentley	d					07 51												08 21							
Farnham	a					07 56												08 26							
	d					07 58												08 28							
Aldershot	d					08 04												08 34							
Ash Vale	d					08 09												08 39							
Brookwood	d	08 23				08 16								08 53				08 46				09 23			
Guildford	d							08 17				08 34							08 47						09 02
Worplesdon	d								←			08 40									←				
Woking	a	08 28		08 17		08 21		08 26	08 28		08 39	08 44		08 58	08 49			08 51	08 57		08 58	09 28			09 11
	d	08 29		08 18		08 22	08 23	08 27	08 29	08 33	08 41	08 46		08 59	08 50			08 52	08 59		08 59	09 29		09 03	09 12
West Byfleet	d	→				08 27				08 37				→				08 57				→		09 07	
Byfleet & New Haw	d									08 40														09 10	
Weybridge	d								08 36	08 43											09 06			09 13	
Walton-on-Thames	d								08 40	08 47											09 10			09 17	
Hersham	d									08 49														09 19	
Esher	d									08 52														09 22	
Surbiton ■	a					08 37			08 46	08 56								09 07			09 16			09 26	
Wimbledon ■ ⊖	a									09 04														09 34	
Earlsfield	a				←					09 08							←							09 38	
Clapham Junction ■	a			08 37	08 42	08 49			08 57	09 12		09 05				09 12	09 12			09 25				09 42	09 31
	a									→														→	
Vauxhall ⊖	a				08 47												09 17								
London Waterloo ■ ⊖	a			08 49	08 52	08 58	08 49	08 51	09 05		09 08	09 13			09 19	09 20	09 22	09 25	09 23	09 34	09 36				09 40

		SW ◇■ ⇆	SW ◇■ ⇆	SW	SW ■	SW ■ ⇆	SW ■	SW		SW ■	SW ■	SW ■	SW ◇■ ⇆	SW ◇■ ⇆	SW	SW ■	SW ■ ⇆	SW ■		SW ■	SW ■	SW	SW ■	SW ◇■ ⇆	SW ◇■ ⇆
Basingstoke	d	08 57								09 17		09 24	09 30	09 35				09 43			09 54			09 57	
Hook	d											09 31									10 01				
Winchfield	d											09 35									10 05				
Fleet	d											09 40						09 54			10 10				
Farnborough (Main)	d									09 30		09 46						10 00			10 16				
Alton	d				08 44											09 14									
Bentley	d				08 51											09 21									
Farnham	a				08 56											09 26									
	d				08 58											09 28									
Aldershot	d				09 04											09 34									
Ash Vale	d				09 09											09 39									
Brookwood	d				09 16							09 53				09 46					10 23				
Guildford	d					09 17					09 34						09 47						10 02		
Worplesdon	d						←				09 40									←					
Woking	a	09 15			09 21	09 25	09 28			09 39	09 44	09 58	09 49			09 51	09 57			09 58	10 28		10 11	10 15	
	d	09 17	09 21		09 22	09 26	09 29	09 33		09 41	09 46	09 59	09 50			09 52	09 59			09 59	10 29	10 03	10 12	10 17	10 21
West Byfleet	d				09 27			09 37				→				09 57					→	10 07			
Byfleet & New Haw	d							09 40														10 10			
Weybridge	d						09 36	09 43												10 06		10 13			
Walton-on-Thames	d						09 40	09 47												10 10		10 17			
Hersham	d							09 49														10 19			
Esher	d							09 52														10 22			
Surbiton ■	a				09 37		09 46	09 56								10 07				10 16		10 26			
Wimbledon ■ ⊖	a							10 04														10 34			
Earlsfield	a			←				10 08							←							10 38			
Clapham Junction ■	a	09 36		09 42	09 48		09 57	10 12			10 05			10 12	10 12			10 25				10 42	10 31	10 36	
	a							→														→			
Vauxhall ⊖	a			09 47											10 17										
London Waterloo ■ ⊖	a	09 49	09 49	09 52	09 57	09 51	10 05			10 07	10 13		10 19	10 20	10 22	10 25	10 23	10 34		10 36			10 40	10 49	10 49

Table 155

Saturdays
until 6 October

Basingstoke, Alton, Guildford and Woking - Waterloo

Network Diagram - see first Page of Table 155

		SW	SW ■	SW ■ ⇆		SW ■	SW	SW ■	SW ■	SW ■	SW ◇■ ⇆	SW ◇■ ⇆	SW	SW ■		SW ■ ⇆	SW ■	SW ■	SW ■	SW	SW ■	SW ◇■ ⇆	SW ◇■ ⇆	SW	
Basingstoke	d							10 17		10 24	10 30	10 35					10 43		10 54			10 57			
Hook	d									10 31									11 01						
Winchfield	d									10 35									11 05						
Fleet	d									10 40							10 54		11 10						
Farnborough (Main)	d							10 30		10 46							11 00		11 16						
Alton	d		09 44											10 14											
Bentley	d		09 51											10 21											
Farnham	a		09 56											10 26											
	d		09 58											10 28											
Aldershot	d		10 04											10 34											
Ash Vale	d		10 09											10 39											
Brookwood	d		10 16							10 53				10 46					11 23						
Guildford	d			10 17					10 34							10 47					11 02				
Worplesdon	d					←			10 40									←							
Woking	a		10 21	10 25		10 28		10 39	10 44	10 58	10 49			10 51		10 57		10 58	11 28		11 11	11 15			
	d		10 22	10 26		10 29	10 33	10 41	10 46	10 59	10 50			10 52		10 59		10 59	11 29	11 03	11 12	11 17	11 21		
West Byfleet	d		10 27				10 37			→				10 57					→	11 07					
Byfleet & New Haw	d						10 40													11 10					
Weybridge	d					10 36	10 43											11 06		11 13					
Walton-on-Thames	d					10 40	10 47											11 10		11 17					
Hersham	d						10 49													11 19					
Esher	d						10 52													11 22					
Surbiton ■	a		10 37			10 46	10 56							11 07				11 16		11 26					
Wimbledon ■ ⊖	a						11 04													11 34					
Earlsfield	a	←					11 08						←							11 38				←	
Clapham Junction ■	a	10 42	10 48			10 57	11 12		11 05			11 12	11 12				11 25			11 42	11 31	11 36		11 42	
	a						→													→					
Vauxhall ⊖	a	10 47											11 17											11 47	
London Waterloo ■ ⊖	a	10 52	10 57	10 51		11 05		11 07	11 13		11 19	11 20	11 22	11 25		11 23	11 34	11 36			11 40	11 49	11 49	11 52	

		SW ■	SW ■ ⇆	SW ■	SW	SW ■	SW ■	SW ■	SW ◇■ ⇆	SW ◇■ ⇆		SW	SW ■	SW ■ ⇆	SW ■	SW ■	SW ■	SW	SW ■	SW ◇■ ⇆		SW ◇■ ⇆	SW	SW ■	SW ■ ⇆
Basingstoke	d					11 17		11 24	11 30	11 35					11 43		11 54			11 57					
Hook	d							11 31									12 01								
Winchfield	d							11 35									12 05								
Fleet	d							11 40							11 54		12 10								
Farnborough (Main)	d					11 30		11 46							12 00		12 16								
Alton	d	10 44											11 15											11 44	
Bentley	d	10 51																						11 51	
Farnham	a	10 56											11 25											11 56	
	d	10 58											11 28											11 58	
Aldershot	d	11 04											11 34											12 04	
Ash Vale	d	11 09											11 39											12 09	
Brookwood	d	11 16						11 53					11 46				12 23							12 16	
Guildford	d		11 17				11 34							11 47					12 02						12 17
Worplesdon	d			←			11 40									←									
Woking	a	11 21	11 25	11 28		11 39	11 44	11 58	11 49				11 51	11 57		11 58	12 28		12 11	12 15				12 21	12 25
	d	11 22	11 26	11 29	11 33	11 41	11 46	11 59	11 50				11 52	11 59		11 59	12 29	12 03	12 12	12 17		12 21		12 22	12 26
West Byfleet	d	11 27			11 37			→					11 57				→	12 07						12 27	
Byfleet & New Haw	d				11 40													12 10							
Weybridge	d			11 36	11 43											12 06		12 13							
Walton-on-Thames	d			11 40	11 47											12 10		12 17							
Hersham	d				11 49													12 19							
Esher	d				11 52													12 22							
Surbiton ■	a	11 37		11 46	11 56								12 07			12 16		12 26						12 37	
Wimbledon ■ ⊖	a				12 04													12 34							
Earlsfield	a				12 08							←						12 38					←		
Clapham Junction ■	a	11 48		11 57	12 12		12 05			12 12		12 12			12 25			12 42	12 31	12 36			12 42	12 48	
	a				→													→							
Vauxhall ⊖	a											12 17											12 47		
London Waterloo ■ ⊖	a	11 57	11 51	12 05		12 07	12 13		12 19	12 21		12 22	12 29	12 27	12 34	12 36			12 43	12 49		12 51	12 52	12 59	12 57

Table 155

Saturdays until 6 October

Basingstoke, Alton, Guildford and Woking - Waterloo

Network Diagram - see first Page of Table 155

	SW ■	SW	SW ■	SW ■	SW ■	SW ◇■ 🍴	SW ◇■ 🍴	SW	SW ■	SW ■ 🍴	SW ■	SW ■	SW ■	SW	SW ■	SW ◇■ 🍴	SW ◇■ 🍴	SW	SW ■	SW ■ 🍴	SW ■	SW
Basingstoke d			12 17		12 24	12 30	12 35				12 43		12 54			12 57						
Hook d					12 31								13 01									
Winchfield d					12 35								13 05									
Fleet d					12 40						12 54		13 10									
Farnborough (Main) d			12 30		12 46						13 00		13 16									
Alton d									12 15										12 44			
Bentley d																			12 51			
Farnham a									12 25										12 56			
d									12 28										12 58			
Aldershot d									12 34										13 04			
Ash Vale d									12 39										13 09			
Brookwood d					12 53				12 46				13 23						13 16			
Guildford d				12 34						12 47					13 02					13 17		
Worplesdon d	←			12 40								←									←	
Woking a	12 28		12 39	12 44	12 58	12 49			12 51	12 57		12 58	13 28		13 11	13 15			13 21	13 25	13 28	
d	12 29	12 33	12 41	12 46	12 59	12 50			12 52	12 59		12 59	13 29	13 03	13 12	13 17	13 21		13 22	13 26	13 29	13 33
West Byfleet d		12 37			→				12 57				→	13 07					13 27			13 37
Byfleet & New Haw d		12 40												13 10								13 40
Weybridge d	12 36	12 43										13 06		13 13							13 36	13 43
Walton-on-Thames d	12 40	12 47										13 10		13 17							13 40	13 47
Hersham d		12 49												13 19								13 49
Esher d		12 52												13 22								13 52
Surbiton ■ a	12 46	12 56							13 07			13 16		13 26					13 37		13 46	13 56
Wimbledon ■ ⊖ a		13 04												13 34								14 04
Earlsfield a		13 08						←						13 38				←				14 08
Clapham Junction ■ a	12 57	13 12		13 05			13 12	13 12			13 25			13 42	13 31	13 36		13 42	13 48		13 57	14 12
a		→												→								→
Vauxhall ⊖ a								13 17										13 47				
London Waterloo ■ ⊖ a	13 05		13 07	13 13		13 19	13 21	13 22	13 29	13 27	13 34	13 36			13 43	13 49	13 51	13 52	13 59	13 57	14 05	

	SW ■	SW ■	SW ■	SW ◇■ 🍴	SW ◇■ 🍴	SW	SW ■	SW ■ 🍴	SW ■	SW ■	SW ■	SW	SW ■	SW ◇■ 🍴	SW ◇■ 🍴	SW	SW ■	SW ■ 🍴	SW ■	SW	SW ■
Basingstoke d	13 17		13 24	13 30	13 35				13 43		13 54			13 57							14 17
Hook d			13 31								14 01										
Winchfield d			13 35								14 05										
Fleet d			13 40						13 54		14 10										
Farnborough (Main) d	13 30		13 46						14 00		14 16										14 30
Alton d							13 15										13 44				
Bentley d																	13 51				
Farnham a							13 25										13 56				
d							13 28										13 58				
Aldershot d							13 34										14 04				
Ash Vale d							13 39										14 09				
Brookwood d			13 53				13 46				14 23						14 16				
Guildford d		13 34						13 47					14 02					14 17			
Worplesdon d		13 40								←									←		
Woking a	13 39	13 44	13 58	13 49			13 51	13 57		13 58	14 28		14 11	14 15			14 21	14 25	14 28		14 39
d	13 41	13 46	13 59	13 50			13 52	13 59		13 59	14 29	14 03	14 12	14 17	14 21		14 22	14 26	14 29	14 33	14 41
West Byfleet d			→				13 57				→	14 07					14 27			14 37	
Byfleet & New Haw d												14 10								14 40	
Weybridge d										14 06		14 13							14 36	14 43	
Walton-on-Thames d										14 10		14 17							14 40	14 47	
Hersham d												14 19								14 49	
Esher d												14 22								14 52	
Surbiton ■ a							14 07			14 16		14 26					14 37		14 46	14 56	
Wimbledon ■ ⊖ a												14 34								15 04	
Earlsfield a						←						14 38				←				15 08	
Clapham Junction ■ a		14 05			14 12	14 12			14 25			14 42	14 31	14 36		14 42	14 48		14 57	15 12	
a												→								→	
Vauxhall ⊖ a						14 17										14 47					
London Waterloo ■ ⊖ a	14 07	14 14		14 19	14 21	14 22	14 29	14 27	14 34	14 36			14 41	14 49	14 51	14 52	14 59	14 57	15 05		15 07

Table 155

Saturdays until 6 October

Basingstoke, Alton, Guildford and Woking - Waterloo

Network Diagram - see first Page of Table 155

	SW ■	SW ■	SW ◇■ 🍴	SW ◇■ 🍴	SW	SW ■	SW ■ 🍴	SW ■	SW ■	SW ■	SW	SW ■	SW ◇■ 🍴	SW ◇■ 🍴	SW	SW ■	SW ■ 🍴	SW ■	SW	SW ■	SW ■	SW ■
Basingstoke d		14 24	14 30	14 35				14 43		14 54			14 57							15 17		15 24
Hook d		14 31								15 01												15 31
Winchfield d		14 35								15 05												15 35
Fleet d		14 40						14 54		15 10												15 40
Farnborough (Main) d		14 46						15 00		15 16										15 30		15 46
Alton d						14 15										14 44						
Bentley d																14 51						
Farnham a						14 25										14 56						
d						14 28										14 58						
Aldershot d						14 34										15 04						
Ash Vale d						14 39										15 09						
Brookwood d		14 53				14 46				15 23						15 16						15 53
Guildford d	14 34						14 47					15 02					15 17				15 34	
Worplesdon d	14 40								←									←			15 40	
Woking a	14 44	14 58	14 49			14 51	14 57		14 58	15 28		15 11	15 15			15 21	15 25	15 28		15 39	15 44	15 58
d	14 46	14 59	14 50			14 52	14 59		14 59	15 29	15 03	15 12	15 17	15 21		15 22	15 26	15 29	15 33	15 41	15 46	15 59
West Byfleet d		→				14 57				→	15 07					15 27			15 37			→
Byfleet & New Haw d											15 10								15 40			
Weybridge d									15 06		15 13							15 36	15 43			
Walton-on-Thames d									15 10		15 17							15 40	15 47			
Hersham d											15 19								15 49			
Esher d											15 22								15 52			
Surbiton ■ a						15 07			15 16		15 26					15 37		15 46	15 56			
Wimbledon ■ ⊖ a											15 34								16 04			
Earlsfield a					←						15 38				←				16 08			
Clapham Junction ■ a	15 05			15 12	15 12			15 25			15 42	15 31	15 36		15 42	15 48		15 57	16 12		16 05	
a											→								→			
Vauxhall ⊖ a					15 17										15 47							
London Waterloo ■ ⊖ a	15 14		15 19	15 21	15 22	15 29	15 27	15 34	15 36			15 41	15 49	15 51	15 52	15 59	15 57	16 05		16 07	16 13	

	SW ◇■ 🍴	SW ◇■ 🍴	SW	SW ■	SW ■ 🍴	SW ■	SW ■	SW ■	SW	SW ■	SW ◇■ 🍴	SW ◇■ 🍴	SW	SW ■	SW ■ 🍴	SW ■	SW	SW ■	SW ■	SW ■	SW ◇■ 🍴
Basingstoke d	15 30	15 35				15 43		15 54			15 57							16 17		16 24	16 30
Hook d								16 01												16 31	
Winchfield d								16 05												16 35	
Fleet d						15 54		16 10												16 40	
Farnborough (Main) d						16 00		16 16										16 30		16 46	
Alton d				15 15										15 44							
Bentley d														15 51							
Farnham a				15 25										15 56							
d				15 28										15 58							
Aldershot d				15 34										16 04							
Ash Vale d				15 39										16 09							
Brookwood d				15 46				16 23						16 16						16 53	
Guildford d					15 47					16 02					16 17				16 34		
Worplesdon d							←									←			16 40		
Woking a	15 49			15 51	15 57		15 58	16 28		16 11	16 15			16 21	16 25	16 28		16 39	16 44	16 58	16 49
d	15 50			15 52	15 59		15 59	16 29	16 03	16 12	16 17	16 21		16 22	16 26	16 29	16 33	16 41	16 46	16 59	16 50
West Byfleet d				15 57				→	16 07					16 27			16 37			→	
Byfleet & New Haw d									16 10								16 40				
Weybridge d							16 06		16 13							16 36	16 43				
Walton-on-Thames d							16 10		16 17							16 40	16 47				
Hersham d									16 19								16 49				
Esher d									16 22								16 52				
Surbiton ■ a				16 07			16 16		16 26					16 37		16 46	16 56				
Wimbledon ■ ⊖ a									16 34								17 04				
Earlsfield a			←						16 38				←				17 08				
Clapham Junction ■ a		16 12	16 12			16 25			16 42	16 31	16 36		16 42	16 48		16 57	17 12		17 05		
a									→								→				
Vauxhall ⊖ a			16 17										16 47								
London Waterloo ■ ⊖ a	16 19	16 20	16 22	16 25	16 23	16 34	16 36			16 40	16 49	16 49	16 52	16 57	16 51	17 05		17 07	17 13		17 19

Table 155

Basingstoke, Alton, Guildford and Woking - Waterloo

Saturdays
until 6 October

Network Diagram - see first Page of Table 155

		SW ◇1 ⌶	SW	SW 1	SW 1 ⌶	SW 1	SW 1	SW 1	SW	SW 1		SW ◇1 ⌶	SW ◇1 ⌶	SW	SW 1	SW 1 ⌶	SW 1	SW	SW 1	SW 1		SW 1	SW ◇1 ⌶	SW ◇1 ⌶	SW
Basingstoke	d	16 35				16 43		16 54				16 57							17 17			17 24	17 30	17 35	
Hook	d							17 01														17 31			
Winchfield	d							17 05														17 35			
Fleet	d					16 54		17 10														17 40			
Farnborough (Main)	d					17 00		17 16											17 30			17 46			
Alton	d			16 15											16 44										
Bentley	d														16 51										
Farnham	a			16 25											16 56										
	d			16 28											16 58										
Aldershot	d			16 34											17 04										
Ash Vale	d			16 39											17 09										
Brookwood	d			16 46				17 23							17 16							17 53			
Guildford	d				16 47					17 02						17 17				17 34					
Worplesdon	d						←										←			17 40					
Woking	a			16 51	16 57		16 58	17 28		17 11		17 15			17 21	17 25	17 28		17 39	17 44		17 58	17 49		
	d			16 52	16 59		16 59	17 29	17 03	17 12		17 17	17 21		17 22	17 26	17 29	17 33	17 41	17 46		17 59	17 50		
West Byfleet	d			16 57				→	17 07						17 27			17 37				→			
Byfleet & New Haw	d								17 10									17 40							
Weybridge	d						17 06		17 13								17 36	17 43							
Walton-on-Thames	d						17 10		17 17								17 40	17 47							
Hersham	d								17 19									17 49							
Esher	d								17 22									17 52							
Surbiton 6	a			17 07			17 16		17 26						17 37		17 46	17 56							
Wimbledon 6 ⊖	a								17 34									18 04							
Earlsfield	a		←						17 38					←				18 08							←
Clapham Junction 10	a	17 12	17 12			17 25			17 42	17 31		17 36		17 42	17 48		17 57	18 12		18 05				18 12	18 12
	a								→									→							
Vauxhall ⊖	a		17 17											17 47											18 17
London Waterloo 15 ⊖	a	17 20	17 22	17 25	17 23	17 34	17 36			17 40		17 49	17 49	17 52	17 57	17 51	18 05		18 07	18 13			18 19	18 20	18 22

		SW 1	SW 1 ⌶	SW 1	SW 1	SW 1		SW	SW 1	SW ◇1 ⌶	SW ◇1 ⌶	SW	SW 1	SW 1	SW 1	SW		SW 1	SW 1	SW 1	SW ◇1 ⌶	SW ◇1 ⌶	SW	SW 1	SW 1 ⌶
Basingstoke	d			17 43		17 54				17 57								18 17		18 24	18 30	18 35			
Hook	d					18 01														18 31					
Winchfield	d					18 05														18 35					
Fleet	d			17 54		18 10														18 40					
Farnborough (Main)	d			18 00		18 16												18 30		18 46					
Alton	d	17 15											17 44											18 15	
Bentley	d												17 51												
Farnham	a	17 25											17 56											18 25	
	d	17 28											17 58											18 28	
Aldershot	d	17 34											18 04											18 34	
Ash Vale	d	17 39											18 09											18 39	
Brookwood	d	17 46				18 23							18 16							18 53				18 46	
Guildford	d		17 47						18 02					18 17					18 34						18 47
Worplesdon	d				←										←				18 40						
Woking	a	17 51	17 57		17 58	18 28			18 11	18 15			18 21	18 25	18 28			18 39	18 44	18 58	18 49			18 51	18 57
	d	17 52	17 59		17 59	18 29		18 03	18 12	18 17	18 21		18 22	18 26	18 29	18 33		18 41	18 46	18 59	18 50			18 52	18 59
West Byfleet	d	17 57				→		18 07					18 27			18 37				→				18 57	
Byfleet & New Haw	d							18 10								18 40									
Weybridge	d				18 06			18 13							18 36	18 43									
Walton-on-Thames	d				18 10			18 17							18 40	18 47									
Hersham	d							18 19								18 49									
Esher	d							18 22								18 52									
Surbiton 6	a	18 07			18 16			18 26					18 37		18 46	18 56								19 07	
Wimbledon 6 ⊖	a							18 34								19 04									
Earlsfield	a							18 38				←				19 08							←		
Clapham Junction 10	a			18 25				18 42	18 31	18 36		18 42	18 48		18 57	19 12			19 05			19 12	19 12		
	a							→								→									
Vauxhall ⊖	a											18 47											19 17		
London Waterloo 15 ⊖	a	18 25	18 23	18 34	18 36				18 40	18 49	18 49	18 52	18 57	18 51	19 05			19 07	19 13		19 19	19 20	19 22	19 25	19 23

Table 155

Basingstoke, Alton, Guildford and Woking - Waterloo

Saturdays
until 6 October

Network Diagram - see first Page of Table 155

		SW 1		SW 1	SW 1	SW	SW 1	SW ◇1 ⌶	SW ◇1 ⌶	SW	SW 1	SW 1		SW 1	SW	SW 1	SW 1	SW 1	SW ◇1 ⌶	SW ◇1 ⌶	SW	SW 1		SW 1	SW 1
Basingstoke	d	18 43			18 54			18 57								19 17		19 24	19 30	19 35					19 43
Hook	d				19 01													19 31							
Winchfield	d				19 05													19 35							
Fleet	d	18 54			19 10													19 40							19 54
Farnborough (Main)	d	19 00			19 16											19 30		19 46							20 00
Alton	d										18 44											19 15			
Bentley	d										18 51														
Farnham	a										18 56											19 25			
	d										18 58											19 28			
Aldershot	d										19 04											19 34			
Ash Vale	d										19 09											19 39			
Brookwood	d				19 23						19 16							19 53				19 46			
Guildford	d						19 02					19 17					19 34							19 47	
Worplesdon	d			←										←			19 40								
Woking	a			18 58	19 28		19 11	19 15			19 21	19 25		19 28		19 39	19 44	19 58	19 49			19 51		19 57	
	d			18 59	19 29	19 03	19 12	19 17	19 21		19 22	19 26		19 29	19 33	19 41	19 46	19 59	19 50			19 52		19 59	
West Byfleet	d				→	19 07					19 27				19 37			→				19 57			
Byfleet & New Haw	d					19 10									19 40										
Weybridge	d			19 06		19 13								19 36	19 43										
Walton-on-Thames	d			19 10		19 17								19 40	19 47										
Hersham	d					19 19									19 49										
Esher	d					19 22									19 52										
Surbiton 6	a			19 16		19 26					19 37			19 46	19 56							20 07			
Wimbledon 6 ⊖	a					19 34									20 04										
Earlsfield	a					19 38				←					20 08						←				
Clapham Junction 10	a	19 25				19 42	19 31	19 36		19 42	19 48			19 57	20 12		20 05			20 12	20 12				20 25
	a					→									→										
Vauxhall ⊖	a									19 47											20 17				
London Waterloo 15 ⊖	a	19 34		19 36			19 40	19 49	19 49	19 52	19 57	19 51		20 05		20 07	20 13		20 19	20 20	20 22	20 25		20 23	20 34

		SW 1	SW	SW 1	SW ◇1 ⌶	SW	SW 1	SW 1		SW 1	SW ◇1 ⌶	SW 1	SW	SW 1	SW 1	SW 1	SW 1	SW ◇1 ⌶		SW 1	SW	SW 1	SW ◇1 ⌶	SW	SW 1
Basingstoke	d									19 54	20 09			20 17			20 24	20 35				20 43			
Hook	d									20 01							20 31								
Winchfield	d									20 05							20 35								
Fleet	d									20 10							20 40					20 54			
Farnborough (Main)	d									20 16				20 30			20 46					21 00			
Alton	d						19 44								20 15										20 44
Bentley	d						19 51																		20 51
Farnham	a						19 56								20 25										20 56
	d						19 58								20 28										20 58
Aldershot	d						20 04								20 34										21 04
Ash Vale	d						20 09								20 39										21 09
Brookwood	d						20 16			20 23					20 46		20 53								21 16
Guildford	d			20 02				20 17								20 39				20 47					
Worplesdon	d	←														20 44									
Woking	a	19 58		20 11			20 21	20 25		20 28	20 29			20 39	20 51	20 52	20 58			20 57		21 09			21 21
	d	19 59	20 03	20 12	20 21		20 22	20 26		20 29	20 30		20 33	20 41	20 52	20 53	20 59			20 59	21 03	21 10	21 21		21 22
West Byfleet	d		20 07				20 27						20 37		20 57						21 07				21 27
Byfleet & New Haw	d		20 10										20 40								21 10				
Weybridge	d	20 06	20 13							20 36			20 43				21 06				21 13				
Walton-on-Thames	d	20 10	20 17							20 40			20 47				21 10				21 17				
Hersham	d		20 19										20 49								21 19				
Esher	d		20 22										20 52								21 22				
Surbiton 6	a	20 16	20 26				20 37			20 46			20 56		21 07		21 16				21 26				21 37
Wimbledon 6 ⊖	a		20 34										21 04								21 34				
Earlsfield	a		20 38			←						←	21 08								21 38			←	
Clapham Junction 10	a		20 42	20 31		20 42	20 48			20 57	20 52	20 57	21 12			21 12		21 16			21 42	21 29		21 42	21 48
	a		→							→											→				
Vauxhall ⊖	a					20 47							21 17											21 47	
London Waterloo 15 ⊖	a	20 36		20 40	20 49	20 52	20 57	20 50			21 04	21 05	21 23	21 07	21 29	21 21	21 34	21 24		21 27		21 38	21 49	21 52	21 57

Table 155

Saturdays until 6 October

Basingstoke, Alton, Guildford and Woking - Waterloo

Network Diagram - see first Page of Table 155

		SW 1	SW 1	SW ◇1	SW 1	SW	SW 1	SW	SW 1	SW 1	SW ◇1	SW 1	SW	SW 1	SW 1	SW	SW 1	SW 1	SW ◇1	SW 1	SW 1	SW
Basingstoke	d		20 54	21 09						21 24	21 35			21 43				21 54	22 09			
Hook	d		21 01							21 31								22 01				
Winchfield	d		21 05							21 35								22 05				
Fleet	d		21 10							21 40				21 54				22 10				
Farnborough (Main)	d		21 16							21 46				22 00				22 16				
Alton	d								21 15								21 44					
Bentley	d																21 51					
Farnham	a								21 25								21 56					
	d								21 28								21 58					
Aldershot	d								21 34								22 04					
Ash Vale	d								21 39								22 09					
Brookwood	d		21 23						21 46	21 53							22 16	22 23				
Guildford	d	21 17					21 39					21 49										22 20
Worplesdon	d						21 44															
Woking	a	21 25	21 28	21 29			21 49		21 51	21 58		21 57		22 09			22 21	22 28	22 28			22 32
	d	21 26	21 29	21 30		21 33	21 50		21 52	21 59		21 59	22 03	22 10	22 21		22 22	22 29	22 29			22 33
West Byfleet	d					21 37			21 57				22 07				22 27					22 37
Byfleet & New Haw	d					21 40							22 10									22 40
Weybridge	d		21 36			21 43				22 06			22 13					22 36				22 43
Walton-on-Thames	d		21 40			21 47				22 10			22 17					22 40				22 47
Hersham	d					21 49							22 19									22 49
Esher	d					21 52							22 22									22 52
Surbiton 6	a		21 46			21 56			22 07	22 16			22 26				22 37	22 46				22 56
Wimbledon 6 ⊖	a					22 04							22 34									23 04
Earlsfield	a				←	22 08		←					22 38			←				←	←	23 08
Clapham Junction 10	a		21 57	21 52	21 57	22 12	22 09	22 12			22 14		22 42	22 29		22 42	22 52	22 57	22 48	22 52	22 57	23 12
	a		→			→							→				→	→				→
Vauxhall ⊖	a							22 17								22 47						
London Waterloo 15 ⊖	a	21 50		22 04	22 07		22 18	22 22	22 27	22 34	22 22	22 24		22 38	22 49	22 52			22 57	23 01	23 05	

		SW 1	SW	SW 1	SW 1	SW ◇1	SW 1	SW	SW 1	SW	SW 1	SW 1	SW 1	SW 1	SW 1	SW 1	SW 1	SW 1
Basingstoke	d				22 24	22 35			22 43			22 54	23 13				23 44	
Hook	d				22 31							23 01					23 51	
Winchfield	d				22 35							23 05					23 55	
Fleet	d				22 40				22 54			23 10					00 01	
Farnborough (Main)	d				22 46				23 00			23 16					00 06	
Alton	d			22 15							22 44				23 15			23 46
Bentley	d										22 51							23 53
Farnham	a			22 25							22 56				23 25			23 58
	d			22 28							22 58				23 28			
Aldershot	d			22 34							23 04				23 34			
Ash Vale	d			22 39							23 09				23 39			
Brookwood	d			22 46	22 53						23 16	23 23			23 46		00 13	
Guildford	d	22 39						22 55								23 39		
Worplesdon	d	22 44					←							←		23 44		
Woking	a	22 49		22 51	22 58	22 53	22 58	23 05	23 09		23 21	23 28	23 31	23 28	23 51	23 49	00 18	
	d	22 50		22 52	22 59	22 55	22 59	23 06	23 10		23 22	23 33	23 32	23 33		23 56	00 20	
West Byfleet	d			22 57	→			23 10			23 27	→		23 37			00 25	
Byfleet & New Haw	d							23 13						23 40				
Weybridge	d						23 06	23 16						23 43			00 29	
Walton-on-Thames	d						23 10	23 20						23 47			00 33	
Hersham	d							23 22						23 49				
Esher	d							23 25						23 52				
Surbiton 6	a			23 07			23 16	23 29			23 37			23 57			00 39	
Wimbledon 6 ⊖	a							23 37						00 06			00 47	
Earlsfield	a		←					23 41		←								
Clapham Junction 10	a	23 09	23 12			23 14		23 44	23 29	23 44	23 48		23 52			00 18	00 53	
	a							→						00 21				
Vauxhall ⊖	a		23 17							23 49				00 30				
London Waterloo 15 ⊖	a	23 18	23 22	23 28		23 22	23 32		23 39	23 54	00 01		00 03	00 35		00 32	01 04	

Table 155

Saturdays from 13 October

Basingstoke, Alton, Guildford and Woking - Waterloo

Network Diagram - see first Page of Table 155

		SW 1	SW 1	SW 1	SW 1	SW 1	SW 1	SW	SW	SW 1	SW	SW 1	SW	SW 1	SW ◇1	SW	SW 1	SW 1	SW	SW 1	SW ◇1	SW	SW 1
Basingstoke	d		22p54	23p13			23p44			04 54		05 54			05 59			06 24			06 30		
Hook	d		23p01				23p51			05 01		06 01						06 31					
Winchfield	d		23p05				23p55			05 05		06 05						06 35					
Fleet	d		23p10				00 01			05 10		06 10						06 40					
Farnborough (Main)	d		23p16				00 06			05 16		06 16						06 46					
Alton	d	22p44																					06 14
Bentley	d	22p51																					06 21
Farnham	a	22p56																					06 26
	d	22p58																					06 28
Aldershot	d	23p04																					06 34
Ash Vale	d	23p09																					06 39
Brookwood	d	23p16	23p23				00 13			05 23		06 23						06 53					06 46
Guildford	d					23p39		04 00			05 14			06 02						06 34			
Worplesdon	d				←	23p44					05 19						←			06 40			
Woking	a	23p21	23p28	23p31	23p28	23p49	00 18	04 08		05 28	05 24	06 28		06 11	06 18		06 28	06 58		06 44	06 49		06 51
	d	23p22	23p33	23p32	23p33	23p56	00 20	04 10	05 27	05 29	05 33	06 29	06 03	06 13	06 19		06 29	06 59	06 33	06 46	06 50		06 52
West Byfleet	d	23p27	→		23p37		00 25		05 32		05 37	→	06 07					→	06 37				06 57
Byfleet & New Haw	d				23p40				05 35		05 40		06 10						06 40				
Weybridge	d				23p43		00 29				05 43		06 13				06 36		06 43				
Walton-on-Thames	d				23p47		00 33				05 47		06 17				06 40		06 47				
Hersham	d				23p49						05 49		06 19						06 49				
Esher	d				23p52						05 52		06 22						06 52				
Surbiton 6	a	23p37			23p57		00 39	04 24		05 40	05 56		06 26				06 46		06 56				07 07
Wimbledon 6 ⊖	a				00 06		00 47	04 31		05 48	06 04		06 34						07 04				
Earlsfield	a										06 08		06 38			←			07 08			←	
Clapham Junction 10	a	23p51		23p55		00 19	00 53	04 43			06 12		06 42	06 32	06 38	06 42	06 57		07 12	07 05		07 12	07 18
	a				00 21				06 43	06 00			→						→				
Vauxhall ⊖	a				00 30				06 49	06 07	06 17					06 47						07 17	
London Waterloo 15 ⊖	a	00 02		00 09	00 35	00 32	01 04	04 53	06 56	06 15	06 22			06 40	06 49	06 52	07 08			07 13	07 19	07 22	07 30

		SW 1	SW 1	SW 1	SW	SW 1	SW ◇1	SW	SW 1	SW ◇1	SW 1	SW 1	SW	SW 1	SW ◇1	SW	SW 1	SW 1	SW 1	SW	SW 1	SW 1	SW 1
Basingstoke	d	06 40		06 54			06 57			07 09		07 24			07 30						07 43		07 54
Hook	d			07 01								07 31											08 01
Winchfield	d			07 05								07 35											08 05
Fleet	d			07 10								07 40									07 54		08 10
Farnborough (Main)	d			07 16								07 46									08 00		08 16
Alton	d								06 44								07 14						
Bentley	d								06 51								07 21						
Farnham	a								06 56								07 26						
	d								06 58								07 28						
Aldershot	d								07 04								07 34						
Ash Vale	d								07 09								07 39						
Brookwood	d			07 23					07 16			07 53					07 46						08 23
Guildford	d					07 02								07 34				07 47				08 02	
Worplesdon	d		←								←			07 40					←				
Woking	a	06 58	06 58	07 28		07 11	07 15		07 21	07 27	07 28	07 58		07 44	07 49		07 51	07 57	07 58		08 09	08 10	08 28
	d	07 00	06 59	07 29	07 03	07 12	07 17		07 22	07 29	07 29	07 59	07 33	07 46	07 50		07 52	07 59	07 59	08 03	08 11	08 13	08 29
West Byfleet	d			→	07 07				07 27			→	07 37				07 57			08 07			→
Byfleet & New Haw	d				07 10								07 40							08 10			
Weybridge	d		07 06		07 13						07 36		07 43						08 06	08 13			
Walton-on-Thames	d		07 10		07 17						07 40		07 47						08 10	08 17			
Hersham	d				07 19								07 49							08 19			
Esher	d				07 22								07 52							08 22			
Surbiton 6	a		07 16		07 26				07 37		07 46		07 56				08 07		08 16	08 26			
Wimbledon 6 ⊖	a				07 34								08 04							08 34			
Earlsfield	a				07 38			←					08 08			←				08 38			
Clapham Junction 10	a	07 23			07 42	07 31	07 36	07 42	07 50		07 57		08 12	08 05		08 12				08 42	08 30	08 33	
	a				→								→							→			
Vauxhall ⊖	a							07 47								08 17							
London Waterloo 15 ⊖	a	07 31	07 33			07 40	07 49	07 52	07 58	07 53	08 05			08 13	08 19	08 22	08 25	08 23	08 34		08 39	08 42	

Table 155

Saturdays
from 13 October

Basingstoke, Alton, Guildford and Woking - Waterloo

Network Diagram - see first Page of Table 155

		SW ◇1 ⌶		SW	SW 1	SW ◇1 ⌶	SW 1 ⌶	SW 1	SW	SW 1	SW 1	SW 1		SW ◇1 ⌶	SW ◇1 ⌶	SW	SW 1	SW 1 ⌶	SW 1	SW 1	SW 1	SW		SW 1	SW ◇1 ⌶
Basingstoke	d	07 57								08 17		08 24		08 30	08 35				08 43		08 54				08 57
Hook	d											08 31									09 01				
Winchfield	d											08 35									09 05				
Fleet	d											08 40							08 54		09 10				
Farnborough (Main)	d									08 30		08 46							09 00		09 16				
Alton	d				07 44												08 14								
Bentley	d				07 51												08 21								
Farnham	a				07 56												08 26								
	d				07 58												08 28								
Aldershot	d				08 04												08 34								
Ash Vale	d				08 09												08 39								
Brookwood	d				08 16							08 53					08 46				09 23				
Guildford	d						08 17				08 34							08 47						09 02	
Worplesdon	d							←			08 40									←					
Woking	a	08 17			08 21		08 26	08 28		08 39	08 44	08 58		08 49			08 51	08 57		08 58	09 28			09 11	09 15
	d	08 18			08 22	08 23	08 27	08 29	08 33	08 41	08 46	08 59		08 50			08 52	08 59		08 59	09 29	09 03		09 12	09 17
West Byfleet	d				08 27				08 37			→					08 57				→	09 07			
Byfleet & New Haw	d								08 40													09 10			
Weybridge	d							08 36	08 43											09 06		09 13			
Walton-on-Thames	d							08 40	08 47											09 10		09 17			
Hersham	d								08 49													09 19			
Esher	d								08 52													09 22			
Surbiton 6	a				08 37			08 46	08 56								09 07			09 16		09 26			
Wimbledon 6 ⊖	a								09 04													09 34			
Earlsfield	a			←					09 08							←						09 38			
Clapham Junction 10	a	08 37		08 42	08 49			08 57	09 12		09 05				09 12	09 12			09 25			09 42		09 31	09 36
	a								→													→			
Vauxhall ⊖	a			08 47												09 17									
London Waterloo 15 ⊖	a	08 49		08 52	08 58	08 49	08 51	09 05		09 08	09 13			09 19	09 20	09 22	09 25	09 23	09 34	09 36				09 40	09 49

		SW ◇1 ⌶	SW	SW 1	SW 1 ⌶	SW 1	SW	SW 1		SW 1	SW 1	SW ◇1 ⌶	SW ◇1 ⌶	SW	SW 1	SW 1 ⌶	SW 1	SW 1		SW 1	SW	SW 1	SW ◇1 ⌶	SW ◇1 ⌶	SW
Basingstoke	d							09 17			09 24	09 30	09 35				09 43			09 54			09 57		
Hook	d										09 31									10 01					
Winchfield	d										09 35									10 05					
Fleet	d										09 40						09 54			10 10					
Farnborough (Main)	d							09 30			09 46						10 00			10 16					
Alton	d			08 44											09 14										
Bentley	d			08 51											09 21										
Farnham	a			08 56											09 26										
	d			08 58											09 28										
Aldershot	d			09 04											09 34										
Ash Vale	d			09 09											09 39										
Brookwood	d			09 16							09 53				09 46					10 23					
Guildford	d				09 17					09 34						09 47						10 02			
Worplesdon	d					←				09 40								←							
Woking	a			09 21	09 25	09 28		09 39		09 44	09 58	09 49			09 51	09 57		09 58		10 28		10 11	10 15		
	d	09 21		09 22	09 26	09 29	09 33	09 41		09 46	09 59	09 50			09 52	09 59		09 59		10 29	10 03	10 12	10 17	10 21	
West Byfleet	d			09 27			09 37				→				09 57					→	10 07				
Byfleet & New Haw	d						09 40														10 10				
Weybridge	d					09 36	09 43											10 06			10 13				
Walton-on-Thames	d					09 40	09 47											10 10			10 17				
Hersham	d						09 49														10 19				
Esher	d						09 52														10 22				
Surbiton 6	a			09 37		09 46	09 56								10 07			10 16			10 26				
Wimbledon 6 ⊖	a						10 04														10 34				
Earlsfield	a		←				10 08							←							10 38				←
Clapham Junction 10	a		09 42	09 48		09 57	10 12			10 05			10 12	10 12			10 25				10 42	10 31	10 36		10 42
	a						→														→				
Vauxhall ⊖	a		09 47											10 17											10 47
London Waterloo 15 ⊖	a	09 49	09 52	09 57	09 51	10 05		10 07		10 13		10 19	10 20	10 22	10 25	10 23	10 34	10 36				10 40	10 49	10 49	10 52

Table 155

Saturdays
from 13 October

Basingstoke, Alton, Guildford and Woking - Waterloo

Network Diagram - see first Page of Table 155

		SW 1	SW 1 ⌶	SW 1		SW	SW 1	SW 1	SW 1	SW ◇1 ⌶	SW ◇1 ⌶	SW	SW 1	SW 1 ⌶		SW 1	SW 1	SW 1	SW	SW 1	SW ◇1 ⌶	SW ◇1 ⌶	SW	SW 1	
Basingstoke	d						10 17		10 24	10 30	10 35					10 43		10 54			10 57				
Hook	d								10 31									11 01							
Winchfield	d								10 35									11 05							
Fleet	d								10 40							10 54		11 10							
Farnborough (Main)	d						10 30		10 46							11 00		11 16							
Alton	d	09 44											10 14											10 44	
Bentley	d	09 51											10 21											10 51	
Farnham	a	09 56											10 26											10 56	
	d	09 58											10 28											10 58	
Aldershot	d	10 04											10 34											11 04	
Ash Vale	d	10 09											10 39											11 09	
Brookwood	d	10 16							10 53				10 46					11 23						11 16	
Guildford	d		10 17					10 34						10 47						11 02					
Worplesdon	d			←				10 40									←								
Woking	a	10 21	10 25	10 28			10 39	10 44	10 58	10 49			10 51	10 57			10 58	11 28		11 11	11 15			11 21	
	d	10 22	10 26	10 29		10 33	10 41	10 46	10 59	10 50			10 52	10 59			10 59	11 29	11 03	11 12	11 17	11 21		11 22	
West Byfleet	d	10 27				10 37			→				10 57					→	11 07					11 27	
Byfleet & New Haw	d					10 40													11 10						
Weybridge	d			10 36		10 43											11 06		11 13						
Walton-on-Thames	d			10 40		10 47											11 10		11 17						
Hersham	d					10 49													11 19						
Esher	d					10 52													11 22						
Surbiton 6	a	10 37		10 46		10 56							11 07				11 16		11 26					11 37	
Wimbledon 6 ⊖	a					11 04													11 34						
Earlsfield	a					11 08						←							11 38				←		
Clapham Junction 10	a	10 48		10 57		11 12		11 05			11 12	11 12				11 25			11 42	11 31	11 36		11 42	11 48	
	a					→													→						
Vauxhall ⊖	a											11 17											11 47		
London Waterloo 15 ⊖	a	10 57	10 51	11 05			11 07	11 13		11 19	11 20	11 22	11 25	11 23		11 34	11 36			11 40	11 49	11 49	11 52	11 57	

		SW 1 ⌶	SW 1	SW	SW 1	SW 1	SW 1	SW ◇1 ⌶	SW ◇1 ⌶	SW		SW 1	SW 1 ⌶	SW 1	SW 1	SW 1	SW	SW 1	SW ◇1 ⌶	SW ◇1 ⌶		SW	SW 1	SW 1 ⌶	SW 1
Basingstoke	d				11 17		11 24	11 30	11 35					11 43		11 54			11 57						
Hook	d						11 31									12 01									
Winchfield	d						11 35									12 05									
Fleet	d						11 40							11 54		12 10									
Farnborough (Main)	d				11 30		11 46							12 00		12 16									
Alton	d											11 15											11 44		
Bentley	d																						11 51		
Farnham	a											11 25											11 56		
	d											11 28											11 58		
Aldershot	d											11 34											12 04		
Ash Vale	d											11 39											12 09		
Brookwood	d						11 53					11 46				12 23							12 16		
Guildford	d	11 17				11 34							11 47					12 02						12 17	
Worplesdon	d		←			11 40									←										←
Woking	a	11 25	11 28		11 39	11 44	11 58	11 49				11 51	11 57		11 58	12 28		12 11	12 15				12 21	12 25	12 28
	d	11 26	11 29	11 33	11 41	11 46	11 59	11 50				11 52	11 59		11 59	12 29	12 03	12 12	12 17	12 21			12 22	12 26	12 29
West Byfleet	d			11 37			→					11 57				→	12 07						12 27		
Byfleet & New Haw	d			11 40													12 10								
Weybridge	d		11 36	11 43											12 06		12 13								12 36
Walton-on-Thames	d		11 40	11 47											12 10		12 17								12 40
Hersham	d			11 49													12 19								
Esher	d			11 52													12 22								
Surbiton 6	a		11 46	11 56								12 07			12 16		12 26						12 37		12 46
Wimbledon 6 ⊖	a			12 04													12 34								
Earlsfield	a			12 08						←							12 38					←			
Clapham Junction 10	a		11 57	12 12		12 05			12 12	12 12				12 25			12 42	12 31	12 36			12 42	12 48		12 57
	a			→													→								
Vauxhall ⊖	a									12 17												12 47			
London Waterloo 15 ⊖	a	11 51	12 05		12 07	12 13		12 19	12 21	12 22		12 29	12 27	12 34	12 36			12 43	12 49	12 51		12 52	12 59	12 57	13 05

Saturdays

from 13 October

Basingstoke, Alton, Guildford and Woking - Waterloo

Network Diagram - see first Page of Table 155

		SW	SW ■1	SW ■1	SW ■1	SW ◇■1 ✠		SW ◇■1 ✠	SW	SW ■1	SW ■1 ✠	SW ■1	SW ■1	SW ■1	SW	SW ■1		SW ◇■1 ✠	SW ◇■1 ✠	SW	SW ■1	SW ■1 ✠	SW ■1	SW	SW ■1
Basingstoke	d		12 17		12 24	12 30		12 35				12 43		12 54				12 57							13 17
Hook	d				12 31									13 01											
Winchfield	d				12 35									13 05											
Fleet	d				12 40							12 54		13 10											
Farnborough (Main)	d		12 30		12 46							13 00		13 16											13 30
Alton	d									12 15											12 44				
Bentley	d																				12 51				
Farnham	a									12 25											12 56				
	d									12 28											12 58				
Aldershot	d									12 34											13 04				
Ash Vale	d									12 39											13 09				
Brookwood	d				12 53					12 46				13 23							13 16				
Guildford	d			12 34							12 47					13 02						13 17			
Worplesdon	d			12 40									←										←		
Woking	a		12 39	12 44	12 58	12 49				12 51	12 57		12 58	13 28		13 11		13 15			13 21	13 25	13 28		13 39
	d	12 33	12 41	12 46	12 59	12 50				12 52	12 59		12 59	13 29	13 03	13 12		13 17	13 21		13 22	13 26	13 29	13 33	13 41
West Byfleet	d	12 37			→					12 57				→	13 07						13 27			13 37	
Byfleet & New Haw	d	12 40													13 10									13 40	
Weybridge	d	12 43											13 06		13 13								13 36	13 43	
Walton-on-Thames	d	12 47											13 10		13 17								13 40	13 47	
Hersham	d	12 49													13 19									13 49	
Esher	d	12 52													13 22									13 52	
Surbiton ■6	a	12 56								13 07			13 16		13 26						13 37		13 46	13 56	
Wimbledon ■6 ⊖	a	13 04													13 34									14 04	
Earlsfield	a	13 08							←						13 38					←				14 08	
Clapham Junction ■10	a	13 12		13 05				13 12	13 12			13 25			13 42	13 31		13 36		13 42	13 48		13 57	14 12	
	a	→													→									→	
Vauxhall ⊖	a								13 17											13 47					
London Waterloo ■15 ⊖	a		13 07	13 13		13 19		13 21	13 22	13 29	13 27	13 34	13 36			13 43		13 49	13 51	13 52	13 59	13 57	14 05		14 07

		SW ■1		SW ■1	SW ◇■1 ✠	SW ◇■1 ✠	SW	SW ■1	SW ■1 ✠	SW ■1	SW ■1	SW ■1		SW	SW ■1	SW ◇■1 ✠	SW ◇■1 ✠	SW	SW ■1	SW ■1 ✠	SW ■1	SW		SW ■1	SW ■1
Basingstoke	d			13 24	13 30	13 35				13 43		13 54				13 57								14 17	
Hook	d			13 31								14 01													
Winchfield	d			13 35								14 05													
Fleet	d			13 40						13 54		14 10													
Farnborough (Main)	d			13 46						14 00		14 16												14 30	
Alton	d							13 15											13 44						
Bentley	d																		13 51						
Farnham	a							13 25											13 56						
	d							13 28											13 58						
Aldershot	d							13 34											14 04						
Ash Vale	d							13 39											14 09						
Brookwood	d			13 53				13 46				14 23							14 16						
Guildford	d	13 34							13 47						14 02					14 17					14 34
Worplesdon	d	13 40									←										←				14 40
Woking	a	13 44		13 58	13 49			13 51	13 57		13 58	14 28			14 11	14 15			14 21	14 25	14 28			14 39	14 44
	d	13 46		13 59	13 50			13 52	13 59		13 59	14 29		14 03	14 12	14 17	14 21		14 22	14 26	14 29	14 33		14 41	14 46
West Byfleet	d			→				13 57				→		14 07					14 27			14 37			
Byfleet & New Haw	d													14 10								14 40			
Weybridge	d										14 06			14 13							14 36	14 43			
Walton-on-Thames	d										14 10			14 17							14 40	14 47			
Hersham	d													14 19								14 49			
Esher	d													14 22								14 52			
Surbiton ■6	a							14 07			14 16			14 26					14 37		14 46	14 56			
Wimbledon ■6 ⊖	a													14 34								15 04			
Earlsfield	a						←							14 38				←				15 08			
Clapham Junction ■10	a	14 05				14 12	14 12			14 25				14 42	14 31	14 36		14 42	14 48		14 57	15 12			15 05
	a													→								→			
Vauxhall ⊖	a						14 17											14 47							
London Waterloo ■15 ⊖	a	14 14			14 19	14 21	14 22	14 29	14 27	14 34	14 36				14 41	14 49	14 51	14 52	14 59	14 57	15 05			15 07	15 14

Table 155

Saturdays

from 13 October

Basingstoke, Alton, Guildford and Woking - Waterloo

Network Diagram - see first Page of Table 155

		SW ■1	SW ◇■1 ✠	SW ◇■1 ✠	SW	SW ■1	SW ■1 ✠	SW ■1		SW ■1	SW ■1	SW	SW ■1	SW ◇■1 ✠	SW ◇■1 ✠	SW	SW ■1	SW ■1 ✠		SW ■1	SW	SW ■1	SW ■1	SW ■1	SW ◇■1 ✠
Basingstoke	d	14 24	14 30	14 35				14 43			14 54			14 57								15 17		15 24	15 30
Hook	d	14 31									15 01													15 31	
Winchfield	d	14 35									15 05													15 35	
Fleet	d	14 40						14 54			15 10													15 40	
Farnborough (Main)	d	14 46						15 00			15 16											15 30		15 46	
Alton	d					14 15											14 44								
Bentley	d																14 51								
Farnham	a					14 25											14 56								
	d					14 28											14 58								
Aldershot	d					14 34											15 04								
Ash Vale	d					14 39											15 09								
Brookwood	d	14 53				14 46					15 23						15 16							15 53	
Guildford	d						14 47						15 02					15 17					15 34		
Worplesdon	d									←										←			15 40		
Woking	a	14 58	14 49			14 51	14 57			14 58	15 28		15 11	15 15			15 21	15 25		15 28		15 39	15 44	15 58	15 49
	d	14 59	14 50			14 52	14 59			14 59	15 29	15 03	15 12	15 17	15 21		15 22	15 26		15 29	15 33	15 41	15 46	15 59	15 50
West Byfleet	d	→				14 57					→	15 07					15 27				15 37			→	
Byfleet & New Haw	d											15 10									15 40				
Weybridge	d									15 06		15 13								15 36	15 43				
Walton-on-Thames	d									15 10		15 17								15 40	15 47				
Hersham	d											15 19									15 49				
Esher	d											15 22									15 52				
Surbiton ■6	a					15 07				15 16		15 26					15 37			15 46	15 56				
Wimbledon ■6 ⊖	a											15 34									16 04				
Earlsfield	a				←							15 38				←					16 08				
Clapham Junction ■10	a			15 12	15 12			15 25				15 42	15 31	15 36		15 42	15 48			15 57	16 12		16 05		
	a											→									→				
Vauxhall ⊖	a				15 17											15 47									
London Waterloo ■15 ⊖	a		15 19	15 21	15 22	15 29	15 27	15 34		15 36			15 41	15 49	15 51	15 52	15 59	15 57		16 05		16 07	16 13		16 19

		SW ◇■1 ✠	SW	SW ■1		SW ■1 ✠	SW ■1	SW ■1	SW ■1	SW	SW ■1	SW ◇■1 ✠	SW ◇■1 ✠	SW		SW ■1	SW ■1 ✠	SW ■1	SW	SW ■1	SW ■1	SW ■1	SW ◇■1 ✠	SW ◇■1 ✠	
Basingstoke	d	15 35					15 43		15 54			15 57								16 17		16 24	16 30	16 35	
Hook	d								16 01													16 31			
Winchfield	d								16 05													16 35			
Fleet	d						15 54		16 10													16 40			
Farnborough (Main)	d						16 00		16 16											16 30		16 46			
Alton	d			15 15												15 44									
Bentley	d															15 51									
Farnham	a			15 25												15 56									
	d			15 28												15 58									
Aldershot	d			15 34												16 04									
Ash Vale	d			15 39												16 09									
Brookwood	d			15 46					16 23							16 16						16 53			
Guildford	d					15 47					16 02						16 17				16 34				
Worplesdon	d							←										←			16 40				
Woking	a			15 51		15 57		15 58	16 28		16 11	16 15				16 21	16 25	16 28		16 39	16 44	16 58	16 49		
	d			15 52		15 59		15 59	16 29	16 03	16 12	16 17	16 21			16 22	16 26	16 29	16 33	16 41	16 46	16 59	16 50		
West Byfleet	d			15 57					→	16 07						16 27			16 37			→			
Byfleet & New Haw	d									16 10									16 40						
Weybridge	d							16 06		16 13								16 36	16 43						
Walton-on-Thames	d							16 10		16 17								16 40	16 47						
Hersham	d									16 19									16 49						
Esher	d									16 22									16 52						
Surbiton ■6	a			16 07				16 16		16 26						16 37		16 46	16 56						
Wimbledon ■6 ⊖	a									16 34									17 04						
Earlsfield	a		←							16 38				←					17 08						
Clapham Junction ■10	a	16 12	16 12				16 25			16 42	16 31	16 36		16 42		16 48		16 57	17 12		17 05			17 12	
	a									→									→						
Vauxhall ⊖	a		16 17											16 47											
London Waterloo ■15 ⊖	a	16 20	16 22	16 25		16 23	16 34	16 36			16 40	16 49	16 49	16 52		16 57	16 51	17 05		17 07	17 13		17 19	17 20	

Table 155

Saturdays
from 13 October

Basingstoke, Alton, Guildford and Woking - Waterloo

Network Diagram - see first Page of Table 155

Station		SW	SW 1	SW 1 ⚒	SW 1	SW 1	SW 1	SW	SW 1	SW ◇1 ⚒		SW ◇1 ⚒	SW	SW 1	SW 1 ⚒	SW 1	SW	SW 1	SW 1	SW 1		SW ◇1 ⚒	SW ◇1 ⚒	SW	SW 1
Basingstoke	d				16 43		16 54			16 57								17 17		17 24		17 30	17 35		
Hook	d						17 01													17 31					
Winchfield	d						17 05													17 35					
Fleet	d				16 54		17 10													17 40					
Farnborough (Main)	d				17 00		17 16											17 30		17 46					
Alton	d		16 15											16 44											17 15
Bentley	d													16 51											
Farnham	a		16 25											16 56											17 25
	d		16 28											16 58											17 28
Aldershot	d		16 34											17 04											17 34
Ash Vale	d		16 39											17 09											17 39
Brookwood	d		16 46				17 23							17 16						17 53					17 46
Guildford	d			16 47					17 02						17 17				17 34						
Worplesdon	d					←										←			17 40						
Woking	a		16 51	16 57		16 58	17 28		17 11	17 15				17 21	17 25	17 28		17 39	17 44	17 58		17 49			17 51
	d		16 52	16 59		16 59	17 29	17 03	17 12	17 17		17 21		17 22	17 26	17 29	17 33	17 41	17 46	17 59		17 50			17 52
West Byfleet	d		16 57				→	17 07						17 27			17 37			→					17 57
Byfleet & New Haw	d							17 10									17 40								
Weybridge	d					17 06		17 13								17 36	17 43								
Walton-on-Thames	d					17 10		17 17								17 40	17 47								
Hersham	d							17 19									17 49								
Esher	d							17 22									17 52								
Surbiton [6]	a		17 07			17 16		17 26						17 37		17 46	17 56								18 07
Wimbledon [6]	⊖ a							17 34									18 04								
Earlsfield	a	←						17 38					←				18 08							←	
Clapham Junction [10]	a	17 12			17 25			17 42	17 31	17 36			17 42	17 48		17 57	18 12		18 05				18 12	18 12	
	a							→									→								
Vauxhall	⊖ a	17 17											17 47											18 17	
London Waterloo [15]	⊖ a	17 22	17 25	17 23	17 34	17 36			17 40	17 49		17 49	17 52	17 57	17 51	18 05		18 07	18 13			18 19	18 20	18 22	18 25

Station		SW 1 ⚒	SW 1	SW 1	SW 1	SW		SW 1	SW ◇1 ⚒	SW ◇1 ⚒	SW	SW 1	SW 1	SW 1	SW	SW 1		SW 1	SW 1	SW ◇1 ⚒	SW ◇1 ⚒	SW	SW 1	SW 1 ⚒	SW 1
Basingstoke	d		17 43		17 54				17 57							18 17			18 24	18 30	18 35				18 43
Hook	d				18 01														18 31						
Winchfield	d				18 05														18 35						
Fleet	d		17 54		18 10														18 40						18 54
Farnborough (Main)	d		18 00		18 16											18 30			18 46						19 00
Alton	d											17 44											18 15		
Bentley	d											17 51													
Farnham	a											17 56											18 25		
	d											17 58											18 28		
Aldershot	d											18 04											18 34		
Ash Vale	d											18 09											18 39		
Brookwood	d				18 23							18 16							18 53				18 46		
Guildford	d	17 47						18 02					18 17					18 34						18 47	
Worplesdon	d			←										←				18 40							
Woking	a	17 57		17 58	18 28			18 11	18 15			18 21	18 25	18 28		18 39		18 44	18 58	18 49			18 51	18 57	
	d	17 59		17 59	18 29	18 03		18 12	18 17	18 21		18 22	18 26	18 29	18 33	18 41		18 46	18 59	18 50			18 52	18 59	
West Byfleet	d				→	18 07						18 27			18 37				→				18 57		
Byfleet & New Haw	d					18 10									18 40										
Weybridge	d			18 06		18 13								18 36	18 43										
Walton-on-Thames	d			18 10		18 17								18 40	18 47										
Hersham	d					18 19									18 49										
Esher	d					18 22									18 52										
Surbiton [6]	a			18 16		18 26						18 37		18 46	18 56								19 07		
Wimbledon [6]	⊖ a					18 34									19 04										
Earlsfield	a					18 38					←				19 08							←			
Clapham Junction [10]	a		18 25			18 42		18 31	18 36		18 42	18 48		18 57	19 12			19 05			19 12	19 12			19 25
	a					→									→										
Vauxhall	⊖ a										18 47											19 17			
London Waterloo [15]	⊖ a	18 23	18 34	18 36				18 40	18 49	18 49	18 52	18 57	18 51	19 05		19 07		19 13		19 19	19 20	19 22	19 25	19 23	19 34

Table 155

Saturdays
from 13 October

Basingstoke, Alton, Guildford and Woking - Waterloo

Network Diagram - see first Page of Table 155

Station		SW 1		SW 1	SW	SW 1	SW ◇1 ⚒	SW ◇1 ⚒	SW	SW 1	SW 1	SW 1		SW	SW 1	SW 1	SW 1	SW ◇1 ⚒	SW ◇1 ⚒	SW	SW 1	SW 1		SW 1	SW 1
Basingstoke	d			18 54			18 57								19 17		19 24	19 30	19 35					19 43	
Hook	d			19 01													19 31								
Winchfield	d			19 05													19 35								
Fleet	d			19 10													19 40							19 54	
Farnborough (Main)	d			19 16											19 30		19 46							20 00	
Alton	d									18 44											19 15				
Bentley	d									18 51															
Farnham	a									18 56											19 25				
	d									18 58											19 28				
Aldershot	d									19 04											19 34				
Ash Vale	d									19 09											19 39				
Brookwood	d			19 23						19 16							19 53				19 46				
Guildford	d					19 02					19 17					19 34						19 47			
Worplesdon	d	←										←				19 40									←
Woking	a	18 58		19 28		19 11	19 15			19 21	19 25	19 28			19 39	19 44	19 58	19 49			19 51	19 57			19 58
	d	18 59		19 29	19 03	19 12	19 17	19 21		19 22	19 26	19 29		19 33	19 41	19 46	19 59	19 50			19 52	19 59			19 59
West Byfleet	d			→	19 07					19 27				19 37			→				19 57				
Byfleet & New Haw	d				19 10									19 40											
Weybridge	d	19 06			19 13							19 36		19 43											20 06
Walton-on-Thames	d	19 10			19 17							19 40		19 47											20 10
Hersham	d				19 19									19 49											
Esher	d				19 22									19 52											
Surbiton [6]	a	19 16			19 26					19 37		19 46		19 56							20 07				20 16
Wimbledon [6]	⊖ a				19 34									20 04											
Earlsfield	a				19 38				←					20 08						←					
Clapham Junction [10]	a				19 42	19 31	19 36		19 42	19 48		19 57		20 12		20 05			20 12	20 12				20 25	
	a				→									→											
Vauxhall	⊖ a								19 47											20 17					
London Waterloo [15]	⊖ a	19 36				19 40	19 49	19 49	19 52	19 57	19 51	20 05			20 07	20 13		20 19	20 20	20 22	20 25	20 23		20 34	20 36

Station		SW	SW 1	SW ◇1 ⚒	SW	SW 1	SW 1	SW 1		SW ◇1 ⚒	SW 1	SW	SW 1	SW 1	SW 1	SW 1	SW ◇1 ⚒	SW 1		SW	SW 1	SW ◇1 ⚒	SW	SW 1	SW 1
Basingstoke	d							19 54		20 09			20 17			20 24	20 35				20 43				
Hook	d							20 01								20 31									
Winchfield	d							20 05								20 35									
Fleet	d							20 10								20 40					20 54				
Farnborough (Main)	d							20 16					20 30			20 46					21 00				
Alton	d					19 44								20 15										20 44	
Bentley	d					19 51																		20 51	
Farnham	a					19 56								20 25										20 56	
	d					19 58								20 28										20 58	
Aldershot	d					20 04								20 34										21 04	
Ash Vale	d					20 09								20 39										21 09	
Brookwood	d					20 16		20 23						20 46		20 53								21 16	
Guildford	d		20 02				20 17								20 39			20 47							21 17
Worplesdon	d														20 44										
Woking	a		20 11			20 21	20 25	20 28		20 29			20 39	20 51	20 52	20 58		20 57			21 09			21 21	21 25
	d	20 03	20 12	20 21		20 22	20 26	20 29		20 30		20 33	20 41	20 52	20 53	20 59		20 59		21 03	21 10	21 21		21 22	21 26
West Byfleet	d	20 07				20 27						20 37		20 57						21 07				21 27	
Byfleet & New Haw	d	20 10										20 40								21 10					
Weybridge	d	20 13						20 36				20 43				21 06				21 13					
Walton-on-Thames	d	20 17						20 40				20 47				21 10				21 17					
Hersham	d	20 19										20 49								21 19					
Esher	d	20 22										20 52								21 22					
Surbiton [6]	a	20 26				20 37		20 46				20 56		21 07		21 16				21 26				21 37	
Wimbledon [6]	⊖ a	20 34										21 04								21 34					
Earlsfield	a	20 38			←						←	21 08								21 38			←		
Clapham Junction [10]	a	20 42	20 31		20 42	20 48		20 57		20 52	20 57	21 12			21 12		21 16			21 42	21 29		21 42	21 48	
	a	→						→												→					
Vauxhall	⊖ a				20 47							21 17											21 47		
London Waterloo [15]	⊖ a		20 40	20 49	20 52	20 57	20 50			21 04	21 05	21 23	21 07	21 29	21 21	21 34	21 24	21 27			21 38	21 49	21 52	21 57	21 50

Table 155

Saturdays from 13 October

Basingstoke, Alton, Guildford and Woking - Waterloo

Network Diagram - see first Page of Table 155

		SW 1	SW ◇1	SW 1		SW	SW 1	SW	SW 1	SW 1	SW ◇1	SW 1	SW	SW 1		SW 1	SW	SW 1	SW 1	SW ◇1	SW 1	SW 1	SW	SW 1
Basingstoke	d	20 54	21 09							21 24	21 35			21 43					21 54	22 09				
Hook	d	21 01								21 31									22 01					
Winchfield	d	21 05								21 35									22 05					
Fleet	d	21 10								21 40				21 54					22 10					
Farnborough (Main)	d	21 16								21 46				22 00					22 16					
Alton	d								21 15									21 44						
Bentley	d																	21 51						
Farnham	a								21 25									21 56						
	d								21 28									21 58						
Aldershot	d								21 34									22 04						
Ash Vale	d								21 39									22 09						
Brookwood	d	21 23							21 46	21 53								22 16	22 23					
Guildford	d						21 39					21 49											22 20	22 39
Worplesdon	d						21 44																	22 44
Woking	a	21 28	21 29				21 49		21 51	21 58		21 57		22 09				22 21	22 28	22 28			22 32	22 49
	d	21 29	21 30			21 33	21 50		21 52	21 59		21 59	22 03	22 10		22 21		22 22	22 29	22 29			22 33	22 50
West Byfleet	d					21 37			21 57				22 07					22 27					22 37	
Byfleet & New Haw	d					21 40							22 10										22 40	
Weybridge	d	21 36				21 43				22 06			22 13						22 36				22 43	
Walton-on-Thames	d	21 40				21 47				22 10			22 17						22 40				22 47	
Hersham	d					21 49							22 19										22 49	
Esher	d					21 52							22 22										22 52	
Surbiton 6	a	21 46				21 56			22 07	22 16			22 26					22 37	22 46				22 56	
Wimbledon 6	⊖ a					22 04							22 34										23 04	
Earlsfield	a			←		22 08		←					22 38				←				←	←	23 08	
Clapham Junction 10	a	21 57	21 52	21 57		22 12	22 09	22 12			22 14		22 42	22 29			22 42	22 52	22 57	22 48	22 52	22 57	23 12	23 09
	a	→				→							→					→	→				→	
Vauxhall	⊖ a							22 17									22 47							
London Waterloo 15	⊖ a		22 04	22 07			22 18	22 22	22 27	22 34	22 22	22 24		22 38		22 49	22 52			22 57	23 01	23 05		23 18

		SW	SW 1	SW 1	SW ◇1	SW 1	SW	SW 1	SW	SW 1		SW 1	SW 1	SW 1	SW 1	SW 1	SW 1	SW 1
Basingstoke	d			22 24	22 35			22 43				22 54	23 13				23 44	
Hook	d			22 31								23 01					23 51	
Winchfield	d			22 35								23 05					23 55	
Fleet	d			22 40				22 54				23 10					00 01	
Farnborough (Main)	d			22 46				23 00				23 16					00 06	
Alton	d		22 15							22 44					23 15			23 46
Bentley	d									22 51								23 53
Farnham	a		22 25							22 56					23 25			23 58
	d		22 28							22 58					23 28			
Aldershot	d		22 34							23 04					23 34			
Ash Vale	d		22 39							23 09					23 39			
Brookwood	d		22 46	22 53						23 16		23 23			23 46		00 13	
Guildford	d						22 55									23 39		
Worplesdon	d					←								←		23 44		
Woking	a		22 51	22 58	22 53	22 58	23 05	23 09		23 21		23 28	23 31	23 28	23 51	23 49	00 18	
	d		22 52	22 59	22 55	22 59	23 06	23 10		23 22		23 33	23 32	23 33		23 56	00 20	
West Byfleet	d		22 57	→			23 10			23 27		→		23 37			00 25	
Byfleet & New Haw	d						23 13							23 40				
Weybridge	d					23 06	23 16							23 43			00 29	
Walton-on-Thames	d					23 10	23 20							23 47			00 33	
Hersham	d						23 22							23 49				
Esher	d						23 25							23 52				
Surbiton 6	a		23 07			23 16	23 29			23 37				23 57			00 39	
Wimbledon 6	⊖ a						23 37							00 06			00 47	
Earlsfield	a	←					23 41		←									
Clapham Junction 10	a	23 12			23 14		23 44	23 29	23 44	23 48			23 52			00 18	00 53	
	a						→							00 21				
Vauxhall	⊖ a	23 17							23 49					00 30				
London Waterloo 15	⊖ a	23 22	23 28		23 22	23 32		23 39	23 54	00 01			00 03	00 35		00 32	01 04	

Table 155

Sundays until 30 September

Basingstoke, Alton, Guildford and Woking - Waterloo

Network Diagram - see first Page of Table 155

		SW 1	SW 1	SW 1	SW 1	SW 1	SW 1	SW	SW 1 A	SW		SW	SW 1	SW 1	SW	SW ◇1	SW 1 B	SW 1 C	SW	SW 1		SW	SW 1	SW	SW 1 D
Basingstoke	d		22p54	23p13			23p44		06 21				07 16			07 20							07 44		
Hook	d		23p01				23p51						07 23												
Winchfield	d		23p05				23p55						07 27												
Fleet	d		23p10				00 01		06 32				07 32												
Farnborough (Main)	d		23p16				00 06		06 38				07 38												
Alton	d	22p44																							
Bentley	d	22p51																							
Farnham	a	22p56																							
	d	22p58												07 30											
Aldershot	d	23p04												07 36											
Ash Vale	d	23p09												07 41											
Brookwood	d	23p16	23p23				00 13						07 45	07 48											
Guildford	d					23p39						06 57			07 27		07 37	07 38						07 57	08 05
Worplesdon	d				←	23p44														←					
Woking	a	23p21	23p28	23p31	23p28	23p49	00 18		06 47			07 05	07 50	07 54	07 35	07 39	07 45	07 45		07 50			08 02	08 05	08 13
	d	23p22	23p33	23p32	23p33	23p56	00 20	06 36	06 48			07 06	07 58		07 36	07 40	07 47	07 47		07 58		07 52	08 04	08 06	08 15
West Byfleet	d	23p27	→		23p37		00 25	06 40				07 10		→	07 40							07 56		08 10	
Byfleet & New Haw	d				23p40			06 43				07 13			07 43							08 00		08 13	
Weybridge	d				23p43		00 29	06 46				07 16			07 46									08 16	
Walton-on-Thames	d				23p47		00 33	06 50				07 20			07 50									08 20	
Hersham	d				23p49			06 52				07 22			07 52									08 22	
Esher	d				23p52			06 55				07 25			07 55									08 25	
Surbiton 6	a	23p37			23p57		00 39	06 59				07 29			07 59					08 09				08 29	
Wimbledon 6	⊖ a				00 06		00 47	07 07				07 37			08 07					08 19				08 37	
Earlsfield	a							07 11		←		07 41			08 11				←					08 41	
Clapham Junction 10	a	23p48		23p52		00 18	00 53	07 15	07 11	07 15		07 45			08 15	08 05	08 10	08 10	08 15	08 27			08 30	08 45	08 40
	a				00 21			→							→							09 01		→	
Vauxhall	⊖ a				00 30					07 20		07 50							08 20			09 08			
London Waterloo 15	⊖ a	00 01		00 03	00 35	00 32	01 04		07 20	07 30		08 00				08 19	08 23	08 23	08 30	08 41		09 13	08 42		08 49

		SW	SW ◇1	SW	SW 1	SW		SW	SW 1	SW 1	SW 1	SW	SW 1	SW	SW ◇1	SW		SW 1	SW	SW	SW 1	SW 1	SW 1	SW	SW 1
Basingstoke	d		08 10						08 16		08 44				09 10						09 16		09 44		
Hook	d								08 23												09 23				
Winchfield	d								08 27												09 27				
Fleet	d								08 32												09 32				
Farnborough (Main)	d								08 38												09 38				
Alton	d									08 15												09 15			
Bentley	d									08 23												09 23			
Farnham	a									08 28												09 28			
	d									08 30												09 30			
Aldershot	d									08 36												09 36			
Ash Vale	d									08 41												09 41			
Brookwood	d								08 45	08 48											09 45	09 48			
Guildford	d			08 27	08 35							08 57	09 05			09 27		09 35						09 57	10 05
Worplesdon	d																								
Woking	a		08 28	08 35	08 42				08 50	08 54	09 02	09 05	09 15		09 28	09 35		09 42			09 50	09 54	10 02	10 05	10 15
	d		08 30	08 36	08 45			08 52	08 58		09 04	09 06	09 15		09 30	09 36		09 45		09 52	09 58		10 04	10 06	10 15
West Byfleet	d			08 40				08 56				09 10				09 40				09 56				10 10	
Byfleet & New Haw	d			08 43				09 00				09 13				09 43				10 00				10 13	
Weybridge	d			08 46								09 16				09 46								10 16	
Walton-on-Thames	d			08 50								09 20				09 50								10 20	
Hersham	d			08 52								09 22				09 52								10 22	
Esher	d			08 55								09 25				09 55								10 25	
Surbiton 6	a			08 59					09 09			09 29				09 59					10 09			10 29	
Wimbledon 6	⊖ a			09 07					09 19			09 37				10 07					10 17			10 37	
Earlsfield	a	←		09 11		←						09 41		←		10 11			←					10 41	
Clapham Junction 10	a	08 45	08 57	09 15	09 06	09 15			09 26		09 30	09 45	09 38	09 45	09 57	10 15		10 04	10 15		10 23		10 27	10 45	10 35
	a			→				10 01				→				→				11 01				→	
Vauxhall	⊖ a	08 50				09 20		10 08						09 50					10 20	11 08					
London Waterloo 15	⊖ a	09 00	09 09		09 19	09 30		10 13	09 39		09 43		09 49	10 00	10 08			10 19	10 30	11 13	10 38		10 42		10 49

A 29 July, 5 August, 12 August, 2 September, 9 September

B 2 September, 9 September

C 29 July, 5 August, 12 August

D until 22 July, 19 August, 26 August, 16 September, 23 September, 30 September

Table 155

Sundays
until 30 September

Basingstoke, Alton, Guildford and Woking - Waterloo

Network Diagram - see first Page of Table 155

		SW ◇1 ✠		SW	SW ◇1 ✠	SW	SW 1 ✠	SW	SW	SW 1	SW 1	SW 1 ✠		SW	SW 1	SW ◇1 ✠	SW	SW ◇1 ✠	SW	SW 1 ✠	SW	SW		SW 1	SW 1
Basingstoke	d	10 00			10 10					10 16		10 44				11 00		11 10						11 16	
Hook	d									10 23														11 23	
Winchfield	d									10 27														11 27	
Fleet	d									10 32														11 32	
Farnborough (Main)	d									10 38														11 38	
Alton	d										10 15														11 15
Bentley	d										10 23														11 23
Farnham	a										10 28														11 28
	d										10 30														11 30
Aldershot	d										10 36														11 36
Ash Vale	d										10 41														11 41
Brookwood	d									10 45	10 48													11 45	11 48
Guildford	d					10 27	10 35							10 57	11 06				11 27	11 35					
Worplesdon	d																								
Woking	a	10 19			10 28	10 35	10 42			10 50	10 54	11 02		11 05	11 13	11 18		11 28	11 35	11 42				11 50	11 54
	d	10 20			10 30	10 36	10 45		10 52	10 58		11 04		11 06	11 15	11 20		11 30	11 36	11 45		11 52		11 58	
West Byfleet	d					10 40			10 56					11 10					11 40			11 56			
Byfleet & New Haw	d					10 43			11 00					11 13					11 43			12 00			
Weybridge	d					10 46								11 16					11 46						
Walton-on-Thames	d					10 50								11 20					11 50						
Hersham	d					10 52								11 22					11 52						
Esher	d					10 55								11 25					11 55						
Surbiton 6	a					10 59				11 09				11 29					11 59					12 09	
Wimbledon 6 ⊖	a					11 07				11 17				11 37					12 07					12 17	
Earlsfield	a			←		11 11		←						11 41			←		12 11		←				
Clapham Junction 10	a	10 40		10 45	10 49	11 15	11 04	11 15		11 23		11 27		11 45	11 34	11 39	11 45	11 49	12 15	12 04	12 15			12 23	
	a					→			12 01					→					→			13 01			
Vauxhall ⊖	a			10 50				11 20	12 08								11 50				12 20	13 08			
London Waterloo 15 ⊖	a	10 54		11 00	11 04		11 19	11 30	12 13	11 38		11 42			11 49	11 54	12 00	12 03		12 19	12 30	13 13		12 39	

		SW 1 ✠	SW	SW 1	SW ◇1 ✠	SW	SW ◇1 ✠	SW		SW 1 ✠	SW	SW	SW 1	SW 1	SW 1 ✠	SW	SW 1	SW ◇1 ✠		SW	SW ◇1 ✠	SW	SW 1 ✠	SW	SW
Basingstoke	d	11 44			12 00		12 10						12 16		12 44			13 00			13 10				
Hook	d												12 23												
Winchfield	d												12 27												
Fleet	d												12 32												
Farnborough (Main)	d												12 38												
Alton	d													12 15											
Bentley	d													12 23											
Farnham	a													12 28											
	d													12 30											
Aldershot	d													12 36											
Ash Vale	d													12 41											
Brookwood	d												12 45	12 48											
Guildford	d		11 57	12 06				12 27		12 35						12 57	13 05					13 27	13 35		
Worplesdon	d																								
Woking	a	12 02	12 05	12 13	12 18		12 28	12 35		12 42			12 50	12 54	13 02	13 05	13 13	13 18			13 28	13 35	13 42		
	d	12 04	12 06	12 15	12 20		12 30	12 36		12 45		12 52	12 58		13 04	13 06	13 15	13 20			13 30	13 36	13 45		13 52
West Byfleet	d		12 10					12 40				12 56				13 10						13 40			13 56
Byfleet & New Haw	d		12 13					12 43				13 00				13 13						13 43			14 00
Weybridge	d		12 16					12 46								13 16						13 46			
Walton-on-Thames	d		12 20					12 50								13 20						13 50			
Hersham	d		12 22					12 52								13 22						13 52			
Esher	d		12 25					12 55								13 25						13 55			
Surbiton 6	a		12 29					12 59					13 09			13 29						13 59			
Wimbledon 6 ⊖	a		12 37					13 07					13 17			13 37						14 07			
Earlsfield	a		12 41			←		13 11			←					13 41				←		14 11		←	
Clapham Junction 10	a	12 27	12 45	12 34	12 39	12 45	12 49	13 15		13 04	13 15		13 23		13 27	13 45	13 34	13 39		13 45	13 49	14 15	14 04	14 15	
	a		→					→				14 01				→						→			15 01
Vauxhall ⊖	a					12 50					13 20	14 08								13 50				14 20	15 08
London Waterloo 15 ⊖	a	12 42		12 49	12 49	13 00	13 04			13 14	13 30	14 13	13 39		13 37		13 44	13 49		14 00	13 59		14 14	14 30	15 13

Table 155

Sundays
until 30 September

Basingstoke, Alton, Guildford and Woking - Waterloo

Network Diagram - see first Page of Table 155

		SW 1	SW 1	SW 1 ✠		SW 1	SW 1	SW	SW 1	SW ◇1 ✠	SW 1	SW	SW ◇1 ✠	SW 1		SW 1	SW	SW 1 ✠	SW	SW	SW 1	SW 1	SW 1 ✠	SW 1	SW 1
Basingstoke	d	13 16		13 44		13 50				14 00			14 10								14 16		14 44	14 50	
Hook	d	13 23																			14 23				
Winchfield	d	13 27																			14 27				
Fleet	d	13 32				14 02															14 32			15 02	
Farnborough (Main)	d	13 38				14 08															14 38			15 08	
Alton	d		13 15				13 45															14 15			14 45
Bentley	d		13 23																			14 23			
Farnham	a		13 28				13 55															14 28			14 55
	d		13 30				14 00															14 30			15 00
Aldershot	d		13 36				14 06															14 36			15 06
Ash Vale	d		13 41				14 11															14 41			15 11
Brookwood	d	13 45	13 48			14 15	14 18														14 45	14 48		15 15	15 18
Guildford	d							13 57	14 05								14 27	14 35							
Worplesdon	d										←														
Woking	a	13 50	13 54	14 02		14 20	14 24	14 05	14 13	14 18	14 20		14 28				14 35	14 42			14 50	14 54	15 02	15 20	15 24
	d	13 58		14 04		14 28		14 06	14 15	14 20	14 28		14 30				14 36	14 45		14 52	14 58		15 04	15 28	
West Byfleet	d					→		14 10									14 40			14 56				→	
Byfleet & New Haw	d							14 13									14 43			15 00					
Weybridge	d							14 16			14 34						14 46								
Walton-on-Thames	d							14 20			14 38						14 50								
Hersham	d							14 22									14 52								
Esher	d							14 25									14 55								
Surbiton 6	a	14 09						14 29			14 45						14 59				15 09				
Wimbledon 6 ⊖	a	14 17						14 37			14 53						15 07				15 17				
Earlsfield	a							14 41				←		←		←	15 11		←						
Clapham Junction 10	a	14 23		14 27				14 45	14 34	14 39	14 59	14 45	14 49	14 59		14 59	15 15	15 04	15 15		15 23		15 27		
	a							→			→						→			16 01					
Vauxhall ⊖	a											14 50							15 20	16 08					
London Waterloo 15 ⊖	a	14 34		14 37					14 44	14 49		14 55	14 59	15 10		15 10		15 14	15 25	16 13	15 34		15 37		

			SW	SW 1	SW ◇1 ✠	SW 1	SW	SW ◇1 ✠	SW 1	SW 1	SW		SW 1 ✠	SW	SW	SW 1	SW 1	SW 1 ✠	SW 1	SW 1	SW		SW 1	SW ◇1 ✠	SW 1
Basingstoke	d				15 00			15 10								15 16		15 44	15 50					16 00	
Hook	d															15 23									
Winchfield	d															15 27									
Fleet	d															15 32			16 02						
Farnborough (Main)	d															15 38			16 08						
Alton	d																15 15			15 45					
Bentley	d																15 23								
Farnham	a																15 28			15 55					
	d																15 30			16 00					
Aldershot	d																15 36			16 06					
Ash Vale	d																15 41			16 11					
Brookwood	d															15 45	15 48		16 15	16 18					
Guildford	d		14 57	15 05							15 27		15 35								15 57		16 05		
Worplesdon	d					←																			←
Woking	a		15 05	15 13	15 18	15 20		15 28			15 35		15 42			15 50	15 54	16 02	16 20	16 24	16 05		16 13	16 18	16 20
	d		15 06	15 15	15 20	15 28		15 30			15 36		15 45		15 52	15 58		16 04	16 28		16 06		16 15	16 20	16 28
West Byfleet	d		15 10								15 40				15 56				→		16 10				
Byfleet & New Haw	d		15 13								15 43				16 00						16 13				
Weybridge	d		15 16			15 34					15 46										16 16				16 34
Walton-on-Thames	d		15 20			15 38					15 50										16 20				16 38
Hersham	d		15 22								15 52										16 22				
Esher	d		15 25								15 55										16 25				
Surbiton 6	a		15 29			15 45					15 59					16 09					16 29				16 45
Wimbledon 6 ⊖	a		15 37			15 53					16 07					16 17					16 37				16 53
Earlsfield	a		15 41				←		←	←	16 11			←							16 41				
Clapham Junction 10	a		15 45	15 34	15 39	15 59	15 45	15 49	15 59	15 59	16 15		16 04	16 15		16 23		16 27			16 45		16 34	16 39	16 59
	a		→			→					→				17 01						→				→
Vauxhall ⊖	a						15 50							16 20	17 08										
London Waterloo 15 ⊖	a			15 44	15 49		15 55	15 59	16 10	16 10			16 14	16 25	17 13	16 34		16 37					16 44	16 49	

Table 155

Sundays
until 30 September

Basingstoke, Alton, Guildford and Woking - Waterloo

Network Diagram - see first Page of Table 155

		SW	SW ◇1 ⌶	SW 1	SW 1	SW	SW 1 ⌶		SW	SW	SW 1	SW 1	SW 1 ⌶	SW 1	SW 1	SW	SW 1		SW ◇1 ⌶	SW 1	SW	SW ◇1 ⌶	SW 1	SW 1	SW
Basingstoke	d		16 10								16 16		16 44	16 50					17 00			17 10			
Hook	d										16 23														
Winchfield	d										16 27														
Fleet	d										16 32			17 02											
Farnborough (Main)	d										16 38			17 08											
Alton	d											16 15			16 45										
Bentley	d											16 23													
Farnham	a											16 28			16 55										
	d											16 30			17 00										
Aldershot	d											16 36			17 06										
Ash Vale	d											16 41			17 11										
Brookwood	d										16 45	16 48		17 15	17 18										
Guildford	d					16 27	16 35									16 57	17 05								17 27
Worplesdon	d																			←					
Woking	a		16 28			16 35	16 42				16 50	16 54	17 02	17 20	17 24	17 05	17 13		17 18	17 20		17 28			17 35
	d		16 30			16 36	16 45			16 52	16 58		17 04	17 28		17 06	17 15		17 20	17 28		17 30			17 36
West Byfleet	d					16 40				16 56				→		17 10									17 40
Byfleet & New Haw	d					16 43				17 00						17 13									17 43
Weybridge	d					16 46										17 16				17 34					17 46
Walton-on-Thames	d					16 50										17 20				17 38					17 50
Hersham	d					16 52										17 22									17 52
Esher	d					16 55										17 25									17 55
Surbiton 6	a					16 59					17 09					17 29				17 45					17 59
Wimbledon 6 ⊖	a					17 07					17 17					17 37				17 53					18 07
Earlsfield	a	←		←	←	17 11			←							17 41					←		←	←	18 11
Clapham Junction 10	a	16 45	16 49	16 59	16 59	17 15	17 04		17 15		17 23		17 27			17 45	17 34		17 39	17 59	17 45	17 49	17 59	17 59	18 15
	a					→				18 01						→				→					→
Vauxhall ⊖	a	16 50							17 20	18 08											17 50				
London Waterloo 15 ⊖	a	16 55	16 59	17 10	17 10		17 14		17 25	18 13	17 34		17 37				17 44		17 49		17 55	17 59	18 10	18 10	

		SW 1 ⌶	SW		SW	SW 1	SW 1	SW 1 ⌶	SW 1	SW 1	SW	SW 1	SW ◇1 ⌶		SW 1	SW	SW ◇1 ⌶	SW 1	SW 1	SW	SW 1 ⌶	SW	SW		
Basingstoke	d					17 16		17 44	17 50				18 00				18 10								
Hook	d					17 23																			
Winchfield	d					17 27																			
Fleet	d					17 32			18 02																
Farnborough (Main)	d					17 38			18 08																
Alton	d						17 15			17 45															
Bentley	d						17 23																		
Farnham	a						17 28			17 55															
	d						17 30			18 00															
Aldershot	d						17 36			18 06															
Ash Vale	d						17 41			18 11															
Brookwood	d					17 45	17 48		18 15	18 18															
Guildford	d	17 35									17 57	18 05								18 27	18 35				
Worplesdon	d														←										
Woking	a	17 42				17 50	17 54	18 02	18 20	18 24	18 05	18 13	18 18		18 20		18 28			18 35	18 42				
	d	17 45			17 52	17 58		18 04	18 28		18 06	18 15	18 20		18 28		18 30			18 36	18 45		18 52		
West Byfleet	d				17 56				→		18 10									18 40			18 56		
Byfleet & New Haw	d				18 00						18 13									18 43			19 00		
Weybridge	d										18 16				18 34					18 46					
Walton-on-Thames	d										18 20				18 38					18 50					
Hersham	d										18 22									18 52					
Esher	d										18 25									18 55					
Surbiton 6	a					18 09					18 29				18 45					18 59					
Wimbledon 6 ⊖	a					18 17					18 37				18 53					19 07					
Earlsfield	a		←								18 41					←		←	←	19 11		←			
Clapham Junction 10	a	18 04	18 15			18 23		18 27			18 45	18 34	18 39		18 59	18 45	18 49	18 59	18 59	19 15	19 04	19 15			
	a				19 01						→				→					→			20 01		
Vauxhall ⊖	a		18 20		19 08											18 50						19 20	20 08		
London Waterloo 15 ⊖	a	18 14	18 25		19 13	18 34		18 37				18 44	18 49			18 55	18 59	19 10	19 10		19 14	19 25	20 13		

Table 155

Sundays
until 30 September

Basingstoke, Alton, Guildford and Woking - Waterloo

Network Diagram - see first Page of Table 155

		SW 1	SW 1	SW 1	SW 1	SW 1	SW	SW 1	SW ◇1 ⌶	SW 1		SW	SW ◇1 ⌶	SW 1	SW 1	SW	SW 1 ⌶	SW	SW	SW 1	SW 1		SW 1	SW 1	SW 1
Basingstoke	d	18 16		18 44	18 50				19 00				19 10							19 16			19 44	19 50	
Hook	d	18 23																		19 23					
Winchfield	d	18 27																		19 27					
Fleet	d	18 32			19 02															19 32				20 02	
Farnborough (Main)	d	18 38			19 08															19 38				20 08	
Alton	d		18 15			18 45															19 15				19 45
Bentley	d		18 23																		19 23				
Farnham	a		18 28			18 55															19 28				19 55
	d		18 30			19 00															19 30				20 00
Aldershot	d		18 36			19 06															19 36				20 06
Ash Vale	d		18 41			19 11															19 41				20 11
Brookwood	d	18 45	18 48		19 15	19 18														19 45	19 48			20 15	20 18
Guildford	d						18 57	19 05								19 27	19 35								
Worplesdon	d									←															
Woking	a	18 50	18 54	19 02	19 20	19 24	19 05	19 13	19 18	19 20			19 28			19 35	19 42			19 50	19 54		20 02	20 20	20 24
	d	18 58		19 04	19 28		19 06	19 15	19 20	19 28			19 30			19 36	19 45		19 52	19 58			20 04	20 28	
West Byfleet	d				→		19 10									19 40			19 56					→	
Byfleet & New Haw	d						19 13									19 43			20 00						
Weybridge	d						19 16			19 34						19 46									
Walton-on-Thames	d						19 20			19 38						19 50									
Hersham	d						19 22									19 52									
Esher	d						19 25									19 55									
Surbiton 6	a	19 09					19 29			19 45						19 59				20 09					
Wimbledon 6 ⊖	a	19 17					19 37			19 53						20 07				20 17					
Earlsfield	a						19 41					←		←	←	20 11		←							
Clapham Junction 10	a	19 23		19 27			19 45	19 34	19 39	19 59		19 45	19 49	19 59	19 59	20 15	20 04	20 15		20 23			20 27		
	a						→			→						→			21 01						
Vauxhall ⊖	a											19 50						20 20	21 08						
London Waterloo 15 ⊖	a	19 34		19 37				19 44	19 49			19 55	19 59	20 10	20 10		20 14	20 25	21 13	20 34			20 37		

		SW	SW 1	SW ◇1 ⌶	SW 1	SW	SW ◇1 ⌶		SW 1	SW 1	SW	SW 1	SW	SW	SW 1	SW 1	SW 1		SW 1	SW 1	SW	SW 1	SW ◇1 ⌶	SW 1	SW
Basingstoke	d			20 00			20 10								20 16		20 44		20 50				21 00		
Hook	d														20 23										
Winchfield	d														20 27										
Fleet	d														20 32				21 02						
Farnborough (Main)	d														20 38				21 08						
Alton	d															20 15				20 45					
Bentley	d															20 23									
Farnham	a															20 28				20 55					
	d															20 30				21 00					
Aldershot	d															20 36				21 06					
Ash Vale	d															20 41				21 11					
Brookwood	d														20 45	20 48			21 15	21 18					
Guildford	d	19 57	20 05								20 27	20 35									20 57	21 05			
Worplesdon	d				←																			←	
Woking	a	20 05	20 13	20 18	20 20		20 28				20 35	20 42			20 50	20 54	21 02		21 20	21 24	21 05	21 13	21 18	21 20	
	d	20 06	20 15	20 20	20 28		20 30				20 36	20 45		20 52	20 58		21 04		21 28		21 06	21 15	21 20	21 28	
West Byfleet	d	20 10									20 40			20 56					→		21 10				
Byfleet & New Haw	d	20 13									20 43			21 00							21 13				
Weybridge	d	20 16			20 34						20 46										21 16			21 34	
Walton-on-Thames	d	20 20			20 38						20 50										21 20			21 38	
Hersham	d	20 22									20 52										21 22				
Esher	d	20 25									20 55										21 25				
Surbiton 6	a	20 29			20 45						20 59				21 09						21 29			21 45	
Wimbledon 6 ⊖	a	20 37			20 53						21 07				21 17						21 37			21 53	
Earlsfield	a	20 41				←			←	←	21 11		←								21 41				←
Clapham Junction 10	a	20 45	20 34	20 39	20 59	20 45	20 49		20 59	20 59	21 15	21 04	21 15		21 23		21 27				21 45	21 34	21 39	21 59	21 45
	a	→			→						→			22 01							→			→	
Vauxhall ⊖	a					20 50							21 20	22 08											21 50
London Waterloo 15 ⊖	a		20 44	20 49		20 55	20 59		21 10	21 10		21 14	21 25	22 13	21 34		21 37					21 44	21 49		21 55

Table 155

Sundays until 30 September

Basingstoke, Alton, Guildford and Woking - Waterloo

Network Diagram - see first Page of Table 155

Station		SW ◇■ ⌶	SW ■		SW ■	SW	SW ■	SW	SW	SW ■	SW ■	SW ■	SW		SW ■	SW	SW ■	SW ■	SW ◇■	SW ■	SW ■	SW	SW ■		SW
Basingstoke	d	21 10								21 16		21 44					21 50		22 10						
Hook	d									21 23															
Winchfield	d									21 27															
Fleet	d									21 32							22 02								
Farnborough (Main)	d									21 38							22 08								
Alton	d										21 15							21 45							
Bentley	d										21 23														
Farnham	a										21 28							21 55							
	d										21 30							22 00							
Aldershot	d										21 36							22 06							
Ash Vale	d										21 41							22 11							
Brookwood	d									21 45	21 48						22 15	22 18							
Guildford	d					21 27	21 35						21 57		22 05							22 27	22 35		
Worplesdon	d																								
Woking	a	21 28				21 35	21 42			21 50	21 54	22 02	22 05		22 13		22 21	22 24	22 28			22 35	22 42		
	d	21 30				21 36	21 45		21 52	21 58		22 04	22 06		22 15		22 28		22 30			22 36	22 45		
West Byfleet	d					21 40			21 56				22 10									22 40			
Byfleet & New Haw	d					21 43			22 00				22 13									22 43			
Weybridge	d					21 46							22 16				22 34					22 46			
Walton-on-Thames	d					21 50							22 20				22 38					22 50			
Hersham	d					21 52							22 22									22 52			
Esher	d					21 55							22 25									22 55			
Surbiton ■	a					21 59				22 09			22 29				22 45					22 59			
Wimbledon ■ ⊖	a					22 07				22 17			22 37				22 53					23 07			
Earlsfield	a		←		←	22 11		←					22 41			←				←	←	23 11			←
Clapham Junction ■	a	21 49	21 59		21 59	22 15	22 04	22 15		22 23		22 27	22 45		22 34	22 45	22 59		22 49	22 59	22 59	23 15	23 04		23 15
	a					→			23 01				→				→					→			
Vauxhall ⊖	a							22 20	23 08							22 50									23 20
London Waterloo ■ ⊖	a	21 59	22 10		22 10		22 14	22 25	23 13	22 34		22 37			22 44	22 55			22 59	23 10	23 10		23 14		23 25

Station		SW	SW ■	SW ■	SW ■	SW	SW ■	SW	SW ■		SW ■	SW ■	SW ■	SW ◇■
Basingstoke	d		22 16		22 44							23 16		23 44
Hook	d		22 23									23 23		
Winchfield	d		22 27									23 27		
Fleet	d		22 32									23 32		
Farnborough (Main)	d		22 38									23 38		
Alton	d			22 15					22 45				23 15	
Bentley	d			22 23									23 23	
Farnham	a			22 28					22 55				23 28	
	d			22 30					23 00				23 30	
Aldershot	d			22 36					23 06				23 36	
Ash Vale	d			22 41					23 11				23 41	
Brookwood	d		22 45	22 48					23 18			23 45	23 48	
Guildford	d					22 57	23 05				23 35			
Worplesdon	d													
Woking	a		22 50	22 54	23 02	23 05	23 13		23 24		23 42	23 50	23 54	00 02
	d	22 52	22 58		23 04	23 06	23 15		23 28		23 45			00 04
West Byfleet	d	22 56				23 10								
Byfleet & New Haw	d	23 00				23 13								
Weybridge	d					23 16			23 34					
Walton-on-Thames	d					23 20			23 38					
Hersham	d					23 22								
Esher	d					23 25								
Surbiton ■	a		23 09			23 29			23 45					
Wimbledon ■ ⊖	a		23 17			23 37			23 53					
Earlsfield	a					23 41		←						
Clapham Junction ■	a		23 23		23 27	23 45	23 34	23 45	23 59		00 04			00 23
	a	00 01				→								
Vauxhall ⊖	a	00 08						23 50						
London Waterloo ■ ⊖	a	00 13	23 34		23 37		23 44	23 55	00 10		00 14			00 33

Table 155

Sundays from 7 October

Basingstoke, Alton, Guildford and Woking - Waterloo

Network Diagram - see first Page of Table 155

Station		SW ■	SW ■	SW ■	SW ■	SW ■	SW ■	SW	SW	SW ■		SW	SW ◇■ ⌶	SW	SW ■	SW	SW ■	SW	SW ■	SW		SW ◇■ ⌶	SW	SW ■	SW
Basingstoke	d		22p54	23p13			23p44			07 16			07 20				07 44					08 10			
Hook	d		23p01				23p51			07 23															
Winchfield	d		23p05				23p55			07 27															
Fleet	d		23p10				00 01			07 32															
Farnborough (Main)	d		23p16				00 06			07 38															
Alton	d	22p44																							
Bentley	d	22p51																							
Farnham	a	22p56																							
	d	22p58																							
Aldershot	d	23p04																							
Ash Vale	d	23p09																							
Brookwood	d	23p16	23p23				00 13			07 45															
Guildford	d					23p39			06 57			07 27						07 57	08 05				08 27	08 35	
Worplesdon	d				←	23p44									←										
Woking	a	23p21	23p28	23p31	23p28	23p49	00 18		07 05	07 50		07 35	07 39		07 50		08 02	08 05	08 13			08 28	08 35	08 42	
	d	23p22	23p33	23p32	23p33	23p56	00 20	06 36	07 06	07 58		07 36	07 40		07 58	07 52	08 04	08 06	08 15			08 30	08 36	08 45	
West Byfleet	d	23p27	→		23p37		00 25	06 40	07 10	→		07 40				07 56		08 10					08 40		
Byfleet & New Haw	d				23p40			06 43	07 13			07 43				08 00		08 13					08 43		
Weybridge	d				23p43		00 29	06 46	07 16			07 46						08 16					08 46		
Walton-on-Thames	d				23p47		00 33	06 50	07 20			07 50						08 20					08 50		
Hersham	d				23p49			06 52	07 22			07 52						08 22					08 52		
Esher	d				23p52			06 55	07 25			07 55						08 25					08 55		
Surbiton ■	a	23p37			23p57		00 39	06 59	07 29			07 59			08 09			08 29					08 59		
Wimbledon ■ ⊖	a				00 06		00 47	07 07	07 37			08 07			08 19			08 37					09 07		
Earlsfield	a							07 11	07 41			08 11		←				08 41		←			09 11		←
Clapham Junction ■	a	23p48		23p52		00 18	00 53	07 15	07 45			08 15	08 05	08 15	08 27		08 30	08 45	08 40	08 45		08 57	09 15	09 06	09 15
	a				00 21							→				09 01		→					→		
Vauxhall ⊖	a				00 30			07 20	07 50					08 20		09 08				08 50					09 20
London Waterloo ■ ⊖	a	00 01		00 03	00 35	00 32	01 04	07 30	08 00				08 19	08 30	08 44	09 13	08 42		08 49	09 00		09 09		09 19	09 30

Station		SW ■	SW	SW ■	SW ■	SW		SW ■	SW	SW ◇■ ⌶	SW	SW ■	SW	SW	SW ■	SW ■		SW ■	SW	SW ■	SW ◇■ ⌶	SW	SW ◇■ ⌶	SW	SW ■ ⌶
Basingstoke	d	08 16			08 44					09 10					09 16			09 44			10 00		10 10		
Hook	d	08 23													09 23										
Winchfield	d	08 27													09 27										
Fleet	d	08 32													09 32										
Farnborough (Main)	d	08 38													09 38										
Alton	d			08 15												09 15									
Bentley	d			08 23												09 23									
Farnham	a			08 28												09 28									
	d			08 30												09 30									
Aldershot	d			08 36												09 36									
Ash Vale	d			08 41												09 41									
Brookwood	d	08 45		08 48											09 45	09 48									
Guildford	d					08 57		09 05			09 27	09 35							09 57	10 05				10 27	10 35
Worplesdon	d																								
Woking	a	08 50		08 54	09 02	09 05		09 15		09 28	09 35	09 42			09 50	09 54		10 02	10 05	10 15	10 19		10 28	10 35	10 42
	d	08 58	08 52		09 04	09 06		09 15		09 30	09 36	09 45		09 52	09 58			10 04	10 06	10 15	10 20		10 30	10 36	10 45
West Byfleet	d		08 56			09 10					09 40			09 56					10 10					10 40	
Byfleet & New Haw	d		09 00			09 13					09 43			10 00					10 13					10 43	
Weybridge	d					09 16					09 46								10 16					10 46	
Walton-on-Thames	d					09 20					09 50								10 20					10 50	
Hersham	d					09 22					09 52								10 22					10 52	
Esher	d					09 25					09 55								10 25					10 55	
Surbiton ■	a	09 09				09 29					09 59				10 09				10 29					10 59	
Wimbledon ■ ⊖	a	09 19				09 37					10 07				10 17				10 37					11 07	
Earlsfield	a					09 41			←		10 11		←						10 41			←		11 11	
Clapham Junction ■	a	09 26			09 30	09 45		09 38	09 45	09 57	10 15	10 04	10 15		10 23			10 27	10 45	10 35	10 40	10 45	10 49	11 15	11 04
	a		10 01			→					→			11 01					→					→	
Vauxhall ⊖	a		10 08						09 50				10 20	11 08								10 50			
London Waterloo ■ ⊖	a	09 42	10 13		09 43			09 49	10 00	10 08		10 19	10 30	11 13	10 38			10 42		10 49	10 54	11 00	11 04		11 19

Table 155

Sundays from 7 October

Basingstoke, Alton, Guildford and Woking - Waterloo

Network Diagram - see first Page of Table 155

	SW		SW	SW ■	SW ■	SW ■ ⌶	SW	SW ■	SW ◇■ ⌶	SW	SW ◇■ ⌶		SW	SW ■ ⌶	SW	SW	SW ■	SW ■	SW ■ ⌶	SW	SW ■		SW ◇■ ⌶	SW
Basingstoke d				10 16		10 44			11 00		11 10						11 16		11 44				12 00	
Hook d				10 23													11 23							
Winchfield d				10 27													11 27							
Fleet d				10 32													11 32							
Farnborough (Main) d				10 38													11 38							
Alton d					10 15													11 15						
Bentley d					10 23													11 23						
Farnham a					10 28													11 28						
d					10 30													11 30						
Aldershot d					10 36													11 36						
Ash Vale d					10 41													11 41						
Brookwood d				10 45	10 48												11 45	11 48						
Guildford d							10 57	11 06					11 27	11 35						11 57	12 06			
Worplesdon d																								
Woking a				10 50	10 54	11 02	11 05	11 13	11 18		11 28		11 35	11 42			11 50	11 54	12 02	12 05	12 13		12 18	
d			10 52	10 58		11 04	11 06	11 15	11 20		11 30		11 36	11 45		11 52	11 58		12 04	12 06	12 15		12 20	
West Byfleet d			10 56				11 10						11 40			11 56				12 10				
Byfleet & New Haw d			11 00				11 13						11 43			12 00				12 13				
Weybridge d							11 16						11 46							12 16				
Walton-on-Thames d							11 20						11 50							12 20				
Hersham d							11 22						11 52							12 22				
Esher d							11 25						11 55							12 25				
Surbiton ■ a				11 09			11 29						11 59				12 09			12 29				
Wimbledon ■ ⊖ a				11 17			11 37						12 07				12 17			12 37				
Earlsfield a	←						11 41			←			12 11		←					12 41				←
Clapham Junction ■ a	11 15			11 23		11 27	11 45	11 34	11 39	11 45	11 49		12 15	12 04	12 15		12 23		12 27	12 45	12 34		12 39	12 45
a			12 01				→						→			13 01				→				
Vauxhall ⊖ a	11 20		12 08							11 50					12 20	13 08								12 50
London Waterloo ■ ⊖ a	11 30		12 13	11 38		11 42		11 49	11 54	12 00	12 03			12 19	12 30	13 13	12 39		12 42		12 49		12 49	13 00

	SW ◇■ ⌶	SW	SW ■ ⌶	SW	SW	SW ■	SW ■		SW ■ ⌶	SW	SW ■	SW ◇■ ⌶	SW	SW ◇■ ⌶	SW	SW ■ ⌶	SW		SW	SW ■	SW ■	SW ■ ⌶	SW ■	SW ■
Basingstoke d	12 10					12 16			12 44			13 00		13 10						13 16		13 44	13 50	
Hook d						12 23														13 23				
Winchfield d						12 27														13 27				
Fleet d						12 32														13 32			14 02	
Farnborough (Main) d						12 38														13 38			14 08	
Alton d							12 15														13 15			13 45
Bentley d							12 23														13 23			
Farnham a							12 28														13 28			13 55
d							12 30														13 30			14 00
Aldershot d							12 36														13 36			14 06
Ash Vale d							12 41														13 41			14 11
Brookwood d						12 45	12 48													13 45	13 48		14 15	14 18
Guildford d		12 27	12 35							12 57	13 05				13 27	13 35								
Worplesdon d																								
Woking a	12 28	12 35	12 42			12 50	12 54		13 02	13 05	13 13	13 18		13 28	13 35	13 42				13 50	13 54	14 02	14 20	14 24
d	12 30	12 36	12 45		12 52	12 58			13 04	13 06	13 15	13 20		13 30	13 36	13 45			13 52	13 58		14 04	14 28	
West Byfleet d		12 40			12 56					13 10					13 40				13 56					→
Byfleet & New Haw d		12 43			13 00					13 13					13 43				14 00					
Weybridge d		12 46								13 16					13 46									
Walton-on-Thames d		12 50								13 20					13 50									
Hersham d		12 52								13 22					13 52									
Esher d		12 55								13 25					13 55									
Surbiton ■ a		12 59				13 09				13 29					13 59					14 09				
Wimbledon ■ ⊖ a		13 07				13 17				13 37					14 07					14 17				
Earlsfield a		13 11		←						13 41			←		14 11		←							
Clapham Junction ■ a	12 49	13 15	13 04	13 15		13 23			13 27	13 45	13 34	13 39	13 45	13 49	14 15	14 04	14 15			14 23		14 27		
a		→			14 01					→					→				15 01					
Vauxhall ⊖ a				13 20	14 08								13 50				14 20		15 08					
London Waterloo ■ ⊖ a	13 04		13 14	13 30	14 13	13 39			13 37		13 44	13 49	14 00	13 59		14 14	14 30		15 13	14 34		14 37		

Table 155

Sundays from 7 October

Basingstoke, Alton, Guildford and Woking - Waterloo

Network Diagram - see first Page of Table 155

	SW	SW ■	SW ◇■ ⌶		SW ■	SW	SW ◇■ ⌶	SW ■	SW ■	SW	SW ■ ⌶	SW	SW		SW ■	SW ■	SW ■ ⌶	SW ■	SW ■	SW	SW ■	SW ◇■ ⌶	SW ■	
Basingstoke d			14 00				14 10								14 16		14 44	14 50				15 00		
Hook d															14 23									
Winchfield d															14 27									
Fleet d															14 32			15 02						
Farnborough (Main) d															14 38			15 08						
Alton d																14 15			14 45					
Bentley d																14 23								
Farnham a																14 28			14 55					
d																14 30			15 00					
Aldershot d																14 36			15 06					
Ash Vale d																14 41			15 11					
Brookwood d															14 45	14 48		15 15	15 18					
Guildford d	13 57	14 05								14 27	14 35									14 57	15 05			
Worplesdon d					←																		←	
Woking a	14 05	14 13	14 18		14 20		14 28			14 35	14 42				14 50	14 54	15 02	15 20	15 24	15 05	15 13	15 18	15 20	
d	14 06	14 15	14 20		14 28		14 30			14 36	14 45		14 52		14 58		15 04	15 28		15 06	15 15	15 20	15 28	
West Byfleet d	14 10									14 40			14 56						→	15 10				
Byfleet & New Haw d	14 13									14 43			15 00							15 13				
Weybridge d	14 16				14 34					14 46										15 16			15 34	
Walton-on-Thames d	14 20				14 38					14 50										15 20			15 38	
Hersham d	14 22									14 52										15 22				
Esher d	14 25									14 55										15 25				
Surbiton ■ a	14 29				14 45					14 59					15 09					15 29			15 45	
Wimbledon ■ ⊖ a	14 37				14 53					15 07					15 17					15 37			15 53	
Earlsfield a	14 41					←		←	←	15 11		←								15 41				
Clapham Junction ■ a	14 45	14 34	14 39		14 59	14 45	14 49	14 59	14 59	15 15	15 04	15 15			15 23		15 27			15 45	15 34	15 39	15 59	
a	→				→					→			16 01							→			→	
Vauxhall ⊖ a						14 50						15 20	16 08											
London Waterloo ■ ⊖ a		14 44	14 49			14 55	14 59	15 10	15 10		15 14	15 25	16 13		15 34		15 37				15 44	15 49		

	SW	SW ◇■ ⌶	SW ■	SW ■	SW	SW ■ ⌶	SW	SW	SW ■	SW ■		SW ■ ⌶	SW ■	SW ■	SW	SW ■	SW ◇■ ⌶	SW ■	SW	SW ◇■ ⌶		SW ■	SW ■	SW
Basingstoke d		15 10							15 16			15 44	15 50				16 00			16 10				
Hook d									15 23															
Winchfield d									15 27															
Fleet d									15 32				16 02											
Farnborough (Main) d									15 38				16 08											
Alton d										15 15				15 45										
Bentley d										15 23														
Farnham a										15 28				15 55										
d										15 30				16 00										
Aldershot d										15 36				16 06										
Ash Vale d										15 41				16 11										
Brookwood d									15 45	15 48			16 15	16 18										
Guildford d					15 27	15 35									15 57	16 05								16 27
Worplesdon d																		←						
Woking a		15 28			15 35	15 42			15 50	15 54		16 02	16 20	16 24	16 05	16 13	16 18	16 20		16 28				16 35
d		15 30			15 36	15 45		15 52	15 58			16 04	16 28		16 06	16 15	16 20	16 28		16 30				16 36
West Byfleet d					15 40			15 56						→	16 10									16 40
Byfleet & New Haw d					15 43			16 00							16 13									16 43
Weybridge d					15 46										16 16			16 34						16 46
Walton-on-Thames d					15 50										16 20			16 38						16 50
Hersham d					15 52										16 22									16 52
Esher d					15 55										16 25									16 55
Surbiton ■ a					15 59				16 09						16 29			16 45						16 59
Wimbledon ■ ⊖ a					16 07				16 17						16 37			16 53						17 07
Earlsfield a	←		←	←	16 11		←								16 41				←			←	←	17 11
Clapham Junction ■ a	15 45	15 49	15 59	15 59	16 15	16 04	16 15		16 23			16 27			16 45	16 34	16 39	16 59	16 45	16 49		16 59	16 59	17 15
a					→			17 01							→			→						→
Vauxhall ⊖ a	15 50						16 20	17 08											16 50					
London Waterloo ■ ⊖ a	15 55	15 59	16 10	16 10		16 14	16 25	17 13	16 34			16 37				16 44	16 49		16 55	16 59		17 10	17 10	

Basingstoke, Alton, Guildford and Woking - Waterloo

Sundays
from 7 October

Network Diagram - see first Page of Table 155

		SW 1 ⌶	SW	SW	SW 1	SW 1	SW 1 ⌶		SW 1	SW 1	SW	SW 1	SW ◇1 ⌶	SW 1	SW	SW ◇1 ⌶	SW 1		SW 1	SW	SW 1 ⌶	SW	SW	SW 1	SW 1
Basingstoke	d				16 16		16 44		16 50				17 00			17 10								17 16	
Hook	d				16 23																			17 23	
Winchfield	d				16 27																			17 27	
Fleet	d				16 32				17 02															17 32	
Farnborough (Main)	d				16 38				17 08															17 38	
Alton	d					16 15				16 45															17 15
Bentley	d					16 23																			17 23
Farnham	a					16 28				16 55															17 28
	d					16 30				17 00															17 30
Aldershot	d					16 36				17 06															17 36
Ash Vale	d					16 41				17 11															17 41
Brookwood	d				16 45	16 48			17 15	17 18														17 45	17 48
Guildford	d	16 35									16 57	17 05								17 27	17 35				
Worplesdon	d													←											
Woking	a	16 42			16 50	16 54	17 02		17 20	17 24	17 05	17 13	17 18	17 20		17 28				17 35	17 42			17 50	17 54
	d	16 45		16 52	16 58		17 04		17 28		17 06	17 15	17 20	17 28		17 30				17 36	17 45		17 52	17 58	
West Byfleet	d			16 56					→		17 10									17 40			17 56		
Byfleet & New Haw	d			17 00							17 13									17 43			18 00		
Weybridge	d										17 16			17 34						17 46					
Walton-on-Thames	d										17 20			17 38						17 50					
Hersham	d										17 22									17 52					
Esher	d										17 25									17 55					
Surbiton 6	a				17 09						17 29			17 45						17 59				18 09	
Wimbledon 6 ⊖	a				17 17						17 37			17 53						18 07				18 17	
Earlsfield	a		←								17 41				←		←		←	18 11		←			
Clapham Junction 10	a	17 04	17 15		17 23		17 27				17 45	17 34	17 39	17 59	17 45	17 49	17 59		17 59	18 15	18 04	18 15		18 23	
	a			18 01							→			→						→			19 01		
Vauxhall ⊖	a		17 20	18 08											17 50							18 20	19 08		
London Waterloo 15 ⊖	a	17 14	17 25	18 13	17 34		17 37					17 44	17 49		17 55	17 59	18 10		18 10		18 14	18 25	19 13	18 34	

		SW 1 ⌶	SW 1	SW 1		SW	SW 1	SW ◇1 ⌶	SW 1	SW	SW ◇1 ⌶	SW 1	SW 1	SW		SW 1 ⌶	SW	SW	SW 1	SW 1	SW 1	SW 1	SW 1	SW	
Basingstoke	d	17 44	17 50					18 00			18 10								18 16		18 44	18 50			
Hook	d																		18 23						
Winchfield	d																		18 27						
Fleet	d		18 02																18 32			19 02			
Farnborough (Main)	d		18 08																18 38			19 08			
Alton	d			17 45																18 15			18 45		
Bentley	d																			18 23					
Farnham	a			17 55																18 28			18 55		
	d			18 00																18 30			19 00		
Aldershot	d			18 06																18 36			19 06		
Ash Vale	d			18 11																18 41			19 11		
Brookwood	d		18 15	18 18															18 45	18 48		19 15	19 18		
Guildford	d					17 57	18 05							18 27		18 35								18 57	
Worplesdon	d								←																
Woking	a	18 02	18 20	18 24		18 05	18 13	18 18	18 20		18 28			18 35		18 42			18 50	18 54	19 02	19 20	19 24	19 05	
	d	18 04	18 28			18 06	18 15	18 20	18 28		18 30			18 36		18 45		18 52	18 58		19 04	19 28		19 06	
West Byfleet	d		→			18 10								18 40				18 56				→		19 10	
Byfleet & New Haw	d					18 13								18 43				19 00						19 13	
Weybridge	d					18 16			18 34					18 46										19 16	
Walton-on-Thames	d					18 20			18 38					18 50										19 20	
Hersham	d					18 22								18 52										19 22	
Esher	d					18 25								18 55										19 25	
Surbiton 6	a					18 29			18 45					18 59					19 09					19 29	
Wimbledon 6 ⊖	a					18 37			18 53					19 07					19 17					19 37	
Earlsfield	a					18 41				←		←	←	19 11			←							19 41	
Clapham Junction 10	a	18 27				18 45	18 34	18 39	18 59	18 45	18 49	18 59	18 59	19 15		19 04	19 15		19 23		19 27			19 45	
	a					→			→					→				20 01						→	
Vauxhall ⊖	a									18 50							19 20	20 08							
London Waterloo 15 ⊖	a	18 37					18 44	18 49		18 55	18 59	19 10	19 10			19 14	19 25	20 13	19 34		19 37				

Basingstoke, Alton, Guildford and Woking - Waterloo

Sundays
from 7 October

Network Diagram - see first Page of Table 155

		SW 1	SW ◇1 ⌶	SW 1	SW	SW ◇1 ⌶	SW 1	SW 1	SW	SW 1 ⌶		SW	SW	SW 1	SW 1	SW 1	SW 1	SW 1	SW	SW 1		SW ◇1 ⌶	SW 1	SW	SW ◇1 ⌶
Basingstoke	d		19 00			19 10								19 16		19 44	19 50					20 00			20 10
Hook	d													19 23											
Winchfield	d													19 27											
Fleet	d													19 32			20 02								
Farnborough (Main)	d													19 38			20 08								
Alton	d														19 15			19 45							
Bentley	d														19 23										
Farnham	a														19 28			19 55							
	d														19 30			20 00							
Aldershot	d														19 36			20 06							
Ash Vale	d														19 41			20 11							
Brookwood	d													19 45	19 48		20 15	20 18							
Guildford	d	19 05							19 27	19 35									19 57	20 05					
Worplesdon	d			←																			←		
Woking	a	19 13	19 18	19 20		19 28			19 35	19 42				19 50	19 54	20 02	20 20	20 24	20 05	20 13		20 18	20 20		20 28
	d	19 15	19 20	19 28		19 30			19 36	19 45			19 52	19 58		20 04	20 28		20 06	20 15		20 20	20 28		20 30
West Byfleet	d								19 40				19 56				→		20 10						
Byfleet & New Haw	d								19 43				20 00						20 13						
Weybridge	d			19 34					19 46										20 16				20 34		
Walton-on-Thames	d			19 38					19 50										20 20				20 38		
Hersham	d								19 52										20 22						
Esher	d								19 55										20 25						
Surbiton 6	a			19 45					19 59					20 09					20 29				20 45		
Wimbledon 6 ⊖	a			19 53					20 07					20 17					20 37				20 53		
Earlsfield	a				←		←	←	20 11			←							20 41					←	
Clapham Junction 10	a	19 34	19 39	19 59	19 45	19 49	19 59	19 59	20 15	20 04		20 15		20 23		20 27			20 45	20 34		20 39	20 59	20 45	20 49
	a			→					→				21 01						→				→		
Vauxhall ⊖	a				19 50							20 20	21 08											20 50	
London Waterloo 15 ⊖	a	19 44	19 49		19 55	19 59	20 10	20 10		20 14		20 25	21 13	20 34		20 37				20 44		20 49		20 55	20 59

		SW 1	SW 1	SW	SW 1	SW		SW	SW 1	SW 1	SW 1	SW 1	SW 1	SW	SW 1	SW ◇1 ⌶		SW 1	SW	SW ◇1 ⌶	SW 1	SW 1	SW	SW 1	SW
Basingstoke	d								20 16		20 44	20 50				21 00				21 10					
Hook	d								20 23																
Winchfield	d								20 27																
Fleet	d								20 32			21 02													
Farnborough (Main)	d								20 38			21 08													
Alton	d									20 15			20 45												
Bentley	d									20 23															
Farnham	a									20 28			20 55												
	d									20 30			21 00												
Aldershot	d									20 36			21 06												
Ash Vale	d									20 41			21 11												
Brookwood	d								20 45	20 48		21 15	21 18												
Guildford	d			20 27	20 35									20 57	21 05								21 27	21 35	
Worplesdon	d																	←							
Woking	a			20 35	20 42				20 50	20 54	21 02	21 20	21 24	21 05	21 13	21 18		21 20		21 28			21 35	21 42	
	d			20 36	20 45			20 52	20 58		21 04	21 28		21 06	21 15	21 20		21 28		21 30			21 36	21 45	
West Byfleet	d			20 40				20 56				→		21 10									21 40		
Byfleet & New Haw	d			20 43				21 00						21 13									21 43		
Weybridge	d			20 46										21 16				21 34					21 46		
Walton-on-Thames	d			20 50										21 20				21 38					21 50		
Hersham	d			20 52										21 22									21 52		
Esher	d			20 55										21 25									21 55		
Surbiton 6	a			20 59					21 09					21 29				21 45					21 59		
Wimbledon 6 ⊖	a			21 07					21 17					21 37				21 53					22 07		
Earlsfield	a	←	←	21 11		←								21 41					←		←	←	22 11		←
Clapham Junction 10	a	20 59	20 59	21 15	21 04	21 15			21 23		21 27			21 45	21 34	21 39		21 59	21 45	21 49	21 59	21 59	22 15	22 04	22 15
	a			→				22 01						→				→					→		
Vauxhall ⊖	a					21 20		22 08											21 50						22 20
London Waterloo 15 ⊖	a	21 10	21 10		21 14	21 25		22 13	21 34		21 37				21 44	21 49			21 55	21 59	22 10	22 10		22 14	22 25

Sundays
from 7 October

Basingstoke, Alton, Guildford and Woking - Waterloo

Network Diagram - see first Page of Table 155

Station		SW	SW ■	SW ■	SW ■	SW	SW ■	SW	SW ■	SW ■	SW ◇■	SW ■	SW ■	SW	SW ■	SW	SW	SW ■	SW ■	SW ■	SW	SW ■
Basingstoke	d		21 16		21 44				21 50		22 10							22 16		22 44		
Hook	d		21 23															22 23				
Winchfield	d		21 27															22 27				
Fleet	d		21 32						22 02									22 32				
Farnborough (Main)	d		21 38						22 08									22 38				
Alton	d			21 15						21 45									22 15			
Bentley	d			21 23															22 23			
Farnham	a			21 28						21 55									22 28			
	d			21 30						22 00									22 30			
Aldershot	d			21 36						22 06									22 36			
Ash Vale	d			21 41						22 11									22 41			
Brookwood	d		21 45	21 48					22 15	22 18								22 45	22 48			
Guildford	d					21 57	22 05							22 27	22 35						22 57	23 05
Worplesdon	d																					
Woking	a		21 50	21 54	22 02	22 05	22 13		22 21	22 24	22 28			22 35	22 42			22 50	22 54	23 02	23 05	23 13
	d	21 52	21 58		22 04	22 06	22 15		22 28		22 30			22 36	22 45		22 52	22 58		23 04	23 06	23 15
West Byfleet	d	21 56				22 10								22 40			22 56				23 10	
Byfleet & New Haw	d	22 00				22 13								22 43			23 00				23 13	
Weybridge	d					22 16			22 34					22 46							23 16	
Walton-on-Thames	d					22 20			22 38					22 50							23 20	
Hersham	d					22 22								22 52							23 22	
Esher	d					22 25								22 55							23 25	
Surbiton 6	a		22 09			22 29			22 45					22 59				23 09			23 29	
Wimbledon 6 ⊖	a		22 17			22 37			22 53					23 07				23 17			23 37	
Earlsfield	a					22 41		←				←	←	23 11		←					23 41	
Clapham Junction 10	a		22 23		22 27	22 45	22 34	22 45	22 59		22 49	22 59	22 59	23 15	23 04	23 15		23 23		23 27	23 45	23 34
	a	23 01				→			→					→			00 01				→	
Vauxhall ⊖	a	23 08						22 50								23 20	00 08					
London Waterloo 15 ⊖	a	23 13	22 34		22 37		22 44	22 55			22 59	23 10	23 10		23 14	23 25	00 13	23 34		23 37		23 44

Station		SW	SW ■	SW ■	SW ■	SW ■	SW ◇■
Basingstoke	d				23 16		23 44
Hook	d				23 23		
Winchfield	d				23 27		
Fleet	d				23 32		
Farnborough (Main)	d				23 38		
Alton	d		22 45			23 15	
Bentley	d					23 23	
Farnham	a		22 55			23 28	
	d		23 00			23 30	
Aldershot	d		23 06			23 36	
Ash Vale	d		23 11			23 41	
Brookwood	d		23 18		23 45	23 48	
Guildford	d			23 35			
Worplesdon	d						
Woking	a		23 24	23 42	23 50	23 54	00 02
	d		23 28	23 45			00 04
West Byfleet	d						
Byfleet & New Haw	d						
Weybridge	d		23 34				
Walton-on-Thames	d		23 38				
Hersham	d						
Esher	d						
Surbiton 6	a		23 45				
Wimbledon 6 ⊖	a		23 53				
Earlsfield	a	←					
Clapham Junction 10	a	23 45	23 59	00 04			00 23
	a						
Vauxhall ⊖	a	23 50					
London Waterloo 15 ⊖	a	23 55	00 10	00 14			00 33

Mondays to Fridays
until 5 October

London - Guildford, Haslemere and Portsmouth

Network Diagram - see first Page of Table 155

Miles	Station		SW MX ■	SW MO ■ A	SW MX ■	SW MO ■ A	SW MX ■	SW MO ■ B	SW MX ■ C	SW ■ D	SW MX ■ C	SW MX ■ E	SW MO ■ F	SW ■ D	SW MX ■ E	SW ■	SW ■	SW ■	SW ■	SW ■	SW ■	SW ■	SW ■ ⚒
0	**London Waterloo** 15 ⊖	d	22p30	22p30	22p45	23p00	23p15	23p30	23p45	23p50		00 05	00 50	00 50	00 50			05 00	05 20	06 15	06 45	07 15	07 30
4	Clapham Junction 10	d		22b39	22b52	23b09	23b22	23b39	23b52	23b59		00u12	00 57	00 57	00u57			05 11	05 29	06u22	06u52	07u23	
24½	**Woking**	a	22p54	23p01	23p11	23p31	23p41	00 01	00 11	00 21		00 31	01 16	01 16	01 19			05 51	06 08	06 41	07 11	07 42	07 54
—		d	22p55	23p02	23p13	23p32	23p43	00 03	00 13	00 23		00 32	01 18	01 18	01 20			05 53	06 11	06 43	07 13	07 44	07 55
26¾	Worplesdon	d			23p18				00 18			00 37							06 16	06 48	07 18	07 49	
30¼	**Guildford**	a	23p03	23p10	23p23	23p40	23p51	00 10	00 24	00 30		00 43	01s26	01s26	01s28			06 00	06 21	06 53	07 23	07 54	08 03
—		d	23p04	23p12	23p25	23p42	23p52	00 12	00 25	00 32		00 45					05 15	06 04	06 30	06 55	07 25	07 56	08 04
33½	Farncombe	d	23p10		23p31	23p48	23p58		00 31			00 51						06 10	06 36	07 01	07 31	08 02	
34½	Godalming	d	23p13		23p34	23p51	00 02		00 34			00 54						06 13	06 39	07 04	07 34	08 05	08 11
36¼	Milford (Surrey)	d			23p38	23p55			00s38			00s58						06 17	06 43	07 08	07 38	08 09	
38½	Witley	d			23p42	23p59			00s43		←	01s02						06 21	06 47	07 12	07 42	08 13	
43	**Haslemere** 4	a	23p24	23p26	23p49	00 06	00 12	00 26	00 49	00 46	00 49	01 09		01s41	01s44		05 29	06 28	06 54	07 19	07 49	08 20	08 24
—		d	23p25	23p27	23p50	00 07	00 13	00 27	00 50	00 47	00 50	01 09					05 30	06 28	06 55	07 20	07 53	08 30	08 25
46¾	Liphook	d			23p55	00 12			→		00s55	01s14					05 35	06 33	07 00	07 25	07 59	→	
51½	Liss	d			00 01	00 18					01s01	01s20					05 41	06 39	07 06	07 31	08 05		
55	Petersfield	d	23p36	23p38	00 06	00 23	00 24	00 38		00 58	01 06	01 26		01s53	01s55		05 46	06 45	07 11	07 36	08 11		08 36
63¼	Rowlands Castle	d			00 16	00 33					01s16	01s35					05 56	06 54	07 21	07 46	08 21		
66½	**Havant**	a	23p48	23p50	00 21	00 38	00 36	00 50		01 10	01 21	01 40	02s00	02s06	02s08		06 01	06 59	07 27	07 51	08 26		08 49
—		d	23p49	23p51	00 22	00 39	00 37	00 51		01 11	01 21	01 41				04 40	06 02	07 00	07 28	07 52	08 27		08 50
67¼	Bedhampton	a			00 24	00 41					01s24	01s43				04 42	06 04	07 02	07 30	07 54	08 29		
70½	Hilsea	a			00 30						01s29	01s49				04 48	06 10	07 08	07 37	08 00	08 35		
72¾	Fratton	a	23p58	23p59	00 34	00 49	00 46	01 00		01 20	01s33	01s53	02s10	02s15	02s17	04 52	06 14	07 12	07 41	08 04	08 39		08 58
73¾	**Portsmouth & Southsea**	a	00 02	00 04	00 38	00 53	00 50	01 04		01 24	01 37	01 57	02s14	02s19	02 21	04 55	06 18	07 16	07 46	08 07	08 43		09 02
74½	**Portsmouth Harbour** ⛴	a	00 07	00 09		00 58	00 55	01 09		01 29			02 19	02 24		04 59	06 22	07 20		08 12	08 48		09 07

Station		SW ■	SW ■	SW ■ ⚒	SW ■	SW ■	SW ■ ⚒	SW ■	SW ■ ⚒	SW ■	SW ■	SW ■ ⚒	SW ■	SW ■ ⚒	SW ■	SW ■	SW ■ ⚒	SW ■	SW ■ ⚒	SW ■	SW ■	SW ■ ⚒	SW ■
London Waterloo 15 ⊖	d		07 45	08 00		08 15	08 30	08 45	09 00		09 15	09 30	09 45	10 00		10 15	10 30	10 45	11 00		11 15	11 30	11 45
Clapham Junction 10	d		07u52			08u22		08u52			09u22		09u52			10u22		10u52			11u22		11u52
Woking	a		08 12	08 24		08 42	08 55	09 11	09 24		09 42	09 54	10 11	10 24		10 41	10 54	11 11	11 24		11 41	11 54	12 11
	d		08 14	08 25		08 44	08 55	09 13	09 25		09 43	09 55	10 13	10 25		10 43	10 55	11 13	11 25		11 43	11 55	12 13
Worplesdon	d		08 19			08 49		09 18					10 18					11 18					12 18
Guildford	a		08 24	08 35		08 54	09 05	09 23	09 33		09 52	10 03	10 23	10 33		10 50	11 03	11 23	11 33		11 50	12 03	12 23
	d		08 26	08 39		08 56	09 07	09 25	09 34		09 54	10 04	10 25	10 34		10 52	11 04	11 25	11 34		11 52	12 04	12 25
Farncombe	d		08 32			09 02		09 31			10 00		10 31			10 58		11 31			11 58		12 31
Godalming	d		08 35			09 05		09 34			10 03		10 34			11 01		11 34			12 01		12 34
Milford (Surrey)	d		08 39			09 09					10 07					11 05					12 05		
Witley	d	←	08 43		←	09 13				←	10 11				←	11 09				←	12 09		
Haslemere 4	a	08 20	08 50	08 54	08 50	09 20	09 24	09 45	09 49	09 45	10 19	10 22	10 45	10 49	10 45	11 16	11 20	11 45	11 49	11 45	12 16	12 20	12 45
	d	08 30	08 58	08 55	08 58		09 25	09 55	09 50	09 55		10 23	10 55	10 50	10 55		11 21	11 55	11 50	11 55		12 21	12 55
Liphook	d	08 35	→		09 03			→		10 00			→		11 00			→		12 00			→
Liss	d	08 41			09 09					10 06					11 06					12 06			
Petersfield	d	08 46		09 06	09 15		09 36		10 01	10 11		10 34		11 01	11 11		11 32		12 01	12 11		12 32	
Rowlands Castle	d	08 56			09 24					10 21					11 21					12 21			
Havant	a	09 04		09 19	09 29		09 49		10 15	10 26		10 49		11 15	11 26		11 49		12 15	12 26		12 49	
	d	09 05		09 20	09 30		09 50		10 16	10 27		10 50		11 16	11 27		11 50		12 16	12 27		12 50	
Bedhampton	a	09 07			09 32					10 29					11 29					12 29			
Hilsea	a	09 13			09 38					10 36					11 36					12 36			
Fratton	a	09 17		09 28	09 42		09 59		10 24	10 40		10 59		11 24	11 40		11 59		12 24	12 40		12 59	
Portsmouth & Southsea	a	09 20		09 32	09 46		10 02		10 28	10 44		11 02		11 28	11 44		12 02		12 28	12 44		13 02	
Portsmouth Harbour ⛴	a	09 26		09 37			10 07		10 33			11 07		11 33			12 07		12 33			13 07	

Station		SW ■ ⚒	SW ■	SW ■	SW ■ ⚒	SW ■	SW ■ ⚒	SW ■	SW ■	SW ■ ⚒	SW ■	SW ■ ⚒	SW ■	SW ■	SW ■ ⚒	SW ■	SW ■ ⚒	SW ■	SW ■	SW ■ ⚒	SW ■	SW ■
London Waterloo 15 ⊖	d	12 00		12 15	12 30	12 45	13 00		13 15	13 30	13 45	14 00		14 15	14 30	14 45	15 00		15 15	15 30		15 45
Clapham Junction 10	d			12u22		12u52			13u22		13u52			14u22		14u52			15u22			15u52
Woking	a	12 24		12 41	12 54	13 11	13 24		13 41	13 54	14 11	14 24		14 41	14 54	15 11	15 24		15 41	15 54		16 11
	d	12 25		12 43	12 55	13 13	13 25		13 43	13 55	14 13	14 25		14 43	14 55	15 13	15 25		15 43	15 55		16 13
Worplesdon	d					13 18					14 18					15 18			15 48			
Guildford	a	12 33		12 50	13 03	13 23	13 33		13 50	14 03	14 23	14 33		14 50	15 03	15 23	15 33		15 53	16 03		16 20
	d	12 34		12 52	13 04	13 25	13 34		13 52	14 04	14 25	14 34		14 52	15 04	15 25	15 34		15 55	16 04		16 22
Farncombe	d			12 58		13 31			13 58		14 31			14 58		15 31			16 01			16 28
Godalming	d			13 01		13 34			14 01		14 34			15 01		15 34			16 04			16 31
Milford (Surrey)	d			13 05					14 05					15 05					16 08			16 35
Witley	d		←	13 09				←	14 09				←	15 09				←	16 12		←	16 39
Haslemere 4	a	12 49	12 45	13 16	13 20	13 45	13 49	13 45	14 16	14 20	14 45	14 49	14 45	15 16	15 20	15 45	15 49	15 45	16 19	16 23	16 19	16 46
	d	12 50	12 55		13 21	13 55	13 50	13 55		14 21	14 55	14 50	14 55		15 21	15 55	15 50	15 55	16 29	16 24	16 29	16 55
Liphook	d		13 00			→		14 00			→		15 00			→		16 00	→		16 34	→
Liss	d		13 06					14 06					15 06					16 06			16 40	
Petersfield	d	13 01	13 11		13 32		14 01	14 11		14 32		15 01	15 11		15 32		16 01	16 11		16 35	16 45	
Rowlands Castle	d		13 21					14 21					15 21					16 21			16 55	
Havant	a	13 15	13 26		13 49		14 15	14 26		14 49		15 14	15 26		15 49		16 15	16 26		16 49	17 03	
	d	13 16	13 27		13 50		14 16	14 27		14 50		15 16	15 27		15 50		16 16	16 27		16 50	17 04	
Bedhampton	a		13 29					14 29					15 29					16 29			17 06	
Hilsea	a		13 36					14 36					15 36					16 36			17 11	
Fratton	a	13 24	13 40		13 59		14 24	14 40		14 58		15 24	15 40		15 59		16 24	16 40		16 59	17 15	
Portsmouth & Southsea	a	13 28	13 44		14 02		14 28	14 44		15 02		15 28	15 44		16 02		16 28	16 44		17 02	17 20	
Portsmouth Harbour ⛴	a	13 33			14 07		14 33			15 07		15 33			16 07		16 33	16 49		17 07	17 26	

A from 21 May until 1 October
B from 21 May until 23 July, 20 August, 27 August, 17 September, 24 September, 1 October
C not from 31 July until 10 August, from 30 August until 7 September
D 30 July, 6 August, 13 August, 3 September, 10 September
E from 31 July until 7 September, not from 14 August until 29 August
F until 23 July, 20 August, 27 August, 17 September, 24 September, 1 October
b Previous night, stops to pick up only

Table 156

London - Guildford, Haslemere and Portsmouth

Network Diagram - see first Page of Table 155

Mondays to Fridays
until 5 October

		SW	SW	SW	SW	SW	SW	SW	SW	SW	SW	SW	SW	SW	SW	SW	SW	SW	SW	SW	SW	SW	SW
		1 ⫪	1	1	1 ⫪	1	1	1 ⫪	1	1	1 ⫪	1	1	1 ⫪	1	1	1	1 ⫪	1	1 ⫪	1	1	1 ⫪
London Waterloo [15] ⊖	d	16 00		16 15	16 30		16 45	17 00		17 15	17 30		17 45	18 00		18 15	18 18	18 30	18 45	19 00		19 15	19 30
Clapham Junction [10]	d			16u22			16u52															19u22	
Woking	a	16 24		16 41	16 54		17 11	17 24		17 38	17 54						18 42	18 57	19 13	19 24		19 43	19 54
	d	16 25		16 43	16 55		17 13	17 25		17 40	17 56						18 43	18 58	19 14	19 25		19 45	19 55
Worplesdon	d			16 48				17 30		17 45	18 00						18 48			19 30			
Guildford	a	16 33		16 53	17 03		17 20	17 36		17 51	18 06		18 21	18 32		18 50	18 54	19 06	19 23	19 36		19 52	20 03
	d	16 34		16 55	17 04		17 22	17 37		17 54	18 08		18 23	18 33		18 51	18 57	19 08	19 24	19 37		19 54	20 04
Farncombe	d			17 01			17 28			18 00			18 29				19 03		19 30			20 00	
Godalming	d			17 04			17 31			18 03	18 15		18 32	18 40			19 06	19 14	19 33			20 03	20 11
Milford (Surrey)	d			17 08			17 35			18 07			18 36				19 10		19 37			20 07	
Witley	d		←	17 12		←	17 39		←	18 11		←	18 40		←		19 14		19 41		←	20 11	
Haslemere [4]	a	16 50	16 46	17 19	17 23	17 19	17 46	17 51	17 46	18 18	18 25	18 18	18 49	18 51	18 49	19 05	19 23	19 25	19 49	19 52	19 49	20 18	20 22
	d	16 51	16 55	17 29	17 24	17 29	17 56	17 52	17 56	18 31	18 26	18 31	18 56	18 52	18 56	19 06		19 26	19 57	19 53	19 57	20 27	20 22
Liphook	d		17 00	→		17 34	→		18 01	→		18 36	→		19 01	19 11			→		20 02	→	
Liss	d		17 06			17 40			18 07			18 42			19 07	19 17					20 08		
Petersfield	d	17 02	17 11		17 35	17 45		18 03	18 12		18 37	18 47		19 03	19 12	19 23		19 37		20 04	20 13		20 33
Rowlands Castle	d		17 21			17 55			18 22			18 57			19 22	19 32					20 23		
Havant	a	17 15	17 26		17 49	18 03		18 19	18 29		18 50	19 02		19 16	19 29	19 40		19 50		20 16	20 28		20 48
	d	17 16	17 27		17 50	18 04		18 20	18 30		18 51	19 03		19 17		19 41		19 51		20 17	20 29		20 49
Bedhampton	a		17 29			18 07			18 32			19 06				19 44					20 31		
Hilsea	a		17 36			18 12			18 39			19 11				19 49					20 37		
Fratton	a	17 24	17 40		17 59	18 16		18 28	18 43		18 59	19 15		19 25		19 55		19 59		20 25	20 41		20 57
Portsmouth & Southsea	a	17 28	17 44		18 02	18 20		18 32	18 46		19 03			19 29				20 03		20 29	20 44		21 01
Portsmouth Harbour ⛴	a	17 35			18 09	18 28		18 39			19 10			19 36				20 10		20 34	20 52		21 06

		SW	SW	SW	SW	SW	SW	SW	SW	SW	SW	SW	SW	SW	SW	SW	SW	SW
		1	1	1 ⫪	1	1	1 ⫪	1	1 ⫪	1	1 ⫪	1	1	1	1	1	1	1 A
London Waterloo [15] ⊖	d		19 45	20 00		20 15	20 30	20 45	21 00		21 30	21 45	22 00		22 30	22 45	23 15	23 45
Clapham Junction [10]	d		19u52			20u22		20u52				21u52				22u52	23u22	23u52
Woking	a		20 11	20 24		20 41	20 54	21 11	21 24		21 54	22 11	22 24		22 54	23 11	23 41	00 11
	d		20 13	20 25		20 43	20 55	21 13	21 25		21 55	22 13	22 25		22 55	23 13	23 43	00 13
Worplesdon	d		20 18					21 18				22 18				23 18		00 18
Guildford	a		20 23	20 33		20 50	21 03	21 23	21 33		22 03	22 23	22 33		23 03	23 23	23 51	00 24
	d		20 25	20 34		20 52	21 04	21 25	21 34		22 04	22 25	22 34		23 04	23 25	23 52	00 25
Farncombe	d		20 31	20 40		20 58		21 31	21 40		22 10	22 31	22 40		23 10	23 31	23 58	00 31
Godalming	d		20 34	20 43		21 01	21 11	21 34	21 43		22 13	22 34	22 43		23 13	23 34	00 02	00 34
Milford (Surrey)	d		20 38			21 05		21 38				22 38				23 38		00s38
Witley	d	←	20 42		←	21 09		21 42		←		22 42		←		23 42		00s43
Haslemere [4]	a	20 18	20 49	20 54	20 49	21 16	21 21	21 49	21 54	21 49	22 24	22 49	22 54	22 49	23 24	23 49	00 12	00 49
	d	20 27	20 59	20 55	20 59		21 22	21 59	21 55	21 59	22 25	22 59	22 55	22 59	23 25	23 50	00 13	00 50
Liphook	d	20 32	→		21 04			→		22 04		→		23 04		23 55		00s55
Liss	d	20 38			21 10					22 10				23 10		00 01		01s01
Petersfield	d	20 43		21 06	21 16		21 33		22 06	22 16	22 36		23 06	23 15	23 36	00 06	00 24	01 06
Rowlands Castle	d	20 53			21 25					22 25				23 25		00 16		01s16
Havant	a	21 00		21 18	21 30		21 45		22 18	22 30	22 48		23 18	23 30	23 48	00 21	00 36	01 21
	d			21 19	21 31		21 46		22 19	22 31	22 49		23 19	23 31	23 49	00 22	00 37	01 21
Bedhampton	a				21 34					22 34				23 33		00 24		01s24
Hilsea	a				21 41					22 39				23 39		00 30		01s29
Fratton	a			21 28	21 45		21 54		22 28	22 43	22 59		23 28	23 43	23 58	00 34	00 46	01s33
Portsmouth & Southsea	a			21 32	21 48		21 58		22 32	22 47	23 04		23 32	23 47	00 02	00 38	00 50	01 37
Portsmouth Harbour ⛴	a			21 37			22 02		22 37		23 08		23 37		00 07		00 55	

Mondays to Fridays
from 8 October

		SW	SW	SW	SW	SW	SW	SW	SW	SW	SW	SW	SW	SW	SW	SW	SW	SW	SW	SW	SW	SW	SW
		MX	MO	MX	MO	MX	MO	MX	MO														
		1	1	1	1	1	1	1	1	1	1	1	1	1	1	1	1 ⫪	1	1	1 ⫪	1	1	1 ⫪
London Waterloo [15] ⊖	d	22p30	22p30	22p45	23p00	23p15	23p30	23p45	00 50			05 00	05 20	06 15	06 45	07 15	07 30		07 45	08 00		08 15	08 30
Clapham Junction [10]	d		22b39	22b52	23b09	23b22	23b39	23b52	00 57			05 11	05 29	06u22	06u52	07u23			07u52			08u22	
Woking	a	22p54	23p01	23p11	23p31	23p41	00 01	00 11	01 16			05 51	06 08	06 41	07 11	07 42	07 54		08 12	08 24		08 42	08 55
	d	22p55	23p02	23p13	23p32	23p43	00 03	00 13	01 18			05 53	06 11	06 43	07 13	07 44	07 55		08 14	08 25		08 44	08 55
Worplesdon	d			23p18				00 18					06 16	06 48	07 18	07 49			08 19			08 49	
Guildford	a	23p03	23p10	23p23	23p40	23p51	00 10	00 24	01s26			06 00	06 21	06 53	07 23	07 54	08 03		08 24	08 35		08 54	09 05
	d	23p04	23p12	23p25	23p42	23p52	00 12	00 25			05 15	06 04	06 30	06 55	07 25	07 56	08 04		08 26	08 39		08 56	09 07
Farncombe	d	23p10		23p31	23p48	23p58		00 31				06 10	06 36	07 01	07 31	08 02			08 32			09 02	
Godalming	d	23p13		23p34	23p51	00 02		00 34				06 13	06 39	07 04	07 34	08 05	08 11		08 35			09 05	
Milford (Surrey)	d			23p38	23p55			00s38				06 17	06 43	07 08	07 38	08 09			08 39			09 09	
Witley	d			23p42	23p59			00s43				06 21	06 47	07 12	07 42	08 13		←	08 43		←	09 13	
Haslemere [4]	a	23p24	23p26	23p49	00 06	00 12	00 26	00 49			05 29	06 28	06 54	07 19	07 49	08 20	08 24	08 20	08 50	08 54	08 50	09 20	09 24
	d	23p25	23p27	23p50	00 07	00 13	00 27	00 50			05 30	06 28	06 55	07 20	07 53	08 30	08 25	08 30	08 58	08 55	08 58		09 25
Liphook	d			23p55	00 12			00s55			05 35	06 33	07 00	07 25	07 59	→		08 35	→		09 03		
Liss	d			00 01	00 18			01s01			05 41	06 39	07 06	07 31	08 05			08 41			09 09		
Petersfield	d	23p36	23p38	00 06	00 23	00 24	00 38	01 06			05 46	06 45	07 11	07 36	08 11		08 36	08 46		09 06	09 15		09 36
Rowlands Castle	d			00 16	00 33			01s16			05 56	06 54	07 21	07 46	08 21			08 56			09 24		
Havant	a	23p48	23p50	00 21	00 38	00 36	00 50	01 21	02s00		06 01	06 59	07 27	07 51	08 26		08 49	09 04		09 19	09 29		09 49
	d	23p49	23p51	00 22	00 39	00 37	00 51	01 21		04 40	06 02	07 00	07 28	07 52	08 27		08 50	09 05		09 20	09 30		09 50
Bedhampton	a			00 24	00 41			01s24		04 42	06 04	07 02	07 30	07 54	08 29			09 07			09 32		
Hilsea	a			00 30				01s29		04 48	06 10	07 08	07 37	08 00	08 35			09 13			09 38		
Fratton	a	23p58	23p59	00 34	00 49	00 46	01 00	01s33	02s10	04 52	06 14	07 12	07 41	08 04	08 39		08 58	09 17		09 28	09 42		09 59
Portsmouth & Southsea	a	00 02	00 04	00 38	00 53	00 50	01 04	01 37	02s14	04 55	06 18	07 16	07 46	08 07	08 43		09 02	09 20		09 32	09 46		10 02
Portsmouth Harbour ⛴	a	00 07	00 09		00 58	00 55	01 09		02 19	04 59	06 22	07 20		08 12	08 48		09 07	09 26		09 37			10 07

A not from 27 July until 10 August, from 29 August until 7 September

b Previous night, stops to pick up only

Table 156

London - Guildford, Haslemere and Portsmouth

Network Diagram - see first Page of Table 155

Mondays to Fridays
from 8 October

		SW	SW	SW	SW	SW	SW	SW	SW	SW	SW	SW	SW	SW	SW	SW	SW	SW	SW	SW	SW	SW	SW
		1	1 ⫪	1	1	1 ⫪	1	1 ⫪	1	1	1 ⫪	1	1 ⫪	1	1	1 ⫪	1	1 ⫪	1	1	1 ⫪	1	1 ⫪
London Waterloo [15] ⊖	d	08 45	09 00		09 15	09 30	09 45	10 00		10 15	10 30	10 45	11 00		11 15	11 30	11 45	12 00		12 15	12 30	12 45	13 00
Clapham Junction [10]	d	08u52			09u22		09u52			10u22		10u52			11u22		11u52			12u22		12u52	
Woking	a	09 11	09 24		09 42	09 54	10 11	10 24		10 41	10 54	11 11	11 24		11 41	11 54	12 11	12 24		12 41	12 54	13 11	13 24
	d	09 13	09 25		09 43	09 55	10 13	10 25		10 43	10 55	11 13	11 25		11 43	11 55	12 13	12 25		12 43	12 55	13 13	13 25
Worplesdon	d	09 18					10 18					11 18					12 18					13 18	
Guildford	a	09 23	09 33		09 52	10 03	10 23	10 33		10 50	11 03	11 23	11 33		11 50	12 03	12 23	12 33		12 50	13 03	13 23	13 33
	d	09 25	09 34		09 54	10 04	10 25	10 34		10 52	11 04	11 25	11 34		11 52	12 04	12 25	12 34		12 52	13 04	13 25	13 34
Farncombe	d	09 31			10 00		10 31			10 58		11 31			11 58		12 31			12 58		13 31	
Godalming	d	09 34			10 03		10 34			11 01		11 34			12 01		12 34			13 01		13 34	
Milford (Surrey)	d				10 07					11 05					12 05					13 05			
Witley	d			←	10 11				←	11 09				←	12 09				←	13 09			
Haslemere [4]	a	09 45	09 49	09 45	10 19	10 22	10 45	10 49	10 45	11 16	11 20	11 45	11 49	11 45	12 16	12 20	12 45	12 49	12 45	13 16	13 20	13 45	13 49
	d	09 55	09 50	09 55		10 23	10 55	10 50	10 55		11 21	11 55	11 50	11 55		12 21	12 55	12 50	12 55		13 21	13 55	13 50
Liphook	d	→		10 00			→		11 00			→		12 00			→		13 00			→	
Liss	d			10 06					11 06					12 06					13 06				
Petersfield	d		10 01	10 11		10 34		11 01	11 11		11 32		12 01	12 11		12 32		13 01	13 11		13 32		14 01
Rowlands Castle	d			10 21					11 21					12 21					13 21				
Havant	a		10 15	10 26		10 49		11 15	11 26		11 49		12 15	12 26		12 49		13 15	13 26		13 49		14 15
	d		10 16	10 27		10 50		11 16	11 27		11 50		12 16	12 27		12 50		13 16	13 27		13 50		14 16
Bedhampton	a			10 29					11 29					12 29					13 29				
Hilsea	a			10 36					11 36					12 36					13 36				
Fratton	a		10 24	10 40		10 59		11 24	11 40		11 59		12 24	12 40		12 59		13 24	13 40		13 59		14 24
Portsmouth & Southsea	a		10 28	10 44		11 02		11 28	11 44		12 02		12 28	12 44		13 02		13 28	13 44		14 02		14 28
Portsmouth Harbour ⛴	a		10 33			11 07		11 33			12 07		12 33			13 07		13 33			14 07		14 33

		SW	SW	SW	SW	SW	SW	SW	SW	SW	SW	SW	SW	SW	SW	SW	SW	SW	SW	SW	SW	SW
		1	1	1 ⫪	1	1 ⫪	1	1	1 ⫪	1	1 ⫪	1	1	1 ⫪	1	1	1 ⫪	1	1	1 ⫪	1	1
London Waterloo [15] ⊖	d		13 15	13 30	13 45	14 00		14 15	14 30	14 45	15 00		15 15	15 30		15 45	16 00		16 15	16 30		16 45
Clapham Junction [10]	d		13u22		13u52			14u22		14u52			15u22			15u52			16u22			16u52
Woking	a		13 41	13 54	14 11	14 24		14 41	14 54	15 11	15 24		15 41	15 54		16 11	16 24		16 41	16 54		17 11
	d		13 43	13 55	14 13	14 25		14 43	14 55	15 13	15 25		15 43	15 55		16 13	16 25		16 43	16 55		17 13
Worplesdon	d				14 18					15 18			15 48						16 48			
Guildford	a		13 50	14 03	14 23	14 33		14 50	15 03	15 23	15 33		15 53	16 03		16 20	16 33		16 53	17 03		17 20
	d		13 52	14 04	14 25	14 34		14 52	15 04	15 25	15 34		15 55	16 04		16 22	16 34		16 55	17 04		17 22
Farncombe	d		13 58		14 31			14 58		15 31			16 01			16 28			17 01			17 28
Godalming	d		14 01		14 34			15 01		15 34			16 04			16 31			17 04			17 31
Milford (Surrey)	d		14 05					15 05					16 08			16 35			17 08			17 35
Witley	d	←	14 09				←	15 09				←	16 12		←	16 39		←	17 12		←	17 39
Haslemere [4]	a	13 45	14 16	14 20	14 45	14 49	14 45	15 16	15 20	15 45	15 49	15 45	16 19	16 23	16 19	16 46	16 50	16 46	17 19	17 23	17 19	17 46
	d	13 55		14 21	14 55	14 50	14 55		15 21	15 55	15 50	15 55	16 29	16 24	16 29	16 55	16 51	16 55	17 29	17 24	17 29	17 56
Liphook	d	14 00			→		15 00			→		16 00	→		16 34	→		17 00	→		17 34	→
Liss	d	14 06					15 06					16 06			16 40			17 06			17 40	
Petersfield	d	14 11		14 32		15 01	15 11		15 32		16 01	16 11		16 35	16 45		17 02	17 11		17 35	17 45	
Rowlands Castle	d	14 21					15 21					16 21			16 55			17 21			17 55	
Havant	a	14 26		14 49		15 14	15 26		15 49		16 15	16 26		16 49	17 03		17 15	17 26		17 49	18 03	
	d	14 27		14 50		15 16	15 27		15 50		16 16	16 27		16 50	17 04		17 16	17 27		17 50	18 04	
Bedhampton	a	14 29					15 29					16 29			17 06			17 29			18 07	
Hilsea	a	14 36					15 36					16 36			17 11			17 36			18 12	
Fratton	a	14 40		14 58		15 24	15 40		15 59		16 24	16 40		16 59	17 15		17 24	17 40		17 59	18 16	
Portsmouth & Southsea	a	14 44		15 02		15 28	15 44		16 02		16 28	16 44		17 02	17 20		17 28	17 44		18 02	18 20	
Portsmouth Harbour ⛴	a			15 07		15 33			16 07		16 33	16 49		17 07	17 26		17 35			18 09	18 28	

		SW	SW	SW	SW	SW	SW	SW	SW	SW	SW	SW	SW	SW	SW	SW	SW	SW	SW	SW	SW	SW	SW
		1 ⫪	1	1	1 ⫪	1	1	1 ⫪	1	1	1	1 ⫪	1	1 ⫪	1	1	1 ⫪	1	1	1 ⫪	1	1	1 ⫪
London Waterloo [15] ⊖	d	17 00		17 15	17 30		17 45	18 00		18 15	18 18	18 30	18 45	19 00		19 15	19 30		19 45	20 00		20 15	20 30
Clapham Junction [10]	d															19u22			19u52			20u22	
Woking	a	17 24		17 38	17 54						18 42	18 57	19 13	19 24		19 43	19 54		20 11	20 24		20 41	20 54
	d	17 25		17 40	17 56						18 43	18 58	19 14	19 25		19 45	19 55		20 13	20 25		20 43	20 55
Worplesdon	d	17 30		17 45	18 00						18 48			19 30					20 18				
Guildford	a	17 36		17 51	18 06		18 21	18 32		18 50	18 54	19 06	19 23	19 36		19 52	20 03		20 23	20 33		20 50	21 03
	d	17 37		17 54	18 08		18 23	18 33		18 51	18 57	19 08	19 24	19 37		19 54	20 04		20 25	20 34		20 52	21 04
Farncombe	d			18 00			18 29				19 03		19 30			20 00			20 31	20 40		20 58	
Godalming	d			18 03	18 15		18 32	18 40			19 06	19 14	19 33			20 03	20 11		20 34	20 43		21 01	21 11
Milford (Surrey)	d			18 07			18 36				19 10		19 37			20 07			20 38			21 05	
Witley	d		←	18 11		←	18 40		←		19 14		19 41		←	20 11		←	20 42		←	21 09	
Haslemere [4]	a	17 51	17 46	18 18	18 25	18 18	18 49	18 51	18 49	19 05	19 23	19 25	19 49	19 52	19 49	20 18	20 22	20 18	20 49	20 54	20 49	21 16	21 21
	d	17 52	17 56	18 31	18 26	18 31	18 56	18 52	18 56	19 06		19 26	19 57	19 53	19 57	20 27	20 22	20 27	20 59	20 55	20 59		21 22
Liphook	d		18 01	→		18 36	→		19 01	19 11			→		20 02	→		20 32	→		21 04		
Liss	d		18 07			18 42			19 07	19 17					20 08			20 38			21 10		
Petersfield	d	18 03	18 12		18 37	18 47		19 03	19 12	19 23		19 37		20 04	20 13		20 33	20 43		21 06	21 16		21 33
Rowlands Castle	d		18 22			18 57			19 22	19 32					20 23			20 53			21 25		
Havant	a	18 19	18 29		18 50	19 02		19 16	19 29	19 40		19 50		20 16	20 28		20 48	21 00		21 18	21 30		21 45
	d	18 20	18 30		18 51	19 03		19 17		19 41		19 51		20 17	20 29		20 49			21 19	21 31		21 46
Bedhampton	a		18 32			19 06				19 44					20 31						21 34		
Hilsea	a		18 39			19 11				19 49					20 37						21 41		
Fratton	a	18 28	18 43		18 59	19 15		19 25		19 55		19 59		20 25	20 41		20 57			21 28	21 45		21 54
Portsmouth & Southsea	a	18 32	18 46		19 03			19 29				20 03		20 29	20 44		21 01			21 32	21 48		21 58
Portsmouth Harbour ⛴	a	18 39			19 10			19 36				20 10		20 34	20 52		21 06			21 37			22 02

London - Guildford, Haslemere and Portsmouth

Mondays to Fridays from 8 October

Network Diagram - see first Page of Table 155

		SW 1	SW 1 ⊼	SW 1	SW 1 ⊼	SW 1	SW 1	SW 1	SW 1	SW 1	SW 1	SW 1
London Waterloo 15 ⊖	d	20 45	21 00		21 30	21 45	22 00		22 30	22 45	23 15	23 45
Clapham Junction 10	d	20u52				21u52				22u52	23u22	23u52
Woking	a	21 11	21 24		21 54	22 11	22 24		22 54	23 11	23 41	00 11
	d	21 13	21 25		21 55	22 13	22 25		22 55	23 13	23 43	00 13
Worplesdon	d	21 18				22 18				23 18		00 18
Guildford	a	21 23	21 33		22 03	22 23	22 33		23 03	23 23	23 51	00 24
	d	21 25	21 34		22 04	22 25	22 34		23 04	23 25	23 52	00 25
Farncombe	d	21 31	21 40		22 10	22 31	22 40		23 10	23 31	23 58	00 31
Godalming	d	21 34	21 43		22 13	22 34	22 43		23 13	23 34	00 02	00 34
Milford (Surrey)	d	21 38				22 38				23 38		00s38
Witley	d	21 42		←		22 42		←		23 42		00s43
Haslemere 4	a	21 49	21 54	21 49	22 24	22 49	22 54	22 49	23 24	23 49	00 12	00 49
	d	21 59	21 55	21 59	22 25	22 59	22 55	22 59	23 25	23 50	00 13	00 50
Liphook	d	→		22 04		→		23 04		23 55		00s55
Liss	d			22 10				23 10		00 01		01s01
Petersfield	d		22 06	22 16	22 36		23 06	23 15	23 36	00 06	00 24	01 06
Rowlands Castle	d			22 25				23 25		00 16		01s16
Havant	a		22 18	22 30	22 48		23 18	23 30	23 48	00 21	00 36	01 21
	d		22 19	22 31	22 49		23 19	23 31	23 49	00 22	00 37	01 21
Bedhampton	a			22 34				23 33		00 24		01s24
Hilsea	a			22 39				23 39		00 30		01s29
Fratton	a		22 28	22 43	22 59		23 28	23 43	23 58	00 34	00 46	01s33
Portsmouth & Southsea	a		22 32	22 47	23 04		23 32	23 47	00 02	00 38	00 50	01 37
Portsmouth Harbour ⛴	a		22 37		23 08		23 37		00 07		00 55	

Saturdays until 6 October

		SW 1	SW 1	SW 1	SW 1 A	SW 1 B	SW 1 B	SW 1	SW 1	SW 1	SW 1	SW 1	SW 1	SW 1	SW 1	SW 1	SW 1	SW 1	SW 1	SW 1	SW 1	SW 1 ⊼	SW 1
London Waterloo 15 ⊖	d	22p30	22p45	23p15	23p45	00§05	00§50			05 00	05 20	06 15	06 45	07 15	07 30	07 45	08 00		08 15	08 30	08 45	09 00	
Clapham Junction 10	d		22b52	23b22	23b52	00u12	00u57			05 11	05 29	06u22	06u52	07u23		07u52			08u22		08u52		
Woking	a	22p54	23p11	23p41	00§11	00§31	01§19			05 51	06 08	06 41	07 11	07 42	07 54	08 11	08 24		08 41	08 54	09 11	09 24	
	d	22p55	23p13	23p43	00§13	00§32	01§20			05 53	06 13	06 43	07 13	07 44	07 55	08 13	08 25		08 43	08 55	09 13	09 25	
Worplesdon	d		23p18		00§18	00§37	§				06 18		07 18			08 18					09 18		
Guildford	a	23p03	23p23	23p51	00§24	00§43	01s28			06 00	06 23	06 51	07 23	07 51	08 03	08 23	08 33		08 50	09 03	09 23	09 33	
	d	23p04	23p25	23p52	00§25	00§45	§		05 15	06 02	06 25	06 53	07 25	07 53	08 04	08 25	08 34		08 52	09 04	09 25	09 34	
Farncombe	d	23p10	23p31	23p58	00§31	00§51	§			06 08	06 31	06 59	07 31	07 59		08 31			08 58		09 31		
Godalming	d	23p13	23p34	00 02	00§34	00§54	§			06 11	06 34	07 02	07 34	08 02		08 34			09 01		09 34		
Milford (Surrey)	d		23p38		00s38	00s58	§			06 15		07 06		08 06					09 05				
Witley	d		23p42		00s43	01s02	§			06 19		07 10		08 10				←	09 09				←
Haslemere 4	a	23p24	23p49	00 12	00§49	01§09	01s44		05 29	06 26	06 44	07 17	07 44	08 17	08 20	08 45	08 49	08 45	09 16	09 20	09 45	09 49	09 45
	d	23p25	23p50	00 13	00§50	01§09	§		05 30		06 45		07 45		08 21	08 55	08 50	08 55		09 21	09 55	09 50	09 55
Liphook	d		23p55		00s55	01s14	§		05 35		06 50		07 50			→		09 00			→		10 00
Liss	d		00 01		01s01	01s20	§		05 41		06 56		07 56					09 06					10 06
Petersfield	d	23p36	00 06	00 24	01§06	01§26	01s55		05 46		07 01		08 01		08 32		09 01	09 11		09 32		10 01	10 11
Rowlands Castle	d		00 16		01s16	01s35	§		05 56		07 11		08 11					09 21					10 21
Havant	a	23p48	00 21	00 36	01§21	01§40	02s08		06 01		07 19		08 16		08 49		09 15	09 26		09 49		10 15	10 26
	d	23p49	00 22	00 37	01§21	01§41	§	04 40	06 02		07 20		08 17		08 50		09 16	09 27		09 50		10 16	10 27
Bedhampton	a		00 24		01s24	01s43	§	04 42	06 04		07 22		08 19					09 29					10 29
Hilsea	a		00 30		01s29	01s49	§	04 48	06 10		07 27		08 25					09 36					10 36
Fratton	a	23p58	00 34	00 46	01s33	01s53	02s17	04 52	06 14		07 31		08 29		08 59		09 24	09 40		09 59		10 24	10 40
Portsmouth & Southsea	a	00 02	00 38	00 50	01§37	01§57	02§21	04 55	06 18		07 35		08 32		09 02		09 28	09 44		10 02		10 28	10 44
Portsmouth Harbour ⛴	a	00 07		00 55				05 00	06 22		07 40		08 37		09 07		09 33			10 07		10 33	

		SW 1	SW 1 ⊼	SW 1	SW 1 ⊼	SW 1	SW 1	SW 1 ⊼	SW 1	SW 1 ⊼	SW 1	SW 1	SW 1 ⊼	SW 1	SW 1 ⊼	SW 1	SW 1	SW 1 ⊼	SW 1	SW 1 ⊼	SW 1	SW 1	SW 1 ⊼
London Waterloo 15 ⊖	d	09 15	09 30	09 45	10 00		10 15	10 30	10 45	11 00		11 15	11 30	11 45	12 00		12 15	12 30	12 45	13 00		13 15	13 30
Clapham Junction 10	d	09u22		09u52			10u22		10u52			11u22		11u52			12u22		12u52			13u22	
Woking	a	09 41	09 54	10 11	10 24		10 41	10 54	11 11	11 24		11 41	11 54	12 11	12 24		12 41	12 54	13 11	13 24		13 41	13 54
	d	09 43	09 55	10 13	10 25		10 43	10 55	11 13	11 25		11 43	11 55	12 13	12 25		12 43	12 55	13 13	13 25		13 43	13 55
Worplesdon	d			10 18					11 18					12 18					13 18				
Guildford	a	09 50	10 03	10 23	10 33		10 50	11 03	11 23	11 33		11 50	12 03	12 23	12 33		12 50	13 03	13 23	13 33		13 50	14 03
	d	09 52	10 04	10 25	10 34		10 52	11 04	11 25	11 34		11 52	12 04	12 25	12 34		12 52	13 04	13 25	13 34		13 52	14 04
Farncombe	d	09 58		10 31			10 58		11 31			11 58		12 31			12 58		13 31			13 58	
Godalming	d	10 01		10 34			11 01		11 34			12 01		12 34			13 01		13 34			14 01	
Milford (Surrey)	d	10 05					11 05					12 05					13 05					14 05	
Witley	d	10 09				←	11 09				←	12 09				←	13 09				←	14 09	
Haslemere 4	a	10 16	10 20	10 45	10 49	10 45	11 16	11 20	11 45	11 49	11 45	12 16	12 20	12 45	12 49	12 45	13 16	13 20	13 45	13 49	13 45	14 16	14 20
	d		10 21	10 55	10 50	10 55		11 21	11 55	11 50	11 55		12 21	12 55	12 50	12 55		13 21	13 55	13 50	13 55		14 21
Liphook	d			→		11 00			→		12 00			→		13 00			→		14 00		
Liss	d					11 06					12 06					13 06					14 06		
Petersfield	d		10 32		11 01	11 11		11 32		12 01	12 11		12 32		13 01	13 11		13 32		14 01	14 11		14 32
Rowlands Castle	d					11 21					12 21					13 21					14 21		
Havant	a		10 49		11 15	11 26		11 49		12 15	12 26		12 49		13 15	13 26		13 49		14 15	14 26		14 49
	d		10 50		11 16	11 27		11 50		12 16	12 27		12 50		13 16	13 27		13 50		14 16	14 27		14 50
Bedhampton	a					11 29					12 29					13 29					14 29		
Hilsea	a					11 36					12 36					13 36					14 36		
Fratton	a		10 59		11 24	11 40		11 59		12 24	12 40		12 59		13 24	13 40		13 59		14 24	14 40		14 59
Portsmouth & Southsea	a		11 02		11 28	11 44		12 02		12 28	12 44		13 02		13 28	13 44		14 02		14 28	14 44		15 02
Portsmouth Harbour ⛴	a		11 07		11 33			12 07		12 33			13 07		13 33			14 07		14 33			15 07

A until 21 July, 18 August, 25 August, 15 September, 22 September, 29 September, 6 October

B 28 July, 4 August, 11 August, 1 September, 8 September

b Previous night, stops to pick up only

London - Guildford, Haslemere and Portsmouth

Saturdays until 6 October

Network Diagram - see first Page of Table 155

		SW 1	SW 1 ⊼	SW 1	SW 1	SW 1 ⊼	SW 1	SW 1 ⊼	SW 1	SW 1	SW 1 ⊼	SW 1	SW 1 ⊼	SW 1	SW 1	SW 1 ⊼	SW 1	SW 1 ⊼	SW 1	SW 1	SW 1 ⊼	SW 1
London Waterloo 15 ⊖	d	13 45	14 00		14 15	14 30	14 45	15 00		15 15	15 30	15 45	16 00		16 15	16 30	16 45	17 00		17 15	17 30	17 45
Clapham Junction 10	d	13u52			14u22		14u52			15u22		15u52			16u22		16u52			17u22		17u52
Woking	a	14 11	14 24		14 41	14 54	15 11	15 24		15 41	15 54	16 11	16 24		16 41	16 54	17 11	17 24		17 41	17 54	18 11
	d	14 13	14 25		14 43	14 55	15 13	15 25		15 43	15 55	16 13	16 25		16 43	16 55	17 13	17 25		17 43	17 55	18 13
Worplesdon	d	14 18					15 18					16 18					17 18					18 18
Guildford	a	14 23	14 33		14 50	15 03	15 23	15 33		15 50	16 03	16 23	16 33		16 50	17 03	17 23	17 33		17 50	18 03	18 23
	d	14 25	14 34		14 52	15 04	15 25	15 34		15 52	16 04	16 25	16 34		16 52	17 04	17 25	17 34		17 52	18 04	18 25
Farncombe	d	14 31			14 58		15 31			15 58		16 31			16 58		17 31			17 58		18 31
Godalming	d	14 34			15 01		15 34			16 01		16 34			17 01		17 34			18 01		18 34
Milford (Surrey)	d				15 05					16 05					17 05					18 05		
Witley	d			←	15 09				←	16 09				←	17 09				←	18 09		
Haslemere 4	a	14 45	14 49	14 45	15 16	15 20	15 45	15 49	15 45	16 16	16 20	16 45	16 49	16 45	17 16	17 20	17 45	17 49	17 45	18 16	18 20	18 45
	d	14 55	14 50	14 55		15 21	15 55	15 50	15 55		16 21	16 55	16 50	16 55		17 21	17 55	17 50	17 55		18 21	18 55
Liphook	d	→		15 00			→		16 00			→		17 00			→		18 00			→
Liss	d			15 06					16 06					17 06					18 06			
Petersfield	d		15 01	15 11		15 32		16 01	16 11		16 32		17 01	17 11		17 32		18 01	18 11		18 32	
Rowlands Castle	d			15 21					16 21					17 21					18 21			
Havant	a		15 14	15 26		15 49		16 15	16 26		16 49		17 15	17 26		17 49		18 15	18 26		18 49	
	d		15 16	15 27		15 50		16 16	16 27		16 50		17 16	17 27		17 50		18 16	18 27		18 50	
Bedhampton	a			15 29					16 29					17 29					18 29			
Hilsea	a			15 36					16 36					17 36					18 36			
Fratton	a		15 24	15 40		15 59		16 24	16 40		16 59		17 24	17 40		17 59		18 24	18 40		18 59	
Portsmouth & Southsea	a		15 28	15 44		16 02		16 28	16 44		17 02		17 28	17 44		18 02		18 28	18 44		19 02	
Portsmouth Harbour ⛴	a		15 33			16 07		16 33			17 07		17 33			18 07		18 33			19 07	

		SW 1 ⊼	SW 1	SW 1	SW 1 ⊼	SW 1	SW 1 ⊼	SW 1	SW 1	SW 1 ⊼	SW 1	SW 1	SW 1	SW 1	SW 1	SW 1	SW 1	SW 1	SW 1	SW 1	SW 1	SW 1	SW 1
London Waterloo 15 ⊖	d	18 00		18 15	18 30	18 45	19 00		19 15	19 30	19 45	20 00		20 15	20 30	20 45	21 00		21 30	21 45	22 00		22 30
Clapham Junction 10	d			18u22		18u52			19u22		19u52			20u22		20u52				21u52			
Woking	a	18 24		18 41	18 54	19 11	19 24		19 41	19 54	20 11	20 24		20 41	20 54	21 11	21 24		21 54	22 11	22 24		22 54
	d	18 25		18 43	18 55	19 13	19 25		19 43	19 55	20 13	20 25		20 43	20 55	21 13	21 25		21 55	22 13	22 25		22 55
Worplesdon	d					19 18					20 18					21 18				22 18			
Guildford	a	18 33		18 50	19 03	19 23	19 33		19 50	20 03	20 23	20 33		20 50	21 03	21 23	21 33		22 03	22 23	22 33		23 03
	d	18 34		18 52	19 04	19 25	19 34		19 52	20 04	20 25	20 34		20 52	21 04	21 25	21 34		22 04	22 25	22 34		23 04
Farncombe	d			18 58		19 31			19 58		20 31			20 58		21 31	21 40		22 10	22 31	22 40		23 10
Godalming	d			19 01		19 34			20 01		20 34			21 01		21 34	21 43		22 13	22 34	22 43		23 13
Milford (Surrey)	d			19 05					20 05					21 05		21 38				22 38			
Witley	d		←	19 09				←	20 09				←	21 09		21 42		←		22 42		←	
Haslemere 4	a	18 49	18 45	19 16	19 20	19 45	19 49	19 45	20 16	20 20	20 45	20 49	20 45	21 16	21 20	21 49	21 54	21 49	22 24	22 49	22 54	22 49	23 24
	d	18 50	18 55		19 21	19 55	19 50	19 55		20 21	20 55	20 50	20 55		21 21	21 59	21 55	21 59	22 25	22 59	22 55	22 59	23 25
Liphook	d		19 00			→		20 00			→		21 00			→		22 04		→		23 04	
Liss	d		19 06					20 06					21 06					22 10				23 10	
Petersfield	d	19 01	19 11		19 32		20 01	20 11		20 32		21 01	21 11		21 32		22 06	22 15	22 36		23 06	23 15	23 36
Rowlands Castle	d		19 21					20 21					21 21					22 25				23 25	
Havant	a	19 15	19 26		19 49		20 15	20 29		20 49		21 15	21 26		21 45		22 18	22 30	22 48		23 18	23 30	23 48
	d	19 16	19 27		19 50		20 16	20 30		20 50		21 16	21 27		21 46		22 19	22 31	22 49		23 19	23 31	23 49
Bedhampton	a		19 29					20 32					21 29					22 33				23 33	
Hilsea	a		19 36					20 41					21 36					22 41				23 41	
Fratton	a	19 24	19 40		19 59		20 24	20 45		20 59		21 24	21 40		21 54		22 28	22 45	22 58		23 28	23 45	23 58
Portsmouth & Southsea	a	19 28	19 44		20 02		20 28	20 48		21 02		21 28	21 43		21 58		22 32	22 49	23 02		23 32	23 48	00 02
Portsmouth Harbour ⛴	a	19 33			20 07		20 33			21 07		21 33			22 03		22 36	22 53	23 08		23 37	23 53	00 07

		SW 1	SW 1	SW 1 A
London Waterloo 15 ⊖	d	22 45	23 15	23§45
Clapham Junction 10	d	22u52	23u22	23u52
Woking	a	23 11	23 41	00§11
	d	23 13	23 43	00§13
Worplesdon	d	23 18		00§18
Guildford	a	23 23	23 51	00§24
	d	23 25	23 52	00§25
Farncombe	d	23 31	23 58	00§31
Godalming	d	23 34	00 02	00§34
Milford (Surrey)	d	23 38		00s38
Witley	d	23 42		00s43
Haslemere 4	a	23 49	00 12	00§49
	d	23 50	00 13	00§50
Liphook	d	23 55		00s55
Liss	d	00 01		01s01
Petersfield	d	00 06	00 24	01§06
Rowlands Castle	d	00 16		01s16
Havant	a	00 21	00 36	01§21
	d	00 22	00 37	01§21
Bedhampton	a	00 24		01s24
Hilsea	a	00 30		01s29
Fratton	a	00 34	00 46	01s33
Portsmouth & Southsea	a	00 38	00 50	01§37
Portsmouth Harbour ⛴	a		00 55	

A until 21 July, 18 August, 25 August, 15 September, 22 September, 29 September, 6 October

London - Guildford, Haslemere and Portsmouth

Network Diagram - see first Page of Table 155

Saturdays from 13 October

		SW ■	SW ■	SW ■	SW ■	SW ■	SW ■	SW ■	SW ■	SW ■	SW ■	SW ■	SW ■	SW ■	SW ■	SW ■	SW ■	SW ■	SW ■	SW ■ ⌶	SW ■	SW ■	SW ■ ⌶
London Waterloo ⊖	d	22p30	22p45	23p15	23p45			05 00	05 20	06 15	06 45	07 15	07 30	07 45	08 00		08 15	08 30	08 45	09 00		09 15	09 30
Clapham Junction	d		22b52	23b22	23b52			05 11	05 29	06u22	06u52	07u23		07u52			08u22		08u52			09u22	
Woking	a	22p54	23p11	23p41	00 11			05 51	06 08	06 41	07 11	07 42	07 54	08 11	08 24		08 41	08 54	09 11	09 24		09 41	09 54
	d	22p55	23p13	23p43	00 13			05 53	06 13	06 43	07 13	07 44	07 55	08 13	08 25		08 43	08 55	09 13	09 25		09 43	09 55
Worplesdon	d		23p18		00 18				06 18		07 18			08 18					09 18				
Guildford	a	23p03	23p23	23p51	00 24			06 00	06 23	06 51	07 23	07 51	08 03	08 23	08 33		08 50	09 03	09 23	09 33		09 50	10 03
	d	23p04	23p25	23p52	00 25		05 15	06 02	06 25	06 53	07 25	07 53	08 04	08 25	08 34		08 52	09 04	09 25	09 34		09 52	10 04
Farncombe	d	23p10	23p31	23p58	00 31			06 08	06 31	06 59	07 31	07 59		08 31			08 58		09 31			09 58	
Godalming	d	23p13	23p34	00 02	00 34			06 11	06 34	07 02	07 34	08 02		08 34			09 01		09 34			10 01	
Milford (Surrey)	d		23p38		00s38			06 15		07 06		08 06					09 05					10 05	
Witley	d		23p42		00s43			06 19		07 10		08 10				←	09 09				←	10 09	
Haslemere	a	23p24	23p49	00 12	00 49		05 29	06 26	06 44	07 17	07 44	08 17	08 20	08 45	08 49	08 45	09 16	09 20	09 45	09 49	09 45	10 16	10 20
	d	23p25	23p50	00 13	00 50		05 30		06 45		07 45		08 21	08 55	08 50	08 55		09 21	09 55	09 50	09 55		10 21
Liphook	d		23p55		00s55		05 35		06 50		07 50			→		09 00			→		10 00		
Liss	d		00 01		01s01		05 41		06 56		07 56					09 06					10 06		
Petersfield	d	23p36	00 06	00 24	01 06		05 46		07 01		08 01		08 32		09 01	09 11		09 32		10 01	10 11		10 32
Rowlands Castle	d		00 16		01s16		05 56		07 11		08 11					09 21					10 21		
Havant	a	23p48	00 21	00 36	01 21		06 01		07 19		08 16		08 49		09 15	09 26		09 49		10 15	10 26		10 49
	d	23p49	00 22	00 37	01 21	04 40	06 02		07 20		08 17		08 50		09 16	09 27		09 50		10 16	10 27		10 50
Bedhampton	a		00 24		01s24	04 42	06 04		07 22		08 19					09 29					10 29		
Hilsea	a		00 30		01s29	04 48	06 10		07 27		08 25					09 36					10 36		
Fratton	a	23p58	00 34	00 46	01s33	04 52	06 14		07 31		08 29		08 59		09 24	09 40		09 59		10 24	10 40		10 59
Portsmouth & Southsea	a	00 02	00 38	00 50	01 37	04 55	06 18		07 35		08 32		09 02		09 28	09 44		10 02		10 28	10 44		11 02
Portsmouth Harbour ⛴	a	00 07		00 55		05 00	06 22		07 40		08 37		09 07		09 33			10 07		10 33			11 07

		SW ■	SW ■ ⌶	SW ■	SW ■	SW ■ ⌶	SW ■	SW ■ ⌶	SW ■	SW ■	SW ■ ⌶	SW ■	SW ■ ⌶	SW ■	SW ■	SW ■ ⌶	SW ■	SW ■ ⌶	SW ■	SW ■	SW ■ ⌶	SW ■	SW ■ ⌶
London Waterloo ⊖	d	09 45	10 00		10 15	10 30	10 45	11 00		11 15	11 30	11 45	12 00		12 15	12 30	12 45	13 00		13 15	13 30	13 45	14 00
Clapham Junction	d	09u52			10u22		10u52			11u22		11u52			12u22		12u52			13u22		13u52	
Woking	a	10 11	10 24		10 41	10 54	11 11	11 24		11 41	11 54	12 11	12 24		12 41	12 54	13 11	13 24		13 41	13 54	14 11	14 24
	d	10 13	10 25		10 43	10 55	11 13	11 25		11 43	11 55	12 13	12 25		12 43	12 55	13 13	13 25		13 43	13 55	14 13	14 25
Worplesdon	d	10 18					11 18					12 18					13 18					14 18	
Guildford	a	10 23	10 33		10 50	11 03	11 23	11 33		11 50	12 03	12 23	12 33		12 50	13 03	13 23	13 33		13 50	14 03	14 23	14 33
	d	10 25	10 34		10 52	11 04	11 25	11 34		11 52	12 04	12 25	12 34		12 52	13 04	13 25	13 34		13 52	14 04	14 25	14 34
Farncombe	d	10 31			10 58		11 31			11 58		12 31			12 58		13 31			13 58		14 31	
Godalming	d	10 34			11 01		11 34			12 01		12 34			13 01		13 34			14 01		14 34	
Milford (Surrey)	d				11 05					12 05					13 05					14 05			
Witley	d			←	11 09				←	12 09				←	13 09				←	14 09			
Haslemere	a	10 45	10 49	10 45	11 16	11 20	11 45	11 49	11 45	12 16	12 20	12 45	12 49	12 45	13 16	13 20	13 45	13 49	13 45	14 16	14 20	14 45	14 49
	d	10 55	10 50	10 55		11 21	11 55	11 50	11 55		12 21	12 55	12 50	12 55		13 21	13 55	13 50	13 55		14 21	14 55	14 50
Liphook	d	→		11 00			→		12 00			→		13 00			→		14 00			→	
Liss	d			11 06					12 06					13 06					14 06				
Petersfield	d		11 01	11 11		11 32		12 01	12 11		12 32		13 01	13 11		13 32		14 01	14 11		14 32		15 01
Rowlands Castle	d			11 21					12 21					13 21					14 21				
Havant	a		11 15	11 26		11 49		12 15	12 26		12 49		13 15	13 26		13 49		14 15	14 26		14 49		15 14
	d		11 16	11 27		11 50		12 16	12 27		12 50		13 16	13 27		13 50		14 16	14 27		14 50		15 16
Bedhampton	a			11 29					12 29					13 29					14 29				
Hilsea	a			11 36					12 36					13 36					14 36				
Fratton	a		11 24	11 40		11 59		12 24	12 40		12 59		13 24	13 40		13 59		14 24	14 40		14 59		15 24
Portsmouth & Southsea	a		11 28	11 44		12 02		12 28	12 44		13 02		13 28	13 44		14 02		14 28	14 44		15 02		15 28
Portsmouth Harbour ⛴	a		11 33			12 07		12 33			13 07		13 33			14 07		14 33			15 07		15 33

		SW ■	SW ■	SW ■ ⌶	SW ■	SW ■ ⌶	SW ■	SW ■	SW ■ ⌶	SW ■	SW ■ ⌶	SW ■	SW ■	SW ■ ⌶	SW ■	SW ■ ⌶	SW ■	SW ■	SW ■ ⌶	SW ■	SW ■ ⌶	SW ■
London Waterloo ⊖	d		14 15	14 30	14 45	15 00		15 15	15 30	15 45	16 00		16 15	16 30	16 45	17 00		17 15	17 30	17 45	18 00	
Clapham Junction	d		14u22		14u52			15u22		15u52			16u22		16u52			17u22		17u52		
Woking	a		14 41	14 54	15 11	15 24		15 41	15 54	16 11	16 24		16 41	16 54	17 11	17 24		17 41	17 54	18 11	18 24	
	d		14 43	14 55	15 13	15 25		15 43	15 55	16 13	16 25		16 43	16 55	17 13	17 25		17 43	17 55	18 13	18 25	
Worplesdon	d				15 18					16 18					17 18					18 18		
Guildford	a		14 50	15 03	15 23	15 33		15 50	16 03	16 23	16 33		16 50	17 03	17 23	17 33		17 50	18 03	18 23	18 33	
	d		14 52	15 04	15 25	15 34		15 52	16 04	16 25	16 34		16 52	17 04	17 25	17 34		17 52	18 04	18 25	18 34	
Farncombe	d		14 58		15 31			15 58		16 31			16 58		17 31			17 58		18 31		
Godalming	d		15 01		15 34			16 01		16 34			17 01		17 34			18 01		18 34		
Milford (Surrey)	d		15 05					16 05					17 05					18 05				
Witley	d	←	15 09				←	16 09				←	17 09				←	18 09				←
Haslemere	a	14 45	15 16	15 20	15 45	15 49	15 45	16 16	16 20	16 45	16 49	16 45	17 16	17 20	17 45	17 49	17 45	18 16	18 20	18 45	18 49	18 45
	d	14 55		15 21	15 55	15 50	15 55		16 21	16 55	16 50	16 55		17 21	17 55	17 50	17 55		18 21	18 55	18 50	18 55
Liphook	d	15 00			→		16 00			→		17 00			→		18 00			→		19 00
Liss	d	15 06					16 06					17 06					18 06					19 06
Petersfield	d	15 11		15 32		16 01	16 11		16 32		17 01	17 11		17 32		18 01	18 11		18 32		19 01	19 11
Rowlands Castle	d	15 21					16 21					17 21					18 21					19 21
Havant	a	15 26		15 49		16 15	16 26		16 49		17 15	17 26		17 49		18 15	18 26		18 49		19 15	19 26
	d	15 27		15 50		16 16	16 27		16 50		17 16	17 27		17 50		18 16	18 27		18 50		19 16	19 27
Bedhampton	a	15 29					16 29					17 29					18 29					19 29
Hilsea	a	15 36					16 36					17 36					18 36					19 36
Fratton	a	15 40		15 59		16 24	16 40		16 59		17 24	17 40		17 59		18 24	18 40		18 59		19 24	19 40
Portsmouth & Southsea	a	15 44		16 02		16 28	16 44		17 02		17 28	17 44		18 02		18 28	18 44		19 02		19 28	19 44
Portsmouth Harbour ⛴	a			16 07		16 33			17 07		17 33			18 07		18 33			19 07		19 33	

b Previous night, stops to pick up only

London - Guildford, Haslemere and Portsmouth

Network Diagram - see first Page of Table 155

Saturdays from 13 October

		SW ■	SW ■ ⌶	SW ■	SW ■ ⌶	SW ■	SW ■	SW ■ ⌶	SW ■	SW ■	SW ■	SW ■	SW ■	SW ■	SW ■	SW ■	SW ■	SW ■	SW ■	SW ■	SW ■	SW ■	SW ■
London Waterloo ⊖	d	18 15	18 30	18 45	19 00		19 15	19 30	19 45	20 00		20 15	20 30	20 45	21 00		21 30	21 45	22 00		22 30	22 45	23 15
Clapham Junction	d	18u22		18u52			19u22		19u52			20u22		20u52				21u52				22u52	23u22
Woking	a	18 41	18 54	19 11	19 24		19 41	19 54	20 11	20 24		20 41	20 54	21 11	21 24		21 54	22 11	22 24		22 54	23 11	23 41
	d	18 43	18 55	19 13	19 25		19 43	19 55	20 13	20 25		20 43	20 55	21 13	21 25		21 55	22 13	22 25		22 55	23 13	23 43
Worplesdon	d			19 18					20 18					21 18				22 18				23 18	
Guildford	a	18 50	19 03	19 23	19 33		19 50	20 03	20 23	20 33		20 50	21 03	21 23	21 33		22 03	22 23	22 33		23 03	23 23	23 51
	d	18 52	19 04	19 25	19 34		19 52	20 04	20 25	20 34		20 52	21 04	21 25	21 34		22 04	22 25	22 34		23 04	23 25	23 52
Farncombe	d	18 58		19 31			19 58		20 31			20 58		21 31	21 40		22 10	22 31	22 40		23 10	23 31	23 58
Godalming	d	19 01		19 34			20 01		20 34			21 01		21 34	21 43		22 13	22 34	22 43		23 13	23 34	00 02
Milford (Surrey)	d	19 05					20 05					21 05		21 38				22 38				23 38	
Witley	d	19 09				←	20 09				←	21 09		21 42		←		22 42		←		23 42	
Haslemere	a	19 16	19 20	19 45	19 49	19 45	20 16	20 20	20 45	20 49	20 45	21 16	21 20	21 49	21 54	21 49	22 24	22 49	22 54	22 49	23 24	23 49	00 12
	d		19 21	19 55	19 50	19 55		20 21	20 55	20 50	20 55		21 21	21 59	21 55	21 59	22 25	22 59	22 55	22 59	23 25	23 50	00 13
Liphook	d			→		20 00			→		21 00			→		22 04		→		23 04		23 55	
Liss	d					20 06					21 06					22 10				23 10		00 01	
Petersfield	d		19 32		20 01	20 11		20 32		21 01	21 11		21 32		22 06	22 15	22 36		23 06	23 15	23 36	00 06	00 24
Rowlands Castle	d					20 21					21 21					22 25				23 25		00 16	
Havant	a		19 49		20 15	20 29		20 49		21 15	21 26		21 45		22 18	22 30	22 48		23 18	23 30	23 48	00 21	00 36
	d		19 50		20 16	20 30		20 50		21 16	21 27		21 46		22 19	22 31	22 49		23 19	23 31	23 49	00 22	00 37
Bedhampton	a					20 32					21 29					22 33				23 33		00 24	
Hilsea	a					20 41					21 36					22 41				23 41		00 30	
Fratton	a		19 59		20 24	20 45		20 59		21 24	21 40		21 54		22 28	22 45	22 58		23 28	23 45	23 58	00 34	00 46
Portsmouth & Southsea	a		20 02		20 28	20 48		21 02		21 28	21 43		21 58		22 32	22 49	23 02		23 32	23 48	00 02	00 38	00 50
Portsmouth Harbour ⛴	a		20 07		20 33			21 07		21 33			22 03		22 36	22 53	23 08		23 37	23 53	00 07		00 55

		SW ■
London Waterloo ⊖	d	23 45
Clapham Junction	d	23u52
Woking	a	00 11
	d	00 13
Worplesdon	d	00 18
Guildford	a	00 24
	d	00 25
Farncombe	d	00 31
Godalming	d	00 34
Milford (Surrey)	d	00s38
Witley	d	00s43
Haslemere	a	00 49
	d	00 50
Liphook	d	00s55
Liss	d	01s01
Petersfield	d	01 06
Rowlands Castle	d	01s16
Havant	a	01 21
	d	01 21
Bedhampton	a	01s24
Hilsea	a	01s29
Fratton	a	01s33
Portsmouth & Southsea	a	01 37
Portsmouth Harbour ⛴	a	

Sundays until 30 September

		SW ■	SW ■	SW ■	SW ■ A	SW ■ B	SW ■ B	SW ■	SW ■	SW ■	SW ■	SW ■	SW ■	SW ■	SW ■	SW ■ ⌶	SW ■	SW ■ ⌶	SW ■	SW ■ ⌶	SW ■	SW ■ ⌶	SW ■
London Waterloo ⊖	d	22p30	22p45	23p15	23p45	00 05	00 50		08 00	08 30	09 00	09 30	10 00	10 30	11 00	11 30	12 00	12 30	13 00	13 30	14 00	14 30	15 00
Clapham Junction	d		22b52	23b22	23b52	00u12	00u57		08u09	08u39	09u09	09u39	10u09	10u39	11u09	11u39	12u09	12u39	13u09	13u39	14u09	14u39	15u09
Woking	a	22p54	23p11	23p41	00 11	00 31	01 19		08 34	09 03	09 34	10 03	10 31	11 01	11 31	12 01	12 31	13 01	13 31	14 01	14 31	15 01	15 31
	d	22p55	23p13	23p43	00 13	00 32	01 20	07 32	08 35	09 04	09 35	10 04	10 32	11 02	11 32	12 02	12 32	13 02	13 32	14 02	14 32	15 02	15 32
Worplesdon	d		23p18		00 18	00 37	⌇																
Guildford	a	23p03	23p23	23p51	00 24	00 43	01s28	07 39	08 43	09 12	09 43	10 12	10 40	11 10	11 40	12 10	12 40	13 10	13 40	14 10	14 40	15 10	15 40
	d	23p04	23p25	23p52	00 25	00 45	⌇	07 41	08 45	09 14	09 45	10 14	10 42	11 12	11 42	12 12	12 42	13 12	13 42	14 12	14 42	15 12	15 42
Farncombe	d	23p10	23p31	23p58	00 31	00 51	⌇	07 48	08 53		09 53		10 48		11 48		12 48		13 48		14 48		15 48
Godalming	d	23p13	23p34	00 02	00 34	00 54	⌇	07 51	08 56		09 56		10 51		11 51		12 51		13 51		14 51		15 51
Milford (Surrey)	d		23p38		00s38	00s58	⌇	07 55	09 00		10 00		10 55		11 55		12 55		13 55		14 55		15 55
Witley	d		23p42		00s43	01s02	⌇	07 59	09 04		10 04		10 59		11 59		12 59		13 59		14 59		15 59
Haslemere	a	23p24	23p49	00 12	00 49	01 09	01s44	08 06	09 11	09 28	10 11	10 28	11 06	11 26	12 06	12 26	13 06	13 26	14 06	14 26	15 06	15 26	16 06
	d	23p25	23p50	00 13	00 50	01 09	⌇	08 07	09 12	09 29	10 12	10 29	11 07	11 27	12 07	12 27	13 07	13 27	14 07	14 27	15 07	15 27	16 07
Liphook	d		23p55		00s55	01s14	⌇	08 12	09 17		10 17		11 12		12 12		13 12		14 12		15 12		16 12
Liss	d		00 01		01s01	01s20	⌇	08 18	09 23		10 23		11 18		12 18		13 18		14 18		15 18		16 18
Petersfield	d	23p36	00 06	00 24	01 06	01 26	01s55	08 23	09 28	09 40	10 28	10 40	11 23	11 38	12 23	12 38	13 23	13 38	14 23	14 38	15 23	15 38	16 23
Rowlands Castle	d		00 16		01s16	01s35	⌇	08 33	09 38		10 38		11 33		12 33		13 33		14 33		15 33		16 33
Havant	a	23p48	00 21	00 36	01 21	01 40	02s08	08 38	09 44	09 52	10 44	10 52	11 38	11 50	12 38	12 50	13 38	13 50	14 38	14 50	15 38	15 50	16 38
	d	23p49	00 22	00 37	01 21	01 41	⌇	08 39	09 45	09 53	10 45	10 53	11 39	11 51	12 39	12 51	13 39	13 51	14 39	14 51	15 39	15 51	16 39
Bedhampton	a		00 24		01s24	01s43	⌇	08 41	09 47		10 47		11 41		12 41		13 41		14 41		15 41		16 41
Hilsea	a		00 30		01s29	01s49	⌇																
Fratton	a	23p58	00 34	00 46	01s33	01s53	02s17	08 49	09 55	10 01	10 55	11 01	11 49	12 00	12 49	13 00	13 49	14 00	14 49	15 00	15 49	16 00	16 49
Portsmouth & Southsea	a	00 02	00 38	00 50	01 37	01 57	02 21	08 53	09 59	10 06	10 59	11 05	11 53	12 04	12 53	13 04	13 53	14 04	14 53	15 04	15 54	16 04	16 53
Portsmouth Harbour ⛴	a	00 07		00 55				08 57	10 04	10 11	11 04	11 11	11 58	12 09	12 58	13 11	13 58	14 11	14 58	15 11	15 58	16 11	16 58

A until 22 July, 19 August, 26 August, 16 September, 23 September, 30 September

B 29 July, 5 August, 12 August, 2 September, 9 September

b Previous night, stops to pick up only

London - Guildford, Haslemere and Portsmouth

Network Diagram - see first Page of Table 155

Sundays until 30 September

		SW [1] T	SW [1]	SW [1] T	SW [1]	SW [1] T	SW [1]	SW [1] T	SW [1]	SW [1] T	SW [1]	SW [1] T	SW [1]	SW [1]	SW [1]	SW [1]	SW [1]	SW [1] A	SW [1] B
London Waterloo [15] ⊖	d	15 30	16 00	16 30	17 00	17 30	18 00	18 30	19 00	19 30	20 00	20 30	21 00	21 30	22 00	22 30	23 00	23 30	23 50
Clapham Junction [10]	d	15u39	16u09	16u39	17u09	17u39	18u09	18u39	19u09	19u39	20u09	20u39	21u09	21u39	22u09	22u39	23u09	23u39	23u59
Woking	a	16 01	16 31	17 01	17 31	18 01	18 31	19 01	19 31	20 01	20 31	21 01	21 31	22 01	22 31	23 01	23 31	00 01	00 21
	d	16 02	16 32	17 02	17 32	18 02	18 32	19 02	19 32	20 02	20 32	21 02	21 32	22 02	22 32	23 02	23 32	00 03	00 23
Worplesdon	d																		
Guildford	a	16 10	16 40	17 10	17 40	18 10	18 40	19 10	19 40	20 10	20 40	21 10	21 40	22 10	22 40	23 10	23 40	00 10	00 30
	d	16 12	16 42	17 12	17 42	18 12	18 42	19 12	19 42	20 12	20 42	21 12	21 42	22 12	22 42	23 12	23 42	00 12	00 32
Farncombe	d		16 48		17 48		18 48		19 48		20 48		21 48		22 48		23 48		
Godalming	d		16 51		17 51		18 51		19 51		20 51		21 51		22 51		23 51		
Milford (Surrey)	d		16 55		17 55		18 55		19 55		20 55		21 55		22 55		23 55		
Witley	d		16 59		17 59		18 59		19 59		20 59		21 59		22 59		23 59		
Haslemere [4]	a	16 26	17 06	17 26	18 06	18 26	19 06	19 26	20 06	20 26	21 06	21 26	22 06	22 26	23 06	23 26	00 06	00 26	00 46
	d	16 27	17 07	17 27	18 07	18 27	19 07	19 27	20 07	20 27	21 07	21 27	22 07	22 27	23 07	23 27	00 07	00 27	00 47
Liphook	d		17 12		18 12		19 12		20 12		21 12		22 12		23 12		00 12		
Liss	d		17 18		18 18		19 18		20 18		21 18		22 18		23 18		00 18		
Petersfield	d	16 38	17 23	17 38	18 23	18 38	19 23	19 38	20 23	20 38	21 23	21 38	22 23	22 38	23 23	23 38	00 23	00 38	00 58
Rowlands Castle	d		17 33		18 33		19 33		20 33		21 33		22 33		23 33		00 33		
Havant	a	16 50	17 38	17 50	18 38	18 50	19 38	19 50	20 38	20 50	21 38	21 50	22 38	22 50	23 38	23 50	00 38	00 50	01 10
	d	16 51	17 39	17 51	18 39	18 51	19 39	19 51	20 39	20 51	21 39	21 51	22 39	22 51	23 39	23 51	00 39	00 51	01 11
Bedhampton	a		17 41		18 41		19 41		20 41		21 41		22 41		23 41		00 41		
Hilsea	a																		
Fratton	a	17 00	17 49	18 00	18 49	19 00	19 49	20 00	20 49	21 00	21 49	22 00	22 49	23 00	23 49	23 59	00 49	01 00	01 20
Portsmouth & Southsea	a	17 04	17 53	18 04	18 53	19 04	19 53	20 04	20 53	21 04	21 53	22 04	22 53	23 04	23 53	00 04	00 53	01 04	01 24
Portsmouth Harbour ⛴	a	17 11	17 58	18 11	18 58	19 11	19 58	20 11	20 58	21 09	21 58	22 11	22 58	23 09	23 58	00 09	00 58	01 09	01 29

Sundays from 7 October

		SW [1]	SW [1]	SW [1]	SW [1]	SW [1]	SW [1]	SW [1]	SW [1]	SW [1]	SW [1]	SW [1]	SW [1]	SW [1] T	SW [1]	SW [1] T	SW [1]	SW [1] T	SW [1]	SW [1] T	SW [1]	SW [1] T	SW [1]
London Waterloo [15] ⊖	d	22p30	22p45	23p15	23p45		08 00	08 30	09 00	09 30	10 00	10 30	11 00	11 30	12 00	12 30	13 00	13 30	14 00	14 30	15 00	15 30	16 00
Clapham Junction [10]	d		22b52	23b22	23b52		08u09	08u39	09u09	09u39	10u09	10u39	11u09	11u39	12u09	12u39	13u09	13u39	14u09	14u39	15u09	15u39	16u09
Woking	a	22p54	23p11	23p41	00 11		08 34	09 03	09 34	10 03	10 31	11 01	11 31	12 01	12 31	13 01	13 31	14 01	14 31	15 01	15 31	16 01	16 31
	d	22p55	23p13	23p43	00 13	07 32	08 35	09 04	09 35	10 04	10 32	11 02	11 32	12 02	12 32	13 02	13 32	14 02	14 32	15 02	15 32	16 02	16 32
Worplesdon	d		23p18		00 18																		
Guildford	a	23p03	23p23	23p51	00 24	07 39	08 43	09 12	09 43	10 12	10 40	11 10	11 40	12 10	12 40	13 10	13 40	14 10	14 40	15 10	15 40	16 10	16 40
	d	23p04	23p25	23p52	00 25	07 41	08 45	09 14	09 45	10 14	10 42	11 12	11 42	12 12	12 42	13 12	13 42	14 12	14 42	15 12	15 42	16 12	16 42
Farncombe	d	23p10	23p31	23p58	00 31	07 48	08 53		09 53		10 48		11 48		12 48		13 48		14 48		15 48		16 48
Godalming	d	23p13	23p34	00 02	00 34	07 51	08 56		09 56		10 51		11 51		12 51		13 51		14 51		15 51		16 51
Milford (Surrey)	d		23p38		00s38	07 55	09 00		10 00		10 55		11 55		12 55		13 55		14 55		15 55		16 55
Witley	d		23p42		00s43	07 59	09 04		10 04		10 59		11 59		12 59		13 59		14 59		15 59		16 59
Haslemere [4]	a	23p24	23p49	00 12	00 49	08 06	09 11	09 28	10 11	10 28	11 06	11 26	12 06	12 26	13 06	13 26	14 06	14 26	15 06	15 26	16 06	16 26	17 06
	d	23p25	23p50	00 13	00 50	08 07	09 12	09 29	10 12	10 29	11 07	11 27	12 07	12 27	13 07	13 27	14 07	14 27	15 07	15 27	16 07	16 27	17 07
Liphook	d		23p55		00s55	08 12	09 17		10 17		11 12		12 12		13 12		14 12		15 12		16 12		17 12
Liss	d		00 01		01s01	08 18	09 23		10 23		11 18		12 18		13 18		14 18		15 18		16 18		17 18
Petersfield	d	23p36	00 06	00 24	01 06	08 23	09 28	09 40	10 28	10 40	11 23	11 38	12 23	12 38	13 23	13 38	14 23	14 38	15 23	15 38	16 23	16 38	17 23
Rowlands Castle	d		00 16		01s16	08 33	09 38		10 38		11 33		12 33		13 33		14 33		15 33		16 33		17 33
Havant	a	23p48	00 21	00 36	01 21	08 38	09 44	09 52	10 44	10 52	11 38	11 50	12 38	12 50	13 38	13 50	14 38	14 50	15 38	15 50	16 38	16 50	17 38
	d	23p49	00 22	00 37	01 21	08 39	09 45	09 53	10 45	10 53	11 39	11 51	12 39	12 51	13 39	13 51	14 39	14 51	15 39	15 51	16 39	16 51	17 39
Bedhampton	a		00 24		01s24	08 41	09 47		10 47		11 41		12 41		13 41		14 41		15 41		16 41		17 41
Hilsea	a		00 30		01s29																		
Fratton	a	23p58	00 34	00 46	01s33	08 49	09 55	10 01	10 55	11 01	11 49	12 00	12 49	13 00	13 49	14 00	14 49	15 00	15 49	16 00	16 49	17 00	17 49
Portsmouth & Southsea	a	00 02	00 38	00 50	01 37	08 53	09 59	10 06	10 59	11 05	11 53	12 04	12 53	13 04	13 53	14 04	14 53	15 04	15 54	16 04	16 53	17 04	17 53
Portsmouth Harbour ⛴	a	00 07		00 55		08 57	10 04	10 11	11 04	11 11	11 58	12 09	12 58	13 11	13 58	14 11	14 58	15 11	15 58	16 11	16 58	17 11	17 58

		SW [1] T	SW [1]	SW [1] T	SW [1]	SW [1] T	SW [1]	SW [1] T	SW [1]	SW [1] T	SW [1]	SW [1]	SW [1]	SW [1]	SW [1]	SW [1]
London Waterloo [15] ⊖	d	16 30	17 00	17 30	18 00	18 30	19 00	19 30	20 00	20 30	21 00	21 30	22 00	22 30	23 00	23 30
Clapham Junction [10]	d	16u39	17u09	17u39	18u09	18u39	19u09	19u39	20u09	20u39	21u09	21u39	22u09	22u39	23u09	23u39
Woking	a	17 01	17 31	18 01	18 31	19 01	19 31	20 01	20 31	21 01	21 31	22 01	22 31	23 01	23 31	00 01
	d	17 02	17 32	18 02	18 32	19 02	19 32	20 02	20 32	21 02	21 32	22 02	22 32	23 02	23 32	00 03
Worplesdon	d															
Guildford	a	17 10	17 40	18 10	18 40	19 10	19 40	20 10	20 40	21 10	21 40	22 10	22 40	23 10	23 40	00 10
	d	17 12	17 42	18 12	18 42	19 12	19 42	20 12	20 42	21 12	21 42	22 12	22 42	23 12	23 42	00 12
Farncombe	d		17 48		18 48		19 48		20 48		21 48		22 48		23 48	
Godalming	d		17 51		18 51		19 51		20 51		21 51		22 51		23 51	
Milford (Surrey)	d		17 55		18 55		19 55		20 55		21 55		22 55		23 55	
Witley	d		17 59		18 59		19 59		20 59		21 59		22 59		23 59	
Haslemere [4]	a	17 26	18 06	18 26	19 06	19 26	20 06	20 26	21 06	21 26	22 06	22 26	23 06	23 26	00 06	00 26
	d	17 27	18 07	18 27	19 07	19 27	20 07	20 27	21 07	21 27	22 07	22 27	23 07	23 27	00 07	00 27
Liphook	d		18 12		19 12		20 12		21 12		22 12		23 12		00 12	
Liss	d		18 18		19 18		20 18		21 18		22 18		23 18		00 18	
Petersfield	d	17 38	18 23	18 38	19 23	19 38	20 23	20 38	21 23	21 38	22 23	22 38	23 23	23 38	00 23	00 38
Rowlands Castle	d		18 33		19 33		20 33		21 33		22 33		23 33		00 33	
Havant	a	17 50	18 38	18 50	19 38	19 50	20 38	20 50	21 38	21 50	22 38	22 50	23 38	23 50	00 38	00 50
	d	17 51	18 39	18 51	19 39	19 51	20 39	20 51	21 39	21 51	22 39	22 51	23 39	23 51	00 39	00 51
Bedhampton	a		18 41		19 41		20 41		21 41		22 41		23 41		00 41	
Hilsea	a															
Fratton	a	18 00	18 49	19 00	19 49	20 00	20 49	21 00	21 49	22 00	22 49	23 00	23 49	23 59	00 49	01 00
Portsmouth & Southsea	a	18 04	18 53	19 04	19 53	20 04	20 53	21 04	21 53	22 04	22 53	23 04	23 53	00 04	00 53	01 04
Portsmouth Harbour ⛴	a	18 11	18 58	19 11	19 58	20 11	20 58	21 09	21 58	22 11	22 58	23 09	23 58	00 09	00 58	01 09

A until 22 July, 19 August, 26 August, 16 September, 23 September, 30 September

B 29 July, 5 August, 12 August, 2 September, 9 September

b Previous night, stops to pick up only

Portsmouth, Haslemere and Guildford - London

Network Diagram - see first Page of Table 155

Mondays to Fridays until 5 October

Miles			SW MX [1]	SW MO [1] A	SW MO [1] A	SW MX [1]	SW [1]	SW [1]	SW [1] T	SW [1]	SW [1]	SW [1] T	SW [1]	SW [1]	SW [1] T	SW [1]	SW [1]	SW [1] T	SW [1]	SW [1]	SW [1] T	SW [1]	SW [1] T
0	Portsmouth Harbour ⛴	d	22p18	22p32	22p48	23p19	04 30		05 19		05 50	06 15			06 42		06 55	07 13		07 29	07 45		08 15
0¾	Portsmouth & Southsea	d	22p24	22p37	22p53	23p24	04 35		05 24		05 55	06 20			06 47		07 00	07 18		07 33	07 50		08 20
1¾	Fratton	d	22p28	22p41	22p57	23p28	04 39		05 28		05 59	06 24			06 51		07 04	07 22		07 37	07 54		08 24
4	Hilsea	d	22p32			23p32	04 43		05 32		06 03			06 42			07 08			07 41			
7¼	Bedhampton	d	22p37		23p04	23p37	04 48		05 37		06 08			06 47			07 13			07 48			
8	Havant	a	22p39	22p49	23p07	23p39	04 50		05 40		06 10	06 33		06 49	06 59		07 15	07 30		07 50	08 03		08 32
—		d	22p40	22p50	23p07	23p40	04 51		05 41		06 11	06 34		06 50	07 00	07 11	07 16	07 32		07 52	08 04		08 34
11¼	Rowlands Castle	d	22p46		23p13	23p46	04 57		05 46		06 16			06 56			07 22			07 57			
19½	Petersfield	d	22p57	23p04	23p24	23p57	05 08		05 57		06 29	06 48		07 07	07 14	07 25	07 33	07 46		08 08	08 18		08 48
23	Liss	d	23p02		23p29	00 02	05 13		06 02		06 34			07 12	07 20		07 38			08 13			
27¾	Liphook	d	23p09		23p36	00 09	05 20		06 09		06 41			07 19	07 27		07 45		←	08 20		←	
31½	Haslemere [4]	a	23p15	23p16	23p41	00 15	05 25		06 15		06 46	07 01		07 25	07 33	07 38	07 51	07 59	07 51	08 26	08 31	08 26	09 01
—		d	23p15	23p17	23p42	00 15	05 26	06 00	06 16	06 30	06 47	07 02	07 10	07 26	07 35	07 40	08 07	08 00	08 07	08 39	08 32	08 39	09 02
36	Witley	d	23p21		23p48	00 21	05 32	06 06		06 36			07 16			07 46	→		08 13	→		08 45	
38¼	Milford (Surrey)	d	23p25		23p52	00 25	05 36	06 11		06 40			07 21			07 50			08 17			08 49	
40	Godalming	d	23p29		23p56	00 29	05 40	06 15		06 44	06 57		07 25	07 35	07 45	07 54			08 21			08 53	
41	Farncombe	d	23p32		23p59	00 32	05 43	06 18		06 47	07 00		07 28	07 38		07 57			08 25			08 57	
44¼	Guildford	a	23p37	23p31	00 04	00 37	05 48	06 23	06 29	06 52	07 06	07 15	07 33	07 43	07 52	08 02		08 13	08 30		08 46	09 02	09 15
—		d	23p39	23p35	00 05		05 50	06 24	06 31	06 53	07 07	07 17	07 34	07 45	07 54	08 03		08 15	08 31		08 54	09 03	09 17
47¾	Worplesdon	d	23p44				05 55	06 30		06 59			07 40	07 50				08 20	08 37				
50½	Woking	a	23p49	23p42	00 13		06 00	06 35	06 39	07 03	07 15	07 25		07 54		08 11		08 26	08 41			09 11	09 27
—		d	23p56	23p45			06 01	06 37	06 41	07 05	07 17	07 26		07 56		08 12		08 27	08 43			09 13	09 28
70½	Clapham Junction [10]	a	00 19	00 04			06 20	06 58	07 02	07 24									09 03			09 32	
74½	London Waterloo [15] ⊖	a	00 33	00 14			06 29	07 08	07 12	07 36	07 45	07 54	08 11	08 24	08 32	08 41		08 55	09 13		09 31	09 43	09 55

		SW [1]	SW [1] T	SW [1]	SW [1] T	SW [1]	SW [1] T	SW [1]	SW [1] T	SW [1]	SW [1] T	SW [1]	SW [1] T	SW [1]	SW [1] T	SW [1]	SW [1] T	SW [1]	SW [1] T	SW [1]	SW [1] T	SW [1]	SW [1] T
Portsmouth Harbour ⛴	d		08 45		09 15	09 18	09 45		10 15		10 45		11 15		11 45		12 15		12 45		13 15		13 45
Portsmouth & Southsea	d	08 24	08 50		09 20	09 24	09 50		10 20	10 24	10 50		11 20	11 24	11 50		12 20	12 24	12 50		13 20	13 24	13 50
Fratton	d	08 28	08 54		09 24	09 28	09 54		10 24	10 28	10 54		11 24	11 28	11 54		12 24	12 28	12 54		13 24	13 28	13 54
Hilsea	d	08 32				09 32				10 32				11 32				12 32				13 32	
Bedhampton	d	08 37				09 37				10 37				11 37				12 37				13 37	
Havant	a	08 40	09 03		09 33	09 39	10 03		10 33	10 39	11 03		11 33	11 39	12 03		12 33	12 39	13 03		13 33	13 39	14 03
	d	08 40	09 04		09 34	09 40	10 04		10 34	10 40	11 04		11 34	11 40	12 04		12 34	12 40	13 04		13 34	13 40	14 04
Rowlands Castle	d	08 46				09 46				10 46				11 46				12 46				13 46	
Petersfield	d	08 57	09 18		09 48	09 57	10 18		10 48	10 57	11 18		11 48	11 57	12 18		12 48	12 57	13 18		13 48	13 57	14 18
Liss	d	09 02				10 02				11 02				12 02				13 02				14 02	
Liphook	d	09 09				10 09				11 09				12 09				13 09				14 09	
Haslemere [4]	a	09 15	09 31		10 01	10 15	10 31		11 01	11 15	11 31		12 01	12 15	12 31		13 01	13 15	13 31		14 01	14 15	14 31
	d	09 15	09 32	09 39	10 02	10 15	10 32	10 39	11 02	11 15	11 32	11 39	12 02	12 15	12 32	12 39	13 02	13 15	13 32	13 39	14 02	14 15	14 32
Witley	d			09 45				10 45				11 45				12 45				13 45			
Milford (Surrey)	d			09 49				10 49				11 49				12 49				13 49			
Godalming	d	09 25		09 53		10 25		10 53		11 25		11 53		12 25		12 53		13 25		13 53		14 25	
Farncombe	d	09 28		09 56		10 28		10 56		11 28		11 56		12 28		12 56		13 28		13 56		14 28	
Guildford	a	09 33	09 45	10 01	10 15	10 33	10 46	11 01	11 15	11 33	11 45	12 01	12 15	12 33	12 45	13 01	13 15	13 33	13 45	14 01	14 15	14 33	14 45
	d	09 34	09 47	10 02	10 17	10 34	10 47	11 02	11 17	11 34	11 47	12 02	12 17	12 34	12 47	13 02	13 17	13 34	13 47	14 02	14 17	14 34	14 47
Worplesdon	d	09 40				10 40				11 40				12 40				13 40				14 40	
Woking	a	09 44	09 59	10 11	10 25	10 44	10 57	11 11	11 25	11 44	11 57	12 11	12 25	12 44	12 57	13 11	13 25	13 44	13 57	14 11	14 25	14 44	14 57
	d	09 46	09 59	10 12	10 26	10 46	10 59	11 12	11 26	11 46	11 59	12 12	12 26	12 46	12 59	13 12	13 26	13 46	13 59	14 12	14 26	14 46	14 59
Clapham Junction [10]	a	10 05		10 31		11 05		11 31		12 05		12 31		13 05		13 31		14 05		14 31		15 05	
London Waterloo [15] ⊖	a	10 13	10 27	10 40	10 51	11 13	11 24	11 40	11 51	12 13	12 23	12 40	12 51	13 13	13 23	13 40	13 51	14 13	14 23	14 40	14 51	15 13	15 23

		SW [1]	SW [1] T	SW [1]	SW [1] T	SW [1]	SW [1] T	SW [1]	SW [1]	SW [1] T	SW [1] T	SW [1]	SW	SW [1] T	SW [1] T	SW [1]	SW [1] T	SW [1] T	SW [1]	SW [1] T	SW [1]	SW [1]	SW [1]
Portsmouth Harbour ⛴	d		14 15		14 45		15 15			15 45	16 15			16 45	17 15	17 18	17 45	18 15		18 45		19 15	
Portsmouth & Southsea	d		14 20	14 24	14 50		15 20	15 24		15 50	16 20	16 24		16 50	17 20	17 24	17 50	18 20	18 24	18 50		19 20	19 24
Fratton	d		14 24	14 28	14 54		15 24	15 28		15 54	16 24	16 28		16 54	17 24	17 28	17 54	18 24	18 28	18 54		19 24	19 28
Hilsea	d			14 32				15 32				16 32				17 32			18 32				19 32
Bedhampton	d			14 37				15 37				16 37				17 37			18 37				19 37
Havant	a		14 33	14 39	15 03		15 33	15 39		16 03	16 33	16 39		17 03	17 33	17 39	18 03	18 33	18 39	19 03		19 33	19 39
	d		14 34	14 40	15 04		15 34	15 40	15 54	16 04	16 34	16 40	16 56	17 04	17 34	17 40	18 04	18 34	18 40	19 04		19 34	19 40
Rowlands Castle	d			14 46				15 46				16 46				17 46			18 46				19 46
Petersfield	d		14 48	14 57	15 18		15 48	15 57	16 10	16 18	16 48	16 57	17 10	17 18	17 48	17 57	18 18	18 48	18 57	19 18		19 48	19 57
Liss	d			15 02				16 02		16 23		17 02		17 23		18 02			19 02				20 02
Liphook	d			15 09				16 09		16 30		17 09		17 30		18 09			19 09				20 09
Haslemere [4]	a		15 01	15 15	15 31		16 01	16 15	16 23	16 36	17 01	17 15	17 32	17 36	18 01	18 15	18 31	19 01	19 15	19 31		20 01	20 15
	d	14 39	15 02	15 15	15 32	15 37	16 02	16 15	16 24	16 37	17 02	17 15		17 37	18 02	18 15	18 32	19 02	19 15	19 32	19 39	20 02	20 15
Witley	d	14 45				15 43			16 30	16 43				17 43			18 38				19 45		20 21
Milford (Surrey)	d	14 49				15 47			16 34	16 47				17 47			18 42				19 49		20 25
Godalming	d	14 53		15 25		15 51		16 25	16 38	16 51		17 25		17 51		18 25	18 46	19 11	19 25		19 53		20 29
Farncombe	d	14 56		15 28		15 54		16 28	16 41	16 54		17 28		17 54		18 28	18 49	19 14	19 28		19 56		20 32
Guildford	a	15 01	15 15	15 33	15 45	15 59	16 15	16 33	16 46	16 59	17 15	17 33	17 47	17 59	18 15	18 33	18 54	19 19	19 33	19 45	20 01	20 15	20 37
	d	15 02	15 17	15 34	15 47	16 00	16 17	16 34	16 47	17 00	17 17	17 34		18 00	18 17	18 34	18 55	19 21	19 34	19 47	20 02	20 17	20 39
Worplesdon	d			15 40		16 06		16 40		17 06		17 40		18 06		18 40			19 40				20 44
Woking	a	15 11	15 25	15 44	15 57	16 11	16 25	16 44	16 57	17 11	17 25	17 44	17 59	18 11		18 44	19 03	19 28	19 45	19 57	20 11	20 25	20 52
	d	15 12	15 26	15 46	15 59	16 12	16 26	16 46	16 59	17 12	17 26	17 46		18 12		18 46	19 05	19 30	19 46	19 59	20 12	20 26	20 53
Clapham Junction [10]	a	15 31		16 05		16 31		17 05		17 31		18 05		18 31		19 05			20 05		20 31		21 12
London Waterloo [15] ⊖	a	15 43	15 51	16 13	16 24	16 40	16 51	17 14	17 27	17 43	17 54	18 14	18 27	18 43	18 59	19 13	19 29	19 59	20 14	20 24	20 40	20 50	21 21

A from 21 May until 1 October

Portsmouth, Haslemere and Guildford - London

Network Diagram - see first Page of Table 155

Mondays to Fridays until 5 October

		SW 1	SW 1	SW 1	SW 1	SW 1	SW 1	SW FO 1 A	SW FX 1 B	SW 1	SW 1
Portsmouth Harbour ⛴	d	19 45	20 15	20 18	20 45	21 18	21 28	22 18	22 18	22 28	23 19
Portsmouth & Southsea	d	19 50	20 20	20 24	20 50	21 24	21 33	22 24	22 24	22 33	23 24
Fratton	d	19 54	20 24	20 28	20 54	21 28	21 37	22 28	22 28	22 37	23 28
Hilsea	d			20 32		21 32	21 41	22 32	22 32	22 41	23 32
Bedhampton	d			20 37		21 37	21 47	22 37	22 37	22 46	23 37
Havant	a	20 03	20 33	20 39	21 03	21 40	21 52	22 39	22 39	22 53	23 39
	d	20 04	20 34	20 40	21 04	21 40		22 40	22 40		23 40
Rowlands Castle	d			20 46		21 46		22 46	22 46		23 46
Petersfield	d	20 18	20 48	20 57	21 18	21 57		22 57	22 57		23 57
Liss	d			21 02		22 02		23 02	23 02		00 02
Liphook	d			21 09		22 09		23 09	23 09		00 09
Haslemere 4	a	20 31	21 01	21 15	21 31	22 15		23 15	23 15		00 15
	d	20 32	21 02	21 15	21 32	22 15		23 15	23 15		00 15
Witley	d			21 21		22 21		23 21	23 21		00 21
Milford (Surrey)	d			21 25		22 25		23 25	23 25		00 25
Godalming	d			21 29		22 29		23 29	23 29		00 29
Farncombe	d			21 32		22 32		23 32	23 32		00 32
Guildford	a	20 45	21 16	21 37	21 45	22 37		23 37	23 37		00 37
	d	20 47	21 17	21 39	21 47	22 39		23 39	23 39		
Worplesdon	d			21 44		22 44		23 44	23 44		
Woking	a	20 56	21 25	21 49	21 57	22 49		23 49	23 49		
	d	20 59	21 26	21 50	21 59	22 50		23 56	23 56		
Clapham Junction 10	a			22 09		23 09		00 19	00 19		
London Waterloo 15 ⊖	a	21 27	21 50	22 18	22 27	23 19		00 32	00 33		

Mondays to Fridays from 8 October

		SW MX 1	SW MO 1	SW MO 1	SW MX 1	SW 1	SW 1	SW 1 ✕	SW 1	SW 1	SW 1 ✕	SW 1	SW 1	SW 1 ✕	SW 1	SW 1	SW 1 ✕	SW 1	SW 1	SW 1 ✕	SW 1	SW 1 ✕	SW 1
Portsmouth Harbour ⛴	d	22p18	22p32	22p48	23p19	04 25		05 14		05 50	06 15			06 42		06 55	07 13		07 29	07 45		08 15	
Portsmouth & Southsea	d	22p24	22p37	22p53	23p24	04 30		05 19		05 55	06 20			06 47		07 00	07 18		07 33	07 50		08 20	08 24
Fratton	d	22p28	22p41	22p57	23p28	04 34		05 23		05 59	06 24			06 51		07 04	07 22		07 37	07 54		08 24	08 28
Hilsea	d	22p32			23p32	04 38		05 27		06 03			06 42			07 08			07 41				08 32
Bedhampton	d	22p37		23p04	23p37	04 43		05 32		06 08			06 47			07 13			07 48				08 37
Havant	a	22p39	22p49	23p07	23p39	04 45		05 35		06 10	06 33		06 49	06 59		07 15	07 30		07 50	08 03		08 32	08 40
	d	22p40	22p50	23p07	23p40	04 46		05 36		06 11	06 34		06 50	07 00	07 11	07 16	07 32		07 52	08 04		08 34	08 40
Rowlands Castle	d	22p46		23p13	23p46	04 52		05 41		06 16			06 56			07 22			07 57				08 46
Petersfield	d	22p57	23p04	23p24	23p57	05 03		05 52		06 29	06 48		07 07	07 14	07 25	07 33	07 46		08 08	08 18		08 48	08 57
Liss	d	23p02		23p29	00 02	05 08		05 57		06 34			07 12	07 20		07 38			08 13				09 02
Liphook	d	23p09		23p36	00 09	05 15		06 04		06 41			07 19	07 27		07 45		←	08 20		←		09 09
Haslemere 4	a	23p15	23p16	23p41	00 15	05 20		06 13		06 46	07 01		07 25	07 33	07 38	07 51	07 59	07 51	08 26	08 31	08 26	09 01	09 15
	d	23p15	23p17	23p42	00 15	05 21	05 57	06 14	06 27	06 47	07 02	07 10	07 26	07 35	07 40	08 07	08 00	08 07	08 39	08 32	08 39	09 02	09 15
Witley	d	23p21		23p48	00 21	05 27	06 03		06 33			07 16			07 46	→		08 13	→		08 45		
Milford (Surrey)	d	23p25		23p52	00 25	05 31	06 08		06 37			07 21			07 50			08 17			08 49		
Godalming	d	23p29		23p56	00 29	05 35	06 12		06 41	06 57		07 25	07 35	07 45	07 54			08 21			08 53		09 25
Farncombe	d	23p32		23p59	00 32	05 38	06 15		06 44	07 00		07 28	07 38		07 57			08 25			08 57		09 28
Guildford	a	23p37	23p31	00 04	00 37	05 48	06 23	06 29	06 52	07 06	07 15	07 33	07 43	07 52	08 02		08 13	08 30		08 46	09 02	09 15	09 33
	d	23p39	23p35	00 05		05 50	06 24	06 31	06 53	07 07	07 17	07 34	07 45	07 54	08 03		08 15	08 31		08 54	09 03	09 17	09 34
Worplesdon	d	23p44				05 55	06 30		06 59			07 40	07 50				08 20	08 37					09 40
Woking	a	23p49	23p42	00 13		06 00	06 35	06 39	07 03	07 15	07 25		07 54		08 11		08 26	08 41			09 11	09 27	09 44
	d	23p56	23p45			06 01	06 37	06 41	07 05	07 17	07 26		07 56		08 12		08 27	08 43			09 13	09 28	09 46
Clapham Junction 10	a	00 19	00 04			06 20	06 58	07 02	07 24									09 03			09 32		10 05
London Waterloo 15 ⊖	a	00 33	00 14			06 29	07 08	07 12	07 36	07 45	07 54	08 11	08 24	08 32	08 41		08 55	09 13		09 31	09 43	09 55	10 13

		SW 1 ✕	SW 1	SW 1 ✕	SW 1	SW 1 ✕	SW 1	SW 1 ✕	SW 1	SW 1 ✕	SW 1	SW 1 ✕	SW 1	SW 1 ✕	SW 1	SW 1 ✕	SW 1	SW 1 ✕	SW 1	SW 1 ✕	SW 1	SW 1 ✕	SW 1
Portsmouth Harbour ⛴	d	08 45		09 15	09 18	09 45		10 15		10 45		11 15		11 45		12 15		12 45		13 15		13 45	
Portsmouth & Southsea	d	08 50		09 20	09 24	09 50		10 20	10 24	10 50		11 20	11 24	11 50		12 20	12 24	12 50		13 20	13 24	13 50	
Fratton	d	08 54		09 24	09 28	09 54		10 24	10 28	10 54		11 24	11 28	11 54		12 24	12 28	12 54		13 24	13 28	13 54	
Hilsea	d				09 32				10 32				11 32				12 32				13 32		
Bedhampton	d				09 37				10 37				11 37				12 37				13 37		
Havant	a	09 03		09 33	09 39	10 03		10 33	10 39	11 03		11 33	11 39	12 03		12 33	12 39	13 03		13 33	13 39	14 03	
	d	09 04		09 34	09 40	10 04		10 34	10 40	11 04		11 34	11 40	12 04		12 34	12 40	13 04		13 34	13 40	14 04	
Rowlands Castle	d				09 46				10 46				11 46				12 46				13 46		
Petersfield	d	09 18		09 48	09 57	10 18		10 48	10 57	11 18		11 48	11 57	12 18		12 48	12 57	13 18		13 48	13 57	14 18	
Liss	d				10 02				11 02				12 02				13 02				14 02		
Liphook	d				10 09				11 09				12 09				13 09				14 09		
Haslemere 4	a	09 31		10 01	10 15	10 31		11 01	11 15	11 31		12 01	12 15	12 31		13 01	13 15	13 31		14 01	14 15	14 31	
	d	09 32	09 39	10 02	10 15	10 32	10 39	11 02	11 15	11 32	11 39	12 02	12 15	12 32	12 39	13 02	13 15	13 32	13 39	14 02	14 15	14 32	14 39
Witley	d		09 45				10 45				11 45				12 45				13 45				14 45
Milford (Surrey)	d		09 49				10 49				11 49				12 49				13 49				14 49
Godalming	d		09 53		10 25		10 53		11 25		11 53		12 25		12 53		13 25		13 53		14 25		14 53
Farncombe	d		09 56		10 28		10 56		11 28		11 56		12 28		12 56		13 28		13 56		14 28		14 56
Guildford	a	09 45	10 01	10 15	10 33	10 46	11 01	11 15	11 33	11 45	12 01	12 15	12 33	12 45	13 01	13 15	13 33	13 45	14 01	14 15	14 33	14 45	15 01
	d	09 47	10 02	10 17	10 34	10 47	11 02	11 17	11 34	11 47	12 02	12 17	12 34	12 47	13 02	13 17	13 34	13 47	14 02	14 17	14 34	14 47	15 02
Worplesdon	d				10 40				11 40				12 40				13 40				14 40		
Woking	a	09 59	10 11	10 25	10 44	10 57	11 11	11 25	11 44	11 57	12 11	12 25	12 44	12 57	13 11	13 25	13 44	13 57	14 11	14 25	14 44	14 57	15 11
	d	09 59	10 12	10 26	10 46	10 59	11 12	11 26	11 46	11 59	12 12	12 26	12 46	12 59	13 12	13 26	13 46	13 59	14 12	14 26	14 46	14 59	15 12
Clapham Junction 10	a		10 31		11 05		11 31		12 05		12 31		13 05		13 31		14 05		14 31		15 05		15 31
London Waterloo 15 ⊖	a	10 27	10 40	10 51	11 13	11 24	11 40	11 51	12 13	12 23	12 40	12 51	13 13	13 23	13 40	13 51	14 13	14 23	14 40	14 51	15 13	15 23	15 43

A until 20 July, 17 August, 24 August, 14 September, 21 September, 28 September, 5 October

B until 19 July, from 23 July until 13 September, not 17 August, 24 August, also FX from 17 September until 4 October

Portsmouth, Haslemere and Guildford - London

Network Diagram - see first Page of Table 155

Mondays to Fridays from 8 October

		SW 1 ✕	SW 1	SW 1 ✕	SW 1	SW 1 ✕	SW 1	SW 1	SW 1 ✕	SW 1 ✕	SW 1	SW	SW 1 ✕	SW 1 ✕	SW 1	SW 1 ✕	SW 1 ✕	SW 1	SW 1 ✕	SW 1	SW 1	SW 1	SW 1
Portsmouth Harbour ⛴	d	14 15		14 45		15 15			15 45	16 15			16 45	17 15	17 18	17 45	18 15		18 45		19 15		19 45
Portsmouth & Southsea	d	14 20	14 24	14 50		15 20	15 24		15 50	16 20	16 24		16 50	17 20	17 24	17 50	18 20	18 24	18 50		19 20	19 24	19 50
Fratton	d	14 24	14 28	14 54		15 24	15 28		15 54	16 24	16 28		16 54	17 24	17 28	17 54	18 24	18 28	18 54		19 24	19 28	19 54
Hilsea	d		14 32				15 32				16 32				17 32			18 32				19 32	
Bedhampton	d		14 37				15 37				16 37				17 37			18 37				19 37	
Havant	a	14 33	14 39	15 03		15 33	15 39		16 03	16 33	16 39		17 03	17 33	17 39	18 03	18 33	18 39	19 03		19 33	19 39	20 03
	d	14 34	14 40	15 04		15 34	15 40	15 54	16 04	16 34	16 40	16 56	17 04	17 34	17 40	18 04	18 34	18 40	19 04		19 34	19 40	20 04
Rowlands Castle	d		14 46				15 46				16 46				17 46			18 46				19 46	
Petersfield	d	14 48	14 57	15 18		15 48	15 57	16 10	16 18	16 48	16 57	17 10	17 18	17 48	17 57	18 18	18 48	18 57	19 18		19 48	19 57	20 18
Liss	d		15 02				16 02		16 23		17 02		17 23		18 02			19 02				20 02	
Liphook	d		15 09				16 09		16 30		17 09		17 30		18 09			19 09				20 09	
Haslemere 4	a	15 01	15 15	15 31		16 01	16 15	16 23	16 36	17 01	17 15	17 32	17 36	18 01	18 15	18 31	19 01	19 15	19 31		20 01	20 15	20 31
	d	15 02	15 15	15 32	15 37	16 02	16 15	16 24	16 37	17 02	17 15		17 37	18 02	18 15	18 32	19 02	19 15	19 32	19 39	20 02	20 15	20 32
Witley	d				15 43			16 30	16 43				17 43			18 38				19 45		20 21	
Milford (Surrey)	d				15 47			16 34	16 47				17 47			18 42				19 49		20 25	
Godalming	d		15 25		15 51		16 25	16 38	16 51		17 25		17 51		18 25	18 46	19 11	19 25		19 53		20 29	
Farncombe	d		15 28		15 54		16 28	16 41	16 54		17 28		17 54		18 28	18 49	19 14	19 28		19 56		20 32	
Guildford	a	15 15	15 33	15 45	15 59	16 15	16 33	16 46	16 59	17 15	17 33	17 47	17 59	18 15	18 33	18 54	19 19	19 33	19 45	20 01	20 15	20 37	20 45
	d	15 17	15 34	15 47	16 00	16 17	16 34	16 47	17 00	17 17	17 34		18 00	18 17	18 34	18 55	19 21	19 34	19 47	20 02	20 17	20 39	20 47
Worplesdon	d		15 40		16 06		16 40		17 06		17 40		18 06		18 40			19 40				20 44	
Woking	a	15 25	15 44	15 57	16 11	16 25	16 44	16 57	17 11	17 25	17 44	17 59	18 11		18 44	19 03	19 28	19 45	19 57	20 11	20 25	20 52	20 56
	d	15 26	15 46	15 59	16 12	16 26	16 46	16 59	17 12	17 26	17 46		18 12		18 46	19 05	19 30	19 46	19 59	20 12	20 26	20 53	20 59
Clapham Junction 10	a		16 05		16 31		17 05		17 31		18 05		18 31		19 05			20 05		20 31		21 12	
London Waterloo 15 ⊖	a	15 51	16 13	16 24	16 40	16 51	17 14	17 27	17 43	17 54	18 14	18 27	18 43	18 59	19 13	19 29	19 59	20 14	20 24	20 40	20 50	21 21	21 27

		SW 1	SW 1	SW 1	SW 1	SW 1	SW FO 1	SW FX 1	SW 1	SW 1
Portsmouth Harbour ⛴	d	20 15	20 18	20 45	21 18	21 28	22 18	22 18	22 28	23 19
Portsmouth & Southsea	d	20 20	20 24	20 50	21 24	21 33	22 24	22 24	22 33	23 24
Fratton	d	20 24	20 28	20 54	21 28	21 37	22 28	22 28	22 37	23 28
Hilsea	d		20 32		21 32	21 41	22 32	22 32	22 41	23 32
Bedhampton	d		20 37		21 37	21 47	22 37	22 37	22 46	23 37
Havant	a	20 33	20 39	21 03	21 40	21 52	22 39	22 39	22 53	23 39
	d	20 34	20 40	21 04	21 40		22 40	22 40		23 40
Rowlands Castle	d		20 46		21 46		22 46	22 46		23 46
Petersfield	d	20 48	20 57	21 18	21 57		22 57	22 57		23 57
Liss	d		21 02		22 02		23 02	23 02		00 02
Liphook	d		21 09		22 09		23 09	23 09		00 09
Haslemere 4	a	21 01	21 15	21 31	22 15		23 15	23 15		00 15
	d	21 02	21 15	21 32	22 15		23 15	23 15		00 15
Witley	d		21 21		22 21		23 21	23 21		00 21
Milford (Surrey)	d		21 25		22 25		23 25	23 25		00 25
Godalming	d		21 29		22 29		23 29	23 29		00 29
Farncombe	d		21 32		22 32		23 32	23 32		00 32
Guildford	a	21 16	21 37	21 45	22 37		23 37	23 37		00 37
	d	21 17	21 39	21 47	22 39		23 39	23 39		
Worplesdon	d		21 44		22 44		23 44	23 44		
Woking	a	21 25	21 49	21 57	22 49		23 49	23 49		
	d	21 26	21 50	21 59	22 50		23 56	23 56		
Clapham Junction 10	a		22 09		23 09		00 19	00 19		
London Waterloo 15 ⊖	a	21 50	22 18	22 27	23 19		00 32	00 33		

Saturdays until 6 October

		SW 1 A	SW 1 B	SW 1	SW 1	SW 1	SW 1	SW 1	SW 1 ✕	SW 1	SW 1 ✕	SW 1	SW 1 ✕	SW 1	SW 1 ✕	SW 1	SW 1 ✕	SW 1	SW 1 ✕	SW 1	SW 1 ✕	SW 1	SW 1 ✕
Portsmouth Harbour ⛴	d	22p18	22p18	23p19	04 43	05 19		06 19	06 45		07 15		07 45		08 15		08 45		09 15		09 45		10 15
Portsmouth & Southsea	d	22p24	22p24	23p24	04 48	05 24		06 24	06 50		07 20	07 24	07 50		08 20	08 24	08 50		09 20	09 24	09 50		10 20
Fratton	d	22p28	22p28	23p28	04 52	05 28		06 28	06 54		07 24	07 28	07 54		08 24	08 28	08 54		09 24	09 28	09 54		10 24
Hilsea	d	22p32	22p32	23p32	04 56	05 32		06 32				07 32				08 32				09 32			
Bedhampton	d	22p37	22p37	23p37	05 01	05 37		06 37				07 37				08 37				09 37			
Havant	a	22p39	22p39	23p39	05 03	05 39		06 40	07 03		07 33	07 39	08 03		08 33	08 39	09 03		09 33	09 39	10 03		10 33
	d	22p40	22p40	23p40	05 04	05 40		06 41	07 04		07 34	07 40	08 04		08 34	08 40	09 04		09 34	09 40	10 04		10 34
Rowlands Castle	d	22p46	22p46	23p46	05 09	05 46		06 46				07 46				08 46				09 46			
Petersfield	d	22p57	22p57	23p57	05 20	05 57		06 57	07 18		07 48	07 57	08 18		08 48	08 57	09 18		09 48	09 57	10 18		10 48
Liss	d	23p02	23p02	00 02	05 25	06 02		07 02				08 02				09 02				10 02			
Liphook	d	23p09	23p09	00 09	05 32	06 09		07 09				08 09				09 09				10 09			
Haslemere 4	a	23p15	23p15	00 15	05 38	06 14		07 14	07 31		08 01	08 14	08 31		09 01	09 15	09 31		10 01	10 15	10 31		11 01
	d	23p15	23p15	00 15	05 39	06 15	06 39	07 15	07 32	07 39	08 02	08 15	08 32	08 39	09 02	09 15	09 32	09 39	10 02	10 15	10 32	10 39	11 02
Witley	d	23p21	23p21	00 21	05 45		06 45			07 45				08 45				09 45				10 45	
Milford (Surrey)	d	23p25	23p25	00 25	05 49		06 49			07 49				08 49				09 49				10 49	
Godalming	d	23p29	23p29	00 29	05 53	06 25	06 53	07 25		07 53		08 25		08 53		09 25		09 53		10 25		10 53	
Farncombe	d	23p32	23p32	00 32	05 56	06 28	06 56	07 28		07 56		08 28		08 56		09 28		09 56		10 28		10 56	
Guildford	a	23p37	23p37	00 37	06 01	06 33	07 01	07 33	07 45	08 01	08 15	08 33	08 45	09 01	09 15	09 33	09 45	10 01	10 15	10 33	10 45	11 01	11 15
	d	23p39	23p39		06 02	06 34	07 02	07 34	07 47	08 02	08 17	08 34	08 47	09 02	09 17	09 34	09 47	10 02	10 17	10 34	10 47	11 02	11 17
Worplesdon	d	23p44	23p44			06 40		07 40				08 40				09 40				10 40			
Woking	a	23p49	23p49		06 11	06 44	07 11	07 44	07 57	08 10	08 26	08 44	08 57	09 11	09 25	09 44	09 57	10 11	10 25	10 44	10 57	11 11	11 25
	d	23p56	23p56		06 13	06 46	07 12	07 46	07 59	08 13	08 27	08 46	08 59	09 12	09 26	09 46	09 59	10 12	10 26	10 46	10 59	11 12	11 26
Clapham Junction 10	a	00 19	00 19		06 32	07 05	07 31	08 05		08 33		09 05		09 31		10 05		10 31		11 05		11 31	
London Waterloo 15 ⊖	a	00 32	00 33		06 40	07 13	07 40	08 13	08 23	08 42	08 51	09 13	09 23	09 40	09 51	10 13	10 23	10 40	10 51	11 13	11 23	11 40	11 51

A until 21 July, 18 August, 25 August, 15 September, 22 September, 29 September, 6 October

B 28 July, 4 August, 11 August, 1 September, 8 September

Table 156

Portsmouth, Haslemere and Guildford - London

Network Diagram - see first Page of Table 155

		SW 1	SW 1 ⚯	SW 1	SW 1 ⚯	SW 1	SW 1 ⚯	SW 1	SW 1 ⚯	SW 1	SW 1 ⚯	SW 1	SW 1 ⚯	SW 1	SW 1 ⚯	SW 1	SW 1 ⚯	SW 1	SW 1 ⚯	SW 1	SW 1 ⚯	SW 1	SW 1 ⚯
Portsmouth Harbour ⛴	d		10 45		11 15		11 45		12 15		12 45		13 15		13 45		14 15		14 45		15 15		15 45
Portsmouth & Southsea	d	10 24	10 50		11 20	11 24	11 50		12 20	12 24	12 50		13 20	13 24	13 50		14 20	14 24	14 50		15 20	15 24	15 50
Fratton	d	10 28	10 54		11 24	11 28	11 54		12 24	12 28	12 54		13 24	13 28	13 54		14 24	14 28	14 54		15 24	15 28	15 54
Hilsea	d	10 32				11 32				12 32				13 32				14 32				15 32	
Bedhampton	d	10 37				11 37				12 37				13 37				14 37				15 37	
Havant	a	10 39	11 03		11 33	11 39	12 03		12 33	12 39	13 03		13 33	13 39	14 03		14 33	14 39	15 03		15 33	15 39	16 03
	d	10 40	11 04		11 34	11 40	12 04		12 34	12 40	13 04		13 34	13 40	14 04		14 34	14 40	15 04		15 34	15 40	16 04
Rowlands Castle	d	10 46				11 46				12 46				13 46				14 46				15 46	
Petersfield	d	10 57	11 18		11 48	11 57	12 18		12 48	12 57	13 18		13 48	13 57	14 18		14 48	14 57	15 18		15 48	15 57	16 18
Liss	d	11 02				12 02				13 02				14 02				15 02				16 02	
Liphook	d	11 09				12 09				13 09				14 09				15 09				16 09	
Haslemere 4	a	11 15	11 31		12 01	12 15	12 31		13 01	13 15	13 31		14 01	14 15	14 31		15 01	15 15	15 31		16 01	16 15	16 31
	d	11 15	11 32	11 39	12 02	12 15	12 32	12 39	13 02	13 15	13 32	13 39	14 02	14 15	14 32	14 39	15 02	15 15	15 32	15 39	16 02	16 15	16 32
Witley	d			11 45				12 45				13 45				14 45				15 45			
Milford (Surrey)	d			11 49				12 49				13 49				14 49				15 49			
Godalming	d	11 25		11 53		12 25		12 53		13 25		13 53		14 25		14 53		15 25		15 53		16 25	
Farncombe	d	11 28		11 56		12 28		12 56		13 28		13 56		14 28		14 56		15 28		15 56		16 28	
Guildford	a	11 33	11 45	12 01	12 15	12 33	12 45	13 01	13 15	13 33	13 45	14 01	14 15	14 33	14 45	15 01	15 15	15 33	15 45	16 01	16 15	16 33	16 45
	d	11 34	11 47	12 02	12 17	12 34	12 47	13 02	13 17	13 34	13 47	14 02	14 17	14 34	14 47	15 02	15 17	15 34	15 47	16 02	16 17	16 34	16 47
Worplesdon	d	11 40				12 40				13 40				14 40				15 40				16 40	
Woking	a	11 44	11 57	12 11	12 25	12 44	12 57	13 11	13 25	13 44	13 57	14 11	14 25	14 44	14 57	15 11	15 25	15 44	15 57	16 11	16 25	16 44	16 57
	d	11 46	11 59	12 12	12 26	12 46	12 59	13 12	13 26	13 46	13 59	14 12	14 26	14 46	14 59	15 12	15 26	15 46	15 59	16 12	16 26	16 46	16 59
Clapham Junction 10	a	12 05		12 31		13 05		13 31		14 05		14 31		15 05		15 31		16 05		16 31		17 05	
London Waterloo 15 ⊖	a	12 13	12 27	12 43	12 57	13 13	13 27	13 43	13 57	14 14	14 27	14 41	14 57	15 14	15 27	15 41	15 57	16 13	16 23	16 40	16 51	17 13	17 23

		SW 1	SW 1 ⚯	SW 1	SW 1 ⚯	SW 1	SW 1	SW 1	SW 1 ⚯	SW 1	SW 1	SW 1	SW 1	SW 1	SW 1	SW 1	SW 1	SW 1	SW 1	SW 1	SW 1	SW 1
Portsmouth Harbour ⛴	d		16 15		16 45			17 18	17 45		18 15		18 45		19 15		19 45	20 15		20 45	21 18	22 18
Portsmouth & Southsea	d		16 20	16 24	16 50		17 10	17 24	17 50		18 20	18 24	18 50		19 20	19 24	19 50	20 20	20 24	20 50	21 24	22 24
Fratton	d		16 24	16 28	16 54		17 14	17 28	17 54		18 24	18 28	18 54		19 24	19 28	19 54	20 24	20 28	20 54	21 28	22 28
Hilsea	d			16 32			17 18	17 32				18 32				19 32			20 32		21 32	22 32
Bedhampton	d			16 37			17 23	17 37				18 37				19 37			20 37		21 37	22 37
Havant	a		16 33	16 39	17 03		17 25	17 39	18 03		18 33	18 39	19 03		19 33	19 39	20 03	20 33	20 39	21 03	21 39	22 39
	d		16 34	16 40	17 04		17 26	17 40	18 04		18 34	18 40	19 04		19 34	19 40	20 04	20 34	20 40	21 04	21 40	22 40
Rowlands Castle	d			16 46			17 32	17 46				18 46				19 46			20 46		21 46	22 46
Petersfield	d		16 48	16 57	17 18		17 43	17 57	18 18		18 48	18 57	19 18		19 48	19 57	20 18	20 48	20 57	21 18	21 57	22 57
Liss	d			17 02			17 48	18 02				19 02				20 02			21 02		22 02	23 02
Liphook	d			17 09			17 55	18 09				19 09				20 09			21 09		22 09	23 09
Haslemere 4	a		17 01	17 15	17 31		18 01	18 15	18 31		19 01	19 15	19 31		20 01	20 15	20 31	21 01	21 15	21 31	22 15	23 15
	d	16 39	17 02	17 15	17 32	17 39	18 02	18 15	18 32	18 39	19 02	19 15	19 32	19 39	20 02	20 15	20 32	21 02	21 15	21 32	22 15	23 15
Witley	d	16 45				17 45				18 45				19 45		20 21			21 21		22 21	23 21
Milford (Surrey)	d	16 49				17 49				18 49				19 49		20 25			21 25		22 25	23 25
Godalming	d	16 53		17 25		17 53		18 25		18 53		19 25		19 53		20 29			21 29		22 29	23 29
Farncombe	d	16 56		17 28		17 56		18 28		18 56		19 28		19 56		20 32			21 32		22 32	23 32
Guildford	a	17 01	17 15	17 33	17 45	18 01	18 15	18 33	18 45	19 01	19 15	19 33	19 45	20 01	20 15	20 37	20 45	21 15	21 37	21 47	22 37	23 37
	d	17 02	17 17	17 34	17 47	18 02	18 17	18 34	18 47	19 02	19 17	19 34	19 47	20 02	20 17	20 39	20 47	21 17	21 39	21 49	22 39	23 39
Worplesdon	d			17 40				18 40				19 40				20 44			21 44		22 44	23 44
Woking	a	17 11	17 25	17 44	17 57	18 11	18 25	18 44	18 57	19 11	19 25	19 44	19 57	20 11	20 25	20 52	20 57	21 25	21 49	21 57	22 49	23 49
	d	17 12	17 26	17 46	17 59	18 12	18 26	18 46	18 59	19 12	19 26	19 46	19 59	20 12	20 26	20 53	20 59	21 26	21 50	21 59	22 50	23 56
Clapham Junction 10	a	17 31		18 05		18 31		19 05		19 31		20 05		20 31		21 12			22 09		23 09	00 18
London Waterloo 15 ⊖	a	17 40	17 51	18 13	18 23	18 40	18 51	19 13	19 23	19 40	19 51	20 13	20 23	20 40	20 50	21 21	21 27	21 50	22 18	22 24	23 18	00 32

		SW 1
Portsmouth Harbour ⛴	d	23 19
Portsmouth & Southsea	d	23 24
Fratton	d	23 28
Hilsea	d	23 32
Bedhampton	d	23 37
Havant	a	23 39
	d	23 40
Rowlands Castle	d	23 46
Petersfield	d	23 57
Liss	d	00 02
Liphook	d	00 09
Haslemere 4	a	00 15
	d	00 15
Witley	d	00 21
Milford (Surrey)	d	00 25
Godalming	d	00 29
Farncombe	d	00 32
Guildford	a	00 37
	d	
Worplesdon	d	
Woking	a	
	d	
Clapham Junction 10	a	
London Waterloo 15 ⊖	a	

Table 156

Portsmouth, Haslemere and Guildford - London

Network Diagram - see first Page of Table 155

		SW 1	SW 1	SW 1	SW 1	SW 1	SW 1	SW 1 ⚯	SW 1	SW 1 ⚯	SW 1	SW 1 ⚯	SW 1	SW 1 ⚯	SW 1	SW 1 ⚯	SW 1	SW 1 ⚯	SW 1	SW 1 ⚯	SW 1	SW 1 ⚯	SW 1
Portsmouth Harbour ⛴	d	22p18	23p19	04 38	05 14		06 19	06 45		07 15		07 45		08 15		08 45		09 15		09 45		10 15	
Portsmouth & Southsea	d	22p24	23p24	04 43	05 19		06 24	06 50		07 20	07 24	07 50		08 20	08 24	08 50		09 20	09 24	09 50		10 20	10 24
Fratton	d	22p28	23p28	04 47	05 23		06 28	06 54		07 24	07 28	07 54		08 24	08 28	08 54		09 24	09 28	09 54		10 24	10 28
Hilsea	d	22p32	23p32	04 51	05 27		06 32				07 32				08 32				09 32				10 32
Bedhampton	d	22p37	23p37	04 56	05 32		06 37				07 37				08 37				09 37				10 37
Havant	a	22p39	23p39	04 58	05 34		06 40	07 03		07 33	07 39	08 03		08 33	08 39	09 03		09 33	09 39	10 03		10 33	10 39
	d	22p40	23p40	04 59	05 35		06 41	07 04		07 34	07 40	08 04		08 34	08 40	09 04		09 34	09 40	10 04		10 34	10 40
Rowlands Castle	d	22p46	23p46	05 04	05 41		06 46				07 46				08 46				09 46				10 46
Petersfield	d	22p57	23p57	05 15	05 52		06 57	07 18		07 48	07 57	08 18		08 48	08 57	09 18		09 48	09 57	10 18		10 48	10 57
Liss	d	23p02	00 02	05 20	05 57		07 02				08 02				09 02				10 02				11 02
Liphook	d	23p09	00 09	05 27	06 04		07 09				08 09				09 09				10 09				11 09
Haslemere 4	a	23p15	00 15	05 33	06 12		07 14	07 31		08 01	08 14	08 31		09 01	09 15	09 31		10 01	10 15	10 31		11 01	11 15
	d	23p15	00 15	05 34	06 13	06 39	07 15	07 32	07 39	08 02	08 15	08 32	08 39	09 02	09 15	09 32	09 39	10 02	10 15	10 32	10 39	11 02	11 15
Witley	d	23p21	00 21	05 40		06 45			07 45				08 45				09 45				10 45		
Milford (Surrey)	d	23p25	00 25	05 44		06 49			07 49				08 49				09 49				10 49		
Godalming	d	23p29	00 29	05 48	06 23	06 53	07 25		07 53		08 25		08 53		09 25		09 53		10 25		10 53		11 25
Farncombe	d	23p32	00 32	05 51	06 26	06 56	07 28		07 56		08 28		08 56		09 28		09 56		10 28		10 56		11 28
Guildford	a	23p37	00 37	06 01	06 33	07 01	07 33	07 45	08 01	08 15	08 33	08 45	09 01	09 15	09 33	09 45	10 01	10 15	10 33	10 45	11 01	11 15	11 33
	d	23p39		06 02	06 34	07 02	07 34	07 47	08 02	08 17	08 34	08 47	09 02	09 17	09 34	09 47	10 02	10 17	10 34	10 47	11 02	11 17	11 34
Worplesdon	d	23p44			06 40		07 40				08 40				09 40				10 40				11 40
Woking	a	23p49		06 11	06 44	07 11	07 44	07 57	08 10	08 26	08 44	08 57	09 11	09 25	09 44	09 57	10 11	10 25	10 44	10 57	11 11	11 25	11 44
	d	23p56		06 13	06 46	07 12	07 46	07 59	08 13	08 27	08 46	08 59	09 12	09 26	09 46	09 59	10 12	10 26	10 46	10 59	11 12	11 26	11 46
Clapham Junction 10	a	00 19		06 32	07 05	07 31	08 05		08 33		09 05		09 31		10 05		10 31		11 05		11 31		12 05
London Waterloo 15 ⊖	a	00 32		06 40	07 13	07 40	08 13	08 23	08 42	08 51	09 13	09 23	09 40	09 51	10 13	10 23	10 40	10 51	11 13	11 23	11 40	11 51	12 13

		SW 1 ⚯	SW 1	SW 1 ⚯	SW 1	SW 1 ⚯	SW 1	SW 1 ⚯	SW 1	SW 1 ⚯	SW 1	SW 1 ⚯	SW 1	SW 1 ⚯	SW 1	SW 1 ⚯	SW 1	SW 1 ⚯	SW 1	SW 1 ⚯	SW 1	SW 1 ⚯	SW 1
Portsmouth Harbour ⛴	d	10 45		11 15		11 45		12 15		12 45		13 15		13 45		14 15		14 45		15 15		15 45	
Portsmouth & Southsea	d	10 50		11 20	11 24	11 50		12 20	12 24	12 50		13 20	13 24	13 50		14 20	14 24	14 50		15 20	15 24	15 50	
Fratton	d	10 54		11 24	11 28	11 54		12 24	12 28	12 54		13 24	13 28	13 54		14 24	14 28	14 54		15 24	15 28	15 54	
Hilsea	d				11 32				12 32				13 32				14 32				15 32		
Bedhampton	d				11 37				12 37				13 37				14 37				15 37		
Havant	a	11 03		11 33	11 39	12 03		12 33	12 39	13 03		13 33	13 39	14 03		14 33	14 39	15 03		15 33	15 39	16 03	
	d	11 04		11 34	11 40	12 04		12 34	12 40	13 04		13 34	13 40	14 04		14 34	14 40	15 04		15 34	15 40	16 04	
Rowlands Castle	d				11 46				12 46				13 46				14 46				15 46		
Petersfield	d	11 18		11 48	11 57	12 18		12 48	12 57	13 18		13 48	13 57	14 18		14 48	14 57	15 18		15 48	15 57	16 18	
Liss	d				12 02				13 02				14 02				15 02				16 02		
Liphook	d				12 09				13 09				14 09				15 09				16 09		
Haslemere 4	a	11 31		12 01	12 15	12 31		13 01	13 15	13 31		14 01	14 15	14 31		15 01	15 15	15 31		16 01	16 15	16 31	
	d	11 32	11 39	12 02	12 15	12 32	12 39	13 02	13 15	13 32	13 39	14 02	14 15	14 32	14 39	15 02	15 15	15 32	15 39	16 02	16 15	16 32	16 39
Witley	d		11 45				12 45				13 45				14 45				15 45				16 45
Milford (Surrey)	d		11 49				12 49				13 49				14 49				15 49				16 49
Godalming	d		11 53		12 25		12 53		13 25		13 53		14 25		14 53		15 25		15 53		16 25		16 53
Farncombe	d		11 56		12 28		12 56		13 28		13 56		14 28		14 56		15 28		15 56		16 28		16 56
Guildford	a	11 45	12 01	12 15	12 33	12 45	13 01	13 15	13 33	13 45	14 01	14 15	14 33	14 45	15 01	15 15	15 33	15 45	16 01	16 15	16 33	16 45	17 01
	d	11 47	12 02	12 17	12 34	12 47	13 02	13 17	13 34	13 47	14 02	14 17	14 34	14 47	15 02	15 17	15 34	15 47	16 02	16 17	16 34	16 47	17 02
Worplesdon	d				12 40				13 40				14 40				15 40				16 40		
Woking	a	11 57	12 11	12 25	12 44	12 57	13 11	13 25	13 44	13 57	14 11	14 25	14 44	14 57	15 11	15 25	15 44	15 57	16 11	16 25	16 44	16 57	17 11
	d	11 59	12 12	12 26	12 46	12 59	13 12	13 26	13 46	13 59	14 12	14 26	14 46	14 59	15 12	15 26	15 46	15 59	16 12	16 26	16 46	16 59	17 12
Clapham Junction 10	a		12 31		13 05		13 31		14 05		14 31		15 05		15 31		16 05		16 31		17 05		17 31
London Waterloo 15 ⊖	a	12 27	12 43	12 57	13 13	13 27	13 43	13 57	14 14	14 27	14 41	14 57	15 14	15 27	15 41	15 57	16 13	16 23	16 40	16 51	17 13	17 23	17 40

		SW 1 ⚯	SW 1	SW 1 ⚯	SW 1	SW 1	SW 1	SW 1 ⚯	SW 1	SW 1	SW 1	SW 1	SW 1	SW 1	SW 1	SW 1	SW 1	SW 1	SW 1	SW 1	SW 1	SW 1
Portsmouth Harbour ⛴	d	16 15		16 45			17 18	17 45		18 15		18 45		19 15		19 45	20 15		20 45	21 18	22 18	23 19
Portsmouth & Southsea	d	16 20	16 24	16 50		17 10	17 24	17 50		18 20	18 24	18 50		19 20	19 24	19 50	20 20	20 24	20 50	21 24	22 24	23 24
Fratton	d	16 24	16 28	16 54		17 14	17 28	17 54		18 24	18 28	18 54		19 24	19 28	19 54	20 24	20 28	20 54	21 28	22 28	23 28
Hilsea	d		16 32			17 18	17 32				18 32				19 32			20 32		21 32	22 32	23 32
Bedhampton	d		16 37			17 23	17 37				18 37				19 37			20 37		21 37	22 37	23 37
Havant	a	16 33	16 39	17 03		17 25	17 39	18 03		18 33	18 39	19 03		19 33	19 39	20 03	20 33	20 39	21 03	21 39	22 39	23 39
	d	16 34	16 40	17 04		17 26	17 40	18 04		18 34	18 40	19 04		19 34	19 40	20 04	20 34	20 40	21 04	21 40	22 40	23 40
Rowlands Castle	d		16 46			17 32	17 46				18 46				19 46			20 46		21 46	22 46	23 46
Petersfield	d	16 48	16 57	17 18		17 43	17 57	18 18		18 48	18 57	19 18		19 48	19 57	20 18	20 48	20 57	21 18	21 57	22 57	23 57
Liss	d		17 02			17 48	18 02				19 02				20 02			21 02		22 02	23 02	00 02
Liphook	d		17 09			17 55	18 09				19 09				20 09			21 09		22 09	23 09	00 09
Haslemere 4	a	17 01	17 15	17 31		18 01	18 15	18 31		19 01	19 15	19 31		20 01	20 15	20 31	21 01	21 15	21 31	22 15	23 15	00 15
	d	17 02	17 15	17 32	17 39	18 02	18 15	18 32	18 39	19 02	19 15	19 32	19 39	20 02	20 15	20 32	21 02	21 15	21 32	22 15	23 15	00 15
Witley	d				17 45				18 45				19 45		20 21			21 21		22 21	23 21	00 21
Milford (Surrey)	d				17 49				18 49				19 49		20 25			21 25		22 25	23 25	00 25
Godalming	d		17 25		17 53		18 25		18 53		19 25		19 53		20 29			21 29		22 29	23 29	00 29
Farncombe	d		17 28		17 56		18 28		18 56		19 28		19 56		20 32			21 32		22 32	23 32	00 32
Guildford	a	17 15	17 33	17 45	18 01	18 15	18 33	18 45	19 01	19 15	19 33	19 45	20 01	20 15	20 37	20 45	21 15	21 37	21 47	22 37	23 37	00 37
	d	17 17	17 34	17 47	18 02	18 17	18 34	18 47	19 02	19 17	19 34	19 47	20 02	20 17	20 39	20 47	21 17	21 39	21 49	22 39	23 39	
Worplesdon	d		17 40				18 40				19 40				20 44			21 44		22 44	23 44	
Woking	a	17 25	17 44	17 57	18 11	18 25	18 44	18 57	19 11	19 25	19 44	19 57	20 11	20 25	20 52	20 57	21 25	21 49	21 57	22 49	23 49	
	d	17 26	17 46	17 59	18 12	18 26	18 46	18 59	19 12	19 26	19 46	19 59	20 12	20 26	20 53	20 59	21 26	21 50	21 59	22 50	23 56	
Clapham Junction 10	a		18 05		18 31		19 05		19 31		20 05		20 31		21 12			22 09		23 09	00 18	
London Waterloo 15 ⊖	a	17 51	18 13	18 23	18 40	18 51	19 13	19 23	19 40	19 51	20 13	20 23	20 40	20 50	21 21	21 27	21 50	22 18	22 24	23 18	00 32	

Table 156

Sundays
until 30 September

Portsmouth, Haslemere and Guildford - London
Network Diagram - see first Page of Table 155

		SW 1	SW 1	SW 1 A	SW 1 B	SW 1 C	SW 1	SW 1	SW 1	SW 1	SW 1 🍴	SW 1	SW 1 🍴	SW 1	SW 1 🍴	SW 1	SW 1 🍴	SW 1	SW 1 🍴	SW 1	SW 1 🍴	SW 1	SW 1 🍴
Portsmouth Harbour ⛴	d	22p18	23p19	06 20	06 20	06 48	07 32	07 48	08 32	08 48	09 32	09 48	10 32	10 48	11 32	11 48	12 32	12 48	13 32	13 48	14 32	14 48	15 32
Portsmouth & Southsea	d	22p24	23p24	06 25	06 25	06 53	07 37	07 53	08 37	08 53	09 37	09 53	10 37	10 53	11 37	11 53	12 37	12 53	13 37	13 53	14 37	14 53	15 37
Fratton	d	22p28	23p28	06 29	06 29	06 57	07 41	07 57	08 41	08 57	09 41	09 57	10 41	10 57	11 41	11 57	12 41	12 57	13 41	13 57	14 41	14 57	15 41
Hilsea	d	22p32	23p32																				
Bedhampton	d	22p37	23p37	06 36	06 36	07 04		08 04		09 04		10 04		11 04		12 04		13 04		14 04		15 04	
Havant	a	22p39	23p39	06 39	06 39	07 07	07 49	08 07	08 49	09 07	09 49	10 07	10 49	11 07	11 49	12 07	12 49	13 07	13 49	14 07	14 49	15 07	15 49
	d	22p40	23p40	06 39	06 39	07 07	07 50	08 07	08 50	09 07	09 50	10 07	10 50	11 07	11 50	12 07	12 50	13 07	13 50	14 07	14 50	15 07	15 50
Rowlands Castle	d	22p46	23p46	06 45	06 45	07 13		08 13		09 13		10 13		11 13		12 13		13 13		14 13		15 13	
Petersfield	d	22p57	23p57	06 56	06 56	07 24	08 04	08 24	09 04	09 24	10 04	10 24	11 04	11 24	12 04	12 24	13 04	13 24	14 04	14 24	15 04	15 24	16 04
Liss	d	23p02	00 02	07 01	07 01	07 29		08 29		09 29		10 29		11 29		12 29		13 29		14 29		15 29	
Liphook	d	23p09	00 09	07 08	07 08	07 36		08 36		09 36		10 36		11 36		12 36		13 36		14 36		15 36	
Haslemere 4	a	23p15	00 15	07 13	07 13	07 41	08 16	08 41	09 16	09 41	10 16	10 41	11 16	11 41	12 16	12 41	13 16	13 41	14 16	14 41	15 16	15 41	16 16
	d	23p15	00 15	07 14	07 14	07 42	08 17	08 42	09 17	09 42	10 17	10 42	11 17	11 42	12 17	12 42	13 17	13 42	14 17	14 42	15 17	15 42	16 17
Witley	d	23p21	00 21	07 20	07 20	07 48		08 48		09 48		10 48		11 48		12 48		13 48		14 48		15 48	
Milford (Surrey)	d	23p25	00 25	07 24	07 24	07 52		08 52		09 52		10 52		11 52		12 52		13 52		14 52		15 52	
Godalming	d	23p29	00 29	07 28	07 28	07 56		08 56		09 56		10 56		11 56		12 56		13 56		14 56		15 56	
Farncombe	d	23p32	00 32	07 31	07 31	07 59		08 59		09 59		10 59		11 59		12 59		13 59		14 59		15 59	
Guildford	a	23p37	00 37	07 36	07 36	08 04	08 31	09 04	09 31	10 04	10 31	11 04	11 31	12 04	12 31	13 04	13 31	14 04	14 31	15 04	15 31	16 04	16 31
	d	23p39		07 38	07 37	08 05	08 35	09 05	09 35	10 05	10 35	11 06	11 35	12 06	12 35	13 05	13 35	14 05	14 35	15 05	15 35	16 05	16 35
Worplesdon	d	23p44																					
Woking	a	23p49		07 45	07 45	08 13	08 42	09 15	09 42	10 15	10 42	11 13	11 42	12 13	12 42	13 13	13 42	14 13	14 42	15 13	15 42	16 13	16 42
	d	23p56		07 47	07 47	08 15	08 45	09 15	09 45	10 15	10 45	11 15	11 45	12 15	12 45	13 15	13 45	14 15	14 45	15 15	15 45	16 15	16 45
Clapham Junction 10	a	00 18		08 10	08 10	08 40	09 06	09 38	10 04	10 35	11 04	11 34	12 04	12 34	13 04	13 34	14 04	14 34	15 04	15 34	16 04	16 34	17 04
London Waterloo 15 ⊖	a	00 32		08 23	08 23	08 49	09 19	09 49	10 19	10 49	11 19	11 49	12 19	12 49	13 14	13 44	14 14	14 44	15 14	15 44	16 14	16 44	17 14

		SW 1	SW 1 🍴	SW 1	SW 1 🍴	SW 1	SW 1 🍴	SW 1	SW 1	SW 1	SW 1	SW 1	SW 1	SW 1	SW 1	SW 1
Portsmouth Harbour ⛴	d	15 48	16 32	16 48	17 32	17 48	18 32	18 48	19 32	19 48	20 32	20 48	21 32	21 48	22 32	22 48
Portsmouth & Southsea	d	15 53	16 37	16 53	17 37	17 53	18 37	18 53	19 37	19 53	20 37	20 53	21 37	21 53	22 37	22 53
Fratton	d	15 57	16 41	16 57	17 41	17 57	18 41	18 57	19 41	19 57	20 41	20 57	21 41	21 57	22 41	22 57
Hilsea	d															
Bedhampton	d	16 04		17 04		18 04		19 04		20 04		21 04		22 04		23 04
Havant	a	16 07	16 49	17 07	17 49	18 07	18 49	19 07	19 49	20 07	20 49	21 07	21 49	22 07	22 49	23 07
	d	16 07	16 50	17 07	17 50	18 07	18 50	19 07	19 50	20 07	20 50	21 07	21 50	22 07	22 50	23 07
Rowlands Castle	d	16 13		17 13		18 13		19 13		20 13		21 13		22 13		23 13
Petersfield	d	16 24	17 04	17 24	18 04	18 24	19 04	19 24	20 04	20 24	21 04	21 24	22 04	22 24	23 04	23 24
Liss	d	16 29		17 29		18 29		19 29		20 29		21 29		22 29		23 29
Liphook	d	16 36		17 36		18 36		19 36		20 36		21 36		22 36		23 36
Haslemere 4	a	16 41	17 16	17 41	18 16	18 41	19 16	19 41	20 16	20 41	21 16	21 41	22 16	22 41	23 16	23 41
	d	16 42	17 17	17 42	18 17	18 42	19 17	19 42	20 17	20 42	21 17	21 42	22 17	22 42	23 17	23 42
Witley	d	16 48		17 48		18 48		19 48		20 48		21 48		22 48		23 48
Milford (Surrey)	d	16 52		17 52		18 52		19 52		20 52		21 52		22 52		23 52
Godalming	d	16 56		17 56		18 56		19 56		20 56		21 56		22 56		23 56
Farncombe	d	16 59		17 59		18 59		19 59		20 59		21 59		22 59		23 59
Guildford	a	17 04	17 31	18 04	18 31	19 04	19 31	20 04	20 31	21 04	21 31	22 04	22 31	23 04	23 31	00 04
	d	17 05	17 35	18 05	18 35	19 05	19 35	20 05	20 35	21 05	21 35	22 05	22 35	23 05	23 35	00 05
Worplesdon	d															
Woking	a	17 13	17 42	18 13	18 42	19 13	19 42	20 13	20 42	21 13	21 42	22 13	22 42	23 13	23 42	00 13
	d	17 15	17 45	18 15	18 45	19 15	19 45	20 15	20 45	21 15	21 45	22 15	22 45	23 15	23 45	
Clapham Junction 10	a	17 34	18 04	18 34	19 04	19 34	20 04	20 34	21 04	21 34	22 04	22 34	23 04	23 34	00 04	
London Waterloo 15 ⊖	a	17 44	18 14	18 44	19 14	19 44	20 14	20 44	21 14	21 44	22 14	22 44	23 14	23 44	00 14	

Sundays
from 7 October

		SW 1	SW 1	SW 1	SW 1	SW 1	SW 1	SW 1	SW 1 🍴	SW 1	SW 1 🍴	SW 1	SW 1 🍴	SW 1	SW 1 🍴	SW 1	SW 1 🍴	SW 1	SW 1 🍴	SW 1	SW 1 🍴	SW 1	SW 1 🍴
Portsmouth Harbour ⛴	d	22p18	23p19	06 43	07 29	07 48	08 29	08 48	09 32	09 48	10 32	10 48	11 32	11 48	12 32	12 48	13 32	13 48	14 32	14 48	15 32	15 48	16 32
Portsmouth & Southsea	d	22p24	23p24	06 48	07 34	07 53	08 34	08 53	09 37	09 53	10 37	10 53	11 37	11 53	12 37	12 53	13 37	13 53	14 37	14 53	15 37	15 53	16 37
Fratton	d	22p28	23p28	06 52	07 38	07 57	08 38	08 57	09 41	09 57	10 41	10 57	11 41	11 57	12 41	12 57	13 41	13 57	14 41	14 57	15 41	15 57	16 41
Hilsea	d	22p32	23p32																				
Bedhampton	d	22p37	23p37	06 59		08 04		09 04		10 04		11 04		12 04		13 04		14 04		15 04		16 04	
Havant	a	22p39	23p39	07 02	07 46	08 07	08 46	09 07	09 49	10 07	10 49	11 07	11 49	12 07	12 49	13 07	13 49	14 07	14 49	15 07	15 49	16 07	16 49
	d	22p40	23p40	07 02	07 47	08 07	08 47	09 07	09 50	10 07	10 50	11 07	11 50	12 07	12 50	13 07	13 50	14 07	14 50	15 07	15 50	16 07	16 50
Rowlands Castle	d	22p46	23p46	07 08		08 13		09 13		10 13		11 13		12 13		13 13		14 13		15 13		16 13	
Petersfield	d	22p57	23p57	07 19	08 01	08 24	09 01	09 24	10 04	10 24	11 04	11 24	12 04	12 24	13 04	13 24	14 04	14 24	15 04	15 24	16 04	16 24	17 04
Liss	d	23p02	00 02	07 24		08 29		09 29		10 29		11 29		12 29		13 29		14 29		15 29		16 29	
Liphook	d	23p09	00 09	07 31		08 36		09 36		10 36		11 36		12 36		13 36		14 36		15 36		16 36	
Haslemere 4	a	23p15	00 15	07 36	08 13	08 41	09 13	09 41	10 16	10 41	11 16	11 41	12 16	12 41	13 16	13 41	14 16	14 41	15 16	15 41	16 16	16 41	17 16
	d	23p15	00 15	07 37	08 14	08 42	09 14	09 42	10 17	10 42	11 17	11 42	12 17	12 42	13 17	13 42	14 17	14 42	15 17	15 42	16 17	16 42	17 17
Witley	d	23p21	00 21	07 43		08 48		09 48		10 48		11 48		12 48		13 48		14 48		15 48		16 48	
Milford (Surrey)	d	23p25	00 25	07 47		08 52		09 52		10 52		11 52		12 52		13 52		14 52		15 52		16 52	
Godalming	d	23p29	00 29	07 51		08 56		09 56		10 56		11 56		12 56		13 56		14 56		15 56		16 56	
Farncombe	d	23p32	00 32	07 54		08 59		09 59		10 59		11 59		12 59		13 59		14 59		15 59		16 59	
Guildford	a	23p37	00 37	08 04	08 31	09 04	09 31	10 04	10 31	11 04	11 31	12 04	12 31	13 04	13 31	14 04	14 31	15 04	15 31	16 04	16 31	17 04	17 31
	d	23p39		08 05	08 35	09 05	09 35	10 05	10 35	11 06	11 35	12 06	12 35	13 05	13 35	14 05	14 35	15 05	15 35	16 05	16 35	17 05	17 35
Worplesdon	d	23p44																					
Woking	a	23p49		08 13	08 42	09 15	09 42	10 15	10 42	11 13	11 42	12 13	12 42	13 13	13 42	14 13	14 42	15 13	15 42	16 13	16 42	17 13	17 42
	d	23p56		08 15	08 45	09 15	09 45	10 15	10 45	11 15	11 45	12 15	12 45	13 15	13 45	14 15	14 45	15 15	15 45	16 15	16 45	17 15	17 45
Clapham Junction 10	a	00 18		08 40	09 06	09 38	10 04	10 35	11 04	11 34	12 04	12 34	13 04	13 34	14 04	14 34	15 04	15 34	16 04	16 34	17 04	17 34	18 04
London Waterloo 15 ⊖	a	00 32		08 49	09 19	09 49	10 19	10 49	11 19	11 49	12 19	12 49	13 14	13 44	14 14	14 44	15 14	15 44	16 14	16 44	17 14	17 44	18 14

A 29 July, 5 August, 12 August
B 2 September, 9 September
C until 22 July, 19 August, 26 August, 16 September, 23 September, 30 September

Table 156

Sundays
from 7 October

Portsmouth, Haslemere and Guildford - London
Network Diagram - see first Page of Table 155

		SW 1	SW 1 🍴	SW 1	SW 1 🍴	SW 1	SW 1	SW 1	SW 1	SW 1	SW 1	SW 1	SW 1	SW 1
Portsmouth Harbour ⛴	d	16 48	17 32	17 48	18 32	18 48	19 32	19 48	20 32	20 48	21 32	21 48	22 32	22 48
Portsmouth & Southsea	d	16 53	17 37	17 53	18 37	18 53	19 37	19 53	20 37	20 53	21 37	21 53	22 37	22 53
Fratton	d	16 57	17 41	17 57	18 41	18 57	19 41	19 57	20 41	20 57	21 41	21 57	22 41	22 57
Hilsea	d													
Bedhampton	d	17 04		18 04		19 04		20 04		21 04		22 04		23 04
Havant	a	17 07	17 49	18 07	18 49	19 07	19 49	20 07	20 49	21 07	21 49	22 07	22 49	23 07
	d	17 07	17 50	18 07	18 50	19 07	19 50	20 07	20 50	21 07	21 50	22 07	22 50	23 07
Rowlands Castle	d	17 13		18 13		19 13		20 13		21 13		22 13		23 13
Petersfield	d	17 24	18 04	18 24	19 04	19 24	20 04	20 24	21 04	21 24	22 04	22 24	23 04	23 24
Liss	d	17 29		18 29		19 29		20 29		21 29		22 29		23 29
Liphook	d	17 36		18 36		19 36		20 36		21 36		22 36		23 36
Haslemere 4	a	17 41	18 16	18 41	19 16	19 41	20 16	20 41	21 16	21 41	22 16	22 41	23 16	23 41
	d	17 42	18 17	18 42	19 17	19 42	20 17	20 42	21 17	21 42	22 17	22 42	23 17	23 42
Witley	d	17 48		18 48		19 48		20 48		21 48		22 48		23 48
Milford (Surrey)	d	17 52		18 52		19 52		20 52		21 52		22 52		23 52
Godalming	d	17 56		18 56		19 56		20 56		21 56		22 56		23 56
Farncombe	d	17 59		18 59		19 59		20 59		21 59		22 59		23 59
Guildford	a	18 04	18 31	19 04	19 31	20 04	20 31	21 04	21 31	22 04	22 31	23 04	23 31	00 04
	d	18 05	18 35	19 05	19 35	20 05	20 35	21 05	21 35	22 05	22 35	23 05	23 35	00 05
Worplesdon	d													
Woking	a	18 13	18 42	19 13	19 42	20 13	20 42	21 13	21 42	22 13	22 42	23 13	23 42	00 13
	d	18 15	18 45	19 15	19 45	20 15	20 45	21 15	21 45	22 15	22 45	23 15	23 45	
Clapham Junction 10	a	18 34	19 04	19 34	20 04	20 34	21 04	21 34	22 04	22 34	23 04	23 34	00 04	
London Waterloo 15 ⊖	a	18 44	19 14	19 44	20 14	20 44	21 14	21 44	22 14	22 44	23 14	23 44	00 14	

Table 157

Havant - Portsmouth Harbour

(Complete service)

Network Diagram - see first Page of Table 155

		SW MX	SW MO A	SW MO A	SW MX	SW MX	SW MX	SW MO A	SW MO B	SW	SW C	SW MX D	SW MX E	SW MO F	SW G	SW MO H	SW I	SW J	SW MX K	SW MX L	SW	SN	SN
Havant	d	23p49	23p51			00 22	00 37	00 39	00 51		01 11	01 21	01 41								04 40	05 21	05 40
Bedhampton	d					00 25		00 41				01s24	01s43								04 43		
Hilsea	d			23p59	00 03	00 30						01s29	01s49								04 48		
Fratton	d	23p59	00 01	00 04	00 08	00 34	00 47	00 50	01 01		01 21	01s33	01s53	02s10	02s10	02s10	02s15	02s15	02s17	02s17	04 52	05 30	05 49
Portsmouth & Southsea	a	00 02	00 04	00 08	00 11	00 38	00 50	00 53	01 04	01s08	01 24	01 37	01 57	02s14	02s14	02s14	02s19	02s19	02 21	02 21	04 55	05 33	05 52
	d	00 03	00 05	00 09	00 13		00 51	00 54	01 05		01 25										04 56	05 33	05 52
Portsmouth Harbour	a	00 07	00 09	00 13	00 16		00 55	00 58	01 09	01 12	01 29			02 19	02 19	02 19	02 24	02 24			04 59	05 37	05 56

		SW	SN	SW	SN	SW	SW	SW	GW ◇	SW	SW	SN	SN	SW	SW	SN	SW	GW ◇	SN	SW	SW	SN	SW
Havant	d	06 02	06 13		06 53		07 00				07 28	07 35	07 41	07 52		07 58			08 22	08 27		08 44	08 50
Bedhampton	d	06 05	06 15		06 56		07 03				07 31	07 37		07 55		08 00			08 25	08 30			
Hilsea	d	06 10	06 20	06 34	07 01	07 05	07 08	07 13		07 35	07 37	07 42		08 00	08 03	08 05	08 09		08 30	08 35	08 45		
Fratton	d	06 15	06 25	06 41	07 05	07 09	07 12	07 17	07 35	07 39	07 42	07 47	07 50	08 04	08 07	08 10	08 13	08 21	08 34	08 40	08 49	08 53	08 59
Portsmouth & Southsea	a	06 18	06 28	06 44	07 08	07 12	07 16	07 22	07 38	07 42	07 46	07 50	07 53	08 07	08 11	08 15	08 19	08 24	08 37	08 43	08 52	08 56	09 02
	d	06 19	06 28	06 45	07 09	07 13	07 17		07 39	07 43			07 53	08 09	08 13	08 17	08 21	08 24	08 38	08 45	08 54	08 57	09 04
Portsmouth Harbour	a	06 22	06 32	06 49	07 12	07 17	07 20		07 45	07 48			07 58	08 12	08 16	08 20	08 24	08 30	08 41	08 48	08 57	09 02	09 07

		SW	SN	SW	SW	SW	SW	GW ◇	SN	SN ◇	SW	SW	SN	SW	SW	SW	GW	SN	SN ◇	SW	SW	SN
Havant	d		09 01	09 05	09 20		09 30		09 33	09 46	09 50		10 07	10 16		10 27		10 32	10 46	10 50		11 05
Bedhampton	d			09 08			09 33		09 36							10 30		10 34				
Hilsea	d	09 05		09 13		09 33	09 38		09 42			10 03			10 33	10 36		10 42			11 03	
Fratton	d	09 10	09 13	09 17	09 29	09 37	09 43	09 42	09 47	09 55	09 59	10 08	10 16	10 25	10 37	10 40	10 42	10 47	10 55	10 59	11 08	11 14
Portsmouth & Southsea	a	09 13	09 17	09 20	09 32	09 42	09 46	09 46	09 50	09 58	10 02	10 11	10 19	10 28	10 42	10 44	10 46	10 50	10 58	11 02	11 11	11 17
	d	09 14	09 18	09 22	09 34			09 46		09 58	10 04	10 12	10 20	10 29			10 46		10 58	11 04	11 12	11 17
Portsmouth Harbour	a	09 18	09 21	09 26	09 37			09 55		10 02	10 07	10 18	10 23	10 33			10 54		11 02	11 07	11 18	11 21

		SW	SW	SW	GW ◇	SN	SN ◇	SW	SW	SN	SW	SW	SW	GW ◇	SN	SN ◇	SW	SW	SN	SW	SW	SW	GW ◇
Havant	d	11 16		11 27		11 32	11 46	11 50		12 05	12 16		12 27		12 32	12 46	12 50		13 05	13 16		13 27	
Bedhampton	d			11 30		11 34							12 30		12 34							13 30	
Hilsea	d		11 33	11 36		11 42			12 03			12 33	12 36		12 42			13 03			13 33	13 36	
Fratton	d	11 25	11 37	11 40	11 42	11 47	11 55	11 59	12 08	12 14	12 25	12 37	12 40	12 42	12 47	12 55	12 59	13 08	13 14	13 25	13 37	13 40	13 42
Portsmouth & Southsea	a	11 28	11 42	11 44	11 46	11 50	11 58	12 02	12 11	12 17	12 28	12 42	12 44	12 46	12 50	12 58	13 02	13 11	13 17	13 28	13 42	13 44	13 46
	d	11 29			11 46		11 58	12 04	12 12	12 17	12 29			12 46		12 58	13 04	13 12	13 17	13 29			13 46
Portsmouth Harbour	a	11 33			11 54		12 02	12 07	12 18	12 21	12 33			12 54		13 02	13 07	13 18	13 21	13 33			13 54

		SN	SN ◇	SW	SW	SN	SW	SW	SW	GW ◇	SN	SN ◇	SW	SW	SN	SW	SW	SW	GW ◇	SN	SN ◇	SW
Havant	d	13 32	13 46	13 50		14 05	14 16		14 27		14 32	14 46	14 50		15 05	15 16		15 27		15 32	15 46	15 50
Bedhampton	d	13 34							14 30		14 34							15 30		15 34		
Hilsea	d	13 42			14 03			14 33	14 36		14 42			15 03			15 33	15 36		15 42		
Fratton	d	13 47	13 55	13 59	14 08	14 14	14 25	14 37	14 40	14 42	14 47	14 55	14 59	15 08	15 14	15 25	15 37	15 40	15 42	15 47	15 55	15 59
Portsmouth & Southsea	a	13 50	13 58	14 02	14 11	14 17	14 28	14 42	14 44	14 46	14 50	14 58	15 02	15 11	15 17	15 28	15 42	15 44	15 46	15 50	15 58	16 02
	d		13 58	14 04	14 12	14 17	14 29			14 46		14 58	15 04	15 12	15 17	15 29			15 46		15 58	16 04
Portsmouth Harbour	a		14 02	14 07	14 18	14 21	14 33			14 54		15 02	15 07	15 18	15 21	15 33			15 54		16 02	16 07

		SW	SN	SN	SW	SW	SW	GW ◇	SN	SN ◇	SW	SW	SN	SW	SN	SW	SW	SW	SW	GW ◇	SN	SW	SN ◇
Havant	d		16 02	16 09	16 16		16 27		16 32	16 46	16 50		17 00	17 04	17 09	17 16			17 27		17 32	17 50	17 54
Bedhampton	d		16 04				16 30		16 34				17 02	17 06					17 30		17 34		17 56
Hilsea	d	16 03				16 33	16 36		16 42			17 03	17 07	17 11				17 33	17 36		17 42		18 01
Fratton	d	16 08	16 12	16 18	16 25	16 37	16 40	16 42	16 47	16 55	16 59	17 08	17 12	17 16	17 19	17 25	17 32	17 37	17 40	17 42	17 47	17 59	18 06
Portsmouth & Southsea	a	16 11	16 15	16 21	16 28	16 40	16 44	16 46	16 50	16 58	17 02	17 11	17 16	17 20	17 22	17 28	17 35	17 42	17 44	17 46	17 50	18 02	18 09
	d	16 12	16 16	16 22	16 29	16 41	16 45	16 46		16 58	17 04	17 12	17 16	17 21		17 30	17 36			17 46		18 04	18 09
Portsmouth Harbour	a	16 18	16 21	16 26	16 33	16 44	16 49	16 54		17 02	17 07	17 18	17 20	17 26		17 35	17 40			17 54		18 09	18 15

		SW	SW	SN	SW	SW	SW	SW	SN	GW ◇	SW	SN ◇	SW	SN	SW	SW	SW	GW	SN	SN ◇	SW	SW	SN
Havant	d		18 04	18 13	18 20			18 30	18 34		18 51	18 54		19 08	19 17				19 33	19 46	19 51		20 07
Bedhampton	d		18 07					18 33	18 36			18 57							19 35				
Hilsea	d	18 04	18 12			18 33		18 39	18 42			19 02	19 05			19 28	19 33		19 43			20 02	
Fratton	d	18 09	18 17	18 22	18 29	18 37	18 40	18 43	18 46	18 48	19 00	19 06	19 09	19 18	19 26	19 33	19 37	19 42	19 47	19 57	20 00	20 08	20 16
Portsmouth & Southsea	a	18 12	18 20	18 25	18 32	18 41	18 43	18 46	18 49	18 52	19 03	19 09	19 12	19 21	19 29	19 36	19 42	19 46	19 50	20 01	20 03	20 11	20 19
	d	18 14	18 22	18 26	18 33		18 45			18 52	19 05		19 14	19 21	19 31	19 38		19 46		20 01	20 05	20 12	
Portsmouth Harbour	a	18 20	18 28	18 31	18 39		18 51			19 00	19 10		19 20	19 26	19 36	19 43		19 54		20 07	20 10	20 20	

A from 21 May
B from 21 May until 23 July, MO from 20 August, not 3 September, 10 September
C 30 July, 6 August, 13 August, 3 September, 10 September
D not from 31 July until 10 August, from 30 August until 7 September
E from 31 July until 7 September, not from 14 August until 29 August
F from 17 September
G 20 August, 27 August
H until 23 July
I 30 July, 6 August, 13 August
J 3 September, 10 September
K from 31 July until 10 August
L from 30 August until 7 September

Table 157

Havant - Portsmouth Harbour

(Complete service)

Network Diagram - see first Page of Table 155

		SW	SW	SW	GW	SW	SN ◇	SW	SN	SW	SW	GW ◇	SW	SW	SN ◇	SW	SN	SW	SW	SW	SN	GW ◇
Havant	d	20 17		20 29		20 49	20 52		21 10	21 19			21 31	21 46	21 49		22 10	22 19		22 31	22 43	
Bedhampton	d			20 32									21 34							22 34		
Hilsea	d		20 33	20 37				21 03			21 33		21 41			22 03			22 33	22 39		
Fratton	d	20 26	20 37	20 41	20 42	20 58	21 02	21 08	21 19	21 29	21 37	21 42	21 45	21 55	21 58	22 08	22 19	22 29	22 37	22 44	22 52	22 56
Portsmouth & Southsea	a	20 29	20 42	20 44	20 46	21 01	21 06	21 11	21 23	21 32	21 40	21 45	21 48	21 58	22 01	22 11	22 22	22 32	22 42	22 47	22 55	22 59
	d	20 31		20 46	20 46	21 03		21 13	21 23	21 33	21 41	21 46		21 58	22 02	22 13	22 22	22 33			22 56	22 59
Portsmouth Harbour	a	20 34		20 52	20 54	21 06		21 16	21 27	21 37	21 45	21 52		22 02	22 05	22 16	22 26	22 37			22 59	23 04

		SW	SN	SW	SW	SW	SW	GW ◇	SN	SW
Havant	d	22 49	23 11	23 19			23 31		23 34	23 49
Bedhampton	d						23 34			
Hilsea	d				23 24	23 33	23 39			
Fratton	d	23 00	23 20	23 29	23 33	23 37	23 44	23 44	23 47	23 59
Portsmouth & Southsea	a	23 04	23 23	23 32	23 36	23 40	23 47	23 48	23 54	00 02
	d	23 05	23 24	23 33	23 36			23 48		00 03
Portsmouth Harbour	a	23 08	23 27	23 37	23 40			23 54		00 07

Saturdays

		SW	SW	SW	SW	SW	SW A	SW B	SW C	SW D	SW	SN ◇	SN	SN	SW	SW	SN	SN	SW	SN	SW	SW	GW
Havant	d	23p49		00 22	00 37		01 21	01 41			04 40	05 34	05 49	05 57	06 02		06 32	06 46		07 04	07 20		
Bedhampton	d			00 25			01s24	01s43			04 43				06 05		06 34				07 22		
Hilsea	d		00 03	00 30			01s29	01s49			04 48				06 10	06 33	06 42		07 03		07 27	07 33	
Fratton	d	23p59	00 08	00 34	00 47		01s33	01s53	02s17	02s17	04 52	05 43	05 58	06 06	06 15	06 37	06 47	06 55	07 08	07 13	07 32	07 37	07 42
Portsmouth & Southsea	a	00 02	00 11	00 38	00 50	01s08	01 37	01 57	02 21	02 21	04 55	05 46	06 01	06 09	06 18	06 42	06 50	06 58	07 11	07 16	07 35	07 42	07 46
	d	00 03	00 13		00 51						04 57		06 01	06 09	06 19			06 58	07 12	07 16	07 36		07 46
Portsmouth Harbour	a	00 07	00 16		00 55	01 12					05 00		06 05	06 16	06 22			07 02	07 16	07 20	07 40		07 52

		SN	SN	SW	SN	SW	SW	GW ◇	SN	SN	SW	SW	SN	SW	SW	SW	GW ◇	SN	SN ◇	SW	SW	SN	SW
Havant	d	07 32	07 46		08 04	08 17			08 32	08 46	08 50		09 04	09 16		09 27		09 32	09 46	09 50		10 07	10 16
Bedhampton	d	07 34				08 20			08 34							09 30		09 34					
Hilsea	d	07 42		08 03		08 25	08 33		08 42			09 04			09 33	09 36		09 42			10 03		
Fratton	d	07 47	07 55	08 08	08 13	08 29	08 37	08 42	08 47	08 55	08 59	09 09	09 13	09 25	09 37	09 40	09 42	09 47	09 55	09 59	10 08	10 16	10 25
Portsmouth & Southsea	a	07 50	07 58	08 11	08 16	08 32	08 42	08 46	08 50	08 58	09 02	09 12	09 16	09 28	09 42	09 44	09 46	09 50	09 58	10 02	10 11	10 19	10 28
	d		07 59	08 13	08 16	08 34		08 46		08 59	09 04	09 13	09 16	09 29			09 46		09 58	10 04	10 12	10 20	10 29
Portsmouth Harbour	a		08 02	08 18	08 20	08 37		08 52		09 02	09 07	09 18	09 20	09 33			09 52		10 02	10 07	10 18	10 23	10 33

		SW	SW	GW ◇	SN	SN ◇	SW	SW	SN	SW	SW	SW	GW ◇	SN	SN ◇	SW	SW	SN	SW	SW	SW	GW ◇
Havant	d		10 27		10 32	10 46	10 50		11 05	11 16		11 27		11 32	11 46	11 50		12 05	12 16		12 27	
Bedhampton	d		10 30		10 34							11 30		11 34							12 30	
Hilsea	d	10 33	10 36		10 43			11 03			11 33	11 36		11 42			12 03			12 33	12 36	
Fratton	d	10 37	10 40	10 42	10 47	10 55	10 59	11 08	11 14	11 25	11 37	11 40	11 42	11 47	11 55	11 59	12 08	12 14	12 25	12 37	12 40	12 42
Portsmouth & Southsea	a	10 42	10 44	10 46	10 50	10 58	11 02	11 11	11 17	11 28	11 42	11 44	11 46	11 50	11 58	12 02	12 11	12 17	12 28	12 42	12 44	12 46
	d			10 46		10 58	11 04	11 12	11 17	11 29			11 46		11 58	12 04	12 12	12 17	12 29			12 46
Portsmouth Harbour	a			10 52		11 02	11 07	11 18	11 21	11 33			11 52		12 02	12 07	12 18	12 21	12 33			12 52

		SN	SN ◇	SW	SW	SN	SW	SW	SW	GW ◇	SN	SN ◇	SW	SW	SN	SW	SW	SW	GW ◇	SN	SN ◇	SW	SW
Havant	d	12 32	12 46	12 50		13 05	13 16		13 27		13 32	13 46	13 50		14 05	14 16		14 27		14 32	14 46	14 50	
Bedhampton	d	12 34							13 30		13 34							14 30		14 34			
Hilsea	d	12 42			13 03			13 33	13 36		13 42			14 03			14 33	14 36		14 42			15 03
Fratton	d	12 47	12 55	12 59	13 08	13 14	13 25	13 37	13 40	13 42	13 47	13 55	13 59	14 08	14 14	14 25	14 37	14 40	14 42	14 47	14 55	14 59	15 08
Portsmouth & Southsea	a	12 50	12 58	13 02	13 11	13 17	13 28	13 42	13 44	13 46	13 50	13 58	14 02	14 11	14 17	14 28	14 42	14 44	14 46	14 50	14 58	15 02	15 11
	d		12 58	13 04	13 12	13 17	13 29			13 46		13 58	14 04	14 12	14 17	14 29			14 46		14 58	15 04	15 12
Portsmouth Harbour	a		13 02	13 07	13 18	13 21	13 33			13 52		14 02	14 07	14 18	14 21	14 33			14 52		15 02	15 07	15 18

		SN	SW	SW	SW	GW ◇	SN	SN ◇	SW	SW	SN	SW	SW	SW	GW ◇	SN	SN ◇	SW	SW	SN	SW	SW
Havant	d	15 05	15 16		15 27		15 32	15 46	15 50		16 05	16 16		16 27		16 32	16 46	16 50		17 05	17 16	
Bedhampton	d				15 30		15 34							16 30		16 34						
Hilsea	d			15 33	15 36		15 42			16 03			16 33	16 36		16 42			17 03			17 33
Fratton	d	15 14	15 25	15 37	15 40	15 42	15 47	15 55	15 59	16 08	16 14	16 25	16 37	16 40	16 42	16 47	16 55	16 59	17 08	17 14	17 25	17 37
Portsmouth & Southsea	a	15 17	15 28	15 42	15 44	15 46	15 50	15 58	16 02	16 11	16 17	16 28	16 40	16 44	16 46	16 50	16 58	17 02	17 11	17 17	17 28	17 42
	d	15 17	15 29			15 46		15 58	16 04	16 12	16 17	16 29	16 41		16 46		16 58	17 04	17 12	17 17	17 29	
Portsmouth Harbour	a	15 21	15 33			15 52		16 02	16 07	16 18	16 21	16 33	16 44		16 52		17 02	17 07	17 18	17 21	17 33	

A until 21 July, from 18 August, not 1 September, 8 September
B 28 July, 4 August, 11 August, 1 September, 8 September
C 1 September, 8 September
D 28 July, 4 August, 11 August

Table 157

Havant - Portsmouth Harbour

(Complete service)

Network Diagram - see first Page of Table 155

Saturdays

	SW ■	GW ◇	SN	SN ◇■	SW ■ ✕	SW ■	SN	SW ■ ✕	SW ■	SW ■	GW ◇	SN	SN ◇■	SW ■ ✕	SW ■	SN	SW ■ ✕	SW ■	SW ■	GW ▪	SN	SN ◇■
Havant d	17 27		17 32	17 46	17 50		18 06	18 16		18 27		18 32	18 46	18 50		19 05	19 16		19 27		19 32	19 46
Bedhampton d	17 30		17 34							18 30		18 34							19 30		19 34	
Hilsea d	17 36		17 42			18 03			18 33	18 36		18 42			19 03			19 33	19 36		19 42	
Fratton d	17 40	17 42	17 47	17 55	17 59	18 08	18 15	18 25	18 37	18 40	18 42	18 47	18 55	18 59	19 08	19 14	19 25	19 37	19 40	19 42	19 47	19 55
Portsmouth & Southsea a	17 44	17 46	17 50	17 58	18 02	18 11	18 18	18 28	18 42	18 44	18 46	18 50	18 58	19 02	19 11	19 17	19 28	19 42	19 44	19 46	19 50	19 58
d		17 46		17 58	18 04	18 12	18 19	18 29			18 46		18 58	19 04	19 12	19 17	19 29			19 46		19 58
Portsmouth Harbour ⛴ a		17 52		18 02	18 07	18 18	18 22	18 33			18 52		19 02	19 07	19 18	19 21	19 33			19 52		20 02

	SW ■ ✕	SW ■	SN ■	SW ■ ✕	SW ■	GW ◇	SW ■	SN ◇■	SW ■ ✕	SW ■	SN ■	SW ■	SW ■	SW ■	GW ◇	SW ■	SN ◇■	SW ■	SN	SW ■	SW ■	GW ◇
Havant d	19 50		20 10	20 16			20 30	20 46	20 50		21 10	21 16		21 27		21 46	21 49		22 10	22 19		
Bedhampton d							20 33							21 30								
Hilsea d		20 03			20 37		20 41			21 03			21 33	21 36				22 03			22 33	
Fratton d	19 59	20 08	20 19	20 25	20 41	20 42	20 45	20 55	20 59	21 08	21 19	21 25	21 37	21 40	21 42	21 55	21 59	22 08	22 19	22 29	22 37	22 42
Portsmouth & Southsea a	20 02	20 11	20 22	20 28	20 44	20 46	20 48	20 58	21 02	21 11	21 22	21 28	21 40	21 43	21 46	21 58	22 02	22 11	22 22	22 32	22 40	22 46
d	20 04	20 12	20 22	20 29		20 46		20 58	21 04	21 12	21 22	21 29	21 41		21 46	22 00	22 03	22 12	22 22	22 33	22 41	22 46
Portsmouth Harbour ⛴ a	20 07	20 18	20 26	20 33		20 52		21 02	21 07	21 18	21 26	21 33	21 45		21 52	22 03	22 06	22 18	22 26	22 36	22 47	22 52

	SW ■	SN	SW ■	SW ■	SN	SW ■	SW ■	GW ◇	SW ■	SN	SW ■
Havant d	22 31	22 43	22 49		23 10	23 19			23 31	23 36	23 49
Bedhampton d	22 34								23 34		
Hilsea d	22 41			23 03			23 33		23 41		
Fratton d	22 45	22 52	22 59	23 08	23 19	23 29	23 37	23 41	23 45	23 48	23 59
Portsmouth & Southsea a	22 49	22 55	23 02	23 11	23 22	23 32	23 40	23 44	23 48	23 51	00 02
d	22 50	22 56	23 03	23 12	23 22	23 33		23 45	23 50		00 03
Portsmouth Harbour ⛴ a	22 53	22 59	23 08	23 18	23 26	23 37		23 52	23 53		00 07

Sundays
until 9 September

	SW ■	SW ■	SW ■	SW ■	SW ■	SW ■ A	SW ■ B	SW ■ C	SW ■ D	SN ■	SW ■	SW ■	SN ■	SW ■	SN ■	SW ■	SW ■	SN ■	SW ■	SN ■	SW ■	SW ■
Havant d	23p49		00 22	00 37		01ʃ21	01ʃ41			07 10			08 11		08 35	08 39		09 11		09 35	09 45	09 53
Bedhampton d			00 25			01s24	01s43								08 37	08 41				09 37	09 47	
Hilsea d		00 03	00 30			01s29	01s49				07 26	08 00		08 26			09 00		09 26			
Fratton d	23p59	00 07	00 34	00 47		01s33	01s53	02s17	02s17	07 19	07 30	08 04	08 20	08 30	08 45	08 50	09 04	09 20	09 30	09 45	09 56	10 02
Portsmouth & Southsea a	00 02	00 11	00 38	00 50	01s08	01ʃ37	01ʃ57	02ʃ21	02ʃ21	07 22	07 33	08 08	08 23	08 33	08 48	08 53	09 08	09 23	09 33	09 48	09 59	10 06
d	00 03	00 12		00 51						07 22		08 09	08 23		08 49	08 54	09 09	09 23		09 49	10 00	10 08
Portsmouth Harbour ⛴ a	00 07	00 16		00 55	01 12					07 26		08 13	08 27		08 52	08 57	09 13	09 27		09 52	10 04	10 11

	SW ■	SN ◇■	SW ■	SN ■	SW ■	SW ■	SW ■	SN ◇■	SW ■	GW ◇	SN ■	SW ■	SW ■	SW ■	SN ◇■	SW ■	GW ◇	SW ■	SN ■	SW ■ ✕	SW ■	SN ◇■
Havant d		10 14		10 35	10 45	10 53		11 14			11 35	11 39	11 51		12 14			12 39	12 35	12 51		13 14
Bedhampton d				10 37	10 47						11 37	11 41						12 41	12 37			
Hilsea d	10 04		10 26				11 04		11 26					12 00		12 26					13 00	
Fratton d	10 08	10 23	10 30	10 45	10 56	11 02	11 08	11 23	11 30	11 41	11 45	11 50	12 01	12 04	12 23	12 30	12 43	12 50	12 54	13 01	13 04	13 23
Portsmouth & Southsea a	10 11	10 26	10 33	10 50	10 59	11 05	11 11	11 26	11 33	11 45	11 49	11 53	12 04	12 08	12 26	12 33	12 46	12 53	12 57	13 04	13 08	13 26
d	10 12	10 27		10 51	11 00	11 07	11 12	11 27		11 45	11 50	11 54	12 05	12 09	12 27		12 46	12 54	12 58	13 05	13 09	13 27
Portsmouth Harbour ⛴ a	10 15	10 30		10 54	11 04	11 11	11 15	11 30		11 52	11 53	11 58	12 09	12 13	12 30		12 52	12 58	13 01	13 11	13 13	13 30

	SW ■	SN ■	SW ■	SW ■ ✕	SW ■	SN ◇■	SW ■	GW ◇ ✕	SN ■	SW ■	SW ■ ✕	SW ■	SN ◇■	SW ■	SN ■	SW ■	SW ■ ✕	SW ■	SN ◇■	SW ■	GW ◇
Havant d		13 35	13 39	13 51		14 14			14 35	14 39	14 51		15 14		15 35	15 39	15 51		16 14		
Bedhampton d		13 37	13 41						14 37	14 41					15 37	15 41					
Hilsea d	13 26				14 00		14 26					15 00		15 26				16 00		16 26	
Fratton d	13 30	13 45	13 50	14 01	14 04	14 23	14 30	14 42	14 45	14 50	15 01	15 04	15 23	15 30	15 45	15 50	16 01	16 04	16 23	16 30	16 42
Portsmouth & Southsea a	13 33	13 48	13 53	14 04	14 08	14 26	14 33	14 45	14 48	14 53	15 04	15 08	15 26	15 33	15 48	15 54	16 04	16 08	16 26	16 33	16 46
d		13 49	13 54	14 05	14 09	14 27		14 45	14 49	14 54	15 05	15 09	15 27		15 49	15 54	16 05	16 09	16 27		16 47
Portsmouth Harbour ⛴ a		13 52	13 58	14 11	14 13	14 30		14 55	14 53	14 58	15 11	15 13	15 30		15 52	15 58	16 11	16 13	16 30		16 52

	SW ■	SN ■	SW ■ ✕	SW ■	SN ◇■	SW ■	GW ◇	SW ■	SN ■	SW ■ ✕	SW ■	SN ◇■	SW ■	GW ◇	SW ■	SN ■	SW ■ ✕	SW ■	SN ◇■	SW ■	GW ◇	SW ■
Havant d	16 39	16 35	16 51		17 14			17 39	17 35	17 51		18 14			18 39	18 35	18 51		19 14			19 39
Bedhampton d	16 41	16 37						17 41	17 37						18 41	18 37						19 41
Hilsea d				17 00		17 26					18 00		18 26					19 00		19 26		
Fratton d	16 50	16 54	17 01	17 04	17 23	17 30	17 42	17 50	17 54	18 01	18 04	18 23	18 30	18 42	18 50	18 54	19 01	19 04	19 23	19 30	19 43	19 50
Portsmouth & Southsea a	16 53	16 57	17 04	17 08	17 26	17 33	17 46	17 53	17 57	18 04	18 08	18 26	18 33	18 45	18 53	18 57	19 04	19 08	19 26	19 33	19 46	19 53
d	16 54	16 58	17 05	17 09	17 27		17 46	17 54	17 58	18 05	18 09	18 27		18 45	18 54	18 58	19 05	19 09	19 27		19 46	19 54
Portsmouth Harbour ⛴ a	16 58	17 01	17 11	17 13	17 30		17 52	17 58	18 01	18 11	18 13	18 30		18 52	18 58	19 01	19 11	19 13	19 30		19 53	19 58

A until 22 July, 19 August, 26 August

B 29 July, 5 August, 12 August, 2 September, 9 September

C 2 September, 9 September

D 29 July, 5 August, 12 August

Table 157

Havant - Portsmouth Harbour

(Complete service)

Network Diagram - see first Page of Table 155

Sundays
until 9 September

	SN ■	SW ■ ✕	SW ■	SN ◇■	SW ■	GW ◇	SN ■	SW ■	SW ■ ✕	SW ■	GW ▪	SN ◇■	SW ■	GW ◇	SN ■	SW ■	SW ■ ✕	SW ■	SN ◇■	SW ■	GW ◇
Havant d	19 35	19 51		20 14			20 35	20 39	20 51			21 15			21 35	21 39	21 51		22 14		
Bedhampton d	19 37						20 37	20 41							21 38	21 41					
Hilsea d			20 00		20 26					21 00			21 26					22 00		22 26	
Fratton d	19 54	20 01	20 04	20 23	20 30	20 41	20 45	20 50	21 01	21 04	21 10	21 24	21 30	21 38	21 46	21 50	22 01	22 04	22 23	22 30	22 40
Portsmouth & Southsea a	19 57	20 04	20 08	20 26	20 33	20 45	20 48	20 53	21 04	21 08	21 15	21 27	21 33	21 41	21 49	21 53	22 04	22 08	22 26	22 33	22 43
d	19 58	20 05	20 09	20 27		20 45	20 49	20 54	21 05	21 09	21 15	21 27		21 42	21 49	21 54	22 05	22 09	22 27		22 44
Portsmouth Harbour ⛴ a	20 01	20 11	20 13	20 30		20 51	20 52	20 58	21 09	21 13	21 26	21 31		21 48	21 53	21 58	22 11	22 13	22 30		22 50

	SN ■	SW ■	GW	SW ■	SW ■	SW ■	SN ◇■	GW ◇	SW ■	SW ■	SW ■
Havant d	22 35	22 39	22 47	22 51			23 22		23 39	23 51	
Bedhampton d	22 37	22 41							23 41		
Hilsea d					23 00	23 24					23 59
Fratton d	22 45	22 50	22 57	23 01	23 04	23 29	23 32	23 43	23 50	00 01	00 04
Portsmouth & Southsea a	22 48	22 53	23 00	23 04	23 08	23 32	23 35	23 46	23 53	00 04	00 08
d	22 49	22 54	23 00	23 05	23 09		23 36	23 47	23 54	00 05	00 09
Portsmouth Harbour ⛴ a	22 52	22 58	23 04	23 09	23 13		23 39	23 54	23 58	00 09	00 13

Sundays
from 16 September

	SW ■	SW ■	SW ■	SW ■	SW ■	SW ■	SN ■	SW ■	SW ■	SN ■	SW ■	SW ■	SN ■	SW ■	SN ■	SW ■	SW ■	SN ■	SW ■	SW ■	SN ◇■	SW ■
Havant d	23p49		00 22	00 37		01 21	07 10			08 11		08 39	08 49		09 11		09 45	09 49	09 53		10 17	
Bedhampton d			00 25			01s24						08 41	08 51				09 47	09 51				
Hilsea d		00 03	00 30			01s29		07 26	08 00		08 26			09 00		09 26				10 04		10 26
Fratton d	23p59	00 07	00 34	00 47		01s33	07 19	07 30	08 04	08 20	08 30	08 50	08 59	09 04	09 20	09 30	09 56	09 59	10 02	10 08	10 26	10 30
Portsmouth & Southsea a	00 02	00 11	00 38	00 50	01s08	01 37	07 22	07 33	08 08	08 23	08 33	08 53	09 03	09 08	09 23	09 33	09 59	10 03	10 06	10 11	10 29	10 33
d	00 03	00 12		00 51			07 22		08 09	08 23		08 54	09 04	09 09	09 23		10 00	10 04	10 08	10 12	10 30	
Portsmouth Harbour ⛴ a	00 07	00 16		00 55	01 12		07 26		08 13	08 27		08 57	09 07	09 13	09 27		10 04	10 07	10 11	10 15	10 35	

	SN ■	SW ■	SW ■	SW ■	SN ◇■	SW ■	GW ◇	SW ■	SN ■	SW ■	SW ■	SN ◇■	SW ■	GW ◇	SW ■	SN ■	SW ■ ✕	SW ■	SN ◇■	SW ■	SW ■	SN ■
Havant d	10 41	10 45	10 53		11 17			11 39	11 44	11 51		12 17			12 39	12 44	12 51		13 17		13 39	13 44
Bedhampton d	10 43	10 47						11 41	11 46						12 41	12 46					13 41	13 46
Hilsea d				11 04		11 26					12 00		12 26					13 00		13 26		
Fratton d	10 51	10 56	11 02	11 08	11 26	11 30	11 41	11 50	11 54	12 01	12 04	12 26	12 30	12 43	12 50	12 54	13 01	13 04	13 26	13 30	13 50	13 54
Portsmouth & Southsea a	10 54	10 59	11 05	11 11	11 29	11 33	11 45	11 53	11 57	12 04	12 08	12 29	12 33	12 46	12 53	12 57	13 04	13 08	13 29	13 33	13 53	13 57
d	10 55	11 00	11 07	11 12	11 30		11 45	11 54	11 58	12 05	12 09	12 30		12 46	12 54	12 58	13 05	13 09	13 30		13 54	13 58
Portsmouth Harbour ⛴ a	10 58	11 04	11 11	11 15	11 35		11 52	11 58	12 01	12 09	12 13	12 35		12 52	12 58	13 01	13 11	13 13	13 35		13 58	14 01

	SW ■ ✕	SW ■	SN ◇■	SW ■	GW ◇ ✕	SW ■	SN ■	SW ■ ✕	SW ■	SN ◇■	SW ■	SW ■	SN ■	SW ■ ✕	SW ■	SN ◇■	SW ■	GW ◇	SW ■	SN ■	SW ■ ✕
Havant d	13 51		14 17			14 39	14 44	14 51		15 17		15 39	15 44	15 51		16 17			16 39	16 44	16 51
Bedhampton d						14 41	14 46					15 41	15 46						16 41	16 46	
Hilsea d		14 00		14 26					15 00		15 26				16 00		16 26				
Fratton d	14 01	14 04	14 26	14 30	14 42	14 50	14 54	15 01	15 04	15 26	15 30	15 50	15 54	16 01	16 04	16 26	16 30	16 42	16 50	16 54	17 01
Portsmouth & Southsea a	14 04	14 08	14 29	14 33	14 45	14 53	14 57	15 04	15 08	15 29	15 33	15 54	15 57	16 04	16 08	16 29	16 33	16 46	16 53	16 57	17 04
d	14 05	14 09	14 30		14 45	14 54	14 58	15 05	15 09	15 30		15 54	15 58	16 05	16 09	16 30		16 47	16 54	16 58	17 05
Portsmouth Harbour ⛴ a	14 11	14 13	14 35		14 55	14 58	15 01	15 11	15 13	15 35		15 58	16 01	16 11	16 13	16 35		16 52	16 58	17 01	17 11

	SW ■	SN ◇■	SW ■	GW ◇	SW ■	SN ■	SW ■ ✕	SW ■	SN ◇■	SW ■	GW ◇	SW ■	SN ■	SW ■ ✕	SW ■	SN ◇■	SW ■	GW ◇	SW ■	SN ■	SW ■ ✕	SW ■
Havant d		17 17			17 39	17 44	17 51		18 17			18 39	18 44	18 51		19 17			19 39	19 44	19 51	
Bedhampton d					17 41	17 46						18 41	18 46						19 41	19 46		
Hilsea d	17 00		17 26					18 00		18 26					19 00		19 26					20 00
Fratton d	17 04	17 26	17 30	17 43	17 50	17 54	18 01	18 04	18 26	18 30	18 42	18 50	18 54	19 01	19 04	19 26	19 30	19 43	19 50	19 54	20 01	20 04
Portsmouth & Southsea a	17 08	17 29	17 33	17 47	17 53	17 57	18 04	18 08	18 29	18 33	18 45	18 53	18 57	19 04	19 08	19 29	19 33	19 46	19 53	19 57	20 04	20 08
d	17 09	17 30		17 47	17 54	17 58	18 05	18 09	18 30		18 45	18 54	18 58	19 05	19 09	19 30		19 46	19 54	19 58	20 05	20 09
Portsmouth Harbour ⛴ a	17 13	17 35		17 52	17 58	18 01	18 11	18 13	18 35		18 52	18 58	19 01	19 11	19 13	19 35		19 53	19 58	20 01	20 11	20 13

	SN ◇■	SW ■	GW ◇	SW ■	SN ■	SW ■ ✕	SW ■	GW ▪	SN ◇■	SW ■	GW ◇	SW ■	SN ■	SW ■ ✕	SW ■	SN ◇■	SW ■	GW ◇	SW ■	SN ■	GW
Havant d	20 17			20 39	20 44	20 51			21 17			21 39	21 44	21 51		22 17			22 39	22 44	22 47
Bedhampton d				20 41	20 46							21 41	21 46						22 41	22 46	
Hilsea d		20 26					21 00			21 26					22 00		22 26				
Fratton d	20 26	20 30	20 41	20 50	20 54	21 01	21 04	21 10	21 26	21 30	21 38	21 50	21 54	22 01	22 04	22 26	22 30	22 40	22 50	22 54	22 57
Portsmouth & Southsea a	20 29	20 33	20 45	20 53	20 57	21 04	21 08	21 15	21 29	21 33	21 41	21 53	21 57	22 04	22 08	22 29	22 33	22 43	22 53	22 57	23 00
d	20 30		20 45	20 54	20 58	21 05	21 09	21 15	21 30		21 42	21 54	21 58	22 05	22 09	22 30		22 44	22 54	22 58	23 00
Portsmouth Harbour ⛴ a	20 35		20 51	20 58	21 01	21 09	21 13	21 26	21 35		21 48	21 58	22 01	22 11	22 13	22 35		22 50	22 58	23 01	23 04

Havant - Portsmouth Harbour

(Complete service)

Sundays from 16 September

Network Diagram - see first Page of Table 155

	SW ■	SW ■	SW ■	SN ◇■	GW ◇	SW ■	SW ■	SW ■
Havant d	22 51			23 22		23 39	23 51	
Bedhampton d						23 41		
Hilsea d		23 00	23 24					23 59
Fratton d	23 01	23 04	23 29	23 32	23 43	23 50	00 01	00 04
Portsmouth & Southsea a	23 04	23 08	23 32	23 35	23 46	23 53	00 04	00 08
d	23 05	23 09		23 36	23 47	23 54	00 05	00 09
Portsmouth Harbour ⛴ a	23 09	23 13		23 39	23 54	23 58	00 09	00 13

Mondays to Fridays

Portsmouth Harbour - Havant

(Complete service)

Network Diagram - see first Page of Table 155

	SW ■ A	SW ■ B	SW ■ A	SW ■ B	SW ■	SW ■ A 🛒	SW ■ B 🛒	SN ■	SW ■		SN ◇■	SW ■	GW ▪ 🛒	SN	SW ■ 🛒	SW ■	SW ■	SW ■ 🛒	SN ◇■		SW ■	SW ■	GW 🛒	GW ◇ 🛒
Portsmouth Harbour ⛴ d	04 25	04 30	04 55	05 00		05 14	05 19	05 33	05 43		05 47	05 50	06 00	06 04	06 15		06 23	06 42	06 46		06 50	06 55	07 01	07 05
Portsmouth & Southsea a	04 28	04 33	04 58	05 03		05 17	05 22	05 36	05 46		05 50	05 53	06 03	06 07	06 18		06 26	06 45	06 49		06 53	06 58	07 04	07 08
d	04 30	04 35	05 00	05 05	05 16	05 19	05 24	05 37	05 48		05 51	05 55	06 04	06 08	06 20	06 23	06 28	06 47	06 50		06 55	07 00	07 05	07 09
Fratton d	04 34	04 39	05 04	05 09	05 20	05 23	05 28	05 41	05 52		05 55	05 59	06a07	06 12	06 24	06 27	06 32	06 51	06 54		06 59	07 04	07 10	07a13
Hilsea d	04 38	04 43	05a08	05a13	05a24	05 27	05 32	05 45	05a56		05 59	06 03				06a31	06a36		06 58		07a03	07 08		
Bedhampton d	04 43	04 48				05 32	05 37	05 50			06 04	06 08							07 03			07 13		
Havant a	04 45	04 50				05 35	05 40	05 52			06 06	06 10		06 20	06 33			06 59	07 05			07 15	07 19	

	SW ■ 🛒	SN	SW ■	SW ■	SW ■		SW ■ 🛒	SW ■	SN	SW ■	SN ◇■	SW ■ 🛒	SW ■	GW ◇ 🛒	SN		SW ■	SW ■ 🛒	SN	SW ■	SN ◇■	SW ■ 🛒	SW ■	GW ◇ 🛒
Portsmouth Harbour ⛴ d	07 13	07 20	07 24	07 29			07 45	07 55		08 05	08 10	08 15		08 23	08 29		08 33	08 45	08 51	08 59	09 12	09 15	09 18	09 23
Portsmouth & Southsea a	07 16	07 23	07 27	07 32			07 48	07 58		08 08	08 13	08 18		08 26	08 32		08 36	08 48	08 54	09 02	09 15	09 18	09 22	09 26
d	07 18	07 24	07 29	07 33	07 38		07 50	08 00	08 03	08 10	08 14	08 20	08 24	08 27	08 33		08 38	08 50	08 55	09 04	09 16	09 20	09 24	09 27
Fratton d	07 22	07 28	07 33	07 37	07 42		07 54	08 04	08 07	08 13	08 18	08 24	08 28	08a31	08 37		08 42	08 54	08 59	09 08	09 20	09 24	09 28	09a31
Hilsea d			07a37	07 41	07a46			08a08	08 11	08a17			08 32				08a46		09 04	09a12			09 32	
Bedhampton d				07 48					08 16				08 37						09 13				09 37	
Havant a	07 30	07 36		07 50			08 03		08 18		08 26	08 32	08 40		08 45			09 03	09 15		09 29	09 33	09 39	

	SN		SW ■	SW ■ 🛒	SN	SW ■	SN ◇■	SW ■ 🛒	SW ■	GW ◇ 🛒	SN		SW ■	SW ■ 🛒	SN	SW ■	SN ◇■	SW ■ 🛒	SW ■	GW ◇ 🛒	SN		SW ■	SW ■ 🛒
Portsmouth Harbour ⛴ d	09 29		09 33	09 45		09 59	10 12	10 15		10 23	10 29		10 33	10 45		10 59	11 12	11 15		11 23	11 29			11 45
Portsmouth & Southsea a	09 32		09 36	09 48		10 02	10 15	10 18		10 26	10 32		10 36	10 48		11 02	11 15	11 18		11 26	11 32			11 48
d	09 33		09 38	09 50	09 59	10 04	10 16	10 20	10 24	10 27	10 33		10 38	10 50	10 59	11 04	11 16	11 20	11 24	11 27	11 33		11 38	11 50
Fratton d	09 37		09 42	09 54	10 04	10 08	10 20	10 24	10 28	10a31	10 37		10 42	10 54	11 04	11 08	11 20	11 24	11 28	11a31	11 37		11 42	11 54
Hilsea d			09a46		10 08	10a12			10 32				10a46		11 08	11a12			11 32				11a46	
Bedhampton d					10 13				10 37						11 13				11 37					
Havant a	09 45			10 03	10 15		10 29	10 33	10 39		10 45			11 03	11 15		11 29	11 33	11 39		11 45			12 03

	SN	SW ■	SN ◇■	SW ■ 🛒	SW ■	GW ◇ 🛒	SN		SW ■	SW ■ 🛒	SN	SW ■	SN ◇■	SW ■ 🛒	SW ■	GW ◇ 🛒	SN		SW ■	SW ■ 🛒	SN	SW ■	SN ◇■	SW ■ 🛒
Portsmouth Harbour ⛴ d		11 59	12 12	12 15		12 23	12 29			12 45		12 59	13 12	13 15		13 23	13 29			13 45		13 59	14 12	14 15
Portsmouth & Southsea a		12 02	12 15	12 18		12 26	12 32			12 48		13 02	13 15	13 18		13 26	13 32			13 48		14 02	14 15	14 18
d	11 59	12 04	12 16	12 20	12 24	12 27	12 33		12 38	12 50	12 59	13 04	13 16	13 20	13 24	13 27	13 33		13 38	13 50	13 59	14 04	14 16	14 20
Fratton d	12 04	12 08	12 20	12 24	12 28	12a31	12 37		12 42	12 54	13 04	13 08	13 20	13 24	13 28	13a31	13 37		13 42	13 54	14 04	14 08	14 20	14 24
Hilsea d	12 08	12a12			12 32				12a46		13 08	13a12			13 32				13a46		14 08	14a12		
Bedhampton d	12 13				12 37						13 13				13 37						14 13			
Havant a	12 15		12 29	12 33	12 39		12 45			13 03	13 15		13 29	13 33	13 39		13 45			14 03	14 15		14 29	14 33

	SW ■	GW ▪ 🛒	SN		SW ■	SW ■ 🛒	SN	SW ■	SN ◇■	SW ■ 🛒	SW ■	GW ▪ 🛒	SN		SW ■	SW ■ 🛒	SN	SW ■	SN ◇■	SW ■ 🛒	SW ■	GW ▪ 🛒	SN	
Portsmouth Harbour ⛴ d		14 23	14 29			14 45		14 59	15 12	15 15		15 23	15 29			15 45		15 59	16 12	16 15		16 23	16 29	
Portsmouth & Southsea a		14 26	14 32			14 48		15 02	15 15	15 18		15 26	15 32			15 48		16 02	16 15	16 18		16 26	16 32	
d	14 24	14 27	14 33		14 38	14 50	14 59	15 04	15 16	15 20	15 24	15 27	15 33		15 38	15 50	15 59	16 04	16 16	16 20	16 24	16 27	16 33	
Fratton d	14 28	14a31	14 37		14 42	14 54	15 04	15 08	15 20	15 24	15 28	15a31	15 37		15 42	15 54	16 04	16 08	16 20	16 24	16 28	16a31	16 37	
Hilsea d	14 32				14a46		15 08	15a12			15 32				15a46		16 08	16a12			16 32			
Bedhampton d	14 37						15 14				15 37						16 13				16 37			
Havant a	14 39		14 45			15 03	15 17		15 29	15 33	15 39		15 45			16 03	16 15		16 29	16 33	16 39		16 45	

	SW ■	SN	SW ■ 🛒	SW ■	SN	SW ■	SN ◇■	SW ■ 🛒	SW ■		GW ◇ 🛒	SN	SW ■	SN	SW ■ 🛒	SN ■	SW ■	SW ■ 🛒	SW ■		GW ◇ 🛒	SN ■	SW ■	SN
Portsmouth Harbour ⛴ d		16 40	16 45	16 49		16 59	17 12	17 15	17 18		17 23	17 29	17 33		17 45		17 59	18 15			18 23	18 28		18 37
Portsmouth & Southsea a		16 44	16 48	16 53		17 02	17 15	17 18	17 22		17 26	17 32	17 36		17 48		18 02	18 18			18 26	18 31		18 40
d	16 38	16 46	16 50	16 55	17 00	17 04	17 16	17 20	17 24		17 27	17 33	17 38	17 46	17 50	17 59	18 04	18 20	18 24		18 27	18 32	18 38	18 42
Fratton d	16 42	16 50	16 54	16 59	17 04	17 08	17 20	17 24	17 28		17a31	17 37	17 42	17 50	17 54	18 04	18 08	18 24	18 28		18a31	18 36	18 42	18 46
Hilsea d	16a46	16 54		17a03	17 08	17a12			17 32				17a46	17 54		18 08	18a12		18 32				18a46	18 50
Bedhampton d					17 14				17 37							18 13			18 37					
Havant a		16 59	17 03		17 17		17 29	17 33	17 39			17 45		17 59	18 03	18 15		18 33	18 39			18 44		18 56

	SW ■ 🛒	SN	SW ■	SW ■	SW ■		GW ◇	SN ■	SW ■	SN ■	SW ■	SN	SW ■	SW ■	SW ■		GW ◇	SN	SW ■	SN ■	SW ■	SW ■	SN ■	SW ■
Portsmouth Harbour ⛴ d	18 45		18 59	19 15			19 23			19 40	19 45		19 59	20 15	20 18		20 23			20 40	20 45	20 59		21 18
Portsmouth & Southsea a	18 48		19 02	19 18			19 26			19 43	19 48		20 02	20 18	20 22		20 26			20 43	20 48	21 02		21 21
d	18 50	18 59	19 04	19 20	19 24		19 27	19 32	19 38	19 44	19 50	19 59	20 04	20 20	20 24		20 27	20 32	20 38	20 44	20 50	21 04	21 15	21 24
Fratton d	18 54	19 04	19 08	19 24	19 28		19a31	19 36	19 42	19 48	19 54	20 04	20 08	20 24	20 28		20a31	20 36	20 42	20 48	20 54	21 08	21 19	21 28
Hilsea d		19 08	19a12		19 32				19a46			20 08	20a12		20 32				20a46			21a12	21 23	21 32
Bedhampton d		19 13			19 37							20 14			20 37								21 28	21 37
Havant a	19 03	19 15		19 33	19 39			19 46		19 56	20 03	20 16		20 33	20 39			20 44		20 56	21 03		21 30	21 40

A from 8 October

B until 5 October

Portsmouth Harbour - Havant

(Complete service)

Network Diagram - see first Page of Table 155

		GW	SW ■	SW ■	SN ■	SW ■	SN	SW ■	SW ■	SW ■	SN	SN	SW ■	SW ■
Portsmouth Harbour	d	21 23	21 28		21 40	21 54	22 15	22 18	22 28	22 33	22 44	23 15	23 19	23 24
Portsmouth & Southsea	a	21 26	21 31		21 43	21 57	22 18	22 21	22 31	22 37	22 47	23 18	23 22	23 27
	d	21 27	21 33	21 38	21 44	21 59	22 19	22 24	22 33	22 38	22 48	23 19	23 24	23 29
Fratton	d	21a31	21 37	21 42	21 48	22 03	22 23	22 28	22 37	22 42	22 52	23 23	23 28	23 33
Hilsea	d		21 41	21a46	21 52	22a07	22 27	22 32	22 41	22a46	22 56	23 27	23 32	23a37
Bedhampton	d		21 47		21 57		22 32	22 37	22 46		23 01	23 33	23 37	
Havant	a		21 52		21 59		22 34	22 39	22 53		23 05	23 36	23 39	

Saturdays

		SW ■ A	SW ■ B	SN ◇■	SW ■	SW ■ A	SW ■ B	SW ■	SN	GW ◇	SN ◇■	SW ■	SN ■	SW ■	SW ■ ⌶	GW	SN	SW ■	SN ◇■	SW ■ ⌶	SW ■	GW ◇ ⌶	SN
Portsmouth Harbour	d	04 38	04 43			05 14	05 19	05 50		06 00	06 12	06 19	06 29		06 45	06 48		06 59	07 12	07 15		07 23	07 29
Portsmouth & Southsea	a	04 41	04 46			05 17	05 22	05 53		06 03	06 15	06 22	06 32		06 48	06 53		07 02	07 15	07 18		07 26	07 32
	d	04 43	04 48	04 56	05 16	05 19	05 24	05 55	05 59	06 04	06 16	06 24	06 33	06 38	06 50	06 54	06 56	07 04	07 16	07 20	07 24	07 27	07 33
Fratton	d	04 47	04 52	05 00	05 20	05 23	05 28	05 59	06 04	06a07	06 20	06 28	06 37	06 42	06 54	06 58	07 01	07 08	07 20	07 24	07 28	07a30	07 37
Hilsea	d	04 51	04 56		05a24	05 27	05 32	06a03	06 08			06 32		06a46			07 05	07a12			07 32		
Bedhampton	d	04 56	05 01			05 32	05 37		06 13			06 37					07 13				07 37		
Havant	a	04 58	05 03	05 08		05 34	05 39		06 15		06 29	06 40	06 45		07 03	07 08	07 15		07 29	07 33	07 39		07 45

		SW ■	SW ■ ⌶	SN	SW ■	SN ◇■	SW ■ ⌶	SW ■	GW ◇ ⌶	SN	SW ■	SW ■ ⌶	SN	SW ■	SN ◇■	SW ■ ⌶	SW ■	GW ◇ ⌶	SN	SW ■	SW ■ ⌶	SN	SW ■
Portsmouth Harbour	d		07 45		07 59	08 12	08 15		08 23	08 29		08 45		08 59	09 12	09 15		09 23	09 29		09 45		09 59
Portsmouth & Southsea	a		07 48		08 02	08 15	08 18		08 26	08 32		08 48		09 02	09 15	09 18		09 26	09 32		09 48		10 02
	d	07 38	07 50	07 59	08 04	08 16	08 20	08 24	08 27	08 33	08 38	08 50	08 59	09 04	09 16	09 20	09 24	09 27	09 33	09 38	09 50	09 59	10 04
Fratton	d	07 42	07 54	08 04	08 08	08 20	08 24	08 28	08a30	08 37	08 42	08 54	09 04	09 08	09 20	09 24	09 28	09a30	09 37	09 42	09 54	10 04	10 08
Hilsea	d	07a46		08 08	08a12			08 32			08a46		09 08	09a12			09 32			09a46		10 08	10a12
Bedhampton	d			08 13				08 37					09 13				09 37					10 13	
Havant	a		08 03	08 15		08 29	08 33	08 39		08 45		09 03	09 15		09 29	09 33	09 39		09 45		10 03	10 15	

		SN ◇■	SW ■ ⌶	SW ■	GW ◇	SN	SW ■	SW ■ ⌶	SN	SW ■	SN ◇■	SW ■ ⌶	SW ■	GW ◇	SN	SW ■	SW ■ ⌶	SN	SW ■	SN ◇■	SW ■ ⌶	SW ■
Portsmouth Harbour	d	10 12	10 15		10 23	10 29		10 45		10 59	11 12	11 15		11 23	11 29		11 45		11 59	12 12	12 15	
Portsmouth & Southsea	a	10 15	10 18		10 26	10 32		10 48		11 02	11 15	11 18		11 26	11 32		11 48		12 02	12 15	12 18	
	d	10 16	10 20	10 24	10 27	10 33	10 38	10 50	10 59	11 04	11 16	11 20	11 24	11 27	11 33	11 38	11 50	11 59	12 04	12 16	12 20	12 24
Fratton	d	10 20	10 24	10 28	10a30	10 37	10 42	10 54	11 04	11 08	11 20	11 24	11 28	11a30	11 37	11 42	11 54	12 04	12 08	12 20	12 24	12 28
Hilsea	d			10 32			10a46		11 08	11a12			11 32			11a46		12 08	12a12			12 32
Bedhampton	d			10 37					11 13				11 37					12 13				12 37
Havant	a	10 29	10 33	10 39		10 45		11 03	11 15		11 29	11 33	11 39		11 45		12 03	12 15		12 29	12 33	12 39

		GW ◇	SN	SW ■	SW ■ ⌶	SN	SW ■	SN ◇■	SW ■ ⌶	SW ■	GW ◇	SN	SW ■	SW ■ ⌶	SN	SW ■	SN ◇■	SW ■ ⌶	SW ■	GW ◇	SN	SW ■	SW ■ ⌶
Portsmouth Harbour	d	12 23	12 29		12 45		12 59	13 12	13 15		13 23	13 29		13 45		13 59	14 12	14 15		14 23	14 29		14 45
Portsmouth & Southsea	a	12 26	12 32		12 48		13 02	13 15	13 18		13 26	13 32		13 48		14 02	14 15	14 18		14 26	14 32		14 48
	d	12 27	12 33	12 38	12 50	12 59	13 04	13 16	13 20	13 24	13 27	13 33	13 38	13 50	13 59	14 04	14 16	14 20	14 24	14 27	14 33	14 38	14 50
Fratton	d	12a30	12 37	12 42	12 54	13 04	13 08	13 20	13 24	13 28	13a30	13 37	13 42	13 54	14 04	14 08	14 20	14 24	14 28	14a30	14 37	14 42	14 54
Hilsea	d			12a46		13 08	13a12			13 32			13a46		14 08	14a12			14 32			14a46	
Bedhampton	d					13 13				13 37					14 13				14 37				
Havant	a		12 45		13 03	13 15		13 29	13 33	13 39		13 45		14 03	14 15		14 29	14 33	14 39		14 45		15 03

		SN	SW ■	SN ◇■	SW ■ ⌶	SW ■	GW ◇	SN	SW ■	SW ■ ⌶	SN	SW ■	SN ◇■	SW ■ ⌶	SW ■	GW ■	SN	SW ■	SW ■ ⌶	SN	SW ■	SW ■
Portsmouth Harbour	d		14 59	15 12	15 15		15 23	15 29		15 45		15 59	16 12	16 15		16 23	16 29		16 45		16 59	
Portsmouth & Southsea	a		15 02	15 15	15 18		15 26	15 32		15 48		16 02	16 15	16 18		16 26	16 32		16 48		17 02	
	d	14 59	15 04	15 16	15 20	15 24	15 27	15 33	15 38	15 50	15 59	16 04	16 16	16 20	16 24	16 27	16 33	16 38	16 50	16 59	17 04	17 10
Fratton	d	15 04	15 08	15 20	15 24	15 28	15a30	15 37	15 42	15 54	16 04	16 08	16 20	16 24	16 28	16a31	16 37	16 42	16 54	17 04	17 08	17 14
Hilsea	d	15 08	15a12			15 32			15a46		16 08	16a12			16 32			16a46		17 08	17a12	17 18
Bedhampton	d	15 14				15 37					16 13				16 37					17 13		17 23
Havant	a	15 17		15 29	15 33	15 39		15 45		16 03	16 15		16 29	16 33	16 39		16 45		17 03	17 15		17 25

		SN ◇■	SW ■	GW ◇	SN	SW ■	SW ■ ⌶	SN ■	SW ■	SN	SW ■	SW ■	GW ◇	SN	SW ■	SW ■	SN	SW ■	SN ■	SW ■	SW ■	GW ◇	SN
Portsmouth Harbour	d	17 12	17 18	17 23	17 29	17 33	17 45		17 59	18 12	18 15		18 23	18 29		18 45		18 59	19 12	19 15		19 23	19 29
Portsmouth & Southsea	a	17 15	17 22	17 26	17 32	17 36	17 48		18 02	18 15	18 18		18 27	18 32		18 48		19 02	19 15	19 18		19 26	19 32
	d	17 16	17 24	17 27	17 33	17 38	17 50	17 59	18 04	18 16	18 20	18 24	18 27	18 33	18 38	18 50	18 59	19 04	19 16	19 20	19 24	19 27	19 33
Fratton	d	17 20	17 28	17a31	17 37	17 42	17 54	18 04	18 08	18 20	18 24	18 28	18a31	18 37	18 42	18 54	19 04	19 08	19 20	19 24	19 28	19a30	19 37
Hilsea	d		17 32			17a46		18 08	18a12			18 32			18a46		19 08	19a12			19 32		
Bedhampton	d		17 37					18 13				18 37					19 13				19 37		
Havant	a	17 29	17 39		17 45		18 03	18 15		18 29	18 33	18 39		18 45		19 03	19 15		19 29	19 33	19 39		19 45

A from 13 October
B until 6 October

Portsmouth Harbour - Havant

(Complete service)

Network Diagram - see first Page of Table 155

		SW ■	SW ■	SN	SW ■	SW ■	SW ■	GW ◇	SN ■	SW ■	SN	SW ■	SW ■	SN ■	SW ■	SW ■	SN ■	SW ■	SN ■	SW ■	SW ■	SN	SN
Portsmouth Harbour	d		19 45		19 59	20 15		20 23	20 28		20 40	20 45	20 59	21 11	21 18		21 40	21 54	22 15	22 18	22 33	22 44	23 15
Portsmouth & Southsea	a		19 48		20 02	20 18		20 26	20 31		20 43	20 48	21 02	21 14	21 21		21 43	21 57	22 18	22 21	22 37	22 47	23 18
	d	19 38	19 50	19 59	20 04	20 20	20 24	20 27	20 32	20 38	20 44	20 50	21 04	21 15	21 24	21 38	21 44	21 59	22 19	22 24	22 38	22 48	23 19
Fratton	d	19 42	19 54	20 04	20 08	20 24	20 28	20a30	20 36	20 42	20 48	20 54	21 08	21 19	21 28	21 42	21 48	22 03	22 23	22 28	22 42	22 52	23 23
Hilsea	d	19a46		20 08	20a12		20 32			20a46	20 52		21a12	21 23	21 32	21a46	21 52	22a07	22 27	22 32	22a46	22 56	23 27
Bedhampton	d			20 13			20 37							21 28	21 37		21 57		22 32	22 37		23 01	23 33
Havant	a		20 03	20 15		20 33	20 39		20 44		20 58	21 03		21 30	21 39		21 59		22 34	22 39		23 05	23 36

		SW ■	SW ■
Portsmouth Harbour	d	23 19	23 24
Portsmouth & Southsea	a	23 22	23 28
	d	23 24	23 29
Fratton	d	23 28	23 33
Hilsea	d	23 32	23a37
Bedhampton	d	23 37	
Havant	a	23 39	

Sundays
until 9 September

		SW ■ A	SW ■	SW ■ B	SN ■	SW ■	SW ■	SW ■	SN ◇■	SW ■	SN ■	SW ■	SW ■	SW ■	SN ◇■	SW ■	SN ■	GW ■	SW ■ ⌶	SW ■ ⌶	SW ■	SN ◇■	SW ■
Portsmouth Harbour	d	06 20	06 37	06 48	07 05	07 17	07 32		07 43	07 48	08 05	08 17	08 32		08 43	08 48	09 05	09 08	09 17	09 32		09 43	09 48
Portsmouth & Southsea	a	06 23	06 40	06 51	07 08	07 20	07 35		07 46	07 51	08 08	08 20	08 35		08 46	08 51	09 08	09 11	09 20	09 35		09 46	09 51
	d	06 25	06 42	06 53	07 09	07 22	07 37	07 42	07 47	07 53	08 09	08 22	08 37	08 42	08 47	08 53	09 09	09 12	09 22	09 37	09 42	09 47	09 53
Fratton	d	06 29	06 46	06 57	07 13	07 26	07 41	07 46	07 51	07 57	08 13	08 26	08 41	08 46	08 51	08 57	09 13	09a15	09 26	09 41	09 46	09 51	09 57
Hilsea	d		06a50			07a30		07a50				08a30		08a50					09a30		09a50		
Bedhampton	d	06 36		07 04	07 21					08 04	08 20					09 04	09 20						10 04
Havant	a	06 39		07 07	07 24		07 49		07 59	08 07	08 23		08 49		08 59	09 07	09 23			09 49		09 59	10 07

		SN ■	SW ■ ⌶	SW ■ ⌶	SW ■	SN ◇■	SW ■	SN ■	GW ◇	SW ■ ⌶	SW ■ ⌶	SW ■	SN ◇■	SW ■	SN ■	SW ■ ⌶	SW ■ ⌶	SW ■	SN ◇■	SW ■	SN ■	GW ◇	SW ■ ⌶
Portsmouth Harbour	d	10 05	10 17	10 32		10 43	10 48	11 05	11 08	11 17	11 32		11 43	11 48	12 05	12 17	12 32		12 43	12 48	13 05	13 08	13 17
Portsmouth & Southsea	a	10 08	10 20	10 35		10 46	10 51	11 08	11 11	11 20	11 35		11 46	11 51	12 08	12 20	12 35		12 46	12 51	13 08	13 11	13 20
	d	10 09	10 22	10 37	10 42	10 47	10 53	11 09	11 12	11 22	11 37	11 42	11 47	11 53	12 09	12 22	12 37	12 42	12 47	12 53	13 09	13 12	13 22
Fratton	d	10 13	10 26	10 41	10 46	10 51	10 57	11 13	11a15	11 26	11 41	11 46	11 51	11 57	12 13	12 26	12 41	12 46	12 51	12 57	13 13	13a15	13 26
Hilsea	d		10a30		10a50					11a30		11a50				12a30		12a50					13a30
Bedhampton	d	10 20					11 04	11 20						12 04	12 20					13 04	13 20		
Havant	a	10 23		10 49		10 59	11 07	11 23			11 49		11 59	12 07	12 23		12 49		12 59	13 07	13 23		

		SW ■ ⌶	SW ■	SN ◇■	SW ■	SN ■	GW ◇	SW ■ ⌶	SW ■ ⌶	SW ■	SN ◇■	SW ■	SN ■	GW ■	SW ■ ⌶	SW ■ ⌶	SW ■	SN ◇■	SW ■	SN ■	GW ◇	SW ■ ⌶
Portsmouth Harbour	d	13 32		13 43	13 48	14 05	14 08	14 17	14 32		14 43	14 48	15 05	15 08	15 17	15 32		15 43	15 48	16 05	16 08	16 17
Portsmouth & Southsea	a	13 35		13 46	13 51	14 08	14 11	14 20	14 35		14 46	14 51	15 08	15 11	15 20	15 35		15 46	15 51	16 08	16 11	16 20
	d	13 37	13 42	13 47	13 53	14 09	14 12	14 22	14 37	14 42	14 47	14 53	15 09	15 12	15 22	15 37	15 42	15 47	15 53	16 09	16 12	16 22
Fratton	d	13 41	13 46	13 51	13 57	14 13	14a15	14 26	14 41	14 46	14 51	14 57	15 13	15a15	15 26	15 41	15 46	15 51	15 57	16 13	16a15	16 26
Hilsea	d		13a50					14a30		14a50					15a30		15a50					16a30
Bedhampton	d				14 04	14 20						15 04	15 20						16 04	16 20		
Havant	a	13 49		13 59	14 07	14 23			14 49		14 59	15 07	15 23			15 49		15 59	16 07	16 23		

		SW ■ ⌶	SW ■	SN ◇■	SW ■	SN ■	GW ◇	SW ■	SW ■ ⌶	SW ■	SN ◇■	SW ■	SN ■	GW ◇	SW ■	SW ■ ⌶	SW ■	SN ◇■	SW ■	SN ■	GW ◇	SW ■	SW ■
Portsmouth Harbour	d	16 32		16 43	16 48	17 05	17 08	17 17	17 32		17 43	17 48	18 05	18 08	18 17	18 32		18 43	18 48	19 05	19 08	19 17	19 32
Portsmouth & Southsea	a	16 35		16 46	16 51	17 08	17 11	17 20	17 35		17 46	17 51	18 08	18 11	18 20	18 35		18 46	18 51	19 08	19 11	19 20	19 35
	d	16 37	16 42	16 47	16 53	17 09	17 12	17 22	17 37	17 42	17 47	17 53	18 09	18 12	18 22	18 37	18 42	18 47	18 53	19 09	19 12	19 22	19 37
Fratton	d	16 41	16 46	16 51	16 57	17 13	17a15	17 26	17 41	17 46	17 51	17 57	18 13	18a15	18 26	18 41	18 46	18 51	18 57	19 13	19a15	19 26	19 41
Hilsea	d		16a50					17a30		17a50					18a30		18a50					19a30	
Bedhampton	d				17 04	17 20						18 04	18 20						19 04	19 20			
Havant	a	16 49		16 59	17 07	17 23			17 49		17 59	18 07	18 23			18 49		18 59	19 07	19 23			19 49

		SW ■	SN ◇■	SW ■	SN ■	GW ◇	SW ■	SW ■	SW ■	SN ■	SW ■	SN ■	SW ■	SW ■	SW ■	SN ■	SW ■	GW	SN ■	SW ■	SW ■	SW ■
Portsmouth Harbour	d		19 43	19 48	20 05	20 08	20 17	20 32		20 43	20 48	21 05	21 17	21 32		21 43	21 48	22 03	22 14	22 17	22 32	
Portsmouth & Southsea	a		19 46	19 51	20 08	20 11	20 20	20 35		20 46	20 51	21 08	21 20	21 35		21 46	21 51	22 11	22 17	22 20	22 35	
	d	19 42	19 47	19 53	20 09	20 12	20 22	20 37	20 42	20 47	20 53	21 09	21 22	21 37	21 42	21 47	21 53	22 12	22 18	22 22	22 37	22 42
Fratton	d	19 46	19 51	19 57	20 13	20a15	20 26	20 41	20 46	20 51	20 57	21 13	21 26	21 41	21 46	21 51	21 57	22a15	22 22	22 26	22 41	22 46
Hilsea	d	19a50					20a30		20a50				21a30		21a50					22a30		22a50
Bedhampton	d			20 04	20 20						21 04	21 20					22 04		22 32			
Havant	a		19 59	20 07	20 23			20 49		20 59	21 07	21 23		21 49		21 59	22 07		22 35		22 49	

A 29 July, 5 August, 12 August, 2 September, 9 September
B until 22 July, 19 August, 26 August

Portsmouth Harbour - Havant

(Complete service)

Sundays until 9 September

Network Diagram - see first Page of Table 155

		SN	SW	SW
		■	■	■
Portsmouth Harbour ⛴	d	22 43	22 48	23 17
Portsmouth & Southsea	a	22 46	22 51	23 20
	d	22 47	22 53	23 22
Fratton	d	22 51	22 57	23 26
Hilsea	d			23a30
Bedhampton	d		23 04	
Havant	a	22 59	23 07	

Sundays from 16 September

		SW	SW	SW	SN	SW	SW	SW	SW	SN		SW	SN	SW	SW	SW	SW	SN	SW	GW		SN	SW	SW	SW
		■	■	■	■	■	■	■	■	◇■		■	■	■	■	■	■	◇■	■	■		■	■	■	■
			A	B			A	B							A	B									
																							⊼	⊼	
Portsmouth Harbour ⛴	d	06 37	06 43	06 48	07 14	07 17	07 29	07 32		07 43		07 48	08 14	08 17	08 29	08 32		08 43	08 48	09 08		09 14	09 17	09 32	
Portsmouth & Southsea	a	06 40	06 46	06 51	07 17	07 20	07 32	07 35		07 46		07 51	08 17	08 20	08 32	08 35		08 46	08 51	09 11		09 17	09 20	09 35	
	d	06 42	06 48	06 53	07 18	07 22	07 34	07 37	07 42	07 47		07 53	08 18	08 22	08 34	08 37	08 42	08 47	08 53	09 12		09 18	09 22	09 37	09 42
Fratton	d	06 46	06 52	06 57	07 22	07 26	07 38	07 41	07 46	07 51		07 57	08 22	08 26	08 38	08 41	08 46	08 51	08 57	09a15		09 22	09 26	09 41	09 46
Hilsea	d	06a50				07a30			07a50					08a30			08a50						09a30		09a50
Bedhampton	d		06 59	07 04	07 30							08 04	08 30						09 04			09 30			
Havant	a		07 02	07 07	07 32		07 46	07 49		07 59		08 07	08 32		08 46	08 49		08 59	09 07			09 32		09 49	

		SN	SW	SN	SW	SW		SW	SN	SW	GW	SN	SW	SW	SW	SN		SW	SN	SW	SW	SW	SN	SW	GW
		◇■	■	■	■	■		■	◇■	■	◇	■	■	■	■	◇■		■	■	■	■	■	◇■	■	◇
					⊼	⊼							⊼	⊼						⊼	⊼				
Portsmouth Harbour ⛴	d	09 43	09 48	10 14	10 17	10 32			10 43	10 48	11 08	11 14	11 17	11 32		11 43		11 48	12 14	12 17	12 32		12 43	12 48	13 08
Portsmouth & Southsea	a	09 46	09 51	10 17	10 20	10 35			10 46	10 51	11 11	11 17	11 20	11 35		11 46		11 51	12 17	12 20	12 35		12 46	12 51	13 11
	d	09 47	09 53	10 18	10 22	10 37		10 42	10 47	10 53	11 12	11 18	11 22	11 37	11 42	11 47		11 53	12 18	12 22	12 37	12 42	12 47	12 53	13 12
Fratton	d	09 51	09 57	10 22	10 26	10 41		10 46	10 51	10 57	11a15	11 22	11 26	11 41	11 46	11 51		11 57	12 22	12 26	12 41	12 46	12 51	12 57	13a15
Hilsea	d				10a30			10a50					11a30		11a50					12a30		12a50			
Bedhampton	d		10 04	10 30						11 04		11 30						12 04	12 30					13 04	
Havant	a	09 59	10 07	10 32		10 49			10 59	11 07		11 32		11 49		11 59		12 07	12 32		12 49		12 59	13 07	

		SN		SW	SW	SW	SN	SW	GW	SN	SW	SW		SW	SN	SW	GW	SN	SW	SW	SW	SN		SW	GW
		■		■	■	■	◇■	■	◇	■	■	■		■	◇■	■	■	■	■	■	■	◇■		■	◇
				⊼	⊼						⊼	⊼							⊼	⊼					
Portsmouth Harbour ⛴	d	13 14		13 17	13 32		13 43	13 48	14 08	14 14	14 17	14 32			14 43	14 48	15 08	15 14	15 17	15 32		15 43		15 48	16 08
Portsmouth & Southsea	a	13 17		13 20	13 35		13 46	13 51	14 11	14 17	14 20	14 35			14 46	14 51	15 11	15 17	15 20	15 35		15 46		15 51	16 11
	d	13 18		13 22	13 37	13 42	13 47	13 53	14 12	14 18	14 22	14 37		14 42	14 47	14 53	15 12	15 18	15 22	15 37	15 42	15 47		15 53	16 12
Fratton	d	13 22		13 26	13 41	13 46	13 51	13 57	14a15	14 22	14 26	14 41		14 46	14 51	14 57	15a15	15 22	15 26	15 41	15 46	15 51		15 57	16a15
Hilsea	d			13a30		13a50					14a30			14a50					15a30		15a50				
Bedhampton	d	13 30						14 04		14 30						15 04		15 30						16 04	
Havant	a	13 32			13 49		13 59	14 07		14 32		14 49			14 59	15 07		15 32		15 49		15 59		16 07	

		SN	SW	SW	SW	SN	SW	GW		SN	SW	SW	SW	SN	SW	GW	SN	SW		SW	SW	SN	SW	GW	SN
		■	■	■	■	◇■	■	◇		■	■	■	■	◇■	■	◇	■	■		■	■	◇■	■	◇	■
			⊼	⊼								⊼								⊼					
Portsmouth Harbour ⛴	d	16 14	16 17	16 32		16 43	16 48	17 08		17 14	17 17	17 32		17 43	17 48	18 08	18 14	18 17		18 32		18 43	18 48	19 08	19 14
Portsmouth & Southsea	a	16 17	16 20	16 35		16 46	16 51	17 11		17 17	17 20	17 35		17 46	17 51	18 11	18 17	18 20		18 35		18 46	18 51	19 11	19 17
	d	16 18	16 22	16 37	16 42	16 47	16 53	17 12		17 18	17 22	17 37	17 42	17 47	17 53	18 12	18 18	18 22		18 37	18 42	18 47	18 53	19 12	19 18
Fratton	d	16 22	16 26	16 41	16 46	16 51	16 57	17a15		17 22	17 26	17 41	17 46	17 51	17 57	18a15	18 22	18 26		18 41	18 46	18 51	18 57	19a15	19 22
Hilsea	d		16a30		16a50						17a30		17a50					18a30			18a50				
Bedhampton	d	16 30					17 04			17 30					18 04		18 30						19 04		19 30
Havant	a	16 32		16 49		16 59	17 07			17 32		17 49		17 59	18 07		18 32			18 49		18 59	19 07		19 32

		SW	SW	SW		SN	SW	GW	SN	SW	SW	SW	SN	SW		SN	SW	SW	SW	SN	SW	GW	SN	SW	
		■	■	■		◇■	■	◇	■	■	■	■	■	■		■	■	■	■	■	■		■	■	
Portsmouth Harbour ⛴	d	19 17	19 32			19 43	19 48	20 08	20 14	20 17	20 32		20 43	20 48		21 14	21 17	21 32		21 43	21 48	22 03	22 14	22 17	
Portsmouth & Southsea	a	19 20	19 35			19 46	19 51	20 11	20 17	20 20	20 35		20 46	20 51		21 17	21 20	21 35		21 46	21 51	22 11	22 17	22 20	
	d	19 22	19 37	19 42		19 47	19 53	20 12	20 18	20 22	20 37	20 42	20 47	20 53		21 18	21 22	21 37	21 42	21 47	21 53	22 12	22 18	22 22	
Fratton	d	19 26	19 41	19 46		19 51	19 57	20a15	20 22	20 26	20 41	20 46	20 51	20 57		21 22	21 26	21 41	21 46	21 51	21 57	22a15	22 22	22 26	
Hilsea	d	19a30		19a50						20a30		20a50					21a30		21a50					22a30	
Bedhampton	d						20 04		20 30					21 04		21 30					22 04		22 32		
Havant	a		19 49			19 59	20 07		20 32		20 49		20 59	21 07		21 32		21 49		21 59	22 07		22 35		

		SW	SW	SN	SW	SW
		■	■	■	■	■
Portsmouth Harbour ⛴	d	22 32		22 43	22 48	23 17
Portsmouth & Southsea	a	22 35		22 46	22 51	23 20
	d	22 37	22 42	22 47	22 53	23 22
Fratton	d	22 41	22 46	22 51	22 57	23 26
Hilsea	d		22a50			23a30
Bedhampton	d				23 04	
Havant	a	22 49		22 59	23 07	

A from 7 October

B 16 September, 23 September, 30 September

Network Diagram for Table 158

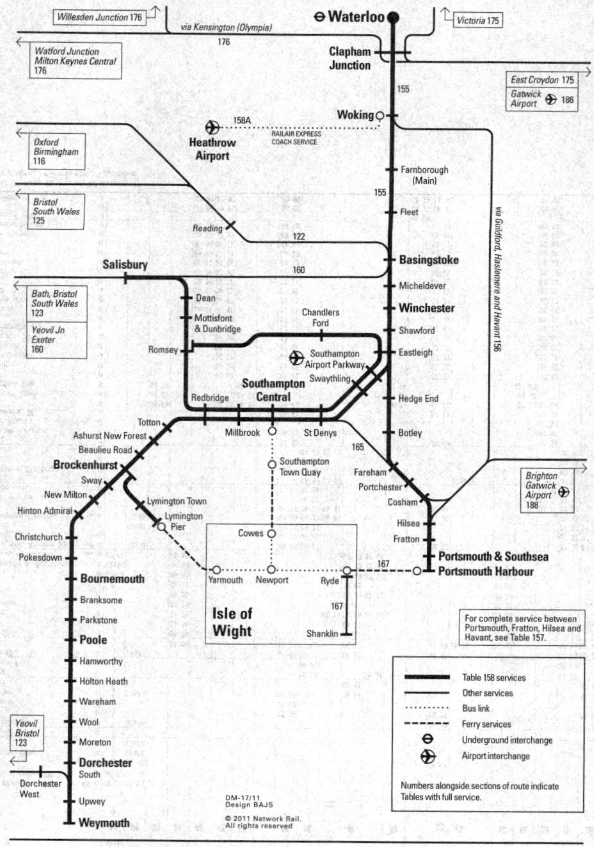

Table 158

Mondays to Fridays
until 5 October

London - Basingstoke, Southampton, Romsey Lymington, Bournemouth and Weymouth

Network Diagram - see first Page of Table 158

Miles	Miles			SW MX ◇■ A ✠	SW MO ◇■ B ✠	SW MX ■	SW MO ◇■ C	SW MO ◇■ C	SW MX ◇■ ✠	SW MO ◇■ C	SW MX ■	SW MX ◇■ ✠	SW MX ■	SW MO ◇■ C ✠	SW ◇■ D ✠	SW MX ◇■	SW MO ■ C	SW MX ■	SW ■	SW MX ■	SW MX ■	SW MX ■ E	SW ■ F
0	—	**London Waterloo** ■15 ⊖	d	21p35	21p35	21p42	21p54		22p05			22p35	22p39	22p54	22p54	23p05	23p07	23p12		23p35	23p48	00 05	00 30
4	—	**Clapham Junction** ■10	d		21b42		22b03		22b12				22b46	23b03	23b03	23b12	23p15	23b19		23b42	23b55	00u12	00u37
24¼	—	**Woking**	d	22p00	22p07	22p19	22p28		22p32			23p00		23p28	23p28	23p32	23p46	23p57		00 03	00 28	00 37	01 00
33¼	—	Farnborough (Main)	d			22p33							23p16				23p59	00 10		00 14	00 41		
36½	—	Fleet	d			22p38							23p21				00 04	00 16		00 20	00 47		
—	—	Reading ■7	d																				
47¾	—	**Basingstoke**	a		22p26	22p58	22p46		22p51				23p33	23p46	23p46	23p53	00 21	00 33		00 33	01 06	00 55	01 18
—	—		d		22p28	23p00	22p48		22p52				23p34	23p48	23p48	23p53				00 35		00 56	01 20
58	—	Micheldever	d			23p10	22p58							23p58	23p58	00 03							
66½	—	**Winchester**	d	22p33	22p44	23p19	23p08		23p09			23p33	23p51	00 08	00 08	00 14				00 51		01 13	01 36
69¾	—	Shawford	d			23p24							23p55										
—	0	**Romsey**	d								23p07												
—	5¼	Chandlers Ford	d								23p14												
73½	0	Eastleigh ■3	a			23p29	23p17		23p17		23p22		00 01	00 18	00 18	00 22				00 59		01 21	01 44
—	—		d			23p30	23p22	23p26	23p18		23p22		00 02	00 22	00 30	00 23			00 30	01 00		01 22	01 45
—	4½	Hedge End	d			23p36		23p32							00s36				00s36				
—	5½	Botley	d			23p40		23p36							00s39				00s39				
—	11	Fareham	d			23p49		23p44							00s47				00s47				
—	14¼	Portchester	d			23p54		23p49							00s53				00s53				
—	16¾	Cosham	d			23p59		23p54							00s57				00s57				
—	18¾	Hilsea	a			00 03		23p59															
—	20½	Fratton	a			00 07		00 04							01s05				01s05				
—	21½	**Portsmouth & Southsea**	a			00 11		00 08							01s08				01s08				
—	22¼	**Portsmouth Harbour** ⛴	a			00 16		00 13							01 12				01 12				
75	—	**Southampton Airport Pkwy** ✈	d	22p42	22p53		23p27		23p22		23p26	23p42	00 06	00 27		00 28				01 05		01 26	01 50
75¾	—	Swaythling	d								23p28												
77¼	—	St Denys	d							←	23p31			00s31		00s32							
79¼	—	**Southampton Central** ⛴	a	22p49	23p00		23p34		23p29	23p34	23p36	23p49	00 13	00 36		00 37				01 12		01 35	01 57
—	—		d	22p51	23p03		23p35		23p31	23p35	23p38	23p51		00 37		00 38						01 37	01 58
80¼	—	Millbrook (Hants)	d				→				23p40												
82	0	Redbridge	d								23p44												
—	6	**Romsey**	d								23p56												
—	9¾	Mottisfont & Dunbridge	d								00 01												
—	13½	Dean	d								00 07												
—	22½	**Salisbury**	a								00 19												
82½	—	Totton	d						23p36	23p41				00s42		00s43						01s42	02s03
85½	—	Ashurst New Forest	d						23p41	23p45													
88	—	Beaulieu Road	d																				
92¾	0	**Brockenhurst** ■3	a	23p04	23p16				23p49	23p53		00 04		00s53		00s54						01s53	02s14
—	—		d	23p05	23p17				23p50	23p54		00 05											
—	4¾	Lymington Town	d																				
—	5¼	**Lymington Pier**	a																				
95½	—	Sway	d						23p54	23p59													
98½	—	New Milton	d		23p24				23p59	00 04				01s01		01s02						02s00	02s22
101	—	Hinton Admiral	d						00 03	00 08													
104¼	—	Christchurch	d						00 08	00 13				01s08		01s09						02s07	02s29
106¼	—	Pokesdown	d						00 11	00 16				01s12		01s13						02s11	02s33
108	—	**Bournemouth**	a	23p25	23p34				00 15	00 20		00 21		01 16		01 17						02 15	02 37
—	—		d	23p29	23p39				00 17	00 22		00 22		01 17		01 18							
110¾	—	Branksome	d	23p35	23p44				00 22	00 27		00 27		01s22		01s23							
112	—	Parkstone (Dorset)	d	23p38	23p47				00 25	00 30		00 30		01s25		01s26							
113¾	—	**Poole** ■4	a	23p41	23p50				00 29	00 34		00 35		01 29		01 30							
—	—		d	23p42	23p51																		
116	—	Hamworthy	d	23p47	23p56																		
118¾	—	Holton Heath	d																				
120¾	—	Wareham	d	23p54	00 03																		
125¾	—	Wool	d	00 01	00 10																		
130¼	—	Moreton (Dorset)	d	00 07	00 17																		
135¾	—	**Dorchester South**	d	00 15	00 25																		
—	—	Dorchester West	d																				
140½	—	Upwey	d	00 21	00 32																		
142¾	—	**Weymouth**	a	00 26	00 36																		

A ✠ to Bournemouth
B from 21 May until 1 October. ✠ to Bournemouth
C from 21 May until 1 October
D 17 September, 24 September, 1 October. ■ to Eastleigh ■ from Eastleigh ✠ to Eastleigh ◇ to Eastleigh
E not from 31 July until 10 August, from 30 August until 7 September
F from 30 July until 10 September, not from 14 August until 29 August
b Previous night, stops to pick up only

Table 158

Mondays to Fridays
until 5 October

London - Basingstoke, Southampton, Romsey Lymington, Bournemouth and Weymouth

Network Diagram - see first Page of Table 158

		SW MO ■ A	SW ■	SW ■	SW ■	SW ■	SW ■	SW ■	SW ■	SW ■	GW ■ ✠	SW ■	GW	SW ■	GW	SW ◇■	SW ■	SW ■	SW ■	SW ■	SW ■	SW ■	GW ◇ ✠
London Waterloo ■15 ⊖	d	00 50	01 05													05 30							
Clapham Junction ■10	d	00 57	01 15													05u37							
Woking	d	01 18	01 49													06 01							
Farnborough (Main)	d		01s58																				
Fleet	d		02s04																				
Reading ■7	d																						
Basingstoke	a		02s16													06 20							
	d								05 40							06 21						06 55	
Micheldever	d								05 50														
Winchester	d		02s33						05 59			06 18				06 38						07 11	
Shawford	d											06 23										07 16	
Romsey	d									05 58			06 38								07 07		
Chandlers Ford	d									06 06											07 14		
Eastleigh ■3	a		02s42						06 07	06 11		06 28				06 47					07 20	07 22	
	d				06 00				06 08	06 13		06 29				06 48	06 50	07 02			07 21	07 24	
Hedge End	d				06 06							06 35						07 08					
Botley	d				06 10							06 39						07 12					
Fareham	d				06 19						06 24	06 50	07 15					07 20					07 29
Portchester	d				06 24							06 55						07 25					
Cosham	d				06 29							07 00	07 23					07 29					
Hilsea	a				06 33							07 05						07 35					
Fratton	a	02s10			06 40							07 09	07 34					07 39					
Portsmouth & Southsea	a	02s14			06 44							07 12	07 38					07 42					
Portsmouth Harbour ⛴	a	02 19			06 49							07 17	07 45					07 48					
Southampton Airport Pkwy ✈	d		02s46						06 13	06 17						06 53					07 25	07 29	
Swaythling	d								06 15	06 20											07 27	07 31	
St Denys	d		02s51						06 18	06 24											07 30	07 34	
Southampton Central ⛴	a		02 56						06 23	06 29	06 45					07 00					07 35	07 39	07 50
	d								06 25	06 30	06 46					07 01				07 19	07 37		07 52
Millbrook (Hants)	d									06 33										07 21	07 40		
Redbridge	d									06 36										07 25	07 43		
Romsey	d									06 44	07 00						07a03				07 51		08 11
Mottisfont & Dunbridge	d									06 49											07 56		
Dean	d									06 55											08 02		
Salisbury	a									07 07	07 18										08 15		08 29
Totton	d								06 30							07 07				07 28			
Ashurst New Forest	d								06 35											07 32			
Beaulieu Road	d																			07 37			
Brockenhurst ■3	a								06 43							07 17				07 43			
	d			05 59			06 16	06 29	06 44					06 59		07 18			07 29	07 44			
Lymington Town	d			06 07				06 37						07 07					07 37				
Lymington Pier	a			06 10				06 40						07 10					07 40				
Sway	d						06 20		06 48							07 23				07 48			
New Milton	d						06 25		06 53							07 28				07 53			
Hinton Admiral	d						06 29		06 57							07 32				07 57			
Christchurch	d						06 34		07 02							07 37				08 02			
Pokesdown	d						06 38		07 06							07 40				08 06			
Bournemouth	a						06 42		07 10							07 44				08 10			
	d					06 11	06 44		07 11							07 46				08 11			
Branksome	d					06 16	06 49		07 16							07 51				08 16			
Parkstone (Dorset)	d					06 19	06 52		07 19							07 54				08 19			
Poole ■4	a					06 23	06 55		07 23							07 57				08 23			
	d					06 24	06 57		07 24							07 58				08 24			
Hamworthy	d					06 29	07 02		07 29							08 03				08 29			
Holton Heath	d					06 33	07 06		07 33							08 07				08 33			
Wareham	d					06 38	07 11		07 38							08 12				08 38			
Wool	d					06 44	07 17		07 44							08 19				08 44			
Moreton (Dorset)	d					06 50	07 23		07 50							08 25				08 50			
Dorchester South	d					06 58	07 31		07 58							08 33				08 58			
Dorchester West	d														08 09								
Upwey	d					07 05	07 38		08 05						08 17	08 40				09 05			
Weymouth	a					07 09	07 42		08 09						08 24	08 44				09 09			

A until 23 July, 20 August, 27 August, 17 September, 24 September, 1 October

Table 158

Mondays to Fridays
until 5 October

London - Basingstoke, Southampton, Romsey Lymington, Bournemouth and Weymouth

Network Diagram - see first Page of Table 158

		SW ■	SW ■	SW ■	SW ◇■	SW ■	GW ◇	GW	SW ■	SW ■	GW ◇	SW ■	SW ■	XC ◇■ ✠	SW ■	SW ■	SW ◇■ A ✠	SW ■	GW ◇ ✠	GW ◇ ✠	SW ■	GW ◇
London Waterloo 15 ⊖	d			06 12	06 30								06 42		07 12		07 35					
Clapham Junction 10	d			06u19	06u37								06u49		07u20							
Woking	d	06 19		06 50	06 57								07 19		07 50		08 00					
Farnborough (Main)	d	06 33		07 04									07 33		08 03							
Fleet	d	06 38		07 09									07 38		08 09							
Reading 7	d													07 46								
Basingstoke	a	06 58		07 28	07 16								07 56	08 08	08 26		08 19					
	d	07 00		07 30	07 18								08 00	08 10			08 20					
Micheldever	d	07 10		07 41									08 10									
Winchester	d	07 19		07 50	07 34								08 19	08 25			08 37					
Shawford	d			07 55									08 24									
Romsey	d					07 13	07 30	07 56				08 07						08 13		08 50		
Chandlers Ford	d											08 14										
Eastleigh 8	a	07 27		08 00	07 43	07 49						08 20	08 30				08 47	08 49				
	d	07 28		08 02	07 44	07 50						08 21	08 31				08 48	08 50				
Hedge End	d	07 34											08 37									
Botley	d	07 38											08 42									
Fareham	d	07 48					08 06						08 51						08 47	09 27		
Portchester	d	07 53											08 56									
Cosham	d	07 58					08 14						09 01							09 35		
Hilsea	a	08 03											09 05									
Fratton	a	08 07					08 20						09 09							09 42		
Portsmouth & Southsea	a	08 11					08 24						09 13							09 46		
Portsmouth Harbour ⛴	a	08 16					08 30						09 18							09 55		
Southampton Airport Pkwy ✈	d			08 06	07 49							08 25		08 33			08 52					
Swaythling	d			08 09								08 27										
St Denys	d			08 12						←		08 30										
Southampton Central ⛴	a			08 17	07 57			08 09		08 17		08 35		08 44			08 59		09 08			
	d			08 19	08 00					08 19	08 23	08 37		08 46			09 01		09 10			
Millbrook (Hants)	d			→						08 21		08 40										
Redbridge	d									08 25		08 43										
Romsey	d					08a03					08 35	08 51						09a03	09 21			
Mottisfont & Dunbridge	d											08 56										
Dean	d											09 02										
Salisbury	a										09 00	09 15							09 39			
Totton	d				08 05					08 28							09 06					
Ashurst New Forest	d									08 32												
Beaulieu Road	d									08 37												
Brockenhurst 8	a				08 16					08 43				08 59			09 17					
	d		07 59		08 17				08 29	08 44				09 00		08 59	09 18				09 29	
Lymington Town	d		08 07						08 37							09 07					09 37	
Lymington Pier	a		08 10						08 40							09 10					09 40	
Sway	d				08 21					08 48							09 22					
New Milton	d				08 26					08 53							09 27					
Hinton Admiral	d				08 30					08 57							09 31					
Christchurch	d				08 35					09 02							09 36					
Pokesdown	d				08 39					09 06							09 40					
Bournemouth	a				08 43					09 10				09 14			09 44					
	d				08 44					09 11							09 45					
Branksome	d				08 49					09 16							09 50					
Parkstone (Dorset)	d				08 52					09 19							09 53					
Poole 4	a				08 56					09 23							09 57					
	d				08 57					09 24							09 58					
Hamworthy	d				09 02					09 29							10 03					
Holton Heath	d									09 33												
Wareham	d				09 09					09 38							10 10					
Wool	d				09 15					09 44												
Moreton (Dorset)	d				09 21					09 50												
Dorchester South	d				09 29					09 58							10 26					
Dorchester West	d																					10 48
Upwey	d				09 36					10 05												10 55
Weymouth	a				09 40					10 09							10 34					11 03

A ✠ to Bournemouth

Table 158

Mondays to Fridays
until 5 October

London - Basingstoke, Southampton, Romsey Lymington, Bournemouth and Weymouth

Network Diagram - see first Page of Table 158

		SW ■ ✠	XC ◇■	SW ■	SW ◇■ A ✠	SW ■ ✠	SW ■	SW ■	XC ◇■ ✠	SW ■	SW ◇■ B ✠	SW ◇■ C ✠	SW ■ ✠	SW ■	GW ◇ ✠	SW ■	SW ■	SW ■	SW ◇■ A ✠	SW ■	GW ◇ D ✠	GW ■ ✠	SW ■
London Waterloo 15 ⊖	d	07 39		07 42	08 05			08 09		08 12	08 35	08 35					08 39	08 42	09 05				
Clapham Junction 10	d	07u46			08u12					08u19							08u46		09u12				
Woking	d			08 19				08 35		08 49	09 00	09 00						09 19					
Farnborough (Main)	d	08 13		08 33				08 45		09 03							09 13	09 33					
Fleet	d	08 19		08 38						09 08							09 19	09 38					
Reading 7	d		08 15						08 46														
Basingstoke	a	08 32	08 40	08 58	08 47			08 58	09 08	09 28							09 31	09 58	09 47				
	d	08 33	08 42		08 49			09 00	09 09								09 33		09 49				
Micheldever	d							09 10															
Winchester	d	08 50	08 57		09 05			09 19	09 24		09 33	09 33					09 49		10 05				
Shawford	d	08 54															09 54						
Romsey	d						09 07							09 19								09 50	10 07
Chandlers Ford	d						09 14																10 14
Eastleigh 8	a	09 00					09 20	09 27						09 50			10 02						10 20
	d	09 01					09 21	09 28						09 51			10 03						10 21
Hedge End	d							09 34															
Botley	d							09 38															
Fareham	d							09 48							09 47						10 15	10 27	
Portchester	d							09 53															
Cosham	d							09 58														10 35	
Hilsea	a							10 03															
Fratton	a							10 07														10 42	
Portsmouth & Southsea	a							10 11														10 46	
Portsmouth Harbour ⛴	a							10 18														10 54	
Southampton Airport Pkwy ✈	d	09 05	09 09		09 14		09 25		09 33		09 42	09 42					10 08		10 14				10 25
Swaythling	d						09 27																10 27
St Denys	d					←	09 30													←			10 30
Southampton Central ⛴	a	09 15	09 17		09 22	09 15	09 35		09 41		09 49	09 49			10 08		10 18		10 22	10 18	10 40		10 35
	d	09 30			09 24	09 30	09 37		09 43		09 51	09 51			10 10		10 30		10 24	10 30	10 42		10 44
Millbrook (Hants)	d	→					09 40										→						10 48
Redbridge	d						09 43																10 51
Romsey	d						09 51							10a03	10 21						10 54		10 59
Mottisfont & Dunbridge	d						09 56																11 04
Dean	d						10 02																11 10
Salisbury	a						10 15								10 39						11 13		11 22
Totton	d					09 35														10 35			
Ashurst New Forest	d					09 40														10 40			
Beaulieu Road	d												←							10 44			
Brockenhurst 8	a				09 37	09 49			09 56		10 04	10 04	09 49						10 37	10 51			
	d				09 38	10 16			09 57		10 05	10 05	10 16			10 12			10 38	11 16			
Lymington Town	d					→										10 20				→			
Lymington Pier	a															10 23							
Sway	d												10 20										
New Milton	d				09 45								10 25						10 45				
Hinton Admiral	d												10 29										
Christchurch	d				09 52								10 34						10 52				
Pokesdown	d				09 56								10 38						10 56				
Bournemouth	a				10 00				10 12		10 20	10 25	10 42						11 00				
	d				10 04						10 24	10 30	10 43						11 04				
Branksome	d										10 29	10 35	10 48										
Parkstone (Dorset)	d										10 32	10 38	10 51										
Poole 4	a				10 13						10 36	10 42	10 55						11 13				
	d				10 14						10 37	10 43							11 14				
Hamworthy	d				10 19						10 42	10 48							11 19				
Holton Heath	d				10 23														11 23				
Wareham	d				10 28						10 49	10 55							11 28				
Wool	d				10 35														11 35				
Moreton (Dorset)	d				10 41														11 41				
Dorchester South	d				10 54						11 05	11 11							11 49				
Dorchester West	d																						
Upwey	d				11 01														11 55				
Weymouth	a				11 06						11 13	11 19							12 00				

A ✠ to Bournemouth

B not from 30 July until 10 August, from 3 September until 7 September. ✠ to Bournemouth

C from 30 July until 10 August, from 3 September until 7 September. ✠ to Bournemouth

D ✠ to Southampton Central

London - Basingstoke, Southampton, Romsey Lymington, Bournemouth and Weymouth

Network Diagram - see first Page of Table 158

		SW	SW	SW	XC	SW		GW	SW	SW	GW	GW	SW	SW	XC	SW		SW	SW	SW	SW	SW	SW	XC	SW
		1	1	1	◇1	1		◇	◇1	1	◇	◇	1	1	◇1	1		◇1	1	1	1	1	1	◇1	1
									A									A							
					🛒				🛒		🛒	🛒			🛒			🛒						🛒	
London Waterloo 15 ⊖	d	09 09				09 12			09 35					09 39		09 42		10 05			10 09				10 12
Clapham Junction 10	d					09u19								09u46				10u12							10u19
Woking	d	09 35				09 49			10 00							10 19					10 35				10 49
Farnborough (Main)	d	09 45				10 03								10 13		10 33					10 45				11 03
Fleet	d					10 08								10 19		10 38									11 08
Reading 7	d				09 46										10 15									10 46	
Basingstoke	a	09 58			10 08	10 28								10 31	10 39	10 58		10 47			10 58			11 08	11 28
	d	10 00			10 10									10 33	10 40			10 49			11 00			11 10	
Micheldever	d	10 10																			11 10				
Winchester	d	10 19			10 25				10 33					10 49	10 55			11 05			11 19			11 25	
Shawford	d													10 54											
Romsey	d		10 19									10 50								11 07		11 20			
Chandlers Ford	d																			11 14					
Eastleigh 3	a	10 27	10 49											10 59						11 20	11 27	11 49			
	d	10 28	10 50											11 00						11 21	11 28	11 50			
Hedge End	d	10 34																			11 34				
Botley	d	10 38																			11 38				
Fareham	d	10 48									10 47	11 27									11 48				
Portchester	d	10 53																			11 53				
Cosham	d	10 58										11 35									11 58				
Hilsea	a	11 03																			12 03				
Fratton	a	11 07										11 42									12 07				
Portsmouth & Southsea	a	11 11										11 46									12 11				
Portsmouth Harbour ⛴	a	11 18										11 54									12 18				
Southampton Airport Pkwy ✈	d				10 33				10 42					11 05	11 09			11 14		11 25				11 33	
Swaythling	d																			11 27					
St Denys	d																		←	11 30					
Southampton Central ⛴	a				10 43				10 49		11 08			11 12	11 16			11 22	11 12	11 35				11 43	
	d				10 45				10 51		11 10			11 30				11 24	11 30	11 37				11 45	
Millbrook (Hants)	d													→						11 40					
Redbridge	d																			11 43					
Romsey	d		11a03								11 21									11 51		12a03			
Mottisfont & Dunbridge	d																			11 56					
Dean	d																			12 02					
Salisbury	a										11 39									12 15					
Totton	d																		11 35						
Ashurst New Forest	d																		11 40						
Beaulieu Road	d									←									11 44						
Brockenhurst 3	a				10 58				11 04	10 51								11 37	11 51					11 58	
	d			10 42	10 59				11 05	11 16			11 12					11 38	12 16				11 42	11 59	
Lymington Town	d			10 50									11 20						→				11 50		
Lymington Pier	a			10 53									11 23										11 53		
Sway	d									11 20															
New Milton	d									11 25								11 45							
Hinton Admiral	d									11 29															
Christchurch	d									11 34								11 52							
Pokesdown	d									11 38								11 56							
Bournemouth	a				11 12				11 20	11 42								12 00						12 12	
	d								11 24	11 43								12 04							
Branksome	d								11 29	11 48															
Parkstone (Dorset)	d								11 32	11 51															
Poole 4	a								11 36	11 55								12 13							
	d								11 37									12 14							
Hamworthy	d								11 42									12 19							
Holton Heath	d																	12 23							
Wareham	d								11 49									12 28							
Wool	d																	12 35							
Moreton (Dorset)	d																	12 41							
Dorchester South	d								12 05									12 49							
Dorchester West	d							11 54																	
Upwey	d							12 02										12 55							
Weymouth	a							12 09	12 13									13 00							

A 🛒 to Bournemouth

London - Basingstoke, Southampton, Romsey Lymington, Bournemouth and Weymouth

Network Diagram - see first Page of Table 158

		SW		SW	GW	GW	GW	SW	SW	SW	SW	SW		GW	SW	SW	SW	SW	XC	SW	GW	SW		SW	GW
		◇1		1	◇	◇		1	1	1	◇1	1		◇	1	1	1	1	◇1	1	◇	◇1		1	◇
		A									A											A			
		🛒			🛒	🛒					🛒								🛒			🛒			🛒
London Waterloo 15 ⊖	d	10 35							10 39	10 42	11 05					11 09				11 12		11 35			
Clapham Junction 10	d								10u46		11u12									11u19					
Woking	d	11 00								11 19						11 35				11 49		12 00			
Farnborough (Main)	d								11 13	11 33						11 45				12 03					
Fleet	d								11 19	11 38										12 08					
Reading 7	d																		11 46						
Basingstoke	a								11 31	11 58	11 47					11 58			12 08	12 28					
	d								11 33		11 49					12 00			12 10						
Micheldever	d															12 10									
Winchester	d	11 33							11 49		12 05					12 19			12 25			12 33			
Shawford	d								11 54																
Romsey	d					11 50	12 10								12 07		12 19								
Chandlers Ford	d														12 14										
Eastleigh 3	a								11 59						12 20	12 27	12 49								
	d								12 00						12 21	12 28	12 50								
Hedge End	d															12 34									
Botley	d															12 38									
Fareham	d				11 47	12 27										12 48									12 47
Portchester	d															12 53									
Cosham	d					12 35										12 58									
Hilsea	a															13 03									
Fratton	a					12 42										13 07									
Portsmouth & Southsea	a					12 46										13 11									
Portsmouth Harbour ⛴	a					12 54										13 18									
Southampton Airport Pkwy ✈	d	11 42							12 05		12 14				12 25				12 33			12 42			
Swaythling	d														12 27										
St Denys	d											←			12 30										
Southampton Central ⛴	a	11 49			12 08		12 22		12 15		12 22	12 15			12 35				12 41			12 49			13 08
	d	11 51			12 10				12 30		12 24	12 30		12 27	12 37				12 43			12 51			13 10
Millbrook (Hants)	d								→						12 40										
Redbridge	d														12 43										
Romsey	d				12 21									12 39	12 51		13a03								13 21
Mottisfont & Dunbridge	d														12 56										
Dean	d														13 02										
Salisbury	a				12 39									13 02	13 15										13 39
Totton	d											12 35													
Ashurst New Forest	d											12 40													
Beaulieu Road	d			←																				←	
Brockenhurst 3	a	12 04		11 51							12 37	12 51							12 56			13 04		12 51	
	d	12 05		12 16				12 12			12 38	13 16						12 42	12 57			13 05		13 16	
Lymington Town	d							12 20				→						12 50							
Lymington Pier	a							12 23										12 53							
Sway	d			12 20																				13 20	
New Milton	d			12 25							12 45													13 25	
Hinton Admiral	d			12 29																				13 29	
Christchurch	d			12 34							12 52													13 34	
Pokesdown	d			12 38							12 56													13 38	
Bournemouth	a	12 20		12 42							13 00								13 10			13 20		13 42	
	d	12 24		12 43							13 04											13 24		13 43	
Branksome	d	12 29		12 48																		13 29		13 48	
Parkstone (Dorset)	d	12 32		12 51																		13 32		13 51	
Poole 4	a	12 36		12 55							13 13											13 36		13 55	
	d	12 37									13 14											13 37			
Hamworthy	d	12 42									13 19											13 42			
Holton Heath	d										13 23														
Wareham	d	12 49									13 28											13 49			
Wool	d										13 35														
Moreton (Dorset)	d										13 41														
Dorchester South	d	13 05									13 49											14 05			
Dorchester West	d																				13 54				
Upwey	d										13 55										14 02				
Weymouth	a	13 13									14 00										14 09	14 13			

A 🛒 to Bournemouth

Table 158

Mondays to Fridays

until 5 October

London - Basingstoke, Southampton, Romsey Lymington, Bournemouth and Weymouth

Network Diagram - see first Page of Table 158

		GW	SW	SW	XC	SW	SW	SW		SW	SW	SW	SW	XC	SW	SW	SW	GW		GW	SW	SW	SW	SW	SW
		◇	1	1	◇1	1	◇1	1		1	1	1	1	◇1	1	◇1	1	◇		◇	1	1	1	◇1	1
							A									A								A	
		🛒			🛒		🛒							🛒		🛒		🛒		🛒				🛒	
London Waterloo 15 ⊖	d			11 39		11 42	12 05				12 09				12 12	12 35						12 39	12 42	13 05	
Clapham Junction 10	d			11u46			12u12								12u19							12u46		13u12	
Woking	d					12 19					12 35				12 49	13 00							13 19		
Farnborough (Main)	d			12 13		12 33					12 45				13 03							13 13	13 33		
Fleet	d			12 19		12 38									13 08							13 19	13 38		
Reading 7	d				12 15									12 46											
Basingstoke	a			12 31	12 39	12 58	12 47				12 58			13 08	13 28							13 31	13 58	13 47	
	d			12 33	12 40		12 49				13 00			13 10								13 33		13 49	
Micheldever	d										13 10														
Winchester	d			12 49	12 55		13 05				13 19			13 25		13 33						13 49		14 05	
Shawford	d			12 54																		13 54			
Romsey	d	12 50								13 07		13 19								13 50					
Chandlers Ford	d									13 14															
Eastleigh 8	a			12 59						13 20	13 27	13 49										13 59			
	d			13 00						13 21	13 28	13 50										14 00			
Hedge End	d										13 34														
Botley	d										13 38														
Fareham	d	13 27									13 48							13 47		14 27					
Portchester	d										13 53														
Cosham	d	13 35									13 58									14 35					
Hilsea	a										14 03														
Fratton	a	13 42									14 07									14 42					
Portsmouth & Southsea	a	13 46									14 11									14 46					
Portsmouth Harbour ⛴	a	13 54									14 18									14 54					
Southampton Airport Pkwy ✈	d			13 05	13 09		13 14			13 25				13 33		13 42						14 05		14 14	
Swaythling	d									13 27															
St Denys	d							←		13 30															←
Southampton Central ⛴	a			13 15	13 17		13 22	13 15		13 35				13 41		13 49		14 08				14 12		14 22	14 12
	d			13 30			13 24	13 30		13 37				13 43		13 51		14 10				14 30		14 24	14 30
Millbrook (Hants)	d			→						13 40												→			
Redbridge	d									13 43															
Romsey	d									13 51		14a03						14 21							
Mottisfont & Dunbridge	d									13 56															
Dean	d									14 02															
Salisbury	a									14 15								14 39							
Totton	d							13 35																	14 35
Ashurst New Forest	d							13 40																	14 40
Beaulieu Road	d																←								
Brockenhurst 3	a						13 37	13 51						13 56		14 04	13 51							14 37	14 51
	d		13 12				13 38	14 16					13 42	13 57		14 05	14 16				14 12			14 38	15 16
Lymington Town	d		13 20					→					13 50								14 20				→
Lymington Pier	a		13 23										13 53								14 23				
Sway	d																14 20								
New Milton	d						13 45										14 25							14 45	
Hinton Admiral	d																14 29								
Christchurch	d						13 52										14 34							14 52	
Pokesdown	d						13 56										14 38							14 56	
Bournemouth	a						14 00							14 10		14 20	14 42							15 00	
	d						14 04									14 24	14 43							15 04	
Branksome	d															14 29	14 48								
Parkstone (Dorset)	d															14 32	14 51								
Poole 4	a						14 13									14 36	14 55							15 13	
	d						14 14									14 37								15 14	
Hamworthy	d						14 19									14 42								15 19	
Holton Heath	d						14 23																	15 23	
Wareham	d						14 28									14 49								15 28	
Wool	d						14 35																	15 35	
Moreton (Dorset)	d						14 41																	15 41	
Dorchester South	d						14 49									15 05								15 49	
Dorchester West	d																								
Upwey	d						14 55																	15 55	
Weymouth	a						15 00									15 13								16 00	

A 🛒 to Bournemouth

Table 158

Mondays to Fridays

until 5 October

London - Basingstoke, Southampton, Romsey Lymington, Bournemouth and Weymouth

Network Diagram - see first Page of Table 158

		GW	SW	SW		SW	XC	SW	SW	SW	GW	SN	SW	GW		SW	SW	XC	SW	SW	SW	SW	SW	SW
		■	1	1		1	◇1	1	◇1	1	■	1	1	◇		1	1	◇1	1	◇1	1	1	1	1
									A											A				
		🛒					🛒		🛒		🛒			🛒				🛒		🛒				
London Waterloo 15 ⊖	d			13 09				13 12	13 35								13 39		13 42	14 05			14 09	
Clapham Junction 10	d							13u19									13u46			14u12				
Woking	d			13 35				13 49	14 00										14 19				14 35	
Farnborough (Main)	d			13 45				14 03									14 13		14 33				14 45	
Fleet	d							14 08									14 19		14 38					
Reading 7	d						13 46											14 15						
Basingstoke	a			13 58			14 08	14 28									14 31	14 39	14 58	14 47			14 58	
	d			14 00			14 10										14 33	14 40		14 49			15 00	
Micheldever	d			14 10																			15 10	
Winchester	d			14 19			14 25		14 33								14 49	14 55		15 05			15 19	
Shawford	d																14 54							
Romsey	d	14 19	14 07										14 13	14 50								15 07		15 19
Chandlers Ford	d		14 14																			15 14		
Eastleigh 8	a		14 20	14 27									14 49				14 59					15 20	15 27	15 49
	d		14 21	14 28								14 41	14 50				15 00					15 21	15 28	15 50
Hedge End	d			14 34																			15 34	
Botley	d			14 38																			15 38	
Fareham	d			14 48							14 47	14a59		15 27									15 48	
Portchester	d			14 53																			15 53	
Cosham	d			14 58										15 35									15 58	
Hilsea	a			15 03																			16 03	
Fratton	a			15 07										15 42									16 07	
Portsmouth & Southsea	a			15 11										15 46									16 11	
Portsmouth Harbour ⛴	a			15 18										15 54									16 18	
Southampton Airport Pkwy ✈	d		14 25				14 35		14 42								15 05	15 09		15 14		15 25		
Swaythling	d		14 27																			15 27		
St Denys	d		14 30																		←	15 30		
Southampton Central ⛴	a	14 32	14 35				14 42		14 49		15 08						15 12	15 17		15 22	15 12	15 35		
	d		14 37				14 43		14 51		15 10						15 30			15 24	15 30	15 37		
Millbrook (Hants)	d		14 40														→					15 40		
Redbridge	d		14 43																			15 43		
Romsey	d		14 51								15 21		15a04									15 51		16a03
Mottisfont & Dunbridge	d		14 56																			15 56		
Dean	d		15 02																			16 02		
Salisbury	a		15 15								15 39											16 15		
Totton	d																				15 35			
Ashurst New Forest	d																				15 40			
Beaulieu Road	d									←														
Brockenhurst 3	a						14 56		15 04	14 51										15 37	15 51			
	d					14 42	14 57		15 05	15 16						15 12				15 38	16 28			
Lymington Town	d					14 50										15 20					→			
Lymington Pier	a					14 53										15 23								
Sway	d									15 20														
New Milton	d									15 25										15 45				
Hinton Admiral	d									15 29														
Christchurch	d									15 34										15 52				
Pokesdown	d									15 38										15 56				
Bournemouth	a						15 11		15 20	15 42										16 00				
	d								15 24	15 43										16 04				
Branksome	d								15 29	15 48														
Parkstone (Dorset)	d								15 32	15 51														
Poole 4	a								15 36	15 55										16 13				
	d								15 37											16 14				
Hamworthy	d								15 42											16 19				
Holton Heath	d																			16 23				
Wareham	d								15 49											16 28				
Wool	d																			16 35				
Moreton (Dorset)	d																			16 41				
Dorchester South	d								16 05											16 49				
Dorchester West	d																							
Upwey	d																			16 55				
Weymouth	a								16 13											17 00				

A 🛒 to Bournemouth

Table 158

Mondays to Fridays
until 5 October

London - Basingstoke, Southampton, Romsey Lymington, Bournemouth and Weymouth

Network Diagram - see first Page of Table 158

		SW	XC	SW	GW	SW	SW	GW	GW	SW	SW	SW	SW	SW	SW	SW	SW	XC	SW	SW	SW	SW	SW
		■	◇■	■	◇	◇■	■	■	◇	■	■	■	◇■	■	■	■	■	◇■	■	■	■	■	■
						A							A										
			✕			✕		✕	✕				✕					✕					
London Waterloo 15 ⊖	d			14 12		14 35					14 39	14 42	15 05				15 09					15 12	
Clapham Junction 10	d			14u19							14u46		15u12									15u19	
Woking	d			14 49		15 00						15 19					15 35					15 49	
Farnborough (Main)	d			15 03							15 13	15 33					15 45					16 03	
Fleet	d			15 08							15 19	15 38										16 08	
Reading 7	d		14 46															15 46					
Basingstoke	a		15 08	15 28							15 31	15 58	15 47				15 58	16 08				16 28	
	d		15 10								15 33		15 49				16 00	16 10			16 24		
Micheldever	d																16 10						
Winchester	d		15 25			15 33					15 49		16 05				16 19	16 25	16 38		16 45		
Shawford	d										15 54								16 43				
Romsey	d								15 50							16 07				16 19			
Chandlers Ford	d															16 14							
Eastleigh 8	a										15 59					16 20	16 27		16 48	16 49	16 53		
	d										16 00					16 21	16 28		16 49	16 50	16 54		
Hedge End	d																16 34				17 00		
Botley	d																16 38				17 04		
Fareham	d							15 47	16 27								16 48				17 12		
Portchester	d																16 53				17 17		
Cosham	d								16 35								16 58				17 22		
Hilsea	a																17 03						
Fratton	a								16 42								17 07				17 31		
Portsmouth & Southsea	a								16 46								17 11				17 35		
Portsmouth Harbour ⛴	a								16 54								17 18				17 40		
Southampton Airport Pkwy ✈	d		15 33			15 42					16 05		16 14			16 25		16 33	16 54				
Swaythling	d															16 27			16 56				
St Denys	d														←	16 30			16 59				
Southampton Central ⛴	a		15 41			15 49		16 08			16 15		16 22		16 15	16 35		16 41	17 04				
	d		15 43			15 51		16 10			16 30		16 24		16 30	16 37		16 43	17 06				
Millbrook (Hants)	d										→					16 40			→				
Redbridge	d															16 43							
Romsey	d							16 21								16 51				17a03			
Mottisfont & Dunbridge	d															16 56							
Dean	d															17 02							
Salisbury	a							16 39								17 15							
Totton	d														16 35								
Ashurst New Forest	d														16 40								
Beaulieu Road	d						←								16 44								
Brockenhurst 3	a		15 56			16 04	15 51						16 37		16 51			16 56					
	d	15 42	15 57			16 05	16 28			16 12			16 38	16 42				16 57					17 12
Lymington Town	d	15 50								16 20				16 50									17 20
Lymington Pier	a	15 53								16 23				16 53									17 23
Sway	d						16 32						16 43										
New Milton	d						16 37						16 48										
Hinton Admiral	d						16 41						16 52										
Christchurch	d						16 46						16 57										
Pokesdown	d						16 50						17 00										
Bournemouth	a		16 10			16 20	16 54						17 04					17 10					
	d					16 24	16 55						17 07										
Branksome	d					16 29	17 00																
Parkstone (Dorset)	d					16 32	17 03																
Poole 4	a					16 36	17 07						17 16										
	d					16 37							17 17										
Hamworthy	d					16 42							17 22										
Holton Heath	d												17 26										
Wareham	d					16 49							17 31										
Wool	d					16 55							17 37										
Moreton (Dorset)	d												17 43										
Dorchester South	d					17 06							17 51										
Dorchester West	d				16 58																		
Upwey	d				17 05								17 58										
Weymouth	a				17 10	17 15							18 02										

A ✕ to Bournemouth

Table 158

Mondays to Fridays
until 5 October

London - Basingstoke, Southampton, Romsey Lymington, Bournemouth and Weymouth

Network Diagram - see first Page of Table 158

		SW		SW	GW	GW	SW	XC	SW	SW	SN	SW	SW	SW	SW	XC	SW	SW	SW	GW	SW	SW	
		◇■		■	■	◇	■	◇■	■	◇■	■	■	■	■	■	◇■	■	■	■	◇	■	◇■	
		A								A												A	
		✕			✕	✕		✕		✕						✕						✕	
London Waterloo 15 ⊖	d	15 35					15 39		15 42	16 05					16 09				16 12			16 35	
Clapham Junction 10	d						15u46			16u12									16u19				
Woking	d	16 00							16 19						16 35				16 49			17u00	
Farnborough (Main)	d						16 13		16 33						16 45				17 03				
Fleet	d						16 19		16 38										17 08				
Reading 7	d							16 15								16 46							
Basingstoke	a						16 31	16 39	16 58	16 47					16 58	17 08			17 30				
	d						16 33	16 40		16 49					17 00	17 10		17 24					
Micheldever	d														17 10			17 34					
Winchester	d	16 33					16 50	17 00		17 05					17 19	17 25		17 44				17 33	
Shawford	d						16 54											17 49					
Romsey	d					16 50								17 07			17 19						
Chandlers Ford	d													17 14									
Eastleigh 8	a						17 00							17 20	17 27		17 49	17 54					
	d						17 01				17 16			17 21	17 28		17 50	17 55					
Hedge End	d														17 34								
Botley	d														17 39								
Fareham	d				16 47	17 27									17 48								
Portchester	d														17 53								
Cosham	d					17 35									17 58								
Hilsea	a														18 04								
Fratton	a					17 42									18 08								
Portsmouth & Southsea	a					17 46									18 12								
Portsmouth Harbour ⛴	a					17 54									18 20								
Southampton Airport Pkwy ✈	d	16 42					17 05			17 14	17 20			17 25		17 33		18 00				17 42	
Swaythling	d													17 27				18 02					
St Denys	d			←									←	17 30				18 05					
Southampton Central ⛴	a	16 49		17 04	17 08		17 13	17 17		17 22	17 28		17 13	17 35		17 41		18 10				17 49	
	d	16 54	16 56	17 06	17 10		17 30			17 24			17 30	17 37		17 43						17 53	17 56
Millbrook (Hants)	d						→							17 40									
Redbridge	d													17 43									
Romsey	d				17 21									17 51			18a03						
Mottisfont & Dunbridge	d													17 56									
Dean	d													18 02									
Salisbury	a				17 39									18 15									
Totton	d		17 01	17a11									17 35										18 01
Ashurst New Forest	d		17 06										17 40										18 06
Beaulieu Road	d												17 44										
Brockenhurst 3	a	17 07	17 14							17 37			17 51			17 56						18 07	18 14
	d	17 08	17 16							17 38		17 42				17 57					18 12	18 08	18 16
Lymington Town	d											17 50									18 20		
Lymington Pier	a											17 53									18 23		
Sway	d		17 20							17 43													18 20
New Milton	d		17 25							17 48													18 25
Hinton Admiral	d		17 29							17 52													18 29
Christchurch	d		17 34							17 57													18 34
Pokesdown	d		17 38							18 00													18 38
Bournemouth	a	17 23	17 42							18 04						18 15						18 22	18 42
	d	17 24	17 43							18 09												18 24	
Branksome	d	17 29	17 48																			18 29	
Parkstone (Dorset)	d	17 32	17 51																			18 32	
Poole 4	a	17 36	17 55							18 18												18 36	
	d	17 37								18 19												18 37	
Hamworthy	d	17 42								18 24												18 42	
Holton Heath	d									18 28													
Wareham	d	17 49								18 33												18 49	
Wool	d	17 55								18 39												18 55	
Moreton (Dorset)	d									18 45													
Dorchester South	d	18 06								18 53												19 06	
Dorchester West	d																			18 58			
Upwey	d									19 00										19 06			
Weymouth	a	18 15								19 06										19 14		19 17	

A ✕ to Bournemouth

Table 158

Mondays to Fridays
until 5 October

London - Basingstoke, Southampton, Romsey Lymington, Bournemouth and Weymouth

Network Diagram - see first Page of Table 158

		GW ◇ ⊼	SW 1	SW 1	SW ◇1 A ⊼	GW ◇ ⊼	SW 1	GW ◇ ⊼	SW 1	SW 1	SW 1	XC ◇1 ⊼	SW 1	SW 1	GW ◇	SW ◇1 A ⊼	GW ◇ ⊼	SW 1	SW 1	SW 1
London Waterloo 15 ⊖	d		16 39	16 42	17 05				17 09				17 12	17 23		17 35		17 39	17 41	17 48
Clapham Junction 10	d		16u46																	
Woking	d			17 19					17 34				17 37	17 52				18 04		18 13
Farnborough (Main)	d		17 13	17 33									17 51	18 08					18 19	
Fleet	d		17 19	17 38									17 56	18 13					18 24	
Reading 7	d											17 46								
Basingstoke	a		17 31	18 00					17 52			18 08	18 16	18 32				18 22	18 45	18 31
	d		17 33						17 54			18 10						18 24		18 33
Micheldever	d								18 04									18 34		
Winchester	d		17 49		18 00				18 14			18 25				18 30		18 44		18 50
Shawford	d		17 54						18 18									18 49		
Romsey	d					17 50	18 07			18 19										
Chandlers Ford	d						18 14													
Eastleigh 8	a		17 59				18 20		18 24	18 49								18 54		18 58
	d		18 01				18 21		18 25	18 50								18 55		18 59
Hedge End	d		18 07						18 31									19 01		
Botley	d		18 11						18 36									19 05		
Fareham	d	17 47	18 23			18 27		18 13	18 45								18 47	19 14		
Portchester	d		18 28						18 50									19 19		
Cosham	d		18 33			18 35			18 55									19 24		
Hilsea	a								19 05									19 28		
Fratton	a		18 40			18 48			19 09									19 32		
Portsmouth & Southsea	a		18 43			18 52			19 12									19 36		
Portsmouth Harbour ⛴	a		18 51			19 00			19 20									19 43		
Southampton Airport Pkwy ✈	d				18 09		18 25					18 33				18 39				19 03
Swaythling	d						18 27													19 06
St Denys	d						18 30													19 09
Southampton Central ⛴	a	18 08			18 16		18 35	18 40				18 44				18 46	19 08			19 18
	d	18 10			18 21 / 18 24		18 37	18 42				18 45				18 51 / 18 54	19 10			
Millbrook (Hants)	d						18 40													
Redbridge	d						18 44													
Romsey	d	18 21					19 00	18 54		19a04							19 21			
Mottisfont & Dunbridge	d						19 05													
Dean	d						19 10													
Salisbury	a	18 39					19 23	19 12									19 39			
Totton	d				18 29											18 59				
Ashurst New Forest	d				18 34											19 04				
Beaulieu Road	d																			
Brockenhurst 3	a				18 42							18 58				19 12				
	d				18 43						18 48	18 59				19 13				
Lymington Town	d										18 56									
Lymington Pier	a										18 59									
Sway	d				18 47											19 17				
New Milton	d				18 52											19 22				
Hinton Admiral	d				18 57											19 26				
Christchurch	d				19 01											19 31				
Pokesdown	d				19 05											19 35				
Bournemouth	a				18 48 / 19 09							19 13				19 20 / 19 39				
	d				18 50 / 19 10											19 21 / 19 40				
Branksome	d				18 55 / 19 15											19 26 / 19 45				
Parkstone (Dorset)	d				18 58 / 19 18											19 29 / 19 48				
Poole 4	a				19 02 / 19 26											19 33 / 19 56				
	d				19 03											19 34				
Hamworthy	d				19 08											19 39				
Holton Heath	d				19 12															
Wareham	d				19 17											19 46				
Wool	d				19 23															
Moreton (Dorset)	d				19 29															
Dorchester South	d				19 37											20 02				
Dorchester West	d														19 54					
Upwey	d				19 44										20 02					
Weymouth	a				19 50										20 10	20 15				

A ⊼ to Bournemouth

Table 158

Mondays to Fridays
until 5 October

London - Basingstoke, Southampton, Romsey Lymington, Bournemouth and Weymouth

Network Diagram - see first Page of Table 158

		XC ◇1 ⊼	SW 1	GW ■ ⊼	SW 1	SW ◇1 A ⊼	SW 1	SW 1	SW 1	SW 1	SW 1	XC ◇1 ⊼	SW 1	SW 1	SW 1	SW 1	SW ◇1 A ⊼	GW ◇	GW ■ ⊼	SW 1	SW 1	SW 1
London Waterloo 15 ⊖	d		17 53			18 05			18 09				18 12		18 23	18 32	18 35				18 39	18 41
Clapham Junction 10	d																				18u46	
Woking	d		18 25						18 35						18 54	19 20					19 06	
Farnborough (Main)	d		18 39										18 48		19 10	19 31						19 20
Fleet	d		18 44										18 54		19 15	19 37						19 26
Reading 7	d	18 15										18 46										
Basingstoke	a	18 47	19 03						18 53			19 08	19 16		19 34	19 59					19 28	19 47
	d	18 48							18 55			19 10		19 24							19 30	
Micheldever	d								19 05												19 40	
Winchester	d	19 09				19 00	19 05		19 14			19 25		19 40			19 30				19 49	
Shawford	d						19 09		19 19					19 45							19 54	
Romsey	d			18 54				19 07		19 19									19 50			
Chandlers Ford	d							19 14														
Eastleigh 8	a	19 27					19 15	19 20	19 25	19 49				19 50							19 59	
	d						19 16	19 21	19 29	19 50				19 51							20 00	
Hedge End	d								19 35					19 57								
Botley	d								19 38					20 01								
Fareham	d			19 27					19 48					20a09				19 47	20 27			
Portchester	d								19 53													
Cosham	d			19 35					19 58													
Hilsea	a								20 02													
Fratton	a			19 42					20 06										20 42			
Portsmouth & Southsea	a			19 46					20 11										20 46			
Portsmouth Harbour ⛴	a			19 54					20 20										20 54			
Southampton Airport Pkwy ✈	d					19 09	19 20	19 25				19 33					19 39				20 05	
Swaythling	d						19 23	19 27														
St Denys	d						19 26	19 30														
Southampton Central ⛴	a					19 18	19 33	19 35				19 41					19 46	20 08			20 16	
	d					19 19		19 37				19 43					19 51 / 19 54	20 10			20 30	
Millbrook (Hants)	d							19 40													→	
Redbridge	d							19 43														
Romsey	d							19 51		20a03								20 21				
Mottisfont & Dunbridge	d							19 56														
Dean	d							20 02														
Salisbury	a							20 15										20 39				
Totton	d					19 25											19 59					
Ashurst New Forest	d																20 04					
Beaulieu Road	d																					
Brockenhurst 3	a					19 35						19 56					20 12					
	d				19 18	19 36					19 48	19 57					20 13			20 18		
Lymington Town	d				19 26						19 56									20 26		
Lymington Pier	a				19 29						19 59									20 29		
Sway	d					19 41											20 17					
New Milton	d					19 46											20 22					
Hinton Admiral	d					19 50											20 26					
Christchurch	d					19 55											20 31					
Pokesdown	d					19 58											20 35					
Bournemouth	a					20 02						20 12					20 20 / 20 39					
	d					20 07											20 21 / 20 40					
Branksome	d					20 12											20 26 / 20 45					
Parkstone (Dorset)	d					20 15											20 29 / 20 48					
Poole 4	a					20 18											20 33 / 20 56					
	d					20 19											20 34					
Hamworthy	d					20 24											20 39					
Holton Heath	d					20 28																
Wareham	d					20 33											20 46					
Wool	d					20 40																
Moreton (Dorset)	d					20 46																
Dorchester South	d					20 54											21 02					
Dorchester West	d																					
Upwey	d					21 00																
Weymouth	a					21 07											21 13					

A ⊼ to Bournemouth

London - Basingstoke, Southampton, Romsey Lymington, Bournemouth and Weymouth

Network Diagram - see first Page of Table 158

		SW ◇1 A 🍴	SW 1	SW 1	SW 1	SW 1	SW 1	XC ◇1 🍴	SW 1	GW ◇	SW ◇1 A 🍴	SW 1	GW ◇	SW 1	SW 1	GW ◇ 🍴	SW 1	GW	SW ◇1 🍴	SW 1	SW 1	SW 1	SW 1
London Waterloo 15 ⊖	d	19 05			19 09				19 12		19 35			19 39	19 42				20 05		20 09		
Clapham Junction 10	d	19u12							19u19					19u46					20u12				
Woking	d				19 35				19 39		20 00				20 19						20 35		
Farnborough (Main)	d				19 45				19 53					20 13	20 33						20 45		
Fleet	d								19 58					20 19	20 38								
Reading 7	d							19 46															
Basingstoke	a	19 47			19 58			20 09	20 16					20 31	20 58				20 47		20 58		
	d	19 49			20 00			20 10						20 33					20 49		21 00		
Micheldever	d				20 10																21 10		
Winchester	d	20 05			20 19			20 25			20 33			20 49					21 05		21 19		
Shawford	d				20 24									20 54							21 24		
Romsey	d			20 07		20 19				20 35						20 50				21 07		21 19	
Chandlers Ford	d			20 14																21 14			
Eastleigh 3	a			20 20	20 29	20 49								20 59						21 20	21 30	21 49	
	d			20 21	20 30	20 50								21 00						21 21	21 30	21 50	
Hedge End	d				20 36																21 36		
Botley	d				20 40																21 40		
Fareham	d				20 49								20 47			21 27					21 48		
Portchester	d				20 54																21 53		
Cosham	d				20 59																21 58		
Hilsea	a				21 03																22 03		
Fratton	a				21 07											21 41					22 08		
Portsmouth & Southsea	a				21 11											21 45					22 11		
Portsmouth Harbour ⛴	a				21 16											21 52					22 16		
Southampton Airport Pkwy ✈	d	20 14		20 25				20 33			20 42			21 05					21 15	21 24			
Swaythling	d			20 27																21 27			
St Denys	d		←	20 30																21 30			
Southampton Central ⛴	a	20 22	20 16	20 35				20 41		20 48	20 49		21 08	21 12					21 24	21 35			
	d	20 24	20 30	20 37				20 43			20 51		21 10					21 20	21 25	21 37			
Millbrook (Hants)	d			20 40																21 40			
Redbridge	d			20 43																21 43			
Romsey	d			20 51		21a03							21 21					21 31		21 51		22a03	
Mottisfont & Dunbridge	d			20 56																21 56			
Dean	d			21 02																22 02			
Salisbury	a			21 15									21 39					21 51		22 15			
Totton	d		20 35								20 56								21 31				
Ashurst New Forest	d		20 40																21 35				
Beaulieu Road	d		20 44									←											
Brockenhurst 3	a	20 37	20 51					20 58			21 07	20 51							21 43				
	d	20 38	21 16				20 48	20 59			21 08	21 16					21 18		21 44				21 48
Lymington Town	d		→				20 56										21 26						21 56
Lymington Pier	a						20 59										21 29						21 59
Sway	d											21 20							21 49				
New Milton	d	20 45										21 25							21 54				
Hinton Admiral	d											21 29							21 58				
Christchurch	d	20 52										21 34							22 03				
Pokesdown	d	20 56										21 38							22 06				
Bournemouth	a	21 00						21 15			21 22	21 42							22 10				
	d	21 04									21 27	21 43							22 12				
Branksome	d										21 32	21 48							22 17				
Parkstone (Dorset)	d										21 35	21 51							22 20				
Poole 4	a	21 13									21 38	21 57							22 23				
	d	21 15									21 39												
Hamworthy	d	21 20									21 44												
Holton Heath	d																						
Wareham	d	21 27									21 51												
Wool	d	21 33									21 58												
Moreton (Dorset)	d	21 39									22 04												
Dorchester South	d	21 47									22 12												
Dorchester West	d																						
Upwey	d	21 54									22 18												
Weymouth	a	21 58									22 23												

A 🍴 to Bournemouth

London - Basingstoke, Southampton, Romsey Lymington, Bournemouth and Weymouth

Network Diagram - see first Page of Table 158

		XC ◇1	SW 1	GW A	GW B	SW ◇1 C 🍴	SW 1	SW 1	GW	SW 1	SW ◇1 🍴	SW 1	XC ◇1	GW ◇	SW 1	SW 1	SW 1	SW ◇1 C 🍴	SW 1	GW ◇	SW 1	SW ◇1 🍴
London Waterloo 15 ⊖	d		20 12			20 35	20 39	20 42			21 05						21 12	21 35	21 39		21 42	22 05
Clapham Junction 10	d		20u19				20u46				21u12						21u19		21u46			22u12
Woking	d		20 49			21 00		21 19			21 32						21 49	22 00			22 19	22 32
Farnborough (Main)	d		21 03				21 13	21 33									22 03		22 13		22 33	
Fleet	d		21 08				21 19	21 38									22 08		22 19		22 38	
Reading 7	d	20 46											21 46									
Basingstoke	a	21 09	21 28				21 31	21 58			21 51		22 09				22 28		22 31		22 58	22 51
	d	21 10					21 33				21 52		22 10			22 21			22 33		23 00	22 52
Micheldever	d						21 43									22 31			22s43		23 10	
Winchester	d	21 25				21 33	21 52				22 09		22 25			22 40		22 33	22 52		23 19	23 09
Shawford	d						21 57									22 45			22 57		23 24	
Romsey	d											22 07		21 50	22 19					22 53		
Chandlers Ford	d											22 14										
Eastleigh 3	a						22 02				22 17	22 21		22 14	22 49	22 50			23 02		23 29	23 17
	d						22 03		22 11		22 18	22 22		22 24	22 50	22 51			23 03		23 30	23 18
Hedge End	d															22 57					23 36	
Botley	d													22 35		23 01					23 40	
Fareham	d													22 42		23 10				23 27	23 49	
Portchester	d															23 15					23 54	
Cosham	d															23 20					23 59	
Hilsea	a															23 24					00 03	
Fratton	a													22 56		23 32				23 44	00 07	
Portsmouth & Southsea	a													22 59		23 36				23 48	00 11	
Portsmouth Harbour ⛴	a													23 04		23 40				23 54	00 16	
Southampton Airport Pkwy ✈	d	21 33				21 42	22 08				22 22	22 26	22 33					22 42	23 08			23 22
Swaythling	d											22 28										
St Denys	d											22 31										
Southampton Central ⛴	a	21 41				21 49	22 18		22 21		22 29	22 36	22 42					22 49	23 17			23 29
	d	21 43				21 51			22 22		22 31	22 38	22 43					22 51				23 31
Millbrook (Hants)	d											22 40										
Redbridge	d											22 44										
Romsey	d								22 34			22a52			23a03							
Mottisfont & Dunbridge	d																					
Dean	d																					
Salisbury	a								22 58													
Totton	d										22 36											23 36
Ashurst New Forest	d										22 41											23 41
Beaulieu Road	d																					
Brockenhurst 3	a	21 56				22 04					22 49		22 56					23 04				23 49
	d	21 57				22 05				22 18	22 50		22 59					23 05				23 50
Lymington Town	d									22 26												
Lymington Pier	a									22 29												
Sway	d										22 54											23 54
New Milton	d										22 59											23 59
Hinton Admiral	d										23 03											00 03
Christchurch	d										23 08											00 08
Pokesdown	d										23 12											00 11
Bournemouth	a	22 16				22 20					23 16		23 21					23 25				00 15
	d					22 24					23 17							23 29				00 17
Branksome	d					22 29					23 22							23 35				00 22
Parkstone (Dorset)	d					22 32					23 25							23 38				00 25
Poole 4	a					22 36					23 29							23 41				00 29
	d					22 37												23 42				
Hamworthy	d					22 42												23 47				
Holton Heath	d																					
Wareham	d					22 49												23 54				
Wool	d					22 55												00 01				
Moreton (Dorset)	d					23 01												00 07				
Dorchester South	d					23 09												00 15				
Dorchester West	d			22 54	22 58																	
Upwey	d			23 02	23 06	23 16												00 21				
Weymouth	a			23 10	23 13	23 20												00 26				

A until 14 September
B from 17 September until 5 October
C 🍴 to Bournemouth

Table 158

Mondays to Fridays

until 5 October

London - Basingstoke, Southampton, Romsey Lymington, Bournemouth and Weymouth

Network Diagram - see first Page of Table 158

		SW	XC	SW	SW	SW	SW	SW	SW	SW	SW	SW
		1	◇1	1	◇1 🛒	1	1	1	◇1	1	1	1
London Waterloo 15 ⊖	d			22 12	22 35		22 39	22 42	23 05	23 12	23 35	23 48
Clapham Junction 10	d			22u19			22u46	22u49	23u12	23u19	23u42	23u55
Woking	d			22 49	23 00			23 19	23 32	23 57	00 03	00 28
Farnborough (Main)	d			23 03			23 16	23 33		00 10	00 14	00 41
Fleet	d			23 08			23 21	23 38		00 16	00 20	00 47
Reading 7	d		22 48									
Basingstoke	a		23 06	23 27			23 33	23 57	23 53	00 33	00 33	01 06
	d		23 10				23 34		23 53		00 35	
Micheldever	d								00 03			
Winchester	d		23 25		23 33		23 51		00 14		00 51	
Shawford	d						23 55					
Romsey	d	23 07				22 58						
Chandlers Ford	d	23 14										
Eastleigh 3	a	23 22				23 34	00 01		00 22		00 59	
	d	23 22				23 36	00 02		00 23		01 00	
Hedge End	d											
Botley	d											
Fareham	d											
Portchester	d											
Cosham	d											
Hilsea	a											
Fratton	a											
Portsmouth & Southsea	a											
Portsmouth Harbour ⛴	a											
Southampton Airport Pkwy ✈	d	23 26	23 37		23 42		00 06		00 28		01 05	
Swaythling	d	23 28										
St Denys	d	23 31							00s32			
Southampton Central ⛴	a	23 36	23 43		23 49		00 13		00 37		01 12	
	d	23 38			23 51				00 38			
Millbrook (Hants)	d	23 40										
Redbridge	d	23 44										
Romsey	d	23 56				23a48						
Mottisfont & Dunbridge	d	00 01										
Dean	d	00 07										
Salisbury	a	00 19										
Totton	d								00s43			
Ashurst New Forest	d											
Beaulieu Road	d											
Brockenhurst 3	a				00 04				00s54			
	d				00 05							
Lymington Town	d											
Lymington Pier	a											
Sway	d											
New Milton	d								01s02			
Hinton Admiral	d											
Christchurch	d								01s09			
Pokesdown	d								01s13			
Bournemouth	a				00 21				01 17			
	d				00 22				01 18			
Branksome	d				00 27				01s23			
Parkstone (Dorset)	d				00 30				01s26			
Poole 4	a				00 35				01 30			
	d											
Hamworthy	d											
Holton Heath	d											
Wareham	d											
Wool	d											
Moreton (Dorset)	d											
Dorchester South	d											
Dorchester West	d											
Upwey	d											
Weymouth	a											

Table 158

Mondays to Fridays

from 8 October

London - Basingstoke, Southampton, Romsey Lymington, Bournemouth and Weymouth

Network Diagram - see first Page of Table 158

		SW MX	SW MO	SW MX	SW MO		SW MX	SW MO	SW MX	SW MX	SW MX	SW MO		SW MX	SW MO	SW MX	SW	SW MX	SW MX	SW MX	SW MO	SW	SW
		◇1 A 🛒	◇1 A 🛒	1	◇1		◇1 🛒	◇1	1	◇1 🛒	1	◇1 🛒		◇1	1	1	1	1	1	1	1	1	1
London Waterloo 15 ⊖	d	21p35	21p35	21p42	21p54		22p05			22p35	22p39	22p54		23p05	23p07	23p12		23p35	23p48	00 05	00 50	01 05	
Clapham Junction 10	d		21b42		22b03		22b12				22b46	23b03		23b12	23p15	23b19		23b42	23b55	00u12	00 57	01 15	
Woking	d	22p00	22p07	22p19	22p28		22p32			23p00		23p28		23p32	23p46	23p57		00 03	00 28	00 37	01 18	01 49	
Farnborough (Main)	d			22p33							23p16				23p59	00 10		00 14	00 41			01s58	
Fleet	d			22p38							23p21				00 04	00 16		00 20	00 47			02s04	
Reading 7	d																						
Basingstoke	a		22p26	22p58	22p46		22p51				23p33	23p46		23p53	00 21	00 33		00 33	01 06	00 55		02s16	
	d		22p28	23p00	22p48		22p52				23p34	23p48		23p53				00 35		00 56			
Micheldever	d			23p10	22p58							23p58		00 03									
Winchester	d	22p33	22p44	23p19	23p08		23p09			23p33	23p51	00 08		00 14				00 51		01 13		02s33	
Shawford	d			23p24							23p55												
Romsey	d								23p07														
Chandlers Ford	d								23p14														
Eastleigh 3	a			23p29	23p17		23p17		23p22		00 01	00 18		00 22				00 59		01 21		02s42	
	d			23p30	23p22	23p26	23p18		23p22		00 02	00 22	00 30	00 23			00 30	01 00		01 22			
Hedge End	d			23p36		23p32							00s36				00s36						
Botley	d			23p40		23p36							00s39				00s39						
Fareham	d			23p49		23p44							00s47				00s47						
Portchester	d			23p54		23p49							00s53				00s53						
Cosham	d			23p59		23p54							00s57				00s57						
Hilsea	a			00 03		23p59																	
Fratton	a			00 07		00 04							01s05				01s05				02s10		
Portsmouth & Southsea	a			00 11		00 08							01s08				01s08				02s14		
Portsmouth Harbour ⛴	a			00 16		00 13							01 12				01 12				02 19		
Southampton Airport Pkwy ✈	d	22p42	22p53		23p27		23p22		23p26	23p42	00 06	00 27		00 28				01 05		01 26		02s46	
Swaythling	d								23p28														
St Denys	d							←	23p31			00s31		00s32								02s51	
Southampton Central ⛴	a	22p49	23p00		23p34		23p29	23p34	23p36	23p49	00 13	00 36		00 37				01 12		01 35		02 56	
	d	22p51	23p03		23p35		23p31	23p35	23p38	23p51		00 37		00 38						01 37			
Millbrook (Hants)	d				→				23p40														
Redbridge	d								23p44														
Romsey	d								23p56														
Mottisfont & Dunbridge	d								00 01														
Dean	d								00 07														
Salisbury	a								00 19														
Totton	d						23p36	23p41				00s42		00s43						01s42			
Ashurst New Forest	d						23p41	23p45															
Beaulieu Road	d																						
Brockenhurst 3	a	23p04	23p16				23p49	23p53		00 04		00s53		00s54						01s53			
	d	23p05	23p17				23p50	23p54		00 05													05 59
Lymington Town	d																						06 07
Lymington Pier	a																						06 10
Sway	d						23p54	23p59															
New Milton	d		23p24				23p59	00 04				01s01		01s02						02s00			
Hinton Admiral	d						00 03	00 08															
Christchurch	d						00 08	00 13				01s08		01s09						02s07			
Pokesdown	d						00 11	00 16				01s12		01s13						02s11			
Bournemouth	a	23p25	23p34				00 15	00 20		00 21		01 16		01 17						02 15			
	d	23p29	23p39				00 17	00 22		00 22		01 17		01 18									
Branksome	d	23p35	23p44				00 22	00 27		00 27		01s22		01s23									
Parkstone (Dorset)	d	23p38	23p47				00 25	00 30		00 30		01s25		01s26									
Poole 4	a	23p41	23p50				00 29	00 34		00 35		01 29		01 30									
	d	23p42	23p51																				
Hamworthy	d	23p47	23p56																				
Holton Heath	d																						
Wareham	d	23p54	00 03																				
Wool	d	00 01	00 10																				
Moreton (Dorset)	d	00 07	00 17																				
Dorchester South	d	00 15	00 25																				
Dorchester West	d																						
Upwey	d	00 21	00 32																				
Weymouth	a	00 26	00 36																				

A 🛒 to Bournemouth

b Previous night, stops to pick up only

London - Basingstoke, Southampton, Romsey Lymington, Bournemouth and Weymouth

Network Diagram - see first Page of Table 158

		SW	SW	SW	SW	SW		SW	GW	SW	GW	SW	GW	SW	SW	SW		SW	SW	SW	SW	GW	SW	SW	SW
		1	1	1	1	1		1	1 🍴	1		1		◇1	1	1		1	1	1	1	◇ 🍴	1	1	1
London Waterloo 15 ⊖	d													05 30											06 12
Clapham Junction 10	d													05u37											06u19
Woking	d													06 01									06 19		06 50
Farnborough (Main)	d																						06 33		07 04
Fleet	d																						06 38		07 09
Reading 7	d																								
Basingstoke	a													06 20									06 58		07 28
	d					05 40								06 21							06 55		07 00		07 30
Micheldever	d					05 50																	07 10		07 41
Winchester	d					05 59				06 18				06 38							07 11		07 19		07 50
Shawford	d									06 23											07 16				07 55
Romsey	d							05 58			06 38									07 07					
Chandlers Ford	d							06 06												07 14					
Eastleigh 3	a					06 07		06 11		06 28				06 47						07 20	07 22		07 27		08 00
	d	06 00				06 08		06 13		06 29				06 48	06 50	07 02				07 21	07 24		07 28		08 02
Hedge End	d	06 06								06 35						07 08							07 34		
Botley	d	06 10								06 39						07 12							07 38		
Fareham	d	06 19							06 24	06 50	07 15					07 20						07 29	07 48		
Portchester	d	06 24								06 55						07 25							07 53		
Cosham	d	06 29								07 00	07 23					07 29							07 58		
Hilsea	a	06 33								07 05						07 35							08 03		
Fratton	a	06 40								07 09	07 34					07 39							08 07		
Portsmouth & Southsea	a	06 44								07 12	07 38					07 42							08 11		
Portsmouth Harbour ⛴	a	06 49								07 17	07 45					07 48							08 16		
Southampton Airport Pkwy ✈	d					06 13		06 17						06 53						07 25	07 29				08 06
Swaythling	d					06 15		06 20												07 27	07 31				08 09
St Denys	d					06 18		06 24												07 30	07 34				08 12
Southampton Central ⛴	a					06 23		06 29	06 45					07 00						07 35	07 39	07 50			08 17
	d					06 25		06 30	06 46					07 01					07 19	07 37		07 52			08 19
Millbrook (Hants)	d							06 33											07 21	07 40					→
Redbridge	d							06 36											07 25	07 43					
Romsey	d							06 44	07 00						07a03					07 51		08 11			
Mottisfont & Dunbridge	d							06 49												07 56					
Dean	d							06 55												08 02					
Salisbury	a							07 07	07 18											08 15		08 29			
Totton	d					06 30								07 07					07 28						
Ashurst New Forest	d					06 35													07 32						
Beaulieu Road	d																		07 37						
Brockenhurst 3	a					06 43								07 17					07 43						
	d			06 16	06 29	06 44						06 59		07 18				07 29	07 44					07 59	
Lymington Town	d				06 37							07 07						07 37						08 07	
Lymington Pier	a				06 40							07 10						07 40						08 10	
Sway	d			06 20		06 48								07 23					07 48						
New Milton	d			06 25		06 53								07 28					07 53						
Hinton Admiral	d			06 29		06 57								07 32					07 57						
Christchurch	d			06 34		07 02								07 37					08 02						
Pokesdown	d			06 38		07 06								07 40					08 06						
Bournemouth	a			06 42		07 10								07 44					08 10						
	d		06 11	06 44		07 11								07 46					08 11						
Branksome	d		06 16	06 49		07 16								07 51					08 16						
Parkstone (Dorset)	d		06 19	06 52		07 19								07 54					08 19						
Poole 4	a		06 23	06 55		07 23								07 57					08 23						
	d		06 24	06 57		07 24								07 58					08 24						
Hamworthy	d		06 29	07 02		07 29								08 03					08 29						
Holton Heath	d		06 33	07 06		07 33								08 07					08 33						
Wareham	d		06 38	07 11		07 38								08 12					08 38						
Wool	d		06 44	07 17		07 44								08 19					08 44						
Moreton (Dorset)	d		06 50	07 23		07 50								08 25					08 50						
Dorchester South	d		06 58	07 31		07 58								08 33					08 58						
Dorchester West	d												08 09												
Upwey	d		07 05	07 38		08 05							08 17	08 40					09 05						
Weymouth	a		07 14	07 42		08 14							08 24	08 44					09 09						

London - Basingstoke, Southampton, Romsey Lymington, Bournemouth and Weymouth

Network Diagram - see first Page of Table 158

		SW		SW	GW	GW	SW	SW	GW	SW	SW	XC		SW	SW	SW	SW	GW	GW	SW	GW	SW		XC	SW
		◇1		1	◇		1	1	◇	1	1	◇1		1	1	◇1	1	◇	◇	1	◇	1		◇1	1
																A									
												🍴				🍴		🍴	🍴			🍴			
London Waterloo 15 ⊖	d	06 30									06 42			07 12		07 35						07 39			07 42
Clapham Junction 10	d	06u37									06u49			07u20								07u46			
Woking	d	06 57									07 19			07 50		08 00									08 19
Farnborough (Main)	d										07 33			08 03								08 13			08 33
Fleet	d										07 38			08 09								08 19			08 38
Reading 7	d											07 46												08 15	
Basingstoke	a	07 16									07 56	08 08		08 26		08 19						08 32		08 40	08 58
	d	07 18									08 00	08 10				08 20						08 33		08 42	
Micheldever	d										08 10														
Winchester	d	07 34									08 19	08 25				08 37						08 50		08 57	
Shawford	d										08 24											08 54			
Romsey	d			07 13	07 30	07 56				08 07							08 13		08 50						
Chandlers Ford	d									08 14															
Eastleigh 3	a	07 43		07 49						08 20	08 30					08 47	08 49					09 00			
	d	07 44		07 50						08 21	08 31					08 48	08 50					09 01			
Hedge End	d										08 37														
Botley	d										08 42														
Fareham	d				08 06						08 51							08 47	09 27						
Portchester	d										08 56														
Cosham	d				08 14						09 01								09 35						
Hilsea	a										09 05														
Fratton	a				08 20						09 09								09 42						
Portsmouth & Southsea	a				08 24						09 13								09 46						
Portsmouth Harbour ⛴	a				08 30						09 18								09 55						
Southampton Airport Pkwy ✈	d	07 49								08 25		08 33				08 52						09 05		09 09	
Swaythling	d									08 27															
St Denys	d							←		08 30															
Southampton Central ⛴	a	07 57				08 09		08 17		08 35		08 44				08 59		09 08				09 15		09 17	
	d	08 00						08 19	08 23	08 37		08 46				09 01		09 10				09 30			
Millbrook (Hants)	d							08 21		08 40												→			
Redbridge	d							08 25		08 43															
Romsey	d			08a03					08 35	08 51							09a03	09 21							
Mottisfont & Dunbridge	d									08 56															
Dean	d									09 02															
Salisbury	a								09 00	09 15								09 39							
Totton	d	08 05						08 28								09 06									
Ashurst New Forest	d							08 32																	
Beaulieu Road	d							08 37																	
Brockenhurst 3	a	08 16						08 43				08 59				09 17									
	d	08 17					08 29	08 44				09 00			08 59	09 18				09 29					
Lymington Town	d						08 37								09 07					09 37					
Lymington Pier	a						08 40								09 10					09 40					
Sway	d	08 21						08 48								09 22									
New Milton	d	08 26						08 53								09 27									
Hinton Admiral	d	08 30						08 57								09 31									
Christchurch	d	08 35						09 02								09 36									
Pokesdown	d	08 39						09 06								09 40									
Bournemouth	a	08 43						09 10				09 14				09 44									
	d	08 44						09 11								09 45									
Branksome	d	08 49						09 16								09 50									
Parkstone (Dorset)	d	08 52						09 19								09 53									
Poole 4	a	08 56						09 23								09 57									
	d	08 57						09 24								09 58									
Hamworthy	d	09 02						09 29								10 03									
Holton Heath	d							09 33																	
Wareham	d	09 09						09 38								10 10									
Wool	d	09 15						09 44																	
Moreton (Dorset)	d	09 21						09 50																	
Dorchester South	d	09 29						09 58								10 26									
Dorchester West	d																				10 48				
Upwey	d	09 36						10 05													10 55				
Weymouth	a	09 40						10 09								10 34					11 03				

A 🍴 to Bournemouth

from 8 October

London - Basingstoke, Southampton, Romsey Lymington, Bournemouth and Weymouth

Network Diagram - see first Page of Table 158

		SW	SW	SW	SW	XC	SW	SW	SW	SW	GW	SW	SW	SW	SW	SW	GW	GW	SW	SW	SW	SW	XC
		◇[1] A 🚌	[1] 🚌	[1]	[1]	◇[1] 🚌	[1]	◇[1] A 🚌	[1] 🚌	[1]	◇ 🚌	[1]	[1]	[1]	◇[1] A 🚌	[1]	◇ B 🚌	■ 🚌	[1]	[1]	[1]	[1]	◇[1] 🚌
London Waterloo [15] ⊖	d	08 05			08 09		08 12	08 35					08 39	08 42	09 05					09 09			
Clapham Junction [10]	d	08u12					08u19						08u46		09u12								
Woking	d				08 35		08 49	09 00						09 19						09 35			
Farnborough (Main)	d				08 45		09 03						09 13	09 33						09 45			
Fleet	d						09 08						09 19	09 38									
Reading [7]	d					08 46																	09 46
Basingstoke	a	08 47			08 58	09 08	09 28						09 31	09 58	09 47					09 58			10 08
	d	08 49			09 00	09 09							09 33		09 49					10 00			10 10
Micheldever	d				09 10															10 10			
Winchester	d	09 05			09 19	09 24		09 33					09 49		10 05					10 19			10 25
Shawford	d												09 54										
Romsey	d			09 07						09 19								09 50	10 07		10 19		
Chandlers Ford	d			09 14															10 14				
Eastleigh [3]	a			09 20	09 27					09 50			10 02						10 20	10 27	10 49		
	d			09 21	09 28					09 51			10 03						10 21	10 28	10 50		
Hedge End	d				09 34															10 34			
Botley	d				09 38															10 38			
Fareham	d				09 48						09 47						10 15	10 27		10 48			
Portchester	d				09 53															10 53			
Cosham	d				09 58													10 35		10 58			
Hilsea	a				10 03															11 03			
Fratton	a				10 07													10 42		11 07			
Portsmouth & Southsea	a				10 11													10 46		11 11			
Portsmouth Harbour ⛴	a				10 18													10 54		11 18			
Southampton Airport Pkwy ✈	d	09 14		09 25		09 33		09 42					10 08		10 14				10 25				10 33
Swaythling	d			09 27															10 27				
St Denys	d		←	09 30												←			10 30				
Southampton Central ⛴	a	09 22	09 15	09 35		09 41		09 49			10 08		10 18		10 22	10 18	10 40		10 35				10 43
	d	09 24	09 30	09 37		09 43		09 51			10 10		10 30		10 24	10 30	10 42		10 44				10 45
Millbrook (Hants)	d			09 40									→						10 48				
Redbridge	d			09 43															10 51				
Romsey	d			09 51						10a03	10 21						10 54		10 59		11a03		
Mottisfont & Dunbridge	d			09 56															11 04				
Dean	d			10 02															11 10				
Salisbury	a			10 15							10 39						11 13		11 22				
Totton	d		09 35													10 35							
Ashurst New Forest	d		09 40													10 40							
Beaulieu Road	d								←							10 44							
Brockenhurst [3]	a	09 37	09 49			09 56		10 04	09 49						10 37	10 51							10 58
	d	09 38	10 16			09 57		10 05	10 16			10 12			10 38	11 16						10 42	10 59
Lymington Town	d		→									10 20				→						10 50	
Lymington Pier	a											10 23										10 53	
Sway	d								10 20														
New Milton	d	09 45							10 25						10 45								
Hinton Admiral	d								10 29														
Christchurch	d	09 52							10 34						10 52								
Pokesdown	d	09 56							10 38						10 56								
Bournemouth	a	10 00				10 12		10 20	10 42						11 00								11 12
	d	10 04						10 24	10 43						11 04								
Branksome	d							10 29	10 48														
Parkstone (Dorset)	d							10 32	10 51														
Poole [4]	a	10 13						10 36	10 55						11 13								
	d	10 14						10 37							11 14								
Hamworthy	d	10 19						10 42							11 19								
Holton Heath	d	10 23													11 23								
Wareham	d	10 28						10 49							11 28								
Wool	d	10 35													11 35								
Moreton (Dorset)	d	10 41													11 41								
Dorchester South	d	10 54						11 05							11 49								
Dorchester West	d																						
Upwey	d	11 01													11 55								
Weymouth	a	11 06						11 13							12 00								

A 🚌 to Bournemouth

B 🚌 to Southampton Central

from 8 October

London - Basingstoke, Southampton, Romsey Lymington, Bournemouth and Weymouth

Network Diagram - see first Page of Table 158

		SW	GW	SW	SW	GW	GW	SW	SW	XC	SW	SW	SW	SW	SW	SW	SW	XC	SW	SW	SW	GW
		[1]	◇	◇[1] A 🚌	[1]	◇ 🚌	◇ 🚌	[1]	[1]	◇[1] 🚌	[1]	◇[1] A 🚌	[1]	[1]	[1]	[1]	[1]	◇[1] 🚌	[1]	◇[1] A 🚌	[1]	◇ 🚌
London Waterloo [15] ⊖	d	09 12		09 35					09 39		09 42	10 05			10 09				10 12	10 35		
Clapham Junction [10]	d	09u19							09u46			10u12							10u19			
Woking	d	09 49		10 00							10 19				10 35				10 49	11 00		
Farnborough (Main)	d	10 03							10 13		10 33				10 45				11 03			
Fleet	d	10 08							10 19		10 38								11 08			
Reading [7]	d									10 15								10 46				
Basingstoke	a	10 28							10 31	10 39	10 58	10 47			10 58			11 08	11 28			
	d								10 33	10 40		10 49			11 00			11 10				
Micheldever	d														11 10							
Winchester	d			10 33					10 49	10 55		11 05			11 19			11 25		11 33		
Shawford	d								10 54													
Romsey	d						10 50							11 07		11 20						
Chandlers Ford	d													11 14								
Eastleigh [3]	a								10 59					11 20	11 27	11 49						
	d								11 00					11 21	11 28	11 50						
Hedge End	d														11 34							
Botley	d														11 38							
Fareham	d					10 47	11 27								11 48							11 47
Portchester	d														11 53							
Cosham	d						11 35								11 58							
Hilsea	a														12 03							
Fratton	a						11 42								12 07							
Portsmouth & Southsea	a						11 46								12 11							
Portsmouth Harbour ⛴	a						11 54								12 18							
Southampton Airport Pkwy ✈	d			10 42					11 05	11 09		11 14		11 25				11 33		11 42		
Swaythling	d													11 27								
St Denys	d												←	11 30								
Southampton Central ⛴	a			10 49		11 08			11 12	11 16		11 22	11 12	11 35				11 43		11 49		12 08
	d			10 51		11 10			11 30			11 24	11 30	11 37				11 45		11 51		12 10
Millbrook (Hants)	d								→					11 40								
Redbridge	d													11 43								
Romsey	d					11 21								11 51		12a03						12 21
Mottisfont & Dunbridge	d													11 56								
Dean	d													12 02								
Salisbury	a					11 39								12 15								12 39
Totton	d												11 35									
Ashurst New Forest	d												11 40									
Beaulieu Road	d				←								11 44								←	
Brockenhurst [3]	a			11 04	10 51							11 37	11 51					11 58		12 04	11 51	
	d			11 05	11 16			11 12				11 38	12 16				11 42	11 59		12 05	12 16	
Lymington Town	d							11 20					→				11 50					
Lymington Pier	a							11 23									11 53					
Sway	d				11 20																12 20	
New Milton	d				11 25							11 45									12 25	
Hinton Admiral	d				11 29																12 29	
Christchurch	d				11 34							11 52									12 34	
Pokesdown	d				11 38							11 56									12 38	
Bournemouth	a			11 20	11 42							12 00						12 12		12 20	12 42	
	d			11 24	11 43							12 04								12 24	12 43	
Branksome	d			11 29	11 48															12 29	12 48	
Parkstone (Dorset)	d			11 32	11 51															12 32	12 51	
Poole [4]	a			11 36	11 55							12 13								12 36	12 55	
	d			11 37								12 14								12 37		
Hamworthy	d			11 42								12 19								12 42		
Holton Heath	d											12 23										
Wareham	d			11 49								12 28								12 49		
Wool	d											12 35										
Moreton (Dorset)	d											12 41										
Dorchester South	d			12 05								12 49								13 05		
Dorchester West	d		11 54																			
Upwey	d		12 02									12 55										
Weymouth	a		12 09	12 13								13 00								13 13		

A 🚌 to Bournemouth

Table 158

Mondays to Fridays
from 8 October

London - Basingstoke, Southampton, Romsey Lymington, Bournemouth and Weymouth

Network Diagram - see first Page of Table 158

		GW ◇ ✠	GW	SW 1	SW 1	SW 1	SW ◇1 A ✠	SW 1	GW ◇	SW 1		SW 1	SW 1	SW 1	XC ◇1 ✠	SW 1	GW ◇	SW ◇1 A ✠	SW 1	GW ◇ ✠		GW ◇ ✠	SW 1	SW 1	XC ◇1 ✠
London Waterloo 15 ⊖	d				10 39	10 42	11 05					11 09				11 12		11 35						11 39	
Clapham Junction 10	d				10u46		11u12									11u19								11u46	
Woking	d					11 19						11 35				11 49		12 00							
Farnborough (Main)	d				11 13	11 33						11 45				12 03								12 13	
Fleet	d				11 19	11 38										12 08								12 19	
Reading 7	d														11 46										12 15
Basingstoke	a				11 31	11 58	11 47					11 58			12 08	12 28								12 31	12 39
	d				11 33		11 49					12 00			12 10									12 33	12 40
Micheldever	d											12 10													
Winchester	d				11 49		12 05					12 19			12 25			12 33						12 49	12 55
Shawford	d				11 54																			12 54	
Romsey	d	11 50	12 10							12 07			12 19									12 50			
Chandlers Ford	d									12 14															
Eastleigh 5	a				11 59					12 20		12 27	12 49											12 59	
	d				12 00					12 21		12 28	12 50											13 00	
Hedge End	d											12 34													
Botley	d											12 38													
Fareham	d	12 27										12 48								12 47		13 27			
Portchester	d											12 53													
Cosham	d	12 35										12 58										13 35			
Hilsea	a											13 03													
Fratton	a	12 42										13 07										13 42			
Portsmouth & Southsea	a	12 46										13 11										13 46			
Portsmouth Harbour ⛴	a	12 54										13 18										13 54			
Southampton Airport Pkwy ✈	d				12 05		12 14			12 25					12 33			12 42						13 05	13 09
Swaythling	d									12 27															
St Denys	d							←		12 30															
Southampton Central ⛴	a		12 22		12 15		12 22	12 15		12 35					12 41			12 49		13 08				13 15	13 17
	d				12 30		12 24	12 30	12 27	12 37					12 43			12 51		13 10				13 30	
Millbrook (Hants)	d				→					12 40														→	
Redbridge	d									12 43															
Romsey	d								12 39	12 51			13a03							13 21					
Mottisfont & Dunbridge	d									12 56															
Dean	d									13 02															
Salisbury	a								13 02	13 15										13 39					
Totton	d							12 35																	
Ashurst New Forest	d							12 40																	
Beaulieu Road	d																		←						
Brockenhurst 3	a						12 37	12 51							12 56			13 04	12 51						
	d			12 12			12 38	13 16						12 42	12 57			13 05	13 16				13 12		
Lymington Town	d			12 20				→						12 50									13 20		
Lymington Pier	a			12 23										12 53									13 23		
Sway	d																		13 20						
New Milton	d						12 45												13 25						
Hinton Admiral	d																		13 29						
Christchurch	d						12 52												13 34						
Pokesdown	d						12 56												13 38						
Bournemouth	a						13 00								13 10			13 20	13 42						
	d						13 04											13 24	13 43						
Branksome	d																	13 29	13 48						
Parkstone (Dorset)	d																	13 32	13 51						
Poole 4	a						13 13											13 36	13 55						
	d						13 14											13 37							
Hamworthy	d						13 19											13 42							
Holton Heath	d						13 23																		
Wareham	d						13 28											13 49							
Wool	d						13 35																		
Moreton (Dorset)	d						13 41																		
Dorchester South	d						13 49											14 05							
Dorchester West	d																13 54								
Upwey	d						13 55										14 02								
Weymouth	a						14 00										14 09	14 13							

A ✠ to Bournemouth

Table 158

Mondays to Fridays
from 8 October

London - Basingstoke, Southampton, Romsey Lymington, Bournemouth and Weymouth

Network Diagram - see first Page of Table 158

		SW 1	SW ◇1 A ✠	SW 1	SW 1	SW 1		SW 1	SW 1	XC ◇1 ✠	SW 1	SW ◇1 A ✠	SW 1	GW ◇ ✠	GW ◇ ✠	SW 1		SW 1	SW 1	SW ◇1 A ✠	SW 1	GW ■ ✠	SW 1	SW 1	SW 1
London Waterloo 15 ⊖	d	11 42	12 05			12 09					12 12	12 35						12 39	12 42	13 05				13 09	
Clapham Junction 10	d		12u12								12u19							12u46		13u12					
Woking	d	12 19				12 35					12 49	13 00							13 19					13 35	
Farnborough (Main)	d	12 33				12 45					13 03							13 13	13 33					13 45	
Fleet	d	12 38									13 08							13 19	13 38						
Reading 7	d									12 46															
Basingstoke	a	12 58	12 47			12 58				13 08	13 28							13 31	13 58	13 47				13 58	
	d		12 49			13 00				13 10								13 33		13 49				14 00	
Micheldever	d					13 10																		14 10	
Winchester	d		13 05			13 19				13 25		13 33						13 49		14 05				14 19	
Shawford	d																	13 54							
Romsey	d				13 07			13 19							13 50							14 19	14 07		
Chandlers Ford	d				13 14																		14 14		
Eastleigh 5	a				13 20	13 27		13 49										13 59					14 20	14 27	
	d				13 21	13 28		13 50										14 00					14 21	14 28	
Hedge End	d					13 34																		14 34	
Botley	d					13 38																		14 38	
Fareham	d					13 48								13 47	14 27									14 48	
Portchester	d					13 53																		14 53	
Cosham	d					13 58									14 35									14 58	
Hilsea	a					14 03																		15 03	
Fratton	a					14 07									14 42									15 07	
Portsmouth & Southsea	a					14 11									14 46									15 11	
Portsmouth Harbour ⛴	a					14 18									14 54									15 18	
Southampton Airport Pkwy ✈	d		13 14		13 25					13 33		13 42						14 05		14 14			14 25		
Swaythling	d				13 27																		14 27		
St Denys	d			←	13 30																←		14 30		
Southampton Central ⛴	a		13 22	13 15	13 35					13 41		13 49		14 08				14 12		14 22	14 12	14 32	14 35		
	d		13 24	13 30	13 37					13 43		13 51		14 10				14 30		14 24	14 30		14 37		
Millbrook (Hants)	d				13 40													→					14 40		
Redbridge	d				13 43																		14 43		
Romsey	d				13 51			14a03						14 21									14 51		
Mottisfont & Dunbridge	d				13 56																		14 56		
Dean	d				14 02																		15 02		
Salisbury	a				14 15									14 39									15 15		
Totton	d			13 35																	14 35				
Ashurst New Forest	d			13 40																	14 40				
Beaulieu Road	d												←												
Brockenhurst 3	a		13 37	13 51						13 56		14 04	13 51							14 37	14 51				
	d		13 38	14 16					13 42	13 57		14 05	14 16			14 12				14 38	15 16				14 42
Lymington Town	d			→					13 50							14 20					→				14 50
Lymington Pier	a								13 53							14 23									14 53
Sway	d												14 20												
New Milton	d		13 45										14 25							14 45					
Hinton Admiral	d												14 29												
Christchurch	d		13 52										14 34							14 52					
Pokesdown	d		13 56										14 38							14 56					
Bournemouth	a		14 00							14 10		14 20	14 42							15 00					
	d		14 04									14 24	14 43							15 04					
Branksome	d											14 29	14 48												
Parkstone (Dorset)	d											14 32	14 51												
Poole 4	a		14 13									14 36	14 55							15 13					
	d		14 14									14 37								15 14					
Hamworthy	d		14 19									14 42								15 19					
Holton Heath	d		14 23																	15 23					
Wareham	d		14 28									14 49								15 28					
Wool	d		14 35																	15 35					
Moreton (Dorset)	d		14 41																	15 41					
Dorchester South	d		14 49									15 05								15 49					
Dorchester West	d																								
Upwey	d		14 55																	15 55					
Weymouth	a		15 00									15 13								16 00					

A ✠ to Bournemouth

Table 158

Mondays to Fridays
from 8 October

London - Basingstoke, Southampton, Romsey Lymington, Bournemouth and Weymouth

Network Diagram - see first Page of Table 158

		XC	SW	SW	SW	GW	SN	SW	GW	SW	SW	XC	SW	SW	SW	SW	SW	SW	SW	XC	SW	GW
		◇1 ⚒	1	◇1 A ⚒	1	■ ⚒	1	1	◇ ⚒	1	1	◇1 ⚒	1	◇1 A ⚒	1	1	1	1	1	◇1 ⚒	1	◇
London Waterloo 15 ⊖	d		13 12	13 35							13 39		13 42	14 05			14 09				14 12	
Clapham Junction 10	d		13u19								13u46			14u12							14u19	
Woking	d		13 49	14 00									14 19				14 35				14 49	
Farnborough (Main)	d		14 03								14 13		14 33				14 45				15 03	
Fleet	d		14 08								14 19		14 38								15 08	
Reading 7	d	13 46										14 15								14 46		
Basingstoke	a	14 08	14 28								14 31	14 39	14 58	14 47			14 58			15 08	15 28	
	d	14 10									14 33	14 40		14 49			15 00			15 10		
Micheldever	d																15 10					
Winchester	d	14 25		14 33							14 49	14 55		15 05			15 19			15 25		
Shawford	d										14 54											
Romsey	d							14 13	14 50							15 07		15 19				
Chandlers Ford	d															15 14						
Eastleigh 8	a							14 49			14 59					15 20	15 27	15 49				
	d						14 41	14 50			15 00					15 21	15 28	15 50				
Hedge End	d																15 34					
Botley	d																15 38					
Fareham	d					14 47	14a59		15 27								15 48					
Portchester	d																15 53					
Cosham	d								15 35								15 58					
Hilsea	a																16 03					
Fratton	a								15 42								16 07					
Portsmouth & Southsea	a								15 46								16 11					
Portsmouth Harbour ⛴	a								15 54								16 18					
Southampton Airport Pkwy ✈	d	14 35		14 42							15 05	15 09		15 14		15 25				15 33		
Swaythling	d															15 27						
St Denys	d														←	15 30						
Southampton Central ⛴	a	14 42		14 49		15 08					15 12	15 17		15 22	15 12	15 35				15 41		
	d	14 43		14 51		15 10					15 30			15 24	15 30	15 37				15 43		
Millbrook (Hants)	d										→					15 40						
Redbridge	d															15 43						
Romsey	d					15 21		15a04								15 51		16a03				
Mottisfont & Dunbridge	d															15 56						
Dean	d															16 02						
Salisbury	a					15 39										16 15						
Totton	d														15 35							
Ashurst New Forest	d														15 40							
Beaulieu Road	d				←																	
Brockenhurst 8	a	14 56		15 04	14 51									15 37	15 51					15 56		
	d	14 57		15 05	15 16					15 12				15 38	16 28				15 42	15 57		
Lymington Town	d									15 20					→				15 50			
Lymington Pier	a									15 23									15 53			
Sway	d				15 20																	
New Milton	d				15 25									15 45								
Hinton Admiral	d				15 29																	
Christchurch	d				15 34									15 52								
Pokesdown	d				15 38									15 56								
Bournemouth	a	15 11		15 20	15 42									16 00						16 10		
	d			15 24	15 43									16 04								
Branksome	d			15 29	15 48																	
Parkstone (Dorset)	d			15 32	15 51																	
Poole 4	a			15 36	15 55									16 13								
	d			15 37										16 14								
Hamworthy	d			15 42										16 19								
Holton Heath	d													16 23								
Wareham	d			15 49										16 28								
Wool	d													16 35								
Moreton (Dorset)	d													16 41								
Dorchester South	d			16 05										16 49								
Dorchester West	d																					16 58
Upwey	d													16 55								17 05
Weymouth	a			16 13										17 00								17 10

A ⚒ to Bournemouth

Table 158

Mondays to Fridays
from 8 October

London - Basingstoke, Southampton, Romsey Lymington, Bournemouth and Weymouth

Network Diagram - see first Page of Table 158

		SW	SW	GW	GW	SW	SW	SW	SW	SW	SW	SW	SW	XC	SW	SW	SW	SW	SW	SW		SW	GW
		◇1 A ⚒	1	■ ⚒	◇ ⚒	1	1	1	◇1 A ⚒	1	1	1	1	◇1 ⚒	1	1	1	1	1	◇1 A ⚒		1	■ ⚒
London Waterloo 15 ⊖	d	14 35					14 39	14 42	15 05				15 09					15 12		15 35			
Clapham Junction 10	d						14u46		15u12									15u19					
Woking	d	15 00						15 19					15 35					15 49		16 00			
Farnborough (Main)	d						15 13	15 33					15 45					16 03					
Fleet	d						15 19	15 38										16 08					
Reading 7	d													15 46									
Basingstoke	a						15 31	15 58	15 47				15 58	16 08				16 28					
	d						15 33		15 49				16 00	16 10			16 24						
Micheldever	d												16 10										
Winchester	d	15 33					15 49		16 05				16 19	16 25	16 38		16 45			16 33			
Shawford	d						15 54								16 43								
Romsey	d				15 50							16 07				16 19							
Chandlers Ford	d											16 14											
Eastleigh 8	a						15 59					16 20	16 27		16 48	16 49	16 53						
	d						16 00					16 21	16 28		16 49	16 50	16 54						
Hedge End	d												16 34				17 00						
Botley	d												16 38				17 04						
Fareham	d			15 47	16 27								16 48				17 12						16 47
Portchester	d												16 53				17 17						
Cosham	d				16 35								16 58				17 22						
Hilsea	a												17 03										
Fratton	a				16 42								17 07				17 31						
Portsmouth & Southsea	a				16 46								17 11				17 35						
Portsmouth Harbour ⛴	a				16 54								17 18				17 40						
Southampton Airport Pkwy ✈	d	15 42					16 05		16 14			16 25		16 33	16 54					16 42			
Swaythling	d											16 27			16 56								
St Denys	d										←	16 30			16 59							←	
Southampton Central ⛴	a	15 49		16 08			16 15		16 22		16 15	16 35		16 41	17 04					16 49		17 04	17 08
	d	15 51		16 10			16 30		16 24		16 30	16 37		16 43	17 06					16 54	16 56	17 06	17 10
Millbrook (Hants)	d						→					16 40			→								
Redbridge	d											16 43											
Romsey	d			16 21								16 51				17a03							17 21
Mottisfont & Dunbridge	d											16 56											
Dean	d											17 02											
Salisbury	a			16 39								17 15											17 39
Totton	d										16 35										17 01	17a11	
Ashurst New Forest	d										16 40										17 06		
Beaulieu Road	d		←								16 44												
Brockenhurst 8	a	16 04	15 51						16 37		16 51			16 56						17 07	17 14		
	d	16 05	16 28			16 12			16 38	16 42				16 57					17 12	17 08	17 16		
Lymington Town	d					16 20				16 50									17 20				
Lymington Pier	a					16 23				16 53									17 23				
Sway	d		16 32						16 43												17 20		
New Milton	d		16 37						16 48												17 25		
Hinton Admiral	d		16 41						16 52												17 29		
Christchurch	d		16 46						16 57												17 34		
Pokesdown	d		16 50						17 00												17 38		
Bournemouth	a	16 20	16 54						17 04					17 10						17 23	17 42		
	d	16 24	16 55						17 07											17 24	17 43		
Branksome	d	16 29	17 00																	17 29	17 48		
Parkstone (Dorset)	d	16 32	17 03																	17 32	17 51		
Poole 4	a	16 36	17 07						17 16											17 36	17 55		
	d	16 37							17 17											17 37			
Hamworthy	d	16 42							17 22											17 42			
Holton Heath	d								17 26														
Wareham	d	16 49							17 31											17 49			
Wool	d	16 55							17 37											17 55			
Moreton (Dorset)	d								17 43														
Dorchester South	d	17 06							17 51											18 06			
Dorchester West	d																						
Upwey	d								17 58														
Weymouth	a	17 15							18 02											18 15			

A ⚒ to Bournemouth

Table 158

Mondays to Fridays
from 8 October

London - Basingstoke, Southampton, Romsey Lymington, Bournemouth and Weymouth

Network Diagram - see first Page of Table 158

		GW ◇ 🍴	SW 1	XC ◇1 🍴	SW 1	SW ◇1 A 🍴	SN 1	SW 1	SW 1	SW 1	SW 1	XC ◇1 🍴	SW 1	SW 1	SW 1	GW ◇	SW 1	SW ◇1 A 🍴		GW ◇ 🍴	SW 1	SW 1
London Waterloo [15] ⊖	d		15 39		15 42	16 05					16 09				16 12			16 35			16 39	16 42
Clapham Junction [10]	d		15u46			16u12									16u19						16u46	
Woking	d				16 19						16 35				16 49			17u00				17 19
Farnborough (Main)	d		16 13		16 33						16 45				17 03						17 13	17 33
Fleet	d		16 19		16 38										17 08						17 19	17 38
Reading [7]	d			16 15								16 46										
Basingstoke	a		16 31	16 39	16 58	16 47					16 58	17 08			17 30						17 31	18 00
	d		16 33	16 40		16 49					17 00	17 10		17 24							17 33	
Micheldever	d										17 10			17 34								
Winchester	d		16 50	17 00		17 05					17 19	17 25		17 44				17 33			17 49	
Shawford	d		16 54											17 49							17 54	
Romsey	d	16 50								17 07			17 19									
Chandlers Ford	d									17 14												
Eastleigh [5]	a		17 00							17 20	17 27		17 49	17 54							17 59	
	d		17 01				17 16			17 21	17 28		17 50	17 55							18 01	
Hedge End	d										17 34										18 07	
Botley	d										17 39										18 11	
Fareham	d	17 27									17 48									17 47	18 23	
Portchester	d										17 53										18 28	
Cosham	d	17 35									17 58										18 33	
Hilsea	a										18 04											
Fratton	a	17 42									18 08										18 40	
Portsmouth & Southsea	a	17 46									18 12										18 43	
Portsmouth Harbour ⛴	a	17 54									18 20										18 51	
Southampton Airport Pkwy ✈	d		17 05			17 14	17 20			17 25		17 33		18 00				17 42				
Swaythling	d									17 27				18 02								
St Denys	d								←	17 30				18 05								
Southampton Central ⛴	a		17 13	17 17		17 22	17 28		17 13	17 35		17 41		18 10				17 49		18 08		
	d		17 30			17 24			17 30	17 37		17 43						17 53	17 56	18 10		
Millbrook (Hants)	d		→							17 40												
Redbridge	d									17 43												
Romsey	d									17 51			18a03							18 21		
Mottisfont & Dunbridge	d									17 56												
Dean	d									18 02												
Salisbury	a									18 15										18 39		
Totton	d								17 35										18 01			
Ashurst New Forest	d								17 40										18 06			
Beaulieu Road	d								17 44													
Brockenhurst [3]	a					17 37			17 51			17 56						18 07	18 14			
	d					17 38		17 42				17 57					18 12	18 08	18 16			
Lymington Town	d							17 50									18 20					
Lymington Pier	a							17 53									18 23					
Sway	d					17 43													18 20			
New Milton	d					17 48													18 25			
Hinton Admiral	d					17 52													18 29			
Christchurch	d					17 57													18 34			
Pokesdown	d					18 00													18 38			
Bournemouth	a					18 04						18 15						18 22	18 42			
	d					18 09												18 24				
Branksome	d																	18 29				
Parkstone (Dorset)	d																	18 32				
Poole [4]	a					18 18												18 36				
	d					18 19												18 37				
Hamworthy	d					18 24												18 42				
Holton Heath	d					18 28																
Wareham	d					18 33												18 49				
Wool	d					18 39												18 55				
Moreton (Dorset)	d					18 45																
Dorchester South	d					18 53												19 06				
Dorchester West	d															18 58						
Upwey	d					19 00										19 06						
Weymouth	a					19 06										19 14		19 17				

A 🍴 to Bournemouth

Table 158

Mondays to Fridays
from 8 October

London - Basingstoke, Southampton, Romsey Lymington, Bournemouth and Weymouth

Network Diagram - see first Page of Table 158

		SW ◇1 A 🍴		GW ◇ 🍴	SW 1	GW ◇ 🍴	SW 1	SW 1	SW 1	XC ◇1 🍴	SW 1	SW 1	GW ◇	SW ◇1 A 🍴		GW ◇ 🍴	SW 1	SW 1	SW 1	XC ◇1 🍴	SW 1	GW ▪ 🍴	SW 1
London Waterloo [15] ⊖	d	17 05					17 09				17 12	17 23		17 35			17 39	17 41	17 48		17 53		
Clapham Junction [10]	d																						
Woking	d						17 34				17 37	17 52					18 04		18 13		18 25		
Farnborough (Main)	d										17 51	18 08						18 19			18 39		
Fleet	d										17 56	18 13						18 24			18 44		
Reading [7]	d									17 46										18 15			
Basingstoke	a						17 52			18 08	18 16	18 32					18 22	18 45	18 31	18 47	19 03		
	d						17 54			18 10							18 24		18 33	18 48			
Micheldever	d						18 04										18 34						
Winchester	d	18 00					18 14			18 25				18 30			18 44		18 50	19 09			
Shawford	d						18 18										18 49						
Romsey	d			17 50	18 07			18 19														18 54	
Chandlers Ford	d				18 14																		
Eastleigh [5]	a				18 20		18 24	18 49									18 54		18 58	19 27			
	d				18 21		18 25	18 50									18 55		18 59				
Hedge End	d						18 31										19 01						
Botley	d						18 36										19 05						
Fareham	d			18 27		18 13	18 45									18 47	19 14					19 27	
Portchester	d						18 50										19 19						
Cosham	d			18 35			18 55										19 24					19 35	
Hilsea	a						19 05										19 28						
Fratton	a			18 48			19 09										19 32					19 42	
Portsmouth & Southsea	a			18 52			19 12										19 36					19 46	
Portsmouth Harbour ⛴	a			19 00			19 20										19 43					19 54	
Southampton Airport Pkwy ✈	d	18 09			18 25					18 33				18 39					19 03				
Swaythling	d				18 27														19 06				
St Denys	d				18 30														19 09				
Southampton Central ⛴	a	18 16			18 35	18 40				18 44				18 46		19 08			19 18				
	d	18 21	18 24		18 37	18 42				18 45				18 51	18 54	19 10							
Millbrook (Hants)	d				18 40																		
Redbridge	d				18 44																		
Romsey	d				19 00	18 54		19a04								19 21							
Mottisfont & Dunbridge	d				19 05																		
Dean	d				19 10																		
Salisbury	a				19 23	19 12										19 39							
Totton	d		18 29												18 59								
Ashurst New Forest	d		18 34												19 04								
Beaulieu Road	d																						
Brockenhurst [3]	a		18 42							18 58					19 12								
	d		18 43						18 48	18 59					19 13								19 18
Lymington Town	d								18 56														19 26
Lymington Pier	a								18 59														19 29
Sway	d		18 47												19 17								
New Milton	d		18 52												19 22								
Hinton Admiral	d		18 57												19 26								
Christchurch	d		19 01												19 31								
Pokesdown	d		19 05												19 35								
Bournemouth	a	18 48	19 09							19 13				19 20	19 39								
	d	18 50	19 10											19 21	19 40								
Branksome	d	18 55	19 15											19 26	19 45								
Parkstone (Dorset)	d	18 58	19 18											19 29	19 48								
Poole [4]	a	19 02	19 26											19 33	19 56								
	d	19 03												19 34									
Hamworthy	d	19 08												19 39									
Holton Heath	d	19 12																					
Wareham	d	19 17												19 46									
Wool	d	19 23																					
Moreton (Dorset)	d	19 29																					
Dorchester South	d	19 37												20 02									
Dorchester West	d												19 54										
Upwey	d	19 44											20 02										
Weymouth	a	19 50											20 10	20 15									

A 🍴 to Bournemouth

Mondays to Fridays
from 8 October

London - Basingstoke, Southampton, Romsey Lymington, Bournemouth and Weymouth

Network Diagram - see first Page of Table 158

		SW ◇■ A 🍴	SW ■	SW ■	SW ■	SW ■	SW ■	XC ◇■ 🍴	SW ■	SW ■	SW ■	SW ■	SW ◇■ A 🍴		GW ◇	GW ■ 🍴	SW ■	SW ■	SW ■	SW ◇■ A 🍴	SW ■	SW ■	SW ■
London Waterloo ⊖	d	18 05			18 09				18 12		18 23	18 32	18 35					18 39	18 41	19 05			19 09
Clapham Junction	d																	18u46		19u12			
Woking	d				18 35						18 54	19 20						19 06					19 35
Farnborough (Main)	d								18 48		19 10	19 31							19 20				19 45
Fleet	d								18 54		19 15	19 37							19 26				
Reading	d							18 46															
Basingstoke	a				18 53			19 08	19 16		19 34	19 59						19 28	19 47	19 47			19 58
	d				18 55			19 10		19 24								19 30		19 49			20 00
Micheldever	d				19 05													19 40					20 10
Winchester	d	19 00	19 05		19 14			19 25		19 40			19 30					19 49		20 05			20 19
Shawford	d		19 09		19 19					19 45								19 54					20 24
Romsey	d			19 07		19 19										19 50						20 07	
Chandlers Ford	d			19 14																		20 14	
Eastleigh	a		19 15	19 20	19 25	19 49				19 50								19 59				20 20	20 29
	d		19 16	19 21	19 29	19 50				19 51								20 00				20 21	20 30
Hedge End	d				19 35					19 57													20 36
Botley	d				19 38					20 01													20 40
Fareham	d				19 48					20a09					19 47	20 27							20 49
Portchester	d				19 53																		20 54
Cosham	d				19 58																		20 59
Hilsea	a				20 02																		21 03
Fratton	a				20 06											20 42							21 07
Portsmouth & Southsea	a				20 11											20 46							21 11
Portsmouth Harbour ⛴	a				20 20											20 54							21 16
Southampton Airport Pkwy ✈	d	19 09	19 20	19 25				19 33					19 39					20 05		20 14		20 25	
Swaythling	d		19 23	19 27																		20 27	
St Denys	d		19 26	19 30																	←	20 30	
Southampton Central ⛴	a	19 18	19 33	19 35				19 41					19 46		20 08			20 16		20 22	20 16	20 35	
	d	19 19		19 37				19 43					19 51	19 54	20 10			20 30		20 24	20 30	20 37	
Millbrook (Hants)	d			19 40														→				20 40	
Redbridge	d			19 43																		20 43	
Romsey	d			19 51		20a03									20 21							20 51	
Mottisfont & Dunbridge	d			19 56																		20 56	
Dean	d			20 02																		21 02	
Salisbury	a			20 15											20 39							21 15	
Totton	d	19 25												19 59							20 35		
Ashurst New Forest	d													20 04							20 40		
Beaulieu Road	d																				20 44		
Brockenhurst	a	19 35						19 56						20 12						20 37	20 51		
	d	19 36					19 48	19 57						20 13			20 18			20 38	21 16		
Lymington Town	d						19 56										20 26				→		
Lymington Pier	a						19 59										20 29						
Sway	d	19 41												20 17									
New Milton	d	19 46												20 22						20 45			
Hinton Admiral	d	19 50												20 26									
Christchurch	d	19 55												20 31						20 52			
Pokesdown	d	19 58												20 35						20 56			
Bournemouth	a	20 02						20 12					20 20	20 39						21 00			
	d	20 07											20 21	20 40						21 04			
Branksome	d	20 12											20 26	20 45									
Parkstone (Dorset)	d	20 15											20 29	20 48									
Poole	a	20 18											20 33	20 56						21 13			
	d	20 19											20 34							21 15			
Hamworthy	d	20 24											20 39							21 20			
Holton Heath	d	20 28																					
Wareham	d	20 33											20 46							21 27			
Wool	d	20 40																		21 33			
Moreton (Dorset)	d	20 46																		21 39			
Dorchester South	d	20 54											21 02							21 47			
Dorchester West	d																						
Upwey	d	21 00																		21 54			
Weymouth	a	21 07											21 13							21 58			

A 🍴 to Bournemouth

Table 158

Mondays to Fridays
from 8 October

London - Basingstoke, Southampton, Romsey Lymington, Bournemouth and Weymouth

Network Diagram - see first Page of Table 158

		SW ■	SW ■	XC ◇■ 🍴	SW ■	GW ◇	SW ◇■ A 🍴	SW ■	GW ◇	SW ■	SW ■	GW ◇ 🍴	SW ■	GW	SW ◇■ 🍴	SW ■	SW ■	SW ■	SW ■	XC ◇■	SW ■	GW
London Waterloo ⊖	d				19 12		19 35			19 39	19 42				20 05		20 09				20 12	
Clapham Junction	d				19u19					19u46					20u12						20u19	
Woking	d				19 39		20 00				20 19						20 35				20 49	
Farnborough (Main)	d				19 53					20 13	20 33						20 45				21 03	
Fleet	d				19 58					20 19	20 38										21 08	
Reading	d			19 46																20 46		
Basingstoke	a			20 09	20 16					20 31	20 58				20 47		20 58			21 09	21 28	
	d			20 10						20 33					20 49		21 00			21 10		
Micheldever	d																21 10					
Winchester	d			20 25			20 33			20 49					21 05		21 19			21 25		
Shawford	d									20 54							21 24					
Romsey	d	20 19				20 35						20 50				21 07		21 19				
Chandlers Ford	d															21 14						
Eastleigh	a	20 49								20 59						21 20	21 30	21 49				
	d	20 50								21 00						21 21	21 30	21 50				
Hedge End	d																21 36					
Botley	d																21 40					
Fareham	d								20 47			21 27					21 48					
Portchester	d																21 53					
Cosham	d																21 58					
Hilsea	a																22 03					
Fratton	a											21 41					22 08					
Portsmouth & Southsea	a											21 45					22 11					
Portsmouth Harbour ⛴	a											21 52					22 16					
Southampton Airport Pkwy ✈	d			20 33			20 42			21 05					21 15	21 24				21 33		
Swaythling	d															21 27						
St Denys	d															21 30						
Southampton Central ⛴	a			20 41		20 48	20 49		21 08	21 12					21 24	21 35				21 41		
	d			20 43			20 51		21 10					21 20	21 25	21 37				21 43		
Millbrook (Hants)	d															21 40						
Redbridge	d															21 43						
Romsey	d	21a03							21 21					21 31		21 51		22a03				
Mottisfont & Dunbridge	d															21 56						
Dean	d															22 02						
Salisbury	a								21 39					21 51		22 15						
Totton	d						20 56								21 31							
Ashurst New Forest	d														21 35							
Beaulieu Road	d							←														
Brockenhurst	a			20 58			21 07	20 51							21 43					21 56		
	d		20 48	20 59			21 08	21 16					21 18		21 44				21 48	21 57		
Lymington Town	d		20 56										21 26						21 56			
Lymington Pier	a		20 59										21 29						21 59			
Sway	d							21 20							21 49							
New Milton	d							21 25							21 54							
Hinton Admiral	d							21 29							21 58							
Christchurch	d							21 34							22 03							
Pokesdown	d							21 38							22 06							
Bournemouth	a			21 15			21 22	21 42							22 10					22 16		
	d						21 27	21 43							22 12							
Branksome	d						21 32	21 48							22 17							
Parkstone (Dorset)	d						21 35	21 51							22 20							
Poole	a						21 38	21 57							22 23							
	d						21 39															
Hamworthy	d						21 44															
Holton Heath	d																					
Wareham	d						21 51															
Wool	d						21 58															
Moreton (Dorset)	d						22 04															
Dorchester South	d						22 12															
Dorchester West	d																					22 58
Upwey	d						22 18															23 06
Weymouth	a						22 23															23 13

A 🍴 to Bournemouth

London - Basingstoke, Southampton, Romsey Lymington, Bournemouth and Weymouth

Network Diagram - see first Page of Table 158

		SW ◇1 A ⌶	SW 1	SW 1	GW	SW 1	SW ◇1 ⌶	SW 1	XC ◇1	GW ◇	SW 1	SW 1	SW 1	SW ◇1 A ⌶	SW 1	GW ◇	SW 1	SW ◇1 ⌶	SW 1	XC ◇1	SW 1	SW ◇1 ⌶	SW 1
London Waterloo 15 ⊖	d	20 35	20 39	20 42			21 05						21 12	21 35	21 39		21 42	22 05			22 12	22 35	
Clapham Junction 10	d		20u46				21u12						21u19		21u46			22u12			22u19		
Woking	d	21 00		21 19			21 32						21 49	22 00			22 19	22 32			22 49	23 00	
Farnborough (Main)	d		21 13	21 33									22 03		22 13		22 33				23 03		
Fleet	d		21 19	21 38									22 08		22 19		22 38				23 08		
Reading 7	d								21 46											22 48			
Basingstoke	a		21 31	21 58			21 51		22 09				22 28		22 31		22 58	22 51		23 06	23 27		
	d		21 33				21 52		22 10			22 21			22 33		23 00	22 52		23 10			
Micheldever	d		21 43									22 31			22s43		23 10						
Winchester	d	21 33	21 52				22 09		22 25			22 40		22 33	22 52		23 19	23 09		23 25		23 33	
Shawford	d		21 57									22 45			22 57		23 24						
Romsey	d							22 07		21 50	22 19					22 53			23 07				22 58
Chandlers Ford	d							22 14											23 14				
Eastleigh 3	a		22 02				22 17	22 21		22 14	22 49	22 50			23 02		23 29	23 17	23 22				23 34
	d		22 03		22 11		22 18	22 22		22 24	22 50	22 51			23 03		23 30	23 18	23 22				23 36
Hedge End	d											22 57					23 36						
Botley	d									22 35		23 01					23 40						
Fareham	d									22 42		23 10				23 27	23 49						
Portchester	d											23 15					23 54						
Cosham	d											23 20					23 59						
Hilsea	a											23 24					00 03						
Fratton	a									22 56		23 32				23 44	00 07						
Portsmouth & Southsea	a									22 59		23 36				23 48	00 11						
Portsmouth Harbour ⛴	a									23 04		23 40				23 54	00 16						
Southampton Airport Pkwy ✈	d	21 42	22 08				22 22	22 26	22 33					22 42	23 08			23 22	23 26	23 37		23 42	
Swaythling	d							22 28											23 28				
St Denys	d							22 31											23 31				
Southampton Central ⛴	a	21 49	22 18		22 21		22 29	22 36	22 42					22 49	23 17			23 29	23 36	23 43		23 49	
	d	21 51			22 22		22 31	22 38	22 43					22 51				23 31	23 38			23 51	
Millbrook (Hants)	d							22 40											23 40				
Redbridge	d							22 44											23 44				
Romsey	d				22 34			22a52			23a03								23 56				23a48
Mottisfont & Dunbridge	d																		00 01				
Dean	d																		00 07				
Salisbury	a				22 58														00 19				
Totton	d						22 36											23 36					
Ashurst New Forest	d						22 41											23 41					
Beaulieu Road	d																						
Brockenhurst 3	a	22 04					22 49		22 56					23 04				23 49				00 04	
	d	22 05				22 18	22 50		22 59					23 05				23 50				00 05	
Lymington Town	d					22 26																	
Lymington Pier	a					22 29																	
Sway	d						22 54											23 54					
New Milton	d						22 59											23 59					
Hinton Admiral	d						23 03											00 03					
Christchurch	d						23 08											00 08					
Pokesdown	d						23 12											00 11					
Bournemouth	a	22 20					23 16		23 21					23 25				00 15				00 21	
	d	22 24					23 17							23 29				00 17				00 22	
Branksome	d	22 29					23 22							23 35				00 22				00 27	
Parkstone (Dorset)	d	22 32					23 25							23 38				00 25				00 30	
Poole 4	a	22 36					23 29							23 41				00 29				00 35	
	d	22 37												23 42									
Hamworthy	d	22 42												23 47									
Holton Heath	d																						
Wareham	d	22 49												23 54									
Wool	d	22 55												00 01									
Moreton (Dorset)	d	23 01												00 07									
Dorchester South	d	23 09												00 15									
Dorchester West	d																						
Upwey	d	23 16												00 21									
Weymouth	a	23 20												00 26									

A ⌶ to Bournemouth

London - Basingstoke, Southampton, Romsey Lymington, Bournemouth and Weymouth

Network Diagram - see first Page of Table 158

		SW 1	SW 1	SW ◇1	SW 1	SW 1	SW 1
London Waterloo 15 ⊖	d	22 39	22 42	23 05	23 12	23 35	23 48
Clapham Junction 10	d	22u46	22u49	23u12	23u19	23u42	23u55
Woking	d		23 19	23 32	23 57	00 03	00 28
Farnborough (Main)	d	23 16	23 33		00 10	00 14	00 41
Fleet	d	23 21	23 38		00 16	00 20	00 47
Reading 7	d						
Basingstoke	a	23 33	23 57	23 53	00 33	00 33	01 06
	d	23 34		23 53		00 35	
Micheldever	d			00 03			
Winchester	d	23 51		00 14		00 51	
Shawford	d	23 55					
Romsey	d						
Chandlers Ford	d						
Eastleigh 3	a	00 01		00 22		00 59	
	d	00 02		00 23		01 00	
Hedge End	d						
Botley	d						
Fareham	d						
Portchester	d						
Cosham	d						
Hilsea	a						
Fratton	a						
Portsmouth & Southsea	a						
Portsmouth Harbour ⛴	a						
Southampton Airport Pkwy ✈	d	00 06		00 28		01 05	
Swaythling	d						
St Denys	d			00s32			
Southampton Central ⛴	a	00 13		00 37		01 12	
	d			00 38			
Millbrook (Hants)	d						
Redbridge	d						
Romsey	d						
Mottisfont & Dunbridge	d						
Dean	d						
Salisbury	a						
Totton	d			00s43			
Ashurst New Forest	d						
Beaulieu Road	d						
Brockenhurst 3	a			00s54			
	d						
Lymington Town	d						
Lymington Pier	a						
Sway	d						
New Milton	d			01s02			
Hinton Admiral	d						
Christchurch	d			01s09			
Pokesdown	d			01s13			
Bournemouth	a			01 17			
	d			01 18			
Branksome	d			01s23			
Parkstone (Dorset)	d			01s26			
Poole 4	a			01 30			
	d						
Hamworthy	d						
Holton Heath	d						
Wareham	d						
Wool	d						
Moreton (Dorset)	d						
Dorchester South	d						
Dorchester West	d						
Upwey	d						
Weymouth	a						

Saturdays
until 6 October

London - Basingstoke, Southampton, Romsey Lymington, Bournemouth and Weymouth

Network Diagram - see first Page of Table 158

		SW	SW	SW	SW	SW	SW	SW	SW	SW	SW	SW	SW	SW	SW	SW	SW	SW	SW	SW	GW	SW	SW
		◇1	1	◇1	1	◇1	1	◇1	1	1	1	1	1	1	1	1	1	1	1	1	◇	1	1
		A 🍴		🍴		🍴							B	C									
London Waterloo 15 ⊖	d	21p35	21p42	22p05		22p35	22p39	23p05	23p12		23p35	23p48	00 05	00 30	01 05								
Clapham Junction 10	d			22b12			22b46	23b12	23b19		23b42	23b55	00u12	00u37	01 15								
Woking	d	22p00	22p19	22p32		23p00		23p32	23p57		00 03	00 28	00 37	01 00	01 42								
Farnborough (Main)	d		22p33				23p16		00 10		00 14	00 41			01s51								
Fleet	d		22p38				23p21		00 16		00 20	00 47			01s57								
Reading 7	d																						
Basingstoke	a		22p58	22p51			23p33	23p53	00 33		00 33	01 06	00 55	01 18	02s09								
	d		23p00	22p52			23p34	23p53			00 35		00 56	01 20									
Micheldever	d		23p10					00 03															
Winchester	d	22p33	23p19	23p09		23p33	23p51	00 14			00 51		01 13	01 36	02s26								
Shawford	d		23p24				23p55																
Romsey	d				23p07															05 58			
Chandlers Ford	d				23p14															06 06			
Eastleigh 8	a		23p29	23p17	23p22		00 01	00 22			00 59		01 21	01 44	02s35					06 11			
	d		23p30	23p18	23p22		00 02	00 23		00 30	01 00		01 22	01 45						06 13		06 28	
Hedge End	d		23p36							00s36												06 34	
Botley	d		23p40							00s39												06 38	
Fareham	d		23p49							00s47											06 28	06 48	
Portchester	d		23p54							00s53												06 53	
Cosham	d		23p59							00s57												06 58	
Hilsea	a		00 03																			07 03	
Fratton	a		00 07							01s05												07 07	
Portsmouth & Southsea	a		00 11							01s08												07 11	
Portsmouth Harbour ⛴	a		00 16							01 12												07 16	
Southampton Airport Pkwy ✈	d	22p42		23p22	23p26	23p42	00 06	00 28			01 05		01 26	01 50	02s39					06 17			
Swaythling	d				23p28															06 20			
St Denys	d				23p31			00s32							02s44					06 23			
Southampton Central ⛴	a	22p49		23p29	23p36	23p49	00 13	00 37			01 12		01 35	01 57	02 49					06 28	06 49		
	d	22p51		23p31	23p38	23p51		00 38					01 37	01 58					06 21	06 30	06 53		
Millbrook (Hants)	d				23p40															06 32			
Redbridge	d				23p44															06 36			
Romsey	d				23p56															06 44	07 11		
Mottisfont & Dunbridge	d				00 01															06 49			
Dean	d				00 07															06 54			
Salisbury	a				00 19															07 07	07 29		
Totton	d			23p36				00s43					01s42	02s03					06 26				
Ashurst New Forest	d			23p41															06 31				
Beaulieu Road	d																						
Brockenhurst 3	a	23p04		23p49		00 04		00s54					01s53	02s14					06 39				
	d	23p05		23p50		00 05											06 12	06 16	06 40				06 42
Lymington Town	d																06 20						06 50
Lymington Pier	a																06 22						06 52
Sway	d			23p54														06 20	06 44				
New Milton	d			23p59				01s02					02s00	02s22				06 25	06 49				
Hinton Admiral	d			00 03														06 29	06 53				
Christchurch	d			00 08				01s09					02s07	02s29				06 34	06 58				
Pokesdown	d			00 11				01s13					02s11	02s33				06 38	07 02				
Bournemouth	a	23p25		00 15		00 21		01 17					02 15	02 37				06 42	07 06				
	d	23p29		00 17		00 22		01 18								06 11		06 44	07 11				
Branksome	d	23p35		00 22		00 27		01s23								06 16		06 49	07 16				
Parkstone (Dorset)	d	23p38		00 25		00 30		01s26								06 19		06 52	07 19				
Poole 4	a	23p41		00 29		00 35		01 30								06 23		06 55	07 23				
	d	23p42														06 24		06 57	07 24				
Hamworthy	d	23p47														06 29		07 02	07 29				
Holton Heath	d															06 33		07 06	07 33				
Wareham	d	23p54														06 38		07 11	07 38				
Wool	d	00 01														06 44		07 17	07 44				
Moreton (Dorset)	d	00 07														06 50		07 23	07 50				
Dorchester South	d	00 15														06 58		07 31	07 58				
Dorchester West	d																						
Upwey	d	00 21														07 05		07 38	08 05				
Weymouth	a	00 26														07 09		07 42	08 09				

A 🍴 to Bournemouth

B until 21 July, 18 August, 25 August, 15 September, 22 September, 29 September, 6 October

C 28 July, 4 August, 11 August, 1 September, 8 September

b Previous night, stops to pick up only

Saturdays
until 6 October

London - Basingstoke, Southampton, Romsey Lymington, Bournemouth and Weymouth

Network Diagram - see first Page of Table 158

		GW	SW	SW	GW	SW	SW	SN	SW	SW	SW	SW	SW	SW	SW	GW	GW	GW	SW	GW	SN	SW	SW
			1	1		◇1	1	1	1	1	1	1	1	◇1	1	◇	◇		1	◇	1	1	1
																🍴							
London Waterloo 15 ⊖	d					05 30					06 12			06 30									06 42
Clapham Junction 10	d					05u37					06u19			06u37									06u49
Woking	d					06 01				06 19	06 49			06 57									07 19
Farnborough (Main)	d									06 33	07 03												07 33
Fleet	d									06 38	07 08												07 38
Reading 7	d																						
Basingstoke	a					06 20				06 58	07 28			07 16									07 58
	d					06 21				07 00				07 18									08 00
Micheldever	d					06 31				07 10													08 10
Winchester	d					06 41				07 19				07 34									08 19
Shawford	d									07 24													08 24
Romsey	d	06 50							07 07						07 13		07 44	07 55				08 07	
Chandlers Ford	d								07 14													08 14	
Eastleigh 8	a					06 50			07 20	07 29				07 42	07 49							08 20	08 30
	d		06 50			06 51		07 14	07 21	07 30				07 43	07 50						08 14	08 21	08 31
Hedge End	d									07 36													08 37
Botley	d									07 40													08 41
Fareham	d	07 27								07 49						07 47	08 27						08 49
Portchester	d									07 54													08 54
Cosham	d	07 35								07 59							08 35						08 59
Hilsea	a									08 03													09 04
Fratton	a	07 42								08 07							08 42						09 08
Portsmouth & Southsea	a	07 46								08 11							08 46						09 12
Portsmouth Harbour ⛴	a	07 52								08 18							08 52						09 18
Southampton Airport Pkwy ✈	d					06 56		07 18	07 25					07 48							08 18	08 25	
Swaythling	d								07 27													08 27	
St Denys	d								07 30													08 30	
Southampton Central ⛴	a					07 03		07 28	07 35					07 56		08 07		08 07			08 28	08 35	
	d					07 05	07 21		07 37					08 00		08 10			08 19	08 27		08 37	
Millbrook (Hants)	d								07 40													08 40	
Redbridge	d								07 43													08 43	
Romsey	d		07a03						07 51						08a03	08 21				08 38		08 51	
Mottisfont & Dunbridge	d								07 56													08 56	
Dean	d								08 02													09 02	
Salisbury	a								08 15							08 40				09 02		09 15	
Totton	d					07 10	07 26							08 05					08 24				
Ashurst New Forest	d						07 31												08 29				
Beaulieu Road	d																		08 33				
Brockenhurst 3	a					07 21	07 39							08 16					08 39				
	d			07 12		07 22	07 40					07 42	08 12	08 17					08 40				
Lymington Town	d			07 20								07 50	08 20										
Lymington Pier	a			07 22								07 52	08 22										
Sway	d					07 26	07 44							08 21					08 45				
New Milton	d					07 31	07 49							08 26					08 50				
Hinton Admiral	d					07 35	07 53							08 30					08 54				
Christchurch	d					07 40	07 58							08 35					08 59				
Pokesdown	d					07 44	08 02							08 39					09 02				
Bournemouth	a					07 48	08 06							08 43					09 06				
	d					07 49	08 11							08 44					09 11				
Branksome	d					07 54	08 16							08 49					09 16				
Parkstone (Dorset)	d					07 57	08 19							08 52					09 19				
Poole 4	a					08 01	08 23							08 56					09 23				
	d					08 02	08 24							08 57					09 24				
Hamworthy	d					08 07	08 29							09 02					09 29				
Holton Heath	d						08 33												09 33				
Wareham	d					08 14	08 38							09 09					09 38				
Wool	d					08 20	08 44							09 15					09 44				
Moreton (Dorset)	d					08 26	08 50							09 21					09 50				
Dorchester South	d					08 34	08 58							09 29					09 58				
Dorchester West	d				08 03																		
Upwey	d				08 11	08 41	09 05							09 36					10 05				
Weymouth	a				08 17	08 45	09 09							09 40					10 09				

Table 158

Saturdays
until 6 October

London - Basingstoke, Southampton, Romsey Lymington, Bournemouth and Weymouth

Network Diagram - see first Page of Table 158

		SW ■		XC ◇■ ✠	SW ■	SW ■	SW ◇■	SW ■	GW ◇ ✠	GW ◇	GW ◇	SW ■		XC ◇■	SW ■	SW ◇■	SW ■	SW ■	SW ■	SW ■	SW ■	XC ◇■ ✠		SW ■	SW ◇■ A ✠
London Waterloo ■15 ⊖	d				07 12		07 35					07 39			07 42	08 05			08 09					08 12	08 35
Clapham Junction ■10	d				07u20							07u46				08u12								08u19	
Woking	d				07 50		08 00								08 19				08 35					08 49	09 00
Farnborough (Main)	d				08 03							08 13			08 33				08 45					09 03	
Fleet	d				08 09							08 19			08 38									09 08	
Reading ■7	d			07 46										08 23								08 46			
Basingstoke	a			08 08	08 28		08 20					08 31		08 40	08 58	08 47			08 58			09 08		09 28	
	d			08 10			08 21					08 33		08 41		08 49			09 00			09 10			
Micheldever	d																		09 10						
Winchester	d			08 25			08 38					08 49		08 56		09 05			09 19			09 25			09 33
Shawford	d											08 54													
Romsey	d							08 19		08 50								09 07		09 19					
Chandlers Ford	d																	09 14							
Eastleigh ■3	a						08 46	08 49				08 59						09 20	09 27	09 49					
	d						08 47	08 50				09 00						09 21	09 28	09 50					
Hedge End	d																		09 34						
Botley	d																		09 38						
Fareham	d								08 47	09 27									09 48						
Portchester	d																		09 53						
Cosham	d									09 35									09 58						
Hilsea	a																		10 03						
Fratton	a									09 42									10 07						
Portsmouth & Southsea	a									09 46									10 11						
Portsmouth Harbour ⛴	a									09 52									10 18						
Southampton Airport Pkwy ✈	d			08 33			08 51					09 05		09 09		09 14		09 25				09 33			09 42
Swaythling	d																	09 27							
St Denys	d																←	09 30							
Southampton Central ⛴	a			08 41			08 58		09 08			09 12		09 17		09 22	09 12	09 35				09 40			09 49
	d			08 43			09 00		09 10			09 30				09 24	09 30	09 37				09 42			09 51
Millbrook (Hants)	d											→						09 40							
Redbridge	d																	09 43							
Romsey	d							09a03	09 21									09 51		10a03					
Mottisfont & Dunbridge	d																	09 56							
Dean	d																	10 02							
Salisbury	a								09 39									10 15							
Totton	d						09 05										09 35								
Ashurst New Forest	d																09 40								
Beaulieu Road	d																09 44								
Brockenhurst ■3	a			08 56			09 16									09 37	09 51					09 57			10 04
	d	08 42		08 58		09 12	09 17									09 38	10 16				09 42	09 58			10 05
Lymington Town	d	08 50				09 20											→				09 50				
Lymington Pier	a	08 52				09 22															09 52				
Sway	d						09 21																		
New Milton	d						09 26									09 45									
Hinton Admiral	d						09 30																		
Christchurch	d						09 35									09 52									
Pokesdown	d						09 39									09 56									
Bournemouth	a			09 14			09 43									10 00						10 11			10 20
	d						09 44									10 04									10 24
Branksome	d						09 49																		10 29
Parkstone (Dorset)	d						09 52																		10 32
Poole ■4	a						09 56									10 13									10 36
	d						09 57									10 14									10 37
Hamworthy	d						10 02									10 19									10 42
Holton Heath	d															10 23									
Wareham	d						10 09									10 28									10 49
Wool	d															10 35									
Moreton (Dorset)	d															10 41									
Dorchester South	d						10 27									10 49									11 05
Dorchester West	d										10 38														
Upwey	d										10 49					10 55									
Weymouth	a						10 35				10 57					11 00									11 13

A not 4 August, 11 August, 1 September. ✠ to Bournemouth

Table 158

Saturdays
until 6 October

London - Basingstoke, Southampton, Romsey Lymington, Bournemouth and Weymouth

Network Diagram - see first Page of Table 158

		SW ◇■ A ✠	SW ■	GW ◇ ✠	GW ◇	SW ■	GW ◇ B	SW ■		SW ■	SW ◇■ C ✠	SW ■	SN ■	SW ■	GW ◇	SW ■	SW ■	SW ■		XC ◇■ ✠	SW ■	GW ◇	SW ◇■ C ✠	SW ■	GW ◇
London Waterloo ■15 ⊖	d	08 35						08 39		08 42	09 05					09 09					09 12		09 35		
Clapham Junction ■10	d							08u46			09u12										09u19				
Woking	d	09 00								09 19						09 35					09 49		10 00		
Farnborough (Main)	d							09 13		09 33						09 45					10 03				
Fleet	d							09 19		09 38											10 08				
Reading ■7	d																			09 46					
Basingstoke	a							09 31		09 58	09 47					09 58				10 08	10 28				
	d							09 33			09 49					10 00				10 10					
Micheldever	d															10 10									
Winchester	d	09 33						09 49			10 05					10 19				10 25			10 33		
Shawford	d							09 54																	
Romsey	d				09 50									10 07			10 19								
Chandlers Ford	d													10 14											
Eastleigh ■3	a							09 59						10 20		10 27	10 49								
	d							10 00					10 14	10 21		10 28	10 50								
Hedge End	d															10 34									
Botley	d															10 38									
Fareham	d			09 47	10 27										10 16	10 48									10 47
Portchester	d															10 53									
Cosham	d				10 35											10 58									
Hilsea	a															11 03									
Fratton	a				10 42											11 07									
Portsmouth & Southsea	a				10 46											11 11									
Portsmouth Harbour ⛴	a				10 52											11 18									
Southampton Airport Pkwy ✈	d	09 42						10 05			10 14		10 18	10 25						10 33			10 42		
Swaythling	d													10 27											
St Denys	d											←		10 30											
Southampton Central ⛴	a	09 49		10 08				10 12			10 22	10 12	10 28	10 35	10 40					10 43			10 49		11 08
	d	09 51		10 10				10 30			10 24	10 30		10 37	10 42					10 45			10 51		11 10
Millbrook (Hants)	d							→						10 40											
Redbridge	d													10 44											
Romsey	d			10 21										10 59	10 53		11a03								11 21
Mottisfont & Dunbridge	d													11 04											
Dean	d													11 10											
Salisbury	a			10 39										11 22	11 12										11 39
Totton	d											10 35													
Ashurst New Forest	d											10 40													
Beaulieu Road	d		←																					←	
Brockenhurst ■3	a	10 04	09 51								10 37	10 51								10 58			11 04	10 51	
	d	10 05	10 16			10 12					10 38	11 16						10 42		10 59			11 05	11 16	
Lymington Town	d					10 20						→						10 50							
Lymington Pier	a					10 22												10 52							
Sway	d		10 20																					11 20	
New Milton	d		10 25								10 45													11 25	
Hinton Admiral	d		10 29																					11 29	
Christchurch	d		10 34								10 52													11 34	
Pokesdown	d		10 38								10 56													11 38	
Bournemouth	a	10 25	10 42								11 00									11 12			11 20	11 42	
	d	10 30	10 43								11 04												11 24	11 43	
Branksome	d	10 35	10 48																				11 29	11 48	
Parkstone (Dorset)	d	10 38	10 51																				11 32	11 51	
Poole ■4	a	10 42	10 55								11 13												11 36	11 55	
	d	10 43									11 14												11 37		
Hamworthy	d	10 48									11 19												11 42		
Holton Heath	d										11 23														
Wareham	d	10 55									11 28												11 49		
Wool	d										11 35														
Moreton (Dorset)	d										11 41														
Dorchester South	d	11 11									11 49												12 05		
Dorchester West	d						11 29															11 54			
Upwey	d										11 55											12 02			
Weymouth	a	11 19					11 42				12 00											12 09	12 13		

A 4 August, 11 August, 1 September. ✠ to Bournemouth

B until 8 September

C ✠ to Bournemouth

Saturdays
until 6 October

London - Basingstoke, Southampton, Romsey Lymington, Bournemouth and Weymouth

Network Diagram - see first Page of Table 158

		GW	SW	SW	XC	SW	SW	SW	SW	SW	SW	SW	XC	SW	SW	SW	GW	GW	GW	SW	SW	SW
		◇	■	■	◇■	■	◇■	■	■	■	■	■	◇■	■	◇■	■	◇	◇		■	■	■
							A								A							
					🍴		🍴						🍴		🍴			🍴				
London Waterloo [15] ⊖	d			09 39		09 42	10 05			10 09				10 12	10 35						10 39	10 42
Clapham Junction [10]	d			09u46			10u12							10u19							10u46	
Woking	d					10 19				10 35				10 49	11 00							11 19
Farnborough (Main)	d			10 13		10 33				10 45				11 03							11 13	11 33
Fleet	d			10 19		10 38								11 08							11 19	11 38
Reading [7]	d				10 15								10 46									
Basingstoke	a			10 31	10 39	10 58	10 47			10 58			11 08	11 28							11 31	11 58
	d			10 33	10 40		10 49			11 00			11 10								11 33	
Micheldever	d									11 10												
Winchester	d			10 49	10 55		11 06			11 19			11 25		11 33						11 49	
Shawford	d			10 54																	11 54	
Romsey	d	10 50							11 07		11 19							11 50	12 04			
Chandlers Ford	d								11 14													
Eastleigh ■	a			10 59					11 20	11 27	11 49										11 59	
	d			11 00					11 21	11 28	11 50										12 00	
Hedge End	d									11 34												
Botley	d									11 38												
Fareham	d	11 27								11 48							11 47	12 27				
Portchester	d									11 53												
Cosham	d	11 35								11 58								12 35				
Hilsea	a									12 03												
Fratton	a	11 42								12 07								12 42				
Portsmouth & Southsea	a	11 46								12 11								12 46				
Portsmouth Harbour ⛴	a	11 52								12 18								12 52				
Southampton Airport Pkwy ✈	d			11 05	11 09		11 15		11 25				11 33		11 42						12 05	
Swaythling	d								11 27													
St Denys	d							←	11 30													
Southampton Central ⛴	a			11 12	11 17		11 22	11 12	11 35				11 41		11 49		12 08		12 20		12 12	
	d			11 30			11 24	11 30	11 37				11 43		11 51		12 10				12 30	
Millbrook (Hants)	d			→					11 40													
Redbridge	d								11 43												→	
Romsey	d								11 51		12a03						12 21					
Mottisfont & Dunbridge	d								11 56													
Dean	d								12 02													
Salisbury	a								12 15								12 39					
Totton	d							11 35														
Ashurst New Forest	d							11 40														
Beaulieu Road	d							11 44								←						
Brockenhurst ■	a						11 37	11 51					11 57		12 04	11 51						
	d		11 12				11 38	12 16				11 42	11 58		12 05	12 16				12 12		
Lymington Town	d		11 20					→				11 50								12 20		
Lymington Pier	a		11 22									11 52								12 22		
Sway	d															12 20						
New Milton	d						11 45									12 25						
Hinton Admiral	d															12 29						
Christchurch	d						11 52									12 34						
Pokesdown	d						11 56									12 38						
Bournemouth	a						12 00						12 11		12 20	12 42						
	d						12 04								12 24	12 43						
Branksome	d														12 29	12 48						
Parkstone (Dorset)	d														12 32	12 51						
Poole ■	a						12 13								12 36	12 55						
	d						12 14								12 37							
Hamworthy	d						12 19								12 42							
Holton Heath	d						12 23															
Wareham	d						12 28								12 49							
Wool	d						12 35															
Moreton (Dorset)	d						12 41															
Dorchester South	d						12 49								13 05							
Dorchester West	d																					
Upwey	d						12 55															
Weymouth	a						13 00								13 13							

A 🍴 to Bournemouth

Saturdays
until 6 October

London - Basingstoke, Southampton, Romsey Lymington, Bournemouth and Weymouth

Network Diagram - see first Page of Table 158

		SW	SW	GW	SN	SW	SW	SW	SW	XC	SW	GW	SW	SW	GW	GW	SW	SW	XC	SW	SW	SW	SW
		◇■	■	◇	■	■	■	■	■	◇■	■	◇	◇■	■	◇	◇	■	■	◇■	■	◇■	■	■
		A											A								A		
		🍴								🍴			🍴			🍴			🍴		🍴		
London Waterloo [15] ⊖	d	11 05					11 09				11 12		11 35					11 39		11 42	12 05		
Clapham Junction [10]	d	11u12									11u19							11u46			12u12		
Woking	d						11 35				11 49		12 00							12 19			
Farnborough (Main)	d						11 45				12 03							12 13		12 33			
Fleet	d										12 08							12 19		12 38			
Reading [7]	d									11 46									12 15				
Basingstoke	a	11 47					11 58			12 08	12 28							12 31	12 40	12 58	12 47		
	d	11 49					12 00			12 10								12 33	12 41		12 49		
Micheldever	d						12 10																
Winchester	d	12 05					12 19			12 25			12 33					12 49	12 56		13 05		
Shawford	d																	12 54					
Romsey	d					12 07		12 19								12 50							13 07
Chandlers Ford	d					12 14																	13 14
Eastleigh ■	a					12 20	12 27	12 49										12 59					13 20
	d				12 14	12 21	12 28	12 50										13 00					13 21
Hedge End	d						12 34																
Botley	d						12 38																
Fareham	d						12 48								12 47	13 27							
Portchester	d						12 53																
Cosham	d						12 58									13 35							
Hilsea	a						13 03																
Fratton	a						13 07									13 42							
Portsmouth & Southsea	a						13 11									13 46							
Portsmouth Harbour ⛴	a						13 18									13 52							
Southampton Airport Pkwy ✈	d	12 14			12 19	12 25				12 33			12 42					13 05	13 09		13 14		13 25
Swaythling	d					12 27																	13 27
St Denys	d		←			12 30																←	13 30
Southampton Central ⛴	a	12 22	12 12		12 28	12 35				12 41			12 49		13 08			13 12	13 17		13 22	13 12	13 35
	d	12 24	12 30	12 27		12 37				12 43			12 51		13 10			13 30			13 24	13 30	13 37
Millbrook (Hants)	d					12 40												→					13 40
Redbridge	d					12 43																	13 43
Romsey	d			12 38		12 51		13a03							13 21								13 51
Mottisfont & Dunbridge	d					12 56																	13 56
Dean	d					13 02																	14 02
Salisbury	a			13 02		13 15									13 39								14 15
Totton	d		12 35																			13 35	
Ashurst New Forest	d		12 40																			13 40	
Beaulieu Road	d													←								13 44	
Brockenhurst ■	a	12 37	12 51							12 57			13 04	12 51							13 37	13 51	
	d	12 38	13 16						12 42	12 58			13 05	13 16			13 12				13 38	14 16	
Lymington Town	d		→						12 50								13 20					→	
Lymington Pier	a								12 52								13 22						
Sway	d													13 20									
New Milton	d	12 45												13 25							13 45		
Hinton Admiral	d													13 29									
Christchurch	d	12 52												13 34							13 52		
Pokesdown	d	12 56												13 38							13 56		
Bournemouth	a	13 00								13 11			13 20	13 42							14 00		
	d	13 04											13 24	13 43							14 04		
Branksome	d												13 29	13 48									
Parkstone (Dorset)	d												13 32	13 51									
Poole ■	a	13 13											13 36	13 55							14 13		
	d	13 14											13 37								14 14		
Hamworthy	d	13 19											13 42								14 19		
Holton Heath	d	13 23																			14 23		
Wareham	d	13 28											13 49								14 28		
Wool	d	13 35																			14 35		
Moreton (Dorset)	d	13 41																			14 41		
Dorchester South	d	13 49											14 05								14 49		
Dorchester West	d											13 54											
Upwey	d	13 55										14 02									14 55		
Weymouth	a	14 00										14 08	14 13								15 00		

A 🍴 to Bournemouth

Table 158

Saturdays until 6 October

London - Basingstoke, Southampton, Romsey Lymington, Bournemouth and Weymouth

Network Diagram - see first Page of Table 158

		SW 1	SW 1	SW 1	XC ◇1 ⌶	SW 1	SW ◇1 A ⌶	SW 1	GW ◇	GW ◇ ⌶	SW 1	SW 1	SW 1	SW ◇1 A ⌶	SW 1	GW ◇	SW 1	SW 1	SW 1	XC ◇1 ⌶	SW 1	SW ◇1 A ⌶	SW 1
London Waterloo 15 ⊖	d	12 09				12 12	12 35					12 39	12 42	13 05				13 09			13 12	13 35	
Clapham Junction 10	d					12u19						12u46		13u12							13u19		
Woking	d	12 35				12 49	13 00						13 19					13 35			13 49	14 00	
Farnborough (Main)	d	12 45				13 03						13 13	13 33					13 45			14 03		
Fleet	d					13 08						13 19	13 38								14 08		
Reading 7	d				12 46															13 46			
Basingstoke	a	12 58			13 08	13 28						13 31	13 58	13 47				13 58		14 08	14 28		
	d	13 00			13 10							13 33		13 49				14 00		14 10			
Micheldever	d	13 10																14 10					
Winchester	d	13 19			13 25		13 33					13 49		14 05				14 19		14 25		14 33	
Shawford	d											13 54											
Romsey	d		13 19							13 50						14 20	14 07						
Chandlers Ford	d																14 14						
Eastleigh 3	a	13 27	13 49									13 59					14 20	14 27					
	d	13 28	13 50									14 00					14 21	14 28					
Hedge End	d	13 34																14 34					
Botley	d	13 38																14 38					
Fareham	d	13 48							13 47	14 27								14 48					
Portchester	d	13 53																14 53					
Cosham	d	13 58								14 35								14 58					
Hilsea	a	14 03																15 03					
Fratton	a	14 07								14 42								15 07					
Portsmouth & Southsea	a	14 11								14 46								15 11					
Portsmouth Harbour ⛴	a	14 18								14 52								15 18					
Southampton Airport Pkwy ✈	d				13 33		13 42					14 05		14 14			14 25			14 33		14 42	
Swaythling	d																14 27						
St Denys	d														←		14 30						
Southampton Central ⛴	a				13 41		13 49		14 08			14 12		14 22	14 12	14 32	14 35			14 41		14 49	
	d				13 43		13 51		14 10			14 30		14 24	14 30		14 37			14 43		14 51	
Millbrook (Hants)	d											→					14 40						
Redbridge	d																14 43						
Romsey	d		14a03						14 21								14 51						
Mottisfont & Dunbridge	d																14 56						
Dean	d																15 02						
Salisbury	a								14 39								15 15						
Totton	d														14 35								
Ashurst New Forest	d														14 40								
Beaulieu Road	d							←															←
Brockenhurst 3	a				13 57		14 04	13 51						14 37	14 51					14 57		15 04	14 51
	d			13 42	13 58		14 05	14 16			14 12			14 38	15 16				14 42	14 58		15 05	15 16
Lymington Town	d			13 50							14 20				→				14 50				
Lymington Pier	a			13 52							14 22								14 52				
Sway	d							14 20															15 20
New Milton	d							14 25						14 45									15 25
Hinton Admiral	d							14 29															15 29
Christchurch	d							14 34						14 52									15 34
Pokesdown	d							14 38						14 56									15 38
Bournemouth	a				14 11		14 20	14 42						15 00						15 11		15 20	15 42
	d						14 24	14 43						15 04								15 24	15 43
Branksome	d						14 29	14 48														15 29	15 48
Parkstone (Dorset)	d						14 32	14 51														15 32	15 51
Poole 4	a						14 36	14 55						15 13								15 36	15 55
	d						14 37							15 14								15 37	
Hamworthy	d						14 42							15 19								15 42	
Holton Heath	d													15 23									
Wareham	d						14 49							15 28								15 49	
Wool	d													15 35									
Moreton (Dorset)	d													15 41									
Dorchester South	d						15 05							15 49								16 05	
Dorchester West	d																						
Upwey	d													15 55									
Weymouth	a						15 13							16 00								16 13	

A ⌶ to Bournemouth

Table 158

Saturdays until 6 October

London - Basingstoke, Southampton, Romsey Lymington, Bournemouth and Weymouth

Network Diagram - see first Page of Table 158

		GW ◇	SN 1	SW 1	GW ◇	SW 1	SW 1	XC ◇1 ⌶	SW 1	SW ◇1 ⌶	SW 1	SW 1	SW 1	SW 1	SW 1	XC ◇1 ⌶	SW 1	GW ◇	SW ◇1 A ⌶	SW 1	GW ◇	GW ◇
London Waterloo 15 ⊖	d						13 39		13 42	14 05			14 09				14 12		14 35			
Clapham Junction 10	d						13u46			14u12							14u19					
Woking	d								14 19				14 35				14 49		15 00			
Farnborough (Main)	d						14 13		14 33				14 45				15 03					
Fleet	d						14 19		14 38								15 08					
Reading 7	d							14 15								14 46						
Basingstoke	a						14 31	14 40	14 58	14 47			14 58			15 08	15 28					
	d						14 33	14 41		14 49			15 00			15 10						
Micheldever	d												15 10									
Winchester	d						14 49	14 56		15 05			15 19			15 25			15 33			
Shawford	d						14 54															
Romsey	d			14 13	14 50							15 07		15 19								15 50
Chandlers Ford	d											15 14										
Eastleigh 3	a			14 49			14 59					15 20	15 27	15 49								
	d		14 41	14 50			15 00					15 21	15 28	15 50								
Hedge End	d												15 34									
Botley	d												15 38									
Fareham	d	14 47	14a59		15 27								15 48								15 47	16 27
Portchester	d												15 53									
Cosham	d				15 35								15 58									16 35
Hilsea	a												16 03									
Fratton	a				15 42								16 07									16 42
Portsmouth & Southsea	a				15 46								16 11									16 46
Portsmouth Harbour ⛴	a				15 52								16 18									16 52
Southampton Airport Pkwy ✈	d						15 05	15 09		15 14		15 25				15 33			15 42			
Swaythling	d											15 27										
St Denys	d										←	15 30										
Southampton Central ⛴	a	15 08					15 12	15 17		15 22	15 12	15 35				15 41			15 49		16 08	
	d	15 10					15 30			15 24	15 30	15 37				15 43			15 51		16 10	
Millbrook (Hants)	d						→					15 40										
Redbridge	d											15 43										
Romsey	d	15 21		15a04								15 51		16a03							16 21	
Mottisfont & Dunbridge	d											15 56										
Dean	d											16 02										
Salisbury	a	15 39										16 15									16 39	
Totton	d										15 35											
Ashurst New Forest	d										15 40											
Beaulieu Road	d										15 44									←		
Brockenhurst 3	a									15 37	15 51					15 57			16 04	15 51		
	d					15 12				15 38	16 16				15 42	15 58			16 05	16 16		
Lymington Town	d					15 20					→				15 50							
Lymington Pier	a					15 22									15 52							
Sway	d																			16 20		
New Milton	d									15 45										16 25		
Hinton Admiral	d																			16 29		
Christchurch	d									15 52										16 34		
Pokesdown	d									15 56										16 38		
Bournemouth	a									16 00						16 11			16 20	16 42		
	d									16 04									16 24	16 43		
Branksome	d																		16 29	16 48		
Parkstone (Dorset)	d																		16 32	16 51		
Poole 4	a									16 13									16 36	16 55		
	d									16 14									16 37			
Hamworthy	d									16 19									16 42			
Holton Heath	d									16 23												
Wareham	d									16 28									16 49			
Wool	d									16 35												
Moreton (Dorset)	d									16 41												
Dorchester South	d									16 49									17 06			
Dorchester West	d																	16 58				
Upwey	d									16 55								17 05				
Weymouth	a									17 00								17 10	17 15			

A ⌶ to Bournemouth

London - Basingstoke, Southampton, Romsey Lymington, Bournemouth and Weymouth

Network Diagram - see first Page of Table 158

		SW	SW	SW	SW	SW	SN	SW	SW	SW	SW	XC	SW	SW	SW	GW	GW	SW	SW	XC	SW	SW	SW
		1	1	1	◇1 A ✕	1	1	1	1	1	1	◇1 ✕	1	◇1 A ✕	1	■	◇	1	1	◇1 ✕	1	◇1 A ✕	1
London Waterloo 15 ⊖	d		14 39	14 42	15 05				15 09				15 12	15 35					15 39		15 42	16 05	
Clapham Junction 10	d		14u46		15u12								15u19						15u46			16u12	
Woking	d			15 19					15 35				15 49	16 00							16 19		
Farnborough (Main)	d		15 13	15 33					15 45				16 03						16 13		16 33		
Fleet	d		15 19	15 38									16 08						16 19		16 38		
Reading 7	d											15 46								16 15			
Basingstoke	a		15 31	15 58	15 47				15 58			16 08	16 28						16 31	16 40	16 58	16 47	
	d		15 33		15 49				16 00			16 10							16 33	16 41		16 49	
Micheldever	d								16 10														
Winchester	d		15 49		16 05				16 19			16 25		16 33					16 49	16 56		17 05	
Shawford	d		15 54																16 54				
Romsey	d							16 07		16 19							16 50						
Chandlers Ford	d							16 14															
Eastleigh 8	a		15 59					16 20	16 27	16 49									16 59				
	d		16 00				16 14	16 21	16 28	16 50									17 00				
Hedge End	d								16 34														
Botley	d								16 38														
Fareham	d								16 48							16 47	17 27						
Portchester	d								16 53														
Cosham	d								16 58								17 35						
Hilsea	a								17 03														
Fratton	a								17 07								17 42						
Portsmouth & Southsea	a								17 11								17 46						
Portsmouth Harbour ⛴	a								17 18								17 52						
Southampton Airport Pkwy ✈	d		16 05		16 14		16 18	16 25				16 33		16 42					17 05	17 09		17 14	
Swaythling	d							16 27															
St Denys	d					←		16 30															←
Southampton Central ⛴	a		16 12		16 22	16 12	16 28	16 35				16 41		16 49		17 08			17 12	17 17		17 22	17 12
	d		16 30		16 24	16 30		16 37				16 43		16 51		17 10			17 30			17 24	17 30
Millbrook (Hants)	d		→					16 40											→				
Redbridge	d							16 43															
Romsey	d							16 51		17a03						17 21							
Mottisfont & Dunbridge	d							16 56															
Dean	d							17 02															
Salisbury	a							17 15								17 39							
Totton	d					16 35																	17 35
Ashurst New Forest	d					16 40																	17 40
Beaulieu Road	d														←								17 44
Brockenhurst 3	a				16 37	16 51						16 57		17 04	16 51							17 37	17 51
	d	16 12			16 38	17 16					16 42	16 58		17 05	17 16			17 12				17 38	18 16
Lymington Town	d	16 20				→					16 50							17 20					→
Lymington Pier	a	16 22									16 52							17 22					
Sway	d														17 20								
New Milton	d				16 45										17 25							17 45	
Hinton Admiral	d														17 29								
Christchurch	d				16 52										17 34							17 52	
Pokesdown	d				16 56										17 38							17 56	
Bournemouth	a				17 00							17 11		17 20	17 42							18 00	
	d				17 04									17 24	17 43							18 04	
Branksome	d													17 29	17 48								
Parkstone (Dorset)	d													17 32	17 51								
Poole 4	a				17 13									17 36	17 55							18 13	
	d				17 14									17 37								18 14	
Hamworthy	d				17 19									17 42								18 19	
Holton Heath	d				17 23																	18 23	
Wareham	d				17 28									17 49								18 28	
Wool	d				17 35																	18 35	
Moreton (Dorset)	d				17 41																	18 41	
Dorchester South	d				17 49									18 05								18 49	
Dorchester West	d																						
Upwey	d				17 55																	18 55	
Weymouth	a				18 00									18 13								19 00	

A ✕ to Bournemouth

London - Basingstoke, Southampton, Romsey Lymington, Bournemouth and Weymouth

Network Diagram - see first Page of Table 158

		SW	SW	SW	SW	XC	SW	SW	GW	SW	SW	GW	GW	SW	SW	SW	SW	SW	SN	SW	SW	SW
		1	1	1	1	◇1 ✕	1	1	◇	◇1 A ✕	1	◇	◇	1	1	1	◇1 B ⊡	1	1	1	1	1
London Waterloo 15 ⊖	d		16 09					16 12		16 35					16 39	16 42	17 05				17 09	
Clapham Junction 10	d							16u19							16u46		17u12					
Woking	d		16 35					16 49		17 00						17 19					17 35	
Farnborough (Main)	d		16 45					17 03							17 13	17 33					17 45	
Fleet	d							17 08							17 19	17 38						
Reading 7	d					16 46																
Basingstoke	a		16 58			17 08		17 28							17 31	17 58	17 47				17 58	
	d		17 00			17 10	17 24								17 33		17 49				18 00	
Micheldever	d		17 10				17 34														18 10	
Winchester	d		17 19			17 25	17 43			17 33					17 49		18 05				18 19	
Shawford	d						17 48								17 54							
Romsey	d	17 07		17 19									17 50							18 07		
Chandlers Ford	d	17 14																		18 14		
Eastleigh 8	a	17 20	17 27	17 49			17 53								17 59					18 20	18 27	
	d	17 21	17 28	17 50			17 54								18 00				18 14	18 21	18 28	
Hedge End	d		17 34																		18 34	
Botley	d		17 38																		18 38	
Fareham	d		17 48									17 47	18 27								18 48	
Portchester	d		17 53																		18 53	
Cosham	d		17 58										18 35								18 58	
Hilsea	a		18 03																		19 03	
Fratton	a		18 07										18 42								19 07	
Portsmouth & Southsea	a		18 11										18 46								19 11	
Portsmouth Harbour ⛴	a		18 18										18 52								19 18	
Southampton Airport Pkwy ✈	d	17 25				17 33	17 59			17 42					18 05		18 14		18 18	18 25		
Swaythling	d	17 27					18 01													18 27		
St Denys	d	17 30					18 04											←		18 30		
Southampton Central ⛴	a	17 35				17 41	18 10			17 49		18 08			18 14		18 22	18 14	18 28	18 35		
	d	17 37				17 43				17 51		18 10			18 30		18 24	18 30		18 37		
Millbrook (Hants)	d	17 40													→					18 40		
Redbridge	d	17 43																		18 44		
Romsey	d	17 51		18a03								18 21								19 00		
Mottisfont & Dunbridge	d	17 56																		19 05		
Dean	d	18 02																		19 10		
Salisbury	a	18 15										18 39								19 23		
Totton	d																	18 35				
Ashurst New Forest	d																	18 40				
Beaulieu Road	d										←											
Brockenhurst 3	a					17 57				18 04	17 51						18 37	18 51				
	d				17 42	17 58				18 05	18 16			18 12			18 38	19 16				18 42
Lymington Town	d				17 50									18 20				→				18 50
Lymington Pier	a				17 52									18 22								18 52
Sway	d										18 20											
New Milton	d										18 25						18 45					
Hinton Admiral	d										18 29											
Christchurch	d										18 34						18 52					
Pokesdown	d										18 38						18 56					
Bournemouth	a					18 11				18 20	18 42						19 00					
	d									18 24	18 43						19 04					
Branksome	d									18 29	18 48											
Parkstone (Dorset)	d									18 32	18 51											
Poole 4	a									18 36	18 55						19 13					
	d									18 37							19 14					
Hamworthy	d									18 42							19 19					
Holton Heath	d																19 23					
Wareham	d									18 49							19 28					
Wool	d																19 35					
Moreton (Dorset)	d																19 41					
Dorchester South	d									19 05							19 49					
Dorchester West	d								18 54													
Upwey	d								19 02								19 55					
Weymouth	a								19 10	19 13							20 00					

A ✕ to Bournemouth

B ⊡ to Bournemouth

Table 158

Saturdays
until 6 October

London - Basingstoke, Southampton, Romsey Lymington, Bournemouth and Weymouth

Network Diagram - see first Page of Table 158

		XC	SW	GW	SW	GW	SW	SW	GW	GW	SW	SW	XC	SW	SW	SW	SW	SW	SW	SW	XC	SW	SW
		◇1 ⌶	1	◇	1	◇	◇1 A ⌶	1	◇	■	1	1	◇1 ⌶	1	◇1 A ⌶	1	1	1	1	1	◇1 ⌶	1	◇1 A ⌶
London Waterloo 15 ⊖	d		17 12				17 35					17 39		17 42	18 05			18 09				18 12	18 35
Clapham Junction 10	d		17u19									17u46			18u12							18u19	
Woking	d		17 49				18 00							18 19				18 35				18 49	19 00
Farnborough (Main)	d		18 03									18 13		18 33				18 45				19 03	
Fleet	d		18 08									18 19		18 38								19 08	
Reading 7	d	17 46											18 15								18 46		
Basingstoke	a	18 08	18 28									18 31	18 40	18 58	18 47			18 58			19 08	19 28	
	d	18 10										18 33	18 41		18 49			19 00			19 10		
Micheldever	d																	19 10					
Winchester	d	18 25					18 33					18 49	18 56		19 05			19 19			19 25		19 33
Shawford	d											18 54											
Romsey	d				18 19					18 50							19 07		19 19				
Chandlers Ford	d																19 14						
Eastleigh 8	a				18 49							18 59					19 20	19 27	19 49				
	d				18 50							19 00					19 21	19 28	19 50				
Hedge End	d																	19 34					
Botley	d																	19 38					
Fareham	d			18 15					18 47	19 27								19 48					
Portchester	d																	19 53					
Cosham	d									19 35								19 58					
Hilsea	a																	20 03					
Fratton	a									19 42								20 07					
Portsmouth & Southsea	a									19 46								20 11					
Portsmouth Harbour ⛴	a									19 52								20 18					
Southampton Airport Pkwy ✈	d	18 33					18 42					19 05	19 09		19 14		19 25				19 33		19 42
Swaythling	d																19 27						
St Denys	d															←	19 30						
Southampton Central ⛴	a	18 40		18 43			18 49		19 08			19 12	19 17		19 22	19 12	19 35				19 41		19 49
	d	18 43		18 45			18 51		19 10			19 30			19 24	19 30	19 37				19 43		19 51
Millbrook (Hants)	d											→					19 40						
Redbridge	d																19 43						
Romsey	d			18 56	19a04				19 21								19 51		20a03				
Mottisfont & Dunbridge	d																19 56						
Dean	d																20 02						
Salisbury	a			19 14					19 39								20 15						
Totton	d															19 35							
Ashurst New Forest	d															19 40							
Beaulieu Road	d							←								19 44							
Brockenhurst 3	a	18 57					19 04	18 51							19 37	19 51					19 57		20 04
	d	18 58					19 05	19 16			19 12				19 38	20 16				19 42	19 58		20 05
Lymington Town	d										19 20					→				19 50			
Lymington Pier	a										19 22									19 52			
Sway	d							19 20															
New Milton	d							19 25							19 45								
Hinton Admiral	d							19 29															
Christchurch	d							19 34							19 52								
Pokesdown	d							19 38							19 56								
Bournemouth	a	19 11					19 20	19 42							20 00						20 11		20 20
	d						19 24	19 43							20 04								20 24
Branksome	d						19 29	19 48															20 29
Parkstone (Dorset)	d						19 32	19 51															20 32
Poole 4	a						19 36	19 55							20 13								20 36
	d						19 37								20 14								20 37
Hamworthy	d						19 42								20 19								20 42
Holton Heath	d														20 23								
Wareham	d						19 49								20 28								20 49
Wool	d														20 35								
Moreton (Dorset)	d														20 41								
Dorchester South	d						20 05								20 49								21 05
Dorchester West	d					19 54																	
Upwey	d					20 01									20 55								
Weymouth	a					20 09	20 13								21 00								21 13

A ⌶ to Bournemouth

Table 158

Saturdays
until 6 October

London - Basingstoke, Southampton, Romsey Lymington, Bournemouth and Weymouth

Network Diagram - see first Page of Table 158

		SW	GW	GW	GW	SW	SW	SW	SW	SW	SN	SW	SW	SW	SW	XC	SW	SW	SW	GW	SW	SW	GW
		1	◇	◇		1	1	1	◇1 A ⌶	1	1	1	1	1	1	◇1 ⌶	1	◇1 A ⌶	1	◇	1	1	◇
London Waterloo 15 ⊖	d						18 39	18 42	19 05				19 09				19 12	19 35			19 39	19 42	
Clapham Junction 10	d						18u46		19u12								19u19				19u46		
Woking	d							19 19					19 35				19 49	20 00				20 19	
Farnborough (Main)	d						19 13	19 33					19 45				20 03				20 13	20 33	
Fleet	d						19 19	19 38									20 08				20 19	20 38	
Reading 7	d															19 46							
Basingstoke	a						19 31	19 58	19 47				19 58			20 08	20 28				20 31	20 58	
	d						19 33		19 49				20 00			20 10					20 33		
Micheldever	d												20 10										
Winchester	d						19 49		20 05				20 19			20 25		20 33			20 49		
Shawford	d						19 54														20 54		
Romsey	d			19 50	20 04							20 07		20 19									20 50
Chandlers Ford	d											20 14											
Eastleigh 8	a						19 59					20 20	20 27	20 49							20 59		
	d						20 00				20 14	20 21	20 28	20 50							21 00		
Hedge End	d												20 34										
Botley	d												20 38										
Fareham	d		19 47	20 28									20 48							20 47			21 27
Portchester	d												20 53										
Cosham	d												20 58										
Hilsea	a												21 03										
Fratton	a			20 42									21 07										21 42
Portsmouth & Southsea	a			20 46									21 11										21 46
Portsmouth Harbour ⛴	a			20 52									21 18										21 52
Southampton Airport Pkwy ✈	d						20 05		20 14		20 18	20 25				20 33		20 42			21 05		
Swaythling	d											20 27											
St Denys	d									←		20 30											
Southampton Central ⛴	a		20 09		20 18		20 14		20 22	20 14	20 26	20 35				20 41		20 49		21 10	21 12		
	d		20 10				20 30		20 24	20 30		20 37				20 43		20 51		21 10			
Millbrook (Hants)	d						→					20 40											
Redbridge	d											20 43											
Romsey	d		20 21									20 51		21a03						21 21			
Mottisfont & Dunbridge	d											20 56											
Dean	d											21 02											
Salisbury	a		20 39									21 15								21 40			
Totton	d									20 35													
Ashurst New Forest	d									20 40													
Beaulieu Road	d	←																	←				
Brockenhurst 3	a	19 51							20 37	20 51						20 57		21 04	20 51				
	d	20 16				20 12			20 38	21 16					20 42	20 58		21 05	21 16				
Lymington Town	d					20 20				→					20 50								
Lymington Pier	a					20 22									20 52								
Sway	d	20 20																	21 20				
New Milton	d	20 25							20 45										21 25				
Hinton Admiral	d	20 29																	21 29				
Christchurch	d	20 34							20 52										21 34				
Pokesdown	d	20 38							20 56										21 38				
Bournemouth	a	20 42							21 00							21 11		21 20	21 42				
	d	20 43							21 04									21 24	21 43				
Branksome	d	20 48																21 29	21 48				
Parkstone (Dorset)	d	20 51																21 32	21 51				
Poole 4	a	20 55							21 13									21 36	21 55				
	d								21 14									21 37					
Hamworthy	d								21 19									21 42					
Holton Heath	d																						
Wareham	d								21 28									21 49					
Wool	d								21 35									21 55					
Moreton (Dorset)	d								21 41									22 01					
Dorchester South	d								21 49									22 09					
Dorchester West	d																						
Upwey	d								21 55									22 16					
Weymouth	a								22 00									22 20					

A ⌶ to Bournemouth

Table 158

Saturdays
until 6 October

London - Basingstoke, Southampton, Romsey Lymington, Bournemouth and Weymouth

Network Diagram - see first Page of Table 158

		SW ■	SW ◇■ 🚌	GW	SW ■	SW ■	SW ■	SW ■	XC ◇■	SW ■	GW ◇	GW A	GW B	SW ◇■ C 🚌	SW ■	SW ■	SW ■	SW ◇■ 🚌	SW ■	XC ◇■ B	XC ◇■ A	SW ■
London Waterloo 15 ⊖	d		20 05			20 09				20 12				20 35	20 39	20 42		21 05				21 12
Clapham Junction 10	d		20u12							20u19					20u46			21u12				21u19
Woking	d					20 35				20 49				21 00		21 19		21 32				21 49
Farnborough (Main)	d					20 45				21 03					21 13	21 33						22 03
Fleet	d									21 08					21 19	21 38						22 08
Reading 7	d								20 46											21 47	21 47	
Basingstoke	a		20 47			20 58			21 08	21 28					21 31	21 58		21 51		22 08	22 09	22 25
	d		20 49			21 00			21 10						21 33	22 00		21 52		22 09	22 10	
Micheldever	d					21 10									21 43	22 10						
Winchester	d		21 05			21 19			21 25					21 33	21 52	22 19		22 09		22 24	22 25	
Shawford	d														21 57							
Romsey	d				21 07		21 19				21 50								22 07			
Chandlers Ford	d				21 14														22 14			
Eastleigh 3	a				21 20	21 27	21 49								22 02	22 27		22 17	22 21			
	d				21 21	21 28	21 50								22 03	22 28		22 18	22 22			
Hedge End	d					21 34										22 34						
Botley	d					21 38										22 38						
Fareham	d					21 48					22 27					22 48						
Portchester	d					21 53										22 53						
Cosham	d					21 58										22 58						
Hilsea	a					22 03										23 03						
Fratton	a					22 07					22 42					23 07						
Portsmouth & Southsea	a					22 11					22 46					23 11						
Portsmouth Harbour ⛴	a					22 18					22 52					23 18						
Southampton Airport Pkwy ✈	d		21 14		21 25				21 33					21 42	22 08			22 22	22 26	22 33	22 34	
Swaythling	d				21 27														22 29			
St Denys	d				21 30														22 32			
Southampton Central ⛴	a		21 22		21 35				21 41					21 49	22 17			22 29	22 36	22 41	22 41	
	d		21 24	21 27	21 37				21 43					21 51				22 31	22 38	22 43	22 43	
Millbrook (Hants)	d				21 40														22 41			
Redbridge	d				21 43														22 45			
Romsey	d			21 38	21 51		22a03												22a52			
Mottisfont & Dunbridge	d				21 56																	
Dean	d				22 02																	
Salisbury	a			22 02	22 15																	
Totton	d		21 29															22 36				
Ashurst New Forest	d		21 34															22 41				
Beaulieu Road	d																					
Brockenhurst 3	a		21 42						21 57					22 04				22 49		22 56	22 56	
	d	21 12	21 43					21 48	21 58					22 05			22 18	22 50		22 59	22 59	
Lymington Town	d	21 20						21 56									22 26					
Lymington Pier	a	21 22						21 58									22 28					
Sway	d		21 47															22 54				
New Milton	d		21 52															22 59				
Hinton Admiral	d		21 56															23 03				
Christchurch	d		22 01															23 08				
Pokesdown	d		22 05															23 12				
Bournemouth	a		22 09						22 15					22 20				23 16		23 20	23 21	
	d		22 10											22 24				23 17				
Branksome	d		22 15											22 29				23 22				
Parkstone (Dorset)	d		22 18											22 32				23 25				
Poole 4	a		22 23											22 36				23 29				
	d													22 37								
Hamworthy	d													22 42								
Holton Heath	d																					
Wareham	d													22 49								
Wool	d													22 55								
Moreton (Dorset)	d													23 01								
Dorchester South	d													23 09								
Dorchester West	d											22 54	22 58									
Upwey	d											23 02	23 06	23 16								
Weymouth	a											23 10	23 13	23 20								

A until 8 September B from 15 September until 6 October C 🚌 to Bournemouth

Table 158

Saturdays
until 6 October

London - Basingstoke, Southampton, Romsey Lymington, Bournemouth and Weymouth

Network Diagram - see first Page of Table 158

		SW ◇■ A 🚌	SW ■	SW ■	GW ◇	SW ■	SW ◇■ 🚌	SW ■	XC ◇■	SW ■	SW ◇■ 🚌	SW ■	SW ■	SW ■	SW ◇■	SW ■	SW ■	SW ■
London Waterloo 15 ⊖	d	21 35		21 39		21 42	22 05			22 12	22 35		22 39	22 42	23 05	23 12	23 35	23 48
Clapham Junction 10	d			21u46			22u12			22u19			22u46	22u49	23u12	23u19	23u42	23u54
Woking	d	22 00				22 19	22 32			22 49	23 00			23 19	23 32	23 57	00 03	00 28
Farnborough (Main)	d			22 13		22 33				23 03			23 16	23 33		00 10	00 14	00 41
Fleet	d			22 19		22 38				23 08			23 21	23 38		00 16	00 20	00 47
Reading 7	d								22 49									
Basingstoke	a			22 31		22 58	22 51		23 07	23 25			23 34	23 55	23 51	00 33	00 33	01 06
	d			22 33		23 00	22 52		23 10				23 36		23 52		00 35	
Micheldever	d			22s43		23 10									00 02			
Winchester	d	22 33		22 53		23 19	23 09		23 25		23 33		23 52		00 12		00 51	
Shawford	d			22 57									23 57					
Romsey	d		22 19		22 50			23 09				23 00						
Chandlers Ford	d							23 16										
Eastleigh 3	a		22 49	23 03		23 27	23 17	23 22				23 35	00 02		00 20		00 59	
	d		22 50	23 04		23 28	23 18	23 23				23 37	00 03		00 21		01 00	
Hedge End	d					23 34												
Botley	d					23 38												
Fareham	d				23 27	23 48												
Portchester	d					23 53												
Cosham	d					23 58												
Hilsea	a					00 03												
Fratton	a				23 40	00 07												
Portsmouth & Southsea	a				23 44	00 11												
Portsmouth Harbour ⛴	a				23 52	00 16												
Southampton Airport Pkwy ✈	d	22 42		23 08			23 22	23 27	23 33		23 42		00 08		00 25		01 05	
Swaythling	d							23 30										
St Denys	d							23 33							00s29			
Southampton Central ⛴	a	22 49		23 17			23 29	23 38	23 41		23 49		00 15		00 34		01 12	
	d	22 51					23 31	23 40			23 51				00 36			
Millbrook (Hants)	d							23 42										
Redbridge	d							23 46										
Romsey	d		23a03					23 57				23a49						
Mottisfont & Dunbridge	d							00 02										
Dean	d							00 08										
Salisbury	a							00 20										
Totton	d						23 36								00s41			
Ashurst New Forest	d						23 41											
Beaulieu Road	d																	
Brockenhurst 3	a	23 04					23 49				00 04				00s52			
	d	23 05					23 50				00 05							
Lymington Town	d																	
Lymington Pier	a																	
Sway	d						23 54											
New Milton	d						23 59								01s00			
Hinton Admiral	d						00 03											
Christchurch	d						00 08								01s07			
Pokesdown	d						00 11								01s11			
Bournemouth	a	23 25					00 15				00 21				01 15			
	d	23 29					00 17				00 22				01 16			
Branksome	d	23 35					00 23				00 27				01s21			
Parkstone (Dorset)	d	23 38					00 26				00 30				01s24			
Poole 4	a	23 41					00 30				00 35				01 29			
	d	23 42																
Hamworthy	d	23 47																
Holton Heath	d																	
Wareham	d	23 54																
Wool	d	00 01																
Moreton (Dorset)	d	00 07																
Dorchester South	d	00 15																
Dorchester West	d																	
Upwey	d	00 21																
Weymouth	a	00 26																

A 🚌 to Bournemouth

London - Basingstoke, Southampton, Romsey Lymington, Bournemouth and Weymouth

Network Diagram - see first Page of Table 158

		SW ◇1 A ⚒	SW 1	SW ◇1 ⚒	SW 1	SW ◇1 ⚒	SW 1	SW ◇1	SW 1	SW 1		SW 1	SW 1	SW 1	SW 1	SW 1	SW 1	SW 1	SW 1	SW 1		GW ◇	SW 1	SW 1	GW
London Waterloo 15 ⊖	d	21p35	21p42	22p05		22p35	22p39	23p05	23p12			23p35	23p48	00 05	01 05										
Clapham Junction 10	d			22b12			22b46	23b12	23b19			23b42	23b55	00u12	01 15										
Woking	d	22p00	22p19	22p32		23p00		23p32	23p57			00 03	00 28	00 37	01 42										
Farnborough (Main)	d		22p33				23p16		00 10			00 14	00 41		01s51										
Fleet	d		22p38				23p21		00 16			00 20	00 47		01s57										
Reading 7	d																								
Basingstoke	a		22p58	22p51			23p33	23p53	00 33			00 33	01 06	00 55	02s09										
	d		23p00	22p52			23p34	23p53				00 35		00 56											
Micheldever	d		23p10					00 03																	
Winchester	d	22p33	23p19	23p09		23p33	23p51	00 14				00 51		01 13	02s26										
Shawford	d		23p24				23p55																		
Romsey	d				23p07															05 58					06 50
Chandlers Ford	d				23p14															06 06					
Eastleigh 8	a		23p29	23p17	23p22		00 01	00 22				00 59		01 21	02s35					06 11					
	d		23p30	23p18	23p22		00 02	00 23		00 30		01 00		01 22						06 13			06 28		
Hedge End	d		23p36							00s36													06 34		
Botley	d		23p40							00s39													06 38		
Fareham	d		23p49							00s47												06 28	06 48		07 27
Portchester	d		23p54							00s53													06 53		
Cosham	d		23p59							00s57													06 58		07 35
Hilsea	a		00 03																				07 03		
Fratton	a		00 07							01s05													07 07		07 42
Portsmouth & Southsea	a		00 11							01s08													07 11		07 46
Portsmouth Harbour ⛴	a		00 16							01 12													07 16		07 52
Southampton Airport Pkwy ✈	d	22p42		23p22	23p26	23p42	00 06	00 28				01 05		01 26	02s39					06 17					
Swaythling	d				23p28															06 20					
St Denys	d				23p31			00s32							02s44					06 23					
Southampton Central ⛴	a	22p49		23p29	23p36	23p49	00 13	00 37				01 12		01 35	02 49					06 28		06 49			
	d	22p51		23p31	23p38	23p51		00 38						01 37					06 21	06 30		06 53			
Millbrook (Hants)	d				23p40															06 32					
Redbridge	d				23p44															06 36					
Romsey	d				23p56															06 44		07 11			
Mottisfont & Dunbridge	d				00 01															06 49					
Dean	d				00 07															06 54					
Salisbury	a				00 19															07 07		07 29			
Totton	d			23p36				00s43						01s42					06 26						
Ashurst New Forest	d			23p41															06 31						
Beaulieu Road	d																								
Brockenhurst 3	a	23p04		23p49		00 04		00s54						01s53					06 39						
	d	23p05		23p50		00 05											06 12	06 16	06 40					06 42	
Lymington Town	d																06 20							06 50	
Lymington Pier	a																06 22							06 52	
Sway	d			23p54														06 20	06 44						
New Milton	d			23p59				01s02						02s00				06 25	06 49						
Hinton Admiral	d			00 03														06 29	06 53						
Christchurch	d			00 08				01s09						02s07				06 34	06 58						
Pokesdown	d			00 11				01s13						02s11				06 38	07 02						
Bournemouth	a	23p25		00 15		00 21		01 17						02 15				06 42	07 06						
	d	23p29		00 17		00 22		01 18								06 11		06 44	07 11						
Branksome	d	23p35		00 22		00 27		01s23								06 16		06 49	07 16						
Parkstone (Dorset)	d	23p38		00 25		00 30		01s26								06 19		06 52	07 19						
Poole 4	a	23p41		00 29		00 35		01 30								06 23		06 55	07 23						
	d	23p42														06 24		06 57	07 24						
Hamworthy	d	23p47														06 29		07 02	07 29						
Holton Heath	d															06 33		07 06	07 33						
Wareham	d	23p54														06 38		07 11	07 38						
Wool	d	00 01														06 44		07 17	07 44						
Moreton (Dorset)	d	00 07														06 50		07 23	07 50						
Dorchester South	d	00 15														06 58		07 31	07 58						
Dorchester West	d																								
Upwey	d	00 21														07 05		07 38	08 05						
Weymouth	a	00 26														07 09		07 42	08 09						

A ⚒ to Bournemouth

b Previous night, stops to pick up only

London - Basingstoke, Southampton, Romsey Lymington, Bournemouth and Weymouth

Network Diagram - see first Page of Table 158

		SW 1	SW 1	GW	SW ◇1	SW 1		SN 1	SW 1	SW 1	SW 1	SW 1	SW 1	SW ◇1	SW 1	GW ◇ ⚒		GW ◇	GW	SW 1	GW ◇	SN 1	SW 1	SW 1	SW 1
London Waterloo 15 ⊖	d				05 30						06 12			06 30										06 42	
Clapham Junction 10	d				05u37						06u19			06u37										06u49	
Woking	d				06 01					06 19	06 49			06 57										07 19	
Farnborough (Main)	d									06 33	07 03													07 33	
Fleet	d									06 38	07 08													07 38	
Reading 7	d																								
Basingstoke	a				06 20					06 58	07 28			07 16										07 58	
	d				06 21					07 00				07 18										08 00	
Micheldever	d				06 31					07 10														08 10	
Winchester	d				06 41					07 19				07 34										08 19	
Shawford	d									07 24														08 24	
Romsey	d								07 07						07 13			07 44	07 55				08 07		
Chandlers Ford	d								07 14														08 14		
Eastleigh 8	a				06 50				07 20	07 29				07 42	07 49								08 20	08 30	
	d	06 50			06 51			07 14	07 21	07 30				07 43	07 50							08 14	08 21	08 31	
Hedge End	d									07 36														08 37	
Botley	d									07 40														08 41	
Fareham	d									07 49						07 47		08 27						08 49	
Portchester	d									07 54														08 54	
Cosham	d									07 59								08 35						08 59	
Hilsea	a									08 03														09 04	
Fratton	a									08 07								08 42						09 08	
Portsmouth & Southsea	a									08 11								08 46						09 12	
Portsmouth Harbour ⛴	a									08 18								08 52						09 18	
Southampton Airport Pkwy ✈	d				06 56			07 18	07 25					07 48								08 18	08 25		
Swaythling	d								07 27														08 27		
St Denys	d								07 30														08 30		
Southampton Central ⛴	a				07 03			07 28	07 35					07 56		08 07			08 07			08 28	08 35		
	d				07 05	07 21			07 37					08 00		08 10				08 19	08 27		08 37		
Millbrook (Hants)	d								07 40														08 40		
Redbridge	d								07 43														08 43		
Romsey	d	07a03							07 51						08a03	08 21					08 38		08 51		
Mottisfont & Dunbridge	d								07 56														08 56		
Dean	d								08 02														09 02		
Salisbury	a								08 15							08 40					09 02		09 15		
Totton	d				07 10	07 26								08 05						08 24					
Ashurst New Forest	d					07 31														08 29					
Beaulieu Road	d																			08 33					
Brockenhurst 3	a				07 21	07 39								08 16						08 39					
	d		07 12		07 22	07 40						07 42	08 12	08 17						08 40					08 42
Lymington Town	d		07 20									07 50	08 20												08 50
Lymington Pier	a		07 22									07 52	08 22												08 52
Sway	d				07 26	07 44								08 21						08 45					
New Milton	d				07 31	07 49								08 26						08 50					
Hinton Admiral	d				07 35	07 53								08 30						08 54					
Christchurch	d				07 40	07 58								08 35						08 59					
Pokesdown	d				07 44	08 02								08 39						09 02					
Bournemouth	a				07 48	08 06								08 43						09 06					
	d				07 49	08 11								08 44						09 11					
Branksome	d				07 54	08 16								08 49						09 16					
Parkstone (Dorset)	d				07 57	08 19								08 52						09 19					
Poole 4	a				08 01	08 23								08 56						09 23					
	d				08 02	08 24								08 57						09 24					
Hamworthy	d				08 07	08 29								09 02						09 29					
Holton Heath	d					08 33														09 33					
Wareham	d				08 14	08 38								09 09						09 38					
Wool	d				08 20	08 44								09 15						09 44					
Moreton (Dorset)	d				08 26	08 50								09 21						09 50					
Dorchester South	d				08 34	08 58								09 29						09 58					
Dorchester West	d			08 03																					
Upwey	d			08 11	08 41	09 05								09 36						10 05					
Weymouth	a			08 17	08 45	09 09								09 40						10 09					

Table 158

Saturdays
from 13 October

London - Basingstoke, Southampton, Romsey Lymington, Bournemouth and Weymouth

Network Diagram - see first Page of Table 158

		XC ◇■ ✠		SW ■	SW ■	SW ◇■	SW ■	GW ◇ ✠	GW ◇	GW ◇	SW ■	XC ◇■		SW ■	SW ◇■	SW ■	SW ■	SW ■	SW ■	SW ■	XC ◇■ ✠	SW ■		SW ◇■ A ✠	SW ■
London Waterloo [15] ⊖	d			07 12		07 35					07 39			07 42	08 05			08 09				08 12		08 35	
Clapham Junction [10]	d			07u20							07u46				08u12							08u19			
Woking	d			07 50		08 00								08 19				08 35				08 49		09 00	
Farnborough (Main)	d			08 03							08 13			08 33				08 45				09 03			
Fleet	d			08 09							08 19			08 38								09 08			
Reading [7]	d	07 46										08 23									08 46				
Basingstoke	a	08 08		08 28		08 20					08 31	08 40		08 58	08 47			08 58			09 08	09 28			
	d	08 10				08 21					08 33	08 41			08 49			09 00			09 10				
Micheldever	d																	09 10							
Winchester	d	08 25				08 38					08 49	08 56			09 05			09 19			09 25			09 33	
Shawford	d										08 54														
Romsey	d						08 19		08 50								09 07		09 19						
Chandlers Ford	d																09 14								
Eastleigh [3]	a					08 46	08 49				08 59						09 20	09 27	09 49						
	d					08 47	08 50				09 00						09 21	09 28	09 50						
Hedge End	d																	09 34							
Botley	d																	09 38							
Fareham	d							08 47	09 27									09 48							
Portchester	d																	09 53							
Cosham	d								09 35									09 58							
Hilsea	a																	10 03							
Fratton	a								09 42									10 07							
Portsmouth & Southsea	a								09 46									10 11							
Portsmouth Harbour ⛴	a								09 52									10 18							
Southampton Airport Pkwy ✈	d	08 33				08 51					09 05	09 09			09 14		09 25				09 33			09 42	
Swaythling	d																09 27								
St Denys	d															←	09 30								
Southampton Central ⛴	a	08 41				08 58		09 08			09 12	09 17			09 22	09 12	09 35				09 40			09 49	
	d	08 43				09 00		09 10			09 30				09 24	09 30	09 37				09 42			09 51	
Millbrook (Hants)	d										→						09 40								
Redbridge	d																09 43								
Romsey	d						09a03	09 21									09 51		10a03						
Mottisfont & Dunbridge	d																09 56								
Dean	d																10 02								
Salisbury	a							09 39									10 15								
Totton	d					09 05										09 35									
Ashurst New Forest	d															09 40									
Beaulieu Road	d															09 44									←
Brockenhurst [3]	a	08 56				09 16									09 37	09 51					09 57			10 04	09 51
	d	08 58			09 12	09 17									09 38	10 16				09 42	09 58			10 05	10 16
Lymington Town	d				09 20											→				09 50					
Lymington Pier	a				09 22															09 52					
Sway	d					09 21																			10 20
New Milton	d					09 26									09 45										10 25
Hinton Admiral	d					09 30																			10 29
Christchurch	d					09 35									09 52										10 34
Pokesdown	d					09 39									09 56										10 38
Bournemouth	a	09 14				09 43									10 00						10 11			10 20	10 42
	d					09 44									10 04									10 24	10 43
Branksome	d					09 49																		10 29	10 48
Parkstone (Dorset)	d					09 52																		10 32	10 51
Poole [4]	a					09 56									10 13									10 36	10 55
	d					09 57									10 14									10 37	
Hamworthy	d					10 02									10 19									10 42	
Holton Heath	d														10 23										
Wareham	d					10 09									10 28									10 49	
Wool	d														10 35										
Moreton (Dorset)	d														10 41										
Dorchester South	d					10 27									10 49									11 05	
Dorchester West	d									10 38															
Upwey	d									10 49					10 55										
Weymouth	a					10 35				10 57					11 00									11 13	

A ✠ to Bournemouth

Table 158

Saturdays
from 13 October

London - Basingstoke, Southampton, Romsey Lymington, Bournemouth and Weymouth

Network Diagram - see first Page of Table 158

		GW ◇ ✠	GW ◇	SW ■	SW ■	SW ■	SW ◇■ A ✠	SW ■		SN ■	SW ■	GW ◇	SW ■	SW ■	SW ■	XC ◇■ ✠	SW ■	GW ◇		SW ◇■ A ✠	SW ■	GW ◇	GW ◇	SW ■	SW ■
London Waterloo [15] ⊖	d				08 39	08 42	09 05						09 09				09 12			09 35					09 39
Clapham Junction [10]	d				08u46		09u12										09u19								09u46
Woking	d					09 19							09 35				09 49			10 00					
Farnborough (Main)	d				09 13	09 33							09 45				10 03								10 13
Fleet	d				09 19	09 38											10 08								10 19
Reading [7]	d															09 46									
Basingstoke	a				09 31	09 58	09 47						09 58			10 08	10 28								10 31
	d				09 33		09 49						10 00			10 10									10 33
Micheldever	d												10 10												
Winchester	d				09 49		10 05						10 19			10 25				10 33					10 49
Shawford	d				09 54																				10 54
Romsey	d		09 50								10 07			10 19									10 50		
Chandlers Ford	d										10 14														
Eastleigh [3]	a				09 59						10 20		10 27	10 49											10 59
	d				10 00					10 14	10 21		10 28	10 50											11 00
Hedge End	d												10 34												
Botley	d												10 38												
Fareham	d	09 47	10 27									10 16	10 48									10 47	11 27		
Portchester	d												10 53												
Cosham	d		10 35										10 58										11 35		
Hilsea	a												11 03												
Fratton	a		10 42										11 07										11 42		
Portsmouth & Southsea	a		10 46										11 11										11 46		
Portsmouth Harbour ⛴	a		10 52										11 18										11 52		
Southampton Airport Pkwy ✈	d				10 05		10 14			10 18	10 25					10 33				10 42					11 05
Swaythling	d										10 27														
St Denys	d							←			10 30														
Southampton Central ⛴	a	10 08			10 12		10 22	10 12		10 28	10 35	10 40				10 43				10 49		11 08			11 12
	d	10 10			10 30		10 24	10 30			10 37	10 42				10 45				10 51		11 10			11 30
Millbrook (Hants)	d				→						10 40														→
Redbridge	d										10 44														
Romsey	d	10 21									10 59	10 53		11a03								11 21			
Mottisfont & Dunbridge	d										11 04														
Dean	d										11 10														
Salisbury	a	10 39									11 22	11 12										11 39			
Totton	d							10 35																	
Ashurst New Forest	d							10 40																	
Beaulieu Road	d																				←				
Brockenhurst [3]	a						10 37	10 51								10 58				11 04	10 51				
	d			10 12			10 38	11 16							10 42	10 59				11 05	11 16			11 12	
Lymington Town	d			10 20				→							10 50									11 20	
Lymington Pier	a			10 22											10 52									11 22	
Sway	d																				11 20				
New Milton	d						10 45														11 25				
Hinton Admiral	d																				11 29				
Christchurch	d						10 52														11 34				
Pokesdown	d						10 56														11 38				
Bournemouth	a						11 00									11 12				11 20	11 42				
	d						11 04													11 24	11 43				
Branksome	d																			11 29	11 48				
Parkstone (Dorset)	d																			11 32	11 51				
Poole [4]	a						11 13													11 36	11 55				
	d						11 14													11 37					
Hamworthy	d						11 19													11 42					
Holton Heath	d						11 23																		
Wareham	d						11 28													11 49					
Wool	d						11 35																		
Moreton (Dorset)	d						11 41																		
Dorchester South	d						11 49													12 05					
Dorchester West	d																	11 54							
Upwey	d						11 55											12 02							
Weymouth	a						12 00											12 09		12 13					

A ✠ to Bournemouth

Table 158

Saturdays
from 13 October

London - Basingstoke, Southampton, Romsey Lymington, Bournemouth and Weymouth

Network Diagram - see first Page of Table 158

		XC ◇1 🛒	SW 1	SW ◇1 A 🛒		SW 1	SW 1	SW 1	SW 1	SW 1	XC ◇1 🛒	SW 1	SW ◇1 A 🛒	SW 1		GW ◇	GW ◇ 🛒	GW	SW 1	SW 1	SW 1	SW ◇1 A 🛒	SW 1	GW ◇
London Waterloo 15 ⊖	d		09 42	10 05				10 09				10 12	10 35							10 39	10 42	11 05		
Clapham Junction 10	d			10u12								10u19								10u46		11u12		
Woking	d		10 19					10 35				10 49	11 00								11 19			
Farnborough (Main)	d		10 33					10 45				11 03								11 13	11 33			
Fleet	d		10 38									11 08								11 19	11 38			
Reading 7	d	10 15									10 46													
Basingstoke	a	10 39	10 58	10 47				10 58			11 08	11 28								11 31	11 58	11 47		
	d	10 40		10 49				11 00			11 10									11 33		11 49		
Micheldever	d							11 10																
Winchester	d	10 55		11 06				11 19			11 25		11 33							11 49		12 05		
Shawford	d																			11 54				
Romsey	d						11 07		11 19								11 50	12 04						
Chandlers Ford	d						11 14																	
Eastleigh 8	a						11 20	11 27	11 49											11 59				
	d						11 21	11 28	11 50											12 00				
Hedge End	d							11 34																
Botley	d							11 38																
Fareham	d							11 48								11 47	12 27							
Portchester	d							11 53																
Cosham	d							11 58									12 35							
Hilsea	a							12 03																
Fratton	a							12 07									12 42							
Portsmouth & Southsea	a							12 11									12 46							
Portsmouth Harbour ⛴	a							12 18									12 52							
Southampton Airport Pkwy ✈	d	11 09		11 15			11 25				11 33		11 42							12 05		12 14		
Swaythling	d						11 27																	
St Denys	d					←	11 30																←	
Southampton Central ⛴	a	11 17		11 22		11 12	11 35				11 41		11 49			12 08		12 20		12 12		12 22	12 12	
	d			11 24		11 30	11 37				11 43		11 51			12 10				12 30		12 24	12 30	12 27
Millbrook (Hants)	d						11 40													→				
Redbridge	d						11 43																	
Romsey	d						11 51		12a03							12 21								12 38
Mottisfont & Dunbridge	d						11 56																	
Dean	d						12 02																	
Salisbury	a						12 15									12 39								13 02
Totton	d					11 35																	12 35	
Ashurst New Forest	d					11 40																	12 40	
Beaulieu Road	d					11 44								←										
Brockenhurst 8	a			11 37		11 51					11 57		12 04	11 51								12 37	12 51	
	d			11 38		12 16				11 42	11 58		12 05	12 16					12 12			12 38	13 16	
Lymington Town	d					→				11 50									12 20				→	
Lymington Pier	a									11 52									12 22					
Sway	d													12 20										
New Milton	d			11 45										12 25								12 45		
Hinton Admiral	d													12 29										
Christchurch	d			11 52										12 34								12 52		
Pokesdown	d			11 56										12 38								12 56		
Bournemouth	a			12 00							12 11		12 20	12 42								13 00		
	d			12 04									12 24	12 43								13 04		
Branksome	d												12 29	12 48										
Parkstone (Dorset)	d												12 32	12 51										
Poole 4	a			12 13									12 36	12 55								13 13		
	d			12 14									12 37									13 14		
Hamworthy	d			12 19									12 42									13 19		
Holton Heath	d			12 23																		13 23		
Wareham	d			12 28									12 49									13 28		
Wool	d			12 35																		13 35		
Moreton (Dorset)	d			12 41																		13 41		
Dorchester South	d			12 49									13 05									13 49		
Dorchester West	d																							
Upwey	d			12 55																		13 55		
Weymouth	a			13 00									13 13									14 00		

A 🛒 to Bournemouth

Table 158

Saturdays
from 13 October

London - Basingstoke, Southampton, Romsey Lymington, Bournemouth and Weymouth

Network Diagram - see first Page of Table 158

		SN 1	SW 1	SW 1	SW 1	SW 1	XC ◇1 🛒	SW 1	GW ◇	SW ◇1 A 🛒		SW 1	GW ◇	GW ◇ 🛒	SW 1	SW 1	XC ◇1 🛒	SW 1	SW ◇1 A 🛒	SW 1		SW 1	SW 1	SW 1	SW 1
London Waterloo 15 ⊖	d			11 09				11 12		11 35						11 39		11 42	12 05				12 09		
Clapham Junction 10	d							11u19								11u46			12u12						
Woking	d			11 35				11 49		12 00								12 19					12 35		
Farnborough (Main)	d			11 45				12 03								12 13		12 33					12 45		
Fleet	d							12 08								12 19		12 38							
Reading 7	d						11 46										12 15								
Basingstoke	a			11 58			12 08	12 28								12 31	12 40	12 58	12 47				12 58		
	d			12 00			12 10									12 33	12 41		12 49				13 00		
Micheldever	d			12 10																			13 10		
Winchester	d			12 19			12 25			12 33						12 49	12 56		13 05				13 19		
Shawford	d															12 54									
Romsey	d		12 07		12 19									12 50								13 07		13 19	
Chandlers Ford	d		12 14																			13 14			
Eastleigh 8	a		12 20	12 27	12 49											12 59						13 20	13 27	13 49	
	d	12 14	12 21	12 28	12 50											13 00						13 21	13 28	13 50	
Hedge End	d			12 34																			13 34		
Botley	d			12 38																			13 38		
Fareham	d			12 48									12 47	13 27									13 48		
Portchester	d			12 53																			13 53		
Cosham	d			12 58										13 35									13 58		
Hilsea	a			13 03																			14 03		
Fratton	a			13 07										13 42									14 07		
Portsmouth & Southsea	a			13 11										13 46									14 11		
Portsmouth Harbour ⛴	a			13 18										13 52									14 18		
Southampton Airport Pkwy ✈	d	12 19	12 25				12 33			12 42						13 05	13 09		13 14			13 25			
Swaythling	d		12 27																			13 27			
St Denys	d		12 30																	←		13 30			
Southampton Central ⛴	a	12 28	12 35				12 41			12 49			13 08			13 12	13 17		13 22	13 12		13 35			
	d		12 37				12 43			12 51			13 10			13 30			13 24	13 30		13 37			
Millbrook (Hants)	d		12 40													→						13 40			
Redbridge	d		12 43																			13 43			
Romsey	d		12 51		13a03								13 21									13 51		14a03	
Mottisfont & Dunbridge	d		12 56																			13 56			
Dean	d		13 02																			14 02			
Salisbury	a		13 15										13 39									14 15			
Totton	d																			13 35					
Ashurst New Forest	d																			13 40					
Beaulieu Road	d											←								13 44					
Brockenhurst 8	a						12 57			13 04		12 51							13 37	13 51					
	d					12 42	12 58			13 05		13 16			13 12				13 38	14 16					13 42
Lymington Town	d					12 50									13 20					→					13 50
Lymington Pier	a					12 52									13 22										13 52
Sway	d											13 20													
New Milton	d											13 25							13 45						
Hinton Admiral	d											13 29													
Christchurch	d											13 34							13 52						
Pokesdown	d											13 38							13 56						
Bournemouth	a						13 11			13 20		13 42							14 00						
	d									13 24		13 43							14 04						
Branksome	d									13 29		13 48													
Parkstone (Dorset)	d									13 32		13 51													
Poole 4	a									13 36		13 55							14 13						
	d									13 37									14 14						
Hamworthy	d									13 42									14 19						
Holton Heath	d																		14 23						
Wareham	d									13 49									14 28						
Wool	d																		14 35						
Moreton (Dorset)	d																		14 41						
Dorchester South	d									14 05									14 49						
Dorchester West	d								13 54																
Upwey	d								14 02										14 55						
Weymouth	a								14 08	14 13									15 00						

A 🛒 to Bournemouth

Table 158

Saturdays from 13 October

London - Basingstoke, Southampton, Romsey Lymington, Bournemouth and Weymouth

Network Diagram - see first Page of Table 158

		XC ◇1 ꟷ	SW 1	SW ◇1 A ꟷ	SW 1	GW ◇		GW ◇ ꟷ	SW 1	SW 1	SW 1	SW ◇1 A ꟷ	SW 1	GW ◇	SW 1	SW 1		SW 1	XC ◇1 ꟷ	SW 1	SW ◇1 A ꟷ	SW 1	GW ◇	SN 1	SW 1
London Waterloo [15] ⊖	d		12 12	12 35						12 39	12 42	13 05				13 09				13 12	13 35				
Clapham Junction [10]	d		12u19							12u46		13u12								13u19					
Woking	d		12 49	13 00							13 19					13 35				13 49	14 00				
Farnborough (Main)	d		13 03							13 13	13 33					13 45				14 03					
Fleet	d		13 08							13 19	13 38									14 08					
Reading [7]	d	12 46																	13 46						
Basingstoke	a	13 08	13 28							13 31	13 58	13 47				13 58			14 08	14 28					
	d	13 10								13 33		13 49				14 00			14 10						
Micheldever	d															14 10									
Winchester	d	13 25		13 33						13 49		14 05				14 19			14 25		14 33				
Shawford	d									13 54															
Romsey	d							13 50						14 20	14 07										14 13
Chandlers Ford	d														14 14										
Eastleigh [3]	a									13 59					14 20	14 27									14 49
	d									14 00					14 21	14 28								14 41	14 50
Hedge End	d															14 34									
Botley	d															14 38									
Fareham	d					13 47		14 27								14 48							14 47	14a59	
Portchester	d															14 53									
Cosham	d							14 35								14 58									
Hilsea	a															15 03									
Fratton	a							14 42								15 07									
Portsmouth & Southsea	a							14 46								15 11									
Portsmouth Harbour ⛴	a							14 52								15 18									
Southampton Airport Pkwy ✈	d	13 33		13 42						14 05		14 14			14 25				14 33		14 42				
Swaythling	d														14 27										
St Denys	d												←		14 30										
Southampton Central ⛴	a	13 41		13 49		14 08				14 12		14 22	14 12	14 32	14 35				14 41		14 49		15 08		
	d	13 43		13 51		14 10				14 30		14 24	14 30		14 37				14 43		14 51		15 10		
Millbrook (Hants)	d									→					14 40										
Redbridge	d														14 43										
Romsey	d					14 21									14 51								15 21		15a04
Mottisfont & Dunbridge	d														14 56										
Dean	d														15 02										
Salisbury	a					14 39									15 15								15 39		
Totton	d												14 35												
Ashurst New Forest	d												14 40												
Beaulieu Road	d				←																	←			
Brockenhurst [3]	a	13 57		14 04	13 51							14 37	14 51						14 57		15 04	14 51			
	d	13 58		14 05	14 16				14 12			14 38	15 16					14 42	14 58		15 05	15 16			
Lymington Town	d								14 20				→					14 50							
Lymington Pier	a								14 22									14 52							
Sway	d				14 20																	15 20			
New Milton	d				14 25							14 45										15 25			
Hinton Admiral	d				14 29																	15 29			
Christchurch	d				14 34							14 52										15 34			
Pokesdown	d				14 38							14 56										15 38			
Bournemouth	a	14 11		14 20	14 42							15 00							15 11		15 20	15 42			
	d			14 24	14 43							15 04									15 24	15 43			
Branksome	d			14 29	14 48																15 29	15 48			
Parkstone (Dorset)	d			14 32	14 51																15 32	15 51			
Poole [4]	a			14 36	14 55							15 13									15 36	15 55			
	d			14 37								15 14									15 37				
Hamworthy	d			14 42								15 19									15 42				
Holton Heath	d											15 23													
Wareham	d			14 49								15 28									15 49				
Wool	d											15 35													
Moreton (Dorset)	d											15 41													
Dorchester South	d			15 05								15 49									16 05				
Dorchester West	d																								
Upwey	d											15 55													
Weymouth	a			15 13								16 00									16 13				

A ꟷ to Bournemouth

Table 158

Saturdays from 13 October

London - Basingstoke, Southampton, Romsey Lymington, Bournemouth and Weymouth

Network Diagram - see first Page of Table 158

		GW ◇		SW 1	SW 1	XC ◇1 ꟷ	SW 1	SW ◇1 ꟷ	SW 1	SW 1	SW 1	SW 1		SW 1	XC ◇1 ꟷ	SW 1	GW ◇	SW ◇1 A ꟷ	SW 1	GW ◇	GW ◇	SW 1		SW 1	SW 1
London Waterloo [15] ⊖	d				13 39		13 42	14 05			14 09					14 12		14 35						14 39	14 42
Clapham Junction [10]	d				13u46			14u12								14u19								14u46	
Woking	d						14 19				14 35					14 49		15 00							15 19
Farnborough (Main)	d				14 13		14 33				14 45					15 03								15 13	15 33
Fleet	d				14 19		14 38									15 08								15 19	15 38
Reading [7]	d					14 15									14 46										
Basingstoke	a				14 31	14 40	14 58	14 47			14 58				15 08	15 28								15 31	15 58
	d				14 33	14 41		14 49			15 00				15 10									15 33	
Micheldever	d										15 10														
Winchester	d				14 49	14 56		15 05			15 19				15 25			15 33						15 49	
Shawford	d				14 54																			15 54	
Romsey	d	14 50								15 07		15 19									15 50				
Chandlers Ford	d									15 14															
Eastleigh [3]	a				14 59					15 20	15 27	15 49												15 59	
	d				15 00					15 21	15 28	15 50												16 00	
Hedge End	d										15 34														
Botley	d										15 38														
Fareham	d	15 27									15 48									15 47	16 27				
Portchester	d										15 53														
Cosham	d	15 35									15 58										16 35				
Hilsea	a										16 03														
Fratton	a	15 42									16 07										16 42				
Portsmouth & Southsea	a	15 46									16 11										16 46				
Portsmouth Harbour ⛴	a	15 52									16 18										16 52				
Southampton Airport Pkwy ✈	d				15 05	15 09		15 14		15 25					15 33			15 42						16 05	
Swaythling	d									15 27															
St Denys	d								←	15 30															
Southampton Central ⛴	a				15 12	15 17		15 22	15 12	15 35					15 41			15 49		16 08				16 12	
	d				15 30			15 24	15 30	15 37					15 43			15 51		16 10				16 30	
Millbrook (Hants)	d				→					15 40														→	
Redbridge	d									15 43															
Romsey	d									15 51		16a03								16 21					
Mottisfont & Dunbridge	d									15 56															
Dean	d									16 02															
Salisbury	a									16 15										16 39					
Totton	d								15 35																
Ashurst New Forest	d								15 40																
Beaulieu Road	d								15 44										←						
Brockenhurst [3]	a							15 37	15 51						15 57			16 04	15 51						
	d			15 12				15 38	16 16					15 42	15 58			16 05	16 16			16 12			
Lymington Town	d			15 20					→					15 50								16 20			
Lymington Pier	a			15 22										15 52								16 22			
Sway	d																		16 20						
New Milton	d							15 45											16 25						
Hinton Admiral	d																		16 29						
Christchurch	d							15 52											16 34						
Pokesdown	d							15 56											16 38						
Bournemouth	a							16 00							16 11			16 20	16 42						
	d							16 04										16 24	16 43						
Branksome	d																	16 29	16 48						
Parkstone (Dorset)	d																	16 32	16 51						
Poole [4]	a							16 13										16 36	16 55						
	d							16 14										16 37							
Hamworthy	d							16 19										16 42							
Holton Heath	d							16 23																	
Wareham	d							16 28										16 49							
Wool	d							16 35																	
Moreton (Dorset)	d							16 41																	
Dorchester South	d							16 49										17 06							
Dorchester West	d																16 58								
Upwey	d							16 55									17 05								
Weymouth	a							17 00									17 10	17 15							

A ꟷ to Bournemouth

London - Basingstoke, Southampton, Romsey Lymington, Bournemouth and Weymouth

Network Diagram - see first Page of Table 158

		SW	SW	SN	SW	SW	SW	SW	XC	SW	SW	SW	GW	GW	SW	SW	XC	SW	SW	SW	SW	SW	SW
		◇■ A ⊼	■	■	■	■	■	■	◇■ ⊼	■	◇■ A ⊼	■	■	◇	■	■	◇■ ⊼	■	◇■ A ⊼	■	■	■	■
London Waterloo ⊖	d	15 05				15 09				15 12	15 35					15 39		15 42	16 05			16 09	
Clapham Junction	d	15u12								15u19						15u46			16u12				
Woking	d					15 35				15 49	16 00							16 19				16 35	
Farnborough (Main)	d					15 45				16 03						16 13		16 33				16 45	
Fleet	d									16 08						16 19		16 38					
Reading ■	d								15 46								16 15						
Basingstoke	a	15 47				15 58			16 08	16 28						16 31	16 40	16 58	16 47			16 58	
	d	15 49				16 00			16 10							16 33	16 41		16 49			17 00	
Micheldever	d					16 10																17 10	
Winchester	d	16 05				16 19			16 25		16 33					16 49	16 56		17 05			17 19	
Shawford	d															16 54							
Romsey	d				16 07		16 19							16 50							17 07		17 19
Chandlers Ford	d				16 14																17 14		
Eastleigh ■	a				16 20	16 27	16 49									16 59					17 20	17 27	17 49
	d			16 14	16 21	16 28	16 50									17 00					17 21	17 28	17 50
Hedge End	d					16 34																17 34	
Botley	d					16 38																17 38	
Fareham	d					16 48							16 47	17 27								17 48	
Portchester	d					16 53																17 53	
Cosham	d					16 58								17 35								17 58	
Hilsea	a					17 03																18 03	
Fratton	a					17 07								17 42								18 07	
Portsmouth & Southsea	a					17 11								17 46								18 11	
Portsmouth Harbour ⛴	a					17 18								17 52								18 18	
Southampton Airport Pkwy ✈	d	16 14		16 18	16 25				16 33		16 42					17 05	17 09		17 14		17 25		
Swaythling	d				16 27																17 27		
St Denys	d		←		16 30															←	17 30		
Southampton Central ⛴	a	16 22	16 12	16 28	16 35				16 41		16 49		17 08			17 12	17 17		17 22	17 12	17 35		
	d	16 24	16 30		16 37				16 43		16 51		17 10			17 30			17 24	17 30	17 37		
Millbrook (Hants)	d				16 40											→					17 40		
Redbridge	d				16 43																17 43		
Romsey	d				16 51		17a03						17 21								17 51		18a03
Mottisfont & Dunbridge	d				16 56																17 56		
Dean	d				17 02																18 02		
Salisbury	a				17 15								17 39								18 15		
Totton	d		16 35																	17 35			
Ashurst New Forest	d		16 40																	17 40			
Beaulieu Road	d											←								17 44			
Brockenhurst ■	a	16 37	16 51						16 57		17 04	16 51							17 37	17 51			
	d	16 38	17 16					16 42	16 58		17 05	17 16			17 12				17 38	18 16			
Lymington Town	d		→					16 50							17 20					→			
Lymington Pier	a							16 52							17 22								
Sway	d											17 20											
New Milton	d	16 45										17 25							17 45				
Hinton Admiral	d											17 29											
Christchurch	d	16 52										17 34							17 52				
Pokesdown	d	16 56										17 38							17 56				
Bournemouth	a	17 00							17 11		17 20	17 42							18 00				
	d	17 04									17 24	17 43							18 04				
Branksome	d										17 29	17 48											
Parkstone (Dorset)	d										17 32	17 51											
Poole ■	a	17 13									17 36	17 55							18 13				
	d	17 14									17 37								18 14				
Hamworthy	d	17 19									17 42								18 19				
Holton Heath	d	17 23																	18 23				
Wareham	d	17 28									17 49								18 28				
Wool	d	17 35																	18 35				
Moreton (Dorset)	d	17 41																	18 41				
Dorchester South	d	17 49									18 05								18 49				
Dorchester West	d																						
Upwey	d	17 55																	18 55				
Weymouth	a	18 00									18 13								19 00				

A ⊼ to Bournemouth

London - Basingstoke, Southampton, Romsey Lymington, Bournemouth and Weymouth

Network Diagram - see first Page of Table 158

		SW	XC	SW	SW	GW	SW	SW	GW	GW	SW	SW	SW	SW	SW	SN	SW	SW	SW	XC	SW	GW
		■	◇■ ⊼	■	■	◇	◇■ A ⊼	■	◇	◇	■	■	■	◇■ B ⊡	■	■	■	■	■	◇■ ⊼	■	◇
London Waterloo ⊖	d				16 12		16 35					16 39	16 42	17 05				17 09			17 12	
Clapham Junction	d				16u19							16u46		17u12							17u19	
Woking	d				16 49		17 00						17 19					17 35			17 49	
Farnborough (Main)	d				17 03							17 13	17 33					17 45			18 03	
Fleet	d				17 08							17 19	17 38								18 08	
Reading ■	d		16 46																	17 46		
Basingstoke	a		17 08		17 28							17 31	17 58	17 47				17 58		18 08	18 28	
	d		17 10	17 24								17 33		17 49				18 00		18 10		
Micheldever	d			17 34														18 10				
Winchester	d		17 25	17 43			17 33					17 49		18 05				18 19		18 25		
Shawford	d			17 48								17 54										
Romsey	d									17 50							18 07					
Chandlers Ford	d																18 14					
Eastleigh ■	a			17 53								17 59					18 20	18 27				
	d			17 54								18 00				18 14	18 21	18 28				
Hedge End	d																	18 34				
Botley	d																	18 38				
Fareham	d								17 47	18 27								18 48				18 15
Portchester	d																	18 53				
Cosham	d									18 35								18 58				
Hilsea	a																	19 03				
Fratton	a									18 42								19 07				
Portsmouth & Southsea	a									18 46								19 11				
Portsmouth Harbour ⛴	a									18 52								19 18				
Southampton Airport Pkwy ✈	d		17 33	17 59			17 42					18 05		18 14		18 18	18 25			18 33		
Swaythling	d			18 01													18 27					
St Denys	d			18 04											←		18 30					
Southampton Central ⛴	a		17 41	18 10			17 49		18 08			18 14		18 22	18 14	18 28	18 35			18 40		18 43
	d		17 43				17 51		18 10			18 30		18 24	18 30		18 37			18 43		18 45
Millbrook (Hants)	d											→					18 40					
Redbridge	d																18 44					
Romsey	d								18 21								19 00					18 56
Mottisfont & Dunbridge	d																19 05					
Dean	d																19 10					
Salisbury	a								18 39								19 23					19 14
Totton	d														18 35							
Ashurst New Forest	d														18 40							
Beaulieu Road	d							←														
Brockenhurst ■	a		17 57				18 04	17 51						18 37	18 51					18 57		
	d	17 42	17 58				18 05	18 16			18 12			18 38	19 16				18 42	18 58		
Lymington Town	d	17 50									18 20				→				18 50			
Lymington Pier	a	17 52									18 22								18 52			
Sway	d							18 20														
New Milton	d							18 25						18 45								
Hinton Admiral	d							18 29														
Christchurch	d							18 34						18 52								
Pokesdown	d							18 38						18 56								
Bournemouth	a		18 11				18 20	18 42						19 00						19 11		
	d						18 24	18 43						19 04								
Branksome	d						18 29	18 48														
Parkstone (Dorset)	d						18 32	18 51														
Poole ■	a						18 36	18 55						19 13								
	d						18 37							19 14								
Hamworthy	d						18 42							19 19								
Holton Heath	d													19 23								
Wareham	d						18 49							19 28								
Wool	d													19 35								
Moreton (Dorset)	d													19 41								
Dorchester South	d						19 05							19 49								
Dorchester West	d					18 54																
Upwey	d					19 02								19 55								
Weymouth	a					19 10	19 13							20 00								

A ⊼ to Bournemouth

B ⊡ to Bournemouth

Saturdays
from 13 October

London - Basingstoke, Southampton, Romsey Lymington, Bournemouth and Weymouth

Network Diagram - see first Page of Table 158

		SW	GW	SW	SW	GW	GW	SW	SW	XC	SW	SW	SW	SW	SW	SW	SW	XC	SW	SW	SW	GW	GW
		■	◇	◇■	■	◇	■	■	■	◇■	■	◇■	■	■	■	■	■	◇■	■	◇■	■	◇	◇
				A ✠						✠		A ✠						✠		A ✠			
London Waterloo ⊖	d			17 35					17 39		17 42	18 05			18 09				18 12	18 35			
Clapham Junction	d								17u46			18u12							18u19				
Woking	d			18 00							18 19				18 35				18 49	19 00			
Farnborough (Main)	d								18 13		18 33				18 45				19 03				
Fleet	d								18 19		18 38								19 08				
Reading	d									18 15								18 46					
Basingstoke	a								18 31	18 40	18 58	18 47			18 58			19 08	19 28				
	d								18 33	18 41		18 49			19 00			19 10					
Micheldever	d														19 10								
Winchester	d			18 33					18 49	18 56		19 05			19 19			19 25		19 33			
Shawford	d								18 54														
Romsey	d	18 19					18 50							19 07		19 19							19 50
Chandlers Ford	d													19 14									
Eastleigh	a	18 49							18 59					19 20	19 27	19 49							
	d	18 50							19 00					19 21	19 28	19 50							
Hedge End	d														19 34								
Botley	d														19 38								
Fareham	d					18 47	19 27								19 48							19 47	20 28
Portchester	d														19 53								
Cosham	d						19 35								19 58								
Hilsea	a														20 03								
Fratton	a						19 42								20 07								20 42
Portsmouth & Southsea	a						19 46								20 11								20 46
Portsmouth Harbour	a						19 52								20 18								20 52
Southampton Airport Pkwy ✈	d			18 42					19 05	19 09		19 14		19 25				19 33		19 42			
Swaythling	d													19 27									
St Denys	d												←	19 30									
Southampton Central	a			18 49		19 08			19 12	19 17		19 22	19 12	19 35				19 41		19 49		20 09	
	d			18 51		19 10			19 30			19 24	19 30	19 37				19 43		19 51		20 10	
Millbrook (Hants)	d								→					19 40									
Redbridge	d													19 43									
Romsey	d	19a04				19 21								19 51		20a03						20 21	
Mottisfont & Dunbridge	d													19 56									
Dean	d													20 02									
Salisbury	a					19 39								20 15								20 39	
Totton	d												19 35										
Ashurst New Forest	d												19 40										
Beaulieu Road	d				←								19 44								←		
Brockenhurst	a			19 04	18 51							19 37	19 51					19 57		20 04	19 51		
	d			19 05	19 16			19 12				19 38	20 16				19 42	19 58		20 05	20 16		
Lymington Town	d							19 20					→				19 50						
Lymington Pier	a							19 22									19 52						
Sway	d				19 20																20 20		
New Milton	d				19 25							19 45									20 25		
Hinton Admiral	d				19 29																20 29		
Christchurch	d				19 34							19 52									20 34		
Pokesdown	d				19 38							19 56									20 38		
Bournemouth	a			19 20	19 42							20 00						20 11		20 20	20 42		
	d			19 24	19 43							20 04								20 24	20 43		
Branksome	d			19 29	19 48															20 29	20 48		
Parkstone (Dorset)	d			19 32	19 51															20 32	20 51		
Poole	a			19 36	19 55							20 13								20 36	20 55		
	d			19 37								20 14								20 37			
Hamworthy	d			19 42								20 19								20 42			
Holton Heath	d											20 23											
Wareham	d			19 49								20 28								20 49			
Wool	d											20 35											
Moreton (Dorset)	d											20 41											
Dorchester South	d			20 05								20 49								21 05			
Dorchester West	d		19 54																				
Upwey	d		20 01									20 55											
Weymouth	a		20 09	20 13								21 00								21 13			

A ✠ to Bournemouth

Saturdays
from 13 October

London - Basingstoke, Southampton, Romsey Lymington, Bournemouth and Weymouth

Network Diagram - see first Page of Table 158

		GW	SW	SW	SW	SW	SW	SN	SW	SW	SW	SW	XC	SW	SW	SW	GW	SW	SW	GW	SW	SW	GW
			■	■	■	◇■	■	■	■	■	■	■	◇■	■	◇■	■	◇	■	■	◇	■	◇■	
						A ✠							✠		A ✠							✠	
London Waterloo ⊖	d			18 39	18 42	19 05				19 09				19 12	19 35			19 39	19 42			20 05	
Clapham Junction	d			18u46		19u12								19u19				19u46				20u12	
Woking	d				19 19					19 35				19 49	20 00				20 19				
Farnborough (Main)	d			19 13	19 33					19 45				20 03				20 13	20 33				
Fleet	d			19 19	19 38									20 08				20 19	20 38				
Reading	d												19 46										
Basingstoke	a			19 31	19 58	19 47				19 58			20 08	20 28				20 31	20 58			20 47	
	d			19 33		19 49				20 00			20 10					20 33				20 49	
Micheldever	d									20 10													
Winchester	d			19 49		20 05				20 19			20 25		20 33			20 49				21 05	
Shawford	d			19 54														20 54					
Romsey	d	20 04							20 07		20 19									20 50			
Chandlers Ford	d								20 14														
Eastleigh	a			19 59					20 20	20 27	20 49							20 59					
	d			20 00				20 14	20 21	20 28	20 50							21 00					
Hedge End	d									20 34													
Botley	d									20 38													
Fareham	d									20 48							20 47			21 27			
Portchester	d									20 53													
Cosham	d									20 58													
Hilsea	a									21 03													
Fratton	a									21 07										21 42			
Portsmouth & Southsea	a									21 11										21 46			
Portsmouth Harbour	a									21 18										21 52			
Southampton Airport Pkwy ✈	d			20 05		20 14		20 18	20 25				20 33		20 42			21 05				21 14	
Swaythling	d								20 27														
St Denys	d						←		20 30														
Southampton Central	a	20 18		20 14		20 22	20 14	20 26	20 35				20 41		20 49		21 10	21 12				21 22	
	d			20 30		20 24	20 30		20 37				20 43		20 51		21 10					21 24	21 27
Millbrook (Hants)	d			→					20 40														
Redbridge	d								20 43														
Romsey	d								20 51		21a03						21 21						21 38
Mottisfont & Dunbridge	d								20 56														
Dean	d								21 02														
Salisbury	a								21 15								21 40						22 02
Totton	d						20 35															21 29	
Ashurst New Forest	d						20 40															21 34	
Beaulieu Road	d															←							
Brockenhurst	a					20 37	20 51						20 57		21 04	20 51						21 42	
	d		20 12			20 38	21 16					20 42	20 58		21 05	21 16					21 12	21 43	
Lymington Town	d		20 20				→					20 50									21 20		
Lymington Pier	a		20 22									20 52									21 22		
Sway	d															21 20						21 47	
New Milton	d					20 45										21 25						21 52	
Hinton Admiral	d															21 29						21 56	
Christchurch	d					20 52										21 34						22 01	
Pokesdown	d					20 56										21 38						22 05	
Bournemouth	a					21 00							21 11		21 20	21 42						22 09	
	d					21 04									21 24	21 43						22 10	
Branksome	d														21 29	21 48						22 15	
Parkstone (Dorset)	d														21 32	21 51						22 18	
Poole	a					21 13									21 36	21 55						22 23	
	d					21 14									21 37								
Hamworthy	d					21 19									21 42								
Holton Heath	d																						
Wareham	d					21 28									21 49								
Wool	d					21 35									21 55								
Moreton (Dorset)	d					21 41									22 01								
Dorchester South	d					21 49									22 09								
Dorchester West	d																						
Upwey	d					21 55									22 16								
Weymouth	a					22 00									22 20								

A ✠ to Bournemouth

London - Basingstoke, Southampton, Romsey Lymington, Bournemouth and Weymouth

Network Diagram - see first Page of Table 158

		SW	SW	SW	SW	XC	SW	GW	GW	SW	SW	SW	SW	SW	SW	XC	SW	SW	SW	SW	GW	SW
		1	1	1	1	◇1	1	◇		◇1 A ⌶	1	1	1	◇1 ⌶	1	◇1	1	◇1 A ⌶	1	1	◇	1
London Waterloo 15 ⊖	d		20 09				20 12			20 35	20 39	20 42		21 05			21 12	21 35		21 39		21 42
Clapham Junction 10	d						20u19				20u46			21u12			21u19			21u46		
Woking	d		20 35				20 49			21 00		21 19		21 32			21 49	22 00				22 19
Farnborough (Main)	d		20 45				21 03				21 13	21 33					22 03			22 13		22 33
Fleet	d						21 08				21 19	21 38					22 08			22 19		22 38
Reading 7	d					20 46										21 47						
Basingstoke	a		20 58			21 08	21 28				21 31	21 58		21 51		22 08	22 25			22 31		22 58
	d		21 00			21 10					21 33	22 00		21 52		22 09				22 33		23 00
Micheldever	d		21 10								21 43	22 10								22s43		23 10
Winchester	d		21 19			21 25				21 33	21 52	22 19		22 09		22 24		22 33		22 53		23 19
Shawford	d										21 57									22 57		
Romsey	d	21 07		21 19				21 50							22 07				22 19		22 50	
Chandlers Ford	d	21 14													22 14							
Eastleigh 8	a	21 20	21 27	21 49							22 02	22 27		22 17	22 21				22 49	23 03		23 27
	d	21 21	21 28	21 50							22 03	22 28		22 18	22 22				22 50	23 04		23 28
Hedge End	d		21 34									22 34										23 34
Botley	d		21 38									22 38										23 38
Fareham	d		21 48					22 27				22 48									23 27	23 48
Portchester	d		21 53									22 53										23 53
Cosham	d		21 58									22 58										23 58
Hilsea	a		22 03									23 03										00 03
Fratton	a		22 07					22 42				23 07									23 40	00 07
Portsmouth & Southsea	a		22 11					22 46				23 11									23 44	00 11
Portsmouth Harbour ⛴	a		22 18					22 52				23 18									23 52	00 16
Southampton Airport Pkwy ✈	d	21 25				21 33				21 42	22 08			22 22	22 26	22 33		22 42		23 08		
Swaythling	d	21 27													22 29							
St Denys	d	21 30													22 32							
Southampton Central ⛴	a	21 35				21 41				21 49	22 17			22 29	22 36	22 41		22 49		23 17		
	d	21 37				21 43				21 51				22 31	22 38	22 43		22 51				
Millbrook (Hants)	d	21 40													22 41							
Redbridge	d	21 43													22 45							
Romsey	d	21 51		22a03											22a52				23a03			
Mottisfont & Dunbridge	d	21 56																				
Dean	d	22 02																				
Salisbury	a	22 15																				
Totton	d													22 36								
Ashurst New Forest	d													22 41								
Beaulieu Road	d																					
Brockenhurst 3	a					21 57				22 04				22 49		22 56		23 04				
	d				21 48	21 58				22 05			22 18	22 50		22 59		23 05				
Lymington Town	d				21 56								22 26									
Lymington Pier	a				21 58								22 28									
Sway	d													22 54								
New Milton	d													22 59								
Hinton Admiral	d													23 03								
Christchurch	d													23 08								
Pokesdown	d													23 12								
Bournemouth	a					22 15				22 20				23 16		23 20		23 25				
	d									22 24				23 17				23 29				
Branksome	d									22 29				23 22				23 35				
Parkstone (Dorset)	d									22 32				23 25				23 38				
Poole 4	a									22 36				23 29				23 41				
	d									22 37								23 42				
Hamworthy	d									22 42								23 47				
Holton Heath	d																					
Wareham	d									22 49								23 54				
Wool	d									22 55								00 01				
Moreton (Dorset)	d									23 01								00 07				
Dorchester South	d									23 09								00 15				
Dorchester West	d								22 58													
Upwey	d								23 06	23 16								00 21				
Weymouth	a								23 13	23 20								00 26				

A ⌶ to Bournemouth

London - Basingstoke, Southampton, Romsey Lymington, Bournemouth and Weymouth

Network Diagram - see first Page of Table 158

		SW	SW	XC	SW	SW	SW	SW	SW	SW	SW	SW	SW
		◇1 ⌶	1	◇1	1	◇1 ⌶	1	1	1	◇1	1	1	1
London Waterloo 15 ⊖	d	22 05			22 12	22 35		22 39	22 42	23 05	23 12	23 35	23 48
Clapham Junction 10	d	22u12			22u19			22u46	22u49	23u12	23u19	23u42	23u54
Woking	d	22 32			22 49	23 00			23 19	23 32	23 57	00 03	00 28
Farnborough (Main)	d				23 03			23 16	23 33		00 10	00 14	00 41
Fleet	d				23 08			23 21	23 38		00 16	00 20	00 47
Reading 7	d			22 49									
Basingstoke	a	22 51		23 07	23 25			23 34	23 55	23 51	00 33	00 33	01 06
	d	22 52		23 10				23 36		23 52		00 35	
Micheldever	d									00 02			
Winchester	d	23 09		23 25		23 33		23 52		00 12		00 51	
Shawford	d							23 57					
Romsey	d		23 09				23 00						
Chandlers Ford	d		23 16										
Eastleigh 8	a	23 17	23 22				23 35	00 02		00 20		00 59	
	d	23 18	23 23				23 37	00 03		00 21		01 00	
Hedge End	d												
Botley	d												
Fareham	d												
Portchester	d												
Cosham	d												
Hilsea	a												
Fratton	a												
Portsmouth & Southsea	a												
Portsmouth Harbour ⛴	a												
Southampton Airport Pkwy ✈	d	23 22	23 27	23 33		23 42		00 08		00 25		01 05	
Swaythling	d		23 30										
St Denys	d		23 33							00s29			
Southampton Central ⛴	a	23 29	23 38	23 41		23 49		00 15		00 34		01 12	
	d	23 31	23 40			23 51				00 36			
Millbrook (Hants)	d		23 42										
Redbridge	d		23 46										
Romsey	d		23 57				23a49						
Mottisfont & Dunbridge	d		00 02										
Dean	d		00 08										
Salisbury	a		00 20										
Totton	d	23 36								00s41			
Ashurst New Forest	d	23 41											
Beaulieu Road	d												
Brockenhurst 3	a	23 49				00 04				00s52			
	d	23 50				00 05							
Lymington Town	d												
Lymington Pier	a												
Sway	d	23 54											
New Milton	d	23 59								01s00			
Hinton Admiral	d	00 03											
Christchurch	d	00 08								01s07			
Pokesdown	d	00 11								01s11			
Bournemouth	a	00 15				00 21				01 15			
	d	00 17				00 22				01 16			
Branksome	d	00 23				00 27				01s21			
Parkstone (Dorset)	d	00 26				00 30				01s24			
Poole 4	a	00 30				00 35				01 29			
Hamworthy	d												
Holton Heath	d												
Wareham	d												
Wool	d												
Moreton (Dorset)	d												
Dorchester South	d												
Dorchester West	d												
Upwey	d												
Weymouth	a												

Table 158

Sundays until 24 June

London - Basingstoke, Southampton, Romsey Lymington, Bournemouth and Weymouth

Network Diagram - see first Page of Table 158

		SW	SW	SW	SW	SW	SW	SW	SW	SW	SW	SW	SW	SW	SW	GW	SW	SW		SW	SN	SW	SW
		◇1	1	◇1	1	◇1	1	◇1	1	1	1	1	1	1	1		1	1		1	◇1	1	1
		A ⊼		⊼		⊼																	
London Waterloo 15 ⊖	d	21p35	21p42	22p05		22p35	22p39	23p05	23p12		23p35	23p48	00 05	01 05									
Clapham Junction 10	d			22b12			22b46	23b12	23b19		23b42	23b54	00u12	01 15									
Woking	d	22p00	22p19	22p32		23p00		23p32	23p57		00 03	00 28	00 37	01 49						07 46			
Farnborough (Main)	d		22p33				23p16		00 10		00 14	00 41		01s58						07 59			
Fleet	d		22p38				23p21		00 16		00 20	00 47		02s04						08 04			
Reading 7	d																						
Basingstoke	a		22p58	22p51			23p34	23p51	00 33		00 33	01 06	00 55	02s16						08 21			
	d		23p00	22p52			23p36	23p52			00 35		00 56					07 48					
Micheldever	d		23p10					00 02										07 58					
Winchester	d	22p33	23p19	23p09		23p33	23p52	00 12			00 51		01 13	02s33				08 08					
Shawford	d						23p57											08 12					
Romsey	d				23p09											08 19							
Chandlers Ford	d				23p16																		
Eastleigh 3	a		23p27	23p17	23p22		00 02	00 20			00 59		01 21	02s42				08 18					
	d		23p28	23p18	23p23		00 03	00 21		00 30	01 00		01 22					08 22	08 26		08 48		
Hedge End	d		23p34							00s36									08 32				
Botley	d		23p38							00s39									08 36				
Fareham	d		23p48							00s47					07 44				08 44		09 02		
Portchester	d		23p53							00s53					07 49				08 49				
Cosham	d		23p58							00s57					07 54				08 54		09a10		
Hilsea	a		00 03												08 00				09 00				
Fratton	a		00 07							01s05					08 04				09 04				
Portsmouth & Southsea	a		00 11							01s08					08 08				09 08				
Portsmouth Harbour ⛴	a		00 16							01 12					08 13				09 13				
Southampton Airport Pkwy ✈	d	22p42		23p22	23p27	23p42	00 08	00 25			01 05		01 26	02s46				08 27					
Swaythling	d				23p30																		
St Denys	d				23p33			00s29						02s51									
Southampton Central ⛴	a	22p49		23p29	23p38	23p49	00 15	00 34			01 12		01 35	02 56		08 29		08 34					
	d	22p51		23p31	23p40	23p51		00 36					01 37					08 35					09 03
Millbrook (Hants)	d				23p42																		
Redbridge	d				23p46																		
Romsey	d				23p57																		
Mottisfont & Dunbridge	d				00 02																		
Dean	d				00 08																		
Salisbury	a				00 20																		
Totton	d			23p36				00s41					01s42					08 41					
Ashurst New Forest	d			23p41														08 45					
Beaulieu Road	d																	08 50					
Brockenhurst 3	a	23p04		23p49		00 04		00s52					01s53					08 56					09 16
	d	23p05		23p50		00 05												08 57				08 59	09 17
Lymington Town	d																					09 07	
Lymington Pier	a																					09 09	
Sway	d			23p54														09 01					
New Milton	d			23p59				01s00					02s00					09 06					09 24
Hinton Admiral	d			00 03														09 10					
Christchurch	d			00 08				01s07					02s07					09 15					
Pokesdown	d			00 11				01s11					02s11					09 19					
Bournemouth	a	23p25		00 15		00 21		01 15					02 15					09 23					09 34
	d	23p29		00 17		00 22		01 16									08 39	09 24					09 39
Branksome	d	23p35		00 23		00 27		01s21									08 44						09 44
Parkstone (Dorset)	d	23p38		00 26		00 30		01s24									08 47						09 47
Poole 4	a	23p41		00 30		00 35		01 29									08 50	09 33					09 50
	d	23p42															08 51						09 51
Hamworthy	d	23p47															08 56						09 56
Holton Heath	d																						
Wareham	d	23p54															09 03						10 03
Wool	d	00 01															09 10						10 10
Moreton (Dorset)	d	00 07															09 16						10 16
Dorchester South	d	00 15															09 24						10 24
Dorchester West	d																						
Upwey	d	00 21															09 31						10 31
Weymouth	a	00 26															09 35						10 35

A ⊼ to Bournemouth

b Previous night, stops to pick up only

Table 158

Sundays until 24 June

London - Basingstoke, Southampton, Romsey Lymington, Bournemouth and Weymouth

Network Diagram - see first Page of Table 158

		SW	SW	SW	GW	SW		SW	SW	GW	SW	SW	SW	SW	SW		SW	XC	SW	GW	SW	SW	SW
		1	1	1	■	◇1		1	1		◇1	1	1	1	◇1		1	◇1 ⊼	1		◇1	1	1
London Waterloo 15 ⊖	d					07 54		08 07			08 35				08 54				09 07		09 35		
Clapham Junction 10	d					08u03		08 15			08u45				09u03				09 15		09u45		
Woking	d					08 28		08 46			09 09				09 28				09 46		10 09		
Farnborough (Main)	d							08 59											09 59				
Fleet	d							09 04											10 04				
Reading 7	d																	09 53					
Basingstoke	a					08 46		09 21			09 28				09 46			10 09	10 21		10 28		
	d					08 48					09 29				09 48			10 10			10 29		
Micheldever	d					08 58									09 58								
Winchester	d					09 08					09 46				10 08			10 25			10 46		
Shawford	d														10 12								
Romsey	d	08 35	08 39									09 35	09 32									10 35	10 32
Chandlers Ford	d	08 42										09 42										10 42	
Eastleigh 3	a	08 47	09 13			09 18						09 48	10 13		10 18							10 48	11 13
	d	08 54	09 15			09 22	09 26					09 54	10 15		10 22	10 26						10 54	11 15
Hedge End	d						09 32									10 32							
Botley	d						09 36									10 36							
Fareham	d				09 32		09 44									10 44							
Portchester	d						09 49									10 49							
Cosham	d						09 54									10 54							
Hilsea	a						10 04									11 04							
Fratton	a						10 08									11 08							
Portsmouth & Southsea	a						10 11									11 11							
Portsmouth Harbour ⛴	a						10 15									11 15							
Southampton Airport Pkwy ✈	d	08 58				09 27					09 55	09 58			10 27			10 34			10 55	10 58	
Swaythling	d	09 01										10 01										11 01	
St Denys	d	09 04										10 04										11 04	
Southampton Central ⛴	a	09 09			09 53	09 34					10 02	10 09			10 34			10 42			11 02	11 09	
	d	09 10			09 54	09 35					10 03	10 10			10 35			10 45			11 03	11 10	
Millbrook (Hants)	d	09 13										10 13										11 13	
Redbridge	d	09 16										10 16										11 16	
Romsey	d	09 24	09a28		10 06							10 24	10a28									11 24	11a28
Mottisfont & Dunbridge	d	09 29																				11 29	
Dean	d	09 35																				11 35	
Salisbury	a	09 48			10 24							10 42										11 48	
Totton	d					09 41									10 41								
Ashurst New Forest	d					09 45									10 45								
Beaulieu Road	d					09 50									10 50								
Brockenhurst 3	a					09 56					10 17				10 56			11 02			11 17		
	d			09 29		09 57			09 59		10 18			10 29	10 57		10 59	11 03			11 18		
Lymington Town	d			09 37					10 07					10 37			11 07						
Lymington Pier	a			09 39					10 09					10 39			11 09						
Sway	d					10 01									11 01								
New Milton	d					10 06					10 25				11 06						11 25		
Hinton Admiral	d					10 10									11 10								
Christchurch	d					10 15									11 15								
Pokesdown	d					10 19									11 19								
Bournemouth	a					10 23					10 35				11 23			11 26			11 35		
	d					10 24					10 39				11 24						11 39		
Branksome	d										10 44										11 44		
Parkstone (Dorset)	d										10 47										11 47		
Poole 4	a					10 33					10 50				11 33						11 50		
	d										10 51										11 51		
Hamworthy	d										10 56										11 56		
Holton Heath	d																						
Wareham	d										11 03										12 03		
Wool	d										11 10										12 10		
Moreton (Dorset)	d										11 16										12 16		
Dorchester South	d										11 24										12 24		
Dorchester West	d									10 26										11 30			
Upwey	d									10 37	11 31									11 37	12 31		
Weymouth	a									10 42	11 35									11 43	12 35		

Table 158

Sundays until 24 June

London - Basingstoke, Southampton, Romsey Lymington, Bournemouth and Weymouth

Network Diagram - see first Page of Table 158

		GW ◇	SW ■	SW ◇■		SW ■	XC ◇■ 🍴	SW ■	GW ◇	SW ◇■ A 🍴	SW ■	SW ■	GW ◇	SW ■	SW ◇■		SW ■	XC ◇■ 🛒	SW ■	GW ◇	SW ◇■ A 🍴	GW ◇
London Waterloo ■ ⊖	d			09 54				10 07		10 35					10 54				11 07		11 35	
Clapham Junction ■	d			10u03				10 15		10u45					11u04				11 15		11u45	
Woking	d			10 28				10 46		11 07					11 28				11 46		12 07	
Farnborough (Main)	d							10 59											11 59			
Fleet	d							11 04											12 04			
Reading ■	d						10 53											11 53				
Basingstoke	a			10 46			11 09	11 21		11 26					11 46			12 09	12 21		12 26	
	d			10 48			11 10			11 28					11 48			12 10			12 28	
Micheldever	d			10 58											11 58							
Winchester	d			11 08			11 25			11 44					12 08			12 25			12 44	
Shawford	d														12 12							
Romsey	d	10 50									11 35	11 32	11 51									12 52
Chandlers Ford	d										11 42											
Eastleigh ■	a			11 18							11 48	12 13			12 18							
	d			11 22	11 26						11 54	12 15			12 22	12 26						
Hedge End	d				11 32											12 32						
Botley	d				11 36											12 36						
Fareham	d	11 26			11 44				11 32				12 28			12 44				12 32		
Portchester	d				11 49											12 49						
Cosham	d	11 34			11 54								12 36			12 54						
Hilsea	a				12 00											13 00						
Fratton	a	11 40			12 04								12 42			13 04						
Portsmouth & Southsea	a	11 45			12 08								12 46			13 08						
Portsmouth Harbour ⛴	a	11 52			12 13								12 52			13 13						
Southampton Airport Pkwy ✈	d			11 27			11 34			11 53	11 58				12 27			12 34			12 53	
Swaythling	d										12 01											
St Denys	d										12 04											
Southampton Central ⛴	a			11 34			11 42		11 53	11 59	12 09				12 34			12 42		12 53	13 00	13 05
	d			11 35			11 45		11 54	12 03	12 10				12 35			12 45		12 54	13 03	
Millbrook (Hants)	d										12 13											
Redbridge	d										12 16											
Romsey	d								12 06		12 24	12a28								13 06		
Mottisfont & Dunbridge	d																					
Dean	d																					
Salisbury	a								12 24		12 42									13 24		
Totton	d			11 41											12 41							
Ashurst New Forest	d			11 45											12 45							
Beaulieu Road	d			11 50											12 50							
Brockenhurst ■	a			11 56			12 02			12 16					12 56			13 02			13 16	
	d		11 29	11 57		11 59	12 03			12 17				12 29	12 57		12 59	13 03			13 17	
Lymington Town	d		11 37			12 07								12 37			13 07					
Lymington Pier	a		11 39			12 09								12 39			13 09					
Sway	d			12 01											13 01							
New Milton	d			12 06						12 24					13 06						13 24	
Hinton Admiral	d			12 10											13 10							
Christchurch	d			12 15											13 15							
Pokesdown	d			12 19											13 19							
Bournemouth	a			12 23			12 26			12 34					13 23			13 26			13 34	
	d			12 24						12 39					13 24						13 39	
Branksome	d									12 44											13 44	
Parkstone (Dorset)	d									12 47											13 47	
Poole ■	a			12 33						12 50					13 33						13 50	
	d									12 51											13 51	
Hamworthy	d									12 56											13 56	
Holton Heath	d																					
Wareham	d									13 03											14 03	
Wool	d									13 10											14 10	
Moreton (Dorset)	d									13 16											14 16	
Dorchester South	d									13 24											14 24	
Dorchester West	d																					
Upwey	d									13 31											14 31	
Weymouth	a									13 35											14 35	

A 🍴 to Bournemouth

Table 158

Sundays until 24 June

London - Basingstoke, Southampton, Romsey Lymington, Bournemouth and Weymouth

Network Diagram - see first Page of Table 158

		SW ■	SW ■	SW ■	SW ◇■ 🍴		SW ■	XC ◇■ 🛒	SW ■	GW ◇	SW ◇■ A 🍴	SW ■	SW ■	GW ◇ 🍴	SW ■	SW ◇■ 🍴		SW ■	XC ◇■ 🛒	SW ■	GW ◇	GW	SW ◇■ A 🍴
London Waterloo ■ ⊖	d				11 54				12 07		12 35					12 54				13 07			13 35
Clapham Junction ■	d				12u04				12 15		12u42					13u03				13 15			13u42
Woking	d				12 28				12 46		13 07					13 28				13 46			14 07
Farnborough (Main)	d								12 59											13 59			
Fleet	d								13 04											14 04			
Reading ■	d							12 53											13 53				
Basingstoke	a				12 46			13 09	13 21		13 26					13 46			14 09	14 21			14 26
	d				12 48			13 10			13 28					13 48			14 10				14 28
Micheldever	d				12 58											13 58							
Winchester	d				13 08			13 25			13 44					14 08			14 25				14 44
Shawford	d															14 12							
Romsey	d	12 35	12 32									13 35	13 32	13 51									
Chandlers Ford	d	12 42										13 42											
Eastleigh ■	a	12 48	13 13		13 18							13 48	14 13			14 18							
	d	12 54	13 15		13 22	13 26						13 54	14 15			14 22	14 26						
Hedge End	d					13 32											14 32						
Botley	d					13 36											14 36						
Fareham	d					13 44				13 32				14 27			14 44				14 32		
Portchester	d					13 49											14 49						
Cosham	d					13 54								14 35			14 54						
Hilsea	a					14 00											15 00						
Fratton	a					14 04								14 41			15 04						
Portsmouth & Southsea	a					14 08								14 45			15 08						
Portsmouth Harbour ⛴	a					14 13								14 55			15 13						
Southampton Airport Pkwy ✈	d	12 58			13 27			13 34			13 53	13 58				14 27			14 34				14 53
Swaythling	d	13 01										14 01											
St Denys	d	13 04										14 04											
Southampton Central ⛴	a	13 09			13 34			13 42		13 53	14 00	14 09				14 34			14 42		14 53		15 00
	d	13 10			13 35			13 45		13 54	14 03	14 10				14 35			14 45		14 54		15 03
Millbrook (Hants)	d	13 13										14 13											
Redbridge	d	13 16										14 16											
Romsey	d	13 24	13a28							14 06		14 24	14a28								15 06		
Mottisfont & Dunbridge	d	13 29																					
Dean	d	13 35																					
Salisbury	a	13 48								14 24		14 42									15 24		
Totton	d				13 41											14 41							
Ashurst New Forest	d				13 45											14 45							
Beaulieu Road	d				13 50											14 50							
Brockenhurst ■	a				13 56			14 01			14 16					14 56			15 02				15 16
	d			13 29	13 57		13 59	14 02			14 17				14 29	14 57		14 59	15 03				15 17
Lymington Town	d			13 37			14 07								14 37			15 07					
Lymington Pier	a			13 39			14 09								14 39			15 09					
Sway	d				14 01											15 01							
New Milton	d				14 06						14 24					15 06							15 24
Hinton Admiral	d				14 10											15 10							
Christchurch	d				14 15											15 15							
Pokesdown	d				14 19											15 19							
Bournemouth	a				14 23			14 26			14 34					15 23			15 26				15 34
	d				14 24						14 39					15 24							15 39
Branksome	d										14 44												15 44
Parkstone (Dorset)	d										14 47												15 47
Poole ■	a				14 33						14 50					15 33							15 50
	d										14 51												15 51
Hamworthy	d										14 56												15 56
Holton Heath	d																						
Wareham	d										15 03												16 03
Wool	d										15 10												16 10
Moreton (Dorset)	d										15 16												16 16
Dorchester South	d										15 24												16 24
Dorchester West	d																					15 40	
Upwey	d										15 31											15 49	16 31
Weymouth	a										15 35											15 54	16 35

A 🍴 to Bournemouth

Table 158

Sundays
until 24 June

London - Basingstoke, Southampton, Romsey Lymington, Bournemouth and Weymouth

Network Diagram - see first Page of Table 158

		SW	SW	GW	SW	SW		SW	XC	SW	GW	SW	SW	SW	GW	SW	SW		SW	XC	SW	GW	SW
		■1	■1	◇	■1	◇■1		■1	◇■1	■1	■	◇■1	■1	■1	◇	■1	◇■1		■1	◇■1	■1	◇	◇■1
												A											A
						🍴			☕			🍴					🍴			☕			🍴
London Waterloo ■15 ⊖	d					13 54				14 07		14 35					14 54				15 07		15 35
Clapham Junction ■10	d					14u03				14 15		14u42					15u03				15 15		15u42
Woking	d					14 28				14 46		15 07					15 28				15 46		16 07
Farnborough (Main)	d									14 59											15 59		
Fleet	d									15 04											16 04		
Reading ■7	d								14 53											15 53			
Basingstoke	a					14 46			15 09	15 21		15 26					15 46			16 09	16 21		16 26
	d					14 48			15 10			15 28					15 48			16 10			16 28
Micheldever	d					14 58											15 58						
Winchester	d					15 08			15 25			15 44					16 08			16 25			16 44
Shawford	d																16 12						
Romsey	d	14 35	14 32	15 10									15 35	15 32	15 51								
Chandlers Ford	d	14 42											15 42										
Eastleigh ■3	a	14 48	15 13			15 18							15 48	16 13			16 18						
	d	14 54	15 15			15 22	15 26						15 54	16 15			16 22	16 26					
Hedge End	d						15 32											16 32					
Botley	d						15 36											16 36					
Fareham	d						15 44				15 32				16 27			16 44				16 32	
Portchester	d						15 49											16 49					
Cosham	d						15 54								16 35			16 54					
Hilsea	a						16 00											17 00					
Fratton	a						16 04								16 42			17 03					
Portsmouth & Southsea	a						16 08								16 46			17 08					
Portsmouth Harbour ⛴	a						16 13								16 52			17 13					
Southampton Airport Pkwy ✈	d	14 58				15 27			15 34			15 53	15 58				16 27			16 34			16 53
Swaythling	d	15 01											16 01										
St Denys	d	15 04											16 04										
Southampton Central ⛴	a	15 09		15 21		15 34			15 42		15 53	16 00	16 09				16 34			16 42		16 53	17 00
	d	15 10				15 35			15 45		15 54	16 03	16 10				16 35			16 45		16 54	17 03
Millbrook (Hants)	d	15 13											16 13										
Redbridge	d	15 16											16 16										
Romsey	d	15 24	15a28								16 06		16 24	16a28								17 06	
Mottisfont & Dunbridge	d	15 29																					
Dean	d	15 35																					
Salisbury	a	15 48									16 24		16 42									17 24	
Totton	d					15 41											16 41						
Ashurst New Forest	d					15 45											16 45						
Beaulieu Road	d					15 50											16 50						
Brockenhurst ■3	a					15 56			16 02			16 16					16 56			17 02			17 16
	d				15 29	15 57		15 59	16 03			16 17				16 29	16 57		16 59	17 03			17 17
Lymington Town	d				15 37			16 07								16 37			17 07				
Lymington Pier	a				15 39			16 09								16 39			17 09				
Sway	d					16 01											17 01						
New Milton	d					16 06						16 24					17 06						17 24
Hinton Admiral	d					16 10											17 10						
Christchurch	d					16 15											17 15						
Pokesdown	d					16 19											17 19						
Bournemouth	a					16 23			16 26			16 34					17 23			17 26			17 34
	d					16 24						16 39					17 24						17 39
Branksome	d											16 44											17 44
Parkstone (Dorset)	d											16 47											17 47
Poole ■4	a					16 33						16 50					17 33						17 50
	d											16 51											17 51
Hamworthy	d											16 56											17 56
Holton Heath	d																						
Wareham	d											17 03											18 03
Wool	d											17 10											18 10
Moreton (Dorset)	d											17 16											18 16
Dorchester South	d											17 24											18 24
Dorchester West	d																						
Upwey	d											17 31											18 31
Weymouth	a											17 35											18 35

A 🍴 to Bournemouth

Table 158

Sundays
until 24 June

London - Basingstoke, Southampton, Romsey Lymington, Bournemouth and Weymouth

Network Diagram - see first Page of Table 158

		SW	SW	SW	GW	GW	SW	SW		SW	XC	SW	GW	SW	SW	SW	SW	GW	SW	SW		SW
		■1	■1	■1	◇	◇	■1	◇■1		■1	◇■1	■1	◇	◇■1	■1	■1	■1	◇	■1	◇■1		■1
														A								
								🍴			☕			🍴						🍴		
London Waterloo ■15 ⊖	d	15 37						15 54				16 07		16 35	16 37					16 54		
Clapham Junction ■10	d	15 46						16u03				16 15		16u42	16 46					17u03		
Woking	d	16 23						16 28				16 46		17 07	17 23					17 28		
Farnborough (Main)	d	16 36										16 59			17 36							
Fleet	d	16 41										17 04			17 41							
Reading ■7	d										16 53											
Basingstoke	a	16 54						16 46			17 09	17 21		17 26	17 54					17 46		
	d							16 48			17 10			17 28						17 48		
Micheldever	d							16 58												17 58		
Winchester	d							17 08			17 25			17 44						18 08		
Shawford	d																			18 12		
Romsey	d		16 35	16 32		16 51										17 35	17 32	17 51				
Chandlers Ford	d		16 42													17 42						
Eastleigh ■3	a		16 48	17 13				17 18								17 48	18 13			18 18		
	d		16 54	17 15				17 22	17 26							17 54	18 15			18 22	18 26	
Hedge End	d								17 32												18 32	
Botley	d								17 36												18 36	
Fareham	d				17 03	17 27			17 44				17 32					18 27			18 44	
Portchester	d								17 49												18 49	
Cosham	d					17 35			17 54									18 35			18 54	
Hilsea	a								18 00												19 00	
Fratton	a					17 41			18 04									18 41			19 03	
Portsmouth & Southsea	a					17 46			18 08									18 45			19 08	
Portsmouth Harbour ⛴	a					17 52			18 13									18 52			19 13	
Southampton Airport Pkwy ✈	d		16 58					17 27			17 34			17 53		17 58				18 27		
Swaythling	d		17 01													18 01						
St Denys	d		17 04													18 04						
Southampton Central ⛴	a		17 09		17 24			17 34			17 40		17 53	18 00		18 09				18 34		
	d		17 10		17 26			17 35			17 45		17 54	18 03		18 10				18 35		
Millbrook (Hants)	d		17 13													18 13						
Redbridge	d		17 16													18 16						
Romsey	d		17 24	17a28	17 39								18 06			18 24	18a28					
Mottisfont & Dunbridge	d		17 29																			
Dean	d		17 35																			
Salisbury	a		17 48		18 00								18 24			18 42						
Totton	d							17 41												18 41		
Ashurst New Forest	d							17 45												18 45		
Beaulieu Road	d							17 50												18 50		
Brockenhurst ■3	a							17 56			18 02			18 16						18 56		
	d						17 29	17 57		17 59	18 03			18 17					18 29	18 57		18 59
Lymington Town	d						17 37			18 07									18 37			19 07
Lymington Pier	a						17 39			18 09									18 39			19 09
Sway	d							18 01												19 01		
New Milton	d							18 06						18 24						19 06		
Hinton Admiral	d							18 10												19 10		
Christchurch	d							18 15												19 15		
Pokesdown	d							18 19												19 19		
Bournemouth	a							18 23			18 26			18 34						19 23		
	d							18 24						18 39						19 24		
Branksome	d													18 44								
Parkstone (Dorset)	d													18 47								
Poole ■4	a							18 33						18 50						19 33		
	d													18 51								
Hamworthy	d													18 56								
Holton Heath	d																					
Wareham	d													19 03								
Wool	d													19 10								
Moreton (Dorset)	d													19 16								
Dorchester South	d													19 24								
Dorchester West	d																					
Upwey	d													19 31								
Weymouth	a													19 35								

A 🍴 to Bournemouth

Table 158

Sundays until 24 June

London - Basingstoke, Southampton, Romsey Lymington, Bournemouth and Weymouth

Network Diagram - see first Page of Table 158

		XC	SW	GW	GW	SW	SW	SW	SW	GW	GW	GW	SW	SW		SW	XC	SW	GW	SW	SW	SN	SW
		◇■	■	◇	◇	◇■	■	■	■	◇	◇	◇	■	◇■		■	◇■	■	◇	◇■	■	◇■	■
		🛒				A 🍴								🍴			🛒			A 🍴			
London Waterloo ⊖	d		17 07			17 35	17 37							17 54				18 07		18 35	18 37		
Clapham Junction	d		17 15			17u42	17 46							18u03				18 15		18u42	18 46		
Woking	d		17 46			18 07	18 23							18 28				18 46		19 07	19 23		
Farnborough (Main)	d		17 59				18 36											18 59			19 36		
Fleet	d		18 04				18 41											19 04			19 41		
Reading	d	17 53															18 53						
Basingstoke	a	18 09	18 21			18 26	18 54							18 46			19 09	19 21		19 26	19 54		
	d	18 10				18 28								18 48			19 10			19 28			
Micheldever	d													18 58									
Winchester	d	18 25				18 44								19 08			19 25			19 44			
Shawford	d																						
Romsey	d							18 35	18 32		18 51	19 14											19 35
Chandlers Ford	d							18 42															19 42
Eastleigh	a							18 48	19 13					19 18									19 48
	d							18 54	19 15					19 22	19 26							19 46	19 54
Hedge End	d														19 32								
Botley	d														19 36								
Fareham	d			18 32						19 03	19 28				19 44				19 32			20 03	
Portchester	d														19 49							20a11	
Cosham	d										19 36				19 54								
Hilsea	a														20 00								
Fratton	a										19 42				20 04								
Portsmouth & Southsea	a										19 46				20 08								
Portsmouth Harbour ⛴	a										19 53				20 13								
Southampton Airport Pkwy ✈	d	18 34				18 53		18 58						19 27			19 34			19 53			19 58
Swaythling	d							19 01															20 01
St Denys	d							19 04															20 04
Southampton Central ⛴	a	18 42		18 53		19 00		19 09		19 24		19 25		19 34			19 40		19 53	20 00			20 09
	d	18 45		18 54		19 03		19 10		19 30				19 35			19 45		19 54	20 03			20 10
Millbrook (Hants)	d							19 13															20 13
Redbridge	d							19 16															20 16
Romsey	d			19 06				19 24	19a28	19 42									20 06				20 24
Mottisfont & Dunbridge	d							19 29															
Dean	d							19 35															
Salisbury	a			19 24				19 48		20 00									20 24				20 42
Totton	d													19 41									
Ashurst New Forest	d													19 45									
Beaulieu Road	d													19 50									
Brockenhurst	a	19 01				19 16								19 56			20 02			20 16			
	d	19 02				19 17							19 29	19 57		19 59	20 03			20 17			
Lymington Town	d												19 37			20 07							
Lymington Pier	a												19 39			20 09							
Sway	d													20 01									
New Milton	d					19 24								20 06						20 24			
Hinton Admiral	d													20 10									
Christchurch	d													20 15									
Pokesdown	d													20 19									
Bournemouth	a	19 26				19 34								20 23			20 26			20 34			
	d					19 39								20 24						20 39			
Branksome	d					19 44														20 44			
Parkstone (Dorset)	d					19 47														20 47			
Poole	a					19 50								20 33						20 50			
	d					19 51														20 51			
Hamworthy	d					19 56														20 56			
Holton Heath	d																						
Wareham	d					20 03														21 03			
Wool	d					20 10														21 10			
Moreton (Dorset)	d					20 17														21 17			
Dorchester South	d					20 25														21 25			
Dorchester West	d				19 47																		
Upwey	d				19 55	20 32														21 32			
Weymouth	a				20 01	20 36														21 36			

A 🍴 to Bournemouth

Table 158

Sundays until 24 June

London - Basingstoke, Southampton, Romsey Lymington, Bournemouth and Weymouth

Network Diagram - see first Page of Table 158

		SW	GW	SW	SW		SW	XC	SW	GW	SW	SW	GW	SN	SW	SW	GW	SW	SW		SW	XC
		■	◇	■	◇■		■	◇■	■	◇	◇■	■	■	◇■	■	■	◇	■	◇■		■	◇■
					🍴			🛒			A 🍴											
London Waterloo ⊖	d				18 54				19 07		19 35	19 37							19 54			
Clapham Junction	d				19u03				19 15		19u42	19 46							20u03			
Woking	d				19 28				19 46		20 07	20 23							20 28			
Farnborough (Main)	d								19 59			20 36										
Fleet	d								20 04			20 41										
Reading	d							19 53														20 53
Basingstoke	a				19 46			20 09	20 21		20 26	20 54							20 46			21 09
	d				19 48			20 10			20 28								20 48			21 10
Micheldever	d				19 58														20 58			
Winchester	d				20 08			20 25			20 44								21 08			21 25
Shawford	d				20 12																	
Romsey	d	19 32	19 50										20 19		20 35	20 32	20 48					
Chandlers Ford	d														20 42							
Eastleigh	a	20 13			20 18										20 48	21 13			21 18			
	d	20 15			20 22	20 26								20 46	20 54	21 15			21 22	21 26		
Hedge End	d					20 32														21 32		
Botley	d					20 36														21 36		
Fareham	d		20 26			20 44				20 32			20 55	21 02			21 25			21 44		
Portchester	d					20 49														21 49		
Cosham	d					20 54								21a10						21 54		
Hilsea	a					21 00														22 00		
Fratton	a		20 41			21 04							21 09				21 38			22 04		
Portsmouth & Southsea	a		20 45			21 08							21 15				21 41			22 08		
Portsmouth Harbour ⛴	a		20 51			21 13							21 26				21 48			22 13		
Southampton Airport Pkwy ✈	d				20 27			20 34			20 53				20 58				21 27			21 34
Swaythling	d														21 01							
St Denys	d														21 04							
Southampton Central ⛴	a				20 34			20 42		20 53	21 00				21 09				21 34			21 43
	d				20 35			20 45		20 54	21 03				21 10				21 35			21 45
Millbrook (Hants)	d														21 13							
Redbridge	d														21 16							
Romsey	d	20a28								21 06					21 24	21a28						
Mottisfont & Dunbridge	d														21 29							
Dean	d														21 35							
Salisbury	a									21 24					21 48							
Totton	d				20 41														21 41			
Ashurst New Forest	d				20 45														21 45			
Beaulieu Road	d				20 50														21 50			
Brockenhurst	a				20 56			21 02			21 16								21 56			22 02
	d			20 29	20 57		20 59	21 03			21 17							21 29	21 57		21 59	22 03
Lymington Town	d			20 37			21 07											21 37			22 07	
Lymington Pier	a			20 39			21 09											21 39			22 09	
Sway	d				21 01														22 01			
New Milton	d				21 06						21 24								22 06			
Hinton Admiral	d				21 10														22 10			
Christchurch	d				21 15														22 15			
Pokesdown	d				21 19														22 19			
Bournemouth	a				21 23			21 26			21 34								22 23			22 26
	d				21 24						21 39								22 24			
Branksome	d										21 44											
Parkstone (Dorset)	d										21 47											
Poole	a				21 33						21 50								22 33			
	d										21 51											
Hamworthy	d										21 56											
Holton Heath	d																					
Wareham	d										22 03											
Wool	d										22 10											
Moreton (Dorset)	d										22 17											
Dorchester South	d										22 25											
Dorchester West	d																					
Upwey	d										22 32											
Weymouth	a										22 36											

A 🍴 to Bournemouth

Table 158

Sundays
until 24 June

London - Basingstoke, Southampton, Romsey Lymington, Bournemouth and Weymouth

Network Diagram - see first Page of Table 158

		SW 1	GW	SW ◇1 A 🚌	SW 1	SW 1	SW 1	GW ◇	SW ◇1		XC ◇1	SW 1	GW	SW ◇1 A 🚌	SW 1	SW 1	SW 1	GW ◇	SW ◇1		SW 1	SW 1	SW ◇1 🚌
London Waterloo 15 ⊖	d	20 07		20 35	20 37				20 54			21 07		21 35	21 37				21 54		22 07	22 37	22 54
Clapham Junction 10	d	20 15		20u42	20 46				21u03			21 15		21u42	21 46				22u03		22 15	22 46	23u03
Woking	d	20 46		21 07	21 23				21 28			21 46		22 07	22 23				22 28		22 46	23 23	23 28
Farnborough (Main)	d	20 59			21 36							21 59			22 36						22 59	23 36	
Fleet	d	21 04			21 41							22 04			22 41						23 04	23 41	
Reading 7	d										21 53												
Basingstoke	a	21 21		21 26	21 54				21 46		22 09	22 21		22 26	22 54				22 46		23 21	23 54	23 46
	d			21 28					21 48		22 10			22 28					22 48				23 48
Micheldever	d								21 58										22 58				23 58
Winchester	d			21 44					22 08		22 25			22 44					23 08				00 08
Shawford	d								22 12														
Romsey	d					21 35	21 32	21 51								22 35	22 28	22 54					
Chandlers Ford	d					21 42										22 42							
Eastleigh 3	a					21 48	22 13		22 18							22 48	23 19		23 17				00 18
	d					21 54	22 15		22 22	22 26						22 54	23 21		23 22	23 26			00 22
Hedge End	d									22 32										23 32			
Botley	d									22 36										23 36			
Fareham	d							22 26		22 44			22 32					23 30		23 44			
Portchester	d									22 49										23 49			
Cosham	d									22 54										23 54			
Hilsea	a									23 00										23 59			
Fratton	a							22 40		23 04								23 43		00 04			
Portsmouth & Southsea	a							22 43		23 08								23 46		00 08			
Portsmouth Harbour ⛴	a							22 50		23 13								23 54		00 13			
Southampton Airport Pkwy ✈	d			21 53		21 58			22 27		22 34			22 53		22 58			23 27				00 27
Swaythling	d					22 01										23 01							
St Denys	d					22 04										23 04							00s31
Southampton Central ⛴	a			22 00		22 09			22 34		22 42		22 53	23 00		23 09			23 34				00 36
	d			22 03		22 10			22 35				22 57	23 03		23 10			23 35				00 37
Millbrook (Hants)	d					22 13										23 13							
Redbridge	d					22 16										23 16							
Romsey	d					22a24	22a31						23 09			23 24	23a33						
Mottisfont & Dunbridge	d															23 29							
Dean	d															23 35							
Salisbury	a												23 27			23 51							
Totton	d								22 41										23 41				00s42
Ashurst New Forest	d								22 45										23 45				
Beaulieu Road	d								22 50														
Brockenhurst 3	a			22 16					22 56					23 16					23 53				00s53
	d			22 17					22 57					23 17					23 54				
Lymington Town	d																						
Lymington Pier	a																						
Sway	d								23 01										23 59				
New Milton	d			22 24					23 06					23 24					00 04				01s01
Hinton Admiral	d								23 10										00 08				
Christchurch	d								23 15										00 13				01s08
Pokesdown	d								23 19										00 16				01s12
Bournemouth	a			22 34					23 23					23 34					00 20				01 16
	d			22 39					23 24					23 39					00 22				01 17
Branksome	d			22 44										23 44					00 27				01s22
Parkstone (Dorset)	d			22 47										23 47					00 30				01s25
Poole 4	a			22 50					23 33					23 50					00 34				01 29
	d			22 51										23 51									
Hamworthy	d			22 56										23 56									
Holton Heath	d																						
Wareham	d			23 03										00 03									
Wool	d			23 10										00 10									
Moreton (Dorset)	d			23 17										00 17									
Dorchester South	d			23 25										00 25									
Dorchester West	d		22 53																				
Upwey	d		23 01	23 32										00 32									
Weymouth	a		23 06	23 36										00 36									

A 🚌 to Bournemouth

Table 158

Sundays
until 24 June

London - Basingstoke, Southampton, Romsey Lymington, Bournemouth and Weymouth

Network Diagram - see first Page of Table 158

		SW 1
London Waterloo 15 ⊖	d	23 07
Clapham Junction 10	d	23 15
Woking	d	23 46
Farnborough (Main)	d	23 59
Fleet	d	00 04
Reading 7	d	
Basingstoke	a	00 21
	d	
Micheldever	d	
Winchester	d	
Shawford	d	
Romsey	d	
Chandlers Ford	d	
Eastleigh 3	a	
	d	
Hedge End	d	
Botley	d	
Fareham	d	
Portchester	d	
Cosham	d	
Hilsea	a	
Fratton	a	
Portsmouth & Southsea	a	
Portsmouth Harbour ⛴	a	
Southampton Airport Pkwy ✈	d	
Swaythling	d	
St Denys	d	
Southampton Central ⛴	a	
	d	
Millbrook (Hants)	d	
Redbridge	d	
Romsey	d	
Mottisfont & Dunbridge	d	
Dean	d	
Salisbury	a	
Totton	d	
Ashurst New Forest	d	
Beaulieu Road	d	
Brockenhurst 3	a	
	d	
Lymington Town	d	
Lymington Pier	a	
Sway	d	
New Milton	d	
Hinton Admiral	d	
Christchurch	d	
Pokesdown	d	
Bournemouth	a	
	d	
Branksome	d	
Parkstone (Dorset)	d	
Poole 4	a	
	d	
Hamworthy	d	
Holton Heath	d	
Wareham	d	
Wool	d	
Moreton (Dorset)	d	
Dorchester South	d	
Dorchester West	d	
Upwey	d	
Weymouth	a	

Table 158

Sundays
1 July to 9 September

London - Basingstoke, Southampton, Romsey Lymington, Bournemouth and Weymouth

Network Diagram - see first Page of Table 158

		SW	SW	SW	SW	SW	SW	SW	SW	SW	SW	SW	SW	SW	SW	SW	GW	SW	SW		SW	SN	SW
		◇1 A ⌶	1	◇1 ⌶	1	◇1 ⌶	1	◇1	1	1	1	1	1 B	1 C	1	1		1	1		1	◇1	1
London Waterloo 15 ⊖	d	21p35	21p42	22p05		22p35	22p39	23p05	23p12		23p35	23p48	00 05	00 30	01 05								
Clapham Junction 10	d			22b12			22b46	23b12	23b19		23b42	23b54	00u12	00u37	01 15								
Woking	d	22p00	22p19	22p32		23p00		23p32	23p57		00 03	00 28	00 37	01 00	01 49						07 46		
Farnborough (Main)	d		22p33				23p16		00 10		00 14	00 41			01s58						07 59		
Fleet	d		22p38				23p21		00 16		00 20	00 47			02s04						08 04		
Reading 7	d																						
Basingstoke	a		22p58	22p51			23p34	23p51	00 33		00 33	01 06	00 55	01 18	02s16						08 21		
	d		23p00	22p52			23p36	23p52			00 35		00 56	01 20					07 48				
Micheldever	d		23p10					00 02											07 58				
Winchester	d	22p33	23p19	23p09		23p33	23p52	00 12			00 51		01 13	01 36	02s33				08 08				
Shawford	d						23p57												08 12				
Romsey	d				23p09												08 19						
Chandlers Ford	d				23p16																		
Eastleigh 8	a		23p27	23p17	23p22		00 02	00 20			00 59		01 21	01 44	02s42				08 18				
	d		23p28	23p18	23p23		00 03	00 21		00 30	01 00		01 22	01 45					08 22	08 26		08 48	
Hedge End	d		23p34							00s36										08 32			
Botley	d		23p38							00s39										08 36			
Fareham	d		23p48							00s47						07 44				08 44		09 02	
Portchester	d		23p53							00s53						07 49				08 49			
Cosham	d		23p58							00s57						07 54				08 54		09a10	
Hilsea	a		00 03													08 00				09 00			
Fratton	a		00 07							01s05						08 04				09 04			
Portsmouth & Southsea	a		00 11							01s08						08 08				09 08			
Portsmouth Harbour ⛴	a		00 16							01 12						08 13				09 13			
Southampton Airport Pkwy ✈	d	22p42		23p22	23p27	23p42	00 08	00 25			01 05		01 26	01 50	02s46				08 27				
Swaythling	d				23p30																		
St Denys	d				23p33			00s29							02s51								
Southampton Central ⛴	a	22p49		23p29	23p38	23p49	00 15	00 34			01 12		01 35	01 57	02 56		08 29		08 34				
	d	22p51		23p31	23p40	23p51		00 36					01 37	01 58					08 35				
Millbrook (Hants)	d				23p42																		
Redbridge	d				23p46																		
Romsey	d				23p57																		
Mottisfont & Dunbridge	d				00 02																		
Dean	d				00 08																		
Salisbury	a				00 20																		
Totton	d			23p36				00s41					01s42	02s03					08 41				
Ashurst New Forest	d			23p41															08 45				
Beaulieu Road	d																		08 50				
Brockenhurst 3	a	23p04		23p49		00 04		00s52					01s53	02s14					08 56				
	d	23p05		23p50		00 05													08 57				08 59
Lymington Town	d																						09 07
Lymington Pier	a																						09 09
Sway	d			23p54															09 01				
New Milton	d			23p59				01s00					02s00	02s22					09 06				
Hinton Admiral	d			00 03															09 10				
Christchurch	d			00 08				01s07					02s07	02s29					09 15				
Pokesdown	d			00 11				01s11					02s11	02s33					09 19				
Bournemouth	a	23p25		00 15		00 21		01 15					02 15	02 37					09 23				
	d	23p29		00 17		00 22		01 16										08 39	09 24				
Branksome	d	23p35		00 23		00 27		01s21										08 44					
Parkstone (Dorset)	d	23p38		00 26		00 30		01s24										08 47					
Poole 4	a	23p41		00 30		00 35		01 29										08 50	09 33				
	d	23p42																08 51					
Hamworthy	d	23p47																08 56					
Holton Heath	d																						
Wareham	d	23p54																09 03					
Wool	d	00 01																09 10					
Moreton (Dorset)	d	00 07																09 16					
Dorchester South	d	00 15																09 24					
Dorchester West	d																						
Upwey	d	00 21																09 31					
Weymouth	a	00 26																09 35					

A ⌶ to Bournemouth
B from 1 July until 22 July, 19 August, 26 August
C 29 July, 5 August, 12 August, 2 September, 9 September
b Previous night, stops to pick up only

Table 158

Sundays
1 July to 9 September

London - Basingstoke, Southampton, Romsey Lymington, Bournemouth and Weymouth

Network Diagram - see first Page of Table 158

		SW	SW	SW	SW	SW	GW	SW		SW	SW	GW	SW	SW	SW	SW	SW		SW	XC	SW	GW	SW
		1 A	1 B	1	1	1	1	◇1		1	1		◇1	1	1	1	◇1		1	◇1 ⌶	1		◇1
London Waterloo 15 ⊖	d		07 35					07 54		08 07			08 35				08 54				09 07		09 35
Clapham Junction 10	d		07u45					08u03		08 15			08u45				09u03				09 15		09u45
Woking	d		08 09					08 28		08 46			09 09				09 28				09 46		10 09
Farnborough (Main)	d									08 59											09 59		
Fleet	d									09 04											10 04		
Reading 7	d																			09 53			
Basingstoke	a		08 27					08 46		09 21			09 28				09 46			10 09	10 21		10 28
	d		08 29					08 48					09 29				09 48			10 10			10 29
Micheldever	d							08 58									09 58						
Winchester	d		08 46					09 08					09 46				10 08			10 25			10 46
Shawford	d																10 12						
Romsey	d			08 35	08 39									09 35	09 32								
Chandlers Ford	d			08 42										09 42									
Eastleigh 8	a			08 47	09 13			09 18						09 48	10 13		10 18						
	d			08 54	09 15			09 22	09 26					09 54	10 15		10 22	10 26					
Hedge End	d								09 32									10 32					
Botley	d								09 36									10 36					
Fareham	d						09 32		09 44									10 44					
Portchester	d								09 49									10 49					
Cosham	d								09 54									10 54					
Hilsea	a								10 04									11 04					
Fratton	a								10 08									11 08					
Portsmouth & Southsea	a								10 11									11 11					
Portsmouth Harbour ⛴	a								10 15									11 15					
Southampton Airport Pkwy ✈	d		08 55	08 58				09 27					09 55	09 58			10 27			10 34			10 55
Swaythling	d			09 01										10 01									
St Denys	d			09 04										10 04									
Southampton Central ⛴	a		09 02	09 09			09 53	09 34					10 02	10 09			10 34			10 42			11 02
	d	09 03	09 03	09 10			09 54	09 35					10 03	10 10			10 35			10 45			11 03
Millbrook (Hants)	d			09 13										10 13									
Redbridge	d			09 16										10 16									
Romsey	d			09 24	09a28		10 06							10 24	10a28								
Mottisfont & Dunbridge	d			09 29																			
Dean	d			09 35																			
Salisbury	a			09 48			10 24							10 42									
Totton	d							09 41									10 41						
Ashurst New Forest	d							09 45									10 45						
Beaulieu Road	d							09 50									10 50						
Brockenhurst 3	a	09 16	09 17					09 56					10 17				10 56			11 02			11 17
	d	09 17	09 18			09 29		09 57			09 59		10 18			10 29	10 57		10 59	11 03			11 18
Lymington Town	d					09 37					10 07					10 37			11 07				
Lymington Pier	a					09 39					10 09					10 39			11 09				
Sway	d							10 01									11 01						
New Milton	d	09 24	09 25					10 06					10 25				11 06						11 25
Hinton Admiral	d							10 10									11 10						
Christchurch	d							10 15									11 15						
Pokesdown	d							10 19									11 19						
Bournemouth	a	09 34	09 35					10 23					10 35				11 23			11 26			11 35
	d	09 39	09 39					10 24					10 39				11 24						11 39
Branksome	d	09 44	09 44										10 44										11 44
Parkstone (Dorset)	d	09 47	09 47										10 47										11 47
Poole 4	a	09 50	09 50					10 33					10 50				11 33						11 50
	d	09 51	09 51										10 51										11 51
Hamworthy	d	09 56	09 56										10 56										11 56
Holton Heath	d																						
Wareham	d	10 03	10 03										11 03										12 03
Wool	d	10 10	10 10										11 10										12 10
Moreton (Dorset)	d	10 16	10 16										11 16										12 16
Dorchester South	d	10 24	10 24										11 24										12 24
Dorchester West	d											10 26										11 30	
Upwey	d	10 31	10 31									10 37	11 31									11 37	12 31
Weymouth	a	10 35	10 35									10 42	11 35									11 43	12 35

A not 29 July, 5 August, 2 September
B 29 July, 5 August, 2 September

London - Basingstoke, Southampton, Romsey Lymington, Bournemouth and Weymouth

Sundays

1 July to 9 September

Network Diagram - see first Page of Table 158

		SW ■	SW ■	GW ◇	SW ■	SW ◇■		SW ■	XC ◇■ 🛒	SW ■	GW ◇	SW ◇■ A 🛒	SW ■	SW ■	GW ◇	SW ■	SW ◇■		SW ■	XC ◇■ 🛒	SW ■	GW ◇
London Waterloo ■15 ⊖	d					09 54				10 07		10 35					10 54				11 07	
Clapham Junction ■10	d					10u03				10 15		10u45					11u04				11 15	
Woking	d					10 28				10 46		11 07					11 28				11 46	
Farnborough (Main)	d									10 59											11 59	
Fleet	d									11 04											12 04	
Reading ■7	d								10 53											11 53		
Basingstoke	a					10 46			11 09	11 21		11 26					11 46			12 09	12 21	
	d					10 48			11 10			11 28					11 48			12 10		
Micheldever	d					10 58											11 58					
Winchester	d					11 08			11 25			11 44					12 08			12 25		
Shawford	d																12 12					
Romsey	d	10 35	10 32	10 50									11 35	11 32	11 51							
Chandlers Ford	d	10 42											11 42									
Eastleigh ■3	a	10 48	11 13			11 18							11 48	12 13			12 18					
	d	10 54	11 15			11 22	11 26						11 54	12 15			12 22	12 26				
Hedge End	d						11 32											12 32				
Botley	d						11 36											12 36				
Fareham	d			11 26			11 44				11 32				12 28			12 44				12 32
Portchester	d						11 49											12 49				
Cosham	d			11 34			11 54								12 36			12 54				
Hilsea	a						12 00											13 00				
Fratton	a			11 40			12 04								12 42			13 04				
Portsmouth & Southsea	a			11 45			12 08								12 46			13 08				
Portsmouth Harbour ⛴	a			11 52			12 13								12 52			13 13				
Southampton Airport Pkwy ✈	d	10 58				11 27			11 34			11 53	11 58				12 27			12 34		
Swaythling	d	11 01											12 01									
St Denys	d	11 04											12 04									
Southampton Central ⛴	a	11 09				11 34			11 42		11 53	11 59	12 09				12 34			12 42		12 53
	d	11 10				11 35			11 45		11 54	12 03	12 10				12 35			12 45		12 54
Millbrook (Hants)	d	11 13											12 13									
Redbridge	d	11 16											12 16									
Romsey	d	11 24	11a28								12 06		12 24	12a28								13 06
Mottisfont & Dunbridge	d	11 29																				
Dean	d	11 35																				
Salisbury	a	11 48									12 24		12 42									13 24
Totton	d					11 41											12 41					
Ashurst New Forest	d					11 45											12 45					
Beaulieu Road	d					11 50											12 50					
Brockenhurst ■3	a					11 56			12 02			12 16					12 56			13 02		
	d				11 29	11 57		11 59	12 03			12 17				12 29	12 57		12 59	13 03		
Lymington Town	d				11 37			12 07								12 37			13 07			
Lymington Pier	a				11 39			12 09								12 39			13 09			
Sway	d					12 01											13 01					
New Milton	d					12 06						12 24					13 06					
Hinton Admiral	d					12 10											13 10					
Christchurch	d					12 15											13 15					
Pokesdown	d					12 19											13 19					
Bournemouth	a					12 23			12 26			12 34					13 23			13 26		
	d					12 24						12 39					13 24					
Branksome	d											12 44										
Parkstone (Dorset)	d											12 47										
Poole ■4	a					12 33						12 50					13 33					
	d											12 51										
Hamworthy	d											12 56										
Holton Heath	d																					
Wareham	d											13 03										
Wool	d											13 10										
Moreton (Dorset)	d											13 16										
Dorchester South	d											13 24										
Dorchester West	d																					
Upwey	d											13 31										
Weymouth	a											13 35										

A 🛒 to Bournemouth

Table 158

London - Basingstoke, Southampton, Romsey Lymington, Bournemouth and Weymouth

Sundays

1 July to 9 September

Network Diagram - see first Page of Table 158

		SW ◇■ A 🛒	GW ◇	SW ■	SW ■	SW ■	SW ◇■ 🛒		SW ■	XC ◇■ 🛒	SW ■	GW ◇	SW ◇■ A 🛒	SW ■	SW ■	GW ◇ 🛒	SW ■	SW ◇■ 🛒		SW ■	XC ◇■ 🛒	SW ■	GW ◇
London Waterloo ■15 ⊖	d	11 35					11 54				12 07		12 35					12 54				13 07	
Clapham Junction ■10	d	11u45					12u04				12 15		12u42					13u03				13 15	
Woking	d	12 07					12 28				12 46		13 07					13 28				13 46	
Farnborough (Main)	d										12 59											13 59	
Fleet	d										13 04											14 04	
Reading ■7	d									12 53											13 53		
Basingstoke	a	12 26					12 46			13 09	13 21		13 26					13 46			14 09	14 21	
	d	12 28					12 48			13 10			13 28					13 48			14 10		
Micheldever	d						12 58											13 58					
Winchester	d	12 44					13 08			13 25			13 44					14 08			14 25		
Shawford	d																	14 12					
Romsey	d		12 52	12 35	12 32									13 35	13 32	13 51							
Chandlers Ford	d			12 42										13 42									
Eastleigh ■3	a			12 48	13 13		13 18							13 48	14 13			14 18					
	d			12 54	13 15		13 22	13 26						13 54	14 15			14 22	14 26				
Hedge End	d							13 32											14 32				
Botley	d							13 36											14 36				
Fareham	d							13 44				13 32				14 27			14 44				14 32
Portchester	d							13 49											14 49				
Cosham	d							13 54								14 35			14 54				
Hilsea	a							14 00											15 00				
Fratton	a							14 04								14 41			15 04				
Portsmouth & Southsea	a							14 08								14 45			15 08				
Portsmouth Harbour ⛴	a							14 13								14 55			15 13				
Southampton Airport Pkwy ✈	d	12 53		12 58			13 27			13 34			13 53	13 58				14 27			14 34		
Swaythling	d			13 01										14 01									
St Denys	d			13 04										14 04									
Southampton Central ⛴	a	13 00	13 05	13 09			13 34			13 42		13 53	14 00	14 09				14 34			14 42		14 53
	d	13 03		13 10			13 35			13 45		13 54	14 03	14 10				14 35			14 45		14 54
Millbrook (Hants)	d			13 13										14 13									
Redbridge	d			13 16										14 16									
Romsey	d			13 24	13a28							14 06		14 24	14a28								15 06
Mottisfont & Dunbridge	d			13 29																			
Dean	d			13 35																			
Salisbury	a			13 48								14 24		14 42									15 24
Totton	d						13 41											14 41					
Ashurst New Forest	d						13 45											14 45					
Beaulieu Road	d						13 50											14 50					
Brockenhurst ■3	a	13 16					13 56			14 01			14 16					14 56			15 02		
	d	13 17				13 29	13 57		13 59	14 02			14 17				14 29	14 57		14 59	15 03		
Lymington Town	d					13 37			14 07								14 37			15 07			
Lymington Pier	a					13 39			14 09								14 39			15 09			
Sway	d						14 01											15 01					
New Milton	d	13 24					14 06						14 24					15 06					
Hinton Admiral	d						14 10											15 10					
Christchurch	d						14 15											15 15					
Pokesdown	d						14 19											15 19					
Bournemouth	a	13 34					14 23			14 26			14 34					15 23			15 26		
	d	13 39					14 24						14 39					15 24					
Branksome	d	13 44											14 44										
Parkstone (Dorset)	d	13 47											14 47										
Poole ■4	a	13 50					14 33						14 50					15 33					
	d	13 51											14 51										
Hamworthy	d	13 56											14 56										
Holton Heath	d																						
Wareham	d	14 03											15 03										
Wool	d	14 10											15 10										
Moreton (Dorset)	d	14 16											15 16										
Dorchester South	d	14 24											15 24										
Dorchester West	d																						
Upwey	d	14 31											15 31										
Weymouth	a	14 35											15 35										

A 🛒 to Bournemouth

Table 158

Sundays
1 July to 9 September

London - Basingstoke, Southampton, Romsey Lymington, Bournemouth and Weymouth

Network Diagram - see first Page of Table 158

		GW	SW	SW	SW	GW	SW	SW		SW	XC	SW	GW	SW	SW	SW	GW	SW	SW		SW	XC	SW
			◇■ A ⌶	■	■	◇	■	◇■ ⌶		■	◇■ ⌶	■	■	◇■ A ⌶	■	■	◇	■	◇■ ⌶		■	◇■ ⌶	■
London Waterloo ⊖	d		13 35					13 54				14 07		14 35					14 54				15 07
Clapham Junction	d		13u42					14u03				14 15		14u42					15u03				15 15
Woking	d		14 07					14 28				14 46		15 07					15 28				15 46
Farnborough (Main)	d											14 59											15 59
Fleet	d											15 04											16 04
Reading ■	d										14 53											15 53	
Basingstoke	a		14 26					14 46			15 09	15 21		15 26					15 46			16 09	16 21
	d		14 28					14 48			15 10			15 28					15 48			16 10	
Micheldever	d							14 58											15 58				
Winchester	d		14 44					15 08			15 25			15 44					16 08			16 25	
Shawford	d																		16 12				
Romsey	d			14 35	14 32	15 10									15 35	15 32	15 51						
Chandlers Ford	d			14 42											15 42								
Eastleigh ■	a			14 48	15 13			15 18							15 48	16 13			16 18				
	d			14 54	15 15			15 22	15 26						15 54	16 15			16 22	16 26			
Hedge End	d								15 32											16 32			
Botley	d								15 36											16 36			
Fareham	d								15 44				15 32				16 27			16 44			
Portchester	d								15 49											16 49			
Cosham	d								15 54								16 35			16 54			
Hilsea	a								16 00											17 00			
Fratton	a								16 04								16 42			17 03			
Portsmouth & Southsea	a								16 08								16 46			17 08			
Portsmouth Harbour ⛴	a								16 13								16 52			17 13			
Southampton Airport Pkwy ✈	d		14 53	14 58				15 27			15 34			15 53	15 58				16 27			16 34	
Swaythling	d			15 01											16 01								
St Denys	d			15 04											16 04								
Southampton Central ⛴	a		15 00	15 09		15 21		15 34			15 42		15 53	16 00	16 09				16 34			16 42	
	d		15 03	15 10				15 35			15 45		15 54	16 03	16 10				16 35			16 45	
Millbrook (Hants)	d			15 13											16 13								
Redbridge	d			15 16											16 16								
Romsey	d			15 24	15a28								16 06		16 24	16a28							
Mottisfont & Dunbridge	d			15 29																			
Dean	d			15 35																			
Salisbury	a			15 48									16 24		16 42								
Totton	d							15 41											16 41				
Ashurst New Forest	d							15 45											16 45				
Beaulieu Road	d							15 50											16 50				
Brockenhurst ■	a		15 16					15 56			16 02			16 16					16 56			17 02	
	d		15 17				15 29	15 57		15 59	16 03			16 17				16 29	16 57		16 59	17 03	
Lymington Town	d						15 37			16 07								16 37			17 07		
Lymington Pier	a						15 39			16 09								16 39			17 09		
Sway	d							16 01											17 01				
New Milton	d		15 24					16 06						16 24					17 06				
Hinton Admiral	d							16 10											17 10				
Christchurch	d							16 15											17 15				
Pokesdown	d							16 19											17 19				
Bournemouth	a		15 34					16 23			16 26			16 34					17 23			17 26	
	d		15 39					16 24						16 39					17 24				
Branksome	d		15 44											16 44									
Parkstone (Dorset)	d		15 47											16 47									
Poole ■	a		15 50					16 33						16 50					17 33				
	d		15 51											16 51									
Hamworthy	d		15 56											16 56									
Holton Heath	d																						
Wareham	d		16 03											17 03									
Wool	d		16 10											17 10									
Moreton (Dorset)	d		16 16											17 16									
Dorchester South	d		16 24											17 24									
Dorchester West	d	15 40																					
Upwey	d	15 49	16 31											17 31									
Weymouth	a	15 54	16 35											17 35									

A ⌶ to Bournemouth

Table 158

Sundays
1 July to 9 September

London - Basingstoke, Southampton, Romsey Lymington, Bournemouth and Weymouth

Network Diagram - see first Page of Table 158

		GW	SW	SW	SW	SW	GW	GW	SW	SW		SW	XC	SW	GW	SW	SW	SW	SW	GW	SW
		◇	◇■ A ⌶	■	■	■	◇	◇	■	◇■ ⌶		■	◇■ ⊐	■	◇	◇■ A ⌶	■	■	■	◇	■
London Waterloo ⊖	d		15 35	15 37						15 54				16 07		16 35	16 37				
Clapham Junction	d		15u42	15 46						16u03				16 15		16u42	16 46				
Woking	d		16 07	16 23						16 28				16 46		17 07	17 23				
Farnborough (Main)	d			16 36										16 59			17 36				
Fleet	d			16 41										17 04			17 41				
Reading ■	d												16 53								
Basingstoke	a		16 26	16 54						16 46			17 09	17 21		17 26	17 54				
	d		16 28							16 48			17 10			17 28					
Micheldever	d									16 58											
Winchester	d		16 44							17 08			17 25			17 44					
Shawford	d																				
Romsey	d				16 35	16 32		16 51										17 35	17 32	17 51	
Chandlers Ford	d				16 42													17 42			
Eastleigh ■	a				16 48	17 13				17 18								17 48	18 13		
	d				16 54	17 15				17 22	17 26							17 54	18 15		
Hedge End	d										17 32										
Botley	d										17 36										
Fareham	d	16 32					17 03	17 27			17 44				17 32					18 27	
Portchester	d										17 49										
Cosham	d							17 35			17 54									18 35	
Hilsea	a										18 00										
Fratton	a							17 41			18 04									18 41	
Portsmouth & Southsea	a							17 46			18 08									18 45	
Portsmouth Harbour ⛴	a							17 52			18 13									18 52	
Southampton Airport Pkwy ✈	d		16 53		16 58					17 27			17 34			17 53		17 58			
Swaythling	d				17 01													18 01			
St Denys	d				17 04													18 04			
Southampton Central ⛴	a	16 53	17 00		17 09		17 24			17 34			17 40		17 53	18 00		18 09			
	d	16 54	17 03		17 10		17 26			17 35			17 45		17 54	18 03		18 10			
Millbrook (Hants)	d				17 13													18 13			
Redbridge	d				17 16													18 16			
Romsey	d	17 06			17 24	17a28	17 39								18 06			18 24	18a28		
Mottisfont & Dunbridge	d				17 29																
Dean	d				17 35																
Salisbury	a	17 24			17 48		18 00								18 24			18 42			
Totton	d									17 41											
Ashurst New Forest	d									17 45											
Beaulieu Road	d									17 50											
Brockenhurst ■	a		17 16							17 56			18 02			18 16					
	d		17 17						17 29	17 57		17 59	18 03			18 17					18 29
Lymington Town	d								17 37			18 07									18 37
Lymington Pier	a								17 39			18 09									18 39
Sway	d									18 01											
New Milton	d		17 24							18 06						18 24					
Hinton Admiral	d									18 10											
Christchurch	d									18 15											
Pokesdown	d									18 19											
Bournemouth	a		17 34							18 23			18 26			18 34					
	d		17 39							18 24						18 39					
Branksome	d		17 44													18 44					
Parkstone (Dorset)	d		17 47													18 47					
Poole ■	a		17 50							18 33						18 50					
	d		17 51													18 51					
Hamworthy	d		17 56													18 56					
Holton Heath	d																				
Wareham	d		18 03													19 03					
Wool	d		18 10													19 10					
Moreton (Dorset)	d		18 16													19 16					
Dorchester South	d		18 24													19 24					
Dorchester West	d																				
Upwey	d		18 31													19 31					
Weymouth	a		18 35													19 35					

A ⌶ to Bournemouth

Table 158

Sundays
1 July to 9 September

London - Basingstoke, Southampton, Romsey Lymington, Bournemouth and Weymouth

Network Diagram - see first Page of Table 158

		SW		SW	XC	SW	GW	GW	SW	SW	SW	SW	GW	GW	GW	SW	SW		SW	XC	SW	GW	SW
		◇■		■	◇■	■	◇	◇	◇■	■	■	■	◇	◇	◇	■	◇■		■	◇■	■	◇	◇■
		🍴			🛒				A 🍴								🍴			🛒			A 🍴
London Waterloo 15 ⊖	d	16 54				17 07			17 35	17 37							17 54				18 07		18 35
Clapham Junction 10	d	17u03				17 15			17u42	17 46							18u03				18 15		18u42
Woking	d	17 28				17 46			18 07	18 23							18 28				18 46		19 07
Farnborough (Main)	d					17 59				18 36											18 59		
Fleet	d					18 04				18 41											19 04		
Reading 7	d				17 53															18 53			
Basingstoke	a	17 46			18 09	18 21			18 26	18 54							18 46			19 09	19 21		19 26
	d	17 48			18 10				18 28								18 48			19 10			19 28
Micheldever	d	17 58															18 58						
Winchester	d	18 08			18 25				18 44								19 08			19 25			19 44
Shawford	d	18 12																					
Romsey	d										18 35	18 32		18 51	19 14								
Chandlers Ford	d										18 42												
Eastleigh 3	a	18 18									18 48	19 13					19 18						
	d	18 22	18 26								18 54	19 15					19 22	19 26					
Hedge End	d		18 32															19 32					
Botley	d		18 36															19 36					
Fareham	d		18 44				18 32						19 03	19 28				19 44				19 32	
Portchester	d		18 49															19 49					
Cosham	d		18 54											19 36				19 54					
Hilsea	a		19 00															20 00					
Fratton	a		19 03											19 42				20 04					
Portsmouth & Southsea	a		19 08											19 46				20 08					
Portsmouth Harbour ⛴	a		19 13											19 53				20 13					
Southampton Airport Pkwy ✈	d	18 27			18 34				18 53		18 58						19 27			19 34			19 53
Swaythling	d										19 01												
St Denys	d										19 04												
Southampton Central ⛴	a	18 34			18 42		18 53		19 00		19 09		19 24		19 25		19 34			19 40		19 53	20 00
	d	18 35			18 45		18 54		19 03		19 10		19 30				19 35			19 45		19 54	20 03
Millbrook (Hants)	d										19 13												
Redbridge	d										19 16												
Romsey	d						19 06				19 24	19a28	19 42									20 06	
Mottisfont & Dunbridge	d										19 29												
Dean	d										19 35												
Salisbury	a						19 24				19 48		20 00									20 24	
Totton	d	18 41															19 41						
Ashurst New Forest	d	18 45															19 45						
Beaulieu Road	d	18 50															19 50						
Brockenhurst 3	a	18 56			19 01				19 16								19 56			20 02			20 16
	d	18 57		18 59	19 02				19 17							19 29	19 57		19 59	20 03			20 17
Lymington Town	d			19 07												19 37			20 07				
Lymington Pier	a			19 09												19 39			20 09				
Sway	d	19 01															20 01						
New Milton	d	19 06							19 24								20 06						20 24
Hinton Admiral	d	19 10															20 10						
Christchurch	d	19 15															20 15						
Pokesdown	d	19 19															20 19						
Bournemouth	a	19 23			19 26				19 34								20 23			20 26			20 34
	d	19 24							19 39								20 24						20 39
Branksome	d								19 44														20 44
Parkstone (Dorset)	d								19 47														20 47
Poole 4	a	19 33							19 50								20 33						20 50
	d								19 51														20 51
Hamworthy	d								19 56														20 56
Holton Heath	d																						
Wareham	d								20 03														21 03
Wool	d								20 10														21 10
Moreton (Dorset)	d								20 17														21 17
Dorchester South	d								20 25														21 25
Dorchester West	d							19 47															
Upwey	d							19 55	20 32														21 32
Weymouth	a							20 01	20 36														21 36

A 🍴 to Bournemouth

Table 158

Sundays
1 July to 9 September

London - Basingstoke, Southampton, Romsey Lymington, Bournemouth and Weymouth

Network Diagram - see first Page of Table 158

		SW	SN	SW	SW	GW	SW	SW		SW	XC	SW	GW	SW	SW	GW	SN	SW	SW	GW	SW	SW	
		■	◇■	■	■	◇	■	◇■		■	◇■	■	◇	◇■	■	■	◇■	■	■	◇	■	◇■	
								🍴			🛒			A 🍴									
London Waterloo 15 ⊖	d	18 37						18 54				19 07		19 35	19 37							19 54	
Clapham Junction 10	d	18 46						19u03				19 15		19u42	19 46							20u03	
Woking	d	19 23						19 28				19 46		20 07	20 23							20 28	
Farnborough (Main)	d	19 36										19 59			20 36								
Fleet	d	19 41										20 04			20 41								
Reading 7	d										19 53												
Basingstoke	a	19 54						19 46			20 09	20 21		20 26	20 54							20 46	
	d							19 48			20 10			20 28								20 48	
Micheldever	d							19 58														20 58	
Winchester	d							20 08			20 25			20 44								21 08	
Shawford	d							20 12															
Romsey	d			19 35	19 32	19 50										20 19		20 35	20 32	20 48			
Chandlers Ford	d			19 42														20 42					
Eastleigh 3	a			19 48	20 13			20 18										20 48	21 13			21 18	
	d		19 46	19 54	20 15			20 22	20 26								20 46	20 54	21 15			21 22	21 26
Hedge End	d								20 32														21 32
Botley	d								20 36														21 36
Fareham	d		20 03			20 26			20 44				20 32			20 55	21 02			21 25			21 44
Portchester	d								20 49														21 49
Cosham	d		20a11						20 54								21a10						21 54
Hilsea	a								21 00														22 00
Fratton	a					20 41			21 04							21 09				21 38			22 04
Portsmouth & Southsea	a					20 45			21 08							21 15				21 41			22 08
Portsmouth Harbour ⛴	a					20 51			21 13							21 26				21 48			22 13
Southampton Airport Pkwy ✈	d			19 58				20 27			20 34			20 53				20 58				21 27	
Swaythling	d			20 01														21 01					
St Denys	d			20 04														21 04					
Southampton Central ⛴	a			20 09				20 34			20 42		20 53	21 00				21 09				21 34	
	d			20 10				20 35			20 45		20 54	21 03				21 10				21 35	
Millbrook (Hants)	d			20 13														21 13					
Redbridge	d			20 16														21 16					
Romsey	d			20 24	20a28								21 06					21 24	21a28				
Mottisfont & Dunbridge	d																	21 29					
Dean	d																	21 35					
Salisbury	a			20 42									21 24					21 48					
Totton	d							20 41														21 41	
Ashurst New Forest	d							20 45														21 45	
Beaulieu Road	d							20 50														21 50	
Brockenhurst 3	a							20 56			21 02			21 16								21 56	
	d						20 29	20 57		20 59	21 03			21 17							21 29	21 57	
Lymington Town	d						20 37			21 07											21 37		
Lymington Pier	a						20 39			21 09											21 39		
Sway	d							21 01														22 01	
New Milton	d							21 06						21 24								22 06	
Hinton Admiral	d							21 10														22 10	
Christchurch	d							21 15														22 15	
Pokesdown	d							21 19														22 19	
Bournemouth	a							21 23			21 26			21 34								22 23	
	d							21 24						21 39								22 24	
Branksome	d													21 44									
Parkstone (Dorset)	d													21 47									
Poole 4	a							21 33						21 50								22 33	
	d													21 51									
Hamworthy	d													21 56									
Holton Heath	d																						
Wareham	d													22 03									
Wool	d													22 10									
Moreton (Dorset)	d													22 17									
Dorchester South	d													22 25									
Dorchester West	d																						
Upwey	d													22 32									
Weymouth	a													22 36									

A 🍴 to Bournemouth

Table 158

Sundays
1 July to 9 September

London - Basingstoke, Southampton, Romsey Lymington, Bournemouth and Weymouth

Network Diagram - see first Page of Table 158

		SW	XC	SW	GW	SW	SW	SW	SW	GW	SW		XC	SW	GW	SW	SW	SW	SW	GW	SW	
		1	◇1	1		◇1 A ⌶	1	1	1	◇	◇1		◇1	1		◇1 A ⌶	1	1	1	◇	◇1	
London Waterloo 15 ⊖	d			20 07		20 35	20 37				20 54			21 07		21 35	21 37				21 54	
Clapham Junction 10	d			20 15		20u42	20 46				21u03			21 15		21u42	21 46				22u03	
Woking	d			20 46		21 07	21 23				21 28			21 46		22 07	22 23				22 28	
Farnborough (Main)	d			20 59			21 36							21 59			22 36					
Fleet	d			21 04			21 41							22 04			22 41					
Reading 7	d		20 53										21 53									
Basingstoke	a		21 09	21 21		21 26	21 54				21 46		22 09	22 21		22 26	22 54				22 46	
	d		21 10			21 28					21 48		22 10			22 28					22 48	
Micheldever	d										21 58										22 58	
Winchester	d		21 25			21 44					22 08		22 25			22 44					23 08	
Shawford	d										22 12											
Romsey	d							21 35	21 32	21 51								22 35	22 28	22 54		
Chandlers Ford	d							21 42										22 42				
Eastleigh 8	a							21 48	22 13		22 18							22 48	23 19		23 17	
	d							21 54	22 15		22 22	22 26						22 54	23 21		23 22	23 26
Hedge End	d											22 32										23 32
Botley	d											22 36										23 36
Fareham	d									22 26		22 44			22 32					23 30		23 44
Portchester	d											22 49										23 49
Cosham	d											22 54										23 54
Hilsea	a											23 00										23 59
Fratton	a									22 40		23 04								23 43		00 04
Portsmouth & Southsea	a									22 43		23 08								23 46		00 08
Portsmouth Harbour ⛴	a									22 50		23 13								23 54		00 13
Southampton Airport Pkwy ✈	d		21 34			21 53		21 58			22 27		22 34			22 53		22 58			23 27	
Swaythling	d							22 01										23 01				
St Denys	d							22 04										23 04				
Southampton Central ⛴	a		21 43			22 00		22 09			22 34		22 42		22 53	23 00		23 09			23 34	
	d		21 45			22 03		22 10			22 35				22 57	23 03		23 10			23 35	
Millbrook (Hants)	d							22 13										23 13				
Redbridge	d							22 16										23 16				
Romsey	d							22a24	22a31						23 09			23 24	23a33			
Mottisfont & Dunbridge	d																	23 29				
Dean	d																	23 35				
Salisbury	a														23 27			23 51				
Totton	d										22 41										23 41	
Ashurst New Forest	d										22 45										23 45	
Beaulieu Road	d										22 50											
Brockenhurst 3	a		22 02			22 16					22 56					23 16					23 53	
	d	21 59	22 03			22 17					22 57					23 17					23 54	
Lymington Town	d	22 07																				
Lymington Pier	a	22 09																				
Sway	d										23 01										23 59	
New Milton	d					22 24					23 06					23 24					00 04	
Hinton Admiral	d										23 10										00 08	
Christchurch	d										23 15										00 13	
Pokesdown	d										23 19										00 16	
Bournemouth	a		22 26			22 34					23 23					23 34					00 20	
	d					22 39					23 24					23 39					00 22	
Branksome	d					22 44										23 44					00 27	
Parkstone (Dorset)	d					22 47										23 47					00 30	
Poole 4	a					22 50					23 33					23 50					00 34	
	d					22 51										23 51						
Hamworthy	d					22 56										23 56						
Holton Heath	d																					
Wareham	d					23 03										00 03						
Wool	d					23 10										00 10						
Moreton (Dorset)	d					23 17										00 17						
Dorchester South	d					23 25										00 25						
Dorchester West	d				22 53																	
Upwey	d				23 01	23 32										00 32						
Weymouth	a				23 06	23 36										00 36						

A ⌶ to Bournemouth

Table 158

Sundays
1 July to 9 September

London - Basingstoke, Southampton, Romsey Lymington, Bournemouth and Weymouth

Network Diagram - see first Page of Table 158

		SW	SW	SW	SW
		1	1	◇1 ⌶	1
London Waterloo 15 ⊖	d	22 07	22 37	22 54	23 07
Clapham Junction 10	d	22 15	22 46	23u03	23 15
Woking	d	22 46	23 23	23 28	23 46
Farnborough (Main)	d	22 59	23 36		23 59
Fleet	d	23 04	23 41		00 04
Reading 7	d				
Basingstoke	a	23 21	23 54	23 46	00 21
	d			23 48	
Micheldever	d			23 58	
Winchester	d			00 08	
Shawford	d				
Romsey	d				
Chandlers Ford	d				
Eastleigh 8	a			00 18	
	d			00 22	
Hedge End	d				
Botley	d				
Fareham	d				
Portchester	d				
Cosham	d				
Hilsea	a				
Fratton	a				
Portsmouth & Southsea	a				
Portsmouth Harbour ⛴	a				
Southampton Airport Pkwy ✈	d			00 27	
Swaythling	d				
St Denys	d			00s31	
Southampton Central ⛴	a			00 36	
	d			00 37	
Millbrook (Hants)	d				
Redbridge	d				
Romsey	d				
Mottisfont & Dunbridge	d				
Dean	d				
Salisbury	a				
Totton	d			00s42	
Ashurst New Forest	d				
Beaulieu Road	d				
Brockenhurst 3	a			00s53	
	d				
Lymington Town	d				
Lymington Pier	a				
Sway	d				
New Milton	d			01s01	
Hinton Admiral	d				
Christchurch	d			01s08	
Pokesdown	d			01s12	
Bournemouth	a			01 16	
	d			01 17	
Branksome	d			01s22	
Parkstone (Dorset)	d			01s25	
Poole 4	a			01 29	
	d				
Hamworthy	d				
Holton Heath	d				
Wareham	d				
Wool	d				
Moreton (Dorset)	d				
Dorchester South	d				
Dorchester West	d				
Upwey	d				
Weymouth	a				

Table 158

Sundays from 16 September

London - Basingstoke, Southampton, Romsey Lymington, Bournemouth and Weymouth

Network Diagram - see first Page of Table 158

		SW	SW	SW	SW	SW	SW	SW	SW	SW		SW	SW	SW	SW	SW	GW	SW	SW			SW	SN	SW	SW
		◇1 A 🍴	1	◇1 🍴	1	◇1 🍴	1	◇1	1	1		1	1	1	1	1		1	1			1	◇1	1	1
London Waterloo 15 ⊖	d	21p35	21p42	22p05		22p35	22p39	23p05	23p12			23p35	23p48	00 05	01 05										
Clapham Junction 10	d			22b12			22b46	23b12	23b19			23b42	23b54	00u12	01 15										
Woking	d	22p00	22p19	22p32		23p00		23p32	23p57			00 03	00 28	00 37	01 49							07 46			
Farnborough (Main)	d		22p33				23p16		00 10			00 14	00 41		01s58							07 59			
Fleet	d		22p38				23p21		00 16			00 20	00 47		02s04							08 04			
Reading 7	d																								
Basingstoke	a		22p58	22p51			23p34	23p51	00 33			00 33	01 06	00 55	02s16							08 21			
	d		23p00	22p52			23p36	23p52				00 35		00 56					07 48						
Micheldever	d		23p10					00 02											07 58						
Winchester	d	22p33	23p19	23p09		23p33	23p52	00 12				00 51		01 13	02s33				08 08						
Shawford	d						23p57												08 12						
Romsey	d				23p09												08 19								
Chandlers Ford	d				23p16																				
Eastleigh 8	a		23p27	23p17	23p22		00 02	00 20				00 59		01 21	02s42				08 18						
	d		23p28	23p18	23p23		00 03	00 21		00 30		01 00		01 22					08 22	08 26			08 48		
Hedge End	d		23p34							00s36										08 32					
Botley	d		23p38							00s39										08 36					
Fareham	d		23p48							00s47						07 44				08 44			09 02		
Portchester	d		23p53							00s53						07 49				08 49					
Cosham	d		23p58							00s57						07 54				08 54			09a10		
Hilsea	a		00 03													08 00				09 00					
Fratton	a		00 07							01s05						08 04				09 04					
Portsmouth & Southsea	a		00 11							01s08						08 08				09 08					
Portsmouth Harbour ⛴	a		00 16							01 12						08 13				09 13					
Southampton Airport Pkwy ✈	d	22p42		23p22	23p27	23p42	00 08	00 25				01 05		01 26	02s46				08 27						
Swaythling	d				23p30																				
St Denys	d				23p33			00s29							02s51										
Southampton Central ⛴	a	22p49		23p29	23p38	23p49	00 15	00 34				01 12		01 35	02 56		08 29		08 34						
	d	22p51		23p31	23p40	23p51		00 36						01 37					08 35						09 03
Millbrook (Hants)	d				23p42																				
Redbridge	d				23p46																				
Romsey	d				23p57																				
Mottisfont & Dunbridge	d				00 02																				
Dean	d				00 08																				
Salisbury	a				00 20																				
Totton	d			23p36				00s41						01s42					08 41						
Ashurst New Forest	d			23p41															08 45						
Beaulieu Road	d																		08 50						
Brockenhurst 3	a	23p04		23p49		00 04		00s52						01s53					08 56						09 16
	d	23p05		23p50		00 05													08 57					08 59	09 17
Lymington Town	d																							09 07	
Lymington Pier	a																							09 09	
Sway	d			23p54															09 01						
New Milton	d			23p59				01s00						02s00					09 06						09 24
Hinton Admiral	d			00 03															09 10						
Christchurch	d			00 08				01s07						02s07					09 15						
Pokesdown	d			00 11				01s11						02s11					09 19						
Bournemouth	a	23p25		00 15		00 21		01 15						02 15					09 23						09 34
	d	23p29		00 17		00 22		01 16										08 39	09 24						09 39
Branksome	d	23p35		00 23		00 27		01s21										08 44							09 44
Parkstone (Dorset)	d	23p38		00 26		00 30		01s24										08 47							09 47
Poole 4	a	23p41		00 30		00 35		01 29										08 50	09 33						09 50
	d	23p42																08 51							09 51
Hamworthy	d	23p47																08 56							09 56
Holton Heath	d																								
Wareham	d	23p54																09 03							10 03
Wool	d	00 01																09 10							10 10
Moreton (Dorset)	d	00 07																09 16							10 16
Dorchester South	d	00 15																09 24							10 24
Dorchester West	d																								
Upwey	d	00 21																09 31							10 31
Weymouth	a	00 26																09 35							10 35

A 🍴 to Bournemouth

b Previous night, stops to pick up only

Table 158

Sundays from 16 September

London - Basingstoke, Southampton, Romsey Lymington, Bournemouth and Weymouth

Network Diagram - see first Page of Table 158

		SW	SW	SW	GW	SW			SW	SW	SW	SW	SW	SW	SW		SW		XC	SW	SW	SW	SW	GW	SW
		1	1	1	■	◇1			1	1	◇1	1	1	1	◇1		1		◇1 🍴	1	◇1	1	1	◇	1
London Waterloo 15 ⊖	d					07 54			08 07		08 35				08 54					09 07	09 35				
Clapham Junction 10	d					08u03			08 15		08u45				09u03					09 15	09u45				
Woking	d					08 28			08 46		09 09				09 28					09 46	10 09				
Farnborough (Main)	d								08 59											09 59					
Fleet	d								09 04											10 04					
Reading 7	d																		09 53						
Basingstoke	a					08 46			09 21		09 28				09 46				10 09	10 21	10 28				
	d					08 48					09 29				09 48				10 10		10 29				
Micheldever	d					08 58									09 58										
Winchester	d					09 08					09 46				10 08				10 25		10 46				
Shawford	d														10 12										
Romsey	d	08 35	08 39									09 35	09 32									10 35	10 32	10 50	
Chandlers Ford	d	08 42										09 42										10 42			
Eastleigh 8	a	08 47	09 13			09 18						09 48	10 13		10 18							10 48	11 13		
	d	08 54	09 15			09 22	09 26					09 54	10 15		10 22	10 26						10 54	11 15		
Hedge End	d						09 32									10 32									
Botley	d						09 36									10 36									
Fareham	d				09 32		09 44									10 44								11 26	
Portchester	d						09 49									10 49									
Cosham	d						09 54									10 54								11 34	
Hilsea	a						10 04									11 04									
Fratton	a						10 08									11 08								11 40	
Portsmouth & Southsea	a						10 11									11 11								11 45	
Portsmouth Harbour ⛴	a						10 15									11 15								11 52	
Southampton Airport Pkwy ✈	d	08 58				09 27					09 55	09 58			10 27				10 34		10 55	10 58			
Swaythling	d	09 01										10 01										11 01			
St Denys	d	09 04										10 04										11 04			
Southampton Central ⛴	a	09 09			09 53	09 34					10 02	10 09			10 34				10 42		11 02	11 09			
	d	09 10			09 54	09 35					10 03	10 10			10 35				10 45		11 03	11 10			
Millbrook (Hants)	d	09 13										10 13										11 13			
Redbridge	d	09 16										10 16										11 16			
Romsey	d	09 24	09a28		10 06							10 24	10a28									11 24	11a28		
Mottisfont & Dunbridge	d	09 29																				11 29			
Dean	d	09 35																				11 35			
Salisbury	a	09 48			10 24							10 42										11 48			
Totton	d					09 41									10 41										
Ashurst New Forest	d					09 45									10 45										
Beaulieu Road	d					09 50									10 50										
Brockenhurst 3	a					09 56					10 17				10 56				11 02		11 17				
	d			09 29		09 57				09 59	10 18			10 29	10 57		10 59		11 03		11 18				11 29
Lymington Town	d			09 37						10 07				10 37			11 07								11 37
Lymington Pier	a			09 39						10 09				10 39			11 09								11 39
Sway	d					10 01									11 01										
New Milton	d					10 06					10 25				11 06						11 25				
Hinton Admiral	d					10 10									11 10										
Christchurch	d					10 15									11 15										
Pokesdown	d					10 19									11 19										
Bournemouth	a					10 23					10 35				11 23				11 26		11 35				
	d					10 24					10 39				11 24						11 39				
Branksome	d										10 44										11 44				
Parkstone (Dorset)	d										10 47										11 47				
Poole 4	a					10 33					10 50				11 33						11 50				
	d										10 51										11 51				
Hamworthy	d										10 56										11 56				
Holton Heath	d																								
Wareham	d										11 03										12 03				
Wool	d										11 10										12 10				
Moreton (Dorset)	d										11 16										12 16				
Dorchester South	d										11 24										12 24				
Dorchester West	d																								
Upwey	d										11 31										12 31				
Weymouth	a										11 35										12 35				

Table 158

Sundays
from 16 September

London - Basingstoke, Southampton, Romsey Lymington, Bournemouth and Weymouth

Network Diagram - see first Page of Table 158

		SW ◇■		SW ■	XC ◇■	SW ■	GW ◇	SW ◇■	SW ■	SW ■	GW ◇	SW ■	SW ◇■		SW ■	XC ◇■	SW ■	GW ◇	SW ◇■	GW ◇	GW ◇	SW ■
					✠			A ✠								⊡			A ✠	B	C	
London Waterloo ⊖	d	09 54				10 07		10 35					10 54				11 07		11 35			
Clapham Junction	d	10u03				10 15		10u45					11u04				11 15		11u45			
Woking	d	10 28				10 46		11 07					11 28				11 46		12 07			
Farnborough (Main)	d					10 59											11 59					
Fleet	d					11 04											12 04					
Reading ■	d				10 53											11 53						
Basingstoke	a	10 46			11 09	11 21		11 26					11 46			12 09	12 21		12 26			
	d	10 48			11 10			11 28					11 48			12 10			12 28			
Micheldever	d	10 58											11 58									
Winchester	d	11 08			11 25			11 44					12 08			12 25			12 44			
Shawford	d												12 12									
Romsey	d								11 35	11 32	11 51									12 52	12 54	12 35
Chandlers Ford	d								11 42													12 42
Eastleigh ■	a	11 18							11 48	12 13			12 18									12 48
	d	11 22	11 26						11 54	12 15			12 22	12 26								12 54
Hedge End	d		11 32											12 32								
Botley	d		11 36											12 36								
Fareham	d		11 44				11 32				12 28			12 44				12 32				
Portchester	d		11 49											12 49								
Cosham	d		11 54								12 36			12 54								
Hilsea	a		12 00											13 00								
Fratton	a		12 04								12 42			13 04								
Portsmouth & Southsea	a		12 08								12 46			13 08								
Portsmouth Harbour	a		12 13								12 52			13 13								
Southampton Airport Pkwy	d	11 27			11 34			11 53	11 58				12 27			12 34			12 53			12 58
Swaythling	d								12 01													13 01
St Denys	d								12 04													13 04
Southampton Central	a	11 34			11 42		11 53	11 59	12 09				12 34			12 42		12 53	13 00	13 05	13 05	13 09
	d	11 35			11 45		11 54	12 03	12 10				12 35			12 45		12 54	13 03			13 10
Millbrook (Hants)	d								12 13													13 13
Redbridge	d								12 16													13 16
Romsey	d						12 06		12 24	12a28								13 06				13 24
Mottisfont & Dunbridge	d																					13 29
Dean	d																					13 35
Salisbury	a						12 24		12 42									13 24				13 48
Totton	d	11 41											12 41									
Ashurst New Forest	d	11 45											12 45									
Beaulieu Road	d	11 50											12 50									
Brockenhurst ■	a	11 56			12 02			12 16					12 56			13 02			13 16			
	d	11 57		11 59	12 03			12 17				12 29	12 57		12 59	13 03			13 17			
Lymington Town	d			12 07								12 37			13 07							
Lymington Pier	a			12 09								12 39			13 09							
Sway	d	12 01											13 01									
New Milton	d	12 06						12 24					13 06						13 24			
Hinton Admiral	d	12 10											13 10									
Christchurch	d	12 15											13 15									
Pokesdown	d	12 19											13 19									
Bournemouth	a	12 23			12 26			12 34					13 23			13 26			13 34			
	d	12 24						12 39					13 24						13 39			
Branksome	d							12 44											13 44			
Parkstone (Dorset)	d							12 47											13 47			
Poole ■	a	12 33						12 50					13 33						13 50			
	d							12 51											13 51			
Hamworthy	d							12 56											13 56			
Holton Heath	d																					
Wareham	d							13 03											14 03			
Wool	d							13 10											14 10			
Moreton (Dorset)	d							13 16											14 16			
Dorchester South	d							13 24											14 24			
Dorchester West	d																					
Upwey	d							13 31											14 31			
Weymouth	a							13 35											14 35			

A ✠ to Bournemouth B from 28 October C from 16 September until 21 October

Table 158

Sundays
from 16 September

London - Basingstoke, Southampton, Romsey Lymington, Bournemouth and Weymouth

Network Diagram - see first Page of Table 158

		SW ■	SW ■	SW ◇■		SW ■	XC ◇■	SW ■	GW ◇	SW ◇■	SW ■	SW ■	GW ◇	SW ■	SW ◇■		SW ■	XC ◇■	SW ■	GW ◇	GW	GW	SW ◇■
				✠			⊡			A ✠			✠		✠			⊡			B	C	A ✠
London Waterloo ⊖	d			11 54				12 07		12 35					12 54				13 07				13 35
Clapham Junction	d			12u04				12 15		12u42					13u03				13 15				13u42
Woking	d			12 28				12 46		13 07					13 28				13 46				14 07
Farnborough (Main)	d							12 59											13 59				
Fleet	d							13 04											14 04				
Reading ■	d						12 53											13 53					
Basingstoke	a			12 46			13 09	13 21		13 26					13 46			14 09	14 21				14 26
	d			12 48			13 10			13 28					13 48			14 10					14 28
Micheldever	d			12 58											13 58								
Winchester	d			13 08			13 25			13 44					14 08			14 25					14 44
Shawford	d														14 12								
Romsey	d	12 32									13 35	13 32	13 51										
Chandlers Ford	d										13 42												
Eastleigh ■	a	13 13		13 18							13 48	14 13			14 18								
	d	13 15		13 22	13 26						13 54	14 15			14 22	14 26							
Hedge End	d				13 32											14 32							
Botley	d				13 36											14 36							
Fareham	d				13 44				13 32				14 27			14 44				14 32			
Portchester	d				13 49											14 49							
Cosham	d				13 54								14 35			14 54							
Hilsea	a				14 00											15 00							
Fratton	a				14 04								14 41			15 04							
Portsmouth & Southsea	a				14 08								14 45			15 08							
Portsmouth Harbour	a				14 13								14 55			15 13							
Southampton Airport Pkwy	d			13 27			13 34			13 53	13 58				14 27			14 34					14 53
Swaythling	d										14 01												
St Denys	d										14 04												
Southampton Central	a			13 34			13 42		13 53	14 00	14 09				14 34			14 42		14 53			15 00
	d			13 35			13 45		13 54	14 03	14 10				14 35			14 45		14 54			15 03
Millbrook (Hants)	d										14 13												
Redbridge	d										14 16												
Romsey	d	13a28							14 06		14 24	14a28								15 06			
Mottisfont & Dunbridge	d																						
Dean	d																						
Salisbury	a								14 24		14 42									15 24			
Totton	d			13 41											14 41								
Ashurst New Forest	d			13 45											14 45								
Beaulieu Road	d			13 50											14 50								
Brockenhurst ■	a			13 56			14 01			14 16					14 56			15 02					15 16
	d		13 29	13 57		13 59	14 02			14 17				14 29	14 57		14 59	15 03					15 17
Lymington Town	d		13 37			14 07								14 37			15 07						
Lymington Pier	a		13 39			14 09								14 39			15 09						
Sway	d			14 01											15 01								
New Milton	d			14 06						14 24					15 06								15 24
Hinton Admiral	d			14 10											15 10								
Christchurch	d			14 15											15 15								
Pokesdown	d			14 19											15 19								
Bournemouth	a			14 23			14 26			14 34					15 23			15 26					15 34
	d			14 24						14 39					15 24								15 39
Branksome	d									14 44													15 44
Parkstone (Dorset)	d									14 47													15 47
Poole ■	a			14 33						14 50					15 33								15 50
	d									14 51													15 51
Hamworthy	d									14 56													15 56
Holton Heath	d																						
Wareham	d									15 03													16 03
Wool	d									15 10													16 10
Moreton (Dorset)	d									15 16													16 16
Dorchester South	d									15 24													16 24
Dorchester West	d																				16 01	16 15	
Upwey	d									15 31											16 10	16 24	16 31
Weymouth	a									15 35											16 15	16 29	16 35

A ✠ to Bournemouth B from 28 October C from 16 September until 21 October

Table 158

Sundays
from 16 September

London - Basingstoke, Southampton, Romsey Lymington, Bournemouth and Weymouth

Network Diagram - see first Page of Table 158

		SW	SW	GW	SW	SW		SW	XC	SW	GW	SW	SW	SW	GW	SW	SW		SW	XC	SW	GW	SW
		■	■	◇	■	◇■		■	◇■	■	■	◇■	■	■	◇	■	◇■		■	◇■	■	◇	◇■
						⊼			⊡			A ⊼					⊼			⊡			A ⊼
London Waterloo 15 ⊖	d					13 54				14 07		14 35					14 54				15 07		15 35
Clapham Junction 10	d					14u03				14 15		14u42					15u03				15 15		15u42
Woking	d					14 28				14 46		15 07					15 28				15 46		16 07
Farnborough (Main)	d									14 59											15 59		
Fleet	d									15 04											16 04		
Reading 7	d								14 53											15 53			
Basingstoke	a					14 46			15 09	15 21		15 26					15 46			16 09	16 21		16 26
	d					14 48			15 10			15 28					15 48			16 10			16 28
Micheldever	d					14 58											15 58						
Winchester	d					15 08			15 25			15 44					16 08			16 25			16 44
Shawford	d																16 12						
Romsey	d	14 35	14 32	15 10									15 35	15 32	15 51								
Chandlers Ford	d	14 42											15 42										
Eastleigh ■	a	14 48	15 13			15 18							15 48	16 13			16 18						
	d	14 54	15 15			15 22	15 26						15 54	16 15			16 22	16 26					
Hedge End	d						15 32											16 32					
Botley	d						15 36											16 36					
Fareham	d						15 44				15 32				16 27			16 44				16 32	
Portchester	d						15 49											16 49					
Cosham	d						15 54								16 35			16 54					
Hilsea	a						16 00											17 00					
Fratton	a						16 04								16 42			17 03					
Portsmouth & Southsea	a						16 08								16 46			17 08					
Portsmouth Harbour ⛴	a						16 13								16 52			17 13					
Southampton Airport Pkwy ✈	d	14 58				15 27			15 34			15 53	15 58				16 27			16 34			16 53
Swaythling	d	15 01											16 01										
St Denys	d	15 04											16 04										
Southampton Central ⛴	a	15 09		15 21		15 34			15 42		15 53	16 00	16 09				16 34			16 42		16 53	17 00
	d	15 10				15 35			15 45		15 54	16 03	16 10				16 35			16 45		16 54	17 03
Millbrook (Hants)	d	15 13											16 13										
Redbridge	d	15 16											16 16										
Romsey	d	15 24	15a28								16 06		16 24	16a28								17 06	
Mottisfont & Dunbridge	d	15 29																					
Dean	d	15 35																					
Salisbury	a	15 48									16 24		16 42									17 24	
Totton	d					15 41											16 41						
Ashurst New Forest	d					15 45											16 45						
Beaulieu Road	d					15 50											16 50						
Brockenhurst 3	a					15 56			16 02			16 16					16 56			17 02			17 16
	d				15 29	15 57		15 59	16 03			16 17				16 29	16 57		16 59	17 03			17 17
Lymington Town	d				15 37			16 07								16 37			17 07				
Lymington Pier	a				15 39			16 09								16 39			17 09				
Sway	d					16 01											17 01						
New Milton	d					16 06						16 24					17 06						17 24
Hinton Admiral	d					16 10											17 10						
Christchurch	d					16 15											17 15						
Pokesdown	d					16 19											17 19						
Bournemouth	a					16 23			16 26			16 34					17 23			17 26			17 34
	d					16 24						16 39					17 24						17 39
Branksome	d											16 44											17 44
Parkstone (Dorset)	d											16 47											17 47
Poole 4	a					16 33						16 50					17 33						17 50
	d											16 51											17 51
Hamworthy	d											16 56											17 56
Holton Heath	d																						
Wareham	d											17 03											18 03
Wool	d											17 10											18 10
Moreton (Dorset)	d											17 16											18 16
Dorchester South	d											17 24											18 24
Dorchester West	d																						
Upwey	d											17 31											18 31
Weymouth	a											17 35											18 35

A ⊼ to Bournemouth

Table 158

Sundays
from 16 September

London - Basingstoke, Southampton, Romsey Lymington, Bournemouth and Weymouth

Network Diagram - see first Page of Table 158

		SW	SW	SW	GW	GW	GW	SW	SW		SW	XC	SW	GW	SW	SW	SW	SW	GW	SW	SW	
		■	■	■	◇	◇	◇	■	◇■		■	◇■	■	◇	◇■	■	■	■	◇	■	◇■	
						A	B		⊼			⊡			C ⊼						⊼	
London Waterloo 15 ⊖	d	15 37							15 54				16 07		16 35	16 37					16 54	
Clapham Junction 10	d	15 46							16u03				16 15		16u42	16 46					17u03	
Woking	d	16 23							16 28				16 46		17 07	17 23					17 28	
Farnborough (Main)	d	16 36											16 59			17 36						
Fleet	d	16 41											17 04			17 41						
Reading 7	d											16 53										
Basingstoke	a	16 54							16 46			17 09	17 21		17 26	17 54					17 46	
	d								16 48			17 10			17 28						17 48	
Micheldever	d								16 58												17 58	
Winchester	d								17 08			17 25			17 44						18 08	
Shawford	d																				18 12	
Romsey	d		16 35	16 32		16 53	16 53										17 35	17 32	17 51			
Chandlers Ford	d		16 42														17 42					
Eastleigh ■	a		16 48	17 13					17 18								17 48	18 13			18 18	
	d		16 54	17 15					17 22	17 26							17 54	18 15			18 22	18 26
Hedge End	d									17 32												18 32
Botley	d									17 36												18 36
Fareham	d				17 03	17 27	17 27			17 44				17 32					18 27			18 44
Portchester	d									17 49												18 49
Cosham	d					17 36	17 35			17 54									18 35			18 54
Hilsea	a									18 00												19 00
Fratton	a					17 42	17 42			18 04									18 41			19 03
Portsmouth & Southsea	a					17 47	17 47			18 08									18 45			19 08
Portsmouth Harbour ⛴	a					17 52	17 52			18 13									18 52			19 13
Southampton Airport Pkwy ✈	d		16 58						17 27			17 34			17 53		17 58				18 27	
Swaythling	d		17 01														18 01					
St Denys	d		17 04														18 04					
Southampton Central ⛴	a		17 09		17 24				17 34			17 40		17 53	18 00		18 09				18 34	
	d		17 10		17 26				17 35			17 45		17 54	18 03		18 10				18 35	
Millbrook (Hants)	d		17 13														18 13					
Redbridge	d		17 16														18 16					
Romsey	d		17 24	17a28	17 39									18 06			18 24	18a28				
Mottisfont & Dunbridge	d		17 29																			
Dean	d		17 35																			
Salisbury	a		17 48		18 00									18 24			18 42					
Totton	d								17 41												18 41	
Ashurst New Forest	d								17 45												18 45	
Beaulieu Road	d								17 50												18 50	
Brockenhurst 3	a								17 56			18 02			18 16						18 56	
	d							17 29	17 57		17 59	18 03			18 17					18 29	18 57	
Lymington Town	d							17 37			18 07									18 37		
Lymington Pier	a							17 39			18 09									18 39		
Sway	d								18 01												19 01	
New Milton	d								18 06						18 24						19 06	
Hinton Admiral	d								18 10												19 10	
Christchurch	d								18 15												19 15	
Pokesdown	d								18 19												19 19	
Bournemouth	a								18 23			18 26			18 34						19 23	
	d								18 24						18 39						19 24	
Branksome	d														18 44							
Parkstone (Dorset)	d														18 47							
Poole 4	a								18 33						18 50						19 33	
	d														18 51							
Hamworthy	d														18 56							
Holton Heath	d																					
Wareham	d														19 03							
Wool	d														19 10							
Moreton (Dorset)	d														19 16							
Dorchester South	d														19 24							
Dorchester West	d																					
Upwey	d														19 31							
Weymouth	a														19 35							

A from 28 October
B from 16 September until 21 October
C ⊼ to Bournemouth

Table 158

Sundays from 16 September

London - Basingstoke, Southampton, Romsey Lymington, Bournemouth and Weymouth

Network Diagram - see first Page of Table 158

		SW	XC	SW	GW	GW	SW	SW	SW	SW	GW	GW	GW	SW	SW		SW	XC	SW	GW	SW	SW	SN
		■	◇■	■	◇	◇	◇■ A	■	■	■	◇	◇	◇	■	◇■		■	◇■	■	◇	◇■ A	■	◇■
London Waterloo ⊖	d			17 07			17 35	17 37							17 54				18 07		18 35	18 37	
Clapham Junction	d			17 15			17u42	17 46							18u03				18 15		18u42	18 46	
Woking	d			17 46			18 07	18 23							18 28				18 46		19 07	19 23	
Farnborough (Main)	d			17 59				18 36											18 59			19 36	
Fleet	d			18 04				18 41											19 04			19 41	
Reading ■	d		17 53															18 53					
Basingstoke	a		18 09	18 21			18 26	18 54							18 46			19 09	19 21		19 26	19 54	
	d		18 10				18 28								18 48			19 10			19 28		
Micheldever	d														18 58								
Winchester	d		18 25				18 44								19 08			19 25			19 44		
Shawford	d																						
Romsey	d								18 35	18 32		18 51	19 14										
Chandlers Ford	d								18 42														
Eastleigh ■	a								18 48	19 13					19 18								
	d								18 54	19 15					19 22	19 26							19 46
Hedge End	d															19 32							
Botley	d															19 36							
Fareham	d				18 32						19 03	19 28				19 44				19 32			20 03
Portchester	d															19 49							
Cosham	d											19 36				19 54							20a11
Hilsea	a															20 00							
Fratton	a											19 42				20 04							
Portsmouth & Southsea	a											19 46				20 08							
Portsmouth Harbour ⛴	a											19 53				20 13							
Southampton Airport Pkwy ✈	d		18 34				18 53		18 58						19 27			19 34			19 53		
Swaythling	d								19 01														
St Denys	d								19 04														
Southampton Central ⛴	a		18 42		18 53		19 00		19 09		19 24		19 25		19 34			19 40		19 53	20 00		
	d		18 45		18 54		19 03		19 10		19 30				19 35			19 45		19 54	20 03		
Millbrook (Hants)	d								19 13														
Redbridge	d								19 16														
Romsey	d				19 06				19 24	19a28	19 42									20 06			
Mottisfont & Dunbridge	d								19 29														
Dean	d								19 35														
Salisbury	a				19 24				19 48		20 00									20 24			
Totton	d														19 41								
Ashurst New Forest	d														19 45								
Beaulieu Road	d														19 50								
Brockenhurst ■	a		19 01				19 16								19 56			20 02			20 16		
	d	18 59	19 02				19 17							19 29	19 57		19 59	20 03			20 17		
Lymington Town	d	19 07												19 37			20 07						
Lymington Pier	a	19 09												19 39			20 09						
Sway	d														20 01								
New Milton	d						19 24								20 06						20 24		
Hinton Admiral	d														20 10								
Christchurch	d														20 15								
Pokesdown	d														20 19								
Bournemouth	a		19 26				19 34								20 23			20 26			20 34		
	d						19 39								20 24						20 39		
Branksome	d						19 44														20 44		
Parkstone (Dorset)	d						19 47														20 47		
Poole ■	a						19 50								20 33						20 50		
	d						19 51														20 51		
Hamworthy	d						19 56														20 56		
Holton Heath	d																						
Wareham	d						20 03														21 03		
Wool	d						20 10														21 10		
Moreton (Dorset)	d						20 17														21 17		
Dorchester South	d						20 25														21 25		
Dorchester West	d					19 47																	
Upwey	d					19 55	20 32														21 32		
Weymouth	a					20 01	20 36														21 36		

A ✕ to Bournemouth

Table 158

Sundays from 16 September

London - Basingstoke, Southampton, Romsey Lymington, Bournemouth and Weymouth

Network Diagram - see first Page of Table 158

		SW	SW	GW	SW	SW		SW	XC	SW	GW	SW	SW	GW	SN	SW	SW	GW	SW	SW		SW
		■	■	◇	■	◇■		■	◇■	■	◇	◇■ A	■	■	◇■	■	■	◇	■	◇■		■
London Waterloo ⊖	d					18 54				19 07		19 35	19 37							19 54		
Clapham Junction	d					19u03				19 15		19u42	19 46							20u03		
Woking	d					19 28				19 46		20 07	20 23							20 28		
Farnborough (Main)	d									19 59			20 36									
Fleet	d									20 04			20 41									
Reading ■	d								19 53													
Basingstoke	a					19 46			20 09	20 21		20 26	20 54							20 46		
	d					19 48			20 10			20 28								20 48		
Micheldever	d					19 58														20 58		
Winchester	d					20 08			20 25			20 44								21 08		
Shawford	d					20 12																
Romsey	d	19 35	19 32	19 50										20 19		20 35	20 32	20 48				
Chandlers Ford	d	19 42														20 42						
Eastleigh ■	a	19 48	20 13			20 18										20 48	21 13			21 18		
	d	19 54	20 15			20 22	20 26								20 46	20 54	21 15			21 22	21 26	
Hedge End	d						20 32														21 32	
Botley	d						20 36														21 36	
Fareham	d			20 26			20 44				20 32			20 55	21 02			21 25			21 44	
Portchester	d						20 49														21 49	
Cosham	d						20 54								21a10						21 54	
Hilsea	a						21 00														22 00	
Fratton	a			20 41			21 04							21 09				21 38			22 04	
Portsmouth & Southsea	a			20 45			21 08							21 15				21 41			22 08	
Portsmouth Harbour ⛴	a			20 51			21 13							21 26				21 48			22 13	
Southampton Airport Pkwy ✈	d	19 58				20 27			20 34			20 53				20 58				21 27		
Swaythling	d	20 01														21 01						
St Denys	d	20 04														21 04						
Southampton Central ⛴	a	20 09				20 34			20 42		20 53	21 00				21 09				21 34		
	d	20 10				20 35			20 45		20 54	21 03				21 10				21 35		
Millbrook (Hants)	d	20 13														21 13						
Redbridge	d	20 16														21 16						
Romsey	d	20 24	20a28								21 06					21 24	21a28					
Mottisfont & Dunbridge	d															21 29						
Dean	d															21 35						
Salisbury	a	20 42									21 24					21 48						
Totton	d					20 41														21 41		
Ashurst New Forest	d					20 45														21 45		
Beaulieu Road	d					20 50														21 50		
Brockenhurst ■	a					20 56			21 02			21 16								21 56		
	d				20 29	20 57		20 59	21 03			21 17							21 29	21 57		21 59
Lymington Town	d				20 37			21 07											21 37			22 07
Lymington Pier	a				20 39			21 09											21 39			22 09
Sway	d					21 01														22 01		
New Milton	d					21 06						21 24								22 06		
Hinton Admiral	d					21 10														22 10		
Christchurch	d					21 15														22 15		
Pokesdown	d					21 19														22 19		
Bournemouth	a					21 23			21 26			21 34								22 23		
	d					21 24						21 39								22 24		
Branksome	d											21 44										
Parkstone (Dorset)	d											21 47										
Poole ■	a					21 33						21 50								22 33		
	d											21 51										
Hamworthy	d											21 56										
Holton Heath	d																					
Wareham	d											22 03										
Wool	d											22 10										
Moreton (Dorset)	d											22 17										
Dorchester South	d											22 25										
Dorchester West	d																					
Upwey	d											22 32										
Weymouth	a											22 36										

A ✕ to Bournemouth

Table 158

Sundays from 16 September

London - Basingstoke, Southampton, Romsey Lymington, Bournemouth and Weymouth

Network Diagram - see first Page of Table 158

		XC	SW	GW	SW	SW	SW	SW	GW	SW		XC	SW	GW	SW	SW	SW	SW	GW	SW		SW	SW
		◇1	1		◇1	1	1	1	◇	◇1		◇1	1		◇1	1	1	1	◇	◇1		1	1
					A ⚒										A ⚒								
London Waterloo 15 ⊖	d		20 07		20 35	20 37				20 54			21 07		21 35	21 37				21 54		22 07	22 37
Clapham Junction 10	d		20 15		20u42	20 46				21u03			21 15		21u42	21 46				22u03		22 15	22 46
Woking	d		20 46		21 07	21 23				21 28			21 46		22 07	22 23				22 28		22 46	23 23
Farnborough (Main)	d		20 59			21 36							21 59			22 36						22 59	23 36
Fleet	d		21 04			21 41							22 04			22 41						23 04	23 41
Reading 7	d	20 53										21 53											
Basingstoke	a	21 09	21 21		21 26	21 54				21 46		22 09	22 21		22 26	22 54				22 46		23 21	23 54
	d	21 10			21 28					21 48		22 10			22 28					22 48			
Micheldever	d									21 58										22 58			
Winchester	d	21 25			21 44					22 08		22 25			22 44					23 08			
Shawford	d									22 12													
Romsey	d						21 35	21 32	21 51								22 35	22 28	22 54				
Chandlers Ford	d						21 42										22 42						
Eastleigh 3	a						21 48	22 13		22 18							22 48	23 19		23 17			
	d						21 54	22 15		22 22	22 26						22 54	23 21		23 22	23 26		
Hedge End	d										22 32										23 32		
Botley	d										22 36										23 36		
Fareham	d								22 26		22 44			22 32					23 30		23 44		
Portchester	d										22 49										23 49		
Cosham	d										22 54										23 54		
Hilsea	a										23 00										23 59		
Fratton	a								22 40		23 04								23 43		00 04		
Portsmouth & Southsea	a								22 43		23 08								23 46		00 08		
Portsmouth Harbour ⛴	a								22 50		23 13								23 54		00 13		
Southampton Airport Pkwy ✈	d	21 34			21 53		21 58			22 27		22 34			22 53		22 58			23 27			
Swaythling	d						22 01										23 01						
St Denys	d						22 04										23 04						
Southampton Central ⛴	a	21 43			22 00		22 09			22 34		22 42		22 53	23 00		23 09			23 34			
	d	21 45			22 03		22 10			22 35				22 57	23 03		23 10			23 35			
Millbrook (Hants)	d						22 13										23 13						
Redbridge	d						22 16										23 16						
Romsey	d						22a24	22a31						23 09			23 24	23a33					
Mottisfont & Dunbridge	d																23 29						
Dean	d																23 35						
Salisbury	a													23 27			23 51						
Totton	d									22 41										23 41			
Ashurst New Forest	d									22 45										23 45			
Beaulieu Road	d									22 50													
Brockenhurst 3	a	22 02			22 16					22 56					23 16					23 53			
	d	22 03			22 17					22 57					23 17					23 54			
Lymington Town	d																						
Lymington Pier	a																						
Sway	d									23 01										23 59			
New Milton	d				22 24					23 06					23 24					00 04			
Hinton Admiral	d									23 10										00 08			
Christchurch	d									23 15										00 13			
Pokesdown	d									23 19										00 16			
Bournemouth	a	22 26			22 34					23 23					23 34					00 20			
	d				22 39					23 24					23 39					00 22			
Branksome	d				22 44										23 44					00 27			
Parkstone (Dorset)	d				22 47										23 47					00 30			
Poole 4	a				22 50					23 33					23 50					00 34			
	d				22 51										23 51								
Hamworthy	d				22 56										23 56								
Holton Heath	d																						
Wareham	d				23 03										00 03								
Wool	d				23 10										00 10								
Moreton (Dorset)	d				23 17										00 17								
Dorchester South	d				23 25										00 25								
Dorchester West	d			22 53																			
Upwey	d			23 01	23 32										00 32								
Weymouth	a			23 06	23 36										00 36								

A ⚒ to Bournemouth

Table 158

Sundays from 16 September

London - Basingstoke, Southampton, Romsey Lymington, Bournemouth and Weymouth

Network Diagram - see first Page of Table 158

		SW		SW
		◇1		1
		⚒		
London Waterloo 15 ⊖	d	22 54		23 07
Clapham Junction 10	d	23u03		23 15
Woking	d	23 28		23 46
Farnborough (Main)	d			23 59
Fleet	d			00 04
Reading 7	d			
Basingstoke	a	23 46		00 21
	d	23 48		
Micheldever	d	23 58		
Winchester	d	00 08		
Shawford	d			
Romsey	d			
Chandlers Ford	d			
Eastleigh 3	a	00 18		
	d	00 22	00 30	
Hedge End	d		00s36	
Botley	d		00s39	
Fareham	d		00s47	
Portchester	d		00s53	
Cosham	d		00s57	
Hilsea	a			
Fratton	a		01s05	
Portsmouth & Southsea	a		01s08	
Portsmouth Harbour ⛴	a		01 12	
Southampton Airport Pkwy ✈	d	00 27		
Swaythling	d			
St Denys	d	00s31		
Southampton Central ⛴	a	00 36		
	d	00 37		
Millbrook (Hants)	d			
Redbridge	d			
Romsey	d			
Mottisfont & Dunbridge	d			
Dean	d			
Salisbury	a			
Totton	d	00s42		
Ashurst New Forest	d			
Beaulieu Road	d			
Brockenhurst 3	a	00s53		
	d			
Lymington Town	d			
Lymington Pier	a			
Sway	d			
New Milton	d	01s01		
Hinton Admiral	d			
Christchurch	d	01s08		
Pokesdown	d	01s12		
Bournemouth	a	01 16		
	d	01 17		
Branksome	d	01s22		
Parkstone (Dorset)	d	01s25		
Poole 4	a	01 29		
	d			
Hamworthy	d			
Holton Heath	d			
Wareham	d			
Wool	d			
Moreton (Dorset)	d			
Dorchester South	d			
Dorchester West	d			
Upwey	d			
Weymouth	a			

Weymouth, Bournemouth, Lymington, Romsey, Southampton and Basingstoke - London

Network Diagram - see first Page of Table 158

Miles	Miles	Station		SW MX [1]	SW MX [1]	SW MO ◇[1] A	SW MX [1] B	SW MX [1] C	SW MO [1] A	SW MX [1]	SW MX ◇[1]	SW MO [1] A	SW MX [1]	SW [1]	SW [1]	XC ◇[1]	GW ◇	SW [1]	SW [1]	SW [1]	SW [1]	SW [1]	SW ◇[1] ⌶
0	—	**Weymouth**	d			20p58	21p10	21p10			22p10	22p58	23p10				05 33						
2¼	—	Upwey	d			21p02	21p14	21p14			22p14	23p02	23p14				05 37						
—	—	Dorchester West	a														05 44						
7	—	**Dorchester South**	d			21p10	21p22	21p22			22p22	23p10	23p22										
12½	—	Moreton (Dorset)	d			21p17	21p28	21p28			22p28	23p17	23p28										
17	—	Wool	d			21p23	21p34	21p34			22p34	23p23	23p34										
22	—	Wareham	d			21p30	21p42	21p42			22p42	23p30	23p42										
24	—	Holton Heath	d																				
26¾	—	Hamworthy	d			21p37	21p48	21p48			22p48	23p37	23p48										
29	—	**Poole [4]**	a			21p41	21p53	21p53			22p53	23p41	23p53										
—	—		d			21p50	21p54	21p54			22p54	23p50	23p54										05 00
30¾	—	Parkstone (Dorset)	d			21p54	21p58	21p58			22p58	23p54											05 04
32	—	Branksome	d			21p57	22p01	22p01			23p01	23p57											05 07
34¾	—	**Bournemouth**	a			22p03	22p07	22p07			23p07	00 03	00 03										05 12
—	—		d			22p06	22p12	22p12			23p12												05 15
36½	—	Pokesdown	d			22p10	22p16	22p16			23p16												05 19
38½	—	Christchurch	d			22p14	22p20	22p20			23p20												05 23
41¾	—	Hinton Admiral	d			22p19	22p25	22p25			23p25												
44¾	—	New Milton	d			22p23	22p29	22p29			23p29												05 30
47¼	—	Sway	d			22p28	22p34	22p34			23p34												
—	0	**Lymington Pier**	d																				
—	0½	Lymington Town	d																				
50	5½	**Brockenhurst [3]**	a			22p33	22p39	22p39			23p39												05 37
—	—		d			22p34	22p40	22p40			23p40												05 38
54¾	—	Beaulieu Road	d			22p39																	
57¼	—	Ashurst New Forest	d			22p43	22p47	22p47			23p47												
60¼	—	Totton	d			22p48	22p52	22p52			23p52												05 49
—	0	**Salisbury**	d															05 35					
—	9	Dean	d															05 47					
—	12¾	Mottisfont & Dunbridge	d															05 53					
—	16½	**Romsey**	d															05 58					
60¾	22½	Redbridge	d																				
62½	—	Millbrook (Hants)	d																				
63½	—	**Southampton Central** ⛴	a			22p53	22p57	22p57			23p57												05 54
—	—		d		22p30	22p55	23p00	23p00			23p59				04 52	05 15					05 42		05 55
65½	—	St Denys	d								00 04				04 57						05 47		
67	—	Swaythling	d								00 07				05 00						05 50		
67¾	—	**Southampton Airport Pkwy** ✈	d		22p38	23p03	23p08	23p08			00 10				05 03	05 22					05 53		06 03
—	0	**Portsmouth Harbour** ⛴	d						23p17	23p24										05 00			
—	0¾	**Portsmouth & Southsea**	d						23p22	23p29										05 05			
—	1¾	Fratton	d						23p26	23p33										05 09			
—	4	Hilsea	d						23p30	23p37										05 13			
—	5½	Cosham	d						23p35	23p42										05 19			
—	8	Portchester	d						23p40	23p47										05 23			
—	11¼	Fareham	d						23p46	23p53										05 29			
—	16¾	Botley	d						23p54	23p59										05 37			
—	17¾	Hedge End	d						23p58	00 05										05 41			
69¾	22¼	Eastleigh [8]	a		22p41	23p09	23p11	23p11	00 04	00 11	00 14				05 06					05 49	05 56		06 07
—	—		d		22p46	23p11	23p12	23p12		00 19					05 07					05 50			06 08
—	24¼	Chandlers Ford	d															06 06					
—	29½	**Romsey**	a															06 44					
73	—	Shawford	d				23p18	23p18							05 13					05 56			
76¼	—	**Winchester**	d		22p55	23p23	23p24	23p24		00a28					05 19	05 31				06 02			06 18
84¾	—	Micheldever	d			23p32	23p33	23p33							05 27					06 10			
95	—	**Basingstoke**	a		23p11	23p42	23p43	23p43							05 38	05 46				06 20			06 34
—	—		d	22p54	23p13	23p44	23p44	23p44						04 54	05 39	05 47			05 54			06 23	06 35
—	—	Reading [7]	a													06 04							
106¾	—	Fleet	d	23p10			00 01	00 02						05 10	05 50				06 10			06 40	
109½	—	Farnborough (Main)	d	23p16			00 06	00 06						05 16	05 56				06 16			06 46	
118½	—	**Woking**	a	23p28	23p31	00 02	00 18	00 18						05 28	06 05				06 28			06 58	06 53
138¾	—	**Clapham Junction [10]**	a	00 21	23p55	00 23	00 53	00 53						06 00	06 25				06 54			07 20	07 14
142¾	—	**London Waterloo [15]** ⊖	a	00 35	00 09	00 33	01 04	01 04						06 12	06 34				07 04			07 31	07 24

A from 21 May until 1 October   B not from 30 August until 7 September   C from 30 August until 7 September

Table 158

Mondays to Fridays
until 5 October

Weymouth, Bournemouth, Lymington, Romsey, Southampton and Basingstoke - London

Network Diagram - see first Page of Table 158

Station		SW [1]	SW [1]	XC ◇[1] ⌶	SW ◇[1] ⌶	SW [1]	SW [1]	SW [1]	SW [1]	GW [1] ⌶	SW [1]	SW [1]	SW [1]	SW [1]	GW	SW ◇[1] ⌶	SW ◇[1] ⌶	SW [1]	SW [1]	XC ◇[1] ⌶	SW [1]	SW [1]
Weymouth	d																					
Upwey	d																					
Dorchester West	a																					
Dorchester South	d																					
Moreton (Dorset)	d																					
Wool	d																					
Wareham	d																					
Holton Heath	d																					
Hamworthy	d																					
Poole [4]	a																					
	d	05 26			05 45												06 11					
Parkstone (Dorset)	d	05 30															06 15					
Branksome	d	05 33															06 18					
Bournemouth	a	05 38			05 54												06 23					
	d	05 40			05 57											06 04	06 25			06 30		
Pokesdown	d	05 44														06 08						
Christchurch	d	05 48														06 12						
Hinton Admiral	d	05 53														06 17						
New Milton	d	05 57														06 21						
Sway	d	06 02														06 26						
Lymington Pier	d					06 14															06 44	
Lymington Town	d					06 16															06 46	
Brockenhurst [3]	a	06 07			06 12	06 25										06 31				06 46	06 55	
	d				06 14											06 33				06 49		
Beaulieu Road	d																					
Ashurst New Forest	d															06 41						
Totton	d										06 12					06 46						
Salisbury	d														06 19							
Dean	d																					
Mottisfont & Dunbridge	d																					
Romsey	d														06 38							
Redbridge	d										06 14											
Millbrook (Hants)	d										06 17											
Southampton Central ⛴	a				06 27						06 24				06 49	06 51	06 55			07 01		
	d			06 15	06 30						06 35			06 43	06 53	07 00			07 10	07 15		
St Denys	d										06 40			06 48								
Swaythling	d										06 43			06 51								
Southampton Airport Pkwy ✈	d			06 22	06 38						06 46	06 50		06 54		07 08			07 18	07 22		
Portsmouth Harbour ⛴	d								05 43	06 00								06 23				
Portsmouth & Southsea	d								05 48	06 04								06 28				
Fratton	d								05 52	06 08								06 32				
Hilsea	d								05 56									06 36				
Cosham	d								06 03	06 15								06 42				
Portchester	d								06 08									06 46				
Fareham	d								06 19	06 24					07a14			06 53				
Botley	d								06 27									07 01				
Hedge End	d								06 31									07 05				
Eastleigh [8]	a								06 37		06 49	06 54		06 58				07 11	07 21			
	d								06 43		06 50			06 59				07 13	07 30			
Chandlers Ford	d										06 55											
Romsey	a									06 59	07 03											
Shawford	d								06 49					07 05					07 36			
Winchester	d			06 31	06 48				06 55			07 05		07 11		07 18		07 22	07 42	07 31		
Micheldever	d								07 04									07 31	→			
Basingstoke	a			06 46					07 14					07 27				07 41		07 46		
	d		06 42	06 47			06 54	07 06	07 17				07 24	07 36				07 47		07 47		07 52
Reading [7]	a			07 04																08 04		
Fleet	d		06 54				07 10	07 22					07 40	07 52								08 09
Farnborough (Main)	d		07 00				07 16	07 28					07 46	07 58								08 16
Woking	a		07 10				07 28					07 40	07 58	08 08				08 05				08 28
Clapham Junction [10]	a																					
London Waterloo [15] ⊖	a		07 41		07 47		07 59	08 06	08 01			08 08	08 29	08 39		08 16		08 34				09 00

until 5 October

Weymouth, Bournemouth, Lymington, Romsey, Southampton and Basingstoke - London

Network Diagram - see first Page of Table 158

		SW ■	SW ◇■ ⌶	SW ◇■ A ⌶	SW ■	SW ■	GW ◇ ⌶	SW ■	XC ◇■ ⌶	SW ■	GW ◇	SW ◇■ ⌶	SW ◇■ A ⌶	GW ◇	SW ■	XC ◇■ ⌶	GW	SW ■
Weymouth	d			05 55									06 25	06 40				
Upwey	d			05 59									06 29	06 45				
Dorchester West	a													06 52				
Dorchester South	d			06 07									06 37					
Moreton (Dorset)	d			06 14									06 44					
Wool	d			06 20									06 50					
Wareham	d			06 27									06 57					
Holton Heath	d			06 31														
Hamworthy	d			06 36									07 04					
Poole ■4	a			06 40									07 08					
	d			06 41									07 11					
Parkstone (Dorset)	d			06 45									07 15					
Branksome	d			06 49									07 19					
Bournemouth	a			06 54									07 24					
	d		06 34	06 56								07 04	07 26			07 30		
Pokesdown	d		06 38									07 08						
Christchurch	d		06 42									07 12						
Hinton Admiral	d		06 47									07 17						
New Milton	d		06 51									07 21						
Sway	d		06 56									07 26						
Lymington Pier	d							07 14										07 44
Lymington Town	d							07 16										07 46
Brockenhurst ■3	a		07 01					07 25				07 31				07 46		07 55
	d		07 03									07 33				07 49		
Beaulieu Road	d																	
Ashurst New Forest	d		07 11									07 41						
Totton	d		07 16									07 46						
Salisbury	d					06 50					07 11						07 36	
Dean	d					07 02												
Mottisfont & Dunbridge	d					07 08												
Romsey	d					07 13					07 30						07 56	
Redbridge	d					07 23												
Millbrook (Hants)	d					07 26												
Southampton Central	a		07 21	07 25		07 29					07 40	07 51	07 55			08 03	08 09	
	d		07 30			07 35				07 38	07 42	08 00				08 15		
St Denys	d					07 40				07 43								
Swaythling	d					07 43				07 46								
Southampton Airport Pkwy	d		07 38			07 46				07 49		08 08				08 22		
Portsmouth Harbour	d				06 50		07 05								07 24			
Portsmouth & Southsea	d				06 55		07 09								07 29			
Fratton	d				06 59		07 13								07 33			
Hilsea	d				07 03										07 37			
Cosham	d				07 08		07 21								07 43			
Portchester	d				07 13										07 48			
Fareham	d				07 20		07 29				08a05				07 54			
Botley	d				07 28										08 01			
Hedge End	d				07 32										08 06			
Eastleigh ■3	a				07 38	07 49				07 53					08 12			
	d				07 43	07 50				07 54					08 13			
Chandlers Ford	d					07 55												
Romsey	a					08 03	08 10											
Shawford	d	←			07 49					08 00					08 20			
Winchester	d	07 42	07 48		07 55				08 01	08 06		08 18			08 26	08 31		
Micheldever	d				08 02													
Basingstoke	a	07 58			08 14				08 16	08 22		08 34			08 42	08 46		
	d	08 05			08 16				08 18	08 24		08 35			08 43	08 47		
Reading ■7	a								08 36							09 04		
Fleet	d	08 22								08 40					08 54			
Farnborough (Main)	d	08 28								08 46					09 00			
Woking	a	08 38			08 34					08 58		08 53						
Clapham Junction ■10	a											09 14			09 26			
London Waterloo ■15 ⊖	a	09 10	08 50		09 03					09 29		09 25			09 38			

A ⌶ from Bournemouth

Table 158

Mondays to Fridays

until 5 October

Weymouth, Bournemouth, Lymington, Romsey, Southampton and Basingstoke - London

Network Diagram - see first Page of Table 158

		SW ■ ⌶	SW ◇■ A ⌶	SW ■	SW ■	SW ■	SW ■	SW ■	GW ◇ ⌶	SW ■	SW ■ ⌶	SW ■	SW ◇■ ⌶	SW ■ ⌶	SW ■	GW ◇ ⌶	SW ■	XC ◇■ ⌶	SW ◇■ A ⌶
Weymouth	d		06 55												07 25				07 55
Upwey	d		06 59												07 29				07 59
Dorchester West	a																		
Dorchester South	d		07 07												07 37				08 07
Moreton (Dorset)	d		07 14												07 44				08 14
Wool	d		07 20												07 50				08 20
Wareham	d		07 27												07 57				08 27
Holton Heath	d		07 31												08 01				08 31
Hamworthy	d		07 36												08 06				08 36
Poole ■4	a		07 40												08 10				08 40
	d	07 20	07 41										07 55		08 11				08 41
Parkstone (Dorset)	d	07 24	07 45										07 59		08 15				08 45
Branksome	d	07 27	07 49										08 02		08 19				08 49
Bournemouth	a	07 32	07 54										08 07		08 24				08 54
	d	07 34	07 59										08 10		08 25			08 45	08 59
Pokesdown	d	07 38											08 14		08 29				
Christchurch	d	07 42											08 18		08 33				
Hinton Admiral	d	07 47											08 24		08 38				
New Milton	d	07 51											08 29		08 42				
Sway	d	07 56											08 34		08 47				
Lymington Pier	d			08 14													08 44		
Lymington Town	d			08 16													08 46		
Brockenhurst ■3	a	08 01	08 14	08 25									08 39		08 52		08 55	08 58	09 14
	d	08 03	08 15										08 41					09 00	09 15
Beaulieu Road	d	08 08																	
Ashurst New Forest	d	08 12											08 48						
Totton	d	08 17											08 53						
Salisbury	d						07 50									08 32			
Dean	d						08 02												
Mottisfont & Dunbridge	d						08 08												
Romsey	d						08 13									08 50			
Redbridge	d						08 21												
Millbrook (Hants)	d						08 25				←								
Southampton Central	a	08 23	08 28				08 27				08 23		08 58			09 04		09 12	09 28
	d	08 48	08 30				08 35				08 48		09 00			09 05		09 15	09 30
St Denys	d	→					08 40				08 53								
Swaythling	d						08 43				08 56								
Southampton Airport Pkwy	d		08 38				08 46				08 59		09 08					09 22	09 38
Portsmouth Harbour	d					07 55		08 05	08 23	08 33									
Portsmouth & Southsea	d					08 00		08 10	08 27	08 38									
Fratton	d					08 04		08 13	08 31	08 42									
Hilsea	d					08 08		08 17		08 46									
Cosham	d					08 13		08 22	08 39	08 51									
Portchester	d					08 18		08 27		08 56									
Fareham	d					08 24		08 33	08 47	09a01						09a27			
Botley	d					08 31		08 41											
Hedge End	d					08 36		08 45											
Eastleigh ■3	a					08 42	08 49	08 51			09 03								
	d					08 43	08 50	08 54			09 14								
Chandlers Ford	d						08 55												
Romsey	a						09 03		09 21										
Shawford	d					08 49					09 19			←					
Winchester	d		08 48			08 56		09 03			09 25		09 18	09 25				09 31	09 48
Micheldever	d					09 04					→								
Basingstoke	a					09 15		09 19					09 35	09 41				09 46	
	d				08 54	09 17						09 24	09 36	09 43				09 47	
Reading ■7	a																	10 04	
Fleet	d				09 10							09 40		09 54					
Farnborough (Main)	d				09 16	09 30						09 46		10 00					
Woking	a		09 22		09 28	09 39						09 58	09 54						10 20
Clapham Junction ■10	a		09 43		09 57								10 15	10 25					
London Waterloo ■15 ⊖	a		09 53		10 05	10 08						10 36	10 23	10 34					10 49

A ⌶ from Bournemouth

Table 158

Mondays to Fridays
until 5 October

Weymouth, Bournemouth, Lymington, Romsey, Southampton and Basingstoke - London

Network Diagram - see first Page of Table 158

		SW	SW	SW	GW	SW	SW	XC	SW	SW	SW	SW	GW	GW	SW	SW	XC	SW	SW	SW
		1	1	1	◇ 🍴	1	1	◇1 🍴	1	1	◇1 A 🍴	1	◇	■ 🍴	1	1	◇1 🍴	◇1 A 🍴	1	1
Weymouth	d										08 20		08 53					09 03		
Upwey	d										08 24		08 58							
Dorchester West	a												09 05							
Dorchester South	d										08 33							09 13		
Moreton (Dorset)	d										08 39									
Wool	d										08 45									
Wareham	d										08 53							09 28		
Holton Heath	d										08 56									
Hamworthy	d										09 01							09 35		
Poole 4	a										09 06							09 39		
	d									08 50	09 07				09 13			09 40		
Parkstone (Dorset)	d									08 54					09 17			09 44		
Branksome	d									08 57					09 20			09 48		
Bournemouth	a									09 02	09 16				09 25			09 53		
	d									09 05	09 18				09 27		09 45	09 55		
Pokesdown	d									09 09	09 22				09 30					
Christchurch	d									09 13	09 26				09 34					
Hinton Admiral	d									09 18					09 39					
New Milton	d									09 22	09 33				09 44					
Sway	d									09 27					09 48					
Lymington Pier	d	09 14														09 44				
Lymington Town	d	09 16														09 46				
Brockenhurst 3	a	09 25								09 32	09 40				09 53	09 55	09 59	10 10		
	d									09 33	09 41				09 54		10 00	10 11		
Beaulieu Road	d																			
Ashurst New Forest	d									09 40										
Totton	d									09 45										
Salisbury	d					08 56								09 32						
Dean	d					09 08														
Mottisfont & Dunbridge	d					09 14														
Romsey	d					09 19								09 50						
Redbridge	d					09 27														
Millbrook (Hants)	d					09 31														
Southampton Central ⛴	a					09 34				09 52	09 55			10 04	10 09		10 12	10 26		
	d					09 36		09 46		09 55	10 00			10 05			10 15	10 30		
St Denys	d					09 41														
Swaythling	d					09 44														
Southampton Airport Pkwy ✈	d					09 46		09 53		10 03	10 08						10 22	10 38		
Portsmouth Harbour ⛴	d			08 59	09 23		09 33													09 59
Portsmouth & Southsea	d			09 04	09 27		09 38													10 04
Fratton	d			09 08	09 31		09 42													10 08
Hilsea	d			09 12			09 46													10 12
Cosham	d			09 17	09 39		09 51													10 17
Portchester	d			09 22			09 56													10 22
Fareham	d			09 28	09 47		10a01							10a27						10 28
Botley	d			09 35																10 35
Hedge End	d			09 40																10 40
Eastleigh 3	a			09 46		09 50				10 06										10 46
	d			09 47		09 51				10 14										10 47
Chandlers Ford	d					09 56														
Romsey	a				10 21	10 03														
Shawford	d									10 19		←								
Winchester	d			09 56				10 03		10 25	10 18	10 25					10 31	10 48		10 56
Micheldever	d			10 05						→										11 05
Basingstoke	a			10 15				10 18			10 34	10 41					10 46			11 15
	d		09 54	10 17				10 19	10 24		10 35	10 43					10 47		10 54	11 17
Reading 7	a							10 36									11 04			
Fleet	d		10 10						10 40			10 54							11 10	
Farnborough (Main)	d		10 16	10 30					10 46			11 00							11 16	11 30
Woking	a		10 28	10 39					10 58									11 19	11 28	11 39
Clapham Junction 10	a		10 57								11 12	11 25							11 57	
London Waterloo 15 ⊖	a		11 05	11 08					11 36		11 20	11 34						11 49	12 06	12 08

A 🍴 from Bournemouth

Table 158

Mondays to Fridays
until 5 October

Weymouth, Bournemouth, Lymington, Romsey, Southampton and Basingstoke - London

Network Diagram - see first Page of Table 158

		GW	SW	SW	SW	SW	SW	SW	SW	GW	XC	SW	SW	SW	SW	GW	SW
		◇ 🍴	1	1	1	1	1	◇1 A 🍴	1	◇ 🍴	◇1 🍴	1	◇1 A 🍴	1	1	◇ 🍴	1
Weymouth	d							09 20					10 03				
Upwey	d							09 24									
Dorchester West	a																
Dorchester South	d							09 33					10 13				
Moreton (Dorset)	d							09 39									
Wool	d							09 45									
Wareham	d							09 53					10 28				
Holton Heath	d							09 56									
Hamworthy	d							10 01					10 35				
Poole 4	a							10 06					10 39				
	d					09 50		10 07					10 40				
Parkstone (Dorset)	d					09 54							10 44				
Branksome	d					09 57							10 48				
Bournemouth	a					10 02		10 17					10 54				
	d					10 05		10 22			10 45		10 59				
Pokesdown	d					10 09		10 26									
Christchurch	d					10 13		10 30									
Hinton Admiral	d					10 18											
New Milton	d					10 22		10 37									
Sway	d					10 27											
Lymington Pier	d						10 27					10 57					
Lymington Town	d						10 29					10 59					
Brockenhurst 3	a					10 32	10 38	10 44			10 58	11 08	11 14				
	d					10 33		10 45			11 00		11 15				
Beaulieu Road	d																
Ashurst New Forest	d					10 40											
Totton	d					10 45											
Salisbury	d		09 56							10 30							10 56
Dean	d		10 08														11 08
Mottisfont & Dunbridge	d		10 14														11 14
Romsey	d		10 19							10 50							11 20
Redbridge	d		10 27														11 27
Millbrook (Hants)	d		10 31														11 31
Southampton Central ⛴	a		10 34			10 53		10 58		11 04	11 12		11 28				11 34
	d		10 35			10 55		11 00		11 05	11 15		11 30				11 35
St Denys	d		10 40														11 40
Swaythling	d		10 43														11 43
Southampton Airport Pkwy ✈	d		10 46			11 03		11 08			11 22		11 38				11 46
Portsmouth Harbour ⛴	d	10 23		10 33											10 59	11 23	
Portsmouth & Southsea	d	10 27		10 38											11 04	11 27	
Fratton	d	10 31		10 42											11 08	11 31	
Hilsea	d			10 46											11 12		
Cosham	d	10 39		10 51											11 17	11 39	
Portchester	d			10 56											11 22		
Fareham	d	10 47		11a01						11a27					11 28	11 47	
Botley	d														11 35		
Hedge End	d														11 40		
Eastleigh 3	a		10 49			11 06									11 46		11 49
	d		10 50			11 14									11 47		11 50
Chandlers Ford	d		10 55														11 55
Romsey	a	11 21	11 03													12 21	12 03
Shawford	d					11 19			←								
Winchester	d					11 25		11 18	11 25		11 31		11 48		11 56		
Micheldever	d					→									12 05		
Basingstoke	a							11 34	11 41		11 46				12 15		
	d				11 24			11 35	11 43		11 47			11 54	12 17		
Reading 7	a										12 04						
Fleet	d				11 40				11 54					12 10			
Farnborough (Main)	d				11 46				12 00					12 16	12 30		
Woking	a				11 58								12 19	12 28	12 39		
Clapham Junction 10	a							12 12	12 25					12 57			
London Waterloo 15 ⊖	a				12 36			12 20	12 34				12 49	13 05	13 07		

A 🍴 from Bournemouth

Weymouth, Bournemouth, Lymington, Romsey, Southampton and Basingstoke - London

Network Diagram - see first Page of Table 158

		XC	SW	SW	SW	SW	SW	GW	XC	GW	SW	SW	GW	SW	SW	GW	SW	SW
		◇■1 ⊼	■1	■1	■1	◇■1 A ⊼	■1	◇ ⊼	◇■1 ⊼		■1	◇■1 A ⊼		■1	■1	◇ ⊼	■1	■1
Weymouth	d					10 20						11 03	11 10					
Upwey	d					10 24							11 15					
Dorchester West	a												11 22					
Dorchester South	d					10 33						11 13						
Moreton (Dorset)	d					10 39												
Wool	d					10 45												
Wareham	d					10 53						11 28						
Holton Heath	d					10 56												
Hamworthy	d					11 01						11 35						
Poole [4]	a					11 06						11 39						
	d			10 50		11 07						11 40						
Parkstone (Dorset)	d			10 54								11 44						
Branksome	d			10 57								11 48						
Bournemouth	a			11 02		11 17						11 54						
	d			11 05		11 22			11 45			11 59						
Pokesdown	d			11 09		11 26												
Christchurch	d			11 13		11 30												
Hinton Admiral	d			11 18														
New Milton	d			11 22		11 37												
Sway	d			11 27														
Lymington Pier	d				11 27						11 57							
Lymington Town	d				11 29						11 59							
Brockenhurst [3]	a			11 32	11 38	11 44			11 58		12 08	12 14						
	d			11 33		11 45			12 00			12 15						
Beaulieu Road	d			11 38														
Ashurst New Forest	d			11 42														
Totton	d			11 47														
Salisbury	d							11 32		11 42							11 56	
Dean	d																12 08	
Mottisfont & Dunbridge	d																12 14	
Romsey	d							11 50		12 10							12 19	
Redbridge	d																12 27	
Millbrook (Hants)	d																12 31	
Southampton Central ⛴	a			11 53		11 58		12 04	12 12	12 22		12 28					12 34	
	d	11 46		11 55		12 00		12 05	12 15			12 30					12 35	
St Denys	d																12 40	
Swaythling	d																12 43	
Southampton Airport Pkwy ✈	d	11 53		12 03		12 08			12 22			12 38					12 46	
Portsmouth Harbour ⛴	d														11 59	12 23		
Portsmouth & Southsea	d														12 04	12 27		
Fratton	d														12 08	12 31		
Hilsea	d														12 12			
Cosham	d														12 17	12 39		
Portchester	d														12 22			
Fareham	d							12a27							12 28	12 47		
Botley	d														12 35			
Hedge End	d														12 40			
Eastleigh [8]	a			12 06											12 46		12 49	
	d			12 14											12 47		12 50	
Chandlers Ford	d																12 55	
Romsey	a															13 21	13 03	
Shawford	d			12 19			←											
Winchester	d	12 02		12 25		12 18	12 25		12 31			12 48			12 56			
Micheldever	d			→											13 05			
Basingstoke	a	12 17				12 34	12 41		12 46						13 15			
	d	12 18	12 24			12 35	12 43		12 47					12 54	13 17			13 24
Reading [7]	a	12 36							13 04									
Fleet	d		12 40				12 54							13 10				13 40
Farnborough (Main)	d		12 46				13 00							13 16	13 30			13 46
Woking	a		12 58									13 19		13 28	13 39			13 58
Clapham Junction [10]	a					13 12	13 25							13 57				
London Waterloo [15] ⊖	a		13 36			13 20	13 34					13 49		14 05	14 07			14 36

A ⊼ from Bournemouth

Weymouth, Bournemouth, Lymington, Romsey, Southampton and Basingstoke - London

Network Diagram - see first Page of Table 158

		SW	SW	SW	SW	GW	XC	SW	SW	SW	SW	GW	SW	XC	SW	SW	SW	SW	SW
		■1	■1	◇■1 A ⊼	■1	◇ ⊼	◇■1 ⊼	■1	◇■1 A ⊼	■1	■1	◇ ⊼	■1	◇■1	■1	■1	■1	◇■1 A ⊼	■1
Weymouth	d			11 20					12 03									12 20	
Upwey	d			11 24														12 24	
Dorchester West	a																		
Dorchester South	d			11 33					12 13									12 33	
Moreton (Dorset)	d			11 39														12 39	
Wool	d			11 45														12 45	
Wareham	d			11 53					12 28									12 53	
Holton Heath	d			11 56														12 56	
Hamworthy	d			12 01					12 35									13 01	
Poole [4]	a			12 06					12 39									13 06	
	d	11 50		12 07					12 40							12 50		13 07	
Parkstone (Dorset)	d	11 54							12 44							12 54			
Branksome	d	11 57							12 48							12 57			
Bournemouth	a	12 02		12 17					12 54							13 02		13 17	
	d	12 05		12 22			12 45		12 59							13 05		13 22	
Pokesdown	d	12 09		12 26												13 09		13 26	
Christchurch	d	12 13		12 30												13 13		13 30	
Hinton Admiral	d	12 18														13 18			
New Milton	d	12 22		12 37												13 22		13 37	
Sway	d	12 27														13 27			
Lymington Pier	d		12 27					12 57									13 27		
Lymington Town	d		12 29					12 59									13 29		
Brockenhurst [3]	a	12 32	12 38	12 44			12 58	13 08	13 14							13 32	13 38	13 44	
	d	12 33		12 45			13 00		13 15							13 33		13 45	
Beaulieu Road	d																		
Ashurst New Forest	d	12 40														13 40			
Totton	d	12 45														13 45			
Salisbury	d					12 32							12 56						
Dean	d												13 08						
Mottisfont & Dunbridge	d												13 14						
Romsey	d					12 50							13 19						
Redbridge	d												13 27						
Millbrook (Hants)	d												13 31						
Southampton Central ⛴	a	12 52		12 58		13 04	13 12		13 28				13 34			13 53		13 58	
	d	12 55		13 00		13 05	13 15		13 30				13 35	13 46		13 55		14 00	
St Denys	d												13 40						
Swaythling	d												13 43						
Southampton Airport Pkwy ✈	d	13 03		13 08			13 22		13 38				13 46	13 53		14 03		14 08	
Portsmouth Harbour ⛴	d										12 59	13 23							
Portsmouth & Southsea	d										13 04	13 27							
Fratton	d										13 08	13 31							
Hilsea	d										13 12								
Cosham	d										13 17	13 39							
Portchester	d										13 22								
Fareham	d					13a27					13 28	13 47							
Botley	d										13 35								
Hedge End	d										13 40								
Eastleigh [8]	a	13 06									13 46		13 49			14 06			
	d	13 14									13 47		13 50			14 14			
Chandlers Ford	d												13 55						
Romsey	a											14 21	14 03						
Shawford	d	13 19			←											14 19			←
Winchester	d	13 25		13 18	13 25		13 31		13 48		13 56			14 03		14 25		14 18	14 25
Micheldever	d	→									14 05					→			
Basingstoke	a			13 34	13 41		13 46				14 15			14 18				14 34	14 41
	d			13 35	13 43		13 47			13 54	14 17			14 19	14 24			14 35	14 43
Reading [7]	a						14 04							14 36					
Fleet	d				13 54					14 10					14 40				14 54
Farnborough (Main)	d				14 00					14 16	14 30				14 46				15 00
Woking	a								14 19	14 28	14 39				14 58				
Clapham Junction [10]	a			14 12	14 25					14 57								15 12	15 25
London Waterloo [15] ⊖	a			14 20	14 34				14 49	15 05	15 08				15 37			15 20	15 34

A ⊼ from Bournemouth

Table 158

Mondays to Fridays

until 5 October

Weymouth, Bournemouth, Lymington, Romsey, Southampton and Basingstoke - London

Network Diagram - see first Page of Table 158

		GW	XC	SW		SW	GW	SW	SW	GW		GW	SW			SW	SW	SW	SW	SW		GW	XC	SW	SW
		◇ ⌶	◇1 ⌶	1		◇1 A ⌶	◇	1	1	■ ⌶		■ ⌶	1			1	1	1	◇1 A ⌶	1		◇ ⌶	◇1 ⌶	1	◇1 A ⌶
Weymouth	d					13 03	13 10												13 20						14 03
Upwey	d						13 15												13 24						
Dorchester West	a						13 22																		
Dorchester South	d					13 13													13 33						14 13
Moreton (Dorset)	d																		13 39						
Wool	d																		13 45						
Wareham	d					13 28													13 53						14 28
Holton Heath	d																		13 56						
Hamworthy	d					13 35													14 01						14 35
Poole 4	a					13 39													14 06						14 39
	d					13 40											13 50		14 07						14 40
Parkstone (Dorset)	d					13 44											13 54								14 44
Branksome	d					13 48											13 57								14 48
Bournemouth	a					13 54											14 02		14 17						14 54
	d		13 45			13 59											14 05		14 22				14 45		14 59
Pokesdown	d																14 09		14 26						
Christchurch	d																14 13		14 30						
Hinton Admiral	d																14 18								
New Milton	d																14 22		14 37						
Sway	d																14 27								
Lymington Pier	d			13 57														14 27						14 57	
Lymington Town	d			13 59														14 29						14 59	
Brockenhurst 3	a		13 58	14 08		14 14											14 32	14 38	14 44				14 58	15 08	15 14
	d		14 00			14 15											14 33		14 45				15 00		15 15
Beaulieu Road	d																								
Ashurst New Forest	d																14 40								
Totton	d																14 45								
Salisbury	d	13 32										13 59	13 50									14 32			
Dean	d												14 02												
Mottisfont & Dunbridge	d												14 08												
Romsey	d	13 50										14 19	14 13									14 50			
Redbridge	d												14 21												
Millbrook (Hants)	d												14 24												
Southampton Central ⛴	a	14 04	14 12			14 28						14 32	14 28				14 53		14 58			15 04	15 12		15 28
	d	14 05	14 15			14 30						14 34	14 35				14 55		15 00			15 05	15 15		15 30
St Denys	d												14 40												
Swaythling	d												14 43												
Southampton Airport Pkwy ✈	d		14 22			14 38							14 46				15 03		15 08				15 22		15 38
Portsmouth Harbour ⛴	d								13 59	14 23															
Portsmouth & Southsea	d								14 04	14 27															
Fratton	d								14 08	14 31															
Hilsea	d								14 12																
Cosham	d								14 17	14 39															
Portchester	d								14 22																
Fareham	d	14a27							14 28	14 47		14a55										15a27			
Botley	d								14 35																
Hedge End	d								14 40																
Eastleigh 3	a								14 46				14 49				15 06								
	d								14 47				14 50				15 14								
Chandlers Ford	d												14 55												
Romsey	a									15 21			15 04												
Shawford	d																15 19			←					
Winchester	d		14 31			14 48			14 56								15 25		15 18	15 25			15 31		15 48
Micheldever	d								15 05								→								
Basingstoke	a		14 46						15 15										15 34	15 41			15 46		
	d		14 47					14 54	15 17							15 24			15 35	15 43			15 47		
Reading 7	a		15 04																				16 04		
Fleet	d							15 10								15 40				15 54					
Farnborough (Main)	d							15 16	15 30							15 46				16 00					
Woking	a					15 19		15 28	15 39							15 58									16 19
Clapham Junction 10	a							15 57											16 12	16 25					
London Waterloo 15 ⊖	a					15 49		16 05	16 07							16 36			16 20	16 34					16 49

A ⌶ from Bournemouth

Table 158

Mondays to Fridays

until 5 October

Weymouth, Bournemouth, Lymington, Romsey, Southampton and Basingstoke - London

Network Diagram - see first Page of Table 158

		SW	SW	GW		SW				XC	SW	SW	SW	SW	SW	GW		XC	SW	SW	GW	SW	SW	GW
		1	1	■ ⌶		1				◇1 ⌶	1	1	1	◇1 A ⌶	1	◇ ⌶		◇1 ⌶	1	◇1 A ⌶	◇	1	1	■ ⌶
Weymouth	d													14 20						15 03	15 08			
Upwey	d													14 24							15 13			
Dorchester West	a																				15 20			
Dorchester South	d													14 33						15 13				
Moreton (Dorset)	d													14 39										
Wool	d													14 45										
Wareham	d													14 53						15 28				
Holton Heath	d													14 56										
Hamworthy	d													15 01						15 35				
Poole 4	a													15 06						15 39				
	d											14 50		15 07						15 40				
Parkstone (Dorset)	d											14 54								15 44				
Branksome	d											14 57								15 48				
Bournemouth	a											15 02		15 17						15 54				
	d											15 05		15 22				15 45		15 59				
Pokesdown	d											15 09		15 26										
Christchurch	d											15 13		15 30										
Hinton Admiral	d											15 18												
New Milton	d											15 22		15 37										
Sway	d											15 27												
Lymington Pier	d												15 27						15 57					
Lymington Town	d												15 29						15 59					
Brockenhurst 3	a											15 32	15 38	15 44				15 58	16 08	16 14				
	d											15 33		15 45				16 00		16 15				
Beaulieu Road	d																							
Ashurst New Forest	d											15 40												
Totton	d											15 45												
Salisbury	d					14 56										15 32								
Dean	d					15 08																		
Mottisfont & Dunbridge	d					15 14																		
Romsey	d					15 19										15 50								
Redbridge	d					15 27																		
Millbrook (Hants)	d					15 31																		
Southampton Central ⛴	a					15 34						15 51		15 58		16 04		16 12		16 28				
	d					15 35				15 47		15 55		16 00		16 05		16 15		16 30				
St Denys	d					15 40																		
Swaythling	d					15 43																		
Southampton Airport Pkwy ✈	d					15 46						16 03		16 08				16 22		16 38				
Portsmouth Harbour ⛴	d		14 59	15 23																			15 59	16 23
Portsmouth & Southsea	d		15 04	15 27																			16 04	16 27
Fratton	d		15 08	15 31																			16 08	16 31
Hilsea	d		15 12																				16 12	
Cosham	d		15 17	15 39																			16 17	16 39
Portchester	d		15 22																				16 22	
Fareham	d		15 28	15 47												16a27							16 28	16 47
Botley	d		15 35																				16 35	
Hedge End	d		15 40																				16 40	
Eastleigh 3	a		15 46			15 49						16 07											16 46	
	d		15 47			15 50						16 14											16 47	
Chandlers Ford	d					15 55																		
Romsey	a			16 21		16 03																		17 21
Shawford	d											16 19			←									
Winchester	d		15 56									16 25		16 18	16 25			16 31		16 48			16 56	
Micheldever	d		16 05									→											17 05	
Basingstoke	a		16 15							16 17				16 34	16 41			16 46					17 15	
	d	15 54	16 17							16 18	16 24			16 35	16 43			16 47				16 54	17 17	
Reading 7	a									16 35								17 03						
Fleet	d	16 10									16 40				16 54							17 10		
Farnborough (Main)	d	16 16	16 30								16 46				17 00							17 16	17 30	
Woking	a	16 28	16 39								16 58									17 20		17 28	17 39	
Clapham Junction 10	a	16 57												17 12	17 25							17 57		
London Waterloo 15 ⊖	a	17 08	17 08								17 35			17 20	17 36					17 50		18 09	18 08	

A ⌶ from Bournemouth

until 5 October

Weymouth, Bournemouth, Lymington, Romsey, Southampton and Basingstoke - London

Network Diagram - see first Page of Table 158

		SW ■				SW ■	SW ■	SW ■	SW ■	SW ◇■ A ⊼	SW ■	GW ◇ ⊼		XC ◇■ ⊼	SW ■	SW ◇■ A ⊼	SW ■	SW ■	GW ◇ ⊼		SW ■			SW ■	SW ■
Weymouth	d									15 20						16 03									
Upwey	d									15 24															
Dorchester West	a																								
Dorchester South	d									15 33						16 13									
Moreton (Dorset)	d									15 39															
Wool	d									15 45															
Wareham	d									15 53						16 28									
Holton Heath	d									15 56															
Hamworthy	d									16 01						16 35									
Poole ■	a									16 06						16 39									
	d							15 50		16 07						16 40									
Parkstone (Dorset)	d							15 54								16 44									
Branksome	d							15 57								16 48									
Bournemouth	a							16 02		16 17						16 54									
	d							16 05		16 22				16 45		16 59									
Pokesdown	d							16 09		16 26															
Christchurch	d							16 13		16 30															
Hinton Admiral	d							16 18																	
New Milton	d							16 22		16 37															
Sway	d							16 27																	
Lymington Pier	d								16 27						16 57										
Lymington Town	d								16 29						16 59										
Brockenhurst ■	a							16 32	16 38	16 44				16 58	17 08	17 14									
	d							16 33		16 45				17 00		17 15								17 20	
Beaulieu Road	d																								
Ashurst New Forest	d							16 40																17 27	
Totton	d							16 45																17 32	
Salisbury	d	15 56										16 32									16 56				
Dean	d	16 08																			17 08				
Mottisfont & Dunbridge	d	16 14																			17 14				
Romsey	d	16 19										16 50									17 19				
Redbridge	d	16 27																			17 27				
Millbrook (Hants)	d	16 31																			17 31				
Southampton Central ⛴	a	16 34						16 51		16 58		17 04		17 12		17 28					17 34			17 41	
	d	16 35						16 52		17 00		17 05		17 15		17 30					17 35				
St Denys	d	16 40						16 57													17 40				
Swaythling	d	16 43						17 00													17 43				
Southampton Airport Pkwy ✈	d	16 46						17 04		17 08				17 22		17 38					17 46				
Portsmouth Harbour ⛴	d					16 49												16 59	17 23						17 33
Portsmouth & Southsea	d					16 55												17 04	17 27						17 38
Fratton	d					16 59												17 08	17 31						17 42
Hilsea	d					17 03												17 12							17 46
Cosham	d					17 08												17 17	17 39						17 51
Portchester	d					17 13												17 22							17 56
Fareham	d					17a18						17a27						17 28	17 47						18a01
Botley	d																	17 35							
Hedge End	d																	17 40							
Eastleigh ■	a	16 49						17 07										17 46			17 49				
	d	16 50						17 14										17 47			17 50				
Chandlers Ford	d	16 55																			17 55				
Romsey	a	17 03																	18 21		18 03				
Shawford	d							17 19			←														
Winchester	d							17 25		17 18	17 25			17 31		17 48		17 56							
Micheldever	d							→										18 05							
Basingstoke	a									17 34	17 42			17 46				18 15							
	d						17 24			17 36	17 43			17 47			17 54	18 17							
Reading ■	a													18 04											
Fleet	d						17 40				17 54						18 10								
Farnborough (Main)	d						17 46				18 00						18 16	18 30							
Woking	a						17 58									18 19	18 28	18 39							
Clapham Junction ■	a									18 12	18 25						18 58								
London Waterloo ■ ⊖	a						18 38			18 23	18 34					18 47	19 06	19 08							

A ⊼ from Bournemouth

until 5 October

Weymouth, Bournemouth, Lymington, Romsey, Southampton and Basingstoke - London

Network Diagram - see first Page of Table 158

			XC ◇■ ⊼	SW ■	SW ■	SW ■	SW ◇■ A ⊼	SW ■		GW ◇ ⊼	XC ◇■ ⊼	SW ■	SW ■	SW ◇■ A ⊼	SW ■	SW ■	GW ◇ ⊼			SW ■			SW ■	SW ■	SW ■
Weymouth	d						16 20							17 04											
Upwey	d						16 24																		
Dorchester West	a																								
Dorchester South	d						16 33							17 14											
Moreton (Dorset)	d						16 39																		
Wool	d						16 45																		
Wareham	d						16 53							17 29											
Holton Heath	d						16 56																		
Hamworthy	d						17 01							17 36											
Poole ■	a						17 06							17 40											
	d				16 50		17 07							17 41										17 50	
Parkstone (Dorset)	d				16 54									17 45										17 54	
Branksome	d				16 57									17 49										17 57	
Bournemouth	a				17 02		17 17							17 54										18 02	
	d				17 05		17 22				17 45			17 59										18 05	
Pokesdown	d				17 09		17 26																	18 09	
Christchurch	d				17 13		17 30																	18 13	
Hinton Admiral	d				17 18																			18 18	
New Milton	d				17 22		17 37																	18 22	
Sway	d				17 27																			18 27	
Lymington Pier	d					17 27						17 57													18 27
Lymington Town	d					17 29						17 59													18 29
Brockenhurst ■	a				17 32	17 38	17 44				17 58	18 08		18 14										18 32	18 38
	d				17 33		17 45				18 00			18 15										18 33	
Beaulieu Road	d																							18 38	
Ashurst New Forest	d				17 40																			18 42	
Totton	d				17 45																			18 47	
Salisbury	d									17 32										17 56					
Dean	d																			18 08					
Mottisfont & Dunbridge	d																			18 14					
Romsey	d									17 50										18 19					
Redbridge	d																			18 27					
Millbrook (Hants)	d																			18 31					
Southampton Central ⛴	a				17 53		17 58			18 04	18 12			18 28						18 34				18 53	
	d		17 46		17 55		18 00			18 05	18 15		18 17	18 30						18 35				18 55	
St Denys	d												18 22							18 40					
Swaythling	d												18 25							18 43					
Southampton Airport Pkwy ✈	d		17 53		18 03		18 08				18 22		18 28	18 38						18 46				19 03	
Portsmouth Harbour ⛴	d															17 59	18 23								
Portsmouth & Southsea	d															18 04	18 27								
Fratton	d															18 08	18 31								
Hilsea	d															18 12									
Cosham	d															18 17	18 39								
Portchester	d															18 22									
Fareham	d									18a27						18 28	18 47								
Botley	d															18 35									
Hedge End	d															18 40									
Eastleigh ■	a				18 06								18 32			18 46				18 49				19 06	
	d				18 14								18 33			18 47				18 50				19 14	
Chandlers Ford	d																			18 55					
Romsey	a																19 21			19 04					
Shawford	d				18 19			←																19 19	
Winchester	d		18 02		18 25		18 18	18 25			18 31		18a41	18 48		18 56								19 25	
Micheldever	d				→											19 05								→	
Basingstoke	a		18 17				18 34	18 41			18 46					19 15									
	d		18 18	18 24			18 35	18 43			18 47				18 54	19 17							19 24		
Reading ■	a		18 36								19 04														
Fleet	d			18 40				18 54							19 10								19 40		
Farnborough (Main)	d			18 46				19 00							19 16	19 30							19 46		
Woking	a			18 58										19 24	19 28	19 39							19 58		
Clapham Junction ■	a						19 12	19 26							19 57										
London Waterloo ■ ⊖	a			19 39			19 20	19 34						19 51	20 05	20 08							20 36		

A ⊼ from Bournemouth

Weymouth, Bournemouth, Lymington, Romsey, Southampton and Basingstoke - London

Network Diagram - see first Page of Table 158

		SW	SW	GW		GW	XC	SW	SW	SW	SW	GW		SW				SW	SW	SW	SW	GW	SW	XC
		◇1	1	◇		■	◇1	◇1	1	1	1	◇		1				1	1	◇1	1	■	1	◇1
		A						A												A				
		⊥				⊥	⊥	⊥												⊥		⊥		
Weymouth	d	17 20		17 30				18 06												18 20				
Upwey	d	17 24		17 35																18 24				
Dorchester West	a			17 42																				
Dorchester South	d	17 33						18 16												18 33				
Moreton (Dorset)	d	17 39																		18 39				
Wool	d	17 45																		18 45				
Wareham	d	17 53						18 31												18 53				
Holton Heath	d	17 56																		18 56				
Hamworthy	d	18 01						18 38												19 01				
Poole 4	a	18 06						18 42												19 06				
	d	18 07						18 43											18 50	19 07				
Parkstone (Dorset)	d							18 47											18 54					
Branksome	d							18 51											18 57					
Bournemouth	a	18 17						18 56											19 02	19 17				
	d	18 22					18 45	18 59											19 05	19 22				19 45
Pokesdown	d	18 26																	19 09	19 26				
Christchurch	d	18 30																	19 13	19 30				
Hinton Admiral	d																		19 18					
New Milton	d	18 37																	19 22	19 37				
Sway	d																		19 27					
Lymington Pier	d								19 03														19 33	
Lymington Town	d								19 05														19 35	
Brockenhurst 3	a	18 44					18 58	19 14	19 14										19 32	19 44			19 44	19 58
	d	18 45					19 00	19 15											19 33	19 45				20 00
Beaulieu Road	d																							
Ashurst New Forest	d																		19 41					
Totton	d																		19 46					
Salisbury	d					18 35								18 56								19 32		
Dean	d													19 08										
Mottisfont & Dunbridge	d													19 14										
Romsey	d					18 54								19 19								19 50		
Redbridge	d													19 27										
Millbrook (Hants)	d													19 31										
Southampton Central ⛴	a	18 58				19 04	19 12	19 28						19 34					19 52	19 58		20 04		20 12
	d	19 00				19 05	19 15	19 30						19 35					19 55	20 00		20 05		20 15
St Denys	d													19 40										
Swaythling	d													19 43										
Southampton Airport Pkwy ✈	d	19 08					19 22	19 38						19 46					20 03	20 08				20 22
Portsmouth Harbour ⛴	d										18 59	19 23												
Portsmouth & Southsea	d										19 04	19 27												
Fratton	d										19 08	19 31												
Hilsea	d										19 12													
Cosham	d										19 17	19 39												
Portchester	d										19 22													
Fareham	d					19a27					19 28	19 47										20a27		
Botley	d										19 35													
Hedge End	d										19 40													
Eastleigh 3	a										19 46			19 49					20 06					
	d										19 47			19 50					20 14					
Chandlers Ford	d													19 55										
Romsey	a											20 21		20 03										
Shawford	d		←																20 19		←			
Winchester	d	19 18	19 25				19 31	19 48			19 56								20 25	20 18	20 25			20 31
Micheldever	d										20 05								→					
Basingstoke	a	19 34	19 41				19 46				20 15									20 34	20 41			20 46
	d	19 35	19 43				19 47			19 54	20 17							20 24		20 36	20 43			20 47
Reading 7	a						20 04																	21 04
Fleet	d		19 54							20 10								20 40			20 54			
Farnborough (Main)	d		20 00							20 16	20 30							20 46			21 00			
Woking	a							20 19		20 28	20 39							20 58			21 09			
Clapham Junction 10	a	20 12	20 25							20 57										21 16	21 29			
London Waterloo 15 ⊖	a	20 20	20 34					20 49		21 05	21 07							21 34		21 24	21 38			

A ⊥ from Bournemouth

Weymouth, Bournemouth, Lymington, Romsey, Southampton and Basingstoke - London

Network Diagram - see first Page of Table 158

		SW	SW	SW	SW	GW		SW				GW	SW	SW	SW	GW	SW	SW				SW	SW	SW
		◇1	1	1	1	◇		1				◇	1	◇1	1	◇	1	1				1	1	1
		A																						
		⊥														⊥								
Weymouth	d	19 06												19 20										
Upwey	d													19 24										
Dorchester West	a																							
Dorchester South	d	19 16												19 37										
Moreton (Dorset)	d													19 43										
Wool	d													19 49										
Wareham	d	19 31												19 57										
Holton Heath	d																							
Hamworthy	d	19 38												20 03										
Poole 4	a	19 42												20 08										
	d	19 43											19 50	20 09										
Parkstone (Dorset)	d	19 47											19 54											
Branksome	d	19 51											19 57											
Bournemouth	a	19 56											20 02	20 18										
	d	19 59											20 05	20 22										
Pokesdown	d												20 09	20 26										
Christchurch	d												20 13	20 30										
Hinton Admiral	d												20 18											
New Milton	d												20 22	20 37										
Sway	d												20 27											
Lymington Pier	d		20 03														20 33	21 03						
Lymington Town	d		20 05														20 35	21 05						
Brockenhurst 3	a	20 14	20 14										20 32	20 44			20 44	21 14						
	d	20 15											20 33	20 45										
Beaulieu Road	d																							
Ashurst New Forest	d												20 40											
Totton	d												20 45											
Salisbury	d							19 56				20 14				20 32								
Dean	d							20 08																
Mottisfont & Dunbridge	d							20 14																
Romsey	d							20 19				20 35				20 50								
Redbridge	d							20 27																
Millbrook (Hants)	d							20 31																
Southampton Central ⛴	a	20 28						20 34				20 48	20 51	20 58		21 04								
	d	20 30						20 35					20 55	21 00		21 05						21 30		
St Denys	d							20 40																
Swaythling	d							20 43																
Southampton Airport Pkwy ✈	d	20 38						20 46					21 03	21 08								21 38		
Portsmouth Harbour ⛴	d				19 59	20 23																		20 59
Portsmouth & Southsea	d				20 04	20 27																		21 04
Fratton	d				20 08	20 31																		21 08
Hilsea	d				20 12																			21 12
Cosham	d				20 17																			21 17
Portchester	d				20 22																			21 22
Fareham	d				20 28	20 47										21a27								21 28
Botley	d				20 35																			21 35
Hedge End	d				20 40																			21 40
Eastleigh 3	a				20 46			20 49					21 06											21 46
	d				20 47			20 50					21 14											21 47
Chandlers Ford	d							20 55																
Romsey	a					21 21		21 03																
Shawford	d				20 53								21 19		←									
Winchester	d	20 48			20 59								21 25	21 18	21 25							21 48		21 56
Micheldever	d				21 07								→											22 05
Basingstoke	a				21 21									21 34	21 41									22 15
	d			20 54	21 24									21 35	21 43								21 54	22 24
Reading 7	a																							
Fleet	d			21 10	21 40										21 54								22 10	22 40
Farnborough (Main)	d			21 16	21 46										22 00								22 16	22 46
Woking	a	21 19		21 28	21 58										22 09							22 19	22 28	22 58
Clapham Junction 10	a			21 57										22 14	22 29								22 57	
London Waterloo 15 ⊖	a	21 49		22 06	22 34									22 22	22 38							22 49	23 08	23 32

A ⊥ from Bournemouth

Table 158

Mondays to Fridays

until 5 October

Weymouth, Bournemouth, Lymington, Romsey, Southampton and Basingstoke - London

Network Diagram - see first Page of Table 158

		SW	GW	SW	SW	SW	GW	GW	SW	SW	SW	SW	SW	SW	SW	SW	SW FX
		1		1	◇1	1		◇	1	1	1	1	1	1	1	1 A	1 B
Weymouth	d				20 10		20 21									21 10	21 10
Upwey	d				20 14		20 26									21 14	21 14
Dorchester West	a						20 33										
Dorchester South	d				20 22											21 22	21 22
Moreton (Dorset)	d				20 28											21 28	21 28
Wool	d				20 34											21 34	21 34
Wareham	d				20 42											21 42	21 42
Holton Heath	d																
Hamworthy	d				20 48											21 48	21 48
Poole 4	a				20 53											21 53	21 53
	d				20 54											21 54	21 54
Parkstone (Dorset)	d				20 58											21 58	21 58
Branksome	d				21 01											22 01	22 01
Bournemouth	a				21 07											22 07	22 07
	d				21 12											22 12	22 12
Pokesdown	d				21 16											22 16	22 16
Christchurch	d				21 20											22 20	22 20
Hinton Admiral	d				21 25											22 25	22 25
New Milton	d				21 29											22 29	22 29
Sway	d				21 34											22 34	22 34
Lymington Pier	d								21 33	22 03							
Lymington Town	d								21 35	22 05							
Brockenhurst 3	a				21 39				21 44	22 14						22 39	22 39
	d				21 40											22 40	22 40
Beaulieu Road	d																
Ashurst New Forest	d				21 47											22 47	22 47
Totton	d				21 52											22 52	22 52
Salisbury	d	20 56						21 32						21 56			
Dean	d	21 08												22 08			
Mottisfont & Dunbridge	d	21 14												22 14			
Romsey	d	21 19						21 50						22 19			
Redbridge	d	21 27												22 27			
Millbrook (Hants)	d	21 31												22 31			
Southampton Central	a	21 34			21 57			22 02						22 34		22 57	22 57
	d	21 35		21 55	22 00			22 04				22 30		22 35		23 00	23 00
St Denys	d	21 40												22 40			
Swaythling	d	21 43												22 43			
Southampton Airport Pkwy	d	21 46		22 03	22 08							22 38		22 46		23 08	23 08
Portsmouth Harbour	d		21 23										21 54		22 33		
Portsmouth & Southsea	d		21 27										21 59		22 38		
Fratton	d		21 31										22 03		22 42		
Hilsea	d												22 07		22 46		
Cosham	d												22 12		22 51		
Portchester	d												22 17		22 56		
Fareham	d		21 48										22 26		23a01		
Botley	d												22 33				
Hedge End	d												22 37				
Eastleigh 3	a	21 49	22 06	22 06				22 14				22 41	22 43	22 49		23 11	23 11
	d	21 50	22 11	22 14								22 46		22 50		23 12	23 12
Chandlers Ford	d	21 55												22 55			
Romsey	a	22 03	22 33											23 03			
Shawford	d			22 20		←										23 18	23 18
Winchester	d			22 26	22 18	22 26						22 55				23 24	23 24
Micheldever	d			→												23 33	23 33
Basingstoke	a				22 34	22 42						23 11				23 43	23 43
	d				22 36	22 43					22 54	23 13				23 44	23 44
Reading 7	a																
Fleet	d					22 54					23 10					00 01	00 02
Farnborough (Main)	d					23 00					23 16					00 06	00 06
Woking	a				22 54	23 09					23 28	23 31				00 18	00 18
Clapham Junction 10	a				23 14	23 29					00 21	23 55				00 53	00 53
London Waterloo 15 ⊖	a				23 23	23 42					00 35	00 09				01 04	01 04

A not 29 August, 30 August, from 3 September until 6 September **B** from 29 August until 6 September

Table 158

Mondays to Fridays

until 5 October

Weymouth, Bournemouth, Lymington, Romsey, Southampton and Basingstoke - London

Network Diagram - see first Page of Table 158

		GW	SW	SW	SW	SW	SW	SW
		◇	1	1	1	1	◇1	1
Weymouth	d						22 10	23 10
Upwey	d						22 14	23 14
Dorchester West	a							
Dorchester South	d						22 22	23 22
Moreton (Dorset)	d						22 28	23 28
Wool	d						22 34	23 34
Wareham	d						22 42	23 42
Holton Heath	d							
Hamworthy	d						22 48	23 48
Poole 4	a						22 53	23 53
	d						22 54	23 54
Parkstone (Dorset)	d						22 58	
Branksome	d						23 01	
Bournemouth	a						23 07	00 03
	d						23 12	
Pokesdown	d						23 16	
Christchurch	d						23 20	
Hinton Admiral	d						23 25	
New Milton	d						23 29	
Sway	d						23 34	
Lymington Pier	d		22 33					
Lymington Town	d		22 35					
Brockenhurst 3	a		22 44				23 39	
	d						23 40	
Beaulieu Road	d							
Ashurst New Forest	d						23 47	
Totton	d						23 52	
Salisbury	d	22 32						
Dean	d							
Mottisfont & Dunbridge	d							
Romsey	d	22 53		22 58	23 07			
Redbridge	d			23 05				
Millbrook (Hants)	d			23 09				
Southampton Central	a	23 04		23 11	23 36		23 57	
	d	23 05		23 20	23 38		23 59	
St Denys	d			23 25			00 04	
Swaythling	d			23 28			00 07	
Southampton Airport Pkwy	d			23 31			00 10	
Portsmouth Harbour	d					23 24		
Portsmouth & Southsea	d					23 29		
Fratton	d					23 33		
Hilsea	d					23 37		
Cosham	d					23 42		
Portchester	d					23 47		
Fareham	d	23a27				23 53		
Botley	d					23 59		
Hedge End	d					00 05		
Eastleigh 3	a			23 34		00 11	00 14	
	d			23 36		00 19		
Chandlers Ford	d			23 41				
Romsey	a			23 48	23 55			
Shawford	d							
Winchester	d					00a28		
Micheldever	d							
Basingstoke	a							
	d							
Reading 7	a							
Fleet	d							
Farnborough (Main)	d							
Woking	a							
Clapham Junction 10	a							
London Waterloo 15 ⊖	a							

Weymouth, Bournemouth, Lymington, Romsey, Southampton and Basingstoke - London

Network Diagram - see first Page of Table 158

		SW MX ■1	SW MX ■1	SW MO ◇■1	SW MX ■1	SW MO ■1	SW MX ■1	SW MX ◇■1	SW MO ■1	SW MX ■1	SW ■1	SW ■1	XC ◇■1	GW ◇	SW ■1	SW ■1	SW ■1	SW ■1	SW ■1	SW ◇■1 🛒	SW ■1	SW ■1	XC ◇■1 🛒
Weymouth	d			20p58	21p10			22p10	22p58	23p10				05 33									
Upwey	d			21p02	21p14			22p14	23p02	23p14				05 37									
Dorchester West	a													05 44									
Dorchester South	d			21p10	21p22			22p22	23p10	23p22													
Moreton (Dorset)	d			21p17	21p28			22p28	23p17	23p28													
Wool	d			21p23	21p34			22p34	23p23	23p34													
Wareham	d			21p30	21p42			22p42	23p30	23p42													
Holton Heath	d																						
Hamworthy	d			21p37	21p48			22p48	23p37	23p48													
Poole ■4	a			21p41	21p53			22p53	23p41	23p53													
	d			21p50	21p54			22p54	23p50	23p54										04 57	05 23		
Parkstone (Dorset)	d			21p54	21p58			22p58	23p54											05 01	05 27		
Branksome	d			21p57	22p01			23p01	23p57											05 04	05 30		
Bournemouth	a			22p03	22p07			23p07	00 03	00 03										05 09	05 36		
	d			22p06	22p12			23p12												05 12	05 38		
Pokesdown	d			22p10	22p16			23p16												05 16	05 42		
Christchurch	d			22p14	22p20			23p20												05 20	05 46		
Hinton Admiral	d			22p19	22p25			23p25													05 51		
New Milton	d			22p23	22p29			23p29												05 27	05 55		
Sway	d			22p28	22p34			23p34													06 00		
Lymington Pier	d																						
Lymington Town	d																						
Brockenhurst ■3	a			22p33	22p39			23p39												05 37	06 07		
	d			22p34	22p40			23p40												05 38			
Beaulieu Road	d			22p39																			
Ashurst New Forest	d			22p43	22p47			23p47												05 49			
Totton	d			22p48	22p52			23p52															
Salisbury	d														05 35								
Dean	d														05 47								
Mottisfont & Dunbridge	d														05 53								
Romsey	d														05 58								
Redbridge	d																						
Millbrook (Hants)	d																						
Southampton Central ⛴	a			22p53	22p57			23p57												05 54			
	d		22p30	22p55	23p00			23p59				04 52	05 15					05 42		05 55			06 15
St Denys	d							00 04				04 57						05 47					
Swaythling	d							00 07				05 00						05 50					
Southampton Airport Pkwy ✈	d		22p38	23p03	23p08			00 10				05 03	05 22					05 53		06 03			06 22
Portsmouth Harbour ⛴	d					23p17	23p24										04 55						
Portsmouth & Southsea	d					23p22	23p29										05 00						
Fratton	d					23p26	23p33										05 04						
Hilsea	d					23p30	23p37										05 08						
Cosham	d					23p35	23p42										05 16						
Portchester	d					23p40	23p47										05 20						
Fareham	d					23p46	23p53										05 26						
Botley	d					23p54	23p59										05 34						
Hedge End	d					23p58	00 05										05 38						
Eastleigh ■8	a		22p41	23p09	23p11	00 04	00 11	00 14				05 06					05 46	05 56		06 07			
	d		22p46	23p11	23p12		00 19					05 07					05 47			06 08			
Chandlers Ford	d														06 06								
Romsey	a														06 44								
Shawford	d				23p18							05 13					05 53						
Winchester	d		22p55	23p23	23p24		00a28					05 19	05 31				05 59			06 18			06 31
Micheldever	d			23p32	23p33							05 27					06 07						
Basingstoke	a		23p11	23p42	23p43							05 38	05 46				06 20			06 34			06 46
	d	22p54	23p13	23p44	23p44						04 54	05 39	05 47			05 54			06 23	06 35		06 42	06 47
Reading ■7	a												06 04										07 04
Fleet	d	23p10			00 01						05 10	05 50				06 10			06 40			06 54	
Farnborough (Main)	d	23p16			00 06						05 16	05 56				06 16			06 46			07 00	
Woking	a	23p28	23p31	00 02	00 18						05 28	06 05				06 28			06 58	06 53		07 10	
Clapham Junction ■10	a	00 21	23p55	00 23	00 53						06 00	06 25				06 54			07 20	07 14			
London Waterloo ■15 ⊖	a	00 35	00 09	00 33	01 04						06 15	06 34				07 04			07 31	07 24		07 41	

Weymouth, Bournemouth, Lymington, Romsey, Southampton and Basingstoke - London

Network Diagram - see first Page of Table 158

		SW ◇■1 🛒	SW ■1	SW ■1	SW ■1	SW ■1	GW ■ 🛒	SW ■1	SW	SW ■1	SW ■1	GW	SW ◇■1 🛒	SW ◇■1 🛒	SW ■1	SW ■1	XC ◇■1 🛒	SW ■1	SW ■1	SW ■1	SW ◇■1 🛒	SW ◇■1 A 🛒
Weymouth	d																					05 50
Upwey	d																					05 54
Dorchester West	a																					
Dorchester South	d																					06 02
Moreton (Dorset)	d																					06 09
Wool	d																					06 15
Wareham	d																					06 22
Holton Heath	d																					06 26
Hamworthy	d																					06 31
Poole ■4	a																					06 38
	d	05 42												06 08								06 39
Parkstone (Dorset)	d													06 12								06 43
Branksome	d													06 15								06 46
Bournemouth	a	05 51												06 23								06 54
	d	05 54											06 04	06 25			06 30				06 34	06 56
Pokesdown	d												06 08								06 38	
Christchurch	d												06 12								06 42	
Hinton Admiral	d												06 17								06 47	
New Milton	d												06 21								06 51	
Sway	d												06 26								06 56	
Lymington Pier	d		06 14															06 44				
Lymington Town	d		06 16															06 46				
Brockenhurst ■3	a	06 12	06 25										06 31				06 46	06 55			07 01	
	d	06 14											06 33				06 49				07 03	
Beaulieu Road	d																					
Ashurst New Forest	d												06 41								07 11	
Totton	d							06 12					06 46								07 16	
Salisbury	d											06 19										
Dean	d																					
Mottisfont & Dunbridge	d																					
Romsey	d											06 38										
Redbridge	d							06 14														
Millbrook (Hants)	d							06 17														
Southampton Central ⛴	a	06 27						06 24				06 49	06 51	06 55			07 01				07 21	07 25
	d	06 30						06 35			06 43	06 53	07 00			07 10	07 15				07 30	
St Denys	d							06 40			06 48											
Swaythling	d							06 43			06 51											
Southampton Airport Pkwy ✈	d	06 38						06 46	06 50		06 54		07 08			07 18	07 22				07 38	
Portsmouth Harbour ⛴	d					05 43	06 00								06 23							
Portsmouth & Southsea	d					05 48	06 04								06 28							
Fratton	d					05 52	06 08								06 32							
Hilsea	d					05 56									06 36							
Cosham	d					06 03	06 15								06 42							
Portchester	d					06 08									06 46							
Fareham	d					06 19	06 24					07a14			06 53							
Botley	d					06 27									07 01							
Hedge End	d					06 31									07 05							
Eastleigh ■8	a					06 37		06 49	06 54		06 58				07 11	07 21						
	d					06 43		06 50			06 59				07 13	07 30						
Chandlers Ford	d							06 55														
Romsey	a						06 59	07 03														
Shawford	d					06 49					07 05					07 36				←		
Winchester	d	06 48				06 55			07 05		07 11		07 18		07 22	07 42 →	07 31			07 42	07 48	
Micheldever	d					07 04									07 31							
Basingstoke	a					07 14					07 27				07 41		07 46			07 58		
	d			06 54	07 06	07 17				07 24	07 36				07 47		07 47		07 52	08 05		
Reading ■7	a																08 04					
Fleet	d			07 10	07 22					07 40	07 52								08 09	08 22		
Farnborough (Main)	d			07 16	07 28					07 46	07 58								08 16	08 28		
Woking	a			07 28					07 40	07 58	08 08				08 05				08 28	08 38		
Clapham Junction ■10	a																					
London Waterloo ■15 ⊖	a	07 47		07 59	08 06	08 01			08 08	08 29	08 39		08 16		08 34				09 00	09 10	08 50	

A 🛒 from Bournemouth

Table 158

Mondays to Fridays

from 8 October

Weymouth, Bournemouth, Lymington, Romsey, Southampton and Basingstoke - London

Network Diagram - see first Page of Table 158

		SW 1	SW 1	GW ◇ ⊼	SW 1	XC ◇1 ⊼	SW 1	GW ◇	SW ◇1 ⊼	SW ◇1 A ⊼	GW ◇	SW 1	XC ◇1 ⊼	GW	SW 1	SW 1 ⊼	SW ◇1 A ⊼
Weymouth	d									06 20	06 40						06 50
Upwey	d									06 24	06 45						06 54
Dorchester West	a										06 52						
Dorchester South	d									06 32							07 02
Moreton (Dorset)	d									06 39							07 09
Wool	d									06 45							07 15
Wareham	d									06 52							07 22
Holton Heath	d																07 26
Hamworthy	d									06 59							07 31
Poole 4	a									07 06							07 38
	d									07 09						07 20	07 39
Parkstone (Dorset)	d									07 13						07 24	07 43
Branksome	d									07 16						07 27	07 46
Bournemouth	a									07 24						07 32	07 54
	d								07 04	07 26			07 30			07 34	07 59
Pokesdown	d								07 08							07 38	
Christchurch	d								07 12							07 42	
Hinton Admiral	d								07 17							07 47	
New Milton	d								07 21							07 51	
Sway	d								07 26							07 56	
Lymington Pier	d				07 14										07 44		
Lymington Town	d				07 16										07 46		
Brockenhurst 3	a				07 25				07 31				07 46		07 55	08 01	08 14
	d								07 33				07 49			08 03	08 15
Beaulieu Road	d															08 08	
Ashurst New Forest	d								07 41							08 12	
Totton	d								07 46							08 17	
Salisbury	d		06 50					07 11						07 36			
Dean	d		07 02														
Mottisfont & Dunbridge	d		07 08														
Romsey	d		07 13					07 30						07 56			
Redbridge	d		07 23														
Millbrook (Hants)	d		07 26														
Southampton Central ⛴	a		07 29					07 40	07 51	07 55			08 03	08 09		08 23	08 28
	d		07 35				07 38	07 42	08 00				08 15			08 48	08 30
St Denys	d		07 40				07 43										
Swaythling	d		07 43				07 46									→	
Southampton Airport Pkwy ✈	d		07 46				07 49		08 08				08 22				08 38
Portsmouth Harbour ⛴	d	06 50		07 05								07 24					
Portsmouth & Southsea	d	06 55		07 09								07 29					
Fratton	d	06 59		07 13								07 33					
Hilsea	d	07 03										07 37					
Cosham	d	07 08		07 21								07 43					
Portchester	d	07 13										07 48					
Fareham	d	07 20		07 29				08a05				07 54					
Botley	d	07 28										08 01					
Hedge End	d	07 32										08 06					
Eastleigh 3	a	07 38	07 49				07 53					08 12					
	d	07 43	07 50				07 54					08 13					
Chandlers Ford	d		07 55														
Romsey	a		08 03	08 10													
Shawford	d	07 49					08 00					08 20					
Winchester	d	07 55				08 01	08 06		08 18			08 26	08 31				08 48
Micheldever	d	08 02															
Basingstoke	a	08 14				08 16	08 22		08 34			08 42	08 46				
	d	08 16				08 18	08 24		08 35			08 43	08 47				
Reading 7	a					08 36							09 04				
Fleet	d						08 40					08 54					
Farnborough (Main)	d						08 46					09 00					
Woking	a	08 34					08 58		08 53								09 22
Clapham Junction 10	a								09 14			09 26					09 43
London Waterloo 15 ⊖	a	09 03					09 29		09 25			09 38					09 53

A ⊼ from Bournemouth

Table 158

Mondays to Fridays

from 8 October

Weymouth, Bournemouth, Lymington, Romsey, Southampton and Basingstoke - London

Network Diagram - see first Page of Table 158

		SW 1	SW 1	SW 1	SW 1	SW 1	GW ◇ ⊼	SW 1	SW 1 ⊼	SW 1	SW ◇1 ⊼	SW 1 ⊼	SW 1	GW ◇ ⊼	SW 1	XC ◇1 ⊼	SW ◇1 A ⊼	SW 1	SW 1	SW 1
Weymouth	d												07 25				07 55			
Upwey	d												07 29				07 59			
Dorchester West	a																			
Dorchester South	d												07 37				08 07			
Moreton (Dorset)	d												07 44				08 14			
Wool	d												07 50				08 20			
Wareham	d												07 57				08 27			
Holton Heath	d												08 01				08 31			
Hamworthy	d												08 06				08 36			
Poole 4	a												08 10				08 40			
	d										07 55		08 11				08 41			
Parkstone (Dorset)	d										07 59		08 15				08 45			
Branksome	d										08 02		08 19				08 49			
Bournemouth	a										08 07		08 24				08 54			
	d										08 10		08 25			08 45	08 59			
Pokesdown	d										08 14		08 29							
Christchurch	d										08 18		08 33							
Hinton Admiral	d										08 24		08 38							
New Milton	d										08 29		08 42							
Sway	d										08 34		08 47							
Lymington Pier	d	08 14													08 44			09 14		
Lymington Town	d	08 16													08 46			09 16		
Brockenhurst 3	a	08 25									08 39		08 52		08 55	08 58	09 14	09 25		
	d										08 41					09 00	09 15			
Beaulieu Road	d																			
Ashurst New Forest	d										08 48									
Totton	d										08 53									
Salisbury	d				07 50									08 32						
Dean	d				08 02															
Mottisfont & Dunbridge	d				08 08															
Romsey	d				08 13									08 50						
Redbridge	d				08 21															
Millbrook (Hants)	d				08 25				←											
Southampton Central ⛴	a				08 27				08 23		08 58			09 04		09 12	09 28			
	d				08 35				08 48		09 00			09 05		09 15	09 30			
St Denys	d				08 40				08 53											
Swaythling	d				08 43				08 56											
Southampton Airport Pkwy ✈	d				08 46				08 59		09 08					09 22	09 38			
Portsmouth Harbour ⛴	d			07 55		08 05	08 23	08 33												08 59
Portsmouth & Southsea	d			08 00		08 10	08 27	08 38												09 04
Fratton	d			08 04		08 13	08 31	08 42												09 08
Hilsea	d			08 08		08 17		08 46												09 12
Cosham	d			08 13		08 22	08 39	08 51												09 17
Portchester	d			08 18		08 27		08 56												09 22
Fareham	d			08 24		08 33	08 47	09a01						09a27						09 28
Botley	d			08 31		08 41														09 35
Hedge End	d			08 36		08 45														09 40
Eastleigh 3	a			08 42	08 49	08 51			09 03											09 46
	d			08 43	08 50	08 54			09 14											09 47
Chandlers Ford	d				08 55															
Romsey	a				09 03		09 21													
Shawford	d			08 49					09 19			←								
Winchester	d			08 56		09 03			09 25		09 18	09 25				09 31	09 48			09 56
Micheldever	d			09 04					→											10 05
Basingstoke	a			09 15		09 19					09 35	09 41				09 46				10 15
	d		08 54	09 17						09 24	09 36	09 43				09 47			09 54	10 17
Reading 7	a															10 04				
Fleet	d		09 10							09 40		09 54							10 10	
Farnborough (Main)	d		09 16	09 30						09 46		10 00							10 16	10 30
Woking	a		09 28	09 39						09 58	09 54						10 20		10 28	10 39
Clapham Junction 10	a		09 57								10 15	10 25							10 57	
London Waterloo 15 ⊖	a		10 05	10 08						10 36	10 23	10 34					10 49		11 05	11 08

A ⊼ from Bournemouth

Weymouth, Bournemouth, Lymington, Romsey, Southampton and Basingstoke - London

Network Diagram - see first Page of Table 158

		GW ◇ ⊼		SW 1		SW 1	SW 1		XC ◇1 ⊼	SW 1	SW 1	SW ◇1 A ⊼	SW 1	GW ◇		GW ■ ⊼	SW 1	SW 1	XC ◇1 ⊼	SW ◇1 A ⊼	SW 1	SW 1	GW ◇ ⊼		
Weymouth	d											08 20		08 53						09 03					
Upwey	d											08 24		08 58											
Dorchester West	a													09 05											
Dorchester South	d											08 33								09 13					
Moreton (Dorset)	d											08 39													
Wool	d											08 45													
Wareham	d											08 53								09 28					
Holton Heath	d											08 56													
Hamworthy	d											09 01								09 35					
Poole 4	a											09 06								09 39					
	d										08 50	09 07					09 13			09 40					
Parkstone (Dorset)	d										08 54						09 17			09 44					
Branksome	d										08 57						09 20			09 48					
Bournemouth	a										09 02	09 16					09 25			09 53					
	d										09 05	09 18					09 27		09 45	09 55					
Pokesdown	d										09 09	09 22					09 30								
Christchurch	d										09 13	09 26					09 34								
Hinton Admiral	d										09 18						09 39								
New Milton	d										09 22	09 33					09 44								
Sway	d										09 27						09 48								
Lymington Pier	d																	09 44							
Lymington Town	d																	09 46							
Brockenhurst 3	a										09 32	09 40					09 53	09 55	09 59	10 10					
	d										09 33	09 41					09 54		10 00	10 11					
Beaulieu Road	d																								
Ashurst New Forest	d										09 40														
Totton	d										09 45														
Salisbury	d			08 56												09 32									
Dean	d			09 08																					
Mottisfont & Dunbridge	d			09 14																					
Romsey	d			09 19		09 07										09 50									
Redbridge	d			09 27																					
Millbrook (Hants)	d			09 31																					
Southampton Central ⛴	a			09 34		09 35					09 52	09 55				10 04	10 09		10 12	10 26					
	d			09 36		09 37			09 46		09 55	10 00				10 05			10 15	10 30					
St Denys	d			09 41																					
Swaythling	d			09 44																					
Southampton Airport Pkwy ✈	d			09 46					09 53		10 03	10 08							10 22	10 38					
Portsmouth Harbour ⛴	d	09 23					09 33															09 59	10 23		
Portsmouth & Southsea	d	09 27					09 38															10 04	10 27		
Fratton	d	09 31					09 42															10 08	10 31		
Hilsea	d						09 46															10 12			
Cosham	d	09 39					09 51															10 17	10 39		
Portchester	d						09 56															10 22			
Fareham	d	09 47					10a01									10a27						10 28	10 47		
Botley	d																					10 35			
Hedge End	d																					10 40			
Eastleigh 3	a			09 50							10 06											10 46			
	d			09 51							10 14											10 47			
Chandlers Ford	d			09 56																					
Romsey	a	10 21		10 03		09 51																	11 21		
Shawford	d										10 19		←												
Winchester	d								10 03		10 25	10 18	10 25						10 31	10 48		10 56			
Micheldever	d										→											11 05			
Basingstoke	a								10 18			10 34	10 41						10 46			11 15			
	d								10 19	10 24		10 35	10 43						10 47		10 54	11 17			
Reading 7	a								10 36										11 04						
Fleet	d									10 40			10 54								11 10				
Farnborough (Main)	d									10 46			11 00								11 16	11 30			
Woking	a									10 58										11 19	11 28	11 39			
Clapham Junction 10	a											11 12	11 25								11 57				
London Waterloo 15 ⊖	a									11 36		11 20	11 34							11 49	12 06	12 08			

A ⊼ from Bournemouth

Table 158 Mondays to Fridays
from 8 October

Weymouth, Bournemouth, Lymington, Romsey, Southampton and Basingstoke - London

Network Diagram - see first Page of Table 158

		SW 1		SW 1		SW 1	SW 1	SW 1	SW ◇1 A ⊼	SW 1		GW ◇ ⊼	XC ◇1 ⊼	SW 1	SW ◇1 A ⊼	SW 1	SW 1	GW ◇ ⊼		SW 1				XC ◇1 ⊼	SW 1
Weymouth	d								09 20						10 03										
Upwey	d								09 24																
Dorchester West	a																								
Dorchester South	d								09 33						10 13										
Moreton (Dorset)	d								09 39																
Wool	d								09 45																
Wareham	d								09 53						10 28										
Holton Heath	d								09 56																
Hamworthy	d								10 01						10 35										
Poole 4	a								10 06						10 39										
	d						09 50		10 07						10 40										
Parkstone (Dorset)	d						09 54								10 44										
Branksome	d						09 57								10 48										
Bournemouth	a						10 02		10 17						10 54										
	d						10 05		10 22				10 45		10 59										
Pokesdown	d						10 09		10 26																
Christchurch	d						10 13		10 30																
Hinton Admiral	d						10 18																		
New Milton	d						10 22		10 37																
Sway	d						10 27																		
Lymington Pier	d							10 27						10 57											
Lymington Town	d							10 29						10 59											
Brockenhurst 3	a						10 32	10 38	10 44				10 58	11 08	11 14										
	d						10 33		10 45				11 00		11 15										
Beaulieu Road	d																								
Ashurst New Forest	d						10 40																		
Totton	d						10 45																		
Salisbury	d	09 56										10 30								10 56					
Dean	d	10 08																		11 08					
Mottisfont & Dunbridge	d	10 14																		11 14					
Romsey	d	10 19										10 50								11 20					
Redbridge	d	10 27																		11 27					
Millbrook (Hants)	d	10 31																		11 31					
Southampton Central ⛴	a	10 34					10 53		10 58			11 04	11 12		11 28					11 34					
	d	10 35					10 55		11 00			11 05	11 15		11 30					11 35				11 46	
St Denys	d	10 40																		11 40					
Swaythling	d	10 43																		11 43					
Southampton Airport Pkwy ✈	d	10 46					11 03		11 08				11 22		11 38					11 46				11 53	
Portsmouth Harbour ⛴	d			10 33													10 59	11 23							
Portsmouth & Southsea	d			10 38													11 04	11 27							
Fratton	d			10 42													11 08	11 31							
Hilsea	d			10 46													11 12								
Cosham	d			10 51													11 17	11 39							
Portchester	d			10 56													11 22								
Fareham	d			11a01								11a27					11 28	11 47							
Botley	d																11 35								
Hedge End	d																11 40								
Eastleigh 3	a	10 49					11 06										11 46			11 49					
	d	10 50					11 14										11 47			11 50					
Chandlers Ford	d	10 55																		11 55					
Romsey	a	11 03																12 21		12 03					
Shawford	d						11 19			←															
Winchester	d						11 25		11 18	11 25			11 31		11 48		11 56							12 02	
Micheldever	d						→										12 05								
Basingstoke	a								11 34	11 41			11 46				12 15							12 17	
	d					11 24			11 35	11 43			11 47			11 54	12 17							12 18	12 24
Reading 7	a												12 04											12 36	
Fleet	d					11 40				11 54						12 10									12 40
Farnborough (Main)	d					11 46				12 00						12 16	12 30								12 46
Woking	a					11 58									12 19	12 28	12 39								12 58
Clapham Junction 10	a								12 12	12 25						12 57									
London Waterloo 15 ⊖	a					12 36			12 20	12 34					12 49	13 05	13 07								13 36

A ⊼ from Bournemouth

Table 158

Mondays to Fridays
from 8 October

Weymouth, Bournemouth, Lymington, Romsey, Southampton and Basingstoke - London

Network Diagram - see first Page of Table 158

		SW	SW	SW	SW	GW	XC	GW	SW	SW	GW	SW	SW	GW	SW	SW	SW	SW	SW
		■	■	◇■ A ⊼	■	◇ ⊼	◇■ ⊼		■	◇■ A ⊼		■	■	◇ ⊼	■	■	■	■	◇■ A ⊼
Weymouth	d			10 20						11 03	11 10								11 20
Upwey	d			10 24							11 15								11 24
Dorchester West	a										11 22								
Dorchester South	d			10 33						11 13									11 33
Moreton (Dorset)	d			10 39															11 39
Wool	d			10 45															11 45
Wareham	d			10 53						11 28									11 53
Holton Heath	d			10 56															11 56
Hamworthy	d			11 01						11 35									12 01
Poole ■	a			11 06						11 39									12 06
	d	10 50		11 07						11 40							11 50		12 07
Parkstone (Dorset)	d	10 54								11 44							11 54		
Branksome	d	10 57								11 48							11 57		
Bournemouth	a	11 02		11 17						11 54							12 02		12 17
	d	11 05		11 22			11 45			11 59							12 05		12 22
Pokesdown	d	11 09		11 26													12 09		12 26
Christchurch	d	11 13		11 30													12 13		12 30
Hinton Admiral	d	11 18															12 18		
New Milton	d	11 22		11 37													12 22		12 37
Sway	d	11 27															12 27		
Lymington Pier	d		11 27						11 57									12 27	
Lymington Town	d		11 29						11 59									12 29	
Brockenhurst ■	a	11 32	11 38	11 44			11 58		12 08	12 14							12 32	12 38	12 44
	d	11 33		11 45			12 00			12 15							12 33		12 45
Beaulieu Road	d	11 38																	
Ashurst New Forest	d	11 42															12 40		
Totton	d	11 47															12 45		
Salisbury	d					11 32		11 42							11 56				
Dean	d														12 08				
Mottisfont & Dunbridge	d														12 14				
Romsey	d					11 50		12 10							12 19				
Redbridge	d														12 27				
Millbrook (Hants)	d														12 31				
Southampton Central ⛴	a	11 53		11 58		12 04	12 12	12 22		12 28					12 34		12 52		12 58
	d	11 55		12 00		12 05	12 15			12 30					12 35		12 55		13 00
St Denys	d														12 40				
Swaythling	d														12 43				
Southampton Airport Pkwy ✈	d	12 03		12 08			12 22			12 38					12 46		13 03		13 08
Portsmouth Harbour ⛴	d											11 59	12 23						
Portsmouth & Southsea	d											12 04	12 27						
Fratton	d											12 08	12 31						
Hilsea	d											12 12							
Cosham	d											12 17	12 39						
Portchester	d											12 22							
Fareham	d					12a27						12 28	12 47						
Botley	d											12 35							
Hedge End	d											12 40							
Eastleigh ■	a	12 06										12 46			12 49		13 06		
	d	12 14										12 47			12 50		13 14		
Chandlers Ford	d														12 55				
Romsey	a												13 21		13 03				
Shawford	d	12 19			←												13 19		
Winchester	d	12 25		12 18	12 25		12 31			12 48		12 56					13 25		13 18
Micheldever	d	→										13 05					→		
Basingstoke	a			12 34	12 41		12 46					13 15							13 34
	d			12 35	12 43		12 47				12 54	13 17				13 24			13 35
Reading ■	a						13 04												
Fleet	d				12 54						13 10					13 40			
Farnborough (Main)	d				13 00						13 16	13 30				13 46			
Woking	a									13 19	13 28	13 39				13 58			
Clapham Junction ■	a			13 12	13 25						13 57								14 12
London Waterloo ■ ⊖	a			13 20	13 34					13 49	14 05	14 07				14 36			14 20

A ⊼ from Bournemouth

Table 158

Mondays to Fridays
from 8 October

Weymouth, Bournemouth, Lymington, Romsey, Southampton and Basingstoke - London

Network Diagram - see first Page of Table 158

		SW	GW	XC	SW	SW	SW	SW	GW	SW	SW	XC	SW	SW	SW	SW	SW	GW	XC	SW
		■	◇ ⊼	◇■ ⊼	■	◇■ A ⊼	■	■	◇ ⊼	■	■	◇■	■	■	■	◇■ A ⊼	■	◇ ⊼	◇■ ⊼	■
Weymouth	d					12 03										12 20				
Upwey	d															12 24				
Dorchester West	a																			
Dorchester South	d					12 13										12 33				
Moreton (Dorset)	d															12 39				
Wool	d															12 45				
Wareham	d					12 28										12 53				
Holton Heath	d															12 56				
Hamworthy	d					12 35										13 01				
Poole ■	a					12 39										13 06				
	d					12 40								12 50		13 07				
Parkstone (Dorset)	d					12 44								12 54						
Branksome	d					12 48								12 57						
Bournemouth	a					12 54								13 02		13 17				
	d			12 45		12 59								13 05		13 22			13 45	
Pokesdown	d													13 09		13 26				
Christchurch	d													13 13		13 30				
Hinton Admiral	d													13 18						
New Milton	d													13 22		13 37				
Sway	d													13 27						
Lymington Pier	d				12 57										13 27					13 57
Lymington Town	d				12 59										13 29					13 59
Brockenhurst ■	a			12 58	13 08	13 14								13 32	13 38	13 44			13 58	14 08
	d			13 00		13 15								13 33		13 45			14 00	
Beaulieu Road	d																			
Ashurst New Forest	d													13 40						
Totton	d													13 45						
Salisbury	d		12 32							12 56								13 32		
Dean	d									13 08										
Mottisfont & Dunbridge	d									13 14										
Romsey	d		12 50							13 19								13 50		
Redbridge	d									13 27										
Millbrook (Hants)	d									13 31										
Southampton Central ⛴	a		13 04	13 12		13 28				13 34				13 53		13 58		14 04	14 12	
	d		13 05	13 15		13 30				13 35	13 44	13 46		13 55		14 00		14 05	14 15	
St Denys	d									13 40	13 49									
Swaythling	d									13 43										
Southampton Airport Pkwy ✈	d			13 22		13 38				13 46		13 53		14 03		14 08			14 22	
Portsmouth Harbour ⛴	d							12 59	13 23											
Portsmouth & Southsea	d							13 04	13 27											
Fratton	d							13 08	13 31											
Hilsea	d							13 12												
Cosham	d							13 17	13 39											
Portchester	d							13 22												
Fareham	d		13a27					13 28	13 47		14a17							14a27		
Botley	d							13 35												
Hedge End	d							13 40												
Eastleigh ■	a							13 46		13 49				14 06						
	d							13 47		13 50				14 14						
Chandlers Ford	d									13 55										
Romsey	a								14 21	14 03										
Shawford	d	←												14 19			←			
Winchester	d	13 25		13 31		13 48		13 56				14 03		14 25		14 18	14 25		14 31	
Micheldever	d							14 05						→						
Basingstoke	a	13 41		13 46				14 15				14 18				14 34	14 41		14 46	
	d	13 43		13 47			13 54	14 17				14 19	14 24			14 35	14 43		14 47	
Reading ■	a			14 04								14 36							15 04	
Fleet	d	13 54					14 10						14 40				14 54			
Farnborough (Main)	d	14 00					14 16	14 30					14 46				15 00			
Woking	a					14 19	14 28	14 39					14 58							
Clapham Junction ■	a	14 25					14 57									15 12	15 25			
London Waterloo ■ ⊖	a	14 34				14 49	15 05	15 08					15 37			15 20	15 34			

A ⊼ from Bournemouth

Table 158

Mondays to Fridays
from 8 October

Weymouth, Bournemouth, Lymington, Romsey, Southampton and Basingstoke - London

Network Diagram - see first Page of Table 158

		SW ◇■ A ⚒	GW ◇	SW ■	SW ■	GW ■ ⚒	GW ■ ⚒		SW ■			SW ■	SW ■	SW ■	SW ◇■ A ⚒	SW ■	GW ◇ ⚒		XC ◇■ ⚒	SW ■	SW ◇■ A ⚒	SW ■	SW ■	GW ■ ⚒
Weymouth	d	13 03	13 10												13 20						14 03			
Upwey	d		13 15												13 24									
Dorchester West	a		13 22																					
Dorchester South	d	13 13													13 33						14 13			
Moreton (Dorset)	d														13 39									
Wool	d														13 45									
Wareham	d	13 28													13 53						14 28			
Holton Heath	d														13 56									
Hamworthy	d	13 35													14 01						14 35			
Poole ■	a	13 39													14 06						14 39			
	d	13 40											13 50		14 07						14 40			
Parkstone (Dorset)	d	13 44											13 54								14 44			
Branksome	d	13 48											13 57								14 48			
Bournemouth	a	13 54											14 02		14 17						14 54			
	d	13 59											14 05		14 22				14 45		14 59			
Pokesdown	d												14 09		14 26									
Christchurch	d												14 13		14 30									
Hinton Admiral	d												14 18											
New Milton	d												14 22		14 37									
Sway	d												14 27											
Lymington Pier	d													14 27						14 57				
Lymington Town	d													14 29						14 59				
Brockenhurst ■	a	14 14											14 32	14 38	14 44				14 58	15 08	15 14			
	d	14 15											14 33		14 45				15 00		15 15			
Beaulieu Road	d																							
Ashurst New Forest	d												14 40											
Totton	d												14 45											
Salisbury	d						13 59		13 50								14 32							
Dean	d								14 02															
Mottisfont & Dunbridge	d								14 08															
Romsey	d						14 19		14 13								14 50							
Redbridge	d								14 21															
Millbrook (Hants)	d								14 24															
Southampton Central ⛴	a	14 28					14 32		14 28				14 53		14 58		15 04		15 12		15 28			
	d	14 30					14 34		14 35				14 55		15 00		15 05		15 15		15 30			
St Denys	d								14 40															
Swaythling	d								14 43															
Southampton Airport Pkwy ✈	d	14 38							14 46				15 03		15 08				15 22		15 38			
Portsmouth Harbour ⛴	d				13 59	14 23																	14 59	15 23
Portsmouth & Southsea	d				14 04	14 27																	15 04	15 27
Fratton	d				14 08	14 31																	15 08	15 31
Hilsea	d				14 12																		15 12	
Cosham	d				14 17	14 39																	15 17	15 39
Portchester	d				14 22																		15 22	
Fareham	d				14 28	14 47	14a55										15a27						15 28	15 47
Botley	d				14 35																		15 35	
Hedge End	d				14 40																		15 40	
Eastleigh ■	a				14 46				14 49				15 06										15 46	
	d				14 47				14 50				15 14										15 47	
Chandlers Ford	d								14 55															
Romsey	a					15 21			15 04															16 21
Shawford	d												15 19			←								
Winchester	d	14 48			14 56								15 25		15 18	15 25			15 31		15 48		15 56	
Micheldever	d				15 05								→										16 05	
Basingstoke	a				15 15										15 34	15 41			15 46				16 15	
	d			14 54	15 17							15 24			15 35	15 43			15 47			15 54	16 17	
Reading ■	a																		16 04					
Fleet	d			15 10								15 40				15 54						16 10		
Farnborough (Main)	d			15 16	15 30							15 46				16 00						16 16	16 30	
Woking	a	15 19		15 28	15 39							15 58									16 19	16 28	16 39	
Clapham Junction ■	a			15 57											16 12	16 25						16 57		
London Waterloo ■ ⊖	a	15 49		16 05	16 07							16 36			16 20	16 34					16 49	17 08	17 08	

A ⚒ from Bournemouth

Table 158

Mondays to Fridays
from 8 October

Weymouth, Bournemouth, Lymington, Romsey, Southampton and Basingstoke - London

Network Diagram - see first Page of Table 158

		SW ■				XC ◇■ ⚒	SW ■	SW ■	SW ■	SW ◇■ A ⚒	SW ■	GW ◇ ⚒	XC ◇■ ⚒		SW ■	SW ◇■ A ⚒	GW ◇	SW ■	SW ■	GW ■ ⚒		SW ■		
Weymouth	d									14 20						15 03	15 08							
Upwey	d									14 24							15 13							
Dorchester West	a																15 20							
Dorchester South	d									14 33						15 13								
Moreton (Dorset)	d									14 39														
Wool	d									14 45														
Wareham	d									14 53						15 28								
Holton Heath	d									14 56														
Hamworthy	d									15 01						15 35								
Poole ■	a									15 06						15 39								
	d							14 50		15 07						15 40								
Parkstone (Dorset)	d							14 54								15 44								
Branksome	d							14 57								15 48								
Bournemouth	a							15 02		15 17						15 54								
	d							15 05		15 22			15 45			15 59								
Pokesdown	d							15 09		15 26														
Christchurch	d							15 13		15 30														
Hinton Admiral	d							15 18																
New Milton	d							15 22		15 37														
Sway	d							15 27																
Lymington Pier	d								15 27						15 57									
Lymington Town	d								15 29						15 59									
Brockenhurst ■	a							15 32	15 38	15 44			15 58		16 08	16 14								
	d							15 33		15 45			16 00			16 15								
Beaulieu Road	d																							
Ashurst New Forest	d							15 40																
Totton	d							15 45																
Salisbury	d	14 56										15 32										15 56		
Dean	d	15 08																				16 08		
Mottisfont & Dunbridge	d	15 14																				16 14		
Romsey	d	15 19										15 50										16 19		
Redbridge	d	15 27																				16 27		
Millbrook (Hants)	d	15 31																				16 31		
Southampton Central ⛴	a	15 34						15 51		15 58		16 04	16 12			16 28						16 34		
	d	15 35				15 47		15 55		16 00		16 05	16 15			16 30						16 35		
St Denys	d	15 40																				16 40		
Swaythling	d	15 43																				16 43		
Southampton Airport Pkwy ✈	d	15 46						16 03		16 08			16 22			16 38						16 46		
Portsmouth Harbour ⛴	d																		15 59	16 23				
Portsmouth & Southsea	d																		16 04	16 27				
Fratton	d																		16 08	16 31				
Hilsea	d																		16 12					
Cosham	d																		16 17	16 39				
Portchester	d																		16 22					
Fareham	d											16a27							16 28	16 47				
Botley	d																		16 35					
Hedge End	d																		16 40					
Eastleigh ■	a	15 49						16 07											16 46			16 49		
	d	15 50						16 14											16 47			16 50		
Chandlers Ford	d	15 55																				16 55		
Romsey	a	16 03																		17 21		17 03		
Shawford	d							16 19			←													
Winchester	d							16 25		16 18	16 25		16 31			16 48			16 56					
Micheldever	d							→											17 05					
Basingstoke	a					16 17				16 34	16 41		16 46						17 15					
	d					16 18	16 24			16 35	16 43		16 47					16 54	17 17					
Reading ■	a					16 35							17 03											
Fleet	d						16 40				16 54							17 10						
Farnborough (Main)	d						16 46				17 00							17 16	17 30					
Woking	a						16 58									17 20		17 28	17 39					
Clapham Junction ■	a									17 12	17 25							17 57						
London Waterloo ■ ⊖	a						17 35			17 20	17 36					17 50		18 09	18 08					

A ⚒ from Bournemouth

Weymouth, Bournemouth, Lymington, Romsey, Southampton and Basingstoke - London

Network Diagram - see first Page of Table 158

		SW	SW	SW	SW	SW	SW	SW	GW	XC	SW	SW	SW	SW	GW	SW	SW	SW	XC	SW
		■	■	■	■	■	◇■	■	◇	◇■	■	◇■	■	■	◇	■	■	■	◇■	■
							A					A								
							⌶		⌶	⌶		⌶			⌶				⌶	
Weymouth	d						15 20					16 03								
Upwey	d						15 24													
Dorchester West	a																			
Dorchester South	d						15 33					16 13								
Moreton (Dorset)	d						15 39													
Wool	d						15 45													
Wareham	d						15 53					16 28								
Holton Heath	d						15 56													
Hamworthy	d						16 01					16 35								
Poole 4	a						16 06					16 39								
	d				15 50		16 07					16 40								
Parkstone (Dorset)	d				15 54							16 44								
Branksome	d				15 57							16 48								
Bournemouth	a				16 02		16 17					16 54								
	d				16 05		16 22			16 45		16 59								
Pokesdown	d				16 09		16 26													
Christchurch	d				16 13		16 30													
Hinton Admiral	d				16 18															
New Milton	d				16 22		16 37													
Sway	d				16 27															
Lymington Pier	d					16 27					16 57									
Lymington Town	d					16 29					16 59									
Brockenhurst 3	a				16 32	16 38	16 44			16 58	17 08	17 14								
	d				16 33		16 45			17 00		17 15					17 20			
Beaulieu Road	d																			
Ashurst New Forest	d				16 40												17 27			
Totton	d				16 45												17 32			
Salisbury	d								16 32							16 56				
Dean	d															17 08				
Mottisfont & Dunbridge	d															17 14				
Romsey	d								16 50							17 19				
Redbridge	d															17 27				
Millbrook (Hants)	d															17 31				
Southampton Central	a				16 51		16 58		17 04	17 12		17 28				17 34	17 41			
	d	16 44			16 52		17 00		17 05	17 15		17 30				17 35			17 46	
St Denys	d	16 49			16 57											17 40				
Swaythling	d				17 00											17 43				
Southampton Airport Pkwy	d				17 04		17 08			17 22		17 38				17 46			17 53	
Portsmouth Harbour	d		16 49											16 59	17 23			17 33		
Portsmouth & Southsea	d		16 55											17 04	17 27			17 38		
Fratton	d		16 59											17 08	17 31			17 42		
Hilsea	d		17 03											17 12				17 46		
Cosham	d		17 08											17 17	17 39			17 51		
Portchester	d		17 13											17 22				17 56		
Fareham	d	17a17	17a18						17a27					17 28	17 47			18a01		
Botley	d													17 35						
Hedge End	d													17 40						
Eastleigh 3	a				17 07									17 46		17 49				
	d				17 14									17 47		17 50				
Chandlers Ford	d															17 55				
Romsey	a														18 21	18 03				
Shawford	d				17 19			←												
Winchester	d				17 25		17 18	17 25		17 31		17 48		17 56					18 02	
Micheldever	d				→									18 05						
Basingstoke	a						17 34	17 42		17 46				18 15					18 17	
	d			17 24			17 36	17 43		17 47			17 54	18 17					18 18	18 24
Reading 7	a									18 04									18 36	
Fleet	d			17 40				17 54					18 10							18 40
Farnborough (Main)	d			17 46				18 00					18 16	18 30						18 46
Woking	a			17 58								18 19	18 28	18 39						18 58
Clapham Junction 10	a						18 12	18 25					18 58							
London Waterloo 15 ⊖	a			18 38			18 23	18 34				18 47	19 06	19 08						19 39

A ⌶ from Bournemouth

Table 158 — Mondays to Fridays from 8 October

Weymouth, Bournemouth, Lymington, Romsey, Southampton and Basingstoke - London

Network Diagram - see first Page of Table 158

		SW	SW	SW	SW	GW	XC	SW	SW	SW	SW	SW	GW	SW	SW	SW	SW	SW	SW	GW
		■	■	◇■	■	◇	◇■	■	■	◇■	■	■	◇	■	■	■	■	◇■	■	◇
				A						A								A		
				⌶		⌶	⌶			⌶			⌶					⌶		
Weymouth	d			16 20						17 04								17 20		17 30
Upwey	d			16 24														17 24		17 35
Dorchester West	a																			17 42
Dorchester South	d			16 33						17 14								17 33		
Moreton (Dorset)	d			16 39														17 39		
Wool	d			16 45														17 45		
Wareham	d			16 53						17 29								17 53		
Holton Heath	d			16 56														17 56		
Hamworthy	d			17 01						17 36								18 01		
Poole 4	a			17 06						17 40								18 06		
	d	16 50		17 07						17 41						17 50		18 07		
Parkstone (Dorset)	d	16 54								17 45						17 54				
Branksome	d	16 57								17 49						17 57				
Bournemouth	a	17 02		17 17						17 54						18 02		18 17		
	d	17 05		17 22			17 45			17 59						18 05		18 22		
Pokesdown	d	17 09		17 26												18 09		18 26		
Christchurch	d	17 13		17 30												18 13		18 30		
Hinton Admiral	d	17 18														18 18				
New Milton	d	17 22		17 37												18 22		18 37		
Sway	d	17 27														18 27				
Lymington Pier	d		17 27					17 57									18 27			
Lymington Town	d		17 29					17 59									18 29			
Brockenhurst 3	a	17 32	17 38	17 44			17 58	18 08		18 14						18 32	18 38	18 44		
	d	17 33		17 45			18 00			18 15						18 33		18 45		
Beaulieu Road	d															18 38				
Ashurst New Forest	d	17 40														18 42				
Totton	d	17 45														18 47				
Salisbury	d					17 32								17 56						
Dean	d													18 08						
Mottisfont & Dunbridge	d													18 14						
Romsey	d					17 50								18 19						
Redbridge	d													18 27						
Millbrook (Hants)	d													18 31						
Southampton Central	a	17 53		17 58		18 04	18 12			18 28				18 34		18 53		18 58		
	d	17 55		18 00		18 05	18 15		18 17	18 30				18 35		18 55		19 00		
St Denys	d								18 22					18 40						
Swaythling	d								18 25					18 43						
Southampton Airport Pkwy	d	18 03		18 08			18 22		18 28	18 38				18 46		19 03		19 08		
Portsmouth Harbour	d											17 59	18 23							
Portsmouth & Southsea	d											18 04	18 27							
Fratton	d											18 08	18 31							
Hilsea	d											18 12								
Cosham	d											18 17	18 39							
Portchester	d											18 22								
Fareham	d					18a27						18 28	18 47							
Botley	d											18 35								
Hedge End	d											18 40								
Eastleigh 3	a	18 06							18 32			18 46		18 49		19 06				
	d	18 14							18 33			18 47		18 50		19 14				
Chandlers Ford	d													18 55						
Romsey	a												19 21	19 04						
Shawford	d	18 19			←											19 19			←	
Winchester	d	18 25		18 18	18 25		18 31		18a41	18 48		18 56				19 25		19 18	19 25	
Micheldever	d	→										19 05				→				
Basingstoke	a			18 34	18 41		18 46					19 15						19 34	19 41	
	d			18 35	18 43		18 47				18 54	19 17			19 24			19 35	19 43	
Reading 7	a						19 04													
Fleet	d				18 54						19 10				19 40				19 54	
Farnborough (Main)	d				19 00						19 16	19 30			19 46				20 00	
Woking	a									19 24	19 28	19 39			19 58					
Clapham Junction 10	a			19 12	19 26						19 57							20 12	20 25	
London Waterloo 15 ⊖	a			19 20	19 34					19 51	20 05	20 08			20 36			20 20	20 34	

A ⌶ from Bournemouth

from 8 October

Weymouth, Bournemouth, Lymington, Romsey, Southampton and Basingstoke - London

Network Diagram - see first Page of Table 158

		GW	XC	SW	SW	SW	SW	GW	SW	SW	SW	SW	SW	GW	SW	XC	SW	SW	SW
		■ ⌶	◇1 ⌶	◇1 A ⌶	1	1	1	◇	1	1	1	◇1 A ⌶	1	■ ⌶	1	◇1	◇1 A ⌶	1	1
Weymouth	d			18 06								18 20					19 06		
Upwey	d											18 24							
Dorchester West	a																		
Dorchester South	d			18 16								18 33					19 16		
Moreton (Dorset)	d											18 39							
Wool	d											18 45							
Wareham	d			18 31								18 53					19 31		
Holton Heath	d											18 56							
Hamworthy	d			18 38								19 01					19 38		
Poole 4	a			18 42								19 06					19 42		
	d			18 43							18 50	19 07					19 43		
Parkstone (Dorset)	d			18 47							18 54						19 47		
Branksome	d			18 51							18 57						19 51		
Bournemouth	a			18 56							19 02	19 17					19 56		
	d		18 45	18 59							19 05	19 22				19 45	19 59		
Pokesdown	d										19 09	19 26							
Christchurch	d										19 13	19 30							
Hinton Admiral	d										19 18								
New Milton	d										19 22	19 37							
Sway	d										19 27								
Lymington Pier	d				19 03										19 33			20 03	
Lymington Town	d				19 05										19 35			20 05	
Brockenhurst 3	a		18 58	19 14	19 14						19 32	19 44			19 44	19 58	20 14	20 14	
	d		19 00	19 15							19 33	19 45				20 00	20 15		
Beaulieu Road	d																		
Ashurst New Forest	d										19 41								
Totton	d										19 46								
Salisbury	d	18 35							18 56					19 32					
Dean	d								19 08										
Mottisfont & Dunbridge	d								19 14										
Romsey	d	18 54							19 19					19 50					
Redbridge	d								19 27										
Millbrook (Hants)	d								19 31										
Southampton Central ⛴	a	19 04	19 12	19 28					19 34		19 52	19 58		20 04		20 12	20 28		
	d	19 05	19 15	19 30					19 35		19 55	20 00		20 05		20 15	20 30		
St Denys	d								19 40										
Swaythling	d								19 43										
Southampton Airport Pkwy ✈	d		19 22	19 38					19 46		20 03	20 08				20 22	20 38		
Portsmouth Harbour ⛴	d						18 59	19 23											
Portsmouth & Southsea	d						19 04	19 27											
Fratton	d						19 08	19 31											
Hilsea	d						19 12												
Cosham	d						19 17	19 39											
Portchester	d						19 22												
Fareham	d	19a27					19 28	19 47						20a27					
Botley	d						19 35												
Hedge End	d						19 40												
Eastleigh 3	a						19 46		19 49		20 06								
	d						19 47		19 50		20 14								
Chandlers Ford	d								19 55										
Romsey	a							20 21	20 03										
Shawford	d										20 19		←						
Winchester	d		19 31	19 48			19 56				20 25	20 18	20 25			20 31	20 48		
Micheldever	d						20 05				→								
Basingstoke	a		19 46				20 15					20 34	20 41			20 46			
	d		19 47			19 54	20 17			20 24		20 36	20 43			20 47			20 54
Reading 7	a		20 04													21 04			
Fleet	d					20 10				20 40			20 54						21 10
Farnborough (Main)	d					20 16	20 30			20 46			21 00						21 16
Woking	a			20 19		20 28	20 39			20 58			21 09				21 19		21 28
Clapham Junction 10	a					20 57						21 16	21 29						21 57
London Waterloo 15 ⊖	a			20 49		21 05	21 07			21 34		21 24	21 38				21 49		22 06

A ⌶ from Bournemouth

from 8 October

Weymouth, Bournemouth, Lymington, Romsey, Southampton and Basingstoke - London

Network Diagram - see first Page of Table 158

		SW	GW	SW	GW	SW	SW	SW	GW	SW	SW	SW	SW	SW	SW	GW
		1	◇	1	◇	1	◇1	1	◇ ⌶	1	1	1	1	1	1	
Weymouth	d						19 20									
Upwey	d						19 24									
Dorchester West	a															
Dorchester South	d						19 37									
Moreton (Dorset)	d						19 43									
Wool	d						19 49									
Wareham	d						19 57									
Holton Heath	d															
Hamworthy	d						20 03									
Poole 4	a						20 08									
	d					19 50	20 09									
Parkstone (Dorset)	d					19 54										
Branksome	d					19 57										
Bournemouth	a					20 02	20 18									
	d					20 05	20 22									
Pokesdown	d					20 09	20 26									
Christchurch	d					20 13	20 30									
Hinton Admiral	d					20 18										
New Milton	d					20 22	20 37									
Sway	d					20 27										
Lymington Pier	d									20 33	21 03					
Lymington Town	d									20 35	21 05					
Brockenhurst 3	a					20 32	20 44			20 44	21 14					
	d					20 33	20 45									
Beaulieu Road	d															
Ashurst New Forest	d					20 40										
Totton	d					20 45										
Salisbury	d			19 56	20 14				20 32						20 56	
Dean	d			20 08											21 08	
Mottisfont & Dunbridge	d			20 14											21 14	
Romsey	d			20 19	20 35				20 50						21 19	
Redbridge	d			20 27											21 27	
Millbrook (Hants)	d			20 31											21 31	
Southampton Central ⛴	a			20 34	20 48	20 51	20 58		21 04						21 34	
	d			20 35		20 55	21 00		21 05			21 30			21 35	
St Denys	d			20 40											21 40	
Swaythling	d			20 43											21 43	
Southampton Airport Pkwy ✈	d			20 46		21 03	21 08					21 38			21 46	
Portsmouth Harbour ⛴	d	19 59	20 23											20 59		21 23
Portsmouth & Southsea	d	20 04	20 27											21 04		21 27
Fratton	d	20 08	20 31											21 08		21 31
Hilsea	d	20 12												21 12		
Cosham	d	20 17												21 17		
Portchester	d	20 22												21 22		
Fareham	d	20 28	20 47						21a27					21 28		21 48
Botley	d	20 35												21 35		
Hedge End	d	20 40												21 40		
Eastleigh 3	a	20 46		20 49		21 06								21 46	21 49	22 06
	d	20 47		20 50		21 14								21 47	21 50	22 11
Chandlers Ford	d			20 55											21 55	
Romsey	a		21 21	21 03											22 03	22 33
Shawford	d	20 53				21 19		←								
Winchester	d	20 59				21 25	21 18	21 25				21 48		21 56		
Micheldever	d	21 07				→								22 05		
Basingstoke	a	21 21					21 34	21 41						22 15		
	d	21 24					21 35	21 43					21 54	22 24		
Reading 7	a															
Fleet	d	21 40						21 54					22 10	22 40		
Farnborough (Main)	d	21 46						22 00					22 16	22 46		
Woking	a	21 58						22 09				22 19	22 28	22 58		
Clapham Junction 10	a						22 14	22 29					22 57			
London Waterloo 15 ⊖	a	22 34					22 22	22 38				22 49	23 08	23 32		

Table 158

Mondays to Fridays

from 8 October

Weymouth, Bournemouth, Lymington, Romsey, Southampton and Basingstoke - London

Network Diagram - see first Page of Table 158

		SW 1	SW ◇1	SW 1	GW	GW ◇	SW 1	SW 1	SW 1	SW 1	SW 1	SW 1	SW 1	SW 1	GW ◇	SW 1	SW 1
Weymouth	d		20 10		20 21									21 10			
Upwey	d		20 14		20 26									21 14			
Dorchester West	a				20 33												
Dorchester South	d		20 22											21 22			
Moreton (Dorset)	d		20 28											21 28			
Wool	d		20 34											21 34			
Wareham	d		20 42											21 42			
Holton Heath	d																
Hamworthy	d		20 48											21 48			
Poole 4	a		20 53											21 53			
	d		20 54											21 54			
Parkstone (Dorset)	d		20 58											21 58			
Branksome	d		21 01											22 01			
Bournemouth	a		21 07											22 07			
	d		21 12											22 12			
Pokesdown	d		21 16											22 16			
Christchurch	d		21 20											22 20			
Hinton Admiral	d		21 25											22 25			
New Milton	d		21 29											22 29			
Sway	d		21 34											22 34			
Lymington Pier	d						21 33	22 03								22 33	
Lymington Town	d						21 35	22 05								22 35	
Brockenhurst 3	a		21 39				21 44	22 14						22 39		22 44	
	d		21 40											22 40			
Beaulieu Road	d																
Ashurst New Forest	d		21 47											22 47			
Totton	d		21 52											22 52			
Salisbury	d					21 32						21 56			22 32		
Dean	d											22 08					
Mottisfont & Dunbridge	d											22 14					
Romsey	d					21 50						22 19			22 53		22 58
Redbridge	d											22 27					23 05
Millbrook (Hants)	d											22 31					23 09
Southampton Central ⛴	a		21 57			22 02						22 34		22 57	23 04		23 11
	d	21 55	22 00			22 04				22 30		22 35		23 00	23 05		23 20
St Denys	d											22 40					23 25
Swaythling	d											22 43					23 28
Southampton Airport Pkwy ✈	d	22 03	22 08							22 38		22 46		23 08			23 31
Portsmouth Harbour ⛴	d										21 54		22 33				
Portsmouth & Southsea	d										21 59		22 38				
Fratton	d										22 03		22 42				
Hilsea	d										22 07		22 46				
Cosham	d										22 12		22 51				
Portchester	d										22 17		22 56				
Fareham	d										22 26		23a01		23a27		
Botley	d										22 33						
Hedge End	d										22 37						
Eastleigh 3	a	22 06				22 14				22 41	22 43	22 49		23 11			23 34
	d	22 14								22 46		22 50		23 12			23 36
Chandlers Ford	d											22 55					23 41
Romsey	a											23 03					23 48
Shawford	d	22 20		←										23 18			
Winchester	d	22 26	22 18	22 26						22 55				23 24			
Micheldever	d	→												23 33			
Basingstoke	a		22 34	22 42						23 11				23 43			
	d		22 36	22 43					22 54	23 13				23 44			
Reading 7	a																
Fleet	d			22 54					23 10					00 01			
Farnborough (Main)	d			23 00					23 16					00 06			
Woking	a		22 54	23 09					23 28	23 31				00 18			
Clapham Junction 10	a		23 14	23 29					00 21	23 55				00 53			
London Waterloo 15 ⊖	a		23 23	23 42					00 35	00 09				01 04			

Table 158

Mondays to Fridays

from 8 October

Weymouth, Bournemouth, Lymington, Romsey, Southampton and Basingstoke - London

Network Diagram - see first Page of Table 158

		SW 1	SW 1	SW ◇1	SW 1
Weymouth	d			22 10	23 10
Upwey	d			22 14	23 14
Dorchester West	a				
Dorchester South	d			22 22	23 22
Moreton (Dorset)	d			22 28	23 28
Wool	d			22 34	23 34
Wareham	d			22 42	23 42
Holton Heath	d				
Hamworthy	d			22 48	23 48
Poole 4	a			22 53	23 53
	d			22 54	23 54
Parkstone (Dorset)	d			22 58	
Branksome	d			23 01	
Bournemouth	a			23 07	00 03
	d			23 12	
Pokesdown	d			23 16	
Christchurch	d			23 20	
Hinton Admiral	d			23 25	
New Milton	d			23 29	
Sway	d			23 34	
Lymington Pier	d				
Lymington Town	d				
Brockenhurst 3	a			23 39	
	d			23 40	
Beaulieu Road	d				
Ashurst New Forest	d			23 47	
Totton	d			23 52	
Salisbury	d				
Dean	d				
Mottisfont & Dunbridge	d				
Romsey	d	23 07			
Redbridge	d				
Millbrook (Hants)	d				
Southampton Central ⛴	a	23 36		23 57	
	d	23 38		23 59	
St Denys	d			00 04	
Swaythling	d			00 07	
Southampton Airport Pkwy ✈	d			00 10	
Portsmouth Harbour ⛴	d		23 24		
Portsmouth & Southsea	d		23 29		
Fratton	d		23 33		
Hilsea	d		23 37		
Cosham	d		23 42		
Portchester	d		23 47		
Fareham	d		23 53		
Botley	d		23 59		
Hedge End	d		00 05		
Eastleigh 3	a		00 11	00 14	
	d		00 19		
Chandlers Ford	d				
Romsey	a	23 55			
Shawford	d				
Winchester	d		00a28		
Micheldever	d				
Basingstoke	a				
	d				
Reading 7	a				
Fleet	d				
Farnborough (Main)	d				
Woking	a				
Clapham Junction 10	a				
London Waterloo 15 ⊖	a				

Table 158

Saturdays
until 6 October

Weymouth, Bournemouth, Lymington, Romsey, Southampton and Basingstoke - London

Network Diagram - see first Page of Table 158

		SW 1	SW 1	SW 1	SW 1	SW ◇1	SW 1	SW 1	XC ◇1	SW 1	SW 1	SW 1	SW 1	SW 1	XC ◇1 ⌶	GW ◇	SW 1	SW 1	SW ◇1 ⌶	SW 1	SW 1	GW ◇	SW 1
Weymouth	d			21p10		22p10	23p10									06 38							
Upwey	d			21p14		22p14	23p14									06 43							
Dorchester West	a															06 50							
Dorchester South	d			21p22		22p22	23p22																
Moreton (Dorset)	d			21p28		22p28	23p28																
Wool	d			21p34		22p34	23p34																
Wareham	d			21p42		22p42	23p42																
Holton Heath	d																						
Hamworthy	d			21p48		22p48	23p48																
Poole 4	a			21p53		22p53	23p53																
	d			21p54		22p54	23p54												05 28				
Parkstone (Dorset)	d			21p58		22p58													05 32				
Branksome	d			22p01		23p01													05 35				
Bournemouth	a			22p07		23p07	00 03												05 40				
	d			22p12		23p12													05 42				
Pokesdown	d			22p16		23p16													05 46				
Christchurch	d			22p20		23p20													05 50				
Hinton Admiral	d			22p25		23p25													05 55				
New Milton	d			22p29		23p29													05 59				
Sway	d			22p34		23p34													06 04				
Lymington Pier	d																						06 27
Lymington Town	d																						06 29
Brockenhurst 3	a			22p39		23p39													06 09				06 37
	d			22p40		23p40													06 10				
Beaulieu Road	d																						
Ashurst New Forest	d			22p47		23p47													06 17				
Totton	d			22p52		23p52													06 22		06 12		
Salisbury	d												05 35										
Dean	d												05 47										
Mottisfont & Dunbridge	d												05 53										
Romsey	d												05 58										
Redbridge	d																				06 14		
Millbrook (Hants)	d																				06 18		
Southampton Central ⛴	a			22p57		23p57													06 27		06 21		
	d		22p30	23p00		23p59			05 09	05 12		05 30		06 00	06 15				06 30		06 35		
St Denys	d					00 04						05 35									06 40		
Swaythling	d					00 07						05 38									06 43		
Southampton Airport Pkwy ✈	d		22p38	23p08		00 10			05 16	05 20		05 41		06 08	06 22				06 38		06 46		
Portsmouth Harbour ⛴	d				23p24													05 50				06 00	
Portsmouth & Southsea	d				23p29													05 55				06 04	
Fratton	d				23p33													05 59				06 08	
Hilsea	d				23p37													06 03					
Cosham	d				23p42						05 09							06 08				06 19	
Portchester	d				23p47						05 14							06 13					
Fareham	d				23p53						05 20							06 19				06 28	
Botley	d				23p59						05 27							06 26					
Hedge End	d				00 05						05 32							06 31					
Eastleigh 3	a		22p41	23p11	00 11	00 14				05 23	05 38	05 45		06 11				06 39	06 41		06 49		
	d		22p46	23p12	00 19					05 24		05 46		06 13				06 47	06 42		06 50		
Chandlers Ford	d												06 06								06 55		
Romsey	a												06 43								07 03	07 10	
Shawford	d			23p18								05 52						06 53		←			
Winchester	d		22p55	23p24	00a28				05 25	05 34		06 00		06 23	06 31			07 00	06 52	07 00			
Micheldever	d			23p33								06 08						→		07 08			
Basingstoke	a		23p11	23p43					05 40	05 50		06 19		06 39	06 46				07 08	07 19			
	d	22p54	23p13	23p44				04 54	05 41	05 54		06 24		06 40	06 47		06 54		07 09	07 24			
Reading 7	a								05 59						07 04								
Fleet	d	23p10		00 01				05 10		06 10		06 40					07 10			07 40			
Farnborough (Main)	d	23p16		00 06				05 16		06 16		06 46					07 16			07 46			
Woking	a	23p28	23p31	00 18				05 28		06 28		06 58		06 58			07 28		07 27	07 58			
Clapham Junction 10	a	00 21	23p55	00 53				06 00		06 57				07 23			07 57						
London Waterloo 15 ⊖	a	00 35	00 09	01 04				06 12		07 05		07 33		07 31			08 05		07 53	08 34			

Table 158

Saturdays
until 6 October

Weymouth, Bournemouth, Lymington, Romsey, Southampton and Basingstoke - London

Network Diagram - see first Page of Table 158

		XC ◇1 ⌶	SW 1	GW	XC ◇1 ⌶	SW 1	SW ◇1 A ⌶	SW 1	SW 1	SW 1	GW ◇ ⌶	XC ◇1 ⌶	SW 1	SW 1	SW 1	SW ◇1 ⌶	SW 1	GW ◇
Weymouth	d																	
Upwey	d																	
Dorchester West	a																	
Dorchester South	d																	
Moreton (Dorset)	d																	
Wool	d																	
Wareham	d						06 10											
Holton Heath	d						06 13											
Hamworthy	d						06 18											
Poole 4	a						06 23											
	d						06 24							06 50		07 07		
Parkstone (Dorset)	d						06 28							06 54				
Branksome	d						06 31							06 57				
Bournemouth	a						06 37							07 02		07 17		
	d	06 25			06 37		06 42							07 05		07 22		
Pokesdown	d						06 46							07 09		07 26		
Christchurch	d						06 50							07 13		07 30		
Hinton Admiral	d						06 55							07 18				
New Milton	d						06 59							07 22		07 37		
Sway	d						07 04							07 27				
Lymington Pier	d					06 57									07 27			
Lymington Town	d					06 59									07 29			
Brockenhurst 3	a	06 38			06 52	07 07	07 09							07 32	07 37	07 44		
	d	06 39			06 55		07 10							07 33		07 45		
Beaulieu Road	d																	
Ashurst New Forest	d						07 17							07 40				
Totton	d						07 22							07 45				
Salisbury	d			06 32						06 50								07 24
Dean	d									07 02								
Mottisfont & Dunbridge	d									07 08								
Romsey	d			06 50						07 13								07 44
Redbridge	d									07 21								
Millbrook (Hants)	d									07 24								
Southampton Central ⛴	a	06 52		07 02	07 07		07 27			07 27				07 52		07 58		08 02
	d	06 53	07 00	07 05	07 15		07 30			07 35		07 47		07 55		08 00		08 05
St Denys	d									07 40								
Swaythling	d									07 43								
Southampton Airport Pkwy ✈	d	07 01	07 08		07 22		07 38			07 46		07 54		08 03		08 08		
Portsmouth Harbour ⛴	d								06 59		07 23							
Portsmouth & Southsea	d								07 04		07 27							
Fratton	d								07 08		07 31							
Hilsea	d								07 12									
Cosham	d								07 17		07 39							
Portchester	d								07 22									
Fareham	d			07a27					07 28		07 47							08a27
Botley	d								07 35									
Hedge End	d								07 40									
Eastleigh 3	a		07 11						07 46	07 49				08 06				
	d		07 14						07 47	07 50				08 14				
Chandlers Ford	d									07 55								
Romsey	a									08 03	08 21							
Shawford	d		07 19											08 19			←	
Winchester	d	07 09	07 25		07 31		07 48		07 56			08 03		08 25		08 18	08 25	
Micheldever	d								08 05					→				
Basingstoke	a	07 24	07 41		07 46				08 15			08 17				08 34	08 41	
	d	07 25	07 43		07 47			07 54	08 17			08 19	08 24			08 35	08 43	
Reading 7	a	07 42			08 04							08 35						
Fleet	d		07 54					08 10					08 40				08 54	
Farnborough (Main)	d		08 00					08 16	08 30				08 46				09 00	
Woking	a		08 09				08 21	08 28	08 39				08 58					
Clapham Junction 10	a		08 30					08 57								09 12	09 25	
London Waterloo 15 ⊖	a		08 39				08 49	09 05	09 08				09 36			09 20	09 34	

A ⌶ from Bournemouth

Saturdays
until 6 October

Weymouth, Bournemouth, Lymington, Romsey, Southampton and Basingstoke - London

Network Diagram - see first Page of Table 158

		GW	XC ◇1 ⌶	SW 1	SW ◇1 A ⌶	SW 1	SW 1	GW ◇ ⌶	SW 1	SW 1	SW 1	SW 1	SW ◇1 A ⌶	SW 1	GW ◇	XC ◇1 ⌶	SW 1	SW ◇1 A ⌶
Weymouth	d				06 55								07 20					08 03
Upwey	d				06 59								07 24					
Dorchester West	a																	
Dorchester South	d				07 07								07 33					08 13
Moreton (Dorset)	d				07 14								07 39					
Wool	d				07 20								07 45					
Wareham	d				07 27								07 53					08 28
Holton Heath	d				07 31								07 56					
Hamworthy	d				07 36								08 01					08 35
Poole 4	a				07 40								08 06					08 39
	d				07 41						07 50		08 07					08 40
Parkstone (Dorset)	d				07 45						07 54							08 44
Branksome	d				07 49						07 57							08 48
Bournemouth	a				07 54						08 02		08 17					08 54
	d		07 45		07 59						08 05		08 22			08 45		08 59
Pokesdown	d										08 09		08 26					
Christchurch	d										08 13		08 30					
Hinton Admiral	d										08 18							
New Milton	d										08 22		08 37					
Sway	d										08 27							
Lymington Pier	d			07 57								08 27					08 57	
Lymington Town	d			07 59								08 29					08 59	
Brockenhurst 3	a		07 58	08 07	08 14						08 32	08 37	08 44			08 58	09 07	09 14
	d		08 00		08 15						08 33		08 45			09 00		09 15
Beaulieu Road	d																	
Ashurst New Forest	d										08 40							
Totton	d										08 45							
Salisbury	d	07 36							07 56						08 32			
Dean	d								08 08									
Mottisfont & Dunbridge	d								08 14									
Romsey	d	07 55							08 19						08 50			
Redbridge	d								08 27									
Millbrook (Hants)	d								08 31									
Southampton Central ⛴	a	08 07	08 12		08 28				08 34		08 52		08 58		09 03	09 12		09 28
	d		08 15		08 30				08 35		08 55		09 00		09 05	09 15		09 30
St Denys	d								08 40									
Swaythling	d								08 43									
Southampton Airport Pkwy ✈	d		08 22		08 38				08 46		09 03		09 08			09 22		09 38
Portsmouth Harbour ⛴	d						07 59	08 23										
Portsmouth & Southsea	d						08 04	08 27										
Fratton	d						08 08	08 31										
Hilsea	d						08 12											
Cosham	d						08 17	08 39										
Portchester	d						08 22											
Fareham	d						08 28	08 47							09a27			
Botley	d						08 35											
Hedge End	d						08 40											
Eastleigh 8	a						08 46		08 49		09 06							
	d						08 47		08 50		09 14							
Chandlers Ford	d								08 55									
Romsey	a							09 21	09 03									
Shawford	d										09 19			←				
Winchester	d		08 31		08 48		08 56				09 25		09 18	09 25		09 31		09 48
Micheldever	d						09 05				→							
Basingstoke	a		08 46				09 15						09 34	09 41		09 46		
	d		08 47			08 54	09 17			09 24			09 35	09 43		09 47		
Reading 7	a		09 04													10 04		
Fleet	d					09 10				09 40				09 54				
Farnborough (Main)	d					09 16	09 30			09 46				10 00				
Woking	a				09 19	09 28	09 39			09 58								10 19
Clapham Junction 10	a					09 57							10 12	10 25				
London Waterloo 15 ⊖	a				09 49	10 05	10 07			10 36			10 20	10 34				10 49

A ⌶ from Bournemouth

Saturdays
until 6 October

Weymouth, Bournemouth, Lymington, Romsey, Southampton and Basingstoke - London

Network Diagram - see first Page of Table 158

		SW 1	SW 1	GW ◇ ⌶	SW 1	XC ◇1 ⌶	SW 1	SW 1	SW 1	SW ◇1 A ⌶	SW 1	GW ◇	GW ◇	XC ◇1 ⌶	SW 1	SW ◇1 A ⌶	SW 1	SW 1	GW ◇
Weymouth	d									08 20		08 46				09 03			
Upwey	d									08 24		08 51							
Dorchester West	a											08 58							
Dorchester South	d									08 33						09 13			
Moreton (Dorset)	d									08 39									
Wool	d									08 45									
Wareham	d									08 53						09 28			
Holton Heath	d									08 56									
Hamworthy	d									09 01						09 35			
Poole 4	a									09 07						09 39			
	d							08 50		09 07						09 40			
Parkstone (Dorset)	d							08 54								09 44			
Branksome	d							08 57								09 48			
Bournemouth	a							09 02		09 17						09 54			
	d							09 05		09 22				09 45		09 59			
Pokesdown	d							09 09		09 26									
Christchurch	d							09 13		09 30									
Hinton Admiral	d							09 18											
New Milton	d							09 22		09 37									
Sway	d							09 27											
Lymington Pier	d								09 27						09 57				
Lymington Town	d								09 29						09 59				
Brockenhurst 3	a							09 32	09 37	09 44				09 58	10 07	10 14			
	d							09 33		09 45				10 00		10 15			
Beaulieu Road	d							09 38											
Ashurst New Forest	d							09 42											
Totton	d							09 47											
Salisbury	d				08 56								09 32						
Dean	d				09 08														
Mottisfont & Dunbridge	d				09 14														
Romsey	d				09 19								09 50						
Redbridge	d				09 27														
Millbrook (Hants)	d				09 31														
Southampton Central ⛴	a				09 34			09 53		09 58			10 03	10 12		10 28			
	d				09 35	09 47		09 55		10 00			10 05	10 15		10 30			
St Denys	d				09 40														
Swaythling	d				09 43														
Southampton Airport Pkwy ✈	d				09 46	09 54		10 03		10 08				10 22		10 38			
Portsmouth Harbour ⛴	d		08 59	09 23														09 59	10 23
Portsmouth & Southsea	d		09 04	09 27														10 04	10 27
Fratton	d		09 08	09 31														10 08	10 31
Hilsea	d		09 12															10 12	
Cosham	d		09 17	09 39														10 17	10 39
Portchester	d		09 22															10 22	
Fareham	d		09 28	09 47									10a27					10 28	10 47
Botley	d		09 35															10 35	
Hedge End	d		09 40															10 40	
Eastleigh 8	a		09 46		09 49			10 06										10 46	
	d		09 47		09 50			10 14										10 47	
Chandlers Ford	d				09 55														
Romsey	a			10 21	10 03														11 21
Shawford	d							10 19			←								
Winchester	d		09 56			10 03		10 25		10 18	10 25			10 31		10 48		10 56	
Micheldever	d		10 05					→										11 05	
Basingstoke	a		10 15			10 17				10 34	10 41			10 46				11 15	
	d	09 54	10 17			10 19	10 24			10 35	10 43			10 47			10 54	11 17	
Reading 7	a					10 34								11 04					
Fleet	d	10 10					10 40				10 54						11 10		
Farnborough (Main)	d	10 16	10 30				10 46				11 00						11 16	11 30	
Woking	a	10 28	10 39				10 58									11 19	11 28	11 39	
Clapham Junction 10	a	10 57								11 12	11 25						11 57		
London Waterloo 15 ⊖	a	11 05	11 07				11 36			11 20	11 34					11 49	12 05	12 07	

A ⌶ from Bournemouth

Table 158

Saturdays
until 6 October

Weymouth, Bournemouth, Lymington, Romsey, Southampton and Basingstoke - London

Network Diagram - see first Page of Table 158

Station		SW ■				SW ■	SW ■	SW ■	SW ◇■ A ⌶	SW ■	GW ◇	XC ◇■ ⌶	SW ■	SW ◇■ A ⌶		SW ■	SW ■	GW ◇		SW ■			XC ◇■ ⌶	SW ■	
Weymouth	d								09 20					10 03											
Upwey	d								09 24																
Dorchester West	a																								
Dorchester South	d								09 33					10 13											
Moreton (Dorset)	d								09 39																
Wool	d								09 45																
Wareham	d								09 53					10 28											
Holton Heath	d								09 56																
Hamworthy	d								10 01					10 35											
Poole [4]	a								10 06					10 39											
	d						09 50		10 07					10 40											
Parkstone (Dorset)	d						09 54							10 44											
Branksome	d						09 57							10 48											
Bournemouth	a						10 02		10 17					10 54											
	d						10 05		10 22			10 45		10 59											
Pokesdown	d						10 09		10 26																
Christchurch	d						10 13		10 30																
Hinton Admiral	d						10 18																		
New Milton	d						10 22		10 37																
Sway	d						10 27																		
Lymington Pier	d							10 27					10 57												
Lymington Town	d							10 29					10 59												
Brockenhurst [3]	a						10 32	10 37	10 44			10 58	11 07	11 14											
	d						10 33		10 45			11 00		11 15											
Beaulieu Road	d																								
Ashurst New Forest	d						10 40																		
Totton	d						10 45																		
Salisbury	d	09 56									10 32									10 56					
Dean	d	10 08																		11 08					
Mottisfont & Dunbridge	d	10 14																		11 14					
Romsey	d	10 19									10 50									11 19					
Redbridge	d	10 27																		11 27					
Millbrook (Hants)	d	10 31																		11 31					
Southampton Central ⛴	a	10 34					10 53		10 58		11 03	11 12		11 28						11 34					
	d	10 35					10 55		11 00		11 05	11 15		11 30						11 35			11 47		
St Denys	d	10 40																		11 40					
Swaythling	d	10 43																		11 43					
Southampton Airport Pkwy ✈	d	10 46					11 03		11 08			11 22		11 38						11 46			11 54		
Portsmouth Harbour ⛴	d																10 59	11 23							
Portsmouth & Southsea	d																11 04	11 27							
Fratton	d																11 08	11 31							
Hilsea	d																11 12								
Cosham	d																11 17	11 39							
Portchester	d																11 22								
Fareham	d										11a27						11 28	11 47							
Botley	d																11 35								
Hedge End	d																11 40								
Eastleigh [3]	a	10 49					11 06										11 46			11 49					
	d	10 50					11 14										11 47			11 50					
Chandlers Ford	d	10 55																		11 55					
Romsey	a	11 03																12 21		12 03					
Shawford	d						11 19			←															
Winchester	d						11 25		11 18	11 25		11 31		11 48			11 56						12 03		
Micheldever	d						→										12 05								
Basingstoke	a								11 34	11 41		11 46					12 15						12 17		
	d					11 24			11 35	11 43		11 47				11 54	12 17						12 19	12 24	
Reading [7]	a											12 04											12 35		
Fleet	d					11 40				11 54						12 10								12 40	
Farnborough (Main)	d					11 46				12 00						12 16	12 30							12 46	
Woking	a					11 58								12 19		12 28	12 39							12 58	
Clapham Junction [10]	a								12 12	12 25						12 57									
London Waterloo [15] ⊖	a					12 36			12 21	12 34				12 51		13 05	13 07							13 36	

A ⌶ from Bournemouth

Table 158

Saturdays
until 6 October

Weymouth, Bournemouth, Lymington, Romsey, Southampton and Basingstoke - London

Network Diagram - see first Page of Table 158

Station		SW ■	SW ■	SW ◇■ A ⌶	SW ■	GW ◇ ⌶	XC ◇■ ⌶	GW	SW ■			SW ◇■ A ⌶	GW ◇	SW ■	SW ■	GW ◇		SW ■				SW ■	SW ■	SW ■	SW ◇■ A ⌶
Weymouth	d			10 20								11 03	11 10												11 20
Upwey	d			10 24									11 15												11 24
Dorchester West	a												11 23												
Dorchester South	d			10 33								11 13													11 33
Moreton (Dorset)	d			10 39																					11 39
Wool	d			10 45																					11 45
Wareham	d			10 53								11 28													11 53
Holton Heath	d			10 56																					11 56
Hamworthy	d			11 01								11 35													12 01
Poole [4]	a			11 06								11 39													12 06
	d	10 50		11 07								11 40											11 50		12 07
Parkstone (Dorset)	d	10 54										11 44											11 54		
Branksome	d	10 57										11 48											11 57		
Bournemouth	a	11 02		11 17								11 54											12 02		12 17
	d	11 05		11 22			11 45					11 59											12 05		12 22
Pokesdown	d	11 09		11 26																			12 09		12 26
Christchurch	d	11 13		11 30																			12 13		12 30
Hinton Admiral	d	11 18																					12 18		
New Milton	d	11 22		11 37																			12 22		12 37
Sway	d	11 27																					12 27		
Lymington Pier	d		11 27						11 57															12 27	
Lymington Town	d		11 29						11 59															12 29	
Brockenhurst [3]	a	11 32	11 37	11 44			11 58		12 07			12 14											12 32	12 37	12 44
	d	11 33		11 45			12 00					12 15											12 33		12 45
Beaulieu Road	d	11 38																							
Ashurst New Forest	d	11 42																					12 40		
Totton	d	11 47																					12 45		
Salisbury	d					11 32		11 43										11 56							
Dean	d																	12 08							
Mottisfont & Dunbridge	d																	12 14							
Romsey	d					11 50		12 04										12 19							
Redbridge	d																	12 27							
Millbrook (Hants)	d																	12 31							
Southampton Central ⛴	a	11 53		11 58		12 03	12 12	12 20				12 28						12 34					12 51		12 58
	d	11 55		12 00		12 05	12 15					12 30						12 35					12 55		13 00
St Denys	d																	12 40							
Swaythling	d																	12 43							
Southampton Airport Pkwy ✈	d	12 03		12 08			12 22					12 38						12 46					13 03		13 08
Portsmouth Harbour ⛴	d														11 59	12 23									
Portsmouth & Southsea	d														12 04	12 27									
Fratton	d														12 08	12 31									
Hilsea	d														12 12										
Cosham	d														12 17	12 39									
Portchester	d														12 22										
Fareham	d					12a27									12 28	12 47									
Botley	d														12 35										
Hedge End	d														12 40										
Eastleigh [3]	a	12 06													12 46			12 49					13 06		
	d	12 14													12 47			12 50					13 14		
Chandlers Ford	d																	12 55							
Romsey	a															13 21		13 03							
Shawford	d	12 19			←																		13 19		
Winchester	d	12 25		12 18	12 25		12 31					12 48			12 56								13 25		13 18
Micheldever	d	→													13 05								→		
Basingstoke	a			12 34	12 41		12 46								13 15										13 34
	d			12 35	12 43		12 47							12 54	13 17							13 24			13 35
Reading [7]	a						13 04																		
Fleet	d				12 54									13 10								13 40			
Farnborough (Main)	d				13 00									13 16	13 30							13 46			
Woking	a											13 19		13 28	13 39							13 58			
Clapham Junction [10]	a			13 12	13 25									13 57											14 12
London Waterloo [15] ⊖	a			13 21	13 34							13 51		14 05	14 07							14 36			14 21

A ⌶ from Bournemouth

Weymouth, Bournemouth, Lymington, Romsey, Southampton and Basingstoke - London

Network Diagram - see first Page of Table 158

		SW ■	GW ◇ ⊼	XC ◇■ ⊼	SW ■	SW ◇■ A ⊼	SW ■	SW ■	GW ◇	SW ■	XC ◇■ ⊼	SW ■	SW ■	SW ■	SW ◇■ A ⊼	SW ■	GW ◇ ⊼	XC ◇■ ⊼	SW ■
Weymouth	d					12 03									12 20				
Upwey	d														12 24				
Dorchester West	a																		
Dorchester South	d					12 13									12 33				
Moreton (Dorset)	d														12 39				
Wool	d														12 45				
Wareham	d					12 28									12 53				
Holton Heath	d														12 56				
Hamworthy	d					12 35									13 01				
Poole ■	a					12 39									13 06				
	d					12 40							12 50		13 07				
Parkstone (Dorset)	d					12 44							12 54						
Branksome	d					12 48							12 57						
Bournemouth	a					12 54							13 02		13 17				
	d			12 45		12 59							13 05		13 22			13 45	
Pokesdown	d												13 09		13 26				
Christchurch	d												13 13		13 30				
Hinton Admiral	d												13 18						
New Milton	d												13 22		13 37				
Sway	d												13 27						
Lymington Pier	d				12 57									13 27					13 57
Lymington Town	d				12 59									13 29					13 59
Brockenhurst ■	a			12 58	13 07	13 14							13 32	13 37	13 44			13 58	14 07
	d			13 00		13 15							13 33		13 45			14 00	
Beaulieu Road	d												13 38						
Ashurst New Forest	d												13 42						
Totton	d												13 47						
Salisbury	d		12 32							12 56							13 32		
Dean	d									13 08									
Mottisfont & Dunbridge	d									13 14									
Romsey	d		12 50							13 19							13 50		
Redbridge	d									13 27									
Millbrook (Hants)	d									13 31									
Southampton Central	a		13 03	13 12		13 28				13 34			13 53		13 58		14 03	14 12	
	d		13 05	13 15		13 30				13 35	13 47		13 55		14 00		14 05	14 15	
St Denys	d									13 40									
Swaythling	d									13 43									
Southampton Airport Pkwy	d			13 22		13 38				13 46	13 54		14 03		14 08			14 22	
Portsmouth Harbour	d							12 59	13 23										
Portsmouth & Southsea	d							13 04	13 27										
Fratton	d							13 08	13 31										
Hilsea	d							13 12											
Cosham	d							13 17	13 39										
Portchester	d							13 22											
Fareham	d		13a27					13 28	13 47								14a27		
Botley	d							13 35											
Hedge End	d							13 40											
Eastleigh ■	a							13 46		13 49			14 06						
	d							13 47		13 50			14 14						
Chandlers Ford	d									13 55									
Romsey	a								14 21	14 03									
Shawford	d	←											14 19			←			
Winchester	d	13 25		13 31		13 48		13 56			14 03		14 25		14 18	14 25		14 31	
Micheldever	d							14 05					→						
Basingstoke	a	13 41		13 46				14 15			14 17				14 34	14 41		14 46	
	d	13 43		13 47			13 54	14 17			14 19	14 24			14 35	14 43		14 47	
Reading ■	a			14 04							14 35							15 04	
Fleet	d	13 54					14 10					14 40				14 54			
Farnborough (Main)	d	14 00					14 16	14 30				14 46				15 00			
Woking	a					14 19	14 28	14 39				14 58							
Clapham Junction ■	a	14 25					14 57								15 12	15 25			
London Waterloo ■ ⊖	a	14 34				14 51	15 05	15 07				15 36			15 21	15 34			

A ⊼ from Bournemouth

Weymouth, Bournemouth, Lymington, Romsey, Southampton and Basingstoke - London

Network Diagram - see first Page of Table 158

		SW ◇■ A ⊼	GW ◇	SW ■	SW ■	GW ◇	GW ◇	SW ■	SW ■	SW ■	SW ■	SW ◇■ A ⊼	SW ■	GW ◇	XC ◇■ ⊼	SW ■	SW ◇■ A ⊼	SW ■	SW ■	GW ◇
Weymouth	d	13 03	13 10									13 20					14 03			
Upwey	d		13 15									13 24								
Dorchester West	a		13 22																	
Dorchester South	d	13 13										13 33					14 13			
Moreton (Dorset)	d											13 39								
Wool	d											13 45								
Wareham	d	13 28										13 53					14 28			
Holton Heath	d											13 56								
Hamworthy	d	13 35										14 01					14 35			
Poole ■	a	13 39										14 06					14 39			
	d	13 40								13 50		14 07					14 40			
Parkstone (Dorset)	d	13 44								13 54							14 44			
Branksome	d	13 48								13 57							14 48			
Bournemouth	a	13 54								14 02		14 17					14 54			
	d	13 59								14 05		14 22			14 45		14 59			
Pokesdown	d									14 09		14 26								
Christchurch	d									14 13		14 30								
Hinton Admiral	d									14 18										
New Milton	d									14 22		14 37								
Sway	d									14 27										
Lymington Pier	d										14 27					14 57				
Lymington Town	d										14 29					14 59				
Brockenhurst ■	a	14 14								14 32	14 37	14 44			14 58	15 07	15 14			
	d	14 15								14 33		14 45			15 00		15 15			
Beaulieu Road	d																			
Ashurst New Forest	d									14 40										
Totton	d									14 45										
Salisbury	d						14 00	13 50						14 32						
Dean	d							14 02												
Mottisfont & Dunbridge	d							14 08												
Romsey	d						14 20	14 13						14 50						
Redbridge	d							14 21												
Millbrook (Hants)	d							14 24												
Southampton Central	a	14 28					14 32	14 28		14 51		14 58		15 03	15 12		15 28			
	d	14 30					14 34	14 35		14 55		15 00		15 05	15 15		15 30			
St Denys	d							14 40												
Swaythling	d							14 43												
Southampton Airport Pkwy	d	14 38						14 46		15 03		15 08			15 22		15 38			
Portsmouth Harbour	d				13 59	14 23													14 59	15 23
Portsmouth & Southsea	d				14 04	14 27													15 04	15 27
Fratton	d				14 08	14 31													15 08	15 31
Hilsea	d				14 12														15 12	
Cosham	d				14 17	14 39													15 17	15 39
Portchester	d				14 22														15 22	
Fareham	d				14 28	14 47	14a54							15a27					15 28	15 47
Botley	d				14 35														15 35	
Hedge End	d				14 40														15 40	
Eastleigh ■	a				14 46			14 49		15 06									15 46	
	d				14 47			14 50		15 14									15 47	
Chandlers Ford	d							14 55												
Romsey	a					15 21		15 04												16 21
Shawford	d									15 19			←							
Winchester	d	14 48			14 56					15 25		15 18	15 25		15 31		15 48		15 56	
Micheldever	d				15 05					→									16 05	
Basingstoke	a				15 15							15 34	15 41		15 46				16 15	
	d			14 54	15 17				15 24			15 35	15 43		15 47			15 54	16 17	
Reading ■	a														16 05					
Fleet	d			15 10					15 40				15 54					16 10		
Farnborough (Main)	d			15 16	15 30				15 46				16 00					16 16	16 30	
Woking	a	15 19		15 28	15 39				15 58								16 19	16 28	16 39	
Clapham Junction ■	a			15 57								16 12	16 25					16 57		
London Waterloo ■ ⊖	a	15 51		16 05	16 07				16 36			16 20	16 34				16 49	17 05	17 07	

A ⊼ from Bournemouth

Saturdays
until 6 October

Weymouth, Bournemouth, Lymington, Romsey, Southampton and Basingstoke - London

Network Diagram - see first Page of Table 158

		SW	XC	SW	SW	SW	SW	SW	GW	XC	SW	SW	GW	SW	SW	GW	SW
		1	◇1	1	1	1	◇1	1	◇	◇1	1	◇1	◇	1	1	1	1
							A					A	B				
			⊼				⊼			⊼		⊼					
Weymouth	d						14 20					15 03	15 08				
Upwey	d						14 24						15 13				
Dorchester West	a												15 20				
Dorchester South	d						14 33					15 13					
Moreton (Dorset)	d						14 39										
Wool	d						14 45										
Wareham	d						14 53					15 28					
Holton Heath	d						14 56										
Hamworthy	d						15 01					15 35					
Poole 4	a						15 06					15 39					
	d				14 50		15 07					15 40					
Parkstone (Dorset)	d				14 54							15 44					
Branksome	d				14 57							15 48					
Bournemouth	a				15 02		15 17					15 54					
	d				15 05		15 22			15 45		15 59					
Pokesdown	d				15 09		15 26										
Christchurch	d				15 13		15 30										
Hinton Admiral	d				15 18												
New Milton	d				15 22		15 37										
Sway	d				15 27												
Lymington Pier	d					15 27					15 57						
Lymington Town	d					15 29					15 59						
Brockenhurst 3	a				15 32	15 37	15 44			15 58	16 07	16 14					
	d				15 33		15 45			16 00		16 15					
Beaulieu Road	d				15 38												
Ashurst New Forest	d				15 42												
Totton	d				15 47												
Salisbury	d	14 56							15 32								15 56
Dean	d	15 08															16 08
Mottisfont & Dunbridge	d	15 14															16 14
Romsey	d	15 19							15 50								16 19
Redbridge	d	15 27															16 27
Millbrook (Hants)	d	15 31															16 31
Southampton Central	a	15 34			15 53		15 58		16 03	16 12		16 28					16 34
	d	15 35	15 47		15 55		16 00		16 05	16 15		16 30					16 35
St Denys	d	15 40															16 40
Swaythling	d	15 43															16 43
Southampton Airport Pkwy	d	15 46	15 54		16 03		16 08			16 22		16 38					16 46
Portsmouth Harbour	d														15 59	16 23	
Portsmouth & Southsea	d														16 04	16 27	
Fratton	d														16 08	16 31	
Hilsea	d														16 12		
Cosham	d														16 17	16 39	
Portchester	d														16 22		
Fareham	d								16a27						16 28	16 47	
Botley	d														16 35		
Hedge End	d														16 40		
Eastleigh 3	a	15 49			16 06										16 46		16 49
	d	15 50			16 14										16 47		16 50
Chandlers Ford	d	15 55															16 55
Romsey	a	16 03														17 21	17 03
Shawford	d				16 19			←									
Winchester	d		16 03		16 25		16 18	16 25		16 31		16 48			16 56		
Micheldever	d				→										17 05		
Basingstoke	a		16 17				16 34	16 41		16 46					17 15		
	d		16 19	16 24			16 35	16 43		16 47				16 54	17 17		
Reading 7	a		16 35							17 04							
Fleet	d			16 40				16 54						17 10			
Farnborough (Main)	d			16 46				17 00						17 16	17 30		
Woking	a			16 58								17 19		17 28	17 39		
Clapham Junction 10	a						17 12	17 25						17 57			
London Waterloo 15 ⊖	a			17 36			17 20	17 34				17 49		18 05	18 07		

A ⊼ from Bournemouth

B from 15 September until 6 October

Saturdays
until 6 October

Weymouth, Bournemouth, Lymington, Romsey, Southampton and Basingstoke - London

Network Diagram - see first Page of Table 158

		SW	SW	SW	SW	SW	GW	XC	SW	SW	GW	SW	SW	GW	SW	SW	XC	SW	SW
		1	1	1	◇1	1	◇	◇1	1	◇1	◇	1	1	◇	1	1	◇1	1	1
					A					A	B								
					⊼			⊼		⊼							⊼		
Weymouth	d				15 20					16 03	16 08								
Upwey	d				15 24						16 13								
Dorchester West	a										16 21								
Dorchester South	d				15 33					16 13									
Moreton (Dorset)	d				15 39														
Wool	d				15 45														
Wareham	d				15 53					16 28									
Holton Heath	d				15 56														
Hamworthy	d				16 01					16 35									
Poole 4	a				16 06					16 39									
	d		15 50		16 07					16 40									16 50
Parkstone (Dorset)	d		15 54							16 44									16 54
Branksome	d		15 57							16 48									16 57
Bournemouth	a		16 02		16 17					16 54									17 02
	d		16 05		16 22			16 45		16 59									17 05
Pokesdown	d		16 09		16 26														17 09
Christchurch	d		16 13		16 30														17 13
Hinton Admiral	d		16 18																17 18
New Milton	d		16 22		16 37														17 22
Sway	d		16 27																17 27
Lymington Pier	d			16 27					16 57										
Lymington Town	d			16 29					16 59										
Brockenhurst 3	a		16 32	16 37	16 44			16 58	17 07	17 14									17 32
	d		16 33		16 45			17 00		17 15									17 33
Beaulieu Road	d																		17 38
Ashurst New Forest	d		16 40																17 42
Totton	d		16 45																17 47
Salisbury	d						16 32								16 56				
Dean	d														17 08				
Mottisfont & Dunbridge	d														17 14				
Romsey	d						16 50								17 19				
Redbridge	d														17 27				
Millbrook (Hants)	d														17 31				
Southampton Central	a		16 51		16 58		17 03	17 12		17 28					17 34				17 53
	d		16 55		17 00		17 05	17 15		17 30					17 35		17 47		17 55
St Denys	d														17 40				
Swaythling	d														17 43				
Southampton Airport Pkwy	d		17 03		17 08			17 22		17 38					17 46		17 54		18 03
Portsmouth Harbour	d												16 59	17 23		17 33			
Portsmouth & Southsea	d												17 04	17 27		17 38			
Fratton	d												17 08	17 31		17 42			
Hilsea	d												17 12			17 46			
Cosham	d												17 17	17 39		17 51			
Portchester	d												17 22			17 56			
Fareham	d						17a27						17 28	17 47		18a01			
Botley	d												17 35						
Hedge End	d												17 40						
Eastleigh 3	a		17 06										17 46		17 49				18 06
	d		17 14										17 47		17 50				18 14
Chandlers Ford	d														17 55				
Romsey	a													18 21	18 03				
Shawford	d		17 19			←													18 19
Winchester	d		17 25		17 18	17 25		17 31		17 48			17 56				18 03		18 25
Micheldever	d		→										18 05						→
Basingstoke	a				17 34	17 41		17 46					18 15				18 17		
	d	17 24			17 35	17 43		17 47				17 54	18 17				18 19	18 24	
Reading 7	a							18 04									18 35		
Fleet	d	17 40				17 54						18 10						18 40	
Farnborough (Main)	d	17 46				18 00						18 16	18 30					18 46	
Woking	a	17 58								18 19		18 28	18 39					18 58	
Clapham Junction 10	a				18 12	18 25						18 57							
London Waterloo 15 ⊖	a	18 36			18 20	18 34				18 49		19 05	19 07					19 36	

A ⊼ from Bournemouth

B until 8 September

Weymouth, Bournemouth, Lymington, Romsey, Southampton and Basingstoke - London

Network Diagram - see first Page of Table 158

		SW	SW	SW	GW	GW	XC	SW	SW	SW	SW	GW	SW	SW	SW	SW	SW	SW	GW	GW
		■	◇■ A ✠	■	◇ B	◇	◇■ ✠	■	◇■ A ✠	■	■	◇	■	■	■	■	◇■ A ✠	■	◇	■
Weymouth	d		16 20		16 55				17 03								17 20		17 28	
Upwey	d		16 24														17 24		17 33	
Dorchester West	a				17 06														17 40	
Dorchester South	d		16 33						17 13								17 33			
Moreton (Dorset)	d		16 39														17 39			
Wool	d		16 45														17 45			
Wareham	d		16 53						17 28								17 53			
Holton Heath	d		16 56														17 56			
Hamworthy	d		17 01						17 35								18 01			
Poole ■	a		17 06						17 39								18 06			
	d		17 07						17 40						17 50		18 07			
Parkstone (Dorset)	d								17 44						17 54					
Branksome	d								17 48						17 57					
Bournemouth	a		17 17						17 54						18 02		18 17			
	d		17 22				17 45		17 59						18 05		18 22			
Pokesdown	d		17 26												18 09		18 26			
Christchurch	d		17 30												18 13		18 30			
Hinton Admiral	d														18 18					
New Milton	d		17 37												18 22		18 37			
Sway	d														18 27					
Lymington Pier	d	17 27						17 57								18 27				
Lymington Town	d	17 29						17 59								18 29				
Brockenhurst ■	a	17 37	17 44				17 58	18 07	18 14						18 32	18 37	18 44			
	d		17 45				18 00		18 15						18 33		18 45			
Beaulieu Road	d																			
Ashurst New Forest	d														18 40					
Totton	d														18 45					
Salisbury	d					17 32							17 56							18 32
Dean	d												18 08							
Mottisfont & Dunbridge	d												18 14							
Romsey	d					17 50							18 19							18 50
Redbridge	d												18 27							
Millbrook (Hants)	d												18 31							
Southampton Central ⛴	a		17 58			18 03	18 12		18 28				18 34		18 51		18 58			19 03
	d		18 00			18 05	18 15		18 30				18 35		18 55		19 00			19 05
St Denys	d												18 40							
Swaythling	d												18 43							
Southampton Airport Pkwy ✈	d		18 08				18 22		18 38				18 46		19 03		19 08			
Portsmouth Harbour ⛴	d										17 59	18 23								
Portsmouth & Southsea	d										18 04	18 27								
Fratton	d										18 08	18 31								
Hilsea	d										18 12									
Cosham	d										18 17	18 39								
Portchester	d										18 22									
Fareham	d					18a27					18 28	18 47								19a27
Botley	d										18 35									
Hedge End	d										18 40									
Eastleigh ■	a										18 46		18 49		19 06					
	d										18 47		18 50		19 14					
Chandlers Ford	d												18 55							
Romsey	a											19 21	19 04							
Shawford	d			←											19 19			←		
Winchester	d		18 18	18 25			18 31		18 48		18 56				19 25		19 18	19 25		
Micheldever	d										19 05				→					
Basingstoke	a		18 34	18 41			18 46				19 15						19 34	19 41		
	d		18 35	18 43			18 47			18 54	19 17			19 24			19 35	19 43		
Reading ■	a						19 04													
Fleet	d			18 54						19 10				19 40				19 54		
Farnborough (Main)	d			19 00						19 16	19 30			19 46				20 00		
Woking	a								19 19	19 28	19 39			19 58						
Clapham Junction ■	a		19 12	19 25						19 57							20 12	20 25		
London Waterloo ■ ⊖	a		19 20	19 34					19 49	20 05	20 07			20 36			20 20	20 34		

A ✠ from Bournemouth

B until 8 September

Weymouth, Bournemouth, Lymington, Romsey, Southampton and Basingstoke - London

Network Diagram - see first Page of Table 158

		XC	SW	SW	SW	SW	GW	SW	SW	SW	SW	SW	SW	GW	XC	GW	SW	SW	SW	SW
		◇■ ✠	■	◇■ A ✠	■	■	◇	■	■	■	■	◇■ A ✠	■	◇	◇■		■	◇■ A ✠	■	■
Weymouth	d			18 06								18 20						19 03		
Upwey	d											18 24								
Dorchester West	a																			
Dorchester South	d			18 16								18 33						19 13		
Moreton (Dorset)	d											18 39								
Wool	d											18 45								
Wareham	d			18 31								18 53						19 28		
Holton Heath	d											18 56								
Hamworthy	d			18 38								19 01						19 35		
Poole ■	a			18 42								19 06						19 39		
	d			18 43						18 50		19 07						19 40		
Parkstone (Dorset)	d			18 47						18 54								19 44		
Branksome	d			18 51						18 57								19 48		
Bournemouth	a			18 56						19 02		19 17						19 54		
	d	18 45		18 59						19 05		19 22			19 45			19 59		
Pokesdown	d									19 09		19 26								
Christchurch	d									19 13		19 30								
Hinton Admiral	d									19 18										
New Milton	d									19 22		19 37								
Sway	d									19 27										
Lymington Pier	d		18 57								19 27						19 57			
Lymington Town	d		18 59								19 29						19 59			
Brockenhurst ■	a	18 58	19 07	19 14						19 32	19 37	19 44			19 58		20 07	20 14		
	d	19 00		19 15						19 33		19 45			20 00			20 15		
Beaulieu Road	d																			
Ashurst New Forest	d									19 40										
Totton	d									19 45										
Salisbury	d							18 56						19 32		19 41				
Dean	d							19 08												
Mottisfont & Dunbridge	d							19 14												
Romsey	d							19 19						19 50		20 04				
Redbridge	d							19 27												
Millbrook (Hants)	d							19 31												
Southampton Central ⛴	a	19 12		19 28				19 34		19 51		19 58		20 02	20 12	20 18		20 28		
	d	19 15		19 30				19 35		19 55		20 00		20 05	20 15			20 30		
St Denys	d							19 40												
Swaythling	d							19 43												
Southampton Airport Pkwy ✈	d	19 22		19 38				19 46		20 03		20 08			20 22			20 38		
Portsmouth Harbour ⛴	d					18 59	19 23													19 59
Portsmouth & Southsea	d					19 04	19 27													20 04
Fratton	d					19 08	19 31													20 08
Hilsea	d					19 12														20 12
Cosham	d					19 17	19 39													20 17
Portchester	d					19 22														20 22
Fareham	d					19 28	19 47							20a27						20 28
Botley	d					19 35														20 35
Hedge End	d					19 40														20 40
Eastleigh ■	a					19 46		19 49		20 06										20 46
	d					19 47		19 50		20 14										20 47
Chandlers Ford	d							19 55												
Romsey	a						20 21	20 03												
Shawford	d									20 19			←							
Winchester	d	19 31		19 48		19 56				20 25		20 18	20 25		20 31			20 48		20 56
Micheldever	d					20 05				→										21 05
Basingstoke	a	19 46				20 15						20 34	20 41		20 46					21 17
	d	19 47			19 54	20 17			20 24			20 35	20 43		20 47				20 54	21 24
Reading ■	a	20 04													21 04					
Fleet	d				20 10				20 40				20 54						21 10	21 40
Farnborough (Main)	d				20 16	20 30			20 46				21 00						21 16	21 46
Woking	a			20 19	20 28	20 39			20 58				21 09					21 19	21 28	21 58
Clapham Junction ■	a				20 57							21 16	21 29						21 57	
London Waterloo ■ ⊖	a			20 49	21 05	21 07			21 34			21 24	21 38					21 49	22 07	22 34

A ✠ from Bournemouth

Saturdays
until 6 October

Weymouth, Bournemouth, Lymington, Romsey, Southampton and Basingstoke - London

Network Diagram - see first Page of Table 158

		GW ◇	SW 1	SW 1	SW 1	SW ◇1	SW 1	GW ◇	SW 1	SW 1	SW 1	SW 1	SW 1	SW 1
Weymouth	d					19 20								
Upwey	d					19 24								
Dorchester West	a													
Dorchester South	d					19 33								
Moreton (Dorset)	d					19 39								
Wool	d					19 45								
Wareham	d					19 53								
Holton Heath	d													
Hamworthy	d					20 01								
Poole 4	a					20 06								
	d			19 50		20 07								
Parkstone (Dorset)	d			19 54										
Branksome	d			19 57										
Bournemouth	a			20 02		20 17								
	d			20 05		20 22								
Pokesdown	d			20 09		20 26								
Christchurch	d			20 13		20 30								
Hinton Admiral	d			20 18										
New Milton	d			20 22		20 37								
Sway	d			20 27										
Lymington Pier	d				20 27				20 57	21 27				
Lymington Town	d				20 29				20 59	21 29				
Brockenhurst 3	a			20 32	20 37	20 44			21 07	21 37				
	d			20 33		20 45								
Beaulieu Road	d													
Ashurst New Forest	d			20 40										
Totton	d			20 45										
Salisbury	d		19 56					20 32						20 56
Dean	d		20 08											21 08
Mottisfont & Dunbridge	d		20 14											21 14
Romsey	d		20 19					20 50						21 19
Redbridge	d		20 27											21 27
Millbrook (Hants)	d		20 31											21 31
Southampton Central ⛴	a		20 34	20 51		20 58		21 03						21 34
	d		20 35	20 55		21 00		21 05			21 30			21 35
St Denys	d		20 40											21 40
Swaythling	d		20 43											21 43
Southampton Airport Pkwy ✈	d		20 46	21 03		21 08					21 38			21 46
Portsmouth Harbour ⛴	d	20 23											20 59	
Portsmouth & Southsea	d	20 27											21 04	
Fratton	d	20 31											21 08	
Hilsea	d												21 12	
Cosham	d												21 17	
Portchester	d												21 22	
Fareham	d	20 47						21a27					21 28	
Botley	d												21 35	
Hedge End	d												21 40	
Eastleigh 8	a		20 49	21 06									21 46	21 49
	d		20 50	21 14									21 47	21 50
Chandlers Ford	d		20 55											21 55
Romsey	a	21 21	21 03											22 03
Shawford	d			21 19			←							
Winchester	d			21 25		21 18	21 25				21 48		21 56	
Micheldever	d			→									22 05	
Basingstoke	a					21 34	21 41						22 15	
	d					21 35	21 43					21 54	22 24	
Reading 7	a													
Fleet	d						21 54					22 10	22 40	
Farnborough (Main)	d						22 00					22 16	22 46	
Woking	a						22 09				22 19	22 28	22 58	
Clapham Junction 10	a					22 14	22 29					22 57		
London Waterloo 15 ⊖	a					22 22	22 38				22 49	23 05	23 32	

Saturdays
until 6 October

Weymouth, Bournemouth, Lymington, Romsey, Southampton and Basingstoke - London

Network Diagram - see first Page of Table 158

		SW 1	SW ◇1	SW 1	GW	SW 1	GW ◇	SW 1	SW 1	SW 1	SW 1	SW 1	SW 1	GW ◇	SW 1	SW 1	SW 1	SW 1	SW 1
Weymouth	d		20 10		20 21								21 10					22 10	23 10
Upwey	d		20 14		20 26								21 14					22 14	23 14
Dorchester West	a				20 33														
Dorchester South	d		20 22										21 22					22 22	23 22
Moreton (Dorset)	d		20 28										21 28					22 28	23 28
Wool	d		20 34										21 34					22 34	23 34
Wareham	d		20 42										21 42					22 42	23 42
Holton Heath	d																		
Hamworthy	d		20 48										21 48					22 48	23 48
Poole 4	a		20 53										21 53					22 53	23 53
	d		20 54										21 54					22 54	23 54
Parkstone (Dorset)	d		20 58										21 58					22 58	
Branksome	d		21 01										22 01					23 01	
Bournemouth	a		21 07										22 07					23 07	00 03
	d		21 12										22 12					23 12	
Pokesdown	d		21 16										22 16					23 16	
Christchurch	d		21 20										22 20					23 20	
Hinton Admiral	d		21 25										22 25					23 25	
New Milton	d		21 29										22 29					23 29	
Sway	d		21 34										22 34					23 34	
Lymington Pier	d							22 03							22 33				
Lymington Town	d							22 05							22 35				
Brockenhurst 3	a		21 39					22 13					22 39		22 43			23 39	
	d		21 40										22 40					23 40	
Beaulieu Road	d																		
Ashurst New Forest	d		21 47										22 47					23 47	
Totton	d		21 52										22 52					23 52	
Salisbury	d						21 32				21 56			22 32					
Dean	d										22 08								
Mottisfont & Dunbridge	d										22 14								
Romsey	d						21 50				22 19			22 50		23 00			
Redbridge	d										22 27					23 08			
Millbrook (Hants)	d										22 31					23 12			
Southampton Central ⛴	a		21 57				22 03				22 34		22 57	23 03		23 15		23 57	
	d	21 55	22 00				22 05			22 30	22 35		23 00	23 05		23 21		23 59	
St Denys	d										22 40					23 26		00 04	
Swaythling	d										22 43					23 29		00 07	
Southampton Airport Pkwy ✈	d	22 03	22 08							22 38	22 46		23 08			23 32		00 10	
Portsmouth Harbour ⛴	d					21 54						22 33					23 24		
Portsmouth & Southsea	d					21 59						22 38					23 29		
Fratton	d					22 03						22 42					23 33		
Hilsea	d					22 07						22 46					23 37		
Cosham	d					22 12						22 51					23 42		
Portchester	d					22 17						22 56					23 47		
Fareham	d					22 23	22a26					23a01		23a26			23 53		
Botley	d					22 30											23 59		
Hedge End	d					22 35											00 05		
Eastleigh 8	a	22 06				22 41				22 41	22 49		23 11			23 35	00 11	00 14	
	d	22 14								22 46	22 50		23 12			23 37	00 21		
Chandlers Ford	d										22 55					23 42			
Romsey	a										23 03					23 49			
Shawford	d	22 19		←									23 18						
Winchester	d	22 25	22 18	22 25						22 55			23 24				00a30		
Micheldever	d	→											23 33						
Basingstoke	a		22 34	22 41						23 11			23 43						
	d		22 35	22 43					22 54	23 13			23 44						
Reading 7	a																		
Fleet	d			22 54					23 10				00 01						
Farnborough (Main)	d			23 00					23 16				00 06						
Woking	a		22 53	23 09					23 28	23 31			00 18						
Clapham Junction 10	a		23 14	23 29					00 21	23 52			00 53						
London Waterloo 15 ⊖	a		23 22	23 39					00 35	00 03			01 04						

Table 158

Saturdays from 13 October

Weymouth, Bournemouth, Lymington, Romsey, Southampton and Basingstoke - London

Network Diagram - see first Page of Table 158

		SW ■	SW ■	SW ■	SW ■	SW ◇■	SW ■	SW ■	XC ◇■	SW ■	SW ■	SW ■	SW ■	SW ■	XC ◇■ ⊼	GW ◇	SW ■	SW ■	SW ◇■ ⊼	SW ■	SW ■	GW ◇	SW ■
Weymouth	d			21p10		22p10	23p10									06 38							
Upwey	d			21p14		22p14	23p14									06 43							
Dorchester West	a															06 50							
Dorchester South	d			21p22		22p22	23p22																
Moreton (Dorset)	d			21p28		22p28	23p28																
Wool	d			21p34		22p34	23p34																
Wareham	d			21p42		22p42	23p42																
Holton Heath	d																						
Hamworthy	d			21p48		22p48	23p48																
Poole ■	a			21p53		22p53	23p53																
	d			21p54		22p54	23p54												05 28				
Parkstone (Dorset)	d			21p58		22p58													05 32				
Branksome	d			22p01		23p01													05 35				
Bournemouth	a			22p07		23p07	00 03												05 40				
	d			22p12		23p12													05 42				
Pokesdown	d			22p16		23p16													05 46				
Christchurch	d			22p20		23p20													05 50				
Hinton Admiral	d			22p25		23p25													05 55				
New Milton	d			22p29		23p29													05 59				
Sway	d			22p34		23p34													06 04				
Lymington Pier	d																						06 27
Lymington Town	d																						06 29
Brockenhurst ■	a			22p39		23p39													06 09				06 37
	d			22p40		23p40													06 10				
Beaulieu Road	d																						
Ashurst New Forest	d			22p47		23p47													06 17				
Totton	d			22p52		23p52													06 22		06 12		
Salisbury	d												05 35										
Dean	d												05 47										
Mottisfont & Dunbridge	d												05 53										
Romsey	d												05 58										
Redbridge	d																				06 14		
Millbrook (Hants)	d																				06 18		
Southampton Central ⛴	a			22p57		23p57													06 27		06 21		
	d		22p30	23p00		23p59			05 09	05 12		05 30		06 00	06 15				06 30		06 35		
St Denys	d					00 04						05 35									06 40		
Swaythling	d					00 07						05 38									06 43		
Southampton Airport Pkwy ✈	d		22p38	23p08		00 10			05 16	05 20		05 41		06 08	06 22				06 38		06 46		
Portsmouth Harbour ⛴	d				23p24													05 50				06 00	
Portsmouth & Southsea	d				23p29													05 55				06 04	
Fratton	d				23p33													05 59				06 08	
Hilsea	d				23p37													06 03					
Cosham	d				23p42						05 09							06 08				06 19	
Portchester	d				23p47						05 14							06 13					
Fareham	d				23p53						05 20							06 19				06 28	
Botley	d				23p59						05 27							06 26					
Hedge End	d				00 05						05 32							06 31					
Eastleigh ■	a		22p41	23p11	00 11	00 14				05 23	05 38	05 45		06 11				06 39	06 41		06 49		
	d		22p46	23p12	00 19					05 24		05 46		06 13				06 47	06 42		06 50		
Chandlers Ford	d												06 06								06 55		
Romsey	a												06 43								07 03	07 10	
Shawford	d			23p18								05 52						06 53		←			
Winchester	d		22p55	23p24	00a28				05 25	05 34		06 00		06 23	06 31			07 00	06 52	07 00			
Micheldever	d			23p33								06 08						→		07 08			
Basingstoke	a		23p11	23p43					05 40	05 50		06 19		06 39	06 46				07 08	07 19			
	d	22p54	23p13	23p44				04 54	05 41	05 54		06 24		06 40	06 47		06 54		07 09	07 24			
Reading ■	a								05 59						07 04								
Fleet	d	23p10		00 01				05 10		06 10		06 40					07 10			07 40			
Farnborough (Main)	d	23p16		00 06				05 16		06 16		06 46					07 16			07 46			
Woking	a	23p28	23p31	00 18				05 28		06 28		06 58		06 58			07 28		07 27	07 58			
Clapham Junction ■	a	00 21	23p55	00 53				06 00		06 57				07 23			07 57						
London Waterloo ■ ⊖	a	00 35	00 09	01 04				06 15		07 08		07 33		07 31			08 05		07 53	08 34			

Table 158

Saturdays from 13 October

Weymouth, Bournemouth, Lymington, Romsey, Southampton and Basingstoke - London

Network Diagram - see first Page of Table 158

		XC ◇■ ⊼	SW ■	GW	XC ◇■ ⊼	SW ■	SW ◇■ A ⊼	SW ■	SW ■	SW ■	GW ◇ ⊼	XC ◇■ ⊼	SW ■	SW ■	SW ■	SW ◇■ ⊼	SW ■	GW ◇
Weymouth	d																	
Upwey	d																	
Dorchester West	a																	
Dorchester South	d																	
Moreton (Dorset)	d																	
Wool	d																	
Wareham	d						06 10											
Holton Heath	d						06 13											
Hamworthy	d						06 18											
Poole ■	a						06 23											
	d						06 24							06 50		07 07		
Parkstone (Dorset)	d						06 28							06 54				
Branksome	d						06 31							06 57				
Bournemouth	a						06 37							07 02		07 17		
	d	06 25			06 37		06 42							07 05		07 22		
Pokesdown	d						06 46							07 09		07 26		
Christchurch	d						06 50							07 13		07 30		
Hinton Admiral	d						06 55							07 18				
New Milton	d						06 59							07 22		07 37		
Sway	d						07 04							07 27				
Lymington Pier	d					06 57									07 27			
Lymington Town	d					06 59									07 29			
Brockenhurst ■	a	06 38			06 52	07 07	07 09							07 32	07 37	07 44		
	d	06 39			06 55		07 10							07 33		07 45		
Beaulieu Road	d																	
Ashurst New Forest	d						07 17							07 40				
Totton	d						07 22							07 45				
Salisbury	d			06 32						06 50								07 24
Dean	d									07 02								
Mottisfont & Dunbridge	d									07 08								
Romsey	d			06 50						07 13								07 44
Redbridge	d									07 21								
Millbrook (Hants)	d									07 24								
Southampton Central ⛴	a	06 52		07 02	07 07		07 27			07 27				07 52		07 58		08 02
	d	06 53	07 00	07 05	07 15		07 30			07 35		07 47		07 55		08 00		08 05
St Denys	d									07 40								
Swaythling	d									07 43								
Southampton Airport Pkwy ✈	d	07 01	07 08		07 22		07 38			07 46		07 54		08 03		08 08		
Portsmouth Harbour ⛴	d								06 59		07 23							
Portsmouth & Southsea	d								07 04		07 27							
Fratton	d								07 08		07 31							
Hilsea	d								07 12									
Cosham	d								07 17		07 39							
Portchester	d								07 22									
Fareham	d			07a27					07 28		07 47							08a27
Botley	d								07 35									
Hedge End	d								07 40									
Eastleigh ■	a		07 11						07 46	07 49				08 06				
	d		07 14						07 47	07 50				08 14				
Chandlers Ford	d									07 55								
Romsey	a									08 03	08 21							
Shawford	d		07 19											08 19			←	
Winchester	d	07 09	07 25		07 31		07 48		07 56			08 03		08 25		08 18	08 25	
Micheldever	d								08 05					→				
Basingstoke	a	07 24	07 41		07 46				08 15			08 17				08 34	08 41	
	d	07 25	07 43		07 47			07 54	08 17			08 19	08 24			08 35	08 43	
Reading ■	a	07 42			08 04							08 35						
Fleet	d		07 54					08 10					08 40				08 54	
Farnborough (Main)	d		08 00					08 16	08 30				08 46				09 00	
Woking	a		08 09				08 21	08 28	08 39				08 58					
Clapham Junction ■	a		08 30					08 57								09 12	09 25	
London Waterloo ■ ⊖	a		08 39				08 49	09 05	09 08				09 36			09 20	09 34	

A ⊼ from Bournemouth

Table 158

Saturdays from 13 October

Weymouth, Bournemouth, Lymington, Romsey, Southampton and Basingstoke - London

Network Diagram - see first Page of Table 158

		GW		XC	SW		SW	SW	SW	GW		SW				SW	SW	SW	SW	SW	GW	XC		SW	SW
				◇■	■		◇■	■	■	◇		■				■	■	■	◇■	■	◇	◇■		■	◇■
							A												A						A
				⌶			⌶			⌶									⌶			⌶			⌶
Weymouth	d						06 50												07 17						08 00
Upwey	d						06 54												07 21						
Dorchester West	a																								
Dorchester South	d						07 02												07 33						08 10
Moreton (Dorset)	d						07 09												07 39						
Wool	d						07 15												07 45						
Wareham	d						07 22												07 53						08 25
Holton Heath	d						07 26												07 56						
Hamworthy	d						07 31												08 01						08 32
Poole [4]	a						07 38												08 06						08 37
	d						07 39										07 50		08 07						08 38
Parkstone (Dorset)	d						07 43										07 54								08 42
Branksome	d						07 46										07 57								08 46
Bournemouth	a						07 54										08 02		08 17						08 54
	d			07 45			07 59										08 05		08 22			08 45			08 59
Pokesdown	d																08 09		08 26						
Christchurch	d																08 13		08 30						
Hinton Admiral	d																08 18								
New Milton	d																08 22		08 37						
Sway	d																08 27								
Lymington Pier	d				07 57													08 27						08 57	
Lymington Town	d				07 59													08 29						08 59	
Brockenhurst [3]	a			07 58	08 07		08 14										08 32	08 37	08 44			08 58		09 07	09 14
	d			08 00			08 15										08 33		08 45			09 00			09 15
Beaulieu Road	d																								
Ashurst New Forest	d																08 40								
Totton	d																08 45								
Salisbury	d	07 36										07 56									08 32				
Dean	d											08 08													
Mottisfont & Dunbridge	d											08 14													
Romsey	d	07 55										08 19									08 50				
Redbridge	d											08 27													
Millbrook (Hants)	d											08 31													
Southampton Central	a	08 07		08 12			08 28					08 34					08 52		08 58		09 03	09 12			09 28
	d			08 15			08 30					08 35					08 55		09 00		09 05	09 15			09 30
St Denys	d											08 40													
Swaythling	d											08 43													
Southampton Airport Pkwy ✈	d			08 22			08 38					08 46					09 03		09 08			09 22			09 38
Portsmouth Harbour	d								07 59	08 23															
Portsmouth & Southsea	d								08 04	08 27															
Fratton	d								08 08	08 31															
Hilsea	d								08 12																
Cosham	d								08 17	08 39															
Portchester	d								08 22																
Fareham	d								08 28	08 47											09a27				
Botley	d								08 35																
Hedge End	d								08 40																
Eastleigh [3]	a								08 46			08 49					09 06								
	d								08 47			08 50					09 14								
Chandlers Ford	d											08 55													
Romsey	a									09 21		09 03													
Shawford	d																09 19			←					
Winchester	d			08 31			08 48		08 56								09 25		09 18	09 25		09 31			09 48
Micheldever	d								09 05								→								
Basingstoke	a			08 46					09 15										09 34	09 41		09 46			
	d			08 47				08 54	09 17							09 24			09 35	09 43		09 47			
Reading [7]	a			09 04																		10 04			
Fleet	d							09 10								09 40				09 54					
Farnborough (Main)	d							09 16	09 30							09 46				10 00					
Woking	a						09 19	09 28	09 39							09 58									10 19
Clapham Junction [10]	a							09 57											10 12	10 25					
London Waterloo [15] ⊖	a						09 49	10 05	10 07							10 36			10 20	10 34					10 49

A ⌶ from Bournemouth

Table 158

Saturdays from 13 October

Weymouth, Bournemouth, Lymington, Romsey, Southampton and Basingstoke - London

Network Diagram - see first Page of Table 158

		SW	SW	GW		SW				XC	SW	SW	SW	SW	SW	GW	GW	XC		SW	SW	SW	SW	GW	
		■	■	◇		■				◇■	■	■	■	◇■	■	◇	◇	◇■		■	◇■	■	■	◇	
														A							A				
				⌶						⌶				⌶				⌶			⌶				
Weymouth	d													08 20		08 46					09 03				
Upwey	d													08 24		08 51									
Dorchester West	a															08 58									
Dorchester South	d													08 33							09 13				
Moreton (Dorset)	d													08 39											
Wool	d													08 45											
Wareham	d													08 53							09 28				
Holton Heath	d													08 56											
Hamworthy	d													09 01							09 35				
Poole [4]	a													09 07							09 39				
	d											08 50		09 07							09 40				
Parkstone (Dorset)	d											08 54									09 44				
Branksome	d											08 57									09 48				
Bournemouth	a											09 02		09 17							09 54				
	d											09 05		09 22				09 45			09 59				
Pokesdown	d											09 09		09 26											
Christchurch	d											09 13		09 30											
Hinton Admiral	d											09 18													
New Milton	d											09 22		09 37											
Sway	d											09 27													
Lymington Pier	d												09 27							09 57					
Lymington Town	d												09 29							09 59					
Brockenhurst [3]	a											09 32	09 37	09 44				09 58		10 07	10 14				
	d											09 33		09 45				10 00			10 15				
Beaulieu Road	d											09 38													
Ashurst New Forest	d											09 42													
Totton	d											09 47													
Salisbury	d					08 56											09 32								
Dean	d					09 08																			
Mottisfont & Dunbridge	d					09 14																			
Romsey	d					09 19											09 50								
Redbridge	d					09 27																			
Millbrook (Hants)	d					09 31																			
Southampton Central	a					09 34						09 53		09 58			10 03	10 12			10 28				
	d					09 35				09 47		09 55		10 00			10 05	10 15			10 30				
St Denys	d					09 40																			
Swaythling	d					09 43																			
Southampton Airport Pkwy ✈	d					09 46				09 54		10 03		10 08				10 22			10 38				
Portsmouth Harbour	d		08 59	09 23																			09 59	10 23	
Portsmouth & Southsea	d		09 04	09 27																			10 04	10 27	
Fratton	d		09 08	09 31																			10 08	10 31	
Hilsea	d		09 12																				10 12		
Cosham	d		09 17	09 39																			10 17	10 39	
Portchester	d		09 22																				10 22		
Fareham	d		09 28	09 47													10a27						10 28	10 47	
Botley	d		09 35																				10 35		
Hedge End	d		09 40																				10 40		
Eastleigh [3]	a		09 46			09 49						10 06											10 46		
	d		09 47			09 50						10 14											10 47		
Chandlers Ford	d					09 55																			
Romsey	a			10 21		10 03																		11 21	
Shawford	d											10 19			←										
Winchester	d		09 56							10 03		10 25		10 18	10 25			10 31			10 48		10 56		
Micheldever	d		10 05									→											11 05		
Basingstoke	a		10 15							10 17				10 34	10 41			10 46					11 15		
	d	09 54	10 17							10 19	10 24			10 35	10 43			10 47				10 54	11 17		
Reading [7]	a									10 34								11 04							
Fleet	d	10 10									10 40				10 54							11 10			
Farnborough (Main)	d	10 16	10 30								10 46				11 00							11 16	11 30		
Woking	a	10 28	10 39								10 58										11 19	11 28	11 39		
Clapham Junction [10]	a	10 57												11 12	11 25							11 57			
London Waterloo [15] ⊖	a	11 05	11 07								11 36			11 20	11 34						11 49	12 05	12 07		

A ⌶ from Bournemouth

Saturdays from 13 October

Weymouth, Bournemouth, Lymington, Romsey, Southampton and Basingstoke - London

Network Diagram - see first Page of Table 158

		SW 1	SW 1	SW 1	SW 1	SW ◇1 A ⌶	SW 1	GW ◇	XC ◇1 ⌶	SW 1	SW ◇1 A ⌶	SW 1	SW 1	GW ◇	SW 1	XC ◇1 ⌶	SW 1
Weymouth	d					09 20					10 03						
Upwey	d					09 24											
Dorchester West	a																
Dorchester South	d					09 33					10 13						
Moreton (Dorset)	d					09 39											
Wool	d					09 45											
Wareham	d					09 53					10 28						
Holton Heath	d					09 56											
Hamworthy	d					10 01					10 35						
Poole 4	a					10 06					10 39						
	d			09 50		10 07					10 40						
Parkstone (Dorset)	d			09 54							10 44						
Branksome	d			09 57							10 48						
Bournemouth	a			10 02		10 17					10 54						
	d			10 05		10 22			10 45		10 59						
Pokesdown	d			10 09		10 26											
Christchurch	d			10 13		10 30											
Hinton Admiral	d			10 18													
New Milton	d			10 22		10 37											
Sway	d			10 27													
Lymington Pier	d				10 27					10 57							
Lymington Town	d				10 29					10 59							
Brockenhurst 3	a			10 32	10 37	10 44			10 58	11 07	11 14						
	d			10 33		10 45			11 00		11 15						
Beaulieu Road	d																
Ashurst New Forest	d			10 40													
Totton	d			10 45													
Salisbury	d	09 56						10 32							10 56		
Dean	d	10 08													11 08		
Mottisfont & Dunbridge	d	10 14													11 14		
Romsey	d	10 19						10 50							11 19		
Redbridge	d	10 27													11 27		
Millbrook (Hants)	d	10 31													11 31		
Southampton Central ⛴	a	10 34		10 53		10 58		11 03	11 12		11 28				11 34		
	d	10 35		10 55		11 00		11 05	11 15		11 30				11 35	11 47	
St Denys	d	10 40													11 40		
Swaythling	d	10 43													11 43		
Southampton Airport Pkwy ✈	d	10 46		11 03		11 08			11 22		11 38				11 46	11 54	
Portsmouth Harbour ⛴	d												10 59	11 23			
Portsmouth & Southsea	d												11 04	11 27			
Fratton	d												11 08	11 31			
Hilsea	d												11 12				
Cosham	d												11 17	11 39			
Portchester	d												11 22				
Fareham	d							11a27					11 28	11 47			
Botley	d												11 35				
Hedge End	d												11 40				
Eastleigh 8	a	10 49		11 06									11 46		11 49		
	d	10 50		11 14									11 47		11 50		
Chandlers Ford	d	10 55													11 55		
Romsey	a	11 03												12 21	12 03		
Shawford	d			11 19			←										
Winchester	d			11 25		11 18	11 25		11 31		11 48		11 56			12 03	
Micheldever	d			→									12 05				
Basingstoke	a					11 34	11 41		11 46				12 15			12 17	
	d		11 24			11 35	11 43		11 47			11 54	12 17			12 19	12 24
Reading 7	a								12 04							12 35	
Fleet	d		11 40				11 54					12 10					12 40
Farnborough (Main)	d		11 46				12 00					12 16	12 30				12 46
Woking	a		11 58								12 19	12 28	12 39				12 58
Clapham Junction 10	a					12 12	12 25					12 57					
London Waterloo 15 ⊖	a		12 36			12 21	12 34				12 51	13 05	13 07				13 36

A ⌶ from Bournemouth

Saturdays from 13 October

Weymouth, Bournemouth, Lymington, Romsey, Southampton and Basingstoke - London

Network Diagram - see first Page of Table 158

		SW 1	SW 1	SW ◇1 A ⌶	SW 1	GW ◇ ⌶	XC ◇1 ⌶	GW	SW 1	SW ◇1 A ⌶	GW ◇	SW 1	SW 1	GW ◇	SW 1	SW 1	SW 1	SW 1	SW ◇1 A ⌶
Weymouth	d			10 20						11 03	11 10								11 20
Upwey	d			10 24							11 15								11 24
Dorchester West	a										11 23								
Dorchester South	d			10 33						11 13									11 33
Moreton (Dorset)	d			10 39															11 39
Wool	d			10 45															11 45
Wareham	d			10 53						11 28									11 53
Holton Heath	d			10 56															11 56
Hamworthy	d			11 01						11 35									12 01
Poole 4	a			11 06						11 39									12 06
	d	10 50		11 07						11 40							11 50		12 07
Parkstone (Dorset)	d	10 54								11 44							11 54		
Branksome	d	10 57								11 48							11 57		
Bournemouth	a	11 02		11 17						11 54							12 02		12 17
	d	11 05		11 22			11 45			11 59							12 05		12 22
Pokesdown	d	11 09		11 26													12 09		12 26
Christchurch	d	11 13		11 30													12 13		12 30
Hinton Admiral	d	11 18															12 18		
New Milton	d	11 22		11 37													12 22		12 37
Sway	d	11 27															12 27		
Lymington Pier	d		11 27						11 57									12 27	
Lymington Town	d		11 29						11 59									12 29	
Brockenhurst 3	a	11 32	11 37	11 44			11 58		12 07	12 14							12 32	12 37	12 44
	d	11 33		11 45			12 00			12 15							12 33		12 45
Beaulieu Road	d	11 38																	
Ashurst New Forest	d	11 42															12 40		
Totton	d	11 47															12 45		
Salisbury	d					11 32		11 43							11 56				
Dean	d														12 08				
Mottisfont & Dunbridge	d														12 14				
Romsey	d					11 50		12 04							12 19				
Redbridge	d														12 27				
Millbrook (Hants)	d														12 31				
Southampton Central ⛴	a	11 53		11 58		12 03	12 12	12 20		12 28					12 34		12 51		12 58
	d	11 55		12 00		12 05	12 15			12 30					12 35		12 55		13 00
St Denys	d														12 40				
Swaythling	d														12 43				
Southampton Airport Pkwy ✈	d	12 03		12 08			12 22			12 38					12 46		13 03		13 08
Portsmouth Harbour ⛴	d												11 59	12 23					
Portsmouth & Southsea	d												12 04	12 27					
Fratton	d												12 08	12 31					
Hilsea	d												12 12						
Cosham	d												12 17	12 39					
Portchester	d												12 22						
Fareham	d					12a27							12 28	12 47					
Botley	d												12 35						
Hedge End	d												12 40						
Eastleigh 8	a	12 06											12 46		12 49		13 06		
	d	12 14											12 47		12 50		13 14		
Chandlers Ford	d														12 55				
Romsey	a													13 21	13 03				
Shawford	d	12 19			←												13 19		
Winchester	d	12 25		12 18	12 25		12 31			12 48			12 56				13 25		13 18
Micheldever	d	→											13 05				→		
Basingstoke	a			12 34	12 41		12 46						13 15						13 34
	d			12 35	12 43		12 47					12 54	13 17			13 24			13 35
Reading 7	a						13 04												
Fleet	d				12 54							13 10				13 40			
Farnborough (Main)	d				13 00							13 16	13 30			13 46			
Woking	a									13 19		13 28	13 39			13 58			
Clapham Junction 10	a			13 12	13 25							13 57							14 12
London Waterloo 15 ⊖	a			13 21	13 34					13 51		14 05	14 07			14 36			14 21

A ⌶ from Bournemouth

Table 158

Saturdays
from 13 October

Weymouth, Bournemouth, Lymington, Romsey, Southampton and Basingstoke - London

Network Diagram - see first Page of Table 158

		SW ■	GW ◇ ⌶	XC ◇■ ⌶	SW ■	SW ◇■ A ⌶	SW ■	SW ■	GW ◇	SW ■	XC ◇■ ⌶	SW ■	SW ■	SW ■	SW ◇■ A ⌶	SW ■	GW ◇ ⌶	XC ◇■ ⌶	SW ■
Weymouth	d					12 03									12 20				
Upwey	d														12 24				
Dorchester West	a																		
Dorchester South	d					12 13									12 33				
Moreton (Dorset)	d														12 39				
Wool	d														12 45				
Wareham	d					12 28									12 53				
Holton Heath	d														12 56				
Hamworthy	d					12 35									13 01				
Poole ■	a					12 39									13 06				
	d					12 40							12 50		13 07				
Parkstone (Dorset)	d					12 44							12 54						
Branksome	d					12 48							12 57						
Bournemouth	a					12 54							13 02		13 17				
	d			12 45		12 59							13 05		13 22			13 45	
Pokesdown	d												13 09		13 26				
Christchurch	d												13 13		13 30				
Hinton Admiral	d												13 18						
New Milton	d												13 22		13 37				
Sway	d												13 27						
Lymington Pier	d				12 57									13 27					13 57
Lymington Town	d				12 59									13 29					13 59
Brockenhurst ■	a			12 58	13 07	13 14							13 32	13 37	13 44			13 58	14 07
	d			13 00		13 15							13 33		13 45			14 00	
Beaulieu Road	d												13 38						
Ashurst New Forest	d												13 42						
Totton	d												13 47						
Salisbury	d		12 32							12 56							13 32		
Dean	d									13 08									
Mottisfont & Dunbridge	d									13 14									
Romsey	d		12 50							13 19							13 50		
Redbridge	d									13 27									
Millbrook (Hants)	d									13 31									
Southampton Central ⛴	a		13 03	13 12		13 28				13 34			13 53		13 58		14 03	14 12	
	d		13 05	13 15		13 30				13 35	13 47		13 55		14 00		14 05	14 15	
St Denys	d									13 40									
Swaythling	d									13 43									
Southampton Airport Pkwy ✈	d			13 22		13 38				13 46	13 54		14 03		14 08			14 22	
Portsmouth Harbour ⛴	d							12 59	13 23										
Portsmouth & Southsea	d							13 04	13 27										
Fratton	d							13 08	13 31										
Hilsea	d							13 12											
Cosham	d							13 17	13 39										
Portchester	d							13 22											
Fareham	d		13a27					13 28	13 47								14a27		
Botley	d							13 35											
Hedge End	d							13 40											
Eastleigh ■	a							13 46		13 49			14 06						
	d							13 47		13 50			14 14						
Chandlers Ford	d									13 55									
Romsey	a								14 21	14 03									
Shawford	d	←											14 19			←			
Winchester	d	13 25		13 31		13 48		13 56			14 03		14 25		14 18	14 25		14 31	
Micheldever	d							14 05					→						
Basingstoke	a	13 41		13 46				14 15			14 17				14 34	14 41		14 46	
	d	13 43		13 47			13 54	14 17			14 19	14 24			14 35	14 43		14 47	
Reading ■	a			14 04							14 35							15 04	
Fleet	d	13 54					14 10					14 40				14 54			
Farnborough (Main)	d	14 00					14 16	14 30				14 46				15 00			
Woking	a					14 19	14 28	14 39				14 58							
Clapham Junction ■	a	14 25					14 57								15 12	15 25			
London Waterloo ■ ⊖	a	14 34				14 51	15 05	15 07				15 36			15 21	15 34			

A ⌶ from Bournemouth

Table 158

Saturdays
from 13 October

Weymouth, Bournemouth, Lymington, Romsey, Southampton and Basingstoke - London

Network Diagram - see first Page of Table 158

		SW ◇■ A ⌶	GW ◇	SW ■	SW ■	GW ◇	GW ◇	SW ■	SW ■	SW ■	SW ■	SW ◇■ A ⌶	SW ■	GW ◇	XC ◇■ ⌶	SW ■	SW ◇■ A ⌶	SW ■	SW ■	GW ◇
Weymouth	d	13 03	13 10									13 20					14 03			
Upwey	d		13 15									13 24								
Dorchester West	a		13 22																	
Dorchester South	d	13 13										13 33					14 13			
Moreton (Dorset)	d											13 39								
Wool	d											13 45								
Wareham	d	13 28										13 53					14 28			
Holton Heath	d											13 56								
Hamworthy	d	13 35										14 01					14 35			
Poole ■	a	13 39										14 06					14 39			
	d	13 40								13 50		14 07					14 40			
Parkstone (Dorset)	d	13 44								13 54							14 44			
Branksome	d	13 48								13 57							14 48			
Bournemouth	a	13 54								14 02		14 17					14 54			
	d	13 59								14 05		14 22			14 45		14 59			
Pokesdown	d									14 09		14 26								
Christchurch	d									14 13		14 30								
Hinton Admiral	d									14 18										
New Milton	d									14 22		14 37								
Sway	d									14 27										
Lymington Pier	d										14 27					14 57				
Lymington Town	d										14 29					14 59				
Brockenhurst ■	a	14 14								14 32	14 37	14 44			14 58	15 07	15 14			
	d	14 15								14 33		14 45			15 00		15 15			
Beaulieu Road	d																			
Ashurst New Forest	d									14 40										
Totton	d									14 45										
Salisbury	d						14 00	13 50						14 32						
Dean	d							14 02												
Mottisfont & Dunbridge	d							14 08												
Romsey	d						14 20	14 13						14 50						
Redbridge	d							14 21												
Millbrook (Hants)	d							14 24												
Southampton Central ⛴	a	14 28					14 32	14 28		14 51		14 58		15 03	15 12		15 28			
	d	14 30					14 34	14 35		14 55		15 00		15 05	15 15		15 30			
St Denys	d							14 40												
Swaythling	d							14 43												
Southampton Airport Pkwy ✈	d	14 38						14 46		15 03		15 08			15 22		15 38			
Portsmouth Harbour ⛴	d				13 59	14 23													14 59	15 23
Portsmouth & Southsea	d				14 04	14 27													15 04	15 27
Fratton	d				14 08	14 31													15 08	15 31
Hilsea	d				14 12														15 12	
Cosham	d				14 17	14 39													15 17	15 39
Portchester	d				14 22														15 22	
Fareham	d				14 28	14 47	14a54							15a27					15 28	15 47
Botley	d				14 35														15 35	
Hedge End	d				14 40														15 40	
Eastleigh ■	a				14 46			14 49		15 06									15 46	
	d				14 47			14 50		15 14									15 47	
Chandlers Ford	d							14 55												
Romsey	a					15 21		15 04												16 21
Shawford	d									15 19			←							
Winchester	d	14 48			14 56					15 25		15 18	15 25		15 31		15 48		15 56	
Micheldever	d				15 05					→									16 05	
Basingstoke	a				15 15							15 34	15 41		15 46				16 15	
	d			14 54	15 17				15 24			15 35	15 43		15 47			15 54	16 17	
Reading ■	a														16 05					
Fleet	d			15 10					15 40				15 54					16 10		
Farnborough (Main)	d			15 16	15 30				15 46				16 00					16 16	16 30	
Woking	a	15 19		15 28	15 39				15 58								16 19	16 28	16 39	
Clapham Junction ■	a			15 57								16 12	16 25					16 57		
London Waterloo ■ ⊖	a	15 51		16 05	16 07				16 36			16 20	16 34				16 49	17 05	17 07	

A ⌶ from Bournemouth

Saturdays
from 13 October

Weymouth, Bournemouth, Lymington, Romsey, Southampton and Basingstoke - London

Network Diagram - see first Page of Table 158

		SW 1	XC ◇1 ✠	SW 1	SW 1	SW 1	SW ◇1 A ✠	SW 1	GW ◇	XC ◇1 ✠	SW 1	SW ◇1 A ✠	GW ◇	SW 1	SW 1	GW 1	SW 1
Weymouth	d						14 20					15 03	15 08				
Upwey	d						14 24						15 13				
Dorchester West	a												15 20				
Dorchester South	d						14 33					15 13					
Moreton (Dorset)	d						14 39										
Wool	d						14 45										
Wareham	d						14 53					15 28					
Holton Heath	d						14 56										
Hamworthy	d						15 01					15 35					
Poole 4	a						15 06					15 39					
	d				14 50		15 07					15 40					
Parkstone (Dorset)	d				14 54							15 44					
Branksome	d				14 57							15 48					
Bournemouth	a				15 02		15 17					15 54					
	d				15 05		15 22			15 45		15 59					
Pokesdown	d				15 09		15 26										
Christchurch	d				15 13		15 30										
Hinton Admiral	d				15 18												
New Milton	d				15 22		15 37										
Sway	d				15 27												
Lymington Pier	d					15 27					15 57						
Lymington Town	d					15 29					15 59						
Brockenhurst 3	a				15 32	15 37	15 44			15 58	16 07	16 14					
	d				15 33		15 45			16 00		16 15					
Beaulieu Road	d				15 38												
Ashurst New Forest	d				15 42												
Totton	d				15 47												
Salisbury	d	14 56							15 32								15 56
Dean	d	15 08															16 08
Mottisfont & Dunbridge	d	15 14															16 14
Romsey	d	15 19							15 50								16 19
Redbridge	d	15 27															16 27
Millbrook (Hants)	d	15 31															16 31
Southampton Central ⛴	a	15 34			15 53		15 58		16 03	16 12		16 28					16 34
	d	15 35	15 47		15 55		16 00		16 05	16 15		16 30					16 35
St Denys	d	15 40															16 40
Swaythling	d	15 43															16 43
Southampton Airport Pkwy ✈	d	15 46	15 54		16 03		16 08			16 22		16 38					16 46
Portsmouth Harbour ⛴	d														15 59	16 23	
Portsmouth & Southsea	d														16 04	16 27	
Fratton	d														16 08	16 31	
Hilsea	d														16 12		
Cosham	d														16 17	16 39	
Portchester	d														16 22		
Fareham	d								16a27						16 28	16 47	
Botley	d														16 35		
Hedge End	d														16 40		
Eastleigh 8	a	15 49			16 06										16 46		16 49
	d	15 50			16 14										16 47		16 50
Chandlers Ford	d	15 55															16 55
Romsey	a	16 03														17 21	17 03
Shawford	d				16 19			←									
Winchester	d		16 03		16 25		16 18	16 25		16 31		16 48			16 56		
Micheldever	d				→										17 05		
Basingstoke	a		16 17				16 34	16 41		16 46					17 15		
	d		16 19	16 24			16 35	16 43		16 47				16 54	17 17		
Reading 7	a		16 35							17 04							
Fleet	d			16 40				16 54						17 10			
Farnborough (Main)	d			16 46				17 00						17 16	17 30		
Woking	a			16 58								17 19		17 28	17 39		
Clapham Junction 10	a						17 12	17 25						17 57			
London Waterloo 15 ⊖	a			17 36			17 20	17 34				17 49		18 05	18 07		

A ✠ from Bournemouth

Saturdays
from 13 October

Weymouth, Bournemouth, Lymington, Romsey, Southampton and Basingstoke - London

Network Diagram - see first Page of Table 158

		SW 1	SW 1	SW 1	SW ◇1 A ✠	SW 1	GW ◇	XC ◇1 ✠	SW 1	SW ◇1 A ✠	SW 1	SW 1	GW ◇	SW 1	SW 1	XC ◇1 ✠	SW 1	SW 1	SW 1
Weymouth	d				15 20					16 03									
Upwey	d				15 24														
Dorchester West	a																		
Dorchester South	d				15 33					16 13									
Moreton (Dorset)	d				15 39														
Wool	d				15 45														
Wareham	d				15 53					16 28									
Holton Heath	d				15 56														
Hamworthy	d				16 01					16 35									
Poole 4	a				16 06					16 39									
	d		15 50		16 07					16 40								16 50	
Parkstone (Dorset)	d		15 54							16 44								16 54	
Branksome	d		15 57							16 48								16 57	
Bournemouth	a		16 02		16 17					16 54								17 02	
	d		16 05		16 22			16 45		16 59								17 05	
Pokesdown	d		16 09		16 26													17 09	
Christchurch	d		16 13		16 30													17 13	
Hinton Admiral	d		16 18															17 18	
New Milton	d		16 22		16 37													17 22	
Sway	d		16 27															17 27	
Lymington Pier	d			16 27					16 57										17 27
Lymington Town	d			16 29					16 59										17 29
Brockenhurst 3	a		16 32	16 37	16 44			16 58	17 07	17 14								17 32	17 37
	d		16 33		16 45			17 00		17 15								17 33	
Beaulieu Road	d																	17 38	
Ashurst New Forest	d		16 40															17 42	
Totton	d		16 45															17 47	
Salisbury	d						16 32							16 56					
Dean	d													17 08					
Mottisfont & Dunbridge	d													17 14					
Romsey	d						16 50							17 19					
Redbridge	d													17 27					
Millbrook (Hants)	d													17 31					
Southampton Central ⛴	a		16 51		16 58		17 03	17 12		17 28				17 34				17 53	
	d		16 55		17 00		17 05	17 15		17 30				17 35		17 47		17 55	
St Denys	d													17 40					
Swaythling	d													17 43					
Southampton Airport Pkwy ✈	d		17 03		17 08			17 22		17 38				17 46		17 54		18 03	
Portsmouth Harbour ⛴	d											16 59	17 23		17 33				
Portsmouth & Southsea	d											17 04	17 27		17 38				
Fratton	d											17 08	17 31		17 42				
Hilsea	d											17 12			17 46				
Cosham	d											17 17	17 39		17 51				
Portchester	d											17 22			17 56				
Fareham	d						17a27					17 28	17 47		18a01				
Botley	d											17 35							
Hedge End	d											17 40							
Eastleigh 8	a		17 06									17 46		17 49				18 06	
	d		17 14									17 47		17 50				18 14	
Chandlers Ford	d													17 55					
Romsey	a												18 21	18 03					
Shawford	d		17 19			←												18 19	
Winchester	d		17 25		17 18	17 25		17 31		17 48		17 56				18 03		18 25	
Micheldever	d		→									18 05						→	
Basingstoke	a				17 34	17 41		17 46				18 15				18 17			
	d	17 24			17 35	17 43		17 47			17 54	18 17				18 19	18 24		
Reading 7	a							18 04								18 35			
Fleet	d	17 40				17 54					18 10						18 40		
Farnborough (Main)	d	17 46				18 00					18 16	18 30					18 46		
Woking	a	17 58								18 19	18 28	18 39					18 58		
Clapham Junction 10	a				18 12	18 25					18 57								
London Waterloo 15 ⊖	a	18 36			18 20	18 34				18 49	19 05	19 07					19 36		

A ✠ from Bournemouth

Table 158

Saturdays from 13 October

Weymouth, Bournemouth, Lymington, Romsey, Southampton and Basingstoke - London

Network Diagram - see first Page of Table 158

		SW ◇■ A 🍴	SW ■	GW ◇	XC ◇■ 🍴	SW ■	SW ◇■ A 🍴	SW ■	SW ■	GW ◇	SW ■	SW ■	SW ■	SW ■	SW ◇■ A 🍴	SW ■	GW ◇	GW ■	XC ◇■ 🍴	SW ■
Weymouth	d	16 20					17 03								17 20		17 28			
Upwey	d	16 24													17 24		17 33			
Dorchester West	a																17 40			
Dorchester South	d	16 33					17 13								17 33					
Moreton (Dorset)	d	16 39													17 39					
Wool	d	16 45													17 45					
Wareham	d	16 53					17 28								17 53					
Holton Heath	d	16 56													17 56					
Hamworthy	d	17 01					17 35								18 01					
Poole ■	a	17 06					17 39								18 06					
	d	17 07					17 40						17 50		18 07					
Parkstone (Dorset)	d						17 44						17 54							
Branksome	d						17 48						17 57							
Bournemouth	a	17 17					17 54						18 02		18 17					
	d	17 22			17 45		17 59						18 05		18 22				18 45	
Pokesdown	d	17 26											18 09		18 26					
Christchurch	d	17 30											18 13		18 30					
Hinton Admiral	d												18 18							
New Milton	d	17 37											18 22		18 37					
Sway	d												18 27							
Lymington Pier	d					17 57								18 27						18 57
Lymington Town	d					17 59								18 29						18 59
Brockenhurst ■	a	17 44			17 58	18 07	18 14						18 32	18 37	18 44				18 58	19 07
	d	17 45			18 00		18 15						18 33		18 45				19 00	
Beaulieu Road	d																			
Ashurst New Forest	d												18 40							
Totton	d												18 45							
Salisbury	d			17 32							17 56							18 32		
Dean	d										18 08									
Mottisfont & Dunbridge	d										18 14									
Romsey	d			17 50							18 19							18 50		
Redbridge	d										18 27									
Millbrook (Hants)	d										18 31									
Southampton Central ⛴	a	17 58		18 03	18 12		18 28				18 34		18 51		18 58			19 03	19 12	
	d	18 00		18 05	18 15		18 30				18 35		18 55		19 00			19 05	19 15	
St Denys	d										18 40									
Swaythling	d										18 43									
Southampton Airport Pkwy ✈	d	18 08			18 22		18 38				18 46		19 03		19 08				19 22	
Portsmouth Harbour ⛴	d								17 59	18 23										
Portsmouth & Southsea	d								18 04	18 27										
Fratton	d								18 08	18 31										
Hilsea	d								18 12											
Cosham	d								18 17	18 39										
Portchester	d								18 22											
Fareham	d			18a27					18 28	18 47								19a27		
Botley	d								18 35											
Hedge End	d								18 40											
Eastleigh ■	a								18 46		18 49		19 06							
	d								18 47		18 50		19 14							
Chandlers Ford	d										18 55									
Romsey	a									19 21	19 04									
Shawford	d		←										19 19			←				
Winchester	d	18 18	18 25		18 31		18 48		18 56				19 25		19 18	19 25			19 31	
Micheldever	d								19 05				→							
Basingstoke	a	18 34	18 41		18 46				19 15						19 34	19 41			19 46	
	d	18 35	18 43		18 47			18 54	19 17			19 24			19 35	19 43			19 47	
Reading ■	a				19 04														20 04	
Fleet	d		18 54					19 10				19 40				19 54				
Farnborough (Main)	d		19 00					19 16	19 30			19 46				20 00				
Woking	a						19 19	19 28	19 39			19 58								
Clapham Junction ■	a	19 12	19 25					19 57							20 12	20 25				
London Waterloo ■ ⊖	a	19 20	19 34				19 49	20 05	20 07			20 36			20 20	20 34				

A 🍴 from Bournemouth

Table 158

Saturdays from 13 October

Weymouth, Bournemouth, Lymington, Romsey, Southampton and Basingstoke - London

Network Diagram - see first Page of Table 158

		SW ◇■ A 🍴	SW ■	SW ■	GW ◇	SW ■	SW ■	SW ■	SW ■	SW ◇■ A 🍴	SW ■	GW ◇	XC ◇■	GW	SW ■	SW ◇■ A 🍴	SW ■	SW ■	GW ◇
Weymouth	d	18 06								18 20						19 03			
Upwey	d									18 24									
Dorchester West	a																		
Dorchester South	d	18 16								18 33						19 13			
Moreton (Dorset)	d									18 39									
Wool	d									18 45									
Wareham	d	18 31								18 53						19 28			
Holton Heath	d									18 56									
Hamworthy	d	18 38								19 01						19 35			
Poole ■	a	18 42								19 06						19 39			
	d	18 43						18 50		19 07						19 40			
Parkstone (Dorset)	d	18 47						18 54								19 44			
Branksome	d	18 51						18 57								19 48			
Bournemouth	a	18 56						19 02		19 17						19 54			
	d	18 59						19 05		19 22			19 45			19 59			
Pokesdown	d							19 09		19 26									
Christchurch	d							19 13		19 30									
Hinton Admiral	d							19 18											
New Milton	d							19 22		19 37									
Sway	d							19 27											
Lymington Pier	d								19 27						19 57				
Lymington Town	d								19 29						19 59				
Brockenhurst ■	a	19 14						19 32	19 37	19 44			19 58		20 07	20 14			
	d	19 15						19 33		19 45			20 00			20 15			
Beaulieu Road	d																		
Ashurst New Forest	d							19 40											
Totton	d							19 45											
Salisbury	d					18 56						19 32		19 41					
Dean	d					19 08													
Mottisfont & Dunbridge	d					19 14													
Romsey	d					19 19						19 50		20 04					
Redbridge	d					19 27													
Millbrook (Hants)	d					19 31													
Southampton Central ⛴	a	19 28				19 34		19 51		19 58		20 02	20 12	20 18		20 28			
	d	19 30				19 35		19 55		20 00		20 05	20 15			20 30			
St Denys	d					19 40													
Swaythling	d					19 43													
Southampton Airport Pkwy ✈	d	19 38				19 46		20 03		20 08			20 22			20 38			
Portsmouth Harbour ⛴	d			18 59	19 23													19 59	20 23
Portsmouth & Southsea	d			19 04	19 27													20 04	20 27
Fratton	d			19 08	19 31													20 08	20 31
Hilsea	d			19 12														20 12	
Cosham	d			19 17	19 39													20 17	
Portchester	d			19 22														20 22	
Fareham	d			19 28	19 47							20a27						20 28	20 47
Botley	d			19 35														20 35	
Hedge End	d			19 40														20 40	
Eastleigh ■	a			19 46		19 49		20 06										20 46	
	d			19 47		19 50		20 14										20 47	
Chandlers Ford	d					19 55													
Romsey	a				20 21	20 03													21 21
Shawford	d							20 19			←								
Winchester	d	19 48		19 56				20 25		20 18	20 25		20 31			20 48		20 56	
Micheldever	d			20 05				→										21 05	
Basingstoke	a			20 15						20 34	20 41		20 46					21 17	
	d		19 54	20 17			20 24			20 35	20 43		20 47				20 54	21 24	
Reading ■	a												21 04						
Fleet	d		20 10				20 40				20 54						21 10	21 40	
Farnborough (Main)	d		20 16	20 30			20 46				21 00						21 16	21 46	
Woking	a	20 19	20 28	20 39			20 58				21 09					21 19	21 28	21 58	
Clapham Junction ■	a		20 57							21 16	21 29						21 57		
London Waterloo ■ ⊖	a	20 49	21 05	21 07			21 34			21 24	21 38					21 49	22 07	22 34	

A 🍴 from Bournemouth

Saturdays
from 13 October

Weymouth, Bournemouth, Lymington, Romsey, Southampton and Basingstoke - London

Network Diagram - see first Page of Table 158

		SW ■	SW ■	SW ■	SW ◇■	SW ■	GW ◇	SW ■	SW ■	SW ■	SW ■	SW ■	SW ■	SW ■	SW ◇■
Weymouth	d				19 20										20 10
Upwey	d				19 24										20 14
Dorchester West	a														
Dorchester South	d				19 33										20 22
Moreton (Dorset)	d				19 39										20 28
Wool	d				19 45										20 34
Wareham	d				19 53										20 42
Holton Heath	d														
Hamworthy	d				20 01										20 48
Poole 4	a				20 06										20 53
	d		19 50		20 07										20 54
Parkstone (Dorset)	d		19 54												20 58
Branksome	d		19 57												21 01
Bournemouth	a		20 02		20 17										21 07
	d		20 05		20 22										21 12
Pokesdown	d		20 09		20 26										21 16
Christchurch	d		20 13		20 30										21 20
Hinton Admiral	d		20 18												21 25
New Milton	d		20 22		20 37										21 29
Sway	d		20 27												21 34
Lymington Pier	d			20 27				20 57	21 27						
Lymington Town	d			20 29				20 59	21 29						
Brockenhurst 3	a		20 32	20 37	20 44			21 07	21 37						21 39
	d		20 33		20 45										21 40
Beaulieu Road	d														
Ashurst New Forest	d		20 40												21 47
Totton	d		20 45												21 52
Salisbury	d	19 56					20 32						20 56		
Dean	d	20 08											21 08		
Mottisfont & Dunbridge	d	20 14											21 14		
Romsey	d	20 19					20 50						21 19		
Redbridge	d	20 27											21 27		
Millbrook (Hants)	d	20 31											21 31		
Southampton Central ⛴	a	20 34	20 51		20 58		21 03						21 34		21 57
	d	20 35	20 55		21 00		21 05			21 30			21 35	21 55	22 00
St Denys	d	20 40											21 40		
Swaythling	d	20 43											21 43		
Southampton Airport Pkwy ✈	d	20 46	21 03		21 08					21 38			21 46	22 03	22 08
Portsmouth Harbour ⛴	d											20 59			
Portsmouth & Southsea	d											21 04			
Fratton	d											21 08			
Hilsea	d											21 12			
Cosham	d											21 17			
Portchester	d											21 22			
Fareham	d						21a27					21 28			
Botley	d											21 35			
Hedge End	d											21 40			
Eastleigh 8	a	20 49	21 06									21 46	21 49	22 06	
	d	20 50	21 14									21 47	21 50	22 14	
Chandlers Ford	d	20 55											21 55		
Romsey	a	21 03											22 03		
Shawford	d		21 19			←								22 19	
Winchester	d		21 25		21 18	21 25				21 48		21 56		22 25	22 18
Micheldever	d		→									22 05		→	
Basingstoke	a				21 34	21 41						22 15			22 34
	d				21 35	21 43					21 54	22 24			22 35
Reading 7	a														
Fleet	d					21 54					22 10	22 40			
Farnborough (Main)	d					22 00					22 16	22 46			
Woking	a					22 09				22 19	22 28	22 58			22 53
Clapham Junction 10	a				22 14	22 29					22 57				23 14
London Waterloo 15 ⊖	a				22 22	22 38				22 49	23 05	23 32			23 22

Saturdays
from 13 October

Weymouth, Bournemouth, Lymington, Romsey, Southampton and Basingstoke - London

Network Diagram - see first Page of Table 158

		SW ■	GW	SW ■	GW ◇	SW ■	SW ■	SW ■	SW ■	SW ■	SW ■	GW ◇	SW ■	SW ■	SW ■	SW ■	SW ■
Weymouth	d		20 21								21 10					22 10	23 10
Upwey	d		20 26								21 14					22 14	23 14
Dorchester West	a		20 33														
Dorchester South	d										21 22					22 22	23 22
Moreton (Dorset)	d										21 28					22 28	23 28
Wool	d										21 34					22 34	23 34
Wareham	d										21 42					22 42	23 42
Holton Heath	d																
Hamworthy	d										21 48					22 48	23 48
Poole 4	a										21 53					22 53	23 53
	d										21 54					22 54	23 54
Parkstone (Dorset)	d										21 58					22 58	
Branksome	d										22 01					23 01	
Bournemouth	a										22 07					23 07	00 03
	d										22 12					23 12	
Pokesdown	d										22 16					23 16	
Christchurch	d										22 20					23 20	
Hinton Admiral	d										22 25					23 25	
New Milton	d										22 29					23 29	
Sway	d										22 34					23 34	
Lymington Pier	d					22 03							22 33				
Lymington Town	d					22 05							22 35				
Brockenhurst 3	a					22 13					22 39		22 43			23 39	
	d										22 40					23 40	
Beaulieu Road	d																
Ashurst New Forest	d										22 47					23 47	
Totton	d										22 52					23 52	
Salisbury	d				21 32				21 56			22 32					
Dean	d								22 08								
Mottisfont & Dunbridge	d								22 14								
Romsey	d				21 50				22 19			22 50		23 00			
Redbridge	d								22 27					23 08			
Millbrook (Hants)	d								22 31					23 12			
Southampton Central ⛴	a				22 03				22 34		22 57	23 03		23 15		23 57	
	d				22 05			22 30	22 35		23 00	23 05		23 21		23 59	
St Denys	d								22 40					23 26		00 04	
Swaythling	d								22 43					23 29		00 07	
Southampton Airport Pkwy ✈	d							22 38	22 46		23 08			23 32		00 10	
Portsmouth Harbour ⛴	d			21 54						22 33					23 24		
Portsmouth & Southsea	d			21 59						22 38					23 29		
Fratton	d			22 03						22 42					23 33		
Hilsea	d			22 07						22 46					23 37		
Cosham	d			22 12						22 51					23 42		
Portchester	d			22 17						22 56					23 47		
Fareham	d			22 23	22a26					23a01		23a26			23 53		
Botley	d			22 30											23 59		
Hedge End	d			22 35											00 05		
Eastleigh 8	a			22 41				22 41	22 49		23 11			23 35	00 11	00 14	
	d							22 46	22 50		23 12			23 37	00 21		
Chandlers Ford	d								22 55					23 42			
Romsey	a								23 03					23 49			
Shawford	d	←									23 18						
Winchester	d	22 25						22 55			23 24				00a30		
Micheldever	d										23 33						
Basingstoke	a	22 41						23 11			23 43						
	d	22 43					22 54	23 13			23 44						
Reading 7	a																
Fleet	d	22 54					23 10				00 01						
Farnborough (Main)	d	23 00					23 16				00 06						
Woking	a	23 09					23 28	23 31			00 18						
Clapham Junction 10	a	23 29					00 21	23 52			00 53						
London Waterloo 15 ⊖	a	23 39					00 35	00 03			01 04						

Table 158

Sundays until 24 June

Weymouth, Bournemouth, Lymington, Romsey, Southampton and Basingstoke - London

Network Diagram - see first Page of Table 158

		SW ■	SW ■	SW ■	SW ■	SW ■	SW ■	SW ■	SW ■	SW ■	SW ■	SW ◇■ A ⌶	SW ■	SW ■	SW ■	SW ◇■ B
Weymouth	d			21p10		22p10	23p10									
Upwey	d			21p14		22p14	23p14									
Dorchester West	a															
Dorchester South	d			21p22		22p22	23p22									
Moreton (Dorset)	d			21p28		22p28	23p28									
Wool	d			21p34		22p34	23p34									
Wareham	d			21p42		22p42	23p42									
Holton Heath	d															
Hamworthy	d			21p48		22p48	23p48									
Poole ■	a			21p53		22p53	23p53									
	d			21p54		22p54	23p54					06 50				07 50
Parkstone (Dorset)	d			21p58		22p58						06 54				07 54
Branksome	d			22p01		23p01						06 57				07 57
Bournemouth	a			22p07		23p07	00 03					07 02				08 02
	d			22p12		23p12						07 06				08 06
Pokesdown	d			22p16		23p16						07 10				08 10
Christchurch	d			22p20		23p20						07 14				08 14
Hinton Admiral	d			22p25		23p25						07 19				08 19
New Milton	d			22p29		23p29						07 23				08 23
Sway	d			22p34		23p34						07 28				08 28
Lymington Pier	d															
Lymington Town	d															
Brockenhurst ■	a			22p39		23p39						07 33				08 33
	d			22p40		23p40						07 34				08 34
Beaulieu Road	d															08 39
Ashurst New Forest	d			22p47		23p47						07 43				08 43
Totton	d			22p52		23p52						07 48				08 48
Salisbury	d													08 08		
Dean	d													08 20		
Mottisfont & Dunbridge	d													08 26		
Romsey	d													08 35		
Redbridge	d															
Millbrook (Hants)	d															
Southampton Central	a			22p57		23p57						07 53				08 53
	d		22p30	23p00		23p59						07 55				08 55
St Denys	d					00 04										
Swaythling	d					00 07										
Southampton Airport Pkwy	d		22p38	23p08		00 10						08 03				09 03
Portsmouth Harbour	d				23p24			06 37			07 17				08 17	
Portsmouth & Southsea	d				23p29			06 42			07 22				08 22	
Fratton	d				23p33			06 46			07 26				08 26	
Hilsea	d				23p37			06 50			07 30				08 30	
Cosham	d				23p42			06 55			07 35				08 35	
Portchester	d				23p47			07 00			07 40				08 40	
Fareham	d				23p53			07a05			07 46				08 46	
Botley	d				23p59						07 54				08 54	
Hedge End	d				00 05						07 58				08 58	
Eastleigh ■	a		22p41	23p11	00 11	00 14					08 04	08 07			09 04	09 07
	d		22p46	23p12	00 21						08 11				09 11	
Chandlers Ford	d													08 42		
Romsey	a													09 24		
Shawford	d			23p18											09 17	
Winchester	d		22p55	23p24	00a30						08 23				09 23	
Micheldever	d			23p33							08 32				09 32	
Basingstoke	a		23p11	23p43							08 42				09 42	
	d	22p54	23p13	23p44					07 16	08 16	08 44		09 16		09 44	
Reading ■	a															
Fleet	d	23p10		00 01					07 32	08 32			09 32			
Farnborough (Main)	d	23p16		00 06					07 38	08 38			09 38			
Woking	a	23p28	23p31	00 18					07 50	08 50	09 02		09 50		10 02	
Clapham Junction ■	a	00 21	23p52	00 53					08 27	09 26	09 30		10 23		10 27	
London Waterloo ■ ⊖	a	00 35	00 03	01 04					08 41	09 39	09 43		10 38		10 42	

A ⌶ to Eastleigh ◇ to Eastleigh

B ◇ to Eastleigh

Table 158

Sundays until 24 June

Weymouth, Bournemouth, Lymington, Romsey, Southampton and Basingstoke - London

Network Diagram - see first Page of Table 158

		SW ■	GW ■	XC ◇■ ⌶	SW ◇■ A ⌶	SW ■	SW ■	SW ■ ⌶	SW ◇■ B ⌶	SW ■	XC ◇■ ⌶	SW ■	SW ◇■ A ⌶	SW ■	SW ■	SW ■ ⌶	SW ◇■ C ⌶	SW ■
Weymouth	d				07 48								08 48					
Upwey	d				07 52								08 52					
Dorchester West	a																	
Dorchester South	d				08 00								09 00					
Moreton (Dorset)	d				08 07								09 07					
Wool	d				08 13								09 13					
Wareham	d				08 20								09 20					
Holton Heath	d																	
Hamworthy	d				08 27								09 27					
Poole ■	a				08 31								09 31					
	d				08 32				08 55				09 32				09 55	
Parkstone (Dorset)	d				08 36								09 36					
Branksome	d				08 40								09 40					
Bournemouth	a				08 46				09 04				09 46				10 04	
	d				08 50				09 06		09 40		09 50				10 06	
Pokesdown	d								09 10								10 10	
Christchurch	d								09 14								10 14	
Hinton Admiral	d								09 19								10 19	
New Milton	d				09 01				09 23				10 01				10 23	
Sway	d								09 28								10 28	
Lymington Pier	d					09 14						09 44		10 14				
Lymington Town	d					09 16						09 46		10 16				
Brockenhurst ■	a				09 08	09 24			09 33		09 53	09 54	10 08	10 24			10 33	
	d				09 09				09 34		09 57		10 09				10 34	
Beaulieu Road	d								09 39								10 39	
Ashurst New Forest	d								09 43								10 43	
Totton	d								09 48								10 48	
Salisbury	d	08 20								09 08								10 13
Dean	d									09 20								
Mottisfont & Dunbridge	d									09 26								
Romsey	d	08 39								09 32								10 32
Redbridge	d	08 46								09 39								10 39
Millbrook (Hants)	d	08 50								09 43								10 43
Southampton Central	a	08 52			09 23				09 53	09 45	10 10		10 23				10 53	10 45
	d	08 59		09 15	09 25				09 55	09 59	10 15		10 25				10 55	10 59
St Denys	d	09 04								10 04								11 04
Swaythling	d	09 07								10 07								11 07
Southampton Airport Pkwy	d	09 10		09 22	09 33				10 03	10 10	10 22		10 33				11 03	11 10
Portsmouth Harbour	d		09 08					09 17								10 17		
Portsmouth & Southsea	d		09 12					09 22								10 22		
Fratton	d		09 16					09 26								10 26		
Hilsea	d							09 30								10 30		
Cosham	d		09 23					09 35								10 35		
Portchester	d							09 40								10 40		
Fareham	d		09 32					09 46								10 46		
Botley	d							09 54								10 54		
Hedge End	d							09 58								10 58		
Eastleigh ■	a	09 13						10 04	10 07	10 13						11 04	11 07	11 13
	d	09 15						10 11		10 15						11 11		11 15
Chandlers Ford	d	09 20								10 20								11 20
Romsey	a	09 28	10 05							10 28								11 28
Shawford	d															11 17		
Winchester	d			09 31	09 42			10 23			10 31		10 42			11 23		
Micheldever	d							10 32								11 32		
Basingstoke	a			09 46	09 58			10 42			10 46		10 58			11 42		
	d			09 47	10 00		10 16	10 44			10 47		11 00		11 16	11 44		
Reading ■	a			10 04							11 04							
Fleet	d						10 32								11 32			
Farnborough (Main)	d						10 38								11 38			
Woking	a				10 19		10 50	11 02					11 18		11 50	12 02		
Clapham Junction ■	a				10 40		11 23	11 27					11 39		12 23	12 27		
London Waterloo ■ ⊖	a				10 54		11 38	11 42					11 54		12 39	12 42		

A ⌶ from Bournemouth

B ⌶ from Eastleigh ◇ to Eastleigh

C ⌶ from Bournemouth ◇ to Eastleigh

Table 158

Sundays until 24 June

Weymouth, Bournemouth, Lymington, Romsey, Southampton and Basingstoke - London

Network Diagram - see first Page of Table 158

		GW	XC	SW	SW	GW	SW	SW	SW	SW	SW	GW	XC	SW	SW	GW	SW	SW
		◇	◇[1]	[1]	◇[1]	◇	[1]	[1]	[1]	◇[1]	[1]	◇	◇[1]	[1]	◇[1]	◇	[1]	[1]
					A					B					A			
			ᴥ		ᴥ				ᴥ	ᴥ			ᴥ		ᴥ			
Weymouth	d				09 48										10 48	11 14		
Upwey	d				09 52										10 52	11 19		
Dorchester West	a															11 27		
Dorchester South	d				10 00										11 00			
Moreton (Dorset)	d				10 07										11 07			
Wool	d				10 13										11 13			
Wareham	d				10 20										11 20			
Holton Heath	d																	
Hamworthy	d				10 27										11 27			
Poole [4]	a				10 31										11 31			
	d				10 32					10 55					11 32			
Parkstone (Dorset)	d				10 36										11 36			
Branksome	d				10 40										11 40			
Bournemouth	a				10 46					11 04					11 46			
	d		10 40		10 50					11 06			11 40		11 50			
Pokesdown	d									11 10								
Christchurch	d									11 14								
Hinton Admiral	d									11 19								
New Milton	d				11 01					11 23					12 01			
Sway	d									11 28								
Lymington Pier	d			10 44			11 14							11 44			12 14	
Lymington Town	d			10 46			11 16							11 46			12 16	
Brockenhurst [3]	a		10 53	10 54	11 08		11 24			11 33			11 53	11 54	12 08		12 24	
	d		10 57		11 09					11 34			11 57		12 09			
Beaulieu Road	d									11 39								
Ashurst New Forest	d									11 43								
Totton	d									11 48								
Salisbury	d	10 32									11 08	11 33						
Dean	d										11 20							
Mottisfont & Dunbridge	d										11 26							
Romsey	d	10 50									11 32	11 51						
Redbridge	d										11 39							
Millbrook (Hants)	d										11 43							
Southampton Central	a	11 02	11 10		11 23					11 53	11 45	12 03	12 10		12 23			
	d	11 04	11 15		11 25					11 55	11 59	12 04	12 15		12 25			
St Denys	d										12 04							
Swaythling	d										12 07							
Southampton Airport Pkwy	d		11 22		11 33					12 03	12 10		12 22		12 33			
Portsmouth Harbour	d					11 08			11 17									
Portsmouth & Southsea	d					11 12			11 22									
Fratton	d					11 16			11 26									
Hilsea	d								11 30									
Cosham	d					11 23			11 35									
Portchester	d								11 40									
Fareham	d	11a26				11 32			11 46			12a28						
Botley	d								11 54									
Hedge End	d								11 58									
Eastleigh [3]	a								12 04	12 07	12 13							
	d								12 11		12 15							
Chandlers Ford	d										12 20							
Romsey	a					12 05					12 28							
Shawford	d																	
Winchester	d		11 31		11 42				12 23				12 31		12 42			
Micheldever	d								12 32									
Basingstoke	a		11 46		11 58				12 42				12 46		12 58			
	d		11 47		12 00			12 16	12 44				12 47		13 00			13 16
Reading [7]	a		12 03										13 04					
Fleet	d							12 32										13 32
Farnborough (Main)	d							12 38										13 38
Woking	a				12 18			12 50	13 02						13 18			13 50
Clapham Junction [10]	a				12 39			13 23	13 27						13 39			14 23
London Waterloo [15] ⊖	a				12 49			13 39	13 37						13 49			14 34

A ᴥ from Bournemouth

B ᴥ from Eastleigh ◇ to Eastleigh

Table 158

Sundays until 24 June

Weymouth, Bournemouth, Lymington, Romsey, Southampton and Basingstoke - London

Network Diagram - see first Page of Table 158

		SW	SW	SW	SW	GW	GW	XC	SW	SW	SW	SW	SW	SW	SW	GW	XC
		[1]	◇[1]	[1]	[1]	◇	◇	◇[1]	[1]	◇[1]	[1]	[1]	[1]	◇[1]	[1]	◇	◇[1]
			A							B				C			
		ᴥ	ᴥ					ᴥ		ᴥ			ᴥ	ᴥ		ᴥ	ᴥ
Weymouth	d									11 48							
Upwey	d									11 52							
Dorchester West	a																
Dorchester South	d									12 00							
Moreton (Dorset)	d									12 07							
Wool	d									12 13							
Wareham	d									12 20							
Holton Heath	d																
Hamworthy	d									12 27							
Poole [4]	a									12 31							
	d		11 55							12 32				12 55			
Parkstone (Dorset)	d									12 36							
Branksome	d									12 40							
Bournemouth	a		12 04							12 46				13 04			
	d		12 06					12 40		12 50				13 06			13 40
Pokesdown	d		12 10											13 10			
Christchurch	d		12 14											13 14			
Hinton Admiral	d		12 19											13 19			
New Milton	d		12 23							13 01				13 23			
Sway	d		12 28											13 28			
Lymington Pier	d				12 44						13 14						
Lymington Town	d				12 46						13 16						
Brockenhurst [3]	a		12 33		12 54			12 53		13 08	13 24			13 33			13 53
	d		12 34					12 57		13 09				13 34			13 57
Beaulieu Road	d		12 39											13 39			
Ashurst New Forest	d		12 43											13 43			
Totton	d		12 48											13 48			
Salisbury	d			12 13			12 33								13 08	13 33	
Dean	d														13 20		
Mottisfont & Dunbridge	d														13 26		
Romsey	d			12 32			12 52								13 32	13 51	
Redbridge	d			12 39											13 39		
Millbrook (Hants)	d			12 43											13 43		
Southampton Central	a		12 53	12 45			13 05	13 10		13 23				13 53	13 45	14 03	14 10
	d		12 55	12 59			13 07	13 15		13 25				13 55	13 59	14 04	14 15
St Denys	d			13 04											14 04		
Swaythling	d			13 07											14 07		
Southampton Airport Pkwy	d		13 03	13 10				13 22		13 33				14 03	14 10		14 22
Portsmouth Harbour	d	12 17				13 08							13 17				
Portsmouth & Southsea	d	12 22				13 12							13 22				
Fratton	d	12 26				13 16							13 26				
Hilsea	d	12 30											13 30				
Cosham	d	12 35				13 23							13 35				
Portchester	d	12 40											13 40				
Fareham	d	12 46				13 32	13a33						13 46			14a26	
Botley	d	12 54											13 54				
Hedge End	d	12 58											13 58				
Eastleigh [3]	a	13 04	13 07	13 13									14 04	14 07	14 13		
	d	13 11		13 15									14 11		14 15		
Chandlers Ford	d			13 20											14 20		
Romsey	a			13 28		14 05									14 28		
Shawford	d	13 17															
Winchester	d	13 23						13 31		13 42			14 23				14 31
Micheldever	d	13 32											14 32				
Basingstoke	a	13 42						13 46		13 58			14 42				14 46
	d	13 44						13 47	13 50	14 00		14 16	14 44				14 47
Reading [7]	a							14 04									15 04
Fleet	d								14 02			14 32					
Farnborough (Main)	d								14 08			14 38					
Woking	a	14 02							14 20	14 18		14 50	15 02				
Clapham Junction [10]	a	14 27							14 59	14 39		15 23	15 27				
London Waterloo [15] ⊖	a	14 37							15 10	14 49		15 34	15 37				

A ᴥ from Bournemouth ◇ to Eastleigh

B ᴥ from Bournemouth

C ᴥ from Eastleigh ◇ to Eastleigh

Table 158

Sundays
until 24 June

Weymouth, Bournemouth, Lymington, Romsey, Southampton and Basingstoke - London

Network Diagram - see first Page of Table 158

		SW	GW	SW	SW	SW	SW	SW	SW	SW	XC	SW	GW	GW	SW	SW	GW	SW	SW
		■	◇	■	◇■ A ✕	■	■	■ ✕	◇■ B ✕	■	◇■ ✕	■	■	◇	■	◇■ A ✕	◇	■	■
Weymouth	d				12 48											13 48	14 15		
Upwey	d				12 52											13 52	14 20		
Dorchester West	a																14 27		
Dorchester South	d				13 00											14 00			
Moreton (Dorset)	d				13 07											14 07			
Wool	d				13 13											14 13			
Wareham	d				13 20											14 20			
Holton Heath	d																		
Hamworthy	d				13 27											14 27			
Poole ■	a				13 31											14 31			
	d				13 32				13 55							14 32			
Parkstone (Dorset)	d				13 36											14 36			
Branksome	d				13 40											14 40			
Bournemouth	a				13 46				14 04							14 46			
	d				13 50				14 06		14 40					14 50			
Pokesdown	d								14 10										
Christchurch	d								14 14										
Hinton Admiral	d								14 19										
New Milton	d				14 01				14 23							15 01			
Sway	d								14 28										
Lymington Pier	d	13 44				14 14						14 44						15 14	
Lymington Town	d	13 46				14 16						14 46						15 16	
Brockenhurst ■	a	13 54			14 08	14 24			14 33		14 53	14 54				15 08		15 24	
	d				14 09				14 34		14 57					15 09			
Beaulieu Road	d								14 39										
Ashurst New Forest	d								14 43										
Totton	d								14 48										
Salisbury	d									14 13				14 48					
Dean	d																		
Mottisfont & Dunbridge	d																		
Romsey	d									14 32				15 10					
Redbridge	d									14 39									
Millbrook (Hants)	d									14 43									
Southampton Central ⛴	a				14 23				14 53	14 45	15 10			15 21		15 23			
	d				14 25				14 55	14 59	15 15			15 22		15 25			
St Denys	d									15 04									
Swaythling	d									15 07									
Southampton Airport Pkwy ✈	d				14 33				15 03	15 10	15 22					15 33			
Portsmouth Harbour ⛴	d		14 08					14 17					15 08						
Portsmouth & Southsea	d		14 12					14 22					15 12						
Fratton	d		14 16					14 26					15 16						
Hilsea	d							14 30											
Cosham	d		14 23					14 35					15 23						
Portchester	d							14 40											
Fareham	d		14 32					14 46					15 32	15a50					
Botley	d							14 54											
Hedge End	d							14 58											
Eastleigh ■	a							15 04	15 07	15 13									
	d								15 11	15 15									
Chandlers Ford	d									15 20									
Romsey	a		15 05							15 28			16 05						
Shawford	d								15 17										
Winchester	d				14 42				15 23		15 31					15 42			
Micheldever	d								15 32										
Basingstoke	a				14 58				15 42		15 46					15 58			
	d			14 50	15 00		15 16		15 44		15 47				15 50	16 00			16 16
Reading ■	a										16 04								
Fleet	d			15 02			15 32								16 02				16 32
Farnborough (Main)	d			15 08			15 38								16 08				16 38
Woking	a			15 20	15 18		15 50		16 02						16 20	16 18			16 50
Clapham Junction ■	a			15 59	15 39		16 23		16 27						16 59	16 39			17 23
London Waterloo ■ ⊖	a			16 10	15 49		16 34		16 37						17 10	16 49			17 34

A ✕ from Bournemouth
B ✕ from Eastleigh ◇ to Eastleigh

Table 158

Sundays
until 24 June

Weymouth, Bournemouth, Lymington, Romsey, Southampton and Basingstoke - London

Network Diagram - see first Page of Table 158

		SW	SW	SW	GW	XC	SW	GW	SW	SW	SW	SW	SW	SW	SW	GW	XC
		■ ✕	◇■ A ✕	■	◇	◇■ ✕	■	◇	■	◇■ B ✕	■	■	■ ✕	◇■ A ✕	■	◇	◇■ ✕
Weymouth	d									14 48							
Upwey	d									14 52							
Dorchester West	a																
Dorchester South	d									15 00							
Moreton (Dorset)	d									15 07							
Wool	d									15 13							
Wareham	d									15 20							
Holton Heath	d																
Hamworthy	d									15 27							
Poole ■	a									15 31							
	d		14 55							15 32				15 55			
Parkstone (Dorset)	d									15 36							
Branksome	d									15 40							
Bournemouth	a		15 04							15 46				16 04			
	d		15 06			15 40				15 50				16 06			16 40
Pokesdown	d		15 10											16 10			
Christchurch	d		15 14											16 14			
Hinton Admiral	d		15 19											16 19			
New Milton	d		15 23							16 01				16 23			
Sway	d		15 28											16 28			
Lymington Pier	d						15 44				16 14						
Lymington Town	d						15 46				16 16						
Brockenhurst ■	a		15 33			15 53	15 54			16 08	16 24			16 33			16 53
	d		15 34			15 57				16 09				16 34			16 57
Beaulieu Road	d		15 39											16 39			
Ashurst New Forest	d		15 43											16 43			
Totton	d		15 48											16 48			
Salisbury	d			15 08	15 33										16 13	16 33	
Dean	d			15 20													
Mottisfont & Dunbridge	d			15 26													
Romsey	d			15 32	15 51										16 32	16 51	
Redbridge	d			15 39											16 39		
Millbrook (Hants)	d			15 43											16 43		
Southampton Central ⛴	a		15 53	15 45	16 03	16 10				16 23				16 53	16 45	17 03	17 10
	d		15 55	15 59	16 05	16 15				16 25				16 55	16 59	17 04	17 15
St Denys	d			16 04											17 04		
Swaythling	d			16 07											17 07		
Southampton Airport Pkwy ✈	d		16 03	16 10		16 22				16 33				17 03	17 10		17 22
Portsmouth Harbour ⛴	d	15 17						16 08					16 17				
Portsmouth & Southsea	d	15 22						16 12					16 22				
Fratton	d	15 26						16 16					16 26				
Hilsea	d	15 30											16 30				
Cosham	d	15 35						16 23					16 35				
Portchester	d	15 40											16 40				
Fareham	d	15 46			16a27			16 32					16 46			17a27	
Botley	d	15 54											16 54				
Hedge End	d	15 58											16 58				
Eastleigh ■	a	16 04	16 07	16 13									17 04	17 07	17 13		
	d		16 11	16 15										17 11	17 15		
Chandlers Ford	d			16 20											17 20		
Romsey	a			16 28				17 05							17 28		
Shawford	d													17 17			
Winchester	d		16 23			16 31				16 42				17 23			17 31
Micheldever	d		16 32											17 32			
Basingstoke	a		16 42			16 46				16 58				17 42			17 46
	d		16 44			16 47			16 50	17 00		17 16		17 44			17 47
Reading ■	a					17 04											18 04
Fleet	d								17 02			17 32					
Farnborough (Main)	d								17 08			17 38					
Woking	a		17 02						17 20	17 18		17 50		18 02			
Clapham Junction ■	a		17 27						17 59	17 39		18 23		18 27			
London Waterloo ■ ⊖	a		17 37						18 10	17 49		18 34		18 37			

A ✕ from Eastleigh ◇ to Eastleigh
B ✕ from Bournemouth

Table 158

Sundays until 24 June

Weymouth, Bournemouth, Lymington, Romsey, Southampton and Basingstoke - London

Network Diagram - see first Page of Table 158

		SW	GW	SW	SW	GW	SW	SW	SW	SW	SW	GW	XC	SW	GW	SW	SW	SW	SW
		[1]	◇	[1]	◇[1] A ⌶	◇	[1]	[1]	[1]	◇[1] B	[1]	◇	◇[1] ⌶	[1]	◇	[1]	◇[1] A ⌶	[1]	[1]
Weymouth	d				15 48	16 10											16 48		
Upwey	d				15 52	16 15											16 52		
Dorchester West	a					16 22													
Dorchester South	d				16 00												17 00		
Moreton (Dorset)	d				16 07												17 07		
Wool	d				16 13												17 13		
Wareham	d				16 20												17 20		
Holton Heath	d																		
Hamworthy	d				16 27												17 27		
Poole [4]	a				16 31												17 31		
	d				16 32					16 55							17 32		
Parkstone (Dorset)	d				16 36												17 36		
Branksome	d				16 40												17 40		
Bournemouth	a				16 46					17 04							17 46		
	d				16 50					17 06			17 40				17 50		
Pokesdown	d									17 10									
Christchurch	d									17 14									
Hinton Admiral	d									17 19									
New Milton	d				17 01					17 23							18 01		
Sway	d									17 28									
Lymington Pier	d	16 44					17 14							17 44				18 14	
Lymington Town	d	16 46					17 16							17 46				18 16	
Brockenhurst [3]	a	16 54			17 08		17 24			17 33			17 53	17 54			18 08	18 24	
	d				17 09					17 34			17 57				18 09		
Beaulieu Road	d									17 39									
Ashurst New Forest	d									17 43									
Totton	d									17 48									
Salisbury	d										17 08	17 33							
Dean	d										17 20								
Mottisfont & Dunbridge	d										17 26								
Romsey	d										17 32	17 51							
Redbridge	d										17 39								
Millbrook (Hants)	d										17 43								
Southampton Central	a				17 23					17 53	17 45	18 03	18 10				18 23		
	d				17 25					17 55	17 59	18 04	18 15				18 25		
St Denys	d										18 04								
Swaythling	d										18 07								
Southampton Airport Pkwy	d				17 33					18 03	18 10		18 22				18 33		
Portsmouth Harbour	d		17 08						17 17						18 08				
Portsmouth & Southsea	d		17 12						17 22						18 12				
Fratton	d		17 16						17 26						18 16				
Hilsea	d								17 30										
Cosham	d		17 23						17 35						18 23				
Portchester	d								17 40										
Fareham	d		17 32						17 46			18a27			18 32				
Botley	d								17 54										
Hedge End	d								17 58										
Eastleigh [3]	a								18 04	18 07	18 13								
	d								18 11		18 15								
Chandlers Ford	d										18 20								
Romsey	a		18 05								18 28				19 05				
Shawford	d																		
Winchester	d				17 42				18 23				18 31				18 42		
Micheldever	d								18 32										
Basingstoke	a				17 58				18 42				18 46				18 58		
	d			17 50	18 00			18 16	18 44				18 47			18 50	19 00		19 16
Reading [7]	a												19 04						
Fleet	d			18 02				18 32								19 02			19 32
Farnborough (Main)	d			18 08				18 38								19 08			19 38
Woking	a			18 20	18 18			18 50	19 02							19 20	19 18		19 50
Clapham Junction [10]	a			18 59	18 39			19 23	19 27							19 59	19 39		20 23
London Waterloo [15] ⊖	a			19 10	18 49			19 34	19 37							20 10	19 49		20 34

A ⌶ from Bournemouth

B ◇ to Eastleigh

Table 158

Sundays until 24 June

Weymouth, Bournemouth, Lymington, Romsey, Southampton and Basingstoke - London

Network Diagram - see first Page of Table 158

		SW	SW	SW	GW	XC	SW	GW	SW	SW	GW	GW	SW	SW	SW	SW	SW	GW
		[1]	◇[1] A	[1]	◇	◇[1] ⌶	[1]	◇	[1]	◇[1] B ⌶	◇	◇	[1]	[1]	[1]	◇[1] A	[1]	◇
Weymouth	d									17 48	17 56							
Upwey	d									17 52	18 01							
Dorchester West	a										18 08							
Dorchester South	d									18 00								
Moreton (Dorset)	d									18 07								
Wool	d									18 13								
Wareham	d									18 20								
Holton Heath	d																	
Hamworthy	d									18 27								
Poole [4]	a									18 31								
	d		17 55							18 32						18 55		
Parkstone (Dorset)	d									18 36								
Branksome	d									18 40								
Bournemouth	a		18 04							18 46						19 04		
	d		18 06			18 40				18 50						19 06		
Pokesdown	d		18 10													19 10		
Christchurch	d		18 14													19 14		
Hinton Admiral	d		18 19													19 19		
New Milton	d		18 23							19 01						19 23		
Sway	d		18 28													19 28		
Lymington Pier	d						18 44						19 14					
Lymington Town	d						18 46						19 16					
Brockenhurst [3]	a		18 33			18 53	18 54			19 08			19 24			19 33		
	d		18 34			18 57				19 09						19 34		
Beaulieu Road	d		18 39													19 39		
Ashurst New Forest	d		18 43													19 43		
Totton	d		18 48													19 48		
Salisbury	d			18 13	18 33							18 56					19 08	19 32
Dean	d																19 20	
Mottisfont & Dunbridge	d																19 26	
Romsey	d			18 32	18 51							19 14					19 32	19 50
Redbridge	d			18 39													19 39	
Millbrook (Hants)	d			18 43													19 43	
Southampton Central	a		18 53	18 45	19 03	19 10				19 23		19 25				19 53	19 45	20 02
	d		18 55	18 59	19 04	19 15				19 25		19 26				19 55	19 59	20 04
St Denys	d			19 04													20 04	
Swaythling	d			19 07													20 07	
Southampton Airport Pkwy	d		19 03	19 10		19 22				19 33						20 03	20 10	
Portsmouth Harbour	d	18 17						19 08							19 17			
Portsmouth & Southsea	d	18 22						19 12							19 22			
Fratton	d	18 26						19 16							19 26			
Hilsea	d	18 30													19 30			
Cosham	d	18 35						19 23							19 35			
Portchester	d	18 40													19 40			
Fareham	d	18 46			19a28			19 32				19a48			19 46			20a26
Botley	d	18 54													19 54			
Hedge End	d	18 58													19 58			
Eastleigh [3]	a	19 04	19 07	19 13											20 04	20 07	20 13	
	d	19 11		19 15											20 11		20 15	
Chandlers Ford	d			19 20													20 20	
Romsey	a			19 28				20 05									20 28	
Shawford	d	19 17																
Winchester	d	19 23				19 31				19 42					20 23			
Micheldever	d	19 32													20 32			
Basingstoke	a	19 42				19 46				19 58					20 42			
	d	19 44				19 47			19 50	20 00				20 16	20 44			
Reading [7]	a					20 04												
Fleet	d								20 02					20 32				
Farnborough (Main)	d								20 08					20 38				
Woking	a	20 02							20 20	20 18				20 50	21 02			
Clapham Junction [10]	a	20 27							20 59	20 39				21 23	21 27			
London Waterloo [15] ⊖	a	20 37							21 10	20 49				21 34	21 37			

A ◇ to Eastleigh

B ⌶ from Bournemouth

Table 158

Sundays until 24 June

Weymouth, Bournemouth, Lymington, Romsey, Southampton and Basingstoke - London

Network Diagram - see first Page of Table 158

		XC	SW	GW	SW	SW	SW	SW	GW	SW	SW	SW	GW	SW	SW	SW	SW
		◇■	■	◇	■	◇■ A ⌶	■	■	■	■	◇■ B	■	◇	■	■	■	■
Weymouth	d					18 48											
Upwey	d					18 52											
Dorchester West	a																
Dorchester South	d					19 00											
Moreton (Dorset)	d					19 07											
Wool	d					19 13											
Wareham	d					19 20											
Holton Heath	d																
Hamworthy	d					19 27											
Poole ■	a					19 31											
	d					19 32					19 55						
Parkstone (Dorset)	d					19 36											
Branksome	d					19 40											
Bournemouth	a					19 46					20 04						
	d	19 40				19 50					20 06						
Pokesdown	d										20 10						
Christchurch	d										20 14						
Hinton Admiral	d										20 19						
New Milton	d					20 01					20 23						
Sway	d										20 28						
Lymington Pier	d		19 44				20 14							20 44	21 14		
Lymington Town	d		19 46				20 16							20 46	21 16		
Brockenhurst ■	a	19 53	19 54			20 08	20 24				20 33			20 54	21 24		
	d	19 57				20 09					20 34						
Beaulieu Road	d										20 39						
Ashurst New Forest	d										20 43						
Totton	d										20 48						
Salisbury	d								20 01			20 13	20 30				
Dean	d																
Mottisfont & Dunbridge	d																
Romsey	d								20 19			20 32	20 48				
Redbridge	d											20 39					
Millbrook (Hants)	d											20 43					
Southampton Central	a	20 10				20 23			20 29		20 53	20 45	20 59				
	d	20 15				20 25			20 31		20 55	20 59	21 02				
St Denys	d											21 04					
Swaythling	d											21 07					
Southampton Airport Pkwy	d	20 22				20 33					21 03	21 10					
Portsmouth Harbour	d			20 08						20 17							
Portsmouth & Southsea	d			20 12						20 22							
Fratton	d			20 16						20 26							
Hilsea	d									20 30							
Cosham	d									20 35							
Portchester	d									20 40							
Fareham	d			20 32					20a54	20 46			21a24				
Botley	d									20 54							
Hedge End	d									20 58							
Eastleigh ■	a									21 04	21 07	21 13					
	d									21 11		21 15					
Chandlers Ford	d											21 20					
Romsey	a			21 05								21 28					
Shawford	d									21 17							
Winchester	d	20 31				20 42				21 23							
Micheldever	d									21 32							
Basingstoke	a	20 46				20 58				21 42							
	d	20 47			20 50	21 00		21 16		21 44						21 50	22 16
Reading ■	a	21 03															
Fleet	d				21 02			21 32								22 02	22 32
Farnborough (Main)	d				21 08			21 38								22 08	22 38
Woking	a				21 20	21 18		21 50		22 02						22 21	22 50
Clapham Junction ■	a				21 59	21 39		22 23		22 27						22 59	23 23
London Waterloo ■ ⊖	a				22 10	21 49		22 34		22 37						23 10	23 34

A ⌶ from Bournemouth

B ◇ to Eastleigh

Table 158

Sundays until 24 June

Weymouth, Bournemouth, Lymington, Romsey, Southampton and Basingstoke - London

Network Diagram - see first Page of Table 158

		SW	SW	GW	SW	GW	SW	GW	SW	SW	SW	SW	SW	GW	SW	SW	SW
		■	◇■ A		■	◇	■		■	■	■	◇■	■	◇	■	■	■
Weymouth	d		19 58	20 09								20 58			21 58	22 58	
Upwey	d		20 02	20 14								21 02			22 02	23 02	
Dorchester West	a			20 21													
Dorchester South	d		20 10									21 10			22 10	23 10	
Moreton (Dorset)	d		20 17									21 17			22 17	23 17	
Wool	d		20 23									21 23			22 23	23 23	
Wareham	d		20 30									21 30			22 30	23 30	
Holton Heath	d																
Hamworthy	d		20 37									21 37			22 37	23 37	
Poole ■	a		20 41									21 41			22 41	23 41	
	d		20 50									21 50			22 50	23 50	
Parkstone (Dorset)	d		20 54									21 54			22 54	23 54	
Branksome	d		20 57									21 57			22 57	23 57	
Bournemouth	a		21 03									22 03			23 03	00 03	
	d		21 06									22 06			23 06		
Pokesdown	d		21 10									22 10			23 10		
Christchurch	d		21 14									22 14			23 14		
Hinton Admiral	d		21 19									22 19			23 19		
New Milton	d		21 23									22 23			23 23		
Sway	d		21 28									22 28			23 28		
Lymington Pier	d						21 44		22 14								
Lymington Town	d						21 46		22 16								
Brockenhurst ■	a		21 33				21 54		22 24			22 33			23 33		
	d		21 34									22 34			23 34		
Beaulieu Road	d		21 39									22 39					
Ashurst New Forest	d		21 43									22 43			23 43		
Totton	d		21 48									22 48			23 48		
Salisbury	d				21 08	21 33								22 36			
Dean	d				21 20												
Mottisfont & Dunbridge	d				21 26												
Romsey	d				21 32	21 51							22 28	22 54			
Redbridge	d				21 39								22 35				
Millbrook (Hants)	d				21 43								22 39				
Southampton Central	a		21 53		21 45	22 03						22 53	22 41	23 05	23 53		
	d		21 55		21 59	22 04						22 55	23 05	23 08			
St Denys	d				22 04								23 10				
Swaythling	d				22 07								23 13				
Southampton Airport Pkwy	d		22 03		22 10							23 03	23 16				
Portsmouth Harbour	d	21 17						22 03		22 17							23 17
Portsmouth & Southsea	d	21 22						22 12		22 22							23 22
Fratton	d	21 26						22 16		22 26							23 26
Hilsea	d	21 30								22 30							23 30
Cosham	d	21 35								22 35							23 35
Portchester	d	21 40								22 40							23 40
Fareham	d	21 46				22a26		22 32		22 46				23a29			23 46
Botley	d	21 54								22 54							23 54
Hedge End	d	21 58								22 58							23 58
Eastleigh ■	a	22 04	22 07		22 13					23 04		23 09	23 19				00 04
	d	22 11			22 15							23 11	23 21				
Chandlers Ford	d				22 20								23 26				
Romsey	a				22 31			23 08					23 33				
Shawford	d																
Winchester	d	22 23										23 23					
Micheldever	d	22 32										23 32					
Basingstoke	a	22 42										23 42					
	d	22 44									23 16	23 44					
Reading ■	a																
Fleet	d										23 32						
Farnborough (Main)	d										23 38						
Woking	a	23 02									23 50	00 02					
Clapham Junction ■	a	23 27										00 23					
London Waterloo ■ ⊖	a	23 37										00 33					

A ◇ to Eastleigh

Table 158

Sundays

1 July to 9 September

Weymouth, Bournemouth, Lymington, Romsey, Southampton and Basingstoke - London

Network Diagram - see first Page of Table 158

		SW ■	SW ■	SW ■	SW ■	SW ■	SW ■	SW ■ A	SW ■	SW ■	SW ■	SW ■	SW ■	SW ◇■ B ⌶	SW ■	SW ■
Weymouth	d			21p10		22p10	23p10									
Upwey	d			21p14		22p14	23p14									
Dorchester West	a															
Dorchester South	d			21p22		22p22	23p22									
Moreton (Dorset)	d			21p28		22p28	23p28									
Wool	d			21p34		22p34	23p34									
Wareham	d			21p42		22p42	23p42									
Holton Heath	d															
Hamworthy	d			21p48		22p48	23p48									
Poole ■	a			21p53		22p53	23p53									
	d			21p54		22p54	23p54							06 50		
Parkstone (Dorset)	d			21p58		22p58								06 54		
Branksome	d			22p01		23p01								06 57		
Bournemouth	a			22p07		23p07	00 03							07 02		
	d			22p12		23p12								07 06		
Pokesdown	d			22p16		23p16								07 10		
Christchurch	d			22p20		23p20								07 14		
Hinton Admiral	d			22p25		23p25								07 19		
New Milton	d			22p29		23p29								07 23		
Sway	d			22p34		23p34								07 28		
Lymington Pier	d															
Lymington Town	d															
Brockenhurst ■	a			22p39		23p39								07 33		
	d			22p40		23p40								07 34		
Beaulieu Road	d															
Ashurst New Forest	d			22p47		23p47								07 43		
Totton	d			22p52		23p52								07 48		
Salisbury	d															08 08
Dean	d															08 20
Mottisfont & Dunbridge	d															08 26
Romsey	d															08 35
Redbridge	d															
Millbrook (Hants)	d															
Southampton Central ⛴	a			22p57		23p57								07 53		
	d		22p30	23p00		23p59		05 40			06 55			07 55		
St Denys	d					00 04										
Swaythling	d					00 07										
Southampton Airport Pkwy ✈	d		22p38	23p08		00 10		05 48			07 03			08 03		
Portsmouth Harbour ⛴	d				23p24				06 37				07 17			
Portsmouth & Southsea	d				23p29				06 42				07 22			
Fratton	d				23p33				06 46				07 26			
Hilsea	d				23p37				06 50				07 30			
Cosham	d				23p42				06 55				07 35			
Portchester	d				23p47				07 00				07 40			
Fareham	d				23p53				07a05				07 46			
Botley	d				23p59								07 54			
Hedge End	d				00 05								07 58			
Eastleigh ■	a		22p41	23p11	00 11	00 14		05 52			07 07		08 04	08 07		
	d		22p46	23p12	00 21			05 53			07 11		08 11			
Chandlers Ford	d															08 42
Romsey	a															09 24
Shawford	d			23p18												
Winchester	d		22p55	23p24	00a30			06 03			07 23		08 23			
Micheldever	d			23p33							07 32		08 32			
Basingstoke	a		23p11	23p43				06 19			07 42		08 42			
	d	22p54	23p13	23p44				06 21		07 16	07 44	08 16	08 44		09 16	
Reading ■	a															
Fleet	d	23p10		00 01				06 32		07 32		08 32			09 32	
Farnborough (Main)	d	23p16		00 06				06 38		07 38		08 38			09 38	
Woking	a	23p28	23p31	00 18				06 47		07 50	08 02	08 50	09 02		09 50	
Clapham Junction ■	a	00 21	23p52	00 53				07 11		08 27	08 30	09 26	09 30		10 23	
London Waterloo ■ ⊖	a	00 35	00 03	01 04				07 20		08 41	08 42	09 39	09 43		10 38	

A 29 July, 5 August, 12 August, 2 September, 9 September

B ⌶ to Eastleigh ◇ to Eastleigh

Table 158

Sundays

1 July to 9 September

Weymouth, Bournemouth, Lymington, Romsey, Southampton and Basingstoke - London

Network Diagram - see first Page of Table 158

		SW ■	SW ◇■ A	SW ■	GW ■	XC ◇■ ⌶	SW ◇■ B ⌶	SW ■	SW ■	SW ■ ⌶	SW ◇■ C ⌶	SW ■	XC ◇■ ⌶	SW ■	SW ◇■ B ⌶	SW ■	SW ■
Weymouth	d						07 48								08 48		
Upwey	d						07 52								08 52		
Dorchester West	a																
Dorchester South	d						08 00								09 00		
Moreton (Dorset)	d						08 07								09 07		
Wool	d						08 13								09 13		
Wareham	d						08 20								09 20		
Holton Heath	d																
Hamworthy	d						08 27								09 27		
Poole ■	a						08 31								09 31		
	d		07 50				08 32				08 55				09 32		
Parkstone (Dorset)	d		07 54				08 36								09 36		
Branksome	d		07 57				08 40								09 40		
Bournemouth	a		08 02				08 46				09 04				09 46		
	d		08 06				08 50				09 06		09 40		09 50		
Pokesdown	d		08 10								09 10						
Christchurch	d		08 14								09 14						
Hinton Admiral	d		08 19								09 19						
New Milton	d		08 23				09 01				09 23				10 01		
Sway	d		08 28								09 28						
Lymington Pier	d							09 14						09 44		10 14	
Lymington Town	d							09 16						09 46		10 16	
Brockenhurst ■	a		08 33				09 08	09 24			09 33		09 53	09 54	10 08	10 24	
	d		08 34				09 09				09 34		09 57		10 09		
Beaulieu Road	d		08 39								09 39						
Ashurst New Forest	d		08 43								09 43						
Totton	d		08 48								09 48						
Salisbury	d			08 20								09 08					
Dean	d											09 20					
Mottisfont & Dunbridge	d											09 26					
Romsey	d			08 39								09 32					
Redbridge	d			08 46								09 39					
Millbrook (Hants)	d			08 50								09 43					
Southampton Central ⛴	a		08 53	08 52			09 23				09 53	09 45	10 10		10 23		
	d		08 55	08 59		09 15	09 25				09 55	09 59	10 15		10 25		
St Denys	d			09 04								10 04					
Swaythling	d			09 07								10 07					
Southampton Airport Pkwy ✈	d		09 03	09 10		09 22	09 33				10 03	10 10	10 22		10 33		
Portsmouth Harbour ⛴	d	08 17			09 08					09 17							
Portsmouth & Southsea	d	08 22			09 12					09 22							
Fratton	d	08 26			09 16					09 26							
Hilsea	d	08 30								09 30							
Cosham	d	08 35			09 23					09 35							
Portchester	d	08 40								09 40							
Fareham	d	08 46			09 32					09 46							
Botley	d	08 54								09 54							
Hedge End	d	08 58								09 58							
Eastleigh ■	a	09 04	09 07	09 13						10 04	10 07	10 13					
	d	09 11		09 15						10 11		10 15					
Chandlers Ford	d			09 20								10 20					
Romsey	a			09 28	10 05							10 28					
Shawford	d	09 17															
Winchester	d	09 23				09 31	09 42			10 23			10 31		10 42		
Micheldever	d	09 32								10 32							
Basingstoke	a	09 42				09 46	09 58			10 42			10 46		10 58		
	d	09 44				09 47	10 00		10 16	10 44			10 47		11 00		11 16
Reading ■	a					10 04							11 04				
Fleet	d								10 32								11 32
Farnborough (Main)	d								10 38								11 38
Woking	a	10 02					10 19		10 50	11 02					11 18		11 50
Clapham Junction ■	a	10 27					10 40		11 23	11 27					11 39		12 23
London Waterloo ■ ⊖	a	10 42					10 54		11 38	11 42					11 54		12 39

A ◇ to Eastleigh

B ⌶ from Bournemouth

C ⌶ from Eastleigh ◇ to Eastleigh

Table 158

Sundays

1 July to 9 September

Weymouth, Bournemouth, Lymington, Romsey, Southampton and Basingstoke - London

Network Diagram - see first Page of Table 158

		SW 1 ⌶	SW ◇1 A ⌶	SW 1	GW ◇	XC ◇1 ⌶	SW 1	SW ◇1 B ⌶	GW ◇	SW 1	SW 1	SW 1 ⌶	SW ◇1 C ⌶	SW 1	GW ◇	XC ◇1 ⌶	SW 1	SW ◇1 B ⌶
Weymouth	d							09 48										10 48
Upwey	d							09 52										10 52
Dorchester West	a																	
Dorchester South	d							10 00										11 00
Moreton (Dorset)	d							10 07										11 07
Wool	d							10 13										11 13
Wareham	d							10 20										11 20
Holton Heath	d																	
Hamworthy	d							10 27										11 27
Poole 4	a							10 31										11 31
	d		09 55					10 32					10 55					11 32
Parkstone (Dorset)	d							10 36										11 36
Branksome	d							10 40										11 40
Bournemouth	a		10 04					10 46					11 04					11 46
	d		10 06			10 40		10 50					11 06			11 40		11 50
Pokesdown	d		10 10										11 10					
Christchurch	d		10 14										11 14					
Hinton Admiral	d		10 19										11 19					
New Milton	d		10 23					11 01					11 23					12 01
Sway	d		10 28										11 28					
Lymington Pier	d						10 44			11 14							11 44	
Lymington Town	d						10 46			11 16							11 46	
Brockenhurst 3	a		10 33			10 53	10 54	11 08		11 24			11 33			11 53	11 54	12 08
	d		10 34			10 57		11 09					11 34			11 57		12 09
Beaulieu Road	d		10 39										11 39					
Ashurst New Forest	d		10 43										11 43					
Totton	d		10 48										11 48					
Salisbury	d			10 13	10 32									11 08	11 33			
Dean	d													11 20				
Mottisfont & Dunbridge	d													11 26				
Romsey	d			10 32	10 50									11 32	11 51			
Redbridge	d			10 39										11 39				
Millbrook (Hants)	d			10 43										11 43				
Southampton Central ⛴	a		10 53	10 45	11 02	11 10		11 23					11 53	11 45	12 03	12 10		12 23
	d		10 55	10 59	11 04	11 15		11 25					11 55	11 59	12 04	12 15		12 25
St Denys	d			11 04										12 04				
Swaythling	d			11 07										12 07				
Southampton Airport Pkwy ✈	d		11 03	11 10		11 22		11 33					12 03	12 10		12 22		12 33
Portsmouth Harbour ⛴	d	10 17							11 08			11 17						
Portsmouth & Southsea	d	10 22							11 12			11 22						
Fratton	d	10 26							11 16			11 26						
Hilsea	d	10 30										11 30						
Cosham	d	10 35							11 23			11 35						
Portchester	d	10 40										11 40						
Fareham	d	10 46			11a26				11 32			11 46			12a28			
Botley	d	10 54										11 54						
Hedge End	d	10 58										11 58						
Eastleigh 8	a	11 04	11 07	11 13								12 04	12 07	12 13				
	d		11 11	11 15									12 11	12 15				
Chandlers Ford	d			11 20										12 20				
Romsey	a			11 28					12 05					12 28				
Shawford	d		11 17															
Winchester	d		11 23			11 31		11 42					12 23			12 31		12 42
Micheldever	d		11 32										12 32					
Basingstoke	a		11 42			11 46		11 58					12 42			12 46		12 58
	d		11 44			11 47		12 00			12 16		12 44			12 47		13 00
Reading 7	a					12 04										13 04		
Fleet	d										12 32							
Farnborough (Main)	d										12 38							
Woking	a		12 02					12 18			12 50		13 02					13 18
Clapham Junction 10	a		12 27					12 39			13 23		13 27					13 39
London Waterloo 15 ⊖	a		12 42					12 49			13 39		13 37					13 49

A ⌶ from Bournemouth ◇ to Eastleigh

B ⌶ from Bournemouth

C ⌶ from Eastleigh ◇ to Eastleigh

Table 158

Sundays

1 July to 9 September

Weymouth, Bournemouth, Lymington, Romsey, Southampton and Basingstoke - London

Network Diagram - see first Page of Table 158

		GW ◇	SW 1	SW 1	SW 1 ⌶	SW ◇1 A ⌶	SW 1	SW 1	GW ◇	GW ◇	XC ◇1 ⌶	SW 1	SW ◇1 B ⌶	SW 1	SW 1	SW 1 ⌶	SW ◇1 C ⌶	SW 1
Weymouth	d	11 14											11 48					
Upwey	d	11 19											11 52					
Dorchester West	a	11 27																
Dorchester South	d												12 00					
Moreton (Dorset)	d												12 07					
Wool	d												12 13					
Wareham	d												12 20					
Holton Heath	d																	
Hamworthy	d												12 27					
Poole 4	a												12 31					
	d					11 55							12 32				12 55	
Parkstone (Dorset)	d												12 36					
Branksome	d												12 40					
Bournemouth	a					12 04							12 46				13 04	
	d					12 06					12 40		12 50				13 06	
Pokesdown	d					12 10											13 10	
Christchurch	d					12 14											13 14	
Hinton Admiral	d					12 19											13 19	
New Milton	d					12 23							13 01				13 23	
Sway	d					12 28											13 28	
Lymington Pier	d		12 14					12 44						13 14				
Lymington Town	d		12 16					12 46						13 16				
Brockenhurst 3	a		12 24			12 33		12 54			12 53		13 08	13 24			13 33	
	d					12 34					12 57		13 09				13 34	
Beaulieu Road	d					12 39											13 39	
Ashurst New Forest	d					12 43											13 43	
Totton	d					12 48											13 48	
Salisbury	d						12 13			12 33								13 08
Dean	d																	13 20
Mottisfont & Dunbridge	d																	13 26
Romsey	d						12 32			12 52								13 32
Redbridge	d						12 39											13 39
Millbrook (Hants)	d						12 43											13 43
Southampton Central ⛴	a					12 53	12 45			13 05	13 10		13 23				13 53	13 45
	d					12 55	12 59			13 07	13 15		13 25				13 55	13 59
St Denys	d						13 04											14 04
Swaythling	d						13 07											14 07
Southampton Airport Pkwy ✈	d					13 03	13 10				13 22		13 33				14 03	14 10
Portsmouth Harbour ⛴	d				12 17				13 08							13 17		
Portsmouth & Southsea	d				12 22				13 12							13 22		
Fratton	d				12 26				13 16							13 26		
Hilsea	d				12 30											13 30		
Cosham	d				12 35				13 23							13 35		
Portchester	d				12 40											13 40		
Fareham	d				12 46				13 32	13a33						13 46		
Botley	d				12 54											13 54		
Hedge End	d				12 58											13 58		
Eastleigh 8	a				13 04	13 07	13 13									14 04	14 07	14 13
	d					13 11	13 15										14 11	14 15
Chandlers Ford	d						13 20											14 20
Romsey	a						13 28		14 05									14 28
Shawford	d					13 17												
Winchester	d					13 23					13 31		13 42				14 23	
Micheldever	d					13 32											14 32	
Basingstoke	a					13 42					13 46		13 58				14 42	
	d			13 16		13 44					13 47	13 50	14 00		14 16		14 44	
Reading 7	a										14 03							
Fleet	d			13 32								14 02			14 32			
Farnborough (Main)	d			13 38								14 08			14 38			
Woking	a			13 50		14 02						14 20	14 18		14 50		15 02	
Clapham Junction 10	a			14 23		14 27						14 59	14 39		15 23		15 27	
London Waterloo 15 ⊖	a			14 34		14 37						15 10	14 49		15 34		15 37	

A ⌶ from Bournemouth ◇ to Eastleigh

B ⌶ from Bournemouth

C ⌶ from Eastleigh ◇ to Eastleigh

Sundays

1 July to 9 September

Weymouth, Bournemouth, Lymington, Romsey, Southampton and Basingstoke - London

Network Diagram - see first Page of Table 158

Station		GW ◇ ⌶	XC ◇[1] ⌶	SW [1]	GW ◇	SW [1]	SW ◇[1] A ⌶	SW [1]	SW [1]	SW [1] ⌶	SW ◇[1] B ⌶	SW [1]	XC ◇[1] ⌶	SW [1]	GW [1]	GW ◇	SW [1]	SW ◇[1] A ⌶	GW ◇
Weymouth	d						12 48											13 48	14 15
Upwey	d						12 52											13 52	14 20
Dorchester West	a																		14 27
Dorchester South	d						13 00											14 00	
Moreton (Dorset)	d						13 07											14 07	
Wool	d						13 13											14 13	
Wareham	d						13 20											14 20	
Holton Heath	d																		
Hamworthy	d						13 27											14 27	
Poole [4]	a						13 31											14 31	
	d						13 32				13 55							14 32	
Parkstone (Dorset)	d						13 36											14 36	
Branksome	d						13 40											14 40	
Bournemouth	a						13 46				14 04							14 46	
	d		13 40				13 50				14 06		14 40					14 50	
Pokesdown	d										14 10								
Christchurch	d										14 14								
Hinton Admiral	d										14 19								
New Milton	d						14 01				14 23							15 01	
Sway	d										14 28								
Lymington Pier	d			13 44				14 14						14 44					
Lymington Town	d			13 46				14 16						14 46					
Brockenhurst [3]	a		13 53	13 54			14 08	14 24			14 33		14 53	14 54				15 08	
	d		13 57				14 09				14 34		14 57					15 09	
Beaulieu Road	d										14 39								
Ashurst New Forest	d										14 43								
Totton	d										14 48								
Salisbury	d	13 33										14 13				14 48			
Dean	d																		
Mottisfont & Dunbridge	d																		
Romsey	d	13 51										14 32				15 10			
Redbridge	d											14 39							
Millbrook (Hants)	d											14 43							
Southampton Central ⛴	a	14 03	14 10				14 23				14 53	14 45	15 10			15 21		15 23	
	d	14 04	14 15				14 25				14 55	14 59	15 15			15 22		15 25	
St Denys	d											15 04							
Swaythling	d											15 07							
Southampton Airport Pkwy ✈	d		14 22				14 33				15 03	15 10	15 22					15 33	
Portsmouth Harbour ⛴	d				14 08					14 17					15 08				
Portsmouth & Southsea	d				14 12					14 22					15 12				
Fratton	d				14 16					14 26					15 16				
Hilsea	d									14 30									
Cosham	d				14 23					14 35					15 23				
Portchester	d									14 40									
Fareham	d	14a26			14 32					14 46					15 32	15a50			
Botley	d									14 54									
Hedge End	d									14 58									
Eastleigh [3]	a									15 04	15 07	15 13							
	d									15 11 (combined)		15 15							
Chandlers Ford	d											15 20							
Romsey	a				15 05							15 28			16 05				
Shawford	d									15 17									
Winchester	d		14 31				14 42			15 23			15 31					15 42	
Micheldever	d									15 32									
Basingstoke	a		14 46				14 58			15 42			15 46					15 58	
	d		14 47			14 50	15 00		15 16	15 44			15 47				15 50	16 00	
Reading [7]	a		15 04										16 04						
Fleet	d					15 02			15 32								16 02		
Farnborough (Main)	d					15 08			15 38								16 08		
Woking	a					15 20	15 18		15 50	16 02							16 20	16 18	
Clapham Junction [10]	a					15 59	15 39		16 23	16 27							16 59	16 39	
London Waterloo [15] ⊖	a					16 10	15 49		16 34	16 37							17 10	16 49	

A ⌶ from Bournemouth

B ⌶ from Eastleigh ◇ to Eastleigh

Sundays

1 July to 9 September

Weymouth, Bournemouth, Lymington, Romsey, Southampton and Basingstoke - London

Network Diagram - see first Page of Table 158

Station		SW [1]	SW [1]	SW [1] ⌶	SW ◇[1] A ⌶	SW [1]	GW ◇	XC ◇[1] ⌶	SW [1]	GW ◇	SW [1]	SW ◇[1] B ⌶	SW [1]	SW [1]	SW [1] ⌶	SW ◇[1] A ⌶	SW [1]
Weymouth	d											14 48					
Upwey	d											14 52					
Dorchester West	a																
Dorchester South	d											15 00					
Moreton (Dorset)	d											15 07					
Wool	d											15 13					
Wareham	d											15 20					
Holton Heath	d																
Hamworthy	d											15 27					
Poole [4]	a											15 31					
	d				14 55							15 32				15 55	
Parkstone (Dorset)	d											15 36					
Branksome	d											15 40					
Bournemouth	a				15 04							15 46				16 04	
	d				15 06			15 40				15 50				16 06	
Pokesdown	d				15 10											16 10	
Christchurch	d				15 14											16 14	
Hinton Admiral	d				15 19											16 19	
New Milton	d				15 23							16 01				16 23	
Sway	d				15 28											16 28	
Lymington Pier	d	15 14							15 44				16 14				
Lymington Town	d	15 16							15 46				16 16				
Brockenhurst [3]	a	15 24			15 33			15 53	15 54			16 08	16 24			16 33	
	d				15 34			15 57				16 09				16 34	
Beaulieu Road	d				15 39											16 39	
Ashurst New Forest	d				15 43											16 43	
Totton	d				15 48											16 48	
Salisbury	d					15 08	15 33										16 13
Dean	d					15 20											
Mottisfont & Dunbridge	d					15 26											
Romsey	d					15 32	15 51										16 32
Redbridge	d					15 39											16 39
Millbrook (Hants)	d					15 43											16 43
Southampton Central ⛴	a				15 53	15 45	16 03	16 10				16 23				16 53	16 45
	d				15 55	15 59	16 05	16 15				16 25				16 55	16 59
St Denys	d					16 04											17 04
Swaythling	d					16 07											17 07
Southampton Airport Pkwy ✈	d				16 03	16 10		16 22				16 33				17 03	17 10
Portsmouth Harbour ⛴	d			15 17						16 08					16 17		
Portsmouth & Southsea	d			15 22						16 12					16 22		
Fratton	d			15 26						16 16					16 26		
Hilsea	d			15 30											16 30		
Cosham	d			15 35						16 23					16 35		
Portchester	d			15 40											16 40		
Fareham	d			15 46			16a27			16 32					16 46		
Botley	d			15 54											16 54		
Hedge End	d			15 58											16 58		
Eastleigh [3]	a			16 04	16 07	16 13									17 04	17 07	17 13
	d			16 11 (combined)		16 15									17 11 (combined)		17 15
Chandlers Ford	d					16 20											17 20
Romsey	a					16 28				17 05							17 28
Shawford	d														17 17		
Winchester	d			16 23				16 31				16 42			17 23		
Micheldever	d			16 32											17 32		
Basingstoke	a			16 42				16 46				16 58			17 42		
	d		16 16	16 44				16 47			16 50	17 00		17 16	17 44		
Reading [7]	a							17 04									
Fleet	d		16 32								17 02			17 32			
Farnborough (Main)	d		16 38								17 08			17 38			
Woking	a		16 50	17 02							17 20	17 18		17 50	18 02		
Clapham Junction [10]	a		17 23	17 27							17 59	17 39		18 23	18 27		
London Waterloo [15] ⊖	a		17 34	17 37							18 10	17 49		18 34	18 37		

A ⌶ from Eastleigh ◇ to Eastleigh

B ⌶ from Bournemouth

Table 158

Sundays

1 July to 9 September

Weymouth, Bournemouth, Lymington, Romsey, Southampton and Basingstoke - London

Network Diagram - see first Page of Table 158

		GW ◇		XC ◇■ 🍴	SW ■	GW ◇	SW ■	SW ◇■ A 🍴	GW ◇		SW ■	SW ■			SW ■	SW ◇■ B	SW ■	GW ◇			XC ◇■ 🍴	SW ■	GW ◇	SW ■	SW ◇■ A 🍴
Weymouth	d							15 48	16 10																16 48
Upwey	d							15 52	16 15																16 52
Dorchester West	a								16 22																
Dorchester South	d							16 00																	17 00
Moreton (Dorset)	d							16 07																	17 07
Wool	d							16 13																	17 13
Wareham	d							16 20																	17 20
Holton Heath	d																								
Hamworthy	d							16 27																	17 27
Poole ■	a							16 31																	17 31
	d							16 32								16 55									17 32
Parkstone (Dorset)	d							16 36																	17 36
Branksome	d							16 40																	17 40
Bournemouth	a							16 46								17 04									17 46
	d			16 40				16 50								17 06					17 40				17 50
Pokesdown	d															17 10									
Christchurch	d															17 14									
Hinton Admiral	d															17 19									
New Milton	d							17 01								17 23									18 01
Sway	d															17 28									
Lymington Pier	d				16 44						17 14											17 44			
Lymington Town	d				16 46						17 16											17 46			
Brockenhurst ■	a			16 53	16 54			17 08			17 24					17 33					17 53	17 54			18 08
	d			16 57				17 09								17 34					17 57				18 09
Beaulieu Road	d															17 39									
Ashurst New Forest	d															17 43									
Totton	d															17 48									
Salisbury	d	16 33															17 08	17 33							
Dean	d																17 20								
Mottisfont & Dunbridge	d																17 26								
Romsey	d	16 51															17 32	17 51							
Redbridge	d																17 39								
Millbrook (Hants)	d																17 43								
Southampton Central ⛴	a	17 03		17 10				17 23								17 53	17 45	18 03			18 10				18 23
	d	17 04		17 15				17 25								17 55	17 59	18 04			18 15				18 25
St Denys	d																18 04								
Swaythling	d																18 07								
Southampton Airport Pkwy ✈	d			17 22				17 33								18 03	18 10				18 22				18 33
Portsmouth Harbour ⛴	d					17 08									17 17								18 08		
Portsmouth & Southsea	d					17 12									17 22								18 12		
Fratton	d					17 16									17 26								18 16		
Hilsea	d														17 30										
Cosham	d					17 23									17 35								18 23		
Portchester	d														17 40										
Fareham	d	17a27				17 32									17 46			18a27					18 32		
Botley	d														17 54										
Hedge End	d														17 58										
Eastleigh ■	a														18 04	18 07	18 13								
	d														18 11		18 15								
Chandlers Ford	d																18 20								
Romsey	a					18 05											18 28						19 05		
Shawford	d																								
Winchester	d			17 31				17 42							18 23						18 31				18 42
Micheldever	d														18 32										
Basingstoke	a			17 46				17 58							18 42						18 46				18 58
	d			17 47			17 50	18 00				18 16			18 44						18 47			18 50	19 00
Reading ■	a			18 04																	19 03				
Fleet	d						18 02					18 32												19 02	
Farnborough (Main)	d						18 08					18 38												19 08	
Woking	a						18 20	18 18				18 50			19 02									19 20	19 18
Clapham Junction ■	a						18 59	18 39				19 23			19 27									19 59	19 39
London Waterloo ■ ⊖	a						19 10	18 49				19 34			19 37									20 10	19 49

A 🍴 from Bournemouth

B ◇ to Eastleigh

Table 158

Sundays

1 July to 9 September

Weymouth, Bournemouth, Lymington, Romsey, Southampton and Basingstoke - London

Network Diagram - see first Page of Table 158

		SW ■	SW ■				SW ■	SW ◇■ A	SW ■	GW ◇		XC ◇■ 🍴	SW ■	GW ◇	SW ■		SW ◇■ B 🍴	GW ◇	GW ◇	SW ■		SW ■		SW ■	SW ◇■ A
Weymouth	d																17 48	17 56							
Upwey	d																17 52	18 01							
Dorchester West	a																	18 08							
Dorchester South	d																18 00								
Moreton (Dorset)	d																18 07								
Wool	d																18 13								
Wareham	d																18 20								
Holton Heath	d																								
Hamworthy	d																18 27								
Poole ■	a																18 31								
	d							17 55									18 32								18 55
Parkstone (Dorset)	d																18 36								
Branksome	d																18 40								
Bournemouth	a							18 04									18 46								19 04
	d							18 06				18 40					18 50								19 06
Pokesdown	d							18 10																	19 10
Christchurch	d							18 14																	19 14
Hinton Admiral	d							18 19																	19 19
New Milton	d							18 23									19 01								19 23
Sway	d							18 28																	19 28
Lymington Pier	d	18 14											18 44							19 14					
Lymington Town	d	18 16											18 46							19 16					
Brockenhurst ■	a	18 24						18 33				18 53	18 54				19 08			19 24					19 33
	d							18 34				18 57					19 09								19 34
Beaulieu Road	d							18 39																	19 39
Ashurst New Forest	d							18 43																	19 43
Totton	d							18 48																	19 48
Salisbury	d								18 13	18 33									18 56						
Dean	d																								
Mottisfont & Dunbridge	d																								
Romsey	d								18 32	18 51									19 14						
Redbridge	d								18 39																
Millbrook (Hants)	d								18 43																
Southampton Central ⛴	a							18 53	18 45	19 03		19 10					19 23		19 25						19 53
	d							18 55	18 59	19 04		19 15					19 25		19 26						19 55
St Denys	d								19 04																
Swaythling	d								19 07																
Southampton Airport Pkwy ✈	d							19 03	19 10			19 22					19 33								20 03
Portsmouth Harbour ⛴	d						18 17							19 08										19 17	
Portsmouth & Southsea	d						18 22							19 12										19 22	
Fratton	d						18 26							19 16										19 26	
Hilsea	d						18 30																	19 30	
Cosham	d						18 35							19 23										19 35	
Portchester	d						18 40																	19 40	
Fareham	d						18 46			19a28				19 32					19a48					19 46	
Botley	d						18 54																	19 54	
Hedge End	d						18 58																	19 58	
Eastleigh ■	a						19 04	19 07	19 13															20 04	20 07
	d						19 11		19 15															20 11	
Chandlers Ford	d								19 20																
Romsey	a								19 28					20 05											
Shawford	d						19 17																		
Winchester	d						19 23					19 31					19 42							20 23	
Micheldever	d						19 32																	20 32	
Basingstoke	a						19 42					19 46					19 58							20 42	
	d		19 16				19 44					19 47			19 50		20 00					20 16		20 44	
Reading ■	a											20 04													
Fleet	d		19 32												20 02							20 32			
Farnborough (Main)	d		19 38												20 08							20 38			
Woking	a		19 50				20 02								20 20		20 18					20 50		21 02	
Clapham Junction ■	a		20 23				20 27								20 59		20 39					21 23		21 27	
London Waterloo ■ ⊖	a		20 34				20 37								21 10		20 49					21 34		21 37	

A ◇ to Eastleigh

B 🍴 from Bournemouth

Weymouth, Bournemouth, Lymington, Romsey, Southampton and Basingstoke - London

Network Diagram - see first Page of Table 158

		SW	GW	XC	SW	GW	SW	SW	SW	SW	GW	SW	SW	SW	GW	SW	SW	SW
		■1	◇	◇■1	■1	◇	■1	◇■1 A ✠	■1	■1	■	■1	◇■1 B	■1	◇	■1	■1	■1
Weymouth	d							18 48										
Upwey	d							18 52										
Dorchester West	a																	
Dorchester South	d							19 00										
Moreton (Dorset)	d							19 07										
Wool	d							19 13										
Wareham	d							19 20										
Holton Heath	d																	
Hamworthy	d							19 27										
Poole 4	a							19 31										
	d							19 32					19 55					
Parkstone (Dorset)	d							19 36										
Branksome	d							19 40										
Bournemouth	a							19 46					20 04					
	d			19 40				19 50					20 06					
Pokesdown	d												20 10					
Christchurch	d												20 14					
Hinton Admiral	d												20 19					
New Milton	d							20 01					20 23					
Sway	d												20 28					
Lymington Pier	d				19 44				20 14							20 44	21 14	
Lymington Town	d				19 46				20 16							20 46	21 16	
Brockenhurst 3	a			19 53	19 54			20 08	20 24				20 33			20 54	21 24	
	d			19 57				20 09					20 34					
Beaulieu Road	d												20 39					
Ashurst New Forest	d												20 43					
Totton	d												20 48					
Salisbury	d	19 08	19 32								20 01			20 13	20 30			
Dean	d	19 20																
Mottisfont & Dunbridge	d	19 26																
Romsey	d	19 32	19 50								20 19			20 32	20 48			
Redbridge	d	19 39												20 39				
Millbrook (Hants)	d	19 43												20 43				
Southampton Central ⛴	a	19 45	20 02	20 10				20 23			20 29		20 53	20 45	20 59			
	d	19 59	20 04	20 15				20 25			20 31		20 55	20 59	21 02			
St Denys	d	20 04												21 04				
Swaythling	d	20 07												21 07				
Southampton Airport Pkwy ✈	d	20 10		20 22				20 33					21 03	21 10				
Portsmouth Harbour ⛴	d					20 08						20 17						
Portsmouth & Southsea	d					20 12						20 22						
Fratton	d					20 16						20 26						
Hilsea	d											20 30						
Cosham	d											20 35						
Portchester	d											20 40						
Fareham	d		20a26			20 32					20a54	20 46			21a24			
Botley	d											20 54						
Hedge End	d											20 58						
Eastleigh 3	a	20 13										21 04	21 07	21 13				
	d	20 15											21 11	21 15				
Chandlers Ford	d	20 20												21 20				
Romsey	a	20 28				21 05								21 28				
Shawford	d												21 17					
Winchester	d			20 31				20 42					21 23					
Micheldever	d												21 32					
Basingstoke	a			20 46				20 58					21 42					
	d			20 47			20 50	21 00		21 16			21 44					21 50
Reading 7	a			21 03														
Fleet	d						21 02			21 32								22 02
Farnborough (Main)	d						21 08			21 38								22 08
Woking	a						21 20	21 18		21 50			22 02					22 21
Clapham Junction 10	a						21 59	21 39		22 23			22 27					22 59
London Waterloo 15 ⊖	a						22 10	21 49		22 34			22 37					23 10

A ✠ from Bournemouth

B ◇ to Eastleigh

Weymouth, Bournemouth, Lymington, Romsey, Southampton and Basingstoke - London

Network Diagram - see first Page of Table 158

		SW	SW	SW	GW	SW	GW	SW	GW	SW	SW	SW	SW	SW	GW	SW	SW	SW	SW
		■1	■1	◇■1 A		■1	◇	■1		■1	■1	■1	◇■1	■1	◇	■1	■1	■1	■1
Weymouth	d			19 58	20 09								20 58			21 58	21 58	22 58	
Upwey	d			20 02	20 14								21 02			22 02	22 02	23 02	
Dorchester West	a				20 21														
Dorchester South	d			20 10									21 10			22 10	22 10	23 10	
Moreton (Dorset)	d			20 17									21 17			22 17	22 17	23 17	
Wool	d			20 23									21 23			22 23	22 23	23 23	
Wareham	d			20 30									21 30			22 30	22 30	23 30	
Holton Heath	d																		
Hamworthy	d			20 37									21 37			22 37	22 37	23 37	
Poole 4	a			20 41									21 41			22 41	22 41	23 41	
	d			20 50									21 50			22 50	22 50	23 50	
Parkstone (Dorset)	d			20 54									21 54			22 54	22 54	23 54	
Branksome	d			20 57									21 57			22 57	22 57	23 57	
Bournemouth	a			21 03									22 03			23 03	23 03	00 03	
	d			21 06									22 06			23 06	23 06		
Pokesdown	d			21 10									22 10			23 10	23 10		
Christchurch	d			21 14									22 14			23 14	23 14		
Hinton Admiral	d			21 19									22 19			23 19	23 19		
New Milton	d			21 23									22 23			23 23	23 23		
Sway	d			21 28									22 28			23 28	23 28		
Lymington Pier	d							21 44		22 14									
Lymington Town	d							21 46		22 16									
Brockenhurst 3	a			21 33				21 54		22 24			22 33			23 33	23 33		
	d			21 34									22 34			23 34	23 34		
Beaulieu Road	d			21 39									22 39						
Ashurst New Forest	d			21 43									22 43			23 43	23 43		
Totton	d			21 48									22 48			23 48	23 48		
Salisbury	d					21 08	21 33								22 36				
Dean	d					21 20													
Mottisfont & Dunbridge	d					21 26													
Romsey	d					21 32	21 51							22 28	22 54				
Redbridge	d					21 39								22 35					
Millbrook (Hants)	d					21 43								22 39					
Southampton Central ⛴	a			21 53		21 45	22 03						22 53	22 41	23 05	23 53	23 53		
	d			21 55		21 59	22 04						22 55	23 05	23 08				
St Denys	d					22 04								23 10					
Swaythling	d					22 07								23 13					
Southampton Airport Pkwy ✈	d			22 03		22 10							23 03	23 16					
Portsmouth Harbour ⛴	d		21 17						22 03		22 17								23 17
Portsmouth & Southsea	d		21 22						22 12		22 22								23 22
Fratton	d		21 26						22 16		22 26								23 26
Hilsea	d		21 30								22 30								23 30
Cosham	d		21 35								22 35								23 35
Portchester	d		21 40								22 40								23 40
Fareham	d		21 46				22a26		22 32		22 46				23a29				23 46
Botley	d		21 54								22 54								23 54
Hedge End	d		21 58								22 58								23 58
Eastleigh 3	a		22 04	22 07		22 13					23 04		23 09	23 19					00 04
	d			22 11		22 15							23 11	23 21					
Chandlers Ford	d					22 20								23 26					
Romsey	a					22 31			23 08					23 33					
Shawford	d																		
Winchester	d			22 23									23 23						
Micheldever	d			22 32									23 32						
Basingstoke	a			22 42									23 42						
	d	22 16		22 44								23 16	23 44						
Reading 7	a																		
Fleet	d	22 32										23 32							
Farnborough (Main)	d	22 38										23 38							
Woking	a	22 50		23 02								23 50	00 02						
Clapham Junction 10	a	23 23		23 27									00 23						
London Waterloo 15 ⊖	a	23 34		23 37									00 33						

A ◇ to Eastleigh

Table 158

Sundays from 16 September

Weymouth, Bournemouth, Lymington, Romsey, Southampton and Basingstoke - London

Network Diagram - see first Page of Table 158

		SW	SW	SW	SW	SW	SW	SW	SW	SW	SW	SW	SW	SW	SW	SW
		■	■	■	■	■	■	■	■ A	■ B	■ A	■ B	■	◇■ C ⌶	■	■
Weymouth	d			21p10		22p10	23p10									
Upwey	d			21p14		22p14	23p14									
Dorchester West	a															
Dorchester South	d			21p22		22p22	23p22									
Moreton (Dorset)	d			21p28		22p28	23p28									
Wool	d			21p34		22p34	23p34									
Wareham	d			21p42		22p42	23p42									
Holton Heath	d															
Hamworthy	d			21p48		22p48	23p48									
Poole ■	a			21p53		22p53	23p53									
	d			21p54		22p54	23p54							06 50		
Parkstone (Dorset)	d			21p58		22p58								06 54		
Branksome	d			22p01		23p01								06 57		
Bournemouth	a			22p07		23p07	00 03							07 02		
	d			22p12		23p12								07 06		
Pokesdown	d			22p16		23p16								07 10		
Christchurch	d			22p20		23p20								07 14		
Hinton Admiral	d			22p25		23p25								07 19		
New Milton	d			22p29		23p29								07 23		
Sway	d			22p34		23p34								07 28		
Lymington Pier	d															
Lymington Town	d															
Brockenhurst ■	a			22p39		23p39								07 33		
	d			22p40		23p40								07 34		
Beaulieu Road	d															
Ashurst New Forest	d			22p47		23p47								07 43		
Totton	d			22p52		23p52								07 48		
Salisbury	d															08 08
Dean	d															08 20
Mottisfont & Dunbridge	d															08 26
Romsey	d															08 35
Redbridge	d															
Millbrook (Hants)	d															
Southampton Central	a			22p57		23p57								07 53		
	d		22p30	23p00		23p59								07 55		
St Denys	d					00 04										
Swaythling	d					00 07										
Southampton Airport Pkwy	d		22p38	23p08		00 10								08 03		
Portsmouth Harbour	d				23p24			06 37					07 17			
Portsmouth & Southsea	d				23p29			06 42					07 22			
Fratton	d				23p33			06 46					07 26			
Hilsea	d				23p37			06 50					07 30			
Cosham	d				23p42			06 55					07 35			
Portchester	d				23p47			07 00					07 40			
Fareham	d				23p53			07a05					07 46			
Botley	d				23p59								07 54			
Hedge End	d				00 05								07 58			
Eastleigh ■	a		22p41	23p11	00 11	00 14							08 04	08 07		
	d		22p46	23p12	00 21									08 11		
Chandlers Ford	d															08 42
Romsey	a															09 24
Shawford	d			23p18												
Winchester	d		22p55	23p24	00a30									08 23		
Micheldever	d			23p33										08 32		
Basingstoke	a		23p11	23p43										08 42		
	d	22p54	23p13	23p44					07 16	07 16	08 16	08 16		08 44	09 16	
Reading ■	a															
Fleet	d	23p10		00 01					07 32	07 32	08 32	08 32			09 32	
Farnborough (Main)	d	23p16		00 06					07 38	07 38	08 38	08 38			09 38	
Woking	a	23p28	23p31	00 18					07 50	07 50	08 50	08 50		09 02	09 50	
Clapham Junction ■	a	00 21	23p52	00 53					08 27	08 27	09 26	09 26		09 30	10 23	
London Waterloo ■ ⊖	a	00 35	00 03	01 04					08 41	08 44	09 39	09 42		09 43	10 38	

A 16 September, 23 September, 30 September
B from 7 October
C ⌶ to Eastleigh ◇ to Eastleigh

Table 158

Sundays from 16 September

Weymouth, Bournemouth, Lymington, Romsey, Southampton and Basingstoke - London

Network Diagram - see first Page of Table 158

		SW	SW	SW	GW	XC	SW	SW	SW	SW	SW	SW	SW	XC	SW	SW	SW	SW	SW
		■	◇■ A	■	■	◇■ ⌶	◇■ B ⌶	◇■ C ⌶	■	■	■ ⌶	◇■ D ⌶	■	◇■ ⌶	■	◇■ B ⌶	◇■ C ⌶	■	■
Weymouth	d						07 43	07 48								08 43	08 48		
Upwey	d						07 47	07 52								08 47	08 52		
Dorchester West	a																		
Dorchester South	d						07 55	08 00								08 55	09 00		
Moreton (Dorset)	d						08 02	08 07								09 02	09 07		
Wool	d						08 08	08 13								09 08	09 13		
Wareham	d						08 15	08 20								09 15	09 20		
Holton Heath	d																		
Hamworthy	d						08 22	08 27								09 22	09 27		
Poole ■	a						08 29	08 31								09 29	09 31		
	d		07 50				08 30	08 32				08 55				09 30	09 32		
Parkstone (Dorset)	d		07 54				08 34	08 36								09 34	09 36		
Branksome	d		07 57				08 37	08 40								09 37	09 40		
Bournemouth	a		08 02				08 46	08 46				09 04				09 46	09 46		
	d		08 06				08 50	08 50				09 06		09 40		09 50	09 50		
Pokesdown	d		08 10									09 10							
Christchurch	d		08 14									09 14							
Hinton Admiral	d		08 19									09 19							
New Milton	d		08 23				09 01	09 01				09 23				10 01	10 01		
Sway	d		08 28									09 28							
Lymington Pier	d								09 14						09 44			10 14	
Lymington Town	d								09 16						09 46			10 16	
Brockenhurst ■	a		08 33				09 08	09 08	09 24			09 33		09 53	09 54	10 08	10 08	10 24	
	d		08 34				09 09	09 09				09 34		09 57		10 09	10 09		
Beaulieu Road	d		08 39									09 39							
Ashurst New Forest	d		08 43									09 43							
Totton	d		08 48									09 48							
Salisbury	d			08 20									09 08						
Dean	d												09 20						
Mottisfont & Dunbridge	d												09 26						
Romsey	d			08 39									09 32						
Redbridge	d			08 46									09 39						
Millbrook (Hants)	d			08 50									09 43						
Southampton Central	a		08 53	08 52			09 23	09 23				09 53	09 45	10 10		10 23	10 23		
	d		08 55	08 59		09 15	09 25	09 25				09 55	09 59	10 15		10 25	10 25		
St Denys	d			09 04									10 04						
Swaythling	d			09 07									10 07						
Southampton Airport Pkwy	d		09 03	09 10		09 22	09 33	09 33				10 03	10 10	10 22		10 33	10 33		
Portsmouth Harbour	d	08 17			09 08						09 17								
Portsmouth & Southsea	d	08 22			09 12						09 22								
Fratton	d	08 26			09 16						09 26								
Hilsea	d	08 30									09 30								
Cosham	d	08 35			09 23						09 35								
Portchester	d	08 40									09 40								
Fareham	d	08 46			09 32						09 46								
Botley	d	08 54									09 54								
Hedge End	d	08 58									09 58								
Eastleigh ■	a	09 04	09 07	09 13							10 04	10 07	10 13						
	d		09 11	09 15								10 11	10 15						
Chandlers Ford	d			09 20									10 20						
Romsey	a			09 28	10 05								10 28						
Shawford	d		09 17																
Winchester	d		09 23			09 31	09 42	09 42				10 23		10 31		10 42	10 42		
Micheldever	d		09 32									10 32							
Basingstoke	a		09 42			09 46	09 58	09 58				10 42		10 46		10 58	10 58		
	d		09 44			09 47	10 00	10 00		10 16		10 44		10 47		11 00	11 00		11 16
Reading ■	a					10 03								11 04					
Fleet	d									10 32									11 32
Farnborough (Main)	d									10 38									11 38
Woking	a		10 02				10 19	10 19		10 50		11 02				11 18	11 18		11 50
Clapham Junction ■	a		10 27				10 40	10 40		11 23		11 27				11 39	11 39		12 23
London Waterloo ■ ⊖	a		10 42				10 54	10 54		11 38		11 42				11 54	11 54		12 39

A ◇ to Eastleigh
B from 7 October. ⌶ from Bournemouth
C 16 September, 23 September, 30 September. ⌶ from Bournemouth
D ⌶ from Eastleigh ◇ to Eastleigh

Weymouth, Bournemouth, Lymington, Romsey, Southampton and Basingstoke - London

Sundays
from 16 September

Network Diagram - see first Page of Table 158

Station		SW ■ ⌶	SW ◇■ A ⌶	SW ■	GW ◇	XC ◇■ ⌶	SW ■	SW ◇■ B ⌶	GW ◇	SW ■	SW ■	SW ■ ⌶	SW ◇■ C ⌶	SW ■	GW ◇	XC ◇■ ⌶	SW ■
Weymouth	d							09 48									
Upwey	d							09 52									
Dorchester West	a																
Dorchester South	d							10 00									
Moreton (Dorset)	d							10 07									
Wool	d							10 13									
Wareham	d							10 20									
Holton Heath	d																
Hamworthy	d							10 27									
Poole ■	a							10 31									
	d		09 55					10 32					10 55				
Parkstone (Dorset)	d							10 36									
Branksome	d							10 40									
Bournemouth	a		10 04					10 46					11 04				
	d		10 06			10 40		10 50					11 06			11 40	
Pokesdown	d		10 10										11 10				
Christchurch	d		10 14										11 14				
Hinton Admiral	d		10 19										11 19				
New Milton	d		10 23					11 01					11 23				
Sway	d		10 28										11 28				
Lymington Pier	d						10 44			11 14							11 44
Lymington Town	d						10 46			11 16							11 46
Brockenhurst ■	a		10 33			10 53	10 54	11 08		11 24			11 33			11 53	11 54
	d		10 34			10 57		11 09					11 34			11 57	
Beaulieu Road	d		10 39										11 39				
Ashurst New Forest	d		10 43										11 43				
Totton	d		10 48										11 48				
Salisbury	d			10 13	10 32									11 08	11 33		
Dean	d													11 20			
Mottisfont & Dunbridge	d													11 26			
Romsey	d			10 32	10 50									11 32	11 51		
Redbridge	d			10 39										11 39			
Millbrook (Hants)	d			10 43										11 43			
Southampton Central ⛴	a		10 53	10 45	11 02	11 10		11 23					11 53	11 45	12 03	12 10	
	d		10 55	10 59	11 04	11 15		11 25					11 55	11 59	12 04	12 15	
St Denys	d			11 04										12 04			
Swaythling	d			11 07										12 07			
Southampton Airport Pkwy ✈	d		11 03	11 10		11 22		11 33					12 03	12 10		12 22	
Portsmouth Harbour ⛴	d	10 17							11 08			11 17					
Portsmouth & Southsea	d	10 22							11 12			11 22					
Fratton	d	10 26							11 16			11 26					
Hilsea	d	10 30										11 30					
Cosham	d	10 35							11 23			11 35					
Portchester	d	10 40										11 40					
Fareham	d	10 46			11a26				11 32			11 46			12a28		
Botley	d	10 54										11 54					
Hedge End	d	10 58										11 58					
Eastleigh ■	a	11 04	11 07	11 13								12 04	12 07	12 13			
	d	11 11		11 15								12 11		12 15			
Chandlers Ford	d			11 20										12 20			
Romsey	a			11 28					12 05					12 28			
Shawford	d	11 17															
Winchester	d	11 23				11 31		11 42				12 23				12 31	
Micheldever	d	11 32										12 32					
Basingstoke	a	11 42				11 46		11 58				12 42				12 46	
	d	11 44				11 47		12 00			12 16	12 44				12 47	
Reading ■	a					12 04										13 04	
Fleet	d										12 32						
Farnborough (Main)	d										12 38						
Woking	a	12 02						12 18			12 50	13 02					
Clapham Junction ■	a	12 27						12 39			13 23	13 27					
London Waterloo ■ ⊖	a	12 42						12 49			13 39	13 37					

A ⌶ from Bournemouth ◇ to Eastleigh
B ⌶ from Bournemouth
C ⌶ from Eastleigh ◇ to Eastleigh

Table 158

Weymouth, Bournemouth, Lymington, Romsey, Southampton and Basingstoke - London

Sundays
from 16 September

Network Diagram - see first Page of Table 158

Station		SW ◇■ A ⌶	SW ■	SW ■	SW ■ ⌶	SW ◇■ B ⌶	SW ■	SW ■	GW ◇	GW ◇ C	GW ◇ D	XC ◇■ ⌶	SW ■	SW ◇■ A ⌶	SW ■	SW ■	SW ■ ⌶	SW ◇■ E ⌶
Weymouth	d	10 48												11 48				
Upwey	d	10 52												11 52				
Dorchester West	a																	
Dorchester South	d	11 00												12 00				
Moreton (Dorset)	d	11 07												12 07				
Wool	d	11 13												12 13				
Wareham	d	11 20												12 20				
Holton Heath	d																	
Hamworthy	d	11 27												12 27				
Poole ■	a	11 31												12 31				
	d	11 32				11 55								12 32				12 55
Parkstone (Dorset)	d	11 36												12 36				
Branksome	d	11 40												12 40				
Bournemouth	a	11 46				12 04								12 46				13 04
	d	11 50				12 06						12 40		12 50				13 06
Pokesdown	d					12 10												13 10
Christchurch	d					12 14												13 14
Hinton Admiral	d					12 19												13 19
New Milton	d	12 01				12 23								13 01				13 23
Sway	d					12 28												13 28
Lymington Pier	d		12 14					12 44							13 14			
Lymington Town	d		12 16					12 46							13 16			
Brockenhurst ■	a	12 08	12 24			12 33		12 54				12 53		13 08	13 24			13 33
	d	12 09				12 34						12 57		13 09				13 34
Beaulieu Road	d					12 39												13 39
Ashurst New Forest	d					12 43												13 43
Totton	d					12 48												13 48
Salisbury	d						12 13			12 33	12 36							
Dean	d																	
Mottisfont & Dunbridge	d																	
Romsey	d						12 32			12 52	12 54							
Redbridge	d						12 39											
Millbrook (Hants)	d						12 43											
Southampton Central ⛴	a	12 23				12 53	12 45			13 05	13 05	13 10		13 23				13 53
	d	12 25				12 55	12 59			13 07	13 07	13 15		13 25				13 55
St Denys	d						13 04											
Swaythling	d						13 07											
Southampton Airport Pkwy ✈	d	12 33				13 03	13 10					13 22		13 33				14 03
Portsmouth Harbour ⛴	d				12 17				13 08								13 17	
Portsmouth & Southsea	d				12 22				13 12								13 22	
Fratton	d				12 26				13 16								13 26	
Hilsea	d				12 30												13 30	
Cosham	d				12 35				13 23								13 35	
Portchester	d				12 40												13 40	
Fareham	d				12 46				13 32	13a33	13a33						13 46	
Botley	d				12 54												13 54	
Hedge End	d				12 58												13 58	
Eastleigh ■	a				13 04	13 07	13 13										14 04	14 07
	d				13 11		13 15										14 11	
Chandlers Ford	d						13 20											
Romsey	a						13 28		14 05									
Shawford	d				13 17													
Winchester	d	12 42			13 23							13 31		13 42			14 23	
Micheldever	d				13 32												14 32	
Basingstoke	a	12 58			13 42							13 46		13 58			14 42	
	d	13 00		13 16	13 44							13 47	13 50	14 00		14 16	14 44	
Reading ■	a											14 02						
Fleet	d			13 32									14 02			14 32		
Farnborough (Main)	d			13 38									14 08			14 38		
Woking	a	13 18		13 50	14 02								14 20	14 18		14 50	15 02	
Clapham Junction ■	a	13 39		14 23	14 27								14 59	14 39		15 23	15 27	
London Waterloo ■ ⊖	a	13 49		14 34	14 37								15 10	14 49		15 34	15 37	

A ⌶ from Bournemouth
B ⌶ from Bournemouth ◇ to Eastleigh
C from 28 October
D from 16 September until 21 October
E ⌶ from Eastleigh ◇ to Eastleigh

Table 158

Sundays from 16 September

Weymouth, Bournemouth, Lymington, Romsey, Southampton and Basingstoke - London

Network Diagram - see first Page of Table 158

		SW	GW	XC	SW	GW	SW	SW	SW	SW	SW	SW	SW	XC	SW	GW	GW	SW
		1	◇	◇1	1	◇	1	◇1	1	1	1	◇1	1	◇1	1	1	◇	1
								A				B						
			⌶	⌶				⌶			⌶	⌶		⌶				
Weymouth	d							12 48										
Upwey	d							12 52										
Dorchester West	a																	
Dorchester South	d							13 00										
Moreton (Dorset)	d							13 07										
Wool	d							13 13										
Wareham	d							13 20										
Holton Heath	d																	
Hamworthy	d							13 27										
Poole 4	a							13 31										
	d							13 32				13 55						
Parkstone (Dorset)	d							13 36										
Branksome	d							13 40										
Bournemouth	a							13 46				14 04						
	d			13 40				13 50				14 06		14 40				
Pokesdown	d											14 10						
Christchurch	d											14 14						
Hinton Admiral	d											14 19						
New Milton	d							14 01				14 23						
Sway	d											14 28						
Lymington Pier	d				13 44				14 14						14 44			
Lymington Town	d				13 46				14 16						14 46			
Brockenhurst 3	a			13 53	13 54			14 08	14 24			14 33		14 53	14 54			
	d			13 57				14 09				14 34		14 57				
Beaulieu Road	d											14 39						
Ashurst New Forest	d											14 43						
Totton	d											14 48						
Salisbury	d	13 08	13 33										14 13				14 48	
Dean	d	13 20																
Mottisfont & Dunbridge	d	13 26																
Romsey	d	13 32	13 51										14 32				15 10	
Redbridge	d	13 39											14 39					
Millbrook (Hants)	d	13 43											14 43					
Southampton Central ⛴	a	13 45	14 03	14 10				14 23				14 53	14 45	15 10			15 21	
	d	13 59	14 04	14 15				14 25				14 55	14 59	15 15			15 22	
St Denys	d	14 04											15 04					
Swaythling	d	14 07											15 07					
Southampton Airport Pkwy ✈	d	14 10		14 22				14 33				15 03	15 10	15 22				
Portsmouth Harbour ⛴	d					14 08					14 17					15 08		
Portsmouth & Southsea	d					14 12					14 22					15 12		
Fratton	d					14 16					14 26					15 16		
Hilsea	d										14 30							
Cosham	d					14 23					14 35					15 23		
Portchester	d										14 40							
Fareham	d		14a26			14 32					14 46					15 32	15a50	
Botley	d										14 54							
Hedge End	d										14 58							
Eastleigh 3	a	14 13									15 04	15 07	15 13					
	d	14 15										15 11	15 15					
Chandlers Ford	d	14 20											15 20					
Romsey	a	14 28				15 05							15 28			16 05		
Shawford	d											15 17						
Winchester	d			14 31				14 42				15 23		15 31				
Micheldever	d											15 32						
Basingstoke	a			14 46				14 58				15 42		15 46				
	d			14 47			14 50	15 00		15 16		15 44		15 47				15 50
Reading 7	a			15 04										16 02				
Fleet	d						15 02			15 32								16 02
Farnborough (Main)	d						15 08			15 38								16 08
Woking	a						15 20	15 18		15 50		16 02						16 20
Clapham Junction 10	a						15 59	15 39		16 23		16 27						16 59
London Waterloo 15 ⊖	a						16 10	15 49		16 34		16 37						17 10

A ⌶ from Bournemouth

B ⌶ from Eastleigh ◇ to Eastleigh

Table 158

Sundays from 16 September

Weymouth, Bournemouth, Lymington, Romsey, Southampton and Basingstoke - London

Network Diagram - see first Page of Table 158

		SW	GW	SW	SW	SW	SW	SW	GW	XC	SW	GW	SW	SW	SW	SW	SW	SW
		◇1	◇	1	1	1	◇1	1	◇	◇1	1	◇	1	◇1	1	1	1	◇1
		A					B							A				B
		⌶				⌶	⌶			⌶				⌶			⌶	⌶
Weymouth	d	13 48	14 00											14 48				
Upwey	d	13 52	14 05											14 52				
Dorchester West	a		14 12															
Dorchester South	d	14 00												15 00				
Moreton (Dorset)	d	14 07												15 07				
Wool	d	14 13												15 13				
Wareham	d	14 20												15 20				
Holton Heath	d																	
Hamworthy	d	14 27												15 27				
Poole 4	a	14 31												15 31				
	d	14 32					14 55							15 32				15 55
Parkstone (Dorset)	d	14 36												15 36				
Branksome	d	14 40												15 40				
Bournemouth	a	14 46					15 04							15 46				16 04
	d	14 50					15 06			15 40				15 50				16 06
Pokesdown	d						15 10											16 10
Christchurch	d						15 14											16 14
Hinton Admiral	d						15 19											16 19
New Milton	d	15 01					15 23							16 01				16 23
Sway	d						15 28											16 28
Lymington Pier	d			15 14							15 44				16 14			
Lymington Town	d			15 16							15 46				16 16			
Brockenhurst 3	a	15 08		15 24			15 33			15 53	15 54			16 08	16 24			16 33
	d	15 09					15 34			15 57				16 09				16 34
Beaulieu Road	d						15 39											16 39
Ashurst New Forest	d						15 43											16 43
Totton	d						15 48											16 48
Salisbury	d							15 08	15 33									
Dean	d							15 20										
Mottisfont & Dunbridge	d							15 26										
Romsey	d							15 32	15 51									
Redbridge	d							15 39										
Millbrook (Hants)	d							15 43										
Southampton Central ⛴	a	15 23					15 53	15 45	16 03	16 10				16 23				16 53
	d	15 25					15 55	15 59	16 05	16 15				16 25				16 55
St Denys	d							16 04										
Swaythling	d							16 07										
Southampton Airport Pkwy ✈	d	15 33					16 03	16 10		16 22				16 33				17 03
Portsmouth Harbour ⛴	d					15 17						16 08					16 17	
Portsmouth & Southsea	d					15 22						16 12					16 22	
Fratton	d					15 26						16 16					16 26	
Hilsea	d					15 30											16 30	
Cosham	d					15 35						16 23					16 35	
Portchester	d					15 40											16 40	
Fareham	d					15 46			16a27			16 32					16 46	
Botley	d					15 54											16 54	
Hedge End	d					15 58											16 58	
Eastleigh 3	a					16 04	16 07	16 13									17 04	17 07
	d						16 11	16 15										17 11
Chandlers Ford	d							16 20										
Romsey	a							16 28				17 05						
Shawford	d																	17 17
Winchester	d	15 42					16 23			16 31				16 42				17 23
Micheldever	d						16 32											17 32
Basingstoke	a	15 58					16 42			16 46				16 58				17 42
	d	16 00			16 16		16 44			16 47			16 50	17 00		17 16		17 44
Reading 7	a									17 04								
Fleet	d				16 32								17 02			17 32		
Farnborough (Main)	d				16 38								17 08			17 38		
Woking	a	16 18			16 50		17 02						17 20	17 18		17 50		18 02
Clapham Junction 10	a	16 39			17 23		17 27						17 59	17 39		18 23		18 27
London Waterloo 15 ⊖	a	16 49			17 34		17 37						18 10	17 49		18 34		18 37

A ⌶ from Bournemouth

B ⌶ from Eastleigh ◇ to Eastleigh

Table 158

Sundays
from 16 September

Weymouth, Bournemouth, Lymington, Romsey, Southampton and Basingstoke - London

Network Diagram - see first Page of Table 158

		SW ■	GW ◇	XC ◇■ ⊼	SW ■	GW ◇	SW ■	SW ◇■ A ⊼	SW ■	SW ■	SW ■	SW ◇■ B	SW ■	GW ◇	XC ◇■ ⊼	SW ■	GW ◇	SW ■	SW ◇■ A ⊼
Weymouth	d							15 48											16 48
Upwey	d							15 52											16 52
Dorchester West	a																		
Dorchester South	d							16 00											17 00
Moreton (Dorset)	d							16 07											17 07
Wool	d							16 13											17 13
Wareham	d							16 20											17 20
Holton Heath	d																		
Hamworthy	d							16 27											17 27
Poole 4	a							16 31											17 31
	d							16 32				16 55							17 32
Parkstone (Dorset)	d							16 36											17 36
Branksome	d							16 40											17 40
Bournemouth	a							16 46				17 04							17 46
	d			16 40				16 50				17 06			17 40				17 50
Pokesdown	d											17 10							
Christchurch	d											17 14							
Hinton Admiral	d											17 19							
New Milton	d							17 01				17 23							18 01
Sway	d											17 28							
Lymington Pier	d				16 44				17 14							17 44			
Lymington Town	d				16 46				17 16							17 46			
Brockenhurst 3	a			16 53	16 54			17 08	17 24			17 33			17 53	17 54			18 08
	d			16 57				17 09				17 34			17 57				18 09
Beaulieu Road	d											17 39							
Ashurst New Forest	d											17 43							
Totton	d											17 48							
Salisbury	d	16 13	16 35										17 08	17 33					
Dean	d												17 20						
Mottisfont & Dunbridge	d												17 26						
Romsey	d	16 32	16 53										17 32	17 51					
Redbridge	d	16 39											17 39						
Millbrook (Hants)	d	16 43											17 43						
Southampton Central ⛴	a	16 45	17 04	17 10				17 23				17 53	17 45	18 03	18 10				18 23
	d	16 59	17 06	17 15				17 25				17 55	17 59	18 04	18 15				18 25
St Denys	d	17 04											18 04						
Swaythling	d	17 07											18 07						
Southampton Airport Pkwy ✈	d	17 10		17 22				17 33				18 03	18 10		18 22				18 33
Portsmouth Harbour ⛴	d					17 08					17 17						18 08		
Portsmouth & Southsea	d					17 12					17 22						18 12		
Fratton	d					17 16					17 26						18 16		
Hilsea	d										17 30								
Cosham	d					17 23					17 35						18 23		
Portchester	d										17 40								
Fareham	d		17a27			17 32					17 46			18a27			18 32		
Botley	d										17 54								
Hedge End	d										17 58								
Eastleigh 3	a	17 13									18 04	18 07	18 13						
	d	17 15									18 11		18 15						
Chandlers Ford	d	17 20											18 20						
Romsey	a	17 28				18 05							18 28				19 05		
Shawford	d																		
Winchester	d			17 31				17 42			18 23				18 31				18 42
Micheldever	d										18 32								
Basingstoke	a			17 46				17 58			18 42				18 46				18 58
	d			17 47			17 50	18 00		18 16	18 44				18 47			18 50	19 00
Reading 7	a			18 04											19 02				
Fleet	d						18 02			18 32								19 02	
Farnborough (Main)	d						18 08			18 38								19 08	
Woking	a						18 20	18 18		18 50	19 02							19 20	19 18
Clapham Junction 10	a						18 59	18 39		19 23	19 27							19 59	19 39
London Waterloo 15 ⊖	a						19 10	18 49		19 34	19 37							20 10	19 49

A ⊼ from Bournemouth
B ◇ to Eastleigh

Table 158

Sundays
from 16 September

Weymouth, Bournemouth, Lymington, Romsey, Southampton and Basingstoke - London

Network Diagram - see first Page of Table 158

		SW ■	SW ■	SW ■	SW ◇■ A	SW ■	GW ◇	XC ◇■ ⊼	SW ■	GW ◇	SW ■	SW ◇■ B ⊼	GW ◇	GW ◇	SW ■	SW ■
Weymouth	d											17 48	17 56			
Upwey	d											17 52	18 01			
Dorchester West	a												18 08			
Dorchester South	d											18 00				
Moreton (Dorset)	d											18 07				
Wool	d											18 13				
Wareham	d											18 20				
Holton Heath	d															
Hamworthy	d											18 27				
Poole 4	a											18 31				
	d				17 55							18 32				
Parkstone (Dorset)	d											18 36				
Branksome	d											18 40				
Bournemouth	a				18 04							18 46				
	d				18 06			18 40				18 50				
Pokesdown	d				18 10											
Christchurch	d				18 14											
Hinton Admiral	d				18 19											
New Milton	d				18 23							19 01				
Sway	d				18 28											
Lymington Pier	d	18 14							18 44						19 14	
Lymington Town	d	18 16							18 46						19 16	
Brockenhurst 3	a	18 24			18 33			18 53	18 54			19 08			19 24	
	d				18 34			18 57				19 09				
Beaulieu Road	d				18 39											
Ashurst New Forest	d				18 43											
Totton	d				18 48											
Salisbury	d					18 13	18 33							18 56		
Dean	d															
Mottisfont & Dunbridge	d															
Romsey	d					18 32	18 51							19 14		
Redbridge	d					18 39										
Millbrook (Hants)	d					18 43										
Southampton Central ⛴	a				18 53	18 45	19 03	19 10				19 23		19 25		
	d				18 55	18 59	19 04	19 15				19 25		19 26		
St Denys	d					19 04										
Swaythling	d					19 07										
Southampton Airport Pkwy ✈	d				19 03	19 10		19 22				19 33				
Portsmouth Harbour ⛴	d			18 17						19 08						
Portsmouth & Southsea	d			18 22						19 12						
Fratton	d			18 26						19 16						
Hilsea	d			18 30												
Cosham	d			18 35						19 23						
Portchester	d			18 40												
Fareham	d			18 46			19a28			19 32				19a48		
Botley	d			18 54												
Hedge End	d			18 58												
Eastleigh 3	a			19 04	19 07	19 13										
	d			19 11		19 15										
Chandlers Ford	d					19 20										
Romsey	a					19 28				20 05						
Shawford	d			19 17												
Winchester	d			19 23				19 31				19 42				
Micheldever	d			19 32												
Basingstoke	a			19 42				19 46				19 58				
	d		19 16	19 44				19 47			19 50	20 00				20 16
Reading 7	a							20 04								
Fleet	d		19 32								20 02					20 32
Farnborough (Main)	d		19 38								20 08					20 38
Woking	a		19 50	20 02							20 20	20 18				20 50
Clapham Junction 10	a		20 23	20 27							20 59	20 39				21 23
London Waterloo 15 ⊖	a		20 34	20 37							21 10	20 49				21 34

A ◇ to Eastleigh
B ⊼ from Bournemouth

Sundays
from 16 September

Weymouth, Bournemouth, Lymington, Romsey, Southampton and Basingstoke - London

Network Diagram - see first Page of Table 158

		SW	SW	SW	GW	XC	SW	GW	SW	SW	SW	SW	GW	SW	SW	SW	GW	SW	SW
		■	◇■ A	■	◇	◇■	■	◇	■	◇■ B ✕	■	■	■	■	◇■ A	■	◇	■	■
Weymouth	d									18 48									
Upwey	d									18 52									
Dorchester West	a																		
Dorchester South	d									19 00									
Moreton (Dorset)	d									19 07									
Wool	d									19 13									
Wareham	d									19 20									
Holton Heath	d																		
Hamworthy	d									19 27									
Poole ■	a									19 31									
	d		18 55							19 32					19 55				
Parkstone (Dorset)	d									19 36									
Branksome	d									19 40									
Bournemouth	a		19 04							19 46					20 04				
	d		19 06			19 40				19 50					20 06				
Pokesdown	d		19 10												20 10				
Christchurch	d		19 14												20 14				
Hinton Admiral	d		19 19												20 19				
New Milton	d		19 23							20 01					20 23				
Sway	d		19 28												20 28				
Lymington Pier	d						19 44				20 14							20 44	21 14
Lymington Town	d						19 46				20 16							20 46	21 16
Brockenhurst ■	a		19 33			19 53	19 54			20 08	20 24				20 33			20 54	21 24
	d		19 34			19 57				20 09					20 34				
Beaulieu Road	d		19 39												20 39				
Ashurst New Forest	d		19 43												20 43				
Totton	d		19 48												20 48				
Salisbury	d			19 08	19 32								20 01			20 13	20 30		
Dean	d			19 20															
Mottisfont & Dunbridge	d			19 26															
Romsey	d			19 32	19 50								20 19			20 32	20 48		
Redbridge	d			19 39												20 39			
Millbrook (Hants)	d			19 43												20 43			
Southampton Central ⛴	a		19 53	19 45	20 02	20 10				20 23			20 29		20 53	20 45	20 59		
	d		19 55	19 59	20 04	20 15				20 25			20 31		20 55	20 59	21 02		
St Denys	d			20 04												21 04			
Swaythling	d			20 07												21 07			
Southampton Airport Pkwy ✈	d		20 03	20 10		20 22				20 33					21 03	21 10			
Portsmouth Harbour ⛴	d	19 17						20 08						20 17					
Portsmouth & Southsea	d	19 22						20 12						20 22					
Fratton	d	19 26						20 16						20 26					
Hilsea	d	19 30												20 30					
Cosham	d	19 35												20 35					
Portchester	d	19 40												20 40					
Fareham	d	19 46			20a26			20 32					20a54	20 46			21a24		
Botley	d	19 54												20 54					
Hedge End	d	19 58												20 58					
Eastleigh ■	a	20 04	20 07	20 13										21 04	21 07	21 13			
	d		20 11	20 15											21 11	21 15			
Chandlers Ford	d			20 20												21 20			
Romsey	a			20 28				21 05								21 28			
Shawford	d														21 17				
Winchester	d		20 23			20 31				20 42					21 23				
Micheldever	d		20 32												21 32				
Basingstoke	a		20 42			20 46				20 58					21 42				
	d		20 44			20 47			20 50	21 00		21 16			21 44				
Reading ■	a					21 03													
Fleet	d								21 02			21 32							
Farnborough (Main)	d								21 08			21 38							
Woking	a		21 02						21 20	21 18		21 50			22 02				
Clapham Junction ■	a		21 27						21 59	21 39		22 23			22 27				
London Waterloo ■ ⊖	a		21 37						22 10	21 49		22 34			22 37				

A ◇ to Eastleigh
B ✕ from Bournemouth

Sundays
from 16 September

Weymouth, Bournemouth, Lymington, Romsey, Southampton and Basingstoke - London

Network Diagram - see first Page of Table 158

		SW	SW	SW	SW	GW	SW	GW	SW	GW	SW	SW	SW	SW	SW	GW	SW	SW	SW
		■	■	■	◇■ A		■	◇	■		■	■	■	◇■	■	◇	■	■	■
Weymouth	d				19 58	20 09								20 58			21 58	22 58	
Upwey	d				20 02	20 14								21 02			22 02	23 02	
Dorchester West	a					20 21													
Dorchester South	d				20 10									21 10			22 10	23 10	
Moreton (Dorset)	d				20 17									21 17			22 17	23 17	
Wool	d				20 23									21 23			22 23	23 23	
Wareham	d				20 30									21 30			22 30	23 30	
Holton Heath	d																		
Hamworthy	d				20 37									21 37			22 37	23 37	
Poole ■	a				20 41									21 41			22 41	23 41	
	d				20 50									21 50			22 50	23 50	
Parkstone (Dorset)	d				20 54									21 54			22 54	23 54	
Branksome	d				20 57									21 57			22 57	23 57	
Bournemouth	a				21 03									22 03			23 03	00 03	
	d				21 06									22 06			23 06		
Pokesdown	d				21 10									22 10			23 10		
Christchurch	d				21 14									22 14			23 14		
Hinton Admiral	d				21 19									22 19			23 19		
New Milton	d				21 23									22 23			23 23		
Sway	d				21 28									22 28			23 28		
Lymington Pier	d								21 44		22 14								
Lymington Town	d								21 46		22 16								
Brockenhurst ■	a				21 33				21 54		22 24			22 33			23 33		
	d				21 34									22 34			23 34		
Beaulieu Road	d				21 39									22 39					
Ashurst New Forest	d				21 43									22 43			23 43		
Totton	d				21 48									22 48			23 48		
Salisbury	d						21 08	21 33								22 36			
Dean	d						21 20												
Mottisfont & Dunbridge	d						21 26												
Romsey	d						21 32	21 51							22 28	22 54			
Redbridge	d						21 39								22 35				
Millbrook (Hants)	d						21 43								22 39				
Southampton Central ⛴	a				21 53		21 45	22 03						22 53	22 41	23 05	23 53		
	d				21 55		21 59	22 04						22 55	23 05	23 08			
St Denys	d						22 04								23 10				
Swaythling	d						22 07								23 13				
Southampton Airport Pkwy ✈	d				22 03		22 10							23 03	23 16				
Portsmouth Harbour ⛴	d			21 17						22 03		22 17							23 17
Portsmouth & Southsea	d			21 22						22 12		22 22							23 22
Fratton	d			21 26						22 16		22 26							23 26
Hilsea	d			21 30								22 30							23 30
Cosham	d			21 35								22 35							23 35
Portchester	d			21 40								22 40							23 40
Fareham	d			21 46				22a26		22 32		22 46				23a29			23 46
Botley	d			21 54								22 54							23 54
Hedge End	d			21 58								22 58							23 58
Eastleigh ■	a			22 04	22 07		22 13					23 04		23 09	23 19				00 04
	d				22 11		22 15							23 11	23 21				
Chandlers Ford	d						22 20								23 26				
Romsey	a						22 31			23 08					23 33				
Shawford	d																		
Winchester	d				22 23									23 23					
Micheldever	d				22 32									23 32					
Basingstoke	a				22 42									23 42					
	d	21 50	22 16		22 44								23 16	23 44					
Reading ■	a																		
Fleet	d	22 02	22 32										23 32						
Farnborough (Main)	d	22 08	22 38										23 38						
Woking	a	22 21	22 50		23 02								23 50	00 02					
Clapham Junction ■	a	22 59	23 23		23 27									00 23					
London Waterloo ■ ⊖	a	23 10	23 34		23 37									00 33					

A ◇ to Eastleigh

Mondays to Saturdays

Woking - Heathrow Railair

Express Coach Service

		SW SX	SW SX	SW SX	SW SX	SW	SW	SW	SW SO	SW SX		SW	SW SO	SW SX	SW SO	SW	SW SX	SW SO	SW	SW SX		SW SO	SW	SW SX	SW
Woking	d		05 20		05 50		06 20		06 50	06 50			07 20	07 20	07 50		07 50	08 20		08 20		08 50		08 50	
Heathrow Terminal 5 Bus	d		05 45		06 15		06 45		07 15	07 25			07 45	08 05	08 15		08 35	08 45		09 05		09 15		09 35	
Heathrow Central Bus Stn	a		06 00		06 30		07 00		07 30	07 40			08 00	08 20	08 30		08 50	09 00		09 20		09 30		09 50	
	d	05 45		06 15		06 45		07 15				07 45				08 30			09 00				09 30		10 00
Heathrow Terminal 5 Bus	a	06 00		06 30		07 00		07 30				08 00				08 45			09 15				09 45		10 15
Woking	a	06 30		07 00		07 30		08 05				08 40				09 25			09 55				10 25		10 50

		SW SO	SW SX	SW	SW	SW		SW	SW	SW	SW	SW	SW	SW	SW	SW		SW	SW	SW	SW	SW	SW	SW	SW
Woking	d	09 35	09 35		10 05			10 35		11 05		11 35		12 05		12 35			13 05		13 35		14 05		14 35
Heathrow Terminal 5 Bus	d	10 00	10 10		10 30			11 00		11 30		12 00		12 30		13 00			13 30		14 00		14 30		15 00
Heathrow Central Bus Stn	a	10 15	10 25		10 45			11 15		11 45		12 15		12 45		13 15			13 45		14 15		14 45		15 15
	d			10 30		11 00			11 30		12 00		12 30		13 00			13 30		14 00		14 30		15 00	
Heathrow Terminal 5 Bus	a			10 45		11 15			11 45		12 15		12 45		13 15			13 45		14 15		14 45		15 15	
Woking	a			11 15		11 45			12 15		12 45		13 15		13 45			14 15		14 45		15 15		15 45	

		SW		SW	SW	SW	SW	SW SO	SW SX	SW	SW SO	SW SX		SW	SW SO	SW SX	SW	SW SO	SW SX	SW	SW SO	SW SX		SW	SW
Woking	d			15 05		15 35		16 05	16 05		16 35	16 35			17 05	17 05		17 35	17 35		18 05	18 05			18 35
Heathrow Terminal 5 Bus	d			15 30		16 00		16 30	16 35		17 00	17 10			17 30	17 40		18 00	18 10		18 30	18 40			19 00
Heathrow Central Bus Stn	a			15 45		16 15		16 45	16 50		17 15	17 25			17 45	17 55		18 15	18 25		18 45	18 55			19 15
	d	15 30			16 00		16 30			17 00				17 30			18 00			18 30				19 00	
Heathrow Terminal 5 Bus	a	15 45			16 15		16 45			17 15				17 45			18 15			18 45				19 15	
Woking	a	16 15			16 45		17 25			18 05				18 35			19 05			19 35				19 55	

		SW	SW SO	SW SX	SW	SW SO	SW SX	SW		SW SO	SW SX	SW SO	SW SX	SW	SW SO	SW SX	SW SO	SW SX		SW SO	SW SX	SW SO	SW SX		
Woking	d		19 05	19 05		19 35	19 35			20 05	20 05	20 35	20 35		21 05	21 05				22 05	22 05				
Heathrow Terminal 5 Bus	d		19 30	19 35		20 00	20 05			20 30	20 35	21 00	21 05		21 30	21 35				22 30	22 35				
Heathrow Central Bus Stn	a		19 45	19 45		20 15	20 15			20 45	20 45	21 15	21 15		21 45	21 45				22 45	22 45				
	d	19 30			20 00			20 30						21 15			22 15	22 15				23 15	23 15		
Heathrow Terminal 5 Bus	a	19 45			20 15			20 45						21 30			22 30	22 30				23 30	23 30		
Woking	a	20 15			20 45			21 15						22 00			22 55	23 00				23 55	23 59		

Sundays

		SW	SW	SW	SW	SW	SW	SW	SW	SW		SW	SW	SW	SW	SW	SW	SW	SW	SW		SW	SW	SW	SW
Woking	d		06 20		06 50		07 20	07 50		08 20			08 50			09 35		10 05		10 35			11 05		11 35
Heathrow Terminal 5 Bus	d		06 45		07 15		07 45	08 15		08 45			09 15			10 00		10 30		11 00			11 30		12 00
Heathrow Central Bus Stn	a		07 00		07 30		08 00	08 30		09 00			09 30			10 15		10 45		11 15			11 45		12 15
	d	06 45		07 15		07 45			08 30			09 00		09 30	10 00		10 30		11 00			11 30		12 00	
Heathrow Terminal 5 Bus	a	07 00		07 30		08 00			08 45			09 15		09 45	10 15		10 45		11 15			11 45		12 15	
Woking	a	07 30		08 00		08 25			09 15			09 45		10 15	10 45		11 15		11 45			12 15		12 45	

		SW	SW	SW	SW	SW		SW	SW	SW	SW	SW	SW	SW	SW	SW		SW	SW	SW	SW	SW	SW	SW	SW
Woking	d		12 05		12 35			13 05		13 35		14 05		14 35		15 05			15 35		16 05		16 35		17 05
Heathrow Terminal 5 Bus	d		12 30		13 00			13 30		14 00		14 30		15 00		15 30			16 00		16 30		17 00		17 30
Heathrow Central Bus Stn	a		12 45		13 15			13 45		14 15		14 45		15 15		15 45			16 15		16 45		17 15		17 45
	d	12 30		13 00		13 30			14 00		14 30		15 00		15 30			16 00		16 30		17 00		17 30	
Heathrow Terminal 5 Bus	a	12 45		13 15		13 45			14 15		14 45		15 15		15 45			16 15		16 45		17 15		17 45	
Woking	a	13 15		13 45		14 15			14 45		15 15		15 45		16 15			16 45		17 15		17 45		18 15	

		SW		SW	SW	SW	SW	SW	SW	SW	SW	SW		SW	SW	SW	SW	SW	SW	SW	SW				
Woking	d			17 35		18 05		18 35		19 05		19 35			20 05	20 35		21 05		22 05					
Heathrow Terminal 5 Bus	d			18 00		18 30		19 00		19 30		20 00			20 30	21 00		21 30		22 30					
Heathrow Central Bus Stn	a			18 15		18 45		19 15		19 45		20 15			20 45	21 15		21 45		22 45					
	d	18 00			18 30		19 00		19 30		20 00			20 30			21 15		22 15		23 15				
Heathrow Terminal 5 Bus	a	18 15			18 45		19 15		19 45		20 15			20 45			21 30		22 30		23 30				
Woking	a	18 45			19 15		19 45		20 15		20 45			21 15			22 00		23 00		23 59				

Network Diagram for Table 160

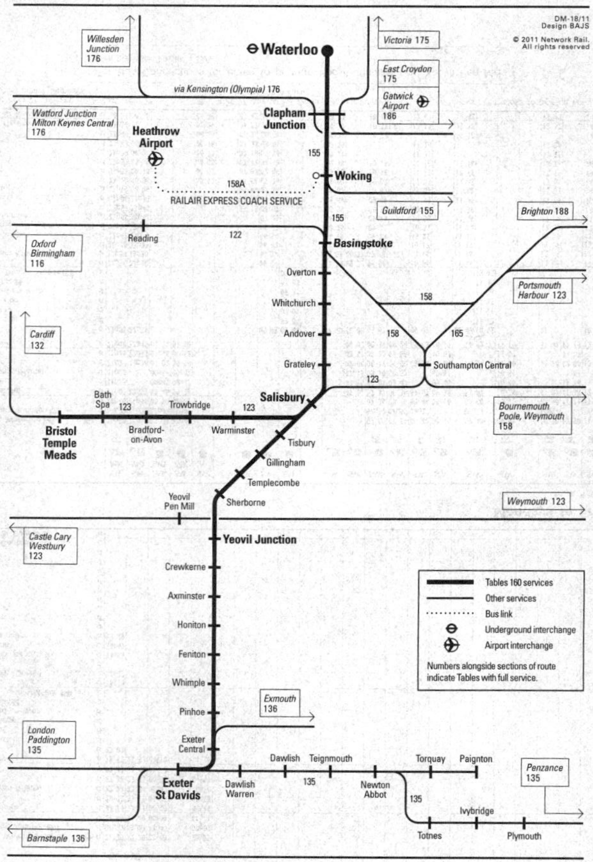

Table 160

Mondays to Fridays

until 5 October

London - Salisbury and Exeter

Network Diagram - see first Page of Table 160

Miles			SW MX ◇1 ⌶	SW MO ◇1 A ⌶	SW MO 1 B	SW MX 1 C	SW MX 1 D	SW 1 E	SW 1	SW 1	SW 1	SW 1	SW ◇1	SW ◇1	SW ◇1 ⌶	SW ◇1 ⌶	SW ◇1 ⌶	SW ◇1 ⌶	SW ◇1 ⌶		SW ◇1 ⌶	SW ◇1 ⌶
0	London Waterloo 15 ⊖	d	20p20	21p15	23p35	23p40	23p55	23p55							07 10	07 50	08 20	08 50	09 20		09 50	10 20
4	Clapham Junction 10	d	20b27	21b22	23b44	23b47	00u02	00u04							07u17	07u57	08u27		09u27			10u27
24½	Woking	d	20p46	21p46	00 08	00 08	00 21	00 28							07 36	08 16	08 46	09 16	09 46		10 16	10 46
47¾	Basingstoke	d	21p07	22p07	00 40	00 28	00 45	01 00						07 22	07 57	08 38	09 07	09 38	10 07		10 38	11 07
55½	Overton	d	21p15		00s49	00s37	00s53	01s09						07 30	08 05	08 47		09 46			10 46	
59¼	Whitchurch (Hants)	d	21p20		00s54	00s42	00s58	01s14						07 35	08 10	08 52		09 51			10 51	
66½	Andover	d	21p29	22p26	01 02	00 50	01 07	01 22						07 44	08 19	09 00	09 24	10 00	10 24		11 00	11 24
72¾	Grateley	d	21p36	22p33	01s10	00s58	01s14	01s30						07 51	08 26	09 08		10 07			11 07	
83¾	Salisbury	a	21p48	22p45	01 22	01 10	01 26	01 42						08 03	08 39	09 20	09 43	10 19	10 42		11 19	11 42
—		d	22p06	22p51							06 08	06 40	07 40	08 08	08 47		09 47		10 47	10 52		11 47
—	Warminster	d										07 00								11 12		
—	Westbury	d										07 09								11 21		
—	Trowbridge	d										07 15								11 27		
—	Bradford-on-Avon	d										07 21								11 33		
—	Bath Spa 7	a										07 33								11 46		
—	Bristol Temple Meads 10	a										07 52								12 05		
96¼	Tisbury	d	22p24	23p10							06 29		07 59	08 27	09 06		10 06		11 06			12 06
105¼	Gillingham (Dorset)	a	22p34	23p20							06 39		08 09	08 37	09 16		10 16		11 16			12 16
—		d	22p35	23p21							06 42		08 11		09 17		10 17		11 17			12 17
112¼	Templecombe	d	22p42	23p28							06 50		08 19		09 25		10 25		11 25			12 25
118¼	Sherborne	d	22p50	23p36							06 57		08 26		09 32		10 32		11 32			12 32
122¾	Yeovil Junction	a	22p55	23p41							07 03		08 32		09 38		10 38		11 38			12 38
—		d	22p57	23p43						06 15	07 07		08 39		09 39		10 39		11 39			12 39
131¾	Crewkerne	d	23p06	23p52						06 24	07 16		08 49		09 49		10 49		11 49			12 49
144¾	Axminster	a	23p19	00 05						06 43	07 35		09 02		10 02		11 02		12 02			13 02
—		d	23p20	00 06					05 52	06 56	07 36		09 03		10 03		11 03		12 03			13 03
155	Honiton	a	23p31	00 18					06 03	07 07	07 49		09 15		10 15		11 15		12 15			13 15
—		d	23p32	00 19					06 08	07 12	07 50		09 16		10 16		11 16		12 16			13 16
159½	Feniton	d	23p38	00 24					06 13	07 18	07 56		09 21				11 21					13 21
163¼	Whimple	d	23p43	00 29					06 18	07 23	08 01		09 26				11 26					13 26
169	Pinhoe	d	23p49						06 25	07 30	08 08		09 33		10 28				12 28			
171¾	Exeter Central	a	23p56						06 29	07 37	08 12		09 37		10 37		11 37		12 37			13 37
172¾	Exeter St Davids 6	a	00 01	00 40					06 35	07 42	08 18		09 42		10 42		11 42		12 42			13 42

		SW ◇1 ⌶	SW ◇1 ⌶	SW ◇1 ⌶	SW ◇1 ⌶		SW ◇1 ⌶	SW ◇1 ⌶	SW ◇1 ⌶	SW ◇1 ⌶	SW ◇1 ⌶	SW ◇1 ⌶	SW ◇1 ⌶	SW ◇1 ⌶	SW ◇1 ⌶	SW ◇1 ⌶	SW ◇1 ⌶	SW ◇1 ⌶	SW ◇1 ⌶	SW ◇1 ⌶		SW ◇1 ⌶	SW ◇1 ⌶
London Waterloo 15 ⊖	d	10 50	11 20	11 50	12 20		12 50	13 20	13 50	14 20	14 50	15 20	15 50	16 20	16 50	17 20	17 50	18 20	18 50	19 20		19 50	20 20
Clapham Junction 10	d		11u27		12u27			13u27		14u27		15u27	15u57	16u27	16u57			18u27		19u27			20u27
Woking	d	11 16	11 46	12 16	12 46		13 16	13 46	14 16	14 46	15 16	15 46	16 16	16 46	17u16	17u46		18 46	19 18	19 46		20 16	20 46
Basingstoke	d	11 38	12 07	12 38	13 07		13 38	14 07	14 38	15 07	15 38	16 07	16 38	17 07	17 38	18 07	18 38	19 07	19 39	20 07		20 38	21 07
Overton	d	11 46		12 46			13 46		14 46		15 46		16 46	17 15	17 46	18 15	18 47	19 15	19 47	20 15		20 46	21 15
Whitchurch (Hants)	d	11 51		12 51			13 51		14 51		15 51		16 51	17 20	17 51	18 20	18 52	19 20	19 52	20 20		20 51	21 20
Andover	d	12 00	12 24	13 00	13 24		14 00	14 24	15 00	15 24	16 00	16 24	17 00	17 29	18 00	18 29	19 00	19 29	20 01	20 29		21 00	21 29
Grateley	d	12 07		13 07			14 07		15 07		16 07		17 07	17 36	18 07	18 36	19 08	19 36	20 08	20 36		21 07	21 36
Salisbury	a	12 19	12 42	13 19	13 43		14 19	14 42	15 19	15 42	16 19	16 42	17 19	17 48	18 19	18 48	19 20	19 48	20 22	20 49		21 19	21 48
	d		12 47		13 47	13 52		14 47	15 23	15 47		16 47	17 23	17 53	18 23	18 53	19 23	19 53		20 53	20 57		22 06
Warminster	d					14 12															21 17		
Westbury	d					14 21															21 25		
Trowbridge	d					14 27															21 31		
Bradford-on-Avon	d					14 33															21 37		
Bath Spa 7	a					14 46															21 50		
Bristol Temple Meads 10	a					15 05															22 06		
Tisbury	d		13 06		14 06			15 06	15 37	16 06		17 06	17 37	18 08	18 37	19 08	19 37	20 08		21 08			22 24
Gillingham (Dorset)	a		13 16		14 16			15 16	15 47	16 16		17 16	17 47	18 18	18 47	19 18	19 48	20 18		21 18			22 34
	d		13 17		14 17			15 17		16 17		17 17		18 19	18 51	19 19	19 51	20 19		21 19			22 35
Templecombe	d		13 25		14 25			15 25		16 25		17 25		18 26	18 58	19 26	19 58	20 26		21 26			22 42
Sherborne	d		13 32		14 32			15 32		16 32		17 32		18 34	19 06	19 34	20 06	20 34		21 34			22 50
Yeovil Junction	a		13 38		14 38			15 38		16 38		17 38		18 39	19 14	19 39	20 14	20 39		21 39			22 55
	d		13 39		14 39			15 39		16 39		17 39		18 41		19 41		20 41		21 41			22 57
Crewkerne	d		13 49		14 49			15 49		16 49		17 49		18 50		19 50		20 50		21 50			23 06
Axminster	a		14 02		15 02			16 02		17 02		18 02		19 03		20 03		21 03		22 03			23 19
	d		14 03		15 03			16 03		17 03		18 03		19 04		20 04		21 04		22 04			23 20
Honiton	a		14 15		15 15			16 15		17 15		18 15		19 16		20 16		21 16		22 16			23 31
	d		14 16		15 16			16 16		17 16		18 18		19 17		20 17		21 17		22 17			23 32
Feniton	d				15 21					17 21				19 22				21 22		22 22			23 38
Whimple	d				15 26					17 26				19 27				21 27		22 27			23 43
Pinhoe	d		14 28					16 28				18 31				20 29				22 34			23 49
Exeter Central	a		14 37		15 37			16 35		17 35		18 38		19 38		20 39		21 37		22 40			23 56
Exeter St Davids 6	a		14 42		15 42			16 42		17 42		18 42		19 45		20 44		21 44		22 45			00 01

A from 21 May until 1 October

B from 21 May until 23 July, 20 August, 27 August, 17 September, 24 September, 1 October

C not from 31 July until 10 August, from 30 August until 7 September

D from 31 July until 7 September, not from 14 August until 29 August

E 30 July, 6 August, 13 August, 3 September, 10 September

b Previous night, stops to pick up only

For Bus Connections for either to or from Yeovil Junction and Yeovil Pen Mill please see Table 123A

Table 160

Mondays to Fridays

until 5 October

London - Salisbury and Exeter

Network Diagram - see first Page of Table 160

		SW ◇1 ⌶	SW 1 ⌶	SW 1 A	SW 1 B
London Waterloo 15 ⊖	d	21 20	22 20	23 40	23 55
Clapham Junction 10	d	21u27	22u27	23u47	00u02
Woking	d	21 49	22 49	00 08	00 21
Basingstoke	d	22 14	23 11	00 28	00 45
Overton	d	22 22	23 19	00s37	00s53
Whitchurch (Hants)	d	22 27	23 24	00s42	00s58
Andover	d	22 36	23 33	00 50	01 07
Grateley	d	22 43	23 40	00s58	01s14
Salisbury	a	22 55	23 52	01 10	01 26
	d	23 03			
Warminster	d				
Westbury	d				
Trowbridge	d				
Bradford-on-Avon	d				
Bath Spa 7	a				
Bristol Temple Meads 10	a				
Tisbury	d	23s16			
Gillingham (Dorset)	a	23s27			
	d				
Templecombe	d	23s35			
Sherborne	d	23s42			
Yeovil Junction	a	23 49			
	d				
Crewkerne	d				
Axminster	a				
	d				
Honiton	a				
	d				
Feniton	d				
Whimple	d				
Pinhoe	d				
Exeter Central	a				
Exeter St Davids 6	a				

Mondays to Fridays

from 8 October

		SW MX ◇1 ⌶	SW MO ◇1 ⌶	SW MO 1	SW MX 1	SW 1	SW 1	SW 1	SW 1	SW ◇1	SW ◇1	SW ◇1 ⌶	SW ◇1 ⌶	SW ◇1 ⌶	SW ◇1 ⌶	SW ◇1 ⌶		SW ◇1 ⌶	SW ◇1 ⌶	SW ◇1 ⌶	SW ◇1 ⌶	SW ◇1 ⌶
London Waterloo 15 ⊖	d	20p20	21p15	23p35	23p40							07 10	07 50	08 20	08 50	09 20		09 50	10 20	10 50	11 20	11 50
Clapham Junction 10	d	20b27	21b22	23b44	23b47							07u17	07u57	08u27		09u27			10u27		11u27	
Woking	d	20p46	21p46	00 08	00 08							07 36	08 16	08 46	09 16	09 46		10 16	10 46	11 16	11 46	12 16
Basingstoke	d	21p07	22p07	00 40	00 28						07 22	07 57	08 38	09 07	09 38	10 07		10 38	11 07	11 38	12 07	12 38
Overton	d	21p15		00s49	00s37						07 30	08 05	08 47		09 46			10 46		11 46		12 46
Whitchurch (Hants)	d	21p20		00s54	00s42						07 35	08 10	08 52		09 51			10 51		11 51		12 51
Andover	d	21p29	22p26	01 02	00 50						07 44	08 19	09 00	09 24	10 00	10 24		11 00	11 24	12 00	12 24	13 00
Grateley	d	21p36	22p33	01s10	00s58						07 51	08 26	09 08		10 07			11 07		12 07		13 07
Salisbury	a	21p48	22p45	01 22	01 10						08 03	08 39	09 20	09 43	10 19	10 42		11 19	11 42	12 19	12 42	13 19
	d	22p06	22p51					06 08	06 40	07 40	08 08	08 47		09 47		10 47	10 52		11 47		12 47	
Warminster	d								07 00								11 12					
Westbury	d								07 09								11 21					
Trowbridge	d								07 15								11 27					
Bradford-on-Avon	d								07 21								11 33					
Bath Spa 7	a								07 33								11 46					
Bristol Temple Meads 10	a								07 52								12 05					
Tisbury	d	22p24	23p10					06 29		07 59	08 27	09 06		10 06		11 06			12 06		13 06	
Gillingham (Dorset)	a	22p34	23p20					06 39		08 09	08 37	09 16		10 16		11 16			12 16		13 16	
	d	22p35	23p21					06 42		08 11		09 17		10 17		11 17			12 17		13 17	
Templecombe	d	22p42	23p28					06 50		08 19		09 25		10 25		11 25			12 25		13 25	
Sherborne	d	22p50	23p36					06 57		08 26		09 32		10 32		11 32			12 32		13 32	
Yeovil Junction	a	22p55	23p41					07 03		08 32		09 38		10 38		11 38			12 38		13 38	
	d	22p57	23p43				06 15	07 07		08 39		09 39		10 39		11 39			12 39		13 39	
Crewkerne	d	23p06	23p52				06 24	07 16		08 49		09 49		10 49		11 49			12 49		13 49	
Axminster	a	23p19	00 05				06 43	07 35		09 02		10 02		11 02		12 02			13 02		14 02	
	d	23p20	00 06			05 52	06 56	07 36		09 03		10 03		11 03		12 03			13 03		14 03	
Honiton	a	23p31	00 18			06 03	07 07	07 49		09 15		10 15		11 15		12 15			13 15		14 15	
	d	23p32	00 19			06 08	07 12	07 50		09 16		10 16		11 16		12 16			13 16		14 16	
Feniton	d	23p38	00 24			06 13	07 18	07 56		09 21				11 21					13 21			
Whimple	d	23p43	00 29			06 18	07 23	08 01		09 26				11 26					13 26			
Pinhoe	d	23p49				06 25	07 30	08 08		09 33		10 28				12 28					14 28	
Exeter Central	a	23p56				06 29	07 37	08 12		09 37		10 37		11 37		12 37			13 37		14 37	
Exeter St Davids 6	a	00 01	00 40			06 35	07 42	08 18		09 42		10 42		11 42		12 42			13 42		14 42	

A not from 27 July until 10 August, from 29 August until 7 September

B from 27 July until 7 September, not from 13 August until 28 August

b Previous night, stops to pick up only

For Bus Connections for either to or from Yeovil Junction and Yeovil Pen Mill please see Table 123A

London - Salisbury and Exeter

Mondays to Fridays
from 8 October

Network Diagram - see first Page of Table 160

		SW ◇■ ✠		SW ◇■ ✠	SW ◇■ ✠	SW ◇■ ✠	SW ◇■ ✠	SW ◇■ ✠	SW ◇■ ✠	SW ◇■ ✠	SW ◇■ ✠	SW ◇■ ✠	SW ◇■ ✠	SW ◇■ ✠	SW ◇■ ✠	SW ◇■ ✠	SW ◇■ ✠		SW ◇■ ✠	SW ◇■ ✠	SW ◇■ ✠	SW ■ ✠	SW ■
London Waterloo ■15 ⊖	d	12 20		12 50	13 20	13 50	14 20	14 50	15 20	15 50	16 20	16 50	17 20	17 50	18 20	18 50	19 20		19 50	20 20	21 20	22 20	23 40
Clapham Junction ■10	d	12u27			13u27		14u27		15u27	15u57	16u27	16u57			18u27		19u27			20u27	21u27	22u27	23u47
Woking	d	12 46		13 16	13 46	14 16	14 46	15 16	15 46	16 16	16 46	17u16	17u46		18 46	19 18	19 46		20 16	20 46	21 49	22 49	00 08
Basingstoke	d	13 07		13 38	14 07	14 38	15 07	15 38	16 07	16 38	17 07	17 38	18 07	18 38	19 07	19 39	20 07		20 38	21 07	22 14	23 11	00 28
Overton	d			13 46		14 46		15 46		16 46	17 15	17 46	18 15	18 47	19 15	19 47	20 15		20 46	21 15	22 22	23 19	00s37
Whitchurch (Hants)	d			13 51		14 51		15 51		16 51	17 20	17 51	18 20	18 52	19 20	19 52	20 20		20 51	21 20	22 27	23 24	00s42
Andover	d	13 24		14 00	14 24	15 00	15 24	16 00	16 24	17 00	17 29	18 00	18 29	19 00	19 29	20 01	20 29		21 00	21 29	22 36	23 33	00 50
Grateley	d			14 07		15 07		16 07		17 07	17 36	18 07	18 36	19 08	19 36	20 08	20 36		21 07	21 36	22 43	23 40	00s58
Salisbury	a	13 43		14 19	14 42	15 19	15 42	16 19	16 42	17 19	17 48	18 19	18 48	19 20	19 48	20 22	20 49		21 19	21 48	22 55	23 52	01 10
	d	13 47	13 52		14 47	15 23	15 47		16 47	17 23	17 53	18 23	18 53	19 23	19 53		20 53	20 57		22 06	23 03		
Warminster	d		14 12															21 17					
Westbury	d		14 21															21 25					
Trowbridge	d		14 27															21 31					
Bradford-on-Avon	d		14 33															21 37					
Bath Spa ■7	a		14 46															21 50					
Bristol Temple Meads ■10	a		15 05															22 06					
Tisbury	d	14 06			15 06	15 37	16 06		17 06	17 37	18 08	18 37	19 08	19 37	20 08		21 08			22 24	23s16		
Gillingham (Dorset)	a	14 16			15 16	15 47	16 16		17 16	17 47	18 18	18 47	19 18	19 48	20 18		21 18			22 34	23s27		
	d	14 17			15 17		16 17		17 17		18 19	18 51	19 19	19 51	20 19		21 19			22 35			
Templecombe	d	14 25			15 25		16 25		17 25		18 26	18 58	19 26	19 58	20 26		21 26			22 42	23s35		
Sherborne	d	14 32			15 32		16 32		17 32		18 34	19 06	19 34	20 06	20 34		21 34			22 50	23s42		
Yeovil Junction	a	14 38			15 38		16 38		17 38		18 39	19 14	19 39	20 14	20 39		21 39			22 55	23 49		
	d	14 39			15 39		16 39		17 39		18 41		19 41		20 41		21 41			22 57			
Crewkerne	d	14 49			15 49		16 49		17 49		18 50		19 50		20 50		21 50			23 06			
Axminster	a	15 02			16 02		17 02		18 02		19 03		20 03		21 03		22 03			23 19			
	d	15 03			16 03		17 03		18 03		19 04		20 04		21 04		22 04			23 20			
Honiton	a	15 15			16 15		17 15		18 15		19 16		20 16		21 16		22 16			23 31			
	d	15 16			16 16		17 16		18 18		19 17		20 17		21 17		22 17			23 32			
Feniton	d	15 21					17 21				19 22				21 22		22 22			23 38			
Whimple	d	15 26					17 26				19 27				21 27		22 27			23 43			
Pinhoe	d				16 28				18 31				20 29				22 34			23 49			
Exeter Central	a	15 37			16 35		17 35		18 38		19 38		20 39		21 37		22 40			23 56			
Exeter St Davids ■6	a	15 42			16 42		17 42		18 42		19 45		20 44		21 44		22 45			00 01			

Saturdays
until 6 October

		SW ◇■ ✠	SW ■ A	SW ■ B	SW ■	SW ■	SW ■	SW ■	SW ◇■	SW ◇■	SW ◇■ ✠	SW ◇■ ✠	SW ◇■ ✠	SW ◇■ ✠	SW ◇■ ✠		SW ◇■ ✠	SW ◇■ ✠	SW ◇■ ✠	SW ◇■ ✠	SW ◇■ ✠
London Waterloo ■15 ⊖	d	20p20	23p40	23p55							07 10	07 50	08 20	08 50	09 20		09 50	10 20	10 50	11 20	11 50
Clapham Junction ■10	d	20b27	23b47	00u02							07u17	07u57	08u27		09u27			10u27		11u27	
Woking	d	20p46	00∫08	00∫21							07 36	08 16	08 46	09 16	09 46		10 16	10 46	11 16	11 46	12 16
Basingstoke	d	21p07	00∫28	00∫45					07 22		07 59	08 38	09 07	09 38	10 07		10 38	11 07	11 38	12 07	12 38
Overton	d	21p15	00s37	00s53					07 30		08 07	08 46		09 46			10 46		11 46		12 46
Whitchurch (Hants)	d	21p20	00s42	00s58					07 35		08 12	08 51		09 51			10 51		11 51		12 51
Andover	d	21p29	00∫50	01∫07					07 44		08 21	09 00	09 24	10 00	10 24		11 00	11 24	12 00	12 24	13 00
Grateley	d	21p36	00s58	01s14					07 51		08 28	09 07		10 07			11 07		12 07		13 07
Salisbury	a	21p48	01∫10	01∫26					08 05		08 42	09 19	09 42	10 19	10 42		11 19	11 42	12 19	12 42	13 19
	d	22p06					06 15	06 40		07 45	08 47		09 47		10 47	10 52		11 47		12 47	
Warminster	d							07 00								11 12					
Westbury	d							07 09								11 21					
Trowbridge	d							07 15								11 27					
Bradford-on-Avon	d							07 21								11 33					
Bath Spa ■7	a							07 33								11 46					
Bristol Temple Meads ■10	a							07 52								12 05					
Tisbury	d	22p24					06 29			07 59	09 06		10 06		11 06			12 06		13 06	
Gillingham (Dorset)	a	22p34					06 39			08 09	09 16		10 16		11 16			12 16		13 16	
	d	22p35					06 42			08 11	09 17		10 17		11 17			12 17		13 17	
Templecombe	d	22p42					06 50			08 19	09 25		10 25		11 25			12 25		13 25	
Sherborne	d	22p50					06 57			08 26	09 32		10 32		11 32			12 32		13 32	
Yeovil Junction	a	22p55					07 03			08 32	09 38		10 38		11 38			12 38		13 38	
	d	22p57				06 15	07 07			08 39	09 39		10 39		11 39			12 39		13 39	
Crewkerne	d	23p06				06 24	07 16			08 49	09 49		10 49		11 49			12 49		13 49	
Axminster	a	23p19				06 43	07 36			09 02	10 02		11 02		12 02			13 02		14 02	
	d	23p20			05 52	06 56	07 38			09 03	10 03		11 03		12 03			13 03		14 03	
Honiton	a	23p31			06 03	07 07	07 51			09 15	10 15		11 15		12 15			13 15		14 15	
	d	23p32			06 08	07 12	07 52			09 16	10 16		11 16		12 16			13 16		14 16	
Feniton	d	23p38			06 13	07 18	07 57			09 21			11 21					13 21			
Whimple	d	23p43			06 18	07 23	08 02			09 26			11 26					13 26			
Pinhoe	d	23p49			06 25	07 30	08 09			09 33	10 28				12 28					14 28	
Exeter Central	a	23p56			06 29	07 37	08 13			09 37	10 37		11 37		12 37			13 37		14 37	
Exeter St Davids ■6	a	00 01			06 35	07 42	08 18			09 42	10 42		11 42		12 42			13 42		14 42	

A until 21 July, 18 August, 25 August, 15 September, 22 September, 29 September, 6 October

B 28 July, 4 August, 11 August, 1 September, 8 September

b Previous night, stops to pick up only

For Bus Connections for either to or from Yeovil Junction and Yeovil Pen Mill please see Table 123A

London - Salisbury and Exeter

Saturdays
until 6 October

Network Diagram - see first Page of Table 160

		SW ◇■ ✠		SW ◇■ ✠	SW ◇■ ✠	SW ◇■ ✠	SW ◇■ ✠	SW ◇■ ✠	SW ◇■ ✠	SW ◇■ ✠	SW ◇■ ✠	SW ◇■ ✠	SW ◇■ ✠	SW ◇■ ✠	SW ◇■ ✠	SW ◇■ ✠	SW ◇■ ✠		SW ◇■ ✠	SW ◇■ ✠	SW ◇■ ✠	SW ■ ✠	SW ■ A
London Waterloo ■15 ⊖	d	12 20		12 50	13 20	13 50	14 20	14 50	15 20	15 50	16 20	16 50	17 20	17 50	18 20	18 50	19 20		19 50	20 20	21 20	22 20	23∫40
Clapham Junction ■10	d	12u27			13u27		14u27		15u27		16u27		17u27		18u27		19u27			20u27	21u27	22u27	23u47
Woking	d	12 46		13 16	13 46	14 16	14 46	15 16	15 46	16 16	16 46	17 16	17 46	18 16	18 46	19 16	19 46		20 16	20 46	21 49	22 49	00∫08
Basingstoke	d	13 07		13 38	14 07	14 38	15 07	15 38	16 07	16 38	17 07	17 38	18 07	18 38	19 07	19 38	20 07		20 38	21 07	22 14	23 11	00∫28
Overton	d			13 46		14 46		15 46		16 46		17 46		18 46		19 46			20 46	21 15	22 22	23 20	00s37
Whitchurch (Hants)	d			13 51		14 51		15 51		16 51		17 51		18 51		19 51			20 51	21 20	22 27	23 25	00s42
Andover	d	13 24		14 00	14 24	15 00	15 24	16 00	16 24	17 00	17 24	18 00	18 24	19 00	19 24	20 00	20 24		21 00	21 29	22 36	23 33	00∫50
Grateley	d			14 07		15 07		16 07		17 07		18 07		19 07		20 07			21 07	21 36	22 43	23 41	00s58
Salisbury	a	13 42		14 19	14 42	15 19	15 42	16 19	16 42	17 19	17 42	18 19	18 43	19 19	19 43	20 19	20 42		21 19	21 48	22 55	23 53	01∫10
	d	13 47	13 52		14 47		15 47		16 47		17 47		18 47		19 47		20 47	20 57		21 53	23 03		
Warminster	d		14 12															21 17					
Westbury	d		14 21															21 25					
Trowbridge	d		14 27															21 31					
Bradford-on-Avon	d		14 33															21 37					
Bath Spa ■7	a		14 46															21 50					
Bristol Temple Meads ■10	a		15 05															22 06					
Tisbury	d	14 06			15 06		16 06		17 06		18 06		19 06		20 06		21 06			22 06	23s16		
Gillingham (Dorset)	a	14 16			15 16		16 16		17 16		18 16		19 16		20 16		21 16			22 16	23s27		
	d	14 17			15 17		16 17		17 17		18 17		19 17		20 17		21 17			22 17			
Templecombe	d	14 25			15 25		16 25		17 25		18 25		19 25		20 25		21 25			22 24	23s35		
Sherborne	d	14 32			15 32		16 32		17 32		18 32		19 32		20 32		21 32			22 32	23s42		
Yeovil Junction	a	14 38			15 38		16 38		17 38		18 38		19 38		20 38		21 38			22 40	23 49		
	d	14 39			15 39		16 39		17 39		18 39		19 39		20 39		21 39						
Crewkerne	d	14 49			15 49		16 49		17 49		18 49		19 49		20 49		21 49						
Axminster	a	15 02			16 02		17 02		18 02		19 02		20 02		21 02		22 02						
	d	15 03			16 03		17 03		18 03		19 03		20 03		21 03		22 03						
Honiton	a	15 15			16 15		17 15		18 15		19 15		20 15		21 15		22 15						
	d	15 16			16 16		17 16		18 16		19 16		20 16		21 16		22 16						
Feniton	d	15 21					17 21				19 21				21 21		22 21						
Whimple	d	15 26					17 26				19 26				21 26		22 26						
Pinhoe	d				16 28				18 28				20 28				22 33						
Exeter Central	a	15 37			16 35		17 37		18 35		19 37		20 39		21 37		22 41						
Exeter St Davids ■6	a	15 42			16 42		17 42		18 42		19 42		20 43		21 42		22 45						

		SW ■ B
London Waterloo ■15 ⊖	d	23∫55
Clapham Junction ■10	d	00u02
Woking	d	00∫21
Basingstoke	d	00∫45
Overton	d	00s53
Whitchurch (Hants)	d	00s58
Andover	d	01∫07
Grateley	d	01s14
Salisbury	a	01∫26
	d	
Warminster	d	
Westbury	d	
Trowbridge	d	
Bradford-on-Avon	d	
Bath Spa ■7	a	
Bristol Temple Meads ■10	a	
Tisbury	d	
Gillingham (Dorset)	a	
	d	
Templecombe	d	
Sherborne	d	
Yeovil Junction	a	
	d	
Crewkerne	d	
Axminster	a	
	d	
Honiton	a	
	d	
Feniton	d	
Whimple	d	
Pinhoe	d	
Exeter Central	a	
Exeter St Davids ■6	a	

A until 21 July, 18 August, 25 August, 15 September, 22 September, 29 September, 6 October

B 28 July, 4 August, 11 August, 1 September, 8 September

For Bus Connections for either to or from Yeovil Junction and Yeovil Pen Mill please see Table 123A

Table 160

London - Salisbury and Exeter

Saturdays from 13 October

Network Diagram - see first Page of Table 160

	SW ◇1 ⌶	SW 1	SW 1	SW 1	SW 1	SW 1	SW ◇1	SW ◇1	SW ◇1 ⌶	SW ◇1 ⌶	SW ◇1 ⌶
London Waterloo 15 ⊖ d	20p20	23p40							07 10	07 50	08 20
Clapham Junction 10 d	20b27	23b47							07u17	07u57	08u27
Woking d	20p46	00 08							07 36	08 16	08 46
Basingstoke d	21p07	00 28					07 22		07 59	08 38	09 07
Overton d	21p15	00s37					07 30		08 07	08 46	
Whitchurch (Hants) d	21p20	00s42					07 35		08 12	08 51	
Andover d	21p29	00 50					07 44		08 21	09 00	09 24
Grateley d	21p36	00s58					07 51		08 28	09 07	
Salisbury a	21p48	01 10					08 05		08 42	09 19	09 42
d	22p06				06 15	06 40		07 45	08 47		09 47
Warminster d						07 00					
Westbury d						07 09					
Trowbridge d						07 15					
Bradford-on-Avon d						07 21					
Bath Spa 7 a						07 33					
Bristol Temple Meads 10 a						07 52					
Tisbury d	22p24				06 29			07 59	09 06		10 06
Gillingham (Dorset) a	22p34				06 39			08 09	09 16		10 16
d	22p35				06 42			08 11	09 17		10 17
Templecombe d	22p42				06 50			08 19	09 25		10 25
Sherborne d	22p50				06 57			08 26	09 32		10 32
Yeovil Junction a	22p55				07 03			08 32	09 38		10 38
d	22p57			06 15	07 07			08 39	09 39		10 39
Crewkerne d	23p06			06 24	07 16			08 49	09 49		10 49
Axminster a	23p19			06 43	07 36			09 02	10 02		11 02
d	23p20		05 52	06 56	07 38			09 03	10 03		11 03
Honiton a	23p31		06 03	07 07	07 51			09 15	10 15		11 15
d	23p32		06 08	07 12	07 52			09 16	10 16		11 16
Feniton d	23p38		06 13	07 18	07 57			09 21			11 21
Whimple d	23p43		06 18	07 23	08 02			09 26			11 26
Pinhoe d	23p49		06 25	07 30	08 09			09 33	10 28		
Exeter Central a	23p56		06 29	07 37	08 13			09 37	10 37		11 37
Exeter St Davids 6 a	00 01		06 35	07 42	08 18			09 42	10 42		11 42

	SW ◇1 ⌶	SW ◇1 ⌶		SW ◇1 ⌶	SW ◇1 ⌶	SW ◇1 ⌶	SW ◇1 ⌶	SW ◇1 ⌶	SW ◇1 ⌶	
London Waterloo 15 ⊖ d	08 50	09 20		09 50	10 20	10 50	11 20	11 50	12 20	
Clapham Junction 10 d		09u27			10u27		11u27		12u27	
Woking d	09 16	09 46		10 16	10 46	11 16	11 46	12 16	12 46	
Basingstoke d	09 38	10 07		10 38	11 07	11 38	12 07	12 38	13 07	
Overton d	09 46			10 46		11 46		12 46		
Whitchurch (Hants) d	09 51			10 51		11 51		12 51		
Andover d	10 00	10 24		11 00	11 24	12 00	12 24	13 00	13 24	
Grateley d	10 07			11 07		12 07		13 07		
Salisbury a	10 19	10 42		11 19	11 42	12 19	12 42	13 19	13 42	
d		10 47	10 52		11 47		12 47		13 47	13 52
Warminster d			11 12							14 12
Westbury d			11 21							14 21
Trowbridge d			11 27							14 27
Bradford-on-Avon d			11 33							14 33
Bath Spa 7 a			11 46							14 46
Bristol Temple Meads 10 a			12 05							15 05
Tisbury d		11 06			12 06		13 06		14 06	
Gillingham (Dorset) a		11 16			12 16		13 16		14 16	
d		11 17			12 17		13 17		14 17	
Templecombe d		11 25			12 25		13 25		14 25	
Sherborne d		11 32			12 32		13 32		14 32	
Yeovil Junction a		11 38			12 38		13 38		14 38	
d		11 39			12 39		13 39		14 39	
Crewkerne d		11 49			12 49		13 49		14 49	
Axminster a		12 02			13 02		14 02		15 02	
d		12 03			13 03		14 03		15 03	
Honiton a		12 15			13 15		14 15		15 15	
d		12 16			13 16		14 16		15 16	
Feniton d					13 21				15 21	
Whimple d					13 26				15 26	
Pinhoe d		12 28					14 28			
Exeter Central a		12 37			13 37		14 37		15 37	
Exeter St Davids 6 a		12 42			13 42		14 42		15 42	

	SW ◇1 ⌶	SW ◇1 ⌶	SW ◇1 ⌶	SW ◇1 ⌶	SW ◇1 ⌶	SW ◇1 ⌶	SW ◇1 ⌶	SW ◇1 ⌶	SW ◇1 ⌶	SW ◇1 ⌶	SW ◇1 ⌶	SW ◇1 ⌶
London Waterloo 15 ⊖ d	12 50	13 20	13 50	14 20	14 50	15 20	15 50	16 20	16 50	17 20	17 50	18 20
Clapham Junction 10 d		13u27		14u27		15u27		16u27		17u27		18u27
Woking d	13 16	13 46	14 16	14 46	15 16	15 46	16 16	16 46	17 16	17 46	18 16	18 46
Basingstoke d	13 38	14 07	14 38	15 07	15 38	16 07	16 38	17 07	17 38	18 07	18 38	19 07
Overton d	13 46		14 46		15 46		16 46		17 46		18 46	
Whitchurch (Hants) d	13 51		14 51		15 51		16 51		17 51		18 51	
Andover d	14 00	14 24	15 00	15 24	16 00	16 24	17 00	17 24	18 00	18 24	19 00	19 24
Grateley d	14 07		15 07		16 07		17 07		18 07		19 07	
Salisbury a	14 19	14 42	15 19	15 42	16 19	16 42	17 19	17 42	18 19	18 43	19 19	19 43
d		14 47		15 47		16 47		17 47		18 47		19 47
Warminster d												
Westbury d												
Trowbridge d												
Bradford-on-Avon d												
Bath Spa 7 a												
Bristol Temple Meads 10 a												
Tisbury d		15 06		16 06		17 06		18 06		19 06		20 06
Gillingham (Dorset) a		15 16		16 16		17 16		18 16		19 16		20 16
d		15 17		16 17		17 17		18 17		19 17		20 17
Templecombe d		15 25		16 25		17 25		18 25		19 25		20 25
Sherborne d		15 32		16 32		17 32		18 32		19 32		20 32
Yeovil Junction a		15 38		16 38		17 38		18 38		19 38		20 38
d		15 39		16 39		17 39		18 39		19 39		20 39
Crewkerne d		15 49		16 49		17 49		18 49		19 49		20 49
Axminster a		16 02		17 02		18 02		19 02		20 02		21 02
d		16 03		17 03		18 03		19 03		20 03		21 03
Honiton a		16 15		17 15		18 15		19 15		20 15		21 15
d		16 16		17 16		18 16		19 16		20 16		21 16
Feniton d				17 21				19 21				21 21
Whimple d				17 26				19 26				21 26
Pinhoe d		16 28				18 28				20 28		
Exeter Central a		16 35		17 37		18 35		19 37		20 39		21 37
Exeter St Davids 6 a		16 42		17 42		18 42		19 42		20 43		21 42

	SW ◇1 ⌶	SW ◇1 ⌶		SW ◇1 ⌶	SW ◇1 ⌶	SW ◇1 ⌶	SW 1 ⌶	SW 1
London Waterloo 15 ⊖ d	18 50	19 20		19 50	20 20	21 20	22 20	23 40
Clapham Junction 10 d		19u27			20u27	21u27	22u27	23u47
Woking d	19 16	19 46		20 16	20 46	21 49	22 49	00 08
Basingstoke d	19 38	20 07		20 38	21 07	22 14	23 11	00 28
Overton d	19 46			20 46	21 15	22 22	23 20	00s37
Whitchurch (Hants) d	19 51			20 51	21 20	22 27	23 25	00s42
Andover d	20 00	20 24		21 00	21 29	22 36	23 33	00 50
Grateley d	20 07			21 07	21 36	22 43	23 41	00s58
Salisbury a	20 19	20 42		21 19	21 48	22 55	23 53	01 10
d		20 47	20 57		21 53	23 03		
Warminster d			21 17					
Westbury d			21 25					
Trowbridge d			21 31					
Bradford-on-Avon d			21 37					
Bath Spa 7 a			21 50					
Bristol Temple Meads 10 a			22 06					
Tisbury d		21 06			22 06	23s16		
Gillingham (Dorset) a		21 16			22 16	23s27		
d		21 17			22 17			
Templecombe d		21 25			22 24	23s35		
Sherborne d		21 32			22 32	23s42		
Yeovil Junction a		21 38			22 40	23 49		
d		21 39						
Crewkerne d		21 49						
Axminster a		22 02						
d		22 03						
Honiton a		22 15						
d		22 16						
Feniton d		22 21						
Whimple d		22 26						
Pinhoe d		22 33						
Exeter Central a		22 41						
Exeter St Davids 6 a		22 45						

b Previous night, stops to pick up only

For Bus Connections for either to or from Yeovil Junction and Yeovil Pen Mill please see Table 123A

Table 160

London - Salisbury and Exeter

Sundays until 30 September

Network Diagram - see first Page of Table 160

	SW 1 A	SW 1 B	SW 1	SW ◇1	SW ◇1 ⌶	SW ◇1 ⌶	SW ◇1 ⌶	SW ◇1 ⌶	SW ◇1 ⌶	
London Waterloo 15 ⊖ d	23p40	23p55			08 15	09 15	10 15	11 15	12 15	
Clapham Junction 10 d	23b47	00u02			08u22	09u22	10u22	11u22	12u22	
Woking d	00∫08	00∫21			08 47	09 47	10 46	11 46	12 46	
Basingstoke d	00∫28	00∫45		08 05	09 08	10 08	11 07	12 07	13 07	
Overton d	00s37	00s53		08 13	09 16		11 15		13 15	
Whitchurch (Hants) d	00s42	00s58		08 18	09 21		11 20		13 20	
Andover d	00∫50	01∫07		08 27	09 30	10 25	11 29	12 24	13 29	
Grateley d	00s58	01s14		08 34		10 32		12 31		
Salisbury a	01∫10	01∫26		08 46	09 46	10 45	11 45	12 45	13 45	
d			07 10	08 51	09 51	10 51	11 51	12 51	13 51	13 55
Warminster d										14 15
Westbury d										14 24
Trowbridge d										14 30
Bradford-on-Avon d										14 36
Bath Spa 7 a										14 49
Bristol Temple Meads 10 a										15 05
Tisbury d			07 24	09 10	10 10	11 10	12 10	13 10	14 10	
Gillingham (Dorset) a			07 34	09 20	10 20	11 20	12 20	13 20	14 20	
d			07 35	09 21	10 21	11 21	12 21	13 21	14 21	
Templecombe d			07 42	09 28	10 28	11 28	12 28	13 28	14 28	
Sherborne d			07 50	09 36	10 36	11 36	12 36	13 36	14 36	
Yeovil Junction a			07 55	09 41	10 41	11 41	12 41	13 41	14 41	
d			07 57	09 43	10 43	11 43	12 43	13 43	14 43	
Crewkerne d			08 06	09 52	10 52	11 52	12 52	13 52	14 52	
Axminster a			08 19	10 05	11 05	12 05	13 05	14 05	15 05	
d			08 20	10 06	11 06	12 06	13 06	14 06	15 06	
Honiton a			08 31	10 18	11 18	12 18	13 18	14 18	15 18	
d			08 35	10 19	11 19	12 19	13 19	14 19	15 19	
Feniton d			08 40		11 24		13 24		15 24	
Whimple d			08 45		11 29		13 29		15 29	
Pinhoe d				10 31		12 31		14 31		
Exeter Central a			08 56	10 40	11 40	12 40	13 40	14 40	15 40	
Exeter St Davids 6 a			09 01	10 45	11 45	12 45	13 45	14 45	15 45	

	SW ◇1 ⌶	SW ◇1 ⌶	SW ◇1 ⌶	SW ◇1 ⌶	SW ◇1 ⌶	SW ◇1 ⌶		SW ◇1 ⌶	SW ◇1 ⌶	SW ◇1 ⌶	SW 1 ⌶	SW 1 A
London Waterloo 15 ⊖ d	13 15	14 15	15 15	16 15	17 15	18 15		19 15	20 15	21 15	22 15	23∫35
Clapham Junction 10 d	13u22	14u22	15u22	16u22	17u22	18u22		19u22	20u22	21u22	22u22	23u44
Woking d	13 46	14 46	15 46	16 46	17 46	18 46		19 46	20 46	21 46	22 46	00∫08
Basingstoke d	14 07	15 07	16 07	17 07	18 07	19 07		20 07	21 07	22 07	23 07	00∫40
Overton d		15 15		17 15		19 15			21 15		23 15	00s49
Whitchurch (Hants) d		15 20		17 20		19 20			21 20		23 20	00s54
Andover d	14 24	15 29	16 24	17 29	18 24	19 29		20 24	21 29	22 26	23 29	01∫02
Grateley d	14 31		16 31		18 31			20 31		22 33	23 36	01s10
Salisbury a	14 45	15 45	16 45	17 45	18 45	19 45		20 45	21 45	22 45	23 48	01∫22
d	14 51	15 51	16 51	17 51	18 51	19 51	19 55	20 51	21 51	22 51		
Warminster d							20 15					
Westbury d							20 23					
Trowbridge d							20 29					
Bradford-on-Avon d							20 35					
Bath Spa 7 a							20 48					
Bristol Temple Meads 10 a							21 04					
Tisbury d	15 10	16 10	17 10	18 10	19 10	20 10		21 10	22 10	23 10		
Gillingham (Dorset) a	15 20	16 20	17 20	18 20	19 20	20 20		21 20	22 20	23 20		
d	15 21	16 21	17 21	18 21	19 21	20 21		21 21	22 21	23 21		
Templecombe d	15 28	16 28	17 28	18 28	19 28	20 28		21 28	22 28	23 28		
Sherborne d	15 36	16 36	17 36	18 36	19 36	20 36		21 36	22 36	23 36		
Yeovil Junction a	15 41	16 41	17 41	18 41	19 41	20 41		21 41	22 42	23 41		
d	15 43	16 43	17 43	18 43	19 43	20 43		21 43		23 43		
Crewkerne d	15 52	16 52	17 52	18 52	19 52	20 52		21 52		23 52		
Axminster a	16 05	17 05	18 05	19 05	20 05	21 05		22 05		00 05		
d	16 06	17 06	18 06	19 06	20 06	21 06		22 06		00 06		
Honiton a	16 18	17 18	18 18	19 18	20 18	21 18		22 18		00 18		
d	16 19	17 19	18 19	19 19	20 19	21 19		22 19		00 19		
Feniton d		17 24		19 24		21 24		22 24		00 24		
Whimple d		17 29		19 29		21 29		22 29		00 29		
Pinhoe d	16 31		18 31		20 31			22 36				
Exeter Central a	16 40	17 40	18 40	19 40	20 40	21 40		22 40				
Exeter St Davids 6 a	16 45	17 45	18 45	19 45	20 45	21 45		22 45		00 40		

	SW 1 B
London Waterloo 15 ⊖ d	23∫55
Clapham Junction 10 d	00u04
Woking d	00∫28
Basingstoke d	01∫00
Overton d	01s09
Whitchurch (Hants) d	01s14
Andover d	01∫22
Grateley d	01s30
Salisbury a	01∫42
Warminster d	
Westbury d	
Trowbridge d	
Bradford-on-Avon d	
Bath Spa 7 a	
Bristol Temple Meads 10 a	
Tisbury d	
Gillingham (Dorset) a	
d	
Templecombe d	
Sherborne d	
Yeovil Junction a	
d	
Crewkerne d	
Axminster a	
d	
Honiton a	
d	
Feniton d	
Whimple d	
Pinhoe d	
Exeter Central a	
Exeter St Davids 6 a	

A until 22 July, 19 August, 26 August, 16 September, 23 September, 30 September

B 29 July, 5 August, 12 August, 2 September, 9 September

b Previous night, stops to pick up only

For Bus Connections for either to or from Yeovil Junction and Yeovil Pen Mill please see Table 123A

Table 160

London - Salisbury and Exeter

Sundays from 7 October

Network Diagram - see first Page of Table 160

		SW	SW	SW	SW	SW	SW	SW	SW		SW	SW	SW	SW	SW	SW		SW	SW	SW	SW	SW
		■	■	◇■	◇■	◇■	◇■	◇■	◇■		◇■	◇■	◇■	◇■	◇■	◇■		◇■	◇■	◇■	■	■
					⌶	⌶	⌶	⌶	⌶		⌶	⌶	⌶	⌶	⌶	⌶		⌶	⌶	⌶	⌶	
London Waterloo 15 ⊖	d	23p40			08 15	09 15	10 15	11 15	12 15		13 15	14 15	15 15	16 15	17 15	18 15		19 15	20 15	21 15	22 15	23 35
Clapham Junction 10	d	23b47			08u22	09u22	10u22	11u22	12u22		13u22	14u22	15u22	16u22	17u22	18u22		19u22	20u22	21u22	22u22	23u44
Woking	d	00 08			08 47	09 47	10 46	11 46	12 46		13 46	14 46	15 46	16 46	17 46	18 46		19 46	20 46	21 46	22 46	00 08
Basingstoke	d	00 28		08 05	09 08	10 08	11 07	12 07	13 07		14 07	15 07	16 07	17 07	18 07	19 07		20 07	21 07	22 07	23 07	00 40
Overton	d	00s37		08 13	09 16		11 15		13 15			15 15		17 15		19 15			21 15		23 15	00s49
Whitchurch (Hants)	d	00s42		08 18	09 21		11 20		13 20			15 20		17 20		19 20			21 20		23 20	00s54
Andover	d	00 50		08 27	09 30	10 25	11 29	12 24	13 29		14 24	15 29	16 24	17 29	18 24	19 29		20 24	21 29	22 26	23 29	01 02
Grateley	d	00s58		08 34		10 32		12 31			14 31		16 31		18 31			20 31		22 33	23 36	01s10
Salisbury	a	01 10		08 46	09 46	10 45	11 45	12 45	13 45		14 45	15 45	16 45	17 45	18 45	19 45		20 45	21 45	22 45	23 48	01 22
	d		07 10	08 51	09 51	10 51	11 51	12 51	13 51	13 55	14 51	15 51	16 51	17 51	18 51	19 51	19 55	20 51	21 51	22 51		
Warminster	d									14 15							20 15					
Westbury	d									14 24							20 23					
Trowbridge	d									14 30							20 29					
Bradford-on-Avon	d									14 36							20 35					
Bath Spa 7	a									14 49							20 48					
Bristol Temple Meads 10	a									15 05							21 04					
Tisbury	d		07 24	09 10	10 10	11 10	12 10	13 10	14 10		15 10	16 10	17 10	18 10	19 10	20 10		21 10	22 10	23 10		
Gillingham (Dorset)	a		07 34	09 20	10 20	11 20	12 20	13 20	14 20		15 20	16 20	17 20	18 20	19 20	20 20		21 20	22 20	23 20		
	d		07 35	09 21	10 21	11 21	12 21	13 21	14 21		15 21	16 21	17 21	18 21	19 21	20 21		21 21	22 21	23 21		
Templecombe	d		07 42	09 28	10 28	11 28	12 28	13 28	14 28		15 28	16 28	17 28	18 28	19 28	20 28		21 28	22 28	23 28		
Sherborne	d		07 50	09 36	10 36	11 36	12 36	13 36	14 36		15 36	16 36	17 36	18 36	19 36	20 36		21 36	22 36	23 36		
Yeovil Junction	a		07 55	09 41	10 41	11 41	12 41	13 41	14 41		15 41	16 41	17 41	18 41	19 41	20 41		21 41	22 42	23 41		
	d		07 57	09 43	10 43	11 43	12 43	13 43	14 43		15 43	16 43	17 43	18 43	19 43	20 43		21 43		23 43		
Crewkerne	d		08 06	09 52	10 52	11 52	12 52	13 52	14 52		15 52	16 52	17 52	18 52	19 52	20 52		21 52		23 52		
Axminster	a		08 19	10 05	11 05	12 05	13 05	14 05	15 05		16 05	17 05	18 05	19 05	20 05	21 05		22 05		00 05		
	d		08 20	10 06	11 06	12 06	13 06	14 06	15 06		16 06	17 06	18 06	19 06	20 06	21 06		22 06		00 06		
Honiton	a		08 31	10 18	11 18	12 18	13 18	14 18	15 18		16 18	17 18	18 18	19 18	20 18	21 18		22 18		00 18		
	d		08 35	10 19	11 19	12 19	13 19	14 19	15 19		16 19	17 19	18 19	19 19	20 19	21 19		22 19		00 19		
Feniton	d		08 40		11 24		13 24		15 24			17 24		19 24		21 24		22 24		00 24		
Whimple	d		08 45		11 29		13 29		15 29			17 29		19 29		21 29		22 29		00 29		
Pinhoe	d			10 31		12 31		14 31			16 31		18 31		20 31			22 36				
Exeter Central	a		08 56	10 40	11 40	12 40	13 40	14 40	15 40		16 40	17 40	18 40	19 40	20 40	21 40		22 40				
Exeter St Davids 6	a		09 01	10 45	11 45	12 45	13 45	14 45	15 45		16 45	17 45	18 45	19 45	20 45	21 45		22 45		00 40		

b Previous night, stops to pick up only

For Bus Connections for either to or from Yeovil Junction and Yeovil Pen Mill please see Table 123A

Table 160

Exeter and Salisbury - London

Mondays to Fridays until 5 October

Network Diagram - see first Page of Table 160

Miles																						
			SW MX	SW MO	SW	SW	SW	SW	SW	SW	SW	SW	SW	SW	SW	SW	SW	SW	SW	SW	SW	SW
			■	■	◇■	◇■	◇■	◇■	◇■	◇■	◇■	◇■	◇■	◇■	◇■	◇■	◇■	◇■	◇■	◇■	◇■	◇■
				A											B							
					⌶	⌶	⌶	⌶	⌶	⌶	⌶	⌶	⌶	⌶	⌶	⌶	⌶	⌶	⌶	⌶	⌶	⌶
0	**Exeter St Davids 6**	d	22p57	23p15					05 10			06 41	07 26			08 26		09 26		10 26		11 26
0¾	**Exeter Central**	d	23p01	23p19					05 14			06 45	07 30			08 30		09 30		10 30		11 30
3½	Pinhoe	d	23p06						05 19			06 50	07 35			08 35		09 35				11 35
9¼	Whimple	d	23p13						05 26			06 57				08 42				10 39		
13	Feniton	d	23p18						05 31			07 02				08 47				10 45		
17½	Honiton	a	23p25	23b34					05 38			07 10	07 47			08 54		09 47		10 51		11 48
—		d	23p32						05 39	06 19		07 11	07 49			08 55		09 53		10 53		11 53
27¾	Axminster	a	23p42	23b45					05 49	06 29		07 21	07 59			09 05		10 03		11 03		12 03
—		d	23p43						05 51	06 30		07 22	08 00			09 06		10 06		11 06		12 06
40¾	Crewkerne	d	23p56	00s11					06 04	06 43		07 35	08 13			09 19		10 19		11 19		12 19
49¾	Yeovil Junction	a	00 04	00s20					06 12	06 52		07 44	08 22			09 27		10 27		11 27		12 27
—		d	00 09				05 15	05 50	06 20	06 53	07 22	07 50	08 29			09 29		10 29		11 29		12 29
54¼	Sherborne	d					05 21	05 56	06 26	07 00	07 28	07 56	08 35			09 35		10 35		11 35		12 35
60¼	Templecombe	d					05 29	06 04	06 34	07 07	07 36	08 04	08 43			09 43		10 43		11 43		12 43
67¾	Gillingham (Dorset)	a					05 36	06 11	06 41	07 14	07 43	08 11	08 50			09 50		10 50		11 50		12 50
—		d					05 37	06 12	06 42	07 15	07 44	08 12	08 51	09 18		09 51		10 51		11 51		12 51
76¼	Tisbury	d					05 47	06 24	06 52	07 26	07 54	08 22	09 01	09 28		10 01		11 01		12 01		13 01
—	Bristol Temple Meads 10	d													08 51							
—	Bath Spa 7	d													09 07							
—	Bradford-on-Avon	d													09 20							
—	Trowbridge	d													09 27							
—	Westbury	d													09 39							
—	Warminster	d													09 46							
88¾	**Salisbury**	a	00 43	00 56			06 02	06 39	07 07	07 40	08 09	08 37	09 16	09 42	10 09	10 16		11 16		12 16		13 16
—																						
—		d			05 15	05 43	06 06	06 45	07 15	07 45	08 15	08 47	09 21	09 47	10 21		10 47	11 21	11 47	12 21	12 47	13 21
99¾	Grateley	d			05 27	05 55	06 19	06 57	07 27	07 57	08 27	08 59		09 59			10 59		11 59		12 59	
106	Andover	d			05 35	06 03	06 26	07 05	07 35	08 05	08 35	09 06	09 38	10 06	10 38		11 06	11 38	12 06	12 38	13 06	13 38
113¾	Whitchurch (Hants)	d			05 43	06 11	06 35	07 13	07 43	08 13	08 43	09 14		10 14			11 14		12 14		13 14	
117	Overton	d			05 49	06 17	06 41	07 19	07 49	08 19	08 49	09 20		10 20			11 20		12 20		13 20	
124¾	**Basingstoke**	a			05 58	06 26	06 49	07 28	07 58	08 28	08 58	09 28	09 55	10 28	10 55		11 28	11 55	12 28	12 55	13 28	13 55
148¾	Woking	a			06 18	06 46			08 18	08 48	09 18	09 49	10 15	10 49	11 15		11 49	12 15	12 49	13 15	13 49	14 15
168¾	Clapham Junction 10	a			06 38		07 28				09 38	10 09	10 36		11 36			12 36		13 36		14 36
172½	**London Waterloo 15** ⊖	a			06 49	07 14	07 39	08 14	08 46	09 17	09 51	10 19	10 49	11 19	11 49		12 19	12 49	13 19	13 49	14 19	14 49

		SW	SW	SW	SW	SW	SW	SW	SW	SW	SW	SW	SW	SW	SW	SW	SW	SW	SW	SW	SW	SW
		◇■	◇■	◇■	◇■	◇■	◇■	◇■	◇■	◇■	◇■	◇■	◇■	◇■	◇■	■	◇■	◇■	◇■	■	■	■
										B												
		⌶	⌶	⌶	⌶	⌶	⌶	⌶	⌶	⌶	⌶	⌶	⌶	⌶	⌶		⌶		⌶			
Exeter St Davids 6	d			12 26		13 26		14 26			15 26		16 26		17 26	17 46	18 26	19 26	20 26	21 23		22 57
Exeter Central	d			12 30		13 30		14 30			15 30		16 30		17 30	17 50	18 30	19 30	20 30	21 30		23 01
Pinhoe	d					13 35					15 35				17 35	17 56		19 35		21 35		23 06
Whimple	d			12 39				14 39					16 39			18 02	18 39		20 39			23 13
Feniton	d			12 45				14 45					16 45			18 08	18 45		20 45			23 18
Honiton	a			12 51		13 48		14 51			15 48		16 51		17 48	18 18	18 51	19 48	20 51	21 47		23 25
	d			12 53		13 53		14 53			15 53		16 53		17 53	18 19	18 53	19 53	20 53	21 53		23 32
Axminster	a			13 03		14 03		15 03			16 03		17 03		18 03	18 29	19 03	20 03	21 03	22 03		23 42
	d			13 06		14 06		15 06			16 06		17 06		18 06		19 06	20 06	21 06	22 06		23 43
Crewkerne	d			13 19		14 19		15 19			16 19		17 19		18 19		19 19	20 19	21 19	22 19		23 56
Yeovil Junction	a			13 27		14 27		15 27			16 27		17 27		18 27		19 27	20 27	21 27	22 27		00 04
	d			13 29		14 29		15 29			16 29		17 29		18 29		19 29	20 29	21 29	22 29		00 09
Sherborne	d			13 35		14 35		15 35			16 35		17 35		18 35		19 35	20 35	21 35	22 35		
Templecombe	d			13 43		14 43		15 43			16 43		17 43		18 43		19 43	20 43	21 43	22 47		
Gillingham (Dorset)	a			13 50		14 50		15 50			16 50		17 50		18 50		19 50	20 50	21 50	22 54		
	d			13 51		14 51		15 51	16 18		16 51		17 51		18 51		19 51	20 51	21 51	22 55		
Tisbury	d			14 01		15 01		16 01	16 28		17 01		18 01		19 01		20 01	21 01	22 01	23 05		
Bristol Temple Meads 10	d		12 51							15 51											22 25	
Bath Spa 7	d		13 07							16 07											22 38	
Bradford-on-Avon	d		13 20							16 22											22 51	
Trowbridge	d		13 27							16 28											22 57	
Westbury	d		13 39							16 39											23 08	
Warminster	d		13 46							16 47											23 15	
Salisbury	a		14 10	14 16		15 16		16 16	16 43	17 09	17 16		18 21		19 23		20 21	21 21	22 16	23 29	23 35	00 43
	d	13 47	14 21		14 47	15 21	15 47	16 21	16 47	17 21		17 47	18 26	18 47	19 26		20 26	21 26	22 26			
Grateley	d	13 59			14 59		15 59		16 59			17 59		18 59	19 38		20 38	21 38	22 38			
Andover	d	14 06	14 38		15 06	15 38	16 06	16 38	17 06	17 38		18 06	18 43	19 06	19 45		20 45	21 45	22 45			
Whitchurch (Hants)	d	14 14			15 14		16 14		17 14			18 14		19 14	19 53		20 53	21 53	22 53			
Overton	d	14 20			15 20		16 20		17 20			18 20		19 20	19 59		20 59	21 59	22 59			
Basingstoke	a	14 28	14 55		15 28	15 55	16 28	16 55	17 29	17 55		18 28	19 00	19 28	20 08		21 08	22 07	23 07			
Woking	a	14 49	15 15		15 49	16 15	16 49	17 15	17 49	18 15		18 49	19 20	19 49	20 29		21 29	22 28				
Clapham Junction 10	a		15 36			16 36		17 36		18 36			19 41		20 52		21 52	22 48				
London Waterloo 15 ⊖	a	15 19	15 49		16 19	16 49	17 19	17 44	18 21	18 45		19 19	19 49	20 19	21 00		22 04	22 58				

A from 21 May until 1 October

B ⌶ from Salisbury

b Previous night, stops to set down only

For Bus Connections for either to or from Yeovil Junction and Yeovil Pen Mill please see Table 123A

Table 160

Exeter and Salisbury - London

Mondays to Fridays
from 8 October

Network Diagram - see first Page of Table 160

		SW MX ■1	SW MO ■1	SW ◇1 ⌶	SW ◇1 ⌶	SW ◇1 ⌶	SW ◇1 ⌶	SW ◇1 ⌶	SW ◇1 ⌶	SW ◇1 ⌶	SW ◇1 ⌶	SW ◇1 ⌶	SW ◇1 ⌶	SW ◇1 A ⌶	SW ◇1 ⌶	SW ◇1 ⌶	SW ◇1 ⌶	SW ◇1 ⌶	SW ◇1 ⌶	SW ◇1 ⌶	SW ◇1 ⌶
Exeter St Davids ■6	d	22p57	23p15					05 10			06 41	07 26			08 26		09 26		10 26		11 26
Exeter Central	d	23p01	23p19					05 14			06 45	07 30			08 30		09 30		10 30		11 30
Pinhoe	d	23p06						05 19			06 50	07 35			08 35		09 35				11 35
Whimple	d	23p13						05 26			06 57				08 42				10 39		
Feniton	d	23p18						05 31			07 02				08 47				10 45		
Honiton	a	23p25	23b34					05 38			07 10	07 47			08 54		09 47		10 51		11 48
	d	23p32						05 39	06 19		07 11	07 49			08 55		09 53		10 53		11 53
Axminster	a	23p42	23b45					05 49	06 29		07 21	07 59			09 05		10 03		11 03		12 03
	d	23p43						05 51	06 30		07 22	08 00			09 06		10 06		11 06		12 06
Crewkerne	d	23p56	00s11					06 04	06 43		07 35	08 13			09 19		10 19		11 19		12 19
Yeovil Junction	a	00 04	00s20					06 12	06 52		07 44	08 22			09 27		10 27		11 27		12 27
	d	00 09				05 12	05 50	06 20	06 53	07 22	07 50	08 29			09 29		10 29		11 29		12 29
Sherborne	d					05 18	05 56	06 26	07 00	07 28	07 56	08 35			09 35		10 35		11 35		12 35
Templecombe	d					05 26	06 04	06 34	07 07	07 36	08 04	08 43			09 43		10 43		11 43		12 43
Gillingham (Dorset)	a					05 33	06 11	06 41	07 14	07 43	08 11	08 50			09 50		10 50		11 50		12 50
	d					05 34	06 12	06 42	07 15	07 44	08 12	08 51	09 18		09 51		10 51		11 51		12 51
Tisbury	d					05 44	06 24	06 52	07 26	07 54	08 22	09 01	09 28		10 01		11 01		12 01		13 01
Bristol Temple Meads ■10	d													08 51							
Bath Spa ■7	d													09 07							
Bradford-on-Avon	d													09 20							
Trowbridge	d													09 27							
Westbury	d													09 39							
Warminster	d													09 46							
Salisbury	a	00 43	00 56			05 59	06 39	07 07	07 40	08 09	08 37	09 16	09 42	10 09	10 16		11 16		12 16		13 16
	d			05 12	05 40	06 03	06 45	07 15	07 45	08 15	08 47	09 21	09 47		10 21	10 47	11 21	11 47	12 21	12 47	13 21
Grateley	d			05 24	05 52	06 16	06 57	07 27	07 57	08 27	08 59		09 59			10 59		11 59		12 59	
Andover	d			05 32	06 00	06 23	07 05	07 35	08 05	08 35	09 06	09 38	10 06		10 38	11 06	11 38	12 06	12 38	13 06	13 38
Whitchurch (Hants)	d			05 40	06 08	06 32	07 13	07 43	08 13	08 43	09 14		10 14			11 14		12 14		13 14	
Overton	d			05 46	06 14	06 38	07 19	07 49	08 19	08 49	09 20		10 20			11 20		12 20		13 20	
Basingstoke	a			05 58	06 26	06 49	07 28	07 58	08 28	08 58	09 28	09 55	10 28		10 55	11 28	11 55	12 28	12 55	13 28	13 55
Woking	a			06 18	06 46			08 18	08 48	09 18	09 49	10 15	10 49		11 15	11 49	12 15	12 49	13 15	13 49	14 15
Clapham Junction ■10	a			06 38		07 28				09 38	10 09	10 36			11 36		12 36		13 36		14 36
London Waterloo ■15 ⊖	a			06 49	07 14	07 39	08 14	08 46	09 17	09 51	10 19	10 49	11 19		11 49	12 19	12 49	13 19	13 49	14 19	14 49

		SW ◇1 ⌶	SW ◇1 ⌶	SW ◇1 ⌶	SW ◇1 ⌶	SW ◇1 ⌶	SW ◇1 ⌶	SW ◇1 ⌶	SW ◇1 ⌶	SW ◇1 A ⌶	SW ◇1 ⌶	SW ◇1 ⌶	SW ◇1 ⌶	SW ◇1 ⌶	SW ◇1 ⌶	SW ■1	SW ◇1 ⌶	SW ◇1	SW ◇1 ⌶	SW ■1	SW ■1	SW ■1
Exeter St Davids ■6	d			12 26		13 26		14 26			15 26		16 26		17 26	17 46	18 26	19 26	20 26	21 23		22 57
Exeter Central	d			12 30		13 30		14 30			15 30		16 30		17 30	17 50	18 30	19 30	20 30	21 30		23 01
Pinhoe	d					13 35					15 35				17 35	17 56		19 35		21 35		23 06
Whimple	d			12 39				14 39					16 39			18 02	18 39		20 39			23 13
Feniton	d			12 45				14 45					16 45			18 08	18 45		20 45			23 18
Honiton	a			12 51		13 48		14 51			15 48		16 51		17 48	18 18	18 51	19 48	20 51	21 47		23 25
	d			12 53		13 53		14 53			15 53		16 53		17 53	18 19	18 53	19 53	20 53	21 53		23 32
Axminster	a			13 03		14 03		15 03			16 03		17 03		18 03	18 29	19 03	20 03	21 03	22 03		23 42
	d			13 06		14 06		15 06			16 06		17 06		18 06		19 06	20 06	21 06	22 06		23 43
Crewkerne	d			13 19		14 19		15 19			16 19		17 19		18 19		19 19	20 19	21 19	22 19		23 56
Yeovil Junction	a			13 27		14 27		15 27			16 27		17 27		18 27		19 27	20 27	21 27	22 27		00 04
	d			13 29		14 29		15 29			16 29		17 29		18 29		19 29	20 29	21 29	22 29		00 09
Sherborne	d			13 35		14 35		15 35			16 35		17 35		18 35		19 35	20 35	21 35	22 35		
Templecombe	d			13 43		14 43		15 43			16 43		17 43		18 43		19 43	20 43	21 43	22 47		
Gillingham (Dorset)	a			13 50		14 50		15 50			16 50		17 50		18 50		19 50	20 50	21 50	22 54		
	d			13 51		14 51		15 51	16 18		16 51		17 51		18 51		19 51	20 51	21 51	22 55		
Tisbury	d			14 01		15 01		16 01	16 28		17 01		18 01		19 01		20 01	21 01	22 01	23 05		
Bristol Temple Meads ■10	d		12 51							15 51											22 25	
Bath Spa ■7	d		13 07							16 07											22 38	
Bradford-on-Avon	d		13 20							16 22											22 51	
Trowbridge	d		13 27							16 28											22 57	
Westbury	d		13 39							16 39											23 08	
Warminster	d		13 46							16 47											23 15	
Salisbury	a		14 10	14 16		15 16		16 16	16 43	17 09	17 16		18 21		19 23		20 21	21 21	22 16	23 29	23 35	00 43
	d	13 47		14 21	14 47	15 21	15 47	16 21	16 47		17 21	17 47	18 26	18 47	19 26		20 26	21 26	22 26			
Grateley	d	13 59			14 59		15 59		16 59			17 59		18 59	19 38		20 38	21 38	22 38			
Andover	d	14 06		14 38	15 06	15 38	16 06	16 38	17 06		17 38	18 06	18 43	19 06	19 45		20 45	21 45	22 45			
Whitchurch (Hants)	d	14 14			15 14		16 14		17 14			18 14		19 14	19 53		20 53	21 53	22 53			
Overton	d	14 20			15 20		16 20		17 20			18 20		19 20	19 59		20 59	21 59	22 59			
Basingstoke	a	14 28		14 55	15 28	15 55	16 28	16 55	17 29		17 55	18 28	19 00	19 28	20 08		21 08	22 07	23 07			
Woking	a	14 49		15 15	15 49	16 15	16 49	17 15	17 49		18 15	18 49	19 20	19 49	20 29		21 29	22 28				
Clapham Junction ■10	a			15 36		16 36		17 36			18 36		19 41		20 52		21 52	22 48				
London Waterloo ■15 ⊖	a	15 19		15 49	16 19	16 49	17 19	17 44	18 21		18 45	19 19	19 49	20 19	21 00		22 04	22 58				

A ⌶ from Salisbury

b Previous night, stops to set down only

For Bus Connections for either to or from Yeovil Junction and Yeovil Pen Mill please see Table 123A

Table 160

Exeter and Salisbury - London

Saturdays
until 6 October

Network Diagram - see first Page of Table 160

		SW ■1	SW ◇1 ⌶	SW ◇1 ⌶	SW ◇1 ⌶	SW ◇1 ⌶	SW ◇1 ⌶	SW ◇1 ⌶	SW ◇1 ⌶	SW ◇1 ⌶	SW ◇1 ⌶	SW ◇1 ⌶	SW ◇1 A ⌶	SW ◇1 ⌶	SW ◇1 ⌶	SW ◇1 ⌶	SW ◇1 ⌶	SW ◇1 ⌶	SW ◇1 ⌶	SW ◇1 ⌶	SW ◇1 ⌶
Exeter St Davids ■6	d	22p57					05 10			06 41	07 26			08 26		09 26		10 26		11 26	
Exeter Central	d	23p01					05 14			06 45	07 30			08 30		09 30		10 30		11 30	
Pinhoe	d	23p06					05 19			06 50	07 35			08 35		09 35				11 35	
Whimple	d	23p13					05 26			06 57				08 42				10 39			
Feniton	d	23p18					05 31			07 02				08 47				10 45			
Honiton	a	23p25					05 38			07 11	07 48			08 54		09 48		10 51		11 48	
	d	23p32					05 39	06 19		07 13	07 53			08 55		09 53		10 53		11 53	
Axminster	a	23p42					05 49	06 29		07 23	08 03			09 05		10 03		11 03		12 03	
	d	23p43					05 51	06 30		07 24	08 06			09 06		10 06		11 06		12 06	
Crewkerne	d	23p56					06 04	06 43		07 37	08 19			09 19		10 19		11 19		12 19	
Yeovil Junction	a	00 04					06 12	06 52		07 45	08 27			09 27		10 27		11 27		12 27	
	d	00 09					06 20	06 53		07 50	08 29			09 29		10 29		11 29		12 29	
Sherborne	d						06 26	07 00		07 56	08 35			09 35		10 35		11 35		12 35	
Templecombe	d						06 34	07 07		08 04	08 43			09 43		10 43		11 43		12 43	
Gillingham (Dorset)	a						06 41	07 14		08 11	08 50			09 50		10 50		11 50		12 50	
	d						06 42	07 15		08 12	08 51			09 51		10 51		11 51		12 51	
Tisbury	d						06 52	07 26		08 22	09 01			10 01		11 01		12 01		13 01	
Bristol Temple Meads ■10	d												08 51								
Bath Spa ■7	d												09 07								
Bradford-on-Avon	d												09 20								
Trowbridge	d												09 27								
Westbury	d												09 39								
Warminster	d												09 46								
Salisbury	a	00 43					07 07	07 40		08 37	09 16		10 09	10 16		11 16		12 16		13 16	
	d		05 15	05 47	06 21	06 47	07 21	07 47	08 21	08 47	09 21	09 47		10 21	10 47	11 21	11 47	12 21	12 47	13 21	13 47
Grateley	d		05 27	05 59		06 59		07 59		08 59		09 59			10 59		11 59		12 59		13 59
Andover	d		05 35	06 06	06 38	07 06	07 38	08 06	08 38	09 06	09 38	10 06		10 38	11 06	11 38	12 06	12 38	13 06	13 38	14 06
Whitchurch (Hants)	d		05 43	06 14		07 14		08 14		09 14		10 14			11 14		12 14		13 14		14 14
Overton	d		05 49	06 20		07 20		08 20		09 20		10 20			11 20		12 20		13 20		14 20
Basingstoke	a		05 58	06 28	06 55	07 28	07 55	08 28	08 55	09 28	09 55	10 28		10 55	11 28	11 55	12 28	12 55	13 28	13 55	14 28
Woking	a		06 18	06 49	07 15	07 49	08 17	08 49	09 15	09 49	10 15	10 49		11 15	11 49	12 15	12 49	13 15	13 49	14 15	14 49
Clapham Junction ■10	a		06 38		07 36		08 37		09 36		10 36			11 36		12 36		13 36		14 36	
London Waterloo ■15 ⊖	a		06 49	07 19	07 49	08 19	08 49	09 19	09 49	10 19	10 49	11 19		11 49	12 19	12 49	13 19	13 49	14 19	14 49	15 19

		SW ◇1 B ⌶	SW ◇1 ⌶	SW ◇1 ⌶	SW ◇1 ⌶	SW ◇1 ⌶	SW ◇1 ⌶	SW ◇1 ⌶	SW ◇1 A ⌶	SW ◇1 ⌶	SW ◇1 ⌶	SW ◇1 ⌶	SW ◇1 ⌶	SW ◇1 ⌶	SW ◇1 ⌶	SW ◇1	SW ◇1 ⌶	SW ■1	SW ■1	SW ■1
Exeter St Davids ■6	d		12 26		13 26		14 26			15 26		16 26		17 26	18 26	19 26	20 26	21 26		22 57
Exeter Central	d		12 30		13 30		14 30			15 30		16 30		17 30	18 30	19 30	20 30	21 30		23 01
Pinhoe	d				13 35					15 35				17 35		19 35		21 35		23 06
Whimple	d		12 39				14 39					16 39		17 42	18 39		20 39			23 13
Feniton	d		12 45				14 45					16 45		17 47	18 45		20 45			23 18
Honiton	a		12 51		13 48		14 51			15 48		16 51		17 54	18 51	19 48	20 51	21 48		23 25
	d		12 53		13 53		14 53			15 53		16 53		17 55	18 53	19 53	20 53	21 53		23 32
Axminster	a		13 03		14 03		15 03			16 03		17 03		18 05	19 03	20 03	21 03	22 03		23 42
	d		13 06		14 06		15 06			16 06		17 06		18 06	19 06	20 06	21 06	22 06		23 43
Crewkerne	d		13 19		14 19		15 19			16 19		17 19		18 19	19 19	20 19	21 19	22 19		23 56
Yeovil Junction	a		13 27		14 27		15 27			16 27		17 27		18 27	19 27	20 27	21 27	22 27		00 04
	d		13 29		14 29		15 29			16 29		17 29		18 29	19 29	20 29	21 29	22 29		00 16
Sherborne	d		13 35		14 35		15 35			16 35		17 35		18 35	19 35	20 35	21 35	22 35		
Templecombe	d		13 43		14 43		15 43			16 43		17 43		18 43	19 43	20 43	21 43	22 43		
Gillingham (Dorset)	a		13 50		14 50		15 50			16 50		17 50		18 50	19 50	20 50	21 50	22 50		
	d		13 51		14 51		15 51			16 51		17 51		18 51	19 51	20 51	21 51	22 51		
Tisbury	d		14 01		15 01		16 01			17 01		18 01		19 01	20 01	21 01	22 01	23 01		
Bristol Temple Meads ■10	d	12 51							15 51										22 23	
Bath Spa ■7	d	13 07							16 07										22 36	
Bradford-on-Avon	d	13 20							16 24										22 47	
Trowbridge	d	13 27							16 30										22 53	
Westbury	d	13 39							16 39										23 04	
Warminster	d	13 46							16 47										23 11	
Salisbury	a	14 10	14 16		15 16		16 16		17 09	17 16		18 16		19 16	20 16	21 16	22 21	23 29	23 34	00 50
	d		14 21	14 47	15 21	15 47	16 21	16 47		17 21	17 47	18 21	18 47	19 26	20 26	21 26	22 26			
Grateley	d			14 59		15 59		16 59			17 59		18 59	19 38	20 38	21 38	22 38			
Andover	d		14 38	15 06	15 38	16 06	16 38	17 06		17 38	18 06	18 38	19 06	19 45	20 45	21 45	22 45			
Whitchurch (Hants)	d			15 14		16 14		17 14			18 14		19 14	19 53	20 53	21 53	22 53			
Overton	d			15 20		16 20		17 20			18 20		19 20	19 59	20 59	21 59	22 59			
Basingstoke	a		14 55	15 28	15 55	16 28	16 55	17 28		17 55	18 28	18 55	19 28	20 08	21 08	22 07	23 07			
Woking	a		15 15	15 49	16 15	16 49	17 15	17 49		18 15	18 49	19 15	19 49	20 29	21 29	22 28				
Clapham Junction ■10	a		15 36		16 36		17 36			18 36		19 36		20 52	21 52	22 48				
London Waterloo ■15 ⊖	a		15 49	16 19	16 49	17 19	17 49	18 19		18 49	19 19	19 49	20 19	21 04	22 04	22 57				

A ⌶ from Salisbury

B 19 May

For Bus Connections for either to or from Yeovil Junction and Yeovil Pen Mill please see Table 123A

Table 160

Exeter and Salisbury - London

Saturdays
from 13 October

Network Diagram - see first Page of Table 160

		SW	SW	SW	SW	SW	SW	SW	SW	SW	SW	SW	SW	SW	SW	SW	SW	SW	SW	SW	SW	SW
		■1	◇■1	◇■1	◇■1	◇■1	◇■1	◇■1	◇■1	◇■1	◇■1	◇■1	◇■1	◇■1	◇■1	◇■1	◇■1	◇■1	◇■1	◇■1	◇■1	◇■1
													A									
			⌶	⌶	⌶	⌶	⌶	⌶	⌶	⌶	⌶	⌶	⌶	⌶	⌶	⌶	⌶	⌶	⌶	⌶	⌶	⌶
Exeter St Davids ■6	d	22p57					05 10			06 41	07 26			08 26		09 26		10 26		11 26		
Exeter Central	d	23p01					05 14			06 45	07 30			08 30		09 30		10 30		11 30		
Pinhoe	d	23p06					05 19			06 50	07 35			08 35		09 35				11 35		
Whimple	d	23p13					05 26			06 57				08 42				10 39				
Feniton	d	23p18					05 31			07 02				08 47				10 45				
Honiton	a	23p25					05 38			07 11	07 48			08 54		09 48		10 51		11 48		
	d	23p32					05 39	06 19		07 13	07 53			08 55		09 53		10 53		11 53		
Axminster	a	23p42					05 49	06 29		07 23	08 03			09 05		10 03		11 03		12 03		
	d	23p43					05 51	06 30		07 24	08 06			09 06		10 06		11 06		12 06		
Crewkerne	d	23p56					06 04	06 43		07 37	08 19			09 19		10 19		11 19		12 19		
Yeovil Junction	a	00 04					06 12	06 52		07 45	08 27			09 27		10 27		11 27		12 27		
	d	00 09					06 20	06 53		07 50	08 29			09 29		10 29		11 29		12 29		
Sherborne	d						06 26	07 00		07 56	08 35			09 35		10 35		11 35		12 35		
Templecombe	d						06 34	07 07		08 04	08 43			09 43		10 43		11 43		12 43		
Gillingham (Dorset)	a						06 41	07 14		08 11	08 50			09 50		10 50		11 50		12 50		
	d						06 42	07 15		08 12	08 51			09 51		10 51		11 51		12 51		
Tisbury	d						06 52	07 26		08 22	09 01			10 01		11 01		12 01		13 01		
Bristol Temple Meads ■10	d												08 51								12 51	
Bath Spa ■7	d												09 07								13 07	
Bradford-on-Avon	d												09 20								13 20	
Trowbridge	d												09 27								13 27	
Westbury	d												09 39								13 39	
Warminster	d												09 46								13 46	
Salisbury	a	00 43					07 07	07 40		08 37	09 16		10 09	10 16		11 16		12 16		13 16	14 10	
	d		05 12	05 44	06 18	06 47	07 21	07 47	08 21	08 47	09 21	09 47	10 21		10 47	11 21	11 47	12 21	12 47	13 21		13 47
Grateley	d		05 24	05 56		06 59		07 59		08 59		09 59			10 59		11 59		12 59			13 59
Andover	d		05 32	06 03	06 35	07 06	07 38	08 06	08 38	09 06	09 38	10 06	10 38		11 06	11 38	12 06	12 38	13 06	13 38		14 06
Whitchurch (Hants)	d		05 40	06 11		07 14		08 14		09 14		10 14			11 14		12 14		13 14			14 14
Overton	d		05 46	06 17		07 20		08 20		09 20		10 20			11 20		12 20		13 20			14 20
Basingstoke	a		05 58	06 28	06 55	07 28	07 55	08 28	08 55	09 28	09 55	10 28	10 55		11 28	11 55	12 28	12 55	13 28	13 55		14 28
Woking	a		06 18	06 49	07 15	07 49	08 17	08 49	09 15	09 49	10 15	10 49	11 15		11 49	12 15	12 49	13 15	13 49	14 15		14 49
Clapham Junction ■10	a		06 38		07 36		08 37		09 36		10 36		11 36			12 36		13 36		14 36		
London Waterloo ■15 ⊖	a		06 49	07 19	07 49	08 19	08 49	09 19	09 49	10 19	10 49	11 19	11 49		12 19	12 49	13 19	13 49	14 19	14 49		15 19

		SW	SW	SW	SW	SW	SW	SW	SW	SW	SW	SW	SW	SW	SW	SW	SW	SW	SW	SW
		◇■1	◇■1	◇■1	◇■1	◇■1	◇■1	◇■1	◇■1	◇■1	◇■1	◇■1	◇■1	◇■1	◇■1	◇■1	◇■1	■1	■1	■1
									A											
		⌶	⌶	⌶	⌶	⌶	⌶	⌶	⌶	⌶	⌶	⌶	⌶	⌶	⌶		⌶			
Exeter St Davids ■6	d		12 26		13 26		14 26			15 26		16 26		17 26	18 26	19 26	20 26	21 26		22 57
Exeter Central	d		12 30		13 30		14 30			15 30		16 30		17 30	18 30	19 30	20 30	21 30		23 01
Pinhoe	d				13 35					15 35				17 35		19 35		21 35		23 06
Whimple	d		12 39				14 39					16 39		17 42	18 39		20 39			23 13
Feniton	d		12 45				14 45					16 45		17 47	18 45		20 45			23 18
Honiton	a		12 51		13 48		14 51			15 48		16 51		17 54	18 51	19 48	20 51	21 48		23 25
	d		12 53		13 53		14 53			15 53		16 53		17 55	18 53	19 53	20 53	21 53		23 32
Axminster	a		13 03		14 03		15 03			16 03		17 03		18 05	19 03	20 03	21 03	22 03		23 42
	d		13 06		14 06		15 06			16 06		17 06		18 06	19 06	20 06	21 06	22 06		23 43
Crewkerne	d		13 19		14 19		15 19			16 19		17 19		18 19	19 19	20 19	21 19	22 19		23 56
Yeovil Junction	a		13 27		14 27		15 27			16 27		17 27		18 27	19 27	20 27	21 27	22 27		00 04
	d		13 29		14 29		15 29			16 29		17 29		18 29	19 29	20 29	21 29	22 29		00 16
Sherborne	d		13 35		14 35		15 35			16 35		17 35		18 35	19 35	20 35	21 35	22 35		
Templecombe	d		13 43		14 43		15 43			16 43		17 43		18 43	19 43	20 43	21 43	22 43		
Gillingham (Dorset)	a		13 50		14 50		15 50			16 50		17 50		18 50	19 50	20 50	21 50	22 50		
	d		13 51		14 51		15 51			16 51		17 51		18 51	19 51	20 51	21 51	22 51		
Tisbury	d		14 01		15 01		16 01			17 01		18 01		19 01	20 01	21 01	22 01	23 01		
Bristol Temple Meads ■10	d	12 51							15 51										22 23	
Bath Spa ■7	d	13 07							16 07										22 36	
Bradford-on-Avon	d	13 20							16 24										22 47	
Trowbridge	d	13 27							16 30										22 53	
Westbury	d	13 39							16 39										23 04	
Warminster	d	13 46							16 47										23 11	
Salisbury	a	14 10	14 16		15 16		16 16		17 09	17 16		18 16		19 16	20 16	21 16	22 21	23 29	23 34	00 50
	d	14 21		14 47	15 21	15 47	16 21	16 47	17 21		17 47	18 21	18 47	19 26	20 26	21 26	22 26			
Grateley	d			14 59		15 59		16 59			17 59		18 59	19 38	20 38	21 38	22 38			
Andover	d	14 38		15 06	15 38	16 06	16 38	17 06	17 38		18 06	18 38	19 06	19 45	20 45	21 45	22 45			
Whitchurch (Hants)	d			15 14		16 14		17 14			18 14		19 14	19 53	20 53	21 53	22 53			
Overton	d			15 20		16 20		17 20			18 20		19 20	19 59	20 59	21 59	22 59			
Basingstoke	a	14 55		15 28	15 55	16 28	16 55	17 28	17 55		18 28	18 55	19 28	20 08	21 08	22 07	23 07			
Woking	a	15 15		15 49	16 15	16 49	17 15	17 49	18 15		18 49	19 15	19 49	20 29	21 29	22 28				
Clapham Junction ■10	a	15 36			16 36		17 36		18 36			19 36		20 52	21 52	22 48				
London Waterloo ■15 ⊖	a	15 49		16 19	16 49	17 19	17 49	18 19	18 49		19 19	19 49	20 19	21 04	22 04	22 57				

A ⌶ from Salisbury

For Bus Connections for either to or from Yeovil Junction and Yeovil Pen Mill please see Table 123A

Table 160

Exeter and Salisbury - London

Sundays
until 30 September

Network Diagram - see first Page of Table 160

		SW	SW	SW	SW	SW	SW	SW	SW	SW	SW	SW	SW	SW	SW	SW	SW	SW	SW	SW	SW	SW	SW
		■1	◇■1	◇■1	◇■1	◇■1	◇■1	◇■1	◇■1	◇■1	◇■1	◇■1	◇■1	◇■1	◇■1	◇■1	◇■1	◇■1	◇■1	◇■1	■1	■1	■1
														A									
			⌶	⌶	⌶	⌶	⌶	⌶	⌶	⌶	⌶	⌶	⌶	⌶	⌶	⌶	⌶	⌶					
Exeter St Davids ■6	d	22p57						09 26	10 26	11 26	12 26	13 26	14 26		15 26	16 26	17 26	18 26	19 26	20 26		21 26	23 15
Exeter Central	d	23p01						09 30	10 30	11 30	12 30	13 30	14 30		15 30	16 30	17 30	18 30	19 30	20 30		21 30	23 19
Pinhoe	d	23p06						09 35		11 35		13 35			15 35		17 35		19 35			21 35	
Whimple	d	23p13						09 42	10 39		12 39		14 39			16 39		18 39		20 39		21 42	
Feniton	d	23p18						09 47	10 45		12 45		14 45			16 45		18 45		20 45		21 47	
Honiton	a	23p25						09 54	10 51	11 48	12 51	13 48	14 51		15 48	16 51	17 48	18 51	19 48	20 51		21 54	23s34
	d	23p32					08 58	09 55	10 53	11 53	12 53	13 53	14 53		15 53	16 53	17 53	18 53	19 53	20 53		21 55	
Axminster	a	23p42					09 08	10 05	11 03	12 03	13 03	14 03	15 03		16 03	17 03	18 03	19 03	20 03	21 03		22 05	23s45
	d	23p43					09 09	10 09	11 09	12 09	13 09	14 09	15 09		16 09	17 09	18 09	19 09	20 09	21 09		22 09	
Crewkerne	d	23p56					09 22	10 22	11 22	12 22	13 22	14 22	15 22		16 22	17 22	18 22	19 22	20 22	21 22		22 22	00s11
Yeovil Junction	a	00 04					09 30	10 30	11 30	12 30	13 30	14 30	15 30		16 30	17 30	18 30	19 30	20 30	21 30		22 30	00s20
	d	00 16			07 32		09 32	10 32	11 32	12 32	13 32	14 32	15 32		16 32	17 32	18 32	19 32	20 32	21 32		22 32	
Sherborne	d				07 38		09 38	10 38	11 38	12 38	13 38	14 38	15 38		16 38	17 38	18 38	19 38	20 38	21 38		22 38	
Templecombe	d				07 46		09 46	10 46	11 46	12 46	13 46	14 46	15 46		16 46	17 46	18 46	19 46	20 46	21 46		22 46	
Gillingham (Dorset)	a				07 53		09 53	10 53	11 53	12 53	13 53	14 53	15 53		16 53	17 53	18 53	19 53	20 53	21 53		22 53	
	d				07 54	08 54	09 54	10 54	11 54	12 54	13 54	14 54	15 54		16 54	17 54	18 54	19 54	20 54	21 54		22 54	
Tisbury	d				08 05	09 05	10 05	11 05	12 05	13 05	14 05	15 05	16 05		17 05	18 05	19 05	20 05	21 05	22 05		23 05	
Bristol Temple Meads ■10	d													16 04							21 35		
Bath Spa ■7	d													16 20							21 49		
Bradford-on-Avon	d													16 31							22 00		
Trowbridge	d													16 37							22 06		
Westbury	d													16 46							22 15		
Warminster	d													16 53							22 22		
Salisbury	a	00 50			08 20	09 20	10 20	11 20	12 20	13 20	14 20	15 20	16 20	17 16	17 20	18 20	19 20	20 20	21 20	22 20	22 46	23 19	00 56
	d		06 45	07 27	08 27	09 27	10 27	11 27	12 27	13 27	14 27	15 27	16 27	17 27		18 27	19 27	20 27	21 27	22 27			
Grateley	d				08 39	09 39		11 39		13 39		15 39		17 39			19 39		21 39	22 39			
Andover	d		07 02	07 44	08 46	09 46	10 44	11 46	12 44	13 46	14 44	15 46	16 44	17 46		18 44	19 46	20 44	21 46	22 46			
Whitchurch (Hants)	d			07 52	08 54		10 52		12 52		14 52		16 52			18 52		20 52		22 54			
Overton	d			07 58	09 00		10 58		12 58		14 58		16 58			18 58		20 58		23 00			
Basingstoke	a		07 19	08 06	09 08	10 02	11 06	12 02	13 06	14 02	15 06	16 02	17 06	18 02		19 06	20 02	21 06	22 03	23 08			
Woking	a		07 39	08 28	09 28	10 28	11 28	12 28	13 28	14 28	15 28	16 28	17 28	18 28		19 28	20 28	21 28	22 28				
Clapham Junction ■10	a		08 05	08 57	09 57	10 49	11 49	12 49	13 49	14 49	15 49	16 49	17 49	18 49		19 49	20 49	21 49	22 49				
London Waterloo ■15 ⊖	a		08 19	09 09	10 08	11 04	12 03	13 04	13 59	14 59	15 59	16 59	17 59	18 59		19 59	20 59	21 59	22 59				

Sundays
from 7 October

		SW	SW	SW	SW	SW	SW	SW	SW	SW	SW	SW	SW	SW	SW	SW	SW	SW	SW	SW	SW	SW	SW
		■1	◇■1	◇■1	◇■1	◇■1	◇■1	◇■1	◇■1	◇■1	◇■1	◇■1	◇■1	◇■1	◇■1	◇■1	◇■1	◇■1	◇■1	◇■1	■1	■1	■1
														A									
			⌶	⌶	⌶	⌶	⌶	⌶	⌶	⌶	⌶	⌶	⌶	⌶	⌶	⌶	⌶	⌶					
Exeter St Davids ■6	d	22p57						09 26	10 26	11 26	12 26	13 26	14 26		15 26	16 26	17 26	18 26	19 26	20 26		21 26	23 15
Exeter Central	d	23p01						09 30	10 30	11 30	12 30	13 30	14 30		15 30	16 30	17 30	18 30	19 30	20 30		21 30	23 19
Pinhoe	d	23p06						09 35		11 35		13 35			15 35		17 35		19 35			21 35	
Whimple	d	23p13						09 42	10 39		12 39		14 39			16 39		18 39		20 39		21 42	
Feniton	d	23p18						09 47	10 45		12 45		14 45			16 45		18 45		20 45		21 47	
Honiton	a	23p25						09 54	10 51	11 48	12 51	13 48	14 51		15 48	16 51	17 48	18 51	19 48	20 51		21 54	23s34
	d	23p32					08 58	09 55	10 53	11 53	12 53	13 53	14 53		15 53	16 53	17 53	18 53	19 53	20 53		21 55	
Axminster	a	23p42					09 08	10 05	11 03	12 03	13 03	14 03	15 03		16 03	17 03	18 03	19 03	20 03	21 03		22 05	23s45
	d	23p43					09 09	10 09	11 09	12 09	13 09	14 09	15 09		16 09	17 09	18 09	19 09	20 09	21 09		22 09	
Crewkerne	d	23p56					09 22	10 22	11 22	12 22	13 22	14 22	15 22		16 22	17 22	18 22	19 22	20 22	21 22		22 22	00s11
Yeovil Junction	a	00 04					09 30	10 30	11 30	12 30	13 30	14 30	15 30		16 30	17 30	18 30	19 30	20 30	21 30		22 30	00s20
	d	00 16			07 32		09 32	10 32	11 32	12 32	13 32	14 32	15 32		16 32	17 32	18 32	19 32	20 32	21 32		22 32	
Sherborne	d				07 38		09 38	10 38	11 38	12 38	13 38	14 38	15 38		16 38	17 38	18 38	19 38	20 38	21 38		22 38	
Templecombe	d				07 46		09 46	10 46	11 46	12 46	13 46	14 46	15 46		16 46	17 46	18 46	19 46	20 46	21 46		22 46	
Gillingham (Dorset)	a				07 53		09 53	10 53	11 53	12 53	13 53	14 53	15 53		16 53	17 53	18 53	19 53	20 53	21 53		22 53	
	d				07 54	08 54	09 54	10 54	11 54	12 54	13 54	14 54	15 54		16 54	17 54	18 54	19 54	20 54	21 54		22 54	
Tisbury	d				08 05	09 05	10 05	11 05	12 05	13 05	14 05	15 05	16 05		17 05	18 05	19 05	20 05	21 05	22 05		23 05	
Bristol Temple Meads ■10	d													16 04							21 35		
Bath Spa ■7	d													16 20							21 49		
Bradford-on-Avon	d													16 31							22 00		
Trowbridge	d													16 37							22 06		
Westbury	d													16 46							22 15		
Warminster	d													16 53							22 22		
Salisbury	a	00 50			08 20	09 20	10 20	11 20	12 20	13 20	14 20	15 20	16 20	17 16	17 20	18 20	19 20	20 20	21 20	22 20	22 46	23 19	00 56
	d		06 42	07 24	08 27	09 27	10 27	11 27	12 27	13 27	14 27	15 27	16 27	17 27		18 27	19 27	20 27	21 27	22 27			
Grateley	d				08 39	09 39		11 39		13 39		15 39		17 39			19 39		21 39	22 39			
Andover	d		06 59	07 41	08 46	09 46	10 44	11 46	12 44	13 46	14 44	15 46	16 44	17 46		18 44	19 46	20 44	21 46	22 46			
Whitchurch (Hants)	d			07 49	08 54		10 52		12 52		14 52		16 52			18 52		20 52		22 54			
Overton	d			07 55	09 00		10 58		12 58		14 58		16 58			18 58		20 58		23 00			
Basingstoke	a		07 19	08 06	09 08	10 02	11 06	12 02	13 06	14 02	15 06	16 02	17 06	18 02		19 06	20 02	21 06	22 03	23 08			
Woking	a		07 39	08 28	09 28	10 28	11 28	12 28	13 28	14 28	15 28	16 28	17 28	18 28		19 28	20 28	21 28	22 28				
Clapham Junction ■10	a		08 05	08 57	09 57	10 49	11 49	12 49	13 49	14 49	15 49	16 49	17 49	18 49		19 49	20 49	21 49	22 49				
London Waterloo ■15 ⊖	a		08 19	09 09	10 08	11 04	12 03	13 04	13 59	14 59	15 59	16 59	17 59	18 59		19 59	20 59	21 59	22 59				

A ⌶ from Salisbury

For Bus Connections for either to or from Yeovil Junction and Yeovil Pen Mill please see Table 123A

Network Diagram for Tables 165, 167

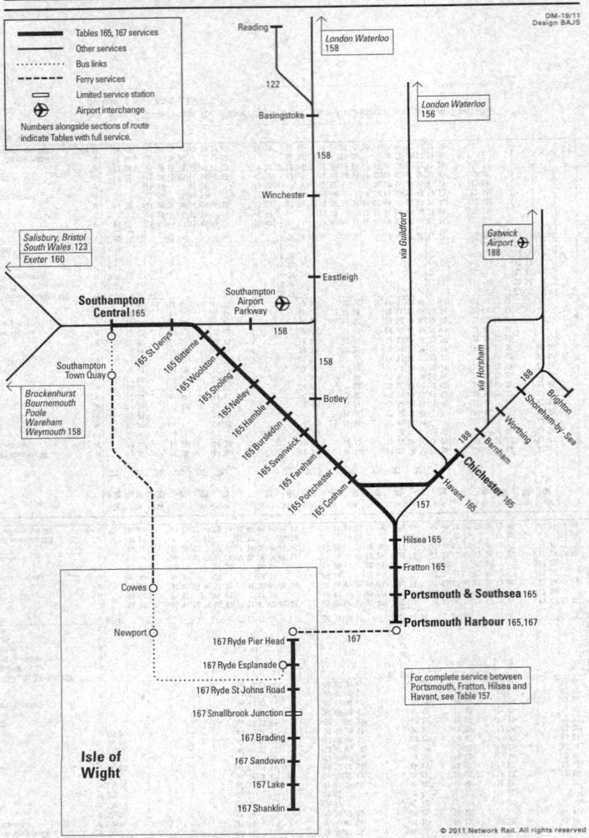

Southampton - Fareham and Portsmouth

Network Diagram - see first Page of Table 165

Miles	Miles			SW MO A	SW MX	SW	SW	SN	SW	SN	SW	SW	GW	SW	SN	SW	SW	SN
0	—	Eastleigh	d	23p26	23p30	00 30			06 00		06 29			07 02		07 28		
1¼	—	Southampton Airport Parkway	d				02s46											
—	—	Southampton Central	d					05 48		06 10		06 21	06 53		07 06		07 17	07 33
3¼	—	St Denys	d				02s51					06 28					07 23	
3¾	—	Bitterne	d									06 30					07 25	
5½	—	Woolston	d					05 57		06 19		06 34			07 15		07 29	
6¼	—	Sholing	d									06 36					07 31	
8	—	Netley	d									06 40					07 35	
8¾	—	Hamble	d									06 42					07 37	
10	—	Bursledon	d									06 45					07 40	
12	—	Swanwick	d					06 06		06 27		06 49			07 24		07 44	07 51
15¾	—	Fareham	a	23p43	23p48	00s47		06 12	06 17	06 33	06 49	06 57	07 14	07 19	07 30	07 46	07 52	07 58
—	—		d	23p44	23p49			06 13	06 19	06 34	06 50	06 58	07 15	07 20	07 31	07 48	07 53	07 58
19	—	Portchester	d	23p49	23p54	00s53		06 18	06 24	06 40	06 55	07 03		07 25	07 36	07 53	07 58	
21½	0	Cosham	d	23p54	23p59	00s57		06 23	06 29	06 44	07 00	07 08	07 23	07 29	07 40	07 58	08 03	08 07
—	4	Havant	a					06 37		06 53					07 46			08 13
—	12¾	Chichester	a					06 58		07 07					08 08			08 27
23	—	Hilsea	a	23p59	00 03				06 33		07 05	07 13		07 35		08 03	08 09	
25¼	—	Fratton	a	00 04	00 07	01s05			06 40		07 09	07 17	07 34	07 39		08 07	08 13	
26¼	—	Portsmouth & Southsea	a	00 08	00 11	01s08			06 44		07 12	07 22	07 38	07 42		08 11	08 19	
27	—	Portsmouth Harbour	a	00 13	00 16	01 12			06 49		07 17		07 45	07 48		08 16	08 24	

		GW	SW	SN	SW	SN	SW	GW	SN	SW	SN	SW	GW	SN	SW	SN	SW	GW	SN	SW	SN	SW	GW
Eastleigh	d				08 31					09 28					10 28					11 28			
Southampton Airport Parkway	d																						
Southampton Central	d	07 42	07 51	08 10		08 33	08 44	09 05	09 10		09 33	09 44	10 05	10 13		10 33	10 44	11 05	11 13		11 33	11 44	12 05
St Denys	d		07 57	08 15			08 49					09 49					10 49					11 49	
Bitterne	d		08 00				08 52					09 52					10 52					11 52	
Woolston	d		08 03				08 55					09 55					10 55					11 55	
Sholing	d		08 06				08 58					09 58					10 58					11 58	
Netley	d		08 10				09 02					10 02					11 02					12 02	
Hamble	d		08 12				09 04					10 04					11 04					12 04	
Bursledon	d		08 15				09 07					10 07					11 07					12 07	
Swanwick	d		08 20	08 28		08 50	09 11		09 28		09 50	10 11		10 32		10 50	11 11		11 33		11 50	12 11	
Fareham	a	08 05	08 27	08 34	08 50	08 56	09 17	09 27	09 36	09 46	09 56	10 17	10 27	10 38	10 46	10 56	11 17	11 27	11 39	11 46	11 56	12 17	12 27
	d	08 06	08 28	08 35	08 51	08 57	09 18	09 27	09 37	09 48	09 56	10 18	10 27	10 39	10 48	10 57	11 18	11 27	11 40	11 48	11 57	12 18	12 27
Portchester	d		08 33	08 40	08 56		09 23		09 42	09 53		10 23		10 44	10 53		11 23		11 45	11 53		12 23	
Cosham	d	08 14	08 38	08 44	09 01	09 05	09 28	09 35	09 46	09 58	10 05	10 28	10 35	10 48	10 58	11 05	11 28	11 35	11 49	11 58	12 05	12 28	12 35
Havant	a			08 50		09 11			09 53		10 11			10 55		11 11			11 55		12 11		
Chichester	a			09 11		09 24			10 10		10 23			11 10		11 24			12 10		12 24		
Hilsea	a		08 45		09 05		09 33			10 03		10 33			11 03		11 33			12 03		12 33	
Fratton	a	08 20	08 49		09 09		09 37	09 42		10 07		10 37	10 42		11 07		11 37	11 42		12 07		12 37	12 42
Portsmouth & Southsea	a	08 24	08 52		09 13		09 42	09 46		10 11		10 42	10 46		11 11		11 42	11 46		12 11		12 42	12 46
Portsmouth Harbour	a	08 30	08 57		09 18			09 55		10 18			10 54		11 18			11 54		12 18			12 54

		SN	SW	SN	SW	GW	SN	SW	SN	SW	GW	SN	SW	GW	SN	SW	GW	SN	SW	SN	SW	GW
Eastleigh	d		12 28					13 28					14 28		14 41				15 28			
Southampton Airport Parkway	d														14n34							
Southampton Central	d	12 13		12 33	12 44	13 05	13 13		13 33	13 44	14 05	14 13		14 34	14n26	14 44	15 05	15 13		15 33	15 44	16 05
St Denys	d				12 49					13 49						14 49					15 49	
Bitterne	d				12 52					13 52						14 52					15 52	
Woolston	d				12 55					13 55						14 55					15 55	
Sholing	d				12 58					13 58						14 58					15 58	
Netley	d				13 02					14 02						15 02					16 02	
Hamble	d				13 04					14 04						15 04					16 04	
Bursledon	d				13 07					14 07						15 07					16 07	
Swanwick	d	12 33		12 50	13 11		13 33		13 50	14 11		14 33				15 11		15 33		15 50	16 11	
Fareham	a	12 39	12 46	12 56	13 17	13 27	13 39	13 46	13 56	14 17	14 27	14 39	14 46	14 55	14 59	15 17	15 27	15 39	15 46	15 56	16 17	16 27
	d	12 40	12 48	12 56	13 18	13 27	13 40	13 48	13 56	14 18	14 27	14 40	14 48	14 56	15 00	15 18	15 27	15 40	15 48	15 57	16 18	16 27
Portchester	d	12 45	12 53		13 23		13 45	13 53		14 23		14 45	14 53			15 23		15 45	15 53		16 23	
Cosham	d	12 49	12 58	13 05	13 28	13 35	13 49	13 58	14 05	14 28	14 35	14 49	14 58	15 04		15 28	15 35	15 49	15 58	16 05	16 28	16 35
Havant	a	12 55		13 11			13 55		14 11			14 55		15 10	15 14			15 57		16 11		
Chichester	a	13 10		13 23			14 10		14 23			15 10		15 21	15 25			16 12		16 24		
Hilsea	a		13 03		13 33			14 03		14 33			15 03			15 33			16 03		16 33	
Fratton	a		13 07		13 37	13 42		14 07		14 37	14 42		15 07			15 37	15 42		16 07		16 37	16 42
Portsmouth & Southsea	a		13 11		13 42	13 46		14 11		14 42	14 46		15 11			15 42	15 46		16 11		16 40	16 46
Portsmouth Harbour	a		13 18			13 54		14 18			14 54		15 18				15 54		16 18		16 44	16 54

A from 21 May until 1 October
B not from 31 July until 10 August, from 30 August until 7 September
C from 30 July until 10 September, not from 14 August until 29 August
n stops at these stations before Eastleigh

Table 165

Southampton - Fareham and Portsmouth

Mondays to Fridays

until 5 October

Network Diagram - see first Page of Table 165

		SN	SW	SW	SN	SW	SW	GW	SN	SW	SN	SW	SW	GW	SN	SW	SN	SW	SW
		◇1	1	1	1	1	1	◇ bike	◇1	1	1	1	1	◇ bike	◇1	1	1	1	1
Eastleigh	d			16 28		16 54				17 28			18 01			18 25		18 55	
Southampton Airport Parkway	d																		
Southampton Central	d	16 12			16 33		16 44	17 05	17 13		17 33	17 44		18 05	18 11		18 33		18 44
St Denys	d						16 49					17 49							18 49
Bitterne	d						16 52					17 52							18 52
Woolston	d						16 55					17 55							18 55
Sholing	d						16 58					17 58							18 58
Netley	d						17 02					18 02							19 02
Hamble	d						17 04					18 04							19 04
Bursledon	d						17 07					18 07							19 07
Swanwick	d	16 29			16 50		17 11		17 33		17 50	18 11			18 28		18 50		19 11
Fareham	a	16 35		16 46	16 56	17 11	17 17	17 27	17 39	17 46	17 56	18 17	18 22	18 27	18 34	18 44	18 56	19 13	19 17
	d	16 36	16 43	16 48	16 57	17 12	17 18	17 27	17 40	17 48	17 56	18 18	18 23	18 27	18 35	18 45	18 56	19 14	19 18
Portchester	d	16 41		16 53		17 17	17 23		17 45	17 53		18 23	18 28		18 40	18 50		19 19	19 23
Cosham	d	16 45		16 58	17 05	17 22	17 28	17 35	17 49	17 58	18 05	18 28	18 33	18 35	18 44	18 55	19 05	19 24	19 28
Havant	a	16 51	16 55		17 11				17 55		18 11				18 50		19 11		
Chichester 4	a	17 08			17 25				18 10		18 24				19 05		19 22		
Hilsea	a			17 03			17 33			18 04		18 33				19 05		19 28	19 33
Fratton	a			17 07		17 31	17 37	17 42		18 08		18 37	18 40	18 48		19 09		19 32	19 37
Portsmouth & Southsea	a			17 11		17 35	17 42	17 46		18 12		18 41	18 43	18 52		19 12		19 36	19 42
Portsmouth Harbour	a			17 18		17 40		17 54		18 20			18 51	19 00		19 20		19 43	

		GW	SN	SW	SN	SW	SW	GW	SN	SW	SN	SW	GW	SN	SW	SN	SW	SN	GW	SN	SW
		■ bike	◇1	1	1	1	1	■ bike	◇1	1	1	1	◇ bike	1	1	1	1	1	◇	1	1
Eastleigh	d			19 29		19 51				20 30					21 30				22 24		22 51
Southampton Airport Parkway	d																				
Southampton Central	d	19 05	19 12		19 33		19 44	20 05	20 11		20 33	20 44	21 05	21 13		21 33	21 44	22 13		22 33	
St Denys	d						19 49					20 49					21 49				
Bitterne	d						19 52					20 52					21 52				
Woolston	d						19 55					20 55					21 55				
Sholing	d						19 58					20 58					21 58				
Netley	d						20 02					21 02					22 02				
Hamble	d						20 04					21 04					22 04				
Bursledon	d						20 07					21 07					22 07				
Swanwick	d		19 29		19 51		20 11		20 28		20 50	21 11		21 33		21 51	22 11	22 30		22 50	
Fareham	a	19 27	19 35	19 46	19 57	20 09	20 17	20 27	20 34	20 48	20 56	21 17	21 27	21 39	21 48	21 57	22 17	22 36	22 42	22 56	23 09
	d	19 27	19 36	19 48	19 57	20 09	20 18	20 27	20 35	20 49	20 57	21 18	21 27	21 40	21 48	21 58	22 18	22 37	22 42	22 57	23 10
Portchester	d		19 41	19 53			20 23		20 40	20 54		21 23		21 45	21 53	22 03	22 23	22 42			23 15
Cosham	d	19 35	19 46	19 58	20 06		20 28		20 44	20 59	21 06	21 28		21 49	21 58	22 07	22 28	22 47		23 05	23 20
Havant	a		19 52		20 12	20 21			20 50		21 12			21 55		22 13		22 56		23 11	
Chichester 4	a		20 06		20 24				21 05		21 24			22 06		22 34		23 11		23 22	
Hilsea	a			20 02			20 33			21 03		21 33			22 03		22 33				23 24
Fratton	a	19 42		20 06			20 37	20 42		21 07		21 37	21 41		22 08		22 37		22 56		23 32
Portsmouth & Southsea	a	19 46		20 11			20 42	20 46		21 11		21 40	21 45		22 11		22 42		22 59		23 36
Portsmouth Harbour	a	19 54		20 20				20 54		21 16		21 45	21 52		22 16				23 04		23 40

		SW	GW	SW
		1	◇	1
Eastleigh	d			23 30
Southampton Airport Parkway	d			
Southampton Central	d	22 44	23 05	
St Denys	d	22 49		
Bitterne	d	22 52		
Woolston	d	22 55		
Sholing	d	22 58		
Netley	d	23 02		
Hamble	d	23 04		
Bursledon	d	23 07		
Swanwick	d	23 11		
Fareham	a	23 17	23 27	23 48
	d	23 18	23 27	23 49
Portchester	d	23 23		23 54
Cosham	d	23 28		23 59
Havant	a			
Chichester 4	a			
Hilsea	a	23 33		00 03
Fratton	a	23 37	23 44	00 07
Portsmouth & Southsea	a	23 40	23 48	00 11
Portsmouth Harbour	a		23 54	00 16

Table 165

Southampton - Fareham and Portsmouth

Mondays to Fridays

from 8 October

Network Diagram - see first Page of Table 165

		SW MO	SW MX	SW	SW	SN	SW	SN	SW	SW	GW	SW	SN	SW	SW	SN	GW	SW	SN
		1	1	1	1	1	1	1	1	1		1	◇1	1	1	1	◇	1	◇1
Eastleigh	d	23p26	23p30	00 30			06 00		06 29			07 02		07 28					
Southampton Airport Parkway	d				02s46														
Southampton Central	d					05 48		06 10		06 21	06 53		07 06		07 17	07 33	07 42	07 51	08 10
St Denys	d				02s51					06 28					07 23			07 57	08 15
Bitterne	d									06 30					07 25			08 00	
Woolston	d					05 57		06 19		06 34			07 15		07 29			08 03	
Sholing	d									06 36					07 31			08 06	
Netley	d									06 40					07 35			08 10	
Hamble	d									06 42					07 37			08 12	
Bursledon	d									06 45					07 40			08 15	
Swanwick	d					06 06		06 27		06 49			07 24		07 44	07 51		08 20	08 28
Fareham	a	23p43	23p48	00s47		06 12	06 17	06 33	06 49	06 57	07 14	07 19	07 30	07 46	07 52	07 58	08 05	08 27	08 34
	d	23p44	23p49			06 13	06 19	06 34	06 50	06 58	07 15	07 20	07 31	07 48	07 53	07 58	08 06	08 28	08 35
Portchester	d	23p49	23p54	00s53		06 18	06 24	06 40	06 55	07 03		07 25	07 36	07 53	07 58			08 33	08 40
Cosham	d	23p54	23p59	00s57		06 23	06 29	06 44	07 00	07 08	07 23	07 29	07 40	07 58	08 03	08 07	08 14	08 38	08 44
Havant	a					06 37		06 53					07 46			08 13			08 50
Chichester 4	a					06 58		07 07					08 08			08 27			09 11
Hilsea	a	23p59	00 03				06 33		07 05	07 13		07 35		08 03	08 09			08 45	
Fratton	a	00 04	00 07	01s05			06 40		07 09	07 17	07 34	07 39		08 07	08 13		08 20	08 49	
Portsmouth & Southsea	a	00 08	00 11	01s08			06 44		07 12	07 22	07 38	07 42		08 11	08 19		08 24	08 52	
Portsmouth Harbour	a	00 13	00 16	01 12			06 49		07 17		07 45	07 48		08 16	08 24		08 30	08 57	

		SW	SN	SW	GW	SN	SW	SN	SW	GW	SN	SW	SN	SW	GW	SN	SW	SN	SW	GW	SN	SW	SN
		1	1	1	◇ bike	◇1	1	1	1	■ bike	◇1	1	1	1	◇ bike	◇1	1	1	1	◇ bike	◇1	1	1
Eastleigh	d	08 31					09 28					10 28					11 28					12 28	
Southampton Airport Parkway	d																						
Southampton Central	d		08 33	08 44	09 05	09 10		09 33	09 44	10 05	10 13		10 33	10 44	11 05	11 13		11 33	11 44	12 05	12 13		12 33
St Denys	d			08 49					09 49					10 49					11 49				
Bitterne	d			08 52					09 52					10 52					11 52				
Woolston	d			08 55					09 55					10 55					11 55				
Sholing	d			08 58					09 58					10 58					11 58				
Netley	d			09 02					10 02					11 02					12 02				
Hamble	d			09 04					10 04					11 04					12 04				
Bursledon	d			09 07					10 07					11 07					12 07				
Swanwick	d		08 50	09 11		09 28		09 50	10 11		10 32		10 50	11 11		11 33		11 50	12 11		12 33		12 50
Fareham	a	08 50	08 56	09 17	09 27	09 36	09 46	09 56	10 17	10 27	10 38	10 46	10 56	11 17	11 27	11 39	11 46	11 56	12 17	12 27	12 39	12 46	12 56
	d	08 51	08 57	09 18	09 27	09 37	09 48	09 56	10 18	10 27	10 39	10 48	10 57	11 18	11 27	11 40	11 48	11 57	12 18	12 27	12 40	12 48	12 56
Portchester	d	08 56		09 23		09 42	09 53		10 23		10 44	10 53		11 23		11 45	11 53		12 23		12 45	12 53	
Cosham	d	09 01	09 05	09 28	09 35	09 46	09 58	10 05	10 28	10 35	10 48	10 58	11 05	11 28	11 35	11 49	11 58	12 05	12 28	12 35	12 49	12 58	13 05
Havant	a		09 11			09 53		10 11			10 55		11 11			11 55		12 11			12 55		13 11
Chichester 4	a		09 24			10 10		10 23			11 10		11 24			12 10		12 24			13 10		13 23
Hilsea	a	09 05		09 33			10 03		10 33			11 03		11 33			12 03		12 33			13 03	
Fratton	a	09 09		09 37	09 42		10 07		10 37	10 42		11 07		11 37	11 42		12 07		12 37	12 42		13 07	
Portsmouth & Southsea	a	09 13		09 42	09 46		10 11		10 42	10 46		11 11		11 42	11 46		12 11		12 42	12 46		13 11	
Portsmouth Harbour	a	09 18			09 55		10 18			10 54		11 18			11 54		12 18			12 54		13 18	

		SW	GW	SN	SW	SN	SW	GW	SN	SW	GW	SN	SW	GW	SN	SW	SN	SW	GW	SN	SW
		1	◇ bike	◇1	1	1	1	◇ bike	◇1	1	■ bike	1	1	◇ bike	◇1	1	1	1	◇ bike	◇1	1
Eastleigh	d				13 28					14 28		14 41				15 28					
Southampton Airport Parkway	d											14n34									
Southampton Central	d	12 44	13 05	13 13		13 33	13 44	14 05	14 13		14 34	14n26	14 44	15 05	15 13		15 33	15 44	16 05	16 12	
St Denys	d	12 49					13 49						14 49					15 49			
Bitterne	d	12 52					13 52						14 52					15 52			
Woolston	d	12 55					13 55						14 55					15 55			
Sholing	d	12 58					13 58						14 58					15 58			
Netley	d	13 02					14 02						15 02					16 02			
Hamble	d	13 04					14 04						15 04					16 04			
Bursledon	d	13 07					14 07						15 07					16 07			
Swanwick	d	13 11		13 33		13 50	14 11		14 33				15 11		15 33		15 50	16 11		16 29	
Fareham	a	13 17	13 27	13 39	13 46	13 56	14 17	14 27	14 39	14 46	14 55	14 59	15 17	15 27	15 39	15 46	15 56	16 17	16 27	16 35	
	d	13 18	13 27	13 40	13 48	13 56	14 18	14 27	14 40	14 48	14 56	15 00	15 18	15 27	15 40	15 48	15 57	16 18	16 27	16 36	16 43
Portchester	d	13 23		13 45	13 53		14 23		14 45	14 53			15 23		15 45	15 53		16 23		16 41	
Cosham	d	13 28	13 35	13 49	13 58	14 05	14 28	14 35	14 49	14 58	15 04		15 28	15 35	15 49	15 58	16 05	16 28	16 35	16 45	
Havant	a			13 55		14 11			14 55		15 10	15 14			15 57		16 11			16 51	16 55
Chichester 4	a			14 10		14 23			15 10		15 21	15 25			16 12		16 24			17 08	
Hilsea	a	13 33			14 03		14 33			15 03			15 33			16 03		16 33			
Fratton	a	13 37	13 42		14 07		14 37	14 42		15 07			15 37	15 42		16 07		16 37	16 42		
Portsmouth & Southsea	a	13 42	13 46		14 11		14 42	14 46		15 11			15 42	15 46		16 11		16 40	16 46		
Portsmouth Harbour	a		13 54		14 18			14 54		15 18				15 54		16 18		16 44	16 54		

n stops at these stations before Eastleigh

Table 165

Southampton - Fareham and Portsmouth

Mondays to Fridays
from 8 October

Network Diagram - see first Page of Table 165

		SW	SN	SW	SW	GW	SN	SW	SN	SW	SW	GW	SN	SW	SN	SW	SW	GW	SN	SW
		■	■	■	■	◇ H	◇■	■	■	■	■	◇ H	◇■	■	■	■	■	■ H	◇■	■
Eastleigh	d	16 28		16 54				17 28			18 01			18 25		18 55				19 29
Southampton Airport Parkway	d																			
Southampton Central	d		16 33		16 44	17 05	17 13		17 33	17 44		18 05	18 11		18 33		18 44	19 05	19 12	
St Denys	d				16 49					17 49							18 49			
Bitterne	d				16 52					17 52							18 52			
Woolston	d				16 55					17 55							18 55			
Sholing	d				16 58					17 58							18 58			
Netley	d				17 02					18 02							19 02			
Hamble	d				17 04					18 04							19 04			
Bursledon	d				17 07					18 07							19 07			
Swanwick	d		16 50		17 11		17 33		17 50	18 11			18 28		18 50		19 11		19 29	
Fareham	a	16 46	16 56	17 11	17 17	17 27	17 39	17 46	17 56	18 17	18 22	18 27	18 34	18 44	18 56	19 13	19 17	19 27	19 35	19 46
	d	16 48	16 57	17 12	17 18	17 27	17 40	17 48	17 56	18 18	18 23	18 27	18 35	18 45	18 56	19 14	19 18	19 27	19 36	19 48
Portchester	d	16 53		17 17	17 23		17 45	17 53		18 23	18 28		18 40	18 50		19 19	19 23		19 41	19 53
Cosham	d	16 58	17 05	17 22	17 28	17 35	17 49	17 58	18 05	18 28	18 33	18 35	18 44	18 55	19 05	19 24	19 28	19 35	19 46	19 58
Havant	a		17 11				17 55		18 11				18 50		19 11				19 52	
Chichester 4	a		17 25				18 10		18 24				19 05		19 22				20 06	
Hilsea	a	17 03			17 33			18 04		18 33				19 05		19 28	19 33			20 02
Fratton	a	17 07		17 31	17 37	17 42		18 08		18 37	18 40	18 48		19 09		19 32	19 37	19 42		20 06
Portsmouth & Southsea	a	17 11		17 35	17 42	17 46		18 12		18 41	18 43	18 52		19 12		19 36	19 42	19 46		20 11
Portsmouth Harbour	a	17 18		17 40		17 54		18 20			18 51	19 00		19 20		19 43		19 54		20 20

		SN	SW	SW	GW	SN	SW	SN	SW	GW	SN	SW	SN	SW	SN	GW	SN	SW	SW	GW
		■	■	■	■ H	◇■	■	■	■	◇ H	■	■	■	■	■	◇	■	■	■	◇
Eastleigh	d		19 51				20 30					21 30				22 24		22 51		
Southampton Airport Parkway	d																			
Southampton Central	d	19 33		19 44	20 05	20 11		20 33	20 44	21 05	21 13		21 33	21 44	22 13		22 33		22 44	23 05
St Denys	d			19 49					20 49					21 49					22 49	
Bitterne	d			19 52					20 52					21 52					22 52	
Woolston	d			19 55					20 55					21 55					22 55	
Sholing	d			19 58					20 58					21 58					22 58	
Netley	d			20 02					21 02					22 02					23 02	
Hamble	d			20 04					21 04					22 04					23 04	
Bursledon	d			20 07					21 07					22 07					23 07	
Swanwick	d	19 51		20 11		20 28		20 50	21 11		21 33		21 51	22 11	22 30		22 50		23 11	
Fareham	a	19 57	20 09	20 17	20 27	20 34	20 48	20 56	21 17	21 27	21 39	21 48	21 57	22 17	22 36	22 42	22 56	23 09	23 17	23 27
	d	19 57	20 09	20 18	20 27	20 35	20 49	20 57	21 18	21 27	21 40	21 48	21 58	22 18	22 37	22 42	22 57	23 10	23 18	23 27
Portchester	d			20 23		20 40	20 54		21 23		21 45	21 53	22 03	22 23	22 42			23 15	23 23	
Cosham	d	20 06		20 28		20 44	20 59	21 06	21 28		21 49	21 58	22 07	22 28	22 47		23 05	23 20	23 28	
Havant	a	20 12	20 21			20 50		21 12			21 55		22 13		22 56		23 11			
Chichester 4	a	20 24				21 05		21 24			22 06		22 34		23 11		23 22			
Hilsea	a			20 33			21 03		21 33			22 03		22 33				23 24	23 33	
Fratton	a			20 37	20 42		21 07		21 37	21 41		22 08		22 37		22 56		23 32	23 37	23 44
Portsmouth & Southsea	a			20 42	20 46		21 11		21 40	21 45		22 11		22 42		22 59		23 36	23 40	23 48
Portsmouth Harbour	a				20 54		21 16		21 45	21 52		22 16				23 04		23 40		23 54

		SW
		■
Eastleigh	d	23 30
Southampton Airport Parkway	d	
Southampton Central	d	
St Denys	d	
Bitterne	d	
Woolston	d	
Sholing	d	
Netley	d	
Hamble	d	
Bursledon	d	
Swanwick	d	
Fareham	a	23 48
	d	23 49
Portchester	d	23 54
Cosham	d	23 59
Havant	a	
Chichester 4	a	
Hilsea	a	00 03
Fratton	a	00 07
Portsmouth & Southsea	a	00 11
Portsmouth Harbour	a	00 16

Table 165

Saturdays

Southampton - Fareham and Portsmouth

Network Diagram - see first Page of Table 165

		SW	SW	SW	SW	SN	SW	SN	SW	GW	SN	SW	SN	SW	GW	SN	SW
		■	■	■	■	◇■	■	■	■		◇■	■	■	■	◇	◇■	■
Eastleigh	d	23p30	00 30				06 28					07 30					08 31
Southampton Airport Parkway	d			02s39													
Southampton Central	d				05 44	06 13		06 33	06 44	07 05	07 13		07 33	07 44	08 05	08 13	
St Denys	d			02s44	05 49				06 49					07 49			
Bitterne	d				05 52				06 52					07 52			
Woolston	d				05 55				06 55					07 55			
Sholing	d				05 58				06 58					07 58			
Netley	d				06 02				07 02					08 02			
Hamble	d				06 04				07 04					08 04			
Bursledon	d				06 07				07 07					08 07			
Swanwick	d				06 11	06 33		06 50	07 11		07 33		07 50	08 11		08 33	
Fareham	a	23p48	00s47		06 17	06 39	06 46	06 56	07 17	07 27	07 39	07 48	07 56	08 17	08 27	08 39	08 48
	d	23p49			06 18	06 40	06 48	06 56	07 18	07 27	07 40	07 49	07 56	08 18	08 27	08 40	08 49
Portchester	d	23p54	00s53		06 23	06 45	06 53		07 23		07 45	07 54		08 23		08 45	08 54
Cosham	d	23p59	00s57		06 28	06 49	06 58	07 05	07 28	07 35	07 49	07 59	08 05	08 28	08 35	08 49	08 59
Havant	a					06 55		07 11			07 55		08 11			08 55	
Chichester 4	a					07 10		07 23			08 10		08 23			09 10	
Hilsea	a	00 03			06 33		07 03		07 33			08 03		08 33			09 04
Fratton	a	00 07	01s05		06 37		07 07		07 37	07 42		08 07		08 37	08 42		09 08
Portsmouth & Southsea	a	00 11	01s08		06 42		07 11		07 42	07 46		08 11		08 42	08 46		09 12
Portsmouth Harbour	a	00 16	01 12				07 16			07 52		08 18			08 52		09 18

		SN	SW	GW	SN	SW	SN	SW	GW	SN	SW	SN	SW	GW	SN	SW	SN	SW	GW	SN	SW
		■	■	◇	◇■	■	■	■	◇	◇■	■	■	■	◇	◇■	■	■	■	◇ H	◇■	■
Eastleigh	d					09 28					10 28					11 28					12 28
Southampton Airport Parkway	d																				
Southampton Central	d	08 33	08 44	09 05	09 13		09 33	09 44	10 05	10 13		10 33	10 44	11 05	11 13		11 33	11 44	12 05	12 13	
St Denys	d		08 49					09 49					10 49					11 49			
Bitterne	d		08 52					09 52					10 52					11 52			
Woolston	d		08 55					09 55					10 55					11 55			
Sholing	d		08 58					09 58					10 58					11 58			
Netley	d		09 02					10 02					11 02					12 02			
Hamble	d		09 04					10 04					11 04					12 04			
Bursledon	d		09 07					10 07					11 07					12 07			
Swanwick	d	08 50	09 11		09 33		09 50	10 11		10 33		10 50	11 11		11 33		11 50	12 11		12 33	
Fareham	a	08 56	09 17	09 27	09 39	09 46	09 56	10 17	10 27	10 39	10 46	10 56	11 17	11 27	11 39	11 46	11 56	12 17	12 27	12 39	12 46
	d	08 56	09 18	09 27	09 40	09 48	09 56	10 18	10 27	10 40	10 48	10 56	11 18	11 27	11 40	11 48	11 56	12 18	12 27	12 40	12 48
Portchester	d		09 23		09 45	09 53		10 23		10 45	10 53		11 23		11 45	11 53		12 23		12 45	12 53
Cosham	d	09 05	09 28	09 35	09 49	09 58	10 05	10 28	10 35	10 49	10 58	11 05	11 28	11 35	11 49	11 58	12 05	12 28	12 35	12 49	12 58
Havant	a	09 11			09 55		10 11			10 55		11 11			11 55		12 11			12 55	
Chichester 4	a	09 23			10 10		10 23			11 10		11 23			12 10		12 23			13 10	
Hilsea	a		09 33			10 03		10 33			11 03		11 33			12 03		12 33			13 03
Fratton	a		09 37	09 42		10 07		10 37	10 42		11 07		11 37	11 42		12 07		12 37	12 42		13 07
Portsmouth & Southsea	a		09 42	09 46		10 11		10 42	10 46		11 11		11 42	11 46		12 11		12 42	12 46		13 11
Portsmouth Harbour	a			09 52		10 18			10 52		11 18			11 52		12 18			12 52		13 18

		SN	SW	GW	SN	SW	SN	SW	GW	SN	SW	GW	SN	SW	GW	SN	SW	SN	SW	GW	SN
		■	■	◇ H	◇■	■	■	■	◇ H	◇■	■	◇	■	■	◇	◇■	■	■	■	◇	◇■
Eastleigh	d					13 28					14 28		14 41				15 28				
Southampton Airport Parkway	d												14n34								
Southampton Central	d	12 33	12 44	13 05	13 13		13 33	13 44	14 05	14 13		14 34	14n26	14 44	15 05	15 13		15 33	15 44	16 05	16 13
St Denys	d		12 49					13 49						14 49					15 49		
Bitterne	d		12 52					13 52						14 52					15 52		
Woolston	d		12 55					13 55						14 55					15 55		
Sholing	d		12 58					13 58						14 58					15 58		
Netley	d		13 02					14 02						15 02					16 02		
Hamble	d		13 04					14 04						15 04					16 04		
Bursledon	d		13 07					14 07						15 07					16 07		
Swanwick	d	12 50	13 11		13 33		13 50	14 11		14 33				15 11		15 33		15 50	16 11		16 33
Fareham	a	12 56	13 17	13 27	13 39	13 46	13 56	14 17	14 27	14 39	14 46	14 54	14 59	15 17	15 27	15 39	15 46	15 56	16 17	16 27	16 39
	d	12 56	13 18	13 27	13 40	13 48	13 56	14 18	14 27	14 40	14 48	14 55	15 00	15 18	15 27	15 40	15 48	15 56	16 18	16 27	16 40
Portchester	d		13 23		13 45	13 53		14 23		14 45	14 53			15 23		15 45	15 53		16 23		16 45
Cosham	d	13 05	13 28	13 35	13 49	13 58	14 05	14 28	14 35	14 49	14 58	15 03		15 28	15 35	15 49	15 58	16 05	16 28	16 35	16 49
Havant	a	13 11			13 55		14 11			14 55		15 10	15 14			15 55		16 11			16 55
Chichester 4	a	13 23			14 10		14 23			15 10		15 21	15 25			16 10		16 23			17 10
Hilsea	a		13 33			14 03		14 33			15 03			15 33			16 03		16 33		
Fratton	a		13 37	13 42		14 07		14 37	14 42		15 07			15 37	15 42		16 07		16 37	16 42	
Portsmouth & Southsea	a		13 42	13 46		14 11		14 42	14 46		15 11			15 42	15 46		16 11		16 40	16 46	
Portsmouth Harbour	a			13 52		14 18			14 52		15 18				15 52		16 18		16 44	16 52	

A until 21 July, from 18 August, not 1 September, 8 September

B 28 July, 4 August, 11 August, 1 September, 8 September

n stops at these stations before Eastleigh

Southampton - Fareham and Portsmouth

Saturdays

Network Diagram - see first Page of Table 165

		SW	SN	SW	GW	SN	SW	SN	SW	GW	SN	SW	SN	SW	GW	SN	SW	SN	SW	GW	SN
		■	■	■	◇	◇■	■	■	■	◇	◇■	■	■	■	■	◇■	■	■	■	◇	◇■
Eastleigh	d	16 28					17 28					18 28					19 28				
Southampton Airport Parkway	d																				
Southampton Central	d		16 33	16 44	17 05	17 13		17 33	17 44	18 05	18 11		18 33	18 44	19 05	19 09		19 33	19 44	20 05	20 11
St Denys	d			16 49					17 49					18 49					19 49		
Bitterne	d			16 52					17 52					18 52					19 52		
Woolston	d			16 55					17 55					18 55					19 55		
Sholing	d			16 58					17 58					18 58					19 58		
Netley	d			17 02					18 02					19 02					20 02		
Hamble	d			17 04					18 04					19 04					20 04		
Bursledon	d			17 07					18 07					19 07					20 07		
Swanwick	d		16 50	17 11		17 33		17 50	18 11		18 28		18 50	19 11		19 28		19 50	20 11		20 28
Fareham	a	16 46	16 56	17 17	17 27	17 39	17 46	17 56	18 17	18 27	18 34	18 46	18 56	19 17	19 27	19 34	19 46	19 56	20 17	20 27	20 34
	d	16 48	16 56	17 18	17 27	17 40	17 48	17 56	18 18	18 27	18 35	18 48	18 56	19 18	19 27	19 35	19 48	19 56	20 18	20 28	20 35
Portchester	d	16 53		17 23		17 45	17 53		18 23		18 40	18 53		19 23		19 40	19 53		20 23		20 40
Cosham	d	16 58	17 05	17 28	17 35	17 49	17 58	18 05	18 28	18 35	18 44	18 58	19 05	19 28	19 35	19 44	19 58	20 05	20 28		20 44
Havant	a		17 11			17 55		18 11			18 50		19 11			19 51		20 11			20 50
Chichester 4	a		17 23			18 10		18 23			19 05		19 23			20 06		20 23			21 05
Hilsea	a	17 03		17 33			18 03		18 33			19 03		19 33			20 03		20 37		
Fratton	a	17 07		17 37	17 42		18 07		18 37	18 42		19 07		19 37	19 42		20 07		20 41	20 42	
Portsmouth & Southsea	a	17 11		17 42	17 46		18 11		18 42	18 46		19 11		19 42	19 46		20 11		20 44	20 46	
Portsmouth Harbour	a	17 18			17 52		18 18			18 52		19 18			19 52		20 18			20 52	

		SW	SN	SW	GW	SN	SW	SN	SW	GW	SN	SW	SN	SW	GW	SW
		■	■	■	◇	■	■	■	■	◇	■	■	■	■	◇	■
Eastleigh	d	20 28					21 28					22 28				23 28
Southampton Airport Parkway	d															
Southampton Central	d		20 33	20 44	21 05	21 13		21 33	21 44	22 05	22 13		22 33	22 44	23 05	
St Denys	d			20 49					21 49					22 49		
Bitterne	d			20 52					21 52					22 52		
Woolston	d			20 55					21 55					22 55		
Sholing	d			20 58					21 58					22 58		
Netley	d			21 02					22 02					23 02		
Hamble	d			21 04					22 04					23 04		
Bursledon	d			21 07					22 07					23 07		
Swanwick	d		20 50	21 11		21 33		21 50	22 11		22 31		22 50	23 11		
Fareham	a	20 46	20 56	21 17	21 27	21 39	21 46	21 56	22 17	22 26	22 38	22 46	22 56	23 17	23 26	23 46
	d	20 48	20 56	21 18	21 27	21 40	21 48	21 57	22 18	22 27	22 39	22 48	23 00	23 18	23 27	23 48
Portchester	d	20 53		21 23		21 45	21 53	22 02	22 23		22 44	22 53		23 23		23 53
Cosham	d	20 58	21 05	21 28		21 49	21 58	22 06	22 28		22 48	22 58	23 08	23 28		23 58
Havant	a		21 11			21 55		22 12			22 54		23 14			
Chichester 4	a		21 23			22 06		22 33			23 09		23 25			
Hilsea	a	21 03		21 33			22 03		22 33			23 03		23 33		00 03
Fratton	a	21 07		21 37	21 42		22 07		22 37	22 42		23 07		23 37	23 40	00 07
Portsmouth & Southsea	a	21 11		21 40	21 46		22 11		22 40	22 46		23 11		23 40	23 44	00 11
Portsmouth Harbour	a	21 18		21 45	21 52		22 18		22 47	22 52		23 18			23 52	00 16

Sundays
until 9 September

		SW	SW	SW	SW	SW	SN	SW	SW	GW	SN	SW	SW	SN	SW	SW	SN	SW	GW
		■	■	■	■	■	◇■	■	■		◇■	■	■	◇■	■	■	◇■	■	◇
Eastleigh	d	23p28	00 30						08 26		08 48		09 26			10 26			
Southampton Airport Parkway	d			02s46							08n36								
Southampton Central	d				06 35		07 29	07 35		08 31	08n27	08 35		09 29	09 35		10 29	10 35	11 04
St Denys	d			02s51	06 41			07 41				08 41			09 41			10 41	
Bitterne	d				06 43			07 43				08 43			09 43			10 43	
Woolston	d				06 47			07 47				08 47			09 47			10 47	
Sholing	d				06 49			07 49				08 49			09 49			10 49	
Netley	d				06 53			07 53				08 53			09 53			10 53	
Hamble	d				06 55			07 55				08 55			09 55			10 55	
Bursledon	d				06 58			07 58				08 58			09 58			10 58	
Swanwick	d				07 02		07 46	08 02				09 02		09 46	10 02		10 46	11 02	
Fareham	a	23p46	00s47		07 09		07 52	08 09	08 43	08 51	09 02	09 09	09 43	09 52	10 09	10 43	10 52	11 09	11 26
	d	23p48			07 10	07 44	07 53	08 10	08 44	08 52	09 02	09 10	09 44	09 53	10 10	10 44	10 53	11 10	11 26
Portchester	d	23p53	00s53		07 15	07 49		08 15	08 49			09 15	09 49		10 15	10 49		11 15	
Cosham	d	23p58	00s57		07 20	07 54	08 02	08 20	08 54	09 00	09 11	09 20	09 54	10 02	10 20	10 54	11 02	11 20	11 34
Havant	a						08 10			09 11	09 17			10 10			11 10		
Chichester 4	a						08 23			09 22	09 29			10 23			11 23		
Hilsea	a	00 03			07 26	08 00		08 26	09 00			09 26	10 04		10 26	11 04		11 26	
Fratton	a	00 07	01s05		07 30	08 04		08 30	09 04			09 30	10 08		10 30	11 08		11 30	11 40
Portsmouth & Southsea	a	00 11	01s08		07 33	08 08		08 33	09 08			09 33	10 11		10 33	11 11		11 33	11 45
Portsmouth Harbour	a	00 16	01 12			08 13			09 13				10 15			11 15			11 52

A until 22 July, 19 August, 26 August

B 29 July, 5 August, 12 August, 2 September, 9 September

n stops at these stations before Eastleigh

Southampton - Fareham and Portsmouth

Sundays
until 9 September

Network Diagram - see first Page of Table 165

		SW	SN	SW	GW	SW	SN	SW	GW	SW	SN	SW	GW	SW	SN	SW	SW	GW	SN	SW	GW	SW	SN
		■	◇■	■	◇	■	◇■	■	◇	■	◇■	■	◇ ✕	■	◇■	■	■	◇	◇■	■	◇	■	◇■
Eastleigh	d	11 26				12 26				13 26				14 26			15 26					16 26	
Southampton Airport Parkway	d																						
Southampton Central	d		11 28	11 35	12 04		12 29	12 35	13 07		13 29	13 35	14 04		14 29	14 35		15 22	15 29	15 35	16 05		16 29
St Denys	d			11 41				12 41				13 41				14 41				15 41			
Bitterne	d			11 43				12 43				13 43				14 43				15 43			
Woolston	d			11 47				12 47				13 47				14 47				15 47			
Sholing	d			11 49				12 49				13 49				14 49				15 49			
Netley	d			11 53				12 53				13 53				14 53				15 53			
Hamble	d			11 55				12 55				13 55				14 55				15 55			
Bursledon	d			11 58				12 58				13 58				14 58				15 58			
Swanwick	d		11 46	12 02			12 46	13 02			13 46	14 02			14 46	15 02			15 46	16 02			16 46
Fareham	a	11 43	11 52	12 09	12 28	12 43	12 52	13 09	13 33	13 43	13 52	14 09	14 26	14 43	14 52	15 09	15 43	15 50	15 57	16 09	16 27	16 43	16 52
	d	11 44	11 53	12 10	12 28	12 44	12 53	13 10	13 34	13 44	13 53	14 10	14 27	14 44	14 53	15 10	15 44	15 51	15 58	16 10	16 27	16 44	16 53
Portchester	d	11 49		12 15		12 49		13 15		13 49		14 15		14 49		15 15	15 49			16 15		16 49	
Cosham	d	11 54	12 02	12 20	12 36	12 54	13 02	13 20	13 42	13 54	14 02	14 20	14 35	14 54	15 02	15 20	15 54	16 01	16 07	16 20	16 35	16 54	17 02
Havant	a		12 10				13 10		14 03		14 10				15 10			16 11	16 15				17 10
Chichester 4	a		12 23				13 23		14 19		14 23				15 23			16 22	16 28				17 23
Hilsea	a	12 00		12 26		13 00		13 26		14 00		14 26		15 00		15 26	16 00			16 26		17 00	
Fratton	a	12 04		12 30	12 42	13 04		13 30		14 04		14 30	14 41	15 04		15 30	16 04			16 30	16 42	17 03	
Portsmouth & Southsea	a	12 08		12 33	12 46	13 08		13 33		14 08		14 33	14 45	15 08		15 33	16 08			16 33	16 46	17 08	
Portsmouth Harbour	a	12 13			12 52	13 13				14 13			14 55	15 13			16 13				16 52	17 13	

		SW	GW	SW	SN	SW	GW	SW	SN	SW	GW	SW	GW	SN	SW	GW	SW	GW	SN	SW	GW	SW
		■	◇	■	◇■	■	◇	■	◇■	■	◇	■	◇	◇■	■	◇	■	■	◇■	■	◇	■
Eastleigh	d			17 26				18 26				19 26		19 46			20 26		20 46			21 26
Southampton Airport Parkway	d													19n38					20n38			
Southampton Central	d	16 35	17 04		17 29	17 35	18 04		18 29	18 35	19 04		19 26	19n30	19 35	20 04		20 31	20n29	20 35	21 02	
St Denys	d	16 41				17 41				18 41					19 41					20 41		
Bitterne	d	16 43				17 43				18 43					19 43					20 43		
Woolston	d	16 47				17 47				18 47					19 47					20 47		
Sholing	d	16 49				17 49				18 49					19 49					20 49		
Netley	d	16 53				17 53				18 53					19 53					20 53		
Hamble	d	16 55				17 55				18 55					19 55					20 55		
Bursledon	d	16 58				17 58				18 58					19 58					20 58		
Swanwick	d	17 02			17 46	18 02			18 46	19 02					20 02					21 02		
Fareham	a	17 09	17 27	17 43	17 52	18 09	18 27	18 43	18 52	19 09	19 28	19 43	19 48	20 02	20 09	20 26	20 43	20 54	21 02	21 10	21 24	21 43
	d	17 10	17 27	17 44	17 53	18 10	18 27	18 44	18 53	19 10	19 28	19 44	19 49	20 03	20 10	20 26	20 44	20 55	21 02	21 10	21 25	21 44
Portchester	d	17 15		17 49		18 15		18 49		19 15		19 49			20 15		20 49			21 15		21 49
Cosham	d	17 20	17 35	17 54	18 02	18 20	18 35	18 54	19 02	19 20	19 36	19 54	19 58	20 12	20 20		20 54		21 11	21 20		21 54
Havant	a				18 10				19 10				20 09	20 18					21 17			
Chichester 4	a				18 23				19 23				20 20	20 30					21 29			
Hilsea	a	17 26		18 00		18 26		19 00		19 26		20 00			20 26		21 00			21 26		22 00
Fratton	a	17 30	17 41	18 04		18 30	18 41	19 03		19 30	19 42	20 04			20 30	20 41	21 04	21 09		21 30	21 38	22 04
Portsmouth & Southsea	a	17 33	17 46	18 08		18 33	18 45	19 08		19 33	19 46	20 08			20 33	20 45	21 08	21 15		21 33	21 41	22 08
Portsmouth Harbour	a		17 52	18 13			18 52	19 13			19 53	20 13				20 51	21 13	21 26			21 48	22 13

		SN	SW	GW	SN	SW	SW	SN	GW	SW
		◇■	■	◇	■	■	■	■	◇	■
Eastleigh	d					22 26				23 26
Southampton Airport Parkway	d									
Southampton Central	d	21 30	21 35	22 04	22 15		22 35	22 52	23 08	
St Denys	d		21 41				22 41			
Bitterne	d		21 43				22 43			
Woolston	d		21 47				22 47			
Sholing	d		21 49				22 49			
Netley	d		21 53				22 53			
Hamble	d		21 55				22 55			
Bursledon	d		21 58				22 58			
Swanwick	d	21 47	22 02		22 32		23 02	23 11		
Fareham	a	21 53	22 09	22 26	22 38	22 43	23 09	23 17	23 29	23 43
	d	21 54	22 10	22 26	22 39	22 44	23 10	23 17	23 30	23 44
Portchester	d		22 15			22 49	23 15			23 49
Cosham	d	22 03	22 20		22 48	22 54	23 20	23 26		23 54
Havant	a	22 10			22 54			23 32		
Chichester 4	a	22 23			23 06			23 44		
Hilsea	a		22 26			23 00	23 24			23 59
Fratton	a		22 30	22 40		23 04	23 28		23 43	00 04
Portsmouth & Southsea	a		22 33	22 43		23 08	23 32		23 46	00 08
Portsmouth Harbour	a			22 50		23 13			23 54	00 13

n stops at these stations before Eastleigh

Table 165

Sundays from 16 September

Southampton - Fareham and Portsmouth

Network Diagram - see first Page of Table 165

		SW	SW	SW	SW	SW	SN	SW	SW	GW	SN	SW	SW	SN	SW	SW	SN	SW	GW	SW
		■	■	■	■	■	◇■	■	■		◇■	■	■	◇■	■	■	◇■	■	◇	■
Eastleigh	d	23p28	00 30						08 26		08 48		09 26			10 26				11 26
Southampton Airport Parkway	d			02s46							08n36									
Southampton Central	d				06 35		07 29	07 35		08 31	08n27	08 35		09 29	09 35		10 29	10 35	11 04	
St Denys	d			02s51	06 41			07 41				08 41			09 41			10 41		
Bitterne	d				06 43			07 43				08 43			09 43			10 43		
Woolston	d				06 47			07 47				08 47			09 47			10 47		
Sholing	d				06 49			07 49				08 49			09 49			10 49		
Netley	d				06 53			07 53				08 53			09 53			10 53		
Hamble	d				06 55			07 55				08 55			09 55			10 55		
Bursledon	d				06 58			07 58				08 58			09 58			10 58		
Swanwick	d				07 02		07 46	08 02				09 02		09 46	10 02		10 46	11 02		
Fareham	a	23p46	00s47		07 09		07 52	08 09	08 43	08 51	09 02	09 09	09 43	09 52	10 09	10 43	10 52	11 09	11 26	11 43
	d	23p48			07 10	07 44	07 53	08 10	08 44	08 52	09 02	09 10	09 44	09 53	10 10	10 44	10 53	11 10	11 26	11 44
Portchester	d	23p53	00s53		07 15	07 49		08 15	08 49			09 15	09 49		10 15	10 49		11 15		11 49
Cosham	d	23p58	00s57		07 20	07 54	08 02	08 20	08 54	09 00	09 11	09 20	09 54	10 02	10 20	10 54	11 02	11 20	11 34	11 54
Havant	a						08 10			09 11	09 17			10 10			11 10			
Chichester ■	a						08 23			09 22	09 29			10 23			11 23			
Hilsea	a	00 03			07 26	08 00		08 26	09 00			09 26	10 04		10 26	11 04		11 26		12 00
Fratton	a	00 07	01s05		07 30	08 04		08 30	09 04			09 30	10 08		10 30	11 08		11 30	11 40	12 04
Portsmouth & Southsea	a	00 11	01s08		07 33	08 08		08 33	09 08			09 33	10 11		10 33	11 11		11 33	11 45	12 08
Portsmouth Harbour	a	00 16	01 12			08 13			09 13				10 15			11 15			11 52	12 13

		SN	SW	GW	SW	SN	SW	GW	SW	SN	SW	GW	SW	SN	SW	SW	GW	SN	SW	GW	SW	SN	SW
		◇■	■	◇	■	◇■	■	◇	■	◇■	■	◇ 🚲	■	◇■	■	■	◇	◇■	■	◇	■	◇■	■
Eastleigh	d				12 26				13 26				14 26			15 26					16 26		
Southampton Airport Parkway	d																						
Southampton Central	d	11 28	11 35	12 04		12 29	12 35	13 07		13 29	13 35	14 04		14 29	14 35		15 22	15 29	15 35	16 05		16 29	16 35
St Denys	d		11 41				12 41				13 41				14 41				15 41				16 41
Bitterne	d		11 43				12 43				13 43				14 43				15 43				16 43
Woolston	d		11 47				12 47				13 47				14 47				15 47				16 47
Sholing	d		11 49				12 49				13 49				14 49				15 49				16 49
Netley	d		11 53				12 53				13 53				14 53				15 53				16 53
Hamble	d		11 55				12 55				13 55				14 55				15 55				16 55
Bursledon	d		11 58				12 58				13 58				14 58				15 58				16 58
Swanwick	d	11 46	12 02			12 46	13 02			13 46	14 02			14 46	15 02			15 46	16 02			16 46	17 02
Fareham	a	11 52	12 09	12 28	12 43	12 52	13 09	13 33	13 43	13 52	14 09	14 26	14 43	14 52	15 09	15 43	15 50	15 57	16 09	16 27	16 43	16 52	17 09
	d	11 53	12 10	12 28	12 44	12 53	13 10	13 34	13 44	13 53	14 10	14 27	14 44	14 53	15 10	15 44	15 51	15 58	16 10	16 27	16 44	16 53	17 10
Portchester	d		12 15		12 49		13 15		13 49		14 15		14 49		15 15	15 49			16 15		16 49		17 15
Cosham	d	12 02	12 20	12 36	12 54	13 02	13 20	13 42	13 54	14 02	14 20	14 35	14 54	15 02	15 20	15 54	16 01	16 07	16 20	16 35	16 54	17 02	17 20
Havant	a	12 10				13 10		14 03		14 10				15 10			16 11	16 15				17 10	
Chichester ■	a	12 23				13 23		14 19		14 23				15 23			16 22	16 28				17 23	
Hilsea	a		12 26		13 00		13 26		14 00		14 26		15 00		15 26	16 00			16 26		17 00		17 26
Fratton	a		12 30	12 42	13 04		13 30		14 04		14 30	14 41	15 04		15 30	16 04			16 30	16 42	17 03		17 30
Portsmouth & Southsea	a		12 33	12 46	13 08		13 33		14 08		14 33	14 45	15 08		15 33	16 08			16 33	16 46	17 08		17 33
Portsmouth Harbour	a			12 52	13 13				14 13			14 55	15 13			16 13				16 52	17 13		

		GW	GW	SW	SN	SW	GW	SW	SN	SW	GW	SW	GW	SN	SW	GW	SW	GW	SN	SW	GW	SW
		◇ A	◇ B	■	◇■	■	◇	■	◇■	■	◇	■	◇	◇■	■	◇	■	■	◇■	■	◇	■
Eastleigh	d			17 26				18 26				19 26		19 46			20 26		20 46			21 26
Southampton Airport Parkway	d													19n38					20n38			
Southampton Central	d	17 06	17 06		17 29	17 35	18 04		18 29	18 35	19 04		19 26	19n30	19 35	20 04		20 31	20n29	20 35	21 02	
St Denys	d					17 41				18 41					19 41					20 41		
Bitterne	d					17 43				18 43					19 43					20 43		
Woolston	d					17 47				18 47					19 47					20 47		
Sholing	d					17 49				18 49					19 49					20 49		
Netley	d					17 53				18 53					19 53					20 53		
Hamble	d					17 55				18 55					19 55					20 55		
Bursledon	d					17 58				18 58					19 58					20 58		
Swanwick	d				17 46	18 02			18 46	19 02					20 02					21 02		
Fareham	a	17 27	17 27	17 43	17 52	18 09	18 27	18 43	18 52	19 09	19 28	19 43	19 48	20 02	20 09	20 26	20 43	20 54	21 02	21 10	21 24	21 43
	d	17 27	17 27	17 44	17 53	18 10	18 27	18 44	18 53	19 10	19 28	19 44	19 49	20 03	20 10	20 26	20 44	20 55	21 02	21 10	21 25	21 44
Portchester	d			17 49		18 15		18 49		19 15		19 49			20 15		20 49			21 15		21 49
Cosham	d	17 36	17 35	17 54	18 02	18 20	18 35	18 54	19 02	19 20	19 36	19 54	19 58	20 12	20 20		20 54		21 11	21 20		21 54
Havant	a				18 10				19 10				20 09	20 18					21 17			
Chichester ■	a				18 23				19 23				20 20	20 30					21 29			
Hilsea	a			18 00		18 26		19 00		19 26		20 00			20 26		21 00			21 26		22 00
Fratton	a	17 42	17 42	18 04		18 30	18 41	19 03		19 30	19 42	20 04			20 30	20 41	21 04	21 09		21 30	21 38	22 04
Portsmouth & Southsea	a	17 47	17 47	18 08		18 33	18 45	19 08		19 33	19 46	20 08			20 33	20 45	21 08	21 15		21 33	21 41	22 08
Portsmouth Harbour	a	17 52	17 52	18 13			18 52	19 13			19 53	20 13				20 51	21 13	21 26			21 48	22 13

A from 28 October

B from 16 September until 21 October

n stops at these stations before Eastleigh

Table 165

Sundays from 16 September

Southampton - Fareham and Portsmouth

Network Diagram - see first Page of Table 165

		SN	SW	GW	SN	SW	SW	SN	GW	SW
		◇■	■	◇	■	■	■	■	◇	■
Eastleigh	d					22 26				23 26
Southampton Airport Parkway	d									
Southampton Central	d	21 30	21 35	22 04	22 15		22 35	22 52	23 08	
St Denys	d		21 41				22 41			
Bitterne	d		21 43				22 43			
Woolston	d		21 47				22 47			
Sholing	d		21 49				22 49			
Netley	d		21 53				22 53			
Hamble	d		21 55				22 55			
Bursledon	d		21 58				22 58			
Swanwick	d	21 47	22 02		22 32		23 02	23 11		
Fareham	a	21 53	22 09	22 26	22 38	22 43	23 09	23 17	23 29	23 43
	d	21 54	22 10	22 26	22 39	22 44	23 10	23 17	23 30	23 44
Portchester	d		22 15			22 49	23 15			23 49
Cosham	d	22 03	22 20		22 48	22 54	23 20	23 26		23 54
Havant	a	22 10			22 54			23 32		
Chichester ■	a	22 23			23 06			23 44		
Hilsea	a		22 26			23 00	23 24			23 59
Fratton	a		22 30	22 40		23 04	23 28		23 43	00 04
Portsmouth & Southsea	a		22 33	22 43		23 08	23 32		23 46	00 08
Portsmouth Harbour	a			22 50		23 13			23 54	00 13

Table 165

Portsmouth and Fareham - Southampton

Mondays to Fridays
until 5 October

Network Diagram - see first Page of Table 165

Miles	Miles			SW	SW MX	SW	SN	SW	SW	GW	SN	SW	SW	SN	SW	GW	SN	SN	SW	SW
				■ A	■	■	■	■	■	■ H	■	■	■	■	■	◇ H	■	■	■	■
0	—	**Portsmouth Harbour** ⛴	d	23p17	23p24	05 00			05 43	06 00			06 23		06 50	07 05			07 24	
0¾	—	**Portsmouth & Southsea**	d	23p22	23p29	05 05		05 16	05 48	06 04		06 23	06 28		06 55	07 09			07 29	07 38
1¾	—	Fratton	d	23p26	23p33	05 09		05 20	05 52	06 08		06 27	06 32		06 59	07 13			07 33	07 42
4	—	Hilsea	d	23p30	23p37	05 13		05 24	05 56			06 31	06 36		07 03				07 37	07 46
—	0	**Chichester** ■	d				05 06				06 09			06 26			07 08	07 13		
—	8¾	Havant	d				05 17				06 20			06 40			07 19	07 31		
5½	12¾	Cosham	d	23p35	23p42	05 19	05 24	05 29	06 03	06 15	06 27	06 36	06 42	06 50	07 08	07 21	07 26	07 38	07 43	07 51
8	—	Portchester	d	23p40	23p47	05 23	05 28	05 34	06 08			06 41	06 46	06 54	07 13		07 30		07 48	07 56
11¼	—	**Fareham**	a	23p45	23p52	05 28	05 33	05 39	06 13	06 23	06 36	06 46	06 51	06 59	07 18	07 28	07 35	07 46	07 53	08 01
—	—		d	23p46	23p53	05 29	05 34	05 40	06 19	06 24	06 37	06 47	06 53	07 00	07 20	07 29	07 36	07 47	07 54	08 03
15	—	Swanwick	d				05 40	05 46			06 43	06 53		07 06			07 42	07 53		08 09
17	—	Bursledon	d					05 50				06 57								08 13
18¼	—	Hamble	d					05 53				07 00								08 16
19	—	Netley	d				05 46	05 55				07 02					07 48	07 59		08 18
20¾	—	Sholing	d					05 59				07 06								08 22
21½	—	Woolston	d				05 50	06 01				07 08					07 52	08 04		08 24
23¼	—	Bitterne	d					06 05				07 12								08 28
—	—	Eastleigh	a	00 04	00 11	05 49			06 37				07 11		07 38				08 12	
—	—	Southampton Airport Parkway	a																	
23¾	—	St Denys	d					06 08				07 15						08 08		08 31
25¼	—	**Southampton Central** ⛴	a				05 59	06 13		06 45	07 02	07 21		07 25		07 50	08 01	08 13		08 38

		SN	SW	SW	GW	SN	SW	SW	SN	GW	SN	SW	GW	SW	SN	GW	SN	SW	SW	SN	GW	SN	SW
		■	■	■	◇ H	■	■	■	◇■	◇ H	■	■	◇ H	■	◇■	◇ H		■	■	◇■	◇ H		■
Portsmouth Harbour ⛴	d		07 55	08 05	08 23		08 33	08 59		09 23		09 33		09 59		10 23		10 33	10 59		11 23		
Portsmouth & Southsea	d		08 00	08 10	08 27		08 38	09 04		09 27		09 38		10 04		10 27		10 38	11 04		11 27		11 38
Fratton	d		08 04	08 13	08 31		08 42	09 08		09 31		09 42		10 08		10 31		10 42	11 08		11 31		11 42
Hilsea	d		08 08	08 17			08 46	09 12				09 46		10 12				10 46	11 12				11 46
Chichester ■	d	07 52				08 22			09 08		09 25		09 47		10 06		10 25			11 05		11 25	
Havant	d	08 03				08 37			09 23		09 39		09 59		10 20		10 37			11 19		11 37	
Cosham	d	08 09	08 13	08 22	08 39	08 45	08 51	09 17	09 30	09 39	09 46	09 51	10 05	10 17	10 28	10 39	10 46	10 51	11 17	11 26	11 39	11 46	11 51
Portchester	d	08 13	08 18	08 27		08 49	08 56	09 22				09 56		10 22	10 32			10 56	11 22	11 30			11 56
Fareham	a	08 18	08 23	08 32	08 46	08 54	09 01	09 27	09 37	09 46	09 53	10 01	10 14	10 27	10 37	10 46	10 53	11 01	11 27	11 35	11 46	11 53	12 01
	d	08 19	08 24	08 33	08 47	08 55	09 03	09 28	09 38	09 47	09 54	10 03	10 15	10 28	10 38	10 47	10 54	11 03	11 28	11 36	11 47	11 54	12 03
Swanwick	d	08 26				09 01	09 09		09 44		10 00	10 09			10 44		11 00	11 09		11 42		12 00	12 09
Bursledon	d	08 29					09 13					10 13						11 13					12 13
Hamble	d	08 32					09 16					10 16						11 16					12 16
Netley	d	08 34					09 18					10 18						11 18					12 18
Sholing	d	08 38					09 22					10 22						11 22					12 22
Woolston	d	08 40					09 24					10 24						11 24					12 24
Bitterne	d	08 43					09 28					10 28						11 28					12 28
Eastleigh	a		08 42	08 51				09 46						10 46					11 46				
Southampton Airport Parkway	a																						
St Denys	d	08 46					09 31					10 31						11 31					12 31
Southampton Central ⛴	a	08 52			09 08	09 19	09 38		10 01	10 08	10 20	10 38	10 40		11 01	11 08	11 19	11 38		12 01	12 08	12 19	12 38

		SW	SN	GW	SN	SW	SW	SN	GW	SN	SW	SW	SN	GW	SN	SW	SW	SN	GW	SN	SW	SW
		■	◇■	◇ H		■	■	◇■	◇ H	■	■	■	◇■	■ H		■	■	◇■	■ H		■	■
Portsmouth Harbour ⛴	d	11 59		12 23			12 59		13 23			13 59		14 23			14 59		15 23			15 59
Portsmouth & Southsea	d	12 04		12 27		12 38	13 04		13 27		13 38	14 04		14 27		14 38	15 04		15 27		15 38	16 04
Fratton	d	12 08		12 31		12 42	13 08		13 31		13 42	14 08		14 31		14 42	15 08		15 31		15 42	16 08
Hilsea	d	12 12				12 46	13 12				13 46	14 12				14 46	15 12				15 46	16 12
Chichester ■	d		12 05		12 25			13 05		13 25			14 05		14 25			15 05		15 25		
Havant	d		12 19		12 37			13 19		13 37			14 19		14 37			15 19		15 37		
Cosham	d	12 17	12 26	12 39	12 46	12 51	13 17	13 26	13 39	13 46	13 51	14 17	14 26	14 39	14 46	14 51	15 17	15 26	15 39	15 46	15 51	16 17
Portchester	d	12 22	12 30			12 56	13 22	13 30			13 56	14 22	14 30			14 56	15 22	15 30			15 56	16 22
Fareham	a	12 27	12 35	12 46	12 53	13 01	13 27	13 35	13 46	13 53	14 01	14 27	14 35	14 46	14 53	15 01	15 27	15 35	15 46	15 53	16 01	16 27
	d	12 28	12 36	12 47	12 54	13 03	13 28	13 36	13 47	13 56	14 03	14 28	14 36	14 47	14 54	15 03	15 28	15 36	15 47	15 54	16 03	16 28
Swanwick	d		12 42		13 00	13 09		13 42		14 02	14 09		14 42		15 00	15 09		15 42		16 00	16 09	
Bursledon	d					13 13					14 13					15 13					16 13	
Hamble	d					13 16					14 16					15 16					16 16	
Netley	d					13 18					14 18					15 18					16 18	
Sholing	d					13 22					14 22					15 22					16 22	
Woolston	d					13 24					14 24					15 24					16 24	
Bitterne	d					13 28					14 28					15 28					16 28	
Eastleigh	a	12 46					13 46			14n37		14 46					15 46					16 46
Southampton Airport Parkway	a									14n33												
St Denys	d					13 31					14 31					15 31					16 31	
Southampton Central ⛴	a		12 59	13 08	13 19	13 38		13 59	14 08	14 19	14 39		14 59	15 08	15 19	15 38		15 59	16 08	16 20	16 38	

A MO from 21 May until 1 October

n stops at these stations after Southampton Central

Table 165

Portsmouth and Fareham - Southampton

Mondays to Fridays
until 5 October

Network Diagram - see first Page of Table 165

		SN	GW	SN	SW	SW	SW	SN	GW	SN	SW	GW	SW	SN	GW	SN	SW	SW	SN	GW	SN	SW	SW
		◇■	■ H	■	■	■	■	◇■	◇ H	■	■	◇ H	■	◇■	◇ H	■	■	■	◇■	◇		■	■
Portsmouth Harbour ⛴	d		16 23			16 49	16 59		17 23		17 33		17 59		18 23			18 59		19 23			19 59
Portsmouth & Southsea	d		16 27		16 38	16 55	17 04		17 27		17 38		18 04		18 27		18 38	19 04		19 27		19 38	20 04
Fratton	d		16 31		16 42	16 59	17 08		17 31		17 42		18 08		18 31		18 42	19 08		19 31		19 42	20 08
Hilsea	d				16 46	17 03	17 12				17 46		18 12				18 46	19 12				19 46	20 12
Chichester ■	d	16 05		16 26				17 05		17 25		17 47		18 05		18 25			19 02		19 20		
Havant	d	16 19		16 38				17 19		17 37		17 58		18 23		18 37			19 20		19 37		
Cosham	d	16 26	16 39	16 46	16 51	17 08	17 17	17 27	17 39	17 46	17 51	18 05	18 17	18 30	18 39	18 44	18 51	19 17	19 29	19 39	19 46	19 51	20 17
Portchester	d	16 30			16 56	17 13	17 22	17 31			17 56		18 22	18 34			18 56	19 22	19 33			19 56	20 22
Fareham	a	16 35	16 46	16 53	17 01	17 18	17 27	17 36	17 46	17 53	18 01	18 12	18 27	18 39	18 46	18 52	19 01	19 27	19 38	19 46	19 54	20 01	20 27
	d	16 36	16 47	16 57	17 03		17 28	17 37	17 47	17 54	18 03	18 13	18 28	18 40	18 47	18 53	19 03	19 28	19 39	19 47	19 55	20 03	20 28
Swanwick	d	16 42			17 09			17 43		18 00	18 09			18 46		18 59	19 09		19 45		20 01	20 09	
Bursledon	d				17 13						18 13						19 13					20 13	
Hamble	d				17 16						18 16						19 16					20 16	
Netley	d				17 18			17 49			18 18						19 18					20 18	
Sholing	d				17 22						18 22						19 22					20 22	
Woolston	d				17 24			17 53			18 24						19 24					20 24	
Bitterne	d				17 28						18 28						19 28					20 28	
Eastleigh	a			17 11			17 46						18 46					19 46					20 46
Southampton Airport Parkway	a			17 20																			
St Denys	d				17 31			17 58			18 31						19 31					20 31	
Southampton Central ⛴	a	17 01	17 08	17 28	17 38			18 03	18 08	18 20	18 38	18 40		19 05	19 08	19 20	19 38		20 03	20 08	20 18	20 38	

		SN	GW	SN	SW	SW	SN	GW	SN	SW	SW	SW	SN	SW	SW	SW
		◇■	◇	■	■	■	◇■		■	■	■	■	◇■	■	■	■
Portsmouth Harbour ⛴	d		20 23			20 59		21 23				21 54		22 33		23 24
Portsmouth & Southsea	d		20 27		20 38	21 04		21 27		21 38		21 59		22 38		23 29
Fratton	d		20 31		20 42	21 08		21 31		21 42		22 03		22 42		23 33
Hilsea	d				20 46	21 12				21 46		22 07		22 46		23 37
Chichester ■	d	20 01		20 26			21 05		21 26				22 05			
Havant	d	20 22		20 37			21 26		21 37		21 58		22 26		22 59	
Cosham	d	20 29		20 45	20 51	21 17	21 34		21 44	21 51	22 05	22 12	22 34	22 51	23 08	23 42
Portchester	d			20 49	20 56	21 22	21 38			21 56		22 17		22 56	23 13	23 47
Fareham	a	20 36	20 46	20 54	21 01	21 27	21 43	21 47	21 51	22 01	22 12	22 25	22 42	23 01	23 18	23 52
	d	20 37	20 47	20 55	21 03	21 28	21 43	21 48	21 52	22 03		22 26	22 43	23 03		23 53
Swanwick	d	20 43		21 01	21 09		21 49		21 58	22 09			22 49	23 09		
Bursledon	d				21 13					22 13				23 13		
Hamble	d				21 16					22 16				23 16		
Netley	d				21 18					22 18				23 18		
Sholing	d				21 22					22 22				23 22		
Woolston	d				21 24		21 58			22 24				23 24		
Bitterne	d				21 28					22 28				23 28		
Eastleigh	a					21 46		22 06				22 43				00 11
Southampton Airport Parkway	a															
St Denys	d				21 31		22 02			22 31				23 31		
Southampton Central ⛴	a	21 01	21 08	21 19	21 38		22 07	22 21	22 16	22 39			23 07	23 39		

Mondays to Fridays
from 8 October

		SW MO	SW MX	SW	SN	SW	SW	GW	SN	SW	SW	SN	SW	GW	SN	SN	SW	SW	SN	SW
		■	■	■	■	■	■	■ H	■	■	■	■	■	◇ H	■	■	■	■	■	■
Portsmouth Harbour ⛴	d	23p17	23p24	04 55			05 43	06 00			06 23		06 50	07 05			07 24			07 55
Portsmouth & Southsea	d	23p22	23p29	05 00		05 16	05 48	06 04		06 23	06 28		06 55	07 09			07 29	07 38		08 00
Fratton	d	23p26	23p33	05 04		05 20	05 52	06 08		06 27	06 32		06 59	07 13			07 33	07 42		08 04
Hilsea	d	23p30	23p37	05 08		05 24	05 56			06 31	06 36		07 03				07 37	07 46		08 08
Chichester ■	d				05 06				06 09			06 26			07 08	07 13			07 52	
Havant	d				05 17				06 20			06 40			07 19	07 31			08 03	
Cosham	d	23p35	23p42	05 16	05 24	05 29	06 03	06 15	06 27	06 36	06 42	06 50	07 08	07 21	07 26	07 38	07 43	07 51	08 09	08 13
Portchester	d	23p40	23p47	05 20	05 28	05 34	06 08			06 41	06 46	06 54	07 13		07 30		07 48	07 56	08 13	08 18
Fareham	a	23p45	23p52	05 25	05 33	05 39	06 13	06 23	06 36	06 46	06 51	06 59	07 18	07 28	07 35	07 46	07 53	08 01	08 18	08 23
	d	23p46	23p53	05 26	05 34	05 40	06 19	06 24	06 37	06 47	06 53	07 00	07 20	07 29	07 36	07 47	07 54	08 03	08 19	08 24
Swanwick	d				05 40	05 46			06 43	06 53		07 06			07 42	07 53		08 09	08 26	
Bursledon	d					05 50				06 57								08 13	08 29	
Hamble	d					05 53				07 00								08 16	08 32	
Netley	d				05 46	05 55				07 02					07 48	07 59		08 18	08 34	
Sholing	d					05 59				07 06								08 22	08 38	
Woolston	d				05 50	06 01				07 08					07 52	08 04		08 24	08 40	
Bitterne	d					06 05				07 12								08 28	08 43	
Eastleigh	a	00 04	00 11	05 46			06 37				07 11		07 38				08 12			08 42
Southampton Airport Parkway	a																			
St Denys	d					06 08				07 15						08 08		08 31	08 46	
Southampton Central ⛴	a				05 59	06 13		06 45	07 02	07 21		07 25		07 50	08 01	08 13		08 38	08 52	

Table 165

Portsmouth and Fareham - Southampton

Mondays to Fridays from 8 October

Network Diagram - see first Page of Table 165

		SW 1	GW ◇ ⊼	SN 1	SW 1	SW 1		SN ◇1	GW ◇ ⊼	SN 1	SW 1	GW ◇ ⊼	SW 1	SN ◇1	GW ◇ ⊼	SN		SW 1	SW 1	SN ◇1	GW ◇ ⊼	SN	SW 1	SW 1	SN ◇1
Portsmouth Harbour	d	08 05	08 23		08 33	08 59			09 23		09 33		09 59		10 23			10 33	10 59		11 23			11 59	
Portsmouth & Southsea	d	08 10	08 27		08 38	09 04			09 27		09 38		10 04		10 27			10 38	11 04		11 27		11 38	12 04	
Fratton	d	08 13	08 31		08 42	09 08			09 31		09 42		10 08		10 31			10 42	11 08		11 31		11 42	12 08	
Hilsea	d	08 17			08 46	09 12					09 46		10 12					10 46	11 12				11 46	12 12	
Chichester 4	d			08 22				09 08		09 25		09 47		10 06		10 25				11 05		11 25			12 05
Havant	d			08 37				09 23		09 39		09 59		10 20		10 37				11 19		11 37			12 19
Cosham	d	08 22	08 39	08 45	08 51	09 17		09 30	09 39	09 46	09 51	10 05	10 17	10 28	10 39	10 46		10 51	11 17	11 26	11 39	11 46	11 51	12 17	12 26
Portchester	d	08 27		08 49	08 56	09 22					09 56		10 22	10 32				10 56	11 22	11 30			11 56	12 22	12 30
Fareham	a	08 32	08 46	08 54	09 01	09 27		09 37	09 46	09 53	10 01	10 14	10 27	10 37	10 46	10 53		11 01	11 27	11 35	11 46	11 53	12 01	12 27	12 35
	d	08 33	08 47	08 55	09 03	09 28		09 38	09 47	09 54	10 03	10 15	10 28	10 38	10 47	10 54		11 03	11 28	11 36	11 47	11 54	12 03	12 28	12 36
Swanwick	d			09 01	09 09			09 44		10 00	10 09			10 44		11 00		11 09		11 42		12 00	12 09		12 42
Bursledon	d				09 13						10 13							11 13					12 13		
Hamble	d				09 16						10 16							11 16					12 16		
Netley	d				09 18						10 18							11 18					12 18		
Sholing	d				09 22						10 22							11 22					12 22		
Woolston	d				09 24						10 24							11 24					12 24		
Bitterne	d				09 28						10 28							11 28					12 28		
Eastleigh	a	08 51				09 46							10 46						11 46					12 46	
Southampton Airport Parkway	a																								
St Denys	d				09 31						10 31							11 31					12 31		
Southampton Central	a		09 08	09 19	09 38			10 01	10 08	10 20	10 38	10 40		11 01	11 08	11 19		11 38		12 01	12 08	12 19	12 38		12 59

		GW ◇ ⊼		SN	SW 1	SW 1	SN ◇1	GW ◇ ⊼	SN 1	SW 1	SW 1	SN ◇1		GW ■ ⊼	SN	SW 1	SW 1	SN ◇1	GW ■ ⊼	SN	SW 1	SW 1		SN ◇1	GW ■ ⊼
Portsmouth Harbour	d	12 23				12 59		13 23			13 59			14 23			14 59		15 23			15 59			16 23
Portsmouth & Southsea	d	12 27			12 38	13 04		13 27		13 38	14 04			14 27		14 38	15 04		15 27		15 38	16 04			16 27
Fratton	d	12 31			12 42	13 08		13 31		13 42	14 08			14 31		14 42	15 08		15 31		15 42	16 08			16 31
Hilsea	d				12 46	13 12				13 46	14 12					14 46	15 12				15 46	16 12			
Chichester 4	d			12 25			13 05		13 25			14 05			14 25			15 05		15 25				16 05	
Havant	d			12 37			13 19		13 37			14 19			14 37			15 19		15 37				16 19	
Cosham	d	12 39		12 46	12 51	13 17	13 26	13 39	13 46	13 51	14 17	14 26		14 39	14 46	14 51	15 17	15 26	15 39	15 46	15 51	16 17		16 26	16 39
Portchester	d				12 56	13 22	13 30			13 56	14 22	14 30				14 56	15 22	15 30			15 56	16 22		16 30	
Fareham	a	12 46		12 53	13 01	13 27	13 35	13 46	13 53	14 01	14 27	14 35		14 46	14 53	15 01	15 27	15 35	15 46	15 53	16 01	16 27		16 35	16 46
	d	12 47		12 54	13 03	13 28	13 36	13 47	13 56	14 03	14 28	14 36		14 47	14 54	15 03	15 28	15 36	15 47	15 54	16 03	16 28		16 36	16 47
Swanwick	d			13 00	13 09		13 42		14 02	14 09		14 42			15 00	15 09		15 42		16 00	16 09			16 42	
Bursledon	d				13 13					14 13						15 13					16 13				
Hamble	d				13 16					14 16						15 16					16 16				
Netley	d				13 18					14 18						15 18					16 18				
Sholing	d				13 22					14 22						15 22					16 22				
Woolston	d				13 24					14 24						15 24					16 24				
Bitterne	d				13 28					14 28						15 28					16 28				
Eastleigh	a					13 46			14n37		14 46						15 46					16 46			
Southampton Airport Parkway	a								14n33																
St Denys	d				13 31					14 31						15 31					16 31				
Southampton Central	a	13 08		13 19	13 38		13 59	14 08	14 19	14 39		14 59		15 08	15 19	15 38		15 59	16 08	16 20	16 38			17 01	17 08

		SN 1	SW 1	SW 1	SW 1	SN ◇1	GW ◇ ⊼	SN 1		SW 1	GW ◇ ⊼	SW 1	SN ◇1	GW ◇ ⊼	SN 1	SW 1	SW 1	SN ◇1		GW ◇	SN	SW 1	SW 1	SN ◇1	GW ◇
Portsmouth Harbour	d			16 49	16 59		17 23			17 33		17 59		18 23			18 59			19 23			19 59		20 23
Portsmouth & Southsea	d		16 38	16 55	17 04		17 27			17 38		18 04		18 27		18 38	19 04			19 27		19 38	20 04		20 27
Fratton	d		16 42	16 59	17 08		17 31			17 42		18 08		18 31		18 42	19 08			19 31		19 42	20 08		20 31
Hilsea	d		16 46	17 03	17 12					17 46		18 12				18 46	19 12					19 46	20 12		
Chichester 4	d	16 26				17 05		17 25			17 47		18 05		18 25			19 02			19 20			20 01	
Havant	d	16 38				17 19		17 37			17 58		18 23		18 37			19 20			19 37			20 22	
Cosham	d	16 46	16 51	17 08	17 17	17 27	17 39	17 46		17 51	18 05	18 17	18 30	18 39	18 44	18 51	19 17	19 29		19 39	19 46	19 51	20 17	20 29	
Portchester	d		16 56	17 13	17 22	17 31				17 56		18 22	18 34			18 56	19 22	19 33				19 56	20 22		
Fareham	a	16 53	17 01	17 18	17 27	17 36	17 46	17 53		18 01	18 12	18 27	18 39	18 46	18 52	19 01	19 27	19 38		19 46	19 54	20 01	20 27	20 36	20 46
	d	16 57	17 03		17 28	17 37	17 47	17 54		18 03	18 13	18 28	18 40	18 47	18 53	19 03	19 28	19 39		19 47	19 55	20 03	20 28	20 37	20 47
Swanwick	d		17 09			17 43		18 00		18 09			18 46		18 59	19 09		19 45			20 01	20 09		20 43	
Bursledon	d		17 13							18 13						19 13						20 13			
Hamble	d		17 16							18 16						19 16						20 16			
Netley	d		17 18			17 49				18 18						19 18						20 18			
Sholing	d		17 22							18 22						19 22						20 22			
Woolston	d		17 24			17 53				18 24						19 24						20 24			
Bitterne	d		17 28							18 28						19 28						20 28			
Eastleigh	a	17 11			17 46							18 46					19 46						20 46		
Southampton Airport Parkway	a	17 20																							
St Denys	d		17 31			17 58				18 31						19 31						20 31			
Southampton Central	a	17 28	17 38			18 03	18 08	18 20		18 38	18 40		19 05	19 08	19 20	19 38		20 03		20 08	20 18	20 38		21 01	21 08

n stops at these stations after Southampton Central

Table 165

Portsmouth and Fareham - Southampton

Mondays to Fridays from 8 October

Network Diagram - see first Page of Table 165

		SN 1	SW 1	SW 1		SN ◇1	GW	SN 1	SW 1	SW 1	SW 1	SN ◇1	SW 1	SW 1		SW 1
Portsmouth Harbour	d			20 59			21 23				21 54		22 33			23 24
Portsmouth & Southsea	d		20 38	21 04			21 27		21 38		21 59		22 38			23 29
Fratton	d		20 42	21 08			21 31		21 42		22 03		22 42			23 33
Hilsea	d		20 46	21 12					21 46		22 07		22 46			23 37
Chichester 4	d	20 26				21 05		21 26				22 05				
Havant	d	20 37				21 26		21 37		21 58		22 26		22 59		
Cosham	d	20 45	20 51	21 17		21 34		21 44	21 51	22 05	22 12	22 34	22 51	23 08		23 42
Portchester	d	20 49	20 56	21 22		21 38			21 56		22 17		22 56	23 13		23 47
Fareham	a	20 54	21 01	21 27		21 43	21 47	21 51	22 01	22 12	22 25	22 42	23 01	23 18		23 52
	d	20 55	21 03	21 28		21 43	21 48	21 52	22 03		22 26	22 43	23 03			23 53
Swanwick	d	21 01	21 09			21 49		21 58	22 09			22 49	23 09			
Bursledon	d		21 13						22 13				23 13			
Hamble	d		21 16						22 16				23 16			
Netley	d		21 18						22 18				23 18			
Sholing	d		21 22						22 22				23 22			
Woolston	d		21 24			21 58			22 24				23 24			
Bitterne	d		21 28						22 28				23 28			
Eastleigh	a			21 46			22 06				22 43					00 11
Southampton Airport Parkway	a															
St Denys	d		21 31			22 02			22 31				23 31			
Southampton Central	a	21 19	21 38			22 07	22 21	22 16	22 39			23 07	23 39			

Saturdays

		SW 1			SW 1	SN 1	SW 1	SN 1	SW 1	GW ◇		SN 1	SN 1	SW 1	SW 1	SN 1	GW ◇ ⊼	SN 1	SW 1	SW 1		SN 1	GW ◇ ⊼	SN	SW 1
Portsmouth Harbour	d	23p24							05 50	06 00					06 59		07 23			07 59			08 23		
Portsmouth & Southsea	d	23p29					05 16		05 55	06 04				06 38	07 04		07 27		07 38	08 04			08 27		08 38
Fratton	d	23p33					05 20		05 59	06 08				06 42	07 08		07 31		07 42	08 08			08 31		08 42
Hilsea	d	23p37					05 24		06 03					06 46	07 12				07 46	08 12					08 46
Chichester 4	d					05 05		05 28				06 06	06 23			07 07		07 25				08 05		08 25	
Havant	d					05 16		05 39				06 24	06 37			07 23		07 37				08 20		08 37	
Cosham	d	23p42			05 09	05 23	05 29	05 49	06 08	06 19		06 30	06 46	06 51	07 17	07 30	07 39	07 46	07 51	08 17		08 28	08 39	08 46	08 51
Portchester	d	23p47			05 14	05 27	05 34		06 13			06 34		06 56	07 22	07 34			07 56	08 22		08 32			08 56
Fareham	a	23p52			05 19	05 32	05 39	05 57	06 18	06 27		06 39	06 53	07 01	07 27	07 39	07 46	07 53	08 01	08 27		08 37	08 46	08 53	09 01
	d	23p53			05 20	05 33	05 40	05 58	06 19	06 28		06 40	06 57	07 03	07 28	07 39	07 47	07 57	08 03	08 28		08 38	08 47	08 54	09 03
Swanwick	d					05 39	05 46	06 04				06 46		07 09		07 45			08 09			08 44		09 00	09 09
Bursledon	d						05 50							07 13					08 13						09 13
Hamble	d						05 53							07 16					08 16						09 16
Netley	d					05 45	05 55							07 18					08 18						09 18
Sholing	d						05 59							07 22					08 22						09 22
Woolston	d					05 49	06 01							07 24					08 24						09 24
Bitterne	d						06 05							07 28					08 28						09 28
Eastleigh	a	00 11			05 38				06 39				07 10		07 46			08 10		08 46					
Southampton Airport Parkway	a												07 17					08 17							
St Denys	d						06 08							07 31					08 31						09 31
Southampton Central	a					05 58	06 13	06 24		06 49		07 05	07 28	07 38		08 03	08 07	08 28	08 38			09 01	09 08	09 19	09 38

		SW 1	SN ◇1	GW ◇ ⊼	SN 1	SW 1		GW ◇	SW 1	SN ◇1	GW ◇	SN	SW 1	SW 1	SN ◇1	GW ◇		SN 1	SW 1	SW 1	SN ◇1	GW ◇	SN	SW 1	SW 1
Portsmouth Harbour	d	08 59		09 23					09 59		10 23			10 59		11 23				11 59		12 23			12 59
Portsmouth & Southsea	d	09 04		09 27		09 38			10 04		10 27		10 38	11 04		11 27			11 38	12 04		12 27		12 38	13 04
Fratton	d	09 08		09 31		09 42			10 08		10 31		10 42	11 08		11 31			11 42	12 08		12 31		12 42	13 08
Hilsea	d	09 12				09 46			10 12				10 46	11 12					11 46	12 12				12 46	13 12
Chichester 4	d		09 05		09 25			09 49		10 05		10 25			11 05			11 25			12 05		12 25		
Havant	d		09 19		09 37			10 00		10 19		10 37			11 19			11 37			12 19		12 37		
Cosham	d	09 17	09 26	09 39	09 46	09 51		10 06	10 17	10 26	10 39	10 46	10 51	11 17	11 26	11 39		11 46	11 51	12 17	12 26	12 39	12 46	12 51	13 17
Portchester	d	09 22	09 30			09 56			10 22	10 30			10 56	11 22	11 30				11 56	12 22	12 30			12 56	13 22
Fareham	a	09 27	09 35	09 46	09 53	10 01		10 15	10 27	10 35	10 46	10 53	11 01	11 27	11 35	11 46		11 53	12 01	12 27	12 35	12 46	12 53	13 01	13 27
	d	09 28	09 36	09 47	09 57	10 03		10 16	10 28	10 36	10 47	10 54	11 03	11 28	11 36	11 47		11 57	12 03	12 28	12 36	12 47	12 54	13 03	13 28
Swanwick	d		09 42			10 09				10 42		11 00	11 09		11 42				12 09		12 42		13 00	13 09	
Bursledon	d					10 13							11 13						12 13					13 13	
Hamble	d					10 16							11 16						12 16					13 16	
Netley	d					10 18							11 18						12 18					13 18	
Sholing	d					10 22							11 22						12 22					13 22	
Woolston	d					10 24							11 24						12 24					13 24	
Bitterne	d					10 28							11 28						12 28					13 28	
Eastleigh	a	09 46			10 10				10 46					11 46				12 10		12 46					13 46
Southampton Airport Parkway	a				10 17													12 18							
St Denys	d					10 31							11 31						12 31					13 31	
Southampton Central	a		09 59	10 08	10 28	10 38		10 40		10 59	11 08	11 19	11 38		11 59	12 08		12 28	12 38		12 59	13 08	13 19	13 38	

Saturdays

Portsmouth and Fareham - Southampton

Network Diagram - see first Page of Table 165

Station		SN	GW	SN	SW	SW	SN	GW	SN	SW	SW
		◇■	◇	■	■	■	◇■	◇		■	■
Portsmouth Harbour ⛴	d		13 23			13 59		14 23			14 59
Portsmouth & Southsea	d		13 27		13 38	14 04		14 27		14 38	15 04
Fratton	d		13 31		13 42	14 08		14 31		14 42	15 08
Hilsea	d				13 46	14 12				14 46	15 12
Chichester ■	d	13 05		13 25			14 05		14 25		
Havant	d	13 19		13 37			14 19		14 37		
Cosham	d	13 26	13 39	13 46	13 51	14 17	14 26	14 39	14 46	14 51	15 17
Portchester	d	13 30			13 56	14 22	14 30			14 56	15 22
Fareham	a	13 35	13 46	13 53	14 01	14 27	14 35	14 46	14 53	15 01	15 27
	d	13 36	13 47	13 56	14 03	14 28	14 36	14 47	14 54	15 03	15 28
Swanwick	d	13 42		14 02	14 09		14 42		15 00	15 09	
Bursledon	d				14 13					15 13	
Hamble	d				14 16					15 16	
Netley	d				14 18					15 18	
Sholing	d				14 22					15 22	
Woolston	d				14 24					15 24	
Bitterne	d				14 28					15 28	
Eastleigh	a			14n37		14 46					15 46
Southampton Airport Parkway	a			14n33							
St Denys	d				14 31					15 31	
Southampton Central ⛴	a	13 59	14 08	14 19	14 39		14 59	15 08	15 19	15 38	

Station		SN	GW	SN	SW	SW	SN	GW	SN	SW	SW	SN
		◇■	◇	■	■	■	◇■	■		■	■	◇■
Portsmouth Harbour ⛴	d		15 23			15 59		16 23			16 59	
Portsmouth & Southsea	d		15 27		15 38	16 04		16 27		16 38	17 04	
Fratton	d		15 31		15 42	16 08		16 31		16 42	17 08	
Hilsea	d				15 46	16 12				16 46	17 12	
Chichester ■	d	15 05		15 25			16 05		16 25			17 05
Havant	d	15 19		15 37			16 19		16 37			17 19
Cosham	d	15 26	15 39	15 46	15 51	16 17	16 26	16 39	16 46	16 51	17 17	17 26
Portchester	d	15 30			15 56	16 22	16 30			16 56	17 22	17 30
Fareham	a	15 35	15 46	15 53	16 01	16 27	16 35	16 46	16 53	17 01	17 27	17 35
	d	15 36	15 47	15 57	16 03	16 28	16 36	16 47	16 54	17 03	17 28	17 36
Swanwick	d	15 42			16 09		16 42		17 00	17 09		17 42
Bursledon	d				16 13					17 13		
Hamble	d				16 16					17 16		
Netley	d				16 18					17 18		
Sholing	d				16 22					17 22		
Woolston	d				16 24					17 24		
Bitterne	d				16 28					17 28		
Eastleigh	a			16 10		16 46					17 46	
Southampton Airport Parkway	a			16 17								
St Denys	d				16 31					17 31		
Southampton Central ⛴	a	15 59	16 08	16 28	16 38		16 59	17 08	17 19	17 38		17 59

Station		GW	SN	SW	GW	SW	SN	GW	SN	SW	SW	SN
		◇	■	■	◇	■	◇■	◇		■	■	◇■
Portsmouth Harbour ⛴	d	17 23		17 33		17 59		18 23			18 59	
Portsmouth & Southsea	d	17 27		17 38		18 04		18 27		18 38	19 04	
Fratton	d	17 31		17 42		18 08		18 31		18 42	19 08	
Hilsea	d			17 46		18 12				18 46	19 12	
Chichester ■	d		17 25		17 46		18 05		18 25			19 05
Havant	d		17 37		18 00		18 19		18 37			19 19
Cosham	d	17 39	17 46	17 51	18 06	18 17	18 26	18 39	18 46	18 51	19 17	19 26
Portchester	d			17 56		18 22	18 30			18 56	19 22	19 30
Fareham	a	17 46	17 53	18 01	18 14	18 27	18 35	18 46	18 53	19 01	19 27	19 35
	d	17 47	17 57	18 03	18 15	18 28	18 36	18 47	18 54	19 03	19 28	19 36
Swanwick	d			18 09			18 42		19 00	19 09		19 42
Bursledon	d			18 13						19 13		
Hamble	d			18 16						19 16		
Netley	d			18 18						19 18		
Sholing	d			18 22						19 22		
Woolston	d			18 24						19 24		
Bitterne	d			18 28						19 28		
Eastleigh	a		18 10			18 46					19 46	
Southampton Airport Parkway	a		18 17									
St Denys	d			18 31						19 31		
Southampton Central ⛴	a	18 08	18 28	18 38	18 43		18 59	19 08	19 19	19 38		19 59

Station		GW	SN	SW	SW	SN	GW	SN	SW	SW	SN	SN
		◇	■	■	■	◇■	◇	■	■	■	◇■	■
Portsmouth Harbour ⛴	d	19 23			19 59		20 23			20 59		
Portsmouth & Southsea	d	19 27		19 38	20 04		20 27		20 38	21 04		
Fratton	d	19 31		19 42	20 08		20 31		20 42	21 08		
Hilsea	d			19 46	20 12				20 46	21 12		
Chichester ■	d		19 25			20 05		20 25			21 05	21 28
Havant	d		19 37			20 26		20 37			21 23	21 40
Cosham	d	19 39	19 46	19 51	20 17	20 32		20 46	20 51	21 17	21 29	21 47
Portchester	d			19 56	20 22	20 36			20 56	21 22	21 33	
Fareham	a	19 46	19 53	20 01	20 27	20 41	20 45	20 53	21 01	21 27	21 38	21 54
	d	19 47	19 57	20 03	20 28	20 42	20 47	20 54	21 03	21 28	21 39	21 55
Swanwick	d			20 09		20 48		21 00	21 09		21 45	22 01
Bursledon	d			20 13					21 13			
Hamble	d			20 16					21 16			
Netley	d			20 18					21 18			
Sholing	d			20 22					21 22			
Woolston	d			20 24					21 24			
Bitterne	d			20 28					21 28			
Eastleigh	a		20 10		20 46					21 46		
Southampton Airport Parkway	a		20 17									
St Denys	d			20 31					21 31			
Southampton Central ⛴	a	20 09	20 26	20 38		21 05	21 10	21 19	21 38		22 02	22 20

Station		SW	SW	SN	SW	SW
		■	■	◇■	■	■
Portsmouth Harbour ⛴	d		21 54		22 33	23 24
Portsmouth & Southsea	d	21 38	21 59		22 38	23 29
Fratton	d	21 42	22 03		22 42	23 33
Hilsea	d	21 46	22 07		22 46	23 37
Chichester ■	d			22 05		
Havant	d			22 26		
Cosham	d	21 51	22 12	22 34	22 51	23 42
Portchester	d	21 56	22 17		22 56	23 47
Fareham	a	22 01	22 22	22 41	23 01	23 52
	d	22 03	22 23	22 42	23 03	23 53
Swanwick	d	22 09		22 48	23 09	
Bursledon	d	22 13			23 13	
Hamble	d	22 16			23 16	
Netley	d	22 18			23 18	
Sholing	d	22 22			23 22	
Woolston	d	22 24			23 24	
Bitterne	d	22 28			23 28	
Eastleigh	a		22 41			00 11
Southampton Airport Parkway	a					
St Denys	d	22 31			23 31	
Southampton Central ⛴	a	22 39		23 05	23 36	

n stops at these stations after Southampton Central

Sundays
until 9 September

Portsmouth and Fareham - Southampton

Network Diagram - see first Page of Table 165

Station		SW	SW	SW	SW	SN	SW	SW	SN	GW	SW	SW
		■	■	■	■	◇■	■	■	◇■	■	■ ☕	■
Portsmouth Harbour ⛴	d	23p24	06 37	07 17			08 17			09 08	09 17	
Portsmouth & Southsea	d	23p29	06 42	07 22	07 42		08 22	08 42		09 12	09 22	09 42
Fratton	d	23p33	06 46	07 26	07 46		08 26	08 46		09 16	09 26	09 46
Hilsea	d	23p37	06 50	07 30	07 50		08 30	08 50			09 30	09 50
Chichester ■	d					07 45			08 44			
Havant	d					07 58			08 58			
Cosham	d	23p42	06 55	07 35	07 55	08 05	08 35	08 55	09 05	09 23	09 35	09 55
Portchester	d	23p47	07 00	07 40	08 00		08 40	09 00			09 40	10 00
Fareham	a	23p52	07 05	07 45	08 05	08 13	08 45	09 05	09 13	09 31	09 45	10 05
	d	23p53	07 06	07 46	08 06	08 14	08 46	09 06	09 14	09 32	09 46	10 06
Swanwick	d		07 12		08 12	08 20		09 12	09 20			10 12
Bursledon	d		07 16		08 16			09 16				10 16
Hamble	d		07 19		08 19			09 19				10 19
Netley	d		07 21		08 21			09 21				10 21
Sholing	d		07 25		08 25			09 25				10 25
Woolston	d		07 27		08 27			09 27				10 27
Bitterne	d		07 31		08 31			09 31				10 31
Eastleigh	a	00 11		08 04			09 04				10 04	
Southampton Airport Parkway	a											
St Denys	d		07 34		08 34			09 34				10 34
Southampton Central ⛴	a		07 40		08 40	08 44		09 40	09 44	09 53		10 40

Station		SN	SW	SW	SN	GW	SW	SW	SN	GW
		◇■	■ ☕	■	◇■	◇	■ ☕	■	◇■	◇
Portsmouth Harbour ⛴	d		10 17			11 08	11 17			
Portsmouth & Southsea	d		10 22	10 42		11 12	11 22	11 42		
Fratton	d		10 26	10 46		11 16	11 26	11 46		
Hilsea	d		10 30	10 50			11 30	11 50		
Chichester ■	d	09 44			10 44				11 44	11 54
Havant	d	09 58			10 58				11 58	12 10
Cosham	d	10 06	10 35	10 55	11 06	11 23	11 35	11 55	12 05	12 23
Portchester	d		10 40	11 00			11 40	12 00		
Fareham	a	10 14	10 45	11 05	11 14	11 31	11 45	12 05	12 13	12 31
	d	10 15	10 46	11 06	11 15	11 32	11 46	12 06	12 14	12 32
Swanwick	d	10 21		11 12	11 21			12 12	12 20	
Bursledon	d			11 16				12 16		
Hamble	d			11 19				12 19		
Netley	d			11 21				12 21		
Sholing	d			11 25				12 25		
Woolston	d			11 27				12 27		
Bitterne	d			11 31				12 31		
Eastleigh	a		11 04				12 04			
Southampton Airport Parkway	a									
St Denys	d			11 34				12 34		
Southampton Central ⛴	a	10 44		11 40	11 45	11 53		12 40	12 44	12 53

Station		SW	SW	SN	GW	SW	SW	SN	GW	SW	SW	SN
		■ ☕	■	◇■	◇	■ ☕	■	◇■	◇	■ ☕	■	◇■
Portsmouth Harbour ⛴	d	12 17			13 08	13 17			14 08	14 17		
Portsmouth & Southsea	d	12 22	12 42		13 12	13 22	13 42		14 12	14 22	14 42	
Fratton	d	12 26	12 46		13 16	13 26	13 46		14 16	14 26	14 46	
Hilsea	d	12 30	12 50			13 30	13 50			14 30	14 50	
Chichester ■	d			12 44				13 44				14 44
Havant	d			12 58				13 58				14 58
Cosham	d	12 35	12 55	13 05	13 23	13 35	13 55	14 05	14 23	14 35	14 55	15 05
Portchester	d	12 40	13 00			13 40	14 00			14 40	15 00	
Fareham	a	12 45	13 05	13 13	13 31	13 45	14 05	14 13	14 31	14 45	15 05	15 13
	d	12 46	13 06	13 14	13 32	13 46	14 06	14 14	14 32	14 46	15 06	15 14
Swanwick	d		13 12	13 20			14 12	14 20			15 12	15 20
Bursledon	d		13 16				14 16				15 16	
Hamble	d		13 19				14 19				15 19	
Netley	d		13 21				14 21				15 21	
Sholing	d		13 25				14 25				15 25	
Woolston	d		13 27				14 27				15 27	
Bitterne	d		13 31				14 31				15 31	
Eastleigh	a	13 04				14 04				15 04		
Southampton Airport Parkway	a											
St Denys	d		13 34				14 34				15 34	
Southampton Central ⛴	a		13 40	13 44	13 53		14 40	14 44	14 53		15 40	15 44

Station		GW	SW	SW	SN	GW	SW	GW	SW	SN	GW	SW
		■	■ ☕	■	◇■	◇	■ ☕	◇	■	◇■	◇	■
Portsmouth Harbour ⛴	d	15 08	15 17			16 08	16 17				17 08	17 17
Portsmouth & Southsea	d	15 12	15 22	15 42		16 12	16 22		16 42		17 12	17 22
Fratton	d	15 16	15 26	15 46		16 16	16 26		16 46		17 16	17 26
Hilsea	d		15 30	15 50			16 30		16 50			17 30
Chichester ■	d				15 44			16 34		16 45		
Havant	d				15 56			16 48		16 59		
Cosham	d	15 23	15 35	15 55	16 04	16 23	16 35	16 55	16 59	17 07	17 23	17 35
Portchester	d		15 40	16 00			16 40		17 03			17 40
Fareham	a	15 31	15 45	16 05	16 12	16 31	16 45	17 02	17 08	17 15	17 31	17 45
	d	15 32	15 46	16 06	16 13	16 32	16 46	17 03	17 09	17 16	17 32	17 46
Swanwick	d			16 12	16 19				17 16	17 24		
Bursledon	d			16 16					17 19			
Hamble	d			16 19					17 23			
Netley	d			16 21					17 25			
Sholing	d			16 25					17 29			
Woolston	d			16 27					17 31			
Bitterne	d			16 31					17 34			
Eastleigh	a		16 04				17 04					18 04
Southampton Airport Parkway	a											
St Denys	d			16 34					17 38			
Southampton Central ⛴	a	15 53		16 40	16 44	16 53		17 24	17 43	17 49	17 53	

Station		SW	SN	GW	SW	GW	SW	SN	GW	SW	SW
		■	◇■	◇	■	◇	■	◇■	◇	■	■
Portsmouth Harbour ⛴	d			18 08	18 17				19 08	19 17	
Portsmouth & Southsea	d	17 42		18 12	18 22		18 42		19 12	19 22	19 42
Fratton	d	17 46		18 16	18 26		18 46		19 16	19 26	19 46
Hilsea	d	17 50			18 30		18 50			19 30	19 50
Chichester ■	d		17 44			18 34		18 45			
Havant	d		17 58			18 48		18 58			
Cosham	d	17 55	18 05	18 23	18 35	18 55	18 59	19 05	19 23	19 35	19 55
Portchester	d	18 00			18 40		19 03			19 40	20 00
Fareham	a	18 05	18 13	18 31	18 45	19 02	19 08	19 13	19 31	19 45	20 05
	d	18 06	18 14	18 32	18 46	19 03	19 09	19 14	19 32	19 46	20 06
Swanwick	d	18 12	18 20				19 16	19 22			20 12
Bursledon	d	18 16					19 19				20 16
Hamble	d	18 19					19 23				20 19
Netley	d	18 21					19 25				20 21
Sholing	d	18 25					19 29				20 25
Woolston	d	18 27					19 31				20 27
Bitterne	d	18 31					19 34				20 31
Eastleigh	a				19 04					20 04	
Southampton Airport Parkway	a										
St Denys	d	18 34					19 38				20 34
Southampton Central ⛴	a	18 40	18 42	18 53		19 24	19 43	19 48	19 53		20 40

Station		SN	GW	SW	SW	SN	SW	SW	SN	GW	SW	SW
		◇■	◇	■	■	◇■	■	■	◇■		■	■
Portsmouth Harbour ⛴	d		20 08	20 17			21 17			22 03	22 17	
Portsmouth & Southsea	d		20 12	20 22	20 42		21 22	21 42		22 12	22 22	22 42
Fratton	d		20 16	20 26	20 46		21 26	21 46		22 16	22 26	22 46
Hilsea	d			20 30	20 50		21 30	21 50			22 30	22 50
Chichester ■	d	19 44				20 44			21 44			
Havant	d	19 58				20 58			21 58			
Cosham	d	20 05		20 35	20 55	21 07	21 35	21 55	22 05		22 35	22 55
Portchester	d			20 40	21 00		21 40	22 00			22 40	23 00
Fareham	a	20 13	20 31	20 45	21 05	21 15	21 45	22 05	22 13	22 31	22 45	23 05
	d	20 14	20 32	20 46	21 06	21 16	21 46	22 06	22 14	22 32	22 46	23 06
Swanwick	d	20 20			21 12	21 22		22 12	22 20			23 12
Bursledon	d				21 16			22 16				23 16
Hamble	d				21 19			22 19				23 19
Netley	d				21 21			22 21				23 21
Sholing	d				21 25			22 25				23 25
Woolston	d				21 27			22 27				23 27
Bitterne	d				21 31			22 31				23 31
Eastleigh	a			21 04			22 04				23 04	
Southampton Airport Parkway	a											
St Denys	d				21 34			22 34				23 34
Southampton Central ⛴	a	20 46	20 53		21 40	21 45		22 40	22 44	22 53		23 40

Table 165

Sundays until 9 September

Portsmouth and Fareham - Southampton

Network Diagram - see first Page of Table 165

	SW
	1
Portsmouth Harbour ⛴ d	23 17
Portsmouth & Southsea d	23 22
Fratton d	23 26
Hilsea d	23 30
Chichester 4 d	
Havant d	
Cosham d	23 35
Portchester d	23 40
Fareham a	23 45
d	23 46
Swanwick d	
Bursledon d	
Hamble d	
Netley d	
Sholing d	
Woolston d	
Bitterne d	
Eastleigh a	00 04
Southampton Airport Parkway a	
St Denys d	
Southampton Central ⛴ a	

Sundays from 16 September

	SW	SW	SW	SW	SN	SW	SW	SN	GW	SW
	1	1	1	1	◇1	1	1	◇1	■	1 🛒
Portsmouth Harbour ⛴ d	23p24	06 37	07 17			08 17			09 08	09 17
Portsmouth & Southsea d	23p29	06 42	07 22	07 42		08 22	08 42		09 12	09 22
Fratton d	23p33	06 46	07 26	07 46		08 26	08 46		09 16	09 26
Hilsea d	23p37	06 50	07 30	07 50		08 30	08 50			09 30
Chichester 4 d					07 45			08 45		
Havant d					07 58			08 58		
Cosham d	23p42	06 55	07 35	07 55	08 05	08 35	08 55	09 05	09 23	09 35
Portchester d	23p47	07 00	07 40	08 00		08 40	09 00			09 40
Fareham a	23p52	07 05	07 45	08 05	08 13	08 45	09 05	09 13	09 31	09 45
d	23p53	07 06	07 46	08 06	08 14	08 46	09 06	09 14	09 32	09 46
Swanwick d		07 12		08 12	08 20		09 12	09 20		
Bursledon d		07 16		08 16			09 16			
Hamble d		07 19		08 19			09 19			
Netley d		07 21		08 21			09 21			
Sholing d		07 25		08 25			09 25			
Woolston d		07 27		08 27			09 27			
Bitterne d		07 31		08 31			09 31			
Eastleigh a	00 11		08 04			09 04				10 04
Southampton Airport Parkway a										
St Denys d		07 34		08 34			09 34			
Southampton Central ⛴ a		07 40		08 40	08 44		09 40	09 44	09 53	

	SW	SN	SW	SW	SN	GW	SW	SW	SN	GW
	1	◇1	1 🛒	1	◇1	◇	1 🛒	1	◇1	◇
Portsmouth Harbour ⛴ d			10 17			11 08	11 17			
Portsmouth & Southsea d	09 42		10 22	10 42		11 12	11 22	11 42		
Fratton d	09 46		10 26	10 46		11 16	11 26	11 46		
Hilsea d	09 50		10 30	10 50			11 30	11 50		
Chichester 4 d		09 45			10 45				11 45	11 54
Havant d		09 58			10 58				11 58	12 10
Cosham d	09 55	10 06	10 35	10 55	11 06	11 23	11 35	11 55	12 05	12 23
Portchester d	10 00		10 40	11 00			11 40	12 00		
Fareham a	10 05	10 14	10 45	11 05	11 14	11 31	11 45	12 05	12 13	12 31
d	10 06	10 15	10 46	11 06	11 15	11 32	11 46	12 06	12 14	12 32
Swanwick d	10 12	10 21		11 12	11 21			12 12	12 20	
Bursledon d	10 16			11 16				12 16		
Hamble d	10 19			11 19				12 19		
Netley d	10 21			11 21				12 21		
Sholing d	10 25			11 25				12 25		
Woolston d	10 27			11 27				12 27		
Bitterne d	10 31			11 31				12 31		
Eastleigh a			11 04				12 04			
Southampton Airport Parkway a										
St Denys d	10 34			11 34				12 34		
Southampton Central ⛴ a	10 40	10 44		11 40	11 45	11 53		12 40	12 44	12 53

	SW	SW	SN	GW	SW	SW	SN	GW	SW	SW	SN
	1 🛒	1	◇1	◇	1 🛒	1	◇1	◇	1 🛒	1	◇1
Portsmouth Harbour ⛴ d	12 17			13 08	13 17			14 08	14 17		
Portsmouth & Southsea d	12 22	12 42		13 12	13 22	13 42		14 12	14 22	14 42	
Fratton d	12 26	12 46		13 16	13 26	13 46		14 16	14 26	14 46	
Hilsea d	12 30	12 50			13 30	13 50			14 30	14 50	
Chichester 4 d			12 45				13 45				14 45
Havant d			12 58				13 58				14 58
Cosham d	12 35	12 55	13 05	13 23	13 35	13 55	14 05	14 23	14 35	14 55	15 05
Portchester d	12 40	13 00			13 40	14 00			14 40	15 00	
Fareham a	12 45	13 05	13 13	13 31	13 45	14 05	14 13	14 31	14 45	15 05	15 13
d	12 46	13 06	13 14	13 32	13 46	14 06	14 14	14 32	14 46	15 06	15 14
Swanwick d		13 12	13 20			14 12	14 20			15 12	15 20
Bursledon d		13 16				14 16				15 16	
Hamble d		13 19				14 19				15 19	
Netley d		13 21				14 21				15 21	
Sholing d		13 25				14 25				15 25	
Woolston d		13 27				14 27				15 27	
Bitterne d		13 31				14 31				15 31	
Eastleigh a	13 04				14 04				15 04		
Southampton Airport Parkway a											
St Denys d		13 34				14 34				15 34	
Southampton Central ⛴ a		13 40	13 44	13 53		14 40	14 44	14 53		15 40	15 44

	GW	SW	SW	SN	GW	SW	GW	SW	SN	GW	SW
	■	1 🛒	1	◇1	◇	1 🛒	◇	1	◇1	◇	1
Portsmouth Harbour ⛴ d	15 08	15 17			16 08	16 17				17 08	17 17
Portsmouth & Southsea d	15 12	15 22	15 42		16 12	16 22		16 42		17 12	17 22
Fratton d	15 16	15 26	15 46		16 16	16 26		16 46		17 16	17 26
Hilsea d		15 30	15 50			16 30		16 50			17 30
Chichester 4 d				15 45			16 34		16 45		
Havant d				15 58			16 48		16 58		
Cosham d	15 23	15 35	15 55	16 05	16 23	16 35	16 55	16 59	17 05	17 23	17 35
Portchester d		15 40	16 00			16 40		17 03			17 40
Fareham a	15 31	15 45	16 05	16 13	16 31	16 45	17 02	17 08	17 14	17 31	17 45
d	15 32	15 46	16 06	16 14	16 32	16 46	17 03	17 09	17 15	17 32	17 46
Swanwick d			16 12	16 20				17 16	17 22		
Bursledon d			16 16					17 19			
Hamble d			16 19					17 23			
Netley d			16 21					17 25			
Sholing d			16 25					17 29			
Woolston d			16 27					17 31			
Bitterne d			16 31					17 34			
Eastleigh a		16 04				17 04					18 04
Southampton Airport Parkway a											
St Denys d			16 34					17 38			
Southampton Central ⛴ a	15 53		16 40	16 44	16 53		17 24	17 43	17 48	17 53	

Table 165

Sundays from 16 September

Portsmouth and Fareham - Southampton

Network Diagram - see first Page of Table 165

	SW	SN	GW	SW	GW	SW	SN	GW	SW	SW	SN
	1	◇1	◇	1	◇	1	◇1	◇	1	1	◇1
Portsmouth Harbour ⛴ d			18 08	18 17				19 08	19 17		
Portsmouth & Southsea d	17 42		18 12	18 22		18 42		19 12	19 22	19 42	
Fratton d	17 46		18 16	18 26		18 46		19 16	19 26	19 46	
Hilsea d	17 50			18 30		18 50			19 30	19 50	
Chichester 4 d		17 45			18 34		18 45				19 45
Havant d		17 58			18 48		18 58				19 58
Cosham d	17 55	18 05	18 23	18 35	18 55	18 59	19 05	19 23	19 35	19 55	20 05
Portchester d	18 00			18 40		19 03			19 40	20 00	
Fareham a	18 05	18 13	18 31	18 45	19 02	19 08	19 13	19 31	19 45	20 05	20 13
d	18 06	18 14	18 32	18 46	19 03	19 09	19 14	19 32	19 46	20 06	20 14
Swanwick d	18 12	18 20				19 16	19 22			20 12	20 20
Bursledon d	18 16					19 19				20 16	
Hamble d	18 19					19 23				20 19	
Netley d	18 21					19 25				20 21	
Sholing d	18 25					19 29				20 25	
Woolston d	18 27					19 31				20 27	
Bitterne d	18 31					19 34				20 31	
Eastleigh a				19 04					20 04		
Southampton Airport Parkway a											
St Denys d	18 34					19 38				20 34	
Southampton Central ⛴ a	18 40	18 42	18 53		19 24	19 43	19 48	19 53		20 40	20 46

	GW	SW	SW	SN	SW	SW	SN	GW	SW	SW
	◇	1	1	◇1	1	1	◇1		1	1
Portsmouth Harbour ⛴ d	20 08	20 17			21 17			22 03	22 17	
Portsmouth & Southsea d	20 12	20 22	20 42		21 22	21 42		22 12	22 22	22 42
Fratton d	20 16	20 26	20 46		21 26	21 46		22 16	22 26	22 46
Hilsea d		20 30	20 50		21 30	21 50			22 30	22 50
Chichester 4 d				20 45			21 45			
Havant d				20 58			21 58			
Cosham d		20 35	20 55	21 07	21 35	21 55	22 05		22 35	22 55
Portchester d		20 40	21 00		21 40	22 00			22 40	23 00
Fareham a	20 31	20 45	21 05	21 15	21 45	22 05	22 13	22 31	22 45	23 05
d	20 32	20 46	21 06	21 16	21 46	22 06	22 14	22 32	22 46	23 06
Swanwick d			21 12	21 22		22 12	22 20			23 12
Bursledon d			21 16			22 16				23 16
Hamble d			21 19			22 19				23 19
Netley d			21 21			22 21				23 21
Sholing d			21 25			22 25				23 25
Woolston d			21 27			22 27				23 27
Bitterne d			21 31			22 31				23 31
Eastleigh a		21 04			22 04				23 04	
Southampton Airport Parkway a										
St Denys d			21 34			22 34				23 34
Southampton Central ⛴ a	20 53		21 40	21 45		22 40	22 44	22 53		23 40

	SW
	1
Portsmouth Harbour ⛴ d	23 17
Portsmouth & Southsea d	23 22
Fratton d	23 26
Hilsea d	23 30
Chichester 4 d	
Havant d	
Cosham d	23 35
Portchester d	23 40
Fareham a	23 45
d	23 46
Swanwick d	
Bursledon d	
Hamble d	
Netley d	
Sholing d	
Woolston d	
Bitterne d	
Eastleigh a	00 04
Southampton Airport Parkway a	
St Denys d	
Southampton Central ⛴ a	

Mondays to Fridays

To and from the Isle of Wight via Portsmouth and Ryde

Network Diagram - see first Page of Table 165

Miles			IL	IL	IL	IL	IL	IL	IL	IL	IL	IL	IL	IL	IL	IL	IL	IL	IL	IL	IL	IL	IL
—	Portsmouth Harbour ⛴	d	05 49	....	06 15	06 40	07 15	07 40	08 15	08 40	09 15	09 40	10 15	10 40	11 15	....	12 15	....	13 15	....	14 15	....	15 15
0	**Ryde Pier Head**	d	05 49	06 07	06 49	07 07	07 49	08 07	08 49	09 07	09 49	10 07	10 49	11 07	11 49	12 07	12 49	13 07	13 49	14 07	14 49	15 07	15 49
—	**Ryde Esplanade**	d	05 51	06 09	06 52	07 09	07 52	08 09	08 52	09 09	09 52	10 09	10 52	11 09	11 52	12 09	12 52	13 09	13 52	14 09	14 52	15 09	15 52
1¼	Ryde St Johns Road	d	05 55	06 13	06 55	07 13	07 55	08 13	08 55	09 13	09 55	10 13	10 55	11 13	11 55	12 13	12 55	13 13	13 55	14 13	14 55	15 13	15 55
2¼	Smallbrook Junction §	d	....	....	....	....	....	....	....	....	....	....	10 58	....	11 58	12 15	12 58	13 15	....	....	14 58	15 15	15 58
4¾	Brading	d	06 02	06 20	07 03	07 20	08 03	08 20	09 03	09 20	10 03	10 20	11 03	11 20	12 03	12 20	13 03	13 20	14 03	14 20	15 03	15 20	16 03
6½	Sandown	d	06 07	06 25	07 07	07 25	08 07	08 25	09 07	09 25	10 07	10 25	11 07	11 25	12 07	12 25	13 07	13 25	14 07	14 25	15 07	15 25	16 07
7¼	Lake	d	06 09	06 27	07 10	07 27	08 10	08 27	09 10	09 27	10 10	10 27	11 10	11 27	12 10	12 27	13 10	13 27	14 10	14 27	15 10	15 27	16 10
8½	**Shanklin**	a	06 12	06 30	07 13	07 30	08 13	08 30	09 13	09 30	10 13	10 30	11 13	11 30	12 13	12 30	13 13	13 30	14 13	14 30	15 13	15 30	16 13

		IL	IL	IL	IL	IL	IL	IL	IL	IL	IL	IL	IL
Portsmouth Harbour ⛴	d	15 40	16 15	16 40	17 15	17 40	18 15	....	19 15	....	20 15	21 15	22 15
Ryde Pier Head	d	16 07	16 49	17 07	17 49	18 07	18 49	19 07	19 49	20 07	20 45	21 45	22 45
Ryde Esplanade	d	16 09	16 52	17 09	17 52	18 09	18 52	19 09	19 52	20 09	20 47	21 47	22 47
Ryde St Johns Road	d	16 13	16 55	17 13	17 55	18 13	18 55	19 13	19 55	20 13	20 51	21 51	22a51
Smallbrook Junction §	d	16 15	....	....	....	....	....	....	....	....	....	....	....
Brading	d	16 20	17 03	17 20	18 03	18 20	19 03	19 20	20 03	20 20	20 57	21 57	....
Sandown	d	16 25	17 07	17 25	18 07	18 25	19 07	19 25	20 07	20 25	21 01	22 01	....
Lake	d	16 27	17 10	17 27	18 10	18 27	19 10	19 27	20 10	20 27	21 04	22 04	....
Shanklin	a	16 30	17 13	17 30	18 13	18 30	19 13	19 30	20 13	20 30	21 07	22 07	....

Saturdays

		IL	IL	IL	IL	IL	IL	IL	IL	IL	IL	IL	IL	IL	IL	IL	IL	IL	IL	IL	IL	IL	IL
Portsmouth Harbour ⛴	d	05 15	....	06 15	06 40	07 15	07 40	08 15	08e40	09 15	09e40	10 15	10e40	11 15	11e40	12 15	12e40	13f15	13e40	14f15	14e40	15 15	15e40
Ryde Pier Head	d	05 49	06 07	06 49	07 07	07 49	08 07	08 49	09 07	09 49	10 07	10 49	11 07	11 49	12 07	12 49	13 07	13 49	14 07	14 49	15 07	15 49	16 07
Ryde Esplanade	d	05 51	06 09	06 52	07 09	07 52	08 09	08 52	09 09	09 52	10 09	10 52	11 09	11 52	12 09	12 52	13 09	13 52	14 09	14 52	15 09	15 52	16 09
Ryde St Johns Road	d	05 55	06 13	06 55	07 13	07 55	08 13	08 55	09 13	09 55	10 13	10 55	11 13	11 55	12 13	12 55	13 13	13 55	14 13	14 55	15 13	15 55	16 13
Smallbrook Junction §	d	....	....	....	....	....	....	....	....	....	....	10 58	....	11 58	12 15	12 58	13 15	....	....	14 58	15 15	15 58	16 15
Brading	d	06 02	06 20	07 03	07 20	08 03	08 20	09 03	09 20	10 03	10 20	11 03	11 20	12 03	12 20	13 03	13 20	14 03	14 20	15 03	15 20	16 03	16 20
Sandown	d	06 07	06 25	07 07	07 25	08 07	08 25	09 07	09 25	10 07	10 25	11 07	11 25	12 07	12 25	13 07	13 25	14 07	14 25	15 07	15 25	16 07	16 25
Lake	d	06 09	06 27	07 10	07 27	08 10	08 27	09 10	09 27	10 10	10 27	11 10	11 27	12 10	12 27	13 10	13 27	14 10	14 27	15 10	15 27	16 10	16 27
Shanklin	a	06 12	06 30	07 13	07 30	08 13	08 30	09 13	09 30	10 13	10 30	11 13	11 30	12 13	12 30	13 13	13 30	14 13	14 30	15 13	15 30	16 13	16 30

		IL	IL	IL	IL	IL	IL	IL	IL	IL	IL	IL
Portsmouth Harbour ⛴	d	16 15	16e40	17 15	17e40	18 15	....	19 15	....	20 15	21 15	22 15
Ryde Pier Head	d	16 49	17 07	17 49	18 07	18 49	19 07	19 49	20 07	20 45	21 45	22 45
Ryde Esplanade	d	16 52	17 09	17 52	18 09	18 52	19 09	19 52	20 09	20 47	21 47	22 47
Ryde St Johns Road	d	16 55	17 13	17 55	18 13	18 55	19 13	19 55	20 13	20 51	21 51	22a51
Smallbrook Junction §	d	....	....	....	....	....	....	....	....	....	....	....
Brading	d	17 03	17 20	18 03	18 20	19 03	19 20	20 03	20 20	20 57	21 57	....
Sandown	d	17 07	17 25	18 07	18 25	19 07	19 25	20 07	20 25	21 01	22 01	....
Lake	d	17 10	17 27	18 10	18 27	19 10	19 27	20 10	20 27	21 04	22 04	....
Shanklin	a	17 13	17 30	18 13	18 30	19 13	19 30	20 13	20 30	21 07	22 07	....

Sundays
until 30 September

		IL	IL	IL	IL	IL	IL	IL	IL	IL	IL	IL	IL	IL	IL	IL	IL	IL	IL	IL	IL	IL	IL
Portsmouth Harbour ⛴	d	....	07 15	....	08 15	....	09 15	09g40	10 15	10g40	11 15	11g40	12 15	12g40	13 15	13g40	14 15	14 40	15 15	15 40	16 15	16 40	17 15
Ryde Pier Head	d	06 49	07 49	....	08 49	09 07	09 49	10 07	10 49	11 07	11 49	12 07	12 49	13 07	13 49	14 07	14 49	15 07	15 49	16 07	16 49	17 07	17 49
Ryde Esplanade	d	06 52	07 52	....	08 52	09 09	09 52	10 09	10 52	11 09	11 52	12 09	12 52	13 09	13 52	14 09	14 52	15 09	15 52	16 09	16 52	17 09	17 52
Ryde St Johns Road	d	06 55	07 55	08 13	08 55	09 13	09 55	10 13	10 55	11 13	11 55	12 13	12 55	13 13	13 55	14 13	14 55	15 13	15 55	16 13	16 55	17 13	17 55
Smallbrook Junction §	d	....	....	....	....	....	....	....	10 58	....	11 58	12 15	12 58	13 15	....	....	14 58	15 15	15 58	16 15	....	....	....
Brading	d	07 03	08 03	08 20	09 03	09 20	10 03	10 20	11 03	11 20	12 03	12 20	13 03	13 20	14 03	14 20	15 03	15 20	16 03	16 20	17 03	17 20	18 03
Sandown	d	07 07	08 07	08 25	09 07	09 25	10 07	10 25	11 07	11 25	12 07	12 25	13 07	13 25	14 07	14 25	15 07	15 25	16 07	16 25	17 07	17 25	18 07
Lake	d	07 10	08 10	08 27	09 10	09 27	10 10	10 27	11 10	11 27	12 10	12 27	13 10	13 27	14 10	14 27	15 10	15 27	16 10	16 27	17 10	17 27	18 10
Shanklin	a	07 13	08 13	08 30	09 13	09 30	10 13	10 30	11 13	11 30	12 13	12 30	13 13	13 30	14 13	14 30	15 13	15 30	16 13	16 30	17 13	17 30	18 13

		IL	IL	IL	IL	IL	IL	IL	IL
Portsmouth Harbour ⛴	d	17 40	18 15	....	19 15	....	20 15	21 15	22 15
Ryde Pier Head	d	18 07	18 49	19 07	19 49	20 07	20 45	21 45	22 45
Ryde Esplanade	d	18 09	18 52	19 09	19 52	20 09	20 47	21 47	22 47
Ryde St Johns Road	d	18 13	18 55	19 13	19 55	20a13	20 51	21 51	22a51
Smallbrook Junction §	d	....	....	....	....	....	....	....	....
Brading	d	18 20	19 03	19 20	20 03	....	20 57	21 57	....
Sandown	d	18 25	19 07	19 25	20 07	....	21 01	22 01	....
Lake	d	18 27	19 10	19 27	20 10	....	21 04	22 04	....
Shanklin	a	18 30	19 13	19 30	20 13	....	21 07	22 07	....

Sundays
from 7 October

		IL	IL	IL	IL	IL	IL	IL	IL	IL	IL	IL	IL	IL	IL	IL	IL	IL	IL	IL	IL	IL	IL
Portsmouth Harbour ⛴	d	....	07 15	08 15	09 15	10 15	11 15	12 15	14 40	13 15	13g40	14 15	14f40	15 15	15f40	16 15	16f40	17 15	17f40	18 15	19 15	20 15	21 15
Ryde Pier Head	d	06 49	07 49	08 49	09 49	10 49	11 49	12 49	13 07	13 49	14 07	14 49	15 07	15 49	16 07	16 49	17 07	17 49	18 07	18 49	19 49	20 45	21 45
Ryde Esplanade	d	06 52	07 52	08 52	09 52	10 52	11 52	12 52	13 09	13 52	14 09	14 52	15 09	15 52	16 09	16 52	17 09	17 52	18 09	18 52	19 52	20 47	21 47
Ryde St Johns Road	d	06 55	07 55	08 55	09 55	10 55	11 55	12 55	13 13	13 55	14 13	14 55	15 13	15 55	16 13	16 55	17 13	17 55	18 13	18 55	19 55	20 51	21 51
Smallbrook Junction §	d	....	....	....	....	10 58	11 58	12 58	13 15	....	....	14 58	15 15	15 58	16 15	....	....	....	....	....	....	....	....
Brading	d	07 03	08 03	09 03	10 03	11 03	12 03	13 03	13 20	14 03	14 20	15 03	15 20	16 03	16 20	17 03	17 20	18 03	18 20	19 03	20 03	20 57	21 57
Sandown	d	07 07	08 07	09 07	10 07	11 07	12 07	13 07	13 25	14 07	14 25	15 07	15 25	16 07	16 25	17 07	17 25	18 07	18 25	19 07	20 07	21 01	22 01
Lake	d	07 10	08 10	09 10	10 10	11 10	12 10	13 10	13 27	14 10	14 27	15 10	15 27	16 10	16 27	17 10	17 27	18 10	18 27	19 10	20 10	21 04	22 04
Shanklin	a	07 13	08 13	09 13	10 13	11 13	12 13	13 13	13 30	14 13	14 30	15 13	15 30	16 13	16 30	17 13	17 30	18 13	18 30	19 13	20 13	21 07	22 07

§ Smallbrook Jn. is only open for access to the I.O.W Steam Railway. For days of operation please enquire locally.

e until 3rd November

f from 10th November

g 3rd June, 10 june, from 29 July until 9 September, 29 October, 4 November

Table 167

Sundays
from 7 October

To and from the Isle of Wight via Portsmouth and Ryde

Network Diagram - see first Page of Table 165

		IL
Portsmouth Harbour ⛴	d	22 15
Ryde Pier Head	d	22 45
Ryde Esplanade	d	22 47
Ryde St Johns Road	d	22a51
Smallbrook Junction §	d	
Brading	d	
Sandown	d	
Lake	d	
Shanklin	a	

Mondays to Fridays

		IL	IL	IL	IL	IL	IL	IL	IL	IL	IL	IL	IL	IL	IL	IL	IL	IL	IL	IL	IL	IL	IL
Shanklin	d	....	....	06 18	06 38	07 18	07 38	08 18	08 38	09 18	09 38	10 18	10 38	11 18	11 38	12 18	12 38	13 18	13 38	14 18	14 38	15 18	15 38
Lake	d	....	....	06 21	06 41	07 21	07 41	08 21	08 41	09 21	09 41	10 21	10 41	11 21	11 41	12 21	12 41	13 21	13 41	14 21	14 41	15 21	15 41
Sandown	d	....	....	06 24	06 44	07 24	07 44	08 24	08 44	09 24	09 44	10 24	10 44	11 24	11 44	12 24	12 44	13 24	13 44	14 24	14 44	15 24	15 44
Brading	d	....	....	06 28	06 48	07 28	07 48	08 28	08 48	09 28	09 48	10 28	10 48	11 28	11 48	12 28	12 48	13 28	13 48	14 28	14 48	15 28	15 48
Smallbrook Junction §	d	....	....	....	....	....	....	....	....	....	....	....	10 53	....	11 53	12 33	12 53	13 33	....	....	14 53	15 33	15 53
Ryde St Johns Road	d	05 35	05 56	06 35	06 55	07 35	07 55	08 35	08 55	09 35	09 55	10 35	10 55	11 35	11 55	12 35	12 55	13 35	13 55	14 35	14 55	15 35	15 55
Ryde Esplanade	d	05 40	06 00	06 40	07 00	07 40	08 00	08 40	09 00	09 40	10 00	10 40	11 00	11 40	12 00	12 40	13 00	13 40	14 00	14 40	15 00	15 40	16 00
Ryde Pier Head	a	05 42	06 02	06 42	07 02	07 42	08 02	08 42	09 02	09 41	10 02	10 42	11 02	11 42	12 02	12 42	13 02	13 42	14 02	14 42	15 02	15 42	16 02
Portsmouth Harbour ⛴	a	06 09	....	07 09	07 32	08 09	08 32	09 09	09 32	10 09	10 32	....	11 32	12 09	....	13 09	....	14 09	....	15 09	....	16 09	16 32

		IL	IL	IL	IL	IL	IL	IL	IL	IL	IL	IL	IL
Shanklin	d	16 18	16 38	17 18	17 38	18 18	18 38	19 18	19 38	20 18	20 38	21 18	22 18
Lake	d	16 21	16 41	17 21	17 41	18 21	18 41	19 21	19 41	20 21	20 41	21 21	22 21
Sandown	d	16 24	16 44	17 24	17 44	18 24	18 44	19 24	19 44	20 24	20 44	21 24	22 24
Brading	d	16 28	16 48	17 28	17 48	18 28	18 48	19 28	19 48	20 28	20 48	21 28	22 28
Smallbrook Junction §	d	16 33	....	....	....	....	....	....	....	....	....	....	....
Ryde St Johns Road	d	16 35	16 55	17 35	17 55	18 35	18 55	19 35	19 55	20 34	20a54	21 34	22 34
Ryde Esplanade	d	16 40	17 00	17 40	18 00	18 40	19 00	19 40	20 00	20 38	....	21 38	22 38
Ryde Pier Head	a	16 42	17 02	17 42	18 02	18 42	19 02	19 42	20 02	20 41	....	21 41	22 41
Portsmouth Harbour ⛴	a	17 09	17 32	18 09	18 32	19 09	19 37	20 09	20 37	21 09	....	22 09	23 09

Saturdays

		IL	IL	IL	IL	IL	IL	IL	IL	IL	IL	IL	IL	IL	IL	IL	IL	IL	IL	IL	IL	IL	IL
Shanklin	d	....	....	06 18	06 38	07 18	07 38	08 18	08 38	09 18	09 38	10 18	10 38	11 18	11 38	12 18	12 38	13 18	13 38	14 18	14 38	15 18	15 38
Lake	d	....	....	06 21	06 41	07 21	07 41	08 21	08 41	09 21	09 41	10 21	10 41	11 21	11 41	12 21	12 41	13 21	13 41	14 21	14 41	15 21	15 41
Sandown	d	....	....	06 24	06 44	07 24	07 44	08 24	08 44	09 24	09 44	10 24	10 44	11 24	11 44	12 24	12 44	13 24	13 44	14 24	14 44	15 24	15 44
Brading	d	....	....	06 28	06 48	07 28	07 48	08 28	08 48	09 28	09 48	10 28	10 48	11 28	11 48	12 28	12 48	13 28	13 48	14 28	14 48	15 28	15 48
Smallbrook Junction §	d	....	....	....	....	....	....	....	....	....	....	....	10 53	....	11 53	12 33	12 53	13 33	....	....	14 53	15 33	15 53
Ryde St Johns Road	d	05 35	05 56	06 35	06 55	07 35	07 55	08 35	08 55	09 35	09 55	10 35	10 55	11 35	11 55	12 35	12 55	13 35	13 55	14 35	14 55	15 35	15 55
Ryde Esplanade	d	05 40	06 00	06 40	07 00	07 40	08 00	08 40	09 00	09 40	10 00	10 40	11 00	11 40	12 00	12 40	13 00	13 40	14 00	14 40	15 00	15 40	16 00
Ryde Pier Head	a	05 42	06 02	06 42	07 02	07 42	08 02	08 42	09 02	09 42	10 02	10 42	11 02	11 42	12 02	12 42	13 02	13 42	14 02	14 42	15 02	15 42	16 02
Portsmouth Harbour ⛴	a	06 09	....	07 09	....	08 09	....	09 09	09e32	10 09	10e32	11 09	11e32	12 09	12e32	13 09	13e32	14g09	14e32	15g09	15e32	16 09	16e32

		IL	IL	IL	IL	IL	IL	IL	IL	IL	IL	IL	IL
Shanklin	d	16 18	16 38	17 18	17 38	18 18	18 38	19 18	19 38	20 18	20 38	21 18	22 18
Lake	d	16 21	16 41	17 21	17 41	18 21	18 41	19 21	19 41	20 21	20 41	21 21	22 21
Sandown	d	16 24	16 44	17 24	17 44	18 24	18 44	19 24	19 44	20 24	20 44	21 24	22 24
Brading	d	16 28	16 48	17 28	17 48	18 28	18 48	19 28	19 48	20 28	20 48	21 28	22 28
Smallbrook Junction §	d	16 33	....	....	....	....	....	....	....	....	....	....	....
Ryde St Johns Road	d	16 35	16 55	17 35	17 55	18 35	18 55	19 35	19 55	20 34	20a54	21 34	22 34
Ryde Esplanade	d	16 40	17 00	17 40	18 00	18 40	19 00	19 40	20 00	20 38	....	21 38	22 38
Ryde Pier Head	a	16 42	17 02	17 42	18 02	18 42	19 02	19 42	20 02	20 41	....	21 41	22 41
Portsmouth Harbour ⛴	a	17 09	17e32	18 09	18e32	19 09	19 37	20 09	....	21 09	....	22 09	23 09

Sundays
until 30 September

		IL	IL	IL	IL	IL	IL	IL	IL	IL	IL	IL	IL	IL	IL	IL	IL	IL	IL	IL	IL	IL	IL
Shanklin	d	....	07 18	08 18	08 38	09 18	09 38	10 18	10 38	11 18	11 38	12 18	12 38	13 18	13 38	14 18	14 38	15 18	15 38	16 18	16 38	17 18	17 38
Lake	d	....	07 21	08 21	08 41	09 21	09 41	10 21	10 41	11 21	11 41	12 21	12 41	13 21	13 41	14 21	14 41	15 21	15 41	16 21	16 41	17 21	17 41
Sandown	d	....	07 24	08 24	08 44	09 24	09 44	10 24	10 44	11 24	11 44	12 24	12 44	13 24	13 44	14 24	14 44	15 24	15 44	16 24	16 44	17 24	17 44
Brading	d	....	07 28	08 28	08 48	09 28	09 48	10 28	10 48	11 28	11 48	12 28	12 48	13 28	13 48	14 28	14 48	15 28	15 48	16 28	16 48	17 28	17 48
Smallbrook Junction §	d	....	....	....	....	....	....	....	10 53	....	11 53	12 33	12 53	13 33	....	....	14 53	15 33	15 53	16 33	....	....	....
Ryde St Johns Road	d	06 35	07 35	08 35	08 55	09 35	09 55	10 35	10 55	11 35	11 55	12 35	12 55	13 35	13 55	14 35	14 55	15 35	15 55	16 35	16 55	17 35	17 55
Ryde Esplanade	d	06 40	07 40	08 40	09 00	09 40	10 00	10 40	11 00	11 40	12 00	12 40	13 00	13 40	14 00	14 40	15 00	15 40	16 00	16 40	17 00	17 40	18 00
Ryde Pier Head	a	06 42	07 42	08 42	09 02	09 42	10 02	10 42	11 02	11 42	12 02	12 42	13 02	13 42	14 02	14 42	15 02	15 42	16 02	16 42	17 02	17 42	18 02
Portsmouth Harbour ⛴	a	....	08 09	09 09	....	10 09	10h32	11 09	11h32	12 09	12h32	13 09	13h32	14 09	14h32	15 09	15 32	16 09	16 32	17 09	17 32	18 09	18 32

		IL	IL	IL	IL	IL	IL	IL
Shanklin	d	18 18	18 38	19 18	19 38	20 18	21 18	22 18
Lake	d	18 21	18 41	19 21	19 41	20 21	21 21	22 21
Sandown	d	18 24	18 44	19 24	19 44	20 24	21 24	22 24
Brading	d	18 28	18 48	19 28	19 48	20 28	21 28	22 28
Smallbrook Junction §	d	....	....	....	....	....	....	....
Ryde St Johns Road	d	18 35	18 55	19 35	19 55	20 34	21 34	22 34
Ryde Esplanade	d	18 40	18 59	19 40	20 00	20 38	21 38	22 38
Ryde Pier Head	a	18 42	19 02	19 42	20 02	20 41	21 41	22 41
Portsmouth Harbour ⛴	a	19 09	19h37	20 09	....	21 09	22 09	23 09

§ Smallbrook Jn. is only open for access to the I.O.W Steam Railway. For days of operation please enquire locally.

e until 3rd November

f from 10th November until 1st December

g from 10th November

h 3rd june, 10 June, from 29 July until 9 September

Table 167

Sundays
from 7 October

To and from the Isle of Wight via Portsmouth and Ryde

Network Diagram - see first Page of Table 165

		IL	IL	IL	IL	IL	IL	IL	IL	IL	IL	IL	IL	IL	IL	IL	IL	IL	IL	IL	IL	IL	IL
Shanklin	d		07 18	08 18	09 18	10 18	11 18	12 18		13 18	13 38	14 18	14 38	15 18	15 38	16 18	16 38	17 18	17 38	18 18	18 38	19 18	20 18
Lake	d		07 21	08 21	09 21	10 21	11 21	12 21		13 21	13 41	14 21	14 41	15 21	15 41	16 21	16 41	17 21	17 41	18 21	18 41	19 21	20 21
Sandown	d		07 24	08 24	09 24	10 24	11 24	12 24		13 24	13 44	14 24	14 44	15 24	15 44	16 24	16 44	17 24	17 44	18 24	18 44	19 24	20 24
Brading	d		07 28	08 28	09 28	10 28	11 28	12 28		13 28	13 48	14 28	14 48	15 28	15 48	16 28	16 48	17 28	17 48	18 28	18 48	19 28	20 28
Smallbrook Junction §	d							12 33		13 33			14 53	15 33	15 53	16 33							
Ryde St Johns Road	d	06 35	07 35	08 35	09 35	10 35	11 35	12 35	12 55	13 35	13 55	14 35	14 55	15 35	15 55	16 35	16 55	17 35	17 55	18 35	18a54	19 35	20 34
Ryde Esplanade	d	06 40	07 40	08 40	09 40	10 40	11 40	12 40	13 00	13 40	14 00	14 40	15 00	15 40	16 00	16 40	17 00	17 40	18 00	18 40		19 40	20 38
Ryde Pier Head	a	06 42	07 42	08 42	09 42	10 42	11 42	12 42	13 02	13 42	14 02	14 42	15 02	15 42	16 02	16 42	17 02	17 42	18 02	18 42		19 42	20 41
Portsmouth Harbour	a		08 09	09 09	10 09	11 09	12 09	13 09	13e32	14 09	14e32	15 09	15f32	16 09	16f32	17 09	17f32	18 09	18f32	19 09		20 09	21 09

		IL	IL
Shanklin	d	21 18	22 18
Lake	d	21 21	22 21
Sandown	d	21 24	22 24
Brading	d	21 28	22 28
Smallbrook Junction §	d		
Ryde St Johns Road	d	21 34	22 34
Ryde Esplanade	d	21 38	22 38
Ryde Pier Head	a	21 41	22 41
Portsmouth Harbour	a	22 09	23 09

§ Smallbrook Jn. is only open for access to the I.O.W Steam Railway. For days of operation please enquire locally.

e 28th October, 4th November
f until 3rd November

Table 175

Mondays to Fridays

London - East Croydon and Purley

COMPLETE SERVICE

		SN MX 1	SN MO	SN MX	SN MX 1	SN MO	SN MO	SN MX 1	SN MO	SN MO 1	FC 1	SN MX ◇1	FC	SN 1	SN MX	SN	SN ◇1	SN ◇1	FC 1	FC	SN MX	SN	SN ◇1
			A			A	A		A	A	B		C				D	D	B	C			
London Victoria 15 ⊖	d				23p47	23p47		23p49	23p50			00 05		00 14		00 16	00 25	00 40				00 42	01 00
Clapham Junction 10	d	23p40			23p53	23p53		23p56	23p56	00 05		00 11		00 20		00 24	00 31	00 46				00 50	01 08
St Pancras International 15 ⊖	d										23p54								00 24				
Farringdon 3 ⊖	d										23p59								00 29				
City Thameslink 3	d																						
London Blackfriars 3 ⊖	d										00 05								00 35				
London Bridge 4 ⊖	d		23p21	23p36			23p39				00 12		00 12		00 06				00 42	00 42	00 36		
New Cross Gate	d			23p41			23p44								00 11						00 41		
Norwood Junction 2	a			23p59			00 02								00 29						00 59		
East Croydon ⇌	a	00 01	00 01	00 03	00 05	00 06	00 06	00 09	00 17	00 22	00 26	00 26	00 26	00 31	00 33	00 44	00 40	00 55	00 56	00 56	01 03	01 10	01 23
South Croydon 4	a			00 06			00 09		00 20						00 37								
Purley Oaks	a			00 09			00 12		00 23						00 40								
Purley 4	a			00 12	00 11		00 15		00 26					00 37	00 43		00 46						01 29

		FC MO 1	FC MX 1	FC 1	SN	SN ◇1	FC 1	SN	SN 1	FC 1	FC 1	SN 1	FC 1	FC	FC 1	FC 1	SN ◇1	FC 1	FC 1	FC 1	FC 1	SN ◇1	FC 1
		A	E	C	D	D	C	D		B	C		B	C	C	B		B	C	B	C		
London Victoria 15 ⊖	d				01 12	01 30		01 42	02 00			03 00					04 00					05 02	
Clapham Junction 10	d				01 18	01 36		01 48	02 08			03 08					04 08					05 08	
St Pancras International 15 ⊖	d	00 54	00 54							01 54			02 54			03 28		03 54		04 24			04 54
Farringdon 3 ⊖	d		00 59																				04 59
City Thameslink 3	d																						
London Blackfriars 3 ⊖	d	01 05	01 05							02 05			03 05			03 39		04 05		04 35			05 04
London Bridge 4 ⊖	d			01 08			01 35				02 05			03 05	03 35				04 05		04 35		
New Cross Gate	d																						
Norwood Junction 2	a																						
East Croydon ⇌	a	01 31	01 31	01 31	01 38	01 45	02 01	02 08	02 23	02 31	02 31	03 23	03 31	03 31	04 01	04 03	04 23	04 31	04 31	05 01	05 01	05 20	05 29
South Croydon 4	a																						
Purley Oaks	a																						
Purley 4	a					01 51			02 29			03 29					04 29					05 25	

		FC 1	SN 1	SN ◇1	FC 1	SN 1	SN ◇1	SN 1	SN	FC 1	SN	SN ◇1	SN 1	SN ◇1	SN 1	FC 1	SN	SN	SN ◇1	SN 1	SN 1	FC 1
London Victoria 15 ⊖	d		05 25	05 32		05 53	06 02				06 13	06 21	06 24	06 32				06 44	06 47	06 51	06 54	
Clapham Junction 10	d		05 33	05 38		05 59	06 08				06 21	06 27	06 30	06 38				06 50	06 53	06 57	07 00	
St Pancras International 15 ⊖	d	05 12			05 32					06 02						06 22						06 38
Farringdon 3 ⊖	d	05 18			05 38					06 08						06 28						06 44
City Thameslink 3	d	05 21			05 41					06 11						06 31						06 47
London Blackfriars 3 ⊖	d	05 24			05 44					06 14						06 34						06 50
London Bridge 4 ⊖	d	05 30			05 50			06 08	06 06	06 20					06 38	06 42	06 36					07 00
New Cross Gate	d								06 11								06 41					
Norwood Junction 2	a		05 50						06 29								06 59					
East Croydon ⇌	a	05 47	05 54	05 48	06 05	06 09	06 17	06 22	06 33	06 33	06 43	06 38	06 40	06 48	06 52	06 54	07 03	07 12	07 03	07 06	07 10	07 14
South Croydon 4	a		05 57						06 36								07 06					
Purley Oaks	a								06 40								07 09					
Purley 4	a			05 53			06 23		06 43		06 51	06 43		06 55			07 12					

		SN 1	SN 1	SN	SN 1	FC 1	SN ◇1	SN 1	SN	SN 1	SN	SN	SN 1	SN 1	SN 1	SN 1	FC 1	SN	SN	SN ◇1	SN	SN 1	SN 1
																						B	C
London Victoria 15 ⊖	d		07 02		07 10		07 17				07 20	07 23			07 32	07 36			07 45	07 47			
Clapham Junction 10	d		07 08		07 16		07 23				07 28	07 30			07 38	07 42			07 51	07 53			
St Pancras International 15 ⊖	d					06 58											07 20						
Farringdon 3 ⊖	d					07 04											07 26						
City Thameslink 3	d					07 07											07 29						
London Blackfriars 3 ⊖	d					07 09											07 32						
London Bridge 4 ⊖	d	07 03		06 54		07 16		07 19	07 06	07 27			07 30	07 33			07 42	07 44			07 36	07 51	07 53
New Cross Gate	d			06 59					07 11					07 38				07 49			07 41		
Norwood Junction 2	a			07 17				07 29	07 29	07 38			07 41								07 59	08 01	
East Croydon ⇌	a	07 16	07 17	07 21	07 26	07 30	07 33	07 33	07 37	07 42	07 49	07 44	07 45	07 48	07 52	07 51	07 54	08 00	08 12	08 02	08 03	08 05	08 05
South Croydon 4	a			07 24					07 40		07 52								08 15		08 06		
Purley Oaks	a			07 28					07 43		07 55								08 18		08 09		
Purley 4	a		07 23	07 31					07 46		07 58	07 52				07 57			08 21		08 12		

		SN ◇1	SN 1	SN 1	SN ◇1	SN 1	SN ◇1	SN 1	FC 1	SN 1	SN	SN	SN	SN ◇1	FC 1	SN 1	SN ◇1	SN 1	SN	SN ◇1	SN 1	SN ◇1
			C																			
London Victoria 15 ⊖	d	07 52			08 02		08 07			08 10			08 15	08 17			08 21			08 32		08 36
Clapham Junction 10	d	07 58			08 08		08 13			08 16			08 23	08 23			08 27			08 38		08 43
St Pancras International 15 ⊖	d								07 44						07 56							
Farringdon 3 ⊖	d								07 50						08 02							
City Thameslink 3	d								07 53						08 05							
London Blackfriars 3 ⊖	d								07 56						08 08							
London Bridge 4 ⊖	d		07 56	08 02		08 00		08 08			08 14	08 06			08 18	08 23		08 25	08 27		08 30	
New Cross Gate	d					08 08						08 11									08 36	
Norwood Junction 2	a		08 07			08 16					08 27	08 29						08 36			08 43	
East Croydon ⇌	a	08 09	08 10	08 15	08 18	08 20	08 22	08 23	08 26	08 26	08 30	08 33	08 44	08 34	08 37	08 37	08 40	08 40	08 42	08 48	08 48	08 52
South Croydon 4	a							08 26				08 36	08 47									
Purley Oaks	a											08 39	08 50									
Purley 4	a					08 25					08 38	08 42	08 54								08 58	

A from 21 May
B from 21 May
C until 18 May
D from 30 July until 7 September, not from 13 August until 29 August
E from 22 May

London - East Croydon and Purley
COMPLETE SERVICE

		FC ■	SN ■	SN	SN	SN ◇■ 🍴	SN ■	SN	SN ◇■	SN ■	SN ◇■ 🍴	SN ■	SN ◇■ 🍴	SN ■	FC ■	SN ■	SN	SN ◇■ 🍴	SN	SN	FC ■	SN ■	SN ◇■ 🍴
London Victoria 15 ⊖	d				08 43	08 47			08 51	08 53	09 02		09 06				09 13	09 17				09 23	09 32
Clapham Junction 10	d				08 51	08 53	08 36			08 59	09 08		09 12				09 21	09 23				09 29	09 38
St Pancras International 15 ⊖	d	08 20													08 48						09 04		
Farringdon 3 ⊖	d	08 26													08 54						09 10		
City Thameslink 3	d	08 29													08 57						09 13		
London Blackfriars 3 ⊖	d	08 32													09 00						09 16		
London Bridge 4 ⊖	d		08 45	08 47				08 36				09 03		09 08	09 12	09 15			09 06	09 20	09 27		
New Cross Gate	d							08 41				09 08							09 12				
Norwood Junction 2	a		08 55					08 59				09 16				09 25			09 30	09 32			
East Croydon	a	08 57	08 59	09 02	09 12	09 03	09 04	09 06	09 07	09 09	09 18	09 20	09 22	09 22	09 24	09 29	09 42	09 32	09 33	09 36	09 39	09 39	09 48
South Croydon 4	a				09 15			09 09									09 45		09 36				
Purley Oaks	a				09 18			09 12									09 48		09 39				
Purley 4	a		09 05	09 09	09 22			09 15				09 26				09 35	09 52		09 42	09 45			

		SN ■	SN ◇■	FC ■	SN ■	SN ■	SN	SN ◇■ 🍴	SN	SN	SN ◇■	FC ■	SN ■	SN ◇■ 🍴	SN ■	SN ◇■ 🍴	SN ■	FC ■	SN ■	SN	SN ◇■ 🍴	SN	SN
London Victoria 15 ⊖	d		09 36				09 43	09 47			09 51		09 53	10 02		10 06				10 13	10 17		
Clapham Junction 10	d		09 42		09 34		09 51	09 53					09 59	10 08		10 12				10 21	10 23		
St Pancras International 15 ⊖	d			09 22								09 40						09 54					
Farringdon 3 ⊖	d			09 28								09 45						09 59					
City Thameslink 3	d			09 31								09 48						10 03					
London Blackfriars 3 ⊖	d			09 34								09 50						10 05					
London Bridge 4 ⊖	d	09 32		09 42		09 45			09 36	09 50		09 57			10 03		10 08	10 12	10 15			10 06	10 20
New Cross Gate	d	09 37							09 41						10 08							10 11	
Norwood Junction 2	a	09 45				09 55			09 59	10 02					10 16				10 25			10 29	10 32
East Croydon	a	09 49	09 52	09 54	09 57	09 59	10 12	10 02	10 03	10 06	10 07	10 09	10 09	10 17	10 20	10 22	10 22	10 24	10 29	10 42	10 32	10 33	10 36
South Croydon 4	a				10 01		10 15		10 06											10 45		10 36	
Purley Oaks	a						10 18		10 09											10 48		10 39	
Purley 4	a	09 56				10 05	10 22		10 12	10 15					10 26				10 35	10 52		10 42	10 45

		FC ■	SN ■	SN ◇■ 🍴	SN ■	SN ◇■	FC ■	SN ■	SN ■	SN	SN ◇■ 🍴	SN	SN	SN ◇■	FC ■	SN ■	SN ◇■	SN ■	SN ◇■	SN ■	FC ■	SN ■
London Victoria 15 ⊖	d		10 23	10 32		10 36				10 43	10 47			10 51		10 53	11 02		11 06			
Clapham Junction 10	d		10 29	10 38		10 42		10 34		10 51	10 53					10 59	11 08		11 12			
St Pancras International 15 ⊖	d	10 09					10 24								10 39						10 54	
Farringdon 3 ⊖	d	10 14					10 29								10 44						10 59	
City Thameslink 3	d	10 18					10 33								10 48						11 03	
London Blackfriars 3 ⊖	d	10 20					10 35								10 50						11 05	
London Bridge 4 ⊖	d	10 27			10 33		10 42		10 45			10 36	10 50		10 57			11 03		11 08	11 12	11 15
New Cross Gate	d				10 38							10 41						11 08				
Norwood Junction 2	a				10 46				10 55			10 59	11 02					11 16				11 25
East Croydon	a	10 39	10 39	10 48	10 50	10 52	10 54	10 57	10 59	11 12	11 02	11 03	11 06	11 07	11 09	11 09	11 17	11 20	11 22	11 23	11 24	11 29
South Croydon 4	a							11 01		11 15		11 06										
Purley Oaks	a									11 18		11 09										
Purley 4	a				10 56				11 06	11 22		11 12	11 15					11 26				11 35

		SN	SN ◇■	SN	SN	FC ■	SN ■	SN ◇■	SN ■	SN ◇■ 🍴	FC ■	SN ■	SN ■	SN	SN ◇■	SN	SN	SN ◇■	FC ■	SN ■	SN ◇■	SN ■	SN ◇■ 🍴
London Victoria 15 ⊖	d	11 13	11 17				11 23	11 32		11 36				11 43	11 47			11 51		11 53	12 02		12 06
Clapham Junction 10	d	11 21	11 23				11 29	11 38		11 42		11 34		11 51	11 53					11 59	12 08		12 12
St Pancras International 15 ⊖	d					11 09					11 24								11 39				
Farringdon 3 ⊖	d					11 14					11 29								11 44				
City Thameslink 3	d					11 18					11 33								11 48				
London Blackfriars 3 ⊖	d					11 20					11 35								11 50				
London Bridge 4 ⊖	d			11 06	11 20	11 27			11 33		11 42		11 45			11 36	11 50		11 57			12 03	
New Cross Gate	d			11 11					11 38							11 41						12 08	
Norwood Junction 2	a			11 29	11 32				11 46				11 55			11 59	12 02					12 16	
East Croydon	a	11 42	11 32	11 33	11 36	11 39	11 39	11 48	11 50	11 52	11 54	11 57	11 59	12 12	12 02	12 03	12 06	12 07	12 09	12 09	12 17	12 20	12 22
South Croydon 4	a	11 45		11 36								12 01		12 15		12 06							
Purley Oaks	a	11 48		11 39										12 18		12 09							
Purley 4	a	11 52		11 42	11 45				11 56				12 05	12 22		12 12	12 15					12 26	

		SN ■	FC ■	SN ■	SN	SN ◇■	SN	SN	FC ■	SN ■	SN ◇■	SN ■	SN ◇■ 🍴	FC ■	SN ■	SN ■	SN	SN ◇■	SN	SN	SN ◇■	FC ■
London Victoria 15 ⊖	d				12 13	12 17				12 23	12 32		12 36				12 43	12 47			12 51	
Clapham Junction 10	d				12 21	12 23				12 29	12 38		12 42		12 34		12 51	12 53				
St Pancras International 15 ⊖	d		11 54						12 09					12 24								12 39
Farringdon 3 ⊖	d		11 59						12 14					12 29								12 44
City Thameslink 3	d		12 03						12 18					12 33								12 48
London Blackfriars 3 ⊖	d		12 05						12 20					12 35								12 50
London Bridge 4 ⊖	d	12 08	12 12	12 15			12 06	12 20	12 27			12 33		12 42		12 45			12 36	12 50		12 57
New Cross Gate	d						12 11					12 38							12 41			
Norwood Junction 2	a			12 25			12 29	12 32				12 46				12 55			12 59	13 02		
East Croydon	a	12 22	12 24	12 29	12 42	12 32	12 33	12 36	12 39	12 39	12 48	12 50	12 52	12 54	12 57	12 59	13 12	13 02	13 03	13 06	13 07	13 09
South Croydon 4	a				12 45		12 36								13 01		13 15		13 06			
Purley Oaks	a				12 48		12 39										13 18		13 09			
Purley 4	a			12 35	12 52		12 42	12 45				12 57				13 05	13 22		13 12	13 15		

		SN ■	SN ◇■	SN ■	SN ◇■ 🍴	SN ■	FC ■	SN ■	SN	SN ◇■	SN	SN	FC ■	SN ■	SN ◇■ 🍴	SN ■	SN ◇■ 🍴	FC ■	SN ■	SN ■	SN	SN ◇■	SN
London Victoria 15 ⊖	d	12 53	13 02		13 06				13 13	13 17				13 23	13 32		13 36				13 43	13 47	
Clapham Junction 10	d	12 59	13 08		13 12				13 21	13 23				13 29	13 38		13 42		13 34		13 51	13 53	
St Pancras International 15 ⊖	d						12 54						13 09					13 24					
Farringdon 3 ⊖	d						12 59						13 14					13 29					
City Thameslink 3	d						13 03						13 18					13 33					
London Blackfriars 3 ⊖	d						13 05						13 20					13 35					
London Bridge 4 ⊖	d			13 03		13 08	13 12	13 15			13 06	13 20	13 27			13 33		13 42		13 45			13 36
New Cross Gate	d			13 08							13 11					13 38							13 41
Norwood Junction 2	a			13 16				13 25			13 29	13 32				13 46				13 55			13 59
East Croydon	a	13 09	13 17	13 20	13 22	13 23	13 24	13 29	13 42	13 32	13 33	13 36	13 39	13 39	13 48	13 50	13 52	13 54	13 57	13 59	14 12	14 02	14 03
South Croydon 4	a								13 45		13 36								14 01		14 15		14 06
Purley Oaks	a								13 48		13 39										14 18		14 09
Purley 4	a			13 26				13 35	13 52		13 42	13 45				13 56				14 05	14 22		14 12

		SN	SN ◇■	FC ■	SN ■	SN ◇■	SN ■	SN ◇■ 🍴	SN ■	FC ■	SN ■	SN	SN ◇■	SN	SN	FC ■	SN ■	SN ◇■ 🍴	SN ■	SN ◇■ 🍴	FC ■	SN ■	SN ■
London Victoria 15 ⊖	d		13 51		13 53	14 02		14 06				14 13	14 17				14 23	14 32		14 36			
Clapham Junction 10	d				13 59	14 08		14 12				14 21	14 23				14 29	14 38		14 42		14 34	
St Pancras International 15 ⊖	d			13 39						13 54						14 09					14 24		
Farringdon 3 ⊖	d			13 44						13 59						14 14					14 29		
City Thameslink 3	d			13 48						14 03						14 18					14 33		
London Blackfriars 3 ⊖	d			13 50						14 05						14 20					14 35		
London Bridge 4 ⊖	d	13 50		13 57			14 03		14 08	14 12	14 15			14 06	14 20	14 27			14 33		14 42		14 45
New Cross Gate	d						14 08							14 11					14 38				
Norwood Junction 2	a	14 02					14 16				14 25			14 29	14 32				14 46				14 55
East Croydon	a	14 06	14 07	14 09	14 09	14 17	14 20	14 22	14 23	14 25	14 29	14 42	14 32	14 33	14 36	14 39	14 40	14 48	14 50	14 52	14 54	14 57	14 59
South Croydon 4	a											14 45		14 36								15 01	
Purley Oaks	a											14 48		14 39									
Purley 4	a	14 15					14 26				14 35	14 52		14 42	14 45				14 56				15 05

		SN	SN ◇■	SN	SN	SN ◇■	FC ■	SN ■	SN ◇■	SN ■	SN ◇■ 🍴	SN ■	FC ■	SN ■	SN	SN ◇■	SN	SN	FC ■	SN ■	SN ◇■	SN ■
London Victoria 15 ⊖	d	14 43	14 47			14 51		14 53	15 02		15 06				15 13	15 17				15 23	15 32	
Clapham Junction 10	d	14 51	14 53					14 59	15 08		15 12				15 21	15 23				15 29	15 38	
St Pancras International 15 ⊖	d						14 39						14 54						15 09			
Farringdon 3 ⊖	d						14 44						14 59						15 14			
City Thameslink 3	d						14 48						15 03						15 18			
London Blackfriars 3 ⊖	d						14 50						15 05						15 20			
London Bridge 4 ⊖	d			14 36	14 50		14 57			15 03		15 08	15 12	15 15			15 06	15 20	15 27			15 33
New Cross Gate	d			14 41						15 08							15 11					15 38
Norwood Junction 2	a			14 59	15 02					15 16				15 25			15 29	15 32				15 46
East Croydon	a	15 12	15 02	15 03	15 06	15 07	15 09	15 09	15 17	15 20	15 22	15 23	15 24	15 29	15 42	15 32	15 33	15 36	15 39	15 40	15 47	15 50
South Croydon 4	a	15 15		15 06											15 45		15 36			15 43		
Purley Oaks	a	15 18		15 09											15 48		15 39					
Purley 4	a	15 22		15 12	15 15					15 26				15 35	15 52		15 42	15 45				15 56

		SN ◇■ 🍴	SN ■	FC ■	SN ■	SN ■	SN	SN ◇■	SN	SN	SN ◇■	FC ■	SN ■	SN ◇■	SN ■	SN ■ 🍴	SN ■	FC ■	SN ■	SN	SN	SN ◇■ 🍴	SN ■
London Victoria 15 ⊖	d	15 36					15 43	15 47			15 51		15 53	16 02		16 06					16 13	16 17	16 19
Clapham Junction 10	d	15 42			15 34		15 51	15 53					15 59	16 08		16 12					16 21	16 23	16 26
St Pancras International 15 ⊖	d			15 24								15 39						15 54					
Farringdon 3 ⊖	d			15 29								15 44						15 59					
City Thameslink 3	d			15 33								15 48						16 03					
London Blackfriars 3 ⊖	d			15 35								15 50						16 05					
London Bridge 4 ⊖	d		15 38	15 42		15 45			15 36	15 50		15 57			16 03		16 08	16 12	16 15	16 06			
New Cross Gate	d								15 41						16 08					16 11			
Norwood Junction 2	a					15 55			15 59	16 02					16 16				16 25	16 29			
East Croydon	a	15 52	15 52	15 54	15 57	15 59	16 12	16 02	16 03	16 06	16 07	16 09	16 09	16 17	16 20	16 22	16 23	16 24	16 29	16 33	16 42	16 33	16 36
South Croydon 4	a				16 01		16 15		16 06				16 12							16 36	16 45		
Purley Oaks	a						16 18		16 09											16 39	16 48		
Purley 4	a					16 05	16 22		16 12	16 15					16 26				16 35	16 42	16 52		

		SN	FC ■	SN ■	SN ◇■ 🍴	SN ■	SN ■ 🍴	SN ■	SN	SN ■	FC ■	SN	SN ◇■ 🍴	SN	SN ■	SN ■	SN ■	SN ■	SN ◇■ 🍴	SN ■	SN ■	FC ■
London Victoria 15 ⊖	d			16 23	16 32		16 36		16 39			16 43	16 47		16 49	16 53			17 02	17 06		
Clapham Junction 10	d			16 29	16 38		16 42		16 45	16 34		16 51	16 53		16 56	16 59			17 08	17 12		
St Pancras International 15 ⊖	d		16 09								16 22											16 46
Farringdon 3 ⊖	d		16 14								16 27											16 51
City Thameslink 3	d		16 18								16 31											16 55
London Blackfriars 3 ⊖	d		16 20								16 36											16 58
London Bridge 4 ⊖	d	16 20	16 27			16 33		16 38			16 43			16 48			16 57	16 59			17 09	
New Cross Gate	d																					
Norwood Junction 2	a	16 32				16 44								17 01				17 10				
East Croydon	a	16 36	16 39	16 39	16 47	16 48	16 52	16 52	16 55	16 58	16 59	17 12	17 03	17 05	17 06	17 09	17 09	17 14	17 17	17 22	17 22	17 26
South Croydon 4	a			16 42					16 58	17 02		17 19		17 08		17 12						
Purley Oaks	a								17 01			17 22		17 11								
Purley 4	a	16 45				16 55			17 05			17 25		17 14				17 20				

London - East Croydon and Purley

COMPLETE SERVICE

		SN	SN 1	SN ◇1	SN	SN 1	SN 1	SN 1	FC 1	SN ◇1	SN 1	SN ◇1 (T)	SN 1	SN	SN 1	SN 1	SN 1	SN ◇1	SN 1	SN	FC 1	SN 1	SN 1 A
London Victoria 15 ⊖	d	17 09		17 17			17 21	17 23		17 32		17 35		17 39				17 47	17 49			17 53	
Clapham Junction 10	d	17 15		17 23			17 27	17 30		17 38		17 42		17 45			17 33	17 53	17 56			18 00	
St Pancras International 15 ⊖	d								17 10												17 28		
Farringdon 3 ⊖	d								17 15												17 33		
City Thameslink 3	d								17 19												17 37		
London Blackfriars 3 ⊖	d								17 22												17 40		
London Bridge 4 ⊖	d		17 15		17 17	17 23					17 32		17 42		17 44	17 47				17 49			17 57
New Cross Gate	d																						
Norwood Junction 2	a				17 30						17 43									18 01			
East Croydon	a	17 27	17 29	17 32	17 34	17 35	17 36	17 40	17 47	17 48	17 49	17 51	17 54	17 55	17 57	17 58	17 59	18 02	18 05	18 05	18 07	18 10	18 11
South Croydon 4	a	17 30	17 32		17 37									17 58	18 01					18 08			
Purley Oaks	a	17 33			17 40									18 01						18 11			
Purley 4	a	17 36			17 44						17 55			18 04						18 14			

		SN 1 B	SN 1 B	SN 1 A	SN ◇1	SN 1	SN ◇1 (T)	FC 1	SN 1	SN	SN 1	SN	SN ◇1	SN	SN 1	SN 1	SN 1	FC 1	SN 1	SN ◇1	SN 1	SN	FC 1
London Victoria 15 ⊖	d				18 02		18 06			18 09			18 17			18 19	18 23			18 32	18 36	18 39	
Clapham Junction 10	d				18 08		18 12			18 15		18 02	18 23			18 26	18 30			18 38	18 42	18 45	
St Pancras International 15 ⊖	d							17 40										18 08					18 20
Farringdon 3 ⊖	d							17 45										18 13					18 25
City Thameslink 3	d							17 49										18 17					18 29
London Blackfriars 3 ⊖	d							17 51										18 20					18 32
London Bridge 4 ⊖	d	17 57	17 59	17 59		18 08			18 12		18 16			18 18	18 23			18 27	18 30				
New Cross Gate	d																						
Norwood Junction 2	a	18 08		18 11										18 30					18 41				
East Croydon	a	18 13	18 14	18 15	18 17	18 21	18 22	18 24	18 24	18 27	18 30	18 32	18 33	18 35	18 36	18 37	18 40	18 41	18 45	18 48	18 52	18 57	19 00
South Croydon 4	a									18 30	18 33	18 35		18 39								19 00	
Purley Oaks	a									18 33		18 38		18 45								19 03	
Purley 4	a	18 19		18 20						18 36		18 40		18 48		18 42			18 50			19 06	

		SN 1	SN 1	SN	SN ◇1 (T)	SN	SN 1	FC 1	SN 1	SN 1	SN ◇1 (T)	SN (T)	SN 1	FC 1	SN 1	SN	SN	SN ◇1 (T)	FC 1	SN 1	SN ◇1 (T)	SN 1
London Victoria 15 ⊖	d			18 45	18 47		18 51		18 53		19 02	19 06			19 10		19 15	19 17		19 23	19 32	
Clapham Junction 10	d		18 34	18 53	18 53		18 57		19 00		19 08	19 12			19 16		19 23	19 23		19 29	19 38	
St Pancras International 15 ⊖	d							18 34						18 54					19 09			
Farringdon 3 ⊖	d							18 40						18 59					19 14			
City Thameslink 3	d							18 43						19 03					19 18			
London Blackfriars 3 ⊖	d							18 46						19 05					19 20			
London Bridge 4 ⊖	d	18 47				18 49		18 57		18 59			19 08	19 12		19 06			19 27			19 33
New Cross Gate	d									19 06						19 11						19 39
Norwood Junction 2	a					19 01				19 13						19 29						19 46
East Croydon	a	19 00	19 02	19 13	19 03	19 05	19 07	19 10	19 10	19 17	19 18	19 22	19 22	19 24	19 27	19 33	19 44	19 33	19 39	19 39	19 48	19 50
South Croydon 4	a	19 03		19 16		19 08										19 36	19 47					
Purley Oaks	a			19 19		19 11										19 39	19 50					
Purley 4	a			19 22		19 14				19 24					19 33	19 42	19 53					19 56

		SN	FC 1	SN 1	SN	SN	SN ◇1 (T)	SN 1	FC 1	SN 1	SN ◇1 (T)	SN 1	SN ◇1	FC 1	SN 1	SN	SN	SN ◇1	SN 1	SN 1	SN ◇1	SN 1	SN ◇1
London Victoria 15 ⊖	d	19 36		19 40		19 45	19 47			19 53	20 02		20 06		20 10		20 15	20 17	20 23		20 32		20 36
Clapham Junction 10	d	19 42		19 46		19 53	19 53			19 59	20 08		20 12		20 16		20 23	20 23	20 29		20 38		20 42
St Pancras International 15 ⊖	d		19 24						19 39					19 54									
Farringdon 3 ⊖	d		19 29						19 44					19 59									
City Thameslink 3	d		19 33						19 48					20 03									
London Blackfriars 3 ⊖	d		19 35						19 50					20 05									
London Bridge 4 ⊖	d		19 42		19 36			19 52	19 57			20 04		20 12		20 06				20 28		20 34	
New Cross Gate	d				19 41											20 11							
Norwood Junction 2	a				19 59			20 03				20 16				20 29						20 45	
East Croydon	a	19 52	19 54	19 57	20 03	20 14	20 03	20 06	20 09	20 09	20 19	20 19	20 22	20 24	20 27	20 33	20 44	20 33	20 39	20 40	20 48	20 49	20 52
South Croydon 4	a				20 06	20 17										20 36	20 47						
Purley Oaks	a				20 09	20 21										20 39	20 50						
Purley 4	a			20 03	20 12	20 24		20 12							20 33	20 42	20 53						

		FC 1	SN 1	SN	SN	SN ◇1	SN 1	SN 1	SN 1	SN 1	SN ◇1	FC 1	SN 1	SN	SN	SN ◇1	SN 1	SN 1	SN 1	SN ◇1	FC 1	SN 1
London Victoria 15 ⊖	d		20 40		20 45	20 47	20 53		21 02		21 06		21 10		21 15	21 17	21 23		21 32	21 36		21 40
Clapham Junction 10	d		20 46		20 53	20 53	20 59		21 08		21 12		21 16		21 23	21 23	21 29		21 38	21 42		21 46
St Pancras International 15 ⊖	d	20 24										20 54									21 24	
Farringdon 3 ⊖	d	20 29										20 59									21 29	
City Thameslink 3	d	20 33										21 03									21 33	
London Blackfriars 3 ⊖	d	20 35										21 05									21 35	
London Bridge 4 ⊖	d	20 42		20 36				20 58		21 04		21 12		21 06				21 26			21 42	
New Cross Gate	d			20 41										21 11								
Norwood Junction 2	a			20 59						21 15				21 29				21 37				
East Croydon	a	20 54	20 57	21 03	21 14	21 03	21 09	21 10	21 18	21 19	21 22	21 24	21 27	21 33	21 44	21 33	21 39	21 41	21 48	21 52	21 54	21 57
South Croydon 4	a			21 06	21 17									21 36	21 47							
Purley Oaks	a			21 09	21 20									21 39	21 50							
Purley 4	a		21 03	21 12	21 23								21 33	21 42	21 53							22 03

A until 18 May
B from 21 May

London - East Croydon and Purley

COMPLETE SERVICE

		SN	SN	SN ◇1	SN 1	SN ◇1	SN 1	SN ◇1	FC 1	SN 1	SN	SN ◇1	SN	SN 1	SN	SN 1	SN	FC 1 A	FC 1 B	SN 1	SN	SN ◇1	SN
London Victoria 15 ⊖	d		21 45	21 47	21 53	22 02		22 06		22 10	22 15	22 17		22 23		22 32	22 36			22 40	22 45	22 47	
Clapham Junction 10	d		21 53	21 53	21 59	22 08		22 12		22 16	22 23	22 23		22 29		22 38	22 42			22 46	22 53	22 53	
St Pancras International 15 ⊖	d								21 54									22 24					
Farringdon 3 ⊖	d								21 59									22 29					
City Thameslink 3	d								22 03									22 33					
London Blackfriars 3 ⊖	d								22 05									22 35					
London Bridge 4 ⊖	d	21 36					22 04		22 12				22 08		22 26			22 42	22 42				22 38
New Cross Gate	d	21 41											22 13										22 43
Norwood Junction 2	a	21 59					22 15						22 31		22 38								23 01
East Croydon	a	22 03	22 14	22 03	22 09	22 18	22 19	22 22	22 24	22 26	22 44	22 33	22 35	22 39	22 42	22 48	22 52	22 54	22 54	22 57	23 14	23 03	23 06
South Croydon 4	a	22 06	22 17								22 47		22 38								23 17		23 09
Purley Oaks	a	22 09	22 20								22 50		22 41								23 20		23 12
Purley 4	a	22 12	22 23							22 33	22 53		22 44							23 03	23 23		23 15

		SN 1	SN	SN ◇1	SN 1	SN ◇1	FC 1 A	FC 1 B	SN 1	SN	SN	SN ◇1	SN 1	SN ◇1	FC 1 A	FC 1 B	SN 1	SN	SN FO	SN 1	SN 1	FC 1 A
London Victoria 15 ⊖	d	22 53		23 02		23 06			23 10		23 15	23 17	23 24	23 32					23 45	23 47	23 49	
Clapham Junction 10	d	22 59		23 08		23 12			23 16		23 23	23 23	23 30	23 38			23 40		23 53	23 53	23 56	
St Pancras International 15 ⊖	d						22 54								23 24							23 54
Farringdon 3 ⊖	d						22 59								23 29							23 59
City Thameslink 3	d						23 03															
London Blackfriars 3 ⊖	d						23 05								23 35							00 05
London Bridge 4 ⊖	d		22 56		23 04		23 12	23 12		23 06					23 42	23 42		23 36				00 12
New Cross Gate	d									23 11								23 41				
Norwood Junction 2	a		23 07		23 15					23 29								23 59				
East Croydon	a	23 09	23 11	23 19	23 19	23 22	23 24	23 24	23 27	23 33	23 44	23 33	23 40	23 51	23 56	23 56	00 01	00 03	00 14	00 05	00 09	00 26
South Croydon 4	a									23 36	23 47							00 06	00 17			
Purley Oaks	a									23 39	23 50							00 09	00 20			
Purley 4	a								23 33	23 42	23 54							00 12	00 23	00 11		

Saturdays

		SN 1	SN	SN	SN 1	SN 1	SN ◇1	FC 1 C	FC D	SN 1	SN	SN	SN ◇1 E	SN ◇1 E	FC 1 C	FC D	SN	SN	SN ◇1	FC 1 C	FC 1 D	SN E	SN ◇1 E
London Victoria 15 ⊖	d			23p45	23p47	23p49	00 05			00 14		00 16	00 25	00 40				00 42	01 00			01 12	01 30
Clapham Junction 10	d	23p40		23p53	23p53	23p56	00 11			00 20		00 24	00 31	00 46				00 50	01 08			01 18	01 36
St Pancras International 15 ⊖	d							23p54							00 24					00 54			
Farringdon 3 ⊖	d							23p59							00 29					00 59			
City Thameslink 3	d																						
London Blackfriars 3 ⊖	d							00 05							00 35					01 05			
London Bridge 4 ⊖	d		23p36					00 12	00 12		00 06				00 42	00 42	00 36				01 05		
New Cross Gate	d		23p41								00 11						00 41						
Norwood Junction 2	a		23p59								00 29						00 59						
East Croydon	a	00 01	00 03	00 14	00 05	00 09	00 24	00 26	00 26	00 31	00 33	00 44	00 40	00 55	00 56	00 56	01 03	01 10	01 21	01 31	01 31	01 38	01 45
South Croydon 4	a		00 06	00 17							00 37	00 50											
Purley Oaks	a		00 09	00 20							00 40	00 53											
Purley 4	a		00 12	00 23	00 11					00 37	00 43	00 56	00 46						01 27				01 51

		FC 1 D	SN E	SN 1	FC 1 C	FC 1 D	SN 1	FC 1 C	FC 1 D	FC 1 D	FC 1	SN ◇1	FC 1 C	FC 1 D	FC 1 C	FC 1 D	SN ◇1	FC 1	FC 1 D	SN 1	SN ◇1	FC 1	FC 1 D
London Victoria 15 ⊖	d		01 42	02 00			03 00					04 00					05 02			05 23	05 32		
Clapham Junction 10	d		01 48	02 08			03 08					04 08					05 08			05 29	05 38		
St Pancras International 15 ⊖	d				01 54			02 54			03 28		03 54		04 24			04 54				05 34	
Farringdon 3 ⊖	d																	04 59				05 39	
City Thameslink 3	d																						
London Blackfriars 3 ⊖	d				02 05			03 05			03 39		04 05		04 35			05 04				05 45	
London Bridge 4 ⊖	d	01 35				02 05			03 05	03 35				04 05		04 35			05 05			05 52	05 52
New Cross Gate	d																						
Norwood Junction 2	a																			05 46			
East Croydon	a	02 02	02 11	02 21	02 31	02 31	03 21	03 31	03 31	04 01	04 03	04 21	04 31	04 31	05 01	05 01	05 21	05 31	05 31	05 49	05 47	06 04	06 04
South Croydon 4	a																			05 52			
Purley Oaks	a																						
Purley 4	a			02 27			03 27					04 27					05 26				05 53		

A from 21 May
B until 18 May
C not 19 May
D 19 May
E 28 July, 4 August, 11 August, 1 September, 8 September

Table 175

Saturdays

London - East Croydon and Purley

COMPLETE SERVICE

		SN 1		SN 1	FC 1	SN 1	FC 1	SN 1	FC 1	FC 1	SN 1	SN		SN	FC 1	FC 1	SN	SN 1	SN 1	SN ◇1	SN 1	FC 1		SN	SN
							A			A						A									
London Victoria 15 ⊖	d	06 02				06 23		06 32									06 43	06 53		07 06					
Clapham Junction 10	d	06 08				06 29		06 38			06 34						06 51	06 59		07 12					
St Pancras International 15 ⊖	d				05 54				06 24						06 39							06 54			
Farringdon 3 ⊖	d				05 59				06 29						06 44							06 59			
City Thameslink 3	d																								
London Blackfriars 3 ⊖	d				06 05				06 35						06 50							07 05			
London Bridge 4 ⊖	d			06 08	06 12		06 27		06 42	06 42		06 36		06 50	06 57	06 57			07 03		07 08	07 12		07 06	07 20
New Cross Gate	d											06 41							07 08					07 11	
Norwood Junction 2	a											06 59		07 02					07 16					07 29	07 32
East Croydon	a	06 17		06 22	06 24	06 39	06 39	06 47	06 54	06 54	06 57	07 03		07 06	07 09	07 09	07 12	07 09	07 20	07 22	07 22	07 24		07 33	07 36
South Croydon 4	a										07 01	07 06					07 15							07 36	
Purley Oaks	a											07 09					07 18							07 39	
Purley 4	a	06 23						06 53				07 12		07 15			07 21		07 26					07 42	07 45

		FC 1	FC 1	SN	SN 1	SN ◇1	SN 1	SN ◇1		FC 1	SN 1	SN 1	SN	SN ◇1	SN	SN	SN ◇1	FC 1		SN 1	FC 1	SN ◇1	SN 1	SN ◇1	SN 1
			A																		A				
London Victoria 15 ⊖	d			07 13	07 23	07 32		07 36					07 43	07 47			07 51			07 53		08 02		08 06	
Clapham Junction 10	d			07 21	07 29	07 38		07 42			07 34		07 51	07 53						07 59		08 08		08 12	
St Pancras International 15 ⊖	d	07 09								07 24								07 39							
Farringdon 3 ⊖	d	07 14								07 29								07 44							
City Thameslink 3	d																								
London Blackfriars 3 ⊖	d	07 20								07 35								07 50							
London Bridge 4 ⊖	d	07 27	07 27				07 33			07 42		07 45			07 36	07 50		07 57			07 57		08 03		08 08
New Cross Gate	d						07 38								07 41								08 08		
Norwood Junction 2	a						07 46					07 55			07 59	08 02							08 16		
East Croydon	a	07 39	07 39	07 42	07 39	07 47	07 50	07 52		07 54	07 57	07 59	08 12	08 02	08 03	08 06	08 07	08 09		08 09	08 09	08 17	08 20	08 22	08 22
South Croydon 4	a			07 45							08 01		08 15		08 06										
Purley Oaks	a			07 48									08 18		08 09										
Purley 4	a			07 51			07 56					08 05	08 21		08 12	08 15							08 26		

		FC 1	SN 1	SN		SN ◇1	SN	SN	FC 1	SN 1	FC 1	SN ◇1	SN 1	SN ◇1		FC 1	SN 1	SN 1	SN	SN ◇1	SN	SN	SN ◇1	FC 1	SN 1
											A														
London Victoria 15 ⊖	d			08 13		08 17				08 23		08 32		08 36					08 43	08 47			08 51		08 53
Clapham Junction 10	d			08 21		08 23				08 29		08 38		08 42			08 34		08 51	08 53					08 59
St Pancras International 15 ⊖	d	07 54							08 09							08 24								08 39	
Farringdon 3 ⊖	d	07 59							08 14							08 29								08 44	
City Thameslink 3	d																								
London Blackfriars 3 ⊖	d	08 05							08 20							08 35								08 50	
London Bridge 4 ⊖	d	08 12	08 15				08 06	08 20	08 27		08 27		08 33			08 42		08 45			08 36	08 50		08 57	
New Cross Gate	d						08 11						08 38								08 41				
Norwood Junction 2	a		08 25				08 29	08 32					08 46					08 55			08 59	09 02			
East Croydon	a	08 24	08 29	08 42		08 32	08 33	08 36	08 39	08 39	08 39	08 47	08 50	08 52		08 54	08 57	08 59	09 12	09 02	09 03	09 06	09 07	09 09	09 09
South Croydon 4	a			08 45			08 36										09 01		09 15		09 06				
Purley Oaks	a			08 48			08 39												09 18		09 09				
Purley 4	a		08 35	08 52			08 42	08 45					08 56					09 05	09 21		09 12	09 15			

			FC 1	SN ◇1	SN 1	SN ◇1 ⌶	SN 1	FC 1	SN 1	SN	SN ◇1		SN	SN	FC 1	SN 1	FC 1	SN ◇1	SN 1	SN ◇1 ⌶	FC 1		SN 1	SN 1	SN
			A														A								
London Victoria 15 ⊖	d			09 02		09 06				09 13	09 17					09 23		09 32		09 36					09 43
Clapham Junction 10	d			09 08		09 12				09 21	09 23					09 29		09 38		09 42			09 34		09 51
St Pancras International 15 ⊖	d							08 54							09 09						09 24				
Farringdon 3 ⊖	d							08 59							09 14						09 29				
City Thameslink 3	d							09 03							09 18						09 33				
London Blackfriars 3 ⊖	d							09 05							09 20						09 35				
London Bridge 4 ⊖	d		08 57		09 03		09 08	09 12	09 15				09 06	09 20	09 27		09 27		09 33		09 42			09 45	
New Cross Gate	d				09 08								09 11						09 38						
Norwood Junction 2	a				09 16				09 25				09 29	09 32					09 46					09 55	
East Croydon	a		09 09	09 17	09 20	09 22	09 22	09 24	09 29	09 42	09 32		09 33	09 36	09 39	09 39	09 39	09 47	09 50	09 52	09 54		09 57	09 59	10 12
South Croydon 4	a									09 45			09 36										10 01		10 15
Purley Oaks	a									09 48			09 39												10 18
Purley 4	a				09 26				09 35	09 51			09 42	09 45					09 56					10 05	10 21

		SN ◇1	SN	SN	SN ◇1	FC 1	and at the same minutes past each hour until	FC 1		SN 1	FC 1	SN ◇1 ⌶	SN 1	SN ◇1 ⌶	SN 1	FC 1	SN 1	SN		SN ◇1	SN	SN	FC 1	SN 1
											A													
London Victoria 15 ⊖	d	09 47			09 51					12 53		13 02		13 06				13 13		13 17				13 23
Clapham Junction 10	d	09 53								12 59		13 08		13 12				13 21		13 23				13 29
St Pancras International 15 ⊖	d					09 39		12 39								12 54							13 09	
Farringdon 3 ⊖	d					09 44		12 44								12 59							13 14	
City Thameslink 3	d					09 48		12 48								13 03							13 18	
London Blackfriars 3 ⊖	d					09 50		12 50								13 05							13 20	
London Bridge 4 ⊖	d		09 36	09 50		09 57		12 57			12 57		13 03		13 08	13 12	13 15				13 06	13 20	13 27	
New Cross Gate	d		09 41										13 08								13 11			
Norwood Junction 2	a		09 59	10 02									13 16				13 25				13 29	13 32		
East Croydon	a	10 02	10 03	10 06	10 07	10 09		13 09		13 09	13 09	13 17	13 20	13 22	13 22	13 24	13 29	13 42		13 32	13 33	13 36	13 39	13 39
South Croydon 4	a		10 06															13 45			13 36			
Purley Oaks	a		10 09															13 48			13 39			
Purley 4	a		10 12	10 15									13 26				13 35	13 51			13 42	13 45		

A 19 May

Table 175

Saturdays

London - East Croydon and Purley

COMPLETE SERVICE

		FC 1	SN ◇1	SN 1	SN ◇1 ⌶		FC 1	SN 1	SN 1	SN	SN ◇1	SN	SN	SN ◇1	FC 1		SN 1	FC 1	SN ◇1 ⌶	SN 1	SN ◇1 ⌶	SN 1	FC 1	SN 1	SN
		A																A							
London Victoria 15 ⊖	d		13 32		13 36					13 43	13 47			13 51			13 53		14 02		14 06				14 13
Clapham Junction 10	d		13 38		13 42			13 34		13 51	13 53						13 59		14 08		14 12				14 21
St Pancras International 15 ⊖	d						13 24								13 39								13 54		
Farringdon 3 ⊖	d						13 29								13 44								13 59		
City Thameslink 3	d						13 33								13 48								14 03		
London Blackfriars 3 ⊖	d						13 35								13 50								14 05		
London Bridge 4 ⊖	d	13 27		13 33			13 42		13 45			13 36	13 50		13 57			13 57		14 03		14 08	14 12	14 15	
New Cross Gate	d			13 38								13 41								14 08					
Norwood Junction 2	a			13 46					13 55			13 59	14 02							14 16				14 25	
East Croydon	a	13 39	13 47	13 50	13 52		13 54	13 57	13 59	14 12	14 02	14 03	14 06	14 07	14 09		14 09	14 09	14 17	14 20	14 22	14 22	14 24	14 29	14 42
South Croydon 4	a							14 01		14 15		14 06													14 45
Purley Oaks	a									14 18		14 09													14 48
Purley 4	a			13 56					14 05	14 22		14 12	14 15							14 26				14 35	14 52

			SN ◇1	SN	SN	FC 1	SN 1	FC 1	SN ◇1	SN 1	SN ◇1 ⌶		FC 1	SN 1	SN 1	SN	SN ◇1	SN	SN	SN ◇1	FC 1		SN 1	FC 1	SN ◇1 ⌶
								A																A	
London Victoria 15 ⊖	d		14 17				14 23		14 32		14 36					14 43	14 47			14 51			14 53		15 02
Clapham Junction 10	d		14 23				14 29		14 38		14 42			14 34		14 51	14 53						14 59		15 08
St Pancras International 15 ⊖	d					14 09							14 24								14 39				
Farringdon 3 ⊖	d					14 14							14 29								14 44				
City Thameslink 3	d					14 18							14 33								14 48				
London Blackfriars 3 ⊖	d					14 20							14 35								14 50				
London Bridge 4 ⊖	d			14 06	14 20	14 27		14 27		14 33			14 42		14 45			14 36	14 50		14 57			14 57	
New Cross Gate	d			14 11						14 38								14 41							
Norwood Junction 2	a			14 29	14 32					14 46					14 55			14 59	15 02						
East Croydon	a		14 32	14 33	14 36	14 39	14 39	14 39	14 47	14 50	14 52		14 54	14 57	14 59	15 12	15 02	15 03	15 06	15 07	15 09		15 09	15 09	15 17
South Croydon 4	a			14 36										15 01		15 15		15 06							
Purley Oaks	a			14 39												15 18		15 09							
Purley 4	a			14 42	14 45					14 56					15 05	15 21		15 12	15 15						

		SN 1	SN ◇1 ⌶	SN 1	FC 1	SN 1	SN		SN ◇1	SN	SN	FC 1	SN 1	FC 1	SN ◇1	SN 1	SN ◇1 ⌶		FC 1	SN 1	SN 1	SN	SN ◇1	SN	SN
														A											
London Victoria 15 ⊖	d		15 06				15 13		15 17				15 23		15 32		15 36					15 43	15 47		
Clapham Junction 10	d		15 12				15 21		15 23				15 29		15 38		15 42			15 34		15 51	15 53		
St Pancras International 15 ⊖	d				14 54							15 09							15 24						
Farringdon 3 ⊖	d				14 59							15 14							15 29						
City Thameslink 3	d				15 03							15 18							15 33						
London Blackfriars 3 ⊖	d				15 05							15 20							15 35						
London Bridge 4 ⊖	d	15 03		15 08	15 12	15 15				15 06	15 20	15 27		15 27		15 33			15 42		15 45			15 36	15 50
New Cross Gate	d	15 08								15 11						15 38								15 41	
Norwood Junction 2	a	15 16				15 25				15 29	15 32					15 46					15 55			15 59	16 02
East Croydon	a	15 20	15 22	15 22	15 24	15 29	15 42		15 32	15 33	15 36	15 39	15 39	15 39	15 47	15 50	15 52		15 54	15 57	15 59	16 12	16 02	16 03	16 06
South Croydon 4	a						15 45			15 36										16 01		16 15		16 06	
Purley Oaks	a						15 48			15 39												16 18		16 09	
Purley 4	a	15 26				15 35	15 51			15 42	15 45					15 56					16 05	16 21		16 12	16 15

		SN ◇1	FC 1		SN 1	FC 1	SN ◇1 ⌶	SN 1	SN ◇1 ⌶	SN 1	FC 1	SN 1	SN		SN ◇1	SN	SN	FC 1	SN 1	FC 1	SN ◇1	SN 1	SN ◇1 ⌶		FC 1
						A														A					
London Victoria 15 ⊖	d	15 51			15 53		16 02		16 06				16 13		16 17				16 23		16 32		16 36		
Clapham Junction 10	d				15 59		16 08		16 12				16 21		16 23				16 29		16 38		16 42		
St Pancras International 15 ⊖	d		15 39								15 54							16 09							16 24
Farringdon 3 ⊖	d		15 44								15 59							16 14							16 29
City Thameslink 3	d		15 48								16 03							16 18							16 33
London Blackfriars 3 ⊖	d		15 50								16 05							16 20							16 35
London Bridge 4 ⊖	d		15 57			15 57		16 03		16 08	16 12	16 15				16 06	16 20	16 27		16 27		16 33			16 42
New Cross Gate	d							16 08								16 11						16 38			
Norwood Junction 2	a							16 16				16 25				16 29	16 32					16 46			
East Croydon	a	16 07	16 09		16 09	16 09	16 17	16 20	16 22	16 22	16 24	16 29	16 42		16 32	16 33	16 36	16 39	16 39	16 39	16 47	16 50	16 52		16 54
South Croydon 4	a												16 45			16 36									
Purley Oaks	a												16 48			16 39									
Purley 4	a							16 26				16 35	16 51			16 42	16 45					16 56			

A 19 May

Table 175

Saturdays

London - East Croydon and Purley
COMPLETE SERVICE

	SN 1	SN 1	SN	SN ◇1	SN	SN	SN ◇1	FC 1	SN 1	FC 1 A	SN ◇1 H	SN 1	SN ◇1 H	SN 1	FC 1	SN 1	SN	SN ◇1	SN	SN	FC 1	SN 1
London Victoria 15 ⊖ d			16 43	16 47			16 51		16 53		17 02		17 06				17 13	17 17				17 23
Clapham Junction 10 d	16 34		16 51	16 53					16 59		17 08		17 12				17 21	17 23				17 29
St Pancras International 15 ⊖ d								16 39							16 54						17 09	
Farringdon 3 ⊖ d								16 44							16 59						17 14	
City Thameslink 3 d								16 48							17 03						17 18	
London Blackfriars 3 ⊖ d								16 50							17 05						17 20	
London Bridge 4 ⊖ d		16 45			16 36	16 50		16 57		16 57		17 03		17 08	17 12	17 15			17 06	17 20	17 27	
New Cross Gate d					16 41							17 08							17 11			
Norwood Junction 2 a		16 55			16 59	17 02						17 16				17 25			17 29	17 32		
East Croydon a	16 57	16 59	17 12	17 02	17 03	17 06	17 07	17 09	17 09	17 09	17 17	17 20	17 22	17 22	17 24	17 29	17 42	17 32	17 33	17 36	17 39	17 39
South Croydon 4 a	17 01		17 15		17 06												17 45		17 36			
Purley Oaks a			17 18		17 09												17 48		17 39			
Purley 4 a		17 05	17 21		17 12	17 15						17 26				17 35	17 51		17 42	17 45		

	FC 1 A	SN ◇1	SN 1	SN ◇1 H	FC 1	SN 1	SN 1	SN	SN ◇1	SN	SN	SN ◇1	FC 1	SN 1	FC 1 A	SN ◇1 H	SN 1	SN ◇1 H	SN 1	FC 1	SN 1	SN
London Victoria 15 ⊖ d		17 32		17 36				17 43	17 47			17 51		17 53		18 02		18 06				18 13
Clapham Junction 10 d		17 38		17 42		17 34		17 51	17 53					17 59		18 08		18 12				18 21
St Pancras International 15 ⊖ d					17 24								17 39							17 54		
Farringdon 3 ⊖ d					17 29								17 44							17 59		
City Thameslink 3 d					17 33								17 48							18 03		
London Blackfriars 3 ⊖ d					17 35								17 50							18 05		
London Bridge 4 ⊖ d	17 27		17 33		17 42		17 45			17 36	17 50		17 57		17 57		18 03		18 08	18 12	18 15	
New Cross Gate d			17 38							17 41							18 08					
Norwood Junction 2 a			17 46				17 56			17 59	18 02						18 16				18 25	
East Croydon a	17 39	17 47	17 50	17 52	17 54	17 57	18 00	18 12	18 02	18 03	18 06	18 07	18 09	18 09	18 09	18 17	18 20	18 22	18 22	18 24	18 29	18 42
South Croydon 4 a						18 01		18 15		18 06												18 45
Purley Oaks a								18 18		18 09												18 48
Purley 4 a			17 56				18 06	18 21		18 12	18 15						18 26				18 35	18 51

	SN ◇1	SN	SN	FC 1	SN 1	FC 1 A	SN ◇1	SN 1	SN ◇1 H	FC 1	SN 1	SN 1	SN	SN ◇1	SN	SN	SN ◇1	FC 1	SN 1	FC 1 A	SN ◇1 H
London Victoria 15 ⊖ d	18 17				18 23		18 32		18 36				18 43	18 47			18 51		18 53		19 02
Clapham Junction 10 d	18 23				18 29		18 38		18 42		18 34		18 51	18 53					18 59		19 08
St Pancras International 15 ⊖ d				18 09						18 24								18 39			
Farringdon 3 ⊖ d				18 14						18 29								18 44			
City Thameslink 3 d				18 18						18 33								18 48			
London Blackfriars 3 ⊖ d				18 20						18 35								18 50			
London Bridge 4 ⊖ d		18 06	18 20	18 27		18 27		18 33		18 42		18 45			18 36	18 50		18 57		18 57	
New Cross Gate d		18 11						18 38							18 41						
Norwood Junction 2 a		18 29	18 32					18 46				18 55			18 59	19 02					
East Croydon a	18 32	18 33	18 36	18 39	18 39	18 39	18 47	18 50	18 52	18 54	18 57	18 59	19 12	19 02	19 03	19 06	19 07	19 09	19 09	19 09	19 17
South Croydon 4 a		18 36									19 01		19 15		19 06						
Purley Oaks a		18 39											19 18		19 09						
Purley 4 a		18 42	18 45					18 56				19 05	19 21		19 12	19 15					

	SN 1	SN ◇1 H	SN 1	FC 1	SN	SN	SN ◇1	SN	FC 1	SN 1	FC 1 A	SN ◇1	SN 1	SN ◇1	FC 1	SN 1	SN	SN ◇1	SN	SN	SN ◇1	FC 1
London Victoria 15 ⊖ d		19 06				19 13	19 17			19 23		19 32		19 36			19 43	19 47			19 51	
Clapham Junction 10 d		19 12				19 21	19 23			19 29		19 38		19 42		19 34	19 51	19 53				
St Pancras International 15 ⊖ d				18 54					19 09						19 24							19 39
Farringdon 3 ⊖ d				18 59					19 14						19 29							19 44
City Thameslink 3 d				19 03					19 18						19 33							19 48
London Blackfriars 3 ⊖ d				19 05					19 20						19 35							19 50
London Bridge 4 ⊖ d	19 03		19 08	19 12	19 06			19 20	19 27		19 27		19 33		19 42				19 36	19 50		19 57
New Cross Gate d	19 08				19 11								19 38						19 41			
Norwood Junction 2 a	19 16				19 29			19 32					19 46						19 59	20 02		
East Croydon a	19 20	19 22	19 22	19 24	19 33	19 42	19 33	19 36	19 39	19 39	19 39	19 47	19 50	19 52	19 54	19 57	20 12	20 02	20 03	20 06	20 07	20 09
South Croydon 4 a					19 36	19 45											20 15		20 06			
Purley Oaks a					19 39	19 48											20 18		20 09			
Purley 4 a	19 26				19 42	19 51		19 45					19 56				20 21		20 12	20 15		

A 19 May

Table 175

Saturdays

London - East Croydon and Purley
COMPLETE SERVICE

	SN 1	FC 1 A	SN ◇1	SN ◇1	SN 1	FC 1	SN 1	SN	SN ◇1	SN	SN	SN ◇1	SN 1	SN ◇1	SN ◇1	FC 1	SN 1	SN 1	SN	SN ◇1	SN
London Victoria 15 ⊖ d	19 53		20 02	20 06			20 10	20 13	20 17			20 21	20 23	20 32	20 36		20 40		20 43	20 47	
Clapham Junction 10 d	19 59		20 08	20 12			20 16	20 21	20 23				20 29	20 38	20 42		20 46	20 34	20 51	20 53	
St Pancras International 15 ⊖ d						19 54										20 24					
Farringdon 3 ⊖ d						19 59										20 29					
City Thameslink 3 d						20 03										20 33					
London Blackfriars 3 ⊖ d						20 05										20 35					
London Bridge 4 ⊖ d		19 57			20 08	20 12				20 06	20 20					20 42					20 36
New Cross Gate d										20 11											20 41
Norwood Junction 2 a					20 19					20 29	20 32										20 59
East Croydon a	20 09	20 09	20 17	20 22	20 22	20 24	20 29	20 42	20 32	20 33	20 36	20 37	20 39	20 47	20 52	20 54	20 57	20 59	21 12	21 02	21 03
South Croydon 4 a								20 45		20 36									21 15		21 06
Purley Oaks a								20 48		20 39									21 18		21 09
Purley 4 a							20 34	20 51		20 42	20 45						21 03		21 21		21 12

	SN	SN 1	SN ◇1	SN ◇1	SN 1	FC 1	SN 1	SN	SN	SN ◇1	SN	SN 1	SN	SN ◇1	FC 1	SN 1	SN	SN ◇1	SN	SN	SN 1	SN ◇1
London Victoria 15 ⊖ d		20 53	21 02	21 06			21 10		21 13	21 17		21 23	21 32	21 36		21 40	21 43	21 47			21 53	22 02
Clapham Junction 10 d		20 59	21 08	21 12			21 16		21 21	21 23		21 29	21 38	21 42		21 46	21 51	21 53			21 59	22 08
St Pancras International 15 ⊖ d						20 54									21 24							
Farringdon 3 ⊖ d						20 59									21 29							
City Thameslink 3 d						21 03																
London Blackfriars 3 ⊖ d						21 05									21 35							
London Bridge 4 ⊖ d	20 50				21 08	21 12		21 06			21 20				21 42				21 36	21 50		
New Cross Gate d								21 11											21 41			
Norwood Junction 2 a	21 02				21 19			21 29			21 32								21 59	22 02		
East Croydon a	21 06	21 09	21 17	21 22	21 22	21 24	21 27	21 33	21 42	21 33	21 36	21 39	21 47	21 52	21 54	21 57	22 12	22 03	22 04	22 07	22 09	22 17
South Croydon 4 a								21 36	21 45								22 15		22 07			
Purley Oaks a								21 39	21 48								22 18		22 10			
Purley 4 a	21 15						21 33	21 42	21 51		21 45					22 03	22 21		22 13	22 16		

	SN ◇1	SN 1	FC 1	SN 1	SN	SN ◇1	SN	SN	SN 1	SN 1	SN ◇1	FC 1	SN 1	SN	SN	SN ◇1	SN	SN 1	SN ◇1	SN 1	SN ◇1	FC 1
London Victoria 15 ⊖ d	22 06			22 10	22 13	22 17			22 23	22 32	22 36		22 40		22 43	22 47		22 53	23 02		23 06	
Clapham Junction 10 d	22 12			22 16	22 21	22 23			22 29	22 38	22 42		22 46		22 51	22 53		22 59	23 08		23 12	
St Pancras International 15 ⊖ d			21 54									22 24										22 54
Farringdon 3 ⊖ d			21 59									22 29										22 59
City Thameslink 3 d																						
London Blackfriars 3 ⊖ d			22 05									22 35										23 05
London Bridge 4 ⊖ d		22 08	22 12				22 06	22 20				22 42		22 36			22 50			23 04		23 12
New Cross Gate d							22 11							22 41								
Norwood Junction 2 a		22 19					22 29	22 32						22 59			23 02			23 15		
East Croydon a	22 22	22 22	22 24	22 27	22 42	22 33	22 35	22 37	22 39	22 47	22 52	22 54	22 57	23 03	23 13	23 03	23 06	23 09	23 17	23 19	23 22	23 24
South Croydon 4 a					22 46		22 38							23 06	23 16							
Purley Oaks a					22 49		22 41							23 09	23 19							
Purley 4 a				22 33	22 52		22 44	22 47					23 03	23 12	23 22		23 15					

	SN 1	SN	SN ◇1	SN	SN 1	SN 1	FC 1	SN	SN	SN 1	SN 1	FC 1
London Victoria 15 ⊖ d	23 10	23 15	23 17		23 24	23 32			23 45	23 47	23 49	
Clapham Junction 10 d	23 16	23 23	23 23		23 30	23 38			23 53	23 53	23 56	
St Pancras International 15 ⊖ d							23 24					23 54
Farringdon 3 ⊖ d							23 29					23 59
City Thameslink 3 d												
London Blackfriars 3 ⊖ d							23 35					00 05
London Bridge 4 ⊖ d				23 06			23 42	23 36				00 12
New Cross Gate d				23 11				23 41				
Norwood Junction 2 a				23 29				23 59				
East Croydon a	23 27	23 44	23 32	23 33	23 40	23 52	23 56	00 03	00 14	00 05	00 09	00 26
South Croydon 4 a		23 47		23 36				00 06	00 17			
Purley Oaks a		23 50		23 39				00 09	00 20			
Purley 4 a	23 33	23 53		23 42				00 13	00 23	00 11		

Sundays
until 24 June

	SN	SN	SN 1	SN 1	SN ◇1	FC 1	SN 1	SN	SN	FC 1	SN	SN	SN 1	FC 1	SN 1	SN 1	SN 1	SN 1	SN ◇1	SN ◇1	SN	SN ◇1
London Victoria 15 ⊖ d		23p45	23p47	23p49	00 05		00 14		00 16			00 42	01 00		02 00	03 00	04 00	05 02	05 47	06 32	06 36	07 02
Clapham Junction 10 d		23p53	23p53	23p56	00 11		00 20		00 24			00 50	01 08		02 08	03 08	04 08	05 08	05 53	06 38	06 42	07 08
St Pancras International 15 ⊖ d						23p54				00 24				00 54								
Farringdon 3 ⊖ d						23p59				00 29												
City Thameslink 3 d																						
London Blackfriars 3 ⊖ d						00 05				00 35				01 05								
London Bridge 4 ⊖ d	23p36					00 12		00 06		00 42	00 36											
New Cross Gate d	23p41							00 11			00 41											
Norwood Junction 2 a	23p59							00 29			00 59											
East Croydon a	00 03	00 14	00 05	00 09	00 24	00 26	00 31	00 33	00 44	00 56	01 03	01 10	01 21	01 31	02 21	03 21	04 21	05 21	06 05	06 51	07 03	07 19
South Croydon 4 a	00 06	00 17						00 37	00 50													
Purley Oaks a	00 09	00 20						00 40	00 53													
Purley 4 a	00 13	00 23	00 11				00 37	00 43	00 56				01 27		02 27	03 27	04 26	05 28		06 56	07 10	07 25

A 19 May

London - East Croydon and Purley

COMPLETE SERVICE

Sundays until 24 June

		SN	FC	SN	SN	SN	FC	SN	SN	SN	SN	SN	SN	FC	SN	SN	SN	SN	SN	SN	FC	SN	SN
		1	1		◇1	1	1		1			◇1	1	1			◇1		◇1	1	1		1
London Victoria 15 ⊖	d			07 06	07 27			07 36	07 40			08 02				08 06	08 17		08 27			08 36	08 40
Clapham Junction 10	d			07 12	07 33			07 42	07 45			08 08				08 12	08 23		08 33			08 42	08 45
St Pancras International 15 ⊖	d						07 24							07 54							08 24		
Farringdon 3 ⊖	d						07 29							07 59							08 29		
City Thameslink 3	d																						
London Blackfriars 3 ⊖	d		06 55				07 34							08 04							08 34		
London Bridge 4 ⊖	d	07 05				07 37	07 41			07 21	07 39		08 05	08 11	07 51			08 09		08 37	08 41		
New Cross Gate	d										07 44							08 14					
Norwood Junction 2	a	07 17				07 48					08 02		08 16					08 32		08 48			
East Croydon ⇌	a	07 21	07 24	07 33	07 42	07 54	07 55	08 03	07 57	08 01	08 07	08 17	08 20	08 25	08 30	08 33	08 32	08 37	08 42	08 54	08 55	09 03	08 57
South Croydon 4	a										08 10							08 40					
Purley Oaks	a										08 13							08 43					
Purley 4	a	07 28		07 40		08 00		08 10			08 16	08 23	08 26			08 40		08 46		09 00		09 10	

		SN	SN	SN	SN	SN	SN	FC	SN	SN	SN	SN	FC	SN	SN	SN	FC	SN	SN	SN	SN	SN
			◇1 ✕		◇1	1	◇1	1			◇1		1	◇1	◇1	1	1		1		◇1 ✕	
London Victoria 15 ⊖	d		08 47		09 02		09 06			09 06	09 17			09 27	09 36			09 36	09 40		09 47	
Clapham Junction 10	d		08 53		09 08		09 12			09 12	09 23			09 33	09 42			09 42	09 45		09 53	
St Pancras International 15 ⊖	d							08 54					09 09				09 24					
Farringdon 3 ⊖	d							08 58					09 14				09 29					
City Thameslink 3	d																					
London Blackfriars 3 ⊖	d							09 04					09 19				09 34					
London Bridge 4 ⊖	d	08 21		08 39		09 05		09 11	08 51			09 09	09 26			09 37	09 41			09 21		09 39
New Cross Gate	d			08 44								09 14										09 44
Norwood Junction 2	a			09 02		09 16						09 32				09 48						10 02
East Croydon ⇌	a	09 01	09 02	09 07	09 17	09 20	09 22	09 25	09 30	09 33	09 32	09 37	09 39	09 42	09 52	09 54	09 55	10 03	09 57	10 01	10 02	10 07
South Croydon 4	a			09 10								09 40										10 10
Purley Oaks	a			09 13								09 43										10 13
Purley 4	a			09 16	09 23	09 26				09 40		09 46				10 00		10 10				10 16

		FC	SN	SN	SN	FC	SN	SN	SN	SN	FC	SN	SN	SN	FC	SN	SN	SN	SN	SN	FC	SN	SN
		1	◇1	1	◇1 ✕	1			◇1		1	◇1	◇1 ✕	1	1		1		◇1 ✕		1	◇1 ✕	1
London Victoria 15 ⊖	d		10 02		10 06			10 06	10 17			10 27	10 36			10 36	10 40		10 47			11 02	
Clapham Junction 10	d		10 08		10 12			10 12	10 23			10 33	10 42			10 42	10 45		10 53			11 08	
St Pancras International 15 ⊖	d	09 39				09 54					10 09				10 24						10 39		
Farringdon 3 ⊖	d	09 44				09 59					10 14				10 29						10 44		
City Thameslink 3	d																						
London Blackfriars 3 ⊖	d	09 49				10 04					10 19				10 34						10 49		
London Bridge 4 ⊖	d	09 56		10 05		10 11	09 51			10 09	10 26			10 37	10 41			10 21		10 39	10 56		11 05
New Cross Gate	d									10 14										10 44			
Norwood Junction 2	a			10 16						10 32				10 48						11 02			11 16
East Croydon ⇌	a	10 09	10 17	10 20	10 22	10 25	10 30	10 33	10 32	10 37	10 39	10 42	10 52	10 54	10 55	11 03	10 57	11 01	11 02	11 07	11 09	11 17	11 20
South Croydon 4	a									10 40										11 10			
Purley Oaks	a									10 43										11 13			
Purley 4	a		10 23	10 26				10 40		10 46				11 00		11 10				11 16		11 23	11 26

		SN	FC		FC	SN	SN	SN	SN	SN	SN	SN	FC	SN	SN	SN	SN	SN	SN	SN	SN	FC
		◇1 ✕	1		1			◇1		◇1	◇1	1	1		1		◇1 ✕		◇1	1	◇1	1
London Victoria 15 ⊖	d	11 06					19 06	19 17		19 27	19 36			19 36	19 40		19 47		20 02		20 06	
Clapham Junction 10	d	11 12		and at the same minutes past each hour until			19 12	19 23		19 33	19 42			19 42	19 45		19 53		20 08		20 12	
St Pancras International 15 ⊖	d		10 54		18 54								19 24									19 54
Farringdon 3 ⊖	d		10 58		18 58								19 29									19 58
City Thameslink 3	d																					
London Blackfriars 3 ⊖	d		11 04		19 04								19 34									20 04
London Bridge 4 ⊖	d		11 11		19 11	18 51			19 09			19 37	19 41			19 21		19 39		20 05		20 11
New Cross Gate	d								19 14									19 44				
Norwood Junction 2	a								19 32			19 48						20 02		20 16		
East Croydon ⇌	a	11 22	11 25		19 25	19 30	19 33	19 32	19 37	19 42	19 52	19 54	19 55	20 03	19 57	20 01	20 02	20 07	20 17	20 20	20 22	20 25
South Croydon 4	a								19 40									20 10				
Purley Oaks	a								19 43									20 13				
Purley 4	a						19 40		19 46			20 00		20 10				20 16	20 23	20 26		

		SN	SN	SN	SN	SN	SN	SN	FC	SN	SN	SN	SN	SN	SN	SN	SN	FC	SN	SN	SN	SN
				◇1		◇1	◇1	1	1		1		◇1		◇1	1	◇1	1			◇1	
London Victoria 15 ⊖	d		20 06	20 17		20 27	20 36			20 36	20 40		20 47		21 02		21 06			21 06	21 17	
Clapham Junction 10	d		20 12	20 23		20 33	20 42			20 42	20 45		20 53		21 08		21 12			21 12	21 23	
St Pancras International 15 ⊖	d								20 24									20 54				
Farringdon 3 ⊖	d								20 29									20 58				
City Thameslink 3	d																					
London Blackfriars 3 ⊖	d								20 34									21 04				
London Bridge 4 ⊖	d	19 51			20 09			20 37	20 41			20 21		20 39		21 05		21 11	20 51			21 09
New Cross Gate	d				20 14									20 44								21 14
Norwood Junction 2	a				20 32			20 48						21 02		21 16						21 32
East Croydon ⇌	a	20 30	20 33	20 32	20 37	20 42	20 52	20 54	20 55	21 03	20 57	21 01	21 02	21 07	21 17	21 20	21 22	21 25	21 30	21 33	21 32	21 37
South Croydon 4	a				20 40									21 10								21 40
Purley Oaks	a				20 43									21 13								21 43
Purley 4	a		20 40		20 46			21 00		21 10				21 16	21 23	21 26				21 40		21 46

London - East Croydon and Purley

COMPLETE SERVICE

Sundays until 24 June

		SN	SN	FC	SN	SN	SN	SN	SN	SN	SN	FC	SN	SN	SN	SN	SN	SN	FC	SN	SN	SN	SN
		◇1	1	1		1		◇1		◇1	1	1			◇1		◇1	1	1		1		◇1
London Victoria 15 ⊖	d	21 27			21 36	21 40		21 47		22 02				22 06	22 17		22 27			22 36	22 40		22 47
Clapham Junction 10	d	21 33			21 42	21 45		21 53		22 08				22 12	22 23		22 33			22 42	22 45		22 53
St Pancras International 15 ⊖	d			21 24								21 54							22 24				
Farringdon 3 ⊖	d			21 29								21 59							22 29				
City Thameslink 3	d																						
London Blackfriars 3 ⊖	d			21 34								22 04							22 34				
London Bridge 4 ⊖	d		21 37	21 41			21 21		21 39		22 05	22 11	21 51			22 09		22 37	22 41			22 21	
New Cross Gate	d								21 44							22 14							
Norwood Junction 2	a		21 48						22 02		22 16					22 32		22 48					
East Croydon ⇌	a	21 42	21 54	21 55	22 03	21 57	22 01	22 02	22 07	22 17	22 20	22 25	22 30	22 33	22 32	22 37	22 42	22 54	22 55	23 03	22 57	23 00	23 03
South Croydon 4	a								22 10							22 40							
Purley Oaks	a								22 13							22 43							
Purley 4	a		22 00		22 10				22 16	22 23	22 26			22 40		22 46		23 00		23 10			

		SN	SN	FC	SN	SN	SN	SN	SN	FC	SN	SN	SN	SN	FC
			1	1			◇1		◇1	1					1
London Victoria 15 ⊖	d		23 04			23 06	23 17		23 32			23 47		23 50	
Clapham Junction 10	d		23 10			23 12	23 23		23 38			23 53		23 56	
St Pancras International 15 ⊖	d			22 54						23 24					23 54
Farringdon 3 ⊖	d			22 59						23 29					23 59
City Thameslink 3	d														
London Blackfriars 3 ⊖	d			23 04						23 34					00 05
London Bridge 4 ⊖	d	22 39		23 11	22 51			23 09		23 41	23 21		23 39		00 12
New Cross Gate	d	22 44						23 14					23 44		
Norwood Junction 2	a	23 02						23 32					00 02		
East Croydon ⇌	a	23 07	23 22	23 25	23 30	23 34	23 37	23 38	23 52	23 56	00 01	00 06	00 06	00 17	00 26
South Croydon 4	a	23 10				23 37							00 09	00 20	
Purley Oaks	a	23 13				23 40							00 12	00 23	
Purley 4	a	23 16	23 28			23 43							00 15	00 26	

Sundays 1 July to 9 September

		SN	SN	SN	SN	SN	FC	SN	SN	SN	SN	SN	FC	SN	SN	SN	FC	SN	SN	SN	SN	SN	SN
				1	1	◇1	1	1			◇1 A	◇1 A	1			1	1	A	◇1 A	A	1	1	1
London Victoria 15 ⊖	d		23p45	23p47	23p49	00 05		00 14		00 16	00 25	00 40			00 42	01 00		01 12	01 30	01 42	02 00	03 00	04 00
Clapham Junction 10	d		23p53	23p53	23p56	00 11		00 20		00 24	00 31	00 46			00 50	01 08		01 18	01 36	01 48	02 08	03 08	04 08
St Pancras International 15 ⊖	d						23p54				≀	≀	00 24				00 54	≀	≀	≀			
Farringdon 3 ⊖	d						23p59				≀	≀	00 29					≀	≀	≀			
City Thameslink 3	d										≀	≀						≀	≀	≀			
London Blackfriars 3 ⊖	d						00 05				≀	≀	00 35				01 05	≀	≀	≀			
London Bridge 4 ⊖	d	23p36					00 12		00 06		≀	≀	00 42	00 36				≀	≀	≀			
New Cross Gate	d	23p41							00 11		≀	≀		00 41				≀	≀	≀			
Norwood Junction 2	a	23p59							00 29		≀	≀		00 59				≀	≀	≀			
East Croydon ⇌	a	00 03	00 14	00 05	00 09	00 24	00 26	00 31	00 33	00 44	00 40	00 55	00 56	01 03	01 10	01 21	01 31	01 38	01 45	02 08	02 21	03 21	04 21
South Croydon 4	a	00 06	00 17						00 37	00 50	≀								≀				
Purley Oaks	a	00 09	00 20						00 40	00 53	≀								≀				
Purley 4	a	00 13	00 23	00 11				00 37	00 43	00 56	00 46					01 27			01 51		02 27	03 27	04 26

		SN	SN	SN	SN	SN	SN	FC	SN	SN	SN	FC	SN	SN	SN	SN	SN	SN	FC	SN	SN	SN	SN
		1	◇1	◇1		◇1	1	1 B		◇1	1	1		1			◇1	1	1			◇1	
London Victoria 15 ⊖	d	05 02	05 47	06 32	06 36	07 02			07 06	07 27			07 36	07 40			08 02				08 06	08 17	
Clapham Junction 10	d	05 08	05 53	06 38	06 42	07 08			07 12	07 33			07 42	07 45			08 08				08 12	08 23	
St Pancras International 15 ⊖	d											07 24							07 54				
Farringdon 3 ⊖	d											07 29							07 59				
City Thameslink 3	d																						
London Blackfriars 3 ⊖	d							06 55				07 34							08 04				
London Bridge 4 ⊖	d						07 05	≀			07 37	07 41			07 21	07 39		08 05	08 11	07 51			08 09
New Cross Gate	d							≀								07 44							08 14
Norwood Junction 2	a						07 17	≀			07 48					08 02		08 16					08 32
East Croydon ⇌	a	05 21	06 05	06 51	07 03	07 19	07 21	07 25	07 33	07 42	07 54	07 55	08 03	07 57	08 01	08 07	08 17	08 20	08 25	08 30	08 33	08 32	08 37
South Croydon 4	a															08 10							08 40
Purley Oaks	a															08 13							08 43
Purley 4	a	05 28		06 56	07 10	07 25	07 28		07 40		08 00		08 10			08 16	08 23	08 26			08 40		08 46

		SN	SN	FC	SN	SN	SN	SN	SN	SN	SN	SN	FC	SN	SN	SN	SN	FC	SN	SN	SN	FC
		◇1	1	1		1		◇1 ✕		◇1	1	◇1	1			◇1		1	◇1	◇1	1	1
London Victoria 15 ⊖	d	08 27			08 36	08 40		08 47		09 02		09 06			09 06	09 17			09 27	09 36		
Clapham Junction 10	d	08 33			08 42	08 45		08 53		09 08		09 12			09 12	09 23			09 33	09 42		
St Pancras International 15 ⊖	d			08 24									08 54					09 09				09 24
Farringdon 3 ⊖	d			08 29									08 58					09 14				09 29
City Thameslink 3	d																					
London Blackfriars 3 ⊖	d			08 34									09 04					09 19				09 34
London Bridge 4 ⊖	d		08 37	08 41			08 21		08 39		09 05		09 11	08 51			09 09	09 26			09 37	09 41
New Cross Gate	d								08 44								09 14					
Norwood Junction 2	a		08 48						09 02		09 16						09 32				09 48	
East Croydon ⇌	a	08 42	08 54	08 55	09 03	08 57	09 01	09 02	09 07	09 17	09 20	09 22	09 25	09 30	09 33	09 32	09 37	09 39	09 42	09 52	09 54	09 55
South Croydon 4	a								09 10								09 40					
Purley Oaks	a								09 13								09 43					
Purley 4	a		09 00		09 10				09 16	09 23	09 26				09 40		09 46				10 00	

A 29 July, 5 August, 12 August, 2 September, 9 September

B from 1 July until 22 July, from 19 August until 9 September

Table 175

Sundays
1 July to 9 September

London - East Croydon and Purley

COMPLETE SERVICE

	SN	SN ■	SN	SN ◇■ H	SN	FC ■		FC ■		SN ◇■	SN ■	SN ◇■ H	FC ■	SN	SN	SN ◇■	SN	SN ◇■		SN ◇■	SN ■	FC ■	SN
London Victoria 15 ⊖ d	09 36	09 40		09 47						19 02		19 06			19 06	19 17		19 27		19 36			19 36
Clapham Junction 10 d	09 42	09 45		09 53			and at the same minutes past each hour until			19 08		19 12			19 12	19 23		19 33		19 42			19 42
St Pancras International 15 ⊖ d						09 39		18 39					18 54									19 24	
Farringdon 3 ⊖ d						09 44		18 44					18 58									19 29	
City Thameslink 3 d																							
London Blackfriars 3 ⊖ d						09 49		18 49					19 04									19 34	
London Bridge 4 ⊖ d			09 21		09 39	09 56		18 56			19 05		19 11	18 51			19 09				19 37	19 41	
New Cross Gate d					09 44												19 14						
Norwood Junction 2 a					10 02						19 16						19 32				19 48		
East Croydon a	10 03	09 57	10 01	10 02	10 07	10 09		19 09		19 17	19 20	19 22	19 25	19 30	19 33	19 32	19 37	19 42		19 52	19 54	19 55	20 03
South Croydon 4 a					10 10												19 40						
Purley Oaks a					10 13												19 43						
Purley 4 a	10 10				10 16					19 23	19 26				19 40		19 46				20 00		20 10

	SN ■	SN	SN ◇■ H	SN	SN ◇■		SN ■	SN ◇■	FC ■	SN	SN	SN ◇■	SN	SN ◇■	SN ◇■		SN ■	FC ■	SN	SN ■	SN	SN ◇■	SN	SN ◇■
London Victoria 15 ⊖ d	19 40		19 47		20 02			20 06			20 06	20 17		20 27	20 36				20 36	20 40		20 47		21 02
Clapham Junction 10 d	19 45		19 53		20 08			20 12			20 12	20 23		20 33	20 42				20 42	20 45		20 53		21 08
St Pancras International 15 ⊖ d									19 54									20 24						
Farringdon 3 ⊖ d									19 58									20 29						
City Thameslink 3 d																								
London Blackfriars 3 ⊖ d									20 04									20 34						
London Bridge 4 ⊖ d		19 21		19 39			20 05		20 11	19 51			20 09				20 37	20 41			20 21		20 39	
New Cross Gate d				19 44									20 14										20 44	
Norwood Junction 2 a				20 02			20 16						20 32				20 48						21 02	
East Croydon a	19 57	20 01	20 02	20 07	20 17		20 20	20 22	20 25	20 30	20 33	20 32	20 37	20 42	20 52		20 54	20 55	21 03	20 57	21 01	21 02	21 07	21 17
South Croydon 4 a				20 10									20 40										21 10	
Purley Oaks a				20 13									20 43										21 13	
Purley 4 a				20 16	20 23		20 26				20 40		20 46				21 00		21 10				21 16	21 23

	SN ■		SN ◇■	FC ■	SN	SN	SN ◇■	SN	SN ◇■	SN ■	FC ■		SN	SN ■	SN	SN ◇■	SN	SN ◇■	SN ■	FC ■	SN		SN	SN ◇■
London Victoria 15 ⊖ d			21 06			21 06	21 17		21 27				21 36	21 40		21 47		22 02					22 06	22 17
Clapham Junction 10 d			21 12			21 12	21 23		21 33				21 42	21 45		21 53		22 08					22 12	22 23
St Pancras International 15 ⊖ d				20 54							21 24									21 54				
Farringdon 3 ⊖ d				20 58							21 29									21 59				
City Thameslink 3 d																								
London Blackfriars 3 ⊖ d				21 04							21 34									22 04				
London Bridge 4 ⊖ d	21 05			21 11	20 51			21 09		21 37	21 41				21 21		21 39		22 05	22 11	21 51			
New Cross Gate d								21 14									21 44							
Norwood Junction 2 a	21 16							21 32		21 48							22 02		22 16					
East Croydon a	21 20		21 22	21 25	21 30	21 33	21 32	21 37	21 42	21 54	21 55		22 03	21 57	22 01	22 02	22 07	22 17	22 20	22 25	22 30		22 33	22 32
South Croydon 4 a								21 40									22 10							
Purley Oaks a								21 43									22 13							
Purley 4 a	21 26					21 40		21 46		22 00			22 10				22 16	22 23	22 26				22 40	

	SN	SN ◇■	SN ■	FC ■	SN	SN ■	SN		SN ◇■	SN	SN ■	FC ■	SN	SN	SN ◇■	SN	SN ◇■		FC ■	SN	SN	SN	SN	FC ■
London Victoria 15 ⊖ d		22 27			22 36	22 40			22 47		23 04			23 06	23 17		23 32				23 47		23 50	
Clapham Junction 10 d		22 33			22 42	22 45			22 53		23 10			23 12	23 23		23 38				23 53		23 56	
St Pancras International 15 ⊖ d				22 24								22 54							23 24					23 54
Farringdon 3 ⊖ d				22 29								22 59							23 29					23 59
City Thameslink 3 d																								
London Blackfriars 3 ⊖ d				22 34								23 04							23 34					00 05
London Bridge 4 ⊖ d	22 09		22 37	22 41			22 21			22 39		23 11	22 51			23 09			23 41	23 21		23 39		00 12
New Cross Gate d	22 14									22 44						23 14						23 44		
Norwood Junction 2 a	22 32		22 48							23 02						23 32						00 02		
East Croydon a	22 37	22 42	22 54	22 55	23 03	22 57	23 00		23 03	23 07	23 22	23 25	23 30	23 34	23 37	23 38	23 52		23 56	00 01	00 06	00 06	00 17	00 26
South Croydon 4 a	22 40									23 10				23 37								00 09	00 20	
Purley Oaks a	22 43									23 13				23 40								00 12	00 23	
Purley 4 a	22 46		23 00		23 10					23 16	23 28			23 43								00 15	00 26	

Sundays
from 16 September

	SN	SN	SN ■	SN ■	SN ◇■	FC ■	SN ■	SN	SN		FC ■	SN	SN	SN ■	FC ■	SN ■	SN ■	SN ■	SN ■		SN ◇■	SN ◇■	SN	SN ◇■
London Victoria 15 ⊖ d		23p45	23p47	23p49	00 05		00 14		00 16				00 42	01 00		02 00	03 00	04 00	05 02		05 47	06 32	06 36	07 02
Clapham Junction 10 d		23p53	23p53	23p56	00 11		00 20		00 24				00 50	01 08		02 08	03 08	04 08	05 08		05 53	06 38	06 42	07 08
St Pancras International 15 ⊖ d						23p54					00 24				00 54									
Farringdon 3 ⊖ d						23p59					00 29													
City Thameslink 3 d																								
London Blackfriars 3 ⊖ d						00 05					00 35				01 05									
London Bridge 4 ⊖ d	23p36					00 12		00 06			00 42	00 36												
New Cross Gate d	23p41							00 11				00 41												
Norwood Junction 2 a	23p59							00 29				00 59												
East Croydon a	00 03	00 14	00 05	00 09	00 24	00 26	00 31	00 33	00 44		00 56	01 03	01 10	01 21	01 31	02 21	03 21	04 21	05 21		06 05	06 51	07 03	07 23
South Croydon 4 a	00 06	00 17						00 37	00 50															
Purley Oaks a	00 09	00 20						00 40	00 53															
Purley 4 a	00 13	00 23	00 11				00 37	00 43	00 56					01 27		02 27	03 27	04 26	05 28			06 56	07 10	07 29

Table 175

Sundays
from 16 September

London - East Croydon and Purley

COMPLETE SERVICE

	FC ■	SN	SN ◇■	SN ■	FC ■		SN ■	SN	SN	SN	SN ◇■	FC ■	SN	SN	SN ◇■		SN	SN ◇■	SN ■	FC ■	SN ■	SN	SN	SN ◇■ H
London Victoria 15 ⊖ d		07 06	07 32				07 34		07 36		08 04			08 06	08 17			08 32			08 34		08 36	08 47
Clapham Junction 10 d		07 12	07 38				07 40		07 42		08 10			08 12	08 23			08 38			08 40		08 42	08 53
St Pancras International 15 ⊖ d					07 24							07 54								08 24				
Farringdon 3 ⊖ d					07 29							07 59								08 29				
City Thameslink 3 d																								
London Blackfriars 3 ⊖ d	06 55				07 34							08 04								08 34				
London Bridge 4 ⊖ d				07 37	07 41			07 21		07 39		08 11	07 51				08 09		08 37	08 41		08 21		
New Cross Gate d										07 44							08 14							
Norwood Junction 2 a				07 47						08 02							08 32		08 47					
East Croydon a	07 25	07 33	07 50	07 54	07 56		07 57	08 01	08 03	08 07	08 23	08 27	08 30	08 33	08 36		08 37	08 50	08 54	08 56	08 57	09 01	09 03	09 06
South Croydon 4 a										08 10							08 40							
Purley Oaks a										08 13							08 43							
Purley 4 a		07 40		08 00					08 10	08 16	08 30			08 40			08 46		09 00				09 10	

	SN		SN ◇■	SN ◇■	FC ■	SN	SN	SN ◇■	SN	FC ■	SN ◇■		SN ■	FC ■	SN ■	SN	SN	SN ◇■ H	SN	FC ■	SN ◇■ H		SN ◇■ H	FC ■
London Victoria 15 ⊖ d			09 02	09 04			09 06	09 17			09 32				09 34		09 36	09 47			10 02		10 04	
Clapham Junction 10 d			09 08	09 10			09 12	09 23			09 38				09 40		09 42	09 53			10 08		10 10	
St Pancras International 15 ⊖ d					08 54					09 09				09 24						09 39				09 54
Farringdon 3 ⊖ d					08 58					09 14				09 29						09 44				09 58
City Thameslink 3 d																								
London Blackfriars 3 ⊖ d					09 04					09 19				09 34						09 49				10 04
London Bridge 4 ⊖ d	08 39				09 11	08 51			09 09	09 26			09 37	09 41		09 21			09 39	09 56				10 11
New Cross Gate d	08 44								09 14										09 44					
Norwood Junction 2 a	09 02								09 32				09 47						10 02					
East Croydon a	09 07		09 21	09 23	09 27	09 30	09 33	09 36	09 37	09 39	09 52		09 54	09 56	09 57	10 01	10 03	10 06	10 07	10 09	10 21		10 23	10 27
South Croydon 4 a	09 10								09 40										10 10					
Purley Oaks a	09 13								09 43										10 13					
Purley 4 a	09 16			09 30			09 40		09 46				10 00				10 10		10 16				10 30	

	SN	SN	SN ◇■	SN	FC ■	SN ◇■	SN ■		FC ■	SN ■	SN	SN	SN ◇■ H	SN	FC ■	SN ◇■ H	SN ◇■ H		FC ■	SN	SN	SN ◇■	SN	FC ■
London Victoria 15 ⊖ d		10 06	10 17			10 32				10 34		10 36	10 47			11 02	11 04				11 06	11 17		
Clapham Junction 10 d		10 12	10 23			10 38				10 40		10 42	10 53			11 08	11 10				11 12	11 23		
St Pancras International 15 ⊖ d					10 09				10 24						10 39				10 54					11 09
Farringdon 3 ⊖ d					10 14				10 29						10 44				10 58					11 14
City Thameslink 3 d																								
London Blackfriars 3 ⊖ d					10 19				10 34						10 49				11 04					11 19
London Bridge 4 ⊖ d	09 51			10 09	10 26		10 37		10 41		10 21			10 39	10 56				11 11	10 51			11 09	11 26
New Cross Gate d				10 14										10 44									11 14	
Norwood Junction 2 a				10 32			10 47							11 02									11 32	
East Croydon a	10 30	10 33	10 36	10 37	10 39	10 52	10 54		10 56	10 57	11 01	11 03	11 06	11 07	11 09	11 21	11 23		11 27	11 30	11 33	11 36	11 37	11 39
South Croydon 4 a				10 40										11 10									11 40	
Purley Oaks a				10 43										11 13									11 43	
Purley 4 a		10 40		10 46			11 00					11 10		11 16			11 30				11 40		11 46	

	SN ◇■	SN ■	FC ■		SN ■	SN	SN	SN ◇■ H	SN	FC ■	SN ◇■ H	SN ◇■ H	FC ■		SN	SN	SN ◇■	SN	FC ■	SN ◇■	SN ■	FC ■	SN ■	
London Victoria 15 ⊖ d	11 32				11 34		11 36	11 47			12 02	12 04				12 06	12 17			12 32			12 34	
Clapham Junction 10 d	11 38				11 40		11 42	11 53			12 08	12 10				12 12	12 23			12 38			12 40	
St Pancras International 15 ⊖ d			11 24							11 39			11 54						12 09			12 24		
Farringdon 3 ⊖ d			11 29							11 44			11 58						12 14			12 29		
City Thameslink 3 d																								
London Blackfriars 3 ⊖ d			11 34							11 49			12 04						12 19			12 34		
London Bridge 4 ⊖ d		11 37	11 41			11 21			11 39	11 56			12 11		11 51			12 09	12 26		12 37	12 41		
New Cross Gate d									11 44									12 14						
Norwood Junction 2 a		11 47							12 02									12 32			12 47			
East Croydon a	11 52	11 54	11 56		11 57	12 01	12 03	12 06	12 07	12 09	12 21	12 23	12 27		12 30	12 33	12 36	12 37	12 42	12 52	12 54	12 56	12 57	
South Croydon 4 a									12 10									12 40						
Purley Oaks a									12 13									12 43						
Purley 4 a		12 00					12 10		12 16			12 30				12 40		12 46			13 00			

	SN	SN	SN ◇■ H	SN	FC ■	SN ◇■ H	SN ◇■ H	FC ■	SN		SN	SN ◇■	SN	FC ■	SN ◇■	SN ■	FC ■	SN ■	SN		SN	SN ◇■ H	SN	FC ■
London Victoria 15 ⊖ d		12 36	12 47			13 02	13 04				13 06	13 17			13 32			13 34			13 36	13 47		
Clapham Junction 10 d		12 42	12 53			13 08	13 10				13 12	13 23			13 38			13 40			13 42	13 53		
St Pancras International 15 ⊖ d					12 39			12 54						13 09			13 24							13 39
Farringdon 3 ⊖ d					12 44			12 58						13 14			13 29							13 44
City Thameslink 3 d																								
London Blackfriars 3 ⊖ d					12 49			13 04						13 19			13 34							13 49
London Bridge 4 ⊖ d	12 21			12 39	12 56			13 11	12 51				13 09	13 26		13 37	13 41		13 21				13 39	13 56
New Cross Gate d				12 44									13 14										13 44	
Norwood Junction 2 a				13 02									13 32			13 47							14 02	
East Croydon a	13 01	13 03	13 06	13 07	13 12	13 21	13 23	13 27	13 30		13 33	13 36	13 37	13 39	13 52	13 54	13 56	13 57	14 01		14 03	14 06	14 07	14 12
South Croydon 4 a				13 10									13 40										14 10	
Purley Oaks a				13 13									13 43										14 13	
Purley 4 a		13 10		13 16			13 30				13 40		13 46			14 00					14 10		14 16	

Table 175

London - East Croydon and Purley

Sundays
from 16 September

COMPLETE SERVICE

		SN ◇1 ⊥	SN ◇1 ⊥	FC 1	SN	SN		SN ◇1	SN	FC 1	SN ◇1	SN 1	FC 1	SN 1	SN	SN		SN ◇1 ⊥	SN	FC 1		FC 1	SN ◇1 ⊥	SN ◇1 ⊥
London Victoria 15 ⊖	d	14 02	14 04			14 06		14 17			14 32			14 34		14 36		14 47					18 02	18 04
Clapham Junction 10	d	14 08	14 10			14 12		14 23			14 38			14 40		14 42		14 53			and at		18 08	18 10
St Pancras International 15 ⊖	d			13 54						14 09			14 24							14 39	the same	17 39		
Farringdon 3 ⊖	d			13 58						14 14			14 29							14 44	minutes	17 44		
City Thameslink 3	d																				past			
London Blackfriars 3 ⊖	d			14 04						14 19			14 34							14 49	each	17 49		
London Bridge 4 ⊖	d			14 11	13 51				14 09	14 26		14 37	14 41		14 21				14 39	14 56	hour until	17 56		
New Cross Gate	d								14 14										14 44					
Norwood Junction 2	a								14 32			14 47							15 02					
East Croydon ⇌	a	14 21	14 23	14 27	14 30	14 33		14 36	14 37	14 39	14 52	14 54	14 56	14 57	15 01	15 03		15 06	15 07	15 09		18 09	18 21	18 23
South Croydon 4	a								14 40										15 10					
Purley Oaks	a								14 43										15 13					
Purley 4	a		14 30			14 40			14 46			15 00				15 10			15 16					18 30

		FC 1		SN	SN	SN ◇1	SN	FC 1	SN ◇1	SN 1	FC 1	SN 1		SN	SN	SN ◇1 ⊥	SN	FC 1	SN ◇1 ⊥	SN ◇1 ⊥	FC 1	SN		SN	SN ◇1
London Victoria 15 ⊖	d				18 06	18 17			18 32			18 34			18 36	18 47			19 02	19 04				19 06	19 17
Clapham Junction 10	d				18 12	18 23			18 38			18 40			18 42	18 53			19 08	19 10				19 12	19 23
St Pancras International 15 ⊖	d	17 54						18 09			18 24							18 39			18 54				
Farringdon 3 ⊖	d	17 58						18 14			18 29							18 44			18 58				
City Thameslink 3	d																								
London Blackfriars 3 ⊖	d	18 04						18 19			18 34							18 49			19 04				
London Bridge 4 ⊖	d	18 11		17 51			18 09	18 26		18 37	18 41			18 21			18 39	18 56			19 11	18 51			
New Cross Gate	d						18 14										18 44								
Norwood Junction 2	a						18 32			18 47							19 02								
East Croydon ⇌	a	18 27		18 30	18 33	18 36	18 37	18 38	18 52	18 54	18 56	18 57		19 01	19 03	19 06	19 07	19 08	19 21	19 23	19 27	19 30		19 33	19 36
South Croydon 4	a						18 40										19 10								
Purley Oaks	a						18 43										19 13								
Purley 4	a				18 40		18 46			19 00					19 10		19 16			19 30				19 40	

		SN	SN ◇1	SN 1	FC 1	SN 1	SN	SN		SN ◇1 ⊥	SN	SN ◇1	SN ◇1	FC 1	SN	SN	SN ◇1	SN		SN ◇1	SN 1	FC 1	SN 1	SN	SN
London Victoria 15 ⊖	d		19 32			19 34		19 36		19 47		20 02	20 04			20 06	20 17			20 32			20 34		20 36
Clapham Junction 10	d		19 38			19 40		19 42		19 53		20 08	20 10			20 12	20 23			20 38			20 40		20 42
St Pancras International 15 ⊖	d				19 24									19 54								20 24			
Farringdon 3 ⊖	d				19 29									19 58								20 29			
City Thameslink 3	d																								
London Blackfriars 3 ⊖	d				19 34									20 04								20 34			
London Bridge 4 ⊖	d	19 09		19 37	19 41		19 21				19 39			20 11	19 51			20 09			20 37	20 41		20 21	
New Cross Gate	d	19 14									19 44							20 14							
Norwood Junction 2	a	19 32		19 47							20 02							20 32			20 47				
East Croydon ⇌	a	19 37	19 50	19 54	19 56	19 57	20 01	20 03		20 06	20 07	20 21	20 23	20 27	20 30	20 33	20 36	20 37		20 50	20 54	20 56	20 57	21 01	21 03
South Croydon 4	a	19 40									20 10							20 40							
Purley Oaks	a	19 43									20 13							20 43							
Purley 4	a	19 46		20 00				20 10			20 16		20 30			20 40		20 46			21 00				21 10

		SN ◇1	SN	SN ◇1		SN ◇1	FC 1	SN	SN	SN ◇1	SN	SN ◇1	SN 1	FC 1		SN 1	SN	SN	SN ◇1	SN	SN ◇1	FC 1	SN	SN
London Victoria 15 ⊖	d	20 47		21 02		21 04			21 06	21 17		21 32				21 34		21 36	21 47		22 04			22 06
Clapham Junction 10	d	20 53		21 08		21 10			21 12	21 23		21 38				21 40		21 42	21 53		22 10			22 12
St Pancras International 15 ⊖	d						20 54							21 24								21 54		
Farringdon 3 ⊖	d						20 58							21 29								21 59		
City Thameslink 3	d																							
London Blackfriars 3 ⊖	d						21 04							21 34								22 04		
London Bridge 4 ⊖	d		20 39				21 11	20 51			21 09		21 37	21 41			21 21			21 39		22 11	21 51	
New Cross Gate	d		20 44								21 14									21 44				
Norwood Junction 2	a		21 02								21 32		21 47							22 02				
East Croydon ⇌	a	21 06	21 07	21 21		21 23	21 27	21 30	21 33	21 36	21 37	21 50	21 54	21 56		21 57	22 01	22 03	22 06	22 07	22 23	22 27	22 30	22 33
South Croydon 4	a		21 10								21 40									22 10				
Purley Oaks	a		21 13								21 43									22 13				
Purley 4	a		21 16			21 30			21 40		21 46		22 00					22 10		22 16	22 30			22 40

		SN ◇1	SN	SN ◇1	SN 1	FC 1	SN 1	SN	SN	SN ◇1		SN	SN 1	FC 1	SN	SN	SN ◇1	SN	SN ◇1	FC 1		SN	SN	SN	SN
London Victoria 15 ⊖	d	22 17		22 32			22 34		22 36	22 47			23 04			23 06	23 17		23 32				23 47		23 50
Clapham Junction 10	d	22 23		22 38			22 40		22 42	22 53			23 10			23 12	23 23		23 38				23 53		23 56
St Pancras International 15 ⊖	d					22 24								22 54						23 24					
Farringdon 3 ⊖	d					22 29								22 59						23 29					
City Thameslink 3	d																								
London Blackfriars 3 ⊖	d					22 34								23 04						23 34					
London Bridge 4 ⊖	d		22 09		22 37	22 41		22 21				22 39		23 11	22 51			23 09		23 41		23 21		23 39	
New Cross Gate	d		22 14									22 44						23 14						23 44	
Norwood Junction 2	a		22 32		22 47							23 02						23 32						00 02	
East Croydon ⇌	a	22 36	22 37	22 50	22 54	22 56	22 57	23 00	23 03	23 06		23 07	23 22	23 26	23 30	23 34	23 37	23 38	23 52	23 56		00 01	00 06	00 06	00 17
South Croydon 4	a		22 40									23 10				23 37								00 09	00 20
Purley Oaks	a		22 43									23 13				23 40								00 12	00 23
Purley 4	a		22 46		23 00				23 10			23 16	23 28			23 43								00 15	00 26

Table 175

London - East Croydon and Purley

Sundays
from 16 September

COMPLETE SERVICE

		FC 1
London Victoria 15 ⊖	d	
Clapham Junction 10	d	
St Pancras International 15 ⊖	d	23 54
Farringdon 3 ⊖	d	23 59
City Thameslink 3	d	
London Blackfriars 3 ⊖	d	00 05
London Bridge 4 ⊖	d	00 12
New Cross Gate	d	
Norwood Junction 2	a	
East Croydon ⇌	a	00 26
South Croydon 4	a	
Purley Oaks	a	
Purley 4	a	

Purley and East Croydon - London

COMPLETE SERVICE

Station		FC MO 1 A	FC MX 1 B	SN MO 1 A	SN MO 1 A	SN MX 1	FC MO 1 C	FC MX 1 D	FC 1 E	FC MX 1 B	SN MO ◇1 A	SN MX ◇1	FC MO 1 E	FC MX 1 B	FC MX 1 D	FC MO 1 C	SN	SN 1	FC F	FC 1 G	SN 1	FC 1 G	FC F
Purley 4	d				23p50	23p49					00 11	00 11						01 22			02 22		
Purley Oaks	d																						
South Croydon 4	d																						
East Croydon	d	23p32	23p32	23p50	23p56	23p58	00 03	00 04	00 04	00 04	00 16	00 17	00 36	00 36	00 36	00 37	00 49	01 28	01 47	01 49	02 28	02 47	02 47
Norwood Junction 2	d																						
New Cross Gate	d																						
London Bridge 4 ⊖	a	23p45	23p45				00 21	00 19	00 21	00 21			00 50	00 51	00 52	00 50				02 14		03 12	
London Blackfriars 3 ⊖	a	23p52	23p52				00 27		00 27	00 28			00 57	00 58		00 57			02 13				03 13
City Thameslink 3	a																						
Farringdon 3 ⊖	a	23p56	23p58				00 33		00 33	00 33													
St Pancras International 15 ⊖	a	00 01	00 02				00 37		00 37	00 37			01 07	01 07		01 07			02 23				03 23
Clapham Junction 10	a			00 01	00 11	00 11					00 29	00 29					01 01	01 40			02 40		
London Victoria 15 ⊖	a			00 08	00 19	00 18					00 37	00 37					01 09	01 49			02 49		

Station		SN 1	FC 1 G	FC F	SN 1	FC	SN	FC 1	SN 1	SN	FC 1	SN	SN	FC 1	SN 1	SN	SN	SN ◇1	SN	SN 1	SN 1	SN	SN 1
Purley 4	d	03 22			04 26		05 07		05 23			05 39			06 00		06 04					06 22	06 25
Purley Oaks	d											05 42					06 07					06 25	
South Croydon 4	d											05 45					06 10					06 28	
East Croydon	d	03 28	03 47	03 47	04 32	04 47	05 13	05 17	05 29	05 33	05 47	05 48	05 51	06 02	06 06	06 11	06 13	06 15	06 17	06 23	06 27	06 31	06 31
Norwood Junction 2	d						05 17			05 37			05 55				06 18					06 37	
New Cross Gate	d						05 34										06 35						
London Bridge 4 ⊖	a		04 12				05 41	05 34			06 02		06 25	06 15			06 44			06 39		06 49	
London Blackfriars 3 ⊖	a			04 13		05 13		05 41			06 10			06 23									
City Thameslink 3	a					05 16		05 44			06 14			06 26									
Farringdon 3 ⊖	a					05 20		05 47			06 18			06 30									
St Pancras International 15 ⊖	a			04 22		05 24		05 52			06 22			06 34									
Clapham Junction 10	a	03 40			04 51				05 48	05 57		06 09			06 18	06 21		06 25	06 37		06 38		06 41
London Victoria 15 ⊖	a	03 49			04 58				05 58	06 06		06 18			06 25	06 28		06 32	06 48		06 45		06 48

Station		FC 1	SN	SN 1	SN 1	FC 1	SN	SN 1	SN	SN 1	SN 1	SN 1	FC 1	SN	SN ◇1	SN 1	SN	FC 1	SN	SN 1	SN 1	SN ◇1 ⌶
Purley 4	d		06 27						06 47		06 54	06 59		07 01					07 17			
Purley Oaks	d		06 30						06 50					07 04					07 20			
South Croydon 4	d		06 33				06 42	06 50	06 53					07 07					07 23		07 25	
East Croydon	d	06 32	06 36	06 39	06 42	06 44	06 45	06 54	06 57	06 59	07 00	07 05	07 09	07 10	07 15	07 15	07 18	07 23	07 26	07 28	07 28	07 31
Norwood Junction 2	d		06 40											07 14								
New Cross Gate	d																					
London Bridge 4 ⊖	a	06 46	06 52	06 55		06 58		07 11		07 14	07 16		07 23	07 28						07 43	07 47	
London Blackfriars 3 ⊖	a	06 52				07 04							07 30					07 51				
City Thameslink 3	a	06 54				07 08							07 32					07 56				
Farringdon 3 ⊖	a	06 58				07 12							07 36					08 00				
St Pancras International 15 ⊖	a	07 02				07 16							07 40					08 04				
Clapham Junction 10	a				06 51		07 05		07 06			07 16			07 24	07 27	07 38		07 36			07 40
London Victoria 15 ⊖	a				07 00		07 16		07 15			07 25			07 33	07 36	07 48		07 46			07 49

Station		SN 1	SN 1	SN ◇1 ⌶	SN	SN 1	SN 1	SN 1	SN	SN	FC 1	SN	SN 1	SN 1	SN ◇1 ⌶	SN 1	SN 1	SN 1	SN 1	SN ◇1	SN	SN 1	SN ◇1 ⌶
Purley 4	d		07 29		07 31	07 37			07 39			07 47				07 55					08 01		
Purley Oaks	d				07 34				07 42			07 50									08 04		
South Croydon 4	d				07 37				07 45			07 53		07 54							08 07		
East Croydon	d	07 32	07 35	07 39	07 40	07 42	07 45	07 46	07 48	07 50	07 54	07 56	07 57	07 59	08 01	08 02	08 03	08 05	08 07	08 08	08 10	08 11	08 13
Norwood Junction 2	d				07 44																08 16		
New Cross Gate	d																						
London Bridge 4 ⊖	a	07 49	07 51		07 58			08 01					08 13	08 16		08 19	08 21	08 23			08 28		
London Blackfriars 3 ⊖	a										08 20												
City Thameslink 3	a										08 23												
Farringdon 3 ⊖	a										08 27												
St Pancras International 15 ⊖	a										08 31												
Clapham Junction 10	a			07 48		07 51	07 55		08 08	08 13		08 06			08 10				08 36	08 17		08 20	08 23
London Victoria 15 ⊖	a			07 57		08 00	08 04		08 19			08 15			08 19					08 26		08 29	08 32

Station		SN 1	SN	SN 1	FC 1	SN 1	SN	SN 1	SN 1	SN ◇1	SN 1	SN 1	SN 1	SN	FC 1	SN	SN ◇1 ⌶	SN 1	SN	SN ◇1 ⌶	SN 1	SN
Purley 4	d			08 15			08 17						08 31			08 33						08 45
Purley Oaks	d						08 20									08 36						08 48
South Croydon 4	d						08 23		08 26					08 35		08 39		08 42				08 51
East Croydon	d	08 15	08 18	08 21	08 23	08 25	08 26	08 27	08 29	08 30	08 32	08 33	08 37	08 39	08 39	08 42	08 43	08 45	08 48	08 50	08 51	08 54
Norwood Junction 2	d															08 47						
New Cross Gate	d																					
London Bridge 4 ⊖	a			08 37		08 41		08 45	08 47		08 52	08 52				09 01					09 06	
London Blackfriars 3 ⊖	a				08 53										09 09							
City Thameslink 3	a				08 56										09 12							
Farringdon 3 ⊖	a				09 00										09 16							
St Pancras International 15 ⊖	a				09 04										09 20							
Clapham Junction 10	a	08 26	08 38				08 36			08 39			08 48	09 04			08 52	08 55	09 08	09 00		09 04
London Victoria 15 ⊖	a	08 35	08 48				08 45			08 48			08 56				09 01	09 04	09 18	09 09		09 13

A from 21 May
B from 22 May
C from 17 September
D until 18 May
E from 21 May until 10 September
F from 21 May
G until 18 May

Purley and East Croydon - London

COMPLETE SERVICE

Station		FC 1	SN 1	SN ◇1	SN 1	SN 1	SN	SN 1	FC 1	SN 1	SN ◇1 ⌶	SN 1	SN	SN	SN ◇1 ⌶	SN 1	SN	SN ◇1	FC 1	SN 1	SN 1	SN ◇1 ⌶	SN ◇1
Purley 4	d				08 52		08 56			09 05			09 08	09 14			09 21				09 32		
Purley Oaks	d						08 59						09 11				09 24						
South Croydon 4	d		08 52				09 02						09 14				09 27						
East Croydon	d	08 54	08 56	08 58	08 59	09 02	09 05	09 08	09 09	09 11	09 14	09 14	09 17	09 20	09 23	09 26	09 30	09 31	09 32	09 33	09 37	09 39	09 43
Norwood Junction 2	d						09 09							09 25			09 35				09 42		
New Cross Gate	d													09 33			09 52						
London Bridge 4 ⊖	a	09 08	09 13		09 15	09 20	09 23							09 41			10 00		09 46	09 51	09 55		
London Blackfriars 3 ⊖	a	09 21							09 37										09 53				
City Thameslink 3	a	09 24							09 40										09 56				
Farringdon 3 ⊖	a	09 27							09 44										10 00				
St Pancras International 15 ⊖	a	09 32							09 48										10 04				
Clapham Junction 10	a			09 07				09 34		09 20	09 23	09 26	09 38		09 32	09 36		09 41				09 48	09 52
London Victoria 15 ⊖	a			09 16						09 27	09 32	09 35	09 48		09 42	09 43		09 50				09 58	09 59

Station		SN 1	SN	FC 1	SN	SN ◇1 ⌶	SN 1	SN	SN ◇1 ⌶	FC 1	SN 1	SN ◇1	SN 1	SN ◇1 ⌶	SN 1	SN	FC 1	SN	SN ◇1 ⌶	SN 1	SN ◇1	SN	FC 1
Purley 4	d		09 38		09 45		09 49	09 51			10 02					10 08		10 15		10 19		10 21	
Purley Oaks	d		09 41					09 54								10 11						10 24	
South Croydon 4	d		09 44					09 57					10 07			10 14						10 27	
East Croydon	d	09 44	09 47	09 47	09 51	09 53	09 55	10 00	10 00	10 02	10 07	10 08	10 10	10 12	10 14	10 17	10 17	10 21	10 23	10 25	10 28	10 30	10 32
Norwood Junction 2	d				09 55		09 59	10 05			10 13							10 25		10 29		10 35	
New Cross Gate	d						10 07	10 22												10 37		10 52	
London Bridge 4 ⊖	a			10 00	10 09		10 13	10 29		10 15	10 25						10 30	10 39		10 43		10 59	10 45
London Blackfriars 3 ⊖	a			10 08						10 23							10 37						10 52
City Thameslink 3	a			10 10						10 26							10 40						10 56
Farringdon 3 ⊖	a			10 14						10 30							10 44						11 00
St Pancras International 15 ⊖	a			10 18						10 34							10 48						11 04
Clapham Junction 10	a	09 55	10 07			10 02			10 09			10 17	10 35	10 21	10 25	10 37			10 32		10 37		
London Victoria 15 ⊖	a	10 05	10 16			10 11			10 16			10 26		10 28	10 35	10 46			10 41		10 45		

Station		SN 1	SN 1	SN ◇1 ⌶	SN 1	SN	FC 1	SN	SN ◇1 ⌶	SN 1	SN	SN ◇1	FC 1	SN 1	SN ◇1	SN 1	SN ◇1	SN 1	SN	FC 1	SN	SN ◇1 ⌶
Purley 4	d		10 33			10 38		10 45		10 49	10 51			11 01					11 08		11 15	
Purley Oaks	d					10 41					10 54								11 11			
South Croydon 4	d					10 44					10 57					11 07			11 14			
East Croydon	d	10 33	10 38	10 42	10 44	10 47	10 47	10 51	10 53	10 55	11 00	11 00	11 02	11 07	11 08	11 11	11 12	11 14	11 17	11 17	11 21	11 23
Norwood Junction 2	d		10 43					10 55		10 59	11 05			11 13							11 25	
New Cross Gate	d									11 07	11 22											
London Bridge 4 ⊖	a	10 49	10 55				11 00	11 09		11 13	11 29		11 15	11 25						11 30	11 39	
London Blackfriars 3 ⊖	a						11 07						11 22							11 37		
City Thameslink 3	a						11 10						11 26							11 40		
Farringdon 3 ⊖	a						11 14						11 30							11 44		
St Pancras International 15 ⊖	a						11 18						11 34							11 48		
Clapham Junction 10	a			10 51	10 55	11 07			11 02			11 09			11 17	11 33	11 21	11 25	11 37			11 32
London Victoria 15 ⊖	a			10 58	11 05	11 16			11 10			11 16			11 24		11 28	11 32				11 40

Station		SN 1	SN ◇1	SN	FC 1	SN 1	SN 1	SN ◇1	SN 1	SN	FC 1	SN	SN ◇1 ⌶	SN 1	SN	SN ◇1	FC 1	SN 1	SN ◇1	SN 1	SN ◇1	SN 1	SN
Purley 4	d	11 19		11 21			11 32			11 38		11 45		11 49	11 51			12 02					12 08
Purley Oaks	d			11 24						11 41					11 54								12 11
South Croydon 4	d			11 27						11 44					11 57					12 07			12 14
East Croydon	d	11 25	11 28	11 30	11 32	11 33	11 37	11 41	11 44	11 47	11 47	11 51	11 53	11 55	12 00	12 00	12 02	12 07	12 08	12 10	12 12	12 14	12 17
Norwood Junction 2	d	11 29		11 35			11 43					11 55		11 59	12 05			12 13					
New Cross Gate	d	11 37		11 52										12 07	12 22								
London Bridge 4 ⊖	a	11 43		11 59	11 45	11 49	11 55				12 00	12 09		12 13	12 29		12 15	12 25					
London Blackfriars 3 ⊖	a				11 52						12 07						12 22						
City Thameslink 3	a				11 56						12 10						12 26						
Farringdon 3 ⊖	a				12 00						12 14						12 30						
St Pancras International 15 ⊖	a				12 04						12 18						12 34						
Clapham Junction 10	a		11 37					11 50	11 55	12 07			12 02			12 09			12 17	12 34	12 21	12 25	12 37
London Victoria 15 ⊖	a		11 44					11 57	12 02				12 10			12 18			12 24		12 28	12 32	

Station		FC 1	SN	SN ◇1 ⌶	SN 1	SN ◇1	SN	FC 1	SN 1	SN 1	SN ◇1	SN 1	SN	FC 1	SN	SN ◇1 ⌶	SN 1	SN	SN ◇1	FC 1	SN 1	SN ◇1
Purley 4	d		12 15		12 19		12 21			12 32			12 38		12 45		12 49	12 51			13 02	
Purley Oaks	d						12 24						12 41					12 54				
South Croydon 4	d						12 27						12 44					12 57				
East Croydon	d	12 17	12 21	12 23	12 25	12 28	12 30	12 32	12 33	12 37	12 41	12 44	12 47	12 47	12 51	12 53	12 55	13 00	13 00	13 02	13 07	13 08
Norwood Junction 2	d		12 25		12 29		12 35			12 43					12 55		12 59	13 05			13 13	
New Cross Gate	d				12 37		12 52										13 07	13 22				
London Bridge 4 ⊖	a	12 30	12 39		12 43		12 59	12 45	12 49	12 55				13 00	13 09		13 13	13 29		13 15	13 25	
London Blackfriars 3 ⊖	a	12 37						12 52						13 07						13 22		
City Thameslink 3	a	12 40						12 56						13 10						13 26		
Farringdon 3 ⊖	a	12 44						13 00						13 14						13 30		
St Pancras International 15 ⊖	a	12 48						13 04						13 18						13 34		
Clapham Junction 10	a			12 32		12 37					12 50	12 55	13 07			13 02			13 09			13 17
London Victoria 15 ⊖	a			12 40		12 44					12 57	13 02	13 16			13 10			13 16			13 24

Purley and East Croydon - London

COMPLETE SERVICE

	SN 1	SN ◇1	SN 1	SN	FC 1	SN	SN ◇1	SN 1	SN ◇1	SN	FC 1	SN 1	SN 1	SN ◇1	SN 1	SN	FC 1	SN	SN ◇1	SN 1	SN	SN ◇1
Purley 4 d				13 08		13 15		13 19		13 21			13 32			13 38		13 45		13 49	13 51	
Purley Oaks d				13 11						13 24						13 41					13 54	
South Croydon 4 d	13 07			13 14						13 27						13 44					13 57	
East Croydon d	13 10	13 12	13 14	13 17	13 17	13 21	13 23	13 25	13 28	13 30	13 32	13 33	13 37	13 41	13 44	13 47	13 47	13 51	13 53	13 55	14 00	14 00
Norwood Junction 2 d						13 25		13 29		13 35			13 43					13 55		13 59	14 05	
New Cross Gate d								13 37		13 52										14 07	14 22	
London Bridge 4 ⊖ a					13 30	13 39		13 43		13 59	13 45	13 49	13 55				14 00	14 09		14 13	14 29	
London Blackfriars 3 ⊖ a					13 37						13 52						14 07					
City Thameslink 3 a					13 40						13 56						14 10					
Farringdon 3 ⊖ a					13 44						14 00						14 14					
St Pancras International 15 ⊖ a					13 48						14 04						14 18					
Clapham Junction 10 a	13 34	13 21	13 25	13 37			13 32		13 37					13 50	13 55	14 07			14 02			14 09
London Victoria 15 ⊖ a		13 28	13 32				13 40		13 44					13 57	14 03				14 10			14 16

	FC 1	SN 1	SN ◇1	SN 1	SN ◇1	SN 1	SN	FC 1	SN	SN ◇1	SN 1	SN ◇1	SN	FC 1	SN 1	SN 1	SN ◇1	SN 1	SN	FC 1	SN	SN ◇1
Purley 4 d		14 02					14 08		14 15		14 19		14 21			14 32			14 38		14 45	
Purley Oaks d							14 11						14 24						14 41			
South Croydon 4 d				14 07			14 14						14 27						14 44			
East Croydon d	14 02	14 08	14 08	14 10	14 12	14 14	14 17	14 17	14 21	14 23	14 25	14 28	14 30	14 32	14 33	14 37	14 41	14 44	14 47	14 47	14 51	14 53
Norwood Junction 2 d		14 13							14 25		14 29		14 35			14 43					14 55	
New Cross Gate d											14 37		14 52									
London Bridge 4 ⊖ a	14 15	14 25						14 30	14 39		14 43		14 59	14 45	14 49	14 55				15 00	15 09	
London Blackfriars 3 ⊖ a	14 22							14 37						14 52						15 07		
City Thameslink 3 a	14 26							14 40						14 56						15 10		
Farringdon 3 ⊖ a	14 29							14 44						15 00						15 14		
St Pancras International 15 ⊖ a	14 34							14 48						15 04						15 18		
Clapham Junction 10 a			14 17	14 34	14 21	14 25	14 37			14 32		14 37					14 50	14 55	15 07			15 02
London Victoria 15 ⊖ a			14 24		14 28	14 32				14 40		14 44					14 57	15 02	15 16			15 10

	SN 1	SN	SN ◇1	FC 1	SN 1	SN ◇1	SN 1	SN ◇1	SN 1	SN	FC 1	SN	SN ◇1	SN 1	SN ◇1	SN	FC 1	SN 1	SN 1	SN ◇1	SN 1
Purley 4 d	14 49	14 51			15 02					15 08		15 15		15 19		15 21			15 32		
Purley Oaks d		14 54								15 11						15 24					
South Croydon 4 d		14 57					15 07			15 14						15 27					
East Croydon d	14 55	15 00	15 00	15 02	15 07	15 08	15 10	15 12	15 14	15 17	15 17	15 21	15 23	15 25	15 28	15 30	15 32	15 33	15 37	15 41	15 44
Norwood Junction 2 d	14 59	15 05			15 13							15 25		15 29		15 35			15 43		
New Cross Gate d	15 07	15 22												15 37		15 52					
London Bridge 4 ⊖ a	15 13	15 29		15 15	15 25						15 30	15 39		15 43		15 59	15 45	15 49	15 55		
London Blackfriars 3 ⊖ a				15 22							15 37						15 52				
City Thameslink 3 a				15 26							15 40						15 56				
Farringdon 3 ⊖ a				15 29							15 44						15 59				
St Pancras International 15 ⊖ a				15 34							15 48						16 04				
Clapham Junction 10 a			15 09			15 17	15 35	15 21	15 25	15 37			15 32		15 37					15 50	15 55
London Victoria 15 ⊖ a			15 20			15 24		15 28	15 35	15 46			15 40		15 46					15 57	16 05

	SN	FC 1	SN	SN ◇1	SN 1	SN	SN ◇1	FC 1	SN 1	SN ◇1	SN 1	SN ◇1	SN 1	SN	FC 1	SN	SN 1	SN ◇1	FC 1	SN	SN ◇1	SN 1
Purley 4 d	15 38		15 45		15 49	15 51			16 02					16 08		16 15	16 18			16 21		
Purley Oaks d	15 41					15 54								16 11						16 24		
South Croydon 4 d	15 44					15 57					16 07			16 14						16 27		
East Croydon d	15 47	15 47	15 51	15 53	15 55	16 00	16 00	16 02	16 07	16 08	16 10	16 12	16 14	16 17	16 17	16 21	16 24	16 24	16 28	16 30	16 30	16 33
Norwood Junction 2 d			15 55		15 59	16 05			16 13							16 25	16 28			16 35		
New Cross Gate d					16 07	16 22											16 36			16 52		
London Bridge 4 ⊖ a		16 00	16 09		16 13	16 29		16 15	16 25							16 39	16 43			17 02		16 47
London Blackfriars 3 ⊖ a		16 07						16 25							16 47				16 55			
City Thameslink 3 a		16 10						16 28							16 54				16 58			
Farringdon 3 ⊖ a		16 13						16 31							16 57				17 01			
St Pancras International 15 ⊖ a		16 17						16 35							17 01				17 05			
Clapham Junction 10 a	16 07			16 02			16 09			16 17	16 34	16 21	16 25	16 37				16 33			16 39	
London Victoria 15 ⊖ a	16 16			16 10			16 16			16 24		16 28	16 35	16 46				16 42			16 46	

	SN ◇1	SN 1	SN ◇1	SN 1	SN	FC 1	SN	SN 1	SN 1	FC 1	SN	SN ◇1	SN 1	FC 1	SN 1	SN ◇1	SN 1	SN	SN	FC 1	SN 1
Purley 4 d		16 34			16 38		16 45		16 49		16 51		17 02					17 08	17 15		17 19
Purley Oaks d					16 41						16 54							17 11			
South Croydon 4 d					16 44						16 57				17 07			17 14			
East Croydon d	16 38	16 40	16 41	16 44	16 47	16 47	16 51	16 54	16 55	16 58	17 00	17 01	17 07	17 09	17 10	17 13	17 14	17 17	17 21	17 23	17 25
Norwood Junction 2 d		16 45					16 55		16 59		17 05		17 12						17 25		17 31
New Cross Gate d									17 06		17 22										17 38
London Bridge 4 ⊖ a		17 00					17 08		17 14		17 35		17 26	17 27					17 37		17 45
London Blackfriars 3 ⊖ a						17 19				17 25				17 35						17 49	
City Thameslink 3 a						17 24				17 28				17 38						17 54	
Farringdon 3 ⊖ a						17 27				17 31				17 41						17 57	
St Pancras International 15 ⊖ a						17 31				17 35				17 45						18 01	
Clapham Junction 10 a	16 47		16 50	16 55	17 07			17 03				17 10			17 34	17 22	17 25	17 37			
London Victoria 15 ⊖ a	16 56		16 58	17 05	17 16			17 10				17 17				17 29	17 35	17 48			

	SN 1	SN	SN ◇1	SN 1	SN 1	SN ◇1	SN 1	SN 1	SN	FC 1	SN	SN 1	SN 1	SN 1	FC 1	SN ◇1	SN	SN 1	SN 1	SN ◇1	SN 1	FC 1
Purley 4 d		17 21							17 38		17 45		17 49				17 59					
Purley Oaks d		17 24							17 41								18 02					
South Croydon 4 d		17 27							17 44								18 05					
East Croydon d	17 26	17 30	17 30	17 36	17 38	17 41	17 41	17 44	17 47	17 47	17 51	17 53	17 55	17 57	17 58	18 02	18 08	18 09	18 10	18 12	18 14	18 16
Norwood Junction 2 d		17 35					17 45				17 55		17 59				18 12					
New Cross Gate d		17 52											18 07									
London Bridge 4 ⊖ a		17 59		17 52			17 58			18 13	18 09		18 16				18 26					
London Blackfriars 3 ⊖ a										18 21					18 25							18 51
City Thameslink 3 a										18 24					18 28							18 54
Farringdon 3 ⊖ a										18 27					18 31							18 57
St Pancras International 15 ⊖ a										18 31					18 35							19 01
Clapham Junction 10 a	17 35		17 39		17 47	17 50		17 55	18 07			18 02		18 06		18 13		18 18	18 35	18 21	18 25	
London Victoria 15 ⊖ a	17 42		17 46		17 54	17 58		18 05	18 16			18 09		18 14		18 20		18 26		18 29	18 35	

	SN	SN	SN 1	SN 1	SN	SN ◇1	FC 1	SN 1	SN 1	SN ◇1	SN 1	SN	FC 1	SN 1	SN 1	SN 1	SN 1	SN	SN ◇1	FC 1	SN 1	SN 1
Purley 4 d	18 08	18 15		18 19	18 21							18 37			18 49			18 51				
Purley Oaks d	18 11				18 24							18 40						18 54				
South Croydon 4 d	18 14				18 27							18 44						18 57				
East Croydon d	18 17	18 21	18 26	18 27	18 30	18 30	18 32	18 36	18 40	18 43	18 44	18 47	18 47	18 53	18 55	18 57	18 57	19 00	19 00	19 02	19 10	19 10
Norwood Junction 2 d		18 29			18 35											19 02		19 05			19 13	
New Cross Gate d					18 52													19 22				
London Bridge 4 ⊖ a		18 41			18 59		18 46	18 50					19 00			19 15		19 29		19 15	19 25	
London Blackfriars 3 ⊖ a							18 55						19 09							19 22		
City Thameslink 3 a							18 58						19 12							19 26		
Farringdon 3 ⊖ a							19 01						19 15							19 30		
St Pancras International 15 ⊖ a							19 05						19 19							19 34		
Clapham Junction 10 a	18 39		18 35	18 38		18 41			18 49	18 52	18 55	19 08		19 02	19 05		19 08		19 11			19 34
London Victoria 15 ⊖ a	18 46		18 42	18 45		18 48			18 56	18 59	19 05	19 15		19 09	19 13		19 15		19 18			

	SN ◇1	SN 1	SN	FC 1	SN ◇1	SN 1	SN ◇1	SN	FC 1	SN 1	SN 1	SN ◇1	SN 1	SN	FC 1	SN ◇1	SN 1	SN	SN 1	FC 1	SN 1
Purley 4 d			19 08			19 19		19 21						19 38			19 53	19 51			
Purley Oaks d			19 11					19 24						19 41				19 54			
South Croydon 4 d			19 14					19 27						19 44				19 57			
East Croydon d	19 12	19 14	19 17	19 17	19 24	19 25	19 29	19 30	19 32	19 33	19 40	19 43	19 44	19 47	19 47	19 54	19 59	20 00	20 01	20 02	20 07
Norwood Junction 2 d								19 35										20 05			
New Cross Gate d								19 52										20 22			
London Bridge 4 ⊖ a				19 30				19 59	19 45	19 49					20 00			20 29		20 15	20 21
London Blackfriars 3 ⊖ a				19 37					19 52						20 07					20 22	
City Thameslink 3 a				19 40					19 56						20 10					20 26	
Farringdon 3 ⊖ a				19 44					20 00						20 14					20 30	
St Pancras International 15 ⊖ a				19 48					20 04						20 18					20 34	
Clapham Junction 10 a	19 21	19 25	19 37		19 33	19 37	19 40				19 49	19 52	19 55	20 07		20 03	20 08		20 11		
London Victoria 15 ⊖ a	19 29	19 35	19 48		19 41	19 44	19 47				19 56	19 59	20 05			20 10	20 15		20 20		

	SN ◇1	SN 1	SN	FC 1	SN ◇1	SN 1	SN ◇1	SN	FC 1	SN 1	SN ◇1	SN 1	SN	FC 1	SN 1	SN ◇1	SN 1	SN	SN ◇1	FC 1	SN ◇1	SN 1
Purley 4 d			20 08			20 18		20 22					20 38				20 49	20 51				
Purley Oaks d			20 11					20 25					20 41					20 54				
South Croydon 4 d			20 14					20 28					20 44					20 57				
East Croydon d	20 11	20 14	20 17	20 17	20 24	20 26	20 30	20 31	20 32	20 34	20 41	20 44	20 47	20 47	20 54	20 54	20 57	21 00	21 00	21 02	21 09	21 14
Norwood Junction 2 d								20 35										21 05				
New Cross Gate d								20 52										21 22				
London Bridge 4 ⊖ a				20 30				20 59	20 45	20 48				21 00	21 09			21 29		21 15		
London Blackfriars 3 ⊖ a				20 37					20 52					21 07						21 22		
City Thameslink 3 a				20 40					20 56					21 10						21 26		
Farringdon 3 ⊖ a				20 44					21 00					21 14						21 30		
St Pancras International 15 ⊖ a				20 48					21 04					21 18						21 34		
Clapham Junction 10 a	20 20	20 25	20 37		20 33	20 37	20 40				20 50	20 55	21 07			21 03	21 07		21 11		21 18	21 25
London Victoria 15 ⊖ a	20 28	20 32	20 46		20 40	20 44	20 50				20 59	21 03	21 18			21 10	21 15		21 18		21 28	21 32

	SN	FC 1	SN ◇1	SN 1	SN	SN ◇1	FC 1	SN 1	SN ◇1	SN 1	SN	SN ◇1	SN 1	SN	SN ◇1	FC 1 A	FC 1 B	SN ◇1	SN 1	SN	SN 1
Purley 4 d	21 08			21 19	21 21						21 38		21 49	21 51						22 08	
Purley Oaks d	21 11				21 24						21 41			21 54						22 11	
South Croydon 4 d	21 14				21 27						21 44			21 57						22 14	
East Croydon d	21 17	21 17	21 24	21 26	21 30	21 30	21 32	21 33	21 42	21 44	21 47	21 54	21 57	22 00	22 00	22 02	22 02	22 09	22 14	22 17	22 18
Norwood Junction 2 d					21 35									22 05							
New Cross Gate d					21 52									22 22							
London Bridge 4 ⊖ a		21 30			21 59		21 45	21 49						22 29		22 15	22 17				22 33
London Blackfriars 3 ⊖ a		21 37					21 52									22 22					
City Thameslink 3 a		21 40					21 56									22 23					
Farringdon 3 ⊖ a		21 44					22 00									22 28					
St Pancras International 15 ⊖ a		21 48					22 04									22 32					
Clapham Junction 10 a	21 37		21 33	21 37		21 40			21 51	21 55	22 07	22 03	22 07		22 10			22 18	22 25	22 37	
London Victoria 15 ⊖ a	21 48		21 40	21 45		21 47			21 58	22 05	22 18	22 11	22 14		22 20			22 26	22 35	22 48	

A from 21 May

B until 18 May

Purley and East Croydon - London

COMPLETE SERVICE

Mondays to Fridays

		SN	SN	SN	SN	FC	FC	SN	SN	SN	SN	SN	SN	SN	SN	FC	FC	SN	SN	SN	SN	FC	FC
		◇1	1		◇1	1	1	1	◇1	1		◇1	1	◇1		1	1	1		1	◇1	1	1
						A	B		⊼							A	B					A	B
Purley 4	d		22 19	22 21							22 38		22 50		22 52				23 08				
Purley Oaks	d			22 24							22 41				22 55				23 11				
South Croydon 4	d			22 27							22 44				22 58				23 14				
East Croydon	d	22 24	22 25	22 30	22 30	22 32	22 32	22 34	22 41	22 44	22 47	22 54	22 56	23 00	23 01	23 02	23 02	23 14	23 17	23 20	23 30	23 32	23 32
Norwood Junction 2	d			22 35											23 06								
New Cross Gate	d			22 52											23 23								
London Bridge 4 ⊖	a			22 59		22 45	22 47	22 49							23 30	23 15	23 17					23 45	23 47
London Blackfriars 3 ⊖	a					22 52										23 22						23 52	
City Thameslink 3	a					22 53																	
Farringdon 3 ⊖	a					22 58										23 28						23 58	
St Pancras International 15 ⊖	a					23 02										23 32						00 02	
Clapham Junction 10	a	22 33	22 37		22 40				22 50	22 55	23 07	23 03	23 06	23 10				23 25	23 37	23 32	23 42		
London Victoria 15 ⊖	a	22 41	22 44		22 50				22 57	23 05	23 16	23 13	23 15	23 20				23 35	23 48	23 40	23 52		

		SN	SN
			1
Purley 4	d	23 34	23 49
Purley Oaks	d	23 37	
South Croydon 4	d	23 40	
East Croydon	d	23 43	23 58
Norwood Junction 2	d	23a47	
New Cross Gate	d		
London Bridge 4 ⊖	a		
London Blackfriars 3 ⊖	a		
City Thameslink 3	a		
Farringdon 3 ⊖	a		
St Pancras International 15 ⊖	a		
Clapham Junction 10	a		00 11
London Victoria 15 ⊖	a		00 18

Saturdays

		FC	SN	FC	FC	SN	FC	FC	SN	SN	FC	FC	SN	FC	FC	SN	FC	FC	SN	FC	FC	FC	FC
		1	1	1	1	◇1	1	1		1	1		1	1		1	1		1	1		1	
		C		D	C		C	D			D			D			D			D		D	
Purley 4	d		23p49			00 11				01 22			02 22			03 22			04 22				
Purley Oaks	d																						
South Croydon 4	d																						
East Croydon	d	23p32	23p58	00 04	00 04	00 17	00 36	00 36	00 49	01 28	01 50	01 50	02 28	02 47	02 47	03 28	03 47	03 47	04 28	04 47	04 47	05 17	05 17
Norwood Junction 2	d																						
New Cross Gate	d																						
London Bridge 4 ⊖	a	23p45		00 19	00 21		00 51	00 52			02 14			03 12			04 12			05 12		05 42	
London Blackfriars 3 ⊖	a	23p52			00 28		00 58					02 13			03 13			04 13			05 13		05 43
City Thameslink 3	a																						
Farringdon 3 ⊖	a	23p58			00 33																05 19		05 49
St Pancras International 15 ⊖	a	00 02			00 37		01 07					02 24			03 23			04 22			05 24		05 54
Clapham Junction 10	a		00 11			00 29			01 01	01 41			02 41			03 41			04 41				
London Victoria 15 ⊖	a		00 18			00 37			01 09	01 49			02 49			03 49			04 50				

		SN	FC	FC	SN	SN	SN	FC	FC	SN	SN	SN	SN	SN	FC	FC	SN	SN	SN	SN	SN	SN	SN
		1	1		◇1	1	◇1	1	1	1		◇1			1	1	◇1	1		1	◇1	1	1
			D						D							D							
Purley 4	d	05 24			05 58					06 19	06 21			06 38				06 49	06 51	07 02			
Purley Oaks	d										06 24			06 41					06 54				
South Croydon 4	d										06 27			06 44					06 57			07 07	
East Croydon	d	05 29	05 47	05 47	06 07	06 10	06 11	06 17	06 17	06 25	06 30	06 41	06 43	06 47	06 47	06 47	06 53	06 55	07 00	07 07	07 10	07 10	07 14
Norwood Junction 2	d									06 29	06 35		06 50					06 59	07 05	07 13			
New Cross Gate	d									06 37	06 52		07 04					07 07	07 22				
London Bridge 4 ⊖	a		06 01	06 02				06 30	06 32	06 43	06 59		07 11		07 00	07 02		07 13	07 29	07 25			
London Blackfriars 3 ⊖	a			06 08				06 37							07 07								
City Thameslink 3	a																						
Farringdon 3 ⊖	a			06 12				06 42							07 12								
St Pancras International 15 ⊖	a			06 16				06 46							07 16								
Clapham Junction 10	a	05 49			06 18	06 34	06 21					06 50		07 07			07 02				07 19	07 34	07 25
London Victoria 15 ⊖	a	05 58			06 26		06 30					06 57		07 16			07 09				07 27		07 32

		SN	FC	FC	SN	SN	SN	SN	FC	FC	SN	SN	SN	SN	SN	FC	FC	SN	SN	SN	SN	SN
			1	1	◇1	1		◇1	1	1	1	1	◇1	1		1	1		◇1	1		◇1
				D						D							D					
Purley 4	d	07 08				07 19	07 21					07 34			07 38			07 45		07 49	07 51	
Purley Oaks	d	07 11					07 24								07 41						07 54	
South Croydon 4	d	07 14					07 27								07 44						07 57	
East Croydon	d	07 17	07 17	07 17	07 23	07 25	07 30	07 30	07 32	07 32	07 33	07 39	07 42	07 44	07 47	07 47	07 47	07 51	07 53	07 55	08 00	08 00
Norwood Junction 2	d					07 29	07 35					07 45						07 55		07 59	08 05	
New Cross Gate	d					07 37	07 52													08 07	08 22	
London Bridge 4 ⊖	a		07 30	07 32		07 43	07 59		07 45	07 47	07 49	07 57				08 00	08 02	08 09		08 13	08 29	
London Blackfriars 3 ⊖	a		07 37						07 52							08 07						
City Thameslink 3	a																					
Farringdon 3 ⊖	a		07 43						07 59							08 13						
St Pancras International 15 ⊖	a		07 48						08 04							08 18						
Clapham Junction 10	a	07 37			07 32			07 39					07 51	07 55	08 07				08 02			08 09
London Victoria 15 ⊖	a	07 46			07 40			07 46					07 58	08 02	08 16				08 10			08 16

A from 21 May
B until 18 May
C not 19 May
D 19 May

Purley and East Croydon - London

COMPLETE SERVICE

Saturdays

		FC	FC	SN	SN	SN	SN	SN	SN	FC	FC	SN	SN	SN	SN	SN	FC	FC	SN	SN	SN	SN	SN
		1	1	1	◇1	1	◇1	1		1	1		◇1	1	◇1		1	1	1	1	◇1	1	
		A									A		⊼					A					
Purley 4	d			08 02					08 08			08 15		08 19		08 21				08 32			08 38
Purley Oaks	d								08 11							08 24							08 41
South Croydon 4	d					08 07			08 14							08 27							08 44
East Croydon	d	08 01	08 02	08 07	08 08	08 10	08 12	08 14	08 17	08 17	08 17	08 21	08 23	08 25	08 28	08 30	08 32	08 32	08 33	08 37	08 40	08 44	08 47
Norwood Junction 2	d			08 13								08 25		08 29		08 35				08 43			
New Cross Gate	d													08 37		08 52							
London Bridge 4 ⊖	a	08 17	08 15	08 25						08 30	08 32	08 39		08 43		08 59	08 45	08 47	08 49	08 55			
London Blackfriars 3 ⊖	a		08 22							08 37							08 52						
City Thameslink 3	a																						
Farringdon 3 ⊖	a		08 29							08 43							08 59						
St Pancras International 15 ⊖	a		08 34							08 48							09 04						
Clapham Junction 10	a				08 17	08 34	08 21	08 25	08 37				08 32		08 37						08 50	08 55	09 07
London Victoria 15 ⊖	a				08 24		08 28	08 32	08 46				08 40		08 44						08 57	09 02	09 16

		FC	FC	SN	SN	SN	SN	SN	FC	FC	SN	SN	SN	SN	SN	SN	FC	FC	SN	SN	SN	SN	SN
		1	1		◇1	1		◇1	1	1	1	◇1	1	◇1	1		1	1		◇1	1	◇1	
			A		⊼				A									A		⊼		⊼	
Purley 4	d			08 45		08 49	08 51				09 02					09 08			09 15		09 19		09 21
Purley Oaks	d						08 54									09 11							09 24
South Croydon 4	d						08 57						09 07			09 14							09 27
East Croydon	d	08 47	08 47	08 51	08 53	08 55	09 00	09 00	09 01	09 02	09 07	09 08	09 10	09 12	09 14	09 17	09 17	09 17	09 21	09 23	09 25	09 28	09 30
Norwood Junction 2	d			08 55		08 59	09 05				09 13								09 25		09 29		09 35
New Cross Gate	d					09 07	09 22														09 37		09 52
London Bridge 4 ⊖	a	09 00	09 02	09 09		09 13	09 29		09 17	09 15	09 25						09 30	09 32	09 39		09 43		09 59
London Blackfriars 3 ⊖	a	09 07								09 22							09 37						
City Thameslink 3	a	09 10								09 26							09 40						
Farringdon 3 ⊖	a	09 14								09 30							09 44						
St Pancras International 15 ⊖	a	09 18								09 34							09 48						
Clapham Junction 10	a				09 02			09 09				09 17	09 34	09 21	09 25	09 37				09 32		09 37	
London Victoria 15 ⊖	a				09 10			09 16				09 24		09 28	09 32	09 46				09 40		09 44	

		FC		FC	FC	SN	SN	SN	SN	SN	FC	FC	SN	SN	SN	SN	SN	FC	FC	SN	SN
		1		1	1	1	1	◇1	1		1	1		◇1	1		◇1	1	1	1	◇1
					A							A		⊼				A			
Purley 4	d		and at the same minutes past each hour until				12 32			12 38			12 45		12 49	12 51				13 02	
Purley Oaks	d									12 41						12 54					
South Croydon 4	d									12 44						12 57					
East Croydon	d	09 32		12 32	12 32	12 33	12 38	12 40	12 44	12 47	12 47	12 47	12 51	12 53	12 55	13 00	13 00	13 01	13 02	13 07	13 08
Norwood Junction 2	d						12 43						12 55		12 59	13 05				13 13	
New Cross Gate	d														13 07	13 22					
London Bridge 4 ⊖	a	09 45		12 45	12 47	12 49	12 55				13 00	13 02	13 09		13 13	13 29		13 17	13 15	13 25	
London Blackfriars 3 ⊖	a	09 52		12 52							13 07								13 22		
City Thameslink 3	a	09 56		12 56							13 10								13 26		
Farringdon 3 ⊖	a	10 00		13 00							13 14								13 30		
St Pancras International 15 ⊖	a	10 04		13 04							13 18								13 34		
Clapham Junction 10	a							12 50	12 55	13 07				13 02			13 09				13 17
London Victoria 15 ⊖	a							12 57	13 02	13 16				13 10			13 16				13 24

		SN	SN	SN	SN	FC	FC	SN	SN	SN	SN	SN	FC	FC	SN	SN		SN	SN	SN	SN	FC
		1	◇1	1		1	1		◇1	1	◇1		1	1	1	1		1	◇1	1		1
							A		⊼		⊼			A								
Purley 4	d				13 08			13 15		13 19		13 21				13 32	and at the same minutes past each hour until	16 32			16 38	
Purley Oaks	d				13 11							13 24									16 41	
South Croydon 4	d	13 07			13 14							13 27									16 44	
East Croydon	d	13 10	13 12	13 14	13 17	13 17	13 17	13 21	13 23	13 25	13 28	13 30	13 32	13 32	13 33	13 37		16 37	16 40	16 44	16 47	16 47
Norwood Junction 2	d							13 25		13 29		13 35				13 43		16 43				
New Cross Gate	d									13 37		13 52										
London Bridge 4 ⊖	a					13 30	13 32	13 39		13 43		13 59	13 45	13 47	13 49	13 55		16 55				17 00
London Blackfriars 3 ⊖	a					13 37							13 52									17 07
City Thameslink 3	a					13 40							13 56									17 10
Farringdon 3 ⊖	a					13 44							14 00									17 14
St Pancras International 15 ⊖	a					13 48							14 04									17 18
Clapham Junction 10	a	13 34	13 21	13 25	13 37				13 32		13 37								16 50	16 55	17 07	
London Victoria 15 ⊖	a		13 28	13 32	13 46				13 40		13 44								16 57	17 02	17 16	

A 19 May

Purley and East Croydon - London

COMPLETE SERVICE

		FC ■1 A	SN	SN ◇■1	SN ■1	SN	SN ◇■1	FC ■1 A	FC ■1	SN ■1	SN ◇■1	SN ■1	SN ◇■1	SN ■1	SN	FC ■1	FC ■1 A	SN	SN ◇■1	SN ■1	SN ◇■1	SN	FC ■1 B
Purley 4	d		16 45		16 49	16 51				17 02					17 08			17 15		17 19		17 21	
Purley Oaks	d					16 54									17 11							17 24	
South Croydon 4	d					16 57						17 07			17 14							17 27	
East Croydon	d	16 47	16 51	16 53	16 55	17 00	17 00	17 01	17 02	17 07	17 08	17 10	17 12	17 14	17 17	17 17	17 17	17 21	17 23	17 25	17 28	17 30	17 31
Norwood Junction 2	d		16 55		16 59	17 05				17 13								17 25		17 29		17 35	
New Cross Gate	d				17 07	17 22														17 37		17 52	
London Bridge 4	a	17 02	17 09		17 13	17 30		17 17	17 15	17 25						17 30	17 32	17 39		17 43		17 59	17 45
London Blackfriars 3	a								17 22							17 37							17 52
City Thameslink 3	a								17 26							17 40							17 56
Farringdon 3	a								17 30							17 44							18 00
St Pancras International 15	a								17 34							17 48							18 04
Clapham Junction 10	a			17 02			17 09				17 17	17 34	17 21	17 25	17 38				17 32		17 37		
London Victoria 15	a			17 10			17 16				17 24		17 28	17 32	17 47				17 40		17 44		

		FC ■1 A	FC ■1 A	SN ■1	SN ■1	SN ◇■1	SN ■1	SN	FC ■1	FC ■1 A	SN	SN ◇■1	SN ■1	SN	SN ◇■1	FC ■1 A	FC ■1	SN ■1	SN ◇■1	SN ■1	SN ◇■1	SN ■1
Purley 4	d				17 32			17 38			17 45		17 49	17 51				18 02				
Purley Oaks	d							17 41						17 54								
South Croydon 4	d							17 44						17 57						18 07		
East Croydon	d	17 32	17 32	17 33	17 37	17 40	17 44	17 47	17 47	17 47	17 51	17 53	17 55	18 00	18 00	18 01	18 02	18 07	18 08	18 10	18 12	18 14
Norwood Junction 2	d				17 43						17 55		17 59	18 05				18 13				
New Cross Gate	d												18 07	18 22								
London Bridge 4	a	17 45	17 47	17 49	17 55				18 00	18 02	18 09		18 13	18 29		18 17	18 15	18 25				
London Blackfriars 3	a	17 52							18 07								18 22					
City Thameslink 3	a	17 56							18 10								18 26					
Farringdon 3	a	18 00							18 14								18 30					
St Pancras International 15	a	18 04							18 18								18 34					
Clapham Junction 10	a					17 50	17 55	18 07				18 02			18 09				18 17	18 34	18 21	18 25
London Victoria 15	a					17 57	18 02	18 16				18 10			18 16				18 24		18 28	18 32

		SN	FC ■1	FC ■1 A	SN	SN ◇■1	SN ■1	SN ◇■1	SN	FC ■1	FC ■1 A	SN ■1	SN ■1	SN ◇■1	SN ■1	SN	FC ■1	FC ■1 A	SN	SN ◇■1	SN ■1	SN	SN ◇■1
Purley 4	d	18 08			18 15		18 19		18 21				18 32			18 38			18 45		18 49	18 51	
Purley Oaks	d	18 11							18 24							18 41						18 54	
South Croydon 4	d	18 14							18 27							18 44						18 57	
East Croydon	d	18 17	18 17	18 17	18 21	18 23	18 25	18 28	18 30	18 32	18 32	18 33	18 37	18 40	18 44	18 47	18 47	18 47	18 51	18 53	18 55	19 00	19 00
Norwood Junction 2	d				18 25		18 29		18 35				18 43						18 55		18 59	19 05	
New Cross Gate	d						18 37		18 52												19 07	19 22	
London Bridge 4	a		18 30	18 32	18 39		18 43		18 59	18 45	18 47	18 49	18 55				19 00	19 02	19 09		19 13	19 29	
London Blackfriars 3	a		18 37							18 52							19 07						
City Thameslink 3	a		18 40							18 56							19 10						
Farringdon 3	a		18 44							19 00							19 14						
St Pancras International 15	a		18 48							19 04							19 18						
Clapham Junction 10	a	18 37				18 32		18 37						18 50	18 55	19 07				19 02			19 09
London Victoria 15	a	18 46				18 40		18 44						18 57	19 02	19 16				19 10			19 16

		FC ■1 A	FC ■1	SN ■1	SN ◇■1	SN ■1	SN ◇■1	SN ■1	SN	FC ■1	FC ■1 A	SN	SN ◇■1	SN ■1	SN ◇■1	SN	FC ■1	FC ■1 A	SN ■1	SN ◇■1	SN ◇■1	SN ■1
Purley 4	d			19 02					19 08			19 15		19 19		19 21						
Purley Oaks	d								19 11							19 24						
South Croydon 4	d					19 07			19 14							19 27						
East Croydon	d	19 01	19 02	19 07	19 08	19 10	19 12	19 14	19 17	19 17	19 17	19 21	19 23	19 25	19 29	19 30	19 32	19 32	19 33	19 38	19 42	19 44
Norwood Junction 2	d			19 13								19 25				19 35						
New Cross Gate	d															19 52						
London Bridge 4	a	19 17	19 15	19 25						19 30	19 32	19 39				19 59	19 45	19 47	19 49			
London Blackfriars 3	a		19 22							19 37							19 52					
City Thameslink 3	a		19 26							19 40							19 56					
Farringdon 3	a		19 30							19 44							20 00					
St Pancras International 15	a		19 34							19 48							20 04					
Clapham Junction 10	a				19 17	19 34	19 21	19 25	19 37				19 32	19 37	19 40					19 47	19 51	19 55
London Victoria 15	a				19 24		19 28	19 32	19 46				19 40	19 44	19 50					19 54	19 58	20 05

		SN	FC ■1	FC ■1 A	SN	SN ◇■1	SN ■1	SN	SN ■1	FC ■1 A	FC ■1	SN ◇■1	SN ■1	SN	FC ■1	FC ■1 A	SN	SN ◇■1	SN ■1	SN	SN ◇■1	FC ■1	FC ■1 A
Purley 4	d	19 38			19 45		19 49	19 51						20 08			20 15		20 19	20 21			
Purley Oaks	d	19 41						19 54						20 11						20 24			
South Croydon 4	d	19 44						19 57						20 14						20 27			
East Croydon	d	19 47	19 47	19 47	19 51	19 53	19 57	20 00	20 00	20 01	20 02	20 12	20 14	20 17	20 17	20 17	20 21	20 23	20 26	20 30	20 30	20 32	20 32
Norwood Junction 2	d				19 55			20 05									20 25			20 35			
New Cross Gate	d							20 22												20 52			
London Bridge 4	a		20 00	20 02	20 09			20 29		20 17	20 15				20 30	20 32	20 39			20 59		20 45	20 47
London Blackfriars 3	a		20 07								20 22				20 37							20 52	
City Thameslink 3	a		20 10								20 26				20 40							20 56	
Farringdon 3	a		20 14								20 30				20 44							21 00	
St Pancras International 15	a		20 18								20 34				20 48							21 04	
Clapham Junction 10	a	20 07				20 02	20 08		20 11			20 21	20 25	20 37				20 32	20 37		20 40		
London Victoria 15	a	20 16				20 10	20 15		20 20			20 28	20 32	20 46				20 40	20 44		20 50		

A 19 May

B not 19 May

Purley and East Croydon - London

COMPLETE SERVICE

		SN ■1	SN ◇■1	SN ■1	SN	FC ■1	FC ■1 A	SN	SN ◇■1	SN ■1	SN	SN ◇■1	FC ■1 A	FC ■1	SN ◇■1	SN ■1	SN	FC ■1	FC ■1 A	SN	SN ◇■1	SN ■1	SN
Purley 4	d				20 38			20 45		20 49	20 51						21 08			21 15		21 19	21 21
Purley Oaks	d				20 41						20 54						21 11						21 24
South Croydon 4	d				20 44						20 57						21 14						21 27
East Croydon	d	20 33	20 42	20 44	20 47	20 47	20 47	20 51	20 53	20 56	21 00	21 00	21 01	21 02	21 09	21 14	21 17	21 17	21 17	21 21	21 23	21 26	21 30
Norwood Junction 2	d							20 55			21 05									21 25			21 35
New Cross Gate	d										21 22												21 52
London Bridge 4	a	20 49				21 00	21 02	21 09			21 29		21 17	21 15				21 30	21 32	21 39			21 59
London Blackfriars 3	a					21 07								21 22				21 37					
City Thameslink 3	a																						
Farringdon 3	a					21 13								21 29				21 43					
St Pancras International 15	a					21 18								21 34				21 48					
Clapham Junction 10	a		20 51	20 55	21 07				21 02	21 07		21 10			21 18	21 25	21 37				21 32	21 37	
London Victoria 15	a		20 58	21 02	21 16				21 10	21 14		21 17			21 26	21 32	21 46				21 40	21 44	

		SN ◇■1	FC ■1	FC ■1 A	SN ■1	SN ◇■1	SN ■1	SN	SN	SN ◇■1	SN ■1	SN	SN ◇■1	FC ■1 A	FC ■1	SN ◇■1	SN ■1	SN	SN	SN ◇■1	SN ■1	SN
Purley 4	d							21 38	21 45		21 49	21 51						22 08	22 15		22 19	22 21
Purley Oaks	d							21 41				21 54						22 11				22 24
South Croydon 4	d							21 44				21 57						22 14				22 27
East Croydon	d	21 31	21 32	21 32	21 33	21 42	21 44	21 47	21 51	21 53	21 56	22 00	22 00	22 01	22 02	22 09	22 14	22 17	22 21	22 23	22 26	22 30
Norwood Junction 2	d								21 55			22 05							22 25			22 35
New Cross Gate	d											22 22										22 52
London Bridge 4	a		21 45	21 47	21 49				22 09			22 29		22 17	22 15				22 39			22 59
London Blackfriars 3	a		21 52												22 22							
City Thameslink 3	a																					
Farringdon 3	a		21 59												22 27							
St Pancras International 15	a		22 04												22 32							
Clapham Junction 10	a	21 40				21 51	21 55	22 07		22 02	22 07		22 10			22 18	22 25	22 37		22 32	22 37	
London Victoria 15	a	21 50				21 58	22 02	22 16		22 13	22 15		22 20			22 26	22 35	22 46		22 40	22 44	

		SN ◇■1	FC ■1	SN ■1	SN ◇■1	SN ■1	SN	SN	SN ■1	SN ◇■1	FC ■1 A	SN	FC ■1	SN ■1	SN	SN	SN ◇■1	FC ■1 B	FC ■1 C	FC ■1 A	SN	SN ■1
Purley 4	d						22 38	22 45	22 50			22 52			23 08	23 15					23 34	23 49
Purley Oaks	d						22 41					22 55			23 11						23 37	
South Croydon 4	d						22 44					22 58			23 14						23 40	
East Croydon	d	22 31	22 32	22 33	22 40	22 44	22 47	22 51	22 56	23 00	23 01	23 01	23 02	23 14	23 17	23 21	23 30	23 32	23 32	23 32	23 43	23 56
Norwood Junction 2	d							22 55				23 06				23 25					23a47	
New Cross Gate	d											23 23										
London Bridge 4	a		22 45	22 49				23 09			23 17	23 30	23 15			23 39		23 44	23 46	23 47		
London Blackfriars 3	a		22 52										23 22					23 52	23 52			
City Thameslink 3	a																					
Farringdon 3	a		22 57										23 28					23 58	23 58			
St Pancras International 15	a		23 02										23 32					00 02	00 02			
Clapham Junction 10	a	22 40			22 49	22 55	23 07		23 06	23 10				23 25	23 37		23 41					00 11
London Victoria 15	a	22 50			22 57	23 05	23 16		23 14	23 20				23 35	23 48		23 52					00 18

Sundays

until 24 June

		FC ■1	SN ■1	FC ■1 D	FC ■1	SN ◇■1	FC ■1	FC ■1 D	SN	SN ■1	SN ■1	SN ■1	SN ■1	SN ◇■1	FC	SN ■1	FC	SN	SN	FC ■1	SN ◇■1	SN	SN
Purley 4	d		23p49			00 11				01 37	02 33	03 33	04 33	05 22		05 56			06 38				07 08
Purley Oaks	d																		06 41				07 11
South Croydon 4	d																		06 44				07 14
East Croydon	d	23p32	23p56	00 04	00 04	00 17	00 36	00 36	00 49	01 43	02 40	03 40	04 40	05 28	05 32	06 02	06 32	06 40	06 47	07 02	07 10	07 12	07 17
Norwood Junction 2	d																		06 52				07 22
New Cross Gate	d																		07 09				07 39
London Bridge 4	a	23p46		00 19	00 21		00 51	00 52											07 17	07 15		07 50	07 48
London Blackfriars 3	a	23p52			00 28		00 58								05 59		06 59			07 22			
City Thameslink 3	a																						
Farringdon 3	a	23p58			00 33															07 27			
St Pancras International 15	a	00 02			00 37		01 07													07 32			
Clapham Junction 10	a		00 11			00 29			01 03	01 54	02 53	03 53	04 53	05 47		06 14		07 00			07 24		
London Victoria 15	a		00 18			00 37			01 10	02 05	03 05	04 05	05 05	05 56		06 22		07 09			07 31		

A 19 May

B from 30 June

C until 23 June

D 20 May

Table 175

Purley and East Croydon - London

COMPLETE SERVICE

Sundays until 24 June

		SN 1	FC 1	SN	SN	SN	SN 1	SN ◇1	FC 1	SN ◇1	SN	SN	SN ◇1	SN	FC 1	SN 1	SN ◇1	SN	SN ◇1	SN	SN 1	SN	SN 1
Purley	d	07 20			07 38	07 47	07 50					08 08	08 14	08 17		08 27				08 38		08 47	08 50
Purley Oaks	d				07 41							08 11								08 41			
South Croydon	d	07 24			07 44							08 14								08 44			
East Croydon	d	07 27	07 32	07 42	07 47	07 53	07 56	08 00	08 02	08 09	08 12	08 17	08 20	08 23	08 32	08 34	08 39	08 42	08 46	08 47	08 50	08 53	08 56
Norwood Junction	d				07 52		08 01					08 22				08 38				08 52			09 01
New Cross Gate	d				08 09							08 39								09 09			
London Bridge	a		07 45	08 19	08 17		08 12		08 15		08 49	08 48			08 45	08 51		09 19		09 18			09 12
London Blackfriars	a		07 52						08 22						08 52								
City Thameslink	a																						
Farringdon	a		07 57						08 27						08 57								
St Pancras International	a		08 02						08 32						09 02								
Clapham Junction	a	07 41				08 12		08 09		08 18			08 32	08 42			08 48		08 55		09 02	09 12	
London Victoria	a	07 48				08 20		08 16		08 25			08 39	08 50			08 55		09 03		09 09	09 20	

		SN ◇1	FC 1	SN ◇1	SN	SN	SN ◇1	SN ◇1	SN	FC 1 A	SN 1	SN ◇1	SN	SN ◇1	FC 1	SN	SN 1	SN	SN 1	SN ◇1	FC 1	SN ◇1
Purley	d					09 08		09 14	09 17		09 27					09 38		09 47	09 50			
Purley Oaks	d					09 11										09 41						
South Croydon	d					09 14										09 44						
East Croydon	d	09 00	09 02	09 09	09 12	09 17	09 17	09 20	09 23	09 32	09 34	09 39	09 42	09 46	09 47	09 47	09 50	09 53	09 56	10 00	10 02	10 09
Norwood Junction	d					09 22					09 38					09 52			10 01			
New Cross Gate	d					09 39										10 09						
London Bridge	a		09 15		09 49	09 48				09 45	09 51		10 19		10 00	10 18			10 12		10 15	
London Blackfriars	a		09 22							09 52					10 07						10 22	
City Thameslink	a																					
Farringdon	a		09 27							09 56					10 14						10 26	
St Pancras International	a		09 32							10 01					10 18						10 31	
Clapham Junction	a	09 09		09 18			09 26	09 32	09 42			09 48		09 55			10 02	10 12		10 09		10 18
London Victoria	a	09 17		09 25			09 33	09 39	09 50			09 55		10 03			10 09	10 20		10 17		10 25

		SN	SN ◇1	FC 1	SN	SN ◇1	SN	FC 1	SN 1	SN ◇1	SN	SN ◇1	FC 1	SN	SN 1	SN	SN 1	SN ◇1	FC 1	SN ◇1	SN	SN ◇1	FC 1
Purley	d				10 08	10 14	10 17		10 27					10 38		10 47	10 50						
Purley Oaks	d				10 11									10 41									
South Croydon	d				10 14									10 44									
East Croydon	d	10 12	10 17	10 17	10 17	10 20	10 23	10 32	10 34	10 39	10 42	10 46	10 47	10 47	10 50	10 53	10 56	11 00	11 02	11 09	11 12	11 17	11 17
Norwood Junction	d				10 22				10 38					10 52			11 01						
New Cross Gate	d				10 39									11 09									
London Bridge	a	10 49		10 30	10 48			10 45	10 51		11 19		11 00	11 18			11 12		11 15		11 49		11 30
London Blackfriars	a			10 37				10 52					11 07						11 22				11 37
City Thameslink	a																						
Farringdon	a			10 44				10 56					11 14						11 26				11 44
St Pancras International	a			10 48				11 01					11 18						11 31				11 48
Clapham Junction	a		10 26			10 32	10 42			10 48		10 55			11 02	11 12		11 09		11 18		11 26	
London Victoria	a		10 33			10 39	10 50			10 55		11 03			11 09	11 20		11 18		11 25		11 33	

		SN	SN ◇1	SN	FC 1	SN 1	SN ◇1	SN	SN ◇1	FC 1	SN	SN 1	SN	SN 1	SN ◇1		SN ◇1	FC 1	SN ◇1	SN	SN ◇1
Purley	d	11 08	11 14	11 17		11 27					11 38		11 47	11 50							
Purley Oaks	d	11 11									11 41										
South Croydon	d	11 14									11 44										
East Croydon	d	11 17	11 20	11 23	11 32	11 34	11 39	11 42	11 46	11 47	11 47	11 50	11 53	11 56	12 00	and at the same minutes past each hour until	18 00	18 02	18 09	18 12	18 17
Norwood Junction	d	11 22				11 38					11 52			12 01							
New Cross Gate	d	11 39									12 09										
London Bridge	a	11 48			11 45	11 51		12 19		12 00	12 18			12 12				18 15		18 49	
London Blackfriars	a				11 52					12 07								18 22			
City Thameslink	a																				
Farringdon	a				11 56					12 14								18 26			
St Pancras International	a				12 01					12 18								18 31			
Clapham Junction	a		11 32	11 42			11 48		11 55			12 02	12 12		12 09		18 09		18 18		18 26
London Victoria	a		11 39	11 50			11 55		12 03			12 09	12 20		12 17		18 17		18 25		18 33

		FC 1	SN	SN ◇1	SN	FC 1	SN 1	SN ◇1	SN	SN ◇1	FC 1	SN	SN 1	SN	SN 1	SN ◇1	FC 1	SN ◇1	SN	SN ◇1	FC 1	SN	SN ◇1
Purley	d		18 08	18 14	18 17		18 27					18 38		18 47	18 50							19 08	19 14
Purley Oaks	d		18 11									18 41										19 11	
South Croydon	d		18 14									18 44										19 14	
East Croydon	d	18 17	18 17	18 20	18 23	18 32	18 34	18 39	18 42	18 46	18 47	18 47	18 50	18 53	18 56	19 00	19 02	19 09	19 12	19 17	19 17	19 17	19 20
Norwood Junction	d		18 22				18 38					18 52			19 01							19 22	
New Cross Gate	d		18 40									19 09										19 39	
London Bridge	a	18 30	18 48			18 45	18 51		19 19		19 00	19 18			19 12		19 15		19 49		19 30	19 48	
London Blackfriars	a	18 37				18 52					19 07						19 22				19 37		
City Thameslink	a																						
Farringdon	a	18 44				18 56					19 14						19 26				19 44		
St Pancras International	a	18 48				19 01					19 18						19 31				19 48		
Clapham Junction	a			18 32	18 42			18 48		18 55			19 02	19 12		19 09		19 18		19 26			19 32
London Victoria	a			18 39	18 50			18 55		19 03			19 09	19 20		19 17		19 25		19 33			19 39

A not 20 May

Table 175

Purley and East Croydon - London

COMPLETE SERVICE

Sundays until 24 June

		SN	FC 1	SN 1	SN ◇1	SN	SN ◇1	SN	SN 1	SN	SN 1	SN ◇1	FC 1	SN ◇1	SN	SN	SN ◇1	SN ◇1	SN	FC 1	SN 1	SN ◇1	SN
Purley	d	19 17		19 27				19 38		19 47	19 50					20 08		20 14	20 17		20 27		
Purley Oaks	d							19 41								20 11							
South Croydon	d							19 44								20 14							
East Croydon	d	19 23	19 32	19 34	19 39	19 42	19 46	19 47	19 50	19 53	19 56	20 00	20 02	20 09	20 12	20 17	20 17	20 20	20 23	20 32	20 34	20 39	20 42
Norwood Junction	d			19 38				19 52			20 01					20 22					20 38		
New Cross Gate	d							20 09								20 39							
London Bridge	a		19 45	19 51		20 19		20 18			20 12		20 15		20 49	20 48				20 45	20 51		21 19
London Blackfriars	a		19 52										20 22							20 52			
City Thameslink	a																						
Farringdon	a		19 56										20 26							20 56			
St Pancras International	a		20 01										20 31							21 01			
Clapham Junction	a	19 42			19 48		19 55		20 02	20 12		20 09		20 18			20 26	20 32	20 42			20 48	
London Victoria	a	19 50			19 55		20 03		20 09	20 20		20 17		20 25			20 33	20 39	20 50			20 55	

		SN ◇1	SN	SN 1	SN	SN 1	SN ◇1	FC 1	SN ◇1	SN	SN	SN ◇1	SN ◇1	SN	FC 1	SN 1	SN ◇1	SN	SN	SN 1	SN	SN 1
Purley	d		20 38		20 47	20 50					21 08		21 14	21 17		21 27			21 38		21 47	21 50
Purley Oaks	d		20 41								21 11								21 41			
South Croydon	d		20 44								21 14								21 44			
East Croydon	d	20 46	20 47	20 50	20 53	20 56	21 00	21 02	21 09	21 12	21 17	21 17	21 20	21 23	21 32	21 34	21 39	21 42	21 47	21 50	21 53	21 56
Norwood Junction	d		20 52			21 01					21 22					21 38			21 52			22 01
New Cross Gate	d		21 09								21 39								22 09			
London Bridge	a		21 18			21 12		21 15		21 49	21 48				21 45	21 51		22 19	22 18			22 12
London Blackfriars	a							21 22							21 52							
City Thameslink	a																					
Farringdon	a							21 26							21 56							
St Pancras International	a							21 31							22 01							
Clapham Junction	a	20 55		21 02	21 12		21 09		21 18			21 26	21 32	21 42			21 48			22 02	22 12	
London Victoria	a	21 03		21 09	21 20		21 17		21 25			21 33	21 39	21 50			21 55			22 09	22 20	

		SN ◇1	FC 1	SN ◇1	SN	SN	SN ◇1	SN	FC 1	SN 1	SN	SN	SN 1	SN	SN 1	SN ◇1	FC 1	SN	SN ◇1	SN	FC 1	SN 1	SN 1
Purley	d					22 08	22 14	22 17		22 27		22 38		22 47	22 50			23 08	23 14	23 17			23 50
Purley Oaks	d					22 11						22 41						23 11		23 20			
South Croydon	d					22 14						22 44						23 14		23 23			
East Croydon	d	22 00	22 02	22 09	22 12	22 17	22 20	22 23	22 32	22 34	22 42	22 47	22 50	22 53	22 56	23 00	23 02	23 17	23 21	23a25	23 32	23 50	23 56
Norwood Junction	d					22 22				22 38		22 52						23a21					
New Cross Gate	d					22 39						23 09											
London Bridge	a		22 15		22 49	22 48			22 45	22 51	23 19	23 18					23 15				23 45		
London Blackfriars	a		22 22						22 52								23 22				23 52		
City Thameslink	a																						
Farringdon	a		22 26						22 56								23 26				23 56		
St Pancras International	a		22 31						23 01								23 31				00 01		
Clapham Junction	a	22 09		22 18			22 32	22 42					23 02	23 12	23 07	23 10			23 31			00 01	00 11
London Victoria	a	22 17		22 25			22 39	22 52					23 09	23 20	23 14	23 20			23 38			00 08	00 19

Sundays 1 July to 9 September

		FC 1	SN 1	FC 1	SN ◇1	FC 1	SN	SN 1	SN 1	SN 1	SN 1	SN ◇1	FC A	FC B	SN 1	FC A	FC B	SN	SN	FC 1	SN ◇1	SN	SN
Purley	d		23p49		00 11			01 37	02 33	03 33	04 33	05 22			05 56				06 38				07 08
Purley Oaks	d																		06 41				07 11
South Croydon	d																		06 44				07 14
East Croydon	d	23p32	23p56	00 04	00 17	00 36	00 49	01 43	02 40	03 40	04 40	05 28	05 32	05 32	06 02	06 32	06 32	06 40	06 47	07 02	07 10	07 12	07 17
Norwood Junction	d																		06 52				07 22
New Cross Gate	d																		07 09				07 39
London Bridge	a	23p44		00 21		00 51													07 17	07 15		07 50	07 48
London Blackfriars	a	23p52		00 28		00 58							05 59	05 59		06 59	06 59			07 22			
City Thameslink	a																07 01						
Farringdon	a	23p58		00 33										06 03						07 26			
St Pancras International	a	00 02		00 37		01 07								06 07			07 09			07 31			
Clapham Junction	a		00 11		00 29		01 03	01 54	02 53	03 53	04 53	05 47			06 14			07 00			07 24		
London Victoria	a		00 18		00 37		01 10	02 05	03 05	04 05	05 05	05 56			06 22			07 09			07 31		

		SN 1	FC 1	SN	SN	SN	SN 1	SN ◇1	FC 1	SN ◇1	SN	SN	SN ◇1	SN	FC 1	SN 1	SN ◇1	SN	SN ◇1	SN	SN 1	SN	SN 1
Purley	d	07 20			07 38	07 47	07 50					08 08	08 14	08 17		08 27				08 38		08 47	08 50
Purley Oaks	d				07 41							08 11								08 41			
South Croydon	d	07 24			07 44							08 14								08 44			
East Croydon	d	07 27	07 32	07 42	07 47	07 53	07 56	08 00	08 02	08 09	08 12	08 17	08 20	08 23	08 32	08 34	08 39	08 42	08 46	08 47	08 50	08 53	08 56
Norwood Junction	d				07 52		08 01					08 22				08 38				08 52			09 01
New Cross Gate	d				08 09							08 39								09 09			
London Bridge	a		07 45	08 19	08 17		08 12		08 15		08 49	08 48			08 45	08 51		09 19		09 18			09 12
London Blackfriars	a		07 52						08 22						08 52								
City Thameslink	a																						
Farringdon	a		07 56						08 26						08 56								
St Pancras International	a		08 01						08 31						09 01								
Clapham Junction	a	07 41				08 12		08 09		08 18			08 32	08 42			08 48		08 55		09 02	09 12	
London Victoria	a	07 48				08 20		08 16		08 25			08 39	08 50			08 55		09 03		09 09	09 20	

A from 1 July until 22 July, from 19 August until 9 September

B 29 July, 5 August, 12 August

Table 175

Sundays
1 July to 9 September

Purley and East Croydon - London

COMPLETE SERVICE

	SN	FC	SN	SN	SN	SN	SN	SN	FC	SN	SN	SN	SN	FC	SN	SN	SN	SN	SN	FC	SN
	◇1	1	◇1 🛒			◇1 🛒	◇1		1	1	◇1		◇1 🛒	1		1		1	◇1	1	◇1 🛒
Purley 4 d					09 08		09 14	09 17		09 27					09 38		09 47	09 50			
Purley Oaks d					09 11										09 41						
South Croydon 4 d					09 14										09 44						
East Croydon d	09 00	09 02	09 09	09 12	09 17	09 17	09 20	09 23	09 32	09 34	09 39	09 42	09 46	09 47	09 47	09 50	09 53	09 56	10 00	10 02	10 09
Norwood Junction 2 d					09 22					09 38					09 52			10 01			
New Cross Gate d					09 39										10 09						
London Bridge 4 ⊖ a		09 15		09 49	09 48				09 45	09 51		10 19		10 00	10 18			10 12		10 15	
London Blackfriars 3 ⊖ a		09 22							09 52					10 07						10 22	
City Thameslink 3 a																					
Farringdon 3 ⊖ a		09 26							09 56					10 14						10 26	
St Pancras International 15 ⊖ a		09 31							10 01					10 18						10 31	
Clapham Junction 10 a	09 09		09 18			09 26	09 32	09 42			09 48		09 55			10 02	10 12		10 09		10 18
London Victoria 15 ⊖ a	09 17		09 25			09 33	09 39	09 50			09 55		10 03			10 09	10 20		10 17		10 25

	SN	SN	FC	SN	SN	SN	FC	SN	SN	SN	SN	FC	SN	SN	SN	SN	SN	FC	SN	SN	SN	FC
		◇1 🛒	1		◇1		1	1	◇1		◇1 🛒	1		1		1	◇1	1	◇1 🛒		◇1 🛒	1
Purley 4 d				10 08	10 14	10 17		10 27					10 38		10 47	10 50						
Purley Oaks d				10 11									10 41									
South Croydon 4 d				10 14									10 44									
East Croydon d	10 12	10 17	10 17	10 17	10 20	10 23	10 32	10 34	10 39	10 42	10 46	10 47	10 47	10 50	10 53	10 56	11 00	11 02	11 09	11 12	11 17	11 17
Norwood Junction 2 d				10 22				10 38					10 52			11 01						
New Cross Gate d				10 39									11 09									
London Bridge 4 ⊖ a	10 49		10 30	10 48			10 45	10 51		11 19		11 00	11 18			11 12		11 15		11 49		11 30
London Blackfriars 3 ⊖ a			10 37				10 52					11 07						11 22				11 37
City Thameslink 3 a																						
Farringdon 3 ⊖ a			10 44				10 56					11 14						11 26				11 44
St Pancras International 15 ⊖ a			10 48				11 01					11 18						11 31				11 48
Clapham Junction 10 a		10 26			10 32	10 42			10 48		10 55			11 02	11 12		11 09		11 18		11 26	
London Victoria 15 ⊖ a		10 33			10 39	10 50			10 55		11 03			11 09	11 20		11 18		11 25		11 33	

	SN	SN	SN	FC	SN	SN	SN	SN	FC	SN	SN	SN	SN	SN		SN	FC	SN	SN	SN
		◇1 🛒		1	1	◇1		◇1 🛒	1		1		1	◇1		◇1	1	◇1 🛒		◇1 🛒
Purley 4 d	11 08	11 14	11 17		11 27					11 38		11 47	11 50		and at the same minutes past each hour until					
Purley Oaks d	11 11									11 41										
South Croydon 4 d	11 14									11 44										
East Croydon d	11 17	11 20	11 23	11 32	11 34	11 39	11 42	11 46	11 47	11 47	11 50	11 53	11 56	12 00		18 00	18 02	18 09	18 12	18 17
Norwood Junction 2 d	11 22				11 38					11 52			12 01							
New Cross Gate d	11 39									12 09										
London Bridge 4 ⊖ a	11 48			11 45	11 51		12 19		12 00	12 18			12 12				18 15		18 49	
London Blackfriars 3 ⊖ a				11 52					12 07								18 22			
City Thameslink 3 a																				
Farringdon 3 ⊖ a				11 56					12 14								18 26			
St Pancras International 15 ⊖ a				12 01					12 18								18 31			
Clapham Junction 10 a		11 32	11 42			11 48		11 55			12 02	12 12		12 09		18 09		18 18		18 26
London Victoria 15 ⊖ a		11 39	11 50			11 55		12 03			12 09	12 20		12 17		18 17		18 25		18 33

	FC	SN	SN	SN	FC	SN	SN	SN	SN	FC	SN	SN	SN	SN	SN	FC	SN	SN	SN	FC	SN	SN
	1		◇1 🛒		1	1	◇1		◇1	1		1		1	◇1	1	◇1 🛒		◇1	1		◇1
Purley 4 d		18 08	18 14	18 17		18 27					18 38		18 47	18 50							19 08	19 14
Purley Oaks d		18 11									18 41										19 11	
South Croydon 4 d		18 14									18 44										19 14	
East Croydon d	18 17	18 17	18 20	18 23	18 32	18 34	18 39	18 42	18 46	18 47	18 47	18 50	18 53	18 56	19 00	19 02	19 09	19 12	19 17	19 17	19 17	19 20
Norwood Junction 2 d		18 22				18 38					18 52			19 01							19 22	
New Cross Gate d		18 40									19 09										19 39	
London Bridge 4 ⊖ a	18 30	18 48			18 45	18 51		19 19		19 00	19 18			19 12		19 15		19 49		19 30	19 48	
London Blackfriars 3 ⊖ a	18 37				18 52					19 07						19 22				19 37		
City Thameslink 3 a																						
Farringdon 3 ⊖ a	18 44				18 56					19 14						19 26				19 44		
St Pancras International 15 ⊖ a	18 48				19 01					19 18						19 31				19 48		
Clapham Junction 10 a			18 32	18 42			18 48		18 55			19 02	19 12		19 09		19 18		19 26			19 32
London Victoria 15 ⊖ a			18 39	18 50			18 55		19 03			19 09	19 20		19 17		19 25		19 33			19 39

	SN	FC	SN	SN	SN	SN	SN	SN	SN	SN	SN	FC	SN	SN	SN	SN	SN	SN	FC	SN	SN	SN
		1	1	◇1		◇1		1		1	◇1	1	◇1			◇1	◇1		1	1	◇1	
Purley 4 d	19 17		19 27				19 38		19 47	19 50					20 08		20 14	20 17		20 27		
Purley Oaks d							19 41								20 11							
South Croydon 4 d							19 44								20 14							
East Croydon d	19 23	19 32	19 34	19 39	19 42	19 46	19 47	19 50	19 53	19 56	20 00	20 02	20 09	20 12	20 17	20 17	20 20	20 23	20 32	20 34	20 39	20 42
Norwood Junction 2 d			19 38				19 52			20 01					20 22					20 38		
New Cross Gate d							20 09								20 39							
London Bridge 4 ⊖ a		19 45	19 51		20 19		20 18			20 12		20 15		20 49	20 48				20 45	20 51		21 19
London Blackfriars 3 ⊖ a		19 52										20 22							20 52			
City Thameslink 3 a																						
Farringdon 3 ⊖ a		19 56										20 26							20 56			
St Pancras International 15 ⊖ a		20 01										20 31							21 01			
Clapham Junction 10 a	19 42			19 48		19 55		20 02	20 12		20 09		20 18			20 26	20 32	20 42			20 48	
London Victoria 15 ⊖ a	19 50			19 55		20 03		20 09	20 20		20 17		20 25			20 33	20 39	20 50			20 55	

Table 175

Sundays
1 July to 9 September

Purley and East Croydon - London

COMPLETE SERVICE

	SN	SN	SN	SN	SN	SN	FC	SN	SN	SN	SN	SN	SN	FC	SN	SN	SN	SN	SN	SN	SN
	◇1		1		1	◇1	1	◇1			◇1	◇1		1	1	◇1			1		1
Purley 4 d		20 38		20 47	20 50					21 08		21 14	21 17		21 27			21 38		21 47	21 50
Purley Oaks d		20 41								21 11								21 41			
South Croydon 4 d		20 44								21 14								21 44			
East Croydon d	20 46	20 47	20 50	20 53	20 56	21 00	21 02	21 09	21 12	21 17	21 17	21 20	21 23	21 32	21 34	21 39	21 42	21 47	21 50	21 53	21 56
Norwood Junction 2 d		20 52			21 01					21 22					21 38			21 52			22 01
New Cross Gate d		21 09								21 39								22 09			
London Bridge 4 ⊖ a		21 18			21 12		21 15		21 49	21 48				21 45	21 51		22 19	22 18			22 12
London Blackfriars 3 ⊖ a							21 22							21 52							
City Thameslink 3 a																					
Farringdon 3 ⊖ a							21 26							21 56							
St Pancras International 15 ⊖ a							21 31							22 01							
Clapham Junction 10 a	20 55		21 02	21 12		21 09		21 18			21 26	21 32	21 42			21 48			22 02	22 12	
London Victoria 15 ⊖ a	21 03		21 09	21 20		21 17		21 25			21 33	21 39	21 50			21 55			22 09	22 20	

	SN	FC	SN	SN	SN	SN	SN	FC	SN	SN	SN	SN	SN	SN	SN	FC	SN	SN	SN	FC	SN	SN
	◇1	1	◇1			◇1		1	1			1		1	◇1	1		◇1		1	1	1
Purley 4 d					22 08	22 14	22 17		22 27		22 38		22 47	22 50			23 08	23 14	23 17			23 50
Purley Oaks d					22 11						22 41						23 11		23 20			
South Croydon 4 d					22 14						22 44						23 14		23 23			
East Croydon d	22 00	22 02	22 09	22 12	22 17	22 20	22 23	22 32	22 34	22 42	22 47	22 50	22 53	22 56	23 00	23 02	23 17	23 21	23a25	23 32	23 50	23 56
Norwood Junction 2 d					22 22				22 38		22 52						23a21					
New Cross Gate d					22 39						23 09											
London Bridge 4 ⊖ a		22 15		22 49	22 48			22 45	22 51	23 19	23 18					23 15				23 45		
London Blackfriars 3 ⊖ a		22 22						22 52								23 22				23 52		
City Thameslink 3 a																						
Farringdon 3 ⊖ a		22 26						22 56								23 26				23 56		
St Pancras International 15 ⊖ a		22 31						23 01								23 31				00 01		
Clapham Junction 10 a	22 09		22 18			22 32	22 42					23 02	23 12	23 07	23 10			23 31			00 01	00 11
London Victoria 15 ⊖ a	22 17		22 25			22 39	22 52					23 09	23 20	23 14	23 20			23 38			00 08	00 19

Sundays
from 16 September

	FC	SN	FC	SN	FC	SN	SN	SN	SN	SN	SN	FC	SN	SN	SN	FC	SN	SN	SN	SN	FC	SN
	1	1	1	◇1	1		1	1	1	1	◇1		1			1	◇1			1	1	
Purley 4 d		23p49		00 11			01 37	02 33	03 33	04 33	05 22		05 56		06 38				07 08	07 20		
Purley Oaks d															06 41				07 11			
South Croydon 4 d															06 44				07 14	07 24		
East Croydon d	23p32	23p56	00 04	00 17	00 36	00 49	01 43	02 40	03 40	04 40	05 28	05 32	06 02	06 40	06 47	07 02	07 10	07 12	07 17	07 27	07 32	07 42
Norwood Junction 2 d															06 52				07 22			
New Cross Gate d															07 09				07 39			
London Bridge 4 ⊖ a	23p44		00 21		00 51										07 17	07 15		07 50	07 48		07 45	08 19
London Blackfriars 3 ⊖ a	23p52		00 28		00 58							05 59				07 22					07 52	
City Thameslink 3 a																						
Farringdon 3 ⊖ a	23p58		00 33													07 26					07 56	
St Pancras International 15 ⊖ a	00 02		00 37		01 07							06 07				07 31					08 01	
Clapham Junction 10 a		00 11		00 29		01 03	01 54	02 53	03 53	04 53	05 47		06 14	07 00			07 24			07 41		
London Victoria 15 ⊖ a		00 18		00 37		01 10	02 05	03 05	04 05	05 05	05 56		06 22	07 09			07 31			07 48		

	SN	SN	SN	SN	FC	SN	SN	SN	SN	SN	FC	SN	SN	SN	SN	SN	SN	SN	FC	SN	SN	SN
			1	◇1	1	◇1 🛒				◇1	1	◇1			1		1	◇1	1	◇1 🛒		◇1 🛒
Purley 4 d	07 38	07 47	07 50					08 08	08 17	08 20				08 38		08 47	08 50					
Purley Oaks d	07 41							08 11						08 41								
South Croydon 4 d	07 44							08 14						08 44								
East Croydon d	07 47	07 53	07 56	08 00	08 01	08 09	08 12	08 17	08 23	08 26	08 32	08 40	08 42	08 47	08 50	08 53	08 56	09 00	09 01	09 10	09 12	09 13
Norwood Junction 2 d	07 52		08 01					08 22						08 52			09 01					
New Cross Gate d	08 09							08 39						09 09								
London Bridge 4 ⊖ a	08 17		08 12		08 15		08 49	08 48			08 45		09 19	09 18			09 12		09 15		09 49	
London Blackfriars 3 ⊖ a					08 22						08 52								09 22			
City Thameslink 3 a																						
Farringdon 3 ⊖ a					08 26						08 56								09 26			
St Pancras International 15 ⊖ a					08 31						09 01								09 31			
Clapham Junction 10 a		08 12		08 11		08 23			08 42	08 37		08 54			09 01	09 12		09 11		09 24		09 27
London Victoria 15 ⊖ a		08 20		08 18		08 30			08 50	08 46		09 01			09 08	09 20		09 18		09 31		09 35

	SN	SN	SN	FC	SN	SN	SN	SN	SN	SN	SN	FC	SN	SN	SN	SN	SN	SN	FC	SN	SN
			◇1 🛒	1	◇1			1		1	◇1	1	◇1 🛒		◇1 🛒			◇1 🛒	1	◇1	
Purley 4 d	09 08	09 17	09 20				09 38		09 47	09 50						10 08	10 17	10 20			
Purley Oaks d	09 11						09 41									10 11					
South Croydon 4 d	09 14						09 44									10 14					
East Croydon d	09 17	09 23	09 26	09 32	09 40	09 42	09 47	09 50	09 53	09 56	10 00	10 01	10 10	10 12	10 13	10 17	10 23	10 26	10 32	10 40	10 42
Norwood Junction 2 d	09 22						09 52			10 01						10 22					
New Cross Gate d	09 39						10 09									10 39					
London Bridge 4 ⊖ a	09 48			09 45		10 19	10 18			10 12		10 15		10 49		10 48			10 45		11 19
London Blackfriars 3 ⊖ a				09 52								10 22							10 52		
City Thameslink 3 a																					
Farringdon 3 ⊖ a				09 56								10 26							10 56		
St Pancras International 15 ⊖ a				10 01								10 31							11 01		
Clapham Junction 10 a		09 42	09 37		09 54			10 01	10 12		10 11		10 24		10 27		10 42	10 37		10 54	
London Victoria 15 ⊖ a		09 50	09 46		10 01			10 08	10 20		10 18		10 31		10 35		10 50	10 46		11 01	

Table 175

Purley and East Croydon - London

COMPLETE SERVICE

		FC	SN	SN	SN	SN	SN	FC	SN	SN	SN	FC	SN	SN	SN	FC	SN	SN	FC	SN	SN	SN	SN
		1		1		1	◇1	1	◇1 ⌶		◇1 ⌶	1			◇1 ⌶	1	◇1		1		1		1
Purley 4	d		10 38		10 47	10 50							11 08	11 17	11 20					11 38		11 47	11 50
Purley Oaks	d		10 41										11 11							11 41			
South Croydon 4	d		10 44										11 14							11 44			
East Croydon	d	10 47	10 47	10 50	10 53	10 56	11 00	11 01	11 10	11 12	11 13	11 17	11 17	11 23	11 26	11 32	11 40	11 42	11 47	11 47	11 50	11 53	11 56
Norwood Junction 2	d		10 52			11 01							11 22							11 52			12 01
New Cross Gate	d		11 09										11 39							12 09			
London Bridge 4 ⊖	a	11 00	11 18			11 12		11 15		11 49		11 30	11 48			11 45		12 19	12 00	12 18			12 12
London Blackfriars 3 ⊖	a	11 07						11 22				11 37				11 52			12 07				
City Thameslink 3	a																						
Farringdon 3 ⊖	a	11 14						11 26				11 44				11 56			12 14				
St Pancras International 15 ⊖	a	11 18						11 31				11 48				12 01			12 18				
Clapham Junction 10	a			11 01	11 12		11 11		11 24		11 27			11 42	11 37		11 54				12 01	12 12	
London Victoria 15 ⊖	a			11 08	11 20		11 18		11 31		11 35			11 50	11 46		12 01				12 08	12 20	

		SN	FC	SN	SN	SN	FC	SN	SN	SN	FC	SN	SN	FC	SN	SN	SN	SN	SN	FC	SN	SN
		◇1	1	◇1 ⌶		◇1 ⌶	1			◇1 ⌶	1	◇1		1		1		1	◇1	1	◇1 ⌶	
Purley 4	d							12 08	12 17	12 20					12 38		12 47	12 50				
Purley Oaks	d							12 11							12 41							
South Croydon 4	d							12 14							12 44							
East Croydon	d	12 00	12 01	12 10	12 12	12 13	12 17	12 17	12 23	12 26	12 32	12 40	12 42	12 47	12 47	12 50	12 53	12 56	13 00	13 01	13 10	13 12
Norwood Junction 2	d							12 22							12 52			13 01				
New Cross Gate	d							12 39							13 09							
London Bridge 4 ⊖	a		12 15		12 49		12 30	12 48			12 45		13 19	13 00	13 18			13 12		13 15		13 49
London Blackfriars 3 ⊖	a		12 22				12 37				12 52			13 07						13 22		
City Thameslink 3	a																					
Farringdon 3 ⊖	a		12 26				12 44				12 56			13 14						13 26		
St Pancras International 15 ⊖	a		12 31				12 48				13 01			13 18						13 31		
Clapham Junction 10	a	12 11		12 24		12 27			12 42	12 37		12 54				13 01	13 12		13 11		13 24	
London Victoria 15 ⊖	a	12 18		12 31		12 35			12 50	12 46		13 01				13 08	13 20		13 18		13 31	

		SN	FC	SN	SN	SN	FC	SN	SN	FC	SN	SN	SN	SN	SN	FC	SN	SN	SN	FC	SN	SN
		◇1 ⌶	1			◇1 ⌶	1	◇1		1		1		1	◇1	1	◇1 ⌶		◇1 ⌶	1		
Purley 4	d			13 08	13 17	13 19					13 38		13 47	13 50							14 08	14 17
Purley Oaks	d			13 11							13 41										14 11	
South Croydon 4	d			13 14							13 44										14 14	
East Croydon	d	13 13	13 17	13 17	13 23	13 26	13 32	13 40	13 42	13 47	13 47	13 50	13 53	13 56	14 00	14 01	14 10	14 12	14 13	14 17	14 17	14 23
Norwood Junction 2	d			13 22							13 52			14 01							14 22	
New Cross Gate	d			13 39							14 09										14 39	
London Bridge 4 ⊖	a		13 30	13 48			13 45		14 19	14 00	14 18			14 12		14 15		14 49		14 30	14 48	
London Blackfriars 3 ⊖	a		13 37				13 52			14 07						14 22				14 37		
City Thameslink 3	a																					
Farringdon 3 ⊖	a		13 44				13 56			14 14						14 26				14 44		
St Pancras International 15 ⊖	a		13 48				14 01			14 18						14 31				14 48		
Clapham Junction 10	a	13 27			13 42	13 37		13 54				14 01	14 12		14 11		14 24		14 27			14 42
London Victoria 15 ⊖	a	13 35			13 50	13 46		14 01				14 08	14 20		14 18		14 31		14 35			14 50

		SN		SN	FC	SN	SN	FC	SN	SN	SN	SN	SN	FC	SN	SN	SN	FC	SN	SN	SN	FC
		◇1 ⌶		◇1 ⌶	1	◇1		1		1		1	◇1	1	◇1 ⌶		◇1 ⌶	1			◇1 ⌶	1
Purley 4	d	14 20	and at the same minutes past each hour until	17 20					17 38		17 47	17 50							18 08	18 17	18 20	
Purley Oaks	d								17 41										18 11			
South Croydon 4	d								17 44										18 14			
East Croydon	d	14 26		17 26	17 32	17 40	17 42	17 47	17 47	17 50	17 53	17 56	18 00	18 01	18 10	18 12	18 13	18 17	18 17	18 23	18 26	18 32
Norwood Junction 2	d								17 52			18 01							18 22			
New Cross Gate	d								18 09										18 40			
London Bridge 4 ⊖	a				17 45		18 19	18 00	18 18			18 12		18 15		18 49		18 30	18 48			18 45
London Blackfriars 3 ⊖	a				17 52			18 07						18 22				18 37				18 52
City Thameslink 3	a																					
Farringdon 3 ⊖	a				17 56			18 14						18 26				18 44				18 56
St Pancras International 15 ⊖	a				18 01			18 18						18 31				18 48				19 01
Clapham Junction 10	a	14 37		17 37		17 54				18 01	18 12		18 11		18 24		18 27			18 42	18 37	
London Victoria 15 ⊖	a	14 46		17 46		18 01				18 08	18 20		18 18		18 31		18 35			18 50	18 46	

		SN	SN	FC	SN	SN	SN	SN	SN	FC	SN	SN	SN	FC	SN	SN	SN	FC	SN	SN	SN	SN
		◇1		1		1		1	◇1	1	◇1 ⌶		◇1	1			◇1	1	◇1			1
Purley 4	d				18 38		18 47	18 50							19 08	19 17	19 20				19 38	
Purley Oaks	d				18 41										19 11						19 41	
South Croydon 4	d				18 44										19 14						19 44	
East Croydon	d	18 40	18 42	18 47	18 47	18 50	18 53	18 56	19 00	19 01	19 10	19 12	19 13	19 17	19 17	19 23	19 26	19 32	19 40	19 42	19 47	19 50
Norwood Junction 2	d				18 52			19 01							19 22						19 52	
New Cross Gate	d				19 09										19 39						20 09	
London Bridge 4 ⊖	a		19 19	19 00	19 18			19 12		19 15		19 49		19 30	19 48			19 45		20 19	20 18	
London Blackfriars 3 ⊖	a			19 07						19 22				19 37				19 52				
City Thameslink 3	a																					
Farringdon 3 ⊖	a			19 14						19 26				19 44				19 56				
St Pancras International 15 ⊖	a			19 18						19 31				19 48				20 01				
Clapham Junction 10	a	18 54				19 01	19 12		19 11		19 24		19 27			19 42	19 37		19 54			20 01
London Victoria 15 ⊖	a	19 01				19 08	19 20		19 18		19 31		19 35			19 50	19 46		20 01			20 08

Table 175

Purley and East Croydon - London

COMPLETE SERVICE

		SN	SN	SN	FC	SN	SN	SN	SN	SN	SN	FC	SN	SN	SN	SN	SN	SN	SN	FC	SN	SN	SN
			1	◇1	1	◇1		◇1			◇1	1	◇1			1		1	◇1	1	◇1		◇1
Purley 4	d	19 47	19 50						20 08	20 17	20 20				20 38		20 47	20 50					
Purley Oaks	d								20 11						20 41								
South Croydon 4	d								20 14						20 44								
East Croydon	d	19 53	19 56	20 00	20 01	20 10	20 12	20 13	20 17	20 23	20 26	20 32	20 40	20 42	20 47	20 50	20 53	20 56	21 00	21 01	21 10	21 12	21 13
Norwood Junction 2	d		20 01						20 22						20 52			21 01					
New Cross Gate	d								20 39						21 09								
London Bridge 4 ⊖	a		20 12		20 15		20 49		20 48			20 45		21 19	21 18			21 12		21 15		21 49	
London Blackfriars 3 ⊖	a				20 22							20 52								21 22			
City Thameslink 3	a																						
Farringdon 3 ⊖	a				20 26							20 56								21 26			
St Pancras International 15 ⊖	a				20 31							21 01								21 31			
Clapham Junction 10	a	20 12		20 11		20 24		20 27		20 42	20 37		20 54			21 01	21 12		21 11		21 24		21 27
London Victoria 15 ⊖	a	20 20		20 18		20 31		20 35		20 50	20 46		21 01			21 08	21 20		21 18		21 31		21 35

		SN	SN	SN	FC	SN	SN	SN	SN	SN	SN	SN	FC	SN	SN	SN	SN	SN	FC	SN	SN	SN	SN
				◇1	1	◇1			1		1	◇1	1	◇1				◇1	1			1	
Purley 4	d	21 08	21 17	21 20				21 38		21 47	21 50					22 08	22 17	22 20			22 38		22 47
Purley Oaks	d	21 11						21 41								22 11					22 41		
South Croydon 4	d	21 14						21 44								22 14					22 44		
East Croydon	d	21 17	21 23	21 26	21 32	21 40	21 42	21 47	21 50	21 53	21 56	22 00	22 01	22 10	22 12	22 17	22 23	22 26	22 32	22 42	22 47	22 50	22 53
Norwood Junction 2	d	21 22						21 52			22 01					22 22					22 52		
New Cross Gate	d	21 39						22 09								22 39					23 09		
London Bridge 4 ⊖	a	21 48			21 45		22 19	22 18			22 12		22 15		22 49	22 48			22 45	23 19	23 18		
London Blackfriars 3 ⊖	a				21 52								22 22						22 52				
City Thameslink 3	a																						
Farringdon 3 ⊖	a				21 56								22 26						22 56				
St Pancras International 15 ⊖	a				22 01								22 31						23 01				
Clapham Junction 10	a		21 42	21 37		21 54			22 01	22 12		22 11		22 24			22 42	22 37				23 01	23 12
London Victoria 15 ⊖	a		21 50	21 46		22 01			22 08	22 20		22 18		22 31			22 52	22 46				23 08	23 20

		SN	SN	FC	SN	SN	SN	FC	SN	SN
		1	◇1	1			◇1	1	1	1
Purley 4	d	22 50			23 08	23 17	23 20			23 50
Purley Oaks	d				23 11	23 20				
South Croydon 4	d				23 14	23 23				
East Croydon	d	22 56	23 00	23 01	23 17	23a25	23 27	23 32	23 50	23 56
Norwood Junction 2	d				23a21					
New Cross Gate	d									
London Bridge 4 ⊖	a			23 15				23 45		
London Blackfriars 3 ⊖	a			23 22				23 52		
City Thameslink 3	a									
Farringdon 3 ⊖	a			23 26				23 56		
St Pancras International 15 ⊖	a			23 31				00 01		
Clapham Junction 10	a	23 07	23 12				23 38		00 01	00 11
London Victoria 15 ⊖	a	23 14	23 20				23 46		00 08	00 19

Network Diagram for Table 176

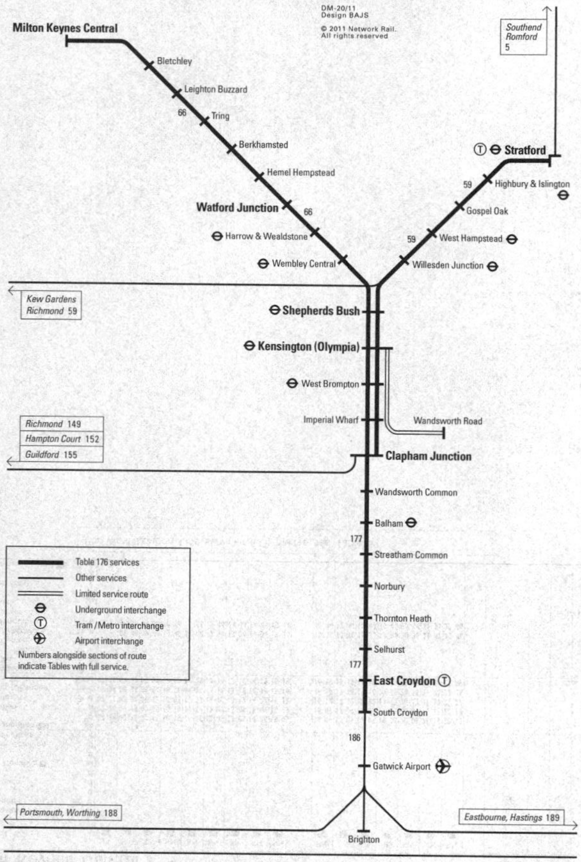

East Croydon, Clapham Junction, Kensington (Olympia) - Watford Junction and Milton Keynes Central

Miles	Miles	Station		SN 1	SN 1	SN 1	SN 1	SN 1	SN	SN 1	SN	SN	SN	SN 1	SN 1	SN 1	SN 1	SN 1	SN 1	SN 1	SN	SN 1	SN
—	—	South Croydon	d									08 35			10 07	11 07	12 07	13 07	14 07	15 07		16 07	
0	—	East Croydon	d						07 50	08 07		08 39		09 08	10 10	11 11	12 10	13 10	14 10	15 10		16 10	
1	—	Selhurst 4	d						07 54	08 13		08 43		09 13	10 14	11 16	12 14	13 13	14 13	15 13		16 13	
1¾	—	Thornton Heath	d						07 56	08 16		08 46		09 16	10 16	11 18	12 16	13 16	14 16	15 16		16 16	
3	—	Norbury	d						07 59	08 20		08 49		09 19	10 19	11 21	12 19	13 19	14 19	15 19		16 19	
4	—	Streatham Common 4	d						08 02	08 23		08 52		09 21	10 22	11 24	12 22	13 21	14 21	15 21		16 21	
5¾	—	Balham 4	d		05 25				08 06	08 28		08 58		09 28	10 29	11 28	12 28	13 28	14 28	15 29		16 28	
6½	—	Wandsworth Common	d						08 08	08 31		09 00		09 30	10 31	11 30	12 30	13 30	14 30	15 31		16 30	
—	—	Wandsworth Road	d																		16 12		
7¾	—	Clapham Junction 10	a		05 29				08 13	08 36		09 04		09 34	10 35	11 33	12 34	13 34	14 34	15 35		16 34	
—	—		d		05 30	05 55	06 38	07 39	08 14	08 39	08 48	09 05	09 24	09 39	10 39	11 39	12 39	13 39	14 39	15 39		16 39	16 49
8¾	—	Imperial Wharf	d	05 07	05 39	06 00	06 42	07 44	08 18	08 44	08 52	09 09	09 28	09 44	10 44	11 44	12 44	13 44	14 44	15 44	16 24	16 44	16 53
9½	—	West Brompton ⊖	d	05 10	05 41	06 03	06 45	07 47	08 21	08 47	08 55	09 12	09 31	09 47	10 47	11 47	12 47	13 47	14 47	15 47	16 26	16 47	16 56
11½	—	Kensington (Olympia) ⊖	d	05 14	05 44	06 07	06 49	07 50	08 25	08 50	08 59	09 15	09 35	09 50	10 50	11 50	12 50	13 50	14 50	15 50	16a29	16 50	16a59
12¾	0	Shepherd's Bush ⊖	d	05 17	05 47	06 10	06 52	07 53	08a27	08 53	09a01	09a18	09a37	09 53	10 53	11 53	12 53	13 53	14 53	15 53		16 53	
—	4	West Hampstead ⊖	a																				
—	6	Gospel Oak	a																				
—	8¾	Highbury & Islington ⊖	a																				
17	—	Wembley Central ⊖	a		06 00	06 24	07 07	08 08		09 08				10 08	11 08	12 08	13 08	14 08	15 08	16 08		17 08	
20½	—	Harrow & Wealdstone ⊖	a	05 33	06 07	06 29	07 12	08 13		09 13				10 13	11 13	12 13	13 13	14 13	15 13	16 13		17 13	
25	—	Watford Junction	a	05 40	06 14	06 36	07 19	08 20		09 20				10 20	11 20	12 20	13 20	14 20	15 20	16 20		17 20	
32	—	Hemel Hempstead	a		06 22		07 27	08 28		09 28				10 28	11 28	12 28	13 28	14 28	15 28	16 28		17 28	
35½	—	Berkhamsted	a		06 26		07 31	08 32		09 32				10 32	11 32	12 32	13 32	14 32	15 32	16 32		17 33	
39¼	—	Tring	a		06 33		07 39	08 39		09 39				10 39	11 39	12 39	13 39	14 39	15 39	16 39		17 38	
47¾	—	Leighton Buzzard	a		06 41		07 50	08 47		09 47				10 47	11 48	12 48	13 48	14 48	15 48	16 47		17 47	
54¼	—	Bletchley	a		06 48		07 57	08 55		09 55				10 57	11 55	12 55	13 55	14 55	15 55	16 55		17 54	
57¼	—	Milton Keynes Central 10	a		06 55		08 03	09 01		10 01				11 02	12 01	13 01	14 01	15 01	16 01	17 00		17 59	

Station		SN	SN 1	SN 1	SN 1	SN 1	SN 1	SN 1
South Croydon	d		17 07					
East Croydon	d		17 10	18 10	19 10			
Selhurst 4	d		17 13	18 13	19 13			
Thornton Heath	d		17 16	18 16	19 16			
Norbury	d		17 19	18 19	19 19			
Streatham Common 4	d		17 21	18 21	19 21			
Balham 4	d		17 28	18 29	19 28			
Wandsworth Common	d		17 30	18 31	19 30			
Wandsworth Road	d							
Clapham Junction 10	a		17 34	18 35	19 34			
	d	17 20	17 39	18 39	19 39	20 39	21 39	22 39
Imperial Wharf	d	17 24	17 44	18 44	19 44	20 44	21 44	22 44
West Brompton ⊖	d	17 27	17 47	18 47	19 47	20 47	21 47	22 47
Kensington (Olympia) ⊖	d	17 30	17 50	18 50	19 50	20 50	21 50	22 50
Shepherd's Bush ⊖	d	17a32	17 53	18 53	19 53	20 53	21 53	22 53
West Hampstead ⊖	a							
Gospel Oak	a							
Highbury & Islington ⊖	a							
Wembley Central ⊖	a		18 08	19 08	20 08	21 08		
Harrow & Wealdstone ⊖	a		18 13	19 13	20 13	21 13	22 16	23 16
Watford Junction	a		18 20	19 20	20 20	21 21	22 23	23 23
Hemel Hempstead	a		18 28	19 28	20 28	21 28		
Berkhamsted	a		18 32	19 33	20 32	21 33		
Tring	a		18 38	19 40	20 39	21 39		
Leighton Buzzard	a		18 46	19 51	20 48	21 50		
Bletchley	a		18 53	20 00	20 55	21 58		
Milton Keynes Central 10	a		19 00	20 06	21 01	22 05		

Saturdays

Station		SN 1	SN 1	SN 1	SN 1	SN 1	SN 1	SN 1	SN 1	SN 1	SN 1	SN 1	SN 1	SN 1	SN 1	SN 1	SN 1	SN 1	SN 1	SN 1	SN 1
South Croydon	d					07 07	08 07	09 07	10 07	11 07	12 07	13 07	14 07	15 07	16 07	17 07	18 07	19 07			
East Croydon	d				06 10	07 10	08 10	09 10	10 10	11 10	12 10	13 10	14 10	15 10	16 10	17 10	18 10	19 10			
Selhurst 4	d				06 13	07 13	08 13	09 13	10 13	11 13	12 13	13 13	14 13	15 13	16 13	17 13	18 13	19 13			
Thornton Heath	d				06 16	07 16	08 16	09 16	10 16	11 16	12 16	13 16	14 16	15 16	16 16	17 16	18 16	19 16			
Norbury	d				06 19	07 19	08 19	09 19	10 19	11 19	12 19	13 19	14 19	15 19	16 19	17 19	18 19	19 19			
Streatham Common 4	d				06 21	07 21	08 21	09 21	10 21	11 21	12 21	13 21	14 21	15 21	16 21	17 21	18 21	19 21			
Balham 4	d		05 33		06 28	07 28	08 28	09 28	10 28	11 28	12 28	13 28	14 28	15 28	16 28	17 28	18 28	19 28			
Wandsworth Common	d				06 30	07 30	08 30	09 30	10 30	11 30	12 30	13 30	14 30	15 30	16 30	17 30	18 30	19 30			
Wandsworth Road	d																				
Clapham Junction 10	a		05 37		06 34	07 34	08 34	09 34	10 34	11 34	12 34	13 34	14 34	15 34	16 34	17 34	18 34	19 34			
	d	05 08	05 38	06 09	06 39	07 39	08 39	09 39	10 39	11 39	12 39	13 39	14 39	15 39	16 39	17 39	18 39	19 38	20 25	21 39	22 39
Imperial Wharf	d	05 12	05 42	06 13	06 44	07 44	08 44	09 44	10 44	11 44	12 44	13 44	14 44	15 44	16 44	17 44	18 44	19 42	20 29	21 44	22 44
West Brompton ⊖	d	05 15	05 45	06 16	06 47	07 47	08 47	09 47	10 47	11 47	12 47	13 47	14 47	15 47	16 47	17 47	18 47	19 45	20 32	21 47	22 47
Kensington (Olympia) ⊖	d	05 19	05 49	06 20	06 50	07 50	08 50	09 50	10 50	11 50	12 50	13 50	14 50	15 50	16 50	17 50	18 50	19 48	20 36	21 50	22 50
Shepherd's Bush ⊖	d	05 22	05 52	06 23	06 53	07 53	08 53	09 53	10 53	11 53	12 53	13 53	14 53	15 53	16 53	17 53	18 53	19 50	20 39	21 53	22 53
West Hampstead ⊖	a																				
Gospel Oak	a																				
Highbury & Islington ⊖	a																				
Wembley Central ⊖	a		06 07	06 38	07 07	08 07	09 07	10 07	11 08	12 07	13 07	14 08	15 07	16 07	17 07	18 07	19 08				
Harrow & Wealdstone ⊖	a	05 40	06 12	06 43	07 12	08 12	09 12	10 12	11 13	12 13	13 12	14 13	15 12	16 12	17 12	18 12	19 13	20 08	21 02	22 13	23 12
Watford Junction	a	05 47	06 19	06 50	07 19	08 19	09 19	10 19	11 20	12 20	13 19	14 20	15 19	16 19	17 19	18 19	19 21	20 15	21 09	22 20	23 19
Hemel Hempstead	a		06 27		07 27	08 27	09 27	10 27	11 28	12 28	13 27	14 28	15 27	16 27	17 27	18 27					
Berkhamsted	a		06 31		07 32	08 31	09 33	10 31	11 33	12 32	13 32	14 32	15 32	16 32	17 32	18 32					
Tring	a		06 37		07 39	08 37	09 38	10 37	11 38	12 37	13 37	14 37	15 37	16 37	17 37	18 37					
Leighton Buzzard	a		06 46		07 47	08 46	09 47	10 47	11 47	12 47	13 47	14 47	15 47	16 47	17 46	18 46					
Bletchley	a		06 54		07 54	08 54	09 54	10 54	11 54	12 54	13 54	14 54	15 54	16 54	17 54	18 54					
Milton Keynes Central 10	a		07 00		08 00	09 00	10 00	11 00	12 00	13 00	14 00	15 00	16 00	17 00	18 00	19 00					

For West London Line services (LO) please see Table 59

Table 176

Sundays

East Croydon, Clapham Junction, Kensington (Olympia) - Watford Junction and Milton Keynes Central

		SN 1	SN 1	SN 1	SN 1	SN 1	SN 1	SN 1	SN 1	SN 1	SN 1	SN 1	SN 1	SN 1	SN 1	SN 1	SN 1
South Croydon	d																
East Croydon ⇌	d																
Selhurst 4	d																
Thornton Heath	d																
Norbury	d																
Streatham Common 4	d																
Balham 4	d																
Wandsworth Common	d																
Wandsworth Road	d																
Clapham Junction 10	a																
	d	07 24	08 15	09 15	10 15	11 15	12 05	13 05	14 05	15 05	16 05	17 05	18 05	19 05	20 05	21 15	22 15
Imperial Wharf	d	07 28	08 19	09 19	10 19	11 19	12 09	13 09	14 09	15 09	16 09	17 09	18 09	19 09	20 09	21 19	22 19
West Brompton ⊖	d	07 31	08 22	09 22	10 22	11 22	12 12	13 12	14 12	15 12	16 12	17 12	18 12	19 12	20 12	21 22	22 22
Kensington (Olympia) ⊖	d	07 34	08 26	09 26	10 26	11 26	12 16	13 16	14 16	15 16	16 16	17 16	18 16	19 16	20 16	21 26	22 26
Shepherd's Bush ⊖	d	07a36	08 29	09 29	10 29	11 29	12 19	13 19	14 19	15 19	16 19	17 19	18 19	19 19	20 19	21 29	22 29
West Hampstead ⊖	a																
Gospel Oak	a																
Highbury & Islington ⊖	a																
Wembley Central ⊖	a																
Harrow & Wealdstone ⊖	a		08 48	09 48	10 48	11 48	12 36	13 36	14 36	15 36	16 36	17 36	18 36	19 36	20 36	21 47	22 48
Watford Junction	a		08 56	09 58	10 56	11 56	12 44	13 44	14 44	15 44	16 44	17 44	18 44	19 43	20 44	21 54	22 56
Hemel Hempstead	a																
Berkhamsted	a																
Tring	a																
Leighton Buzzard	a																
Bletchley	a																
Milton Keynes Central 10	a																

For West London Line services (LO) please see Table 59

Table 176

Mondays to Fridays

Milton Keynes Central, Watford Junction, Kensington (Olympia) - Clapham Junction and East Croydon

Miles	Miles			SN MX 1	SN 1 A	SN MX 1	SN 1	SN 1	SN 1	SN	SN	SN 1	SN	SN	SN 1	SN 1	SN 1	SN 1	SN 1	SN 1	SN 1	SN	SN
0	—	**Milton Keynes Central** 10	d	22p11					07 01			08 13			09 13	10 13	11 13	12 13	13 13	14 13	15 13		
3	—	Bletchley	d	22p15					07 05			08 17			09 17	10 17	11 17	12 17	13 17	14 17	15 17		
9½	—	Leighton Buzzard	d	22p22					07 13			08 24			09 24	10 24	11 24	12 24	13 24	14 24	15 24		
18	—	Tring	d	22p34					07 22			08 34			09 34	10 34	11 34	12 34	13 34	14 34	15 34		
21¾	—	Berkhamsted	d	22p39					07 26			08 39			09 39	10 39	11 39	12 39	13 39	14 39	15 39		
25¼	—	Hemel Hempstead	d	22p43					07 31			08 43			09 43	10 43	11 43	12 43	13 43	14 43	15 43		
32¼	—	**Watford Junction**	d	22p53	23p17	23p29	05 54	06 53	07 38			08 51			09 51	10 51	11 51	12 51	13 51	14 51	15 51		
36¾	—	Harrow & Wealdstone ⊖	d	23p00	23p23	23p35	06 00	06 59	07 45			08 58			09 58	10 59	11 59	12 59	13 59	14 59	15 59		
40¼	—	Wembley Central ⊖	d				06 05	07 04	07 49			09 05			10 05	11 04	12 04	13 04	14 04	15 04	16 05		
—	4¾	Highbury & Islington ⊖	d																				
—	7½	Gospel Oak	d																				
—	9½	West Hampstead ⊖	d																				
44½	13½	**Shepherd's Bush** ⊖	d	23p21	23p45	23p54	06 19	07 19	08 04	08 31	09 06	09 18	09 33		10 21	11 19	12 19	13 19	14 19	15 22	16 19		
45¾	—	**Kensington (Olympia)** ⊖	d	23p23	23p48	23p56	06 22	07 22	08 07	08 33	09 09	09 21	09 35	10 02	10 24	11 21	12 22	13 22	14 22	15 24	16 22	16 34	17 04
47¾	—	West Brompton ⊖	d	23p26	23p50	23p59	06 25	07 25	08 10	08 35	09 12	09 23	09 37	10 04	10 27	11 23	12 25	13 25	14 25	15 26	16 25	16 36	17 06
48½	—	Imperial Wharf	d	23p28	23p53	00 02	06 27	07 27	08 13	08 38	09 15	09 26	09 40	10 07	10 29	11 26	12 27	13 28	14 28	15 29	16 27	16 39	17 09
49½	—	**Clapham Junction** 10	a	23p33	23p58	00 07	06 32	07 32	08 17	08 43	09 19	09 31	09 45		10 34	11 30	12 32	13 32	14 32	15 33	16 32	16 43	17 13
—	—		d	23p40	00 05				08 36			09 34			10 34	11 34	12 34	13 34	14 34	15 34	16 34		
—	—	Wandsworth Road	a											10 20									
50¾	—	Wandsworth Common	a						08 39			09 37			10 37	11 37	12 37	13 37	14 37	15 37	16 37		
51½	—	Balham 4	a	23p44					08 42			09 41			10 40	11 40	12 40	13 40	14 40	15 40	16 40		
53¼	—	Streatham Common 4	a	23p48					08 46			09 45			10 45	11 45	12 45	13 45	14 45	15 45	16 45		
54¼	—	Norbury	a	23p51					08 48			09 48			10 48	11 48	12 48	13 48	14 48	15 48	16 48		
55½	—	Thornton Heath	a	23p54					08 51			09 51			10 51	11 51	12 51	13 51	14 51	15 51	16 51		
56¼	—	Selhurst 4	a	23p56					08 54			09 53			10 53	11 53	12 53	13 53	14 53	15 53	16 54		
57¼	—	**East Croydon** ⇌	a	00 01	00 22				09 04			09 57			10 57	11 57	12 57	13 57	14 57	15 57	16 58		
—	—	**South Croydon**	a									10 01			11 01	12 01	13 01	14 01	15 01	16 01	17 02		

		SN 1	SN	SN 1	SN 1	SN 1	SN 1	SN 1	SN 1	SN 1	SN 1
Milton Keynes Central 10	d	16 13		17 13	18 13	19 15	20 13	21 13		22 11	
Bletchley	d	16 17		17 17	18 17	19 19	20 17	21 17		22 15	
Leighton Buzzard	d	16 24		17 24	18 24	19 26	20 24	21 24		22 22	
Tring	d	16 34		17 34	18 34	19 36	20 34	21 34		22 34	
Berkhamsted	d	16 39		17 39	18 39	19 41	20 39	21 39		22 39	
Hemel Hempstead	d	16 43		17 43	18 43	19 45	20 43	21 43		22 43	
Watford Junction	d	16 51		17 51	18 51	19 54	20 51	21 51	22 27	22 53	23 29
Harrow & Wealdstone ⊖	d	16 59		17 59	18 59	20 01	20 59	21 59	22 33	23 00	23 35
Wembley Central ⊖	d	17 05		18 05	19 05	20 06	21 04				
Highbury & Islington ⊖	d										
Gospel Oak	d										
West Hampstead ⊖	d										
Shepherd's Bush ⊖	d	17 19	17 45	18 19	19 18	20 21	21 22	22 23	22 49	23 21	23 54
Kensington (Olympia) ⊖	d	17 22	17 47	18 22	19 20	20 23	21 24	22 25	22 51	23 23	23 56
West Brompton ⊖	d	17 25	17 50	18 25	19 23	20 25	21 27	22 27	22 54	23 26	23 59
Imperial Wharf	d	17 28	17 53	18 27	19 25	20 28	21 29	22 30	22 56	23 28	00 02
Clapham Junction 10	a	17 32	17 57	18 32	19 30	20 33	21 34	22 34	23 01	23 33	00 07
	d	17 33	18 02	18 34	19 34					23 40	
Wandsworth Road	a										
Wandsworth Common	a	17 36	18 05	18 37	19 37						
Balham 4	a	17 39	18 08	18 40	19 40					23 44	
Streatham Common 4	a	17 46	18 15	18 46	19 45					23 48	
Norbury	a	17 48	18 18	18 49	19 48					23 51	
Thornton Heath	a	17 51	18 21	18 52	19 51					23 54	
Selhurst 4	a	17 54	18 24	18 54	19 53					23 56	
East Croydon ⇌	a	17 59	18 32	19 02						00 01	
South Croydon	a		18 35								

A MO from 21 May

For West London Line services (LO) please see Table 59

Saturdays

Milton Keynes Central, Watford Junction, Kensington (Olympia) - Clapham Junction and East Croydon

		SN	SN	SN	SN	SN	SN	SN	SN	SN	SN	SN	SN	SN	SN	SN	SN	SN	SN	SN	SN	SN	SN
		1	1	1	1	1	1	1	1	1	1	1	1	1	1	1	1	1	1	1	1	1	1
Milton Keynes Central 10	d	22p11				07 13	08 13	09 13	10 13	11 13	12 13	13 13	14 13	15 13	16 13	17 13	18 13		19 13				
Bletchley	d	22p15				07 17	08 17	09 17	10 17	11 17	12 17	13 17	14 17	15 17	16 17	17 17	18 17		19 17				
Leighton Buzzard	d	22p22				07 24	08 24	09 24	10 24	11 24	12 24	13 24	14 24	15 24	16 24	17 24	18 24		19 24				
Tring	d	22p34				07 34	08 34	09 34	10 34	11 34	12 34	13 34	14 34	15 34	16 34	17 34	18 34		19 34				
Berkhamsted	d	22p39				07 39	08 39	09 39	10 39	11 39	12 39	13 39	14 39	15 39	16 39	17 39	18 39		19 39				
Hemel Hempstead	d	22p43				07 43	08 43	09 43	10 43	11 43	12 43	13 43	14 43	15 43	16 43	17 43	18 43		19 43				
Watford Junction	d	22p53	23p29	05 52	06 55	07 52	08 52	09 52	10 52	11 52	12 52	13 52	14 52	15 52	16 52	17 52	18 52	19 31	19 51	20 43	21 43	22 48	23 25
Harrow & Wealdstone ⊖	d	23p00	23p35	05 58	07 01	07 59	08 59	09 59	10 59	11 59	12 59	13 59	14 59	15 59	16 59	17 59	18 59	19 38	19 58	20 50	21 50	22 55	23 31
Wembley Central ⊖	d				07 06	08 04	09 04	10 04	11 04	12 04	13 04	14 04	15 04	16 04	17 04	18 04	19 04	19 43					
Highbury & Islington ⊖	d																						
Gospel Oak	d																						
West Hampstead ⊖	d																						
Shepherd's Bush ⊖	d	23p21	23p54	06 20	07 19	08 19	09 19	10 19	11 19	12 19	13 19	14 19	15 19	16 19	17 19	18 19	19 19	19 57	20 19	21 07	22 07	23 14	23 49
Kensington (Olympia) ⊖	d	23p23	23p56	06 23	07 22	08 22	09 22	10 22	11 22	12 22	13 22	14 22	15 22	16 22	17 22	18 22	19 22	20 00	20 22	21 10	22 10	23 16	23 51
West Brompton ⊖	d	23p26	23p59	06 26	07 25	08 25	09 25	10 25	11 25	12 25	13 25	14 25	15 25	16 25	17 25	18 25	19 25	20 03	20 25	21 13	22 13	23 19	23 54
Imperial Wharf	d	23p28	00 02	06 28	07 27	08 27	09 27	10 27	11 27	12 27	13 27	14 27	15 27	16 27	17 27	18 27	19 27	20 05	20 27	21 15	22 15	23 21	23 57
Clapham Junction 10	a	23p33	00 07	06 33	07 33	08 33	09 33	10 33	11 33	12 33	13 33	14 33	15 33	16 33	17 32	18 32	19 32	20 10	20 32	21 20	22 20	23 26	00 02
	d	23p40		06 34	07 34	08 34	09 34	10 34	11 34	12 34	13 34	14 34	15 34	16 34	17 34	18 34	19 34		20 34				
Wandsworth Road	a																						
Wandsworth Common	a			06 37	07 37	08 37	09 37	10 37	11 37	12 37	13 37	14 37	15 37	16 37	17 37	18 37	19 37		20 37				
Balham 4	a	23p44		06 40	07 40	08 40	09 40	10 40	11 40	12 40	13 40	14 40	15 40	16 40	17 40	18 40	19 40		20 40				
Streatham Common 4	a	23p48		06 45	07 45	08 45	09 45	10 45	11 45	12 45	13 45	14 45	15 45	16 45	17 45	18 45	19 45		20 45				
Norbury	a	23p51		06 48	07 48	08 48	09 48	10 48	11 48	12 48	13 48	14 48	15 48	16 48	17 48	18 48	19 48		20 48				
Thornton Heath	a	23p54		06 51	07 51	08 51	09 51	10 51	11 51	12 51	13 51	14 51	15 51	16 51	17 51	18 51	19 51		20 51				
Selhurst 4	a	23p56		06 53	07 53	08 53	09 53	10 53	11 53	12 53	13 53	14 53	15 53	16 53	17 53	18 53	19 53		20 53				
East Croydon	a	00 01		06 57	07 57	08 57	09 57	10 57	11 57	12 57	13 57	14 57	15 57	16 57	17 57	18 57	19 57		20 59				
South Croydon	a			07 01	08 01	09 01	10 01	11 01	12 01	13 01	14 01	15 01	16 01	17 01	18 01	19 01							

Sundays

		SN	SN	SN	SN	SN	SN	SN	SN	SN	SN	SN	SN	SN	SN	SN	SN	SN	SN
		1	1	1	1	1	1	1	1	1	1	1	1	1	1	1	1	1	1
Milton Keynes Central 10	d																		
Bletchley	d																		
Leighton Buzzard	d																		
Tring	d																		
Berkhamsted	d																		
Hemel Hempstead	d																		
Watford Junction	d	23p25			09 17	10 17	11 22	12 22	13 22	14 22	15 22	16 22	17 22	18 22	19 22	20 22	21 17	22 17	23 17
Harrow & Wealdstone ⊖	d	23p31			09 23	10 23	11 28	12 29	13 28	14 28	15 28	16 28	17 28	18 28	19 28	20 28	21 23	22 23	23 23
Wembley Central ⊖	d																		
Highbury & Islington ⊖	d																		
Gospel Oak	d																		
West Hampstead ⊖	d																		
Shepherd's Bush ⊖	d	23p49	07 47	08 50	09 45	10 45	11 45	12 45	13 45	14 45	15 45	16 45	17 45	18 45	19 45	20 45	21 45	22 45	23 45
Kensington (Olympia) ⊖	d	23p51	07 49	08 53	09 48	10 48	11 48	12 48	13 48	14 48	15 48	16 48	17 48	18 48	19 48	20 48	21 48	22 48	23 48
West Brompton ⊖	d	23p54	07 51	08 56	09 50	10 50	11 50	12 50	13 50	14 50	15 50	16 50	17 50	18 50	19 50	20 50	21 50	22 50	23 50
Imperial Wharf	d	23p57	07 54	08 58	09 53	10 53	11 53	12 53	13 53	14 53	15 53	16 53	17 53	18 53	19 53	20 53	21 53	22 53	23 53
Clapham Junction 10	a	00 02	07 58	09 03	09 58	10 58	11 58	12 58	13 58	14 58	15 58	16 58	17 58	18 58	19 58	20 58	21 58	22 58	23 58
	d																		00 05
Wandsworth Road	a																		
Wandsworth Common	a																		
Balham 4	a																		
Streatham Common 4	a																		
Norbury	a																		
Thornton Heath	a																		
Selhurst 4	a																		
East Croydon	a																		00 22
South Croydon	a																		

For West London Line services (LO) please see Table 59

Network Diagram for Tables 177, 178, 179, 181, 182 | also 175 ⊙

DM-21/11
Design BAJS

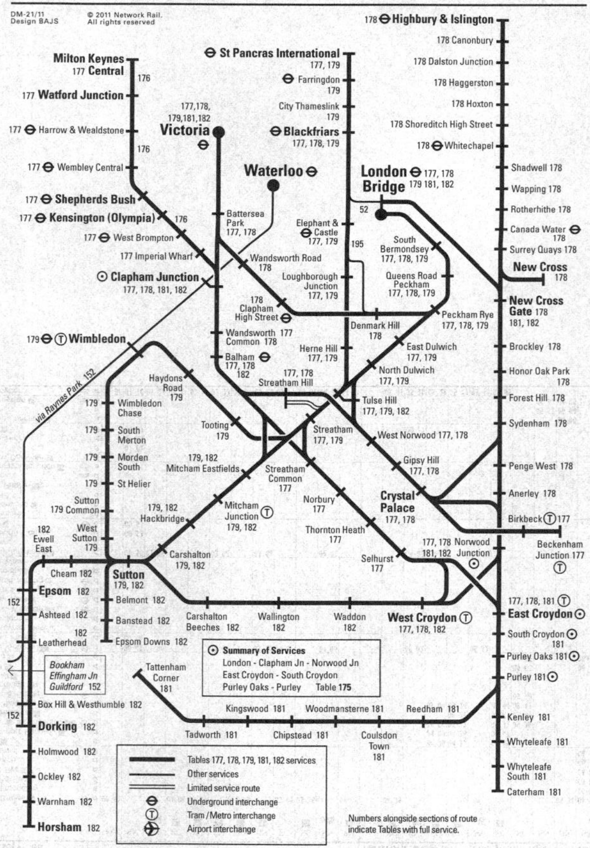

Luton, Milton Keynes Central and London East and West Croydon via Tulse Hill - Crystal Palace - Norbury

Local Services

Network Diagram - see first Page of Table 177

Miles	Miles	Miles	Miles	Miles			SN 1	SN	SN	SN	SN	SN 1	SN 1	SN	SN	SN	FC	SN ◇1	SN	SN	FC	SN 1	SN	SN
							A	A	A	A	A	A	A	A	A	A	A	A	A	A				A
—	0	—	—	0	London Bridge 4 ⊖	d			23p36	23p33					23p48		23p59		00 06	00 03	00 12			00 36
—	1¾	—	—	1¾	South Bermondsey	d				23p37					23p52					00 07				
—	2¾	—	—	2¾	Queens Rd Peckham	d				23p39					23p54					00 09				
—	3½	—	—	3½	Peckham Rye 4	d				23p42					23p57					00 12				
—	4¼	—	—	4¼	East Dulwich	d				23p45					00 01					00 15				
—	4¾	—	—	4¾	North Dulwich	d				23p47					00 03					00 17				
—	—	—	—	—	Luton 10	d																		
—	—	—	—	—	Luton Airport Parkway 7	d																		
—	—	—	—	—	St Pancras International 15 ⊖	d																		
—	—	—	—	—	City Thameslink 3	d																		
—	—	—	—	—	London Blackfriars 3 ⊖	d																		
—	—	—	—	—	Elephant & Castle ⊖	d																		
—	—	—	—	—	Loughborough Jn.	d																		
—	—	—	—	—	Herne Hill 4	d																		
—	6	—	—	6	Tulse Hill 3	d				23p51					00 06		00 09			00 21				
—	7½	—	—	—	Streatham 4	d									00 10		00a13							
0	—	0	0	—	London Victoria 15 ⊖	d		23p34			23p38	23p47	23p49	23p51		23p54		00 05				00 14	00 16	
1¼	—	1¼	1¼	—	Battersea Park 4	d		23p38			23p42			23p55		23p58							00 20	
—	—	—	—	—	Milton Keynes Central	d	22p11																	
—	—	—	—	—	Watford Junction	d	22p53																	
—	—	—	—	—	Harrow & Wealdstone ⊖	d	23p00																	
—	—	—	—	—	Wembley Central ⊖	d																		
—	—	—	—	—	Shepherd's Bush ⊖	d	23p21																	
—	—	—	—	—	Kensington (Olympia) ⊖	d	23p23																	
—	—	—	—	—	West Brompton ⊖	d	23p26																	
—	—	—	—	—	Imperial Wharf	d	23p28																	
2¾	—	2¾	2¾	—	Clapham Junction 10	d	23p40	23p42			23p46	23p53	23p56	23p59		00 02		00 11				00 20	00 24	
—	—	—	—	—	Latchmere	d																		
4	—	4	4	—	Wandsworth Common	d		23p45			23p49			00 02		00 05							00 27	
4¾	—	4¾	4¾	—	Balham 4 ⊖	d	23p44	23p47			23p51			00 04		00 07							00 29	
5¾	—	5¾	—	—	Streatham Hill	d					23p54					00 10								
7	—	7	—	6½	West Norwood 4	d				23p54	23p58					00 14				00 24				
8	—	8	—	7½	Gipsy Hill	d				23p57	00 01					00 17				00 27				
8¾	—	8¾	—	8¼	Crystal Palace 4	d				23p59	00 03					00a19				00 29				
—	—	10¼	—	—	Birkbeck	d																		
—	—	11¾	—	—	Beckenham Junction 4	a																		
—	8	—	6½	—	Streatham Common 4	d	23p48	23p51						00 08	00 13								00 33	
—	9	—	7½	—	Norbury	d	23p51	23p54						00 11	00 15								00 36	
—	10¼	—	8¾	—	Thornton Heath	d	23p54	23p57						00 14	00 18								00 39	
—	11	—	9½	—	Selhurst 4	d	23p57	23p59						00 17	00 21								00 41	
10¼	—	—	—	9¾	Norwood Junction 2	a			23p59	00 04	00 08								00 29	00 34				00 59
—	—	—	—	—		d			23p59		00 09								00 30					01 00
—	12	—	—	—	West Croydon 4	a		00 03			00 14			00 21	00 28									
11½	—	—	10½	11	East Croydon	a	00 01		00 03			00 05	00 09					00 26	00 33		00 26	00 31	00 44	01 03

A not 14 May

Luton, Milton Keynes Central and London East and West Croydon via Tulse Hill - Crystal Palace - Norbury

Local Services

Network Diagram - see first Page of Table 177

		FC	SN	SN ◇1	FC 1	FC 1	SN 1	FC 1	SN 1	FC	FC 1	SN ◇1	FC 1	FC 1	SN ◇1	FC 1	FC 1	SN ◇1	FC 1	FC	SN	SN	SN	SN
London Bridge 4 ⊖	d	00 42			01 08	01 35		02 05		03 05	03 35		04 05	04 35								05 36	06 00	
South Bermondsey	d																						06 04	
Queens Rd Peckham	d																						06 06	
Peckham Rye 4	d																						06 09	
East Dulwich	d																						06 12	
North Dulwich	d																						06 14	
Luton 10	d															04 06	04 33		04 45					
Luton Airport Parkway 7	d															04 09	04 35		04 47					
St Pancras International 15 ⊖	d															04 54	05 12		05 32	05 36				
City Thameslink 3	d																05 21		05 41	05 44				
London Blackfriars 3 ⊖	d															05 04	05 24		05 44	05 47				
Elephant & Castle ⊖	d																			05 50				
Loughborough Jn.	d																							
Herne Hill 4	d																			05 57				
Tulse Hill 3	d																			06 02			06 18	
Streatham 4	d																			06a05			06a21	
London Victoria 15 ⊖	d		00 42	01 00			02 00		03 00			04 00			05 02			05 32						06 00
Battersea Park 4	d		00 46																					06 04
Milton Keynes Central	d																							
Watford Junction	d																							
Harrow & Wealdstone ⊖	d																							
Wembley Central ⊖	d																							
Shepherd's Bush ⊖	d																							
Kensington (Olympia) ⊖	d																							
West Brompton ⊖	d																							
Imperial Wharf	d																							
Clapham Junction 10	d		00 50	01 08			02 08		03 08			04 08			05 08			05 38						06 08
Latchmere	d																							
Wandsworth Common	d		00 53																					06 11
Balham 4 ⊖	d		00 55																					06 13
Streatham Hill	d																							
West Norwood 4	d																							
Gipsy Hill	d																							
Crystal Palace 4	d																							
Birkbeck	d																							
Beckenham Junction 4	a																							
Streatham Common 4	d		00 59																					06 17
Norbury	d		01 02																					06 20
Thornton Heath	d		01 05																					06 23
Selhurst 4	d		01 07												05 17									06 26
Norwood Junction 2	a																					06 00		
	d																				05 53	06 00		
West Croydon 4	a																				05 57	06 05		06 31
East Croydon	a	00 56	01 10	01 23	01 31	02 01	02 23	02 31	03 23	03 31	04 01	04 23	04 31	05 01	05 20	05 29	05 47	05 48	06 05					

Table 177

Mondays to Fridays

until 18 May

Luton, Milton Keynes Central and London East and West Croydon via Tulse Hill - Crystal Palace - Norbury

Local Services

Network Diagram - see first Page of Table 177

		SN	FC	SN	SN		SN	SN	SN	SN	SN	SN	SN	SN	SN	FC	SN	SN	FC	SN	SN		SN	SN	SN
		◇[1]	[1]									◇[1]			◇[1]	[1]									◇[1]
London Bridge [4] ⊖	d			06 06					06 11	06 18	06 19		06 30					06 33		06 36					
South Bermondsey	d								06 15	06 22			06 34					06 37							
Queens Rd Peckham	d								06 18	06 24			06 36					06 39							
Peckham Rye [4]	d								06 20	06 27			06 39					06 42							
East Dulwich	d									06 30			06 42					06 45							
North Dulwich	d									06 32			06 44					06 47							
Luton [10]	d		05 24													05 44			05 48						
Luton Airport Parkway [7]	d		05 27													05 46			05 50						
St Pancras International [15] ⊖	d		06 02													06 22			06 34						
City Thameslink [3]	d		06 11													06 31			06 43						
London Blackfriars [3] ⊖	d		06 14													06 34			06 46						
Elephant & Castle ⊖	d																		06 49						
Loughborough Jn.	d																		06 53						
Herne Hill [4]	d																		06 57						
Tulse Hill [3]	d									06 36			06 48					06 50	07 02						
Streatham [4]	d									06 39			06a51						07a05						
London Victoria [15] ⊖	d	06 02			06 07		06 13	06 19				06 21		06 30	06 32						06 36		06 41	06 44	06 47
Battersea Park [4]	d				06 11		06 17	06 23	06a32					06 34							06 40		06a45		
Milton Keynes Central	d																								
Watford Junction	d																								
Harrow & Wealdstone ⊖	d																								
Wembley Central ⊖	d																								
Shepherd's Bush ⊖	d																								
Kensington (Olympia) ⊖	d																								
West Brompton ⊖	d																								
Imperial Wharf	d																								
Clapham Junction [10]	d	06 08			06 15		06 21	06 27				06 27		06 38	06 38						06 44			06 50	06 53
Latchmere	d																								
Wandsworth Common	d				06 18		06 24	06 30						06 41							06 47			06 53	
Balham [4] ⊖	d				06 20		06 26	06 32						06 44							06 49			06 56	
Streatham Hill	d				06 23			06 35									06 42				06 53				
West Norwood [4]	d				06 27			06 39									06 45	06 53			06 56				
Gipsy Hill	d				06 30			06 42			06a41						06 48	06 56			06 59				
Crystal Palace [4]	d				06 32			06a44									06a51	06 59			07 02				
Birkbeck 🚋	d																	07 03							
Beckenham Junction [4] 🚋	a																	07 06							
Streatham Common [4]	d						06 30			06 42				06 48										07 00	
Norbury	d						06 33			06 45				06 50										07 02	
Thornton Heath	d						06 36			06 48				06 53										07 05	
Selhurst [4]	d						06 39			06 51				06 56										07 09	
Norwood Junction [2]	a			06 29	06 37															06 59	07 07				
	d			06 30	06 39															07 00	07 09				
West Croydon [4] 🚋	a				06 44					06 56				07 02							07 13				
East Croydon 🚋	a	06 17	06 33	06 33			06 43					06 38			06 48	06 54				07 03				07 12	07 03

Table 177

Mondays to Fridays

until 18 May

Luton, Milton Keynes Central and London East and West Croydon via Tulse Hill - Crystal Palace - Norbury

Local Services

Network Diagram - see first Page of Table 177

		SN	SN	SN	SN	SN	FC	SN	SN	SN	FC	SN	SN		SN	FC	SN	SN	SN	SN	SN	SN	SN	SN	SN
						[1]	[1]		[1]		[1]					[1]				◇[1]					
London Bridge [4] ⊖	d		06 41	06 48	06 51					06 54		06 58			07 03		07 06						07 11	07 16	07 21
South Bermondsey	d		06 45	06 52								07 02			07 07								07 15	07 20	
Queens Rd Peckham	d		06 48	06 54								07 04			07 09								07 17	07 22	
Peckham Rye [4]	d		06 50	06 57								07 07			07 12								07 20	07 25	
East Dulwich	d			07 00								07 10			07 15									07 28	
North Dulwich	d			07 02								07 12			07 17									07 30	
Luton [10]	d						06 04				06 22					06 34									
Luton Airport Parkway [7]	d						06 06				06 24														
St Pancras International [15] ⊖	d						06 38				06 58					07 04									
City Thameslink [3]	d						06 47				07 07					07 13									
London Blackfriars [3] ⊖	d						06 50				07 09					07 16									
Elephant & Castle ⊖	d															07 19									
Loughborough Jn.	d															07 23									
Herne Hill [4]	d															07 27									
Tulse Hill [3]	d			07 07								07 16			07 20	07 31								07 34	
Streatham [4]	d			07 10								07a19				07a34								07 37	
London Victoria [15] ⊖	d	06 49				06 51		07 00	07 02									07 06	07 11	07 17	07 17	07 20			
Battersea Park [4]	d	06 53	07a02					07 04										07 10	07a15		07 21	07 24	07a32		
Milton Keynes Central	d																								
Watford Junction	d																								
Harrow & Wealdstone ⊖	d																								
Wembley Central ⊖	d																								
Shepherd's Bush ⊖	d																								
Kensington (Olympia) ⊖	d																								
West Brompton ⊖	d																								
Imperial Wharf	d																								
Clapham Junction [10]	d	06 57				06 57		07 08	07 08									07 14		07 23	07 25	07 28			
Latchmere	d																								
Wandsworth Common	d	07 00						07 11										07 17				07 31			
Balham [4] ⊖	d	07 02						07 13										07 20			07 29	07 33			
Streatham Hill	d	07 05											07 12					07 23			07 32				
West Norwood [4]	d	07 09											07 15		07 23			07 27			07 38				
Gipsy Hill	d	07 12			07a15								07 18		07 26			07 30			07 41				07a45
Crystal Palace [4]	d	07a14											07a21		07 29			07 32			07a43				
Birkbeck 🚋	d														07 33										
Beckenham Junction [4] 🚋	a														07 36										
Streatham Common [4]	d			07 13				07 18														07 37		07 40	
Norbury	d			07 16				07 21														07 40		07 43	
Thornton Heath	d			07 19				07 24														07 43		07 46	
Selhurst [4]	d			07 21				07 27														07 46		07 51	
Norwood Junction [2]	a									07 17							07 29	07 38							
	d									07 18							07 31	07 39							
West Croydon [4] 🚋	a			07 26				07 32										07 44						07 56	
East Croydon 🚋	a					07 06	07 14		07 17	07 21	07 30						07 37			07 33		07 49			

Luton, Milton Keynes Central and London East and West Croydon via Tulse Hill - Crystal Palace - Norbury

Local Services

Network Diagram - see first Page of Table 177

		SN	SN	SN	SN		SN	SN	SN	SN	FC	FC	FC	SN	SN	SN	SN	SN	SN	SN	SN		FC	SN	SN
		1					1		1	1	1	1					1							◇1	
London Bridge [4] ⊖	d	07 27		07 29			07 30	07 33	07 33					07 36	07 41	07 44	07 56				07 47				
South Bermondsey	d			07 33				07 37							07 45										
Queens Rd Peckham	d			07 35				07 39							07 47										
Peckham Rye [4]	d			07 38				07 42							07 50						07 53				
East Dulwich	d			07 41				07 45													07 56				
North Dulwich	d			07 43				07 47													07 58				
Luton [10]	d										06 46	06 54	06 43										06 50		
Luton Airport Parkway [7]	d										06 48		06 45										06 52		
St Pancras International [15] ⊖	d										07 20	07 24	07 28										07 32		
City Thameslink [3]	d										07 29	07 33	07 37										07 41		
London Blackfriars [3] ⊖	d										07 32	07 36	07 40										07 44		
Elephant & Castle ⊖	d											07a39	07a43										07 47		
Loughborough Jn.	d																						07 51		
Herne Hill [4]	d																						07 57		
Tulse Hill [3]	d			07 47				07 50													08 02		08 05		
Streatham [4]	d			07a51																	08 05		08a08		
London Victoria [15] ⊖	d		07 23		07 30					07 36								07 36	07 41	07 45				07 47	07 52
Battersea Park [4]	d				07 34										08a02			07 40	07a45						
Milton Keynes Central	d																								
Watford Junction	d																								
Harrow & Wealdstone ⊖	d																								
Wembley Central ⊖	d																								
Shepherd's Bush ⊖	d																								
Kensington (Olympia) ⊖	d																								
West Brompton ⊖	d																								
Imperial Wharf	d																								
Clapham Junction [10]	d		07 30		07 38					07 42								07 44		07 51				07 53	07 58
Latchmere	d																								
Wandsworth Common	d				07 41													07 47		07 54					
Balham [4] ⊖	d				07 44													07 50		07 57					08 03
Streatham Hill	d																	07 53							08 06
West Norwood [4]	d							07 53										07 58							08 09
Gipsy Hill	d							07 56										08 01							08 12
Crystal Palace [4]	d							07 59										08 04							08a15
Birkbeck	d							08 03																	
Beckenham Junction [4]	a							08 06																	
Streatham Common [4]	d				07 48															08 01	08 08				
Norbury	d				07 50															08 03	08 11				
Thornton Heath	d				07 53															08 06	08 14				
Selhurst [4]	d				07 56															08 09	08 17				
Norwood Junction [2]	a	07 38					07 41							07 59			08 07	08 08							
	d	07 38					07 42							08 00			08 07	08 09							
West Croydon [4]	a				08 02													08 14			08 23				
East Croydon	a	07 42	07 44				07 45		07 48	07 51	07 54			08 03		08 00	08 10			08 12				08 02	

Luton, Milton Keynes Central and London East and West Croydon via Tulse Hill - Crystal Palace - Norbury

Local Services

Network Diagram - see first Page of Table 177

		SN	SN	SN	SN	SN	SN	FC	SN	SN	SN	SN	SN		SN	SN	SN	SN	SN	FC	SN	SN	SN	SN	SN
			1	◇1	1		◇1	1								1			◇1	1	◇1				
London Bridge [4] ⊖	d	07 51	07 53		08 00					08 03	08 06	08 14	08 06			08 08								08 10	08 17
South Bermondsey	d									08 07	08 11													08 14	
Queens Rd Peckham	d									08 09	08 13													08 16	
Peckham Rye [4]	d									08 12	08 16													08 19	08 23
East Dulwich	d									08 15	08 19														08 26
North Dulwich	d									08 17	08 21														08 28
Luton [10]	d							07 14												07 22					
Luton Airport Parkway [7]	d																			07 25					
St Pancras International [15] ⊖	d							07 44												07 56					
City Thameslink [3]	d							07 53												08 05					
London Blackfriars [3] ⊖	d							07 56												08 08					
Elephant & Castle ⊖	d																								
Loughborough Jn.	d																								
Herne Hill [4]	d																								
Tulse Hill [3]	d							08 10		08 21	08 25														08 32
Streatham [4]	d										08a28														08 36
London Victoria [15] ⊖	d			07 52		08 03	08 07								08 07		08 11	08 15	08 17		08 21		08 22		
Battersea Park [4]	d					08 07									08 11		08a15	08 19					08 26	08a32	
Milton Keynes Central	d																								
Watford Junction	d																								
Harrow & Wealdstone ⊖	d																								
Wembley Central ⊖	d																								
Shepherd's Bush ⊖	d																								
Kensington (Olympia) ⊖	d																								
West Brompton ⊖	d																								
Imperial Wharf	d																								
Clapham Junction [10]	d			07 58		08 11	08 13								08 16			08 23	08 23		08 27		08 30		
Latchmere	d																								
Wandsworth Common	d					08 14									08 19			08 26					08 33		
Balham [4] ⊖	d					08 16									08 21			08 28					08 35		
Streatham Hill	d								08 15						08 24							08 35	08 38		
West Norwood [4]	d								08 19	08 24					08 28							08 38	08 42		
Gipsy Hill	d	08a15							08 22	08 27					08 31							08 41	08 45		
Crystal Palace [4]	d								08a24	08 29					08 34							08a44	08a47		
Birkbeck	d									08 33															
Beckenham Junction [4]	a									08 37															
Streatham Common [4]	d					08 20												08 32							08 39
Norbury	d					08 23												08 35							08 41
Thornton Heath	d					08 26												08 38							08 44
Selhurst [4]	d					08 32												08 41							08 47
Norwood Junction [2]	a				08 16							08 27	08 29		08 38										
	d				08 16							08 27	08 30		08 39										
West Croydon [4]	a					08 36									08 44										08 53
East Croydon	a		08 05	08 09	08 20		08 22	08 26				08 30	08 33			08 23		08 44	08 34	08 37	08 40				

Table 177

Mondays to Fridays
until 18 May

Luton, Milton Keynes Central and London East and West Croydon via Tulse Hill - Crystal Palace - Norbury

Local Services

Network Diagram - see first Page of Table 177

		FC	SN	SN 1	SN	SN	SN	SN 1	SN 1	SN	SN ◇1	SN	SN ◇1	FC 1	FC 1	SN 1	SN	SN	SN	SN	SN ◇1	SN	SN ◇1
London Bridge 4 ⊖	d		08 21	08 23	08 24		08 27	08 30				08 33				08 45	08 36						
South Bermondsey	d				08 28							08 37											
Queens Rd Peckham	d				08 30							08 39											
Peckham Rye 4	d				08 33							08 42											
East Dulwich	d				08 36							08 45											
North Dulwich	d				08 38							08 47											
Luton 10	d	07 30												07 50	07 57								
Luton Airport Parkway 7	d	07 32													07 59								
St Pancras International 15 ⊖	d	08 12												08 20	08 32								
City Thameslink 3	d	08 21												08 29	08 41								
London Blackfriars 3 ⊖	d	08 24												08 32	08 44								
Elephant & Castle ⊖	d	08 27													08 47								
Loughborough Jn.	d	08 31													08 51								
Herne Hill 4	d	08 36													08 57								
Tulse Hill 3	d	08 40			08 47							08 50			09 01								
Streatham 4	d	08a44			08a50										09a05								
London Victoria 15 ⊖	d					08 26				08 31	08 32		08 36					08 36	08 41	08 43	08 47	08 49	08 51
Battersea Park 4	d									08 36								08 40	08a45	08 47		08 53	
Milton Keynes Central	d								07 01														
Watford Junction	d								07 38														
Harrow & Wealdstone ⊖	d								07 45														
Wembley Central ⊖	d								07 49														
Shepherd's Bush ⊖	d								08 04														
Kensington (Olympia) ⊖	d								08 07														
West Brompton ⊖	d								08 10														
Imperial Wharf	d								08 13														
Clapham Junction 10	d					08 33			08 36	08 40	08 38		08 43					08 44		08 51	08 53	08 57	
Latchmere	d																						
Wandsworth Common	d					08 36			08 39	08 43								08 47		08 54		09 00	
Balham 4 ⊖	d					08 38			08 42	08 46								08 50		08 56		09 02	
Streatham Hill	d																	08 53				09 05	
West Norwood 4	d											08 53						08 57				09 09	
Gipsy Hill	d		08a43									08 56						09 00				09 12	
Crystal Palace 4	d											08 59						09 02				09a14	
Birkbeck	d											09 03											
Beckenham Junction 4	a											09 06											
Streatham Common 4	d					08 42			08 46	08 51										09 00			
Norbury	d					08 45			08 48	08 54										09 03			
Thornton Heath	d					08 48			08 51	08 57										09 06			
Selhurst 4	d					08 51			08 54	09 00										09 09			
Norwood Junction 2	a							08 43								08 55	08 59	09 07					
	d							08 44								08 56	09 00	09 09					
West Croydon 4	a					08 55				09 05								09 13					
East Croydon	a			08 37			08 42	08 48	09 04		08 48		08 52	08 57		08 59	09 06			09 12	09 03		09 07

Table 177

Mondays to Fridays
until 18 May

Luton, Milton Keynes Central and London East and West Croydon via Tulse Hill - Crystal Palace - Norbury

Local Services

Network Diagram - see first Page of Table 177

		SN	SN	SN	SN	SN	SN	SN	SN 1	SN 1	SN	SN	SN	SN	SN ◇1	FC 1	FC	SN	SN	SN ◇1	FC 1	SN	SN	SN
London Bridge 4 ⊖	d		08 41	08 47	08 48	08 51	09 03		09 03	09 15	09 06	09 11	09 20											09 18
South Bermondsey	d		08 45		08 52		09 07					09 15												09 22
Queens Rd Peckham	d		08 48		08 54		09 09					09 18												09 24
Peckham Rye 4	d		08 50		08 57		09 12					09 20												09 27
East Dulwich	d				09 00		09 15																	09 30
North Dulwich	d				09 02		09 17																	09 32
Luton 10	d															08 12					08 28			
Luton Airport Parkway 7	d															08 15					08 30			
St Pancras International 15 ⊖	d															08 48	08 56				09 04			
City Thameslink 3	d															08 57	09 05				09 13			
London Blackfriars 3 ⊖	d															09 00	09 08				09 16			
Elephant & Castle ⊖	d																09 12							
Loughborough Jn.	d																09 16							
Herne Hill 4	d																09 25							
Tulse Hill 3	d				09 05		09 20										09 31							09 35
Streatham 4	d				09 09												09a35							09 39
London Victoria 15 ⊖	d	08 52						09 03						09 05	09 06			09 11	09 13	09 17		09 19	09 22	
Battersea Park 4	d	08 56	09a02					09 07				09a32		09 10				09a15	09 17			09 23		
Milton Keynes Central	d																							
Watford Junction	d																							
Harrow & Wealdstone ⊖	d																							
Wembley Central ⊖	d																							
Shepherd's Bush ⊖	d																							
Kensington (Olympia) ⊖	d																							
West Brompton ⊖	d																							
Imperial Wharf	d																							
Clapham Junction 10	d	09 00						09 11						09 14	09 12				09 21	09 23		09 27	09 30	
Latchmere	d																							
Wandsworth Common	d	09 03						09 14						09 17					09 24			09 30	09 33	
Balham 4 ⊖	d	09 05						09 16						09 20					09 26			09 32	09 35	
Streatham Hill	d													09 23								09 35		
West Norwood 4	d						09 23							09 27								09 40		
Gipsy Hill	d					09a14	09 26							09 30								09 43		
Crystal Palace 4	d						09 29							09 32								09a46		
Birkbeck	d						09 33																	
Beckenham Junction 4	a						09 36																	
Streatham Common 4	d	09 09			09 13			09 20											09 30				09 39	09 42
Norbury	d	09 12			09 15			09 23											09 33				09 42	09 45
Thornton Heath	d	09 15			09 18			09 26											09 36				09 45	09 48
Selhurst 4	d	09 18			09 21			09 29											09 39				09 48	09 51
Norwood Junction 2	a								09 16	09 25	09 30		09 32	09 37										
	d								09 16	09 26	09 30		09 33	09 39										
West Croydon 4	a	09 22			09 26			09 33						09 43									09 52	09 56
East Croydon	a			09 02					09 20	09 29	09 33		09 36		09 22	09 24			09 42	09 32	09 39			

Table 177

Mondays to Fridays
until 18 May

Luton, Milton Keynes Central and London East and West Croydon via Tulse Hill - Crystal Palace - Norbury

Local Services

Network Diagram - see first Page of Table 177

		SN 1	SN	SN ◇1	SN 1		SN	SN	SN 1	SN	SN	SN	SN	SN ◇1	FC 1	FC	SN	SN	SN ◇1	SN	SN ◇1		FC 1	SN	SN
London Bridge ⊖	d		09 22		09 32		09 33		09 45	09 36	09 41	09 50													09 48
South Bermondsey	d						09 37				09 45														09 52
Queens Rd Peckham	d						09 39				09 48														09 54
Peckham Rye	d						09 42				09 50														09 57
East Dulwich	d						09 45																		10 00
North Dulwich	d						09 47																		10 02
Luton	d														08 48	08 54							09 04		
Luton Airport Parkway	d														08 50	08 56							09 06		
St Pancras International ⊖	d														09 22	09 34							09 40		
City Thameslink	d														09 31	09 43							09 48		
London Blackfriars ⊖	d														09 34	09 46							09 50		
Elephant & Castle ⊖	d															09 49									
Loughborough Jn.	d															09 53									
Herne Hill	d															09 57									
Tulse Hill	d						09 50									10 01									10 05
Streatham	d															10a05									10 09
London Victoria ⊖	d			09 32				09 33					09 35	09 36			09 41	09 43	09 47	09 49	09 51			09 53	
Battersea Park	d							09 37			10a02		09 40				09a45	09 47		09 53					
Milton Keynes Central	d	08 13																							
Watford Junction	d	08 51																							
Harrow & Wealdstone ⊖	d	08 58																							
Wembley Central ⊖	d	09 05																							
Shepherd's Bush ⊖	d	09 18																							
Kensington (Olympia) ⊖	d	09 21																							
West Brompton ⊖	d	09 23																							
Imperial Wharf	d	09 26																							
Clapham Junction	d	09 34		09 38				09 41					09 44	09 42				09 51	09 53	09 57				10 00	
Latchmere	d																								
Wandsworth Common	d	09 37						09 44					09 47					09 54		10 00				10 03	
Balham ⊖	d	09 41						09 46					09 50					09 56		10 02				10 05	
Streatham Hill	d												09 53							10 05					
West Norwood	d						09 53						09 57							10 10					
Gipsy Hill	d		09a46				09 56						10 00							10 13					
Crystal Palace	d						09 59						10 02							10a16					
Birkbeck	d						10 03																		
Beckenham Junction	a						10 06																		
Streatham Common	d	09 45						09 50										10 00						10 09	10 12
Norbury	d	09 48						09 53										10 03						10 12	10 15
Thornton Heath	d	09 51						09 56										10 06						10 15	10 18
Selhurst	d	09 54						09 59										10 09						10 18	10 21
Norwood Junction	a				09 45				09 55	09 59		10 02	10 07												
	d				09 45				09 56	10 00		10 03	10 09												
West Croydon	a							10 03					10 13											10 22	10 26
East Croydon	a	09 57		09 48	09 49				09 59	10 03		10 06		09 52	09 54			10 12	10 02		10 07		10 09		

Table 177

Mondays to Fridays
until 18 May

Luton, Milton Keynes Central and London East and West Croydon via Tulse Hill - Crystal Palace - Norbury

Local Services

Network Diagram - see first Page of Table 177

		SN	SN	SN	SN 1	SN ◇1	FC 1	FC	SN 1	SN	SN	SN	SN		SN	SN	SN ◇1	FC 1	SN	SN	SN	SN 1	SN	SN ◇1	SN
London Bridge ⊖	d	09 52	10 03		10 03				10 15	10 06	10 11	10 20									10 18		10 22		10 33
South Bermondsey	d		10 07								10 15										10 22				10 37
Queens Rd Peckham	d		10 09								10 18										10 24				10 39
Peckham Rye	d		10 12								10 20										10 27				10 42
East Dulwich	d		10 15																		10 30				10 45
North Dulwich	d		10 17																		10 32				10 47
Luton	d						09 18	09 14										09 34							
Luton Airport Parkway	d						09 20	09 16										09 36							
St Pancras International ⊖	d						09 54	10 04										10 09							
City Thameslink	d						10 03	10 13										10 18							
London Blackfriars ⊖	d						10 05	10 16										10 20							
Elephant & Castle ⊖	d							10 19																	
Loughborough Jn.	d							10 23																	
Herne Hill	d							10 27																	
Tulse Hill	d		10 20					10 31													10 35				10 50
Streatham	d							10a35													10 39				
London Victoria ⊖	d			10 03		10 06							10 06		10 11	10 13	10 17		10 19	10 23				10 32	
Battersea Park	d			10 07							10a32		10 10		10a15	10 17			10 23						
Milton Keynes Central	d																					09 13			
Watford Junction	d																					09 51			
Harrow & Wealdstone ⊖	d																					09 58			
Wembley Central ⊖	d																					10 05			
Shepherd's Bush ⊖	d																					10 21			
Kensington (Olympia) ⊖	d																					10 24			
West Brompton ⊖	d																					10 27			
Imperial Wharf	d																					10 29			
Clapham Junction	d			10 11		10 12							10 14			10 21	10 23		10 27	10 30		10 34		10 38	
Latchmere	d																								
Wandsworth Common	d			10 14									10 17			10 24			10 30	10 33		10 37			
Balham ⊖	d			10 16									10 20			10 26			10 32	10 35		10 40			
Streatham Hill	d												10 23						10 35						
West Norwood	d		10 23										10 27						10 40						10 53
Gipsy Hill	d	10a15	10 26										10 30						10 43				10a45		10 56
Crystal Palace	d		10 29										10 32						10a46						10 59
Birkbeck	d		10 33																						11 03
Beckenham Junction	a		10 36																						11 06
Streatham Common	d			10 20												10 30				10 39	10 42	10 45			
Norbury	d			10 23												10 33				10 42	10 45	10 48			
Thornton Heath	d			10 26												10 36				10 45	10 48	10 51			
Selhurst	d			10 29												10 39				10 48	10 51	10 54			
Norwood Junction	a				10 16				10 25	10 29		10 32	10 37												
	d				10 16				10 26	10 30		10 33	10 39												
West Croydon	a			10 33									10 43							10 52	10 56				
East Croydon	a				10 20	10 22	10 24		10 29	10 33		10 36				10 42	10 32	10 39				10 57		10 48	

Luton, Milton Keynes Central and London East and West Croydon via Tulse Hill - Crystal Palace - Norbury

Local Services

Network Diagram - see first Page of Table 177

Station		SN	SN 1	SN ◇1	FC 1		FC	SN 1	SN	SN	SN	SN	SN	SN	SN ◇1	SN	SN ◇1	FC 1	SN	SN	SN		SN	SN	SN 1
London Bridge 4 ⊖	d		10 33					10 45	10 36	10 41	10 50									10 48	10 52		11 03		11 03
South Bermondsey	d									10 45										10 52			11 07		
Queens Rd Peckham	d									10 48										10 54			11 09		
Peckham Rye 4	d									10 50										10 57			11 12		
East Dulwich	d																			11 00			11 15		
North Dulwich	d																			11 02			11 17		
Luton 10	d				09 48		09 44											10 04							
Luton Airport Parkway 7	d				09 50		09 46											10 06							
St Pancras International 15 ⊖	d				10 24		10 34											10 39							
City Thameslink 3	d				10 33		10 43											10 48							
London Blackfriars 3 ⊖	d				10 35		10 46											10 50							
Elephant & Castle ⊖	d						10 49																		
Loughborough Jn.	d						10 53																		
Herne Hill 4	d						10 57																		
Tulse Hill 3	d						11 01													11 05			11 20		
Streatham 4	d						11a05													11 09					
London Victoria 15 ⊖	d	10 33		10 36								10 36	10 41	10 43	10 47	10 49	10 51		10 53					11 03	
Battersea Park 4	d	10 37								11a02		10 40	10a45	10 47		10 53								11 07	
Milton Keynes Central	d																								
Watford Junction	d																								
Harrow & Wealdstone ⊖	d																								
Wembley Central ⊖	d																								
Shepherd's Bush ⊖	d																								
Kensington (Olympia) ⊖	d																								
West Brompton ⊖	d																								
Imperial Wharf	d																								
Clapham Junction 10	d	10 41		10 42								10 44		10 51	10 53	10 57			11 00					11 11	
Latchmere	d																								
Wandsworth Common	d	10 44										10 47		10 54		11 00			11 03					11 14	
Balham 4 ⊖	d	10 46										10 50		10 56		11 02			11 05					11 16	
Streatham Hill	d											10 53				11 05									
West Norwood 4	d											10 57				11 10							11 23		
Gipsy Hill	d											11 00				11 13					11a15		11 26		
Crystal Palace 4	d											11 02				11a16							11 29		
Birkbeck	d																						11 33		
Beckenham Junction 4	a																						11 36		
Streatham Common 4	d	10 50												11 00					11 09	11 12				11 20	
Norbury	d	10 53												11 03					11 12	11 15				11 23	
Thornton Heath	d	10 56												11 06					11 15	11 18				11 26	
Selhurst 4	d	10 59												11 09					11 18	11 21				11 29	
Norwood Junction 2	a		10 46					10 55	10 59		11 02	11 07													11 16
	d		10 46					10 56	11 00		11 03	11 09													11 16
West Croydon 4	a	11 03										11 13							11 22	11 26				11 33	
East Croydon	a		10 50	10 52	10 54			10 59	11 03		11 06			11 12	11 02		11 07	11 09							11 20

Table 177

Mondays to Fridays
until 18 May

Luton, Milton Keynes Central and London East and West Croydon via Tulse Hill - Crystal Palace - Norbury

Local Services

Network Diagram - see first Page of Table 177

Station		SN ◇1	FC 1	FC	SN 1	SN	SN	SN	SN	SN	SN	SN ◇1	FC 1		SN	SN	SN	SN 1	SN	SN ◇1	SN	SN	SN 1	SN ◇1	FC 1
London Bridge 4 ⊖	d				11 15	11 06	11 11	11 20									11 18		11 22		11 33		11 33		
South Bermondsey	d						11 15										11 22				11 37				
Queens Rd Peckham	d						11 18										11 24				11 39				
Peckham Rye 4	d						11 20										11 27				11 42				
East Dulwich	d																11 30				11 45				
North Dulwich	d																11 32				11 47				
Luton 10	d		10 18	10 14									10 34												10 49
Luton Airport Parkway 7	d		10 20	10 16									10 36												10 51
St Pancras International 15 ⊖	d		10 54	11 04									11 09												11 24
City Thameslink 3	d		11 03	11 13									11 18												11 33
London Blackfriars 3 ⊖	d		11 05	11 16									11 20												11 35
Elephant & Castle ⊖	d			11 19																					
Loughborough Jn.	d			11 23																					
Herne Hill 4	d			11 27																					
Tulse Hill 3	d			11 31													11 35				11 50				
Streatham 4	d			11a35													11 39								
London Victoria 15 ⊖	d	11 06							11 06	11 11	11 13	11 17			11 19	11 23				11 32		11 33		11 36	
Battersea Park 4	d						11a32		11 10	11a15	11 17				11 23							11 37			
Milton Keynes Central	d																	10 13							
Watford Junction	d																	10 51							
Harrow & Wealdstone ⊖	d																	10 59							
Wembley Central ⊖	d																	11 04							
Shepherd's Bush ⊖	d																	11 19							
Kensington (Olympia) ⊖	d																	11 21							
West Brompton ⊖	d																	11 23							
Imperial Wharf	d																	11 26							
Clapham Junction 10	d	11 12							11 14		11 21	11 23			11 27	11 30		11 34		11 38		11 41		11 42	
Latchmere	d																								
Wandsworth Common	d								11 17		11 24				11 30	11 33		11 37				11 44			
Balham 4 ⊖	d								11 20		11 26				11 32	11 35		11 40				11 46			
Streatham Hill	d								11 23						11 35										
West Norwood 4	d								11 27						11 40						11 53				
Gipsy Hill	d								11 30						11 43				11a45		11 56				
Crystal Palace 4	d								11 32						11a46						11 59				
Birkbeck	d																				12 03				
Beckenham Junction 4	a																				12 06				
Streatham Common 4	d										11 30					11 39	11 42	11 45				11 50			
Norbury	d										11 33					11 42	11 45	11 48				11 53			
Thornton Heath	d										11 36					11 45	11 48	11 51				11 56			
Selhurst 4	d										11 39					11 48	11 51	11 54				11 59			
Norwood Junction 2	a				11 25	11 29		11 32	11 37														11 46		
	d				11 26	11 30		11 33	11 39														11 46		
West Croydon 4	a								11 43							11 52	11 56					12 03			
East Croydon	a	11 22	11 24		11 29	11 33		11 36			11 42	11 32	11 39					11 57		11 48			11 50	11 52	11 54

Table 177

Mondays to Fridays
until 18 May

Luton, Milton Keynes Central and London East and West Croydon via Tulse Hill - Crystal Palace - Norbury

Local Services

Network Diagram - see first Page of Table 177

Station		FC	SN ■	SN	SN		SN	SN	SN	SN	SN ◇■	SN	SN ◇■	FC ■	SN	SN	SN	SN	SN	SN ■	SN ◇■		FC ■	FC	SN ■
London Bridge ■ ⊖	d		11 45	11 36	11 41		11 50									11 48	11 52	12 03		12 03					12 15
South Bermondsey	d				11 45											11 52		12 07							
Queens Rd Peckham	d				11 48											11 54		12 09							
Peckham Rye ■	d				11 50											11 57		12 12							
East Dulwich	d															12 00		12 15							
North Dulwich	d															12 02		12 17							
Luton ■	d	10 44												11 04									11 18	11 14	
Luton Airport Parkway ■	d	10 46												11 06									11 20	11 16	
St Pancras International ■ ⊖	d	11 34												11 39									11 54	12 04	
City Thameslink ■	d	11 43												11 48									12 03	12 13	
London Blackfriars ■ ⊖	d	11 46												11 50									12 05	12 16	
Elephant & Castle ⊖	d	11 49																						12 19	
Loughborough Jn.	d	11 53																						12 23	
Herne Hill ■	d	11 57																						12 27	
Tulse Hill ■	d	12 01														12 05		12 20						12 31	
Streatham ■	d	12a05														12 09								12a35	
London Victoria ■ ⊖	d							11 36	11 41	11 43	11 47	11 49	11 51						12 03		12 06				
Battersea Park ■	d				12a02			11 40	11a45	11 47		11 53							12 07						
Milton Keynes Central	d																								
Watford Junction	d																								
Harrow & Wealdstone ⊖	d																								
Wembley Central ⊖	d																								
Shepherd's Bush ⊖	d																								
Kensington (Olympia) ⊖	d																								
West Brompton ⊖	d																								
Imperial Wharf	d																								
Clapham Junction ■	d							11 44		11 51	11 53	11 57			12 00				12 11		12 12				
Latchmere	d																								
Wandsworth Common	d							11 47		11 54		12 00			12 03				12 14						
Balham ■ ⊖	d							11 50		11 56		12 02			12 05				12 16						
Streatham Hill	d							11 53				12 05													
West Norwood ■	d							11 57				12 10						12 23							
Gipsy Hill	d							12 00				12 13					12a15	12 26							
Crystal Palace ■	d							12 02				12a16						12 29							
Birkbeck	d																	12 33							
Beckenham Junction ■	a																	12 36							
Streatham Common ■	d									12 00					12 09	12 12			12 20						
Norbury	d									12 03					12 12	12 15			12 23						
Thornton Heath	d									12 06					12 15	12 18			12 26						
Selhurst ■	d									12 09					12 18	12 21			12 29						
Norwood Junction ■	a		11 55	11 59			12 02	12 07												12 16					12 25
	d		11 56	12 00			12 03	12 09												12 16					12 26
West Croydon ■	a							12 13							12 22	12 26			12 33						
East Croydon	a		11 59	12 03			12 06			12 12	12 02		12 07	12 09						12 20	12 22		12 24		12 29

Table 177

Mondays to Fridays
until 18 May

Luton, Milton Keynes Central and London East and West Croydon via Tulse Hill - Crystal Palace - Norbury

Local Services

Network Diagram - see first Page of Table 177

Station		SN	SN	SN	SN	SN	SN	SN ◇■	FC ■	SN	SN	SN	SN ■		SN	SN ◇■	SN	SN	SN ■	SN ◇■	FC ■	FC	SN ■	SN	SN
London Bridge ■ ⊖	d	12 06	12 11	12 20								12 18			12 22		12 33		12 33				12 45	12 36	12 41
South Bermondsey	d		12 15									12 22					12 37								12 45
Queens Rd Peckham	d		12 18									12 24					12 39								12 48
Peckham Rye ■	d		12 20									12 27					12 42								12 50
East Dulwich	d											12 30					12 45								
North Dulwich	d											12 32					12 47								
Luton ■	d								11 34												11 48	11 44			
Luton Airport Parkway ■	d								11 36												11 50	11 46			
St Pancras International ■ ⊖	d								12 09												12 24	12 34			
City Thameslink ■	d								12 18												12 33	12 43			
London Blackfriars ■ ⊖	d								12 20												12 35	12 46			
Elephant & Castle ⊖	d																					12 49			
Loughborough Jn.	d																					12 53			
Herne Hill ■	d																					12 57			
Tulse Hill ■	d											12 35					12 50					13 01			
Streatham ■	d											12 39										13a05			
London Victoria ■ ⊖	d				12 06	12 11	12 13	12 17		12 19						12 32		12 33		12 36					
Battersea Park ■	d		12a32		12 10	12a15	12 17			12 23								12 37							13a02
Milton Keynes Central	d												11 13												
Watford Junction	d												11 51												
Harrow & Wealdstone ⊖	d												11 59												
Wembley Central ⊖	d												12 04												
Shepherd's Bush ⊖	d												12 19												
Kensington (Olympia) ⊖	d												12 22												
West Brompton ⊖	d												12 25												
Imperial Wharf	d												12 27												
Clapham Junction ■	d				12 14		12 21	12 23		12 27	12 30		12 34			12 38		12 41		12 42					
Latchmere	d																								
Wandsworth Common	d				12 17		12 24			12 30	12 33		12 37					12 44							
Balham ■ ⊖	d				12 20		12 26			12 32	12 35		12 40					12 46							
Streatham Hill	d				12 23					12 35															
West Norwood ■	d				12 27					12 40							12 53								
Gipsy Hill	d				12 30					12 43					12a45		12 56								
Crystal Palace ■	d				12 32					12a46							12 59								
Birkbeck	d																13 03								
Beckenham Junction ■	a																13 06								
Streatham Common ■	d						12 30				12 39	12 42	12 45					12 50							
Norbury	d						12 33				12 42	12 45	12 48					12 53							
Thornton Heath	d						12 36				12 45	12 48	12 51					12 56							
Selhurst ■	d						12 39				12 48	12 51	12 54					12 59							
Norwood Junction ■	a	12 29		12 32	12 37														12 46				12 55	12 59	
	d	12 30		12 33	12 39														12 46				12 56	13 00	
West Croydon ■	a				12 43						12 52	12 56						13 03							
East Croydon	a	12 33		12 36			12 42	12 32	12 39				12 57			12 48			12 50	12 52	12 54		12 59	13 03	

Table 177

Mondays to Fridays
until 18 May

Luton, Milton Keynes Central and London East and West Croydon via Tulse Hill - Crystal Palace - Norbury

Local Services

Network Diagram - see first Page of Table 177

		SN	SN	SN	SN		SN	SN	SN	FC	SN	SN	SN	SN	SN	SN	SN	FC	FC	SN	SN		SN	SN	SN
							◇1		◇1	1						1	◇1	1		1					
London Bridge 4 ⊖	d	12 50										12 48	12 52	13 03		13 03				13 15	13 06		13 11	13 20	
South Bermondsey	d											12 52		13 07									13 15		
Queens Rd Peckham	d											12 54		13 09									13 18		
Peckham Rye 4	d											12 57		13 12									13 20		
East Dulwich	d											13 00		13 15											
North Dulwich	d											13 02		13 17											
Luton 10	d									12 04								12 18	12 14						
Luton Airport Parkway 7	d									12 06								12 20	12 16						
St Pancras International 15 ⊖	d									12 39								12 54	13 04						
City Thameslink 3	d									12 48								13 03	13 13						
London Blackfriars 3 ⊖	d									12 50								13 05	13 16						
Elephant & Castle ⊖	d																		13 19						
Loughborough Jn.	d																		13 23						
Herne Hill 4	d																		13 27						
Tulse Hill 3	d											13 05		13 20					13 31						
Streatham 4	d											13 09							13a35						
London Victoria 15 ⊖	d		12 36	12 41	12 43		12 47	12 49	12 51						13 03		13 06								13 06
Battersea Park 4	d		12 40	12a45	12 47			12 53							13 07								13a32		13 10
Milton Keynes Central	d																								
Watford Junction	d																								
Harrow & Wealdstone ⊖	d																								
Wembley Central ⊖	d																								
Shepherd's Bush ⊖	d																								
Kensington (Olympia) ⊖	d																								
West Brompton ⊖	d																								
Imperial Wharf	d																								
Clapham Junction 10	d		12 44		12 51		12 53	12 57			13 00				13 11		13 12								13 14
Latchmere	d																								
Wandsworth Common	d		12 47		12 54			13 00			13 03				13 14										13 17
Balham 4 ⊖	d		12 50		12 56			13 02			13 05				13 16										13 20
Streatham Hill	d		12 53					13 05																	13 23
West Norwood 4	d		12 57					13 10						13 23											13 27
Gipsy Hill	d		13 00					13 13					13a15	13 26											13 30
Crystal Palace 4	d		13 02					13a16						13 29											13 32
Birkbeck	d													13 33											
Beckenham Junction 4	a													13 36											
Streatham Common 4	d				13 00						13 09	13 12			13 20										
Norbury	d				13 03						13 12	13 15			13 23										
Thornton Heath	d				13 06						13 15	13 18			13 26										
Selhurst 4	d				13 09						13 18	13 21			13 29										
Norwood Junction 2	a	13 02	13 07													13 16				13 25	13 29			13 32	13 37
	d	13 03	13 09													13 16				13 26	13 30			13 33	13 39
West Croydon 4	a		13 13								13 22	13 26			13 33										13 43
East Croydon	a	13 06			13 12		13 02		13 07	13 09						13 20	13 22	13 24		13 29	13 33			13 36	

Table 177

Mondays to Fridays
until 18 May

Luton, Milton Keynes Central and London East and West Croydon via Tulse Hill - Crystal Palace - Norbury

Local Services

Network Diagram - see first Page of Table 177

		SN	SN	SN	FC	SN	SN	SN	SN	SN	SN	SN	SN		SN	SN	FC	FC	SN	SN	SN	SN	SN	SN	SN
				◇1	1				1		◇1				1	◇1	1		1						
London Bridge 4 ⊖	d							13 18		13 22		13 33			13 33				13 45	13 36	13 41	13 50			
South Bermondsey	d							13 22				13 37									13 45				
Queens Rd Peckham	d							13 24				13 39									13 48				
Peckham Rye 4	d							13 27				13 42									13 50				
East Dulwich	d							13 30				13 45													
North Dulwich	d							13 32				13 47													
Luton 10	d				12 34												12 48	12 44							
Luton Airport Parkway 7	d				12 36												12 50	12 46							
St Pancras International 15 ⊖	d				13 09												13 24	13 34							
City Thameslink 3	d				13 18												13 33	13 43							
London Blackfriars 3 ⊖	d				13 20												13 35	13 46							
Elephant & Castle ⊖	d																	13 49							
Loughborough Jn.	d																	13 53							
Herne Hill 4	d																	13 57							
Tulse Hill 3	d							13 35				13 50						14 01							
Streatham 4	d							13 39										14a05							
London Victoria 15 ⊖	d	13 11	13 13	13 17		13 19	13 23				13 32		13 33			13 36							13 36	13 41	13 43
Battersea Park 4	d	13a15	13 17			13 23							13 37								14a02		13 40	13a45	13 47
Milton Keynes Central	d								12 13																
Watford Junction	d								12 51																
Harrow & Wealdstone ⊖	d								12 59																
Wembley Central ⊖	d								13 04																
Shepherd's Bush ⊖	d								13 19																
Kensington (Olympia) ⊖	d								13 22																
West Brompton ⊖	d								13 25																
Imperial Wharf	d								13 28																
Clapham Junction 10	d		13 21	13 23		13 27	13 30		13 34		13 38		13 41			13 42							13 44		13 51
Latchmere	d																								
Wandsworth Common	d		13 24			13 30	13 33		13 37				13 44										13 47		13 54
Balham 4 ⊖	d		13 26			13 32	13 35		13 40				13 46										13 50		13 56
Streatham Hill	d					13 35																	13 53		
West Norwood 4	d					13 40						13 53											13 57		
Gipsy Hill	d					13 43				13a45		13 56											14 00		
Crystal Palace 4	d					13a46						13 59											14 02		
Birkbeck	d											14 03													
Beckenham Junction 4	a											14 06													
Streatham Common 4	d		13 30				13 39	13 42	13 45				13 50												14 00
Norbury	d		13 33				13 42	13 45	13 48				13 53												14 03
Thornton Heath	d		13 36				13 45	13 48	13 51				13 56												14 06
Selhurst 4	d		13 39				13 48	13 51	13 54				13 59												14 09
Norwood Junction 2	a														13 46				13 55	13 59		14 02	14 07		
	d														13 46				13 56	14 00		14 03	14 09		
West Croydon 4	a						13 52	13 56					14 03										14 13		
East Croydon	a		13 42	13 32	13 39				13 57		13 48				13 50	13 52	13 54		13 59	14 03		14 06			14 12

Table 177

Mondays to Fridays
until 18 May

Luton, Milton Keynes Central and London East and West Croydon via Tulse Hill - Crystal Palace - Norbury

Local Services

Network Diagram - see first Page of Table 177

		SN ◇1	SN	SN ◇1	FC 1		SN	SN	SN	SN	SN	SN 1	SN ◇1	FC 1	FC	SN 1	SN	SN	SN	SN	SN		SN	SN ◇1	FC 1
London Bridge 4 ⊖	d							13 48	13 52	14 03		14 03				14 15	14 06	14 11	14 20						
South Bermondsey	d							13 52		14 07								14 15							
Queens Rd Peckham	d							13 54		14 09								14 18							
Peckham Rye 4	d							13 57		14 12								14 20							
East Dulwich	d							14 00		14 15															
North Dulwich	d							14 02		14 17															
Luton 10	d				13 04									13 18	13 14										13 34
Luton Airport Parkway 7	d				13 06									13 20	13 16										13 36
St Pancras International 15 ⊖	d				13 39									13 54	14 04										14 09
City Thameslink 3	d				13 48									14 03	14 13										14 18
London Blackfriars 3 ⊖	d				13 50									14 05	14 16										14 20
Elephant & Castle ⊖	d														14 19										
Loughborough Jn.	d														14 23										
Herne Hill 4	d														14 27										
Tulse Hill 3	d							14 05		14 20					14 31										
Streatham 4	d							14 09							14a35										
London Victoria 15 ⊖	d	13 47	13 49	13 51							14 03		14 06							14 06	14 11		14 13	14 17	
Battersea Park 4	d		13 53								14 07							14a32		14 10	14a15		14 17		
Milton Keynes Central	d																								
Watford Junction	d																								
Harrow & Wealdstone ⊖	d																								
Wembley Central ⊖	d																								
Shepherd's Bush ⊖	d																								
Kensington (Olympia) ⊖	d																								
West Brompton ⊖	d																								
Imperial Wharf	d																								
Clapham Junction 10	d	13 53	13 57				14 00				14 11		14 12							14 14			14 21	14 23	
Latchmere	d																								
Wandsworth Common	d		14 00				14 03				14 14									14 17			14 24		
Balham 4 ⊖	d		14 02				14 05				14 16									14 20			14 26		
Streatham Hill	d		14 05																	14 23					
West Norwood 4	d		14 10							14 23										14 27					
Gipsy Hill	d		14 13						14a15	14 26										14 30					
Crystal Palace 4	d		14a16							14 29										14 32					
Birkbeck ⇌	d									14 33															
Beckenham Junction 4 ⇌	a									14 36															
Streatham Common 4	d						14 09	14 12			14 20												14 30		
Norbury	d						14 12	14 15			14 23												14 33		
Thornton Heath	d						14 15	14 18			14 26												14 36		
Selhurst 4	d						14 18	14 21			14 29												14 39		
Norwood Junction 2	a											14 16				14 25	14 29		14 32	14 37					
	d											14 16				14 26	14 30		14 33	14 39					
West Croydon 4 ⇌	a						14 22	14 26			14 33									14 43					
East Croydon ⇌	a	14 02		14 07	14 09							14 20	14 22	14 25		14 29	14 33		14 36				14 42	14 32	14 39

Table 177

Mondays to Fridays
until 18 May

Luton, Milton Keynes Central and London East and West Croydon via Tulse Hill - Crystal Palace - Norbury

Local Services

Network Diagram - see first Page of Table 177

		SN	SN	SN	SN 1	SN	SN ◇1	SN	SN	SN 1	SN ◇1	FC 1	FC		SN 1	SN	SN	SN	SN	SN	SN	SN ◇1	SN	SN ◇1	FC 1
London Bridge 4 ⊖	d			14 18		14 22		14 33		14 33					14 45	14 36	14 41	14 50							
South Bermondsey	d			14 22				14 37									14 45								
Queens Rd Peckham	d			14 24				14 39									14 48								
Peckham Rye 4	d			14 27				14 42									14 50								
East Dulwich	d			14 30				14 45																	
North Dulwich	d			14 32				14 47																	
Luton 10	d											13 48	13 44												14 04
Luton Airport Parkway 7	d											13 50	13 46												14 06
St Pancras International 15 ⊖	d											14 24	14 34												14 39
City Thameslink 3	d											14 33	14 43												14 48
London Blackfriars 3 ⊖	d											14 35	14 46												14 50
Elephant & Castle ⊖	d												14 49												
Loughborough Jn.	d												14 53												
Herne Hill 4	d												14 57												
Tulse Hill 3	d			14 35				14 50					15 01												
Streatham 4	d			14 39									15a05												
London Victoria 15 ⊖	d	14 19					14 32		14 33		14 36								14 36	14 41	14 43	14 47	14 49	14 51	
Battersea Park 4	d	14 23							14 37								15a02		14 40	14a45	14 47		14 53		
Milton Keynes Central	d				13 13																				
Watford Junction	d				13 51																				
Harrow & Wealdstone ⊖	d				13 59																				
Wembley Central ⊖	d				14 04																				
Shepherd's Bush ⊖	d				14 19																				
Kensington (Olympia) ⊖	d				14 22																				
West Brompton ⊖	d				14 25																				
Imperial Wharf	d				14 28																				
Clapham Junction 10	d	14 27	14 30		14 34		14 38		14 41		14 42								14 44		14 51	14 53	14 57		
Latchmere	d																								
Wandsworth Common	d	14 30	14 33		14 37				14 44										14 47		14 54		15 00		
Balham 4 ⊖	d	14 32	14 35		14 40				14 46										14 50		14 56		15 02		
Streatham Hill	d	14 35																	14 53				15 05		
West Norwood 4	d	14 40						14 53											14 57				15 10		
Gipsy Hill	d	14 43				14a45		14 56											15 00				15 13		
Crystal Palace 4	d	14a46						14 59											15 02				15a16		
Birkbeck ⇌	d							15 03																	
Beckenham Junction 4 ⇌	a							15 06																	
Streatham Common 4	d		14 39	14 42	14 45				14 50												15 00				
Norbury	d		14 42	14 45	14 48				14 53												15 03				
Thornton Heath	d		14 45	14 48	14 51				14 56												15 06				
Selhurst 4	d		14 48	14 51	14 54				14 59												15 09				
Norwood Junction 2	a									14 46					14 55	14 59		15 02	15 07						
	d									14 46					14 56	15 00		15 03	15 09						
West Croydon 4 ⇌	a		14 52	14 56					15 03										15 13						
East Croydon ⇌	a				14 57		14 48			14 50	14 52	14 54			14 59	15 03		15 06			15 12	15 02		15 07	15 09

Table 177

Mondays to Fridays
until 18 May

Luton, Milton Keynes Central and London East and West Croydon via Tulse Hill - Crystal Palace - Norbury

Local Services

Network Diagram - see first Page of Table 177

		SN	SN	SN	SN		SN	SN	SN	FC	FC	SN	SN	SN	SN	SN	SN	SN	SN	FC	SN		SN	SN	SN
								1	◇1 🚲	1		1							◇1	1					1
London Bridge 4 ⊖	d		14 48	14 52	15 03			15 03				15 15	15 06	15 11	15 20									15 18	
South Bermondsey	d		14 52		15 07									15 15										15 22	
Queens Rd Peckham	d		14 54		15 09									15 18										15 24	
Peckham Rye 4	d		14 57		15 12									15 20										15 27	
East Dulwich	d		15 00		15 15																			15 30	
North Dulwich	d		15 02		15 17																			15 32	
Luton 10	d									14 18	14 14									14 34					
Luton Airport Parkway 7	d									14 20	14 16									14 36					
St Pancras International 15 ⊖	d									14 54	15 04									15 09					
City Thameslink 3	d									15 03	15 13									15 18					
London Blackfriars 3 ⊖	d									15 05	15 16									15 20					
Elephant & Castle ⊖	d										15 19														
Loughborough Jn.	d										15 23														
Herne Hill 4	d										15 27														
Tulse Hill 3	d		15 05		15 20						15 31													15 35	
Streatham 4	d		15 09								15a35													15 39	
London Victoria 15 ⊖	d						15 03		15 06							15 06	15 11	15 13	15 17		15 19		15 23		
Battersea Park 4	d						15 07							15a32		15 10	15a15	15 17			15 23				
Milton Keynes Central	d																								14 13
Watford Junction	d																								14 51
Harrow & Wealdstone ⊖	d																								14 59
Wembley Central ⊖	d																								15 04
Shepherd's Bush ⊖	d																								15 22
Kensington (Olympia) ⊖	d																								15 24
West Brompton ⊖	d																								15 26
Imperial Wharf	d																								15 29
Clapham Junction 10	d	15 00					15 11		15 12							15 14		15 21	15 23		15 27		15 30		15 34
Latchmere	d																								
Wandsworth Common	d	15 03					15 14									15 17		15 24			15 30		15 33		15 37
Balham 4 ⊖	d	15 05					15 16									15 20		15 26			15 32		15 35		15 40
Streatham Hill	d															15 23					15 35				
West Norwood 4	d				15 23											15 27					15 40				
Gipsy Hill	d			15a15	15 26											15 30					15 43				
Crystal Palace 4	d				15 29											15 32					15a46				
Birkbeck 🚋	d				15 33																				
Beckenham Junction 4 🚋	a				15 36																				
Streatham Common 4	d	15 09	15 12				15 20											15 30					15 39	15 42	15 45
Norbury	d	15 12	15 15				15 23											15 33					15 42	15 45	15 48
Thornton Heath	d	15 15	15 18				15 26											15 36					15 45	15 48	15 51
Selhurst 4	d	15 18	15 21				15 29											15 39					15 48	15 51	15 54
Norwood Junction 2	a							15 16				15 25	15 29		15 32	15 37									
	d							15 16				15 26	15 30		15 33	15 39									
West Croydon 4 🚋	a	15 22	15 26				15 33									15 43							15 52	15 56	
East Croydon 🚋	a							15 20	15 22	15 24		15 29	15 33		15 36			15 42	15 32	15 39					15 57

Table 177

Mondays to Fridays
until 18 May

Luton, Milton Keynes Central and London East and West Croydon via Tulse Hill - Crystal Palace - Norbury

Local Services

Network Diagram - see first Page of Table 177

		SN	SN	SN	SN	SN	SN	FC	FC	SN	SN	SN	SN		SN	SN	SN	SN	SN	SN	FC	SN	SN	SN	SN
			◇1			1	◇1 🚲	1		1								◇1		◇1	1				
London Bridge 4 ⊖	d	15 22		15 33		15 33				15 45	15 36	15 41	15 50										15 48	15 52	16 03
South Bermondsey	d			15 37								15 45											15 52		16 07
Queens Rd Peckham	d			15 39								15 48											15 54		16 09
Peckham Rye 4	d			15 42								15 50											15 57		16 12
East Dulwich	d			15 45																			16 00		16 15
North Dulwich	d			15 47																			16 02		16 17
Luton 10	d							14 48	14 44												15 04				
Luton Airport Parkway 7	d							14 50	14 46												15 06				
St Pancras International 15 ⊖	d							15 24	15 34												15 39				
City Thameslink 3	d							15 33	15 43												15 48				
London Blackfriars 3 ⊖	d							15 35	15 46												15 50				
Elephant & Castle ⊖	d								15 49																
Loughborough Jn.	d								15 53																
Herne Hill 4	d								15 57																
Tulse Hill 3	d			15 50					16 01														16 05		16 20
Streatham 4	d								16a05														16 09		
London Victoria 15 ⊖	d		15 32		15 33		15 36								15 36	15 41	15 43	15 47	15 49	15 51		15 53			
Battersea Park 4	d				15 37							16a02			15 40	15a45	15 47		15 53						
Milton Keynes Central	d																								
Watford Junction	d																								
Harrow & Wealdstone ⊖	d																								
Wembley Central ⊖	d																								
Shepherd's Bush ⊖	d																								
Kensington (Olympia) ⊖	d																								
West Brompton ⊖	d																								
Imperial Wharf	d																								
Clapham Junction 10	d		15 38		15 41		15 42								15 44		15 51	15 53	15 57			16 00			
Latchmere	d																								
Wandsworth Common	d				15 44										15 47		15 54		16 00			16 03			
Balham 4 ⊖	d				15 46										15 50		15 56		16 02			16 05			
Streatham Hill	d														15 53				16 05						
West Norwood 4	d			15 53											15 57				16 10						16 23
Gipsy Hill	d	15a45		15 56											16 00				16 13					16a15	16 26
Crystal Palace 4	d			15 59											16 02				16a16						16 29
Birkbeck 🚋	d			16 03																					16 33
Beckenham Junction 4 🚋	a			16 06																					16 38
Streatham Common 4	d				15 50												16 00					16 09	16 12		
Norbury	d				15 53												16 03					16 12	16 15		
Thornton Heath	d				15 56												16 06					16 15	16 18		
Selhurst 4	d				15 59												16 09					16 18	16 21		
Norwood Junction 2	a					15 46				15 55	15 59		16 02		16 07										
	d					15 46				15 56	16 00		16 03		16 09										
West Croydon 4 🚋	a				16 03										16 13							16 22	16 26		
East Croydon 🚋	a		15 47			15 50	15 52	15 54		15 59	16 03		16 06				16 12	16 02		16 07	16 09				

Table 177

Mondays to Fridays
until 18 May

Luton, Milton Keynes Central and London East and West Croydon via Tulse Hill - Crystal Palace - Norbury

Local Services

Network Diagram - see first Page of Table 177

		SN	SN ■	SN ■ 🚲	FC ■		FC	SN ■	SN	SN	SN	SN	SN	SN	SN ◇■ 🚲	SN	SN ■	FC ■	SN	SN ■	SN		SN ◇■ 🚲	SN	SN
London Bridge ⊖	d		16 03					16 15	16 06	16 11	16 20					16 18					16 22			16 33	
South Bermondsey	d									16 15						16 22								16 37	
Queens Rd Peckham	d									16 18						16 24								16 39	
Peckham Rye	d									16 20						16 27								16 42	
East Dulwich	d															16 30								16 45	
North Dulwich	d															16 32								16 47	
Luton	d				15 18		15 14											15 34							
Luton Airport Parkway	d				15 20		15 16											15 36							
St Pancras International ⊖	d				15 54		16 04											16 09							
City Thameslink	d				16 03		16 13											16 18							
London Blackfriars ⊖	d				16 05		16 16											16 20							
Elephant & Castle ⊖	d						16 19																		
Loughborough Jn.	d						16 23																		
Herne Hill	d						16 27																		
Tulse Hill	d						16 32									16 35								16 50	
Streatham	d						16a35									16 39									
London Victoria ⊖	d	16 03		16 06								16 07	16 11	16 13	16 17		16 19		16 19				16 32		16 33
Battersea Park	d	16 07								16a32		16 11	16a15	16 17					16 23						16 37
Milton Keynes Central	d																			15 13					
Watford Junction	d																			15 51					
Harrow & Wealdstone ⊖	d																			15 59					
Wembley Central ⊖	d																			16 05					
Shepherd's Bush ⊖	d																			16 19					
Kensington (Olympia) ⊖	d																			16 22					
West Brompton ⊖	d																			16 25					
Imperial Wharf	d																			16 27					
Clapham Junction	d	16 11		16 12								16 15		16 21	16 23		16 26		16 27	16 34			16 38		16 41
Latchmere	d																								
Wandsworth Common	d	16 14										16 18		16 24					16 30	16 37					16 44
Balham ⊖	d	16 16										16 20		16 26					16 32	16 40					16 46
Streatham Hill	d											16 23							16 35						
West Norwood	d											16 27							16 39					16 53	
Gipsy Hill	d											16 30							16 44		16a45			16 56	
Crystal Palace	d											16 32							16a46					16 59	
Birkbeck 🚋	d																							17 03	
Beckenham Junction 🚋	a																							17 08	
Streatham Common	d	16 20												16 30		16 42				16 45					16 50
Norbury	d	16 23												16 33		16 45				16 48					16 53
Thornton Heath	d	16 26												16 36		16 48				16 51					16 56
Selhurst	d	16 29												16 39		16 51				16 55					16 59
Norwood Junction	a		16 16					16 25	16 29		16 32	16 37													
	d		16 16					16 26	16 30		16 33	16 39													
West Croydon 🚋	a	16 33										16 43				16 57									17 03
East Croydon 🚋	a		16 20	16 22	16 24			16 29	16 33		16 36			16 42	16 33		16 36	16 39		16 58			16 47		

Table 177

Mondays to Fridays
until 18 May

Luton, Milton Keynes Central and London East and West Croydon via Tulse Hill - Crystal Palace - Norbury

Local Services

Network Diagram - see first Page of Table 177

		SN ■	SN	SN ■ 🚲	SN	SN	SN	SN	FC ■	FC	FC ■	SN	SN		SN ◇■ 🚲	SN	SN ■	SN	SN	SN ■	SN	SN ■	SN	SN	SN
London Bridge ⊖	d	16 33	16 36		16 41	16 48										16 48			16 52	16 57	16 58	16 59	17 03		17 05
South Bermondsey	d				16 45											16 52					17 02				
Queens Rd Peckham	d				16 48											16 54					17 04				
Peckham Rye	d				16 50											16 57					17 07				
East Dulwich	d															17 00					17 10				
North Dulwich	d															17 02					17 12				
Luton	d								15 48	15 44	16 04														
Luton Airport Parkway	d								15 50	15 46	16 06														
St Pancras International ⊖	d								16 22	16 34	16 40														
City Thameslink	d								16 31	16 43	16 49														
London Blackfriars ⊖	d								16 36	16 46	16 52														
Elephant & Castle ⊖	d									16 49	16 56														
Loughborough Jn.	d									16 53	17 00														
Herne Hill	d									16 57	17a04														
Tulse Hill	d									17 02						17 05					17 17				
Streatham	d									17a05						17 09									
London Victoria ⊖	d			16 36			16 37	16 39				16 41	16 43		16 47		16 49	16 49						17 01	
Battersea Park	d				17a02		16 41					16a45	16 47					16 53						17 05	
Milton Keynes Central	d																								
Watford Junction	d																								
Harrow & Wealdstone ⊖	d																								
Wembley Central ⊖	d																								
Shepherd's Bush ⊖	d																								
Kensington (Olympia) ⊖	d																								
West Brompton ⊖	d																								
Imperial Wharf	d																								
Clapham Junction	d			16 42			16 45	16 45					16 51		16 53		16 56	16 57						17 09	
Latchmere	d																								
Wandsworth Common	d						16 48						16 54					17 00						17 12	
Balham ⊖	d						16 50						16 56					17 03						17 14	
Streatham Hill	d						16 53											17 06							
West Norwood	d						16 57											17 09			17 20				
Gipsy Hill	d						17 00											17 12	17a15		17 23				
Crystal Palace	d						17 03											17a15			17 26				
Birkbeck 🚋	d																				17 30				
Beckenham Junction 🚋	a																				17 35				
Streatham Common	d												17 00			17 12								17 18	
Norbury	d												17 03			17 15								17 21	
Thornton Heath	d												17 06			17 18								17 24	
Selhurst	d												17 09			17 21								17 27	
Norwood Junction	a	16 44	16 59			17 01	17 07															17 10	17 16		17 29
	d	16 44	17 00			17 02	17 09															17 10	17 16		17 30
West Croydon 🚋	a		17 07				17 13									17 27							17 21	17 32	17 37
East Croydon 🚋	a	16 48		16 52		17 05		16 55	16 59				17 12		17 03		17 06			17 09		17 14			

Table 177

Mondays to Fridays
until 18 May

Luton, Milton Keynes Central and London East and West Croydon via Tulse Hill - Crystal Palace - Norbury

Local Services

Network Diagram - see first Page of Table 177

		SN 1	FC 1	FC	SN	SN	SN	SN	SN	SN	SN ◇1	SN	SN 1	SN	SN	SN 1	FC 1	SN 1	SN	SN	SN ◇1	SN 1	SN
London Bridge 4 ⊖	d				17 11	17 17						17 18			17 19	17 23			17 28	17 29		17 32	
South Bermondsey	d				17 15							17 22							17 32				
Queens Rd Peckham	d				17 18							17 24							17 35				
Peckham Rye 4	d				17 20							17 27							17 37				
East Dulwich	d											17 30							17 40				
North Dulwich	d											17 32							17 42				
Luton 10	d		16 14	16 16													16 34						
Luton Airport Parkway 7	d		16 17	16 18													16 36						
St Pancras International 15 ⊖	d		16 46	17 02													17 10						
City Thameslink 3	d		16 55	17 11													17 19						
London Blackfriars 3 ⊖	d		16 58	17 14													17 22						
Elephant & Castle ⊖	d		17 02	17 18																			
Loughborough Jn.	d			17 22																			
Herne Hill 4	d			17 26																			
Tulse Hill 3	d			17 31								17 36							17 46				
Streatham 4	d			17a35								17 39											
London Victoria 15 ⊖	d	17 06					17 06	17 09	17 11	17 13	17 17		17 21	17 22							17 32		17 33
Battersea Park 4	d				17a32		17 10		17a15	17 17				17 26									17 37
Milton Keynes Central	d																	16 13					
Watford Junction	d																	16 51					
Harrow & Wealdstone ⊖	d																	16 59					
Wembley Central ⊖	d																	17 05					
Shepherd's Bush ⊖	d																	17 19					
Kensington (Olympia) ⊖	d																	17 22					
West Brompton ⊖	d																	17 25					
Imperial Wharf	d																	17 28					
Clapham Junction 10	d	17 12					17 14	17 15		17 21	17 23		17 27	17 30				17 33			17 38		17 41
Latchmere	d																						
Wandsworth Common	d						17 17			17 24				17 33				17 36					17 44
Balham 4 ⊖	d						17 19			17 26				17 35				17 39					17 46
Streatham Hill	d						17 22							17 38									
West Norwood 4	d						17 27							17 42					17 49				
Gipsy Hill	d						17 30							17 45	17a46				17 52				
Crystal Palace 4	d						17 33							17a47					17 54				
Birkbeck	d																		17 58				
Beckenham Junction 4	a																		18 04				
Streatham Common 4	d									17 30		17 42						17 46					17 50
Norbury	d									17 33		17 45						17 48					17 53
Thornton Heath	d									17 36		17 48						17 51					17 56
Selhurst 4	d									17a40		17 50						17 55					17 59
Norwood Junction 2	a					17 30	17 37													17 41		17 43	
	d					17 30	17 38													17 43		17 44	
West Croydon 4	a						17 43					17 57								17 47			
East Croydon	a	17 22	17 26			17 34		17 27			17 32		17 36			17 35	17 47	17 59			17 48	17 49	18 03

Table 177

Mondays to Fridays
until 18 May

Luton, Milton Keynes Central and London East and West Croydon via Tulse Hill - Crystal Palace - Norbury

Local Services

Network Diagram - see first Page of Table 177

		SN ◇1	SN	SN	SN 1	FC 1	FC	SN	SN	SN	SN	SN	SN	SN ◇1	SN 1	SN	SN	SN 1	SN	SN 1	SN	SN	SN	SN
London Bridge 4 ⊖	d		17 36	17 41	17 42			17 48	17 49							17 53		17 57	17 58	17 59		18 02		18 06
South Bermondsey	d			17 45				17 52											18 02					
Queens Rd Peckham	d			17 47				17 54											18 04					
Peckham Rye 4	d			17 50				17 57											18 07					
East Dulwich	d							18 00											18 10					
North Dulwich	d							18 02											18 12					
Luton 10	d					16 50	16 46																	
Luton Airport Parkway 7	d					16 52	16 48																	
St Pancras International 15 ⊖	d					17 28	17 32																	
City Thameslink 3	d					17 37	17 41																	
London Blackfriars 3 ⊖	d					17 40	17 44																	
Elephant & Castle ⊖	d						17 48																	
Loughborough Jn.	d						17 52																	
Herne Hill 4	d						17 57																	
Tulse Hill 3	d						18 02	18 05											18 17					
Streatham 4	d						18a05	18 09																
London Victoria 15 ⊖	d	17 35								17 37	17 39	17 41	17 45	17 47	17 49		17 52						18 03	
Battersea Park 4	d			18a02						17 41		17a45	17 49				17 56						18 07	
Milton Keynes Central	d																							
Watford Junction	d																							
Harrow & Wealdstone ⊖	d																							
Wembley Central ⊖	d																							
Shepherd's Bush ⊖	d																				17 45			
Kensington (Olympia) ⊖	d																				17 47			
West Brompton ⊖	d																				17 50			
Imperial Wharf	d																				17 53			
Clapham Junction 10	d	17 42								17 45	17 45		17 53	17 53	17 56		18 00				18 02		18 11	
Latchmere	d																							
Wandsworth Common	d									17 48			17 56				18 03				18 05		18 14	
Balham 4 ⊖	d									17 50			17 58				18 05				18 08		18 16	
Streatham Hill	d									17 53							18 08							
West Norwood 4	d									17 57							18 14		18 20					
Gipsy Hill	d									18 00						18a15	18 17		18 23					
Crystal Palace 4	d									18 02							18a19		18 26					
Birkbeck	d																		18 30					
Beckenham Junction 4	a																		18 35					
Streatham Common 4	d							18 12					18 02								18 15		18 20	
Norbury	d							18 14					18 05								18 18		18 23	
Thornton Heath	d							18 17					18 08								18 21		18 26	
Selhurst 4	d							18 21					18a12								18 26		18 29	
Norwood Junction 2	a		17 59						18 01	18 08										18 11		18 15		18 29
	d		18 00						18 02	18 09										18 11		18 16		18 32
West Croydon 4	a		18 08					18 27		18 14												18 20	18 34	18 39
East Croydon	a	17 51			17 54	18 07			18 05		17 55			18 02	18 05			18 11		18 15	18 32			

Table 177

Mondays to Fridays
until 18 May

Luton, Milton Keynes Central and London East and West Croydon via Tulse Hill - Crystal Palace - Norbury

Local Services

Network Diagram - see first Page of Table 177

		SN ◇1 ✕	FC 1	FC	FC		SN	SN 1	SN	SN	SN	SN	SN	SN ◇1	SN	SN	SN 1	SN 1	FC 1	SN	SN		SN 1	SN 1	SN
London Bridge 4 ⊖	d						18 11	18 12	18 18						18 18	18 21	18 23				18 28		18 30		18 32
South Bermondsey	d						18 15								18 22						18 32				
Queens Rd Peckham	d						18 18								18 24						18 34				
Peckham Rye 4	d						18 20								18 27						18 37				
East Dulwich	d														18 30						18 40				
North Dulwich	d														18 32						18 42				
Luton 10	d			17 10	17 22														17 30						
Luton Airport Parkway 7	d			17 12	17 24														17 33						
St Pancras International 15 ⊖	d		17 40	17 44	18 04														18 08						
City Thameslink 3	d		17 49	17 53	18 13														18 17						
London Blackfriars 3 ⊖	d		17 51	17 56	18 16														18 20						
Elephant & Castle ⊖	d		17 55	18 00	18 20																				
Loughborough Jn.	d				18 24																				
Herne Hill 4	d			18a06	18 28																				
Tulse Hill 3	d				18 32										18 35						18 48				
Streatham 4	d				18a35										18 39										
London Victoria 15 ⊖	d	18 06								18 07	18 09	18 11	18 13	18 17				18 19		18 22					
Battersea Park 4	d						18a32			18 11		18a15	18 17							18 26					
Milton Keynes Central	d																							17 13	
Watford Junction	d																							17 51	
Harrow & Wealdstone ⊖	d																							17 59	
Wembley Central ⊖	d																							18 05	
Shepherd's Bush ⊖	d																							18 19	
Kensington (Olympia) ⊖	d																							18 22	
West Brompton ⊖	d																							18 25	
Imperial Wharf	d																							18 27	
Clapham Junction 10	d	18 12								18 15	18 15		18 21	18 23				18 26		18 30				18 34	
Latchmere	d																								
Wandsworth Common	d									18 18			18 24							18 33				18 37	
Balham 4 ⊖	d									18 20			18 26							18 35				18 40	
Streatham Hill	d									18 23										18 38					
West Norwood 4	d									18 27										18 42	18 51				
Gipsy Hill	d									18 30						18a45				18 45	18 54				
Crystal Palace 4	d									18 33										18a47	18 57				
Birkbeck	d																				19 01				
Beckenham Junction 4	a																				19 06				
Streatham Common 4	d												18 30		18 42									18 46	
Norbury	d												18 33		18 44									18 49	
Thornton Heath	d												18 36		18 47									18 52	
Selhurst 4	d												18a40		18 51									18 56	
Norwood Junction 2	a								18 30	18 37													18 41		18 45
	d								18 31	18 39													18 42		18 46
West Croydon 4	a									18 44					18 57										18 50
East Croydon	a	18 22	18 24					18 24	18 35		18 27			18 33			18 36	18 37	18 41				18 45	19 02	

Table 177

Mondays to Fridays
until 18 May

Luton, Milton Keynes Central and London East and West Croydon via Tulse Hill - Crystal Palace - Norbury

Local Services

Network Diagram - see first Page of Table 177

		SN ◇1	SN	SN	SN 1	SN	SN	SN	SN	FC 1	SN	SN	SN ◇1 ✕		SN	SN	SN 1	FC 1	FC	SN	SN 1	SN	SN	SN ✕	FC 1
London Bridge 4 ⊖	d			18 36		18 41	18 49								18 48	18 51					18 59		18 57		
South Bermondsey	d					18 45									18 52								19 01		
Queens Rd Peckham	d					18 48									18 54								19 03		
Peckham Rye 4	d					18 50									18 57								19 06		
East Dulwich	d														19 00								19 09		
North Dulwich	d														19 02								19 11		
Luton 10	d									17 46								18 00							18 18
Luton Airport Parkway 7	d									17 48								18 02							18 20
St Pancras International 15 ⊖	d									18 20								18 34	18 38						18 54
City Thameslink 3	d									18 29								18 43	18 47						19 03
London Blackfriars 3 ⊖	d									18 32								18 46	18 50						19 05
Elephant & Castle ⊖	d									18 36									18 54						
Loughborough Jn.	d																		18 58						
Herne Hill 4	d																		19 02						
Tulse Hill 3	d														19 05				19 09				19 14		
Streatham 4	d														19 09				19a13						
London Victoria 15 ⊖	d	18 32	18 32		18 36			18 36	18 39		18 41	18 45	18 47				18 51			18 52		18 59		19 06	
Battersea Park 4	d		18 36			19a02		18 40			18a45	18 49								18 56		19 04			
Milton Keynes Central	d																								
Watford Junction	d																								
Harrow & Wealdstone ⊖	d																								
Wembley Central ⊖	d																								
Shepherd's Bush ⊖	d																								
Kensington (Olympia) ⊖	d																								
West Brompton ⊖	d																								
Imperial Wharf	d																								
Clapham Junction 10	d	18 38	18 40		18 42			18 44	18 45			18 53	18 53				18 57			19 00		19 08		19 12	
Latchmere	d																								
Wandsworth Common	d		18 43					18 47				18 56								19 03		19 11			
Balham 4 ⊖	d		18 45					18 49				18 58								19 05		19 14			
Streatham Hill	d							18 52												19 08					
West Norwood 4	d							18 56												19 12			19 17		
Gipsy Hill	d							18 59								19a15				19 15			19 20		
Crystal Palace 4	d							19 01												19a19			19 23		
Birkbeck	d																								
Beckenham Junction 4	a																								
Streatham Common 4	d		18 50									19 02			19 12							19 18			
Norbury	d		18 52									19 05			19 15							19 20			
Thornton Heath	d		18 55									19 08			19 18							19 23			
Selhurst 4	d		19 00									19 10			19 21							19 27			
Norwood Junction 2	a			18 59			19 01	19 06													19 13		19 27		
	d			19 02			19 02	19 09													19 14		19 28		
West Croydon 4	a		19 04	19 09				19 14							19 27							19 32	19 35		
East Croydon	a	18 48			18 52		19 05		18 57	19 00		19 13	19 03				19 07	19 10			19 17			19 22	19 24

until 18 May

Luton, Milton Keynes Central and London East and West Croydon via Tulse Hill - Crystal Palace - Norbury

Local Services

Network Diagram - see first Page of Table 177

Station		SN	SN	SN	FC		SN 1	SN	SN	SN ◇1	FC 1	SN	SN	SN	SN	SN	SN	SN ◇1	SN 1	SN	SN		FC 1	SN	SN 1
London Bridge 4 ⊖	d	19 06		19 08									19 11	19 18	19 22	19 31			19 33	19 28				19 36	19 52
South Bermondsey	d			19 12									19 15	19 22						19 32					
Queens Rd Peckham	d			19 14									19 18	19 24						19 34					
Peckham Rye 4	d			19 17									19 20	19 27						19 37					
East Dulwich	d			19 20										19 30						19 40					
North Dulwich	d			19 22										19 32						19 42					
Luton 10	d				18 22						18 34												18 48		
Luton Airport Parkway 7	d				18 24						18 36												18 50		
St Pancras International 15 ⊖	d				19 04						19 09												19 24		
City Thameslink 3	d				19 13						19 18												19 33		
London Blackfriars 3 ⊖	d				19 16						19 20												19 35		
Elephant & Castle ⊖	d				19 19																				
Loughborough Jn.	d				19 23																				
Herne Hill 4	d				19 27																				
Tulse Hill 3	d			19 27	19 31									19 35						19 46					
Streatham 4	d				19a35									19 39											
London Victoria 15 ⊖	d		19 06				19 10	19 11	19 15	19 17		19 22					19 30	19 32			19 36				
Battersea Park 4	d		19 10					19a15	19 19			19 26	19a32				19 34								
Milton Keynes Central	d																								
Watford Junction	d																								
Harrow & Wealdstone ⊖	d																								
Wembley Central ⊖	d																								
Shepherd's Bush ⊖	d																								
Kensington (Olympia) ⊖	d																								
West Brompton ⊖	d																								
Imperial Wharf	d																								
Clapham Junction 10	d		19 14				19 16		19 23	19 23		19 30					19 38	19 38			19 42				
Latchmere	d																								
Wandsworth Common	d		19 17						19 26			19 33					19 41								
Balham 4 ⊖	d		19 20						19 28			19 35					19 44								
Streatham Hill	d		19 23									19 38													
West Norwood 4	d		19 27	19 30								19 42								19 49					
Gipsy Hill	d		19 30	19 33								19 45			19a45					19 52					
Crystal Palace 4	d		19 32	19 35								19a47								19 54					
Birkbeck	d			19 39																					
Beckenham Junction 4	a			19 43																					
Streatham Common 4	d								19 32					19 42			19 48								
Norbury	d								19 35					19 45			19 51								
Thornton Heath	d								19 38					19 48			19 54								
Selhurst 4	d								19 41					19 51			19 57								
Norwood Junction 2	a	19 29	19 37													19 44			19 46	19 59				19 59	20 03
	d	19 30	19 39													19 44			19 47	20 02				20 00	20 03
West Croydon 4	a		19 44											19 56		19 49	20 02			20 07					
East Croydon	a	19 33					19 27		19 44	19 33	19 39							19 48	19 50		19 52		19 54	20 03	20 06

Table 177

Mondays to Fridays

until 18 May

Luton, Milton Keynes Central and London East and West Croydon via Tulse Hill - Crystal Palace - Norbury

Local Services

Network Diagram - see first Page of Table 177

Station		SN	SN	FC	SN 1	SN	SN	SN ◇1	FC 1	SN	SN	SN	SN		SN	SN	SN ◇1	FC 1	FC	SN	SN	SN 1	SN	SN	SN ◇1
London Bridge 4 ⊖	d		19 38								19 41	19 48	19 54			20 03				20 06					
South Bermondsey	d		19 42								19 45	19 52				20 07									
Queens Rd Peckham	d		19 44								19 48	19 54				20 09									
Peckham Rye 4	d		19 47								19 50	19 57				20 12									
East Dulwich	d		19 50									20 00				20 15									
North Dulwich	d		19 52									20 02				20 17									
Luton 10	d			18 54					19 04									19 18	19 24						
Luton Airport Parkway 7	d			18 57					19 06									19 20	19 27						
St Pancras International 15 ⊖	d			19 34					19 39									19 54	20 04						
City Thameslink 3	d			19 43					19 48									20 03	20 13						
London Blackfriars 3 ⊖	d			19 46					19 50									20 05	20 16						
Elephant & Castle ⊖	d			19 49															20 19						
Loughborough Jn.	d			19 53															20 23						
Herne Hill 4	d			19 57															20 27						
Tulse Hill 3	d		19 57	20 01								20 05				20 21			20 31						
Streatham 4	d			20a05								20 09							20a35						
London Victoria 15 ⊖	d	19 36			19 40	19 41	19 45	19 47		19 52					20 00		20 06				20 06	20 10	20 11	20 15	20 17
Battersea Park 4	d	19 40				19a45	19 49			19 56	20a02				20 04						20 10		20a15	20 19	
Milton Keynes Central	d																								
Watford Junction	d																								
Harrow & Wealdstone ⊖	d																								
Wembley Central ⊖	d																								
Shepherd's Bush ⊖	d																								
Kensington (Olympia) ⊖	d																								
West Brompton ⊖	d																								
Imperial Wharf	d																								
Clapham Junction 10	d	19 44			19 46		19 53	19 53		20 00					20 08		20 12				20 14	20 16		20 23	20 23
Latchmere	d																								
Wandsworth Common	d	19 47					19 56			20 03					20 11						20 17			20 26	
Balham 4 ⊖	d	19 50					19 59			20 05					20 14						20 20			20 28	
Streatham Hill	d	19 53								20 08											20 23				
West Norwood 4	d	19 57	20 00							20 12						20 24					20 27				
Gipsy Hill	d	20 00	20 03							20 15			20a16			20 27					20 30				
Crystal Palace 4	d	20 02	20 05							20a17						20 29					20 33				
Birkbeck	d		20 09													20 33									
Beckenham Junction 4	a		20 13													20 37									
Streatham Common 4	d						20 03					20 12			20 18									20 32	
Norbury	d						20 05					20 15			20 20									20 35	
Thornton Heath	d						20 08					20 18			20 23									20 38	
Selhurst 4	d						20 11					20 21			20 27									20 41	
Norwood Junction 2	a	20 07																		20 29	20 37				
	d	20 09																		20 30	20 39				
West Croydon 4	a	20 13										20 26			20 32						20 43				
East Croydon	a				19 57		20 14	20 03	20 09								20 22	20 24		20 33		20 27		20 44	20 33

Luton, Milton Keynes Central and London East and West Croydon via Tulse Hill - Crystal Palace - Norbury

Local Services

Network Diagram - see first Page of Table 177

		SN	SN	SN	SN	SN ■	SN	SN ◇■	SN	SN ■	SN ◇■	FC ■	FC	SN	SN	SN ■	SN	SN	SN ◇■	SN	SN	SN	SN
London Bridge ■ ⊖	d		20 11	20 18	20 22	20 28			20 33	20 34				20 36							20 41	20 48	20 52
South Bermondsey	d		20 15	20 22					20 37												20 45	20 52	
Queens Rd Peckham	d		20 18	20 24					20 39												20 48	20 54	
Peckham Rye ■	d		20 20	20 27					20 42												20 50	20 57	
East Dulwich	d			20 30					20 45													21 00	
North Dulwich	d			20 32					20 47													21 02	
Luton ■	d											19 50	19 46										
Luton Airport Parkway ■	d											19 52	19 48										
St Pancras International ■ ⊖	d											20 24	20 34										
City Thameslink ■	d											20 33	20 43										
London Blackfriars ■ ⊖	d											20 35	20 46										
Elephant & Castle ⊖	d												20 49										
Loughborough Jn.	d												20 53										
Herne Hill ■	d												20 57										
Tulse Hill ■	d			20 35					20 51				21 01									21 05	
Streatham ■	d			20 39									21a05									21 09	
London Victoria ■ ⊖	d	20 22					20 30	20 32			20 36				20 36	20 40	20 41	20 45	20 47	20 52			
Battersea Park ■	d	20 26	20a32				20 34								20 40		20a45	20 49		20 56	21a02		
Milton Keynes Central	d																						
Watford Junction	d																						
Harrow & Wealdstone ⊖	d																						
Wembley Central ⊖	d																						
Shepherd's Bush ⊖	d																						
Kensington (Olympia) ⊖	d																						
West Brompton ⊖	d																						
Imperial Wharf	d																						
Clapham Junction ■	d	20 30					20 38	20 38			20 42				20 44	20 46		20 53	20 53	21 00			
Latchmere	d																						
Wandsworth Common	d	20 33					20 41								20 47			20 56		21 03			
Balham ■ ⊖	d	20 35					20 44								20 50			20 58		21 05			
Streatham Hill	d	20 38													20 53					21 08			
West Norwood ■	d	20 42							20 54						20 57					21 12			
Gipsy Hill	d	20 45			20a45				20 57						21 00					21 15			21a15
Crystal Palace ■	d	20a47							20 59						21 03					21a17			
Birkbeck	d								21 03														
Beckenham Junction ■	a								21 07														
Streatham Common ■	d			20 42			20 48											21 02				21 12	
Norbury	d			20 45			20 50											21 05				21 15	
Thornton Heath	d			20 48			20 53											21 08				21 18	
Selhurst ■	d			20 51			20 57											21 11				21 21	
Norwood Junction ■	a									20 45				20 59	21 07								
	d									20 45				21 00	21 09								
West Croydon ■	a			20 56			21 02								21 13							21 26	
East Croydon	a					20 40		20 48		20 49	20 52	20 54		21 03		20 57		21 14	21 03				

Table 177 Mondays to Fridays until 18 May

Luton, Milton Keynes Central and London East and West Croydon via Tulse Hill - Crystal Palace - Norbury

Local Services

Network Diagram - see first Page of Table 177

		SN ■	SN	SN ■	SN	SN ◇■	FC ■	FC	SN	SN	SN ■	SN	SN	SN ◇■	SN	SN	SN	SN	SN ■	SN	SN	SN ◇■	FC ■	FC
London Bridge ■ ⊖	d	20 58			21 03				21 06							21 11	21 18	21 22	21 26		21 33			
South Bermondsey	d				21 07											21 15	21 22				21 37			
Queens Rd Peckham	d				21 09											21 18	21 24				21 39			
Peckham Rye ■	d				21 12											21 20	21 27				21 42			
East Dulwich	d				21 15												21 30				21 45			
North Dulwich	d				21 17												21 32				21 47			
Luton ■	d						20 16	20 20															20 46	20 50
Luton Airport Parkway ■	d						20 18	20 22															20 48	20 52
St Pancras International ■ ⊖	d						20 54	21 06															21 24	21 36
City Thameslink ■	d						21 03	21 13															21 33	21 43
London Blackfriars ■ ⊖	d						21 05	21 16															21 35	21 46
Elephant & Castle ⊖	d							21 19																21 49
Loughborough Jn.	d							21 23																21 53
Herne Hill ■	d							21 27																21 57
Tulse Hill ■	d				21 21			21 31									21 35				21 51			22 01
Streatham ■	d							21a35									21 39							22a05
London Victoria ■ ⊖	d		21 00	21 02		21 06				21 06	21 10	21 11	21 15	21 17	21 23					21 30		21 36		
Battersea Park ■	d		21 04							21 10		21a15	21 19		21 27	21a32				21 34				
Milton Keynes Central	d																							
Watford Junction	d																							
Harrow & Wealdstone ⊖	d																							
Wembley Central ⊖	d																							
Shepherd's Bush ⊖	d																							
Kensington (Olympia) ⊖	d																							
West Brompton ⊖	d																							
Imperial Wharf	d																							
Clapham Junction ■	d		21 08	21 08		21 12				21 14	21 16		21 23	21 23	21 31					21 38		21 42		
Latchmere	d																							
Wandsworth Common	d		21 11							21 17			21 26		21 34					21 41				
Balham ■ ⊖	d		21 14							21 20			21 29		21 36					21 44				
Streatham Hill	d									21 23					21 39									
West Norwood ■	d				21 24					21 27					21 43						21 54			
Gipsy Hill	d				21 27					21 30					21 46			21a45			21 57			
Crystal Palace ■	d				21 29					21 33					21a48						21 59			
Birkbeck	d				21 33																22 03			
Beckenham Junction ■	a				21 37																22 07			
Streatham Common ■	d		21 18										21 33				21 42			21 48				
Norbury	d		21 20										21 35				21 45			21 50				
Thornton Heath	d		21 23										21 38				21 48			21 53				
Selhurst ■	d		21 27										21 41				21 51			21 57				
Norwood Junction ■	a								21 29	21 37									21 37					
	d								21 30	21 39									21 38					
West Croydon ■	a		21 32							21 43							21 56			22 02				
East Croydon	a	21 10		21 18		21 22	21 24		21 33		21 27		21 44	21 33					21 41			21 52	21 54	

Table 177

Mondays to Fridays
until 18 May

Luton, Milton Keynes Central and London East and West Croydon via Tulse Hill - Crystal Palace - Norbury

Local Services

Network Diagram - see first Page of Table 177

		SN	SN	SN ■	SN		SN	SN ◇■	SN	SN	SN	SN	SN	SN ◇■	SN	SN ◇■	FC ■	FC	SN	SN	SN ■		SN	SN	SN
London Bridge ⊖	d	21 36								21 41	21 48	21 52			22 03				22 08						
South Bermondsey	d									21 45	21 52				22 07										
Queens Rd Peckham	d									21 48	21 54				22 09										
Peckham Rye	d									21 50	21 57				22 12										
East Dulwich	d										22 00				22 15										
North Dulwich	d										22 02				22 17										
Luton	d																21 16	21 20							
Luton Airport Parkway	d																21 18	21 22							
St Pancras International ⊖	d																21 54	22 06							
City Thameslink	d																22 03	22 13							
London Blackfriars ⊖	d																22 05	22 16							
Elephant & Castle ⊖	d																	22 19							
Loughborough Jn.	d																	22 23							
Herne Hill	d																	22 27							
Tulse Hill	d										22 05				22 21			22 31							
Streatham	d										22 09							22a35							
London Victoria ⊖	d		21 36	21 40	21 41		21 45	21 47	21 52				22 00	22 02		22 06				22 06	22 10		22 11	22 15	22 22
Battersea Park	d		21 40		21a45		21 49		21 56	22a02			22 04							22 10			22a15	22 19	22 26
Milton Keynes Central	d																								
Watford Junction	d																								
Harrow & Wealdstone ⊖	d																								
Wembley Central ⊖	d																								
Shepherd's Bush ⊖	d																								
Kensington (Olympia) ⊖	d																								
West Brompton ⊖	d																								
Imperial Wharf	d																								
Clapham Junction	d		21 44	21 46			21 53	21 53	22 00				22 08	22 08		22 12				22 14	22 16			22 23	22 30
Latchmere	d																								
Wandsworth Common	d		21 47				21 56		22 03				22 11							22 17				22 26	22 33
Balham ⊖	d		21 50				21 58		22 05				22 14							22 20				22 28	22 35
Streatham Hill	d		21 53						22 08											22 23					22 38
West Norwood	d		21 57						22 12						22 24					22 27					22 42
Gipsy Hill	d		22 00						22 15			22a15			22 27					22 30					22 45
Crystal Palace	d		22 03						22a17						22 29					22 33					22a47
Birkbeck	d														22 35										
Beckenham Junction	a														22 38										
Streatham Common	d						22 02				22 12		22 18											22 32	
Norbury	d						22 05				22 15		22 20											22 35	
Thornton Heath	d						22 08				22 18		22 23											22 38	
Selhurst	d						22 11				22 21		22 27											22 41	
Norwood Junction	a	21 59	22 07																22 31	22 37					
	d	22 00	22 09																22 32	22 39					
West Croydon	a		22 13								22 26		22 32							22 43					
East Croydon	a	22 03		21 57			22 14	22 03						22 18		22 22	22 24		22 35		22 26			22 44	

Table 177

Mondays to Fridays
until 18 May

Luton, Milton Keynes Central and London East and West Croydon via Tulse Hill - Crystal Palace - Norbury

Local Services

Network Diagram - see first Page of Table 177

		SN	SN	SN	SN	SN	SN ■	SN	SN	SN	SN	FC ■	SN		SN	SN ■	SN	SN	SN ◇■	SN	SN	SN	SN	FC	SN ◇■
London Bridge ⊖	d	22 11	22 18	22 23	22 26			22 33		22 38	22 41	22 42	22 56							22 48	22 52			23 01	
South Bermondsey	d	22 15	22 22					22 37			22 45									22 52					
Queens Rd Peckham	d	22 18	22 24					22 39			22 48									22 54					
Peckham Rye	d	22 20	22 27					22 42			22 50									22 57					
East Dulwich	d		22 30					22 45												23 00					
North Dulwich	d		22 32					22 47												23 02					
Luton	d																								
Luton Airport Parkway	d																								
St Pancras International ⊖	d																								
City Thameslink	d																								
London Blackfriars ⊖	d																								
Elephant & Castle ⊖	d																								
Loughborough Jn.	d																								
Herne Hill	d																								
Tulse Hill	d		22 35					22 51												23 05				23 11	
Streatham	d		22 39																	23 09				23a15	
London Victoria ⊖	d					22 30	22 32		22 36						22 36	22 40	22 41	22 45	22 47			22 52	23 00		23 02
Battersea Park	d	22a32				22 34					23a02				22 40		22a45	22 49				22 56	23 04		
Milton Keynes Central	d																								
Watford Junction	d																								
Harrow & Wealdstone ⊖	d																								
Wembley Central ⊖	d																								
Shepherd's Bush ⊖	d																								
Kensington (Olympia) ⊖	d																								
West Brompton ⊖	d																								
Imperial Wharf	d																								
Clapham Junction	d					22 38	22 38		22 42						22 46	22 46		22 53	22 53			23 00	23 08		23 08
Latchmere	d																								
Wandsworth Common	d					22 41									22 49			22 56				23 03	23 11		
Balham ⊖	d					22 44									22 52			22 58				23 05	23 14		
Streatham Hill	d														22 55							23 08			
West Norwood	d							22 54							22 58							23 12			
Gipsy Hill	d			22a45				22 57							23 01						23a15	23 15			
Crystal Palace	d							22 59							23 04							23a17			
Birkbeck	d							23 03																	
Beckenham Junction	a							23 07																	
Streatham Common	d		22 42			22 48												23 02		23 12			23 18		
Norbury	d		22 45			22 50												23 05		23 15			23 20		
Thornton Heath	d		22 48			22 53												23 08		23 18			23 23		
Selhurst	d		22 51			22 57												23 11		23 21			23 27		
Norwood Junction	a				22 38					23 01			23 07		23 08										
	d				22 38					23 02			23 07		23 09										
West Croydon	a		22 56			23 02									23 13					23 26			23 32		
East Croydon	a				22 42		22 48		22 52	23 06		22 54	23 11			22 57		23 14	23 03						23 19

Table 177

Mondays to Fridays
until 18 May

Luton, Milton Keynes Central and London East and West Croydon via Tulse Hill - Crystal Palace - Norbury

Local Services

Network Diagram - see first Page of Table 177

Station		SN ◇1	SN	SN	SN		SN 1	SN	SN	SN ◇1	SN	SN	FC 1	SN	SN	FC	SN ◇1	SN	SN	FC 1	SN 1		SN	SN	SN A
London Bridge 4 ⊖	d		23 06	23 05								23 11	23 12	23 18	23 22	23 29		23 36	23 33	23 42					
South Bermondsey	d			23 09								23 15		23 22					23 37						
Queens Rd Peckham	d			23 11								23 18		23 24					23 39						
Peckham Rye 4	d			23 14								23 20		23 27					23 42						
East Dulwich	d			23 17										23 30					23 45						
North Dulwich	d			23 19										23 32					23 47						
Luton 10	d																								
Luton Airport Parkway 7	d																								
St Pancras International 15 ⊖	d																								
City Thameslink 3	d																								
London Blackfriars 3 ⊖	d																								
Elephant & Castle ⊖	d																								
Loughborough Jn.	d																								
Herne Hill 4	d																								
Tulse Hill 5	d			23 23										23 35		23 41			23 51						
Streatham 4	d													23 39		23a45									
London Victoria 15 ⊖	d	23 06			23 06		23 10	23 11	23 15	23 17	23 22						23 32						23 34	23 38	23 45
Battersea Park 4	d				23 10			23a15	23 19		23 26	23a32											23 38	23 42	23 49
Milton Keynes Central	d																				22 11				
Watford Junction	d																				22 53				
Harrow & Wealdstone ⊖	d																				23 00				
Wembley Central ⊖	d																								
Shepherd's Bush ⊖	d																				23 21				
Kensington (Olympia) ⊖	d																				23 23				
West Brompton ⊖	d																				23 26				
Imperial Wharf	d																				23 28				
Clapham Junction 10	d	23 12			23 14		23 16		23 23	23 23	23 30						23 38				23 40		23 42	23 46	23 53
Latchmere	d																								
Wandsworth Common	d				23 17				23 26		23 33												23 45	23 49	23 56
Balham 4 ⊖	d				23 20				23 28		23 35										23 44		23 47	23 51	23 58
Streatham Hill	d				23 23						23 38													23 54	
West Norwood 4	d			23 26	23 29						23 42								23 54					23 58	
Gipsy Hill	d			23 29	23 32						23 45				23a45				23 57					00 01	
Crystal Palace 4	d			23 31	23 35						23a47								23 59					00 03	
Birkbeck 🚊	d																								
Beckenham Junction 4 🚊	a																								
Streatham Common 4	d								23 32					23 42							23 48		23 51		00 02
Norbury	d								23 35					23 45							23 51		23 54		00 05
Thornton Heath	d								23 38					23 48							23 54		23 57		00 08
Selhurst 4	d								23 41					23 51							23 57		23 59		00 11
Norwood Junction 2	a		23 29	23 36	23 39													23 59	00 04					00 08	
	d		23 30		23 40													23 59						00 09	
West Croydon 4 🚊	a				23 44									23 56									00 03	00 14	
East Croydon 🚊	a	23 22	23 33				23 27		23 44	23 33			23 24				23 51	00 03		23 56	00 01				00 14

A 18 May

Table 177

Mondays to Fridays
until 18 May

Luton, Milton Keynes Central and London East and West Croydon via Tulse Hill - Crystal Palace - Norbury

Local Services

Network Diagram - see first Page of Table 177

Station		SN 1	SN 1	SN A	SN	SN	SN	SN B	FC
London Bridge 4 ⊖	d				23 48	23 52			23 59
South Bermondsey	d				23 52				
Queens Rd Peckham	d				23 54				
Peckham Rye 4	d				23 57				
East Dulwich	d				00 01				
North Dulwich	d				00 03				
Luton 10	d								
Luton Airport Parkway 7	d								
St Pancras International 15 ⊖	d								
City Thameslink 3	d								
London Blackfriars 3 ⊖	d								
Elephant & Castle ⊖	d								
Loughborough Jn.	d								
Herne Hill 4	d								
Tulse Hill 5	d				00 06				00 09
Streatham 4	d				00 10				00a13
London Victoria 15 ⊖	d	23 47	23 49	23 51			23 54	23 59	
Battersea Park 4	d			23 55			23 58	00 03	
Milton Keynes Central	d								
Watford Junction	d								
Harrow & Wealdstone ⊖	d								
Wembley Central ⊖	d								
Shepherd's Bush ⊖	d								
Kensington (Olympia) ⊖	d								
West Brompton ⊖	d								
Imperial Wharf	d								
Clapham Junction 10	d	23 53	23 56	23 59			00 02	00 07	
Latchmere	d								
Wandsworth Common	d			00 02			00 05	00 10	
Balham 4 ⊖	d			00 04			00 07	00 12	
Streatham Hill	d						00 10		
West Norwood 4	d						00 14		
Gipsy Hill	d					00a15	00 17		
Crystal Palace 4	d						00a19		
Birkbeck 🚊	d								
Beckenham Junction 4 🚊	a								
Streatham Common 4	d			00 08	00 13			00 16	
Norbury	d			00 11	00 15			00 19	
Thornton Heath	d			00 14	00 18			00 22	
Selhurst 4	d			00 17	00 21			00 25	
Norwood Junction 2	a								
	d								
West Croydon 4 🚊	a			00 21	00 28			00 30	
East Croydon 🚊	a	00 05	00 09						

A not 18 May

B 18 May

Table 177

Mondays to Fridays
from 21 May

Luton, Milton Keynes Central and London East and West Croydon via Tulse Hill - Crystal Palace - Norbury

Local Services

Network Diagram - see first Page of Table 177

	SN MX ■	SN MO	SN MX	SN MX	SN MO	SN MX	FC MX	SN MX	SN MX ■	SN MO	SN MX ■	SN MO	SN MO ■	FC MX ■ A	FC MO ■ B	SN MX	SN MX	SN MX	SN MO	SN MX ◇■	SN ■	SN MX	SN MX
London Bridge ⊖ d		23p21		23p36	23p39	23p33											23p48					00 06	00 03
South Bermondsey d		23p25				23p37											23p52						00 07
Queens Rd Peckham d		23p27				23p39											23p54						00 09
Peckham Rye d		23p30				23p42											23p57						00 12
East Dulwich d		23p33				23p45											00 01						00 15
North Dulwich d		23p35				23p47											00 03						00 17
Luton d							22p46							23p06	23p07								
Luton Airport Parkway d							22p49							23p09	23p09								
St Pancras International ⊖ d							23p36							23p54	23p54								
City Thameslink d																							
London Blackfriars ⊖ d							23p46							00 05	00 05								
Elephant & Castle ⊖ d							23p49																
Loughborough Jn. d																							
Herne Hill d							23p57																
Tulse Hill d		23p39				23p51	00 01										00 06						00 21
Streatham d		23p42					00a05										00 10						
London Victoria ⊖ d			23p34					23p38	23p47	23p47	23p49	23p50				23p51		23p54	23p54	00 05	00 14		
Battersea Park d			23p38					23p42								23p55		23p58	23p58				
Milton Keynes Central d	22p11																						
Watford Junction d	22p53																						
Harrow & Wealdstone ⊖ d	23p00												23p17										
Wembley Central ⊖ d													23p23										
Shepherd's Bush ⊖ d	23p21												23p45										
Kensington (Olympia) ⊖ d	23p23												23p48										
West Brompton ⊖ d	23p26												23p50										
Imperial Wharf d	23p28												23p53										
Clapham Junction d	23p40		23p42					23p46	23p53	23p53	23p56	23p56	00 05			23p59		00 02	00 02	00 11	00 20		
Latchmere d																							
Wandsworth Common d			23p45					23p49				23p59				00 02		00 05	00 05				
Balham ⊖ d	23p44		23p47					23p51				00 02				00 04		00 07	00 07				
Streatham Hill d								23p54										00 10	00 11				
West Norwood d						23p54		23p58										00 14	00 14				00 24
Gipsy Hill d						23p57		00 01										00 17	00 17				00 27
Crystal Palace d						23p59		00 03										00a19	00 20				00 29
Birkbeck d																							
Beckenham Junction a																							
Streatham Common d	23p48	23p48	23p51									00 06				00 08	00 13						
Norbury d	23p51	23p51	23p54									00 08				00 11	00 15						
Thornton Heath d	23p54	23p54	23p57									00 11				00 14	00 18						
Selhurst d	23p57	23p57	23p59									00 14				00 17	00 21						
Norwood Junction a				23p59	00 02	00 04		00 08											00 25			00 29	00 34
Norwood Junction d				23p59	00 03			00 09														00 30	
West Croydon a			00 03					00 14								00 21	00 28						
East Croydon a	00 01	00 01		00 03	00 06				00 05	00 06	00 09	00 17	00 22	00 26	00 26					00 26	00 31	00 33	

A from 22 May until 22 June, from 26 June

B from 21 May until 25 June

Table 177

Mondays to Fridays
from 21 May

Luton, Milton Keynes Central and London East and West Croydon via Tulse Hill - Crystal Palace - Norbury

Local Services

Network Diagram - see first Page of Table 177

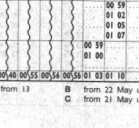

	SN	SN ◇■ A	SN ◇■ A	FC MX ■ B	FC MO ■ C	SN MX	SN	SN ◇■	FC MX ■ B	FC MO ■ C	SN A	SN ◇■ A	SN A	SN ■	FC ■	SN ■	FC ■	FC ■	SN ◇■	FC ■	FC ■	SN ◇■
London Bridge ⊖ d						00 36																
South Bermondsey d																						
Queens Rd Peckham d																						
Peckham Rye d																						
East Dulwich d																						
North Dulwich d																						
Luton d				23p36	23p37				00 06	00 07					01 06		02 06			03 06		
Luton Airport Parkway d				23p39	23p39				00 09	00 09					01 09		02 09			03 09		
St Pancras International ⊖ d				00 24	00 24				00 54	00 54					01 54		02 54	03 28		03 54	04 24	
City Thameslink d																						
London Blackfriars ⊖ d				00 35	00 35				01 05	01 05					02 05		03 05	03 39		04 05	04 35	
Elephant & Castle ⊖ d																						
Loughborough Jn. d																						
Herne Hill d																						
Tulse Hill d																						
Streatham d																						
London Victoria ⊖ d	00 16	00 25	00 40				00 42	01 00			01 12	01 30	01 42	02 00		03 00			04 00			05 02
Battersea Park d	00 20						00 46															
Milton Keynes Central d																						
Watford Junction d																						
Harrow & Wealdstone ⊖ d																						
Wembley Central ⊖ d																						
Shepherd's Bush ⊖ d																						
Kensington (Olympia) ⊖ d																						
West Brompton ⊖ d																						
Imperial Wharf d																						
Clapham Junction d	00 24	00 31	00 46				00 50	01 08			01 18	01 36	01 48	02 08		03 08			04 08			05 08
Latchmere d																						
Wandsworth Common d	00 27						00 53															
Balham ⊖ d	00 29						00 55				01 23		01 53									
Streatham Hill d																						
West Norwood d																						
Gipsy Hill d																						
Crystal Palace d																						
Birkbeck d																						
Beckenham Junction a																						
Streatham Common d	00 33						00 59				01 27		01 57									
Norbury d	00 36						01 02				01 29		01 59									
Thornton Heath d	00 39						01 05				01 32		02 02									
Selhurst d	00 41						01 07				01 35		02 05									05 17
Norwood Junction a						00 59																
Norwood Junction d						01 00																
West Croydon a																						
East Croydon a	00 44	00 40	00 55	00 56	00 56	01 03	01 10	01 23	01 31	01 31	01 38	01 45	02 08	02 23	02 31	03 23	03 31	04 03	04 23	04 31	05 01	05 20

A from 30 July until 7 September, not from 13 August until 29 August

B from 22 May until 22 June, from 26 June

C from 21 May until 25 June

Table 177

Mondays to Fridays
from 21 May

Luton, Milton Keynes Central and London East and West Croydon via Tulse Hill - Crystal Palace - Norbury

Local Services

Network Diagram - see first Page of Table 177

		FC ■	FC ■	SN ◇■	FC ■	FC	SN	SN	SN	SN	SN ◇■	FC ■	SN	SN	SN	SN		SN	SN	SN	SN ◇■	SN	SN	SN ◇■	FC ■
London Bridge ■ ⊖	d							05 36	06 00				06 06					06 11	06 18	06 19		06 30			
South Bermondsey	d								06 04									06 15	06 22			06 34			
Queens Rd Peckham	d								06 06									06 18	06 24			06 36			
Peckham Rye ■	d								06 09									06 20	06 27			06 39			
East Dulwich	d								06 12										06 30			06 42			
North Dulwich	d								06 14										06 32			06 44			
Luton ■	d	04 06	04 32		04 44							05 24													05 44
Luton Airport Parkway ■	d	04 09	04 35		04 47							05 27													05 46
St Pancras International ■ ⊖	d	04 54	05 12		05 32	05 36						06 02													06 22
City Thameslink ■	d		05 21		05 41	05 44						06 11													06 31
London Blackfriars ■ ⊖	d	05 04	05 24		05 44	05 47						06 14													06 34
Elephant & Castle ⊖	d					05 50																			
Loughborough Jn.	d																								
Herne Hill ■	d					05 57													06 36			06 48			
Tulse Hill ■	d					06 02			06 18										06 39			06a51			
Streatham ■	d					06a05			06a21																
London Victoria ■ ⊖	d			05 32						06 00	06 02			06 07	06 13	06 19					06 21		06 30	06 32	
Battersea Park ■	d									06 04				06 11	06 17	06 23		06a32					06 34		
Milton Keynes Central	d																								
Watford Junction	d																								
Harrow & Wealdstone ⊖	d																								
Wembley Central ⊖	d																								
Shepherd's Bush ⊖	d																								
Kensington (Olympia) ⊖	d																								
West Brompton ⊖	d																								
Imperial Wharf	d																								
Clapham Junction ■	d			05 38						06 08	06 08			06 15	06 21	06 27					06 27		06 38	06 38	
Latchmere	d																								
Wandsworth Common	d									06 11				06 18	06 24	06 30							06 41		
Balham ■ ⊖	d									06 13				06 20	06 26	06 32							06 44		
Streatham Hill	d													06 23		06 35									
West Norwood ■	d													06 27		06 39				06a41					
Gipsy Hill	d													06 30		06 42									
Crystal Palace ■	d													06 32		06a44									
Birkbeck	d																								
Beckenham Junction ■	a																								
Streatham Common ■	d									06 17					06 30				06 42				06 48		
Norbury	d									06 20					06 33				06 45				06 50		
Thornton Heath	d									06 23					06 36				06 48				06 53		
Selhurst ■	d									06 26					06 39				06 51				06 56		
Norwood Junction ■	a							06 00					06 29	06 37											
	d						05 53	06 00					06 30	06 39											
West Croydon ■	a						05 57	06 05		06 31				06 44					06 56				07 02		
East Croydon	a	05 29	05 47	05 48	06 05						06 17	06 33	06 33		06 43						06 38			06 48	06 54

Table 177

Mondays to Fridays
from 21 May

Luton, Milton Keynes Central and London East and West Croydon via Tulse Hill - Crystal Palace - Norbury

Local Services

Network Diagram - see first Page of Table 177

		SN	SN	FC	SN	SN	SN	SN		SN ◇■	SN	SN	SN	SN	SN ■	FC ■	SN	SN ■	SN	FC ■	SN	SN	SN	FC ■ A
London Bridge ■ ⊖	d		06 33		06 36							06 41	06 48	06 51					06 54		06 58		07 03	
South Bermondsey	d		06 37									06 45	06 52								07 02		07 07	
Queens Rd Peckham	d		06 39									06 48	06 54								07 04		07 09	
Peckham Rye ■	d		06 42									06 50	06 57								07 07		07 12	
East Dulwich	d		06 45										07 00								07 10		07 15	
North Dulwich	d		06 47										07 02								07 12		07 17	
Luton ■	d			05 48												06 04				06 22				06 32
Luton Airport Parkway ■	d			05 50												06 06				06 24				
St Pancras International ■ ⊖	d			06 34												06 38				06 58				07 04
City Thameslink ■	d			06 43												06 47				07 07				07 13
London Blackfriars ■ ⊖	d			06 46												06 50				07 09				07 16
Elephant & Castle ⊖	d			06 49																				07 19
Loughborough Jn.	d			06 53																				07 23
Herne Hill ■	d			06 57																				07 27
Tulse Hill ■	d		06 50	07 02									07 07								07 16		07 20	07 31
Streatham ■	d			07a05									07 10								07a19			07a34
London Victoria ■ ⊖	d					06 36	06 41	06 44		06 47	06 49				06 51		07 00	07 02						
Battersea Park ■	d					06 40	06a45				06 53	07a02					07 04							
Milton Keynes Central	d																							
Watford Junction	d																							
Harrow & Wealdstone ⊖	d																							
Wembley Central ⊖	d																							
Shepherd's Bush ⊖	d																							
Kensington (Olympia) ⊖	d																							
West Brompton ⊖	d																							
Imperial Wharf	d																							
Clapham Junction ■	d					06 44		06 50		06 53	06 57				06 57		07 08	07 08						
Latchmere	d																							
Wandsworth Common	d					06 47		06 53			07 00						07 11							
Balham ■ ⊖	d					06 49		06 56			07 02						07 13							
Streatham Hill	d	06 42				06 53					07 05											07 12		
West Norwood ■	d	06 45	06 53			06 56					07 09											07 15	07 23	
Gipsy Hill	d	06 48	06 56			06 59					07 12			07a15								07 18	07 26	
Crystal Palace ■	d	06a51	06 59			07 02					07a14											07a21	07 29	
Birkbeck	d		07 03																				07 33	
Beckenham Junction ■	a		07 06																				07 36	
Streatham Common ■	d							07 00					07 13				07 18							
Norbury	d							07 02					07 16				07 21							
Thornton Heath	d							07 05					07 19				07 24							
Selhurst ■	d							07 09					07 21				07 27							
Norwood Junction ■	a				06 59	07 07													07 17					
	d				07 00	07 09													07 18					
West Croydon ■	a					07 13							07 26				07 32							
East Croydon	a				07 03			07 12		07 03					07 06	07 14		07 17	07 21	07 30				

A from 8 October

Luton, Milton Keynes Central and London East and West Croydon via Tulse Hill - Crystal Palace - Norbury

Local Services

Network Diagram - see first Page of Table 177

		FC ■ A	SN	SN	SN	SN ◇■	SN	SN	SN	SN	SN	SN ■	SN	SN	SN	SN ■		SN	SN ■	SN ■	FC ■	FC ■	FC	SN	SN
London Bridge ■ ⊖	d		07 06						07 11	07 16	07 21	07 27		07 29		07 30		07 33	07 33					07 36	07 41
South Bermondsey	d								07 15	07 20				07 33				07 37							07 45
Queens Rd Peckham	d								07 17	07 22				07 35				07 39							07 47
Peckham Rye ■	d								07 20	07 25				07 38				07 42							07 50
East Dulwich	d									07 28				07 41				07 45							
North Dulwich	d									07 30				07 43				07 47							
Luton ■	d	06 34																			06 46	06 54	06 43		
Luton Airport Parkway ■	d																				06 48		06 45		
St Pancras International ■ ⊖	d	07 04																			07 20	07 24	07 28		
City Thameslink ■	d	07 13																			07 29	07 33	07 37		
London Blackfriars ■ ⊖	d	07 16																			07 32	07 36	07 40		
Elephant & Castle ⊖	d	07 19																				07a39	07a43		
Loughborough Jn.	d	07 23																							
Herne Hill ■	d	07 27																							
Tulse Hill ■	d	07 31								07 34				07 47				07 50							
Streatham ■	d	07a34								07 37				07a51											
London Victoria ■ ⊖	d			07 06	07 11	07 17	07 17	07 20					07 23		07 30					07 36					
Battersea Park ■	d			07 10	07a15		07 21	07 24	07a32						07 34										08a02
Milton Keynes Central	d																								
Watford Junction	d																								
Harrow & Wealdstone ⊖	d																								
Wembley Central ⊖	d																								
Shepherd's Bush ⊖	d																								
Kensington (Olympia) ⊖	d																								
West Brompton ⊖	d																								
Imperial Wharf	d																								
Clapham Junction ■	d			07 14		07 23	07 25	07 28					07 30		07 38					07 42					
Latchmere	d																								
Wandsworth Common	d			07 17				07 31							07 41										
Balham ■ ⊖	d			07 20			07 29	07 33							07 44										
Streatham Hill	d			07 23			07 32																		
West Norwood ■	d			07 27			07 38											07 53							
Gipsy Hill	d			07 30			07 41				07a45							07 56							
Crystal Palace ■	d			07 32			07a43											07 59							
Birkbeck	d																	08 03							
Beckenham Junction ■	a																	08 06							
Streatham Common ■	d							07 37		07 40					07 48										
Norbury	d							07 40		07 43					07 50										
Thornton Heath	d							07 43		07 46					07 53										
Selhurst ■	d							07 46		07 51					07 56										
Norwood Junction ■	a		07 29	07 38								07 38				07 41									
	d		07 31	07 39								07 38				07 42								07 59	
West Croydon ■	a			07 44						07 56					08 02									08 00	
East Croydon	a		07 37			07 33		07 49				07 42	07 44			07 45			07 48	07 51	07 54			08 03	

A from 21 May until 5 October

Luton, Milton Keynes Central and London East and West Croydon via Tulse Hill - Crystal Palace - Norbury

Local Services

Network Diagram - see first Page of Table 177

		SN	SN ■	SN	SN	SN	SN	FC		SN ◇■	SN	SN ◇■	SN	SN ■	SN	SN ◇■	FC ■	SN	SN	SN	SN	SN	SN	SN ■	
London Bridge ■ ⊖	d	07 44	07 51				07 47						07 53	08 00					08 03	08 06	08 14	08 06		08 08	
South Bermondsey	d																		08 07	08 11					
Queens Rd Peckham	d																		08 09	08 13					
Peckham Rye ■	d						07 53												08 12	08 16					
East Dulwich	d						07 56												08 15	08 19					
North Dulwich	d						07 58												08 17	08 21					
Luton ■	d							06 50									07 14								
Luton Airport Parkway ■	d							06 52																	
St Pancras International ■ ⊖	d							07 32									07 44								
City Thameslink ■	d							07 41									07 53								
London Blackfriars ■ ⊖	d							07 44									07 56								
Elephant & Castle ⊖	d							07 47																	
Loughborough Jn.	d							07 51																	
Herne Hill ■	d							07 57																	
Tulse Hill ■	d						08 02	08 05									08 10		08 21	08 25					
Streatham ■	d						08 05	08a08												08a28					
London Victoria ■ ⊖	d			07 36	07 41	07 45				07 47	07 52	07 52			08 03	08 07							08 07		
Battersea Park ■	d			07 40	07a45										08 07								08 11		
Milton Keynes Central	d																								
Watford Junction	d																								
Harrow & Wealdstone ⊖	d																								
Wembley Central ⊖	d																								
Shepherd's Bush ⊖	d																								
Kensington (Olympia) ⊖	d																								
West Brompton ⊖	d																								
Imperial Wharf	d																								
Clapham Junction ■	d			07 44		07 51				07 53	07 58	07 58			08 11	08 13							08 16		
Latchmere	d																								
Wandsworth Common	d			07 47		07 54									08 14								08 19		
Balham ■ ⊖	d			07 50		07 57					08 03				08 16								08 21		
Streatham Hill	d			07 53							08 06							08 15					08 24		
West Norwood ■	d			07 58							08 09							08 19	08 24				08 28		
Gipsy Hill	d			08 01							08 12		08a15					08 22	08 27				08 31		
Crystal Palace ■	d			08 04							08a15							08a24	08 29				08 34		
Birkbeck	d																		08 33						
Beckenham Junction ■	a																		08 37						
Streatham Common ■	d					08 01	08 08								08 20										
Norbury	d					08 03	08 11								08 23										
Thornton Heath	d					08 06	08 14								08 26										
Selhurst ■	d					08 09	08 17								08 32										
Norwood Junction ■	a		08 01	08 08										08 16							08 27	08 29	08 38		
	d		08 02	08 09										08 16							08 27	08 30	08 39		
West Croydon ■	a			08 14			08 23								08 36								08 44		
East Croydon	a	08 00	08 05			08 12				08 02		08 09		08 20		08 22	08 26				08 30	08 33		08 23	

Table 177

Mondays to Fridays
from 21 May

Luton, Milton Keynes Central and London East and West Croydon via Tulse Hill - Crystal Palace - Norbury

Local Services

Network Diagram - see first Page of Table 177

		SN	SN	SN ◇1	FC 1	SN ◇1	SN	SN	SN	SN	FC	SN	SN 1	SN	SN	SN		SN 1	SN 1	SN	SN ◇1 H	SN	SN ◇1 H	FC 1	FC 1
London Bridge 4 ⊖	d								08 10	08 17		08 21	08 23	08 24		08 27		08 30				08 33			
South Bermondsey	d								08 14					08 28								08 37			
Queens Rd Peckham	d								08 16					08 30								08 39			
Peckham Rye 4	d								08 19	08 23				08 33								08 42			
East Dulwich	d									08 26				08 36								08 45			
North Dulwich	d									08 28				08 38								08 47			
Luton 10	d				07 22						07 30													07 50	07 57
Luton Airport Parkway 7	d				07 25						07 32														07 59
St Pancras International 15 ⊖	d				07 56						08 12													08 20	08 32
City Thameslink 3	d				08 05						08 21													08 29	08 41
London Blackfriars 3 ⊖	d				08 08						08 24													08 32	08 44
Elephant & Castle ⊖	d										08 27														08 47
Loughborough Jn.	d										08 31														08 51
Herne Hill 4	d										08 36														08 57
Tulse Hill 3	d									08 32	08 40			08 47								08 50			09 01
Streatham 4	d									08 36	08a44			08a50											09a05
London Victoria 15 ⊖	d	08 11	08 15	08 17		08 21		08 22							08 26					08 31	08 32		08 36		
Battersea Park 4	d	08a15	08 19					08 26	08a32											08 36					
Milton Keynes Central	d																		07 01						
Watford Junction	d																		07 38						
Harrow & Wealdstone ⊖	d																		07 45						
Wembley Central ⊖	d																		07 49						
Shepherd's Bush ⊖	d																		08 04						
Kensington (Olympia) ⊖	d																		08 07						
West Brompton ⊖	d																		08 10						
Imperial Wharf	d																		08 13						
Clapham Junction 10	d		08 23	08 23		08 27		08 30							08 33				08 36	08 40	08 38		08 43		
Latchmere	d																								
Wandsworth Common	d		08 26					08 33							08 36				08 39	08 43					
Balham 4 ⊖	d		08 28					08 35							08 38				08 42	08 46					
Streatham Hill	d						08 35	08 38																	
West Norwood 4	d						08 38	08 42														08 53			
Gipsy Hill	d						08 41	08 45				08a43										08 56			
Crystal Palace 4	d						08a44	08a47														08 59			
Birkbeck	d																					09 03			
Beckenham Junction 4	a																					09 06			
Streatham Common 4	d		08 32							08 39					08 42				08 46	08 51					
Norbury	d		08 35							08 41					08 45				08 48	08 54					
Thornton Heath	d		08 38							08 44					08 48				08 51	08 57					
Selhurst 4	d		08 41							08 47					08 51				08 54	09 00					
Norwood Junction 2	a																	08 43							
	d																	08 44							
West Croydon 4	a									08 53					08 55					09 05					
East Croydon	a		08 44	08 34	08 37	08 40							08 37			08 42		08 48	09 04		08 48		08 52	08 57	

Table 177

Mondays to Fridays
from 21 May

Luton, Milton Keynes Central and London East and West Croydon via Tulse Hill - Crystal Palace - Norbury

Local Services

Network Diagram - see first Page of Table 177

		SN 1	SN	SN	SN	SN	SN ◇1 H	SN		SN ◇1	SN	SN	SN	SN	SN	SN	SN	SN 1	SN 1	SN	SN	SN	SN	SN ◇1 H
London Bridge 4 ⊖	d	08 45	08 36									08 41	08 47	08 48	08 51	09 03		09 03	09 15	09 06	09 11	09 20		
South Bermondsey	d											08 45		08 52		09 07					09 15			
Queens Rd Peckham	d											08 48		08 54		09 09					09 18			
Peckham Rye 4	d											08 50		08 57		09 12					09 20			
East Dulwich	d													09 00		09 15								
North Dulwich	d													09 02		09 17								
Luton 10	d																							
Luton Airport Parkway 7	d																							
St Pancras International 15 ⊖	d																							
City Thameslink 3	d																							
London Blackfriars 3 ⊖	d																							
Elephant & Castle ⊖	d																							
Loughborough Jn.	d																							
Herne Hill 4	d																							
Tulse Hill 3	d													09 05		09 20								
Streatham 4	d													09 09										
London Victoria 15 ⊖	d			08 36	08 41	08 43	08 47	08 49		08 51	08 52						09 03						09 05	09 06
Battersea Park 4	d			08 40	08a45	08 47		08 53			08 56	09a02					09 07				09a32		09 10	
Milton Keynes Central	d																							
Watford Junction	d																							
Harrow & Wealdstone ⊖	d																							
Wembley Central ⊖	d																							
Shepherd's Bush ⊖	d																							
Kensington (Olympia) ⊖	d																							
West Brompton ⊖	d																							
Imperial Wharf	d																							
Clapham Junction 10	d			08 44		08 51	08 53	08 57			09 00						09 11						09 14	09 12
Latchmere	d																							
Wandsworth Common	d			08 47		08 54		09 00			09 03						09 14						09 17	
Balham 4 ⊖	d			08 50		08 56		09 02			09 05						09 16						09 20	
Streatham Hill	d			08 53				09 05															09 23	
West Norwood 4	d			08 57				09 09								09 23							09 27	
Gipsy Hill	d			09 00				09 12							09a14	09 26							09 30	
Crystal Palace 4	d			09 02				09a14								09 29							09 32	
Birkbeck	d															09 33								
Beckenham Junction 4	a															09 36								
Streatham Common 4	d					09 00					09 09			09 13			09 20							
Norbury	d					09 03					09 12			09 15			09 23							
Thornton Heath	d					09 06					09 15			09 18			09 26							
Selhurst 4	d					09 09					09 18			09 21			09 29							
Norwood Junction 2	a	08 55	08 59	09 07														09 16	09 25	09 30		09 32	09 37	
	d	08 56	09 00	09 09														09 16	09 26	09 30		09 33	09 39	
West Croydon 4	a			09 13							09 22			09 26			09 33						09 43	
East Croydon	a	08 59	09 06			09 12	09 03			09 07			09 02					09 20	09 29	09 33		09 36		09 22

Table 177

Mondays to Fridays

from 21 May

Luton, Milton Keynes Central and London East and West Croydon via Tulse Hill - Crystal Palace - Norbury

Local Services

Network Diagram - see first Page of Table 177

		FC ■	FC	SN	SN	SN ◇■ ⊼	FC ■	SN	SN	SN	SN ■	SN	SN ◇■ ⊼	SN ■	SN	SN		SN ■	SN	SN	SN	SN	SN ◇■	FC ■	FC
London Bridge ■ ⊖	d									09 18		09 22		09 32	09 33			09 45	09 36	09 41	09 50				
South Bermondsey	d									09 22					09 37					09 45					
Queens Rd Peckham	d									09 24					09 39					09 48					
Peckham Rye ■	d									09 27					09 42					09 50					
East Dulwich	d									09 30					09 45										
North Dulwich	d									09 32					09 47										
Luton ■	d	08 12					08 28																	08 48	08 54
Luton Airport Parkway ■	d	08 15					08 30																	08 50	08 56
St Pancras International ■ ⊖	d	08 48	08 56				09 04																	09 22	09 34
City Thameslink ■	d	08 57	09 05				09 13																	09 31	09 43
London Blackfriars ■ ⊖	d	09 00	09 08				09 16																	09 34	09 46
Elephant & Castle ⊖	d		09 12																						09 49
Loughborough Jn.	d		09 16																						09 53
Herne Hill ■	d		09 25																						09 57
Tulse Hill ■	d		09 31							09 35					09 50										10 01
Streatham ■	d		09a35							09 39															10a05
London Victoria ■ ⊖	d			09 11	09 13	09 17		09 19	09 22				09 32			09 33						09 35	09 36		
Battersea Park ■	d			09a15	09 17			09 23								09 37				10a02		09 40			
Milton Keynes Central	d										08 13														
Watford Junction	d										08 51														
Harrow & Wealdstone ⊖	d										08 58														
Wembley Central ⊖	d										09 05														
Shepherd's Bush ⊖	d										09 18														
Kensington (Olympia) ⊖	d										09 21														
West Brompton ⊖	d										09 23														
Imperial Wharf	d										09 26														
Clapham Junction ■	d				09 21	09 23		09 27	09 30		09 34		09 38			09 41						09 44	09 42		
Latchmere	d																								
Wandsworth Common	d				09 24			09 30	09 33		09 37					09 44						09 47			
Balham ■ ⊖	d				09 26			09 32	09 35		09 41					09 46						09 50			
Streatham Hill	d							09 35														09 53			
West Norwood ■	d							09 40							09 53							09 57			
Gipsy Hill	d							09 43				09a46			09 56							10 00			
Crystal Palace ■	d							09a46							09 59							10 02			
Birkbeck ⇌	d														10 03										
Beckenham Junction ■ ⇌	a														10 06										
Streatham Common ■	d				09 30				09 39	09 42	09 45					09 50									
Norbury	d				09 33				09 42	09 45	09 48					09 53									
Thornton Heath	d				09 36				09 45	09 48	09 51					09 56									
Selhurst ■	d				09 39				09 48	09 51	09 54					09 59									
Norwood Junction ■	a													09 45				09 55	09 59		10 02	10 07			
	d													09 45				09 56	10 00		10 03	10 09			
West Croydon ■ ⇌	a								09 52	09 56						10 03						10 13			
East Croydon ⇌	a	09 24			09 42	09 32	09 39				09 57		09 48	09 49				09 59	10 03		10 06		09 52	09 54	

Table 177

Mondays to Fridays

from 21 May

Luton, Milton Keynes Central and London East and West Croydon via Tulse Hill - Crystal Palace - Norbury

Local Services

Network Diagram - see first Page of Table 177

		SN	SN	SN ◇■ ⊼	SN	SN ◇■	FC ■	SN		SN	SN	SN	SN	SN ■	SN ◇■ ⊼	FC ■	FC	SN ■	SN	SN	SN	SN	SN	SN
London Bridge ■ ⊖	d									09 48	09 52	10 03		10 03				10 15	10 06	10 11	10 20			
South Bermondsey	d									09 52		10 07								10 15				
Queens Rd Peckham	d									09 54		10 09								10 18				
Peckham Rye ■	d									09 57		10 12								10 20				
East Dulwich	d									10 00		10 15												
North Dulwich	d									10 02		10 17												
Luton ■	d						09 04									09 18	09 14							
Luton Airport Parkway ■	d						09 06									09 20	09 16							
St Pancras International ■ ⊖	d						09 40									09 54	10 04							
City Thameslink ■	d						09 48									10 03	10 13							
London Blackfriars ■ ⊖	d						09 50									10 05	10 16							
Elephant & Castle ⊖	d																10 19							
Loughborough Jn.	d																10 23							
Herne Hill ■	d																10 27							
Tulse Hill ■	d									10 05		10 20					10 31							
Streatham ■	d									10 09							10a35							
London Victoria ■ ⊖	d	09 41	09 43	09 47	09 49	09 51		09 53					10 03		10 06							10 06	10 11	10 13
Battersea Park ■	d	09a45	09 47		09 53								10 07							10a32		10 10	10a15	10 17
Milton Keynes Central	d																							
Watford Junction	d																							
Harrow & Wealdstone ⊖	d																							
Wembley Central ⊖	d																							
Shepherd's Bush ⊖	d																							
Kensington (Olympia) ⊖	d																							
West Brompton ⊖	d																							
Imperial Wharf	d																							
Clapham Junction ■	d		09 51	09 53	09 57			10 00					10 11		10 12							10 14		10 21
Latchmere	d																							
Wandsworth Common	d		09 54		10 00			10 03					10 14									10 17		10 24
Balham ■ ⊖	d		09 56		10 02			10 05					10 16									10 20		10 26
Streatham Hill	d				10 05																	10 23		
West Norwood ■	d				10 10							10 23										10 27		
Gipsy Hill	d				10 13						10a15	10 26										10 30		
Crystal Palace ■	d				10a16							10 29										10 32		
Birkbeck ⇌	d											10 33												
Beckenham Junction ■ ⇌	a											10 36												
Streatham Common ■	d		10 00					10 09		10 12			10 20											10 30
Norbury	d		10 03					10 12		10 15			10 23											10 33
Thornton Heath	d		10 06					10 15		10 18			10 26											10 36
Selhurst ■	d		10 09					10 18		10 21			10 29											10 39
Norwood Junction ■	a													10 16				10 25	10 29		10 32	10 37		
	d													10 16				10 26	10 30		10 33	10 39		
West Croydon ■ ⇌	a							10 22		10 26			10 33									10 43		
East Croydon ⇌	a		10 12	10 02		10 07	10 09							10 20	10 22	10 24		10 29	10 33		10 36			10 42

Table 177

Mondays to Fridays
from 21 May

Luton, Milton Keynes Central and London East and West Croydon via Tulse Hill - Crystal Palace - Norbury

Local Services

Network Diagram - see first Page of Table 177

		SN ◇1 H	FC 1	SN	SN	SN	SN 1	SN	SN ◇1 H	SN	SN	SN 1	SN ◇1	FC 1	FC	SN 1		SN	SN	SN	SN	SN	SN	SN ◇1 H	SN
London Bridge 4 ⊖	d					10 18		10 22		10 33		10 33				10 45		10 36	10 41	10 50					
South Bermondsey	d					10 22				10 37									10 45						
Queens Rd Peckham	d					10 24				10 39									10 48						
Peckham Rye 4	d					10 27				10 42									10 50						
East Dulwich	d					10 30				10 45															
North Dulwich	d					10 32				10 47															
Luton 10	d		09 34											09 48	09 44										
Luton Airport Parkway 7	d		09 36											09 50	09 46										
St Pancras International 15 ⊖	d		10 09											10 24	10 34										
City Thameslink 3	d		10 18											10 33	10 43										
London Blackfriars 3 ⊖	d		10 20											10 35	10 46										
Elephant & Castle ⊖	d														10 49										
Loughborough Jn.	d														10 53										
Herne Hill 4	d														10 57										
Tulse Hill 3	d					10 35				10 50					11 01										
Streatham 4	d					10 39									11a05										
London Victoria 15 ⊖	d	10 17		10 19	10 23				10 32		10 33		10 36								10 36	10 41	10 43	10 47	10 49
Battersea Park 4	d			10 23							10 37								11a02		10 40	10a45	10 47		10 53
Milton Keynes Central	d						09 13																		
Watford Junction	d						09 51																		
Harrow & Wealdstone ⊖	d						09 58																		
Wembley Central ⊖	d						10 05																		
Shepherd's Bush ⊖	d						10 21																		
Kensington (Olympia) ⊖	d						10 24																		
West Brompton ⊖	d						10 27																		
Imperial Wharf	d						10 29																		
Clapham Junction 10	d	10 23		10 27	10 30		10 34		10 38		10 41		10 42								10 44		10 51	10 53	10 57
Latchmere	d																								
Wandsworth Common	d			10 30	10 33		10 37				10 44										10 47		10 54		11 00
Balham 4 ⊖	d			10 32	10 35		10 40				10 46										10 50		10 56		11 02
Streatham Hill	d			10 35																	10 53				11 05
West Norwood 4	d			10 40						10 53											10 57				11 10
Gipsy Hill	d			10 43				10a45		10 56											11 00				11 13
Crystal Palace 4	d			10a46						10 59											11 02				11a16
Birkbeck	d									11 03															
Beckenham Junction 4	a									11 06															
Streatham Common 4	d				10 39	10 42	10 45				10 50												11 00		
Norbury	d				10 42	10 45	10 48				10 53												11 03		
Thornton Heath	d				10 45	10 48	10 51				10 56												11 06		
Selhurst 4	d				10 48	10 51	10 54				10 59												11 09		
Norwood Junction 2	a											10 46				10 55		10 59		11 02	11 07				
	d											10 46				10 56		11 00		11 03	11 09				
West Croydon 4	a				10 52	10 56					11 03										11 13				
East Croydon	a	10 32	10 39				10 57		10 48			10 50	10 52	10 54		10 59		11 03		11 06			11 12	11 02	

Table 177

Mondays to Fridays
from 21 May

Luton, Milton Keynes Central and London East and West Croydon via Tulse Hill - Crystal Palace - Norbury

Local Services

Network Diagram - see first Page of Table 177

		SN ◇1	FC 1	SN	SN	SN	SN	SN		SN 1	SN ◇1	FC 1	FC	SN 1	SN	SN	SN	SN	SN	SN	SN ◇1	FC 1	SN	SN
London Bridge 4 ⊖	d				10 48	10 52	11 03			11 03				11 15	11 06	11 11	11 20							
South Bermondsey	d				10 52		11 07									11 15								
Queens Rd Peckham	d				10 54		11 09									11 18								
Peckham Rye 4	d				10 57		11 12									11 20								
East Dulwich	d				11 00		11 15																	
North Dulwich	d				11 02		11 17																	
Luton 10	d		10 04									10 18	10 14									10 34		
Luton Airport Parkway 7	d		10 06									10 20	10 16									10 36		
St Pancras International 15 ⊖	d		10 39									10 54	11 04									11 09		
City Thameslink 3	d		10 48									11 03	11 13									11 18		
London Blackfriars 3 ⊖	d		10 50									11 05	11 16									11 20		
Elephant & Castle ⊖	d												11 19											
Loughborough Jn.	d												11 23											
Herne Hill 4	d												11 27											
Tulse Hill 3	d				11 05		11 20						11 31											
Streatham 4	d				11 09								11a35											
London Victoria 15 ⊖	d	10 51		10 53				11 03			11 06							11 06	11 11	11 13	11 17		11 19	11 23
Battersea Park 4	d							11 07								11a32		11 10	11a15	11 17			11 23	
Milton Keynes Central	d																							
Watford Junction	d																							
Harrow & Wealdstone ⊖	d																							
Wembley Central ⊖	d																							
Shepherd's Bush ⊖	d																							
Kensington (Olympia) ⊖	d																							
West Brompton ⊖	d																							
Imperial Wharf	d																							
Clapham Junction 10	d			11 00				11 11			11 12							11 14		11 21	11 23		11 27	11 30
Latchmere	d																							
Wandsworth Common	d			11 03				11 14										11 17		11 24			11 30	11 33
Balham 4 ⊖	d			11 05				11 16										11 20		11 26			11 32	11 35
Streatham Hill	d																	11 23					11 35	
West Norwood 4	d						11 23											11 27					11 40	
Gipsy Hill	d					11a15	11 26											11 30					11 43	
Crystal Palace 4	d						11 29											11 32					11a46	
Birkbeck	d						11 33																	
Beckenham Junction 4	a						11 36																	
Streatham Common 4	d			11 09	11 12			11 20												11 30				11 39
Norbury	d			11 12	11 15			11 23												11 33				11 42
Thornton Heath	d			11 15	11 18			11 26												11 36				11 45
Selhurst 4	d			11 18	11 21			11 29												11 39				11 48
Norwood Junction 2	a									11 16				11 25	11 29		11 32	11 37						
	d									11 16				11 26	11 30		11 33	11 39						
West Croydon 4	a			11 22	11 26			11 33										11 43						11 52
East Croydon	a	11 07	11 09							11 20	11 22	11 24		11 29	11 33		11 36			11 42	11 32	11 39		

Luton, Milton Keynes Central and London East and West Croydon via Tulse Hill - Crystal Palace - Norbury

Local Services

Network Diagram - see first Page of Table 177

		SN	SN 1	SN	SN ◇1	SN	SN	SN 1	SN ◇1	FC 1	FC	SN 1	SN	SN	SN	SN		SN	SN	SN ◇1	SN	SN ◇1	FC 1	SN	SN
London Bridge 4 ⊖	d	11 18		11 22		11 33		11 33				11 45	11 36	11 41	11 50										11 48
South Bermondsey	d	11 22				11 37								11 45											11 52
Queens Rd Peckham	d	11 24				11 39								11 48											11 54
Peckham Rye 4	d	11 27				11 42								11 50											11 57
East Dulwich	d	11 30				11 45																			12 00
North Dulwich	d	11 32				11 47																			12 02
Luton 10	d									10 49	10 44												11 04		
Luton Airport Parkway 7	d									10 51	10 46												11 06		
St Pancras International 15 ⊖	d									11 24	11 34												11 39		
City Thameslink 3	d									11 33	11 43												11 48		
London Blackfriars 3 ⊖	d									11 35	11 46												11 50		
Elephant & Castle ⊖	d										11 49														
Loughborough Jn.	d										11 53														
Herne Hill 4	d										11 57														
Tulse Hill 3	d	11 35				11 50					12 01														12 05
Streatham 4	d	11 39									12a05														12 09
London Victoria 15 ⊖	d				11 32		11 33		11 36							11 36		11 41	11 43	11 47	11 49	11 51			
Battersea Park 4	d						11 37							12a02		11 40		11a45	11 47		11 53				
Milton Keynes Central	d		10 13																						
Watford Junction	d		10 51																						
Harrow & Wealdstone ⊖	d		10 59																						
Wembley Central ⊖	d		11 04																						
Shepherd's Bush ⊖	d		11 19																						
Kensington (Olympia) ⊖	d		11 21																						
West Brompton ⊖	d		11 23																						
Imperial Wharf	d		11 26																						
Clapham Junction 10	d		11 34		11 38		11 41		11 42							11 44			11 51	11 53	11 57			12 00	
Latchmere	d																								
Wandsworth Common	d		11 37				11 44									11 47			11 54		12 00			12 03	
Balham 4 ⊖	d		11 40				11 46									11 50			11 56		12 02			12 05	
Streatham Hill	d															11 53					12 05				
West Norwood 4	d					11 53										11 57					12 10				
Gipsy Hill	d			11a45		11 56										12 00					12 13				
Crystal Palace 4	d					11 59										12 02					12a16				
Birkbeck	d					12 03																			
Beckenham Junction 4	a					12 06																			
Streatham Common 4	d	11 42	11 45				11 50												12 00					12 09	12 12
Norbury	d	11 45	11 48				11 53												12 03					12 12	12 15
Thornton Heath	d	11 48	11 51				11 56												12 06					12 15	12 18
Selhurst 4	d	11 51	11 54				11 59												12 09					12 18	12 21
Norwood Junction 2	a							11 46				11 55	11 59		12 02	12 07									
	d							11 46				11 56	12 00		12 03	12 09									
West Croydon 4	a	11 56					12 03									12 13								12 22	12 26
East Croydon	a		11 57		11 48			11 50	11 52	11 54		11 59	12 03		12 06				12 12	12 02		12 07	12 09		

Table 177

Mondays to Fridays

from 21 May

Luton, Milton Keynes Central and London East and West Croydon via Tulse Hill - Crystal Palace - Norbury

Local Services

Network Diagram - see first Page of Table 177

		SN	SN	SN	SN 1	SN ◇1	FC 1	FC		SN 1	SN	SN	SN	SN	SN	SN	SN ◇1	FC 1	SN	SN	SN	SN 1	SN	SN ◇1
London Bridge 4 ⊖	d	11 52	12 03		12 03					12 15	12 06	12 11	12 20								12 18		12 22	
South Bermondsey	d		12 07									12 15									12 22			
Queens Rd Peckham	d		12 09									12 18									12 24			
Peckham Rye 4	d		12 12									12 20									12 27			
East Dulwich	d		12 15																		12 30			
North Dulwich	d		12 17																		12 32			
Luton 10	d						11 18	11 14										11 34						
Luton Airport Parkway 7	d						11 20	11 16										11 36						
St Pancras International 15 ⊖	d						11 54	12 04										12 09						
City Thameslink 3	d						12 03	12 13										12 18						
London Blackfriars 3 ⊖	d						12 05	12 16										12 20						
Elephant & Castle ⊖	d							12 19																
Loughborough Jn.	d							12 23																
Herne Hill 4	d							12 27																
Tulse Hill 3	d		12 20					12 31													12 35			
Streatham 4	d							12a35													12 39			
London Victoria 15 ⊖	d			12 03		12 06								12 06	12 11	12 13	12 17		12 19					12 32
Battersea Park 4	d			12 07								12a32		12 10	12a15	12 17			12 23					
Milton Keynes Central	d																					11 13		
Watford Junction	d																					11 51		
Harrow & Wealdstone ⊖	d																					11 59		
Wembley Central ⊖	d																					12 04		
Shepherd's Bush ⊖	d																					12 19		
Kensington (Olympia) ⊖	d																					12 22		
West Brompton ⊖	d																					12 25		
Imperial Wharf	d																					12 27		
Clapham Junction 10	d			12 11		12 12								12 14		12 21	12 23		12 27	12 30		12 34		12 38
Latchmere	d																							
Wandsworth Common	d			12 14										12 17		12 24			12 30	12 33		12 37		
Balham 4 ⊖	d			12 16										12 20		12 26			12 32	12 35		12 40		
Streatham Hill	d													12 23					12 35					
West Norwood 4	d		12 23											12 27					12 40					
Gipsy Hill	d	12a15	12 26											12 30					12 43				12a45	
Crystal Palace 4	d		12 29											12 32					12a46					
Birkbeck	d		12 33																					
Beckenham Junction 4	a		12 36																					
Streatham Common 4	d			12 20												12 30				12 39	12 42	12 45		
Norbury	d			12 23												12 33				12 42	12 45	12 48		
Thornton Heath	d			12 26												12 36				12 45	12 48	12 51		
Selhurst 4	d			12 29												12 39				12 48	12 51	12 54		
Norwood Junction 2	a				12 16					12 25	12 29		12 32	12 37										
	d				12 16					12 26	12 30		12 33	12 39										
West Croydon 4	a			12 33										12 43						12 52	12 56			
East Croydon	a				12 20	12 22	12 24			12 29	12 33		12 36			12 42	12 32	12 39				12 57		12 48

Table 177

Mondays to Fridays
from 21 May

Luton, Milton Keynes Central and London East and West Croydon via Tulse Hill - Crystal Palace - Norbury

Local Services

Network Diagram - see first Page of Table 177

		SN	SN	SN ■	SN ◇■ H	FC ■	FC	SN ■	SN	SN	SN	SN	SN	SN	SN ◇■	SN		SN ◇■	FC ■	SN	SN	SN	SN	SN	SN ■
London Bridge ■ ⊖	d	12 33		12 33				12 45	12 36	12 41	12 50										12 48	12 52	13 03		13 03
South Bermondsey	d	12 37								12 45											12 52		13 07		
Queens Rd Peckham	d	12 39								12 48											12 54		13 09		
Peckham Rye ■	d	12 42								12 50											12 57		13 12		
East Dulwich	d	12 45																			13 00		13 15		
North Dulwich	d	12 47																			13 02		13 17		
Luton ■	d					11 48	11 44												12 04						
Luton Airport Parkway ■	d					11 50	11 46												12 06						
St Pancras International ■ ⊖	d					12 24	12 34												12 39						
City Thameslink ■	d					12 33	12 43												12 48						
London Blackfriars ■ ⊖	d					12 35	12 46												12 50						
Elephant & Castle ⊖	d						12 49																		
Loughborough Jn.	d						12 53																		
Herne Hill ■	d						12 57														13 05		13 20		
Tulse Hill ■	d	12 50					13 01														13 09				
Streatham ■	d						13a05																		
London Victoria ■ ⊖	d		12 33		12 36							12 36	12 41	12 43	12 47	12 49		12 51						13 03	
Battersea Park ■	d		12 37							13a02		12 40	12a45	12 47		12 53								13 07	
Milton Keynes Central	d																								
Watford Junction	d																								
Harrow & Wealdstone ⊖	d																								
Wembley Central ⊖	d																								
Shepherd's Bush ⊖	d																								
Kensington (Olympia) ⊖	d																								
West Brompton ⊖	d																								
Imperial Wharf	d																								
Clapham Junction ■	d		12 41		12 42							12 44		12 51	12 53	12 57				13 00				13 11	
Latchmere	d																								
Wandsworth Common	d		12 44									12 47		12 54		13 00				13 03				13 14	
Balham ■ ⊖	d		12 46									12 50		12 56		13 02				13 05				13 16	
Streatham Hill	d											12 53				13 05									
West Norwood ■	d	12 53										12 57				13 10							13 23		
Gipsy Hill	d	12 56										13 00				13 13						13a15	13 26		
Crystal Palace ■	d	12 59										13 02				13a16							13 29		
Birkbeck	d	13 03																					13 33		
Beckenham Junction ■	a	13 06																					13 36		
Streatham Common ■	d		12 50											13 00						13 09	13 12			13 20	
Norbury	d		12 53											13 03						13 12	13 15			13 23	
Thornton Heath	d		12 56											13 06						13 15	13 18			13 26	
Selhurst ■	d		12 59											13 09						13 18	13 21			13 29	
Norwood Junction ■	a			12 46				12 55	12 59		13 02	13 07													13 16
	d			12 46				12 56	13 00		13 03	13 09													13 16
West Croydon ■	a		13 03									13 13								13 22	13 26			13 33	
East Croydon	a			12 50	12 52	12 54		12 59	13 03		13 06			13 12	13 02			13 07	13 09						13 20

Table 177

Mondays to Fridays
from 21 May

Luton, Milton Keynes Central and London East and West Croydon via Tulse Hill - Crystal Palace - Norbury

Local Services

Network Diagram - see first Page of Table 177

		SN ◇■ H	FC ■	FC	SN ■	SN	SN	SN		SN	SN	SN	SN ◇■	FC ■	SN	SN	SN	SN ■	SN	SN ◇■ H	SN	SN	SN ■	SN ◇■ H
London Bridge ■ ⊖	d				13 15	13 06	13 11	13 20									13 18		13 22		13 33		13 33	
South Bermondsey	d						13 15										13 22				13 37			
Queens Rd Peckham	d						13 18										13 24				13 39			
Peckham Rye ■	d						13 20										13 27				13 42			
East Dulwich	d																13 30				13 45			
North Dulwich	d																13 32				13 47			
Luton ■	d		12 18	12 14										12 34										
Luton Airport Parkway ■	d		12 20	12 16										12 36										
St Pancras International ■ ⊖	d		12 54	13 04										13 09										
City Thameslink ■	d		13 03	13 13										13 18										
London Blackfriars ■ ⊖	d		13 05	13 16										13 20										
Elephant & Castle ⊖	d			13 19																				
Loughborough Jn.	d			13 23																				
Herne Hill ■	d			13 27																				
Tulse Hill ■	d			13 31													13 35				13 50			
Streatham ■	d			13a35													13 39							
London Victoria ■ ⊖	d	13 06								13 06	13 11	13 13	13 17		13 19	13 23				13 32		13 33		13 36
Battersea Park ■	d						13a32			13 10	13a15	13 17			13 23							13 37		
Milton Keynes Central	d																	12 13						
Watford Junction	d																	12 51						
Harrow & Wealdstone ⊖	d																	12 59						
Wembley Central ⊖	d																	13 04						
Shepherd's Bush ⊖	d																	13 19						
Kensington (Olympia) ⊖	d																	13 22						
West Brompton ⊖	d																	13 25						
Imperial Wharf	d																	13 28						
Clapham Junction ■	d	13 12								13 14		13 21	13 23		13 27	13 30		13 34		13 38		13 41		13 42
Latchmere	d																							
Wandsworth Common	d									13 17		13 24			13 30	13 33		13 37				13 44		
Balham ■ ⊖	d									13 20		13 26			13 32	13 35		13 40				13 46		
Streatham Hill	d									13 23					13 35									
West Norwood ■	d									13 27					13 40						13 53			
Gipsy Hill	d									13 30					13 43				13a45		13 56			
Crystal Palace ■	d									13 32					13a46						13 59			
Birkbeck	d																				14 03			
Beckenham Junction ■	a																				14 06			
Streatham Common ■	d											13 30				13 39	13 42	13 45				13 50		
Norbury	d											13 33				13 42	13 45	13 48				13 53		
Thornton Heath	d											13 36				13 45	13 48	13 51				13 56		
Selhurst ■	d											13 39				13 48	13 51	13 54				13 59		
Norwood Junction ■	a				13 25	13 29		13 32		13 37													13 46	
	d				13 26	13 30		13 33		13 39													13 46	
West Croydon ■	a									13 43						13 52	13 56					14 03		
East Croydon	a	13 22	13 24		13 29	13 33		13 36				13 42	13 32	13 39				13 57		13 48			13 50	13 52

Luton, Milton Keynes Central and London East and West Croydon via Tulse Hill - Crystal Palace - Norbury

Local Services

Network Diagram - see first Page of Table 177

		FC ■	FC	SN ■	SN	SN	SN	SN	SN	SN	SN ◇■	SN	SN ◇■	FC ■	SN	SN		SN	SN	SN	SN ■	SN ◇■	FC ■	FC	SN ■
London Bridge ⊖	d			13 45	13 36	13 41	13 50									13 48		13 52	14 03		14 03				14 15
South Bermondsey	d					13 45										13 52			14 07						
Queens Rd Peckham	d					13 48										13 54			14 09						
Peckham Rye	d					13 50										13 57			14 12						
East Dulwich	d															14 00			14 15						
North Dulwich	d															14 02			14 17						
Luton	d	12 48	12 44											13 04									13 18	13 14	
Luton Airport Parkway	d	12 50	12 46											13 06									13 20	13 16	
St Pancras International ⊖	d	13 24	13 34											13 39									13 54	14 04	
City Thameslink	d	13 33	13 43											13 48									14 03	14 13	
London Blackfriars ⊖	d	13 35	13 46											13 50									14 05	14 16	
Elephant & Castle ⊖	d		13 49																					14 19	
Loughborough Jn.	d		13 53																					14 23	
Herne Hill	d		13 57																					14 27	
Tulse Hill	d		14 01													14 05			14 20					14 31	
Streatham	d		14a05													14 09								14a35	
London Victoria ⊖	d							13 36	13 41	13 43	13 47	13 49	13 51							14 03		14 06			
Battersea Park	d					14a02		13 40	13a45	13 47		13 53								14 07					
Milton Keynes Central	d																								
Watford Junction	d																								
Harrow & Wealdstone ⊖	d																								
Wembley Central ⊖	d																								
Shepherd's Bush ⊖	d																								
Kensington (Olympia) ⊖	d																								
West Brompton ⊖	d																								
Imperial Wharf	d																								
Clapham Junction	d							13 44		13 51	13 53	13 57			14 00					14 11		14 12			
Latchmere	d																								
Wandsworth Common	d							13 47		13 54		14 00			14 03					14 14					
Balham ⊖	d							13 50		13 56		14 02			14 05					14 16					
Streatham Hill	d							13 53				14 05													
West Norwood	d							13 57				14 10							14 23						
Gipsy Hill	d							14 00				14 13						14a15	14 26						
Crystal Palace	d							14 02				14a16							14 29						
Birkbeck	d																		14 33						
Beckenham Junction	a																		14 36						
Streatham Common	d									14 00					14 09	14 12				14 20					
Norbury	d									14 03					14 12	14 15				14 23					
Thornton Heath	d									14 06					14 15	14 18				14 26					
Selhurst	d									14 09					14 18	14 21				14 29					
Norwood Junction	a			13 55	13 59		14 02	14 07													14 16				14 25
	d			13 56	14 00		14 03	14 09													14 16				14 26
West Croydon	a							14 13							14 22	14 26				14 33					
East Croydon	a	13 54		13 59	14 03		14 06			14 12	14 02		14 07	14 09							14 20	14 22	14 25		14 29

Luton, Milton Keynes Central and London East and West Croydon via Tulse Hill - Crystal Palace - Norbury

Local Services

Network Diagram - see first Page of Table 177

		SN	SN	SN	SN	SN	SN	SN ◇■		FC ■	SN	SN	SN	SN ■	SN	SN ◇■	SN	SN	SN ■	SN ◇■	FC ■	FC	SN ■	SN
London Bridge ⊖	d	14 06	14 11	14 20									14 18		14 22		14 33		14 33				14 45	14 36
South Bermondsey	d		14 15										14 22				14 37							
Queens Rd Peckham	d		14 18										14 24				14 39							
Peckham Rye	d		14 20										14 27				14 42							
East Dulwich	d												14 30				14 45							
North Dulwich	d												14 32				14 47							
Luton	d									13 34											13 48	13 44		
Luton Airport Parkway	d									13 36											13 50	13 46		
St Pancras International ⊖	d									14 09											14 24	14 34		
City Thameslink	d									14 18											14 33	14 43		
London Blackfriars ⊖	d									14 20											14 35	14 46		
Elephant & Castle ⊖	d																					14 49		
Loughborough Jn.	d																					14 53		
Herne Hill	d																					14 57		
Tulse Hill	d												14 35				14 50					15 01		
Streatham	d												14 39									15a05		
London Victoria ⊖	d				14 06	14 11	14 13	14 17			14 19					14 32		14 33		14 36				
Battersea Park	d		14a32		14 10	14a15	14 17				14 23							14 37						
Milton Keynes Central	d													13 13										
Watford Junction	d													13 51										
Harrow & Wealdstone ⊖	d													13 59										
Wembley Central ⊖	d													14 04										
Shepherd's Bush ⊖	d													14 19										
Kensington (Olympia) ⊖	d													14 22										
West Brompton ⊖	d													14 25										
Imperial Wharf	d													14 28										
Clapham Junction	d				14 14		14 21	14 23			14 27	14 30		14 34		14 38		14 41		14 42				
Latchmere	d																							
Wandsworth Common	d				14 17		14 24				14 30	14 33		14 37				14 44						
Balham ⊖	d				14 20		14 26				14 32	14 35		14 40				14 46						
Streatham Hill	d				14 23						14 35													
West Norwood	d				14 27						14 40						14 53							
Gipsy Hill	d				14 30						14 43				14a45		14 56							
Crystal Palace	d				14 32						14a46						14 59							
Birkbeck	d																15 03							
Beckenham Junction	a																15 06							
Streatham Common	d						14 30					14 39	14 42	14 45				14 50						
Norbury	d						14 33					14 42	14 45	14 48				14 53						
Thornton Heath	d						14 36					14 45	14 48	14 51				14 56						
Selhurst	d						14 39					14 48	14 51	14 54				14 59						
Norwood Junction	a	14 29		14 32	14 37														14 46				14 55	14 59
	d	14 30		14 33	14 39														14 46				14 56	15 00
West Croydon	a				14 43							14 52	14 56					15 03						
East Croydon	a	14 33		14 36			14 42	14 32		14 39				14 57		14 48			14 50	14 52	14 54		14 59	15 03

Table 177

Mondays to Fridays
from 21 May

Luton, Milton Keynes Central and London East and West Croydon via Tulse Hill - Crystal Palace - Norbury

Local Services

Network Diagram - see first Page of Table 177

		SN	SN	SN	SN	SN	SN ◇1	SN	SN ◇1	FC 1	SN	SN	SN	SN	SN	SN 1		SN ◇1	FC 1	FC	SN 1	SN	SN	SN	SN
London Bridge 4 ⊖	d	14 41	14 50									14 48	14 52	15 03		15 03					15 15	15 06	15 11	15 20	
South Bermondsey	d	14 45										14 52		15 07									15 15		
Queens Rd Peckham	d	14 48										14 54		15 09									15 18		
Peckham Rye 4	d	14 50										14 57		15 12									15 20		
East Dulwich	d											15 00		15 15											
North Dulwich	d											15 02		15 17											
Luton 10	d									14 04									14 18	14 14					
Luton Airport Parkway 7	d									14 06									14 20	14 16					
St Pancras International 15 ⊖	d									14 39									14 54	15 04					
City Thameslink 3	d									14 48									15 03	15 13					
London Blackfriars 3 ⊖	d									14 50									15 05	15 16					
Elephant & Castle ⊖	d																			15 19					
Loughborough Jn.	d																			15 23					
Herne Hill 4	d																			15 27					
Tulse Hill 3	d											15 05		15 20						15 31					
Streatham 4	d											15 09								15a35					
London Victoria 15 ⊖	d			14 36	14 41	14 43	14 47	14 49	14 51						15 03			15 06							15 06
Battersea Park 4	d	15a02		14 40	14a45	14 47		14 53							15 07								15a32		15 10
Milton Keynes Central	d																								
Watford Junction	d																								
Harrow & Wealdstone ⊖	d																								
Wembley Central ⊖	d																								
Shepherd's Bush ⊖	d																								
Kensington (Olympia) ⊖	d																								
West Brompton ⊖	d																								
Imperial Wharf	d																								
Clapham Junction 10	d			14 44		14 51	14 53	14 57			15 00				15 11			15 12							15 14
Latchmere	d																								
Wandsworth Common	d			14 47		14 54		15 00			15 03				15 14										15 17
Balham 4 ⊖	d			14 50		14 56		15 02			15 05				15 16										15 20
Streatham Hill	d			14 53				15 05																	15 23
West Norwood 4	d			14 57				15 10						15 23											15 27
Gipsy Hill	d			15 00				15 13					15a15	15 26											15 30
Crystal Palace 4	d			15 02				15a16						15 29											15 32
Birkbeck	d													15 33											
Beckenham Junction 4	a													15 36											
Streatham Common 4	d					15 00					15 09	15 12			15 20										
Norbury	d					15 03					15 12	15 15			15 23										
Thornton Heath	d					15 06					15 15	15 18			15 26										
Selhurst 4	d					15 09					15 18	15 21			15 29										
Norwood Junction 2	a		15 02	15 07												15 16					15 25	15 29		15 32	15 37
	d		15 03	15 09												15 16					15 26	15 30		15 33	15 39
West Croydon 4	a			15 13							15 22	15 26			15 33										15 43
East Croydon	a		15 06			15 12	15 02		15 07	15 09						15 20		15 22	15 24		15 29	15 33		15 36	

Table 177

Mondays to Fridays
from 21 May

Luton, Milton Keynes Central and London East and West Croydon via Tulse Hill - Crystal Palace - Norbury

Local Services

Network Diagram - see first Page of Table 177

		SN	SN	SN ◇1	FC 1	SN	SN	SN		SN 1	SN	SN ◇1	SN	SN	SN 1	SN ◇1	FC 1	FC	SN 1	SN	SN	SN	SN	SN
London Bridge 4 ⊖	d							15 18			15 22		15 33		15 33				15 45	15 36	15 41	15 50		
South Bermondsey	d							15 22					15 37								15 45			
Queens Rd Peckham	d							15 24					15 39								15 48			
Peckham Rye 4	d							15 27					15 42								15 50			
East Dulwich	d							15 30					15 45											
North Dulwich	d							15 32					15 47											
Luton 10	d				14 34												14 48	14 44						
Luton Airport Parkway 7	d				14 36												14 50	14 46						
St Pancras International 15 ⊖	d				15 09												15 24	15 34						
City Thameslink 3	d				15 18												15 33	15 43						
London Blackfriars 3 ⊖	d				15 20												15 35	15 46						
Elephant & Castle ⊖	d																	15 49						
Loughborough Jn.	d																	15 53						
Herne Hill 4	d																	15 57						
Tulse Hill 3	d							15 35					15 50					16 01						
Streatham 4	d							15 39										16a05						
London Victoria 15 ⊖	d	15 11	15 13	15 17		15 19	15 23					15 32		15 33		15 36							15 36	15 41
Battersea Park 4	d	15a15	15 17			15 23								15 37							16a02		15 40	15a45
Milton Keynes Central	d									14 13														
Watford Junction	d									14 51														
Harrow & Wealdstone ⊖	d									14 59														
Wembley Central ⊖	d									15 04														
Shepherd's Bush ⊖	d									15 22														
Kensington (Olympia) ⊖	d									15 24														
West Brompton ⊖	d									15 26														
Imperial Wharf	d									15 29														
Clapham Junction 10	d		15 21	15 23		15 27	15 30			15 34		15 38		15 41		15 42							15 44	
Latchmere	d																							
Wandsworth Common	d		15 24			15 30	15 33			15 37				15 44									15 47	
Balham 4 ⊖	d		15 26			15 32	15 35			15 40				15 46									15 50	
Streatham Hill	d					15 35																	15 53	
West Norwood 4	d					15 40							15 53										15 57	
Gipsy Hill	d					15 43					15a45		15 56										16 00	
Crystal Palace 4	d					15a46							15 59										16 02	
Birkbeck	d												16 03											
Beckenham Junction 4	a												16 06											
Streatham Common 4	d		15 30				15 39	15 42		15 45				15 50										
Norbury	d		15 33				15 42	15 45		15 48				15 53										
Thornton Heath	d		15 36				15 45	15 48		15 51				15 56										
Selhurst 4	d		15 39				15 48	15 51		15 54				15 59										
Norwood Junction 2	a														15 46				15 55	15 59		16 02	16 07	
	d														15 46				15 56	16 00		16 03	16 09	
West Croydon 4	a						15 52	15 56						16 03									16 13	
East Croydon	a		15 42	15 32	15 39					15 57		15 47			15 50	15 52	15 54		15 59	16 03		16 06		

Table 177

Mondays to Fridays

from 21 May

Luton, Milton Keynes Central and London East and West Croydon via Tulse Hill - Crystal Palace - Norbury

Local Services

Network Diagram - see first Page of Table 177

		SN	SN ◇1	SN	SN ◇1	FC 1	SN	SN	SN	SN	SN	SN 1	SN 1 ⌘	FC 1	FC	SN 1		SN	SN	SN	SN	SN	SN	SN ◇1 ⌘	SN
London Bridge ⊖	d							15 48	15 52	16 03		16 03				16 15		16 06	16 11	16 20					16 18
South Bermondsey	d							15 52		16 07									16 15						16 22
Queens Rd Peckham	d							15 54		16 09									16 18						16 24
Peckham Rye	d							15 57		16 12									16 20						16 27
East Dulwich	d							16 00		16 15															16 30
North Dulwich	d							16 02		16 17															16 32
Luton	d					15 04								15 18	15 14										
Luton Airport Parkway	d					15 06								15 20	15 16										
St Pancras International ⊖	d					15 39								15 54	16 04										
City Thameslink	d					15 48								16 03	16 13										
London Blackfriars ⊖	d					15 50								16 05	16 16										
Elephant & Castle ⊖	d														16 19										
Loughborough Jn.	d														16 23										
Herne Hill	d														16 27										
Tulse Hill	d							16 05		16 20					16 32										16 35
Streatham	d							16 09							16a35										16 39
London Victoria ⊖	d	15 43	15 47	15 49	15 51		15 53				16 03		16 06								16 07	16 11	16 13	16 17	
Battersea Park	d	15 47		15 53							16 07								16a32		16 11	16a15	16 17		
Milton Keynes Central	d																								
Watford Junction	d																								
Harrow & Wealdstone ⊖	d																								
Wembley Central ⊖	d																								
Shepherd's Bush ⊖	d																								
Kensington (Olympia) ⊖	d																								
West Brompton ⊖	d																								
Imperial Wharf	d																								
Clapham Junction	d	15 51	15 53	15 57			16 00				16 11		16 12								16 15		16 21	16 23	
Latchmere	d																								
Wandsworth Common	d	15 54		16 00			16 03				16 14										16 18		16 24		
Balham ⊖	d	15 56		16 02			16 05				16 16										16 20		16 26		
Streatham Hill	d			16 05																	16 23				
West Norwood	d			16 10						16 23											16 27				
Gipsy Hill	d			16 13					16a15	16 26											16 30				
Crystal Palace	d			16a16						16 29											16 32				
Birkbeck	d									16 33															
Beckenham Junction	a									16 38															
Streatham Common	d	16 00					16 09	16 12			16 20												16 30		16 42
Norbury	d	16 03					16 12	16 15			16 23												16 33		16 45
Thornton Heath	d	16 06					16 15	16 18			16 26												16 36		16 48
Selhurst	d	16 09					16 18	16 21			16 29												16 39		16 51
Norwood Junction	a											16 16				16 25		16 29		16 32	16 37				
	d											16 16				16 26		16 30		16 33	16 39				
West Croydon	a						16 22	16 26			16 33										16 43				16 57
East Croydon	a	16 12	16 02		16 07	16 09						16 20	16 22	16 24		16 29		16 33		16 36			16 42	16 33	

Table 177

Mondays to Fridays

from 21 May

Luton, Milton Keynes Central and London East and West Croydon via Tulse Hill - Crystal Palace - Norbury

Local Services

Network Diagram - see first Page of Table 177

		SN 1	FC 1	SN	SN 1	SE 1 A	SN	SN ◇1 ⌘		SN	SN	SN 1	SN	SN 1 ⌘	SN	SN	SN	SN	FC 1	FC	FC 1	SN	SN	SN ◇1 ⌘
London Bridge ⊖	d						16 22			16 33		16 33	16 36		16 41	16 48								
South Bermondsey	d									16 37					16 45									
Queens Rd Peckham	d									16 39					16 48									
Peckham Rye	d									16 42					16 50									
East Dulwich	d									16 45														
North Dulwich	d									16 47														
Luton	d		15 34																15 48	15 44	16 04			
Luton Airport Parkway	d		15 36																15 50	15 46	16 06			
St Pancras International ⊖	d		16 09																16 22	16 34	16 40			
City Thameslink	d		16 18																16 31	16 43	16 49			
London Blackfriars ⊖	d		16 20			16 20													16 36	16 46	16 52			
Elephant & Castle ⊖	d					16a23														16 49	16 56			
Loughborough Jn.	d																			16 53	17 00			
Herne Hill	d																			16 57	17a04			
Tulse Hill	d									16 50										17 02				
Streatham	d																			17a05				
London Victoria ⊖	d	16 19		16 19				16 32			16 33			16 36			16 37	16 39				16 41	16 43	16 47
Battersea Park	d			16 23							16 37				17a02		16 41					16a45	16 47	
Milton Keynes Central	d				15 13																			
Watford Junction	d				15 51																			
Harrow & Wealdstone ⊖	d				15 59																			
Wembley Central ⊖	d				16 05																			
Shepherd's Bush ⊖	d				16 19																			
Kensington (Olympia) ⊖	d				16 22																			
West Brompton ⊖	d				16 25																			
Imperial Wharf	d				16 27																			
Clapham Junction	d	16 26		16 27	16 34			16 38			16 41			16 42			16 45	16 45					16 51	16 53
Latchmere	d																							
Wandsworth Common	d			16 30	16 37						16 44						16 48						16 54	
Balham ⊖	d			16 32	16 40						16 46						16 50						16 56	
Streatham Hill	d			16 35													16 53							
West Norwood	d			16 39						16 53							16 57							
Gipsy Hill	d			16 44			16a45			16 56							17 00							
Crystal Palace	d			16a46						16 59							17 03							
Birkbeck	d									17 03														
Beckenham Junction	a									17 08														
Streatham Common	d				16 45						16 50												17 00	
Norbury	d				16 48						16 53												17 03	
Thornton Heath	d				16 51						16 56												17 06	
Selhurst	d				16 55						16 59												17 09	
Norwood Junction	a											16 44	16 59			17 01	17 07							
	d											16 44	17 00			17 02	17 09							
West Croydon	a										17 03		17 07				17 13							
East Croydon	a	16 36	16 39		16 58			16 47				16 48		16 52		17 05		16 55	16 59				17 12	17 03

A from 21 May until 27 July

Table 177

Mondays to Fridays
from 21 May

Luton, Milton Keynes Central and London East and West Croydon via Tulse Hill - Crystal Palace - Norbury

Local Services

Network Diagram - see first Page of Table 177

		SN	SN ■	SN	SN	SN ■	SN	SN ■	SN	SN	SN	SN ■	FC ■	FC	SN	SN		SN	SN	SN	SN	SN ◇■	SN	SN ■	SN
London Bridge ⊖	d	16 48			16 52	16 57	16 58	16 59	17 03		17 05				17 11	17 17							17 18		
South Bermondsey	d	16 52					17 02								17 15								17 22		
Queens Rd Peckham	d	16 54					17 04								17 18								17 24		
Peckham Rye	d	16 57					17 07								17 20								17 27		
East Dulwich	d	17 00					17 10																17 30		
North Dulwich	d	17 02					17 12																17 32		
Luton	d												16 14	16 16											
Luton Airport Parkway	d												16 17	16 18											
St Pancras International ⊖	d												16 46	17 02											
City Thameslink	d												16 55	17 11											
London Blackfriars ⊖	d												16 58	17 14											
Elephant & Castle ⊖	d												17 02	17 18											
Loughborough Jn.	d													17 22											
Herne Hill	d													17 26									17 36		
Tulse Hill	d	17 05					17 17							17 31									17 39		
Streatham	d	17 09												17a35											
London Victoria ⊖	d		16 49	16 49						17 01		17 06						17 06	17 09	17 11	17 13	17 17		17 21	17 22
Battersea Park	d			16 53						17 05					17a32			17 10		17a15	17 17				17 26
Milton Keynes Central	d																								
Watford Junction	d																								
Harrow & Wealdstone ⊖	d																								
Wembley Central ⊖	d																								
Shepherd's Bush ⊖	d																								
Kensington (Olympia) ⊖	d																								
West Brompton ⊖	d																								
Imperial Wharf	d																								
Clapham Junction	d		16 56	16 57						17 09		17 12						17 14	17 15		17 21	17 23		17 27	17 30
Latchmere	d																								
Wandsworth Common	d			17 00						17 12								17 17			17 24				17 33
Balham ⊖	d			17 03						17 14								17 19			17 26				17 35
Streatham Hill	d			17 06														17 22							17 38
West Norwood	d			17 09			17 20											17 27							17 42
Gipsy Hill	d			17 12	17a15		17 23											17 30							17 45
Crystal Palace	d			17a15			17 26											17 33							17a47
Birkbeck	d						17 30																		
Beckenham Junction	a						17 35																		
Streatham Common	d	17 12								17 18											17 30		17 42		
Norbury	d	17 15								17 21											17 33		17 45		
Thornton Heath	d	17 18								17 24											17 36		17 48		
Selhurst	d	17 21								17 27											17a40		17 50		
Norwood Junction	a							17 10	17 16		17 29					17 30		17 37							
	d							17 10	17 16		17 30					17 30		17 38							
West Croydon	a	17 27							17 21	17 32	17 37							17 43					17 57		
East Croydon	a		17 06			17 09		17 14				17 22	17 26			17 34			17 27			17 32		17 36	

Table 177

Mondays to Fridays
from 21 May

Luton, Milton Keynes Central and London East and West Croydon via Tulse Hill - Crystal Palace - Norbury

Local Services

Network Diagram - see first Page of Table 177

		SN	SN ■	FC ■	SN ■	SN	SN	SN ◇■		SN ■	SN	SN ◇■	SN	SN	SN ■	FC ■	FC	SN	SN	SN	SN	SN	SN	SN ◇■
London Bridge ⊖	d	17 19	17 23			17 28	17 29			17 32			17 36	17 41	17 42			17 48	17 49					
South Bermondsey	d					17 32								17 45				17 52						
Queens Rd Peckham	d					17 35								17 47				17 54						
Peckham Rye	d					17 37								17 50				17 57						
East Dulwich	d					17 40												18 00						
North Dulwich	d					17 42												18 02						
Luton	d			16 34												16 50	16 46							
Luton Airport Parkway	d			16 36												16 52	16 48							
St Pancras International ⊖	d			17 10												17 28	17 32							
City Thameslink	d			17 19												17 37	17 41							
London Blackfriars ⊖	d			17 22												17 40	17 44							
Elephant & Castle ⊖	d																17 48							
Loughborough Jn.	d																17 52							
Herne Hill	d																17 57							
Tulse Hill	d					17 46											18 02	18 05						
Streatham	d																18a05	18 09						
London Victoria ⊖	d							17 32			17 33	17 35								17 37	17 39	17 41	17 45	17 47
Battersea Park	d										17 37			18a02						17 41		17a45	17 49	
Milton Keynes Central	d				16 13																			
Watford Junction	d				16 51																			
Harrow & Wealdstone ⊖	d				16 59																			
Wembley Central ⊖	d				17 05																			
Shepherd's Bush ⊖	d				17 19																			
Kensington (Olympia) ⊖	d				17 22																			
West Brompton ⊖	d				17 25																			
Imperial Wharf	d				17 28																			
Clapham Junction	d				17 33			17 38			17 41	17 42								17 45	17 45		17 53	17 53
Latchmere	d																							
Wandsworth Common	d				17 36						17 44									17 48			17 56	
Balham ⊖	d				17 39						17 46									17 50			17 58	
Streatham Hill	d																			17 53				
West Norwood	d					17 49														17 57				
Gipsy Hill	d	17a46				17 52														18 00				
Crystal Palace	d					17 54														18 02				
Birkbeck	d					17 58																		
Beckenham Junction	a					18 04																		
Streatham Common	d				17 46						17 50							18 12					18 02	
Norbury	d				17 48						17 53							18 14					18 05	
Thornton Heath	d				17 51						17 56							18 17					18 08	
Selhurst	d				17 55						17 59							18 21					18a12	
Norwood Junction	a						17 41			17 43			17 59						18 01	18 08				
	d						17 43			17 44			18 00						18 02	18 09				
West Croydon	a						17 47				18 03		18 08					18 27		18 14				
East Croydon	a		17 35	17 47	17 59			17 48		17 49		17 51			17 54	18 07			18 05		17 55			18 02

Table 177

Mondays to Fridays

from 21 May

Luton, Milton Keynes Central and London East and West Croydon via Tulse Hill - Crystal Palace - Norbury

Local Services

Network Diagram - see first Page of Table 177

		SN [1]	SN	SN	SN [1]	SN	SN [1]	SN	SN	SN	SN	SN ◇[1]	FC [1]	FC	FC	SN		SN [1]	SN	SN	SN	SN	SN	SN ◇[1]	SN
London Bridge [4] ⊖	d		17 53		17 57	17 58	17 59		18 02		18 06					18 11		18 12	18 18						18 18
South Bermondsey	d					18 02										18 15									18 22
Queens Rd Peckham	d					18 04										18 18									18 24
Peckham Rye [4]	d					18 07										18 20									18 27
East Dulwich	d					18 10																			18 30
North Dulwich	d					18 12																			18 32
Luton [10]	d													17 10	17 22										
Luton Airport Parkway [7]	d													17 12	17 24										
St Pancras International [15] ⊖	d												17 40	17 44	18 04										
City Thameslink [3]	d												17 49	17 53	18 13										
London Blackfriars [3] ⊖	d												17 51	17 56	18 16										
Elephant & Castle ⊖	d												17 55	18 00	18 20										
Loughborough Jn.	d														18 24										
Herne Hill [4]	d													18a06	18 28										
Tulse Hill [3]	d					18 17									18 32										18 35
Streatham [4]	d														18a35										18 39
London Victoria [15] ⊖	d	17 49		17 52						18 03		18 06								18 07	18 09	18 11	18 13	18 17	
Battersea Park [4]	d			17 56						18 07						18a32				18 11		18a15	18 17		
Milton Keynes Central	d																								
Watford Junction	d																								
Harrow & Wealdstone ⊖	d																								
Wembley Central ⊖	d																								
Shepherd's Bush ⊖	d							17 45																	
Kensington (Olympia) ⊖	d							17 47																	
West Brompton ⊖	d							17 50																	
Imperial Wharf	d							17 53																	
Clapham Junction [10]	d	17 56		18 00				18 02		18 11		18 12								18 15	18 15		18 21	18 23	
Latchmere	d																								
Wandsworth Common	d			18 03				18 05		18 14										18 18			18 24		
Balham [4] ⊖	d			18 05				18 08		18 16										18 20			18 26		
Streatham Hill	d			18 08																18 23					
West Norwood [4]	d			18 14		18 20														18 27					
Gipsy Hill	d		18a15	18 17		18 23														18 30					
Crystal Palace [4]	d			18a19		18 26														18 33					
Birkbeck	d					18 30																			
Beckenham Junction [4]	a					18 35																			
Streatham Common [4]	d							18 15		18 20													18 30		18 42
Norbury	d							18 18		18 23													18 33		18 44
Thornton Heath	d							18 21		18 26													18 36		18 47
Selhurst [4]	d							18 26		18 29													18a40		18 51
Norwood Junction [2]	a				18 08				18 15		18 29								18 30	18 37					
	d				18 08				18 16		18 32								18 31	18 39					
West Croydon [4]	a								18 20	18 34	18 39									18 44					18 57
East Croydon	a	18 05			18 13		18 14	18 32				18 22	18 24					18 24	18 35		18 27			18 33	

Table 177

Mondays to Fridays

from 21 May

Luton, Milton Keynes Central and London East and West Croydon via Tulse Hill - Crystal Palace - Norbury

Local Services

Network Diagram - see first Page of Table 177

		SN	SN [1]	SN [1]	FC [1]	SN	SN	SN [1]		SN [1]	SN	SN ◇[1]	SN	SN	SN [1]	SN	SN	SN	SN	FC [1]	SN	SN	SN ◇[1]	SN
London Bridge [4] ⊖	d	18 21	18 23				18 28	18 30			18 32			18 36		18 41	18 49							18 48
South Bermondsey	d						18 32									18 45								18 52
Queens Rd Peckham	d						18 34									18 48								18 54
Peckham Rye [4]	d						18 37									18 50								18 57
East Dulwich	d						18 40																	19 00
North Dulwich	d						18 42																	19 02
Luton [10]	d				17 30															17 46				
Luton Airport Parkway [7]	d				17 33															17 48				
St Pancras International [15] ⊖	d				18 08															18 20				
City Thameslink [3]	d				18 17															18 29				
London Blackfriars [3] ⊖	d				18 20															18 32				
Elephant & Castle ⊖	d																			18 36				
Loughborough Jn.	d																							
Herne Hill [4]	d																							
Tulse Hill [3]	d						18 48																	19 05
Streatham [4]	d																							19 09
London Victoria [15] ⊖	d			18 19		18 22						18 32	18 32		18 36			18 36	18 39		18 41	18 45	18 47	
Battersea Park [4]	d					18 26							18 36			19a02		18 40			18a45	18 49		
Milton Keynes Central	d									17 13														
Watford Junction	d									17 51														
Harrow & Wealdstone ⊖	d									17 59														
Wembley Central ⊖	d									18 05														
Shepherd's Bush ⊖	d									18 19														
Kensington (Olympia) ⊖	d									18 22														
West Brompton ⊖	d									18 25														
Imperial Wharf	d									18 27														
Clapham Junction [10]	d			18 26		18 30				18 34		18 38	18 40		18 42			18 44	18 45			18 53	18 53	
Latchmere	d																							
Wandsworth Common	d					18 33				18 37			18 43					18 47				18 56		
Balham [4] ⊖	d					18 35				18 40			18 45					18 49				18 58		
Streatham Hill	d					18 38												18 52						
West Norwood [4]	d					18 42	18 51											18 56						
Gipsy Hill	d	18a45				18 45	18 54											18 59						
Crystal Palace [4]	d					18a47	18 57											19 01						
Birkbeck	d						19 01																	
Beckenham Junction [4]	a						19 06																	
Streatham Common [4]	d									18 46			18 50									19 02		19 12
Norbury	d									18 49			18 52									19 05		19 15
Thornton Heath	d									18 52			18 55									19 08		19 18
Selhurst [4]	d									18 56			19 00									19 10		19 21
Norwood Junction [2]	a							18 41			18 45			18 59			19 01	19 06						
	d							18 42			18 46			19 02			19 02	19 09						
West Croydon [4]	a										18 50		19 04	19 09				19 14						19 27
East Croydon	a		18 36	18 37	18 41			18 45		19 02		18 48			18 52		19 05		18 57	19 00		19 13	19 03	

Table 177

Mondays to Fridays
from 21 May

Luton, Milton Keynes Central and London East and West Croydon via Tulse Hill - Crystal Palace - Norbury

Local Services

Network Diagram - see first Page of Table 177

	SN	SN ■	FC ■	FC	SN	SE ■ A	SN ■	SN	SN	SN	FC ■	SN	SN	SN	FC		SN ■	SN	SN	SN ◇■	FC ■	SN	SN	SN
London Bridge ■ ⊖ d	18 51						18 59		18 57			19 06		19 08									19 11	19 18
South Bermondsey d									19 01					19 12									19 15	19 22
Queens Rd Peckham d									19 03					19 14									19 18	19 24
Peckham Rye ■ d									19 06					19 17									19 20	19 27
East Dulwich d									19 09					19 20										19 30
North Dulwich d									19 11					19 22										19 32
Luton ■ d			18 00								18 18				18 22						18 34			
Luton Airport Parkway ■ d			18 02								18 20				18 24						18 36			
St Pancras International ■ ⊖ d			18 34	18 38							18 54				19 04						19 09			
City Thameslink ■ d			18 43	18 47							19 03				19 13						19 18			
London Blackfriars ■ ⊖ d			18 46	18 50		18 55					19 05				19 16						19 20			
Elephant & Castle ⊖ d				18 54		18a58									19 19									
Loughborough Jn. d				18 58											19 23									
Herne Hill ■ d				19 02											19 27									
Tulse Hill ■ d				19 09					19 14					19 27	19 31									19 35
Streatham ■ d				19a13											19a35									19 39
London Victoria ■ ⊖ d		18 51			18 52			18 59		19 06			19 06				19 10	19 11	19 15	19 17		19 22		
Battersea Park ■ d					18 56			19 04					19 10					19a15	19 19			19 26	19a32	
Milton Keynes Central d																								
Watford Junction d																								
Harrow & Wealdstone ⊖ d																								
Wembley Central ⊖ d																								
Shepherd's Bush ⊖ d																								
Kensington (Olympia) ⊖ d																								
West Brompton ⊖ d																								
Imperial Wharf d																								
Clapham Junction ■ d		18 57			19 00			19 08		19 12			19 14				19 16		19 23	19 23		19 30		
Latchmere d																								
Wandsworth Common d					19 03			19 11					19 17						19 26			19 33		
Balham ■ ⊖ d					19 05			19 14					19 20						19 28			19 35		
Streatham Hill d					19 08								19 23									19 38		
West Norwood ■ d					19 12				19 17				19 27	19 30								19 42		
Gipsy Hill d	19a15				19 15				19 20				19 30	19 33								19 45		
Crystal Palace ■ d					19a19				19 23				19 32	19 35								19a47		
Birkbeck ⇌ d														19 39										
Beckenham Junction ■ ⇌ a														19 43										
Streatham Common ■ d								19 18											19 32					19 42
Norbury d								19 20											19 35					19 45
Thornton Heath d								19 23											19 38					19 48
Selhurst ■ d								19 27											19 41					19 51
Norwood Junction ■ a							19 13		19 27			19 29	19 37											
d							19 14		19 28			19 30	19 39											
West Croydon ■ ⇌ a								19 32	19 35				19 44											19 56
East Croydon ⇌ a		19 07	19 10				19 17			19 22	19 24	19 33					19 27		19 44	19 33	19 39			

A from 21 May until 27 July

Table 177

Mondays to Fridays
from 21 May

Luton, Milton Keynes Central and London East and West Croydon via Tulse Hill - Crystal Palace - Norbury

Local Services

Network Diagram - see first Page of Table 177

	SN	SN	SN	SN ◇■	SN ■	SN	SN		FC ■	SN	SN ■	SN	SN	FC	SN ■	SN	SN	SN ◇■	FC ■	SN	SN	SN	SN
London Bridge ■ ⊖ d	19 22	19 31			19 33	19 28				19 36	19 52		19 38								19 41	19 48	19 54
South Bermondsey d						19 32							19 42								19 45	19 52	
Queens Rd Peckham d						19 34							19 44								19 48	19 54	
Peckham Rye ■ d						19 37							19 47								19 50	19 57	
East Dulwich d						19 40							19 50									20 00	
North Dulwich d						19 42							19 52									20 02	
Luton ■ d									18 48					18 54					19 04				
Luton Airport Parkway ■ d									18 50					18 57					19 06				
St Pancras International ■ ⊖ d									19 24					19 34					19 39				
City Thameslink ■ d									19 33					19 43					19 48				
London Blackfriars ■ ⊖ d									19 35					19 46					19 50				
Elephant & Castle ⊖ d														19 49									
Loughborough Jn. d														19 53									
Herne Hill ■ d														19 57									
Tulse Hill ■ d						19 46							19 57	20 01								20 05	
Streatham ■ d														20a05								20 09	
London Victoria ■ ⊖ d			19 30	19 32			19 36					19 36			19 40	19 41	19 45	19 47		19 52			
Battersea Park ■ d			19 34									19 40				19a45	19 49			19 56	20a02		
Milton Keynes Central d																							
Watford Junction d																							
Harrow & Wealdstone ⊖ d																							
Wembley Central ⊖ d																							
Shepherd's Bush ⊖ d																							
Kensington (Olympia) ⊖ d																							
West Brompton ⊖ d																							
Imperial Wharf d																							
Clapham Junction ■ d			19 38	19 38			19 42					19 44			19 46		19 53	19 53		20 00			
Latchmere d																							
Wandsworth Common d			19 41									19 47					19 56			20 03			
Balham ■ ⊖ d			19 44									19 50					19 59			20 05			
Streatham Hill d												19 53								20 08			
West Norwood ■ d						19 49						19 57	20 00							20 12			
Gipsy Hill d	19a45					19 52						20 00	20 03							20 15			20a16
Crystal Palace ■ d						19 54						20 02	20 05							20a17			
Birkbeck ⇌ d													20 09										
Beckenham Junction ■ ⇌ a													20 13										
Streatham Common ■ d			19 48														20 03					20 12	
Norbury d			19 51														20 05					20 15	
Thornton Heath d			19 54														20 08					20 18	
Selhurst ■ d			19 57														20 11					20 21	
Norwood Junction ■ a		19 44			19 46	19 59				19 59	20 03	20 07											
d		19 44			19 47	20 02				20 00	20 03	20 09											
West Croydon ■ ⇌ a		19 49	20 02			20 07						20 13										20 26	
East Croydon ⇌ a				19 48	19 50		19 52		19 54	20 03	20 06				19 57		20 14	20 03	20 09				

Luton, Milton Keynes Central and London East and West Croydon via Tulse Hill - Crystal Palace - Norbury

Local Services

Network Diagram - see first Page of Table 177

		SN	SN	SN ◇■	FC ■	FC	SN	SN	SN ■	SN	SN	SN ◇■	SN	SN	SN	SN		SN ■	SN	SN ◇■	SN	SN ■	SN ◇■	FC ■	FC
London Bridge ⊖	d		20 03				20 06							20 11	20 18	20 22		20 28			20 33	20 34			
South Bermondsey	d		20 07											20 15	20 22						20 37				
Queens Rd Peckham	d		20 09											20 18	20 24						20 39				
Peckham Rye	d		20 12											20 20	20 27						20 42				
East Dulwich	d		20 15												20 30						20 45				
North Dulwich	d		20 17												20 32						20 47				
Luton	d				19 18	19 24																		19 50	19 46
Luton Airport Parkway	d				19 20	19 27																		19 52	19 48
St Pancras International ⊖	d				19 54	20 04																		20 24	20 34
City Thameslink	d				20 03	20 13																		20 33	20 43
London Blackfriars ⊖	d				20 05	20 16																		20 35	20 46
Elephant & Castle ⊖	d					20 19																			20 49
Loughborough Jn.	d					20 23																			20 53
Herne Hill	d					20 27																			20 57
Tulse Hill	d		20 21			20 31									20 35						20 51				21 01
Streatham	d					20a35									20 39										21a05
London Victoria ⊖	d	20 00		20 06				20 06	20 10	20 11	20 15	20 17	20 22						20 30	20 32			20 36		
Battersea Park	d	20 04						20 10		20a15	20 19		20 26	20a32					20 34						
Milton Keynes Central	d																								
Watford Junction	d																								
Harrow & Wealdstone ⊖	d																								
Wembley Central ⊖	d																								
Shepherd's Bush ⊖	d																								
Kensington (Olympia) ⊖	d																								
West Brompton ⊖	d																								
Imperial Wharf	d																								
Clapham Junction	d	20 08		20 12				20 14	20 16		20 23	20 23	20 30						20 38	20 38			20 42		
Latchmere	d																								
Wandsworth Common	d	20 11						20 17			20 26		20 33						20 41						
Balham ⊖	d	20 14						20 20			20 28		20 35						20 44						
Streatham Hill	d							20 23					20 38												
West Norwood	d		20 24					20 27					20 42								20 54				
Gipsy Hill	d		20 27					20 30					20 45			20a45					20 57				
Crystal Palace	d		20 29					20 33					20a47								20 59				
Birkbeck ⇌	d		20 33																		21 03				
Beckenham Junction ⇌	a		20 37																		21 07				
Streatham Common	d	20 18									20 32				20 42				20 48						
Norbury	d	20 20									20 35				20 45				20 50						
Thornton Heath	d	20 23									20 38				20 48				20 53						
Selhurst	d	20 27									20 41				20 51				20 57						
Norwood Junction	a						20 29	20 37														20 45			
	d						20 30	20 39														20 45			
West Croydon ⇌	a	20 32						20 43							20 56				21 02						
East Croydon ⇌	a			20 22	20 24		20 33		20 27		20 44	20 33						20 40		20 48		20 49	20 52	20 54	

Table 177 Mondays to Fridays from 21 May

Luton, Milton Keynes Central and London East and West Croydon via Tulse Hill - Crystal Palace - Norbury

Local Services

Network Diagram - see first Page of Table 177

		SN	SN	SN ■	SN	SN	SN ◇■	SN		SN	SN	SN	SN ■	SN	SN ■	SN	SN ◇■	FC ■	FC	SN	SN	SN ■	SN	SN	
London Bridge ⊖	d	20 36								20 41	20 48	20 52	20 58			21 03				21 06					
South Bermondsey	d									20 45	20 52					21 07									
Queens Rd Peckham	d									20 48	20 54					21 09									
Peckham Rye	d									20 50	20 57					21 12									
East Dulwich	d										21 00					21 15									
North Dulwich	d										21 02					21 17									
Luton	d																	20 16	20 20						
Luton Airport Parkway	d																	20 18	20 22						
St Pancras International ⊖	d																	20 54	21 06						
City Thameslink	d																	21 03	21 13						
London Blackfriars ⊖	d																	21 05	21 16						
Elephant & Castle ⊖	d																		21 19						
Loughborough Jn.	d																		21 23						
Herne Hill	d																		21 27						
Tulse Hill	d										21 05					21 21			21 31						
Streatham	d										21 09								21a35						
London Victoria ⊖	d		20 36	20 40	20 41	20 45	20 47	20 52						21 00	21 02		21 06				21 06	21 10	21 11	21 15	
Battersea Park	d		20 40		20a45	20 49		20 56		21a02				21 04							21 10		21a15	21 19	
Milton Keynes Central	d																								
Watford Junction	d																								
Harrow & Wealdstone ⊖	d																								
Wembley Central ⊖	d																								
Shepherd's Bush ⊖	d																								
Kensington (Olympia) ⊖	d																								
West Brompton ⊖	d																								
Imperial Wharf	d																								
Clapham Junction	d		20 44	20 46		20 53	20 53	21 00						21 08	21 08		21 12				21 14	21 16		21 23	
Latchmere	d																								
Wandsworth Common	d		20 47			20 56		21 03						21 11							21 17			21 26	
Balham ⊖	d		20 50			20 58		21 05						21 14							21 20			21 29	
Streatham Hill	d		20 53					21 08													21 23				
West Norwood	d		20 57					21 12								21 24					21 27				
Gipsy Hill	d		21 00					21 15				21a15				21 27					21 30				
Crystal Palace	d		21 03					21a17								21 29					21 33				
Birkbeck ⇌	d															21 33									
Beckenham Junction ⇌	a															21 37									
Streatham Common	d					21 02					21 12			21 18										21 33	
Norbury	d					21 05					21 15			21 20										21 35	
Thornton Heath	d					21 08					21 18			21 23										21 38	
Selhurst	d					21 11					21 21			21 27										21 41	
Norwood Junction	a	20 59	21 07																	21 29	21 37				
	d	21 00	21 09																	21 30	21 39				
West Croydon ⇌	a		21 13								21 26			21 32							21 43				
East Croydon ⇌	a	21 03		20 57		21 14	21 03						21 10		21 18		21 22	21 24		21 33		21 27		21 44	

Table 177

Mondays to Fridays

from 21 May

Luton, Milton Keynes Central and London East and West Croydon via Tulse Hill - Crystal Palace - Norbury

Local Services

Network Diagram - see first Page of Table 177

		SN	SN	SN	SN	SN	SN	SN	SN	SN	FC	FC	SN	SN	SN	SN		SN	SN	SN	SN	SN	SN	SN	SN
		◇1					1			◇1	1				1				◇1						◇1
London Bridge 4 ⊖	d			21 11	21 18	21 22	21 26		21 33				21 36								21 41	21 48	21 52		
South Bermondsey	d			21 15	21 22				21 37												21 45	21 52			
Queens Rd Peckham	d			21 18	21 24				21 39												21 48	21 54			
Peckham Rye 4	d			21 20	21 27				21 42												21 50	21 57			
East Dulwich	d				21 30				21 45													22 00			
North Dulwich	d				21 32				21 47													22 02			
Luton 10	d										20 46	20 50													
Luton Airport Parkway 7	d										20 48	20 52													
St Pancras International 15 ⊖	d										21 24	21 36													
City Thameslink 3	d										21 33	21 43													
London Blackfriars 3 ⊖	d										21 35	21 46													
Elephant & Castle ⊖	d											21 49													
Loughborough Jn.	d											21 53													
Herne Hill 4	d											21 57													
Tulse Hill 3	d				21 35				21 51			22 01										22 05			
Streatham 4	d				21 39							22a05										22 09			
London Victoria 15 ⊖	d	21 17	21 23					21 30		21 36				21 36	21 40	21 41		21 45	21 47	21 52				22 00	22 02
Battersea Park 4	d		21 27	21a32				21 34						21 40		21a45		21 49		21 56	22a02			22 04	
Milton Keynes Central	d																								
Watford Junction	d																								
Harrow & Wealdstone ⊖	d																								
Wembley Central ⊖	d																								
Shepherd's Bush ⊖	d																								
Kensington (Olympia) ⊖	d																								
West Brompton ⊖	d																								
Imperial Wharf	d																								
Clapham Junction 10	d	21 23	21 31					21 38		21 42				21 44	21 46			21 53	21 53	22 00				22 08	22 08
Latchmere	d																								
Wandsworth Common	d		21 34					21 41						21 47				21 56		22 03				22 11	
Balham 4 ⊖	d		21 36					21 44						21 50				21 58		22 05				22 14	
Streatham Hill	d		21 39											21 53						22 08					
West Norwood 4	d		21 43						21 54					21 57						22 12					
Gipsy Hill	d		21 46			21a45			21 57					22 00						22 15			22a15		
Crystal Palace 4	d		21a48						21 59					22 03						22a17					
Birkbeck	d								22 03																
Beckenham Junction 4	a								22 07																
Streatham Common 4	d				21 42			21 48										22 02				22 12		22 18	
Norbury	d				21 45			21 50										22 05				22 15		22 20	
Thornton Heath	d				21 48			21 53										22 08				22 18		22 23	
Selhurst 4	d				21 51			21 57										22 11				22 21		22 27	
Norwood Junction 2	a						21 37						21 59	22 07											
	d						21 38						22 00	22 09											
West Croydon 4	a				21 56			22 02						22 13								22 26		22 32	
East Croydon	a	21 33					21 41			21 52	21 54		22 03		21 57			22 14	22 03						22 18

Table 177

Mondays to Fridays

from 21 May

Luton, Milton Keynes Central and London East and West Croydon via Tulse Hill - Crystal Palace - Norbury

Local Services

Network Diagram - see first Page of Table 177

		SN	SN	FC	FC	SN	SN	SN		SN	SN	SN	SN	SN	SN	SN	SN	SN	SN	SN	FC	FC	SN	SN
			◇1	1				1										1			1			
London Bridge 4 ⊖	d	22 03				22 08							22 11	22 18	22 23	22 26			22 33				22 38	22 41
South Bermondsey	d	22 07											22 15	22 22					22 37					22 45
Queens Rd Peckham	d	22 09											22 18	22 24					22 39					22 48
Peckham Rye 4	d	22 12											22 20	22 27					22 42					22 50
East Dulwich	d	22 15												22 30					22 45					
North Dulwich	d	22 17												22 32					22 47					
Luton 10	d			21 16	21 20																21 46	21 50		
Luton Airport Parkway 7	d			21 18	21 22																21 48	21 52		
St Pancras International 15 ⊖	d			21 54	22 06																22 24	22 36		
City Thameslink 3	d			22 03	22 13																22 33	22 43		
London Blackfriars 3 ⊖	d			22 05	22 16																22 35	22 46		
Elephant & Castle ⊖	d				22 19																	22 49		
Loughborough Jn.	d				22 23																	22 53		
Herne Hill 4	d				22 27																	22 57		
Tulse Hill 3	d	22 21			22 31									22 35					22 51			23 01		
Streatham 4	d				22a35									22 39								23a05		
London Victoria 15 ⊖	d		22 06				22 06	22 10		22 11	22 15	22 22					22 30	22 32		22 36				
Battersea Park 4	d						22 10			22a15	22 19	22 26	22a32				22 34							23a02
Milton Keynes Central	d																							
Watford Junction	d																							
Harrow & Wealdstone ⊖	d																							
Wembley Central ⊖	d																							
Shepherd's Bush ⊖	d																							
Kensington (Olympia) ⊖	d																							
West Brompton ⊖	d																							
Imperial Wharf	d																							
Clapham Junction 10	d		22 12				22 14	22 16			22 23	22 30					22 38	22 38		22 42				
Latchmere	d																							
Wandsworth Common	d						22 17				22 26	22 33					22 41							
Balham 4 ⊖	d						22 20				22 28	22 35					22 44							
Streatham Hill	d						22 23					22 38												
West Norwood 4	d	22 24					22 27					22 42							22 54					
Gipsy Hill	d	22 27					22 30					22 45			22a45				22 57					
Crystal Palace 4	d	22 29					22 33					22a47							22 59					
Birkbeck	d	22 35																	23 03					
Beckenham Junction 4	a	22 38																	23 07					
Streatham Common 4	d										22 32			22 42			22 48							
Norbury	d										22 35			22 45			22 50							
Thornton Heath	d										22 38			22 48			22 53							
Selhurst 4	d										22 41			22 51			22 57							
Norwood Junction 2	a					22 31	22 37									22 38							23 01	
	d					22 32	22 39									22 38							23 02	
West Croydon 4	a						22 43							22 56			23 02							
East Croydon	a		22 22	22 24		22 35		22 26			22 44					22 42		22 48		22 52	22 54		23 06	

Table 177

Mondays to Fridays
from 21 May

Luton, Milton Keynes Central and London East and West Croydon via Tulse Hill - Crystal Palace - Norbury

Local Services

Network Diagram - see first Page of Table 177

		SN	SN	SN	SN	SN	SN	SN	SN	SN	SN	SN	SN	FC	SN	SN		FC	SN	SN	SN	SN	SN	SN	SN
				■			◇■					◇■	◇■	■						■			◇■		
London Bridge ■	⊖ d	22 56						22 48	22 52						23 06	23 05									23 11
South Bermondsey	d							22 52								23 09									23 15
Queens Rd Peckham	d							22 54								23 11									23 18
Peckham Rye ■	d							22 57								23 14									23 20
East Dulwich	d							23 00								23 17									
North Dulwich	d							23 02								23 19									
Luton ■	d													22 16				22 20							
Luton Airport Parkway ■	d													22 18				22 22							
St Pancras International ■	⊖ d													22 54				23 06							
City Thameslink ■	d													23 03											
London Blackfriars ■	⊖ d													23 05				23 16							
Elephant & Castle	⊖ d																	23 19							
Loughborough Jn.	d																	23s23							
Herne Hill ■	d																	23 27							
Tulse Hill ■	d							23 05								23 23		23 31							
Streatham ■	d							23 09										23a35							
London Victoria ■	⊖ d		22 36	22 40	22 41	22 45	22 47			22 52	23 00	23 02	23 06						23 06	23 10	23 11	23 15	23 17	23 22	
Battersea Park ■	d		22 40		22a45	22 49				22 56	23 04								23 10		23a15	23 19		23 26	23a32
Milton Keynes Central	d																								
Watford Junction	d																								
Harrow & Wealdstone	⊖ d																								
Wembley Central	⊖ d																								
Shepherd's Bush	⊖ d																								
Kensington (Olympia)	⊖ d																								
West Brompton	⊖ d																								
Imperial Wharf	d																								
Clapham Junction ■	d		22 46	22 46		22 53	22 53			23 00	23 08	23 08	23 12						23 14	23 16		23 23	23 23	23 30	
Latchmere	d																								
Wandsworth Common	d		22 49			22 56				23 03	23 11								23 17			23 26		23 33	
Balham ■	⊖ d		22 52			22 58				23 05	23 14								23 20			23 28		23 35	
Streatham Hill	d		22 55							23 08									23 23					23 38	
West Norwood ■	d		22 58							23 12						23 26			23 29					23 42	
Gipsy Hill	d		23 01						23a15	23 15						23 29			23 32					23 45	
Crystal Palace ■	d		23 04							23a17						23 31			23 35					23a47	
Birkbeck	⇌ d																								
Beckenham Junction ■	⇌ a																								
Streatham Common ■	d					23 02		23 12			23 18											23 32			
Norbury	d					23 05		23 15			23 20											23 35			
Thornton Heath	d					23 08		23 18			23 23											23 38			
Selhurst ■	d					23 11		23 21			23 27											23 41			
Norwood Junction ■	a	23 07	23 08												23 29	23 36			23 39						
	d	23 07	23 09												23 30				23 40						
West Croydon ■	⇌ a		23 13					23 26			23 32								23 44						
East Croydon	⇌ a	23 11		22 57		23 14	23 03					23 19	23 22	23 24	23 33					23 27		23 44	23 33		

Table 177

Mondays to Fridays
from 21 May

Luton, Milton Keynes Central and London East and West Croydon via Tulse Hill - Crystal Palace - Norbury

Local Services

Network Diagram - see first Page of Table 177

		SN	SN	SN	FC	SN	SN	SN		SN	FC	SN	SN	SN	SN	FC	FC	SN	SN	SN	SN	SN			
													FO					FX				FO			
				◇■	■	■								■	■	■	■								
London Bridge ■	⊖ d	23 18	23 22					23 36		23 33									23 48	23 52					
South Bermondsey	d	23 22								23 37									23 52						
Queens Rd Peckham	d	23 24								23 39									23 54						
Peckham Rye ■	d	23 27								23 42									23 57						
East Dulwich	d	23 30								23 45									00 01						
North Dulwich	d	23 32								23 47									00 03						
Luton ■	d				22 40						22 46					23 06	23 36								
Luton Airport Parkway ■	d				22 42						22 49					23 09	23 39								
St Pancras International ■	⊖ d				23 24						23 36					23 54	00 24								
City Thameslink ■	d																								
London Blackfriars ■	⊖ d				23 35						23 46					00 05	00 35								
Elephant & Castle	⊖ d										23 49														
Loughborough Jn.	d																								
Herne Hill ■	d										23 57														
Tulse Hill ■	d	23 35								23 51	00 01								00 06						
Streatham ■	d	23 39									00a05								00 10						
London Victoria ■	⊖ d			23 32			23 34					23 38	23 45	23 47	23 49			23 51			23 54	23 59			
Battersea Park ■	d						23 38					23 42	23 49					23 55			23 58	00 03			
Milton Keynes Central	d					22 11																			
Watford Junction	d					22 53																			
Harrow & Wealdstone	⊖ d					23 00																			
Wembley Central	⊖ d																								
Shepherd's Bush	⊖ d					23 21																			
Kensington (Olympia)	⊖ d					23 23																			
West Brompton	⊖ d					23 26																			
Imperial Wharf	d					23 28																			
Clapham Junction ■	d			23 38		23 40	23 42					23 46	23 53	23 53	23 56			23 59			00 02	00 07			
Latchmere	d																								
Wandsworth Common	d						23 45					23 49	23 56					00 02			00 05	00 10			
Balham ■	⊖ d					23 44	23 47					23 51	23 58					00 04			00 07	00 12			
Streatham Hill	d											23 54									00 10				
West Norwood ■	d									23 54		23 58									00 14				
Gipsy Hill	d		23a45							23 57		00 01								00a15	00 17				
Crystal Palace ■	d									23 59		00 03									00a19				
Birkbeck	⇌ d																								
Beckenham Junction ■	⇌ a																								
Streatham Common ■	d	23 42				23 48	23 51						00 02					00 08	00 13			00 16			
Norbury	d	23 45				23 51	23 54						00 05					00 11	00 15			00 19			
Thornton Heath	d	23 48				23 54	23 57						00 08					00 14	00 18			00 22			
Selhurst ■	d	23 51				23 57	23 59						00 11					00 17	00 21			00 25			
Norwood Junction ■	a							23 59		00 04		00 08													
	d							23 59				00 09													
West Croydon ■	⇌ a	23 56					00 03					00 14						00 21	00 28			00 30			
East Croydon	⇌ a			23 51	23 56	00 01		00 03					00 14	00 05	00 09	00 26	00 56								

Table 177

Saturdays

Luton, Milton Keynes Central and London East and West Croydon via Tulse Hill - Crystal Palace - Norbury

Local Services

Network Diagram - see first Page of Table 177

		SN	SN	SN	SN	FC	SN	SN	SN	SN	SN	SN	SN	FC	SN	FC		SN	SN	SN	FC	SN	SN	SN	SN
		■							■		■				◇■	■						■			
						A								B		A					B				
London Bridge ■ ⊖	d			23p36	23p33					23p48				23p59				00 06	00 03		00 12			00 18	
South Bermondsey	d				23p37					23p52									00 07					00 22	
Queens Rd Peckham	d				23p39					23p54									00 09					00 24	
Peckham Rye ■	d				23p42					23p57									00 12					00 27	
East Dulwich	d				23p45					00 01									00 15					00 30	
North Dulwich	d				23p47					00 03									00 17					00 32	
Luton ■	d					22p46										23p06									
Luton Airport Parkway ■	d					22p49										23p09									
St Pancras International ■ ⊖	d					23p36										23p54									
City Thameslink ■	d																								
London Blackfriars ■ ⊖	d					23p46										00 05									
Elephant & Castle ⊖	d					23p49																			
Loughborough Jn.	d																								
Herne Hill ■	d					23p57																			
Tulse Hill ■	d				23p51	00 01				00 06				00 09					00 21					00 35	
Streatham ■	d					00a05				00 10				00a13										00 39	
London Victoria ■ ⊖	d		23p34				23p38	23p45	23p47		23p49	23p54	23p59		00 05					00 07		00 14	00 16		00 22
Battersea Park ■	d		23p38				23p42	23p49				23p58	00 03							00 11			00 20		00 26
Milton Keynes Central	d	22p11																							
Watford Junction	d	22p53																							
Harrow & Wealdstone ⊖	d	23p00																							
Wembley Central ⊖	d																								
Shepherd's Bush ⊖	d	23p21																							
Kensington (Olympia) ⊖	d	23p23																							
West Brompton ⊖	d	23p26																							
Imperial Wharf	d	23p28																							
Clapham Junction ■	d	23p40	23p42				23p46	23p53	23p53		23p56	00 02	00 07		00 11					00 15		00 20	00 24		00 30
Latchmere	d																								
Wandsworth Common	d		23p45				23p49	23p56				00 05	00 10							00 18			00 27		00 33
Balham ■ ⊖	d	23p44	23p47				23p51	23p58				00 07	00 12							00 20			00 29		00 35
Streatham Hill	d						23p54					00 10								00 23					00 38
West Norwood ■	d				23p54		23p58					00 14							00 24	00 28					00 42
Gipsy Hill	d				23p57		00 01					00 17							00 27	00 31					00 45
Crystal Palace ■	d				23p59		00 03					00a19							00 29	00 33					00 47
Birkbeck	d																								
Beckenham Junction ■	a																								
Streatham Common ■	d	23p48	23p51					00 02		00 13			00 16										00 33	00 42	
Norbury	d	23p51	23p54					00 05		00 15			00 19										00 36	00 45	
Thornton Heath	d	23p54	23p57					00 08		00 18			00 22										00 39	00 48	
Selhurst ■	d	23p57	23p59					00 11		00 21			00 25										00 41	00 51	
Norwood Junction ■	a			23p59	00 04		00 08											00 29	00 34	00 38					00 52
	d			23p59			00 09											00 30		00 38					00 52
West Croydon ■	a		00 03				00 14			00 28			00 30							00 43				00 55	00 58
East Croydon	a	00 01		00 03				00 14	00 05		00 09				00 24	00 26		00 33			00 26	00 31	00 44		

A not 19 May

B 19 May

Table 177

Saturdays

Luton, Milton Keynes Central and London East and West Croydon via Tulse Hill - Crystal Palace - Norbury

Local Services

Network Diagram - see first Page of Table 177

		SN	SN	SN	SN	SN	SN	FC		FC	SN	SN	FC	FC	SN	SN	FC	SN	SN	FC	FC	SN	FC	FC
		◇■					◇■	■				◇■	■	■		◇■	■		■	■	■	■	■	■
		A					A	B		C			B	C	A	A	C	A		B	C		B	C
London Bridge ■ ⊖	d			00 36	00 33					00 42				01 05			01 35				02 05			03 05
South Bermondsey	d				00 37																			
Queens Rd Peckham	d				00 39																			
Peckham Rye ■	d				00 42																			
East Dulwich	d				00 45																			
North Dulwich	d				00 47																			
Luton ■	d							23p36					00 06							01 06			02 06	
Luton Airport Parkway ■	d							23p39					00 09							01 09			02 09	
St Pancras International ■ ⊖	d							00 24					00 54							01 54			02 54	
City Thameslink ■	d																							
London Blackfriars ■ ⊖	d							00 35					01 05							02 05			03 05	
Elephant & Castle ⊖	d																							
Loughborough Jn.	d																							
Herne Hill ■	d																							
Tulse Hill ■	d				00 51																			
Streatham ■	d																							
London Victoria ■ ⊖	d	00 25	00 34			00 37	00 40				00 42	01 00			01 12	01 30		01 42	02 00			03 00		
Battersea Park ■	d		00 38			00 41					00 46													
Milton Keynes Central	d																							
Watford Junction	d																							
Harrow & Wealdstone ⊖	d																							
Wembley Central ⊖	d																							
Shepherd's Bush ⊖	d																							
Kensington (Olympia) ⊖	d																							
West Brompton ⊖	d																							
Imperial Wharf	d																							
Clapham Junction ■	d	00 31	00 42			00 45	00 46				00 50	01 08			01 18	01 36		01 48	02 08			03 08		
Latchmere	d																							
Wandsworth Common	d		00 45			00 48					00 53													
Balham ■ ⊖	d		00 47			00 50					00 55				01 23			01 53						
Streatham Hill	d					00 53																		
West Norwood ■	d				00 54	00 58																		
Gipsy Hill	d				00 57	01 01																		
Crystal Palace ■	d				00 59	01 03																		
Birkbeck	d																							
Beckenham Junction ■	a																							
Streatham Common ■	d		00 51								00 59				01 27			02 00						
Norbury	d		00 54								01 02				01 29			02 02						
Thornton Heath	d		00 57								01 05				01 32			02 05						
Selhurst ■	d		01 00								01 07				01 35			02 08						
Norwood Junction ■	a			00 59	01 04	01 08																		
	d			01 00		01 08																		
West Croydon ■	a		01 04			01 13																		
East Croydon	a	00 40		01 03			00 55	00 56		00 56	01 10	01 21	01 31	01 31	01 38	01 45	02 02	02 11	02 21	02 31	02 31	03 21	03 31	03 31

A 28 July, 4 August, 11 August, 1 September, 8 September

B not 19 May

C 19 May

Table 177

Saturdays

Luton, Milton Keynes Central and London East and West Croydon via Tulse Hill - Crystal Palace - Norbury

Local Services

Network Diagram - see first Page of Table 177

		FC	FC	SN	FC	FC	FC	FC	SN	FC	FC	SN	FC	FC	SN	FC	SN	FC	SN	SN	FC	SN	SN	FC
		1	1	◇1	1	1	1	1	◇1	1	1	◇1	1	1	1	1					1	1	1	1
		A			B	A	B	A			A			A							A			
London Bridge 4 ⊖	d	03 35				04 05		04 35			05 05			05 52			06 11				06 27			
South Bermondsey	d																06 15							
Queens Rd Peckham	d																06 18							
Peckham Rye 4	d																06 20							
East Dulwich	d																							
North Dulwich	d																							
Luton 10	d				03 06		03 36			04 06			04 46			05 16								05 46
Luton Airport Parkway 7	d				03 09		03 39			04 09			04 49			05 19								05 49
St Pancras International 15 ⊖	d		03 28		03 54		04 24			04 54			05 34			05 54								06 24
City Thameslink 3	d																							
London Blackfriars 3 ⊖	d		03 39		04 05		04 35			05 04			05 45			06 05		06 16						06 35
Elephant & Castle ⊖	d																	06 19						
Loughborough Jn.	d																							
Herne Hill 4	d																	06 27						
Tulse Hill 3	d																	06 31						
Streatham 4	d																	06a35						
London Victoria 15 ⊖	d			04 00					05 02			05 32			06 02				06 23				06 32	
Battersea Park 4	d																06a32							
Milton Keynes Central	d																							
Watford Junction	d																							
Harrow & Wealdstone ⊖	d																					05 52		
Wembley Central ⊖	d																					05 58		
Shepherd's Bush ⊖	d																					06 20		
Kensington (Olympia) ⊖	d																					06 23		
West Brompton ⊖	d																					06 26		
Imperial Wharf	d																					06 28		
Clapham Junction 10	d			04 08					05 08			05 38			06 08				06 30			06 34	06 38	
Latchmere	d																							
Wandsworth Common	d																		06 33			06 37		
Balham 4 ⊖	d																		06 35			06 40		
Streatham Hill	d																							
West Norwood 4	d																							
Gipsy Hill	d																							
Crystal Palace 4	d																							
Birkbeck	d																							
Beckenham Junction 4	a																							
Streatham Common 4	d																		06 39			06 45		
Norbury	d																		06 42			06 48		
Thornton Heath	d																		06 45			06 51		
Selhurst 4	d																		06 48			06 54		
Norwood Junction 2	a																							
	d																			06 33				
West Croydon 4	a																		06 52					
East Croydon	a	04 01	04 03	04 21	04 31	04 31	05 01	05 01	05 21	05 31	05 31	05 47	06 04	06 04	06 17	06 24				06 36	06 39	06 57	06 47	06 54

A 19 May

B not 19 May

Table 177

Saturdays

Luton, Milton Keynes Central and London East and West Croydon via Tulse Hill - Crystal Palace - Norbury

Local Services

Network Diagram - see first Page of Table 177

		FC	SN	SN	SN	SN	FC	SN	SN	SN	FC	SN	FC	SN	SN	FC	FC	SN	SN	SN	FC	SN	SN
							1				1		1	1	◇1	1					1		
							A						A										
London Bridge 4 ⊖	d		06 36			06 41	06 42		06 48	06 50			06 57	07 03				07 06	07 11	07 20			
South Bermondsey	d					06 45			06 52										07 15				
Queens Rd Peckham	d					06 48			06 54										07 18				
Peckham Rye 4	d					06 50			06 57										07 20				
East Dulwich	d								07 00														
North Dulwich	d								07 02														
Luton 10	d										06 04					06 18					06 34		
Luton Airport Parkway 7	d										06 06					06 20					06 36		
St Pancras International 15 ⊖	d	06 34									06 39					06 54	07 04				07 09		
City Thameslink 3	d																						
London Blackfriars 3 ⊖	d	06 46									06 50					07 05	07 16				07 20		
Elephant & Castle ⊖	d	06 49															07 19						
Loughborough Jn.	d	06 53															07 23						
Herne Hill 4	d	06 57															07 27						
Tulse Hill 3	d	07 01							07 05								07 31						
Streatham 4	d	07a05							07 09								07a35						
London Victoria 15 ⊖	d			06 41	06 43			06 53							07 06							07 06	07 11
Battersea Park 4	d			06a45	06 47	07a02													07a32			07 11	07a15
Milton Keynes Central	d																						
Watford Junction	d																						
Harrow & Wealdstone ⊖	d																						
Wembley Central ⊖	d																						
Shepherd's Bush ⊖	d																						
Kensington (Olympia) ⊖	d																						
West Brompton ⊖	d																						
Imperial Wharf	d																						
Clapham Junction 10	d				06 51			07 00							07 12							07 14	
Latchmere	d																						
Wandsworth Common	d				06 54			07 03														07 18	
Balham 4 ⊖	d				06 56			07 05														07 20	
Streatham Hill	d											06 53										07 23	
West Norwood 4	d											06 57										07 27	
Gipsy Hill	d											07 00										07 30	
Crystal Palace 4	d											07 02										07 32	
Birkbeck	d																						
Beckenham Junction 4	a																						
Streatham Common 4	d				07 00			07 09	07 12														
Norbury	d				07 03			07 12	07 15														
Thornton Heath	d				07 06			07 15	07 18														
Selhurst 4	d				07 09			07 18	07 21														
Norwood Junction 2	a		06 59							07 02		07 07		07 16				07 29		07 32		07 37	
	d		07 00							07 03		07 09		07 16				07 30		07 33		07 39	
West Croydon 4	a							07 22	07 26			07 14										07 43	
East Croydon	a		07 03		07 12		06 54			07 06	07 09		07 09	07 20	07 22	07 24		07 33		07 36	07 39		

A 19 May

Luton, Milton Keynes Central and London East and West Croydon via Tulse Hill - Crystal Palace - Norbury

Local Services

Network Diagram - see first Page of Table 177

Station		SN	SN	SN	FC	SN	SN	SN	SN	SN	SN	FC	FC	SN	SN	SN		SN	SN	SN	SN	SN	SN	SN	FC
					■ A	■	◇■			■	◇■	■		■								◇■		◇■	■
London Bridge ■ ⊖	d			07 18	07 27			07 33		07 33				07 45	07 36	07 41		07 50							
South Bermondsey	d			07 22				07 37								07 45									
Queens Rd Peckham	d			07 24				07 39								07 48									
Peckham Rye ■	d			07 27				07 42								07 50									
East Dulwich	d			07 30				07 45																	
North Dulwich	d			07 32				07 47																	
Luton ■	d											06 48													07 04
Luton Airport Parkway ■	d											06 50													07 06
St Pancras International ■ ⊖	d											07 24	07 34												07 39
City Thameslink ■	d																								
London Blackfriars ■ ⊖	d											07 35	07 46												07 50
Elephant & Castle ⊖	d												07 49												
Loughborough Jn.	d												07 53												
Herne Hill ■	d												07 57												
Tulse Hill ■	d			07 35				07 50					08 01												
Streatham ■	d			07 39									08a05												
London Victoria ■ ⊖	d	07 13	07 23				07 32		07 33		07 36								07 36	07 41	07 43	07 47	07 49	07 51	
Battersea Park ■	d	07 17							07 37							08a02			07 40	07a45	07 47		07 53		
Milton Keynes Central	d																								
Watford Junction	d					06 55																			
Harrow & Wealdstone ⊖	d					07 01																			
Wembley Central ⊖	d					07 06																			
Shepherd's Bush ⊖	d					07 19																			
Kensington (Olympia) ⊖	d					07 22																			
West Brompton ⊖	d					07 25																			
Imperial Wharf	d					07 27																			
Clapham Junction ■	d	07 21	07 30			07 34	07 38		07 41		07 42								07 44		07 51	07 53	07 57		
Latchmere	d																								
Wandsworth Common	d	07 24	07 33			07 37			07 44										07 47		07 54		08 00		
Balham ■ ⊖	d	07 26	07 35			07 40			07 46										07 50		07 56		08 02		
Streatham Hill	d																		07 53				08 05		
West Norwood ■	d							07 53											07 57				08 10		
Gipsy Hill	d							07 56											08 00				08 13		
Crystal Palace ■	d							07 59											08 02				08a16		
Birkbeck	d							08 03																	
Beckenham Junction ■	a							08 06																	
Streatham Common ■	d	07 30	07 39	07 42		07 45			07 50												08 00				
Norbury	d	07 33	07 42	07 45		07 48			07 53												08 03				
Thornton Heath	d	07 36	07 45	07 48		07 51			07 56												08 06				
Selhurst ■	d	07 39	07 48	07 51		07 54			07 59												08 09				
Norwood Junction ■	a									07 46				07 55	07 59			08 02	08 07						
	d									07 46				07 56	08 00			08 03	08 09						
West Croydon ■	a		07 52	07 56					08 03										08 13						
East Croydon	a	07 42			07 39	07 57	07 47			07 50	07 52	07 54		07 59	08 03			08 06			08 12	08 02		08 07	08 09

A 19 May

Luton, Milton Keynes Central and London East and West Croydon via Tulse Hill - Crystal Palace - Norbury

Local Services

Network Diagram - see first Page of Table 177

Station		SN	SN	FC	SN	SN	SN	SN		FC	FC	SN	SN	SN	SN	SN	SN	SN	SN	FC	SN	SN	SN	SN	
				■ A			■	◇■		■		■							◇■	■					
London Bridge ■ ⊖	d		07 48	07 57	08 03		08 03					08 15	08 06	08 11	08 20								08 18	08 22	
South Bermondsey	d		07 52		08 07									08 15									08 22		
Queens Rd Peckham	d		07 54		08 09									08 18									08 24		
Peckham Rye ■	d		07 57		08 12									08 20									08 27		
East Dulwich	d		08 00		08 15																		08 30		
North Dulwich	d		08 02		08 17																		08 32		
Luton ■	d									07 18	07 14									07 34					
Luton Airport Parkway ■	d									07 20	07 16									07 36					
St Pancras International ■ ⊖	d									07 54	08 04									08 09					
City Thameslink ■	d																								
London Blackfriars ■ ⊖	d									08 05	08 16									08 20					
Elephant & Castle ⊖	d										08 19														
Loughborough Jn.	d										08 23														
Herne Hill ■	d										08 27														
Tulse Hill ■	d		08 05		08 20						08 31												08 35		
Streatham ■	d		08 09								08a35												08 39		
London Victoria ■ ⊖	d	07 53				08 03		08 06								08 06	08 11	08 13	08 17		08 19	08 23			
Battersea Park ■	d					08 07								08a32		08 10	08a15	08 17			08 23				
Milton Keynes Central	d																								
Watford Junction	d																								
Harrow & Wealdstone ⊖	d																								
Wembley Central ⊖	d																								
Shepherd's Bush ⊖	d																								
Kensington (Olympia) ⊖	d																								
West Brompton ⊖	d																								
Imperial Wharf	d																								
Clapham Junction ■	d	08 00				08 11		08 12								08 14		08 21	08 23		08 27	08 30			
Latchmere	d																								
Wandsworth Common	d	08 03				08 14										08 17		08 24			08 30	08 33			
Balham ■ ⊖	d	08 05				08 16										08 20		08 26			08 32	08 35			
Streatham Hill	d															08 23					08 35				
West Norwood ■	d				08 23											08 27					08 40				
Gipsy Hill	d				08 26											08 30					08 43			08a45	
Crystal Palace ■	d				08 29											08 32					08a46				
Birkbeck	d				08 33																				
Beckenham Junction ■	a				08 36																				
Streatham Common ■	d	08 09	08 12			08 20												08 30				08 39	08 42		
Norbury	d	08 12	08 15			08 23												08 33				08 42	08 45		
Thornton Heath	d	08 15	08 18			08 26												08 36				08 45	08 48		
Selhurst ■	d	08 18	08 21			08 29												08 39				08 48	08 51		
Norwood Junction ■	a						08 16					08 25	08 29		08 32	08 37									
	d						08 16					08 26	08 30		08 33	08 39									
West Croydon ■	a	08 22	08 26			08 33										08 43						08 52	08 56		
East Croydon	a			08 09			08 20	08 22		08 24		08 29	08 33		08 36			08 42	08 32	08 39					

A 19 May

Table 177

Luton, Milton Keynes Central and London East and West Croydon via Tulse Hill - Crystal Palace - Norbury

Local Services

Network Diagram - see first Page of Table 177

		FC ■ A	SN ■	SN ◇■	SN	SN	SN ■	SN ◇■	FC ■	FC	SN ■	SN	SN	SN	SN	SN		SN	SN ◇■	SN	SN ◇■	FC ■	SN	SN	SN
London Bridge ⊖	d	08 27			08 33		08 33				08 45	08 36	08 41	08 50										08 48	08 52
South Bermondsey	d				08 37								08 45											08 52	
Queens Rd Peckham	d				08 39								08 48											08 54	
Peckham Rye	d				08 42								08 50											08 57	
East Dulwich	d				08 45																			09 00	
North Dulwich	d				08 47																			09 02	
Luton	d								07 48	07 44												08 04			
Luton Airport Parkway	d								07 50	07 46												08 06			
St Pancras International ⊖	d								08 24	08 34												08 39			
City Thameslink	d																								
London Blackfriars ⊖	d								08 35	08 46												08 50			
Elephant & Castle ⊖	d									08 49															
Loughborough Jn.	d									08 53															
Herne Hill	d									08 57															
Tulse Hill	d				08 50					09 01														09 05	
Streatham	d									09a05														09 09	
London Victoria ⊖	d			08 32		08 33		08 36							08 36	08 41		08 43	08 47	08 49	08 51		08 53		
Battersea Park	d					08 37							09a02		08 40	08a45		08 47		08 53					
Milton Keynes Central	d		07 13																						
Watford Junction	d		07 52																						
Harrow & Wealdstone ⊖	d		07 59																						
Wembley Central ⊖	d		08 04																						
Shepherd's Bush ⊖	d		08 19																						
Kensington (Olympia) ⊖	d		08 22																						
West Brompton ⊖	d		08 25																						
Imperial Wharf	d		08 27																						
Clapham Junction	d		08 34	08 38		08 41		08 42							08 44			08 51	08 53	08 57			09 00		
Latchmere	d																								
Wandsworth Common	d		08 37			08 44									08 47			08 54		09 00			09 03		
Balham ⊖	d		08 40			08 46									08 50			08 56		09 02			09 05		
Streatham Hill	d														08 53					09 05					
West Norwood	d				08 53										08 57					09 10					
Gipsy Hill	d				08 56										09 00					09 13					
Crystal Palace	d				08 59										09 02					09a16					09a15
Birkbeck	d				09 03																				
Beckenham Junction	a				09 06																				
Streatham Common	d		08 45			08 50												09 00					09 09	09 12	
Norbury	d		08 48			08 53												09 03					09 12	09 15	
Thornton Heath	d		08 51			08 56												09 06					09 15	09 18	
Selhurst	d		08 54			08 59												09 09					09 18	09 21	
Norwood Junction	a						08 46				08 55	08 59		09 02	09 07										
	d						08 46				08 56	09 00		09 03	09 09										
West Croydon	a					09 03									09 13								09 22	09 26	
East Croydon	a	08 39	08 57	08 47			08 50	08 52	08 54		08 59	09 03		09 06				09 12	09 02		09 07	09 09			

A 19 May

Table 177

Luton, Milton Keynes Central and London East and West Croydon via Tulse Hill - Crystal Palace - Norbury

Local Services

Network Diagram - see first Page of Table 177

		FC ■ A	SN	SN	SN ■	SN ◇■	FC ■	FC		SN ■	SN	SN	SN	SN	SN	SN	SN ◇■	FC ■	SN	SN	SN	SN	FC ■ A	SN ■	
London Bridge ⊖	d	08 57	09 03		09 03					09 15	09 06	09 11	09 20								09 18	09 22	09 27		
South Bermondsey	d		09 07									09 15									09 22				
Queens Rd Peckham	d		09 09									09 18									09 24				
Peckham Rye	d		09 12									09 20									09 27				
East Dulwich	d		09 15																		09 30				
North Dulwich	d		09 17																		09 32				
Luton	d						08 18	08 14										08 34							
Luton Airport Parkway	d						08 20	08 16										08 36							
St Pancras International ⊖	d						08 54	09 04										09 09							
City Thameslink	d						09 03	09 13										09 18							
London Blackfriars ⊖	d						09 05	09 16										09 20							
Elephant & Castle ⊖	d							09 19																	
Loughborough Jn.	d							09 23																	
Herne Hill	d							09 27																	
Tulse Hill	d		09 20					09 31													09 35				
Streatham	d							09a35													09 39				
London Victoria ⊖	d			09 03		09 06								09 06	09 11	09 13	09 17		09 19	09 23					
Battersea Park	d			09 07								09a32		09 10	09a15	09 17			09 23						
Milton Keynes Central	d																							08 13	
Watford Junction	d																							08 52	
Harrow & Wealdstone ⊖	d																							08 59	
Wembley Central ⊖	d																							09 04	
Shepherd's Bush ⊖	d																							09 19	
Kensington (Olympia) ⊖	d																							09 22	
West Brompton ⊖	d																							09 25	
Imperial Wharf	d																							09 27	
Clapham Junction	d			09 11		09 12								09 14		09 21	09 23		09 27	09 30				09 34	
Latchmere	d																								
Wandsworth Common	d			09 14										09 17		09 24			09 30	09 33				09 37	
Balham ⊖	d			09 16										09 20		09 26			09 32	09 35				09 40	
Streatham Hill	d													09 23					09 35						
West Norwood	d		09 23											09 27					09 40						
Gipsy Hill	d		09 26											09 30					09 43			09a45			
Crystal Palace	d		09 29											09 32					09a46						
Birkbeck	d		09 33																						
Beckenham Junction	a		09 36																						
Streatham Common	d			09 20												09 30				09 39	09 42			09 45	
Norbury	d			09 23												09 33				09 42	09 45			09 48	
Thornton Heath	d			09 26												09 36				09 45	09 48			09 51	
Selhurst	d			09 29												09 39				09 48	09 51			09 54	
Norwood Junction	a				09 16					09 25	09 29		09 32	09 37											
	d				09 16					09 26	09 30		09 33	09 39											
West Croydon	a			09 33										09 43						09 52	09 56				
East Croydon	a	09 09			09 20	09 22	09 24			09 29	09 33		09 36			09 42	09 32	09 39					09 39	09 57	

A 19 May

Table 177

Luton, Milton Keynes Central and London East and West Croydon via Tulse Hill - Crystal Palace - Norbury

Local Services

Network Diagram - see first Page of Table 177

		SN ◇1	SN	SN	SN 1	SN ◇1	FC 1	FC	SN 1	SN	SN	SN	SN	SN	SN	SN ◇1		SN	SN ◇1	FC 1		FC 1	SN	SN
London Bridge ⊖	d		09 33		09 33				09 45	09 36	09 41	09 50									and at the same minutes past each hour until			16 48
South Bermondsey	d		09 37								09 45													16 52
Queens Rd Peckham	d		09 39								09 48													16 54
Peckham Rye	d		09 42								09 50													16 57
East Dulwich	d		09 45																					17 00
North Dulwich	d		09 47																					17 02
Luton	d						08 48	08 44												09 04		16 04		
Luton Airport Parkway	d						08 50	08 46												09 06		16 06		
St Pancras International ⊖	d						09 24	09 34												09 39		16 39		
City Thameslink	d						09 33	09 43												09 48		16 48		
London Blackfriars ⊖	d						09 35	09 46												09 50		16 50		
Elephant & Castle ⊖	d							09 49																
Loughborough Jn.	d							09 53																
Herne Hill	d							09 57																
Tulse Hill	d		09 50					10 01																17 05
Streatham	d							10a05																17 09
London Victoria ⊖	d	09 32		09 33		09 36							09 36	09 41	09 43	09 47		09 49	09 51				16 53	
Battersea Park	d			09 37							10a02		09 40	09a45	09 47			09 53						
Milton Keynes Central	d																							
Watford Junction	d																							
Harrow & Wealdstone ⊖	d																							
Wembley Central ⊖	d																							
Shepherd's Bush ⊖	d																							
Kensington (Olympia) ⊖	d																							
West Brompton ⊖	d																							
Imperial Wharf	d																							
Clapham Junction	d	09 38		09 41		09 42							09 44		09 51	09 53		09 57					17 00	
Latchmere	d																							
Wandsworth Common	d			09 44									09 47		09 54			10 00					17 03	
Balham ⊖	d			09 46									09 50		09 56			10 02					17 05	
Streatham Hill	d												09 53					10 05						
West Norwood	d		09 53										09 57					10 10						
Gipsy Hill	d		09 56										10 00					10 13						
Crystal Palace	d		09 59										10 02					10a16						
Birkbeck	d		10 03																					
Beckenham Junction	a		10 06																					
Streatham Common	d			09 50											10 00								17 09	17 12
Norbury	d			09 53											10 03								17 12	17 15
Thornton Heath	d			09 56											10 06								17 15	17 18
Selhurst	d			09 59											10 09								17 18	17 21
Norwood Junction	a				09 46				09 55	09 59		10 02	10 07											
	d				09 46				09 56	10 00		10 03	10 09											
West Croydon	a			10 03									10 13										17 22	17 26
East Croydon	a	09 47			09 50	09 52	09 54		09 59	10 03		10 06			10 12	10 02			10 07	10 09		17 09		

Table 177

Luton, Milton Keynes Central and London East and West Croydon via Tulse Hill - Crystal Palace - Norbury

Local Services

Network Diagram - see first Page of Table 177

		SN	FC 1 A	SN	SN	SN 1	SN ◇1	FC 1		FC	SN 1	SN	SN	SN	SN	SN	SN	SN ◇1	FC 1	SN	SN	SN	SN	FC 1 A
London Bridge ⊖	d	16 52	16 57	17 03		17 03					17 15	17 06	17 11	17 20								17 18	17 22	17 27
South Bermondsey	d			17 07									17 15									17 22		
Queens Rd Peckham	d			17 09									17 18									17 24		
Peckham Rye	d			17 12									17 20									17 27		
East Dulwich	d			17 15																		17 30		
North Dulwich	d			17 17																		17 32		
Luton	d							16 18		16 14									16 34					
Luton Airport Parkway	d							16 20		16 16									16 36					
St Pancras International ⊖	d							16 54		17 04									17 09					
City Thameslink	d							17 03		17 13									17 18					
London Blackfriars ⊖	d							17 05		17 16									17 20					
Elephant & Castle ⊖	d									17 19														
Loughborough Jn.	d									17 23														
Herne Hill	d									17 27														
Tulse Hill	d			17 20						17 31												17 35		
Streatham	d									17a35												17 39		
London Victoria ⊖	d				17 03		17 06								17 06	17 11	17 13	17 17		17 19	17 23			
Battersea Park	d				17 07								17a32		17 10	17a15	17 17			17 23				
Milton Keynes Central	d																							
Watford Junction	d																							
Harrow & Wealdstone ⊖	d																							
Wembley Central ⊖	d																							
Shepherd's Bush ⊖	d																							
Kensington (Olympia) ⊖	d																							
West Brompton ⊖	d																							
Imperial Wharf	d																							
Clapham Junction	d				17 11		17 12								17 14		17 21	17 23		17 27	17 30			
Latchmere	d																							
Wandsworth Common	d				17 14										17 17		17 24			17 30	17 33			
Balham ⊖	d				17 16										17 20		17 26			17 32	17 35			
Streatham Hill	d														17 23					17 35				
West Norwood	d			17 23											17 27					17 40				
Gipsy Hill	d	17a15		17 26											17 30					17 43			17a45	
Crystal Palace	d			17 29											17 32					17a46				
Birkbeck	d			17 33																				
Beckenham Junction	a			17 36																				
Streatham Common	d				17 20												17 30				17 39	17 42		
Norbury	d				17 23												17 33				17 42	17 45		
Thornton Heath	d				17 26												17 36				17 45	17 48		
Selhurst	d				17 29												17 39				17 48	17 51		
Norwood Junction	a					17 16					17 25	17 29		17 32	17 37									
	d					17 16					17 26	17 30		17 33	17 39									
West Croydon	a				17 33										17 43						17 52	17 56		
East Croydon	a		17 09			17 20	17 22	17 24			17 29	17 33		17 36			17 42	17 32	17 39					17 39

A 19 May

Table 177

Luton, Milton Keynes Central and London East and West Croydon via Tulse Hill - Crystal Palace - Norbury

Local Services

Network Diagram - see first Page of Table 177

		SN	SN	SN	SN	SN	SN	FC	FC	SN	SN	SN	SN	SN	SN	SN		SN	SN	SN	FC	SN	SN	SN	FC
		1	◇1			1	◇1	1		1								◇1		◇1	1				1
																									A
London Bridge 4 ⊖	d			17 33		17 33				17 45	17 36	17 41	17 50										17 48	17 52	17 57
South Bermondsey	d			17 37								17 45											17 52		
Queens Rd Peckham	d			17 39								17 48											17 54		
Peckham Rye 4	d			17 42								17 50											17 57		
East Dulwich	d			17 45																			18 00		
North Dulwich	d			17 47																			18 02		
Luton 10	d							16 48	16 44												17 04				
Luton Airport Parkway 7	d							16 50	16 46												17 06				
St Pancras International 15 ⊖	d							17 24	17 34												17 39				
City Thameslink 3	d							17 33	17 43												17 48				
London Blackfriars 3 ⊖	d							17 35	17 46												17 50				
Elephant & Castle ⊖	d								17 49																
Loughborough Jn.	d								17 53																
Herne Hill 4	d								17 57																
Tulse Hill 3	d			17 50					18 01														18 05		
Streatham 4	d								18a05														18 09		
London Victoria 15 ⊖	d		17 32		17 33		17 36							17 36	17 41	17 43		17 47	17 49	17 51		17 53			
Battersea Park 4	d				17 37							18a02		17 40	17a45	17 47			17 53						
Milton Keynes Central	d	16 13																							
Watford Junction	d	16 52																							
Harrow & Wealdstone ⊖	d	16 59																							
Wembley Central ⊖	d	17 04																							
Shepherd's Bush ⊖	d	17 19																							
Kensington (Olympia) ⊖	d	17 22																							
West Brompton ⊖	d	17 25																							
Imperial Wharf	d	17 27																							
Clapham Junction 10	d	17 34	17 38		17 41		17 42							17 44		17 51		17 53	17 57			18 00			
Latchmere	d																								
Wandsworth Common	d	17 37			17 44									17 47		17 54			18 00			18 03			
Balham 4 ⊖	d	17 40			17 46									17 50		17 56			18 02			18 05			
Streatham Hill	d													17 53					18 05						
West Norwood 4	d			17 53										17 57					18 10						
Gipsy Hill	d			17 56										18 00					18 13						
Crystal Palace 4	d			17 59										18 02					18a16					18a15	
Birkbeck	d			18 03																					
Beckenham Junction 4	a			18 06																					
Streatham Common 4	d	17 45			17 50											18 00						18 09	18 12		
Norbury	d	17 48			17 53											18 03						18 12	18 15		
Thornton Heath	d	17 51			17 56											18 06						18 15	18 18		
Selhurst 4	d	17 54			17 59											18 09						18 18	18 21		
Norwood Junction 2	a					17 46				17 56	17 59		18 02	18 07											
	d					17 46				17 56	18 00		18 03	18 09											
West Croydon 4	a				18 03									18 13								18 22	18 26		
East Croydon	a	17 57	17 47			17 50	17 52	17 54		18 00	18 03		18 06			18 12		18 02		18 07	18 09				18 09

A 19 May

Table 177

Luton, Milton Keynes Central and London East and West Croydon via Tulse Hill - Crystal Palace - Norbury

Local Services

Network Diagram - see first Page of Table 177

		SN	SN	SN	SN	FC	FC	SN		SN	SN	SN	SN	SN	SN	SN	FC	SN	SN	SN	SN	FC	SN	SN
				1	◇1	1		1								◇1	1					1	1	◇1
																						A		
London Bridge 4 ⊖	d	18 03		18 03				18 15		18 06	18 11	18 20								18 18	18 22	18 27		
South Bermondsey	d	18 07									18 15									18 22				
Queens Rd Peckham	d	18 09									18 18									18 24				
Peckham Rye 4	d	18 12									18 20									18 27				
East Dulwich	d	18 15																		18 30				
North Dulwich	d	18 17																		18 32				
Luton 10	d					17 18	17 14										17 34							
Luton Airport Parkway 7	d					17 20	17 16										17 36							
St Pancras International 15 ⊖	d					17 54	18 04										18 09							
City Thameslink 3	d					18 03	18 13										18 18							
London Blackfriars 3 ⊖	d					18 05	18 16										18 20							
Elephant & Castle ⊖	d						18 19																	
Loughborough Jn.	d						18 23																	
Herne Hill 4	d						18 27																	
Tulse Hill 3	d	18 20					18 31													18 35				
Streatham 4	d						18a35													18 39				
London Victoria 15 ⊖	d		18 03		18 06								18 06	18 11	18 13	18 17		18 19	18 23					18 32
Battersea Park 4	d		18 07								18a32		18 10	18a15	18 17			18 23						
Milton Keynes Central	d																						17 13	
Watford Junction	d																						17 52	
Harrow & Wealdstone ⊖	d																						17 59	
Wembley Central ⊖	d																						18 04	
Shepherd's Bush ⊖	d																						18 19	
Kensington (Olympia) ⊖	d																						18 22	
West Brompton ⊖	d																						18 25	
Imperial Wharf	d																						18 27	
Clapham Junction 10	d		18 11		18 12								18 14		18 21	18 23		18 27	18 30				18 34	18 38
Latchmere	d																							
Wandsworth Common	d		18 14										18 17		18 24			18 30	18 33				18 37	
Balham 4 ⊖	d		18 16										18 20		18 26			18 32	18 35				18 40	
Streatham Hill	d												18 23					18 35						
West Norwood 4	d	18 23											18 27					18 40						
Gipsy Hill	d	18 26											18 30					18 43						
Crystal Palace 4	d	18 29											18 32					18a46			18a45			
Birkbeck	d	18 33																						
Beckenham Junction 4	a	18 36																						
Streatham Common 4	d		18 20												18 30				18 39	18 42			18 45	
Norbury	d		18 23												18 33				18 42	18 45			18 48	
Thornton Heath	d		18 26												18 36				18 45	18 48			18 51	
Selhurst 4	d		18 29												18 39				18 48	18 51			18 54	
Norwood Junction 2	a			18 16				18 25		18 29		18 32	18 37											
	d			18 16				18 26		18 30		18 33	18 39											
West Croydon 4	a		18 33										18 43						18 52	18 56				
East Croydon	a			18 20	18 22	18 24		18 29		18 33		18 36			18 42	18 32	18 39					18 39	18 57	18 47

A 19 May

Table 177

Luton, Milton Keynes Central and London East and West Croydon via Tulse Hill - Crystal Palace - Norbury

Local Services

Network Diagram - see first Page of Table 177

		SN	SN	SN ■	SN ◇■	FC ■	FC	SN ■	SN	SN	SN	SN	SN	SN	SN ◇■	SN		SN ◇■	FC ■	SN	SN	SN	FC ■ A	SN	SN
London Bridge ■ ⊖	d	18 33		18 33				18 45	18 36	18 41	18 50										18 48	18 52	18 57	19 03	
South Bermondsey	d	18 37								18 45											18 52			19 07	
Queens Rd Peckham	d	18 39								18 48											18 54			19 09	
Peckham Rye ■	d	18 42								18 50											18 57			19 12	
East Dulwich	d	18 45																			19 00			19 15	
North Dulwich	d	18 47																			19 02			19 17	
Luton ■	d					17 48	17 44												18 04						
Luton Airport Parkway ■	d					17 50	17 46												18 06						
St Pancras International ■ ⊖	d					18 24	18 34												18 39						
City Thameslink ■	d					18 33	18 43												18 48						
London Blackfriars ■ ⊖	d					18 35	18 46												18 50						
Elephant & Castle ⊖	d						18 49																		
Loughborough Jn.	d						18 53																		
Herne Hill ■	d						18 57																		
Tulse Hill ■	d	18 50					19 01														19 05			19 20	
Streatham ■	d						19a05														19 09				
London Victoria ■ ⊖	d		18 33		18 36							18 36	18 41	18 43	18 47	18 49		18 51		18 53					19 03
Battersea Park ■	d		18 37							19a02		18 40	18a45	18 47		18 53									19 07
Milton Keynes Central	d																								
Watford Junction	d																								
Harrow & Wealdstone ⊖	d																								
Wembley Central ⊖	d																								
Shepherd's Bush ⊖	d																								
Kensington (Olympia) ⊖	d																								
West Brompton ⊖	d																								
Imperial Wharf	d																								
Clapham Junction ■	d		18 41		18 42							18 44		18 51	18 53	18 57				19 00					19 11
Latchmere	d																								
Wandsworth Common	d		18 44									18 47		18 54		19 00				19 03					19 14
Balham ■ ⊖	d		18 46									18 50		18 56		19 02				19 05					19 16
Streatham Hill	d											18 53				19 05									
West Norwood ■	d	18 53										18 57				19 10								19 23	
Gipsy Hill	d	18 56										19 00				19 13						19a15		19 26	
Crystal Palace ■	d	18 59										19 02				19a16								19 29	
Birkbeck 🚊	d	19 03																						19 33	
Beckenham Junction ■ 🚊	a	19 06																						19 36	
Streatham Common ■	d		18 50											19 00						19 09	19 12				19 20
Norbury	d		18 53											19 03						19 12	19 15				19 23
Thornton Heath	d		18 56											19 06						19 15	19 18				19 26
Selhurst ■	d		18 59											19 09						19 18	19 21				19 29
Norwood Junction ■	a			18 46				18 55	18 59		19 02	19 07													
	d			18 46				18 56	19 00		19 03	19 09													
West Croydon ■ 🚊	a		19 03									19 13								19 22	19 26				19 33
East Croydon 🚊	a			18 50	18 52	18 54		18 59	19 03		19 06			19 12	19 02			19 07	19 09				19 09		

A 19 May

Table 177

Saturdays

Luton, Milton Keynes Central and London East and West Croydon via Tulse Hill - Crystal Palace - Norbury

Local Services

Network Diagram - see first Page of Table 177

		SN ■	SN ◇■	FC ■	FC	SN	SN	SN		SN	SN	SN	SN ◇■	FC ■	SN	SN	SN	SN	FC ■ A	SN ■	SN ◇■	SN	SN	SN ■
London Bridge ■ ⊖	d	19 03				19 06	19 11	19 20									19 18	19 22	19 27			19 33		19 33
South Bermondsey	d						19 15										19 22					19 37		
Queens Rd Peckham	d						19 18										19 24					19 39		
Peckham Rye ■	d						19 20										19 27					19 42		
East Dulwich	d																19 30					19 45		
North Dulwich	d																19 32					19 47		
Luton ■	d			18 18	18 14									18 34										
Luton Airport Parkway ■	d			18 20	18 16									18 36										
St Pancras International ■ ⊖	d			18 54	19 04									19 09										
City Thameslink ■	d			19 03	19 13									19 18										
London Blackfriars ■ ⊖	d			19 05	19 16									19 20										
Elephant & Castle ⊖	d				19 19																			
Loughborough Jn.	d				19 23																			
Herne Hill ■	d				19 27																			
Tulse Hill ■	d				19 31												19 35					19 50		
Streatham ■	d				19a35												19 39							
London Victoria ■ ⊖	d		19 06							19 06	19 11	19 13	19 17		19 19	19 23					19 32		19 33	
Battersea Park ■	d						19a32			19 10	19a15	19 17			19 23								19 37	
Milton Keynes Central	d																			18 13				
Watford Junction	d																			18 52				
Harrow & Wealdstone ⊖	d																			18 59				
Wembley Central ⊖	d																			19 04				
Shepherd's Bush ⊖	d																			19 19				
Kensington (Olympia) ⊖	d																			19 22				
West Brompton ⊖	d																			19 25				
Imperial Wharf	d																			19 27				
Clapham Junction ■	d		19 12							19 14		19 21	19 23		19 27	19 30				19 34	19 38		19 41	
Latchmere	d																							
Wandsworth Common	d									19 17		19 24			19 30	19 33				19 37			19 44	
Balham ■ ⊖	d									19 20		19 26			19 32	19 35				19 40			19 46	
Streatham Hill	d									19 23					19 35									
West Norwood ■	d									19 27					19 40							19 53		
Gipsy Hill	d									19 30					19 43			19a45				19 56		
Crystal Palace ■	d									19 32					19a46							19 59		
Birkbeck 🚊	d																					20 03		
Beckenham Junction ■ 🚊	a																					20 06		
Streatham Common ■	d											19 30				19 39	19 42			19 45			19 50	
Norbury	d											19 33				19 42	19 45			19 48			19 53	
Thornton Heath	d											19 36				19 45	19 48			19 51			19 56	
Selhurst ■	d											19 39				19 48	19 51			19 54			19 59	
Norwood Junction ■	a	19 16				19 29		19 32		19 37														19 46
	d	19 16				19 30		19 33		19 39														19 46
West Croydon ■ 🚊	a									19 43						19 52	19 56						20 03	
East Croydon 🚊	a	19 20	19 22	19 24		19 33		19 36				19 42	19 33	19 39					19 39	19 57	19 47			19 50

A 19 May

Table 177

Luton, Milton Keynes Central and London East and West Croydon via Tulse Hill - Crystal Palace - Norbury

Local Services

Network Diagram - see first Page of Table 177

		SN ◇■	FC ■	FC	SN	SN	SN	SN	SN	SN	SN ◇■	SN	SN ◇■	FC ■	SN	SN		SN	FC ■ A	SN	SN	SN ◇■	FC ■	FC	SN
London Bridge	d				19 36	19 41	19 50									19 48		19 52	19 57	20 03					20 06
South Bermondsey	d					19 45										19 52				20 07					
Queens Rd Peckham	d					19 48										19 54				20 09					
Peckham Rye	d					19 50										19 57				20 12					
East Dulwich	d															20 00				20 15					
North Dulwich	d															20 02				20 17					
Luton	d		18 48	18 44										19 04									19 18	19 14	
Luton Airport Parkway	d		18 50	18 46										19 06									19 20	19 16	
St Pancras International	d		19 24	19 34										19 39									19 54	20 04	
City Thameslink	d		19 33	19 43										19 48									20 03	20 13	
London Blackfriars	d		19 35	19 46										19 50									20 05	20 16	
Elephant & Castle	d			19 49																				20 19	
Loughborough Jn.	d			19 53																				20 23	
Herne Hill	d			19 57																				20 27	
Tulse Hill	d			20 01												20 05				20 20				20 31	
Streatham	d			20a05												20 09								20a35	
London Victoria	d	19 36						19 36	19 41	19 43	19 47	19 49	19 51		19 53						20 03	20 06			
Battersea Park	d					20a02		19 40	19a45	19 47		19 53									20 07				
Milton Keynes Central	d																								
Watford Junction	d																								
Harrow & Wealdstone	d																								
Wembley Central	d																								
Shepherd's Bush	d																								
Kensington (Olympia)	d																								
West Brompton	d																								
Imperial Wharf	d																								
Clapham Junction	d	19 42						19 44		19 51	19 53	19 57			20 00						20 11	20 12			
Latchmere	d																								
Wandsworth Common	d							19 47		19 54		20 00			20 03						20 14				
Balham	d							19 50		19 56		20 02			20 05						20 16				
Streatham Hill	d							19 53				20 05													
West Norwood	d							19 57				20 10								20 23					
Gipsy Hill	d							20 00				20 13						20a15		20 26					
Crystal Palace	d							20 02				20a16								20 29					
Birkbeck	d																			20 33					
Beckenham Junction	a																			20 36					
Streatham Common	d									20 00					20 09	20 12					20 20				
Norbury	d									20 03					20 12	20 15					20 23				
Thornton Heath	d									20 06					20 15	20 18					20 26				
Selhurst	d									20 09					20 18	20 21					20 29				
Norwood Junction	a				19 59		20 02	20 07																	20 29
	d				20 00		20 03	20 09																	20 30
West Croydon	a							20 14							20 24	20 27					20 33				
East Croydon	a	19 52	19 54		20 03		20 06			20 12	20 02		20 07	20 09					20 09			20 22	20 24		20 33

A 19 May

Table 177

Luton, Milton Keynes Central and London East and West Croydon via Tulse Hill - Crystal Palace - Norbury

Local Services

Network Diagram - see first Page of Table 177

		SN	SN	SN	SN ■	SN	SN	SN ◇■		SN	SN ◇■	SN	SN	SN ■	SN	SN ◇■	SN	SN	SN ◇■	FC ■	FC	SN	SN	SN
London Bridge	d	20 11	20 20										20 18		20 22		20 33					20 36	20 41	20 50
South Bermondsey	d	20 15											20 22				20 37						20 45	
Queens Rd Peckham	d	20 18											20 24				20 39						20 48	
Peckham Rye	d	20 20											20 27				20 42						20 50	
East Dulwich	d												20 30				20 45							
North Dulwich	d												20 32				20 47							
Luton	d																			19 46	19 50			
Luton Airport Parkway	d																			19 48	19 52			
St Pancras International	d																			20 24	20 36			
City Thameslink	d																			20 33	20 43			
London Blackfriars	d																			20 35	20 46			
Elephant & Castle	d																				20 49			
Loughborough Jn.	d																				20 53			
Herne Hill	d																				20 57			
Tulse Hill	d												20 35				20 50				21 01			
Streatham	d												20 39								21a05			
London Victoria	d			20 06	20 10	20 11	20 13	20 17		20 19	20 21	20 23				20 32		20 33	20 36					
Battersea Park	d	20a32		20 10		20a15	20 17			20 23								20 37					21a02	
Milton Keynes Central	d													19 13										
Watford Junction	d													19 51										
Harrow & Wealdstone	d													19 58										
Wembley Central	d																							
Shepherd's Bush	d													20 19										
Kensington (Olympia)	d													20 22										
West Brompton	d													20 25										
Imperial Wharf	d													20 27										
Clapham Junction	d			20 14	20 16		20 21	20 23		20 27		20 30		20 34		20 38		20 41	20 42					
Latchmere	d																							
Wandsworth Common	d			20 17			20 24			20 30		20 33		20 37				20 44						
Balham	d			20 20			20 26			20 32		20 35		20 40				20 46						
Streatham Hill	d			20 23						20 35														
West Norwood	d			20 27						20 40							20 53							
Gipsy Hill	d			20 30						20 43					20a45		20 56							
Crystal Palace	d			20 32						20a46							20 59							
Birkbeck	d																21 03							
Beckenham Junction	a																21 06							
Streatham Common	d						20 30					20 39	20 42	20 45				20 50						
Norbury	d						20 33					20 42	20 45	20 48				20 53						
Thornton Heath	d						20 36					20 45	20 48	20 51				20 56						
Selhurst	d						20 39					20 48	20 51	20 55				20 59						
Norwood Junction	a		20 32	20 37																		20 59		21 02
	d		20 33	20 39																		21 00		21 03
West Croydon	a			20 44								20 54	20 56					21 03						
East Croydon	a		20 36		20 29		20 42	20 32			20 37			20 59		20 47			20 52	20 54		21 03		21 06

Table 177

Luton, Milton Keynes Central and London East and West Croydon via Tulse Hill - Crystal Palace - Norbury

Local Services

Network Diagram - see first Page of Table 177

		SN	SN 1	SN	SN	SN ◇1	SN	SN	SN	SN	SN ◇1	SN	SN	SN ◇1	FC 1	FC		SN	SN	SN	SN	SN 1	SN	SN	SN ◇1
London Bridge ⊖	d								20 48	20 52		21 03						21 06	21 11	21 20					
South Bermondsey	d								20 52			21 07							21 15						
Queens Rd Peckham	d								20 54			21 09							21 18						
Peckham Rye	d								20 57			21 12							21 20						
East Dulwich	d								21 00			21 15													
North Dulwich	d								21 02			21 17													
Luton	d														20 16	20 20									
Luton Airport Parkway	d														20 18	20 22									
St Pancras International ⊖	d														20 54	21 06									
City Thameslink	d														21 03										
London Blackfriars ⊖	d														21 05	21 16									
Elephant & Castle ⊖	d															21 19									
Loughborough Jn.	d															21 23									
Herne Hill	d															21 27									
Tulse Hill	d								21 05			21 20				21 31									
Streatham	d								21 09							21a35									
London Victoria ⊖	d	20 36	20 40	20 41	20 43	20 47	20 49	20 53			21 02		21 03	21 06							21 06	21 10	21 11	21 13	21 17
Battersea Park	d	20 40		20a45	20 47		20 53						21 07						21a32		21 10		21a15	21 17	
Milton Keynes Central	d																								
Watford Junction	d																								
Harrow & Wealdstone ⊖	d																								
Wembley Central ⊖	d																								
Shepherd's Bush ⊖	d																								
Kensington (Olympia) ⊖	d																								
West Brompton ⊖	d																								
Imperial Wharf	d																								
Clapham Junction	d	20 44	20 46		20 51	20 53	20 57	21 00			21 08		21 11	21 12							21 14	21 16		21 21	21 23
Latchmere	d																								
Wandsworth Common	d	20 47			20 54		21 00	21 03					21 14								21 17			21 24	
Balham ⊖	d	20 50			20 56		21 02	21 05					21 16								21 20			21 26	
Streatham Hill	d	20 53					21 05														21 23				
West Norwood	d	20 57					21 10					21 23									21 27				
Gipsy Hill	d	21 00					21 13			21a15		21 26									21 30				
Crystal Palace	d	21 02					21a16					21 29									21 32				
Birkbeck	d											21 33													
Beckenham Junction	a											21 36													
Streatham Common	d				21 00			21 09	21 12				21 20											21 30	
Norbury	d				21 03			21 12	21 15				21 23											21 33	
Thornton Heath	d				21 06			21 15	21 18				21 26											21 36	
Selhurst	d				21 09			21 18	21 21				21 29											21 39	
Norwood Junction	a	21 07																21 29		21 32	21 37				
	d	21 09																21 30		21 33	21 39				
West Croydon	a	21 14						21 24	21 26				21 33								21 44				
East Croydon	a		20 57		21 12	21 02					21 17			21 22	21 24			21 33		21 36		21 27		21 42	21 33

Table 177

Luton, Milton Keynes Central and London East and West Croydon via Tulse Hill - Crystal Palace - Norbury

Local Services

Network Diagram - see first Page of Table 177

		SN	SN	SN	SN	SN	SN	SN ◇1		FC 1	FC	SN	SN	SN	SN	SN 1	SN	SN	SN ◇1	SN	SN	SN	SN	SN ◇1
London Bridge ⊖	d			21 18	21 22	21 33						21 36	21 41	21 50								21 48	21 52	
South Bermondsey	d			21 22		21 37							21 45									21 52		
Queens Rd Peckham	d			21 24		21 39							21 48									21 54		
Peckham Rye	d			21 27		21 42							21 50									21 57		
East Dulwich	d			21 30		21 45																22 00		
North Dulwich	d			21 32		21 47																22 02		
Luton	d									20 46	20 50													
Luton Airport Parkway	d									20 48	20 52													
St Pancras International ⊖	d									21 24	21 36													
City Thameslink	d																							
London Blackfriars ⊖	d									21 35	21 46													
Elephant & Castle ⊖	d										21 49													
Loughborough Jn	d										21 53													
Herne Hill	d										21 57													
Tulse Hill	d			21 35		21 50					22 01											22 05		
Streatham	d			21 39							22a05											22 09		
London Victoria ⊖	d	21 19	21 23				21 33	21 36							21 36	21 40	21 41	21 43	21 47	21 49	21 53			22 02
Battersea Park	d	21 23					21 37						22a02		21 40		21a45	21 47		21 53				
Milton Keynes Central	d																							
Watford Junction	d																							
Harrow & Wealdstone ⊖	d																							
Wembley Central ⊖	d																							
Shepherd's Bush ⊖	d																							
Kensington (Olympia) ⊖	d																							
West Brompton ⊖	d																							
Imperial Wharf	d																							
Clapham Junction	d	21 27	21 30				21 41	21 42							21 44	21 46		21 51	21 53	21 57	22 00			22 08
Latchmere	d																							
Wandsworth Common	d	21 30	21 33				21 44								21 47			21 54		22 00	22 03			
Balham ⊖	d	21 32	21 35				21 46								21 50			21 56		22 02	22 05			
Streatham Hill	d	21 35													21 53					22 05				
West Norwood	d	21 40				21 53									21 57					22 10				
Gipsy Hill	d	21 43			21a45	21 56									22 00					22 13			22a15	
Crystal Palace	d	21a46				21 59									22 02					22a16				
Birkbeck	d					22 03																		
Beckenham Junction	a					22 06																		
Streatham Common	d		21 39	21 42			21 50											22 00			22 09	22 12		
Norbury	d		21 42	21 45			21 53											22 03			22 12	22 15		
Thornton Heath	d		21 45	21 48			21 56											22 06			22 15	22 18		
Selhurst	d		21 48	21 51			21 59											22 09			22 18	22 21		
Norwood Junction	a											21 59		22 02	22 07									
	d											22 00		22 03	22 09									
West Croydon	a		21 54	21 56			22 03								22 13						22 22	22 26		
East Croydon	a							21 52		21 54		22 04		22 07		21 57		22 12	22 03					22 17

Table 177

Saturdays

Luton, Milton Keynes Central and London East and West Croydon via Tulse Hill - Crystal Palace - Norbury

Local Services

Network Diagram - see first Page of Table 177

		SN	SN	SN ◇1	FC 1	FC	SN	SN	SN	SN	SN 1	SN	SN	SN	SN	SN		SN	SN 1	SN	SN	SN ◇1	FC 1	FC	SN
London Bridge 4 ⊖	d	22 03					22 06	22 11	22 20							22 18		22 22		22 33					22 36
South Bermondsey	d	22 07						22 15								22 22				22 37					
Queens Rd Peckham	d	22 09						22 18								22 24				22 39					
Peckham Rye 4	d	22 12						22 20								22 27				22 42					
East Dulwich	d	22 15														22 30				22 45					
North Dulwich	d	22 17														22 32				22 47					
Luton 10	d				21 16	21 20																	21 46	21 50	
Luton Airport Parkway 7	d				21 18	21 22																	21 48	21 52	
St Pancras International 15 ⊖	d				21 54	22 06																	22 24	22 36	
City Thameslink 3	d																								
London Blackfriars 3 ⊖	d				22 05	22 16																	22 35	22 46	
Elephant & Castle ⊖	d					22 19																		22 49	
Loughborough Jn.	d					22 23																		22 53	
Herne Hill 4	d					22 27																		22 57	
Tulse Hill 3	d	22 20				22 31										22 35				22 50				23 01	
Streatham 4	d					22a35										22 39								23a05	
London Victoria 15 ⊖	d		22 03	22 06						22 06	22 10	22 11	22 13	22 19	22 23				22 32		22 33	22 36			
Battersea Park 4	d		22 07					22a32		22 10		22a15	22 17	22 23							22 37				
Milton Keynes Central	d																								
Watford Junction	d																								
Harrow & Wealdstone ⊖	d																								
Wembley Central ⊖	d																								
Shepherd's Bush ⊖	d																								
Kensington (Olympia) ⊖	d																								
West Brompton ⊖	d																								
Imperial Wharf	d																								
Clapham Junction 10	d		22 11	22 12						22 14	22 16		22 21	22 27	22 30				22 38		22 41	22 42			
Latchmere	d																								
Wandsworth Common	d		22 14							22 17			22 24	22 30	22 33						22 44				
Balham 4 ⊖	d		22 16							22 20			22 26	22 32	22 35						22 46				
Streatham Hill	d									22 23				22 35											
West Norwood 4	d	22 23								22 27				22 40						22 53					
Gipsy Hill	d	22 26								22 30				22 43				22a45		22 56					
Crystal Palace 4	d	22 29								22 32				22a46						22 59					
Birkbeck	d	22 33																		23 03					
Beckenham Junction 4	a	22 36																		23 06					
Streatham Common 4	d		22 20										22 30		22 39	22 42					22 50				
Norbury	d		22 23										22 33		22 42	22 45					22 53				
Thornton Heath	d		22 26										22 36		22 45	22 48					22 56				
Selhurst 4	d		22 29										22 39		22 48	22 51					22 59				
Norwood Junction 2	a						22 29		22 32	22 37															22 59
	d						22 30		22 33	22 39															23 00
West Croydon 4	a		22 33							22 43					22 52	22 56					23 03				
East Croydon	a			22 22	22 24		22 35		22 37		22 27		22 42						22 47			22 52	22 54		23 03

Table 177

Saturdays

Luton, Milton Keynes Central and London East and West Croydon via Tulse Hill - Crystal Palace - Norbury

Local Services

Network Diagram - see first Page of Table 177

		SN	SN	SN	SN 1	SN	SN	SN ◇1		SN	SN	SN	SN	SN ◇1	SN	SN ◇1	FC 1 A	FC 1 B	SN	SN	FC B	FC A	SN	SN 1
London Bridge 4 ⊖	d	22 41	22 50									22 48	22 52						23 06	23 03				
South Bermondsey	d	22 45										22 52								23 07				
Queens Rd Peckham	d	22 48										22 54								23 09				
Peckham Rye 4	d	22 50										22 57								23 12				
East Dulwich	d											23 00								23 15				
North Dulwich	d											23 02								23 17				
Luton 10	d																22 15	22 16			22 20			
Luton Airport Parkway 7	d																22 18	22 18			22 22			
St Pancras International 15 ⊖	d																22 54	22 54			23 06	23 06		
City Thameslink 3	d																							
London Blackfriars 3 ⊖	d																23 05	23 05			23 16	23 16		
Elephant & Castle ⊖	d																				23 19	23 19		
Loughborough Jn.	d																				23 23	23 23		
Herne Hill 4	d																				23 27	23 27		
Tulse Hill 3	d											23 05								23 21	23 31	23 31		
Streatham 4	d											23 09									23a35	23a35		
London Victoria 15 ⊖	d			22 36	22 40	22 41	22 43	22 47		22 49	22 53			23 02	23 03	23 06							23 06	23 10
Battersea Park 4	d	23a02		22 40		22a45	22 47			22 53					23 07								23 10	
Milton Keynes Central	d																							
Watford Junction	d																							
Harrow & Wealdstone ⊖	d																							
Wembley Central ⊖	d																							
Shepherd's Bush ⊖	d																							
Kensington (Olympia) ⊖	d																							
West Brompton ⊖	d																							
Imperial Wharf	d																							
Clapham Junction 10	d			22 44	22 46		22 51	22 53		22 57	23 00			23 08	23 11	23 12							23 14	23 16
Latchmere	d																							
Wandsworth Common	d			22 47			22 54			23 00	23 03				23 14								23 17	
Balham 4 ⊖	d			22 50			22 56			23 02	23 05				23 16								23 20	
Streatham Hill	d			22 53						23 05													23 23	
West Norwood 4	d			22 57						23 10										23 24			23 27	
Gipsy Hill	d			23 00						23 13			23a15							23 27			23 30	
Crystal Palace 4	d			23 03						23a16										23 29			23 32	
Birkbeck	d																							
Beckenham Junction 4	a																							
Streatham Common 4	d						23 00				23 09	23 12			23 20									
Norbury	d						23 03				23 12	23 15			23 23									
Thornton Heath	d						23 06				23 15	23 18			23 26									
Selhurst 4	d						23 09				23 18	23 21			23 29									
Norwood Junction 2	a		23 02	23 07															23 29	23 34			23 37	
	d		23 03	23 09															23 30				23 39	
West Croydon 4	a			23 13							23 22	23 26			23 33								23 43	
East Croydon	a		23 06		22 57		23 13	23 03						23 17		23 22	23 24	23 24	23 33					23 27

A until 23 June

B from 30 June

Table 177

Saturdays

Luton, Milton Keynes Central and London East and West Croydon via Tulse Hill - Crystal Palace - Norbury

Local Services

Network Diagram - see first Page of Table 177

		SN	SN	SN	SN	SN	SN	SN	SN	FC	FC	SN	SN	SN	FC	FC		SN	SN	SN	SN	SN	FC	FC	SN
				◇■					■	■ A	■ B				A	B				■		■	■	■	
London Bridge ■ ⊖	d					23 11	23 18	23 22					23 36	23 33							23 48				23 52
South Bermondsey	d					23 15	23 22							23 37							23 52				
Queens Rd Peckham	d					23 18	23 24							23 39							23 54				
Peckham Rye ■	d					23 20	23 27							23 42							23 57				
East Dulwich	d						23 30							23 45							00 01				
North Dulwich	d						23 32							23 47							00 03				
Luton ■	d									22 40	22 42				22 46								23 06	23 36	
Luton Airport Parkway ■	d									22 42	22 45				22 49								23 09	23 39	
St Pancras International ■ ⊖	d									23 24	23 24				23 36	23 36							23 54	00 24	
City Thameslink ■	d																								
London Blackfriars ■ ⊖	d									23 35	23 35				23 46	23 46							00 05	00 35	
Elephant & Castle ⊖	d														23 49	23 49									
Loughborough Jn.	d																								
Herne Hill ■	d														23 57	23 57									
Tulse Hill ■	d						23 35							23 51	00 01	00 01					00 06				
Streatham ■	d						23 39								00a05	00a05					00 10				
London Victoria ■ ⊖	d	23 11	23 15	23 17	23 19				23 32			23 34						23 38	23 45	23 47		23 49			
Battersea Park ■	d	23a15	23 19		23 23	23a32						23 38						23 42	23 49						
Milton Keynes Central	d																								
Watford Junction	d																								
Harrow & Wealdstone ⊖	d																								
Wembley Central ⊖	d																								
Shepherd's Bush ⊖	d																								
Kensington (Olympia) ⊖	d																								
West Brompton ⊖	d																								
Imperial Wharf	d																								
Clapham Junction ■	d		23 23	23 23	23 27				23 38			23 42						23 46	23 53	23 53		23 56			
Latchmere	d																								
Wandsworth Common	d		23 26		23 30							23 45						23 49	23 56						
Balham ■ ⊖	d		23 28		23 32							23 47						23 51	23 58						
Streatham Hill	d				23 35													23 54							
West Norwood ■	d				23 40									23 54				23 58							
Gipsy Hill	d				23 43			23a45						23 57				00 01							00a15
Crystal Palace ■	d				23a46									23 59				00 03							
Birkbeck 🚊	d																								
Beckenham Junction ■ 🚊	a																								
Streatham Common ■	d		23 32				23 42					23 51							00 02		00 13				
Norbury	d		23 35				23 45					23 54							00 05		00 15				
Thornton Heath	d		23 38				23 48					23 57							00 08		00 18				
Selhurst ■	d		23 41				23 51					23 59							00 11		00 21				
Norwood Junction ■	a												23 59	00 04				00 08							
	d												23 59					00 09							
West Croydon ■ 🚊	a						23 56					00 03						00 14			00 27				
East Croydon 🚊	a		23 44	23 32					23 52	23 56	23 56		00 03						00 14	00 05		00 09	00 26	00 56	

A from 30 June

B until 23 June

Table 177

Saturdays

Luton, Milton Keynes Central and London East and West Croydon via Tulse Hill - Crystal Palace - Norbury

Local Services

Network Diagram - see first Page of Table 177

		SN	SN
London Bridge ■ ⊖	d		
South Bermondsey	d		
Queens Rd Peckham	d		
Peckham Rye ■	d		
East Dulwich	d		
North Dulwich	d		
Luton ■	d		
Luton Airport Parkway ■	d		
St Pancras International ■ ⊖	d		
City Thameslink ■	d		
London Blackfriars ■ ⊖	d		
Elephant & Castle ⊖	d		
Loughborough Jn.	d		
Herne Hill ■	d		
Tulse Hill ■	d		
Streatham ■	d		
London Victoria ■ ⊖	d	23 54	23 59
Battersea Park ■	d	23 58	00 03
Milton Keynes Central	d		
Watford Junction	d		
Harrow & Wealdstone ⊖	d		
Wembley Central ⊖	d		
Shepherd's Bush ⊖	d		
Kensington (Olympia) ⊖	d		
West Brompton ⊖	d		
Imperial Wharf	d		
Clapham Junction ■	d	00 02	00 07
Latchmere	d		
Wandsworth Common	d	00 05	00 10
Balham ■ ⊖	d	00 07	00 12
Streatham Hill	d	00 10	
West Norwood ■	d	00 14	
Gipsy Hill	d	00 17	
Crystal Palace ■	d	00a19	
Birkbeck 🚊	d		
Beckenham Junction ■ 🚊	a		
Streatham Common ■	d		00 16
Norbury	d		00 19
Thornton Heath	d		00 22
Selhurst ■	d		00 25
Norwood Junction ■	a		
	d		
West Croydon ■ 🚊	a		00 30
East Croydon 🚊	a		

Table 177

Luton, Milton Keynes Central and London East and West Croydon via Tulse Hill - Crystal Palace - Norbury

Sundays until 24 June

Local Services

Network Diagram - see first Page of Table 177

		SN	SN	SN	FC	SN	SN	SN ■	SN	SN ■	SN	SN	SN ◇■	FC ■	SN	SN	SN	SN ■	SN	FC ■	SN	SN	SN	SN
London Bridge 4 ⊖	d		23p36	23p33					23p48						00 06	00 03					00 18			00 36
South Bermondsey	d			23p37					23p52							00 07					00 22			
Queens Rd Peckham	d			23p39					23p54							00 09					00 24			
Peckham Rye 4	d			23p42					23p57							00 12					00 27			
East Dulwich	d			23p45					00 01							00 15					00 30			
North Dulwich	d			23p47					00 03							00 17					00 32			
Luton 10	d													23p06						23p36				
Luton Airport Parkway 7	d													23p09						23p39				
St Pancras International 15 ⊖	d				23p36									23p54						00 24				
City Thameslink 3	d																							
London Blackfriars 3 ⊖	d				23p46									00 05						00 35				
Elephant & Castle ⊖	d				23p49																			
Loughborough Jn.	d																							
Herne Hill 4	d				23p57																			
Tulse Hill 3	d			23p51	00 01				00 06							00 21					00 35			
Streatham 4	d				00a05				00 10												00 39			
London Victoria 15 ⊖	d	23p34				23p38	23p45	23p47		23p49	23p54	23p59	00 05				00 07	00 14	00 16			00 22	00 34	
Battersea Park 4	d	23p38				23p42	23p49				23p58	00 03					00 11		00 20			00 26	00 38	
Milton Keynes Central	d																							
Watford Junction	d																							
Harrow & Wealdstone ⊖	d																							
Wembley Central ⊖	d																							
Shepherd's Bush ⊖	d																							
Kensington (Olympia) ⊖	d																							
West Brompton ⊖	d																							
Imperial Wharf	d																							
Clapham Junction 10	d	23p42				23p46	23p53	23p53		23p56	00 02	00 07	00 11				00 15	00 20	00 24			00 30	00 42	
Latchmere	d																							
Wandsworth Common	d	23p45				23p49	23p56				00 05	00 10					00 18		00 27			00 33	00 45	
Balham 4 ⊖	d	23p47				23p51	23p58				00 07	00 12					00 20		00 29			00 35	00 47	
Streatham Hill	d					23p54					00 10						00 23					00 38		
West Norwood 4	d			23p54		23p58					00 14					00 24	00 28					00 42		
Gipsy Hill	d			23p57		00 01					00 17					00 27	00 31					00 45		
Crystal Palace 4	d			23p59		00 03					00a19					00 29	00 33					00 47		
Birkbeck	d																							
Beckenham Junction 4	a																							
Streatham Common 4	d	23p51					00 02		00 13			00 16							00 33		00 42		00 51	
Norbury	d	23p54					00 05		00 15			00 19							00 36		00 45		00 54	
Thornton Heath	d	23p57					00 08		00 18			00 22							00 39		00 48		00 57	
Selhurst 4	d	23p59					00 11		00 21			00 25							00 41		00 51		01 00	
Norwood Junction 2	a		23p59	00 04		00 08									00 29	00 34	00 38					00 52		00 59
	d		23p59			00 09									00 30		00 38					00 52		01 00
West Croydon 4	a	00 03				00 14			00 27			00 30					00 43				00 55	00 58	01 04	
East Croydon	a		00 03				00 14	00 05		00 09			00 24	00 26	00 33			00 31	00 44	00 56				01 03

Table 177

Luton, Milton Keynes Central and London East and West Croydon via Tulse Hill - Crystal Palace - Norbury

Sundays until 24 June

Local Services

Network Diagram - see first Page of Table 177

		SN	SN	SN	SN ■	FC ■	SN ■	SN ■	SN ■	SN ■	SN ◇■	SN ◇■	SN	SN	SN ■	FC ■	SN	SN	SN	SN	SN	SN ■	SN
London Bridge 4 ⊖	d	00 33													07 05			07 11		07 21	07 24	07 37	
South Bermondsey	d	00 37																07 15		07 25			
Queens Rd Peckham	d	00 39																07 18		07 27			
Peckham Rye 4	d	00 42																07 20		07 30			
East Dulwich	d	00 45																		07 33			
North Dulwich	d	00 47																		07 35			
Luton 10	d					00 06																	
Luton Airport Parkway 7	d					00 09																	
St Pancras International 15 ⊖	d					00 54																	
City Thameslink 3	d																						
London Blackfriars 3 ⊖	d					01 05										06 55							
Elephant & Castle ⊖	d																						
Loughborough Jn.	d																						
Herne Hill 4	d																						
Tulse Hill 3	d	00 51																		07 39			
Streatham 4	d																			07 42			
London Victoria 15 ⊖	d		00 37	00 42	01 00		02 00	03 00	04 00	05 02	05 47	06 32	06 36	06 49			07 06		07 19				07 24
Battersea Park 4	d		00 41	00 46										06 53				07a32					07 28
Milton Keynes Central	d																						
Watford Junction	d																						
Harrow & Wealdstone ⊖	d																						
Wembley Central ⊖	d																						
Shepherd's Bush ⊖	d																						
Kensington (Olympia) ⊖	d																						
West Brompton ⊖	d																						
Imperial Wharf	d																						
Clapham Junction 10	d		00 45	00 50	01 08		02 08	03 08	04 08	05 08	05 53	06 38	06 42	06 57			07 12		07 26				07 32
Latchmere	d																						
Wandsworth Common	d		00 48	00 53										07 00									07 35
Balham 4 ⊖	d		00 50	00 55									06 47	07 02			07 17		07 30				07 37
Streatham Hill	d		00 53																				07 41
West Norwood 4	d	00 54	00 58																				07 46
Gipsy Hill	d	00 57	01 01																				07 49
Crystal Palace 4	d	00 59	01 03																				07 51
Birkbeck	d																						
Beckenham Junction 4	a																						
Streatham Common 4	d			00 59									06 51	07 06			07 21		07 34	07 48			
Norbury	d			01 02									06 54	07 09			07 24		07 37	07 51			
Thornton Heath	d			01 05									06 57	07 12			07 27		07 40	07 54			
Selhurst 4	d			01 07									07 00	07 16			07 30		07 43	07 57			
Norwood Junction 2	a	01 04	01 08												07 17						07 44	07 48	07 56
	d		01 08												07 17						07 48	07 48	07 57
West Croydon 4	a		01 13											07 20					07 48		07 55		08 01
East Croydon	a			01 10	01 21	01 31	02 21	03 21	04 21	05 21	06 05	06 51	07 03		07 21	07 24	07 33			08 01		07 54	

Table 177

Sundays
until 24 June

Luton, Milton Keynes Central and London East and West Croydon via Tulse Hill - Crystal Palace - Norbury

Local Services

Network Diagram - see first Page of Table 177

		SN ◇■	FC ■	SN	SN	SN	SN	SN	SN	SN	SN	SN ■	FC ■	SN	SN	SN		SN	SN ◇■	SN	SN	SN	SN	SN	SN ■
London Bridge ⊖	d			07 36		07 39		07 41		07 51	07 54	08 05			08 06					08 09	08 11		08 21	08 24	08 37
South Bermondsey	d			07 40				07 45		07 55					08 10						08 15		08 25		
Queens Rd Peckham	d			07 42				07 48		07 57					08 12						08 18		08 27		
Peckham Rye	d			07 45				07 50		08 00					08 15						08 20		08 30		
East Dulwich	d			07 48						08 03					08 18								08 33		
North Dulwich	d			07 50						08 05					08 20								08 35		
Luton	d		06 37										07 07												
Luton Airport Parkway	d		06 39										07 09												
St Pancras International ⊖	d		07 24										07 54												
City Thameslink	d																								
London Blackfriars ⊖	d		07 34										08 04												
Elephant & Castle ⊖	d																								
Loughborough Jn.	d																								
Herne Hill	d																								
Tulse Hill	d			07 54						08 09					08 24								08 39		
Streatham	d									08 12													08 42		
London Victoria ⊖	d	07 27			07 36		07 41		07 49					07 54		08 06		08 11	08 17			08 19			
Battersea Park	d						07a45	08a02						07 58				08a15			08a32				
Milton Keynes Central	d																								
Watford Junction	d																								
Harrow & Wealdstone ⊖	d																								
Wembley Central ⊖	d																								
Shepherd's Bush ⊖	d																								
Kensington (Olympia) ⊖	d																								
West Brompton ⊖	d																								
Imperial Wharf	d																								
Clapham Junction	d	07 33			07 42				07 56					08 02		08 12			08 23			08 26			
Latchmere	d																								
Wandsworth Common	d													08 05											
Balham ⊖	d				07 47				08 00					08 07		08 17						08 30			
Streatham Hill	d													08 11											
West Norwood	d			07 57										08 16	08 27										
Gipsy Hill	d			08 00										08 19	08 30										
Crystal Palace	d			08a02										08 21	08a32										
Birkbeck	d																								
Beckenham Junction	a																								
Streatham Common	d				07 51				08 04	08 18						08 21						08 34	08 48		
Norbury	d				07 54				08 07	08 21						08 24						08 37	08 51		
Thornton Heath	d				07 57				08 10	08 24						08 27						08 40	08 54		
Selhurst	d				08 00				08 13	08 27						08 30						08 43	08 57		
Norwood Junction	a					08 02					08 14	08 16		08 26						08 32				08 44	08 48
	d					08 03					08 16	08 16		08 27						08 33				08 46	08 48
West Croydon	a								08 18		08 24			08 31								08 48		08 54	
East Croydon	a	07 42	07 55		08 03	08 07				08 30		08 20	08 25			08 33			08 32	08 37			09 01		08 54

Table 177

Sundays
until 24 June

Luton, Milton Keynes Central and London East and West Croydon via Tulse Hill - Crystal Palace - Norbury

Local Services

Network Diagram - see first Page of Table 177

		SN	SN ◇■	FC ■	SN	SN	SN	SN ◇■ H		SN	SN	SN	SN	SN	SN ■	SN	SN	SN ◇■	FC ■	FC	SN	SN	SN ◇■	SN	
London Bridge ⊖	d				08 36					08 39	08 41		08 51	08 54	09 05		09 06							09 09	
South Bermondsey	d				08 40						08 45		08 55				09 10								
Queens Rd Peckham	d				08 42						08 48		08 57				09 12								
Peckham Rye	d				08 45						08 50		09 00				09 15								
East Dulwich	d				08 48								09 03				09 18								
North Dulwich	d				08 50								09 05				09 20								
Luton	d			07 37															08 14	08 18					
Luton Airport Parkway	d			07 39															08 17	08 21					
St Pancras International ⊖	d			08 24															08 54	09 05					
City Thameslink	d																								
London Blackfriars ⊖	d			08 34															09 04	09 15					
Elephant & Castle ⊖	d																			09 18					
Loughborough Jn.	d																			09 22					
Herne Hill	d																			09 26					
Tulse Hill	d				08 54								09 09				09 24			09 30					
Streatham	d												09 12							09a34					
London Victoria ⊖	d	08 24	08 27			08 36	08 41	08 47				08 49				08 54		09 06			09 06	09 11	09 17		
Battersea Park	d	08 28					08a45				09a02					08 58						09a15			
Milton Keynes Central	d																								
Watford Junction	d																								
Harrow & Wealdstone ⊖	d																								
Wembley Central ⊖	d																								
Shepherd's Bush ⊖	d																								
Kensington (Olympia) ⊖	d																								
West Brompton ⊖	d																								
Imperial Wharf	d																								
Clapham Junction	d	08 32	08 33			08 42		08 53				08 56				09 02		09 12			09 12		09 23		
Latchmere	d																								
Wandsworth Common	d	08 35														09 05									
Balham ⊖	d	08 37				08 47						09 00				09 07					09 17				
Streatham Hill	d	08 41														09 11									
West Norwood	d	08 46			08 57											09 16	09 27								
Gipsy Hill	d	08 49			09 00											09 19	09 30								
Crystal Palace	d	08 51			09a02											09 21	09a32								
Birkbeck	d																								
Beckenham Junction	a																								
Streatham Common	d					08 51						09 04	09 18								09 21				
Norbury	d					08 54						09 07	09 21								09 24				
Thornton Heath	d					08 57						09 10	09 24								09 27				
Selhurst	d					09 00						09 13	09 27								09 30				
Norwood Junction	a	08 56								09 02				09 14	09 16	09 26								09 32	
	d	08 57								09 03				09 16	09 16	09 27								09 33	
West Croydon	a	09 01										09 18		09 24		09 31									
East Croydon	a		08 42	08 55		09 03		09 02		09 07			09 30		09 20			09 22	09 25		09 33		09 32	09 37	

Table 177

Sundays until 24 June

Luton, Milton Keynes Central and London East and West Croydon via Tulse Hill - Crystal Palace - Norbury

Local Services

Network Diagram - see first Page of Table 177

		FC ■	SN	SN	SN	SN	SN ■	SN	SN ◇■	SN	SN ◇■	FC ■	FC	SN	SN	SN ◇■ H		SN	FC ■	SN	SN	SN	SN	SN ■	SN
London Bridge ■ ⊖	d		09 11		09 21	09 24	09 37			09 36								09 39		09 41		09 51	09 54	10 05	
South Bermondsey	d		09 15		09 25					09 40										09 45		09 55			
Queens Rd Peckham	d		09 18		09 27					09 42										09 48		09 57			
Peckham Rye ■	d		09 20		09 30					09 45										09 50		10 00			
East Dulwich	d				09 33					09 48												10 03			
North Dulwich	d				09 35					09 50												10 05			
Luton ■	d	08 30										08 44	08 48						09 00						
Luton Airport Parkway ■	d	08 33										08 47	08 51						09 03						
St Pancras International ■ ⊖	d	09 09										09 24	09 35						09 39						
City Thameslink ■	d																								
London Blackfriars ■ ⊖	d	09 19										09 34	09 45						09 49						
Elephant & Castle ⊖	d												09 48												
Loughborough Jn.	d												09 52												
Herne Hill ■	d												09 56												
Tulse Hill ■	d				09 39					09 54			10 00									10 09			
Streatham ■	d				09 42								10a04									10 12			
London Victoria ■ ⊖	d			09 19				09 24	09 27		09 36			09 36	09 41	09 47					09 49				09 54
Battersea Park ■	d		09a32					09 28							09a45					10a02					09 58
Milton Keynes Central	d																								
Watford Junction	d																								
Harrow & Wealdstone ⊖	d																								
Wembley Central ⊖	d																								
Shepherd's Bush ⊖	d																								
Kensington (Olympia) ⊖	d																								
West Brompton ⊖	d																								
Imperial Wharf	d																								
Clapham Junction ■	d			09 26				09 32	09 33		09 42			09 42		09 53					09 56				10 02
Latchmere	d																								
Wandsworth Common	d							09 35																	10 05
Balham ■ ⊖	d			09 30				09 37						09 47							10 00				10 07
Streatham Hill	d							09 41																	10 11
West Norwood ■	d							09 46		09 57															10 16
Gipsy Hill	d							09 49		10 00															10 19
Crystal Palace ■	d							09 51		10a02															10 21
Birkbeck	d																								
Beckenham Junction ■	a																								
Streatham Common ■	d			09 34	09 48									09 51							10 04	10 18			
Norbury	d			09 37	09 51									09 54							10 07	10 21			
Thornton Heath	d			09 40	09 54									09 57							10 10	10 24			
Selhurst ■	d			09 43	09 57									10 00							10 13	10 27			
Norwood Junction ■	a					09 44	09 48	09 56										10 02					10 14	10 16	10 26
	d					09 46	09 48	09 57										10 03					10 16	10 16	10 27
West Croydon ■	a			09 48		09 54		10 01													10 18		10 24		10 31
East Croydon	a	09 39			10 01		09 54		09 42		09 52	09 55		10 03		10 02		10 07	10 09			10 30		10 20	

Table 177

Sundays until 24 June

Luton, Milton Keynes Central and London East and West Croydon via Tulse Hill - Crystal Palace - Norbury

Local Services

Network Diagram - see first Page of Table 177

		SN	SN ◇■ H	FC ■	FC	SN	SN	SN ◇■		SN	FC ■	SN	SN	SN	SN	SN ■	SN	SN ◇■	SN	SN ◇■ H	FC ■	FC	SN	SN	
London Bridge ■ ⊖	d	10 06								10 09		10 11		10 21	10 24	10 37			10 36						
South Bermondsey	d	10 10										10 15		10 25					10 40						
Queens Rd Peckham	d	10 12										10 18		10 27					10 42						
Peckham Rye ■	d	10 15										10 20		10 30					10 45						
East Dulwich	d	10 18												10 33					10 48						
North Dulwich	d	10 20												10 35					10 50						
Luton ■	d			09 14	09 18						09 30										09 44	09 48			
Luton Airport Parkway ■	d			09 17	09 21						09 32										09 47	09 51			
St Pancras International ■ ⊖	d			09 54	10 05						10 09										10 24	10 35			
City Thameslink ■	d																								
London Blackfriars ■ ⊖	d			10 04	10 15						10 19										10 34	10 45			
Elephant & Castle ⊖	d				10 18																	10 48			
Loughborough Jn.	d				10 22																	10 52			
Herne Hill ■	d				10 26																	10 56			
Tulse Hill ■	d	10 24			10 30									10 39					10 54			11 00			
Streatham ■	d				10a34									10 42								11a04			
London Victoria ■ ⊖	d		10 06			10 06	10 11	10 17					10 19				10 24	10 27		10 36			10 36	10 41	
Battersea Park ■	d						10a15					10a32					10 28							10a45	
Milton Keynes Central	d																								
Watford Junction	d																								
Harrow & Wealdstone ⊖	d																								
Wembley Central ⊖	d																								
Shepherd's Bush ⊖	d																								
Kensington (Olympia) ⊖	d																								
West Brompton ⊖	d																								
Imperial Wharf	d																								
Clapham Junction ■	d		10 12			10 12		10 23					10 26				10 32	10 33		10 42			10 42		
Latchmere	d																								
Wandsworth Common	d																10 35								
Balham ■ ⊖	d					10 17							10 30				10 37						10 47		
Streatham Hill	d																10 41								
West Norwood ■	d	10 27															10 46		10 57						
Gipsy Hill	d	10 30															10 49		11 00						
Crystal Palace ■	d	10a32															10 51		11a02						
Birkbeck	d																								
Beckenham Junction ■	a																								
Streatham Common ■	d					10 21							10 34	10 48									10 51		
Norbury	d					10 24							10 37	10 51									10 54		
Thornton Heath	d					10 27							10 40	10 54									10 57		
Selhurst ■	d					10 30							10 43	10 57									11 00		
Norwood Junction ■	a									10 32					10 44	10 48	10 56								
	d									10 33					10 46	10 48	10 57								
West Croydon ■	a												10 48		10 54		11 01								
East Croydon	a		10 22	10 25		10 33		10 32		10 37	10 39			11 01		10 54		10 42		10 52	10 55		11 03		

Table 177

Sundays until 24 June

Luton, Milton Keynes Central and London East and West Croydon via Tulse Hill - Crystal Palace - Norbury

Local Services

Network Diagram - see first Page of Table 177

		SN ◇■ H	SN	FC ■	SN	SN	SN	SN	SN ■	SN	SN	SN ◇■ H	FC ■	FC	SN	SN		SN ◇■	SN	FC ■	SN	SN	SN	SN	SN ■
London Bridge [4] ⊖	d		10 39		10 41		10 51	10 54	11 05		11 06								11 09		11 11		11 21	11 24	11 37
South Bermondsey	d				10 45		10 55				11 10										11 15		11 25		
Queens Rd Peckham	d				10 48		10 57				11 12										11 18		11 27		
Peckham Rye [4]	d				10 50		11 00				11 15										11 20		11 30		
East Dulwich	d						11 03				11 18												11 33		
North Dulwich	d						11 05				11 20												11 35		
Luton [10]	d			10 00									10 14							10 30					
Luton Airport Parkway [7]	d			10 02									10 17							10 32					
St Pancras International [15] ⊖	d			10 39									10 54	11 05						11 09					
City Thameslink [3]	d																								
London Blackfriars [3] ⊖	d			10 49									11 04	11 15						11 19					
Elephant & Castle ⊖	d													11 18											
Loughborough Jn.	d													11 22											
Herne Hill [4]	d													11 26											
Tulse Hill [3]	d						11 09				11 24			11 30									11 39		
Streatham [4]	d						11 12							11a34									11 42		
London Victoria [15] ⊖	d	10 47				10 49				10 54		11 06			11 06	11 11		11 17				11 19			
Battersea Park [4]	d				11a02					10 58						11a15					11a32				
Milton Keynes Central	d																								
Watford Junction	d																								
Harrow & Wealdstone ⊖	d																								
Wembley Central ⊖	d																								
Shepherd's Bush ⊖	d																								
Kensington (Olympia) ⊖	d																								
West Brompton ⊖	d																								
Imperial Wharf	d																								
Clapham Junction [10]	d	10 53				10 56				11 02		11 12			11 12			11 23				11 26			
Latchmere	d																								
Wandsworth Common	d									11 05															
Balham [4] ⊖	d					11 00				11 07					11 17							11 30			
Streatham Hill	d									11 11															
West Norwood [4]	d									11 16	11 27														
Gipsy Hill	d									11 19	11 30														
Crystal Palace [4]	d									11 21	11a32														
Birkbeck ⇌	d																								
Beckenham Junction [4] ⇌	a																								
Streatham Common [4]	d					11 04	11 18								11 21							11 34	11 48		
Norbury	d					11 07	11 21								11 24							11 37	11 51		
Thornton Heath	d					11 10	11 24								11 27							11 40	11 54		
Selhurst [4]	d					11 13	11 27								11 30							11 43	11 57		
Norwood Junction [2]	a		11 02					11 14	11 16	11 26									11 32					11 44	11 48
	d		11 03					11 16	11 16	11 27									11 33					11 46	11 48
West Croydon [4] ⇌	a					11 18		11 24		11 31												11 48		11 54	
East Croydon ⇌	a	11 02	11 07	11 09			11 30		11 20			11 22	11 25		11 33			11 32	11 37	11 39			12 01		11 54

Table 177

Sundays until 24 June

Luton, Milton Keynes Central and London East and West Croydon via Tulse Hill - Crystal Palace - Norbury

Local Services

Network Diagram - see first Page of Table 177

		SN	SN ◇■	SN	SN ◇■ H	FC ■	FC	SN		SN	SN ◇■ H	SN	FC ■	SN	SN	SN	SN	SN ■	SN	SN	SN ◇■ H	FC ■	FC	SN
London Bridge [4] ⊖	d			11 36								11 39		11 41		11 51	11 54	12 05		12 06				
South Bermondsey	d			11 40										11 45		11 55				12 10				
Queens Rd Peckham	d			11 42										11 48		11 57				12 12				
Peckham Rye [4]	d			11 45										11 50		12 00				12 15				
East Dulwich	d			11 48												12 03				12 18				
North Dulwich	d			11 50												12 05				12 20				
Luton [10]	d					10 44							11 00									11 14		
Luton Airport Parkway [7]	d					10 47							11 02									11 17		
St Pancras International [15] ⊖	d					11 24	11 35						11 39									11 54	12 05	
City Thameslink [3]	d																							
London Blackfriars [3] ⊖	d					11 34	11 45						11 49									12 04	12 15	
Elephant & Castle ⊖	d						11 48																12 18	
Loughborough Jn.	d						11 52																12 22	
Herne Hill [4]	d						11 56																12 26	
Tulse Hill [3]	d			11 54			12 00									12 09				12 24			12 30	
Streatham [4]	d						12a04									12 12							12a34	
London Victoria [15] ⊖	d	11 24	11 27		11 36			11 36		11 41	11 47				11 49				11 54		12 06			12 06
Battersea Park [4]	d	11 28								11a45				12a02					11 58					
Milton Keynes Central	d																							
Watford Junction	d																							
Harrow & Wealdstone ⊖	d																							
Wembley Central ⊖	d																							
Shepherd's Bush ⊖	d																							
Kensington (Olympia) ⊖	d																							
West Brompton ⊖	d																							
Imperial Wharf	d																							
Clapham Junction [10]	d	11 32	11 33		11 42			11 42			11 53				11 56				12 02		12 12			12 12
Latchmere	d																							
Wandsworth Common	d	11 35																	12 05					
Balham [4] ⊖	d	11 37						11 47							12 00				12 07					12 17
Streatham Hill	d	11 41																	12 11					
West Norwood [4]	d	11 46		11 57															12 16	12 27				
Gipsy Hill	d	11 49		12 00															12 19	12 30				
Crystal Palace [4]	d	11 51		12a02															12 21	12a32				
Birkbeck ⇌	d																							
Beckenham Junction [4] ⇌	a																							
Streatham Common [4]	d							11 51							12 04	12 18								12 21
Norbury	d							11 54							12 07	12 21								12 24
Thornton Heath	d							11 57							12 10	12 24								12 27
Selhurst [4]	d							12 00							12 13	12 27								12 30
Norwood Junction [2]	a	11 56										12 02					12 14	12 16	12 26					
	d	11 57										12 03					12 16	12 16	12 27					
West Croydon [4] ⇌	a	12 01													12 18		12 24		12 31					
East Croydon ⇌	a		11 42		11 52	11 55		12 03			12 02	12 07	12 09			12 30		12 20			12 22	12 25		12 33

Table 177

Sundays
until 24 June

Luton, Milton Keynes Central and London East and West Croydon via Tulse Hill - Crystal Palace - Norbury

Local Services

Network Diagram - see first Page of Table 177

		SN	SN ◇1	SN	FC 1	SN	SN	SN	SN	SN 1	SN	SN ◇1	SN	SN ◇1	FC 1	FC		SN	SN	SN ◇1	SN	FC 1	SN	SN	SN
London Bridge 4 ⊖	d			12 09		12 11		12 21	12 24	12 37			12 36								12 39		12 41		12 51
South Bermondsey	d					12 15		12 25					12 40										12 45		12 55
Queens Rd Peckham	d					12 18		12 27					12 42										12 48		12 57
Peckham Rye 4	d					12 20		12 30					12 45										12 50		13 00
East Dulwich	d							12 33					12 48												13 03
North Dulwich	d							12 35					12 50												13 05
Luton 10	d				11 30										11 44							12 00			
Luton Airport Parkway 7	d				11 32										11 47							12 02			
St Pancras International 15 ⊖	d				12 09										12 24	12 35						12 39			
City Thameslink 3	d																								
London Blackfriars 3 ⊖	d				12 19										12 34	12 45						12 49			
Elephant & Castle ⊖	d															12 48									
Loughborough Jn.	d															12 52									
Herne Hill 4	d															12 56									
Tulse Hill 3	d							12 39					12 54			13 00									13 09
Streatham 4	d							12 42								13a04									13 12
London Victoria 15 ⊖	d	12 11	12 17				12 19				12 24	12 27		12 36				12 36	12 41	12 47				12 49	
Battersea Park 4	d	12a15				12a32					12 28								12a45				13a02		
Milton Keynes Central	d																								
Watford Junction	d																								
Harrow & Wealdstone ⊖	d																								
Wembley Central ⊖	d																								
Shepherd's Bush ⊖	d																								
Kensington (Olympia) ⊖	d																								
West Brompton ⊖	d																								
Imperial Wharf	d																								
Clapham Junction 10	d		12 23				12 26				12 32	12 33		12 42				12 42		12 53				12 56	
Latchmere	d																								
Wandsworth Common	d										12 35														
Balham 4 ⊖	d						12 30				12 37							12 47						13 00	
Streatham Hill	d										12 41														
West Norwood 4	d										12 46		12 57												
Gipsy Hill	d										12 49		13 00												
Crystal Palace 4	d										12 51		13a02												
Birkbeck	d																								
Beckenham Junction 4	a																								
Streatham Common 4	d						12 34	12 48										12 51						13 04	13 18
Norbury	d						12 37	12 51										12 54						13 07	13 21
Thornton Heath	d						12 40	12 54										12 57						13 10	13 24
Selhurst 4	d						12 43	12 57										13 00						13 13	13 27
Norwood Junction 2	a			12 32					12 44	12 48	12 56										13 02				
	d			12 33					12 46	12 48	12 57										13 03				
West Croydon 4	a						12 48		12 54		13 01													13 18	
East Croydon	a		12 32	12 37	12 39			13 01		12 54		12 42		12 52	12 55			13 03		13 02	13 07	13 09			13 30

Table 177

Sundays
until 24 June

Luton, Milton Keynes Central and London East and West Croydon via Tulse Hill - Crystal Palace - Norbury

Local Services

Network Diagram - see first Page of Table 177

		SN	SN 1	SN	SN	SN ◇1	FC 1	FC		SN	SN	SN ◇1	SN	FC 1	SN	SN	SN	SN	SN 1	SN	SN ◇1	SN	SN ◇1	FC 1
London Bridge 4 ⊖	d	12 54	13 05		13 06								13 09		13 11		13 21	13 24	13 37			13 36		
South Bermondsey	d				13 10										13 15		13 25					13 40		
Queens Rd Peckham	d				13 12										13 18		13 27					13 42		
Peckham Rye 4	d				13 15										13 20		13 30					13 45		
East Dulwich	d				13 18												13 33					13 48		
North Dulwich	d				13 20												13 35					13 50		
Luton 10	d						12 14							12 30										12 44
Luton Airport Parkway 7	d						12 17							12 32										12 47
St Pancras International 15 ⊖	d						12 54	13 05						13 09										13 24
City Thameslink 3	d																							
London Blackfriars 3 ⊖	d						13 04	13 15						13 19										13 34
Elephant & Castle ⊖	d							13 18																
Loughborough Jn.	d							13 22																
Herne Hill 4	d							13 26																
Tulse Hill 3	d				13 24			13 30									13 39					13 54		
Streatham 4	d							13a34									13 42							
London Victoria 15 ⊖	d			12 54		13 06				13 06	13 11	13 17				13 19				13 24	13 27		13 36	
Battersea Park 4	d			12 58							13a15				13a32					13 28				
Milton Keynes Central	d																							
Watford Junction	d																							
Harrow & Wealdstone ⊖	d																							
Wembley Central ⊖	d																							
Shepherd's Bush ⊖	d																							
Kensington (Olympia) ⊖	d																							
West Brompton ⊖	d																							
Imperial Wharf	d																							
Clapham Junction 10	d			13 02		13 12				13 12		13 23				13 26				13 32	13 33		13 42	
Latchmere	d																							
Wandsworth Common	d			13 05																13 35				
Balham 4 ⊖	d			13 07						13 17						13 30				13 37				
Streatham Hill	d			13 11																13 41				
West Norwood 4	d			13 16	13 27															13 46		13 57		
Gipsy Hill	d			13 19	13 30															13 49		14 00		
Crystal Palace 4	d			13 21	13a32															13 51		14a02		
Birkbeck	d																							
Beckenham Junction 4	a																							
Streatham Common 4	d									13 21						13 34	13 48							
Norbury	d									13 24						13 37	13 51							
Thornton Heath	d									13 27						13 40	13 54							
Selhurst 4	d									13 30						13 43	13 57							
Norwood Junction 2	a	13 14	13 16	13 26									13 32					13 44	13 48	13 56				
	d	13 16	13 16	13 27									13 33					13 46	13 48	13 57				
West Croydon 4	a	13 24		13 31												13 48		13 54		14 01				
East Croydon	a		13 20			13 22	13 25			13 33		13 32	13 37	13 39			14 01		13 54		13 42		13 52	13 55

Table 177

Sundays
until 24 June

Luton, Milton Keynes Central and London East and West Croydon via Tulse Hill - Crystal Palace - Norbury

Local Services

Network Diagram - see first Page of Table 177

		FC	SN	SN	SN ◇1	SN	FC 1	SN	SN	SN	SN	SN 1	SN	SN	SN ◇1	FC 1		FC	SN	SN	SN ◇1	SN	FC 1	SN	SN
London Bridge 4 ⊖	d					13 39		13 41		13 51	13 54	14 05		14 06								14 09		14 11	
South Bermondsey	d							13 45		13 55				14 10										14 15	
Queens Rd Peckham	d							13 48		13 57				14 12										14 18	
Peckham Rye 4	d							13 50		14 00				14 15										14 20	
East Dulwich	d									14 03				14 18											
North Dulwich	d									14 05				14 20											
Luton 10	d						13 00									13 14							13 30		
Luton Airport Parkway 7	d						13 03									13 17							13 32		
St Pancras International 15 ⊖	d	13 35					13 39									13 54		14 05					14 09		
City Thameslink 3	d																								
London Blackfriars 3 ⊖	d	13 45					13 49									14 04		14 15					14 19		
Elephant & Castle ⊖	d	13 48																14 18							
Loughborough Jn.	d	13 52																14 22							
Herne Hill 4	d	13 56																14 26							
Tulse Hill 3	d	14 00								14 09				14 24				14 30							
Streatham 4	d	14a04								14 12								14a34							
London Victoria 15 ⊖	d		13 36	13 41	13 47				13 49				13 54		14 06				14 06	14 11	14 17				14 19
Battersea Park 4	d			13a45				14a02					13 58							14a15				14a32	
Milton Keynes Central	d																								
Watford Junction	d																								
Harrow & Wealdstone ⊖	d																								
Wembley Central ⊖	d																								
Shepherd's Bush ⊖	d																								
Kensington (Olympia) ⊖	d																								
West Brompton ⊖	d																								
Imperial Wharf	d																								
Clapham Junction 10	d		13 42		13 53				13 56				14 02		14 12				14 12		14 23				14 26
Latchmere	d																								
Wandsworth Common	d												14 05												
Balham 4 ⊖	d		13 47						14 00				14 07						14 17						14 30
Streatham Hill	d												14 11												
West Norwood 4	d												14 16	14 27											
Gipsy Hill	d												14 19	14 30											
Crystal Palace 4	d												14 21	14a32											
Birkbeck	d																								
Beckenham Junction 4	a																								
Streatham Common 4	d		13 51						14 04	14 18									14 21						14 34
Norbury	d		13 54						14 07	14 21									14 24						14 37
Thornton Heath	d		13 57						14 10	14 24									14 27						14 40
Selhurst 4	d		14 00						14 13	14 27									14 30						14 43
Norwood Junction 2	a					14 02					14 14	14 16	14 26									14 32			
	d					14 03					14 16	14 16	14 27									14 33			
West Croydon 4	a								14 18		14 24		14 31												14 48
East Croydon	a		14 03		14 02	14 07	14 09			14 30		14 20			14 22	14 25			14 33		14 32	14 37	14 39		

Table 177

Sundays
until 24 June

Luton, Milton Keynes Central and London East and West Croydon via Tulse Hill - Crystal Palace - Norbury

Local Services

Network Diagram - see first Page of Table 177

		SN	SN	SN 1	SN	SN ◇1	SN	SN ◇1		FC 1	FC	SN	SN	SN ◇1	SN	FC 1		FC 1	SN	SN	SN	SN	SN 1
London Bridge 4 ⊖	d	14 21	14 24	14 37			14 36								14 39				17 41		17 51	17 54	18 05
South Bermondsey	d	14 25					14 40												17 45		17 55		
Queens Rd Peckham	d	14 27					14 42												17 48		17 57		
Peckham Rye 4	d	14 30					14 45												17 50		18 00		
East Dulwich	d	14 33					14 48														18 03		
North Dulwich	d	14 35					14 50														18 05		
Luton 10	d									13 44						14 00		17 00					
Luton Airport Parkway 7	d									13 47						14 02		17 02					
St Pancras International 15 ⊖	d									14 24	14 35					14 39		17 39					
City Thameslink 3	d																						
London Blackfriars 3 ⊖	d									14 34	14 45					14 49		17 49					
Elephant & Castle ⊖	d										14 48												
Loughborough Jn.	d										14 52												
Herne Hill 4	d										14 56												
Tulse Hill 3	d	14 39					14 54				15 00										18 09		
Streatham 4	d	14 42									15a04										18 12		
London Victoria 15 ⊖	d				14 24	14 27		14 36				14 36	14 41	14 47			and at the same minutes past each hour until			17 49			
Battersea Park 4	d				14 28								14a45						18a02				
Milton Keynes Central	d																						
Watford Junction	d																						
Harrow & Wealdstone ⊖	d																						
Wembley Central ⊖	d																						
Shepherd's Bush ⊖	d																						
Kensington (Olympia) ⊖	d																						
West Brompton ⊖	d																						
Imperial Wharf	d																						
Clapham Junction 10	d				14 32	14 33		14 42				14 42		14 53						17 56			
Latchmere	d																						
Wandsworth Common	d				14 35																		
Balham 4 ⊖	d				14 37							14 47								18 00			
Streatham Hill	d				14 41																		
West Norwood 4	d				14 46		14 57																
Gipsy Hill	d				14 49		15 00																
Crystal Palace 4	d				14 51		15a02																
Birkbeck	d																						
Beckenham Junction 4	a																						
Streatham Common 4	d	14 48										14 51								18 04	18 18		
Norbury	d	14 51										14 54								18 07	18 21		
Thornton Heath	d	14 54										14 57								18 10	18 24		
Selhurst 4	d	14 57										15 00								18 13	18 27		
Norwood Junction 2	a		14 44	14 48	14 56										15 02							18 14	18 16
	d		14 46	14 48	14 57										15 03							18 16	18 16
West Croydon 4	a		14 54		15 01															18 18		18 24	
East Croydon	a	15 01		14 54		14 42		14 52		14 55		15 03		15 02	15 07	15 09		18 09			18 30		18 20

Table 177

Sundays until 24 June

Luton, Milton Keynes Central and London East and West Croydon via Tulse Hill - Crystal Palace - Norbury

Local Services

Network Diagram - see first Page of Table 177

		SN	SN	SN	FC	FC	SN	SN	SN	SN	FC	SN	SN	SN	SN	SN		SN	SN	SN	SN	FC	FC	SN	SN
				◇1	1				◇1		1					1			◇1		◇1	1			
London Bridge 4 ⊖	d		18 06							18 09		18 11		18 21	18 24	18 37				18 36					
South Bermondsey	d		18 10									18 15		18 25						18 40					
Queens Rd Peckham	d		18 12									18 18		18 27						18 42					
Peckham Rye 4	d		18 15									18 20		18 30						18 45					
East Dulwich	d		18 18											18 33						18 48					
North Dulwich	d		18 20											18 35						18 50					
Luton 10	d				17 14						17 23											17 44			
Luton Airport Parkway 7	d				17 17						17 26											17 47			
St Pancras International 15 ⊖	d				17 54	18 05					18 09											18 24	18 35		
City Thameslink 3	d																								
London Blackfriars 3 ⊖	d				18 04	18 15					18 19											18 34	18 45		
Elephant & Castle ⊖	d					18 18																	18 48		
Loughborough Jn.	d					18 22																	18 52		
Herne Hill 4	d					18 26																	18 56		
Tulse Hill 3	d		18 24			18 30								18 39						18 54			19 00		
Streatham 4	d					18a34								18 42									19a04		
London Victoria 15 ⊖	d	17 54		18 06			18 06	18 11	18 17				18 19					18 24	18 27		18 36			18 36	18 41
Battersea Park 4	d	17 58						18a15				18a32						18 28							18a45
Milton Keynes Central	d																								
Watford Junction	d																								
Harrow & Wealdstone ⊖	d																								
Wembley Central ⊖	d																								
Shepherd's Bush ⊖	d																								
Kensington (Olympia) ⊖	d																								
West Brompton ⊖	d																								
Imperial Wharf	d																								
Clapham Junction 10	d	18 02		18 12			18 12		18 23				18 26					18 32	18 33		18 42			18 42	
Latchmere	d																								
Wandsworth Common	d	18 05																18 35							
Balham 4 ⊖	d	18 07					18 17						18 30					18 37						18 47	
Streatham Hill	d	18 11																18 41							
West Norwood 4	d	18 16	18 27															18 46		18 57					
Gipsy Hill	d	18 19	18 30															18 49		19 00					
Crystal Palace 4	d	18 21	18a32															18 51		19a02					
Birkbeck	d																								
Beckenham Junction 4	a																								
Streatham Common 4	d						18 21						18 34	18 48										18 51	
Norbury	d						18 24						18 37	18 51										18 54	
Thornton Heath	d						18 27						18 40	18 54										18 57	
Selhurst 4	d						18 30						18 43	18 57										19 00	
Norwood Junction 2	a	18 26								18 32					18 44	18 48		18 56							
	d	18 27								18 33					18 46	18 48		18 57							
West Croydon 4	a	18 31											18 48		18 54			19 01							
East Croydon	a			18 22	18 25		18 33		18 32	18 37	18 39			19 01		18 54			18 42		18 52	18 55		19 03	

Table 177

Sundays until 24 June

Luton, Milton Keynes Central and London East and West Croydon via Tulse Hill - Crystal Palace - Norbury

Local Services

Network Diagram - see first Page of Table 177

		SN	SN	FC	SN	SN	SN	SN		SN	SN	SN	SN	FC	FC	SN	SN	SN	SN	SN	SN	SN	SN	SN	
		◇1		1						1			◇1	1				◇1						1	
London Bridge 4 ⊖	d		18 39		18 41		18 51	18 54		19 05		19 06							19 09	19 11		19 21	19 24	19 37	
South Bermondsey	d				18 45		18 55					19 10								19 15		19 25			
Queens Rd Peckham	d				18 48		18 57					19 12								19 18		19 27			
Peckham Rye 4	d				18 50		19 00					19 15								19 20		19 30			
East Dulwich	d						19 03					19 18										19 33			
North Dulwich	d						19 05					19 20										19 35			
Luton 10	d			17 53										18 14											
Luton Airport Parkway 7	d			17 56										18 17											
St Pancras International 15 ⊖	d			18 39										18 54	19 05										
City Thameslink 3	d																								
London Blackfriars 3 ⊖	d			18 49										19 04	19 15										
Elephant & Castle ⊖	d														19 18										
Loughborough Jn.	d														19 22										
Herne Hill 4	d														19 26										
Tulse Hill 3	d						19 09					19 24			19 30							19 39			
Streatham 4	d						19 12								19a34							19 42			
London Victoria 15 ⊖	d	18 47				18 49					18 54		19 06			19 06	19 11	19 17			19 19				
Battersea Park 4	d				19a02						18 58						19a15			19a32					
Milton Keynes Central	d																								
Watford Junction	d																								
Harrow & Wealdstone ⊖	d																								
Wembley Central ⊖	d																								
Shepherd's Bush ⊖	d																								
Kensington (Olympia) ⊖	d																								
West Brompton ⊖	d																								
Imperial Wharf	d																								
Clapham Junction 10	d	18 53				18 56					19 02		19 12			19 12		19 23			19 26				
Latchmere	d																								
Wandsworth Common	d										19 05														
Balham 4 ⊖	d					19 00					19 07					19 17					19 30				
Streatham Hill	d										19 11														
West Norwood 4	d										19 16	19 27													
Gipsy Hill	d										19 19	19 30													
Crystal Palace 4	d										19 21	19a32													
Birkbeck	d																								
Beckenham Junction 4	a																								
Streatham Common 4	d					19 04	19 18									19 21					19 34	19 48			
Norbury	d					19 07	19 21									19 24					19 37	19 51			
Thornton Heath	d					19 10	19 24									19 27					19 40	19 54			
Selhurst 4	d					19 13	19 27									19 30					19 43	19 57			
Norwood Junction 2	a		19 02					19 14		19 16	19 26								19 32				19 44	19 48	
	d		19 03					19 16		19 16	19 27								19 33				19 46	19 48	
West Croydon 4	a					19 18		19 24			19 31										19 48		19 54		
East Croydon	a	19 02	19 07	19 09			19 30			19 20			19 22	19 25		19 33		19 32	19 37			20 01		19 54	

Table 177

Sundays until 24 June

Luton, Milton Keynes Central and London East and West Croydon via Tulse Hill - Crystal Palace - Norbury

Local Services

Network Diagram - see first Page of Table 177

		SN	SN ◇1	SN	SN ◇1	FC 1	FC	SN	SN	SN ◇1	SN	SN	SN	SN	SN	SN 1		SN	SN	SN ◇1	FC 1	FC	SN	SN	SN ◇1
London Bridge ⊖	d			19 36							19 39	19 41		19 51	19 54	20 05			20 06						
South Bermondsey	d			19 40								19 45		19 55					20 10						
Queens Rd Peckham	d			19 42								19 48		19 57					20 12						
Peckham Rye	d			19 45								19 50		20 00					20 15						
East Dulwich	d			19 48										20 03					20 18						
North Dulwich	d			19 50										20 05					20 20						
Luton	d					18 44															19 14				
Luton Airport Parkway	d					18 47															19 17				
St Pancras International ⊖	d					19 24	19 35														19 54	20 05			
City Thameslink	d																								
London Blackfriars ⊖	d					19 34	19 45														20 04	20 15			
Elephant & Castle ⊖	d						19 48															20 18			
Loughborough Jn.	d						19 52															20 22			
Herne Hill	d						19 56															20 26			
Tulse Hill	d			19 54			20 00							20 09					20 24			20 30			
Streatham	d						20a04							20 12								20a34			
London Victoria ⊖	d	19 24	19 27		19 36			19 36	19 41	19 47			19 49					19 54		20 06			20 06	20 11	20 17
Battersea Park	d	19 28							19a45			20a02						19 58						20a15	
Milton Keynes Central	d																								
Watford Junction	d																								
Harrow & Wealdstone ⊖	d																								
Wembley Central ⊖	d																								
Shepherd's Bush ⊖	d																								
Kensington (Olympia) ⊖	d																								
West Brompton ⊖	d																								
Imperial Wharf	d																								
Clapham Junction	d	19 32	19 33		19 42			19 42		19 53			19 56					20 02		20 12			20 12		20 23
Latchmere	d																								
Wandsworth Common	d	19 35																20 05							
Balham ⊖	d	19 37						19 47					20 00					20 07					20 17		
Streatham Hill	d	19 41																20 11							
West Norwood	d	19 46		19 57														20 16	20 27						
Gipsy Hill	d	19 49		20 00														20 19	20 30						
Crystal Palace	d	19 51		20a02														20 21	20a32						
Birkbeck ⇌	d																								
Beckenham Junction ⇌	a																								
Streatham Common	d							19 51					20 04	20 18									20 21		
Norbury	d							19 54					20 07	20 21									20 24		
Thornton Heath	d							19 57					20 10	20 24									20 27		
Selhurst	d							20 00					20 13	20 27									20 30		
Norwood Junction	a	19 56									20 02				20 14	20 16		20 26							
	d	19 57									20 03				20 16	20 16		20 27							
West Croydon ⇌	a	20 01											20 18		20 24			20 31							
East Croydon ⇌	a		19 42		19 52	19 55		20 03		20 02	20 07			20 30		20 20				20 22	20 25		20 33		20 32

Table 177

Sundays until 24 June

Luton, Milton Keynes Central and London East and West Croydon via Tulse Hill - Crystal Palace - Norbury

Local Services

Network Diagram - see first Page of Table 177

		SN	SN	SN	SN	SN	SN 1	SN		SN ◇1	SN	SN ◇1	FC 1	FC	SN	SN	SN ◇1	SN	SN	SN	SN	SN	SN 1	SN	
London Bridge ⊖	d	20 09	20 11		20 21	20 24	20 37				20 36							20 39	20 41		20 51	20 54	21 05		
South Bermondsey	d		20 15		20 25						20 40								20 45		20 55				
Queens Rd Peckham	d		20 18		20 27						20 42								20 48		20 57				
Peckham Rye	d		20 20		20 30						20 45								20 50		21 00				
East Dulwich	d				20 33						20 48										21 03				
North Dulwich	d				20 35						20 50										21 05				
Luton	d												19 44												
Luton Airport Parkway	d												19 47												
St Pancras International ⊖	d												20 24	20 35											
City Thameslink	d																								
London Blackfriars ⊖	d												20 34	20 45											
Elephant & Castle ⊖	d													20 48											
Loughborough Jn.	d													20 52											
Herne Hill	d													20 56											
Tulse Hill	d				20 39						20 54			21 00							21 09				
Streatham	d				20 42									21a04							21 12				
London Victoria ⊖	d			20 19				20 24		20 27		20 36			20 36	20 41	20 47			20 49				20 54	
Battersea Park	d		20a32					20 28								20a45			21a02					20 58	
Milton Keynes Central	d																								
Watford Junction	d																								
Harrow & Wealdstone ⊖	d																								
Wembley Central ⊖	d																								
Shepherd's Bush ⊖	d																								
Kensington (Olympia) ⊖	d																								
West Brompton ⊖	d																								
Imperial Wharf	d																								
Clapham Junction	d			20 26				20 32		20 33		20 42			20 42		20 53			20 56				21 02	
Latchmere	d																								
Wandsworth Common	d							20 35																21 05	
Balham ⊖	d			20 30				20 37							20 47					21 00				21 07	
Streatham Hill	d							20 41																21 11	
West Norwood	d							20 46			20 57													21 16	
Gipsy Hill	d							20 49			21 00													21 19	
Crystal Palace	d							20 51			21a02													21 21	
Birkbeck ⇌	d																								
Beckenham Junction ⇌	a																								
Streatham Common	d			20 34	20 48										20 51					21 04	21 18				
Norbury	d			20 37	20 51										20 54					21 07	21 21				
Thornton Heath	d			20 40	20 54										20 57					21 10	21 24				
Selhurst	d			20 43	20 57										21 00					21 13	21 27				
Norwood Junction	a	20 32				20 44	20 48	20 56										21 02				21 14	21 16	21 26	
	d	20 33				20 46	20 48	20 57										21 03				21 16	21 16	21 27	
West Croydon ⇌	a			20 48		20 54		21 01												21 18		21 24		21 31	
East Croydon ⇌	a	20 37			21 01		20 54			20 42		20 52	20 55		21 03		21 02	21 07			21 30		21 20		

Table 177

Sundays until 24 June

Luton, Milton Keynes Central and London East and West Croydon via Tulse Hill - Crystal Palace - Norbury

Local Services

Network Diagram - see first Page of Table 177

		SN	SN	FC	FC	SN	SN	SN	SN	SN	SN	SN	SN	SN	SN	SN		FC	SN	SN	SN	SN	SN	SN	SN
			◇1	1				◇1						1		◇1		1				◇1			
London Bridge ⊖	d	21 06							21 09	21 11		21 21	21 24	21 37					21 36				21 39	21 41	
South Bermondsey	d	21 10								21 15		21 25							21 40					21 45	
Queens Rd Peckham	d	21 12								21 18		21 27							21 42					21 48	
Peckham Rye	d	21 15								21 20		21 30							21 45					21 50	
East Dulwich	d	21 18										21 33							21 48						
North Dulwich	d	21 20										21 35							21 50						
Luton	d			20 14														20 37							
Luton Airport Parkway	d			20 17														20 39							
St Pancras International ⊖	d			20 54	21 05													21 24							
City Thameslink	d																								
London Blackfriars ⊖	d			21 04	21 15													21 34							
Elephant & Castle ⊖	d				21 18																				
Loughborough Jn.	d				21 22																				
Herne Hill	d				21 26																				
Tulse Hill	d	21 24			21 30							21 39							21 54						
Streatham	d				21a34							21 42													
London Victoria ⊖	d		21 06			21 06	21 11	21 17			21 19				21 24	21 27				21 36	21 41	21 47			21 49
Battersea Park	d						21a15			21a32					21 28						21a45			22a02	
Milton Keynes Central	d																								
Watford Junction	d																								
Harrow & Wealdstone ⊖	d																								
Wembley Central ⊖	d																								
Shepherd's Bush ⊖	d																								
Kensington (Olympia) ⊖	d																								
West Brompton ⊖	d																								
Imperial Wharf	d																								
Clapham Junction	d		21 12			21 12		21 23			21 26				21 32	21 33				21 42		21 53			21 56
Latchmere	d																								
Wandsworth Common	d														21 35										
Balham ⊖	d					21 17					21 30				21 38					21 47					22 00
Streatham Hill	d														21 41										
West Norwood	d	21 27													21 46				21 57						
Gipsy Hill	d	21 30													21 49				22 00						
Crystal Palace	d	21a32													21 51				22a02						
Birkbeck	d																								
Beckenham Junction	a																								
Streatham Common	d					21 21					21 34	21 48								21 51					22 04
Norbury	d					21 24					21 37	21 51								21 54					22 07
Thornton Heath	d					21 27					21 40	21 54								21 57					22 10
Selhurst	d					21 30					21 43	21 57								22 00					22 13
Norwood Junction	a								21 32				21 44	21 48	21 56								22 02		
	d								21 33				21 46	21 48	21 57								22 03		
West Croydon	a										21 48		21 54		22 01										22 18
East Croydon	a		21 22	21 25		21 33		21 32	21 37			22 01		21 54		21 42		21 55		22 03		22 02	22 07		

Table 177

Sundays until 24 June

Luton, Milton Keynes Central and London East and West Croydon via Tulse Hill - Crystal Palace - Norbury

Local Services

Network Diagram - see first Page of Table 177

		SN	SN	SN	FC	SN	SN	SN		SN	SN	SN	SN	SN	SN	SN	SN	SN	FC	SN	SN	SN	SN	SN	
				1	1						◇1					1		◇1	1				◇1		
London Bridge ⊖	d	21 51	21 54	22 05			22 06					22 09	22 11		22 21	22 37				22 36				22 39	
South Bermondsey	d	21 55					22 10						22 15		22 25					22 40					
Queens Rd Peckham	d	21 57					22 12						22 18		22 27					22 42					
Peckham Rye	d	22 00					22 15						22 20		22 30					22 45					
East Dulwich	d	22 03					22 18								22 33					22 48					
North Dulwich	d	22 05					22 20								22 35					22 50					
Luton	d				21 07														21 37						
Luton Airport Parkway	d				21 09														21 39						
St Pancras International ⊖	d				21 54														22 24						
City Thameslink	d																								
London Blackfriars ⊖	d				22 04														22 34						
Elephant & Castle ⊖	d																								
Loughborough Jn.	d																								
Herne Hill	d																								
Tulse Hill	d	22 09					22 24								22 39					22 54					
Streatham	d	22 12													22 42										
London Victoria ⊖	d					21 54		22 06		22 11	22 17			22 19			22 24	22 27			22 36	22 41	22 47		
Battersea Park	d					21 58				22a15			22a32				22 28					22a45			
Milton Keynes Central	d																								
Watford Junction	d																								
Harrow & Wealdstone ⊖	d																								
Wembley Central ⊖	d																								
Shepherd's Bush ⊖	d																								
Kensington (Olympia) ⊖	d																								
West Brompton ⊖	d																								
Imperial Wharf	d																								
Clapham Junction	d					22 02		22 12			22 23			22 26			22 32	22 33			22 42		22 53		
Latchmere	d																								
Wandsworth Common	d					22 05											22 35								
Balham ⊖	d					22 07		22 17						22 30			22 38				22 47				
Streatham Hill	d					22 11											22 41								
West Norwood	d					22 16	22 27										22 46			22 57					
Gipsy Hill	d					22 19	22 30										22 49			23 00					
Crystal Palace	d					22 21	22a32										22 51			23a02					
Birkbeck	d																								
Beckenham Junction	a																								
Streatham Common	d	22 18						22 21						22 34	22 48						22 51				
Norbury	d	22 21						22 24						22 37	22 51						22 54				
Thornton Heath	d	22 24						22 27						22 40	22 54						22 57				
Selhurst	d	22 27						22 30						22 43	22 57						23 00				
Norwood Junction	a		22 14	22 16		22 26						22 32				22 48	22 56							23 02	
	d		22 16	22 16		22 27						22 33				22 48	22 57							23 03	
West Croydon	a		22 24			22 31								22 48			23 01								
East Croydon	a	22 30		22 20	22 25			22 33			22 32	22 37			23 00	22 54		22 42	22 55		23 03		23 03	23 07	

Table 177

Sundays until 24 June

Luton, Milton Keynes Central and London East and West Croydon via Tulse Hill - Crystal Palace - Norbury

Local Services

Network Diagram - see first Page of Table 177

		SN	SN	SN	SN 1	FC 1	SN	SN	SN	SN	SN ◇1	SN	SN	SN	SN	SN ◇1		FC 1	SN	SN	SN	SN	SN	SN 1	FC 1
London Bridge 4 ⊖	d			22 41			22 51	23 06				23 09			23 11				23 21		23 39				
South Bermondsey	d			22 45			22 55	23 10							23 15				23 25						
Queens Rd Peckham	d			22 48			22 57	23 12							23 18				23 27						
Peckham Rye 4	d			22 50			23 00	23 15							23 20				23 30						
East Dulwich	d						23 03	23 18											23 33						
North Dulwich	d						23 05	23 20											23 35						
Luton 10	d					22 07												22 37							23 07
Luton Airport Parkway 7	d					22 09												22 39							23 09
St Pancras International 15 ⊖	d					22 54												23 24							23 54
City Thameslink 3	d																								
London Blackfriars 3 ⊖	d					23 04												23 34							00 05
Elephant & Castle ⊖	d																								
Loughborough Jn.	d																								
Herne Hill 4	d																								
Tulse Hill 3	d						23 09	23 24											23 39						
Streatham 4	d						23 12												23 42						
London Victoria 15 ⊖	d	22 49	22 54		23 04				23 06	23 11	23 17		23 19	23 24		23 32				23 36		23 47	23 50		
Battersea Park 4	d		22 58	23a02						23a15			23 23	23 28	23a32					23 40					
Milton Keynes Central	d																								
Watford Junction	d																							23 17	
Harrow & Wealdstone ⊖	d																							23 23	
Wembley Central ⊖	d																								
Shepherd's Bush ⊖	d																							23 45	
Kensington (Olympia) ⊖	d																							23 48	
West Brompton ⊖	d																							23 50	
Imperial Wharf	d																							23 53	
Clapham Junction 10	d	22 56	23 02		23 10				23 12		23 23		23 27	23 32		23 38				23 44		23 53	23 56	00 05	
Latchmere	d																								
Wandsworth Common	d		23 05										23 30	23 35						23 47			23 59		
Balham 4 ⊖	d	23 00	23 07						23 17				23 32	23 37						23 49			00 02		
Streatham Hill	d		23 11											23 41											
West Norwood 4	d		23 16					23 27						23 44											
Gipsy Hill	d		23 19					23 30						23 47											
Crystal Palace 4	d		23 21					23a32						23 50											
Birkbeck	d																								
Beckenham Junction 4	a																								
Streatham Common 4	d	23 04					23 18		23 21				23 36						23 48	23 53			00 06		
Norbury	d	23 07					23 21		23 24				23 39						23 51	23 56			00 08		
Thornton Heath	d	23 10					23 24		23 27				23 42						23 54	23 59			00 11		
Selhurst 4	d	23 13					23 27		23 30				23 45			23 48			23 57	00a01			00 14		
Norwood Junction 2	a		23 26									23 32		23 54							00 02				
	d		23 27									23 33		23 55							00 03				
West Croydon 4	a	23 18	23 31										23 49	23 59											
East Croydon	a				23 22	23 25	23 30		23 34		23 37	23 38				23 52		23 56	00 01		00 06	00 06	00 17	00 22	00 26

Table 177

Sundays until 24 June

Luton, Milton Keynes Central and London East and West Croydon via Tulse Hill - Crystal Palace - Norbury

Local Services

Network Diagram - see first Page of Table 177

		FC 1	SN
London Bridge 4 ⊖	d		
South Bermondsey	d		
Queens Rd Peckham	d		
Peckham Rye 4	d		
East Dulwich	d		
North Dulwich	d		
Luton 10	d	23 37	
Luton Airport Parkway 7	d	23 39	
St Pancras International 15 ⊖	d	00 24	
City Thameslink 3	d		
London Blackfriars 3 ⊖	d	00 35	
Elephant & Castle ⊖	d		
Loughborough Jn.	d		
Herne Hill 4	d		
Tulse Hill 3	d		
Streatham 4	d		
London Victoria 15 ⊖	d		23 54
Battersea Park 4	d		23 58
Milton Keynes Central	d		
Watford Junction	d		
Harrow & Wealdstone ⊖	d		
Wembley Central ⊖	d		
Shepherd's Bush ⊖	d		
Kensington (Olympia) ⊖	d		
West Brompton ⊖	d		
Imperial Wharf	d		
Clapham Junction 10	d		00 02
Latchmere	d		
Wandsworth Common	d		00 05
Balham 4 ⊖	d		00 07
Streatham Hill	d		00 11
West Norwood 4	d		00 14
Gipsy Hill	d		00 17
Crystal Palace 4	d		00 20
Birkbeck	d		
Beckenham Junction 4	a		
Streatham Common 4	d		
Norbury	d		
Thornton Heath	d		
Selhurst 4	d		
Norwood Junction 2	a		00 25
	d		
West Croydon 4	a		
East Croydon	a	00 56	

Table 177

Sundays
1 July to 9 September

Luton, Milton Keynes Central and London East and West Croydon via Tulse Hill - Crystal Palace - Norbury

Local Services

Network Diagram - see first Page of Table 177

		SN	SN	SN	FC	SN	SN	SN	SN	SN	SN	SN	SN	FC	SN	SN		SN	SN	SN	SN	SN	SN	SN	SN
								1		1			◇1	1					1				◇1 A		
London Bridge 4 ⊖	d		23p36	23p33					23p48						00 06	00 03					00 18				00 36
South Bermondsey	d			23p37					23p52							00 07					00 22				
Queens Rd Peckham	d			23p39					23p54							00 09					00 24				
Peckham Rye 4	d			23p42					23p57							00 12					00 27				
East Dulwich	d			23p45					00 01							00 15					00 30				
North Dulwich	d			23p47					00 03							00 17					00 32				
Luton 10	d				22p46									23p06											
Luton Airport Parkway 7	d				22p49									23p09											
St Pancras International 15 ⊖	d				23p36									23p54											
City Thameslink 3	d																								
London Blackfriars 3 ⊖	d				23p46									00 05											
Elephant & Castle ⊖	d				23p49																				
Loughborough Jn.	d																								
Herne Hill 4	d				23p57																				
Tulse Hill 3	d			23p51	00 01				00 06							00 21					00 35				
Streatham 4	d				00a05				00 10												00 39				
London Victoria 15 ⊖	d	23p34				23p38	23p45	23p47		23p49	23p54	23p59	00 05					00 07	00 14	00 16		00 22	00 25	00 34	
Battersea Park 4	d	23p38				23p42	23p49				23p58	00 03						00 11		00 20		00 26		00 38	
Milton Keynes Central	d																								
Watford Junction	d																								
Harrow & Wealdstone ⊖	d																								
Wembley Central ⊖	d																								
Shepherd's Bush ⊖	d																								
Kensington (Olympia) ⊖	d																								
West Brompton ⊖	d																								
Imperial Wharf	d																								
Clapham Junction 10	d	23p42				23p46	23p53	23p53		23p56	00 02	00 07	00 11					00 15	00 20	00 24		00 30	00 31	00 42	
Latchmere	d																								
Wandsworth Common	d	23p45				23p49	23p56				00 05	00 10						00 18		00 27		00 33		00 45	
Balham 4 ⊖	d	23p47				23p51	23p58				00 07	00 12						00 20		00 29		00 35		00 47	
Streatham Hill	d					23p54					00 10							00 23				00 38			
West Norwood 4	d			23p54		23p58					00 14					00 24		00 28				00 42			
Gipsy Hill	d			23p57		00 01					00 17					00 27		00 31				00 45			
Crystal Palace 4	d			23p59		00 03					00a19					00 29		00 33				00 47			
Birkbeck	d																								
Beckenham Junction 4	a																								
Streatham Common 4	d	23p51					00 02		00 13			00 16								00 33	00 42			00 51	
Norbury	d	23p54					00 05		00 15			00 19								00 36	00 45			00 54	
Thornton Heath	d	23p57					00 08		00 18			00 22								00 39	00 48			00 57	
Selhurst 4	d	23p59					00 11		00 21			00 25								00 41	00 51			01 00	
Norwood Junction 2	a		23p59	00 04		00 08									00 29	00 34		00 38				00 52			00 59
	d		23p59			00 09									00 30			00 38				00 52			01 00
West Croydon 4	a	00 03				00 14			00 27			00 30						00 43			00 55	00 58		01 04	
East Croydon	a		00 03				00 14	00 05		00 09			00 24	00 26	00 33				00 31	00 44			00 40		01 03

A 29 July, 5 August, 12 August, 2 September, 9 September

Table 177

Sundays
1 July to 9 September

Luton, Milton Keynes Central and London East and West Croydon via Tulse Hill - Crystal Palace - Norbury

Local Services

Network Diagram - see first Page of Table 177

		SN	SN	SN	FC	SN	SN	FC		SN	SN	SN	SN	SN	SN	SN	SN	SN	SN	SN	SN	FC	SN	SN
				◇1 A	1		1	1		A	◇1 A	A	1	1	1	1	◇1	◇1			1	1 B		
London Bridge 4 ⊖	d	00 33																			07 05			07 11
South Bermondsey	d	00 37																						07 15
Queens Rd Peckham	d	00 39																						07 18
Peckham Rye 4	d	00 42																						07 20
East Dulwich	d	00 45																						
North Dulwich	d	00 47																						
Luton 10	d				23p36			00 06																
Luton Airport Parkway 7	d				23p39			00 09																
St Pancras International 15 ⊖	d				00 24			00 54																
City Thameslink 3	d																							
London Blackfriars 3 ⊖	d				00 35			01 05														06 55		
Elephant & Castle ⊖	d																							
Loughborough Jn.	d																							
Herne Hill 4	d																							
Tulse Hill 3	d	00 51																						
Streatham 4	d																							
London Victoria 15 ⊖	d		00 37	00 40		00 42	01 00			01 12	01 30	01 42	02 00	03 00	04 00	05 02	05 47	06 32	06 36	06 49			07 06	
Battersea Park 4	d		00 41			00 46														06 53				07a32
Milton Keynes Central	d																							
Watford Junction	d																							
Harrow & Wealdstone ⊖	d																							
Wembley Central ⊖	d																							
Shepherd's Bush ⊖	d																							
Kensington (Olympia) ⊖	d																							
West Brompton ⊖	d																							
Imperial Wharf	d																							
Clapham Junction 10	d		00 45	00 46		00 50	01 08			01 18	01 36	01 48	02 08	03 08	04 08	05 08	05 53	06 38	06 42	06 57			07 12	
Latchmere	d																							
Wandsworth Common	d		00 48			00 53														07 00				
Balham 4 ⊖	d		00 50			00 55				01 23		01 53							06 47	07 02			07 17	
Streatham Hill	d		00 53																					
West Norwood 4	d	00 54	00 58																					
Gipsy Hill	d	00 57	01 01																					
Crystal Palace 4	d	00 59	01 03																					
Birkbeck	d																							
Beckenham Junction 4	a																							
Streatham Common 4	d					00 59				01 27		01 57							06 51	07 06			07 21	
Norbury	d					01 02				01 29		01 59							06 54	07 09			07 24	
Thornton Heath	d					01 05				01 32		02 02							06 57	07 12			07 27	
Selhurst 4	d					01 07				01 35		02 05							07 00	07 16			07 30	
Norwood Junction 2	a	01 04	01 08																		07 17			
	d		01 08																		07 17			
West Croydon 4	a		01 13																	07 20				
East Croydon	a			00 55	00 56	01 10	01 21	01 31		01 38	01 45	02 08	02 21	03 21	04 21	05 21	06 05	06 51	07 03		07 21	07 25	07 33	

A 29 July, 5 August, 12 August, 2 September, 9 September

B from 1 July until 22 July, from 19 August until 9 September

Luton, Milton Keynes Central and London East and West Croydon via Tulse Hill - Crystal Palace - Norbury

Local Services

Network Diagram - see first Page of Table 177

		SN	SN	SN	SN ■	SN	SN ◇■	FC ■	SN	SN	SN	SN	SN	SN	SN	SN		SN ■	FC ■	SN	SN	SN	SN	SN ◇■	SN
London Bridge ■ ⊖	d		07 21	07 24	07 37				07 36		07 39		07 41		07 51	07 54		08 05			08 06				08 09
South Bermondsey	d		07 25						07 40				07 45		07 55						08 10				
Queens Rd Peckham	d		07 27						07 42				07 48		07 57						08 12				
Peckham Rye ■	d		07 30						07 45				07 50		08 00						08 15				
East Dulwich	d		07 33						07 48						08 03						08 18				
North Dulwich	d		07 35						07 50						08 05						08 20				
Luton ■	d							06 36											07 06						
Luton Airport Parkway ■	d							06 39											07 09						
St Pancras International ■ ⊖	d							07 24											07 54						
City Thameslink ■	d																								
London Blackfriars ■ ⊖	d							07 34											08 04						
Elephant & Castle ⊖	d																								
Loughborough Jn.	d																								
Herne Hill ■	d																				08 24				
Tulse Hill ■	d		07 39						07 54						08 09										
Streatham ■	d		07 42												08 12										
London Victoria ■ ⊖	d	07 19				07 24	07 27			07 36		07 41		07 49						07 54		08 06	08 11	08 17	
Battersea Park ■	d					07 28						07a45	08a02							07 58			08a15		
Milton Keynes Central	d																								
Watford Junction	d																								
Harrow & Wealdstone ⊖	d																								
Wembley Central ⊖	d																								
Shepherd's Bush ⊖	d																								
Kensington (Olympia) ⊖	d																								
West Brompton ⊖	d																								
Imperial Wharf	d																								
Clapham Junction ■	d	07 26				07 32	07 33			07 42				07 56						08 02		08 12		08 23	
Latchmere	d																								
Wandsworth Common	d					07 35														08 05					
Balham ■ ⊖	d	07 30				07 37				07 47				08 00						08 07		08 17			
Streatham Hill	d					07 41														08 11					
West Norwood ■	d					07 46			07 57											08 16	08 27				
Gipsy Hill	d					07 49			08 00											08 19	08 30				
Crystal Palace ■	d					07 51			08a02											08 21	08a32				
Birkbeck	d																								
Beckenham Junction ■	a																								
Streatham Common ■	d	07 34	07 48							07 51				08 04	08 18							08 21			
Norbury	d	07 37	07 51							07 54				08 07	08 21							08 24			
Thornton Heath	d	07 40	07 54							07 57				08 10	08 24							08 27			
Selhurst ■	d	07 43	07 57							08 00				08 13	08 27							08 30			
Norwood Junction ■	a			07 44	07 48	07 56					08 02					08 14		08 16		08 26					08 32
	d			07 48	07 48	07 57					08 03					08 16		08 16		08 27					08 33
West Croydon ■	a	07 48		07 55		08 01								08 18		08 24				08 31					
East Croydon	a		08 01		07 54		07 42	07 55		08 03	08 07				08 30			08 20	08 25			08 33		08 32	08 37

Table 177

Sundays
1 July to 9 September

Luton, Milton Keynes Central and London East and West Croydon via Tulse Hill - Crystal Palace - Norbury

Local Services

Network Diagram - see first Page of Table 177

		SN	SN	SN	SN	SN ■	SN	SN ◇■		FC ■	SN	SN	SN	SN ◇■	SN	SN	SN	SN	SN	SN ■	SN	SN	SN ◇■	FC ■	
London Bridge ■ ⊖	d	08 11		08 21	08 24	08 37					08 36				08 39	08 41		08 51	08 54	09 05		09 06			
South Bermondsey	d	08 15		08 25							08 40					08 45		08 55				09 10			
Queens Rd Peckham	d	08 18		08 27							08 42					08 48		08 57				09 12			
Peckham Rye ■	d	08 20		08 30							08 45					08 50		09 00				09 15			
East Dulwich	d			08 33							08 48							09 03				09 18			
North Dulwich	d			08 35							08 50							09 05				09 20			
Luton ■	d									07 36														08 14	
Luton Airport Parkway ■	d									07 39														08 17	
St Pancras International ■ ⊖	d									08 24														08 54	
City Thameslink ■	d																								
London Blackfriars ■ ⊖	d									08 34														09 04	
Elephant & Castle ⊖	d																								
Loughborough Jn.	d																								
Herne Hill ■	d																								
Tulse Hill ■	d			08 39							08 54							09 09				09 24			
Streatham ■	d			08 42														09 12							
London Victoria ■ ⊖	d		08 19				08 24	08 27				08 36	08 41	08 47			08 49				08 54		09 06		
Battersea Park ■	d	08a32					08 28						08a45			09a02					08 58				
Milton Keynes Central	d																								
Watford Junction	d																								
Harrow & Wealdstone ⊖	d																								
Wembley Central ⊖	d																								
Shepherd's Bush ⊖	d																								
Kensington (Olympia) ⊖	d																								
West Brompton ⊖	d																								
Imperial Wharf	d																								
Clapham Junction ■	d		08 26				08 32	08 33				08 42		08 53			08 56				09 02		09 12		
Latchmere	d																								
Wandsworth Common	d						08 35														09 05				
Balham ■ ⊖	d		08 30				08 37					08 47					09 00				09 07				
Streatham Hill	d						08 41														09 11				
West Norwood ■	d						08 46				08 57										09 16	09 27			
Gipsy Hill	d						08 49				09 00										09 19	09 30			
Crystal Palace ■	d						08 51				09a02										09 21	09a32			
Birkbeck	d																								
Beckenham Junction ■	a																								
Streatham Common ■	d		08 34	08 48								08 51					09 04	09 18							
Norbury	d		08 37	08 51								08 54					09 07	09 21							
Thornton Heath	d		08 40	08 54								08 57					09 10	09 24							
Selhurst ■	d		08 43	08 57								09 00					09 13	09 27							
Norwood Junction ■	a				08 44	08 48	08 56								09 02				09 14	09 16	09 26				
	d				08 46	08 48	08 57								09 03				09 16	09 16	09 27				
West Croydon ■	a		08 48		08 54		09 01										09 18		09 24		09 31				
East Croydon	a			09 01		08 54		08 42		08 55		09 03		09 02	09 07			09 30		09 20			09 22	09 25	

Table 177

Sundays
1 July to 9 September

Luton, Milton Keynes Central and London East and West Croydon via Tulse Hill - Crystal Palace - Norbury

Local Services

Network Diagram - see first Page of Table 177

		FC	SN	SN	SN ◇1	SN	FC 1	SN	SN	SN	SN	SN 1	SN	SN ◇1	SN	SN ◇1	FC 1	FC	SN	SN	SN ◇1 ⌶	SN
London Bridge 4 ⊖	d					09 09		09 11		09 21	09 24	09 37			09 36							09 39
South Bermondsey	d							09 15		09 25					09 40							
Queens Rd Peckham	d							09 18		09 27					09 42							
Peckham Rye 4	d							09 20		09 30					09 45							
East Dulwich	d									09 33					09 48							
North Dulwich	d									09 35					09 50							
Luton 10	d	08 18					08 30										08 44	08 48				
Luton Airport Parkway 7	d	08 21					08 33										08 47	08 51				
St Pancras International 15 ⊖	d	09 05					09 09										09 24	09 35				
City Thameslink 3	d																					
London Blackfriars 3 ⊖	d	09 15					09 19										09 34	09 45				
Elephant & Castle ⊖	d	09 18																09 48				
Loughborough Jn	d	09 22																09 52				
Herne Hill 4	d	09 26																09 56				
Tulse Hill 3	d	09 30								09 39					09 54			10 00				
Streatham 4	d	09a34								09 42								10a04				
London Victoria 15 ⊖	d		09 06	09 11	09 17				09 19				09 24	09 27		09 36			09 36	09 41	09 47	
Battersea Park 4	d			09a15				09a32					09 28							09a45		
Milton Keynes Central	d																					
Watford Junction	d																					
Harrow & Wealdstone ⊖	d																					
Wembley Central ⊖	d																					
Shepherd's Bush ⊖	d																					
Kensington (Olympia) ⊖	d																					
West Brompton ⊖	d																					
Imperial Wharf	d																					
Clapham Junction 10	d		09 12		09 23				09 26				09 32	09 33		09 42			09 42		09 53	
Latchmere	d																					
Wandsworth Common	d												09 35									
Balham 4 ⊖	d		09 17						09 30				09 37						09 47			
Streatham Hill	d												09 41									
West Norwood 4	d												09 46		09 57							
Gipsy Hill	d												09 49		10 00							
Crystal Palace 4	d												09 51		10a02							
Birkbeck 🚋	d																					
Beckenham Junction 4 🚋	a																					
Streatham Common 4	d		09 21						09 34	09 48												
Norbury	d		09 24						09 37	09 51									09 51			
Thornton Heath	d		09 27						09 40	09 54									09 54			
Selhurst 4	d		09 30						09 43	09 57									09 57			
Norwood Junction 2	a					09 32					09 44	09 48	09 56						10 00			
	d					09 33					09 46	09 48	09 57									10 02
West Croydon 4 🚋	a								09 48		09 54		10 01									10 03
East Croydon 🚋	a		09 33		09 32	09 37	09 39			10 01		09 54		09 42		09 52	09 55		10 03		10 02	10 07

Table 177

Sundays
1 July to 9 September

Luton, Milton Keynes Central and London East and West Croydon via Tulse Hill - Crystal Palace - Norbury

Local Services

Network Diagram - see first Page of Table 177

		FC 1		FC 1	SN	SN	SN	SN	SN 1	SN	SN	SN ◇1 ⌶	FC 1	FC	SN	SN	SN ◇1	SN	SN	SN	SN	SN	SN 1
London Bridge 4 ⊖	d				18 41		18 51	18 54	19 05		19 06							19 09	19 11		19 21	19 24	19 37
South Bermondsey	d				18 45		18 55				19 10								19 15		19 25		
Queens Rd Peckham	d				18 48		18 57				19 12								19 18		19 27		
Peckham Rye 4	d				18 50		19 00				19 15								19 20		19 30		
East Dulwich	d						19 03				19 18										19 33		
North Dulwich	d						19 05				19 20										19 35		
Luton 10	d	09 00		18 00									18 14	18 18									
Luton Airport Parkway 7	d	09 03		18 03									18 17	18 21									
St Pancras International 15 ⊖	d	09 39		18 39									18 54	19 05									
City Thameslink 3	d																						
London Blackfriars 3 ⊖	d	09 49		18 49									19 04	19 15									
Elephant & Castle ⊖	d													19 18									
Loughborough Jn	d													19 22									
Herne Hill 4	d													19 26									
Tulse Hill 3	d						19 09				19 24			19 30							19 39		
Streatham 4	d						19 12							19a34							19 42		
London Victoria 15 ⊖	d		and at the same minutes past each hour until			18 49				18 54		19 06			19 06	19 11	19 17			19 19			
Battersea Park 4	d				19a02					18 58						19a15			19a32				
Milton Keynes Central	d																						
Watford Junction	d																						
Harrow & Wealdstone ⊖	d																						
Wembley Central ⊖	d																						
Shepherd's Bush ⊖	d																						
Kensington (Olympia) ⊖	d																						
West Brompton ⊖	d																						
Imperial Wharf	d																						
Clapham Junction 10	d					18 56				19 02		19 12			19 12		19 23			19 26			
Latchmere	d																						
Wandsworth Common	d									19 05													
Balham 4 ⊖	d					19 00				19 07					19 17					19 30			
Streatham Hill	d									19 11													
West Norwood 4	d									19 16	19 27												
Gipsy Hill	d									19 19	19 30												
Crystal Palace 4	d									19 21	19a32												
Birkbeck 🚋	d																						
Beckenham Junction 4 🚋	a																						
Streatham Common 4	d					19 04	19 18								19 21					19 34	19 48		
Norbury	d					19 07	19 21								19 24					19 37	19 51		
Thornton Heath	d					19 10	19 24								19 27					19 40	19 54		
Selhurst 4	d					19 13	19 27								19 30					19 43	19 57		
Norwood Junction 2	a							19 14	19 16	19 26								19 32				19 44	19 48
	d							19 16	19 16	19 27								19 33				19 46	19 48
West Croydon 4 🚋	a					19 18		19 24		19 31										19 48		19 54	
East Croydon 🚋	a	10 09		19 09			19 30		19 20			19 22	19 25		19 33		19 32	19 37			20 01		19 54

Table 177

Sundays
1 July to 9 September

Luton, Milton Keynes Central and London East and West Croydon via Tulse Hill - Crystal Palace - Norbury

Local Services

Network Diagram - see first Page of Table 177

		SN		SN ◇■	SN	SN ◇■	FC ■	FC	SN	SN	SN ◇■	SN	SN	SN	SN	SN	SN ■	SN		SN	SN ◇■	FC ■	FC	SN	SN
London Bridge ⊖	d				19 36							19 39	19 41		19 51	19 54	20 05			20 06					
South Bermondsey	d				19 40								19 45		19 55					20 10					
Queens Rd Peckham	d				19 42								19 48		19 57					20 12					
Peckham Rye	d				19 45								19 50		20 00					20 15					
East Dulwich	d				19 48										20 03					20 18					
North Dulwich	d				19 50										20 05					20 20					
Luton	d						18 44	18 48														19 14	19 18		
Luton Airport Parkway	d						18 47	18 51														19 17	19 21		
St Pancras International ⊖	d						19 24	19 35														19 54	20 05		
City Thameslink	d																								
London Blackfriars ⊖	d						19 34	19 45														20 04	20 15		
Elephant & Castle ⊖	d							19 48															20 18		
Loughborough Jn.	d							19 52															20 22		
Herne Hill	d							19 56															20 26		
Tulse Hill	d				19 54			20 00							20 09					20 24			20 30		
Streatham	d							20a04							20 12								20a34		
London Victoria ⊖	d	19 24		19 27		19 36			19 36	19 41	19 47			19 49				19 54			20 06			20 06	20 11
Battersea Park	d	19 28								19a45			20a02					19 58							20a15
Milton Keynes Central	d																								
Watford Junction	d																								
Harrow & Wealdstone ⊖	d																								
Wembley Central ⊖	d																								
Shepherd's Bush ⊖	d																								
Kensington (Olympia) ⊖	d																								
West Brompton ⊖	d																								
Imperial Wharf	d																								
Clapham Junction	d	19 32		19 33		19 42			19 42		19 53			19 56				20 02			20 12			20 12	
Latchmere	d																								
Wandsworth Common	d	19 35																20 05							
Balham ⊖	d	19 37							19 47					20 00				20 07						20 17	
Streatham Hill	d	19 41																20 11							
West Norwood	d	19 46			19 57													20 16		20 27					
Gipsy Hill	d	19 49			20 00													20 19		20 30					
Crystal Palace	d	19 51			20a02													20 21		20a32					
Birkbeck	d																								
Beckenham Junction	a																								
Streatham Common	d								19 51					20 04	20 18									20 21	
Norbury	d								19 54					20 07	20 21									20 24	
Thornton Heath	d								19 57					20 10	20 24									20 27	
Selhurst	d								20 00					20 13	20 27									20 30	
Norwood Junction	a	19 56										20 02				20 14	20 16	20 26							
	d	19 57										20 03				20 16	20 16	20 27							
West Croydon	a	20 01												20 18		20 24		20 31							
East Croydon	a			19 42		19 52	19 55		20 03		20 02	20 07			20 30		20 20				20 22	20 25		20 33	

Table 177

Sundays
1 July to 9 September

Luton, Milton Keynes Central and London East and West Croydon via Tulse Hill - Crystal Palace - Norbury

Local Services

Network Diagram - see first Page of Table 177

		SN ◇■	SN	SN	SN	SN	SN	SN ■	SN	SN ◇■		SN	SN ◇■	FC ■	FC	SN	SN	SN ◇■	SN	SN	SN	SN	SN	SN ■	SN
London Bridge ⊖	d		20 09	20 11		20 21	20 24	20 37				20 36							20 39	20 41		20 51	20 54	21 05	
South Bermondsey	d			20 15		20 25						20 40								20 45		20 55			
Queens Rd Peckham	d			20 18		20 27						20 42								20 48		20 57			
Peckham Rye	d			20 20		20 30						20 45								20 50		21 00			
East Dulwich	d					20 33						20 48										21 03			
North Dulwich	d					20 35						20 50										21 05			
Luton	d													19 44	19 48										
Luton Airport Parkway	d													19 47	19 51										
St Pancras International ⊖	d													20 24	20 35										
City Thameslink	d																								
London Blackfriars ⊖	d													20 34	20 45										
Elephant & Castle ⊖	d														20 48										
Loughborough Jn.	d														20 52										
Herne Hill	d														20 56										
Tulse Hill	d					20 39						20 54			21 00							21 09			
Streatham	d					20 42									21a04							21 12			
London Victoria ⊖	d	20 17			20 19				20 24	20 27			20 36			20 36	20 41	20 47			20 49				20 54
Battersea Park	d			20a32					20 28								20a45			21a02					20 58
Milton Keynes Central	d																								
Watford Junction	d																								
Harrow & Wealdstone ⊖	d																								
Wembley Central ⊖	d																								
Shepherd's Bush ⊖	d																								
Kensington (Olympia) ⊖	d																								
West Brompton ⊖	d																								
Imperial Wharf	d																								
Clapham Junction	d	20 23			20 26				20 32	20 33			20 42			20 42		20 53			20 56				21 02
Latchmere	d																								
Wandsworth Common	d								20 35																21 05
Balham ⊖	d				20 30				20 37							20 47					21 00				21 07
Streatham Hill	d								20 41																21 11
West Norwood	d								20 46			20 57													21 16
Gipsy Hill	d								20 49			21 00													21 19
Crystal Palace	d								20 51			21a02													21 21
Birkbeck	d																								
Beckenham Junction	a																								
Streatham Common	d				20 34	20 48										20 51					21 04	21 18			
Norbury	d				20 37	20 51										20 54					21 07	21 21			
Thornton Heath	d				20 40	20 54										20 57					21 10	21 24			
Selhurst	d				20 43	20 57										21 00					21 13	21 27			
Norwood Junction	a		20 32				20 44	20 48	20 56										21 02				21 14	21 16	21 26
	d		20 33				20 46	20 48	20 57										21 03				21 16	21 16	21 27
West Croydon	a				20 48		20 54		21 01												21 18		21 24		21 31
East Croydon	a	20 32	20 37			21 01		20 54		20 42			20 52	20 55		21 03		21 02	21 07			21 30		21 20	

Table 177

Sundays
1 July to 9 September

Luton, Milton Keynes Central and London East and West Croydon via Tulse Hill - Crystal Palace - Norbury

Local Services

Network Diagram - see first Page of Table 177

		SN		SN ◇1	FC 1	FC	SN	SN	SN ◇1	SN	SN	SN	SN	SN	SN 1	SN	SN ◇1	FC 1		SN	SN	SN	SN ◇1	SN	SN
London Bridge ⊖	d	21 06								21 09	21 11		21 21	21 24	21 37					21 36				21 39	21 41
South Bermondsey	d	21 10									21 15		21 25							21 40					21 45
Queens Rd Peckham	d	21 12									21 18		21 27							21 42					21 48
Peckham Rye	d	21 15									21 20		21 30							21 45					21 50
East Dulwich	d	21 18											21 33							21 48					
North Dulwich	d	21 20											21 35							21 50					
Luton	d				20 14	20 18												20 36							
Luton Airport Parkway	d				20 17	20 21												20 39							
St Pancras International ⊖	d				20 54	21 05												21 24							
City Thameslink	d																								
London Blackfriars ⊖	d				21 04	21 15												21 34							
Elephant & Castle ⊖	d					21 18																			
Loughborough Jn.	d					21 22																			
Herne Hill	d					21 26																			
Tulse Hill	d	21 24				21 30							21 39							21 54					
Streatham	d					21a34							21 42												
London Victoria ⊖	d			21 06			21 06	21 11	21 17			21 19				21 24	21 27				21 36	21 41	21 47		
Battersea Park	d							21a15			21a32					21 28						21a45			22a02
Milton Keynes Central	d																								
Watford Junction	d																								
Harrow & Wealdstone ⊖	d																								
Wembley Central ⊖	d																								
Shepherd's Bush ⊖	d																								
Kensington (Olympia) ⊖	d																								
West Brompton ⊖	d																								
Imperial Wharf	d																								
Clapham Junction	d			21 12			21 12		21 23			21 26				21 32	21 33				21 42		21 53		
Latchmere	d																								
Wandsworth Common	d															21 35									
Balham ⊖	d						21 17					21 30				21 38					21 47				
Streatham Hill	d															21 41									
West Norwood	d	21 27														21 46				21 57					
Gipsy Hill	d	21 30														21 49				22 00					
Crystal Palace	d	21a32														21 51				22a02					
Birkbeck	d																								
Beckenham Junction	a																								
Streatham Common	d						21 21					21 34	21 48								21 51				
Norbury	d						21 24					21 37	21 51								21 54				
Thornton Heath	d						21 27					21 40	21 54								21 57				
Selhurst	d						21 30					21 43	21 57								22 00				
Norwood Junction	a									21 32				21 44	21 48	21 56								22 02	
	d									21 33				21 46	21 48	21 57								22 03	
West Croydon	a											21 48		21 54		22 01									
East Croydon	a			21 22	21 25		21 33		21 32	21 37			22 01		21 54		21 42	21 55			22 03		22 02	22 07	

Table 177

Sundays
1 July to 9 September

Luton, Milton Keynes Central and London East and West Croydon via Tulse Hill - Crystal Palace - Norbury

Local Services

Network Diagram - see first Page of Table 177

		SN	SN	SN	SN 1	FC 1	SN	SN	SN	SN		SN ◇1	SN	SN	SN	SN	SN 1	SN	SN ◇1	FC 1	SN	SN	SN	SN ◇1	SN
London Bridge ⊖	d		21 51	21 54	22 05			22 06					22 09	22 11		22 21	22 37				22 36				22 39
South Bermondsey	d		21 55					22 10						22 15		22 25					22 40				
Queens Rd Peckham	d		21 57					22 12						22 18		22 27					22 42				
Peckham Rye	d		22 00					22 15						22 20		22 30					22 45				
East Dulwich	d		22 03					22 18								22 33					22 48				
North Dulwich	d		22 05					22 20								22 35					22 50				
Luton	d					21 06														21 36					
Luton Airport Parkway	d					21 09														21 39					
St Pancras International ⊖	d					21 54														22 24					
City Thameslink	d																								
London Blackfriars ⊖	d					22 04														22 34					
Elephant & Castle ⊖	d																								
Loughborough Jn.	d																								
Herne Hill	d																								
Tulse Hill	d		22 09					22 24								22 39					22 54				
Streatham	d		22 12													22 42									
London Victoria ⊖	d	21 49					21 54		22 06	22 11		22 17			22 19			22 24	22 27			22 36	22 41	22 47	
Battersea Park	d						21 58			22a15				22a32				22 28					22a45		
Milton Keynes Central	d																								
Watford Junction	d																								
Harrow & Wealdstone ⊖	d																								
Wembley Central ⊖	d																								
Shepherd's Bush ⊖	d																								
Kensington (Olympia) ⊖	d																								
West Brompton ⊖	d																								
Imperial Wharf	d																								
Clapham Junction	d	21 56					22 02		22 12			22 23			22 26			22 32	22 33			22 42		22 53	
Latchmere	d																								
Wandsworth Common	d						22 05											22 35							
Balham ⊖	d	22 00					22 07		22 17						22 30			22 38				22 47			
Streatham Hill	d						22 11											22 41							
West Norwood	d						22 16	22 27										22 46			22 57				
Gipsy Hill	d						22 19	22 30										22 49			23 00				
Crystal Palace	d						22 21	22a32										22 51			23a02				
Birkbeck	d																								
Beckenham Junction	a																								
Streatham Common	d	22 04	22 18						22 21						22 34	22 48						22 51			
Norbury	d	22 07	22 21						22 24						22 37	22 51						22 54			
Thornton Heath	d	22 10	22 24						22 27						22 40	22 54						22 57			
Selhurst	d	22 13	22 27						22 30						22 43	22 57						23 00			
Norwood Junction	a			22 14	22 16		22 26						22 32				22 48	22 56							23 02
	d			22 16	22 16		22 27						22 33				22 48	22 57							23 03
West Croydon	a	22 18		22 24			22 31								22 48			23 01							
East Croydon	a		22 30		22 20	22 25			22 33			22 32	22 37			23 00	22 54		22 42	22 55		23 03		23 03	23 07

Table 177

Sundays
1 July to 9 September

Luton, Milton Keynes Central and London East and West Croydon via Tulse Hill - Crystal Palace - Norbury

Local Services

Network Diagram - see first Page of Table 177

		SN		SN	SN	SN ■1	FC ■1	SN	SN	SN	SN	SN ◇■1	SN	SN	SN	SN	SN ◇■1	FC ■1		SN	SN	SN	SN	SN	SN ■1
London Bridge 4 ⊖	d				22 41			22 51	23 06				23 09			23 11				23 21		23 39			
South Bermondsey	d				22 45			22 55	23 10							23 15				23 25					
Queens Rd Peckham	d				22 48			22 57	23 12							23 18				23 27					
Peckham Rye 4	d				22 50			23 00	23 15							23 20				23 30					
East Dulwich	d							23 03	23 18											23 33					
North Dulwich	d							23 05	23 20											23 35					
Luton 10	d						22 06											22 36							
Luton Airport Parkway 7	d						22 09											22 39							
St Pancras International 15 ⊖	d						22 54											23 24							
City Thameslink 3	d																								
London Blackfriars 3 ⊖	d						23 04											23 34							
Elephant & Castle ⊖	d																								
Loughborough Jn.	d																								
Herne Hill 4	d																								
Tulse Hill 3	d							23 09	23 24											23 39					
Streatham 4	d							23 12												23 42					
London Victoria 15 ⊖	d	22 49		22 54		23 04				23 06	23 11	23 17		23 19	23 24		23 32				23 36		23 47	23 50	
Battersea Park 4	d			22 58	23a02						23a15			23 23	23 28	23a32					23 40				
Milton Keynes Central	d																								
Watford Junction	d																								23 17
Harrow & Wealdstone ⊖	d																								23 23
Wembley Central ⊖	d																								
Shepherd's Bush ⊖	d																								23 45
Kensington (Olympia) ⊖	d																								23 48
West Brompton ⊖	d																								23 50
Imperial Wharf	d																								23 53
Clapham Junction 10	d	22 56		23 02		23 10				23 12		23 23		23 27	23 32		23 38				23 44		23 53	23 56	00 05
Latchmere	d																								
Wandsworth Common	d			23 05										23 30	23 35						23 47			23 59	
Balham 4 ⊖	d	23 00		23 07						23 17				23 32	23 37						23 49			00 02	
Streatham Hill	d			23 11											23 41										
West Norwood 4	d			23 16					23 27						23 44										
Gipsy Hill	d			23 19					23 30						23 47										
Crystal Palace 4	d			23 21					23a32						23 50										
Birkbeck	d																								
Beckenham Junction 4	a																								
Streatham Common 4	d	23 04						23 18		23 21				23 36						23 48	23 53			00 06	
Norbury	d	23 07						23 21		23 24				23 39						23 51	23 56			00 08	
Thornton Heath	d	23 10						23 24		23 27				23 42						23 54	23 59			00 11	
Selhurst 4	d	23 13						23 27		23 30				23 45			23 48			23 57	00a01			00 14	
Norwood Junction 2	a			23 26									23 32		23 54							00 02			
	d			23 27									23 33		23 55							00 03			
West Croydon 4	a	23 18		23 31										23 49	23 59										
East Croydon	a					23 22	23 25	23 30		23 34		23 37	23 38				23 52	23 56		00 01		00 06	00 06	00 17	00 22

Table 177

Sundays
1 July to 9 September

Luton, Milton Keynes Central and London East and West Croydon via Tulse Hill - Crystal Palace - Norbury

Local Services

Network Diagram - see first Page of Table 177

		FC ■1	FC ■1	SN
London Bridge 4 ⊖	d			
South Bermondsey	d			
Queens Rd Peckham	d			
Peckham Rye 4	d			
East Dulwich	d			
North Dulwich	d			
Luton 10	d	23 06	23 36	
Luton Airport Parkway 7	d	23 09	23 39	
St Pancras International 15 ⊖	d	23 54	00 24	
City Thameslink 3	d			
London Blackfriars 3 ⊖	d	00 05	00 35	
Elephant & Castle ⊖	d			
Loughborough Jn.	d			
Herne Hill 4	d			
Tulse Hill 3	d			
Streatham 4	d			
London Victoria 15 ⊖	d			23 54
Battersea Park 4	d			23 58
Milton Keynes Central	d			
Watford Junction	d			
Harrow & Wealdstone ⊖	d			
Wembley Central ⊖	d			
Shepherd's Bush ⊖	d			
Kensington (Olympia) ⊖	d			
West Brompton ⊖	d			
Imperial Wharf	d			
Clapham Junction 10	d			00 02
Latchmere	d			
Wandsworth Common	d			00 05
Balham 4 ⊖	d			00 07
Streatham Hill	d			00 11
West Norwood 4	d			00 14
Gipsy Hill	d			00 17
Crystal Palace 4	d			00 20
Birkbeck	d			
Beckenham Junction 4	a			
Streatham Common 4	d			
Norbury	d			
Thornton Heath	d			
Selhurst 4	d			
Norwood Junction 2	a			00 25
	d			
West Croydon 4	a			
East Croydon	a	00 26	00 56	

Table 177

Sundays
from 16 September

Luton, Milton Keynes Central and London East and West Croydon via Tulse Hill - Crystal Palace - Norbury

Local Services

Network Diagram - see first Page of Table 177

		SN	SN	SN	FC	SN	SN	SN 1	SN	SN 1	SN	SN	SN ◇1	FC 1	SN	SN		SN	SN 1	SN	FC 1	SN	SN	SN	SN
London Bridge 4 ⊖	d		23p36	23p33					23p48						00 06	00 03						00 18			00 36
South Bermondsey	d			23p37					23p52							00 07						00 22			
Queens Rd Peckham	d			23p39					23p54							00 09						00 24			
Peckham Rye 4	d			23p42					23p57							00 12						00 27			
East Dulwich	d			23p45					00 01							00 15						00 30			
North Dulwich	d			23p47					00 03							00 17						00 32			
Luton 10	d				22p46									23p06							23p36				
Luton Airport Parkway 7	d				22p49									23p09							23p39				
St Pancras International 15 ⊖	d				23p36									23p54							00 24				
City Thameslink 3	d																								
London Blackfriars 3 ⊖	d				23p46									00 05							00 35				
Elephant & Castle ⊖	d				23p49																				
Loughborough Jn.	d																								
Herne Hill 4	d				23p57																				
Tulse Hill 3	d			23p51	00 01				00 06							00 21						00 35			
Streatham 4	d				00a05				00 10													00 39			
London Victoria 15 ⊖	d	23p34				23p38	23p45	23p47		23p49	23p54	23p59	00 05					00 07	00 14	00 16			00 22	00 34	
Battersea Park 4	d	23p38				23p42	23p49				23p58	00 03						00 11		00 20			00 26	00 38	
Milton Keynes Central	d																								
Watford Junction	d																								
Harrow & Wealdstone ⊖	d																								
Wembley Central ⊖	d																								
Shepherd's Bush ⊖	d																								
Kensington (Olympia) ⊖	d																								
West Brompton ⊖	d																								
Imperial Wharf	d																								
Clapham Junction 10	d	23p42				23p46	23p53	23p53		23p56	00 02	00 07	00 11					00 15	00 20	00 24			00 30	00 42	
Latchmere	d																								
Wandsworth Common	d	23p45				23p49	23p56				00 05	00 10						00 18		00 27			00 33	00 45	
Balham 4 ⊖	d	23p47				23p51	23p58				00 07	00 12						00 20		00 29			00 35	00 47	
Streatham Hill	d					23p54					00 10							00 23					00 38		
West Norwood 4	d			23p54		23p58					00 14					00 24		00 28					00 42		
Gipsy Hill	d			23p57		00 01					00 17					00 27		00 31					00 45		
Crystal Palace 4	d			23p59		00 03					00a19					00 29		00 33					00 47		
Birkbeck	d																								
Beckenham Junction 4	a																								
Streatham Common 4	d	23p51					00 02		00 13			00 16								00 33		00 42		00 51	
Norbury	d	23p54					00 05		00 15			00 19								00 36		00 45		00 54	
Thornton Heath	d	23p57					00 08		00 18			00 22								00 39		00 48		00 57	
Selhurst 4	d	23p59					00 11		00 21			00 25								00 41		00 51		01 00	
Norwood Junction 2	a		23p59	00 04		00 08									00 29	00 34		00 38					00 52		00 59
	d		23p59			00 09									00 30			00 38					00 52		01 00
West Croydon 4	a	00 03				00 14			00 27			00 30						00 43				00 55	00 58	01 04	
East Croydon	a		00 03				00 14	00 05		00 09			00 24	00 26	00 33				00 31	00 44	00 56				01 03

Table 177

Sundays
from 16 September

Luton, Milton Keynes Central and London East and West Croydon via Tulse Hill - Crystal Palace - Norbury

Local Services

Network Diagram - see first Page of Table 177

		SN	SN	SN	SN 1	FC 1	SN 1	SN 1		SN 1	SN 1	SN ◇1	SN ◇1	SN	SN	FC 1	SN	SN	SN	SN	SN	SN 1	SN	SN ◇1
London Bridge 4 ⊖	d	00 33																07 11		07 21	07 24	07 37		
South Bermondsey	d	00 37																07 15		07 25				
Queens Rd Peckham	d	00 39																07 18		07 27				
Peckham Rye 4	d	00 42																07 20		07 30				
East Dulwich	d	00 45																		07 33				
North Dulwich	d	00 47																		07 35				
Luton 10	d					00 06																		
Luton Airport Parkway 7	d					00 09																		
St Pancras International 15 ⊖	d					00 54																		
City Thameslink 3	d																							
London Blackfriars 3 ⊖	d					01 05										06 55								
Elephant & Castle ⊖	d																							
Loughborough Jn.	d																							
Herne Hill 4	d																							
Tulse Hill 3	d	00 51																		07 39				
Streatham 4	d																			07 42				
London Victoria 15 ⊖	d		00 37	00 42	01 00		02 00	03 00		04 00	05 02	05 47	06 32	06 36	06 49		07 06		07 19				07 24	07 32
Battersea Park 4	d		00 41	00 46											06 53			07a32					07 28	
Milton Keynes Central	d																							
Watford Junction	d																							
Harrow & Wealdstone ⊖	d																							
Wembley Central ⊖	d																							
Shepherd's Bush ⊖	d																							
Kensington (Olympia) ⊖	d																							
West Brompton ⊖	d																							
Imperial Wharf	d																							
Clapham Junction 10	d		00 45	00 50	01 08		02 08	03 08		04 08	05 08	05 53	06 38	06 42	06 57		07 12		07 26				07 32	07 38
Latchmere	d																							
Wandsworth Common	d		00 48	00 53											07 00								07 35	
Balham 4 ⊖	d		00 50	00 55										06 47	07 02		07 17		07 30				07 37	
Streatham Hill	d		00 53																				07 41	
West Norwood 4	d	00 54	00 58																				07 46	
Gipsy Hill	d	00 57	01 01																				07 49	
Crystal Palace 4	d	00 59	01 03																				07 51	
Birkbeck	d																							
Beckenham Junction 4	a																							
Streatham Common 4	d			00 59										06 51	07 06		07 21		07 34	07 48				
Norbury	d			01 02										06 54	07 09		07 24		07 37	07 51				
Thornton Heath	d			01 05										06 57	07 12		07 27		07 40	07 54				
Selhurst 4	d			01 07										07 00	07 16		07 30		07 43	07 57				
Norwood Junction 2	a	01 04	01 08																		07 44	07 47	07 56	
	d		01 08																		07 48	07 48	07 57	
West Croydon 4	a		01 13												07 20				07 48		07 55		08 01	
East Croydon	a			01 10	01 21	01 31	02 21	03 21		04 21	05 21	06 05	06 51	07 03		07 25	07 33			08 01		07 54		07 50

Table 177

Sundays from 16 September

Luton, Milton Keynes Central and London East and West Croydon via Tulse Hill - Crystal Palace - Norbury

Local Services

Network Diagram - see first Page of Table 177

		FC 1	SN	SN	SN	FC 1	SN	SN	SN	SN	SN	SN	SN	SN	SN	SN ◇1		SN	SN	SN	SN	SN	SN 1	SN	SN ◇1
London Bridge ⊖	d		07 36		07 39			07 41		07 51	07 54		08 06					08 09	08 11		08 21	08 24	08 37		
South Bermondsey	d		07 40					07 45		07 55			08 10						08 15		08 25				
Queens Rd Peckham	d		07 42					07 48		07 57			08 12						08 18		08 27				
Peckham Rye	d		07 45					07 50		08 00			08 15						08 20		08 30				
East Dulwich	d		07 48							08 03			08 18								08 33				
North Dulwich	d		07 50							08 05			08 20								08 35				
Luton	d	06 36				07 06																			
Luton Airport Parkway	d	06 39				07 09																			
St Pancras International ⊖	d	07 24				07 54																			
City Thameslink	d																								
London Blackfriars ⊖	d	07 34				08 04																			
Elephant & Castle ⊖	d																								
Loughborough Jn.	d																								
Herne Hill	d																								
Tulse Hill	d		07 54							08 09			08 24								08 39				
Streatham	d									08 12											08 42				
London Victoria ⊖	d			07 36			07 41		07 49			07 54		08 06	08 11	08 17				08 19				08 24	08 32
Battersea Park	d						07a45	08a02				07 58			08a15				08a32					08 28	
Milton Keynes Central	d																								
Watford Junction	d																								
Harrow & Wealdstone ⊖	d																								
Wembley Central ⊖	d																								
Shepherd's Bush ⊖	d																								
Kensington (Olympia) ⊖	d																								
West Brompton ⊖	d																								
Imperial Wharf	d																								
Clapham Junction	d			07 42					07 56			08 02		08 12		08 23				08 26				08 32	08 38
Latchmere	d																								
Wandsworth Common	d											08 05												08 35	
Balham ⊖	d			07 47					08 00			08 07		08 17						08 30				08 37	
Streatham Hill	d											08 11												08 41	
West Norwood	d		07 57									08 16	08 27											08 46	
Gipsy Hill	d		08 00									08 19	08 30											08 49	
Crystal Palace	d		08a02									08 21	08a32											08 51	
Birkbeck	d																								
Beckenham Junction	a																								
Streatham Common	d			07 51					08 04	08 18				08 21						08 34	08 48				
Norbury	d			07 54					08 07	08 21				08 24						08 37	08 51				
Thornton Heath	d			07 57					08 10	08 24				08 27						08 40	08 54				
Selhurst	d			08 00					08 13	08 27				08 30						08 43	08 57				
Norwood Junction	a				08 02						08 14	08 26						08 32				08 44	08 47	08 56	
	d				08 03						08 16	08 27						08 33				08 46	08 48	08 57	
West Croydon	a								08 18		08 24	08 31								08 48		08 54		09 01	
East Croydon	a	07 56		08 03	08 07	08 27				08 30				08 33		08 36		08 37			09 01		08 54		08 50

Table 177

Sundays from 16 September

Luton, Milton Keynes Central and London East and West Croydon via Tulse Hill - Crystal Palace - Norbury

Local Services

Network Diagram - see first Page of Table 177

		FC 1	SN	SN	SN	SN ◇1	SN	SN		SN	SN	SN	SN	SN ◇1	FC 1	SN	FC	SN	SN	SN ◇1	SN	FC 1	SN	SN
London Bridge ⊖	d		08 36				08 39	08 41			08 51	08 54				09 06					09 09		09 11	
South Bermondsey	d		08 40					08 45			08 55					09 10							09 15	
Queens Rd Peckham	d		08 42					08 48			08 57					09 12							09 18	
Peckham Rye	d		08 45					08 50			09 00					09 15							09 20	
East Dulwich	d		08 48								09 03					09 18								
North Dulwich	d		08 50								09 05					09 20								
Luton	d	07 36													08 14		08 18					08 30		
Luton Airport Parkway	d	07 39													08 17		08 21					08 33		
St Pancras International ⊖	d	08 24													08 54		09 05					09 09		
City Thameslink	d																							
London Blackfriars ⊖	d	08 34													09 04		09 15					09 19		
Elephant & Castle ⊖	d																09 18							
Loughborough Jn.	d																09 22							
Herne Hill	d																09 26							
Tulse Hill	d		08 54								09 09					09 24	09 30							
Streatham	d										09 12						09a34							
London Victoria ⊖	d			08 36	08 41	08 47				08 49			08 54	09 02				09 06	09 11	09 17				09 19
Battersea Park	d				08a45			09a02					08 58						09a15				09a32	
Milton Keynes Central	d																							
Watford Junction	d																							
Harrow & Wealdstone ⊖	d																							
Wembley Central ⊖	d																							
Shepherd's Bush ⊖	d																							
Kensington (Olympia) ⊖	d																							
West Brompton ⊖	d																							
Imperial Wharf	d																							
Clapham Junction	d			08 42		08 53				08 56			09 02	09 08				09 12		09 23				09 26
Latchmere	d																							
Wandsworth Common	d												09 05											
Balham ⊖	d			08 47						09 00			09 07					09 17						09 30
Streatham Hill	d												09 11											
West Norwood	d		08 57										09 16			09 27								
Gipsy Hill	d		09 00										09 19			09 30								
Crystal Palace	d		09a02										09 21			09a32								
Birkbeck	d																							
Beckenham Junction	a																							
Streatham Common	d			08 51						09 04	09 18							09 21						09 34
Norbury	d			08 54						09 07	09 21							09 24						09 37
Thornton Heath	d			08 57						09 10	09 24							09 27						09 40
Selhurst	d			09 00						09 13	09 27							09 30						09 43
Norwood Junction	a						09 02					09 14	09 26								09 32			
	d						09 03					09 16	09 27								09 33			
West Croydon	a									09 18		09 24	09 31											09 48
East Croydon	a	08 56		09 03		09 06	09 07				09 30			09 21	09 27			09 33		09 36	09 37	09 39		

Table 177

Luton, Milton Keynes Central and London East and West Croydon via Tulse Hill - Crystal Palace - Norbury

Sundays
from 16 September

Local Services

Network Diagram - see first Page of Table 177

		SN	SN	SN	SN	SN	FC	SN	FC	SN	SN	SN	SN	FC	SN	SN		SN	SN	SN	SN	FC	SN	FC	SN
				■		◇■	■					◇■ H		■							◇■ H	■			
London Bridge ■ ⊖	d	09 21	09 24	09 37				09 36					09 39		09 41			09 51	09 54				10 06		
South Bermondsey	d	09 25						09 40							09 45			09 55					10 10		
Queens Rd Peckham	d	09 27						09 42							09 48			09 57					10 12		
Peckham Rye ■	d	09 30						09 45							09 50			10 00					10 15		
East Dulwich	d	09 33						09 48										10 03					10 18		
North Dulwich	d	09 35						09 50										10 05					10 20		
Luton ■	d						08 44		08 48					09 00								09 14		09 18	
Luton Airport Parkway ■	d						08 47		08 51					09 03								09 17		09 21	
St Pancras International ■ ⊖	d						09 24		09 35					09 39								09 54		10 05	
City Thameslink ■	d																								
London Blackfriars ■ ⊖	d						09 34		09 45					09 49								10 04		10 15	
Elephant & Castle ⊖	d								09 48															10 18	
Loughborough Jn.	d								09 52															10 22	
Herne Hill ■	d								09 56															10 26	
Tulse Hill ■	d	09 39						09 54	10 00									10 09					10 24	10 30	
Streatham ■	d	09 42							10a04									10 12						10a34	
London Victoria ■ ⊖	d				09 24	09 32				09 36	09 41	09 47				09 49				09 54	10 02				10 06
Battersea Park ■	d				09 28						09a45				10a02					09 58					
Milton Keynes Central	d																								
Watford Junction	d																								
Harrow & Wealdstone ⊖	d																								
Wembley Central ⊖	d																								
Shepherd's Bush ⊖	d																								
Kensington (Olympia) ⊖	d																								
West Brompton ⊖	d																								
Imperial Wharf	d																								
Clapham Junction ■	d				09 32	09 38				09 42		09 53				09 56				10 02	10 08				10 12
Latchmere	d																								
Wandsworth Common	d				09 35															10 05					
Balham ■ ⊖	d				09 37					09 47						10 00				10 07					10 17
Streatham Hill	d				09 41															10 11					
West Norwood ■	d				09 46			09 57												10 16			10 27		
Gipsy Hill	d				09 49			10 00												10 19			10 30		
Crystal Palace ■	d				09 51			10a02												10 21			10a32		
Birkbeck	d																								
Beckenham Junction ■	a																								
Streatham Common ■	d	09 48								09 51						10 04		10 18							10 21
Norbury	d	09 51								09 54						10 07		10 21							10 24
Thornton Heath	d	09 54								09 57						10 10		10 24							10 27
Selhurst ■	d	09 57								10 00						10 13		10 27							10 30
Norwood Junction ■	a		09 44	09 47	09 56								10 02						10 14	10 26					
	d		09 46	09 48	09 57								10 03						10 16	10 27					
West Croydon ■	a		09 54		10 01											10 18			10 24	10 31					
East Croydon	a	10 01		09 54		09 52	09 56			10 03		10 06	10 07	10 09				10 30			10 21	10 27			10 33

Table 177

Luton, Milton Keynes Central and London East and West Croydon via Tulse Hill - Crystal Palace - Norbury

Sundays
from 16 September

Local Services

Network Diagram - see first Page of Table 177

		SN	SN	SN	FC	SN	SN	SN		SN	SN	SN	SN	FC	SN	FC	SN	SN	SN	SN	FC	SN	SN	SN
			◇■		■						■		◇■	■					◇■ H		■			
London Bridge ■ ⊖	d			10 09		10 11		10 21		10 24	10 37				10 36					10 39		10 41		10 51
South Bermondsey	d					10 15		10 25							10 40							10 45		10 55
Queens Rd Peckham	d					10 18		10 27							10 42							10 48		10 57
Peckham Rye ■	d					10 20		10 30							10 45							10 50		11 00
East Dulwich	d							10 33							10 48									11 03
North Dulwich	d							10 35							10 50									11 05
Luton ■	d				09 30									09 44		09 48					10 00			
Luton Airport Parkway ■	d				09 33									09 47		09 51					10 03			
St Pancras International ■ ⊖	d				10 09									10 24		10 35					10 39			
City Thameslink ■	d																							
London Blackfriars ■ ⊖	d				10 19									10 34		10 45					10 49			
Elephant & Castle ⊖	d															10 48								
Loughborough Jn.	d															10 52								
Herne Hill ■	d															10 56								
Tulse Hill ■	d							10 39							10 54	11 00								11 09
Streatham ■	d							10 42								11a04								11 12
London Victoria ■ ⊖	d	10 11	10 17				10 19					10 24	10 32				10 36	10 41	10 47				10 49	
Battersea Park ■	d	10a15				10a32						10 28						10a45				11a02		
Milton Keynes Central	d																							
Watford Junction	d																							
Harrow & Wealdstone ⊖	d																							
Wembley Central ⊖	d																							
Shepherd's Bush ⊖	d																							
Kensington (Olympia) ⊖	d																							
West Brompton ⊖	d																							
Imperial Wharf	d																							
Clapham Junction ■	d		10 23				10 26					10 32	10 38				10 42		10 53				10 56	
Latchmere	d																							
Wandsworth Common	d											10 35												
Balham ■ ⊖	d						10 30					10 37					10 47						11 00	
Streatham Hill	d											10 41												
West Norwood ■	d											10 46			10 57									
Gipsy Hill	d											10 49			11 00									
Crystal Palace ■	d											10 51			11a02									
Birkbeck	d																							
Beckenham Junction ■	a																							
Streatham Common ■	d						10 34	10 48									10 51						11 04	11 18
Norbury	d						10 37	10 51									10 54						11 07	11 21
Thornton Heath	d						10 40	10 54									10 57						11 10	11 24
Selhurst ■	d						10 43	10 57									11 00						11 13	11 27
Norwood Junction ■	a			10 32						10 44	10 47	10 56								11 02				
	d			10 33						10 46	10 48	10 57								11 03				
West Croydon ■	a						10 48			10 54		11 01											11 18	
East Croydon	a		10 36	10 37	10 39			11 01			10 54		10 52	10 56			11 03		11 06	11 07	11 09			11 30

Table 177

Sundays from 16 September

Luton, Milton Keynes Central and London East and West Croydon via Tulse Hill - Crystal Palace - Norbury

Local Services

Network Diagram - see first Page of Table 177

		SN	SN	SN ◇[1]	FC [1]	SN	FC	SN	SN	SN ◇[1]	SN	FC [1]	SN	SN	SN	SN		SN [1]	SN	SN ◇[1]	FC [1]	SN	FC	SN	SN
London Bridge [4] ⊖	d	10 54				11 06					11 09		11 11		11 21	11 24		11 37				11 36			
South Bermondsey	d					11 10							11 15		11 25							11 40			
Queens Rd Peckham	d					11 12							11 18		11 27							11 42			
Peckham Rye [4]	d					11 15							11 20		11 30							11 45			
East Dulwich	d					11 18									11 33							11 48			
North Dulwich	d					11 20									11 35							11 50			
Luton [10]	d				10 14		10 18					10 30									10 44		10 48		
Luton Airport Parkway [7]	d				10 17		10 21					10 33									10 47		10 51		
St Pancras International [15] ⊖	d				10 54		11 05					11 09									11 24		11 35		
City Thameslink [3]	d																								
London Blackfriars [3] ⊖	d				11 04		11 15					11 19									11 34		11 45		
Elephant & Castle ⊖	d						11 18																11 48		
Loughborough Jn.	d						11 22																11 52		
Herne Hill [4]	d						11 26																11 56		
Tulse Hill [3]	d					11 24	11 30								11 39							11 54	12 00		
Streatham [4]	d						11a34								11 42								12a04		
London Victoria [15] ⊖	d		10 54	11 02				11 06	11 11	11 17				11 19					11 24	11 32				11 36	11 41
Battersea Park [4]	d		10 58						11a15				11a32						11 28						11a45
Milton Keynes Central	d																								
Watford Junction	d																								
Harrow & Wealdstone ⊖	d																								
Wembley Central ⊖	d																								
Shepherd's Bush ⊖	d																								
Kensington (Olympia) ⊖	d																								
West Brompton ⊖	d																								
Imperial Wharf	d																								
Clapham Junction [10]	d		11 02	11 08				11 12		11 23				11 26					11 32	11 38				11 42	
Latchmere	d																								
Wandsworth Common	d		11 05																11 35						
Balham [4] ⊖	d		11 07					11 17						11 30					11 37					11 47	
Streatham Hill	d		11 11																11 41						
West Norwood [4]	d		11 16			11 27													11 46			11 57			
Gipsy Hill	d		11 19			11 30													11 49			12 00			
Crystal Palace [4]	d		11 21			11a32													11 51			12a02			
Birkbeck	d																								
Beckenham Junction [4]	a																								
Streatham Common [4]	d							11 21						11 34	11 48									11 51	
Norbury	d							11 24						11 37	11 51									11 54	
Thornton Heath	d							11 27						11 40	11 54									11 57	
Selhurst [4]	d							11 30						11 43	11 57									12 00	
Norwood Junction [2]	a	11 14	11 26								11 32					11 44		11 47	11 56						
	d	11 16	11 27								11 33					11 46		11 48	11 57						
West Croydon [4]	a	11 24	11 31											11 48		11 54			12 01						
East Croydon	a			11 21	11 27			11 33		11 36	11 37	11 39			12 01			11 54		11 52	11 56			12 03	

Table 177

Sundays from 16 September

Luton, Milton Keynes Central and London East and West Croydon via Tulse Hill - Crystal Palace - Norbury

Local Services

Network Diagram - see first Page of Table 177

		SN ◇[1]	SN	FC [1]	SN	SN	SN	SN		SN	SN ◇[1]	FC [1]	SN	FC	SN	SN	SN ◇[1]	SN	FC [1]	SN	SN	SN	SN	SN [1]	
London Bridge [4] ⊖	d		11 39		11 41		11 51	11 54					12 06					12 09		12 11		12 21	12 24	12 37	
South Bermondsey	d				11 45		11 55						12 10							12 15		12 25			
Queens Rd Peckham	d				11 48		11 57						12 12							12 18		12 27			
Peckham Rye [4]	d				11 50		12 00						12 15							12 20		12 30			
East Dulwich	d						12 03						12 18									12 33			
North Dulwich	d						12 05						12 20									12 35			
Luton [10]	d			11 00								11 14		11 18					11 30						
Luton Airport Parkway [7]	d			11 03								11 17		11 21					11 33						
St Pancras International [15] ⊖	d			11 39								11 54		12 05					12 09						
City Thameslink [3]	d																								
London Blackfriars [3] ⊖	d			11 49								12 04		12 15					12 19						
Elephant & Castle ⊖	d													12 18											
Loughborough Jn.	d													12 22											
Herne Hill [4]	d													12 26											
Tulse Hill [3]	d						12 09						12 24	12 30								12 39			
Streatham [4]	d						12 12							12a34								12 42			
London Victoria [15] ⊖	d	11 47				11 49				11 54	12 02				12 06	12 11	12 17				12 19				
Battersea Park [4]	d				12a02					11 58						12a15				12a32					
Milton Keynes Central	d																								
Watford Junction	d																								
Harrow & Wealdstone ⊖	d																								
Wembley Central ⊖	d																								
Shepherd's Bush ⊖	d																								
Kensington (Olympia) ⊖	d																								
West Brompton ⊖	d																								
Imperial Wharf	d																								
Clapham Junction [10]	d	11 53				11 56				12 02	12 08				12 12		12 23				12 26				
Latchmere	d																								
Wandsworth Common	d									12 05															
Balham [4] ⊖	d					12 00				12 07					12 17						12 30				
Streatham Hill	d									12 11															
West Norwood [4]	d									12 16			12 27												
Gipsy Hill	d									12 19			12 30												
Crystal Palace [4]	d									12 21			12a32												
Birkbeck	d																								
Beckenham Junction [4]	a																								
Streatham Common [4]	d					12 04	12 18								12 21						12 34	12 48			
Norbury	d					12 07	12 21								12 24						12 37	12 51			
Thornton Heath	d					12 10	12 24								12 27						12 40	12 54			
Selhurst [4]	d					12 13	12 27								12 30						12 43	12 57			
Norwood Junction [2]	a		12 02					12 14		12 26								12 32					12 44	12 47	
	d		12 03					12 16		12 27								12 33					12 46	12 48	
West Croydon [4]	a					12 18		12 24		12 31											12 48		12 54		
East Croydon	a	12 06	12 07	12 09			12 30				12 21	12 27			12 33		12 36	12 37	12 42			13 01		12 54	

Sundays
from 16 September

Luton, Milton Keynes Central and London East and West Croydon via Tulse Hill - Crystal Palace - Norbury

Local Services

Network Diagram - see first Page of Table 177

		SN	SN ◇1	FC 1	SN	FC	SN	SN	SN ◇1	SN	FC 1	SN	SN	SN	SN	SN		SN ◇1	FC 1	SN	FC	SN	SN	SN ◇1	SN
London Bridge 4 ⊖	d				12 36					12 39		12 41		12 51	12 54					13 06					13 09
South Bermondsey	d				12 40							12 45		12 55						13 10					
Queens Rd Peckham	d				12 42							12 48		12 57						13 12					
Peckham Rye 4	d				12 45							12 50		13 00						13 15					
East Dulwich	d				12 48									13 03						13 18					
North Dulwich	d				12 50									13 05						13 20					
Luton 10	d			11 44		11 48					12 00								12 14		12 18				
Luton Airport Parkway 7	d			11 47		11 51					12 03								12 17		12 21				
St Pancras International 15 ⊖	d			12 24		12 35					12 39								12 54		13 05				
City Thameslink 3	d																								
London Blackfriars 3 ⊖	d			12 34		12 45					12 49								13 04		13 15				
Elephant & Castle ⊖	d					12 48															13 18				
Loughborough Jn.	d					12 52															13 22				
Herne Hill 4	d					12 56															13 26				
Tulse Hill 3	d				12 54	13 00								13 09						13 24	13 30				
Streatham 4	d					13a04								13 12							13a34				
London Victoria 15 ⊖	d	12 24	12 32				12 36	12 41	12 47				12 49			12 54		13 02				13 06	13 11	13 17	
Battersea Park 4	d	12 28						12a45				13a02				12 58							13a15		
Milton Keynes Central	d																								
Watford Junction	d																								
Harrow & Wealdstone ⊖	d																								
Wembley Central ⊖	d																								
Shepherd's Bush ⊖	d																								
Kensington (Olympia) ⊖	d																								
West Brompton ⊖	d																								
Imperial Wharf	d																								
Clapham Junction 10	d	12 32	12 38				12 42		12 53				12 56			13 02		13 08				13 12		13 23	
Latchmere	d																								
Wandsworth Common	d	12 35														13 05									
Balham 4 ⊖	d	12 37					12 47						13 00			13 07						13 17			
Streatham Hill	d	12 41														13 11									
West Norwood 4	d	12 46			12 57											13 16				13 27					
Gipsy Hill	d	12 49			13 00											13 19				13 30					
Crystal Palace 4	d	12 51			13a02											13 21				13a32					
Birkbeck 🚋	d																								
Beckenham Junction 4 🚋	a																								
Streatham Common 4	d						12 51						13 04	13 18								13 21			
Norbury	d						12 54						13 07	13 21								13 24			
Thornton Heath	d						12 57						13 10	13 24								13 27			
Selhurst 4	d						13 00						13 13	13 27								13 30			
Norwood Junction 2	a	12 56								13 02					13 14	13 26									13 32
	d	12 57								13 03					13 16	13 27									13 33
West Croydon 4 🚋	a	13 01												13 18	13 24	13 31									
East Croydon 🚋	a		12 52	12 56			13 03		13 06	13 07	13 12			13 30				13 21	13 27			13 33		13 36	13 37

Sundays
from 16 September

Luton, Milton Keynes Central and London East and West Croydon via Tulse Hill - Crystal Palace - Norbury

Local Services

Network Diagram - see first Page of Table 177

		FC 1	SN	SN	SN	SN	SN 1	SN		SN ◇1	FC 1	SN	FC	SN	SN	SN ◇1	SN	FC 1	SN	SN	SN	SN	SN	SN ◇1
London Bridge 4 ⊖	d		13 11		13 21	13 24	13 37					13 36					13 39		13 41		13 51	13 54		
South Bermondsey	d		13 15		13 25							13 40							13 45		13 55			
Queens Rd Peckham	d		13 18		13 27							13 42							13 48		13 57			
Peckham Rye 4	d		13 20		13 30							13 45							13 50		14 00			
East Dulwich	d				13 33							13 48									14 03			
North Dulwich	d				13 35							13 50									14 05			
Luton 10	d	12 30									12 44		12 48					13 00						
Luton Airport Parkway 7	d	12 33									12 47		12 51					13 03						
St Pancras International 15 ⊖	d	13 09									13 24		13 35					13 39						
City Thameslink 3	d																							
London Blackfriars 3 ⊖	d	13 19									13 34		13 45					13 49						
Elephant & Castle ⊖	d												13 48											
Loughborough Jn.	d												13 52											
Herne Hill 4	d												13 56											
Tulse Hill 3	d				13 39							13 54	14 00								14 09			
Streatham 4	d				13 42								14a04								14 12			
London Victoria 15 ⊖	d			13 19				13 24		13 32				13 36	13 41	13 47				13 49			13 54	14 02
Battersea Park 4	d		13a32					13 28							13a45				14a02				13 58	
Milton Keynes Central	d																							
Watford Junction	d																							
Harrow & Wealdstone ⊖	d																							
Wembley Central ⊖	d																							
Shepherd's Bush ⊖	d																							
Kensington (Olympia) ⊖	d																							
West Brompton ⊖	d																							
Imperial Wharf	d																							
Clapham Junction 10	d			13 26				13 32		13 38				13 42		13 53				13 56			14 02	14 08
Latchmere	d																							
Wandsworth Common	d							13 35															14 05	
Balham 4 ⊖	d			13 30				13 37						13 47						14 00			14 07	
Streatham Hill	d							13 41															14 11	
West Norwood 4	d							13 46				13 57											14 16	
Gipsy Hill	d							13 49				14 00											14 19	
Crystal Palace 4	d							13 51				14a02											14 21	
Birkbeck 🚋	d																							
Beckenham Junction 4 🚋	a																							
Streatham Common 4	d			13 34	13 48									13 51						14 04	14 18			
Norbury	d			13 37	13 51									13 54						14 07	14 21			
Thornton Heath	d			13 40	13 54									13 57						14 10	14 24			
Selhurst 4	d			13 43	13 57									14 00						14 13	14 27			
Norwood Junction 2	a					13 44	13 47	13 56									14 02					14 14	14 26	
	d					13 46	13 48	13 57									14 03					14 16	14 27	
West Croydon 4 🚋	a			13 48		13 54		14 01												14 18		14 24	14 31	
East Croydon 🚋	a	13 39			14 01		13 54			13 52	13 56			14 03		14 06	14 07	14 12			14 30			14 21

Luton, Milton Keynes Central and London East and West Croydon via Tulse Hill - Crystal Palace - Norbury

Local Services

Network Diagram - see first Page of Table 177

		FC	SN	FC	SN	SN	SN ◇	SN	FC	SN	SN	SN	SN	SN	SN	SN ◇		FC	SN	FC	SN	SN	SN ◇	SN
London Bridge ⊖	d		14 06					14 09		14 11		14 21	14 24	14 37					14 36					14 39
South Bermondsey	d		14 10							14 15		14 25							14 40					
Queens Rd Peckham	d		14 12							14 18		14 27							14 42					
Peckham Rye	d		14 15							14 20		14 30							14 45					
East Dulwich	d		14 18									14 33							14 48					
North Dulwich	d		14 20									14 35							14 50					
Luton	d	13 14		13 18					13 30									13 44		13 48				
Luton Airport Parkway	d	13 17		13 21					13 33									13 47		13 51				
St Pancras International ⊖	d	13 54		14 05					14 09									14 24		14 35				
City Thameslink	d																							
London Blackfriars ⊖	d	14 04		14 15					14 19									14 34		14 45				
Elephant & Castle ⊖	d			14 18																14 48				
Loughborough Jn.	d			14 22																14 52				
Herne Hill	d			14 26																14 56				
Tulse Hill	d		14 24	14 30								14 39							14 54	15 00				
Streatham	d			14a34								14 42								15a04				
London Victoria ⊖	d				14 06	14 11	14 17				14 19				14 24	14 32					14 36	14 41	14 47	
Battersea Park	d					14a15				14a32					14 28							14a45		
Milton Keynes Central	d																							
Watford Junction	d																							
Harrow & Wealdstone ⊖	d																							
Wembley Central ⊖	d																							
Shepherd's Bush ⊖	d																							
Kensington (Olympia) ⊖	d																							
West Brompton ⊖	d																							
Imperial Wharf	d																							
Clapham Junction	d				14 12		14 23				14 26				14 32	14 38					14 42		14 53	
Latchmere	d																							
Wandsworth Common	d														14 35									
Balham ⊖	d				14 17						14 30				14 37						14 47			
Streatham Hill	d														14 41									
West Norwood	d		14 27												14 46				14 57					
Gipsy Hill	d		14 30												14 49				15 00					
Crystal Palace	d		14a32												14 51				15a02					
Birkbeck	d																							
Beckenham Junction	a																							
Streatham Common	d				14 21						14 34	14 48									14 51			
Norbury	d				14 24						14 37	14 51									14 54			
Thornton Heath	d				14 27						14 40	14 54									14 57			
Selhurst	d				14 30						14 43	14 57									15 00			
Norwood Junction	a							14 32					14 44	14 47	14 56									15 02
	d							14 33					14 46	14 48	14 57									15 03
West Croydon	a										14 48		14 54		15 01						15 03			
East Croydon	a	14 27			14 33		14 36	14 37	14 39			15 01		14 54		14 52		14 56					15 06	15 07

Luton, Milton Keynes Central and London East and West Croydon via Tulse Hill - Crystal Palace - Norbury

Local Services

Network Diagram - see first Page of Table 177

		FC		FC	SN	SN	SN	SN		SN	SN ◇	FC	SN	FC	SN	SN	SN ◇	SN	FC	SN	SN	SN	SN	SN
London Bridge ⊖	d				17 41		17 51	17 54					18 06					18 09		18 11		18 21	18 24	18 37
South Bermondsey	d				17 45		17 55						18 10							18 15		18 25		
Queens Rd Peckham	d				17 48		17 57						18 12							18 18		18 27		
Peckham Rye	d				17 50		18 00						18 15							18 20		18 30		
East Dulwich	d						18 03						18 18									18 33		
North Dulwich	d						18 05						18 20									18 35		
Luton	d	14 00		17 00								17 14		17 18					17 30					
Luton Airport Parkway	d	14 03		17 03								17 17		17 21					17 33					
St Pancras International ⊖	d	14 39		17 39								17 54		18 05					18 09					
City Thameslink	d																							
London Blackfriars ⊖	d	14 49		17 49								18 04		18 15					18 19					
Elephant & Castle ⊖	d													18 18										
Loughborough Jn.	d													18 22										
Herne Hill	d													18 26										
Tulse Hill	d						18 09						18 24	18 30								18 39		
Streatham	d						18 12							18a34								18 42		
London Victoria ⊖	d		and at			17 49				17 54	18 02				18 06	18 11	18 17				18 19			
Battersea Park	d		the same		18a02					17 58						18a15				18a32				
Milton Keynes Central	d		minutes																					
Watford Junction	d		past																					
Harrow & Wealdstone ⊖	d		each																					
Wembley Central ⊖	d		hour until																					
Shepherd's Bush ⊖	d																							
Kensington (Olympia) ⊖	d																							
West Brompton ⊖	d																							
Imperial Wharf	d																							
Clapham Junction	d					17 56				18 02	18 08				18 12		18 23				18 26			
Latchmere	d																							
Wandsworth Common	d									18 05														
Balham ⊖	d					18 00				18 07					18 17						18 30			
Streatham Hill	d									18 11														
West Norwood	d									18 16			18 27											
Gipsy Hill	d									18 19			18 30											
Crystal Palace	d									18 21			18a32											
Birkbeck	d																							
Beckenham Junction	a																							
Streatham Common	d					18 04	18 18								18 21						18 34	18 48		
Norbury	d					18 07	18 21								18 24						18 37	18 51		
Thornton Heath	d					18 10	18 24								18 27						18 40	18 54		
Selhurst	d					18 13	18 27								18 30						18 43	18 57		
Norwood Junction	a							18 14		18 26								18 32					18 44	18 47
	d							18 16		18 27								18 33					18 46	18 48
West Croydon	a					18 18		18 24		18 31											18 48		18 54	
East Croydon	a	15 09		18 09			18 30				18 21	18 27			18 33		18 36	18 37	18 38			19 01		18 54

Table 177

Sundays
from 16 September

Luton, Milton Keynes Central and London East and West Croydon via Tulse Hill - Crystal Palace - Norbury

Local Services

Network Diagram - see first Page of Table 177

	SN	SN ◇1	FC 1	SN	FC	SN	SN	SN ◇1	SN	FC 1	SN	SN	SN	SN	SN		SN ◇1	FC 1	SN	FC	SN	SN	SN ◇1
London Bridge ⊖ d				18 36					18 39		18 41		18 51	18 54					19 06				
South Bermondsey d				18 40							18 45		18 55						19 10				
Queens Rd Peckham d				18 42							18 48		18 57						19 12				
Peckham Rye d				18 45							18 50		19 00						19 15				
East Dulwich d				18 48									19 03						19 18				
North Dulwich d				18 50									19 05						19 20				
Luton d			17 44		17 48					18 00								18 14		18 18			
Luton Airport Parkway d			17 47		17 51					18 03								18 17		18 21			
St Pancras International ⊖ d			18 24		18 35					18 39								18 54		19 05			
City Thameslink d																							
London Blackfriars ⊖ d			18 34		18 45					18 49								19 04		19 15			
Elephant & Castle ⊖ d					18 48															19 18			
Loughborough Jn. d					18 52															19 22			
Herne Hill d					18 56															19 26			
Tulse Hill d				18 54	19 00								19 09						19 24	19 30			
Streatham d					19a04								19 12							19a34			
London Victoria ⊖ d	18 24	18 32				18 36	18 41	18 47				18 49			18 54		19 02				19 06	19 11	19 17
Battersea Park d	18 28						18a45				19a02				18 58							19a15	
Milton Keynes Central d																							
Watford Junction d																							
Harrow & Wealdstone ⊖ d																							
Wembley Central ⊖ d																							
Shepherd's Bush ⊖ d																							
Kensington (Olympia) ⊖ d																							
West Brompton ⊖ d																							
Imperial Wharf d																							
Clapham Junction d	18 32	18 38				18 42		18 53				18 56			19 02		19 08				19 12		19 23
Latchmere d																							
Wandsworth Common d	18 35														19 05								
Balham ⊖ d	18 37					18 47						19 00			19 07						19 17		
Streatham Hill d	18 41														19 11								
West Norwood d	18 46			18 57											19 16				19 27				
Gipsy Hill d	18 49			19 00											19 19				19 30				
Crystal Palace d	18 51			19a02											19 21				19a32				
Birkbeck d																							
Beckenham Junction a																							
Streatham Common d						18 51						19 04	19 18								19 21		
Norbury d						18 54						19 07	19 21								19 24		
Thornton Heath d						18 57						19 10	19 24								19 27		
Selhurst d						19 00						19 13	19 27								19 30		
Norwood Junction a	18 56								19 02					19 14	19 26								
Norwood Junction d	18 57								19 03					19 16	19 27								
West Croydon a	19 01											19 18		19 24	19 31								
East Croydon a		18 52	18 56			19 03		19 06	19 07	19 08			19 30				19 21	19 27			19 33		19 36

Table 177

Sundays
from 16 September

Luton, Milton Keynes Central and London East and West Croydon via Tulse Hill - Crystal Palace - Norbury

Local Services

Network Diagram - see first Page of Table 177

	SN	SN	SN	SN	SN	SN 1	SN	SN ◇1		FC 1	SN	FC	SN	SN	SN ◇1	SN	SN	SN	SN	SN	SN	SN ◇1	FC 1	SN
London Bridge ⊖ d	19 09	19 11		19 21	19 24	19 37					19 36					19 39	19 41		19 51	19 54				20 06
South Bermondsey d		19 15		19 25							19 40						19 45		19 55					20 10
Queens Rd Peckham d		19 18		19 27							19 42						19 48		19 57					20 12
Peckham Rye d		19 20		19 30							19 45						19 50		20 00					20 15
East Dulwich d				19 33							19 48								20 03					20 18
North Dulwich d				19 35							19 50								20 05					20 20
Luton d										18 44		18 48											19 14	
Luton Airport Parkway d										18 47		18 51											19 17	
St Pancras International ⊖ d										19 24		19 35											19 54	
City Thameslink d																								
London Blackfriars ⊖ d										19 34		19 45											20 04	
Elephant & Castle ⊖ d												19 48												
Loughborough Jn. d												19 52												
Herne Hill d												19 56												
Tulse Hill d				19 39							19 54	20 00							20 09					20 24
Streatham d				19 42								20a04							20 12					
London Victoria ⊖ d			19 19				19 24	19 32					19 36	19 41	19 47			19 49			19 54	20 02		
Battersea Park d		19a32					19 28							19a45			20a02				19 58			
Milton Keynes Central d																								
Watford Junction d																								
Harrow & Wealdstone ⊖ d																								
Wembley Central ⊖ d																								
Shepherd's Bush ⊖ d																								
Kensington (Olympia) ⊖ d																								
West Brompton ⊖ d																								
Imperial Wharf d																								
Clapham Junction d			19 26				19 32	19 38					19 42		19 53			19 56			20 02	20 08		
Latchmere d																								
Wandsworth Common d							19 35														20 05			
Balham ⊖ d			19 30				19 37						19 47					20 00			20 07			
Streatham Hill d							19 41														20 11			
West Norwood d							19 46				19 57										20 16			20 27
Gipsy Hill d							19 49				20 00										20 19			20 30
Crystal Palace d							19 51				20a02										20 21			20a32
Birkbeck d																								
Beckenham Junction a																								
Streatham Common d			19 34	19 48									19 51					20 04	20 18					
Norbury d			19 37	19 51									19 54					20 07	20 21					
Thornton Heath d			19 40	19 54									19 57					20 10	20 24					
Selhurst d			19 43	19 57									20 00					20 13	20 27					
Norwood Junction a	19 32				19 44	19 47	19 56									20 02				20 14	20 26			
Norwood Junction d	19 33				19 46	19 48	19 57									20 03				20 16	20 27			
West Croydon a			19 48		19 54		20 01											20 18		20 24	20 31			
East Croydon a	19 37			20 01		19 54		19 50		19 56			20 03		20 06	20 07			20 30			20 21	20 27	

Table 177

Sundays from 16 September

Luton, Milton Keynes Central and London East and West Croydon via Tulse Hill - Crystal Palace - Norbury

Local Services

Network Diagram - see first Page of Table 177

		FC	SN	SN	SN ◇1	SN	SN	SN	SN	SN	SN 1	SN	SN ◇1	FC 1	SN	FC	SN	SN	SN ◇1	SN	SN	SN	SN
London Bridge	d					20 09	20 11		20 21	20 24	20 37				20 36					20 39	20 41		20 51
South Bermondsey	d						20 15		20 25						20 40						20 45		20 55
Queens Rd Peckham	d						20 18		20 27						20 42						20 48		20 57
Peckham Rye	d						20 20		20 30						20 45						20 50		21 00
East Dulwich	d								20 33						20 48								21 03
North Dulwich	d								20 35						20 50								21 05
Luton	d	19 18												19 44		19 48							
Luton Airport Parkway	d	19 21												19 47		19 51							
St Pancras International	d	20 05												20 24		20 35							
City Thameslink	d																						
London Blackfriars	d	20 15												20 34		20 45							
Elephant & Castle	d	20 18														20 48							
Loughborough Jn.	d	20 22														20 52							
Herne Hill	d	20 26														20 56							
Tulse Hill	d	20 30							20 39						20 54	21 00							21 09
Streatham	d	20a34							20 42							21a04							21 12
London Victoria	d		20 06	20 11	20 17			20 19				20 24	20 32				20 36	20 41	20 47			20 49	
Battersea Park	d			20a15			20a32					20 28						20a45			21a02		
Milton Keynes Central	d																						
Watford Junction	d																						
Harrow & Wealdstone	d																						
Wembley Central	d																						
Shepherd's Bush	d																						
Kensington (Olympia)	d																						
West Brompton	d																						
Imperial Wharf	d																						
Clapham Junction	d		20 12		20 23			20 26				20 32	20 38				20 42		20 53			20 56	
Latchmere	d																						
Wandsworth Common	d											20 35											
Balham	d		20 17					20 30				20 37					20 47					21 00	
Streatham Hill	d											20 41											
West Norwood	d											20 46			20 57								
Gipsy Hill	d											20 49			21 00								
Crystal Palace	d											20 51			21a02								
Birkbeck	d																						
Beckenham Junction	a																						
Streatham Common	d		20 21					20 34	20 48								20 51					21 04	21 18
Norbury	d		20 24					20 37	20 51								20 54					21 07	21 21
Thornton Heath	d		20 27					20 40	20 54								20 57					21 10	21 24
Selhurst	d		20 30					20 43	20 57								21 00					21 13	21 27
Norwood Junction	a					20 32				20 44	20 47	20 56								21 02			
	d					20 33				20 46	20 48	20 57								21 03			
West Croydon	a							20 48		20 54		21 01										21 18	
East Croydon	a		20 33		20 36	20 37			21 01		20 54		20 50	20 56			21 03		21 06	21 07			21 30

Table 177

Sundays from 16 September

Luton, Milton Keynes Central and London East and West Croydon via Tulse Hill - Crystal Palace - Norbury

Local Services

Network Diagram - see first Page of Table 177

		SN	SN	SN ◇1	FC 1	SN	FC	SN	SN	SN ◇1	SN	SN	SN	SN	SN	SN 1	SN	SN ◇1	FC 1	SN	SN	SN	SN ◇1	SN
London Bridge	d	20 54				21 06					21 09	21 11		21 21	21 24	21 37				21 36				21 39
South Bermondsey	d					21 10						21 15		21 25						21 40				
Queens Rd Peckham	d					21 12						21 18		21 27						21 42				
Peckham Rye	d					21 15						21 20		21 30						21 45				
East Dulwich	d					21 18								21 33						21 48				
North Dulwich	d					21 20								21 35						21 50				
Luton	d				20 14		20 18												20 36					
Luton Airport Parkway	d				20 17		20 21												20 39					
St Pancras International	d				20 54		21 05												21 24					
City Thameslink	d																							
London Blackfriars	d				21 04		21 15												21 34					
Elephant & Castle	d						21 18																	
Loughborough Jn.	d						21 22																	
Herne Hill	d						21 26																	
Tulse Hill	d					21 24	21 30							21 39						21 54				
Streatham	d						21a34							21 42										
London Victoria	d		20 54	21 02				21 06	21 11	21 17			21 19				21 24	21 32			21 36	21 41	21 47	
Battersea Park	d		20 58						21a15			21a32					21 28					21a45		
Milton Keynes Central	d																							
Watford Junction	d																							
Harrow & Wealdstone	d																							
Wembley Central	d																							
Shepherd's Bush	d																							
Kensington (Olympia)	d																							
West Brompton	d																							
Imperial Wharf	d																							
Clapham Junction	d		21 02	21 08				21 12		21 23			21 26				21 32	21 38			21 42		21 53	
Latchmere	d																							
Wandsworth Common	d		21 05														21 35							
Balham	d		21 07					21 17					21 30				21 38				21 47			
Streatham Hill	d		21 11														21 41							
West Norwood	d		21 16			21 27											21 46			21 57				
Gipsy Hill	d		21 19			21 30											21 49			22 00				
Crystal Palace	d		21 21			21a32											21 51			22a02				
Birkbeck	d																							
Beckenham Junction	a																							
Streatham Common	d							21 21					21 34	21 48							21 51			
Norbury	d							21 24					21 37	21 51							21 54			
Thornton Heath	d							21 27					21 40	21 54							21 57			
Selhurst	d							21 30					21 43	21 57							22 00			
Norwood Junction	a	21 14	21 26								21 32				21 44	21 47	21 56							22 02
	d	21 16	21 27								21 33				21 46	21 48	21 57							22 03
West Croydon	a	21 24	21 31										21 48		21 54		22 01							
East Croydon	a			21 21	21 27			21 33		21 36	21 37			22 01		21 54		21 50	21 56		22 03		22 06	22 07

Table 177

Sundays from 16 September

Luton, Milton Keynes Central and London East and West Croydon via Tulse Hill - Crystal Palace - Norbury

Local Services

Network Diagram - see first Page of Table 177

		FC ■	SN	SN	SN	SN	SN	SN	SN	SN	SN ◇■	SN	SN	SN	SN	SN ■	SN	SN ◇■	FC ■	SN	SN	SN	SN ◇■
London Bridge ■ ⊖	d		21 41		21 51	21 54		22 06				22 09	22 11		22 21	22 37				22 36			
South Bermondsey	d		21 45		21 55			22 10					22 15		22 25					22 40			
Queens Rd Peckham	d		21 48		21 57			22 12					22 18		22 27					22 42			
Peckham Rye ■	d		21 50		22 00			22 15					22 20		22 30					22 45			
East Dulwich	d				22 03			22 18							22 33					22 48			
North Dulwich	d				22 05			22 20							22 35					22 50			
Luton ■	d	21 06																	21 36				
Luton Airport Parkway ■	d	21 09																	21 39				
St Pancras International ■ ⊖	d	21 54																	22 24				
City Thameslink ■	d																						
London Blackfriars ■ ⊖	d	22 04																	22 34				
Elephant & Castle ⊖	d																						
Loughborough Jn.	d																						
Herne Hill ■	d																						
Tulse Hill ■	d				22 09			22 24							22 39					22 54			
Streatham ■	d				22 12										22 42								
London Victoria ■ ⊖	d			21 49			21 54		22 06	22 11	22 17			22 19			22 24	22 32			22 36	22 41	22 47
Battersea Park ■	d		22a02				21 58			22a15			22a32				22 28					22a45	
Milton Keynes Central	d																						
Watford Junction	d																						
Harrow & Wealdstone ⊖	d																						
Wembley Central ⊖	d																						
Shepherd's Bush ⊖	d																						
Kensington (Olympia) ⊖	d																						
West Brompton ⊖	d																						
Imperial Wharf	d																						
Clapham Junction ■	d			21 56			22 02		22 12		22 23			22 26			22 32	22 38			22 42		22 53
Latchmere	d																						
Wandsworth Common	d						22 05										22 35						
Balham ■ ⊖	d			22 00			22 07		22 17					22 30			22 38				22 47		
Streatham Hill	d						22 11										22 41						
West Norwood ■	d						22 16	22 27									22 46			22 57			
Gipsy Hill	d						22 19	22 30									22 49			23 00			
Crystal Palace ■	d						22 21	22a32									22 51			23a02			
Birkbeck 🚋	d																						
Beckenham Junction ■ 🚋	a																						
Streatham Common ■	d			22 04	22 18				22 21					22 34	22 48						22 51		
Norbury	d			22 07	22 21				22 24					22 37	22 51						22 54		
Thornton Heath	d			22 10	22 24				22 27					22 40	22 54						22 57		
Selhurst ■	d			22 13	22 27				22 30					22 43	22 57						23 00		
Norwood Junction ■	a					22 14	22 26					22 32				22 47	22 56						
	d					22 16	22 27					22 33				22 48	22 57						
West Croydon ■ 🚋	a			22 18		22 24	22 31							22 48			23 01						
East Croydon 🚋	a	22 27			22 30				22 33		22 36	22 37			23 00	22 54		22 50	22 56		23 03		23 06

Table 177

Sundays from 16 September

Luton, Milton Keynes Central and London East and West Croydon via Tulse Hill - Crystal Palace - Norbury

Local Services

Network Diagram - see first Page of Table 177

		SN	SN	SN	SN	SN ■	FC ■	SN	SN	SN	SN	SN ◇■	SN	SN	SN	SN	SN ◇■	FC ■	SN	SN	SN	SN	SN	SN ■
London Bridge ■ ⊖	d	22 39			22 41			22 51	23 06				23 09			23 11			23 21		23 39			
South Bermondsey	d				22 45			22 55	23 10							23 15			23 25					
Queens Rd Peckham	d				22 48			22 57	23 12							23 18			23 27					
Peckham Rye ■	d				22 50			23 00	23 15							23 20			23 30					
East Dulwich	d							23 03	23 18										23 33					
North Dulwich	d							23 05	23 20										23 35					
Luton ■	d						22 06											22 36						
Luton Airport Parkway ■	d						22 09											22 39						
St Pancras International ■ ⊖	d						22 54											23 24						
City Thameslink ■	d																							
London Blackfriars ■ ⊖	d						23 04											23 34						
Elephant & Castle ⊖	d																							
Loughborough Jn.	d																							
Herne Hill ■	d																							
Tulse Hill ■	d							23 09	23 24										23 39					
Streatham ■	d							23 12											23 42					
London Victoria ■ ⊖	d		22 49	22 54		23 04				23 06	23 11	23 17		23 19	23 24		23 32			23 36		23 47	23 50	
Battersea Park ■	d			22 58	23a02						23a15			23 23	23 28	23a32				23 40				
Milton Keynes Central	d																							
Watford Junction	d																							23 17
Harrow & Wealdstone ⊖	d																							23 23
Wembley Central ⊖	d																							
Shepherd's Bush ⊖	d																							23 45
Kensington (Olympia) ⊖	d																							23 48
West Brompton ⊖	d																							23 50
Imperial Wharf	d																							23 53
Clapham Junction ■	d		22 56	23 02		23 10				23 12		23 23		23 27	23 32		23 38			23 44		23 53	23 56	00 05
Latchmere	d																							
Wandsworth Common	d			23 05										23 30	23 35					23 47			23 59	
Balham ■ ⊖	d		23 00	23 07						23 17				23 32	23 37					23 49			00 02	
Streatham Hill	d			23 11											23 41									
West Norwood ■	d			23 16					23 27						23 44									
Gipsy Hill	d			23 19					23 30						23 47									
Crystal Palace ■	d			23 21					23a32						23 50									
Birkbeck 🚋	d																							
Beckenham Junction ■ 🚋	a																							
Streatham Common ■	d		23 04					23 18		23 21				23 36					23 48	23 53			00 06	
Norbury	d		23 07					23 21		23 24				23 39					23 51	23 56			00 08	
Thornton Heath	d		23 10					23 24		23 27				23 42					23 54	23 59			00 11	
Selhurst ■	d		23 13					23 27		23 30				23 45			23 48		23 57	00a01			00 14	
Norwood Junction ■	a	23 02		23 26									23 32		23 54						00 02			
	d	23 03		23 27									23 33		23 55						00 03			
West Croydon ■ 🚋	a		23 18	23 31										23 49	23 59									
East Croydon 🚋	a	23 07				23 22	23 26	23 30		23 34		23 37	23 38				23 52	23 56	00 01		00 06	00 06	00 17	00 22

Table 177

Sundays from 16 September

Luton, Milton Keynes Central and London East and West Croydon via Tulse Hill - Crystal Palace - Norbury

Local Services

Network Diagram - see first Page of Table 177

Station		FC ■	FC ■	SN
London Bridge ■ ⊖	d			
South Bermondsey	d			
Queens Rd Peckham	d			
Peckham Rye ■	d			
East Dulwich	d			
North Dulwich	d			
Luton ■	d	23 06	23 36	
Luton Airport Parkway ■	d	23 09	23 39	
St Pancras International ■ ⊖	d	23 54	00 24	
City Thameslink ■	d			
London Blackfriars ■ ⊖	d	00 05	00 35	
Elephant & Castle ⊖	d			
Loughborough Jn	d			
Herne Hill ■	d			
Tulse Hill ■	d			
Streatham ■	d			
London Victoria ■ ⊖	d			23 54
Battersea Park ■	d			23 58
Milton Keynes Central	d			
Watford Junction	d			
Harrow & Wealdstone ⊖	d			
Wembley Central ⊖	d			
Shepherd's Bush ⊖	d			
Kensington (Olympia) ⊖	d			
West Brompton ⊖	d			
Imperial Wharf	d			
Clapham Junction ■	d			00 02
Latchmere	d			
Wandsworth Common	d			00 05
Balham ■ ⊖	d			00 07
Streatham Hill	d			00 11
West Norwood ■	d			00 14
Gipsy Hill	d			00 17
Crystal Palace ■	d			00 20
Birkbeck 🚋	d			
Beckenham Junction ■ 🚋	a			
Streatham Common ■	d			
Norbury	d			
Thornton Heath	d			
Selhurst ■	d			
Norwood Junction ■	a			00 25
	d			
West Croydon ■ 🚋	a			
East Croydon 🚋	a	00 26	00 56	

Table 177

Mondays to Fridays until 18 May

East and West Croydon, London Milton Keynes Central and Luton via Norbury Crystal Palace - Tulse Hill

Local Services

Network Diagram - see first Page of Table 177

Miles	Miles	Miles	Miles	Miles	Station		SN	SN	SN ■	SN	SN	SN	SN ■	FC ■	SN ■	FC ■	SN ■	FC ■	SN ■	FC	SN		FC ■	SN	FC
							A	A	A	A	A														
0	—	—	0	0	**East Croydon** 🚋	d			23p58			00 49	01 28	01 49	02 28	02 47	03 28	03 47	04 32	04 47	05 13		05 17	05 33	
—	0	—	—	—	**West Croydon** ■ 🚋	d																			
1¾	—	—	—	1¾	Norwood Junction ■	a															05 17			05 37	
—	—	—	—	—		d															05 17			05 37	
—	1	—	1	—	Selhurst ■	d																			05 36
—	1¾	—	1¾	—	Thornton Heath	d																			05 38
—	3	—	3	—	Norbury	d																			05 40
—	4	—	4	—	Streatham Common ■	d																			05 43
—	—	0	—	—	Beckenham Junction ■ 🚋	d																			
—	—	1½	—	—	Birkbeck 🚋	d																			
2¾	—	3	—	2¾	**Crystal Palace** ■	d	23p43	23p51		00 13	00 21													05 41	
3½	—	3¾	—	3½	Gipsy Hill	d	23p45			00 15														05 43	
4½	—	4¾	—	4½	West Norwood ■	d	23p48			00 18														05 46	
5¾	—	6	—	—	Streatham Hill	d	23p52			00 22														05 50	
6¾	—	7	5¾	—	Balham ■ ⊖	d	23p55			00 25														05 53	
7½	—	7¾	6½	—	Wandsworth Common	d	23p58			00 27															
—	—	—	—	—	Latchmere	d																			
8¾	—	9	7¾	—	Clapham Junction ■	d	00 02		00 12	00 31		01 01	01 41		02 41		03 41		04 51					05 57	
—	—	—	—	—	Imperial Wharf	d																			
—	—	—	—	—	West Brompton ⊖	d																			
—	—	—	—	—	Kensington (Olympia) ⊖	d																			
—	—	—	—	—	Shepherd's Bush ⊖	d																			
—	—	—	—	—	Wembley Central ⊖	d																			
—	—	—	—	—	Harrow & Wealdstone ⊖	d																			
—	—	—	—	—	Watford Junction	d																			
—	—	—	—	—	Milton Keynes Central ■	a																			
10¼	—	10½	9¼	—	Battersea Park ■	d	00 05			00 35														06 01	
11½	—	11¾	10¼	—	**London Victoria** ■ ⊖	a	00 10		00 18	00 42		01 09	01 49		02 49		03 49		04 58					06 06	
—	4½	—	—	—	Streatham ■	d																			05 46
—	6	—	—	5	Tulse Hill ■	d																			05 50
—	—	—	—	—	Herne Hill ■	a																			05 54
—	—	—	—	—	Loughborough Jn	a																			
—	—	—	—	—	Elephant & Castle ⊖	a																			06 00
—	—	—	—	—	London Blackfriars ■ ⊖	a														05 13			05 41		06 03
—	—	—	—	—	City Thameslink ■	a														05 16			05 44		06 06
—	—	—	—	—	St Pancras International ■ ⊖	a														05 24			05 52		06 14
—	—	—	—	—	Luton Airport Parkway ■	a														06 09			06 35		07 00
—	—	—	—	—	**Luton** ■	a														06 12			06 38		07 03
—	7¼	—	—	6¼	North Dulwich	d																			
—	7¾	—	—	6¾	East Dulwich	d																			
—	8½	—	—	7½	Peckham Rye ■	d																			
—	9¼	—	—	8¼	Queens Rd Peckham	d																			
—	10¼	—	—	9¼	South Bermondsey	d																			
—	12	—	—	11	**London Bridge** ■ ⊖	a		00 11			00 41			02 14		03 12		04 12			05 41				

A not 14 May

East and West Croydon, London Milton Keynes Central and Luton via Norbury Crystal Palace - Tulse Hill

Local Services

Network Diagram - see first Page of Table 177

		SN	FC ■	SN	SN	FC	SN	SN ■	SN	SN ◇■	SN	SN	SN		SN ■	SN ■	FC	SN	SN	SN	SN	SN	SN ■	SN	SN
East Croydon	d		05 47	05 48	05 51			06 06	06 13	06 15			06 17		06 23	06 31					06 31	06 36	06 42		
West Croydon	d	05 45					06 01				06 15									06 26					
Norwood Junction	a	05 50			05 55				06 17		06 19										06 35	06 40			
	d	05 50			05 55				06 18		06 20								06 23		06 37	06 40			
Selhurst	d			05 52		05 56	06 06	06 09					06 20							06 31					
Thornton Heath	d			05 54		05 58	06 08						06 22							06 33					
Norbury	d			05 57		06 00	06 11						06 25							06 36					
Streatham Common	d			05 59		06 03	06 13						06 27							06 38					
Beckenham Junction	d																								
Birkbeck	d																								
Crystal Palace	d				05 59														06 27					06 39	06 44
Gipsy Hill	d				06 01														06 29					06 41	
West Norwood	d				06 04														06 32					06 44	
Streatham Hill	d																		06 36					06 48	
Balham ⊖	d			06 03			06 17						06 31						06 39	06 42				06 51	
Wandsworth Common	d			06 05			06 19						06 33						06 41	06 44					
Latchmere	d																								
Clapham Junction	d			06 09			06 23	06 18		06 25			06 37			06 41			06 45	06 48			06 51	06 56	
Imperial Wharf	d																								
West Brompton ⊖	d																								
Kensington (Olympia) ⊖	d																								
Shepherd's Bush ⊖	d																								
Wembley Central ⊖	d																								
Harrow & Wealdstone ⊖	d																								
Watford Junction	d																								
Milton Keynes Central	a																								
Battersea Park	d			06 13			06 27					06 32	06 41					06 45	06 48	06 52					
London Victoria ⊖	a			06 18			06 31	06 25		06 32		06 36	06 48			06 48			06 53	06 58			07 00	07 05	
Streatham	d					06 06											06 38								
Tulse Hill	d				06 08	06 10											06 42								
Herne Hill	a					06 14											06 46								
Loughborough Jn	a					06 19											06 49								
Elephant & Castle ⊖	a					06 23											06 53								
London Blackfriars ⊖	a		06 10			06 27											06 57								
City Thameslink	a		06 14			06 32											07 00								
St Pancras International ⊖	a		06 22			06 40											07 08								
Luton Airport Parkway	a		06 55			07 23											07 49								
Luton	a		06 58			07 26											07 53								
North Dulwich	d				06 11																				
East Dulwich	d				06 13																				
Peckham Rye	d				06 15													06 56							
Queens Rd Peckham	d				06 18													06 59							
South Bermondsey	d				06 20													07 01							
London Bridge ⊖	a	06 14			06 25				06 44		06 33				06 39			07 08			06 49	06 52			07 06

Table 177

Mondays to Fridays
until 18 May

East and West Croydon, London Milton Keynes Central and Luton via Norbury Crystal Palace - Tulse Hill

Local Services

Network Diagram - see first Page of Table 177

		SN	SN	SN	SN		SN	SN	SN ■	SN	SN ■	SN	SN	SN ■	SN	SN	SN ◇■	FC	SN	SN	SN		SN	SN	SN
East Croydon	d						06 57	06 45	06 59		07 00			07 05		07 10	07 15								07 26
West Croydon	d	06 31		06 45											06 58				07 01	07 13					
Norwood Junction	a			06 49												07 14				07 17					
	d		06 47	06 50									06 53			07 14				07 18					
Selhurst	d	06 35						06 48							07 02				07 05						
Thornton Heath	d	06 37						06 50							07 04				07 07						
Norbury	d	06 40						06 53							07 07				07 10						
Streatham Common	d	06 43						06 56							07 10				07 13						
Beckenham Junction	d																								
Birkbeck	d																								
Crystal Palace	d		06 51							06 51			06 57										07 13	07 14	
Gipsy Hill	d		06 53										06 59										07 15		
West Norwood	d		06 56										07 02										07 18		
Streatham Hill	d												07 06										07 22		
Balham ⊖	d							07 00					07 09		07 14								07 25		
Wandsworth Common	d							07 02					07 11		07 16								07 27		
Latchmere	d																								
Clapham Junction	d						07 07	07 06					07 15	07 17	07 20		07 24						07 31		07 37
Imperial Wharf	d																								
West Brompton ⊖	d																								
Kensington (Olympia) ⊖	d																								
Shepherd's Bush ⊖	d																								
Wembley Central ⊖	d																								
Harrow & Wealdstone ⊖	d																								
Watford Junction	d																								
Milton Keynes Central	a																								
Battersea Park	d				07 02			07 09				07 15	07 18		07 23						07 32		07 35		
London Victoria ⊖	a				07 08		07 15	07 16					07 25	07 25	07 30		07 33				07 38		07 41		07 46
Streatham	d	06 46																07 16	07 19						
Tulse Hill	d	06 50	07 00															07 20	07 24						
Herne Hill	a																	07 23							
Loughborough Jn	a																	07 27							
Elephant & Castle ⊖	a																	07 31							
London Blackfriars ⊖	a																	07 35							
City Thameslink	a																	07 38							
St Pancras International ⊖	a																	07 46							
Luton Airport Parkway	a																	08 20							
Luton	a																	08 23							
North Dulwich	d	06 53	07 03																07 27						
East Dulwich	d	06 55	07 05																07 29						
Peckham Rye	d	06 59	07 08									07 26							07 31						
Queens Rd Peckham	d	07 02	07 10									07 29							07 34						
South Bermondsey	d	07 04	07 13									07 31							07 36						
London Bridge ⊖	a	07 11	07 19	07 04					07 14	07 16	07 16	07 38				07 28			07 43	07 32				07 36	

Table 177

Mondays to Fridays
until 18 May

East and West Croydon, London Milton Keynes Central and Luton via Norbury Crystal Palace - Tulse Hill

Local Services

Network Diagram - see first Page of Table 177

		SN	SN ■	SN	SN	SN ◇■	SN ■	FC	SN	SN	SN ◇■	SN	SN		SN ■	SN ■	SN	SN	SN	SN	SN	SN	SN	SN	SN
East Croydon	d	07 18	07 28			07 31	07 35				07 39		07 40		07 42	07 46							07 56	07 48	07 50
West Croydon	d									07 17		07 28					07 31	07 34	07 44						
Norwood Junction	a									07 21			07 44						07 48						
	d									07 22			07 44						07 49						
Selhurst	d	07 21										07 32					07 35	07 38						07 51	07 54
Thornton Heath	d	07 23										07 34					07 37	07 40						07 53	07 56
Norbury	d	07 26										07 37					07 40	07 43						07 56	07 59
Streatham Common	d	07 28										07 40					07 43	07 46						07 59	08 02
Beckenham Junction	d			07 13																					
Birkbeck	d			07 16																					
Crystal Palace	d			07 20	07 21					07 26											07 43	07 44			
Gipsy Hill	d			07 22						07 28											07 45				
West Norwood	d			07 25						07 31											07 48				
Streatham Hill	d									07 35											07 52				
Balham	d	07 32								07 39		07 44						07 50			07 55			08 03	08 06
Wandsworth Common	d	07 34								07 41		07 46						07 52			07 57			08 05	08 08
Latchmere	d																								
Clapham Junction	d	07 38				07 41				07 45	07 48	07 50			07 51			07 56			08 01		08 07	08 09	08 14
Imperial Wharf	d																								08 18
West Brompton	d																								08 21
Kensington (Olympia)	d																								08 25
Shepherd's Bush	d																								08a27
Wembley Central	d																								
Harrow & Wealdstone	d																								
Watford Junction	d																								
Milton Keynes Central	a																								
Battersea Park	d	07 42							07 45	07 48		07 53						07 59		08 02	08 05			08 12	
London Victoria	a	07 48				07 49				07 57	07 57	08 00			08 00			08 06		08 08	08 11		08 15	08 19	
Streatham	d							07 38									07 46								
Tulse Hill	d			07 29				07 43									07 52								
Herne Hill	a							07 46																	
Loughborough Jn	a							07 50																	
Elephant & Castle	a							07 54																	
London Blackfriars	a							07 58																	
City Thameslink	a							08 00																	
St Pancras International	a							08 08																	
Luton Airport Parkway	a																								
Luton	a																								
North Dulwich	d			07 32													07 55								
East Dulwich	d			07 34													07 57								
Peckham Rye	d			07 36					07 56								07 59								
Queens Rd Peckham	d			07 39					07 59								08 02								
South Bermondsey	d			07 41					08 01								08 04								
London Bridge	a		07 43	07 48	07 45		07 51		08 08				07 58			08 01	08 11		08 05			08 07			

Table 177

Mondays to Fridays
until 18 May

East and West Croydon, London Milton Keynes Central and Luton via Norbury Crystal Palace - Tulse Hill

Local Services

Network Diagram - see first Page of Table 177

		SN ■	SN	SN	SN ◇■		SN ■	SN ■	FC	SN	SN	SN ◇■	SN ■	SN	SN	SN ◇■	SN	SN	SN	SN ■	SN		SN	SN	SN
East Croydon	d	07 57			08 01		08 02	08 03				08 08	08 11			08 13				08 07	08 10				08 26
West Croydon	d										07 47			07 58	08 01		08 05						08 15		
Norwood Junction	a										07 51										08 16		08 20		
	d										07 52										08 16		08 20		
Selhurst	d													08 02	08 05		08 09			08 13					
Thornton Heath	d													08 04	08 07		08 11			08 16					
Norbury	d													08 07	08 10		08 14			08 20					
Streatham Common	d													08 10	08 13		08 17			08 23					
Beckenham Junction	d		07 42																						
Birkbeck	d		07 45																						
Crystal Palace	d		07 49	07 52							07 56								08 13					08 15	
Gipsy Hill	d		07 51								07 58								08 15						
West Norwood	d		07 54								08 01								08 18						
Streatham Hill	d										08 05								08 22						
Balham	d										08 09			08 14			08 21		08 25	08 28					
Wandsworth Common	d										08 11			08 16					08 27	08 31					
Latchmere	d																								
Clapham Junction	d				08 11						08 16	08 18	08 21	08 20		08 24	08 26		08 31	08 39					08 37
Imperial Wharf	d																			08 44					
West Brompton	d																			08 47					
Kensington (Olympia)	d																			08 50					
Shepherd's Bush	d																			08 53					
Wembley Central	d																			09 08					
Harrow & Wealdstone	d																			09 13					
Watford Junction	d																			09 20					
Milton Keynes Central	a																			10 01					
Battersea Park	d									08 15	08 19			08 23				08 32	08 35						
London Victoria	a				08 19						08 26	08 26	08 29	08 30		08 32	08 36	08 39	08 41						08 45
Streatham	d								08 09						08 16										
Tulse Hill	d		07 59						08 13						08 22										
Herne Hill	a								08 17																
Loughborough Jn	a								08 23																
Elephant & Castle	a								08 27																
London Blackfriars	a								08 32																
City Thameslink	a								08 35																
St Pancras International	a								08 43																
Luton Airport Parkway	a								09 29																
Luton	a								09 34																
North Dulwich	d		08 02												08 25										
East Dulwich	d		08 04												08 27										
Peckham Rye	d		08 06							08 26					08 29										
Queens Rd Peckham	d		08 09							08 29					08 32										
South Bermondsey	d		08 11							08 31					08 34										
London Bridge	a	08 13	08 18	08 15			08 19	08 21		08 38					08 41						08 28		08 35	08 37	

Table 177

Mondays to Fridays
until 18 May

East and West Croydon, London Milton Keynes Central and Luton via Norbury Crystal Palace - Tulse Hill

Local Services

Network Diagram - see first Page of Table 177

Station		SN	SN	SN	SN	SN	SN	SN	SN	FC	SN	SN	SN		SN	SN	SN	SN	SN	SN	SN	SN	SN	SN	SN
			■	■			◇■	■	■									◇■ ✕			◇■ ✕				◇■
East Croydon	d	08 18	08 21	08 27			08 30	08 33	08 37							08 39	08 42	08 43			08 50			08 54	08 58
West Croydon	d											08 19	08 26		08 31				08 44						
Norwood Junction	a											08 24					08 46		08 49						
	d											08 25					08 47		08 49						
Selhurst	d	08 21											08 31		08 35	08 43									
Thornton Heath	d	08 23											08 33		08 37	08 46									
Norbury	d	08 26											08 36		08 40	08 49									
Streatham Common	d	08 28											08 38		08 43	08 52									
Beckenham Junction	d				08 12																				
Birkbeck	d				08 15																				
Crystal Palace	d				08 19	08 24						08 29										08 40	08 44		
Gipsy Hill	d				08 21							08 31										08 43			
West Norwood	d				08 24							08 34										08 46			
Streatham Hill	d											08 38										08 49			
Balham ⊖	d	08 32										08 41	08 43			08 58						08 55			
Wandsworth Common	d	08 34										08 43	08 45			09 00						08 57			
Latchmere	d																								
Clapham Junction	d	08 38					08 40		08 48			08 47	08 50			09 05		08 53			09 01	09 01		09 04	09 08
Imperial Wharf	d															09 09									
West Brompton ⊖	d															09 12									
Kensington (Olympia) ⊖	d															09 15									
Shepherd's Bush ⊖	d															09a18									
Wembley Central ⊖	d																								
Harrow & Wealdstone ⊖	d																								
Watford Junction	d																								
Milton Keynes Central	a																								
Battersea Park	d	08 42									08 45	08 50	08 53							09 02		09 05			
London Victoria ⊖	a	08 48					08 48		08 56			08 57	09 00					09 01		09 08	09 09	09 11		09 13	09 16
Streatham	d									08 39					08 50										
Tulse Hill	d				08 28					08 43					08 55										
Herne Hill	a									08 47															
Loughborough Jn	a									08 50															
Elephant & Castle ⊖	a									08 57															
London Blackfriars ⊖	a									09 01															
City Thameslink	a									09 04															
St Pancras International ⊖	a									09 12															
Luton Airport Parkway	a									09 58															
Luton	a									10 03															
North Dulwich	d				08 31										08 58										
East Dulwich	d				08 33										09 00										
Peckham Rye	d				08 36						08 56				09 02										
Queens Rd Peckham	d				08 38						08 59				09 05										
South Bermondsey	d				08 41						09 01				09 07										
London Bridge ⊖	a		08 37	08 45	08 48	08 47		08 52			09 08				09 14		09 01		09 04				09 06		

Table 177

Mondays to Fridays
until 18 May

East and West Croydon, London Milton Keynes Central and Luton via Norbury Crystal Palace - Tulse Hill

Local Services

Network Diagram - see first Page of Table 177

Station		SN	SN	SN	SN		SN	FC	SN	SN	SN	SN	SN	SN	SN	SN	SN	SN	SN	SN	SN		SN	SN	SN
			■				■					■			■	◇■ ✕					◇■ ✕			◇■	
East Croydon	d	08 48	08 51				08 59				09 05	09 11			09 08	09 14					09 23		09 17	09 31	
West Croydon	d									08 49			08 57	09 01											
Norwood Junction	a									08 53	09 09														
	d									08 54	09 09														
Selhurst	d	08 51											09 01	09 05	09 13								09 21		
Thornton Heath	d	08 53											09 03	09 07	09 16								09 23		
Norbury	d	08 56											09 06	09 10	09 19								09 26		
Streatham Common	d	08 58											09 09	09 13	09 21								09 28		
Beckenham Junction	d			08 43																					
Birkbeck	d			08 46																					
Crystal Palace	d			08 50	08 51					08 58								09 11	09 14	09 21					
Gipsy Hill	d			08 52						09 00								09 14							
West Norwood	d			08 55						09 03								09 17							
Streatham Hill	d									09 07								09 21							
Balham ⊖	d	09 02								09 10			09 13		09 28			09 25					09 32		
Wandsworth Common	d	09 04								09 12			09 15		09 30			09 27					09 34		
Latchmere	d																								
Clapham Junction	d	09 08								09 16		09 21	09 19		09 39	09 24		09 31			09 33		09 38	09 41	
Imperial Wharf	d														09 44										
West Brompton ⊖	d														09 47										
Kensington (Olympia) ⊖	d														09 50										
Shepherd's Bush ⊖	d														09 53										
Wembley Central ⊖	d														10 08										
Harrow & Wealdstone ⊖	d														10 13										
Watford Junction	d														10 20										
Milton Keynes Central	a														11 02										
Battersea Park	d	09 12							09 15	09 19			09 22				09 32	09 35					09 42		09 45
London Victoria ⊖	a	09 18								09 27		09 27	09 31			09 32	09 38	09 42			09 42		09 48	09 50	
Streatham	d							09 08						09 20											
Tulse Hill	d			08 59				09 16						09 26											
Herne Hill	a							09 19																	
Loughborough Jn	a							09 23																	
Elephant & Castle ⊖	a							09 29																	
London Blackfriars ⊖	a							09 33																	
City Thameslink	a							09 36																	
St Pancras International ⊖	a							09 44																	
Luton Airport Parkway	a							10 29																	
Luton	a							10 33																	
North Dulwich	d			09 02										09 29											
East Dulwich	d			09 04										09 31											
Peckham Rye	d			09 07					09 26					09 33											09 56
Queens Rd Peckham	d			09 09					09 29					09 36											09 59
South Bermondsey	d			09 12					09 31					09 38											10 01
London Bridge ⊖	a		09 06	09 19	09 14		09 15		09 38		09 23			09 44					09 37	09 43					10 06

East and West Croydon, London Milton Keynes Central and Luton via Norbury Crystal Palace - Tulse Hill

Local Services

Network Diagram - see first Page of Table 177

		SN	SN	SN	SN	SN	SN	FC	SN	SN	SN	SN	SN		SN	SN	SN	SN	SN	SN	SN	SN	SN	SN	SN
					1				◇1 ⌶			◇1							◇1 ⌶				1		
East Croydon ⇌	d		09 20	09 30	09 37				09 39			09 43					09 47		10 00			09 51	09 55		10 00
West Croydon 4 ⇌	d	09 15								09 28	09 31		09 35								09 45			09 58	
Norwood Junction 2	a	09 19	09 24	09 34	09 41																09 50	09 55	09 59		10 04
	d	09 22	09 25	09 35	09 42																09 52	09 55	09 59		10 05
Selhurst 4	d									09 32	09 35		09 39				09 50							10 02	
Thornton Heath	d									09 34	09 37		09 41				09 52							10 04	
Norbury	d									09 37	09 40		09 44				09 55							10 07	
Streatham Common 4	d									09 40	09 43		09 47				09 58							10 10	
Beckenham Junction 4 ⇌	d					09 23																			
Birkbeck ⇌	d					09 26																			
Crystal Palace 4	d	09 26				09 30	09 36									09 43		09 51			09 56				
Gipsy Hill	d	09 28				09 32										09 46					09 58				
West Norwood 4	d	09 31				09 35										09 49					10 01				
Streatham Hill	d	09 35														09 52					10 05				
Balham 4 ⊖	d	09 41								09 44			09 52			09 56	10 02				10 09			10 14	
Wandsworth Common	d	09 43								09 46			09 54			09 58	10 04				10 11			10 16	
Latchmere	d																								
Clapham Junction 10	d	09 47							09 48	09 50		09 52	09 58			10 02	10 08		10 09		10 15			10 20	
Imperial Wharf	d																								
West Brompton ⊖	d																								
Kensington (Olympia) ⊖	d																								
Shepherd's Bush ⊖	d																								
Wembley Central ⊖	d																								
Harrow & Wealdstone ⊖	d																								
Watford Junction	d																								
Milton Keynes Central 10	a																								
Battersea Park 4	d	09 50								09 53					10 03	10 05	10 11			10 15	10 19			10 23	
London Victoria 15 ⊖	a	09 58							09 58	09 58		09 59	10 05		10 07	10 11	10 16		10 16		10 24			10 28	
Streatham 4	d							09 38			09 46														
Tulse Hill 3	d					09 39		09 42			09 54														
Herne Hill 4	a							09 46																	
Loughborough Jn	a							09 50																	
Elephant & Castle ⊖	a							09 54																	
London Blackfriars 3 ⊖	a							09 59																	
City Thameslink 3	a							10 02																	
St Pancras International 15 ⊖	a							10 10																	
Luton Airport Parkway 7	a							10 58																	
Luton 10	a							11 03																	
North Dulwich	d					09 42					09 57														
East Dulwich	d					09 44					09 59														
Peckham Rye 4	d					09 47					10 01									10 26					
Queens Rd Peckham	d					09 49					10 04									10 29					
South Bermondsey	d					09 52					10 06									10 31					
London Bridge 4 ⊖	a		09 41	10 00	09 55	09 58	09 59				10 11							10 11		10 36		10 09	10 13		10 29

East and West Croydon, London Milton Keynes Central and Luton via Norbury Crystal Palace - Tulse Hill

Local Services

Network Diagram - see first Page of Table 177

		SN	SN	FC	SN		SN	SN	SN	SN	SN	SN	SN	SN	SN	SN	SN	SN	SN	SN	SN		SN	FC	SN
		1					◇1 ⌶				1		◇1					1			1				
East Croydon ⇌	d	10 07					10 12				10 10		10 28	10 17			10 21	10 25		10 30	10 38				
West Croydon 4 ⇌	d				10 01			10 04								10 15			10 28						10 31
Norwood Junction 2	a	10 12														10 19	10 25	10 29		10 34	10 42				
	d	10 13														10 22	10 25	10 29		10 35	10 43				
Selhurst 4	d				10 05			10 09			10 14			10 20					10 32						10 35
Thornton Heath	d				10 07			10 11			10 16			10 22					10 34						10 37
Norbury	d				10 10			10 14			10 19			10 25					10 37						10 40
Streatham Common 4	d				10 13			10 17			10 22			10 28					10 40						10 43
Beckenham Junction 4 ⇌	d		09 53																				10 23		
Birkbeck ⇌	d		09 56																				10 26		
Crystal Palace 4	d		10 00							10 13		10 21				10 26							10 30		
Gipsy Hill	d		10 02							10 15						10 29							10 32		
West Norwood 4	d		10 05							10 18						10 32							10 35		
Streatham Hill	d									10 22						10 35									
Balham 4 ⊖	d							10 21		10 25	10 29			10 32		10 39			10 44						
Wandsworth Common	d							10 23		10 27	10 31			10 34		10 41			10 46						
Latchmere	d																								
Clapham Junction 10	d						10 21	10 27		10 31	10 39		10 38	10 38		10 45			10 50						
Imperial Wharf	d										10 44														
West Brompton ⊖	d										10 47														
Kensington (Olympia) ⊖	d										10 50														
Shepherd's Bush ⊖	d										10 53														
Wembley Central ⊖	d										11 08														
Harrow & Wealdstone ⊖	d										11 13														
Watford Junction	d										11 20														
Milton Keynes Central 10	a										12 01														
Battersea Park 4	d								10 32	10 35				10 41	10 45	10 49			10 53						
London Victoria 15 ⊖	a						10 28	10 34	10 36	10 39			10 45	10 46		10 53			10 58						
Streatham 4	d			10 08	10 16																			10 38	10 46
Tulse Hill 3	d		10 09	10 12	10 24																		10 39	10 42	10 54
Herne Hill 4	a			10 16																				10 46	
Loughborough Jn	a			10 19																				10 49	
Elephant & Castle ⊖	a			10 23																				10 53	
London Blackfriars 3 ⊖	a			10 27																				10 57	
City Thameslink 3	a			10 32																				11 02	
St Pancras International 15 ⊖	a			10 40																				11 10	
Luton Airport Parkway 7	a			11 27																				11 55	
Luton 10	a			11 31																				11 59	
North Dulwich	d		10 12		10 27																		10 42		10 57
East Dulwich	d		10 14		10 29																		10 44		10 59
Peckham Rye 4	d		10 17		10 31										10 56								10 47		11 01
Queens Rd Peckham	d		10 19		10 34										10 59								10 49		11 04
South Bermondsey	d		10 22		10 36										11 01								10 52		11 06
London Bridge 4 ⊖	a	10 25	10 26		10 41							10 41			11 06		10 39	10 43		10 59	10 55		10 56		11 11

Table 177

Mondays to Fridays
until 18 May

East and West Croydon, London
Milton Keynes Central and Luton via Norbury
Crystal Palace - Tulse Hill

Local Services

Network Diagram - see first Page of Table 177

		SN ◇1 ✠	SN	SN	SN	SN	SN	SN ◇1	SN	SN	SN	SN 1	SN	SN	SN 1	SN	FC	SN	SN ◇1	SN	SN	SN	SN 1	SN
East Croydon	d	10 42				10 47		11 00			10 51	10 55		11 00	11 07				11 12				11 11	11 17
West Croydon	d		10 34							10 45			10 58					11 01		11 04				
Norwood Junction	a									10 49	10 55	10 59		11 04	11 12									
	d									10 52	10 55	10 59		11 05	11 13									
Selhurst	d		10 39			10 50							11 02					11 05		11 09			11 16	11 20
Thornton Heath	d		10 41			10 52							11 04					11 07		11 11			11 18	11 22
Norbury	d		10 44			10 55							11 07					11 10		11 14			11 21	11 25
Streatham Common	d		10 47			10 58							11 10					11 13		11 17			11 24	11 28
Beckenham Junction	d															10 53								
Birkbeck	d															10 56								
Crystal Palace	d				10 43		10 51			10 56						11 00						11 13		
Gipsy Hill	d				10 45					10 59						11 02						11 15		
West Norwood	d				10 48					11 02						11 05						11 18		
Streatham Hill	d				10 52					11 05												11 22		
Balham ⊖	d		10 51		10 55	11 02				11 09			11 14							11 21		11 25	11 28	11 32
Wandsworth Common	d		10 53		10 57	11 04				11 11			11 16							11 23		11 27	11 30	11 34
Latchmere	d																							
Clapham Junction	d	10 51	10 57		11 01	11 08		11 10		11 15			11 20						11 21	11 27		11 31	11 39	11 38
Imperial Wharf	d																						11 44	
West Brompton ⊖	d																						11 47	
Kensington (Olympia) ⊖	d																						11 50	
Shepherd's Bush ⊖	d																						11 53	
Wembley Central ⊖	d																						12 08	
Harrow & Wealdstone ⊖	d																						12 13	
Watford Junction	d																						12 20	
Milton Keynes Central	a																						13 01	
Battersea Park	d			11 02	11 05	11 11			11 15	11 18			11 23								11 32	11 35		
London Victoria ⊖	a	10 58	11 04	11 06	11 09	11 16		11 16		11 23			11 28						11 28	11 34	11 36	11 39		11a41
Streatham	d																11 08	11 16						
Tulse Hill	d															11 09	11 12	11 24						
Herne Hill	a																11 16							
Loughborough Jn	a																11 19							
Elephant & Castle ⊖	a																11 23							
London Blackfriars ⊖	a																11 27							
City Thameslink	a																11 32							
St Pancras International ⊖	a																11 40							
Luton Airport Parkway	a																12 25							
Luton	a																12 29							
North Dulwich	d															11 12		11 27						
East Dulwich	d															11 14		11 29						
Peckham Rye	d								11 26							11 17		11 31						
Queens Rd Peckham	d								11 29							11 19		11 34						
South Bermondsey	d								11 31							11 22		11 36						
London Bridge ⊖	a						11 11		11 36		11 09	11 13		11 29	11 25	11 26		11 41						

Table 177

Mondays to Fridays
until 18 May

East and West Croydon, London
Milton Keynes Central and Luton via Norbury
Crystal Palace - Tulse Hill

Local Services

Network Diagram - see first Page of Table 177

		SN	SN ◇1	SN	SN	SN	SN 1	SN	SN 1	SN	FC	SN ◇1	SN	SN	SN	SN	SN	SN	SN	SN ◇1	SN	SN	SN
East Croydon	d		11 28			11 21	11 25	11 30	11 37			11 41						11 47		12 00			11 51
West Croydon	d				11 15								11 28	11 31	11 34							11 45	
Norwood Junction	a				11 19	11 25	11 29	11 34	11 42													11 49	11 55
	d				11 22	11 25	11 29	11 35	11 43													11 52	11 55
Selhurst	d												11 32	11 35	11 39			11 50					
Thornton Heath	d												11 34	11 37	11 41			11 52					
Norbury	d												11 37	11 40	11 44			11 55					
Streatham Common	d												11 40	11 43	11 47			11 58					
Beckenham Junction	d									11 23													
Birkbeck	d									11 26													
Crystal Palace	d	11 21			11 26					11 30							11 43		11 51			11 56	
Gipsy Hill	d				11 29					11 32							11 45					11 59	
West Norwood	d				11 32					11 35							11 48					12 02	
Streatham Hill	d				11 35												11 52					12 05	
Balham ⊖	d				11 40								11 44		11 51		11 55	12 02				12 09	
Wandsworth Common	d				11 42								11 46		11 53		11 57	12 04				12 11	
Latchmere	d																						
Clapham Junction	d		11 37		11 46							11 50	11 50		11 57		12 01	12 08		12 12		12 15	
Imperial Wharf	d																						
West Brompton ⊖	d																						
Kensington (Olympia) ⊖	d																						
Shepherd's Bush ⊖	d																						
Wembley Central ⊖	d																						
Harrow & Wealdstone ⊖	d																						
Watford Junction	d																						
Milton Keynes Central	a																						
Battersea Park	d			11 45	11 49								11 53			12 02	12 05	12a11			12 15	12 18	
London Victoria ⊖	a		11 44		11 54							11 57	11 58		12 04	12 07	12 09			12 18		12 23	
Streatham	d										11 38			11 46									
Tulse Hill	d									11 39	11 42			11 54									
Herne Hill	a										11 46												
Loughborough Jn	a										11 49												
Elephant & Castle ⊖	a										11 53												
London Blackfriars ⊖	a										11 57												
City Thameslink	a										12 02												
St Pancras International ⊖	a										12 10												
Luton Airport Parkway	a										12 55												
Luton	a										12 57												
North Dulwich	d									11 42				11 57									
East Dulwich	d									11 44				11 59									
Peckham Rye	d			11 56						11 47				12 01							12 26		
Queens Rd Peckham	d			11 59						11 49				12 04							12 29		
South Bermondsey	d			12 01						11 52				12 06							12 31		
London Bridge ⊖	a	11 41		12 06		11 39	11 43	11 59	11 55	11 56				12 11					12 14		12 36		12 09

Table 177

Mondays to Fridays
until 18 May

East and West Croydon, London
Milton Keynes Central and Luton via Norbury
Crystal Palace - Tulse Hill

Local Services

Network Diagram - see first Page of Table 177

		SN	SN	SN	SN	SN	FC	SN	SN	SN	SN	SN	SN		SN	SN	SN	SN	SN	SN	SN	SN	SN	SN	FC
		■			■				◇■				■				◇■				■		■		
East Croydon	d	11 55		12 00	12 07				12 12				12 10		12 17		12 28			12 21	12 25	12 30	12 37		
West Croydon [4]	d		11 58					12 01		12 04									12 15						
Norwood Junction [2]	a	11 59		12 04	12 12														12 19	12 25	12 29	12 34	12 42		
	d	11 59		12 05	12 13														12 22	12 25	12 29	12 35	12 43		
Selhurst [4]	d		12 02					12 05		12 09			12 14		12 20										
Thornton Heath	d		12 04					12 07		12 11			12 16		12 22										
Norbury	d		12 07					12 10		12 14			12 19		12 25										
Streatham Common [4]	d		12 10					12 13		12 17			12 22		12 28										
Beckenham Junction [4]	d					11 53																		12 23	
Birkbeck	d					11 56																		12 26	
Crystal Palace [4]	d					12 00						12 13				12 21			12 26					12 30	
Gipsy Hill	d					12 02						12 15							12 29					12 32	
West Norwood [4]	d					12 05						12 18							12 32					12 35	
Streatham Hill	d											12 22							12 35						
Balham [4] ⊖	d		12 14							12 21		12 25	12 28		12 32				12 39						
Wandsworth Common	d		12 16							12 23		12 27	12 30		12 34				12 41						
Latchmere	d																								
Clapham Junction [10]	d		12 20						12 22	12 27		12 31	12 39		12 38		12 37		12 45						
Imperial Wharf	d												12 44												
West Brompton ⊖	d												12 47												
Kensington (Olympia) ⊖	d												12 50												
Shepherd's Bush ⊖	d												12 53												
Wembley Central ⊖	d												13 08												
Harrow & Wealdstone ⊖	d												13 13												
Watford Junction	d												13 20												
Milton Keynes Central [10]	a												14 01												
Battersea Park [4]	d		12 23								12 32	12 35			12a41			12 45	12 48						
London Victoria [15] ⊖	a		12 28						12 28	12 34	12 36	12 39					12 44		12 53						
Streatham [4]	d						12 08	12 16																	12 38
Tulse Hill [3]	d					12 09	12 12	12 24																12 39	12 42
Herne Hill [4]	a						12 16																		12 46
Loughborough Jn	a						12 19																		12 49
Elephant & Castle ⊖	a						12 23																		12 53
London Blackfriars [3] ⊖	a						12 27																		12 57
City Thameslink [3]	a						12 32																		13 02
St Pancras International [15] ⊖	a						12 40																		13 10
Luton Airport Parkway [7]	a						13 25																		13 55
Luton [10]	a						13 29																		13 59
North Dulwich	d					12 12		12 27																12 42	
East Dulwich	d					12 14		12 29																12 44	
Peckham Rye [4]	d					12 17		12 31										12 56						12 47	
Queens Rd Peckham	d					12 19		12 34										12 59						12 49	
South Bermondsey	d					12 22		12 36										13 01						12 52	
London Bridge [4] ⊖	a	12 13		12 29	12 25	12 26		12 41								12 41		13 06		12 39	12 43	12 59	12 55	12 56	

Table 177

Mondays to Fridays
until 18 May

East and West Croydon, London
Milton Keynes Central and Luton via Norbury
Crystal Palace - Tulse Hill

Local Services

Network Diagram - see first Page of Table 177

		SN	SN	SN	SN		SN	SN	SN	SN	SN	SN	SN	SN	SN	SN	SN	SN	SN	FC	SN		SN	SN	SN
		◇■									◇■				■			■					◇■		
East Croydon	d	12 41							12 47		13 00			12 51	12 55		13 00	13 07					13 12		
West Croydon [4]	d		12 28	12 31	12 34								12 45			12 58					13 01			13 04	
Norwood Junction [2]	a												12 49	12 55	12 59		13 04	13 12							
	d												12 52	12 55	12 59		13 05	13 13							
Selhurst [4]	d		12 32	12 35	12 39				12 50							13 02					13 05			13 09	
Thornton Heath	d		12 34	12 37	12 41				12 52							13 04					13 07			13 11	
Norbury	d		12 37	12 40	12 44				12 55							13 07					13 10			13 14	
Streatham Common [4]	d		12 40	12 43	12 47				12 58							13 10					13 13			13 17	
Beckenham Junction [4]	d																		12 53						
Birkbeck	d																		12 56						
Crystal Palace [4]	d							12 43		12 51			12 56						13 00						
Gipsy Hill	d							12 45					12 59						13 02						
West Norwood [4]	d							12 48					13 02						13 05						
Streatham Hill	d							12 52					13 05												
Balham [4] ⊖	d		12 44		12 51			12 55	13 02				13 09			13 14								13 21	
Wandsworth Common	d		12 46		12 53			12 57	13 04				13 11			13 16								13 23	
Latchmere	d																								
Clapham Junction [10]	d	12 50	12 50		12 57			13 01	13 08		13 10		13 15			13 20							13 21	13 27	
Imperial Wharf	d																								
West Brompton ⊖	d																								
Kensington (Olympia) ⊖	d																								
Shepherd's Bush ⊖	d																								
Wembley Central ⊖	d																								
Harrow & Wealdstone ⊖	d																								
Watford Junction	d																								
Milton Keynes Central [10]	a																								
Battersea Park [4]	d		12 53				13 02	13 05	13 11			13 15	13 18			13 23									13 32
London Victoria [15] ⊖	a	12 57	12 58		13 04		13 06	13 09	13 16		13 16		13 23			13 28							13 28	13 34	13 36
Streatham [4]	d			12 46																13 08	13 16				
Tulse Hill [3]	d			12 54															13 09	13 12	13 24				
Herne Hill [4]	a																			13 16					
Loughborough Jn	a																			13 19					
Elephant & Castle ⊖	a																			13 23					
London Blackfriars [3] ⊖	a																			13 27					
City Thameslink [3]	a																			13 32					
St Pancras International [15] ⊖	a																			13 40					
Luton Airport Parkway [7]	a																			14 25					
Luton [10]	a																			14 29					
North Dulwich	d			12 57															13 12		13 27				
East Dulwich	d			12 59															13 14		13 29				
Peckham Rye [4]	d			13 01								13 26							13 17		13 31				
Queens Rd Peckham	d			13 04								13 29							13 19		13 34				
South Bermondsey	d			13 06								13 31							13 22		13 36				
London Bridge [4] ⊖	a			13 11						13 11		13 36		13 09	13 13		13 29	13 25	13 26		13 41				

Table 177

Mondays to Fridays

until 18 May

East and West Croydon, London Milton Keynes Central and Luton via Norbury Crystal Palace - Tulse Hill

Local Services

Network Diagram - see first Page of Table 177

		SN	SN ■1	SN	SN	SN ◇■1	SN	SN	SN	SN ■1	SN	SN ■1	SN		FC	SN ◇■1	SN	SN	SN	SN	SN	SN	SN	SN ◇■1	SN
East Croydon	d		13 10	13 17		13 28			13 21	13 25	13 30	13 37				13 41						13 47		14 00	
West Croydon 4	d							13 15									13 28	13 31	13 34						
Norwood Junction 2	a							13 19	13 25	13 29	13 34	13 42													
	d							13 22	13 25	13 29	13 35	13 43													
Selhurst 4	d		13 13	13 20													13 32	13 35	13 39			13 50			
Thornton Heath	d		13 16	13 22													13 34	13 37	13 41			13 52			
Norbury	d		13 19	13 25													13 37	13 40	13 44			13 55			
Streatham Common 4	d		13 21	13 28													13 40	13 43	13 47			13 58			
Beckenham Junction 4	d												13 23												
Birkbeck	d												13 26												
Crystal Palace 4	d	13 13			13 21			13 26					13 30								13 43		13 51		
Gipsy Hill	d	13 15						13 29					13 32								13 45				
West Norwood 4	d	13 18						13 32					13 35								13 48				
Streatham Hill	d	13 22						13 35													13 52				
Balham 4 ⊖	d	13 25	13 28	13 32				13 39									13 44		13 51		13 55	14 02			
Wandsworth Common	d	13 27	13 30	13 34				13 41									13 46		13 53		13 57	14 04			
Latchmere	d																								
Clapham Junction 10	d	13 31	13 39	13 38		13 37		13 45								13 50	13 50		13 57		14 01	14 08		14 10	
Imperial Wharf	d		13 44																						
West Brompton ⊖	d		13 47																						
Kensington (Olympia) ⊖	d		13 50																						
Shepherd's Bush ⊖	d		13 53																						
Wembley Central ⊖	d		14 08																						
Harrow & Wealdstone ⊖	d		14 13																						
Watford Junction	d		14 20																						
Milton Keynes Central 10	a		15 01																						
Battersea Park 4	d	13 35		13a41			13 45	13 48									13 53			14 02	14 05	14a11			14 15
London Victoria 15 ⊖	a	13 39				13 44		13 53								13 57	13 58		14 04	14 06	14 09			14 16	
Streatham 4	d														13 38			13 46							
Tulse Hill 3	d												13 39		13 42			13 54							
Herne Hill 4	a														13 46										
Loughborough Jn	a														13 49										
Elephant & Castle ⊖	a														13 53										
London Blackfriars 3 ⊖	a														13 57										
City Thameslink 3	a														14 02										
St Pancras International 15 ⊖	a														14 10										
Luton Airport Parkway 7	a														14 55										
Luton 10	a														14 59										
North Dulwich	d												13 42					13 57							
East Dulwich	d												13 44					13 59							
Peckham Rye 4	d						13 56						13 47					14 01							
Queens Rd Peckham	d						13 59						13 49					14 04							14 26
South Bermondsey	d						14 01						13 52					14 06							14 29
London Bridge 4 ⊖	a				13 44		14 06		13 39	13 43	13 59	13 55	13 56					14 11					14 11		14 36

Table 177

Mondays to Fridays

until 18 May

East and West Croydon, London Milton Keynes Central and Luton via Norbury Crystal Palace - Tulse Hill

Local Services

Network Diagram - see first Page of Table 177

		SN	SN	SN ■1	SN		SN	SN ■1	SN	FC	SN	SN ◇■1	SN	SN	SN	SN ■1	SN	SN	SN ◇■1	SN	SN		SN	SN ■1	SN
East Croydon	d		13 51	13 55			14 00	14 08				14 12				14 10	14 17		14 28				14 21	14 25	14 30
West Croydon 4	d	13 45			13 58						14 01		14 04								14 15				
Norwood Junction 2	a	13 49	13 55	13 59			14 04	14 12													14 19		14 25	14 29	14 34
	d	13 52	13 55	13 59			14 05	14 13													14 22		14 25	14 29	14 35
Selhurst 4	d				14 02						14 05		14 09			14 13	14 20								
Thornton Heath	d				14 04						14 07		14 11			14 16	14 22								
Norbury	d				14 07						14 10		14 14			14 19	14 25								
Streatham Common 4	d				14 10						14 13		14 17			14 21	14 28								
Beckenham Junction 4	d								13 53																
Birkbeck	d								13 56																
Crystal Palace 4	d	13 56							14 00						14 13			14 21			14 26				
Gipsy Hill	d	13 59							14 02						14 15						14 29				
West Norwood 4	d	14 02							14 05						14 18						14 32				
Streatham Hill	d	14 05													14 22						14 35				
Balham 4 ⊖	d	14 09			14 14								14 21		14 25	14 28	14 32				14 39				
Wandsworth Common	d	14 11			14 16								14 23		14 27	14 30	14 34				14 41				
Latchmere	d																								
Clapham Junction 10	d	14 15			14 20							14 21	14 27		14 31	14 39	14 38		14 37		14 45				
Imperial Wharf	d															14 44									
West Brompton ⊖	d															14 47									
Kensington (Olympia) ⊖	d															14 50									
Shepherd's Bush ⊖	d															14 53									
Wembley Central ⊖	d															15 08									
Harrow & Wealdstone ⊖	d															15 13									
Watford Junction	d															15 20									
Milton Keynes Central 10	a															16 01									
Battersea Park 4	d	14 18			14 23									14 32	14 35		14a41			14 45	14 48				
London Victoria 15 ⊖	a	14 23			14 28							14 28	14 34	14 36	14 39				14 44		14 53				
Streatham 4	d									14 08	14 16														
Tulse Hill 3	d								14 09	14 12	14 24														
Herne Hill 4	a									14 16															
Loughborough Jn	a									14 19															
Elephant & Castle ⊖	a									14 23															
London Blackfriars 3 ⊖	a									14 27															
City Thameslink 3	a									14 32															
St Pancras International 15 ⊖	a									14 40															
Luton Airport Parkway 7	a									15 25															
Luton 10	a									15 29															
North Dulwich	d								14 12		14 27														
East Dulwich	d								14 14		14 29														
Peckham Rye 4	d								14 17		14 31									14 56					
Queens Rd Peckham	d								14 19		14 34									14 59					
South Bermondsey	d								14 22		14 36									15 01					
London Bridge 4 ⊖	a		14 09	14 13			14 29	14 25	14 26		14 41							14 41		15 06			14 39	14 43	14 59

Table 177

Mondays to Fridays

until 18 May

East and West Croydon, London Milton Keynes Central and Luton via Norbury Crystal Palace - Tulse Hill

Local Services

Network Diagram - see first Page of Table 177

		SN ■	SN	FC	SN ◇■	SN	SN	SN	SN	SN	SN	SN	SN ◇■		SN	SN	SN	SN ■	SN	SN	SN ■	SN	FC	SN	SN ◇■
East Croydon	d	14 37			14 41						14 47		15 00				14 51	14 55		15 00	15 07				15 12
West Croydon ■	d					14 28	14 31	14 34								14 45			14 58					15 01	
Norwood Junction ■	a	14 42														14 49	14 55	14 59		15 04	15 12				
	d	14 43														14 52	14 55	14 59		15 05	15 13				
Selhurst ■	d					14 32	14 35	14 39			14 50								15 02					15 05	
Thornton Heath	d					14 34	14 37	14 41			14 52								15 04					15 07	
Norbury	d					14 37	14 40	14 44			14 55								15 07					15 10	
Streatham Common ■	d					14 40	14 43	14 47			14 58								15 10					15 13	
Beckenham Junction ■	d		14 23																			14 53			
Birkbeck	d		14 26																			14 56			
Crystal Palace ■	d		14 30							14 43		14 51				14 56						15 00			
Gipsy Hill	d		14 32							14 45						14 59						15 02			
West Norwood ■	d		14 35							14 48						15 02						15 05			
Streatham Hill	d									14 52						15 05									
Balham ■ ⊖	d					14 44		14 51		14 55	15 02					15 09			15 14						
Wandsworth Common	d					14 46		14 53		14 57	15 04					15 11			15 16						
Latchmere	d																								
Clapham Junction ■	d				14 50	14 50		14 57		15 01	15 08		15 10			15 15			15 20						15 21
Imperial Wharf	d																								
West Brompton ⊖	d																								
Kensington (Olympia) ⊖	d																								
Shepherd's Bush ⊖	d																								
Wembley Central ⊖	d																								
Harrow & Wealdstone ⊖	d																								
Watford Junction	d																								
Milton Keynes Central ■	a																								
Battersea Park ■	d					14 53			15 02	15 05	15 11				15 15	15 18			15 23						
London Victoria ■ ⊖	a				14 57	14 58		15 04	15 06	15 09	15 16		15 20			15 24			15 28						15 28
Streatham ■	d			14 38			14 46																15 08	15 16	
Tulse Hill ■	d		14 39	14 42			14 54															15 09	15 12	15 24	
Herne Hill ■	a			14 46																			15 16		
Loughborough Jn	a			14 49																			15 19		
Elephant & Castle ⊖	a			14 53																			15 23		
London Blackfriars ■ ⊖	a			14 57																			15 27		
City Thameslink ■	a			15 02																			15 32		
St Pancras International ■ ⊖	a			15 10																			15 40		
Luton Airport Parkway ■	a			15 55																			16 25		
Luton ■	a			15 59																			16 29		
North Dulwich	d		14 42				14 57															15 12		15 27	
East Dulwich	d		14 44				14 59															15 14		15 29	
Peckham Rye ■	d		14 47				15 01								15 26							15 17		15 31	
Queens Rd Peckham	d		14 49				15 04								15 29							15 19		15 34	
South Bermondsey	d		14 52				15 06								15 31							15 22		15 36	
London Bridge ■ ⊖	a	14 55	14 56				15 11					15 11			15 36		15 09	15 13		15 29	15 25	15 26		15 41	

Table 177

Mondays to Fridays

until 18 May

East and West Croydon, London Milton Keynes Central and Luton via Norbury Crystal Palace - Tulse Hill

Local Services

Network Diagram - see first Page of Table 177

		SN	SN	SN	SN ■		SN	SN	SN ◇■	SN	SN	SN	SN ■	SN	SN ■	SN	FC	SN ◇■ ✕	SN	SN	SN		SN	SN	SN
East Croydon	d				15 10		15 17		15 28			15 21	15 25	15 30	15 37			15 41							15 47
West Croydon ■	d	15 04									15 15								15 28	15 31	15 34				
Norwood Junction ■	a										15 19	15 25	15 29	15 34	15 42										
	d										15 22	15 25	15 29	15 35	15 43										
Selhurst ■	d	15 09			15 13		15 20												15 32	15 35	15 39				15 50
Thornton Heath	d	15 11			15 16		15 22												15 34	15 37	15 41				15 52
Norbury	d	15 14			15 19		15 25												15 37	15 40	15 44				15 55
Streatham Common ■	d	15 17			15 21		15 28												15 40	15 43	15 47				15 58
Beckenham Junction ■	d															15 23									
Birkbeck	d															15 26									
Crystal Palace ■	d			15 13				15 21			15 26					15 30								15 43	
Gipsy Hill	d			15 15							15 29					15 32								15 45	
West Norwood ■	d			15 18							15 32					15 35								15 48	
Streatham Hill	d			15 22							15 35													15 52	
Balham ■ ⊖	d	15 21		15 25	15 29		15 32				15 39								15 44		15 51			15 55	16 02
Wandsworth Common	d	15 23		15 27	15 31		15 34				15 41								15 46		15 53			15 57	16 04
Latchmere	d																								
Clapham Junction ■	d	15 27		15 31	15 39		15 38		15 38		15 45							15 50	15 50		15 57			16 01	16 08
Imperial Wharf	d				15 44																				
West Brompton ⊖	d				15 47																				
Kensington (Olympia) ⊖	d				15 50																				
Shepherd's Bush ⊖	d				15 53																				
Wembley Central ⊖	d				16 08																				
Harrow & Wealdstone ⊖	d				16 13																				
Watford Junction	d				16 20																				
Milton Keynes Central ■	a				17 00																				
Battersea Park ■	d		15 32	15 35			15 41			15 45	15 49								15 53				16 02	16 05	16 11
London Victoria ■ ⊖	a	15 34	15 36	15 39			15 46		15 46		15 54							15 57	15 58		16 04		16 06	16 10	16 16
Streatham ■	d																15 38			15 46					
Tulse Hill ■	d															15 39	15 42			15 54					
Herne Hill ■	a																15 46								
Loughborough Jn	a																15 49								
Elephant & Castle ⊖	a																15 53								
London Blackfriars ■ ⊖	a																15 57								
City Thameslink ■	a																16 02								
St Pancras International ■ ⊖	a																16 10								
Luton Airport Parkway ■	a																16 57								
Luton ■	a																17 01								
North Dulwich	d															15 42				15 57					
East Dulwich	d															15 44				15 59					
Peckham Rye ■	d									15 56						15 47				16 01					
Queens Rd Peckham	d									15 59						15 49				16 04					
South Bermondsey	d									16 01						15 52				16 06					
London Bridge ■ ⊖	a							15 41		16 06		15 39	15 43	15 59	15 55	15 56				16 11					

Table 177

Mondays to Fridays

until 18 May

East and West Croydon, London Milton Keynes Central and Luton via Norbury Crystal Palace - Tulse Hill

Local Services

Network Diagram - see first Page of Table 177

		SN	SN	SN ◇■ ⛌	SN	SN	SN	SN ■	SN	SN	SN ■	SN	FC		SN	SN ◇■ ⛌	SN	SN	SN	SN ■	SN	SN	SN ◇■ ⛌	SN	SN
East Croydon	d			16 00			15 51	15 55		16 00	16 07					16 12				16 10	16 17		16 30		
West Croydon ■	d					15 45			15 58						16 01		16 04								16 15
Norwood Junction ■	a					15 49	15 55	15 59		16 04	16 12														16 20
	d					15 52	15 55	15 59		16 05	16 13														16 22
Selhurst ■	d								16 02						16 05		16 09			16 13	16 20				
Thornton Heath	d								16 04						16 07		16 11			16 16	16 22				
Norbury	d								16 07						16 10		16 14			16 19	16 25				
Streatham Common ■	d								16 10						16 13		16 17			16 21	16 28				
Beckenham Junction ■	d											15 53													
Birkbeck	d											15 56													
Crystal Palace ■	d	15 51				15 56						16 00							16 13			16 21			16 26
Gipsy Hill	d					15 59						16 02							16 15						16 29
West Norwood ■	d					16 02						16 05							16 18						16 32
Streatham Hill	d		15 56			16 05													16 22						16 35
Balham ■ ⊖	d					16 09			16 14								16 21		16 25	16 28	16 32				16 39
Wandsworth Common	d					16 11			16 16								16 23		16 27	16 30	16 34				16 41
Latchmere	d																								
Clapham Junction ■	d			16 09		16 15			16 20							16 21	16 27		16 31	16 39	16 38		16 40		16 45
Imperial Wharf	d																			16 44					
West Brompton ⊖	d																			16 47					
Kensington (Olympia) ⊖	d																			16 50					
Shepherd's Bush ⊖	d																			16 53					
Wembley Central ⊖	d																			17 08					
Harrow & Wealdstone ⊖	d																			17 13					
Watford Junction	d																			17 21					
Milton Keynes Central ■	a																			17 59					
Battersea Park ■	d				16 15	16 18			16 23									16 32	16 35		16 41			16 45	16 49
London Victoria ■ ⊖	a			16 16		16 23			16 28							16 28	16 34	16 38	16 40		16 46		16 46		16 55
Streatham ■	d												16 08		16 16										
Tulse Hill ■	d		16 00									16 09	16 12		16 24										
Herne Hill ■	a												16 16												
Loughborough Jn	a												16 19												
Elephant & Castle ⊖	a												16 23												
London Blackfriars ■ ⊖	a												16 29												
City Thameslink ■	a												16 32												
St Pancras International ■ ⊖	a												16 39												
Luton Airport Parkway ■	a												17 25												
Luton ■	a												17 29												
North Dulwich	d		16 03									16 12			16 27										
East Dulwich	d		16 05									16 14			16 29										
Peckham Rye ■	d		16 07		16 26							16 17			16 31									16 56	
Queens Rd Peckham	d		16 10		16 29							16 19			16 34									16 59	
South Bermondsey	d		16 12		16 31							16 22			16 36									17 01	
London Bridge ■ ⊖	a	16 11	16 17		16 38		16 09	16 13		16 29	16 25	16 26			16 41							16 41		17 08	

Table 177

Mondays to Fridays

until 18 May

East and West Croydon, London Milton Keynes Central and Luton via Norbury Crystal Palace - Tulse Hill

Local Services

Network Diagram - see first Page of Table 177

		SN	SN ■	SN	SN		SN	FC	SN ■	SN	SN ◇■ ⛌	SN	SN	SN	SN	SN	SN ◇■	SN	SN	SN	SN ■		SN	SN	SN ■
East Croydon	d	16 21	16 24				16 30		16 40		16 41				16 47		17 01			16 51	16 55			17 00	17 07
West Croydon ■	d				16 28					16 31		16 34							16 45				16 58		
Norwood Junction ■	a	16 25	16 28				16 34		16 44										16 50	16 55	16 59			17 04	17 11
	d	16 25	16 28				16 35		16 45										16 52	16 55	16 59			17 05	17 12
Selhurst ■	d				16 32					16 35		16 39			16 50								17 02		
Thornton Heath	d				16 34					16 37		16 41			16 52								17 04		
Norbury	d				16 37					16 40		16 44			16 55								17 07		
Streatham Common ■	d				16 40					16 43		16 47			16 58								17 10		
Beckenham Junction ■	d			16 23																					
Birkbeck	d			16 26																					
Crystal Palace ■	d			16 30										16 43		16 50			16 56						
Gipsy Hill	d			16 32										16 45					16 59						
West Norwood ■	d			16 35										16 48					17 02						
Streatham Hill	d													16 52					17 05						
Balham ■ ⊖	d				16 44							16 51		16 55	17 02				17 09				17 14		
Wandsworth Common	d				16 46							16 53		16 57	17 04				17 11				17 16		
Latchmere	d																								
Clapham Junction ■	d				16 50						16 51	16 57		17 01	17 08		17 11		17 15				17 20		
Imperial Wharf	d																								
West Brompton ⊖	d																								
Kensington (Olympia) ⊖	d																								
Shepherd's Bush ⊖	d																								
Wembley Central ⊖	d																								
Harrow & Wealdstone ⊖	d																								
Watford Junction	d																								
Milton Keynes Central ■	a																								
Battersea Park ■	d				16 53								17 02	17 05	17 11			17 15	17 18				17 23		
London Victoria ■ ⊖	a				16 58						16 58	17 04	17 08	17 10	17 16		17 17		17 23				17 28		
Streatham ■	d							16 40		16 46															
Tulse Hill ■	d			16 39				16 46		16 53															
Herne Hill ■	a							16 50																	
Loughborough Jn	a							16 53																	
Elephant & Castle ⊖	a							16 59																	
London Blackfriars ■ ⊖	a							17 03																	
City Thameslink ■	a							17 06																	
St Pancras International ■ ⊖	a							17 13																	
Luton Airport Parkway ■	a																								
Luton ■	a																								
North Dulwich	d			16 42						16 56															
East Dulwich	d			16 44						16 58															
Peckham Rye ■	d			16 47						17 00								17 26							
Queens Rd Peckham	d			16 49						17 03								17 29							
South Bermondsey	d			16 52						17 05								17 31							
London Bridge ■ ⊖	a	16 39	16 43	16 56			17 02		17 00	17 10						17 12		17 38		17 08	17 14			17 35	17 26

East and West Croydon, London Milton Keynes Central and Luton via Norbury Crystal Palace - Tulse Hill

Local Services

Network Diagram - see first Page of Table 177

		SN	FC	SN	SN ◇1	SN	SN	SN	SN	SN 1	SN	SN	SN ◇1	SN	SN 1	FC	SN	SN	SN	SN 1	SN	SN	SN	SN ◇1
East Croydon	d				17 13					17 10			17 30	17 17	17 38				17 21	17 25			17 30	17 41
West Croydon 4	d			17 01		17 04	17 12											17 18			17 28			
Norwood Junction 2	a																	17 22	17 25	17 30			17 34	
	d																	17 23	17 25	17 31		17 32	17 35	
Selhurst 4	d			17 05		17 09				17 13				17 20							17 32			
Thornton Heath	d			17 07		17 11				17 16				17 22							17 34			
Norbury	d			17 10		17 14				17 19				17 25							17 37			
Streatham Common 4	d			17 13		17 17				17 21				17 28							17 40			
Beckenham Junction 4	d	16 53									17 11													
Birkbeck	d	16 56									17 14													
Crystal Palace 4	d	17 00							17 13		17 18	17 21						17 27				17 36		
Gipsy Hill	d	17 02							17 15		17 20							17 29				17 38		
West Norwood 4	d	17 05							17 18		17 23							17 32				17 41		
Streatham Hill	d								17 22									17 36						
Balham 4 ⊖	d					17 21			17 25	17 28				17 32				17 39			17 44			
Wandsworth Common	d					17 23			17 27	17 30				17 34				17 41			17 46			
Latchmere	d																							
Clapham Junction 10	d				17 23	17 27			17 31	17 39			17 40	17 38	17 48			17 45			17 50			17 51
Imperial Wharf	d									17 44														
West Brompton ⊖	d									17 47														
Kensington (Olympia) ⊖	d									17 50														
Shepherd's Bush ⊖	d									17 53														
Wembley Central ⊖	d									18 08														
Harrow & Wealdstone ⊖	d									18 13														
Watford Junction	d									18 20														
Milton Keynes Central 10	a									19 00														
Battersea Park 4	d							17 32	17 35					17 41			17 45	17 48			17 53			
London Victoria 15 ⊖	a				17 29	17 34		17 38	17 42				17 46	17 48	17 54			17 55			17 58			17 58
Streatham 4	d		17 10	17 16												17 40								
Tulse Hill 3	d	17 09	17 16	17 22							17 27					17 44						17 45		
Herne Hill 4	a		17 20													17 47								
Loughborough Jn	a		17 24													17 51								
Elephant & Castle ⊖	a		17 28													17 55								
London Blackfriars 3 ⊖	a		17 31													17 59								
City Thameslink 3	a		17 34													18 02								
St Pancras International 15 ⊖	a		17 41													18 09								
Luton Airport Parkway 7	a		18 27													18 58								
Luton 10	a		18 31													19 01								
North Dulwich	d	17 12		17 25							17 30											17 48		
East Dulwich	d	17 14		17 27							17 32											17 50		
Peckham Rye 4	d	17 17		17 29							17 35						17 57					17 53		
Queens Rd Peckham	d	17 19		17 32							17 37						17 59					17 55		
South Bermondsey	d	17 22		17 34							17 40						18 02					17 58		
London Bridge 4 ⊖	a	17 27		17 40			17 28				17 44	17 43					18 08		17 37	17 45		18 02	17 59	

East and West Croydon, London Milton Keynes Central and Luton via Norbury Crystal Palace - Tulse Hill

Local Services

Network Diagram - see first Page of Table 177

		SN 1	SN	SN	SN	SN	SN	SN	SN	SN	SN ◇1	FC	SN	SN	SN 1	SN	SN 1	SN	SN	SN 1	SN ◇1	SN	SN
East Croydon	d	17 41					17 47	17 51			18 02				17 55	18 08	18 09			18 10	18 12		
West Croydon 4	d		17 31	17 42										17 48				17 58	18 01			18 13	
Norwood Junction 2	a	17 45						17 55						17 54	17 59	18 12							
	d	17 45						17 55						17 55	17 59	18 12							
Selhurst 4	d		17 35				17 50											18 02	18 05	18 13			
Thornton Heath	d		17 37				17 52											18 04	18 07	18 16			
Norbury	d		17 40				17 55											18 07	18 10	18 19			
Streatham Common 4	d		17 43				17 58											18 10	18 13	18 21			
Beckenham Junction 4	d									17 48													
Birkbeck	d									17 51													
Crystal Palace 4	d					17 44			17 48	17 55				17 59									
Gipsy Hill	d					17 46				17 57				18 01									
West Norwood 4	d					17 49				18 00				18 04									
Streatham Hill	d					17 53								18 08									
Balham 4 ⊖	d					17 56	18 02							18 11				18 14		18 29			
Wandsworth Common	d					17 58	18 04							18 13				18 16		18 31			
Latchmere	d																						
Clapham Junction 10	d					18 02	18 08				18 13			18 17			18 19	18 20		18 39	18 22		
Imperial Wharf	d																			18 44			
West Brompton ⊖	d																			18 47			
Kensington (Olympia) ⊖	d																			18 50			
Shepherd's Bush ⊖	d																			18 53			
Wembley Central ⊖	d																			19 08			
Harrow & Wealdstone ⊖	d																			19 13			
Watford Junction	d																			19 21			
Milton Keynes Central 10	a																			20 06			
Battersea Park 4	d				18 02	18 06	18 11						18 15	18 20				18 23					
London Victoria 15 ⊖	a				18 08	18 12	18 16				18 20			18 25			18 26	18 28			18 29		
Streatham 4	d		17 46									18 10							18 16				18 20
Tulse Hill 3	d		17 54							18 05		18 16							18 20				18 24
Herne Hill 4	a											18 19											
Loughborough Jn	a											18 23											
Elephant & Castle ⊖	a											18 27											
London Blackfriars 3 ⊖	a											18 31											
City Thameslink 3	a											18 34											
St Pancras International 15 ⊖	a											18 41											
Luton Airport Parkway 7	a											19 30											
Luton 10	a											19 33											
North Dulwich	d		17 57							18 08									18 23				18 27
East Dulwich	d		17 59							18 10									18 25				18 29
Peckham Rye 4	d		18 01							18 12			18 26						18 29				18 32
Queens Rd Peckham	d		18 04							18 15			18 29						18 32				18 35
South Bermondsey	d		18 06							18 17			18 31						18 34				18 37
London Bridge 4 ⊖	a	17 58	18 11	18 00				18 09	18 13	18 22			18 38		18 16	18 26			18 39			18 29	18 42

Table 177

Mondays to Fridays
until 18 May

East and West Croydon, London Milton Keynes Central and Luton via Norbury Crystal Palace - Tulse Hill

Local Services

Network Diagram - see first Page of Table 177

		SN	SN	SN	SN	SN 1	SN	SN ◇1 ⌶	FC	SN	SN	SN	SN		SN 1	SN	SN	SN ◇1 ⌶	SN	SN	SN	SN 1	SN	SN	SN
East Croydon ⇌	d					18 27	18 17	18 30				18 21	18 30		18 40			18 43				18 55	18 47		
West Croydon 4 ⇌	d										18 18					18 28	18 31								
Norwood Junction 2	a										18 23	18 28	18 34												
	d										18 24	18 29	18 35												
Selhurst 4	d						18 20									18 32	18 36						18 51		
Thornton Heath	d						18 22									18 34	18 38						18 53		
Norbury	d						18 25									18 37	18 41						18 56		
Streatham Common 4	d						18 28									18 40	18 44						18 58		
Beckenham Junction 4 ⇌	d			18 11																					18 44
Birkbeck ⇌	d			18 14																					18 47
Crystal Palace 4	d		18 13	18 18	18 20						18 28									18 43	18 51				18 51
Gipsy Hill	d		18 15	18 20							18 30									18 45					18 53
West Norwood 4	d		18 18	18 23							18 33									18 48					18 56
Streatham Hill	d		18 22								18 37									18 52					
Balham 4 ⊖	d		18 25				18 33				18 40					18 44				18 55			19 02		
Wandsworth Common	d		18 27				18 35				18 42					18 46				18 57			19 04		
Latchmere	d																								
Clapham Junction 10	d		18 32			18 38	18 39	18 41			18 46				18 50	18 50		18 53		19 01		19 06	19 08		
Imperial Wharf	d																								
West Brompton ⊖	d																								
Kensington (Olympia) ⊖	d																								
Shepherd's Bush ⊖	d																								
Wembley Central ⊖	d																								
Harrow & Wealdstone ⊖	d																								
Watford Junction	d																								
Milton Keynes Central 10	a																								
Battersea Park 4	d	18 32	18 35							18 45	18 49								19 02	19 05					
London Victoria 15 ⊖	a	18 39	18 42			18 45	18 46	18 48			18 54				18 56	18 57		18 59	19 08	19 12		19 13	19 15		
Streatham 4	d								18 40								18 47							18 56	
Tulse Hill 3	d			18 28					18 44								18 54							19 00	19 07
Herne Hill 4	a								18 47																
Loughborough Jn	a								18 51																
Elephant & Castle ⊖	a								18 55																
London Blackfriars 3 ⊖	a								18 59																
City Thameslink 3	a								19 02																
St Pancras International 15 ⊖	a								19 09																
Luton Airport Parkway 7	a								19 54																
Luton 10	a								19 57																
North Dulwich	d			18 31													18 57							19 03	19 10
East Dulwich	d			18 33													18 59							19 05	19 12
Peckham Rye 4	d			18 36						18 57							19 01							19 07	19 14
Queens Rd Peckham	d			18 38						19 00							19 04							19 10	19 17
South Bermondsey	d			18 41						19 02							19 06							19 12	19 19
London Bridge 4 ⊖	a			18 45	18 45					19 09		18 41	18 59				19 11				19 13			19 17	19 24

Table 177

Mondays to Fridays
until 18 May

East and West Croydon, London Milton Keynes Central and Luton via Norbury Crystal Palace - Tulse Hill

Local Services

Network Diagram - see first Page of Table 177

		SN ◇1	FC	SN	SN		SN	SN	SN 1	SN	SN 1	SN ◇1 ⌶	SN	SN	SN	SN 1	SN	SN ◇1	SN	SN	SN		SN	SN	SN 1
East Croydon ⇌	d	19 00						19 00	19 10		19 10	19 12				19 25		19 29	19 17					19 30	19 40
West Croydon 4 ⇌	d				18 47		18 58			19 01											19 17				
Norwood Junction 2	a				18 51			19 04	19 13												19 21			19 34	
	d				18 52			19 05	19 13												19 22			19 35	
Selhurst 4	d						19 02			19 05	19 13								19 20						
Thornton Heath	d						19 04			19 07	19 16								19 22						
Norbury	d						19 07			19 10	19 19								19 25						
Streatham Common 4	d						19 10			19 13	19 21								19 28						
Beckenham Junction 4 ⇌	d																						19 25		
Birkbeck ⇌	d																						19 28		
Crystal Palace 4	d				18 56									19 13	19 21						19 26		19 32		
Gipsy Hill	d				18 59									19 15							19 29		19 34		
West Norwood 4	d				19 02									19 18							19 32		19 37		
Streatham Hill	d				19 05									19 22							19 35				
Balham 4 ⊖	d				19 09		19 14				19 28			19 25					19 32		19 39				
Wandsworth Common	d				19 11		19 16				19 30			19 27					19 34		19 41				
Latchmere	d																								
Clapham Junction 10	d	19 12			19 15		19 20				19 39	19 22		19 31		19 38		19 41	19 38		19 45				19 50
Imperial Wharf	d										19 44														
West Brompton ⊖	d										19 47														
Kensington (Olympia) ⊖	d										19 50														
Shepherd's Bush ⊖	d										19 53														
Wembley Central ⊖	d										20 08														
Harrow & Wealdstone ⊖	d										20 13														
Watford Junction	d										20 20														
Milton Keynes Central 10	a										21 01														
Battersea Park 4	d			19 15	19 18		19 23						19 32	19 35					19 41	19 45	19 48				
London Victoria 15 ⊖	a	19 18			19 25		19 28					19 29	19 36	19 41		19 44		19 47	19 48		19 54				19 56
Streatham 4	d		19 10							19 16							19 26								
Tulse Hill 3	d		19 14							19 22							19 31						19 41		
Herne Hill 4	a		19 17																						
Loughborough Jn	a		19 20																						
Elephant & Castle ⊖	a		19 24																						
London Blackfriars 3 ⊖	a		19 28																						
City Thameslink 3	a		19 32																						
St Pancras International 15 ⊖	a		19 40																						
Luton Airport Parkway 7	a		20 25																						
Luton 10	a		20 29																						
North Dulwich	d									19 25							19 34						19 44		
East Dulwich	d									19 27							19 36						19 46		
Peckham Rye 4	d			19 26						19 29							19 38			19 56			19 49		
Queens Rd Peckham	d			19 29						19 32							19 41			19 59			19 51		
South Bermondsey	d			19 31						19 34							19 43			20 01			19 54		
London Bridge 4 ⊖	a			19 36				19 29	19 25	19 41					19 41		19 51			20 06			19 58	19 59	

East and West Croydon, London Milton Keynes Central and Luton via Norbury Crystal Palace - Tulse Hill

Local Services

Network Diagram - see first Page of Table 177

		SN	FC	SN ◇1	FC 1	SN	SN	SN	SN	SN	SN 1	SN 1	SN		SN	SN	SN	SN	FC	SN	SN ◇1	SN	SN	SN	SN 1
East Croydon ⇌	d			19 43	19 47					19 47	19 59	20 01						20 00			20 11				20 26
West Croydon 4 ⇌	d	19 28							19 31						19 47		19 58			20 01					
Norwood Junction 2	a														19 51			20 04							
	d														19 52			20 05							
Selhurst 4	d	19 32							19 35	19 50							20 02			20 05					
Thornton Heath	d	19 34							19 37	19 52							20 04			20 07					
Norbury	d	19 37							19 40	19 55							20 07			20 10					
Streatham Common 4	d	19 40							19 43	19 58							20 10			20 13					
Beckenham Junction 4 ⇌	d															19 54									
Birkbeck ⇌	d															19 57									
Crystal Palace 4	d						19 43	19 51							19 56	20 01							20 13	20 21	
Gipsy Hill	d						19 45								19 58	20 03							20 16		
West Norwood 4	d						19 48								20 01	20 06							20 19		
Streatham Hill	d						19 52								20 05								20 22		
Balham 4 ⊖	d	19 45					19 55			20 02					20 08		20 14						20 25		
Wandsworth Common	d	19 47					19 57			20 04					20 10		20 16						20 27		
Latchmere	d																								
Clapham Junction 10	d	19 51		19 53			20 01			20 08	20 08	20 11			20 14		20 20				20 21		20 31		20 37
Imperial Wharf	d																								
West Brompton ⊖	d																								
Kensington (Olympia) ⊖	d																								
Shepherd's Bush ⊖	d																								
Wembley Central ⊖	d																								
Harrow & Wealdstone ⊖	d																								
Watford Junction	d																								
Milton Keynes Central 10	a																								
Battersea Park 4	d	19 54				20 02	20 05			20a11			20 15		20 18		20 23					20 32	20 35		
London Victoria 15 ⊖	a	19 59		19 59		20 06	20 09				20 15	20 20			20 22		20 28				20 28	20 36	20 39		20 44
Streatham 4	d		19 40						19 46										20 06	20 17					
Tulse Hill 3	d		19 44						19 54							20 11			20 12	20 24					
Herne Hill 4	a		19 47																20 16						
Loughborough Jn	a		19 50																20 19						
Elephant & Castle ⊖	a		19 54																20 23						
London Blackfriars 3 ⊖	a		19 58		20 07														20 27						
City Thameslink 3	a		20 02		20 10														20 32						
St Pancras International 15 ⊖	a		20 10		20 18														20 40						
Luton Airport Parkway 7	a		20 55		20 50														21 25						
Luton 10	a		20 59		20 53														21 29						
North Dulwich	d								19 57							20 14				20 27					
East Dulwich	d								19 59							20 16				20 29					
Peckham Rye 4	d								20 01				20 26			20 18				20 31					
Queens Rd Peckham	d								20 04				20 29			20 21				20 34					
South Bermondsey	d								20 06				20 31			20 23				20 36					
London Bridge 4 ⊖	a							20 11	20 14				20 36			20 28		20 29		20 41				20 41	

Table 177 Mondays to Fridays
until 18 May

East and West Croydon, London Milton Keynes Central and Luton via Norbury Crystal Palace - Tulse Hill

Local Services

Network Diagram - see first Page of Table 177

		SN	SN ◇1	SN	SN		SN	SN	FC	SN	SN ◇1	SN	SN	SN	SN	SN 1	SN	SN	SN	SN	SN		FC	SN	SN ◇1
East Croydon ⇌	d	20 17	20 30					20 31			20 41					20 57	20 47				21 00				21 09
West Croydon 4 ⇌	d				20 18					20 31		20 35							20 45					21 01	
Norwood Junction 2	a				20 22			20 35											20 49		21 04				
	d				20 23			20 35											20 52		21 05				
Selhurst 4	d	20 20								20 35		20 39					20 50							21 05	
Thornton Heath	d	20 22								20 37		20 41					20 52							21 07	
Norbury	d	20 25								20 40		20 44					20 55							21 10	
Streatham Common 4	d	20 28								20 43		20 47					20 58							21 13	
Beckenham Junction 4 ⇌	d						20 24													20 53					
Birkbeck ⇌	d						20 27													20 56					
Crystal Palace 4	d				20 27		20 31							20 43	20 51				20 56	21 00					
Gipsy Hill	d				20 29		20 33							20 45					20 59	21 02					
West Norwood 4	d				20 32		20 36							20 48					21 02	21 05					
Streatham Hill	d				20 36									20 52					21 05						
Balham 4 ⊖	d	20 32			20 39							20 51		20 56			21 02		21 08						
Wandsworth Common	d	20 34			20 41							20 53		20 58			21 04		21 10						
Latchmere	d																								
Clapham Junction 10	d	20 38	20 41		20 45						20 51	20 57		21 03		21 08	21 08		21 14						21 18
Imperial Wharf	d																								
West Brompton ⊖	d																								
Kensington (Olympia) ⊖	d																								
Shepherd's Bush ⊖	d																								
Wembley Central ⊖	d																								
Harrow & Wealdstone ⊖	d																								
Watford Junction	d																								
Milton Keynes Central 10	a																								
Battersea Park 4	d	20 41		20 45	20 48								21 02	21 06			21 11	21 15	21 18						
London Victoria 15 ⊖	a	20 46	20 50		20 53						20 59	21 04	21 06	21 11		21 15	21 18		21 22						21 28
Streatham 4	d								20 36	20 46													21 06	21 16	
Tulse Hill 3	d						20 40		20 42	20 54										21 09			21 12	21 24	
Herne Hill 4	a								20 46														21 16		
Loughborough Jn	a								20 49														21 19		
Elephant & Castle ⊖	a								20 53														21 23		
London Blackfriars 3 ⊖	a								20 57														21 27		
City Thameslink 3	a								21 02														21 32		
St Pancras International 15 ⊖	a								21 10														21 40		
Luton Airport Parkway 7	a								21 55														22 25		
Luton 10	a								21 59														22 29		
North Dulwich	d						20 43			20 57										21 12				21 27	
East Dulwich	d						20 45			20 59										21 14				21 29	
Peckham Rye 4	d			20 56			20 48			21 01								21 26		21 17				21 31	
Queens Rd Peckham	d			20 59			20 50			21 04								21 29		21 19				21 34	
South Bermondsey	d			21 01			20 53			21 06								21 31		21 22				21 36	
London Bridge 4 ⊖	a			21 06			20 57	20 59		21 11					21 11			21 36		21 26	21 29			21 41	

Table 177

Mondays to Fridays

until 18 May

East and West Croydon, London Milton Keynes Central and Luton via Norbury Crystal Palace - Tulse Hill

Local Services

Network Diagram - see first Page of Table 177

		SN	SN	SN	SN	SN 1	SN ◇1	SN	SN	SN	SN	SN	SN ◇1		FC	SN	SN	SN	SN	SN	SN 1	SN	SN	SN	SN
East Croydon	d					21 26	21 30	21 17				21 30	21 42								21 57	21 47			
West Croydon 4	d	21 04								21 18						21 31	21 34							21 48	
Norwood Junction 2	a									21 22		21 34												21 52	
	d									21 23		21 35												21 53	
Selhurst 4	d	21 09						21 20								21 35	21 39					21 50			
Thornton Heath	d	21 11						21 22								21 37	21 41					21 52			
Norbury	d	21 14						21 25								21 40	21 44					21 55			
Streatham Common 4	d	21 17						21 28								21 43	21 47					21 58			
Beckenham Junction 4	d										21 23														21 53
Birkbeck	d										21 26														21 56
Crystal Palace 4	d			21 13	21 21					21 27	21 30								21 43	21 51				21 57	22 00
Gipsy Hill	d			21 15						21 29	21 32								21 45					21 59	22 02
West Norwood 4	d			21 18						21 32	21 35								21 48					22 02	22 05
Streatham Hill	d			21 22						21 36									21 52					22 06	
Balham 4 ⊖	d	21 21		21 26				21 32		21 39							21 51		21 56			22 02		22 09	
Wandsworth Common	d	21 23		21 28				21 34		21 41							21 53		21 58			22 04		22 11	
Latchmere	d																								
Clapham Junction 10	d	21 27		21 33		21 38	21 41	21 38		21 45			21 51				21 57		22 03		22 08	22 08		22 15	
Imperial Wharf	d																								
West Brompton ⊖	d																								
Kensington (Olympia) ⊖	d																								
Shepherd's Bush ⊖	d																								
Wembley Central ⊖	d																								
Harrow & Wealdstone ⊖	d																								
Watford Junction	d																								
Milton Keynes Central 10	a																								
Battersea Park 4	d		21 32	21 36				21 41	21 45	21 48								22 02	22 06			22 11	22 15	22 18	
London Victoria 15 ⊖	a	21 34	21 36	21 41		21 45	21 47	21 48		21 53			21 58				22 04	22 06	22 11		22 14	22 18		22 23	
Streatham 4	d														21 49	21 46									
Tulse Hill 3	d										21 39				21 53	21 54									22 09
Herne Hill 4	a														21 56										
Loughborough Jn	a														22 00										
Elephant & Castle ⊖	a														22 04										
London Blackfriars 3 ⊖	a														22 07										
City Thameslink 3	a														22 10										
St Pancras International 15 ⊖	a														22 17										
Luton Airport Parkway 7	a														23 01										
Luton 10	a														23 04										
North Dulwich	d										21 42					21 57									22 12
East Dulwich	d										21 44					21 59									22 14
Peckham Rye 4	d								21 56		21 47					22 01							22 26		22 17
Queens Rd Peckham	d								21 59		21 49					22 04							22 29		22 19
South Bermondsey	d								22 01		21 52					22 06							22 31		22 22
London Bridge 4 ⊖	a				21 43				22 06		21 56	21 59				22 11				22 13			22 36		22 26

Table 177

Mondays to Fridays

until 18 May

East and West Croydon, London Milton Keynes Central and Luton via Norbury Crystal Palace - Tulse Hill

Local Services

Network Diagram - see first Page of Table 177

		SN	SN	SN ◇1	SN		SN	SN	SN	SN	SN 1	SN	SN ◇1	FC	SN	SN	SN	SN	SN ◇1 H	SN	SN		SN	SN	SN 1
East Croydon	d	22 00		22 09							22 25	22 17	22 30				22 30		22 41						22 56
West Croydon 4	d		22 01		22 04											22 18		22 31		22 34					
Norwood Junction 2	a	22 04														22 22	22 34								
	d	22 05														22 23	22 35								
Selhurst 4	d		22 05		22 09							22 20						22 35		22 39					
Thornton Heath	d		22 07		22 11							22 22						22 37		22 41					
Norbury	d		22 10		22 14							22 25						22 40		22 44					
Streatham Common 4	d		22 13		22 17							22 28						22 43		22 47					
Beckenham Junction 4	d									22 15															
Birkbeck	d									22 18															
Crystal Palace 4	d							22 13	22 21	22 22						22 27							22 43	22 51	
Gipsy Hill	d							22 15		22 24						22 29							22 45		
West Norwood 4	d							22 18		22 27						22 32							22 48		
Streatham Hill	d							22 22								22 36							22 52		
Balham 4 ⊖	d				22 21			22 26				22 32				22 39				22 51			22 56		
Wandsworth Common	d				22 23			22 28				22 34				22 41				22 53			22 58		
Latchmere	d																								
Clapham Junction 10	d			22 18	22 27			22 33			22 38	22 38	22 41			22 45			22 51	22 57			23 03		23 07
Imperial Wharf	d																								
West Brompton ⊖	d																								
Kensington (Olympia) ⊖	d																								
Shepherd's Bush ⊖	d																								
Wembley Central ⊖	d																								
Harrow & Wealdstone ⊖	d																								
Watford Junction	d																								
Milton Keynes Central 10	a																								
Battersea Park 4	d						22 32	22 36				22 41			22 45	22 48					23 02		23 07		
London Victoria 15 ⊖	a			22 26	22 34		22 36	22 41			22 44	22 48	22 50			22 53			22 57	23 04	23 06		23 14		23 15
Streatham 4	d		22 16											22 40				22 46							
Tulse Hill 3	d		22 24							22 35				22 44				22 54							
Herne Hill 4	a																								
Loughborough Jn	a																								
Elephant & Castle ⊖	a																								
London Blackfriars 3 ⊖	a																								
City Thameslink 3	a																								
St Pancras International 15 ⊖	a																								
Luton Airport Parkway 7	a																								
Luton 10	a																								
North Dulwich	d		22 27							22 38								22 57							
East Dulwich	d		22 29							22 40								22 59							
Peckham Rye 4	d		22 31							22 43					22 56			23 01							
Queens Rd Peckham	d		22 34							22 45					22 59			23 04							
South Bermondsey	d		22 36							22 48					23 01			23 06							
London Bridge 4 ⊖	a	22 29	22 41						22 45	22 52				22 55	23 06		22 59	23 11						23 11	

Table 177

Mondays to Fridays

until 18 May

East and West Croydon, London Milton Keynes Central and Luton via Norbury Crystal Palace - Tulse Hill

Local Services

Network Diagram - see first Page of Table 177

		SN	SN	SN	SN	SN	SN	SN	SN	SN	SN	SN	SN ◇		SN	SN	SN	SN	SN	SN
East Croydon	d	22 47				23 01					23 17		23 30				23 43			23 58
West Croydon	d			22 48			23 01	23 04							23 18					
Norwood Junction	a			22 52		23 05									23 22		23 47			
	d			22 53		23 06									23 23					
Selhurst	d	22 50					23 05	23 09			23 20									
Thornton Heath	d	22 52					23 07	23 11			23 22									
Norbury	d	22 55					23 10	23 14			23 25									
Streatham Common	d	22 58					23 13	23 17			23 28									
Beckenham Junction	d				22 53											23 23				
Birkbeck	d				22 56											23 26				
Crystal Palace	d			22 57	23 00					23 13		23 21			23 27	23 30		23 43	23 51	
Gipsy Hill	d			22 59	23 02					23 15					23 29	23 32		23 45		
West Norwood	d			23 02	23 05					23 18					23 32	23 35		23 48		
Streatham Hill	d			23 06						23 22					23 36			23 52		
Balham	d	23 02		23 09				23 21		23 26	23 32				23 40			23 55		
Wandsworth Common	d	23 04		23 11				23 23		23 28	23 34				23 42			23 58		
Latchmere	d																			
Clapham Junction	d	23 08		23 15				23 27		23 33	23 38		23 42		23 46			00 02		00 12
Imperial Wharf	d																			
West Brompton	d																			
Kensington (Olympia)	d																			
Shepherd's Bush	d																			
Wembley Central	d																			
Harrow & Wealdstone	d																			
Watford Junction	d																			
Milton Keynes Central	a																			
Battersea Park	d	23 11	23 15	23 19					23 32	23 37	23 41				23 49			00 05		
London Victoria	a	23 16		23 25				23 34	23 37	23 41	23 48		23 52		23 54			00 10		00 18
Streatham	d						23 16													
Tulse Hill	d				23 09		23 24									23 39				
Herne Hill	a																			
Loughborough Jn	a																			
Elephant & Castle	a																			
London Blackfriars	a																			
City Thameslink	a																			
St Pancras International	a																			
Luton Airport Parkway	a																			
Luton	a																			
North Dulwich	d				23 12		23 27									23 42				
East Dulwich	d				23 14		23 29									23 44				
Peckham Rye	d		23 26		23 17		23 31									23 47				
Queens Rd Peckham	d		23 29		23 19		23 34									23 49				
South Bermondsey	d		23 31		23 22		23 36									23 52				
London Bridge	a		23 36		23 26	23 30	23 41					23 45				23 56			00 11	

Table 177

Mondays to Fridays

from 21 May

East and West Croydon, London Milton Keynes Central and Luton via Norbury Crystal Palace - Tulse Hill

Local Services

Network Diagram - see first Page of Table 177

		FC MX	FC MX	SN MO	SN MO	SN MX	SN MX	SN MX	SN MO	SN MO	SN MX	SN MX	SN	SN	FC MX A	FC MO B		SN	FC MX A	FC MO B	SN	FC	SN	FC	SN
East Croydon	d							23p58		23p56			00 49	01 28	01 47	01 47		02 28	02 47	02 47	03 28	03 47	04 32	04 47	05 13
West Croydon	d			23p37					23p52																
Norwood Junction	a																								05 17
	d																								05 17
Selhurst	d			23p41					23p56	00 01															
Thornton Heath	d			23p43					23p58																
Norbury	d			23p46					00 01																
Streatham Common	d			23p49					00 04																
Beckenham Junction	d																								
Birkbeck	d																								
Crystal Palace	d				23p37	23p43	23p51				00 13	00 21													
Gipsy Hill	d				23p39	23p45					00 15														
West Norwood	d				23p42	23p48					00 18														
Streatham Hill	d					23p52					00 22														
Balham	d			23p53		23p55			00 08		00 25														
Wandsworth Common	d					23p58					00 27														
Latchmere	d																								
Clapham Junction	d			23p58		00 02		00 12	00 12	00 12	00 31		01 01	01 41				02 41			03 41		04 51		
Imperial Wharf	d																								
West Brompton	d																								
Kensington (Olympia)	d																								
Shepherd's Bush	d																								
Wembley Central	d																								
Harrow & Wealdstone	d																								
Watford Junction	d																								
Milton Keynes Central	a																								
Battersea Park	d					00 05					00 35														
London Victoria	a			00 04		00 10		00 18	00 19	00 19	00 42		01 09	01 49				02 49			03 49		04 58		
Streatham	d	22p49	23p19																						
Tulse Hill	d	22p53	23p23		23p46																				
Herne Hill	a	22p56	23p26																						
Loughborough Jn	a	23p00																							
Elephant & Castle	a	23p04	23p33																						
London Blackfriars	a	23p07	23p37												02 13	02 13			03 13	03 13		04 13		05 13	
City Thameslink	a																							05 16	
St Pancras International	a	23p17	23p47												02 23	02 23			03 23	03 23		04 22		05 24	
Luton Airport Parkway	a	00 02	00 32												03 09	03 10			04 09	04 10		05 09		06 09	
Luton	a	00 05	00 35												03 12	03 13			04 12	04 13		05 12		06 12	
North Dulwich	d				23p49																				
East Dulwich	d				23p51																				
Peckham Rye	d				23p53																				
Queens Rd Peckham	d				23p56																				
South Bermondsey	d				23p58																				
London Bridge	a				00 03		00 11					00 41													05 41

A from 22 May until 22 June, from 26 June B from 21 May until 25 June

Table 177

Mondays to Fridays
from 21 May

East and West Croydon, London
Milton Keynes Central and Luton via Norbury
Crystal Palace - Tulse Hill

Local Services

Network Diagram - see first Page of Table 177

		FC 1	SN	FC	SN	FC 1	SN	SN		FC	SN	SN 1	SN	SN ◇1	SN	SN	SN	SN 1	SN 1	FC	SN	SN	SN	SN	
East Croydon	d	05 17	05 33			05 47	05 48	05 51				06 06	06 13	06 15			06 17	06 23	06 31					06 31	
West Croydon 4	d				05 45						06 01				06 15								06 26		
Norwood Junction 2	a		05 37		05 50			05 55					06 17		06 19									06 35	
	d		05 37		05 50			05 55					06 18		06 20							06 23		06 37	
Selhurst 4	d			05 36			05 52			05 56	06 06	06 09					06 20						06 31		
Thornton Heath	d			05 38			05 54			05 58	06 08						06 22						06 33		
Norbury	d			05 40			05 57			06 00	06 11						06 25						06 36		
Streatham Common 4	d			05 43			05 59			06 03	06 13						06 27						06 38		
Beckenham Junction 4	d																								
Birkbeck	d																								
Crystal Palace 4	d		05 41					05 59														06 27			
Gipsy Hill	d		05 43					06 01														06 29			
West Norwood 4	d		05 46					06 04														06 32			
Streatham Hill	d		05 50																			06 36			
Balham 4 ⊖	d		05 53				06 03				06 17						06 31					06 39	06 42		
Wandsworth Common	d						06 05				06 19						06 33					06 41	06 44		
Latchmere	d																								
Clapham Junction 10	d		05 57				06 09				06 23	06 18		06 25			06 37		06 41			06 45	06 48		
Imperial Wharf	d																								
West Brompton ⊖	d																								
Kensington (Olympia) ⊖	d																								
Shepherd's Bush ⊖	d																								
Wembley Central ⊖	d																								
Harrow & Wealdstone ⊖	d																								
Watford Junction	d																								
Milton Keynes Central 10	a																								
Battersea Park 4	d		06 01				06 13				06 27					06 32	06 41				06 45	06 48	06 52		
London Victoria 15 ⊖	a		06 06				06 18				06 31	06 25		06 32		06 36	06 48		06 48			06 53	06 58		
Streatham 4	d			05 46						06 06										06 38					
Tulse Hill 3	d			05 50				06 08		06 10										06 42					
Herne Hill 4	a			05 54						06 14										06 46					
Loughborough Jn	a									06 19										06 49					
Elephant & Castle ⊖	a			06 00						06 23										06 53					
London Blackfriars 3 ⊖	a	05 41		06 03		06 10				06 27										06 57					
City Thameslink 3	a	05 44		06 06		06 14				06 32										07 00					
St Pancras International 15 ⊖	a	05 52		06 14		06 22				06 40										07 08					
Luton Airport Parkway 7	a	06 35		07 00		06 55				07 23										07 49					
Luton 10	a	06 38		07 03		06 58				07 26										07 53					
North Dulwich	d							06 11																	
East Dulwich	d							06 13																	
Peckham Rye 4	d							06 15													06 56				
Queens Rd Peckham	d							06 18													06 59				
South Bermondsey	d							06 20													07 01				
London Bridge 4 ⊖	a				06 14			06 25					06 44		06 33			06 39			07 08			06 49	

Table 177

Mondays to Fridays
from 21 May

East and West Croydon, London
Milton Keynes Central and Luton via Norbury
Crystal Palace - Tulse Hill

Local Services

Network Diagram - see first Page of Table 177

		SN	SN 1	SN	SN	SN	SN	SN	SN	SN	SN	SN 1	SN	SN 1	SN	SN		SN 1	SN	SN	SN ◇1	FC	SN	SN	SN
East Croydon	d	06 36	06 42							06 57	06 45	06 59		07 00				07 05		07 10	07 15				
West Croydon 4	d					06 31		06 45											06 58				07 01	07 13	
Norwood Junction 2	a	06 40						06 49												07 14				07 17	
	d	06 40					06 47	06 50								06 53				07 14				07 18	
Selhurst 4	d					06 35					06 48								07 02				07 05		
Thornton Heath	d					06 37					06 50								07 04				07 07		
Norbury	d					06 40					06 53								07 07				07 10		
Streatham Common 4	d					06 43					06 56								07 10				07 13		
Beckenham Junction 4	d																								
Birkbeck	d																								
Crystal Palace 4	d			06 39	06 44		06 51						06 51			06 57									
Gipsy Hill	d			06 41			06 53									06 59									
West Norwood 4	d			06 44			06 56									07 02									
Streatham Hill	d			06 48												07 06									
Balham 4 ⊖	d			06 51							07 00					07 09			07 14						
Wandsworth Common	d										07 02					07 11			07 16						
Latchmere	d																								
Clapham Junction 10	d		06 51	06 56						07 07	07 06					07 15		07 17	07 20		07 24				
Imperial Wharf	d																								
West Brompton ⊖	d																								
Kensington (Olympia) ⊖	d																								
Shepherd's Bush ⊖	d																								
Wembley Central ⊖	d																								
Harrow & Wealdstone ⊖	d																								
Watford Junction	d																								
Milton Keynes Central 10	a																								
Battersea Park 4	d								07 02		07 09				07 15	07 18			07 23						07 32
London Victoria 15 ⊖	a		07 00	07 05					07 08	07 15	07 16					07 25		07 25	07 30		07 33				07 38
Streatham 4	d					06 46																07 16	07 19		
Tulse Hill 3	d					06 50	07 00															07 20	07 24		
Herne Hill 4	a																					07 23			
Loughborough Jn	a																					07 27			
Elephant & Castle ⊖	a																					07 31			
London Blackfriars 3 ⊖	a																					07 35			
City Thameslink 3	a																					07 38			
St Pancras International 15 ⊖	a																					07 46			
Luton Airport Parkway 7	a																					08 20			
Luton 10	a																					08 23			
North Dulwich	d					06 53	07 03																07 27		
East Dulwich	d					06 55	07 05																07 29		
Peckham Rye 4	d					06 59	07 08								07 26								07 31		
Queens Rd Peckham	d					07 02	07 10								07 29								07 34		
South Bermondsey	d					07 04	07 13								07 31								07 36		
London Bridge 4 ⊖	a	06 52			07 06	07 11	07 19	07 04				07 14	07 16	07 16	07 38					07 28			07 43	07 32	

East and West Croydon, London Milton Keynes Central and Luton via Norbury Crystal Palace - Tulse Hill

Local Services

Network Diagram - see first Page of Table 177

	SN	SN	SN	SN	SN [1]	SN	SN	SN ◇[1]	SN [1]	FC	SN	SN	SN ◇[1]	SN	SN	SN [1]	SN [1]	SN	SN	SN	SN	SN
East Croydon ⇌ d			07 26	07 18	07 28			07 31	07 35				07 39		07 40	07 42	07 46					
West Croydon [4] ⇌ d												07 17		07 28				07 31	07 34	07 44		
Norwood Junction [2] a												07 21			07 44					07 48		
d												07 22			07 44					07 49		
Selhurst [4] d				07 21										07 32				07 35	07 38			
Thornton Heath d				07 23										07 34				07 37	07 40			
Norbury d				07 26										07 37				07 40	07 43			
Streatham Common [4] d				07 28										07 40				07 43	07 46			
Beckenham Junction [4] ⇌ d						07 13																
Birkbeck ⇌ d						07 16																
Crystal Palace [4] d	07 13	07 14				07 20	07 21					07 26										07 43
Gipsy Hill d	07 15					07 22						07 28										07 45
West Norwood [4] d	07 18					07 25						07 31										07 48
Streatham Hill d	07 22											07 35										07 52
Balham [4] ⊖ d	07 25			07 32								07 39		07 44					07 50			07 55
Wandsworth Common d	07 27			07 34								07 41		07 46					07 52			07 57
Latchmere d																						
Clapham Junction [10] d	07 31		07 37	07 38				07 41				07 45	07 48	07 50		07 51			07 56			08 01
Imperial Wharf d																						
West Brompton ⊖ d																						
Kensington (Olympia) ⊖ d																						
Shepherd's Bush ⊖ d																						
Wembley Central ⊖ d																						
Harrow & Wealdstone ⊖ d																						
Watford Junction d																						
Milton Keynes Central [10] a																						
Battersea Park [4] d	07 35			07 42							07 45	07 48		07 53					07 59		08 02	08 05
London Victoria [15] ⊖ a	07 41		07 46	07 48				07 49				07 57	07 57	08 00		08 00			08 06		08 08	08 11
Streatham [4] d										07 38								07 46				
Tulse Hill [3] d						07 29				07 43								07 52				
Herne Hill [4] a										07 46												
Loughborough Jn a										07 50												
Elephant & Castle ⊖ a										07 54												
London Blackfriars [3] ⊖ a										07 58												
City Thameslink [3] a										08 00												
St Pancras International [15] ⊖ a										08 08												
Luton Airport Parkway [7] a																						
Luton [10] a																						
North Dulwich d						07 32												07 55				
East Dulwich d						07 34												07 57				
Peckham Rye [4] d						07 36					07 55							07 59				
Queens Rd Peckham d						07 39					07 59							08 02				
South Bermondsey d						07 41					08 01							08 04				
London Bridge [4] ⊖ a		07 36			07 43	07 48	07 45		07 51		08 08				07 58		08 01	08 11		08 05		

East and West Croydon, London Milton Keynes Central and Luton via Norbury Crystal Palace - Tulse Hill

Local Services

Network Diagram - see first Page of Table 177

	SN	SN	SN	SN	SN [1]	SN	SN	SN ◇[1]	SN [1]	SN [1]	FC	SN	SN	SN ◇[1]	SN [1]	SN	SN	SN ◇[1]	SN	SN	SN	SN [1]	SN
East Croydon ⇌ d		07 56	07 48	07 50	07 57			08 01	08 02	08 03				08 08	08 11			08 13				08 07	08 10
West Croydon [4] ⇌ d													07 47			07 58	08 01		08 05				
Norwood Junction [2] a													07 51										08 16
d													07 52										08 16
Selhurst [4] d			07 51	07 54												08 02	08 05		08 09			08 13	
Thornton Heath d			07 53	07 56												08 04	08 07		08 11			08 16	
Norbury d			07 56	07 59												08 07	08 10		08 14			08 20	
Streatham Common [4] d			07 59	08 02												08 10	08 13		08 17			08 23	
Beckenham Junction [4] ⇌ d						07 42																	
Birkbeck ⇌ d						07 45																	
Crystal Palace [4] d	07 44					07 49	07 52						07 56								08 13		
Gipsy Hill d						07 51							07 58								08 15		
West Norwood [4] d						07 54							08 01								08 18		
Streatham Hill d													08 05								08 22		
Balham [4] ⊖ d			08 03	08 06									08 09			08 14			08 21		08 25	08 28	
Wandsworth Common d			08 05	08 08									08 11			08 16					08 27	08 31	
Latchmere d																							
Clapham Junction [10] d		08 07	08 09	08 14				08 11					08 16	08 18	08 21	08 20		08 24	08 26		08 31	08 39	
Imperial Wharf d				08 18																		08 44	
West Brompton ⊖ d				08 21																		08 47	
Kensington (Olympia) ⊖ d				08 25																		08 50	
Shepherd's Bush ⊖ d				08a27																		08 53	
Wembley Central ⊖ d																						09 08	
Harrow & Wealdstone ⊖ d																						09 13	
Watford Junction d																						09 20	
Milton Keynes Central [10] a																						10 01	
Battersea Park [4] d			08 12									08 15	08 19			08 23				08 32	08 35		
London Victoria [15] ⊖ a		08 15	08 19					08 19					08 26	08 26	08 29	08 30		08 32	08 36	08 39	08 41		
Streatham [4] d											08 09						08 16						
Tulse Hill [3] d						07 59					08 13						08 22						
Herne Hill [4] a											08 17												
Loughborough Jn a											08 23												
Elephant & Castle ⊖ a											08 27												
London Blackfriars [3] ⊖ a											08 32												
City Thameslink [3] a											08 35												
St Pancras International [15] ⊖ a											08 43												
Luton Airport Parkway [7] a											09 29												
Luton [10] a											09 34												
North Dulwich d						08 02											08 25						
East Dulwich d						08 04											08 27						
Peckham Rye [4] d						08 06						08 26					08 29						
Queens Rd Peckham d						08 09						08 29					08 32						
South Bermondsey d						08 11						08 31					08 34						
London Bridge [4] ⊖ a	08 07				08 13	08 18	08 15		08 19	08 21		08 38					08 41						08 28

East and West Croydon, London Milton Keynes Central and Luton via Norbury Crystal Palace - Tulse Hill

Local Services

Network Diagram - see first Page of Table 177

		SN	SN	SN	SN	SN ■1	SN ■1	SN		SN	SN ◇■1	SN ■1	SN ■1	FC	SN	SN	SN	SN	SN	SN	SN ◇■1 🚌	SN	SN	SN ◇■1 🚌
East Croydon 🚊	d			08 26	08 18	08 21	08 27				08 30	08 33	08 37						08 39	08 42	08 43			08 50
West Croydon 4 🚊	d	08 15														08 19	08 26	08 31				08 44		
Norwood Junction 2	a	08 20														08 24				08 46		08 49		
	d	08 20														08 25				08 47		08 49		
Selhurst 4	d				08 21												08 31	08 35	08 43					
Thornton Heath	d				08 23												08 33	08 37	08 46					
Norbury	d				08 26												08 36	08 40	08 49					
Streatham Common 4	d				08 28												08 38	08 43	08 52					
Beckenham Junction 4 🚊	d							08 12																
Birkbeck 🚊	d							08 15																
Crystal Palace 4	d		08 15					08 19		08 24						08 29								
Gipsy Hill	d							08 21								08 31								
West Norwood 4	d							08 24								08 34								
Streatham Hill	d															08 38								
Balham 4 ⊖	d				08 32											08 41	08 43		08 58					
Wandsworth Common	d				08 34											08 43	08 45		09 00					
Latchmere	d																							
Clapham Junction 10	d			08 37	08 38						08 40		08 48			08 47	08 50		09 05		08 53			09 01
Imperial Wharf	d																		09 09					
West Brompton ⊖	d																		09 12					
Kensington (Olympia) ⊖	d																		09 15					
Shepherd's Bush ⊖	d																		09a18					
Wembley Central ⊖	d																							
Harrow & Wealdstone ⊖	d																							
Watford Junction	d																							
Milton Keynes Central 10	a																							
Battersea Park 4	d				08 42										08 45	08 50	08 53						09 02	
London Victoria 15 ⊖	a			08 45	08 48						08 48		08 56			08 57	09 00				09 01		09 08	09 09
Streatham 4	d													08 39										
Tulse Hill 3	d							08 28						08 43				08 50						
Herne Hill 4	a													08 47				08 55						
Loughborough Jn	a													08 50										
Elephant & Castle ⊖	a													08 57										
London Blackfriars 3 ⊖	a													09 01										
City Thameslink 3	a													09 04										
St Pancras International 15 ⊖	a													09 12										
Luton Airport Parkway 7	a													09 58										
Luton 10	a													10 03										
North Dulwich	d							08 31										08 58						
East Dulwich	d							08 33										09 00						
Peckham Rye 4	d							08 36							08 56			09 02						
Queens Rd Peckham	d							08 38							08 59			09 05						
South Bermondsey	d							08 41							09 01			09 07						
London Bridge 4 ⊖	a	08 35	08 37			08 37	08 45	08 48		08 47		08 52			09 08			09 14		09 01		09 04		

East and West Croydon, London Milton Keynes Central and Luton via Norbury Crystal Palace - Tulse Hill

Local Services

Network Diagram - see first Page of Table 177

		SN	SN	SN	SN ◇■1	SN	SN ■1	SN	SN	SN ■1	FC	SN	SN	SN	SN ■1	SN		SN	SN ■1	SN ◇■1 🚌	SN	SN	SN	SN	SN ◇■1 🚌
East Croydon 🚊	d			08 54	08 58	08 48	08 51			08 59				09 05	09 11				09 08	09 14					09 23
West Croydon 4 🚊	d												08 49			08 57		09 01							
Norwood Junction 2	a												08 53	09 09											
	d												08 54	09 09											
Selhurst 4	d					08 51										09 01		09 05	09 13						
Thornton Heath	d					08 53										09 03		09 07	09 16						
Norbury	d					08 56										09 06		09 10	09 19						
Streatham Common 4	d					08 58										09 09		09 13	09 21						
Beckenham Junction 4 🚊	d							08 43																	
Birkbeck 🚊	d							08 46																	
Crystal Palace 4	d	08 40	08 44					08 50	08 51				08 58									09 11	09 14	09 21	
Gipsy Hill	d	08 43						08 52					09 00									09 14			
West Norwood 4	d	08 46						08 55					09 03									09 17			
Streatham Hill	d	08 49											09 07									09 21			
Balham 4 ⊖	d	08 55				09 02							09 10			09 13			09 28			09 25			
Wandsworth Common	d	08 57				09 04							09 12			09 15			09 30			09 27			
Latchmere	d																								
Clapham Junction 10	d	09 01		09 04	09 08	09 08							09 16		09 21	09 19			09 39	09 24		09 31			09 33
Imperial Wharf	d																		09 44						
West Brompton ⊖	d																		09 47						
Kensington (Olympia) ⊖	d																		09 50						
Shepherd's Bush ⊖	d																		09 53						
Wembley Central ⊖	d																		10 08						
Harrow & Wealdstone ⊖	d																		10 13						
Watford Junction	d																		10 20						
Milton Keynes Central 10	a																		11 02						
Battersea Park 4	d	09 05				09 12						09 15	09 19			09 22					09 32	09 35			
London Victoria 15 ⊖	a	09 11		09 13	09 16	09 18							09 27		09 27	09 31				09 32	09 38	09 42			09 42
Streatham 4	d										09 08							09 20							
Tulse Hill 3	d							08 59			09 16							09 26							
Herne Hill 4	a										09 19														
Loughborough Jn	a										09 23														
Elephant & Castle ⊖	a										09 29														
London Blackfriars 3 ⊖	a										09 33														
City Thameslink 3	a										09 36														
St Pancras International 15 ⊖	a										09 44														
Luton Airport Parkway 7	a										10 29														
Luton 10	a										10 33														
North Dulwich	d							09 02										09 29							
East Dulwich	d							09 04										09 31							
Peckham Rye 4	d							09 07				09 26						09 33							
Queens Rd Peckham	d							09 09				09 29						09 36							
South Bermondsey	d							09 12				09 31						09 38							
London Bridge 4 ⊖	a		09 06				09 06	09 19	09 14	09 15		09 38		09 23				09 44					09 37	09 43	

East and West Croydon, London Milton Keynes Central and Luton via Norbury Crystal Palace - Tulse Hill

Local Services

Network Diagram - see first Page of Table 177

		SN	SN ◇1	SN	SN	SN	SN	SN 1		SN	SN	FC	SN ◇1 ⌶	SN	SN	SN ◇1	SN	SN	SN	SN	SN	SN ◇1 ⌶	SN	SN
East Croydon	d	09 17	09 31			09 20	09 30	09 37					09 39			09 43				09 47		10 00		
West Croydon	d				09 15									09 28	09 31		09 35							09 45
Norwood Junction	a				09 19	09 24	09 34	09 41																09 50
	d				09 22	09 25	09 35	09 42																09 52
Selhurst	d	09 21												09 32	09 35		09 39			09 50				
Thornton Heath	d	09 23												09 34	09 37		09 41			09 52				
Norbury	d	09 26												09 37	09 40		09 44			09 55				
Streatham Common	d	09 28												09 40	09 43		09 47			09 58				
Beckenham Junction	d									09 23														
Birkbeck	d									09 26														
Crystal Palace	d				09 26					09 30	09 36								09 43		09 51			09 56
Gipsy Hill	d				09 28					09 32									09 46					09 58
West Norwood	d				09 31					09 35									09 49					10 01
Streatham Hill	d				09 35														09 52					10 05
Balham ⊖	d	09 32			09 41									09 44			09 52		09 56	10 02				10 09
Wandsworth Common	d	09 34			09 43									09 46			09 54		09 58	10 04				10 11
Latchmere	d																							
Clapham Junction	d	09 38	09 41		09 47								09 48	09 50		09 52	09 58		10 02	10 08		10 09		10 15
Imperial Wharf	d																							
West Brompton ⊖	d																							
Kensington (Olympia) ⊖	d																							
Shepherd's Bush ⊖	d																							
Wembley Central ⊖	d																							
Harrow & Wealdstone ⊖	d																							
Watford Junction	d																							
Milton Keynes Central	a																							
Battersea Park	d	09 42		09 45	09 50									09 53				10 03	10 05	10 11			10 15	10 19
London Victoria ⊖	a	09 48	09 50		09 58								09 58	09 58		09 59	10 05	10 07	10 11	10 16		10 16		10 24
Streatham	d											09 38			09 46									
Tulse Hill	d									09 39		09 42			09 54									
Herne Hill	a											09 46												
Loughborough Jn	a											09 50												
Elephant & Castle ⊖	a											09 54												
London Blackfriars ⊖	a											09 59												
City Thameslink	a											10 02												
St Pancras International ⊖	a											10 10												
Luton Airport Parkway	a											10 58												
Luton	a											11 03												
North Dulwich	d									09 42					09 57									
East Dulwich	d									09 44					09 59									
Peckham Rye	d			09 56						09 47					10 01								10 26	
Queens Rd Peckham	d			09 59						09 49					10 04								10 29	
South Bermondsey	d			10 01						09 52					10 06								10 31	
London Bridge ⊖	a			10 06		09 41	10 00	09 55		09 58	09 59				10 11						10 11		10 36	

Table 177

Mondays to Fridays
from 21 May

East and West Croydon, London Milton Keynes Central and Luton via Norbury Crystal Palace - Tulse Hill

Local Services

Network Diagram - see first Page of Table 177

		SN	SN 1	SN	SN	SN 1	SN	FC	SN	SN ◇1 ⌶	SN	SN	SN	SN 1	SN	SN ◇1		SN	SN	SN	SN	SN 1	SN	SN	SN 1
East Croydon	d	09 51	09 55		10 00	10 07				10 12				10 10		10 28		10 17			10 21	10 25		10 30	10 38
West Croydon	d			09 58					10 01		10 04									10 15			10 28		
Norwood Junction	a	09 55	09 59		10 04	10 12														10 19	10 25	10 29		10 34	10 42
	d	09 55	09 59		10 05	10 13														10 22	10 25	10 29		10 35	10 43
Selhurst	d			10 02					10 05		10 09			10 14				10 20					10 32		
Thornton Heath	d			10 04					10 07		10 11			10 16				10 22					10 34		
Norbury	d			10 07					10 10		10 14			10 19				10 25					10 37		
Streatham Common	d			10 10					10 13		10 17			10 22				10 28					10 40		
Beckenham Junction	d						09 53																		
Birkbeck	d						09 56																		
Crystal Palace	d						10 00						10 13		10 21					10 26					
Gipsy Hill	d						10 02						10 15							10 29					
West Norwood	d						10 05						10 18							10 32					
Streatham Hill	d												10 22							10 35					
Balham ⊖	d			10 14							10 21		10 25	10 29				10 32		10 39			10 44		
Wandsworth Common	d			10 16							10 23		10 27	10 31				10 34		10 41			10 46		
Latchmere	d																								
Clapham Junction	d			10 20						10 21	10 27		10 31	10 39		10 38		10 38		10 45			10 50		
Imperial Wharf	d													10 44											
West Brompton ⊖	d													10 47											
Kensington (Olympia) ⊖	d													10 50											
Shepherd's Bush ⊖	d													10 53											
Wembley Central ⊖	d													11 08											
Harrow & Wealdstone ⊖	d													11 13											
Watford Junction	d													11 20											
Milton Keynes Central	a													12 01											
Battersea Park	d			10 23								10 32	10 35					10 41	10 45	10 49			10 53		
London Victoria ⊖	a			10 28						10 28	10 34	10 36	10 39			10 45		10 46		10 53			10 58		
Streatham	d							10 08	10 16																
Tulse Hill	d						10 09	10 12	10 24																
Herne Hill	a							10 16																	
Loughborough Jn	a							10 19																	
Elephant & Castle ⊖	a							10 23																	
London Blackfriars ⊖	a							10 27																	
City Thameslink	a							10 32																	
St Pancras International ⊖	a							10 40																	
Luton Airport Parkway	a							11 27																	
Luton	a							11 31																	
North Dulwich	d						10 12		10 27																
East Dulwich	d						10 14		10 29																
Peckham Rye	d						10 17		10 31										10 56						
Queens Rd Peckham	d						10 19		10 34										10 59						
South Bermondsey	d						10 22		10 36										11 01						
London Bridge ⊖	a	10 09	10 13		10 29	10 25	10 26		10 41						10 41				11 06		10 39	10 43		10 59	10 55

Table 177

Mondays to Fridays
from 21 May

East and West Croydon, London Milton Keynes Central and Luton via Norbury Crystal Palace - Tulse Hill

Local Services

Network Diagram - see first Page of Table 177

		SN	FC	SN	SN ◇1	SN	SN	SN		SN	SN	SN ◇1	SN	SN	SN	SN 1	SN	SN	SN 1	SN	FC	SN	SN ◇1	SN
East Croydon	d				10 42					10 47		11 00			10 51	10 55		11 00	11 07				11 12	
West Croydon	d			10 31		10 34								10 45			10 58					11 01		11 04
Norwood Junction	a													10 49	10 55	10 59		11 04	11 12					
	d													10 52	10 55	10 59		11 05	11 13					
Selhurst	d			10 35		10 39				10 50							11 02					11 05		11 09
Thornton Heath	d			10 37		10 41				10 52							11 04					11 07		11 11
Norbury	d			10 40		10 44				10 55							11 07					11 10		11 14
Streatham Common	d			10 43		10 47				10 58							11 10					11 13		11 17
Beckenham Junction	d	10 23																		10 53				
Birkbeck	d	10 26																		10 56				
Crystal Palace	d	10 30						10 43			10 51			10 56						11 00				
Gipsy Hill	d	10 32						10 45						10 59						11 02				
West Norwood	d	10 35						10 48						11 02						11 05				
Streatham Hill	d							10 52						11 05										
Balham ⊖	d					10 51		10 55		11 02				11 09			11 14							11 21
Wandsworth Common	d					10 53		10 57		11 04				11 11			11 16							11 23
Latchmere	d																							
Clapham Junction	d				10 51	10 57		11 01		11 08		11 10		11 15			11 20						11 21	11 27
Imperial Wharf	d																							
West Brompton ⊖	d																							
Kensington (Olympia) ⊖	d																							
Shepherd's Bush ⊖	d																							
Wembley Central ⊖	d																							
Harrow & Wealdstone ⊖	d																							
Watford Junction	d																							
Milton Keynes Central	a																							
Battersea Park	d						11 02	11 05		11 11			11 15	11 18			11 23							
London Victoria ⊖	a				10 58	11 04	11 06	11 09		11 16		11 16		11 23			11 28						11 28	11 34
Streatham	d		10 38	10 46																	11 08	11 16		
Tulse Hill	d	10 39	10 42	10 54																11 09	11 12	11 24		
Herne Hill	a		10 46																		11 16			
Loughborough Jn	a		10 49																		11 19			
Elephant & Castle ⊖	a		10 53																		11 23			
London Blackfriars ⊖	a		10 57																		11 27			
City Thameslink	a		11 02																		11 32			
St Pancras International ⊖	a		11 10																		11 40			
Luton Airport Parkway	a		11 55																		12 25			
Luton	a		11 59																		12 29			
North Dulwich	d	10 42		10 57																11 12		11 27		
East Dulwich	d	10 44		10 59																11 14		11 29		
Peckham Rye	d	10 47		11 01									11 26							11 17		11 31		
Queens Rd Peckham	d	10 49		11 04									11 29							11 19		11 34		
South Bermondsey	d	10 52		11 06									11 31							11 22		11 36		
London Bridge ⊖	a	10 56		11 11							11 11		11 36		11 09	11 13		11 29	11 25	11 26		11 41		

Table 177

Mondays to Fridays
from 21 May

East and West Croydon, London Milton Keynes Central and Luton via Norbury Crystal Palace - Tulse Hill

Local Services

Network Diagram - see first Page of Table 177

		SN	SN	SN 1	SN	SN	SN ◇1	SN	SN	SN	SN 1	SN	SN 1	SN	FC	SN ◇1		SN	SN	SN	SN	SN	SN	SN	SN ◇1
East Croydon	d			11 11	11 17		11 28			11 21	11 25	11 30	11 37			11 41							11 47		12 00
West Croydon	d								11 15									11 28	11 31	11 34					
Norwood Junction	a								11 19	11 25	11 29	11 34	11 42												
	d								11 22	11 25	11 29	11 35	11 43												
Selhurst	d			11 16	11 20													11 32	11 35	11 39			11 50		
Thornton Heath	d			11 18	11 22													11 34	11 37	11 41			11 52		
Norbury	d			11 21	11 25													11 37	11 40	11 44			11 55		
Streatham Common	d			11 24	11 28													11 40	11 43	11 47			11 58		
Beckenham Junction	d													11 23											
Birkbeck	d													11 26											
Crystal Palace	d		11 13			11 21			11 26					11 30								11 43		11 51	
Gipsy Hill	d		11 15						11 29					11 32								11 45			
West Norwood	d		11 18						11 32					11 35								11 48			
Streatham Hill	d		11 22						11 35													11 52			
Balham ⊖	d		11 25	11 28	11 32				11 40									11 44		11 51		11 55	12 02		
Wandsworth Common	d		11 27	11 30	11 34				11 42									11 46		11 53		11 57	12 04		
Latchmere	d																								
Clapham Junction	d		11 31	11 39	11 38		11 37		11 46							11 50		11 50		11 57		12 01	12 08		12 12
Imperial Wharf	d			11 44																					
West Brompton ⊖	d			11 47																					
Kensington (Olympia) ⊖	d			11 50																					
Shepherd's Bush ⊖	d			11 53																					
Wembley Central ⊖	d			12 08																					
Harrow & Wealdstone ⊖	d			12 13																					
Watford Junction	d			12 20																					
Milton Keynes Central	a			13 01																					
Battersea Park	d	11 32	11 35		11a41			11 45	11 49									11 53			12 02	12 05	12a11		
London Victoria ⊖	a	11 36	11 39				11 44		11 54							11 57		11 58		12 04	12 07	12 09			12 18
Streatham	d														11 38				11 46						
Tulse Hill	d													11 39	11 42				11 54						
Herne Hill	a														11 46										
Loughborough Jn	a														11 49										
Elephant & Castle ⊖	a														11 53										
London Blackfriars ⊖	a														11 57										
City Thameslink	a														12 02										
St Pancras International ⊖	a														12 10										
Luton Airport Parkway	a														12 55										
Luton	a														12 57										
North Dulwich	d													11 42					11 57						
East Dulwich	d													11 44					11 59						
Peckham Rye	d							11 56						11 47					12 01						
Queens Rd Peckham	d							11 59						11 49					12 04						
South Bermondsey	d							12 01						11 52					12 06						
London Bridge ⊖	a					11 41		12 06		11 39	11 43	11 59	11 55	11 56					12 11					12 14	

Table 177

Mondays to Fridays
from 21 May

East and West Croydon, London Milton Keynes Central and Luton via Norbury Crystal Palace - Tulse Hill

Local Services

Network Diagram - see first Page of Table 177

		SN	SN	SN	SN [1]	SN	SN	SN [1]	SN	FC	SN	SN ◇[1]	SN	SN	SN	SN [1]	SN	SN	SN ◇[1]	SN	SN	SN	SN [1]
East Croydon	d			11 51	11 55		12 00	12 07				12 12				12 10	12 17		12 28			12 21	12 25
West Croydon [4]	d		11 45			11 58					12 01		12 04								12 15		
Norwood Junction [2]	a		11 49	11 55	11 59		12 04	12 12													12 19	12 25	12 29
	d		11 52	11 55	11 59		12 05	12 13													12 22	12 25	12 29
Selhurst [4]	d					12 02					12 05		12 09			12 14	12 20						
Thornton Heath	d					12 04					12 07		12 11			12 16	12 22						
Norbury	d					12 07					12 10		12 14			12 19	12 25						
Streatham Common [4]	d					12 10					12 13		12 17			12 22	12 28						
Beckenham Junction [4]	d								11 53														
Birkbeck	d								11 56														
Crystal Palace [4]	d		11 56						12 00						12 13			12 21			12 26		
Gipsy Hill	d		11 59						12 02						12 15						12 29		
West Norwood [4]	d		12 02						12 05						12 18						12 32		
Streatham Hill	d		12 05												12 22						12 35		
Balham [4] ⊖	d		12 09			12 14							12 21		12 25	12 28	12 32				12 39		
Wandsworth Common	d		12 11			12 16							12 23		12 27	12 30	12 34				12 41		
Latchmere	d																						
Clapham Junction [10]	d		12 15			12 20						12 22	12 27		12 31	12 39	12 38		12 37		12 45		
Imperial Wharf	d															12 44							
West Brompton ⊖	d															12 47							
Kensington (Olympia) ⊖	d															12 50							
Shepherd's Bush ⊖	d															12 53							
Wembley Central ⊖	d															13 08							
Harrow & Wealdstone ⊖	d															13 13							
Watford Junction	d															13 20							
Milton Keynes Central [10]	a															14 01							
Battersea Park [4]	d	12 15	12 18			12 23								12 32	12 35		12a41			12 45	12 48		
London Victoria [15] ⊖	a		12 23			12 28						12 28	12 34	12 36	12 39				12 44		12 53		
Streatham [4]	d									12 08	12 16												
Tulse Hill [3]	d								12 09	12 12	12 24												
Herne Hill [4]	a									12 16													
Loughborough Jn	a									12 19													
Elephant & Castle ⊖	a									12 23													
London Blackfriars [3] ⊖	a									12 27													
City Thameslink [3]	a									12 32													
St Pancras International [15] ⊖	a									12 40													
Luton Airport Parkway [7]	a									13 25													
Luton [10]	a									13 29													
North Dulwich	d								12 12		12 27												
East Dulwich	d								12 14		12 29												
Peckham Rye [4]	d	12 26							12 17		12 31									12 56			
Queens Rd Peckham	d	12 29							12 19		12 34									12 59			
South Bermondsey	d	12 31							12 22		12 36									13 01			
London Bridge [4] ⊖	a	12 36		12 09	12 13		12 29	12 25	12 26		12 41							12 41		13 06		12 39	12 43

Table 177

Mondays to Fridays
from 21 May

East and West Croydon, London Milton Keynes Central and Luton via Norbury Crystal Palace - Tulse Hill

Local Services

Network Diagram - see first Page of Table 177

		SN	SN [1]	SN	FC	SN ◇[1]	SN	SN	SN	SN	SN	SN	SN	SN ◇[1]	SN	SN	SN	SN [1]	SN	SN	SN [1]	SN	FC	SN
East Croydon	d	12 30	12 37			12 41						12 47		13 00			12 51	12 55		13 00	13 07			
West Croydon [4]	d						12 28	12 31	12 34							12 45			12 58					13 01
Norwood Junction [2]	a	12 34	12 42													12 49	12 55	12 59		13 04	13 12			
	d	12 35	12 43													12 52	12 55	12 59		13 05	13 13			
Selhurst [4]	d						12 32	12 35	12 39			12 50							13 02					13 05
Thornton Heath	d						12 34	12 37	12 41			12 52							13 04					13 07
Norbury	d						12 37	12 40	12 44			12 55							13 07					13 10
Streatham Common [4]	d						12 40	12 43	12 47			12 58							13 10					13 13
Beckenham Junction [4]	d			12 23																		12 53		
Birkbeck	d			12 26																		12 56		
Crystal Palace [4]	d			12 30							12 43		12 51			12 56						13 00		
Gipsy Hill	d			12 32							12 45					12 59						13 02		
West Norwood [4]	d			12 35							12 48					13 02						13 05		
Streatham Hill	d										12 52					13 05								
Balham [4] ⊖	d						12 44		12 51		12 55	13 02				13 09			13 14					
Wandsworth Common	d						12 46		12 53		12 57	13 04				13 11			13 16					
Latchmere	d																							
Clapham Junction [10]	d					12 50	12 50		12 57		13 01	13 08		13 10		13 15			13 20					
Imperial Wharf	d																							
West Brompton ⊖	d																							
Kensington (Olympia) ⊖	d																							
Shepherd's Bush ⊖	d																							
Wembley Central ⊖	d																							
Harrow & Wealdstone ⊖	d																							
Watford Junction	d																							
Milton Keynes Central [10]	a																							
Battersea Park [4]	d						12 53			13 02	13 05	13 11			13 15	13 18			13 23					
London Victoria [15] ⊖	a					12 57	12 58		13 04	13 06	13 09	13 16		13 16		13 23			13 28					
Streatham [4]	d				12 38			12 46															13 08	13 16
Tulse Hill [3]	d			12 39	12 42			12 54														13 09	13 12	13 24
Herne Hill [4]	a				12 46																		13 16	
Loughborough Jn	a				12 49																		13 19	
Elephant & Castle ⊖	a				12 53																		13 23	
London Blackfriars [3] ⊖	a				12 57																		13 27	
City Thameslink [3]	a				13 02																		13 32	
St Pancras International [15] ⊖	a				13 10																		13 40	
Luton Airport Parkway [7]	a				13 55																		14 25	
Luton [10]	a				13 59																		14 29	
North Dulwich	d			12 42				12 57														13 12		13 27
East Dulwich	d			12 44				12 59														13 14		13 29
Peckham Rye [4]	d			12 47				13 01							13 26							13 17		13 31
Queens Rd Peckham	d			12 49				13 04							13 29							13 19		13 34
South Bermondsey	d			12 52				13 06							13 31							13 22		13 36
London Bridge [4] ⊖	a	12 59	12 55	12 56				13 11					13 11		13 36		13 09	13 13		13 29	13 25	13 26		13 41

Table 177

Mondays to Fridays

from 21 May

East and West Croydon, London Milton Keynes Central and Luton via Norbury Crystal Palace - Tulse Hill

Local Services

Network Diagram - see first Page of Table 177

		SN ◇1	SN	SN	SN	SN 1	SN	SN		SN ◇1	SN	SN	SN	SN 1	SN	SN 1	SN	FC	SN ◇1	SN	SN	SN	SN	SN
East Croydon ⇌	d	13 12				13 10	13 17			13 28			13 21	13 25	13 30	13 37			13 41					
West Croydon 4 ⇌	d		13 04									13 15								13 28	13 31	13 34		
Norwood Junction 2	a											13 19	13 25	13 29	13 34	13 42								
	d											13 22	13 25	13 29	13 35	13 43								
Selhurst 4	d		13 09			13 13	13 20													13 32	13 35	13 39		
Thornton Heath	d		13 11			13 16	13 22													13 34	13 37	13 41		
Norbury	d		13 14			13 19	13 25													13 37	13 40	13 44		
Streatham Common 4	d		13 17			13 21	13 28													13 40	13 43	13 47		
Beckenham Junction 4 ⇌	d																13 23							
Birkbeck ⇌	d																13 26							
Crystal Palace 4	d				13 13			13 21				13 26					13 30							13 43
Gipsy Hill	d				13 15							13 29					13 32							13 45
West Norwood 4	d				13 18							13 32					13 35							13 48
Streatham Hill	d				13 22							13 35												13 52
Balham 4 ⊖	d		13 21		13 25	13 28	13 32					13 39								13 44		13 51		13 55
Wandsworth Common	d		13 23		13 27	13 30	13 34					13 41								13 46		13 53		13 57
Latchmere	d																							
Clapham Junction 10	d	13 21	13 27		13 31	13 39	13 38			13 37		13 45							13 50	13 50		13 57		14 01
Imperial Wharf	d					13 44																		
West Brompton ⊖	d					13 47																		
Kensington (Olympia) ⊖	d					13 50																		
Shepherd's Bush ⊖	d					13 53																		
Wembley Central ⊖	d					14 08																		
Harrow & Wealdstone ⊖	d					14 13																		
Watford Junction	d					14 20																		
Milton Keynes Central 10	a					15 01																		
Battersea Park 4	d			13 32	13 35		13a41				13 45	13 48								13 53			14 02	14 05
London Victoria 15 ⊖	a	13 28	13 34	13 36	13 39					13 44		13 53							13 57	13 58		14 04	14 06	14 09
Streatham 4	d																	13 38			13 46			
Tulse Hill 3	d																13 39	13 42			13 54			
Herne Hill 4	a																	13 46						
Loughborough Jn	a																	13 49						
Elephant & Castle ⊖	a																	13 53						
London Blackfriars 3 ⊖	a																	13 57						
City Thameslink 3	a																	14 02						
St Pancras International 15 ⊖	a																	14 10						
Luton Airport Parkway 7	a																	14 55						
Luton 10	a																	14 59						
North Dulwich	d																13 42				13 57			
East Dulwich	d																13 44				13 59			
Peckham Rye 4	d										13 56						13 47				14 01			
Queens Rd Peckham	d										13 59						13 49				14 04			
South Bermondsey	d										14 01						13 52				14 06			
London Bridge 4 ⊖	a							13 44			14 06		13 39	13 43	13 59	13 55	13 56				14 11			

Table 177

Mondays to Fridays

from 21 May

East and West Croydon, London Milton Keynes Central and Luton via Norbury Crystal Palace - Tulse Hill

Local Services

Network Diagram - see first Page of Table 177

		SN	SN	SN ◇1	SN	SN	SN	SN 1	SN	SN	SN 1	SN	FC	SN	SN ◇1	SN		SN	SN	SN 1	SN	SN	SN ◇1	SN	SN
East Croydon ⇌	d	13 47		14 00			13 51	13 55		14 00	14 08				14 12					14 10	14 17		14 28		
West Croydon 4 ⇌	d					13 45			13 58					14 01		14 04									14 15
Norwood Junction 2	a					13 49	13 55	13 59		14 04	14 12														14 19
	d					13 52	13 55	13 59		14 05	14 13														14 22
Selhurst 4	d	13 50							14 02					14 05		14 09				14 13	14 20				
Thornton Heath	d	13 52							14 04					14 07		14 11				14 16	14 22				
Norbury	d	13 55							14 07					14 10		14 14				14 19	14 25				
Streatham Common 4	d	13 58							14 10					14 13		14 17				14 21	14 28				
Beckenham Junction 4 ⇌	d											13 53													
Birkbeck ⇌	d											13 56													
Crystal Palace 4	d		13 51			13 56						14 00							14 13			14 21			14 26
Gipsy Hill	d					13 59						14 02							14 15						14 29
West Norwood 4	d					14 02						14 05							14 18						14 32
Streatham Hill	d					14 05													14 22						14 35
Balham 4 ⊖	d	14 02				14 09			14 14							14 21			14 25	14 28	14 32				14 39
Wandsworth Common	d	14 04				14 11			14 16							14 23			14 27	14 30	14 34				14 41
Latchmere	d																								
Clapham Junction 10	d	14 08		14 10		14 15			14 20						14 21	14 27			14 31	14 39	14 38		14 37		14 45
Imperial Wharf	d																			14 44					
West Brompton ⊖	d																			14 47					
Kensington (Olympia) ⊖	d																			14 50					
Shepherd's Bush ⊖	d																			14 53					
Wembley Central ⊖	d																			15 08					
Harrow & Wealdstone ⊖	d																			15 13					
Watford Junction	d																			15 20					
Milton Keynes Central 10	a																			16 01					
Battersea Park 4	d	14a11			14 15	14 18			14 23									14 32	14 35		14a41			14 45	14 48
London Victoria 15 ⊖	a			14 16		14 23			14 28						14 28	14 34		14 36	14 39				14 44		14 53
Streatham 4	d												14 08	14 16											
Tulse Hill 3	d											14 09	14 12	14 24											
Herne Hill 4	a												14 16												
Loughborough Jn	a												14 19												
Elephant & Castle ⊖	a												14 23												
London Blackfriars 3 ⊖	a												14 27												
City Thameslink 3	a												14 32												
St Pancras International 15 ⊖	a												14 40												
Luton Airport Parkway 7	a												15 25												
Luton 10	a												15 29												
North Dulwich	d											14 12		14 27											
East Dulwich	d											14 14		14 29											
Peckham Rye 4	d				14 26							14 17		14 31										14 56	
Queens Rd Peckham	d				14 29							14 19		14 34										14 59	
South Bermondsey	d				14 31							14 22		14 36										15 01	
London Bridge 4 ⊖	a		14 11		14 36		14 09	14 13		14 29	14 25	14 26		14 41								14 41		15 06	

Table 177

Mondays to Fridays
from 21 May

East and West Croydon, London Milton Keynes Central and Luton via Norbury Crystal Palace - Tulse Hill

Local Services

Network Diagram - see first Page of Table 177

		SN	SN ■	SN	SN ■	SN	FC	SN ◇■		SN	SN	SN	SN	SN	SN	SN	SN ◇■	SN	SN	SN	SN ■	SN	SN	SN ■
East Croydon ⇌	d	14 21	14 25	14 30	14 37			14 41							14 47		15 00			14 51	14 55		15 00	15 07
West Croydon ■ ⇌	d									14 28	14 31	14 34							14 45			14 58		
Norwood Junction ■	a	14 25	14 29	14 34	14 42														14 49	14 55	14 59		15 04	15 12
	d	14 25	14 29	14 35	14 43														14 52	14 55	14 59		15 05	15 13
Selhurst ■	d									14 32	14 35	14 39			14 50							15 02		
Thornton Heath	d									14 34	14 37	14 41			14 52							15 04		
Norbury	d									14 37	14 40	14 44			14 55							15 07		
Streatham Common ■	d									14 40	14 43	14 47			14 58							15 10		
Beckenham Junction ■ ⇌	d					14 23																		
Birkbeck ⇌	d					14 26																		
Crystal Palace ■	d					14 30								14 43		14 51			14 56					
Gipsy Hill	d					14 32								14 45					14 59					
West Norwood ■	d					14 35								14 48					15 02					
Streatham Hill	d													14 52					15 05					
Balham ■ ⊖	d									14 44		14 51		14 55	15 02				15 09			15 14		
Wandsworth Common	d									14 46		14 53		14 57	15 04				15 11			15 16		
Latchmere	d																							
Clapham Junction ■	d							14 50		14 50		14 57		15 01	15 08		15 10		15 15			15 20		
Imperial Wharf	d																							
West Brompton ⊖	d																							
Kensington (Olympia) ⊖	d																							
Shepherd's Bush ⊖	d																							
Wembley Central ⊖	d																							
Harrow & Wealdstone ⊖	d																							
Watford Junction	d																							
Milton Keynes Central ■	a																							
Battersea Park ■	d									14 53			15 02	15 05	15 11			15 15	15 18			15 23		
London Victoria ■ ⊖	a							14 57		14 58		15 04	15 06	15 09	15 16		15 20		15 24			15 28		
Streatham ■	d						14 38				14 46													
Tulse Hill ■	d					14 39	14 42				14 54													
Herne Hill ■	a						14 46																	
Loughborough Jn	a						14 49																	
Elephant & Castle ⊖	a						14 53																	
London Blackfriars ■ ⊖	a						14 57																	
City Thameslink ■	a						15 02																	
St Pancras International ■ ⊖	a						15 10																	
Luton Airport Parkway ■	a						15 55																	
Luton ■	a						15 59																	
North Dulwich	d					14 42					14 57													
East Dulwich	d					14 44					14 59													
Peckham Rye ■	d					14 47					15 01							15 26						
Queens Rd Peckham	d					14 49					15 04							15 29						
South Bermondsey	d					14 52					15 06							15 31						
London Bridge ■ ⊖	a	14 39	14 43	14 59	14 55	14 56					15 11					15 11		15 36		15 09	15 13		15 29	15 25

Table 177

Mondays to Fridays
from 21 May

East and West Croydon, London Milton Keynes Central and Luton via Norbury Crystal Palace - Tulse Hill

Local Services

Network Diagram - see first Page of Table 177

		SN	FC	SN	SN ◇■	SN	SN	SN	SN ■	SN	SN	SN ◇■	SN	SN	SN	SN ■		SN	SN ■	SN	FC	SN ◇■	SN	SN	SN
East Croydon ⇌	d				15 12				15 10	15 17		15 28			15 21	15 25		15 30	15 37			15 41			
West Croydon ■ ⇌	d			15 01		15 04								15 15									15 28	15 31	15 34
Norwood Junction ■	a													15 19	15 25	15 29		15 34	15 42						
	d													15 22	15 25	15 29		15 35	15 43						
Selhurst ■	d			15 05		15 09			15 13	15 20													15 32	15 35	15 39
Thornton Heath	d			15 07		15 11			15 16	15 22													15 34	15 37	15 41
Norbury	d			15 10		15 14			15 19	15 25													15 37	15 40	15 44
Streatham Common ■	d			15 13		15 17			15 21	15 28													15 40	15 43	15 47
Beckenham Junction ■ ⇌	d	14 53																		15 23					
Birkbeck ⇌	d	14 56																		15 26					
Crystal Palace ■	d	15 00						15 13			15 21			15 26						15 30					
Gipsy Hill	d	15 02						15 15						15 29						15 32					
West Norwood ■	d	15 05						15 18						15 32						15 35					
Streatham Hill	d							15 22						15 35											
Balham ■ ⊖	d					15 21		15 25	15 29	15 32				15 39									15 44		15 51
Wandsworth Common	d					15 23		15 27	15 31	15 34				15 41									15 46		15 53
Latchmere	d																								
Clapham Junction ■	d				15 21	15 27		15 31	15 39	15 38		15 38		15 45								15 50	15 50		15 57
Imperial Wharf	d								15 44																
West Brompton ⊖	d								15 47																
Kensington (Olympia) ⊖	d								15 50																
Shepherd's Bush ⊖	d								15 53																
Wembley Central ⊖	d								16 08																
Harrow & Wealdstone ⊖	d								16 13																
Watford Junction	d								16 20																
Milton Keynes Central ■	a								17 00																
Battersea Park ■	d						15 32	15 35		15 41			15 45	15 49									15 53		
London Victoria ■ ⊖	a				15 28	15 34	15 36	15 39		15 46		15 46		15 54								15 57	15 58		16 04
Streatham ■	d		15 08	15 16																	15 38			15 46	
Tulse Hill ■	d	15 09	15 12	15 24																15 39	15 42			15 54	
Herne Hill ■	a		15 16																		15 46				
Loughborough Jn	a		15 19																		15 49				
Elephant & Castle ⊖	a		15 23																		15 53				
London Blackfriars ■ ⊖	a		15 27																		15 57				
City Thameslink ■	a		15 32																		16 02				
St Pancras International ■ ⊖	a		15 40																		16 10				
Luton Airport Parkway ■	a		16 25																		16 57				
Luton ■	a		16 29																		17 01				
North Dulwich	d	15 12		15 27																15 42				15 57	
East Dulwich	d	15 14		15 29																15 44				15 59	
Peckham Rye ■	d	15 17		15 31									15 56							15 47				16 01	
Queens Rd Peckham	d	15 19		15 34									15 59							15 49				16 04	
South Bermondsey	d	15 22		15 36									16 01							15 52				16 06	
London Bridge ■ ⊖	a	15 26		15 41							15 41		16 06		15 39	15 43		15 59	15 55	15 56				16 11	

Table 177

Mondays to Fridays
from 21 May

East and West Croydon, London
Milton Keynes Central and Luton via Norbury
Crystal Palace - Tulse Hill

Local Services

Network Diagram - see first Page of Table 177

		SN	SN	SN	SN	SN	SN ◇1 ⌶	SN		SN	SN	SN 1	SN	SN	SN 1	SN	FC	SN	SN ◇1 ⌶	SN	SN	SN	SN 1	SN
East Croydon ⇌	d			15 47			16 00				15 51	15 55		16 00	16 07				16 12				16 10	16 17
West Croydon 4 ⇌	d									15 45			15 58					16 01		16 04				
Norwood Junction 2	a									15 49	15 55	15 59		16 04	16 12									
	d									15 52	15 55	15 59		16 05	16 13									
Selhurst 4	d			15 50									16 02					16 05		16 09			16 13	16 20
Thornton Heath	d			15 52									16 04					16 07		16 11			16 16	16 22
Norbury	d			15 55									16 07					16 10		16 14			16 19	16 25
Streatham Common 4	d			15 58									16 10					16 13		16 17			16 21	16 28
Beckenham Junction 4 ⇌	d															15 53								
Birkbeck ⇌	d															15 56								
Crystal Palace 4	d		15 43		15 51					15 56						16 00						16 13		
Gipsy Hill	d		15 45							15 59						16 02						16 15		
West Norwood 4	d		15 48							16 02						16 05						16 18		
Streatham Hill	d		15 52			15 56				16 05												16 22		
Balham 4 ⊖	d		15 55	16 02						16 09			16 14							16 21		16 25	16 28	16 32
Wandsworth Common	d		15 57	16 04						16 11			16 16							16 23		16 27	16 30	16 34
Latchmere	d																							
Clapham Junction 10	d		16 01	16 08			16 09			16 15			16 20						16 21	16 27		16 31	16 39	16 38
Imperial Wharf	d																						16 44	
West Brompton ⊖	d																						16 47	
Kensington (Olympia) ⊖	d																						16 50	
Shepherd's Bush ⊖	d																						16 53	
Wembley Central ⊖	d																						17 08	
Harrow & Wealdstone ⊖	d																						17 13	
Watford Junction	d																						17 21	
Milton Keynes Central 10	a																						17 59	
Battersea Park 4	d	16 02	16 05	16 11				16 15		16 18			16 23								16 32	16 35		16 41
London Victoria 15 ⊖	a	16 06	16 10	16 16			16 16			16 23			16 28						16 28	16 34	16 38	16 40		16 46
Streatham 4	d																16 08	16 16						
Tulse Hill 3	d					16 00										16 09	16 12	16 24						
Herne Hill 4	a																16 16							
Loughborough Jn	a																16 19							
Elephant & Castle ⊖	a																16 23							
London Blackfriars 3 ⊖	a																16 29							
City Thameslink 3	a																16 32							
St Pancras International 15 ⊖	a																16 39							
Luton Airport Parkway 7	a																17 25							
Luton 10	a																17 29							
North Dulwich	d					16 03										16 12		16 27						
East Dulwich	d					16 05										16 14		16 29						
Peckham Rye 4	d					16 07		16 26								16 17		16 31						
Queens Rd Peckham	d					16 10		16 29								16 19		16 34						
South Bermondsey	d					16 12		16 31								16 22		16 36						
London Bridge 4 ⊖	a				16 11	16 17		16 38			16 09	16 13		16 29	16 25	16 26		16 41						

Table 177

Mondays to Fridays
from 21 May

East and West Croydon, London
Milton Keynes Central and Luton via Norbury
Crystal Palace - Tulse Hill

Local Services

Network Diagram - see first Page of Table 177

		SN	SN ◇1 ⌶	SN	SN	SN	SN 1	SN	SN	SN	FC	SN 1	SN	SN ◇1 ⌶	SN	SN		SN	SN	SN	SN ◇1	SN	SN	SN	SN 1
East Croydon ⇌	d		16 30			16 21	16 24			16 30		16 40		16 41					16 47		17 01			16 51	16 55
West Croydon 4 ⇌	d				16 15				16 28				16 31		16 34								16 45		
Norwood Junction 2	a				16 20	16 25	16 28			16 34		16 44											16 50	16 55	16 59
	d				16 22	16 25	16 28			16 35		16 45											16 52	16 55	16 59
Selhurst 4	d								16 32				16 35		16 39				16 50						
Thornton Heath	d								16 34				16 37		16 41				16 52						
Norbury	d								16 37				16 40		16 44				16 55						
Streatham Common 4	d								16 40				16 43		16 47				16 58						
Beckenham Junction 4 ⇌	d							16 23																	
Birkbeck ⇌	d							16 26																	
Crystal Palace 4	d	16 21			16 26			16 30										16 43		16 50			16 56		
Gipsy Hill	d				16 29			16 32										16 45					16 59		
West Norwood 4	d				16 32			16 35										16 48					17 02		
Streatham Hill	d				16 35													16 52					17 05		
Balham 4 ⊖	d				16 39				16 44						16 51			16 55	17 02				17 09		
Wandsworth Common	d				16 41				16 46						16 53			16 57	17 04				17 11		
Latchmere	d																								
Clapham Junction 10	d		16 40		16 45				16 50					16 51	16 57			17 01	17 08		17 11		17 15		
Imperial Wharf	d																								
West Brompton ⊖	d																								
Kensington (Olympia) ⊖	d																								
Shepherd's Bush ⊖	d																								
Wembley Central ⊖	d																								
Harrow & Wealdstone ⊖	d																								
Watford Junction	d																								
Milton Keynes Central 10	a																								
Battersea Park 4	d			16 45	16 49				16 53							17 02		17 05	17 11			17 15	17 18		
London Victoria 15 ⊖	a		16 46		16 55				16 58					16 58	17 04	17 08		17 10	17 16		17 17		17 23		
Streatham 4	d										16 40		16 46												
Tulse Hill 3	d							16 39			16 46		16 53												
Herne Hill 4	a										16 50														
Loughborough Jn	a										16 53														
Elephant & Castle ⊖	a										16 59														
London Blackfriars 3 ⊖	a										17 03														
City Thameslink 3	a										17 06														
St Pancras International 15 ⊖	a										17 13														
Luton Airport Parkway 7	a																								
Luton 10	a																								
North Dulwich	d							16 42					16 56												
East Dulwich	d							16 44					16 58												
Peckham Rye 4	d			16 56				16 47					17 00									17 26			
Queens Rd Peckham	d			16 59				16 49					17 03									17 29			
South Bermondsey	d			17 01				16 52					17 05									17 31			
London Bridge 4 ⊖	a	16 41		17 08		16 39	16 43	16 56		17 02		17 00	17 10							17 12		17 38		17 08	17 14

Table 177

Mondays to Fridays
from 21 May

East and West Croydon, London Milton Keynes Central and Luton via Norbury Crystal Palace - Tulse Hill

Local Services

Network Diagram - see first Page of Table 177

Station		SN	SN	SN ■	SN	FC	SN	SN ◇■		SN	SN	SN	SN	SN ■	SN	SN	SN ◇■	SN	SN ■	FC	SN	SN	SN	SN ■
East Croydon	d		17 00	17 07				17 13						17 10			17 30	17 17	17 38				17 21	17 25
West Croydon	d	16 58					17 01			17 04	17 12											17 18		
Norwood Junction	a		17 04	17 11																		17 22	17 25	17 30
	d		17 05	17 12																		17 23	17 25	17 31
Selhurst	d	17 02					17 05			17 09				17 13				17 20						
Thornton Heath	d	17 04					17 07			17 11				17 16				17 22						
Norbury	d	17 07					17 10			17 14				17 19				17 25						
Streatham Common	d	17 10					17 13			17 17				17 21				17 28						
Beckenham Junction	d				16 53										17 11									
Birkbeck	d				16 56										17 14									
Crystal Palace	d				17 00								17 13		17 18	17 21						17 27		
Gipsy Hill	d				17 02								17 15		17 20							17 29		
West Norwood	d				17 05								17 18		17 23							17 32		
Streatham Hill	d												17 22									17 36		
Balham ⊖	d	17 14								17 21			17 25	17 28				17 32				17 39		
Wandsworth Common	d	17 16								17 23			17 27	17 30				17 34				17 41		
Latchmere	d																							
Clapham Junction	d	17 20						17 23		17 27			17 31	17 39			17 40	17 38	17 48			17 45		
Imperial Wharf	d													17 44										
West Brompton ⊖	d													17 47										
Kensington (Olympia) ⊖	d													17 50										
Shepherd's Bush ⊖	d													17 53										
Wembley Central ⊖	d													18 08										
Harrow & Wealdstone ⊖	d													18 13										
Watford Junction	d													18 20										
Milton Keynes Central	a													19 00										
Battersea Park	d	17 23										17 32	17 35					17 41			17 45	17 48		
London Victoria ⊖	a	17 28						17 29		17 34		17 38	17 42				17 46	17 48	17 54			17 55		
Streatham	d					17 10	17 16													17 40				
Tulse Hill	d				17 09	17 16	17 22								17 27					17 44				
Herne Hill	a					17 20														17 47				
Loughborough Jn	a					17 24														17 51				
Elephant & Castle ⊖	a					17 28														17 55				
London Blackfriars ⊖	a					17 31														17 59				
City Thameslink	a					17 34														18 02				
St Pancras International ⊖	a					17 41														18 09				
Luton Airport Parkway	a					18 27														18 58				
Luton	a					18 31														19 01				
North Dulwich	d				17 12		17 25								17 30									
East Dulwich	d				17 14		17 27								17 32						17 57			
Peckham Rye	d				17 17		17 29								17 35						17 59			
Queens Rd Peckham	d				17 19		17 32								17 37						18 02			
South Bermondsey	d				17 22		17 34								17 40						18 08			
London Bridge ⊖	a		17 35	17 26	17 27		17 40				17 28				17 44	17 43							17 37	17 45

Table 177

Mondays to Fridays
from 21 May

East and West Croydon, London Milton Keynes Central and Luton via Norbury Crystal Palace - Tulse Hill

Local Services

Network Diagram - see first Page of Table 177

Station		SN	SN	SN	SN ◇■	SN ■	SN	SN	SN	SN	SN	SN	SN	SN	SN ◇■	FC		SN	SN	SN ■	SN	SN ■	SN	SN	SN ■
East Croydon	d			17 30	17 41	17 41					17 47	17 51			18 02					17 55	18 08	18 09			18 10
West Croydon	d	17 28					17 31	17 42											17 48				17 58	18 01	
Norwood Junction	a			17 34		17 45						17 55							17 54	17 59	18 12				
	d		17 32	17 35		17 45						17 55							17 55	17 59	18 12				
Selhurst	d	17 32					17 35				17 50												18 02	18 05	18 13
Thornton Heath	d	17 34					17 37				17 52												18 04	18 07	18 16
Norbury	d	17 37					17 40				17 55												18 07	18 10	18 19
Streatham Common	d	17 40					17 43				17 58												18 10	18 13	18 21
Beckenham Junction	d													17 48											
Birkbeck	d													17 51											
Crystal Palace	d		17 36							17 44			17 48	17 55					17 59						
Gipsy Hill	d		17 38							17 46				17 57					18 01						
West Norwood	d		17 41							17 49				18 00					18 04						
Streatham Hill	d									17 53									18 08						
Balham ⊖	d	17 44								17 56	18 02								18 11				18 14		18 29
Wandsworth Common	d	17 46								17 58	18 04								18 13				18 16		18 31
Latchmere	d																								
Clapham Junction	d	17 50			17 51					18 02	18 08				18 13				18 17			18 19	18 20		18 39
Imperial Wharf	d																								18 44
West Brompton ⊖	d																								18 47
Kensington (Olympia) ⊖	d																								18 50
Shepherd's Bush ⊖	d																								18 53
Wembley Central ⊖	d																								19 08
Harrow & Wealdstone ⊖	d																								19 13
Watford Junction	d																								19 21
Milton Keynes Central	a																								20 06
Battersea Park	d	17 53							18 02	18 06	18 11							18 15	18 20				18 23		
London Victoria ⊖	a	17 58			17 58				18 08	18 12	18 16				18 20				18 25			18 26	18 28		
Streatham	d						17 46									18 10								18 16	
Tulse Hill	d		17 45				17 54							18 05		18 16								18 20	
Herne Hill	a															18 19									
Loughborough Jn	a															18 23									
Elephant & Castle ⊖	a															18 27									
London Blackfriars ⊖	a															18 31									
City Thameslink	a															18 34									
St Pancras International ⊖	a															18 41									
Luton Airport Parkway	a															19 30									
Luton	a															19 33									
North Dulwich	d		17 48				17 57							18 08										18 23	
East Dulwich	d		17 50				17 59							18 10										18 25	
Peckham Rye	d		17 53				18 01							18 12				18 26						18 29	
Queens Rd Peckham	d		17 55				18 04							18 15				18 29						18 32	
South Bermondsey	d		17 58				18 06							18 17				18 31						18 34	
London Bridge ⊖	a		18 02	17 59		17 58	18 11	18 00				18 09	18 13	18 22				18 38		18 16	18 26			18 39	

East and West Croydon, London
Milton Keynes Central and Luton via Norbury
Crystal Palace - Tulse Hill

Local Services

Network Diagram - see first Page of Table 177

		SN ◇1	SN	SN	SN	SN	SN	SN		SN 1	SN	SN ◇1	FC	SN	SN	SN	SN	SN 1	SN	SN	SN ◇1	SN	SN	SN	
East Croydon ⇌	d	18 12								18 27	18 17	18 30				18 21	18 30	18 40			18 43				
West Croydon 4 ⇌	d		18 13												18 18				18 28	18 31					
Norwood Junction 2	a														18 23	18 28	18 34								
	d														18 24	18 29	18 35								
Selhurst 4	d										18 20								18 32	18 36					
Thornton Heath	d										18 22								18 34	18 38					
Norbury	d										18 25								18 37	18 41					
Streatham Common 4	d										18 28								18 40	18 44					
Beckenham Junction 4 ⇌	d						18 11																		
Birkbeck ⇌	d						18 14																		
Crystal Palace 4	d					18 13	18 18	18 20							18 28								18 43	18 51	
Gipsy Hill	d					18 15	18 20								18 30								18 45		
West Norwood 4	d					18 18	18 23								18 33								18 48		
Streatham Hill	d					18 22									18 37								18 52		
Balham 4 ⊖	d					18 25					18 33				18 40				18 44				18 55		
Wandsworth Common	d					18 27					18 35				18 42				18 46				18 57		
Latchmere	d																								
Clapham Junction 10	d	18 22				18 32				18 38	18 39	18 41			18 46			18 50	18 50		18 53		19 01		
Imperial Wharf	d																								
West Brompton ⊖	d																								
Kensington (Olympia) ⊖	d																								
Shepherd's Bush ⊖	d																								
Wembley Central ⊖	d																								
Harrow & Wealdstone ⊖	d																								
Watford Junction	d																								
Milton Keynes Central 10	a																								
Battersea Park 4	d				18 32	18 35								18 45	18 49							19 02	19 05		
London Victoria 15 ⊖	a	18 29			18 39	18 42				18 45	18 46	18 48			18 54			18 56	18 57		18 59	19 08	19 12		
Streatham 4	d			18 20									18 40							18 47					
Tulse Hill 3	d			18 24			18 28						18 44							18 54					
Herne Hill 4	a												18 47												
Loughborough Jn	a												18 51												
Elephant & Castle ⊖	a												18 55												
London Blackfriars 3 ⊖	a												18 59												
City Thameslink 3	a												19 02												
St Pancras International 15 ⊖	a												19 09												
Luton Airport Parkway 7	a												19 54												
Luton 10	a												19 57												
North Dulwich	d			18 27			18 31													18 57					
East Dulwich	d			18 29			18 33													18 59					
Peckham Rye 4	d			18 32			18 36							18 57						19 01					
Queens Rd Peckham	d			18 35			18 38							19 00						19 04					
South Bermondsey	d			18 37			18 41							19 02						19 06					
London Bridge 4 ⊖	a		18 29	18 42			18 45	18 45						19 09		18 41	18 59			19 11				19 13	

East and West Croydon, London
Milton Keynes Central and Luton via Norbury
Crystal Palace - Tulse Hill

Local Services

Network Diagram - see first Page of Table 177

		SN 1	SN	SN	SN	SN ◇1	FC	SN	SN	SN	SN	SN 1	SN	SN 1	SN ◇1	SN		SN	SN	SN 1	SN	SN ◇1	SN	SN	SN
East Croydon ⇌	d	18 55	18 47			19 00					19 00	19 10		19 10	19 12					19 25		19 29	19 17		
West Croydon 4 ⇌	d								18 47	18 58			19 01												19 17
Norwood Junction 2	a								18 51		19 04	19 13													19 21
	d								18 52		19 05	19 13													19 22
Selhurst 4	d		18 51							19 02			19 05	19 13									19 20		
Thornton Heath	d		18 53							19 04			19 07	19 16									19 22		
Norbury	d		18 56							19 07			19 10	19 19									19 25		
Streatham Common 4	d		18 58							19 10			19 13	19 21									19 28		
Beckenham Junction 4 ⇌	d				18 44																				
Birkbeck ⇌	d				18 47																				
Crystal Palace 4	d				18 51				18 56									19 13	19 21						19 26
Gipsy Hill	d				18 53				18 59									19 15							19 29
West Norwood 4	d				18 56				19 02									19 18							19 32
Streatham Hill	d								19 05									19 22							19 35
Balham 4 ⊖	d		19 02						19 09	19 14				19 28				19 25					19 32		19 39
Wandsworth Common	d		19 04						19 11	19 16				19 30				19 27					19 34		19 41
Latchmere	d																								
Clapham Junction 10	d	19 06	19 08			19 12			19 15	19 20				19 39	19 22			19 31		19 38		19 41	19 38		19 45
Imperial Wharf	d													19 44											
West Brompton ⊖	d													19 47											
Kensington (Olympia) ⊖	d													19 50											
Shepherd's Bush ⊖	d													19 53											
Wembley Central ⊖	d													20 08											
Harrow & Wealdstone ⊖	d													20 13											
Watford Junction	d													20 20											
Milton Keynes Central 10	a													21 01											
Battersea Park 4	d							19 15	19 18	19 23						19 32		19 35					19 41	19 45	19 48
London Victoria 15 ⊖	a	19 13	19 15			19 18			19 25	19 28					19 29	19 36		19 41		19 44		19 47	19 48		19 54
Streatham 4	d			18 56			19 10						19 16								19 26				
Tulse Hill 3	d			19 00	19 07		19 14						19 22								19 31				
Herne Hill 4	a						19 17																		
Loughborough Jn	a						19 20																		
Elephant & Castle ⊖	a						19 24																		
London Blackfriars 3 ⊖	a						19 28																		
City Thameslink 3	a						19 32																		
St Pancras International 15 ⊖	a						19 40																		
Luton Airport Parkway 7	a						20 25																		
Luton 10	a						20 29																		
North Dulwich	d			19 03	19 10								19 25								19 34				
East Dulwich	d			19 05	19 12								19 27								19 36				
Peckham Rye 4	d			19 07	19 14			19 26					19 29								19 38			19 56	
Queens Rd Peckham	d			19 10	19 17			19 29					19 32								19 41			19 59	
South Bermondsey	d			19 12	19 19			19 31					19 34								19 43			20 01	
London Bridge 4 ⊖	a			19 17	19 24			19 36			19 29	19 25	19 41						19 41		19 51			20 06	

East and West Croydon, London Milton Keynes Central and Luton via Norbury Crystal Palace - Tulse Hill

Local Services

Network Diagram - see first Page of Table 177

		SN	SN	SN 1	SN	FC	SN ◇1	FC 1		SN	SN	SN	SN	SN	SN 1	SN 1	SN	SN	SN	SN	SN	FC	SN	SN ◇1
East Croydon	d		19 30	19 40			19 43	19 47						19 47	19 59	20 01					20 00			20 11
West Croydon 4	d				19 28								19 31					19 47		19 58			20 01	
Norwood Junction 2	a		19 34															19 51			20 04			
	d		19 35															19 52			20 05			
Selhurst 4	d				19 32								19 35	19 50						20 02			20 05	
Thornton Heath	d				19 34								19 37	19 52						20 04			20 07	
Norbury	d				19 37								19 40	19 55						20 07			20 10	
Streatham Common 4	d				19 40								19 43	19 58						20 10			20 13	
Beckenham Junction 4	d	19 25																	19 54					
Birkbeck	d	19 28																	19 57					
Crystal Palace 4	d	19 32									19 43	19 51						19 56	20 01					
Gipsy Hill	d	19 34									19 45							19 58	20 03					
West Norwood 4	d	19 37									19 48							20 01	20 06					
Streatham Hill	d										19 52							20 05						
Balham 4 ⊖	d				19 45						19 55			20 02				20 08		20 14				
Wandsworth Common	d				19 47						19 57			20 04				20 10		20 16				
Latchmere	d																							
Clapham Junction 10	d			19 50	19 51		19 53				20 01			20 08	20 08	20 11		20 14		20 20				20 21
Imperial Wharf	d																							
West Brompton ⊖	d																							
Kensington (Olympia) ⊖	d																							
Shepherd's Bush ⊖	d																							
Wembley Central ⊖	d																							
Harrow & Wealdstone ⊖	d																							
Watford Junction	d																							
Milton Keynes Central 10	a																							
Battersea Park 4	d				19 54					20 02	20 05			20a11			20 15	20 18		20 23				
London Victoria 15 ⊖	a			19 56	19 59		19 59			20 06	20 09				20 15	20 20		20 22		20 28				20 28
Streatham 4	d					19 40							19 46									20 06	20 17	
Tulse Hill 3	d	19 41				19 44							19 54						20 11			20 12	20 24	
Herne Hill 4	a					19 47																20 16		
Loughborough Jn	a					19 50																20 19		
Elephant & Castle ⊖	a					19 54																20 23		
London Blackfriars 3 ⊖	a					19 58		20 07														20 27		
City Thameslink 3	a					20 02		20 10														20 32		
St Pancras International 15 ⊖	a					20 10		20 18														20 40		
Luton Airport Parkway 7	a					20 55		20 50														21 25		
Luton 10	a					20 59		20 53														21 29		
North Dulwich	d	19 44											19 57						20 14				20 27	
East Dulwich	d	19 46											19 59						20 16				20 29	
Peckham Rye 4	d	19 49											20 01				20 26		20 18				20 31	
Queens Rd Peckham	d	19 51											20 04				20 29		20 21				20 34	
South Bermondsey	d	19 54											20 06				20 31		20 23				20 36	
London Bridge 4 ⊖	a	19 58	19 59									20 11	20 14				20 36		20 28		20 29		20 41	

East and West Croydon, London Milton Keynes Central and Luton via Norbury Crystal Palace - Tulse Hill

Local Services

Network Diagram - see first Page of Table 177

		SN	SN	SN	SN 1	SN	SN ◇1	SN	SN	SN	SN	FC	SN	SN ◇1	SN	SN		SN	SN	SN 1	SN	SN	SN	SN	SN
East Croydon	d				20 26	20 17	20 30				20 31			20 41						20 57	20 47				21 00
West Croydon 4	d								20 18				20 31		20 35								20 45		
Norwood Junction 2	a								20 22		20 35												20 49		21 04
	d								20 23		20 35												20 52		21 05
Selhurst 4	d					20 20							20 35		20 39						20 50				
Thornton Heath	d					20 22							20 37		20 41						20 52				
Norbury	d					20 25							20 40		20 44						20 55				
Streatham Common 4	d					20 28							20 43		20 47						20 58				
Beckenham Junction 4	d									20 24														20 53	
Birkbeck	d									20 27														20 56	
Crystal Palace 4	d		20 13	20 21					20 27	20 31								20 43	20 51				20 56	21 00	
Gipsy Hill	d		20 16						20 29	20 33								20 45					20 59	21 02	
West Norwood 4	d		20 19						20 32	20 36								20 48					21 02	21 05	
Streatham Hill	d		20 22						20 36									20 52					21 05		
Balham 4 ⊖	d		20 25			20 32			20 39						20 51			20 56			21 02		21 08		
Wandsworth Common	d		20 27			20 34			20 41						20 53			20 58			21 04		21 10		
Latchmere	d																								
Clapham Junction 10	d		20 31		20 37	20 38	20 41		20 45					20 51	20 57			21 03		21 08	21 08		21 14		
Imperial Wharf	d																								
West Brompton ⊖	d																								
Kensington (Olympia) ⊖	d																								
Shepherd's Bush ⊖	d																								
Wembley Central ⊖	d																								
Harrow & Wealdstone ⊖	d																								
Watford Junction	d																								
Milton Keynes Central 10	a																								
Battersea Park 4	d	20 32	20 35			20 41		20 45	20 48							21 02		21 06			21 11	21 15	21 18		
London Victoria 15 ⊖	a	20 36	20 39		20 44	20 46	20 50		20 53					20 59	21 04	21 06		21 11		21 15	21 18		21 22		
Streatham 4	d											20 36	20 46												
Tulse Hill 3	d									20 40		20 42	20 54											21 09	
Herne Hill 4	a											20 46													
Loughborough Jn	a											20 49													
Elephant & Castle ⊖	a											20 53													
London Blackfriars 3 ⊖	a											20 57													
City Thameslink 3	a											21 02													
St Pancras International 15 ⊖	a											21 10													
Luton Airport Parkway 7	a											21 55													
Luton 10	a											21 59													
North Dulwich	d									20 43			20 57											21 12	
East Dulwich	d									20 45			20 59											21 14	
Peckham Rye 4	d							20 56		20 48			21 01									21 26		21 17	
Queens Rd Peckham	d							20 59		20 50			21 04									21 29		21 19	
South Bermondsey	d							21 01		20 53			21 06									21 31		21 22	
London Bridge 4 ⊖	a			20 41				21 06		20 57	20 59		21 11						21 11			21 36		21 26	21 29

East and West Croydon, London Milton Keynes Central and Luton via Norbury Crystal Palace - Tulse Hill

Local Services

Network Diagram - see first Page of Table 177

Station		FC	SN	SN ◇[1]	SN	SN	SN	SN	SN [1]	SN ◇[1]	SN	SN	SN	SN	SN	SN ◇[1]	FC	SN	SN	SN	SN	SN	SN [1]
East Croydon	d			21 09					21 26	21 30	21 17				21 30	21 42							21 57
West Croydon [4]	d		21 01		21 04								21 18					21 31	21 34				
Norwood Junction [2]	a												21 22		21 34								
	d												21 23		21 35								
Selhurst [4]	d		21 05		21 09						21 20							21 35	21 39				
Thornton Heath	d		21 07		21 11						21 22							21 37	21 41				
Norbury	d		21 10		21 14						21 25							21 40	21 44				
Streatham Common [4]	d		21 13		21 17						21 28							21 43	21 47				
Beckenham Junction [4]	d													21 23									
Birkbeck	d													21 26									
Crystal Palace [4]	d						21 13	21 21					21 27	21 30							21 43	21 51	
Gipsy Hill	d						21 15						21 29	21 32							21 45		
West Norwood [4]	d						21 18						21 32	21 35							21 48		
Streatham Hill	d						21 22						21 36								21 52		
Balham [4] ⊖	d				21 21		21 26				21 32		21 39						21 51		21 56		
Wandsworth Common	d				21 23		21 28				21 34		21 41						21 53		21 58		
Latchmere	d																						
Clapham Junction [10]	d			21 18	21 27		21 33		21 38	21 41	21 38		21 45			21 51			21 57		22 03		22 08
Imperial Wharf	d																						
West Brompton ⊖	d																						
Kensington (Olympia) ⊖	d																						
Shepherd's Bush ⊖	d																						
Wembley Central ⊖	d																						
Harrow & Wealdstone ⊖	d																						
Watford Junction	d																						
Milton Keynes Central [10]	a																						
Battersea Park [4]	d					21 32	21 36				21 41	21 45	21 48							22 02	22 06		
London Victoria [15] ⊖	a			21 28	21 34	21 36	21 41		21 45	21 47	21 48		21 53			21 58			22 04	22 06	22 11		22 14
Streatham [4]	d	21 06	21 16														21 49	21 46					
Tulse Hill [3]	d	21 12	21 24											21 39			21 53	21 54					
Herne Hill [4]	a	21 16															21 56						
Loughborough Jn	a	21 19															22 00						
Elephant & Castle ⊖	a	21 23															22 04						
London Blackfriars [3] ⊖	a	21 27															22 07						
City Thameslink [3]	a	21 32															22 10						
St Pancras International [15] ⊖	a	21 40															22 17						
Luton Airport Parkway [7]	a	22 25															23 01						
Luton [10]	a	22 29															23 04						
North Dulwich	d		21 27											21 42				21 57					
East Dulwich	d		21 29											21 44				21 59					
Peckham Rye [4]	d		21 31									21 56		21 47				22 01					
Queens Rd Peckham	d		21 34									21 59		21 49				22 04					
South Bermondsey	d		21 36									22 01		21 52				22 06					
London Bridge [4] ⊖	a		21 41					21 43				22 06		21 56	21 59			22 11				22 13	

East and West Croydon, London Milton Keynes Central and Luton via Norbury Crystal Palace - Tulse Hill

Local Services

Network Diagram - see first Page of Table 177

Station		SN	SN	SN	SN	SN	SN ◇[1]	FC	SN	SN	SN	SN	SN	SN	SN [1]	SN	SN ◇[1]	SN	SN	SN	SN ◇[1]	FC	SN	SN
East Croydon	d	21 47				22 00	22 09								22 25	22 17	22 30			22 30	22 41			
West Croydon [4]	d			21 48					22 01	22 04									22 18				22 31	22 34
Norwood Junction [2]	a			21 52		22 04													22 22	22 34				
	d			21 53		22 05													22 23	22 35				
Selhurst [4]	d	21 50							22 05	22 09						22 20							22 35	22 39
Thornton Heath	d	21 52							22 07	22 11						22 22							22 37	22 41
Norbury	d	21 55							22 10	22 14						22 25							22 40	22 44
Streatham Common [4]	d	21 58							22 13	22 17						22 28							22 43	22 47
Beckenham Junction [4]	d				21 53									22 15										
Birkbeck	d				21 56									22 18										
Crystal Palace [4]	d			21 57	22 00							22 13	22 21	22 22					22 27					
Gipsy Hill	d			21 59	22 02							22 15		22 24					22 29					
West Norwood [4]	d			22 02	22 05							22 18		22 27					22 32					
Streatham Hill	d			22 06								22 22							22 36					
Balham [4] ⊖	d	22 02		22 09						22 21		22 26				22 32			22 39					22 51
Wandsworth Common	d	22 04		22 11						22 23		22 28				22 34			22 41					22 53
Latchmere	d																							
Clapham Junction [10]	d	22 08		22 15			22 18			22 27		22 33			22 38	22 38	22 41		22 45		22 51			22 57
Imperial Wharf	d																							
West Brompton ⊖	d																							
Kensington (Olympia) ⊖	d																							
Shepherd's Bush ⊖	d																							
Wembley Central ⊖	d																							
Harrow & Wealdstone ⊖	d																							
Watford Junction	d																							
Milton Keynes Central [10]	a																							
Battersea Park [4]	d	22 11	22 15	22 18							22 32	22 36				22 41		22 45	22 48					
London Victoria [15] ⊖	a	22 18		22 23			22 26			22 34	22 36	22 41			22 44	22 48	22 50		22 53		22 57			23 04
Streatham [4]	d							22 19	22 16													22 49	22 46	
Tulse Hill [3]	d				22 09			22 23	22 24					22 35								22 53	22 54	
Herne Hill [4]	a							22 26														22 56		
Loughborough Jn	a							22 30														23 00		
Elephant & Castle ⊖	a							22 34														23 04		
London Blackfriars [3] ⊖	a							22 37														23 07		
City Thameslink [3]	a							22 40																
St Pancras International [15] ⊖	a							22 47														23 17		
Luton Airport Parkway [7]	a							23 32														00 02		
Luton [10]	a							23 35														00 05		
North Dulwich	d				22 12				22 27					22 38									22 57	
East Dulwich	d				22 14				22 29					22 40									22 59	
Peckham Rye [4]	d		22 26		22 17				22 31					22 43				22 56					23 01	
Queens Rd Peckham	d		22 29		22 19				22 34					22 45				22 59					23 04	
South Bermondsey	d		22 31		22 22				22 36					22 48				23 01					23 06	
London Bridge [4] ⊖	a		22 36		22 26	22 29			22 41				22 45	22 52				23 06		22 59			23 11	

Table 177

Mondays to Fridays
from 21 May

East and West Croydon, London Milton Keynes Central and Luton via Norbury Crystal Palace - Tulse Hill

Local Services

Network Diagram - see first Page of Table 177

		SN	SN	SN	SN ■	SN	SN	SN		SN	SN	FC	SN	SN	SN	SN	SN	SN	SN ◇■	SN	SN	SN	SN	SN
East Croydon	d				22 56	22 47					23 01						23 17		23 30			23 43		
West Croydon ■	d							22 48					23 01	23 04						23 18		23 47		
Norwood Junction ■	a							22 52			23 05									23 22				
	d							22 53			23 06									23 23				
Selhurst ■	d					22 50							23 05	23 09			23 20							
Thornton Heath	d					22 52							23 07	23 11			23 22							
Norbury	d					22 55							23 10	23 14			23 25							
Streatham Common ■	d					22 58							23 13	23 17			23 28							
Beckenham Junction ■	d									22 53											23 23			
Birkbeck	d									22 56											23 26			
Crystal Palace ■	d		22 43	22 51				22 57		23 00						23 13		23 21		23 27	23 30		23 43	23 51
Gipsy Hill	d		22 45					22 59		23 02						23 15				23 29	23 32		23 45	
West Norwood ■	d		22 48					23 02		23 05						23 18				23 32	23 35		23 48	
Streatham Hill	d		22 52					23 06								23 22				23 36			23 52	
Balham ■ ⊖	d		22 56			23 02		23 09						23 21		23 26	23 32			23 40			23 55	
Wandsworth Common	d		22 58			23 04		23 11						23 23		23 28	23 34			23 42			23 58	
Latchmere	d																							
Clapham Junction ■	d		23 03		23 07	23 08		23 15						23 27		23 33	23 38		23 42	23 46			00 02	
Imperial Wharf	d																							
West Brompton ⊖	d																							
Kensington (Olympia) ⊖	d																							
Shepherd's Bush ⊖	d																							
Wembley Central ⊖	d																							
Harrow & Wealdstone ⊖	d																							
Watford Junction	d																							
Milton Keynes Central ■	a																							
Battersea Park ■	d	23 02	23 07			23 11	23 15	23 19							23 32	23 37	23 41			23 49			00 05	
London Victoria ■ ⊖	a	23 06	23 14		23 15	23 16		23 25						23 34	23 37	23 41	23 48		23 52	23 54			00 10	
Streatham ■	d											23 19	23 16											
Tulse Hill ■	d									23 09		23 23	23 24								23 39			
Herne Hill ■	a											23 26												
Loughborough Jn	a																							
Elephant & Castle ⊖	a											23 33												
London Blackfriars ■ ⊖	a											23 37												
City Thameslink ■	a																							
St Pancras International ■ ⊖	a											23 47												
Luton Airport Parkway ■	a											00 32												
Luton ■	a											00 35												
North Dulwich	d									23 12			23 27								23 42			
East Dulwich	d									23 14			23 29								23 44			
Peckham Rye ■	d						23 26			23 17			23 31								23 47			
Queens Rd Peckham	d						23 29			23 19			23 34								23 49			
South Bermondsey	d						23 31			23 22			23 36								23 52			
London Bridge ■ ⊖	a			23 11			23 36			23 26	23 30		23 41					23 45			23 56			00 11

Table 177

Mondays to Fridays
from 21 May

East and West Croydon, London Milton Keynes Central and Luton via Norbury Crystal Palace - Tulse Hill

Local Services

Network Diagram - see first Page of Table 177

		SN ■
East Croydon	d	23 58
West Croydon ■	d	
Norwood Junction ■	a	
	d	
Selhurst ■	d	
Thornton Heath	d	
Norbury	d	
Streatham Common ■	d	
Beckenham Junction ■	d	
Birkbeck	d	
Crystal Palace ■	d	
Gipsy Hill	d	
West Norwood ■	d	
Streatham Hill	d	
Balham ■ ⊖	d	
Wandsworth Common	d	
Latchmere	d	
Clapham Junction ■	d	00 12
Imperial Wharf	d	
West Brompton ⊖	d	
Kensington (Olympia) ⊖	d	
Shepherd's Bush ⊖	d	
Wembley Central ⊖	d	
Harrow & Wealdstone ⊖	d	
Watford Junction	d	
Milton Keynes Central ■	a	
Battersea Park ■	d	
London Victoria ■ ⊖	a	00 18
Streatham ■	d	
Tulse Hill ■	d	
Herne Hill ■	a	
Loughborough Jn	a	
Elephant & Castle ⊖	a	
London Blackfriars ■ ⊖	a	
City Thameslink ■	a	
St Pancras International ■ ⊖	a	
Luton Airport Parkway ■	a	
Luton ■	a	
North Dulwich	d	
East Dulwich	d	
Peckham Rye ■	d	
Queens Rd Peckham	d	
South Bermondsey	d	
London Bridge ■ ⊖	a	

Table 177

Saturdays

East and West Croydon, London Milton Keynes Central and Luton via Norbury Crystal Palace - Tulse Hill

Local Services

Network Diagram - see first Page of Table 177

		FC	FC	SN	SN	SN	SN	SN	SN	SN	FC	FC	SN	FC	FC	SN		FC	FC	SN	FC	FC	FC	FC	FC
						[1]				[1]	[1]		[1]	[1]		[1]		[1]		[1]	[1]		[1]		[1]
		A	A								B			B				B			B		B		B
East Croydon	d					23p58			00 49	01 28	01 50	01 50	02 28	02 47	02 47	03 28		03 47	03 47	04 28	04 47	04 47	05 17	05 17	05 47
West Croydon [4]	d																								
Norwood Junction [2]	a																								
	d																								
Selhurst [4]	d																								
Thornton Heath	d																								
Norbury	d																								
Streatham Common [4]	d																								
Beckenham Junction [4]	d																								
Birkbeck	d																								
Crystal Palace [4]	d			23p43	23p51		00 13	00 21																	
Gipsy Hill	d			23p45			00 15																		
West Norwood [4]	d			23p48			00 18																		
Streatham Hill	d			23p52			00 22																		
Balham [4]	d			23p55			00 25																		
Wandsworth Common	d			23p58			00 27																		
Latchmere	d																								
Clapham Junction [10]	d			00 02		00 12	00 31		01 01	01 41			02 41			03 41				04 41					
Imperial Wharf	d																								
West Brompton	d																								
Kensington (Olympia)	d																								
Shepherd's Bush	d																								
Wembley Central	d																								
Harrow & Wealdstone	d																								
Watford Junction	d																								
Milton Keynes Central [10]	a																								
Battersea Park [4]	d			00 05			00 35																		
London Victoria [15]	a			00 10		00 18	00 42		01 09	01 49			02 49			03 49				04 50					
Streatham [4]	d	22p49	23p19																						
Tulse Hill [3]	d	22p53	23p23																						
Herne Hill [4]	a	22p56	23p26																						
Loughborough Jn	a	23p00																							
Elephant & Castle	a	23p04	23p33																						
London Blackfriars [3]	a	23p07	23p37									02 13			03 13				04 13			05 13		05 43	
City Thameslink [3]	a																								
St Pancras International [15]	a	23p17	23p47									02 24			03 23				04 22			05 24		05 54	
Luton Airport Parkway [7]	a	00 02	00 32									03 09			04 09				05 09			06 09		06 37	
Luton [10]	a	00 05	00 35									03 12			04 12				05 12			06 12		06 40	
North Dulwich	d																								
East Dulwich	d																								
Peckham Rye [4]	d																								
Queens Rd Peckham	d																								
South Bermondsey	d																								
London Bridge [4]	a				00 11			00 41			02 14			03 12				04 12			05 12		05 42		06 01

A not 19 May

B 19 May

Table 177

Saturdays

East and West Croydon, London Milton Keynes Central and Luton via Norbury Crystal Palace - Tulse Hill

Local Services

Network Diagram - see first Page of Table 177

		FC	FC	FC	SN	SN	SN	FC		FC	SN	SN	SN	SN	SN	SN	SN	SN	FC	FC	SN	SN	SN	FC
							◇[1]				[1]				[1]		◇[1]							
		A						A												A				
East Croydon	d		05 47				06 07				06 10				06 25	06 30	06 41				06 43		06 47	
West Croydon [4]	d													06 18										
Norwood Junction [2]	a													06 22	06 29	06 34					06 49			
	d				05 52									06 23	06 29	06 35		06 41			06 50			
Selhurst [4]	d	05 39		05 39		06 01		06 09		06 09	06 13								06 39	06 39			06 50	
Thornton Heath	d	05 41		05 41		06 03		06 11		06 11	06 16								06 41	06 41			06 52	
Norbury	d	05 43		05 43		06 06		06 13		06 13	06 19								06 43	06 43			06 55	
Streatham Common [4]	d	05 46		05 46		06 08		06 16		06 16	06 21								06 46	06 46			06 58	
Beckenham Junction [4]	d																							
Birkbeck	d																							
Crystal Palace [4]	d				05 56									06 27				06 45						
Gipsy Hill	d				05 59									06 29				06 47						
West Norwood [4]	d				06 02									06 32				06 50						
Streatham Hill	d				06 05									06 36										
Balham [4]	d				06 09	06 12					06 28			06 39									07 02	
Wandsworth Common	d				06 11	06 14					06 30			06 41									07 04	
Latchmere	d																							
Clapham Junction [10]	d				06 15	06 18	06 19				06 39			06 45			06 50						07 08	
Imperial Wharf	d										06 44													
West Brompton	d										06 47													
Kensington (Olympia)	d										06 50													
Shepherd's Bush	d										06 53													
Wembley Central	d										07 07													
Harrow & Wealdstone	d										07 12													
Watford Junction	d										07 19													
Milton Keynes Central [10]	a										08 00													
Battersea Park [4]	d				06 18	06 22						06 32	06 45	06 48								07 02	07 11	
London Victoria [15]	a				06 23	06 26	06 26					06 36		06 53			06 57					07 06	07 16	
Streatham [4]	d	05 49		05 49				06 19		06 19									06 49	06 49				07 08
Tulse Hill [3]	d	05 55		05 55				06 23		06 25								06 54	06 55	06 57				07 12
Herne Hill [4]	a			05 59						06 29									06 59	07 01				07 16
Loughborough Jn	a									06 34									07 04					07 19
Elephant & Castle	a			06 08						06 38									07 08					07 23
London Blackfriars [3]	a		06 08	06 12						06 42									07 12					07 27
City Thameslink [3]	a																							
St Pancras International [15]	a		06 16	06 23						06 53									07 23					07 40
Luton Airport Parkway [7]	a		06 50	07 07						07 37									08 07					08 25
Luton [10]	a		06 53	07 11						07 41									08 10					08 29
North Dulwich	d																	06 57						
East Dulwich	d																	06 59						
Peckham Rye [4]	d												06 56					07 01						
Queens Rd Peckham	d												06 59					07 04						
South Bermondsey	d												07 01					07 06						
London Bridge [4]	a	06 09						06 35					07 06		06 43	06 59		07 14			07 11			

A 19 May

East and West Croydon, London
Milton Keynes Central and Luton via Norbury
Crystal Palace - Tulse Hill

Local Services

Network Diagram - see first Page of Table 177

Station		SN	SN	SN ■	SN	SN ■	SN ◇■	SN	FC A	SN	SN ■	SN	SN	SN	SN ◇■	FC		SN	SN	SN ■	SN	SN	SN ■	FC A	SN
East Croydon	d			06 55	07 00	07 07	07 10				07 10			07 17	07 30					07 25		07 30	07 39		
West Croydon	d		06 45					06 58		07 01		07 15									07 28				07 31
Norwood Junction	a		06 52	06 59	07 04	07 12						07 19								07 29		07 34	07 44		
	d		06 53	06 59	07 05	07 13						07 20							07 23	07 29		07 35	07 45		
Selhurst	d							07 02		07 05	07 13			07 20							07 32				07 35
Thornton Heath	d							07 04		07 07	07 16			07 22							07 34				07 37
Norbury	d							07 07		07 10	07 19			07 25							07 37				07 40
Streatham Common	d							07 10		07 13	07 21			07 28							07 40				07 43
Beckenham Junction	d																								
Birkbeck	d																								
Crystal Palace	d		06 57																07 27						
Gipsy Hill	d		06 59																07 29						
West Norwood	d		07 02																07 32						
Streatham Hill	d		07 06																07 36						
Balham	d		07 09					07 14			07 28			07 32					07 39		07 44				
Wandsworth Common	d		07 11					07 16			07 30			07 34					07 41		07 46				
Latchmere	d																								
Clapham Junction	d		07 15				07 19	07 20			07 39			07 38	07 39				07 45		07 50				
Imperial Wharf	d										07 44														
West Brompton	d										07 47														
Kensington (Olympia)	d										07 50														
Shepherd's Bush	d										07 53														
Wembley Central	d										08 07														
Harrow & Wealdstone	d										08 12														
Watford Junction	d										08 19														
Milton Keynes Central	a										09 00														
Battersea Park	d	07 15	07 19					07 23					07 32	07 41				07 45	07 48		07 53				
London Victoria	a		07 24				07 27	07 28					07 36	07 46	07 46				07 53		07 58				
Streatham	d								07 10	07 16						07 38								07 40	07 46
Tulse Hill	d								07 17	07 24						07 42								07 47	07 54
Herne Hill	a															07 46									
Loughborough Jn	a															07 49									
Elephant & Castle	a															07 53									
London Blackfriars	a															07 57									
City Thameslink	a																								
St Pancras International	a															08 10									
Luton Airport Parkway	a															08 55									
Luton	a															08 59									
North Dulwich	d									07 27															07 57
East Dulwich	d									07 29															07 59
Peckham Rye	d	07 26								07 31								07 56							08 01
Queens Rd Peckham	d	07 29								07 34								07 59							08 04
South Bermondsey	d	07 31								07 36								08 01							08 06
London Bridge	a	07 36		07 13	07 29	07 25			07 30	07 41		07 41						08 06		07 43		07 59	07 57	08 00	08 11

A 19 May

Table 177 Saturdays

East and West Croydon, London
Milton Keynes Central and Luton via Norbury
Crystal Palace - Tulse Hill

Local Services

Network Diagram - see first Page of Table 177

Station		SN ◇■	SN	SN	SN	SN	SN ◇■	FC		SN	SN	SN	SN ■	SN	SN	SN ■	FC A	SN	SN ■	SN ◇■	SN	SN	SN	SN ◇■
East Croydon	d	07 42				07 47	08 00					07 51	07 55		08 00	08 07			08 10	08 12				08 28
West Croydon	d		07 45											07 58				08 01						
Norwood Junction	a		07 49									07 55	07 59		08 04	08 12								
	d		07 50								07 53	07 55	07 59		08 05	08 13								
Selhurst	d					07 50								08 02				08 05	08 13					
Thornton Heath	d					07 52								08 04				08 07	08 16					
Norbury	d					07 55								08 07				08 10	08 19					
Streatham Common	d					07 58								08 10				08 13	08 21					
Beckenham Junction	d																							
Birkbeck	d																							
Crystal Palace	d				07 43						07 57											08 13	08 21	
Gipsy Hill	d				07 45						07 59											08 15		
West Norwood	d				07 48						08 02											08 18		
Streatham Hill	d				07 52						08 06											08 22		
Balham	d				07 55	08 02					08 09			08 14					08 28			08 25		
Wandsworth Common	d				07 57	08 04					08 11			08 16					08 30			08 27		
Latchmere	d																							
Clapham Junction	d	07 51			08 01	08 08	08 10				08 15			08 20					08 39	08 21		08 31		08 37
Imperial Wharf	d																		08 44					
West Brompton	d																		08 47					
Kensington (Olympia)	d																		08 50					
Shepherd's Bush	d																		08 53					
Wembley Central	d																		09 07					
Harrow & Wealdstone	d																		09 12					
Watford Junction	d																		09 19					
Milton Keynes Central	a																		10 00					
Battersea Park	d			08 02	08 05	08 11				08 15	08 18			08 23							08 32	08 35		
London Victoria	a	07 58		08 06	08 09	08 16	08 16				08 23			08 28						08 28	08 36	08 39		08 44
Streatham	d							08 08									08 10	08 16						
Tulse Hill	d							08 12									08 17	08 24						
Herne Hill	a							08 16																
Loughborough Jn	a							08 19																
Elephant & Castle	a							08 23																
London Blackfriars	a							08 27																
City Thameslink	a																							
St Pancras International	a							08 40																
Luton Airport Parkway	a							09 25																
Luton	a							09 29																
North Dulwich	d																	08 27						
East Dulwich	d																	08 29						
Peckham Rye	d									08 26								08 31						
Queens Rd Peckham	d									08 29								08 34						
South Bermondsey	d									08 31								08 36						
London Bridge	a		08 11							08 36		08 09	08 13		08 29	08 25	08 30	08 41					08 41	

A 19 May

Table 177

Saturdays

East and West Croydon, London
Milton Keynes Central and Luton via Norbury
Crystal Palace - Tulse Hill

Local Services

Network Diagram - see first Page of Table 177

		SN	SN	SN	SN	SN ■	SN	SN ■	SN	FC	SN ◇■	SN	FC A	SN	SN	SN		SN	SN	SN	SN ◇■	SN	SN	SN	SN ■
East Croydon	d	08 17			08 21	08 25	08 30	08 37			08 40								08 47		09 00			08 51	08 55
West Croydon	d			08 15								08 28		08 31	08 34								08 45		
Norwood Junction	a			08 19	08 25	08 29	08 34	08 42															08 49	08 55	08 59
	d			08 22	08 25	08 29	08 35	08 43															08 52	08 55	08 59
Selhurst	d	08 20										08 32		08 35	08 39				08 50						
Thornton Heath	d	08 22										08 34		08 37	08 41				08 52						
Norbury	d	08 25										08 37		08 40	08 44				08 55						
Streatham Common	d	08 28										08 40		08 43	08 47				08 58						
Beckenham Junction	d								08 23																
Birkbeck	d								08 26																
Crystal Palace	d			08 26					08 30									08 43		08 51			08 56		
Gipsy Hill	d			08 29					08 32									08 45					08 58		
West Norwood	d			08 32					08 35									08 48					09 01		
Streatham Hill	d			08 35														08 52					09 06		
Balham ⊖	d	08 32		08 39								08 44			08 51			08 55	09 02				09 09		
Wandsworth Common	d	08 34		08 41								08 46			08 53			08 57	09 04				09 11		
Latchmere	d																								
Clapham Junction	d	08 38		08 45							08 50	08 50			08 57			09 01	09 08		09 10		09 15		
Imperial Wharf	d																								
West Brompton ⊖	d																								
Kensington (Olympia) ⊖	d																								
Shepherd's Bush ⊖	d																								
Wembley Central ⊖	d																								
Harrow & Wealdstone ⊖	d																								
Watford Junction	d																								
Milton Keynes Central	a																								
Battersea Park	d	08 41	08 45	08 48								08 53				09 02		09 05	09 11			09 15	09 18		
London Victoria ⊖	a	08 46		08 53							08 57	08 58			09 04	09 06		09 09	09 16		09 16		09 23		
Streatham	d									08 38			08 40	08 46											
Tulse Hill	d								08 39	08 42			08 47	08 54											
Herne Hill	a									08 46															
Loughborough Jn	a									08 49															
Elephant & Castle ⊖	a									08 53															
London Blackfriars ⊖	a									08 57															
City Thameslink	a									09 02															
St Pancras International ⊖	a									09 10															
Luton Airport Parkway	a									09 55															
Luton	a									09 59															
North Dulwich	d								08 42					08 57											
East Dulwich	d								08 44					08 59											
Peckham Rye	d		08 56						08 46					09 01								09 26			
Queens Rd Peckham	d		08 59						08 49					09 04								09 29			
South Bermondsey	d		09 01						08 51					09 06								09 31			
London Bridge ⊖	a		09 06		08 39	08 43	08 59	08 55	08 56				09 00	09 11						09 11		09 36		09 09	09 13

A 19 May

Table 177

Saturdays

East and West Croydon, London
Milton Keynes Central and Luton via Norbury
Crystal Palace - Tulse Hill

Local Services

Network Diagram - see first Page of Table 177

		SN	SN	SN ■	SN	FC	FC A	SN		SN ◇■	SN	SN	SN	SN ■	SN	SN ◇■	SN	SN	SN	SN	SN ■	SN	SN ■	SN	
East Croydon	d		09 00	09 07						09 12				09 10		09 28	09 17			09 21	09 25	09 30	09 37		
West Croydon	d	08 58						09 01			09 04								09 15						
Norwood Junction	a		09 04	09 12															09 19	09 25	09 29	09 34	09 42		
	d		09 05	09 13															09 22	09 25	09 29	09 35	09 43		
Selhurst	d	09 02						09 05			09 09			09 13			09 20								
Thornton Heath	d	09 04						09 07			09 11			09 16			09 22								
Norbury	d	09 07						09 10			09 14			09 19			09 25								
Streatham Common	d	09 10						09 13			09 17			09 21			09 28								
Beckenham Junction	d				08 53																			09 23	
Birkbeck	d				08 56																			09 26	
Crystal Palace	d				09 00								09 13		09 21				09 26					09 30	
Gipsy Hill	d				09 02								09 15						09 29					09 32	
West Norwood	d				09 05								09 18						09 32					09 35	
Streatham Hill	d												09 22						09 35						
Balham ⊖	d	09 14									09 21		09 25	09 28			09 32		09 39						
Wandsworth Common	d	09 16									09 23		09 27	09 30			09 34		09 41						
Latchmere	d																								
Clapham Junction	d	09 20								09 21	09 27		09 32	09 39		09 37	09 38		09 45						
Imperial Wharf	d													09 44											
West Brompton ⊖	d													09 47											
Kensington (Olympia) ⊖	d													09 50											
Shepherd's Bush ⊖	d													09 53											
Wembley Central ⊖	d													10 07											
Harrow & Wealdstone ⊖	d													10 12											
Watford Junction	d													10 19											
Milton Keynes Central	a													11 00											
Battersea Park	d	09 23										09 32	09 36				09 41	09 45	09 48						
London Victoria ⊖	a	09 28								09 28	09 34	09 36	09 40			09 44	09 46		09 53						
Streatham	d					09 08	09 10	09 16																	
Tulse Hill	d				09 09	09 12	09 17	09 24																09 39	
Herne Hill	a					09 16																			
Loughborough Jn	a					09 19																			
Elephant & Castle ⊖	a					09 23																			
London Blackfriars ⊖	a					09 27																			
City Thameslink	a					09 32																			
St Pancras International ⊖	a					09 40																			
Luton Airport Parkway	a					10 25																			
Luton	a					10 29																			
North Dulwich	d				09 12			09 27																09 42	
East Dulwich	d				09 14			09 29																09 44	
Peckham Rye	d				09 16			09 31										09 56						09 46	
Queens Rd Peckham	d				09 19			09 34										09 59						09 49	
South Bermondsey	d				09 21			09 36										10 01						09 51	
London Bridge ⊖	a		09 29	09 25	09 26		09 30	09 41							09 41			10 06		09 39	09 43	09 59	09 55	09 56	

A 19 May

Table 177

Saturdays

East and West Croydon, London Milton Keynes Central and Luton via Norbury Crystal Palace - Tulse Hill

Local Services

Network Diagram - see first Page of Table 177

		FC	SN ◇1	SN	FC A	SN	SN	SN	SN	SN	SN	SN ◇1	SN	SN	SN	SN 1		SN	SN	SN 1	SN	FC	FC A	SN	SN ◇1
East Croydon	d		09 40							09 47		10 00			09 51	09 55			10 00	10 07					10 12
West Croydon 4	d			09 28		09 31	09 34							09 45				09 58						10 01	
Norwood Junction 2	a													09 49	09 55	09 59			10 04	10 12					
	d													09 52	09 55	09 59			10 05	10 13					
Selhurst 4	d			09 32		09 35	09 39			09 50								10 02						10 05	
Thornton Heath	d			09 34		09 37	09 41			09 52								10 04						10 07	
Norbury	d			09 37		09 40	09 44			09 55								10 07						10 10	
Streatham Common 4	d			09 40		09 43	09 47			09 58								10 10						10 13	
Beckenham Junction 4	d																				09 53				
Birkbeck	d																				09 56				
Crystal Palace 4	d								09 43		09 51			09 56							10 00				
Gipsy Hill	d								09 45					09 59							10 02				
West Norwood 4	d								09 48					10 02							10 05				
Streatham Hill	d								09 52					10 05											
Balham 4 ⊖	d			09 44			09 51		09 55	10 02				10 09				10 14							
Wandsworth Common	d			09 46			09 53		09 57	10 04				10 11				10 16							
Latchmere	d																								
Clapham Junction 10	d		09 50	09 50			09 57		10 01	10 08		10 10		10 15				10 20							10 21
Imperial Wharf	d																								
West Brompton ⊖	d																								
Kensington (Olympia) ⊖	d																								
Shepherd's Bush ⊖	d																								
Wembley Central ⊖	d																								
Harrow & Wealdstone ⊖	d																								
Watford Junction	d																								
Milton Keynes Central 10	a																								
Battersea Park 4	d			09 53				10 02	10 05	10 11			10 15	10 18				10 23							
London Victoria 15 ⊖	a		09 57	09 58			10 04	10 06	10 09	10 16		10 16		10 23				10 28							10 28
Streatham 4	d	09 38			09 40	09 46																10 08	10 10	10 16	
Tulse Hill 3	d	09 42			09 47	09 54															10 09	10 12	10 17	10 24	
Herne Hill 4	a	09 46																				10 16			
Loughborough Jn	a	09 49																				10 19			
Elephant & Castle ⊖	a	09 53																				10 23			
London Blackfriars 3 ⊖	a	09 57																				10 27			
City Thameslink 3	a	10 02																				10 32			
St Pancras International 15 ⊖	a	10 10																				10 40			
Luton Airport Parkway 7	a	10 55																				11 25			
Luton 10	a	10 59																				11 29			
North Dulwich	d					09 57															10 12			10 27	
East Dulwich	d					09 59															10 14			10 29	
Peckham Rye 4	d					10 01							10 26								10 16			10 31	
Queens Rd Peckham	d					10 04							10 29								10 19			10 34	
South Bermondsey	d					10 06							10 3								10 21			10 36	
London Bridge 4 ⊖	a				10 00	10 11					10 11		10 36		10 09	10 13			10 29	10 25	10 26		10 30	10 41	

A 19 May

Table 177

Saturdays

East and West Croydon, London Milton Keynes Central and Luton via Norbury Crystal Palace - Tulse Hill

Local Services

Network Diagram - see first Page of Table 177

		SN	SN	SN	SN 1	SN	SN ◇1	SN		SN	SN	SN	SN 1	SN	SN 1	SN	FC	SN ◇1	SN	FC A	SN	SN	SN	SN
East Croydon	d				10 10		10 28	10 17				10 21	10 25	10 30	10 37			10 40						
West Croydon 4	d	10 04									10 15								10 28		10 31	10 34		
Norwood Junction 2	a										10 19	10 25	10 29	10 34	10 42									
	d										10 22	10 25	10 29	10 35	10 43									
Selhurst 4	d	10 09			10 13			10 20											10 32		10 35	10 39		
Thornton Heath	d	10 11			10 16			10 22											10 34		10 37	10 41		
Norbury	d	10 14			10 19			10 25											10 37		10 40	10 44		
Streatham Common 4	d	10 17			10 21			10 28											10 40		10 43	10 47		
Beckenham Junction 4	d															10 23								
Birkbeck	d															10 26								
Crystal Palace 4	d			10 13		10 21					10 26					10 30								10 43
Gipsy Hill	d			10 15							10 29					10 32								10 45
West Norwood 4	d			10 18							10 32					10 35								10 48
Streatham Hill	d			10 22							10 35													10 52
Balham 4 ⊖	d	10 21		10 25	10 28			10 32			10 39								10 44			10 51		10 55
Wandsworth Common	d	10 23		10 27	10 30			10 34			10 41								10 46			10 53		10 57
Latchmere	d																							
Clapham Junction 10	d	10 27		10 31	10 39		10 37	10 38			10 45							10 50	10 50			10 57		11 01
Imperial Wharf	d				10 44																			
West Brompton ⊖	d				10 47																			
Kensington (Olympia) ⊖	d				10 50																			
Shepherd's Bush ⊖	d				10 53																			
Wembley Central ⊖	d				11 08																			
Harrow & Wealdstone ⊖	d				11 13																			
Watford Junction	d				11 20																			
Milton Keynes Central 10	a				12 00																			
Battersea Park 4	d		10 32	10 35				10 41		10 45	10 48								10 53				11 02	11 05
London Victoria 15 ⊖	a	10 34	10 36	10 39			10 44	10 46			10 53							10 57	10 58			11 04	11 06	11 09
Streatham 4	d																10 38			10 40	10 46			
Tulse Hill 3	d															10 39	10 42			10 47	10 54			
Herne Hill 4	a																10 46							
Loughborough Jn	a																10 49							
Elephant & Castle ⊖	a																10 53							
London Blackfriars 3 ⊖	a																10 57							
City Thameslink 3	a																11 02							
St Pancras International 15 ⊖	a																11 10							
Luton Airport Parkway 7	a																11 55							
Luton 10	a																11 59							
North Dulwich	d															10 42					10 57			
East Dulwich	d															10 44					10 59			
Peckham Rye 4	d									10 56						10 46					11 01			
Queens Rd Peckham	d									10 59						10 49					11 04			
South Bermondsey	d									11 01						10 51					11 06			
London Bridge 4 ⊖	a					10 41				11 06		10 39	10 43	10 59	10 55	10 56				11 00	11 11			

A 19 May

Table 177

Saturdays

East and West Croydon, London Milton Keynes Central and Luton via Norbury Crystal Palace - Tulse Hill

Local Services

Network Diagram - see first Page of Table 177

Station		SN	SN	SN ◇1	SN	SN	SN	SN 1	SN	SN	SN 1	SN	FC	FC A	SN	SN ◇1		SN	SN	SN	SN 1	SN	SN ◇1	SN	SN
East Croydon	d	10 47		11 00			10 51	10 55		11 00	11 07					11 12					11 10		11 28	11 17	
West Croydon 4	d					10 45			10 58						11 01			11 04							
Norwood Junction 2	a					10 49	10 55	10 59		11 04	11 12														
	d					10 52	10 55	10 59		11 05	11 13														
Selhurst 4	d	10 50							11 02						11 05			11 09			11 13			11 20	
Thornton Heath	d	10 52							11 04						11 07			11 11			11 16			11 22	
Norbury	d	10 55							11 07						11 10			11 14			11 19			11 25	
Streatham Common 4	d	10 58							11 10						11 13			11 17			11 21			11 28	
Beckenham Junction 4	d											10 53													
Birkbeck	d											10 56													
Crystal Palace 4	d		10 51			10 56						11 00								11 13		11 21			
Gipsy Hill	d					10 59						11 02								11 15					
West Norwood 4	d					11 02						11 05								11 18					
Streatham Hill	d					11 05														11 22					
Balham 4 ⊖	d	11 02				11 09			11 14									11 21		11 25	11 28			11 32	
Wandsworth Common	d	11 04				11 11			11 16									11 23		11 27	11 30			11 34	
Latchmere	d																								
Clapham Junction 10	d	11 08		11 10		11 15			11 20							11 21		11 27		11 31	11 39		11 37	11 38	
Imperial Wharf	d																				11 44				
West Brompton ⊖	d																				11 47				
Kensington (Olympia) ⊖	d																				11 50				
Shepherd's Bush ⊖	d																				11 53				
Wembley Central ⊖	d																				12 07				
Harrow & Wealdstone ⊖	d																				12 13				
Watford Junction	d																				12 20				
Milton Keynes Central 10	a																				13 00				
Battersea Park 4	d	11 11			11 15	11 18			11 23										11 32	11 35				11 41	11 45
London Victoria 15 ⊖	a	11 16		11 16		11 23			11 28							11 28		11 34	11 36	11 39			11 44	11 46	
Streatham 4	d												11 08	11 10	11 16										
Tulse Hill 3	d											11 09	11 12	11 17	11 24										
Herne Hill 4	a												11 16												
Loughborough Jn	a												11 19												
Elephant & Castle ⊖	a												11 23												
London Blackfriars 3 ⊖	a												11 27												
City Thameslink 3	a												11 32												
St Pancras International 15 ⊖	a												11 40												
Luton Airport Parkway 7	a												12 25												
Luton 10	a												12 29												
North Dulwich	d											11 12			11 27										
East Dulwich	d											11 14			11 29										
Peckham Rye 4	d				11 26							11 16			11 31										11 56
Queens Rd Peckham	d				11 29							11 19			11 34										11 59
South Bermondsey	d				11 31							11 21			11 36										12 01
London Bridge 4 ⊖	a		11 11		11 36		11 09	11 13		11 29	11 25	11 26		11 30	11 41							11 41			12 06

A 19 May

Table 177

Saturdays

East and West Croydon, London Milton Keynes Central and Luton via Norbury Crystal Palace - Tulse Hill

Local Services

Network Diagram - see first Page of Table 177

Station		SN	SN	SN 1	SN	SN 1	SN	FC		SN ◇1	SN	FC A	SN	SN	SN	SN	SN	SN	SN ◇1	SN	SN	SN	SN 1	SN
East Croydon	d		11 21	11 25	11 30	11 37				11 40							11 47		12 00			11 51	11 55	
West Croydon 4	d	11 15									11 28		11 31	11 34							11 45			11 58
Norwood Junction 2	a	11 19	11 25	11 29	11 34	11 42															11 49	11 55	11 59	
	d	11 22	11 25	11 29	11 35	11 43															11 52	11 55	11 59	
Selhurst 4	d										11 32		11 35	11 39			11 50							12 02
Thornton Heath	d										11 34		11 37	11 41			11 52							12 04
Norbury	d										11 37		11 40	11 44			11 55							12 07
Streatham Common 4	d										11 40		11 43	11 47			11 58							12 10
Beckenham Junction 4	d						11 23																	
Birkbeck	d						11 26																	
Crystal Palace 4	d	11 26					11 30									11 43		11 51			11 56			
Gipsy Hill	d	11 29					11 32									11 45					11 59			
West Norwood 4	d	11 32					11 35									11 48					12 02			
Streatham Hill	d	11 35														11 52					12 05			
Balham 4 ⊖	d	11 39									11 44			11 51		11 55	12 02				12 09			12 14
Wandsworth Common	d	11 41									11 46			11 53		11 57	12 04				12 11			12 16
Latchmere	d																							
Clapham Junction 10	d	11 45								11 50	11 50			11 57		12 01	12 08		12 10		12 15			12 20
Imperial Wharf	d																							
West Brompton ⊖	d																							
Kensington (Olympia) ⊖	d																							
Shepherd's Bush ⊖	d																							
Wembley Central ⊖	d																							
Harrow & Wealdstone ⊖	d																							
Watford Junction	d																							
Milton Keynes Central 10	a																							
Battersea Park 4	d	11 48									11 53				12 02	12 05	12 11			12 15	12 18			12 23
London Victoria 15 ⊖	a	11 53								11 57	11 58			12 04	12 06	12 09	12 16		12 16		12 23			12 28
Streatham 4	d							11 38				11 40	11 46											
Tulse Hill 3	d						11 39	11 42				11 47	11 54											
Herne Hill 4	a							11 46																
Loughborough Jn	a							11 49																
Elephant & Castle ⊖	a							11 53																
London Blackfriars 3 ⊖	a							11 57																
City Thameslink 3	a							12 02																
St Pancras International 15 ⊖	a							12 10																
Luton Airport Parkway 7	a							12 55																
Luton 10	a							12 59																
North Dulwich	d						11 42						11 57											
East Dulwich	d						11 44						11 59											
Peckham Rye 4	d						11 46						12 01							12 26				
Queens Rd Peckham	d						11 49						12 04							12 29				
South Bermondsey	d						11 51						12 06							12 31				
London Bridge 4 ⊖	a		11 39	11 43	11 59	11 55	11 56					12 00	12 11					12 11		12 36		12 09	12 13	

A 19 May

East and West Croydon, London Milton Keynes Central and Luton via Norbury Crystal Palace - Tulse Hill

Local Services

Network Diagram - see first Page of Table 177

		SN	SN ■	SN	FC	FC A	SN	SN ◇■	SN	SN	SN	SN ■	SN	SN ◇■	SN	SN		SN	SN	SN ■	SN	SN ■	SN	FC	SN ◇■
East Croydon	d	12 00	12 07					12 12				12 10		12 28	12 17				12 21	12 25	12 30	12 38			12 40
West Croydon	d						12 01		12 04									12 15							
Norwood Junction	a	12 04	12 12															12 19	12 25	12 29	12 34	12 42			
	d	12 05	12 13															12 22	12 25	12 29	12 35	12 43			
Selhurst	d						12 05		12 09			12 13			12 20										
Thornton Heath	d						12 07		12 11			12 16			12 22										
Norbury	d						12 10		12 14			12 19			12 25										
Streatham Common	d						12 13		12 17			12 21			12 28										
Beckenham Junction	d			11 53																			12 23		
Birkbeck	d			11 56																			12 26		
Crystal Palace	d			12 00							12 13		12 21					12 26					12 30		
Gipsy Hill	d			12 02							12 15							12 29					12 32		
West Norwood	d			12 05							12 18							12 32					12 35		
Streatham Hill	d										12 22							12 35							
Balham ⊖	d								12 21		12 25	12 28			12 32			12 39							
Wandsworth Common	d								12 23		12 27	12 30			12 34			12 41							
Latchmere	d																								12 50
Clapham Junction	d							12 21	12 27		12 31	12 39		12 37	12 38			12 45							
Imperial Wharf	d											12 44													
West Brompton ⊖	d											12 47													
Kensington (Olympia) ⊖	d											12 50													
Shepherd's Bush ⊖	d											12 53													
Wembley Central ⊖	d											13 07													
Harrow & Wealdstone ⊖	d											13 12													
Watford Junction	d											13 19													
Milton Keynes Central	a											14 00													
Battersea Park	d									12 32	12 35				12 41	12 45		12 48							12 57
London Victoria ⊖	a							12 28	12 34	12 36	12 39			12 44	12 46			12 53							
Streatham	d				12 08	12 10	12 16																	12 38	
Tulse Hill	d			12 09	12 12	12 17	12 24																12 39	12 42	
Herne Hill	a				12 16																			12 46	
Loughborough Jn	a				12 19																			12 49	
Elephant & Castle ⊖	a				12 23																			12 53	
London Blackfriars ⊖	a				12 27																			12 57	
City Thameslink	a				12 32																			13 02	
St Pancras International ⊖	a				12 40																			13 10	
Luton Airport Parkway	a				13 25																			13 55	
Luton	a				13 29																			13 59	
North Dulwich	d			12 12			12 27																12 42		
East Dulwich	d			12 14			12 29																12 44		
Peckham Rye	d			12 16			12 31									12 56							12 46		
Queens Rd Peckham	d			12 19			12 34									12 59							12 49		
South Bermondsey	d			12 21			12 36									13 01							12 51		
London Bridge ⊖	a	12 29	12 25	12 26		12 30	12 41						12 44			13 06			12 39	12 43	12 59	12 55	12 56		

A 19 May

Table 177 Saturdays

East and West Croydon, London Milton Keynes Central and Luton via Norbury Crystal Palace - Tulse Hill

Local Services

Network Diagram - see first Page of Table 177

		SN	FC A	SN	SN	SN	SN	SN		SN	SN ◇■	SN	SN	SN	SN ■	SN	SN	SN ■	SN	FC	FC A	SN	SN ◇■	SN
East Croydon	d							12 47			13 00			12 51	12 55		13 00	13 07					13 12	
West Croydon	d	12 28		12 31	12 34								12 45			12 58						13 01		13 04
Norwood Junction	a												12 49	12 55	12 59		13 04	13 12						
	d												12 52	12 55	12 59		13 05	13 13						
Selhurst	d	12 32		12 35	12 39			12 50								13 02						13 05		13 09
Thornton Heath	d	12 34		12 37	12 41			12 52								13 04						13 07		13 11
Norbury	d	12 37		12 40	12 44			12 55								13 07						13 10		13 14
Streatham Common	d	12 40		12 43	12 47			12 57								13 10						13 13		13 17
Beckenham Junction	d																		12 53					
Birkbeck	d																		12 56					
Crystal Palace	d						12 43			12 51			12 56						13 00					
Gipsy Hill	d						12 45						12 59						13 02					
West Norwood	d						12 48						13 02						13 05					
Streatham Hill	d						12 52						13 05											
Balham ⊖	d	12 44			12 51		12 55	13 01					13 09			13 14								13 21
Wandsworth Common	d	12 46			12 53		12 57	13 03					13 11			13 16								13 23
Latchmere	d																							
Clapham Junction	d	12 50			12 57		13 01	13 07			13 10		13 15			13 20							13 21	13 27
Imperial Wharf	d																							
West Brompton ⊖	d																							
Kensington (Olympia) ⊖	d																							
Shepherd's Bush ⊖	d																							
Wembley Central ⊖	d																							
Harrow & Wealdstone ⊖	d																							
Watford Junction	d																							
Milton Keynes Central	a																							
Battersea Park	d	12 53				13 02	13 05	13 11				13 15	13 18			13 23								
London Victoria ⊖	a	12 58			13 04	13 06	13 09	13 16			13 16		13 23			13 28							13 28	13 34
Streatham	d		12 40	12 46																13 08	13 10	13 16		
Tulse Hill	d		12 47	12 54															13 09	13 12	13 17	13 24		
Herne Hill	a																			13 16				
Loughborough Jn	a																			13 19				
Elephant & Castle ⊖	a																			13 23				
London Blackfriars ⊖	a																			13 27				
City Thameslink	a																			13 32				
St Pancras International ⊖	a																			13 40				
Luton Airport Parkway	a																			14 25				
Luton	a																			14 29				
North Dulwich	d			12 57															13 12			13 27		
East Dulwich	d			12 59															13 14			13 29		
Peckham Rye	d			13 01								13 26							13 16			13 31		
Queens Rd Peckham	d			13 04								13 29							13 19			13 34		
South Bermondsey	d			13 06								13 31							13 21			13 36		
London Bridge ⊖	a		13 00	13 11						13 11		13 36		13 09	13 13		13 29	13 25	13 26		13 30	13 41		

A 19 May

Table 177

East and West Croydon, London Milton Keynes Central and Luton via Norbury Crystal Palace - Tulse Hill

Local Services

Network Diagram - see first Page of Table 177

		SN	SN	SN 1	SN	SN ◇1	SN	SN	SN	SN	SN 1	SN	SN 1	SN	FC	SN ◇1		SN	FC A	SN	SN	SN	SN	SN	SN
East Croydon	d			13 10		13 28	13 17			13 21	13 25	13 30	13 37			13 40								13 47	
West Croydon 4	d								13 15									13 28		13 31	13 34				
Norwood Junction 2	a								13 19	13 25	13 29	13 34	13 42												
	d								13 22	13 25	13 29	13 35	13 43												
Selhurst 4	d			13 13			13 20											13 32		13 35	13 39			13 50	
Thornton Heath	d			13 16			13 22											13 34		13 37	13 41			13 52	
Norbury	d			13 19			13 25											13 37		13 40	13 44			13 55	
Streatham Common 4	d			13 21			13 28											13 40		13 43	13 47			13 58	
Beckenham Junction 4	d													13 23											
Birkbeck	d													13 26											
Crystal Palace 4	d		13 13		13 21				13 26					13 30									13 43		13 51
Gipsy Hill	d		13 15						13 29					13 32									13 45		
West Norwood 4	d		13 18						13 32					13 35									13 48		
Streatham Hill	d		13 22						13 35														13 52		
Balham 4 ⊖	d		13 25	13 28			13 32		13 39									13 44			13 51		13 55	14 02	
Wandsworth Common	d		13 27	13 30			13 34		13 41									13 46			13 53		13 57	14 04	
Latchmere	d																								
Clapham Junction 10	d		13 31	13 39		13 37	13 38		13 45							13 50		13 50			13 57		14 01	14 08	
Imperial Wharf	d			13 44																					
West Brompton ⊖	d			13 47																					
Kensington (Olympia) ⊖	d			13 50																					
Shepherd's Bush ⊖	d			13 53																					
Wembley Central ⊖	d			14 08																					
Harrow & Wealdstone ⊖	d			14 13																					
Watford Junction	d			14 20																					
Milton Keynes Central 10	a			15 00																					
Battersea Park 4	d	13 32	13 35				13 41	13 45	13 48									13 53				14 02	14 05	14 11	
London Victoria 15 ⊖	a	13 36	13 39			13 44	13 46		13 53							13 57		13 58			14 04	14 06	14 09	14 16	
Streatham 4	d														13 38				13 40	13 46					
Tulse Hill 3	d													13 39	13 42				13 47	13 54					
Herne Hill 4	a														13 46										
Loughborough Jn	a														13 49										
Elephant & Castle ⊖	a														13 53										
London Blackfriars 3 ⊖	a														13 57										
City Thameslink 3	a														14 02										
St Pancras International 15 ⊖	a														14 10										
Luton Airport Parkway 7	a														14 55										
Luton 10	a														14 59										
North Dulwich	d													13 42						13 57					
East Dulwich	d													13 44						13 59					
Peckham Rye 4	d							13 56						13 46						14 01					
Queens Rd Peckham	d							13 59						13 49						14 04					
South Bermondsey	d							14 01						13 51						14 06					
London Bridge 4 ⊖	a				13 44			14 06		13 39	13 43	13 59	13 55	13 56					14 00	14 11					14 11

A 19 May

Table 177

East and West Croydon, London Milton Keynes Central and Luton via Norbury Crystal Palace - Tulse Hill

Local Services

Network Diagram - see first Page of Table 177

		SN ◇1	SN	SN	SN	SN 1	SN	SN		SN 1	SN	FC	FC A	SN	SN ◇1	SN	SN	SN	SN 1	SN	SN ◇1	SN	SN	SN
East Croydon	d	14 00			13 51	13 55		14 00		14 07					14 12				14 10		14 28	14 17		
West Croydon 4	d			13 45			13 58							14 01		14 04								14 15
Norwood Junction 2	a			13 49	13 55	13 59		14 04		14 12														14 19
	d			13 52	13 55	13 59		14 05		14 13														14 22
Selhurst 4	d						14 02							14 05		14 09			14 13			14 20		
Thornton Heath	d						14 04							14 07		14 11			14 16			14 22		
Norbury	d						14 07							14 10		14 14			14 19			14 25		
Streatham Common 4	d						14 10							14 13		14 17			14 21			14 28		
Beckenham Junction 4	d										13 53													
Birkbeck	d										13 56													
Crystal Palace 4	d			13 56							14 00							14 13		14 21				14 26
Gipsy Hill	d			13 59							14 02							14 15						14 29
West Norwood 4	d			14 02							14 05							14 18						14 32
Streatham Hill	d			14 05														14 22						14 35
Balham 4 ⊖	d			14 09			14 14									14 21		14 25	14 28			14 32		14 39
Wandsworth Common	d			14 11			14 16									14 23		14 27	14 30			14 34		14 41
Latchmere	d																							
Clapham Junction 10	d	14 10		14 15			14 20								14 21	14 27		14 31	14 39		14 37	14 38		14 45
Imperial Wharf	d																		14 44					
West Brompton ⊖	d																		14 47					
Kensington (Olympia) ⊖	d																		14 50					
Shepherd's Bush ⊖	d																		14 53					
Wembley Central ⊖	d																		15 07					
Harrow & Wealdstone ⊖	d																		15 12					
Watford Junction	d																		15 19					
Milton Keynes Central 10	a																		16 00					
Battersea Park 4	d		14 15	14 18			14 23										14 32	14 35				14 41	14 45	14 48
London Victoria 15 ⊖	a	14 16		14 23			14 28								14 28	14 34	14 36	14 39			14 44	14 46		14 53
Streatham 4	d											14 08	14 10	14 16										
Tulse Hill 3	d										14 09	14 12	14 17	14 24										
Herne Hill 4	a											14 16												
Loughborough Jn	a											14 19												
Elephant & Castle ⊖	a											14 23												
London Blackfriars 3 ⊖	a											14 27												
City Thameslink 3	a											14 32												
St Pancras International 15 ⊖	a											14 40												
Luton Airport Parkway 7	a											15 25												
Luton 10	a											15 29												
North Dulwich	d										14 12			14 27										
East Dulwich	d										14 14			14 29										
Peckham Rye 4	d		14 26								14 16			14 31									14 56	
Queens Rd Peckham	d		14 29								14 19			14 34									14 59	
South Bermondsey	d		14 31								14 21			14 36									15 01	
London Bridge 4 ⊖	a		14 36		14 09	14 13		14 29		14 25	14 26		14 30	14 41						14 44			15 06	

A 19 May

Table 177

East and West Croydon, London
Milton Keynes Central and Luton via Norbury
Crystal Palace - Tulse Hill

Local Services

Network Diagram - see first Page of Table 177

		SN	SN ■1	SN	SN ■1	SN	FC	SN ◇■1	SN	FC A	SN	SN	SN	SN	SN	SN		SN ◇■1	SN	SN	SN	SN ■1	SN	SN	SN ■1
East Croydon	d	14 21	14 25	14 30	14 37			14 40							14 47			15 00			14 51	14 55		15 00	15 07
West Croydon	d								14 28		14 31	14 34								14 45			14 58		
Norwood Junction	a	14 25	14 29	14 34	14 42															14 49	14 55	14 59		15 04	15 12
	d	14 25	14 29	14 35	14 43															14 52	14 55	14 59		15 05	15 13
Selhurst	d								14 32		14 35	14 39			14 50								15 02		
Thornton Heath	d								14 34		14 37	14 41			14 52								15 04		
Norbury	d								14 37		14 40	14 44			14 55								15 07		
Streatham Common	d								14 40		14 43	14 47			14 58								15 10		
Beckenham Junction	d					14 23																			
Birkbeck	d					14 26																			
Crystal Palace	d					14 30								14 43		14 51				14 56					
Gipsy Hill	d					14 32								14 45						14 59					
West Norwood	d					14 35								14 48						15 02					
Streatham Hill	d													14 52						15 05					
Balham	d								14 44			14 51		14 55	15 02					15 09			15 14		
Wandsworth Common	d								14 46			14 53		14 57	15 04					15 11			15 16		
Latchmere	d																								
Clapham Junction	d							14 50	14 50			14 57		15 01	15 08			15 10		15 15			15 20		
Imperial Wharf	d																								
West Brompton	d																								
Kensington (Olympia)	d																								
Shepherd's Bush	d																								
Wembley Central	d																								
Harrow & Wealdstone	d																								
Watford Junction	d																								
Milton Keynes Central	a																								
Battersea Park	d								14 53				15 02	15 05	15 11				15 15	15 18			15 23		
London Victoria	a							14 57	14 58			15 04	15 06	15 09	15 16			15 16		15 23			15 28		
Streatham	d						14 38			14 40	14 46														
Tulse Hill	d					14 39	14 42			14 47	14 54														
Herne Hill	a						14 46																		
Loughborough Jn	a						14 49																		
Elephant & Castle	a						14 53																		
London Blackfriars	a						14 57																		
City Thameslink	a						15 02																		
St Pancras International	a						15 10																		
Luton Airport Parkway	a						15 55																		
Luton	a						15 59																		
North Dulwich	d					14 42					14 57														
East Dulwich	d					14 44					14 59														
Peckham Rye	d					14 46					15 01								15 26						
Queens Rd Peckham	d					14 49					15 04								15 29						
South Bermondsey	d					14 51					15 06								15 31						
London Bridge	a	14 39	14 43	14 59	14 55	14 56				15 00	15 11					15 11			15 36		15 09	15 13		15 29	15 25

A 19 May

Table 177

East and West Croydon, London
Milton Keynes Central and Luton via Norbury
Crystal Palace - Tulse Hill

Local Services

Network Diagram - see first Page of Table 177

		SN	FC	FC A	SN	SN ◇■1	SN	SN		SN	SN ■1	SN	SN ◇■1	SN	SN	SN	SN	SN ■1	SN	SN ■1	SN	FC	SN ◇■1	SN	
East Croydon	d					15 12					15 10		15 28	15 17			15 21	15 25	15 30	15 37			15 40		
West Croydon	d				15 01		15 04									15 15								15 28	
Norwood Junction	a															15 19	15 25	15 29	15 34	15 42					
	d															15 22	15 25	15 29	15 35	15 43					
Selhurst	d				15 05		15 09				15 13			15 20										15 32	
Thornton Heath	d				15 07		15 11				15 16			15 22										15 34	
Norbury	d				15 10		15 14				15 19			15 25										15 37	
Streatham Common	d				15 13		15 17				15 21			15 28										15 40	
Beckenham Junction	d	14 53																			15 23				
Birkbeck	d	14 56																			15 26				
Crystal Palace	d	15 00								15 13		15 21				15 26					15 30				
Gipsy Hill	d	15 02								15 15						15 29					15 32				
West Norwood	d	15 05								15 18						15 32					15 35				
Streatham Hill	d									15 22						15 35									
Balham	d						15 21			15 25	15 28			15 32		15 39								15 44	
Wandsworth Common	d						15 23			15 27	15 30			15 34		15 41								15 46	
Latchmere	d																								
Clapham Junction	d					15 21	15 27			15 31	15 39		15 37	15 38		15 45							15 50	15 50	
Imperial Wharf	d										15 44														
West Brompton	d										15 47														
Kensington (Olympia)	d										15 50														
Shepherd's Bush	d										15 53														
Wembley Central	d										16 07														
Harrow & Wealdstone	d										16 12														
Watford Junction	d										16 19														
Milton Keynes Central	a										17 00														
Battersea Park	d							15 32		15 35				15 41	15 45	15 48								15 53	
London Victoria	a					15 28	15 34	15 36		15 39			15 44	15 46		15 53							15 57	15 58	
Streatham	d		15 08	15 10	15 16																	15 38			
Tulse Hill	d	15 09	15 12	15 17	15 24																15 39	15 42			
Herne Hill	a		15 16																			15 46			
Loughborough Jn	a		15 19																			15 49			
Elephant & Castle	a		15 23																			15 53			
London Blackfriars	a		15 27																			15 57			
City Thameslink	a		15 32																			16 02			
St Pancras International	a		15 40																			16 10			
Luton Airport Parkway	a		16 25																			16 55			
Luton	a		16 29																			16 59			
North Dulwich	d	15 12			15 27																15 42				
East Dulwich	d	15 14			15 29																15 44				
Peckham Rye	d	15 16			15 31										15 56						15 46				
Queens Rd Peckham	d	15 19			15 34										15 59						15 49				
South Bermondsey	d	15 21			15 36										16 01						15 51				
London Bridge	a	15 26		15 30	15 41							15 44			16 06		15 39	15 43	15 59	15 55	15 56				

A 19 May

Table 177

Saturdays

East and West Croydon, London
Milton Keynes Central and Luton via Norbury
Crystal Palace - Tulse Hill

Local Services

Network Diagram - see first Page of Table 177

		FC	SN	SN	SN	SN	SN	SN	SN	SN	SN	SN	SN	SN	SN	SN	SN	FC	FC	SN	SN	SN	SN	SN
		A							◇1				1			1			A		◇1			
East Croydon	d						15 47		16 00			15 51	15 55		16 00	16 07					16 12			
West Croydon	d		15 31	15 34							15 45			15 58						16 01		16 04		
Norwood Junction	a										15 49	15 55	15 59		16 04	16 12								
	d										15 52	15 55	15 59		16 05	16 13								
Selhurst	d		15 35	15 39			15 50							16 02						16 05		16 09		
Thornton Heath	d		15 37	15 41			15 52							16 04						16 07		16 11		
Norbury	d		15 40	15 44			15 55							16 07						16 10		16 14		
Streatham Common	d		15 43	15 47			15 58							16 10						16 13		16 17		
Beckenham Junction	d																15 53							
Birkbeck	d																15 56							
Crystal Palace	d					15 43		15 51			15 56						16 00							16 13
Gipsy Hill	d					15 45					15 59						16 02							16 15
West Norwood	d					15 48					16 02						16 05							16 18
Streatham Hill	d					15 52					16 05													16 22
Balham	d			15 51		15 55	16 02				16 09			16 14								16 21		16 25
Wandsworth Common	d			15 53		15 57	16 04				16 11			16 16								16 23		16 27
Latchmere	d																							
Clapham Junction	d			15 57		16 01	16 08		16 10		16 15			16 20							16 21	16 27		16 31
Imperial Wharf	d																							
West Brompton	d																							
Kensington (Olympia)	d																							
Shepherd's Bush	d																							
Wembley Central	d																							
Harrow & Wealdstone	d																							
Watford Junction	d																							
Milton Keynes Central	a																							
Battersea Park	d				16 02	16 05	16 11			16 15	16 18			16 23									16 32	16 35
London Victoria	a			16 04	16 06	16 09	16 16		16 16		16 23			16 28							16 28	16 34	16 36	16 39
Streatham	d	15 40	15 46															16 08	16 10	16 16				
Tulse Hill	d	15 47	15 54														16 09	16 12	16 17	16 24				
Herne Hill	a																	16 16						
Loughborough Jn	a																	16 19						
Elephant & Castle	a																	16 23						
London Blackfriars	a																	16 27						
City Thameslink	a																	16 32						
St Pancras International	a																	16 40						
Luton Airport Parkway	a																	17 25						
Luton	a																	17 29						
North Dulwich	d		15 57														16 12			16 27				
East Dulwich	d		15 59														16 14			16 29				
Peckham Rye	d		16 01							16 26							16 16			16 31				
Queens Rd Peckham	d		16 04							16 29							16 19			16 34				
South Bermondsey	d		16 06							16 31							16 21			16 36				
London Bridge	a	16 00	16 11					16 11		16 36		16 09	16 13		16 29	16 25	16 26		16 30	16 41				

A 19 May

Table 177

Saturdays

East and West Croydon, London
Milton Keynes Central and Luton via Norbury
Crystal Palace - Tulse Hill

Local Services

Network Diagram - see first Page of Table 177

		SN	SN	SN	SN	SN	SN	SN	SN	SN	SN	SN	FC	SN	SN	FC	SN	SN	SN	SN	SN	SN	SN
		1		◇1					1		1			◇1		A							◇1
East Croydon	d	16 10		16 28	16 17			16 21	16 25	16 30	16 37			16 40							16 47		17 00
West Croydon	d						16 15								16 28		16 31	16 34					
Norwood Junction	a						16 19	16 25	16 29	16 34	16 42												
	d						16 22	16 25	16 29	16 35	16 43												
Selhurst	d	16 13			16 20										16 32		16 35	16 39			16 50		
Thornton Heath	d	16 16			16 22										16 34		16 37	16 41			16 52		
Norbury	d	16 19			16 25										16 37		16 40	16 44			16 55		
Streatham Common	d	16 21			16 28										16 40		16 43	16 47			16 58		
Beckenham Junction	d											16 23											
Birkbeck	d											16 26											
Crystal Palace	d		16 21				16 26					16 30								16 43		16 51	
Gipsy Hill	d						16 29					16 32								16 45			
West Norwood	d						16 32					16 35								16 48			
Streatham Hill	d						16 35													16 52			
Balham	d	16 28			16 32		16 39								16 44			16 51		16 55	17 02		
Wandsworth Common	d	16 30			16 34		16 41								16 46			16 53		16 57	17 04		
Latchmere	d																						
Clapham Junction	d	16 39		16 37	16 38		16 45							16 50	16 50			16 57		17 01	17 08		17 10
Imperial Wharf	d	16 44																					
West Brompton	d	16 47																					
Kensington (Olympia)	d	16 50																					
Shepherd's Bush	d	16 53																					
Wembley Central	d	17 07																					
Harrow & Wealdstone	d	17 12																					
Watford Junction	d	17 19																					
Milton Keynes Central	a	18 00																					
Battersea Park	d				16 41	16 45	16 48								16 53				17 02	17 05	17 11		
London Victoria	a			16 44	16 46		16 53							16 57	16 58			17 04	17 06	17 09	17 16		17 16
Streatham	d												16 38			16 40	16 46						
Tulse Hill	d											16 39	16 42			16 47	16 54						
Herne Hill	a												16 46										
Loughborough Jn	a												16 49										
Elephant & Castle	a												16 53										
London Blackfriars	a												16 57										
City Thameslink	a												17 02										
St Pancras International	a												17 10										
Luton Airport Parkway	a												17 55										
Luton	a												17 59										
North Dulwich	d											16 42					16 57						
East Dulwich	d											16 44					16 59						
Peckham Rye	d					16 56						16 46					17 01						
Queens Rd Peckham	d					16 59						16 49					17 04						
South Bermondsey	d					17 01						16 51					17 06						
London Bridge	a		16 41			17 06		16 39	16 43	16 59	16 55	16 56				17 00	17 11					17 11	

A 19 May

Table 177

Saturdays

East and West Croydon, London Milton Keynes Central and Luton via Norbury Crystal Palace - Tulse Hill

Local Services

Network Diagram - see first Page of Table 177

		SN	SN	SN	SN	SN	SN	SN	SN	FC	FC	SN	SN	SN	SN	SN		SN	SN	SN	SN	SN	SN	SN	SN
					■			■			A		◇■					■		◇■					■
East Croydon	d			16 51	16 55		17 00	17 07					17 12					17 10		17 28	17 17			17 21	17 25
West Croydon 4	d		16 45			16 58						17 01		17 04									17 15		
Norwood Junction 2	a		16 50	16 55	16 59		17 04	17 12															17 19	17 25	17 29
	d		16 52	16 55	16 59		17 05	17 13															17 22	17 25	17 29
Selhurst 4	d					17 02						17 05		17 09				17 13			17 20				
Thornton Heath	d					17 04						17 07		17 11				17 16			17 22				
Norbury	d					17 07						17 10		17 14				17 19			17 25				
Streatham Common 4	d					17 10						17 13		17 17				17 21			17 28				
Beckenham Junction 4	d								16 53																
Birkbeck	d								16 56																
Crystal Palace 4	d		16 56						17 00							17 13			17 21				17 26		
Gipsy Hill	d		16 59						17 02							17 15							17 29		
West Norwood 4	d		17 02						17 05							17 18							17 32		
Streatham Hill	d		17 05													17 22							17 35		
Balham 4	d		17 09			17 14								17 21		17 25		17 28			17 33		17 39		
Wandsworth Common	d		17 11			17 16								17 23		17 27		17 30			17 35		17 41		
Latchmere	d																								
Clapham Junction 10	d		17 15			17 20							17 21	17 27		17 31		17 39		17 37	17 39		17 45		
Imperial Wharf	d																	17 44							
West Brompton	d																	17 47							
Kensington (Olympia)	d																	17 50							
Shepherd's Bush	d																	17 53							
Wembley Central	d																	18 07							
Harrow & Wealdstone	d																	18 12							
Watford Junction	d																	18 19							
Milton Keynes Central 10	a																	19 00							
Battersea Park 4	d	17 15	17 18			17 23									17 32	17 35					17 42	17 45	17 48		
London Victoria 15	a		17 23			17 28							17 28	17 34	17 36	17 39				17 44	17 47		17 53		
Streatham 4	d									17 08	17 10	17 16													
Tulse Hill 3	d								17 09	17 12	17 17	17 24													
Herne Hill 4	a									17 16															
Loughborough Jn	a									17 19															
Elephant & Castle	a									17 23															
London Blackfriars 3	a									17 27															
City Thameslink 3	a									17 32															
St Pancras International 15	a									17 40															
Luton Airport Parkway 7	a									18 25															
Luton 10	a									18 29															
North Dulwich	d								17 12			17 27													
East Dulwich	d								17 14			17 29													
Peckham Rye 4	d	17 26							17 16			17 31										17 56			
Queens Rd Peckham	d	17 29							17 19			17 34										17 59			
South Bermondsey	d	17 31							17 21			17 36										18 01			
London Bridge 4	a	17 36		17 09	17 13		17 30	17 25	17 26		17 30	17 41							17 41			18 06		17 39	17 43

A 19 May

Table 177

Saturdays

East and West Croydon, London Milton Keynes Central and Luton via Norbury Crystal Palace - Tulse Hill

Local Services

Network Diagram - see first Page of Table 177

		SN	SN	SN	FC	SN	SN	FC		SN	SN	SN	SN	SN	SN	SN	SN	SN	SN	SN	SN	SN	SN	SN	
			■			◇■		A								◇■				■			■		
East Croydon	d	17 30	17 37			17 40								17 47		18 00			17 51	17 55		18 00	18 07		
West Croydon 4	d						17 28			17 31	17 34							17 45			17 58				
Norwood Junction 2	a	17 34	17 42															17 49	17 55	17 59		18 04	18 12		
	d	17 35	17 43															17 52	17 55	17 59		18 05	18 13		
Selhurst 4	d						17 32			17 35	17 39			17 50							18 02				
Thornton Heath	d						17 34			17 37	17 41			17 52							18 04				
Norbury	d						17 37			17 40	17 44			17 55							18 07				
Streatham Common 4	d						17 40			17 43	17 47			17 58							18 10				
Beckenham Junction 4	d			17 23																				17 53	
Birkbeck	d			17 26																				17 56	
Crystal Palace 4	d			17 30									17 43		17 51			17 56						18 00	
Gipsy Hill	d			17 32									17 45					17 59						18 02	
West Norwood 4	d			17 35									17 48					18 02						18 05	
Streatham Hill	d												17 52					18 05							
Balham 4	d						17 44				17 51		17 55	18 02				18 09			18 14				
Wandsworth Common	d						17 46				17 53		17 57	18 04				18 11			18 16				
Latchmere	d																								
Clapham Junction 10	d					17 50	17 50				17 57		18 01	18 08		18 10		18 15			18 20				
Imperial Wharf	d																								
West Brompton	d																								
Kensington (Olympia)	d																								
Shepherd's Bush	d																								
Wembley Central	d																								
Harrow & Wealdstone	d																								
Watford Junction	d																								
Milton Keynes Central 10	a																								
Battersea Park 4	d						17 53					18 02	18 05	18 11			18 15	18 18			18 23				
London Victoria 15	a					17 57	17 58				18 04	18 06	18 09	18 16		18 16		18 23			18 28				
Streatham 4	d				17 38			17 40		17 46															
Tulse Hill 3	d			17 39	17 42			17 47		17 54														18 09	
Herne Hill 4	a				17 46																				
Loughborough Jn	a				17 49																				
Elephant & Castle	a				17 53																				
London Blackfriars 3	a				17 57																				
City Thameslink 3	a				18 02																				
St Pancras International 15	a				18 10																				
Luton Airport Parkway 7	a				18 55																				
Luton 10	a				18 59																				
North Dulwich	d			17 42						17 57														18 12	
East Dulwich	d			17 44						17 59														18 14	
Peckham Rye 4	d			17 46						18 01							18 26							18 16	
Queens Rd Peckham	d			17 49						18 04							18 29							18 19	
South Bermondsey	d			17 51						18 06							18 31							18 21	
London Bridge 4	a	17 59	17 55	17 56				18 00		18 11					18 11		18 36		18 09	18 13		18 29	18 25	18 26	

A 19 May

Table 177

East and West Croydon, London
Milton Keynes Central and Luton via Norbury
Crystal Palace - Tulse Hill

Local Services

Network Diagram - see first Page of Table 177

		FC	FC	SN	SN	SN	SN	SN	SN	SN	SN	SN	SN	SN	SN	SN		SN	SN	SN	FC	SN	SN	FC	SN
					◇1				1		◇1 ᴛ					1			1			◇1			
			A																					A	
East Croydon	d				18 12				18 10		18 28	18 17			18 21	18 25		18 30	18 37			18 40			
West Croydon 4	d			18 01		18 04								18 15									18 28		18 31
Norwood Junction 2	a													18 19	18 25	18 29		18 34	18 42						
	d													18 22	18 25	18 29		18 35	18 43						
Selhurst 4	d			18 05		18 09			18 13			18 20											18 32		18 35
Thornton Heath	d			18 07		18 11			18 16			18 22											18 34		18 37
Norbury	d			18 10		18 14			18 19			18 25											18 37		18 40
Streatham Common 4	d			18 13		18 17			18 21			18 28											18 40		18 43
Beckenham Junction 4	d																			18 23					
Birkbeck	d																			18 26					
Crystal Palace 4	d							18 13		18 21				18 26						18 30					
Gipsy Hill	d							18 15						18 29						18 32					
West Norwood 4	d							18 18						18 32						18 35					
Streatham Hill	d							18 22						18 35											
Balham 4 ⊖	d					18 21		18 25	18 28			18 32		18 39									18 44		
Wandsworth Common	d					18 23		18 27	18 30			18 34		18 41									18 46		
Latchmere	d																								
Clapham Junction 10	d				18 21	18 27		18 31	18 39		18 37	18 38		18 45								18 50	18 50		
Imperial Wharf	d								18 44																
West Brompton ⊖	d								18 47																
Kensington (Olympia) ⊖	d								18 50																
Shepherd's Bush ⊖	d								18 53																
Wembley Central ⊖	d								19 08																
Harrow & Wealdstone ⊖	d								19 13																
Watford Junction	d								19a21																
Milton Keynes Central 10	a																								
Battersea Park 4	d						18 32	18 35				18 41	18 45	18 48									18 53		
London Victoria 15 ⊖	a				18 28	18 34	18 36	18 39			18 44	18 46		18 53								18 57	18 58		
Streatham 4	d	18 08	18 10	18 16																	18 38			18 40	18 46
Tulse Hill 3	d	18 12	18 17	18 24																18 39	18 42			18 47	18 54
Herne Hill 4	a	18 16																			18 46				
Loughborough Jn	a	18 19																			18 49				
Elephant & Castle ⊖	a	18 23																			18 53				
London Blackfriars 3 ⊖	a	18 27																			18 57				
City Thameslink 3	a	18 32																			19 02				
St Pancras International 15 ⊖	a	18 40																			19 10				
Luton Airport Parkway 7	a	19 25																			19 55				
Luton 10	a	19 29																			19 59				
North Dulwich	d			18 27																18 42					18 57
East Dulwich	d			18 29																18 44					18 59
Peckham Rye 4	d			18 31									18 56							18 46					19 01
Queens Rd Peckham	d			18 34									18 59							18 49					19 04
South Bermondsey	d			18 36									19 01							18 51					19 06
London Bridge 4 ⊖	a		18 30	18 41						18 41			19 06		18 39	18 43		18 59	18 55	18 56				19 00	19 11

A 19 May

Table 177

East and West Croydon, London
Milton Keynes Central and Luton via Norbury
Crystal Palace - Tulse Hill

Local Services

Network Diagram - see first Page of Table 177

		SN	SN	SN	SN	SN	SN	SN		SN	SN	SN	SN	SN	SN	SN	FC	FC	SN	SN	SN	SN	SN	SN	
							◇1					1			1					◇1				1	
																		A							
East Croydon	d				18 47		19 00				18 51	18 55		19 00	19 07					19 12				19 10	
West Croydon 4	d	18 34								18 45			18 58						19 01		19 04				
Norwood Junction 2	a									18 49	18 55	18 59		19 04	19 12										
	d									18 52	18 55	18 59		19 05	19 13										
Selhurst 4	d	18 39			18 50								19 02						19 05		19 09			19 13	
Thornton Heath	d	18 41			18 52								19 04						19 07		19 11			19 16	
Norbury	d	18 44			18 55								19 07						19 10		19 14			19 19	
Streatham Common 4	d	18 47			18 58								19 10						19 13		19 17			19 21	
Beckenham Junction 4	d															18 53									
Birkbeck	d															18 56									
Crystal Palace 4	d			18 43		18 51				18 56						19 00							19 13		
Gipsy Hill	d			18 45						18 59						19 02							19 15		
West Norwood 4	d			18 48						19 02						19 05							19 18		
Streatham Hill	d			18 52						19 05													19 22		
Balham 4 ⊖	d	18 51		18 55	19 02					19 09			19 14								19 21		19 25	19 28	
Wandsworth Common	d	18 53		18 57	19 04					19 11			19 16								19 23		19 27	19 30	
Latchmere	d																								
Clapham Junction 10	d	18 57		19 01	19 08		19 10			19 15			19 20							19 21	19 27		19 31	19 38	
Imperial Wharf	d																							19 42	
West Brompton ⊖	d																							19 45	
Kensington (Olympia) ⊖	d																							19 48	
Shepherd's Bush ⊖	d																							19 50	
Wembley Central ⊖	d																								
Harrow & Wealdstone ⊖	d																							20 08	
Watford Junction	d																							20a15	
Milton Keynes Central 10	a																								
Battersea Park 4	d		19 02	19 05	19 11			19 15		19 18			19 23									19 32	19 35		
London Victoria 15 ⊖	a	19 04	19 06	19 09	19 16		19 16			19 23			19 28							19 28	19 34	19 36	19 39		
Streatham 4	d																19 08	19 10	19 16						
Tulse Hill 3	d															19 09	19 12	19 17	19 24						
Herne Hill 4	a																19 16								
Loughborough Jn	a																19 19								
Elephant & Castle ⊖	a																19 23								
London Blackfriars 3 ⊖	a																19 27								
City Thameslink 3	a																19 32								
St Pancras International 15 ⊖	a																19 40								
Luton Airport Parkway 7	a																20 25								
Luton 10	a																20 29								
North Dulwich	d															19 12			19 27						
East Dulwich	d															19 14			19 29						
Peckham Rye 4	d							19 26								19 16			19 31						
Queens Rd Peckham	d							19 29								19 19			19 34						
South Bermondsey	d							19 31								19 21			19 36						
London Bridge 4 ⊖	a					19 11		19 36			19 09	19 13		19 29	19 25	19 26		19 30	19 41						

A 19 May

Table 177

East and West Croydon, London Milton Keynes Central and Luton via Norbury Crystal Palace - Tulse Hill

Local Services

Network Diagram - see first Page of Table 177

		SN	SN ■	SN	SN ◇■	SN	SN	SN	SN	SN	SN	FC	FC A	SN	SN ◇■	SN		SN	SN	SN	SN ■	SN	SN ■	SN	SN
East Croydon ⇌	d		19 25	19 17	19 29			19 21			19 30				19 42						19 57	19 47	20 00		
West Croydon ■ ⇌	d						19 15			19 28				19 31		19 34									19 45
Norwood Junction ■	a						19 19	19 25			19 34														19 49
	d						19 22	19 25			19 35														19 52
Selhurst ■	d			19 20						19 32				19 35		19 39						19 50			
Thornton Heath	d			19 22						19 34				19 37		19 41						19 52			
Norbury	d			19 25						19 37				19 40		19 44						19 55			
Streatham Common ■	d			19 28						19 40				19 43		19 47						19 58			
Beckenham Junction ■ ⇌	d								19 23																
Birkbeck ⇌	d								19 26																
Crystal Palace ■	d	19 21					19 26		19 30										19 43	19 51					19 56
Gipsy Hill	d						19 29		19 32										19 45						19 59
West Norwood ■	d						19 32		19 35										19 48						20 02
Streatham Hill	d						19 35												19 52						20 05
Balham ■ ⊖	d			19 32			19 39			19 44						19 51			19 55			20 02			20 09
Wandsworth Common	d			19 34			19 41			19 46						19 53			19 57			20 04			20 11
Latchmere	d																								
Clapham Junction ■	d		19 37	19 38	19 40		19 45			19 50					19 51	19 57			20 01		20 09	20 08	20 12		20 15
Imperial Wharf	d																								
West Brompton ⊖	d																								
Kensington (Olympia) ⊖	d																								
Shepherd's Bush ⊖	d																								
Wembley Central ⊖	d																								
Harrow & Wealdstone ⊖	d																								
Watford Junction	d																								
Milton Keynes Central ■	a																								
Battersea Park ■	d			19 41		19 45	19 48			19 53								20 02	20 05			20 11		20 15	20 18
London Victoria ■ ⊖	a		19 44	19 46	19 50		19 53			19 58					19 58	20 04		20 06	20 09		20 15	20 16	20 20		20 23
Streatham ■	d											19 38	19 40	19 46											
Tulse Hill ■	d								19 39			19 42	19 47	19 54											
Herne Hill ■	a											19 46													
Loughborough Jn	a											19 49													
Elephant & Castle ⊖	a											19 53													
London Blackfriars ■ ⊖	a											19 57													
City Thameslink ■	a											20 02													
St Pancras International ■ ⊖	a											20 10													
Luton Airport Parkway ■	a											20 55													
Luton ■	a											20 59													
North Dulwich	d								19 42					19 57											
East Dulwich	d								19 44					19 59											
Peckham Rye ■	d					19 56			19 46					20 01										20 26	
Queens Rd Peckham	d					19 59			19 49					20 04										20 29	
South Bermondsey	d					20 01			19 51					20 06										20 31	
London Bridge ■ ⊖	a	19 41				20 06		19 39	19 56		19 59		20 00	20 11						20 11				20 36	

A 19 May

Table 177

East and West Croydon, London Milton Keynes Central and Luton via Norbury Crystal Palace - Tulse Hill

Local Services

Network Diagram - see first Page of Table 177

		SN	SN	SN	SN	FC	FC A	SN		SN ◇■	SN	SN	SN	SN	SN ■	SN	SN ◇■	SN	SN	SN	SN	SN	SN	FC B
East Croydon ⇌	d	19 51			20 00					20 12					20 26	20 17	20 30			20 21			20 30	
West Croydon ■ ⇌	d			19 58				20 01			20 04								20 15			20 28		
Norwood Junction ■	a	19 55			20 04														20 19	20 25			20 34	
	d	19 55			20 05														20 22	20 25			20 35	
Selhurst ■	d			20 02				20 05			20 09					20 20						20 32		
Thornton Heath	d			20 04				20 07			20 11					20 22						20 34		
Norbury	d			20 07				20 10			20 14					20 25						20 37		
Streatham Common ■	d			20 10				20 13			20 17					20 28						20 40		
Beckenham Junction ■ ⇌	d		19 53																		20 23			
Birkbeck ⇌	d		19 56																		20 26			
Crystal Palace ■	d		20 00										20 13	20 21					20 26		20 30			
Gipsy Hill	d		20 03										20 15						20 29		20 33			
West Norwood ■	d		20 06										20 18						20 32		20 36			
Streatham Hill	d												20 22						20 35					
Balham ■ ⊖	d			20 14							20 21		20 25			20 32			20 39			20 44		
Wandsworth Common	d			20 16							20 23		20 27			20 34			20 41			20 46		
Latchmere	d																							
Clapham Junction ■	d			20 20						20 21	20 27		20 31		20 37	20 38	20 41		20 45			20 50		
Imperial Wharf	d																							
West Brompton ⊖	d																							
Kensington (Olympia) ⊖	d																							
Shepherd's Bush ⊖	d																							
Wembley Central ⊖	d																							
Harrow & Wealdstone ⊖	d																							
Watford Junction	d																							
Milton Keynes Central ■	a																							
Battersea Park ■	d			20 23								20 32	20 35			20 41		20 45	20 48			20 53		
London Victoria ■ ⊖	a			20 28						20 28	20 34	20 36	20 39		20 44	20 46	20 50		20 53			20 58		
Streatham ■	d					20 08	20 10	20 16																20 38
Tulse Hill ■	d		20 09			20 12	20 17	20 24													20 39			20 42
Herne Hill ■	a					20 16																		20 46
Loughborough Jn	a					20 19																		20 49
Elephant & Castle ⊖	a					20 23																		20 53
London Blackfriars ■ ⊖	a					20 27																		20 57
City Thameslink ■	a					20 32																		
St Pancras International ■ ⊖	a					20 40																		21 10
Luton Airport Parkway ■	a					21 25																		
Luton ■	a					21 29																		
North Dulwich	d		20 12					20 27													20 42			
East Dulwich	d		20 14					20 29													20 44			
Peckham Rye ■	d		20 16					20 31										20 56			20 46			
Queens Rd Peckham	d		20 19					20 34										20 59			20 49			
South Bermondsey	d		20 21					20 36										21 01			20 51			
London Bridge ■ ⊖	a	20 09	20 26		20 29		20 30	20 41						20 41				21 06		20 39	20 56		20 59	

A 19 May

B until 23 June

Table 177

Saturdays

East and West Croydon, London
Milton Keynes Central and Luton via Norbury
Crystal Palace - Tulse Hill

Local Services

Network Diagram - see first Page of Table 177

Station		FC A	FC B	SN	SN ◇1	SN	SN	SN	SN	SN 1	SN	SN	SN	SN	SN	SN		FC C	FC A	SN ◇1	SN	FC B	SN	SN	SN
East Croydon	d				20 42					20 56	20 47			20 51		21 00				21 09					
West Croydon 4	d			20 31		20 34							20 45								20 58		21 02	21 04	
Norwood Junction 2	a												20 49	20 55		21 04									
	d												20 52	20 55		21 05									
Selhurst 4	d			20 35		20 39					20 50										21 02		21 06	21 09	
Thornton Heath	d			20 37		20 41					20 52										21 04		21 08	21 11	
Norbury	d			20 40		20 44					20 55										21 07		21 11	21 14	
Streatham Common 4	d			20 43		20 47					20 58										21 10		21 14	21 17	
Beckenham Junction 4	d														20 53										
Birkbeck	d														20 56										
Crystal Palace 4	d							20 43	20 51				20 56		21 00										
Gipsy Hill	d							20 45					20 59		21 02										
West Norwood 4	d							20 48					21 02		21 05										
Streatham Hill	d							20 52					21 05												
Balham 4	⊖ d					20 51		20 55			21 02		21 09								21 14			21 21	
Wandsworth Common	d					20 53		20 57			21 04		21 11								21 16			21 23	
Latchmere	d																								
Clapham Junction 10	d				20 51	20 57		21 01		21 07	21 08		21 15							21 18	21 20			21 27	
Imperial Wharf	d																								
West Brompton	⊖ d																								
Kensington (Olympia)	⊖ d																								
Shepherd's Bush	⊖ d																								
Wembley Central	⊖ d																								
Harrow & Wealdstone	⊖ d																								
Watford Junction	d																								
Milton Keynes Central 10	a																								
Battersea Park 4	d						21 02	21 05			21 11	21 15	21 18								21 23				21 32
London Victoria 15	⊖ a				20 58	21 04	21 06	21 09		21 14	21 16		21 23							21 26	21 28			21 34	21 36
Streatham 4	d	20 38	20 40	20 46														21 08	21 08			21 10	21 17		
Tulse Hill 3	d	20 42	20 47	20 54											21 09			21 12	21 12			21 17	21 24		
Herne Hill 4	a	20 46																21 16	21 16						
Loughborough Jn	a	20 49																21 19	21 19						
Elephant & Castle	⊖ a	20 53																21 23	21 23						
London Blackfriars 3	⊖ a	20 57																21 27	21 27						
City Thameslink 3	a																								
St Pancras International 15	⊖ a	21 10																21 40	21 40						
Luton Airport Parkway 7	a	21 55																	22 25						
Luton 10	a	21 59																	22 29						
North Dulwich	d			20 57											21 12								21 27		
East Dulwich	d			20 59											21 14								21 29		
Peckham Rye 4	d			21 01								21 26			21 16								21 31		
Queens Rd Peckham	d			21 04								21 29			21 19								21 34		
South Bermondsey	d			21 06								21 31			21 21								21 36		
London Bridge 4	⊖ a		21 00	21 11					21 13			21 36		21 09	21 26	21 29						21 30	21 41		

A from 30 June B 19 May C until 23 June

Table 177

Saturdays

East and West Croydon, London
Milton Keynes Central and Luton via Norbury
Crystal Palace - Tulse Hill

Local Services

Network Diagram - see first Page of Table 177

Station		SN	SN	SN 1	SN	SN ◇1	SN	SN		SN	SN	SN	SN	FC A	SN ◇1	FC B	FC C	SN	SN	SN	SN	SN	SN 1	SN
East Croydon	d			21 26	21 17	21 31				21 21			21 30		21 42								21 56	21 47
West Croydon 4	d							21 15				21 28						21 31	21 34					
Norwood Junction 2	a							21 19		21 25			21 34											
	d							21 22		21 25			21 35											
Selhurst 4	d				21 20							21 32						21 35	21 39					21 50
Thornton Heath	d				21 22							21 34						21 37	21 41					21 52
Norbury	d				21 25							21 37						21 40	21 44					21 55
Streatham Common 4	d				21 28							21 40						21 43	21 47					21 58
Beckenham Junction 4	d										21 23													
Birkbeck	d										21 26													
Crystal Palace 4	d	21 13	21 21					21 26			21 30										21 43	21 51		
Gipsy Hill	d	21 15						21 29			21 32										21 45			
West Norwood 4	d	21 18						21 32			21 35										21 48			
Streatham Hill	d	21 22						21 35													21 52			
Balham 4	⊖ d	21 25			21 32			21 39				21 44							21 51		21 55			22 02
Wandsworth Common	d	21 27			21 34			21 41				21 46							21 53		21 57			22 04
Latchmere	d																							
Clapham Junction 10	d	21 31		21 37	21 38	21 41		21 45				21 50			21 51				21 57		22 01		22 07	22 08
Imperial Wharf	d																							
West Brompton	⊖ d																							
Kensington (Olympia)	⊖ d																							
Shepherd's Bush	⊖ d																							
Wembley Central	⊖ d																							
Harrow & Wealdstone	⊖ d																							
Watford Junction	d																							
Milton Keynes Central 10	a																							
Battersea Park 4	d	21 35			21 41		21 45	21 48				21 53								22 02	22 05			22 11
London Victoria 15	⊖ a	21 39		21 44	21 46	21 50		21 53				21 58			21 58				22 04	22 06	22 09		22 15	22 16
Streatham 4	d													21 40		21 49	21 49	21 46						
Tulse Hill 3	d										21 39			21 47		21 53	21 53	21 54						
Herne Hill 4	a															21 56	21 56							
Loughborough Jn	a															22 00	22 00							
Elephant & Castle	⊖ a															22 04	22 04							
London Blackfriars 3	⊖ a															22 07	22 07							
City Thameslink 3	a																							
St Pancras International 15	⊖ a															22 17	22 17							
Luton Airport Parkway 7	a															23 01	23 02							
Luton 10	a															23 04	23 05							
North Dulwich	d										21 42							21 57						
East Dulwich	d										21 44							21 59						
Peckham Rye 4	d						21 56				21 46							22 01						
Queens Rd Peckham	d						21 59				21 49							22 04						
South Bermondsey	d						22 01				21 51							22 06						
London Bridge 4	⊖ a		21 43				22 06			21 39	21 56		21 59	22 00				22 11				22 13		

A 19 May B from 30 June C until 23 June

East and West Croydon, London
Milton Keynes Central and Luton via Norbury
Crystal Palace - Tulse Hill

Local Services

Network Diagram - see first Page of Table 177

		SN	SN	SN	SN	SN	SN	SN	FC	FC	SN	SN	SN	SN	SN	SN		SN	SN	SN	SN	SN	SN	SN	SN
							◇1		A							1			◇1						◇1
East Croydon	d			21 51		22 00	22 09									22 26		22 17	22 31			22 21		22 30	22 40
West Croydon	d		21 45					21 58			22 01	22 04									22 15				
Norwood Junction	a		21 49	21 55		22 04															22 19	22 25		22 34	
	d		21 52	21 55		22 05															22 22	22 25		22 35	
Selhurst	d							22 02			22 05	22 10						22 20							
Thornton Heath	d							22 04			22 07	22 12						22 22							
Norbury	d							22 07			22 10	22 15						22 25							
Streatham Common	d							22 10			22 13	22 17						22 28							
Beckenham Junction	d				21 53																		22 23		
Birkbeck	d				21 56																		22 26		
Crystal Palace	d		21 56		22 00									22 13	22 21						22 26		22 30		
Gipsy Hill	d		21 59		22 02									22 15							22 29		22 32		
West Norwood	d		22 02		22 05									22 18							22 32		22 35		
Streatham Hill	d		22 05											22 22							22 35				
Balham	d		22 09					22 14				22 22		22 25				22 32			22 39				
Wandsworth Common	d		22 11					22 16				22 24		22 27				22 34			22 41				
Latchmere	d																								
Clapham Junction	d		22 15				22 18	22 20				22 27		22 31		22 37		22 38	22 41		22 45				22 50
Imperial Wharf	d																								
West Brompton	d																								
Kensington (Olympia)	d																								
Shepherd's Bush	d																								
Wembley Central	d																								
Harrow & Wealdstone	d																								
Watford Junction	d																								
Milton Keynes Central	a																								
Battersea Park	d	22 15	22 18					22 23					22 32	22 35				22 41		22 45	22 48				
London Victoria	a		22 23				22 26	22 28				22 34	22 36	22 39		22 44		22 46	22 50		22 53				22 57
Streatham	d								22 10	22 19	22 16														
Tulse Hill	d				22 09				22 17	22 23	22 24												22 39		
Herne Hill	a									22 26															
Loughborough Jn	a									22 30															
Elephant & Castle	a									22 34															
London Blackfriars	a									22 37															
City Thameslink	a																								
St Pancras International	a									22 47															
Luton Airport Parkway	a									23 32															
Luton	a									23 35															
North Dulwich	d				22 12						22 27												22 42		
East Dulwich	d				22 14						22 29												22 44		
Peckham Rye	d	22 26			22 16						22 31									22 56			22 46		
Queens Rd Peckham	d	22 29			22 19						22 34									22 59			22 49		
South Bermondsey	d	22 31			22 21						22 36									23 01			22 51		
London Bridge	a	22 36		22 09	22 26	22 29			22 30		22 41				22 43					23 06		22 39	22 56	22 59	

A 19 May

East and West Croydon, London
Milton Keynes Central and Luton via Norbury
Crystal Palace - Tulse Hill

Local Services

Network Diagram - see first Page of Table 177

		SN	FC	FC	SN	SN	SN	SN		SN	SN	SN	SN	SN	SN	SN	SN	SN	FC	SN	SN	SN	SN	SN	
			A								1														
East Croydon	d										22 56	22 47			22 51			23 01						23 17	
West Croydon	d	22 28			22 31	22 34								22 45			22 58			23 01	23 04				
Norwood Junction	a													22 49	22 55			23 05							
	d													22 52	22 55			23 06							
Selhurst	d	22 32			22 35	22 39						22 50					23 02			23 05	23 09			23 20	
Thornton Heath	d	22 34			22 37	22 41						22 52					23 04			23 07	23 11			23 22	
Norbury	d	22 37			22 40	22 44						22 55					23 07			23 10	23 14			23 25	
Streatham Common	d	22 40			22 43	22 47						22 58					23 10			23 13	23 17			23 28	
Beckenham Junction	d															22 53									
Birkbeck	d															22 56									
Crystal Palace	d							22 43		22 51				22 56		23 00							23 13		
Gipsy Hill	d							22 45						22 59		23 02							23 15		
West Norwood	d							22 48						23 02		23 05							23 18		
Streatham Hill	d							22 52						23 05									23 22		
Balham	d	22 44				22 51		22 55				23 02		23 09			23 14				23 21		23 25	23 32	
Wandsworth Common	d	22 46				22 53		22 57				23 04		23 11			23 16				23 23		23 27	23 34	
Latchmere	d																								
Clapham Junction	d	22 50				22 57		23 01			23 07	23 08		23 15			23 20				23 27		23 31	23 38	
Imperial Wharf	d																								
West Brompton	d																								
Kensington (Olympia)	d																								
Shepherd's Bush	d																								
Wembley Central	d																								
Harrow & Wealdstone	d																								
Watford Junction	d																								
Milton Keynes Central	a																								
Battersea Park	d	22 53					23 02	23 05				23 11	23 15	23 18			23 23					23 32	23 35	23 41	
London Victoria	a	22 58				23 04	23 06	23 09			23 14	23 16		23 24			23 29				23 34	23 37	23 41	23 48	
Streatham	d		22 40	22 49	22 46														23 19	23 19					
Tulse Hill	d		22 47	22 53	22 54											23 09			23 23	23 24					
Herne Hill	a			22 56															23 26						
Loughborough Jn	a			23 00																					
Elephant & Castle	a			23 04															23 33						
London Blackfriars	a			23 07															23 37						
City Thameslink	a																								
St Pancras International	a			23 17															23 47						
Luton Airport Parkway	a			00 02															00 32						
Luton	a			00 05															00 35						
North Dulwich	d				22 57											23 12				23 27					
East Dulwich	d				22 59											23 14				23 29					
Peckham Rye	d				23 01								23 26			23 16				23 31					
Queens Rd Peckham	d				23 04								23 29			23 19				23 34					
South Bermondsey	d				23 06								23 31			23 21				23 36					
London Bridge	a		23 00		23 11					23 13			23 36		23 09	23 26		23 30		23 41					

A 19 May

Table 177

Saturdays

East and West Croydon, London
Milton Keynes Central and Luton via Norbury
Crystal Palace - Tulse Hill

Local Services

Network Diagram - see first Page of Table 177

		SN	SN ◇1	SN	SN	SN	SN	SN	SN	SN	SN	SN 1
East Croydon	d		23 30		23 21				23 43			23 56
West Croydon 4	d			23 15			23 28	23 34				
Norwood Junction 2	a			23 19	23 25				23 47			
	d			23 22	23 25							
Selhurst 4	d						23 32	23 39				
Thornton Heath	d						23 34	23 41				
Norbury	d						23 37	23 44				
Streatham Common 4	d						23 40	23 46				
Beckenham Junction 4	d					23 23						
Birkbeck	d					23 26						
Crystal Palace 4	d	23 21		23 26		23 30				23 43	23 51	
Gipsy Hill	d			23 29		23 32				23 45		
West Norwood 4	d			23 32		23 35				23 48		
Streatham Hill	d			23 35						23 52		
Balham 4 ⊖	d			23 39			23 44	23 50		23 55		
Wandsworth Common	d			23 41			23 46	23 52		23 57		
Latchmere	d											
Clapham Junction 10	d		23 42	23 45			23 50	23 56		00 02		00 12
Imperial Wharf	d											
West Brompton ⊖	d											
Kensington (Olympia) ⊖	d											
Shepherd's Bush ⊖	d											
Wembley Central ⊖	d											
Harrow & Wealdstone ⊖	d											
Watford Junction	d											
Milton Keynes Central 10	a											
Battersea Park 4	d			23 49			23 53			00 05		
London Victoria 15 ⊖	a		23 52	23 53			23 58	00 04		00 10		00 18
Streatham 4	d											
Tulse Hill 3	d					23 39						
Herne Hill 4	a											
Loughborough Jn	a											
Elephant & Castle ⊖	a											
London Blackfriars 3 ⊖	a											
City Thameslink 3	a											
St Pancras International 15 ⊖	a											
Luton Airport Parkway 7	a											
Luton 10	a											
North Dulwich	d					23 42						
East Dulwich	d					23 44						
Peckham Rye 4	d					23 46						
Queens Rd Peckham	d					23 49						
South Bermondsey	d					23 51						
London Bridge 4 ⊖	a	23 43			23 39	23 56					00 11	

Table 177

Sundays
until 24 June

East and West Croydon, London
Milton Keynes Central and Luton via Norbury
Crystal Palace - Tulse Hill

Local Services

Network Diagram - see first Page of Table 177

		FC	FC	SN	SN	SN	SN 1	SN	SN	SN	SN 1	SN 1	SN 1	SN 1	FC	SN 1		SN	SN	SN	SN	SN	SN	SN	SN
East Croydon	d						23p56			00 49	01 43	02 40	03 40	04 40	05 32	06 02		06 40	06 47					07 12	07 17
West Croydon 4	d			23p34																		07 07			
Norwood Junction 2	a																		06 51						07 21
	d																		06 52		06 57				07 22
Selhurst 4	d			23p39														06 43		06 47		07 11		07 15	
Thornton Heath	d			23p41														06 45		06 49		07 13		07 17	
Norbury	d			23p44														06 48		06 52		07 16		07 20	
Streatham Common 4	d			23p46														06 51		06 55		07 19		07 23	
Beckenham Junction 4	d																								
Birkbeck	d																								
Crystal Palace 4	d				23p43	23p51		00 13	00 21												07 01		07 07		
Gipsy Hill	d				23p45			00 15													07 03		07 09		
West Norwood 4	d				23p48			00 18													07 06		07 12		
Streatham Hill	d				23p52			00 22													07 10				
Balham 4 ⊖	d			23p50	23p55			00 26										06 55			07 13	07 23			
Wandsworth Common	d			23p52	23p57			00 28										06 57			07 15				
Latchmere	d																								
Clapham Junction 10	d			23p56	00 02		00 12	00 32		01 03	01 54	02 53	03 53	04 53		06 15		07 00			07 19	07 27			
Imperial Wharf	d																								
West Brompton ⊖	d																								
Kensington (Olympia) ⊖	d																								
Shepherd's Bush ⊖	d																								
Wembley Central ⊖	d																								
Harrow & Wealdstone ⊖	d																								
Watford Junction	d																								
Milton Keynes Central 10	a																								
Battersea Park 4	d				00 05			00 35										07 04			07 23				
London Victoria 15 ⊖	a			00 04	00 10		00 18	00 42		01 10	02 05	03 05	04 05	05 05		06 22		07 09			07 27	07 34			
Streatham 4	d	22p49	23p19																	06 58				07 28	
Tulse Hill 3	d	22p53	23p23																	07 02			07 16	07 32	
Herne Hill 4	a	22p56	23p26																						
Loughborough Jn	a	23p00																							
Elephant & Castle ⊖	a	23p04	23p33																						
London Blackfriars 3 ⊖	a	23p07	23p37												05 59										
City Thameslink 3	a																								
St Pancras International 15 ⊖	a	23p17	23p47																						
Luton Airport Parkway 7	a	00 02	00 32																						
Luton 10	a	00 05	00 35																						
North Dulwich	d																			07 05			07 19	07 35	
East Dulwich	d																			07 07			07 21	07 37	
Peckham Rye 4	d																			07 09			07 23	07 39	
Queens Rd Peckham	d																			07 12			07 26	07 42	
South Bermondsey	d																			07 14			07 28	07 44	
London Bridge 4 ⊖	a					00 11			00 41										07 17	07 19			07 33	07 50	07 48

Table 177

East and West Croydon, London
Milton Keynes Central and Luton via Norbury
Crystal Palace - Tulse Hill

Local Services

Network Diagram - see first Page of Table 177

		SN	SN 1	SN	SN	SN	SN	SN		SN	SN	SN	SN	SN ◇1 H	SN	SN	SN 1	SN	SN	SN	SN	SN	SN	SN ◇1
East Croydon ⇌	d		07 27							07 42	07 47		07 53	08 09			07 56				08 12	08 17		08 20
West Croydon 4 ⇌	d				07 22	07 34	07 37									07 52		08 04	08 07					
Norwood Junction 2	a				07 26	07 39					07 51					07 56	08 00	08 09				08 21		
	d				07 27	07 40					07 52					07 57	08 01	08 10				08 22		
Selhurst 4	d		07 31				07 41			07 46			07 57						08 11		08 16			
Thornton Heath	d						07 43			07 48			07 59						08 13		08 18			
Norbury	d						07 46			07 51			08 02						08 16		08 21			
Streatham Common 4	d						07 49			07 53			08 04						08 19		08 23			
Beckenham Junction 4 ⇌	d																							
Birkbeck ⇌	d																							
Crystal Palace 4	d				07 31			07 37								08 01				08 07				
Gipsy Hill	d				07 33			07 39								08 03				08 09				
West Norwood 4	d				07 36			07 42								08 06				08 12				
Streatham Hill	d				07 40											08 10								
Balham 4 ⊖	d				07 43		07 53						08 08			08 13			08 23					
Wandsworth Common	d				07 45											08 15								
Latchmere	d																							
Clapham Junction 10	d		07 41		07 49		07 57						08 13	08 19		08 19			08 27					08 32
Imperial Wharf	d																							
West Brompton ⊖	d																							
Kensington (Olympia) ⊖	d																							
Shepherd's Bush ⊖	d																							
Wembley Central ⊖	d																							
Harrow & Wealdstone ⊖	d																							
Watford Junction	d																							
Milton Keynes Central 10	a																							
Battersea Park 4	d	07 32		07 45	07 53							08 02			08 15	08 23							08 32	
London Victoria 15 ⊖	a	07 36	07 48		07 57		08 04					08 06	08 20	08 25		08 27			08 34				08 36	08 39
Streatham 4	d									07 58											08 28			
Tulse Hill 3	d							07 46		08 02										08 16	08 32			
Herne Hill 4	a																							
Loughborough Jn	a																							
Elephant & Castle ⊖	a																							
London Blackfriars 3 ⊖	a																							
City Thameslink 3	a																							
St Pancras International 15 ⊖	a																							
Luton Airport Parkway 7	a																							
Luton 10	a																							
North Dulwich	d							07 49		08 05										08 19	08 35			
East Dulwich	d							07 51		08 07										08 21	08 37			
Peckham Rye 4	d			07 56				07 53		08 10					08 26					08 23	08 40			
Queens Rd Peckham	d			07 59				07 56		08 12					08 29					08 26	08 42			
South Bermondsey	d			08 01				07 58		08 15					08 31					08 28	08 45			
London Bridge 4 ⊖	a			08 06		08 01		08 03		08 19	08 17				08 36		08 12	08 31		08 33	08 49	08 48		

Table 177

East and West Croydon, London
Milton Keynes Central and Luton via Norbury
Crystal Palace - Tulse Hill

Local Services

Network Diagram - see first Page of Table 177

		SN	SN ◇1	SN	SN	SN 1	SN	SN	SN	SN	SN	SN	SN	SN ◇1 H	SN	SN		SN 1	SN	SN	SN	SN	SN	SN	SN ◇1
East Croydon ⇌	d	08 23	08 39			08 34				08 42	08 47		08 53	09 09				08 56				09 12	09 17		09 20
West Croydon 4 ⇌	d				08 22		08 34	08 37								08 52			09 04	09 07					
Norwood Junction 2	a				08 26	08 38	08 39				08 51					08 56		09 00	09 09				09 21		
	d				08 27	08 38	08 40				08 52					08 57		09 01	09 10				09 22		
Selhurst 4	d	08 26						08 41		08 46			08 57							09 11		09 16			
Thornton Heath	d	08 28						08 43		08 48			08 59							09 13		09 18			
Norbury	d	08 31						08 46		08 51			09 02							09 16		09 21			
Streatham Common 4	d	08 34						08 49		08 53			09 04							09 19		09 23			
Beckenham Junction 4 ⇌	d																								
Birkbeck ⇌	d																								
Crystal Palace 4	d				08 31				08 37							09 01					09 07				
Gipsy Hill	d				08 33				08 39							09 03					09 09				
West Norwood 4	d				08 36				08 42							09 06					09 12				
Streatham Hill	d				08 40											09 10									
Balham 4 ⊖	d	08 38			08 43			08 53					09 08			09 13				09 23					
Wandsworth Common	d				08 45											09 15									
Latchmere	d																								
Clapham Junction 10	d	08 42	08 48		08 49			08 57					09 13	09 19		09 19				09 27					09 32
Imperial Wharf	d																								
West Brompton ⊖	d																								
Kensington (Olympia) ⊖	d																								
Shepherd's Bush ⊖	d																								
Wembley Central ⊖	d																								
Harrow & Wealdstone ⊖	d																								
Watford Junction	d																								
Milton Keynes Central 10	a																								
Battersea Park 4	d			08 45	08 52							09 02			09 15	09 23								09 32	
London Victoria 15 ⊖	a	08 50	08 55		08 57			09 04				09 06	09 20	09 25		09 27				09 34				09 36	09 39
Streatham 4	d									08 58												09 28			
Tulse Hill 3	d								08 46	09 02											09 16	09 32			
Herne Hill 4	a																								
Loughborough Jn	a																								
Elephant & Castle ⊖	a																								
London Blackfriars 3 ⊖	a																								
City Thameslink 3	a																								
St Pancras International 15 ⊖	a																								
Luton Airport Parkway 7	a																								
Luton 10	a																								
North Dulwich	d								08 49	09 05											09 19	09 35			
East Dulwich	d								08 51	09 07											09 21	09 37			
Peckham Rye 4	d			08 56					08 53	09 10					09 26						09 23	09 40			
Queens Rd Peckham	d			08 59					08 56	09 12					09 29						09 26	09 42			
South Bermondsey	d			09 01					08 58	09 15					09 31						09 28	09 45			
London Bridge 4 ⊖	a			09 06		08 51	09 01		09 03	09 19	09 18				09 36			09 12	09 31		09 33	09 49	09 48		

Table 177

Sundays until 24 June

East and West Croydon, London Milton Keynes Central and Luton via Norbury Crystal Palace - Tulse Hill

Local Services

Network Diagram - see first Page of Table 177

		SN	SN ◇1	SN	SN	SN 1	SN	SN	SN	SN	SN	FC 1	SN	SN	FC	SN ◇1 ⌶	SN	SN	SN 1	SN	SN	SN	SN
East Croydon	d	09 23	09 39			09 34				09 42	09 47	09 47		09 53		10 09			09 56				10 12
West Croydon 4	d				09 22		09 34	09 37										09 52		10 04	10 07		
Norwood Junction 2	a				09 26	09 38	09 39				09 51							09 56	10 00	10 09			
	d				09 27	09 38	09 40				09 52							09 57	10 01	10 10			
Selhurst 4	d	09 26						09 41		09 46				09 57							10 11		10 16
Thornton Heath	d	09 28						09 43		09 48				09 59							10 13		10 18
Norbury	d	09 31						09 46		09 51				10 02							10 16		10 21
Streatham Common 4	d	09 34						09 49		09 53				10 04							10 19		10 23
Beckenham Junction 4	d																						
Birkbeck	d																						
Crystal Palace 4	d				09 31				09 37									10 01				10 07	
Gipsy Hill	d				09 33				09 39									10 03				10 09	
West Norwood 4	d				09 36				09 42									10 06				10 12	
Streatham Hill	d				09 40													10 10					
Balham 4	⊖ d	09 38			09 43			09 53						10 08				10 13			10 23		
Wandsworth Common	d				09 45													10 15					
Latchmere	d																						
Clapham Junction 10	d	09 42	09 48		09 49			09 57						10 13		10 19		10 19			10 27		
Imperial Wharf	d																						
West Brompton	⊖ d																						
Kensington (Olympia)	⊖ d																						
Shepherd's Bush	⊖ d																						
Wembley Central	⊖ d																						
Harrow & Wealdstone	⊖ d																						
Watford Junction	d																						
Milton Keynes Central 10	a																						
Battersea Park 4	d			09 45	09 53								10 02				10 15	10 22					
London Victoria 15	⊖ a	09 50	09 55		09 57			10 04					10 06	10 20		10 25		10 27			10 34		
Streatham 4	d									09 58					10 06								10 28
Tulse Hill 3	d								09 46	10 02					10 10							10 16	10 32
Herne Hill 4	a														10 14								
Loughborough Jn	a														10 17								
Elephant & Castle	⊖ a														10 21								
London Blackfriars 3	⊖ a											10 07			10 25								
City Thameslink 3	a																						
St Pancras International 15	⊖ a											10 18			10 35								
Luton Airport Parkway 7	a																						
Luton 10	a																						
North Dulwich	d								09 49	10 05												10 19	10 35
East Dulwich	d								09 51	10 07												10 21	10 37
Peckham Rye 4	d			09 56					09 53	10 10							10 26					10 23	10 40
Queens Rd Peckham	d			09 59					09 56	10 12							10 29					10 26	10 42
South Bermondsey	d			10 01					09 58	10 15							10 31					10 28	10 45
London Bridge 4	⊖ a			10 06		09 51	10 01		10 03	10 19	10 18						10 36		10 12	10 31		10 33	10 49

Table 177

Sundays until 24 June

East and West Croydon, London Milton Keynes Central and Luton via Norbury Crystal Palace - Tulse Hill

Local Services

Network Diagram - see first Page of Table 177

		SN	FC 1	SN	SN ◇1	SN	FC	SN ◇1	SN	SN	SN 1	SN	SN	SN	SN	SN	FC 1	SN	SN	FC	SN ◇1 ⌶	SN	SN	SN 1
East Croydon	d	10 17	10 17		10 20	10 23		10 39			10 34				10 42	10 47	10 47		10 53		11 09			10 56
West Croydon 4	d									10 22		10 34	10 37										10 52	
Norwood Junction 2	a	10 21								10 26	10 38	10 39				10 51							10 56	11 00
	d	10 22								10 27	10 38	10 40				10 52							10 57	11 01
Selhurst 4	d					10 26							10 41		10 46				10 57					
Thornton Heath	d					10 28							10 43		10 48				10 59					
Norbury	d					10 31							10 46		10 51				11 02					
Streatham Common 4	d					10 34							10 49		10 53				11 04					
Beckenham Junction 4	d																							
Birkbeck	d																							
Crystal Palace 4	d									10 31				10 37									11 01	
Gipsy Hill	d									10 33				10 39									11 03	
West Norwood 4	d									10 36				10 42									11 06	
Streatham Hill	d									10 40													11 10	
Balham 4	⊖ d					10 38				10 43			10 53						11 08				11 13	
Wandsworth Common	d									10 45													11 15	
Latchmere	d																							
Clapham Junction 10	d				10 32	10 42		10 49		10 49			10 57						11 13		11 19		11 19	
Imperial Wharf	d																							
West Brompton	⊖ d																							
Kensington (Olympia)	⊖ d																							
Shepherd's Bush	⊖ d																							
Wembley Central	⊖ d																							
Harrow & Wealdstone	⊖ d																							
Watford Junction	d																							
Milton Keynes Central 10	a																							
Battersea Park 4	d			10 32					10 45	10 52								11 02				11 15	11 22	
London Victoria 15	⊖ a			10 36	10 39	10 50		10 55		10 57			11 04					11 06	11 20		11 25		11 27	
Streatham 4	d						10 36								10 58					11 06				
Tulse Hill 3	d						10 40							10 46	11 02					11 10				
Herne Hill 4	a						10 44													11 14				
Loughborough Jn	a						10 47													11 17				
Elephant & Castle	⊖ a						10 51													11 21				
London Blackfriars 3	⊖ a		10 37				10 55										11 07			11 25				
City Thameslink 3	a																							
St Pancras International 15	⊖ a		10 48				11 05										11 18			11 35				
Luton Airport Parkway 7	a		11 20														11 54							
Luton 10	a		11 23														11 57							
North Dulwich	d													10 49	11 05									
East Dulwich	d													10 51	11 07									
Peckham Rye 4	d								10 56					10 53	11 10							11 26		
Queens Rd Peckham	d								10 59					10 56	11 12							11 29		
South Bermondsey	d								11 01					10 58	11 15							11 31		
London Bridge 4	⊖ a	10 48							11 06		10 51	11 01		11 03	11 19	11 18						11 36		11 12

Table 177

Sundays until 24 June

East and West Croydon, London
Milton Keynes Central and Luton via Norbury
Crystal Palace - Tulse Hill

Local Services

Network Diagram - see first Page of Table 177

		SN	SN	SN	SN	SN	FC 1	SN		SN ◇1 H	SN	FC	SN ◇1	SN	SN	SN 1	SN	SN	SN	SN	SN	FC 1	SN	SN
East Croydon ⇌	d				11 12	11 17	11 17			11 20	11 23		11 39			11 34				11 42	11 47	11 47		11 53
West Croydon 4 ⇌	d	11 04	11 07												11 22		11 34	11 37						
Norwood Junction 2	a	11 09				11 21									11 26	11 38	11 39				11 51			
	d	11 10				11 22									11 27	11 38	11 40				11 52			
Selhurst 4	d		11 11		11 16						11 26							11 41		11 46				11 57
Thornton Heath	d		11 13		11 18						11 28							11 43		11 48				11 59
Norbury	d		11 16		11 21						11 31							11 46		11 51				12 02
Streatham Common 4	d		11 19		11 23						11 34							11 49		11 53				12 04
Beckenham Junction 4 ⇌	d																							
Birkbeck ⇌	d																							
Crystal Palace 4	d			11 07											11 31				11 37					
Gipsy Hill	d			11 09											11 33				11 39					
West Norwood 4	d			11 12											11 36				11 42					
Streatham Hill	d														11 40									
Balham 4 ⊖	d		11 23								11 38				11 43			11 53						12 08
Wandsworth Common	d														11 45									
Latchmere	d																							
Clapham Junction 10	d		11 27							11 32	11 42		11 48		11 49			11 57						12 13
Imperial Wharf	d																							
West Brompton ⊖	d																							
Kensington (Olympia) ⊖	d																							
Shepherd's Bush ⊖	d																							
Wembley Central ⊖	d																							
Harrow & Wealdstone ⊖	d																							
Watford Junction	d																							
Milton Keynes Central 10	a																							
Battersea Park 4	d							11 32						11 45	11 52								12 02	
London Victoria 15 ⊖	a		11 34					11 36		11 39	11 50		11 55		11 57			12 04					12 06	12 20
Streatham 4	d				11 28							11 36								11 58				
Tulse Hill 3	d			11 16	11 32							11 40							11 46	12 02				
Herne Hill 4	a											11 44												
Loughborough Jn	a											11 47												
Elephant & Castle ⊖	a											11 51												
London Blackfriars 3 ⊖	a						11 37					11 55										12 07		
City Thameslink 3	a																							
St Pancras International 15 ⊖	a						11 48					12 05										12 18		
Luton Airport Parkway 7	a						12 24															12 54		
Luton 10	a						12 27															12 57		
North Dulwich	d			11 19	11 35														11 49	12 05				
East Dulwich	d			11 21	11 37														11 51	12 07				
Peckham Rye 4	d			11 23	11 40									11 56					11 53	12 10				
Queens Rd Peckham	d			11 26	11 42									11 59					11 56	12 12				
South Bermondsey	d			11 28	11 45									12 01					11 58	12 15				
London Bridge 4 ⊖	a	11 31		11 33	11 49	11 48								12 06		11 51	12 01		12 03	12 19	12 18			

Table 177

Sundays until 24 June

East and West Croydon, London
Milton Keynes Central and Luton via Norbury
Crystal Palace - Tulse Hill

Local Services

Network Diagram - see first Page of Table 177

		FC	SN ◇1 H	SN	SN	SN 1	SN	SN	SN	SN	SN	FC 1	SN	SN ◇1 H	SN	FC		SN ◇1	SN	SN	SN 1	SN	SN	SN	SN
East Croydon ⇌	d		12 09			11 56				12 12	12 17	12 17		12 20	12 23			12 39			12 34				12 42
West Croydon 4 ⇌	d				11 52		12 04	12 07												12 22		12 34	12 37		
Norwood Junction 2	a				11 56	12 00	12 09				12 21									12 26	12 38	12 39			
	d				11 57	12 01	12 10				12 22									12 27	12 38	12 40			
Selhurst 4	d							12 11		12 16					12 26								12 41		12 46
Thornton Heath	d							12 13		12 18					12 28								12 43		12 48
Norbury	d							12 16		12 21					12 31								12 46		12 51
Streatham Common 4	d							12 19		12 23					12 34								12 49		12 53
Beckenham Junction 4 ⇌	d																								
Birkbeck ⇌	d																								
Crystal Palace 4	d				12 01				12 07											12 31				12 37	
Gipsy Hill	d				12 03				12 09											12 33				12 39	
West Norwood 4	d				12 06				12 12											12 36				12 42	
Streatham Hill	d				12 10															12 40					
Balham 4 ⊖	d				12 13			12 23							12 38					12 43			12 53		
Wandsworth Common	d				12 15															12 45					
Latchmere	d																								
Clapham Junction 10	d		12 19		12 19			12 27						12 32	12 42			12 48		12 49			12 57		
Imperial Wharf	d																								
West Brompton ⊖	d																								
Kensington (Olympia) ⊖	d																								
Shepherd's Bush ⊖	d																								
Wembley Central ⊖	d																								
Harrow & Wealdstone ⊖	d																								
Watford Junction	d																								
Milton Keynes Central 10	a																								
Battersea Park 4	d			12 15	12 22								12 32						12 45	12 52					
London Victoria 15 ⊖	a		12 25		12 27			12 34					12 36	12 39	12 50			12 55		12 57			13 04		
Streatham 4	d	12 06								12 28						12 36									12 58
Tulse Hill 3	d	12 10							12 16	12 32						12 40								12 46	13 02
Herne Hill 4	a	12 14														12 44									
Loughborough Jn	a	12 17														12 47									
Elephant & Castle ⊖	a	12 21														12 51									
London Blackfriars 3 ⊖	a	12 25										12 37				12 55									
City Thameslink 3	a																								
St Pancras International 15 ⊖	a	12 35										12 48				13 05									
Luton Airport Parkway 7	a											13 24													
Luton 10	a											13 27													
North Dulwich	d								12 19	12 35														12 49	13 05
East Dulwich	d								12 21	12 37														12 51	13 07
Peckham Rye 4	d			12 26					12 23	12 40									12 56					12 53	13 10
Queens Rd Peckham	d			12 29					12 26	12 42									12 59					12 56	13 12
South Bermondsey	d			12 31					12 28	12 45									13 01					12 58	13 15
London Bridge 4 ⊖	a			12 36		12 12	12 31		12 33	12 49	12 48								13 06		12 51	13 01		13 03	13 19

Table 177

Sundays
until 24 June

East and West Croydon, London
Milton Keynes Central and Luton via Norbury
Crystal Palace - Tulse Hill

Local Services

Network Diagram - see first Page of Table 177

		SN	FC 1	SN	SN	FC	SN ◇1 ✠	SN	SN	SN 1	SN	SN	SN	SN	SN	FC 1	SN	SN ◇1 ✠	SN	FC	SN ◇1	SN	SN
East Croydon	d	12 47	12 47		12 53		13 09			12 56				13 12	13 17	13 17		13 20	13 23		13 39		
West Croydon 4	d								12 52		13 04	13 07											13 22
Norwood Junction 2	a	12 51							12 56	13 00	13 09				13 21								13 26
	d	12 52							12 57	13 01	13 10				13 22								13 27
Selhurst 4	d				12 57							13 11		13 16					13 26				
Thornton Heath	d				12 59							13 13		13 18					13 28				
Norbury	d				13 02							13 16		13 21					13 31				
Streatham Common 4	d				13 04							13 19		13 23					13 34				
Beckenham Junction 4	d																						
Birkbeck	d																						
Crystal Palace 4	d								13 01				13 07										13 31
Gipsy Hill	d								13 03				13 09										13 33
West Norwood 4	d								13 06				13 12										13 36
Streatham Hill	d								13 10														13 40
Balham 4	d				13 08				13 13			13 23							13 38				13 43
Wandsworth Common	d								13 15														13 45
Latchmere	d																						
Clapham Junction 10	d				13 13		13 19		13 19			13 27						13 32	13 42		13 48		13 49
Imperial Wharf	d																						
West Brompton	d																						
Kensington (Olympia)	d																						
Shepherd's Bush	d																						
Wembley Central	d																						
Harrow & Wealdstone	d																						
Watford Junction	d																						
Milton Keynes Central 10	a																						
Battersea Park 4	d			13 02				13 15	13 23								13 32					13 45	13 52
London Victoria 15	a			13 06	13 20		13 25		13 27			13 34					13 36	13 39	13 50		13 55		13 57
Streatham 4	d					13 06								13 28						13 36			
Tulse Hill 3	d					13 10							13 16	13 32						13 40			
Herne Hill 4	a					13 14														13 44			
Loughborough Jn	a					13 17														13 47			
Elephant & Castle	a					13 21														13 51			
London Blackfriars 3	a		13 07			13 25										13 37				13 55			
City Thameslink 3	a																						
St Pancras International 15	a		13 18			13 35										13 48				14 05			
Luton Airport Parkway 7	a		13 54													14 24							
Luton 10	a		13 57													14 27							
North Dulwich	d												13 19	13 35									
East Dulwich	d												13 21	13 37									
Peckham Rye 4	d							13 26					13 23	13 40									
Queens Rd Peckham	d							13 29					13 26	13 42								13 56	
South Bermondsey	d							13 31					13 28	13 45								13 59	
London Bridge 4	a	13 18						13 36		13 12	13 31		13 33	13 49	13 48							14 06	

Table 177

Sundays
until 24 June

East and West Croydon, London
Milton Keynes Central and Luton via Norbury
Crystal Palace - Tulse Hill

Local Services

Network Diagram - see first Page of Table 177

		SN 1	SN	SN	SN	SN	SN	FC 1	SN	SN	FC	SN ◇1 ✠	SN	SN	SN 1	SN	SN	SN	SN	SN	FC 1	SN	SN ◇1 ✠	SN
East Croydon	d	13 34				13 42	13 47	13 47		13 53		14 09			13 56				14 12	14 17	14 17		14 20	14 23
West Croydon 4	d		13 34	13 37										13 52		14 04	14 07							
Norwood Junction 2	a	13 38	13 39				13 51							13 56	14 00	14 09				14 21				
	d	13 38	13 40				13 52							13 57	14 01	14 10				14 22				
Selhurst 4	d			13 41		13 46				13 57							14 11		14 16					14 26
Thornton Heath	d			13 43		13 48				13 59							14 13		14 18					14 28
Norbury	d			13 46		13 51				14 02							14 16		14 21					14 31
Streatham Common 4	d			13 49		13 53				14 04							14 19		14 23					14 34
Beckenham Junction 4	d																							
Birkbeck	d																							
Crystal Palace 4	d				13 37									14 01				14 07						
Gipsy Hill	d				13 39									14 03				14 09						
West Norwood 4	d				13 42									14 06				14 12						
Streatham Hill	d													14 10										
Balham 4	d			13 53						14 08				14 13			14 23							14 38
Wandsworth Common	d													14 15										
Latchmere	d																							
Clapham Junction 10	d			13 57						14 13		14 19		14 19			14 27						14 32	14 42
Imperial Wharf	d																							
West Brompton	d																							
Kensington (Olympia)	d																							
Shepherd's Bush	d																							
Wembley Central	d																							
Harrow & Wealdstone	d																							
Watford Junction	d																							
Milton Keynes Central 10	a																							
Battersea Park 4	d								14 02				14 15	14 23								14 32		
London Victoria 15	a			14 04					14 06	14 20		14 25		14 27			14 34					14 36	14 39	14 50
Streatham 4	d					13 58					14 06								14 28					
Tulse Hill 3	d				13 46	14 02					14 10							14 16	14 32					
Herne Hill 4	a										14 14													
Loughborough Jn	a										14 17													
Elephant & Castle	a										14 21													
London Blackfriars 3	a							14 07			14 25										14 37			
City Thameslink 3	a																							
St Pancras International 15	a							14 18			14 35										14 48			
Luton Airport Parkway 7	a							14 54													15 24			
Luton 10	a							14 57													15 27			
North Dulwich	d				13 49	14 05												14 19	14 35					
East Dulwich	d				13 51	14 07												14 21	14 37					
Peckham Rye 4	d				13 53	14 10							14 26					14 23	14 40					
Queens Rd Peckham	d				13 56	14 12							14 29					14 26	14 42					
South Bermondsey	d				13 58	14 15							14 31					14 28	14 45					
London Bridge 4	a	13 51	14 01		14 03	14 19	14 18						14 36		14 12	14 31		14 33	14 49	14 48				

Table 177

Sundays until 24 June

East and West Croydon, London
Milton Keynes Central and Luton via Norbury
Crystal Palace - Tulse Hill

Local Services

Network Diagram - see first Page of Table 177

		FC	SN ◇1	SN	SN	SN 1	SN	SN		SN	SN	SN	FC 1	SN	SN	FC	SN ◇1	SN	SN	SN 1	SN	SN	SN	SN
East Croydon	d		14 39			14 34					14 42	14 47	14 47		14 53		15 09			14 56				15 12
West Croydon 4	d				14 22		14 34	14 37											14 52		15 04	15 07		
Norwood Junction 2	a				14 26	14 38	14 39					14 51							14 56	15 00	15 09			
	d				14 27	14 38	14 40					14 52							14 57	15 01	15 10			
Selhurst 4	d							14 41			14 46				14 57							15 11		15 16
Thornton Heath	d							14 43			14 48				14 59							15 13		15 18
Norbury	d							14 46			14 51				15 02							15 16		15 21
Streatham Common 4	d							14 49			14 53				15 04							15 19		15 23
Beckenham Junction 4	d																							
Birkbeck	d																							
Crystal Palace 4	d				14 31					14 37									15 01				15 07	
Gipsy Hill	d				14 33					14 39									15 03				15 09	
West Norwood 4	d				14 36					14 42									15 06				15 12	
Streatham Hill	d				14 40														15 10					
Balham 4 ⊖	d				14 43			14 53							15 08				15 13			15 23		
Wandsworth Common	d				14 45														15 15					
Latchmere	d																							
Clapham Junction 10	d		14 48		14 49			14 57							15 13		15 19		15 19			15 27		
Imperial Wharf	d																							
West Brompton ⊖	d																							
Kensington (Olympia) ⊖	d																							
Shepherd's Bush ⊖	d																							
Wembley Central ⊖	d																							
Harrow & Wealdstone ⊖	d																							
Watford Junction	d																							
Milton Keynes Central 10	a																							
Battersea Park 4	d			14 45	14 52									15 02				15 15	15 23					
London Victoria 15 ⊖	a		14 55		14 57			15 04						15 06	15 20		15 25		15 27			15 34		
Streatham 4	d	14 36									14 58					15 06								15 28
Tulse Hill 3	d	14 40								14 46	15 02					15 10							15 16	15 32
Herne Hill 4	a	14 44														15 14								
Loughborough Jn	a	14 47														15 17								
Elephant & Castle ⊖	a	14 51														15 21								
London Blackfriars 3 ⊖	a	14 55											15 07			15 25								
City Thameslink 3	a																							
St Pancras International 15 ⊖	a	15 05											15 18			15 35								
Luton Airport Parkway 7	a												15 54											
Luton 10	a												15 57											
North Dulwich	d									14 49	15 05												15 19	15 35
East Dulwich	d									14 51	15 07												15 21	15 37
Peckham Rye 4	d			14 56						14 53	15 10							15 26					15 23	15 40
Queens Rd Peckham	d			14 59						14 56	15 12							15 29					15 26	15 42
South Bermondsey	d			15 01						14 58	15 15							15 31					15 28	15 45
London Bridge 4 ⊖	a			15 06		14 51	15 01			15 03	15 19	15 18						15 36		15 12	15 31		15 33	15 49

Table 177

Sundays until 24 June

East and West Croydon, London
Milton Keynes Central and Luton via Norbury
Crystal Palace - Tulse Hill

Local Services

Network Diagram - see first Page of Table 177

		SN	FC 1	SN	SN ◇1	SN	FC	SN ◇1	SN	SN	SN 1	SN	SN	SN	SN	SN		FC 1	SN	SN	FC	SN ◇1	SN	SN	SN 1
East Croydon	d	15 17	15 17		15 20	15 23		15 39			15 34				15 42	15 47		15 47		15 53		16 09			15 56
West Croydon 4	d									15 22		15 34	15 37											15 52	
Norwood Junction 2	a	15 21								15 26	15 38	15 39				15 51								15 56	16 00
	d	15 22								15 27	15 38	15 40				15 52								15 57	16 01
Selhurst 4	d					15 26							15 41		15 46					15 57					
Thornton Heath	d					15 28							15 43		15 48					15 59					
Norbury	d					15 31							15 46		15 51					16 02					
Streatham Common 4	d					15 34							15 49		15 53					16 04					
Beckenham Junction 4	d																								
Birkbeck	d																								
Crystal Palace 4	d									15 31				15 37										16 01	
Gipsy Hill	d									15 33				15 39										16 03	
West Norwood 4	d									15 36				15 42										16 06	
Streatham Hill	d									15 40														16 10	
Balham 4 ⊖	d					15 38				15 43			15 53							16 08				16 13	
Wandsworth Common	d									15 45														16 15	
Latchmere	d																								
Clapham Junction 10	d				15 32	15 42		15 49		15 49			15 57							16 13		16 19		16 19	
Imperial Wharf	d																								
West Brompton ⊖	d																								
Kensington (Olympia) ⊖	d																								
Shepherd's Bush ⊖	d																								
Wembley Central ⊖	d																								
Harrow & Wealdstone ⊖	d																								
Watford Junction	d																								
Milton Keynes Central 10	a																								
Battersea Park 4	d			15 32					15 45	15 52									16 02				16 15	16 23	
London Victoria 15 ⊖	a			15 36	15 39	15 50		15 55		15 57			16 04						16 06	16 20		16 25		16 27	
Streatham 4	d						15 36								15 58						16 06				
Tulse Hill 3	d						15 40							15 46	16 02						16 10				
Herne Hill 4	a						15 44														16 14				
Loughborough Jn	a						15 47														16 17				
Elephant & Castle ⊖	a						15 51														16 21				
London Blackfriars 3 ⊖	a		15 37				15 55											16 07			16 25				
City Thameslink 3	a																								
St Pancras International 15 ⊖	a		15 48				16 05											16 18			16 35				
Luton Airport Parkway 7	a		16 24															16 56							
Luton 10	a		16 27															16 59							
North Dulwich	d													15 49	16 05										
East Dulwich	d													15 51	16 07										
Peckham Rye 4	d								15 56					15 53	16 10								16 26		
Queens Rd Peckham	d								15 59					15 56	16 12								16 29		
South Bermondsey	d								16 01					15 58	16 15								16 31		
London Bridge 4 ⊖	a	15 48							16 06		15 51	16 01		16 03	16 19	16 18							16 36		16 12

Table 177

Sundays until 24 June

East and West Croydon, London
Milton Keynes Central and Luton via Norbury
Crystal Palace - Tulse Hill

Local Services

Network Diagram - see first Page of Table 177

		SN	SN	SN	SN	SN	FC 1	SN	SN ◇1	SN	FC	SN ◇1	SN	SN	SN 1	SN	SN	SN	SN	SN	FC 1	SN	SN
East Croydon	d				16 12	16 17	16 17		16 20	16 23		16 39			16 34				16 42	16 47	16 47		16 53
West Croydon 4	d	16 04	16 07											16 22		16 34	16 37						
Norwood Junction 2	a	16 09				16 21								16 26	16 38	16 39				16 51			
	d	16 10				16 22								16 27	16 38	16 40				16 52			
Selhurst 4	d		16 11		16 16					16 26							16 41		16 46				16 57
Thornton Heath	d		16 13		16 18					16 28							16 43		16 48				16 59
Norbury	d		16 16		16 21					16 31							16 46		16 51				17 02
Streatham Common 4	d		16 19		16 23					16 34							16 49		16 53				17 04
Beckenham Junction 4	d																						
Birkbeck	d																						
Crystal Palace 4	d			16 07										16 31				16 37					
Gipsy Hill	d			16 09										16 33				16 39					
West Norwood 4	d			16 12										16 36				16 42					
Streatham Hill	d													16 40									
Balham 4 ⊖	d		16 23							16 38				16 43			16 53						17 08
Wandsworth Common	d													16 45									
Latchmere	d																						
Clapham Junction 10	d		16 27						16 32	16 42		16 48		16 49			16 57						17 13
Imperial Wharf	d																						
West Brompton ⊖	d																						
Kensington (Olympia) ⊖	d																						
Shepherd's Bush ⊖	d																						
Wembley Central ⊖	d																						
Harrow & Wealdstone ⊖	d																						
Watford Junction	d																						
Milton Keynes Central 10	a																						
Battersea Park 4	d							16 32					16 45	16 52								17 02	
London Victoria 15 ⊖	a		16 34					16 36	16 39	16 50		16 55		16 57			17 04					17 06	17 20
Streatham 4	d				16 28						16 36								16 58				
Tulse Hill 3	d			16 16	16 32						16 40							16 46	17 02				
Herne Hill 4	a										16 44												
Loughborough Jn	a										16 47												
Elephant & Castle ⊖	a										16 51												
London Blackfriars 3 ⊖	a						16 37				16 55										17 07		
City Thameslink 3	a																						
St Pancras International 15 ⊖	a						16 48				17 05										17 18		
Luton Airport Parkway 7	a						17 26														17 56		
Luton 10	a						17 29														17 59		
North Dulwich	d			16 19	16 35													16 49	17 05				
East Dulwich	d			16 21	16 37													16 51	17 07				
Peckham Rye 4	d			16 23	16 40								16 56					16 53	17 10				
Queens Rd Peckham	d			16 26	16 42								16 59					16 56	17 12				
South Bermondsey	d			16 28	16 45								17 01					16 58	17 15				
London Bridge 4 ⊖	a	16 31		16 33	16 49	16 48							17 06		16 51	17 01		17 03	17 19	17 18			

Table 177

Sundays until 24 June

East and West Croydon, London
Milton Keynes Central and Luton via Norbury
Crystal Palace - Tulse Hill

Local Services

Network Diagram - see first Page of Table 177

		FC	SN ◇1	SN	SN	SN 1	SN	SN	SN	SN	SN	FC 1	SN	SN ◇1	SN	FC	SN ◇1	SN	SN	SN 1	SN	SN	SN	SN
East Croydon	d		17 09			16 56				17 12	17 17	17 17		17 20	17 23		17 39			17 34				17 42
West Croydon 4	d				16 52		17 04	17 07											17 22		17 34	17 37		
Norwood Junction 2	a				16 56	17 00	17 09				17 21								17 26	17 38	17 39			
	d				16 57	17 01	17 10				17 22								17 27	17 38	17 40			
Selhurst 4	d							17 11		17 16					17 26							17 41		17 46
Thornton Heath	d							17 13		17 18					17 28							17 43		17 48
Norbury	d							17 16		17 21					17 31							17 46		17 51
Streatham Common 4	d							17 19		17 23					17 34							17 49		17 53
Beckenham Junction 4	d																							
Birkbeck	d																							
Crystal Palace 4	d				17 01				17 07										17 31				17 37	
Gipsy Hill	d				17 03				17 09										17 33				17 39	
West Norwood 4	d				17 06				17 12										17 36				17 42	
Streatham Hill	d				17 10														17 40					
Balham 4 ⊖	d				17 13			17 23							17 38				17 43			17 53		
Wandsworth Common	d				17 15														17 45					
Latchmere	d																							
Clapham Junction 10	d		17 19		17 19			17 27						17 32	17 42		17 48		17 49			17 57		
Imperial Wharf	d																							
West Brompton ⊖	d																							
Kensington (Olympia) ⊖	d																							
Shepherd's Bush ⊖	d																							
Wembley Central ⊖	d																							
Harrow & Wealdstone ⊖	d																							
Watford Junction	d																							
Milton Keynes Central 10	a																							
Battersea Park 4	d			17 15	17 23								17 32					17 45	17 52					
London Victoria 15 ⊖	a		17 25		17 27			17 34					17 36	17 39	17 50		17 55		17 57			18 04		
Streatham 4	d	17 06								17 28						17 36								17 58
Tulse Hill 3	d	17 10							17 16	17 32						17 40							17 46	18 02
Herne Hill 4	a	17 14														17 44								
Loughborough Jn	a	17 17														17 47								
Elephant & Castle ⊖	a	17 21														17 51								
London Blackfriars 3 ⊖	a	17 25										17 37				17 55								
City Thameslink 3	a																							
St Pancras International 15 ⊖	a	17 35										17 48				18 05								
Luton Airport Parkway 7	a											18 26												
Luton 10	a											18 29												
North Dulwich	d								17 19	17 35													17 49	18 05
East Dulwich	d								17 21	17 37													17 51	18 07
Peckham Rye 4	d			17 26					17 23	17 40								17 56					17 53	18 10
Queens Rd Peckham	d			17 29					17 26	17 42								17 59					17 56	18 12
South Bermondsey	d			17 31					17 28	17 45								18 01					17 58	18 15
London Bridge 4 ⊖	a			17 36		17 12	17 31		17 33	17 49	17 48							18 06		17 51	18 01		18 03	18 19

Table 177

Sundays until 24 June

East and West Croydon, London Milton Keynes Central and Luton via Norbury Crystal Palace - Tulse Hill

Local Services

Network Diagram - see first Page of Table 177

Station		SN	FC 1	SN	SN	FC	SN ◇1 ⌶	SN		SN	SN 1	SN	SN	SN	SN	SN	FC 1	SN	SN ◇1 ⌶	SN	FC	SN ◇1	SN	SN
East Croydon (tram)	d	17 47	17 47		17 53		18 09				17 56				18 12	18 17	18 17		18 20	18 23		18 39		
West Croydon 4 (tram)	d									17 52		18 04	18 07											18 22
Norwood Junction 2	a	17 51								17 56	18 00	18 09				18 21								18 26
	d	17 52								17 57	18 01	18 10				18 22								18 27
Selhurst 4	d				17 57								18 11		18 16					18 26				
Thornton Heath	d				17 59								18 13		18 18					18 28				
Norbury	d				18 02								18 16		18 21					18 31				
Streatham Common 4	d				18 04								18 19		18 23					18 34				
Beckenham Junction 4 (tram)	d																							
Birkbeck (tram)	d																							
Crystal Palace 4	d									18 01				18 07										18 31
Gipsy Hill	d									18 03				18 09										18 33
West Norwood 4	d									18 06				18 12										18 36
Streatham Hill	d									18 10														18 40
Balham 4 ⊖	d				18 08					18 13			18 23							18 38				18 43
Wandsworth Common	d									18 15														18 45
Latchmere	d																							
Clapham Junction 10	d				18 13		18 19			18 19			18 27						18 32	18 42		18 48		18 49
Imperial Wharf	d																							
West Brompton ⊖	d																							
Kensington (Olympia) ⊖	d																							
Shepherd's Bush ⊖	d																							
Wembley Central ⊖	d																							
Harrow & Wealdstone ⊖	d																							
Watford Junction	d																							
Milton Keynes Central 10	a																							
Battersea Park 4	d			18 02				18 15		18 23								18 32					18 45	18 52
London Victoria 15 ⊖	a			18 06	18 20		18 25			18 27			18 34					18 36	18 39	18 50		18 55		18 57
Streatham 4	d					18 06									18 28						18 36			
Tulse Hill 3	d					18 10								18 16	18 32						18 40			
Herne Hill 4	a					18 14															18 44			
Loughborough Jn	a					18 17															18 47			
Elephant & Castle ⊖	a					18 21															18 51			
London Blackfriars 3 ⊖	a		18 07			18 25											18 37				18 55			
City Thameslink 3	a																							
St Pancras International 15 ⊖	a		18 18			18 35											18 48				19 05			
Luton Airport Parkway 7	a		18 56														19 26							
Luton 10	a		18 59														19 29							
North Dulwich	d													18 19	18 35									
East Dulwich	d													18 21	18 37								18 56	
Peckham Rye 4	d							18 26						18 23	18 40								18 59	
Queens Rd Peckham	d							18 29						18 26	18 42								19 01	
South Bermondsey	d							18 31						18 28	18 45								19 06	
London Bridge 4 ⊖	a	18 18						18 36			18 12	18 31		18 33	18 49	18 48								

Table 177

Sundays until 24 June

East and West Croydon, London Milton Keynes Central and Luton via Norbury Crystal Palace - Tulse Hill

Local Services

Network Diagram - see first Page of Table 177

Station		SN 1	SN	SN	SN	SN	SN	FC 1	SN	SN	FC	SN ◇1 ⌶	SN	SN	SN 1	SN		SN	SN	SN	SN	FC 1	SN	SN ◇1	SN
East Croydon (tram)	d	18 34				18 42	18 47	18 47		18 53		19 09			18 56					19 12	19 17	19 17		19 20	19 23
West Croydon 4 (tram)	d		18 34	18 37										18 52		19 04		19 07							
Norwood Junction 2	a	18 38	18 39				18 51							18 56	19 00	19 09					19 21				
	d	18 38	18 40				18 52							18 57	19 01	19 10					19 22				
Selhurst 4	d			18 41		18 46				18 57								19 11		19 16					19 26
Thornton Heath	d			18 43		18 48				18 59								19 13		19 18					19 28
Norbury	d			18 46		18 51				19 02								19 16		19 21					19 31
Streatham Common 4	d			18 49		18 53				19 04								19 19		19 23					19 34
Beckenham Junction 4 (tram)	d																								
Birkbeck (tram)	d																								
Crystal Palace 4	d				18 37									19 01					19 07						
Gipsy Hill	d				18 39									19 03					19 09						
West Norwood 4	d				18 42									19 06					19 12						
Streatham Hill	d													19 10											
Balham 4 ⊖	d			18 53						19 08				19 13				19 23							19 38
Wandsworth Common	d													19 15											
Latchmere	d																								
Clapham Junction 10	d			18 57						19 13		19 19		19 19				19 27						19 32	19 42
Imperial Wharf	d																								
West Brompton ⊖	d																								
Kensington (Olympia) ⊖	d																								
Shepherd's Bush ⊖	d																								
Wembley Central ⊖	d																								
Harrow & Wealdstone ⊖	d																								
Watford Junction	d																								
Milton Keynes Central 10	a																								
Battersea Park 4	d								19 02				19 15	19 23									19 32		
London Victoria 15 ⊖	a			19 04					19 06	19 20		19 25		19 27				19 34					19 36	19 39	19 50
Streatham 4	d					18 58					19 06									19 28					
Tulse Hill 3	d				18 46	19 02					19 10								19 16	19 32					
Herne Hill 4	a										19 14														
Loughborough Jn	a										19 17														
Elephant & Castle ⊖	a										19 21														
London Blackfriars 3 ⊖	a							19 07			19 25											19 37			
City Thameslink 3	a																								
St Pancras International 15 ⊖	a							19 18			19 35											19 48			
Luton Airport Parkway 7	a							19 56														20 26			
Luton 10	a							19 59														20 29			
North Dulwich	d				18 49	19 05													19 19	19 35					
East Dulwich	d				18 51	19 07													19 21	19 37					
Peckham Rye 4	d				18 53	19 10							19 26						19 23	19 40					
Queens Rd Peckham	d				18 56	19 12							19 29						19 26	19 42					
South Bermondsey	d				18 58	19 15							19 31						19 28	19 45					
London Bridge 4 ⊖	a	18 51	19 01		19 03	19 19	19 18						19 36		19 12	19 31			19 33	19 49	19 48				

Table 177

Sundays
until 24 June

East and West Croydon, London Milton Keynes Central and Luton via Norbury Crystal Palace - Tulse Hill

Local Services

Network Diagram - see first Page of Table 177

		FC	SN ◇1	SN	SN	SN 1	SN	SN	SN	SN	SN	SN	SN	FC	SN ◇1	SN	SN	SN 1	SN	SN	SN	SN	SN
East Croydon	d		19 39			19 34				19 42	19 47		19 53		20 09			19 56				20 12	20 17
West Croydon [4]	d				19 22		19 34	19 37									19 52		20 04	20 07			
Norwood Junction [2]	a				19 26	19 38	19 39				19 51						19 56	20 00	20 09				20 21
	d				19 27	19 38	19 40				19 52						19 57	20 01	20 10				20 22
Selhurst [4]	d							19 41		19 46			19 57							20 11		20 16	
Thornton Heath	d							19 43		19 48			19 59							20 13		20 18	
Norbury	d							19 46		19 51			20 02							20 16		20 21	
Streatham Common [4]	d							19 49		19 53			20 04							20 19		20 23	
Beckenham Junction [4]	d																						
Birkbeck	d																						
Crystal Palace [4]	d				19 31				19 37								20 01				20 07		
Gipsy Hill	d				19 33				19 39								20 03				20 09		
West Norwood [4]	d				19 36				19 42								20 06				20 12		
Streatham Hill	d				19 40												20 10						
Balham [4] ⊖	d				19 43			19 53					20 08				20 13			20 23			
Wandsworth Common	d				19 45												20 15						
Latchmere	d																						
Clapham Junction [10]	d		19 48		19 49			19 57					20 13		20 19		20 19			20 27			
Imperial Wharf	d																						
West Brompton ⊖	d																						
Kensington (Olympia) ⊖	d																						
Shepherd's Bush ⊖	d																						
Wembley Central ⊖	d																						
Harrow & Wealdstone ⊖	d																						
Watford Junction	d																						
Milton Keynes Central [10]	a																						
Battersea Park [4]	d			19 45	19 52							20 02				20 15	20 22						
London Victoria [15] ⊖	a		19 55		19 57			20 04				20 06	20 20		20 25		20 27			20 34			
Streatham [4]	d	19 36								19 58				20 06								20 28	
Tulse Hill [3]	d	19 40							19 46	20 02				20 10							20 16	20 32	
Herne Hill [4]	a	19 44												20 14									
Loughborough Jn	a	19 47												20 17									
Elephant & Castle ⊖	a	19 51												20 21									
London Blackfriars [3] ⊖	a	19 55												20 25									
City Thameslink [3]	a																						
St Pancras International [15] ⊖	a	20 13												20 43									
Luton Airport Parkway [7]	a	20 58												21 28									
Luton [10]	a	21 01												21 31									
North Dulwich	d								19 49	20 05											20 19	20 35	
East Dulwich	d								19 51	20 07											20 21	20 37	
Peckham Rye [4]	d			19 56					19 53	20 10						20 26					20 23	20 40	
Queens Rd Peckham	d			19 59					19 56	20 12						20 29					20 26	20 42	
South Bermondsey	d			20 01					19 58	20 15						20 31					20 28	20 45	
London Bridge [4] ⊖	a			20 06		19 51	20 01		20 03	20 19	20 18					20 36		20 12	20 31		20 33	20 49	20 48

Table 177

Sundays
until 24 June

East and West Croydon, London Milton Keynes Central and Luton via Norbury Crystal Palace - Tulse Hill

Local Services

Network Diagram - see first Page of Table 177

		SN	SN ◇1	SN	FC	SN ◇1	SN	SN	SN 1	SN	SN	SN	SN	SN	SN	SN	FC	SN ◇1	SN	SN	SN 1	SN	SN	SN
East Croydon	d		20 20	20 23		20 39			20 34				20 42	20 47		20 53		21 09			20 56			
West Croydon [4]	d							20 22		20 34	20 37									20 52		21 04	21 07	
Norwood Junction [2]	a							20 26	20 38	20 39				20 51						20 56	21 00	21 09		
	d							20 27	20 38	20 40				20 52						20 57	21 01	21 10		
Selhurst [4]	d			20 26							20 41		20 46			20 57							21 11	
Thornton Heath	d			20 28							20 43		20 48			20 59							21 13	
Norbury	d			20 31							20 46		20 51			21 02							21 16	
Streatham Common [4]	d			20 34							20 49		20 53			21 04							21 19	
Beckenham Junction [4]	d																							
Birkbeck	d																							
Crystal Palace [4]	d							20 31				20 37								21 01				21 07
Gipsy Hill	d							20 33				20 39								21 03				21 09
West Norwood [4]	d							20 36				20 42								21 06				21 12
Streatham Hill	d							20 40												21 10				
Balham [4] ⊖	d			20 38				20 43			20 53					21 08				21 13			21 23	
Wandsworth Common	d							20 45												21 15				
Latchmere	d																							
Clapham Junction [10]	d		20 32	20 42		20 48		20 49			20 57					21 13		21 19		21 19			21 27	
Imperial Wharf	d																							
West Brompton ⊖	d																							
Kensington (Olympia) ⊖	d																							
Shepherd's Bush ⊖	d																							
Wembley Central ⊖	d																							
Harrow & Wealdstone ⊖	d																							
Watford Junction	d																							
Milton Keynes Central [10]	a																							
Battersea Park [4]	d	20 32					20 45	20 52							21 02				21 15	21 23				
London Victoria [15] ⊖	a	20 36	20 39	20 50		20 55		20 57			21 04				21 06	21 20		21 25		21 27			21 34	
Streatham [4]	d				20 36								20 58				21 06							
Tulse Hill [3]	d				20 40							20 46	21 02				21 10							21 16
Herne Hill [4]	a				20 44												21 14							
Loughborough Jn	a				20 47												21 17							
Elephant & Castle ⊖	a				20 51												21 21							
London Blackfriars [3] ⊖	a				20 55												21 25							
City Thameslink [3]	a																							
St Pancras International [15] ⊖	a				21 13												21 43							
Luton Airport Parkway [7]	a				21 58												22 28							
Luton [10]	a				22 01												22 31							
North Dulwich	d											20 49	21 05											21 19
East Dulwich	d											20 51	21 07											21 21
Peckham Rye [4]	d						20 56					20 53	21 10						21 26					21 23
Queens Rd Peckham	d						20 59					20 56	21 12						21 29					21 26
South Bermondsey	d						21 01					20 58	21 15						21 31					21 28
London Bridge [4] ⊖	a						21 06		20 51	21 01		21 03	21 19	21 18					21 36		21 12	21 31		21 33

Table 177

Sundays
until 24 June

East and West Croydon, London Milton Keynes Central and Luton via Norbury Crystal Palace - Tulse Hill

Local Services

Network Diagram - see first Page of Table 177

		SN	SN	SN	SN ◇1	SN	FC	SN ◇1		SN	SN	SN 1	SN	SN	SN	SN	SN	SN	SN	SN ◇1	SN	SN	SN 1	SN
East Croydon ⇌	d	21 12	21 17		21 20	21 23		21 39				21 34				21 42	21 47		21 53	22 09			21 56	
West Croydon 4 ⇌	d										21 22		21 34	21 37								21 52		22 04
Norwood Junction 2	a		21 21								21 26	21 38	21 39				21 51					21 56	22 00	22 09
	d		21 22								21 27	21 38	21 40				21 52					21 57	22 01	22 10
Selhurst 4	d	21 16				21 26								21 41		21 46			21 56					
Thornton Heath	d	21 18				21 28								21 43		21 48			21 58					
Norbury	d	21 21				21 31								21 46		21 51			22 01					
Streatham Common 4	d	21 23				21 34								21 49		21 53			22 04					
Beckenham Junction 4 ⇌	d																							
Birkbeck ⇌	d																							
Crystal Palace 4	d										21 31				21 37							22 01		
Gipsy Hill	d										21 33				21 39							22 03		
West Norwood 4	d										21 36				21 42							22 06		
Streatham Hill	d										21 40											22 10		
Balham 4 ⊖	d					21 38					21 43			21 53					22 08			22 13		
Wandsworth Common	d										21 45											22 15		
Latchmere	d																							
Clapham Junction 10	d				21 32	21 42		21 48			21 49			21 57					22 12	22 19		22 19		
Imperial Wharf	d																							
West Brompton ⊖	d																							
Kensington (Olympia) ⊖	d																							
Shepherd's Bush ⊖	d																							
Wembley Central ⊖	d																							
Harrow & Wealdstone ⊖	d																							
Watford Junction	d																							
Milton Keynes Central 10	a																							
Battersea Park 4	d			21 32						21 45	21 53							22 02			22 15	22 23		
London Victoria 15 ⊖	a			21 36	21 39	21 50		21 55			21 57			22 04				22 06	22 20	22 25		22 27		
Streatham 4	d	21 28					21 36									21 58								
Tulse Hill 3	d	21 32					21 40								21 46	22 02								
Herne Hill 4	a						21 44																	
Loughborough Jn	a						21 47																	
Elephant & Castle ⊖	a						21 51																	
London Blackfriars 3 ⊖	a						21 55																	
City Thameslink 3	a																							
St Pancras International 15 ⊖	a						22 13																	
Luton Airport Parkway 7	a						22 58																	
Luton 10	a						23 01																	
North Dulwich	d	21 35													21 49	22 05								
East Dulwich	d	21 37													21 51	22 07								
Peckham Rye 4	d	21 40								21 56					21 53	22 10					22 26			
Queens Rd Peckham	d	21 42								21 59					21 56	22 12					22 29			
South Bermondsey	d	21 45								22 01					21 58	22 15					22 31			
London Bridge 4 ⊖	a	21 49	21 48							22 06		21 51	22 01		22 03	22 19	22 18				22 36		22 12	22 31

Table 177

Sundays
until 24 June

East and West Croydon, London Milton Keynes Central and Luton via Norbury Crystal Palace - Tulse Hill

Local Services

Network Diagram - see first Page of Table 177

		SN	SN	SN	SN	SN	SN ◇1	SN	SN	SN	SN 1	SN	SN	SN	SN	SN		SN	SN	SN 1	SN	SN	SN	SN	SN
East Croydon ⇌	d			22 12	22 17		22 20	22 23			22 34				22 42	22 47			22 53	22 56					23 17
West Croydon 4 ⇌	d	22 07								22 22		22 34	22 37									22 52	23 07		
Norwood Junction 2	a				22 21					22 26	22 38	22 39				22 51						22 56			23 21
	d				22 22					22 27	22 38	22 40				22 52						22 57			
Selhurst 4	d	22 11		22 16				22 26					22 41		22 46				22 57	22 59			23 11		
Thornton Heath	d	22 13		22 18				22 28					22 43		22 48				22 59				23 13		
Norbury	d	22 16		22 21				22 31					22 46		22 51				23 02				23 16		
Streatham Common 4	d	22 19		22 23				22 34					22 49		22 53				23 04				23 19		
Beckenham Junction 4 ⇌	d																								
Birkbeck ⇌	d																								
Crystal Palace 4	d		22 07							22 31				22 37								23 01		23 07	
Gipsy Hill	d		22 09							22 33				22 39								23 03		23 09	
West Norwood 4	d		22 12							22 36				22 42								23 06		23 12	
Streatham Hill	d									22 40												23 10			
Balham 4 ⊖	d	22 23						22 38		22 43			22 53						23 08			23 13	23 23		
Wandsworth Common	d									22 45												23 15			
Latchmere	d																								
Clapham Junction 10	d	22 27					22 32	22 42		22 49			22 57						23 13	23 08		23 19	23 27		
Imperial Wharf	d																								
West Brompton ⊖	d																								
Kensington (Olympia) ⊖	d																								
Shepherd's Bush ⊖	d																								
Wembley Central ⊖	d																								
Harrow & Wealdstone ⊖	d																								
Watford Junction	d																								
Milton Keynes Central 10	a																								
Battersea Park 4	d					22 32			22 45	22 53								23 02			23 15	23 23			
London Victoria 15 ⊖	a	22 34				22 36	22 39	22 52		22 57			23 04					23 06	23 20	23 14		23 27	23 34		
Streatham 4	d			22 28											22 58										
Tulse Hill 3	d		22 16	22 32										22 46	23 02									23 16	
Herne Hill 4	a																								
Loughborough Jn	a																								
Elephant & Castle ⊖	a																								
London Blackfriars 3 ⊖	a																								
City Thameslink 3	a																								
St Pancras International 15 ⊖	a																								
Luton Airport Parkway 7	a																								
Luton 10	a																								
North Dulwich	d		22 19	22 35										22 49	23 05									23 19	
East Dulwich	d		22 21	22 37										22 51	23 07									23 21	
Peckham Rye 4	d		22 23	22 40					22 56					22 53	23 10						23 26			23 23	
Queens Rd Peckham	d		22 26	22 42					22 59					22 56	23 12						23 29			23 26	
South Bermondsey	d		22 28	22 45					23 01					22 58	23 15						23 31			23 28	
London Bridge 4 ⊖	a		22 33	22 49	22 48				23 06		22 51	23 01		23 03	23 19	23 18					23 36			23 33	

Table 177

Sundays
until 24 June

East and West Croydon, London
Milton Keynes Central and Luton via Norbury
Crystal Palace - Tulse Hill

Local Services

Network Diagram - see first Page of Table 177

		SN	SN ◇1	SN	SN	SN	SN	SN		SN 1
East Croydon	d		23 21		23 26					23 56
West Croydon 4	d			23 22		23 37		23 52		
Norwood Junction 2	a			23 26						
	d			23 27						
Selhurst 4	d				23a29	23 41		23 56		00 01
Thornton Heath	d					23 43		23 58		
Norbury	d					23 46		00 01		
Streatham Common 4	d					23 49		00 04		
Beckenham Junction 4	d									
Birkbeck	d									
Crystal Palace 4	d			23 31			23 37			
Gipsy Hill	d			23 33			23 39			
West Norwood 4	d			23 36			23 42			
Streatham Hill	d			23 40						
Balham 4 ⊖	d			23 43		23 53		00 08		
Wandsworth Common	d			23 45						
Latchmere	d									
Clapham Junction 10	d		23 32	23 49		23 58		00 12		00 12
Imperial Wharf	d									
West Brompton ⊖	d									
Kensington (Olympia) ⊖	d									
Shepherd's Bush ⊖	d									
Wembley Central ⊖	d									
Harrow & Wealdstone ⊖	d									
Watford Junction	d									
Milton Keynes Central 10	a									
Battersea Park 4	d	23 32		23 53						
London Victoria 15 ⊖	a	23 37	23 38	23 57		00 04		00 19		00 19
Streatham 4	d									
Tulse Hill 3	d						23 46			
Herne Hill 4	a									
Loughborough Jn	a									
Elephant & Castle ⊖	a									
London Blackfriars 3 ⊖	a									
City Thameslink 3	a									
St Pancras International 15 ⊖	a									
Luton Airport Parkway 7	a									
Luton 10	a									
North Dulwich	d						23 49			
East Dulwich	d						23 51			
Peckham Rye 4	d						23 53			
Queens Rd Peckham	d						23 56			
South Bermondsey	d						23 58			
London Bridge 4 ⊖	a						00 03			

Table 177

Sundays
1 July to 9 September

East and West Croydon, London
Milton Keynes Central and Luton via Norbury
Crystal Palace - Tulse Hill

Local Services

Network Diagram - see first Page of Table 177

		FC	FC	SN	SN	SN	SN 1	SN	SN	SN	SN 1	SN 1	SN 1	SN 1	FC A	FC B		SN 1	SN	SN	SN	SN	SN	SN	SN
East Croydon	d						23p56			00 49	01 43	02 40	03 40	04 40	05 32	05 32		06 02	06 40	06 47					07 12
West Croydon 4	d			23p34																			07 07		
Norwood Junction 2	a																			06 51					
	d																			06 52		06 57			
Selhurst 4	d			23p39															06 43		06 47		07 11		07 15
Thornton Heath	d			23p41															06 45		06 49		07 13		07 17
Norbury	d			23p44															06 48		06 52		07 16		07 20
Streatham Common 4	d			23p46															06 51		06 55		07 19		07 23
Beckenham Junction 4	d																								
Birkbeck	d																								
Crystal Palace 4	d				23p43	23p51		00 13	00 21													07 01		07 07	
Gipsy Hill	d				23p45			00 15														07 03		07 09	
West Norwood 4	d				23p48			00 18														07 06		07 12	
Streatham Hill	d				23p52			00 22														07 10			
Balham 4 ⊖	d			23p50	23p55			00 26											06 55			07 13	07 23		
Wandsworth Common	d			23p52	23p57			00 28											06 57			07 15			
Latchmere	d																								
Clapham Junction 10	d			23p56	00 02		00 12	00 32		01 03	01 54	02 53	03 53	04 53				06 15	07 00			07 19	07 27		
Imperial Wharf	d																								
West Brompton ⊖	d																								
Kensington (Olympia) ⊖	d																								
Shepherd's Bush ⊖	d																								
Wembley Central ⊖	d																								
Harrow & Wealdstone ⊖	d																								
Watford Junction	d																								
Milton Keynes Central 10	a																								
Battersea Park 4	d				00 05			00 35											07 04			07 23			
London Victoria 15 ⊖	a			00 04	00 10		00 18	00 42		01 10	02 05	03 05	04 05	05 05				06 22	07 09			07 27	07 34		
Streatham 4	d	22p49	23p19																		06 58				07 28
Tulse Hill 3	d	22p53	23p23																		07 02			07 16	07 32
Herne Hill 4	a	22p56	23p26																						
Loughborough Jn	a	23p00																							
Elephant & Castle ⊖	a	23p04	23p33																						
London Blackfriars 3 ⊖	a	23p07	23p37												05 59	05 59									
City Thameslink 3	a																								
St Pancras International 15 ⊖	a	23p17	23p47													06 07									
Luton Airport Parkway 7	a	00 02	00 32													06 53									
Luton 10	a	00 05	00 35													06 56									
North Dulwich	d																				07 05			07 19	07 35
East Dulwich	d																				07 07			07 21	07 37
Peckham Rye 4	d																				07 09			07 23	07 39
Queens Rd Peckham	d																				07 12			07 26	07 42
South Bermondsey	d																				07 14			07 28	07 44
London Bridge 4 ⊖	a					00 11			00 41											07 17	07 19			07 33	07 50

A from 1 July until 22 July, from 19 August until 9 September

B 29 July, 5 August, 12 August

East and West Croydon, London
Milton Keynes Central and Luton via Norbury
Crystal Palace - Tulse Hill

Local Services

Network Diagram - see first Page of Table 177

		SN	SN	SN	SN	SN	SN	SN		SN	SN	SN	SN	SN	SN	SN	SN	SN	SN	SN	SN	SN	SN	SN
				1											◇1			1						
East Croydon	d	07 17		07 27							07 42	07 47		07 53	08 09			07 56				08 12	08 17	
West Croydon 4	d					07 22	07 34	07 37									07 52		08 04	08 07				
Norwood Junction 2	a	07 21				07 26	07 39					07 51					07 56	08 00	08 09				08 21	
	d	07 22				07 27	07 40					07 52					07 57	08 01	08 10				08 22	
Selhurst 4	d			07 31				07 41			07 46			07 57						08 11		08 16		
Thornton Heath	d							07 43			07 48			07 59						08 13		08 18		
Norbury	d							07 46			07 51			08 02						08 16		08 21		
Streatham Common 4	d							07 49			07 53			08 04						08 19		08 23		
Beckenham Junction 4	d																							
Birkbeck	d																							
Crystal Palace 4	d					07 31				07 37							08 01				08 07			
Gipsy Hill	d					07 33				07 39							08 03				08 09			
West Norwood 4	d					07 36				07 42							08 06				08 12			
Streatham Hill	d					07 40											08 10							
Balham 4	⊖ d					07 43		07 53						08 08			08 13			08 23				
Wandsworth Common	d					07 45											08 15							
Latchmere	d																							
Clapham Junction 10	d			07 41		07 49		07 57						08 13	08 19		08 19			08 27				
Imperial Wharf	d																							
West Brompton	⊖ d																							
Kensington (Olympia)	⊖ d																							
Shepherd's Bush	⊖ d																							
Wembley Central	⊖ d																							
Harrow & Wealdstone	⊖ d																							
Watford Junction	d																							
Milton Keynes Central 10	a																							
Battersea Park 4	d		07 32		07 45	07 53							08 02			08 15	08 23							08 32
London Victoria 15	⊖ a		07 36	07 48		07 57		08 04					08 06	08 20	08 25		08 27			08 34				08 36
Streatham 4	d										07 58											08 28		
Tulse Hill 3	d									07 46	08 02										08 16	08 32		
Herne Hill 4	a																							
Loughborough Jn	a																							
Elephant & Castle	⊖ a																							
London Blackfriars 3	⊖ a																							
City Thameslink 3	a																							
St Pancras International 15	⊖ a																							
Luton Airport Parkway 7	a																							
Luton 10	a																							
North Dulwich	d									07 49	08 05										08 19	08 35		
East Dulwich	d									07 51	08 07										08 21	08 37		
Peckham Rye 4	d				07 56					07 53	08 10					08 26					08 23	08 40		
Queens Rd Peckham	d				07 59					07 56	08 12					08 29					08 26	08 42		
South Bermondsey	d				08 01					07 58	08 15					08 31					08 28	08 45		
London Bridge 4	⊖ a	07 48			08 06		08 01			08 03	08 19	08 17				08 36		08 12	08 31		08 33	08 49	08 48	

East and West Croydon, London
Milton Keynes Central and Luton via Norbury
Crystal Palace - Tulse Hill

Local Services

Network Diagram - see first Page of Table 177

		SN	SN	SN	SN	SN	SN	SN	SN	SN	SN	SN	SN	SN	SN	SN		SN	SN	SN	SN	SN	SN	SN	SN
		◇1		◇1			1								◇1				1						
East Croydon	d	08 20	08 23	08 39			08 34				08 42	08 47		08 53	09 09				08 56				09 12	09 17	
West Croydon 4	d					08 22		08 34	08 37									08 52		09 04	09 07				
Norwood Junction 2	a					08 26	08 38	08 39				08 51						08 56	09 00	09 09				09 21	
	d					08 27	08 38	08 40				08 52						08 57	09 01	09 10				09 22	
Selhurst 4	d		08 26						08 41		08 46			08 57							09 11		09 16		
Thornton Heath	d		08 28						08 43		08 48			08 59							09 13		09 18		
Norbury	d		08 31						08 46		08 51			09 02							09 16		09 21		
Streatham Common 4	d		08 34						08 49		08 53			09 04							09 19		09 23		
Beckenham Junction 4	d																								
Birkbeck	d																								
Crystal Palace 4	d					08 31				08 37								09 01				09 07			
Gipsy Hill	d					08 33				08 39								09 03				09 09			
West Norwood 4	d					08 36				08 42								09 06				09 12			
Streatham Hill	d					08 40												09 10							
Balham 4	⊖ d		08 38			08 43			08 53					09 08				09 13			09 23				
Wandsworth Common	d					08 45												09 15							
Latchmere	d																								
Clapham Junction 10	d	08 32	08 42	08 48		08 49			08 57					09 13	09 19			09 19			09 27				
Imperial Wharf	d																								
West Brompton	⊖ d																								
Kensington (Olympia)	⊖ d																								
Shepherd's Bush	⊖ d																								
Wembley Central	⊖ d																								
Harrow & Wealdstone	⊖ d																								
Watford Junction	d																								
Milton Keynes Central 10	a																								
Battersea Park 4	d				08 45	08 52							09 02			09 15		09 23							09 32
London Victoria 15	⊖ a	08 39	08 50	08 55		08 57			09 04				09 06	09 20	09 25			09 27			09 34				09 36
Streatham 4	d										08 58												09 28		
Tulse Hill 3	d									08 46	09 02											09 16	09 32		
Herne Hill 4	a																								
Loughborough Jn	a																								
Elephant & Castle	⊖ a																								
London Blackfriars 3	⊖ a																								
City Thameslink 3	a																								
St Pancras International 15	⊖ a																								
Luton Airport Parkway 7	a																								
Luton 10	a																								
North Dulwich	d									08 49	09 05											09 19	09 35		
East Dulwich	d									08 51	09 07											09 21	09 37		
Peckham Rye 4	d				08 56					08 53	09 10					09 26						09 23	09 40		
Queens Rd Peckham	d				08 59					08 56	09 12					09 29						09 26	09 42		
South Bermondsey	d				09 01					08 58	09 15					09 31						09 28	09 45		
London Bridge 4	⊖ a				09 06		08 51	09 01		09 03	09 19	09 18				09 36			09 12	09 31		09 33	09 49	09 48	

Table 177

Sundays

1 July to 9 September

East and West Croydon, London
Milton Keynes Central and Luton via Norbury
Crystal Palace - Tulse Hill

Local Services

Network Diagram - see first Page of Table 177

		SN ◇1	SN	SN ◇1	SN	SN	SN 1	SN	SN	SN	SN	SN	FC 1	SN	SN	FC	SN ◇1	SN	SN	SN 1	SN	SN	SN
East Croydon	d	09 20	09 23	09 39			09 34				09 42	09 47	09 47		09 53		10 09			09 56			
West Croydon	d					09 22		09 34	09 37										09 52		10 04	10 07	
Norwood Junction	a					09 26	09 38	09 39				09 51							09 56	10 00	10 09		
	d					09 27	09 38	09 40				09 52							09 57	10 01	10 10		
Selhurst	d		09 26						09 41		09 46				09 57							10 11	
Thornton Heath	d		09 28						09 43		09 48				09 59							10 13	
Norbury	d		09 31						09 46		09 51				10 02							10 16	
Streatham Common	d		09 34						09 49		09 53				10 04							10 19	
Beckenham Junction	d																						
Birkbeck	d																						
Crystal Palace	d					09 31				09 37									10 01				10 07
Gipsy Hill	d					09 33				09 39									10 03				10 09
West Norwood	d					09 36				09 42									10 06				10 12
Streatham Hill	d					09 40													10 10				
Balham	d		09 38			09 43			09 53						10 08				10 13			10 23	
Wandsworth Common	d					09 45													10 15				
Latchmere	d																						
Clapham Junction	d	09 32	09 42	09 48		09 49			09 57						10 13		10 19		10 19			10 27	
Imperial Wharf	d																						
West Brompton	d																						
Kensington (Olympia)	d																						
Shepherd's Bush	d																						
Wembley Central	d																						
Harrow & Wealdstone	d																						
Watford Junction	d																						
Milton Keynes Central	a																						
Battersea Park	d				09 45	09 53								10 02				10 15	10 22				
London Victoria	a	09 39	09 50	09 55		09 57			10 04					10 06	10 20		10 25		10 27			10 34	
Streatham	d										09 58					10 06							
Tulse Hill	d									09 46	10 02					10 10							10 16
Herne Hill	a															10 14							
Loughborough Jn	a															10 17							
Elephant & Castle	a															10 21							
London Blackfriars	a												10 07			10 25							
City Thameslink	a																						
St Pancras International	a												10 18			10 35							
Luton Airport Parkway	a															11 20							
Luton	a															11 24							
North Dulwich	d									09 49	10 05												10 19
East Dulwich	d									09 51	10 07												10 21
Peckham Rye	d				09 56					09 53	10 10							10 26					10 23
Queens Rd Peckham	d				09 59					09 56	10 12							10 29					10 26
South Bermondsey	d				10 01					09 58	10 15							10 31					10 28
London Bridge	a				10 06		09 51	10 01		10 03	10 19	10 18						10 36		10 12	10 31		10 33

Table 177

Sundays

1 July to 9 September

East and West Croydon, London
Milton Keynes Central and Luton via Norbury
Crystal Palace - Tulse Hill

Local Services

Network Diagram - see first Page of Table 177

		SN	SN	FC 1	SN	SN ◇1	SN	FC	SN ◇1	SN	SN	SN 1	SN	SN	SN	SN	SN	FC 1	SN	SN	FC	SN ◇1	SN	SN
East Croydon	d	10 12	10 17	10 17		10 20	10 23		10 39			10 34				10 42	10 47	10 47		10 53		11 09		
West Croydon	d										10 22		10 34	10 37										10 52
Norwood Junction	a		10 21								10 26	10 38	10 39				10 51							10 56
	d		10 22								10 27	10 38	10 40				10 52							10 57
Selhurst	d	10 16					10 26							10 41		10 46				10 57				
Thornton Heath	d	10 18					10 28							10 43		10 48				10 59				
Norbury	d	10 21					10 31							10 46		10 51				11 02				
Streatham Common	d	10 23					10 34							10 49		10 53				11 04				
Beckenham Junction	d																							
Birkbeck	d																							
Crystal Palace	d										10 31				10 37									11 01
Gipsy Hill	d										10 33				10 39									11 03
West Norwood	d										10 36				10 42									11 06
Streatham Hill	d										10 40													11 10
Balham	d						10 38				10 43			10 53						11 08				11 13
Wandsworth Common	d										10 45													11 15
Latchmere	d																							
Clapham Junction	d					10 32	10 42		10 49		10 49			10 57						11 13		11 19		11 19
Imperial Wharf	d																							
West Brompton	d																							
Kensington (Olympia)	d																							
Shepherd's Bush	d																							
Wembley Central	d																							
Harrow & Wealdstone	d																							
Watford Junction	d																							
Milton Keynes Central	a																							
Battersea Park	d				10 32					10 45	10 52								11 02				11 15	11 22
London Victoria	a				10 36	10 39	10 50		10 55		10 57			11 04					11 06	11 20		11 25		11 27
Streatham	d	10 28						10 36								10 58					11 06			
Tulse Hill	d	10 32						10 40							10 46	11 02					11 10			
Herne Hill	a							10 44													11 14			
Loughborough Jn	a							10 47													11 17			
Elephant & Castle	a							10 51													11 21			
London Blackfriars	a			10 37				10 55										11 07			11 25			
City Thameslink	a																							
St Pancras International	a			10 48				11 05										11 18			11 35			
Luton Airport Parkway	a			11 24				11 50										11 54			12 20			
Luton	a			11 27				11 54										11 57			12 24			
North Dulwich	d	10 35													10 49	11 05								
East Dulwich	d	10 37													10 51	11 07								
Peckham Rye	d	10 40								10 56					10 53	11 10							11 26	
Queens Rd Peckham	d	10 42								10 59					10 56	11 12							11 29	
South Bermondsey	d	10 45								11 01					10 58	11 15							11 31	
London Bridge	a	10 49	10 48							11 06		10 51	11 01		11 03	11 19	11 18						11 36	

Table 177

Sundays
1 July to 9 September

East and West Croydon, London Milton Keynes Central and Luton via Norbury Crystal Palace - Tulse Hill

Local Services

Network Diagram - see first Page of Table 177

		SN 1	SN	SN	SN	SN	SN	FC 1		SN	SN ◇1	SN	FC	SN ◇1	SN	SN	SN 1	SN	SN	SN	SN	SN	FC 1	SN
East Croydon	d	10 56				11 12	11 17	11 17			11 20	11 23		11 39			11 34				11 42	11 47	11 47	
West Croydon 4	d		11 04	11 07												11 22		11 34	11 37					
Norwood Junction 2	a	11 00	11 09				11 21									11 26	11 38	11 39				11 51		
	d	11 01	11 10				11 22									11 27	11 38	11 40				11 52		
Selhurst 4	d			11 11		11 16						11 26							11 41		11 46			
Thornton Heath	d			11 13		11 18						11 28							11 43		11 48			
Norbury	d			11 16		11 21						11 31							11 46		11 51			
Streatham Common 4	d			11 19		11 23						11 34							11 49		11 53			
Beckenham Junction 4	d																							
Birkbeck	d																							
Crystal Palace 4	d				11 07											11 31				11 37				
Gipsy Hill	d				11 09											11 33				11 39				
West Norwood 4	d				11 12											11 36				11 42				
Streatham Hill	d															11 40								
Balham 4 ⊖	d			11 23								11 38				11 43			11 53					
Wandsworth Common	d															11 45								
Latchmere	d																							
Clapham Junction 10	d			11 27							11 32	11 42		11 48		11 49			11 57					
Imperial Wharf	d																							
West Brompton ⊖	d																							
Kensington (Olympia) ⊖	d																							
Shepherd's Bush ⊖	d																							
Wembley Central ⊖	d																							
Harrow & Wealdstone ⊖	d																							
Watford Junction	d																							
Milton Keynes Central 10	a																							
Battersea Park 4	d									11 32					11 45	11 52								12 02
London Victoria 15 ⊖	a			11 34						11 36	11 39	11 50		11 55		11 57			12 04					12 06
Streatham 4	d					11 28							11 36								11 58			
Tulse Hill 3	d				11 16	11 32							11 40							11 46	12 02			
Herne Hill 4	a												11 44											
Loughborough Jn	a												11 47											
Elephant & Castle ⊖	a												11 51											
London Blackfriars 3 ⊖	a							11 37					11 55										12 07	
City Thameslink 3	a																							
St Pancras International 15 ⊖	a							11 48					12 05										12 18	
Luton Airport Parkway 7	a							12 24					12 50										12 54	
Luton 10	a							12 27					12 54										12 57	
North Dulwich	d				11 19	11 35														11 49	12 05			
East Dulwich	d				11 21	11 37														11 51	12 07			
Peckham Rye 4	d				11 23	11 40									11 56					11 53	12 10			
Queens Rd Peckham	d				11 26	11 42									11 59					11 56	12 12			
South Bermondsey	d				11 28	11 45									12 01					11 58	12 15			
London Bridge 4 ⊖	a	11 12	11 31		11 33	11 49	11 48								12 06		11 51	12 01		12 03	12 19	12 18		

Table 177

Sundays
1 July to 9 September

East and West Croydon, London Milton Keynes Central and Luton via Norbury Crystal Palace - Tulse Hill

Local Services

Network Diagram - see first Page of Table 177

		SN	FC	SN ◇1	SN	SN	SN 1	SN	SN	SN	SN	SN	FC 1	SN	SN ◇1	SN		FC	SN ◇1	SN	SN	SN 1	SN	SN	SN
East Croydon	d	11 53		12 09			11 56				12 12	12 17	12 17		12 20	12 23			12 39			12 34			
West Croydon 4	d					11 52		12 04	12 07												12 22		12 34	12 37	
Norwood Junction 2	a					11 56	12 00	12 09				12 21									12 26	12 38	12 39		
	d					11 57	12 01	12 10				12 22									12 27	12 38	12 40		
Selhurst 4	d	11 57							12 11		12 16					12 26								12 41	
Thornton Heath	d	11 59							12 13		12 18					12 28								12 43	
Norbury	d	12 02							12 16		12 21					12 31								12 46	
Streatham Common 4	d	12 04							12 19		12 23					12 34								12 49	
Beckenham Junction 4	d																								
Birkbeck	d																								
Crystal Palace 4	d					12 01				12 07											12 31				12 37
Gipsy Hill	d					12 03				12 09											12 33				12 39
West Norwood 4	d					12 06				12 12											12 36				12 42
Streatham Hill	d					12 10															12 40				
Balham 4 ⊖	d	12 08				12 13			12 23							12 38					12 43			12 53	
Wandsworth Common	d					12 15															12 45				
Latchmere	d																								
Clapham Junction 10	d	12 13		12 19		12 19			12 27						12 32	12 42			12 48		12 49			12 57	
Imperial Wharf	d																								
West Brompton ⊖	d																								
Kensington (Olympia) ⊖	d																								
Shepherd's Bush ⊖	d																								
Wembley Central ⊖	d																								
Harrow & Wealdstone ⊖	d																								
Watford Junction	d																								
Milton Keynes Central 10	a																								
Battersea Park 4	d				12 15	12 22								12 32						12 45	12 52				
London Victoria 15 ⊖	a	12 20		12 25		12 27			12 34					12 36	12 39	12 50			12 55		12 57			13 04	
Streatham 4	d		12 06								12 28							12 36							
Tulse Hill 3	d		12 10							12 16	12 32							12 40							12 46
Herne Hill 4	a		12 14															12 44							
Loughborough Jn	a		12 17															12 47							
Elephant & Castle ⊖	a		12 21															12 51							
London Blackfriars 3 ⊖	a		12 25										12 37					12 55							
City Thameslink 3	a																								
St Pancras International 15 ⊖	a		12 35										12 48					13 05							
Luton Airport Parkway 7	a		13 20										13 24					13 50							
Luton 10	a		13 24										13 27					13 54							
North Dulwich	d									12 19	12 35														12 49
East Dulwich	d									12 21	12 37														12 51
Peckham Rye 4	d				12 26					12 23	12 40									12 56					12 53
Queens Rd Peckham	d				12 29					12 26	12 42									12 59					12 56
South Bermondsey	d				12 31					12 28	12 45									13 01					12 58
London Bridge 4 ⊖	a				12 36		12 12	12 31		12 33	12 49	12 48								13 06		12 51	13 01		13 03

Table 177

Sundays

1 July to 9 September

East and West Croydon, London Milton Keynes Central and Luton via Norbury Crystal Palace - Tulse Hill

Local Services

Network Diagram - see first Page of Table 177

		SN	SN	FC [1]	SN	SN	FC	SN ◇[1] ⊼		SN	SN	SN [1]	SN	SN	SN	SN	SN	FC [1]	SN	SN ◇[1] ⊼	SN	FC	SN ◇[1]	SN
East Croydon (tram)	d	12 42	12 47	12 47		12 53		13 09				12 56				13 12	13 17	13 17		13 20	13 23		13 39	
West Croydon [4] (tram)	d										12 52		13 04	13 07										
Norwood Junction [2]	a		12 51								12 56	13 00	13 09				13 21							
	d		12 52								12 57	13 01	13 10				13 22							
Selhurst [4]	d	12 46				12 57								13 11		13 16					13 26			
Thornton Heath	d	12 48				12 59								13 13		13 18					13 28			
Norbury	d	12 51				13 02								13 16		13 21					13 31			
Streatham Common [4]	d	12 53				13 04								13 19		13 23					13 34			
Beckenham Junction [4] (tram)	d																							
Birkbeck (tram)	d																							
Crystal Palace [4]	d										13 01				13 07									
Gipsy Hill	d										13 03				13 09									
West Norwood [4]	d										13 06				13 12									
Streatham Hill	d										13 10													
Balham [4] ⊖	d					13 08					13 13			13 23							13 38			
Wandsworth Common	d										13 15													
Latchmere	d																							
Clapham Junction [10]	d					13 13		13 19			13 19			13 27						13 32	13 42		13 48	
Imperial Wharf	d																							
West Brompton ⊖	d																							
Kensington (Olympia) ⊖	d																							
Shepherd's Bush ⊖	d																							
Wembley Central ⊖	d																							
Harrow & Wealdstone ⊖	d																							
Watford Junction	d																							
Milton Keynes Central [10]	a																							
Battersea Park [4]	d				13 02					13 15	13 23								13 32					13 45
London Victoria [15] ⊖	a				13 06	13 20		13 25			13 27			13 34					13 36	13 39	13 50		13 55	
Streatham [4]	d	12 58					13 06									13 28						13 36		
Tulse Hill [3]	d	13 02					13 10								13 16	13 32						13 40		
Herne Hill [4]	a						13 14															13 44		
Loughborough Jn	a						13 17															13 47		
Elephant & Castle ⊖	a						13 21															13 51		
London Blackfriars [3] ⊖	a			13 07			13 25											13 37				13 55		
City Thameslink [3]	a																							
St Pancras International [15] ⊖	a			13 18			13 35											13 48				14 05		
Luton Airport Parkway [7]	a			13 54			14 20											14 24				14 50		
Luton [10]	a			13 57			14 24											14 27				14 54		
North Dulwich	d	13 05													13 19	13 35								
East Dulwich	d	13 07													13 21	13 37								
Peckham Rye [4]	d	13 10								13 26					13 23	13 40								13 56
Queens Rd Peckham	d	13 12								13 29					13 26	13 42								13 59
South Bermondsey	d	13 15								13 31					13 28	13 45								14 01
London Bridge [4] ⊖	a	13 19	13 18							13 36		13 12	13 31		13 33	13 49	13 48							14 06

Table 177

Sundays

1 July to 9 September

East and West Croydon, London Milton Keynes Central and Luton via Norbury Crystal Palace - Tulse Hill

Local Services

Network Diagram - see first Page of Table 177

		SN	SN [1]	SN	SN	SN	SN	SN	FC [1]	SN	SN	FC	SN ◇[1] ⊼	SN	SN	SN [1]		SN	SN	SN	SN	SN	FC [1]	SN	SN ◇[1] ⊼
East Croydon (tram)	d		13 34				13 42	13 47	13 47		13 53		14 09			13 56					14 12	14 17	14 17		14 20
West Croydon [4] (tram)	d	13 22		13 34	13 37										13 52			14 04	14 07						
Norwood Junction [2]	a	13 26	13 38	13 39				13 51							13 56	14 00		14 09				14 21			
	d	13 27	13 38	13 40				13 52							13 57	14 01		14 10				14 22			
Selhurst [4]	d				13 41		13 46				13 57								14 11		14 16				
Thornton Heath	d				13 43		13 48				13 59								14 13		14 18				
Norbury	d				13 46		13 51				14 02								14 16		14 21				
Streatham Common [4]	d				13 49		13 53				14 04								14 19		14 23				
Beckenham Junction [4] (tram)	d																								
Birkbeck (tram)	d																								
Crystal Palace [4]	d	13 31				13 37									14 01					14 07					
Gipsy Hill	d	13 33				13 39									14 03					14 09					
West Norwood [4]	d	13 36				13 42									14 06					14 12					
Streatham Hill	d	13 40													14 10										
Balham [4] ⊖	d	13 43			13 53						14 08				14 13				14 23						
Wandsworth Common	d	13 45													14 15										
Latchmere	d																								
Clapham Junction [10]	d	13 49			13 57						14 13		14 19		14 19				14 27						14 32
Imperial Wharf	d																								
West Brompton ⊖	d																								
Kensington (Olympia) ⊖	d																								
Shepherd's Bush ⊖	d																								
Wembley Central ⊖	d																								
Harrow & Wealdstone ⊖	d																								
Watford Junction	d																								
Milton Keynes Central [10]	a																								
Battersea Park [4]	d	13 52								14 02				14 15	14 23									14 32	
London Victoria [15] ⊖	a	13 57			14 04					14 06	14 20		14 25		14 27				14 34					14 36	14 39
Streatham [4]	d						13 58					14 06									14 28				
Tulse Hill [3]	d					13 46	14 02					14 10								14 16	14 32				
Herne Hill [4]	a											14 14													
Loughborough Jn	a											14 17													
Elephant & Castle ⊖	a											14 21													
London Blackfriars [3] ⊖	a								14 07			14 25											14 37		
City Thameslink [3]	a																								
St Pancras International [15] ⊖	a								14 18			14 35											14 48		
Luton Airport Parkway [7]	a								14 54			15 20											15 24		
Luton [10]	a								14 57			15 24											15 27		
North Dulwich	d					13 49	14 05													14 19	14 35				
East Dulwich	d					13 51	14 07													14 21	14 37				
Peckham Rye [4]	d					13 53	14 10							14 26						14 23	14 40				
Queens Rd Peckham	d					13 56	14 12							14 29						14 26	14 42				
South Bermondsey	d					13 58	14 15							14 31						14 28	14 45				
London Bridge [4] ⊖	a		13 51	14 01		14 03	14 19	14 18						14 36		14 12		14 31		14 33	14 49	14 48			

Table 177

Sundays
1 July to 9 September

East and West Croydon, London Milton Keynes Central and Luton via Norbury Crystal Palace - Tulse Hill

Local Services

Network Diagram - see first Page of Table 177

		SN	FC	SN ◇1	SN	SN	SN 1	SN		SN	SN	SN	SN	FC 1	SN	SN	FC	SN ◇1 ⌶	SN	SN	SN 1	SN	SN	SN
East Croydon	d	14 23		14 39			14 34					14 42	14 47	14 47		14 53		15 09			14 56			
West Croydon 4	d					14 22		14 34		14 37										14 52		15 04	15 07	
Norwood Junction 2	a					14 26	14 38	14 39					14 51							14 56	15 00	15 09		
	d					14 27	14 38	14 40					14 52							14 57	15 01	15 10		
Selhurst 4	d	14 26								14 41		14 46				14 57							15 11	
Thornton Heath	d	14 28								14 43		14 48				14 59							15 13	
Norbury	d	14 31								14 46		14 51				15 02							15 16	
Streatham Common 4	d	14 34								14 49		14 53				15 04							15 19	
Beckenham Junction 4	d																							
Birkbeck	d																							
Crystal Palace 4	d					14 31					14 37									15 01				15 07
Gipsy Hill	d					14 33					14 39									15 03				15 09
West Norwood 4	d					14 36					14 42									15 06				15 12
Streatham Hill	d					14 40														15 10				
Balham 4 ⊖	d	14 38				14 43				14 53						15 08				15 13			15 23	
Wandsworth Common	d					14 45														15 15				
Latchmere	d																							
Clapham Junction 10	d	14 42		14 48		14 49				14 57						15 13		15 19		15 19			15 27	
Imperial Wharf	d																							
West Brompton ⊖	d																							
Kensington (Olympia) ⊖	d																							
Shepherd's Bush ⊖	d																							
Wembley Central ⊖	d																							
Harrow & Wealdstone ⊖	d																							
Watford Junction	d																							
Milton Keynes Central 10	a																							
Battersea Park 4	d				14 45	14 52									15 02				15 15	15 23				
London Victoria 15 ⊖	a	14 50		14 55		14 57				15 04					15 06	15 20		15 25		15 27			15 34	
Streatham 4	d		14 36									14 58					15 06							
Tulse Hill 3	d		14 40								14 46	15 02					15 10							15 16
Herne Hill 4	a		14 44														15 14							
Loughborough Jn	a		14 47														15 17							
Elephant & Castle ⊖	a		14 51														15 21							
London Blackfriars 3 ⊖	a		14 55											15 07			15 25							
City Thameslink 3	a																							
St Pancras International 15 ⊖	a		15 05											15 18			15 35							
Luton Airport Parkway 7	a		15 50											15 54			16 20							
Luton 10	a		15 54											15 57			16 24							
North Dulwich	d										14 49	15 05												15 19
East Dulwich	d										14 51	15 07												15 21
Peckham Rye 4	d				14 56						14 53	15 10							15 26					15 23
Queens Rd Peckham	d				14 59						14 56	15 12							15 29					15 26
South Bermondsey	d				15 01						14 58	15 15							15 31					15 28
London Bridge 4 ⊖	a				15 06		14 51	15 01			15 03	15 19	15 18						15 36		15 12	15 31		15 33

Table 177

Sundays
1 July to 9 September

East and West Croydon, London Milton Keynes Central and Luton via Norbury Crystal Palace - Tulse Hill

Local Services

Network Diagram - see first Page of Table 177

		SN	SN	FC 1	SN	SN ◇1 ⌶	SN	FC	SN ◇1	SN	SN	SN 1	SN	SN	SN	SN		SN	FC 1	SN	SN	FC	SN ◇1 ⌶	SN	SN
East Croydon	d	15 12	15 17	15 17		15 20	15 23		15 39			15 34				15 42		15 47	15 47		15 53		16 09		
West Croydon 4	d										15 22		15 34	15 37											15 52
Norwood Junction 2	a		15 21								15 26	15 38	15 39					15 51							15 56
	d		15 22								15 27	15 38	15 40					15 52							15 57
Selhurst 4	d	15 16					15 26							15 41		15 46					15 57				
Thornton Heath	d	15 18					15 28							15 43		15 48					15 59				
Norbury	d	15 21					15 31							15 46		15 51					16 02				
Streatham Common 4	d	15 23					15 34							15 49		15 53					16 04				
Beckenham Junction 4	d																								
Birkbeck	d																								
Crystal Palace 4	d										15 31				15 37										16 01
Gipsy Hill	d										15 33				15 39										16 03
West Norwood 4	d										15 36				15 42										16 06
Streatham Hill	d										15 40														16 10
Balham 4 ⊖	d						15 38				15 43			15 53							16 08				16 13
Wandsworth Common	d										15 45														16 15
Latchmere	d																								
Clapham Junction 10	d					15 32	15 42		15 49		15 49			15 57							16 13		16 19		16 19
Imperial Wharf	d																								
West Brompton ⊖	d																								
Kensington (Olympia) ⊖	d																								
Shepherd's Bush ⊖	d																								
Wembley Central ⊖	d																								
Harrow & Wealdstone ⊖	d																								
Watford Junction	d																								
Milton Keynes Central 10	a																								
Battersea Park 4	d				15 32					15 45	15 52									16 02				16 15	16 23
London Victoria 15 ⊖	a				15 36	15 39	15 50		15 55		15 57			16 04						16 06	16 20		16 25		16 27
Streatham 4	d	15 28						15 36								15 58						16 06			
Tulse Hill 3	d	15 32						15 40							15 46	16 02						16 10			
Herne Hill 4	a							15 44														16 14			
Loughborough Jn	a							15 47														16 17			
Elephant & Castle ⊖	a							15 51														16 21			
London Blackfriars 3 ⊖	a			15 37				15 55											16 07			16 25			
City Thameslink 3	a																								
St Pancras International 15 ⊖	a			15 48				16 05											16 18			16 35			
Luton Airport Parkway 7	a			16 24				16 50											16 54			17 20			
Luton 10	a			16 27				16 54											16 57			17 24			
North Dulwich	d	15 35													15 49	16 05									
East Dulwich	d	15 37													15 51	16 07									
Peckham Rye 4	d	15 40								15 56					15 53	16 10								16 26	
Queens Rd Peckham	d	15 42								15 59					15 56	16 12								16 29	
South Bermondsey	d	15 45								16 01					15 58	16 15								16 31	
London Bridge 4 ⊖	a	15 49	15 48							16 06		15 51	16 01		16 03	16 19		16 18						16 36	

Table 177

Sundays
1 July to 9 September

East and West Croydon, London Milton Keynes Central and Luton via Norbury Crystal Palace - Tulse Hill

Local Services

Network Diagram - see first Page of Table 177

		SN	SN	SN	SN	SN	SN	FC		SN	SN	SN	FC	SN	SN	SN	SN	SN	SN	SN	SN	SN	FC	SN
		1						1			◇1 🚌			◇1			1						1	
East Croydon	d	15 56				16 12	16 17	16 17			16 20	16 23		16 39			16 34				16 42	16 47	16 47	
West Croydon 4	d		16 04	16 07												16 22		16 34	16 37					
Norwood Junction 2	a	16 00	16 09				16 21									16 26	16 38	16 39				16 51		
	d	16 01	16 10				16 22									16 27	16 38	16 40				16 52		
Selhurst 4	d			16 11		16 16						16 26							16 41		16 46			
Thornton Heath	d			16 13		16 18						16 28							16 43		16 48			
Norbury	d			16 16		16 21						16 31							16 46		16 51			
Streatham Common 4	d			16 19		16 23						16 34							16 49		16 53			
Beckenham Junction 4	d																							
Birkbeck	d																							
Crystal Palace 4	d				16 07											16 31				16 37				
Gipsy Hill	d				16 09											16 33				16 39				
West Norwood 4	d				16 12											16 36				16 42				
Streatham Hill	d															16 40								
Balham 4 ⊖	d			16 23								16 38				16 43			16 53					
Wandsworth Common	d															16 45								
Latchmere	d																							
Clapham Junction 10	d			16 27							16 32	16 42		16 48		16 49			16 57					
Imperial Wharf	d																							
West Brompton ⊖	d																							
Kensington (Olympia) ⊖	d																							
Shepherd's Bush ⊖	d																							
Wembley Central ⊖	d																							
Harrow & Wealdstone ⊖	d																							
Watford Junction	d																							
Milton Keynes Central 10	a																							
Battersea Park 4	d									16 32					16 45	16 52								17 02
London Victoria 15 ⊖	a			16 34						16 36	16 39	16 50		16 55		16 57			17 04					17 06
Streatham 4	d					16 28							16 36								16 58			
Tulse Hill 3	d				16 16	16 32							16 40							16 46	17 02			
Herne Hill 4	a												16 44											
Loughborough Jn	a												16 47											
Elephant & Castle ⊖	a												16 51											
London Blackfriars 3 ⊖	a							16 37					16 55											
City Thameslink 3	a																						17 07	
St Pancras International 15 ⊖	a							16 48					17 05										17 18	
Luton Airport Parkway 7	a							17 24					17 50										17 54	
Luton 10	a							17 27					17 54										17 57	
North Dulwich	d				16 19	16 35														16 49	17 05			
East Dulwich	d				16 21	16 37														16 51	17 07			
Peckham Rye 4	d				16 23	16 40									16 56					16 53	17 10			
Queens Rd Peckham	d				16 26	16 42									16 59					16 56	17 12			
South Bermondsey	d				16 28	16 45									17 01					16 58	17 15			
London Bridge 4 ⊖	a	16 12	16 31		16 33	16 49	16 48								17 06		16 51	17 01		17 03	17 19	17 18		

Table 177

Sundays
1 July to 9 September

East and West Croydon, London Milton Keynes Central and Luton via Norbury Crystal Palace - Tulse Hill

Local Services

Network Diagram - see first Page of Table 177

		SN	FC	SN	SN	SN	SN	SN	SN	SN	SN	SN	FC	SN	SN	SN		FC	SN	SN	SN	SN	SN	SN	SN
				◇1 🚌			1						1		◇1 🚌				◇1			1			
East Croydon	d	16 53		17 09			16 56				17 12	17 17	17 17		17 20	17 23			17 39			17 34			
West Croydon 4	d					16 52		17 04	17 07												17 22		17 34	17 37	
Norwood Junction 2	a					16 56	17 00	17 09				17 21									17 26	17 38	17 39		
	d					16 57	17 01	17 10				17 22									17 27	17 38	17 40		
Selhurst 4	d	16 57							17 11		17 16					17 26								17 41	
Thornton Heath	d	16 59							17 13		17 18					17 28								17 43	
Norbury	d	17 02							17 16		17 21					17 31								17 46	
Streatham Common 4	d	17 04							17 19		17 23					17 34								17 49	
Beckenham Junction 4	d																								
Birkbeck	d																								
Crystal Palace 4	d					17 01				17 07											17 31				17 37
Gipsy Hill	d					17 03				17 09											17 33				17 39
West Norwood 4	d					17 06				17 12											17 36				17 42
Streatham Hill	d					17 10															17 40				
Balham 4 ⊖	d	17 08				17 13			17 23							17 38					17 43			17 53	
Wandsworth Common	d					17 15															17 45				
Latchmere	d																								
Clapham Junction 10	d	17 13		17 19		17 19			17 27						17 32	17 42			17 48		17 49			17 57	
Imperial Wharf	d																								
West Brompton ⊖	d																								
Kensington (Olympia) ⊖	d																								
Shepherd's Bush ⊖	d																								
Wembley Central ⊖	d																								
Harrow & Wealdstone ⊖	d																								
Watford Junction	d																								
Milton Keynes Central 10	a																								
Battersea Park 4	d				17 15	17 23								17 32						17 45	17 52				
London Victoria 15 ⊖	a	17 20		17 25		17 27			17 34					17 36	17 39	17 50			17 55		17 57			18 04	
Streatham 4	d		17 06								17 28							17 36							
Tulse Hill 3	d		17 10							17 16	17 32							17 40							17 46
Herne Hill 4	a		17 14															17 44							
Loughborough Jn	a		17 17															17 47							
Elephant & Castle ⊖	a		17 21															17 51							
London Blackfriars 3 ⊖	a		17 25										17 37					17 55							
City Thameslink 3	a																								
St Pancras International 15 ⊖	a		17 35										17 48					18 05							
Luton Airport Parkway 7	a		18 20										18 24					18 50							
Luton 10	a		18 24										18 27					18 54							
North Dulwich	d									17 19	17 35														17 49
East Dulwich	d									17 21	17 37														17 51
Peckham Rye 4	d				17 26					17 23	17 40									17 56					17 53
Queens Rd Peckham	d				17 29					17 26	17 42									17 59					17 56
South Bermondsey	d				17 31					17 28	17 45									18 01					17 58
London Bridge 4 ⊖	a				17 36		17 12	17 31		17 33	17 49	17 48								18 06		17 51	18 01		18 03

Table 177

Sundays
1 July to 9 September

East and West Croydon, London Milton Keynes Central and Luton via Norbury Crystal Palace - Tulse Hill

Local Services

Network Diagram - see first Page of Table 177

Station		SN	SN	FC ■	SN	SN	FC	SN ◇■ ⚒		SN	SN	SN ■	SN	SN	SN	SN	SN	FC ■	SN	SN ◇■ ⚒	SN	FC	SN ◇■	SN
East Croydon ⇌	d	17 42	17 47	17 47		17 53		18 09				17 56				18 12	18 17	18 17		18 20	18 23		18 39	
West Croydon ■ ⇌	d										17 52		18 04	18 07										
Norwood Junction ■	a		17 51								17 56	18 00	18 09				18 21							
	d		17 52								17 57	18 01	18 10				18 22							
Selhurst ■	d	17 46				17 57								18 11		18 16					18 26			
Thornton Heath	d	17 48				17 59								18 13		18 18					18 28			
Norbury	d	17 51				18 02								18 16		18 21					18 31			
Streatham Common ■	d	17 53				18 04								18 19		18 23					18 34			
Beckenham Junction ■ ⇌	d																							
Birkbeck ⇌	d																							
Crystal Palace ■	d										18 01				18 07									
Gipsy Hill	d										18 03				18 09									
West Norwood ■	d										18 06				18 12									
Streatham Hill	d										18 10													
Balham ■ ⊖	d					18 08					18 13			18 23							18 38			
Wandsworth Common	d										18 15													
Latchmere	d																							
Clapham Junction ■	d					18 13		18 19			18 19			18 27						18 32	18 42		18 48	
Imperial Wharf	d																							
West Brompton ⊖	d																							
Kensington (Olympia) ⊖	d																							
Shepherd's Bush ⊖	d																							
Wembley Central ⊖	d																							
Harrow & Wealdstone ⊖	d																							
Watford Junction	d																							
Milton Keynes Central ■	a																							
Battersea Park ■	d				18 02					18 15	18 23								18 32					18 45
London Victoria ■ ⊖	a				18 06	18 20		18 25			18 27			18 34					18 36	18 39	18 50		18 55	
Streatham ■	d	17 58					18 06									18 28						18 36		
Tulse Hill ■	d	18 02					18 10								18 16	18 32						18 40		
Herne Hill ■	a						18 14															18 44		
Loughborough Jn	a						18 17															18 47		
Elephant & Castle ⊖	a						18 21															18 51		
London Blackfriars ■ ⊖	a			18 07			18 25											18 37				18 55		
City Thameslink ■	a																							
St Pancras International ■ ⊖	a			18 18			18 35											18 48				19 05		
Luton Airport Parkway ■	a			18 54			19 20											19 24				19 50		
Luton ■	a			18 57			19 24											19 27				19 54		
North Dulwich	d	18 05													18 19	18 35								
East Dulwich	d	18 07													18 21	18 37								
Peckham Rye ■	d	18 10								18 26					18 23	18 40								18 56
Queens Rd Peckham	d	18 12								18 29					18 26	18 42								18 59
South Bermondsey	d	18 15								18 31					18 28	18 45								19 01
London Bridge ■ ⊖	a	18 19	18 18							18 36		18 12	18 31		18 33	18 49	18 48							19 06

Table 177

Sundays
1 July to 9 September

East and West Croydon, London Milton Keynes Central and Luton via Norbury Crystal Palace - Tulse Hill

Local Services

Network Diagram - see first Page of Table 177

Station		SN	SN ■	SN	SN	SN	SN	SN	FC ■	SN	SN	FC	SN ◇■ ⚒	SN	SN	SN ■		SN	SN	SN	SN	SN	FC ■	SN	SN ◇■
East Croydon ⇌	d		18 34				18 42	18 47	18 47		18 53		19 09			18 56					19 12	19 17	19 17		19 20
West Croydon ■ ⇌	d	18 22		18 34	18 37										18 52			19 04	19 07						
Norwood Junction ■	a	18 26	18 38	18 39				18 51							18 56	19 00		19 09				19 21			
	d	18 27	18 38	18 40				18 52							18 57	19 01		19 10				19 22			
Selhurst ■	d				18 41		18 46				18 57								19 11		19 16				
Thornton Heath	d				18 43		18 48				18 59								19 13		19 18				
Norbury	d				18 46		18 51				19 02								19 16		19 21				
Streatham Common ■	d				18 49		18 53				19 04								19 19		19 23				
Beckenham Junction ■ ⇌	d																								
Birkbeck ⇌	d																								
Crystal Palace ■	d	18 31				18 37									19 01					19 07					
Gipsy Hill	d	18 33				18 39									19 03					19 09					
West Norwood ■	d	18 36				18 42									19 06					19 12					
Streatham Hill	d	18 40													19 10										
Balham ■ ⊖	d	18 43			18 53						19 08				19 13				19 23						
Wandsworth Common	d	18 45													19 15										
Latchmere	d																								
Clapham Junction ■	d	18 49			18 57						19 13		19 19		19 19				19 27						19 32
Imperial Wharf	d																								
West Brompton ⊖	d																								
Kensington (Olympia) ⊖	d																								
Shepherd's Bush ⊖	d																								
Wembley Central ⊖	d																								
Harrow & Wealdstone ⊖	d																								
Watford Junction	d																								
Milton Keynes Central ■	a																								
Battersea Park ■	d	18 52								19 02				19 15	19 23									19 32	
London Victoria ■ ⊖	a	18 57			19 04					19 06	19 20		19 25		19 27				19 34					19 36	19 39
Streatham ■	d						18 58					19 06									19 28				
Tulse Hill ■	d					18 46	19 02					19 10								19 16	19 32				
Herne Hill ■	a											19 14													
Loughborough Jn	a											19 17													
Elephant & Castle ⊖	a											19 21													
London Blackfriars ■ ⊖	a								19 07			19 25											19 37		
City Thameslink ■	a																								
St Pancras International ■ ⊖	a								19 18			19 35											19 48		
Luton Airport Parkway ■	a								19 54			20 20											20 24		
Luton ■	a								19 57			20 23											20 27		
North Dulwich	d					18 49	19 05													19 19	19 35				
East Dulwich	d					18 51	19 07													19 21	19 37				
Peckham Rye ■	d					18 53	19 10							19 26						19 23	19 40				
Queens Rd Peckham	d					18 56	19 12							19 29						19 26	19 42				
South Bermondsey	d					18 58	19 15							19 31						19 28	19 45				
London Bridge ■ ⊖	a		18 51	19 01		19 03	19 19	19 18						19 36		19 12		19 31		19 33	19 49	19 48			

Table 177

Sundays
1 July to 9 September

East and West Croydon, London
Milton Keynes Central and Luton via Norbury
Crystal Palace - Tulse Hill

Local Services

Network Diagram - see first Page of Table 177

		SN	FC	SN ◇1	SN	SN	SN 1	SN		SN	SN	SN	SN	SN	SN	FC	SN ◇1	SN	SN	SN 1	SN	SN	SN	SN
East Croydon ⇌	d	19 23		19 39			19 34					19 42	19 47		19 53		20 09			19 56				20 12
West Croydon 4 ⇌	d					19 22		19 34		19 37									19 52		20 04	20 07		
Norwood Junction 2	a					19 26	19 38	19 39					19 51						19 56	20 00	20 09			
	d					19 27	19 38	19 40					19 52						19 57	20 01	20 10			
Selhurst 4	d	19 26								19 41		19 46			19 57							20 11		20 16
Thornton Heath	d	19 28								19 43		19 48			19 59							20 13		20 18
Norbury	d	19 31								19 46		19 51			20 02							20 16		20 21
Streatham Common 4	d	19 34								19 49		19 53			20 04							20 19		20 23
Beckenham Junction 4 ⇌	d																							
Birkbeck ⇌	d																							
Crystal Palace 4	d					19 31					19 37								20 01				20 07	
Gipsy Hill	d					19 33					19 39								20 03				20 09	
West Norwood 4	d					19 36					19 42								20 06				20 12	
Streatham Hill	d					19 40													20 10					
Balham 4 ⊖	d	19 38				19 43				19 53					20 08				20 13			20 23		
Wandsworth Common	d					19 45													20 15					
Latchmere	d																							
Clapham Junction 10	d	19 42		19 48		19 49				19 57					20 13		20 19		20 19			20 27		
Imperial Wharf	d																							
West Brompton ⊖	d																							
Kensington (Olympia) ⊖	d																							
Shepherd's Bush ⊖	d																							
Wembley Central ⊖	d																							
Harrow & Wealdstone ⊖	d																							
Watford Junction	d																							
Milton Keynes Central 10	a																							
Battersea Park 4	d				19 45	19 52								20 02				20 15	20 22					
London Victoria 15 ⊖	a	19 50		19 55		19 57				20 04				20 06	20 20		20 25		20 27			20 34		
Streatham 4	d		19 36									19 58				20 06								
Tulse Hill 3	d		19 40								19 46	20 02				20 10								20 28
Herne Hill 4	a		19 44													20 14							20 16	20 32
Loughborough Jn	a		19 47													20 17								
Elephant & Castle ⊖	a		19 51													20 21								
London Blackfriars 3 ⊖	a		19 55													20 25								
City Thameslink 3	a																							
St Pancras International 15 ⊖	a		20 05													20 35								
Luton Airport Parkway 7	a		20 50													21 20								
Luton 10	a		20 53													21 23								
North Dulwich	d										19 49	20 05											20 19	20 35
East Dulwich	d										19 51	20 07											20 21	20 37
Peckham Rye 4	d				19 56						19 53	20 10						20 26					20 23	20 40
Queens Rd Peckham	d				19 59						19 56	20 12						20 29					20 26	20 42
South Bermondsey	d				20 01						19 58	20 15						20 31					20 28	20 45
London Bridge 4 ⊖	a				20 06		19 51	20 01			20 03	20 19	20 18					20 36		20 12	20 31		20 33	20 49

Table 177

Sundays
1 July to 9 September

East and West Croydon, London
Milton Keynes Central and Luton via Norbury
Crystal Palace - Tulse Hill

Local Services

Network Diagram - see first Page of Table 177

		SN	SN	SN ◇1	SN	FC	SN ◇1	SN	SN	SN 1	SN	SN	SN	SN	SN	SN		SN	FC	SN ◇1	SN	SN	SN 1	SN	SN
East Croydon ⇌	d	20 17		20 20	20 23		20 39			20 34				20 42	20 47			20 53		21 09			20 56		
West Croydon 4 ⇌	d								20 22		20 34	20 37										20 52		21 04	21 07
Norwood Junction 2	a	20 21							20 26	20 38	20 39				20 51							20 56	21 00	21 09	
	d	20 22							20 27	20 38	20 40				20 52							20 57	21 01	21 10	
Selhurst 4	d				20 26							20 41		20 46				20 57							21 11
Thornton Heath	d				20 28							20 43		20 48				20 59							21 13
Norbury	d				20 31							20 46		20 51				21 02							21 16
Streatham Common 4	d				20 34							20 49		20 53				21 04							21 19
Beckenham Junction 4 ⇌	d																								
Birkbeck ⇌	d																								
Crystal Palace 4	d								20 31				20 37									21 01			
Gipsy Hill	d								20 33				20 39									21 03			
West Norwood 4	d								20 36				20 42									21 06			
Streatham Hill	d								20 40													21 10			
Balham 4 ⊖	d				20 38				20 43			20 53						21 08				21 13			21 23
Wandsworth Common	d								20 45													21 15			
Latchmere	d																								
Clapham Junction 10	d			20 32	20 42		20 48		20 49			20 57						21 13		21 19		21 19			21 27
Imperial Wharf	d																								
West Brompton ⊖	d																								
Kensington (Olympia) ⊖	d																								
Shepherd's Bush ⊖	d																								
Wembley Central ⊖	d																								
Harrow & Wealdstone ⊖	d																								
Watford Junction	d																								
Milton Keynes Central 10	a																								
Battersea Park 4	d		20 32					20 45	20 52							21 02					21 15	21 23			
London Victoria 15 ⊖	a		20 36	20 39	20 50		20 55		20 57			21 04				21 06		21 20		21 25		21 27			21 34
Streatham 4	d					20 36								20 58					21 06						
Tulse Hill 3	d					20 40							20 46	21 02					21 10						
Herne Hill 4	a					20 44													21 14						
Loughborough Jn	a					20 47													21 17						
Elephant & Castle ⊖	a					20 51													21 21						
London Blackfriars 3 ⊖	a					20 55													21 25						
City Thameslink 3	a																								
St Pancras International 15 ⊖	a					21 05													21 35						
Luton Airport Parkway 7	a					21 50													22 20						
Luton 10	a					21 53													22 23						
North Dulwich	d												20 49	21 05											
East Dulwich	d												20 51	21 07											
Peckham Rye 4	d							20 56					20 53	21 10							21 26				
Queens Rd Peckham	d							20 59					20 56	21 12							21 29				
South Bermondsey	d							21 01					20 58	21 15							21 31				
London Bridge 4 ⊖	a	20 48						21 06		20 51	21 01		21 03	21 19	21 18						21 36		21 12	21 31	

Table 177

Sundays
1 July to 9 September

East and West Croydon, London
Milton Keynes Central and Luton via Norbury
Crystal Palace - Tulse Hill

Local Services

Network Diagram - see first Page of Table 177

		SN	SN	SN	SN	SN ◇1	SN	FC		SN ◇1	SN	SN	SN 1	SN	SN	SN	SN	SN	SN	SN	SN ◇1	SN	SN	SN 1	
East Croydon	d		21 12	21 17		21 20	21 23			21 39			21 34				21 42	21 47		21 53	22 09			21 56	
West Croydon 4	d											21 22		21 34	21 37								21 52		
Norwood Junction 2	a			21 21								21 26	21 38	21 39				21 51					21 56	22 00	
	d			21 22								21 27	21 38	21 40				21 52					21 57	22 01	
Selhurst 4	d		21 16				21 26								21 41		21 46			21 56					
Thornton Heath	d		21 18				21 28								21 43		21 48			21 58					
Norbury	d		21 21				21 31								21 46		21 51			22 01					
Streatham Common 4	d		21 23				21 34								21 49		21 53			22 04					
Beckenham Junction 4	d																								
Birkbeck	d																								
Crystal Palace 4	d	21 07										21 31				21 37							22 01		
Gipsy Hill	d	21 09										21 33				21 39							22 03		
West Norwood 4	d	21 12										21 36				21 42							22 06		
Streatham Hill	d											21 40											22 10		
Balham 4 ⊖	d						21 38					21 43			21 53					22 08			22 13		
Wandsworth Common	d											21 45											22 15		
Latchmere	d																								
Clapham Junction 10	d					21 32	21 42			21 48		21 49			21 57					22 12	22 19		22 19		
Imperial Wharf	d																								
West Brompton ⊖	d																								
Kensington (Olympia) ⊖	d																								
Shepherd's Bush ⊖	d																								
Wembley Central ⊖	d																								
Harrow & Wealdstone ⊖	d																								
Watford Junction	d																								
Milton Keynes Central 10	a																								
Battersea Park 4	d				21 32						21 45	21 53							22 02			22 15	22 23		
London Victoria 15 ⊖	a				21 36	21 39	21 50			21 55		21 57			22 04				22 06	22 20	22 25		22 27		
Streatham 4	d		21 28					21 36									21 58								
Tulse Hill 3	d	21 16	21 32					21 40								21 46	22 02								
Herne Hill 4	a							21 44																	
Loughborough Jn	a							21 47																	
Elephant & Castle ⊖	a							21 51																	
London Blackfriars 3 ⊖	a							21 55																	
City Thameslink 3	a																								
St Pancras International 15 ⊖	a							22 05																	
Luton Airport Parkway 7	a							22 50																	
Luton 10	a							22 53																	
North Dulwich	d	21 19	21 35													21 49	22 05								
East Dulwich	d	21 21	21 37													21 51	22 07								
Peckham Rye 4	d	21 23	21 40								21 56					21 53	22 10					22 26			
Queens Rd Peckham	d	21 26	21 42								21 59					21 56	22 12					22 29			
South Bermondsey	d	21 28	21 45								22 01					21 58	22 15					22 31			
London Bridge 4 ⊖	a	21 33	21 49	21 48							22 06		21 51	22 01		22 03	22 19	22 18				22 36		22 12	

Table 177

Sundays
1 July to 9 September

East and West Croydon, London
Milton Keynes Central and Luton via Norbury
Crystal Palace - Tulse Hill

Local Services

Network Diagram - see first Page of Table 177

		SN	SN	SN	SN	SN	SN	SN ◇1	SN	SN	SN	SN 1	SN	SN	SN	SN		SN	SN	SN	SN 1	SN	SN	SN	SN
East Croydon	d				22 12	22 17		22 20	22 23			22 34				22 42		22 47		22 53	22 56				
West Croydon 4	d	22 04	22 07								22 22		22 34	22 37									22 52	23 07	
Norwood Junction 2	a	22 09				22 21					22 26	22 38	22 39					22 51					22 56		
	d	22 10				22 22					22 27	22 38	22 40					22 52					22 57		
Selhurst 4	d		22 11		22 16				22 26					22 41		22 46				22 57	22 59			23 11	
Thornton Heath	d		22 13		22 18				22 28					22 43		22 48				22 59				23 13	
Norbury	d		22 16		22 21				22 31					22 46		22 51				23 02				23 16	
Streatham Common 4	d		22 19		22 23				22 34					22 49		22 53				23 04				23 19	
Beckenham Junction 4	d																								
Birkbeck	d																								
Crystal Palace 4	d			22 07							22 31				22 37								23 01		23 07
Gipsy Hill	d			22 09							22 33				22 39								23 03		23 09
West Norwood 4	d			22 12							22 36				22 42								23 06		23 12
Streatham Hill	d										22 40												23 10		
Balham 4 ⊖	d		22 23						22 38		22 43			22 53						23 08			23 13	23 23	
Wandsworth Common	d										22 45												23 15		
Latchmere	d																								
Clapham Junction 10	d		22 27					22 32	22 42		22 49			22 57						23 13	23 08		23 19	23 27	
Imperial Wharf	d																								
West Brompton ⊖	d																								
Kensington (Olympia) ⊖	d																								
Shepherd's Bush ⊖	d																								
Wembley Central ⊖	d																								
Harrow & Wealdstone ⊖	d																								
Watford Junction	d																								
Milton Keynes Central 10	a																								
Battersea Park 4	d						22 32			22 45	22 53								23 02			23 15	23 23		
London Victoria 15 ⊖	a		22 34				22 36	22 39	22 52		22 57			23 04					23 06	23 20	23 14		23 27	23 34	
Streatham 4	d				22 28											22 58									
Tulse Hill 3	d			22 16	22 32										22 46	23 02									23 16
Herne Hill 4	a																								
Loughborough Jn	a																								
Elephant & Castle ⊖	a																								
London Blackfriars 3 ⊖	a																								
City Thameslink 3	a																								
St Pancras International 15 ⊖	a																								
Luton Airport Parkway 7	a																								
Luton 10	a																								
North Dulwich	d			22 19	22 35										22 49	23 05									23 19
East Dulwich	d			22 21	22 37										22 51	23 07									23 21
Peckham Rye 4	d			22 23	22 40					22 56					22 53	23 10						23 26			23 23
Queens Rd Peckham	d			22 26	22 42					22 59					22 56	23 12						23 29			23 26
South Bermondsey	d			22 28	22 45					23 01					22 58	23 15						23 31			23 28
London Bridge 4 ⊖	a	22 31		22 33	22 49	22 48				23 06		22 51	23 01		23 03	23 19		23 18				23 36			23 33

Sundays
1 July to 9 September

East and West Croydon, London Milton Keynes Central and Luton via Norbury Crystal Palace - Tulse Hill

Local Services

Network Diagram - see first Page of Table 177

		SN	SN	SN ◇1	SN	SN	SN	SN	SN	SN 1
East Croydon ⇌	d	23 17		23 21		23 26				23 56
West Croydon 4 ⇌	d				23 22		23 37		23 52	
Norwood Junction 2	a	23 21			23 26					
	d				23 27					
Selhurst 4	d					23a29	23 41		23 56	00 01
Thornton Heath	d						23 43		23 58	
Norbury	d						23 46		00 01	
Streatham Common 4	d						23 49		00 04	
Beckenham Junction 4 ⇌	d									
Birkbeck ⇌	d									
Crystal Palace 4	d				23 31			23 37		
Gipsy Hill	d				23 33			23 39		
West Norwood 4	d				23 36			23 42		
Streatham Hill	d				23 40					
Balham 4 ⊖	d				23 43		23 53		00 08	
Wandsworth Common	d				23 45					
Latchmere	d									
Clapham Junction 10	d			23 32	23 49		23 58		00 12	00 12
Imperial Wharf	d									
West Brompton ⊖	d									
Kensington (Olympia) ⊖	d									
Shepherd's Bush ⊖	d									
Wembley Central ⊖	d									
Harrow & Wealdstone ⊖	d									
Watford Junction	d									
Milton Keynes Central 10	a									
Battersea Park 4	d		23 32		23 53					
London Victoria 15 ⊖	a		23 37	23 38	23 57		00 04		00 19	00 19
Streatham 4	d									
Tulse Hill 3	d							23 46		
Herne Hill 4	a									
Loughborough Jn	a									
Elephant & Castle ⊖	a									
London Blackfriars 3 ⊖	a									
City Thameslink 3	a									
St Pancras International 15 ⊖	a									
Luton Airport Parkway 7	a									
Luton 10	a									
North Dulwich	d							23 49		
East Dulwich	d							23 51		
Peckham Rye 4	d							23 53		
Queens Rd Peckham	d							23 56		
South Bermondsey	d							23 58		
London Bridge 4 ⊖	a							00 03		

Sundays
from 16 September

East and West Croydon, London Milton Keynes Central and Luton via Norbury Crystal Palace - Tulse Hill

Local Services

Network Diagram - see first Page of Table 177

		FC	FC	SN	SN	SN	SN 1	SN	SN	SN	SN 1	SN 1	SN 1	SN 1	FC	SN 1	SN	SN	SN	SN	SN	SN	SN	SN
East Croydon ⇌	d						23p56			00 49	01 43	02 40	03 40	04 40	05 32	06 02	06 40	06 47					07 12	07 17
West Croydon 4 ⇌	d			23p34																	07 07			
Norwood Junction 2	a																	06 51						07 21
	d																	06 52		06 57				07 22
Selhurst 4	d			23p39													06 43		06 47		07 11		07 15	
Thornton Heath	d			23p41													06 45		06 49		07 13		07 17	
Norbury	d			23p44													06 48		06 52		07 16		07 20	
Streatham Common 4	d			23p46													06 51		06 55		07 19		07 23	
Beckenham Junction 4 ⇌	d																							
Birkbeck ⇌	d																							
Crystal Palace 4	d				23p43	23p51		00 13	00 21											07 01		07 07		
Gipsy Hill	d				23p45			00 15												07 03		07 09		
West Norwood 4	d				23p48			00 18												07 06		07 12		
Streatham Hill	d				23p52			00 22												07 10				
Balham 4 ⊖	d			23p50	23p55			00 26									06 55			07 13	07 23			
Wandsworth Common	d			23p52	23p57			00 28									06 57			07 15				
Latchmere	d																							
Clapham Junction 10	d			23p56	00 02		00 12	00 32		01 03	01 54	02 53	03 53	04 53		06 15	07 00			07 19	07 27			
Imperial Wharf	d																							
West Brompton ⊖	d																							
Kensington (Olympia) ⊖	d																							
Shepherd's Bush ⊖	d																							
Wembley Central ⊖	d																							
Harrow & Wealdstone ⊖	d																							
Watford Junction	d																							
Milton Keynes Central 10	a																							
Battersea Park 4	d				00 05			00 35									07 04				07 23			
London Victoria 15 ⊖	a			00 04	00 10		00 18	00 42		01 10	02 05	03 05	04 05	05 05		06 22	07 09				07 27	07 34		
Streatham 4	d	22p49	23p19																06 58					07 28
Tulse Hill 3	d	22p53	23p23																07 02			07 16	07 32	
Herne Hill 4	a	22p56	23p26																					
Loughborough Jn	a	23p00																						
Elephant & Castle ⊖	a	23p04	23p33																					
London Blackfriars 3 ⊖	a	23p07	23p37												05 59									
City Thameslink 3	a																							
St Pancras International 15 ⊖	a	23p17	23p47												06 07									
Luton Airport Parkway 7	a	00 02	00 32												06 53									
Luton 10	a	00 05	00 35												06 56									
North Dulwich	d																		07 05			07 19	07 35	
East Dulwich	d																		07 07			07 21	07 37	
Peckham Rye 4	d																		07 09			07 23	07 39	
Queens Rd Peckham	d																		07 12			07 26	07 42	
South Bermondsey	d																		07 14			07 28	07 44	
London Bridge 4 ⊖	a					00 11			00 41									07 17	07 19			07 33	07 50	07 48

Table 177

Sundays from 16 September

East and West Croydon, London Milton Keynes Central and Luton via Norbury Crystal Palace - Tulse Hill

Local Services

Network Diagram - see first Page of Table 177

		SN	SN 1	SN	SN	SN	SN	SN		SN	SN	SN	SN	SN	SN	SN 1	SN	SN	SN ◇1 H	SN	SN	SN	SN	SN ◇1
East Croydon ⇌	d		07 27							07 42	07 47		07 53			07 56			08 09		08 12	08 17		08 26
West Croydon 4 ⇌	d				07 22	07 34	07 37								07 52		08 04			08 07				
Norwood Junction 2	a				07 26	07 39					07 51				07 56	08 00	08 09					08 21		
	d				07 27	07 40					07 52				07 57	08 01	08 10					08 22		
Selhurst 4	d		07 31				07 41			07 46			07 57							08 11	08 16			
Thornton Heath	d						07 43			07 48			07 59							08 13	08 18			
Norbury	d						07 46			07 51			08 02							08 16	08 21			
Streatham Common 4	d						07 49			07 53			08 04							08 19	08 23			
Beckenham Junction 4 ⇌	d																							
Birkbeck ⇌	d																							
Crystal Palace 4	d				07 31			07 37							08 01			08 07						
Gipsy Hill	d				07 33			07 39							08 03			08 09						
West Norwood 4	d				07 36			07 42							08 06			08 12						
Streatham Hill	d				07 40										08 10									
Balham 4 ⊖	d				07 43		07 53						08 08		08 13					08 23				
Wandsworth Common	d				07 45										08 15									
Latchmere	d																							
Clapham Junction 10	d		07 41		07 49		07 57						08 13		08 19				08 24	08 27				08 38
Imperial Wharf	d																							
West Brompton ⊖	d																							
Kensington (Olympia) ⊖	d																							
Shepherd's Bush ⊖	d																							
Wembley Central ⊖	d																							
Harrow & Wealdstone ⊖	d																							
Watford Junction	d																							
Milton Keynes Central 10	a																							
Battersea Park 4	d	07 32		07 45	07 53							08 02		08 15	08 23								08 32	
London Victoria 15 ⊖	a	07 36	07 48		07 57		08 04					08 06	08 20		08 27				08 30	08 34			08 36	08 46
Streatham 4	d									07 58											08 28			
Tulse Hill 3	d							07 46		08 02								08 16			08 32			
Herne Hill 4	a																							
Loughborough Jn	a																							
Elephant & Castle ⊖	a																							
London Blackfriars 3 ⊖	a																							
City Thameslink 3	a																							
St Pancras International 15 ⊖	a																							
Luton Airport Parkway 7	a																							
Luton 10	a																							
North Dulwich	d							07 49		08 05								08 19			08 35			
East Dulwich	d							07 51		08 07								08 21			08 37			
Peckham Rye 4	d			07 56				07 53		08 10				08 26				08 23			08 40			
Queens Rd Peckham	d			07 59				07 56		08 12				08 29				08 26			08 42			
South Bermondsey	d			08 01				07 58		08 15				08 31				08 28			08 45			
London Bridge 4 ⊖	a			08 06		08 01		08 03		08 19	08 17			08 36		08 12	08 31	08 33			08 49	08 48		

Table 177

Sundays from 16 September

East and West Croydon, London Milton Keynes Central and Luton via Norbury Crystal Palace - Tulse Hill

Local Services

Network Diagram - see first Page of Table 177

		SN	SN	SN	SN	SN	SN ◇1	SN	SN	SN	SN	SN	SN	SN	SN 1	SN		SN	SN ◇1 H	SN	SN	SN	SN	SN ◇1 H	SN
East Croydon ⇌	d	08 23					08 40		08 42	08 47		08 53			08 56				09 10		09 12	09 17		09 26	09 23
West Croydon 4 ⇌	d			08 22	08 34			08 37						08 52		09 04				09 07					
Norwood Junction 2	a			08 26	08 39					08 51				08 56	09 00	09 09						09 21			
	d			08 27	08 40					08 52				08 57	09 01	09 10						09 22			
Selhurst 4	d	08 26						08 41	08 46			08 57								09 11	09 16				09 26
Thornton Heath	d	08 28						08 43	08 48			08 59								09 13	09 18				09 28
Norbury	d	08 31						08 46	08 51			09 02								09 16	09 21				09 31
Streatham Common 4	d	08 34						08 49	08 53			09 04								09 19	09 23				09 34
Beckenham Junction 4 ⇌	d																								
Birkbeck ⇌	d																								
Crystal Palace 4	d			08 31		08 37								09 01				09 07							
Gipsy Hill	d			08 33		08 39								09 03				09 09							
West Norwood 4	d			08 36		08 42								09 06				09 12							
Streatham Hill	d			08 40										09 10											
Balham 4 ⊖	d	08 38		08 43				08 53				09 08		09 13						09 23					09 38
Wandsworth Common	d			08 45										09 15											
Latchmere	d																								
Clapham Junction 10	d	08 42		08 49			08 55	08 57				09 13		09 19					09 25	09 27				09 38	09 42
Imperial Wharf	d																								
West Brompton ⊖	d																								
Kensington (Olympia) ⊖	d																								
Shepherd's Bush ⊖	d																								
Wembley Central ⊖	d																								
Harrow & Wealdstone ⊖	d																								
Watford Junction	d																								
Milton Keynes Central 10	a																								
Battersea Park 4	d		08 45	08 52							09 02		09 15	09 23									09 32		
London Victoria 15 ⊖	a	08 50		08 57			09 01	09 04			09 06	09 20		09 27					09 31	09 34			09 36	09 46	09 50
Streatham 4	d								08 58												09 28				
Tulse Hill 3	d					08 46			09 02									09 16			09 32				
Herne Hill 4	a																								
Loughborough Jn	a																								
Elephant & Castle ⊖	a																								
London Blackfriars 3 ⊖	a																								
City Thameslink 3	a																								
St Pancras International 15 ⊖	a																								
Luton Airport Parkway 7	a																								
Luton 10	a																								
North Dulwich	d					08 49			09 05									09 19			09 35				
East Dulwich	d					08 51			09 07									09 21			09 37				
Peckham Rye 4	d		08 56			08 53			09 10				09 26					09 23			09 40				
Queens Rd Peckham	d		08 59			08 56			09 12				09 29					09 26			09 42				
South Bermondsey	d		09 01			08 58			09 15				09 31					09 28			09 45				
London Bridge 4 ⊖	a		09 06		09 01	09 03			09 19	09 18			09 36		09 12	09 31		09 33			09 49	09 48			

Table 177

Sundays
from 16 September

East and West Croydon, London
Milton Keynes Central and Luton via Norbury
Crystal Palace - Tulse Hill

Local Services

Network Diagram - see first Page of Table 177

		SN	SN	SN	SN	SN ◇1	SN	SN		SN	SN	SN	FC	SN	SN	SN 1	SN	SN	SN ◇1 H	SN	SN	SN	SN	SN ◇1 H	
East Croydon	d					09 40		09 42		09 47		09 53				09 56			10 10		10 12	10 17		10 26	
West Croydon 4	d		09 22	09 34			09 37								09 52		10 04			10 07					
Norwood Junction 2	a		09 26	09 39						09 51					09 56	10 00	10 09					10 21			
	d		09 27	09 40						09 52					09 57	10 01	10 10					10 22			
Selhurst 4	d						09 41	09 46				09 57								10 11	10 16				
Thornton Heath	d						09 43	09 48				09 59								10 13	10 18				
Norbury	d						09 46	09 51				10 02								10 16	10 21				
Streatham Common 4	d						09 49	09 53				10 04								10 19	10 23				
Beckenham Junction 4	d																								
Birkbeck	d																								
Crystal Palace 4	d		09 31		09 37										10 01			10 07							
Gipsy Hill	d		09 33		09 39										10 03			10 09							
West Norwood 4	d		09 36		09 42										10 06			10 12							
Streatham Hill	d		09 40												10 10										
Balham 4 ⊖	d		09 43				09 53					10 08			10 13					10 23					
Wandsworth Common	d		09 45												10 15										
Latchmere	d																								
Clapham Junction 10	d		09 49			09 55	09 57					10 13			10 19				10 25	10 27				10 38	
Imperial Wharf	d																								
West Brompton ⊖	d																								
Kensington (Olympia) ⊖	d																								
Shepherd's Bush ⊖	d																								
Wembley Central ⊖	d																								
Harrow & Wealdstone ⊖	d																								
Watford Junction	d																								
Milton Keynes Central 10	a																								
Battersea Park 4	d	09 45	09 53								10 02			10 15	10 22								10 32		
London Victoria 15 ⊖	a		09 57			10 01	10 04				10 06	10 20			10 27				10 31	10 34			10 36	10 46	
Streatham 4	d							09 58					10 06								10 28				
Tulse Hill 3	d				09 46			10 02					10 10					10 16			10 32				
Herne Hill 4	a												10 14												
Loughborough Jn	a												10 17												
Elephant & Castle ⊖	a												10 21												
London Blackfriars 3 ⊖	a												10 25												
City Thameslink 3	a																								
St Pancras International 15 ⊖	a												10 35												
Luton Airport Parkway 7	a												11 20												
Luton 10	a												11 24												
North Dulwich	d				09 49			10 05										10 19			10 35				
East Dulwich	d				09 51			10 07										10 21			10 37				
Peckham Rye 4	d	09 56			09 53			10 10						10 26				10 23			10 40				
Queens Rd Peckham	d	09 59			09 56			10 12						10 29				10 26			10 42				
South Bermondsey	d	10 01			09 58			10 15						10 31				10 28			10 45				
London Bridge 4 ⊖	a	10 06		10 01	10 03			10 19		10 18				10 36		10 12	10 31	10 33			10 49	10 48			

Table 177

Sundays
from 16 September

East and West Croydon, London
Milton Keynes Central and Luton via Norbury
Crystal Palace - Tulse Hill

Local Services

Network Diagram - see first Page of Table 177

		SN	FC	SN	SN	SN	SN	SN ◇1	SN	SN	SN	FC 1	SN	SN	FC	SN		SN	SN 1	SN	SN	SN ◇1 H	SN	SN	SN
East Croydon	d	10 23						10 40		10 42	10 47	10 47		10 53					10 56			11 10		11 12	11 17
West Croydon 4	d				10 22	10 34			10 37									10 52		11 04			11 07		
Norwood Junction 2	a				10 26	10 39					10 51							10 56	11 00	11 09					11 21
	d				10 27	10 40					10 52							10 57	11 01	11 10					11 22
Selhurst 4	d	10 26							10 41	10 46				10 57									11 11	11 16	
Thornton Heath	d	10 28							10 43	10 48				10 59									11 13	11 18	
Norbury	d	10 31							10 46	10 51				11 02									11 16	11 21	
Streatham Common 4	d	10 34							10 49	10 53				11 04									11 19	11 23	
Beckenham Junction 4	d																								
Birkbeck	d																								
Crystal Palace 4	d				10 31		10 37											11 01			11 07				
Gipsy Hill	d				10 33		10 39											11 03			11 09				
West Norwood 4	d				10 36		10 42											11 06			11 12				
Streatham Hill	d				10 40													11 10							
Balham 4 ⊖	d	10 38			10 43				10 53					11 08				11 13					11 23		
Wandsworth Common	d				10 45													11 15							
Latchmere	d																								
Clapham Junction 10	d	10 42			10 49			10 55	10 57					11 13				11 19				11 25	11 27		
Imperial Wharf	d																								
West Brompton ⊖	d																								
Kensington (Olympia) ⊖	d																								
Shepherd's Bush ⊖	d																								
Wembley Central ⊖	d																								
Harrow & Wealdstone ⊖	d																								
Watford Junction	d																								
Milton Keynes Central 10	a																								
Battersea Park 4	d			10 45	10 52								11 02			11 15		11 22							
London Victoria 15 ⊖	a	10 50			10 57			11 01	11 04				11 06	11 20				11 27				11 31	11 34		
Streatham 4	d		10 36							10 58					11 06									11 28	
Tulse Hill 3	d		10 40				10 46			11 02					11 10						11 16			11 32	
Herne Hill 4	a		10 44												11 14										
Loughborough Jn	a		10 47												11 17										
Elephant & Castle ⊖	a		10 51												11 21										
London Blackfriars 3 ⊖	a		10 55									11 07			11 25										
City Thameslink 3	a																								
St Pancras International 15 ⊖	a		11 05									11 18			11 35										
Luton Airport Parkway 7	a		11 50									11 54			12 20										
Luton 10	a		11 54									11 57			12 24										
North Dulwich	d						10 49			11 05											11 19			11 35	
East Dulwich	d						10 51			11 07											11 21			11 37	
Peckham Rye 4	d			10 56			10 53			11 10						11 26					11 23			11 40	
Queens Rd Peckham	d			10 59			10 56			11 12						11 29					11 26			11 42	
South Bermondsey	d			11 01			10 58			11 15						11 31					11 28			11 45	
London Bridge 4 ⊖	a			11 06		11 01	11 03			11 19	11 18					11 36		11 12	11 31		11 33			11 49	11 48

Table 177

Sundays from 16 September

East and West Croydon, London
Milton Keynes Central and Luton via Norbury
Crystal Palace - Tulse Hill

Local Services

Network Diagram - see first Page of Table 177

Station		FC 1	SN	SN ◇1	SN	FC	SN	SN		SN	SN	SN ◇1	SN	SN	SN	FC 1	SN	SN	FC	SN	SN	SN 1	SN	SN
East Croydon	d	11 17		11 26	11 23							11 40		11 42	11 47	11 47		11 53				11 56		
West Croydon 4	d							11 22		11 34			11 37								11 52		12 04	
Norwood Junction 2	a							11 26		11 39					11 51						11 56	12 00	12 09	
	d							11 27		11 40					11 52						11 57	12 01	12 10	
Selhurst 4	d				11 26								11 41	11 46				11 57						
Thornton Heath	d				11 28								11 43	11 48				11 59						
Norbury	d				11 31								11 46	11 51				12 02						
Streatham Common 4	d				11 34								11 49	11 53				12 04						
Beckenham Junction 4	d																							
Birkbeck	d																							
Crystal Palace 4	d							11 31			11 37										12 01			12 07
Gipsy Hill	d							11 33			11 39										12 03			12 09
West Norwood 4	d							11 36			11 42										12 06			12 12
Streatham Hill	d							11 40													12 10			
Balham 4	d				11 38			11 43					11 53					12 08			12 13			
Wandsworth Common	d							11 45													12 15			
Latchmere	d																							
Clapham Junction 10	d			11 38	11 42			11 49				11 55	11 57					12 13			12 19			
Imperial Wharf	d																							
West Brompton	d																							
Kensington (Olympia)	d																							
Shepherd's Bush	d																							
Wembley Central	d																							
Harrow & Wealdstone	d																							
Watford Junction	d																							
Milton Keynes Central 10	a																							
Battersea Park 4	d		11 32				11 45	11 52									12 02			12 15	12 22			
London Victoria 15	a		11 36	11 46	11 50			11 57				12 01	12 04				12 06	12 20			12 27			
Streatham 4	d					11 36								11 58					12 06					
Tulse Hill 3	d					11 40					11 46			12 02					12 10					12 16
Herne Hill 4	a					11 44													12 14					
Loughborough Jn	a					11 47													12 17					
Elephant & Castle	a					11 51													12 21					
London Blackfriars 3	a	11 37				11 55										12 07			12 25					
City Thameslink 3	a																							
St Pancras International 15	a	11 48				12 05										12 18			12 35					
Luton Airport Parkway 7	a	12 24				12 50										12 54			13 20					
Luton 10	a	12 27				12 54										12 57			13 24					
North Dulwich	d										11 49			12 05										12 19
East Dulwich	d										11 51			12 07										12 21
Peckham Rye 4	d						11 56				11 53			12 10						12 26				12 23
Queens Rd Peckham	d						11 59				11 56			12 12						12 29				12 26
South Bermondsey	d						12 01				11 58			12 15						12 31				12 28
London Bridge 4	a						12 06			12 01	12 03			12 19	12 18					12 36		12 12	12 31	12 33

Table 177

Sundays from 16 September

East and West Croydon, London
Milton Keynes Central and Luton via Norbury
Crystal Palace - Tulse Hill

Local Services

Network Diagram - see first Page of Table 177

Station		SN ◇1	SN	SN	SN	FC 1	SN	SN ◇1	SN	FC	SN	SN	SN	SN	SN ◇1	SN		SN	SN	FC 1	SN	SN	FC	SN
East Croydon	d	12 10		12 12	12 17	12 17		12 26	12 23						12 40			12 42	12 47	12 47		12 53		
West Croydon 4	d		12 07									12 22	12 34			12 37								
Norwood Junction 2	a				12 21							12 26	12 39						12 51					
	d				12 22							12 27	12 40						12 52					
Selhurst 4	d		12 11	12 16					12 26							12 41		12 46				12 57		
Thornton Heath	d		12 13	12 18					12 28							12 43		12 48				12 59		
Norbury	d		12 16	12 21					12 31							12 46		12 51				13 02		
Streatham Common 4	d		12 19	12 23					12 34							12 49		12 53				13 04		
Beckenham Junction 4	d																							
Birkbeck	d																							
Crystal Palace 4	d											12 31		12 37										
Gipsy Hill	d											12 33		12 39										
West Norwood 4	d											12 36		12 42										
Streatham Hill	d											12 40												
Balham 4	d		12 23						12 38			12 43				12 53						13 08		
Wandsworth Common	d											12 45												
Latchmere	d																							
Clapham Junction 10	d	12 25	12 27					12 38	12 42			12 49			12 55	12 57						13 13		
Imperial Wharf	d																							
West Brompton	d																							
Kensington (Olympia)	d																							
Shepherd's Bush	d																							
Wembley Central	d																							
Harrow & Wealdstone	d																							
Watford Junction	d																							
Milton Keynes Central 10	a																							
Battersea Park 4	d						12 32				12 45	12 52									13 02			13 15
London Victoria 15	a	12 31	12 34				12 36	12 46	12 50			12 57			13 01	13 04					13 06	13 20		
Streatham 4	d			12 28						12 36								12 58					13 06	
Tulse Hill 3	d			12 32						12 40				12 46				13 02					13 10	
Herne Hill 4	a									12 44													13 14	
Loughborough Jn	a									12 47													13 17	
Elephant & Castle	a									12 51													13 21	
London Blackfriars 3	a					12 37				12 55										13 07			13 25	
City Thameslink 3	a																							
St Pancras International 15	a					12 48				13 05										13 18			13 35	
Luton Airport Parkway 7	a					13 24				13 50										13 54			14 20	
Luton 10	a					13 27				13 54										13 57			14 24	
North Dulwich	d			12 35										12 49				13 05						
East Dulwich	d			12 37										12 51				13 07						
Peckham Rye 4	d			12 40							12 56			12 53				13 10						13 26
Queens Rd Peckham	d			12 42							12 59			12 56				13 12						13 29
South Bermondsey	d			12 45							13 01			12 58				13 15						13 31
London Bridge 4	a			12 49	12 48						13 06		13 01	13 03				13 19	13 18					13 36

Table 177

Sundays
from 16 September

East and West Croydon, London Milton Keynes Central and Luton via Norbury Crystal Palace - Tulse Hill

Local Services

Network Diagram - see first Page of Table 177

		SN		SN	SN 1	SN	SN	SN ◇1		SN	SN	SN	FC 1	SN	SN ◇1	SN	FC	SN	SN	SN	SN	SN ◇1	SN	SN
East Croydon	d				17 56			18 10			18 12	18 17	18 17		18 26	18 23						18 40		18 42
West Croydon 4	d	12 52		17 52		18 04				18 07									18 22	18 34			18 37	
Norwood Junction 2	a	12 56		17 56	18 00	18 09						18 21							18 26	18 39				
	d	12 57		17 57	18 01	18 10						18 22							18 27	18 40				
Selhurst 4	d									18 11	18 16					18 26							18 41	18 46
Thornton Heath	d									18 13	18 18					18 28							18 43	18 48
Norbury	d									18 16	18 21					18 31							18 46	18 51
Streatham Common 4	d									18 19	18 23					18 34							18 49	18 53
Beckenham Junction 4	d																							
Birkbeck	d																							
Crystal Palace 4	d	13 01		18 01			18 07												18 31		18 37			
Gipsy Hill	d	13 03		18 03			18 09												18 33		18 39			
West Norwood 4	d	13 06		18 06			18 12												18 36		18 42			
Streatham Hill	d	13 10		18 10															18 40					
Balham 4 ⊖	d	13 13		18 13						18 23						18 38			18 43				18 53	
Wandsworth Common	d	13 15		18 15															18 45					
Latchmere	d																							
Clapham Junction 10	d	13 19	and at the same minutes past each hour until	18 19				18 25		18 27					18 38	18 42			18 49			18 55	18 57	
Imperial Wharf	d																							
West Brompton ⊖	d																							
Kensington (Olympia) ⊖	d																							
Shepherd's Bush ⊖	d																							
Wembley Central ⊖	d																							
Harrow & Wealdstone ⊖	d																							
Watford Junction	d																							
Milton Keynes Central 10	a																							
Battersea Park 4	d	13 23		18 23										18 32				18 45	18 52					
London Victoria 15 ⊖	a	13 27		18 27				18 31		18 34				18 36	18 46	18 50			18 57			19 01	19 04	
Streatham 4	d										18 28						18 36							18 58
Tulse Hill 3	d						18 16				18 32						18 40				18 46			19 02
Herne Hill 4	a																18 44							
Loughborough Jn	a																18 47							
Elephant & Castle ⊖	a																18 51							
London Blackfriars 3 ⊖	a												18 37				18 55							
City Thameslink 3	a																							
St Pancras International 15 ⊖	a												18 48				19 05							
Luton Airport Parkway 7	a												19 24				19 50							
Luton 10	a												19 27				19 54							
North Dulwich	d						18 19				18 35										18 49			19 05
East Dulwich	d						18 21				18 37										18 51			19 07
Peckham Rye 4	d						18 23				18 40							18 56			18 53			19 10
Queens Rd Peckham	d						18 26				18 42							18 59			18 56			19 12
South Bermondsey	d						18 28				18 45							19 01			18 58			19 15
London Bridge 4 ⊖	a				18 12	18 31	18 33				18 49	18 48						19 06		19 01	19 03			19 19

Table 177

Sundays
from 16 September

East and West Croydon, London Milton Keynes Central and Luton via Norbury Crystal Palace - Tulse Hill

Local Services

Network Diagram - see first Page of Table 177

			SN	FC 1	SN	SN	FC	SN	SN	SN 1	SN	SN	SN ◇1	SN	SN	SN	FC 1		SN	SN ◇1	SN	FC	SN	SN	SN
East Croydon	d		18 47	18 47		18 53				18 56			19 10		19 12	19 17	19 17			19 26	19 23				
West Croydon 4	d								18 52		19 04			19 07										19 22	19 34
Norwood Junction 2	a		18 51						18 56	19 00	19 09					19 21								19 26	19 39
	d		18 52						18 57	19 01	19 10					19 22								19 27	19 40
Selhurst 4	d					18 57								19 11	19 16						19 26				
Thornton Heath	d					18 59								19 13	19 18						19 28				
Norbury	d					19 02								19 16	19 21						19 31				
Streatham Common 4	d					19 04								19 19	19 23						19 34				
Beckenham Junction 4	d																								
Birkbeck	d																								
Crystal Palace 4	d								19 01			19 07												19 31	
Gipsy Hill	d								19 03			19 09												19 33	
West Norwood 4	d								19 06			19 12												19 36	
Streatham Hill	d								19 10															19 40	
Balham 4 ⊖	d					19 08			19 13					19 23							19 38			19 43	
Wandsworth Common	d								19 15															19 45	
Latchmere	d																								
Clapham Junction 10	d					19 13			19 19				19 25	19 27						19 38	19 42			19 49	
Imperial Wharf	d																								
West Brompton ⊖	d																								
Kensington (Olympia) ⊖	d																								
Shepherd's Bush ⊖	d																								
Wembley Central ⊖	d																								
Harrow & Wealdstone ⊖	d																								
Watford Junction	d																								
Milton Keynes Central 10	a																								
Battersea Park 4	d				19 02			19 15	19 23										19 32				19 45	19 52	
London Victoria 15 ⊖	a				19 06	19 20			19 27				19 31	19 34					19 36	19 46	19 50			19 57	
Streatham 4	d						19 06								19 28							19 36			
Tulse Hill 3	d						19 10					19 16			19 32							19 40			
Herne Hill 4	a						19 14															19 44			
Loughborough Jn	a						19 17															19 47			
Elephant & Castle ⊖	a						19 21															19 51			
London Blackfriars 3 ⊖	a			19 07			19 25										19 37					19 55			
City Thameslink 3	a																								
St Pancras International 15 ⊖	a			19 18			19 35										19 48					20 05			
Luton Airport Parkway 7	a			19 54			20 20										20 24					20 50			
Luton 10	a			19 57			20 23										20 27					20 53			
North Dulwich	d											19 19			19 35										
East Dulwich	d											19 21			19 37										
Peckham Rye 4	d							19 26				19 23			19 40								19 56		
Queens Rd Peckham	d							19 29				19 26			19 42								19 59		
South Bermondsey	d							19 31				19 28			19 45								20 01		
London Bridge 4 ⊖	a		19 18					19 36		19 12	19 31	19 33			19 49	19 48							20 06		20 01

Table 177

Sundays
from 16 September

East and West Croydon, London
Milton Keynes Central and Luton via Norbury
Crystal Palace - Tulse Hill

Local Services

Network Diagram - see first Page of Table 177

		SN	SN ◇1	SN	SN	SN	SN	SN	FC		SN	SN	SN 1	SN	SN	SN ◇1	SN	SN	SN	SN	SN ◇1	SN	FC	SN	SN
East Croydon ⇌	d		19 40		19 42	19 47		19 53					19 56			20 10		20 12	20 17		20 26	20 23			
West Croydon 4 ⇌	d			19 37								19 52		20 04			20 07								20 22
Norwood Junction 2	a					19 51						19 56	20 00	20 09					20 21						20 26
	d					19 52						19 57	20 01	20 10					20 22						20 27
Selhurst 4	d			19 41	19 46			19 57									20 11	20 16				20 26			
Thornton Heath	d			19 43	19 48			19 59									20 13	20 18				20 28			
Norbury	d			19 46	19 51			20 02									20 16	20 21				20 31			
Streatham Common 4	d			19 49	19 53			20 04									20 19	20 23				20 34			
Beckenham Junction 4 ⇌	d																								
Birkbeck ⇌	d																								
Crystal Palace 4	d	19 37										20 01			20 07										20 31
Gipsy Hill	d	19 39										20 03			20 09										20 33
West Norwood 4	d	19 42										20 06			20 12										20 36
Streatham Hill	d											20 10													20 40
Balham 4 ⊖	d			19 53				20 08				20 13					20 23					20 38			20 43
Wandsworth Common	d											20 15													20 45
Latchmere	d																								
Clapham Junction 10	d		19 55	19 57				20 13				20 19				20 25	20 27				20 38	20 42			20 49
Imperial Wharf	d																								
West Brompton ⊖	d																								
Kensington (Olympia) ⊖	d																								
Shepherd's Bush ⊖	d																								
Wembley Central ⊖	d																								
Harrow & Wealdstone ⊖	d																								
Watford Junction	d																								
Milton Keynes Central 10	a																								
Battersea Park 4	d						20 02				20 15	20 22								20 32				20 45	20 52
London Victoria 15 ⊖	a		20 01	20 04			20 06	20 20				20 27				20 31	20 34			20 36	20 46	20 50			20 57
Streatham 4	d				19 58				20 06									20 28					20 36		
Tulse Hill 3	d	19 46			20 02				20 10						20 16			20 32					20 40		
Herne Hill 4	a								20 14														20 44		
Loughborough Jn	a								20 17														20 47		
Elephant & Castle ⊖	a								20 21														20 51		
London Blackfriars 3 ⊖	a								20 25														20 55		
City Thameslink 3	a																								
St Pancras International 15 ⊖	a								20 35														21 05		
Luton Airport Parkway 7	a								21 20														21 50		
Luton 10	a								21 23														21 53		
North Dulwich	d	19 49			20 05										20 19			20 35							
East Dulwich	d	19 51			20 07										20 21			20 37							
Peckham Rye 4	d	19 53			20 10						20 26				20 23			20 40						20 56	
Queens Rd Peckham	d	19 56			20 12						20 29				20 26			20 42						20 59	
South Bermondsey	d	19 58			20 15						20 31				20 28			20 45						21 01	
London Bridge 4 ⊖	a	20 03			20 19	20 18					20 36		20 12	20 31	20 33			20 49	20 48					21 06	

Table 177

Sundays
from 16 September

East and West Croydon, London
Milton Keynes Central and Luton via Norbury
Crystal Palace - Tulse Hill

Local Services

Network Diagram - see first Page of Table 177

			SN	SN	SN ◇1	SN	SN	SN	SN	SN	FC	SN	SN	SN 1	SN	SN	SN ◇1		SN	SN	SN	SN	SN ◇1	SN	FC
East Croydon ⇌	d				20 40		20 42	20 47		20 53				20 56			21 10			21 12	21 17		21 26	21 23	
West Croydon 4 ⇌	d		20 34			20 37							20 52		21 04				21 07						
Norwood Junction 2	a		20 39					20 51					20 56	21 00	21 09						21 21				
	d		20 40					20 52					20 57	21 01	21 10						21 22				
Selhurst 4	d					20 41	20 46			20 57									21 11	21 16				21 26	
Thornton Heath	d					20 43	20 48			20 59									21 13	21 18				21 28	
Norbury	d					20 46	20 51			21 02									21 16	21 21				21 31	
Streatham Common 4	d					20 49	20 53			21 04									21 19	21 23				21 34	
Beckenham Junction 4 ⇌	d																								
Birkbeck ⇌	d																								
Crystal Palace 4	d			20 37									21 01			21 07									
Gipsy Hill	d			20 39									21 03			21 09									
West Norwood 4	d			20 42									21 06			21 12									
Streatham Hill	d												21 10												
Balham 4 ⊖	d					20 53				21 08			21 13						21 23					21 38	
Wandsworth Common	d												21 15												
Latchmere	d																								
Clapham Junction 10	d				20 55	20 57				21 13			21 19				21 25		21 27				21 38	21 42	
Imperial Wharf	d																								
West Brompton ⊖	d																								
Kensington (Olympia) ⊖	d																								
Shepherd's Bush ⊖	d																								
Wembley Central ⊖	d																								
Harrow & Wealdstone ⊖	d																								
Watford Junction	d																								
Milton Keynes Central 10	a																								
Battersea Park 4	d								21 02			21 15	21 23									21 32			
London Victoria 15 ⊖	a				21 01	21 04			21 06	21 20			21 27				21 31		21 34			21 36	21 46	21 50	
Streatham 4	d						20 58				21 06									21 28					21 36
Tulse Hill 3	d			20 46			21 02				21 10					21 16				21 32					21 40
Herne Hill 4	a										21 14														21 44
Loughborough Jn	a										21 17														21 47
Elephant & Castle ⊖	a										21 21														21 51
London Blackfriars 3 ⊖	a										21 25														21 55
City Thameslink 3	a																								
St Pancras International 15 ⊖	a										21 35														22 05
Luton Airport Parkway 7	a										22 20														22 50
Luton 10	a										22 23														22 53
North Dulwich	d			20 49			21 05									21 19				21 35					
East Dulwich	d			20 51			21 07									21 21				21 37					
Peckham Rye 4	d			20 53			21 10					21 26				21 23				21 40					
Queens Rd Peckham	d			20 56			21 12					21 29				21 26				21 42					
South Bermondsey	d			20 58			21 15					21 31				21 28				21 45					
London Bridge 4 ⊖	a		21 01	21 03			21 19	21 18				21 36		21 12	21 31	21 33				21 49	21 48				

Table 177

Sundays from 16 September

East and West Croydon, London Milton Keynes Central and Luton via Norbury Crystal Palace - Tulse Hill

Local Services

Network Diagram - see first Page of Table 177

		SN	SN	SN	SN	SN ◇1	SN	SN	SN	SN	SN	SN	SN	SN 1	SN	SN	SN ◇1	SN	SN	SN	SN	SN ◇1	SN	SN
East Croydon	d					21 40		21 42	21 47		21 53			21 56			22 10		22 12	22 17		22 26	22 23	
West Croydon 4	d		21 22	21 34			21 37						21 52		22 04			22 07						
Norwood Junction 2	a		21 26	21 39					21 51				21 56	22 00	22 09					22 21				
	d		21 27	21 40					21 52				21 57	22 01	22 10					22 22				
Selhurst 4	d						21 41	21 46			21 56							22 11	22 16				22 26	
Thornton Heath	d						21 43	21 48			21 58							22 13	22 18				22 28	
Norbury	d						21 46	21 51			22 01							22 16	22 21				22 31	
Streatham Common 4	d						21 49	21 53			22 04							22 19	22 23				22 34	
Beckenham Junction 4	d																							
Birkbeck	d																							
Crystal Palace 4	d		21 31		21 37								22 01			22 07								
Gipsy Hill	d		21 33		21 39								22 03			22 09								
West Norwood 4	d		21 36		21 42								22 06			22 12								
Streatham Hill	d		21 40										22 10											
Balham 4 ⊖	d		21 43				21 53				22 08		22 13					22 23					22 38	
Wandsworth Common	d		21 45										22 15											
Latchmere	d																							
Clapham Junction 10	d		21 49			21 55	21 57				22 12		22 19				22 25	22 27				22 38	22 42	
Imperial Wharf	d																							
West Brompton ⊖	d																							
Kensington (Olympia) ⊖	d																							
Shepherd's Bush ⊖	d																							
Wembley Central ⊖	d																							
Harrow & Wealdstone ⊖	d																							
Watford Junction	d																							
Milton Keynes Central 10	a																							
Battersea Park 4	d	21 45	21 53							22 02		22 15	22 23								22 32			22 45
London Victoria 15 ⊖	a		21 57			22 01	22 04			22 06	22 20		22 27				22 31	22 34			22 36	22 46	22 52	
Streatham 4	d							21 58											22 28					
Tulse Hill 3	d				21 46			22 02								22 16			22 32					
Herne Hill 4	a																							
Loughborough Jn	a																							
Elephant & Castle ⊖	a																							
London Blackfriars 3 ⊖	a																							
City Thameslink 3	a																							
St Pancras International 15 ⊖	a																							
Luton Airport Parkway 7	a																							
Luton 10	a																							
North Dulwich	d				21 49			22 05								22 19			22 35					
East Dulwich	d				21 51			22 07								22 21			22 37					
Peckham Rye 4	d	21 56			21 53			22 10				22 26				22 23			22 40					22 56
Queens Rd Peckham	d	21 59			21 56			22 12				22 29				22 26			22 42					22 59
South Bermondsey	d	22 01			21 58			22 15				22 31				22 28			22 45					23 01
London Bridge 4 ⊖	a	22 06		22 01	22 03			22 19	22 18			22 36		22 12	22 31	22 33			22 49	22 48				23 06

Table 177

Sundays from 16 September

East and West Croydon, London Milton Keynes Central and Luton via Norbury Crystal Palace - Tulse Hill

Local Services

Network Diagram - see first Page of Table 177

		SN	SN	SN	SN	SN	SN	SN	SN	SN 1	SN	SN	SN	SN	SN	SN	SN	SN ◇1	SN	SN	SN	SN	SN 1
East Croydon	d					22 42	22 47		22 53	22 56					23 17	23 26		23 27					23 56
West Croydon 4	d	22 22	22 34	22 37								22 52	23 07						23 22	23 37		23 52	
Norwood Junction 2	a	22 26	22 39				22 51					22 56			23 21				23 26				
	d	22 27	22 40				22 52					22 57							23 27				
Selhurst 4	d			22 41		22 46			22 57	22 59			23 11			23a29				23 41		23 56	00 01
Thornton Heath	d			22 43		22 48			22 59				23 13							23 43		23 58	
Norbury	d			22 46		22 51			23 02				23 16							23 46		00 01	
Streatham Common 4	d			22 49		22 53			23 04				23 19							23 49		00 04	
Beckenham Junction 4	d																						
Birkbeck	d																						
Crystal Palace 4	d	22 31			22 37							23 01		23 07					23 31		23 37		
Gipsy Hill	d	22 33			22 39							23 03		23 09					23 33		23 39		
West Norwood 4	d	22 36			22 42							23 06		23 12					23 36		23 42		
Streatham Hill	d	22 40										23 10							23 40				
Balham 4 ⊖	d	22 43		22 53					23 08			23 13	23 23						23 43	23 53		00 08	
Wandsworth Common	d	22 45										23 15							23 45				
Latchmere	d																						
Clapham Junction 10	d	22 49		22 57					23 13	23 08		23 19	23 27					23 39	23 49	23 58		00 12	00 12
Imperial Wharf	d																						
West Brompton ⊖	d																						
Kensington (Olympia) ⊖	d																						
Shepherd's Bush ⊖	d																						
Wembley Central ⊖	d																						
Harrow & Wealdstone ⊖	d																						
Watford Junction	d																						
Milton Keynes Central 10	a																						
Battersea Park 4	d	22 53						23 02			23 15	23 23					23 32		23 53				
London Victoria 15 ⊖	a	22 57		23 04				23 06	23 20	23 14		23 27	23 34				23 37	23 46	23 57	00 04		00 19	00 19
Streatham 4	d					22 58																	
Tulse Hill 3	d				22 46	23 02								23 16							23 46		
Herne Hill 4	a																						
Loughborough Jn	a																						
Elephant & Castle ⊖	a																						
London Blackfriars 3 ⊖	a																						
City Thameslink 3	a																						
St Pancras International 15 ⊖	a																						
Luton Airport Parkway 7	a																						
Luton 10	a																						
North Dulwich	d				22 49	23 05								23 19							23 49		
East Dulwich	d				22 51	23 07								23 21							23 51		
Peckham Rye 4	d				22 53	23 10					23 26			23 23							23 53		
Queens Rd Peckham	d				22 56	23 12					23 29			23 26							23 56		
South Bermondsey	d				22 58	23 15					23 31			23 28							23 58		
London Bridge 4 ⊖	a		23 01		23 03	23 19	23 18				23 36			23 33							00 03		

London Bridge to London Victoria - Croydon and East London Line

Network Diagram - see first Page of Table 177

Miles	Miles	Miles	Miles	Miles			SN MX	SN MX	SN MO A	SN MX	LO MO A	LO MX	SN MX	LO MX	LO MX		SN MX	SN MX	LO MX	LO MX B	SN MX	SE	SE	SN	SN
0	0	0	—	—	**London Bridge** 4 ⊖	d	23p22	23p36	23p39				23p52				00 03	00 06			00 36			06 00	
—	—	—	—	—	**Highbury & Islington**	a																			
—	—	—	—	—		d					23p23	23p25		23p35	23p42				23p56	00 10					
—	—	—	—	—	Canonbury	d					23p25	23p27		23p37	23p44				23p58	00 12					
—	—	—	0	—	Dalston Junction Stn ELL	d					23p28	23p30		23p40	23p47				00 02	00 15					
—	—	—	0½	—	Haggerston	d					23p29	23p31		23p41	23p48				00 03	00 16					
—	—	—	1	—	Hoxton	d					23p31	23p33		23p43	23p50				00 05	00 18					
—	—	—	1¾	—	Shoreditch High Street	d					23p34	23p36		23p46	23p53				00 08	00 21					
—	—	—	2½	—	Whitechapel	d					23p36	23p38		23p48	23p55				00 10	00 23					
—	—	—	3¼	—	Shadwell	d					23p38	23p40		23p50	23p57				00 12	00 25					
—	—	—	3¾	—	Wapping	d					23p40	23p42		23p52	23p59				00 14	00 27					
—	—	—	4	—	Rotherhithe	d					23p42	23p44		23p54	00 01				00 16	00 29					
—	—	—	4¼	—	Canada Water	d					23p44	23p46		23p56	00 03				00 18	00 31					
—	—	—	4½	—	Surrey Quays	d					23p45	23p47		23p57	00 05				00 19	00 32					
—	—	—	5¾	—	**New Cross ELL**	a																			
—	2¾	2¾	5¾	—	**New Cross Gate** 4	a	23p27	23p41	23p44		23p49	23p51	23p57	00 01	00 08			00 11	00 23	00 36	00 41				
—	—	—	—	—		d	23p27	23p41	23p44		23p50	23p52	23p57	00 02				00 11			00 41				
—	3¾	3¾	—	—	Brockley	d	23p30	23p44	23p47		23p52	23p54	00 01	00 04				00 14			00 44				
—	4¾	4¾	—	—	Honor Oak Park	d	23p33	23p47	23p50		23p55	23p57	00 04	00 07				00 17			00 47				
—	5¾	5¾	—	—	Forest Hill 4	d	23p35	23p49	23p52		23p58	23p59	00 06	00 10				00 19			00 49				
—	6½	6½	—	—	Sydenham	d	23p38	23p52	23p55		00 01	00 02	00 09	00 12				00 22			00 52				
—	7¾	—	—	—	**Crystal Palace** 4	d	23p43			00 03		00a07	00 13												05 59
—	8½	—	—	—	Gipsy Hill	d	23p45						00 15												06 01
—	9½	—	—	—	West Norwood 4	d	23p48						00 18												06 04
—	10¾	—	—	—	Streatham Hill	d	23p52						00 22												
—	11¾	—	—	—	Balham 4 ⊖	d	23p55						00 25												
—	12½	—	—	—	Wandsworth Common	d	23p58						00 27												
—	13¾	—	—	—	Clapham Junction 10	d	00 02						00 31												
1¾	—	—	—	—	South Bermondsey	d											00 07							06 04	
2¾	—	—	—	—	Queens Rd Peckham	d											00 09							06 06	
3½	—	—	0	0	Peckham Rye 4	d											00 12					05 04	06 04	06a09	06a15
4¼	—	—	0¾	0¾	Denmark Hill 4	d																05 07	06 07		
—	—	—	—	4½	**London Blackfriars** 3 ⊖	a																05 17	06 17		
6¼	—	—	—	—	Clapham High Street ⊖	d																			
6¾	—	—	—	—	Wandsworth Road	d																			
7½	15¼	—	—	—	Battersea Park 4	d	00 05						00 35												
8¾	16½	—	5	—	**London Victoria** 15 ⊖	a	00 10						00 42												
—	—	7¼	—	—	Penge West	d		23p54	23p57		00 03			00 15				00 24			00 54				
—	—	7½	—	—	Anerley	d		23p56	23p59		00 05			00 17				00 26			00 56				
—	—	8¾	—	0	Norwood Junction 2	d		23p59	00 03	00 09	00 08			00 20			00a34	00 30			01 00				
—	—	—	—	1¾	**West Croydon** 4	a				00 14	00 15			00 27											
—	—	10	—	—	**East Croydon**	a		00 03	00 06									00 33			01 03				

		LO	LO	LO	LO	LO	SN	SN	LO	LO		SN	LO	LO	SN	SN	SE	SN	LO	SN		SN	LO	LO
London Bridge 4 ⊖	d						06 06	06 11				06 19			06 30	06 33				06 36		06 41		
Highbury & Islington	a																							
	d			05 35						05 55			06 05											06 25
Canonbury	d			05 37						05 57			06 07											06 27
Dalston Junction Stn ELL	d			05 40	05 50					06 00			06 10	06 20										06 30
Haggerston	d			05 41	05 51					06 01			06 11	06 21										06 31
Hoxton	d			05 43	05 53					06 03			06 13	06 23										06 33
Shoreditch High Street	d			05 46	05 56					06 06			06 16	06 26										06 36
Whitechapel	d			05 48	05 58					06 08			06 18	06 28										06 38
Shadwell	d			05 50	06 00					06 10			06 20	06 30										06 40
Wapping	d			05 52	06 02					06 12			06 22	06 32										06 42
Rotherhithe	d			05 54	06 04					06 14			06 24	06 34										06 44
Canada Water	d			05 56	06 06					06 16			06 26	06 36										06 46
Surrey Quays	d			05 57	06 07					06 17			06 27	06 37										06 47
New Cross ELL	a				06 12									06 42										
New Cross Gate 4	a			06 01			06 11			06 21		06 25	06 31							06 41				06 51
	d	05 47	05 52	06 02		06 07	06 11		06 17	06 22		06 25	06 32						06 37	06 41			06 47	06 52
Brockley	d	05 49	05 54	06 04		06 09	06 14		06 19	06 24		06 27	06 34						06 39	06 44			06 49	06 54
Honor Oak Park	d	05 52	05 57	06 07		06 12	06 17		06 22	06 27		06 30	06 37						06 42	06 47			06 52	06 57
Forest Hill 4	d	05 55	06 00	06 10		06 15	06 19		06 25	06 30		06 33	06 40						06 45	06 49			06 55	07 00
Sydenham	d	05 57	06 02	06 12		06 17	06 22		06 27	06 32		06 35	06 42						06 47	06 52			06 57	07 02
Crystal Palace 4	d		06a07			06a22				06a37		06 39						06 51	06a52					07a07
Gipsy Hill	d											06 41						06 53						
West Norwood 4	d											06 44						06 56						
Streatham Hill	d											06 48												
Balham 4 ⊖	d											06 51												
Wandsworth Common	d																							
Clapham Junction 10	d											06 56												
South Bermondsey	d							06 15							06 34	06 37						06 45		
Queens Rd Peckham	d							06 18							06 36	06 39						06 48		
Peckham Rye 4	d							06 20							06a39	06a42	06 47	07a08				06 50		
Denmark Hill 4	d							06 23									06 50					06 53		
London Blackfriars 3 ⊖	a																							
Clapham High Street ⊖	d							06 28														06 58		
Wandsworth Road	d							06 29														06 59		
Battersea Park 4	d							06 32														07 02		
London Victoria 15 ⊖	a							06 36				07 05					07 04					07 08		
Penge West	d	06 00		06 15			06 24		06 30				06 45							06 54			07 00	
Anerley	d	06 02		06 17			06 26		06 32				06 47							06 56			07 02	
Norwood Junction 2	d	06 05		06 20			06 30		06 35				06 50							07 00			07 05	
West Croydon 4	a	06 13		06 30					06 41				07 00										07 11	
East Croydon	a						06 33													07 03				

A from 21 May until 23 July

B until 26 July

Table 178

Mondays to Fridays

until 27 July

London Bridge to London Victoria - Croydon and East London Line

Network Diagram - see first Page of Table 177

		LO	SN	SN	LO	SN	SN		SN	LO	LO	SN	LO	LO	LO	SN	SE		SN	LO	SN	SN	SN	LO	LO
London Bridge 4 ⊖	d		06 51	06 54		06 58	07 03					07 06				07 11			07 21		07 29	07 33			
Highbury & Islington	a																								
	d				06 33					06 40			06 48	06 55						07 03				07 10	
Canonbury	d				06 35					06 42			06 50	06 57						07 05				07 12	
Dalston Junction Stn ELL	d	06 35			06 40					06 45	06 50		06 55	07 00	07 05					07 10				07 15	07 20
Haggerston	d	06 36			06 41					06 46	06 51		06 56	07 01	07 06					07 11				07 16	07 21
Hoxton	d	06 38			06 43					06 48	06 53		06 58	07 03	07 08					07 13				07 18	07 23
Shoreditch High Street	d	06 41			06 46					06 51	06 56		07 01	07 06	07 11					07 16				07 21	07 26
Whitechapel	d	06 43			06 48					06 53	06 58		07 03	07 08	07 13					07 18				07 23	07 28
Shadwell	d	06 45			06 50					06 55	07 00		07 05	07 10	07 15					07 20				07 25	07 30
Wapping	d	06 47			06 52					06 57	07 02		07 07	07 12	07 17					07 22				07 27	07 32
Rotherhithe	d	06 49			06 54					06 59	07 04		07 09	07 14	07 19					07 24				07 29	07 34
Canada Water	d	06 51			06 56					07 01	07 06		07 11	07 16	07 21					07 26				07 31	07 36
Surrey Quays	d	06 52			06 57					07 02	07 07		07 12	07 17	07 22					07 27				07 32	07 37
New Cross ELL	a	06 57									07 12				07 27										07 42
New Cross Gate 4	a		06 56	06 59	07 00					07 06		07 11	07 15	07 21					07 26	07 31				07 36	
	d		06 56	06 59	07 02					07 07		07 11	07 17	07 22					07 26	07 32				07 37	
Brockley	d		06 59	07 02	07 04					07 09		07 14	07 19	07 24					07 29	07 34				07 39	
Honor Oak Park	d		07 02	07 05	07 07					07 12		07 17	07 22	07 27					07 32	07 37				07 42	
Forest Hill 4	d		07 04	07 07	07 10					07 15		07 19	07 25	07 30					07 34	07 40				07 45	
Sydenham	d		07 07	07 10	07 12					07 17		07 22	07 27	07 32					07 37	07 42				07 47	
Crystal Palace 4	d		07 13						07 20	07a22				07a37					07 43				07 49	07a52	
Gipsy Hill	d		07 15						07 22										07 45				07 51		
West Norwood 4	d		07 18						07 25										07 48				07 54		
Streatham Hill	d		07 22																07 52						
Balham 4 ⊖	d		07 25																07 55						
Wandsworth Common	d		07 27																07 57						
Clapham Junction 10	d		07 31																08 01						
South Bermondsey	d					07 02	07 07									07 15					07 33	07 37			
Queens Rd Peckham	d					07 04	07 09									07 17					07 35	07 39			
Peckham Rye 4	d					07a07	07a12		07a36							07 20	07 23				07a38	07a42	08a06		
Denmark Hill 4	d															07 23	07 29								
London Blackfriars 3 ⊖	a																								
Clapham High Street ⊖	d															07 28									
Wandsworth Road	d															07 29									
Battersea Park 4	d		07 35													07 32			08 05						
London Victoria 15 ⊖	a		07 41													07 38	07 42		08 11						
Penge West	d			07 12	07 15							07 24	07 30							07 45					
Anerley	d			07 14	07 17							07 26	07 32							07 47					
Norwood Junction 2	d			07 18	07 20							07 31	07 35							07 50					
West Croydon 4	a				07 30								07 42							08 00					
East Croydon	a			07 21								07 37													

		SN	LO		SN	SN	LO	LO	SE	SN A	SN B	LO	SN		SE	SN	SN	LO	LO	SN	LO	LO	LO		SN
London Bridge 4 ⊖	d	07 36			07 41	07 44				07 51	07 53		08 03			08 06				08 06					08 10
Highbury & Islington	a																								
	d		07 18				07 25					07 33						07 40			07 48	07 55			
Canonbury	d		07 20				07 27					07 35						07 42			07 50	07 57			
Dalston Junction Stn ELL	d		07 25				07 30	07 35				07 40						07 45	07 50		07 55	08 00	08 05		
Haggerston	d		07 26				07 31	07 36				07 41						07 46	07 51		07 56	08 01	08 06		
Hoxton	d		07 28				07 33	07 38				07 43						07 48	07 53		07 58	08 03	08 08		
Shoreditch High Street	d		07 31				07 36	07 41				07 46						07 51	07 56		08 01	08 06	08 11		
Whitechapel	d		07 33				07 38	07 43				07 48						07 53	07 58		08 03	08 08	08 13		
Shadwell	d		07 35				07 40	07 45				07 50						07 55	08 00		08 05	08 10	08 15		
Wapping	d		07 37				07 42	07 47				07 52						07 57	08 02		08 07	08 12	08 17		
Rotherhithe	d		07 39				07 44	07 49				07 54						07 59	08 04		08 09	08 14	08 19		
Canada Water	d		07 41				07 46	07 51				07 56						08 01	08 06		08 11	08 16	08 21		
Surrey Quays	d		07 42				07 47	07 52				07 57						08 02	08 07		08 12	08 17	08 22		
New Cross ELL	a							07 57											08 12				08 27		
New Cross Gate 4	a	07 41	07 45			07 49	07 51			07 56	07 58	08 01						08 06		08 11	08 16	08 21			
	d	07 41	07 47			07 49	07 52			07 56	07 58	08 02						08 07		08 11	08 17	08 22			
Brockley	d	07 44	07 49				07 54			07 59	08 01	08 04						08 09		08 14	08 19	08 24			
Honor Oak Park	d	07 47	07 52				07 57			08 02	08 04	08 07						08 12		08 17	08 22	08 27			
Forest Hill 4	d	07 49	07 55				08 00			08 04	08 06	08 10						08 15		08 19	08 25	08 30			
Sydenham	d	07 52	07 57				08 02			08 07	08 09	08 12						08 17		08 22	08 27	08 32			
Crystal Palace 4	d						08a07			08 13	08 13						08 19	08a22				08a37			
Gipsy Hill	d									08 15	08 15						08 21								
West Norwood 4	d									08 18	08 18						08 24								
Streatham Hill	d									08 22	08 22														
Balham 4 ⊖	d									08 25	08 25														
Wandsworth Common	d									08 27	08 27														
Clapham Junction 10	d									08 31	08 31														
South Bermondsey	d				07 45								08 07			08 11									08 14
Queens Rd Peckham	d				07 47								08 09			08 13									08 16
Peckham Rye 4	d				07 50				07 54				08a12		08 13	08a16	08a36								08 19
Denmark Hill 4	d				07 53				07 59						08 17										08 22
London Blackfriars 3 ⊖	a																								
Clapham High Street ⊖	d				07 58																				08 27
Wandsworth Road	d				07 59																				08 29
Battersea Park 4	d				08 02					08 35	08 35														08 32
London Victoria 15 ⊖	a				08 08				08 11	08 41	08 41				08 29										08 39
Penge West	d	07 54	08 00									08 15								08 24	08 30				
Anerley	d	07 56	08 02									08 17								08 26	08 32				
Norwood Junction 2	d	08 00	08 05									08 20								08 30	08 35				
West Croydon 4	a		08 12									08 30									08 43				
East Croydon	a	08 03				08 00														08 33					

A until 18 May

B from 21 May until 27 July

Table 178

Mondays to Fridays

until 27 July

London Bridge to London Victoria - Croydon and East London Line

Network Diagram - see first Page of Table 177

		SE 1	SE	SN	LO	SN	SN	LO	LO	SN	LO	LO	LO	SN	SE	SE	SN	LO	LO	LO	SN	SN	LO
London Bridge 4 ⊖	d			08 21		08 33				08 36				08 41	07b37		08 51				09 03	09 06	
Highbury & Islington	a																						
	d				08 03			08 10			08 18	08 25						08 33	08 40				08 48
Canonbury	d				08 05			08 12			08 20	08 27						08 35	08 42				08 50
Dalston Junction Stn ELL	d				08 10			08 15	08 20		08 25	08 30	08 35					08 40	08 46	08 50			08 55
Haggerston	d				08 11			08 16	08 21		08 26	08 31	08 36					08 41	08 47	08 51			08 56
Hoxton	d				08 13			08 18	08 23		08 28	08 33	08 38					08 43	08 49	08 53			08 58
Shoreditch High Street	d				08 16			08 21	08 26		08 31	08 36	08 41					08 46	08 52	08 56			09 01
Whitechapel	d				08 18			08 23	08 28		08 33	08 38	08 43					08 48	08 54	08 58			09 03
Shadwell	d				08 20			08 25	08 30		08 35	08 40	08 45					08 50	08 56	09 00			09 05
Wapping	d				08 22			08 27	08 32		08 37	08 42	08 47					08 52	08 58	09 02			09 07
Rotherhithe	d				08 24			08 29	08 34		08 39	08 44	08 49					08 54	09 00	09 04			09 09
Canada Water	d				08 26			08 31	08 36		08 41	08 46	08 51					08 56	09 02	09 06			09 11
Surrey Quays	d				08 27			08 32	08 37		08 42	08 47	08 52					08 57	09 03	09 07			09 12
New Cross ELL	a								08 42				08 57							09 12			
New Cross Gate 4	a			08 26	08 31			08 36		08 41	08 46	08 51					08 57	09 01	09 07			09 12	09 16
	d			08 26	08 32			08 37		08 41	08 47	08 52					08 57	09 02	09 08			09 12	09 17
Brockley	d			08 29	08 34			08 39		08 44	08 49	08 54					09 00	09 04	09 10			09 14	09 19
Honor Oak Park	d			08 32	08 37			08 42		08 47	08 52	08 57					09 03	09 07	09 13			09 17	09 22
Forest Hill 4	d			08 34	08 40			08 45		08 49	08 55	09 00					09 05	09 10	09 16			09 20	09 25
Sydenham	d			08 37	08 42			08 47		08 52	08 57	09 02					09 08	09 12	09 18			09 22	09 27
Crystal Palace 4	d			08 40			08 50	08a52				09a07					09 11		09a23				
Gipsy Hill	d			08 43			08 52										09 14						
West Norwood 4	d			08 46			08 55										09 17						
Streatham Hill	d			08 49													09 21						
Balham 4 ⊖	d			08 55													09 25						
Wandsworth Common	d			08 57													09 27						
Clapham Junction 10	d			09 01													09 31						
South Bermondsey	d					08 37								08 45							09 07		
Queens Rd Peckham	d					08 39								08 48							09 09		
Peckham Rye 4	d		08 33			08a42	09a07							08 50	08 55	08 55					09a12		
Denmark Hill 4	d	08 30	08 36											08 53	09 02	09 02							
London Blackfriars 3 ⊖	a																						
Clapham High Street ⊖	d													08 58									
Wandsworth Road	d													08 59									
Battersea Park 4	d			09 05										09 02			09 35						
London Victoria 15 ⊖	a	08 42	08 49	09 11										09 08	09 11	09 11	09 42						
Penge West	d				08 45					08 54	09 00							09 15				09 25	09 30
Anerley	d				08 47					08 56	09 02							09 17				09 27	09 32
Norwood Junction 2	d				08 50					09 00	09 05							09 20				09 30	09 35
West Croydon 4	a				09 00						09 12							09 30					09 42
East Croydon	a									09 06												09 33	

		SE	SN	SN	LO	LO	SN	LO	LO	LO	SN	SN	LO	SE	SN	SN	LO	LO	SN	LO	LO	LO	SN
London Bridge 4 ⊖	d		09 11				09 22				09 33	09 36			09 41				09 52				10 03
Highbury & Islington	a																						
	d				08 55			09 03	09 10				09 18				09 25			09 33	09 40		
Canonbury	d				08 57			09 05	09 12				09 20				09 27			09 35	09 42		
Dalston Junction Stn ELL	d				09 01	09 05		09 10	09 15	09 20			09 25				09 30	09 35		09 40	09 45	09 50	
Haggerston	d				09 02	09 06		09 11	09 16	09 21			09 26				09 31	09 36		09 41	09 46	09 51	
Hoxton	d				09 04	09 08		09 13	09 18	09 23			09 28				09 33	09 38		09 43	09 48	09 53	
Shoreditch High Street	d				09 07	09 11		09 16	09 21	09 26			09 31				09 36	09 41		09 46	09 51	09 56	
Whitechapel	d				09 09	09 13		09 18	09 23	09 28			09 33				09 38	09 43		09 48	09 53	09 58	
Shadwell	d				09 11	09 15		09 20	09 25	09 30			09 35				09 40	09 45		09 50	09 55	10 00	
Wapping	d				09 13	09 17		09 22	09 27	09 32			09 37				09 42	09 47		09 52	09 57	10 02	
Rotherhithe	d				09 15	09 19		09 24	09 29	09 34			09 39				09 44	09 49		09 54	09 59	10 04	
Canada Water	d				09 17	09 21		09 26	09 31	09 36			09 41				09 46	09 51		09 56	10 01	10 06	
Surrey Quays	d				09 18	09 22		09 27	09 32	09 37			09 42				09 47	09 52		09 57	10 02	10 07	
New Cross ELL	a					09 27				09 42								09 57				10 12	
New Cross Gate 4	a				09 22		09 28	09 30	09 36			09 41	09 46				09 51		09 57	10 01	10 06		
	d				09 23		09 28	09 32	09 37			09 41	09 47				09 52		09 57	10 02	10 07		
Brockley	d				09 25		09 30	09 34	09 39			09 44	09 49				09 54		10 00	10 04	10 09		
Honor Oak Park	d				09 28		09 33	09 37	09 42			09 47	09 52				09 57		10 03	10 07	10 12		
Forest Hill 4	d				09 31		09 36	09 40	09 45			09 49	09 55				10 00		10 05	10 10	10 15		
Sydenham	d				09 33		09 38	09 42	09 47			09 52	09 57				10 02		10 08	10 12	10 17		
Crystal Palace 4	d			09 30	09a38		09 43		09a52							10 00	10a07		10 13		10a22		
Gipsy Hill	d			09 32			09 46									10 02			10 15				
West Norwood 4	d			09 35			09 49									10 05			10 18				
Streatham Hill	d						09 52												10 22				
Balham 4 ⊖	d						09 56												10 25				
Wandsworth Common	d						09 58												10 27				
Clapham Junction 10	d						10 02												10 31				
South Bermondsey	d		09 15								09 37				09 45								10 07
Queens Rd Peckham	d		09 18								09 39				09 48								10 09
Peckham Rye 4	d	09 14	09 20	09a47							09a42			09 45	09 50	10a17							10a12
Denmark Hill 4	d	09 17	09 23											09 49	09 53								
London Blackfriars 3 ⊖	a																						
Clapham High Street ⊖	d		09 28												09 58								
Wandsworth Road	d		09 29												09 59								
Battersea Park 4	d		09 32				10 05								10 03				10 35				
London Victoria 15 ⊖	a	09 29	09 38				10 11							10 00	10 07				10 39				
Penge West	d							09 45				09 54	10 00							10 15			
Anerley	d							09 47				09 56	10 02							10 17			
Norwood Junction 2	d							09 50				10 00	10 05							10 20			
West Croydon 4	a							10 00					10 12							10 30			
East Croydon	a											10 03											

b London Bridge-I

London Bridge to London Victoria - Croydon and East London Line

Network Diagram - see first Page of Table 177

Station		SN	LO	SE	SN	SN	LO	LO	SN	LO	LO	LO	SN	SN	LO	SE	SN	SN	LO	LO	SN	LO
London Bridge 4 ⊖	d	10 06			10 11				10 22				10 33	10 36			10 41				10 52	
Highbury & Islington	a																					
	d		09 48				09 55			10 03	10 10				10 18				10 25			10 33
Canonbury	d		09 50				09 57			10 05	10 12				10 20				10 27			10 35
Dalston Junction Stn ELL	d		09 55				10 00	10 05		10 10	10 15	10 20			10 25				10 30	10 35		10 40
Haggerston	d		09 56				10 01	10 06		10 11	10 16	10 21			10 26				10 31	10 36		10 41
Hoxton	d		09 58				10 03	10 08		10 13	10 18	10 23			10 28				10 33	10 38		10 43
Shoreditch High Street	d		10 01				10 06	10 11		10 16	10 21	10 26			10 31				10 36	10 41		10 46
Whitechapel	d		10 03				10 08	10 13		10 18	10 23	10 28			10 33				10 38	10 43		10 48
Shadwell	d		10 05				10 10	10 15		10 20	10 25	10 30			10 35				10 40	10 45		10 50
Wapping	d		10 07				10 12	10 17		10 22	10 27	10 32			10 37				10 42	10 47		10 52
Rotherhithe	d		10 09				10 14	10 19		10 24	10 29	10 34			10 39				10 44	10 49		10 54
Canada Water	d		10 11				10 16	10 21		10 26	10 31	10 36			10 41				10 46	10 51		10 56
Surrey Quays	d		10 12				10 17	10 22		10 27	10 32	10 37			10 42				10 47	10 52		10 57
New Cross ELL	a							10 27				10 42								10 57		
New Cross Gate 4	a	10 11	10 16				10 21		10 27	10 31	10 36			10 41	10 46				10 51		10 57	11 01
	d	10 11	10 17				10 22		10 27	10 32	10 37			10 41	10 47				10 52		10 57	11 02
Brockley	d	10 14	10 19				10 24		10 30	10 34	10 39			10 44	10 49				10 54		11 00	11 04
Honor Oak Park	d	10 17	10 22				10 27		10 33	10 37	10 42			10 47	10 52				10 57		11 03	11 07
Forest Hill 4	d	10 19	10 25				10 30		10 35	10 40	10 45			10 49	10 55				11 00		11 05	11 10
Sydenham	d	10 22	10 27				10 32		10 38	10 42	10 47			10 52	10 57				11 02		11 08	11 12
Crystal Palace 4	d					10 30	10a37		10 43		10a52							11 00	11a07		11 13	
Gipsy Hill	d					10 32			10 45									11 02			11 15	
West Norwood 4	d					10 35			10 48									11 05			11 18	
Streatham Hill	d								10 52												11 22	
Balham 4 ⊖	d								10 55												11 25	
Wandsworth Common	d								10 57												11 27	
Clapham Junction 10	d								11 01												11 31	
South Bermondsey	d				10 15								10 37				10 45					
Queens Rd Peckham	d				10 18								10 39				10 48					
Peckham Rye 4	d			10 15	10 20	10a47							10a42			10 45	10 50	11a17				
Denmark Hill 4	d			10 19	10 23											10 49	10 53					
London Blackfriars 3 ⊖	a																					
Clapham High Street ⊖	d				10 28												10 58					
Wandsworth Road	d				10 29												10 59					
Battersea Park 4	d				10 32				11 05								11 02				11 35	
London Victoria 15 ⊖	a			10 28	10 36				11 09							10 58	11 06				11 39	
Penge West	d	10 24	10 30							10 45				10 54	11 00							11 15
Anerley	d	10 26	10 32							10 47				10 56	11 02							11 17
Norwood Junction 2	d	10 30	10 35							10 50				11 00	11 05							11 20
West Croydon 4	a		10 42							11 00					11 12							11 30
East Croydon	a	10 33												11 03								

Station		LO	LO	SN	SN	LO	SE	SN	SN	LO	LO	SN	LO	LO	LO	SN	SN	LO	SE	SN	SN	LO	LO
London Bridge 4 ⊖	d			11 03	11 06			11 11				11 22				11 33	11 36			11 41			
Highbury & Islington	a																						
	d	10 40				10 48				10 55			11 03	11 10				11 18				11 25	
Canonbury	d	10 42				10 50				10 57			11 05	11 12				11 20				11 27	
Dalston Junction Stn ELL	d	10 45	10 50			10 55				11 00	11 05		11 10	11 15	11 20			11 25				11 30	11 35
Haggerston	d	10 46	10 51			10 56				11 01	11 06		11 11	11 16	11 21			11 26				11 31	11 36
Hoxton	d	10 48	10 53			10 58				11 03	11 08		11 13	11 18	11 23			11 28				11 33	11 38
Shoreditch High Street	d	10 51	10 56			11 01				11 06	11 11		11 16	11 21	11 26			11 31				11 36	11 41
Whitechapel	d	10 53	10 58			11 03				11 08	11 13		11 18	11 23	11 28			11 33				11 38	11 43
Shadwell	d	10 55	11 00			11 05				11 10	11 15		11 20	11 25	11 30			11 35				11 40	11 45
Wapping	d	10 57	11 02			11 07				11 12	11 17		11 22	11 27	11 32			11 37				11 42	11 47
Rotherhithe	d	10 59	11 04			11 09				11 14	11 19		11 24	11 29	11 34			11 39				11 44	11 49
Canada Water	d	11 01	11 06			11 11				11 16	11 21		11 26	11 31	11 36			11 41				11 46	11 51
Surrey Quays	d	11 02	11 07			11 12				11 17	11 22		11 27	11 32	11 37			11 42				11 47	11 52
New Cross ELL	a		11 12								11 27				11 42								11 57
New Cross Gate 4	a	11 06			11 11	11 16				11 21		11 27	11 31	11 36			11 41	11 46				11 51	
	d	11 07			11 11	11 17				11 22		11 27	11 32	11 37			11 41	11 47				11 52	
Brockley	d	11 09			11 14	11 19				11 24		11 30	11 34	11 39			11 44	11 49				11 54	
Honor Oak Park	d	11 12			11 17	11 22				11 27		11 33	11 37	11 42			11 47	11 52				11 57	
Forest Hill 4	d	11 15			11 19	11 25				11 30		11 35	11 40	11 45			11 49	11 55				12 00	
Sydenham	d	11 17			11 22	11 27				11 32		11 38	11 42	11 47			11 52	11 57				12 02	
Crystal Palace 4	d	11a22							11 30	11a37		11 43		11a52							12 00	12a07	
Gipsy Hill	d								11 32			11 45									12 02		
West Norwood 4	d								11 35			11 48									12 05		
Streatham Hill	d											11 52											
Balham 4 ⊖	d											11 55											
Wandsworth Common	d											11 57											
Clapham Junction 10	d											12 01											
South Bermondsey	d			11 07				11 15								11 37				11 45			
Queens Rd Peckham	d			11 09				11 18								11 39				11 48			
Peckham Rye 4	d			11a12			11 15	11 20	11a47							11a42			11 45	11 50	12a17		
Denmark Hill 4	d						11 19	11 23											11 49	11 54			
London Blackfriars 3 ⊖	a																						
Clapham High Street ⊖	d							11 28												11 58			
Wandsworth Road	d							11 29												12 00			
Battersea Park 4	d							11 32				12 05								12 02			
London Victoria 15 ⊖	a						11 28	11 36				12 09							11 58	12 07			
Penge West	d				11 24	11 30							11 45				11 54	12 00					
Anerley	d				11 26	11 32							11 47				11 56	12 02					
Norwood Junction 2	d				11 30	11 35							11 50				12 00	12 05					
West Croydon 4	a					11 42							12 00					12 12					
East Croydon	a				11 33												12 03						

London Bridge to London Victoria - Croydon and East London Line

Network Diagram - see first Page of Table 177

Station		SN	LO		LO	LO	SN	SN	LO	SE	SN	SN	LO		LO	SN	LO	LO	LO	SN	SN	LO	SE		SN
London Bridge 4 ⊖	d	11 52					12 03	12 06			12 11					12 22				12 33	12 36				12 41
Highbury & Islington	a																								
	d		11 33		11 40				11 48				11 55				12 03	12 10				12 18			
Canonbury	d		11 35		11 42				11 50				11 57				12 05	12 12				12 20			
Dalston Junction Stn ELL	d		11 40		11 45	11 50			11 55				12 00		12 05		12 10	12 15	12 20			12 25			
Haggerston	d		11 41		11 46	11 51			11 56				12 01		12 06		12 11	12 16	12 21			12 26			
Hoxton	d		11 43		11 48	11 53			11 58				12 03		12 08		12 13	12 18	12 23			12 28			
Shoreditch High Street	d		11 46		11 51	11 56			12 01				12 06		12 11		12 16	12 21	12 26			12 31			
Whitechapel	d		11 48		11 53	11 58			12 03				12 08		12 13		12 18	12 23	12 28			12 33			
Shadwell	d		11 50		11 55	12 00			12 05				12 10		12 15		12 20	12 25	12 30			12 35			
Wapping	d		11 52		11 57	12 02			12 07				12 12		12 17		12 22	12 27	12 32			12 37			
Rotherhithe	d		11 54		11 59	12 04			12 09				12 14		12 19		12 24	12 29	12 34			12 39			
Canada Water	d		11 56		12 01	12 06			12 11				12 16		12 21		12 26	12 31	12 36			12 41			
Surrey Quays	d		11 57		12 02	12 07			12 12				12 17		12 22		12 27	12 32	12 37			12 42			
New Cross ELL	a					12 12									12 27				12 42						
New Cross Gate 4	a	11 57	12 01		12 06			12 11	12 16				12 21			12 27	12 31	12 36			12 41	12 46			
	d	11 57	12 02		12 07			12 11	12 17				12 22			12 27	12 32	12 37			12 41	12 47			
Brockley	d	12 00	12 04		12 09			12 14	12 19				12 24			12 30	12 34	12 39			12 44	12 49			
Honor Oak Park	d	12 03	12 07		12 12			12 17	12 22				12 27			12 33	12 37	12 42			12 47	12 52			
Forest Hill 4	d	12 05	12 10		12 15			12 19	12 25				12 30			12 35	12 40	12 45			12 49	12 55			
Sydenham	d	12 08	12 12		12 17			12 22	12 27				12 32			12 38	12 42	12 47			12 52	12 57			
Crystal Palace 4	d	12 13			12a22							12 30	12a37			12 43		12a52							
Gipsy Hill	d	12 15										12 32				12 45									
West Norwood 4	d	12 18										12 35				12 48									
Streatham Hill	d	12 22														12 52									
Balham 4 ⊖	d	12 25														12 55									
Wandsworth Common	d	12 27														12 57									
Clapham Junction 10	d	12 31														13 01									
South Bermondsey	d						12 07				12 15									12 37					12 45
Queens Rd Peckham	d						12 09				12 18									12 39					12 48
Peckham Rye 4	d						12a12			12 15	12 20	12a47								12a42			12 45		12 50
Denmark Hill 4	d									12 19	12 23												12 49		12 53
London Blackfriars 3 ⊖	a																								
Clapham High Street ⊖	d										12 28														12 58
Wandsworth Road	d										12 29														12 59
Battersea Park 4	d	12 35									12 32					13 05									13 02
London Victoria 15 ⊖	a	12 39								12 28	12 36					13 09							12 58		13 06
Penge West	d		12 15					12 24	12 30								12 45				12 54	13 00			
Anerley	d		12 17					12 26	12 32								12 47				12 56	13 02			
Norwood Junction 2	d		12 20					12 30	12 35								12 50				13 00	13 05			
West Croydon 4	a		12 30						12 42								13 00					13 12			
East Croydon	a							12 33													13 03				

Station		SN	LO	LO	SN	LO	LO	LO	SN		SN	LO	SE	SN	SN	LO	LO	SN	LO		LO	LO	SN	SN	LO
London Bridge 4 ⊖	d				12 52				13 03		13 06			13 11				13 22					13 33	13 36	
Highbury & Islington	a																								
	d		12 25			12 33	12 40					12 48				12 55			13 03		13 10				13 18
Canonbury	d		12 27			12 35	12 42					12 50				12 57			13 05		13 12				13 20
Dalston Junction Stn ELL	d		12 30	12 35		12 40	12 45	12 50				12 55				13 00	13 05		13 10		13 15	13 20			13 25
Haggerston	d		12 31	12 36		12 41	12 46	12 51				12 56				13 01	13 06		13 11		13 16	13 21			13 26
Hoxton	d		12 33	12 38		12 43	12 48	12 53				12 58				13 03	13 08		13 13		13 18	13 23			13 28
Shoreditch High Street	d		12 36	12 41		12 46	12 51	12 56				13 01				13 06	13 11		13 16		13 21	13 26			13 31
Whitechapel	d		12 38	12 43		12 48	12 53	12 58				13 03				13 08	13 13		13 18		13 23	13 28			13 33
Shadwell	d		12 40	12 45		12 50	12 55	13 00				13 05				13 10	13 15		13 20		13 25	13 30			13 35
Wapping	d		12 42	12 47		12 52	12 57	13 02				13 07				13 12	13 17		13 22		13 27	13 32			13 37
Rotherhithe	d		12 44	12 49		12 54	12 59	13 04				13 09				13 14	13 19		13 24		13 29	13 34			13 39
Canada Water	d		12 46	12 51		12 56	13 01	13 06				13 11				13 16	13 21		13 26		13 31	13 36			13 41
Surrey Quays	d		12 47	12 52		12 57	13 02	13 07				13 12				13 17	13 22		13 27		13 32	13 37			13 42
New Cross ELL	a			12 57				13 12									13 27					13 42			
New Cross Gate 4	a		12 51		12 57	13 01	13 06				13 11	13 16				13 21		13 27	13 31		13 36			13 41	13 46
	d		12 52		12 57	13 02	13 07				13 11	13 17				13 22		13 27	13 32		13 37			13 41	13 47
Brockley	d		12 54		13 00	13 04	13 09				13 14	13 19				13 24		13 30	13 34		13 39			13 44	13 49
Honor Oak Park	d		12 57		13 03	13 07	13 12				13 17	13 22				13 27		13 33	13 37		13 42			13 47	13 52
Forest Hill 4	d		13 00		13 05	13 10	13 15				13 19	13 25				13 30		13 35	13 40		13 45			13 49	13 55
Sydenham	d		13 02		13 08	13 12	13 17				13 22	13 27				13 32		13 38	13 42		13 47			13 52	13 57
Crystal Palace 4	d	13 00	13a07		13 13		13a22								13 30	13a37		13 43			13a52				
Gipsy Hill	d	13 02			13 15										13 32			13 45							
West Norwood 4	d	13 05			13 18										13 35			13 48							
Streatham Hill	d				13 22													13 52							
Balham 4 ⊖	d				13 25													13 55							
Wandsworth Common	d				13 27													13 57							
Clapham Junction 10	d				13 31													14 01							
South Bermondsey	d								13 07					13 15									13 37		
Queens Rd Peckham	d								13 09					13 18									13 39		
Peckham Rye 4	d	13a17							13a12				13 15	13 20	13a47								13a42		
Denmark Hill 4	d												13 19	13 23											
London Blackfriars 3 ⊖	a																								
Clapham High Street ⊖	d													13 28											
Wandsworth Road	d													13 29											
Battersea Park 4	d				13 35									13 32				14 05							
London Victoria 15 ⊖	a				13 39								13 28	13 36				14 09							
Penge West	d					13 15					13 24	13 30							13 45					13 54	14 00
Anerley	d					13 17					13 26	13 32							13 47					13 56	14 02
Norwood Junction 2	d					13 20					13 30	13 35							13 50					14 00	14 05
West Croydon 4	a					13 30						13 42							14 00						14 12
East Croydon	a										13 33													14 03	

Table 178

Mondays to Fridays

until 27 July

London Bridge to London Victoria - Croydon and East London Line

Network Diagram - see first Page of Table 177

		SE	SN	SN	LO		LO	SN	LO	LO	LO	SN	SN	LO	SE		SN	SN	LO	LO	SN	LO	LO	LO	SN
London Bridge 4 ⊖	d		13 41					13 52				14 03	14 06				14 11				14 22				14 33
Highbury & Islington	a																								
	d				13 25				13 33	13 40				13 48					13 55			14 03	14 10		
Canonbury	d				13 27				13 35	13 42				13 50					13 57			14 05	14 12		
Dalston Junction Stn ELL	d				13 30		13 35		13 40	13 45	13 50			13 55					14 00	14 05		14 10	14 15	14 20	
Haggerston	d				13 31		13 36		13 41	13 46	13 51			13 56					14 01	14 06		14 11	14 16	14 21	
Hoxton	d				13 33		13 38		13 43	13 48	13 53			13 58					14 03	14 08		14 13	14 18	14 23	
Shoreditch High Street	d				13 36		13 41		13 46	13 51	13 56			14 01					14 06	14 11		14 16	14 21	14 26	
Whitechapel	d				13 38		13 43		13 48	13 53	13 58			14 03					14 08	14 13		14 18	14 23	14 28	
Shadwell	d				13 40		13 45		13 50	13 55	14 00			14 05					14 10	14 15		14 20	14 25	14 30	
Wapping	d				13 42		13 47		13 52	13 57	14 02			14 07					14 12	14 17		14 22	14 27	14 32	
Rotherhithe	d				13 44		13 49		13 54	13 59	14 04			14 09					14 14	14 19		14 24	14 29	14 34	
Canada Water	d				13 46		13 51		13 56	14 01	14 06			14 11					14 16	14 21		14 26	14 31	14 36	
Surrey Quays	d				13 47		13 52		13 57	14 02	14 07			14 12					14 17	14 22		14 27	14 32	14 37	
New Cross ELL	a						13 57				14 12									14 27				14 42	
New Cross Gate 4	a				13 51			13 57	14 01	14 06			14 11	14 16					14 21		14 27	14 31	14 36		
	d				13 52			13 57	14 02	14 07			14 11	14 17					14 22		14 27	14 32	14 37		
Brockley	d				13 54			14 00	14 04	14 09			14 14	14 19					14 24		14 30	14 34	14 39		
Honor Oak Park	d				13 57			14 03	14 07	14 12			14 17	14 22					14 27		14 33	14 37	14 42		
Forest Hill 4	d				14 00			14 05	14 10	14 15			14 19	14 25					14 30		14 35	14 40	14 45		
Sydenham	d				14 02			14 08	14 12	14 17			14 22	14 27					14 32		14 38	14 42	14 47		
Crystal Palace 4	d			14 00	14a07			14 13		14a22								14 30	14a37		14 43		14a52		
Gipsy Hill	d			14 02				14 15										14 32			14 45				
West Norwood 4	d			14 05				14 18										14 35			14 48				
Streatham Hill	d							14 22													14 52				
Balham 4 ⊖	d							14 25													14 55				
Wandsworth Common	d							14 27													14 57				
Clapham Junction 10	d							14 31													15 01				
South Bermondsey	d		13 45									14 07					14 15								14 37
Queens Rd Peckham	d		13 48									14 09					14 18								14 39
Peckham Rye 4	d	13 45	13 50	14a17								14a12			14 15		14 20	14a47							14a42
Denmark Hill 4	d	13 49	13 53												14 19		14 23								
London Blackfriars 3 ⊖	a																								
Clapham High Street ⊖	d		13 58														14 28								
Wandsworth Road	d		13 59														14 29								
Battersea Park 4	d		14 02					14 35									14 32				15 05				
London Victoria 15 ⊖	a	13 58	14 06					14 39							14 28		14 36				15 09				
Penge West	d								14 15				14 24	14 30								14 45			
Anerley	d								14 17				14 26	14 32								14 47			
Norwood Junction 2	d								14 20				14 30	14 35								14 50			
West Croydon 4	a								14 30					14 42								15 00			
East Croydon	a												14 33												

			SN	LO	SE	SN	SN	LO	LO	SN	LO		LO	LO	SN	SN	LO	SE	SN	SN	LO		LO	SN	LO
London Bridge 4 ⊖	d		14 36			14 41				14 52					15 03	15 06			15 11					15 22	
Highbury & Islington	a																								
	d			14 18				14 25			14 33		14 40				14 48				14 55				15 03
Canonbury	d			14 20				14 27			14 35		14 42				14 50				14 57				15 05
Dalston Junction Stn ELL	d			14 25				14 30	14 35		14 40		14 45	14 50			14 55				15 00		15 05		15 10
Haggerston	d			14 26				14 31	14 36		14 41		14 46	14 51			14 56				15 01		15 06		15 11
Hoxton	d			14 28				14 33	14 38		14 43		14 48	14 53			14 58				15 03		15 08		15 13
Shoreditch High Street	d			14 31				14 36	14 41		14 46		14 51	14 56			15 01				15 06		15 11		15 16
Whitechapel	d			14 33				14 38	14 43		14 48		14 53	14 58			15 03				15 08		15 13		15 18
Shadwell	d			14 35				14 40	14 45		14 50		14 55	15 00			15 05				15 10		15 15		15 20
Wapping	d			14 37				14 42	14 47		14 52		14 57	15 02			15 07				15 12		15 17		15 22
Rotherhithe	d			14 39				14 44	14 49		14 54		14 59	15 04			15 09				15 14		15 19		15 24
Canada Water	d			14 41				14 46	14 51		14 56		15 01	15 06			15 11				15 16		15 21		15 26
Surrey Quays	d			14 42				14 47	14 52		14 57		15 02	15 07			15 12				15 17		15 22		15 27
New Cross ELL	a								14 57					15 12									15 27		
New Cross Gate 4	a		14 41	14 46				14 51		14 57	15 01		15 06			15 11	15 16				15 21			15 27	15 31
	d		14 41	14 47				14 52		14 57	15 02		15 07			15 11	15 17				15 22			15 27	15 32
Brockley	d		14 44	14 49				14 54		15 00	15 04		15 09			15 14	15 19				15 24			15 30	15 34
Honor Oak Park	d		14 47	14 52				14 57		15 03	15 07		15 12			15 17	15 22				15 27			15 33	15 37
Forest Hill 4	d		14 49	14 55				15 00		15 05	15 10		15 15			15 19	15 25				15 30			15 35	15 40
Sydenham	d		14 52	14 57				15 02		15 08	15 12		15 17			15 22	15 27				15 32			15 38	15 42
Crystal Palace 4	d						15 00	15a07		15 13			15a22							15 30	15a37			15 43	
Gipsy Hill	d						15 02			15 15										15 32				15 45	
West Norwood 4	d						15 05			15 18										15 35				15 48	
Streatham Hill	d									15 22														15 52	
Balham 4 ⊖	d									15 25														15 55	
Wandsworth Common	d									15 27														15 57	
Clapham Junction 10	d									15 31														16 01	
South Bermondsey	d					14 45									15 07				15 15						
Queens Rd Peckham	d					14 48									15 09				15 18						
Peckham Rye 4	d				14 45	14 50	15a17								15a12			15 15	15 20	15a47					
Denmark Hill 4	d				14 49	14 53												15 19	15 23						
London Blackfriars 3 ⊖	a																								
Clapham High Street ⊖	d					14 58													15 28						
Wandsworth Road	d					14 59													15 29						
Battersea Park 4	d					15 02				15 35									15 32					16 05	
London Victoria 15 ⊖	a				14 58	15 06				15 39								15 28	15 36					16 10	
Penge West	d		14 54	15 00							15 15					15 24	15 30								15 45
Anerley	d		14 56	15 02							15 17					15 26	15 32								15 47
Norwood Junction 2	d		15 00	15 05							15 20					15 30	15 35								15 50
West Croydon 4	a			15 12							15 30						15 42								16 00
East Croydon	a		15 03													15 33									

Table 178

Mondays to Fridays

until 27 July

London Bridge to London Victoria - Croydon and East London Line

Network Diagram - see first Page of Table 177

		LO	LO	SN	SN	LO	SE		SN	SN	SN	LO	LO	SN	LO	LO	LO		SN	SN	LO	SE	SN	SN	LO
London Bridge 4 ⊖	d			15 33	15 36				15 41					15 52					16 03	16 06			16 11		
Highbury & Islington	a																								
	d	15 10				15 18						15 25			15 33	15 40					15 48				15 55
Canonbury	d	15 12				15 20						15 27			15 35	15 42					15 50				15 57
Dalston Junction Stn ELL	d	15 15	15 20			15 25						15 30	15 35		15 40	15 45	15 50				15 55				16 00
Haggerston	d	15 16	15 21			15 26						15 31	15 36		15 41	15 46	15 51				15 56				16 01
Hoxton	d	15 18	15 23			15 28						15 33	15 38		15 43	15 48	15 53				15 58				16 03
Shoreditch High Street	d	15 21	15 26			15 31						15 36	15 41		15 46	15 51	15 56				16 01				16 06
Whitechapel	d	15 23	15 28			15 33						15 38	15 43		15 48	15 53	15 58				16 03				16 08
Shadwell	d	15 25	15 30			15 35						15 40	15 45		15 50	15 55	16 00				16 05				16 10
Wapping	d	15 27	15 32			15 37						15 42	15 47		15 52	15 57	16 02				16 07				16 12
Rotherhithe	d	15 29	15 34			15 39						15 44	15 49		15 54	15 59	16 04				16 09				16 14
Canada Water	d	15 31	15 36			15 41						15 46	15 51		15 56	16 01	16 06				16 11				16 16
Surrey Quays	d	15 32	15 37			15 42						15 47	15 52		15 57	16 02	16 07				16 12				16 17
New Cross ELL	a		15 42										15 57				16 12								
New Cross Gate 4	a	15 36			15 41	15 46						15 51		15 57	16 01	16 06				16 11	16 16				16 21
	d	15 37			15 41	15 47						15 52		15 57	16 02	16 07				16 11	16 17				16 22
Brockley	d	15 39			15 44	15 49						15 54		16 00	16 04	16 09				16 14	16 19				16 24
Honor Oak Park	d	15 42			15 47	15 52						15 57		16 03	16 07	16 12				16 17	16 22				16 27
Forest Hill 4	d	15 45			15 49	15 55						16 00		16 05	16 10	16 15				16 19	16 25				16 30
Sydenham	d	15 47			15 52	15 57						16 02		16 08	16 12	16 17				16 22	16 27				16 32
Crystal Palace 4	d	15a52									16 00	16a07		16 13		16a22								16 30	16a37
Gipsy Hill	d										16 02			16 15										16 32	
West Norwood 4	d										16 05			16 18										16 35	
Streatham Hill	d									15 56				16 22											
Balham 4 ⊖	d													16 25											
Wandsworth Common	d													16 27											
Clapham Junction 10	d													16 31											
South Bermondsey	d			15 37					15 45										16 07				16 15		
Queens Rd Peckham	d			15 39					15 48										16 09				16 18		
Peckham Rye 4	d			15a42			15 45		15 50	16a07	16a17								16a12			16 15	16 20	16a47	
Denmark Hill 4	d						15 49		15 53													16 19	16 23		
London Blackfriars 3 ⊖	a																								
Clapham High Street ⊖	d								15 58														16 28		
Wandsworth Road	d								15 59														16 29		
Battersea Park 4	d								16 02					16 35									16 32		
London Victoria 15 ⊖	a						15 58		16 06					16 40								16 28	16 38		
Penge West	d				15 54	16 00									16 15					16 24	16 30				
Anerley	d				15 56	16 02									16 17					16 26	16 32				
Norwood Junction 2	d				16 00	16 05									16 20					16 30	16 35				
West Croydon 4	a					16 12									16 30						16 42				
East Croydon	a				16 03															16 33					

		LO	SN		LO	LO	LO	SN	SN	LO	SE	SN	SN		LO	LO	SN	LO	SN	SE	SN	LO	LO		SN
London Bridge 4 ⊖	d		16 22					16 33	16 36			16 41					16 52		16 58						17 05
Highbury & Islington	a																								
	d				16 03	16 10				16 18					16 25			16 33				16 40			
Canonbury	d				16 05	16 12				16 20					16 27			16 35				16 42			
Dalston Junction Stn ELL	d	16 05			16 10	16 15	16 20			16 25					16 30	16 35		16 40				16 45	16 50		
Haggerston	d	16 06			16 11	16 16	16 21			16 26					16 31	16 36		16 41				16 46	16 51		
Hoxton	d	16 08			16 13	16 18	16 23			16 28					16 33	16 38		16 43				16 48	16 53		
Shoreditch High Street	d	16 11			16 16	16 21	16 26			16 31					16 36	16 41		16 46				16 51	16 56		
Whitechapel	d	16 13			16 18	16 23	16 28			16 33					16 38	16 43		16 48				16 53	16 58		
Shadwell	d	16 15			16 20	16 25	16 30			16 35					16 40	16 45		16 50				16 55	17 00		
Wapping	d	16 17			16 22	16 27	16 32			16 37					16 42	16 47		16 52				16 57	17 02		
Rotherhithe	d	16 19			16 24	16 29	16 34			16 39					16 44	16 49		16 54				16 59	17 04		
Canada Water	d	16 21			16 26	16 31	16 36			16 41					16 46	16 51		16 56				17 01	17 06		
Surrey Quays	d	16 22			16 27	16 32	16 37			16 42					16 47	16 52		16 57				17 02	17 07		
New Cross ELL	a	16 27					16 42									16 57							17 12		
New Cross Gate 4	a		16 27		16 31	16 36			16 41	16 46					16 51		16 57	17 01				17 06			17 11
	d		16 27		16 32	16 37			16 41	16 47					16 52		16 57	17 02				17 07			17 11
Brockley	d		16 30		16 34	16 39			16 44	16 49					16 54		17 00	17 04				17 09			17 14
Honor Oak Park	d		16 33		16 37	16 42			16 47	16 52					16 57		17 03	17 07				17 12			17 17
Forest Hill 4	d		16 35		16 40	16 45			16 49	16 55					17 00		17 05	17 10				17 15			17 19
Sydenham	d		16 38		16 42	16 47			16 52	16 57					17 02		17 08	17 12				17 17			17 22
Crystal Palace 4	d		16 43			16a52							17 00		17a07		17 13				17 18	17a22			
Gipsy Hill	d		16 45										17 02				17 15				17 20				
West Norwood 4	d		16 48										17 05				17 18				17 23				
Streatham Hill	d		16 52														17 22								
Balham 4 ⊖	d		16 55														17 25								
Wandsworth Common	d		16 57														17 27								
Clapham Junction 10	d		17 01														17 31								
South Bermondsey	d							16 37				16 45							17 02						
Queens Rd Peckham	d							16 39				16 48							17 04						
Peckham Rye 4	d							16a42			16 45	16 50	17a17						17a07	17 15	17a35				
Denmark Hill 4	d										16 49	16 53								17 19					
London Blackfriars 3 ⊖	a																								
Clapham High Street ⊖	d											16 58													
Wandsworth Road	d											16 59													
Battersea Park 4	d		17 05									17 02					17 35								
London Victoria 15 ⊖	a		17 10								17 01	17 08					17 42			17 28					
Penge West	d				16 45				16 54	17 00								17 15							17 24
Anerley	d				16 47				16 56	17 02								17 17							17 26
Norwood Junction 2	d				16 50				17 00	17 05								17 20							17 30
West Croydon 4	a				17 00				17 07	17 12								17 30							17 37
East Croydon	a																								

Table 178

Mondays to Fridays

until 27 July

London Bridge to London Victoria - Croydon and East London Line

Network Diagram - see first Page of Table 177

Station		LO	SN	SN	LO	LO	SN	LO A	LO B		LO	LO	SN	SN	LO	SE	SN	SN	LO		LO	SN	LO	SN	SE
London Bridge 4 ⊖	d		17 11				17 19						17 28	17 36			17 41					17 53		17 58	
Highbury & Islington	a																								
	d	16 48			16 55			17 03	17 03		17 10				17 18				17 25				17 33		
Canonbury	d	16 50			16 57			17 05	17 05		17 12				17 20				17 27				17 35		
Dalston Junction Stn ELL	d	16 55			17 00	17 05		17 10	17 10		17 15	17 20			17 25				17 30		17 35		17 40		
Haggerston	d	16 56			17 01	17 06		17 11	17 11		17 16	17 21			17 26				17 31		17 36		17 41		
Hoxton	d	16 58			17 03	17 08		17 13	17 13		17 18	17 23			17 28				17 33		17 38		17 43		
Shoreditch High Street	d	17 01			17 06	17 11		17 16	17 16		17 21	17 26			17 31				17 36		17 41		17 46		
Whitechapel	d	17 03			17 08	17 13		17 18	17 18		17 23	17 28			17 33				17 38		17 43		17 48		
Shadwell	d	17 05			17 10	17 15		17 20	17 20		17 25	17 30			17 35				17 40		17 45		17 50		
Wapping	d	17 07			17 12	17 17		17 22	17 22		17 27	17 32			17 37				17 42		17 47		17 52		
Rotherhithe	d	17 09			17 14	17 19		17 24	17 24		17 29	17 34			17 39				17 44		17 49		17 54		
Canada Water	d	17 11			17 16	17 21		17 26	17 26		17 31	17 36			17 41				17 46		17 51		17 56		
Surrey Quays	d	17 12			17 17	17 22		17 27	17 27		17 32	17 37			17 42				17 47		17 52		17 57		
New Cross ELL	a					17 27						17 42									17 57				
New Cross Gate 4	a	17 16			17 21		17 26	17 30	17 31		17 36			17 41	17 46				17 51			17 58	18 01		
	d	17 17			17 22		17 26	17 32	17 32		17 37			17 41	17 47				17 52			17 58	18 02		
Brockley	d	17 19			17 24		17 29	17 34	17 34		17 39			17 44	17 49				17 54			18 01	18 04		
Honor Oak Park	d	17 22			17 27		17 32	17 37	17 37		17 42			17 47	17 52				17 57			18 04	18 07		
Forest Hill 4	d	17 25			17 30		17 34	17 40	17 40		17 45			17 49	17 55				18 00			18 06	18 10		
Sydenham	d	17 27			17 32		17 37	17 42	17 42		17 47			17 52	17 57				18 02			18 09	18 12		
Crystal Palace 4	d			17 36	17a37		17 44				17a52							17 55	18a07			18 13			
Gipsy Hill	d			17 38			17 46											17 57				18 15			
West Norwood 4	d			17 41			17 49											18 00				18 18			
Streatham Hill	d						17 53															18 22			
Balham 4 ⊖	d						17 56															18 25			
Wandsworth Common	d						17 58															18 27			
Clapham Junction 10	d						18 02															18 32			
South Bermondsey	d		17 15										17 32				17 45							18 02	
Queens Rd Peckham	d		17 18										17 35				17 47							18 04	
Peckham Rye 4	d		17 20	17a53									17a37			17 45	17 50	18a12						18a07	18 15
Denmark Hill 4	d		17 23													17 49	17 53								18 19
London Blackfriars 3 ⊖	a																								
Clapham High Street ⊖	d		17 28														17 58								
Wandsworth Road	d		17 29														17 59								
Battersea Park 4	d		17 32				18 06										18 02					18 35			
London Victoria 15 ⊖	a		17 38				18 12									17 59	18 08					18 42			18 29
Penge West	d	17 30						17 45	17 45					17 54	18 00								18 15		
Anerley	d	17 32						17 47	17 47					17 56	18 02								18 17		
Norwood Junction 2	d	17 35						17 50	17 50					18 00	18 05								18 20		
West Croydon 4	a	17 42						18 01	18 01					18 08	18 12								18 30		
East Croydon	a																								

Station		SN	LO	LO	SN		LO	LO	LO	SN	SN	LO A	LO B	SN	SE		SN	LO	LO	SN	LO	LO	LO	SN	SE
London Bridge 4 ⊖	d				18 06					18 11	18 21			18 28						18 36				18 41	
Highbury & Islington	a																								
	d		17 40				17 48	17 55				18 03	18 03					18 10			18 18	18 25			
Canonbury	d		17 42				17 50	17 57				18 05	18 05					18 12			18 20	18 27			
Dalston Junction Stn ELL	d		17 45	17 50			17 55	18 00	18 05			18 10	18 10					18 15	18 20		18 25	18 30	18 35		
Haggerston	d		17 46	17 51			17 56	18 01	18 06			18 11	18 11					18 16	18 21		18 26	18 31	18 36		
Hoxton	d		17 48	17 53			17 58	18 03	18 08			18 13	18 13					18 18	18 23		18 28	18 33	18 38		
Shoreditch High Street	d		17 51	17 56			18 01	18 06	18 11			18 16	18 16					18 21	18 26		18 31	18 36	18 41		
Whitechapel	d		17 53	17 58			18 03	18 08	18 13			18 18	18 18					18 23	18 28		18 33	18 38	18 43		
Shadwell	d		17 55	18 00			18 05	18 10	18 15			18 20	18 20					18 25	18 30		18 35	18 40	18 45		
Wapping	d		17 57	18 02			18 07	18 12	18 17			18 22	18 22					18 27	18 32		18 37	18 42	18 47		
Rotherhithe	d		17 59	18 04			18 09	18 14	18 19			18 24	18 24					18 29	18 34		18 39	18 44	18 49		
Canada Water	d		18 01	18 06			18 11	18 16	18 21			18 26	18 26					18 31	18 36		18 41	18 46	18 51		
Surrey Quays	d		18 02	18 07			18 12	18 17	18 22			18 27	18 27					18 32	18 37		18 42	18 47	18 52		
New Cross ELL	a			18 12					18 27										18 42				18 57		
New Cross Gate 4	a		18 06		18 11		18 16	18 21			18 26	18 30	18 31					18 36		18 41	18 46	18 51			
	d		18 07		18 11		18 17	18 22			18 26	18 32	18 32					18 37		18 41	18 47	18 52			
Brockley	d		18 09		18 14		18 19	18 24			18 29	18 34	18 34					18 39		18 44	18 49	18 54			
Honor Oak Park	d		18 12		18 17		18 22	18 27			18 32	18 37	18 37					18 42		18 47	18 52	18 57			
Forest Hill 4	d		18 15		18 19		18 25	18 30			18 34	18 40	18 40					18 45		18 49	18 55	19 00			
Sydenham	d		18 17		18 22		18 27	18 32			18 37	18 42	18 42					18 47		18 52	18 57	19 02			
Crystal Palace 4	d	18 18	18a22					18a37			18 43						18 51	18a52				19a07			
Gipsy Hill	d	18 20									18 45						18 53								
West Norwood 4	d	18 23									18 48						18 56								
Streatham Hill	d										18 52														
Balham 4 ⊖	d										18 55														
Wandsworth Common	d										18 57														
Clapham Junction 10	d										19 01														
South Bermondsey	d									18 15				18 32										18 45	
Queens Rd Peckham	d									18 18				18 34										18 48	
Peckham Rye 4	d	18a36								18 20				18a37	18 45		19a14							18 50	
Denmark Hill 4	d									18 23					18 49									18 53	18 59
London Blackfriars 3 ⊖	a																								
Clapham High Street ⊖	d									18 28														18 58	
Wandsworth Road	d									18 29														18 59	
Battersea Park 4	d									18 32	19 05													19 02	
London Victoria 15 ⊖	a									18 39	19 12				18 58									19 08	19 13
Penge West	d				18 24		18 30					18 45	18 45							18 54	19 00				
Anerley	d				18 26		18 32					18 47	18 47							18 56	19 02				
Norwood Junction 2	d				18 32		18 35					18 50	18 50							19 02	19 05				
West Croydon 4	a				18 39		18 42					19 01	19 01							19 09	19 12				
East Croydon	a																								

A not 27 July

B 27 July

London Bridge to London Victoria - Croydon and East London Line

Network Diagram - see first Page of Table 177

		SN	LO	LO	LO	SN	SN	LO	SE	SN	SN	SE	SN	LO	LO	SN	LO	LO	LO	SN	SN	LO
London Bridge 4 ⊖	d	18 51				18 57	19 06			19 08	19 11					19 22				19 28	19 36	
Highbury & Islington	a																					
	d		18 33	18 40				18 48						18 55			19 03	19 10				19 18
Canonbury	d		18 35	18 42				18 50						18 57			19 05	19 12				19 20
Dalston Junction Stn ELL	d		18 40	18 45	18 50			18 55						19 00	19 05		19 10	19 15	19 20			19 25
Haggerston	d		18 41	18 46	18 51			18 56						19 01	19 06		19 11	19 16	19 21			19 26
Hoxton	d		18 43	18 48	18 53			18 58						19 03	19 08		19 13	19 18	19 23			19 28
Shoreditch High Street	d		18 46	18 51	18 56			19 01						19 06	19 11		19 16	19 21	19 26			19 31
Whitechapel	d		18 48	18 53	18 58			19 03						19 08	19 13		19 18	19 23	19 28			19 33
Shadwell	d		18 50	18 55	19 00			19 05						19 10	19 15		19 20	19 25	19 30			19 35
Wapping	d		18 52	18 57	19 02			19 07						19 12	19 17		19 22	19 27	19 32			19 37
Rotherhithe	d		18 54	18 59	19 04			19 09						19 14	19 19		19 24	19 29	19 34			19 39
Canada Water	d		18 56	19 01	19 06			19 11						19 16	19 21		19 26	19 31	19 36			19 41
Surrey Quays	d		18 57	19 02	19 07			19 12						19 17	19 22		19 27	19 32	19 37			19 42
New Cross ELL	a				19 12										19 27				19 42			
New Cross Gate 4	a	18 56	19 01	19 06			19 11	19 16						19 21		19 27	19 31	19 36			19 41	19 46
	d	18 56	19 02	19 07			19 11	19 17						19 22		19 27	19 32	19 37			19 41	19 47
Brockley	d	18 59	19 04	19 09			19 14	19 19						19 24		19 30	19 34	19 39			19 44	19 49
Honor Oak Park	d	19 02	19 07	19 12			19 17	19 22						19 27		19 33	19 37	19 42			19 47	19 52
Forest Hill 4	d	19 04	19 10	19 15			19 19	19 25						19 30		19 35	19 40	19 45			19 49	19 55
Sydenham	d	19 07	19 12	19 17			19 22	19 27						19 32		19 38	19 42	19 47			19 52	19 57
Crystal Palace 4	d	19 13		19a22									19 32	19a37		19 43		19a52				
Gipsy Hill	d	19 15											19 34			19 45						
West Norwood 4	d	19 18											19 37			19 48						
Streatham Hill	d	19 22														19 52						
Balham 4 ⊖	d	19 25														19 55						
Wandsworth Common	d	19 27														19 57						
Clapham Junction 10	d	19 31														20 01						
South Bermondsey	d					19 01				19 12	19 15									19 32		
Queens Rd Peckham	d					19 03				19 14	19 18									19 34		
Peckham Rye 4	d					19 06			19 15	19a17	19 20		19a49							19 37		
Denmark Hill 4	d								19 19		19 23	19 28										
London Blackfriars 3 ⊖	a																					
Clapham High Street ⊖	d										19 28											
Wandsworth Road	d										19 29											
Battersea Park 4	d	19 35									19 32					20 05						
London Victoria 15 ⊖	a	19 41							19 28		19 36	19 43				20 09						
Penge West	d		19 15				19 24	19 30									19 45				19 54	20 00
Anerley	d		19 17				19 26	19 32									19 47				19 56	20 02
Norwood Junction 2	d		19 20			19 28	19 30	19 35									19 50			20 02	20 00	20 05
West Croydon 4	a		19 30			19 35		19 42									20 00			20 07		20 12
East Croydon	a						19 33														20 03	

		SN	SN	SN	LO	LO	SN	LO A	LO B	LO	LO	SN	SN	LO	SN	SN	LO	LO	SN	LO	LO	LO	SN
London Bridge 4 ⊖	d	19 38	19 41				19 54					20 03	20 06		20 11				20 22				20 33
Highbury & Islington	a																						
	d				19 25			19 33	19 33	19 40				19 48			19 55			20 03	20 10		
Canonbury	d				19 27			19 35	19 35	19 42				19 50			19 57			20 05	20 12		
Dalston Junction Stn ELL	d				19 30	19 35		19 40	19 40	19 45	19 50			19 55			20 00	20 05		20 10	20 15	20 20	
Haggerston	d				19 31	19 36		19 41	19 41	19 46	19 51			19 56			20 01	20 06		20 11	20 16	20 21	
Hoxton	d				19 33	19 38		19 43	19 43	19 48	19 53			19 58			20 03	20 08		20 13	20 18	20 23	
Shoreditch High Street	d				19 36	19 41		19 46	19 46	19 51	19 56			20 01			20 06	20 11		20 16	20 21	20 26	
Whitechapel	d				19 38	19 43		19 48	19 48	19 53	19 58			20 03			20 08	20 13		20 18	20 23	20 28	
Shadwell	d				19 40	19 45		19 50	19 50	19 55	20 00			20 05			20 10	20 15		20 20	20 25	20 30	
Wapping	d				19 42	19 47		19 52	19 52	19 57	20 02			20 07			20 12	20 17		20 22	20 27	20 32	
Rotherhithe	d				19 44	19 49		19 54	19 54	19 59	20 04			20 09			20 14	20 19		20 24	20 29	20 34	
Canada Water	d				19 46	19 51		19 56	19 56	20 01	20 06			20 11			20 16	20 21		20 26	20 31	20 36	
Surrey Quays	d				19 47	19 52		19 57	19 57	20 02	20 07			20 12			20 17	20 22		20 27	20 32	20 37	
New Cross ELL	a					19 57					20 12							20 27				20 42	
New Cross Gate 4	a				19 51		19 59	20 00	20 01	20 06			20 11	20 16			20 21		20 27	20 31	20 36		
	d				19 52		19 59	20 02	20 02	20 07			20 11	20 17			20 22		20 27	20 32	20 37		
Brockley	d				19 54		20 02	20 04	20 04	20 09			20 14	20 19			20 24		20 30	20 34	20 39		
Honor Oak Park	d				19 57		20 05	20 07	20 07	20 12			20 17	20 22			20 27		20 33	20 37	20 42		
Forest Hill 4	d				20 00		20 07	20 10	20 10	20 15			20 19	20 25			20 30		20 35	20 40	20 45		
Sydenham	d				20 02		20 10	20 12	20 12	20 17			20 22	20 27			20 32		20 38	20 42	20 47		
Crystal Palace 4	d			20 01	20a07		20 13			20a22						20 31	20a37		20 43		20a52		
Gipsy Hill	d			20 03			20 16									20 33			20 45				
West Norwood 4	d			20 06			20 19									20 36			20 48				
Streatham Hill	d						20 22												20 52				
Balham 4 ⊖	d						20 25												20 56				
Wandsworth Common	d						20 27												20 58				
Clapham Junction 10	d						20 31												21 03				
South Bermondsey	d	19 42	19 45									20 07			20 15								20 37
Queens Rd Peckham	d	19 44	19 48									20 09			20 18								20 39
Peckham Rye 4	d	19a47	19 50	20a18								20a12			20 20	20a48							20a42
Denmark Hill 4	d		19 53												20 23								
London Blackfriars 3 ⊖	a																						
Clapham High Street ⊖	d		19 58												20 28								
Wandsworth Road	d		19 59												20 29								
Battersea Park 4	d		20 02				20 35								20 32				21 06				
London Victoria 15 ⊖	a		20 06				20 39								20 36				21 11				
Penge West	d							20 15	20 15				20 24	20 30						20 45			
Anerley	d							20 17	20 17				20 26	20 32						20 47			
Norwood Junction 2	d							20 20	20 20				20 30	20 35						20 50			
West Croydon 4	a							20 29	20 29					20 42						21 00			
East Croydon	a												20 33										

A not 27 July

B 27 July

Table 178

Mondays to Fridays

until 27 July

London Bridge to London Victoria - Croydon and East London Line

Network Diagram - see first Page of Table 177

		SN	LO		SN	SN	LO	LO	SN	LO	LO	LO	SN		SN	LO	SE A	SN	SE B	SN	LO	LO	SN		LO
London Bridge 4 ⊖	d	20 36			20 41				20 52				21 03		21 06			21 11					21 22		
Highbury & Islington	a																								
	d		20 18				20 25			20 33	20 40					20 48					20 55				21 03
Canonbury	d		20 20				20 27			20 35	20 42					20 50					20 57				21 05
Dalston Junction Stn ELL	d		20 25				20 30	20 35		20 40	20 45	20 50				20 55					21 00	21 05			21 10
Haggerston	d		20 26				20 31	20 36		20 41	20 46	20 51				20 56					21 01	21 06			21 11
Hoxton	d		20 28				20 33	20 38		20 43	20 48	20 53				20 58					21 03	21 08			21 13
Shoreditch High Street	d		20 31				20 36	20 41		20 46	20 51	20 56				21 01					21 06	21 11			21 16
Whitechapel	d		20 33				20 38	20 43		20 48	20 53	20 58				21 03					21 08	21 13			21 18
Shadwell	d		20 35				20 40	20 45		20 50	20 55	21 00				21 05					21 10	21 15			21 20
Wapping	d		20 37				20 42	20 47		20 52	20 57	21 02				21 07					21 12	21 17			21 22
Rotherhithe	d		20 39				20 44	20 49		20 54	20 59	21 04				21 09					21 14	21 19			21 24
Canada Water	d		20 41				20 46	20 51		20 56	21 01	21 06				21 11					21 16	21 21			21 26
Surrey Quays	d		20 42				20 47	20 52		20 57	21 02	21 07				21 12					21 17	21 22			21 27
New Cross ELL	a							20 57				21 12										21 27			
New Cross Gate 4	a	20 41	20 46				20 51		20 57	21 01	21 06				21 11	21 16					21 21		21 27		21 31
	d	20 41	20 47				20 52		20 57	21 02	21 07				21 11	21 17					21 22		21 27		21 32
Brockley	d	20 44	20 49				20 54		21 00	21 04	21 09				21 14	21 19					21 24		21 30		21 34
Honor Oak Park	d	20 47	20 52				20 57		21 03	21 07	21 12				21 17	21 22					21 27		21 33		21 37
Forest Hill 4	d	20 49	20 55				21 00		21 05	21 10	21 15				21 19	21 25					21 30		21 35		21 40
Sydenham	d	20 52	20 57				21 02		21 08	21 12	21 17				21 22	21 27					21 32		21 38		21 42
Crystal Palace 4	d					21 00	21a07		21 13		21a22									21 30	21a37		21 43		
Gipsy Hill	d					21 02			21 15											21 32			21 45		
West Norwood 4	d					21 05			21 18											21 35			21 48		
Streatham Hill	d								21 22														21 52		
Balham 4 ⊖	d								21 26														21 56		
Wandsworth Common	d								21 28														21 58		
Clapham Junction 10	d								21 33														22 03		
South Bermondsey	d				20 45								21 07					21 15							
Queens Rd Peckham	d				20 48								21 09					21 18							
Peckham Rye 4	d				20 50	21a17							21a12				21 20	21 20	21 20	21a47					
Denmark Hill 4	d				20 53												21 23	21 23	21 24						
London Blackfriars 3 ⊖	a																		21 34						
Clapham High Street ⊖	d				20 58													21 28							
Wandsworth Road	d				20 59													21 29							
Battersea Park 4	d				21 02				21 36									21 32					22 06		
London Victoria 15 ⊖	a				21 06				21 41								21 33	21 36					22 11		
Penge West	d	20 54	21 00							21 15					21 24	21 30									21 45
Anerley	d	20 56	21 02							21 17					21 26	21 32									21 47
Norwood Junction 2	d	21 00	21 05							21 20					21 30	21 35									21 50
West Croydon 4	a		21 12							21 30						21 42									22 00
East Croydon	a	21 03													21 33										

		LO	LO	SN	SN	LO	SE A	SN	SE B		SN	LO	LO	SN	LO	LO	LO	SN	SN		LO	SE A	SN	SE B	SN
London Bridge 4 ⊖	d			21 33	21 36			21 41						21 52				22 03	22 08				22 11		
Highbury & Islington	a																								
	d	21 10				21 18						21 25			21 33	21 40					21 48				
Canonbury	d	21 12				21 20						21 27			21 35	21 42					21 50				
Dalston Junction Stn ELL	d	21 15	21 20			21 25						21 30	21 35		21 40	21 45	21 50				21 55				
Haggerston	d	21 16	21 21			21 26						21 31	21 36		21 41	21 46	21 51				21 56				
Hoxton	d	21 18	21 23			21 28						21 33	21 38		21 43	21 48	21 53				21 58				
Shoreditch High Street	d	21 21	21 26			21 31						21 36	21 41		21 46	21 51	21 56				22 01				
Whitechapel	d	21 23	21 28			21 33						21 38	21 43		21 48	21 53	21 58				22 03				
Shadwell	d	21 25	21 30			21 35						21 40	21 45		21 50	21 55	22 00				22 05				
Wapping	d	21 27	21 32			21 37						21 42	21 47		21 52	21 57	22 02				22 07				
Rotherhithe	d	21 29	21 34			21 39						21 44	21 49		21 54	21 59	22 04				22 09				
Canada Water	d	21 31	21 36			21 41						21 46	21 51		21 56	22 01	22 06				22 11				
Surrey Quays	d	21 32	21 37			21 42						21 47	21 52		21 57	22 02	22 07				22 12				
New Cross ELL	a		21 42										21 57				22 13								
New Cross Gate 4	a	21 36			21 41	21 46						21 51		21 57	22 01	22 06			22 13		22 16				
	d	21 37			21 41	21 47						21 52		21 57	22 02	22 07			22 13		22 17				
Brockley	d	21 39			21 44	21 49						21 54		22 00	22 04	22 09			22 16		22 19				
Honor Oak Park	d	21 42			21 47	21 52						21 57		22 03	22 07	22 12			22 19		22 22				
Forest Hill 4	d	21 45			21 49	21 55						22 00		22 05	22 10	22 15			22 21		22 25				
Sydenham	d	21 47			21 52	21 57						22 02		22 08	22 12	22 17			22 24		22 27				
Crystal Palace 4	d	21a52									22 00	22a07		22 13		22a22									22 22
Gipsy Hill	d										22 02			22 15											22 24
West Norwood 4	d										22 05			22 18											22 27
Streatham Hill	d													22 22											
Balham 4 ⊖	d													22 26											
Wandsworth Common	d													22 28											
Clapham Junction 10	d													22 33											
South Bermondsey	d			21 37				21 45										22 07					22 15		
Queens Rd Peckham	d			21 39				21 48										22 09					22 18		
Peckham Rye 4	d			21a42			21 50	21 50	21 50		22a17							22a12				22 20	22 20	22 20	22a43
Denmark Hill 4	d						21 53	21 53	21 54													22 23	22 23	22 24	
London Blackfriars 3 ⊖	a								22 04															22 34	
Clapham High Street ⊖	d							21 58															22 28		
Wandsworth Road	d							21 59															22 29		
Battersea Park 4	d							22 02						22 36									22 32		
London Victoria 15 ⊖	a						22 03	22 06						22 41								22 33	22 36		
Penge West	d				21 54	22 00									22 15				22 26		22 30				
Anerley	d				21 56	22 02									22 17				22 28		22 32				
Norwood Junction 2	d				22 00	22 05									22 20				22 32		22 35				
West Croydon 4	a					22 12									22 30						22 42				
East Croydon	a				22 03														22 35						

A until 18 May

B from 21 May until 27 July

London Bridge to London Victoria - Croydon and East London Line

Network Diagram - see first Page of Table 177

		LO	SN	LO A	LO B		LO A	LO	SN	SN	LO A	SE C	SN	SE D	SN		LO	SN	LO A	LO B	LO A	LO	SN	SN	LO A
London Bridge 4 ⊖	d		22 23						22 33	22 38			22 41					22 52					23 05	23 06	
Highbury & Islington	a																								
	d	21 55		22 03	22 05		22 10				22 18						22 25		22 33	22 35	22 40				22 48
Canonbury	d	21 57		22 05	22 07		22 12				22 20						22 27		22 35	22 37	22 42				22 50
Dalston Junction Stn ELL	d	22 00		22 08	22 10		22 15	22 20			22 25						22 30		22 38	22 40	22 45	22 50			22 55
Haggerston	d	22 01		22 09	22 11		22 16	22 21			22 26						22 31		22 39	22 41	22 46	22 51			22 56
Hoxton	d	22 03		22 11	22 13		22 18	22 23			22 28						22 33		22 41	22 43	22 48	22 53			22 58
Shoreditch High Street	d	22 06		22 14	22 16		22 21	22 26			22 31						22 36		22 44	22 46	22 51	22 56			23 01
Whitechapel	d	22 08		22 16	22 18		22 23	22 28			22 33						22 38		22 46	22 48	22 53	22 58			23 03
Shadwell	d	22 10		22 18	22 20		22 25	22 30			22 35						22 40		22 48	22 50	22 55	23 00			23 05
Wapping	d	22 12		22 20	22 22		22 27	22 32			22 37						22 42		22 50	22 52	22 57	23 02			23 07
Rotherhithe	d	22 14		22 22	22 24		22 29	22 34			22 39						22 44		22 52	22 54	22 59	23 04			23 09
Canada Water	d	22 16		22 24	22 26		22 31	22 36			22 41						22 46		22 54	22 56	23 01	23 06			23 11
Surrey Quays	d	22 17		22 25	22 27		22 32	22 37			22 42						22 47		22 55	22 57	23 02	23 07			23 12
New Cross ELL	a							22 42														23 12			
New Cross Gate 4	a	22 21	22 28	22 29	22 31		22 36			22 43	22 46						22 51	22 57	22 59	23 01	23 06			23 11	23 16
	d	22 22	22 28	22 30	22 32		22 37			22 43	22 47						22 52	22 57	23 00	23 02	23 07			23 11	23 17
Brockley	d	22 24	22 31	22 32	22 34		22 39			22 46	22 49						22 54	23 00	23 02	23 04	23 09			23 14	23 19
Honor Oak Park	d	22 27	22 34	22 35	22 37		22 42			22 49	22 52						22 57	23 03	23 05	23 07	23 12			23 17	23 22
Forest Hill 4	d	22 30	22 36	22 38	22 40		22 45			22 51	22 55						23 00	23 05	23 08	23 10	23 15			23 19	23 25
Sydenham	d	22 32	22 39	22 40	22 42		22 47			22 54	22 57						23 02	23 08	23 10	23 12	23 17			23 22	23 27
Crystal Palace 4	d	22a37	22 43				22a52								23 00		23a07	23 13			23a22				
Gipsy Hill	d		22 45												23 02			23 15							
West Norwood 4	d		22 48												23 05			23 18							
Streatham Hill	d		22 52															23 22							
Balham 4 ⊖	d		22 56															23 26							
Wandsworth Common	d		22 58															23 28							
Clapham Junction 10	d		23 03															23 33							
South Bermondsey	d								22 37				22 45										23 09		
Queens Rd Peckham	d								22 39				22 48										23 11		
Peckham Rye 4	d								22a42			22 50	22 50	22 50	23a17								23 14		
Denmark Hill 4	d											22 53	22 53	22 54											
London Blackfriars 3 ⊖	a													23 04											
Clapham High Street ⊖	d												22 58												
Wandsworth Road	d												22 59												
Battersea Park 4	d		23 07										23 02					23 37							
London Victoria 15 ⊖	a		23 14									23 03	23 06					23 41							
Penge West	d			22 43	22 45					22 56	23 00								23 13	23 15				23 24	23 30
Anerley	d			22 45	22 47					22 58	23 02								23 15	23 17				23 26	23 32
Norwood Junction 2	d			22 48	22 50					23 02	23 05								23 18	23 20			23a36	23 30	23 35
West Croydon 4	a			23 00	23 00						23 12								23 30	23 30					23 42
East Croydon	a									23 06														23 33	

			SE C	SN	SE D	SN	LO	SN	LO A	LO B	LO A		LO	SN	SN	LO A	LO	SN	LO A	LO B	LO A		LO B	LO A	LO A
London Bridge 4 ⊖	d			23 11				23 22						23 33	23 36			23 52							
Highbury & Islington	a																								
	d						22 55		23 03	23 05	23 10					23 18	23 25		23 33	23 35	23 40		23 42	23 48	23 55
Canonbury	d						22 57		23 05	23 07	23 12					23 20	23 27		23 35	23 37	23 42		23 44	23 50	23 57
Dalston Junction Stn ELL	d						23 00		23 08	23 10	23 15		23 20			23 25	23 30		23 38	23 40	23 45		23 47	23 55	00 01
Haggerston	d						23 01		23 09	23 11	23 16		23 21			23 26	23 31		23 39	23 41	23 46		23 48	23 56	00 02
Hoxton	d						23 03		23 11	23 13	23 18		23 23			23 28	23 33		23 41	23 43	23 48		23 50	23 58	00 04
Shoreditch High Street	d						23 06		23 14	23 16	23 21		23 26			23 31	23 36		23 44	23 46	23 51		23 53	00 01	00 07
Whitechapel	d						23 08		23 16	23 18	23 23		23 28			23 33	23 38		23 46	23 48	23 53		23 55	00 03	00 09
Shadwell	d						23 10		23 18	23 20	23 25		23 30			23 35	23 40		23 48	23 50	23 55		23 57	00 05	00 11
Wapping	d						23 12		23 20	23 22	23 27		23 32			23 37	23 42		23 50	23 52	23 57		23 59	00 07	00 13
Rotherhithe	d						23 14		23 22	23 24	23 29		23 34			23 39	23 44		23 52	23 54	23 59		00 01	00 09	00 15
Canada Water	d						23 16		23 24	23 26	23 31		23 36			23 41	23 46		23 54	23 56	00 02		00 03	00 11	00 17
Surrey Quays	d						23 17		23 25	23 27	23 32		23 37			23 42	23 47		23 55	23 57	00 03		00 05	00 12	00 18
New Cross ELL	a												23 42												
New Cross Gate 4	a						23 21	23 27	23 29	23 31	23 36				23 41	23 46	23 51	23 57	23 58	00 01	00 07		00 08	00 16	00 22
	d						23 22	23 27	23 30	23 32	23 37				23 41	23 47	23 52	23 57	23 59	00 02	00 08			00 17	00 23
Brockley	d						23 24	23 30	23 32	23 34	23 39				23 44	23 49	23 54	00 01	00 03	00 04	00 10			00 19	00 25
Honor Oak Park	d						23 27	23 33	23 35	23 37	23 42				23 47	23 52	23 57	00 04	00 06	00 07	00 13			00 22	00 28
Forest Hill 4	d						23 30	23 35	23 38	23 40	23 45				23 49	23 55	23 59	00 06	00 09	00 10	00 16			00 25	00 31
Sydenham	d						23 32	23 38	23 40	23 42	23 47				23 52	23 57	00 02	00 09	00 11	00 12	00 18			00 27	00 33
Crystal Palace 4	d					23 30	23a37	23 43			23a52						00a07	00 13			00a23				00a38
Gipsy Hill	d					23 32		23 45										00 15							
West Norwood 4	d					23 35		23 48										00 18							
Streatham Hill	d							23 52										00 22							
Balham 4 ⊖	d							23 55										00 25							
Wandsworth Common	d							23 58										00 27							
Clapham Junction 10	d							00 02										00 31							
South Bermondsey	d			23 15										23 37											
Queens Rd Peckham	d			23 18										23 39											
Peckham Rye 4	d		23 20	23 20	23 20	23a47								23 42											
Denmark Hill 4	d		23 23	23 23	23 24																				
London Blackfriars 3 ⊖	a				23 34																				
Clapham High Street ⊖	d			23 28																					
Wandsworth Road	d			23 29																					
Battersea Park 4	d			23 32				00 05										00 35							
London Victoria 15 ⊖	a		23 33	23 37				00 10										00 42							
Penge West	d								23 43	23 45					23 54	00 01			00 14	00 15				00 30	
Anerley	d								23 45	23 47					23 56	00 03			00 16	00 17				00 32	
Norwood Junction 2	d								23 48	23 50				00a04	23 59	00 06			00 19	00 20				00 35	
West Croydon 4	a								23 59	23 59						00 13			00 26	00 27				00 42	
East Croydon	a														00 03										

A 27 July
B not 27 July
C until 18 May
D from 21 May until 27 July

Table 178

Mondays to Fridays

until 27 July

London Bridge to London Victoria - Croydon and East London Line

Network Diagram - see first Page of Table 177

		LO A
London Bridge 4 ⊖	d	
Highbury & Islington	a	
	d	23 56
Canonbury	d	23 58
Dalston Junction Stn ELL	d	00 02
Haggerston	d	00 03
Hoxton	d	00 05
Shoreditch High Street	d	00 08
Whitechapel	d	00 10
Shadwell	d	00 12
Wapping	d	00 14
Rotherhithe	d	00 16
Canada Water	d	00 18
Surrey Quays	d	00 19
New Cross ELL	a	
New Cross Gate 4	a	00 23
	d	
Brockley	d	
Honor Oak Park	d	
Forest Hill 4	d	
Sydenham	d	
Crystal Palace 4	d	
Gipsy Hill	d	
West Norwood 4	d	
Streatham Hill	d	
Balham 4 ⊖	d	
Wandsworth Common	d	
Clapham Junction 10	d	
South Bermondsey	d	
Queens Rd Peckham	d	
Peckham Rye 4	d	
Denmark Hill 4	d	
London Blackfriars 3 ⊖	a	
Clapham High Street ⊖	d	
Wandsworth Road	d	
Battersea Park 4	d	
London Victoria 15 ⊖	a	
Penge West	d	
Anerley	d	
Norwood Junction 2	d	
West Croydon 4	a	
East Croydon	a	

A not 27 July

30 July to 10 August

London Bridge to London Victoria - Croydon and East London Line

Network Diagram - see first Page of Table 177

Station		SN A	LO MO	SN A	SN MO	LO A	SN A	LO MO	LO A	LO MO		SN A	LO A	LO MO	LO A	LO MO	SN A	SN A	LO A	LO MO		LO A	LO MO	LO A	LO MO
London Bridge 4 ⊖	d	23p22		23p36	23p39							23p52					00 03	00 06							
Highbury & Islington	a																								
	d		23p06			23p18		23p21	23p25	23p28			23p33	23p36	23p40	23p43			23p48	23p51		23p55	23p58	00 03	00 06
Canonbury	d		23p08			23p20		23p23	23p27	23p30			23p35	23p38	23p42	23p45			23p50	23p53		23p57	00 01	00 05	00 08
Dalston Junction Stn ELL	d		23p11			23p25		23p28	23p30	23p33			23p38	23p41	23p45	23p48			23p55	23p58		00 01	00 04	00 10	00 13
Haggerston	d		23p12			23p26		23p29	23p31	23p34			23p39	23p42	23p46	23p49			23p56	23p59		00 02	00 06	00 11	00 14
Hoxton	d		23p14			23p28		23p31	23p33	23p36			23p41	23p44	23p48	23p51			23p58	00 01		00 04	00 08	00 13	00 16
Shoreditch High Street	d		23p17			23p31		23p34	23p36	23p39			23p44	23p47	23p51	23p54			00 01	00 04		00 07	00 10	00 16	00 19
Whitechapel	d		23p19			23p33		23p36	23p38	23p41			23p46	23p49	23p53	23p56			00 03	00 06		00 09	00 13	00 18	00 21
Shadwell	d		23p21			23p35		23p38	23p40	23p43			23p48	23p51	23p55	23p58			00 05	00 08		00 11	00 15	00 20	00 23
Wapping	d		23p23			23p37		23p40	23p42	23p45			23p50	23p53	23p57	00 01			00 07	00 10		00 13	00 17	00 22	00 25
Rotherhithe	d		23p25			23p39		23p42	23p44	23p47			23p52	23p55	23p59	00 03			00 09	00 12		00 15	00 18	00 24	00 27
Canada Water	d		23p27			23p41		23p44	23p46	23p49			23p54	23p57	00 02	00 05			00 11	00 14		00 17	00 20	00 26	00 29
Surrey Quays	d		23p28			23p42		23p45	23p47	23p50			23p55	23p58	00 03	00 06			00 12	00 15		00 18	00 22	00 27	00 30
New Cross ELL	a																								
New Cross Gate 4	a	23p27	23p32	23p41	23p44	23p46		23p49	23p51	23p54		23p57	23p58	00 02	00 07	00 10		00 11	00 16	00 19		00 22	00 25	00 31	00 34
	d	23p27	23p33	23p41	23p44	23p47		23p50	23p52	23p55		23p57	23p59	00 03	00 08	00 11		00 11	00 17	00 20		00 23	00 26	00 32	00 35
Brockley	d	23p30	23p35	23p44	23p47	23p49		23p52	23p54	23p57		00 01	00 03	00 06	00 10	00 13		00 14	00 19	00 22		00 25	00 29	00 34	00 37
Honor Oak Park	d	23p33	23p38	23p47	23p50	23p52		23p55	23p57	00 01		00 04	00 06	00 09	00 13	00 16		00 17	00 22	00 25		00 28	00 32	00 37	00 40
Forest Hill 4	d	23p35	23p41	23p49	23p52	23p55		23p58	23p59	00 04		00 06	00 09	00 12	00 16	00 19		00 19	00 25	00 28		00 31	00 34	00 40	00 43
Sydenham	d	23p38	23p43	23p52	23p55	23p57		00 01	00 02	00 06		00 09	00 11	00 14	00 18	00 21		00 22	00 27	00 30		00 33	00 37	00 42	00 45
Crystal Palace 4	d	23p43					00 03		00a07	00a11		00 13			00a23	00a26						00a38	00a41		
Gipsy Hill	d	23p45										00 15													
West Norwood 4	d	23p48										00 18													
Streatham Hill	d	23p52										00 22													
Balham 4 ⊖	d	23p55										00 25													
Wandsworth Common	d	23p58										00 27													
Clapham Junction 10	d	00 02										00 31													
South Bermondsey	d																00 07								
Queens Rd Peckham	d																00 09								
Peckham Rye 4	d																00 12								
Denmark Hill 4	d																								
London Blackfriars 3 ⊖	a																								
Clapham High Street ⊖	d																								
Wandsworth Road	d																								
Battersea Park 4	d	00 05										00 35													
London Victoria 15 ⊖	a	00 10										00 42													
Penge West	d		23p46	23p54	23p57	00 01		00 04					00 14	00 17				00 24	00 30	00 33				00 45	00 48
Anerley	d		23p48	23p56	23p59	00 03		00 06					00 16	00 19				00 26	00 32	00 35				00 47	00 50
Norwood Junction 2	d		23p55	23p59	00 03	00 06	00 09	00 09					00 19	00 22			00a34	00 30	00 35	00 38				00 50	00 53
West Croydon 4	a		00 03			00 13	00 14	00 16					00 26	00 29					00 42	00 45				00 57	01 00
East Croydon	a			00 03	00 06													00 33							

Station		LO A	LO MO	SN A	LO A	LO MO		LO A	LO MO	LO A	LO MO	LO A	LO MO	LO A	LO MO	LO A		LO MO	LO A	LO MO	LO A	LO MO	LO A	LO MO	SE
London Bridge 4 ⊖	d			00 36																					
Highbury & Islington	a																								
	d	00 10	00 13		00 18	00 21		00 25	00 28	00 33	00 36	00 40	00 43	00 48	00 51	00 55		00 58	01 03	01 06	01 10	01 13	01 25	01 28	
Canonbury	d	00 12	00 15		00 20	00 23		00 27	00 30	00 35	00 38	00 42	00 45	00 50	00 53	00 57		01 00	01 05	01 08	01 12	01 15	01 27	01 30	
Dalston Junction Stn ELL	d	00 15	00 18		00 25	00 28		00 30	00 33	00 40	00 43	00 45	00 48	00 55	00 58	01 00		01 03	01 10	01 13	01 15	01 18	01 32	01 35	
Haggerston	d	00 16	00 19		00 26	00 29		00 31	00 34	00 41	00 44	00 46	00 49	00 56	00 59	01 01		01 04	01 11	01 14	01 16	01 19	01 33	01 36	
Hoxton	d	00 18	00 21		00 28	00 31		00 33	00 36	00 43	00 46	00 48	00 51	00 58	01 01	01 03		01 06	01 13	01 16	01 18	01 21	01 35	01 38	
Shoreditch High Street	d	00 21	00 24		00 31	00 34		00 36	00 39	00 46	00 49	00 51	00 54	01 01	01 04	01 06		01 09	01 16	01 19	01 21	01 24	01 38	01 41	
Whitechapel	d	00 23	00 26		00 33	00 36		00 38	00 41	00 48	00 51	00 53	00 56	01 03	01 06	01 08		01 11	01 18	01 21	01 23	01 26	01 40	01 43	
Shadwell	d	00 25	00 28		00 35	00 38		00 40	00 43	00 50	00 53	00 55	00 58	01 05	01 08	01 10		01 13	01 20	01 23	01 25	01 28	01 42	01 45	
Wapping	d	00 27	00 30		00 37	00 40		00 42	00 45	00 52	00 55	00 57	01 00	01 07	01 10	01 12		01 15	01 22	01 25	01 27	01 30	01 44	01 47	
Rotherhithe	d	00 29	00 32		00 39	00 42		00 44	00 47	00 54	00 57	00 59	01 02	01 09	01 12	01 14		01 17	01 24	01 27	01 29	01 32	01 46	01 49	
Canada Water	d	00 31	00 34		00 41	00 44		00 46	00 49	00 56	00 59	01 01	01 04	01 11	01 14	01 16		01 19	01 26	01 29	01 31	01 34	01 48	01 51	
Surrey Quays	d	00 32	00 35		00 42	00 45		00 47	00 50	00 57	01 00	01 02	01 05	01 12	01 15	01 17		01 20	01 27	01 30	01 32	01 35	01 49	01 52	
New Cross ELL	a																								
New Cross Gate 4	a	00 36	00 39	00 41	00 47	00 50		00 51	00 54	01 02	01 05	01 06	01 09	01 16	01 19	01 21		01 24	01 31	01 34	01 36	01 39	01 53	01 56	
	d	00 37	00 40	00 41	00 47	00 50		00 52	00 55	01 03	01 06	01 07	01 10	01 17	01 20	01 22		01 25	01 32	01 35	01 37	01 40	01 54	01 57	
Brockley	d	00 39	00 42	00 44	00 49	00 52		00 54	00 57	01 05	01 08	01 09	01 12	01 19	01 22	01 24		01 27	01 34	01 37	01 39	01 42	01 56	01 59	
Honor Oak Park	d	00 42	00 45	00 47	00 52	00 55		00 57	01 00	01 08	01 11	01 12	01 15	01 22	01 25	01 27		01 30	01 37	01 40	01 42	01 45	01 59	02 02	
Forest Hill 4	d	00 45	00 48	00 49	00 55	00 58		00 59	01 02	01 11	01 14	01 15	01 18	01 25	01 28	01 30		01 33	01 40	01 43	01 45	01 48	02 02	02 05	
Sydenham	d	00 47	00 50	00 52	00 57	01 00		01 02	01 05	01 13	01 16	01 17	01 20	01 27	01 30	01 32		01 35	01 42	01 45	01 47	01 50	02 04	02 07	
Crystal Palace 4	d	00a52	00a55					01a07	01a10			01a22	01a25			01a37		01a40			01a52	01a55			
Gipsy Hill	d																								
West Norwood 4	d																								
Streatham Hill	d																								
Balham 4 ⊖	d																								
Wandsworth Common	d																								
Clapham Junction 10	d																								
South Bermondsey	d																								
Queens Rd Peckham	d																								
Peckham Rye 4	d																								05 04
Denmark Hill 4	d																								05 07
London Blackfriars 3 ⊖	a																								05 17
Clapham High Street ⊖	d																								
Wandsworth Road	d																								
Battersea Park 4	d																								
London Victoria 15 ⊖	a																								
Penge West	d			00 54	01 00	01 03				01 16	01 19			01 30	01 33				01 45	01 48			02 07	02 10	
Anerley	d			00 56	01 02	01 05				01 18	01 21			01 32	01 35				01 47	01 50			02 09	02 12	
Norwood Junction 2	d			01 00	01 05	01 08				01 21	01 24			01 35	01 38				01 50	01 53			02 12	02 15	
West Croydon 4	a				01 14	01 17				01 28	01 31			01 42	01 45				01 57	02 00			02 19	02 22	
East Croydon	a			01 03																					

A not 30 July, 6 August

London Bridge to London Victoria - Croydon and East London Line

Network Diagram - see first Page of Table 177

		SE		SN	SN	LO	LO	LO	LO	LO	SN	SN		LO	LO	SN	LO	LO	SN	SN	SE	SN		LO	SN
London Bridge 4 ⊖	d			06 00							06 06	06 11				06 19			06 30	06 33					06 36
Highbury & Islington	a																								
	d							05 35							05 55		06 05								
Canonbury	d							05 37							05 57		06 07								
Dalston Junction Stn ELL	d							05 40	05 50						06 00		06 10	06 20							
Haggerston	d							05 41	05 51						06 01		06 11	06 21							
Hoxton	d							05 43	05 53						06 03		06 13	06 23							
Shoreditch High Street	d							05 46	05 56						06 06		06 16	06 26							
Whitechapel	d							05 48	05 58						06 08		06 18	06 28							
Shadwell	d							05 50	06 00						06 10		06 20	06 30							
Wapping	d							05 52	06 02						06 12		06 22	06 32							
Rotherhithe	d							05 54	06 04						06 14		06 24	06 34							
Canada Water	d							05 56	06 06						06 16		06 26	06 36							
Surrey Quays	d							05 57	06 07						06 17		06 27	06 37							
New Cross ELL	a								06 12									06 42							
New Cross Gate 4	a							06 01			06 11				06 21	06 25	06 31								06 41
	d					05 47	05 52	06 02		06 07	06 11			06 17	06 22	06 25	06 32							06 37	06 41
Brockley	d					05 49	05 54	06 04		06 09	06 14			06 19	06 24	06 27	06 34							06 39	06 44
Honor Oak Park	d					05 52	05 57	06 07		06 12	06 17			06 22	06 27	06 30	06 37							06 42	06 47
Forest Hill 4	d					05 55	06 00	06 10		06 15	06 19			06 25	06 30	06 33	06 40							06 45	06 49
Sydenham	d					05 57	06 02	06 12		06 17	06 22			06 27	06 32	06 35	06 42							06 47	06 52
Crystal Palace 4	d				05 59		06a07			06a22					06a37	06 39						06 51		06a52	
Gipsy Hill	d				06 01											06 41						06 53			
West Norwood 4	d				06 04											06 44						06 56			
Streatham Hill	d															06 48									
Balham 4 ⊖	d															06 51									
Wandsworth Common	d																								
Clapham Junction 10	d															06 56									
South Bermondsey	d			06 04								06 15							06 34	06 37					
Queens Rd Peckham	d			06 06								06 18							06 36	06 39					
Peckham Rye 4	d	06 04		06a09	06a15							06 20							06a39	06a42	06 47	07a08			
Denmark Hill 4	d	06 07										06 23									06 50				
London Blackfriars 3 ⊖	a	06 17																							
Clapham High Street ⊖	d											06 28													
Wandsworth Road	d											06 29													
Battersea Park 4	d											06 32													
London Victoria 15 ⊖	a											06 36				07 05					07 04				
Penge West	d					06 00		06 15			06 24			06 30			06 45								06 54
Anerley	d					06 02		06 17			06 26			06 32			06 47								06 56
Norwood Junction 2	d					06 05		06 20			06 30			06 35			06 50								07 00
West Croydon 4	a					06 13		06 30						06 41			07 00								
East Croydon	a										06 33														07 03

		SN	LO	LO	LO	SN	SN	LO		SN	SN	SN	LO	LO	SN	LO	LO	LO		SN	SE	SN	LO	SN	SN
London Bridge 4 ⊖	d	06 41				06 51	06 54			06 58	07 03				07 06					07 11		07 21		07 29	07 33
Highbury & Islington	a																								
	d			06 25				06 33					06 40			06 48	06 55						07 03		
Canonbury	d			06 27				06 35					06 42			06 50	06 57						07 05		
Dalston Junction Stn ELL	d			06 30	06 35			06 40					06 45	06 50		06 55	07 00	07 05					07 10		
Haggerston	d			06 31	06 36			06 41					06 46	06 51		06 56	07 01	07 06					07 11		
Hoxton	d			06 33	06 38			06 43					06 48	06 53		06 58	07 03	07 08					07 13		
Shoreditch High Street	d			06 36	06 41			06 46					06 51	06 56		07 01	07 06	07 11					07 16		
Whitechapel	d			06 38	06 43			06 48					06 53	06 58		07 03	07 08	07 13					07 18		
Shadwell	d			06 40	06 45			06 50					06 55	07 00		07 05	07 10	07 15					07 20		
Wapping	d			06 42	06 47			06 52					06 57	07 02		07 07	07 12	07 17					07 22		
Rotherhithe	d			06 44	06 49			06 54					06 59	07 04		07 09	07 14	07 19					07 24		
Canada Water	d			06 46	06 51			06 56					07 01	07 06		07 11	07 16	07 21					07 26		
Surrey Quays	d			06 47	06 52			06 57					07 02	07 07		07 12	07 17	07 22					07 27		
New Cross ELL	a				06 57									07 12				07 27							
New Cross Gate 4	a			06 51		06 56	06 59	07 00					07 06		07 11	07 15	07 21					07 26	07 31		
	d		06 47	06 52		06 56	06 59	07 02					07 07		07 11	07 17	07 22					07 26	07 32		
Brockley	d		06 49	06 54		06 59	07 02	07 04					07 09		07 14	07 19	07 24					07 29	07 34		
Honor Oak Park	d		06 52	06 57		07 02	07 05	07 07					07 12		07 17	07 22	07 27					07 32	07 37		
Forest Hill 4	d		06 55	07 00		07 04	07 07	07 10					07 15		07 19	07 25	07 30					07 34	07 40		
Sydenham	d		06 57	07 02		07 07	07 10	07 12					07 17		07 22	07 27	07 32					07 37	07 42		
Crystal Palace 4	d			07a07		07 13						07 20	07a22				07a37					07 43			
Gipsy Hill	d					07 15						07 22										07 45			
West Norwood 4	d					07 18						07 25										07 48			
Streatham Hill	d					07 22																07 52			
Balham 4 ⊖	d					07 25																07 55			
Wandsworth Common	d					07 27																07 57			
Clapham Junction 10	d					07 31																08 01			
South Bermondsey	d	06 45								07 02	07 07									07 15				07 33	07 37
Queens Rd Peckham	d	06 48								07 04	07 09									07 17				07 35	07 39
Peckham Rye 4	d	06 50								07a07	07a12	07a36								07 20	07 23			07a38	07a42
Denmark Hill 4	d	06 53																		07 23	07 29				
London Blackfriars 3 ⊖	a																								
Clapham High Street ⊖	d	06 58																		07 28					
Wandsworth Road	d	06 59																		07 29					
Battersea Park 4	d	07 02				07 35														07 32		08 05			
London Victoria 15 ⊖	a	07 08				07 41														07 38	07 42	08 11			
Penge West	d		07 00				07 12	07 15							07 24	07 30							07 45		
Anerley	d		07 02				07 14	07 17							07 26	07 32							07 47		
Norwood Junction 2	d		07 05				07 18	07 20							07 31	07 35							07 50		
West Croydon 4	a		07 11					07 30								07 42							08 00		
East Croydon	a						07 21								07 37										

London Bridge to London Victoria - Croydon and East London Line

Network Diagram - see first Page of Table 177

		SN	LO	LO		SN	LO	SN	SN	LO	LO	SE	SN	LO		SN	SE	SN	SN	LO	LO	SN	LO	LO	
London Bridge 4 ⊖	d					07 36		07 41	07 44				07 53			08 03		08 06				08 06			
Highbury & Islington	a																								
	d		07 10				07 18			07 25				07 33						07 40			07 48	07 55	
Canonbury	d		07 12				07 20			07 27				07 35						07 42			07 50	07 57	
Dalston Junction Stn ELL	d		07 15	07 20			07 25			07 30	07 35			07 40						07 45	07 50		07 55	08 00	
Haggerston	d		07 16	07 21			07 26			07 31	07 36			07 41						07 46	07 51		07 56	08 01	
Hoxton	d		07 18	07 23			07 28			07 33	07 38			07 43						07 48	07 53		07 58	08 03	
Shoreditch High Street	d		07 21	07 26			07 31			07 36	07 41			07 46						07 51	07 56		08 01	08 06	
Whitechapel	d		07 23	07 28			07 33			07 38	07 43			07 48						07 53	07 58		08 03	08 08	
Shadwell	d		07 25	07 30			07 35			07 40	07 45			07 50						07 55	08 00		08 05	08 10	
Wapping	d		07 27	07 32			07 37			07 42	07 47			07 52						07 57	08 02		08 07	08 12	
Rotherhithe	d		07 29	07 34			07 39			07 44	07 49			07 54						07 59	08 04		08 09	08 14	
Canada Water	d		07 31	07 36			07 41			07 46	07 51			07 56						08 01	08 06		08 11	08 16	
Surrey Quays	d		07 32	07 37			07 42			07 47	07 52			07 57						08 02	08 07		08 12	08 17	
New Cross ELL	a			07 42							07 57										08 12				
New Cross Gate 4	a		07 36			07 41	07 45		07 49	07 51			07 58	08 01						08 06		08 11	08 16	08 21	
	d		07 37			07 41	07 47		07 49	07 52			07 58	08 02						08 07		08 11	08 17	08 22	
Brockley	d		07 39			07 44	07 49			07 54			08 01	08 04						08 09		08 14	08 19	08 24	
Honor Oak Park	d		07 42			07 47	07 52			07 57			08 04	08 07						08 12		08 17	08 22	08 27	
Forest Hill 4	d		07 45			07 49	07 55			08 00			08 06	08 10						08 15		08 19	08 25	08 30	
Sydenham	d		07 47			07 52	07 57			08 02			08 09	08 12						08 17		08 22	08 27	08 32	
Crystal Palace 4	d	07 49	07a52							08a07			08 13						08 19	08a22				08a37	
Gipsy Hill	d	07 51											08 15						08 21						
West Norwood 4	d	07 54											08 18						08 24						
Streatham Hill	d												08 22												
Balham 4 ⊖	d												08 25												
Wandsworth Common	d												08 27												
Clapham Junction 10	d												08 31												
South Bermondsey	d							07 45								08 07		08 11							
Queens Rd Peckham	d							07 47								08 09		08 13							
Peckham Rye 4	d	08a06						07 50				07 54				08a12	08 13	08a16	08a36						
Denmark Hill 4	d							07 53				07 59					08 17								
London Blackfriars 3 ⊖	a																								
Clapham High Street ⊖	d							07 58																	
Wandsworth Road	d							07 59																	
Battersea Park 4	d							08 02					08 35												
London Victoria 15 ⊖	a							08 08				08 11	08 41				08 29								
Penge West	d					07 54	08 00							08 15								08 24	08 30		
Anerley	d					07 56	08 02							08 17								08 26	08 32		
Norwood Junction 2	d					08 00	08 05							08 20								08 30	08 35		
West Croydon 4	a						08 12							08 30									08 43		
East Croydon	a					08 03			08 00													08 33			

		LO	SN	SE 1	SE	SN	LO	SN	SN	LO		LO	SN	LO	LO	LO	SN	SE	SE	SN		LO	LO	LO	SN
London Bridge 4 ⊖	d		08 10			08 21		08 33					08 36				08 41	07b37		08 51					09 03
Highbury & Islington	a																								
	d						08 03			08 10				08 18	08 25							08 33	08 40		
Canonbury	d						08 05			08 12				08 20	08 27							08 35	08 42		
Dalston Junction Stn ELL	d	08 05					08 10			08 15		08 20		08 25	08 30	08 35						08 40	08 46	08 50	
Haggerston	d	08 06					08 11			08 16		08 21		08 26	08 31	08 36						08 41	08 47	08 51	
Hoxton	d	08 08					08 13			08 18		08 23		08 28	08 33	08 38						08 43	08 49	08 53	
Shoreditch High Street	d	08 11					08 16			08 21		08 26		08 31	08 36	08 41						08 46	08 52	08 56	
Whitechapel	d	08 13					08 18			08 23		08 28		08 33	08 38	08 43						08 48	08 54	08 58	
Shadwell	d	08 15					08 20			08 25		08 30		08 35	08 40	08 45						08 50	08 56	09 00	
Wapping	d	08 17					08 22			08 27		08 32		08 37	08 42	08 47						08 52	08 58	09 02	
Rotherhithe	d	08 19					08 24			08 29		08 34		08 39	08 44	08 49						08 54	09 00	09 04	
Canada Water	d	08 21					08 26			08 31		08 36		08 41	08 46	08 51						08 56	09 02	09 06	
Surrey Quays	d	08 22					08 27			08 32		08 37		08 42	08 47	08 52						08 57	09 03	09 07	
New Cross ELL	a	08 27										08 42				08 57								09 12	
New Cross Gate 4	a					08 26	08 31			08 36			08 41	08 46	08 51					08 57		09 01	09 07		
	d					08 26	08 32			08 37			08 41	08 47	08 52					08 57		09 02	09 08		
Brockley	d					08 29	08 34			08 39			08 44	08 49	08 54					09 00		09 04	09 10		
Honor Oak Park	d					08 32	08 37			08 42			08 47	08 52	08 57					09 03		09 07	09 13		
Forest Hill 4	d					08 34	08 40			08 45			08 49	08 55	09 00					09 05		09 10	09 16		
Sydenham	d					08 37	08 42			08 47			08 52	08 57	09 02					09 08		09 12	09 18		
Crystal Palace 4	d					08 40			08 50	08a52					09a07					09 11			09a23		
Gipsy Hill	d					08 43			08 52											09 14					
West Norwood 4	d					08 46			08 55											09 17					
Streatham Hill	d					08 49														09 21					
Balham 4 ⊖	d					08 55														09 25					
Wandsworth Common	d					08 57														09 27					
Clapham Junction 10	d					09 01														09 31					
South Bermondsey	d		08 14					08 37									08 45								09 07
Queens Rd Peckham	d		08 16					08 39									08 48								09 09
Peckham Rye 4	d		08 19		08 33			08a42	09a07								08 50	08 55	08 55						09a12
Denmark Hill 4	d		08 22	08 30	08 36												08 53	09 02	09 02						
London Blackfriars 3 ⊖	a																								
Clapham High Street ⊖	d		08 27														08 58								
Wandsworth Road	d		08 29														08 59								
Battersea Park 4	d		08 32			09 05											09 02			09 35					
London Victoria 15 ⊖	a		08 39	08 42	08 49	09 11											09 08	09 14	09 14	09 42					
Penge West	d						08 45						08 54	09 00								09 15			
Anerley	d						08 47						08 56	09 02								09 17			
Norwood Junction 2	d						08 50						09 00	09 05								09 20			
West Croydon 4	a						09 00							09 12								09 30			
East Croydon	a												09 06												

b London Bridge-1

London Bridge to London Victoria - Croydon and East London Line

Network Diagram - see first Page of Table 177

		SN	LO	SE	SN	SN		LO	LO	SN	LO	LO	LO	SN	SN	LO		SE	SN	SN	LO	LO	SN	LO	LO
London Bridge 4 ⊖	d	09 06			09 11					09 22				09 33	09 36				09 41				09 52		
Highbury & Islington	a																								
	d		08 48					08 55			09 03	09 10				09 18					09 25			09 33	09 40
Canonbury	d		08 50					08 57			09 05	09 12				09 20					09 27			09 35	09 42
Dalston Junction Stn ELL	d		08 55					09 01	09 05		09 10	09 15	09 20			09 25					09 30	09 35		09 40	09 45
Haggerston	d		08 56					09 02	09 06		09 11	09 16	09 21			09 26					09 31	09 36		09 41	09 46
Hoxton	d		08 58					09 04	09 08		09 13	09 18	09 23			09 28					09 33	09 38		09 43	09 48
Shoreditch High Street	d		09 01					09 07	09 11		09 16	09 21	09 26			09 31					09 36	09 41		09 46	09 51
Whitechapel	d		09 03					09 09	09 13		09 18	09 23	09 28			09 33					09 38	09 43		09 48	09 53
Shadwell	d		09 05					09 11	09 15		09 20	09 25	09 30			09 35					09 40	09 45		09 50	09 55
Wapping	d		09 07					09 13	09 17		09 22	09 27	09 32			09 37					09 42	09 47		09 52	09 57
Rotherhithe	d		09 09					09 15	09 19		09 24	09 29	09 34			09 39					09 44	09 49		09 54	09 59
Canada Water	d		09 11					09 17	09 21		09 26	09 31	09 36			09 41					09 46	09 51		09 56	10 01
Surrey Quays	d		09 12					09 18	09 22		09 27	09 32	09 37			09 42					09 47	09 52		09 57	10 02
New Cross ELL	a								09 27				09 42									09 57			
New Cross Gate 4	a	09 12	09 16					09 22		09 28	09 30	09 36			09 41	09 46					09 51		09 57	10 01	10 06
	d	09 12	09 17					09 23		09 28	09 32	09 37			09 41	09 47					09 52		09 57	10 02	10 07
Brockley	d	09 14	09 19					09 25		09 30	09 34	09 39			09 44	09 49					09 54		10 00	10 04	10 09
Honor Oak Park	d	09 17	09 22					09 28		09 33	09 37	09 42			09 47	09 52					09 57		10 03	10 07	10 12
Forest Hill 4	d	09 20	09 25					09 31		09 36	09 40	09 45			09 49	09 55					10 00		10 05	10 10	10 15
Sydenham	d	09 22	09 27					09 33		09 38	09 42	09 47			09 52	09 57					10 02		10 08	10 12	10 17
Crystal Palace 4	d					09 30		09a38		09 43		09a52								10 00	10a07		10 13		10a22
Gipsy Hill	d					09 32				09 46										10 02			10 15		
West Norwood 4	d					09 35				09 49										10 05			10 18		
Streatham Hill	d									09 52													10 22		
Balham 4 ⊖	d									09 56													10 25		
Wandsworth Common	d									09 58													10 27		
Clapham Junction 10	d									10 02													10 31		
South Bermondsey	d				09 15									09 37					09 45						
Queens Rd Peckham	d				09 18									09 39					09 48						
Peckham Rye 4	d			09 14	09 20	09a47								09a42				09 45	09 50	10a17					
Denmark Hill 4	d			09 17	09 23													09 49	09 53						
London Blackfriars 3 ⊖	a																								
Clapham High Street ⊖	d				09 28														09 58						
Wandsworth Road	d				09 29														09 59						
Battersea Park 4	d				09 32					10 05									10 03				10 35		
London Victoria 15 ⊖	a			09 29	09 38					10 11								10 00	10 07				10 39		
Penge West	d	09 25	09 30								09 45				09 54	10 00								10 15	
Anerley	d	09 27	09 32								09 47				09 56	10 02								10 17	
Norwood Junction 2	d	09 30	09 35								09 50				10 00	10 05								10 20	
West Croydon 4	a		09 42								10 00					10 12								10 30	
East Croydon	a	09 33													10 03										

		LO		SN	SN	LO	SE	SN	SN	LO	LO	SN		LO	LO	LO	SN	SN	LO	SE	SN	SN		LO	LO
London Bridge 4 ⊖	d			10 03	10 06			10 11				10 22					10 33	10 36			10 41				
Highbury & Islington	a																								
	d					09 48				09 55				10 03	10 10				10 18					10 25	
Canonbury	d					09 50				09 57				10 05	10 12				10 20					10 27	
Dalston Junction Stn ELL	d	09 50				09 55				10 00	10 05			10 10	10 15	10 20			10 25					10 30	10 35
Haggerston	d	09 51				09 56				10 01	10 06			10 11	10 16	10 21			10 26					10 31	10 36
Hoxton	d	09 53				09 58				10 03	10 08			10 13	10 18	10 23			10 28					10 33	10 38
Shoreditch High Street	d	09 56				10 01				10 06	10 11			10 16	10 21	10 26			10 31					10 36	10 41
Whitechapel	d	09 58				10 03				10 08	10 13			10 18	10 23	10 28			10 33					10 38	10 43
Shadwell	d	10 00				10 05				10 10	10 15			10 20	10 25	10 30			10 35					10 40	10 45
Wapping	d	10 02				10 07				10 12	10 17			10 22	10 27	10 32			10 37					10 42	10 47
Rotherhithe	d	10 04				10 09				10 14	10 19			10 24	10 29	10 34			10 39					10 44	10 49
Canada Water	d	10 06				10 11				10 16	10 21			10 26	10 31	10 36			10 41					10 46	10 51
Surrey Quays	d	10 07				10 12				10 17	10 22			10 27	10 32	10 37			10 42					10 47	10 52
New Cross ELL	a	10 12									10 27					10 42									10 57
New Cross Gate 4	a				10 11	10 16				10 21		10 27		10 31	10 36			10 41	10 46					10 51	
	d				10 11	10 17				10 22		10 27		10 32	10 37			10 41	10 47					10 52	
Brockley	d				10 14	10 19				10 24		10 30		10 34	10 39			10 44	10 49					10 54	
Honor Oak Park	d				10 17	10 22				10 27		10 33		10 37	10 42			10 47	10 52					10 57	
Forest Hill 4	d				10 19	10 25				10 30		10 35		10 40	10 45			10 49	10 55					11 00	
Sydenham	d				10 22	10 27				10 32		10 38		10 42	10 47			10 52	10 57					11 02	
Crystal Palace 4	d								10 30	10a37		10 43			10a52							11 00		11a07	
Gipsy Hill	d								10 32			10 45										11 02			
West Norwood 4	d								10 35			10 48										11 05			
Streatham Hill	d											10 52													
Balham 4 ⊖	d											10 55													
Wandsworth Common	d											10 57													
Clapham Junction 10	d											11 01													
South Bermondsey	d			10 07				10 15									10 37				10 45				
Queens Rd Peckham	d			10 09				10 18									10 39				10 48				
Peckham Rye 4	d			10a12			10 15	10 20	10a47								10a42			10 45	10 50	11a17			
Denmark Hill 4	d						10 19	10 23												10 49	10 53				
London Blackfriars 3 ⊖	a																								
Clapham High Street ⊖	d							10 28													10 58				
Wandsworth Road	d							10 29													10 59				
Battersea Park 4	d							10 32				11 05									11 02				
London Victoria 15 ⊖	a						10 31	10 36				11 09								11 03	11 06				
Penge West	d				10 24	10 30								10 45				10 54	11 00						
Anerley	d				10 26	10 32								10 47				10 56	11 02						
Norwood Junction 2	d				10 30	10 35								10 50				11 00	11 05						
West Croydon 4	a					10 42								11 00					11 12						
East Croydon	a				10 33													11 03							

30 July to 10 August

London Bridge to London Victoria - Croydon and East London Line

Network Diagram - see first Page of Table 177

Station		SN	LO	LO	LO	SN	SN	LO		SE	SN	SN	LO	LO	SN	LO	LO	LO		SN	SN	LO	SE	SN	SN
London Bridge 4 ⊖	d	10 52				11 03	11 06				11 11				11 22					11 33	11 36			11 41	
Highbury & Islington	a																								
	d		10 33	10 40				10 48					10 55			11 03	11 10					11 18			
Canonbury	d		10 35	10 42				10 50					10 57			11 05	11 12					11 20			
Dalston Junction Stn ELL	d		10 40	10 45	10 50			10 55					11 00	11 05		11 10	11 15	11 20				11 25			
Haggerston	d		10 41	10 46	10 51			10 56					11 01	11 06		11 11	11 16	11 21				11 26			
Hoxton	d		10 43	10 48	10 53			10 58					11 03	11 08		11 13	11 18	11 23				11 28			
Shoreditch High Street	d		10 46	10 51	10 56			11 01					11 06	11 11		11 16	11 21	11 26				11 31			
Whitechapel	d		10 48	10 53	10 58			11 03					11 08	11 13		11 18	11 23	11 28				11 33			
Shadwell	d		10 50	10 55	11 00			11 05					11 10	11 15		11 20	11 25	11 30				11 35			
Wapping	d		10 52	10 57	11 02			11 07					11 12	11 17		11 22	11 27	11 32				11 37			
Rotherhithe	d		10 54	10 59	11 04			11 09					11 14	11 19		11 24	11 29	11 34				11 39			
Canada Water	d		10 56	11 01	11 06			11 11					11 16	11 21		11 26	11 31	11 36				11 41			
Surrey Quays	d		10 57	11 02	11 07			11 12					11 17	11 22		11 27	11 32	11 37				11 42			
New Cross ELL	a				11 12									11 27				11 42							
New Cross Gate 4	a	10 57	11 01	11 06			11 11	11 16					11 21		11 27	11 31	11 36				11 41	11 46			
	d	10 57	11 02	11 07			11 11	11 17					11 22		11 27	11 32	11 37				11 41	11 47			
Brockley	d	11 00	11 04	11 09			11 14	11 19					11 24		11 30	11 34	11 39				11 44	11 49			
Honor Oak Park	d	11 03	11 07	11 12			11 17	11 22					11 27		11 33	11 37	11 42				11 47	11 52			
Forest Hill 4	d	11 05	11 10	11 15			11 19	11 25					11 30		11 35	11 40	11 45				11 49	11 55			
Sydenham	d	11 08	11 12	11 17			11 22	11 27					11 32		11 38	11 42	11 47				11 52	11 57			
Crystal Palace 4	d	11 13		11a22								11 30	11a37		11 43		11a52								12 00
Gipsy Hill	d	11 15										11 32			11 45										12 02
West Norwood 4	d	11 18										11 35			11 48										12 05
Streatham Hill	d	11 22													11 52										
Balham 4 ⊖	d	11 25													11 55										
Wandsworth Common	d	11 27													11 57										
Clapham Junction 10	d	11 31													12 01										
South Bermondsey	d					11 07					11 15									11 37				11 45	
Queens Rd Peckham	d					11 09					11 18									11 39				11 48	
Peckham Rye 4	d					11a12				11 15	11 20	11a47								11a42			11 45	11 50	12a17
Denmark Hill 4	d									11 19	11 23												11 49	11 54	
London Blackfriars 3 ⊖	a																								
Clapham High Street ⊖	d										11 28													11 58	
Wandsworth Road	d										11 29													12 00	
Battersea Park 4	d	11 35									11 32				12 05									12 02	
London Victoria 15 ⊖	a	11 39								11 31	11 36				12 09								12 03	12 07	
Penge West	d		11 15				11 24	11 30								11 45					11 54	12 00			
Anerley	d		11 17				11 26	11 32								11 47					11 56	12 02			
Norwood Junction 2	d		11 20				11 30	11 35								11 50					12 00	12 05			
West Croydon 4 🚊	a		11 30					11 42								12 00						12 12			
East Croydon 🚊	a						11 33														12 03				

Station		LO	LO	SN		LO	LO	LO	SN	SN	LO	SE	SN	SN		LO	LO	SN	LO	LO	LO	SN	SN	LO	
London Bridge 4 ⊖	d			11 52					12 03	12 06			12 11					12 22				12 33	12 36		
Highbury & Islington	a																								
	d	11 25				11 33	11 40				11 48					11 55			12 03	12 10				12 18	
Canonbury	d	11 27				11 35	11 42				11 50					11 57			12 05	12 12				12 20	
Dalston Junction Stn ELL	d	11 30	11 35			11 40	11 45	11 50			11 55					12 00	12 05		12 10	12 15	12 20			12 25	
Haggerston	d	11 31	11 36			11 41	11 46	11 51			11 56					12 01	12 06		12 11	12 16	12 21			12 26	
Hoxton	d	11 33	11 38			11 43	11 48	11 53			11 58					12 03	12 08		12 13	12 18	12 23			12 28	
Shoreditch High Street	d	11 36	11 41			11 46	11 51	11 56			12 01					12 06	12 11		12 16	12 21	12 26			12 31	
Whitechapel	d	11 38	11 43			11 48	11 53	11 58			12 03					12 08	12 13		12 18	12 23	12 28			12 33	
Shadwell	d	11 40	11 45			11 50	11 55	12 00			12 05					12 10	12 15		12 20	12 25	12 30			12 35	
Wapping	d	11 42	11 47			11 52	11 57	12 02			12 07					12 12	12 17		12 22	12 27	12 32			12 37	
Rotherhithe	d	11 44	11 49			11 54	11 59	12 04			12 09					12 14	12 19		12 24	12 29	12 34			12 39	
Canada Water	d	11 46	11 51			11 56	12 01	12 06			12 11					12 16	12 21		12 26	12 31	12 36			12 41	
Surrey Quays	d	11 47	11 52			11 57	12 02	12 07			12 12					12 17	12 22		12 27	12 32	12 37			12 42	
New Cross ELL	a		11 57					12 12									12 27				12 42				
New Cross Gate 4	a	11 51		11 57		12 01	12 06			12 11	12 16					12 21		12 27	12 31	12 36			12 41	12 46	
	d	11 52		11 57		12 02	12 07			12 11	12 17					12 22		12 27	12 32	12 37			12 41	12 47	
Brockley	d	11 54		12 00		12 04	12 09			12 14	12 19					12 24		12 30	12 34	12 39			12 44	12 49	
Honor Oak Park	d	11 57		12 03		12 07	12 12			12 17	12 22					12 27		12 33	12 37	12 42			12 47	12 52	
Forest Hill 4	d	12 00		12 05		12 10	12 15			12 19	12 25					12 30		12 35	12 40	12 45			12 49	12 55	
Sydenham	d	12 02		12 08		12 12	12 17			12 22	12 27					12 32		12 38	12 42	12 47			12 52	12 57	
Crystal Palace 4	d	12a07		12 13			12a22							12 30		12a37		12 43		12a52					
Gipsy Hill	d			12 15										12 32				12 45							
West Norwood 4	d			12 18										12 35				12 48							
Streatham Hill	d			12 22														12 52							
Balham 4 ⊖	d			12 25														12 55							
Wandsworth Common	d			12 27														12 57							
Clapham Junction 10	d			12 31														13 01							
South Bermondsey	d								12 07				12 15									12 37			
Queens Rd Peckham	d								12 09				12 18									12 39			
Peckham Rye 4	d								12a12			12 15	12 20	12a47								12a42			
Denmark Hill 4	d											12 19	12 23												
London Blackfriars 3 ⊖	a																								
Clapham High Street ⊖	d												12 28												
Wandsworth Road	d												12 29												
Battersea Park 4	d			12 35									12 32					13 05							
London Victoria 15 ⊖	a			12 39								12 31	12 36					13 09							
Penge West	d					12 15				12 24	12 30								12 45				12 54	13 00	
Anerley	d					12 17				12 26	12 32								12 47				12 56	13 02	
Norwood Junction 2	d					12 20				12 30	12 35								12 50				13 00	13 05	
West Croydon 4 🚊	a					12 30					12 42								13 00					13 12	
East Croydon 🚊	a									12 33													13 03		

Table 178

Mondays to Fridays

30 July to 10 August

London Bridge to London Victoria - Croydon and East London Line

Network Diagram - see first Page of Table 177

Station		SE	SN	SN	LO	LO	SN	LO	LO	LO	SN	SN	LO	SE	SN	SN	LO	LO	SN	LO	LO	LO	SN
London Bridge 4 ⊖	d		12 41				12 52				13 03	13 06			13 11				13 22				13 33
Highbury & Islington	a																						
	d				12 25			12 33	12 40				12 48				12 55			13 03	13 10		
Canonbury	d				12 27			12 35	12 42				12 50				12 57			13 05	13 12		
Dalston Junction Stn ELL	d				12 30	12 35		12 40	12 45	12 50			12 55				13 00	13 05		13 10	13 15	13 20	
Haggerston	d				12 31	12 36		12 41	12 46	12 51			12 56				13 01	13 06		13 11	13 16	13 21	
Hoxton	d				12 33	12 38		12 43	12 48	12 53			12 58				13 03	13 08		13 13	13 18	13 23	
Shoreditch High Street	d				12 36	12 41		12 46	12 51	12 56			13 01				13 06	13 11		13 16	13 21	13 26	
Whitechapel	d				12 38	12 43		12 48	12 53	12 58			13 03				13 08	13 13		13 18	13 23	13 28	
Shadwell	d				12 40	12 45		12 50	12 55	13 00			13 05				13 10	13 15		13 20	13 25	13 30	
Wapping	d				12 42	12 47		12 52	12 57	13 02			13 07				13 12	13 17		13 22	13 27	13 32	
Rotherhithe	d				12 44	12 49		12 54	12 59	13 04			13 09				13 14	13 19		13 24	13 29	13 34	
Canada Water	d				12 46	12 51		12 56	13 01	13 06			13 11				13 16	13 21		13 26	13 31	13 36	
Surrey Quays	d				12 47	12 52		12 57	13 02	13 07			13 12				13 17	13 22		13 27	13 32	13 37	
New Cross ELL	a					12 57				13 12								13 27				13 42	
New Cross Gate 4	a				12 51		12 57	13 01	13 06			13 11	13 16				13 21		13 27	13 31	13 36		
	d				12 52		12 57	13 02	13 07			13 11	13 17				13 22		13 27	13 32	13 37		
Brockley	d				12 54		13 00	13 04	13 09			13 14	13 19				13 24		13 30	13 34	13 39		
Honor Oak Park	d				12 57		13 03	13 07	13 12			13 17	13 22				13 27		13 33	13 37	13 42		
Forest Hill 4	d				13 00		13 05	13 10	13 15			13 19	13 25				13 30		13 35	13 40	13 45		
Sydenham	d				13 02		13 08	13 12	13 17			13 22	13 27				13 32		13 38	13 42	13 47		
Crystal Palace 4	d			13 00	13a07		13 13		13a22							13 30	13a37		13 43		13a52		
Gipsy Hill	d			13 02			13 15									13 32			13 45				
West Norwood 4	d			13 05			13 18									13 35			13 48				
Streatham Hill	d						13 22												13 52				
Balham 4 ⊖	d						13 25												13 55				
Wandsworth Common	d						13 27												13 57				
Clapham Junction 10	d						13 31												14 01				
South Bermondsey	d		12 45								13 07				13 15								13 37
Queens Rd Peckham	d		12 48								13 09				13 18								13 39
Peckham Rye 4	d	12 45	12 50	13a17							13a12			13 15	13 20	13a47							13a42
Denmark Hill 4	d	12 49	12 53											13 19	13 23								
London Blackfriars 3 ⊖	a																						
Clapham High Street ⊖	d		12 58												13 28								
Wandsworth Road	d		12 59												13 29								
Battersea Park 4	d		13 02				13 35								13 32				14 05				
London Victoria 15 ⊖	a	13 01	13 06				13 39							13 31	13 36				14 09				
Penge West	d							13 15				13 24	13 30							13 45			
Anerley	d							13 17				13 26	13 32							13 47			
Norwood Junction 2	d							13 20				13 30	13 35							13 50			
West Croydon 4	a							13 30					13 42							14 00			
East Croydon	a											13 33											

Station		SN	LO	SE	SN	SN	LO	LO	SN	LO	LO	LO	SN	SN	LO	SE	SN	SN	LO	LO	SN	LO	LO
London Bridge 4 ⊖	d	13 36			13 41				13 52				14 03	14 06			14 11				14 22		
Highbury & Islington	a																						
	d		13 18				13 25			13 33	13 40				13 48				13 55			14 03	14 10
Canonbury	d		13 20				13 27			13 35	13 42				13 50				13 57			14 05	14 12
Dalston Junction Stn ELL	d		13 25				13 30	13 35		13 40	13 45	13 50			13 55				14 00	14 05		14 10	14 15
Haggerston	d		13 26				13 31	13 36		13 41	13 46	13 51			13 56				14 01	14 06		14 11	14 16
Hoxton	d		13 28				13 33	13 38		13 43	13 48	13 53			13 58				14 03	14 08		14 13	14 18
Shoreditch High Street	d		13 31				13 36	13 41		13 46	13 51	13 56			14 01				14 06	14 11		14 16	14 21
Whitechapel	d		13 33				13 38	13 43		13 48	13 53	13 58			14 03				14 08	14 13		14 18	14 23
Shadwell	d		13 35				13 40	13 45		13 50	13 55	14 00			14 05				14 10	14 15		14 20	14 25
Wapping	d		13 37				13 42	13 47		13 52	13 57	14 02			14 07				14 12	14 17		14 22	14 27
Rotherhithe	d		13 39				13 44	13 49		13 54	13 59	14 04			14 09				14 14	14 19		14 24	14 29
Canada Water	d		13 41				13 46	13 51		13 56	14 01	14 06			14 11				14 16	14 21		14 26	14 31
Surrey Quays	d		13 42				13 47	13 52		13 57	14 02	14 07			14 12				14 17	14 22		14 27	14 32
New Cross ELL	a							13 57				14 12								14 27			
New Cross Gate 4	a	13 41	13 46				13 51		13 57	14 01	14 06			14 11	14 16				14 21		14 27	14 31	14 36
	d	13 41	13 47				13 52		13 57	14 02	14 07			14 11	14 17				14 22		14 27	14 32	14 37
Brockley	d	13 44	13 49				13 54		14 00	14 04	14 09			14 14	14 19				14 24		14 30	14 34	14 39
Honor Oak Park	d	13 47	13 52				13 57		14 03	14 07	14 12			14 17	14 22				14 27		14 33	14 37	14 42
Forest Hill 4	d	13 49	13 55				14 00		14 05	14 10	14 15			14 19	14 25				14 30		14 35	14 40	14 45
Sydenham	d	13 52	13 57				14 02		14 08	14 12	14 17			14 22	14 27				14 32		14 38	14 42	14 47
Crystal Palace 4	d					14 00	14a07		14 13		14a22							14 30	14a37		14 43		14a52
Gipsy Hill	d					14 02			14 15									14 32			14 45		
West Norwood 4	d					14 05			14 18									14 35			14 48		
Streatham Hill	d								14 22												14 52		
Balham 4 ⊖	d								14 25												14 55		
Wandsworth Common	d								14 27												14 57		
Clapham Junction 10	d								14 31												15 01		
South Bermondsey	d				13 45								14 07				14 15						
Queens Rd Peckham	d				13 48								14 09				14 18						
Peckham Rye 4	d			13 45	13 50	14a17							14a12			14 15	14 20	14a47					
Denmark Hill 4	d			13 49	13 53											14 19	14 23						
London Blackfriars 3 ⊖	a																						
Clapham High Street ⊖	d				13 58												14 28						
Wandsworth Road	d				13 59												14 29						
Battersea Park 4	d				14 02				14 35								14 32				15 05		
London Victoria 15 ⊖	a			14 01	14 06				14 39							14 31	14 36				15 09		
Penge West	d	13 54	14 00							14 15				14 24	14 30							14 45	
Anerley	d	13 56	14 02							14 17				14 26	14 32							14 47	
Norwood Junction 2	d	14 00	14 05							14 20				14 30	14 35							14 50	
West Croydon 4	a		14 12							14 30					14 42							15 00	
East Croydon	a	14 03												14 33									

30 July to 10 August

London Bridge to London Victoria - Croydon and East London Line

Network Diagram - see first Page of Table 177

		LO		SN	SN	LO	SE	SN	SN	LO	LO	SN		LO	LO	LO	SN	SN	LO	SE	SN	SN		LO	LO
London Bridge ■4 ⊖	d			14 33	14 36			14 41				14 52					15 03	15 06			15 11				
Highbury & Islington	a																								
	d					14 18				14 25				14 33	14 40				14 48					14 55	
Canonbury	d					14 20				14 27				14 35	14 42				14 50					14 57	
Dalston Junction Stn ELL	d	14 20				14 25				14 30	14 35			14 40	14 45	14 50			14 55					15 00	15 05
Haggerston	d	14 21				14 26				14 31	14 36			14 41	14 46	14 51			14 56					15 01	15 06
Hoxton	d	14 23				14 28				14 33	14 38			14 43	14 48	14 53			14 58					15 03	15 08
Shoreditch High Street	d	14 26				14 31				14 36	14 41			14 46	14 51	14 56			15 01					15 06	15 11
Whitechapel	d	14 28				14 33				14 38	14 43			14 48	14 53	14 58			15 03					15 08	15 13
Shadwell	d	14 30				14 35				14 40	14 45			14 50	14 55	15 00			15 05					15 10	15 15
Wapping	d	14 32				14 37				14 42	14 47			14 52	14 57	15 02			15 07					15 12	15 17
Rotherhithe	d	14 34				14 39				14 44	14 49			14 54	14 59	15 04			15 09					15 14	15 19
Canada Water	d	14 36				14 41				14 46	14 51			14 56	15 01	15 06			15 11					15 16	15 21
Surrey Quays	d	14 37				14 42				14 47	14 52			14 57	15 02	15 07			15 12					15 17	15 22
New Cross ELL	a	14 42									14 57					15 12									15 27
New Cross Gate ■4	a				14 41	14 46				14 51		14 57		15 01	15 06			15 11	15 16					15 21	
	d				14 41	14 47				14 52		14 57		15 02	15 07			15 11	15 17					15 22	
Brockley	d				14 44	14 49				14 54		15 00		15 04	15 09			15 14	15 19					15 24	
Honor Oak Park	d				14 47	14 52				14 57		15 03		15 07	15 12			15 17	15 22					15 27	
Forest Hill ■4	d				14 49	14 55				15 00		15 05		15 10	15 15			15 19	15 25					15 30	
Sydenham	d				14 52	14 57				15 02		15 08		15 12	15 17			15 22	15 27					15 32	
Crystal Palace ■4	d								15 00	15a07		15 13			15a22							15 30		15a37	
Gipsy Hill	d								15 02			15 15										15 32			
West Norwood ■4	d								15 05			15 18										15 35			
Streatham Hill	d											15 22													
Balham ■4 ⊖	d											15 25													
Wandsworth Common	d											15 27													
Clapham Junction ■10	d											15 31													
South Bermondsey	d			14 37				14 45									15 07				15 15				
Queens Rd Peckham	d			14 39				14 48									15 09				15 18				
Peckham Rye ■4	d			14a42			14 45	14 50	15a17								15a12			15 15	15 20	15a47			
Denmark Hill ■4	d						14 49	14 53												15 19	15 23				
London Blackfriars ■3 ⊖	a																								
Clapham High Street ⊖	d							14 58													15 28				
Wandsworth Road	d							14 59													15 29				
Battersea Park ■4	d							15 02				15 35									15 32				
London Victoria ■15 ⊖	a						15 01	15 06				15 39								15 31	15 36				
Penge West	d				14 54	15 00								15 15				15 24	15 30						
Anerley	d				14 56	15 02								15 17				15 26	15 32						
Norwood Junction ■2	d				15 00	15 05								15 20				15 30	15 35						
West Croydon ■4	a					15 12								15 30					15 42						
East Croydon	a				15 03													15 33							

		SN	LO	LO	LO	SN	SN	LO		SE	SN	SN	SN	LO	LO	SN	LO	LO		LO	SN	SN	LO	SE	SN
London Bridge ■4 ⊖	d	15 22				15 33	15 36				15 41					15 52					16 03	16 06			16 11
Highbury & Islington	a																								
	d		15 03	15 10				15 18						15 25			15 33	15 40					15 48		
Canonbury	d		15 05	15 12				15 20						15 27			15 35	15 42					15 50		
Dalston Junction Stn ELL	d		15 10	15 15	15 20			15 25						15 30	15 35		15 40	15 45		15 50			15 55		
Haggerston	d		15 11	15 16	15 21			15 26						15 31	15 36		15 41	15 46		15 51			15 56		
Hoxton	d		15 13	15 18	15 23			15 28						15 33	15 38		15 43	15 48		15 53			15 58		
Shoreditch High Street	d		15 16	15 21	15 26			15 31						15 36	15 41		15 46	15 51		15 56			16 01		
Whitechapel	d		15 18	15 23	15 28			15 33						15 38	15 43		15 48	15 53		15 58			16 03		
Shadwell	d		15 20	15 25	15 30			15 35						15 40	15 45		15 50	15 55		16 00			16 05		
Wapping	d		15 22	15 27	15 32			15 37						15 42	15 47		15 52	15 57		16 02			16 07		
Rotherhithe	d		15 24	15 29	15 34			15 39						15 44	15 49		15 54	15 59		16 04			16 09		
Canada Water	d		15 26	15 31	15 36			15 41						15 46	15 51		15 56	16 01		16 06			16 11		
Surrey Quays	d		15 27	15 32	15 37			15 42						15 47	15 52		15 57	16 02		16 07			16 12		
New Cross ELL	a				15 42										15 57					16 12					
New Cross Gate ■4	a	15 27	15 31	15 36			15 41	15 46						15 51		15 57	16 01	16 06				16 11	16 16		
	d	15 27	15 32	15 37			15 41	15 47						15 52		15 57	16 02	16 07				16 11	16 17		
Brockley	d	15 30	15 34	15 39			15 44	15 49						15 54		16 00	16 04	16 09				16 14	16 19		
Honor Oak Park	d	15 33	15 37	15 42			15 47	15 52						15 57		16 03	16 07	16 12				16 17	16 22		
Forest Hill ■4	d	15 35	15 40	15 45			15 49	15 55						16 00		16 05	16 10	16 15				16 19	16 25		
Sydenham	d	15 38	15 42	15 47			15 52	15 57						16 02		16 08	16 12	16 17				16 22	16 27		
Crystal Palace ■4	d	15 43		15a52									16 00	16a07		16 13		16a22							
Gipsy Hill	d	15 45											16 02			16 15									
West Norwood ■4	d	15 48											16 05			16 18									
Streatham Hill	d	15 52										15 56				16 22									
Balham ■4 ⊖	d	15 55														16 25									
Wandsworth Common	d	15 57														16 27									
Clapham Junction ■10	d	16 01														16 31									
South Bermondsey	d					15 37					15 45										16 07				16 15
Queens Rd Peckham	d					15 39					15 48										16 09				16 18
Peckham Rye ■4	d					15a42				15 45	15 50	16a07	16a17								16a12			16 15	16 20
Denmark Hill ■4	d									15 49	15 53													16 19	16 23
London Blackfriars ■3 ⊖	a																								
Clapham High Street ⊖	d										15 58														16 28
Wandsworth Road	d										15 59														16 29
Battersea Park ■4	d	16 05									16 02					16 35									16 32
London Victoria ■15 ⊖	a	16 10								16 01	16 06					16 40								16 31	16 38
Penge West	d		15 45				15 54	16 00									16 15					16 24	16 30		
Anerley	d		15 47				15 56	16 02									16 17					16 26	16 32		
Norwood Junction ■2	d		15 50				16 00	16 05									16 20					16 30	16 35		
West Croydon ■4	a		16 00					16 12									16 30						16 42		
East Croydon	a						16 03															16 33			

Mondays to Fridays

30 July to 10 August

London Bridge to London Victoria - Croydon and East London Line

Network Diagram - see first Page of Table 177

		SE	SN	LO		LO	SN	LO	LO	LO	SN	SN	LO	SE		SN	SN	LO	LO	SN	LO	SN	SE	SN
London Bridge 4 ⊖	d						16 22				16 33	16 36				16 41				16 52		16 58		
Highbury & Islington	a																							
	d			15 55				16 03	16 10				16 18					16 25			16 33			
Canonbury	d			15 57				16 05	16 12				16 20					16 27			16 35			
Dalston Junction Stn ELL	d			16 00		16 05		16 10	16 15	16 20			16 25					16 30	16 35		16 40			
Haggerston	d			16 01		16 06		16 11	16 16	16 21			16 26					16 31	16 36		16 41			
Hoxton	d			16 03		16 08		16 13	16 18	16 23			16 28					16 33	16 38		16 43			
Shoreditch High Street	d			16 06		16 11		16 16	16 21	16 26			16 31					16 36	16 41		16 46			
Whitechapel	d			16 08		16 13		16 18	16 23	16 28			16 33					16 38	16 43		16 48			
Shadwell	d			16 10		16 15		16 20	16 25	16 30			16 35					16 40	16 45		16 50			
Wapping	d			16 12		16 17		16 22	16 27	16 32			16 37					16 42	16 47		16 52			
Rotherhithe	d			16 14		16 19		16 24	16 29	16 34			16 39					16 44	16 49		16 54			
Canada Water	d			16 16		16 21		16 26	16 31	16 36			16 41					16 46	16 51		16 56			
Surrey Quays	d			16 17		16 22		16 27	16 32	16 37			16 42					16 47	16 52		16 57			
New Cross ELL	a					16 27				16 42									16 57					
New Cross Gate 4	a			16 21			16 27	16 31	16 36			16 41	16 46					16 51		16 57	17 01			
	d			16 22			16 27	16 32	16 37			16 41	16 47					16 52		16 57	17 02			
Brockley	d			16 24			16 30	16 34	16 39			16 44	16 49					16 54		17 00	17 04			
Honor Oak Park	d			16 27			16 33	16 37	16 42			16 47	16 52					16 57		17 03	17 07			
Forest Hill 4	d			16 30			16 35	16 40	16 45			16 49	16 55					17 00		17 05	17 10			
Sydenham	d			16 32			16 38	16 42	16 47			16 52	16 57					17 02		17 08	17 12			
Crystal Palace 4	d		16 30	16a37			16 43		16a52								17 00	17a07		17 13				17 18
Gipsy Hill	d		16 32				16 45										17 02			17 15				17 20
West Norwood 4	d		16 35				16 48										17 05			17 18				17 23
Streatham Hill	d						16 52													17 22				
Balham 4 ⊖	d						16 55													17 25				
Wandsworth Common	d						16 57													17 27				
Clapham Junction 10	d						17 01													17 31				
South Bermondsey	d										16 37					16 45						17 02		
Queens Rd Peckham	d										16 39					16 48						17 04		
Peckham Rye 4	d		16a47								16a42			16 45		16 50	17a17					17a07	17 15	17a35
Denmark Hill 4	d	16 28												16 49		16 53							17 19	
London Blackfriars 3 ⊖	a																							
Clapham High Street ⊖	d															16 58								
Wandsworth Road	d															16 59								
Battersea Park 4	d						17 05									17 02				17 35				
London Victoria 15 ⊖	a	16 44					17 10							17 04		17 08				17 42			17 31	
Penge West	d							16 45				16 54	17 00								17 15			
Anerley	d							16 47				16 56	17 02								17 17			
Norwood Junction 2	d							16 50				17 00	17 05								17 20			
West Croydon 4	a							17 00				17 07	17 12								17 30			
East Croydon	a																							

		LO	LO	SN	LO	SN	SN	LO	LO	SN		LO	LO	LO	SN	SN	LO	SE	SN	SN		LO	LO	SN	LO
London Bridge 4 ⊖	d			17 05		17 11				17 19					17 28	17 36			17 41					17 53	
Highbury & Islington	a																								
	d	16 40			16 48			16 55				17 03	17 10				17 18					17 25			17 33
Canonbury	d	16 42			16 50			16 57				17 05	17 12				17 20					17 27			17 35
Dalston Junction Stn ELL	d	16 45	16 50		16 55			17 00	17 05			17 10	17 15	17 20			17 25					17 30	17 35		17 40
Haggerston	d	16 46	16 51		16 56			17 01	17 06			17 11	17 16	17 21			17 26					17 31	17 36		17 41
Hoxton	d	16 48	16 53		16 58			17 03	17 08			17 13	17 18	17 23			17 28					17 33	17 38		17 43
Shoreditch High Street	d	16 51	16 56		17 01			17 06	17 11			17 16	17 21	17 26			17 31					17 36	17 41		17 46
Whitechapel	d	16 53	16 58		17 03			17 08	17 13			17 18	17 23	17 28			17 33					17 38	17 43		17 48
Shadwell	d	16 55	17 00		17 05			17 10	17 15			17 20	17 25	17 30			17 35					17 40	17 45		17 50
Wapping	d	16 57	17 02		17 07			17 12	17 17			17 22	17 27	17 32			17 37					17 42	17 47		17 52
Rotherhithe	d	16 59	17 04		17 09			17 14	17 19			17 24	17 29	17 34			17 39					17 44	17 49		17 54
Canada Water	d	17 01	17 06		17 11			17 16	17 21			17 26	17 31	17 36			17 41					17 46	17 51		17 56
Surrey Quays	d	17 02	17 07		17 12			17 17	17 22			17 27	17 32	17 37			17 42					17 47	17 52		17 57
New Cross ELL	a		17 12						17 27					17 42									17 57		
New Cross Gate 4	a	17 06		17 11	17 16			17 21		17 26		17 31	17 36			17 41	17 46					17 51		17 58	18 01
	d	17 07		17 11	17 17			17 22		17 26		17 32	17 37			17 41	17 47					17 52		17 58	18 02
Brockley	d	17 09		17 14	17 19			17 24		17 29		17 34	17 39			17 44	17 49					17 54		18 01	18 04
Honor Oak Park	d	17 12		17 17	17 22			17 27		17 32		17 37	17 42			17 47	17 52					17 57		18 04	18 07
Forest Hill 4	d	17 15		17 19	17 25			17 30		17 34		17 40	17 45			17 49	17 55					18 00		18 06	18 10
Sydenham	d	17 17		17 22	17 27			17 32		17 37		17 42	17 47			17 52	17 57					18 02		18 09	18 12
Crystal Palace 4	d	17a22					17 36	17a37		17 44			17a52							17 55		18a07		18 13	
Gipsy Hill	d						17 38			17 46										17 57				18 15	
West Norwood 4	d						17 41			17 49										18 00				18 18	
Streatham Hill	d									17 53														18 22	
Balham 4 ⊖	d									17 56														18 25	
Wandsworth Common	d									17 58														18 27	
Clapham Junction 10	d									18 02														18 32	
South Bermondsey	d					17 15									17 32				17 45						
Queens Rd Peckham	d					17 18									17 35				17 47						
Peckham Rye 4	d					17 20	17a53								17a37			17 45	17 50	18a12					
Denmark Hill 4	d					17 23												17 49	17 53						
London Blackfriars 3 ⊖	a																								
Clapham High Street ⊖	d					17 28													17 58						
Wandsworth Road	d					17 29													17 59						
Battersea Park 4	d					17 32				18 06									18 02					18 35	
London Victoria 15 ⊖	a					17 38				18 12								18 02	18 08					18 42	
Penge West	d			17 24	17 30							17 45				17 54	18 00								18 15
Anerley	d			17 26	17 32							17 47				17 56	18 02								18 17
Norwood Junction 2	d			17 30	17 35							17 50				18 00	18 05								18 20
West Croydon 4	a			17 37	17 42							18 01				18 08	18 12								18 30
East Croydon	a																								

London Bridge to London Victoria - Croydon and East London Line

Network Diagram - see first Page of Table 177

Station		SN	SE	SN	LO	LO		SN	LO	LO	LO	SN	SN	LO	SN	SE		SN	LO	LO	SN	LO	LO	LO	SN
London Bridge [4] ⊖	d	17 58						18 06				18 11	18 21		18 28						18 36				18 41
Highbury & Islington	a																								
	d				17 40				17 48	17 55				18 03					18 10			18 18	18 25		
Canonbury	d				17 42				17 50	17 57				18 05					18 12			18 20	18 27		
Dalston Junction Stn ELL	d				17 45	17 50			17 55	18 00	18 05			18 10					18 15	18 20		18 25	18 30	18 35	
Haggerston	d				17 46	17 51			17 56	18 01	18 06			18 11					18 16	18 21		18 26	18 31	18 36	
Hoxton	d				17 48	17 53			17 58	18 03	18 08			18 13					18 18	18 23		18 28	18 33	18 38	
Shoreditch High Street	d				17 51	17 56			18 01	18 06	18 11			18 16					18 21	18 26		18 31	18 36	18 41	
Whitechapel	d				17 53	17 58			18 03	18 08	18 13			18 18					18 23	18 28		18 33	18 38	18 43	
Shadwell	d				17 55	18 00			18 05	18 10	18 15			18 20					18 25	18 30		18 35	18 40	18 45	
Wapping	d				17 57	18 02			18 07	18 12	18 17			18 22					18 27	18 32		18 37	18 42	18 47	
Rotherhithe	d				17 59	18 04			18 09	18 14	18 19			18 24					18 29	18 34		18 39	18 44	18 49	
Canada Water	d				18 01	18 06			18 11	18 16	18 21			18 26					18 31	18 36		18 41	18 46	18 51	
Surrey Quays	d				18 02	18 07			18 12	18 17	18 22			18 27					18 32	18 37		18 42	18 47	18 52	
New Cross ELL	a					18 12					18 27									18 42				18 57	
New Cross Gate [4]	a				18 06			18 11	18 16	18 21			18 26	18 31					18 36		18 41	18 46	18 51		
	d				18 07			18 11	18 17	18 22			18 26	18 32					18 37		18 41	18 47	18 52		
Brockley	d				18 09			18 14	18 19	18 24			18 29	18 34					18 39		18 44	18 49	18 54		
Honor Oak Park	d				18 12			18 17	18 22	18 27			18 32	18 37					18 42		18 47	18 52	18 57		
Forest Hill [4]	d				18 15			18 19	18 25	18 30			18 34	18 40					18 45		18 49	18 55	19 00		
Sydenham	d				18 17			18 22	18 27	18 32			18 37	18 42					18 47		18 52	18 57	19 02		
Crystal Palace [4]	d			18 18	18a22					18a37			18 43					18 51	18a52				19a07		
Gipsy Hill	d			18 20									18 45					18 53							
West Norwood [4]	d			18 23									18 48					18 56							
Streatham Hill	d												18 52												
Balham [4] ⊖	d												18 55												
Wandsworth Common	d												18 57												
Clapham Junction [10]	d												19 01												
South Bermondsey	d	18 02										18 15			18 32										18 45
Queens Rd Peckham	d	18 04										18 18			18 34										18 48
Peckham Rye [4]	d	18a07	18 15	18a36								18 20			18a37	18 45		19a14							18 50
Denmark Hill [4]	d		18 19									18 23				18 49									18 53
London Blackfriars [3] ⊖	a																								
Clapham High Street ⊖	d											18 28													18 58
Wandsworth Road	d											18 29													18 59
Battersea Park [4]	d											18 32	19 05												19 02
London Victoria [15] ⊖	a		18 32									18 39	19 12			19 01									19 08
Penge West	d							18 24	18 30					18 45							18 54	19 00			
Anerley	d							18 26	18 32					18 47							18 56	19 02			
Norwood Junction [2]	d							18 32	18 35					18 50							19 02	19 05			
West Croydon [4] ⇌	a							18 39	18 42					19 01							19 09	19 12			
East Croydon ⇌	a																								

Station		SE		SN	LO	LO	LO	SN	SN	LO	SE	SN		SN	SE	SN	LO	LO	SN	LO	LO	LO		SN	SN
London Bridge [4] ⊖	d			18 51				18 57	19 06			19 08		19 11					19 22					19 28	19 36
Highbury & Islington	a																								
	d				18 33	18 40				18 48							18 55			19 03	19 10				
Canonbury	d				18 35	18 42				18 50							18 57			19 05	19 12				
Dalston Junction Stn ELL	d				18 40	18 45	18 50			18 55							19 00	19 05		19 10	19 15	19 20			
Haggerston	d				18 41	18 46	18 51			18 56							19 01	19 06		19 11	19 16	19 21			
Hoxton	d				18 43	18 48	18 53			18 58							19 03	19 08		19 13	19 18	19 23			
Shoreditch High Street	d				18 46	18 51	18 56			19 01							19 06	19 11		19 16	19 21	19 26			
Whitechapel	d				18 48	18 53	18 58			19 03							19 08	19 13		19 18	19 23	19 28			
Shadwell	d				18 50	18 55	19 00			19 05							19 10	19 15		19 20	19 25	19 30			
Wapping	d				18 52	18 57	19 02			19 07							19 12	19 17		19 22	19 27	19 32			
Rotherhithe	d				18 54	18 59	19 04			19 09							19 14	19 19		19 24	19 29	19 34			
Canada Water	d				18 56	19 01	19 06			19 11							19 16	19 21		19 26	19 31	19 36			
Surrey Quays	d				18 57	19 02	19 07			19 12							19 17	19 22		19 27	19 32	19 37			
New Cross ELL	a						19 12											19 27				19 42			
New Cross Gate [4]	a			18 56	19 01	19 06			19 11	19 16							19 21		19 27	19 31	19 36				19 41
	d			18 56	19 02	19 07			19 11	19 17							19 22		19 27	19 32	19 37				19 41
Brockley	d			18 59	19 04	19 09			19 14	19 19							19 24		19 30	19 34	19 39				19 44
Honor Oak Park	d			19 02	19 07	19 12			19 17	19 22							19 27		19 33	19 37	19 42				19 47
Forest Hill [4]	d			19 04	19 10	19 15			19 19	19 25							19 30		19 35	19 40	19 45				19 49
Sydenham	d			19 07	19 12	19 17			19 22	19 27							19 32		19 38	19 42	19 47				19 52
Crystal Palace [4]	d			19 13		19a22										19 32	19a37		19 43		19a52				
Gipsy Hill	d			19 15												19 34			19 45						
West Norwood [4]	d			19 18												19 37			19 48						
Streatham Hill	d			19 22															19 52						
Balham [4] ⊖	d			19 25															19 55						
Wandsworth Common	d			19 27															19 57						
Clapham Junction [10]	d			19 31															20 01						
South Bermondsey	d							19 01				19 12		19 15										19 32	
Queens Rd Peckham	d							19 03				19 14		19 18										19 34	
Peckham Rye [4]	d							19 06			19 15	19a17		19 20		19a49								19 37	
Denmark Hill [4]	d	18 59									19 19			19 23	19 28										
London Blackfriars [3] ⊖	a																								
Clapham High Street ⊖	d													19 28											
Wandsworth Road	d													19 29											
Battersea Park [4]	d			19 35										19 32					20 05						
London Victoria [15] ⊖	a	19 13		19 41							19 31			19 36	19 43				20 09						
Penge West	d				19 15				19 24	19 30										19 45					19 54
Anerley	d				19 17				19 26	19 32										19 47					19 56
Norwood Junction [2]	d				19 20			19 28	19 30	19 35										19 50				20 02	20 00
West Croydon [4] ⇌	a				19 30			19 35		19 42										20 00				20 07	
East Croydon ⇌	a								19 33																20 03

London Bridge to London Victoria - Croydon and East London Line

Network Diagram - see first Page of Table 177

Station		LO	SN	SN	SN	LO	LO	SE		SN	LO	LO	LO	SN	SN	LO	SN	SN		LO	LO	SN	LO	LO	LO
London Bridge [4] ⊖	d		19 38	19 41						19 54				20 03	20 06		20 11					20 22			
Highbury & Islington	a																								
	d	19 18				19 25					19 33	19 40				19 48				19 55			20 03	20 10	
Canonbury	d	19 20				19 27					19 35	19 42				19 50				19 57			20 05	20 12	
Dalston Junction Stn ELL	d	19 25				19 30	19 35				19 40	19 45	19 50			19 55				20 00	20 05		20 10	20 15	20 20
Haggerston	d	19 26				19 31	19 36				19 41	19 46	19 51			19 56				20 01	20 06		20 11	20 16	20 21
Hoxton	d	19 28				19 33	19 38				19 43	19 48	19 53			19 58				20 03	20 08		20 13	20 18	20 23
Shoreditch High Street	d	19 31				19 36	19 41				19 46	19 51	19 56			20 01				20 06	20 11		20 16	20 21	20 26
Whitechapel	d	19 33				19 38	19 43				19 48	19 53	19 58			20 03				20 08	20 13		20 18	20 23	20 28
Shadwell	d	19 35				19 40	19 45				19 50	19 55	20 00			20 05				20 10	20 15		20 20	20 25	20 30
Wapping	d	19 37				19 42	19 47				19 52	19 57	20 02			20 07				20 12	20 17		20 22	20 27	20 32
Rotherhithe	d	19 39				19 44	19 49				19 54	19 59	20 04			20 09				20 14	20 19		20 24	20 29	20 34
Canada Water	d	19 41				19 46	19 51				19 56	20 01	20 06			20 11				20 16	20 21		20 26	20 31	20 36
Surrey Quays	d	19 42				19 47	19 52				19 57	20 02	20 07			20 12				20 17	20 22		20 27	20 32	20 37
New Cross ELL	a						19 57						20 12								20 27				20 42
New Cross Gate [4]	a	19 46				19 51				19 59	20 01	20 06			20 11	20 16				20 21		20 27	20 31	20 36	
	d	19 47				19 52				19 59	20 02	20 07			20 11	20 17				20 22		20 27	20 32	20 37	
Brockley	d	19 49				19 54				20 02	20 04	20 09			20 14	20 19				20 24		20 30	20 34	20 39	
Honor Oak Park	d	19 52				19 57				20 05	20 07	20 12			20 17	20 22				20 27		20 33	20 37	20 42	
Forest Hill [4]	d	19 55				20 00				20 07	20 10	20 15			20 19	20 25				20 30		20 35	20 40	20 45	
Sydenham	d	19 57				20 02				20 10	20 12	20 17			20 22	20 27				20 32		20 38	20 42	20 47	
Crystal Palace [4]	d				20 01	20a07				20 13		20a22						20 31		20a37		20 43		20a52	
Gipsy Hill	d				20 03					20 16								20 33				20 45			
West Norwood [4]	d				20 06					20 19								20 36				20 48			
Streatham Hill	d									20 22												20 52			
Balham [4] ⊖	d									20 25												20 56			
Wandsworth Common	d									20 27												20 58			
Clapham Junction [10]	d									20 31												21 03			
South Bermondsey	d		19 42	19 45										20 07			20 15								
Queens Rd Peckham	d		19 44	19 48										20 09			20 18								
Peckham Rye [4]	d		19a47	19 50	20a18									20a12			20 20	20a48							
Denmark Hill [4]	d			19 53				20 18									20 23								
London Blackfriars [3] ⊖	a																								
Clapham High Street ⊖	d			19 58													20 28								
Wandsworth Road	d			19 59													20 29								
Battersea Park [4]	d			20 02						20 35							20 32					21 06			
London Victoria [15] ⊖	a			20 06				20 31		20 39							20 36					21 11			
Penge West	d	20 00									20 15				20 24	20 30							20 45		
Anerley	d	20 02									20 17				20 26	20 32							20 47		
Norwood Junction [2]	d	20 05									20 20				20 30	20 35							20 50		
West Croydon [4] 🚋	a	20 12									20 29					20 42							21 00		
East Croydon 🚋	a														20 33										

Station		SN	SN	LO		SN	SN	LO	LO	SE	SN	LO	LO	LO		SN	SN	LO	SN	SE	SN	LO	LO	SN	
London Bridge [4] ⊖	d	20 33	20 36			20 41					20 52					21 03	21 06		21 11					21 22	
Highbury & Islington	a																								
	d			20 18				20 25				20 33	20 40					20 48				20 55			
Canonbury	d			20 20				20 27				20 35	20 42					20 50				20 57			
Dalston Junction Stn ELL	d			20 25				20 30	20 35			20 40	20 45	20 50				20 55				21 00	21 05		
Haggerston	d			20 26				20 31	20 36			20 41	20 46	20 51				20 56				21 01	21 06		
Hoxton	d			20 28				20 33	20 38			20 43	20 48	20 53				20 58				21 03	21 08		
Shoreditch High Street	d			20 31				20 36	20 41			20 46	20 51	20 56				21 01				21 06	21 11		
Whitechapel	d			20 33				20 38	20 43			20 48	20 53	20 58				21 03				21 08	21 13		
Shadwell	d			20 35				20 40	20 45			20 50	20 55	21 00				21 05				21 10	21 15		
Wapping	d			20 37				20 42	20 47			20 52	20 57	21 02				21 07				21 12	21 17		
Rotherhithe	d			20 39				20 44	20 49			20 54	20 59	21 04				21 09				21 14	21 19		
Canada Water	d			20 41				20 46	20 51			20 56	21 01	21 06				21 11				21 16	21 21		
Surrey Quays	d			20 42				20 47	20 52			20 57	21 02	21 07				21 12				21 17	21 22		
New Cross ELL	a								20 57					21 12									21 27		
New Cross Gate [4]	a		20 41	20 46				20 51			20 57	21 01	21 06				21 11	21 16				21 21		21 27	
	d		20 41	20 47				20 52			20 57	21 02	21 07				21 11	21 17				21 22		21 27	
Brockley	d		20 44	20 49				20 54			21 00	21 04	21 09				21 14	21 19				21 24		21 30	
Honor Oak Park	d		20 47	20 52				20 57			21 03	21 07	21 12				21 17	21 22				21 27		21 33	
Forest Hill [4]	d		20 49	20 55				21 00			21 05	21 10	21 15				21 19	21 25				21 30		21 35	
Sydenham	d		20 52	20 57				21 02			21 08	21 12	21 17				21 22	21 27				21 32		21 38	
Crystal Palace [4]	d						21 00	21a07			21 13		21a22								21 30	21a37		21 43	
Gipsy Hill	d						21 02				21 15										21 32			21 45	
West Norwood [4]	d						21 05				21 18										21 35			21 48	
Streatham Hill	d										21 22													21 52	
Balham [4] ⊖	d										21 26													21 56	
Wandsworth Common	d										21 28													21 58	
Clapham Junction [10]	d										21 33													22 03	
South Bermondsey	d	20 37				20 45										21 07			21 15						
Queens Rd Peckham	d	20 39				20 48										21 09			21 18						
Peckham Rye [4]	d	20a42				20 50	21a17									21a12			21 20	21 20	21a47				
Denmark Hill [4]	d					20 53				21 18									21 23	21 24					
London Blackfriars [3] ⊖	a																			21 37					
Clapham High Street ⊖	d					20 58													21 28						
Wandsworth Road	d					20 59													21 29						
Battersea Park [4]	d					21 02					21 36								21 32					22 06	
London Victoria [15] ⊖	a					21 06				21 31	21 41								21 36					22 11	
Penge West	d		20 54	21 00								21 15					21 24	21 30							
Anerley	d		20 56	21 02								21 17					21 26	21 32							
Norwood Junction [2]	d		21 00	21 05								21 20					21 30	21 35							
West Croydon [4] 🚋	a			21 12								21 30						21 42							
East Croydon 🚋	a		21 03														21 33								

30 July to 10 August

London Bridge to London Victoria - Croydon and East London Line

Network Diagram - see first Page of Table 177

Station		LO	LO	LO	SN	SN	LO	SN	SE	SE		SN	LO	LO	SE	SN	LO	LO	LO	SN		SN	LO	SN	SE
London Bridge	d				21 33	21 36		21 41								21 52				22 03		22 08		22 11	
Highbury & Islington	a																								
	d	21 03	21 10				21 18						21 25				21 33	21 40					21 48		
Canonbury	d	21 05	21 12				21 20						21 27				21 35	21 42					21 50		
Dalston Junction Stn ELL	d	21 10	21 15	21 20			21 25						21 30	21 35			21 40	21 45	21 50				21 55		
Haggerston	d	21 11	21 16	21 21			21 26						21 31	21 36			21 41	21 46	21 51				21 56		
Hoxton	d	21 13	21 18	21 23			21 28						21 33	21 38			21 43	21 48	21 53				21 58		
Shoreditch High Street	d	21 16	21 21	21 26			21 31						21 36	21 41			21 46	21 51	21 56				22 01		
Whitechapel	d	21 18	21 23	21 28			21 33						21 38	21 43			21 48	21 53	21 58				22 03		
Shadwell	d	21 20	21 25	21 30			21 35						21 40	21 45			21 50	21 55	22 00				22 05		
Wapping	d	21 22	21 27	21 32			21 37						21 42	21 47			21 52	21 57	22 02				22 07		
Rotherhithe	d	21 24	21 29	21 34			21 39						21 44	21 49			21 54	21 59	22 04				22 09		
Canada Water	d	21 26	21 31	21 36			21 41						21 46	21 51			21 56	22 01	22 06				22 11		
Surrey Quays	d	21 27	21 32	21 37			21 42						21 47	21 52			21 57	22 02	22 07				22 12		
New Cross ELL	a			21 42										21 57					22 13						
New Cross Gate	a	21 31	21 36			21 41	21 46						21 51			21 57	22 01	22 06				22 13	22 16		
	d	21 32	21 37			21 41	21 47						21 52			21 57	22 02	22 07				22 13	22 17		
Brockley	d	21 34	21 39			21 44	21 49						21 54			22 00	22 04	22 09				22 16	22 19		
Honor Oak Park	d	21 37	21 42			21 47	21 52						21 57			22 03	22 07	22 12				22 19	22 22		
Forest Hill	d	21 40	21 45			21 49	21 55						22 00			22 05	22 10	22 15				22 21	22 25		
Sydenham	d	21 42	21 47			21 52	21 57						22 02			22 08	22 12	22 17				22 24	22 27		
Crystal Palace	d		21a52									22 00	22a07			22 13		22a22							
Gipsy Hill	d											22 02				22 15									
West Norwood	d											22 05				22 18									
Streatham Hill	d															22 22									
Balham	d															22 26									
Wandsworth Common	d															22 28									
Clapham Junction	d															22 33									
South Bermondsey	d				21 37			21 45												22 07				22 15	
Queens Rd Peckham	d				21 39			21 48												22 09				22 18	
Peckham Rye	d				21a42			21 50	21 50			22a17								22a12				22 20	22 20
Denmark Hill	d							21 53	21 54	21 59					22 17									22 23	22 24
London Blackfriars	a								22 04																22 34
Clapham High Street	d							21 58																22 28	
Wandsworth Road	d							21 59																22 29	
Battersea Park	d							22 02								22 36								22 32	
London Victoria	a							22 06		22 14					22 31	22 41								22 36	
Penge West	d	21 45				21 54	22 00										22 15					22 26	22 30		
Anerley	d	21 47				21 56	22 02										22 17					22 28	22 32		
Norwood Junction	d	21 50				22 00	22 05										22 20					22 32	22 35		
West Croydon	a	22 00					22 12										22 30						22 42		
East Croydon	a					22 03																22 35			

Station		SN	LO	SN	LO	LO		LO	SN	SN	LO	SN	SE	SE A	SN	LO		SN	LO	LO	LO	SN	SN	LO	SN
London Bridge	d			22 23					22 33	22 38		22 41						22 52				23 05	23 06		23 11
Highbury & Islington	a																								
	d		21 55		22 03	22 10					22 18					22 25			22 33	22 40				22 48	
Canonbury	d		21 57		22 05	22 12					22 20					22 27			22 35	22 42				22 50	
Dalston Junction Stn ELL	d		22 00		22 08	22 15		22 20			22 25					22 30			22 38	22 45	22 50			22 55	
Haggerston	d		22 01		22 09	22 16		22 21			22 26					22 31			22 39	22 46	22 51			22 56	
Hoxton	d		22 03		22 11	22 18		22 23			22 28					22 33			22 41	22 48	22 53			22 58	
Shoreditch High Street	d		22 06		22 14	22 21		22 26			22 31					22 36			22 44	22 51	22 56			23 01	
Whitechapel	d		22 08		22 16	22 23		22 28			22 33					22 38			22 46	22 53	22 58			23 03	
Shadwell	d		22 10		22 18	22 25		22 30			22 35					22 40			22 48	22 55	23 00			23 05	
Wapping	d		22 12		22 20	22 27		22 32			22 37					22 42			22 50	22 57	23 02			23 07	
Rotherhithe	d		22 14		22 22	22 29		22 34			22 39					22 44			22 52	22 59	23 04			23 09	
Canada Water	d		22 16		22 24	22 31		22 36			22 41					22 46			22 54	23 01	23 06			23 11	
Surrey Quays	d		22 17		22 25	22 32		22 37			22 42					22 47			22 55	23 02	23 07			23 12	
New Cross ELL	a							22 42													23 12				
New Cross Gate	a		22 21	22 28	22 29	22 36				22 43	22 46					22 51		22 57	22 59	23 06			23 11	23 16	
	d		22 22	22 28	22 30	22 37				22 43	22 47					22 52		22 57	23 00	23 07			23 11	23 17	
Brockley	d		22 24	22 31	22 32	22 39				22 46	22 49					22 54		23 00	23 02	23 09			23 14	23 19	
Honor Oak Park	d		22 27	22 34	22 35	22 42				22 49	22 52					22 57		23 03	23 05	23 12			23 17	23 22	
Forest Hill	d		22 30	22 36	22 38	22 45				22 51	22 55					23 00		23 05	23 08	23 15			23 19	23 25	
Sydenham	d		22 32	22 39	22 40	22 47				22 54	22 57					23 02		23 08	23 10	23 17			23 22	23 27	
Crystal Palace	d	22 22	22a37	22 43		22a52									23 00	23a07		23 13		23a22					
Gipsy Hill	d	22 24		22 45											23 02			23 15							
West Norwood	d	22 27		22 48											23 05			23 18							
Streatham Hill	d			22 52														23 22							
Balham	d			22 56														23 26							
Wandsworth Common	d			22 58														23 28							
Clapham Junction	d			23 03														23 33							
South Bermondsey	d								22 37			22 45										23 09			23 15
Queens Rd Peckham	d								22 39			22 48										23 11			23 18
Peckham Rye	d	22a43							22a42			22 50	22 50		23a17							23 14			23 20
Denmark Hill	d											22 53	22 54	22 59											23 23
London Blackfriars	a												23 04												
Clapham High Street	d											22 58													23 28
Wandsworth Road	d											22 59													23 29
Battersea Park	d			23 07								23 02						23 37							23 32
London Victoria	a			23 14								23 06		23 14				23 41							23 37
Penge West	d				22 43					22 56	23 00								23 13				23 24	23 30	
Anerley	d				22 45					22 58	23 02								23 15				23 26	23 32	
Norwood Junction	d				22 48					23 02	23 05								23 18			23a36	23 30	23 35	
West Croydon	a				23 00						23 12								23 30					23 42	
East Croydon	a									23 06													23 33		

A not 3 August, 10 August

30 July to 10 August

London Bridge to London Victoria - Croydon and East London Line

Network Diagram - see first Page of Table 177

		SE		SN	LO	SN	LO	LO	LO	SN	SN	LO		LO	SN	LO	LO	LO	LO
London Bridge 4 ⊖	d					23 22				23 33	23 36				23 52				
Highbury & Islington	a																		
	d				22 55		23 03	23 10				23 18		23 25		23 33	23 40	23 48	23 55
Canonbury	d				22 57		23 05	23 12				23 20		23 27		23 35	23 42	23 50	23 57
Dalston Junction Stn ELL	d				23 00		23 08	23 15	23 20			23 25		23 30		23 38	23 45	23 55	00 01
Haggerston	d				23 01		23 09	23 16	23 21			23 26		23 31		23 39	23 46	23 56	00 02
Hoxton	d				23 03		23 11	23 18	23 23			23 28		23 33		23 41	23 48	23 58	00 04
Shoreditch High Street	d				23 06		23 14	23 21	23 26			23 31		23 36		23 44	23 51	00 01	00 07
Whitechapel	d				23 08		23 16	23 23	23 28			23 33		23 38		23 46	23 53	00 03	00 09
Shadwell	d				23 10		23 18	23 25	23 30			23 35		23 40		23 48	23 55	00 05	00 11
Wapping	d				23 12		23 20	23 27	23 32			23 37		23 42		23 50	23 57	00 07	00 13
Rotherhithe	d				23 14		23 22	23 29	23 34			23 39		23 44		23 52	23 59	00 09	00 15
Canada Water	d				23 16		23 24	23 31	23 36			23 41		23 46		23 54	00 02	00 11	00 17
Surrey Quays	d				23 17		23 25	23 32	23 37			23 42		23 47		23 55	00 03	00 12	00 18
New Cross ELL	a								23 42										
New Cross Gate 4	a				23 21	23 27	23 29	23 36			23 41	23 46		23 51	23 57	23 58	00 07	00 16	00 22
	d				23 22	23 27	23 30	23 37			23 41	23 47		23 52	23 57	23 59	00 08	00 17	00 23
Brockley	d				23 24	23 30	23 32	23 39			23 44	23 49		23 54	00 01	00 03	00 10	00 19	00 25
Honor Oak Park	d				23 27	23 33	23 35	23 42			23 47	23 52		23 57	00 04	00 06	00 13	00 22	00 28
Forest Hill 4	d				23 30	23 35	23 38	23 45			23 49	23 55		23 59	00 06	00 09	00 16	00 25	00 31
Sydenham	d				23 32	23 38	23 40	23 47			23 52	23 57		00 02	00 09	00 11	00 18	00 27	00 33
Crystal Palace 4	d			23 30	23a37	23 43		23a52						00a07	00 13		00a23		00a38
Gipsy Hill	d			23 32		23 45									00 15				
West Norwood 4	d			23 35		23 48									00 18				
Streatham Hill	d					23 52									00 22				
Balham 4 ⊖	d					23 55									00 25				
Wandsworth Common	d					23 58									00 27				
Clapham Junction 10	d					00 02									00 31				
South Bermondsey	d									23 37									
Queens Rd Peckham	d									23 39									
Peckham Rye 4	d	23 20		23a47						23 42									
Denmark Hill 4	d	23 24																	
London Blackfriars 3 ⊖	a	23 34																	
Clapham High Street ⊖	d																		
Wandsworth Road	d																		
Battersea Park 4	d					00 05									00 35				
London Victoria 15 ⊖	a					00 10									00 42				
Penge West	d						23 43				23 54	00 01				00 14		00 30	
Anerley	d						23 45				23 56	00 03				00 16		00 32	
Norwood Junction 2	d						23 48			00a04	23 59	00 06				00 19		00 35	
West Croydon 4	a						23 59					00 13				00 26		00 42	
East Croydon	a										00 03								

Mondays to Fridays

13 August to 28 August

		SN MX	LO A	SN MX	SN MO	SN MX	LO A	LO B	LO MX	LO A		SN MX	LO MX	LO A	LO MX	LO A	SN MX	SN MX	LO A	LO MX		LO A	LO A	LO MX	LO A
London Bridge 4 ⊖	d	23p22		23p36	23p39							23p52					00 03	00 06							
Highbury & Islington	a																								
	d		23p06				23p21	23p23	23p25	23p28			23p35	23p36	23p42	23p43			23p51	23p56		23p58	00 06	00 10	00 13
Canonbury	d		23p08				23p23	23p25	23p27	23p30			23p37	23p38	23p44	23p45			23p53	23p58		00 01	00 08	00 12	00 15
Dalston Junction Stn ELL	d		23p11				23p28	23p28	23p30	23p33			23p40	23p41	23p47	23p48			23p58	00 02		00 04	00 13	00 15	00 18
Haggerston	d		23p12				23p29	23p29	23p31	23p34			23p41	23p42	23p48	23p49			23p59	00 03		00 06	00 14	00 16	00 19
Hoxton	d		23p14				23p31	23p31	23p33	23p36			23p43	23p44	23p50	23p51			00 01	00 05		00 08	00 16	00 18	00 21
Shoreditch High Street	d		23p17				23p34	23p34	23p36	23p39			23p46	23p47	23p53	23p54			00 04	00 08		00 10	00 19	00 21	00 24
Whitechapel	d		23p19				23p36	23p36	23p38	23p41			23p48	23p49	23p55	23p56			00 06	00 10		00 13	00 21	00 23	00 26
Shadwell	d		23p21				23p38	23p38	23p40	23p43			23p50	23p51	23p57	23p58			00 08	00 12		00 15	00 23	00 25	00 28
Wapping	d		23p23				23p40	23p40	23p42	23p45			23p52	23p53	23p59	00 01			00 10	00 14		00 17	00 25	00 27	00 30
Rotherhithe	d		23p25				23p42	23p42	23p44	23p47			23p54	23p55	00 01	00 03			00 12	00 16		00 18	00 27	00 29	00 32
Canada Water	d		23p27				23p44	23p44	23p46	23p49			23p56	23p57	00 03	00 05			00 14	00 18		00 20	00 29	00 31	00 34
Surrey Quays	d		23p28				23p45	23p45	23p47	23p50			23p57	23p58	00 05	00 06			00 15	00 19		00 22	00 30	00 32	00 35
New Cross ELL	a																								
New Cross Gate 4	a	23p27	23p32	23p41	23p44		23p49	23p49	23p51	23p54		23p57	00 01	00 02	00 08	00 10		00 11	00 19	00 23		00 25	00 34	00 36	00 39
	d	23p27	23p33	23p41	23p44		23p50	23p50	23p52	23p55		23p57	00 02	00 03		00 11		00 11	00 20			00 26	00 35		00 40
Brockley	d	23p30	23p35	23p44	23p47		23p52	23p52	23p54	23p57		00 01	00 04	00 06		00 13		00 14	00 22			00 29	00 37		00 42
Honor Oak Park	d	23p33	23p38	23p47	23p50		23p55	23p55	23p57	00 01		00 04	00 07	00 09		00 16		00 17	00 25			00 32	00 40		00 45
Forest Hill 4	d	23p35	23p41	23p49	23p52		23p58	23p58	23p59	00 04		00 06	00 10	00 12		00 19		00 19	00 28			00 34	00 43		00 48
Sydenham	d	23p38	23p43	23p52	23p55		00 01	00 01	00 02	00 06		00 09	00 12	00 14		00 21		00 22	00 30			00 37	00 45		00 50
Crystal Palace 4	d	23p43				00 03			00a07	00a11		00 13				00a26						00a41			00a55
Gipsy Hill	d	23p45										00 15													
West Norwood 4	d	23p48										00 18													
Streatham Hill	d	23p52										00 22													
Balham 4 ⊖	d	23p55										00 25													
Wandsworth Common	d	23p58										00 27													
Clapham Junction 10	d	00 02										00 31													
South Bermondsey	d																00 07								
Queens Rd Peckham	d																00 09								
Peckham Rye 4	d																00 12								
Denmark Hill 4	d																								
London Blackfriars 3 ⊖	a																								
Clapham High Street ⊖	d																								
Wandsworth Road	d																								
Battersea Park 4	d	00 05										00 35													
London Victoria 15 ⊖	a	00 10										00 42													
Penge West	d		23p46	23p54	23p57		00 04	00 03					00 15	00 17				00 24	00 33				00 48		
Anerley	d		23p48	23p56	23p59		00 06	00 05					00 17	00 19				00 26	00 35				00 50		
Norwood Junction 2	d		23p55	23p59	00 03	00 09	00 09	00 08					00 20	00 22			00a34	00 30	00 38				00 53		
West Croydon 4	a		00 03			00 14	00 16	00 15					00 27	00 29					00 45				01 00		
East Croydon	a			00 03	00 06													00 33							

A 13 August

B 20 August, 27 August

Table 178 **Mondays to Fridays**

13 August to 28 August

London Bridge to London Victoria - Croydon and East London Line

Network Diagram - see first Page of Table 177

		SN MX	LO A	LO A	LO A	LO A		LO A	LO A	LO A	LO A	LO A	SE	SE	SN	SN		LO	LO	LO	LO	LO	SN	SN	LO
London Bridge 4 ⊖	d	00 36													06 00								06 06	06 11	
Highbury & Islington	a																								
	d		00 21	00 28	00 36	00 43		00 51	00 58	01 06	01 13	01 28								05 35					
Canonbury	d		00 23	00 30	00 38	00 45		00 53	01 00	01 08	01 15	01 30								05 37					
Dalston Junction Stn ELL	d		00 28	00 33	00 43	00 48		00 58	01 03	01 13	01 18	01 35								05 40	05 50				
Haggerston	d		00 29	00 34	00 44	00 49		00 59	01 04	01 14	01 19	01 36								05 41	05 51				
Hoxton	d		00 31	00 36	00 46	00 51		01 01	01 06	01 16	01 21	01 38								05 43	05 53				
Shoreditch High Street	d		00 34	00 39	00 49	00 54		01 04	01 09	01 19	01 24	01 41								05 46	05 56				
Whitechapel	d		00 36	00 41	00 51	00 56		01 06	01 11	01 21	01 26	01 43								05 48	05 58				
Shadwell	d		00 38	00 43	00 53	00 58		01 08	01 13	01 23	01 28	01 45								05 50	06 00				
Wapping	d		00 40	00 45	00 55	01 00		01 10	01 15	01 25	01 30	01 47								05 52	06 02				
Rotherhithe	d		00 42	00 47	00 57	01 02		01 12	01 17	01 27	01 32	01 49								05 54	06 04				
Canada Water	d		00 44	00 49	00 59	01 04		01 14	01 19	01 29	01 34	01 51								05 56	06 06				
Surrey Quays	d		00 45	00 50	01 00	01 05		01 15	01 20	01 30	01 35	01 52								05 57	06 07				
New Cross ELL	a																				06 12				
New Cross Gate 4	a	00 41	00 50	00 54	01 05	01 09		01 19	01 24	01 34	01 39	01 56								06 01			06 11		
	d	00 41	00 50	00 55	01 06	01 10		01 20	01 25	01 35	01 40	01 57						05 47	05 52	06 02		06 07	06 11		06 17
Brockley	d	00 44	00 52	00 57	01 08	01 12		01 22	01 27	01 37	01 42	01 59						05 49	05 54	06 04		06 09	06 14		06 19
Honor Oak Park	d	00 47	00 55	01 00	01 11	01 15		01 25	01 30	01 40	01 45	02 02						05 52	05 57	06 07		06 12	06 17		06 22
Forest Hill 4	d	00 49	00 58	01 02	01 14	01 18		01 28	01 33	01 43	01 48	02 05						05 55	06 00	06 10		06 15	06 19		06 25
Sydenham	d	00 52	01 00	01 05	01 16	01 20		01 30	01 35	01 45	01 50	02 07						05 57	06 02	06 12		06 17	06 22		06 27
Crystal Palace 4	d			01a10		01a25			01a40		01a55					05 59			06a07			06a22			
Gipsy Hill	d															06 01									
West Norwood 4	d															06 04									
Streatham Hill	d																								
Balham 4 ⊖	d																								
Wandsworth Common	d																								
Clapham Junction 10	d																								
South Bermondsey	d														06 04									06 15	
Queens Rd Peckham	d														06 06									06 18	
Peckham Rye 4	d												05 04	06 04	06a09	06a15								06 20	
Denmark Hill 4	d												05 07	06 07										06 23	
London Blackfriars 3 ⊖	a												05 17	06 17											
Clapham High Street ⊖	d																							06 28	
Wandsworth Road	d																							06 29	
Battersea Park 4	d																							06 32	
London Victoria 15 ⊖	a																							06 36	
Penge West	d	00 54	01 03		01 19			01 33		01 48		02 10						06 00		06 15			06 24		06 30
Anerley	d	00 56	01 05		01 21			01 35		01 50		02 12						06 02		06 17			06 26		06 32
Norwood Junction 2	d	01 00	01 08		01 24			01 38		01 53		02 15						06 05		06 20			06 30		06 35
West Croydon 4	a		01 17		01 31			01 45		02 00		02 22						06 13		06 30					06 41
East Croydon	a	01 03																					06 33		

		LO		SN	LO	LO	SN	SN	SE	SN	LO	SN		SN	LO	LO	LO	SN	SN	LO	SN	SN		SN	LO
London Bridge 4 ⊖	d			06 19			06 30	06 33				06 36		06 41				06 51	06 54		06 58	07 03			
Highbury & Islington	a																								
	d	05 55			06 05											06 25				06 33					06 40
Canonbury	d	05 57			06 07											06 27				06 35					06 42
Dalston Junction Stn ELL	d	06 00			06 10	06 20										06 30	06 35			06 40					06 45
Haggerston	d	06 01			06 11	06 21										06 31	06 36			06 41					06 46
Hoxton	d	06 03			06 13	06 23										06 33	06 38			06 43					06 48
Shoreditch High Street	d	06 06			06 16	06 26										06 36	06 41			06 46					06 51
Whitechapel	d	06 08			06 18	06 28										06 38	06 43			06 48					06 53
Shadwell	d	06 10			06 20	06 30										06 40	06 45			06 50					06 55
Wapping	d	06 12			06 22	06 32										06 42	06 47			06 52					06 57
Rotherhithe	d	06 14			06 24	06 34										06 44	06 49			06 54					06 59
Canada Water	d	06 16			06 26	06 36										06 46	06 51			06 56					07 01
Surrey Quays	d	06 17			06 27	06 37										06 47	06 52			06 57					07 02
New Cross ELL	a					06 42											06 57								
New Cross Gate 4	a	06 21		06 25	06 31							06 41				06 51		06 56	06 59	07 00					07 06
	d	06 22		06 25	06 32						06 37	06 41			06 47	06 52		06 56	06 59	07 02					07 07
Brockley	d	06 24		06 27	06 34						06 39	06 44			06 49	06 54		06 59	07 02	07 04					07 09
Honor Oak Park	d	06 27		06 30	06 37						06 42	06 47			06 52	06 57		07 02	07 05	07 07					07 12
Forest Hill 4	d	06 30		06 33	06 40						06 45	06 49			06 55	07 00		07 04	07 07	07 10					07 15
Sydenham	d	06 32		06 35	06 42						06 47	06 52			06 57	07 02		07 07	07 10	07 12					07 17
Crystal Palace 4	d	06a37		06 39						06 51	06a52					07a07		07 13						07 20	07a22
Gipsy Hill	d			06 41						06 53								07 15						07 22	
West Norwood 4	d			06 44						06 56								07 18						07 25	
Streatham Hill	d			06 48														07 22							
Balham 4 ⊖	d			06 51														07 25							
Wandsworth Common	d																	07 27							
Clapham Junction 10	d			06 56														07 31							
South Bermondsey	d						06 34	06 37						06 45							07 02	07 07			
Queens Rd Peckham	d						06 36	06 39						06 48							07 04	07 09			
Peckham Rye 4	d						06a39	06a42	06 47	07a08				06 50							07a07	07a12		07a36	
Denmark Hill 4	d								06 50					06 53											
London Blackfriars 3 ⊖	a																								
Clapham High Street ⊖	d													06 58											
Wandsworth Road	d													06 59											
Battersea Park 4	d													07 02				07 35							
London Victoria 15 ⊖	a			07 05					07 04					07 08				07 41							
Penge West	d				06 45							06 54			07 00				07 12	07 15					
Anerley	d				06 47							06 56			07 02				07 14	07 17					
Norwood Junction 2	d				06 50							07 00			07 05				07 18	07 20					
West Croydon 4	a				07 00										07 11					07 30					
East Croydon	a											07 03							07 21						

A 13 August

Table 178

Mondays to Fridays

13 August to 28 August

London Bridge to London Victoria - Croydon and East London Line

Network Diagram - see first Page of Table 177

		LO	SN	LO	LO	LO	SN	SE		SN	LO	SN	SN	SN	LO	LO	SN	LO		SN	SN	LO	LO	SE	SN
London Bridge 4 ⊖	d		07 06				07 11			07 21		07 29	07 33				07 36			07 41	07 44				07 53
Highbury & Islington	a																								
	d			06 48	06 55						07 03				07 10			07 18				07 25			
Canonbury	d			06 50	06 57						07 05				07 12			07 20				07 27			
Dalston Junction Stn ELL	d	06 50		06 55	07 00	07 05					07 10				07 15	07 20		07 25				07 30	07 35		
Haggerston	d	06 51		06 56	07 01	07 06					07 11				07 16	07 21		07 26				07 31	07 36		
Hoxton	d	06 53		06 58	07 03	07 08					07 13				07 18	07 23		07 28				07 33	07 38		
Shoreditch High Street	d	06 56		07 01	07 06	07 11					07 16				07 21	07 26		07 31				07 36	07 41		
Whitechapel	d	06 58		07 03	07 08	07 13					07 18				07 23	07 28		07 33				07 38	07 43		
Shadwell	d	07 00		07 05	07 10	07 15					07 20				07 25	07 30		07 35				07 40	07 45		
Wapping	d	07 02		07 07	07 12	07 17					07 22				07 27	07 32		07 37				07 42	07 47		
Rotherhithe	d	07 04		07 09	07 14	07 19					07 24				07 29	07 34		07 39				07 44	07 49		
Canada Water	d	07 06		07 11	07 16	07 21					07 26				07 31	07 36		07 41				07 46	07 51		
Surrey Quays	d	07 07		07 12	07 17	07 22					07 27				07 32	07 37		07 42				07 47	07 52		
New Cross ELL	a	07 12				07 27										07 42							07 57		
New Cross Gate 4	a		07 11	07 15	07 21					07 26	07 31				07 36		07 41	07 45			07 49	07 51			07 58
	d		07 11	07 17	07 22					07 26	07 32				07 37		07 41	07 47			07 49	07 52			07 58
Brockley	d		07 14	07 19	07 24					07 29	07 34				07 39		07 44	07 49				07 54			08 01
Honor Oak Park	d		07 17	07 22	07 27					07 32	07 37				07 42		07 47	07 52				07 57			08 04
Forest Hill 4	d		07 19	07 25	07 30					07 34	07 40				07 45		07 49	07 55				08 00			08 06
Sydenham	d		07 22	07 27	07 32					07 37	07 42				07 47		07 52	07 57				08 02			08 09
Crystal Palace 4	d				07a37					07 43				07 49	07a52							08a07			08 13
Gipsy Hill	d									07 45				07 51											08 15
West Norwood 4	d									07 48				07 54											08 18
Streatham Hill	d									07 52															08 22
Balham 4 ⊖	d									07 55															08 25
Wandsworth Common	d									07 57															08 27
Clapham Junction 10	d									08 01															08 31
South Bermondsey	d						07 15					07 33	07 37							07 45					
Queens Rd Peckham	d						07 17					07 35	07 39							07 47					
Peckham Rye 4	d						07 20	07 23				07a38	07a42	08a06						07 50				07 54	
Denmark Hill 4	d						07 23	07 29												07 53				07 59	
London Blackfriars 3 ⊖	a																								
Clapham High Street ⊖	d						07 28													07 58					
Wandsworth Road	d						07 29													07 59					
Battersea Park 4	d						07 32			08 05										08 02					08 35
London Victoria 15 ⊖	a						07 38	07 42		08 11										08 08				08 11	08 41
Penge West	d		07 24	07 30							07 45						07 54	08 00							
Anerley	d		07 26	07 32							07 47						07 56	08 02							
Norwood Junction 2	d		07 31	07 35							07 50						08 00	08 05							
West Croydon 4	a			07 42							08 00							08 12							
East Croydon	a		07 37														08 03				08 00				

		LO	SN	SE		SN	SN	LO	LO	SN	LO	LO	LO	SN		SE 1	SE	SN	LO	SN	SN	LO	LO	SN	
London Bridge 4 ⊖	d		08 03			08 06				08 06				08 10				08 21		08 33				08 36	
Highbury & Islington	a																								
	d	07 33						07 40			07 48	07 55							08 03			08 10			
Canonbury	d	07 35						07 42			07 50	07 57							08 05			08 12			
Dalston Junction Stn ELL	d	07 40						07 45	07 50		07 55	08 00	08 05						08 10			08 15	08 20		
Haggerston	d	07 41						07 46	07 51		07 56	08 01	08 06						08 11			08 16	08 21		
Hoxton	d	07 43						07 48	07 53		07 58	08 03	08 08						08 13			08 18	08 23		
Shoreditch High Street	d	07 46						07 51	07 56		08 01	08 06	08 11						08 16			08 21	08 26		
Whitechapel	d	07 48						07 53	07 58		08 03	08 08	08 13						08 18			08 23	08 28		
Shadwell	d	07 50						07 55	08 00		08 05	08 10	08 15						08 20			08 25	08 30		
Wapping	d	07 52						07 57	08 02		08 07	08 12	08 17						08 22			08 27	08 32		
Rotherhithe	d	07 54						07 59	08 04		08 09	08 14	08 19						08 24			08 29	08 34		
Canada Water	d	07 56						08 01	08 06		08 11	08 16	08 21						08 26			08 31	08 36		
Surrey Quays	d	07 57						08 02	08 07		08 12	08 17	08 22						08 27			08 32	08 37		
New Cross ELL	a								08 12				08 27										08 42		
New Cross Gate 4	a	08 01						08 06		08 11	08 16	08 21						08 26	08 31			08 36		08 41	
	d	08 02						08 07		08 11	08 17	08 22						08 26	08 32			08 37		08 41	
Brockley	d	08 04						08 09		08 14	08 19	08 24						08 29	08 34			08 39		08 44	
Honor Oak Park	d	08 07						08 12		08 17	08 22	08 27						08 32	08 37			08 42		08 47	
Forest Hill 4	d	08 10						08 15		08 19	08 25	08 30						08 34	08 40			08 45		08 49	
Sydenham	d	08 12						08 17		08 22	08 27	08 32						08 37	08 42			08 47		08 52	
Crystal Palace 4	d						08 19	08a22				08a37						08 40			08 50	08a52			
Gipsy Hill	d						08 21											08 43			08 52				
West Norwood 4	d						08 24											08 46			08 55				
Streatham Hill	d																	08 49							
Balham 4 ⊖	d																	08 55							
Wandsworth Common	d																	08 57							
Clapham Junction 10	d																	09 01							
South Bermondsey	d		08 07			08 11								08 14						08 37					
Queens Rd Peckham	d		08 09			08 13								08 16						08 39					
Peckham Rye 4	d		08a12	08 13		08a16	08a36							08 19			08 33			08a42	09a07				
Denmark Hill 4	d			08 17										08 22		08 30	08 36								
London Blackfriars 3 ⊖	a																								
Clapham High Street ⊖	d													08 27											
Wandsworth Road	d													08 29											
Battersea Park 4	d													08 32				09 05							
London Victoria 15 ⊖	a			08 29										08 39		08 42	08 49	09 11							
Penge West	d	08 15								08 24	08 30								08 45					08 54	
Anerley	d	08 17								08 26	08 32								08 47					08 56	
Norwood Junction 2	d	08 20								08 30	08 35								08 50					09 00	
West Croydon 4	a	08 30									08 43								09 00						
East Croydon	a									08 33														09 06	

13 August to 28 August

London Bridge to London Victoria - Croydon and East London Line

Network Diagram - see first Page of Table 177

		LO	LO	LO	SN	SE	SE	SN	LO	LO		LO	SN	SN	LO	SE	SN	SN	LO	LO		SN	LO	LO	LO
London Bridge 4 ⊖	d				08 41	07b37		08 51					09 03	09 06			09 11					09 22			
Highbury & Islington	a																								
	d	08 18	08 25						08 33	08 40					08 48				08 55				09 03	09 10	
Canonbury	d	08 20	08 27						08 35	08 42					08 50				08 57				09 05	09 12	
Dalston Junction Stn ELL	d	08 25	08 30	08 35					08 40	08 46		08 50			08 55				09 01	09 05			09 10	09 15	09 20
Haggerston	d	08 26	08 31	08 36					08 41	08 47		08 51			08 56				09 02	09 06			09 11	09 16	09 21
Hoxton	d	08 28	08 33	08 38					08 43	08 49		08 53			08 58				09 04	09 08			09 13	09 18	09 23
Shoreditch High Street	d	08 31	08 36	08 41					08 46	08 52		08 56			09 01				09 07	09 11			09 16	09 21	09 26
Whitechapel	d	08 33	08 38	08 43					08 48	08 54		08 58			09 03				09 09	09 13			09 18	09 23	09 28
Shadwell	d	08 35	08 40	08 45					08 50	08 56		09 00			09 05				09 11	09 15			09 20	09 25	09 30
Wapping	d	08 37	08 42	08 47					08 52	08 58		09 02			09 07				09 13	09 17			09 22	09 27	09 32
Rotherhithe	d	08 39	08 44	08 49					08 54	09 00		09 04			09 09				09 15	09 19			09 24	09 29	09 34
Canada Water	d	08 41	08 46	08 51					08 56	09 02		09 06			09 11				09 17	09 21			09 26	09 31	09 36
Surrey Quays	d	08 42	08 47	08 52					08 57	09 03		09 07			09 12				09 18	09 22			09 27	09 32	09 37
New Cross ELL	a			08 57								09 12								09 27					09 42
New Cross Gate 4	a	08 46	08 51					08 57	09 01	09 07				09 12	09 16				09 22			09 28	09 30	09 36	
	d	08 47	08 52					08 57	09 02	09 08				09 12	09 17				09 23			09 28	09 32	09 37	
Brockley	d	08 49	08 54					09 00	09 04	09 10				09 14	09 19				09 25			09 30	09 34	09 39	
Honor Oak Park	d	08 52	08 57					09 03	09 07	09 13				09 17	09 22				09 28			09 33	09 37	09 42	
Forest Hill 4	d	08 55	09 00					09 05	09 10	09 16				09 20	09 25				09 31			09 36	09 40	09 45	
Sydenham	d	08 57	09 02					09 08	09 12	09 18				09 22	09 27				09 33			09 38	09 42	09 47	
Crystal Palace 4	d		09a07					09 11		09a23								09 30	09a38			09 43		09a52	
Gipsy Hill	d							09 14										09 32				09 46			
West Norwood 4	d							09 17										09 35				09 49			
Streatham Hill	d							09 21														09 52			
Balham 4 ⊖	d							09 25														09 56			
Wandsworth Common	d							09 27														09 58			
Clapham Junction 10	d							09 31														10 02			
South Bermondsey	d				08 45								09 07				09 15								
Queens Rd Peckham	d				08 48								09 09				09 18								
Peckham Rye 4	d				08 50	08 55	08 55						09a12			09 14	09 20	09a47							
Denmark Hill 4	d				08 53	09 02	09 02									09 17	09 23								
London Blackfriars 3 ⊖	a																								
Clapham High Street ⊖	d				08 58												09 28								
Wandsworth Road	d				08 59												09 29								
Battersea Park 4	d				09 02			09 35									09 32					10 05			
London Victoria 15 ⊖	a				09 08	09 11	09 11	09 42								09 29	09 38					10 11			
Penge West	d	09 00							09 15					09 25	09 30								09 45		
Anerley	d	09 02							09 17					09 27	09 32								09 47		
Norwood Junction 2	d	09 05							09 20					09 30	09 35								09 50		
West Croydon 4	a	09 12							09 30						09 42								10 00		
East Croydon	a													09 33											

		SN	SN	LO	SE	SN		SN	LO	LO	SN	LO	LO	LO	SN	SN		LO	SE	SN	SN	LO	LO	SN	LO
London Bridge 4 ⊖	d	09 33	09 36			09 41					09 52				10 03	10 06				10 11				10 22	
Highbury & Islington	a																								
	d			09 18					09 25			09 33	09 40					09 48				09 55			10 03
Canonbury	d			09 20					09 27			09 35	09 42					09 50				09 57			10 05
Dalston Junction Stn ELL	d			09 25					09 30	09 35		09 40	09 45	09 50				09 55				10 00	10 05		10 10
Haggerston	d			09 26					09 31	09 36		09 41	09 46	09 51				09 56				10 01	10 06		10 11
Hoxton	d			09 28					09 33	09 38		09 43	09 48	09 53				09 58				10 03	10 08		10 13
Shoreditch High Street	d			09 31					09 36	09 41		09 46	09 51	09 56				10 01				10 06	10 11		10 16
Whitechapel	d			09 33					09 38	09 43		09 48	09 53	09 58				10 03				10 08	10 13		10 18
Shadwell	d			09 35					09 40	09 45		09 50	09 55	10 00				10 05				10 10	10 15		10 20
Wapping	d			09 37					09 42	09 47		09 52	09 57	10 02				10 07				10 12	10 17		10 22
Rotherhithe	d			09 39					09 44	09 49		09 54	09 59	10 04				10 09				10 14	10 19		10 24
Canada Water	d			09 41					09 46	09 51		09 56	10 01	10 06				10 11				10 16	10 21		10 26
Surrey Quays	d			09 42					09 47	09 52		09 57	10 02	10 07				10 12				10 17	10 22		10 27
New Cross ELL	a									09 57				10 12									10 27		
New Cross Gate 4	a		09 41	09 46					09 51		09 57	10 01	10 06			10 11		10 16				10 21		10 27	10 31
	d		09 41	09 47					09 52		09 57	10 02	10 07			10 11		10 17				10 22		10 27	10 32
Brockley	d		09 44	09 49					09 54		10 00	10 04	10 09			10 14		10 19				10 24		10 30	10 34
Honor Oak Park	d		09 47	09 52					09 57		10 03	10 07	10 12			10 17		10 22				10 27		10 33	10 37
Forest Hill 4	d		09 49	09 55					10 00		10 05	10 10	10 15			10 19		10 25				10 30		10 35	10 40
Sydenham	d		09 52	09 57					10 02		10 08	10 12	10 17			10 22		10 27				10 32		10 38	10 42
Crystal Palace 4	d							10 00	10a07		10 13		10a22								10 30	10a37		10 43	
Gipsy Hill	d							10 02			10 15										10 32			10 45	
West Norwood 4	d							10 05			10 18										10 35			10 48	
Streatham Hill	d										10 22													10 52	
Balham 4 ⊖	d										10 25													10 55	
Wandsworth Common	d										10 27													10 57	
Clapham Junction 10	d										10 31													11 01	
South Bermondsey	d	09 37				09 45									10 07					10 15					
Queens Rd Peckham	d	09 39				09 48									10 09					10 18					
Peckham Rye 4	d	09a42			09 45	09 50		10a17							10a12				10 15	10 20	10a47				
Denmark Hill 4	d				09 49	09 53													10 19	10 23					
London Blackfriars 3 ⊖	a																								
Clapham High Street ⊖	d					09 58														10 28					
Wandsworth Road	d					09 59														10 29					
Battersea Park 4	d					10 03					10 35									10 32				11 05	
London Victoria 15 ⊖	a				10 00	10 07					10 39								10 28	10 36				11 09	
Penge West	d		09 54	10 00								10 15				10 24		10 30							10 45
Anerley	d		09 56	10 02								10 17				10 26		10 32							10 47
Norwood Junction 2	d		10 00	10 05								10 20				10 30		10 35							10 50
West Croydon 4	a			10 12								10 30						10 42							11 00
East Croydon	a		10 03													10 33									

b London Bridge-I

London Bridge to London Victoria - Croydon and East London Line

Network Diagram - see first Page of Table 177

Station		LO		LO	SN	SN	LO	SE	SN	SN	LO	LO		SN	LO	LO	LO	SN	SN	LO	SE	SN		SN	LO
London Bridge 4 ⊖	d				10 33	10 36			10 41					10 52				11 03	11 06			11 11			
Highbury & Islington	a																								
	d	10 10					10 18				10 25				10 33	10 40				10 48					10 55
Canonbury	d	10 12					10 20				10 27				10 35	10 42				10 50					10 57
Dalston Junction Stn ELL	d	10 15		10 20			10 25				10 30	10 35			10 40	10 45	10 50			10 55					11 00
Haggerston	d	10 16		10 21			10 26				10 31	10 36			10 41	10 46	10 51			10 56					11 01
Hoxton	d	10 18		10 23			10 28				10 33	10 38			10 43	10 48	10 53			10 58					11 03
Shoreditch High Street	d	10 21		10 26			10 31				10 36	10 41			10 46	10 51	10 56			11 01					11 06
Whitechapel	d	10 23		10 28			10 33				10 38	10 43			10 48	10 53	10 58			11 03					11 08
Shadwell	d	10 25		10 30			10 35				10 40	10 45			10 50	10 55	11 00			11 05					11 10
Wapping	d	10 27		10 32			10 37				10 42	10 47			10 52	10 57	11 02			11 07					11 12
Rotherhithe	d	10 29		10 34			10 39				10 44	10 49			10 54	10 59	11 04			11 09					11 14
Canada Water	d	10 31		10 36			10 41				10 46	10 51			10 56	11 01	11 06			11 11					11 16
Surrey Quays	d	10 32		10 37			10 42				10 47	10 52			10 57	11 02	11 07			11 12					11 17
New Cross ELL	a			10 42								10 57					11 12								
New Cross Gate 4	a	10 36				10 41	10 46				10 51			10 57	11 01	11 06			11 11	11 16					11 21
	d	10 37				10 41	10 47				10 52			10 57	11 02	11 07			11 11	11 17					11 22
Brockley	d	10 39				10 44	10 49				10 54			11 00	11 04	11 09			11 14	11 19					11 24
Honor Oak Park	d	10 42				10 47	10 52				10 57			11 03	11 07	11 12			11 17	11 22					11 27
Forest Hill 4	d	10 45				10 49	10 55				11 00			11 05	11 10	11 15			11 19	11 25					11 30
Sydenham	d	10 47				10 52	10 57				11 02			11 08	11 12	11 17			11 22	11 27					11 32
Crystal Palace 4	d	10a52								11 00	11a07			11 13		11a22								11 30	11a37
Gipsy Hill	d									11 02				11 15										11 32	
West Norwood 4	d									11 05				11 18										11 35	
Streatham Hill	d													11 22											
Balham 4 ⊖	d													11 25											
Wandsworth Common	d													11 27											
Clapham Junction 10	d													11 31											
South Bermondsey	d				10 37				10 45									11 07				11 15			
Queens Rd Peckham	d				10 39				10 48									11 09				11 18			
Peckham Rye 4	d				10a42			10 45	10 50	11a17								11a12			11 15	11 20		11a47	
Denmark Hill 4	d							10 49	10 53												11 19	11 23			
London Blackfriars 3 ⊖	a																								
Clapham High Street ⊖	d								10 58													11 28			
Wandsworth Road	d								10 59													11 29			
Battersea Park 4	d								11 02					11 35								11 32			
London Victoria 15 ⊖	a							10 58	11 06					11 39							11 28	11 36			
Penge West	d					10 54	11 00								11 15				11 24	11 30					
Anerley	d					10 56	11 02								11 17				11 26	11 32					
Norwood Junction 2	d					11 00	11 05								11 20				11 30	11 35					
West Croydon 4	a						11 12								11 30					11 42					
East Croydon	a					11 03													11 33						

Station		LO	SN	LO	LO	LO	SN	SN		LO	SE	SN	SN	LO	LO	SN	LO	LO		LO	SN	SN	LO	SE	SN
London Bridge 4 ⊖	d		11 22				11 33	11 36				11 41				11 52					12 03	12 06			12 11
Highbury & Islington	a																								
	d			11 03	11 10					11 18				11 25			11 33	11 40					11 48		
Canonbury	d			11 05	11 12					11 20				11 27			11 35	11 42					11 50		
Dalston Junction Stn ELL	d	11 05		11 10	11 15	11 20				11 25				11 30	11 35		11 40	11 45		11 50			11 55		
Haggerston	d	11 06		11 11	11 16	11 21				11 26				11 31	11 36		11 41	11 46		11 51			11 56		
Hoxton	d	11 08		11 13	11 18	11 23				11 28				11 33	11 38		11 43	11 48		11 53			11 58		
Shoreditch High Street	d	11 11		11 16	11 21	11 26				11 31				11 36	11 41		11 46	11 51		11 56			12 01		
Whitechapel	d	11 13		11 18	11 23	11 28				11 33				11 38	11 43		11 48	11 53		11 58			12 03		
Shadwell	d	11 15		11 20	11 25	11 30				11 35				11 40	11 45		11 50	11 55		12 00			12 05		
Wapping	d	11 17		11 22	11 27	11 32				11 37				11 42	11 47		11 52	11 57		12 02			12 07		
Rotherhithe	d	11 19		11 24	11 29	11 34				11 39				11 44	11 49		11 54	11 59		12 04			12 09		
Canada Water	d	11 21		11 26	11 31	11 36				11 41				11 46	11 51		11 56	12 01		12 06			12 11		
Surrey Quays	d	11 22		11 27	11 32	11 37				11 42				11 47	11 52		11 57	12 02		12 07			12 12		
New Cross ELL	a	11 27				11 42									11 57					12 12					
New Cross Gate 4	a		11 27	11 31	11 36			11 41		11 46				11 51		11 57	12 01	12 06				12 11	12 16		
	d		11 27	11 32	11 37			11 41		11 47				11 52		11 57	12 02	12 07				12 11	12 17		
Brockley	d		11 30	11 34	11 39			11 44		11 49				11 54		12 00	12 04	12 09				12 14	12 19		
Honor Oak Park	d		11 33	11 37	11 42			11 47		11 52				11 57		12 03	12 07	12 12				12 17	12 22		
Forest Hill 4	d		11 35	11 40	11 45			11 49		11 55				12 00		12 05	12 10	12 15				12 19	12 25		
Sydenham	d		11 38	11 42	11 47			11 52		11 57				12 02		12 08	12 12	12 17				12 22	12 27		
Crystal Palace 4	d		11 43		11a52								12 00	12a07		12 13		12a22							
Gipsy Hill	d		11 45										12 02			12 15									
West Norwood 4	d		11 48										12 05			12 18									
Streatham Hill	d		11 52													12 22									
Balham 4 ⊖	d		11 55													12 25									
Wandsworth Common	d		11 57													12 27									
Clapham Junction 10	d		12 01													12 31									
South Bermondsey	d						11 37					11 45									12 07				12 15
Queens Rd Peckham	d						11 39					11 48									12 09				12 18
Peckham Rye 4	d						11a42				11 45	11 50	12a17								12a12			12 15	12 20
Denmark Hill 4	d										11 49	11 54												12 19	12 23
London Blackfriars 3 ⊖	a																								
Clapham High Street ⊖	d											11 58													12 28
Wandsworth Road	d											12 00													12 29
Battersea Park 4	d		12 05									12 02				12 35									12 32
London Victoria 15 ⊖	a		12 09								11 58	12 07				12 39								12 28	12 36
Penge West	d			11 45				11 54		12 00							12 15					12 24	12 30		
Anerley	d			11 47				11 56		12 02							12 17					12 26	12 32		
Norwood Junction 2	d			11 50				12 00		12 05							12 20					12 30	12 35		
West Croydon 4	a			12 00						12 12							12 30						12 42		
East Croydon	a							12 03														12 33			

13 August to 28 August

London Bridge to London Victoria - Croydon and East London Line

Network Diagram - see first Page of Table 177

		SN	LO	LO		SN	LO	LO	LO	SN	SN	LO	SE	SN		SN	LO	LO	SN	LO	LO	LO	SN	SN
London Bridge 4 ⊖	d					12 22				12 33	12 36			12 41					12 52				13 03	13 06
Highbury & Islington	a																							
	d		11 55				12 03	12 10				12 18					12 25			12 33	12 40			
Canonbury	d		11 57				12 05	12 12				12 20					12 27			12 35	12 42			
Dalston Junction Stn ELL	d		12 00	12 05			12 10	12 15	12 20			12 25					12 30	12 35		12 40	12 45	12 50		
Haggerston	d		12 01	12 06			12 11	12 16	12 21			12 26					12 31	12 36		12 41	12 46	12 51		
Hoxton	d		12 03	12 08			12 13	12 18	12 23			12 28					12 33	12 38		12 43	12 48	12 53		
Shoreditch High Street	d		12 06	12 11			12 16	12 21	12 26			12 31					12 36	12 41		12 46	12 51	12 56		
Whitechapel	d		12 08	12 13			12 18	12 23	12 28			12 33					12 38	12 43		12 48	12 53	12 58		
Shadwell	d		12 10	12 15			12 20	12 25	12 30			12 35					12 40	12 45		12 50	12 55	13 00		
Wapping	d		12 12	12 17			12 22	12 27	12 32			12 37					12 42	12 47		12 52	12 57	13 02		
Rotherhithe	d		12 14	12 19			12 24	12 29	12 34			12 39					12 44	12 49		12 54	12 59	13 04		
Canada Water	d		12 16	12 21			12 26	12 31	12 36			12 41					12 46	12 51		12 56	13 01	13 06		
Surrey Quays	d		12 17	12 22			12 27	12 32	12 37			12 42					12 47	12 52		12 57	13 02	13 07		
New Cross ELL	a			12 27					12 42									12 57				13 12		
New Cross Gate 4	a		12 21			12 27	12 31	12 36			12 41	12 46					12 51		12 57	13 01	13 06			13 11
	d		12 22			12 27	12 32	12 37			12 41	12 47					12 52		12 57	13 02	13 07			13 11
Brockley	d		12 24			12 30	12 34	12 39			12 44	12 49					12 54		13 00	13 04	13 09			13 14
Honor Oak Park	d		12 27			12 33	12 37	12 42			12 47	12 52					12 57		13 03	13 07	13 12			13 17
Forest Hill 4	d		12 30			12 35	12 40	12 45			12 49	12 55					13 00		13 05	13 10	13 15			13 19
Sydenham	d		12 32			12 38	12 42	12 47			12 52	12 57					13 02		13 08	13 12	13 17			13 22
Crystal Palace 4	d	12 30	12a37			12 43		12a52								13 00	13a07		13 13		13a22			
Gipsy Hill	d	12 32				12 45										13 02			13 15					
West Norwood 4	d	12 35				12 48										13 05			13 18					
Streatham Hill	d					12 52													13 22					
Balham 4 ⊖	d					12 55													13 25					
Wandsworth Common	d					12 57													13 27					
Clapham Junction 10	d					13 01													13 31					
South Bermondsey	d									12 37				12 45									13 07	
Queens Rd Peckham	d									12 39				12 48									13 09	
Peckham Rye 4	d	12a47								12a42			12 45	12 50		13a17							13a12	
Denmark Hill 4	d												12 49	12 53										
London Blackfriars 3 ⊖	a																							
Clapham High Street ⊖	d													12 58										
Wandsworth Road	d													12 59										
Battersea Park 4	d					13 05								13 02					13 35					
London Victoria 15 ⊖	a					13 09							12 58	13 06					13 39					
Penge West	d						12 45				12 54	13 00								13 15				13 24
Anerley	d						12 47				12 56	13 02								13 17				13 26
Norwood Junction 2	d						12 50				13 00	13 05								13 20				13 30
West Croydon 4	a						13 00					13 12								13 30				
East Croydon	a										13 03													13 33

		LO	SE	SN	SN	LO	LO	SN	LO	LO		LO	SN	SN	LO	SE	SN	SN	LO	LO		SN	LO	LO	LO
London Bridge 4 ⊖	d			13 11				13 22					13 33	13 36			13 41					13 52			
Highbury & Islington	a																								
	d	12 48				12 55			13 03	13 10					13 18				13 25				13 33	13 40	
Canonbury	d	12 50				12 57			13 05	13 12					13 20				13 27				13 35	13 42	
Dalston Junction Stn ELL	d	12 55				13 00	13 05		13 10	13 15		13 20			13 25				13 30	13 35			13 40	13 45	13 50
Haggerston	d	12 56				13 01	13 06		13 11	13 16		13 21			13 26				13 31	13 36			13 41	13 46	13 51
Hoxton	d	12 58				13 03	13 08		13 13	13 18		13 23			13 28				13 33	13 38			13 43	13 48	13 53
Shoreditch High Street	d	13 01				13 06	13 11		13 16	13 21		13 26			13 31				13 36	13 41			13 46	13 51	13 56
Whitechapel	d	13 03				13 08	13 13		13 18	13 23		13 28			13 33				13 38	13 43			13 48	13 53	13 58
Shadwell	d	13 05				13 10	13 15		13 20	13 25		13 30			13 35				13 40	13 45			13 50	13 55	14 00
Wapping	d	13 07				13 12	13 17		13 22	13 27		13 32			13 37				13 42	13 47			13 52	13 57	14 02
Rotherhithe	d	13 09				13 14	13 19		13 24	13 29		13 34			13 39				13 44	13 49			13 54	13 59	14 04
Canada Water	d	13 11				13 16	13 21		13 26	13 31		13 36			13 41				13 46	13 51			13 56	14 01	14 06
Surrey Quays	d	13 12				13 17	13 22		13 27	13 32		13 37			13 42				13 47	13 52			13 57	14 02	14 07
New Cross ELL	a						13 27					13 42								13 57					14 12
New Cross Gate 4	a	13 16				13 21		13 27	13 31	13 36				13 41	13 46				13 51			13 57	14 01	14 06	
	d	13 17				13 22		13 27	13 32	13 37				13 41	13 47				13 52			13 57	14 02	14 07	
Brockley	d	13 19				13 24		13 30	13 34	13 39				13 44	13 49				13 54			14 00	14 04	14 09	
Honor Oak Park	d	13 22				13 27		13 33	13 37	13 42				13 47	13 52				13 57			14 03	14 07	14 12	
Forest Hill 4	d	13 25				13 30		13 35	13 40	13 45				13 49	13 55				14 00			14 05	14 10	14 15	
Sydenham	d	13 27				13 32		13 38	13 42	13 47				13 52	13 57				14 02			14 08	14 12	14 17	
Crystal Palace 4	d				13 30	13a37		13 43		13a52								14 00	14a07			14 13		14a22	
Gipsy Hill	d				13 32			13 45										14 02				14 15			
West Norwood 4	d				13 35			13 48										14 05				14 18			
Streatham Hill	d							13 52														14 22			
Balham 4 ⊖	d							13 55														14 25			
Wandsworth Common	d							13 57														14 27			
Clapham Junction 10	d							14 01														14 31			
South Bermondsey	d			13 15									13 37				13 45								
Queens Rd Peckham	d			13 18									13 39				13 48								
Peckham Rye 4	d		13 15	13 20	13a47								13a42			13 45	13 50	14a17							
Denmark Hill 4	d		13 19	13 23												13 49	13 53								
London Blackfriars 3 ⊖	a																								
Clapham High Street ⊖	d			13 28													13 58								
Wandsworth Road	d			13 29													13 59								
Battersea Park 4	d			13 32				14 05									14 02					14 35			
London Victoria 15 ⊖	a		13 28	13 36				14 09								13 58	14 06					14 39			
Penge West	d	13 30							13 45					13 54	14 00								14 15		
Anerley	d	13 32							13 47					13 56	14 02								14 17		
Norwood Junction 2	d	13 35							13 50					14 00	14 05								14 20		
West Croydon 4	a	13 42							14 00						14 12								14 30		
East Croydon	a													14 03											

Table 178

London Bridge to London Victoria - Croydon and East London Line

Mondays to Fridays

13 August to 28 August

Network Diagram - see first Page of Table 177

		SN	SN	LO	SE	SN		SN	LO	LO	SN	LO	LO	LO	SN	SN		LO	SE	SN	SN	LO	LO	SN	LO
London Bridge [4] ⊖	d	14 03	14 06			14 11					14 22				14 33	14 36				14 41				14 52	
Highbury & Islington	a																								
	d			13 48					13 55			14 03	14 10					14 18				14 25			14 33
Canonbury	d			13 50					13 57			14 05	14 12					14 20				14 27			14 35
Dalston Junction Stn ELL	d			13 55					14 00	14 05		14 10	14 15	14 20				14 25				14 30	14 35		14 40
Haggerston	d			13 56					14 01	14 06		14 11	14 16	14 21				14 26				14 31	14 36		14 41
Hoxton	d			13 58					14 03	14 08		14 13	14 18	14 23				14 28				14 33	14 38		14 43
Shoreditch High Street	d			14 01					14 06	14 11		14 16	14 21	14 26				14 31				14 36	14 41		14 46
Whitechapel	d			14 03					14 08	14 13		14 18	14 23	14 28				14 33				14 38	14 43		14 48
Shadwell	d			14 05					14 10	14 15		14 20	14 25	14 30				14 35				14 40	14 45		14 50
Wapping	d			14 07					14 12	14 17		14 22	14 27	14 32				14 37				14 42	14 47		14 52
Rotherhithe	d			14 09					14 14	14 19		14 24	14 29	14 34				14 39				14 44	14 49		14 54
Canada Water	d			14 11					14 16	14 21		14 26	14 31	14 36				14 41				14 46	14 51		14 56
Surrey Quays	d			14 12					14 17	14 22		14 27	14 32	14 37				14 42				14 47	14 52		14 57
New Cross ELL	a									14 27				14 42									14 57		
New Cross Gate [4]	a		14 11	14 16					14 21		14 27	14 31	14 36			14 41		14 46				14 51		14 57	15 01
	d		14 11	14 17					14 22		14 27	14 32	14 37			14 41		14 47				14 52		14 57	15 02
Brockley	d		14 14	14 19					14 24		14 30	14 34	14 39			14 44		14 49				14 54		15 00	15 04
Honor Oak Park	d		14 17	14 22					14 27		14 33	14 37	14 42			14 47		14 52				14 57		15 03	15 07
Forest Hill [4]	d		14 19	14 25					14 30		14 35	14 40	14 45			14 49		14 55				15 00		15 05	15 10
Sydenham	d		14 22	14 27					14 32		14 38	14 42	14 47			14 52		14 57				15 02		15 08	15 12
Crystal Palace [4]	d							14 30	14a37		14 43		14a52								15 00	15a07		15 13	
Gipsy Hill	d							14 32			14 45										15 02			15 15	
West Norwood [4]	d							14 35			14 48										15 05			15 18	
Streatham Hill	d										14 52													15 22	
Balham [4] ⊖	d										14 55													15 25	
Wandsworth Common	d										14 57													15 27	
Clapham Junction [10]	d										15 01													15 31	
South Bermondsey	d	14 07				14 15									14 37					14 45					
Queens Rd Peckham	d	14 09				14 18									14 39					14 48					
Peckham Rye [4]	d	14a12			14 15	14 20		14a47							14a42				14 45	14 50	15a17				
Denmark Hill [4]	d				14 19	14 23													14 49	14 53					
London Blackfriars [3] ⊖	a																								
Clapham High Street ⊖	d					14 28														14 58					
Wandsworth Road	d					14 29														14 59					
Battersea Park [4]	d					14 32					15 05									15 02				15 35	
London Victoria [15] ⊖	a				14 28	14 36					15 09								14 58	15 06				15 39	
Penge West	d		14 24	14 30								14 45				14 54		15 00							15 15
Anerley	d		14 26	14 32								14 47				14 56		15 02							15 17
Norwood Junction [2]	d		14 30	14 35								14 50				15 00		15 05							15 20
West Croydon [4]	a			14 42								15 00						15 12							15 30
East Croydon	a		14 33													15 03									

		LO		LO	SN	SN	LO	SE	SN	SN	LO	LO		SN	LO	LO	LO	SN	SN	LO	SE	SN		SN	SN
London Bridge [4] ⊖	d				15 03	15 06			15 11					15 22				15 33	15 36			15 41			
Highbury & Islington	a																								
	d	14 40					14 48				14 55				15 03	15 10				15 18					
Canonbury	d	14 42					14 50				14 57				15 05	15 12				15 20					
Dalston Junction Stn ELL	d	14 45		14 50			14 55				15 00	15 05			15 10	15 15	15 20			15 25					
Haggerston	d	14 46		14 51			14 56				15 01	15 06			15 11	15 16	15 21			15 26					
Hoxton	d	14 48		14 53			14 58				15 03	15 08			15 13	15 18	15 23			15 28					
Shoreditch High Street	d	14 51		14 56			15 01				15 06	15 11			15 16	15 21	15 26			15 31					
Whitechapel	d	14 53		14 58			15 03				15 08	15 13			15 18	15 23	15 28			15 33					
Shadwell	d	14 55		15 00			15 05				15 10	15 15			15 20	15 25	15 30			15 35					
Wapping	d	14 57		15 02			15 07				15 12	15 17			15 22	15 27	15 32			15 37					
Rotherhithe	d	14 59		15 04			15 09				15 14	15 19			15 24	15 29	15 34			15 39					
Canada Water	d	15 01		15 06			15 11				15 16	15 21			15 26	15 31	15 36			15 41					
Surrey Quays	d	15 02		15 07			15 12				15 17	15 22			15 27	15 32	15 37			15 42					
New Cross ELL	a			15 12								15 27					15 42								
New Cross Gate [4]	a	15 06				15 11	15 16				15 21			15 27	15 31	15 36			15 41	15 46					
	d	15 07				15 11	15 17				15 22			15 27	15 32	15 37			15 41	15 47					
Brockley	d	15 09				15 14	15 19				15 24			15 30	15 34	15 39			15 44	15 49					
Honor Oak Park	d	15 12				15 17	15 22				15 27			15 33	15 37	15 42			15 47	15 52					
Forest Hill [4]	d	15 15				15 19	15 25				15 30			15 35	15 40	15 45			15 49	15 55					
Sydenham	d	15 17				15 22	15 27				15 32			15 38	15 42	15 47			15 52	15 57					
Crystal Palace [4]	d	15a22								15 30	15a37			15 43		15a52									
Gipsy Hill	d									15 32				15 45											16 00
West Norwood [4]	d									15 35				15 48											16 02
Streatham Hill	d													15 52											16 05
Balham [4] ⊖	d													15 55										15 56	
Wandsworth Common	d													15 57											
Clapham Junction [10]	d													16 01											
South Bermondsey	d				15 07				15 15									15 37				15 45			
Queens Rd Peckham	d				15 09				15 18									15 39				15 48			
Peckham Rye [4]	d				15a12			15 15	15 20	15a47								15a42			15 45	15 50		16a07	16a17
Denmark Hill [4]	d							15 19	15 23												15 49	15 53			
London Blackfriars [3] ⊖	a																								
Clapham High Street ⊖	d								15 28													15 58			
Wandsworth Road	d								15 29													15 59			
Battersea Park [4]	d								15 32					16 05								16 02			
London Victoria [15] ⊖	a							15 28	15 36					16 10							15 58	16 06			
Penge West	d					15 24	15 30								15 45				15 54	16 00					
Anerley	d					15 26	15 32								15 47				15 56	16 02					
Norwood Junction [2]	d					15 30	15 35								15 50				16 00	16 05					
West Croydon [4]	a						15 42								16 00					16 12					
East Croydon	a					15 33													16 03						

13 August to 28 August

London Bridge to London Victoria - Croydon and East London Line

Network Diagram - see first Page of Table 177

		LO	LO	SN	LO	LO	LO	SN		SN	LO	SE	SN	SN	LO	LO	SN	LO		LO	LO	SN	SN	LO	SE
London Bridge 4 ⊖	d			15 52				16 03		16 06			16 11				16 22					16 33	16 36		
Highbury & Islington	a																								
	d	15 25			15 33	15 40					15 48				15 55			16 03		16 10				16 18	
Canonbury	d	15 27			15 35	15 42					15 50				15 57			16 05		16 12				16 20	
Dalston Junction Stn ELL	d	15 30	15 35		15 40	15 45	15 50				15 55				16 00	16 05		16 10		16 15	16 20			16 25	
Haggerston	d	15 31	15 36		15 41	15 46	15 51				15 56				16 01	16 06		16 11		16 16	16 21			16 26	
Hoxton	d	15 33	15 38		15 43	15 48	15 53				15 58				16 03	16 08		16 13		16 18	16 23			16 28	
Shoreditch High Street	d	15 36	15 41		15 46	15 51	15 56				16 01				16 06	16 11		16 16		16 21	16 26			16 31	
Whitechapel	d	15 38	15 43		15 48	15 53	15 58				16 03				16 08	16 13		16 18		16 23	16 28			16 33	
Shadwell	d	15 40	15 45		15 50	15 55	16 00				16 05				16 10	16 15		16 20		16 25	16 30			16 35	
Wapping	d	15 42	15 47		15 52	15 57	16 02				16 07				16 12	16 17		16 22		16 27	16 32			16 37	
Rotherhithe	d	15 44	15 49		15 54	15 59	16 04				16 09				16 14	16 19		16 24		16 29	16 34			16 39	
Canada Water	d	15 46	15 51		15 56	16 01	16 06				16 11				16 16	16 21		16 26		16 31	16 36			16 41	
Surrey Quays	d	15 47	15 52		15 57	16 02	16 07				16 12				16 17	16 22		16 27		16 32	16 37			16 42	
New Cross ELL	a		15 57				16 12									16 27					16 42				
New Cross Gate 4	a	15 51		15 57	16 01	16 06				16 11	16 16				16 21		16 27	16 31		16 36			16 41	16 46	
	d	15 52		15 57	16 02	16 07				16 11	16 17				16 22		16 27	16 32		16 37			16 41	16 47	
Brockley	d	15 54		16 00	16 04	16 09				16 14	16 19				16 24		16 30	16 34		16 39			16 44	16 49	
Honor Oak Park	d	15 57		16 03	16 07	16 12				16 17	16 22				16 27		16 33	16 37		16 42			16 47	16 52	
Forest Hill 4	d	16 00		16 05	16 10	16 15				16 19	16 25				16 30		16 35	16 40		16 45			16 49	16 55	
Sydenham	d	16 02		16 08	16 12	16 17				16 22	16 27				16 32		16 38	16 42		16 47			16 52	16 57	
Crystal Palace 4	d	16a07		16 13		16a22								16 30	16a37		16 43			16a52					
Gipsy Hill	d			16 15										16 32			16 45								
West Norwood 4	d			16 18										16 35			16 48								
Streatham Hill	d			16 22													16 52								
Balham 4 ⊖	d			16 25													16 55								
Wandsworth Common	d			16 27													16 57								
Clapham Junction 10	d			16 31													17 01								
South Bermondsey	d							16 07					16 15									16 37			
Queens Rd Peckham	d							16 09					16 18									16 39			
Peckham Rye 4	d							16a12				16 15	16 20	16a47								16a42			16 45
Denmark Hill 4	d											16 19	16 23												16 49
London Blackfriars 3 ⊖	a																								
Clapham High Street ⊖	d												16 28												
Wandsworth Road	d												16 29												
Battersea Park 4	d			16 35									16 32				17 05								
London Victoria 15 ⊖	a			16 40								16 28	16 38				17 10								17 01
Penge West	d				16 15					16 24	16 30							16 45					16 54	17 00	
Anerley	d				16 17					16 26	16 32							16 47					16 56	17 02	
Norwood Junction 2	d				16 20					16 30	16 35							16 50					17 00	17 05	
West Croydon 4	a				16 30						16 42							17 00					17 07	17 12	
East Croydon	a									16 33															

		SN	SN	LO		LO	SN	LO	SN	SE	SN	LO	LO	SN		LO	SN	SN	LO	LO	SN	LO	LO	LO
London Bridge 4 ⊖	d	16 41					16 52		16 58					17 05			17 11				17 19			
Highbury & Islington	a																							
	d			16 25				16 33				16 40				16 48			16 55			17 03	17 10	
Canonbury	d			16 27				16 35				16 42				16 50			16 57			17 05	17 12	
Dalston Junction Stn ELL	d			16 30		16 35		16 40				16 45	16 50			16 55			17 00	17 05		17 10	17 15	17 20
Haggerston	d			16 31		16 36		16 41				16 46	16 51			16 56			17 01	17 06		17 11	17 16	17 21
Hoxton	d			16 33		16 38		16 43				16 48	16 53			16 58			17 03	17 08		17 13	17 18	17 23
Shoreditch High Street	d			16 36		16 41		16 46				16 51	16 56			17 01			17 06	17 11		17 16	17 21	17 26
Whitechapel	d			16 38		16 43		16 48				16 53	16 58			17 03			17 08	17 13		17 18	17 23	17 28
Shadwell	d			16 40		16 45		16 50				16 55	17 00			17 05			17 10	17 15		17 20	17 25	17 30
Wapping	d			16 42		16 47		16 52				16 57	17 02			17 07			17 12	17 17		17 22	17 27	17 32
Rotherhithe	d			16 44		16 49		16 54				16 59	17 04			17 09			17 14	17 19		17 24	17 29	17 34
Canada Water	d			16 46		16 51		16 56				17 01	17 06			17 11			17 16	17 21		17 26	17 31	17 36
Surrey Quays	d			16 47		16 52		16 57				17 02	17 07			17 12			17 17	17 22		17 27	17 32	17 37
New Cross ELL	a					16 57							17 12							17 27				17 42
New Cross Gate 4	a			16 51			16 57	17 01				17 06		17 11		17 16			17 21		17 26	17 30	17 36	
	d			16 52			16 57	17 02				17 07		17 11		17 17			17 22		17 26	17 32	17 37	
Brockley	d			16 54			17 00	17 04				17 09		17 14		17 19			17 24		17 29	17 34	17 39	
Honor Oak Park	d			16 57			17 03	17 07				17 12		17 17		17 22			17 27		17 32	17 37	17 42	
Forest Hill 4	d			17 00			17 05	17 10				17 15		17 19		17 25			17 30		17 34	17 40	17 45	
Sydenham	d			17 02			17 08	17 12				17 17		17 22		17 27			17 32		17 37	17 42	17 47	
Crystal Palace 4	d		17 00	17a07			17 13				17 18	17a22						17 36	17a37		17 44		17a52	
Gipsy Hill	d		17 02				17 15				17 20							17 38			17 46			
West Norwood 4	d		17 05				17 18				17 23							17 41			17 49			
Streatham Hill	d						17 22														17 53			
Balham 4 ⊖	d						17 25														17 56			
Wandsworth Common	d						17 27														17 58			
Clapham Junction 10	d						17 31														18 02			
South Bermondsey	d	16 45							17 02								17 15							
Queens Rd Peckham	d	16 48							17 04								17 18							
Peckham Rye 4	d	16 50	17a17						17a07	17 15	17a35						17 20	17a53						
Denmark Hill 4	d	16 53								17 19							17 23							
London Blackfriars 3 ⊖	a																							
Clapham High Street ⊖	d	16 58															17 28							
Wandsworth Road	d	16 59															17 29							
Battersea Park 4	d	17 02					17 35										17 32				18 06			
London Victoria 15 ⊖	a	17 08					17 42			17 28							17 38				18 12			
Penge West	d							17 15						17 24		17 30						17 45		
Anerley	d							17 17						17 26		17 32						17 47		
Norwood Junction 2	d							17 20						17 30		17 35						17 50		
West Croydon 4	a							17 30						17 37		17 42						18 01		
East Croydon	a																							

London Bridge to London Victoria - Croydon and East London Line

Network Diagram - see first Page of Table 177

		SN	SN	LO	SE	SN	SN	LO	LO	SN		LO	SN	SE	SN	LO	LO	SN	LO	LO		LO	SN	SN	LO
London Bridge 4 ⊖	d	17 28	17 36			17 41				17 53			17 58					18 06					18 11	18 21	
Highbury & Islington	a																								
	d			17 18				17 25				17 33				17 40			17 48	17 55					18 03
Canonbury	d			17 20				17 27				17 35				17 42			17 50	17 57					18 05
Dalston Junction Stn ELL	d			17 25				17 30	17 35			17 40				17 45	17 50		17 55	18 00		18 05			18 10
Haggerston	d			17 26				17 31	17 36			17 41				17 46	17 51		17 56	18 01		18 06			18 11
Hoxton	d			17 28				17 33	17 38			17 43				17 48	17 53		17 58	18 03		18 08			18 13
Shoreditch High Street	d			17 31				17 36	17 41			17 46				17 51	17 56		18 01	18 06		18 11			18 16
Whitechapel	d			17 33				17 38	17 43			17 48				17 53	17 58		18 03	18 08		18 13			18 18
Shadwell	d			17 35				17 40	17 45			17 50				17 55	18 00		18 05	18 10		18 15			18 20
Wapping	d			17 37				17 42	17 47			17 52				17 57	18 02		18 07	18 12		18 17			18 22
Rotherhithe	d			17 39				17 44	17 49			17 54				17 59	18 04		18 09	18 14		18 19			18 24
Canada Water	d			17 41				17 46	17 51			17 56				18 01	18 06		18 11	18 16		18 21			18 26
Surrey Quays	d			17 42				17 47	17 52			17 57				18 02	18 07		18 12	18 17		18 22			18 27
New Cross ELL	a								17 57								18 12					18 27			
New Cross Gate 4	a		17 41	17 46				17 51		17 58		18 01				18 06		18 11	18 16	18 21				18 26	18 30
	d		17 41	17 47				17 52		17 58		18 02				18 07		18 11	18 17	18 22				18 26	18 32
Brockley	d		17 44	17 49				17 54		18 01		18 04				18 09		18 14	18 19	18 24				18 29	18 34
Honor Oak Park	d		17 47	17 52				17 57		18 04		18 07				18 12		18 17	18 22	18 27				18 32	18 37
Forest Hill 4	d		17 49	17 55				18 00		18 06		18 10				18 15		18 19	18 25	18 30				18 34	18 40
Sydenham	d		17 52	17 57				18 02		18 09		18 12				18 17		18 22	18 27	18 32				18 37	18 42
Crystal Palace 4	d						17 55	18a07		18 13					18 18	18a22				18a37				18 43	
Gipsy Hill	d						17 57			18 15					18 20									18 45	
West Norwood 4	d						18 00			18 18					18 23									18 48	
Streatham Hill	d									18 22														18 52	
Balham 4 ⊖	d									18 25														18 55	
Wandsworth Common	d									18 27														18 57	
Clapham Junction 10	d									18 32														19 01	
South Bermondsey	d	17 32				17 45							18 02										18 15		
Queens Rd Peckham	d	17 35				17 47							18 04										18 18		
Peckham Rye 4	d	17a37			17 45	17 50	18a12						18a07	18 15	18a36								18 20		
Denmark Hill 4	d				17 49	17 53								18 19									18 23		
London Blackfriars 3 ⊖	a																								
Clapham High Street ⊖	d					17 58																	18 28		
Wandsworth Road	d					17 59																	18 29		
Battersea Park 4	d					18 02				18 35													18 32	19 05	
London Victoria 15 ⊖	a				17 59	18 08				18 42				18 29									18 39	19 12	
Penge West	d		17 54	18 00								18 15						18 24	18 30						18 45
Anerley	d		17 56	18 02								18 17						18 26	18 32						18 47
Norwood Junction 2	d		18 00	18 05								18 20						18 32	18 35						18 50
West Croydon 4	a		18 08	18 12								18 30						18 39	18 42						19 01
East Croydon	a																								

		SN	SE	SN	LO	LO		SN	LO	LO	LO	SN	SE	SN	LO	LO		LO	SN	SN	LO	SE	SN	SN	SE
London Bridge 4 ⊖	d	18 28						18 36				18 41		18 51					18 57	19 06			19 08	19 11	
Highbury & Islington	a																								
	d				18 10				18 18	18 25					18 33	18 40					18 48				
Canonbury	d				18 12				18 20	18 27					18 35	18 42					18 50				
Dalston Junction Stn ELL	d				18 15	18 20			18 25	18 30	18 35				18 40	18 45		18 50			18 55				
Haggerston	d				18 16	18 21			18 26	18 31	18 36				18 41	18 46		18 51			18 56				
Hoxton	d				18 18	18 23			18 28	18 33	18 38				18 43	18 48		18 53			18 58				
Shoreditch High Street	d				18 21	18 26			18 31	18 36	18 41				18 46	18 51		18 56			19 01				
Whitechapel	d				18 23	18 28			18 33	18 38	18 43				18 48	18 53		18 58			19 03				
Shadwell	d				18 25	18 30			18 35	18 40	18 45				18 50	18 55		19 00			19 05				
Wapping	d				18 27	18 32			18 37	18 42	18 47				18 52	18 57		19 02			19 07				
Rotherhithe	d				18 29	18 34			18 39	18 44	18 49				18 54	18 59		19 04			19 09				
Canada Water	d				18 31	18 36			18 41	18 46	18 51				18 56	19 01		19 06			19 11				
Surrey Quays	d				18 32	18 37			18 42	18 47	18 52				18 57	19 02		19 07			19 12				
New Cross ELL	a					18 42					18 57							19 12							
New Cross Gate 4	a				18 36			18 41	18 46	18 51				18 56	19 01	19 06				19 11	19 16				
	d				18 37			18 41	18 47	18 52				18 56	19 02	19 07				19 11	19 17				
Brockley	d				18 39			18 44	18 49	18 54				18 59	19 04	19 09				19 14	19 19				
Honor Oak Park	d				18 42			18 47	18 52	18 57				19 02	19 07	19 12				19 17	19 22				
Forest Hill 4	d				18 45			18 49	18 55	19 00				19 04	19 10	19 15				19 19	19 25				
Sydenham	d				18 47			18 52	18 57	19 02				19 07	19 12	19 17				19 22	19 27				
Crystal Palace 4	d			18 51	18a52					19a07				19 13		19a22									
Gipsy Hill	d			18 53										19 15											
West Norwood 4	d			18 56										19 18											
Streatham Hill	d													19 22											
Balham 4 ⊖	d													19 25											
Wandsworth Common	d													19 27											
Clapham Junction 10	d													19 31											
South Bermondsey	d	18 32										18 45							19 01				19 12	19 15	
Queens Rd Peckham	d	18 34										18 48							19 03				19 14	19 18	
Peckham Rye 4	d	18a37	18 45	19a14								18 50							19 06			19 15	19a17	19 20	
Denmark Hill 4	d		18 49									18 53	18 59									19 19		19 23	19 28
London Blackfriars 3 ⊖	a																								
Clapham High Street ⊖	d											18 58												19 28	
Wandsworth Road	d											18 59												19 29	
Battersea Park 4	d											19 02		19 35										19 32	
London Victoria 15 ⊖	a		18 58									19 08	19 13	19 41								19 28		19 36	19 43
Penge West	d							18 54	19 00						19 15					19 24	19 30				
Anerley	d							18 56	19 02						19 17					19 26	19 32				
Norwood Junction 2	d							19 02	19 05						19 20				19 28	19 30	19 35				
West Croydon 4	a							19 09	19 12						19 30				19 35		19 42				
East Croydon	a																			19 33					

13 August to 28 August

London Bridge to London Victoria - Croydon and East London Line

Network Diagram - see first Page of Table 177

Station		SN		LO	LO	SN	LO	LO	LO	SN	SN	LO		SN	SN	SN	LO	LO	SN	LO	LO	LO		SN	SN
London Bridge 4 ⊖	d					19 22				19 28	19 36			19 38	19 41				19 54					20 03	20 06
Highbury & Islington	a																								
	d			18 55			19 03	19 10				19 18					19 25			19 33	19 40				
Canonbury	d			18 57			19 05	19 12				19 20					19 27			19 35	19 42				
Dalston Junction Stn ELL	d			19 00	19 05		19 10	19 15	19 20			19 25					19 30	19 35		19 40	19 45	19 50			
Haggerston	d			19 01	19 06		19 11	19 16	19 21			19 26					19 31	19 36		19 41	19 46	19 51			
Hoxton	d			19 03	19 08		19 13	19 18	19 23			19 28					19 33	19 38		19 43	19 48	19 53			
Shoreditch High Street	d			19 06	19 11		19 16	19 21	19 26			19 31					19 36	19 41		19 46	19 51	19 56			
Whitechapel	d			19 08	19 13		19 18	19 23	19 28			19 33					19 38	19 43		19 48	19 53	19 58			
Shadwell	d			19 10	19 15		19 20	19 25	19 30			19 35					19 40	19 45		19 50	19 55	20 00			
Wapping	d			19 12	19 17		19 22	19 27	19 32			19 37					19 42	19 47		19 52	19 57	20 02			
Rotherhithe	d			19 14	19 19		19 24	19 29	19 34			19 39					19 44	19 49		19 54	19 59	20 04			
Canada Water	d			19 16	19 21		19 26	19 31	19 36			19 41					19 46	19 51		19 56	20 01	20 06			
Surrey Quays	d			19 17	19 22		19 27	19 32	19 37			19 42					19 47	19 52		19 57	20 02	20 07			
New Cross ELL	a				19 27				19 42									19 57				20 12			
New Cross Gate 4	a			19 21		19 27	19 31	19 36			19 41	19 46					19 51		19 59	20 00	20 06				20 11
	d			19 22		19 27	19 32	19 37			19 41	19 47					19 52		19 59	20 02	20 07				20 11
Brockley	d			19 24		19 30	19 34	19 39			19 44	19 49					19 54		20 02	20 04	20 09				20 14
Honor Oak Park	d			19 27		19 33	19 37	19 42			19 47	19 52					19 57		20 05	20 07	20 12				20 17
Forest Hill 4	d			19 30		19 35	19 40	19 45			19 49	19 55					20 00		20 07	20 10	20 15				20 19
Sydenham	d			19 32		19 38	19 42	19 47			19 52	19 57					20 02		20 10	20 12	20 17				20 22
Crystal Palace 4	d	19 32		19a37		19 43		19a52								20 01	20a07		20 13		20a22				
Gipsy Hill	d	19 34				19 45										20 03			20 16						
West Norwood 4	d	19 37				19 48										20 06			20 19						
Streatham Hill	d					19 52													20 22						
Balham 4 ⊖	d					19 55													20 25						
Wandsworth Common	d					19 57													20 27						
Clapham Junction 10	d					20 01													20 31						
South Bermondsey	d									19 32				19 42	19 45									20 07	
Queens Rd Peckham	d									19 34				19 44	19 48									20 09	
Peckham Rye 4	d	19a49								19 37				19a47	19 50	20a18								20a12	
Denmark Hill 4	d														19 53										
London Blackfriars 3 ⊖	a																								
Clapham High Street ⊖	d														19 58										
Wandsworth Road	d														19 59										
Battersea Park 4	d					20 05									20 02				20 35						
London Victoria 15 ⊖	a					20 09									20 06				20 39						
Penge West	d						19 45				19 54	20 00								20 15					20 24
Anerley	d						19 47				19 56	20 02								20 17					20 26
Norwood Junction 2	d						19 50			20 02	20 00	20 05								20 20					20 30
West Croydon 4	a						20 00			20 07		20 12								20 29					
East Croydon	a										20 03														20 33

Station		LO	SN	SN	LO	LO	SN	LO		LO	LO	SN	SN	LO	SN	SN	LO	LO		SN	LO	LO	LO	SN	SN
London Bridge 4 ⊖	d		20 11				20 22					20 33	20 36		20 41					20 52				21 03	21 06
Highbury & Islington	a																								
	d	19 48			19 55			20 03		20 10				20 18			20 25				20 33	20 40			
Canonbury	d	19 50			19 57			20 05		20 12				20 20			20 27				20 35	20 42			
Dalston Junction Stn ELL	d	19 55			20 00	20 05		20 10		20 15	20 20			20 25			20 30	20 35			20 40	20 45	20 50		
Haggerston	d	19 56			20 01	20 06		20 11		20 16	20 21			20 26			20 31	20 36			20 41	20 46	20 51		
Hoxton	d	19 58			20 03	20 08		20 13		20 18	20 23			20 28			20 33	20 38			20 43	20 48	20 53		
Shoreditch High Street	d	20 01			20 06	20 11		20 16		20 21	20 26			20 31			20 36	20 41			20 46	20 51	20 56		
Whitechapel	d	20 03			20 08	20 13		20 18		20 23	20 28			20 33			20 38	20 43			20 48	20 53	20 58		
Shadwell	d	20 05			20 10	20 15		20 20		20 25	20 30			20 35			20 40	20 45			20 50	20 55	21 00		
Wapping	d	20 07			20 12	20 17		20 22		20 27	20 32			20 37			20 42	20 47			20 52	20 57	21 02		
Rotherhithe	d	20 09			20 14	20 19		20 24		20 29	20 34			20 39			20 44	20 49			20 54	20 59	21 04		
Canada Water	d	20 11			20 16	20 21		20 26		20 31	20 36			20 41			20 46	20 51			20 56	21 01	21 06		
Surrey Quays	d	20 12			20 17	20 22		20 27		20 32	20 37			20 42			20 47	20 52			20 57	21 02	21 07		
New Cross ELL	a					20 27					20 42							20 57					21 12		
New Cross Gate 4	a	20 16			20 21		20 27	20 31		20 36			20 41	20 46			20 51			20 57	21 01	21 06			21 11
	d	20 17			20 22		20 27	20 32		20 37			20 41	20 47			20 52			20 57	21 02	21 07			21 11
Brockley	d	20 19			20 24		20 30	20 34		20 39			20 44	20 49			20 54			21 00	21 04	21 09			21 14
Honor Oak Park	d	20 22			20 27		20 33	20 37		20 42			20 47	20 52			20 57			21 03	21 07	21 12			21 17
Forest Hill 4	d	20 25			20 30		20 35	20 40		20 45			20 49	20 55			21 00			21 05	21 10	21 15			21 19
Sydenham	d	20 27			20 32		20 38	20 42		20 47			20 52	20 57			21 02			21 08	21 12	21 17			21 22
Crystal Palace 4	d			20 31	20a37		20 43			20a52						21 00	21a07			21 13		21a22			
Gipsy Hill	d			20 33			20 45									21 02				21 15					
West Norwood 4	d			20 36			20 48									21 05				21 18					
Streatham Hill	d						20 52													21 22					
Balham 4 ⊖	d						20 56													21 26					
Wandsworth Common	d						20 58													21 28					
Clapham Junction 10	d						21 03													21 33					
South Bermondsey	d		20 15									20 37			20 45									21 07	
Queens Rd Peckham	d		20 18									20 39			20 48									21 09	
Peckham Rye 4	d		20 20	20a48								20a42			20 50	21a17								21a12	
Denmark Hill 4	d		20 23												20 53										
London Blackfriars 3 ⊖	a																								
Clapham High Street ⊖	d		20 28												20 58										
Wandsworth Road	d		20 29												20 59										
Battersea Park 4	d		20 32				21 06								21 02					21 36					
London Victoria 15 ⊖	a		20 36				21 11								21 06					21 41					
Penge West	d	20 30						20 45					20 54	21 00							21 15				21 24
Anerley	d	20 32						20 47					20 56	21 02							21 17				21 26
Norwood Junction 2	d	20 35						20 50					21 00	21 05							21 20				21 30
West Croydon 4	a	20 42						21 00						21 12							21 30				
East Croydon	a												21 03												21 33

Table 178

Mondays to Fridays

13 August to 28 August

London Bridge to London Victoria - Croydon and East London Line

Network Diagram - see first Page of Table 177

		LO	SN	SE	SN	LO	LO	SN	LO	LO	LO	SN	SN	LO	SN	SE	SN	LO	LO	SN	LO	LO
London Bridge 4 ⊖	d		21 11					21 22				21 33	21 36		21 41					21 52		
Highbury & Islington	a																					
	d	20 48				20 55			21 03	21 10				21 18				21 25			21 33	21 40
Canonbury	d	20 50				20 57			21 05	21 12				21 20				21 27			21 35	21 42
Dalston Junction Stn ELL	d	20 55				21 00	21 05		21 10	21 15	21 20			21 25				21 30	21 35		21 40	21 45
Haggerston	d	20 56				21 01	21 06		21 11	21 16	21 21			21 26				21 31	21 36		21 41	21 46
Hoxton	d	20 58				21 03	21 08		21 13	21 18	21 23			21 28				21 33	21 38		21 43	21 48
Shoreditch High Street	d	21 01				21 06	21 11		21 16	21 21	21 26			21 31				21 36	21 41		21 46	21 51
Whitechapel	d	21 03				21 08	21 13		21 18	21 23	21 28			21 33				21 38	21 43		21 48	21 53
Shadwell	d	21 05				21 10	21 15		21 20	21 25	21 30			21 35				21 40	21 45		21 50	21 55
Wapping	d	21 07				21 12	21 17		21 22	21 27	21 32			21 37				21 42	21 47		21 52	21 57
Rotherhithe	d	21 09				21 14	21 19		21 24	21 29	21 34			21 39				21 44	21 49		21 54	21 59
Canada Water	d	21 11				21 16	21 21		21 26	21 31	21 36			21 41				21 46	21 51		21 56	22 01
Surrey Quays	d	21 12				21 17	21 22		21 27	21 32	21 37			21 42				21 47	21 52		21 57	22 02
New Cross ELL	a						21 27				21 42								21 57			
New Cross Gate 4	a	21 16				21 21		21 27	21 31	21 36			21 41	21 46				21 51		21 57	22 01	22 06
	d	21 17				21 22		21 27	21 32	21 37			21 41	21 47				21 52		21 57	22 02	22 07
Brockley	d	21 19				21 24		21 30	21 34	21 39			21 44	21 49				21 54		22 00	22 04	22 09
Honor Oak Park	d	21 22				21 27		21 33	21 37	21 42			21 47	21 52				21 57		22 03	22 07	22 12
Forest Hill 4	d	21 25				21 30		21 35	21 40	21 45			21 49	21 55				22 00		22 05	22 10	22 15
Sydenham	d	21 27				21 32		21 38	21 42	21 47			21 52	21 57				22 02		22 08	22 12	22 17
Crystal Palace 4	d				21 30	21a37		21 43		21a52							22 00	22a07		22 13		22a22
Gipsy Hill	d				21 32			21 45									22 02			22 15		
West Norwood 4	d				21 35			21 48									22 05			22 18		
Streatham Hill	d							21 52												22 22		
Balham 4 ⊖	d							21 56												22 26		
Wandsworth Common	d							21 58												22 28		
Clapham Junction 10	d							22 03												22 33		
South Bermondsey	d		21 15									21 37			21 45							
Queens Rd Peckham	d		21 18									21 39			21 48							
Peckham Rye 4	d		21 20	21 20	21a47							21a42			21 50	21 50	22a17					
Denmark Hill 4	d		21 23	21 24											21 53	21 54						
London Blackfriars 3 ⊖	a			21 34												22 04						
Clapham High Street ⊖	d		21 28												21 58							
Wandsworth Road	d		21 29												21 59							
Battersea Park 4	d		21 32					22 06							22 02					22 36		
London Victoria 15 ⊖	a		21 36					22 11							22 06					22 41		
Penge West	d	21 30							21 45				21 54	22 00							22 15	
Anerley	d	21 32							21 47				21 56	22 02							22 17	
Norwood Junction 2	d	21 35							21 50				22 00	22 05							22 20	
West Croydon 4	a	21 42							22 00					22 12							22 30	
East Croydon	a												22 03									

		LO	SN	SN	LO	SN	SE	SN	LO	SN	LO	LO	SN	SN	SN	SE	SN	LO	SN	LO	LO	SN	SN
London Bridge 4 ⊖	d		22 03	22 08		22 11				22 23			22 33	22 38	22 41				22 52			23 05	23 06
Highbury & Islington	a																						
	d				21 48				21 55		22 05							22 25		22 35			
Canonbury	d				21 50				21 57		22 07							22 27		22 37			
Dalston Junction Stn ELL	d	21 50			21 55				22 00		22 10	22 20						22 30		22 40	22 50		
Haggerston	d	21 51			21 56				22 01		22 11	22 21						22 31		22 41	22 51		
Hoxton	d	21 53			21 58				22 03		22 13	22 23						22 33		22 43	22 53		
Shoreditch High Street	d	21 56			22 01				22 06		22 16	22 26						22 36		22 46	22 56		
Whitechapel	d	21 58			22 03				22 08		22 18	22 28						22 38		22 48	22 58		
Shadwell	d	22 00			22 05				22 10		22 20	22 30						22 40		22 50	23 00		
Wapping	d	22 02			22 07				22 12		22 22	22 32						22 42		22 52	23 02		
Rotherhithe	d	22 04			22 09				22 14		22 24	22 34						22 44		22 54	23 04		
Canada Water	d	22 06			22 11				22 16		22 26	22 36						22 46		22 56	23 06		
Surrey Quays	d	22 07			22 12				22 17		22 27	22 37						22 47		22 57	23 07		
New Cross ELL	a	22 13										22 42									23 12		
New Cross Gate 4	a			22 13	22 16				22 21	22 28	22 31			22 43				22 51	22 57	23 01			23 11
	d			22 13	22 17				22 22	22 28	22 32			22 43				22 52	22 57	23 02			23 11
Brockley	d			22 16	22 19				22 24	22 31	22 34			22 46				22 54	23 00	23 04			23 14
Honor Oak Park	d			22 19	22 22				22 27	22 34	22 37			22 49				22 57	23 03	23 07			23 17
Forest Hill 4	d			22 21	22 25				22 30	22 36	22 40			22 51				23 00	23 05	23 10			23 19
Sydenham	d			22 24	22 27				22 32	22 39	22 42			22 54				23 02	23 08	23 12			23 22
Crystal Palace 4	d							22 22	22a37	22 43							23 00	23a07	23 13				
Gipsy Hill	d							22 24		22 45							23 02		23 15				
West Norwood 4	d							22 27		22 48							23 05		23 18				
Streatham Hill	d									22 52									23 22				
Balham 4 ⊖	d									22 56									23 26				
Wandsworth Common	d									22 58									23 28				
Clapham Junction 10	d									23 03									23 33				
South Bermondsey	d		22 07			22 15							22 37		22 45							23 09	
Queens Rd Peckham	d		22 09			22 18							22 39		22 48							23 11	
Peckham Rye 4	d		22a12			22 20	22 20	22a43					22a42		22 50	22 50	23a17					23 14	
Denmark Hill 4	d					22 23	22 24								22 53	22 54							
London Blackfriars 3 ⊖	a						22 34									23 04							
Clapham High Street ⊖	d					22 28									22 58								
Wandsworth Road	d					22 29									22 59								
Battersea Park 4	d					22 32				23 07					23 02				23 37				
London Victoria 15 ⊖	a					22 36				23 14					23 06				23 41				
Penge West	d			22 26	22 30						22 45			22 56						23 15			23 24
Anerley	d			22 28	22 32						22 47			22 58						23 17			23 26
Norwood Junction 2	d			22 32	22 35						22 50			23 02						23 20		23a36	23 30
West Croydon 4	a				22 42						23 00									23 30			
East Croydon	a			22 35										23 06									23 33

Table 178

Mondays to Fridays

13 August to 28 August

London Bridge to London Victoria - Croydon and East London Line

Network Diagram - see first Page of Table 177

		SN	SE	SN	LO	SN		LO	LO	SN	SN	LO	SN	LO	LO	LO
London Bridge 4 ⊖	d	23 11				23 22				23 33	23 36		23 52			
Highbury & Islington	a															
	d				22 55			23 05				23 25		23 35	23 42	23 56
Canonbury	d				22 57			23 07				23 27		23 37	23 44	23 58
Dalston Junction Stn ELL	d				23 00			23 10	23 20			23 30		23 40	23 47	00 02
Haggerston	d				23 01			23 11	23 21			23 31		23 41	23 48	00 03
Hoxton	d				23 03			23 13	23 23			23 33		23 43	23 50	00 05
Shoreditch High Street	d				23 06			23 16	23 26			23 36		23 46	23 53	00 08
Whitechapel	d				23 08			23 18	23 28			23 38		23 48	23 55	00 10
Shadwell	d				23 10			23 20	23 30			23 40		23 50	23 57	00 12
Wapping	d				23 12			23 22	23 32			23 42		23 52	23 59	00 14
Rotherhithe	d				23 14			23 24	23 34			23 44		23 54	00 01	00 16
Canada Water	d				23 16			23 26	23 36			23 46		23 56	00 03	00 18
Surrey Quays	d				23 17			23 27	23 37			23 47		23 57	00 05	00 19
New Cross ELL	a								23 42							
New Cross Gate 4	a				23 21	23 27		23 31			23 41	23 51	23 57	00 01	00 08	00 23
	d				23 22	23 27		23 32			23 41	23 52	23 57	00 02		
Brockley	d				23 24	23 30		23 34			23 44	23 54	00 01	00 04		
Honor Oak Park	d				23 27	23 33		23 37			23 47	23 57	00 04	00 07		
Forest Hill 4	d				23 30	23 35		23 40			23 49	23 59	00 06	00 10		
Sydenham	d				23 32	23 38		23 42			23 52	00 02	00 09	00 12		
Crystal Palace 4	d			23 30	23a37	23 43						00a07	00 13			
Gipsy Hill	d			23 32		23 45							00 15			
West Norwood 4	d			23 35		23 48							00 18			
Streatham Hill	d					23 52							00 22			
Balham 4 ⊖	d					23 55							00 25			
Wandsworth Common	d					23 58							00 27			
Clapham Junction 10	d					00 02							00 31			
South Bermondsey	d	23 15								23 37						
Queens Rd Peckham	d	23 18								23 39						
Peckham Rye 4	d	23 20	23 20	23a47						23 42						
Denmark Hill 4	d	23 23	23 24													
London Blackfriars 3 ⊖	a		23 34													
Clapham High Street ⊖	d	23 28														
Wandsworth Road	d	23 29														
Battersea Park 4	d	23 32				00 05							00 35			
London Victoria 15 ⊖	a	23 37				00 10							00 42			
Penge West	d							23 45			23 54			00 15		
Anerley	d							23 47			23 56			00 17		
Norwood Junction 2	d							23 50		00a04	23 59			00 20		
West Croydon 4	a							23 59						00 27		
East Croydon	a										00 03					

Mondays to Fridays

29 August to 7 September

		SN A	LO B	SN A	SN B	LO C	SN A	LO B	LO A	LO B	SN A	LO C	LO D	LO B	LO C	LO D	LO B	SN A	SN A	LO C	LO B	LO C	LO D
London Bridge 4 ⊖	d	23p22		23p36	23p39						23p52							00 03	00 06				
Highbury & Islington	a																						
	d		23p06			23p18		23p21	23p25	23p28		23p33	23p35	23p36	23p40	23p42	23p43			23p48	23p51	23p55	23p56
Canonbury	d		23p08			23p20		23p23	23p27	23p30		23p35	23p37	23p38	23p42	23p44	23p45			23p50	23p53	23p57	23p58
Dalston Junction Stn ELL	d		23p11			23p25		23p28	23p30	23p33		23p38	23p40	23p41	23p45	23p47	23p48			23p55	23p58	00 01	00 02
Haggerston	d		23p12			23p26		23p29	23p31	23p34		23p39	23p41	23p42	23p46	23p48	23p49			23p56	23p59	00 02	00 03
Hoxton	d		23p14			23p28		23p31	23p33	23p36		23p41	23p43	23p44	23p48	23p50	23p51			23p58	00 01	00 04	00 05
Shoreditch High Street	d		23p17			23p31		23p34	23p36	23p39		23p44	23p46	23p47	23p51	23p53	23p54			00 01	00 04	00 07	00 08
Whitechapel	d		23p19			23p33		23p36	23p38	23p41		23p46	23p48	23p49	23p53	23p55	23p56			00 03	00 06	00 09	00 10
Shadwell	d		23p21			23p35		23p38	23p40	23p43		23p48	23p50	23p51	23p55	23p57	23p58			00 05	00 08	00 11	00 12
Wapping	d		23p23			23p37		23p40	23p42	23p45		23p50	23p52	23p53	23p57	23p59	00 01			00 07	00 10	00 13	00 14
Rotherhithe	d		23p25			23p39		23p42	23p44	23p47		23p52	23p54	23p55	23p59	00 01	00 03			00 09	00 12	00 15	00 16
Canada Water	d		23p27			23p41		23p44	23p46	23p49		23p54	23p56	23p57	00 02	00 03	00 05			00 11	00 14	00 17	00 18
Surrey Quays	d		23p28			23p42		23p45	23p47	23p50		23p55	23p57	23p58	00 03	00 05	00 06			00 12	00 15	00 18	00 19
New Cross ELL	a																						
New Cross Gate 4	a	23p27	23p32	23p41	23p44	23p46		23p49	23p51	23p54	23p57	23p58	00 01	00 02	00 07	00 08	00 10		00 11	00 16	00 19	00 22	00 23
	d	23p27	23p33	23p41	23p44	23p47		23p50	23p52	23p55	23p57	23p59	00 02	00 03	00 08		00 11		00 11	00 17	00 20	00 23	
Brockley	d	23p30	23p35	23p44	23p47	23p49		23p52	23p54	23p57	00 01	00 03	00 04	00 06	00 10		00 13		00 14	00 19	00 22	00 25	
Honor Oak Park	d	23p33	23p38	23p47	23p50	23p52		23p55	23p57	00 01	00 04	00 06	00 07	00 09	00 13		00 16		00 17	00 22	00 25	00 28	
Forest Hill 4	d	23p35	23p41	23p49	23p52	23p55		23p58	23p59	00 04	00 06	00 09	00 10	00 12	00 16		00 19		00 19	00 25	00 28	00 31	
Sydenham	d	23p38	23p43	23p52	23p55	23p57		00 01	00 02	00 06	00 09	00 11	00 12	00 14	00 18		00 21		00 22	00 27	00 30	00 33	
Crystal Palace 4	d	23p43					00 03		00a07	00a11	00 13				00a23		00a26					00a38	
Gipsy Hill	d	23p45									00 15												
West Norwood 4	d	23p48									00 18												
Streatham Hill	d	23p52									00 22												
Balham 4 ⊖	d	23p55									00 25												
Wandsworth Common	d	23p58									00 27												
Clapham Junction 10	d	00 02									00 31												
South Bermondsey	d																	00 07					
Queens Rd Peckham	d																	00 09					
Peckham Rye 4	d																	00 12					
Denmark Hill 4	d																						
London Blackfriars 3 ⊖	a																						
Clapham High Street ⊖	d																						
Wandsworth Road	d																						
Battersea Park 4	d	00 05									00 35												
London Victoria 15 ⊖	a	00 10									00 42												
Penge West	d		23p46	23p54	23p57	00 01		00 04				00 14	00 15	00 17					00 24	00 30	00 33		
Anerley	d		23p48	23p56	23p59	00 03		00 06				00 16	00 17	00 19					00 26	00 32	00 35		
Norwood Junction 2	d		23p55	23p59	00 03	00 06	00 09	00 09				00 19	00 20	00 22				00a34	00 30	00 35	00 38		
West Croydon 4	a		00 03			00 13	00 14	00 16				00 26	00 27	00 29						00 42	00 45		
East Croydon	a			00 03	00 06														00 33				

A not 3 September
B 3 September
C not 29 August, 3 September
D 29 August

Table 178

Mondays to Fridays

29 August to 7 September

London Bridge to London Victoria - Croydon and East London Line

Network Diagram - see first Page of Table 177

		LO A	LO B	LO A	LO B	LO A		SN C	LO B	LO A	LO B	LO A	LO B	LO A	LO B	LO A		LO B	LO A	LO B	LO A	LO B	LO A	LO B	LO A
London Bridge 4 ⊖	d							00 36																	
Highbury & Islington	a																								
	d	23p58	00 03	00 06	00 10	00 13			00 18	00 21	00 25	00 28	00 33	00 36	00 40	00 43		00 48	00 51	00 55	00 58	01 03	01 06	01 10	01 13
Canonbury	d	00 01	00 05	00 08	00 12	00 15			00 20	00 23	00 27	00 30	00 35	00 38	00 42	00 45		00 50	00 53	00 57	01 00	01 05	01 08	01 12	01 15
Dalston Junction Stn ELL	d	00 04	00 10	00 13	00 15	00 18			00 25	00 28	00 30	00 33	00 40	00 43	00 45	00 48		00 55	00 58	01 00	01 03	01 10	01 13	01 15	01 18
Haggerston	d	00 06	00 11	00 14	00 16	00 19			00 26	00 29	00 31	00 34	00 41	00 44	00 46	00 49		00 56	00 59	01 01	01 04	01 11	01 14	01 16	01 19
Hoxton	d	00 08	00 13	00 16	00 18	00 21			00 28	00 31	00 33	00 36	00 43	00 46	00 48	00 51		00 58	01 01	01 03	01 06	01 13	01 16	01 18	01 21
Shoreditch High Street	d	00 10	00 16	00 19	00 21	00 24			00 31	00 34	00 36	00 39	00 46	00 49	00 51	00 54		01 01	01 04	01 06	01 09	01 16	01 19	01 21	01 24
Whitechapel	d	00 13	00 18	00 21	00 23	00 26			00 33	00 36	00 38	00 41	00 48	00 51	00 53	00 56		01 03	01 06	01 08	01 11	01 18	01 21	01 23	01 26
Shadwell	d	00 15	00 20	00 23	00 25	00 28			00 35	00 38	00 40	00 43	00 50	00 53	00 55	00 58		01 05	01 08	01 10	01 13	01 20	01 23	01 25	01 28
Wapping	d	00 17	00 22	00 25	00 27	00 30			00 37	00 40	00 42	00 45	00 52	00 55	00 57	01 00		01 07	01 10	01 12	01 15	01 22	01 25	01 27	01 30
Rotherhithe	d	00 18	00 24	00 27	00 29	00 32			00 39	00 42	00 44	00 47	00 54	00 57	00 59	01 02		01 09	01 12	01 14	01 17	01 24	01 27	01 29	01 32
Canada Water	d	00 20	00 26	00 29	00 31	00 34			00 41	00 44	00 46	00 49	00 56	00 59	01 01	01 04		01 11	01 14	01 16	01 19	01 26	01 29	01 31	01 34
Surrey Quays	d	00 22	00 27	00 30	00 32	00 35			00 42	00 45	00 47	00 50	00 57	01 00	01 02	01 05		01 12	01 15	01 17	01 20	01 27	01 30	01 32	01 35
New Cross ELL	a																								
New Cross Gate 4	a	00 25	00 31	00 34	00 36	00 39		00 41	00 47	00 50	00 51	00 54	01 02	01 05	01 06	01 09		01 16	01 19	01 21	01 24	01 31	01 34	01 36	01 39
	d	00 26	00 32	00 35	00 37	00 40		00 41	00 47	00 50	00 52	00 55	01 03	01 06	01 07	01 10		01 17	01 20	01 22	01 25	01 32	01 35	01 37	01 40
Brockley	d	00 29	00 34	00 37	00 39	00 42		00 44	00 49	00 52	00 54	00 57	01 05	01 08	01 09	01 12		01 19	01 22	01 24	01 27	01 34	01 37	01 39	01 42
Honor Oak Park	d	00 32	00 37	00 40	00 42	00 45		00 47	00 52	00 55	00 57	01 00	01 08	01 11	01 12	01 15		01 22	01 25	01 27	01 30	01 37	01 40	01 42	01 45
Forest Hill 4	d	00 34	00 40	00 43	00 45	00 48		00 49	00 55	00 58	00 59	01 02	01 11	01 14	01 15	01 18		01 25	01 28	01 30	01 33	01 40	01 43	01 45	01 48
Sydenham	d	00 37	00 42	00 45	00 47	00 50		00 52	00 57	01 00	01 02	01 05	01 13	01 16	01 17	01 20		01 27	01 30	01 32	01 35	01 42	01 45	01 47	01 50
Crystal Palace 4	d	00a41			00a52	00a55					01a07	01a10			01a22	01a25				01a37	01a40			01a52	01a55
Gipsy Hill	d																								
West Norwood 4	d																								
Streatham Hill	d																								
Balham 4 ⊖	d																								
Wandsworth Common	d																								
Clapham Junction 10	d																								
South Bermondsey	d																								
Queens Rd Peckham	d																								
Peckham Rye 4	d																								
Denmark Hill 4	d																								
London Blackfriars 3 ⊖	a																								
Clapham High Street ⊖	d																								
Wandsworth Road	d																								
Battersea Park 4	d																								
London Victoria 15 ⊖	a																								
Penge West	d		00 45	00 48				00 54	01 00	01 03			01 16	01 19				01 30	01 33			01 45	01 48		
Anerley	d		00 47	00 50				00 56	01 02	01 05			01 18	01 21				01 32	01 35			01 47	01 50		
Norwood Junction 2	d		00 50	00 53				01 00	01 05	01 08			01 21	01 24				01 35	01 38			01 50	01 53		
West Croydon 4	a		00 57	01 00					01 14	01 17			01 28	01 31				01 42	01 45			01 57	02 00		
East Croydon	a							01 03																	

		LO B		LO A	SE	SE	SN	SN	LO	LO	LO	LO		LO	SN	SN	LO	LO	SN	LO	LO	SN		SN	SE
London Bridge 4 ⊖	d						06 00								06 06	06 11			06 19			06 30		06 33	
Highbury & Islington	a																								
	d	01 25		01 28							05 35							05 55		06 05					
Canonbury	d	01 27		01 30							05 37							05 57		06 07					
Dalston Junction Stn ELL	d	01 32		01 35							05 40	05 50						06 00		06 10	06 20				
Haggerston	d	01 33		01 36							05 41	05 51						06 01		06 11	06 21				
Hoxton	d	01 35		01 38							05 43	05 53						06 03		06 13	06 23				
Shoreditch High Street	d	01 38		01 41							05 46	05 56						06 06		06 16	06 26				
Whitechapel	d	01 40		01 43							05 48	05 58						06 08		06 18	06 28				
Shadwell	d	01 42		01 45							05 50	06 00						06 10		06 20	06 30				
Wapping	d	01 44		01 47							05 52	06 02						06 12		06 22	06 32				
Rotherhithe	d	01 46		01 49							05 54	06 04						06 14		06 24	06 34				
Canada Water	d	01 48		01 51							05 56	06 06						06 16		06 26	06 36				
Surrey Quays	d	01 49		01 52							05 57	06 07						06 17		06 27	06 37				
New Cross ELL	a											06 12									06 42				
New Cross Gate 4	a	01 53		01 56							06 01				06 11			06 21	06 25	06 31					
	d	01 54		01 57					05 47	05 52	06 02			06 07	06 11		06 17	06 22	06 25	06 32					
Brockley	d	01 56		01 59					05 49	05 54	06 04			06 09	06 14		06 19	06 24	06 27	06 34					
Honor Oak Park	d	01 59		02 02					05 52	05 57	06 07			06 12	06 17		06 22	06 27	06 30	06 37					
Forest Hill 4	d	02 02		02 05					05 55	06 00	06 10			06 15	06 19		06 25	06 30	06 33	06 40					
Sydenham	d	02 04		02 07					05 57	06 02	06 12			06 17	06 22		06 27	06 32	06 35	06 42					
Crystal Palace 4	d							05 59		06a07				06a22				06a37	06 39						
Gipsy Hill	d							06 01											06 41						
West Norwood 4	d							06 04											06 44						
Streatham Hill	d																		06 48						
Balham 4 ⊖	d																		06 51						
Wandsworth Common	d																								
Clapham Junction 10	d																		06 56						
South Bermondsey	d						06 04									06 15						06 34		06 37	
Queens Rd Peckham	d						06 06									06 18						06 36		06 39	
Peckham Rye 4	d				05 04	06 04	06a09	06a15								06 20						06a39		06a42	06 47
Denmark Hill 4	d				05 07	06 07										06 23									06 50
London Blackfriars 3 ⊖	a				05 17	06 17																			
Clapham High Street ⊖	d															06 28									
Wandsworth Road	d															06 29									
Battersea Park 4	d															06 32									
London Victoria 15 ⊖	a															06 36			07 05						07 04
Penge West	d	02 07		02 10					06 00		06 15				06 24		06 30			06 45					
Anerley	d	02 09		02 12					06 02		06 17				06 26		06 32			06 47					
Norwood Junction 2	d	02 12		02 15					06 05		06 20				06 30		06 35			06 50					
West Croydon 4	a	02 19		02 22					06 13		06 30						06 41			07 00					
East Croydon	a														06 33										

A 3 September

B not 29 August, 3 September

C not 3 September

London Bridge to London Victoria - Croydon and East London Line

Network Diagram - see first Page of Table 177

		SN	LO	SN	SN	LO	LO	LO	SN	SN	LO	SN	SN	SN	LO	LO	SN	LO	LO	LO	SN	SE	SN
London Bridge 4 ⊖	d			06 36	06 41				06 51	06 54		06 58	07 03				07 06				07 11		07 21
Highbury & Islington	a																						
	d						06 25				06 33				06 40			06 48	06 55				
Canonbury	d						06 27				06 35				06 42			06 50	06 57				
Dalston Junction Stn ELL	d						06 30	06 35			06 40				06 45	06 50		06 55	07 00	07 05			
Haggerston	d						06 31	06 36			06 41				06 46	06 51		06 56	07 01	07 06			
Hoxton	d						06 33	06 38			06 43				06 48	06 53		06 58	07 03	07 08			
Shoreditch High Street	d						06 36	06 41			06 46				06 51	06 56		07 01	07 06	07 11			
Whitechapel	d						06 38	06 43			06 48				06 53	06 58		07 03	07 08	07 13			
Shadwell	d						06 40	06 45			06 50				06 55	07 00		07 05	07 10	07 15			
Wapping	d						06 42	06 47			06 52				06 57	07 02		07 07	07 12	07 17			
Rotherhithe	d						06 44	06 49			06 54				06 59	07 04		07 09	07 14	07 19			
Canada Water	d						06 46	06 51			06 56				07 01	07 06		07 11	07 16	07 21			
Surrey Quays	d						06 47	06 52			06 57				07 02	07 07		07 12	07 17	07 22			
New Cross ELL	a							06 57								07 12				07 27			
New Cross Gate 4	a			06 41			06 51		06 56	06 59	07 00				07 06		07 11	07 15	07 21				07 26
	d		06 37	06 41		06 47	06 52		06 56	06 59	07 02				07 07		07 11	07 17	07 22				07 26
Brockley	d		06 39	06 44		06 49	06 54		06 59	07 02	07 04				07 09		07 14	07 19	07 24				07 29
Honor Oak Park	d		06 42	06 47		06 52	06 57		07 02	07 05	07 07				07 12		07 17	07 22	07 27				07 32
Forest Hill 4	d		06 45	06 49		06 55	07 00		07 04	07 07	07 10				07 15		07 19	07 25	07 30				07 34
Sydenham	d		06 47	06 52		06 57	07 02		07 07	07 10	07 12				07 17		07 22	07 27	07 32				07 37
Crystal Palace 4	d	06 51	06a52				07a07		07 13					07 20	07a22				07a37				07 43
Gipsy Hill	d	06 53							07 15					07 22									07 45
West Norwood 4	d	06 56							07 18					07 25									07 48
Streatham Hill	d								07 22														07 52
Balham 4 ⊖	d								07 25														07 55
Wandsworth Common	d								07 27														07 57
Clapham Junction 10	d								07 31														08 01
South Bermondsey	d				06 45							07 02	07 07								07 15		
Queens Rd Peckham	d				06 48							07 04	07 09								07 17		
Peckham Rye 4	d	07a08			06 50							07a07	07a12	07a36							07 20	07 23	
Denmark Hill 4	d				06 53																07 23	07 29	
London Blackfriars 3 ⊖	a																						
Clapham High Street ⊖	d				06 58																07 28		
Wandsworth Road	d				06 59																07 29		
Battersea Park 4	d				07 02				07 35												07 32		08 05
London Victoria 15 ⊖	a				07 08				07 41												07 38	07 42	08 11
Penge West	d			06 54		07 00				07 12	07 15						07 24	07 30					
Anerley	d			06 56		07 02				07 14	07 17						07 26	07 32					
Norwood Junction 2	d			07 00		07 05				07 18	07 20						07 31	07 35					
West Croydon 4	a					07 11					07 30							07 42					
East Croydon	a			07 03						07 21							07 37						

		LO	SN	SN	SN	LO	LO	SN	LO	SN	SN	LO	LO	SE	SN	LO	SN	SE	SN	SN	LO	LO
London Bridge 4 ⊖	d		07 29	07 33				07 36		07 41	07 44				07 53		08 03		08 06			
Highbury & Islington	a																					
	d	07 03				07 10			07 18			07 25				07 33					07 40	
Canonbury	d	07 05				07 12			07 20			07 27				07 35					07 42	
Dalston Junction Stn ELL	d	07 10				07 15	07 20		07 25			07 30	07 35			07 40					07 45	07 50
Haggerston	d	07 11				07 16	07 21		07 26			07 31	07 36			07 41					07 46	07 51
Hoxton	d	07 13				07 18	07 23		07 28			07 33	07 38			07 43					07 48	07 53
Shoreditch High Street	d	07 16				07 21	07 26		07 31			07 36	07 41			07 46					07 51	07 56
Whitechapel	d	07 18				07 23	07 28		07 33			07 38	07 43			07 48					07 53	07 58
Shadwell	d	07 20				07 25	07 30		07 35			07 40	07 45			07 50					07 55	08 00
Wapping	d	07 22				07 27	07 32		07 37			07 42	07 47			07 52					07 57	08 02
Rotherhithe	d	07 24				07 29	07 34		07 39			07 44	07 49			07 54					07 59	08 04
Canada Water	d	07 26				07 31	07 36		07 41			07 46	07 51			07 56					08 01	08 06
Surrey Quays	d	07 27				07 32	07 37		07 42			07 47	07 52			07 57					08 02	08 07
New Cross ELL	a						07 42						07 57									08 12
New Cross Gate 4	a	07 31				07 36		07 41	07 45		07 49	07 51			07 58	08 01					08 06	
	d	07 32				07 37		07 41	07 47		07 49	07 52			07 58	08 02					08 07	
Brockley	d	07 34				07 39		07 44	07 49			07 54			08 01	08 04					08 09	
Honor Oak Park	d	07 37				07 42		07 47	07 52			07 57			08 04	08 07					08 12	
Forest Hill 4	d	07 40				07 45		07 49	07 55			08 00			08 06	08 10					08 15	
Sydenham	d	07 42				07 47		07 52	07 57			08 02			08 09	08 12					08 17	
Crystal Palace 4	d				07 49	07a52						08a07			08 13					08 19	08a22	
Gipsy Hill	d				07 51										08 15					08 21		
West Norwood 4	d				07 54										08 18					08 24		
Streatham Hill	d														08 22							
Balham 4 ⊖	d														08 25							
Wandsworth Common	d														08 27							
Clapham Junction 10	d														08 31							
South Bermondsey	d		07 33	07 37						07 45							08 07		08 11			
Queens Rd Peckham	d		07 35	07 39						07 47							08 09		08 13			
Peckham Rye 4	d		07a38	07a42	08a06					07 50				07 54			08a12	08 13	08a16	08a36		
Denmark Hill 4	d									07 53				07 59				08 17				
London Blackfriars 3 ⊖	a																					
Clapham High Street ⊖	d									07 58												
Wandsworth Road	d									07 59												
Battersea Park 4	d									08 02					08 35							
London Victoria 15 ⊖	a									08 08				08 11	08 41			08 29				
Penge West	d	07 45						07 54	08 00							08 15						
Anerley	d	07 47						07 56	08 02							08 17						
Norwood Junction 2	d	07 50						08 00	08 05							08 20						
West Croydon 4	a	08 00							08 12							08 30						
East Croydon	a							08 03			08 00											

Table 178

Mondays to Fridays

29 August to 7 September

London Bridge to London Victoria - Croydon and East London Line

Network Diagram - see first Page of Table 177

		SN	LO	LO	LO	SN	SE 1	SE	SN	LO		SN	SN	LO	LO	SN	LO	LO	LO	SN		SE	SE	SN	LO
London Bridge 4 ⊖	d	08 06				08 10			08 21			08 33				08 36				08 41		07b37		08 51	
Highbury & Islington	a																								
	d		07 48	07 55						08 03				08 10			08 18	08 25							08 33
Canonbury	d		07 50	07 57						08 05				08 12			08 20	08 27							08 35
Dalston Junction Stn ELL	d		07 55	08 00	08 05					08 10				08 15	08 20		08 25	08 30	08 35						08 40
Haggerston	d		07 56	08 01	08 06					08 11				08 16	08 21		08 26	08 31	08 36						08 41
Hoxton	d		07 58	08 03	08 08					08 13				08 18	08 23		08 28	08 33	08 38						08 43
Shoreditch High Street	d		08 01	08 06	08 11					08 16				08 21	08 26		08 31	08 36	08 41						08 46
Whitechapel	d		08 03	08 08	08 13					08 18				08 23	08 28		08 33	08 38	08 43						08 48
Shadwell	d		08 05	08 10	08 15					08 20				08 25	08 30		08 35	08 40	08 45						08 50
Wapping	d		08 07	08 12	08 17					08 22				08 27	08 32		08 37	08 42	08 47						08 52
Rotherhithe	d		08 09	08 14	08 19					08 24				08 29	08 34		08 39	08 44	08 49						08 54
Canada Water	d		08 11	08 16	08 21					08 26				08 31	08 36		08 41	08 46	08 51						08 56
Surrey Quays	d		08 12	08 17	08 22					08 27				08 32	08 37		08 42	08 47	08 52						08 57
New Cross ELL	a				08 27										08 42				08 57						
New Cross Gate 4	a	08 11	08 16	08 21					08 26	08 31				08 36		08 41	08 46	08 51						08 57	09 01
	d	08 11	08 17	08 22					08 26	08 32				08 37		08 41	08 47	08 52						08 57	09 02
Brockley	d	08 14	08 19	08 24					08 29	08 34				08 39		08 44	08 49	08 54						09 00	09 04
Honor Oak Park	d	08 17	08 22	08 27					08 32	08 37				08 42		08 47	08 52	08 57						09 03	09 07
Forest Hill 4	d	08 19	08 25	08 30					08 34	08 40				08 45		08 49	08 55	09 00						09 05	09 10
Sydenham	d	08 22	08 27	08 32					08 37	08 42				08 47		08 52	08 57	09 02						09 08	09 12
Crystal Palace 4	d			08a37					08 40				08 50	08a52				09a07						09 11	
Gipsy Hill	d								08 43				08 52											09 14	
West Norwood 4	d								08 46				08 55											09 17	
Streatham Hill	d								08 49															09 21	
Balham 4 ⊖	d								08 55															09 25	
Wandsworth Common	d								08 57															09 27	
Clapham Junction 10	d								09 01															09 31	
South Bermondsey	d					08 14						08 37								08 45					
Queens Rd Peckham	d					08 16						08 39								08 48					
Peckham Rye 4	d					08 19		08 33				08a42	09a07							08 50		08 55	08 55		
Denmark Hill 4	d					08 22	08 30	08 36												08 53		09 02	09 02		
London Blackfriars 3 ⊖	a																								
Clapham High Street ⊖	d					08 27														08 58					
Wandsworth Road	d					08 29														08 59					
Battersea Park 4	d					08 32			09 05											09 02				09 35	
London Victoria 15 ⊖	a					08 39	08 42	08 49	09 11											09 08		09 11	09 11	09 42	
Penge West	d	08 24	08 30							08 45						08 54	09 00								09 15
Anerley	d	08 26	08 32							08 47						08 56	09 02								09 17
Norwood Junction 2	d	08 30	08 35							08 50						09 00	09 05								09 20
West Croydon 4	a		08 43							09 00							09 12								09 30
East Croydon	a	08 33														09 06									

		LO	LO	SN	SN	LO		SE	SN	SN	LO	LO	SN	LO	LO	LO		SN	SN	LO	SE	SN	SN	LO	LO
London Bridge 4 ⊖	d			09 03	09 06				09 11				09 22					09 33	09 36			09 41			
Highbury & Islington	a																								
	d	08 40				08 48					08 55			09 03	09 10					09 18				09 25	
Canonbury	d	08 42				08 50					08 57			09 05	09 12					09 20				09 27	
Dalston Junction Stn ELL	d	08 46	08 50			08 55					09 01	09 05		09 10	09 15	09 20				09 25				09 30	09 35
Haggerston	d	08 47	08 51			08 56					09 02	09 06		09 11	09 16	09 21				09 26				09 31	09 36
Hoxton	d	08 49	08 53			08 58					09 04	09 08		09 13	09 18	09 23				09 28				09 33	09 38
Shoreditch High Street	d	08 52	08 56			09 01					09 07	09 11		09 16	09 21	09 26				09 31				09 36	09 41
Whitechapel	d	08 54	08 58			09 03					09 09	09 13		09 18	09 23	09 28				09 33				09 38	09 43
Shadwell	d	08 56	09 00			09 05					09 11	09 15		09 20	09 25	09 30				09 35				09 40	09 45
Wapping	d	08 58	09 02			09 07					09 13	09 17		09 22	09 27	09 32				09 37				09 42	09 47
Rotherhithe	d	09 00	09 04			09 09					09 15	09 19		09 24	09 29	09 34				09 39				09 44	09 49
Canada Water	d	09 02	09 06			09 11					09 17	09 21		09 26	09 31	09 36				09 41				09 46	09 51
Surrey Quays	d	09 03	09 07			09 12					09 18	09 22		09 27	09 32	09 37				09 42				09 47	09 52
New Cross ELL	a		09 12									09 27				09 42									09 57
New Cross Gate 4	a	09 07			09 12	09 16					09 22		09 28	09 30	09 36				09 41	09 46				09 51	
	d	09 08			09 12	09 17					09 23		09 28	09 32	09 37				09 41	09 47				09 52	
Brockley	d	09 10			09 14	09 19					09 25		09 30	09 34	09 39				09 44	09 49				09 54	
Honor Oak Park	d	09 13			09 17	09 22					09 28		09 33	09 37	09 42				09 47	09 52				09 57	
Forest Hill 4	d	09 16			09 20	09 25					09 31		09 36	09 40	09 45				09 49	09 55				10 00	
Sydenham	d	09 18			09 22	09 27					09 33		09 38	09 42	09 47				09 52	09 57				10 02	
Crystal Palace 4	d	09a23								09 30	09a38		09 43		09a52								10 00	10a07	
Gipsy Hill	d									09 32			09 46										10 02		
West Norwood 4	d									09 35			09 49										10 05		
Streatham Hill	d												09 52												
Balham 4 ⊖	d												09 56												
Wandsworth Common	d												09 58												
Clapham Junction 10	d												10 02												
South Bermondsey	d			09 07					09 15									09 37				09 45			
Queens Rd Peckham	d			09 09					09 18									09 39				09 48			
Peckham Rye 4	d			09a12				09 14	09 20	09a47								09a42			09 45	09 50	10a17		
Denmark Hill 4	d							09 17	09 23												09 49	09 53			
London Blackfriars 3 ⊖	a																								
Clapham High Street ⊖	d								09 28													09 58			
Wandsworth Road	d								09 29													09 59			
Battersea Park 4	d								09 32				10 05									10 03			
London Victoria 15 ⊖	a							09 29	09 38				10 11								10 00	10 07			
Penge West	d				09 25	09 30								09 45					09 54	10 00					
Anerley	d				09 27	09 32								09 47					09 56	10 02					
Norwood Junction 2	d				09 30	09 35								09 50					10 00	10 05					
West Croydon 4	a					09 42								10 00						10 12					
East Croydon	a				09 33														10 03						

b London Bridge-l

London Bridge to London Victoria - Croydon and East London Line

Network Diagram - see first Page of Table 177

		SN		LO	LO	LO	SN	SN	LO	SE	SN	SN		LO	LO	SN	LO	LO	LO	SN	SN	LO		SE	SN
London Bridge 4 ⊖	d	09 52					10 03	10 06			10 11					10 22				10 33	10 36				10 41
Highbury & Islington	a																								
	d			09 33	09 40				09 48					09 55			10 03	10 10				10 18			
Canonbury	d			09 35	09 42				09 50					09 57			10 05	10 12				10 20			
Dalston Junction Stn ELL	d			09 40	09 45	09 50			09 55					10 00	10 05		10 10	10 15	10 20			10 25			
Haggerston	d			09 41	09 46	09 51			09 56					10 01	10 06		10 11	10 16	10 21			10 26			
Hoxton	d			09 43	09 48	09 53			09 58					10 03	10 08		10 13	10 18	10 23			10 28			
Shoreditch High Street	d			09 46	09 51	09 56			10 01					10 06	10 11		10 16	10 21	10 26			10 31			
Whitechapel	d			09 48	09 53	09 58			10 03					10 08	10 13		10 18	10 23	10 28			10 33			
Shadwell	d			09 50	09 55	10 00			10 05					10 10	10 15		10 20	10 25	10 30			10 35			
Wapping	d			09 52	09 57	10 02			10 07					10 12	10 17		10 22	10 27	10 32			10 37			
Rotherhithe	d			09 54	09 59	10 04			10 09					10 14	10 19		10 24	10 29	10 34			10 39			
Canada Water	d			09 56	10 01	10 06			10 11					10 16	10 21		10 26	10 31	10 36			10 41			
Surrey Quays	d			09 57	10 02	10 07			10 12					10 17	10 22		10 27	10 32	10 37			10 42			
New Cross ELL	a					10 12									10 27				10 42						
New Cross Gate 4	a	09 57		10 01	10 06			10 11	10 16					10 21		10 27	10 31	10 36			10 41	10 46			
	d	09 57		10 02	10 07			10 11	10 17					10 22		10 27	10 32	10 37			10 41	10 47			
Brockley	d	10 00		10 04	10 09			10 14	10 19					10 24		10 30	10 34	10 39			10 44	10 49			
Honor Oak Park	d	10 03		10 07	10 12			10 17	10 22					10 27		10 33	10 37	10 42			10 47	10 52			
Forest Hill 4	d	10 05		10 10	10 15			10 19	10 25					10 30		10 35	10 40	10 45			10 49	10 55			
Sydenham	d	10 08		10 12	10 17			10 22	10 27					10 32		10 38	10 42	10 47			10 52	10 57			
Crystal Palace 4	d	10 13			10a22							10 30		10a37		10 43		10a52							
Gipsy Hill	d	10 15										10 32				10 45									
West Norwood 4	d	10 18										10 35				10 48									
Streatham Hill	d	10 22														10 52									
Balham 4 ⊖	d	10 25														10 55									
Wandsworth Common	d	10 27														10 57									
Clapham Junction 10	d	10 31														11 01									
South Bermondsey	d						10 07				10 15									10 37					10 45
Queens Rd Peckham	d						10 09				10 18									10 39					10 48
Peckham Rye 4	d						10a12			10 15	10 20	10a47								10a42				10 45	10 50
Denmark Hill 4	d									10 19	10 23													10 49	10 53
London Blackfriars 3 ⊖	a																								
Clapham High Street ⊖	d										10 28														10 58
Wandsworth Road	d										10 29														10 59
Battersea Park 4	d	10 35									10 32					11 05									11 02
London Victoria 15 ⊖	a	10 39								10 28	10 36					11 09								10 58	11 06
Penge West	d			10 15				10 24	10 30								10 45				10 54	11 00			
Anerley	d			10 17				10 26	10 32								10 47				10 56	11 02			
Norwood Junction 2	d			10 20				10 30	10 35								10 50				11 00	11 05			
West Croydon 4	a			10 30					10 42								11 00					11 12			
East Croydon	a							10 33													11 03				

		SN	LO	LO	SN	LO	LO	LO		SN	SN	LO	SE	SN	SN	LO	LO	SN		LO	LO	LO	SN	SN	LO
London Bridge 4 ⊖	d				10 52					11 03	11 06			11 11				11 22					11 33	11 36	
Highbury & Islington	a																								
	d		10 25			10 33	10 40					10 48				10 55				11 03	11 10				11 18
Canonbury	d		10 27			10 35	10 42					10 50				10 57				11 05	11 12				11 20
Dalston Junction Stn ELL	d		10 30	10 35		10 40	10 45	10 50				10 55				11 00	11 05			11 10	11 15	11 20			11 25
Haggerston	d		10 31	10 36		10 41	10 46	10 51				10 56				11 01	11 06			11 11	11 16	11 21			11 26
Hoxton	d		10 33	10 38		10 43	10 48	10 53				10 58				11 03	11 08			11 13	11 18	11 23			11 28
Shoreditch High Street	d		10 36	10 41		10 46	10 51	10 56				11 01				11 06	11 11			11 16	11 21	11 26			11 31
Whitechapel	d		10 38	10 43		10 48	10 53	10 58				11 03				11 08	11 13			11 18	11 23	11 28			11 33
Shadwell	d		10 40	10 45		10 50	10 55	11 00				11 05				11 10	11 15			11 20	11 25	11 30			11 35
Wapping	d		10 42	10 47		10 52	10 57	11 02				11 07				11 12	11 17			11 22	11 27	11 32			11 37
Rotherhithe	d		10 44	10 49		10 54	10 59	11 04				11 09				11 14	11 19			11 24	11 29	11 34			11 39
Canada Water	d		10 46	10 51		10 56	11 01	11 06				11 11				11 16	11 21			11 26	11 31	11 36			11 41
Surrey Quays	d		10 47	10 52		10 57	11 02	11 07				11 12				11 17	11 22			11 27	11 32	11 37			11 42
New Cross ELL	a			10 57				11 12									11 27					11 42			
New Cross Gate 4	a		10 51		10 57	11 01	11 06				11 11	11 16				11 21		11 27		11 31	11 36			11 41	11 46
	d		10 52		10 57	11 02	11 07				11 11	11 17				11 22		11 27		11 32	11 37			11 41	11 47
Brockley	d		10 54		11 00	11 04	11 09				11 14	11 19				11 24		11 30		11 34	11 39			11 44	11 49
Honor Oak Park	d		10 57		11 03	11 07	11 12				11 17	11 22				11 27		11 33		11 37	11 42			11 47	11 52
Forest Hill 4	d		11 00		11 05	11 10	11 15				11 19	11 25				11 30		11 35		11 40	11 45			11 49	11 55
Sydenham	d		11 02		11 08	11 12	11 17				11 22	11 27				11 32		11 38		11 42	11 47			11 52	11 57
Crystal Palace 4	d	11 00	11a07		11 13		11a22								11 30	11a37		11 43			11a52				
Gipsy Hill	d	11 02			11 15										11 32			11 45							
West Norwood 4	d	11 05			11 18										11 35			11 48							
Streatham Hill	d				11 22													11 52							
Balham 4 ⊖	d				11 25													11 55							
Wandsworth Common	d				11 27													11 57							
Clapham Junction 10	d				11 31													12 01							
South Bermondsey	d									11 07				11 15									11 37		
Queens Rd Peckham	d									11 09				11 18									11 39		
Peckham Rye 4	d	11a17								11a12			11 15	11 20	11a47								11a42		
Denmark Hill 4	d												11 19	11 23											
London Blackfriars 3 ⊖	a																								
Clapham High Street ⊖	d													11 28											
Wandsworth Road	d													11 29											
Battersea Park 4	d				11 35									11 32				12 05							
London Victoria 15 ⊖	a				11 39								11 28	11 36				12 09							
Penge West	d					11 15					11 24	11 30								11 45				11 54	12 00
Anerley	d					11 17					11 26	11 32								11 47				11 56	12 02
Norwood Junction 2	d					11 20					11 30	11 35								11 50				12 00	12 05
West Croydon 4	a					11 30						11 42								12 00					12 12
East Croydon	a										11 33													12 03	

Mondays to Fridays

29 August to 7 September

London Bridge to London Victoria - Croydon and East London Line

Network Diagram - see first Page of Table 177

		SE	SN	SN		LO	LO	SN	LO	LO	LO	SN	SN	LO		SE	SN	SN	LO	LO	SN	LO	LO	LO	
London Bridge 4 ⊖	d		11 41					11 52				12 03	12 06				12 11				12 22				
Highbury & Islington	a																								
	d					11 25			11 33	11 40				11 48					11 55			12 03	12 10		
Canonbury	d					11 27			11 35	11 42				11 50					11 57			12 05	12 12		
Dalston Junction Stn ELL	d					11 30	11 35		11 40	11 45	11 50			11 55					12 00	12 05		12 10	12 15	12 20	
Haggerston	d					11 31	11 36		11 41	11 46	11 51			11 56					12 01	12 06		12 11	12 16	12 21	
Hoxton	d					11 33	11 38		11 43	11 48	11 53			11 58					12 03	12 08		12 13	12 18	12 23	
Shoreditch High Street	d					11 36	11 41		11 46	11 51	11 56			12 01					12 06	12 11		12 16	12 21	12 26	
Whitechapel	d					11 38	11 43		11 48	11 53	11 58			12 03					12 08	12 13		12 18	12 23	12 28	
Shadwell	d					11 40	11 45		11 50	11 55	12 00			12 05					12 10	12 15		12 20	12 25	12 30	
Wapping	d					11 42	11 47		11 52	11 57	12 02			12 07					12 12	12 17		12 22	12 27	12 32	
Rotherhithe	d					11 44	11 49		11 54	11 59	12 04			12 09					12 14	12 19		12 24	12 29	12 34	
Canada Water	d					11 46	11 51		11 56	12 01	12 06			12 11					12 16	12 21		12 26	12 31	12 36	
Surrey Quays	d					11 47	11 52		11 57	12 02	12 07			12 12					12 17	12 22		12 27	12 32	12 37	
New Cross ELL	a						11 57				12 12									12 27				12 42	
New Cross Gate 4	a					11 51		11 57	12 01	12 06			12 11	12 16					12 21		12 27	12 31	12 36		
	d					11 52		11 57	12 02	12 07			12 11	12 17					12 22		12 27	12 32	12 37		
Brockley	d					11 54		12 00	12 04	12 09			12 14	12 19					12 24		12 30	12 34	12 39		
Honor Oak Park	d					11 57		12 03	12 07	12 12			12 17	12 22					12 27		12 33	12 37	12 42		
Forest Hill 4	d					12 00		12 05	12 10	12 15			12 19	12 25					12 30		12 35	12 40	12 45		
Sydenham	d					12 02		12 08	12 12	12 17			12 22	12 27					12 32		12 38	12 42	12 47		
Crystal Palace 4	d			12 00		12a07		12 13		12a22								12 30	12a37		12 43		12a52		
Gipsy Hill	d			12 02				12 15										12 32			12 45				
West Norwood 4	d			12 05				12 18										12 35			12 48				
Streatham Hill	d							12 22													12 52				
Balham 4 ⊖	d							12 25													12 55				
Wandsworth Common	d							12 27													12 57				
Clapham Junction 10	d							12 31													13 01				
South Bermondsey	d		11 45									12 07					12 15								
Queens Rd Peckham	d		11 48									12 09					12 18								
Peckham Rye 4	d	11 45	11 50	12a17								12a12				12 15	12 20	12a47							
Denmark Hill 4	d	11 49	11 54													12 19	12 23								
London Blackfriars 3 ⊖	a																								
Clapham High Street ⊖	d		11 58														12 28								
Wandsworth Road	d		12 00														12 29								
Battersea Park 4	d		12 02					12 35									12 32				13 05				
London Victoria 15 ⊖	a	11 58	12 07					12 39								12 28	12 36				13 09				
Penge West	d								12 15				12 24	12 30								12 45			
Anerley	d								12 17				12 26	12 32								12 47			
Norwood Junction 2	d								12 20				12 30	12 35								12 50			
West Croydon 4	a								12 30					12 42								13 00			
East Croydon	a												12 33												

		SN	SN	LO	SE	SN	SN	LO	LO	SN		LO	LO	LO	SN	SN	LO	SE	SN	SN		LO	LO	SN	LO
London Bridge 4 ⊖	d	12 33	12 36			12 41				12 52					13 03	13 06			13 11					13 22	
Highbury & Islington	a																								
	d			12 18				12 25				12 33	12 40				12 48					12 55			13 03
Canonbury	d			12 20				12 27				12 35	12 42				12 50					12 57			13 05
Dalston Junction Stn ELL	d			12 25				12 30	12 35			12 40	12 45	12 50			12 55					13 00	13 05		13 10
Haggerston	d			12 26				12 31	12 36			12 41	12 46	12 51			12 56					13 01	13 06		13 11
Hoxton	d			12 28				12 33	12 38			12 43	12 48	12 53			12 58					13 03	13 08		13 13
Shoreditch High Street	d			12 31				12 36	12 41			12 46	12 51	12 56			13 01					13 06	13 11		13 16
Whitechapel	d			12 33				12 38	12 43			12 48	12 53	12 58			13 03					13 08	13 13		13 18
Shadwell	d			12 35				12 40	12 45			12 50	12 55	13 00			13 05					13 10	13 15		13 20
Wapping	d			12 37				12 42	12 47			12 52	12 57	13 02			13 07					13 12	13 17		13 22
Rotherhithe	d			12 39				12 44	12 49			12 54	12 59	13 04			13 09					13 14	13 19		13 24
Canada Water	d			12 41				12 46	12 51			12 56	13 01	13 06			13 11					13 16	13 21		13 26
Surrey Quays	d			12 42				12 47	12 52			12 57	13 02	13 07			13 12					13 17	13 22		13 27
New Cross ELL	a								12 57					13 12									13 27		
New Cross Gate 4	a		12 41	12 46				12 51		12 57		13 01	13 06			13 11	13 16					13 21		13 27	13 31
	d		12 41	12 47				12 52		12 57		13 02	13 07			13 11	13 17					13 22		13 27	13 32
Brockley	d		12 44	12 49				12 54		13 00		13 04	13 09			13 14	13 19					13 24		13 30	13 34
Honor Oak Park	d		12 47	12 52				12 57		13 03		13 07	13 12			13 17	13 22					13 27		13 33	13 37
Forest Hill 4	d		12 49	12 55				13 00		13 05		13 10	13 15			13 19	13 25					13 30		13 35	13 40
Sydenham	d		12 52	12 57				13 02		13 08		13 12	13 17			13 22	13 27					13 32		13 38	13 42
Crystal Palace 4	d						13 00	13a07		13 13			13a22							13 30		13a37		13 43	
Gipsy Hill	d						13 02			13 15										13 32				13 45	
West Norwood 4	d						13 05			13 18										13 35				13 48	
Streatham Hill	d									13 22														13 52	
Balham 4 ⊖	d									13 25														13 55	
Wandsworth Common	d									13 27														13 57	
Clapham Junction 10	d									13 31														14 01	
South Bermondsey	d	12 37				12 45									13 07				13 15						
Queens Rd Peckham	d	12 39				12 48									13 09				13 18						
Peckham Rye 4	d	12a42			12 45	12 50	13a17								13a12			13 15	13 20	13a47					
Denmark Hill 4	d				12 49	12 53												13 19	13 23						
London Blackfriars 3 ⊖	a																								
Clapham High Street ⊖	d					12 58													13 28						
Wandsworth Road	d					12 59													13 29						
Battersea Park 4	d					13 02				13 35									13 32					14 05	
London Victoria 15 ⊖	a				12 58	13 06				13 39								13 28	13 36					14 09	
Penge West	d		12 54	13 00								13 15				13 24	13 30								13 45
Anerley	d		12 56	13 02								13 17				13 26	13 32								13 47
Norwood Junction 2	d		13 00	13 05								13 20				13 30	13 35								13 50
West Croydon 4	a			13 12								13 30					13 42								14 00
East Croydon	a		13 03													13 33									

London Bridge to London Victoria - Croydon and East London Line

Network Diagram - see first Page of Table 177

		LO	LO	SN	SN	LO		SE	SN	SN	LO	LO	SN	LO	LO	LO		SN	SN	LO	SE	SN	SN	LO	LO
London Bridge 4 ⊖	d			13 33	13 36				13 41				13 52					14 03	14 06			14 11			
Highbury & Islington	a																								
	d	13 10				13 18					13 25			13 33	13 40					13 48				13 55	
Canonbury	d	13 12				13 20					13 27			13 35	13 42					13 50				13 57	
Dalston Junction Stn ELL	d	13 15	13 20			13 25					13 30	13 35		13 40	13 45	13 50				13 55				14 00	14 05
Haggerston	d	13 16	13 21			13 26					13 31	13 36		13 41	13 46	13 51				13 56				14 01	14 06
Hoxton	d	13 18	13 23			13 28					13 33	13 38		13 43	13 48	13 53				13 58				14 03	14 08
Shoreditch High Street	d	13 21	13 26			13 31					13 36	13 41		13 46	13 51	13 56				14 01				14 06	14 11
Whitechapel	d	13 23	13 28			13 33					13 38	13 43		13 48	13 53	13 58				14 03				14 08	14 13
Shadwell	d	13 25	13 30			13 35					13 40	13 45		13 50	13 55	14 00				14 05				14 10	14 15
Wapping	d	13 27	13 32			13 37					13 42	13 47		13 52	13 57	14 02				14 07				14 12	14 17
Rotherhithe	d	13 29	13 34			13 39					13 44	13 49		13 54	13 59	14 04				14 09				14 14	14 19
Canada Water	d	13 31	13 36			13 41					13 46	13 51		13 56	14 01	14 06				14 11				14 16	14 21
Surrey Quays	d	13 32	13 37			13 42					13 47	13 52		13 57	14 02	14 07				14 12				14 17	14 22
New Cross ELL	a		13 42									13 57				14 12									14 27
New Cross Gate 4	a	13 36			13 41	13 46					13 51		13 57	14 01	14 06				14 11	14 16				14 21	
	d	13 37			13 41	13 47					13 52		13 57	14 02	14 07				14 11	14 17				14 22	
Brockley	d	13 39			13 44	13 49					13 54		14 00	14 04	14 09				14 14	14 19				14 24	
Honor Oak Park	d	13 42			13 47	13 52					13 57		14 03	14 07	14 12				14 17	14 22				14 27	
Forest Hill 4	d	13 45			13 49	13 55					14 00		14 05	14 10	14 15				14 19	14 25				14 30	
Sydenham	d	13 47			13 52	13 57					14 02		14 08	14 12	14 17				14 22	14 27				14 32	
Crystal Palace 4	d	13a52								14 00	14a07		14 13		14a22								14 30	14a37	
Gipsy Hill	d									14 02			14 15										14 32		
West Norwood 4	d									14 05			14 18										14 35		
Streatham Hill	d												14 22												
Balham 4 ⊖	d												14 25												
Wandsworth Common	d												14 27												
Clapham Junction 10	d												14 31												
South Bermondsey	d			13 37					13 45									14 07				14 15			
Queens Rd Peckham	d			13 39					13 48									14 09				14 18			
Peckham Rye 4	d			13a42				13 45	13 50	14a17								14a12			14 15	14 20	14a47		
Denmark Hill 4	d							13 49	13 53												14 19	14 23			
London Blackfriars 3 ⊖	a																								
Clapham High Street ⊖	d								13 58													14 28			
Wandsworth Road	d								13 59													14 29			
Battersea Park 4	d								14 02				14 35									14 32			
London Victoria 15 ⊖	a							13 58	14 06				14 39								14 28	14 36			
Penge West	d				13 54	14 00								14 15					14 24	14 30					
Anerley	d				13 56	14 02								14 17					14 26	14 32					
Norwood Junction 2	d				14 00	14 05								14 20					14 30	14 35					
West Croydon 4	a					14 12								14 30						14 42					
East Croydon	a				14 03														14 33						

		SN		LO	LO	LO	SN	SN	LO	SE	SN	SN		LO	LO	SN	LO	LO	LO	SN	SN	LO		SE	SN
London Bridge 4 ⊖	d	14 22					14 33	14 36			14 41					14 52				15 03	15 06				15 11
Highbury & Islington	a																								
	d			14 03	14 10				14 18					14 25			14 33	14 40				14 48			
Canonbury	d			14 05	14 12				14 20					14 27			14 35	14 42				14 50			
Dalston Junction Stn ELL	d			14 10	14 15	14 20			14 25					14 30	14 35		14 40	14 45	14 50			14 55			
Haggerston	d			14 11	14 16	14 21			14 26					14 31	14 36		14 41	14 46	14 51			14 56			
Hoxton	d			14 13	14 18	14 23			14 28					14 33	14 38		14 43	14 48	14 53			14 58			
Shoreditch High Street	d			14 16	14 21	14 26			14 31					14 36	14 41		14 46	14 51	14 56			15 01			
Whitechapel	d			14 18	14 23	14 28			14 33					14 38	14 43		14 48	14 53	14 58			15 03			
Shadwell	d			14 20	14 25	14 30			14 35					14 40	14 45		14 50	14 55	15 00			15 05			
Wapping	d			14 22	14 27	14 32			14 37					14 42	14 47		14 52	14 57	15 02			15 07			
Rotherhithe	d			14 24	14 29	14 34			14 39					14 44	14 49		14 54	14 59	15 04			15 09			
Canada Water	d			14 26	14 31	14 36			14 41					14 46	14 51		14 56	15 01	15 06			15 11			
Surrey Quays	d			14 27	14 32	14 37			14 42					14 47	14 52		14 57	15 02	15 07			15 12			
New Cross ELL	a					14 42									14 57				15 12						
New Cross Gate 4	a	14 27		14 31	14 36			14 41	14 46					14 51		14 57	15 01	15 06			15 11	15 16			
	d	14 27		14 32	14 37			14 41	14 47					14 52		14 57	15 02	15 07			15 11	15 17			
Brockley	d	14 30		14 34	14 39			14 44	14 49					14 54		15 00	15 04	15 09			15 14	15 19			
Honor Oak Park	d	14 33		14 37	14 42			14 47	14 52					14 57		15 03	15 07	15 12			15 17	15 22			
Forest Hill 4	d	14 35		14 40	14 45			14 49	14 55					15 00		15 05	15 10	15 15			15 19	15 25			
Sydenham	d	14 38		14 42	14 47			14 52	14 57					15 02		15 08	15 12	15 17			15 22	15 27			
Crystal Palace 4	d	14 43			14a52							15 00		15a07		15 13		15a22							
Gipsy Hill	d	14 45										15 02				15 15									
West Norwood 4	d	14 48										15 05				15 18									
Streatham Hill	d	14 52														15 22									
Balham 4 ⊖	d	14 55														15 25									
Wandsworth Common	d	14 57														15 27									
Clapham Junction 10	d	15 01														15 31									
South Bermondsey	d						14 37				14 45									15 07					15 15
Queens Rd Peckham	d						14 39				14 48									15 09					15 18
Peckham Rye 4	d						14a42			14 45	14 50	15a17								15a12				15 15	15 20
Denmark Hill 4	d									14 49	14 53													15 19	15 23
London Blackfriars 3 ⊖	a																								
Clapham High Street ⊖	d										14 58														15 28
Wandsworth Road	d										14 59														15 29
Battersea Park 4	d	15 05									15 02					15 35									15 32
London Victoria 15 ⊖	a	15 09								14 58	15 06					15 39								15 28	15 36
Penge West	d			14 45				14 54	15 00								15 15				15 24	15 30			
Anerley	d			14 47				14 56	15 02								15 17				15 26	15 32			
Norwood Junction 2	d			14 50				15 00	15 05								15 20				15 30	15 35			
West Croydon 4	a			15 00					15 12								15 30					15 42			
East Croydon	a							15 03													15 33				

London Bridge to London Victoria - Croydon and East London Line

Network Diagram - see first Page of Table 177

		SN	LO	LO	SN	LO	LO	LO		SN	SN	LO	SE	SN	SN	SN	LO	LO		SN	LO	LO	LO	SN	SN
London Bridge 4 ⊖	d				15 22					15 33	15 36			15 41						15 52				16 03	16 06
Highbury & Islington	a																								
	d		14 55			15 03	15 10					15 18					15 25				15 33	15 40			
Canonbury	d		14 57			15 05	15 12					15 20					15 27				15 35	15 42			
Dalston Junction Stn ELL	d		15 00	15 05		15 10	15 15	15 20				15 25					15 30	15 35			15 40	15 45	15 50		
Haggerston	d		15 01	15 06		15 11	15 16	15 21				15 26					15 31	15 36			15 41	15 46	15 51		
Hoxton	d		15 03	15 08		15 13	15 18	15 23				15 28					15 33	15 38			15 43	15 48	15 53		
Shoreditch High Street	d		15 06	15 11		15 16	15 21	15 26				15 31					15 36	15 41			15 46	15 51	15 56		
Whitechapel	d		15 08	15 13		15 18	15 23	15 28				15 33					15 38	15 43			15 48	15 53	15 58		
Shadwell	d		15 10	15 15		15 20	15 25	15 30				15 35					15 40	15 45			15 50	15 55	16 00		
Wapping	d		15 12	15 17		15 22	15 27	15 32				15 37					15 42	15 47			15 52	15 57	16 02		
Rotherhithe	d		15 14	15 19		15 24	15 29	15 34				15 39					15 44	15 49			15 54	15 59	16 04		
Canada Water	d		15 16	15 21		15 26	15 31	15 36				15 41					15 46	15 51			15 56	16 01	16 06		
Surrey Quays	d		15 17	15 22		15 27	15 32	15 37				15 42					15 47	15 52			15 57	16 02	16 07		
New Cross ELL	a			15 27				15 42										15 57					16 12		
New Cross Gate 4	a		15 21		15 27	15 31	15 36				15 41	15 46					15 51			15 57	16 01	16 06			16 11
	d		15 22		15 27	15 32	15 37				15 41	15 47					15 52			15 57	16 02	16 07			16 11
Brockley	d		15 24		15 30	15 34	15 39				15 44	15 49					15 54			16 00	16 04	16 09			16 14
Honor Oak Park	d		15 27		15 33	15 37	15 42				15 47	15 52					15 57			16 03	16 07	16 12			16 17
Forest Hill 4	d		15 30		15 35	15 40	15 45				15 49	15 55					16 00			16 05	16 10	16 15			16 19
Sydenham	d		15 32		15 38	15 42	15 47				15 52	15 57					16 02			16 08	16 12	16 17			16 22
Crystal Palace 4	d	15 30	15a37		15 43		15a52									16 00	16a07			16 13		16a22			
Gipsy Hill	d	15 32			15 45											16 02				16 15					
West Norwood 4	d	15 35			15 48											16 05				16 18					
Streatham Hill	d				15 52															16 22					
Balham 4 ⊖	d				15 55										15 56					16 25					
Wandsworth Common	d				15 57															16 27					
Clapham Junction 10	d				16 01															16 31					
South Bermondsey	d									15 37				15 45										16 07	
Queens Rd Peckham	d									15 39				15 48										16 09	
Peckham Rye 4	d	15a47								15a42			15 45	15 50	16a07	16a17								16a12	
Denmark Hill 4	d												15 49	15 53											
London Blackfriars 3 ⊖	a																								
Clapham High Street ⊖	d													15 58											
Wandsworth Road	d													15 59											
Battersea Park 4	d				16 05									16 02						16 35					
London Victoria 15 ⊖	a				16 10								15 58	16 06						16 40					
Penge West	d					15 45					15 54	16 00									16 15				16 24
Anerley	d					15 47					15 56	16 02									16 17				16 26
Norwood Junction 2	d					15 50					16 00	16 05									16 20				16 30
West Croydon 4 🚋	a					16 00						16 12									16 30				
East Croydon 🚋	a										16 03														16 33

		LO	SE	SN		SN	LO	LO	SN	LO	LO	LO	SN	SN		LO	SE	SN	SN	LO	LO	SN	LO	SN	
London Bridge 4 ⊖	d			16 11					16 22				16 33	16 36				16 41				16 52		16 58	
Highbury & Islington	a																								
	d	15 48					15 55			16 03	16 10					16 18				16 25			16 33		
Canonbury	d	15 50					15 57			16 05	16 12					16 20				16 27			16 35		
Dalston Junction Stn ELL	d	15 55					16 00	16 05		16 10	16 15	16 20				16 25				16 30	16 35		16 40		
Haggerston	d	15 56					16 01	16 06		16 11	16 16	16 21				16 26				16 31	16 36		16 41		
Hoxton	d	15 58					16 03	16 08		16 13	16 18	16 23				16 28				16 33	16 38		16 43		
Shoreditch High Street	d	16 01					16 06	16 11		16 16	16 21	16 26				16 31				16 36	16 41		16 46		
Whitechapel	d	16 03					16 08	16 13		16 18	16 23	16 28				16 33				16 38	16 43		16 48		
Shadwell	d	16 05					16 10	16 15		16 20	16 25	16 30				16 35				16 40	16 45		16 50		
Wapping	d	16 07					16 12	16 17		16 22	16 27	16 32				16 37				16 42	16 47		16 52		
Rotherhithe	d	16 09					16 14	16 19		16 24	16 29	16 34				16 39				16 44	16 49		16 54		
Canada Water	d	16 11					16 16	16 21		16 26	16 31	16 36				16 41				16 46	16 51		16 56		
Surrey Quays	d	16 12					16 17	16 22		16 27	16 32	16 37				16 42				16 47	16 52		16 57		
New Cross ELL	a							16 27				16 42									16 57				
New Cross Gate 4	a	16 16					16 21		16 27	16 31	16 36			16 41		16 46				16 51		16 57	17 01		
	d	16 17					16 22		16 27	16 32	16 37			16 41		16 47				16 52		16 57	17 02		
Brockley	d	16 19					16 24		16 30	16 34	16 39			16 44		16 49				16 54		17 00	17 04		
Honor Oak Park	d	16 22					16 27		16 33	16 37	16 42			16 47		16 52				16 57		17 03	17 07		
Forest Hill 4	d	16 25					16 30		16 35	16 40	16 45			16 49		16 55				17 00		17 05	17 10		
Sydenham	d	16 27					16 32		16 38	16 42	16 47			16 52		16 57				17 02		17 08	17 12		
Crystal Palace 4	d					16 30	16a37		16 43		16a52								17 00	17a07		17 13			
Gipsy Hill	d					16 32			16 45										17 02			17 15			
West Norwood 4	d					16 35			16 48										17 05			17 18			
Streatham Hill	d								16 52													17 22			
Balham 4 ⊖	d								16 55													17 25			
Wandsworth Common	d								16 57													17 27			
Clapham Junction 10	d								17 01													17 31			
South Bermondsey	d			16 15									16 37					16 45						17 02	
Queens Rd Peckham	d			16 18									16 39					16 48						17 04	
Peckham Rye 4	d		16 15	16 20		16a47							16a42				16 45	16 50	17a17					17a07	
Denmark Hill 4	d		16 19	16 23													16 49	16 53							
London Blackfriars 3 ⊖	a																								
Clapham High Street ⊖	d			16 28														16 58							
Wandsworth Road	d			16 29														16 59							
Battersea Park 4	d			16 32					17 05									17 02				17 35			
London Victoria 15 ⊖	a		16 28	16 38					17 10								17 01	17 08				17 42			
Penge West	d	16 30								16 45				16 54		17 00							17 15		
Anerley	d	16 32								16 47				16 56		17 02							17 17		
Norwood Junction 2	d	16 35								16 50				17 00		17 05							17 20		
West Croydon 4 🚋	a	16 42								17 00				17 07		17 12							17 30		
East Croydon 🚋	a																								

29 August to 7 September

London Bridge to London Victoria - Croydon and East London Line

Network Diagram - see first Page of Table 177

Station		SE	SN	LO	LO	SN	LO	SN	SN	LO		LO	SN	LO	LO	LO	SN	SN	LO	SE		SN	SN	LO	LO
London Bridge 4 ⊖	d					17 05		17 11					17 19				17 28	17 36				17 41			
Highbury & Islington	a																								
	d			16 40			16 48			16 55				17 03	17 10				17 18					17 25	
Canonbury	d			16 42			16 50			16 57				17 05	17 12				17 20					17 27	
Dalston Junction Stn ELL	d			16 45	16 50		16 55			17 00		17 05		17 10	17 15	17 20			17 25					17 30	17 35
Haggerston	d			16 46	16 51		16 56			17 01		17 06		17 11	17 16	17 21			17 26					17 31	17 36
Hoxton	d			16 48	16 53		16 58			17 03		17 08		17 13	17 18	17 23			17 28					17 33	17 38
Shoreditch High Street	d			16 51	16 56		17 01			17 06		17 11		17 16	17 21	17 26			17 31					17 36	17 41
Whitechapel	d			16 53	16 58		17 03			17 08		17 13		17 18	17 23	17 28			17 33					17 38	17 43
Shadwell	d			16 55	17 00		17 05			17 10		17 15		17 20	17 25	17 30			17 35					17 40	17 45
Wapping	d			16 57	17 02		17 07			17 12		17 17		17 22	17 27	17 32			17 37					17 42	17 47
Rotherhithe	d			16 59	17 04		17 09			17 14		17 19		17 24	17 29	17 34			17 39					17 44	17 49
Canada Water	d			17 01	17 06		17 11			17 16		17 21		17 26	17 31	17 36			17 41					17 46	17 51
Surrey Quays	d			17 02	17 07		17 12			17 17		17 22		17 27	17 32	17 37			17 42					17 47	17 52
New Cross ELL	a				17 12							17 27				17 42									17 57
New Cross Gate 4	a			17 06		17 11	17 16			17 21			17 26	17 31	17 36			17 41	17 46					17 51	
	d			17 07		17 11	17 17			17 22			17 26	17 32	17 37			17 41	17 47					17 52	
Brockley	d			17 09		17 14	17 19			17 24			17 29	17 34	17 39			17 44	17 49					17 54	
Honor Oak Park	d			17 12		17 17	17 22			17 27			17 32	17 37	17 42			17 47	17 52					17 57	
Forest Hill 4	d			17 15		17 19	17 25			17 30			17 34	17 40	17 45			17 49	17 55					18 00	
Sydenham	d			17 17		17 22	17 27			17 32			17 37	17 42	17 47			17 52	17 57					18 02	
Crystal Palace 4	d		17 18	17a22					17 36	17a37			17 44		17a52								17 55	18a07	
Gipsy Hill	d		17 20						17 38				17 46										17 57		
West Norwood 4	d		17 23						17 41				17 49										18 00		
Streatham Hill	d												17 53												
Balham 4 ⊖	d												17 56												
Wandsworth Common	d												17 58												
Clapham Junction 10	d												18 02												
South Bermondsey	d							17 15									17 32					17 45			
Queens Rd Peckham	d							17 18									17 35					17 47			
Peckham Rye 4	d	17 15	17a35					17 20	17a53								17a37			17 45		17 50	18a12		
Denmark Hill 4	d	17 19						17 23												17 49		17 53			
London Blackfriars 3 ⊖	a																								
Clapham High Street ⊖	d							17 28														17 58			
Wandsworth Road	d							17 29														17 59			
Battersea Park 4	d							17 32					18 06									18 02			
London Victoria 15 ⊖	a	17 28						17 38					18 12							17 59		18 08			
Penge West	d					17 24	17 30							17 45				17 54	18 00						
Anerley	d					17 26	17 32							17 47				17 56	18 02						
Norwood Junction 2	d					17 30	17 35							17 50				18 00	18 05						
West Croydon 4	a					17 37	17 42							18 01				18 08	18 12						
East Croydon	a																								

Station		SN	LO	SN	SE	SN		LO	LO	SN	LO	LO	LO	SN	SN	LO		SN	SE	SN	LO	LO	SN	LO	LO
London Bridge 4 ⊖	d	17 53		17 58						18 06				18 11	18 21			18 28					18 36		
Highbury & Islington	a																								
	d		17 33					17 40			17 48	17 55				18 03					18 10			18 18	18 25
Canonbury	d		17 35					17 42			17 50	17 57				18 05					18 12			18 20	18 27
Dalston Junction Stn ELL	d		17 40					17 45	17 50		17 55	18 00	18 05			18 10					18 15	18 20		18 25	18 30
Haggerston	d		17 41					17 46	17 51		17 56	18 01	18 06			18 11					18 16	18 21		18 26	18 31
Hoxton	d		17 43					17 48	17 53		17 58	18 03	18 08			18 13					18 18	18 23		18 28	18 33
Shoreditch High Street	d		17 46					17 51	17 56		18 01	18 06	18 11			18 16					18 21	18 26		18 31	18 36
Whitechapel	d		17 48					17 53	17 58		18 03	18 08	18 13			18 18					18 23	18 28		18 33	18 38
Shadwell	d		17 50					17 55	18 00		18 05	18 10	18 15			18 20					18 25	18 30		18 35	18 40
Wapping	d		17 52					17 57	18 02		18 07	18 12	18 17			18 22					18 27	18 32		18 37	18 42
Rotherhithe	d		17 54					17 59	18 04		18 09	18 14	18 19			18 24					18 29	18 34		18 39	18 44
Canada Water	d		17 56					18 01	18 06		18 11	18 16	18 21			18 26					18 31	18 36		18 41	18 46
Surrey Quays	d		17 57					18 02	18 07		18 12	18 17	18 22			18 27					18 32	18 37		18 42	18 47
New Cross ELL	a								18 12				18 27									18 42			
New Cross Gate 4	a	17 58	18 01					18 06		18 11	18 16	18 21			18 26	18 31					18 36		18 41	18 46	18 51
	d	17 58	18 02					18 07		18 11	18 17	18 22			18 26	18 32					18 37		18 41	18 47	18 52
Brockley	d	18 01	18 04					18 09		18 14	18 19	18 24			18 29	18 34					18 39		18 44	18 49	18 54
Honor Oak Park	d	18 04	18 07					18 12		18 17	18 22	18 27			18 32	18 37					18 42		18 47	18 52	18 57
Forest Hill 4	d	18 06	18 10					18 15		18 19	18 25	18 30			18 34	18 40					18 45		18 49	18 55	19 00
Sydenham	d	18 09	18 12					18 17		18 22	18 27	18 32			18 37	18 42					18 47		18 52	18 57	19 02
Crystal Palace 4	d	18 13				18 18		18a22				18a37			18 43					18 51	18a52				19a07
Gipsy Hill	d	18 15				18 20									18 45					18 53					
West Norwood 4	d	18 18				18 23									18 48					18 56					
Streatham Hill	d	18 22													18 52										
Balham 4 ⊖	d	18 25													18 55										
Wandsworth Common	d	18 27													18 57										
Clapham Junction 10	d	18 32													19 01										
South Bermondsey	d			18 02										18 15				18 32							
Queens Rd Peckham	d			18 04										18 18				18 34							
Peckham Rye 4	d			18a07	18 15	18a36								18 20				18a37	18 45	19a14					
Denmark Hill 4	d				18 19									18 23					18 49						
London Blackfriars 3 ⊖	a																								
Clapham High Street ⊖	d													18 28											
Wandsworth Road	d													18 29											
Battersea Park 4	d	18 35												18 32	19 05										
London Victoria 15 ⊖	a	18 42			18 29									18 39	19 12				18 58						
Penge West	d		18 15							18 24	18 30					18 45							18 54	19 00	
Anerley	d		18 17							18 26	18 32					18 47							18 56	19 02	
Norwood Junction 2	d		18 20							18 32	18 35					18 50							19 02	19 05	
West Croydon 4	a		18 30							18 39	18 42					19 01							19 09	19 12	
East Croydon	a																								

Table 178

Mondays to Fridays

29 August to 7 September

London Bridge to London Victoria - Croydon and East London Line

Network Diagram - see first Page of Table 177

Station		LO		SN	SE	SN	LO	LO	LO	SN	SN	LO		SE	SN	SN	SE	SN	LO	LO	SN	LO		LO	LO
London Bridge 4 ⊖	d			18 41		18 51				18 57	19 06				19 08	19 11					19 22				
Highbury & Islington	a																								
	d						18 33	18 40				18 48							18 55			19 03		19 10	
Canonbury	d						18 35	18 42				18 50							18 57			19 05		19 12	
Dalston Junction Stn ELL	d	18 35					18 40	18 45	18 50			18 55							19 00	19 05		19 10		19 15	19 20
Haggerston	d	18 36					18 41	18 46	18 51			18 56							19 01	19 06		19 11		19 16	19 21
Hoxton	d	18 38					18 43	18 48	18 53			18 58							19 03	19 08		19 13		19 18	19 23
Shoreditch High Street	d	18 41					18 46	18 51	18 56			19 01							19 06	19 11		19 16		19 21	19 26
Whitechapel	d	18 43					18 48	18 53	18 58			19 03							19 08	19 13		19 18		19 23	19 28
Shadwell	d	18 45					18 50	18 55	19 00			19 05							19 10	19 15		19 20		19 25	19 30
Wapping	d	18 47					18 52	18 57	19 02			19 07							19 12	19 17		19 22		19 27	19 32
Rotherhithe	d	18 49					18 54	18 59	19 04			19 09							19 14	19 19		19 24		19 29	19 34
Canada Water	d	18 51					18 56	19 01	19 06			19 11							19 16	19 21		19 26		19 31	19 36
Surrey Quays	d	18 52					18 57	19 02	19 07			19 12							19 17	19 22		19 27		19 32	19 37
New Cross ELL	a	18 57							19 12											19 27					19 42
New Cross Gate 4	a					18 56	19 01	19 06			19 11	19 16							19 21		19 27	19 31		19 36	
	d					18 56	19 02	19 07			19 11	19 17							19 22		19 27	19 32		19 37	
Brockley	d					18 59	19 04	19 09			19 14	19 19							19 24		19 30	19 34		19 39	
Honor Oak Park	d					19 02	19 07	19 12			19 17	19 22							19 27		19 33	19 37		19 42	
Forest Hill 4	d					19 04	19 10	19 15			19 19	19 25							19 30		19 35	19 40		19 45	
Sydenham	d					19 07	19 12	19 17			19 22	19 27							19 32		19 38	19 42		19 47	
Crystal Palace 4	d					19 13		19a22										19 32	19a37		19 43			19a52	
Gipsy Hill	d					19 15												19 34			19 45				
West Norwood 4	d					19 18												19 37			19 48				
Streatham Hill	d					19 22															19 52				
Balham 4 ⊖	d					19 25															19 55				
Wandsworth Common	d					19 27															19 57				
Clapham Junction 10	d					19 31															20 01				
South Bermondsey	d			18 45						19 01					19 12	19 15									
Queens Rd Peckham	d			18 48						19 03					19 14	19 18									
Peckham Rye 4	d			18 50						19 06				19 15	19a17	19 20		19a49							
Denmark Hill 4	d			18 53	18 59									19 19		19 23	19 28								
London Blackfriars 3 ⊖	a																								
Clapham High Street ⊖	d			18 58												19 28									
Wandsworth Road	d			18 59												19 29									
Battersea Park 4	d			19 02		19 35										19 32					20 05				
London Victoria 15 ⊖	a			19 08	19 13	19 41								19 28		19 36	19 43				20 09				
Penge West	d						19 15				19 24	19 30										19 45			
Anerley	d						19 17				19 26	19 32										19 47			
Norwood Junction 2	d						19 20			19 28	19 30	19 35										19 50			
West Croydon 4	a						19 30			19 35		19 42										20 00			
East Croydon	a										19 33														

Station		SN	SN	LO	SN	SN	SN	LO		LO	SN	LO	LO	LO	SN	SN	LO	SN		SN	LO	LO	SN	LO	LO
London Bridge 4 ⊖	d	19 28	19 36		19 38	19 41					19 54				20 03	20 06		20 11					20 22		
Highbury & Islington	a																								
	d			19 18				19 25				19 33	19 40				19 48				19 55			20 03	20 10
Canonbury	d			19 20				19 27				19 35	19 42				19 50				19 57			20 05	20 12
Dalston Junction Stn ELL	d			19 25				19 30		19 35		19 40	19 45	19 50			19 55				20 00	20 05		20 10	20 15
Haggerston	d			19 26				19 31		19 36		19 41	19 46	19 51			19 56				20 01	20 06		20 11	20 16
Hoxton	d			19 28				19 33		19 38		19 43	19 48	19 53			19 58				20 03	20 08		20 13	20 18
Shoreditch High Street	d			19 31				19 36		19 41		19 46	19 51	19 56			20 01				20 06	20 11		20 16	20 21
Whitechapel	d			19 33				19 38		19 43		19 48	19 53	19 58			20 03				20 08	20 13		20 18	20 23
Shadwell	d			19 35				19 40		19 45		19 50	19 55	20 00			20 05				20 10	20 15		20 20	20 25
Wapping	d			19 37				19 42		19 47		19 52	19 57	20 02			20 07				20 12	20 17		20 22	20 27
Rotherhithe	d			19 39				19 44		19 49		19 54	19 59	20 04			20 09				20 14	20 19		20 24	20 29
Canada Water	d			19 41				19 46		19 51		19 56	20 01	20 06			20 11				20 16	20 21		20 26	20 31
Surrey Quays	d			19 42				19 47		19 52		19 57	20 02	20 07			20 12				20 17	20 22		20 27	20 32
New Cross ELL	a									19 57				20 12								20 27			
New Cross Gate 4	a		19 41	19 46				19 51			19 59	20 01	20 06			20 11	20 16				20 21		20 27	20 31	20 36
	d		19 41	19 47				19 52			19 59	20 02	20 07			20 11	20 17				20 22		20 27	20 32	20 37
Brockley	d		19 44	19 49				19 54			20 02	20 04	20 09			20 14	20 19				20 24		20 30	20 34	20 39
Honor Oak Park	d		19 47	19 52				19 57			20 05	20 07	20 12			20 17	20 22				20 27		20 33	20 37	20 42
Forest Hill 4	d		19 49	19 55				20 00			20 07	20 10	20 15			20 19	20 25				20 30		20 35	20 40	20 45
Sydenham	d		19 52	19 57				20 02			20 10	20 12	20 17			20 22	20 27				20 32		20 38	20 42	20 47
Crystal Palace 4	d						20 01	20a07			20 13		20a22							20 31	20a37		20 43		20a52
Gipsy Hill	d						20 03				20 16									20 33			20 45		
West Norwood 4	d						20 06				20 19									20 36			20 48		
Streatham Hill	d										20 22												20 52		
Balham 4 ⊖	d										20 25												20 56		
Wandsworth Common	d										20 27												20 58		
Clapham Junction 10	d										20 31												21 03		
South Bermondsey	d	19 32			19 42	19 45									20 07			20 15							
Queens Rd Peckham	d	19 34			19 44	19 48									20 09			20 18							
Peckham Rye 4	d	19 37			19a47	19 50	20a18								20a12			20 20		20a48					
Denmark Hill 4	d					19 53												20 23							
London Blackfriars 3 ⊖	a																								
Clapham High Street ⊖	d					19 58												20 28							
Wandsworth Road	d					19 59												20 29							
Battersea Park 4	d					20 02					20 35							20 32					21 06		
London Victoria 15 ⊖	a					20 06					20 39							20 36					21 11		
Penge West	d		19 54	20 00								20 15				20 24	20 30							20 45	
Anerley	d		19 56	20 02								20 17				20 26	20 32							20 47	
Norwood Junction 2	d	20 02	20 00	20 05								20 20				20 30	20 35							20 50	
West Croydon 4	a	20 07		20 12								20 29					20 42							21 00	
East Croydon	a		20 03													20 33									

29 August to 7 September

London Bridge to London Victoria - Croydon and East London Line

Network Diagram - see first Page of Table 177

		LO	SN	SN		LO	SN	SN	LO	LO	SN	LO	LO	LO		SN	SN	LO	SN	SE	SN	LO	LO	SN	
London Bridge 4 ⊖	d		20 33	20 36			20 41				20 52					21 03	21 06		21 11					21 22	
Highbury & Islington	a																								
	d					20 18			20 25			20 33	20 40					20 48				20 55			
Canonbury	d					20 20			20 27			20 35	20 42					20 50				20 57			
Dalston Junction Stn ELL	d	20 20				20 25			20 30	20 35		20 40	20 45	20 50				20 55				21 00	21 05		
Haggerston	d	20 21				20 26			20 31	20 36		20 41	20 46	20 51				20 56				21 01	21 06		
Hoxton	d	20 23				20 28			20 33	20 38		20 43	20 48	20 53				20 58				21 03	21 08		
Shoreditch High Street	d	20 26				20 31			20 36	20 41		20 46	20 51	20 56				21 01				21 06	21 11		
Whitechapel	d	20 28				20 33			20 38	20 43		20 48	20 53	20 58				21 03				21 08	21 13		
Shadwell	d	20 30				20 35			20 40	20 45		20 50	20 55	21 00				21 05				21 10	21 15		
Wapping	d	20 32				20 37			20 42	20 47		20 52	20 57	21 02				21 07				21 12	21 17		
Rotherhithe	d	20 34				20 39			20 44	20 49		20 54	20 59	21 04				21 09				21 14	21 19		
Canada Water	d	20 36				20 41			20 46	20 51		20 56	21 01	21 06				21 11				21 16	21 21		
Surrey Quays	d	20 37				20 42			20 47	20 52		20 57	21 02	21 07				21 12				21 17	21 22		
New Cross ELL	a	20 42								20 57				21 12									21 27		
New Cross Gate 4	a			20 41		20 46			20 51		20 57	21 01	21 06				21 11	21 16				21 21		21 27	
	d			20 41		20 47			20 52		20 57	21 02	21 07				21 11	21 17				21 22		21 27	
Brockley	d			20 44		20 49			20 54		21 00	21 04	21 09				21 14	21 19				21 24		21 30	
Honor Oak Park	d			20 47		20 52			20 57		21 03	21 07	21 12				21 17	21 22				21 27		21 33	
Forest Hill 4	d			20 49		20 55			21 00		21 05	21 10	21 15				21 19	21 25				21 30		21 35	
Sydenham	d			20 52		20 57			21 02		21 08	21 12	21 17				21 22	21 27				21 32		21 38	
Crystal Palace 4	d							21 00	21a07		21 13		21a22								21 30	21a37		21 43	
Gipsy Hill	d							21 02			21 15										21 32			21 45	
West Norwood 4	d							21 05			21 18										21 35			21 48	
Streatham Hill	d										21 22													21 52	
Balham 4 ⊖	d										21 26													21 56	
Wandsworth Common	d										21 28													21 58	
Clapham Junction 10	d										21 33													22 03	
South Bermondsey	d		20 37				20 45									21 07			21 15						
Queens Rd Peckham	d		20 39				20 48									21 09			21 18						
Peckham Rye 4	d		20a42				20 50	21a17								21a12			21 20	21 20	21a47				
Denmark Hill 4	d						20 53												21 23	21 24					
London Blackfriars 3 ⊖	a																			21 34					
Clapham High Street ⊖	d						20 58												21 28						
Wandsworth Road	d						20 59												21 29						
Battersea Park 4	d						21 02				21 36								21 32					22 06	
London Victoria 15 ⊖	a						21 06				21 41								21 36					22 11	
Penge West	d			20 54		21 00						21 15					21 24	21 30							
Anerley	d			20 56		21 02						21 17					21 26	21 32							
Norwood Junction 2	d			21 00		21 05						21 20					21 30	21 35							
West Croydon 4	a					21 12						21 30						21 42							
East Croydon	a			21 03													21 33								

		LO	LO	LO	SN	SN	LO	SN	SE	SN		LO	LO	SN	LO	LO	LO	SN	SN	LO		SN	SE	SN	LO
London Bridge 4 ⊖	d				21 33	21 36		21 41						21 52				22 03	22 08			22 11			
Highbury & Islington	a																								
	d	21 03	21 10				21 18					21 25			21 33	21 40				21 48					21 55
Canonbury	d	21 05	21 12				21 20					21 27			21 35	21 42				21 50					21 57
Dalston Junction Stn ELL	d	21 10	21 15	21 20			21 25					21 30	21 35		21 40	21 45	21 50			21 55					22 00
Haggerston	d	21 11	21 16	21 21			21 26					21 31	21 36		21 41	21 46	21 51			21 56					22 01
Hoxton	d	21 13	21 18	21 23			21 28					21 33	21 38		21 43	21 48	21 53			21 58					22 03
Shoreditch High Street	d	21 16	21 21	21 26			21 31					21 36	21 41		21 46	21 51	21 56			22 01					22 06
Whitechapel	d	21 18	21 23	21 28			21 33					21 38	21 43		21 48	21 53	21 58			22 03					22 08
Shadwell	d	21 20	21 25	21 30			21 35					21 40	21 45		21 50	21 55	22 00			22 05					22 10
Wapping	d	21 22	21 27	21 32			21 37					21 42	21 47		21 52	21 57	22 02			22 07					22 12
Rotherhithe	d	21 24	21 29	21 34			21 39					21 44	21 49		21 54	21 59	22 04			22 09					22 14
Canada Water	d	21 26	21 31	21 36			21 41					21 46	21 51		21 56	22 01	22 06			22 11					22 16
Surrey Quays	d	21 27	21 32	21 37			21 42					21 47	21 52		21 57	22 02	22 07			22 12					22 17
New Cross ELL	a			21 42									21 57				22 13								
New Cross Gate 4	a	21 31	21 36			21 41	21 46					21 51		21 57	22 01	22 06			22 13	22 16					22 21
	d	21 32	21 37			21 41	21 47					21 52		21 57	22 02	22 07			22 13	22 17					22 22
Brockley	d	21 34	21 39			21 44	21 49					21 54		22 00	22 04	22 09			22 16	22 19					22 24
Honor Oak Park	d	21 37	21 42			21 47	21 52					21 57		22 03	22 07	22 12			22 19	22 22					22 27
Forest Hill 4	d	21 40	21 45			21 49	21 55					22 00		22 05	22 10	22 15			22 21	22 25					22 30
Sydenham	d	21 42	21 47			21 52	21 57					22 02		22 08	22 12	22 17			22 24	22 27					22 32
Crystal Palace 4	d		21a52							22 00		22a07		22 13		22a22								22 22	22a37
Gipsy Hill	d									22 02				22 15										22 24	
West Norwood 4	d									22 05				22 18										22 27	
Streatham Hill	d													22 22											
Balham 4 ⊖	d													22 26											
Wandsworth Common	d													22 28											
Clapham Junction 10	d													22 33											
South Bermondsey	d				21 37			21 45										22 07				22 15			
Queens Rd Peckham	d				21 39			21 48										22 09				22 18			
Peckham Rye 4	d				21a42			21 50	21 50	22a17								22a12				22 20	22 20	22a43	
Denmark Hill 4	d							21 53	21 54													22 23	22 24		
London Blackfriars 3 ⊖	a								22 04														22 34		
Clapham High Street ⊖	d							21 58														22 28			
Wandsworth Road	d							21 59														22 29			
Battersea Park 4	d							22 02						22 36								22 32			
London Victoria 15 ⊖	a							22 06						22 41								22 36			
Penge West	d	21 45				21 54	22 00								22 15				22 26	22 30					
Anerley	d	21 47				21 56	22 02								22 17				22 28	22 32					
Norwood Junction 2	d	21 50				22 00	22 05								22 20				22 32	22 35					
West Croydon 4	a	22 00					22 12								22 30					22 42					
East Croydon	a					22 03													22 35						

Table 178

Mondays to Fridays

29 August to 7 September

London Bridge to London Victoria - Croydon and East London Line

Network Diagram - see first Page of Table 177

		SN	LO	LO	LO	SN		SN	LO	SN	SE	SN	LO	SN	LO	LO		LO	SN	SN	LO	SN	SE	SN	LO
London Bridge 4 ⊖	d	22 23				22 33		22 38		22 41				22 52					23 05	23 06		23 11			
Highbury & Islington	a																								
	d		22 03	22 10					22 18				22 25		22 33	22 40					22 48				22 55
Canonbury	d		22 05	22 12					22 20				22 27		22 35	22 42					22 50				22 57
Dalston Junction Stn ELL	d		22 08	22 15	22 20				22 25				22 30		22 38	22 45		22 50			22 55				23 00
Haggerston	d		22 09	22 16	22 21				22 26				22 31		22 39	22 46		22 51			22 56				23 01
Hoxton	d		22 11	22 18	22 23				22 28				22 33		22 41	22 48		22 53			22 58				23 03
Shoreditch High Street	d		22 14	22 21	22 26				22 31				22 36		22 44	22 51		22 56			23 01				23 06
Whitechapel	d		22 16	22 23	22 28				22 33				22 38		22 46	22 53		22 58			23 03				23 08
Shadwell	d		22 18	22 25	22 30				22 35				22 40		22 48	22 55		23 00			23 05				23 10
Wapping	d		22 20	22 27	22 32				22 37				22 42		22 50	22 57		23 02			23 07				23 12
Rotherhithe	d		22 22	22 29	22 34				22 39				22 44		22 52	22 59		23 04			23 09				23 14
Canada Water	d		22 24	22 31	22 36				22 41				22 46		22 54	23 01		23 06			23 11				23 16
Surrey Quays	d		22 25	22 32	22 37				22 42				22 47		22 55	23 02		23 07			23 12				23 17
New Cross ELL	a				22 42													23 12							
New Cross Gate 4	a	22 28	22 29	22 36				22 43	22 46				22 51	22 57	22 59	23 06				23 11	23 16				23 21
	d	22 28	22 30	22 37				22 43	22 47				22 52	22 57	23 00	23 07				23 11	23 17				23 22
Brockley	d	22 31	22 32	22 39				22 46	22 49				22 54	23 00	23 02	23 09				23 14	23 19				23 24
Honor Oak Park	d	22 34	22 35	22 42				22 49	22 52				22 57	23 03	23 05	23 12				23 17	23 22				23 27
Forest Hill 4	d	22 36	22 38	22 45				22 51	22 55				23 00	23 05	23 08	23 15				23 19	23 25				23 30
Sydenham	d	22 39	22 40	22 47				22 54	22 57				23 02	23 08	23 10	23 17				23 22	23 27				23 32
Crystal Palace 4	d	22 43		22a52								23 00	23a07	23 13		23a22								23 30	23a37
Gipsy Hill	d	22 45										23 02		23 15										23 32	
West Norwood 4	d	22 48										23 05		23 18										23 35	
Streatham Hill	d	22 52												23 22											
Balham 4 ⊖	d	22 56												23 26											
Wandsworth Common	d	22 58												23 28											
Clapham Junction 10	d	23 03												23 33											
South Bermondsey	d					22 37				22 45									23 09			23 15			
Queens Rd Peckham	d					22 39				22 48									23 11			23 18			
Peckham Rye 4	d					22a42				22 50	22 50	23a17							23 14			23 20	23 20	23a47	
Denmark Hill 4	d									22 53	22 54											23 23	23 24		
London Blackfriars 3 ⊖	a										23 04												23 34		
Clapham High Street ⊖	d									22 58												23 28			
Wandsworth Road	d									22 59												23 29			
Battersea Park 4	d	23 07								23 02				23 37								23 32			
London Victoria 15 ⊖	a	23 14								23 06				23 41								23 37			
Penge West	d		22 43					22 56	23 00						23 13					23 24	23 30				
Anerley	d		22 45					22 58	23 02						23 15					23 26	23 32				
Norwood Junction 2	d		22 48					23 02	23 05						23 18				23a36	23 30	23 35				
West Croydon 4	a		23 00						23 12						23 30						23 42				
East Croydon	a							23 06												23 33					

		SN		LO	LO	LO	SN	SN	LO	LO	SN	LO		LO	LO	LO
London Bridge 4 ⊖	d	23 22					23 33	23 36			23 52					
Highbury & Islington	a															
	d			23 03	23 10				23 18	23 25		23 33		23 40	23 48	23 55
Canonbury	d			23 05	23 12				23 20	23 27		23 35		23 42	23 50	23 57
Dalston Junction Stn ELL	d			23 08	23 15	23 20			23 25	23 30		23 38		23 45	23 55	00 01
Haggerston	d			23 09	23 16	23 21			23 26	23 31		23 39		23 46	23 56	00 02
Hoxton	d			23 11	23 18	23 23			23 28	23 33		23 41		23 48	23 58	00 04
Shoreditch High Street	d			23 14	23 21	23 26			23 31	23 36		23 44		23 51	00 01	00 07
Whitechapel	d			23 16	23 23	23 28			23 33	23 38		23 46		23 53	00 03	00 09
Shadwell	d			23 18	23 25	23 30			23 35	23 40		23 48		23 55	00 05	00 11
Wapping	d			23 20	23 27	23 32			23 37	23 42		23 50		23 57	00 07	00 13
Rotherhithe	d			23 22	23 29	23 34			23 39	23 44		23 52		23 59	00 09	00 15
Canada Water	d			23 24	23 31	23 36			23 41	23 46		23 54		00 02	00 11	00 17
Surrey Quays	d			23 25	23 32	23 37			23 42	23 47		23 55		00 03	00 12	00 18
New Cross ELL	a					23 42										
New Cross Gate 4	a	23 27		23 29	23 36			23 41	23 46	23 51	23 57	23 58		00 07	00 16	00 22
	d	23 27		23 30	23 37			23 41	23 47	23 52	23 57	23 59		00 08	00 17	00 23
Brockley	d	23 30		23 32	23 39			23 44	23 49	23 54	00 01	00 03		00 10	00 19	00 25
Honor Oak Park	d	23 33		23 35	23 42			23 47	23 52	23 57	00 04	00 06		00 13	00 22	00 28
Forest Hill 4	d	23 35		23 38	23 45			23 49	23 55	23 59	00 06	00 09		00 16	00 25	00 31
Sydenham	d	23 38		23 40	23 47			23 52	23 57	00 02	00 09	00 11		00 18	00 27	00 33
Crystal Palace 4	d	23 43			23a52					00a07	00 13			00a23		00a38
Gipsy Hill	d	23 45									00 15					
West Norwood 4	d	23 48									00 18					
Streatham Hill	d	23 52									00 22					
Balham 4 ⊖	d	23 55									00 25					
Wandsworth Common	d	23 58									00 27					
Clapham Junction 10	d	00 02									00 31					
South Bermondsey	d						23 37									
Queens Rd Peckham	d						23 39									
Peckham Rye 4	d						23 42									
Denmark Hill 4	d															
London Blackfriars 3 ⊖	a															
Clapham High Street ⊖	d															
Wandsworth Road	d															
Battersea Park 4	d	00 05									00 35					
London Victoria 15 ⊖	a	00 10									00 42					
Penge West	d			23 43				23 54	00 01			00 14			00 30	
Anerley	d			23 45				23 56	00 03			00 16			00 32	
Norwood Junction 2	d			23 48			00a04	23 59	00 06			00 19			00 35	
West Croydon 4	a			23 59					00 13			00 26			00 42	
East Croydon	a							00 03								

London Bridge to London Victoria - Croydon and East London Line

Network Diagram - see first Page of Table 177

		SN	LO	SN	SN	SN	LO	LO	LO	LO		SN	LO	LO	LO	LO	SN	SN	LO	LO		LO	LO	LO	LO
		MX		MX	MO	MX		MO	MX			MX	MX		MX		MX	MX		MX				MX	
			A				A	B		A				A		A			A			A	A		A
London Bridge 4 ⊖	d	23p22		23p36	23p39							23p52					00 03	00 06							
Highbury & Islington	a																								
	d		23p06				23p21	23p23	23p25	23p28			23p35	23p36	23p42	23p43			23p51	23p56		23p58	00 06	00 10	00 13
Canonbury	d		23p08				23p23	23p25	23p27	23p30			23p37	23p38	23p44	23p45			23p53	23p58		00 01	00 08	00 12	00 15
Dalston Junction Stn ELL	d		23p11				23p28	23p28	23p30	23p33			23p40	23p41	23p47	23p48			23p58	00 02		00 04	00 13	00 15	00 18
Haggerston	d		23p12				23p29	23p29	23p31	23p34			23p41	23p42	23p48	23p49			23p59	00 03		00 06	00 14	00 16	00 19
Hoxton	d		23p14				23p31	23p31	23p33	23p36			23p43	23p44	23p50	23p51			00 01	00 05		00 08	00 16	00 18	00 21
Shoreditch High Street	d		23p17				23p34	23p34	23p36	23p39			23p46	23p47	23p53	23p54			00 04	00 08		00 10	00 19	00 21	00 24
Whitechapel	d		23p19				23p36	23p36	23p38	23p41			23p48	23p49	23p55	23p56			00 06	00 10		00 13	00 21	00 23	00 26
Shadwell	d		23p21				23p38	23p38	23p40	23p43			23p50	23p51	23p57	23p58			00 08	00 12		00 15	00 23	00 25	00 28
Wapping	d		23p23				23p40	23p40	23p42	23p45			23p52	23p53	23p59	00 01			00 10	00 14		00 17	00 25	00 27	00 30
Rotherhithe	d		23p25				23p42	23p42	23p44	23p47			23p54	23p55	00 01	00 03			00 12	00 16		00 18	00 27	00 29	00 32
Canada Water	d		23p27				23p44	23p44	23p46	23p49			23p56	23p57	00 03	00 05			00 14	00 18		00 20	00 29	00 31	00 34
Surrey Quays	d		23p28				23p45	23p45	23p47	23p50			23p57	23p58	00 05	00 06			00 15	00 19		00 22	00 30	00 32	00 35
New Cross ELL	a																								
New Cross Gate 4	a	23p27	23p32	23p41	23p44		23p49	23p49	23p51	23p54		23p57	00 01	00 02	00 08	00 10		00 11	00 19	00 23		00 25	00 34	00 36	00 39
	d	23p27	23p33	23p41	23p44		23p50	23p50	23p52	23p55		23p57	00 02	00 03		00 11		00 11	00 20			00 26	00 35		00 40
Brockley	d	23p30	23p35	23p44	23p47		23p52	23p52	23p54	23p57		00 01	00 04	00 06		00 13		00 14	00 22			00 29	00 37		00 42
Honor Oak Park	d	23p33	23p38	23p47	23p50		23p55	23p55	23p57	00 01		00 04	00 07	00 09		00 16		00 17	00 25			00 32	00 40		00 45
Forest Hill 4	d	23p35	23p41	23p49	23p52		23p58	23p58	23p59	00 04		00 06	00 10	00 12		00 19		00 19	00 28			00 34	00 43		00 48
Sydenham	d	23p38	23p43	23p52	23p55		00 01	00 01	00 02	00 06		00 09	00 12	00 14		00 21		00 22	00 30			00 37	00 45		00 50
Crystal Palace 4	d	23p43				00 03			00a07	00a11		00 13				00a26						00a41			00a55
Gipsy Hill	d	23p45										00 15													
West Norwood 4	d	23p48										00 18													
Streatham Hill	d	23p52										00 22													
Balham 4 ⊖	d	23p55										00 25													
Wandsworth Common	d	23p58										00 27													
Clapham Junction 10	d	00 02										00 31													
South Bermondsey	d																00 07								
Queens Rd Peckham	d																00 09								
Peckham Rye 4	d																00 12								
Denmark Hill 4	d																								
London Blackfriars 3 ⊖	a																								
Clapham High Street ⊖	d																								
Wandsworth Road	d																								
Battersea Park 4	d	00 05										00 35													
London Victoria 15 ⊖	a	00 10										00 42													
Penge West	d		23p46	23p54	23p57		00 04	00 03					00 15	00 17				00 24	00 33				00 48		
Anerley	d		23p48	23p56	23p59		00 06	00 05					00 17	00 19				00 26	00 35				00 50		
Norwood Junction 2	d		23p55	23p59	00 03	00 09	00 09	00 08					00 20	00 22			00a34	00 30	00 38				00 53		
West Croydon 4	a		00 03			00 14	00 16	00 15					00 27	00 29					00 45				01 00		
East Croydon	a			00 03	00 06													00 33							

		SN	LO	LO	LO	LO		LO	LO	LO	LO	LO	SE	SE	SN	SN		LO	LO	LO	LO	LO	SN	SN	LO
		MX																							
			A	A	A	A		A	A	A	A	A													
London Bridge 4 ⊖	d	00 36													06 00								06 06	06 11	
Highbury & Islington	a																								
	d		00 21	00 28	00 36	00 43		00 51	00 58	01 06	01 13	01 28								05 35					
Canonbury	d		00 23	00 30	00 38	00 45		00 53	01 00	01 08	01 15	01 30								05 37					
Dalston Junction Stn ELL	d		00 28	00 33	00 43	00 48		00 58	01 03	01 13	01 18	01 35								05 40	05 50				
Haggerston	d		00 29	00 34	00 44	00 49		00 59	01 04	01 14	01 19	01 36								05 41	05 51				
Hoxton	d		00 31	00 36	00 46	00 51		01 01	01 06	01 16	01 21	01 38								05 43	05 53				
Shoreditch High Street	d		00 34	00 39	00 49	00 54		01 04	01 09	01 19	01 24	01 41								05 46	05 56				
Whitechapel	d		00 36	00 41	00 51	00 56		01 06	01 11	01 21	01 26	01 43								05 48	05 58				
Shadwell	d		00 38	00 43	00 53	00 58		01 08	01 13	01 23	01 28	01 45								05 50	06 00				
Wapping	d		00 40	00 45	00 55	01 00		01 10	01 15	01 25	01 30	01 47								05 52	06 02				
Rotherhithe	d		00 42	00 47	00 57	01 02		01 12	01 17	01 27	01 32	01 49								05 54	06 04				
Canada Water	d		00 44	00 49	00 59	01 04		01 14	01 19	01 29	01 34	01 51								05 56	06 06				
Surrey Quays	d		00 45	00 50	01 00	01 05		01 15	01 20	01 30	01 35	01 52								05 57	06 07				
New Cross ELL	a																				06 12				
New Cross Gate 4	a	00 41	00 50	00 54	01 05	01 09		01 19	01 24	01 34	01 39	01 56								06 01			06 11		
	d	00 41	00 50	00 55	01 06	01 10		01 20	01 25	01 35	01 40	01 57						05 47	05 52	06 02		06 07	06 11		06 17
Brockley	d	00 44	00 52	00 57	01 08	01 12		01 22	01 27	01 37	01 42	01 59						05 49	05 54	06 04		06 09	06 14		06 19
Honor Oak Park	d	00 47	00 55	01 00	01 11	01 15		01 25	01 30	01 40	01 45	02 02						05 52	05 57	06 07		06 12	06 17		06 22
Forest Hill 4	d	00 49	00 58	01 02	01 14	01 18		01 28	01 33	01 43	01 48	02 05						05 55	06 00	06 10		06 15	06 19		06 25
Sydenham	d	00 52	01 00	01 05	01 16	01 20		01 30	01 35	01 45	01 50	02 07						05 57	06 02	06 12		06 17	06 22		06 27
Crystal Palace 4	d			01a10		01a25			01a40		01a55					05 59			06a07			06a22			
Gipsy Hill	d															06 01									
West Norwood 4	d															06 04									
Streatham Hill	d																								
Balham 4 ⊖	d																								
Wandsworth Common	d																								
Clapham Junction 10	d																								
South Bermondsey	d														06 04									06 15	
Queens Rd Peckham	d														06 06									06 18	
Peckham Rye 4	d												05 04	06 04	06a09	06a15								06 20	
Denmark Hill 4	d												05 07	06 07										06 23	
London Blackfriars 3 ⊖	a												05 17	06 17											
Clapham High Street ⊖	d																							06 28	
Wandsworth Road	d																							06 29	
Battersea Park 4	d																							06 32	
London Victoria 15 ⊖	a																							06 36	
Penge West	d	00 54	01 03		01 19			01 33		01 48		02 10						06 00		06 15			06 24		06 30
Anerley	d	00 56	01 05		01 21			01 35		01 50		02 12						06 02		06 17			06 26		06 32
Norwood Junction 2	d	01 00	01 08		01 24			01 38		01 53		02 15						06 05		06 20			06 30		06 35
West Croydon 4	a		01 17		01 31			01 45		02 00		02 22						06 13		06 30					06 41
East Croydon	a	01 03																					06 33		

A 10 September

B from 17 September

Table 178

Mondays to Fridays

from 10 September

London Bridge to London Victoria - Croydon and East London Line

Network Diagram - see first Page of Table 177

		LO		SN	LO	LO	SN	SN	SE	SN	LO	SN		SN	LO	LO	LO	SN	SN	LO	SN	SN		SN	LO
London Bridge 4 ⊖	d			06 19			06 30	06 33				06 36		06 41				06 51	06 54		06 58	07 03			
Highbury & Islington	a																								
	d	05 55			06 05											06 25				06 33					06 40
Canonbury	d	05 57			06 07											06 27				06 35					06 42
Dalston Junction Stn ELL	d	06 00			06 10	06 20										06 30	06 35			06 40					06 45
Haggerston	d	06 01			06 11	06 21										06 31	06 36			06 41					06 46
Hoxton	d	06 03			06 13	06 23										06 33	06 38			06 43					06 48
Shoreditch High Street	d	06 06			06 16	06 26										06 36	06 41			06 46					06 51
Whitechapel	d	06 08			06 18	06 28										06 38	06 43			06 48					06 53
Shadwell	d	06 10			06 20	06 30										06 40	06 45			06 50					06 55
Wapping	d	06 12			06 22	06 32										06 42	06 47			06 52					06 57
Rotherhithe	d	06 14			06 24	06 34										06 44	06 49			06 54					06 59
Canada Water	d	06 16			06 26	06 36										06 46	06 51			06 56					07 01
Surrey Quays	d	06 17			06 27	06 37										06 47	06 52			06 57					07 02
New Cross ELL	a					06 42											06 57								
New Cross Gate 4	a	06 21		06 25	06 31							06 41				06 51		06 56	06 59	07 00					07 06
	d	06 22		06 25	06 32						06 37	06 41			06 47	06 52		06 56	06 59	07 02					07 07
Brockley	d	06 24		06 27	06 34						06 39	06 44			06 49	06 54		06 59	07 02	07 04					07 09
Honor Oak Park	d	06 27		06 30	06 37						06 42	06 47			06 52	06 57		07 02	07 05	07 07					07 12
Forest Hill 4	d	06 30		06 33	06 40						06 45	06 49			06 55	07 00		07 04	07 07	07 10					07 15
Sydenham	d	06 32		06 35	06 42						06 47	06 52			06 57	07 02		07 07	07 10	07 12					07 17
Crystal Palace 4	d	06a37		06 39						06 51	06a52					07a07		07 13						07 20	07a22
Gipsy Hill	d			06 41						06 53								07 15						07 22	
West Norwood 4	d			06 44						06 56								07 18						07 25	
Streatham Hill	d			06 48														07 22							
Balham 4 ⊖	d			06 51														07 25							
Wandsworth Common	d																	07 27							
Clapham Junction 10	d			06 56														07 31							
South Bermondsey	d						06 34	06 37						06 45							07 02	07 07			
Queens Rd Peckham	d						06 36	06 39						06 48							07 04	07 09			
Peckham Rye 4	d						06a39	06a42	06 47	07a08				06 50							07a07	07a12		07a36	
Denmark Hill 4	d								06 50					06 53											
London Blackfriars 3 ⊖	a																								
Clapham High Street ⊖	d													06 58											
Wandsworth Road	d													06 59											
Battersea Park 4	d													07 02				07 35							
London Victoria 15 ⊖	a			07 05					07 04					07 08				07 41							
Penge West	d				06 45							06 54			07 00				07 12	07 15					
Anerley	d				06 47							06 56			07 02				07 14	07 17					
Norwood Junction 2	d				06 50							07 00			07 05				07 18	07 20					
West Croydon 4	a				07 00										07 11					07 30					
East Croydon	a											07 03							07 21						

		LO	SN	LO	LO	LO	SN	SE		SN	LO	SN	SN	SN	LO	LO	SN	LO		SN	SN	LO	LO	SE	SN
London Bridge 4 ⊖	d		07 06				07 11			07 21		07 29	07 33				07 36			07 41	07 44				07 53
Highbury & Islington	a																								
	d			06 48	06 55						07 03				07 10			07 18				07 25			
Canonbury	d			06 50	06 57						07 05				07 12			07 20				07 27			
Dalston Junction Stn ELL	d	06 50		06 55	07 00	07 05					07 10				07 15	07 20		07 25				07 30	07 35		
Haggerston	d	06 51		06 56	07 01	07 06					07 11				07 16	07 21		07 26				07 31	07 36		
Hoxton	d	06 53		06 58	07 03	07 08					07 13				07 18	07 23		07 28				07 33	07 38		
Shoreditch High Street	d	06 56		07 01	07 06	07 11					07 16				07 21	07 26		07 31				07 36	07 41		
Whitechapel	d	06 58		07 03	07 08	07 13					07 18				07 23	07 28		07 33				07 38	07 43		
Shadwell	d	07 00		07 05	07 10	07 15					07 20				07 25	07 30		07 35				07 40	07 45		
Wapping	d	07 02		07 07	07 12	07 17					07 22				07 27	07 32		07 37				07 42	07 47		
Rotherhithe	d	07 04		07 09	07 14	07 19					07 24				07 29	07 34		07 39				07 44	07 49		
Canada Water	d	07 06		07 11	07 16	07 21					07 26				07 31	07 36		07 41				07 46	07 51		
Surrey Quays	d	07 07		07 12	07 17	07 22					07 27				07 32	07 37		07 42				07 47	07 52		
New Cross ELL	a	07 12				07 27										07 42							07 57		
New Cross Gate 4	a		07 11	07 15	07 21					07 26	07 31				07 36		07 41	07 45			07 49	07 51			07 58
	d		07 11	07 17	07 22					07 26	07 32				07 37		07 41	07 47			07 49	07 52			07 58
Brockley	d		07 14	07 19	07 24					07 29	07 34				07 39		07 44	07 49				07 54			08 01
Honor Oak Park	d		07 17	07 22	07 27					07 32	07 37				07 42		07 47	07 52				07 57			08 04
Forest Hill 4	d		07 19	07 25	07 30					07 34	07 40				07 45		07 49	07 55				08 00			08 06
Sydenham	d		07 22	07 27	07 32					07 37	07 42				07 47		07 52	07 57				08 02			08 09
Crystal Palace 4	d				07a37					07 43				07 49	07a52							08a07			08 13
Gipsy Hill	d									07 45				07 51											08 15
West Norwood 4	d									07 48				07 54											08 18
Streatham Hill	d									07 52															08 22
Balham 4 ⊖	d									07 55															08 25
Wandsworth Common	d									07 57															08 27
Clapham Junction 10	d									08 01															08 31
South Bermondsey	d						07 15					07 33	07 37							07 45					
Queens Rd Peckham	d						07 17					07 35	07 39							07 47					
Peckham Rye 4	d						07 20	07 23				07a38	07a42	08a06						07 50				07 54	
Denmark Hill 4	d						07 23	07 29												07 53				07 59	
London Blackfriars 3 ⊖	a																								
Clapham High Street ⊖	d						07 28													07 58					
Wandsworth Road	d						07 29													07 59					
Battersea Park 4	d						07 32			08 05										08 02					08 35
London Victoria 15 ⊖	a						07 38	07 42		08 11										08 08				08 11	08 41
Penge West	d		07 24	07 30							07 45						07 54	08 00							
Anerley	d		07 26	07 32							07 47						07 56	08 02							
Norwood Junction 2	d		07 31	07 35							07 50						08 00	08 05							
West Croydon 4	a			07 42							08 00							08 12							
East Croydon	a		07 37														08 03				08 00				

London Bridge to London Victoria - Croydon and East London Line

Network Diagram - see first Page of Table 177

	LO	SN	SE		SN	SN	LO	LO	SN	LO	LO	LO	SN		SE [1]	SE	SN	LO	SN	SN	LO	LO	SN	
London Bridge [4] ⊖ d		08 03			08 06				08 06				08 10				08 21		08 33				08 36	
Highbury & Islington a																								
d	07 33						07 40			07 48	07 55							08 03			08 10			
Canonbury d	07 35						07 42			07 50	07 57							08 05			08 12			
Dalston Junction Stn ELL d	07 40						07 45	07 50		07 55	08 00	08 05						08 10			08 15	08 20		
Haggerston d	07 41						07 46	07 51		07 56	08 01	08 06						08 11			08 16	08 21		
Hoxton d	07 43						07 48	07 53		07 58	08 03	08 08						08 13			08 18	08 23		
Shoreditch High Street d	07 46						07 51	07 56		08 01	08 06	08 11						08 16			08 21	08 26		
Whitechapel d	07 48						07 53	07 58		08 03	08 08	08 13						08 18			08 23	08 28		
Shadwell d	07 50						07 55	08 00		08 05	08 10	08 15						08 20			08 25	08 30		
Wapping d	07 52						07 57	08 02		08 07	08 12	08 17						08 22			08 27	08 32		
Rotherhithe d	07 54						07 59	08 04		08 09	08 14	08 19						08 24			08 29	08 34		
Canada Water d	07 56						08 01	08 06		08 11	08 16	08 21						08 26			08 31	08 36		
Surrey Quays d	07 57						08 02	08 07		08 12	08 17	08 22						08 27			08 32	08 37		
New Cross ELL a								08 12				08 27										08 42		
New Cross Gate [4] a	08 01						08 06		08 11	08 16	08 21						08 26	08 31			08 36		08 41	
d	08 02						08 07		08 11	08 17	08 22						08 26	08 32			08 37		08 41	
Brockley d	08 04						08 09		08 14	08 19	08 24						08 29	08 34			08 39		08 44	
Honor Oak Park d	08 07						08 12		08 17	08 22	08 27						08 32	08 37			08 42		08 47	
Forest Hill [4] d	08 10						08 15		08 19	08 25	08 30						08 34	08 40			08 45		08 49	
Sydenham d	08 12						08 17		08 22	08 27	08 32						08 37	08 42			08 47		08 52	
Crystal Palace [4] d						08 19	08a22				08a37						08 40			08 50	08a52			
Gipsy Hill d						08 21											08 43			08 52				
West Norwood [4] d						08 24											08 46			08 55				
Streatham Hill d																	08 49							
Balham [4] ⊖ d																	08 55							
Wandsworth Common d																	08 57							
Clapham Junction [10] d																	09 01							
South Bermondsey d		08 07			08 11								08 14						08 37					
Queens Rd Peckham d		08 09			08 13								08 16						08 39					
Peckham Rye [4] d		08a12	08 13		08a16	08a36							08 19			08 33			08a42	09a07				
Denmark Hill [4] d			08 17										08 22		08 30	08 36								
London Blackfriars [3] ⊖ a																								
Clapham High Street ⊖ d													08 27											
Wandsworth Road d													08 29											
Battersea Park [4] d													08 32				09 05							
London Victoria [15] ⊖ a			08 29										08 39		08 42	08 49	09 11							
Penge West d	08 15								08 24	08 30								08 45					08 54	
Anerley d	08 17								08 26	08 32								08 47					08 56	
Norwood Junction [2] d	08 20								08 30	08 35								08 50					09 00	
West Croydon [4] a	08 30									08 43								09 00						
East Croydon a									08 33														09 06	

	LO	LO	LO	SN	SE	SE	SN	LO	LO		LO	SN	SN	LO	SE	SN	SN	LO	LO		SN	LO	LO	LO
London Bridge [4] ⊖ d				08 41	07b37		08 51					09 03	09 06			09 11					09 22			
Highbury & Islington a																								
d	08 18	08 25						08 33	08 40					08 48				08 55				09 03	09 10	
Canonbury d	08 20	08 27						08 35	08 42					08 50				08 57				09 05	09 12	
Dalston Junction Stn ELL d	08 25	08 30	08 35					08 40	08 46		08 50			08 55				09 01	09 05			09 10	09 15	09 20
Haggerston d	08 26	08 31	08 36					08 41	08 47		08 51			08 56				09 02	09 06			09 11	09 16	09 21
Hoxton d	08 28	08 33	08 38					08 43	08 49		08 53			08 58				09 04	09 08			09 13	09 18	09 23
Shoreditch High Street d	08 31	08 36	08 41					08 46	08 52		08 56			09 01				09 07	09 11			09 16	09 21	09 26
Whitechapel d	08 33	08 38	08 43					08 48	08 54		08 58			09 03				09 09	09 13			09 18	09 23	09 28
Shadwell d	08 35	08 40	08 45					08 50	08 56		09 00			09 05				09 11	09 15			09 20	09 25	09 30
Wapping d	08 37	08 42	08 47					08 52	08 58		09 02			09 07				09 13	09 17			09 22	09 27	09 32
Rotherhithe d	08 39	08 44	08 49					08 54	09 00		09 04			09 09				09 15	09 19			09 24	09 29	09 34
Canada Water d	08 41	08 46	08 51					08 56	09 02		09 06			09 11				09 17	09 21			09 26	09 31	09 36
Surrey Quays d	08 42	08 47	08 52					08 57	09 03		09 07			09 12				09 18	09 22			09 27	09 32	09 37
New Cross ELL a			08 57								09 12								09 27					09 42
New Cross Gate [4] a	08 46	08 51					08 57	09 01	09 07				09 12	09 16				09 22			09 28	09 30	09 36	
d	08 47	08 52					08 57	09 02	09 08				09 12	09 17				09 23			09 28	09 32	09 37	
Brockley d	08 49	08 54					09 00	09 04	09 10				09 14	09 19				09 25			09 30	09 34	09 39	
Honor Oak Park d	08 52	08 57					09 03	09 07	09 13				09 17	09 22				09 28			09 33	09 37	09 42	
Forest Hill [4] d	08 55	09 00					09 05	09 10	09 16				09 20	09 25				09 31			09 36	09 40	09 45	
Sydenham d	08 57	09 02					09 08	09 12	09 18				09 22	09 27				09 33			09 38	09 42	09 47	
Crystal Palace [4] d		09a07					09 11		09a23								09 30	09a38			09 43		09a52	
Gipsy Hill d							09 14										09 32				09 46			
West Norwood [4] d							09 17										09 35				09 49			
Streatham Hill d							09 21														09 52			
Balham [4] ⊖ d							09 25														09 56			
Wandsworth Common d							09 27														09 58			
Clapham Junction [10] d							09 31														10 02			
South Bermondsey d				08 45								09 07				09 15								
Queens Rd Peckham d				08 48								09 09				09 18								
Peckham Rye [4] d				08 50	08 55	08 55						09a12			09 14	09 20	09a47							
Denmark Hill [4] d				08 53	09 02	09 02									09 17	09 23								
London Blackfriars [3] ⊖ a																								
Clapham High Street ⊖ d				08 58												09 28								
Wandsworth Road d				08 59												09 29								
Battersea Park [4] d				09 02			09 35									09 32					10 05			
London Victoria [15] ⊖ a				09 08	09 11	09 11	09 42								09 29	09 38					10 11			
Penge West d	09 00							09 15					09 25	09 30								09 45		
Anerley d	09 02							09 17					09 27	09 32								09 47		
Norwood Junction [2] d	09 05							09 20					09 30	09 35								09 50		
West Croydon [4] a	09 12							09 30						09 42								10 00		
East Croydon a													09 33											

b London Bridge-1

Table 178

Mondays to Fridays

from 10 September

London Bridge to London Victoria - Croydon and East London Line

Network Diagram - see first Page of Table 177

		SN	SN	LO	SE	SN		SN	LO	LO	SN	LO	LO	LO	SN	SN		LO	SE	SN	SN	LO	LO	SN	LO
London Bridge 4 ⊖	d	09 33	09 36			09 41					09 52				10 03	10 06				10 11				10 22	
Highbury & Islington	a																								
	d			09 18					09 25			09 33	09 40					09 48				09 55			10 03
Canonbury	d			09 20					09 27			09 35	09 42					09 50				09 57			10 05
Dalston Junction Stn ELL	d			09 25					09 30	09 35		09 40	09 45	09 50				09 55				10 00	10 05		10 10
Haggerston	d			09 26					09 31	09 36		09 41	09 46	09 51				09 56				10 01	10 06		10 11
Hoxton	d			09 28					09 33	09 38		09 43	09 48	09 53				09 58				10 03	10 08		10 13
Shoreditch High Street	d			09 31					09 36	09 41		09 46	09 51	09 56				10 01				10 06	10 11		10 16
Whitechapel	d			09 33					09 38	09 43		09 48	09 53	09 58				10 03				10 08	10 13		10 18
Shadwell	d			09 35					09 40	09 45		09 50	09 55	10 00				10 05				10 10	10 15		10 20
Wapping	d			09 37					09 42	09 47		09 52	09 57	10 02				10 07				10 12	10 17		10 22
Rotherhithe	d			09 39					09 44	09 49		09 54	09 59	10 04				10 09				10 14	10 19		10 24
Canada Water	d			09 41					09 46	09 51		09 56	10 01	10 06				10 11				10 16	10 21		10 26
Surrey Quays	d			09 42					09 47	09 52		09 57	10 02	10 07				10 12				10 17	10 22		10 27
New Cross ELL	a									09 57				10 12									10 27		
New Cross Gate 4	a		09 41	09 46					09 51		09 57	10 01	10 06			10 11		10 16				10 21		10 27	10 31
	d		09 41	09 47					09 52		09 57	10 02	10 07			10 11		10 17				10 22		10 27	10 32
Brockley	d		09 44	09 49					09 54		10 00	10 04	10 09			10 14		10 19				10 24		10 30	10 34
Honor Oak Park	d		09 47	09 52					09 57		10 03	10 07	10 12			10 17		10 22				10 27		10 33	10 37
Forest Hill 4	d		09 49	09 55					10 00		10 05	10 10	10 15			10 19		10 25				10 30		10 35	10 40
Sydenham	d		09 52	09 57					10 02		10 08	10 12	10 17			10 22		10 27				10 32		10 38	10 42
Crystal Palace 4	d							10 00	10a07		10 13		10a22								10 30	10a37		10 43	
Gipsy Hill	d							10 02			10 15										10 32			10 45	
West Norwood 4	d							10 05			10 18										10 35			10 48	
Streatham Hill	d										10 22													10 52	
Balham 4 ⊖	d										10 25													10 55	
Wandsworth Common	d										10 27													10 57	
Clapham Junction 10	d										10 31													11 01	
South Bermondsey	d	09 37				09 45									10 07					10 15					
Queens Rd Peckham	d	09 39				09 48									10 09					10 18					
Peckham Rye 4	d	09a42			09 45	09 50		10a17							10a12				10 15	10 20	10a47				
Denmark Hill 4	d				09 49	09 53													10 19	10 23					
London Blackfriars 3 ⊖	a																								
Clapham High Street ⊖	d					09 58														10 28					
Wandsworth Road	d					09 59														10 29					
Battersea Park 4	d					10 03					10 35									10 32				11 05	
London Victoria 15 ⊖	a				10 00	10 07					10 39								10 28	10 36				11 09	
Penge West	d		09 54	10 00								10 15				10 24		10 30							10 45
Anerley	d		09 56	10 02								10 17				10 26		10 32							10 47
Norwood Junction 2	d		10 00	10 05								10 20				10 30		10 35							10 50
West Croydon 4	a			10 12								10 30						10 42							11 00
East Croydon	a		10 03													10 33									

		LO		LO	SN	SN	LO	SE	SN	SN	LO	LO		SN	LO	LO	LO	SN	SN	LO	SE	SN		SN	LO
London Bridge 4 ⊖	d				10 33	10 36			10 41					10 52				11 03	11 06			11 11			
Highbury & Islington	a																								
	d	10 10					10 18				10 25				10 33	10 40				10 48					10 55
Canonbury	d	10 12					10 20				10 27				10 35	10 42				10 50					10 57
Dalston Junction Stn ELL	d	10 15		10 20			10 25				10 30	10 35			10 40	10 45	10 50			10 55					11 00
Haggerston	d	10 16		10 21			10 26				10 31	10 36			10 41	10 46	10 51			10 56					11 01
Hoxton	d	10 18		10 23			10 28				10 33	10 38			10 43	10 48	10 53			10 58					11 03
Shoreditch High Street	d	10 21		10 26			10 31				10 36	10 41			10 46	10 51	10 56			11 01					11 06
Whitechapel	d	10 23		10 28			10 33				10 38	10 43			10 48	10 53	10 58			11 03					11 08
Shadwell	d	10 25		10 30			10 35				10 40	10 45			10 50	10 55	11 00			11 05					11 10
Wapping	d	10 27		10 32			10 37				10 42	10 47			10 52	10 57	11 02			11 07					11 12
Rotherhithe	d	10 29		10 34			10 39				10 44	10 49			10 54	10 59	11 04			11 09					11 14
Canada Water	d	10 31		10 36			10 41				10 46	10 51			10 56	11 01	11 06			11 11					11 16
Surrey Quays	d	10 32		10 37			10 42				10 47	10 52			10 57	11 02	11 07			11 12					11 17
New Cross ELL	a			10 42								10 57					11 12								
New Cross Gate 4	a	10 36				10 41	10 46				10 51			10 57	11 01	11 06			11 11	11 16					11 21
	d	10 37				10 41	10 47				10 52			10 57	11 02	11 07			11 11	11 17					11 22
Brockley	d	10 39				10 44	10 49				10 54			11 00	11 04	11 09			11 14	11 19					11 24
Honor Oak Park	d	10 42				10 47	10 52				10 57			11 03	11 07	11 12			11 17	11 22					11 27
Forest Hill 4	d	10 45				10 49	10 55				11 00			11 05	11 10	11 15			11 19	11 25					11 30
Sydenham	d	10 47				10 52	10 57				11 02			11 08	11 12	11 17			11 22	11 27					11 32
Crystal Palace 4	d	10a52								11 00	11a07			11 13		11a22								11 30	11a37
Gipsy Hill	d									11 02				11 15										11 32	
West Norwood 4	d									11 05				11 18										11 35	
Streatham Hill	d													11 22											
Balham 4 ⊖	d													11 25											
Wandsworth Common	d													11 27											
Clapham Junction 10	d													11 31											
South Bermondsey	d				10 37				10 45									11 07				11 15			
Queens Rd Peckham	d				10 39				10 48									11 09				11 18			
Peckham Rye 4	d				10a42			10 45	10 50	11a17								11a12			11 15	11 20		11a47	
Denmark Hill 4	d							10 49	10 53												11 19	11 23			
London Blackfriars 3 ⊖	a																								
Clapham High Street ⊖	d								10 58													11 28			
Wandsworth Road	d								10 59													11 29			
Battersea Park 4	d								11 02					11 35								11 32			
London Victoria 15 ⊖	a							10 58	11 06					11 39							11 28	11 36			
Penge West	d					10 54	11 00								11 15				11 24	11 30					
Anerley	d					10 56	11 02								11 17				11 26	11 32					
Norwood Junction 2	d					11 00	11 05								11 20				11 30	11 35					
West Croydon 4	a						11 12								11 30					11 42					
East Croydon	a					11 03													11 33						

Table 178

Mondays to Fridays

from 10 September

London Bridge to London Victoria - Croydon and East London Line

Network Diagram - see first Page of Table 177

Station		LO	SN	LO	LO	LO	SN	SN		LO	SE	SN	SN	LO	LO	SN	LO	LO		LO	SN	SN	LO	SE	SN
London Bridge 4 ⊖	d		11 22				11 33	11 36				11 41				11 52					12 03	12 06			12 11
Highbury & Islington	a																								
	d			11 03	11 10					11 18				11 25			11 33	11 40					11 48		
Canonbury	d			11 05	11 12					11 20				11 27			11 35	11 42					11 50		
Dalston Junction Stn ELL	d	11 05		11 10	11 15	11 20				11 25				11 30	11 35		11 40	11 45		11 50			11 55		
Haggerston	d	11 06		11 11	11 16	11 21				11 26				11 31	11 36		11 41	11 46		11 51			11 56		
Hoxton	d	11 08		11 13	11 18	11 23				11 28				11 33	11 38		11 43	11 48		11 53			11 58		
Shoreditch High Street	d	11 11		11 16	11 21	11 26				11 31				11 36	11 41		11 46	11 51		11 56			12 01		
Whitechapel	d	11 13		11 18	11 23	11 28				11 33				11 38	11 43		11 48	11 53		11 58			12 03		
Shadwell	d	11 15		11 20	11 25	11 30				11 35				11 40	11 45		11 50	11 55		12 00			12 05		
Wapping	d	11 17		11 22	11 27	11 32				11 37				11 42	11 47		11 52	11 57		12 02			12 07		
Rotherhithe	d	11 19		11 24	11 29	11 34				11 39				11 44	11 49		11 54	11 59		12 04			12 09		
Canada Water	d	11 21		11 26	11 31	11 36				11 41				11 46	11 51		11 56	12 01		12 06			12 11		
Surrey Quays	d	11 22		11 27	11 32	11 37				11 42				11 47	11 52		11 57	12 02		12 07			12 12		
New Cross ELL	a	11 27				11 42									11 57					12 12					
New Cross Gate 4	a		11 27	11 31	11 36			11 41		11 46				11 51		11 57	12 01	12 06				12 11	12 16		
	d		11 27	11 32	11 37			11 41		11 47				11 52		11 57	12 02	12 07				12 11	12 17		
Brockley	d		11 30	11 34	11 39			11 44		11 49				11 54		12 00	12 04	12 09				12 14	12 19		
Honor Oak Park	d		11 33	11 37	11 42			11 47		11 52				11 57		12 03	12 07	12 12				12 17	12 22		
Forest Hill 4	d		11 35	11 40	11 45			11 49		11 55				12 00		12 05	12 10	12 15				12 19	12 25		
Sydenham	d		11 38	11 42	11 47			11 52		11 57				12 02		12 08	12 12	12 17				12 22	12 27		
Crystal Palace 4	d		11 43		11a52								12 00	12a07		12 13		12a22							
Gipsy Hill	d		11 45										12 02			12 15									
West Norwood 4	d		11 48										12 05			12 18									
Streatham Hill	d		11 52													12 22									
Balham 4 ⊖	d		11 55													12 25									
Wandsworth Common	d		11 57													12 27									
Clapham Junction 10	d		12 01													12 31									
South Bermondsey	d						11 37					11 45									12 07				12 15
Queens Rd Peckham	d						11 39					11 48									12 09				12 18
Peckham Rye 4	d						11a42				11 45	11 50	12a17								12a12			12 15	12 20
Denmark Hill 4	d										11 49	11 54												12 19	12 23
London Blackfriars 3 ⊖	a																								
Clapham High Street ⊖	d											11 58													12 28
Wandsworth Road	d											12 00													12 29
Battersea Park 4	d		12 05									12 02				12 35									12 32
London Victoria 15 ⊖	a		12 09								11 58	12 07				12 39								12 28	12 36
Penge West	d			11 45				11 54		12 00							12 15					12 24	12 30		
Anerley	d			11 47				11 56		12 02							12 17					12 26	12 32		
Norwood Junction 2	d			11 50				12 00		12 05							12 20					12 30	12 35		
West Croydon 4	a			12 00						12 12							12 30						12 42		
East Croydon	a							12 03														12 33			

Station		SN	LO	LO		SN	LO	LO	LO	SN	SN	LO	SE	SN		SN	LO	LO	SN	LO	LO	LO	SN	SN	
London Bridge 4 ⊖	d					12 22				12 33	12 36			12 41					12 52				13 03	13 06	
Highbury & Islington	a																								
	d		11 55				12 03	12 10				12 18					12 25			12 33	12 40				
Canonbury	d		11 57				12 05	12 12				12 20					12 27			12 35	12 42				
Dalston Junction Stn ELL	d		12 00	12 05			12 10	12 15	12 20			12 25					12 30	12 35		12 40	12 45	12 50			
Haggerston	d		12 01	12 06			12 11	12 16	12 21			12 26					12 31	12 36		12 41	12 46	12 51			
Hoxton	d		12 03	12 08			12 13	12 18	12 23			12 28					12 33	12 38		12 43	12 48	12 53			
Shoreditch High Street	d		12 06	12 11			12 16	12 21	12 26			12 31					12 36	12 41		12 46	12 51	12 56			
Whitechapel	d		12 08	12 13			12 18	12 23	12 28			12 33					12 38	12 43		12 48	12 53	12 58			
Shadwell	d		12 10	12 15			12 20	12 25	12 30			12 35					12 40	12 45		12 50	12 55	13 00			
Wapping	d		12 12	12 17			12 22	12 27	12 32			12 37					12 42	12 47		12 52	12 57	13 02			
Rotherhithe	d		12 14	12 19			12 24	12 29	12 34			12 39					12 44	12 49		12 54	12 59	13 04			
Canada Water	d		12 16	12 21			12 26	12 31	12 36			12 41					12 46	12 51		12 56	13 01	13 06			
Surrey Quays	d		12 17	12 22			12 27	12 32	12 37			12 42					12 47	12 52		12 57	13 02	13 07			
New Cross ELL	a			12 27					12 42									12 57				13 12			
New Cross Gate 4	a		12 21			12 27	12 31	12 36			12 41	12 46					12 51		12 57	13 01	13 06			13 11	
	d		12 22			12 27	12 32	12 37			12 41	12 47					12 52		12 57	13 02	13 07			13 11	
Brockley	d		12 24			12 30	12 34	12 39			12 44	12 49					12 54		13 00	13 04	13 09			13 14	
Honor Oak Park	d		12 27			12 33	12 37	12 42			12 47	12 52					12 57		13 03	13 07	13 12			13 17	
Forest Hill 4	d		12 30			12 35	12 40	12 45			12 49	12 55					13 00		13 05	13 10	13 15			13 19	
Sydenham	d		12 32			12 38	12 42	12 47			12 52	12 57					13 02		13 08	13 12	13 17			13 22	
Crystal Palace 4	d	12 30	12a37			12 43		12a52								13 00	13a07		13 13		13a22				
Gipsy Hill	d	12 32				12 45										13 02			13 15						
West Norwood 4	d	12 35				12 48										13 05			13 18						
Streatham Hill	d					12 52													13 22						
Balham 4 ⊖	d					12 55													13 25						
Wandsworth Common	d					12 57													13 27						
Clapham Junction 10	d					13 01													13 31						
South Bermondsey	d									12 37				12 45									13 07		
Queens Rd Peckham	d									12 39				12 48									13 09		
Peckham Rye 4	d	12a47								12a42			12 45	12 50		13a17							13a12		
Denmark Hill 4	d												12 49	12 53											
London Blackfriars 3 ⊖	a																								
Clapham High Street ⊖	d													12 58											
Wandsworth Road	d													12 59											
Battersea Park 4	d					13 05								13 02					13 35						
London Victoria 15 ⊖	a					13 09							12 58	13 06					13 39						
Penge West	d						12 45				12 54	13 00								13 15				13 24	
Anerley	d						12 47				12 56	13 02								13 17				13 26	
Norwood Junction 2	d						12 50				13 00	13 05								13 20				13 30	
West Croydon 4	a						13 00					13 12								13 30					
East Croydon	a										13 03													13 33	

London Bridge to London Victoria - Croydon and East London Line

Network Diagram - see first Page of Table 177

Station		LO	SE	SN	SN	LO	LO	SN	LO	LO		LO	SN	SN	LO	SE	SN	SN	LO	LO		SN	LO	LO	LO
London Bridge [4] ⊖	d			13 11				13 22					13 33	13 36			13 41					13 52			
Highbury & Islington	a																								
	d	12 48				12 55			13 03	13 10					13 18				13 25				13 33	13 40	
Canonbury	d	12 50				12 57			13 05	13 12					13 20				13 27				13 35	13 42	
Dalston Junction Stn ELL	d	12 55				13 00	13 05		13 10	13 15		13 20			13 25				13 30	13 35			13 40	13 45	13 50
Haggerston	d	12 56				13 01	13 06		13 11	13 16		13 21			13 26				13 31	13 36			13 41	13 46	13 51
Hoxton	d	12 58				13 03	13 08		13 13	13 18		13 23			13 28				13 33	13 38			13 43	13 48	13 53
Shoreditch High Street	d	13 01				13 06	13 11		13 16	13 21		13 26			13 31				13 36	13 41			13 46	13 51	13 56
Whitechapel	d	13 03				13 08	13 13		13 18	13 23		13 28			13 33				13 38	13 43			13 48	13 53	13 58
Shadwell	d	13 05				13 10	13 15		13 20	13 25		13 30			13 35				13 40	13 45			13 50	13 55	14 00
Wapping	d	13 07				13 12	13 17		13 22	13 27		13 32			13 37				13 42	13 47			13 52	13 57	14 02
Rotherhithe	d	13 09				13 14	13 19		13 24	13 29		13 34			13 39				13 44	13 49			13 54	13 59	14 04
Canada Water	d	13 11				13 16	13 21		13 26	13 31		13 36			13 41				13 46	13 51			13 56	14 01	14 06
Surrey Quays	d	13 12				13 17	13 22		13 27	13 32		13 37			13 42				13 47	13 52			13 57	14 02	14 07
New Cross ELL	a						13 27					13 42								13 57					14 12
New Cross Gate [4]	a	13 16				13 21		13 27	13 31	13 36				13 41	13 46				13 51			13 57	14 01	14 06	
	d	13 17				13 22		13 27	13 32	13 37				13 41	13 47				13 52			13 57	14 02	14 07	
Brockley	d	13 19				13 24		13 30	13 34	13 39				13 44	13 49				13 54			14 00	14 04	14 09	
Honor Oak Park	d	13 22				13 27		13 33	13 37	13 42				13 47	13 52				13 57			14 03	14 07	14 12	
Forest Hill [4]	d	13 25				13 30		13 35	13 40	13 45				13 49	13 55				14 00			14 05	14 10	14 15	
Sydenham	d	13 27				13 32		13 38	13 42	13 47				13 52	13 57				14 02			14 08	14 12	14 17	
Crystal Palace [4]	d				13 30	13a37		13 43		13a52								14 00	14a07			14 13		14a22	
Gipsy Hill	d				13 32			13 45										14 02				14 15			
West Norwood [4]	d				13 35			13 48										14 05				14 18			
Streatham Hill	d							13 52														14 22			
Balham [4] ⊖	d							13 55														14 25			
Wandsworth Common	d							13 57														14 27			
Clapham Junction [10]	d							14 01														14 31			
South Bermondsey	d			13 15									13 37				13 45								
Queens Rd Peckham	d			13 18									13 39				13 48								
Peckham Rye [4]	d		13 15	13 20	13a47								13a42			13 45	13 50	14a17							
Denmark Hill [4]	d		13 19	13 23												13 49	13 53								
London Blackfriars [3] ⊖	a																								
Clapham High Street ⊖	d			13 28													13 58								
Wandsworth Road	d			13 29													13 59								
Battersea Park [4]	d			13 32				14 05									14 02					14 35			
London Victoria [15] ⊖	a		13 28	13 36				14 09								13 58	14 06					14 39			
Penge West	d	13 30							13 45					13 54	14 00								14 15		
Anerley	d	13 32							13 47					13 56	14 02								14 17		
Norwood Junction [2]	d	13 35							13 50					14 00	14 05								14 20		
West Croydon [4] 🚋	a	13 42							14 00						14 12								14 30		
East Croydon 🚋	a													14 03											

Station		SN	SN	LO	SE	SN		SN	LO	LO	SN	LO	LO	LO	SN	SN		LO	SE	SN	SN	LO	LO	SN	LO
London Bridge [4] ⊖	d	14 03	14 06			14 11					14 22				14 33	14 36				14 41				14 52	
Highbury & Islington	a																								
	d			13 48					13 55			14 03	14 10					14 18				14 25			14 33
Canonbury	d			13 50					13 57			14 05	14 12					14 20				14 27			14 35
Dalston Junction Stn ELL	d			13 55					14 00	14 05		14 10	14 15	14 20				14 25				14 30	14 35		14 40
Haggerston	d			13 56					14 01	14 06		14 11	14 16	14 21				14 26				14 31	14 36		14 41
Hoxton	d			13 58					14 03	14 08		14 13	14 18	14 23				14 28				14 33	14 38		14 43
Shoreditch High Street	d			14 01					14 06	14 11		14 16	14 21	14 26				14 31				14 36	14 41		14 46
Whitechapel	d			14 03					14 08	14 13		14 18	14 23	14 28				14 33				14 38	14 43		14 48
Shadwell	d			14 05					14 10	14 15		14 20	14 25	14 30				14 35				14 40	14 45		14 50
Wapping	d			14 07					14 12	14 17		14 22	14 27	14 32				14 37				14 42	14 47		14 52
Rotherhithe	d			14 09					14 14	14 19		14 24	14 29	14 34				14 39				14 44	14 49		14 54
Canada Water	d			14 11					14 16	14 21		14 26	14 31	14 36				14 41				14 46	14 51		14 56
Surrey Quays	d			14 12					14 17	14 22		14 27	14 32	14 37				14 42				14 47	14 52		14 57
New Cross ELL	a									14 27				14 42									14 57		
New Cross Gate [4]	a		14 11	14 16					14 21		14 27	14 31	14 36			14 41		14 46				14 51		14 57	15 01
	d		14 11	14 17					14 22		14 27	14 32	14 37			14 41		14 47				14 52		14 57	15 02
Brockley	d		14 14	14 19					14 24		14 30	14 34	14 39			14 44		14 49				14 54		15 00	15 04
Honor Oak Park	d		14 17	14 22					14 27		14 33	14 37	14 42			14 47		14 52				14 57		15 03	15 07
Forest Hill [4]	d		14 19	14 25					14 30		14 35	14 40	14 45			14 49		14 55				15 00		15 05	15 10
Sydenham	d		14 22	14 27					14 32		14 38	14 42	14 47			14 52		14 57				15 02		15 08	15 12
Crystal Palace [4]	d							14 30	14a37		14 43		14a52								15 00	15a07		15 13	
Gipsy Hill	d							14 32			14 45										15 02			15 15	
West Norwood [4]	d							14 35			14 48										15 05			15 18	
Streatham Hill	d										14 52													15 22	
Balham [4] ⊖	d										14 55													15 25	
Wandsworth Common	d										14 57													15 27	
Clapham Junction [10]	d										15 01													15 31	
South Bermondsey	d	14 07				14 15									14 37					14 45					
Queens Rd Peckham	d	14 09				14 18									14 39					14 48					
Peckham Rye [4]	d	14a12			14 15	14 20		14a47							14a42				14 45	14 50	15a17				
Denmark Hill [4]	d				14 19	14 23													14 49	14 53					
London Blackfriars [3] ⊖	a																								
Clapham High Street ⊖	d					14 28														14 58					
Wandsworth Road	d					14 29														14 59					
Battersea Park [4]	d					14 32					15 05									15 02				15 35	
London Victoria [15] ⊖	a				14 28	14 36					15 09								14 58	15 06				15 39	
Penge West	d		14 24	14 30								14 45				14 54		15 00							15 15
Anerley	d		14 26	14 32								14 47				14 56		15 02							15 17
Norwood Junction [2]	d		14 30	14 35								14 50				15 00		15 05							15 20
West Croydon [4] 🚋	a			14 42								15 00						15 12							15 30
East Croydon 🚋	a		14 33													15 03									

from 10 September

London Bridge to London Victoria - Croydon and East London Line

Network Diagram - see first Page of Table 177

Station		LO		LO	SN	SN	LO	SE	SN	SN	LO	LO		SN	LO	LO	LO	SN	SN	LO	SE	SN		SN	SN
London Bridge ■4 ⊖	d				15 03	15 06			15 11					15 22				15 33	15 36			15 41			
Highbury & Islington	a																								
	d	14 40					14 48				14 55				15 03	15 10				15 18					
Canonbury	d	14 42					14 50				14 57				15 05	15 12				15 20					
Dalston Junction Stn ELL	d	14 45		14 50			14 55				15 00	15 05			15 10	15 15	15 20			15 25					
Haggerston	d	14 46		14 51			14 56				15 01	15 06			15 11	15 16	15 21			15 26					
Hoxton	d	14 48		14 53			14 58				15 03	15 08			15 13	15 18	15 23			15 28					
Shoreditch High Street	d	14 51		14 56			15 01				15 06	15 11			15 16	15 21	15 26			15 31					
Whitechapel	d	14 53		14 58			15 03				15 08	15 13			15 18	15 23	15 28			15 33					
Shadwell	d	14 55		15 00			15 05				15 10	15 15			15 20	15 25	15 30			15 35					
Wapping	d	14 57		15 02			15 07				15 12	15 17			15 22	15 27	15 32			15 37					
Rotherhithe	d	14 59		15 04			15 09				15 14	15 19			15 24	15 29	15 34			15 39					
Canada Water	d	15 01		15 06			15 11				15 16	15 21			15 26	15 31	15 36			15 41					
Surrey Quays	d	15 02		15 07			15 12				15 17	15 22			15 27	15 32	15 37			15 42					
New Cross ELL	a			15 12								15 27					15 42								
New Cross Gate ■4	a	15 06				15 11	15 16				15 21			15 27	15 31	15 36			15 41	15 46					
	d	15 07				15 11	15 17				15 22			15 27	15 32	15 37			15 41	15 47					
Brockley	d	15 09				15 14	15 19				15 24			15 30	15 34	15 39			15 44	15 49					
Honor Oak Park	d	15 12				15 17	15 22				15 27			15 33	15 37	15 42			15 47	15 52					
Forest Hill ■4	d	15 15				15 19	15 25				15 30			15 35	15 40	15 45			15 49	15 55					
Sydenham	d	15 17				15 22	15 27				15 32			15 38	15 42	15 47			15 52	15 57					
Crystal Palace ■4	d	15a22								15 30	15a37			15 43		15a52									16 00
Gipsy Hill	d									15 32				15 45											16 02
West Norwood ■4	d									15 35				15 48											16 05
Streatham Hill	d													15 52										15 56	
Balham ■4 ⊖	d													15 55											
Wandsworth Common	d													15 57											
Clapham Junction ■10	d													16 01											
South Bermondsey	d				15 07				15 15									15 37				15 45			
Queens Rd Peckham	d				15 09				15 18									15 39				15 48			
Peckham Rye ■4	d				15a12			15 15	15 20	15a47								15a42			15 45	15 50		16a07	16a17
Denmark Hill ■4	d							15 19	15 23												15 49	15 53			
London Blackfriars ■3 ⊖	a																								
Clapham High Street ⊖	d								15 28													15 58			
Wandsworth Road	d								15 29													15 59			
Battersea Park ■4	d								15 32					16 05								16 02			
London Victoria ■15 ⊖	a							15 28	15 36					16 10							15 58	16 06			
Penge West	d					15 24	15 30								15 45				15 54	16 00					
Anerley	d					15 26	15 32								15 47				15 56	16 02					
Norwood Junction ■2	d					15 30	15 35								15 50				16 00	16 05					
West Croydon ■4	a						15 42								16 00					16 12					
East Croydon	a					15 33													16 03						

Station		LO	LO	SN	LO	LO	LO	SN		SN	LO	SE	SN	SN	LO	LO	SN	LO		LO	LO	SN	SN	LO	SE
London Bridge ■4 ⊖	d			15 52				16 03		16 06			16 11				16 22					16 33	16 36		
Highbury & Islington	a																								
	d	15 25			15 33	15 40					15 48				15 55			16 03		16 10				16 18	
Canonbury	d	15 27			15 35	15 42					15 50				15 57			16 05		16 12				16 20	
Dalston Junction Stn ELL	d	15 30	15 35		15 40	15 45	15 50				15 55				16 00	16 05		16 10		16 15	16 20			16 25	
Haggerston	d	15 31	15 36		15 41	15 46	15 51				15 56				16 01	16 06		16 11		16 16	16 21			16 26	
Hoxton	d	15 33	15 38		15 43	15 48	15 53				15 58				16 03	16 08		16 13		16 18	16 23			16 28	
Shoreditch High Street	d	15 36	15 41		15 46	15 51	15 56				16 01				16 06	16 11		16 16		16 21	16 26			16 31	
Whitechapel	d	15 38	15 43		15 48	15 53	15 58				16 03				16 08	16 13		16 18		16 23	16 28			16 33	
Shadwell	d	15 40	15 45		15 50	15 55	16 00				16 05				16 10	16 15		16 20		16 25	16 30			16 35	
Wapping	d	15 42	15 47		15 52	15 57	16 02				16 07				16 12	16 17		16 22		16 27	16 32			16 37	
Rotherhithe	d	15 44	15 49		15 54	15 59	16 04				16 09				16 14	16 19		16 24		16 29	16 34			16 39	
Canada Water	d	15 46	15 51		15 56	16 01	16 06				16 11				16 16	16 21		16 26		16 31	16 36			16 41	
Surrey Quays	d	15 47	15 52		15 57	16 02	16 07				16 12				16 17	16 22		16 27		16 32	16 37			16 42	
New Cross ELL	a		15 57				16 12									16 27					16 42				
New Cross Gate ■4	a	15 51		15 57	16 01	16 06				16 11	16 16				16 21		16 27	16 31		16 36			16 41	16 46	
	d	15 52		15 57	16 02	16 07				16 11	16 17				16 22		16 27	16 32		16 37			16 41	16 47	
Brockley	d	15 54		16 00	16 04	16 09				16 14	16 19				16 24		16 30	16 34		16 39			16 44	16 49	
Honor Oak Park	d	15 57		16 03	16 07	16 12				16 17	16 22				16 27		16 33	16 37		16 42			16 47	16 52	
Forest Hill ■4	d	16 00		16 05	16 10	16 15				16 19	16 25				16 30		16 35	16 40		16 45			16 49	16 55	
Sydenham	d	16 02		16 08	16 12	16 17				16 22	16 27				16 32		16 38	16 42		16 47			16 52	16 57	
Crystal Palace ■4	d	16a07		16 13		16a22								16 30	16a37		16 43			16a52					
Gipsy Hill	d			16 15										16 32			16 45								
West Norwood ■4	d			16 18										16 35			16 48								
Streatham Hill	d			16 22													16 52								
Balham ■4 ⊖	d			16 25													16 55								
Wandsworth Common	d			16 27													16 57								
Clapham Junction ■10	d			16 31													17 01								
South Bermondsey	d							16 07					16 15									16 37			
Queens Rd Peckham	d							16 09					16 18									16 39			
Peckham Rye ■4	d							16a12				16 15	16 20	16a47								16a42			16 45
Denmark Hill ■4	d											16 19	16 23												16 49
London Blackfriars ■3 ⊖	a																								
Clapham High Street ⊖	d												16 28												
Wandsworth Road	d												16 29												
Battersea Park ■4	d			16 35									16 32				17 05								
London Victoria ■15 ⊖	a			16 40								16 28	16 38				17 10								17 01
Penge West	d				16 15					16 24	16 30							16 45					16 54	17 00	
Anerley	d				16 17					16 26	16 32							16 47					16 56	17 02	
Norwood Junction ■2	d				16 20					16 30	16 35							16 50					17 00	17 05	
West Croydon ■4	a				16 30						16 42							17 00					17 07	17 12	
East Croydon	a									16 33															

London Bridge to London Victoria - Croydon and East London Line

Network Diagram - see first Page of Table 177

Station		SN	SN	LO		LO	SN	LO	SN	SE	SN	LO	LO	SN		LO	SN	SN	LO	LO	SN	LO	LO	LO	
London Bridge 4 ⊖	d	16 41					16 52		16 58					17 05			17 11				17 19				
Highbury & Islington	a																								
	d			16 25				16 33				16 40				16 48			16 55			17 03	17 10		
Canonbury	d			16 27				16 35				16 42				16 50			16 57			17 05	17 12		
Dalston Junction Stn ELL	d			16 30		16 35		16 40				16 45	16 50			16 55			17 00	17 05		17 10	17 15	17 20	
Haggerston	d			16 31		16 36		16 41				16 46	16 51			16 56			17 01	17 06		17 11	17 16	17 21	
Hoxton	d			16 33		16 38		16 43				16 48	16 53			16 58			17 03	17 08		17 13	17 18	17 23	
Shoreditch High Street	d			16 36		16 41		16 46				16 51	16 56			17 01			17 06	17 11		17 16	17 21	17 26	
Whitechapel	d			16 38		16 43		16 48				16 53	16 58			17 03			17 08	17 13		17 18	17 23	17 28	
Shadwell	d			16 40		16 45		16 50				16 55	17 00			17 05			17 10	17 15		17 20	17 25	17 30	
Wapping	d			16 42		16 47		16 52				16 57	17 02			17 07			17 12	17 17		17 22	17 27	17 32	
Rotherhithe	d			16 44		16 49		16 54				16 59	17 04			17 09			17 14	17 19		17 24	17 29	17 34	
Canada Water	d			16 46		16 51		16 56				17 01	17 06			17 11			17 16	17 21		17 26	17 31	17 36	
Surrey Quays	d			16 47		16 52		16 57				17 02	17 07			17 12			17 17	17 22		17 27	17 32	17 37	
New Cross ELL	a					16 57							17 12							17 27				17 42	
New Cross Gate 4	a			16 51			16 57	17 01				17 06		17 11		17 16			17 21		17 26	17 30	17 36		
	d			16 52			16 57	17 02				17 07		17 11		17 17			17 22		17 26	17 32	17 37		
Brockley	d			16 54			17 00	17 04				17 09		17 14		17 19			17 24		17 29	17 34	17 39		
Honor Oak Park	d			16 57			17 03	17 07				17 12		17 17		17 22			17 27		17 32	17 37	17 42		
Forest Hill 4	d			17 00			17 05	17 10				17 15		17 19		17 25			17 30		17 34	17 40	17 45		
Sydenham	d			17 02			17 08	17 12				17 17		17 22		17 27			17 32		17 37	17 42	17 47		
Crystal Palace 4	d		17 00	17a07			17 13				17 18	17a22						17 36	17a37		17 44		17a52		
Gipsy Hill	d		17 02				17 15				17 20							17 38			17 46				
West Norwood 4	d		17 05				17 18				17 23							17 41			17 49				
Streatham Hill	d						17 22														17 53				
Balham 4 ⊖	d						17 25														17 56				
Wandsworth Common	d						17 27														17 58				
Clapham Junction 10	d						17 31														18 02				
South Bermondsey	d	16 45							17 02								17 15								
Queens Rd Peckham	d	16 48							17 04								17 18								
Peckham Rye 4	d	16 50	17a17						17a07	17 15	17a35						17 20	17a53							
Denmark Hill 4	d	16 53								17 19							17 23								
London Blackfriars 3 ⊖	a																								
Clapham High Street ⊖	d	16 58															17 28								
Wandsworth Road	d	16 59															17 29								
Battersea Park 4	d	17 02					17 35										17 32				18 06				
London Victoria 15 ⊖	a	17 08					17 42			17 28							17 38				18 12				
Penge West	d							17 15						17 24		17 30						17 45			
Anerley	d							17 17						17 26		17 32						17 47			
Norwood Junction 2	d							17 20						17 30		17 35						17 50			
West Croydon 4	a							17 30						17 37		17 42						18 01			
East Croydon	a																								

Station		SN	SN	LO	SE	SN	SN	LO	LO	SN		LO	SN	SE	SN	LO	LO	SN	LO	LO		LO	SN	SN	LO
London Bridge 4 ⊖	d	17 28	17 36			17 41				17 53			17 58					18 06					18 11	18 21	
Highbury & Islington	a																								
	d			17 18				17 25				17 33				17 40			17 48	17 55					18 03
Canonbury	d			17 20				17 27				17 35				17 42			17 50	17 57					18 05
Dalston Junction Stn ELL	d			17 25				17 30	17 35			17 40				17 45	17 50		17 55	18 00		18 05			18 10
Haggerston	d			17 26				17 31	17 36			17 41				17 46	17 51		17 56	18 01		18 06			18 11
Hoxton	d			17 28				17 33	17 38			17 43				17 48	17 53		17 58	18 03		18 08			18 13
Shoreditch High Street	d			17 31				17 36	17 41			17 46				17 51	17 56		18 01	18 06		18 11			18 16
Whitechapel	d			17 33				17 38	17 43			17 48				17 53	17 58		18 03	18 08		18 13			18 18
Shadwell	d			17 35				17 40	17 45			17 50				17 55	18 00		18 05	18 10		18 15			18 20
Wapping	d			17 37				17 42	17 47			17 52				17 57	18 02		18 07	18 12		18 17			18 22
Rotherhithe	d			17 39				17 44	17 49			17 54				17 59	18 04		18 09	18 14		18 19			18 24
Canada Water	d			17 41				17 46	17 51			17 56				18 01	18 06		18 11	18 16		18 21			18 26
Surrey Quays	d			17 42				17 47	17 52			17 57				18 02	18 07		18 12	18 17		18 22			18 27
New Cross ELL	a								17 57								18 12					18 27			
New Cross Gate 4	a		17 41	17 46				17 51		17 58		18 01				18 06		18 11	18 16	18 21				18 26	18 30
	d		17 41	17 47				17 52		17 58		18 02				18 07		18 11	18 17	18 22				18 26	18 32
Brockley	d		17 44	17 49				17 54		18 01		18 04				18 09		18 14	18 19	18 24				18 29	18 34
Honor Oak Park	d		17 47	17 52				17 57		18 04		18 07				18 12		18 17	18 22	18 27				18 32	18 37
Forest Hill 4	d		17 49	17 55				18 00		18 06		18 10				18 15		18 19	18 25	18 30				18 34	18 40
Sydenham	d		17 52	17 57				18 02		18 09		18 12				18 17		18 22	18 27	18 32				18 37	18 42
Crystal Palace 4	d						17 55	18a07		18 13					18 18	18a22				18a37				18 43	
Gipsy Hill	d						17 57			18 15					18 20									18 45	
West Norwood 4	d						18 00			18 18					18 23									18 48	
Streatham Hill	d									18 22														18 52	
Balham 4 ⊖	d									18 25														18 55	
Wandsworth Common	d									18 27														18 57	
Clapham Junction 10	d									18 32														19 01	
South Bermondsey	d	17 32				17 45							18 02										18 15		
Queens Rd Peckham	d	17 35				17 47							18 04										18 18		
Peckham Rye 4	d	17a37			17 45	17 50	18a12						18a07	18 15	18a36								18 20		
Denmark Hill 4	d				17 49	17 53								18 19									18 23		
London Blackfriars 3 ⊖	a																								
Clapham High Street ⊖	d					17 58																	18 28		
Wandsworth Road	d					17 59																	18 29		
Battersea Park 4	d					18 02				18 35													18 32	19 05	
London Victoria 15 ⊖	a				17 59	18 08				18 42				18 29									18 39	19 12	
Penge West	d		17 54	18 00								18 15						18 24	18 30						18 45
Anerley	d		17 56	18 02								18 17						18 26	18 32						18 47
Norwood Junction 2	d		18 00	18 05								18 20						18 32	18 35						18 50
West Croydon 4	a		18 08	18 12								18 30						18 39	18 42						19 01
East Croydon	a																								

from 10 September

London Bridge to London Victoria - Croydon and East London Line

Network Diagram - see first Page of Table 177

		SN	SE	SN	LO	LO		SN	LO	LO	LO	SN	SE	SN	LO	LO		LO	SN	SN	LO	SE	SN	SN	SE
London Bridge 4 ⊖	d	18 28						18 36				18 41		18 51					18 57	19 06			19 08	19 11	
Highbury & Islington	a																								
	d				18 10				18 18	18 25					18 33	18 40					18 48				
Canonbury	d				18 12				18 20	18 27					18 35	18 42					18 50				
Dalston Junction Stn ELL	d				18 15	18 20			18 25	18 30	18 35				18 40	18 45		18 50			18 55				
Haggerston	d				18 16	18 21			18 26	18 31	18 36				18 41	18 46		18 51			18 56				
Hoxton	d				18 18	18 23			18 28	18 33	18 38				18 43	18 48		18 53			18 58				
Shoreditch High Street	d				18 21	18 26			18 31	18 36	18 41				18 46	18 51		18 56			19 01				
Whitechapel	d				18 23	18 28			18 33	18 38	18 43				18 48	18 53		18 58			19 03				
Shadwell	d				18 25	18 30			18 35	18 40	18 45				18 50	18 55		19 00			19 05				
Wapping	d				18 27	18 32			18 37	18 42	18 47				18 52	18 57		19 02			19 07				
Rotherhithe	d				18 29	18 34			18 39	18 44	18 49				18 54	18 59		19 04			19 09				
Canada Water	d				18 31	18 36			18 41	18 46	18 51				18 56	19 01		19 06			19 11				
Surrey Quays	d				18 32	18 37			18 42	18 47	18 52				18 57	19 02		19 07			19 12				
New Cross ELL	a					18 42					18 57							19 12							
New Cross Gate 4	a				18 36			18 41	18 46	18 51				18 56	19 01	19 06				19 11	19 16				
	d				18 37			18 41	18 47	18 52				18 56	19 02	19 07				19 11	19 17				
Brockley	d				18 39			18 44	18 49	18 54				18 59	19 04	19 09				19 14	19 19				
Honor Oak Park	d				18 42			18 47	18 52	18 57				19 02	19 07	19 12				19 17	19 22				
Forest Hill 4	d				18 45			18 49	18 55	19 00				19 04	19 10	19 15				19 19	19 25				
Sydenham	d				18 47			18 52	18 57	19 02				19 07	19 12	19 17				19 22	19 27				
Crystal Palace 4	d			18 51	18a52					19a07				19 13		19a22									
Gipsy Hill	d			18 53										19 15											
West Norwood 4	d			18 56										19 18											
Streatham Hill	d													19 22											
Balham 4 ⊖	d													19 25											
Wandsworth Common	d													19 27											
Clapham Junction 10	d													19 31											
South Bermondsey	d	18 32										18 45							19 01				19 12	19 15	
Queens Rd Peckham	d	18 34										18 48							19 03				19 14	19 18	
Peckham Rye 4	d	18a37	18 45	19a14								18 50							19 06			19 15	19a17	19 20	
Denmark Hill 4	d		18 49									18 53	18 59									19 19		19 23	19 28
London Blackfriars 3 ⊖	a																								
Clapham High Street ⊖	d											18 58												19 28	
Wandsworth Road	d											18 59												19 29	
Battersea Park 4	d											19 02		19 35										19 32	
London Victoria 15 ⊖	a		18 58									19 08	19 13	19 41								19 28		19 36	19 43
Penge West	d							18 54	19 00						19 15					19 24	19 30				
Anerley	d							18 56	19 02						19 17					19 26	19 32				
Norwood Junction 2	d							19 02	19 05						19 20				19 28	19 30	19 35				
West Croydon 4	a							19 09	19 12						19 30				19 35		19 42				
East Croydon	a																			19 33					

		SN		LO	LO	SN	LO	LO	LO	SN	SN	LO		SN	SN	SN	LO	LO	SN	LO	LO	LO		SN	SN
London Bridge 4 ⊖	d					19 22				19 28	19 36			19 38	19 41				19 54					20 03	20 06
Highbury & Islington	a																								
	d			18 55			19 03	19 10				19 18					19 25			19 33	19 40				
Canonbury	d			18 57			19 05	19 12				19 20					19 27			19 35	19 42				
Dalston Junction Stn ELL	d			19 00	19 05		19 10	19 15	19 20			19 25					19 30	19 35		19 40	19 45	19 50			
Haggerston	d			19 01	19 06		19 11	19 16	19 21			19 26					19 31	19 36		19 41	19 46	19 51			
Hoxton	d			19 03	19 08		19 13	19 18	19 23			19 28					19 33	19 38		19 43	19 48	19 53			
Shoreditch High Street	d			19 06	19 11		19 16	19 21	19 26			19 31					19 36	19 41		19 46	19 51	19 56			
Whitechapel	d			19 08	19 13		19 18	19 23	19 28			19 33					19 38	19 43		19 48	19 53	19 58			
Shadwell	d			19 10	19 15		19 20	19 25	19 30			19 35					19 40	19 45		19 50	19 55	20 00			
Wapping	d			19 12	19 17		19 22	19 27	19 32			19 37					19 42	19 47		19 52	19 57	20 02			
Rotherhithe	d			19 14	19 19		19 24	19 29	19 34			19 39					19 44	19 49		19 54	19 59	20 04			
Canada Water	d			19 16	19 21		19 26	19 31	19 36			19 41					19 46	19 51		19 56	20 01	20 06			
Surrey Quays	d			19 17	19 22		19 27	19 32	19 37			19 42					19 47	19 52		19 57	20 02	20 07			
New Cross ELL	a				19 27				19 42									19 57				20 12			
New Cross Gate 4	a			19 21		19 27	19 31	19 36			19 41	19 46					19 51		19 59	20 00	20 06				20 11
	d			19 22		19 27	19 32	19 37			19 41	19 47					19 52		19 59	20 02	20 07				20 11
Brockley	d			19 24		19 30	19 34	19 39			19 44	19 49					19 54		20 02	20 04	20 09				20 14
Honor Oak Park	d			19 27		19 33	19 37	19 42			19 47	19 52					19 57		20 05	20 07	20 12				20 17
Forest Hill 4	d			19 30		19 35	19 40	19 45			19 49	19 55					20 00		20 07	20 10	20 15				20 19
Sydenham	d			19 32		19 38	19 42	19 47			19 52	19 57					20 02		20 10	20 12	20 17				20 22
Crystal Palace 4	d	19 32		19a37		19 43		19a52								20 01	20a07		20 13		20a22				
Gipsy Hill	d	19 34				19 45										20 03			20 16						
West Norwood 4	d	19 37				19 48										20 06			20 19						
Streatham Hill	d					19 52													20 22						
Balham 4 ⊖	d					19 55													20 25						
Wandsworth Common	d					19 57													20 27						
Clapham Junction 10	d					20 01													20 31						
South Bermondsey	d									19 32				19 42	19 45									20 07	
Queens Rd Peckham	d									19 34				19 44	19 48									20 09	
Peckham Rye 4	d	19a49								19 37				19a47	19 50	20a18								20a12	
Denmark Hill 4	d														19 53										
London Blackfriars 3 ⊖	a																								
Clapham High Street ⊖	d														19 58										
Wandsworth Road	d														19 59										
Battersea Park 4	d					20 05									20 02				20 35						
London Victoria 15 ⊖	a					20 09									20 06				20 39						
Penge West	d						19 45				19 54	20 00								20 15					20 24
Anerley	d						19 47				19 56	20 02								20 17					20 26
Norwood Junction 2	d						19 50			20 02	20 00	20 05								20 20					20 30
West Croydon 4	a						20 00			20 07		20 12								20 29					
East Croydon	a										20 03														20 33

Table 178

Mondays to Fridays

from 10 September

London Bridge to London Victoria - Croydon and East London Line

Network Diagram - see first Page of Table 177

		LO	SN	SN	LO	LO	SN	LO		LO	LO	SN	SN	LO	SN	SN	LO	LO		SN	LO	LO	LO	SN	SN
London Bridge 4 ⊖	d		20 11				20 22					20 33	20 36		20 41					20 52				21 03	21 06
Highbury & Islington	a																								
	d	19 48			19 55			20 03		20 10				20 18			20 25				20 33	20 40			
Canonbury	d	19 50			19 57			20 05		20 12				20 20			20 27				20 35	20 42			
Dalston Junction Stn ELL	d	19 55			20 00	20 05		20 10		20 15	20 20			20 25			20 30	20 35			20 40	20 45	20 50		
Haggerston	d	19 56			20 01	20 06		20 11		20 16	20 21			20 26			20 31	20 36			20 41	20 46	20 51		
Hoxton	d	19 58			20 03	20 08		20 13		20 18	20 23			20 28			20 33	20 38			20 43	20 48	20 53		
Shoreditch High Street	d	20 01			20 06	20 11		20 16		20 21	20 26			20 31			20 36	20 41			20 46	20 51	20 56		
Whitechapel	d	20 03			20 08	20 13		20 18		20 23	20 28			20 33			20 38	20 43			20 48	20 53	20 58		
Shadwell	d	20 05			20 10	20 15		20 20		20 25	20 30			20 35			20 40	20 45			20 50	20 55	21 00		
Wapping	d	20 07			20 12	20 17		20 22		20 27	20 32			20 37			20 42	20 47			20 52	20 57	21 02		
Rotherhithe	d	20 09			20 14	20 19		20 24		20 29	20 34			20 39			20 44	20 49			20 54	20 59	21 04		
Canada Water	d	20 11			20 16	20 21		20 26		20 31	20 36			20 41			20 46	20 51			20 56	21 01	21 06		
Surrey Quays	d	20 12			20 17	20 22		20 27		20 32	20 37			20 42			20 47	20 52			20 57	21 02	21 07		
New Cross ELL	a					20 27					20 42							20 57					21 12		
New Cross Gate 4	a	20 16			20 21		20 27	20 31		20 36			20 41	20 46			20 51			20 57	21 01	21 06			21 11
	d	20 17			20 22		20 27	20 32		20 37			20 41	20 47			20 52			20 57	21 02	21 07			21 11
Brockley	d	20 19			20 24		20 30	20 34		20 39			20 44	20 49			20 54			21 00	21 04	21 09			21 14
Honor Oak Park	d	20 22			20 27		20 33	20 37		20 42			20 47	20 52			20 57			21 03	21 07	21 12			21 17
Forest Hill 4	d	20 25			20 30		20 35	20 40		20 45			20 49	20 55			21 00			21 05	21 10	21 15			21 19
Sydenham	d	20 27			20 32		20 38	20 42		20 47			20 52	20 57			21 02			21 08	21 12	21 17			21 22
Crystal Palace 4	d			20 31	20a37		20 43			20a52						21 00	21a07			21 13		21a22			
Gipsy Hill	d			20 33			20 45									21 02				21 15					
West Norwood 4	d			20 36			20 48									21 05				21 18					
Streatham Hill	d						20 52													21 22					
Balham 4 ⊖	d						20 56													21 26					
Wandsworth Common	d						20 58													21 28					
Clapham Junction 10	d						21 03													21 33					
South Bermondsey	d		20 15									20 37			20 45									21 07	
Queens Rd Peckham	d		20 18									20 39			20 48									21 09	
Peckham Rye 4	d		20 20	20a48								20a42			20 50	21a17								21a12	
Denmark Hill 4	d		20 23												20 53										
London Blackfriars 3 ⊖	a																								
Clapham High Street ⊖	d		20 28												20 58										
Wandsworth Road	d		20 29												20 59										
Battersea Park 4	d		20 32				21 06								21 02					21 36					
London Victoria 15 ⊖	a		20 36				21 11								21 06					21 41					
Penge West	d	20 30						20 45					20 54	21 00							21 15				21 24
Anerley	d	20 32						20 47					20 56	21 02							21 17				21 26
Norwood Junction 2	d	20 35						20 50					21 00	21 05							21 20				21 30
West Croydon 4	a	20 42						21 00						21 12							21 30				
East Croydon	a												21 03												21 33

		LO	SN	SE		SN	LO	LO	SN	LO	LO	LO	SN	SN		LO	SN	SE	SN	LO	LO	SN	LO	LO	
London Bridge 4 ⊖	d		21 11						21 22				21 33	21 36			21 41					21 52			
Highbury & Islington	a																								
	d	20 48					20 55			21 03	21 10					21 18				21 25			21 33	21 40	
Canonbury	d	20 50					20 57			21 05	21 12					21 20				21 27			21 35	21 42	
Dalston Junction Stn ELL	d	20 55					21 00	21 05		21 10	21 15	21 20				21 25				21 30	21 35		21 40	21 45	
Haggerston	d	20 56					21 01	21 06		21 11	21 16	21 21				21 26				21 31	21 36		21 41	21 46	
Hoxton	d	20 58					21 03	21 08		21 13	21 18	21 23				21 28				21 33	21 38		21 43	21 48	
Shoreditch High Street	d	21 01					21 06	21 11		21 16	21 21	21 26				21 31				21 36	21 41		21 46	21 51	
Whitechapel	d	21 03					21 08	21 13		21 18	21 23	21 28				21 33				21 38	21 43		21 48	21 53	
Shadwell	d	21 05					21 10	21 15		21 20	21 25	21 30				21 35				21 40	21 45		21 50	21 55	
Wapping	d	21 07					21 12	21 17		21 22	21 27	21 32				21 37				21 42	21 47		21 52	21 57	
Rotherhithe	d	21 09					21 14	21 19		21 24	21 29	21 34				21 39				21 44	21 49		21 54	21 59	
Canada Water	d	21 11					21 16	21 21		21 26	21 31	21 36				21 41				21 46	21 51		21 56	22 01	
Surrey Quays	d	21 12					21 17	21 22		21 27	21 32	21 37				21 42				21 47	21 52		21 57	22 02	
New Cross ELL	a							21 27				21 42									21 57				
New Cross Gate 4	a	21 16					21 21		21 27	21 31	21 36			21 41		21 46				21 51		21 57	22 01	22 06	
	d	21 17					21 22		21 27	21 32	21 37			21 41		21 47				21 52		21 57	22 02	22 07	
Brockley	d	21 19					21 24		21 30	21 34	21 39			21 44		21 49				21 54		22 00	22 04	22 09	
Honor Oak Park	d	21 22					21 27		21 33	21 37	21 42			21 47		21 52				21 57		22 03	22 07	22 12	
Forest Hill 4	d	21 25					21 30		21 35	21 40	21 45			21 49		21 55				22 00		22 05	22 10	22 15	
Sydenham	d	21 27					21 32		21 38	21 42	21 47			21 52		21 57				22 02		22 08	22 12	22 17	
Crystal Palace 4	d					21 30	21a37		21 43		21a52								22 00	22a07		22 13		22a22	
Gipsy Hill	d					21 32			21 45										22 02			22 15			
West Norwood 4	d					21 35			21 48										22 05			22 18			
Streatham Hill	d								21 52													22 22			
Balham 4 ⊖	d								21 56													22 26			
Wandsworth Common	d								21 58													22 28			
Clapham Junction 10	d								22 03													22 33			
South Bermondsey	d		21 15										21 37				21 45								
Queens Rd Peckham	d		21 18										21 39				21 48								
Peckham Rye 4	d		21 20	21 20		21a47							21a42				21 50	21 50	22a17						
Denmark Hill 4	d		21 23	21 24													21 53	21 54							
London Blackfriars 3 ⊖	a			21 34														22 04							
Clapham High Street ⊖	d		21 28														21 58								
Wandsworth Road	d		21 29														21 59								
Battersea Park 4	d		21 32						22 06								22 02					22 36			
London Victoria 15 ⊖	a		21 36						22 11								22 06					22 41			
Penge West	d	21 30								21 45				21 54		22 00							22 15		
Anerley	d	21 32								21 47				21 56		22 02							22 17		
Norwood Junction 2	d	21 35								21 50				22 00		22 05							22 20		
West Croydon 4	a	21 42								22 00						22 12							22 30		
East Croydon	a													22 03											

London Bridge to London Victoria - Croydon and East London Line

Network Diagram - see first Page of Table 177

		LO	SN	SN	LO	SN	SE	SN	LO	SN		LO	LO	SN	SN	SN	SE	SN	LO	SN		LO	LO	SN	SN
London Bridge	d		22 03	22 08		22 11				22 23				22 33	22 38	22 41				22 52				23 05	23 06
Highbury & Islington	a																								
	d				21 48				21 55			22 05							22 25			22 35			
Canonbury	d				21 50				21 57			22 07							22 27			22 37			
Dalston Junction Stn ELL	d	21 50			21 55				22 00			22 10	22 20						22 30			22 40	22 50		
Haggerston	d	21 51			21 56				22 01			22 11	22 21						22 31			22 41	22 51		
Hoxton	d	21 53			21 58				22 03			22 13	22 23						22 33			22 43	22 53		
Shoreditch High Street	d	21 56			22 01				22 06			22 16	22 26						22 36			22 46	22 56		
Whitechapel	d	21 58			22 03				22 08			22 18	22 28						22 38			22 48	22 58		
Shadwell	d	22 00			22 05				22 10			22 20	22 30						22 40			22 50	23 00		
Wapping	d	22 02			22 07				22 12			22 22	22 32						22 42			22 52	23 02		
Rotherhithe	d	22 04			22 09				22 14			22 24	22 34						22 44			22 54	23 04		
Canada Water	d	22 06			22 11				22 16			22 26	22 36						22 46			22 56	23 06		
Surrey Quays	d	22 07			22 12				22 17			22 27	22 37						22 47			22 57	23 07		
New Cross ELL	a	22 13											22 42										23 12		
New Cross Gate	a			22 13	22 16				22 21	22 28		22 31			22 43				22 51	22 57		23 01			23 11
	d			22 13	22 17				22 22	22 28		22 32			22 43				22 52	22 57		23 02			23 11
Brockley	d			22 16	22 19				22 24	22 31		22 34			22 46				22 54	23 00		23 04			23 14
Honor Oak Park	d			22 19	22 22				22 27	22 34		22 37			22 49				22 57	23 03		23 07			23 17
Forest Hill	d			22 21	22 25				22 30	22 36		22 40			22 51				23 00	23 05		23 10			23 19
Sydenham	d			22 24	22 27				22 32	22 39		22 42			22 54				23 02	23 08		23 12			23 22
Crystal Palace	d							22 22	22a37	22 43								23 00	23a07	23 13					
Gipsy Hill	d							22 24		22 45								23 02		23 15					
West Norwood	d							22 27		22 48								23 05		23 18					
Streatham Hill	d									22 52										23 22					
Balham	d									22 56										23 26					
Wandsworth Common	d									22 58										23 28					
Clapham Junction	d									23 03										23 33					
South Bermondsey	d		22 07			22 15								22 37		22 45								23 09	
Queens Rd Peckham	d		22 09			22 18								22 39		22 48								23 11	
Peckham Rye	d		22a12			22 20	22 20	22a43						22a42		22 50	22 50	23a17						23 14	
Denmark Hill	d					22 23	22 24									22 53	22 54								
London Blackfriars	a						22 34										23 04								
Clapham High Street	d					22 28										22 58									
Wandsworth Road	d					22 29										22 59									
Battersea Park	d					22 32				23 07						23 02				23 37					
London Victoria	a					22 36				23 14						23 06				23 41					
Penge West	d			22 26	22 30							22 45			22 56							23 15			23 24
Anerley	d			22 28	22 32							22 47			22 58							23 17			23 26
Norwood Junction	d			22 32	22 35							22 50			23 02							23 20		23a36	23 30
West Croydon	a				22 42							23 00										23 30			
East Croydon	a			22 35											23 06										23 33

		SN	SE	SN	LO	SN		LO	LO	SN	SN	LO	SN	LO	LO	LO
London Bridge	d	23 11				23 22				23 33	23 36		23 52			
Highbury & Islington	a															
	d				22 55			23 05				23 25		23 35	23 42	23 56
Canonbury	d				22 57			23 07				23 27		23 37	23 44	23 58
Dalston Junction Stn ELL	d				23 00			23 10	23 20			23 30		23 40	23 47	00 02
Haggerston	d				23 01			23 11	23 21			23 31		23 41	23 48	00 03
Hoxton	d				23 03			23 13	23 23			23 33		23 43	23 50	00 05
Shoreditch High Street	d				23 06			23 16	23 26			23 36		23 46	23 53	00 08
Whitechapel	d				23 08			23 18	23 28			23 38		23 48	23 55	00 10
Shadwell	d				23 10			23 20	23 30			23 40		23 50	23 57	00 12
Wapping	d				23 12			23 22	23 32			23 42		23 52	23 59	00 14
Rotherhithe	d				23 14			23 24	23 34			23 44		23 54	00 01	00 16
Canada Water	d				23 16			23 26	23 36			23 46		23 56	00 03	00 18
Surrey Quays	d				23 17			23 27	23 37			23 47		23 57	00 05	00 19
New Cross ELL	a								23 42							
New Cross Gate	a				23 21	23 27		23 31			23 41	23 51	23 57	00 01	00 08	00 23
	d				23 22	23 27		23 32			23 41	23 52	23 57	00 02		
Brockley	d				23 24	23 30		23 34			23 44	23 54	00 01	00 04		
Honor Oak Park	d				23 27	23 33		23 37			23 47	23 57	00 04	00 07		
Forest Hill	d				23 30	23 35		23 40			23 49	23 59	00 06	00 10		
Sydenham	d				23 32	23 38		23 42			23 52	00 02	00 09	00 12		
Crystal Palace	d			23 30	23a37	23 43						00a07	00 13			
Gipsy Hill	d			23 32		23 45							00 15			
West Norwood	d			23 35		23 48							00 18			
Streatham Hill	d					23 52							00 22			
Balham	d					23 55							00 25			
Wandsworth Common	d					23 58							00 27			
Clapham Junction	d					00 02							00 31			
South Bermondsey	d	23 15								23 37						
Queens Rd Peckham	d	23 18								23 39						
Peckham Rye	d	23 20	23 20	23a47						23 42						
Denmark Hill	d	23 23	23 24													
London Blackfriars	a		23 34													
Clapham High Street	d	23 28														
Wandsworth Road	d	23 29														
Battersea Park	d	23 32				00 05							00 35			
London Victoria	a	23 37				00 10							00 42			
Penge West	d							23 45			23 54			00 15		
Anerley	d							23 47			23 56			00 17		
Norwood Junction	d							23 50		00a04	23 59			00 20		
West Croydon	a							23 59						00 27		
East Croydon	a										00 03					

Table 178

Saturdays

until 21 July

London Bridge to London Victoria - Croydon and East London Line

Network Diagram - see first Page of Table 177

Station		SN	SN	SN	LO	SN	LO	LO	SN	SN		LO	LO	SN	SN	SN	SN	SN	SE A	SN		SE B	LO	LO	LO
London Bridge 4 ⊖	d	23p22	23p36			23p52			00 03	00 06						00 33	00 36			06 11					
Highbury & Islington	a																								
	d				23p25		23p35	23p42				23p56	00 10												05 35
Canonbury	d				23p27		23p37	23p44				23p58	00 12												05 37
Dalston Junction Stn ELL	d				23p30		23p40	23p47				00 02	00 15												05 40
Haggerston	d				23p31		23p41	23p48				00 03	00 16												05 41
Hoxton	d				23p33		23p43	23p50				00 05	00 18												05 43
Shoreditch High Street	d				23p36		23p46	23p53				00 08	00 21												05 46
Whitechapel	d				23p38		23p48	23p55				00 10	00 23												05 48
Shadwell	d				23p40		23p50	23p57				00 12	00 25												05 50
Wapping	d				23p42		23p52	23p59				00 14	00 27												05 52
Rotherhithe	d				23p44		23p54	00 01				00 16	00 29												05 54
Canada Water	d				23p46		23p56	00 03				00 18	00 31												05 56
Surrey Quays	d				23p47		23p57	00 05				00 19	00 32												05 57
New Cross ELL	a																								
New Cross Gate 4	a	23p27	23p41		23p51	23p57	00 01	00 08		00 11		00 23	00 36				00 41								06 01
	d	23p27	23p41		23p52	23p57	00 02			00 11							00 41						05 47	05 52	06 02
Brockley	d	23p30	23p44		23p54	00 01	00 04			00 14							00 44						05 49	05 54	06 04
Honor Oak Park	d	23p33	23p47		23p57	00 04	00 07			00 17							00 47						05 52	05 57	06 07
Forest Hill 4	d	23p35	23p49		23p59	00 06	00 10			00 19							00 49						05 55	06 00	06 10
Sydenham	d	23p38	23p52		00 02	00 09	00 12			00 22							00 52						05 57	06 02	06 12
Crystal Palace 4	d	23p43		00 03	00a07	00 13								00 33	00 47			01 03						06a07	
Gipsy Hill	d	23p45				00 15																			
West Norwood 4	d	23p48				00 18																			
Streatham Hill	d	23p52				00 22																			
Balham 4 ⊖	d	23p55				00 25																			
Wandsworth Common	d	23p58				00 27																			
Clapham Junction 10	d	00 02				00 31																			
South Bermondsey	d								00 07							00 37				06 15					
Queens Rd Peckham	d								00 09							00 39				06 18					
Peckham Rye 4	d								00 12							00 42			06 13	06 20		06 20			
Denmark Hill 4	d																		06 17	06 23		06 24			
London Blackfriars 3 ⊖	a																					06 34			
Clapham High Street ⊖	d																			06 28					
Wandsworth Road	d																			06 29					
Battersea Park 4	d	00 05				00 35														06 32					
London Victoria 15 ⊖	a	00 10				00 42													06 26	06 36					
Penge West	d		23p54				00 15			00 24							00 54						06 00		06 15
Anerley	d		23p56				00 17			00 26							00 56						06 02		06 17
Norwood Junction 2	d		23p59	00 09			00 20		00a34	00 30				00 38	00 52	01a04	01 00	01 08					06 06		06 18
West Croydon 4	a			00 14			00 27							00 43	00 58			01 13					06 12		06 30
East Croydon	a		00 03							00 33							01 03								

Station		LO	SE A	SE B	LO	LO		LO	LO	LO	SN	LO	SN	SN	SE A	SE B		SE A	SE B	LO	LO	LO	LO	LO	LO
London Bridge 4 ⊖	d												06 36	06 41											
Highbury & Islington	a																								
	d							05 55	06 05												06 25		06 33	06 40	
Canonbury	d							05 57	06 07												06 27		06 35	06 42	
Dalston Junction Stn ELL	d	05 50						06 00	06 10	06 20											06 30	06 35	06 40	06 45	06 50
Haggerston	d	05 51						06 01	06 11	06 21											06 31	06 36	06 41	06 46	06 51
Hoxton	d	05 53						06 03	06 13	06 23											06 33	06 38	06 43	06 48	06 53
Shoreditch High Street	d	05 56						06 06	06 16	06 26											06 36	06 41	06 46	06 51	06 56
Whitechapel	d	05 58						06 08	06 18	06 28											06 38	06 43	06 48	06 53	06 58
Shadwell	d	06 00						06 10	06 20	06 30											06 40	06 45	06 50	06 55	07 00
Wapping	d	06 02						06 12	06 22	06 32											06 42	06 47	06 52	06 57	07 02
Rotherhithe	d	06 04						06 14	06 24	06 34											06 44	06 49	06 54	06 59	07 04
Canada Water	d	06 06						06 16	06 26	06 36											06 46	06 51	06 56	07 01	07 06
Surrey Quays	d	06 07						06 17	06 27	06 37											06 47	06 52	06 57	07 02	07 07
New Cross ELL	a	06 12								06 42												06 57			07 12
New Cross Gate 4	a							06 21	06 31				06 41								06 51		07 01	07 06	
	d				06 07	06 17		06 22	06 32			06 37	06 41							06 47	06 52		07 02	07 07	
Brockley	d				06 09	06 19		06 24	06 34			06 39	06 44							06 49	06 54		07 04	07 09	
Honor Oak Park	d				06 12	06 22		06 27	06 37			06 42	06 47							06 52	06 57		07 07	07 12	
Forest Hill 4	d				06 15	06 25		06 30	06 40			06 45	06 49							06 55	07 00		07 10	07 15	
Sydenham	d				06 17	06 27		06 32	06 42			06 47	06 52							06 57	07 02		07 12	07 17	
Crystal Palace 4	d				06a22			06a37			06 45	06a52									07a07			07a22	
Gipsy Hill	d										06 47														
West Norwood 4	d										06 50														
Streatham Hill	d																								
Balham 4 ⊖	d																								
Wandsworth Common	d																								
Clapham Junction 10	d																								
South Bermondsey	d													06 45											
Queens Rd Peckham	d													06 48											
Peckham Rye 4	d		06 43	06 50							07a01			06 50	07 13	07 15		07 17	07 20						
Denmark Hill 4	d		06 47	06 54										06 53	07 17	07 19		07 21	07 24						
London Blackfriars 3 ⊖	a			07 04															07 34						
Clapham High Street ⊖	d													06 58											
Wandsworth Road	d													06 59											
Battersea Park 4	d													07 02											
London Victoria 15 ⊖	a		06 56											07 06	07 26	07 28		07 30							
Penge West	d					06 30			06 45				06 54							07 00			07 15		
Anerley	d					06 32			06 47				06 56							07 02			07 17		
Norwood Junction 2	d					06 35			06 50				07 00							07 05			07 20		
West Croydon 4	a					06 41			07 00											07 11			07 30		
East Croydon	a												07 03												

A 19 May

B not 19 May

Table 178

Saturdays
until 21 July

London Bridge to London Victoria - Croydon and East London Line

Network Diagram - see first Page of Table 177

		SN		LO	LO	LO	LO	LO	SN	LO	SN	SN		LO	LO	LO	LO	LO	LO	SE A	SE B	SE A		SN	SE B
London Bridge 4 ⊖	d	07 06							07 11		07 33	07 36												07 41	
Highbury & Islington	a																								
	d			06 48	06 55		07 03	07 10						07 18	07 25		07 33	07 40							
Canonbury	d			06 50	06 57		07 05	07 12						07 20	07 27		07 35	07 42							
Dalston Junction Stn ELL	d			06 55	07 00	07 05	07 10	07 15		07 20				07 25	07 30	07 35	07 40	07 45	07 50						
Haggerston	d			06 56	07 01	07 06	07 11	07 16		07 21				07 26	07 31	07 36	07 41	07 46	07 51						
Hoxton	d			06 58	07 03	07 08	07 13	07 18		07 23				07 28	07 33	07 38	07 43	07 48	07 53						
Shoreditch High Street	d			07 01	07 06	07 11	07 16	07 21		07 26				07 31	07 36	07 41	07 46	07 51	07 56						
Whitechapel	d			07 03	07 08	07 13	07 18	07 23		07 28				07 33	07 38	07 43	07 48	07 53	07 58						
Shadwell	d			07 05	07 10	07 15	07 20	07 25		07 30				07 35	07 40	07 45	07 50	07 55	08 00						
Wapping	d			07 07	07 12	07 17	07 22	07 27		07 32				07 37	07 42	07 47	07 52	07 57	08 02						
Rotherhithe	d			07 09	07 14	07 19	07 24	07 29		07 34				07 39	07 44	07 49	07 54	07 59	08 04						
Canada Water	d			07 11	07 16	07 21	07 26	07 31		07 36				07 41	07 46	07 51	07 56	08 01	08 06						
Surrey Quays	d			07 12	07 17	07 22	07 27	07 32		07 37				07 42	07 47	07 52	07 57	08 02	08 07						
New Cross ELL	a					07 27				07 42						07 57			08 12						
New Cross Gate 4	a	07 11		07 16	07 21		07 31	07 36				07 41		07 46	07 51		08 01	08 06							
	d	07 11		07 17	07 22		07 32	07 37				07 41		07 47	07 52		08 02	08 07							
Brockley	d	07 14		07 19	07 24		07 34	07 39				07 44		07 49	07 54		08 04	08 09							
Honor Oak Park	d	07 17		07 22	07 27		07 37	07 42				07 47		07 52	07 57		08 07	08 12							
Forest Hill 4	d	07 19		07 25	07 30		07 40	07 45				07 49		07 55	08 00		08 10	08 15							
Sydenham	d	07 22		07 27	07 32		07 42	07 47				07 52		07 57	08 02		08 12	08 17							
Crystal Palace 4	d				07a37			07a52							08a07			08a22							
Gipsy Hill	d																								
West Norwood 4	d																								
Streatham Hill	d																								
Balham 4 ⊖	d																								
Wandsworth Common	d																								
Clapham Junction 10	d																								
South Bermondsey	d								07 15		07 37													07 45	
Queens Rd Peckham	d								07 18		07 39													07 48	
Peckham Rye 4	d								07 20		07a42									07 43	07 45	07 47		07 50	07 50
Denmark Hill 4	d								07 23											07 47	07 49	07 51		07 53	07 54
London Blackfriars 3 ⊖	a																								08 04
Clapham High Street ⊖	d								07 28															07 58	
Wandsworth Road	d								07 29															07 59	
Battersea Park 4	d								07 32															08 02	
London Victoria 15 ⊖	a								07 36											07 56	07 58	08 00		08 06	
Penge West	d	07 24		07 30			07 45					07 54		08 00			08 15								
Anerley	d	07 26		07 32			07 47					07 56		08 02			08 17								
Norwood Junction 2	d	07 30		07 35			07 50					08 00		08 05			08 20								
West Croydon 4	a			07 41			08 00							08 11			08 30								
East Croydon	a	07 33										08 03													

		SN	SN	LO	SE A	SE B	SE A	SN		SE B	SN	LO	LO	SN	LO	LO	LO	SN		SN	LO	SE A	SE B	SE A	SN
London Bridge 4 ⊖	d	08 03	08 06					08 11						08 22				08 33		08 36					08 41
Highbury & Islington	a																								
	d			07 48								07 55			08 03	08 10					08 18				
Canonbury	d			07 50								07 57			08 05	08 12					08 20				
Dalston Junction Stn ELL	d			07 55								08 00	08 05		08 10	08 15	08 20				08 25				
Haggerston	d			07 56								08 01	08 06		08 11	08 16	08 21				08 26				
Hoxton	d			07 58								08 03	08 08		08 13	08 18	08 23				08 28				
Shoreditch High Street	d			08 01								08 06	08 11		08 16	08 21	08 26				08 31				
Whitechapel	d			08 03								08 08	08 13		08 18	08 23	08 28				08 33				
Shadwell	d			08 05								08 10	08 15		08 20	08 25	08 30				08 35				
Wapping	d			08 07								08 12	08 17		08 22	08 27	08 32				08 37				
Rotherhithe	d			08 09								08 14	08 19		08 24	08 29	08 34				08 39				
Canada Water	d			08 11								08 16	08 21		08 26	08 31	08 36				08 41				
Surrey Quays	d			08 12								08 17	08 22		08 27	08 32	08 37				08 42				
New Cross ELL	a												08 27				08 42								
New Cross Gate 4	a		08 11	08 16								08 21		08 27	08 31	08 36				08 41	08 46				
	d		08 11	08 17								08 22		08 27	08 32	08 37				08 41	08 47				
Brockley	d		08 14	08 19								08 24		08 30	08 34	08 39				08 44	08 49				
Honor Oak Park	d		08 17	08 22								08 27		08 33	08 37	08 42				08 47	08 52				
Forest Hill 4	d		08 19	08 25								08 30		08 35	08 40	08 45				08 49	08 55				
Sydenham	d		08 22	08 27								08 32		08 38	08 42	08 47				08 52	08 57				
Crystal Palace 4	d										08 30	08a37		08 43		08a52									
Gipsy Hill	d										08 32			08 45											
West Norwood 4	d										08 35			08 48											
Streatham Hill	d													08 52											
Balham 4 ⊖	d													08 55											
Wandsworth Common	d													08 57											
Clapham Junction 10	d													09 01											
South Bermondsey	d	08 07						08 15										08 37							08 45
Queens Rd Peckham	d	08 09						08 18										08 39							08 48
Peckham Rye 4	d	08a12			08 13	08 15	08 17	08 20		08 20	08a46							08a42				08 43	08 45	08 47	08 50
Denmark Hill 4	d				08 17	08 19	08 21	08 23		08 24												08 47	08 49	08 51	08 53
London Blackfriars 3 ⊖	a									08 34															
Clapham High Street ⊖	d							08 28																	08 58
Wandsworth Road	d							08 29																	08 59
Battersea Park 4	d							08 32						09 05											09 02
London Victoria 15 ⊖	a				08 26	08 28	08 30	08 36						09 09								08 56	08 58	09 00	09 06
Penge West	d		08 24	08 30											08 45					08 54	09 00				
Anerley	d		08 26	08 32											08 47					08 56	09 02				
Norwood Junction 2	d		08 30	08 35											08 50					09 00	09 05				
West Croydon 4	a			08 41											09 00						09 12				
East Croydon	a		08 33																	09 03					

A 19 May

B not 19 May

Table 178

Saturdays
until 21 July

London Bridge to London Victoria - Croydon and East London Line

Network Diagram - see first Page of Table 177

		SE A	SN	LO		LO	SN	LO	LO	LO	SN	SN	LO	SE B		SE A	SE B	SN	SE A	SN	LO	LO	SN	LO	
London Bridge 4 ⊖	d						08 52				09 03	09 06						09 11					09 22		
Highbury & Islington	a																								
	d			08 25				08 33	08 40				08 48								08 55			09 03	
Canonbury	d			08 27				08 35	08 42				08 50								08 57			09 05	
Dalston Junction Stn ELL	d			08 30		08 35		08 40	08 45	08 50			08 55								09 00	09 05		09 10	
Haggerston	d			08 31		08 36		08 41	08 46	08 51			08 56								09 01	09 06		09 11	
Hoxton	d			08 33		08 38		08 43	08 48	08 53			08 58								09 03	09 08		09 13	
Shoreditch High Street	d			08 36		08 41		08 46	08 51	08 56			09 01								09 06	09 11		09 16	
Whitechapel	d			08 38		08 43		08 48	08 53	08 58			09 03								09 08	09 13		09 18	
Shadwell	d			08 40		08 45		08 50	08 55	09 00			09 05								09 10	09 15		09 20	
Wapping	d			08 42		08 47		08 52	08 57	09 02			09 07								09 12	09 17		09 22	
Rotherhithe	d			08 44		08 49		08 54	08 59	09 04			09 09								09 14	09 19		09 24	
Canada Water	d			08 46		08 51		08 56	09 01	09 06			09 11								09 16	09 21		09 26	
Surrey Quays	d			08 47		08 52		08 57	09 02	09 07			09 12								09 17	09 22		09 27	
New Cross ELL	a					08 57				09 12												09 27			
New Cross Gate 4	a			08 51			08 57	09 01	09 06			09 11	09 16								09 21		09 27	09 31	
	d			08 52			08 57	09 02	09 07			09 11	09 17								09 22		09 27	09 32	
Brockley	d			08 54			09 00	09 04	09 09			09 14	09 19								09 24		09 30	09 34	
Honor Oak Park	d			08 57			09 03	09 07	09 12			09 17	09 22								09 27		09 33	09 37	
Forest Hill 4	d			09 00			09 05	09 10	09 15			09 19	09 25								09 30		09 35	09 40	
Sydenham	d			09 02			09 08	09 12	09 17			09 22	09 27								09 32		09 38	09 42	
Crystal Palace 4	d		09 00	09a07			09 13		09a22											09 30	09a37		09 43		
Gipsy Hill	d		09 02				09 15													09 32			09 45		
West Norwood 4	d		09 05				09 18													09 35			09 48		
Streatham Hill	d						09 22																09 52		
Balham 4 ⊖	d						09 25																09 55		
Wandsworth Common	d						09 27																09 57		
Clapham Junction 10	d						09 32																10 01		
South Bermondsey	d										09 07							09 15							
Queens Rd Peckham	d										09 09							09 18							
Peckham Rye 4	d	08 50	09a16								09a12			09 13		09 15	09 17	09 20	09 20	09a46					
Denmark Hill 4	d	08 54												09 17		09 19	09 21	09 23	09 24						
London Blackfriars 3 ⊖	a	09 04																	09 34						
Clapham High Street ⊖	d																	09 28							
Wandsworth Road	d																	09 29							
Battersea Park 4	d						09 36											09 32					10 05		
London Victoria 15 ⊖	a						09 40							09 26		09 28	09 30	09 36					10 09		
Penge West	d							09 15				09 24	09 30											09 45	
Anerley	d							09 17				09 26	09 32											09 47	
Norwood Junction 2	d							09 20				09 30	09 35											09 50	
West Croydon 4	a							09 30					09 42											10 00	
East Croydon	a											09 33													

		LO	LO	SN	SN	LO	SE B	SE A	SE B	SN		SE A	SN	LO	LO	SN		SN	LO		LO	LO	SN	SN
London Bridge 4 ⊖	d			09 33	09 36					09 41						09 52		16 52					17 03	17 06
Highbury & Islington	a																							
	d	09 10				09 18								09 25					16 33		16 40			
Canonbury	d	09 12				09 20								09 27					16 35		16 42			
Dalston Junction Stn ELL	d	09 15	09 20			09 25								09 30	09 35				16 40		16 45	16 50		
Haggerston	d	09 16	09 21			09 26								09 31	09 36				16 41		16 46	16 51		
Hoxton	d	09 18	09 23			09 28								09 33	09 38				16 43		16 48	16 53		
Shoreditch High Street	d	09 21	09 26			09 31								09 36	09 41				16 46		16 51	16 56		
Whitechapel	d	09 23	09 28			09 33								09 38	09 43				16 48		16 53	16 58		
Shadwell	d	09 25	09 30			09 35								09 40	09 45				16 50		16 55	17 00		
Wapping	d	09 27	09 32			09 37								09 42	09 47				16 52		16 57	17 02		
Rotherhithe	d	09 29	09 34			09 39								09 44	09 49				16 54		16 59	17 04		
Canada Water	d	09 31	09 36			09 41								09 46	09 51				16 56		17 01	17 06		
Surrey Quays	d	09 32	09 37			09 42								09 47	09 52				16 57		17 02	17 07		
New Cross ELL	a		09 42												09 57							17 12		
New Cross Gate 4	a	09 36			09 41	09 46								09 51		09 57		16 57	17 01		17 06			17 11
	d	09 37			09 41	09 47								09 52		09 57		16 57	17 02		17 07			17 11
Brockley	d	09 39			09 44	09 49								09 54		10 00	and at the same minutes past each hour until	17 00	17 04		17 09			17 14
Honor Oak Park	d	09 42			09 47	09 52								09 57		10 03		17 03	17 07		17 12			17 17
Forest Hill 4	d	09 45			09 49	09 55								10 00		10 05		17 05	17 10		17 15			17 19
Sydenham	d	09 47			09 52	09 57								10 02		10 08		17 08	17 12		17 17			17 22
Crystal Palace 4	d	09a52											10 00	10a07		10 13		17 13			17a22			
Gipsy Hill	d												10 02			10 15		17 15						
West Norwood 4	d												10 05			10 18		17 18						
Streatham Hill	d															10 22		17 22						
Balham 4 ⊖	d															10 25		17 25						
Wandsworth Common	d															10 27		17 27						
Clapham Junction 10	d															10 31		17 31						
South Bermondsey	d			09 37						09 45													17 07	
Queens Rd Peckham	d			09 39						09 48													17 09	
Peckham Rye 4	d			09a42			09 43	09 45	09 47	09 50		09 50	10a16										17a12	
Denmark Hill 4	d						09 47	09 49	09 51	09 53		09 54												
London Blackfriars 3 ⊖	a											10 04												
Clapham High Street ⊖	d									09 58														
Wandsworth Road	d									09 59														
Battersea Park 4	d									10 02						10 35		17 35						
London Victoria 15 ⊖	a						09 56	09 58	10 00	10 06						10 39		17 39						
Penge West	d				09 54	10 00													17 15					17 24
Anerley	d				09 56	10 02													17 17					17 26
Norwood Junction 2	d				10 00	10 05													17 20					17 30
West Croydon 4	a					10 12													17 30					
East Croydon	a				10 03																			17 33

A not 19 May

B 19 May

London Bridge to London Victoria - Croydon and East London Line

Network Diagram - see first Page of Table 177

		LO	SE A	SE B	SE A	SN		SE B	SN	LO	LO	SN	LO	LO	LO	SN		SN	LO	SE A	SE B	SE A	SN	SE B	SN
London Bridge 4 ⊖	d					17 11						17 22				17 33		17 36					17 41		
Highbury & Islington	a																								
	d	16 48								16 55			17 03	17 10					17 18						
Canonbury	d	16 50								16 57			17 05	17 12					17 20						
Dalston Junction Stn ELL	d	16 55								17 00	17 05		17 10	17 15	17 20				17 25						
Haggerston	d	16 56								17 01	17 06		17 11	17 16	17 21				17 26						
Hoxton	d	16 58								17 03	17 08		17 13	17 18	17 23				17 28						
Shoreditch High Street	d	17 01								17 06	17 11		17 16	17 21	17 26				17 31						
Whitechapel	d	17 03								17 08	17 13		17 18	17 23	17 28				17 33						
Shadwell	d	17 05								17 10	17 15		17 20	17 25	17 30				17 35						
Wapping	d	17 07								17 12	17 17		17 22	17 27	17 32				17 37						
Rotherhithe	d	17 09								17 14	17 19		17 24	17 29	17 34				17 39						
Canada Water	d	17 11								17 16	17 21		17 26	17 31	17 36				17 41						
Surrey Quays	d	17 12								17 17	17 22		17 27	17 32	17 37				17 42						
New Cross ELL	a										17 27				17 42										
New Cross Gate 4	a	17 16								17 21		17 27	17 31	17 36				17 41	17 46						
	d	17 17								17 22		17 27	17 32	17 37				17 41	17 47						
Brockley	d	17 19								17 24		17 30	17 34	17 39				17 44	17 49						
Honor Oak Park	d	17 22								17 27		17 33	17 37	17 42				17 47	17 52						
Forest Hill 4	d	17 25								17 30		17 35	17 40	17 45				17 49	17 55						
Sydenham	d	17 27								17 32		17 38	17 42	17 47				17 52	17 57						
Crystal Palace 4	d								17 30	17a37		17 43		17a52											18 00
Gipsy Hill	d								17 32			17 45													18 02
West Norwood 4	d								17 35			17 48													18 05
Streatham Hill	d											17 52													
Balham 4 ⊖	d											17 55													
Wandsworth Common	d											17 57													
Clapham Junction 10	d											18 01													
South Bermondsey	d					17 15										17 37							17 45		
Queens Rd Peckham	d					17 18										17 39							17 48		
Peckham Rye 4	d		17 13	17 15	17 17	17 20		17 20	17a46							17a42				17 43	17 45	17 47	17 50	17 50	18a16
Denmark Hill 4	d		17 17	17 19	17 21	17 23		17 24												17 47	17 49	17 51	17 53	17 54	
London Blackfriars 3 ⊖	a							17 34																18 04	
Clapham High Street ⊖	d					17 28																	17 58		
Wandsworth Road	d					17 29																	17 59		
Battersea Park 4	d					17 32						18 05											18 02		
London Victoria 15 ⊖	a		17 26	17 28	17 30	17 36						18 09								17 56	17 58	18 00	18 06		
Penge West	d	17 30											17 45					17 54	18 00						
Anerley	d	17 32											17 47					17 56	18 02						
Norwood Junction 2	d	17 35											17 50					18 00	18 05						
West Croydon 4	a	17 42											18 00						18 11						
East Croydon	a																	18 03							

		LO		LO	SN	LO	LO	LO	SN	SN	LO	SE A		SE B	SE A	SN	SE B	SN	LO	LO	SN	LO		LO	LO
London Bridge 4 ⊖	d				17 52				18 03	18 06						18 11					18 22				
Highbury & Islington	a																								
	d	17 25				17 33	17 40				17 48								17 55			18 03		18 10	
Canonbury	d	17 27				17 35	17 42				17 50								17 57			18 05		18 12	
Dalston Junction Stn ELL	d	17 30		17 35		17 40	17 45	17 50			17 55								18 00	18 05		18 10		18 15	18 20
Haggerston	d	17 31		17 36		17 41	17 46	17 51			17 56								18 01	18 06		18 11		18 16	18 21
Hoxton	d	17 33		17 38		17 43	17 48	17 53			17 58								18 03	18 08		18 13		18 18	18 23
Shoreditch High Street	d	17 36		17 41		17 46	17 51	17 56			18 01								18 06	18 11		18 16		18 21	18 26
Whitechapel	d	17 38		17 43		17 48	17 53	17 58			18 03								18 08	18 13		18 18		18 23	18 28
Shadwell	d	17 40		17 45		17 50	17 55	18 00			18 05								18 10	18 15		18 20		18 25	18 30
Wapping	d	17 42		17 47		17 52	17 57	18 02			18 07								18 12	18 17		18 22		18 27	18 32
Rotherhithe	d	17 44		17 49		17 54	17 59	18 04			18 09								18 14	18 19		18 24		18 29	18 34
Canada Water	d	17 46		17 51		17 56	18 01	18 06			18 11								18 16	18 21		18 26		18 31	18 36
Surrey Quays	d	17 47		17 52		17 57	18 02	18 07			18 12								18 17	18 22		18 27		18 32	18 37
New Cross ELL	a			17 57				18 12												18 27					18 42
New Cross Gate 4	a	17 51			17 57	18 01	18 06			18 11	18 16								18 21		18 27	18 31		18 36	
	d	17 52			17 57	18 02	18 07			18 11	18 17								18 22		18 27	18 32		18 37	
Brockley	d	17 54			18 00	18 04	18 09			18 14	18 19								18 24		18 30	18 34		18 39	
Honor Oak Park	d	17 57			18 03	18 07	18 12			18 17	18 22								18 27		18 33	18 37		18 42	
Forest Hill 4	d	18 00			18 05	18 10	18 15			18 19	18 25								18 30		18 35	18 40		18 45	
Sydenham	d	18 02			18 08	18 12	18 17			18 22	18 27								18 32		18 38	18 42		18 47	
Crystal Palace 4	d	18a07			18 13		18a22											18 30	18a37		18 43			18a52	
Gipsy Hill	d				18 15													18 32			18 45				
West Norwood 4	d				18 18													18 35			18 48				
Streatham Hill	d				18 22																18 52				
Balham 4 ⊖	d				18 25																18 55				
Wandsworth Common	d				18 27																18 57				
Clapham Junction 10	d				18 31																19 01				
South Bermondsey	d								18 07							18 15									
Queens Rd Peckham	d								18 09							18 18									
Peckham Rye 4	d								18a12			18 13		18 15	18 17	18 20	18 20	18a46							
Denmark Hill 4	d											18 17		18 19	18 21	18 23	18 24								
London Blackfriars 3 ⊖	a																18 34								
Clapham High Street ⊖	d															18 28									
Wandsworth Road	d															18 29									
Battersea Park 4	d				18 35											18 32					19 05				
London Victoria 15 ⊖	a				18 39							18 26		18 28	18 30	18 36					19 09				
Penge West	d					18 15				18 24	18 30											18 45			
Anerley	d					18 17				18 26	18 32											18 47			
Norwood Junction 2	d					18 20				18 30	18 35											18 50			
West Croydon 4	a					18 30					18 41											19 00			
East Croydon	a									18 33															

A 19 May

B not 19 May

Table 178

Saturdays

until 21 July

London Bridge to London Victoria - Croydon and East London Line

Network Diagram - see first Page of Table 177

		SN	SN	LO	SE A	SE B	SE A	SN		SE B	SN	LO	LO	SN	LO	LO	LO	SN		SN	LO	SE A	SE B	SE A	SN
London Bridge 4 ⊖	d	18 33	18 36					18 41						18 52				19 03		19 06					19 11
Highbury & Islington	a																								
	d			18 18								18 25			18 33	18 40					18 48				
Canonbury	d			18 20								18 27			18 35	18 42					18 50				
Dalston Junction Stn ELL	d			18 25								18 30	18 35		18 40	18 45	18 50				18 55				
Haggerston	d			18 26								18 31	18 36		18 41	18 46	18 51				18 56				
Hoxton	d			18 28								18 33	18 38		18 43	18 48	18 53				18 58				
Shoreditch High Street	d			18 31								18 36	18 41		18 46	18 51	18 56				19 01				
Whitechapel	d			18 33								18 38	18 43		18 48	18 53	18 58				19 03				
Shadwell	d			18 35								18 40	18 45		18 50	18 55	19 00				19 05				
Wapping	d			18 37								18 42	18 47		18 52	18 57	19 02				19 07				
Rotherhithe	d			18 39								18 44	18 49		18 54	18 59	19 04				19 09				
Canada Water	d			18 41								18 46	18 51		18 56	19 01	19 06				19 11				
Surrey Quays	d			18 42								18 47	18 52		18 57	19 02	19 07				19 12				
New Cross ELL	a												18 57				19 12								
New Cross Gate 4	a		18 41	18 46								18 51		18 57	19 01	19 06				19 11	19 16				
	d		18 41	18 47								18 52		18 57	19 02	19 07				19 11	19 17				
Brockley	d		18 44	18 49								18 54		19 00	19 04	19 09				19 14	19 19				
Honor Oak Park	d		18 47	18 52								18 57		19 03	19 07	19 12				19 17	19 22				
Forest Hill 4	d		18 49	18 55								19 00		19 05	19 10	19 15				19 19	19 25				
Sydenham	d		18 52	18 57								19 02		19 08	19 12	19 17				19 22	19 27				
Crystal Palace 4	d										19 00	19a07		19 13		19a22									
Gipsy Hill	d										19 02			19 15											
West Norwood 4	d										19 05			19 18											
Streatham Hill	d													19 22											
Balham 4 ⊖	d													19 25											
Wandsworth Common	d													19 27											
Clapham Junction 10	d													19 31											
South Bermondsey	d	18 37						18 45										19 07							19 15
Queens Rd Peckham	d	18 39						18 48										19 09							19 18
Peckham Rye 4	d	18a42			18 43	18 45	18 47	18 50		18 50	19a16							19a12				19 13	19 15	19 17	19 20
Denmark Hill 4	d				18 47	18 49	18 51	18 53		18 54												19 17	19 19	19 21	19 23
London Blackfriars 3 ⊖	a									19 04															
Clapham High Street ⊖	d							18 58																	19 28
Wandsworth Road	d							18 59																	19 29
Battersea Park 4	d							19 02						19 35											19 32
London Victoria 15 ⊖	a				18 56	18 58	19 00	19 06						19 39								19 26	19 28	19 30	19 36
Penge West	d		18 54	19 00											19 15					19 24	19 30				
Anerley	d		18 56	19 02											19 17					19 26	19 32				
Norwood Junction 2	d		19 00	19 05											19 20					19 30	19 35				
West Croydon 4	a			19 11											19 30						19 41				
East Croydon	a		19 03																	19 33					

		SE B	SN	LO		LO	SN	LO	LO	LO	SN	SN	LO	SE A		SN	SE B	SN	LO	LO	SN	LO	LO	LO	
London Bridge 4 ⊖	d						19 22				19 33	19 36				19 41					19 52				
Highbury & Islington	a																								
	d			18 55				19 03	19 10				19 18						19 25			19 33	19 40		
Canonbury	d			18 57				19 05	19 12				19 20						19 27			19 35	19 42		
Dalston Junction Stn ELL	d			19 00		19 05		19 10	19 15	19 20			19 25						19 30	19 35		19 40	19 45	19 50	
Haggerston	d			19 01		19 06		19 11	19 16	19 21			19 26						19 31	19 36		19 41	19 46	19 51	
Hoxton	d			19 03		19 08		19 13	19 18	19 23			19 28						19 33	19 38		19 43	19 48	19 53	
Shoreditch High Street	d			19 06		19 11		19 16	19 21	19 26			19 31						19 36	19 41		19 46	19 51	19 56	
Whitechapel	d			19 08		19 13		19 18	19 23	19 28			19 33						19 38	19 43		19 48	19 53	19 58	
Shadwell	d			19 10		19 15		19 20	19 25	19 30			19 35						19 40	19 45		19 50	19 55	20 00	
Wapping	d			19 12		19 17		19 22	19 27	19 32			19 37						19 42	19 47		19 52	19 57	20 02	
Rotherhithe	d			19 14		19 19		19 24	19 29	19 34			19 39						19 44	19 49		19 54	19 59	20 04	
Canada Water	d			19 16		19 21		19 26	19 31	19 36			19 41						19 46	19 51		19 56	20 01	20 06	
Surrey Quays	d			19 17		19 22		19 27	19 32	19 37			19 42						19 47	19 52		19 57	20 02	20 07	
New Cross ELL	a					19 27				19 42										19 57				20 12	
New Cross Gate 4	a			19 21			19 27	19 31	19 36			19 41	19 46						19 51		19 57	20 01	20 06		
	d			19 22			19 27	19 32	19 37			19 41	19 47						19 52		19 57	20 02	20 07		
Brockley	d			19 24			19 30	19 34	19 39			19 44	19 49						19 54		20 00	20 04	20 09		
Honor Oak Park	d			19 27			19 33	19 37	19 42			19 47	19 52						19 57		20 03	20 07	20 12		
Forest Hill 4	d			19 30			19 35	19 40	19 45			19 49	19 55						20 00		20 05	20 10	20 15		
Sydenham	d			19 32			19 38	19 42	19 47			19 52	19 57						20 02		20 08	20 12	20 17		
Crystal Palace 4	d		19 30	19a37			19 43		19a52									20 00	20a07		20 13		20a22		
Gipsy Hill	d		19 32				19 45											20 03			20 15				
West Norwood 4	d		19 35				19 48											20 06			20 18				
Streatham Hill	d						19 52														20 22				
Balham 4 ⊖	d						19 55														20 25				
Wandsworth Common	d						19 57														20 27				
Clapham Junction 10	d						20 01														20 31				
South Bermondsey	d										19 37					19 45									
Queens Rd Peckham	d										19 39					19 48									
Peckham Rye 4	d	19 20	19a46								19a42			19 43		19 50	19 50	20a16							
Denmark Hill 4	d	19 24												19 47		19 53	19 54								
London Blackfriars 3 ⊖	a	19 34															20 04								
Clapham High Street ⊖	d															19 58									
Wandsworth Road	d															19 59									
Battersea Park 4	d						20 05									20 02					20 35				
London Victoria 15 ⊖	a						20 09							19 56		20 06					20 39				
Penge West	d							19 45				19 54	20 00									20 15			
Anerley	d							19 47				19 56	20 02									20 17			
Norwood Junction 2	d							19 50				20 00	20 05									20 20			
West Croydon 4	a							20 00					20 15									20 30			
East Croydon	a											20 03													

A 19 May

B not 19 May

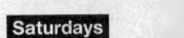

London Bridge to London Victoria - Croydon and East London Line

Network Diagram - see first Page of Table 177

		SN	SN	LO	SE A	SN	SE B	SN	LO	LO		SN	LO	LO	LO	SN	SN	LO	SE A	SN		SE B	SN	LO	LO
London Bridge [4] ⊖	d	20 03	20 06			20 11						20 22				20 33	20 36			20 41					
Highbury & Islington	a																								
	d			19 48					19 55				20 03	20 10				20 18						20 25	
Canonbury	d			19 50					19 57				20 05	20 12				20 20						20 27	
Dalston Junction Stn ELL	d			19 55					20 00	20 05			20 10	20 15	20 20			20 25						20 30	20 35
Haggerston	d			19 56					20 01	20 06			20 11	20 16	20 21			20 26						20 31	20 36
Hoxton	d			19 58					20 03	20 08			20 13	20 18	20 23			20 28						20 33	20 38
Shoreditch High Street	d			20 01					20 06	20 11			20 16	20 21	20 26			20 31						20 36	20 41
Whitechapel	d			20 03					20 08	20 13			20 18	20 23	20 28			20 33						20 38	20 43
Shadwell	d			20 05					20 10	20 15			20 20	20 25	20 30			20 35						20 40	20 45
Wapping	d			20 07					20 12	20 17			20 22	20 27	20 32			20 37						20 42	20 47
Rotherhithe	d			20 09					20 14	20 19			20 24	20 29	20 34			20 39						20 44	20 49
Canada Water	d			20 11					20 16	20 21			20 26	20 31	20 36			20 41						20 46	20 51
Surrey Quays	d			20 12					20 17	20 22			20 27	20 32	20 37			20 42						20 47	20 52
New Cross ELL	a									20 27					20 42										20 57
New Cross Gate [4]	a		20 11	20 16					20 21			20 27	20 31	20 36			20 41	20 46						20 51	
	d		20 11	20 17					20 22			20 27	20 32	20 37			20 41	20 47						20 52	
Brockley	d		20 14	20 19					20 24			20 30	20 34	20 39			20 44	20 49						20 54	
Honor Oak Park	d		20 17	20 22					20 27			20 33	20 37	20 42			20 47	20 52						20 57	
Forest Hill [4]	d		20 19	20 25					20 30			20 35	20 40	20 45			20 49	20 55						21 00	
Sydenham	d		20 22	20 27					20 32			20 38	20 42	20 47			20 52	20 57						21 02	
Crystal Palace [4]	d							20 30	20a37			20 43		20a52									21 00	21a07	
Gipsy Hill	d							20 33				20 45											21 02		
West Norwood [4]	d							20 36				20 48											21 05		
Streatham Hill	d											20 52													
Balham [4] ⊖	d											20 55													
Wandsworth Common	d											20 57													
Clapham Junction [10]	d											21 01													
South Bermondsey	d	20 07				20 15										20 37				20 45					
Queens Rd Peckham	d	20 09				20 18										20 39				20 48					
Peckham Rye [4]	d	20a12			20 13	20 20	20 20	20a46								20a42			20 43	20 50		20 50	21a16		
Denmark Hill [4]	d				20 17	20 23	20 24												20 47	20 53		20 54			
London Blackfriars [3] ⊖	a						20 34															21 04			
Clapham High Street ⊖	d					20 28														20 58					
Wandsworth Road	d					20 29														20 59					
Battersea Park [4]	d					20 32						21 05								21 02					
London Victoria [15] ⊖	a				20 26	20 36						21 09							20 56	21 06					
Penge West	d		20 24	20 30									20 45				20 54	21 00							
Anerley	d		20 26	20 32									20 47				20 56	21 02							
Norwood Junction [2]	d		20 30	20 35									20 50				21 00	21 05							
West Croydon [4]	a			20 45									21 00					21 15							
East Croydon	a		20 33														21 03								

		SN	LO	LO	LO	SN		SN	LO	SE A	SN	SE B	SN	LO	LO	SN		LO	LO	LO	SN	SN	LO	SE A	SN
London Bridge [4] ⊖	d	20 52				21 03		21 06			21 11					21 22					21 33	21 36			21 41
Highbury & Islington	a																								
	d		20 33	20 40					20 48					20 55				21 03	21 10				21 18		
Canonbury	d		20 35	20 42					20 50					20 57				21 05	21 12				21 20		
Dalston Junction Stn ELL	d		20 40	20 45	20 50				20 55					21 00	21 05			21 10	21 15	21 20			21 25		
Haggerston	d		20 41	20 46	20 51				20 56					21 01	21 06			21 11	21 16	21 21			21 26		
Hoxton	d		20 43	20 48	20 53				20 58					21 03	21 08			21 13	21 18	21 23			21 28		
Shoreditch High Street	d		20 46	20 51	20 56				21 01					21 06	21 11			21 16	21 21	21 26			21 31		
Whitechapel	d		20 48	20 53	20 58				21 03					21 08	21 13			21 18	21 23	21 28			21 33		
Shadwell	d		20 50	20 55	21 00				21 05					21 10	21 15			21 20	21 25	21 30			21 35		
Wapping	d		20 52	20 57	21 02				21 07					21 12	21 17			21 22	21 27	21 32			21 37		
Rotherhithe	d		20 54	20 59	21 04				21 09					21 14	21 19			21 24	21 29	21 34			21 39		
Canada Water	d		20 56	21 01	21 06				21 11					21 16	21 21			21 26	21 31	21 36			21 41		
Surrey Quays	d		20 57	21 02	21 07				21 12					21 17	21 22			21 27	21 32	21 37			21 42		
New Cross ELL	a				21 12										21 27					21 42					
New Cross Gate [4]	a	20 57	21 01	21 06				21 11	21 16					21 21		21 27		21 31	21 36			21 41	21 46		
	d	20 57	21 02	21 07				21 11	21 17					21 22		21 27		21 32	21 37			21 41	21 47		
Brockley	d	21 00	21 04	21 09				21 14	21 19					21 24		21 30		21 34	21 39			21 44	21 49		
Honor Oak Park	d	21 03	21 07	21 12				21 17	21 22					21 27		21 33		21 37	21 42			21 47	21 52		
Forest Hill [4]	d	21 05	21 10	21 15				21 19	21 25					21 30		21 35		21 40	21 45			21 49	21 55		
Sydenham	d	21 08	21 12	21 17				21 22	21 27					21 32		21 38		21 42	21 47			21 52	21 57		
Crystal Palace [4]	d	21 13		21a22									21 30	21a37		21 43			21a52						
Gipsy Hill	d	21 15											21 32			21 45									
West Norwood [4]	d	21 18											21 35			21 48									
Streatham Hill	d	21 22														21 52									
Balham [4] ⊖	d	21 25														21 55									
Wandsworth Common	d	21 27														21 57									
Clapham Junction [10]	d	21 31														22 01									
South Bermondsey	d					21 07					21 15										21 37				21 45
Queens Rd Peckham	d					21 09					21 18										21 39				21 48
Peckham Rye [4]	d					21a12				21 13	21 20	21 20	21a46								21a42			21 43	21 50
Denmark Hill [4]	d									21 17	21 23	21 24												21 47	21 53
London Blackfriars [3] ⊖	a											21 34													
Clapham High Street ⊖	d										21 28														21 58
Wandsworth Road	d										21 29														21 59
Battersea Park [4]	d	21 35									21 32					22 05									22 02
London Victoria [15] ⊖	a	21 39								21 26	21 36					22 09								21 56	22 06
Penge West	d		21 15					21 24	21 30									21 45				21 54	22 00		
Anerley	d		21 17					21 26	21 32									21 47				21 56	22 02		
Norwood Junction [2]	d		21 20					21 30	21 35									21 50				22 00	22 05		
West Croydon [4]	a		21 30						21 45									22 00					22 12		
East Croydon	a							21 33														22 04			

A 19 May

B not 19 May

Table 178

Saturdays

until 21 July

London Bridge to London Victoria - Croydon and East London Line

Network Diagram - see first Page of Table 177

		SE A		SN	LO	LO	SN	LO	LO	LO	SN	SN		LO	SE B	SN	SE A	SN	LO	SN	LO	LO		SN	SN
London Bridge 4 ⊖	d						21 52				22 03	22 06				22 11				22 22				22 33	22 36
Highbury & Islington	a																								
	d				21 25			21 33	21 40					21 48					21 55		22 05				
Canonbury	d				21 27			21 35	21 42					21 50					21 57		22 07				
Dalston Junction Stn ELL	d				21 30	21 35		21 40	21 45	21 50				21 55					22 00		22 10	22 20			
Haggerston	d				21 31	21 36		21 41	21 46	21 51				21 56					22 01		22 11	22 21			
Hoxton	d				21 33	21 38		21 43	21 48	21 53				21 58					22 03		22 13	22 23			
Shoreditch High Street	d				21 36	21 41		21 46	21 51	21 56				22 01					22 06		22 16	22 26			
Whitechapel	d				21 38	21 43		21 48	21 53	21 58				22 03					22 08		22 18	22 28			
Shadwell	d				21 40	21 45		21 50	21 55	22 00				22 05					22 10		22 20	22 30			
Wapping	d				21 42	21 47		21 52	21 57	22 02				22 07					22 12		22 22	22 32			
Rotherhithe	d				21 44	21 49		21 54	21 59	22 04				22 09					22 14		22 24	22 34			
Canada Water	d				21 46	21 51		21 56	22 01	22 06				22 11					22 16		22 26	22 36			
Surrey Quays	d				21 47	21 52		21 57	22 02	22 07				22 12					22 17		22 27	22 37			
New Cross ELL	a					21 57				22 13												22 42			
New Cross Gate 4	a				21 51		21 57	22 01	22 06			22 11		22 16					22 21	22 27	22 31				22 41
	d				21 52		21 57	22 02	22 07			22 11		22 17					22 22	22 27	22 32				22 41
Brockley	d				21 54		22 00	22 04	22 09			22 14		22 19					22 24	22 30	22 34				22 44
Honor Oak Park	d				21 57		22 03	22 07	22 12			22 17		22 22					22 27	22 33	22 37				22 47
Forest Hill 4	d				22 00		22 05	22 10	22 15			22 19		22 25					22 30	22 35	22 40				22 49
Sydenham	d				22 02		22 08	22 12	22 17			22 22		22 27					22 32	22 38	22 42				22 52
Crystal Palace 4	d			22 00	22a07		22 13		22a22									22 30	22a37	22 43					
Gipsy Hill	d			22 02			22 15											22 32		22 45					
West Norwood 4	d			22 05			22 18											22 35		22 48					
Streatham Hill	d						22 22													22 52					
Balham 4 ⊖	d						22 25													22 55					
Wandsworth Common	d						22 27													22 57					
Clapham Junction 10	d						22 31													23 01					
South Bermondsey	d										22 07					22 15								22 37	
Queens Rd Peckham	d										22 09					22 18								22 39	
Peckham Rye 4	d	21 50		22a16							22a12				22 13	22 20	22 20	22a46						22a42	
Denmark Hill 4	d	21 54													22 17	22 23	22 24								
London Blackfriars 3 ⊖	a	22 04															22 34								
Clapham High Street ⊖	d															22 28									
Wandsworth Road	d															22 29									
Battersea Park 4	d						22 35									22 32				23 05					
London Victoria 15 ⊖	a						22 39								22 26	22 36				23 09					
Penge West	d							22 15				22 24		22 30							22 45				22 54
Anerley	d							22 17				22 26		22 32							22 47				22 56
Norwood Junction 2	d							22 20				22 30		22 35							22 50				23 00
West Croydon 4	a							22 30						22 42							23 00				
East Croydon	a											22 35													23 03

		SE B	SN	SE A	SN	LO	SN	LO		LO	SN	SN	SE B	SN	SE A	SN	LO	SN		LO	LO	SN	SN	LO	SN
London Bridge 4 ⊖	d		22 41				22 52				23 03	23 06		23 11				23 22				23 33	23 36		23 52
Highbury & Islington	a																								
	d					22 25		22 35									22 55			23 05				23 25	
Canonbury	d					22 27		22 37									22 57			23 07				23 27	
Dalston Junction Stn ELL	d					22 30		22 40		22 50							23 00			23 10	23 20			23 30	
Haggerston	d					22 31		22 41		22 51							23 01			23 11	23 21			23 31	
Hoxton	d					22 33		22 43		22 53							23 03			23 13	23 23			23 33	
Shoreditch High Street	d					22 36		22 46		22 56							23 06			23 16	23 26			23 36	
Whitechapel	d					22 38		22 48		22 58							23 08			23 18	23 28			23 38	
Shadwell	d					22 40		22 50		23 00							23 10			23 20	23 30			23 40	
Wapping	d					22 42		22 52		23 02							23 12			23 22	23 32			23 42	
Rotherhithe	d					22 44		22 54		23 04							23 14			23 24	23 34			23 44	
Canada Water	d					22 46		22 56		23 06							23 16			23 26	23 36			23 46	
Surrey Quays	d					22 47		22 57		23 07							23 17			23 27	23 37			23 47	
New Cross ELL	a									23 12											23 42				
New Cross Gate 4	a					22 51	22 57	23 01				23 11					23 21	23 27		23 31			23 41	23 51	23 57
	d					22 52	22 57	23 02				23 11					23 22	23 27		23 32			23 41	23 52	23 57
Brockley	d					22 54	23 00	23 04				23 14					23 24	23 30		23 34			23 44	23 54	00 01
Honor Oak Park	d					22 57	23 03	23 07				23 17					23 27	23 33		23 37			23 47	23 57	00 04
Forest Hill 4	d					23 00	23 05	23 10				23 19					23 30	23 35		23 40			23 49	23 59	00 06
Sydenham	d					23 02	23 08	23 12				23 22					23 32	23 38		23 42			23 52	00 02	00 09
Crystal Palace 4	d				23 00	23a07	23 13									23 30	23a37	23 43						00a07	00 13
Gipsy Hill	d				23 02		23 15									23 32		23 45							00 15
West Norwood 4	d				23 05		23 18									23 35		23 48							00 18
Streatham Hill	d						23 22											23 52							00 22
Balham 4 ⊖	d						23 25											23 55							00 26
Wandsworth Common	d						23 27											23 57							00 28
Clapham Junction 10	d						23 31											00 02							00 32
South Bermondsey	d		22 45								23 07			23 15								23 37			
Queens Rd Peckham	d		22 48								23 09			23 18								23 39			
Peckham Rye 4	d	22 43	22 50	22 50	23a16						23 12		23 13	23 20	23 20	23a46						23 42			
Denmark Hill 4	d	22 47	22 53	22 54									23 17	23 23	23 24										
London Blackfriars 3 ⊖	a			23 04											23 34										
Clapham High Street ⊖	d		22 58											23 28											
Wandsworth Road	d		22 59											23 29											
Battersea Park 4	d		23 02				23 35							23 32				00 05							00 35
London Victoria 15 ⊖	a	22 56	23 06				23 41						23 26	23 37				00 10							00 42
Penge West	d							23 15				23 24								23 45			23 54		
Anerley	d							23 17				23 26								23 47			23 56		
Norwood Junction 2	d							23 20			23a34	23 30								23 50		00a04	23 59		
West Croydon 4	a							23 30												23 59					
East Croydon	a											23 33											00 03		

A not 19 May

B 19 May

Table 178

Saturdays
until 21 July

London Bridge to London Victoria - Croydon and East London Line

Network Diagram - see first Page of Table 177

		LO	LO	LO
London Bridge [4] ⊖	d			
Highbury & Islington	a			
	d	23 35	23 42	23 56
Canonbury	d	23 37	23 44	23 58
Dalston Junction Stn ELL	d	23 40	23 47	00 02
Haggerston	d	23 41	23 48	00 03
Hoxton	d	23 43	23 50	00 05
Shoreditch High Street	d	23 46	23 53	00 08
Whitechapel	d	23 48	23 55	00 10
Shadwell	d	23 50	23 57	00 12
Wapping	d	23 52	23 59	00 14
Rotherhithe	d	23 54	00 01	00 16
Canada Water	d	23 56	00 03	00 18
Surrey Quays	d	23 57	00 05	00 19
New Cross ELL	a			
New Cross Gate [4]	a	00 02	00 08	00 23
	d	00 02		
Brockley	d	00 04		
Honor Oak Park	d	00 07		
Forest Hill [4]	d	00 10		
Sydenham	d	00 12		
Crystal Palace [4]	d			
Gipsy Hill	d			
West Norwood [4]	d			
Streatham Hill	d			
Balham [4] ⊖	d			
Wandsworth Common	d			
Clapham Junction [10]	d			
South Bermondsey	d			
Queens Rd Peckham	d			
Peckham Rye [4]	d			
Denmark Hill [4]	d			
London Blackfriars [3] ⊖	a			
Clapham High Street ⊖	d			
Wandsworth Road	d			
Battersea Park [4]	d			
London Victoria [15] ⊖	a			
Penge West	d	00 15		
Anerley	d	00 17		
Norwood Junction [2]	d	00 20		
West Croydon [4]	a	00 27		
East Croydon	a			

Saturdays
28 July to 11 August

		SN	SN	LO	SN	LO	SN	LO	LO	SN		SN	LO	SN	LO	LO	SN	LO	SN	SN		LO	SN	LO	LO
London Bridge [4] ⊖	d	23p22	23p36				23p52			00 03		00 06							00 33	00 36					
Highbury & Islington	a																								
	d			23p18		23p25		23p33	23p40				23p48		23p55	00 03		00 10				00 18		00 25	00 33
Canonbury	d			23p20		23p27		23p35	23p42				23p50		23p57	00 05		00 12				00 20		00 27	00 35
Dalston Junction Stn ELL	d			23p25		23p30		23p38	23p45				23p55		00 01	00 09		00 15				00 25		00 30	00 40
Haggerston	d			23p26		23p31		23p39	23p46				23p56		00 02	00 10		00 16				00 26		00 31	00 41
Hoxton	d			23p28		23p33		23p41	23p48				23p58		00 04	00 12		00 18				00 28		00 33	00 43
Shoreditch High Street	d			23p31		23p36		23p44	23p51				00 01		00 07	00 15		00 21				00 31		00 36	00 46
Whitechapel	d			23p33		23p38		23p46	23p53				00 03		00 09	00 17		00 23				00 33		00 38	00 48
Shadwell	d			23p35		23p40		23p48	23p55				00 05		00 11	00 19		00 25				00 35		00 40	00 50
Wapping	d			23p37		23p42		23p50	23p57				00 07		00 13	00 21		00 27				00 37		00 42	00 52
Rotherhithe	d			23p39		23p44		23p52	23p59				00 09		00 15	00 23		00 29				00 39		00 44	00 54
Canada Water	d			23p41		23p46		23p54	00 02				00 11		00 17	00 25		00 31				00 41		00 46	00 56
Surrey Quays	d			23p42		23p47		23p55	00 03				00 12		00 18	00 26		00 32				00 42		00 47	00 57
New Cross ELL	a																								
New Cross Gate [4]	a	23p27	23p41	23p46		23p51	23p57	23p58	00 07			00 11	00 16		00 22	00 30		00 36		00 41		00 47		00 51	01 02
	d	23p27	23p41	23p47		23p52	23p57	23p59	00 08			00 11	00 17		00 23	00 31		00 37		00 41		00 47		00 52	01 03
Brockley	d	23p30	23p44	23p49		23p54	00 01	00 03	00 10			00 14	00 19		00 25	00 33		00 39		00 44		00 49		00 54	01 05
Honor Oak Park	d	23p33	23p47	23p52		23p57	00 04	00 06	00 13			00 17	00 22		00 28	00 36		00 42		00 47		00 52		00 57	01 08
Forest Hill [4]	d	23p35	23p49	23p55		23p59	00 06	00 09	00 16			00 19	00 25		00 31	00 39		00 45		00 49		00 55		00 59	01 11
Sydenham	d	23p38	23p52	23p57		00 02	00 09	00 11	00 18			00 22	00 27		00 33	00 41		00 47		00 52		00 57		01 02	01 13
Crystal Palace [4]	d	23p43			00 03	00a07	00 13		00a23					00 33	00a38		00 47	00a52					01 03	01a07	
Gipsy Hill	d	23p45					00 15																		
West Norwood [4]	d	23p48					00 18																		
Streatham Hill	d	23p52					00 22																		
Balham [4] ⊖	d	23p55					00 25																		
Wandsworth Common	d	23p58					00 27																		
Clapham Junction [10]	d	00 02					00 31																		
South Bermondsey	d									00 07									00 37						
Queens Rd Peckham	d									00 09									00 39						
Peckham Rye [4]	d									00 12									00 42						
Denmark Hill [4]	d																								
London Blackfriars [3] ⊖	a																								
Clapham High Street ⊖	d																								
Wandsworth Road	d																								
Battersea Park [4]	d	00 05					00 35																		
London Victoria [15] ⊖	a	00 10					00 42																		
Penge West	d		23p54	00 01				00 14				00 24	00 30			00 44				00 54		01 00			01 16
Anerley	d		23p56	00 03				00 16				00 26	00 32			00 46				00 56		01 02			01 18
Norwood Junction [2]	d		23p59	00 06	00 09			00 19		00a34		00 30	00 35	00 38		00 49	00 52		01a04	01 00		01 05	01 08		01 21
West Croydon [4]	a			00 13	00 14			00 26					00 42	00 43		00 56	00 58					01 14	01 13		01 28
East Croydon	a		00 03									00 33								01 03					

Table 178

Saturdays

28 July to 11 August

London Bridge to London Victoria - Croydon and East London Line

Network Diagram - see first Page of Table 177

		LO	LO	LO	LO	LO		LO	SN	SE	LO	LO	LO	LO	SE	LO		LO	LO	LO	LO	SN	LO	SN	SN
London Bridge 4 ⊖	d								06 11															06 36	06 41
Highbury & Islington	a																								
	d	00 40	00 48	00 55	01 03	01 10		01 25					05 35						05 55	06 05					
Canonbury	d	00 42	00 50	00 57	01 05	01 12		01 27					05 37						05 57	06 07					
Dalston Junction Stn ELL	d	00 45	00 55	01 00	01 10	01 15		01 32					05 40	05 50					06 00	06 10	06 20				
Haggerston	d	00 46	00 56	01 01	01 11	01 16		01 33					05 41	05 51					06 01	06 11	06 21				
Hoxton	d	00 48	00 58	01 03	01 13	01 18		01 35					05 43	05 53					06 03	06 13	06 23				
Shoreditch High Street	d	00 51	01 01	01 06	01 16	01 21		01 38					05 46	05 56					06 06	06 16	06 26				
Whitechapel	d	00 53	01 03	01 08	01 18	01 23		01 40					05 48	05 58					06 08	06 18	06 28				
Shadwell	d	00 55	01 05	01 10	01 20	01 25		01 42					05 50	06 00					06 10	06 20	06 30				
Wapping	d	00 57	01 07	01 12	01 22	01 27		01 44					05 52	06 02					06 12	06 22	06 32				
Rotherhithe	d	00 59	01 09	01 14	01 24	01 29		01 46					05 54	06 04					06 14	06 24	06 34				
Canada Water	d	01 01	01 11	01 16	01 26	01 31		01 48					05 56	06 06					06 16	06 26	06 36				
Surrey Quays	d	01 02	01 12	01 17	01 27	01 32		01 49					05 57	06 07					06 17	06 27	06 37				
New Cross ELL	a													06 12							06 42				
New Cross Gate 4	a	01 06	01 16	01 21	01 31	01 36		01 53					06 01						06 21	06 31				06 41	
	d	01 07	01 17	01 22	01 32	01 37		01 54			05 47	05 52	06 02			06 07		06 17	06 22	06 32			06 37	06 41	
Brockley	d	01 09	01 19	01 24	01 34	01 39		01 56			05 49	05 54	06 04			06 09		06 19	06 24	06 34			06 39	06 44	
Honor Oak Park	d	01 12	01 22	01 27	01 37	01 42		01 59			05 52	05 57	06 07			06 12		06 22	06 27	06 37			06 42	06 47	
Forest Hill 4	d	01 15	01 25	01 30	01 40	01 45		02 02			05 55	06 00	06 10			06 15		06 25	06 30	06 40			06 45	06 49	
Sydenham	d	01 17	01 27	01 32	01 42	01 47		02 04			05 57	06 02	06 12			06 17		06 27	06 32	06 42			06 47	06 52	
Crystal Palace 4	d	01a22		01a37		01a52						06a07				06a22			06a37			06 45	06a52		
Gipsy Hill	d																					06 47			
West Norwood 4	d																					06 50			
Streatham Hill	d																								
Balham 4 ⊖	d																								
Wandsworth Common	d																								
Clapham Junction 10	d																								
South Bermondsey	d								06 15																06 45
Queens Rd Peckham	d								06 18																06 48
Peckham Rye 4	d								06 20	06 20					06 50							07a01			06 50
Denmark Hill 4	d								06 23	06 24					06 54										06 53
London Blackfriars 3 ⊖	a									06 34					07 04										
Clapham High Street ⊖	d								06 28																06 58
Wandsworth Road	d								06 29																06 59
Battersea Park 4	d								06 32																07 02
London Victoria 15 ⊖	a								06 36																07 06
Penge West	d		01 30		01 45			02 07			06 00		06 15					06 30		06 45				06 54	
Anerley	d		01 32		01 47			02 09			06 02		06 17					06 32		06 47				06 56	
Norwood Junction 2	d		01 35		01 50			02 12			06 06		06 20					06 35		06 50				07 00	
West Croydon 4	a		01 42		01 57			02 19			06 13		06 30					06 41		07 00					
East Croydon	a																							07 03	

		SE		SE	LO	LO	LO	LO	LO	LO	SN	LO		LO	LO	LO	LO	SN	LO	SN	SN	LO		LO	LO
London Bridge 4 ⊖	d										07 06							07 11		07 33	07 36				
Highbury & Islington	a																								
	d					06 25		06 33	06 40			06 48		06 55		07 03	07 10					07 18		07 25	
Canonbury	d					06 27		06 35	06 42			06 50		06 57		07 05	07 12					07 20		07 27	
Dalston Junction Stn ELL	d					06 30	06 35	06 40	06 45	06 50		06 55		07 00	07 05	07 10	07 15		07 20			07 25		07 30	07 35
Haggerston	d					06 31	06 36	06 41	06 46	06 51		06 56		07 01	07 06	07 11	07 16		07 21			07 26		07 31	07 36
Hoxton	d					06 33	06 38	06 43	06 48	06 53		06 58		07 03	07 08	07 13	07 18		07 23			07 28		07 33	07 38
Shoreditch High Street	d					06 36	06 41	06 46	06 51	06 56		07 01		07 06	07 11	07 16	07 21		07 26			07 31		07 36	07 41
Whitechapel	d					06 38	06 43	06 48	06 53	06 58		07 03		07 08	07 13	07 18	07 23		07 28			07 33		07 38	07 43
Shadwell	d					06 40	06 45	06 50	06 55	07 00		07 05		07 10	07 15	07 20	07 25		07 30			07 35		07 40	07 45
Wapping	d					06 42	06 47	06 52	06 57	07 02		07 07		07 12	07 17	07 22	07 27		07 32			07 37		07 42	07 47
Rotherhithe	d					06 44	06 49	06 54	06 59	07 04		07 09		07 14	07 19	07 24	07 29		07 34			07 39		07 44	07 49
Canada Water	d					06 46	06 51	06 56	07 01	07 06		07 11		07 16	07 21	07 26	07 31		07 36			07 41		07 46	07 51
Surrey Quays	d					06 47	06 52	06 57	07 02	07 07		07 12		07 17	07 22	07 27	07 32		07 37			07 42		07 47	07 52
New Cross ELL	a						06 57			07 12					07 27				07 42						07 57
New Cross Gate 4	a					06 51		07 00	07 06		07 11	07 15		07 21		07 31	07 36				07 41	07 45		07 51	
	d				06 47	06 52		07 02	07 07		07 11	07 17		07 22		07 32	07 37				07 41	07 47		07 52	
Brockley	d				06 49	06 54		07 04	07 09		07 14	07 19		07 24		07 34	07 39				07 44	07 49		07 54	
Honor Oak Park	d				06 52	06 57		07 07	07 12		07 17	07 22		07 27		07 37	07 42				07 47	07 52		07 57	
Forest Hill 4	d				06 55	07 00		07 10	07 15		07 19	07 25		07 30		07 40	07 45				07 49	07 55		08 00	
Sydenham	d				06 57	07 02		07 12	07 17		07 22	07 27		07 32		07 42	07 47				07 52	07 57		08 02	
Crystal Palace 4	d					07a07			07a22					07a37			07a52							08a07	
Gipsy Hill	d																								
West Norwood 4	d																								
Streatham Hill	d																								
Balham 4 ⊖	d																								
Wandsworth Common	d																								
Clapham Junction 10	d																								
South Bermondsey	d																	07 15		07 37					
Queens Rd Peckham	d																	07 18		07 39					
Peckham Rye 4	d	07 17		07 20														07 20		07a42					
Denmark Hill 4	d	07 21		07 24														07 23							
London Blackfriars 3 ⊖	a			07 34																					
Clapham High Street ⊖	d																	07 28							
Wandsworth Road	d																	07 29							
Battersea Park 4	d																	07 32							
London Victoria 15 ⊖	a	07 33																07 36							
Penge West	d				07 00			07 15			07 24	07 30				07 45					07 54	08 00			
Anerley	d				07 02			07 17			07 26	07 32				07 47					07 56	08 02			
Norwood Junction 2	d				07 05			07 20			07 30	07 35				07 50					08 00	08 05			
West Croydon 4	a				07 11			07 30				07 42				08 00						08 12			
East Croydon	a										07 33										08 03				

Table 178

Saturdays

28 July to 11 August

London Bridge to London Victoria - Croydon and East London Line

Network Diagram - see first Page of Table 177

	LO	LO	LO	SE	SN	SE	SN		SN	LO	SE	SN	SE	SN	LO	LO	SN		LO	LO	LO	SN	SN	LO
London Bridge 4 ⊖ d					07 41		08 03		08 06			08 11					08 22					08 33	08 36	
Highbury & Islington a																								
d	07 33	07 40								07 48					07 55				08 03	08 10				08 18
Canonbury d	07 35	07 42								07 50					07 57				08 05	08 12				08 20
Dalston Junction Stn ELL d	07 40	07 45	07 50							07 55					08 00	08 05			08 10	08 15	08 20			08 25
Haggerston d	07 41	07 46	07 51							07 56					08 01	08 06			08 11	08 16	08 21			08 26
Hoxton d	07 43	07 48	07 53							07 58					08 03	08 08			08 13	08 18	08 23			08 28
Shoreditch High Street d	07 46	07 51	07 56							08 01					08 06	08 11			08 16	08 21	08 26			08 31
Whitechapel d	07 48	07 53	07 58							08 03					08 08	08 13			08 18	08 23	08 28			08 33
Shadwell d	07 50	07 55	08 00							08 05					08 10	08 15			08 20	08 25	08 30			08 35
Wapping d	07 52	07 57	08 02							08 07					08 12	08 17			08 22	08 27	08 32			08 37
Rotherhithe d	07 54	07 59	08 04							08 09					08 14	08 19			08 24	08 29	08 34			08 39
Canada Water d	07 56	08 01	08 06							08 11					08 16	08 21			08 26	08 31	08 36			08 41
Surrey Quays d	07 57	08 02	08 07							08 12					08 17	08 22			08 27	08 32	08 37			08 42
New Cross ELL a			08 12													08 27					08 42			
New Cross Gate 4 a	08 01	08 06							08 11	08 16					08 21		08 27		08 31	08 36			08 41	08 46
d	08 02	08 07							08 11	08 16					08 22		08 27		08 32	08 37			08 41	08 47
Brockley d	08 04	08 09							08 14	08 17					08 24		08 30		08 34	08 39			08 44	08 49
Honor Oak Park d	08 07	08 12							08 17	08 20					08 27		08 33		08 37	08 42			08 47	08 52
Forest Hill 4 d	08 10	08 15							08 19	08 24					08 30		08 35		08 40	08 45			08 49	08 55
Sydenham d	08 12	08 17							08 22	08 25					08 32		08 38		08 42	08 47			08 52	08 57
Crystal Palace 4 d		08a22												08 30	08a37		08 43			08a52				
Gipsy Hill d														08 32			08 45							
West Norwood 4 d														08 35			08 48							
Streatham Hill d																	08 52							
Balham 4 ⊖ d																	08 55							
Wandsworth Common d																	08 57							
Clapham Junction 10 d																	09 01							
South Bermondsey d					07 45		08 07					08 15										08 37		
Queens Rd Peckham d					07 48		08 09					08 18										08 39		
Peckham Rye 4 d				07 47	07 50	07 50	08a12				08 17	08 20	08 20	08a46								08a42		
Denmark Hill 4 d				07 51	07 53	07 54					08 21	08 23	08 24											
London Blackfriars 3 ⊖ a						08 04							08 34											
Clapham High Street ⊖ d					07 58							08 28												
Wandsworth Road d					07 59							08 29												
Battersea Park 4 d					08 02							08 32					09 05							
London Victoria 15 ⊖ a				08 03	08 06						08 33	08 36					09 09							
Penge West d	08 15								08 24	08 29									08 45				08 54	09 00
Anerley d	08 17								08 26	08 31									08 47				08 56	09 02
Norwood Junction 2 d	08 20								08 30	08 34									08 50				09 00	09 05
West Croydon 4 a	08 30									08 41									09 00					09 12
East Croydon a									08 33														09 03	

	SE	SN	SE		SN	LO	LO	SN	LO	LO	LO	SN	SN		LO	SE	SN	SE	SN	LO	LO	SN	LO	
London Bridge 4 ⊖ d		08 41						08 52				09 03	09 06				09 11					09 22		
Highbury & Islington a																								
d						08 25			08 33	08 40					08 48					08 55			09 03	
Canonbury d						08 27			08 35	08 42					08 50					08 57			09 05	
Dalston Junction Stn ELL d						08 30	08 35		08 40	08 45	08 50				08 55					09 00	09 05		09 10	
Haggerston d						08 31	08 36		08 41	08 46	08 51				08 56					09 01	09 06		09 11	
Hoxton d						08 33	08 38		08 43	08 48	08 53				08 58					09 03	09 08		09 13	
Shoreditch High Street d						08 36	08 41		08 46	08 51	08 56				09 01					09 06	09 11		09 16	
Whitechapel d						08 38	08 43		08 48	08 53	08 58				09 03					09 08	09 13		09 18	
Shadwell d						08 40	08 45		08 50	08 55	09 00				09 05					09 10	09 15		09 20	
Wapping d						08 42	08 47		08 52	08 57	09 02				09 07					09 12	09 17		09 22	
Rotherhithe d						08 44	08 49		08 54	08 59	09 04				09 09					09 14	09 19		09 24	
Canada Water d						08 46	08 51		08 56	09 01	09 06				09 11					09 16	09 21		09 26	
Surrey Quays d						08 47	08 52		08 57	09 02	09 07				09 12					09 17	09 22		09 27	
New Cross ELL a							08 57				09 12										09 27			
New Cross Gate 4 a						08 51		08 57	09 01	09 06			09 11		09 16					09 21		09 27	09 30	
d						08 52		08 57	09 02	09 07			09 11		09 17					09 22		09 27	09 32	
Brockley d						08 54		09 00	09 04	09 09			09 14		09 19					09 24		09 30	09 34	
Honor Oak Park d						08 57		09 03	09 07	09 12			09 17		09 22					09 27		09 33	09 37	
Forest Hill 4 d						09 00		09 05	09 10	09 15			09 19		09 25					09 30		09 35	09 40	
Sydenham d						09 02		09 08	09 12	09 17			09 22		09 27					09 32		09 38	09 42	
Crystal Palace 4 d					09 00	09a07		09 13		09a22									09 30	09a37		09 43		
Gipsy Hill d					09 02			09 15											09 32			09 45		
West Norwood 4 d					09 05			09 18											09 35			09 48		
Streatham Hill d								09 22														09 52		
Balham 4 ⊖ d								09 25														09 55		
Wandsworth Common d								09 27														09 57		
Clapham Junction 10 d								09 32														10 01		
South Bermondsey d		08 45										09 07					09 15							
Queens Rd Peckham d		08 48										09 09					09 18							
Peckham Rye 4 d	08 47	08 50	08 50		09a16							09a12				09 17	09 20	09 20	09a46					
Denmark Hill 4 d	08 51	08 53	08 54													09 21	09 23	09 24						
London Blackfriars 3 ⊖ a			09 04															09 34						
Clapham High Street ⊖ d		08 58															09 28							
Wandsworth Road d		08 59															09 29							
Battersea Park 4 d		09 02						09 36									09 32					10 05		
London Victoria 15 ⊖ a	09 03	09 06						09 40								09 33	09 36					10 09		
Penge West d									09 15				09 24		09 30								09 45	
Anerley d									09 17				09 26		09 32								09 47	
Norwood Junction 2 d									09 20				09 30		09 35								09 50	
West Croydon 4 a									09 30						09 42								10 00	
East Croydon a													09 33											

Table 178

Saturdays

28 July to 11 August

London Bridge to London Victoria - Croydon and East London Line

Network Diagram - see first Page of Table 177

		LO	LO	SN	SN	LO	SE	SN	SE	SN		LO	LO	SN	
London Bridge 4 ⊖	d			09 33	09 36			09 41						09 52	
Highbury & Islington	a														
	d	09 10				09 18						09 25			
Canonbury	d	09 12				09 20						09 27			
Dalston Junction Stn ELL	d	09 15	09 20			09 25						09 30	09 35		
Haggerston	d	09 16	09 21			09 26						09 31	09 36		
Hoxton	d	09 18	09 23			09 28						09 33	09 38		
Shoreditch High Street	d	09 21	09 26			09 31						09 36	09 41		
Whitechapel	d	09 23	09 28			09 33						09 38	09 43		
Shadwell	d	09 25	09 30			09 35						09 40	09 45		
Wapping	d	09 27	09 32			09 37						09 42	09 47		
Rotherhithe	d	09 29	09 34			09 39						09 44	09 49		
Canada Water	d	09 31	09 36			09 41						09 46	09 51		
Surrey Quays	d	09 32	09 37			09 42						09 47	09 52		
New Cross ELL	a		09 42										09 57		
New Cross Gate 4	a	09 36			09 41	09 46						09 51		09 57	
	d	09 37			09 41	09 47						09 52		09 57	
Brockley	d	09 39			09 44	09 49						09 54		10 00	and at
Honor Oak Park	d	09 42			09 47	09 52						09 57		10 03	the same
Forest Hill 4	d	09 45			09 49	09 55						10 00		10 05	minutes
Sydenham	d	09 47			09 52	09 57						10 02		10 08	past
Crystal Palace 4	d	09a52								10 00		10a07		10 13	each
Gipsy Hill	d									10 02				10 15	hour until
West Norwood 4	d									10 05				10 18	
Streatham Hill	d													10 22	
Balham 4 ⊖	d													10 25	
Wandsworth Common	d													10 27	
Clapham Junction 10	d													10 31	
South Bermondsey	d			09 37				09 45							
Queens Rd Peckham	d			09 39				09 48							
Peckham Rye 4	d			09a42			09 47	09 50	09 50	10a16					
Denmark Hill 4	d						09 51	09 53	09 54						
London Blackfriars 3 ⊖	a								10 04						
Clapham High Street ⊖	d							09 58							
Wandsworth Road	d							09 59							
Battersea Park 4	d							10 02						10 35	
London Victoria 15 ⊖	a						10 03	10 06						10 39	
Penge West	d				09 54	10 00									
Anerley	d				09 56	10 02									
Norwood Junction 2	d				10 00	10 05									
West Croydon 4	a					10 12									
East Croydon	a				10 03										

		SN	LO	LO	LO		SN	SN	LO	SE
London Bridge 4 ⊖	d	18 52					19 03	19 06		
Highbury & Islington	a									
	d		18 33	18 40					18 48	
Canonbury	d		18 35	18 42					18 50	
Dalston Junction Stn ELL	d		18 40	18 45	18 50				18 55	
Haggerston	d		18 41	18 46	18 51				18 56	
Hoxton	d		18 43	18 48	18 53				18 58	
Shoreditch High Street	d		18 46	18 51	18 56				19 01	
Whitechapel	d		18 48	18 53	18 58				19 03	
Shadwell	d		18 50	18 55	19 00				19 05	
Wapping	d		18 52	18 57	19 02				19 07	
Rotherhithe	d		18 54	18 59	19 04				19 09	
Canada Water	d		18 56	19 01	19 06				19 11	
Surrey Quays	d		18 57	19 02	19 07				19 12	
New Cross ELL	a				19 12					
New Cross Gate 4	a	18 57	19 01	19 06				19 11	19 16	
	d	18 57	19 02	19 07				19 11	19 17	
Brockley	d	19 00	19 04	19 09				19 14	19 19	
Honor Oak Park	d	19 03	19 07	19 12				19 17	19 22	
Forest Hill 4	d	19 05	19 10	19 15				19 19	19 25	
Sydenham	d	19 08	19 12	19 17				19 22	19 27	
Crystal Palace 4	d	19 13		19a22						
Gipsy Hill	d	19 15								
West Norwood 4	d	19 18								
Streatham Hill	d	19 22								
Balham 4 ⊖	d	19 25								
Wandsworth Common	d	19 27								
Clapham Junction 10	d	19 31								
South Bermondsey	d						19 07			
Queens Rd Peckham	d						19 09			
Peckham Rye 4	d						19a12			19 17
Denmark Hill 4	d									19 21
London Blackfriars 3 ⊖	a									
Clapham High Street ⊖	d									
Wandsworth Road	d									
Battersea Park 4	d	19 35								
London Victoria 15 ⊖	a	19 39								19 33
Penge West	d		19 15					19 24	19 30	
Anerley	d		19 17					19 26	19 32	
Norwood Junction 2	d		19 20					19 30	19 35	
West Croydon 4	a		19 30						19 42	
East Croydon	a							19 33		

		SN	SE	SN	LO	LO		SN	LO	LO	LO	SN	SN
London Bridge 4 ⊖	d	19 11						19 22				19 33	19 36
Highbury & Islington	a												
	d				18 55				19 03	19 10			
Canonbury	d				18 57				19 05	19 12			
Dalston Junction Stn ELL	d				19 00	19 05			19 10	19 15	19 20		
Haggerston	d				19 01	19 06			19 11	19 16	19 21		
Hoxton	d				19 03	19 08			19 13	19 18	19 23		
Shoreditch High Street	d				19 06	19 11			19 16	19 21	19 26		
Whitechapel	d				19 08	19 13			19 18	19 23	19 28		
Shadwell	d				19 10	19 15			19 20	19 25	19 30		
Wapping	d				19 12	19 17			19 22	19 27	19 32		
Rotherhithe	d				19 14	19 19			19 24	19 29	19 34		
Canada Water	d				19 16	19 21			19 26	19 31	19 36		
Surrey Quays	d				19 17	19 22			19 27	19 32	19 37		
New Cross ELL	a					19 27					19 42		
New Cross Gate 4	a				19 21			19 27	19 31	19 36			19 41
	d				19 22			19 27	19 32	19 37			19 41
Brockley	d				19 24			19 30	19 34	19 39			19 44
Honor Oak Park	d				19 27			19 33	19 37	19 42			19 47
Forest Hill 4	d				19 30			19 35	19 40	19 45			19 49
Sydenham	d				19 32			19 38	19 42	19 47			19 52
Crystal Palace 4	d			19 30	19a37			19 43		19a52			
Gipsy Hill	d			19 32				19 45					
West Norwood 4	d			19 35				19 48					
Streatham Hill	d							19 52					
Balham 4 ⊖	d							19 55					
Wandsworth Common	d							19 57					
Clapham Junction 10	d							20 01					
South Bermondsey	d	19 15										19 37	
Queens Rd Peckham	d	19 18										19 39	
Peckham Rye 4	d	19 20	19 20	19a46								19a42	
Denmark Hill 4	d	19 23	19 24										
London Blackfriars 3 ⊖	a		19 34										
Clapham High Street ⊖	d	19 28											
Wandsworth Road	d	19 29											
Battersea Park 4	d	19 32						20 05					
London Victoria 15 ⊖	a	19 36						20 09					
Penge West	d								19 45				19 54
Anerley	d								19 47				19 56
Norwood Junction 2	d								19 50				20 00
West Croydon 4	a								20 00				
East Croydon	a												20 03

		LO	SN	SE		SN	LO	LO	SN	LO	LO	LO	SN
London Bridge 4 ⊖	d		19 41						19 52				20 03
Highbury & Islington	a												
	d	19 18					19 25			19 33	19 40		
Canonbury	d	19 20					19 27			19 35	19 42		
Dalston Junction Stn ELL	d	19 25					19 30	19 35		19 40	19 45	19 50	
Haggerston	d	19 26					19 31	19 36		19 41	19 46	19 51	
Hoxton	d	19 28					19 33	19 38		19 43	19 48	19 53	
Shoreditch High Street	d	19 31					19 36	19 41		19 46	19 51	19 56	
Whitechapel	d	19 33					19 38	19 43		19 48	19 53	19 58	
Shadwell	d	19 35					19 40	19 45		19 50	19 55	20 00	
Wapping	d	19 37					19 42	19 47		19 52	19 57	20 02	
Rotherhithe	d	19 39					19 44	19 49		19 54	19 59	20 04	
Canada Water	d	19 41					19 46	19 51		19 56	20 01	20 06	
Surrey Quays	d	19 42					19 47	19 52		19 57	20 02	20 07	
New Cross ELL	a							19 57				20 12	
New Cross Gate 4	a	19 46					19 51		19 57	20 01	20 06		
	d	19 47					19 52		19 57	20 02	20 07		
Brockley	d	19 49					19 54		20 00	20 04	20 09		
Honor Oak Park	d	19 52					19 57		20 03	20 07	20 12		
Forest Hill 4	d	19 55					20 00		20 05	20 10	20 15		
Sydenham	d	19 57					20 02		20 08	20 12	20 17		
Crystal Palace 4	d					20 00	20a07		20 13		20a22		
Gipsy Hill	d					20 03			20 15				
West Norwood 4	d					20 06			20 18				
Streatham Hill	d								20 22				
Balham 4 ⊖	d								20 25				
Wandsworth Common	d								20 27				
Clapham Junction 10	d								20 31				
South Bermondsey	d		19 45										20 07
Queens Rd Peckham	d		19 48										20 09
Peckham Rye 4	d		19 50	19 50		20a16							20a12
Denmark Hill 4	d		19 53	19 54									
London Blackfriars 3 ⊖	a			20 04									
Clapham High Street ⊖	d		19 58										
Wandsworth Road	d		19 59										
Battersea Park 4	d		20 02						20 35				
London Victoria 15 ⊖	a		20 06						20 39				
Penge West	d	20 00								20 15			
Anerley	d	20 02								20 17			
Norwood Junction 2	d	20 05								20 20			
West Croydon 4	a	20 12								20 30			
East Croydon	a												

Table 178

Saturdays

28 July to 11 August

London Bridge to London Victoria - Croydon and East London Line

Network Diagram - see first Page of Table 177

Station		SN		LO	SN	SE	SN	LO	LO	SN	LO	LO		LO	SN	SN	LO	SN	SE	SN	LO	LO		SN	LO
London Bridge 4 ⊖	d	20 06			20 11					20 22					20 33	20 36		20 41						20 52	
Highbury & Islington	a																								
	d			19 48				19 55			20 03	20 10					20 18				20 25				20 33
Canonbury	d			19 50				19 57			20 05	20 12					20 20				20 27				20 35
Dalston Junction Stn ELL	d			19 55				20 00	20 05		20 10	20 15		20 20			20 25				20 30	20 35			20 40
Haggerston	d			19 56				20 01	20 06		20 11	20 16		20 21			20 26				20 31	20 36			20 41
Hoxton	d			19 58				20 03	20 08		20 13	20 18		20 23			20 28				20 33	20 38			20 43
Shoreditch High Street	d			20 01				20 06	20 11		20 16	20 21		20 26			20 31				20 36	20 41			20 46
Whitechapel	d			20 03				20 08	20 13		20 18	20 23		20 28			20 33				20 38	20 43			20 48
Shadwell	d			20 05				20 10	20 15		20 20	20 25		20 30			20 35				20 40	20 45			20 50
Wapping	d			20 07				20 12	20 17		20 22	20 27		20 32			20 37				20 42	20 47			20 52
Rotherhithe	d			20 09				20 14	20 19		20 24	20 29		20 34			20 39				20 44	20 49			20 54
Canada Water	d			20 11				20 16	20 21		20 26	20 31		20 36			20 41				20 46	20 51			20 56
Surrey Quays	d			20 12				20 17	20 22		20 27	20 32		20 37			20 42				20 47	20 52			20 57
New Cross ELL	a								20 27					20 42								20 57			
New Cross Gate 4	a	20 11		20 16				20 21		20 27	20 31	20 36				20 41	20 46				20 51			20 57	21 01
	d	20 11		20 17				20 22		20 27	20 32	20 37				20 41	20 47				20 52			20 57	21 02
Brockley	d	20 14		20 19				20 24		20 30	20 34	20 39				20 44	20 49				20 54			21 00	21 04
Honor Oak Park	d	20 17		20 22				20 27		20 33	20 37	20 42				20 47	20 52				20 57			21 03	21 07
Forest Hill 4	d	20 19		20 25				20 30		20 35	20 40	20 45				20 49	20 55				21 00			21 05	21 10
Sydenham	d	20 22		20 27				20 32		20 38	20 42	20 47				20 52	20 57				21 02			21 08	21 12
Crystal Palace 4	d						20 30	20a37		20 43		20a52								21 00	21a07			21 13	
Gipsy Hill	d						20 33			20 45										21 02				21 15	
West Norwood 4	d						20 36			20 48										21 05				21 18	
Streatham Hill	d									20 52														21 22	
Balham 4 ⊖	d									20 55														21 25	
Wandsworth Common	d									20 57														21 27	
Clapham Junction 10	d									21 01														21 31	
South Bermondsey	d				20 15										20 37			20 45							
Queens Rd Peckham	d				20 18										20 39			20 48							
Peckham Rye 4	d				20 20	20 20	20a46								20a42			20 50	20 50	21a16					
Denmark Hill 4	d				20 23	20 24												20 53	20 54						
London Blackfriars 3 ⊖	a					20 34													21 04						
Clapham High Street ⊖	d				20 28													20 58							
Wandsworth Road	d				20 29													20 59							
Battersea Park 4	d				20 32					21 05								21 02						21 35	
London Victoria 15 ⊖	a				20 36					21 09								21 06						21 39	
Penge West	d	20 24		20 30							20 45					20 54	21 00								21 15
Anerley	d	20 26		20 32							20 47					20 56	21 02								21 17
Norwood Junction 2	d	20 30		20 35							20 50					21 00	21 05								21 20
West Croydon 4	a			20 42							21 00						21 12								21 30
East Croydon	a	20 33														21 03									

Station		LO	LO	SN	SN	LO	SN	SE		SN	LO	LO	SN	LO	LO	LO	SN	SN		LO	SN	SE	SN	LO	LO
London Bridge 4 ⊖	d			21 03	21 06		21 11						21 22				21 33	21 36			21 41				
Highbury & Islington	a																								
	d	20 40				20 48					20 55			21 03	21 10					21 18				21 25	
Canonbury	d	20 42				20 50					20 57			21 05	21 12					21 20				21 27	
Dalston Junction Stn ELL	d	20 45	20 50			20 55					21 00	21 05		21 10	21 15	21 20				21 25				21 30	21 35
Haggerston	d	20 46	20 51			20 56					21 01	21 06		21 11	21 16	21 21				21 26				21 31	21 36
Hoxton	d	20 48	20 53			20 58					21 03	21 08		21 13	21 18	21 23				21 28				21 33	21 38
Shoreditch High Street	d	20 51	20 56			21 01					21 06	21 11		21 16	21 21	21 26				21 31				21 36	21 41
Whitechapel	d	20 53	20 58			21 03					21 08	21 13		21 18	21 23	21 28				21 33				21 38	21 43
Shadwell	d	20 55	21 00			21 05					21 10	21 15		21 20	21 25	21 30				21 35				21 40	21 45
Wapping	d	20 57	21 02			21 07					21 12	21 17		21 22	21 27	21 32				21 37				21 42	21 47
Rotherhithe	d	20 59	21 04			21 09					21 14	21 19		21 24	21 29	21 34				21 39				21 44	21 49
Canada Water	d	21 01	21 06			21 11					21 16	21 21		21 26	21 31	21 36				21 41				21 46	21 51
Surrey Quays	d	21 02	21 07			21 12					21 17	21 22		21 27	21 32	21 37				21 42				21 47	21 52
New Cross ELL	a		21 12									21 27				21 42									21 57
New Cross Gate 4	a	21 06			21 11	21 16					21 21		21 27	21 31	21 36			21 41		21 46				21 51	
	d	21 07			21 11	21 17					21 22		21 27	21 32	21 37			21 41		21 47				21 52	
Brockley	d	21 09			21 14	21 19					21 24		21 30	21 34	21 39			21 44		21 49				21 54	
Honor Oak Park	d	21 12			21 17	21 22					21 27		21 33	21 37	21 42			21 47		21 52				21 57	
Forest Hill 4	d	21 15			21 19	21 25					21 30		21 35	21 40	21 45			21 49		21 55				22 00	
Sydenham	d	21 17			21 22	21 27					21 32		21 38	21 42	21 47			21 52		21 57				22 02	
Crystal Palace 4	d	21a22								21 30	21a37		21 43		21a52								22 00	22a07	
Gipsy Hill	d									21 32			21 45										22 02		
West Norwood 4	d									21 35			21 48										22 05		
Streatham Hill	d												21 52												
Balham 4 ⊖	d												21 55												
Wandsworth Common	d												21 57												
Clapham Junction 10	d												22 01												
South Bermondsey	d			21 07			21 15										21 37				21 45				
Queens Rd Peckham	d			21 09			21 18										21 39				21 48				
Peckham Rye 4	d			21a12			21 20	21 20		21a46							21a42				21 50	21 50	22a16		
Denmark Hill 4	d						21 23	21 24													21 53	21 54			
London Blackfriars 3 ⊖	a							21 34														22 04			
Clapham High Street ⊖	d						21 28														21 58				
Wandsworth Road	d						21 29														21 59				
Battersea Park 4	d						21 32						22 05								22 02				
London Victoria 15 ⊖	a						21 36						22 09								22 06				
Penge West	d				21 24	21 30								21 45				21 54		22 00					
Anerley	d				21 26	21 32								21 47				21 56		22 02					
Norwood Junction 2	d				21 30	21 35								21 50				22 00		22 05					
West Croydon 4	a					21 42								22 00						22 12					
East Croydon	a				21 33													22 04							

Table 178

Saturdays

28 July to 11 August

London Bridge to London Victoria - Croydon and East London Line

Network Diagram - see first Page of Table 177

		SN	LO	LO		LO	SN	SN	LO	SN	SE	SN	LO	SN		LO	LO	LO	SN	SN	LO	SN	SE	SN	
London Bridge 4 ⊖	d	21 52					22 03	22 06		22 11				22 22					22 33	22 36		22 41			
Highbury & Islington	a																								
	d		21 33	21 40					21 48				21 55			22 03	22 10				22 18				
Canonbury	d		21 35	21 42					21 50				21 57			22 05	22 12				22 20				
Dalston Junction Stn ELL	d		21 40	21 45		21 50			21 55				22 00			22 08	22 15	22 20			22 25				
Haggerston	d		21 41	21 46		21 51			21 56				22 01			22 09	22 16	22 21			22 26				
Hoxton	d		21 43	21 48		21 53			21 58				22 03			22 11	22 18	22 23			22 28				
Shoreditch High Street	d		21 46	21 51		21 56			22 01				22 06			22 14	22 21	22 26			22 31				
Whitechapel	d		21 48	21 53		21 58			22 03				22 08			22 16	22 23	22 28			22 33				
Shadwell	d		21 50	21 55		22 00			22 05				22 10			22 18	22 25	22 30			22 35				
Wapping	d		21 52	21 57		22 02			22 07				22 12			22 20	22 27	22 32			22 37				
Rotherhithe	d		21 54	21 59		22 04			22 09				22 14			22 22	22 29	22 34			22 39				
Canada Water	d		21 56	22 01		22 06			22 11				22 16			22 24	22 31	22 36			22 41				
Surrey Quays	d		21 57	22 02		22 07			22 12				22 17			22 25	22 32	22 37			22 42				
New Cross ELL	a					22 13												22 42							
New Cross Gate 4	a	21 57	22 01	22 06				22 11	22 16				22 21	22 27		22 29	22 36			22 41	22 46				
	d	21 57	22 02	22 07				22 11	22 17				22 22	22 27		22 30	22 37			22 41	22 47				
Brockley	d	22 00	22 04	22 09				22 14	22 19				22 24	22 30		22 32	22 39			22 44	22 49				
Honor Oak Park	d	22 03	22 07	22 12				22 17	22 22				22 27	22 33		22 35	22 42			22 47	22 52				
Forest Hill 4	d	22 05	22 10	22 15				22 19	22 25				22 30	22 35		22 38	22 45			22 49	22 55				
Sydenham	d	22 08	22 12	22 17				22 22	22 27				22 32	22 38		22 40	22 47			22 52	22 57				
Crystal Palace 4	d	22 13		22a22								22 30	22a37	22 43			22a52							23 00	
Gipsy Hill	d	22 15										22 32		22 45										23 02	
West Norwood 4	d	22 18										22 35		22 48										23 05	
Streatham Hill	d	22 22												22 52											
Balham 4 ⊖	d	22 25												22 55											
Wandsworth Common	d	22 27												22 57											
Clapham Junction 10	d	22 31												23 01											
South Bermondsey	d						22 07			22 15									22 37			22 45			
Queens Rd Peckham	d						22 09			22 18									22 39			22 48			
Peckham Rye 4	d						22a12			22 20	22 20	22a46							22a42			22 50	22 50	23a16	
Denmark Hill 4	d									22 23	22 24											22 53	22 54		
London Blackfriars 3 ⊖	a										22 34												23 04		
Clapham High Street ⊖	d									22 28												22 58			
Wandsworth Road	d									22 29												22 59			
Battersea Park 4	d	22 35								22 32				23 05								23 02			
London Victoria 15 ⊖	a	22 39								22 36				23 09								23 06			
Penge West	d		22 15					22 24	22 30							22 43				22 54	23 00				
Anerley	d		22 17					22 26	22 32							22 45				22 56	23 02				
Norwood Junction 2	d		22 20					22 30	22 35							22 48				23 00	23 05				
West Croydon 4	a		22 30						22 42							23 00					23 12				
East Croydon	a							22 35												23 03					

		LO	SN	LO	LO	LO	SN	SN	LO	SN		SE	SN	LO	SN	LO	LO	LO	SN	SN		LO	LO	SN	LO
London Bridge 4 ⊖	d		22 52				23 03	23 06		23 11					23 22				23 33	23 36				23 52	
Highbury & Islington	a																								
	d	22 25		22 33	22 40				22 48					22 55		23 03	23 10					23 18	23 25		23 33
Canonbury	d	22 27		22 35	22 42				22 50					22 57		23 05	23 12					23 20	23 27		23 35
Dalston Junction Stn ELL	d	22 30		22 38	22 45	22 50			22 55					23 00		23 08	23 15	23 20				23 25	23 30		23 38
Haggerston	d	22 31		22 39	22 46	22 51			22 56					23 01		23 09	23 16	23 21				23 26	23 31		23 39
Hoxton	d	22 33		22 41	22 48	22 53			22 58					23 03		23 11	23 18	23 23				23 28	23 33		23 41
Shoreditch High Street	d	22 36		22 44	22 51	22 56			23 01					23 06		23 14	23 21	23 26				23 31	23 36		23 44
Whitechapel	d	22 38		22 46	22 53	22 58			23 03					23 08		23 16	23 23	23 28				23 33	23 38		23 46
Shadwell	d	22 40		22 48	22 55	23 00			23 05					23 10		23 18	23 25	23 30				23 35	23 40		23 48
Wapping	d	22 42		22 50	22 57	23 02			23 07					23 12		23 20	23 27	23 32				23 37	23 42		23 50
Rotherhithe	d	22 44		22 52	22 59	23 04			23 09					23 14		23 22	23 29	23 34				23 39	23 44		23 52
Canada Water	d	22 46		22 54	23 01	23 06			23 11					23 16		23 24	23 31	23 36				23 41	23 46		23 54
Surrey Quays	d	22 47		22 55	23 02	23 07			23 12					23 17		23 25	23 32	23 37				23 42	23 47		23 55
New Cross ELL	a					23 12												23 42							
New Cross Gate 4	a	22 51	22 57	22 59	23 06			23 11	23 16					23 21	23 27	23 29	23 36			23 41		23 46	23 51	23 57	23 58
	d	22 52	22 57	23 00	23 07			23 11	23 17					23 22	23 27	23 30	23 37			23 41		23 47	23 52	23 57	23 59
Brockley	d	22 54	23 00	23 02	23 09			23 14	23 19					23 24	23 30	23 32	23 39			23 44		23 49	23 54	00 01	00 03
Honor Oak Park	d	22 57	23 03	23 05	23 12			23 17	23 22					23 27	23 33	23 35	23 42			23 47		23 52	23 57	00 04	00 06
Forest Hill 4	d	23 00	23 05	23 08	23 15			23 19	23 25					23 30	23 35	23 38	23 45			23 49		23 55	23 59	00 06	00 09
Sydenham	d	23 02	23 08	23 10	23 17			23 22	23 27					23 32	23 38	23 40	23 47			23 52		23 57	00 02	00 09	00 11
Crystal Palace 4	d	23a07	23 13		23a22								23 30	23a37	23 43		23a52						00a07	00 13	
Gipsy Hill	d		23 15										23 32		23 45									00 15	
West Norwood 4	d		23 18										23 35		23 48									00 18	
Streatham Hill	d		23 22												23 52									00 22	
Balham 4 ⊖	d		23 25												23 55									00 26	
Wandsworth Common	d		23 27												23 57									00 28	
Clapham Junction 10	d		23 31												00 02									00 32	
South Bermondsey	d						23 07			23 15									23 37						
Queens Rd Peckham	d						23 09			23 18									23 39						
Peckham Rye 4	d						23 12			23 20		23 20	23a46						23 42						
Denmark Hill 4	d									23 23		23 24													
London Blackfriars 3 ⊖	a											23 34													
Clapham High Street ⊖	d									23 28															
Wandsworth Road	d									23 29															
Battersea Park 4	d		23 35							23 32					00 05									00 35	
London Victoria 15 ⊖	a		23 41							23 37					00 10									00 42	
Penge West	d			23 13				23 24	23 30							23 43				23 54		00 01			00 14
Anerley	d			23 15				23 26	23 32							23 45				23 56		00 03			00 16
Norwood Junction 2	d			23 18			23a34	23 30	23 35							23 48			00a04	23 59		00 06			00 19
West Croydon 4	a			23 30					23 42							23 59						00 13			00 26
East Croydon	a							23 33												00 03					

Table 178

Saturdays

28 July to 11 August

London Bridge to London Victoria - Croydon and East London Line

Network Diagram - see first Page of Table 177

		LO	LO	LO
London Bridge	d			
Highbury & Islington	a			
	d	23 40	23 48	23 55
Canonbury	d	23 42	23 50	23 57
Dalston Junction Stn ELL	d	23 45	23 55	00 01
Haggerston	d	23 46	23 56	00 02
Hoxton	d	23 48	23 58	00 04
Shoreditch High Street	d	23 51	00 01	00 07
Whitechapel	d	23 53	00 03	00 09
Shadwell	d	23 55	00 05	00 11
Wapping	d	23 57	00 07	00 13
Rotherhithe	d	23 59	00 09	00 15
Canada Water	d	00 02	00 11	00 17
Surrey Quays	d	00 03	00 12	00 18
New Cross ELL	a			
New Cross Gate	a	00 07	00 16	00 22
	d	00 08	00 17	00 23
Brockley	d	00 10	00 19	00 25
Honor Oak Park	d	00 13	00 22	00 28
Forest Hill	d	00 16	00 25	00 31
Sydenham	d	00 18	00 27	00 33
Crystal Palace	d	00a23		00a38
Gipsy Hill	d			
West Norwood	d			
Streatham Hill	d			
Balham	d			
Wandsworth Common	d			
Clapham Junction	d			
South Bermondsey	d			
Queens Rd Peckham	d			
Peckham Rye	d			
Denmark Hill	d			
London Blackfriars	a			
Clapham High Street	d			
Wandsworth Road	d			
Battersea Park	d			
London Victoria	a			
Penge West	d		00 30	
Anerley	d		00 32	
Norwood Junction	d		00 35	
West Croydon	a		00 42	
East Croydon	a			

Saturdays

18 August to 25 August

		SN	SN	SN	LO	SN	LO	LO	SN	SN		LO	LO	SN	SN	SN	SN	SN	SN	SE		LO	LO	LO	LO
London Bridge	d	23p22	23p36			23p52			00 03	00 06						00 33	00 36		06 11						
Highbury & Islington	a																								
	d				23p25		23p35	23p42				23p56	00 10											05 35	
Canonbury	d				23p27		23p37	23p44				23p58	00 12											05 37	
Dalston Junction Stn ELL	d				23p30		23p40	23p47				00 02	00 15											05 40	05 50
Haggerston	d				23p31		23p41	23p48				00 03	00 16											05 41	05 51
Hoxton	d				23p33		23p43	23p50				00 05	00 18											05 43	05 53
Shoreditch High Street	d				23p36		23p46	23p53				00 08	00 21											05 46	05 56
Whitechapel	d				23p38		23p48	23p55				00 10	00 23											05 48	05 58
Shadwell	d				23p40		23p50	23p57				00 12	00 25											05 50	06 00
Wapping	d				23p42		23p52	23p59				00 14	00 27											05 52	06 02
Rotherhithe	d				23p44		23p54	00 01				00 16	00 29											05 54	06 04
Canada Water	d				23p46		23p56	00 03				00 18	00 31											05 56	06 06
Surrey Quays	d				23p47		23p57	00 05				00 19	00 32											05 57	06 07
New Cross ELL	a																								06 12
New Cross Gate	a	23p27	23p41		23p51	23p57	00 01	00 08		00 11		00 23	00 36				00 41							06 01	
	d	23p27	23p41		23p52	23p57	00 02			00 11							00 41					05 47	05 52	06 02	
Brockley	d	23p30	23p44		23p54	00 01	00 04			00 14							00 44					05 49	05 54	06 04	
Honor Oak Park	d	23p33	23p47		23p57	00 04	00 07			00 17							00 47					05 52	05 57	06 07	
Forest Hill	d	23p35	23p49		23p59	00 06	00 10			00 19							00 49					05 55	06 00	06 10	
Sydenham	d	23p38	23p52		00 02	00 09	00 12			00 22							00 52					05 57	06 02	06 12	
Crystal Palace	d	23p43		00 03	00a07	00 13								00 33	00 47			01 03					06a07		
Gipsy Hill	d	23p45				00 15																			
West Norwood	d	23p48				00 18																			
Streatham Hill	d	23p52				00 22																			
Balham	d	23p55				00 25																			
Wandsworth Common	d	23p58				00 27																			
Clapham Junction	d	00 02				00 31																			
South Bermondsey	d								00 07							00 37			06 15						
Queens Rd Peckham	d								00 09							00 39			06 18						
Peckham Rye	d								00 12							00 42			06 20	06 20					
Denmark Hill	d																		06 23	06 24					
London Blackfriars	a																			06 34					
Clapham High Street	d																		06 28						
Wandsworth Road	d																		06 29						
Battersea Park	d	00 05				00 35													06 32						
London Victoria	a	00 10				00 42													06 36						
Penge West	d		23p54					00 15		00 24							00 54					06 00		06 15	
Anerley	d		23p56					00 17		00 26							00 56					06 02		06 17	
Norwood Junction	d		23p59	00 09				00 20	00a34	00 30				00 38	00 52	01a04	01 00	01 08				06 06		06 18	
West Croydon	a			00 14				00 27						00 43	00 58			01 13				06 12		06 30	
East Croydon	a		00 03							00 33							01 03								

Table 178

Saturdays

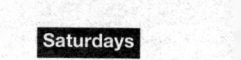

18 August to 25 August

London Bridge to London Victoria - Croydon and East London Line

Network Diagram - see first Page of Table 177

		SE	LO	LO	LO	LO		LO	SN	LO	SN	SN	SE	SE	LO	LO		LO	LO	LO	LO	SN	LO	LO	LO
London Bridge [4] ⊖	d										06 36	06 41										07 06			
Highbury & Islington	a																								
	d				05 55	06 05										06 25			06 33	06 40			06 48	06 55	
Canonbury	d				05 57	06 07										06 27			06 35	06 42			06 50	06 57	
Dalston Junction Stn ELL	d				06 00	06 10		06 20								06 30		06 35	06 40	06 45	06 50		06 55	07 00	07 05
Haggerston	d				06 01	06 11		06 21								06 31		06 36	06 41	06 46	06 51		06 56	07 01	07 06
Hoxton	d				06 03	06 13		06 23								06 33		06 38	06 43	06 48	06 53		06 58	07 03	07 08
Shoreditch High Street	d				06 06	06 16		06 26								06 36		06 41	06 46	06 51	06 56		07 01	07 06	07 11
Whitechapel	d				06 08	06 18		06 28								06 38		06 43	06 48	06 53	06 58		07 03	07 08	07 13
Shadwell	d				06 10	06 20		06 30								06 40		06 45	06 50	06 55	07 00		07 05	07 10	07 15
Wapping	d				06 12	06 22		06 32								06 42		06 47	06 52	06 57	07 02		07 07	07 12	07 17
Rotherhithe	d				06 14	06 24		06 34								06 44		06 49	06 54	06 59	07 04		07 09	07 14	07 19
Canada Water	d				06 16	06 26		06 36								06 46		06 51	06 56	07 01	07 06		07 11	07 16	07 21
Surrey Quays	d				06 17	06 27		06 37								06 47		06 52	06 57	07 02	07 07		07 12	07 17	07 22
New Cross ELL	a							06 42										06 57			07 12				07 27
New Cross Gate [4]	a				06 21	06 31					06 41					06 51			07 01	07 06		07 11	07 16	07 21	
	d		06 07	06 17	06 22	06 32				06 37	06 41				06 47	06 52			07 02	07 07		07 11	07 17	07 22	
Brockley	d		06 09	06 19	06 24	06 34				06 39	06 44				06 49	06 54			07 04	07 09		07 14	07 19	07 24	
Honor Oak Park	d		06 12	06 22	06 27	06 37				06 42	06 47				06 52	06 57			07 07	07 12		07 17	07 22	07 27	
Forest Hill [4]	d		06 15	06 25	06 30	06 40				06 45	06 49				06 55	07 00			07 10	07 15		07 19	07 25	07 30	
Sydenham	d		06 17	06 27	06 32	06 42				06 47	06 52				06 57	07 02			07 12	07 17		07 22	07 27	07 32	
Crystal Palace [4]	d		06a22		06a37				06 45	06a52						07a07				07a22				07a37	
Gipsy Hill	d								06 47																
West Norwood [4]	d								06 50																
Streatham Hill	d																								
Balham [4] ⊖	d																								
Wandsworth Common	d																								
Clapham Junction [10]	d																								
South Bermondsey	d											06 45													
Queens Rd Peckham	d											06 48													
Peckham Rye [4]	d	06 50							07a01			06 50	07 15	07 20											
Denmark Hill [4]	d	06 54										06 53	07 19	07 24											
London Blackfriars [3] ⊖	a	07 04												07 34											
Clapham High Street ⊖	d											06 58													
Wandsworth Road	d											06 59													
Battersea Park [4]	d											07 02													
London Victoria [15] ⊖	a											07 06	07 28												
Penge West	d			06 30		06 45					06 54				07 00				07 15			07 24	07 30		
Anerley	d			06 32		06 47					06 56				07 02				07 17			07 26	07 32		
Norwood Junction [2]	d			06 35		06 50					07 00				07 05				07 20			07 30	07 35		
West Croydon [4] 🚋	a			06 41		07 00									07 11				07 30				07 41		
East Croydon 🚋	a										07 03											07 33			

		LO		LO	SN	LO	SN	SN	LO	LO	LO	LO		LO	LO	SE	SN	SE	SN	SN	LO	SE		SN	SE
London Bridge [4] ⊖	d				07 11		07 33	07 36									07 41		08 03	08 06				08 11	
Highbury & Islington	a																								
	d	07 03		07 10					07 18	07 25		07 33		07 40							07 48				
Canonbury	d	07 05		07 12					07 20	07 27		07 35		07 42							07 50				
Dalston Junction Stn ELL	d	07 10		07 15		07 20			07 25	07 30	07 35	07 40		07 45	07 50						07 55				
Haggerston	d	07 11		07 16		07 21			07 26	07 31	07 36	07 41		07 46	07 51						07 56				
Hoxton	d	07 13		07 18		07 23			07 28	07 33	07 38	07 43		07 48	07 53						07 58				
Shoreditch High Street	d	07 16		07 21		07 26			07 31	07 36	07 41	07 46		07 51	07 56						08 01				
Whitechapel	d	07 18		07 23		07 28			07 33	07 38	07 43	07 48		07 53	07 58						08 03				
Shadwell	d	07 20		07 25		07 30			07 35	07 40	07 45	07 50		07 55	08 00						08 05				
Wapping	d	07 22		07 27		07 32			07 37	07 42	07 47	07 52		07 57	08 02						08 07				
Rotherhithe	d	07 24		07 29		07 34			07 39	07 44	07 49	07 54		07 59	08 04						08 09				
Canada Water	d	07 26		07 31		07 36			07 41	07 46	07 51	07 56		08 01	08 06						08 11				
Surrey Quays	d	07 27		07 32		07 37			07 42	07 47	07 52	07 57		08 02	08 07						08 12				
New Cross ELL	a					07 42					07 57				08 12										
New Cross Gate [4]	a	07 31		07 36				07 41	07 46	07 51		08 01		08 06						08 11	08 16				
	d	07 32		07 37				07 41	07 47	07 52		08 02		08 07						08 11	08 17				
Brockley	d	07 34		07 39				07 44	07 49	07 54		08 04		08 09						08 14	08 19				
Honor Oak Park	d	07 37		07 42				07 47	07 52	07 57		08 07		08 12						08 17	08 22				
Forest Hill [4]	d	07 40		07 45				07 49	07 55	08 00		08 10		08 15						08 19	08 25				
Sydenham	d	07 42		07 47				07 52	07 57	08 02		08 12		08 17						08 22	08 27				
Crystal Palace [4]	d			07a52						08a07				08a22											
Gipsy Hill	d																								
West Norwood [4]	d																								
Streatham Hill	d																								
Balham [4] ⊖	d																								
Wandsworth Common	d																								
Clapham Junction [10]	d																								
South Bermondsey	d				07 15		07 37										07 45		08 07					08 15	
Queens Rd Peckham	d				07 18		07 39										07 48		08 09					08 18	
Peckham Rye [4]	d				07 20		07a42									07 45	07 50	07 50	08a12			08 15		08 20	08 20
Denmark Hill [4]	d				07 23											07 49	07 53	07 54				08 19		08 23	08 24
London Blackfriars [3] ⊖	a																	08 04							08 34
Clapham High Street ⊖	d				07 28												07 58							08 28	
Wandsworth Road	d				07 29												07 59							08 29	
Battersea Park [4]	d				07 32												08 02							08 32	
London Victoria [15] ⊖	a				07 36											07 58	08 06					08 28		08 36	
Penge West	d	07 45						07 54	08 00			08 15								08 24	08 30				
Anerley	d	07 47						07 56	08 02			08 17								08 26	08 32				
Norwood Junction [2]	d	07 50						08 00	08 05			08 20								08 30	08 35				
West Croydon [4] 🚋	a	08 00							08 11			08 30									08 41				
East Croydon 🚋	a							08 03												08 33					

Table 178

Saturdays

18 August to 25 August

London Bridge to London Victoria - Croydon and East London Line

Network Diagram - see first Page of Table 177

		SN	LO	LO	SN	LO	LO	LO		SN	SN	LO	SE	SN	SE	SN	LO	LO		SN	LO	LO	LO	SN	SN
London Bridge 4 ⊖	d				08 22					08 33	08 36			08 41						08 52				09 03	09 06
Highbury & Islington	a																								
	d		07 55			08 03	08 10					08 18					08 25				08 33	08 40			
Canonbury	d		07 57			08 05	08 12					08 20					08 27				08 35	08 42			
Dalston Junction Stn ELL	d		08 00	08 05		08 10	08 15	08 20				08 25					08 30	08 35			08 40	08 45	08 50		
Haggerston	d		08 01	08 06		08 11	08 16	08 21				08 26					08 31	08 36			08 41	08 46	08 51		
Hoxton	d		08 03	08 08		08 13	08 18	08 23				08 28					08 33	08 38			08 43	08 48	08 53		
Shoreditch High Street	d		08 06	08 11		08 16	08 21	08 26				08 31					08 36	08 41			08 46	08 51	08 56		
Whitechapel	d		08 08	08 13		08 18	08 23	08 28				08 33					08 38	08 43			08 48	08 53	08 58		
Shadwell	d		08 10	08 15		08 20	08 25	08 30				08 35					08 40	08 45			08 50	08 55	09 00		
Wapping	d		08 12	08 17		08 22	08 27	08 32				08 37					08 42	08 47			08 52	08 57	09 02		
Rotherhithe	d		08 14	08 19		08 24	08 29	08 34				08 39					08 44	08 49			08 54	08 59	09 04		
Canada Water	d		08 16	08 21		08 26	08 31	08 36				08 41					08 46	08 51			08 56	09 01	09 06		
Surrey Quays	d		08 17	08 22		08 27	08 32	08 37				08 42					08 47	08 52			08 57	09 02	09 07		
New Cross ELL	a			08 27				08 42										08 57					09 12		
New Cross Gate 4	a		08 21		08 27	08 31	08 36				08 41	08 46					08 51			08 57	09 01	09 06			09 11
	d		08 22		08 27	08 32	08 37				08 41	08 47					08 52			08 57	09 02	09 07			09 11
Brockley	d		08 24		08 30	08 34	08 39				08 44	08 49					08 54			09 00	09 04	09 09			09 14
Honor Oak Park	d		08 27		08 33	08 37	08 42				08 47	08 52					08 57			09 03	09 07	09 12			09 17
Forest Hill 4	d		08 30		08 35	08 40	08 45				08 49	08 55					09 00			09 05	09 10	09 15			09 19
Sydenham	d		08 32		08 38	08 42	08 47				08 52	08 57					09 02			09 08	09 12	09 17			09 22
Crystal Palace 4	d	08 30	08a37		08 43		08a52									09 00	09a07			09 13		09a22			
Gipsy Hill	d	08 32			08 45											09 02				09 15					
West Norwood 4	d	08 35			08 48											09 05				09 18					
Streatham Hill	d				08 52															09 22					
Balham 4 ⊖	d				08 55															09 25					
Wandsworth Common	d				08 57															09 27					
Clapham Junction 10	d				09 01															09 32					
South Bermondsey	d									08 37				08 45										09 07	
Queens Rd Peckham	d									08 39				08 48										09 09	
Peckham Rye 4	d	08a46								08a42			08 45	08 50	08 50	09a16								09a12	
Denmark Hill 4	d												08 49	08 53	08 54										
London Blackfriars 3 ⊖	a														09 04										
Clapham High Street ⊖	d													08 58											
Wandsworth Road	d													08 59											
Battersea Park 4	d				09 05									09 02						09 36					
London Victoria 15 ⊖	a				09 09								08 58	09 06						09 40					
Penge West	d					08 45					08 54	09 00									09 15				09 24
Anerley	d					08 47					08 56	09 02									09 17				09 26
Norwood Junction 2	d					08 50					09 00	09 05									09 20				09 30
West Croydon 4	a					09 00						09 12									09 30				
East Croydon	a										09 03														09 33

		LO	SE	SN		SE	SN	LO	LO	SN	LO	LO	LO	SN		SN	LO	SE	SN	SE	SN	LO	LO		
London Bridge 4 ⊖	d			09 11						09 22				09 33		09 36			09 41						
Highbury & Islington	a																								
	d	08 48						08 55			09 03	09 10					09 18					09 25			
Canonbury	d	08 50						08 57			09 05	09 12					09 20					09 27			
Dalston Junction Stn ELL	d	08 55						09 00	09 05		09 10	09 15	09 20				09 25					09 30	09 35		
Haggerston	d	08 56						09 01	09 06		09 11	09 16	09 21				09 26					09 31	09 36		
Hoxton	d	08 58						09 03	09 08		09 13	09 18	09 23				09 28					09 33	09 38		
Shoreditch High Street	d	09 01						09 06	09 11		09 16	09 21	09 26				09 31					09 36	09 41		
Whitechapel	d	09 03						09 08	09 13		09 18	09 23	09 28				09 33					09 38	09 43		
Shadwell	d	09 05						09 10	09 15		09 20	09 25	09 30				09 35					09 40	09 45		
Wapping	d	09 07						09 12	09 17		09 22	09 27	09 32				09 37					09 42	09 47		
Rotherhithe	d	09 09						09 14	09 19		09 24	09 29	09 34				09 39					09 44	09 49		
Canada Water	d	09 11						09 16	09 21		09 26	09 31	09 36				09 41					09 46	09 51		
Surrey Quays	d	09 12						09 17	09 22		09 27	09 32	09 37				09 42					09 47	09 52		
New Cross ELL	a								09 27				09 42										09 57		
New Cross Gate 4	a	09 16						09 21		09 27	09 31	09 36				09 41	09 46					09 51			
	d	09 17						09 22		09 27	09 32	09 37				09 41	09 47					09 52			
Brockley	d	09 19						09 24		09 30	09 34	09 39				09 44	09 49					09 54			
Honor Oak Park	d	09 22						09 27		09 33	09 37	09 42				09 47	09 52					09 57			
Forest Hill 4	d	09 25						09 30		09 35	09 40	09 45				09 49	09 55					10 00			
Sydenham	d	09 27						09 32		09 38	09 42	09 47				09 52	09 57					10 02			
Crystal Palace 4	d						09 30	09a37		09 43		09a52									10 00	10a07			
Gipsy Hill	d						09 32			09 45											10 02				
West Norwood 4	d						09 35			09 48											10 05				
Streatham Hill	d									09 52															
Balham 4 ⊖	d									09 55															
Wandsworth Common	d									09 57															
Clapham Junction 10	d									10 01															
South Bermondsey	d			09 15										09 37					09 45						
Queens Rd Peckham	d			09 18										09 39					09 48						
Peckham Rye 4	d		09 15	09 20		09 20	09a46							09a42				09 45	09 50	09 50	10a16				
Denmark Hill 4	d		09 19	09 23		09 24												09 49	09 53	09 54					
London Blackfriars 3 ⊖	a					09 34														10 04					
Clapham High Street ⊖	d			09 28															09 58						
Wandsworth Road	d			09 29															09 59						
Battersea Park 4	d			09 32						10 05									10 02						
London Victoria 15 ⊖	a		09 28	09 36						10 09								09 58	10 06						
Penge West	d	09 30									09 45					09 54	10 00								
Anerley	d	09 32									09 47					09 56	10 02								
Norwood Junction 2	d	09 35									09 50					10 00	10 05								
West Croydon 4	a	09 42									10 00						10 12								
East Croydon	a															10 03									

Table 178

Saturdays

18 August to 25 August

London Bridge to London Victoria - Croydon and East London Line

Network Diagram - see first Page of Table 177

		SN		SN		LO	LO	LO	SN	SN	LO	SE	SN	SE		SN	LO	LO	SN	LO	LO	LO	SN	SN
London Bridge 4 ⊖	d	09 52		16 52					17 03	17 06			17 11						17 22				17 33	17 36
Highbury & Islington	a																							
	d					16 33	16 40				16 48						16 55			17 03	17 10			
Canonbury	d					16 35	16 42				16 50						16 57			17 05	17 12			
Dalston Junction Stn ELL	d					16 40	16 45	16 50			16 55						17 00	17 05		17 10	17 15	17 20		
Haggerston	d					16 41	16 46	16 51			16 56						17 01	17 06		17 11	17 16	17 21		
Hoxton	d					16 43	16 48	16 53			16 58						17 03	17 08		17 13	17 18	17 23		
Shoreditch High Street	d					16 46	16 51	16 56			17 01						17 06	17 11		17 16	17 21	17 26		
Whitechapel	d					16 48	16 53	16 58			17 03						17 08	17 13		17 18	17 23	17 28		
Shadwell	d					16 50	16 55	17 00			17 05						17 10	17 15		17 20	17 25	17 30		
Wapping	d					16 52	16 57	17 02			17 07						17 12	17 17		17 22	17 27	17 32		
Rotherhithe	d					16 54	16 59	17 04			17 09						17 14	17 19		17 24	17 29	17 34		
Canada Water	d					16 56	17 01	17 06			17 11						17 16	17 21		17 26	17 31	17 36		
Surrey Quays	d					16 57	17 02	17 07			17 12						17 17	17 22		17 27	17 32	17 37		
New Cross ELL	a							17 12										17 27				17 42		
New Cross Gate 4	a	09 57		16 57		17 01	17 06			17 11	17 16						17 21		17 27	17 31	17 36			17 41
	d	09 57		16 57		17 02	17 07			17 11	17 17						17 22		17 27	17 32	17 37			17 41
Brockley	d	10 00	and at the same minutes past each hour until	17 00		17 04	17 09			17 14	17 19						17 24		17 30	17 34	17 39			17 44
Honor Oak Park	d	10 03		17 03		17 07	17 12			17 17	17 22						17 27		17 33	17 37	17 42			17 47
Forest Hill 4	d	10 05		17 05		17 10	17 15			17 19	17 25						17 30		17 35	17 40	17 45			17 49
Sydenham	d	10 08		17 08		17 12	17 17			17 22	17 27						17 32		17 38	17 42	17 47			17 52
Crystal Palace 4	d	10 13		17 13			17a22									17 30	17a37		17 43		17a52			
Gipsy Hill	d	10 15		17 15												17 32			17 45					
West Norwood 4	d	10 18		17 18												17 35			17 48					
Streatham Hill	d	10 22		17 22															17 52					
Balham 4 ⊖	d	10 25		17 25															17 55					
Wandsworth Common	d	10 27		17 27															17 57					
Clapham Junction 10	d	10 31		17 31															18 01					
South Bermondsey	d								17 07				17 15										17 37	
Queens Rd Peckham	d								17 09				17 18										17 39	
Peckham Rye 4	d								17a12			17 15	17 20	17 20		17a46							17a42	
Denmark Hill 4	d											17 19	17 23	17 24										
London Blackfriars 3 ⊖	a													17 34										
Clapham High Street ⊖	d												17 28											
Wandsworth Road	d												17 29											
Battersea Park 4	d	10 35		17 35									17 32						18 05					
London Victoria 15 ⊖	a	10 39		17 39								17 28	17 36						18 09					
Penge West	d					17 15				17 24	17 30									17 45				17 54
Anerley	d					17 17				17 26	17 32									17 47				17 56
Norwood Junction 2	d					17 20				17 30	17 35									17 50				18 00
West Croydon 4	a					17 30					17 42									18 00				
East Croydon	a									17 33														18 03

			LO	SE	SN	SE	SN	LO	LO	SN	LO		LO	LO	SN	SN	LO	SE	SN	SE	SN		LO	LO	SN
London Bridge 4 ⊖	d				17 41					17 52					18 03	18 06			18 11						18 22
Highbury & Islington	a																								
	d		17 18					17 25			17 33		17 40				17 48						17 55		
Canonbury	d		17 20					17 27			17 35		17 42				17 50						17 57		
Dalston Junction Stn ELL	d		17 25					17 30	17 35		17 40		17 45	17 50			17 55						18 00	18 05	
Haggerston	d		17 26					17 31	17 36		17 41		17 46	17 51			17 56						18 01	18 06	
Hoxton	d		17 28					17 33	17 38		17 43		17 48	17 53			17 58						18 03	18 08	
Shoreditch High Street	d		17 31					17 36	17 41		17 46		17 51	17 56			18 01						18 06	18 11	
Whitechapel	d		17 33					17 38	17 43		17 48		17 53	17 58			18 03						18 08	18 13	
Shadwell	d		17 35					17 40	17 45		17 50		17 55	18 00			18 05						18 10	18 15	
Wapping	d		17 37					17 42	17 47		17 52		17 57	18 02			18 07						18 12	18 17	
Rotherhithe	d		17 39					17 44	17 49		17 54		17 59	18 04			18 09						18 14	18 19	
Canada Water	d		17 41					17 46	17 51		17 56		18 01	18 06			18 11						18 16	18 21	
Surrey Quays	d		17 42					17 47	17 52		17 57		18 02	18 07			18 12						18 17	18 22	
New Cross ELL	a								17 57					18 12										18 27	
New Cross Gate 4	a		17 46					17 51		17 57	18 01		18 06			18 11	18 16						18 21		18 27
	d		17 47					17 52		17 57	18 02		18 07			18 11	18 17						18 22		18 27
Brockley	d		17 49					17 54		18 00	18 04		18 09			18 14	18 19						18 24		18 30
Honor Oak Park	d		17 52					17 57		18 03	18 07		18 12			18 17	18 22						18 27		18 33
Forest Hill 4	d		17 55					18 00		18 05	18 10		18 15			18 19	18 25						18 30		18 35
Sydenham	d		17 57					18 02		18 08	18 12		18 17			18 22	18 27						18 32		18 38
Crystal Palace 4	d						18 00	18a07		18 13			18a22								18 30		18a37		18 43
Gipsy Hill	d						18 02			18 15											18 32				18 45
West Norwood 4	d						18 05			18 18											18 35				18 48
Streatham Hill	d									18 22															18 52
Balham 4 ⊖	d									18 25															18 55
Wandsworth Common	d									18 27															18 57
Clapham Junction 10	d									18 31															19 01
South Bermondsey	d				17 45										18 07				18 15						
Queens Rd Peckham	d				17 48										18 09				18 18						
Peckham Rye 4	d			17 45	17 50	17 50	18a16								18a12			18 15	18 20	18 20	18a46				
Denmark Hill 4	d			17 49	17 53	17 54												18 19	18 23	18 24					
London Blackfriars 3 ⊖	a					18 04														18 34					
Clapham High Street ⊖	d				17 58														18 28						
Wandsworth Road	d				17 59														18 29						
Battersea Park 4	d				18 02					18 35									18 32						19 05
London Victoria 15 ⊖	a			17 58	18 06					18 39								18 28	18 36						19 09
Penge West	d		18 00								18 15					18 24	18 30								
Anerley	d		18 02								18 17					18 26	18 32								
Norwood Junction 2	d		18 05								18 20					18 30	18 35								
West Croydon 4	a		18 11								18 30						18 41								
East Croydon	a															18 33									

London Bridge to London Victoria - Croydon and East London Line

Network Diagram - see first Page of Table 177

		LO	LO	LO	SN	SN	LO	SE	SN	SE	SN	LO	LO	SN	LO	LO	LO	SN	SN	LO	SE	SN	SE
London Bridge 4 ⊖	d				18 33	18 36			18 41					18 52				19 03	19 06			19 11	
Highbury & Islington	a																						
	d	18 03	18 10				18 18					18 25			18 33	18 40				18 48			
Canonbury	d	18 05	18 12				18 20					18 27			18 35	18 42				18 50			
Dalston Junction Stn ELL	d	18 10	18 15	18 20			18 25					18 30	18 35		18 40	18 45	18 50			18 55			
Haggerston	d	18 11	18 16	18 21			18 26					18 31	18 36		18 41	18 46	18 51			18 56			
Hoxton	d	18 13	18 18	18 23			18 28					18 33	18 38		18 43	18 48	18 53			18 58			
Shoreditch High Street	d	18 16	18 21	18 26			18 31					18 36	18 41		18 46	18 51	18 56			19 01			
Whitechapel	d	18 18	18 23	18 28			18 33					18 38	18 43		18 48	18 53	18 58			19 03			
Shadwell	d	18 20	18 25	18 30			18 35					18 40	18 45		18 50	18 55	19 00			19 05			
Wapping	d	18 22	18 27	18 32			18 37					18 42	18 47		18 52	18 57	19 02			19 07			
Rotherhithe	d	18 24	18 29	18 34			18 39					18 44	18 49		18 54	18 59	19 04			19 09			
Canada Water	d	18 26	18 31	18 36			18 41					18 46	18 51		18 56	19 01	19 06			19 11			
Surrey Quays	d	18 27	18 32	18 37			18 42					18 47	18 52		18 57	19 02	19 07			19 12			
New Cross ELL	a			18 42									18 57				19 12						
New Cross Gate 4	a	18 31	18 36			18 41	18 46					18 51		18 57	19 01	19 06			19 11	19 16			
	d	18 32	18 37			18 41	18 47					18 52		18 57	19 02	19 07			19 11	19 17			
Brockley	d	18 34	18 39			18 44	18 49					18 54		19 00	19 04	19 09			19 14	19 19			
Honor Oak Park	d	18 37	18 42			18 47	18 52					18 57		19 03	19 07	19 12			19 17	19 22			
Forest Hill 4	d	18 40	18 45			18 49	18 55					19 00		19 05	19 10	19 15			19 19	19 25			
Sydenham	d	18 42	18 47			18 52	18 57					19 02		19 08	19 12	19 17			19 22	19 27			
Crystal Palace 4	d		18a52								19 00	19a07		19 13		19a22							
Gipsy Hill	d										19 02			19 15									
West Norwood 4	d										19 05			19 18									
Streatham Hill	d													19 22									
Balham 4 ⊖	d													19 25									
Wandsworth Common	d													19 27									
Clapham Junction 10	d													19 31									
South Bermondsey	d				18 37				18 45									19 07				19 15	
Queens Rd Peckham	d				18 39				18 48									19 09				19 18	
Peckham Rye 4	d				18a42			18 45	18 50	18 50	19a16							19a12			19 15	19 20	19 20
Denmark Hill 4	d							18 49	18 53	18 54											19 19	19 23	19 24
London Blackfriars 3 ⊖	a									19 04													19 34
Clapham High Street ⊖	d								18 58													19 28	
Wandsworth Road	d								18 59													19 29	
Battersea Park 4	d								19 02					19 35								19 32	
London Victoria 15 ⊖	a							18 58	19 06					19 39							19 28	19 36	
Penge West	d	18 45				18 54	19 00								19 15				19 24	19 30			
Anerley	d	18 47				18 56	19 02								19 17				19 26	19 32			
Norwood Junction 2	d	18 50				19 00	19 05								19 20				19 30	19 35			
West Croydon 4	a	19 00					19 11								19 30					19 41			
East Croydon	a					19 03													19 33				

		SN	LO	LO	SN	LO	LO	LO	SN	SN	LO	SN	SE	SN	LO	LO	SN	LO	LO	LO	SN	SN
London Bridge 4 ⊖	d				19 22				19 33	19 36		19 41					19 52				20 03	20 06
Highbury & Islington	a																					
	d		18 55			19 03	19 10				19 18				19 25			19 33	19 40			
Canonbury	d		18 57			19 05	19 12				19 20				19 27			19 35	19 42			
Dalston Junction Stn ELL	d		19 00	19 05		19 10	19 15	19 20			19 25				19 30	19 35		19 40	19 45	19 50		
Haggerston	d		19 01	19 06		19 11	19 16	19 21			19 26				19 31	19 36		19 41	19 46	19 51		
Hoxton	d		19 03	19 08		19 13	19 18	19 23			19 28				19 33	19 38		19 43	19 48	19 53		
Shoreditch High Street	d		19 06	19 11		19 16	19 21	19 26			19 31				19 36	19 41		19 46	19 51	19 56		
Whitechapel	d		19 08	19 13		19 18	19 23	19 28			19 33				19 38	19 43		19 48	19 53	19 58		
Shadwell	d		19 10	19 15		19 20	19 25	19 30			19 35				19 40	19 45		19 50	19 55	20 00		
Wapping	d		19 12	19 17		19 22	19 27	19 32			19 37				19 42	19 47		19 52	19 57	20 02		
Rotherhithe	d		19 14	19 19		19 24	19 29	19 34			19 39				19 44	19 49		19 54	19 59	20 04		
Canada Water	d		19 16	19 21		19 26	19 31	19 36			19 41				19 46	19 51		19 56	20 01	20 06		
Surrey Quays	d		19 17	19 22		19 27	19 32	19 37			19 42				19 47	19 52		19 57	20 02	20 07		
New Cross ELL	a			19 27				19 42								19 57				20 12		
New Cross Gate 4	a		19 21		19 27	19 31	19 36			19 41	19 46				19 51		19 57	20 01	20 06			20 11
	d		19 22		19 27	19 32	19 37			19 41	19 47				19 52		19 57	20 02	20 07			20 11
Brockley	d		19 24		19 30	19 34	19 39			19 44	19 49				19 54		20 00	20 04	20 09			20 14
Honor Oak Park	d		19 27		19 33	19 37	19 42			19 47	19 52				19 57		20 03	20 07	20 12			20 17
Forest Hill 4	d		19 30		19 35	19 40	19 45			19 49	19 55				20 00		20 05	20 10	20 15			20 19
Sydenham	d		19 32		19 38	19 42	19 47			19 52	19 57				20 02		20 08	20 12	20 17			20 22
Crystal Palace 4	d	19 30	19a37		19 43		19a52							20 00	20a07		20 13		20a22			
Gipsy Hill	d	19 32			19 45									20 03			20 15					
West Norwood 4	d	19 35			19 48									20 06			20 18					
Streatham Hill	d				19 52												20 22					
Balham 4 ⊖	d				19 55												20 25					
Wandsworth Common	d				19 57												20 27					
Clapham Junction 10	d				20 01												20 31					
South Bermondsey	d								19 37			19 45									20 07	
Queens Rd Peckham	d								19 39			19 48									20 09	
Peckham Rye 4	d	19a46							19a42			19 50	19 50	20a16							20a12	
Denmark Hill 4	d											19 53	19 54									
London Blackfriars 3 ⊖	a												20 04									
Clapham High Street ⊖	d											19 58										
Wandsworth Road	d											19 59										
Battersea Park 4	d				20 05							20 02					20 35					
London Victoria 15 ⊖	a				20 09							20 06					20 39					
Penge West	d					19 45				19 54	20 00							20 15				20 24
Anerley	d					19 47				19 56	20 02							20 17				20 26
Norwood Junction 2	d					19 50				20 00	20 05							20 20				20 30
West Croydon 4	a					20 00					20 15							20 30				
East Croydon	a									20 03												20 33

Table 178

Saturdays

18 August to 25 August

London Bridge to London Victoria - Croydon and East London Line

Network Diagram - see first Page of Table 177

		LO	SN	SE	SN	LO	LO	SN	LO		LO	LO	SN	SN	LO	SN	SE	SN	LO		LO	SN	LO	LO	LO
London Bridge 4 ⊖	d		20 11					20 22					20 33	20 36		20 41						20 52			
Highbury & Islington	a																								
	d	19 48				19 55			20 03		20 10				20 18				20 25				20 33	20 40	
Canonbury	d	19 50				19 57			20 05		20 12				20 20				20 27				20 35	20 42	
Dalston Junction Stn ELL	d	19 55				20 00	20 05		20 10		20 15	20 20			20 25				20 30		20 35		20 40	20 45	20 50
Haggerston	d	19 56				20 01	20 06		20 11		20 16	20 21			20 26				20 31		20 36		20 41	20 46	20 51
Hoxton	d	19 58				20 03	20 08		20 13		20 18	20 23			20 28				20 33		20 38		20 43	20 48	20 53
Shoreditch High Street	d	20 01				20 06	20 11		20 16		20 21	20 26			20 31				20 36		20 41		20 46	20 51	20 56
Whitechapel	d	20 03				20 08	20 13		20 18		20 23	20 28			20 33				20 38		20 43		20 48	20 53	20 58
Shadwell	d	20 05				20 10	20 15		20 20		20 25	20 30			20 35				20 40		20 45		20 50	20 55	21 00
Wapping	d	20 07				20 12	20 17		20 22		20 27	20 32			20 37				20 42		20 47		20 52	20 57	21 02
Rotherhithe	d	20 09				20 14	20 19		20 24		20 29	20 34			20 39				20 44		20 49		20 54	20 59	21 04
Canada Water	d	20 11				20 16	20 21		20 26		20 31	20 36			20 41				20 46		20 51		20 56	21 01	21 06
Surrey Quays	d	20 12				20 17	20 22		20 27		20 32	20 37			20 42				20 47		20 52		20 57	21 02	21 07
New Cross ELL	a						20 27					20 42									20 57				21 12
New Cross Gate 4	a	20 16				20 21		20 27	20 31		20 36			20 41	20 46				20 51			20 57	21 01	21 06	
	d	20 17				20 22		20 27	20 32		20 37			20 41	20 47				20 52			20 57	21 02	21 07	
Brockley	d	20 19				20 24		20 30	20 34		20 39			20 44	20 49				20 54			21 00	21 04	21 09	
Honor Oak Park	d	20 22				20 27		20 33	20 37		20 42			20 47	20 52				20 57			21 03	21 07	21 12	
Forest Hill 4	d	20 25				20 30		20 35	20 40		20 45			20 49	20 55				21 00			21 05	21 10	21 15	
Sydenham	d	20 27				20 32		20 38	20 42		20 47			20 52	20 57				21 02			21 08	21 12	21 17	
Crystal Palace 4	d				20 30	20a37		20 43			20a52							21 00	21a07			21 13		21a22	
Gipsy Hill	d				20 33			20 45										21 02				21 15			
West Norwood 4	d				20 36			20 48										21 05				21 18			
Streatham Hill	d							20 52														21 22			
Balham 4 ⊖	d							20 55														21 25			
Wandsworth Common	d							20 57														21 27			
Clapham Junction 10	d							21 01														21 31			
South Bermondsey	d		20 15										20 37			20 45									
Queens Rd Peckham	d		20 18										20 39			20 48									
Peckham Rye 4	d		20 20	20 20	20a46								20a42			20 50	20 50	21a16							
Denmark Hill 4	d		20 23	20 24												20 53	20 54								
London Blackfriars 3 ⊖	a			20 34													21 04								
Clapham High Street ⊖	d		20 28													20 58									
Wandsworth Road	d		20 29													20 59									
Battersea Park 4	d		20 32					21 05								21 02						21 35			
London Victoria 15 ⊖	a		20 36					21 09								21 06						21 39			
Penge West	d	20 30							20 45					20 54	21 00								21 15		
Anerley	d	20 32							20 47					20 56	21 02								21 17		
Norwood Junction 2	d	20 35							20 50					21 00	21 05								21 20		
West Croydon 4	a	20 45							21 00						21 15								21 30		
East Croydon	a													21 03											

		SN	SN	LO	SN		SE	SN	LO	LO	SN	LO	LO	LO	SN		SN	LO	SN	SE	SN	LO	LO	SN	LO
London Bridge 4 ⊖	d	21 03	21 06		21 11						21 22				21 33		21 36		21 41					21 52	
Highbury & Islington	a																								
	d			20 48					20 55			21 03	21 10					21 18				21 25			21 33
Canonbury	d			20 50					20 57			21 05	21 12					21 20				21 27			21 35
Dalston Junction Stn ELL	d			20 55					21 00	21 05		21 10	21 15	21 20				21 25				21 30	21 35		21 40
Haggerston	d			20 56					21 01	21 06		21 11	21 16	21 21				21 26				21 31	21 36		21 41
Hoxton	d			20 58					21 03	21 08		21 13	21 18	21 23				21 28				21 33	21 38		21 43
Shoreditch High Street	d			21 01					21 06	21 11		21 16	21 21	21 26				21 31				21 36	21 41		21 46
Whitechapel	d			21 03					21 08	21 13		21 18	21 23	21 28				21 33				21 38	21 43		21 48
Shadwell	d			21 05					21 10	21 15		21 20	21 25	21 30				21 35				21 40	21 45		21 50
Wapping	d			21 07					21 12	21 17		21 22	21 27	21 32				21 37				21 42	21 47		21 52
Rotherhithe	d			21 09					21 14	21 19		21 24	21 29	21 34				21 39				21 44	21 49		21 54
Canada Water	d			21 11					21 16	21 21		21 26	21 31	21 36				21 41				21 46	21 51		21 56
Surrey Quays	d			21 12					21 17	21 22		21 27	21 32	21 37				21 42				21 47	21 52		21 57
New Cross ELL	a									21 27				21 42									21 57		
New Cross Gate 4	a		21 11	21 16					21 21		21 27	21 31	21 36				21 41	21 46				21 51		21 57	22 01
	d		21 11	21 17					21 22		21 27	21 32	21 37				21 41	21 47				21 52		21 57	22 02
Brockley	d		21 14	21 19					21 24		21 30	21 34	21 39				21 44	21 49				21 54		22 00	22 04
Honor Oak Park	d		21 17	21 22					21 27		21 33	21 37	21 42				21 47	21 52				21 57		22 03	22 07
Forest Hill 4	d		21 19	21 25					21 30		21 35	21 40	21 45				21 49	21 55				22 00		22 05	22 10
Sydenham	d		21 22	21 27					21 32		21 38	21 42	21 47				21 52	21 57				22 02		22 08	22 12
Crystal Palace 4	d							21 30	21a37		21 43		21a52								22 00	22a07		22 13	
Gipsy Hill	d							21 32			21 45										22 02			22 15	
West Norwood 4	d							21 35			21 48										22 05			22 18	
Streatham Hill	d										21 52													22 22	
Balham 4 ⊖	d										21 55													22 25	
Wandsworth Common	d										21 57													22 27	
Clapham Junction 10	d										22 01													22 31	
South Bermondsey	d	21 07			21 15										21 37				21 45						
Queens Rd Peckham	d	21 09			21 18										21 39				21 48						
Peckham Rye 4	d	21a12			21 20		21 20	21a46							21a42				21 50	21 50	22a16				
Denmark Hill 4	d				21 23		21 24												21 53	21 54					
London Blackfriars 3 ⊖	a						21 34													22 04					
Clapham High Street ⊖	d				21 28														21 58						
Wandsworth Road	d				21 29														21 59						
Battersea Park 4	d				21 32						22 05								22 02					22 35	
London Victoria 15 ⊖	a				21 36						22 09								22 06					22 39	
Penge West	d		21 24	21 30								21 45					21 54	22 00							22 15
Anerley	d		21 26	21 32								21 47					21 56	22 02							22 17
Norwood Junction 2	d		21 30	21 35								21 50					22 00	22 05							22 20
West Croydon 4	a			21 45								22 00						22 12							22 30
East Croydon	a		21 33														22 04								

Table 178

Saturdays

18 August to 25 August

London Bridge to London Victoria - Croydon and East London Line

Network Diagram - see first Page of Table 177

			LO	LO	SN	SN	LO	SN	SE	SN	LO		SN	LO	LO	SN	SN	SN	SE	SN	LO		SN	LO	LO
London Bridge [4] ⊖	d				22 03	22 06		22 11					22 22			22 33	22 36	22 41					22 52		
Highbury & Islington	a																								
	d		21 40				21 48				21 55			22 05							22 25			22 35	
Canonbury	d		21 42				21 50				21 57			22 07							22 27			22 37	
Dalston Junction Stn ELL	d		21 45	21 50			21 55				22 00			22 10	22 20						22 30			22 40	22 50
Haggerston	d		21 46	21 51			21 56				22 01			22 11	22 21						22 31			22 41	22 51
Hoxton	d		21 48	21 53			21 58				22 03			22 13	22 23						22 33			22 43	22 53
Shoreditch High Street	d		21 51	21 56			22 01				22 06			22 16	22 26						22 36			22 46	22 56
Whitechapel	d		21 53	21 58			22 03				22 08			22 18	22 28						22 38			22 48	22 58
Shadwell	d		21 55	22 00			22 05				22 10			22 20	22 30						22 40			22 50	23 00
Wapping	d		21 57	22 02			22 07				22 12			22 22	22 32						22 42			22 52	23 02
Rotherhithe	d		21 59	22 04			22 09				22 14			22 24	22 34						22 44			22 54	23 04
Canada Water	d		22 01	22 06			22 11				22 16			22 26	22 36						22 46			22 56	23 06
Surrey Quays	d		22 02	22 07			22 12				22 17			22 27	22 37						22 47			22 57	23 07
New Cross ELL	a			22 13											22 42										23 12
New Cross Gate [4]	a		22 06			22 11	22 16				22 21		22 27	22 31			22 41				22 51		22 57	23 01	
	d		22 07			22 11	22 17				22 22		22 27	22 32			22 41				22 52		22 57	23 02	
Brockley	d		22 09			22 14	22 19				22 24		22 30	22 34			22 44				22 54		23 00	23 04	
Honor Oak Park	d		22 12			22 17	22 22				22 27		22 33	22 37			22 47				22 57		23 03	23 07	
Forest Hill [4]	d		22 15			22 19	22 25				22 30		22 35	22 40			22 49				23 00		23 05	23 10	
Sydenham	d		22 17			22 22	22 27				22 32		22 38	22 42			22 52				23 02		23 08	23 12	
Crystal Palace [4]	d		22a22							22 30	22a37		22 43							23 00	23a07		23 13		
Gipsy Hill	d									22 32			22 45							23 02			23 15		
West Norwood [4]	d									22 35			22 48							23 05			23 18		
Streatham Hill	d												22 52										23 22		
Balham [4] ⊖	d												22 55										23 25		
Wandsworth Common	d												22 57										23 27		
Clapham Junction [10]	d												23 01										23 31		
South Bermondsey	d				22 07			22 15								22 37		22 45							
Queens Rd Peckham	d				22 09			22 18								22 39		22 48							
Peckham Rye [4]	d				22a12			22 20	22 20	22a46						22a42		22 50	22 50	23a16					
Denmark Hill [4]	d							22 23	22 24									22 53	22 54						
London Blackfriars [3] ⊖	a								22 34										23 04						
Clapham High Street ⊖	d							22 28										22 58							
Wandsworth Road	d							22 29										22 59							
Battersea Park [4]	d							22 32					23 05					23 02					23 35		
London Victoria [15] ⊖	a							22 36					23 09					23 06					23 41		
Penge West	d					22 24	22 30							22 45			22 54							23 15	
Anerley	d					22 26	22 32							22 47			22 56							23 17	
Norwood Junction [2]	d					22 30	22 35							22 50			23 00							23 20	
West Croydon [4]	a						22 42							23 00										23 30	
East Croydon	a					22 35											23 03								

		SN	SN	SN	SE	SN	LO		SN	LO	LO	SN	SN	LO	SN	LO	LO		LO
London Bridge [4] ⊖	d	23 03	23 06	23 11					23 22			23 33	23 36		23 52				
Highbury & Islington	a																		
	d						22 55			23 05				23 25		23 35	23 42		23 56
Canonbury	d						22 57			23 07				23 27		23 37	23 44		23 58
Dalston Junction Stn ELL	d						23 00			23 10	23 20			23 30		23 40	23 47		00 02
Haggerston	d						23 01			23 11	23 21			23 31		23 41	23 48		00 03
Hoxton	d						23 03			23 13	23 23			23 33		23 43	23 50		00 05
Shoreditch High Street	d						23 06			23 16	23 26			23 36		23 46	23 53		00 08
Whitechapel	d						23 08			23 18	23 28			23 38		23 48	23 55		00 10
Shadwell	d						23 10			23 20	23 30			23 40		23 50	23 57		00 12
Wapping	d						23 12			23 22	23 32			23 42		23 52	23 59		00 14
Rotherhithe	d						23 14			23 24	23 34			23 44		23 54	00 01		00 16
Canada Water	d						23 16			23 26	23 36			23 46		23 56	00 03		00 18
Surrey Quays	d						23 17			23 27	23 37			23 47		23 57	00 05		00 19
New Cross ELL	a										23 42								
New Cross Gate [4]	a		23 11				23 21		23 27	23 31			23 41	23 51	23 57	00 02	00 08		00 23
	d		23 11				23 22		23 27	23 32			23 41	23 52	23 57	00 02			
Brockley	d		23 14				23 24		23 30	23 34			23 44	23 54	00 01	00 04			
Honor Oak Park	d		23 17				23 27		23 33	23 37			23 47	23 57	00 04	00 07			
Forest Hill [4]	d		23 19				23 30		23 35	23 40			23 49	23 59	00 06	00 10			
Sydenham	d		23 22				23 32		23 38	23 42			23 52	00 02	00 09	00 12			
Crystal Palace [4]	d					23 30	23a37		23 43					00a07	00 13				
Gipsy Hill	d					23 32			23 45						00 15				
West Norwood [4]	d					23 35			23 48						00 18				
Streatham Hill	d								23 52						00 22				
Balham [4] ⊖	d								23 55						00 26				
Wandsworth Common	d								23 57						00 28				
Clapham Junction [10]	d								00 02						00 32				
South Bermondsey	d	23 07		23 15								23 37							
Queens Rd Peckham	d	23 09		23 18								23 39							
Peckham Rye [4]	d	23 12		23 20	23 20	23a46						23 42							
Denmark Hill [4]	d			23 23	23 24														
London Blackfriars [3] ⊖	a				23 34														
Clapham High Street ⊖	d			23 28															
Wandsworth Road	d			23 29															
Battersea Park [4]	d			23 32					00 05						00 35				
London Victoria [15] ⊖	a			23 37					00 10						00 42				
Penge West	d		23 24							23 45			23 54			00 15			
Anerley	d		23 26							23 47			23 56			00 17			
Norwood Junction [2]	d	23a34	23 30							23 50		00a04	23 59			00 20			
West Croydon [4]	a									23 59						00 27			
East Croydon	a		23 33										00 03						

Table 178

Saturdays

1 September to 8 September

London Bridge to London Victoria - Croydon and East London Line

Network Diagram - see first Page of Table 177

		SN	SN	LO	SN	LO	SN	LO	LO	SN		SN	LO	SN	LO	LO	SN	LO	SN	SN		LO	SN	LO	LO
London Bridge 4 ⊖	d	23p22	23p36				23p52			00 03		00 06							00 33	00 36					
Highbury & Islington	a																								
	d			23p18		23p25		23p33	23p40				23p48		23p55	00 03		00 10				00 18		00 25	00 33
Canonbury	d			23p20		23p27		23p35	23p42				23p50		23p57	00 05		00 12				00 20		00 27	00 35
Dalston Junction Stn ELL	d			23p25		23p30		23p38	23p45				23p55		00 01	00 09		00 15				00 25		00 30	00 40
Haggerston	d			23p26		23p31		23p39	23p46				23p56		00 02	00 10		00 16				00 26		00 31	00 41
Hoxton	d			23p28		23p33		23p41	23p48				23p58		00 04	00 12		00 18				00 28		00 33	00 43
Shoreditch High Street	d			23p31		23p36		23p44	23p51				00 01		00 07	00 15		00 21				00 31		00 36	00 46
Whitechapel	d			23p33		23p38		23p46	23p53				00 03		00 09	00 17		00 23				00 33		00 38	00 48
Shadwell	d			23p35		23p40		23p48	23p55				00 05		00 11	00 19		00 25				00 35		00 40	00 50
Wapping	d			23p37		23p42		23p50	23p57				00 07		00 13	00 21		00 27				00 37		00 42	00 52
Rotherhithe	d			23p39		23p44		23p52	23p59				00 09		00 15	00 23		00 29				00 39		00 44	00 54
Canada Water	d			23p41		23p46		23p54	00 02				00 11		00 17	00 25		00 31				00 41		00 46	00 56
Surrey Quays	d			23p42		23p47		23p55	00 03				00 12		00 18	00 26		00 32				00 42		00 47	00 57
New Cross ELL	a																								
New Cross Gate 4	a	23p27	23p41	23p46		23p51	23p57	23p58	00 07			00 11	00 16		00 22	00 30		00 36		00 41		00 47		00 51	01 02
	d	23p27	23p41	23p47		23p52	23p57	23p59	00 08			00 11	00 17		00 23	00 31		00 37		00 41		00 47		00 52	01 03
Brockley	d	23p30	23p44	23p49		23p54	00 01	00 03	00 10			00 14	00 19		00 25	00 33		00 39		00 44		00 49		00 54	01 05
Honor Oak Park	d	23p33	23p47	23p52		23p57	00 04	00 06	00 13			00 17	00 22		00 28	00 36		00 42		00 47		00 52		00 57	01 08
Forest Hill 4	d	23p35	23p49	23p55		23p59	00 06	00 09	00 16			00 19	00 25		00 31	00 39		00 45		00 49		00 55		00 59	01 11
Sydenham	d	23p38	23p52	23p57		00 02	00 09	00 11	00 18			00 22	00 27		00 33	00 41		00 47		00 52		00 57		01 02	01 13
Crystal Palace 4	d	23p43			00 03	00a07	00 13		00a23					00 33	00a38		00 47	00a52					01 03	01a07	
Gipsy Hill	d	23p45					00 15																		
West Norwood 4	d	23p48					00 18																		
Streatham Hill	d	23p52					00 22																		
Balham 4 ⊖	d	23p55					00 25																		
Wandsworth Common	d	23p58					00 27																		
Clapham Junction 10	d	00 02					00 31																		
South Bermondsey	d									00 07									00 37						
Queens Rd Peckham	d									00 09									00 39						
Peckham Rye 4	d									00 12									00 42						
Denmark Hill 4	d																								
London Blackfriars 3 ⊖	a																								
Clapham High Street ⊖	d																								
Wandsworth Road	d																								
Battersea Park 4	d	00 05					00 35																		
London Victoria 15 ⊖	a	00 10					00 42																		
Penge West	d		23p54	00 01				00 14				00 24	00 30			00 44				00 54		01 00			01 16
Anerley	d		23p56	00 03				00 16				00 26	00 32			00 46				00 56		01 02			01 18
Norwood Junction 2	d		23p59	00 06	00 09			00 19		00a34		00 30	00 35	00 38		00 49	00 52		01a04	01 00		01 05	01 08		01 21
West Croydon 4	a			00 13	00 14			00 26					00 42	00 43		00 56	00 58					01 14	01 13		01 28
East Croydon	a		00 03									00 33								01 03					

		LO	LO	LO	LO	LO		LO	SN	SE	LO	LO	LO	LO	SE	LO		LO	LO	LO	LO	SN	LO	SN	SN
London Bridge 4 ⊖	d								06 11															06 36	06 41
Highbury & Islington	a																								
	d	00 40	00 48	00 55	01 03	01 10		01 25					05 35						05 55	06 05					
Canonbury	d	00 42	00 50	00 57	01 05	01 12		01 27					05 37						05 57	06 07					
Dalston Junction Stn ELL	d	00 45	00 55	01 00	01 10	01 15		01 32					05 40	05 50					06 00	06 10	06 20				
Haggerston	d	00 46	00 56	01 01	01 11	01 16		01 33					05 41	05 51					06 01	06 11	06 21				
Hoxton	d	00 48	00 58	01 03	01 13	01 18		01 35					05 43	05 53					06 03	06 13	06 23				
Shoreditch High Street	d	00 51	01 01	01 06	01 16	01 21		01 38					05 46	05 56					06 06	06 16	06 26				
Whitechapel	d	00 53	01 03	01 08	01 18	01 23		01 40					05 48	05 58					06 08	06 18	06 28				
Shadwell	d	00 55	01 05	01 10	01 20	01 25		01 42					05 50	06 00					06 10	06 20	06 30				
Wapping	d	00 57	01 07	01 12	01 22	01 27		01 44					05 52	06 02					06 12	06 22	06 32				
Rotherhithe	d	00 59	01 09	01 14	01 24	01 29		01 46					05 54	06 04					06 14	06 24	06 34				
Canada Water	d	01 01	01 11	01 16	01 26	01 31		01 48					05 56	06 06					06 16	06 26	06 36				
Surrey Quays	d	01 02	01 12	01 17	01 27	01 32		01 49					05 57	06 07					06 17	06 27	06 37				
New Cross ELL	a													06 12							06 42				
New Cross Gate 4	a	01 06	01 16	01 21	01 31	01 36		01 53					06 01						06 21	06 31				06 41	
	d	01 07	01 17	01 22	01 32	01 37		01 54			05 47	05 52	06 02			06 07		06 17	06 22	06 32			06 37	06 41	
Brockley	d	01 09	01 19	01 24	01 34	01 39		01 56			05 49	05 54	06 04			06 09		06 19	06 24	06 34			06 39	06 44	
Honor Oak Park	d	01 12	01 22	01 27	01 37	01 42		01 59			05 52	05 57	06 07			06 12		06 22	06 27	06 37			06 42	06 47	
Forest Hill 4	d	01 15	01 25	01 30	01 40	01 45		02 02			05 55	06 00	06 10			06 15		06 25	06 30	06 40			06 45	06 49	
Sydenham	d	01 17	01 27	01 32	01 42	01 47		02 04			05 57	06 02	06 12			06 17		06 27	06 32	06 42			06 47	06 52	
Crystal Palace 4	d	01a22		01a37		01a52						06a07				06a22			06a37			06 45	06a52		
Gipsy Hill	d																					06 47			
West Norwood 4	d																					06 50			
Streatham Hill	d																								
Balham 4 ⊖	d																								
Wandsworth Common	d																								
Clapham Junction 10	d																								
South Bermondsey	d								06 15																06 45
Queens Rd Peckham	d								06 18																06 48
Peckham Rye 4	d								06 20	06 20					06 50							07a01			06 50
Denmark Hill 4	d								06 23	06 24					06 54										06 53
London Blackfriars 3 ⊖	a									06 34					07 04										
Clapham High Street ⊖	d								06 28																06 58
Wandsworth Road	d								06 29																06 59
Battersea Park 4	d								06 32																07 02
London Victoria 15 ⊖	a								06 36																07 06
Penge West	d		01 30		01 45			02 07			06 00		06 15					06 30		06 45				06 54	
Anerley	d		01 32		01 47			02 09			06 02		06 17					06 32		06 47				06 56	
Norwood Junction 2	d		01 35		01 50			02 12			06 06		06 20					06 35		06 50				07 00	
West Croydon 4	a		01 42		01 57			02 19			06 13		06 30					06 41		07 00					
East Croydon	a																							07 03	

1 September to 8 September

London Bridge to London Victoria - Croydon and East London Line

Network Diagram - see first Page of Table 177

		SE		SE	LO	LO	LO	LO	LO	LO	SN	LO		LO	LO	LO	LO	SN	LO	SN	SN	LO		LO	LO
London Bridge 4 ⊖	d										07 06							07 11		07 33	07 36				
Highbury & Islington	a																								
	d					06 25		06 33	06 40			06 48		06 55		07 03	07 10					07 18		07 25	
Canonbury	d					06 27		06 35	06 42			06 50		06 57		07 05	07 12					07 20		07 27	
Dalston Junction Stn ELL	d					06 30	06 35	06 40	06 45	06 50		06 55		07 00	07 05	07 10	07 15		07 20			07 25		07 30	07 35
Haggerston	d					06 31	06 36	06 41	06 46	06 51		06 56		07 01	07 06	07 11	07 16		07 21			07 26		07 31	07 36
Hoxton	d					06 33	06 38	06 43	06 48	06 53		06 58		07 03	07 08	07 13	07 18		07 23			07 28		07 33	07 38
Shoreditch High Street	d					06 36	06 41	06 46	06 51	06 56		07 01		07 06	07 11	07 16	07 21		07 26			07 31		07 36	07 41
Whitechapel	d					06 38	06 43	06 48	06 53	06 58		07 03		07 08	07 13	07 18	07 23		07 28			07 33		07 38	07 43
Shadwell	d					06 40	06 45	06 50	06 55	07 00		07 05		07 10	07 15	07 20	07 25		07 30			07 35		07 40	07 45
Wapping	d					06 42	06 47	06 52	06 57	07 02		07 07		07 12	07 17	07 22	07 27		07 32			07 37		07 42	07 47
Rotherhithe	d					06 44	06 49	06 54	06 59	07 04		07 09		07 14	07 19	07 24	07 29		07 34			07 39		07 44	07 49
Canada Water	d					06 46	06 51	06 56	07 01	07 06		07 11		07 16	07 21	07 26	07 31		07 36			07 41		07 46	07 51
Surrey Quays	d					06 47	06 52	06 57	07 02	07 07		07 12		07 17	07 22	07 27	07 32		07 37			07 42		07 47	07 52
New Cross ELL	a						06 57			07 12					07 27				07 42						07 57
New Cross Gate 4	a					06 51		07 00	07 06		07 11	07 15		07 21		07 31	07 36				07 41	07 45		07 51	
	d				06 47	06 52		07 02	07 07		07 11	07 17		07 22		07 32	07 37				07 41	07 47		07 52	
Brockley	d				06 49	06 54		07 04	07 09		07 14	07 19		07 24		07 34	07 39				07 44	07 49		07 54	
Honor Oak Park	d				06 52	06 57		07 07	07 12		07 17	07 22		07 27		07 37	07 42				07 47	07 52		07 57	
Forest Hill 4	d				06 55	07 00		07 10	07 15		07 19	07 25		07 30		07 40	07 45				07 49	07 55		08 00	
Sydenham	d				06 57	07 02		07 12	07 17		07 22	07 27		07 32		07 42	07 47				07 52	07 57		08 02	
Crystal Palace 4	d					07a07			07a22					07a37			07a52							08a07	
Gipsy Hill	d																								
West Norwood 4	d																								
Streatham Hill	d																								
Balham 4 ⊖	d																								
Wandsworth Common	d																								
Clapham Junction 10	d																								
South Bermondsey	d																	07 15		07 37					
Queens Rd Peckham	d																	07 18		07 39					
Peckham Rye 4	d	07 15		07 20														07 20		07a42					
Denmark Hill 4	d	07 19		07 24														07 23							
London Blackfriars 3 ⊖	a			07 34																					
Clapham High Street ⊖	d																	07 28							
Wandsworth Road	d																	07 29							
Battersea Park 4	d																	07 32							
London Victoria 15 ⊖	a	07 28																07 36							
Penge West	d				07 00			07 15			07 24	07 30				07 45					07 54	08 00			
Anerley	d				07 02			07 17			07 26	07 32				07 47					07 56	08 02			
Norwood Junction 2	d				07 05			07 20			07 30	07 35				07 50					08 00	08 05			
West Croydon 4	a				07 11			07 30				07 42				08 00						08 12			
East Croydon	a										07 33										08 03				

		LO	LO	LO	SE	SN	SE	SN		SN	LO	SE	SN	SE	SN	LO	LO	SN		LO	LO	LO	SN	SN	LO
London Bridge 4 ⊖	d					07 41		08 03		08 06			08 11					08 22					08 33	08 36	
Highbury & Islington	a																								
	d	07 33	07 40								07 48					07 55				08 03	08 10				08 18
Canonbury	d	07 35	07 42								07 50					07 57				08 05	08 12				08 20
Dalston Junction Stn ELL	d	07 40	07 45	07 50							07 55					08 00	08 05			08 10	08 15	08 20			08 25
Haggerston	d	07 41	07 46	07 51							07 56					08 01	08 06			08 11	08 16	08 21			08 26
Hoxton	d	07 43	07 48	07 53							07 58					08 03	08 08			08 13	08 18	08 23			08 28
Shoreditch High Street	d	07 46	07 51	07 56							08 01					08 06	08 11			08 16	08 21	08 26			08 31
Whitechapel	d	07 48	07 53	07 58							08 03					08 08	08 13			08 18	08 23	08 28			08 33
Shadwell	d	07 50	07 55	08 00							08 05					08 10	08 15			08 20	08 25	08 30			08 35
Wapping	d	07 52	07 57	08 02							08 07					08 12	08 17			08 22	08 27	08 32			08 37
Rotherhithe	d	07 54	07 59	08 04							08 09					08 14	08 19			08 24	08 29	08 34			08 39
Canada Water	d	07 56	08 01	08 06							08 11					08 16	08 21			08 26	08 31	08 36			08 41
Surrey Quays	d	07 57	08 02	08 07							08 12					08 17	08 22			08 27	08 32	08 37			08 42
New Cross ELL	a			08 12													08 27					08 42			
New Cross Gate 4	a	08 01	08 06							08 11	08 16					08 21		08 27		08 31	08 36			08 41	08 46
	d	08 02	08 07							08 11	08 16					08 22		08 27		08 32	08 37			08 41	08 47
Brockley	d	08 04	08 09							08 14	08 17					08 24		08 30		08 34	08 39			08 44	08 49
Honor Oak Park	d	08 07	08 12							08 17	08 20					08 27		08 33		08 37	08 42			08 47	08 52
Forest Hill 4	d	08 10	08 15							08 19	08 24					08 30		08 35		08 40	08 45			08 49	08 55
Sydenham	d	08 12	08 17							08 22	08 25					08 32		08 38		08 42	08 47			08 52	08 57
Crystal Palace 4	d		08a22												08 30	08a37		08 43			08a52				
Gipsy Hill	d														08 32			08 45							
West Norwood 4	d														08 35			08 48							
Streatham Hill	d																	08 52							
Balham 4 ⊖	d																	08 55							
Wandsworth Common	d																	08 57							
Clapham Junction 10	d																	09 01							
South Bermondsey	d					07 45		08 07					08 15										08 37		
Queens Rd Peckham	d					07 48		08 09					08 18										08 39		
Peckham Rye 4	d				07 45	07 50	07 50	08a12				08 15	08 20	08 20	08a46								08a42		
Denmark Hill 4	d				07 49	07 53	07 54					08 19	08 23	08 24											
London Blackfriars 3 ⊖	a						08 04							08 34											
Clapham High Street ⊖	d					07 58							08 28												
Wandsworth Road	d					07 59							08 29												
Battersea Park 4	d					08 02							08 32					09 05							
London Victoria 15 ⊖	a				07 58	08 06						08 28	08 36					09 09							
Penge West	d	08 15								08 24	08 29									08 45				08 54	09 00
Anerley	d	08 17								08 26	08 31									08 47				08 56	09 02
Norwood Junction 2	d	08 20								08 30	08 34									08 50				09 00	09 05
West Croydon 4	a	08 30									08 41									09 00					09 12
East Croydon	a									08 33														09 03	

Table 178

Saturdays

1 September to 8 September

London Bridge to London Victoria - Croydon and East London Line

Network Diagram - see first Page of Table 177

Station		SE	SN	SE		SN	LO	LO	SN	LO	LO	LO	SN	SN		LO	SE	SN	SE	SN	LO	LO	SN	LO	
London Bridge 4 ⊖	d		08 41						08 52				09 03	09 06				09 11					09 22		
Highbury & Islington	a																								
	d						08 25			08 33	08 40					08 48					08 55			09 03	
Canonbury	d						08 27			08 35	08 42					08 50					08 57			09 05	
Dalston Junction Stn ELL	d						08 30	08 35		08 40	08 45	08 50				08 55					09 00	09 05		09 10	
Haggerston	d						08 31	08 36		08 41	08 46	08 51				08 56					09 01	09 06		09 11	
Hoxton	d						08 33	08 38		08 43	08 48	08 53				08 58					09 03	09 08		09 13	
Shoreditch High Street	d						08 36	08 41		08 46	08 51	08 56				09 01					09 06	09 11		09 16	
Whitechapel	d						08 38	08 43		08 48	08 53	08 58				09 03					09 08	09 13		09 18	
Shadwell	d						08 40	08 45		08 50	08 55	09 00				09 05					09 10	09 15		09 20	
Wapping	d						08 42	08 47		08 52	08 57	09 02				09 07					09 12	09 17		09 22	
Rotherhithe	d						08 44	08 49		08 54	08 59	09 04				09 09					09 14	09 19		09 24	
Canada Water	d						08 46	08 51		08 56	09 01	09 06				09 11					09 16	09 21		09 26	
Surrey Quays	d						08 47	08 52		08 57	09 02	09 07				09 12					09 17	09 22		09 27	
New Cross ELL	a							08 57				09 12										09 27			
New Cross Gate 4	a						08 51		08 57	09 01	09 06			09 11		09 16					09 21		09 27	09 30	
	d						08 52		08 57	09 02	09 07			09 11		09 17					09 22		09 27	09 32	
Brockley	d						08 54		09 00	09 04	09 09			09 14		09 19					09 24		09 30	09 34	
Honor Oak Park	d						08 57		09 03	09 07	09 12			09 17		09 22					09 27		09 33	09 37	
Forest Hill 4	d						09 00		09 05	09 10	09 15			09 19		09 25					09 30		09 35	09 40	
Sydenham	d						09 02		09 08	09 12	09 17			09 22		09 27					09 32		09 38	09 42	
Crystal Palace 4	d					09 00	09a07		09 13		09a22									09 30	09a37		09 43		
Gipsy Hill	d					09 02			09 15											09 32			09 45		
West Norwood 4	d					09 05			09 18											09 35			09 48		
Streatham Hill	d								09 22														09 52		
Balham 4 ⊖	d								09 25														09 55		
Wandsworth Common	d								09 27														09 57		
Clapham Junction 10	d								09 32														10 01		
South Bermondsey	d		08 45										09 07					09 15							
Queens Rd Peckham	d		08 48										09 09					09 18							
Peckham Rye 4	d	08 45	08 50	08 50		09a16							09a12				09 15	09 20	09 20	09a46					
Denmark Hill 4	d	08 49	08 53	08 54													09 19	09 23	09 24						
London Blackfriars 3 ⊖	a			09 04															09 34						
Clapham High Street ⊖	d		08 58															09 28							
Wandsworth Road	d		08 59															09 29							
Battersea Park 4	d		09 02						09 36									09 32					10 05		
London Victoria 15 ⊖	a	08 58	09 06						09 40								09 28	09 36					10 09		
Penge West	d									09 15				09 24		09 30								09 45	
Anerley	d									09 17				09 26		09 32								09 47	
Norwood Junction 2	d									09 20				09 30		09 35								09 50	
West Croydon 4	a									09 30						09 42								10 00	
East Croydon	a													09 33											

Station		LO	LO	SN	SN	LO	SE	SN	SE	SN		LO	LO	SN		SN	LO	LO	LO		SN	SN	LO	SE
London Bridge 4 ⊖	d			09 33	09 36			09 41						09 52		18 52					19 03	19 06		
Highbury & Islington	a																							
	d	09 10				09 18						09 25					18 33	18 40					18 48	
Canonbury	d	09 12				09 20						09 27					18 35	18 42					18 50	
Dalston Junction Stn ELL	d	09 15	09 20			09 25						09 30	09 35				18 40	18 45	18 50				18 55	
Haggerston	d	09 16	09 21			09 26						09 31	09 36				18 41	18 46	18 51				18 56	
Hoxton	d	09 18	09 23			09 28						09 33	09 38				18 43	18 48	18 53				18 58	
Shoreditch High Street	d	09 21	09 26			09 31						09 36	09 41				18 46	18 51	18 56				19 01	
Whitechapel	d	09 23	09 28			09 33						09 38	09 43				18 48	18 53	18 58				19 03	
Shadwell	d	09 25	09 30			09 35						09 40	09 45				18 50	18 55	19 00				19 05	
Wapping	d	09 27	09 32			09 37						09 42	09 47				18 52	18 57	19 02				19 07	
Rotherhithe	d	09 29	09 34			09 39						09 44	09 49				18 54	18 59	19 04				19 09	
Canada Water	d	09 31	09 36			09 41						09 46	09 51				18 56	19 01	19 06				19 11	
Surrey Quays	d	09 32	09 37			09 42						09 47	09 52				18 57	19 02	19 07				19 12	
New Cross ELL	a		09 42										09 57						19 12					
New Cross Gate 4	a	09 36			09 41	09 46						09 51		09 57		18 57	19 01	19 06				19 11	19 16	
	d	09 37			09 41	09 47						09 52		09 57		18 57	19 02	19 07				19 11	19 17	
Brockley	d	09 39			09 44	09 49						09 54		10 00	and at the same minutes past each hour until	19 00	19 04	19 09				19 14	19 19	
Honor Oak Park	d	09 42			09 47	09 52						09 57		10 03		19 03	19 07	19 12				19 17	19 22	
Forest Hill 4	d	09 45			09 49	09 55						10 00		10 05		19 05	19 10	19 15				19 19	19 25	
Sydenham	d	09 47			09 52	09 57						10 02		10 08		19 08	19 12	19 17				19 22	19 27	
Crystal Palace 4	d	09a52								10 00		10a07		10 13		19 13		19a22						
Gipsy Hill	d									10 02				10 15		19 15								
West Norwood 4	d									10 05				10 18		19 18								
Streatham Hill	d													10 22		19 22								
Balham 4 ⊖	d													10 25		19 25								
Wandsworth Common	d													10 27		19 27								
Clapham Junction 10	d													10 31		19 31								
South Bermondsey	d			09 37				09 45													19 07			
Queens Rd Peckham	d			09 39				09 48													19 09			
Peckham Rye 4	d			09a42			09 45	09 50	09 50	10a16											19a12			19 15
Denmark Hill 4	d						09 49	09 53	09 54															19 19
London Blackfriars 3 ⊖	a								10 04															
Clapham High Street ⊖	d							09 58																
Wandsworth Road	d							09 59																
Battersea Park 4	d							10 02						10 35		19 35								
London Victoria 15 ⊖	a						09 58	10 06						10 39		19 39								19 28
Penge West	d				09 54	10 00											19 15					19 24	19 30	
Anerley	d				09 56	10 02											19 17					19 26	19 32	
Norwood Junction 2	d				10 00	10 05											19 20					19 30	19 35	
West Croydon 4	a					10 12											19 30						19 42	
East Croydon	a				10 03																	19 33		

Table 178

1 September to 8 September

London Bridge to London Victoria - Croydon and East London Line

Network Diagram - see first Page of Table 177

		SN	SE	SN	LO	LO		SN	LO	LO	LO	SN	SN	LO	SN	SE		SN	LO	LO	SN	LO	LO	LO	SN
London Bridge 4 ⊖	d	19 11						19 22				19 33	19 36		19 41						19 52				20 03
Highbury & Islington	a																								
	d				18 55				19 03	19 10				19 18					19 25			19 33	19 40		
Canonbury	d				18 57				19 05	19 12				19 20					19 27			19 35	19 42		
Dalston Junction Stn ELL	d				19 00	19 05			19 10	19 15	19 20			19 25					19 30	19 35		19 40	19 45	19 50	
Haggerston	d				19 01	19 06			19 11	19 16	19 21			19 26					19 31	19 36		19 41	19 46	19 51	
Hoxton	d				19 03	19 08			19 13	19 18	19 23			19 28					19 33	19 38		19 43	19 48	19 53	
Shoreditch High Street	d				19 06	19 11			19 16	19 21	19 26			19 31					19 36	19 41		19 46	19 51	19 56	
Whitechapel	d				19 08	19 13			19 18	19 23	19 28			19 33					19 38	19 43		19 48	19 53	19 58	
Shadwell	d				19 10	19 15			19 20	19 25	19 30			19 35					19 40	19 45		19 50	19 55	20 00	
Wapping	d				19 12	19 17			19 22	19 27	19 32			19 37					19 42	19 47		19 52	19 57	20 02	
Rotherhithe	d				19 14	19 19			19 24	19 29	19 34			19 39					19 44	19 49		19 54	19 59	20 04	
Canada Water	d				19 16	19 21			19 26	19 31	19 36			19 41					19 46	19 51		19 56	20 01	20 06	
Surrey Quays	d				19 17	19 22			19 27	19 32	19 37			19 42					19 47	19 52		19 57	20 02	20 07	
New Cross ELL	a					19 27					19 42									19 57				20 12	
New Cross Gate 4	a				19 21			19 27	19 31	19 36			19 41	19 46					19 51		19 57	20 01	20 06		
	d				19 22			19 27	19 32	19 37			19 41	19 47					19 52		19 57	20 02	20 07		
Brockley	d				19 24			19 30	19 34	19 39			19 44	19 49					19 54		20 00	20 04	20 09		
Honor Oak Park	d				19 27			19 33	19 37	19 42			19 47	19 52					19 57		20 03	20 07	20 12		
Forest Hill 4	d				19 30			19 35	19 40	19 45			19 49	19 55					20 00		20 05	20 10	20 15		
Sydenham	d				19 32			19 38	19 42	19 47			19 52	19 57					20 02		20 08	20 12	20 17		
Crystal Palace 4	d			19 30	19a37			19 43		19a52								20 00	20a07		20 13		20a22		
Gipsy Hill	d			19 32				19 45										20 03			20 15				
West Norwood 4	d			19 35				19 48										20 06			20 18				
Streatham Hill	d							19 52													20 22				
Balham 4 ⊖	d							19 55													20 25				
Wandsworth Common	d							19 57													20 27				
Clapham Junction 10	d							20 01													20 31				
South Bermondsey	d	19 15										19 37			19 45										20 07
Queens Rd Peckham	d	19 18										19 39			19 48										20 09
Peckham Rye 4	d	19 20	19 20	19a46								19a42			19 50	19 50		20a16							20a12
Denmark Hill 4	d	19 23	19 24												19 53	19 54									
London Blackfriars 3 ⊖	a		19 34													20 04									
Clapham High Street ⊖	d	19 28													19 58										
Wandsworth Road	d	19 29													19 59										
Battersea Park 4	d	19 32						20 05							20 02						20 35				
London Victoria 15 ⊖	a	19 36						20 09							20 06						20 39				
Penge West	d								19 45				19 54	20 00								20 15			
Anerley	d								19 47				19 56	20 02								20 17			
Norwood Junction 2	d								19 50				20 00	20 05								20 20			
West Croydon 4	a								20 00					20 12								20 30			
East Croydon	a												20 03												

		SN		LO	SN	SE	SN	LO	LO	SN	LO	LO		LO	SN	SN	LO	SN	SE	SN	LO	LO		SN	LO
London Bridge 4 ⊖	d	20 06			20 11					20 22					20 33	20 36		20 41						20 52	
Highbury & Islington	a																								
	d			19 48				19 55			20 03	20 10					20 18				20 25				20 33
Canonbury	d			19 50				19 57			20 05	20 12					20 20				20 27				20 35
Dalston Junction Stn ELL	d			19 55				20 00	20 05		20 10	20 15		20 20			20 25				20 30	20 35			20 40
Haggerston	d			19 56				20 01	20 06		20 11	20 16		20 21			20 26				20 31	20 36			20 41
Hoxton	d			19 58				20 03	20 08		20 13	20 18		20 23			20 28				20 33	20 38			20 43
Shoreditch High Street	d			20 01				20 06	20 11		20 16	20 21		20 26			20 31				20 36	20 41			20 46
Whitechapel	d			20 03				20 08	20 13		20 18	20 23		20 28			20 33				20 38	20 43			20 48
Shadwell	d			20 05				20 10	20 15		20 20	20 25		20 30			20 35				20 40	20 45			20 50
Wapping	d			20 07				20 12	20 17		20 22	20 27		20 32			20 37				20 42	20 47			20 52
Rotherhithe	d			20 09				20 14	20 19		20 24	20 29		20 34			20 39				20 44	20 49			20 54
Canada Water	d			20 11				20 16	20 21		20 26	20 31		20 36			20 41				20 46	20 51			20 56
Surrey Quays	d			20 12				20 17	20 22		20 27	20 32		20 37			20 42				20 47	20 52			20 57
New Cross ELL	a								20 27					20 42								20 57			
New Cross Gate 4	a	20 11		20 16				20 21		20 27	20 31	20 36				20 41	20 46				20 51			20 57	21 01
	d	20 11		20 17				20 22		20 27	20 32	20 37				20 41	20 47				20 52			20 57	21 02
Brockley	d	20 14		20 19				20 24		20 30	20 34	20 39				20 44	20 49				20 54			21 00	21 04
Honor Oak Park	d	20 17		20 22				20 27		20 33	20 37	20 42				20 47	20 52				20 57			21 03	21 07
Forest Hill 4	d	20 19		20 25				20 30		20 35	20 40	20 45				20 49	20 55				21 00			21 05	21 10
Sydenham	d	20 22		20 27				20 32		20 38	20 42	20 47				20 52	20 57				21 02			21 08	21 12
Crystal Palace 4	d						20 30	20a37		20 43		20a52								21 00	21a07			21 13	
Gipsy Hill	d						20 33			20 45										21 02				21 15	
West Norwood 4	d						20 36			20 48										21 05				21 18	
Streatham Hill	d									20 52														21 22	
Balham 4 ⊖	d									20 55														21 25	
Wandsworth Common	d									20 57														21 27	
Clapham Junction 10	d									21 01														21 31	
South Bermondsey	d				20 15										20 37			20 45							
Queens Rd Peckham	d				20 18										20 39			20 48							
Peckham Rye 4	d				20 20	20 20	20a46								20a42			20 50	20 50	21a16					
Denmark Hill 4	d				20 23	20 24												20 53	20 54						
London Blackfriars 3 ⊖	a					20 34													21 04						
Clapham High Street ⊖	d				20 28													20 58							
Wandsworth Road	d				20 29													20 59							
Battersea Park 4	d				20 32					21 05								21 02						21 35	
London Victoria 15 ⊖	a				20 36					21 09								21 06						21 39	
Penge West	d	20 24		20 30							20 45					20 54	21 00								21 15
Anerley	d	20 26		20 32							20 47					20 56	21 02								21 17
Norwood Junction 2	d	20 30		20 35							20 50					21 00	21 05								21 20
West Croydon 4	a			20 42							21 00						21 12								21 30
East Croydon	a	20 33														21 03									

Saturdays

1 September to 8 September

London Bridge to London Victoria - Croydon and East London Line

Network Diagram - see first Page of Table 177

		LO	LO	SN	SN	LO	SN	SE	SN	LO	LO	SN	LO	LO	LO	SN	SN	LO	SN	SE	SN	LO	LO
London Bridge 4 ⊖	d			21 03	21 06		21 11					21 22				21 33	21 36		21 41				
Highbury & Islington	a																						
	d	20 40				20 48				20 55			21 03	21 10				21 18				21 25	
Canonbury	d	20 42				20 50				20 57			21 05	21 12				21 20				21 27	
Dalston Junction Stn ELL	d	20 45	20 50			20 55				21 00	21 05		21 10	21 15	21 20			21 25				21 30	21 35
Haggerston	d	20 46	20 51			20 56				21 01	21 06		21 11	21 16	21 21			21 26				21 31	21 36
Hoxton	d	20 48	20 53			20 58				21 03	21 08		21 13	21 18	21 23			21 28				21 33	21 38
Shoreditch High Street	d	20 51	20 56			21 01				21 06	21 11		21 16	21 21	21 26			21 31				21 36	21 41
Whitechapel	d	20 53	20 58			21 03				21 08	21 13		21 18	21 23	21 28			21 33				21 38	21 43
Shadwell	d	20 55	21 00			21 05				21 10	21 15		21 20	21 25	21 30			21 35				21 40	21 45
Wapping	d	20 57	21 02			21 07				21 12	21 17		21 22	21 27	21 32			21 37				21 42	21 47
Rotherhithe	d	20 59	21 04			21 09				21 14	21 19		21 24	21 29	21 34			21 39				21 44	21 49
Canada Water	d	21 01	21 06			21 11				21 16	21 21		21 26	21 31	21 36			21 41				21 46	21 51
Surrey Quays	d	21 02	21 07			21 12				21 17	21 22		21 27	21 32	21 37			21 42				21 47	21 52
New Cross ELL	a		21 12								21 27				21 42								21 57
New Cross Gate 4	a	21 06			21 11	21 16				21 21		21 27	21 31	21 36			21 41	21 46				21 51	
	d	21 07			21 11	21 17				21 22		21 27	21 32	21 37			21 41	21 47				21 52	
Brockley	d	21 09			21 14	21 19				21 24		21 30	21 34	21 39			21 44	21 49				21 54	
Honor Oak Park	d	21 12			21 17	21 22				21 27		21 33	21 37	21 42			21 47	21 52				21 57	
Forest Hill 4	d	21 15			21 19	21 25				21 30		21 35	21 40	21 45			21 49	21 55				22 00	
Sydenham	d	21 17			21 22	21 27				21 32		21 38	21 42	21 47			21 52	21 57				22 02	
Crystal Palace 4	d	21a22							21 30	21a37		21 43		21a52							22 00	22a07	
Gipsy Hill	d								21 32			21 45									22 02		
West Norwood 4	d								21 35			21 48									22 05		
Streatham Hill	d											21 52											
Balham 4 ⊖	d											21 55											
Wandsworth Common	d											21 57											
Clapham Junction 10	d											22 01											
South Bermondsey	d			21 07			21 15									21 37			21 45				
Queens Rd Peckham	d			21 09			21 18									21 39			21 48				
Peckham Rye 4	d			21a12			21 20	21 20	21a46							21a42			21 50	21 50	22a16		
Denmark Hill 4	d						21 23	21 24											21 53	21 54			
London Blackfriars 3 ⊖	a							21 34												22 04			
Clapham High Street ⊖	d						21 28												21 58				
Wandsworth Road	d						21 29												21 59				
Battersea Park 4	d						21 32					22 05							22 02				
London Victoria 15 ⊖	a						21 36					22 09							22 06				
Penge West	d				21 24	21 30							21 45				21 54	22 00					
Anerley	d				21 26	21 32							21 47				21 56	22 02					
Norwood Junction 2	d				21 30	21 35							21 50				22 00	22 05					
West Croydon 4 🚋	a					21 42							22 00					22 12					
East Croydon 🚋	a				21 33												22 04						

		SN	LO	LO	LO	SN	SN	LO	SN	SE	SN	LO	SN	LO	LO	LO	SN	SN	LO	SN	SE	SN
London Bridge 4 ⊖	d	21 52				22 03	22 06		22 11				22 22				22 33	22 36		22 41		
Highbury & Islington	a																					
	d		21 33	21 40				21 48				21 55		22 03	22 10				22 18			
Canonbury	d		21 35	21 42				21 50				21 57		22 05	22 12				22 20			
Dalston Junction Stn ELL	d		21 40	21 45	21 50			21 55				22 00		22 08	22 15	22 20			22 25			
Haggerston	d		21 41	21 46	21 51			21 56				22 01		22 09	22 16	22 21			22 26			
Hoxton	d		21 43	21 48	21 53			21 58				22 03		22 11	22 18	22 23			22 28			
Shoreditch High Street	d		21 46	21 51	21 56			22 01				22 06		22 14	22 21	22 26			22 31			
Whitechapel	d		21 48	21 53	21 58			22 03				22 08		22 16	22 23	22 28			22 33			
Shadwell	d		21 50	21 55	22 00			22 05				22 10		22 18	22 25	22 30			22 35			
Wapping	d		21 52	21 57	22 02			22 07				22 12		22 20	22 27	22 32			22 37			
Rotherhithe	d		21 54	21 59	22 04			22 09				22 14		22 22	22 29	22 34			22 39			
Canada Water	d		21 56	22 01	22 06			22 11				22 16		22 24	22 31	22 36			22 41			
Surrey Quays	d		21 57	22 02	22 07			22 12				22 17		22 25	22 32	22 37			22 42			
New Cross ELL	a				22 13											22 42						
New Cross Gate 4	a	21 57	22 01	22 06			22 11	22 16				22 21	22 27	22 29	22 36			22 41	22 46			
	d	21 57	22 02	22 07			22 11	22 17				22 22	22 27	22 30	22 37			22 41	22 47			
Brockley	d	22 00	22 04	22 09			22 14	22 19				22 24	22 30	22 32	22 39			22 44	22 49			
Honor Oak Park	d	22 03	22 07	22 12			22 17	22 22				22 27	22 33	22 35	22 42			22 47	22 52			
Forest Hill 4	d	22 05	22 10	22 15			22 19	22 25				22 30	22 35	22 38	22 45			22 49	22 55			
Sydenham	d	22 08	22 12	22 17			22 22	22 27				22 32	22 38	22 40	22 47			22 52	22 57			
Crystal Palace 4	d	22 13		22a22							22 30	22a37	22 43		22a52							23 00
Gipsy Hill	d	22 15									22 32		22 45									23 02
West Norwood 4	d	22 18									22 35		22 48									23 05
Streatham Hill	d	22 22											22 52									
Balham 4 ⊖	d	22 25											22 55									
Wandsworth Common	d	22 27											22 57									
Clapham Junction 10	d	22 31											23 01									
South Bermondsey	d					22 07			22 15								22 37			22 45		
Queens Rd Peckham	d					22 09			22 18								22 39			22 48		
Peckham Rye 4	d					22a12			22 20	22 20	22a46						22a42			22 50	22 50	23a16
Denmark Hill 4	d								22 23	22 24										22 53	22 54	
London Blackfriars 3 ⊖	a									22 34											23 04	
Clapham High Street ⊖	d								22 28											22 58		
Wandsworth Road	d								22 29											22 59		
Battersea Park 4	d	22 35							22 32				23 05							23 02		
London Victoria 15 ⊖	a	22 39							22 36				23 09							23 06		
Penge West	d		22 15				22 24	22 30						22 43				22 54	23 00			
Anerley	d		22 17				22 26	22 32						22 45				22 56	23 02			
Norwood Junction 2	d		22 20				22 30	22 35						22 48				23 00	23 05			
West Croydon 4 🚋	a		22 30					22 42						23 00					23 12			
East Croydon 🚋	a						22 35											23 03				

Table 178

Saturdays

1 September to 8 September

London Bridge to London Victoria - Croydon and East London Line

Network Diagram - see first Page of Table 177

		LO	SN	LO	LO	LO	SN	SN	LO	SN		SE	SN	LO	SN	LO	LO	LO	SN	SN		LO	LO	SN	LO
London Bridge 4 ⊖	d		22 52				23 03	23 06		23 11					23 22				23 33	23 36				23 52	
Highbury & Islington	a																								
	d	22 25		22 33	22 40				22 48					22 55		23 03	23 10					23 18	23 25		23 33
Canonbury	d	22 27		22 35	22 42				22 50					22 57		23 05	23 12					23 20	23 27		23 35
Dalston Junction Stn ELL	d	22 30		22 38	22 45	22 50			22 55					23 00		23 08	23 15	23 20				23 25	23 30		23 38
Haggerston	d	22 31		22 39	22 46	22 51			22 56					23 01		23 09	23 16	23 21				23 26	23 31		23 39
Hoxton	d	22 33		22 41	22 48	22 53			22 58					23 03		23 11	23 18	23 23				23 28	23 33		23 41
Shoreditch High Street	d	22 36		22 44	22 51	22 56			23 01					23 06		23 14	23 21	23 26				23 31	23 36		23 44
Whitechapel	d	22 38		22 46	22 53	22 58			23 03					23 08		23 16	23 23	23 28				23 33	23 38		23 46
Shadwell	d	22 40		22 48	22 55	23 00			23 05					23 10		23 18	23 25	23 30				23 35	23 40		23 48
Wapping	d	22 42		22 50	22 57	23 02			23 07					23 12		23 20	23 27	23 32				23 37	23 42		23 50
Rotherhithe	d	22 44		22 52	22 59	23 04			23 09					23 14		23 22	23 29	23 34				23 39	23 44		23 52
Canada Water	d	22 46		22 54	23 01	23 06			23 11					23 16		23 24	23 31	23 36				23 41	23 46		23 54
Surrey Quays	d	22 47		22 55	23 02	23 07			23 12					23 17		23 25	23 32	23 37				23 42	23 47		23 55
New Cross ELL	a					23 12												23 42							
New Cross Gate 4	a	22 51	22 57	22 59	23 06			23 11	23 16					23 21	23 27	23 29	23 36			23 41		23 46	23 51	23 57	23 58
	d	22 52	22 57	23 00	23 07			23 11	23 17					23 22	23 27	23 30	23 37			23 41		23 47	23 52	23 57	23 59
Brockley	d	22 54	23 00	23 02	23 09			23 14	23 19					23 24	23 30	23 32	23 39			23 44		23 49	23 54	00 01	00 03
Honor Oak Park	d	22 57	23 03	23 05	23 12			23 17	23 22					23 27	23 33	23 35	23 42			23 47		23 52	23 57	00 04	00 06
Forest Hill 4	d	23 00	23 05	23 08	23 15			23 19	23 25					23 30	23 35	23 38	23 45			23 49		23 55	23 59	00 06	00 09
Sydenham	d	23 02	23 08	23 10	23 17			23 22	23 27					23 32	23 38	23 40	23 47			23 52		23 57	00 02	00 09	00 11
Crystal Palace 4	d	23a07	23 13		23a22								23 30	23a37	23 43		23a52						00a07	00 13	
Gipsy Hill	d		23 15										23 32		23 45									00 15	
West Norwood 4	d		23 18										23 35		23 48									00 18	
Streatham Hill	d		23 22												23 52									00 22	
Balham 4 ⊖	d		23 25												23 55									00 26	
Wandsworth Common	d		23 27												23 57									00 28	
Clapham Junction 10	d		23 31												00 02									00 32	
South Bermondsey	d						23 07			23 15									23 37						
Queens Rd Peckham	d						23 09			23 18									23 39						
Peckham Rye 4	d						23 12			23 20		23 20	23a46						23 42						
Denmark Hill 4	d									23 23		23 24													
London Blackfriars 3 ⊖	a											23 34													
Clapham High Street ⊖	d									23 28															
Wandsworth Road	d									23 29															
Battersea Park 4	d		23 35							23 32					00 05									00 35	
London Victoria 15 ⊖	a		23 41							23 37					00 10									00 42	
Penge West	d			23 13				23 24	23 30							23 43				23 54		00 01			00 14
Anerley	d			23 15				23 26	23 32							23 45				23 56		00 03			00 16
Norwood Junction 2	d			23 18			23a34	23 30	23 35							23 48			00a04	23 59		00 06			00 19
West Croydon 4 🚋	a			23 30					23 42							23 59						00 13			00 26
East Croydon 🚋	a							23 33												00 03					

		LO	LO	LO
London Bridge 4 ⊖	d			
Highbury & Islington	a			
	d	23 40	23 48	23 55
Canonbury	d	23 42	23 50	23 57
Dalston Junction Stn ELL	d	23 45	23 55	00 01
Haggerston	d	23 46	23 56	00 02
Hoxton	d	23 48	23 58	00 04
Shoreditch High Street	d	23 51	00 01	00 07
Whitechapel	d	23 53	00 03	00 09
Shadwell	d	23 55	00 05	00 11
Wapping	d	23 57	00 07	00 13
Rotherhithe	d	23 59	00 09	00 15
Canada Water	d	00 02	00 11	00 17
Surrey Quays	d	00 03	00 12	00 18
New Cross ELL	a			
New Cross Gate 4	a	00 07	00 16	00 22
	d	00 08	00 17	00 23
Brockley	d	00 10	00 19	00 25
Honor Oak Park	d	00 13	00 22	00 28
Forest Hill 4	d	00 16	00 25	00 31
Sydenham	d	00 18	00 27	00 33
Crystal Palace 4	d	00a23		00a38
Gipsy Hill	d			
West Norwood 4	d			
Streatham Hill	d			
Balham 4 ⊖	d			
Wandsworth Common	d			
Clapham Junction 10	d			
South Bermondsey	d			
Queens Rd Peckham	d			
Peckham Rye 4	d			
Denmark Hill 4	d			
London Blackfriars 3 ⊖	a			
Clapham High Street ⊖	d			
Wandsworth Road	d			
Battersea Park 4	d			
London Victoria 15 ⊖	a			
Penge West	d		00 30	
Anerley	d		00 32	
Norwood Junction 2	d		00 35	
West Croydon 4 🚋	a		00 42	
East Croydon 🚋	a			

Table 178

Saturdays

from 15 September

London Bridge to London Victoria - Croydon and East London Line

Network Diagram - see first Page of Table 177

		SN	SN	SN	LO	SN	LO	LO	SN	SN		LO	LO	SN	SN	SN	SN	SN	SN	SE		LO	LO	LO	LO
London Bridge 4 ⊖	d	23p22	23p36			23p52			00 03	00 06						00 33	00 36		06 11						
Highbury & Islington	a																								
	d				23p25		23p35	23p42				23p56	00 10											05 35	
Canonbury	d				23p27		23p37	23p44				23p58	00 12											05 37	
Dalston Junction Stn ELL	d				23p30		23p40	23p47				00 02	00 15											05 40	05 50
Haggerston	d				23p31		23p41	23p48				00 03	00 16											05 41	05 51
Hoxton	d				23p33		23p43	23p50				00 05	00 18											05 43	05 53
Shoreditch High Street	d				23p36		23p46	23p53				00 08	00 21											05 46	05 56
Whitechapel	d				23p38		23p48	23p55				00 10	00 23											05 48	05 58
Shadwell	d				23p40		23p50	23p57				00 12	00 25											05 50	06 00
Wapping	d				23p42		23p52	23p59				00 14	00 27											05 52	06 02
Rotherhithe	d				23p44		23p54	00 01				00 16	00 29											05 54	06 04
Canada Water	d				23p46		23p56	00 03				00 18	00 31											05 56	06 06
Surrey Quays	d				23p47		23p57	00 05				00 19	00 32											05 57	06 07
New Cross ELL	a																								06 12
New Cross Gate 4	a	23p27	23p41		23p51	23p57	00 01	00 08		00 11		00 23	00 36				00 41							06 01	
	d	23p27	23p41		23p52	23p57	00 02			00 11							00 41					05 47	05 52	06 02	
Brockley	d	23p30	23p44		23p54	00 01	00 04			00 14							00 44					05 49	05 54	06 04	
Honor Oak Park	d	23p33	23p47		23p57	00 04	00 07			00 17							00 47					05 52	05 57	06 07	
Forest Hill 4	d	23p35	23p49		23p59	00 06	00 10			00 19							00 49					05 55	06 00	06 10	
Sydenham	d	23p38	23p52		00 02	00 09	00 12			00 22							00 52					05 57	06 02	06 12	
Crystal Palace 4	d	23p43		00 03	00a07	00 13								00 33	00 47			01 03					06a07		
Gipsy Hill	d	23p45				00 15																			
West Norwood 4	d	23p48				00 18																			
Streatham Hill	d	23p52				00 22																			
Balham 4 ⊖	d	23p55				00 25																			
Wandsworth Common	d	23p58				00 27																			
Clapham Junction 10	d	00 02				00 31																			
South Bermondsey	d								00 07							00 37			06 15						
Queens Rd Peckham	d								00 09							00 39			06 18						
Peckham Rye 4	d								00 12							00 42			06 20	06 20					
Denmark Hill 4	d																		06 23	06 24					
London Blackfriars 3 ⊖	a																			06 34					
Clapham High Street ⊖	d																		06 28						
Wandsworth Road	d																		06 29						
Battersea Park 4	d	00 05				00 35													06 32						
London Victoria 15 ⊖	a	00 10				00 42													06 36						
Penge West	d		23p54				00 15			00 24							00 54					06 00		06 15	
Anerley	d		23p56				00 17			00 26							00 56					06 02		06 17	
Norwood Junction 2	d		23p59	00 09			00 20		00a34	00 30				00 38	00 52	01a04	01 00	01 08				06 06		06 18	
West Croydon 4 🚋	a			00 14			00 27							00 43	00 58			01 13				06 12		06 30	
East Croydon 🚋	a		00 03							00 33							01 03								

		SE	LO	LO	LO	LO		LO	SN	LO	SN	SN	SE	SE	LO	LO		LO	LO	LO	LO	SN	LO	LO	LO
London Bridge 4 ⊖	d										06 36	06 41										07 06			
Highbury & Islington	a																								
	d				05 55	06 05										06 25			06 33	06 40			06 48	06 55	
Canonbury	d				05 57	06 07										06 27			06 35	06 42			06 50	06 57	
Dalston Junction Stn ELL	d				06 00	06 10		06 20								06 30		06 35	06 40	06 45	06 50		06 55	07 00	07 05
Haggerston	d				06 01	06 11		06 21								06 31		06 36	06 41	06 46	06 51		06 56	07 01	07 06
Hoxton	d				06 03	06 13		06 23								06 33		06 38	06 43	06 48	06 53		06 58	07 03	07 08
Shoreditch High Street	d				06 06	06 16		06 26								06 36		06 41	06 46	06 51	06 56		07 01	07 06	07 11
Whitechapel	d				06 08	06 18		06 28								06 38		06 43	06 48	06 53	06 58		07 03	07 08	07 13
Shadwell	d				06 10	06 20		06 30								06 40		06 45	06 50	06 55	07 00		07 05	07 10	07 15
Wapping	d				06 12	06 22		06 32								06 42		06 47	06 52	06 57	07 02		07 07	07 12	07 17
Rotherhithe	d				06 14	06 24		06 34								06 44		06 49	06 54	06 59	07 04		07 09	07 14	07 19
Canada Water	d				06 16	06 26		06 36								06 46		06 51	06 56	07 01	07 06		07 11	07 16	07 21
Surrey Quays	d				06 17	06 27		06 37								06 47		06 52	06 57	07 02	07 07		07 12	07 17	07 22
New Cross ELL	a							06 42										06 57			07 12				07 27
New Cross Gate 4	a				06 21	06 31					06 41					06 51			07 01	07 06		07 11	07 16	07 21	
	d		06 07	06 17	06 22	06 32				06 37	06 41				06 47	06 52			07 02	07 07		07 11	07 17	07 22	
Brockley	d		06 09	06 19	06 24	06 34				06 39	06 44				06 49	06 54			07 04	07 09		07 14	07 19	07 24	
Honor Oak Park	d		06 12	06 22	06 27	06 37				06 42	06 47				06 52	06 57			07 07	07 12		07 17	07 22	07 27	
Forest Hill 4	d		06 15	06 25	06 30	06 40				06 45	06 49				06 55	07 00			07 10	07 15		07 19	07 25	07 30	
Sydenham	d		06 17	06 27	06 32	06 42				06 47	06 52				06 57	07 02			07 12	07 17		07 22	07 27	07 32	
Crystal Palace 4	d		06a22		06a37				06 45	06a52						07a07				07a22				07a37	
Gipsy Hill	d								06 47																
West Norwood 4	d								06 50																
Streatham Hill	d																								
Balham 4 ⊖	d																								
Wandsworth Common	d																								
Clapham Junction 10	d																								
South Bermondsey	d											06 45													
Queens Rd Peckham	d											06 48													
Peckham Rye 4	d	06 50							07a01			06 50	07 15	07 20											
Denmark Hill 4	d	06 54										06 53	07 19	07 24											
London Blackfriars 3 ⊖	a	07 04												07 34											
Clapham High Street ⊖	d											06 58													
Wandsworth Road	d											06 59													
Battersea Park 4	d											07 02													
London Victoria 15 ⊖	a											07 06	07 28												
Penge West	d			06 30		06 45					06 54				07 00				07 15			07 24	07 30		
Anerley	d			06 32		06 47					06 56				07 02				07 17			07 26	07 32		
Norwood Junction 2	d			06 35		06 50					07 00				07 05				07 20			07 30	07 35		
West Croydon 4 🚋	a			06 41		07 00									07 11				07 30				07 41		
East Croydon 🚋	a										07 03											07 33			

Table 178

Saturdays

from 15 September

London Bridge to London Victoria - Croydon and East London Line

Network Diagram - see first Page of Table 177

Station		LO		LO	SN	LO	SN	SN	LO	LO	LO	LO		LO	LO	SE	SN	SE	SN	SN	LO	SE		SN	SE
London Bridge 4 ⊖	d				07 11		07 33	07 36									07 41		08 03	08 06				08 11	
Highbury & Islington	a																								
	d	07 03		07 10					07 18	07 25		07 33		07 40							07 48				
Canonbury	d	07 05		07 12					07 20	07 27		07 35		07 42							07 50				
Dalston Junction Stn ELL	d	07 10		07 15		07 20			07 25	07 30	07 35	07 40		07 45	07 50						07 55				
Haggerston	d	07 11		07 16		07 21			07 26	07 31	07 36	07 41		07 46	07 51						07 56				
Hoxton	d	07 13		07 18		07 23			07 28	07 33	07 38	07 43		07 48	07 53						07 58				
Shoreditch High Street	d	07 16		07 21		07 26			07 31	07 36	07 41	07 46		07 51	07 56						08 01				
Whitechapel	d	07 18		07 23		07 28			07 33	07 38	07 43	07 48		07 53	07 58						08 03				
Shadwell	d	07 20		07 25		07 30			07 35	07 40	07 45	07 50		07 55	08 00						08 05				
Wapping	d	07 22		07 27		07 32			07 37	07 42	07 47	07 52		07 57	08 02						08 07				
Rotherhithe	d	07 24		07 29		07 34			07 39	07 44	07 49	07 54		07 59	08 04						08 09				
Canada Water	d	07 26		07 31		07 36			07 41	07 46	07 51	07 56		08 01	08 06						08 11				
Surrey Quays	d	07 27		07 32		07 37			07 42	07 47	07 52	07 57		08 02	08 07						08 12				
New Cross ELL	a					07 42					07 57				08 12										
New Cross Gate 4	a	07 31		07 36				07 41	07 46	07 51		08 01		08 06						08 11	08 16				
	d	07 32		07 37				07 41	07 47	07 52		08 02		08 07						08 11	08 17				
Brockley	d	07 34		07 39				07 44	07 49	07 54		08 04		08 09						08 14	08 19				
Honor Oak Park	d	07 37		07 42				07 47	07 52	07 57		08 07		08 12						08 17	08 22				
Forest Hill 4	d	07 40		07 45				07 49	07 55	08 00		08 10		08 15						08 19	08 25				
Sydenham	d	07 42		07 47				07 52	07 57	08 02		08 12		08 17						08 22	08 27				
Crystal Palace 4	d			07a52						08a07				08a22											
Gipsy Hill	d																								
West Norwood 4	d																								
Streatham Hill	d																								
Balham 4 ⊖	d																								
Wandsworth Common	d																								
Clapham Junction 10	d																								
South Bermondsey	d				07 15		07 37										07 45		08 07					08 15	
Queens Rd Peckham	d				07 18		07 39										07 48		08 09					08 18	
Peckham Rye 4	d				07 20		07a42									07 45	07 50	07 50	08a12			08 15		08 20	08 20
Denmark Hill 4	d				07 23											07 49	07 53	07 54				08 19		08 23	08 24
London Blackfriars 3 ⊖	a																	08 04							08 34
Clapham High Street ⊖	d				07 28												07 58							08 28	
Wandsworth Road	d				07 29												07 59							08 29	
Battersea Park 4	d				07 32												08 02							08 32	
London Victoria 15 ⊖	a				07 36											07 58	08 06					08 28		08 36	
Penge West	d	07 45						07 54	08 00			08 15								08 24	08 30				
Anerley	d	07 47						07 56	08 02			08 17								08 26	08 32				
Norwood Junction 2	d	07 50						08 00	08 05			08 20								08 30	08 35				
West Croydon 4	a	08 00							08 11			08 30									08 41				
East Croydon	a							08 03												08 33					

Station		SN	LO	LO	SN	LO	LO	LO		SN	SN	LO	SE	SN	SE	SN	LO	LO		SN	LO	LO	LO	SN	SN
London Bridge 4 ⊖	d				08 22					08 33	08 36			08 41						08 52				09 03	09 06
Highbury & Islington	a																								
	d		07 55			08 03	08 10					08 18					08 25				08 33	08 40			
Canonbury	d		07 57			08 05	08 12					08 20					08 27				08 35	08 42			
Dalston Junction Stn ELL	d		08 00	08 05		08 10	08 15	08 20				08 25					08 30	08 35			08 40	08 45	08 50		
Haggerston	d		08 01	08 06		08 11	08 16	08 21				08 26					08 31	08 36			08 41	08 46	08 51		
Hoxton	d		08 03	08 08		08 13	08 18	08 23				08 28					08 33	08 38			08 43	08 48	08 53		
Shoreditch High Street	d		08 06	08 11		08 16	08 21	08 26				08 31					08 36	08 41			08 46	08 51	08 56		
Whitechapel	d		08 08	08 13		08 18	08 23	08 28				08 33					08 38	08 43			08 48	08 53	08 58		
Shadwell	d		08 10	08 15		08 20	08 25	08 30				08 35					08 40	08 45			08 50	08 55	09 00		
Wapping	d		08 12	08 17		08 22	08 27	08 32				08 37					08 42	08 47			08 52	08 57	09 02		
Rotherhithe	d		08 14	08 19		08 24	08 29	08 34				08 39					08 44	08 49			08 54	08 59	09 04		
Canada Water	d		08 16	08 21		08 26	08 31	08 36				08 41					08 46	08 51			08 56	09 01	09 06		
Surrey Quays	d		08 17	08 22		08 27	08 32	08 37				08 42					08 47	08 52			08 57	09 02	09 07		
New Cross ELL	a			08 27				08 42										08 57					09 12		
New Cross Gate 4	a		08 21		08 27	08 31	08 36				08 41	08 46					08 51			08 57	09 01	09 06			09 11
	d		08 22		08 27	08 32	08 37				08 41	08 47					08 52			08 57	09 02	09 07			09 11
Brockley	d		08 24		08 30	08 34	08 39				08 44	08 49					08 54			09 00	09 04	09 09			09 14
Honor Oak Park	d		08 27		08 33	08 37	08 42				08 47	08 52					08 57			09 03	09 07	09 12			09 17
Forest Hill 4	d		08 30		08 35	08 40	08 45				08 49	08 55					09 00			09 05	09 10	09 15			09 19
Sydenham	d		08 32		08 38	08 42	08 47				08 52	08 57					09 02			09 08	09 12	09 17			09 22
Crystal Palace 4	d	08 30	08a37		08 43		08a52									09 00	09a07			09 13		09a22			
Gipsy Hill	d	08 32			08 45											09 02				09 15					
West Norwood 4	d	08 35			08 48											09 05				09 18					
Streatham Hill	d				08 52															09 22					
Balham 4 ⊖	d				08 55															09 25					
Wandsworth Common	d				08 57															09 27					
Clapham Junction 10	d				09 01															09 32					
South Bermondsey	d									08 37				08 45										09 07	
Queens Rd Peckham	d									08 39				08 48										09 09	
Peckham Rye 4	d	08a46								08a42			08 45	08 50	08 50	09a16								09a12	
Denmark Hill 4	d												08 49	08 53	08 54										
London Blackfriars 3 ⊖	a														09 04										
Clapham High Street ⊖	d													08 58											
Wandsworth Road	d													08 59											
Battersea Park 4	d				09 05									09 02						09 36					
London Victoria 15 ⊖	a				09 09								08 58	09 06						09 40					
Penge West	d					08 45					08 54	09 00									09 15				09 24
Anerley	d					08 47					08 56	09 02									09 17				09 26
Norwood Junction 2	d					08 50					09 00	09 05									09 20				09 30
West Croydon 4	a					09 00						09 12									09 30				
East Croydon	a										09 03														09 33

Table 178

Saturdays

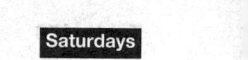

from 15 September

London Bridge to London Victoria - Croydon and East London Line

Network Diagram - see first Page of Table 177

		LO	SE	SN		SE	SN	LO	LO	SN	LO	LO	LO	SN		SN	LO	SE	SN	SE	SN	LO	LO		
London Bridge [4] ⊖	d			09 11						09 22				09 33		09 36			09 41						
Highbury & Islington	a																								
	d	08 48						08 55			09 03	09 10					09 18					09 25			
Canonbury	d	08 50						08 57			09 05	09 12					09 20					09 27			
Dalston Junction Stn ELL	d	08 55						09 00	09 05		09 10	09 15	09 20				09 25					09 30	09 35		
Haggerston	d	08 56						09 01	09 06		09 11	09 16	09 21				09 26					09 31	09 36		
Hoxton	d	08 58						09 03	09 08		09 13	09 18	09 23				09 28					09 33	09 38		
Shoreditch High Street	d	09 01						09 06	09 11		09 16	09 21	09 26				09 31					09 36	09 41		
Whitechapel	d	09 03						09 08	09 13		09 18	09 23	09 28				09 33					09 38	09 43		
Shadwell	d	09 05						09 10	09 15		09 20	09 25	09 30				09 35					09 40	09 45		
Wapping	d	09 07						09 12	09 17		09 22	09 27	09 32				09 37					09 42	09 47		
Rotherhithe	d	09 09						09 14	09 19		09 24	09 29	09 34				09 39					09 44	09 49		
Canada Water	d	09 11						09 16	09 21		09 26	09 31	09 36				09 41					09 46	09 51		
Surrey Quays	d	09 12						09 17	09 22		09 27	09 32	09 37				09 42					09 47	09 52		
New Cross ELL	a								09 27				09 42										09 57		
New Cross Gate [4]	a	09 16						09 21		09 27	09 31	09 36				09 41	09 46					09 51			
	d	09 17						09 22		09 27	09 32	09 37				09 41	09 47					09 52			
Brockley	d	09 19						09 24		09 30	09 34	09 39				09 44	09 49					09 54			
Honor Oak Park	d	09 22						09 27		09 33	09 37	09 42				09 47	09 52					09 57			
Forest Hill [4]	d	09 25						09 30		09 35	09 40	09 45				09 49	09 55					10 00			
Sydenham	d	09 27						09 32		09 38	09 42	09 47				09 52	09 57					10 02			
Crystal Palace [4]	d						09 30	09a37		09 43		09a52									10 00	10a07			
Gipsy Hill	d						09 32			09 45											10 02				
West Norwood [4]	d						09 35			09 48											10 05				
Streatham Hill	d									09 52															
Balham [4] ⊖	d									09 55															
Wandsworth Common	d									09 57															
Clapham Junction [10]	d									10 01															
South Bermondsey	d			09 15										09 37					09 45						
Queens Rd Peckham	d			09 18										09 39					09 48						
Peckham Rye [4]	d		09 15	09 20		09 20	09a46							09a42				09 45	09 50	09 50	10a16				
Denmark Hill [4]	d		09 19	09 23		09 24												09 49	09 53	09 54					
London Blackfriars [3] ⊖	a					09 34														10 04					
Clapham High Street ⊖	d			09 28															09 58						
Wandsworth Road	d			09 29															09 59						
Battersea Park [4]	d			09 32						10 05									10 02						
London Victoria [15] ⊖	a		09 28	09 36						10 09								09 58	10 06						
Penge West	d	09 30									09 45					09 54	10 00								
Anerley	d	09 32									09 47					09 56	10 02								
Norwood Junction [2]	d	09 35									09 50					10 00	10 05								
West Croydon [4]	a	09 42									10 00						10 12								
East Croydon	a															10 03									

		SN		SN		LO	LO	LO	SN	SN	LO	SE	SN	SE		SN	LO	LO	SN	LO	LO	LO	SN	SN
London Bridge [4] ⊖	d	09 52		16 52					17 03	17 06			17 11						17 22				17 33	17 36
Highbury & Islington	a																							
	d					16 33	16 40				16 48						16 55			17 03	17 10			
Canonbury	d					16 35	16 42				16 50						16 57			17 05	17 12			
Dalston Junction Stn ELL	d					16 40	16 45	16 50			16 55						17 00	17 05		17 10	17 15	17 20		
Haggerston	d					16 41	16 46	16 51			16 56						17 01	17 06		17 11	17 16	17 21		
Hoxton	d					16 43	16 48	16 53			16 58						17 03	17 08		17 13	17 18	17 23		
Shoreditch High Street	d					16 46	16 51	16 56			17 01						17 06	17 11		17 16	17 21	17 26		
Whitechapel	d					16 48	16 53	16 58			17 03						17 08	17 13		17 18	17 23	17 28		
Shadwell	d					16 50	16 55	17 00			17 05						17 10	17 15		17 20	17 25	17 30		
Wapping	d					16 52	16 57	17 02			17 07						17 12	17 17		17 22	17 27	17 32		
Rotherhithe	d					16 54	16 59	17 04			17 09						17 14	17 19		17 24	17 29	17 34		
Canada Water	d					16 56	17 01	17 06			17 11						17 16	17 21		17 26	17 31	17 36		
Surrey Quays	d					16 57	17 02	17 07			17 12						17 17	17 22		17 27	17 32	17 37		
New Cross ELL	a							17 12										17 27				17 42		
New Cross Gate [4]	a	09 57		16 57		17 01	17 06			17 11	17 16						17 21		17 27	17 31	17 36			17 41
	d	09 57		16 57		17 02	17 07			17 11	17 17						17 22		17 27	17 32	17 37			17 41
Brockley	d	10 00	and at the same minutes past each hour until	17 00		17 04	17 09			17 14	17 19						17 24		17 30	17 34	17 39			17 44
Honor Oak Park	d	10 03		17 03		17 07	17 12			17 17	17 22						17 27		17 33	17 37	17 42			17 47
Forest Hill [4]	d	10 05		17 05		17 10	17 15			17 19	17 25						17 30		17 35	17 40	17 45			17 49
Sydenham	d	10 08		17 08		17 12	17 17			17 22	17 27						17 32		17 38	17 42	17 47			17 52
Crystal Palace [4]	d	10 13		17 13			17a22									17 30	17a37		17 43		17a52			
Gipsy Hill	d	10 15		17 15												17 32			17 45					
West Norwood [4]	d	10 18		17 18												17 35			17 48					
Streatham Hill	d	10 22		17 22															17 52					
Balham [4] ⊖	d	10 25		17 25															17 55					
Wandsworth Common	d	10 27		17 27															17 57					
Clapham Junction [10]	d	10 31		17 31															18 01					
South Bermondsey	d								17 07				17 15										17 37	
Queens Rd Peckham	d								17 09				17 18										17 39	
Peckham Rye [4]	d								17a12			17 15	17 20	17 20		17a46							17a42	
Denmark Hill [4]	d											17 19	17 23	17 24										
London Blackfriars [3] ⊖	a													17 34										
Clapham High Street ⊖	d												17 28											
Wandsworth Road	d												17 29											
Battersea Park [4]	d	10 35		17 35									17 32						18 05					
London Victoria [15] ⊖	a	10 39		17 39								17 28	17 36						18 09					
Penge West	d					17 15				17 24	17 30									17 45				17 54
Anerley	d					17 17				17 26	17 32									17 47				17 56
Norwood Junction [2]	d					17 20				17 30	17 35									17 50				18 00
West Croydon [4]	a					17 30					17 42									18 00				
East Croydon	a									17 33														18 03

Table 178

Saturdays

from 15 September

London Bridge to London Victoria - Croydon and East London Line

Network Diagram - see first Page of Table 177

		LO	SE	SN	SE	SN	LO	LO	SN	LO		LO	LO	SN	SN	LO	SE	SN	SE	SN		LO	LO	SN
London Bridge 4 ⊖	d			17 41					17 52					18 03	18 06			18 11						18 22
Highbury & Islington	a																							
	d	17 18					17 25			17 33		17 40				17 48						17 55		
Canonbury	d	17 20					17 27			17 35		17 42				17 50						17 57		
Dalston Junction Stn ELL	d	17 25					17 30	17 35		17 40		17 45	17 50			17 55						18 00	18 05	
Haggerston	d	17 26					17 31	17 36		17 41		17 46	17 51			17 56						18 01	18 06	
Hoxton	d	17 28					17 33	17 38		17 43		17 48	17 53			17 58						18 03	18 08	
Shoreditch High Street	d	17 31					17 36	17 41		17 46		17 51	17 56			18 01						18 06	18 11	
Whitechapel	d	17 33					17 38	17 43		17 48		17 53	17 58			18 03						18 08	18 13	
Shadwell	d	17 35					17 40	17 45		17 50		17 55	18 00			18 05						18 10	18 15	
Wapping	d	17 37					17 42	17 47		17 52		17 57	18 02			18 07						18 12	18 17	
Rotherhithe	d	17 39					17 44	17 49		17 54		17 59	18 04			18 09						18 14	18 19	
Canada Water	d	17 41					17 46	17 51		17 56		18 01	18 06			18 11						18 16	18 21	
Surrey Quays	d	17 42					17 47	17 52		17 57		18 02	18 07			18 12						18 17	18 22	
New Cross ELL	a							17 57					18 12										18 27	
New Cross Gate 4	a	17 46					17 51		17 57	18 01		18 06			18 11	18 16						18 21		18 27
	d	17 47					17 52		17 57	18 02		18 07			18 11	18 17						18 22		18 27
Brockley	d	17 49					17 54		18 00	18 04		18 09			18 14	18 19						18 24		18 30
Honor Oak Park	d	17 52					17 57		18 03	18 07		18 12			18 17	18 22						18 27		18 33
Forest Hill 4	d	17 55					18 00		18 05	18 10		18 15			18 19	18 25						18 30		18 35
Sydenham	d	17 57					18 02		18 08	18 12		18 17			18 22	18 27						18 32		18 38
Crystal Palace 4	d					18 00	18a07		18 13			18a22								18 30		18a37		18 43
Gipsy Hill	d					18 02			18 15											18 32				18 45
West Norwood 4	d					18 05			18 18											18 35				18 48
Streatham Hill	d								18 22															18 52
Balham 4 ⊖	d								18 25															18 55
Wandsworth Common	d								18 27															18 57
Clapham Junction 10	d								18 31															19 01
South Bermondsey	d			17 45										18 07				18 15						
Queens Rd Peckham	d			17 48										18 09				18 18						
Peckham Rye 4	d		17 45	17 50	17 50	18a16								18a12			18 15	18 20	18 20	18a46				
Denmark Hill 4	d		17 49	17 53	17 54												18 19	18 23	18 24					
London Blackfriars 3 ⊖	a				18 04														18 34					
Clapham High Street ⊖	d			17 58														18 28						
Wandsworth Road	d			17 59														18 29						
Battersea Park 4	d			18 02					18 35									18 32						19 05
London Victoria 15 ⊖	a		17 58	18 06					18 39								18 28	18 36						19 09
Penge West	d	18 00								18 15					18 24	18 30								
Anerley	d	18 02								18 17					18 26	18 32								
Norwood Junction 2	d	18 05								18 20					18 30	18 35								
West Croydon 4	a	18 11								18 30						18 41								
East Croydon	a														18 33									

		LO	LO	LO	SN	SN	LO		SE	SN	SE	SN	LO	LO	SN	LO	LO		LO	SN	SN	LO	SE	SN	SE
London Bridge 4 ⊖	d				18 33	18 36				18 41					18 52					19 03	19 06			19 11	
Highbury & Islington	a																								
	d	18 03	18 10				18 18						18 25			18 33	18 40					18 48			
Canonbury	d	18 05	18 12				18 20						18 27			18 35	18 42					18 50			
Dalston Junction Stn ELL	d	18 10	18 15	18 20			18 25						18 30	18 35		18 40	18 45		18 50			18 55			
Haggerston	d	18 11	18 16	18 21			18 26						18 31	18 36		18 41	18 46		18 51			18 56			
Hoxton	d	18 13	18 18	18 23			18 28						18 33	18 38		18 43	18 48		18 53			18 58			
Shoreditch High Street	d	18 16	18 21	18 26			18 31						18 36	18 41		18 46	18 51		18 56			19 01			
Whitechapel	d	18 18	18 23	18 28			18 33						18 38	18 43		18 48	18 53		18 58			19 03			
Shadwell	d	18 20	18 25	18 30			18 35						18 40	18 45		18 50	18 55		19 00			19 05			
Wapping	d	18 22	18 27	18 32			18 37						18 42	18 47		18 52	18 57		19 02			19 07			
Rotherhithe	d	18 24	18 29	18 34			18 39						18 44	18 49		18 54	18 59		19 04			19 09			
Canada Water	d	18 26	18 31	18 36			18 41						18 46	18 51		18 56	19 01		19 06			19 11			
Surrey Quays	d	18 27	18 32	18 37			18 42						18 47	18 52		18 57	19 02		19 07			19 12			
New Cross ELL	a			18 42										18 57					19 12						
New Cross Gate 4	a	18 31	18 36			18 41	18 46						18 51		18 57	19 01	19 06				19 11	19 16			
	d	18 32	18 37			18 41	18 47						18 52		18 57	19 02	19 07				19 11	19 17			
Brockley	d	18 34	18 39			18 44	18 49						18 54		19 00	19 04	19 09				19 14	19 19			
Honor Oak Park	d	18 37	18 42			18 47	18 52						18 57		19 03	19 07	19 12				19 17	19 22			
Forest Hill 4	d	18 40	18 45			18 49	18 55						19 00		19 05	19 10	19 15				19 19	19 25			
Sydenham	d	18 42	18 47			18 52	18 57						19 02		19 08	19 12	19 17				19 22	19 27			
Crystal Palace 4	d		18a52									19 00	19a07		19 13		19a22								
Gipsy Hill	d											19 02			19 15										
West Norwood 4	d											19 05			19 18										
Streatham Hill	d														19 22										
Balham 4 ⊖	d														19 25										
Wandsworth Common	d														19 27										
Clapham Junction 10	d														19 31										
South Bermondsey	d				18 37					18 45										19 07				19 15	
Queens Rd Peckham	d				18 39					18 48										19 09				19 18	
Peckham Rye 4	d				18a42				18 45	18 50	18 50	19a16								19a12			19 15	19 20	19 20
Denmark Hill 4	d								18 49	18 53	18 54												19 19	19 23	19 24
London Blackfriars 3 ⊖	a										19 04														19 34
Clapham High Street ⊖	d									18 58														19 28	
Wandsworth Road	d									18 59														19 29	
Battersea Park 4	d									19 02					19 35									19 32	
London Victoria 15 ⊖	a								18 58	19 06					19 39								19 28	19 36	
Penge West	d	18 45				18 54	19 00									19 15					19 24	19 30			
Anerley	d	18 47				18 56	19 02									19 17					19 26	19 32			
Norwood Junction 2	d	18 50				19 00	19 05									19 20					19 30	19 35			
West Croydon 4	a	19 00					19 11									19 30						19 41			
East Croydon	a					19 03															19 33				

Table 178

Saturdays

from 15 September

London Bridge to London Victoria - Croydon and East London Line

Network Diagram - see first Page of Table 177

		SN	LO		LO	SN	LO	LO	LO	SN	SN	LO	SN		SE	SN	LO	LO	SN	LO	LO	LO	SN		SN
London Bridge 4 ⊖	d					19 22				19 33	19 36		19 41						19 52				20 03		20 06
Highbury & Islington	a																								
	d		18 55				19 03	19 10				19 18					19 25			19 33	19 40				
Canonbury	d		18 57				19 05	19 12				19 20					19 27			19 35	19 42				
Dalston Junction Stn ELL	d		19 00		19 05		19 10	19 15	19 20			19 25					19 30	19 35		19 40	19 45	19 50			
Haggerston	d		19 01		19 06		19 11	19 16	19 21			19 26					19 31	19 36		19 41	19 46	19 51			
Hoxton	d		19 03		19 08		19 13	19 18	19 23			19 28					19 33	19 38		19 43	19 48	19 53			
Shoreditch High Street	d		19 06		19 11		19 16	19 21	19 26			19 31					19 36	19 41		19 46	19 51	19 56			
Whitechapel	d		19 08		19 13		19 18	19 23	19 28			19 33					19 38	19 43		19 48	19 53	19 58			
Shadwell	d		19 10		19 15		19 20	19 25	19 30			19 35					19 40	19 45		19 50	19 55	20 00			
Wapping	d		19 12		19 17		19 22	19 27	19 32			19 37					19 42	19 47		19 52	19 57	20 02			
Rotherhithe	d		19 14		19 19		19 24	19 29	19 34			19 39					19 44	19 49		19 54	19 59	20 04			
Canada Water	d		19 16		19 21		19 26	19 31	19 36			19 41					19 46	19 51		19 56	20 01	20 06			
Surrey Quays	d		19 17		19 22		19 27	19 32	19 37			19 42					19 47	19 52		19 57	20 02	20 07			
New Cross ELL	a				19 27				19 42									19 57				20 12			
New Cross Gate 4	a		19 21			19 27	19 31	19 36			19 41	19 46					19 51		19 57	20 01	20 06				20 11
	d		19 22			19 27	19 32	19 37			19 41	19 47					19 52		19 57	20 02	20 07				20 11
Brockley	d		19 24			19 30	19 34	19 39			19 44	19 49					19 54		20 00	20 04	20 09				20 14
Honor Oak Park	d		19 27			19 33	19 37	19 42			19 47	19 52					19 57		20 03	20 07	20 12				20 17
Forest Hill 4	d		19 30			19 35	19 40	19 45			19 49	19 55					20 00		20 05	20 10	20 15				20 19
Sydenham	d		19 32			19 38	19 42	19 47			19 52	19 57					20 02		20 08	20 12	20 17				20 22
Crystal Palace 4	d	19 30	19a37			19 43		19a52								20 00	20a07		20 13		20a22				
Gipsy Hill	d	19 32				19 45										20 03			20 15						
West Norwood 4	d	19 35				19 48										20 06			20 18						
Streatham Hill	d					19 52													20 22						
Balham 4 ⊖	d					19 55													20 25						
Wandsworth Common	d					19 57													20 27						
Clapham Junction 10	d					20 01													20 31						
South Bermondsey	d									19 37			19 45										20 07		
Queens Rd Peckham	d									19 39			19 48										20 09		
Peckham Rye 4	d	19a46								19a42			19 50		19 50	20a16							20a12		
Denmark Hill 4	d												19 53		19 54										
London Blackfriars 3 ⊖	a														20 04										
Clapham High Street ⊖	d												19 58												
Wandsworth Road	d												19 59												
Battersea Park 4	d					20 05							20 02						20 35						
London Victoria 15 ⊖	a					20 09							20 06						20 39						
Penge West	d						19 45				19 54	20 00								20 15					20 24
Anerley	d						19 47				19 56	20 02								20 17					20 26
Norwood Junction 2	d						19 50				20 00	20 05								20 20					20 30
West Croydon 4	a						20 00					20 15								20 30					
East Croydon	a										20 03														20 33

		LO	SN	SE	SN	LO	LO	SN	LO		LO	LO	SN	SN	LO	SN	SE	SN	LO		LO	SN	LO	LO	LO
London Bridge 4 ⊖	d		20 11					20 22					20 33	20 36		20 41						20 52			
Highbury & Islington	a																								
	d	19 48				19 55			20 03		20 10				20 18				20 25				20 33	20 40	
Canonbury	d	19 50				19 57			20 05		20 12				20 20				20 27				20 35	20 42	
Dalston Junction Stn ELL	d	19 55				20 00	20 05		20 10		20 15	20 20			20 25				20 30		20 35		20 40	20 45	20 50
Haggerston	d	19 56				20 01	20 06		20 11		20 16	20 21			20 26				20 31		20 36		20 41	20 46	20 51
Hoxton	d	19 58				20 03	20 08		20 13		20 18	20 23			20 28				20 33		20 38		20 43	20 48	20 53
Shoreditch High Street	d	20 01				20 06	20 11		20 16		20 21	20 26			20 31				20 36		20 41		20 46	20 51	20 56
Whitechapel	d	20 03				20 08	20 13		20 18		20 23	20 28			20 33				20 38		20 43		20 48	20 53	20 58
Shadwell	d	20 05				20 10	20 15		20 20		20 25	20 30			20 35				20 40		20 45		20 50	20 55	21 00
Wapping	d	20 07				20 12	20 17		20 22		20 27	20 32			20 37				20 42		20 47		20 52	20 57	21 02
Rotherhithe	d	20 09				20 14	20 19		20 24		20 29	20 34			20 39				20 44		20 49		20 54	20 59	21 04
Canada Water	d	20 11				20 16	20 21		20 26		20 31	20 36			20 41				20 46		20 51		20 56	21 01	21 06
Surrey Quays	d	20 12				20 17	20 22		20 27		20 32	20 37			20 42				20 47		20 52		20 57	21 02	21 07
New Cross ELL	a						20 27					20 42									20 57				21 12
New Cross Gate 4	a	20 16				20 21		20 27	20 31		20 36			20 41	20 46				20 51			20 57	21 01	21 06	
	d	20 17				20 22		20 27	20 32		20 37			20 41	20 47				20 52			20 57	21 02	21 07	
Brockley	d	20 19				20 24		20 30	20 34		20 39			20 44	20 49				20 54			21 00	21 04	21 09	
Honor Oak Park	d	20 22				20 27		20 33	20 37		20 42			20 47	20 52				20 57			21 03	21 07	21 12	
Forest Hill 4	d	20 25				20 30		20 35	20 40		20 45			20 49	20 55				21 00			21 05	21 10	21 15	
Sydenham	d	20 27				20 32		20 38	20 42		20 47			20 52	20 57				21 02			21 08	21 12	21 17	
Crystal Palace 4	d				20 30	20a37		20 43			20a52							21 00	21a07			21 13		21a22	
Gipsy Hill	d				20 33			20 45										21 02				21 15			
West Norwood 4	d				20 36			20 48										21 05				21 18			
Streatham Hill	d							20 52														21 22			
Balham 4 ⊖	d							20 55														21 25			
Wandsworth Common	d							20 57														21 27			
Clapham Junction 10	d							21 01														21 31			
South Bermondsey	d		20 15										20 37			20 45									
Queens Rd Peckham	d		20 18										20 39			20 48									
Peckham Rye 4	d		20 20	20 20	20a46								20a42			20 50	20 50	21a16							
Denmark Hill 4	d		20 23	20 24												20 53	20 54								
London Blackfriars 3 ⊖	a			20 34													21 04								
Clapham High Street ⊖	d		20 28													20 58									
Wandsworth Road	d		20 29													20 59									
Battersea Park 4	d		20 32					21 05								21 02						21 35			
London Victoria 15 ⊖	a		20 36					21 09								21 06						21 39			
Penge West	d	20 30							20 45					20 54	21 00								21 15		
Anerley	d	20 32							20 47					20 56	21 02								21 17		
Norwood Junction 2	d	20 35							20 50					21 00	21 05								21 20		
West Croydon 4	a	20 45							21 00						21 15								21 30		
East Croydon	a													21 03											

Table 178

Saturdays

from 15 September

London Bridge to London Victoria - Croydon and East London Line

Network Diagram - see first Page of Table 177

		SN	SN	LO	SN		SE	SN	LO	LO	SN	LO	LO	LO	SN		SN	LO	SN	SE	SN	LO	LO	SN	LO
London Bridge 4 ⊖	d	21 03	21 06		21 11						21 22				21 33		21 36		21 41					21 52	
Highbury & Islington	a																								
	d			20 48					20 55			21 03	21 10					21 18				21 25			21 33
Canonbury	d			20 50					20 57			21 05	21 12					21 20				21 27			21 35
Dalston Junction Stn ELL	d			20 55					21 00	21 05		21 10	21 15	21 20				21 25				21 30	21 35		21 40
Haggerston	d			20 56					21 01	21 06		21 11	21 16	21 21				21 26				21 31	21 36		21 41
Hoxton	d			20 58					21 03	21 08		21 13	21 18	21 23				21 28				21 33	21 38		21 43
Shoreditch High Street	d			21 01					21 06	21 11		21 16	21 21	21 26				21 31				21 36	21 41		21 46
Whitechapel	d			21 03					21 08	21 13		21 18	21 23	21 28				21 33				21 38	21 43		21 48
Shadwell	d			21 05					21 10	21 15		21 20	21 25	21 30				21 35				21 40	21 45		21 50
Wapping	d			21 07					21 12	21 17		21 22	21 27	21 32				21 37				21 42	21 47		21 52
Rotherhithe	d			21 09					21 14	21 19		21 24	21 29	21 34				21 39				21 44	21 49		21 54
Canada Water	d			21 11					21 16	21 21		21 26	21 31	21 36				21 41				21 46	21 51		21 56
Surrey Quays	d			21 12					21 17	21 22		21 27	21 32	21 37				21 42				21 47	21 52		21 57
New Cross ELL	a									21 27				21 42									21 57		
New Cross Gate 4	a		21 11	21 16					21 21		21 27	21 31	21 36				21 41	21 46				21 51		21 57	22 01
	d		21 11	21 17					21 22		21 27	21 32	21 37				21 41	21 47				21 52		21 57	22 02
Brockley	d		21 14	21 19					21 24		21 30	21 34	21 39				21 44	21 49				21 54		22 00	22 04
Honor Oak Park	d		21 17	21 22					21 27		21 33	21 37	21 42				21 47	21 52				21 57		22 03	22 07
Forest Hill 4	d		21 19	21 25					21 30		21 35	21 40	21 45				21 49	21 55				22 00		22 05	22 10
Sydenham	d		21 22	21 27					21 32		21 38	21 42	21 47				21 52	21 57				22 02		22 08	22 12
Crystal Palace 4	d							21 30	21a37		21 43		21a52								22 00	22a07		22 13	
Gipsy Hill	d							21 32			21 45										22 02			22 15	
West Norwood 4	d							21 35			21 48										22 05			22 18	
Streatham Hill	d										21 52													22 22	
Balham 4 ⊖	d										21 55													22 25	
Wandsworth Common	d										21 57													22 27	
Clapham Junction 10	d										22 01													22 31	
South Bermondsey	d	21 07			21 15										21 37				21 45						
Queens Rd Peckham	d	21 09			21 18										21 39				21 48						
Peckham Rye 4	d	21a12			21 20		21 20	21a46							21a42				21 50	21 50	22a16				
Denmark Hill 4	d				21 23		21 24												21 53	21 54					
London Blackfriars 3 ⊖	a						21 34													22 04					
Clapham High Street ⊖	d				21 28														21 58						
Wandsworth Road	d				21 29														21 59						
Battersea Park 4	d				21 32						22 05								22 02					22 35	
London Victoria 15 ⊖	a				21 36						22 09								22 06					22 39	
Penge West	d		21 24	21 30								21 45					21 54	22 00							22 15
Anerley	d		21 26	21 32								21 47					21 56	22 02							22 17
Norwood Junction 2	d		21 30	21 35								21 50					22 00	22 05							22 20
West Croydon 4	a			21 45								22 00						22 12							22 30
East Croydon	a		21 33														22 04								

			LO	LO	SN	SN	LO	SN	SE	SN	LO		SN	LO	LO	SN	SN	SN	SE	SN	LO		SN	LO	LO
London Bridge 4 ⊖	d				22 03	22 06		22 11					22 22			22 33	22 36	22 41					22 52		
Highbury & Islington	a																								
	d		21 40				21 48				21 55			22 05							22 25			22 35	
Canonbury	d		21 42				21 50				21 57			22 07							22 27			22 37	
Dalston Junction Stn ELL	d		21 45	21 50			21 55				22 00			22 10	22 20						22 30			22 40	22 50
Haggerston	d		21 46	21 51			21 56				22 01			22 11	22 21						22 31			22 41	22 51
Hoxton	d		21 48	21 53			21 58				22 03			22 13	22 23						22 33			22 43	22 53
Shoreditch High Street	d		21 51	21 56			22 01				22 06			22 16	22 26						22 36			22 46	22 56
Whitechapel	d		21 53	21 58			22 03				22 08			22 18	22 28						22 38			22 48	22 58
Shadwell	d		21 55	22 00			22 05				22 10			22 20	22 30						22 40			22 50	23 00
Wapping	d		21 57	22 02			22 07				22 12			22 22	22 32						22 42			22 52	23 02
Rotherhithe	d		21 59	22 04			22 09				22 14			22 24	22 34						22 44			22 54	23 04
Canada Water	d		22 01	22 06			22 11				22 16			22 26	22 36						22 46			22 56	23 06
Surrey Quays	d		22 02	22 07			22 12				22 17			22 27	22 37						22 47			22 57	23 07
New Cross ELL	a			22 13											22 42										23 12
New Cross Gate 4	a		22 06			22 11	22 16				22 21		22 27	22 31			22 41				22 51		22 57	23 01	
	d		22 07			22 11	22 17				22 22		22 27	22 32			22 41				22 52		22 57	23 02	
Brockley	d		22 09			22 14	22 19				22 24		22 30	22 34			22 44				22 54		23 00	23 04	
Honor Oak Park	d		22 12			22 17	22 22				22 27		22 33	22 37			22 47				22 57		23 03	23 07	
Forest Hill 4	d		22 15			22 19	22 25				22 30		22 35	22 40			22 49				23 00		23 05	23 10	
Sydenham	d		22 17			22 22	22 27				22 32		22 38	22 42			22 52				23 02		23 08	23 12	
Crystal Palace 4	d		22a22							22 30	22a37		22 43							23 00	23a07		23 13		
Gipsy Hill	d									22 32			22 45							23 02			23 15		
West Norwood 4	d									22 35			22 48							23 05			23 18		
Streatham Hill	d												22 52										23 22		
Balham 4 ⊖	d												22 55										23 25		
Wandsworth Common	d												22 57										23 27		
Clapham Junction 10	d												23 01										23 31		
South Bermondsey	d				22 07			22 15								22 37		22 45							
Queens Rd Peckham	d				22 09			22 18								22 39		22 48							
Peckham Rye 4	d				22a12			22 20	22 20	22a46						22a42		22 50	22 50	23a16					
Denmark Hill 4	d							22 23	22 24									22 53	22 54						
London Blackfriars 3 ⊖	a								22 34										23 04						
Clapham High Street ⊖	d							22 28										22 58							
Wandsworth Road	d							22 29										22 59							
Battersea Park 4	d							22 32					23 05					23 02					23 35		
London Victoria 15 ⊖	a							22 36					23 09					23 06					23 41		
Penge West	d					22 24	22 30							22 45			22 54							23 15	
Anerley	d					22 26	22 32							22 47			22 56							23 17	
Norwood Junction 2	d					22 30	22 35							22 50			23 00							23 20	
West Croydon 4	a						22 42							23 00										23 30	
East Croydon	a					22 35											23 03								

Table 178

Saturdays
from 15 September

London Bridge to London Victoria - Croydon and East London Line

Network Diagram - see first Page of Table 177

		SN	SN	SN	SE	SN	LO		SN	LO	LO	SN	SN	LO	SN	LO	LO		LO
London Bridge 4 ⊖	d	23 03	23 06	23 11					23 22			23 33	23 36		23 52				
Highbury & Islington	a																		
	d						22 55			23 05				23 25		23 35	23 42		23 56
Canonbury	d						22 57			23 07				23 27		23 37	23 44		23 58
Dalston Junction Stn ELL	d						23 00			23 10	23 20			23 30		23 40	23 47		00 02
Haggerston	d						23 01			23 11	23 21			23 31		23 41	23 48		00 03
Hoxton	d						23 03			23 13	23 23			23 33		23 43	23 50		00 05
Shoreditch High Street	d						23 06			23 16	23 26			23 36		23 46	23 53		00 08
Whitechapel	d						23 08			23 18	23 28			23 38		23 48	23 55		00 10
Shadwell	d						23 10			23 20	23 30			23 40		23 50	23 57		00 12
Wapping	d						23 12			23 22	23 32			23 42		23 52	23 59		00 14
Rotherhithe	d						23 14			23 24	23 34			23 44		23 54	00 01		00 16
Canada Water	d						23 16			23 26	23 36			23 46		23 56	00 03		00 18
Surrey Quays	d						23 17			23 27	23 37			23 47		23 57	00 05		00 19
New Cross ELL	a										23 42								
New Cross Gate 4	a		23 11				23 21		23 27	23 31			23 41	23 51	23 57	00 02	00 08		00 23
	d		23 11				23 22		23 27	23 32			23 41	23 52	23 57	00 02			
Brockley	d		23 14				23 24		23 30	23 34			23 44	23 54	00 01	00 04			
Honor Oak Park	d		23 17				23 27		23 33	23 37			23 47	23 57	00 04	00 07			
Forest Hill 4	d		23 19				23 30		23 35	23 40			23 49	23 59	00 06	00 10			
Sydenham	d		23 22				23 32		23 38	23 42			23 52	00 02	00 09	00 12			
Crystal Palace 4	d					23 30	23a37		23 43					00a07	00 13				
Gipsy Hill	d					23 32			23 45						00 15				
West Norwood 4	d					23 35			23 48						00 18				
Streatham Hill	d								23 52						00 22				
Balham 4 ⊖	d								23 55						00 26				
Wandsworth Common	d								23 57						00 28				
Clapham Junction 10	d								00 02						00 32				
South Bermondsey	d	23 07		23 15								23 37							
Queens Rd Peckham	d	23 09		23 18								23 39							
Peckham Rye 4	d	23 12		23 20	23 20	23a46						23 42							
Denmark Hill 4	d			23 23	23 24														
London Blackfriars 3 ⊖	a				23 34														
Clapham High Street ⊖	d			23 28															
Wandsworth Road	d			23 29															
Battersea Park 4	d			23 32					00 05						00 35				
London Victoria 15 ⊖	a			23 37					00 10						00 42				
Penge West	d		23 24							23 45			23 54			00 15			
Anerley	d		23 26							23 47			23 56			00 17			
Norwood Junction 2	d	23a34	23 30							23 50		00a04	23 59			00 20			
West Croydon 4 (tram)	a									23 59						00 27			
East Croydon (tram)	a		23 33										00 03						

Sundays
until 22 July

		SN	SN	SN	LO	SN	LO	LO	SN	SN		LO	LO	SN	SN	SN	SN	SN	SE	SN		SN	SE	LO	LO
London Bridge 4 ⊖	d	23p22	23p36			23p52			00 03	00 06						00 33	00 36			07 11					
Highbury & Islington	a																								
	d				23p25		23p35	23p42				23p56	00 10												06 51
Canonbury	d				23p27		23p37	23p44				23p58	00 12												06 53
Dalston Junction Stn ELL	d				23p30		23p40	23p47				00 02	00 15												06 56
Haggerston	d				23p31		23p41	23p48				00 03	00 16												06 57
Hoxton	d				23p33		23p43	23p50				00 05	00 18												06 59
Shoreditch High Street	d				23p36		23p46	23p53				00 08	00 21												07 02
Whitechapel	d				23p38		23p48	23p55				00 10	00 23												07 04
Shadwell	d				23p40		23p50	23p57				00 12	00 25												07 06
Wapping	d				23p42		23p52	23p59				00 14	00 27												07 08
Rotherhithe	d				23p44		23p54	00 01				00 16	00 29												07 10
Canada Water	d				23p46		23p56	00 03				00 18	00 31												07 12
Surrey Quays	d				23p47		23p57	00 05				00 19	00 32												07 13
New Cross ELL	a																								
New Cross Gate 4	a	23p27	23p41		23p51	23p57	00 02	00 08		00 11		00 23	00 36				00 41								07 17
	d	23p27	23p41		23p52	23p57	00 02			00 11							00 41							07 04	07 18
Brockley	d	23p30	23p44		23p54	00 01	00 04			00 14							00 44							07 06	07 20
Honor Oak Park	d	23p33	23p47		23p57	00 04	00 07			00 17							00 47							07 09	07 23
Forest Hill 4	d	23p35	23p49		23p59	00 06	00 10			00 19							00 49							07 12	07 26
Sydenham	d	23p38	23p52		00 02	00 09	00 12			00 22							00 52							07 14	07 28
Crystal Palace 4	d	23p43		00 03	00a07	00 13								00 33	00 47			01 03				07 07			07a33
Gipsy Hill	d	23p45				00 15																07 09			
West Norwood 4	d	23p48				00 18																07 12			
Streatham Hill	d	23p52				00 22																			
Balham 4 ⊖	d	23p55				00 26																			
Wandsworth Common	d	23p57				00 28																			
Clapham Junction 10	d	00 02				00 32																			
South Bermondsey	d								00 07							00 37				07 15					
Queens Rd Peckham	d								00 09							00 39				07 18					
Peckham Rye 4	d								00 12							00 42			07 09	07 20		07a23	07 39		
Denmark Hill 4	d																		07 13	07 23			07 43		
London Blackfriars 3 ⊖	a																		07 23				07 53		
Clapham High Street ⊖	d																			07 28					
Wandsworth Road	d																			07 29					
Battersea Park 4	d	00 05				00 35														07 32					
London Victoria 15 ⊖	a	00 10				00 42														07 36					
Penge West	d		23p54				00 15			00 24							00 54							07 17	
Anerley	d		23p56				00 17			00 26							00 56							07 19	
Norwood Junction 2	d		23p59	00 09			00 20		00a34	00 30				00 38	00 52	01a04	01 00	01 08						07 22	
West Croydon 4 (tram)	a			00 14			00 27							00 43	00 58			01 13						07 29	
East Croydon (tram)	a		00 03							00 33							01 03								

Table 178

Sundays
until 22 July

London Bridge to London Victoria - Croydon and East London Line

Network Diagram - see first Page of Table 177

		SN	LO	SN	SN	SN		SN	LO	SN	LO	SE	SN	SN	SN	SN		LO	SN	LO	LO	SE	SN	SN	SN
London Bridge 4 ⊖	d	07 24		07 36	07 39	07 41				07 54			08 06	08 09	08 11				08 24				08 36	08 39	08 41
Highbury & Islington	a																								
	d		07 05						07 21		07 35							07 51		08 05	08 15				
Canonbury	d		07 07						07 23		07 37							07 53		08 07	08 17				
Dalston Junction Stn ELL	d		07 12						07 26		07 42							07 56		08 12	08 22				
Haggerston	d		07 13						07 27		07 43							07 57		08 13	08 23				
Hoxton	d		07 15						07 29		07 45							07 59		08 15	08 25				
Shoreditch High Street	d		07 18						07 32		07 48							08 02		08 18	08 28				
Whitechapel	d		07 20						07 34		07 50							08 04		08 20	08 30				
Shadwell	d		07 22						07 36		07 52							08 06		08 22	08 32				
Wapping	d		07 24						07 38		07 54							08 08		08 24	08 34				
Rotherhithe	d		07 26						07 40		07 56							08 10		08 26	08 36				
Canada Water	d		07 28						07 42		07 58							08 12		08 28	08 38				
Surrey Quays	d		07 29						07 43		07 59							08 13		08 29	08 39				
New Cross ELL	a																				08 45				
New Cross Gate 4	a	07 29	07 33		07 44				07 47	07 59	08 03			08 14				08 17	08 29	08 33				08 44	
	d	07 29	07 34		07 44				07 48	07 59	08 03			08 14				08 18	08 29	08 34				08 44	
Brockley	d	07 32	07 36		07 47				07 50	08 02	08 06			08 17				08 20	08 32	08 36				08 47	
Honor Oak Park	d	07 35	07 39		07 50				07 53	08 05	08 09			08 20				08 23	08 35	08 39				08 50	
Forest Hill 4	d	07 37	07 42		07 52				07 56	08 07	08 12			08 22				08 26	08 37	08 42				08 52	
Sydenham	d	07 40	07 44		07 55				07 58	08 10	08 14			08 25				08 28	08 40	08 44				08 55	
Crystal Palace 4	d							07 37	08a03							08 07		08a33							
Gipsy Hill	d							07 39								08 09									
West Norwood 4	d							07 42								08 12									
Streatham Hill	d																								
Balham 4 ⊖	d																								
Wandsworth Common	d																								
Clapham Junction 10	d																								
South Bermondsey	d			07 40		07 45							08 10		08 15								08 40		08 45
Queens Rd Peckham	d			07 42		07 48							08 12		08 18								08 42		08 48
Peckham Rye 4	d			07a45		07 50		07a53				08 09	08a15		08 20	08a23						08 39	08a45		08 50
Denmark Hill 4	d					07 53						08 13			08 23							08 43			08 53
London Blackfriars 3 ⊖	a											08 23										08 53			
Clapham High Street ⊖	d					07 58									08 28										08 58
Wandsworth Road	d					07 59									08 29										08 59
Battersea Park 4	d					08 02									08 32										09 02
London Victoria 15 ⊖	a					08 06									08 36										09 06
Penge West	d		07 47		07 57						08 17			08 27						08 47				08 57	
Anerley	d		07 49		07 59						08 19			08 29						08 49				08 59	
Norwood Junction 2	d	07 48	07 52		08 03					08 16	08 22			08 33					08 46	08 52				09 03	
West Croydon 4	a	07 55	07 59							08 24	08 28								08 54	08 58					
East Croydon	a				08 07									08 37										09 07	

		SN		LO	LO	SN	LO	LO	SE	SN	SN	SN		SN	LO	LO	SN	LO	LO	SE	SN	SN		SN	SN
London Bridge 4 ⊖	d					08 54				09 06	09 09	09 11					09 24				09 36	09 39		09 41	
Highbury & Islington	a																								
	d			08 21	08 30		08 35	08 45							08 51	09 00		09 05	09 15						
Canonbury	d			08 23	08 32		08 37	08 47							08 53	09 02		09 07	09 17						
Dalston Junction Stn ELL	d			08 26	08 37		08 42	08 52							08 56	09 07		09 12	09 22						
Haggerston	d			08 27	08 38		08 43	08 53							08 57	09 08		09 13	09 23						
Hoxton	d			08 29	08 40		08 45	08 55							08 59	09 10		09 15	09 25						
Shoreditch High Street	d			08 32	08 43		08 48	08 58							09 02	09 13		09 18	09 28						
Whitechapel	d			08 34	08 45		08 50	09 00							09 04	09 15		09 20	09 30						
Shadwell	d			08 36	08 47		08 52	09 02							09 06	09 17		09 22	09 32						
Wapping	d			08 38	08 49		08 54	09 04							09 08	09 19		09 24	09 34						
Rotherhithe	d			08 40	08 51		08 56	09 06							09 10	09 21		09 26	09 36						
Canada Water	d			08 42	08 53		08 58	09 08							09 12	09 23		09 28	09 38						
Surrey Quays	d			08 43	08 54		08 59	09 09							09 13	09 24		09 29	09 39						
New Cross ELL	a				09 00			09 15								09 30			09 45						
New Cross Gate 4	a			08 47		08 59	09 03				09 14				09 17		09 29	09 33				09 44			
	d			08 48		08 59	09 04				09 14				09 18		09 29	09 34				09 44			
Brockley	d			08 50		09 02	09 06				09 17				09 20		09 32	09 36				09 47			
Honor Oak Park	d			08 53		09 05	09 09				09 20				09 23		09 35	09 39				09 50			
Forest Hill 4	d			08 56		09 07	09 12				09 22				09 26		09 37	09 42				09 52			
Sydenham	d			08 58		09 10	09 14				09 25				09 28		09 40	09 44				09 55			
Crystal Palace 4	d	08 37		09a03										09 07	09a33										09 37
Gipsy Hill	d	08 39												09 09											09 39
West Norwood 4	d	08 42												09 12											09 42
Streatham Hill	d																								
Balham 4 ⊖	d																								
Wandsworth Common	d																								
Clapham Junction 10	d																								
South Bermondsey	d									09 10		09 15									09 40			09 45	
Queens Rd Peckham	d									09 12		09 18									09 42			09 48	
Peckham Rye 4	d	08a53							09 09	09a15		09 20		09a23						09 39	09a45			09 50	09a53
Denmark Hill 4	d								09 13			09 23								09 43				09 53	
London Blackfriars 3 ⊖	a								09 23											09 53					
Clapham High Street ⊖	d											09 28												09 58	
Wandsworth Road	d											09 29												09 59	
Battersea Park 4	d											09 32												10 02	
London Victoria 15 ⊖	a											09 36												10 06	
Penge West	d						09 17				09 27							09 47				09 57			
Anerley	d						09 19				09 29							09 49				09 59			
Norwood Junction 2	d					09 16	09 22				09 33						09 46	09 52				10 03			
West Croydon 4	a					09 24	09 28										09 54	09 58							
East Croydon	a										09 37											10 07			

Table 178

Sundays until 22 July

London Bridge to London Victoria - Croydon and East London Line

Network Diagram - see first Page of Table 177

		LO	LO	SN	LO	LO	SE	SN		SN	SN	SN	LO	LO	SN	LO	LO	SE		SN	SN	SN	SN	LO	LO
London Bridge 4 ⊖	d			09 54				10 06		10 09	10 11				10 24					10 36	10 39	10 41			
Highbury & Islington	a																								
	d	09 21	09 30		09 35	09 45							09 51	10 00		10 05	10 15							10 21	10 30
Canonbury	d	09 23	09 32		09 37	09 47							09 53	10 02		10 07	10 17							10 23	10 32
Dalston Junction Stn ELL	d	09 26	09 37		09 42	09 52							09 56	10 07		10 12	10 22							10 26	10 37
Haggerston	d	09 27	09 38		09 43	09 53							09 57	10 08		10 13	10 23							10 27	10 38
Hoxton	d	09 29	09 40		09 45	09 55							09 59	10 10		10 15	10 25							10 29	10 40
Shoreditch High Street	d	09 32	09 43		09 48	09 58							10 02	10 13		10 18	10 28							10 32	10 43
Whitechapel	d	09 34	09 45		09 50	10 00							10 04	10 15		10 20	10 30							10 34	10 45
Shadwell	d	09 36	09 47		09 52	10 02							10 06	10 17		10 22	10 32							10 36	10 47
Wapping	d	09 38	09 49		09 54	10 04							10 08	10 19		10 24	10 34							10 38	10 49
Rotherhithe	d	09 40	09 51		09 56	10 06							10 10	10 21		10 26	10 36							10 40	10 51
Canada Water	d	09 42	09 53		09 58	10 08							10 12	10 23		10 28	10 38							10 42	10 53
Surrey Quays	d	09 43	09 54		09 59	10 09							10 13	10 24		10 29	10 39							10 43	10 54
New Cross ELL	a		10 00			10 15								10 30			10 45								11 00
New Cross Gate 4	a	09 47		09 59	10 03					10 14			10 17		10 29	10 33					10 44			10 47	
	d	09 48		09 59	10 04					10 14			10 18		10 29	10 34					10 44			10 48	
Brockley	d	09 50		10 02	10 06					10 17			10 20		10 32	10 36					10 47			10 50	
Honor Oak Park	d	09 53		10 05	10 09					10 20			10 23		10 35	10 39					10 50			10 53	
Forest Hill 4	d	09 56		10 07	10 12					10 22			10 26		10 37	10 42					10 52			10 56	
Sydenham	d	09 58		10 10	10 14					10 25			10 28		10 40	10 44					10 55			10 58	
Crystal Palace 4	d	10a03										10 07	10a33										10 37	11a03	
Gipsy Hill	d											10 09											10 39		
West Norwood 4	d											10 12											10 42		
Streatham Hill	d																								
Balham 4 ⊖	d																								
Wandsworth Common	d																								
Clapham Junction 10	d																								
South Bermondsey	d							10 10			10 15									10 40		10 45			
Queens Rd Peckham	d							10 12			10 18									10 42		10 48			
Peckham Rye 4	d						10 09	10a15			10 20	10a23						10 39		10a45		10 50	10a53		
Denmark Hill 4	d						10 13				10 23							10 43				10 53			
London Blackfriars 3 ⊖	a						10 23											10 53							
Clapham High Street ⊖	d										10 28											10 58			
Wandsworth Road	d										10 29											10 59			
Battersea Park 4	d										10 32											11 02			
London Victoria 15 ⊖	a										10 36											11 06			
Penge West	d				10 17					10 27						10 47					10 57				
Anerley	d				10 19					10 29						10 49					10 59				
Norwood Junction 2	d			10 16	10 22					10 33					10 46	10 52					11 03				
West Croydon 4	a			10 24	10 28										10 54	10 58									
East Croydon	a									10 37											11 07				

		SN	LO	LO		SE	SN	SN	SN	SN	LO	LO	SN	LO		LO	SE	SN	SN	SN	SN	LO	LO	SN	
London Bridge 4 ⊖	d	10 54					11 06	11 09	11 11				11 24					11 36	11 39	11 41				11 54	
Highbury & Islington	a																								
	d		10 35	10 45							10 51	11 00		11 05		11 15						11 21	11 30		
Canonbury	d		10 37	10 47							10 53	11 02		11 07		11 17						11 23	11 32		
Dalston Junction Stn ELL	d		10 42	10 52							10 56	11 07		11 12		11 22						11 26	11 37		
Haggerston	d		10 43	10 53							10 57	11 08		11 13		11 23						11 27	11 38		
Hoxton	d		10 45	10 55							10 59	11 10		11 15		11 25						11 29	11 40		
Shoreditch High Street	d		10 48	10 58							11 02	11 13		11 18		11 28						11 32	11 43		
Whitechapel	d		10 50	11 00							11 04	11 15		11 20		11 30						11 34	11 45		
Shadwell	d		10 52	11 02							11 06	11 17		11 22		11 32						11 36	11 47		
Wapping	d		10 54	11 04							11 08	11 19		11 24		11 34						11 38	11 49		
Rotherhithe	d		10 56	11 06							11 10	11 21		11 26		11 36						11 40	11 51		
Canada Water	d		10 58	11 08							11 12	11 23		11 28		11 38						11 42	11 53		
Surrey Quays	d		10 59	11 09							11 13	11 24		11 29		11 39						11 43	11 54		
New Cross ELL	a			11 15								11 30				11 45							12 00		
New Cross Gate 4	a	10 59	11 03					11 14			11 17		11 29	11 33					11 44			11 47		11 59	
	d	10 59	11 04					11 14			11 18		11 29	11 34					11 44			11 48		11 59	
Brockley	d	11 02	11 06					11 17			11 20		11 32	11 36					11 47			11 50		12 02	
Honor Oak Park	d	11 05	11 09					11 20			11 23		11 35	11 39					11 50			11 53		12 05	
Forest Hill 4	d	11 07	11 12					11 22			11 26		11 37	11 42					11 52			11 56		12 07	
Sydenham	d	11 10	11 14					11 25			11 28		11 40	11 44					11 55			11 58		12 10	
Crystal Palace 4	d									11 07	11a33										11 37	12a03			
Gipsy Hill	d									11 09											11 39				
West Norwood 4	d									11 12											11 42				
Streatham Hill	d																								
Balham 4 ⊖	d																								
Wandsworth Common	d																								
Clapham Junction 10	d																								
South Bermondsey	d						11 10		11 15									11 40		11 45					
Queens Rd Peckham	d						11 12		11 18									11 42		11 48					
Peckham Rye 4	d					11 09	11a15		11 20	11a23							11 39	11a45		11 50	11a53				
Denmark Hill 4	d					11 13			11 23								11 43			11 53					
London Blackfriars 3 ⊖	a					11 23											11 53								
Clapham High Street ⊖	d								11 28											11 58					
Wandsworth Road	d								11 29											11 59					
Battersea Park 4	d								11 32											12 02					
London Victoria 15 ⊖	a								11 36											12 06					
Penge West	d		11 17					11 27						11 47					11 57						
Anerley	d		11 19					11 29						11 49					11 59						
Norwood Junction 2	d	11 16	11 22					11 33					11 46	11 52					12 03					12 16	
West Croydon 4	a	11 24	11 28										11 54	11 58										12 24	
East Croydon	a							11 37											12 07						

Table 178

Sundays

until 22 July

London Bridge to London Victoria - Croydon and East London Line

Network Diagram - see first Page of Table 177

Station		LO	SE	SN	SN	LO	LO	SN	LO	SN		SE	SN	LO	LO	SN	LO	LO	LO	SN		SN	LO	SN	SE
London Bridge 4 ⊖	d			12 06				12 09		12 11						12 24				12 36		12 39		12 41	
Highbury & Islington	a																								
	d	11 35				11 43			11 51					11 58			12 06	12 13					12 21		
Canonbury	d	11 37				11 45			11 53					12 00			12 08	12 15					12 23		
Dalston Junction Stn ELL	d	11 42				11 48	11 52		11 58					12 03	12 08		12 13	12 18	12 23				12 28		
Haggerston	d	11 43				11 49	11 53		11 59					12 04	12 09		12 14	12 19	12 24				12 29		
Hoxton	d	11 45				11 51	11 55		12 01					12 06	12 11		12 16	12 21	12 26				12 31		
Shoreditch High Street	d	11 48				11 54	11 58		12 04					12 09	12 14		12 19	12 24	12 29				12 34		
Whitechapel	d	11 50				11 56	12 00		12 06					12 11	12 16		12 21	12 26	12 31				12 36		
Shadwell	d	11 52				11 58	12 02		12 08					12 13	12 18		12 23	12 28	12 33				12 38		
Wapping	d	11 54				12 00	12 04		12 10					12 15	12 20		12 25	12 30	12 35				12 40		
Rotherhithe	d	11 56				12 02	12 06		12 12					12 17	12 22		12 27	12 32	12 37				12 42		
Canada Water	d	11 58				12 04	12 08		12 14					12 19	12 24		12 29	12 34	12 39				12 44		
Surrey Quays	d	11 59				12 05	12 09		12 15					12 20	12 25		12 30	12 35	12 40				12 45		
New Cross ELL	a						12 14								12 30				12 45						
New Cross Gate 4	a	12 03				12 09		12 14	12 19					12 24		12 29	12 34	12 39				12 44	12 49		
	d	12 04				12 10		12 14	12 20					12 25		12 29	12 35	12 40				12 44	12 50		
Brockley	d	12 06				12 12		12 17	12 22					12 27		12 32	12 37	12 42				12 47	12 52		
Honor Oak Park	d	12 09				12 15		12 20	12 25					12 30		12 35	12 40	12 45				12 50	12 55		
Forest Hill 4	d	12 12				12 18		12 22	12 28					12 33		12 37	12 43	12 48				12 52	12 58		
Sydenham	d	12 14				12 20		12 25	12 30					12 35		12 40	12 45	12 50				12 55	13 00		
Crystal Palace 4	d				12 07	12a25							12 37	12a40				12a55							
Gipsy Hill	d				12 09								12 39												
West Norwood 4	d				12 12								12 42												
Streatham Hill	d																								
Balham 4 ⊖	d																								
Wandsworth Common	d																								
Clapham Junction 10	d																								
South Bermondsey	d			12 10						12 15										12 40				12 45	
Queens Rd Peckham	d			12 12						12 18										12 42				12 48	
Peckham Rye 4	d		12 09	12a15	12a23					12 20		12 39	12a53							12a45				12 50	13 09
Denmark Hill 4	d		12 13							12 23		12 43												12 53	13 13
London Blackfriars 3 ⊖	a		12 23									12 53													13 23
Clapham High Street ⊖	d									12 28														12 58	
Wandsworth Road	d									12 29														12 59	
Battersea Park 4	d									12 32														13 02	
London Victoria 15 ⊖	a									12 36														13 06	
Penge West	d	12 17						12 27	12 33								12 48					12 57	13 03		
Anerley	d	12 19						12 29	12 35								12 50					12 59	13 05		
Norwood Junction 2	d	12 22						12 33	12 38							12 46	12 53					13 03	13 08		
West Croydon 4	a	12 28							12 45							12 54	12 59						13 15		
East Croydon	a							12 37														13 07			

Station		SN	LO	LO	SN	LO		LO	LO	SN		SN	SN	LO	SN		SE	SN	LO	LO	SN	LO	LO	LO
London Bridge 4 ⊖	d				12 54					13 06		17 06	17 09		17 11						17 24			
Highbury & Islington	a																							
	d		12 28			12 36		12 43						16 51					16 58			17 06	17 13	
Canonbury	d		12 30			12 38		12 45						16 53					17 00			17 08	17 15	
Dalston Junction Stn ELL	d		12 33	12 38		12 43		12 48	12 53					16 58					17 03	17 08		17 13	17 18	17 23
Haggerston	d		12 34	12 39		12 44		12 49	12 54					16 59					17 04	17 09		17 14	17 19	17 24
Hoxton	d		12 36	12 41		12 46		12 51	12 56					17 01					17 06	17 11		17 16	17 21	17 26
Shoreditch High Street	d		12 39	12 44		12 49		12 54	12 59					17 04					17 09	17 14		17 19	17 24	17 29
Whitechapel	d		12 41	12 46		12 51		12 56	13 01					17 06					17 11	17 16		17 21	17 26	17 31
Shadwell	d		12 43	12 48		12 53		12 58	13 03					17 08					17 13	17 18		17 23	17 28	17 33
Wapping	d		12 45	12 50		12 55		13 00	13 05					17 10					17 15	17 20		17 25	17 30	17 35
Rotherhithe	d		12 47	12 52		12 57		13 02	13 07					17 12					17 17	17 22		17 27	17 32	17 37
Canada Water	d		12 49	12 54		12 59		13 04	13 09					17 14					17 19	17 24		17 29	17 34	17 39
Surrey Quays	d		12 50	12 55		13 00		13 05	13 10					17 15					17 20	17 25		17 30	17 35	17 40
New Cross ELL	a			13 00					13 15											17 30				17 45
New Cross Gate 4	a		12 54		12 59	13 04		13 09					17 14	17 19					17 24		17 29	17 34	17 39	
	d		12 55		12 59	13 05		13 10					17 14	17 20					17 25		17 29	17 35	17 40	
Brockley	d		12 57		13 02	13 07		13 12			and at the same minutes past each hour until		17 17	17 22					17 27		17 32	17 37	17 42	
Honor Oak Park	d		13 00		13 05	13 10		13 15					17 20	17 25					17 30		17 35	17 40	17 45	
Forest Hill 4	d		13 03		13 07	13 13		13 18					17 22	17 28					17 33		17 37	17 43	17 48	
Sydenham	d		13 05		13 10	13 15		13 20					17 25	17 30					17 35		17 40	17 45	17 50	
Crystal Palace 4	d	13 07	13a10					13a25										17 37	17a40				17a55	
Gipsy Hill	d	13 09																17 39						
West Norwood 4	d	13 12																17 42						
Streatham Hill	d																							
Balham 4 ⊖	d																							
Wandsworth Common	d																							
Clapham Junction 10	d																							
South Bermondsey	d									13 10		17 10			17 15									
Queens Rd Peckham	d									13 12		17 12			17 18									
Peckham Rye 4	d	13a23								13a15		17a15			17 20		17 39	17a53						
Denmark Hill 4	d														17 23		17 43							
London Blackfriars 3 ⊖	a																17 53							
Clapham High Street ⊖	d														17 28									
Wandsworth Road	d														17 29									
Battersea Park 4	d														17 32									
London Victoria 15 ⊖	a														17 36									
Penge West	d					13 18							17 27	17 33								17 48		
Anerley	d					13 20							17 29	17 35								17 50		
Norwood Junction 2	d				13 16	13 23							17 33	17 38							17 46	17 53		
West Croydon 4	a				13 24	13 29								17 45							17 54	17 59		
East Croydon	a												17 37											

Table 178

Sundays

until 22 July

London Bridge to London Victoria - Croydon and East London Line

Network Diagram - see first Page of Table 177

		SN		SN	LO	SN	SE	SN	LO	LO	SN	LO		LO	LO	SN	SN	LO	SN	SE	SN	LO		LO	SN
London Bridge ■4 ⊖	d	17 36		17 39		17 41					17 54					18 06	18 09		18 11						18 24
Highbury & Islington	a																								
	d				17 21				17 28			17 36		17 43				17 51				17 58			
Canonbury	d				17 23				17 30			17 38		17 45				17 53				18 00			
Dalston Junction Stn ELL	d				17 28				17 33	17 38		17 43		17 48	17 53			17 58				18 03		18 08	
Haggerston	d				17 29				17 34	17 39		17 44		17 49	17 54			17 59				18 04		18 09	
Hoxton	d				17 31				17 36	17 41		17 46		17 51	17 56			18 01				18 06		18 11	
Shoreditch High Street	d				17 34				17 39	17 44		17 49		17 54	17 59			18 04				18 09		18 14	
Whitechapel	d				17 36				17 41	17 46		17 51		17 56	18 01			18 06				18 11		18 16	
Shadwell	d				17 38				17 43	17 48		17 53		17 58	18 03			18 08				18 13		18 18	
Wapping	d				17 40				17 45	17 50		17 55		18 00	18 05			18 10				18 15		18 20	
Rotherhithe	d				17 42				17 47	17 52		17 57		18 02	18 07			18 12				18 17		18 22	
Canada Water	d				17 44				17 49	17 54		17 59		18 04	18 09			18 14				18 19		18 24	
Surrey Quays	d				17 45				17 50	17 55		18 00		18 05	18 10			18 15				18 20		18 25	
New Cross ELL	a									18 00					18 15									18 30	
New Cross Gate ■4	a			17 44	17 49				17 54		17 59	18 04		18 09			18 14	18 19				18 24			18 29
	d			17 44	17 50				17 55		17 59	18 05		18 10			18 14	18 20				18 25			18 29
Brockley	d			17 47	17 52				17 57		18 02	18 07		18 12			18 17	18 22				18 27			18 32
Honor Oak Park	d			17 50	17 55				18 00		18 05	18 10		18 15			18 20	18 25				18 30			18 35
Forest Hill ■4	d			17 52	17 58				18 03		18 07	18 13		18 18			18 22	18 28				18 33			18 37
Sydenham	d			17 55	18 00				18 05		18 10	18 15		18 20			18 25	18 30				18 35			18 40
Crystal Palace ■4	d							18 07	18a10					18a25							18 37	18a40			
Gipsy Hill	d							18 09													18 39				
West Norwood ■4	d							18 12													18 42				
Streatham Hill	d																								
Balham ■4 ⊖	d																								
Wandsworth Common	d																								
Clapham Junction ■10	d																								
South Bermondsey	d	17 40				17 45										18 10			18 15						
Queens Rd Peckham	d	17 42				17 48										18 12			18 18						
Peckham Rye ■4	d	17a45				17 50	18 09	18a23								18a15			18 20	18 39	18a53				
Denmark Hill ■4	d					17 53	18 13												18 23	18 43					
London Blackfriars ■3 ⊖	a						18 23													18 53					
Clapham High Street ⊖	d					17 58													18 28						
Wandsworth Road	d					17 59													18 29						
Battersea Park ■4	d					18 02													18 32						
London Victoria ■15 ⊖	a					18 06													18 36						
Penge West	d			17 57	18 03							18 18					18 27	18 33							
Anerley	d			17 59	18 05							18 20					18 29	18 35							
Norwood Junction ■2	d			18 03	18 08						18 16	18 23					18 33	18 38							18 46
West Croydon ■4 🚌	a				18 14						18 24	18 29						18 44							18 54
East Croydon 🚌	a			18 07													18 37								

		LO	LO	LO	SN	SN	LO	SN		SE	SN	LO	LO	SN	LO	LO	LO	SN		SN	LO	SN	SE	SN	LO
London Bridge ■4 ⊖	d				18 36	18 39		18 41						18 54				19 06		19 09		19 11			
Highbury & Islington	a																								
	d	18 06	18 13				18 21					18 28			18 36	18 43					18 51				18 58
Canonbury	d	18 08	18 15				18 23					18 30			18 38	18 45					18 53				19 00
Dalston Junction Stn ELL	d	18 13	18 18	18 23			18 28					18 33	18 38		18 43	18 48	18 53				18 58				19 03
Haggerston	d	18 14	18 19	18 24			18 29					18 34	18 39		18 44	18 49	18 54				18 59				19 04
Hoxton	d	18 16	18 21	18 26			18 31					18 36	18 41		18 46	18 51	18 56				19 01				19 06
Shoreditch High Street	d	18 19	18 24	18 29			18 34					18 39	18 44		18 49	18 54	18 59				19 04				19 09
Whitechapel	d	18 21	18 26	18 31			18 36					18 41	18 46		18 51	18 56	19 01				19 06				19 11
Shadwell	d	18 23	18 28	18 33			18 38					18 43	18 48		18 53	18 58	19 03				19 08				19 13
Wapping	d	18 25	18 30	18 35			18 40					18 45	18 50		18 55	19 00	19 05				19 10				19 15
Rotherhithe	d	18 27	18 32	18 37			18 42					18 47	18 52		18 57	19 02	19 07				19 12				19 17
Canada Water	d	18 29	18 34	18 39			18 44					18 49	18 54		18 59	19 04	19 09				19 14				19 19
Surrey Quays	d	18 30	18 35	18 40			18 45					18 50	18 55		19 00	19 05	19 10				19 15				19 20
New Cross ELL	a			18 45									19 00				19 15								
New Cross Gate ■4	a	18 34	18 39			18 44	18 49					18 54		18 59	19 04	19 09				19 14	19 19				19 24
	d	18 35	18 40			18 44	18 50					18 55		18 59	19 05	19 10				19 14	19 20				19 25
Brockley	d	18 37	18 42			18 47	18 52					18 57		19 02	19 07	19 12				19 17	19 22				19 27
Honor Oak Park	d	18 40	18 45			18 50	18 55					19 00		19 05	19 10	19 15				19 20	19 25				19 30
Forest Hill ■4	d	18 43	18 48			18 52	18 58					19 03		19 07	19 13	19 18				19 22	19 28				19 33
Sydenham	d	18 45	18 50			18 55	19 00					19 05		19 10	19 15	19 20				19 25	19 30				19 35
Crystal Palace ■4	d		18a55								19 07	19a10				19a25								19 37	19a40
Gipsy Hill	d										19 09													19 39	
West Norwood ■4	d										19 12													19 42	
Streatham Hill	d																								
Balham ■4 ⊖	d																								
Wandsworth Common	d																								
Clapham Junction ■10	d																								
South Bermondsey	d				18 40			18 45										19 10				19 15			
Queens Rd Peckham	d				18 42			18 48										19 12				19 18			
Peckham Rye ■4	d				18a45			18 50		19 09	19a23							19a15				19 20	19 39	19a53	
Denmark Hill ■4	d							18 53		19 13												19 23	19 43		
London Blackfriars ■3 ⊖	a									19 23													19 53		
Clapham High Street ⊖	d							18 58														19 28			
Wandsworth Road	d							18 59														19 29			
Battersea Park ■4	d							19 02														19 32			
London Victoria ■15 ⊖	a							19 06														19 36			
Penge West	d	18 48				18 57	19 03								19 18					19 27	19 33				
Anerley	d	18 50				18 59	19 05								19 20					19 29	19 35				
Norwood Junction ■2	d	18 53				19 03	19 08							19 16	19 23					19 33	19 38				
West Croydon ■4 🚌	a	18 59					19 14							19 24	19 29						19 44				
East Croydon 🚌	a					19 07														19 37					

Table 178

Sundays

until 22 July

London Bridge to London Victoria - Croydon and East London Line

Network Diagram - see first Page of Table 177

		LO	SN	LO		LO	LO	SN	SN	LO	SN	SE	SN	LO		LO	SN	LO	LO	LO	SN	SN	LO	SN	
London Bridge [4] ⊖	d		19 24					19 36	19 39		19 41						19 54				20 06	20 09		20 11	
Highbury & Islington	a																								
	d			19 06		19 13				19 21				19 28				19 36	19 43				19 51		
Canonbury	d			19 08		19 15				19 23				19 30				19 38	19 45				19 53		
Dalston Junction Stn ELL	d	19 08		19 13		19 18	19 23			19 28				19 33		19 38		19 43	19 48	19 53			19 58		
Haggerston	d	19 09		19 14		19 19	19 24			19 29				19 34		19 39		19 44	19 49	19 54			19 59		
Hoxton	d	19 11		19 16		19 21	19 26			19 31				19 36		19 41		19 46	19 51	19 56			20 01		
Shoreditch High Street	d	19 14		19 19		19 24	19 29			19 34				19 39		19 44		19 49	19 54	19 59			20 04		
Whitechapel	d	19 16		19 21		19 26	19 31			19 36				19 41		19 46		19 51	19 56	20 01			20 06		
Shadwell	d	19 18		19 23		19 28	19 33			19 38				19 43		19 48		19 53	19 58	20 03			20 08		
Wapping	d	19 20		19 25		19 30	19 35			19 40				19 45		19 50		19 55	20 00	20 05			20 10		
Rotherhithe	d	19 22		19 27		19 32	19 37			19 42				19 47		19 52		19 57	20 02	20 07			20 12		
Canada Water	d	19 24		19 29		19 34	19 39			19 44				19 49		19 54		19 59	20 04	20 09			20 14		
Surrey Quays	d	19 25		19 30		19 35	19 40			19 45				19 50		19 55		20 00	20 05	20 10			20 15		
New Cross ELL	a	19 30					19 45									20 00				20 15					
New Cross Gate [4]	a		19 29	19 34		19 39			19 44	19 49				19 54			19 59	20 04	20 09			20 14	20 19		
	d		19 29	19 35		19 40			19 44	19 50				19 55			19 59	20 05	20 10			20 14	20 20		
Brockley	d		19 32	19 37		19 42			19 47	19 52				19 57			20 02	20 07	20 12			20 17	20 22		
Honor Oak Park	d		19 35	19 40		19 45			19 50	19 55				20 00			20 05	20 10	20 15			20 20	20 25		
Forest Hill [4]	d		19 37	19 43		19 48			19 52	19 58				20 03			20 07	20 13	20 18			20 22	20 28		
Sydenham	d		19 40	19 45		19 50			19 55	20 00				20 05			20 10	20 15	20 20			20 25	20 30		
Crystal Palace [4]	d					19a55							20 07	20a10					20a25						
Gipsy Hill	d												20 09												
West Norwood [4]	d												20 12												
Streatham Hill	d																								
Balham [4] ⊖	d																								
Wandsworth Common	d																								
Clapham Junction [10]	d																								
South Bermondsey	d							19 40			19 45										20 10			20 15	
Queens Rd Peckham	d							19 42			19 48										20 12			20 18	
Peckham Rye [4]	d							19a45			19 50	20 09	20a23								20a15			20 20	
Denmark Hill [4]	d										19 53	20 13												20 23	
London Blackfriars [3] ⊖	a											20 23													
Clapham High Street ⊖	d										19 58													20 28	
Wandsworth Road	d										19 59													20 29	
Battersea Park [4]	d										20 02													20 32	
London Victoria [15] ⊖	a										20 06													20 36	
Penge West	d			19 48					19 57	20 03								20 18				20 27	20 33		
Anerley	d			19 50					19 59	20 05								20 20				20 29	20 35		
Norwood Junction [2]	d		19 46	19 53					20 03	20 08							20 16	20 23				20 33	20 38		
West Croydon [4]	a		19 54	19 59						20 15							20 24	20 29					20 45		
East Croydon	a								20 07													20 37			

		SE	SN	LO	LO	SN	LO	LO	LO	SN		SN	LO	SN	SE	SN	LO	LO	SN	LO		LO	LO	SN	SN
London Bridge [4] ⊖	d					20 24				20 36		20 39		20 41					20 54					21 06	21 09
Highbury & Islington	a																								
	d			19 58			20 06	20 13					20 21				20 28			20 36		20 43			
Canonbury	d			20 00			20 08	20 15					20 23				20 30			20 38		20 45			
Dalston Junction Stn ELL	d			20 03	20 08		20 13	20 18	20 23				20 28				20 33	20 38		20 43		20 48	20 53		
Haggerston	d			20 04	20 09		20 14	20 19	20 24				20 29				20 34	20 39		20 44		20 49	20 54		
Hoxton	d			20 06	20 11		20 16	20 21	20 26				20 31				20 36	20 41		20 46		20 51	20 56		
Shoreditch High Street	d			20 09	20 14		20 19	20 24	20 29				20 34				20 39	20 44		20 49		20 54	20 59		
Whitechapel	d			20 11	20 16		20 21	20 26	20 31				20 36				20 41	20 46		20 51		20 56	21 01		
Shadwell	d			20 13	20 18		20 23	20 28	20 33				20 38				20 43	20 48		20 53		20 58	21 03		
Wapping	d			20 15	20 20		20 25	20 30	20 35				20 40				20 45	20 50		20 55		21 00	21 05		
Rotherhithe	d			20 17	20 22		20 27	20 32	20 37				20 42				20 47	20 52		20 57		21 02	21 07		
Canada Water	d			20 19	20 24		20 29	20 34	20 39				20 44				20 49	20 54		20 59		21 04	21 09		
Surrey Quays	d			20 20	20 25		20 30	20 35	20 40				20 45				20 50	20 55		21 00		21 05	21 10		
New Cross ELL	a				20 30				20 45									21 00					21 15		
New Cross Gate [4]	a			20 24		20 29	20 34	20 39				20 44	20 49				20 54		20 59	21 04		21 09			21 14
	d			20 25		20 29	20 35	20 40				20 44	20 50				20 55		20 59	21 05		21 10			21 14
Brockley	d			20 27		20 32	20 37	20 42				20 47	20 52				20 57		21 02	21 07		21 12			21 17
Honor Oak Park	d			20 30		20 35	20 40	20 45				20 50	20 55				21 00		21 05	21 10		21 15			21 20
Forest Hill [4]	d			20 33		20 37	20 43	20 48				20 52	20 58				21 03		21 07	21 13		21 18			21 22
Sydenham	d			20 35		20 40	20 45	20 50				20 55	21 00				21 05		21 10	21 15		21 20			21 25
Crystal Palace [4]	d		20 37	20a40				20a55								21 07	21a10					21a25			
Gipsy Hill	d		20 39													21 09									
West Norwood [4]	d		20 42													21 12									
Streatham Hill	d																								
Balham [4] ⊖	d																								
Wandsworth Common	d																								
Clapham Junction [10]	d																								
South Bermondsey	d									20 40				20 45										21 10	
Queens Rd Peckham	d									20 42				20 48										21 12	
Peckham Rye [4]	d	20 39	20a53							20a45				20 50	21 09	21a23								21a15	
Denmark Hill [4]	d	20 43												20 53	21 13										
London Blackfriars [3] ⊖	a	20 53													21 23										
Clapham High Street ⊖	d													20 58											
Wandsworth Road	d													20 59											
Battersea Park [4]	d													21 02											
London Victoria [15] ⊖	a													21 06											
Penge West	d						20 48					20 57	21 03							21 18					21 27
Anerley	d						20 50					20 59	21 05							21 20					21 29
Norwood Junction [2]	d					20 46	20 53					21 03	21 08						21 16	21 23					21 33
West Croydon [4]	a					20 54	20 59						21 15						21 24	21 29					
East Croydon	a											21 07													21 37

Table 178

Sundays
until 22 July

London Bridge to London Victoria - Croydon and East London Line

Network Diagram - see first Page of Table 177

Station		LO	SN	SE	SN	LO		LO	SN	LO	LO	LO	SN	SN	LO	SN		SE	SN	LO	LO	SN	LO	LO	LO
London Bridge [4] ⊖	d		21 11						21 24				21 36	21 39		21 41						21 54			
Highbury & Islington	a																								
	d	20 51				20 58				21 06	21 13				21 21					21 28			21 36	21 43	
Canonbury	d	20 53				21 00				21 08	21 15				21 23					21 30			21 38	21 45	
Dalston Junction Stn ELL	d	20 58				21 03		21 08		21 13	21 18	21 23			21 28					21 33	21 38		21 43	21 48	21 53
Haggerston	d	20 59				21 04		21 09		21 14	21 19	21 24			21 29					21 34	21 39		21 44	21 49	21 54
Hoxton	d	21 01				21 06		21 11		21 16	21 21	21 26			21 31					21 36	21 41		21 46	21 51	21 56
Shoreditch High Street	d	21 04				21 09		21 14		21 19	21 24	21 29			21 34					21 39	21 44		21 49	21 54	21 59
Whitechapel	d	21 06				21 11		21 16		21 21	21 26	21 31			21 36					21 41	21 46		21 51	21 56	22 01
Shadwell	d	21 08				21 13		21 18		21 23	21 28	21 33			21 38					21 43	21 48		21 53	21 58	22 03
Wapping	d	21 10				21 15		21 20		21 25	21 30	21 35			21 40					21 45	21 50		21 55	22 00	22 05
Rotherhithe	d	21 12				21 17		21 22		21 27	21 32	21 37			21 42					21 47	21 52		21 57	22 02	22 07
Canada Water	d	21 14				21 19		21 24		21 29	21 34	21 39			21 44					21 49	21 54		21 59	22 04	22 09
Surrey Quays	d	21 15				21 20		21 25		21 30	21 35	21 40			21 45					21 50	21 55		22 00	22 05	22 10
New Cross ELL	a							21 30				21 45									22 00				22 16
New Cross Gate [4]	a	21 19				21 24			21 29	21 34	21 39			21 44	21 49					21 54		21 59	22 04	22 09	
	d	21 20				21 25			21 29	21 35	21 40			21 44	21 50					21 55		21 59	22 05	22 10	
Brockley	d	21 22				21 27			21 32	21 37	21 42			21 47	21 52					21 57		22 02	22 07	22 12	
Honor Oak Park	d	21 25				21 30			21 35	21 40	21 45			21 50	21 55					22 00		22 05	22 10	22 15	
Forest Hill [4]	d	21 28				21 33			21 37	21 43	21 48			21 52	21 58					22 03		22 07	22 13	22 18	
Sydenham	d	21 30				21 35			21 40	21 45	21 50			21 55	22 00					22 05		22 10	22 15	22 20	
Crystal Palace [4]	d				21 37	21a40					21a55								22 07	22a10				22a25	
Gipsy Hill	d				21 39														22 09						
West Norwood [4]	d				21 42														22 12						
Streatham Hill	d																								
Balham [4] ⊖	d																								
Wandsworth Common	d																								
Clapham Junction [10]	d																								
South Bermondsey	d		21 15										21 40			21 45									
Queens Rd Peckham	d		21 18										21 42			21 48									
Peckham Rye [4]	d		21 20	21 39	21a53								21a45			21 50		22 09	22a23						
Denmark Hill [4]	d		21 23	21 43												21 53		22 13							
London Blackfriars [3] ⊖	a			21 53														22 23							
Clapham High Street ⊖	d		21 28													21 58									
Wandsworth Road	d		21 29													21 59									
Battersea Park [4]	d		21 32													22 02									
London Victoria [15] ⊖	a		21 36													22 06									
Penge West	d	21 33								21 48				21 57	22 03								22 18		
Anerley	d	21 35								21 50				21 59	22 05								22 20		
Norwood Junction [2]	d	21 38							21 46	21 53				22 03	22 08							22 16	22 23		
West Croydon [4]	a	21 45							21 54	21 59					22 15							22 24	22 29		
East Croydon	a													22 07											

Station		SN		SN	LO	LO	SN	SE	SN	SN	LO	SN		LO	LO	SN	SE	SN	SN	LO	SN	LO		LO	SN
London Bridge [4] ⊖	d	22 06		22 09			22 11		22 36			22 39				22 41		23 06			23 09				23 11
Highbury & Islington	a																								
	d				21 51						22 13			22 23						22 43		22 53			
Canonbury	d				21 53						22 15			22 25						22 45		22 55			
Dalston Junction Stn ELL	d				21 58	22 08					22 18			22 28	22 38					22 48		22 58		23 08	
Haggerston	d				21 59	22 09					22 19			22 29	22 39					22 49		22 59		23 09	
Hoxton	d				22 01	22 11					22 21			22 31	22 41					22 51		23 01		23 11	
Shoreditch High Street	d				22 04	22 14					22 24			22 34	22 44					22 54		23 04		23 14	
Whitechapel	d				22 06	22 16					22 26			22 36	22 46					22 56		23 06		23 16	
Shadwell	d				22 08	22 18					22 28			22 38	22 48					22 58		23 08		23 18	
Wapping	d				22 10	22 20					22 30			22 40	22 50					23 00		23 10		23 20	
Rotherhithe	d				22 12	22 22					22 32			22 42	22 52					23 02		23 12		23 22	
Canada Water	d				22 14	22 24					22 34			22 44	22 54					23 04		23 14		23 24	
Surrey Quays	d				22 15	22 25					22 35			22 45	22 55					23 05		23 15		23 25	
New Cross ELL	a					22 30									23 00									23 30	
New Cross Gate [4]	a			22 14	22 19						22 39	22 44		22 49						23 09	23 14	23 19			
	d			22 14	22 20						22 40	22 44		22 50						23 10	23 14	23 20			
Brockley	d			22 17	22 22						22 42	22 47		22 52						23 12	23 17	23 22			
Honor Oak Park	d			22 20	22 25						22 45	22 50		22 55						23 15	23 20	23 25			
Forest Hill [4]	d			22 22	22 28						22 48	22 52		22 58						23 18	23 22	23 28			
Sydenham	d			22 25	22 30						22 50	22 55		23 00						23 20	23 25	23 30			
Crystal Palace [4]	d									22 37	22a55								23 07	23a25					
Gipsy Hill	d									22 39									23 09						
West Norwood [4]	d									22 42									23 12						
Streatham Hill	d																								
Balham [4] ⊖	d																								
Wandsworth Common	d																								
Clapham Junction [10]	d																								
South Bermondsey	d	22 10					22 15		22 40							22 45		23 10							23 15
Queens Rd Peckham	d	22 12					22 18		22 42							22 48		23 12							23 18
Peckham Rye [4]	d	22a15					22 20	22 39	22a45	22a53						22 50	23 09	23a15	23a23						23 20
Denmark Hill [4]	d						22 23	22 43								22 53	23 13								23 23
London Blackfriars [3] ⊖	a							22 53									23 23								
Clapham High Street ⊖	d						22 28									22 58									23 28
Wandsworth Road	d						22 29									22 59									23 29
Battersea Park [4]	d						22 32									23 02									23 32
London Victoria [15] ⊖	a						22 36									23 06									23 37
Penge West	d			22 27	22 33							22 57		23 03							23 27	23 33			
Anerley	d			22 29	22 35							22 59		23 05							23 29	23 35			
Norwood Junction [2]	d			22 33	22 38							23 03		23 08							23 33	23 38			
West Croydon [4]	a				22 45									23 14								23 44			
East Croydon	a			22 37								23 07									23 38				

Sundays
until 22 July

London Bridge to London Victoria - Croydon and East London Line

Network Diagram - see first Page of Table 177

		SN	SN	LO	SN	LO
London Bridge 4 ⊖	d				23 39	
Highbury & Islington	a					
	d			23 13		23 23
Canonbury	d			23 15		23 25
Dalston Junction Stn ELL	d			23 18		23 28
Haggerston	d			23 19		23 29
Hoxton	d			23 21		23 31
Shoreditch High Street	d			23 24		23 34
Whitechapel	d			23 26		23 36
Shadwell	d			23 28		23 38
Wapping	d			23 30		23 40
Rotherhithe	d			23 32		23 42
Canada Water	d			23 34		23 44
Surrey Quays	d			23 35		23 45
New Cross ELL	a					
New Cross Gate 4	a			23 39	23 44	23 49
	d			23 40	23 44	23 50
Brockley	d			23 42	23 47	23 52
Honor Oak Park	d			23 45	23 50	23 55
Forest Hill 4	d			23 48	23 52	23 58
Sydenham	d			23 50	23 55	00 01
Crystal Palace 4	d	23 37	23 50	23a55		
Gipsy Hill	d	23 39				
West Norwood 4	d	23 42				
Streatham Hill	d					
Balham 4 ⊖	d					
Wandsworth Common	d					
Clapham Junction 10	d					
South Bermondsey	d					
Queens Rd Peckham	d					
Peckham Rye 4	d	23a53				
Denmark Hill 4	d					
London Blackfriars 3 ⊖	a					
Clapham High Street ⊖	d					
Wandsworth Road	d					
Battersea Park 4	d					
London Victoria 15 ⊖	a					
Penge West	d				23 57	00 03
Anerley	d				23 59	00 05
Norwood Junction 2	d		23 55		00 03	00 08
West Croydon 4	a		23 59			00 15
East Croydon	a				00 06	

Sundays
29 July to 12 August

		SN	SN	LO	SN	LO	SN	LO	LO	SN		SN	LO	SN	LO	LO	SN	LO	SN	SN		SN	LO	LO	LO
London Bridge 4 ⊖	d	23p22	23p36				23p52			00 03		00 06							00 33	00 36					
Highbury & Islington	a																								
	d			23p18		23p25		23p33	23p40				23p48		23p55	00 03		00 10					00 18	00 25	00 33
Canonbury	d			23p20		23p27		23p35	23p42				23p50		23p57	00 05		00 12					00 20	00 27	00 35
Dalston Junction Stn ELL	d			23p25		23p30		23p38	23p45				23p55		00 01	00 09		00 15					00 25	00 30	00 40
Haggerston	d			23p26		23p31		23p39	23p46				23p56		00 02	00 10		00 16					00 26	00 31	00 41
Hoxton	d			23p28		23p33		23p41	23p48				23p58		00 04	00 12		00 18					00 28	00 33	00 43
Shoreditch High Street	d			23p31		23p36		23p44	23p51				00 01		00 07	00 15		00 21					00 31	00 36	00 46
Whitechapel	d			23p33		23p38		23p46	23p53				00 03		00 09	00 17		00 23					00 33	00 38	00 48
Shadwell	d			23p35		23p40		23p48	23p55				00 05		00 11	00 19		00 25					00 35	00 40	00 50
Wapping	d			23p37		23p42		23p50	23p57				00 07		00 13	00 21		00 27					00 37	00 42	00 52
Rotherhithe	d			23p39		23p44		23p52	23p59				00 09		00 15	00 23		00 29					00 39	00 44	00 54
Canada Water	d			23p41		23p46		23p54	00 02				00 11		00 17	00 25		00 31					00 41	00 46	00 56
Surrey Quays	d			23p42		23p47		23p55	00 03				00 12		00 18	00 26		00 32					00 42	00 47	00 57
New Cross ELL	a																								
New Cross Gate 4	a	23p27	23p41	23p46		23p51	23p57	23p58	00 07			00 11	00 16		00 22	00 30		00 36		00 41			00 47	00 51	01 02
	d	23p27	23p41	23p47		23p52	23p57	23p59	00 08			00 11	00 17		00 23	00 31		00 37		00 41			00 47	00 52	01 03
Brockley	d	23p30	23p44	23p49		23p54	00 01	00 03	00 10			00 14	00 19		00 25	00 33		00 39		00 44			00 49	00 54	01 05
Honor Oak Park	d	23p33	23p47	23p52		23p57	00 04	00 06	00 13			00 17	00 22		00 28	00 36		00 42		00 47			00 52	00 57	01 08
Forest Hill 4	d	23p35	23p49	23p55		23p59	00 06	00 09	00 16			00 19	00 25		00 31	00 39		00 45		00 49			00 55	00 59	01 11
Sydenham	d	23p38	23p52	23p57		00 02	00 09	00 11	00 18			00 22	00 27		00 33	00 41		00 47		00 52			00 57	01 02	01 13
Crystal Palace 4	d	23p43			00 03	00a07	00 13		00a23					00 33	00a38		00 47	00a52				01 03		01a07	
Gipsy Hill	d	23p45					00 15																		
West Norwood 4	d	23p48					00 18																		
Streatham Hill	d	23p52					00 22																		
Balham 4 ⊖	d	23p55					00 26																		
Wandsworth Common	d	23p57					00 28																		
Clapham Junction 10	d	00 02					00 32																		
South Bermondsey	d									00 07									00 37						
Queens Rd Peckham	d									00 09									00 39						
Peckham Rye 4	d									00 12									00 42						
Denmark Hill 4	d																								
London Blackfriars 3 ⊖	a																								
Clapham High Street ⊖	d																								
Wandsworth Road	d																								
Battersea Park 4	d	00 05					00 35																		
London Victoria 15 ⊖	a	00 10					00 42																		
Penge West	d		23p54	00 01				00 14				00 24	00 30			00 44				00 54			01 00		01 16
Anerley	d		23p56	00 03				00 16				00 26	00 32			00 46				00 56			01 02		01 18
Norwood Junction 2	d		23p59	00 06	00 09			00 19		00a34		00 30	00 35	00 38		00 49	00 52		01a04	01 00		01 08	01 10		01 21
West Croydon 4	a			00 13	00 14			00 26					00 42	00 43		00 56	00 58					01 13	01 18		01 28
East Croydon	a		00 03									00 33								01 03					

Table 178

Sundays

29 July to 12 August

London Bridge to London Victoria - Croydon and East London Line

Network Diagram - see first Page of Table 177

		LO	LO	LO	LO	LO		LO	SE	LO	LO	LO	LO	SE	LO	LO		LO	LO	LO	SE	SN	SE	LO	SN
London Bridge 4 ⊖	d																					07 11			
Highbury & Islington	a																								
	d	00 40	00 48	00 55	01 03	01 10		01 25				05 38						05 58	06 08						
Canonbury	d	00 42	00 50	00 57	01 05	01 12		01 27				05 40						06 00	06 10						
Dalston Junction Stn ELL	d	00 45	00 55	01 00	01 10	01 15		01 32				05 43	05 53					06 03	06 13	06 23					
Haggerston	d	00 46	00 56	01 01	01 11	01 16		01 33				05 44	05 54					06 04	06 14	06 24					
Hoxton	d	00 48	00 58	01 03	01 13	01 18		01 35				05 46	05 56					06 06	06 16	06 26					
Shoreditch High Street	d	00 51	01 01	01 06	01 16	01 21		01 38				05 49	05 59					06 09	06 19	06 29					
Whitechapel	d	00 53	01 03	01 08	01 18	01 23		01 40				05 51	06 01					06 11	06 21	06 31					
Shadwell	d	00 55	01 05	01 10	01 20	01 25		01 42				05 53	06 03					06 13	06 23	06 33					
Wapping	d	00 57	01 07	01 12	01 22	01 27		01 44				05 55	06 05					06 15	06 25	06 35					
Rotherhithe	d	00 59	01 09	01 14	01 24	01 29		01 46				05 57	06 07					06 17	06 27	06 37					
Canada Water	d	01 01	01 11	01 16	01 26	01 31		01 48				05 59	06 09					06 19	06 29	06 39					
Surrey Quays	d	01 02	01 12	01 17	01 27	01 32		01 49				06 00	06 10					06 20	06 30	06 40					
New Cross ELL	a												06 15							06 45					
New Cross Gate 4	a	01 06	01 16	01 21	01 31	01 36		01 53				06 04						06 24	06 34						
	d	01 07	01 17	01 22	01 32	01 37		01 54		05 50	05 55	06 05			06 10	06 20		06 25	06 35					06 40	
Brockley	d	01 09	01 19	01 24	01 34	01 39		01 56		05 52	05 57	06 07			06 12	06 22		06 27	06 37					06 42	
Honor Oak Park	d	01 12	01 22	01 27	01 37	01 42		01 59		05 55	06 00	06 10			06 15	06 25		06 30	06 40					06 45	
Forest Hill 4	d	01 15	01 25	01 30	01 40	01 45		02 02		05 58	06 03	06 13			06 18	06 28		06 33	06 43					06 48	
Sydenham	d	01 17	01 27	01 32	01 42	01 47		02 04		06 00	06 05	06 15			06 20	06 30		06 35	06 45					06 50	
Crystal Palace 4	d	01a22		01a37		01a52					06a10				06a25			06a40						06a55	07 07
Gipsy Hill	d																								07 09
West Norwood 4	d																								07 12
Streatham Hill	d																								
Balham 4 ⊖	d																								
Wandsworth Common	d																								
Clapham Junction 10	d																								
South Bermondsey	d																					07 15			
Queens Rd Peckham	d																					07 18			
Peckham Rye 4	d								06 20					06 50							07 17	07 20	07 20		07a23
Denmark Hill 4	d								06 24					06 54							07 21	07 23	07 24		
London Blackfriars 3 ⊖	a								06 34					07 04									07 34		
Clapham High Street ⊖	d																					07 28			
Wandsworth Road	d																					07 29			
Battersea Park 4	d																					07 32			
London Victoria 15 ⊖	a																				07 33	07 36			
Penge West	d		01 30		01 45			02 07		06 03		06 18				06 33			06 48						
Anerley	d		01 32		01 47			02 09		06 05		06 20				06 35			06 50						
Norwood Junction 2	d		01 35		01 50			02 12		06 08		06 23				06 38			06 53						
West Croydon 4 🚋	a		01 42		01 57			02 19		06 16		06 33				06 44			06 59						
East Croydon 🚋	a																								

		LO		LO	LO	LO	LO	LO	LO	SN	LO	LO		SN	LO	LO	LO	SN	SN	LO	SE	SN		SE	SN
London Bridge 4 ⊖	d													07 24				07 36	07 39			07 41			
Highbury & Islington	a																								
	d			06 28		06 36	06 43		06 51		06 58				07 06	07 13				07 21					
Canonbury	d			06 30		06 38	06 45		06 53		07 00				07 08	07 15				07 23					
Dalston Junction Stn ELL	d			06 33	06 38	06 43	06 48	06 53	06 58		07 03	07 08			07 13	07 18	07 23			07 28					
Haggerston	d			06 34	06 39	06 44	06 49	06 54	06 59		07 04	07 09			07 14	07 19	07 24			07 29					
Hoxton	d			06 36	06 41	06 46	06 51	06 56	07 01		07 06	07 11			07 16	07 21	07 26			07 31					
Shoreditch High Street	d			06 39	06 44	06 49	06 54	06 59	07 04		07 09	07 14			07 19	07 24	07 29			07 34					
Whitechapel	d			06 41	06 46	06 51	06 56	07 01	07 06		07 11	07 16			07 21	07 26	07 31			07 36					
Shadwell	d			06 43	06 48	06 53	06 58	07 03	07 08		07 13	07 18			07 23	07 28	07 33			07 38					
Wapping	d			06 45	06 50	06 55	07 00	07 05	07 10		07 15	07 20			07 25	07 30	07 35			07 40					
Rotherhithe	d			06 47	06 52	06 57	07 02	07 07	07 12		07 17	07 22			07 27	07 32	07 37			07 42					
Canada Water	d			06 49	06 54	06 59	07 04	07 09	07 14		07 19	07 24			07 29	07 34	07 39			07 44					
Surrey Quays	d			06 50	06 55	07 00	07 05	07 10	07 15		07 20	07 25			07 30	07 35	07 40			07 45					
New Cross ELL	a				07 00			07 15				07 30					07 45								
New Cross Gate 4	a			06 54		07 03	07 09		07 18		07 24			07 29	07 34	07 39			07 44	07 48					
	d	06 50		06 55		07 05	07 10		07 20		07 25			07 29	07 35	07 40			07 44	07 50					
Brockley	d	06 52		06 57		07 07	07 12		07 22		07 27			07 32	07 37	07 42			07 47	07 52					
Honor Oak Park	d	06 55		07 00		07 10	07 15		07 25		07 30			07 35	07 40	07 45			07 50	07 55					
Forest Hill 4	d	06 58		07 03		07 13	07 18		07 28		07 33			07 37	07 43	07 48			07 52	07 58					
Sydenham	d	07 00		07 05		07 15	07 20		07 30		07 35			07 40	07 45	07 50			07 55	08 00					
Crystal Palace 4	d			07a10			07a25			07 37	07a40					07a55									08 07
Gipsy Hill	d									07 39															08 09
West Norwood 4	d									07 42															08 12
Streatham Hill	d																								
Balham 4 ⊖	d																								
Wandsworth Common	d																								
Clapham Junction 10	d																								
South Bermondsey	d																	07 40				07 45			
Queens Rd Peckham	d																	07 42				07 48			
Peckham Rye 4	d									07a53								07a45			07 47	07 50		07 50	08a23
Denmark Hill 4	d																				07 51	07 53		07 54	
London Blackfriars 3 ⊖	a																							08 04	
Clapham High Street ⊖	d																					07 58			
Wandsworth Road	d																					07 59			
Battersea Park 4	d																					08 02			
London Victoria 15 ⊖	a																				08 03	08 06			
Penge West	d	07 03					07 18								07 48				07 57	08 03					
Anerley	d	07 05					07 20								07 50				07 59	08 05					
Norwood Junction 2	d	07 08					07 23							07 48	07 53				08 03	08 08					
West Croydon 4 🚋	a	07 14					07 35		07 46					07 55	08 00					08 15					
East Croydon 🚋	a																		08 07						

Table 178

Sundays

29 July to 12 August

London Bridge to London Victoria - Croydon and East London Line

Network Diagram - see first Page of Table 177

		LO	LO	SN	LO	LO	LO	SN		SN	LO	SE	SN	SE	SN	LO	LO	SN		LO	LO	LO	SN	SN	LO
London Bridge 4 ⊖	d			07 54				08 06		08 09			08 11					08 24					08 36	08 39	
Highbury & Islington	a																								
	d	07 28			07 36	07 43					07 51					07 58				08 06	08 13				08 21
Canonbury	d	07 30			07 38	07 45					07 53					08 00				08 08	08 15				08 23
Dalston Junction Stn ELL	d	07 33	07 38		07 43	07 48	07 53				07 58					08 03	08 08			08 13	08 18	08 23			08 28
Haggerston	d	07 34	07 39		07 44	07 49	07 54				07 59					08 04	08 09			08 14	08 19	08 24			08 29
Hoxton	d	07 36	07 41		07 46	07 51	07 56				08 01					08 06	08 11			08 16	08 21	08 26			08 31
Shoreditch High Street	d	07 39	07 44		07 49	07 54	07 59				08 04					08 09	08 14			08 19	08 24	08 29			08 34
Whitechapel	d	07 41	07 46		07 51	07 56	08 01				08 06					08 11	08 16			08 21	08 26	08 31			08 36
Shadwell	d	07 43	07 48		07 53	07 58	08 03				08 08					08 13	08 18			08 23	08 28	08 33			08 38
Wapping	d	07 45	07 50		07 55	08 00	08 05				08 10					08 15	08 20			08 25	08 30	08 35			08 40
Rotherhithe	d	07 47	07 52		07 57	08 02	08 07				08 12					08 17	08 22			08 27	08 32	08 37			08 42
Canada Water	d	07 49	07 54		07 59	08 04	08 09				08 14					08 19	08 24			08 29	08 34	08 39			08 44
Surrey Quays	d	07 50	07 55		08 00	08 05	08 10				08 15					08 20	08 25			08 30	08 35	08 40			08 45
New Cross ELL	a		08 00				08 15										08 30					08 45			
New Cross Gate 4	a	07 54		07 59	08 04	08 09				08 14	08 19					08 24		08 29		08 34	08 39			08 44	08 49
	d	07 55		07 59	08 05	08 10				08 14	08 20					08 25		08 29		08 35	08 40			08 44	08 50
Brockley	d	07 57		08 02	08 07	08 12				08 17	08 22					08 27		08 32		08 37	08 42			08 47	08 52
Honor Oak Park	d	08 00		08 05	08 10	08 15				08 20	08 25					08 30		08 35		08 40	08 45			08 50	08 55
Forest Hill 4	d	08 03		08 07	08 13	08 18				08 22	08 28					08 33		08 37		08 43	08 48			08 52	08 58
Sydenham	d	08 05		08 10	08 15	08 20				08 25	08 30					08 35		08 40		08 45	08 50			08 55	09 00
Crystal Palace 4	d	08a10				08a25									08 37	08a40					08a55				
Gipsy Hill	d														08 39										
West Norwood 4	d														08 42										
Streatham Hill	d																								
Balham 4 ⊖	d																								
Wandsworth Common	d																								
Clapham Junction 10	d																								
South Bermondsey	d							08 10					08 15										08 40		
Queens Rd Peckham	d							08 12					08 18										08 42		
Peckham Rye 4	d							08a15				08 17	08 20	08 20	08a53								08a45		
Denmark Hill 4	d											08 21	08 23	08 24											
London Blackfriars 3 ⊖	a													08 34											
Clapham High Street ⊖	d												08 28												
Wandsworth Road	d												08 29												
Battersea Park 4	d												08 32												
London Victoria 15 ⊖	a											08 33	08 36												
Penge West	d				08 18					08 27	08 33									08 48				08 57	09 03
Anerley	d				08 20					08 29	08 35									08 50				08 59	09 05
Norwood Junction 2	d			08 16	08 23					08 33	08 38							08 46		08 53				09 03	09 08
West Croydon 4	a			08 24	08 29						08 47							08 54		08 59					09 15
East Croydon	a									08 37														09 07	

		SE	SN	SE		SN	LO	LO	SN	LO	LO	LO	SN	SN		LO	SE	SN	SE	SN	LO	LO	SN	LO	LO
London Bridge 4 ⊖	d		08 41						08 54				09 06	09 09				09 11					09 24		
Highbury & Islington	a																								
	d						08 28			08 36	08 43					08 51					08 58			09 06	09 13
Canonbury	d						08 30			08 38	08 45					08 53					09 00			09 08	09 15
Dalston Junction Stn ELL	d						08 33	08 38		08 43	08 48	08 53				08 58					09 03	09 08		09 13	09 18
Haggerston	d						08 34	08 39		08 44	08 49	08 54				08 59					09 04	09 09		09 14	09 19
Hoxton	d						08 36	08 41		08 46	08 51	08 56				09 01					09 06	09 11		09 16	09 21
Shoreditch High Street	d						08 39	08 44		08 49	08 54	08 59				09 04					09 09	09 14		09 19	09 24
Whitechapel	d						08 41	08 46		08 51	08 56	09 01				09 06					09 11	09 16		09 21	09 26
Shadwell	d						08 43	08 48		08 53	08 58	09 03				09 08					09 13	09 18		09 23	09 28
Wapping	d						08 45	08 50		08 55	09 00	09 05				09 10					09 15	09 20		09 25	09 30
Rotherhithe	d						08 47	08 52		08 57	09 02	09 07				09 12					09 17	09 22		09 27	09 32
Canada Water	d						08 49	08 54		08 59	09 04	09 09				09 14					09 19	09 24		09 29	09 34
Surrey Quays	d						08 50	08 55		09 00	09 05	09 10				09 15					09 20	09 25		09 30	09 35
New Cross ELL	a							09 00				09 15										09 30			
New Cross Gate 4	a						08 54		08 59	09 04	09 09			09 14		09 19					09 24		09 29	09 33	09 39
	d						08 55		08 59	09 05	09 10			09 14		09 20					09 25		09 29	09 34	09 40
Brockley	d						08 57		09 02	09 07	09 12			09 17		09 22					09 27		09 32	09 35	09 42
Honor Oak Park	d						09 00		09 05	09 10	09 15			09 20		09 25					09 30		09 35	09 38	09 45
Forest Hill 4	d						09 03		09 07	09 13	09 18			09 22		09 28					09 33		09 37	09 42	09 48
Sydenham	d						09 05		09 10	09 15	09 20			09 25		09 30					09 35		09 40	09 43	09 50
Crystal Palace 4	d					09 07	09a10				09a25									09 37	09a40				09a55
Gipsy Hill	d					09 09														09 39					
West Norwood 4	d					09 12														09 42					
Streatham Hill	d																								
Balham 4 ⊖	d																								
Wandsworth Common	d																								
Clapham Junction 10	d																								
South Bermondsey	d		08 45										09 10					09 15							
Queens Rd Peckham	d		08 48										09 12					09 18							
Peckham Rye 4	d	08 47	08 50	08 50		09a23							09a15				09 17	09 20	09 20	09a53					
Denmark Hill 4	d	08 51	08 53	08 54													09 21	09 23	09 24						
London Blackfriars 3 ⊖	a			09 04															09 34						
Clapham High Street ⊖	d		08 58															09 28							
Wandsworth Road	d		08 59															09 29							
Battersea Park 4	d		09 02															09 32							
London Victoria 15 ⊖	a	09 03	09 06														09 33	09 36							
Penge West	d									09 18				09 27		09 33								09 47	
Anerley	d									09 20				09 29		09 35								09 49	
Norwood Junction 2	d								09 16	09 23				09 33		09 38							09 46	09 52	
West Croydon 4	a								09 24	09 29						09 45							09 54	09 59	
East Croydon	a													09 37											

Table 178

Sundays

29 July to 12 August

London Bridge to London Victoria - Croydon and East London Line

Network Diagram - see first Page of Table 177

		LO	SN	SN	LO	SE	SN	SE	SN	LO		LO	SN	LO	LO	LO	SN	SN	LO	SE		SN	SE	SN
London Bridge 4 ⊖	d		09 36	09 39			09 41						09 54				10 06	10 09				10 11		
Highbury & Islington	a																							
	d				09 21					09 28				09 36	09 43				09 51					
Canonbury	d				09 23					09 30				09 38	09 45				09 53					
Dalston Junction Stn ELL	d	09 23			09 28					09 33		09 38		09 43	09 48	09 53			09 58					
Haggerston	d	09 24			09 29					09 34		09 39		09 44	09 49	09 54			09 59					
Hoxton	d	09 26			09 31					09 36		09 41		09 46	09 51	09 56			10 01					
Shoreditch High Street	d	09 29			09 34					09 39		09 44		09 49	09 54	09 59			10 04					
Whitechapel	d	09 31			09 36					09 41		09 46		09 51	09 56	10 01			10 06					
Shadwell	d	09 33			09 38					09 43		09 48		09 53	09 58	10 03			10 08					
Wapping	d	09 35			09 40					09 45		09 50		09 55	10 00	10 05			10 10					
Rotherhithe	d	09 37			09 42					09 47		09 52		09 57	10 02	10 07			10 12					
Canada Water	d	09 39			09 44					09 49		09 54		09 59	10 04	10 09			10 14					
Surrey Quays	d	09 40			09 45					09 50		09 55		10 00	10 05	10 10			10 15					
New Cross ELL	a	09 45										10 00				10 15								
New Cross Gate 4	a			09 44	09 49					09 54			09 59	10 04	10 09			10 14	10 19					
	d			09 44	09 50					09 55			09 59	10 05	10 10			10 14	10 20					
Brockley	d			09 47	09 52					09 57			10 02	10 07	10 12			10 17	10 22					
Honor Oak Park	d			09 50	09 55					10 00			10 05	10 10	10 15			10 20	10 25					
Forest Hill 4	d			09 52	09 58					10 03			10 07	10 13	10 18			10 22	10 28					
Sydenham	d			09 55	10 00					10 05			10 10	10 15	10 20			10 25	10 30					
Crystal Palace 4	d								10 07	10a10					10a25									10 37
Gipsy Hill	d								10 09															10 39
West Norwood 4	d								10 12															10 42
Streatham Hill	d																							
Balham 4 ⊖	d																							
Wandsworth Common	d																							
Clapham Junction 10	d																							
South Bermondsey	d		09 40				09 45										10 10					10 15		
Queens Rd Peckham	d		09 42				09 48										10 12					10 18		
Peckham Rye 4	d		09a45			09 47	09 50	09 50	10a23								10a15			10 17		10 20	10 20	10a53
Denmark Hill 4	d					09 51	09 53	09 54												10 21		10 23	10 24	
London Blackfriars 3 ⊖	a							10 04															10 34	
Clapham High Street ⊖	d						09 58															10 28		
Wandsworth Road	d						09 59															10 29		
Battersea Park 4	d						10 02															10 32		
London Victoria 15 ⊖	a					10 03	10 06													10 33		10 36		
Penge West	d			09 57	10 03									10 18				10 27	10 33					
Anerley	d			09 59	10 05									10 20				10 29	10 35					
Norwood Junction 2	d			10 03	10 08								10 16	10 23				10 33	10 38					
West Croydon 4	a				10 15								10 24	10 29					10 45					
East Croydon	a			10 07														10 37						

		LO	LO	SN	LO		LO		LO	LO	SN	SN	LO	SE	SN	SE	SN		LO	LO	SN	LO	LO	LO
London Bridge 4 ⊖	d			10 24							16 36	16 39			16 41						16 54			
Highbury & Islington	a																							
	d	09 58			10 06		16 06		16 13				16 21						16 28			16 36	16 43	
Canonbury	d	10 00			10 08		16 08		16 15				16 23						16 30			16 38	16 45	
Dalston Junction Stn ELL	d	10 03	10 08		10 13		16 13		16 18	16 23			16 28						16 33	16 38		16 43	16 48	16 53
Haggerston	d	10 04	10 09		10 14		16 14		16 19	16 24			16 29						16 34	16 39		16 44	16 49	16 54
Hoxton	d	10 06	10 11		10 16		16 16		16 21	16 26			16 31						16 36	16 41		16 46	16 51	16 56
Shoreditch High Street	d	10 09	10 14		10 19		16 19		16 24	16 29			16 34						16 39	16 44		16 49	16 54	16 59
Whitechapel	d	10 11	10 16		10 21		16 21		16 26	16 31			16 36						16 41	16 46		16 51	16 56	17 01
Shadwell	d	10 13	10 18		10 23		16 23		16 28	16 33			16 38						16 43	16 48		16 53	16 58	17 03
Wapping	d	10 15	10 20		10 25		16 25		16 30	16 35			16 40						16 45	16 50		16 55	17 00	17 05
Rotherhithe	d	10 17	10 22		10 27		16 27		16 32	16 37			16 42						16 47	16 52		16 57	17 02	17 07
Canada Water	d	10 19	10 24		10 29		16 29		16 34	16 39			16 44						16 49	16 54		16 59	17 04	17 09
Surrey Quays	d	10 20	10 25		10 30		16 30		16 35	16 40			16 45						16 50	16 55		17 00	17 05	17 10
New Cross ELL	a		10 30							16 45										17 00				17 15
New Cross Gate 4	a	10 24		10 29	10 34		16 34		16 39			16 44	16 49						16 54		16 59	17 04	17 09	
	d	10 25		10 29	10 35		16 35		16 40			16 44	16 50						16 55		16 59	17 05	17 10	
Brockley	d	10 27		10 32	10 37	and at	16 37		16 42			16 47	16 52						16 57		17 02	17 07	17 12	
Honor Oak Park	d	10 30		10 35	10 40	the same	16 40		16 45			16 50	16 55						17 00		17 05	17 10	17 15	
Forest Hill 4	d	10 33		10 37	10 43	minutes	16 43		16 48			16 52	16 58						17 03		17 07	17 13	17 18	
Sydenham	d	10 35		10 40	10 45	past	16 45		16 50			16 55	17 00						17 05		17 10	17 15	17 20	
Crystal Palace 4	d	10a40				each			16a55								17 07		17a10				17a25	
Gipsy Hill	d					hour until											17 09							
West Norwood 4	d																17 12							
Streatham Hill	d																							
Balham 4 ⊖	d																							
Wandsworth Common	d																							
Clapham Junction 10	d																							
South Bermondsey	d										16 40				16 45									
Queens Rd Peckham	d										16 42				16 48									
Peckham Rye 4	d										16a45			16 47	16 50	16 50	17a23							
Denmark Hill 4	d													16 51	16 53	16 54								
London Blackfriars 3 ⊖	a															17 04								
Clapham High Street ⊖	d														16 58									
Wandsworth Road	d														16 59									
Battersea Park 4	d														17 02									
London Victoria 15 ⊖	a													17 03	17 06									
Penge West	d				10 48		16 48					16 57	17 03									17 18		
Anerley	d				10 50		16 50					16 59	17 05									17 20		
Norwood Junction 2	d			10 46	10 53		16 53					17 03	17 08								17 16	17 23		
West Croydon 4	a			10 54	10 59		16 59						17 15								17 24	17 29		
East Croydon	a											17 07												

29 July to 12 August

London Bridge to London Victoria - Croydon and East London Line

Network Diagram - see first Page of Table 177

		SN	SN	LO		SE	SN	SE	SN	LO	LO	SN	LO	LO		LO	SN	SN	LO	SE	SN	SE	SN	LO
London Bridge 4 ⊖	d	17 06	17 09				17 11					17 24					17 36	17 39			17 41			
Highbury & Islington	a																							
	d			16 51						16 58			17 06	17 13					17 21					17 28
Canonbury	d			16 53						17 00			17 08	17 15					17 23					17 30
Dalston Junction Stn ELL	d			16 58						17 03	17 08		17 13	17 18		17 23			17 28					17 33
Haggerston	d			16 59						17 04	17 09		17 14	17 19		17 24			17 29					17 34
Hoxton	d			17 01						17 06	17 11		17 16	17 21		17 26			17 31					17 36
Shoreditch High Street	d			17 04						17 09	17 14		17 19	17 24		17 29			17 34					17 39
Whitechapel	d			17 06						17 11	17 16		17 21	17 26		17 31			17 36					17 41
Shadwell	d			17 08						17 13	17 18		17 23	17 28		17 33			17 38					17 43
Wapping	d			17 10						17 15	17 20		17 25	17 30		17 35			17 40					17 45
Rotherhithe	d			17 12						17 17	17 22		17 27	17 32		17 37			17 42					17 47
Canada Water	d			17 14						17 19	17 24		17 29	17 34		17 39			17 44					17 49
Surrey Quays	d			17 15						17 20	17 25		17 30	17 35		17 40			17 45					17 50
New Cross ELL	a										17 30					17 45								
New Cross Gate 4	a		17 14	17 19						17 24		17 29	17 32	17 39				17 44	17 49					17 54
	d		17 14	17 20						17 25		17 29	17 33	17 40				17 44	17 50					17 55
Brockley	d		17 17	17 22						17 27		17 32	17 35	17 42				17 47	17 52					17 57
Honor Oak Park	d		17 20	17 25						17 30		17 35	17 38	17 45				17 50	17 55					18 00
Forest Hill 4	d		17 22	17 28						17 33		17 37	17 41	17 48				17 52	17 58					18 03
Sydenham	d		17 25	17 30						17 35		17 40	17 43	17 50				17 55	18 00					18 05
Crystal Palace 4	d								17 37	17a40				17a55									18 07	18a10
Gipsy Hill	d								17 39														18 09	
West Norwood 4	d								17 42														18 12	
Streatham Hill	d																							
Balham 4 ⊖	d																							
Wandsworth Common	d																							
Clapham Junction 10	d																							
South Bermondsey	d	17 10					17 15										17 40				17 45			
Queens Rd Peckham	d	17 12					17 18										17 42				17 48			
Peckham Rye 4	d	17a15				17 17	17 20	17 20	17a53								17a45			17 47	17 50	17 50	18a23	
Denmark Hill 4	d					17 21	17 23	17 24												17 51	17 53	17 54		
London Blackfriars 3 ⊖	a							17 34														18 04		
Clapham High Street ⊖	d						17 28														17 58			
Wandsworth Road	d						17 29														17 59			
Battersea Park 4	d						17 32														18 02			
London Victoria 15 ⊖	a					17 33	17 36													18 03	18 06			
Penge West	d		17 27	17 33									17 46					17 57	18 03					
Anerley	d		17 29	17 35									17 48					17 59	18 05					
Norwood Junction 2	d		17 33	17 38								17 46	17 51					18 03	18 08					
West Croydon 4	a			17 45								17 54	17 59						18 15					
East Croydon	a		17 37															18 07						

		LO	SN	LO	LO	LO	SN	SN	LO	SE		SN	SE	SN	LO	LO	SN	LO	LO	LO		SN	SN	LO	SE
London Bridge 4 ⊖	d		17 54				18 06	18 09				18 11					18 24					18 36	18 39		
Highbury & Islington	a																								
	d			17 36	17 43				17 51						17 58			18 06	18 13					18 21	
Canonbury	d			17 38	17 45				17 53						18 00			18 08	18 15					18 23	
Dalston Junction Stn ELL	d	17 38		17 43	17 48	17 53			17 58						18 03	18 08		18 13	18 18	18 23				18 28	
Haggerston	d	17 39		17 44	17 49	17 54			17 59						18 04	18 09		18 14	18 19	18 24				18 29	
Hoxton	d	17 41		17 46	17 51	17 56			18 01						18 06	18 11		18 16	18 21	18 26				18 31	
Shoreditch High Street	d	17 44		17 49	17 54	17 59			18 04						18 09	18 14		18 19	18 24	18 29				18 34	
Whitechapel	d	17 46		17 51	17 56	18 01			18 06						18 11	18 16		18 21	18 26	18 31				18 36	
Shadwell	d	17 48		17 53	17 58	18 03			18 08						18 13	18 18		18 23	18 28	18 33				18 38	
Wapping	d	17 50		17 55	18 00	18 05			18 10						18 15	18 20		18 25	18 30	18 35				18 40	
Rotherhithe	d	17 52		17 57	18 02	18 07			18 12						18 17	18 22		18 27	18 32	18 37				18 42	
Canada Water	d	17 54		17 59	18 04	18 09			18 14						18 19	18 24		18 29	18 34	18 39				18 44	
Surrey Quays	d	17 55		18 00	18 05	18 10			18 15						18 20	18 25		18 30	18 35	18 40				18 45	
New Cross ELL	a	18 00				18 15										18 30				18 45					
New Cross Gate 4	a		17 59	18 04	18 09			18 14	18 19						18 24		18 29	18 32	18 39				18 44	18 49	
	d		17 59	18 05	18 10			18 14	18 20						18 25		18 29	18 33	18 40				18 44	18 50	
Brockley	d		18 02	18 07	18 12			18 17	18 22						18 27		18 32	18 35	18 42				18 47	18 52	
Honor Oak Park	d		18 05	18 10	18 15			18 20	18 25						18 30		18 35	18 38	18 45				18 50	18 55	
Forest Hill 4	d		18 07	18 13	18 18			18 22	18 28						18 33		18 37	18 41	18 48				18 52	18 58	
Sydenham	d		18 10	18 15	18 20			18 25	18 30						18 35		18 40	18 43	18 50				18 55	19 00	
Crystal Palace 4	d				18a25									18 37	18a40				18a55						
Gipsy Hill	d													18 39											
West Norwood 4	d													18 42											
Streatham Hill	d																								
Balham 4 ⊖	d																								
Wandsworth Common	d																								
Clapham Junction 10	d																								
South Bermondsey	d						18 10					18 15										18 40			
Queens Rd Peckham	d						18 12					18 18										18 42			
Peckham Rye 4	d						18a15			18 17		18 20	18 20	18a53								18a45			18 47
Denmark Hill 4	d									18 21		18 23	18 24												18 51
London Blackfriars 3 ⊖	a												18 34												
Clapham High Street ⊖	d											18 28													
Wandsworth Road	d											18 29													
Battersea Park 4	d											18 32													
London Victoria 15 ⊖	a									18 33		18 36													19 03
Penge West	d			18 18				18 27	18 33									18 46					18 57	19 03	
Anerley	d			18 20				18 29	18 35									18 48					18 59	19 05	
Norwood Junction 2	d		18 16	18 23				18 33	18 38								18 46	18 51					19 03	19 08	
West Croydon 4	a		18 24	18 29					18 45								18 54	18 59						19 15	
East Croydon	a							18 37															19 07		

Table 178

Sundays

29 July to 12 August

London Bridge to London Victoria - Croydon and East London Line

Network Diagram - see first Page of Table 177

		SN	SE	SN	LO	LO		SN	LO	LO	LO	SN	SN	LO	SE	SN		SE	SN	LO	LO	SN	LO	LO	LO
London Bridge 4 ⊖	d	18 41						18 54				19 06	19 09			19 11						19 24			
Highbury & Islington	a																								
	d				18 28				18 36	18 43				18 51						18 58			19 06	19 13	
Canonbury	d				18 30				18 38	18 45				18 53						19 00			19 08	19 15	
Dalston Junction Stn ELL	d				18 33	18 38			18 43	18 48	18 53			18 58						19 03	19 08		19 13	19 18	19 23
Haggerston	d				18 34	18 39			18 44	18 49	18 54			18 59						19 04	19 09		19 14	19 19	19 24
Hoxton	d				18 36	18 41			18 46	18 51	18 56			19 01						19 06	19 11		19 16	19 21	19 26
Shoreditch High Street	d				18 39	18 44			18 49	18 54	18 59			19 04						19 09	19 14		19 19	19 24	19 29
Whitechapel	d				18 41	18 46			18 51	18 56	19 01			19 06						19 11	19 16		19 21	19 26	19 31
Shadwell	d				18 43	18 48			18 53	18 58	19 03			19 08						19 13	19 18		19 23	19 28	19 33
Wapping	d				18 45	18 50			18 55	19 00	19 05			19 10						19 15	19 20		19 25	19 30	19 35
Rotherhithe	d				18 47	18 52			18 57	19 02	19 07			19 12						19 17	19 22		19 27	19 32	19 37
Canada Water	d				18 49	18 54			18 59	19 04	19 09			19 14						19 19	19 24		19 29	19 34	19 39
Surrey Quays	d				18 50	18 55			19 00	19 05	19 10			19 15						19 20	19 25		19 30	19 35	19 40
New Cross ELL	a					19 00					19 15										19 30				19 45
New Cross Gate 4	a				18 54			18 59	19 04	19 09			19 14	19 19						19 24		19 29	19 34	19 39	
	d				18 55			18 59	19 05	19 10			19 14	19 20						19 25		19 29	19 35	19 40	
Brockley	d				18 57			19 02	19 07	19 12			19 17	19 22						19 27		19 32	19 37	19 42	
Honor Oak Park	d				19 00			19 05	19 10	19 15			19 20	19 25						19 30		19 35	19 40	19 45	
Forest Hill 4	d				19 03			19 07	19 13	19 18			19 22	19 28						19 33		19 37	19 43	19 48	
Sydenham	d				19 05			19 10	19 15	19 20			19 25	19 30						19 35		19 40	19 45	19 50	
Crystal Palace 4	d			19 07	19a10					19a25									19 37	19a40				19a55	
Gipsy Hill	d			19 09															19 39						
West Norwood 4	d			19 12															19 42						
Streatham Hill	d																								
Balham 4 ⊖	d																								
Wandsworth Common	d																								
Clapham Junction 10	d																								
South Bermondsey	d	18 45										19 10				19 15									
Queens Rd Peckham	d	18 48										19 12				19 18									
Peckham Rye 4	d	18 50	18 50	19a23								19a15			19 17	19 20		19 20	19a53						
Denmark Hill 4	d	18 53	18 54												19 21	19 23		19 24							
London Blackfriars 3 ⊖	a		19 04															19 34							
Clapham High Street ⊖	d	18 58														19 28									
Wandsworth Road	d	18 59														19 29									
Battersea Park 4	d	19 02														19 32									
London Victoria 15 ⊖	a	19 06													19 33	19 36									
Penge West	d								19 18				19 27	19 33									19 48		
Anerley	d								19 20				19 29	19 35									19 50		
Norwood Junction 2	d							19 16	19 23				19 33	19 38								19 46	19 53		
West Croydon 4	a							19 24	19 29					19 45								19 54	19 59		
East Croydon	a												19 37												

		SN		SN	LO	SN	SE	SN	LO	LO	SN	LO		LO	LO	SN	SN	LO	SN	SE	SN	LO		LO	SN
London Bridge 4 ⊖	d	19 36		19 39		19 41					19 54					20 06	20 09		20 11						20 24
Highbury & Islington	a																								
	d				19 21				19 28			19 36		19 43				19 51				19 58			
Canonbury	d				19 23				19 30			19 38		19 45				19 53				20 00			
Dalston Junction Stn ELL	d				19 28				19 33	19 38		19 43		19 48	19 53			19 58				20 03		20 08	
Haggerston	d				19 29				19 34	19 39		19 44		19 49	19 54			19 59				20 04		20 09	
Hoxton	d				19 31				19 36	19 41		19 46		19 51	19 56			20 01				20 06		20 11	
Shoreditch High Street	d				19 34				19 39	19 44		19 49		19 54	19 59			20 04				20 09		20 14	
Whitechapel	d				19 36				19 41	19 46		19 51		19 56	20 01			20 06				20 11		20 16	
Shadwell	d				19 38				19 43	19 48		19 53		19 58	20 03			20 08				20 13		20 18	
Wapping	d				19 40				19 45	19 50		19 55		20 00	20 05			20 10				20 15		20 20	
Rotherhithe	d				19 42				19 47	19 52		19 57		20 02	20 07			20 12				20 17		20 22	
Canada Water	d				19 44				19 49	19 54		19 59		20 04	20 09			20 14				20 19		20 24	
Surrey Quays	d				19 45				19 50	19 55		20 00		20 05	20 10			20 15				20 20		20 25	
New Cross ELL	a									20 00					20 15									20 30	
New Cross Gate 4	a			19 44	19 49				19 54		19 59	20 04		20 09			20 14	20 19				20 24			20 29
	d			19 44	19 50				19 55		19 59	20 05		20 10			20 14	20 20				20 25			20 29
Brockley	d			19 47	19 52				19 57		20 02	20 07		20 12			20 17	20 22				20 27			20 32
Honor Oak Park	d			19 50	19 55				20 00		20 05	20 10		20 15			20 20	20 25				20 30			20 35
Forest Hill 4	d			19 52	19 58				20 03		20 07	20 13		20 18			20 22	20 28				20 33			20 37
Sydenham	d			19 55	20 00				20 05		20 10	20 15		20 20			20 25	20 30				20 35			20 40
Crystal Palace 4	d							20 07	20a10					20a25							20 37	20a40			
Gipsy Hill	d							20 09													20 39				
West Norwood 4	d							20 12													20 42				
Streatham Hill	d																								
Balham 4 ⊖	d																								
Wandsworth Common	d																								
Clapham Junction 10	d																								
South Bermondsey	d	19 40				19 45										20 10			20 15						
Queens Rd Peckham	d	19 42				19 48										20 12			20 18						
Peckham Rye 4	d	19a45				19 50	19 50	20a23								20a15			20 20	20 20	20a53				
Denmark Hill 4	d					19 53	19 54												20 23	20 24					
London Blackfriars 3 ⊖	a						20 04													20 34					
Clapham High Street ⊖	d					19 58													20 28						
Wandsworth Road	d					19 59													20 29						
Battersea Park 4	d					20 02													20 32						
London Victoria 15 ⊖	a					20 06													20 36						
Penge West	d			19 57	20 03							20 18					20 27	20 33							
Anerley	d			19 59	20 05							20 20					20 29	20 35							
Norwood Junction 2	d			20 03	20 08						20 16	20 23					20 33	20 38							20 46
West Croydon 4	a				20 15						20 24	20 30						20 45							20 54
East Croydon	a			20 07													20 37								

29 July to 12 August

London Bridge to London Victoria - Croydon and East London Line

Network Diagram - see first Page of Table 177

		LO	LO	LO	SN	SN	LO	SE		SN	SE	SN	LO	LO	SN	LO	LO	LO		SN	SN	LO	SN	SE	SN
London Bridge 4 ⊖	d				20 36	20 39				20 41					20 54					21 06	21 09		21 11		
Highbury & Islington	a																								
	d	20 06	20 13				20 21						20 28			20 36	20 43					20 51			
Canonbury	d	20 08	20 15				20 23						20 30			20 38	20 45					20 53			
Dalston Junction Stn ELL	d	20 13	20 18	20 23			20 28						20 33	20 38		20 43	20 48	20 53				20 58			
Haggerston	d	20 14	20 19	20 24			20 29						20 34	20 39		20 44	20 49	20 54				20 59			
Hoxton	d	20 16	20 21	20 26			20 31						20 36	20 41		20 46	20 51	20 56				21 01			
Shoreditch High Street	d	20 19	20 24	20 29			20 34						20 39	20 44		20 49	20 54	20 59				21 04			
Whitechapel	d	20 21	20 26	20 31			20 36						20 41	20 46		20 51	20 56	21 01				21 06			
Shadwell	d	20 23	20 28	20 33			20 38						20 43	20 48		20 53	20 58	21 03				21 08			
Wapping	d	20 25	20 30	20 35			20 40						20 45	20 50		20 55	21 00	21 05				21 10			
Rotherhithe	d	20 27	20 32	20 37			20 42						20 47	20 52		20 57	21 02	21 07				21 12			
Canada Water	d	20 29	20 34	20 39			20 44						20 49	20 54		20 59	21 04	21 09				21 14			
Surrey Quays	d	20 30	20 35	20 40			20 45						20 50	20 55		21 00	21 05	21 10				21 15			
New Cross ELL	a			20 45										21 00				21 15							
New Cross Gate 4	a	20 34	20 39			20 44	20 49						20 54		20 59	21 04	21 09				21 14	21 19			
	d	20 35	20 40			20 44	20 50						20 55		20 59	21 05	21 10				21 14	21 20			
Brockley	d	20 37	20 42			20 47	20 52						20 57		21 02	21 07	21 12				21 17	21 22			
Honor Oak Park	d	20 40	20 45			20 50	20 55						21 00		21 05	21 10	21 15				21 20	21 25			
Forest Hill 4	d	20 43	20 48			20 52	20 58						21 03		21 07	21 13	21 18				21 22	21 28			
Sydenham	d	20 45	20 50			20 55	21 00						21 05		21 10	21 15	21 20				21 25	21 30			
Crystal Palace 4	d		20a55									21 07	21a10				21a25								21 37
Gipsy Hill	d											21 09													21 39
West Norwood 4	d											21 12													21 42
Streatham Hill	d																								
Balham 4 ⊖	d																								
Wandsworth Common	d																								
Clapham Junction 10	d																								
South Bermondsey	d				20 40					20 45										21 10			21 15		
Queens Rd Peckham	d				20 42					20 48										21 12			21 18		
Peckham Rye 4	d				20a45					20 50	20 50	21a23								21a15			21 20	21 20	21a53
Denmark Hill 4	d							20 40		20 53	20 54												21 23	21 24	
London Blackfriars 3 ⊖	a										21 04													21 34	
Clapham High Street ⊖	d									20 58													21 28		
Wandsworth Road	d									20 59													21 29		
Battersea Park 4	d									21 02													21 32		
London Victoria 15 ⊖	a							20 53		21 06													21 36		
Penge West	d	20 48				20 57	21 03									21 18					21 27	21 33			
Anerley	d	20 50				20 59	21 05									21 20					21 29	21 35			
Norwood Junction 2	d	20 53				21 03	21 08								21 16	21 23					21 33	21 38			
West Croydon 4	a	20 59					21 15								21 24	21 29						21 45			
East Croydon	a					21 07															21 37				

		LO	LO	SN		LO	LO	LO	SN	SN	LO	SN	SE	SN		LO	LO	SN	LO	LO	LO	SN	SN	LO	
London Bridge 4 ⊖	d			21 24					21 36	21 39		21 41						21 54				22 06	22 09		
Highbury & Islington	a																								
	d	20 58				21 06	21 13				21 21					21 28			21 36	21 43				21 51	
Canonbury	d	21 00				21 08	21 15				21 23					21 30			21 38	21 45				21 53	
Dalston Junction Stn ELL	d	21 03	21 08			21 13	21 18	21 23			21 28					21 33	21 38		21 43	21 48	21 53			21 58	
Haggerston	d	21 04	21 09			21 14	21 19	21 24			21 29					21 34	21 39		21 44	21 49	21 54			21 59	
Hoxton	d	21 06	21 11			21 16	21 21	21 26			21 31					21 36	21 41		21 46	21 51	21 56			22 01	
Shoreditch High Street	d	21 09	21 14			21 19	21 24	21 29			21 34					21 39	21 44		21 49	21 54	21 59			22 04	
Whitechapel	d	21 11	21 16			21 21	21 26	21 31			21 36					21 41	21 46		21 51	21 56	22 01			22 06	
Shadwell	d	21 13	21 18			21 23	21 28	21 33			21 38					21 43	21 48		21 53	21 58	22 03			22 08	
Wapping	d	21 15	21 20			21 25	21 30	21 35			21 40					21 45	21 50		21 55	22 00	22 05			22 10	
Rotherhithe	d	21 17	21 22			21 27	21 32	21 37			21 42					21 47	21 52		21 57	22 02	22 07			22 12	
Canada Water	d	21 19	21 24			21 29	21 34	21 39			21 44					21 49	21 54		21 59	22 04	22 09			22 14	
Surrey Quays	d	21 20	21 25			21 30	21 35	21 40			21 45					21 50	21 55		22 00	22 05	22 10			22 15	
New Cross ELL	a		21 30					21 45									22 00				22 16				
New Cross Gate 4	a	21 24		21 29		21 34	21 39			21 44	21 49					21 54		21 59	22 04	22 09			22 14	22 19	
	d	21 25		21 29		21 35	21 40			21 44	21 50					21 55		21 59	22 05	22 10			22 14	22 20	
Brockley	d	21 27		21 32		21 37	21 42			21 47	21 52					21 57		22 02	22 07	22 12			22 17	22 22	
Honor Oak Park	d	21 30		21 35		21 40	21 45			21 50	21 55					22 00		22 05	22 10	22 15			22 20	22 25	
Forest Hill 4	d	21 33		21 37		21 43	21 48			21 52	21 58					22 03		22 07	22 13	22 18			22 22	22 28	
Sydenham	d	21 35		21 40		21 45	21 50			21 55	22 00					22 05		22 10	22 15	22 20			22 25	22 30	
Crystal Palace 4	d	21a40					21a55							22 07		22a10				22a25					
Gipsy Hill	d													22 09											
West Norwood 4	d													22 12											
Streatham Hill	d																								
Balham 4 ⊖	d																								
Wandsworth Common	d																								
Clapham Junction 10	d																								
South Bermondsey	d								21 40			21 45										22 10			
Queens Rd Peckham	d								21 42			21 48										22 12			
Peckham Rye 4	d								21a45			21 50	21 50	22a23								22a15			
Denmark Hill 4	d											21 53	21 54												
London Blackfriars 3 ⊖	a												22 04												
Clapham High Street ⊖	d											21 58													
Wandsworth Road	d											21 59													
Battersea Park 4	d											22 02													
London Victoria 15 ⊖	a											22 06													
Penge West	d					21 48				21 57	22 03								22 18				22 27	22 33	
Anerley	d					21 50				21 59	22 05								22 20				22 29	22 35	
Norwood Junction 2	d			21 46		21 53				22 03	22 08							22 16	22 23				22 33	22 38	
West Croydon 4	a			21 54		21 59					22 15							22 24	22 29					22 45	
East Croydon	a									22 07													22 37		

Table 178

Sundays

29 July to 12 August

London Bridge to London Victoria - Croydon and East London Line

Network Diagram - see first Page of Table 177

Station		SN	SE	SN	SE	SN	LO	LO	LO	LO		SN	LO	SN	SN	SE	SN	LO	LO	LO		LO	SN	LO	SN
London Bridge 4 ⊖	d	22 11		22 36								22 39		22 41	23 06								23 09		23 11
Highbury & Islington	a																								
	d						21 58	22 06	22 13				22 21					22 28	22 36	22 43				22 51	
Canonbury	d						22 00	22 08	22 15				22 23					22 30	22 38	22 45				22 53	
Dalston Junction Stn ELL	d						22 03	22 11	22 18	22 23			22 28					22 33	22 41	22 48		22 53		22 58	
Haggerston	d						22 04	22 12	22 19	22 24			22 29					22 34	22 42	22 49		22 54		22 59	
Hoxton	d						22 06	22 14	22 21	22 26			22 31					22 36	22 44	22 51		22 56		23 01	
Shoreditch High Street	d						22 09	22 17	22 24	22 29			22 34					22 39	22 47	22 54		22 59		23 04	
Whitechapel	d						22 11	22 19	22 26	22 31			22 36					22 41	22 49	22 56		23 01		23 06	
Shadwell	d						22 13	22 21	22 28	22 33			22 38					22 43	22 51	22 58		23 03		23 08	
Wapping	d						22 15	22 23	22 30	22 35			22 40					22 45	22 53	23 00		23 05		23 10	
Rotherhithe	d						22 17	22 25	22 32	22 37			22 42					22 47	22 55	23 02		23 07		23 12	
Canada Water	d						22 19	22 27	22 34	22 39			22 44					22 49	22 57	23 04		23 09		23 14	
Surrey Quays	d						22 20	22 28	22 35	22 40			22 45					22 50	22 58	23 05		23 10		23 15	
New Cross ELL	a									22 45												23 15			
New Cross Gate 4	a						22 24	22 32	22 39			22 44	22 49					22 54	23 02	23 09			23 14	23 19	
	d						22 25	22 33	22 40			22 44	22 50					22 55	23 03	23 10			23 14	23 20	
Brockley	d						22 27	22 35	22 42			22 47	22 52					22 57	23 05	23 12			23 17	23 22	
Honor Oak Park	d						22 30	22 38	22 45			22 50	22 55					23 00	23 08	23 15			23 20	23 25	
Forest Hill 4	d						22 33	22 41	22 48			22 52	22 58					23 03	23 11	23 18			23 22	23 28	
Sydenham	d						22 35	22 43	22 50			22 55	23 00					23 05	23 13	23 20			23 25	23 30	
Crystal Palace 4	d					22 37	22a40		22a55								23 07	23a10		23a25					
Gipsy Hill	d					22 39											23 09								
West Norwood 4	d					22 42											23 12								
Streatham Hill	d																								
Balham 4 ⊖	d																								
Wandsworth Common	d																								
Clapham Junction 10	d																								
South Bermondsey	d	22 15		22 40										22 45	23 10										23 15
Queens Rd Peckham	d	22 18		22 42										22 48	23 12										23 18
Peckham Rye 4	d	22 20	22 20	22a45	22 50	22a53								22 50	23a15	23 20	23a23								23 20
Denmark Hill 4	d	22 23	22 24		22 54									22 53		23 24									23 23
London Blackfriars 3 ⊖	a		22 34		23 04											23 34									
Clapham High Street ⊖	d	22 28												22 58											23 28
Wandsworth Road	d	22 29												22 59											23 29
Battersea Park 4	d	22 32												23 02											23 32
London Victoria 15 ⊖	a	22 36												23 06											23 37
Penge West	d							22 46				22 57	23 03						23 16				23 27	23 33	
Anerley	d							22 48				22 59	23 05						23 18				23 29	23 35	
Norwood Junction 2	d							22 51				23 03	23 08						23 21				23 33	23 38	
West Croydon 4	a							22 59					23 15						23 29					23 45	
East Croydon	a											23 07											23 38		

Station		SN	LO	SN	LO	LO		LO	SN	LO	LO	LO	LO	LO	LO
London Bridge 4 ⊖	d								23 39						
Highbury & Islington	a														
	d		22 58		23 06	23 13				23 21	23 28	23 36	23 43	23 51	23 58
Canonbury	d		23 00		23 08	23 15				23 23	23 30	23 38	23 45	23 53	00 01
Dalston Junction Stn ELL	d		23 03		23 11	23 18		23 23		23 28	23 33	23 41	23 48	23 58	00 04
Haggerston	d		23 04		23 12	23 19		23 24		23 29	23 34	23 42	23 49	23 59	00 06
Hoxton	d		23 06		23 14	23 21		23 26		23 31	23 36	23 44	23 51	00 01	00 08
Shoreditch High Street	d		23 09		23 17	23 24		23 29		23 34	23 39	23 47	23 54	00 04	00 10
Whitechapel	d		23 11		23 19	23 26		23 31		23 36	23 41	23 49	23 56	00 06	00 13
Shadwell	d		23 13		23 21	23 28		23 33		23 38	23 43	23 51	23 58	00 08	00 15
Wapping	d		23 15		23 23	23 30		23 35		23 40	23 45	23 53	00 01	00 10	00 17
Rotherhithe	d		23 17		23 25	23 32		23 37		23 42	23 47	23 55	00 03	00 12	00 18
Canada Water	d		23 19		23 27	23 34		23 39		23 44	23 49	23 57	00 05	00 14	00 20
Surrey Quays	d		23 20		23 28	23 35		23 40		23 45	23 50	23 58	00 06	00 15	00 22
New Cross ELL	a							23 45							
New Cross Gate 4	a		23 24		23 32	23 39			23 44	23 49	23 54	00 02	00 10	00 19	00 25
	d		23 25		23 33	23 40			23 44	23 50	23 55	00 03	00 11	00 20	00 26
Brockley	d		23 27		23 35	23 42			23 47	23 52	23 57	00 06	00 13	00 22	00 29
Honor Oak Park	d		23 30		23 38	23 45			23 50	23 55	00 01	00 09	00 16	00 25	00 32
Forest Hill 4	d		23 33		23 41	23 48			23 52	23 58	00 04	00 12	00 19	00 28	00 34
Sydenham	d		23 35		23 43	23 50			23 55	00 01	00 06	00 14	00 21	00 30	00 37
Crystal Palace 4	d	23 37	23a40	23 50		23a55					00a11		00a26		00a41
Gipsy Hill	d	23 39													
West Norwood 4	d	23 42													
Streatham Hill	d														
Balham 4 ⊖	d														
Wandsworth Common	d														
Clapham Junction 10	d														
South Bermondsey	d														
Queens Rd Peckham	d														
Peckham Rye 4	d	23a53													
Denmark Hill 4	d														
London Blackfriars 3 ⊖	a														
Clapham High Street ⊖	d														
Wandsworth Road	d														
Battersea Park 4	d														
London Victoria 15 ⊖	a														
Penge West	d				23 46				23 57	00 04		00 17		00 33	
Anerley	d				23 48				23 59	00 06		00 19		00 35	
Norwood Junction 2	d			23 55	23 55				00 03	00 09		00 22		00 38	
West Croydon 4	a			23 59	00 03					00 16		00 29		00 45	
East Croydon	a								00 06						

Table 178

Sundays

19 August to 26 August

London Bridge to London Victoria - Croydon and East London Line

Network Diagram - see first Page of Table 177

		SN	SN	SN	LO	SN	LO	LO	SN	SN		LO	LO	SN	SN	SN	SN	SN	SE	SN		SN	SE	LO	LO
London Bridge 4 ⊖	d	23p22	23p36			23p52			00 03	00 06						00 33	00 36			07 11					
Highbury & Islington	a																								
	d				23p25		23p35	23p42				23p56	00 10												06 51
Canonbury	d				23p27		23p37	23p44				23p58	00 12												06 53
Dalston Junction Stn ELL	d				23p30		23p40	23p47				00 02	00 15												06 56
Haggerston	d				23p31		23p41	23p48				00 03	00 16												06 57
Hoxton	d				23p33		23p43	23p50				00 05	00 18												06 59
Shoreditch High Street	d				23p36		23p46	23p53				00 08	00 21												07 02
Whitechapel	d				23p38		23p48	23p55				00 10	00 23												07 04
Shadwell	d				23p40		23p50	23p57				00 12	00 25												07 06
Wapping	d				23p42		23p52	23p59				00 14	00 27												07 08
Rotherhithe	d				23p44		23p54	00 01				00 16	00 29												07 10
Canada Water	d				23p46		23p56	00 03				00 18	00 31												07 12
Surrey Quays	d				23p47		23p57	00 05				00 19	00 32												07 13
New Cross ELL	a																								
New Cross Gate 4	a	23p27	23p41		23p51	23p57	00 02	00 08		00 11		00 23	00 36				00 41								07 17
	d	23p27	23p41		23p52	23p57	00 02			00 11							00 41							07 04	07 18
Brockley	d	23p30	23p44		23p54	00 01	00 04			00 14							00 44							07 06	07 20
Honor Oak Park	d	23p33	23p47		23p57	00 04	00 07			00 17							00 47							07 09	07 23
Forest Hill 4	d	23p35	23p49		23p59	00 06	00 10			00 19							00 49							07 12	07 26
Sydenham	d	23p38	23p52		00 02	00 09	00 12			00 22							00 52							07 14	07 28
Crystal Palace 4	d	23p43		00 03	00a07	00 13								00 33	00 47			01 03				07 07			07a33
Gipsy Hill	d	23p45				00 15																07 09			
West Norwood 4	d	23p48				00 18																07 12			
Streatham Hill	d	23p52				00 22																			
Balham 4 ⊖	d	23p55				00 26																			
Wandsworth Common	d	23p57				00 28																			
Clapham Junction 10	d	00 02				00 32																			
South Bermondsey	d								00 07							00 37				07 15					
Queens Rd Peckham	d								00 09							00 39				07 18					
Peckham Rye 4	d								00 12							00 42			07 09	07 20		07a23	07 39		
Denmark Hill 4	d																		07 13	07 23			07 43		
London Blackfriars 3 ⊖	a																		07 23				07 53		
Clapham High Street ⊖	d																			07 28					
Wandsworth Road	d																			07 29					
Battersea Park 4	d	00 05				00 35														07 32					
London Victoria 15 ⊖	a	00 10				00 42														07 36					
Penge West	d		23p54				00 15			00 24							00 54							07 17	
Anerley	d		23p56				00 17			00 26							00 56							07 19	
Norwood Junction 2	d		23p59	00 09			00 20		00a34	00 30				00 38	00 52	01a04	01 00	01 08						07 22	
West Croydon 4	a			00 14			00 27							00 43	00 58			01 13						07 29	
East Croydon	a		00 03							00 33							01 03								

		SN	LO	SN	SN	SN		SN	LO	SN	LO	SE	SN	SN	SN	SN		LO	SN	LO	LO	SE	SN	SN	SN
London Bridge 4 ⊖	d	07 24		07 36	07 39	07 41				07 54			08 06	08 09	08 11				08 24				08 36	08 39	08 41
Highbury & Islington	a																								
	d		07 05						07 21		07 35							07 51		08 05	08 15				
Canonbury	d		07 07						07 23		07 37							07 53		08 07	08 17				
Dalston Junction Stn ELL	d		07 12						07 26		07 42							07 56		08 12	08 22				
Haggerston	d		07 13						07 27		07 43							07 57		08 13	08 23				
Hoxton	d		07 15						07 29		07 45							07 59		08 15	08 25				
Shoreditch High Street	d		07 18						07 32		07 48							08 02		08 18	08 28				
Whitechapel	d		07 20						07 34		07 50							08 04		08 20	08 30				
Shadwell	d		07 22						07 36		07 52							08 06		08 22	08 32				
Wapping	d		07 24						07 38		07 54							08 08		08 24	08 34				
Rotherhithe	d		07 26						07 40		07 56							08 10		08 26	08 36				
Canada Water	d		07 28						07 42		07 58							08 12		08 28	08 38				
Surrey Quays	d		07 29						07 43		07 59							08 13		08 29	08 39				
New Cross ELL	a																				08 45				
New Cross Gate 4	a	07 29	07 33		07 44				07 47	07 59	08 03			08 14				08 17	08 29	08 33				08 44	
	d	07 29	07 34		07 44				07 48	07 59	08 03			08 14				08 18	08 29	08 34				08 44	
Brockley	d	07 32	07 36		07 47				07 50	08 02	08 06			08 17				08 20	08 32	08 36				08 47	
Honor Oak Park	d	07 35	07 39		07 50				07 53	08 05	08 09			08 20				08 23	08 35	08 39				08 50	
Forest Hill 4	d	07 37	07 42		07 52				07 56	08 07	08 12			08 22				08 26	08 37	08 42				08 52	
Sydenham	d	07 40	07 44		07 55				07 58	08 10	08 14			08 25				08 28	08 40	08 44				08 55	
Crystal Palace 4	d							07 37	08a03							08 07		08a33							
Gipsy Hill	d							07 39								08 09									
West Norwood 4	d							07 42								08 12									
Streatham Hill	d																								
Balham 4 ⊖	d																								
Wandsworth Common	d																								
Clapham Junction 10	d																								
South Bermondsey	d			07 40		07 45							08 10		08 15								08 40		08 45
Queens Rd Peckham	d			07 42		07 48							08 12		08 18								08 42		08 48
Peckham Rye 4	d			07a45		07 50		07a53				08 09	08a15		08 20	08a23						08 39	08a45		08 50
Denmark Hill 4	d					07 53						08 13			08 23							08 43			08 53
London Blackfriars 3 ⊖	a											08 23										08 53			
Clapham High Street ⊖	d					07 58									08 28										08 58
Wandsworth Road	d					07 59									08 29										08 59
Battersea Park 4	d					08 02									08 32										09 02
London Victoria 15 ⊖	a					08 06									08 36										09 06
Penge West	d		07 47		07 57						08 17			08 27						08 47				08 57	
Anerley	d		07 49		07 59						08 19			08 29						08 49				08 59	
Norwood Junction 2	d	07 48	07 52		08 03					08 16	08 22			08 33					08 46	08 52				09 03	
West Croydon 4	a	07 55	07 59							08 24	08 28								08 54	08 58					
East Croydon	a				08 07									08 37										09 07	

Table 178

Sundays

19 August to 26 August

London Bridge to London Victoria - Croydon and East London Line

Network Diagram - see first Page of Table 177

		SN		LO	LO	SN	LO	LO	SE	SN	SN	SN		SN	LO	LO	SN	LO	LO	SE	SN	SN		SN	SN
London Bridge 4 ⊖	d					08 54				09 06	09 09	09 11					09 24				09 36	09 39		09 41	
Highbury & Islington	a																								
	d			08 21	08 30		08 35	08 45							08 51	09 00		09 05	09 15						
Canonbury	d			08 23	08 32		08 37	08 47							08 53	09 02		09 07	09 17						
Dalston Junction Stn ELL	d			08 26	08 37		08 42	08 52							08 56	09 07		09 12	09 22						
Haggerston	d			08 27	08 38		08 43	08 53							08 57	09 08		09 13	09 23						
Hoxton	d			08 29	08 40		08 45	08 55							08 59	09 10		09 15	09 25						
Shoreditch High Street	d			08 32	08 43		08 48	08 58							09 02	09 13		09 18	09 28						
Whitechapel	d			08 34	08 45		08 50	09 00							09 04	09 15		09 20	09 30						
Shadwell	d			08 36	08 47		08 52	09 02							09 06	09 17		09 22	09 32						
Wapping	d			08 38	08 49		08 54	09 04							09 08	09 19		09 24	09 34						
Rotherhithe	d			08 40	08 51		08 56	09 06							09 10	09 21		09 26	09 36						
Canada Water	d			08 42	08 53		08 58	09 08							09 12	09 23		09 28	09 38						
Surrey Quays	d			08 43	08 54		08 59	09 09							09 13	09 24		09 29	09 39						
New Cross ELL	a				09 00			09 15								09 30			09 45						
New Cross Gate 4	a			08 47		08 59	09 03				09 14				09 17		09 29	09 33				09 44			
	d			08 48		08 59	09 04				09 14				09 18		09 29	09 34				09 44			
Brockley	d			08 50		09 02	09 06				09 17				09 20		09 32	09 36				09 47			
Honor Oak Park	d			08 53		09 05	09 09				09 20				09 23		09 35	09 39				09 50			
Forest Hill 4	d			08 56		09 07	09 12				09 22				09 26		09 37	09 42				09 52			
Sydenham	d			08 58		09 10	09 14				09 25				09 28		09 40	09 44				09 55			
Crystal Palace 4	d	08 37		09a03										09 07	09a33										09 37
Gipsy Hill	d	08 39												09 09											09 39
West Norwood 4	d	08 42												09 12											09 42
Streatham Hill	d																								
Balham 4 ⊖	d																								
Wandsworth Common	d																								
Clapham Junction 10	d																								
South Bermondsey	d									09 10		09 15									09 40			09 45	
Queens Rd Peckham	d									09 12		09 18									09 42			09 48	
Peckham Rye 4	d	08a53							09 09	09a15		09 20		09a23						09 39	09a45			09 50	09a53
Denmark Hill 4	d								09 13			09 23								09 43				09 53	
London Blackfriars 3 ⊖	a								09 23											09 53					
Clapham High Street ⊖	d											09 28												09 58	
Wandsworth Road	d											09 29												09 59	
Battersea Park 4	d											09 32												10 02	
London Victoria 15 ⊖	a											09 36												10 06	
Penge West	d						09 17				09 27							09 47				09 57			
Anerley	d						09 19				09 29							09 49				09 59			
Norwood Junction 2	d					09 16	09 22				09 33						09 46	09 52				10 03			
West Croydon 4	a					09 24	09 28										09 54	09 58							
East Croydon	a										09 37											10 07			

		LO	LO	SN	LO	LO	SE	SN		SN	SN	SN	LO	LO	SN	LO	LO	SE		SN	SN	SN	SN	LO	LO
London Bridge 4 ⊖	d			09 54				10 06		10 09	10 11				10 24					10 36	10 39	10 41			
Highbury & Islington	a																								
	d	09 21	09 30		09 35	09 45							09 51	10 00		10 05	10 15							10 21	10 30
Canonbury	d	09 23	09 32		09 37	09 47							09 53	10 02		10 07	10 17							10 23	10 32
Dalston Junction Stn ELL	d	09 26	09 37		09 42	09 52							09 56	10 07		10 12	10 22							10 26	10 37
Haggerston	d	09 27	09 38		09 43	09 53							09 57	10 08		10 13	10 23							10 27	10 38
Hoxton	d	09 29	09 40		09 45	09 55							09 59	10 10		10 15	10 25							10 29	10 40
Shoreditch High Street	d	09 32	09 43		09 48	09 58							10 02	10 13		10 18	10 28							10 32	10 43
Whitechapel	d	09 34	09 45		09 50	10 00							10 04	10 15		10 20	10 30							10 34	10 45
Shadwell	d	09 36	09 47		09 52	10 02							10 06	10 17		10 22	10 32							10 36	10 47
Wapping	d	09 38	09 49		09 54	10 04							10 08	10 19		10 24	10 34							10 38	10 49
Rotherhithe	d	09 40	09 51		09 56	10 06							10 10	10 21		10 26	10 36							10 40	10 51
Canada Water	d	09 42	09 53		09 58	10 08							10 12	10 23		10 28	10 38							10 42	10 53
Surrey Quays	d	09 43	09 54		09 59	10 09							10 13	10 24		10 29	10 39							10 43	10 54
New Cross ELL	a		10 00			10 15								10 30			10 45								11 00
New Cross Gate 4	a	09 47		09 59	10 03					10 14			10 17		10 29	10 33					10 44			10 47	
	d	09 48		09 59	10 04					10 14			10 18		10 29	10 34					10 44			10 48	
Brockley	d	09 50		10 02	10 06					10 17			10 20		10 32	10 36					10 47			10 50	
Honor Oak Park	d	09 53		10 05	10 09					10 20			10 23		10 35	10 39					10 50			10 53	
Forest Hill 4	d	09 56		10 07	10 12					10 22			10 26		10 37	10 42					10 52			10 56	
Sydenham	d	09 58		10 10	10 14					10 25			10 28		10 40	10 44					10 55			10 58	
Crystal Palace 4	d	10a03										10 07	10a33										10 37	11a03	
Gipsy Hill	d											10 09											10 39		
West Norwood 4	d											10 12											10 42		
Streatham Hill	d																								
Balham 4 ⊖	d																								
Wandsworth Common	d																								
Clapham Junction 10	d																								
South Bermondsey	d							10 10			10 15									10 40		10 45			
Queens Rd Peckham	d							10 12			10 18									10 42		10 48			
Peckham Rye 4	d						10 09	10a15			10 20	10a23						10 39		10a45		10 50	10a53		
Denmark Hill 4	d						10 13				10 23							10 43				10 53			
London Blackfriars 3 ⊖	a						10 23											10 53							
Clapham High Street ⊖	d										10 28											10 58			
Wandsworth Road	d										10 29											10 59			
Battersea Park 4	d										10 32											11 02			
London Victoria 15 ⊖	a										10 36											11 06			
Penge West	d				10 17					10 27						10 47					10 57				
Anerley	d				10 19					10 29						10 49					10 59				
Norwood Junction 2	d			10 16	10 22					10 33					10 46	10 52					11 03				
West Croydon 4	a			10 24	10 28										10 54	10 58									
East Croydon	a									10 37											11 07				

Table 178

Sundays

19 August to 26 August

London Bridge to London Victoria - Croydon and East London Line

Network Diagram - see first Page of Table 177

		SN	LO	LO		SE	SN	SN	SN	SN	LO	LO	SN	LO		LO	SE	SN	SN	SN	SN	LO	LO	SN	
London Bridge ■ ⊖	d	10 54					11 06	11 09	11 11				11 24					11 36	11 39	11 41				11 54	
Highbury & Islington	a																								
	d		10 35	10 45							10 51	11 00		11 05		11 15						11 21	11 30		
Canonbury	d		10 37	10 47							10 53	11 02		11 07		11 17						11 23	11 32		
Dalston Junction Stn ELL	d		10 42	10 52							10 56	11 07		11 12		11 22						11 26	11 37		
Haggerston	d		10 43	10 53							10 57	11 08		11 13		11 23						11 27	11 38		
Hoxton	d		10 45	10 55							10 59	11 10		11 15		11 25						11 29	11 40		
Shoreditch High Street	d		10 48	10 58							11 02	11 13		11 18		11 28						11 32	11 43		
Whitechapel	d		10 50	11 00							11 04	11 15		11 20		11 30						11 34	11 45		
Shadwell	d		10 52	11 02							11 06	11 17		11 22		11 32						11 36	11 47		
Wapping	d		10 54	11 04							11 08	11 19		11 24		11 34						11 38	11 49		
Rotherhithe	d		10 56	11 06							11 10	11 21		11 26		11 36						11 40	11 51		
Canada Water	d		10 58	11 08							11 12	11 23		11 28		11 38						11 42	11 53		
Surrey Quays	d		10 59	11 09							11 13	11 24		11 29		11 39						11 43	11 54		
New Cross ELL	a			11 15								11 30				11 45							12 00		
New Cross Gate ■	a	10 59	11 03					11 14			11 17		11 29	11 33					11 44			11 47		11 59	
	d	10 59	11 04					11 14			11 18		11 29	11 34					11 44			11 48		11 59	
Brockley	d	11 02	11 06					11 17			11 20		11 32	11 36					11 47			11 50		12 02	
Honor Oak Park	d	11 05	11 09					11 20			11 23		11 35	11 39					11 50			11 53		12 05	
Forest Hill ■	d	11 07	11 12					11 22			11 26		11 37	11 42					11 52			11 56		12 07	
Sydenham	d	11 10	11 14					11 25			11 28		11 40	11 44					11 55			11 58		12 10	
Crystal Palace ■	d									11 07	11a33										11 37	12a03			
Gipsy Hill	d									11 09											11 39				
West Norwood ■	d									11 12											11 42				
Streatham Hill	d																								
Balham ■ ⊖	d																								
Wandsworth Common	d																								
Clapham Junction ■	d																								
South Bermondsey	d						11 10		11 15									11 40		11 45					
Queens Rd Peckham	d						11 12		11 18									11 42		11 48					
Peckham Rye ■	d					11 09	11a15		11 20	11a23							11 39	11a45		11 50	11a53				
Denmark Hill ■	d					11 13			11 23								11 43			11 53					
London Blackfriars ■ ⊖	a					11 23											11 53								
Clapham High Street ⊖	d								11 28											11 58					
Wandsworth Road	d								11 29											11 59					
Battersea Park ■	d								11 32											12 02					
London Victoria ■ ⊖	a								11 36											12 06					
Penge West	d		11 17					11 27						11 47					11 57						
Anerley	d		11 19					11 29						11 49					11 59						
Norwood Junction ■	d	11 16	11 22					11 33					11 46	11 52					12 03					12 16	
West Croydon ■	a	11 24	11 28										11 54	11 58										12 24	
East Croydon	a							11 37											12 07						

		LO	SE	SN	SN	LO	LO	SN	LO	SN		SE	SN	LO	LO	SN	LO	LO	LO	SN		SN	LO	SN	SE
London Bridge ■ ⊖	d			12 06				12 09		12 11						12 24				12 36		12 39		12 41	
Highbury & Islington	a																								
	d	11 35				11 43			11 51					11 58			12 06	12 13					12 21		
Canonbury	d	11 37				11 45			11 53					12 00			12 08	12 15					12 23		
Dalston Junction Stn ELL	d	11 42				11 48	11 52		11 58					12 03	12 08		12 13	12 18	12 23				12 28		
Haggerston	d	11 43				11 49	11 53		11 59					12 04	12 09		12 14	12 19	12 24				12 29		
Hoxton	d	11 45				11 51	11 55		12 01					12 06	12 11		12 16	12 21	12 26				12 31		
Shoreditch High Street	d	11 48				11 54	11 58		12 04					12 09	12 14		12 19	12 24	12 29				12 34		
Whitechapel	d	11 50				11 56	12 00		12 06					12 11	12 16		12 21	12 26	12 31				12 36		
Shadwell	d	11 52				11 58	12 02		12 08					12 13	12 18		12 23	12 28	12 33				12 38		
Wapping	d	11 54				12 00	12 04		12 10					12 15	12 20		12 25	12 30	12 35				12 40		
Rotherhithe	d	11 56				12 02	12 06		12 12					12 17	12 22		12 27	12 32	12 37				12 42		
Canada Water	d	11 58				12 04	12 08		12 14					12 19	12 24		12 29	12 34	12 39				12 44		
Surrey Quays	d	11 59				12 05	12 09		12 15					12 20	12 25		12 30	12 35	12 40				12 45		
New Cross ELL	a						12 14								12 30				12 45						
New Cross Gate ■	a	12 03				12 09		12 14	12 19					12 24		12 29	12 34	12 39				12 44	12 49		
	d	12 04				12 10		12 14	12 20					12 25		12 29	12 35	12 40				12 44	12 50		
Brockley	d	12 06				12 12		12 17	12 22					12 27		12 32	12 37	12 42				12 47	12 52		
Honor Oak Park	d	12 09				12 15		12 20	12 25					12 30		12 35	12 40	12 45				12 50	12 55		
Forest Hill ■	d	12 12				12 18		12 22	12 28					12 33		12 37	12 43	12 48				12 52	12 58		
Sydenham	d	12 14				12 20		12 25	12 30					12 35		12 40	12 45	12 50				12 55	13 00		
Crystal Palace ■	d				12 07	12a25							12 37	12a40				12a55							
Gipsy Hill	d				12 09								12 39												
West Norwood ■	d				12 12								12 42												
Streatham Hill	d																								
Balham ■ ⊖	d																								
Wandsworth Common	d																								
Clapham Junction ■	d																								
South Bermondsey	d			12 10						12 15										12 40				12 45	
Queens Rd Peckham	d			12 12						12 18										12 42				12 48	
Peckham Rye ■	d		12 09	12a15	12a23					12 20		12 39	12a53							12a45				12 50	13 09
Denmark Hill ■	d		12 13							12 23		12 43												12 53	13 13
London Blackfriars ■ ⊖	a		12 23									12 53													13 23
Clapham High Street ⊖	d									12 28														12 58	
Wandsworth Road	d									12 29														12 59	
Battersea Park ■	d									12 32														13 02	
London Victoria ■ ⊖	a									12 36														13 06	
Penge West	d	12 17						12 27	12 33								12 48					12 57	13 03		
Anerley	d	12 19						12 29	12 35								12 50					12 59	13 05		
Norwood Junction ■	d	12 22						12 33	12 38							12 46	12 53					13 03	13 08		
West Croydon ■	a	12 28							12 45							12 54	12 59						13 15		
East Croydon	a							12 37														13 07			

Table 178

Sundays

19 August to 26 August

London Bridge to London Victoria - Croydon and East London Line

Network Diagram - see first Page of Table 177

		SN	LO	LO	SN	LO		LO	LO	SN		SN	SN	LO	SN		SE	SN	LO	LO	SN	LO	LO	LO
London Bridge 4 ⊖	d				12 54					13 06		17 06	17 09		17 11						17 24			
Highbury & Islington	a																							
	d		12 28			12 36		12 43						16 51					16 58			17 06	17 13	
Canonbury	d		12 30			12 38		12 45						16 53					17 00			17 08	17 15	
Dalston Junction Stn ELL	d		12 33	12 38		12 43		12 48	12 53					16 58					17 03	17 08		17 13	17 18	17 23
Haggerston	d		12 34	12 39		12 44		12 49	12 54					16 59					17 04	17 09		17 14	17 19	17 24
Hoxton	d		12 36	12 41		12 46		12 51	12 56					17 01					17 06	17 11		17 16	17 21	17 26
Shoreditch High Street	d		12 39	12 44		12 49		12 54	12 59					17 04					17 09	17 14		17 19	17 24	17 29
Whitechapel	d		12 41	12 46		12 51		12 56	13 01					17 06					17 11	17 16		17 21	17 26	17 31
Shadwell	d		12 43	12 48		12 53		12 58	13 03					17 08					17 13	17 18		17 23	17 28	17 33
Wapping	d		12 45	12 50		12 55		13 00	13 05					17 10					17 15	17 20		17 25	17 30	17 35
Rotherhithe	d		12 47	12 52		12 57		13 02	13 07					17 12					17 17	17 22		17 27	17 32	17 37
Canada Water	d		12 49	12 54		12 59		13 04	13 09					17 14					17 19	17 24		17 29	17 34	17 39
Surrey Quays	d		12 50	12 55		13 00		13 05	13 10					17 15					17 20	17 25		17 30	17 35	17 40
New Cross ELL	a			13 00					13 15											17 30				17 45
New Cross Gate 4	a		12 54		12 59	13 04		13 09					17 14	17 19					17 24		17 29	17 34	17 39	
	d		12 55		12 59	13 05		13 10					17 14	17 20					17 25		17 29	17 35	17 40	
Brockley	d		12 57		13 02	13 07		13 12			and at the same minutes past each hour until		17 17	17 22					17 27		17 32	17 37	17 42	
Honor Oak Park	d		13 00		13 05	13 10		13 15					17 20	17 25					17 30		17 35	17 40	17 45	
Forest Hill 4	d		13 03		13 07	13 13		13 18					17 22	17 28					17 33		17 37	17 43	17 48	
Sydenham	d		13 05		13 10	13 15		13 20					17 25	17 30					17 35		17 40	17 45	17 50	
Crystal Palace 4	d	13 07	13a10					13a25										17 37	17a40				17a55	
Gipsy Hill	d	13 09																17 39						
West Norwood 4	d	13 12																17 42						
Streatham Hill	d																							
Balham 4 ⊖	d																							
Wandsworth Common	d																							
Clapham Junction 10	d																							
South Bermondsey	d									13 10		17 10			17 15									
Queens Rd Peckham	d									13 12		17 12			17 18									
Peckham Rye 4	d	13a23								13a15		17a15			17 20		17 39	17a53						
Denmark Hill 4	d														17 23		17 43							
London Blackfriars 3 ⊖	a																17 53							
Clapham High Street ⊖	d														17 28									
Wandsworth Road	d														17 29									
Battersea Park 4	d														17 32									
London Victoria 15 ⊖	a														17 36									
Penge West	d					13 18							17 27	17 33								17 48		
Anerley	d					13 20							17 29	17 35								17 50		
Norwood Junction 2	d				13 16	13 23							17 33	17 38							17 46	17 53		
West Croydon 4	a				13 24	13 29								17 45							17 54	17 59		
East Croydon	a												17 37											

		SN		SN	LO	SN	SE	SN	LO	LO	SN	LO		LO	LO	SN	SN	LO	SN	SE	SN	LO		LO	SN
London Bridge 4 ⊖	d	17 36		17 39		17 41					17 54					18 06	18 09		18 11						18 24
Highbury & Islington	a																								
	d				17 21				17 28			17 36		17 43				17 51				17 58			
Canonbury	d				17 23				17 30			17 38		17 45				17 53				18 00			
Dalston Junction Stn ELL	d				17 28				17 33	17 38		17 43		17 48	17 53			17 58				18 03		18 08	
Haggerston	d				17 29				17 34	17 39		17 44		17 49	17 54			17 59				18 04		18 09	
Hoxton	d				17 31				17 36	17 41		17 46		17 51	17 56			18 01				18 06		18 11	
Shoreditch High Street	d				17 34				17 39	17 44		17 49		17 54	17 59			18 04				18 09		18 14	
Whitechapel	d				17 36				17 41	17 46		17 51		17 56	18 01			18 06				18 11		18 16	
Shadwell	d				17 38				17 43	17 48		17 53		17 58	18 03			18 08				18 13		18 18	
Wapping	d				17 40				17 45	17 50		17 55		18 00	18 05			18 10				18 15		18 20	
Rotherhithe	d				17 42				17 47	17 52		17 57		18 02	18 07			18 12				18 17		18 22	
Canada Water	d				17 44				17 49	17 54		17 59		18 04	18 09			18 14				18 19		18 24	
Surrey Quays	d				17 45				17 50	17 55		18 00		18 05	18 10			18 15				18 20		18 25	
New Cross ELL	a									18 00					18 15									18 30	
New Cross Gate 4	a			17 44	17 49				17 54		17 59	18 04		18 09			18 14	18 19				18 24			18 29
	d			17 44	17 50				17 55		17 59	18 05		18 10			18 14	18 20				18 25			18 29
Brockley	d			17 47	17 52				17 57		18 02	18 07		18 12			18 17	18 22				18 27			18 32
Honor Oak Park	d			17 50	17 55				18 00		18 05	18 10		18 15			18 20	18 25				18 30			18 35
Forest Hill 4	d			17 52	17 58				18 03		18 07	18 13		18 18			18 22	18 28				18 33			18 37
Sydenham	d			17 55	18 00				18 05		18 10	18 15		18 20			18 25	18 30				18 35			18 40
Crystal Palace 4	d							18 07	18a10					18a25							18 37	18a40			
Gipsy Hill	d							18 09													18 39				
West Norwood 4	d							18 12													18 42				
Streatham Hill	d																								
Balham 4 ⊖	d																								
Wandsworth Common	d																								
Clapham Junction 10	d																								
South Bermondsey	d	17 40				17 45										18 10			18 15						
Queens Rd Peckham	d	17 42				17 48										18 12			18 18						
Peckham Rye 4	d	17a45				17 50	18 09	18a23								18a15			18 20	18 39	18a53				
Denmark Hill 4	d					17 53	18 13												18 23	18 43					
London Blackfriars 3 ⊖	a						18 23													18 53					
Clapham High Street ⊖	d					17 58													18 28						
Wandsworth Road	d					17 59													18 29						
Battersea Park 4	d					18 02													18 32						
London Victoria 15 ⊖	a					18 06													18 36						
Penge West	d			17 57	18 03							18 18					18 27	18 33							
Anerley	d			17 59	18 05							18 20					18 29	18 35							
Norwood Junction 2	d			18 03	18 08						18 16	18 23					18 33	18 38							18 46
West Croydon 4	a				18 14						18 24	18 29						18 44							18 54
East Croydon	a			18 07													18 37								

Table 178

Sundays

19 August to 26 August

London Bridge to London Victoria - Croydon and East London Line

Network Diagram - see first Page of Table 177

Station		LO	LO	LO	SN	SN	LO	SN		SE	SN	LO	LO	SN	LO	LO	LO	SN		SN	LO	SN	SE	SN	LO
London Bridge 4 ⊖	d				18 36	18 39		18 41						18 54				19 06		19 09		19 11			
Highbury & Islington	a																								
	d	18 06	18 13				18 21					18 28			18 36	18 43					18 51				18 58
Canonbury	d	18 08	18 15				18 23					18 30			18 38	18 45					18 53				19 00
Dalston Junction Stn ELL	d	18 13	18 18	18 23			18 28					18 33	18 38		18 43	18 48	18 53				18 58				19 03
Haggerston	d	18 14	18 19	18 24			18 29					18 34	18 39		18 44	18 49	18 54				18 59				19 04
Hoxton	d	18 16	18 21	18 26			18 31					18 36	18 41		18 46	18 51	18 56				19 01				19 06
Shoreditch High Street	d	18 19	18 24	18 29			18 34					18 39	18 44		18 49	18 54	18 59				19 04				19 09
Whitechapel	d	18 21	18 26	18 31			18 36					18 41	18 46		18 51	18 56	19 01				19 06				19 11
Shadwell	d	18 23	18 28	18 33			18 38					18 43	18 48		18 53	18 58	19 03				19 08				19 13
Wapping	d	18 25	18 30	18 35			18 40					18 45	18 50		18 55	19 00	19 05				19 10				19 15
Rotherhithe	d	18 27	18 32	18 37			18 42					18 47	18 52		18 57	19 02	19 07				19 12				19 17
Canada Water	d	18 29	18 34	18 39			18 44					18 49	18 54		18 59	19 04	19 09				19 14				19 19
Surrey Quays	d	18 30	18 35	18 40			18 45					18 50	18 55		19 00	19 05	19 10				19 15				19 20
New Cross ELL	a			18 45									19 00				19 15								
New Cross Gate 4	a	18 34	18 39			18 44	18 49					18 54		18 59	19 04	19 09				19 14	19 19				19 24
	d	18 35	18 40			18 44	18 50					18 55		18 59	19 05	19 10				19 14	19 20				19 25
Brockley	d	18 37	18 42			18 47	18 52					18 57		19 02	19 07	19 12				19 17	19 22				19 27
Honor Oak Park	d	18 40	18 45			18 50	18 55					19 00		19 05	19 10	19 15				19 20	19 25				19 30
Forest Hill 4	d	18 43	18 48			18 52	18 58					19 03		19 07	19 13	19 18				19 22	19 28				19 33
Sydenham	d	18 45	18 50			18 55	19 00					19 05		19 10	19 15	19 20				19 25	19 30				19 35
Crystal Palace 4	d		18a55								19 07	19a10				19a25								19 37	19a40
Gipsy Hill	d										19 09													19 39	
West Norwood 4	d										19 12													19 42	
Streatham Hill	d																								
Balham 4 ⊖	d																								
Wandsworth Common	d																								
Clapham Junction 10	d																								
South Bermondsey	d				18 40			18 45										19 10				19 15			
Queens Rd Peckham	d				18 42			18 48										19 12				19 18			
Peckham Rye 4	d				18a45			18 50		19 09	19a23							19a15				19 20	19 39	19a53	
Denmark Hill 4	d							18 53		19 13												19 23	19 43		
London Blackfriars 3 ⊖	a									19 23													19 53		
Clapham High Street ⊖	d							18 58														19 28			
Wandsworth Road	d							18 59														19 29			
Battersea Park 4	d							19 02														19 32			
London Victoria 15 ⊖	a							19 06														19 36			
Penge West	d	18 48				18 57	19 03								19 18					19 27	19 33				
Anerley	d	18 50				18 59	19 05								19 20					19 29	19 35				
Norwood Junction 2	d	18 53				19 03	19 08							19 16	19 23					19 33	19 38				
West Croydon 4	a	18 59					19 14							19 24	19 29						19 44				
East Croydon	a					19 07														19 37					

Station		LO	SN	LO		LO	LO	SN	SN	LO	SN	SE	SN	LO		LO	SN	LO	LO	LO	SN	SN	LO	SN	
London Bridge 4 ⊖	d		19 24					19 36	19 39		19 41						19 54				20 06	20 09		20 11	
Highbury & Islington	a																								
	d			19 06		19 13				19 21				19 28				19 36	19 43				19 51		
Canonbury	d			19 08		19 15				19 23				19 30				19 38	19 45				19 53		
Dalston Junction Stn ELL	d	19 08		19 13		19 18	19 23			19 28				19 33		19 38		19 43	19 48	19 53			19 58		
Haggerston	d	19 09		19 14		19 19	19 24			19 29				19 34		19 39		19 44	19 49	19 54			19 59		
Hoxton	d	19 11		19 16		19 21	19 26			19 31				19 36		19 41		19 46	19 51	19 56			20 01		
Shoreditch High Street	d	19 14		19 19		19 24	19 29			19 34				19 39		19 44		19 49	19 54	19 59			20 04		
Whitechapel	d	19 16		19 21		19 26	19 31			19 36				19 41		19 46		19 51	19 56	20 01			20 06		
Shadwell	d	19 18		19 23		19 28	19 33			19 38				19 43		19 48		19 53	19 58	20 03			20 08		
Wapping	d	19 20		19 25		19 30	19 35			19 40				19 45		19 50		19 55	20 00	20 05			20 10		
Rotherhithe	d	19 22		19 27		19 32	19 37			19 42				19 47		19 52		19 57	20 02	20 07			20 12		
Canada Water	d	19 24		19 29		19 34	19 39			19 44				19 49		19 54		19 59	20 04	20 09			20 14		
Surrey Quays	d	19 25		19 30		19 35	19 40			19 45				19 50		19 55		20 00	20 05	20 10			20 15		
New Cross ELL	a	19 30					19 45									20 00				20 15					
New Cross Gate 4	a		19 29	19 34		19 39			19 44	19 49				19 54			19 59	20 04	20 09			20 14	20 19		
	d		19 29	19 35		19 40			19 44	19 50				19 55			19 59	20 05	20 10			20 14	20 20		
Brockley	d		19 32	19 37		19 42			19 47	19 52				19 57			20 02	20 07	20 12			20 17	20 22		
Honor Oak Park	d		19 35	19 40		19 45			19 50	19 55				20 00			20 05	20 10	20 15			20 20	20 25		
Forest Hill 4	d		19 37	19 43		19 48			19 52	19 58				20 03			20 07	20 13	20 18			20 22	20 28		
Sydenham	d		19 40	19 45		19 50			19 55	20 00				20 05			20 10	20 15	20 20			20 25	20 30		
Crystal Palace 4	d					19a55							20 07	20a10					20a25						
Gipsy Hill	d												20 09												
West Norwood 4	d												20 12												
Streatham Hill	d																								
Balham 4 ⊖	d																								
Wandsworth Common	d																								
Clapham Junction 10	d																								
South Bermondsey	d							19 40			19 45										20 10			20 15	
Queens Rd Peckham	d							19 42			19 48										20 12			20 18	
Peckham Rye 4	d							19a45			19 50	20 09	20a23								20a15			20 20	
Denmark Hill 4	d										19 53	20 13												20 23	
London Blackfriars 3 ⊖	a											20 23													
Clapham High Street ⊖	d										19 58													20 28	
Wandsworth Road	d										19 59													20 29	
Battersea Park 4	d										20 02													20 32	
London Victoria 15 ⊖	a										20 06													20 36	
Penge West	d			19 48					19 57	20 03								20 18				20 27	20 33		
Anerley	d			19 50					19 59	20 05								20 20				20 29	20 35		
Norwood Junction 2	d		19 46	19 53					20 03	20 08							20 16	20 23				20 33	20 38		
West Croydon 4	a		19 54	19 59						20 15							20 24	20 29					20 45		
East Croydon	a								20 07													20 37			

Table 178

Sundays

19 August to 26 August

London Bridge to London Victoria - Croydon and East London Line

Network Diagram - see first Page of Table 177

Station		SE	SN	LO	LO	SN	LO	LO	LO	SN		SN	LO	SN	SE	SN	LO	LO	SN	LO		LO	LO	SN	SN
London Bridge 4 ⊖	d					20 24				20 36		20 39		20 41					20 54					21 06	21 09
Highbury & Islington	a																								
	d			19 58			20 06	20 13					20 21				20 28			20 36		20 43			
Canonbury	d			20 00			20 08	20 15					20 23				20 30			20 38		20 45			
Dalston Junction Stn ELL	d			20 03	20 08		20 13	20 18	20 23				20 28				20 33	20 38		20 43		20 48	20 53		
Haggerston	d			20 04	20 09		20 14	20 19	20 24				20 29				20 34	20 39		20 44		20 49	20 54		
Hoxton	d			20 06	20 11		20 16	20 21	20 26				20 31				20 36	20 41		20 46		20 51	20 56		
Shoreditch High Street	d			20 09	20 14		20 19	20 24	20 29				20 34				20 39	20 44		20 49		20 54	20 59		
Whitechapel	d			20 11	20 16		20 21	20 26	20 31				20 36				20 41	20 46		20 51		20 56	21 01		
Shadwell	d			20 13	20 18		20 23	20 28	20 33				20 38				20 43	20 48		20 53		20 58	21 03		
Wapping	d			20 15	20 20		20 25	20 30	20 35				20 40				20 45	20 50		20 55		21 00	21 05		
Rotherhithe	d			20 17	20 22		20 27	20 32	20 37				20 42				20 47	20 52		20 57		21 02	21 07		
Canada Water	d			20 19	20 24		20 29	20 34	20 39				20 44				20 49	20 54		20 59		21 04	21 09		
Surrey Quays	d			20 20	20 25		20 30	20 35	20 40				20 45				20 50	20 55		21 00		21 05	21 10		
New Cross ELL	a				20 30				20 45									21 00					21 15		
New Cross Gate 4	a			20 24		20 29	20 34	20 39				20 44	20 49				20 54		20 59	21 04		21 09			21 14
	d			20 25		20 29	20 35	20 40				20 44	20 50				20 55		20 59	21 05		21 10			21 14
Brockley	d			20 27		20 32	20 37	20 42				20 47	20 52				20 57		21 02	21 07		21 12			21 17
Honor Oak Park	d			20 30		20 35	20 40	20 45				20 50	20 55				21 00		21 05	21 10		21 15			21 20
Forest Hill 4	d			20 33		20 37	20 43	20 48				20 52	20 58				21 03		21 07	21 13		21 18			21 22
Sydenham	d			20 35		20 40	20 45	20 50				20 55	21 00				21 05		21 10	21 15		21 20			21 25
Crystal Palace 4	d		20 37	20a40				20a55								21 07	21a10					21a25			
Gipsy Hill	d		20 39													21 09									
West Norwood 4	d		20 42													21 12									
Streatham Hill	d																								
Balham 4 ⊖	d																								
Wandsworth Common	d																								
Clapham Junction 10	d																								
South Bermondsey	d									20 40				20 45										21 10	
Queens Rd Peckham	d									20 42				20 48										21 12	
Peckham Rye 4	d	20 39	20a53							20a45				20 50	21 09	21a23								21a15	
Denmark Hill 4	d	20 43												20 53	21 13										
London Blackfriars 3 ⊖	a	20 53													21 23										
Clapham High Street ⊖	d													20 58											
Wandsworth Road	d													20 59											
Battersea Park 4	d													21 02											
London Victoria 15 ⊖	a													21 06											
Penge West	d						20 48					20 57	21 03							21 18					21 27
Anerley	d						20 50					20 59	21 05							21 20					21 29
Norwood Junction 2	d					20 46	20 53					21 03	21 08						21 16	21 23					21 33
West Croydon 4 🚌	a					20 54	20 59						21 15						21 24	21 29					
East Croydon 🚌	a											21 07													21 37

Station		LO	SN	SE	SN	LO		LO	SN	LO	LO	LO	SN	SN	LO	SN		SE	SN	LO	LO	SN	LO	LO	LO
London Bridge 4 ⊖	d		21 11						21 24				21 36	21 39		21 41						21 54			
Highbury & Islington	a																								
	d	20 51				20 58				21 06	21 13				21 21					21 28			21 36	21 43	
Canonbury	d	20 53				21 00				21 08	21 15				21 23					21 30			21 38	21 45	
Dalston Junction Stn ELL	d	20 58				21 03		21 08		21 13	21 18	21 23			21 28					21 33	21 38		21 43	21 48	21 53
Haggerston	d	20 59				21 04		21 09		21 14	21 19	21 24			21 29					21 34	21 39		21 44	21 49	21 54
Hoxton	d	21 01				21 06		21 11		21 16	21 21	21 26			21 31					21 36	21 41		21 46	21 51	21 56
Shoreditch High Street	d	21 04				21 09		21 14		21 19	21 24	21 29			21 34					21 39	21 44		21 49	21 54	21 59
Whitechapel	d	21 06				21 11		21 16		21 21	21 26	21 31			21 36					21 41	21 46		21 51	21 56	22 01
Shadwell	d	21 08				21 13		21 18		21 23	21 28	21 33			21 38					21 43	21 48		21 53	21 58	22 03
Wapping	d	21 10				21 15		21 20		21 25	21 30	21 35			21 40					21 45	21 50		21 55	22 00	22 05
Rotherhithe	d	21 12				21 17		21 22		21 27	21 32	21 37			21 42					21 47	21 52		21 57	22 02	22 07
Canada Water	d	21 14				21 19		21 24		21 29	21 34	21 39			21 44					21 49	21 54		21 59	22 04	22 09
Surrey Quays	d	21 15				21 20		21 25		21 30	21 35	21 40			21 45					21 50	21 55		22 00	22 05	22 10
New Cross ELL	a							21 30				21 45									22 00				22 16
New Cross Gate 4	a	21 19				21 24			21 29	21 34	21 39			21 44	21 49					21 54		21 59	22 04	22 09	
	d	21 20				21 25			21 29	21 35	21 40			21 44	21 50					21 55		21 59	22 05	22 10	
Brockley	d	21 22				21 27			21 32	21 37	21 42			21 47	21 52					21 57		22 02	22 07	22 12	
Honor Oak Park	d	21 25				21 30			21 35	21 40	21 45			21 50	21 55					22 00		22 05	22 10	22 15	
Forest Hill 4	d	21 28				21 33			21 37	21 43	21 48			21 52	21 58					22 03		22 07	22 13	22 18	
Sydenham	d	21 30				21 35			21 40	21 45	21 50			21 55	22 00					22 05		22 10	22 15	22 20	
Crystal Palace 4	d				21 37	21a40					21a55								22 07	22a10				22a25	
Gipsy Hill	d				21 39														22 09						
West Norwood 4	d				21 42														22 12						
Streatham Hill	d																								
Balham 4 ⊖	d																								
Wandsworth Common	d																								
Clapham Junction 10	d																								
South Bermondsey	d		21 15										21 40			21 45									
Queens Rd Peckham	d		21 18										21 42			21 48									
Peckham Rye 4	d		21 20	21 39	21a53								21a45			21 50		22 09	22a23						
Denmark Hill 4	d		21 23	21 43												21 53		22 13							
London Blackfriars 3 ⊖	a			21 53														22 23							
Clapham High Street ⊖	d		21 28													21 58									
Wandsworth Road	d		21 29													21 59									
Battersea Park 4	d		21 32													22 02									
London Victoria 15 ⊖	a		21 36													22 06									
Penge West	d	21 33								21 48				21 57	22 03								22 18		
Anerley	d	21 35								21 50				21 59	22 05								22 20		
Norwood Junction 2	d	21 38							21 46	21 53				22 03	22 08							22 16	22 23		
West Croydon 4 🚌	a	21 45							21 54	21 59					22 15							22 24	22 29		
East Croydon 🚌	a													22 07											

Table 178

Sundays

19 August to 26 August

London Bridge to London Victoria - Croydon and East London Line

Network Diagram - see first Page of Table 177

Station		SN		SN	LO	LO	SN	SE	SN	SN	LO	SN		LO	LO	SN	SE	SN	SN	LO	SN	LO		LO	SN
London Bridge 4 ⊖	d	22 06		22 09			22 11		22 36			22 39				22 41		23 06			23 09				23 11
Highbury & Islington	a																								
	d				21 51						22 13			22 23						22 43		22 53			
Canonbury	d				21 53						22 15			22 25						22 45		22 55			
Dalston Junction Stn ELL	d				21 58	22 08					22 18			22 28	22 38					22 48		22 58		23 08	
Haggerston	d				21 59	22 09					22 19			22 29	22 39					22 49		22 59		23 09	
Hoxton	d				22 01	22 11					22 21			22 31	22 41					22 51		23 01		23 11	
Shoreditch High Street	d				22 04	22 14					22 24			22 34	22 44					22 54		23 04		23 14	
Whitechapel	d				22 06	22 16					22 26			22 36	22 46					22 56		23 06		23 16	
Shadwell	d				22 08	22 18					22 28			22 38	22 48					22 58		23 08		23 18	
Wapping	d				22 10	22 20					22 30			22 40	22 50					23 00		23 10		23 20	
Rotherhithe	d				22 12	22 22					22 32			22 42	22 52					23 02		23 12		23 22	
Canada Water	d				22 14	22 24					22 34			22 44	22 54					23 04		23 14		23 24	
Surrey Quays	d				22 15	22 25					22 35			22 45	22 55					23 05		23 15		23 25	
New Cross ELL	a					22 30									23 00									23 30	
New Cross Gate 4	a			22 14	22 19						22 39	22 44		22 49						23 09	23 14	23 19			
	d			22 14	22 20						22 40	22 44		22 50						23 10	23 14	23 20			
Brockley	d			22 17	22 22						22 42	22 47		22 52						23 12	23 17	23 22			
Honor Oak Park	d			22 20	22 25						22 45	22 50		22 55						23 15	23 20	23 25			
Forest Hill 4	d			22 22	22 28						22 48	22 52		22 58						23 18	23 22	23 28			
Sydenham	d			22 25	22 30						22 50	22 55		23 00						23 20	23 25	23 30			
Crystal Palace 4	d									22 37	22a55								23 07	23a25					
Gipsy Hill	d									22 39									23 09						
West Norwood 4	d									22 42									23 12						
Streatham Hill	d																								
Balham 4 ⊖	d																								
Wandsworth Common	d																								
Clapham Junction 10	d																								
South Bermondsey	d	22 10					22 15		22 40							22 45		23 10							23 15
Queens Rd Peckham	d	22 12					22 18		22 42							22 48		23 12							23 18
Peckham Rye 4	d	22a15					22 20	22 39	22a45	22a53						22 50	23 09	23a15	23a23						23 20
Denmark Hill 4	d						22 23	22 43								22 53	23 13								23 23
London Blackfriars 3 ⊖	a							22 53									23 23								
Clapham High Street ⊖	d						22 28									22 58									23 28
Wandsworth Road	d						22 29									22 59									23 29
Battersea Park 4	d						22 32									23 02									23 32
London Victoria 15 ⊖	a						22 36									23 06									23 37
Penge West	d			22 27	22 33							22 57		23 03							23 27	23 33			
Anerley	d			22 29	22 35							22 59		23 05							23 29	23 35			
Norwood Junction 2	d			22 33	22 38							23 03		23 08							23 33	23 38			
West Croydon 4	a				22 45									23 14								23 44			
East Croydon	a			22 37								23 07									23 38				

Station		SN	SN	LO	SN	LO
London Bridge 4 ⊖	d				23 39	
Highbury & Islington	a					
	d			23 13		23 23
Canonbury	d			23 15		23 25
Dalston Junction Stn ELL	d			23 18		23 28
Haggerston	d			23 19		23 29
Hoxton	d			23 21		23 31
Shoreditch High Street	d			23 24		23 34
Whitechapel	d			23 26		23 36
Shadwell	d			23 28		23 38
Wapping	d			23 30		23 40
Rotherhithe	d			23 32		23 42
Canada Water	d			23 34		23 44
Surrey Quays	d			23 35		23 45
New Cross ELL	a					
New Cross Gate 4	a			23 39	23 44	23 49
	d			23 40	23 44	23 50
Brockley	d			23 42	23 47	23 52
Honor Oak Park	d			23 45	23 50	23 55
Forest Hill 4	d			23 48	23 52	23 58
Sydenham	d			23 50	23 55	00 01
Crystal Palace 4	d	23 37	23 50	23a55		
Gipsy Hill	d	23 39				
West Norwood 4	d	23 42				
Streatham Hill	d					
Balham 4 ⊖	d					
Wandsworth Common	d					
Clapham Junction 10	d					
South Bermondsey	d					
Queens Rd Peckham	d					
Peckham Rye 4	d	23a53				
Denmark Hill 4	d					
London Blackfriars 3 ⊖	a					
Clapham High Street ⊖	d					
Wandsworth Road	d					
Battersea Park 4	d					
London Victoria 15 ⊖	a					
Penge West	d				23 57	00 03
Anerley	d				23 59	00 05
Norwood Junction 2	d		23 55		00 03	00 08
West Croydon 4	a		23 59			00 15
East Croydon	a				00 06	

London Bridge to London Victoria - Croydon and East London Line

Network Diagram - see first Page of Table 177

		SN A	LO B	SN A	SN B	LO A	SN A	LO B	LO A	LO B		SN A	LO A	LO B	LO A	LO B	SN A	SN A	LO A	LO B		LO A	LO B	LO A	LO B
London Bridge 4 ⊖	d	23p22		23p36	23p39							23p52					00 03	00 06							
Highbury & Islington	a																								
	d		23p06			23p18		23p21	23p25	23p28			23p33	23p36	23p40	23p43			23p48	23p51		23p55	23p58	00 03	00 06
Canonbury	d		23p08			23p20		23p23	23p27	23p30			23p35	23p38	23p42	23p45			23p50	23p53		23p57	00 01	00 05	00 08
Dalston Junction Stn ELL	d		23p11			23p25		23p28	23p30	23p33			23p38	23p41	23p45	23p48			23p55	23p58		00 01	00 04	00 10	00 13
Haggerston	d		23p12			23p26		23p29	23p31	23p34			23p39	23p42	23p46	23p49			23p56	23p59		00 02	00 06	00 11	00 14
Hoxton	d		23p14			23p28		23p31	23p33	23p36			23p41	23p44	23p48	23p51			23p58	00 01		00 04	00 08	00 13	00 16
Shoreditch High Street	d		23p17			23p31		23p34	23p36	23p39			23p44	23p47	23p51	23p54			00 01	00 04		00 07	00 10	00 16	00 19
Whitechapel	d		23p19			23p33		23p36	23p38	23p41			23p46	23p49	23p53	23p56			00 03	00 06		00 09	00 13	00 18	00 21
Shadwell	d		23p21			23p35		23p38	23p40	23p43			23p48	23p51	23p55	23p58			00 05	00 08		00 11	00 15	00 20	00 23
Wapping	d		23p23			23p37		23p40	23p42	23p45			23p50	23p53	23p57	00 01			00 07	00 10		00 13	00 17	00 22	00 25
Rotherhithe	d		23p25			23p39		23p42	23p44	23p47			23p52	23p55	23p59	00 03			00 09	00 12		00 15	00 18	00 24	00 27
Canada Water	d		23p27			23p41		23p44	23p46	23p49			23p54	23p57	00 02	00 05			00 11	00 14		00 17	00 20	00 26	00 29
Surrey Quays	d		23p28			23p42		23p45	23p47	23p50			23p55	23p58	00 03	00 06			00 12	00 15		00 18	00 22	00 27	00 30
New Cross ELL	a																								
New Cross Gate 4	a	23p27	23p32	23p41	23p44	23p46		23p49	23p51	23p54		23p57	23p58	00 02	00 07	00 10		00 11	00 16	00 19		00 22	00 25	00 31	00 34
	d	23p27	23p33	23p41	23p44	23p47		23p50	23p52	23p55		23p57	23p59	00 03	00 08	00 11		00 11	00 17	00 20		00 23	00 26	00 32	00 35
Brockley	d	23p30	23p35	23p44	23p47	23p49		23p52	23p54	23p57		00 01	00 03	00 06	00 10	00 13		00 14	00 19	00 22		00 25	00 29	00 34	00 37
Honor Oak Park	d	23p33	23p38	23p47	23p50	23p52		23p55	23p57	00 01		00 04	00 06	00 09	00 13	00 16		00 17	00 22	00 25		00 28	00 32	00 37	00 40
Forest Hill 4	d	23p35	23p41	23p49	23p52	23p55		23p58	23p59	00 04		00 06	00 09	00 12	00 16	00 19		00 19	00 25	00 28		00 31	00 34	00 40	00 43
Sydenham	d	23p38	23p43	23p52	23p55	23p57		00 01	00 02	00 06		00 09	00 11	00 14	00 18	00 21		00 22	00 27	00 30		00 33	00 37	00 42	00 45
Crystal Palace 4	d	23p43					00 03		00a07	00a11		00 13			00a23	00a26						00a38	00a41		
Gipsy Hill	d	23p45										00 15													
West Norwood 4	d	23p48										00 18													
Streatham Hill	d	23p52										00 22													
Balham 4 ⊖	d	23p55										00 25													
Wandsworth Common	d	23p58										00 27													
Clapham Junction 10	d	00 02										00 31													
South Bermondsey	d																00 07								
Queens Rd Peckham	d																00 09								
Peckham Rye 4	d																00 12								
Denmark Hill 4	d																								
London Blackfriars 3 ⊖	a																								
Clapham High Street ⊖	d																								
Wandsworth Road	d																								
Battersea Park 4	d	00 05										00 35													
London Victoria 15 ⊖	a	00 10										00 42													
Penge West	d		23p46	23p54	23p57	00 01		00 04					00 14	00 17				00 24	00 30	00 33				00 45	00 48
Anerley	d		23p48	23p56	23p59	00 03		00 06					00 16	00 19				00 26	00 32	00 35				00 47	00 50
Norwood Junction 2	d		23p55	23p59	00 03	00 06	00 09	00 09					00 19	00 22			00a34	00 30	00 35	00 38				00 50	00 53
West Croydon 4	a		00 03			00 13	00 14	00 16					00 26	00 29					00 42	00 45				00 57	01 00
East Croydon	a			00 03	00 06													00 33							

		LO A	LO B	SN A	LO A	LO B		LO A	LO B	LO A	LO B	LO A	LO B	LO A	LO B	LO A		LO B	LO A	LO B	LO A	LO B	LO A	LO B	SE
London Bridge 4 ⊖	d			00 36																					
Highbury & Islington	a																								
	d	00 10	00 13		00 18	00 21		00 25	00 28	00 33	00 36	00 40	00 43	00 48	00 51	00 55		00 58	01 03	01 06	01 10	01 13	01 25	01 28	
Canonbury	d	00 12	00 15		00 20	00 23		00 27	00 30	00 35	00 38	00 42	00 45	00 50	00 53	00 57		01 00	01 05	01 08	01 12	01 15	01 27	01 30	
Dalston Junction Stn ELL	d	00 15	00 18		00 25	00 28		00 30	00 33	00 40	00 43	00 45	00 48	00 55	00 58	01 00		01 03	01 10	01 13	01 15	01 18	01 32	01 35	
Haggerston	d	00 16	00 19		00 26	00 29		00 31	00 34	00 41	00 44	00 46	00 49	00 56	00 59	01 01		01 04	01 11	01 14	01 16	01 19	01 33	01 36	
Hoxton	d	00 18	00 21		00 28	00 31		00 33	00 36	00 43	00 46	00 48	00 51	00 58	01 01	01 03		01 06	01 13	01 16	01 18	01 21	01 35	01 38	
Shoreditch High Street	d	00 21	00 24		00 31	00 34		00 36	00 39	00 46	00 49	00 51	00 54	01 01	01 04	01 06		01 09	01 16	01 19	01 21	01 24	01 38	01 41	
Whitechapel	d	00 23	00 26		00 33	00 36		00 38	00 41	00 48	00 51	00 53	00 56	01 03	01 06	01 08		01 11	01 18	01 21	01 23	01 26	01 40	01 43	
Shadwell	d	00 25	00 28		00 35	00 38		00 40	00 43	00 50	00 53	00 55	00 58	01 05	01 08	01 10		01 13	01 20	01 23	01 25	01 28	01 42	01 45	
Wapping	d	00 27	00 30		00 37	00 40		00 42	00 45	00 52	00 55	00 57	01 00	01 07	01 10	01 12		01 15	01 22	01 25	01 27	01 30	01 44	01 47	
Rotherhithe	d	00 29	00 32		00 39	00 42		00 44	00 47	00 54	00 57	00 59	01 02	01 09	01 12	01 14		01 17	01 24	01 27	01 29	01 32	01 46	01 49	
Canada Water	d	00 31	00 34		00 41	00 44		00 46	00 49	00 56	00 59	01 01	01 04	01 11	01 14	01 16		01 19	01 26	01 29	01 31	01 34	01 48	01 51	
Surrey Quays	d	00 32	00 35		00 42	00 45		00 47	00 50	00 57	01 00	01 02	01 05	01 12	01 15	01 17		01 20	01 27	01 30	01 32	01 35	01 49	01 52	
New Cross ELL	a																								
New Cross Gate 4	a	00 36	00 39	00 41	00 47	00 50		00 51	00 54	01 02	01 05	01 06	01 09	01 16	01 19	01 21		01 24	01 31	01 34	01 36	01 39	01 53	01 56	
	d	00 37	00 40	00 41	00 47	00 50		00 52	00 55	01 03	01 06	01 07	01 10	01 17	01 20	01 22		01 25	01 32	01 35	01 37	01 40	01 54	01 57	
Brockley	d	00 39	00 42	00 44	00 49	00 52		00 54	00 57	01 05	01 08	01 09	01 12	01 19	01 22	01 24		01 27	01 34	01 37	01 39	01 42	01 56	01 59	
Honor Oak Park	d	00 42	00 45	00 47	00 52	00 55		00 57	01 00	01 08	01 11	01 12	01 15	01 22	01 25	01 27		01 30	01 37	01 40	01 42	01 45	01 59	02 02	
Forest Hill 4	d	00 45	00 48	00 49	00 55	00 58		00 59	01 02	01 11	01 14	01 15	01 18	01 25	01 28	01 30		01 33	01 40	01 43	01 45	01 48	02 02	02 05	
Sydenham	d	00 47	00 50	00 52	00 57	01 00		01 02	01 05	01 13	01 16	01 17	01 20	01 27	01 30	01 32		01 35	01 42	01 45	01 47	01 50	02 04	02 07	
Crystal Palace 4	d	00a52	00a55					01a07	01a10			01a22	01a25			01a37		01a40			01a52	01a55			
Gipsy Hill	d																								
West Norwood 4	d																								
Streatham Hill	d																								
Balham 4 ⊖	d																								
Wandsworth Common	d																								
Clapham Junction 10	d																								
South Bermondsey	d																								
Queens Rd Peckham	d																								
Peckham Rye 4	d																								05 04
Denmark Hill 4	d																								05 07
London Blackfriars 3 ⊖	a																								05 17
Clapham High Street ⊖	d																								
Wandsworth Road	d																								
Battersea Park 4	d																								
London Victoria 15 ⊖	a																								
Penge West	d			00 54	01 00	01 03				01 16	01 19			01 30	01 33				01 45	01 48			02 07	02 10	
Anerley	d			00 56	01 02	01 05				01 18	01 21			01 32	01 35				01 47	01 50			02 09	02 12	
Norwood Junction 2	d			01 00	01 05	01 08				01 21	01 24			01 35	01 38				01 50	01 53			02 12	02 15	
West Croydon 4	a				01 14	01 17				01 28	01 31			01 42	01 45				01 57	02 00			02 19	02 22	
East Croydon	a			01 03																					

A not 3 September **B** 3 September

3 September to 7 September

London Bridge to London Victoria - Croydon and East London Line

Network Diagram - see first Page of Table 177

Station		SE		SN	SN	LO	LO	LO	LO	LO	SN	SN		LO	LO	SN	LO	LO	SN	SN	SE	SN		LO	SN
London Bridge 4 ⊖	d			06 00							06 06	06 11				06 19			06 30	06 33					06 36
Highbury & Islington	a																								
	d							05 35							05 55		06 05								
Canonbury	d							05 37							05 57		06 07								
Dalston Junction Stn ELL	d							05 40	05 50						06 00		06 10	06 20							
Haggerston	d							05 41	05 51						06 01		06 11	06 21							
Hoxton	d							05 43	05 53						06 03		06 13	06 23							
Shoreditch High Street	d							05 46	05 56						06 06		06 16	06 26							
Whitechapel	d							05 48	05 58						06 08		06 18	06 28							
Shadwell	d							05 50	06 00						06 10		06 20	06 30							
Wapping	d							05 52	06 02						06 12		06 22	06 32							
Rotherhithe	d							05 54	06 04						06 14		06 24	06 34							
Canada Water	d							05 56	06 06						06 16		06 26	06 36							
Surrey Quays	d							05 57	06 07						06 17		06 27	06 37							
New Cross ELL	a								06 12									06 42							
New Cross Gate 4	a							06 01			06 11				06 21	06 25	06 31								06 41
	d					05 47	05 52	06 02		06 07	06 11			06 17	06 22	06 25	06 32							06 37	06 41
Brockley	d					05 49	05 54	06 04		06 09	06 14			06 19	06 24	06 27	06 34							06 39	06 44
Honor Oak Park	d					05 52	05 57	06 07		06 12	06 17			06 22	06 27	06 30	06 37							06 42	06 47
Forest Hill 4	d					05 55	06 00	06 10		06 15	06 19			06 25	06 30	06 33	06 40							06 45	06 49
Sydenham	d					05 57	06 02	06 12		06 17	06 22			06 27	06 32	06 35	06 42							06 47	06 52
Crystal Palace 4	d				05 59		06a07			06a22					06a37	06 39						06 51		06a52	
Gipsy Hill	d				06 01											06 41						06 53			
West Norwood 4	d				06 04											06 44						06 56			
Streatham Hill	d															06 48									
Balham 4 ⊖	d															06 51									
Wandsworth Common	d																								
Clapham Junction 10	d															06 56									
South Bermondsey	d			06 04								06 15							06 34	06 37					
Queens Rd Peckham	d			06 06								06 18							06 36	06 39					
Peckham Rye 4	d	06 04		06a09	06a15							06 20							06a39	06a42	06 47	07a08			
Denmark Hill 4	d	06 07										06 23									06 50				
London Blackfriars 3 ⊖	a	06 17																							
Clapham High Street ⊖	d											06 28													
Wandsworth Road	d											06 29													
Battersea Park 4	d											06 32													
London Victoria 15 ⊖	a											06 36				07 05					07 04				
Penge West	d					06 00		06 15			06 24			06 30			06 45								06 54
Anerley	d					06 02		06 17			06 26			06 32			06 47								06 56
Norwood Junction 2	d					06 05		06 20			06 30			06 35			06 50								07 00
West Croydon 4	a					06 13		06 30						06 41			07 00								
East Croydon	a										06 33														07 03

Station		SN	LO	LO	LO	SN	SN	LO		SN	SN	SN	LO	LO	SN	LO	LO	LO		SN	SE	SN	LO	SN	SN
London Bridge 4 ⊖	d	06 41				06 51	06 54			06 58	07 03				07 06					07 11		07 21		07 29	07 33
Highbury & Islington	a																								
	d			06 25				06 33					06 40			06 48	06 55						07 03		
Canonbury	d			06 27				06 35					06 42			06 50	06 57						07 05		
Dalston Junction Stn ELL	d			06 30	06 35			06 40					06 45	06 50		06 55	07 00	07 05					07 10		
Haggerston	d			06 31	06 36			06 41					06 46	06 51		06 56	07 01	07 06					07 11		
Hoxton	d			06 33	06 38			06 43					06 48	06 53		06 58	07 03	07 08					07 13		
Shoreditch High Street	d			06 36	06 41			06 46					06 51	06 56		07 01	07 06	07 11					07 16		
Whitechapel	d			06 38	06 43			06 48					06 53	06 58		07 03	07 08	07 13					07 18		
Shadwell	d			06 40	06 45			06 50					06 55	07 00		07 05	07 10	07 15					07 20		
Wapping	d			06 42	06 47			06 52					06 57	07 02		07 07	07 12	07 17					07 22		
Rotherhithe	d			06 44	06 49			06 54					06 59	07 04		07 09	07 14	07 19					07 24		
Canada Water	d			06 46	06 51			06 56					07 01	07 06		07 11	07 16	07 21					07 26		
Surrey Quays	d			06 47	06 52			06 57					07 02	07 07		07 12	07 17	07 22					07 27		
New Cross ELL	a				06 57									07 12				07 27							
New Cross Gate 4	a			06 51		06 56	06 59	07 00					07 06		07 11	07 15	07 21					07 26	07 31		
	d		06 47	06 52		06 56	06 59	07 02					07 07		07 11	07 17	07 22					07 26	07 32		
Brockley	d		06 49	06 54		06 59	07 02	07 04					07 09		07 14	07 19	07 24					07 29	07 34		
Honor Oak Park	d		06 52	06 57		07 02	07 05	07 07					07 12		07 17	07 22	07 27					07 32	07 37		
Forest Hill 4	d		06 55	07 00		07 04	07 07	07 10					07 15		07 19	07 25	07 30					07 34	07 40		
Sydenham	d		06 57	07 02		07 07	07 10	07 12					07 17		07 22	07 27	07 32					07 37	07 42		
Crystal Palace 4	d			07a07		07 13						07 20	07a22				07a37					07 43			
Gipsy Hill	d					07 15						07 22										07 45			
West Norwood 4	d					07 18						07 25										07 48			
Streatham Hill	d					07 22																07 52			
Balham 4 ⊖	d					07 25																07 55			
Wandsworth Common	d					07 27																07 57			
Clapham Junction 10	d					07 31																08 01			
South Bermondsey	d	06 45								07 02	07 07									07 15				07 33	07 37
Queens Rd Peckham	d	06 48								07 04	07 09									07 17				07 35	07 39
Peckham Rye 4	d	06 50								07a07	07a12	07a36								07 20	07 23			07a38	07a42
Denmark Hill 4	d	06 53																		07 23	07 29				
London Blackfriars 3 ⊖	a																								
Clapham High Street ⊖	d	06 58																		07 28					
Wandsworth Road	d	06 59																		07 29					
Battersea Park 4	d	07 02				07 35														07 32		08 05			
London Victoria 15 ⊖	a	07 08				07 41														07 38	07 42	08 11			
Penge West	d		07 00				07 12	07 15							07 24	07 30							07 45		
Anerley	d		07 02				07 14	07 17							07 26	07 32							07 47		
Norwood Junction 2	d		07 05				07 18	07 20							07 31	07 35							07 50		
West Croydon 4	a		07 11					07 30								07 42							08 00		
East Croydon	a						07 21								07 37										

Table 178

Mondays to Fridays

3 September to 7 September

London Bridge to London Victoria - Croydon and East London Line

Network Diagram - see first Page of Table 177

		SN	LO	LO		SN	LO	SN	SN	LO	LO	SE	SN	LO		SN	SE	SN	SN	LO	LO	SN	LO	LO	
London Bridge 4 ⊖	d					07 36		07 41	07 44				07 53			08 03		08 06				08 06			
Highbury & Islington	a																								
	d		07 10				07 18			07 25				07 33						07 40			07 48	07 55	
Canonbury	d		07 12				07 20			07 27				07 35						07 42			07 50	07 57	
Dalston Junction Stn ELL	d		07 15	07 20			07 25			07 30	07 35			07 40						07 45	07 50		07 55	08 00	
Haggerston	d		07 16	07 21			07 26			07 31	07 36			07 41						07 46	07 51		07 56	08 01	
Hoxton	d		07 18	07 23			07 28			07 33	07 38			07 43						07 48	07 53		07 58	08 03	
Shoreditch High Street	d		07 21	07 26			07 31			07 36	07 41			07 46						07 51	07 56		08 01	08 06	
Whitechapel	d		07 23	07 28			07 33			07 38	07 43			07 48						07 53	07 58		08 03	08 08	
Shadwell	d		07 25	07 30			07 35			07 40	07 45			07 50						07 55	08 00		08 05	08 10	
Wapping	d		07 27	07 32			07 37			07 42	07 47			07 52						07 57	08 02		08 07	08 12	
Rotherhithe	d		07 29	07 34			07 39			07 44	07 49			07 54						07 59	08 04		08 09	08 14	
Canada Water	d		07 31	07 36			07 41			07 46	07 51			07 56						08 01	08 06		08 11	08 16	
Surrey Quays	d		07 32	07 37			07 42			07 47	07 52			07 57						08 02	08 07		08 12	08 17	
New Cross ELL	a			07 42							07 57										08 12				
New Cross Gate 4	a		07 36			07 41	07 45		07 49	07 51			07 58	08 01						08 06		08 11	08 16	08 21	
	d		07 37			07 41	07 47		07 49	07 52			07 58	08 02						08 07		08 11	08 17	08 22	
Brockley	d		07 39			07 44	07 49			07 54			08 01	08 04						08 09		08 14	08 19	08 24	
Honor Oak Park	d		07 42			07 47	07 52			07 57			08 04	08 07						08 12		08 17	08 22	08 27	
Forest Hill 4	d		07 45			07 49	07 55			08 00			08 06	08 10						08 15		08 19	08 25	08 30	
Sydenham	d		07 47			07 52	07 57			08 02			08 09	08 12						08 17		08 22	08 27	08 32	
Crystal Palace 4	d	07 49	07a52							08a07			08 13						08 19	08a22				08a37	
Gipsy Hill	d	07 51											08 15						08 21						
West Norwood 4	d	07 54											08 18						08 24						
Streatham Hill	d												08 22												
Balham 4 ⊖	d												08 25												
Wandsworth Common	d												08 27												
Clapham Junction 10	d												08 31												
South Bermondsey	d							07 45								08 07		08 11							
Queens Rd Peckham	d							07 47								08 09		08 13							
Peckham Rye 4	d	08a06						07 50				07 54				08a12	08 13	08a16	08a36						
Denmark Hill 4	d							07 53				07 59					08 17								
London Blackfriars 3 ⊖	a																								
Clapham High Street ⊖	d							07 58																	
Wandsworth Road	d							07 59																	
Battersea Park 4	d							08 02					08 35												
London Victoria 15 ⊖	a							08 08				08 11	08 41				08 29								
Penge West	d					07 54	08 00							08 15								08 24	08 30		
Anerley	d					07 56	08 02							08 17								08 26	08 32		
Norwood Junction 2	d					08 00	08 05							08 20								08 30	08 35		
West Croydon 4	a						08 12							08 30									08 43		
East Croydon	a					08 03			08 00													08 33			

		LO	SN	SE 1	SE	SN	LO	SN	SN	LO		LO	SN	LO	LO	LO	SN	SE	SE	SN		LO	LO	LO	SN
London Bridge 4 ⊖	d		08 10			08 21		08 33					08 36				08 41	07b37		08 51					09 03
Highbury & Islington	a																								
	d						08 03			08 10				08 18	08 25							08 33	08 40		
Canonbury	d						08 05			08 12				08 20	08 27							08 35	08 42		
Dalston Junction Stn ELL	d	08 05					08 10			08 15		08 20		08 25	08 30	08 35						08 40	08 46	08 50	
Haggerston	d	08 06					08 11			08 16		08 21		08 26	08 31	08 36						08 41	08 47	08 51	
Hoxton	d	08 08					08 13			08 18		08 23		08 28	08 33	08 38						08 43	08 49	08 53	
Shoreditch High Street	d	08 11					08 16			08 21		08 26		08 31	08 36	08 41						08 46	08 52	08 56	
Whitechapel	d	08 13					08 18			08 23		08 28		08 33	08 38	08 43						08 48	08 54	08 58	
Shadwell	d	08 15					08 20			08 25		08 30		08 35	08 40	08 45						08 50	08 56	09 00	
Wapping	d	08 17					08 22			08 27		08 32		08 37	08 42	08 47						08 52	08 58	09 02	
Rotherhithe	d	08 19					08 24			08 29		08 34		08 39	08 44	08 49						08 54	09 00	09 04	
Canada Water	d	08 21					08 26			08 31		08 36		08 41	08 46	08 51						08 56	09 02	09 06	
Surrey Quays	d	08 22					08 27			08 32		08 37		08 42	08 47	08 52						08 57	09 03	09 07	
New Cross ELL	a	08 27										08 42				08 57								09 12	
New Cross Gate 4	a					08 26	08 31			08 36			08 41	08 46	08 51					08 57		09 01	09 07		
	d					08 26	08 32			08 37			08 41	08 47	08 52					08 57		09 02	09 08		
Brockley	d					08 29	08 34			08 39			08 44	08 49	08 54					09 00		09 04	09 10		
Honor Oak Park	d					08 32	08 37			08 42			08 47	08 52	08 57					09 03		09 07	09 13		
Forest Hill 4	d					08 34	08 40			08 45			08 49	08 55	09 00					09 05		09 10	09 16		
Sydenham	d					08 37	08 42			08 47			08 52	08 57	09 02					09 08		09 12	09 18		
Crystal Palace 4	d					08 40			08 50	08a52					09a07					09 11			09a23		
Gipsy Hill	d					08 43			08 52											09 14					
West Norwood 4	d					08 46			08 55											09 17					
Streatham Hill	d					08 49														09 21					
Balham 4 ⊖	d					08 55														09 25					
Wandsworth Common	d					08 57														09 27					
Clapham Junction 10	d					09 01														09 31					
South Bermondsey	d		08 14					08 37									08 45								09 07
Queens Rd Peckham	d		08 16					08 39									08 48								09 09
Peckham Rye 4	d		08 19		08 33			08a42	09a07								08 50	08 55	08 55						09a12
Denmark Hill 4	d		08 22	08 30	08 36												08 53	09 02	09 02						
London Blackfriars 3 ⊖	a																								
Clapham High Street ⊖	d		08 27														08 58								
Wandsworth Road	d		08 29														08 59								
Battersea Park 4	d		08 32			09 05											09 02			09 35					
London Victoria 15 ⊖	a		08 39	08 42	08 49	09 11											09 08	09 11	09 11	09 42					
Penge West	d						08 45						08 54	09 00								09 15			
Anerley	d						08 47						08 56	09 02								09 17			
Norwood Junction 2	d						08 50						09 00	09 05								09 20			
West Croydon 4	a						09 00							09 12								09 30			
East Croydon	a												09 06												

b London Bridge-l

3 September to 7 September

London Bridge to London Victoria - Croydon and East London Line

Network Diagram - see first Page of Table 177

		SN	LO	SE	SN	SN		LO	LO	SN	LO	LO	LO	SN	SN	LO		SE	SN	SN	LO	LO	SN	LO	LO
London Bridge 4	⊖ d	09 06			09 11					09 22				09 33	09 36				09 41				09 52		
Highbury & Islington	a																								
	d		08 48					08 55			09 03	09 10				09 18					09 25			09 33	09 40
Canonbury	d		08 50					08 57			09 05	09 12				09 20					09 27			09 35	09 42
Dalston Junction Stn ELL	d		08 55					09 01	09 05		09 10	09 15	09 20			09 25					09 30	09 35		09 40	09 45
Haggerston	d		08 56					09 02	09 06		09 11	09 16	09 21			09 26					09 31	09 36		09 41	09 46
Hoxton	d		08 58					09 04	09 08		09 13	09 18	09 23			09 28					09 33	09 38		09 43	09 48
Shoreditch High Street	d		09 01					09 07	09 11		09 16	09 21	09 26			09 31					09 36	09 41		09 46	09 51
Whitechapel	d		09 03					09 09	09 13		09 18	09 23	09 28			09 33					09 38	09 43		09 48	09 53
Shadwell	d		09 05					09 11	09 15		09 20	09 25	09 30			09 35					09 40	09 45		09 50	09 55
Wapping	d		09 07					09 13	09 17		09 22	09 27	09 32			09 37					09 42	09 47		09 52	09 57
Rotherhithe	d		09 09					09 15	09 19		09 24	09 29	09 34			09 39					09 44	09 49		09 54	09 59
Canada Water	d		09 11					09 17	09 21		09 26	09 31	09 36			09 41					09 46	09 51		09 56	10 01
Surrey Quays	d		09 12					09 18	09 22		09 27	09 32	09 37			09 42					09 47	09 52		09 57	10 02
New Cross ELL	a								09 27				09 42									09 57			
New Cross Gate 4	a	09 12	09 16					09 22		09 28	09 30	09 36			09 41	09 46					09 51		09 57	10 01	10 06
	d	09 12	09 17					09 23		09 28	09 32	09 37			09 41	09 47					09 52		09 57	10 02	10 07
Brockley	d	09 14	09 19					09 25		09 30	09 34	09 39			09 44	09 49					09 54		10 00	10 04	10 09
Honor Oak Park	d	09 17	09 22					09 28		09 33	09 37	09 42			09 47	09 52					09 57		10 03	10 07	10 12
Forest Hill 4	d	09 20	09 25					09 31		09 36	09 40	09 45			09 49	09 55					10 00		10 05	10 10	10 15
Sydenham	d	09 22	09 27					09 33		09 38	09 42	09 47			09 52	09 57					10 02		10 08	10 12	10 17
Crystal Palace 4	d					09 30		09a38		09 43		09a52								10 00	10a07		10 13		10a22
Gipsy Hill	d					09 32				09 46										10 02			10 15		
West Norwood 4	d					09 35				09 49										10 05			10 18		
Streatham Hill	d									09 52													10 22		
Balham 4	⊖ d									09 56													10 25		
Wandsworth Common	d									09 58													10 27		
Clapham Junction 10	d									10 02													10 31		
South Bermondsey	d				09 15									09 37					09 45						
Queens Rd Peckham	d				09 18									09 39					09 48						
Peckham Rye 4	d			09 14	09 20	09a47								09a42				09 45	09 50	10a17					
Denmark Hill 4	d			09 17	09 23													09 49	09 53						
London Blackfriars 3	⊖ a																								
Clapham High Street	⊖ d				09 28														09 58						
Wandsworth Road	d				09 29														09 59						
Battersea Park 4	d				09 32					10 05									10 03				10 35		
London Victoria 15	⊖ a			09 29	09 38					10 11								10 00	10 07				10 39		
Penge West	d	09 25	09 30								09 45				09 54	10 00								10 15	
Anerley	d	09 27	09 32								09 47				09 56	10 02								10 17	
Norwood Junction 2	d	09 30	09 35								09 50				10 00	10 05								10 20	
West Croydon 4	a		09 42								10 00					10 12								10 30	
East Croydon	a	09 33													10 03										

		LO		SN	SN	LO	SE	SN	SN	LO	LO	SN		LO	LO	LO	SN	SN	LO	SE	SN	SN		LO	LO
London Bridge 4	⊖ d			10 03	10 06			10 11				10 22					10 33	10 36			10 41				
Highbury & Islington	a																								
	d					09 48				09 55				10 03	10 10				10 18					10 25	
Canonbury	d					09 50				09 57				10 05	10 12				10 20					10 27	
Dalston Junction Stn ELL	d	09 50				09 55				10 00	10 05			10 10	10 15	10 20			10 25					10 30	10 35
Haggerston	d	09 51				09 56				10 01	10 06			10 11	10 16	10 21			10 26					10 31	10 36
Hoxton	d	09 53				09 58				10 03	10 08			10 13	10 18	10 23			10 28					10 33	10 38
Shoreditch High Street	d	09 56				10 01				10 06	10 11			10 16	10 21	10 26			10 31					10 36	10 41
Whitechapel	d	09 58				10 03				10 08	10 13			10 18	10 23	10 28			10 33					10 38	10 43
Shadwell	d	10 00				10 05				10 10	10 15			10 20	10 25	10 30			10 35					10 40	10 45
Wapping	d	10 02				10 07				10 12	10 17			10 22	10 27	10 32			10 37					10 42	10 47
Rotherhithe	d	10 04				10 09				10 14	10 19			10 24	10 29	10 34			10 39					10 44	10 49
Canada Water	d	10 06				10 11				10 16	10 21			10 26	10 31	10 36			10 41					10 46	10 51
Surrey Quays	d	10 07				10 12				10 17	10 22			10 27	10 32	10 37			10 42					10 47	10 52
New Cross ELL	a	10 12									10 27					10 42									10 57
New Cross Gate 4	a				10 11	10 16				10 21		10 27		10 31	10 36			10 41	10 46					10 51	
	d				10 11	10 17				10 22		10 27		10 32	10 37			10 41	10 47					10 52	
Brockley	d				10 14	10 19				10 24		10 30		10 34	10 39			10 44	10 49					10 54	
Honor Oak Park	d				10 17	10 22				10 27		10 33		10 37	10 42			10 47	10 52					10 57	
Forest Hill 4	d				10 19	10 25				10 30		10 35		10 40	10 45			10 49	10 55					11 00	
Sydenham	d				10 22	10 27				10 32		10 38		10 42	10 47			10 52	10 57					11 02	
Crystal Palace 4	d								10 30	10a37		10 43			10a52							11 00		11a07	
Gipsy Hill	d								10 32			10 45										11 02			
West Norwood 4	d								10 35			10 48										11 05			
Streatham Hill	d											10 52													
Balham 4	⊖ d											10 55													
Wandsworth Common	d											10 57													
Clapham Junction 10	d											11 01													
South Bermondsey	d			10 07				10 15									10 37				10 45				
Queens Rd Peckham	d			10 09				10 18									10 39				10 48				
Peckham Rye 4	d			10a12			10 15	10 20	10a47								10a42			10 45	10 50	11a17			
Denmark Hill 4	d						10 19	10 23												10 49	10 53				
London Blackfriars 3	⊖ a																								
Clapham High Street	⊖ d							10 28													10 58				
Wandsworth Road	d							10 29													10 59				
Battersea Park 4	d							10 32				11 05									11 02				
London Victoria 15	⊖ a						10 28	10 36				11 09								10 58	11 06				
Penge West	d				10 24	10 30								10 45				10 54	11 00						
Anerley	d				10 26	10 32								10 47				10 56	11 02						
Norwood Junction 2	d				10 30	10 35								10 50				11 00	11 05						
West Croydon 4	a					10 42								11 00					11 12						
East Croydon	a				10 33													11 03							

Table 178

London Bridge to London Victoria - Croydon and East London Line

Mondays to Fridays

3 September to 7 September

Network Diagram - see first Page of Table 177

Station		SN	LO	LO	LO	SN	SN	LO		SE	SN	SN	LO	LO	SN	LO	LO	LO		SN	SN	LO	SE	SN	SN
London Bridge 4 ⊖	d	10 52				11 03	11 06				11 11				11 22					11 33	11 36			11 41	
Highbury & Islington	a																								
	d		10 33	10 40				10 48					10 55			11 03	11 10					11 18			
Canonbury	d		10 35	10 42				10 50					10 57			11 05	11 12					11 20			
Dalston Junction Stn ELL	d		10 40	10 45	10 50			10 55					11 00	11 05		11 10	11 15	11 20				11 25			
Haggerston	d		10 41	10 46	10 51			10 56					11 01	11 06		11 11	11 16	11 21				11 26			
Hoxton	d		10 43	10 48	10 53			10 58					11 03	11 08		11 13	11 18	11 23				11 28			
Shoreditch High Street	d		10 46	10 51	10 56			11 01					11 06	11 11		11 16	11 21	11 26				11 31			
Whitechapel	d		10 48	10 53	10 58			11 03					11 08	11 13		11 18	11 23	11 28				11 33			
Shadwell	d		10 50	10 55	11 00			11 05					11 10	11 15		11 20	11 25	11 30				11 35			
Wapping	d		10 52	10 57	11 02			11 07					11 12	11 17		11 22	11 27	11 32				11 37			
Rotherhithe	d		10 54	10 59	11 04			11 09					11 14	11 19		11 24	11 29	11 34				11 39			
Canada Water	d		10 56	11 01	11 06			11 11					11 16	11 21		11 26	11 31	11 36				11 41			
Surrey Quays	d		10 57	11 02	11 07			11 12					11 17	11 22		11 27	11 32	11 37				11 42			
New Cross ELL	a				11 12									11 27				11 42							
New Cross Gate 4	a	10 57	11 01	11 06			11 11	11 16					11 21		11 27	11 31	11 36				11 41	11 46			
	d	10 57	11 02	11 07			11 11	11 17					11 22		11 27	11 32	11 37				11 41	11 47			
Brockley	d	11 00	11 04	11 09			11 14	11 19					11 24		11 30	11 34	11 39				11 44	11 49			
Honor Oak Park	d	11 03	11 07	11 12			11 17	11 22					11 27		11 33	11 37	11 42				11 47	11 52			
Forest Hill 4	d	11 05	11 10	11 15			11 19	11 25					11 30		11 35	11 40	11 45				11 49	11 55			
Sydenham	d	11 08	11 12	11 17			11 22	11 27					11 32		11 38	11 42	11 47				11 52	11 57			
Crystal Palace 4	d	11 13		11a22								11 30	11a37		11 43		11a52								12 00
Gipsy Hill	d	11 15										11 32			11 45										12 02
West Norwood 4	d	11 18										11 35			11 48										12 05
Streatham Hill	d	11 22													11 52										
Balham 4 ⊖	d	11 25													11 55										
Wandsworth Common	d	11 27													11 57										
Clapham Junction 10	d	11 31													12 01										
South Bermondsey	d					11 07					11 15									11 37				11 45	
Queens Rd Peckham	d					11 09					11 18									11 39				11 48	
Peckham Rye 4	d					11a12				11 15	11 20	11a47								11a42			11 45	11 50	12a17
Denmark Hill 4	d									11 19	11 23												11 49	11 54	
London Blackfriars 3 ⊖	a																								
Clapham High Street ⊖	d										11 28													11 58	
Wandsworth Road	d										11 29													12 00	
Battersea Park 4	d	11 35									11 32				12 05									12 02	
London Victoria 15 ⊖	a	11 39								11 28	11 36				12 09								11 58	12 07	
Penge West	d		11 15				11 24	11 30								11 45					11 54	12 00			
Anerley	d		11 17				11 26	11 32								11 47					11 56	12 02			
Norwood Junction 2	d		11 20				11 30	11 35								11 50					12 00	12 05			
West Croydon 4	a		11 30					11 42								12 00						12 12			
East Croydon	a						11 33														12 03				

Station		LO	LO	SN		LO	LO	LO	SN	SN	LO	SE	SN	SN		LO	LO	SN	LO	LO	LO	SN	SN	LO	
London Bridge 4 ⊖	d			11 52					12 03	12 06			12 11					12 22				12 33	12 36		
Highbury & Islington	a																								
	d	11 25				11 33	11 40				11 48					11 55			12 03	12 10				12 18	
Canonbury	d	11 27				11 35	11 42				11 50					11 57			12 05	12 12				12 20	
Dalston Junction Stn ELL	d	11 30	11 35			11 40	11 45	11 50			11 55					12 00	12 05		12 10	12 15	12 20			12 25	
Haggerston	d	11 31	11 36			11 41	11 46	11 51			11 56					12 01	12 06		12 11	12 16	12 21			12 26	
Hoxton	d	11 33	11 38			11 43	11 48	11 53			11 58					12 03	12 08		12 13	12 18	12 23			12 28	
Shoreditch High Street	d	11 36	11 41			11 46	11 51	11 56			12 01					12 06	12 11		12 16	12 21	12 26			12 31	
Whitechapel	d	11 38	11 43			11 48	11 53	11 58			12 03					12 08	12 13		12 18	12 23	12 28			12 33	
Shadwell	d	11 40	11 45			11 50	11 55	12 00			12 05					12 10	12 15		12 20	12 25	12 30			12 35	
Wapping	d	11 42	11 47			11 52	11 57	12 02			12 07					12 12	12 17		12 22	12 27	12 32			12 37	
Rotherhithe	d	11 44	11 49			11 54	11 59	12 04			12 09					12 14	12 19		12 24	12 29	12 34			12 39	
Canada Water	d	11 46	11 51			11 56	12 01	12 06			12 11					12 16	12 21		12 26	12 31	12 36			12 41	
Surrey Quays	d	11 47	11 52			11 57	12 02	12 07			12 12					12 17	12 22		12 27	12 32	12 37			12 42	
New Cross ELL	a		11 57					12 12									12 27				12 42				
New Cross Gate 4	a	11 51		11 57		12 01	12 06			12 11	12 16					12 21		12 27	12 31	12 36			12 41	12 46	
	d	11 52		11 57		12 02	12 07			12 11	12 17					12 22		12 27	12 32	12 37			12 41	12 47	
Brockley	d	11 54		12 00		12 04	12 09			12 14	12 19					12 24		12 30	12 34	12 39			12 44	12 49	
Honor Oak Park	d	11 57		12 03		12 07	12 12			12 17	12 22					12 27		12 33	12 37	12 42			12 47	12 52	
Forest Hill 4	d	12 00		12 05		12 10	12 15			12 19	12 25					12 30		12 35	12 40	12 45			12 49	12 55	
Sydenham	d	12 02		12 08		12 12	12 17			12 22	12 27					12 32		12 38	12 42	12 47			12 52	12 57	
Crystal Palace 4	d	12a07		12 13			12a22							12 30		12a37		12 43		12a52					
Gipsy Hill	d			12 15										12 32				12 45							
West Norwood 4	d			12 18										12 35				12 48							
Streatham Hill	d			12 22														12 52							
Balham 4 ⊖	d			12 25														12 55							
Wandsworth Common	d			12 27														12 57							
Clapham Junction 10	d			12 31														13 01							
South Bermondsey	d								12 07				12 15									12 37			
Queens Rd Peckham	d								12 09				12 18									12 39			
Peckham Rye 4	d								12a12			12 15	12 20	12a47								12a42			
Denmark Hill 4	d											12 19	12 23												
London Blackfriars 3 ⊖	a																								
Clapham High Street ⊖	d												12 28												
Wandsworth Road	d												12 29												
Battersea Park 4	d			12 35									12 32					13 05							
London Victoria 15 ⊖	a			12 39								12 28	12 36					13 09							
Penge West	d					12 15				12 24	12 30								12 45				12 54	13 00	
Anerley	d					12 17				12 26	12 32								12 47				12 56	13 02	
Norwood Junction 2	d					12 20				12 30	12 35								12 50				13 00	13 05	
West Croydon 4	a					12 30					12 42								13 00					13 12	
East Croydon	a									12 33													13 03		

London Bridge to London Victoria - Croydon and East London Line

Network Diagram - see first Page of Table 177

		SE	SN	SN	LO	LO	SN	LO	LO	LO		SN	SN	LO	SE	SN	SN	LO	LO	SN		LO	LO	LO	SN
London Bridge 4 ⊖	d		12 41				12 52					13 03	13 06			13 11				13 22					13 33
Highbury & Islington	a																								
	d				12 25			12 33	12 40					12 48				12 55				13 03	13 10		
Canonbury	d				12 27			12 35	12 42					12 50				12 57				13 05	13 12		
Dalston Junction Stn ELL	d				12 30	12 35		12 40	12 45	12 50				12 55				13 00	13 05			13 10	13 15	13 20	
Haggerston	d				12 31	12 36		12 41	12 46	12 51				12 56				13 01	13 06			13 11	13 16	13 21	
Hoxton	d				12 33	12 38		12 43	12 48	12 53				12 58				13 03	13 08			13 13	13 18	13 23	
Shoreditch High Street	d				12 36	12 41		12 46	12 51	12 56				13 01				13 06	13 11			13 16	13 21	13 26	
Whitechapel	d				12 38	12 43		12 48	12 53	12 58				13 03				13 08	13 13			13 18	13 23	13 28	
Shadwell	d				12 40	12 45		12 50	12 55	13 00				13 05				13 10	13 15			13 20	13 25	13 30	
Wapping	d				12 42	12 47		12 52	12 57	13 02				13 07				13 12	13 17			13 22	13 27	13 32	
Rotherhithe	d				12 44	12 49		12 54	12 59	13 04				13 09				13 14	13 19			13 24	13 29	13 34	
Canada Water	d				12 46	12 51		12 56	13 01	13 06				13 11				13 16	13 21			13 26	13 31	13 36	
Surrey Quays	d				12 47	12 52		12 57	13 02	13 07				13 12				13 17	13 22			13 27	13 32	13 37	
New Cross ELL	a					12 57				13 12									13 27					13 42	
New Cross Gate 4	a				12 51		12 57	13 01	13 06				13 11	13 16				13 21		13 27		13 31	13 36		
	d				12 52		12 57	13 02	13 07				13 11	13 17				13 22		13 27		13 32	13 37		
Brockley	d				12 54		13 00	13 04	13 09				13 14	13 19				13 24		13 30		13 34	13 39		
Honor Oak Park	d				12 57		13 03	13 07	13 12				13 17	13 22				13 27		13 33		13 37	13 42		
Forest Hill 4	d				13 00		13 05	13 10	13 15				13 19	13 25				13 30		13 35		13 40	13 45		
Sydenham	d				13 02		13 08	13 12	13 17				13 22	13 27				13 32		13 38		13 42	13 47		
Crystal Palace 4	d			13 00	13a07		13 13		13a22								13 30	13a37		13 43			13a52		
Gipsy Hill	d			13 02			13 15										13 32			13 45					
West Norwood 4	d			13 05			13 18										13 35			13 48					
Streatham Hill	d						13 22													13 52					
Balham 4 ⊖	d						13 25													13 55					
Wandsworth Common	d						13 27													13 57					
Clapham Junction 10	d						13 31													14 01					
South Bermondsey	d		12 45									13 07				13 15									13 37
Queens Rd Peckham	d		12 48									13 09				13 18									13 39
Peckham Rye 4	d	12 45	12 50	13a17								13a12			13 15	13 20	13a47								13a42
Denmark Hill 4	d	12 49	12 53												13 19	13 23									
London Blackfriars 3 ⊖	a																								
Clapham High Street ⊖	d		12 58													13 28									
Wandsworth Road	d		12 59													13 29									
Battersea Park 4	d		13 02				13 35									13 32				14 05					
London Victoria 15 ⊖	a	12 58	13 06				13 39								13 28	13 36				14 09					
Penge West	d							13 15					13 24	13 30								13 45			
Anerley	d							13 17					13 26	13 32								13 47			
Norwood Junction 2	d							13 20					13 30	13 35								13 50			
West Croydon 4	a							13 30						13 42								14 00			
East Croydon	a												13 33												

		SN	LO	SE	SN	SN		LO	LO	SN	LO	LO	LO	SN	SN	LO		SE	SN	SN	LO	LO	SN	LO	LO
London Bridge 4 ⊖	d	13 36			13 41					13 52				14 03	14 06				14 11				14 22		
Highbury & Islington	a																								
	d		13 18					13 25			13 33	13 40				13 48					13 55			14 03	14 10
Canonbury	d		13 20					13 27			13 35	13 42				13 50					13 57			14 05	14 12
Dalston Junction Stn ELL	d		13 25					13 30	13 35		13 40	13 45	13 50			13 55					14 00	14 05		14 10	14 15
Haggerston	d		13 26					13 31	13 36		13 41	13 46	13 51			13 56					14 01	14 06		14 11	14 16
Hoxton	d		13 28					13 33	13 38		13 43	13 48	13 53			13 58					14 03	14 08		14 13	14 18
Shoreditch High Street	d		13 31					13 36	13 41		13 46	13 51	13 56			14 01					14 06	14 11		14 16	14 21
Whitechapel	d		13 33					13 38	13 43		13 48	13 53	13 58			14 03					14 08	14 13		14 18	14 23
Shadwell	d		13 35					13 40	13 45		13 50	13 55	14 00			14 05					14 10	14 15		14 20	14 25
Wapping	d		13 37					13 42	13 47		13 52	13 57	14 02			14 07					14 12	14 17		14 22	14 27
Rotherhithe	d		13 39					13 44	13 49		13 54	13 59	14 04			14 09					14 14	14 19		14 24	14 29
Canada Water	d		13 41					13 46	13 51		13 56	14 01	14 06			14 11					14 16	14 21		14 26	14 31
Surrey Quays	d		13 42					13 47	13 52		13 57	14 02	14 07			14 12					14 17	14 22		14 27	14 32
New Cross ELL	a								13 57				14 12									14 27			
New Cross Gate 4	a	13 41	13 46					13 51		13 57	14 01	14 06			14 11	14 16					14 21		14 27	14 31	14 36
	d	13 41	13 47					13 52		13 57	14 02	14 07			14 11	14 17					14 22		14 27	14 32	14 37
Brockley	d	13 44	13 49					13 54		14 00	14 04	14 09			14 14	14 19					14 24		14 30	14 34	14 39
Honor Oak Park	d	13 47	13 52					13 57		14 03	14 07	14 12			14 17	14 22					14 27		14 33	14 37	14 42
Forest Hill 4	d	13 49	13 55					14 00		14 05	14 10	14 15			14 19	14 25					14 30		14 35	14 40	14 45
Sydenham	d	13 52	13 57					14 02		14 08	14 12	14 17			14 22	14 27					14 32		14 38	14 42	14 47
Crystal Palace 4	d					14 00		14a07		14 13		14a22								14 30	14a37		14 43		14a52
Gipsy Hill	d					14 02				14 15										14 32			14 45		
West Norwood 4	d					14 05				14 18										14 35			14 48		
Streatham Hill	d									14 22													14 52		
Balham 4 ⊖	d									14 25													14 55		
Wandsworth Common	d									14 27													14 57		
Clapham Junction 10	d									14 31													15 01		
South Bermondsey	d				13 45									14 07					14 15						
Queens Rd Peckham	d				13 48									14 09					14 18						
Peckham Rye 4	d			13 45	13 50	14a17								14a12				14 15	14 20	14a47					
Denmark Hill 4	d			13 49	13 53													14 19	14 23						
London Blackfriars 3 ⊖	a																								
Clapham High Street ⊖	d				13 58														14 28						
Wandsworth Road	d				13 59														14 29						
Battersea Park 4	d				14 02					14 35									14 32				15 05		
London Victoria 15 ⊖	a			13 58	14 06					14 39								14 28	14 36				15 09		
Penge West	d	13 54	14 00								14 15				14 24	14 30								14 45	
Anerley	d	13 56	14 02								14 17				14 26	14 32								14 47	
Norwood Junction 2	d	14 00	14 05								14 20				14 30	14 35								14 50	
West Croydon 4	a		14 12								14 30					14 42								15 00	
East Croydon	a	14 03													14 33										

Table 178

Mondays to Fridays

3 September to 7 September

London Bridge to London Victoria - Croydon and East London Line

Network Diagram - see first Page of Table 177

Station		LO		SN	SN	LO	SE	SN	SN	LO	LO	SN		LO	LO	LO	SN	SN	LO	SE	SN	SN		LO	LO
London Bridge 4 ⊖	d			14 33	14 36			14 41				14 52					15 03	15 06			15 11				
Highbury & Islington	a																								
	d					14 18				14 25				14 33	14 40				14 48					14 55	
Canonbury	d					14 20				14 27				14 35	14 42				14 50					14 57	
Dalston Junction Stn ELL	d	14 20				14 25				14 30	14 35			14 40	14 45	14 50			14 55					15 00	15 05
Haggerston	d	14 21				14 26				14 31	14 36			14 41	14 46	14 51			14 56					15 01	15 06
Hoxton	d	14 23				14 28				14 33	14 38			14 43	14 48	14 53			14 58					15 03	15 08
Shoreditch High Street	d	14 26				14 31				14 36	14 41			14 46	14 51	14 56			15 01					15 06	15 11
Whitechapel	d	14 28				14 33				14 38	14 43			14 48	14 53	14 58			15 03					15 08	15 13
Shadwell	d	14 30				14 35				14 40	14 45			14 50	14 55	15 00			15 05					15 10	15 15
Wapping	d	14 32				14 37				14 42	14 47			14 52	14 57	15 02			15 07					15 12	15 17
Rotherhithe	d	14 34				14 39				14 44	14 49			14 54	14 59	15 04			15 09					15 14	15 19
Canada Water	d	14 36				14 41				14 46	14 51			14 56	15 01	15 06			15 11					15 16	15 21
Surrey Quays	d	14 37				14 42				14 47	14 52			14 57	15 02	15 07			15 12					15 17	15 22
New Cross ELL	a	14 42									14 57					15 12									15 27
New Cross Gate 4	a				14 41	14 46				14 51		14 57		15 01	15 06			15 11	15 16					15 21	
	d				14 41	14 47				14 52		14 57		15 02	15 07			15 11	15 17					15 22	
Brockley	d				14 44	14 49				14 54		15 00		15 04	15 09			15 14	15 19					15 24	
Honor Oak Park	d				14 47	14 52				14 57		15 03		15 07	15 12			15 17	15 22					15 27	
Forest Hill 4	d				14 49	14 55				15 00		15 05		15 10	15 15			15 19	15 25					15 30	
Sydenham	d				14 52	14 57				15 02		15 08		15 12	15 17			15 22	15 27					15 32	
Crystal Palace 4	d								15 00	15a07		15 13			15a22							15 30		15a37	
Gipsy Hill	d								15 02			15 15										15 32			
West Norwood 4	d								15 05			15 18										15 35			
Streatham Hill	d											15 22													
Balham 4 ⊖	d											15 25													
Wandsworth Common	d											15 27													
Clapham Junction 10	d											15 31													
South Bermondsey	d			14 37				14 45									15 07				15 15				
Queens Rd Peckham	d			14 39				14 48									15 09				15 18				
Peckham Rye 4	d			14a42			14 45	14 50	15a17								15a12			15 15	15 20	15a47			
Denmark Hill 4	d						14 49	14 53												15 19	15 23				
London Blackfriars 3 ⊖	a																								
Clapham High Street ⊖	d							14 58													15 28				
Wandsworth Road	d							14 59													15 29				
Battersea Park 4	d							15 02				15 35									15 32				
London Victoria 15 ⊖	a						14 58	15 06				15 39								15 28	15 36				
Penge West	d				14 54	15 00								15 15				15 24	15 30						
Anerley	d				14 56	15 02								15 17				15 26	15 32						
Norwood Junction 2	d				15 00	15 05								15 20				15 30	15 35						
West Croydon 4	a					15 12								15 30					15 42						
East Croydon	a				15 03													15 33							

Station		SN	LO	LO	LO	SN	SN	LO		SE	SN	SN	SN	LO	LO	SN	LO	LO		LO	SN	SN	LO	SE	SN
London Bridge 4 ⊖	d	15 22				15 33	15 36				15 41					15 52					16 03	16 06			16 11
Highbury & Islington	a																								
	d		15 03	15 10				15 18						15 25			15 33	15 40					15 48		
Canonbury	d		15 05	15 12				15 20						15 27			15 35	15 42					15 50		
Dalston Junction Stn ELL	d		15 10	15 15	15 20			15 25						15 30	15 35		15 40	15 45		15 50			15 55		
Haggerston	d		15 11	15 16	15 21			15 26						15 31	15 36		15 41	15 46		15 51			15 56		
Hoxton	d		15 13	15 18	15 23			15 28						15 33	15 38		15 43	15 48		15 53			15 58		
Shoreditch High Street	d		15 16	15 21	15 26			15 31						15 36	15 41		15 46	15 51		15 56			16 01		
Whitechapel	d		15 18	15 23	15 28			15 33						15 38	15 43		15 48	15 53		15 58			16 03		
Shadwell	d		15 20	15 25	15 30			15 35						15 40	15 45		15 50	15 55		16 00			16 05		
Wapping	d		15 22	15 27	15 32			15 37						15 42	15 47		15 52	15 57		16 02			16 07		
Rotherhithe	d		15 24	15 29	15 34			15 39						15 44	15 49		15 54	15 59		16 04			16 09		
Canada Water	d		15 26	15 31	15 36			15 41						15 46	15 51		15 56	16 01		16 06			16 11		
Surrey Quays	d		15 27	15 32	15 37			15 42						15 47	15 52		15 57	16 02		16 07			16 12		
New Cross ELL	a				15 42										15 57					16 12					
New Cross Gate 4	a	15 27	15 31	15 36			15 41	15 46						15 51		15 57	16 01	16 06				16 11	16 16		
	d	15 27	15 32	15 37			15 41	15 47						15 52		15 57	16 02	16 07				16 11	16 17		
Brockley	d	15 30	15 34	15 39			15 44	15 49						15 54		16 00	16 04	16 09				16 14	16 19		
Honor Oak Park	d	15 33	15 37	15 42			15 47	15 52						15 57		16 03	16 07	16 12				16 17	16 22		
Forest Hill 4	d	15 35	15 40	15 45			15 49	15 55						16 00		16 05	16 10	16 15				16 19	16 25		
Sydenham	d	15 38	15 42	15 47			15 52	15 57						16 02		16 08	16 12	16 17				16 22	16 27		
Crystal Palace 4	d	15 43		15a52									16 00	16a07		16 13		16a22							
Gipsy Hill	d	15 45											16 02			16 15									
West Norwood 4	d	15 48											16 05			16 18									
Streatham Hill	d	15 52										15 56				16 22									
Balham 4 ⊖	d	15 55														16 25									
Wandsworth Common	d	15 57														16 27									
Clapham Junction 10	d	16 01														16 31									
South Bermondsey	d					15 37					15 45										16 07				16 15
Queens Rd Peckham	d					15 39					15 48										16 09				16 18
Peckham Rye 4	d					15a42				15 45	15 50	16a07	16a17								16a12			16 15	16 20
Denmark Hill 4	d									15 49	15 53													16 19	16 23
London Blackfriars 3 ⊖	a																								
Clapham High Street ⊖	d										15 58														16 28
Wandsworth Road	d										15 59														16 29
Battersea Park 4	d	16 05									16 02					16 35									16 32
London Victoria 15 ⊖	a	16 10								15 58	16 06					16 40								16 28	16 38
Penge West	d		15 45				15 54	16 00									16 15					16 24	16 30		
Anerley	d		15 47				15 56	16 02									16 17					16 26	16 32		
Norwood Junction 2	d		15 50				16 00	16 05									16 20					16 30	16 35		
West Croydon 4	a		16 00					16 12									16 30						16 42		
East Croydon	a						16 03															16 33			

3 September to 7 September

London Bridge to London Victoria - Croydon and East London Line

Network Diagram - see first Page of Table 177

Station		SN	LO	LO		SN	LO	LO	LO	SN	SN	LO	SE	SN		SN	LO	LO	SN	LO	SN	SE	SN	LO	
London Bridge 4 ⊖	d					16 22				16 33	16 36			16 41					16 52		16 58				
Highbury & Islington	a																								
	d		15 55				16 03	16 10				16 18					16 25			16 33				16 40	
Canonbury	d		15 57				16 05	16 12				16 20					16 27			16 35				16 42	
Dalston Junction Stn ELL	d		16 00	16 05			16 10	16 15	16 20			16 25					16 30	16 35		16 40				16 45	
Haggerston	d		16 01	16 06			16 11	16 16	16 21			16 26					16 31	16 36		16 41				16 46	
Hoxton	d		16 03	16 08			16 13	16 18	16 23			16 28					16 33	16 38		16 43				16 48	
Shoreditch High Street	d		16 06	16 11			16 16	16 21	16 26			16 31					16 36	16 41		16 46				16 51	
Whitechapel	d		16 08	16 13			16 18	16 23	16 28			16 33					16 38	16 43		16 48				16 53	
Shadwell	d		16 10	16 15			16 20	16 25	16 30			16 35					16 40	16 45		16 50				16 55	
Wapping	d		16 12	16 17			16 22	16 27	16 32			16 37					16 42	16 47		16 52				16 57	
Rotherhithe	d		16 14	16 19			16 24	16 29	16 34			16 39					16 44	16 49		16 54				16 59	
Canada Water	d		16 16	16 21			16 26	16 31	16 36			16 41					16 46	16 51		16 56				17 01	
Surrey Quays	d		16 17	16 22			16 27	16 32	16 37			16 42					16 47	16 52		16 57				17 02	
New Cross ELL	a			16 27					16 42									16 57							
New Cross Gate 4	a		16 21			16 27	16 31	16 36			16 41	16 46					16 51		16 57	17 01				17 06	
	d		16 22			16 27	16 32	16 37			16 41	16 47					16 52		16 57	17 02				17 07	
Brockley	d		16 24			16 30	16 34	16 39			16 44	16 49					16 54		17 00	17 04				17 09	
Honor Oak Park	d		16 27			16 33	16 37	16 42			16 47	16 52					16 57		17 03	17 07				17 12	
Forest Hill 4	d		16 30			16 35	16 40	16 45			16 49	16 55					17 00		17 05	17 10				17 15	
Sydenham	d		16 32			16 38	16 42	16 47			16 52	16 57					17 02		17 08	17 12				17 17	
Crystal Palace 4	d	16 30	16a37			16 43		16a52								17 00	17a07		17 13				17 18	17a22	
Gipsy Hill	d	16 32				16 45										17 02			17 15				17 20		
West Norwood 4	d	16 35				16 48										17 05			17 18				17 23		
Streatham Hill	d					16 52													17 22						
Balham 4 ⊖	d					16 55													17 25						
Wandsworth Common	d					16 57													17 27						
Clapham Junction 10	d					17 01													17 31						
South Bermondsey	d									16 37				16 45							17 02				
Queens Rd Peckham	d									16 39				16 48							17 04				
Peckham Rye 4	d	16a47								16a42			16 45	16 50		17a17					17a07	17 15	17a35		
Denmark Hill 4	d												16 49	16 53								17 19			
London Blackfriars 3 ⊖	a																								
Clapham High Street ⊖	d													16 58											
Wandsworth Road	d													16 59											
Battersea Park 4	d					17 05								17 02					17 35						
London Victoria 15 ⊖	a					17 10							17 01	17 08					17 42			17 28			
Penge West	d						16 45				16 54	17 00								17 15					
Anerley	d						16 47				16 56	17 02								17 17					
Norwood Junction 2	d						16 50				17 00	17 05								17 20					
West Croydon 4	a						17 00				17 07	17 12								17 30					
East Croydon	a																								

Station		LO	SN	LO	SN	SN	LO	LO	SN	LO		LO	LO	SN	SN	LO	SE	SN	SN	LO		LO	SN	LO	SN
London Bridge 4 ⊖	d		17 05		17 11				17 19					17 28	17 36			17 41					17 53		17 58
Highbury & Islington	a																								
	d			16 48			16 55			17 03		17 10				17 18				17 25				17 33	
Canonbury	d			16 50			16 57			17 05		17 12				17 20				17 27				17 35	
Dalston Junction Stn ELL	d	16 50		16 55			17 00	17 05		17 10		17 15	17 20			17 25				17 30		17 35		17 40	
Haggerston	d	16 51		16 56			17 01	17 06		17 11		17 16	17 21			17 26				17 31		17 36		17 41	
Hoxton	d	16 53		16 58			17 03	17 08		17 13		17 18	17 23			17 28				17 33		17 38		17 43	
Shoreditch High Street	d	16 56		17 01			17 06	17 11		17 16		17 21	17 26			17 31				17 36		17 41		17 46	
Whitechapel	d	16 58		17 03			17 08	17 13		17 18		17 23	17 28			17 33				17 38		17 43		17 48	
Shadwell	d	17 00		17 05			17 10	17 15		17 20		17 25	17 30			17 35				17 40		17 45		17 50	
Wapping	d	17 02		17 07			17 12	17 17		17 22		17 27	17 32			17 37				17 42		17 47		17 52	
Rotherhithe	d	17 04		17 09			17 14	17 19		17 24		17 29	17 34			17 39				17 44		17 49		17 54	
Canada Water	d	17 06		17 11			17 16	17 21		17 26		17 31	17 36			17 41				17 46		17 51		17 56	
Surrey Quays	d	17 07		17 12			17 17	17 22		17 27		17 32	17 37			17 42				17 47		17 52		17 57	
New Cross ELL	a	17 12						17 27					17 42									17 57			
New Cross Gate 4	a		17 11	17 16			17 21		17 26	17 31		17 36			17 41	17 46				17 51			17 58	18 01	
	d		17 11	17 17			17 22		17 26	17 32		17 37			17 41	17 47				17 52			17 58	18 02	
Brockley	d		17 14	17 19			17 24		17 29	17 34		17 39			17 44	17 49				17 54			18 01	18 04	
Honor Oak Park	d		17 17	17 22			17 27		17 32	17 37		17 42			17 47	17 52				17 57			18 04	18 07	
Forest Hill 4	d		17 19	17 25			17 30		17 34	17 40		17 45			17 49	17 55				18 00			18 06	18 10	
Sydenham	d		17 22	17 27			17 32		17 37	17 42		17 47			17 52	17 57				18 02			18 09	18 12	
Crystal Palace 4	d					17 36	17a37		17 44			17a52							17 55	18a07			18 13		
Gipsy Hill	d					17 38			17 46										17 57				18 15		
West Norwood 4	d					17 41			17 49										18 00				18 18		
Streatham Hill	d								17 53														18 22		
Balham 4 ⊖	d								17 56														18 25		
Wandsworth Common	d								17 58														18 27		
Clapham Junction 10	d								18 02														18 32		
South Bermondsey	d				17 15									17 32				17 45							18 02
Queens Rd Peckham	d				17 18									17 35				17 47							18 04
Peckham Rye 4	d				17 20	17a53								17a37			17 45	17 50	18a12						18a07
Denmark Hill 4	d				17 23												17 49	17 53							
London Blackfriars 3 ⊖	a																								
Clapham High Street ⊖	d				17 28													17 58							
Wandsworth Road	d				17 29													17 59							
Battersea Park 4	d				17 32				18 06									18 02					18 35		
London Victoria 15 ⊖	a				17 38				18 12								17 59	18 08					18 42		
Penge West	d		17 24	17 30						17 45					17 54	18 00								18 15	
Anerley	d		17 26	17 32						17 47					17 56	18 02								18 17	
Norwood Junction 2	d		17 30	17 35						17 50					18 00	18 05								18 20	
West Croydon 4	a		17 37	17 42						18 01					18 08	18 12								18 30	
East Croydon	a																								

3 September to 7 September

London Bridge to London Victoria - Croydon and East London Line

Network Diagram - see first Page of Table 177

Station		SE	SN	LO	LO	SN	LO	LO	LO	SN	SN	LO	SN	SE	SN	LO	LO	SN	LO	LO	LO	SN	SE
London Bridge 4 ⊖	d					18 06				18 11	18 21		18 28					18 36				18 41	
Highbury & Islington	a																						
	d			17 40			17 48	17 55				18 03				18 10			18 18	18 25			
Canonbury	d			17 42			17 50	17 57				18 05				18 12			18 20	18 27			
Dalston Junction Stn ELL	d			17 45	17 50		17 55	18 00	18 05			18 10				18 15	18 20		18 25	18 30	18 35		
Haggerston	d			17 46	17 51		17 56	18 01	18 06			18 11				18 16	18 21		18 26	18 31	18 36		
Hoxton	d			17 48	17 53		17 58	18 03	18 08			18 13				18 18	18 23		18 28	18 33	18 38		
Shoreditch High Street	d			17 51	17 56		18 01	18 06	18 11			18 16				18 21	18 26		18 31	18 36	18 41		
Whitechapel	d			17 53	17 58		18 03	18 08	18 13			18 18				18 23	18 28		18 33	18 38	18 43		
Shadwell	d			17 55	18 00		18 05	18 10	18 15			18 20				18 25	18 30		18 35	18 40	18 45		
Wapping	d			17 57	18 02		18 07	18 12	18 17			18 22				18 27	18 32		18 37	18 42	18 47		
Rotherhithe	d			17 59	18 04		18 09	18 14	18 19			18 24				18 29	18 34		18 39	18 44	18 49		
Canada Water	d			18 01	18 06		18 11	18 16	18 21			18 26				18 31	18 36		18 41	18 46	18 51		
Surrey Quays	d			18 02	18 07		18 12	18 17	18 22			18 27				18 32	18 37		18 42	18 47	18 52		
New Cross ELL	a				18 12				18 27								18 42				18 57		
New Cross Gate 4	a			18 06		18 11	18 16	18 21			18 26	18 31				18 36		18 41	18 46	18 51			
	d			18 07		18 11	18 17	18 22			18 26	18 32				18 37		18 41	18 47	18 52			
Brockley	d			18 09		18 14	18 19	18 24			18 29	18 34				18 39		18 44	18 49	18 54			
Honor Oak Park	d			18 12		18 17	18 22	18 27			18 32	18 37				18 42		18 47	18 52	18 57			
Forest Hill 4	d			18 15		18 19	18 25	18 30			18 34	18 40				18 45		18 49	18 55	19 00			
Sydenham	d			18 17		18 22	18 27	18 32			18 37	18 42				18 47		18 52	18 57	19 02			
Crystal Palace 4	d		18 18	18a22				18a37			18 43				18 51	18a52				19a07			
Gipsy Hill	d		18 20								18 45				18 53								
West Norwood 4	d		18 23								18 48				18 56								
Streatham Hill	d										18 52												
Balham 4 ⊖	d										18 55												
Wandsworth Common	d										18 57												
Clapham Junction 10	d										19 01												
South Bermondsey	d									18 15			18 32									18 45	
Queens Rd Peckham	d									18 18			18 34									18 48	
Peckham Rye 4	d	18 15	18a36							18 20			18a37	18 45	19a14							18 50	
Denmark Hill 4	d	18 19								18 23				18 49								18 53	18 59
London Blackfriars 3 ⊖	a																						
Clapham High Street ⊖	d									18 28												18 58	
Wandsworth Road	d									18 29												18 59	
Battersea Park 4	d									18 32	19 05											19 02	
London Victoria 15 ⊖	a	18 29								18 39	19 12			18 58								19 08	19 13
Penge West	d					18 24	18 30					18 45						18 54	19 00				
Anerley	d					18 26	18 32					18 47						18 56	19 02				
Norwood Junction 2	d					18 32	18 35					18 50						19 02	19 05				
West Croydon 4 🚌	a					18 39	18 42					19 01						19 09	19 12				
East Croydon 🚌	a																						

Station		SN	LO	LO	LO	SN	SN	LO	SE	SN	SN	SE	SN	LO	LO	SN	LO	LO	LO	SN	SN	LO
London Bridge 4 ⊖	d	18 51				18 57	19 06			19 08	19 11					19 22				19 28	19 36	
Highbury & Islington	a																					
	d		18 33	18 40				18 48						18 55			19 03	19 10				19 18
Canonbury	d		18 35	18 42				18 50						18 57			19 05	19 12				19 20
Dalston Junction Stn ELL	d		18 40	18 45	18 50			18 55						19 00	19 05		19 10	19 15	19 20			19 25
Haggerston	d		18 41	18 46	18 51			18 56						19 01	19 06		19 11	19 16	19 21			19 26
Hoxton	d		18 43	18 48	18 53			18 58						19 03	19 08		19 13	19 18	19 23			19 28
Shoreditch High Street	d		18 46	18 51	18 56			19 01						19 06	19 11		19 16	19 21	19 26			19 31
Whitechapel	d		18 48	18 53	18 58			19 03						19 08	19 13		19 18	19 23	19 28			19 33
Shadwell	d		18 50	18 55	19 00			19 05						19 10	19 15		19 20	19 25	19 30			19 35
Wapping	d		18 52	18 57	19 02			19 07						19 12	19 17		19 22	19 27	19 32			19 37
Rotherhithe	d		18 54	18 59	19 04			19 09						19 14	19 19		19 24	19 29	19 34			19 39
Canada Water	d		18 56	19 01	19 06			19 11						19 16	19 21		19 26	19 31	19 36			19 41
Surrey Quays	d		18 57	19 02	19 07			19 12						19 17	19 22		19 27	19 32	19 37			19 42
New Cross ELL	a				19 12										19 27				19 42			
New Cross Gate 4	a	18 56	19 01	19 06			19 11	19 16						19 21		19 27	19 31	19 36			19 41	19 46
	d	18 56	19 02	19 07			19 11	19 17						19 22		19 27	19 32	19 37			19 41	19 47
Brockley	d	18 59	19 04	19 09			19 14	19 19						19 24		19 30	19 34	19 39			19 44	19 49
Honor Oak Park	d	19 02	19 07	19 12			19 17	19 22						19 27		19 33	19 37	19 42			19 47	19 52
Forest Hill 4	d	19 04	19 10	19 15			19 19	19 25						19 30		19 35	19 40	19 45			19 49	19 55
Sydenham	d	19 07	19 12	19 17			19 22	19 27						19 32		19 38	19 42	19 47			19 52	19 57
Crystal Palace 4	d	19 13		19a22									19 32	19a37		19 43		19a52				
Gipsy Hill	d	19 15											19 34			19 45						
West Norwood 4	d	19 18											19 37			19 48						
Streatham Hill	d	19 22														19 52						
Balham 4 ⊖	d	19 25														19 55						
Wandsworth Common	d	19 27														19 57						
Clapham Junction 10	d	19 31														20 01						
South Bermondsey	d					19 01				19 12	19 15									19 32		
Queens Rd Peckham	d					19 03				19 14	19 18									19 34		
Peckham Rye 4	d					19 06			19 15	19a17	19 20		19a49							19 37		
Denmark Hill 4	d								19 19		19 23	19 28										
London Blackfriars 3 ⊖	a																					
Clapham High Street ⊖	d										19 28											
Wandsworth Road	d										19 29											
Battersea Park 4	d	19 35									19 32					20 05						
London Victoria 15 ⊖	a	19 41							19 28		19 36	19 43				20 09						
Penge West	d		19 15				19 24	19 30									19 45				19 54	20 00
Anerley	d		19 17				19 26	19 32									19 47				19 56	20 02
Norwood Junction 2	d		19 20			19 28	19 30	19 35									19 50			20 02	20 00	20 05
West Croydon 4 🚌	a		19 30			19 35		19 42									20 00			20 07		20 12
East Croydon 🚌	a						19 33														20 03	

3 September to 7 September

London Bridge to London Victoria - Croydon and East London Line

Network Diagram - see first Page of Table 177

		SN	SN	SN	LO	LO	SN	LO		LO	LO	SN	SN	LO	SN	SN	LO	LO		SN	LO	LO	LO	SN	SN
London Bridge 4 ⊖	d	19 38	19 41				19 54					20 03	20 06		20 11					20 22				20 33	20 36
Highbury & Islington	a																								
	d				19 25			19 33		19 40				19 48			19 55				20 03	20 10			
Canonbury	d				19 27			19 35		19 42				19 50			19 57				20 05	20 12			
Dalston Junction Stn ELL	d				19 30	19 35		19 40		19 45	19 50			19 55			20 00	20 05			20 10	20 15	20 20		
Haggerston	d				19 31	19 36		19 41		19 46	19 51			19 56			20 01	20 06			20 11	20 16	20 21		
Hoxton	d				19 33	19 38		19 43		19 48	19 53			19 58			20 03	20 08			20 13	20 18	20 23		
Shoreditch High Street	d				19 36	19 41		19 46		19 51	19 56			20 01			20 06	20 11			20 16	20 21	20 26		
Whitechapel	d				19 38	19 43		19 48		19 53	19 58			20 03			20 08	20 13			20 18	20 23	20 28		
Shadwell	d				19 40	19 45		19 50		19 55	20 00			20 05			20 10	20 15			20 20	20 25	20 30		
Wapping	d				19 42	19 47		19 52		19 57	20 02			20 07			20 12	20 17			20 22	20 27	20 32		
Rotherhithe	d				19 44	19 49		19 54		19 59	20 04			20 09			20 14	20 19			20 24	20 29	20 34		
Canada Water	d				19 46	19 51		19 56		20 01	20 06			20 11			20 16	20 21			20 26	20 31	20 36		
Surrey Quays	d				19 47	19 52		19 57		20 02	20 07			20 12			20 17	20 22			20 27	20 32	20 37		
New Cross ELL	a					19 57					20 12							20 27					20 42		
New Cross Gate 4	a				19 51		19 59	20 01		20 06			20 11	20 16			20 21			20 27	20 31	20 36			20 41
	d				19 52		19 59	20 02		20 07			20 11	20 17			20 22			20 27	20 32	20 37			20 41
Brockley	d				19 54		20 02	20 04		20 09			20 14	20 19			20 24			20 30	20 34	20 39			20 44
Honor Oak Park	d				19 57		20 05	20 07		20 12			20 17	20 22			20 27			20 33	20 37	20 42			20 47
Forest Hill 4	d				20 00		20 07	20 10		20 15			20 19	20 25			20 30			20 35	20 40	20 45			20 49
Sydenham	d				20 02		20 10	20 12		20 17			20 22	20 27			20 32			20 38	20 42	20 47			20 52
Crystal Palace 4	d			20 01	20a07		20 13			20a22						20 31	20a37			20 43		20a52			
Gipsy Hill	d			20 03			20 16									20 33				20 45					
West Norwood 4	d			20 06			20 19									20 36				20 48					
Streatham Hill	d						20 22													20 52					
Balham 4 ⊖	d						20 25													20 56					
Wandsworth Common	d						20 27													20 58					
Clapham Junction 10	d						20 31													21 03					
South Bermondsey	d	19 42	19 45									20 07			20 15									20 37	
Queens Rd Peckham	d	19 44	19 48									20 09			20 18									20 39	
Peckham Rye 4	d	19a47	19 50	20a18								20a12			20 20	20a48								20a42	
Denmark Hill 4	d		19 53												20 23										
London Blackfriars 3 ⊖	a																								
Clapham High Street ⊖	d		19 58												20 28										
Wandsworth Road	d		19 59												20 29										
Battersea Park 4	d		20 02				20 35								20 32					21 06					
London Victoria 15 ⊖	a		20 06				20 39								20 36					21 11					
Penge West	d							20 15					20 24	20 30							20 45				20 54
Anerley	d							20 17					20 26	20 32							20 47				20 56
Norwood Junction 2	d							20 20					20 30	20 35							20 50				21 00
West Croydon 4	a							20 29						20 42							21 00				
East Croydon	a												20 33												21 03

		LO	SN	SN		LO	LO	SN	LO	LO	LO	SN	SN	LO		SN	SE	SN	LO	LO	SN	LO	LO	LO	
London Bridge 4 ⊖	d		20 41					20 52				21 03	21 06			21 11					21 22				
Highbury & Islington	a																								
	d	20 18				20 25			20 33	20 40				20 48					20 55			21 03	21 10		
Canonbury	d	20 20				20 27			20 35	20 42				20 50					20 57			21 05	21 12		
Dalston Junction Stn ELL	d	20 25				20 30	20 35		20 40	20 45	20 50			20 55					21 00	21 05		21 10	21 15	21 20	
Haggerston	d	20 26				20 31	20 36		20 41	20 46	20 51			20 56					21 01	21 06		21 11	21 16	21 21	
Hoxton	d	20 28				20 33	20 38		20 43	20 48	20 53			20 58					21 03	21 08		21 13	21 18	21 23	
Shoreditch High Street	d	20 31				20 36	20 41		20 46	20 51	20 56			21 01					21 06	21 11		21 16	21 21	21 26	
Whitechapel	d	20 33				20 38	20 43		20 48	20 53	20 58			21 03					21 08	21 13		21 18	21 23	21 28	
Shadwell	d	20 35				20 40	20 45		20 50	20 55	21 00			21 05					21 10	21 15		21 20	21 25	21 30	
Wapping	d	20 37				20 42	20 47		20 52	20 57	21 02			21 07					21 12	21 17		21 22	21 27	21 32	
Rotherhithe	d	20 39				20 44	20 49		20 54	20 59	21 04			21 09					21 14	21 19		21 24	21 29	21 34	
Canada Water	d	20 41				20 46	20 51		20 56	21 01	21 06			21 11					21 16	21 21		21 26	21 31	21 36	
Surrey Quays	d	20 42				20 47	20 52		20 57	21 02	21 07			21 12					21 17	21 22		21 27	21 32	21 37	
New Cross ELL	a						20 57				21 12									21 27				21 42	
New Cross Gate 4	a	20 46				20 51		20 57	21 01	21 06			21 11	21 16					21 21		21 27	21 31	21 36		
	d	20 47				20 52		20 57	21 02	21 07			21 11	21 17					21 22		21 27	21 32	21 37		
Brockley	d	20 49				20 54		21 00	21 04	21 09			21 14	21 19					21 24		21 30	21 34	21 39		
Honor Oak Park	d	20 52				20 57		21 03	21 07	21 12			21 17	21 22					21 27		21 33	21 37	21 42		
Forest Hill 4	d	20 55				21 00		21 05	21 10	21 15			21 19	21 25					21 30		21 35	21 40	21 45		
Sydenham	d	20 57				21 02		21 08	21 12	21 17			21 22	21 27					21 32		21 38	21 42	21 47		
Crystal Palace 4	d			21 00		21a07		21 13		21a22								21 30	21a37		21 43		21a52		
Gipsy Hill	d			21 02				21 15										21 32			21 45				
West Norwood 4	d			21 05				21 18										21 35			21 48				
Streatham Hill	d							21 22													21 52				
Balham 4 ⊖	d							21 26													21 56				
Wandsworth Common	d							21 28													21 58				
Clapham Junction 10	d							21 33													22 03				
South Bermondsey	d		20 45									21 07				21 15									
Queens Rd Peckham	d		20 48									21 09				21 18									
Peckham Rye 4	d		20 50	21a17								21a12				21 20	21 20	21a47							
Denmark Hill 4	d		20 53													21 23	21 24								
London Blackfriars 3 ⊖	a																21 34								
Clapham High Street ⊖	d		20 58													21 28									
Wandsworth Road	d		20 59													21 29									
Battersea Park 4	d		21 02					21 36								21 32					22 06				
London Victoria 15 ⊖	a		21 06					21 41								21 36					22 11				
Penge West	d	21 00							21 15				21 24	21 30								21 45			
Anerley	d	21 02							21 17				21 26	21 32								21 47			
Norwood Junction 2	d	21 05							21 20				21 30	21 35								21 50			
West Croydon 4	a	21 12							21 30					21 42								22 00			
East Croydon	a												21 33												

Table 178

Mondays to Fridays

3 September to 7 September

London Bridge to London Victoria - Croydon and East London Line

Network Diagram - see first Page of Table 177

		SN	SN	LO	SN	SE	SN	LO	LO	SN		LO	LO	LO	SN	SN	LO	SN	SE	SN		LO	SN	LO	LO
London Bridge 4 ⊖	d	21 33	21 36		21 41					21 52					22 03	22 08		22 11					22 23		
Highbury & Islington	a																								
	d			21 18				21 25				21 33	21 40				21 48					21 55		22 03	22 10
Canonbury	d			21 20				21 27				21 35	21 42				21 50					21 57		22 05	22 12
Dalston Junction Stn ELL	d			21 25				21 30	21 35			21 40	21 45	21 50			21 55					22 00		22 08	22 15
Haggerston	d			21 26				21 31	21 36			21 41	21 46	21 51			21 56					22 01		22 09	22 16
Hoxton	d			21 28				21 33	21 38			21 43	21 48	21 53			21 58					22 03		22 11	22 18
Shoreditch High Street	d			21 31				21 36	21 41			21 46	21 51	21 56			22 01					22 06		22 14	22 21
Whitechapel	d			21 33				21 38	21 43			21 48	21 53	21 58			22 03					22 08		22 16	22 23
Shadwell	d			21 35				21 40	21 45			21 50	21 55	22 00			22 05					22 10		22 18	22 25
Wapping	d			21 37				21 42	21 47			21 52	21 57	22 02			22 07					22 12		22 20	22 27
Rotherhithe	d			21 39				21 44	21 49			21 54	21 59	22 04			22 09					22 14		22 22	22 29
Canada Water	d			21 41				21 46	21 51			21 56	22 01	22 06			22 11					22 16		22 24	22 31
Surrey Quays	d			21 42				21 47	21 52			21 57	22 02	22 07			22 12					22 17		22 25	22 32
New Cross ELL	a								21 57					22 13											
New Cross Gate 4	a		21 41	21 46				21 51		21 57		22 01	22 06			22 13	22 16					22 21	22 28	22 29	22 36
	d		21 41	21 47				21 52		21 57		22 02	22 07			22 13	22 17					22 22	22 28	22 30	22 37
Brockley	d		21 44	21 49				21 54		22 00		22 04	22 09			22 16	22 19					22 24	22 31	22 32	22 39
Honor Oak Park	d		21 47	21 52				21 57		22 03		22 07	22 12			22 19	22 22					22 27	22 34	22 35	22 42
Forest Hill 4	d		21 49	21 55				22 00		22 05		22 10	22 15			22 21	22 25					22 30	22 36	22 38	22 45
Sydenham	d		21 52	21 57				22 02		22 08		22 12	22 17			22 24	22 27					22 32	22 39	22 40	22 47
Crystal Palace 4	d						22 00	22a07		22 13			22a22							22 22		22a37	22 43		22a52
Gipsy Hill	d						22 02			22 15										22 24			22 45		
West Norwood 4	d						22 05			22 18										22 27			22 48		
Streatham Hill	d									22 22													22 52		
Balham 4 ⊖	d									22 26													22 56		
Wandsworth Common	d									22 28													22 58		
Clapham Junction 10	d									22 33													23 03		
South Bermondsey	d	21 37			21 45										22 07			22 15							
Queens Rd Peckham	d	21 39			21 48										22 09			22 18							
Peckham Rye 4	d	21a42			21 50	21 50	22a17								22a12			22 20	22 20	22a43					
Denmark Hill 4	d				21 53	21 54												22 23	22 24						
London Blackfriars 3 ⊖	a					22 04													22 34						
Clapham High Street ⊖	d				21 58													22 28							
Wandsworth Road	d				21 59													22 29							
Battersea Park 4	d				22 02					22 36								22 32					23 07		
London Victoria 15 ⊖	a				22 06					22 41								22 36					23 14		
Penge West	d		21 54	22 00								22 15				22 26	22 30							22 43	
Anerley	d		21 56	22 02								22 17				22 28	22 32							22 45	
Norwood Junction 2	d		22 00	22 05								22 20				22 32	22 35							22 48	
West Croydon 4	a			22 12								22 30					22 42							23 00	
East Croydon	a		22 03													22 35									

		LO	SN	SN	LO	SN		SE	SN	LO	SN	LO	LO	LO	SN	SN		LO	SN	SE	SN	LO	SN	LO	LO
London Bridge 4 ⊖	d		22 33	22 38		22 41					22 52				23 05	23 06			23 11				23 22		
Highbury & Islington	a																								
	d				22 18					22 25		22 33	22 40					22 48				22 55		23 03	23 10
Canonbury	d				22 20					22 27		22 35	22 42					22 50				22 57		23 05	23 12
Dalston Junction Stn ELL	d	22 20			22 25					22 30		22 38	22 45	22 50				22 55				23 00		23 08	23 15
Haggerston	d	22 21			22 26					22 31		22 39	22 46	22 51				22 56				23 01		23 09	23 16
Hoxton	d	22 23			22 28					22 33		22 41	22 48	22 53				22 58				23 03		23 11	23 18
Shoreditch High Street	d	22 26			22 31					22 36		22 44	22 51	22 56				23 01				23 06		23 14	23 21
Whitechapel	d	22 28			22 33					22 38		22 46	22 53	22 58				23 03				23 08		23 16	23 23
Shadwell	d	22 30			22 35					22 40		22 48	22 55	23 00				23 05				23 10		23 18	23 25
Wapping	d	22 32			22 37					22 42		22 50	22 57	23 02				23 07				23 12		23 20	23 27
Rotherhithe	d	22 34			22 39					22 44		22 52	22 59	23 04				23 09				23 14		23 22	23 29
Canada Water	d	22 36			22 41					22 46		22 54	23 01	23 06				23 11				23 16		23 24	23 31
Surrey Quays	d	22 37			22 42					22 47		22 55	23 02	23 07				23 12				23 17		23 25	23 32
New Cross ELL	a	22 42												23 12											
New Cross Gate 4	a			22 43	22 46					22 51	22 57	22 59	23 06			23 11		23 16				23 21	23 27	23 29	23 36
	d			22 43	22 47					22 52	22 57	23 00	23 07			23 11		23 17				23 22	23 27	23 30	23 37
Brockley	d			22 46	22 49					22 54	23 00	23 02	23 09			23 14		23 19				23 24	23 30	23 32	23 39
Honor Oak Park	d			22 49	22 52					22 57	23 03	23 05	23 12			23 17		23 22				23 27	23 33	23 35	23 42
Forest Hill 4	d			22 51	22 55					23 00	23 05	23 08	23 15			23 19		23 25				23 30	23 35	23 38	23 45
Sydenham	d			22 54	22 57					23 02	23 08	23 10	23 17			23 22		23 27				23 32	23 38	23 40	23 47
Crystal Palace 4	d								23 00	23a07	23 13		23a22								23 30	23a37	23 43		23a52
Gipsy Hill	d								23 02		23 15										23 32		23 45		
West Norwood 4	d								23 05		23 18										23 35		23 48		
Streatham Hill	d										23 22												23 52		
Balham 4 ⊖	d										23 26												23 55		
Wandsworth Common	d										23 28												23 58		
Clapham Junction 10	d										23 33												00 02		
South Bermondsey	d		22 37			22 45									23 09				23 15						
Queens Rd Peckham	d		22 39			22 48									23 11				23 18						
Peckham Rye 4	d		22a42			22 50		22 50	23a17						23 14				23 20	23 20	23a47				
Denmark Hill 4	d					22 53		22 54											23 23	23 24					
London Blackfriars 3 ⊖	a							23 04												23 34					
Clapham High Street ⊖	d					22 58													23 28						
Wandsworth Road	d					22 59													23 29						
Battersea Park 4	d					23 02					23 37								23 32				00 05		
London Victoria 15 ⊖	a					23 06					23 41								23 37				00 10		
Penge West	d			22 56	23 00							23 13				23 24		23 30						23 43	
Anerley	d			22 58	23 02							23 15				23 26		23 32						23 45	
Norwood Junction 2	d			23 02	23 05							23 18			23a36	23 30		23 35						23 48	
West Croydon 4	a				23 12							23 30						23 42						23 59	
East Croydon	a			23 06												23 33									

3 September to 7 September

London Bridge to London Victoria - Croydon and East London Line

Network Diagram - see first Page of Table 177

		LO		SN	SN	LO	LO	SN	LO	LO	LO	LO
London Bridge 4 ⊖	d			23 33	23 36			23 52				
Highbury & Islington	a											
	d					23 18	23 25		23 33	23 40	23 48	23 55
Canonbury	d					23 20	23 27		23 35	23 42	23 50	23 57
Dalston Junction Stn ELL	d	23 20				23 25	23 30		23 38	23 45	23 55	00 01
Haggerston	d	23 21				23 26	23 31		23 39	23 46	23 56	00 02
Hoxton	d	23 23				23 28	23 33		23 41	23 48	23 58	00 04
Shoreditch High Street	d	23 26				23 31	23 36		23 44	23 51	00 01	00 07
Whitechapel	d	23 28				23 33	23 38		23 46	23 53	00 03	00 09
Shadwell	d	23 30				23 35	23 40		23 48	23 55	00 05	00 11
Wapping	d	23 32				23 37	23 42		23 50	23 57	00 07	00 13
Rotherhithe	d	23 34				23 39	23 44		23 52	23 59	00 09	00 15
Canada Water	d	23 36				23 41	23 46		23 54	00 02	00 11	00 17
Surrey Quays	d	23 37				23 42	23 47		23 55	00 03	00 12	00 18
New Cross ELL	a	23 42										
New Cross Gate 4	a				23 41	23 46	23 51	23 57	23 58	00 07	00 16	00 22
	d				23 41	23 47	23 52	23 57	23 59	00 08	00 17	00 23
Brockley	d				23 44	23 49	23 54	00 01	00 03	00 10	00 19	00 25
Honor Oak Park	d				23 47	23 52	23 57	00 04	00 06	00 13	00 22	00 28
Forest Hill 4	d				23 49	23 55	23 59	00 06	00 09	00 16	00 25	00 31
Sydenham	d				23 52	23 57	00 02	00 09	00 11	00 18	00 27	00 33
Crystal Palace 4	d						00a07	00 13		00a23		00a38
Gipsy Hill	d							00 15				
West Norwood 4	d							00 18				
Streatham Hill	d							00 22				
Balham 4 ⊖	d							00 25				
Wandsworth Common	d							00 27				
Clapham Junction 10	d							00 31				
South Bermondsey	d			23 37								
Queens Rd Peckham	d			23 39								
Peckham Rye 4	d			23 42								
Denmark Hill 4	d											
London Blackfriars 3 ⊖	a											
Clapham High Street ⊖	d											
Wandsworth Road	d											
Battersea Park 4	d							00 35				
London Victoria 15 ⊖	a							00 42				
Penge West	d				23 54	00 01			00 14		00 30	
Anerley	d				23 56	00 03			00 16		00 32	
Norwood Junction 2	d			00a04	23 59	00 06			00 19		00 35	
West Croydon 4	a					00 13			00 26		00 42	
East Croydon	a				00 03							

Sundays

from 16 September

		SN	SN	SN	LO	SN	LO	LO	SN	SN		LO	LO	SN	SN	SN	SN	SN	SE	SN		SN	SE	LO	LO
London Bridge 4 ⊖	d	23p22	23p36			23p52			00 03	00 06						00 33	00 36			07 11					
Highbury & Islington	a																								
	d				23p25		23p35	23p42				23p56	00 10												06 51
Canonbury	d				23p27		23p37	23p44				23p58	00 12												06 53
Dalston Junction Stn ELL	d				23p30		23p40	23p47				00 02	00 15												06 56
Haggerston	d				23p31		23p41	23p48				00 03	00 16												06 57
Hoxton	d				23p33		23p43	23p50				00 05	00 18												06 59
Shoreditch High Street	d				23p36		23p46	23p53				00 08	00 21												07 02
Whitechapel	d				23p38		23p48	23p55				00 10	00 23												07 04
Shadwell	d				23p40		23p50	23p57				00 12	00 25												07 06
Wapping	d				23p42		23p52	23p59				00 14	00 27												07 08
Rotherhithe	d				23p44		23p54	00 01				00 16	00 29												07 10
Canada Water	d				23p46		23p56	00 03				00 18	00 31												07 12
Surrey Quays	d				23p47		23p57	00 05				00 19	00 32												07 13
New Cross ELL	a																								
New Cross Gate 4	a	23p27	23p41		23p51	23p57	00 02	00 08		00 11		00 23	00 36				00 41								07 17
	d	23p27	23p41		23p52	23p57	00 02			00 11							00 41							07 04	07 18
Brockley	d	23p30	23p44		23p54	00 01	00 04			00 14							00 44							07 06	07 20
Honor Oak Park	d	23p33	23p47		23p57	00 04	00 07			00 17							00 47							07 09	07 23
Forest Hill 4	d	23p35	23p49		23p59	00 06	00 10			00 19							00 49							07 12	07 26
Sydenham	d	23p38	23p52		00 02	00 09	00 12			00 22							00 52							07 14	07 28
Crystal Palace 4	d	23p43		00 03	00a07	00 13								00 33	00 47			01 03				07 07			07a33
Gipsy Hill	d	23p45				00 15																07 09			
West Norwood 4	d	23p48				00 18																07 12			
Streatham Hill	d	23p52				00 22																			
Balham 4 ⊖	d	23p55				00 26																			
Wandsworth Common	d	23p57				00 28																			
Clapham Junction 10	d	00 02				00 32																			
South Bermondsey	d								00 07							00 37				07 15					
Queens Rd Peckham	d								00 09							00 39				07 18					
Peckham Rye 4	d								00 12							00 42			07 09	07 20		07a23	07 39		
Denmark Hill 4	d																		07 13	07 23			07 43		
London Blackfriars 3 ⊖	a																		07 23				07 53		
Clapham High Street ⊖	d																			07 28					
Wandsworth Road	d																			07 29					
Battersea Park 4	d	00 05				00 35														07 32					
London Victoria 15 ⊖	a	00 10				00 42														07 36					
Penge West	d		23p54				00 15			00 24							00 54							07 17	
Anerley	d		23p56				00 17			00 26							00 56							07 19	
Norwood Junction 2	d		23p59	00 09			00 20		00a34	00 30				00 38	00 52	01a04	01 00	01 08						07 22	
West Croydon 4	a			00 14			00 27							00 43	00 58			01 13						07 29	
East Croydon	a		00 03							00 33							01 03								

Table 178 **Sundays**

from 16 September

London Bridge to London Victoria - Croydon and East London Line

Network Diagram - see first Page of Table 177

		SN	LO	SN	SN	SN		SN	LO	SN	LO	SE	SN	SN	SN	SN		LO	SN	LO	LO	SE	SN	SN	SN
London Bridge 4 ⊖	d	07 24		07 36	07 39	07 41				07 54			08 06	08 09	08 11				08 24				08 36	08 39	08 41
Highbury & Islington	a																								
	d		07 05						07 21		07 35							07 51		08 05	08 15				
Canonbury	d		07 07						07 23		07 37							07 53		08 07	08 17				
Dalston Junction Stn ELL	d		07 12						07 26		07 42							07 56		08 12	08 22				
Haggerston	d		07 13						07 27		07 43							07 57		08 13	08 23				
Hoxton	d		07 15						07 29		07 45							07 59		08 15	08 25				
Shoreditch High Street	d		07 18						07 32		07 48							08 02		08 18	08 28				
Whitechapel	d		07 20						07 34		07 50							08 04		08 20	08 30				
Shadwell	d		07 22						07 36		07 52							08 06		08 22	08 32				
Wapping	d		07 24						07 38		07 54							08 08		08 24	08 34				
Rotherhithe	d		07 26						07 40		07 56							08 10		08 26	08 36				
Canada Water	d		07 28						07 42		07 58							08 12		08 28	08 38				
Surrey Quays	d		07 29						07 43		07 59							08 13		08 29	08 39				
New Cross ELL	a																				08 45				
New Cross Gate 4	a	07 29	07 33		07 44				07 47	07 59	08 03			08 14				08 17	08 29	08 33				08 44	
	d	07 29	07 34		07 44				07 48	07 59	08 03			08 14				08 18	08 29	08 34				08 44	
Brockley	d	07 32	07 36		07 47				07 50	08 02	08 06			08 17				08 20	08 32	08 36				08 47	
Honor Oak Park	d	07 35	07 39		07 50				07 53	08 05	08 09			08 20				08 23	08 35	08 39				08 50	
Forest Hill 4	d	07 37	07 42		07 52				07 56	08 07	08 12			08 22				08 26	08 37	08 42				08 52	
Sydenham	d	07 40	07 44		07 55				07 58	08 10	08 14			08 25				08 28	08 40	08 44				08 55	
Crystal Palace 4	d							07 37	08a03							08 07		08a33							
Gipsy Hill	d							07 39								08 09									
West Norwood 4	d							07 42								08 12									
Streatham Hill	d																								
Balham 4 ⊖	d																								
Wandsworth Common	d																								
Clapham Junction 10	d																								
South Bermondsey	d			07 40		07 45							08 10		08 15								08 40		08 45
Queens Rd Peckham	d			07 42		07 48							08 12		08 18								08 42		08 48
Peckham Rye 4	d			07a45		07 50		07a53				08 09	08a15		08 20	08a23						08 39	08a45		08 50
Denmark Hill 4	d					07 53						08 13			08 23							08 43			08 53
London Blackfriars 3 ⊖	a											08 23										08 53			
Clapham High Street ⊖	d					07 58									08 28										08 58
Wandsworth Road	d					07 59									08 29										08 59
Battersea Park 4	d					08 02									08 32										09 02
London Victoria 15 ⊖	a					08 06									08 36										09 06
Penge West	d		07 47		07 57						08 17			08 27						08 47				08 57	
Anerley	d		07 49		07 59						08 19			08 29						08 49				08 59	
Norwood Junction 2	d	07 48	07 52		08 03					08 16	08 22			08 33					08 46	08 52				09 03	
West Croydon 4	a	07 55	07 59							08 24	08 28								08 54	08 58					
East Croydon	a				08 07									08 37										09 07	

		SN		LO	LO	SN	LO	LO	SE	SN	SN	SN		SN	LO	LO	SN	LO	LO	SE	SN	SN		SN	SN
London Bridge 4 ⊖	d					08 54				09 06	09 09	09 11					09 24				09 36	09 39		09 41	
Highbury & Islington	a																								
	d			08 21	08 30		08 35	08 45							08 51	09 00		09 05	09 15						
Canonbury	d			08 23	08 32		08 37	08 47							08 53	09 02		09 07	09 17						
Dalston Junction Stn ELL	d			08 26	08 37		08 42	08 52							08 56	09 07		09 12	09 22						
Haggerston	d			08 27	08 38		08 43	08 53							08 57	09 08		09 13	09 23						
Hoxton	d			08 29	08 40		08 45	08 55							08 59	09 10		09 15	09 25						
Shoreditch High Street	d			08 32	08 43		08 48	08 58							09 02	09 13		09 18	09 28						
Whitechapel	d			08 34	08 45		08 50	09 00							09 04	09 15		09 20	09 30						
Shadwell	d			08 36	08 47		08 52	09 02							09 06	09 17		09 22	09 32						
Wapping	d			08 38	08 49		08 54	09 04							09 08	09 19		09 24	09 34						
Rotherhithe	d			08 40	08 51		08 56	09 06							09 10	09 21		09 26	09 36						
Canada Water	d			08 42	08 53		08 58	09 08							09 12	09 23		09 28	09 38						
Surrey Quays	d			08 43	08 54		08 59	09 09							09 13	09 24		09 29	09 39						
New Cross ELL	a				09 00			09 15								09 30			09 45						
New Cross Gate 4	a			08 47		08 59	09 03				09 14				09 17		09 29	09 33				09 44			
	d			08 48		08 59	09 04				09 14				09 18		09 29	09 34				09 44			
Brockley	d			08 50		09 02	09 06				09 17				09 20		09 32	09 36				09 47			
Honor Oak Park	d			08 53		09 05	09 09				09 20				09 23		09 35	09 39				09 50			
Forest Hill 4	d			08 56		09 07	09 12				09 22				09 26		09 37	09 42				09 52			
Sydenham	d			08 58		09 10	09 14				09 25				09 28		09 40	09 44				09 55			
Crystal Palace 4	d	08 37		09a03										09 07	09a33										09 37
Gipsy Hill	d	08 39												09 09											09 39
West Norwood 4	d	08 42												09 12											09 42
Streatham Hill	d																								
Balham 4 ⊖	d																								
Wandsworth Common	d																								
Clapham Junction 10	d																								
South Bermondsey	d									09 10		09 15									09 40			09 45	
Queens Rd Peckham	d									09 12		09 18									09 42			09 48	
Peckham Rye 4	d	08a53							09 09	09a15		09 20		09a23						09 39	09a45			09 50	09a53
Denmark Hill 4	d								09 13			09 23								09 43				09 53	
London Blackfriars 3 ⊖	a								09 23											09 53					
Clapham High Street ⊖	d											09 28												09 58	
Wandsworth Road	d											09 29												09 59	
Battersea Park 4	d											09 32												10 02	
London Victoria 15 ⊖	a											09 36												10 06	
Penge West	d						09 17				09 27							09 47				09 57			
Anerley	d						09 19				09 29							09 49				09 59			
Norwood Junction 2	d					09 16	09 22				09 33						09 46	09 52				10 03			
West Croydon 4	a					09 24	09 28										09 54	09 58							
East Croydon	a										09 37											10 07			

Table 178

Sundays

from 16 September

London Bridge to London Victoria - Croydon and East London Line

Network Diagram - see first Page of Table 177

		LO	LO	SN	LO	LO	SE	SN		SN	SN	SN	LO	LO	SN	LO	LO	SE		SN	SN	SN	SN	LO	LO
London Bridge 4 ⊖	d			09 54				10 06		10 09	10 11				10 24					10 36	10 39	10 41			
Highbury & Islington	a																								
	d	09 21	09 30		09 35	09 45							09 51	10 00		10 05	10 15							10 21	10 30
Canonbury	d	09 23	09 32		09 37	09 47							09 53	10 02		10 07	10 17							10 23	10 32
Dalston Junction Stn ELL	d	09 26	09 37		09 42	09 52							09 56	10 07		10 12	10 22							10 26	10 37
Haggerston	d	09 27	09 38		09 43	09 53							09 57	10 08		10 13	10 23							10 27	10 38
Hoxton	d	09 29	09 40		09 45	09 55							09 59	10 10		10 15	10 25							10 29	10 40
Shoreditch High Street	d	09 32	09 43		09 48	09 58							10 02	10 13		10 18	10 28							10 32	10 43
Whitechapel	d	09 34	09 45		09 50	10 00							10 04	10 15		10 20	10 30							10 34	10 45
Shadwell	d	09 36	09 47		09 52	10 02							10 06	10 17		10 22	10 32							10 36	10 47
Wapping	d	09 38	09 49		09 54	10 04							10 08	10 19		10 24	10 34							10 38	10 49
Rotherhithe	d	09 40	09 51		09 56	10 06							10 10	10 21		10 26	10 36							10 40	10 51
Canada Water	d	09 42	09 53		09 58	10 08							10 12	10 23		10 28	10 38							10 42	10 53
Surrey Quays	d	09 43	09 54		09 59	10 09							10 13	10 24		10 29	10 39							10 43	10 54
New Cross ELL	a		10 00			10 15								10 30			10 45								11 00
New Cross Gate 4	a	09 47		09 59	10 03					10 14			10 17		10 29	10 33					10 44			10 47	
	d	09 48		09 59	10 04					10 14			10 18		10 29	10 34					10 44			10 48	
Brockley	d	09 50		10 02	10 06					10 17			10 20		10 32	10 36					10 47			10 50	
Honor Oak Park	d	09 53		10 05	10 09					10 20			10 23		10 35	10 39					10 50			10 53	
Forest Hill 4	d	09 56		10 07	10 12					10 22			10 26		10 37	10 42					10 52			10 56	
Sydenham	d	09 58		10 10	10 14					10 25			10 28		10 40	10 44					10 55			10 58	
Crystal Palace 4	d	10a03										10 07	10a33										10 37	11a03	
Gipsy Hill	d											10 09											10 39		
West Norwood 4	d											10 12											10 42		
Streatham Hill	d																								
Balham 4 ⊖	d																								
Wandsworth Common	d																								
Clapham Junction 10	d																								
South Bermondsey	d							10 10			10 15									10 40		10 45			
Queens Rd Peckham	d							10 12			10 18									10 42		10 48			
Peckham Rye 4	d						10 09	10a15			10 20	10a23						10 39		10a45		10 50	10a53		
Denmark Hill 4	d						10 13				10 23							10 43				10 53			
London Blackfriars 3 ⊖	a						10 23											10 53							
Clapham High Street ⊖	d										10 28											10 58			
Wandsworth Road	d										10 29											10 59			
Battersea Park 4	d										10 32											11 02			
London Victoria 15 ⊖	a										10 36											11 06			
Penge West	d				10 17					10 27						10 47					10 57				
Anerley	d				10 19					10 29						10 49					10 59				
Norwood Junction 2	d			10 16	10 22					10 33					10 46	10 52					11 03				
West Croydon 4 🚌	a			10 24	10 28										10 54	10 58									
East Croydon 🚌	a									10 37											11 07				

		SN	LO	LO		SE	SN	SN	SN	SN	LO	LO	SN	LO		LO	SE	SN	SN	SN	SN	LO	LO	SN	
London Bridge 4 ⊖	d	10 54					11 06	11 09	11 11				11 24					11 36	11 39	11 41				11 54	
Highbury & Islington	a																								
	d		10 35	10 45							10 51	11 00		11 05		11 15						11 21	11 30		
Canonbury	d		10 37	10 47							10 53	11 02		11 07		11 17						11 23	11 32		
Dalston Junction Stn ELL	d		10 42	10 52							10 56	11 07		11 12		11 22						11 26	11 37		
Haggerston	d		10 43	10 53							10 57	11 08		11 13		11 23						11 27	11 38		
Hoxton	d		10 45	10 55							10 59	11 10		11 15		11 25						11 29	11 40		
Shoreditch High Street	d		10 48	10 58							11 02	11 13		11 18		11 28						11 32	11 43		
Whitechapel	d		10 50	11 00							11 04	11 15		11 20		11 30						11 34	11 45		
Shadwell	d		10 52	11 02							11 06	11 17		11 22		11 32						11 36	11 47		
Wapping	d		10 54	11 04							11 08	11 19		11 24		11 34						11 38	11 49		
Rotherhithe	d		10 56	11 06							11 10	11 21		11 26		11 36						11 40	11 51		
Canada Water	d		10 58	11 08							11 12	11 23		11 28		11 38						11 42	11 53		
Surrey Quays	d		10 59	11 09							11 13	11 24		11 29		11 39						11 43	11 54		
New Cross ELL	a			11 15								11 30				11 45							12 00		
New Cross Gate 4	a	10 59	11 03					11 14			11 17		11 29	11 33					11 44			11 47		11 59	
	d	10 59	11 04					11 14			11 18		11 29	11 34					11 44			11 48		11 59	
Brockley	d	11 02	11 06					11 17			11 20		11 32	11 36					11 47			11 50		12 02	
Honor Oak Park	d	11 05	11 09					11 20			11 23		11 35	11 39					11 50			11 53		12 05	
Forest Hill 4	d	11 07	11 12					11 22			11 26		11 37	11 42					11 52			11 56		12 07	
Sydenham	d	11 10	11 14					11 25			11 28		11 40	11 44					11 55			11 58		12 10	
Crystal Palace 4	d									11 07	11a33										11 37	12a03			
Gipsy Hill	d									11 09											11 39				
West Norwood 4	d									11 12											11 42				
Streatham Hill	d																								
Balham 4 ⊖	d																								
Wandsworth Common	d																								
Clapham Junction 10	d																								
South Bermondsey	d						11 10		11 15									11 40		11 45					
Queens Rd Peckham	d						11 12		11 18									11 42		11 48					
Peckham Rye 4	d					11 09	11a15		11 20	11a23							11 39	11a45		11 50	11a53				
Denmark Hill 4	d					11 13			11 23								11 43			11 53					
London Blackfriars 3 ⊖	a					11 23											11 53								
Clapham High Street ⊖	d								11 28											11 58					
Wandsworth Road	d								11 29											11 59					
Battersea Park 4	d								11 32											12 02					
London Victoria 15 ⊖	a								11 36											12 06					
Penge West	d		11 17					11 27						11 47					11 57						
Anerley	d		11 19					11 29						11 49					11 59						
Norwood Junction 2	d	11 16	11 22					11 33					11 46	11 52					12 03					12 16	
West Croydon 4 🚌	a	11 24	11 28										11 54	11 58										12 24	
East Croydon 🚌	a							11 37											12 07						

Table 178

Sundays

from 16 September

London Bridge to London Victoria - Croydon and East London Line

Network Diagram - see first Page of Table 177

		LO	SE	SN	SN	LO	LO	SN	LO	SN		SE	SN	LO	LO	SN	LO	LO	LO	SN		SN	LO	SN	SE
London Bridge 4 ⊖	d			12 06				12 09		12 11						12 24				12 36		12 39		12 41	
Highbury & Islington	a																								
	d	11 35				11 43			11 51					11 58			12 06	12 13					12 21		
Canonbury	d	11 37				11 45			11 53					12 00			12 08	12 15					12 23		
Dalston Junction Stn ELL	d	11 42				11 48	11 52		11 58					12 03	12 08		12 13	12 18	12 23				12 28		
Haggerston	d	11 43				11 49	11 53		11 59					12 04	12 09		12 14	12 19	12 24				12 29		
Hoxton	d	11 45				11 51	11 55		12 01					12 06	12 11		12 16	12 21	12 26				12 31		
Shoreditch High Street	d	11 48				11 54	11 58		12 04					12 09	12 14		12 19	12 24	12 29				12 34		
Whitechapel	d	11 50				11 56	12 00		12 06					12 11	12 16		12 21	12 26	12 31				12 36		
Shadwell	d	11 52				11 58	12 02		12 08					12 13	12 18		12 23	12 28	12 33				12 38		
Wapping	d	11 54				12 00	12 04		12 10					12 15	12 20		12 25	12 30	12 35				12 40		
Rotherhithe	d	11 56				12 02	12 06		12 12					12 17	12 22		12 27	12 32	12 37				12 42		
Canada Water	d	11 58				12 04	12 08		12 14					12 19	12 24		12 29	12 34	12 39				12 44		
Surrey Quays	d	11 59				12 05	12 09		12 15					12 20	12 25		12 30	12 35	12 40				12 45		
New Cross ELL	a						12 14								12 30				12 45						
New Cross Gate 4	a	12 03				12 09		12 14	12 19					12 24		12 29	12 34	12 39				12 44	12 49		
	d	12 04				12 10		12 14	12 20					12 25		12 29	12 35	12 40				12 44	12 50		
Brockley	d	12 06				12 12		12 17	12 22					12 27		12 32	12 37	12 42				12 47	12 52		
Honor Oak Park	d	12 09				12 15		12 20	12 25					12 30		12 35	12 40	12 45				12 50	12 55		
Forest Hill 4	d	12 12				12 18		12 22	12 28					12 33		12 37	12 43	12 48				12 52	12 58		
Sydenham	d	12 14				12 20		12 25	12 30					12 35		12 40	12 45	12 50				12 55	13 00		
Crystal Palace 4	d				12 07	12a25							12 37	12a40				12a55							
Gipsy Hill	d				12 09								12 39												
West Norwood 4	d				12 12								12 42												
Streatham Hill	d																								
Balham 4 ⊖	d																								
Wandsworth Common	d																								
Clapham Junction 10	d																								
South Bermondsey	d			12 10						12 15										12 40				12 45	
Queens Rd Peckham	d			12 12						12 18										12 42				12 48	
Peckham Rye 4	d		12 09	12a15	12a23					12 20		12 39	12a53							12a45				12 50	13 09
Denmark Hill 4	d		12 13							12 23		12 43												12 53	13 13
London Blackfriars 3 ⊖	a		12 23									12 53													13 23
Clapham High Street ⊖	d									12 28														12 58	
Wandsworth Road	d									12 29														12 59	
Battersea Park 4	d									12 32														13 02	
London Victoria 15 ⊖	a									12 36														13 06	
Penge West	d	12 17						12 27	12 33								12 48					12 57	13 03		
Anerley	d	12 19						12 29	12 35								12 50					12 59	13 05		
Norwood Junction 2	d	12 22						12 33	12 38							12 46	12 53					13 03	13 08		
West Croydon 4	a	12 28							12 45							12 54	12 59						13 15		
East Croydon	a							12 37														13 07			

		SN	LO	LO	SN	LO		LO	LO	SN	and at the same minutes past each hour until	SN	SN	LO	SN		SE	SN	LO	LO	SN	LO	LO	LO
London Bridge 4 ⊖	d				12 54					13 06		17 06	17 09		17 11						17 24			
Highbury & Islington	a																							
	d		12 28			12 36		12 43						16 51					16 58			17 06	17 13	
Canonbury	d		12 30			12 38		12 45						16 53					17 00			17 08	17 15	
Dalston Junction Stn ELL	d		12 33	12 38		12 43		12 48	12 53					16 58					17 03	17 08		17 13	17 18	17 23
Haggerston	d		12 34	12 39		12 44		12 49	12 54					16 59					17 04	17 09		17 14	17 19	17 24
Hoxton	d		12 36	12 41		12 46		12 51	12 56					17 01					17 06	17 11		17 16	17 21	17 26
Shoreditch High Street	d		12 39	12 44		12 49		12 54	12 59					17 04					17 09	17 14		17 19	17 24	17 29
Whitechapel	d		12 41	12 46		12 51		12 56	13 01					17 06					17 11	17 16		17 21	17 26	17 31
Shadwell	d		12 43	12 48		12 53		12 58	13 03					17 08					17 13	17 18		17 23	17 28	17 33
Wapping	d		12 45	12 50		12 55		13 00	13 05					17 10					17 15	17 20		17 25	17 30	17 35
Rotherhithe	d		12 47	12 52		12 57		13 02	13 07					17 12					17 17	17 22		17 27	17 32	17 37
Canada Water	d		12 49	12 54		12 59		13 04	13 09					17 14					17 19	17 24		17 29	17 34	17 39
Surrey Quays	d		12 50	12 55		13 00		13 05	13 10					17 15					17 20	17 25		17 30	17 35	17 40
New Cross ELL	a			13 00					13 15											17 30				17 45
New Cross Gate 4	a		12 54		12 59	13 04		13 09					17 14	17 19					17 24		17 29	17 34	17 39	
	d		12 55		12 59	13 05		13 10					17 14	17 20					17 25		17 29	17 35	17 40	
Brockley	d		12 57		13 02	13 07		13 12					17 17	17 22					17 27		17 32	17 37	17 42	
Honor Oak Park	d		13 00		13 05	13 10		13 15					17 20	17 25					17 30		17 35	17 40	17 45	
Forest Hill 4	d		13 03		13 07	13 13		13 18					17 22	17 28					17 33		17 37	17 43	17 48	
Sydenham	d		13 05		13 10	13 15		13 20					17 25	17 30					17 35		17 40	17 45	17 50	
Crystal Palace 4	d	13 07	13a10					13a25										17 37	17a40				17a55	
Gipsy Hill	d	13 09																17 39						
West Norwood 4	d	13 12																17 42						
Streatham Hill	d																							
Balham 4 ⊖	d																							
Wandsworth Common	d																							
Clapham Junction 10	d																							
South Bermondsey	d									13 10		17 10			17 15									
Queens Rd Peckham	d									13 12		17 12			17 18									
Peckham Rye 4	d	13a23								13a15		17a15			17 20		17 39	17a53						
Denmark Hill 4	d														17 23		17 43							
London Blackfriars 3 ⊖	a																17 53							
Clapham High Street ⊖	d														17 28									
Wandsworth Road	d														17 29									
Battersea Park 4	d														17 32									
London Victoria 15 ⊖	a														17 36									
Penge West	d					13 18							17 27	17 33								17 48		
Anerley	d					13 20							17 29	17 35								17 50		
Norwood Junction 2	d				13 16	13 23							17 33	17 38							17 46	17 53		
West Croydon 4	a				13 24	13 29								17 45							17 54	17 59		
East Croydon	a												17 37											

Table 178

Sundays
from 16 September

London Bridge to London Victoria - Croydon and East London Line

Network Diagram - see first Page of Table 177

		SN		SN	LO	SN	SE	SN	LO	LO	SN	LO		LO	LO	SN	SN	LO	SN	SE	SN	LO		LO	SN
London Bridge 4 ⊖	d	17 36		17 39		17 41					17 54					18 06	18 09		18 11						18 24
Highbury & Islington	a																								
	d				17 21				17 28			17 36		17 43				17 51				17 58			
Canonbury	d				17 23				17 30			17 38		17 45				17 53				18 00			
Dalston Junction Stn ELL	d				17 28				17 33	17 38		17 43		17 48	17 53			17 58				18 03		18 08	
Haggerston	d				17 29				17 34	17 39		17 44		17 49	17 54			17 59				18 04		18 09	
Hoxton	d				17 31				17 36	17 41		17 46		17 51	17 56			18 01				18 06		18 11	
Shoreditch High Street	d				17 34				17 39	17 44		17 49		17 54	17 59			18 04				18 09		18 14	
Whitechapel	d				17 36				17 41	17 46		17 51		17 56	18 01			18 06				18 11		18 16	
Shadwell	d				17 38				17 43	17 48		17 53		17 58	18 03			18 08				18 13		18 18	
Wapping	d				17 40				17 45	17 50		17 55		18 00	18 05			18 10				18 15		18 20	
Rotherhithe	d				17 42				17 47	17 52		17 57		18 02	18 07			18 12				18 17		18 22	
Canada Water	d				17 44				17 49	17 54		17 59		18 04	18 09			18 14				18 19		18 24	
Surrey Quays	d				17 45				17 50	17 55		18 00		18 05	18 10			18 15				18 20		18 25	
New Cross ELL	a									18 00					18 15									18 30	
New Cross Gate 4	a			17 44	17 49				17 54		17 59	18 04		18 09			18 14	18 19				18 24			18 29
	d			17 44	17 50				17 55		17 59	18 05		18 10			18 14	18 20				18 25			18 29
Brockley	d			17 47	17 52				17 57		18 02	18 07		18 12			18 17	18 22				18 27			18 32
Honor Oak Park	d			17 50	17 55				18 00		18 05	18 10		18 15			18 20	18 25				18 30			18 35
Forest Hill 4	d			17 52	17 58				18 03		18 07	18 13		18 18			18 22	18 28				18 33			18 37
Sydenham	d			17 55	18 00				18 05		18 10	18 15		18 20			18 25	18 30				18 35			18 40
Crystal Palace 4	d							18 07	18a10					18a25							18 37	18a40			
Gipsy Hill	d							18 09													18 39				
West Norwood 4	d							18 12													18 42				
Streatham Hill	d																								
Balham 4 ⊖	d																								
Wandsworth Common	d																								
Clapham Junction 10	d																								
South Bermondsey	d	17 40				17 45										18 10			18 15						
Queens Rd Peckham	d	17 42				17 48										18 12			18 18						
Peckham Rye 4	d	17a45				17 50	18 09	18a23								18a15			18 20	18 39	18a53				
Denmark Hill 4	d					17 53	18 13												18 23	18 43					
London Blackfriars 3 ⊖	a						18 23													18 53					
Clapham High Street ⊖	d					17 58													18 28						
Wandsworth Road	d					17 59													18 29						
Battersea Park 4	d					18 02													18 32						
London Victoria 15 ⊖	a					18 06													18 36						
Penge West	d			17 57	18 03							18 18					18 27	18 33							
Anerley	d			17 59	18 05							18 20					18 29	18 35							
Norwood Junction 2	d			18 03	18 08						18 16	18 23					18 33	18 38							18 46
West Croydon 4	a				18 14						18 24	18 29						18 44							18 54
East Croydon	a			18 07													18 37								

		LO	LO	LO	SN	SN	LO	SN		SE	SN	LO	LO	SN	LO	LO	LO	SN		SN	LO	SN	SE	SN	LO
London Bridge 4 ⊖	d				18 36	18 39		18 41						18 54				19 06		19 09		19 11			
Highbury & Islington	a																								
	d	18 06	18 13				18 21					18 28			18 36	18 43					18 51				18 58
Canonbury	d	18 08	18 15				18 23					18 30			18 38	18 45					18 53				19 00
Dalston Junction Stn ELL	d	18 13	18 18	18 23			18 28					18 33	18 38		18 43	18 48	18 53				18 58				19 03
Haggerston	d	18 14	18 19	18 24			18 29					18 34	18 39		18 44	18 49	18 54				18 59				19 04
Hoxton	d	18 16	18 21	18 26			18 31					18 36	18 41		18 46	18 51	18 56				19 01				19 06
Shoreditch High Street	d	18 19	18 24	18 29			18 34					18 39	18 44		18 49	18 54	18 59				19 04				19 09
Whitechapel	d	18 21	18 26	18 31			18 36					18 41	18 46		18 51	18 56	19 01				19 06				19 11
Shadwell	d	18 23	18 28	18 33			18 38					18 43	18 48		18 53	18 58	19 03				19 08				19 13
Wapping	d	18 25	18 30	18 35			18 40					18 45	18 50		18 55	19 00	19 05				19 10				19 15
Rotherhithe	d	18 27	18 32	18 37			18 42					18 47	18 52		18 57	19 02	19 07				19 12				19 17
Canada Water	d	18 29	18 34	18 39			18 44					18 49	18 54		18 59	19 04	19 09				19 14				19 19
Surrey Quays	d	18 30	18 35	18 40			18 45					18 50	18 55		19 00	19 05	19 10				19 15				19 20
New Cross ELL	a			18 45									19 00				19 15								
New Cross Gate 4	a	18 34	18 39			18 44	18 49					18 54		18 59	19 04	19 09				19 14	19 19				19 24
	d	18 35	18 40			18 44	18 50					18 55		18 59	19 05	19 10				19 14	19 20				19 25
Brockley	d	18 37	18 42			18 47	18 52					18 57		19 02	19 07	19 12				19 17	19 22				19 27
Honor Oak Park	d	18 40	18 45			18 50	18 55					19 00		19 05	19 10	19 15				19 20	19 25				19 30
Forest Hill 4	d	18 43	18 48			18 52	18 58					19 03		19 07	19 13	19 18				19 22	19 28				19 33
Sydenham	d	18 45	18 50			18 55	19 00					19 05		19 10	19 15	19 20				19 25	19 30				19 35
Crystal Palace 4	d		18a55								19 07	19a10				19a25								19 37	19a40
Gipsy Hill	d										19 09													19 39	
West Norwood 4	d										19 12													19 42	
Streatham Hill	d																								
Balham 4 ⊖	d																								
Wandsworth Common	d																								
Clapham Junction 10	d																								
South Bermondsey	d				18 40			18 45										19 10				19 15			
Queens Rd Peckham	d				18 42			18 48										19 12				19 18			
Peckham Rye 4	d				18a45			18 50		19 09	19a23							19a15				19 20	19 39	19a53	
Denmark Hill 4	d							18 53		19 13												19 23	19 43		
London Blackfriars 3 ⊖	a									19 23													19 53		
Clapham High Street ⊖	d							18 58														19 28			
Wandsworth Road	d							18 59														19 29			
Battersea Park 4	d							19 02														19 32			
London Victoria 15 ⊖	a							19 06														19 36			
Penge West	d	18 48				18 57	19 03								19 18					19 27	19 33				
Anerley	d	18 50				18 59	19 05								19 20					19 29	19 35				
Norwood Junction 2	d	18 53				19 03	19 08							19 16	19 23					19 33	19 38				
West Croydon 4	a	18 59					19 14							19 24	19 29						19 44				
East Croydon	a					19 07														19 37					

Table 178

Sundays
from 16 September

London Bridge to London Victoria - Croydon and East London Line

Network Diagram - see first Page of Table 177

		LO	SN	LO		LO	LO	SN	SN	LO	SN	SE	SN	LO		LO	SN	LO	LO	LO	SN	SN	LO	SN	
London Bridge 4 ⊖	d		19 24					19 36	19 39		19 41						19 54				20 06	20 09		20 11	
Highbury & Islington	a																								
	d			19 06		19 13				19 21				19 28				19 36	19 43				19 51		
Canonbury	d			19 08		19 15				19 23				19 30				19 38	19 45				19 53		
Dalston Junction Stn ELL	d	19 08		19 13		19 18	19 23			19 28				19 33		19 38		19 43	19 48	19 53			19 58		
Haggerston	d	19 09		19 14		19 19	19 24			19 29				19 34		19 39		19 44	19 49	19 54			19 59		
Hoxton	d	19 11		19 16		19 21	19 26			19 31				19 36		19 41		19 46	19 51	19 56			20 01		
Shoreditch High Street	d	19 14		19 19		19 24	19 29			19 34				19 39		19 44		19 49	19 54	19 59			20 04		
Whitechapel	d	19 16		19 21		19 26	19 31			19 36				19 41		19 46		19 51	19 56	20 01			20 06		
Shadwell	d	19 18		19 23		19 28	19 33			19 38				19 43		19 48		19 53	19 58	20 03			20 08		
Wapping	d	19 20		19 25		19 30	19 35			19 40				19 45		19 50		19 55	20 00	20 05			20 10		
Rotherhithe	d	19 22		19 27		19 32	19 37			19 42				19 47		19 52		19 57	20 02	20 07			20 12		
Canada Water	d	19 24		19 29		19 34	19 39			19 44				19 49		19 54		19 59	20 04	20 09			20 14		
Surrey Quays	d	19 25		19 30		19 35	19 40			19 45				19 50		19 55		20 00	20 05	20 10			20 15		
New Cross ELL	a	19 30					19 45									20 00				20 15					
New Cross Gate 4	a		19 29	19 34		19 39			19 44	19 49				19 54			19 59	20 04	20 09			20 14	20 19		
	d		19 29	19 35		19 40			19 44	19 50				19 55			19 59	20 05	20 10			20 14	20 20		
Brockley	d		19 32	19 37		19 42			19 47	19 52				19 57			20 02	20 07	20 12			20 17	20 22		
Honor Oak Park	d		19 35	19 40		19 45			19 50	19 55				20 00			20 05	20 10	20 15			20 20	20 25		
Forest Hill 4	d		19 37	19 43		19 48			19 52	19 58				20 03			20 07	20 13	20 18			20 22	20 28		
Sydenham	d		19 40	19 45		19 50			19 55	20 00				20 05			20 10	20 15	20 20			20 25	20 30		
Crystal Palace 4	d					19a55							20 07	20a10					20a25						
Gipsy Hill	d												20 09												
West Norwood 4	d												20 12												
Streatham Hill	d																								
Balham 4 ⊖	d																								
Wandsworth Common	d																								
Clapham Junction 10	d																								
South Bermondsey	d							19 40			19 45										20 10			20 15	
Queens Rd Peckham	d							19 42			19 48										20 12			20 18	
Peckham Rye 4	d							19a45			19 50	20 09	20a23								20a15			20 20	
Denmark Hill 4	d										19 53	20 13												20 23	
London Blackfriars 3 ⊖	a											20 23													
Clapham High Street ⊖	d										19 58													20 28	
Wandsworth Road	d										19 59													20 29	
Battersea Park 4	d										20 02													20 32	
London Victoria 15 ⊖	a										20 06													20 36	
Penge West	d			19 48					19 57	20 03								20 18				20 27	20 33		
Anerley	d			19 50					19 59	20 05								20 20				20 29	20 35		
Norwood Junction 2	d		19 46	19 53					20 03	20 08							20 16	20 23				20 33	20 38		
West Croydon 4	a		19 54	19 59						20 15							20 24	20 29					20 45		
East Croydon	a								20 07													20 37			

		SE	SN	LO	LO	SN	LO	LO	LO	SN		SN	LO	SN	SE	SN	LO	LO	SN	LO		LO	LO	SN	SN
London Bridge 4 ⊖	d					20 24				20 36		20 39		20 41					20 54					21 06	21 09
Highbury & Islington	a																								
	d			19 58			20 06	20 13					20 21				20 28			20 36		20 43			
Canonbury	d			20 00			20 08	20 15					20 23				20 30			20 38		20 45			
Dalston Junction Stn ELL	d			20 03	20 08		20 13	20 18	20 23				20 28				20 33	20 38		20 43		20 48	20 53		
Haggerston	d			20 04	20 09		20 14	20 19	20 24				20 29				20 34	20 39		20 44		20 49	20 54		
Hoxton	d			20 06	20 11		20 16	20 21	20 26				20 31				20 36	20 41		20 46		20 51	20 56		
Shoreditch High Street	d			20 09	20 14		20 19	20 24	20 29				20 34				20 39	20 44		20 49		20 54	20 59		
Whitechapel	d			20 11	20 16		20 21	20 26	20 31				20 36				20 41	20 46		20 51		20 56	21 01		
Shadwell	d			20 13	20 18		20 23	20 28	20 33				20 38				20 43	20 48		20 53		20 58	21 03		
Wapping	d			20 15	20 20		20 25	20 30	20 35				20 40				20 45	20 50		20 55		21 00	21 05		
Rotherhithe	d			20 17	20 22		20 27	20 32	20 37				20 42				20 47	20 52		20 57		21 02	21 07		
Canada Water	d			20 19	20 24		20 29	20 34	20 39				20 44				20 49	20 54		20 59		21 04	21 09		
Surrey Quays	d			20 20	20 25		20 30	20 35	20 40				20 45				20 50	20 55		21 00		21 05	21 10		
New Cross ELL	a				20 30				20 45									21 00					21 15		
New Cross Gate 4	a			20 24		20 29	20 34	20 39				20 44	20 49				20 54		20 59	21 04		21 09			21 14
	d			20 25		20 29	20 35	20 40				20 44	20 50				20 55		20 59	21 05		21 10			21 14
Brockley	d			20 27		20 32	20 37	20 42				20 47	20 52				20 57		21 02	21 07		21 12			21 17
Honor Oak Park	d			20 30		20 35	20 40	20 45				20 50	20 55				21 00		21 05	21 10		21 15			21 20
Forest Hill 4	d			20 33		20 37	20 43	20 48				20 52	20 58				21 03		21 07	21 13		21 18			21 22
Sydenham	d			20 35		20 40	20 45	20 50				20 55	21 00				21 05		21 10	21 15		21 20			21 25
Crystal Palace 4	d		20 37	20a40				20a55								21 07	21a10					21a25			
Gipsy Hill	d		20 39													21 09									
West Norwood 4	d		20 42													21 12									
Streatham Hill	d																								
Balham 4 ⊖	d																								
Wandsworth Common	d																								
Clapham Junction 10	d																								
South Bermondsey	d									20 40				20 45										21 10	
Queens Rd Peckham	d									20 42				20 48										21 12	
Peckham Rye 4	d	20 39	20a53							20a45				20 50	21 09	21a23								21a15	
Denmark Hill 4	d	20 43												20 53	21 13										
London Blackfriars 3 ⊖	a	20 53													21 23										
Clapham High Street ⊖	d													20 58											
Wandsworth Road	d													20 59											
Battersea Park 4	d													21 02											
London Victoria 15 ⊖	a													21 06											
Penge West	d						20 48					20 57	21 03							21 18					21 27
Anerley	d						20 50					20 59	21 05							21 20					21 29
Norwood Junction 2	d					20 46	20 53					21 03	21 08						21 16	21 23					21 33
West Croydon 4	a					20 54	20 59						21 15						21 24	21 29					
East Croydon	a											21 07													21 37

London Bridge to London Victoria - Croydon and East London Line

Network Diagram - see first Page of Table 177

		LO	SN	SE	SN	LO		LO	SN	LO	LO	LO	SN	SN	LO	SN		SE	SN	LO	LO	SN	LO	LO	LO
London Bridge 4 ⊖	d		21 11						21 24				21 36	21 39		21 41						21 54			
Highbury & Islington	a																								
	d	20 51				20 58				21 06	21 13				21 21					21 28			21 36	21 43	
Canonbury	d	20 53				21 00				21 08	21 15				21 23					21 30			21 38	21 45	
Dalston Junction Stn ELL	d	20 58				21 03		21 08		21 13	21 18	21 23			21 28					21 33	21 38		21 43	21 48	21 53
Haggerston	d	20 59				21 04		21 09		21 14	21 19	21 24			21 29					21 34	21 39		21 44	21 49	21 54
Hoxton	d	21 01				21 06		21 11		21 16	21 21	21 26			21 31					21 36	21 41		21 46	21 51	21 56
Shoreditch High Street	d	21 04				21 09		21 14		21 19	21 24	21 29			21 34					21 39	21 44		21 49	21 54	21 59
Whitechapel	d	21 06				21 11		21 16		21 21	21 26	21 31			21 36					21 41	21 46		21 51	21 56	22 01
Shadwell	d	21 08				21 13		21 18		21 23	21 28	21 33			21 38					21 43	21 48		21 53	21 58	22 03
Wapping	d	21 10				21 15		21 20		21 25	21 30	21 35			21 40					21 45	21 50		21 55	22 00	22 05
Rotherhithe	d	21 12				21 17		21 22		21 27	21 32	21 37			21 42					21 47	21 52		21 57	22 02	22 07
Canada Water	d	21 14				21 19		21 24		21 29	21 34	21 39			21 44					21 49	21 54		21 59	22 04	22 09
Surrey Quays	d	21 15				21 20		21 25		21 30	21 35	21 40			21 45					21 50	21 55		22 00	22 05	22 10
New Cross ELL	a							21 30				21 45									22 00				22 16
New Cross Gate 4	a	21 19				21 24			21 29	21 34	21 39			21 44	21 49					21 54		21 59	22 04	22 09	
	d	21 20				21 25			21 29	21 35	21 40			21 44	21 50					21 55		21 59	22 05	22 10	
Brockley	d	21 22				21 27			21 32	21 37	21 42			21 47	21 52					21 57		22 02	22 07	22 12	
Honor Oak Park	d	21 25				21 30			21 35	21 40	21 45			21 50	21 55					22 00		22 05	22 10	22 15	
Forest Hill 4	d	21 28				21 33			21 37	21 43	21 48			21 52	21 58					22 03		22 07	22 13	22 18	
Sydenham	d	21 30				21 35			21 40	21 45	21 50			21 55	22 00					22 05		22 10	22 15	22 20	
Crystal Palace 4	d				21 37	21a40					21a55								22 07	22a10				22a25	
Gipsy Hill	d				21 39														22 09						
West Norwood 4	d				21 42														22 12						
Streatham Hill	d																								
Balham 4 ⊖	d																								
Wandsworth Common	d																								
Clapham Junction 10	d																								
South Bermondsey	d		21 15										21 40			21 45									
Queens Rd Peckham	d		21 18										21 42			21 48									
Peckham Rye 4	d		21 20	21 39	21a53								21a45			21 50		22 09	22a23						
Denmark Hill 4	d		21 23	21 43												21 53		22 13							
London Blackfriars 3 ⊖	a			21 53														22 23							
Clapham High Street ⊖	d		21 28													21 58									
Wandsworth Road	d		21 29													21 59									
Battersea Park 4	d		21 32													22 02									
London Victoria 15 ⊖	a		21 36													22 06									
Penge West	d	21 33								21 48				21 57	22 03								22 18		
Anerley	d	21 35								21 50				21 59	22 05								22 20		
Norwood Junction 2	d	21 38							21 46	21 53				22 03	22 08							22 16	22 23		
West Croydon 4	a	21 45							21 54	21 59					22 15							22 24	22 29		
East Croydon	a													22 07											

		SN		SN	LO	LO	SN	SE	SN	SN	LO	SN		LO	LO	SN	SE	SN	SN	LO	SN	LO		LO	SN
London Bridge 4 ⊖	d	22 06		22 09			22 11		22 36			22 39				22 41		23 06			23 09				23 11
Highbury & Islington	a																								
	d				21 51						22 13			22 23						22 43		22 53			
Canonbury	d				21 53						22 15			22 25						22 45		22 55			
Dalston Junction Stn ELL	d				21 58	22 08					22 18			22 28	22 38					22 48		22 58		23 08	
Haggerston	d				21 59	22 09					22 19			22 29	22 39					22 49		22 59		23 09	
Hoxton	d				22 01	22 11					22 21			22 31	22 41					22 51		23 01		23 11	
Shoreditch High Street	d				22 04	22 14					22 24			22 34	22 44					22 54		23 04		23 14	
Whitechapel	d				22 06	22 16					22 26			22 36	22 46					22 56		23 06		23 16	
Shadwell	d				22 08	22 18					22 28			22 38	22 48					22 58		23 08		23 18	
Wapping	d				22 10	22 20					22 30			22 40	22 50					23 00		23 10		23 20	
Rotherhithe	d				22 12	22 22					22 32			22 42	22 52					23 02		23 12		23 22	
Canada Water	d				22 14	22 24					22 34			22 44	22 54					23 04		23 14		23 24	
Surrey Quays	d				22 15	22 25					22 35			22 45	22 55					23 05		23 15		23 25	
New Cross ELL	a					22 30									23 00									23 30	
New Cross Gate 4	a			22 14	22 19						22 39	22 44		22 49						23 09	23 14	23 19			
	d			22 14	22 20						22 40	22 44		22 50						23 10	23 14	23 20			
Brockley	d			22 17	22 22						22 42	22 47		22 52						23 12	23 17	23 22			
Honor Oak Park	d			22 20	22 25						22 45	22 50		22 55						23 15	23 20	23 25			
Forest Hill 4	d			22 22	22 28						22 48	22 52		22 58						23 18	23 22	23 28			
Sydenham	d			22 25	22 30						22 50	22 55		23 00						23 20	23 25	23 30			
Crystal Palace 4	d									22 37	22a55								23 07	23a25					
Gipsy Hill	d									22 39									23 09						
West Norwood 4	d									22 42									23 12						
Streatham Hill	d																								
Balham 4 ⊖	d																								
Wandsworth Common	d																								
Clapham Junction 10	d																								
South Bermondsey	d	22 10					22 15		22 40							22 45		23 10							23 15
Queens Rd Peckham	d	22 12					22 18		22 42							22 48		23 12							23 18
Peckham Rye 4	d	22a15					22 20	22 39	22a45	22a53						22 50	23 09	23a15	23a23						23 20
Denmark Hill 4	d						22 23	22 43								22 53	23 13								23 23
London Blackfriars 3 ⊖	a							22 53									23 23								
Clapham High Street ⊖	d						22 28									22 58									23 28
Wandsworth Road	d						22 29									22 59									23 29
Battersea Park 4	d						22 32									23 02									23 32
London Victoria 15 ⊖	a						22 36									23 06									23 37
Penge West	d			22 27	22 33							22 57		23 03							23 27	23 33			
Anerley	d			22 29	22 35							22 59		23 05							23 29	23 35			
Norwood Junction 2	d			22 33	22 38							23 03		23 08							23 33	23 38			
West Croydon 4	a				22 45									23 14								23 44			
East Croydon	a			22 37								23 07									23 38				

Table 178

Sundays

from 16 September

London Bridge to London Victoria - Croydon and East London Line

Network Diagram - see first Page of Table 177

Station		SN	SN	LO	SN	LO
London Bridge 4 ⊖	d				23 39	
Highbury & Islington	a					
	d			23 13		23 23
Canonbury	d			23 15		23 25
Dalston Junction Stn ELL	d			23 18		23 28
Haggerston	d			23 19		23 29
Hoxton	d			23 21		23 31
Shoreditch High Street	d			23 24		23 34
Whitechapel	d			23 26		23 36
Shadwell	d			23 28		23 38
Wapping	d			23 30		23 40
Rotherhithe	d			23 32		23 42
Canada Water	d			23 34		23 44
Surrey Quays	d			23 35		23 45
New Cross ELL	a					
New Cross Gate 4	a			23 39	23 44	23 49
	d			23 40	23 44	23 50
Brockley	d			23 42	23 47	23 52
Honor Oak Park	d			23 45	23 50	23 55
Forest Hill 4	d			23 48	23 52	23 58
Sydenham	d			23 50	23 55	00 01
Crystal Palace 4	d	23 37	23 50	23a55		
Gipsy Hill	d	23 39				
West Norwood 4	d	23 42				
Streatham Hill	d					
Balham 4 ⊖	d					
Wandsworth Common	d					
Clapham Junction 10	d					
South Bermondsey	d					
Queens Rd Peckham	d					
Peckham Rye 4	d	23a53				
Denmark Hill 4	d					
London Blackfriars 3 ⊖	a					
Clapham High Street ⊖	d					
Wandsworth Road	d					
Battersea Park 4	d					
London Victoria 15 ⊖	a					
Penge West	d				23 57	00 03
Anerley	d				23 59	00 05
Norwood Junction 2	d		23 55		00 03	00 08
West Croydon 4 🚋	a		23 59			00 15
East Croydon 🚋	a				00 06	

until 27 July

East London Line and Croydon - London Victoria to London Bridge

Network Diagram - see first Page of Table 177

Miles	Miles	Miles	Miles	Miles			LO MX	LO MX	LO MX	SN MO A	SN MX	SN MX	SN MX	SN	SE		LO B	LO C	SN	LO B	LO C	LO B	LO C	LO B	LO C
—	—	0	—	—	East Croydon	d								05 13					05 51						
—	—	—	—	0	West Croydon [4]	d		23p22									05 39	05 39						05 52	05 52
—	—	1¼	—	1¾	Norwood Junction [2]	d		23p28						05 17			05 43	05 43	05 55					05 58	05 58
—	—	2½	—	—	Anerley	d		23p31						05 20			05 46	05 46						06 01	06 01
—	—	2¾	—	—	Penge West	d		23p33						05 22			05 48	05 48						06 03	06 03
0	0	—	0	—	London Victoria [15] ⊖	d					23p22	23p54													
1¼	1¼	—	—	—	Battersea Park [4]	d					23p26	23p58													
2	—	—	—	—	Wandsworth Road	d																			
2½	—	—	—	—	Clapham High Street ⊖	d																			
—	—	—	—	0	London Blackfriars [3] ⊖	d									05 28										
4½	—	—	4¼	3¾	Denmark Hill [4]	d									05 39										
5¼	—	—	5	4¼	Peckham Rye [4]	d				23p53			00 12		05a41				06 15						
6	—	—	—	—	Queens Rd Peckham	d				23p56									06 18						
7	—	—	—	—	South Bermondsey	d				23p58									06 20						
—	2¾	—	—	—	Clapham Junction [10]	d					23p30	00 02													
—	4	—	—	—	Wandsworth Common	d					23p33	00 05													
—	4¾	—	—	—	Balham [4] ⊖	d					23p35	00 07													
—	5¾	—	—	—	Streatham Hill	d					23p38	00 10													
—	7	—	—	—	West Norwood [4]	d					23p42	00 14	00 24												
—	8	—	—	—	Gipsy Hill	d					23p45	00 17	00 27												
—	8¾	—	—	—	Crystal Palace [4]	d			23p43		23p51	00 21	00a29									05 58	05 58		
—	10	3½	—	—	Sydenham	d		23p36	23p46		23p54	00 24		05 24			05 51	05 51				06 01	06 01	06 06	06 06
—	10¾	4¼	—	—	Forest Hill [4]	d		23p38	23p49		23p57	00 27		05 27			05 53	05 53				06 04	06 04	06 08	06 08
—	11¾	5¼	—	—	Honor Oak Park	d		23p41	23p51		23p59	00 29		05 29			05 56	05 56				06 06	06 06	06 11	06 11
—	12¾	6¼	—	—	Brockley	d		23p43	23p54		00 02	00 32		05 32			05 58	05 58				06 09	06 09	06 13	06 13
—	13¾	7¼	—	—	New Cross Gate [4]	a		23p46	23p56		00 04	00 34		05 34			06 01	06 01				06 11	06 11	06 16	06 16
—	—	—	—	—		d		23p46	23p56		00 04	00 34		05 34			06 01	06 01				06 11	06 11	06 16	06 16
—	—	—	0	—	New Cross ELL	d	23p36													06 06	06 06				
—	—	—	1¼	—	Surrey Quays	d	23p40	23p49	23p59								06 05	06 05		06 10	06 10	06 15	06 15	06 19	06 19
—	—	—	1½	—	Canada Water	d	23p42	23p51	00 02								06 07	06 07		06 12	06 12	06 17	06 17	06 21	06 21
—	—	—	1¾	—	Rotherhithe	d	23p43	23p53	00 03								06 08	06 08		06 13	06 13	06 18	06 18	06 23	06 23
—	—	—	2	—	Wapping	d	23p45	23p54	00 05								06 10	06 10		06 15	06 15	06 20	06 20	06 24	06 24
—	—	—	2½	—	Shadwell	d	23p47	23p56	00 07								06 12	06 12		06 17	06 17	06 22	06 22	06 26	06 26
—	—	—	3¼	—	Whitechapel	d	23p49	23p59	00 09								06 14	06 14		06 19	06 19	06 24	06 24	06 29	06 29
—	—	—	4	—	Shoreditch High Street	d	23p51	00 01	00 11								06 16	06 16		06 21	06 21	06 26	06 26	06 31	06 31
—	—	—	4¾	—	Hoxton	d	23p53	00 03	00 13								06 18	06 18		06 23	06 23	06 28	06 28	06 33	06 33
—	—	—	5¼	—	Haggerston	d	23p55	00 05	00 15								06 20	06 20		06 25	06 25	06 30	06 30	06 35	06 35
—	—	—	5¾	—	Dalston Junction Stn ELL	a	00 02	00 07	00 17								06 22	06 22		06 28	06 32	06 32	06 32	06 37	06 37
—	—	—	—	—	Canonbury	d		00 12	00 20								06 27	06 27				06 35	06 35	06 42	06 42
—	—	—	—	—	Highbury & Islington	a		00 19	00 28								06 32	06 35				06 40	06 43	06 46	06 49
—	—	—	—	—		d																			
8¾	16½	10	—	—	London Bridge [4] ⊖	a				00 03	00 11	00 41		05 41					06 25						

		LO B	LO C	LO B	LO C	LO B	LO C	SN	LO B	LO C		LO B	LO C	LO B	LO C	SN	LO B	LO C	LO B	LO C		SN	SN	LO B
East Croydon	d							06 13																
West Croydon [4]	d					06 09	06 09							06 22	06 22									
Norwood Junction [2]	d					06 13	06 13	06 18						06 28	06 28	06 32								
Anerley	d					06 16	06 16	06 21						06 31	06 31	06 35								
Penge West	d					06 18	06 18	06 23						06 33	06 33	06 37								
London Victoria [15] ⊖	d																					06 19		
Battersea Park [4]	d																					06 23		
Wandsworth Road	d																							
Clapham High Street ⊖	d																							
London Blackfriars [3] ⊖	d																							
Denmark Hill [4]	d																							
Peckham Rye [4]	d																							
Queens Rd Peckham	d																							
South Bermondsey	d																							
Clapham Junction [10]	d																					06 27		
Wandsworth Common	d																					06 30		
Balham [4] ⊖	d																					06 32		
Streatham Hill	d																					06 35	06 42	
West Norwood [4]	d																					06 39	06 45	
Gipsy Hill	d																					06 42	06 48	
Crystal Palace [4]	d			06 13	06 13							06 28	06 28						06 41	06 41		06 44	06 51	06 58
Sydenham	d			06 16	06 16	06 21	06 21	06 25				06 31	06 31	06 36	06 36	06 39			06 44	06 44		06 48	06 54	07 01
Forest Hill [4]	d			06 19	06 19	06 23	06 23	06 28				06 34	06 34	06 38	06 38	06 42			06 47	06 47		06 50	06 57	07 04
Honor Oak Park	d			06 21	06 21	06 26	06 26	06 30				06 36	06 36	06 41	06 41	06 44			06 49	06 49		06 53	06 59	07 06
Brockley	d			06 24	06 24	06 28	06 28	06 33				06 39	06 39	06 43	06 43	06 47			06 52	06 52		06 55	07 02	07 09
New Cross Gate [4]	a			06 26	06 26	06 31	06 31	06 35				06 41	06 41	06 46	06 46	06 49			06 54	06 54		06 58	07 04	07 11
	d			06 26	06 26	06 31	06 31	06 35				06 41	06 41	06 46	06 46	06 49			06 54	06 54		06 58	07 04	07 11
New Cross ELL	d	06 21	06 21						06 36	06 36							06 51	06 51						
Surrey Quays	d	06 25	06 25	06 30	06 30	06 35	06 35		06 40	06 40		06 45	06 45	06 49	06 49		06 55	06 55	07 00	07 00				07 15
Canada Water	d	06 27	06 27	06 32	06 32	06 37	06 37		06 42	06 42		06 47	06 47	06 51	06 51		06 57	06 57	07 02	07 02				07 17
Rotherhithe	d	06 28	06 28	06 33	06 33	06 38	06 38		06 43	06 43		06 48	06 48	06 53	06 53		06 58	06 58	07 03	07 03				07 18
Wapping	d	06 30	06 30	06 35	06 35	06 40	06 40		06 45	06 45		06 50	06 50	06 54	06 54		07 00	07 00	07 05	07 05				07 20
Shadwell	d	06 32	06 32	06 37	06 37	06 42	06 42		06 47	06 47		06 52	06 52	06 56	06 56		07 02	07 02	07 07	07 07				07 22
Whitechapel	d	06 34	06 34	06 39	06 39	06 44	06 44		06 49	06 49		06 54	06 54	06 59	06 59		07 04	07 04	07 09	07 09				07 24
Shoreditch High Street	d	06 36	06 36	06 41	06 41	06 46	06 46		06 51	06 51		06 56	06 56	07 01	07 01		07 06	07 06	07 11	07 11				07 26
Hoxton	d	06 38	06 38	06 43	06 43	06 48	06 48		06 53	06 53		06 58	06 58	07 03	07 03		07 08	07 08	07 13	07 13				07 28
Haggerston	d	06 40	06 40	06 45	06 45	06 50	06 50		06 55	06 55		07 00	07 00	07 05	07 05		07 10	07 10	07 15	07 15				07 30
Dalston Junction Stn ELL	a	06 43	06 47	06 47	06 47	06 52	06 52		06 58	07 02		07 02	07 02	07 07	07 07		07 13	07 17	07 17	07 17				07 32
Canonbury	d			06 50	06 50	06 57	06 57					07 05	07 05	07 12	07 12				07 20	07 20				07 35
Highbury & Islington	a			06 56	06 59	07 02	07 05					07 10	07 13	07 16	07 19				07 25	07 28				07 40
	d																							
London Bridge [4] ⊖	a							06 44								07 00						07 06	07 16	

A from 21 May until 23 July

B not 27 July

C 27 July

Table 178

Mondays to Fridays

until 27 July

East London Line and Croydon - London Victoria to London Bridge

Network Diagram - see first Page of Table 177

		LO A	SN	SE	SN	SN	LO B		LO A	SN	LO B	LO A	LO B	LO A	SN	LO B	LO A		LO B	LO A	SN	SN	SN	SN	SN
East Croydon	d																								
West Croydon 4	d					06 31	06 39		06 39				06 52	06 52											07 01
Norwood Junction 2	d						06 43		06 43	06 47			06 58	06 58	07 02										
Anerley	d						06 46		06 46				07 01	07 01	07 05										
Penge West	d						06 48		06 48				07 03	07 03	07 07										
London Victoria 15	d				06 41																06 49			07 11	
Battersea Park 4	d				06 45																06 53			07 15	
Wandsworth Road	d				06 47																			07 17	
Clapham High Street	d				06 49																			07 19	
London Blackfriars 3	d			06 42																					
Denmark Hill 4	d			06 52	06 54																			07 24	
Peckham Rye 4	d		06 42	06a55	06 56	06 59				07 08													07 12	07 26	07 31
Queens Rd Peckham	d				06 59	07 02				07 10														07 29	07 34
South Bermondsey	d				07 01	07 04				07 13														07 31	07 36
Clapham Junction 10	d																				06 57				
Wandsworth Common	d																				07 00				
Balham 4	d																				07 02				
Streatham Hill	d																				07 05	07 12			
West Norwood 4	d		06 53																		07 09	07 15	07 23		
Gipsy Hill	d		06 56																		07 12	07 18	07 26		
Crystal Palace 4	d	06 58	06a59																07 11	07 11	07 14	07 21	07a29		
Sydenham	d	07 01					06 51		06 51				07 06	07 06	07 09				07 14	07 14	07 18	07 24			
Forest Hill 4	d	07 04					06 53		06 53				07 08	07 08	07 12				07 17	07 17	07 20	07 27			
Honor Oak Park	d	07 06					06 56		06 56				07 11	07 11	07 14				07 19	07 19	07 23	07 29			
Brockley	d	07 09					06 58		06 58				07 13	07 13	07 17				07 22	07 22	07 25	07 32			
New Cross Gate 4	a	07 11					07 01		07 01				07 16	07 16	07 19				07 24	07 24	07 28	07 34			
	d	07 11					07 01		07 01				07 16	07 16	07 19				07 24	07 24	07 28	07 34			
New Cross ELL	d										07 06	07 06				07 21	07 21								
Surrey Quays	d	07 15					07 05		07 05		07 10	07 10	07 19	07 19		07 25	07 25		07 30	07 30					
Canada Water	d	07 17					07 07		07 07		07 12	07 12	07 21	07 21		07 27	07 27		07 32	07 32					
Rotherhithe	d	07 18					07 08		07 08		07 13	07 13	07 23	07 23		07 28	07 28		07 33	07 33					
Wapping	d	07 20					07 10		07 10		07 15	07 15	07 24	07 24		07 30	07 30		07 35	07 35					
Shadwell	d	07 22					07 12		07 12		07 17	07 17	07 26	07 26		07 32	07 32		07 37	07 37					
Whitechapel	d	07 24					07 14		07 14		07 19	07 19	07 29	07 29		07 34	07 34		07 39	07 39					
Shoreditch High Street	d	07 26					07 16		07 16		07 21	07 21	07 31	07 31		07 36	07 36		07 41	07 41					
Hoxton	d	07 28					07 18		07 18		07 23	07 23	07 33	07 33		07 38	07 38		07 43	07 43					
Haggerston	d	07 30					07 20		07 20		07 25	07 25	07 35	07 35		07 40	07 40		07 45	07 45					
Dalston Junction Stn ELL	a	07 32					07 23		07 23		07 28	07 32	07 37	07 37		07 43	07 47		07 47	07 47					
Canonbury	d	07 35					07 27		07 27				07 42	07 42					07 50	07 50					
Highbury & Islington	a	07 43					07 32		07 35				07 46	07 49					07 55	07 58					
	d																								
London Bridge 4	a				07 08	07 11				07 19					07 30						07 36	07 45		07 38	07 43

		LO B	LO A		SN	SN	LO B	LO A	LO B	LO A	LO B	LO A	SN		LO B	LO A	LO B	LO A	SN	SN	SN	SN	SE		SN
East Croydon	d																								
West Croydon 4	d	07 09	07 09		07 17						07 22	07 22													07 31
Norwood Junction 2	d	07 13	07 13		07 22						07 28	07 28	07 32												
Anerley	d	07 16	07 16								07 31	07 31	07 35												
Penge West	d	07 18	07 18								07 33	07 33	07 37												
London Victoria 15	d																		07 17			07 41	07 43		
Battersea Park 4	d																		07 21			07 45			
Wandsworth Road	d																					07 47			
Clapham High Street	d																					07 49			
London Blackfriars 3	d																								
Denmark Hill 4	d																					07 54	07 53		
Peckham Rye 4	d					07 36															07 42	07 56	07a56		07 59
Queens Rd Peckham	d					07 39																07 59			08 02
South Bermondsey	d					07 41																08 01			08 04
Clapham Junction 10	d																		07 25						
Wandsworth Common	d																								
Balham 4	d																		07 29						
Streatham Hill	d																		07 32						
West Norwood 4	d																		07 38		07 53				
Gipsy Hill	d																		07 41		07 56				
Crystal Palace 4	d				07a26				07 28	07 28							07 41	07 41	07 44	07 52	07a59				
Sydenham	d	07 21	07 21						07 31	07 31	07 36	07 36	07 39				07 44	07 44	07 48	07 56					
Forest Hill 4	d	07 23	07 23						07 34	07 34	07 38	07 38	07 42				07 47	07 47	07 50	07 58					
Honor Oak Park	d	07 26	07 26						07 36	07 36	07 41	07 41	07 44				07 49	07 49	07 53	08 01					
Brockley	d	07 28	07 28						07 39	07 39	07 43	07 43	07 47				07 52	07 52	07 55	08 03					
New Cross Gate 4	a	07 31	07 31						07 41	07 41	07 46	07 46	07 49				07 54	07 54	07 58	08 06					
	d	07 31	07 31						07 41	07 41	07 46	07 46	07 49				07 54	07 54	07 58	08 06					
New Cross ELL	d						07 36	07 36							07 51	07 51									
Surrey Quays	d	07 35	07 35				07 40	07 40	07 45	07 45	07 49	07 49			07 55	07 55	08 00	08 00							
Canada Water	d	07 37	07 37				07 42	07 42	07 47	07 47	07 51	07 51			07 57	07 57	08 02	08 02							
Rotherhithe	d	07 38	07 38				07 43	07 43	07 48	07 48	07 53	07 53			07 58	07 58	08 03	08 03							
Wapping	d	07 40	07 40				07 45	07 45	07 50	07 50	07 54	07 54			08 00	08 00	08 05	08 05							
Shadwell	d	07 42	07 42				07 47	07 47	07 52	07 52	07 56	07 56			08 02	08 02	08 07	08 07							
Whitechapel	d	07 44	07 44				07 49	07 49	07 54	07 54	07 59	07 59			08 04	08 04	08 09	08 09							
Shoreditch High Street	d	07 46	07 46				07 51	07 51	07 56	07 56	08 01	08 01			08 06	08 06	08 11	08 11							
Hoxton	d	07 48	07 48				07 53	07 53	07 58	07 58	08 03	08 03			08 08	08 08	08 13	08 13							
Haggerston	d	07 50	07 50				07 55	07 55	08 00	08 00	08 05	08 05			08 10	08 10	08 15	08 15							
Dalston Junction Stn ELL	a	07 53	07 53				07 58	08 02	08 02	08 02	08 07	08 07			08 13	08 17	08 17	08 17							
Canonbury	d	07 57	07 57						08 05	08 05	08 12	08 12					08 20	08 20							
Highbury & Islington	a	08 02	08 05						08 10	08 13	08 16	08 19					08 25	08 28							
	d																								
London Bridge 4	a					07 48							07 58						08 07	08 15		08 08			08 11

A 27 July

B not 27 July

East London Line and Croydon - London Victoria to London Bridge

Network Diagram - see first Page of Table 177

Station		LO A	LO B	SN	SN	LO A	LO B	LO A	LO B		LO A	LO A	LO B	SN	LO A	LO B	LO A	LO B	SN		SN	LO A	LO A	LO B	SN
East Croydon	d																								
West Croydon 4	d	07 39	07 39	07 47								07 52	07 52												
Norwood Junction 2	d	07 43	07 43	07 52								07 58	07 58	08 02											
Anerley	d	07 46	07 46									08 01	08 01	08 05											
Penge West	d	07 48	07 48									08 03	08 03	08 07											
London Victoria 15 ⊖	d																		07 52						
Battersea Park 4	d																								
Wandsworth Road	d																								
Clapham High Street ⊖	d																								
London Blackfriars 3 ⊖	d																								
Denmark Hill 4	d																								
Peckham Rye 4	d				08 06																				08 12
Queens Rd Peckham	d				08 09																				
South Bermondsey	d				08 11																				
Clapham Junction 10	d																		07 58						
Wandsworth Common	d																								
Balham 4 ⊖	d																		08 03						
Streatham Hill	d																		08 06		08 15				
West Norwood 4	d																		08 09		08 19				08 24
Gipsy Hill	d																		08 12		08 22				08 27
Crystal Palace 4	d			07a56				07 58	07 58								08 11	08 11	08 15		08 24		08 28	08 28	08a29
Sydenham	d	07 51	07 51					08 01	08 01			08 06	08 06	08 09			08 14	08 14	08 18		08 28		08 31	08 31	
Forest Hill 4	d	07 53	07 53					08 04	08 04			08 08	08 08	08 12			08 17	08 17	08 21		08 30		08 34	08 34	
Honor Oak Park	d	07 56	07 56					08 06	08 06			08 11	08 11	08 14			08 19	08 19	08 23		08 33		08 36	08 36	
Brockley	d	07 58	07 58					08 09	08 09			08 13	08 13	08 17			08 22	08 22	08 26		08 35		08 39	08 39	
New Cross Gate 4	a	08 01	08 01					08 11	08 11			08 16	08 16	08 19			08 24	08 24	08 28		08 38		08 41	08 41	
	d	08 01	08 01					08 11	08 11			08 16	08 16	08 19			08 24	08 24	08 28		08 38		08 41	08 41	
New Cross ELL	d					08 06	08 06								08 21	08 21									
Surrey Quays	d	08 05	08 05			08 10	08 10	08 15	08 15		08 19	08 21	08 21		08 25	08 25	08 30	08 30				08 34	08 45	08 45	
Canada Water	d	08 07	08 07			08 12	08 12	08 17	08 17		08 21	08 23	08 23		08 27	08 27	08 32	08 32				08 36	08 47	08 47	
Rotherhithe	d	08 08	08 08			08 13	08 13	08 18	08 18		08 22	08 25	08 25		08 28	08 28	08 33	08 33				08 37	08 48	08 48	
Wapping	d	08 10	08 10			08 15	08 15	08 20	08 20		08 24	08 26	08 26		08 30	08 30	08 35	08 35				08 39	08 50	08 50	
Shadwell	d	08 12	08 12			08 17	08 17	08 22	08 22		08 26	08 28	08 28		08 32	08 32	08 37	08 37				08 41	08 52	08 52	
Whitechapel	d	08 14	08 14			08 19	08 19	08 24	08 24		08 28	08 31	08 31		08 34	08 34	08 39	08 39				08 43	08 54	08 54	
Shoreditch High Street	d	08 16	08 16			08 21	08 21	08 26	08 26		08 30	08 33	08 33		08 36	08 36	08 41	08 41				08 45	08 56	08 56	
Hoxton	d	08 18	08 18			08 23	08 23	08 28	08 28		08 32	08 35	08 35		08 38	08 38	08 43	08 43				08 47	08 58	08 58	
Haggerston	d	08 20	08 20			08 25	08 25	08 30	08 30		08 34	08 37	08 37		08 40	08 40	08 45	08 45				08 49	09 00	09 00	
Dalston Junction Stn ELL	a	08 23	08 23			08 28	08 32	08 32	08 32		08 37	08 39	08 39		08 43	08 47	08 47	08 47				08 52	09 02	09 02	
Canonbury	d	08 27	08 27					08 35	08 35			08 42	08 42				08 50	08 50					09 05	09 05	
Highbury & Islington	a	08 32	08 35					08 40	08 43			08 46	08 49				08 55	08 58					09 10	09 13	
	d																								
London Bridge 4 ⊖	a				08 18									08 28					08 37		08 47				

Station		SE	SN	SN	LO A		LO B	SN	SN	LO A	LO B	LO A	LO B	SN	LO A		LO B	LO A	LO B	SN	SN	LO A	LO B	SN	SE
East Croydon	d																								
West Croydon 4	d			08 01	08 09		08 09	08 19				08 23	08 23												
Norwood Junction 2	d				08 13		08 13	08 25				08 28	08 28	08 32											
Anerley	d				08 16		08 16					08 31	08 31	08 35											
Penge West	d				08 18		08 18					08 33	08 33	08 37											
London Victoria 15 ⊖	d	08 09	08 11																		08 22				08 39
Battersea Park 4	d		08 15																		08 26				
Wandsworth Road	d		08 17																						
Clapham High Street ⊖	d		08 19																						
London Blackfriars 3 ⊖	d																								
Denmark Hill 4	d	08 18	08 24																						08 48
Peckham Rye 4	d	08a21	08 26	08 29					08 36															08 42	08a51
Queens Rd Peckham	d		08 29	08 32					08 38																
South Bermondsey	d		08 31	08 34					08 41																
Clapham Junction 10	d																				08 30				
Wandsworth Common	d																				08 33				
Balham 4 ⊖	d																				08 35				
Streatham Hill	d																			08 35	08 38				
West Norwood 4	d																			08 38	08 42			08 53	
Gipsy Hill	d																			08 41	08 45			08 56	
Crystal Palace 4	d							08a29										08 41	08 41	08 44	08 51	08 58	08 58	08a59	
Sydenham	d				08 21		08 21					08 36	08 36	08 39				08 44	08 44	08 47	08 54	09 01	09 01		
Forest Hill 4	d				08 23		08 23					08 38	08 38	08 42				08 47	08 47	08 50	08 57	09 04	09 04		
Honor Oak Park	d				08 26		08 26					08 41	08 41	08 44				08 49	08 49	08 52	08 59	09 06	09 06		
Brockley	d				08 28		08 28					08 43	08 43	08 47				08 52	08 52	08 55	09 02	09 09	09 09		
New Cross Gate 4	a				08 31		08 31					08 46	08 46	08 49				08 54	08 54	08 57	09 04	09 11	09 11		
	d				08 31		08 31					08 46	08 46	08 49				08 54	08 54	08 57	09 04	09 11	09 11		
New Cross ELL	d									08 36	08 36				08 51		08 51								
Surrey Quays	d				08 37		08 37			08 40	08 40	08 49	08 49		08 55		08 55	09 00	09 00			09 15	09 15		
Canada Water	d				08 39		08 39			08 42	08 42	08 51	08 51		08 57		08 57	09 02	09 02			09 17	09 17		
Rotherhithe	d				08 40		08 40			08 43	08 43	08 53	08 53		08 58		08 58	09 03	09 03			09 18	09 18		
Wapping	d				08 42		08 42			08 45	08 45	08 54	08 54		09 00		09 00	09 05	09 05			09 20	09 20		
Shadwell	d				08 44		08 44			08 47	08 47	08 56	08 56		09 02		09 02	09 07	09 07			09 22	09 22		
Whitechapel	d				08 46		08 46			08 49	08 49	08 59	08 59		09 04		09 04	09 09	09 09			09 24	09 24		
Shoreditch High Street	d				08 48		08 48			08 51	08 51	09 01	09 01		09 06		09 06	09 11	09 11			09 26	09 26		
Hoxton	d				08 50		08 50			08 53	08 53	09 03	09 03		09 08		09 08	09 13	09 13			09 28	09 28		
Haggerston	d				08 52		08 52			08 55	08 55	09 05	09 05		09 10		09 10	09 15	09 15			09 30	09 30		
Dalston Junction Stn ELL	a				08 55		08 55			08 58	09 02	09 07	09 07		09 13		09 17	09 17	09 17			09 32	09 32		
Canonbury	d				08 57		08 57					09 12	09 12					09 20	09 20			09 35	09 35		
Highbury & Islington	a				09 02		09 05					09 16	09 19					09 25	09 28			09 40	09 43		
	d																								
London Bridge 4 ⊖	a		08 38	08 41					08 48					08 58						09 06	09 14				

A not 27 July

B 27 July

Table 178

Mondays to Fridays

until 27 July

East London Line and Croydon - London Victoria to London Bridge

Network Diagram - see first Page of Table 177

			SN	SN	LO A	LO B	SN	LO A	LO B	LO A	LO B		SN	SN	LO A	LO B	LO A	LO B	SN	SN	LO A		LO B	SN	SE
East Croydon	d																								
West Croydon 4	d			08 31	08 39	08 39	08 49			08 53	08 53														
Norwood Junction 2	d				08 43	08 43	08 54			08 58	08 58			09 02											
Anerley	d				08 46	08 46				09 01	09 01			09 05											
Penge West	d				08 48	08 48				09 03	09 03			09 07											
London Victoria 15 ⊖	d		08 41																08 49						09 09
Battersea Park 4	d		08 45																08 53						
Wandsworth Road	d		08 47																						
Clapham High Street ⊖	d		08 49																						
London Blackfriars 3 ⊖	d																								
Denmark Hill 4	d		08 54																						09 18
Peckham Rye 4	d		08 56	09 02									09 07											09 12	09a21
Queens Rd Peckham	d		08 59	09 05									09 09												
South Bermondsey	d		09 01	09 07									09 12												
Clapham Junction 10	d																		08 57						
Wandsworth Common	d																		09 00						
Balham 4 ⊖	d																		09 02						
Streatham Hill	d																		09 05						
West Norwood 4	d																		09 09					09 23	
Gipsy Hill	d																		09 12					09 26	
Crystal Palace 4	d						08a58										09 11	09 11	09 14	09 21	09 28		09 28	09a29	
Sydenham	d				08 51	08 51				09 06	09 06			09 09			09 14	09 14	09 18	09 24	09 31		09 31		
Forest Hill 4	d				08 53	08 53				09 08	09 08			09 12			09 17	09 17	09 20	09 27	09 34		09 34		
Honor Oak Park	d				08 56	08 56				09 11	09 11			09 14			09 19	09 19	09 23	09 29	09 36		09 36		
Brockley	d				08 58	08 58				09 13	09 13			09 17			09 22	09 22	09 25	09 32	09 39		09 39		
New Cross Gate 4	a				09 01	09 01				09 16	09 16			09 19			09 24	09 24	09 28	09 34	09 41		09 41		
	d				09 01	09 01				09 16	09 16			09 19			09 24	09 24	09 28	09 34	09 41		09 41		
New Cross ELL	d							09 06	09 06						09 21	09 21									
Surrey Quays	d				09 05	09 05		09 10	09 10	09 19	09 19				09 25	09 25	09 30	09 30			09 45		09 45		
Canada Water	d				09 07	09 07		09 12	09 12	09 21	09 21				09 27	09 27	09 32	09 32			09 47		09 47		
Rotherhithe	d				09 08	09 08		09 13	09 13	09 23	09 23				09 28	09 28	09 33	09 33			09 48		09 48		
Wapping	d				09 10	09 10		09 15	09 15	09 24	09 24				09 30	09 30	09 35	09 35			09 50		09 50		
Shadwell	d				09 12	09 12		09 17	09 17	09 26	09 26				09 32	09 32	09 37	09 37			09 52		09 52		
Whitechapel	d				09 14	09 14		09 19	09 19	09 29	09 29				09 34	09 34	09 39	09 39			09 54		09 54		
Shoreditch High Street	d				09 16	09 16		09 21	09 21	09 31	09 31				09 36	09 36	09 41	09 41			09 56		09 56		
Hoxton	d				09 18	09 18		09 23	09 23	09 33	09 33				09 38	09 38	09 43	09 43			09 58		09 58		
Haggerston	d				09 20	09 20		09 25	09 25	09 35	09 35				09 40	09 40	09 45	09 45			10 00		10 00		
Dalston Junction Stn ELL	a				09 23	09 23		09 28	09 32	09 37	09 37				09 43	09 47	09 47	09 47			10 02		10 02		
Canonbury	d				09 27	09 27				09 42	09 42						09 50	09 50			10 05		10 05		
Highbury & Islington	a				09 32	09 35				09 46	09 49						09 55	09 58			10 10		10 13		
	d																								
London Bridge 4 ⊖	a		09 08	09 14									09 19	09 29					09 37	09 43					

		SN	SN	LO A	LO B	SN	LO A		LO B	LO A	LO B	SN	SN	LO A	LO B	LO A	LO B		SN	LO A	LO B	SN	SN	SE	SN
East Croydon	d					09 20							09 30												
West Croydon 4	d		09 01	09 09	09 09					09 22	09 22														
Norwood Junction 2	d			09 14	09 14	09 25				09 28	09 28		09 35												
Anerley	d			09 17	09 17					09 31	09 31		09 38												
Penge West	d			09 19	09 19					09 33	09 33		09 40												
London Victoria 15 ⊖	d	09 11																	09 19					09 39	09 41
Battersea Park 4	d	09 15																	09 23						09 45
Wandsworth Road	d	09 17																							09 47
Clapham High Street ⊖	d	09 19																							09 49
London Blackfriars 3 ⊖	d																								
Denmark Hill 4	d	09 24																						09 48	09 54
Peckham Rye 4	d	09 26	09 33																			09 42	09 47	09a51	09 56
Queens Rd Peckham	d	09 29	09 36																				09 49		09 59
South Bermondsey	d	09 31	09 38																				09 52		10 01
Clapham Junction 10	d																		09 27						
Wandsworth Common	d																		09 30						
Balham 4 ⊖	d																		09 32						
Streatham Hill	d																		09 35						
West Norwood 4	d																		09 40			09 53			
Gipsy Hill	d																		09 43			09 56			
Crystal Palace 4	d											09 36				09 43	09 43		09 51	09 58	09 58	09a59			
Sydenham	d			09 21	09 21					09 36	09 36	09 39	09 42			09 46	09 46		09 54	10 01	10 01				
Forest Hill 4	d			09 23	09 23					09 38	09 38	09 42	09 45			09 49	09 49		09 57	10 04	10 04				
Honor Oak Park	d			09 26	09 26					09 41	09 41	09 44	09 47			09 51	09 51		09 59	10 06	10 06				
Brockley	d			09 28	09 28					09 43	09 43	09 47	09 50			09 54	09 54		10 02	10 09	10 09				
New Cross Gate 4	a			09 31	09 31	09 32				09 46	09 46	09 49	09 52			09 56	09 56		10 04	10 11	10 11				
	d			09 31	09 31	09 33				09 46	09 46	09 49	09 52			09 56	09 56		10 04	10 11	10 11				
New Cross ELL	d						09 36		09 36					09 51	09 51										
Surrey Quays	d			09 35	09 35		09 40		09 40	09 49	09 49			09 55	09 55	10 00	10 00			10 15	10 15				
Canada Water	d			09 37	09 37		09 42		09 42	09 51	09 51			09 57	09 57	10 02	10 02			10 17	10 17				
Rotherhithe	d			09 38	09 38		09 43		09 43	09 53	09 53			09 58	09 58	10 03	10 03			10 18	10 18				
Wapping	d			09 40	09 40		09 45		09 45	09 54	09 54			10 00	10 00	10 05	10 05			10 20	10 20				
Shadwell	d			09 42	09 42		09 47		09 47	09 56	09 56			10 02	10 02	10 07	10 07			10 22	10 22				
Whitechapel	d			09 44	09 44		09 49		09 49	09 59	09 59			10 04	10 04	10 09	10 09			10 24	10 24				
Shoreditch High Street	d			09 46	09 46		09 51		09 51	10 01	10 01			10 06	10 06	10 11	10 11			10 26	10 26				
Hoxton	d			09 48	09 48		09 53		09 53	10 03	10 03			10 08	10 08	10 13	10 13			10 28	10 28				
Haggerston	d			09 50	09 50		09 55		09 55	10 05	10 05			10 10	10 10	10 15	10 15			10 30	10 30				
Dalston Junction Stn ELL	a			09 53	09 53		09 58		10 02	10 07	10 07			10 13	10 17	10 17	10 17			10 32	10 32				
Canonbury	d			09 57	09 57					10 12	10 12					10 20	10 20			10 35	10 35				
Highbury & Islington	a			10 02	10 05					10 16	10 19					10 25	10 28			10 40	10 43				
	d																								
London Bridge 4 ⊖	a	09 38	09 44			09 41						09 59	10 00						10 11				09 58		10 06

A not 27 July

B 27 July

Table 178

Mondays to Fridays

until 27 July

East London Line and Croydon - London Victoria to London Bridge

Network Diagram - see first Page of Table 177

Station		SN	LO A		LO B	LO A	LO B	LO A	LO B	SN	LO A	LO B	LO A		LO B	SN	LO A	LO B	SN	SN	SE	SN	SN		LO A
East Croydon	d									10 00															
West Croydon 4	d	09 31	09 39		09 39			09 52	09 52														10 01		10 09
Norwood Junction 2	d		09 43		09 43			09 58	09 58	10 05															10 13
Anerley	d		09 46		09 46			10 01	10 01	10 08															10 16
Penge West	d		09 48		09 48			10 03	10 03	10 10															10 18
London Victoria 15 ⊖	d															09 49					10 09	10 11			
Battersea Park 4	d															09 53						10 15			
Wandsworth Road	d																					10 17			
Clapham High Street ⊖	d																					10 19			
London Blackfriars 3 ⊖	d																								
Denmark Hill 4	d																				10 18	10 24			
Peckham Rye 4	d	10 01																	10 12	10 17	10a21	10 26	10 31		
Queens Rd Peckham	d	10 04																		10 19		10 29	10 34		
South Bermondsey	d	10 06																		10 22		10 31	10 36		
Clapham Junction 10	d															09 57									
Wandsworth Common	d															10 00									
Balham 4 ⊖	d															10 02									
Streatham Hill	d															10 05									
West Norwood 4	d															10 10			10 23						
Gipsy Hill	d															10 13			10 26						
Crystal Palace 4	d												10 13		10 13	10 21	10 28	10 28	10a29						
Sydenham	d		09 51		09 51			10 06	10 06	10 12			10 16		10 16	10 24	10 31	10 31							10 21
Forest Hill 4	d		09 53		09 53			10 08	10 08	10 15			10 19		10 19	10 27	10 34	10 34							10 23
Honor Oak Park	d		09 56		09 56			10 11	10 11	10 17			10 21		10 21	10 29	10 36	10 36							10 26
Brockley	d		09 58		09 58			10 13	10 13	10 20			10 24		10 24	10 32	10 39	10 39							10 28
New Cross Gate 4	a		10 01		10 01			10 16	10 16	10 22			10 26		10 26	10 34	10 41	10 41							10 31
	d		10 01		10 01			10 16	10 16	10 22			10 26		10 26	10 34	10 41	10 41							10 31
New Cross ELL	d					10 06	10 06				10 21	10 21													
Surrey Quays	d		10 05		10 05	10 10	10 10	10 19	10 19		10 25	10 25	10 30		10 30		10 45	10 45							10 35
Canada Water	d		10 07		10 07	10 12	10 12	10 21	10 21		10 27	10 27	10 32		10 32		10 47	10 47							10 37
Rotherhithe	d		10 08		10 08	10 13	10 13	10 23	10 23		10 28	10 28	10 33		10 33		10 48	10 48							10 38
Wapping	d		10 10		10 10	10 15	10 15	10 24	10 24		10 30	10 30	10 35		10 35		10 50	10 50							10 40
Shadwell	d		10 12		10 12	10 17	10 17	10 26	10 26		10 32	10 32	10 37		10 37		10 52	10 52							10 42
Whitechapel	d		10 14		10 14	10 19	10 19	10 29	10 29		10 34	10 34	10 39		10 39		10 54	10 54							10 44
Shoreditch High Street	d		10 16		10 16	10 21	10 21	10 31	10 31		10 36	10 36	10 41		10 41		10 56	10 56							10 46
Hoxton	d		10 18		10 18	10 23	10 23	10 33	10 33		10 38	10 38	10 43		10 43		10 58	10 58							10 48
Haggerston	d		10 20		10 20	10 25	10 25	10 35	10 35		10 40	10 40	10 45		10 45		11 00	11 00							10 50
Dalston Junction Stn ELL	a		10 22		10 22	10 28	10 32	10 37	10 37		10 43	10 47	10 47		10 47		11 02	11 02							10 52
Canonbury	d		10 27		10 27			10 42	10 42				10 50		10 50		11 05	11 05							10 57
Highbury & Islington	a		10 32		10 35			10 46	10 49				10 55		10 58		11 10	11 13							11 02
	d																								
London Bridge 4 ⊖	a	10 11								10 29						10 41				10 26		10 36	10 41		

Station		LO B	LO A	LO B	LO A	LO B	SN	LO A	LO B		LO A	LO B	SN	LO A	LO B	SN	SN	SE	SN		SN	LO A	LO B	LO A	LO B
East Croydon	d						10 30																		
West Croydon 4	d	10 09			10 22	10 22															10 31	10 39	10 39		
Norwood Junction 2	d	10 13			10 28	10 28	10 35															10 43	10 43		
Anerley	d	10 16			10 31	10 31	10 38															10 46	10 46		
Penge West	d	10 18			10 33	10 33	10 40															10 48	10 48		
London Victoria 15 ⊖	d												10 19					10 39	10 41						
Battersea Park 4	d												10 23						10 45						
Wandsworth Road	d																		10 47						
Clapham High Street ⊖	d																		10 49						
London Blackfriars 3 ⊖	d																								
Denmark Hill 4	d																	10 48	10 54						
Peckham Rye 4	d															10 42	10 47	10a51	10 56		11 01				
Queens Rd Peckham	d																10 49		10 59		11 04				
South Bermondsey	d																10 52		11 01		11 06				
Clapham Junction 10	d												10 27												
Wandsworth Common	d												10 30												
Balham 4 ⊖	d												10 32												
Streatham Hill	d												10 35												
West Norwood 4	d												10 40			10 53									
Gipsy Hill	d												10 43			10 56									
Crystal Palace 4	d										10 43	10 43	10 51	10 58	10 58	10a59									
Sydenham	d	10 21			10 36	10 36	10 42				10 46	10 46	10 54	11 01	11 01							10 51	10 51		
Forest Hill 4	d	10 23			10 38	10 38	10 45				10 49	10 49	10 57	11 04	11 04							10 53	10 53		
Honor Oak Park	d	10 26			10 41	10 41	10 47				10 51	10 51	10 59	11 06	11 06							10 56	10 56		
Brockley	d	10 28			10 43	10 43	10 50				10 54	10 54	11 02	11 09	11 09							10 58	10 58		
New Cross Gate 4	a	10 31			10 46	10 46	10 52				10 56	10 56	11 04	11 11	11 11							11 01	11 01		
	d	10 31			10 46	10 46	10 52				10 56	10 56	11 04	11 11	11 11							11 01	11 01		
New Cross ELL	d		10 36	10 36				10 51	10 51															11 06	11 06
Surrey Quays	d	10 35	10 40	10 40	10 49	10 49		10 55	10 55		11 00	11 00		11 15	11 15							11 05	11 05	11 10	11 10
Canada Water	d	10 37	10 42	10 42	10 51	10 51		10 57	10 57		11 02	11 02		11 17	11 17							11 07	11 07	11 12	11 12
Rotherhithe	d	10 38	10 43	10 43	10 53	10 53		10 58	10 58		11 03	11 03		11 18	11 18							11 08	11 08	11 13	11 13
Wapping	d	10 40	10 45	10 45	10 54	10 54		11 00	11 00		11 05	11 05		11 20	11 20							11 10	11 10	11 15	11 15
Shadwell	d	10 42	10 47	10 47	10 56	10 56		11 02	11 02		11 07	11 07		11 22	11 22							11 12	11 12	11 17	11 17
Whitechapel	d	10 44	10 49	10 49	10 59	10 59		11 04	11 04		11 09	11 09		11 24	11 24							11 14	11 14	11 19	11 19
Shoreditch High Street	d	10 46	10 51	10 51	11 01	11 01		11 06	11 06		11 11	11 11		11 26	11 26							11 16	11 16	11 21	11 21
Hoxton	d	10 48	10 53	10 53	11 03	11 03		11 08	11 08		11 13	11 13		11 28	11 28							11 18	11 18	11 23	11 23
Haggerston	d	10 50	10 55	10 55	11 05	11 05		11 10	11 10		11 15	11 15		11 30	11 30							11 20	11 20	11 25	11 25
Dalston Junction Stn ELL	a	10 52	10 58	11 02	11 07	11 07		11 13	11 17		11 17	11 17		11 32	11 32							11 22	11 22	11 28	11 32
Canonbury	d	10 57			11 12	11 12					11 20	11 20		11 35	11 35							11 27	11 27		
Highbury & Islington	a	11 05			11 16	11 19					11 25	11 28		11 40	11 43							11 32	11 35		
	d																								
London Bridge 4 ⊖	a						10 59						11 11				10 56		11 06		11 11				

A not 27 July

B 27 July

East London Line and Croydon - London Victoria to London Bridge

Network Diagram - see first Page of Table 177

		LO A	LO B	SN	LO A		LO B	LO A	LO B	SN	LO A	LO B	SN	SN	SE		SN	SN	LO A	LO B	LO A	LO B	LO A	LO B	SN
East Croydon	d			11 00																					11 30
West Croydon	d	10 52	10 52															11 01	11 09	11 09			11 22	11 22	
Norwood Junction	d	10 58	10 58	11 05															11 13	11 13			11 28	11 28	11 35
Anerley	d	11 01	11 01	11 08															11 16	11 16			11 31	11 31	11 38
Penge West	d	11 03	11 03	11 10															11 18	11 18			11 33	11 33	11 40
London Victoria	d									10 49					11 09		11 11								
Battersea Park	d									10 53							11 15								
Wandsworth Road	d																11 17								
Clapham High Street	d																11 19								
London Blackfriars	d																								
Denmark Hill	d														11 18		11 24								
Peckham Rye	d												11 12	11 17	11a21		11 26	11 31							
Queens Rd Peckham	d													11 19			11 29	11 34							
South Bermondsey	d													11 22			11 31	11 36							
Clapham Junction	d									10 57															
Wandsworth Common	d									11 00															
Balham	d									11 02															
Streatham Hill	d									11 05															
West Norwood	d									11 10			11 23												
Gipsy Hill	d									11 13			11 26												
Crystal Palace	d							11 13	11 13	11 21	11 28	11 28	11a29												
Sydenham	d	11 06	11 06	11 12				11 16	11 16	11 24	11 31	11 31							11 21	11 21			11 36	11 36	11 42
Forest Hill	d	11 08	11 08	11 15				11 19	11 19	11 27	11 34	11 34							11 23	11 23			11 38	11 38	11 45
Honor Oak Park	d	11 11	11 11	11 17				11 21	11 21	11 29	11 36	11 36							11 26	11 26			11 41	11 41	11 47
Brockley	d	11 13	11 13	11 20				11 24	11 24	11 32	11 39	11 39							11 28	11 28			11 43	11 43	11 50
New Cross Gate	a	11 16	11 16	11 22				11 26	11 26	11 34	11 41	11 41							11 31	11 31			11 46	11 46	11 52
	d	11 16	11 16	11 22				11 26	11 26	11 34	11 41	11 41							11 31	11 31			11 46	11 46	11 52
New Cross ELL	d				11 21		11 21														11 36	11 36			
Surrey Quays	d	11 19	11 19		11 25		11 25	11 30	11 30		11 45	11 45							11 35	11 35	11 40	11 40	11 49	11 49	
Canada Water	d	11 21	11 21		11 27		11 27	11 32	11 32		11 47	11 47							11 37	11 37	11 42	11 42	11 51	11 51	
Rotherhithe	d	11 23	11 23		11 28		11 28	11 33	11 33		11 48	11 48							11 38	11 38	11 43	11 43	11 53	11 53	
Wapping	d	11 24	11 24		11 30		11 30	11 35	11 35		11 50	11 50							11 40	11 40	11 45	11 45	11 54	11 54	
Shadwell	d	11 26	11 26		11 32		11 32	11 37	11 37		11 52	11 52							11 42	11 42	11 47	11 47	11 56	11 56	
Whitechapel	d	11 29	11 29		11 34		11 34	11 39	11 39		11 54	11 54							11 44	11 44	11 49	11 49	11 59	11 59	
Shoreditch High Street	d	11 31	11 31		11 36		11 36	11 41	11 41		11 56	11 56							11 46	11 46	11 51	11 51	12 01	12 01	
Hoxton	d	11 33	11 33		11 38		11 38	11 43	11 43		11 58	11 58							11 48	11 48	11 53	11 53	12 03	12 03	
Haggerston	d	11 35	11 35		11 40		11 40	11 45	11 45		12 00	12 00							11 50	11 50	11 55	11 55	12 05	12 05	
Dalston Junction Stn ELL	a	11 37	11 37		11 43		11 47	11 47	11 47		12 02	12 02							11 52	11 52	11 58	12 02	12 07	12 07	
Canonbury	d	11 42	11 42					11 50	11 50		12 05	12 05							11 57	11 57			12 12	12 12	
Highbury & Islington	a	11 46	11 49					11 55	11 58		12 10	12 13							12 02	12 05			12 16	12 19	
	d																								
London Bridge	a			11 29						11 41				11 26			11 36	11 41							11 59

			LO A	LO B	LO A	LO B	SN	LO A	LO B	SN	SN		SE	SN	SN	LO A	LO B	LO A	LO B	LO A	LO B		SN	LO A	LO B
East Croydon	d																						12 00		
West Croydon	d														11 31	11 39	11 39			11 52	11 52				
Norwood Junction	d															11 43	11 43			11 58	11 58		12 05		
Anerley	d															11 46	11 46			12 01	12 01		12 08		
Penge West	d															11 48	11 48			12 03	12 03		12 10		
London Victoria	d						11 19						11 39	11 41											
Battersea Park	d						11 23							11 45											
Wandsworth Road	d													11 47											
Clapham High Street	d													11 49											
London Blackfriars	d																								
Denmark Hill	d												11 48	11 54											
Peckham Rye	d									11 42	11 47		11a51	11 56	12 01										
Queens Rd Peckham	d										11 49			11 59	12 04										
South Bermondsey	d										11 52			12 01	12 06										
Clapham Junction	d						11 27																		
Wandsworth Common	d						11 30																		
Balham	d						11 32																		
Streatham Hill	d						11 35																		
West Norwood	d						11 40			11 53															
Gipsy Hill	d						11 43			11 56															
Crystal Palace	d				11 43	11 43	11 51	11 58	11 58	11a59															
Sydenham	d				11 46	11 46	11 54	12 01	12 01							11 51	11 51			12 06	12 06		12 12		
Forest Hill	d				11 49	11 49	11 57	12 04	12 04							11 53	11 53			12 08	12 08		12 15		
Honor Oak Park	d				11 51	11 51	11 59	12 06	12 06							11 56	11 56			12 11	12 11		12 17		
Brockley	d				11 54	11 54	12 02	12 09	12 09							11 58	11 58			12 13	12 13		12 20		
New Cross Gate	a				11 56	11 56	12 04	12 11	12 11							12 01	12 01			12 16	12 16		12 22		
	d				11 56	11 56	12 04	12 11	12 11							12 01	12 01			12 16	12 16		12 22		
New Cross ELL	d		11 51	11 51														12 06	12 06					12 21	12 21
Surrey Quays	d		11 55	11 55	12 00	12 00		12 15	12 15							12 05	12 05	12 10	12 10	12 19	12 19			12 25	12 25
Canada Water	d		11 57	11 57	12 02	12 02		12 17	12 17							12 07	12 07	12 12	12 12	12 21	12 21			12 27	12 27
Rotherhithe	d		11 58	11 58	12 03	12 03		12 18	12 18							12 08	12 08	12 13	12 13	12 23	12 23			12 28	12 28
Wapping	d		12 00	12 00	12 05	12 05		12 20	12 20							12 10	12 10	12 15	12 15	12 24	12 24			12 30	12 30
Shadwell	d		12 02	12 02	12 07	12 07		12 22	12 22							12 12	12 12	12 17	12 17	12 26	12 26			12 32	12 32
Whitechapel	d		12 04	12 04	12 09	12 09		12 24	12 24							12 14	12 14	12 19	12 19	12 29	12 29			12 34	12 34
Shoreditch High Street	d		12 06	12 06	12 11	12 11		12 26	12 26							12 16	12 16	12 21	12 21	12 31	12 31			12 36	12 36
Hoxton	d		12 08	12 08	12 13	12 13		12 28	12 28							12 18	12 18	12 23	12 23	12 33	12 33			12 38	12 38
Haggerston	d		12 10	12 10	12 15	12 15		12 30	12 30							12 20	12 20	12 25	12 25	12 35	12 35			12 40	12 40
Dalston Junction Stn ELL	a		12 13	12 17	12 17	12 17		12 32	12 32							12 22	12 22	12 28	12 32	12 37	12 37			12 43	12 47
Canonbury	d				12 20	12 20		12 35	12 35							12 27	12 27			12 42	12 42				
Highbury & Islington	a				12 25	12 28		12 40	12 43							12 32	12 35			12 46	12 49				
	d																								
London Bridge	a						12 14				11 56			12 06	12 11								12 29		

A not 27 July

B 27 July

East London Line and Croydon - London Victoria to London Bridge

Network Diagram - see first Page of Table 177

Station		LO A	LO B	SN	LO A	LO B	SN		SN	SE	SN	SN	LO A	LO B	LO A	LO B	LO A		LO B	SN	LO A	LO B	LO A	LO B	SN
East Croydon	d																			12 30					
West Croydon 4	d											12 01	12 09	12 09			12 22		12 22						
Norwood Junction 2	d												12 13	12 13			12 28		12 28	12 35					
Anerley	d												12 16	12 16			12 31		12 31	12 38					
Penge West	d												12 18	12 18			12 33		12 33	12 40					
London Victoria 15 ⊖	d			11 49						12 09	12 11														12 19
Battersea Park 4	d			11 53							12 15														12 23
Wandsworth Road	d										12 17														
Clapham High Street ⊖	d										12 19														
London Blackfriars 3 ⊖	d																								
Denmark Hill 4	d									12 18	12 24														
Peckham Rye 4	d						12 12		12 17	12a21	12 26	12 31													
Queens Rd Peckham	d								12 19		12 29	12 34													
South Bermondsey	d								12 22		12 31	12 36													
Clapham Junction 10	d			11 57																					12 27
Wandsworth Common	d			12 00																					12 30
Balham 4 ⊖	d			12 02																					12 32
Streatham Hill	d			12 05																					12 35
West Norwood 4	d			12 10			12 23																		12 40
Gipsy Hill	d			12 13			12 26																		12 43
Crystal Palace 4	d	12 13	12 13	12 21	12 28	12 28	12a29																12 43	12 43	12 51
Sydenham	d	12 16	12 16	12 24	12 31	12 31							12 21	12 21			12 36		12 36	12 42			12 46	12 46	12 54
Forest Hill 4	d	12 19	12 19	12 27	12 34	12 34							12 23	12 23			12 38		12 38	12 45			12 49	12 49	12 57
Honor Oak Park	d	12 21	12 21	12 29	12 36	12 36							12 26	12 26			12 41		12 41	12 47			12 51	12 51	12 59
Brockley	d	12 24	12 24	12 32	12 39	12 39							12 28	12 28			12 43		12 43	12 50			12 54	12 54	13 02
New Cross Gate 4	a	12 26	12 26	12 34	12 41	12 41							12 31	12 31			12 46		12 46	12 52			12 56	12 56	13 04
	d	12 26	12 26	12 34	12 41	12 41							12 31	12 31			12 46		12 46	12 52			12 56	12 56	13 04
New Cross ELL	d														12 36	12 36					12 51	12 51			
Surrey Quays	d	12 30	12 30		12 45	12 45							12 35	12 35	12 40	12 40	12 49		12 49		12 55	12 55	13 00	13 00	
Canada Water	d	12 32	12 32		12 47	12 47							12 37	12 37	12 42	12 42	12 51		12 51		12 57	12 57	13 02	13 02	
Rotherhithe	d	12 33	12 33		12 48	12 48							12 38	12 38	12 43	12 43	12 53		12 53		12 58	12 58	13 03	13 03	
Wapping	d	12 35	12 35		12 50	12 50							12 40	12 40	12 45	12 45	12 54		12 54		13 00	13 00	13 05	13 05	
Shadwell	d	12 37	12 37		12 52	12 52							12 42	12 42	12 47	12 47	12 56		12 56		13 02	13 02	13 07	13 07	
Whitechapel	d	12 39	12 39		12 54	12 54							12 44	12 44	12 49	12 49	12 59		12 59		13 04	13 04	13 09	13 09	
Shoreditch High Street	d	12 41	12 41		12 56	12 56							12 46	12 46	12 51	12 51	13 01		13 01		13 06	13 06	13 11	13 11	
Hoxton	d	12 43	12 43		12 58	12 58							12 48	12 48	12 53	12 53	13 03		13 03		13 08	13 08	13 13	13 13	
Haggerston	d	12 45	12 45		13 00	13 00							12 50	12 50	12 55	12 55	13 05		13 05		13 10	13 10	13 15	13 15	
Dalston Junction Stn ELL	a	12 47	12 47		13 02	13 02							12 52	12 52	12 58	13 02	13 07		13 07		13 13	13 17	13 17	13 17	
Canonbury	d	12 50	12 50		13 05	13 05							12 57	12 57			13 12		13 12				13 20	13 20	
Highbury & Islington	a	12 55	12 58		13 10	13 13							13 02	13 05			13 16		13 19				13 25	13 28	
	d																								
London Bridge 4 ⊖	a			12 41					12 26		12 36	12 41								12 59					13 11

Station		LO A	LO B		SN	SN	SE	SN	SN	LO A	LO B	LO A	LO B		LO A	LO B	SN	LO A	LO B	LO A	LO B	SN	LO A		LO B
East Croydon	d																13 00								
West Croydon 4	d								12 31	12 39	12 39				12 52	12 52									
Norwood Junction 2	d									12 43	12 43				12 58	12 58	13 05								
Anerley	d									12 46	12 46				13 01	13 01	13 08								
Penge West	d									12 48	12 48				13 03	13 03	13 10								
London Victoria 15 ⊖	d						12 39	12 41														12 49			
Battersea Park 4	d							12 45														12 53			
Wandsworth Road	d							12 47																	
Clapham High Street ⊖	d							12 49																	
London Blackfriars 3 ⊖	d																								
Denmark Hill 4	d						12 48	12 54																	
Peckham Rye 4	d				12 42	12 47	12a51	12 56	13 01																
Queens Rd Peckham	d					12 49		12 59	13 04																
South Bermondsey	d					12 52		13 01	13 06																
Clapham Junction 10	d																					12 57			
Wandsworth Common	d																					13 00			
Balham 4 ⊖	d																					13 02			
Streatham Hill	d																					13 05			
West Norwood 4	d				12 53																	13 10			
Gipsy Hill	d				12 56																	13 13			
Crystal Palace 4	d	12 58	12 58		12a59															13 13	13 13	13 21	13 28		13 28
Sydenham	d	13 01	13 01							12 51	12 51				13 06	13 06	13 12			13 16	13 16	13 24	13 31		13 31
Forest Hill 4	d	13 04	13 04							12 53	12 53				13 08	13 08	13 15			13 19	13 19	13 27	13 34		13 34
Honor Oak Park	d	13 06	13 06							12 56	12 56				13 11	13 11	13 17			13 21	13 21	13 29	13 36		13 36
Brockley	d	13 09	13 09							12 58	12 58				13 13	13 13	13 20			13 24	13 24	13 32	13 39		13 39
New Cross Gate 4	a	13 11	13 11							13 01	13 01				13 16	13 16	13 22			13 26	13 26	13 34	13 41		13 41
	d	13 11	13 11							13 01	13 01				13 16	13 16	13 22			13 26	13 26	13 34	13 41		13 41
New Cross ELL	d											13 06	13 06					13 21	13 21						
Surrey Quays	d	13 15	13 15							13 05	13 05	13 10	13 10		13 19	13 19		13 25	13 25	13 30	13 30		13 45		13 45
Canada Water	d	13 17	13 17							13 07	13 07	13 12	13 12		13 21	13 21		13 27	13 27	13 32	13 32		13 47		13 47
Rotherhithe	d	13 18	13 18							13 08	13 08	13 13	13 13		13 23	13 23		13 28	13 28	13 33	13 33		13 48		13 48
Wapping	d	13 20	13 20							13 10	13 10	13 15	13 15		13 24	13 24		13 30	13 30	13 35	13 35		13 50		13 50
Shadwell	d	13 22	13 22							13 12	13 12	13 17	13 17		13 26	13 26		13 32	13 32	13 37	13 37		13 52		13 52
Whitechapel	d	13 24	13 24							13 14	13 14	13 19	13 19		13 29	13 29		13 34	13 34	13 39	13 39		13 54		13 54
Shoreditch High Street	d	13 26	13 26							13 16	13 16	13 21	13 21		13 31	13 31		13 36	13 36	13 41	13 41		13 56		13 56
Hoxton	d	13 28	13 28							13 18	13 18	13 23	13 23		13 33	13 33		13 38	13 38	13 43	13 43		13 58		13 58
Haggerston	d	13 30	13 30							13 20	13 20	13 25	13 25		13 35	13 35		13 40	13 40	13 45	13 45		14 00		14 00
Dalston Junction Stn ELL	a	13 32	13 32							13 22	13 22	13 28	13 32		13 37	13 37		13 43	13 47	13 47	13 47		14 02		14 02
Canonbury	d	13 35	13 35							13 27	13 27				13 42	13 42				13 50	13 50		14 05		14 05
Highbury & Islington	a	13 40	13 43							13 32	13 35				13 46	13 49				13 55	13 58		14 10		14 13
	d																								
London Bridge 4 ⊖	a					12 56		13 06	13 11								13 29					13 44			

A not 27 July

B 27 July

Table 178

Mondays to Fridays

until 27 July

East London Line and Croydon - London Victoria to London Bridge

Network Diagram - see first Page of Table 177

		SN	SN	SE	SN	SN	LO A	LO B	LO A		LO B	LO A	LO B	SN	LO A	LO B	LO A	LO B	SN		LO A	LO B	SN	SN	SE
East Croydon	d													13 30											
West Croydon 4	d					13 01	13 09	13 09				13 22	13 22												
Norwood Junction 2	d						13 13	13 13				13 28	13 28	13 35											
Anerley	d						13 16	13 16				13 31	13 31	13 38											
Penge West	d						13 18	13 18				13 33	13 33	13 40											
London Victoria 15 ⊖	d			13 09	13 11														13 19						13 39
Battersea Park 4	d				13 15														13 23						
Wandsworth Road	d				13 17																				
Clapham High Street ⊖	d				13 19																				
London Blackfriars 3 ⊖	d																								
Denmark Hill 4	d			13 18	13 24																				13 48
Peckham Rye 4	d	13 12	13 17	13a21	13 26	13 31																	13 42	13 47	13a51
Queens Rd Peckham	d		13 19		13 29	13 34																		13 49	
South Bermondsey	d		13 22		13 31	13 36																		13 52	
Clapham Junction 10	d																		13 27						
Wandsworth Common	d																		13 30						
Balham 4 ⊖	d																		13 32						
Streatham Hill	d																		13 35						
West Norwood 4	d	13 23																	13 40				13 53		
Gipsy Hill	d	13 26																	13 43				13 56		
Crystal Palace 4	d	13a29															13 43	13 43	13 51		13 58	13 58	13a59		
Sydenham	d						13 21	13 21				13 36	13 36	13 42			13 46	13 46	13 54		14 01	14 01			
Forest Hill 4	d						13 23	13 23				13 38	13 38	13 45			13 49	13 49	13 57		14 04	14 04			
Honor Oak Park	d						13 26	13 26				13 41	13 41	13 47			13 51	13 51	13 59		14 06	14 06			
Brockley	d						13 28	13 28				13 43	13 43	13 50			13 54	13 54	14 02		14 09	14 09			
New Cross Gate 4	a						13 31	13 31				13 46	13 46	13 52			13 56	13 56	14 04		14 11	14 11			
	d						13 31	13 31				13 46	13 46	13 52			13 56	13 56	14 04		14 11	14 11			
New Cross ELL	d								13 36		13 36				13 51	13 51									
Surrey Quays	d						13 35	13 35	13 40		13 40	13 49	13 49		13 55	13 55	14 00	14 00			14 15	14 15			
Canada Water	d						13 37	13 37	13 42		13 42	13 51	13 51		13 57	13 57	14 02	14 02			14 17	14 17			
Rotherhithe	d						13 38	13 38	13 43		13 43	13 53	13 53		13 58	13 58	14 03	14 03			14 18	14 18			
Wapping	d						13 40	13 40	13 45		13 45	13 54	13 54		14 00	14 00	14 05	14 05			14 20	14 20			
Shadwell	d						13 42	13 42	13 47		13 47	13 56	13 56		14 02	14 02	14 07	14 07			14 22	14 22			
Whitechapel	d						13 44	13 44	13 49		13 49	13 59	13 59		14 04	14 04	14 09	14 09			14 24	14 24			
Shoreditch High Street	d						13 46	13 46	13 51		13 51	14 01	14 01		14 06	14 06	14 11	14 11			14 26	14 26			
Hoxton	d						13 48	13 48	13 53		13 53	14 03	14 03		14 08	14 08	14 13	14 13			14 28	14 28			
Haggerston	d						13 50	13 50	13 55		13 55	14 05	14 05		14 10	14 10	14 15	14 15			14 30	14 30			
Dalston Junction Stn ELL	a						13 52	13 52	13 58		14 02	14 07	14 07		14 13	14 17	14 17	14 17			14 32	14 32			
Canonbury	d						13 57	13 57				14 12	14 12				14 20	14 20			14 35	14 35			
Highbury & Islington	a						14 02	14 05				14 16	14 19				14 25	14 28			14 40	14 43			
	d																								
London Bridge 4 ⊖	a		13 26		13 36	13 41								13 59					14 11					13 56	

		SN	SN	LO A	LO B		LO A	LO B	LO A	LO B	SN	LO A	LO B	LO A	LO B		SN	LO A	LO B	SN	SN	SE	SN	SN	LO A
East Croydon	d										14 00														
West Croydon 4	d		13 31	13 39	13 39				13 52	13 52														14 01	14 09
Norwood Junction 2	d			13 43	13 43				13 58	13 58	14 05														14 13
Anerley	d			13 46	13 46				14 01	14 01	14 08														14 16
Penge West	d			13 48	13 48				14 03	14 03	14 10														14 18
London Victoria 15 ⊖	d	13 41															13 49					14 09	14 11		
Battersea Park 4	d	13 45															13 53						14 15		
Wandsworth Road	d	13 47																					14 17		
Clapham High Street ⊖	d	13 49																					14 19		
London Blackfriars 3 ⊖	d																								
Denmark Hill 4	d	13 54																				14 18	14 24		
Peckham Rye 4	d	13 56	14 01																	14 12	14 17	14a21	14 26	14 31	
Queens Rd Peckham	d	13 59	14 04																		14 19		14 29	14 34	
South Bermondsey	d	14 01	14 06																		14 22		14 31	14 36	
Clapham Junction 10	d																13 57								
Wandsworth Common	d																14 00								
Balham 4 ⊖	d																14 02								
Streatham Hill	d																14 05								
West Norwood 4	d																14 10			14 23					
Gipsy Hill	d																14 13			14 26					
Crystal Palace 4	d													14 13	14 13		14 21	14 28	14 28	14a29					
Sydenham	d			13 51	13 51				14 06	14 06	14 12			14 16	14 16		14 24	14 31	14 31						14 21
Forest Hill 4	d			13 53	13 53				14 08	14 08	14 15			14 19	14 19		14 27	14 34	14 34						14 23
Honor Oak Park	d			13 56	13 56				14 11	14 11	14 17			14 21	14 21		14 29	14 36	14 36						14 26
Brockley	d			13 58	13 58				14 13	14 13	14 20			14 24	14 24		14 32	14 39	14 39						14 28
New Cross Gate 4	a			14 01	14 01				14 16	14 16	14 22			14 26	14 26		14 34	14 41	14 41						14 31
	d			14 01	14 01				14 16	14 16	14 22			14 26	14 26		14 34	14 41	14 41						14 31
New Cross ELL	d						14 06	14 06				14 21	14 21												
Surrey Quays	d			14 05	14 05		14 10	14 10	14 19	14 19		14 25	14 25	14 30	14 30			14 45	14 45						14 35
Canada Water	d			14 07	14 07		14 12	14 12	14 21	14 21		14 27	14 27	14 32	14 32			14 47	14 47						14 37
Rotherhithe	d			14 08	14 08		14 13	14 13	14 23	14 23		14 28	14 28	14 33	14 33			14 48	14 48						14 38
Wapping	d			14 10	14 10		14 15	14 15	14 24	14 24		14 30	14 30	14 35	14 35			14 50	14 50						14 40
Shadwell	d			14 12	14 12		14 17	14 17	14 26	14 26		14 32	14 32	14 37	14 37			14 52	14 52						14 42
Whitechapel	d			14 14	14 14		14 19	14 19	14 29	14 29		14 34	14 34	14 39	14 39			14 54	14 54						14 44
Shoreditch High Street	d			14 16	14 16		14 21	14 21	14 31	14 31		14 36	14 36	14 41	14 41			14 56	14 56						14 46
Hoxton	d			14 18	14 18		14 23	14 23	14 33	14 33		14 38	14 38	14 43	14 43			14 58	14 58						14 48
Haggerston	d			14 20	14 20		14 25	14 25	14 35	14 35		14 40	14 40	14 45	14 45			15 00	15 00						14 50
Dalston Junction Stn ELL	a			14 22	14 22		14 28	14 32	14 37	14 37		14 43	14 47	14 47	14 47			15 02	15 02						14 52
Canonbury	d			14 27	14 27				14 42	14 42				14 50	14 50			15 05	15 05						14 57
Highbury & Islington	a			14 32	14 35				14 46	14 49				14 55	14 58			15 10	15 13						15 02
	d																								
London Bridge 4 ⊖	a	14 06	14 11								14 29						14 41				14 26		14 36	14 41	

A not 27 July

B 27 July

East London Line and Croydon - London Victoria to London Bridge

Network Diagram - see first Page of Table 177

Station		LO A	LO B	LO A	LO B	LO A	SN	LO B	LO A	LO B	LO A	SN	LO B	LO A	SN	SN	SE	SN	SN	LO B	LO A	LO B
East Croydon	d						14 30															
West Croydon 4	d	14 09			14 22	14 22													14 31	14 39	14 39	
Norwood Junction 2	d	14 13			14 28	14 28	14 35													14 43	14 43	
Anerley	d	14 16			14 31	14 31	14 38													14 46	14 46	
Penge West	d	14 18			14 33	14 33	14 40													14 48	14 48	
London Victoria 15	d											14 19					14 39	14 41				
Battersea Park 4	d											14 23						14 45				
Wandsworth Road	d																	14 47				
Clapham High Street	d																	14 49				
London Blackfriars 3	d																					
Denmark Hill 4	d																14 48	14 54				
Peckham Rye 4	d														14 42	14 47	14a51	14 56	15 01			
Queens Rd Peckham	d															14 49		14 59	15 04			
South Bermondsey	d															14 52		15 01	15 06			
Clapham Junction 10	d											14 27										
Wandsworth Common	d											14 30										
Balham 4	d											14 32										
Streatham Hill	d											14 35										
West Norwood 4	d											14 40			14 53							
Gipsy Hill	d											14 43			14 56							
Crystal Palace 4	d									14 43	14 43	14 51	14 58	14 58	14a59							
Sydenham	d	14 21			14 36	14 36	14 42			14 46	14 46	14 54	15 01	15 01						14 51	14 51	
Forest Hill 4	d	14 23			14 38	14 38	14 45			14 49	14 49	14 57	15 04	15 04						14 53	14 53	
Honor Oak Park	d	14 26			14 41	14 41	14 47			14 51	14 51	14 59	15 06	15 06						14 56	14 56	
Brockley	d	14 28			14 43	14 43	14 50			14 54	14 54	15 02	15 09	15 09						14 58	14 58	
New Cross Gate 4	a	14 31			14 46	14 46	14 52			14 56	14 56	15 04	15 11	15 11						15 01	15 01	
	d	14 31			14 46	14 46	14 52			14 56	14 56	15 04	15 11	15 11						15 01	15 01	
New Cross ELL	d		14 36	14 36				14 51	14 51													15 06
Surrey Quays	d	14 35	14 40	14 40	14 49	14 49		14 55	14 55	15 00	15 00		15 15	15 15						15 05	15 05	15 10
Canada Water	d	14 37	14 42	14 42	14 51	14 51		14 57	14 57	15 02	15 02		15 17	15 17						15 07	15 07	15 12
Rotherhithe	d	14 38	14 43	14 43	14 53	14 53		14 58	14 58	15 03	15 03		15 18	15 18						15 08	15 08	15 13
Wapping	d	14 40	14 45	14 45	14 54	14 54		15 00	15 00	15 05	15 05		15 20	15 20						15 10	15 10	15 15
Shadwell	d	14 42	14 47	14 47	14 56	14 56		15 02	15 02	15 07	15 07		15 22	15 22						15 12	15 12	15 17
Whitechapel	d	14 44	14 49	14 49	14 59	14 59		15 04	15 04	15 09	15 09		15 24	15 24						15 14	15 14	15 19
Shoreditch High Street	d	14 46	14 51	14 51	15 01	15 01		15 06	15 06	15 11	15 11		15 26	15 26						15 16	15 16	15 21
Hoxton	d	14 48	14 53	14 53	15 03	15 03		15 08	15 08	15 13	15 13		15 28	15 28						15 18	15 18	15 23
Haggerston	d	14 50	14 55	14 55	15 05	15 05		15 10	15 10	15 15	15 15		15 30	15 30						15 20	15 20	15 25
Dalston Junction Stn ELL	a	14 52	14 58	15 02	15 07	15 07		15 13	15 17	15 17	15 17		15 32	15 32						15 22	15 22	15 28
Canonbury	d	14 57			15 12	15 12				15 20	15 20		15 35	15 35						15 27	15 27	
Highbury & Islington	a	15 05			15 16	15 19				15 25	15 28		15 40	15 43						15 32	15 35	
	d																					
London Bridge 4	a						14 59					15 11				14 56		15 06	15 11			

Station		LO A	LO B	LO A	SN	LO B	LO A	LO B	LO A	SN	LO B	LO A	SN	SN	SE	SN	SN	LO B	LO A	LO B	LO A	LO B	LO A
East Croydon	d				15 00																		
West Croydon 4	d		14 52	14 52													15 01	15 09	15 09			15 22	15 22
Norwood Junction 2	d		14 58	14 58	15 05													15 13	15 13			15 28	15 28
Anerley	d		15 01	15 01	15 08													15 16	15 16			15 31	15 31
Penge West	d		15 03	15 03	15 10													15 18	15 18			15 33	15 33
London Victoria 15	d									14 49					15 09	15 11							
Battersea Park 4	d									14 53						15 15							
Wandsworth Road	d															15 17							
Clapham High Street	d															15 19							
London Blackfriars 3	d																						
Denmark Hill 4	d														15 18	15 24							
Peckham Rye 4	d												15 12	15 17	15a21	15 26	15 31						
Queens Rd Peckham	d													15 19		15 29	15 34						
South Bermondsey	d													15 22		15 31	15 36						
Clapham Junction 10	d									14 57													
Wandsworth Common	d									15 00													
Balham 4	d									15 02													
Streatham Hill	d									15 05													
West Norwood 4	d									15 10			15 23										
Gipsy Hill	d									15 13			15 26										
Crystal Palace 4	d							15 13	15 13	15 21	15 28	15 28	15a29										
Sydenham	d		15 06	15 06	15 12			15 16	15 16	15 24	15 31	15 31						15 21	15 21			15 36	15 36
Forest Hill 4	d		15 08	15 08	15 15			15 19	15 19	15 27	15 34	15 34						15 23	15 23			15 38	15 38
Honor Oak Park	d		15 11	15 11	15 17			15 21	15 21	15 29	15 36	15 36						15 26	15 26			15 41	15 41
Brockley	d		15 13	15 13	15 20			15 24	15 24	15 32	15 39	15 39						15 28	15 28			15 43	15 43
New Cross Gate 4	a		15 16	15 16	15 22			15 26	15 26	15 34	15 41	15 41						15 31	15 31			15 46	15 46
	d		15 16	15 16	15 22			15 26	15 26	15 34	15 41	15 41						15 31	15 31			15 46	15 46
New Cross ELL	d	15 06				15 21	15 21													15 36	15 36		
Surrey Quays	d	15 10	15 19	15 19		15 25	15 25	15 30	15 30		15 45	15 45						15 35	15 35	15 40	15 40	15 49	15 49
Canada Water	d	15 12	15 21	15 21		15 27	15 27	15 32	15 32		15 47	15 47						15 37	15 37	15 42	15 42	15 51	15 51
Rotherhithe	d	15 13	15 23	15 23		15 28	15 28	15 33	15 33		15 48	15 48						15 38	15 38	15 43	15 43	15 53	15 53
Wapping	d	15 15	15 24	15 24		15 30	15 30	15 35	15 35		15 50	15 50						15 40	15 40	15 45	15 45	15 54	15 54
Shadwell	d	15 17	15 26	15 26		15 32	15 32	15 37	15 37		15 52	15 52						15 42	15 42	15 47	15 47	15 56	15 56
Whitechapel	d	15 19	15 29	15 29		15 34	15 34	15 39	15 39		15 54	15 54						15 44	15 44	15 49	15 49	15 59	15 59
Shoreditch High Street	d	15 21	15 31	15 31		15 36	15 36	15 41	15 41		15 56	15 56						15 46	15 46	15 51	15 51	16 01	16 01
Hoxton	d	15 23	15 33	15 33		15 38	15 38	15 43	15 43		15 58	15 58						15 48	15 48	15 53	15 53	16 03	16 03
Haggerston	d	15 25	15 35	15 35		15 40	15 40	15 45	15 45		16 00	16 00						15 50	15 50	15 55	15 55	16 05	16 05
Dalston Junction Stn ELL	a	15 32	15 37	15 37		15 43	15 47	15 47	15 47		16 02	16 02						15 52	15 52	15 58	16 02	16 07	16 07
Canonbury	d		15 42	15 42				15 50	15 50		16 05	16 05						15 57	15 57			16 12	16 12
Highbury & Islington	a		15 46	15 49				15 55	15 58		16 10	16 13						16 02	16 05			16 16	16 19
	d																						
London Bridge 4	a				15 29					15 41				15 26		15 36	15 41						

A 27 July

B not 27 July

Table 178

Mondays to Fridays

until 27 July

East London Line and Croydon - London Victoria to London Bridge

Network Diagram - see first Page of Table 177

		SN	LO A		LO B	LO A	LO B	SN	LO A	LO B	SN	SN	SE		SN	SN	LO A	LO B	LO A	LO B	LO A	LO B	SN		SN
East Croydon	d	15 30																							16 00
West Croydon 4	d															15 31	15 39	15 39			15 52	15 52			
Norwood Junction 2	d	15 35															15 43	15 43			15 58	15 58			16 05
Anerley	d	15 38															15 46	15 46			16 01	16 01			16 08
Penge West	d	15 40															15 48	15 48			16 03	16 03			16 10
London Victoria 15 ⊖	d							15 19					15 39		15 41										
Battersea Park 4	d							15 23							15 45										
Wandsworth Road	d														15 47										
Clapham High Street ⊖	d														15 49										
London Blackfriars 3 ⊖	d																								
Denmark Hill 4	d												15 48		15 54										
Peckham Rye 4	d										15 42	15 47	15a51		15 56	16 01							16 07		
Queens Rd Peckham	d											15 49			15 59	16 04							16 10		
South Bermondsey	d											15 52			16 01	16 06							16 12		
Clapham Junction 10	d							15 27																	
Wandsworth Common	d							15 30																	
Balham 4 ⊖	d							15 32																	
Streatham Hill	d							15 35																	
West Norwood 4	d							15 40			15 53														
Gipsy Hill	d							15 43			15 56														
Crystal Palace 4	d					15 43	15 43	15 51	15 58	15 58	15a59														
Sydenham	d	15 42				15 46	15 46	15 54	16 01	16 01							15 51	15 51			16 06	16 06			16 12
Forest Hill 4	d	15 45				15 49	15 49	15 57	16 04	16 04							15 53	15 53			16 08	16 08			16 15
Honor Oak Park	d	15 47				15 51	15 51	15 59	16 06	16 06							15 56	15 56			16 11	16 11			16 17
Brockley	d	15 50				15 54	15 54	16 02	16 09	16 09							15 58	15 58			16 13	16 13			16 20
New Cross Gate 4	a	15 52				15 56	15 56	16 04	16 11	16 11							16 01	16 01			16 16	16 16			16 22
	d	15 52				15 56	15 56	16 04	16 11	16 11							16 01	16 01			16 16	16 16			16 22
New Cross ELL	d		15 51		15 51														16 06	16 06					
Surrey Quays	d		15 55		15 55	16 00	16 00		16 15	16 15							16 05	16 05	16 10	16 10	16 19	16 19			
Canada Water	d		15 57		15 57	16 02	16 02		16 17	16 17							16 07	16 07	16 12	16 12	16 21	16 21			
Rotherhithe	d		15 58		15 58	16 03	16 03		16 18	16 18							16 08	16 08	16 13	16 13	16 23	16 23			
Wapping	d		16 00		16 00	16 05	16 05		16 20	16 20							16 10	16 10	16 15	16 15	16 24	16 24			
Shadwell	d		16 02		16 02	16 07	16 07		16 22	16 22							16 12	16 12	16 17	16 17	16 26	16 26			
Whitechapel	d		16 04		16 04	16 09	16 09		16 24	16 24							16 14	16 14	16 19	16 19	16 29	16 29			
Shoreditch High Street	d		16 06		16 06	16 11	16 11		16 26	16 26							16 16	16 16	16 21	16 21	16 31	16 31			
Hoxton	d		16 08		16 08	16 13	16 13		16 28	16 28							16 18	16 18	16 23	16 23	16 33	16 33			
Haggerston	d		16 10		16 10	16 15	16 15		16 30	16 30							16 20	16 20	16 25	16 25	16 35	16 35			
Dalston Junction Stn ELL	a		16 13		16 17	16 17	16 17		16 32	16 32							16 22	16 22	16 28	16 32	16 37	16 37			
Canonbury	d					16 20	16 20		16 35	16 35							16 27	16 27			16 42	16 42			
Highbury & Islington	a					16 25	16 28		16 40	16 43							16 32	16 35			16 46	16 49			
	d																								
London Bridge 4 ⊖	a	15 59						16 11				15 56			16 06	16 11							16 17		16 29

		LO A	LO B	LO A	LO B	SN	LO A	LO B	SN		SN	SE	SN	SN	LO A	LO B	LO A	LO B	LO A		LO B	SN	LO A	LO B	LO A
East Croydon	d																					16 30			
West Croydon 4	d													16 01	16 09	16 09			16 22		16 22				
Norwood Junction 2	d														16 13	16 13			16 28		16 28	16 35			
Anerley	d														16 16	16 16			16 31		16 31	16 38			
Penge West	d														16 18	16 18			16 33		16 33	16 40			
London Victoria 15 ⊖	d					15 49						16 09	16 11												
Battersea Park 4	d					15 53							16 15												
Wandsworth Road	d												16 17												
Clapham High Street ⊖	d												16 19												
London Blackfriars 3 ⊖	d																								
Denmark Hill 4	d											16 18	16 24												
Peckham Rye 4	d								16 12		16 17	16a21	16 26	16 31											
Queens Rd Peckham	d										16 19		16 29	16 34											
South Bermondsey	d										16 22		16 31	16 36											
Clapham Junction 10	d					15 57																			
Wandsworth Common	d					16 00																			
Balham 4 ⊖	d					16 02																			
Streatham Hill	d					16 05																			
West Norwood 4	d					16 10			16 23																
Gipsy Hill	d					16 13			16 26																
Crystal Palace 4	d			16 13	16 13	16 21	16 28	16 28	16a29																16 43
Sydenham	d			16 16	16 16	16 24	16 31	16 31							16 21	16 21			16 36		16 36	16 42			16 46
Forest Hill 4	d			16 19	16 19	16 27	16 34	16 34							16 23	16 23			16 38		16 38	16 45			16 49
Honor Oak Park	d			16 21	16 21	16 29	16 36	16 36							16 26	16 26			16 41		16 41	16 47			16 51
Brockley	d			16 24	16 24	16 32	16 39	16 39							16 28	16 28			16 43		16 43	16 50			16 54
New Cross Gate 4	a			16 26	16 26	16 34	16 41	16 41							16 31	16 31			16 46		16 46	16 52			16 56
	d			16 26	16 26	16 34	16 41	16 41							16 31	16 31			16 46		16 46	16 52			16 56
New Cross ELL	d	16 21	16 21														16 36	16 36					16 51	16 51	
Surrey Quays	d	16 25	16 25	16 30	16 30		16 45	16 45							16 35	16 35	16 40	16 40	16 49		16 49		16 55	16 55	17 00
Canada Water	d	16 27	16 27	16 32	16 32		16 47	16 47							16 37	16 37	16 42	16 42	16 51		16 51		16 57	16 57	17 02
Rotherhithe	d	16 28	16 28	16 33	16 33		16 48	16 48							16 38	16 38	16 43	16 43	16 53		16 53		16 58	16 58	17 03
Wapping	d	16 30	16 30	16 35	16 35		16 50	16 50							16 40	16 40	16 45	16 45	16 54		16 54		17 00	17 00	17 05
Shadwell	d	16 32	16 32	16 37	16 37		16 52	16 52							16 42	16 42	16 47	16 47	16 56		16 56		17 02	17 02	17 07
Whitechapel	d	16 34	16 34	16 39	16 39		16 54	16 54							16 44	16 44	16 49	16 49	16 59		16 59		17 04	17 04	17 09
Shoreditch High Street	d	16 36	16 36	16 41	16 41		16 56	16 56							16 46	16 46	16 51	16 51	17 01		17 01		17 06	17 06	17 11
Hoxton	d	16 38	16 38	16 43	16 43		16 58	16 58							16 48	16 48	16 53	16 53	17 03		17 03		17 08	17 08	17 13
Haggerston	d	16 40	16 40	16 45	16 45		17 00	17 00							16 50	16 50	16 55	16 55	17 05		17 05		17 10	17 10	17 15
Dalston Junction Stn ELL	a	16 43	16 47	16 47	16 47		17 02	17 02							16 52	16 52	16 58	17 02	17 07		17 07		17 13	17 17	17 17
Canonbury	d			16 50	16 50		17 05	17 05							16 57	16 57			17 12		17 12				17 20
Highbury & Islington	a			16 55	16 58		17 10	17 13							17 02	17 05			17 16		17 19				17 25
	d																								
London Bridge 4 ⊖	a					16 41					16 26		16 38	16 41								17 02			

A not 27 July

B 27 July

East London Line and Croydon - London Victoria to London Bridge

Network Diagram - see first Page of Table 177

	LO A	SN	LO B	LO A		SN	SN	SE	SN	SN	LO B	LO A	LO B	LO A		LO B	LO A	SN	LO B	LO A	LO B	LO A	SN	SN
East Croydon d																		17 00						
West Croydon 4 d										16 31	16 39	16 39				16 52	16 52							
Norwood Junction 2 d											16 43	16 43				16 58	16 58	17 05						
Anerley d											16 46	16 46				17 01	17 01	17 08						
Penge West d											16 48	16 48				17 03	17 03	17 10						
London Victoria 15 ⊖ d		16 19						16 39	16 41														16 49	
Battersea Park 4 d		16 23							16 45														16 53	
Wandsworth Road d									16 47															
Clapham High Street ⊖ d									16 49															
London Blackfriars 3 ⊖ d																								
Denmark Hill 4 d								16 48	16 54															
Peckham Rye 4 d						16 42	16 47	16a51	16 56	17 00														17 07
Queens Rd Peckham d							16 49		16 59	17 03														
South Bermondsey d							16 52		17 01	17 05														
Clapham Junction 10 d		16 27																					16 57	
Wandsworth Common d		16 30																					17 00	
Balham 4 ⊖ d		16 32																					17 03	
Streatham Hill d		16 35																					17 06	
West Norwood 4 d		16 39				16 53																	17 09	17 20
Gipsy Hill d		16 44				16 56																	17 12	17 23
Crystal Palace 4 d	16 43	16 50	16 58	16 58		16a59															17 13	17 13	17 21	17a26
Sydenham d	16 46	16 54	17 01	17 01							16 51	16 51				17 06	17 06	17 12			17 16	17 16	17 24	
Forest Hill 4 d	16 49	16 56	17 04	17 04							16 53	16 53				17 08	17 08	17 15			17 19	17 19	17 27	
Honor Oak Park d	16 51	16 59	17 06	17 06							16 56	16 56				17 11	17 11	17 17			17 21	17 21	17 29	
Brockley d	16 54	17 01	17 09	17 09							16 58	16 58				17 13	17 13	17 20			17 24	17 24	17 32	
New Cross Gate 4 a	16 56	17 04	17 11	17 11							17 01	17 01				17 16	17 16	17 22			17 26	17 26	17 34	
d	16 56	17 04	17 11	17 11							17 01	17 01				17 16	17 16	17 22			17 26	17 26	17 34	
New Cross ELL d													17 06	17 06					17 21	17 21				
Surrey Quays d	17 00		17 15	17 15							17 05	17 05	17 10	17 10		17 19	17 19		17 25	17 25	17 30	17 30		
Canada Water d	17 02		17 17	17 17							17 07	17 07	17 12	17 12		17 21	17 21		17 27	17 27	17 32	17 32		
Rotherhithe d	17 03		17 18	17 18							17 08	17 08	17 13	17 13		17 23	17 23		17 28	17 28	17 33	17 33		
Wapping d	17 05		17 20	17 20							17 10	17 10	17 15	17 15		17 24	17 24		17 30	17 30	17 35	17 35		
Shadwell d	17 07		17 22	17 22							17 12	17 12	17 17	17 17		17 26	17 26		17 32	17 32	17 37	17 37		
Whitechapel d	17 09		17 24	17 24							17 14	17 14	17 19	17 19		17 29	17 29		17 34	17 34	17 39	17 39		
Shoreditch High Street d	17 11		17 26	17 26							17 16	17 16	17 21	17 21		17 31	17 31		17 36	17 36	17 41	17 41		
Hoxton d	17 13		17 28	17 28							17 18	17 18	17 23	17 23		17 33	17 33		17 38	17 38	17 43	17 43		
Haggerston d	17 15		17 30	17 30							17 20	17 20	17 25	17 25		17 35	17 35		17 40	17 40	17 45	17 45		
Dalston Junction Stn ELL a	17 17		17 32	17 32							17 22	17 22	17 28	17 32		17 37	17 37		17 43	17 47	17 47	17 47		
Canonbury d	17 20		17 35	17 35							17 27	17 27				17 42	17 42				17 50	17 50		
Highbury & Islington a	17 28		17 40	17 43							17 32	17 35				17 46	17 49				17 55	17 58		
d																								
London Bridge 4 ⊖ a		17 12					16 56		17 08	17 10								17 35					17 43	

		SE	SN	SN	SN	LO B	LO A	SN	SN	LO B		LO A	LO B	LO A	LO B	LO A	LO B	LO A	LO B	LO A		SN	SN	SE
East Croydon d																								
West Croydon 4 d					17 01	17 09	17 09	17 12							17 22	17 22								
Norwood Junction 2 d						17 13	17 13								17 28	17 28								
Anerley d						17 16	17 16								17 31	17 31								
Penge West d						17 18	17 18								17 33	17 33								
London Victoria 15 ⊖ d		17 04		17 11																		17 22		17 34
Battersea Park 4 d				17 15																		17 26		
Wandsworth Road d				17 17																				
Clapham High Street ⊖ d				17 19																				
London Blackfriars 3 ⊖ d																								
Denmark Hill 4 d		17 13		17 24																				17 43
Peckham Rye 4 d		17a16	17 17	17 26	17 29				17 35														17 37	17a46
Queens Rd Peckham d			17 19	17 29	17 32				17 37															
South Bermondsey d			17 22	17 31	17 34				17 40															
Clapham Junction 10 d																						17 30		
Wandsworth Common d																						17 33		
Balham 4 ⊖ d																						17 35		
Streatham Hill d																						17 38		
West Norwood 4 d																						17 42	17 49	
Gipsy Hill d																						17 45	17 52	
Crystal Palace 4 d													17 28	17 28					17 43	17 43		17 48	17a54	
Sydenham d						17 21	17 21						17 31	17 31	17 36	17 36			17 46	17 46		17 54		
Forest Hill 4 d						17 23	17 23						17 34	17 34	17 38	17 38			17 49	17 49		17 57		
Honor Oak Park d						17 26	17 26						17 36	17 36	17 41	17 41			17 51	17 51		17 59		
Brockley d						17 28	17 28						17 39	17 39	17 43	17 43			17 54	17 54		18 02		
New Cross Gate 4 a						17 31	17 31						17 41	17 41	17 46	17 46			17 56	17 56		18 04		
d						17 31	17 31						17 41	17 41	17 46	17 46			17 56	17 56		18 04		
New Cross ELL d										17 36		17 36					17 51	17 51						
Surrey Quays d						17 35	17 35			17 40		17 40	17 45	17 45	17 49	17 49	17 55	17 55	18 00	18 00				
Canada Water d						17 37	17 37			17 42		17 42	17 47	17 47	17 51	17 51	17 57	17 57	18 02	18 02				
Rotherhithe d						17 38	17 38			17 43		17 43	17 48	17 48	17 53	17 53	17 58	17 58	18 03	18 03				
Wapping d						17 40	17 40			17 45		17 45	17 50	17 50	17 54	17 54	18 00	18 00	18 05	18 05				
Shadwell d						17 42	17 42			17 47		17 47	17 52	17 52	17 56	17 56	18 02	18 02	18 07	18 07				
Whitechapel d						17 44	17 44			17 49		17 49	17 54	17 54	17 59	17 59	18 04	18 04	18 09	18 09				
Shoreditch High Street d						17 46	17 46			17 51		17 51	17 56	17 56	18 01	18 01	18 06	18 06	18 11	18 11				
Hoxton d						17 48	17 48			17 53		17 53	17 58	17 58	18 03	18 03	18 08	18 08	18 13	18 13				
Haggerston d						17 50	17 50			17 55		17 55	18 00	18 00	18 05	18 05	18 10	18 10	18 15	18 15				
Dalston Junction Stn ELL a						17 52	17 52			17 58		18 02	18 02	18 02	18 07	18 07	18 13	18 17	18 17	18 17				
Canonbury d						17 57	17 57						18 05	18 05	18 12	18 12			18 20	18 20				
Highbury & Islington a						18 02	18 05						18 10	18 13	18 16	18 19			18 25	18 28				
d																								
London Bridge 4 ⊖ a			17 27	17 38	17 40			17 28	17 44													18 13		

A 27 July

B not 27 July

Table 178

Mondays to Fridays

until 27 July

East London Line and Croydon - London Victoria to London Bridge

Network Diagram - see first Page of Table 177

		SN	SN	SN	SN	LO A	LO B		SN	LO A	LO B	LO A	LO B	LO A	LO B	SN	LO A		LO B	LO A	LO B	SN	SN	SE	SN
East Croydon	d		17 30																						
West Croydon 4	d				17 31	17 39	17 39		17 42					17 52	17 52										
Norwood Junction 2	d	17 32	17 35			17 43	17 43							17 58	17 58	18 04									
Anerley	d		17 38			17 46	17 46							18 01	18 01	18 07									
Penge West	d		17 40			17 48	17 48							18 03	18 03	18 09									
London Victoria 15 ⊖	d			17 41																		17 52		17 56	
Battersea Park 4	d			17 45																		17 56			
Wandsworth Road	d			17 47																					
Clapham High Street ⊖	d			17 49																					
London Blackfriars 3 ⊖	d																								
Denmark Hill 4	d			17 54																				18 06	
Peckham Rye 4	d	17 53		17 57	18 01																		18 07	18a08	18 12
Queens Rd Peckham	d	17 55		17 59	18 04																				18 15
South Bermondsey	d	17 58		18 02	18 06																				18 17
Clapham Junction 10	d																					18 00			
Wandsworth Common	d																					18 03			
Balham 4 ⊖	d																					18 05			
Streatham Hill	d																					18 08			
West Norwood 4	d																					18 14	18 20		
Gipsy Hill	d																					18 17	18 23		
Crystal Palace 4	d										17 58	17 58								18 13	18 13	18 20	18a26		
Sydenham	d		17 42			17 51	17 51				18 01	18 01	18 06	18 06	18 11					18 16	18 16	18 24			
Forest Hill 4	d		17 45			17 53	17 53				18 04	18 04	18 08	18 08	18 14					18 19	18 19	18 27			
Honor Oak Park	d		17 47			17 56	17 56				18 06	18 06	18 11	18 11	18 16					18 21	18 21	18 29			
Brockley	d		17 50			17 58	17 58				18 09	18 09	18 13	18 13	18 19					18 24	18 24	18 32			
New Cross Gate 4	a		17 52			18 01	18 01				18 11	18 11	18 16	18 16	18 21					18 26	18 26	18 34			
	d		17 52			18 01	18 01				18 11	18 11	18 16	18 16	18 21					18 26	18 26	18 34			
New Cross ELL	d									18 06	18 06						18 21		18 21						
Surrey Quays	d					18 05	18 05			18 10	18 10	18 15	18 15	18 19	18 19		18 25		18 25	18 30	18 30				
Canada Water	d					18 07	18 07			18 12	18 12	18 17	18 17	18 21	18 21		18 27		18 27	18 32	18 32				
Rotherhithe	d					18 08	18 08			18 13	18 13	18 18	18 18	18 23	18 23		18 28		18 28	18 33	18 33				
Wapping	d					18 10	18 10			18 15	18 15	18 20	18 20	18 24	18 24		18 30		18 30	18 35	18 35				
Shadwell	d					18 12	18 12			18 17	18 17	18 22	18 22	18 26	18 26		18 32		18 32	18 37	18 37				
Whitechapel	d					18 14	18 14			18 19	18 19	18 24	18 24	18 29	18 29		18 34		18 34	18 39	18 39				
Shoreditch High Street	d					18 16	18 16			18 21	18 21	18 26	18 26	18 31	18 31		18 36		18 36	18 41	18 41				
Hoxton	d					18 18	18 18			18 23	18 23	18 28	18 28	18 33	18 33		18 38		18 38	18 43	18 43				
Haggerston	d					18 20	18 20			18 25	18 25	18 30	18 30	18 35	18 35		18 40		18 40	18 45	18 45				
Dalston Junction Stn ELL	a					18 23	18 23			18 28	18 32	18 32	18 32	18 37	18 37		18 43		18 47	18 47	18 47				
Canonbury	d					18 27	18 27					18 35	18 35	18 42	18 42					18 50	18 50				
Highbury & Islington	a					18 32	18 35					18 40	18 43	18 46	18 49					18 55	18 58				
	d																								
London Bridge 4 ⊖	a	18 02	17 59	18 08	18 11				18 00							18 31						18 45			18 22

		SN	SN		LO A	LO B	SN	LO A	LO B	LO A	LO B	LO A	LO B		LO A	LO B	SE	SN	SN	SN	LO A	LO B	SN		SN
East Croydon	d																			18 30					
West Croydon 4	d		18 01		18 09	18 09	18 13					18 22	18 22												
Norwood Junction 2	d				18 13	18 13						18 28	18 28							18 35					
Anerley	d				18 16	18 16						18 31	18 31							18 38					
Penge West	d				18 18	18 18						18 33	18 33							18 40					
London Victoria 15 ⊖	d	18 11															18 18						18 22		
Battersea Park 4	d	18 15																					18 26		
Wandsworth Road	d	18 17																							
Clapham High Street ⊖	d	18 19																							
London Blackfriars 3 ⊖	d																								
Denmark Hill 4	d	18 24															18 28								
Peckham Rye 4	d	18 26	18 29														18a31	18 32	18 36						18 37
Queens Rd Peckham	d	18 29	18 32															18 35	18 38						
South Bermondsey	d	18 31	18 34															18 37	18 41						
Clapham Junction 10	d																						18 30		
Wandsworth Common	d																						18 33		
Balham 4 ⊖	d																						18 35		
Streatham Hill	d																						18 38		
West Norwood 4	d																						18 42		18 51
Gipsy Hill	d																						18 45		18 54
Crystal Palace 4	d									18 28	18 28										18 43	18 43	18 51		18a57
Sydenham	d				18 21	18 21				18 31	18 31	18 36	18 36							18 42	18 46	18 46	18 54		
Forest Hill 4	d				18 23	18 23				18 34	18 34	18 38	18 38							18 45	18 49	18 49	18 57		
Honor Oak Park	d				18 26	18 26				18 36	18 36	18 41	18 41							18 47	18 51	18 51	18 59		
Brockley	d				18 28	18 28				18 39	18 39	18 43	18 43							18 50	18 54	18 54	19 02		
New Cross Gate 4	a				18 31	18 31				18 41	18 41	18 46	18 46							18 52	18 56	18 56	19 04		
	d				18 31	18 31				18 41	18 41	18 46	18 46							18 52	18 56	18 56	19 04		
New Cross ELL	d							18 36	18 36						18 51	18 51									
Surrey Quays	d				18 35	18 35		18 40	18 40	18 45	18 45	18 49	18 49		18 55	18 55					19 00	19 00			
Canada Water	d				18 37	18 37		18 42	18 42	18 47	18 47	18 51	18 51		18 57	18 57					19 02	19 02			
Rotherhithe	d				18 38	18 38		18 43	18 43	18 48	18 48	18 53	18 53		18 58	18 58					19 03	19 03			
Wapping	d				18 40	18 40		18 45	18 45	18 50	18 50	18 54	18 54		19 00	19 00					19 05	19 05			
Shadwell	d				18 42	18 42		18 47	18 47	18 52	18 52	18 56	18 56		19 02	19 02					19 07	19 07			
Whitechapel	d				18 44	18 44		18 49	18 49	18 54	18 54	18 59	18 59		19 04	19 04					19 09	19 09			
Shoreditch High Street	d				18 46	18 46		18 51	18 51	18 56	18 56	19 01	19 01		19 06	19 06					19 11	19 11			
Hoxton	d				18 48	18 48		18 53	18 53	18 58	18 58	19 03	19 03		19 08	19 08					19 13	19 13			
Haggerston	d				18 50	18 50		18 55	18 55	19 00	19 00	19 05	19 05		19 10	19 10					19 15	19 15			
Dalston Junction Stn ELL	a				18 52	18 52		18 58	19 02	19 02	19 02	19 07	19 07		19 13	19 17					19 17	19 17			
Canonbury	d				18 57	18 57				19 05	19 05	19 12	19 12								19 20	19 20			
Highbury & Islington	a				19 02	19 05				19 10	19 13	19 16	19 19								19 25	19 28			
	d																								
London Bridge 4 ⊖	a	18 38	18 39				18 29										18 42	18 45	18 59				19 13		

A not 27 July

B 27 July

Table 178

Mondays to Fridays

until 27 July

East London Line and Croydon - London Victoria to London Bridge

Network Diagram - see first Page of Table 177

		SE	SN	SN	LO A	LO B	LO A	LO B	LO A		LO B	LO A	LO B	SN	LO A	LO B	LO A	LO B	SN		SN	SN	SN	LO A	LO B
East Croydon	d													19 00											
West Croydon 4	d			18 31	18 39	18 39						18 52	18 52												
Norwood Junction 2	d				18 43	18 43						18 58	18 58	19 05											
Anerley	d				18 46	18 46						19 01	19 01	19 08											
Penge West	d				18 48	18 48						19 03	19 03	19 10											
London Victoria 15 ⊖	d	18 39	18 41																18 52						
Battersea Park 4	d		18 45																18 56						
Wandsworth Road	d		18 47																						
Clapham High Street ⊖	d		18 49																						
London Blackfriars 3 ⊖	d																								
Denmark Hill 4	d	18 48	18 54																						
Peckham Rye 4	d	18a51	18 57	19 01																	19 06	19 07	19 14		
Queens Rd Peckham	d		19 00	19 04																		19 10	19 17		
South Bermondsey	d		19 02	19 06																		19 12	19 19		
Clapham Junction 10	d																		19 00						
Wandsworth Common	d																		19 03						
Balham 4 ⊖	d																		19 05						
Streatham Hill	d																		19 08						
West Norwood 4	d																		19 12		19 17				
Gipsy Hill	d																		19 15		19 20				
Crystal Palace 4	d								18 58		18 58						19 13	19 13	19 21		19a23			19 28	19 28
Sydenham	d				18 51	18 51			19 01		19 01	19 06	19 06	19 12			19 16	19 16	19 24					19 31	19 31
Forest Hill 4	d				18 53	18 53			19 04		19 04	19 08	19 08	19 15			19 19	19 19	19 27					19 34	19 34
Honor Oak Park	d				18 56	18 56			19 06		19 06	19 11	19 11	19 17			19 21	19 21	19 29					19 36	19 36
Brockley	d				18 58	18 58			19 09		19 09	19 13	19 13	19 20			19 24	19 24	19 32					19 39	19 39
New Cross Gate 4	a				19 01	19 01			19 11		19 11	19 16	19 16	19 22			19 26	19 26	19 34					19 41	19 41
	d				19 01	19 01			19 11		19 11	19 16	19 16	19 22			19 26	19 26	19 34					19 41	19 41
New Cross ELL	d						19 06	19 06							19 21	19 21									
Surrey Quays	d				19 05	19 05	19 10	19 10	19 15		19 15	19 19	19 19		19 25	19 25	19 30	19 30						19 45	19 45
Canada Water	d				19 07	19 07	19 12	19 12	19 17		19 17	19 21	19 21		19 27	19 27	19 32	19 32						19 47	19 47
Rotherhithe	d				19 08	19 08	19 13	19 13	19 18		19 18	19 23	19 23		19 28	19 28	19 33	19 33						19 48	19 48
Wapping	d				19 10	19 10	19 15	19 15	19 20		19 20	19 24	19 24		19 30	19 30	19 35	19 35						19 50	19 50
Shadwell	d				19 12	19 12	19 17	19 17	19 22		19 22	19 26	19 26		19 32	19 32	19 37	19 37						19 52	19 52
Whitechapel	d				19 14	19 14	19 19	19 19	19 24		19 24	19 29	19 29		19 34	19 34	19 39	19 39						19 54	19 54
Shoreditch High Street	d				19 16	19 16	19 21	19 21	19 26		19 26	19 31	19 31		19 36	19 36	19 41	19 41						19 56	19 56
Hoxton	d				19 18	19 18	19 23	19 23	19 28		19 28	19 33	19 33		19 38	19 38	19 43	19 43						19 58	19 58
Haggerston	d				19 20	19 20	19 25	19 25	19 30		19 30	19 35	19 35		19 40	19 40	19 45	19 45						20 00	20 00
Dalston Junction Stn ELL	a				19 22	19 22	19 28	19 32	19 32		19 32	19 37	19 37		19 43	19 47	19 47	19 47						20 02	20 02
Canonbury	d				19 27	19 27			19 35		19 35	19 42	19 42				19 50	19 50						20 05	20 05
Highbury & Islington	a				19 32	19 35			19 40		19 43	19 46	19 49				19 55	19 58						20 10	20 13
	d																								
London Bridge 4 ⊖	a		19 09	19 11										19 29					19 41			19 17	19 24		

		SN	SE	SN	SN		LO A	LO B	LO A	LO B	LO A	LO B	SN	LO A	LO B		LO A	LO B	SN	SN	SN	LO A	LO B	SN	SN
East Croydon	d												19 30												
West Croydon 4	d				19 01		19 09	19 09			19 22	19 22													
Norwood Junction 2	d						19 13	19 13			19 28	19 28	19 35												
Anerley	d						19 16	19 16			19 31	19 31	19 38												
Penge West	d						19 18	19 18			19 33	19 33	19 40												
London Victoria 15 ⊖	d		19 09	19 11															19 22						
Battersea Park 4	d			19 15															19 26						
Wandsworth Road	d			19 17																					
Clapham High Street ⊖	d			19 19																					
London Blackfriars 3 ⊖	d																								
Denmark Hill 4	d		19 18	19 24																					
Peckham Rye 4	d	19 17	19a21	19 26	19 29															19 37	19 38			19 47	19 49
Queens Rd Peckham	d			19 29	19 32																19 41				19 51
South Bermondsey	d			19 31	19 34																19 43				19 54
Clapham Junction 10	d																		19 30						
Wandsworth Common	d																		19 33						
Balham 4 ⊖	d																		19 35						
Streatham Hill	d																		19 38						
West Norwood 4	d	19 30																	19 42	19 49				20 00	
Gipsy Hill	d	19 33																	19 45	19 52				20 03	
Crystal Palace 4	d	19a35															19 43	19 43	19 51	19a54		19 58	19 58	20a05	
Sydenham	d						19 21	19 21			19 36	19 36	19 42				19 46	19 46	19 54			20 01	20 01		
Forest Hill 4	d						19 23	19 23			19 38	19 38	19 45				19 49	19 49	19 57			20 04	20 04		
Honor Oak Park	d						19 26	19 26			19 41	19 41	19 47				19 51	19 51	19 59			20 06	20 06		
Brockley	d						19 28	19 28			19 43	19 43	19 50				19 54	19 54	20 02			20 09	20 09		
New Cross Gate 4	a						19 31	19 31			19 46	19 46	19 52				19 56	19 56	20 04			20 11	20 11		
	d						19 31	19 31			19 46	19 46	19 52				19 56	19 56	20 04			20 11	20 11		
New Cross ELL	d								19 36	19 36				19 51	19 51										
Surrey Quays	d						19 35	19 35	19 40	19 40	19 49	19 49		19 55	19 55		20 00	20 00				20 15	20 15		
Canada Water	d						19 37	19 37	19 42	19 42	19 51	19 51		19 57	19 57		20 02	20 02				20 17	20 17		
Rotherhithe	d						19 38	19 38	19 43	19 43	19 53	19 53		19 58	19 58		20 03	20 03				20 18	20 18		
Wapping	d						19 40	19 40	19 45	19 45	19 54	19 54		20 00	20 00		20 05	20 05				20 20	20 20		
Shadwell	d						19 42	19 42	19 47	19 47	19 56	19 56		20 02	20 02		20 07	20 07				20 22	20 22		
Whitechapel	d						19 44	19 44	19 49	19 49	19 59	19 59		20 04	20 04		20 09	20 09				20 24	20 24		
Shoreditch High Street	d						19 46	19 46	19 51	19 51	20 01	20 01		20 06	20 06		20 11	20 11				20 26	20 26		
Hoxton	d						19 48	19 48	19 53	19 53	20 03	20 03		20 08	20 08		20 13	20 13				20 28	20 28		
Haggerston	d						19 50	19 50	19 55	19 55	20 05	20 05		20 10	20 10		20 15	20 15				20 30	20 30		
Dalston Junction Stn ELL	a						19 52	19 52	19 58	20 02	20 07	20 07		20 13	20 17		20 17	20 17				20 32	20 32		
Canonbury	d						19 57	19 57			20 12	20 12					20 20	20 20				20 35	20 35		
Highbury & Islington	a						20 02	20 05			20 16	20 19					20 25	20 28				20 40	20 43		
	d																								
London Bridge 4 ⊖	a			19 36	19 41								19 59						20 11		19 51				19 58

A not 27 July

B 27 July

Table 178

Mondays to Fridays

until 27 July

East London Line and Croydon - London Victoria to London Bridge

Network Diagram - see first Page of Table 177

		SE	SN	SN	LO A	LO B	LO A	LO B	LO A	LO B	SN	LO A	LO B	LO A	LO B	SN	LO A	LO B	SN	SN	SN	SN
East Croydon	d										20 00											
West Croydon 4	d			19 31	19 39	19 39			19 52	19 52												20 01
Norwood Junction 2	d				19 43	19 43			19 58	19 58	20 05											
Anerley	d				19 46	19 46			20 01	20 01	20 08											
Penge West	d				19 48	19 48			20 03	20 03	20 10											
London Victoria 15 ⊖	d	19 39	19 41													19 52					20 11	
Battersea Park 4	d		19 45													19 56					20 15	
Wandsworth Road	d		19 47																		20 17	
Clapham High Street ⊖	d		19 49																		20 19	
London Blackfriars 3 ⊖	d																					
Denmark Hill 4	d	19 48	19 54																		20 24	
Peckham Rye 4	d	19a51	19 56	20 01															20 12	20 18	20 26	20 31
Queens Rd Peckham	d		19 59	20 04																20 21	20 29	20 34
South Bermondsey	d		20 01	20 06																20 23	20 31	20 36
Clapham Junction 10	d															20 00						
Wandsworth Common	d															20 03						
Balham 4 ⊖	d															20 05						
Streatham Hill	d															20 08						
West Norwood 4	d															20 12			20 24			
Gipsy Hill	d															20 15			20 27			
Crystal Palace 4	d													20 13	20 13	20 21	20 28	20 28	20a29			
Sydenham	d				19 51	19 51			20 06	20 06	20 12			20 16	20 16	20 24	20 31	20 31				
Forest Hill 4	d				19 53	19 53			20 08	20 08	20 15			20 19	20 19	20 27	20 34	20 34				
Honor Oak Park	d				19 56	19 56			20 11	20 11	20 17			20 21	20 21	20 29	20 36	20 36				
Brockley	d				19 58	19 58			20 13	20 13	20 20			20 24	20 24	20 32	20 39	20 39				
New Cross Gate 4	a				20 01	20 01			20 16	20 16	20 22			20 26	20 26	20 34	20 41	20 41				
	d				20 01	20 01			20 16	20 16	20 22			20 26	20 26	20 34	20 41	20 41				
New Cross ELL	d						20 06	20 06				20 21	20 21									
Surrey Quays	d				20 05	20 05	20 10	20 10	20 19	20 19		20 25	20 25	20 30	20 30		20 45	20 45				
Canada Water	d				20 07	20 07	20 12	20 12	20 21	20 21		20 27	20 27	20 32	20 32		20 47	20 47				
Rotherhithe	d				20 08	20 08	20 13	20 13	20 23	20 23		20 28	20 28	20 33	20 33		20 48	20 48				
Wapping	d				20 10	20 10	20 15	20 15	20 24	20 24		20 30	20 30	20 35	20 35		20 50	20 50				
Shadwell	d				20 12	20 12	20 17	20 17	20 26	20 26		20 32	20 32	20 37	20 37		20 52	20 52				
Whitechapel	d				20 14	20 14	20 19	20 19	20 29	20 29		20 34	20 34	20 39	20 39		20 54	20 54				
Shoreditch High Street	d				20 16	20 16	20 21	20 21	20 31	20 31		20 36	20 36	20 41	20 41		20 56	20 56				
Hoxton	d				20 18	20 18	20 23	20 23	20 33	20 33		20 38	20 38	20 43	20 43		20 58	20 58				
Haggerston	d				20 20	20 20	20 25	20 25	20 35	20 35		20 40	20 40	20 45	20 45		21 00	21 00				
Dalston Junction Stn ELL	a				20 22	20 22	20 28	20 32	20 37	20 37		20 43	20 47	20 47	20 47		21 02	21 02				
Canonbury	d				20 27	20 27			20 42	20 42				20 50	20 50		21 05	21 05				
Highbury & Islington	a				20 32	20 35			20 46	20 49				20 55	20 58		21 10	21 13				
	d																					
London Bridge 4 ⊖	a		20 06	20 14							20 29					20 41				20 28	20 36	20 41

		LO A	LO B	LO A	LO B	LO A	LO B	SN	LO A	LO B	LO A	LO B	SN	LO A	LO B	SN	SN	SN	SN	LO A	LO B	LO A	LO B
East Croydon	d							20 31															
West Croydon 4	d	20 09	20 09			20 22	20 22												20 31	20 39	20 39		
Norwood Junction 2	d	20 13	20 13			20 28	20 28	20 35												20 43	20 43		
Anerley	d	20 16	20 16			20 31	20 31	20 38												20 46	20 46		
Penge West	d	20 18	20 18			20 33	20 33	20 40												20 48	20 48		
London Victoria 15 ⊖	d												20 22					20 41					
Battersea Park 4	d												20 26					20 45					
Wandsworth Road	d																	20 47					
Clapham High Street ⊖	d																	20 49					
London Blackfriars 3 ⊖	d																						
Denmark Hill 4	d																	20 54					
Peckham Rye 4	d															20 42	20 48	20 56	21 01				
Queens Rd Peckham	d																20 50	20 59	21 04				
South Bermondsey	d																20 53	21 01	21 06				
Clapham Junction 10	d												20 30										
Wandsworth Common	d												20 33										
Balham 4 ⊖	d												20 35										
Streatham Hill	d												20 38										
West Norwood 4	d												20 42			20 54							
Gipsy Hill	d												20 45			20 57							
Crystal Palace 4	d										20 43	20 43	20 51	20 58	20 58	20a59							
Sydenham	d	20 21	20 21			20 36	20 36	20 42			20 46	20 46	20 54	21 01	21 01					20 51	20 51		
Forest Hill 4	d	20 23	20 23			20 38	20 38	20 45			20 49	20 49	20 57	21 04	21 04					20 53	20 53		
Honor Oak Park	d	20 26	20 26			20 41	20 41	20 47			20 51	20 51	20 59	21 06	21 06					20 56	20 56		
Brockley	d	20 28	20 28			20 43	20 43	20 50			20 54	20 54	21 02	21 09	21 09					20 58	20 58		
New Cross Gate 4	a	20 31	20 31			20 46	20 46	20 52			20 56	20 56	21 04	21 11	21 11					21 01	21 01		
	d	20 31	20 31			20 46	20 46	20 52			20 56	20 56	21 04	21 11	21 11					21 01	21 01		
New Cross ELL	d			20 36	20 36				20 51	20 51												21 06	21 06
Surrey Quays	d	20 35	20 35	20 40	20 40	20 49	20 49		20 55	20 55	21 00	21 00		21 15	21 15					21 05	21 05	21 10	21 10
Canada Water	d	20 37	20 37	20 42	20 42	20 51	20 51		20 57	20 57	21 02	21 02		21 17	21 17					21 07	21 07	21 12	21 12
Rotherhithe	d	20 38	20 38	20 43	20 43	20 53	20 53		20 58	20 58	21 03	21 03		21 18	21 18					21 08	21 08	21 13	21 13
Wapping	d	20 40	20 40	20 45	20 45	20 54	20 54		21 00	21 00	21 05	21 05		21 20	21 20					21 10	21 10	21 15	21 15
Shadwell	d	20 42	20 42	20 47	20 47	20 56	20 56		21 02	21 02	21 07	21 07		21 22	21 22					21 12	21 12	21 17	21 17
Whitechapel	d	20 44	20 44	20 49	20 49	20 59	20 59		21 04	21 04	21 09	21 09		21 24	21 24					21 14	21 14	21 19	21 19
Shoreditch High Street	d	20 46	20 46	20 51	20 51	21 01	21 01		21 06	21 06	21 11	21 11		21 26	21 26					21 16	21 16	21 21	21 21
Hoxton	d	20 48	20 48	20 53	20 53	21 03	21 03		21 08	21 08	21 13	21 13		21 28	21 28					21 18	21 18	21 23	21 23
Haggerston	d	20 50	20 50	20 55	20 55	21 05	21 05		21 10	21 10	21 15	21 15		21 30	21 30					21 20	21 20	21 25	21 25
Dalston Junction Stn ELL	a	20 52	20 52	20 58	21 02	21 07	21 07		21 13	21 17	21 17	21 17		21 32	21 32					21 22	21 22	21 28	21 32
Canonbury	d	20 57	20 57			21 12	21 12				21 20	21 20		21 35	21 35					21 27	21 27		
Highbury & Islington	a	21 02	21 05			21 16	21 19				21 25	21 28		21 40	21 43					21 32	21 35		
	d																						
London Bridge 4 ⊖	a							20 59					21 11				20 57	21 06	21 11				

A not 27 July

B 27 July

Table 178

Mondays to Fridays

until 27 July

East London Line and Croydon - London Victoria to London Bridge

Network Diagram - see first Page of Table 177

Station		LO A	LO B		SN	LO A	LO B	LO A	LO B	SN	LO A	LO B	SN		SN	SN	SN	LO A	LO B	LO A	LO B	LO A	LO B		SN
East Croydon	d				21 00																				21 30
West Croydon 4	d	20 52	20 52														21 01	21 09	21 09			21 22	21 22		
Norwood Junction 2	d	20 58	20 58		21 05													21 13	21 13			21 28	21 28		21 35
Anerley	d	21 01	21 01		21 08													21 16	21 16			21 31	21 31		21 38
Penge West	d	21 03	21 03		21 10													21 18	21 18			21 33	21 33		21 40
London Victoria 15 ⊖	d									20 52						21 11									
Battersea Park 4	d									20 56						21 15									
Wandsworth Road	d															21 17									
Clapham High Street ⊖	d															21 19									
London Blackfriars 3 ⊖	d																								
Denmark Hill 4	d															21 24									
Peckham Rye 4	d												21 12		21 17	21 26	21 31								
Queens Rd Peckham	d														21 19	21 29	21 34								
South Bermondsey	d														21 22	21 31	21 36								
Clapham Junction 10	d									21 00															
Wandsworth Common	d									21 03															
Balham 4 ⊖	d									21 05															
Streatham Hill	d									21 08															
West Norwood 4	d									21 12			21 24												
Gipsy Hill	d									21 15			21 27												
Crystal Palace 4	d							21 13	21 13	21 21	21 28	21 28	21a29												
Sydenham	d	21 06	21 06		21 12			21 16	21 16	21 27	21 31	21 31						21 21	21 21			21 36	21 36		21 42
Forest Hill 4	d	21 08	21 08		21 15			21 19	21 19	21 29	21 34	21 34						21 23	21 23			21 38	21 38		21 45
Honor Oak Park	d	21 11	21 11		21 17			21 21	21 21	21 32	21 36	21 36						21 26	21 26			21 41	21 41		21 47
Brockley	d	21 13	21 13		21 20			21 24	21 24	21 34	21 39	21 39						21 28	21 28			21 43	21 43		21 50
New Cross Gate 4	a	21 16	21 16		21 22			21 26	21 26	21 37	21 41	21 41						21 31	21 31			21 46	21 46		21 52
	d	21 16	21 16		21 22			21 26	21 26	21 37	21 41	21 41						21 31	21 31			21 46	21 46		21 52
New Cross ELL	d					21 21	21 21													21 36	21 36				
Surrey Quays	d	21 19	21 19			21 25	21 25	21 30	21 30		21 45	21 45						21 35	21 35	21 40	21 40	21 49	21 49		
Canada Water	d	21 21	21 21			21 27	21 27	21 32	21 32		21 47	21 47						21 37	21 37	21 42	21 42	21 51	21 51		
Rotherhithe	d	21 23	21 23			21 28	21 28	21 33	21 33		21 48	21 48						21 38	21 38	21 43	21 43	21 53	21 53		
Wapping	d	21 24	21 24			21 30	21 30	21 35	21 35		21 50	21 50						21 40	21 40	21 45	21 45	21 54	21 54		
Shadwell	d	21 26	21 26			21 32	21 32	21 37	21 37		21 52	21 52						21 42	21 42	21 47	21 47	21 56	21 56		
Whitechapel	d	21 29	21 29			21 34	21 34	21 39	21 39		21 54	21 54						21 44	21 44	21 49	21 49	21 59	21 59		
Shoreditch High Street	d	21 31	21 31			21 36	21 36	21 41	21 41		21 56	21 56						21 46	21 46	21 51	21 51	22 01	22 01		
Hoxton	d	21 33	21 33			21 38	21 38	21 43	21 43		21 58	21 58						21 48	21 48	21 53	21 53	22 03	22 03		
Haggerston	d	21 35	21 35			21 40	21 40	21 45	21 45		22 00	22 00						21 50	21 50	21 55	21 55	22 05	22 05		
Dalston Junction Stn ELL	a	21 37	21 37			21 43	21 47	21 47	21 47		22 02	22 02						21 52	21 52	21 58	22 02	22 07	22 07		
Canonbury	d	21 42	21 42					21 50	21 50		22 05	22 05						21 57	21 57			22 12	22 12		
Highbury & Islington	a	21 46	21 49					21 55	21 58		22 10	22 13						22 02	22 05			22 16	22 19		
	d																								
London Bridge 4 ⊖	a				21 29					21 43					21 26	21 36	21 41								21 59

Station		LO A	LO B	LO A	LO B	SN	LO A	LO B	SN		SN	SE C	SN	SE D	SN	LO A	LO B	LO A	LO B		LO A	LO B	SN	LO A	LO B
East Croydon	d																						22 00		
West Croydon 4	d														21 31	21 39	21 39				21 52	21 52			
Norwood Junction 2	d															21 43	21 43				21 58	21 58	22 05		
Anerley	d															21 46	21 46				22 01	22 01	22 08		
Penge West	d															21 48	21 48				22 03	22 03	22 10		
London Victoria 15 ⊖	d					21 23							21 41	21 43											
Battersea Park 4	d					21 27							21 45												
Wandsworth Road	d												21 47												
Clapham High Street ⊖	d												21 49												
London Blackfriars 3 ⊖	d											21 42													
Denmark Hill 4	d											21 52	21 54	21 52											
Peckham Rye 4	d								21 42		21 47	21a55	21 56	21a55	22 01										
Queens Rd Peckham	d										21 49		21 59		22 04										
South Bermondsey	d										21 52		22 01		22 06										
Clapham Junction 10	d					21 31																			
Wandsworth Common	d					21 34																			
Balham 4 ⊖	d					21 36																			
Streatham Hill	d					21 39																			
West Norwood 4	d					21 43			21 54																
Gipsy Hill	d					21 46			21 57																
Crystal Palace 4	d			21 43	21 43	21 51	21 58	21 58	21a59															22 13	22 13
Sydenham	d			21 46	21 46	21 54	22 01	22 01								21 51	21 51				22 06	22 06	22 12	22 16	22 16
Forest Hill 4	d			21 49	21 49	21 57	22 04	22 04								21 53	21 53				22 08	22 08	22 15	22 19	22 19
Honor Oak Park	d			21 51	21 51	21 59	22 06	22 06								21 56	21 56				22 11	22 11	22 17	22 21	22 21
Brockley	d			21 54	21 54	22 02	22 09	22 09								21 58	21 58				22 13	22 13	22 20	22 24	22 24
New Cross Gate 4	a			21 56	21 56	22 04	22 11	22 11								22 01	22 01				22 16	22 16	22 22	22 26	22 26
	d			21 56	21 56	22 04	22 11	22 11								22 01	22 01				22 16	22 16	22 22	22 26	22 26
New Cross ELL	d	21 51	21 51															22 06	22 06						
Surrey Quays	d	21 55	21 55	22 00	22 00		22 15	22 15								22 05	22 05	22 10	22 10		22 19	22 19		22 30	22 30
Canada Water	d	21 57	21 57	22 02	22 02		22 17	22 17								22 07	22 07	22 12	22 12		22 21	22 21		22 32	22 32
Rotherhithe	d	21 58	21 58	22 03	22 03		22 18	22 18								22 08	22 08	22 13	22 13		22 23	22 23		22 33	22 33
Wapping	d	22 00	22 00	22 05	22 05		22 20	22 20								22 10	22 10	22 15	22 15		22 24	22 24		22 35	22 35
Shadwell	d	22 02	22 02	22 07	22 07		22 22	22 22								22 12	22 12	22 17	22 17		22 26	22 26		22 37	22 37
Whitechapel	d	22 04	22 04	22 09	22 09		22 24	22 24								22 14	22 14	22 19	22 19		22 29	22 29		22 39	22 39
Shoreditch High Street	d	22 06	22 06	22 11	22 11		22 26	22 26								22 16	22 16	22 21	22 21		22 31	22 31		22 41	22 41
Hoxton	d	22 08	22 08	22 13	22 13		22 28	22 28								22 18	22 18	22 23	22 23		22 33	22 33		22 43	22 43
Haggerston	d	22 10	22 10	22 15	22 15		22 30	22 30								22 20	22 20	22 25	22 25		22 35	22 35		22 45	22 45
Dalston Junction Stn ELL	a	22 13	22 17	22 17	22 17		22 32	22 32								22 22	22 22	22 29	22 33		22 37	22 37		22 47	22 47
Canonbury	d			22 20	22 20		22 35	22 35								22 27	22 27				22 42	22 42		22 50	22 50
Highbury & Islington	a			22 25	22 28		22 40	22 43								22 32	22 35				22 46	22 49		22 55	22 58
	d																								
London Bridge 4 ⊖	a					22 13					21 56		22 06		22 11								22 29		

A not 27 July
B 27 July
C from 21 May until 27 July
D until 18 May

Table 178

Mondays to Fridays

until 27 July

East London Line and Croydon - London Victoria to London Bridge

Network Diagram - see first Page of Table 177

Station		SN	LO A	LO B	SN		SN	SE C	SN	SE D	SN	LO A	LO B	LO A	LO B		LO A	LO B	SN	LO A	LO B	SN	SN	SN	SE C
East Croydon	d																		22 30						
West Croydon 4	d										22 01	22 09	22 09				22 22	22 22							
Norwood Junction 2	d											22 13	22 13				22 28	22 28	22 35						
Anerley	d											22 16	22 16				22 31	22 31	22 38						
Penge West	d											22 18	22 18				22 33	22 33	22 40						
London Victoria 15 ⊖	d	21 52							22 11	22 13												22 22			
Battersea Park 4	d	21 56							22 15													22 26			
Wandsworth Road	d								22 17																
Clapham High Street ⊖	d								22 19																
London Blackfriars 3 ⊖	d							22 12																	22 42
Denmark Hill 4	d							22 22	22 24	22 22															22 52
Peckham Rye 4	d				22 12		22 17	22a25	22 26	22a25	22 31												22 42	22 43	22a55
Queens Rd Peckham	d						22 19		22 29		22 34													22 45	
South Bermondsey	d						22 22		22 31		22 36													22 48	
Clapham Junction 10	d	22 00																				22 30			
Wandsworth Common	d	22 03																				22 33			
Balham 4 ⊖	d	22 05																				22 35			
Streatham Hill	d	22 08																				22 38			
West Norwood 4	d	22 12			22 24																	22 42	22 54		
Gipsy Hill	d	22 15			22 27																	22 45	22 57		
Crystal Palace 4	d	22 21	22 28	22 28	22a29															22 43	22 43	22 51	22a59		
Sydenham	d	22 24	22 31	22 31								22 21	22 21				22 36	22 36	22 42	22 46	22 46	22 54			
Forest Hill 4	d	22 27	22 34	22 34								22 23	22 23				22 38	22 38	22 45	22 49	22 49	22 57			
Honor Oak Park	d	22 29	22 36	22 36								22 26	22 26				22 41	22 41	22 47	22 51	22 51	22 59			
Brockley	d	22 32	22 39	22 39								22 28	22 28				22 43	22 43	22 50	22 54	22 54	23 02			
New Cross Gate 4	a	22 34	22 41	22 41								22 31	22 31				22 46	22 46	22 52	22 56	22 56	23 04			
	d	22 34	22 41	22 41								22 31	22 31				22 46	22 46	22 52	22 56	22 56	23 04			
New Cross ELL	d													22 36	22 36										
Surrey Quays	d		22 45	22 45								22 35	22 35	22 40	22 40		22 49	22 49		23 00	23 00				
Canada Water	d		22 47	22 47								22 37	22 37	22 42	22 42		22 51	22 51		23 02	23 02				
Rotherhithe	d		22 48	22 48								22 38	22 38	22 43	22 43		22 53	22 53		23 03	23 03				
Wapping	d		22 50	22 50								22 40	22 40	22 45	22 45		22 54	22 54		23 05	23 05				
Shadwell	d		22 52	22 52								22 42	22 42	22 47	22 47		22 56	22 56		23 07	23 07				
Whitechapel	d		22 54	22 54								22 44	22 44	22 49	22 49		22 59	22 59		23 09	23 09				
Shoreditch High Street	d		22 56	22 56								22 46	22 46	22 51	22 51		23 01	23 01		23 11	23 11				
Hoxton	d		22 58	22 58								22 48	22 48	22 53	22 53		23 03	23 03		23 13	23 13				
Haggerston	d		23 00	23 00								22 50	22 50	22 55	22 55		23 05	23 05		23 15	23 15				
Dalston Junction Stn ELL	a		23 02	23 02								22 52	22 52	22 58	23 02		23 07	23 07		23 17	23 17				
Canonbury	d		23 05	23 05								22 57	22 57				23 12	23 12		23 20	23 20				
Highbury & Islington	a		23 10	23 13								23 02	23 05				23 16	23 19		23 25	23 28				
	d																								
London Bridge 4 ⊖	a	22 45					22 26		22 36		22 41								22 59			23 11		22 52	

Station			SN	SE D	SN	LO A	LO B	LO A	LO B	LO A	LO B		SN	LO A	LO B	SN	SN	SN	SE C	SN	LO B		LO A	SE D	SN
East Croydon	d												23 01												
West Croydon 4	d				22 31	22 39	22 39			22 52	22 52														23 01
Norwood Junction 2	d					22 43	22 43			22 58	22 58		23 06												
Anerley	d					22 46	22 46			23 01	23 01		23 09												
Penge West	d					22 48	22 48			23 03	23 03		23 11												
London Victoria 15 ⊖	d		22 41	22 43												22 52				23 11				23 13	
Battersea Park 4	d		22 45													22 56				23 15					
Wandsworth Road	d		22 47																	23 17					
Clapham High Street ⊖	d		22 49																	23 19					
London Blackfriars 3 ⊖	d																		23 12						
Denmark Hill 4	d		22 54	22 52															23 22	23 24				23 22	
Peckham Rye 4	d		22 56	22a55	23 01												23 14	23 17	23a25	23 26				23a25	23 31
Queens Rd Peckham	d		22 59		23 04													23 19		23 29					23 34
South Bermondsey	d		23 01		23 06													23 22		23 31					23 36
Clapham Junction 10	d															23 00									
Wandsworth Common	d															23 03									
Balham 4 ⊖	d															23 05									
Streatham Hill	d															23 08									
West Norwood 4	d															23 12	23 26								
Gipsy Hill	d															23 15	23 29								
Crystal Palace 4	d													23 13	23 13	23 21	23a31								
Sydenham	d					22 51	22 51			23 06	23 06		23 13	23 16	23 16	23 24									
Forest Hill 4	d					22 53	22 53			23 08	23 08		23 16	23 19	23 19	23 27									
Honor Oak Park	d					22 56	22 56			23 11	23 11		23 18	23 21	23 21	23 29									
Brockley	d					22 58	22 58			23 13	23 13		23 21	23 24	23 24	23 32									
New Cross Gate 4	a					23 01	23 01			23 16	23 16		23 23	23 26	23 26	23 34									
	d					23 01	23 01			23 16	23 16		23 23	23 26	23 26	23 34									
New Cross ELL	d							23 06	23 06												23 36		23 36		
Surrey Quays	d					23 05	23 05	23 10	23 10	23 19	23 19			23 30	23 30						23 40		23 40		
Canada Water	d					23 07	23 07	23 12	23 12	23 21	23 21			23 32	23 32						23 42		23 42		
Rotherhithe	d					23 08	23 08	23 13	23 13	23 23	23 23			23 33	23 33						23 43		23 43		
Wapping	d					23 10	23 10	23 15	23 15	23 24	23 24			23 35	23 35						23 45		23 45		
Shadwell	d					23 12	23 12	23 17	23 17	23 26	23 26			23 37	23 37						23 47		23 47		
Whitechapel	d					23 14	23 14	23 19	23 19	23 29	23 29			23 39	23 39						23 49		23 49		
Shoreditch High Street	d					23 16	23 16	23 21	23 21	23 31	23 31			23 41	23 41						23 51		23 51		
Hoxton	d					23 18	23 18	23 23	23 23	23 33	23 33			23 43	23 43						23 53		23 53		
Haggerston	d					23 20	23 20	23 25	23 25	23 35	23 35			23 45	23 45						23 55		23 55		
Dalston Junction Stn ELL	a					23 22	23 22	23 28	23 32	23 37	23 37			23 47	23 47						23 58		00 02		
Canonbury	d					23 27	23 27			23 42	23 44			23 50	23 50						00 01				
Highbury & Islington	a					23 32	23 35			23 46	23 51			23 55	23 58						00 10				
	d																								
London Bridge 4 ⊖	a		23 06		23 11								23 30			23 45		23 26		23 36					23 41

A not 27 July
B 27 July
C from 21 May until 27 July
D until 18 May

until 27 July

East London Line and Croydon - London Victoria to London Bridge

Network Diagram - see first Page of Table 177

		LO A	LO B	LO	SN	SN	SN		SE C	SE D	SN
East Croydon	d										
West Croydon 4	d	23 22	23 22								
Norwood Junction 2	d	23 28	23 28								
Anerley	d	23 31	23 31								
Penge West	d	23 33	23 33								
London Victoria 15 ⊖	d				23 22					23 43	23 54
Battersea Park 4	d				23 26						23 58
Wandsworth Road	d										
Clapham High Street ⊖	d										
London Blackfriars 3 ⊖	d								23 42		
Denmark Hill 4	d								23 52	23 52	
Peckham Rye 4	d					23 42	23 47		23a55	23a55	
Queens Rd Peckham	d						23 49				
South Bermondsey	d						23 52				
Clapham Junction 10	d				23 30						00 02
Wandsworth Common	d				23 33						00 05
Balham 4 ⊖	d				23 35						00 07
Streatham Hill	d				23 38						00 10
West Norwood 4	d				23 42	23 54					00 14
Gipsy Hill	d				23 45	23 57					00 17
Crystal Palace 4	d			23 43	23 51	23a59					00 21
Sydenham	d	23 36	23 36	23 46	23 54						00 24
Forest Hill 4	d	23 38	23 38	23 49	23 57						00 27
Honor Oak Park	d	23 41	23 41	23 51	23 59						00 29
Brockley	d	23 43	23 43	23 54	00 02						00 32
New Cross Gate 4	a	23 46	23 46	23 56	00 04						00 34
	d	23 46	23 46	23 56	00 04						00 34
New Cross ELL	d										
Surrey Quays	d	23 49	23 49	23 59							
Canada Water	d	23 51	23 51	00 02							
Rotherhithe	d	23 53	23 53	00 03							
Wapping	d	23 54	23 54	00 05							
Shadwell	d	23 56	23 56	00 07							
Whitechapel	d	23 59	23 59	00 09							
Shoreditch High Street	d	00 01	00 01	00 11							
Hoxton	d	00 03	00 03	00 13							
Haggerston	d	00 05	00 05	00 15							
Dalston Junction Stn ELL	a	00 07	00 07	00 17							
Canonbury	d	00 11	00 12	00 20							
Highbury & Islington	a	00 18	00 19	00 28							
	d										
London Bridge 4 ⊖	a				00 11		23 56				00 41

A 27 July
B not 27 July
C from 21 May until 27 July
D until 18 May

Table 178

Mondays to Fridays

30 July to 10 August

East London Line and Croydon - London Victoria to London Bridge

Network Diagram - see first Page of Table 177

		LO MO	LO A	LO MO	LO A	LO MO	LO A	LO MO	SN MO	SN A		SN A	SN A	SN	LO	LO	LO	SE	SE	SN		LO	LO	LO	LO
East Croydon ⇌	d													05 13						05 51					
West Croydon 4 ⇌	d				23p22	23p25									05 39							05 52			06 09
Norwood Junction 2	d				23p28	23p31								05 17	05 43					05 55		05 58			06 13
Anerley	d				23p31	23p34								05 20	05 46							06 01			06 16
Penge West	d				23p33	23p36								05 22	05 48							06 03			06 18
London Victoria 15 ⊖	d				≀					23p22		23p54						00 56							
Battersea Park 4	d				≀					23p26		23p58													
Wandsworth Road	d				≀					≀		≀													
Clapham High Street ⊖	d				≀					≀		≀													
London Blackfriars 3 ⊖	d				≀					≀		≀							05 28						
Denmark Hill 4	d				≀					≀		≀						01 06	05 39						
Peckham Rye 4	d				≀				23p53	≀		≀	00∫12					01a08	05a41	06 15					
Queens Rd Peckham	d				≀				23p56	≀		≀	≀							06 18					
South Bermondsey	d				≀				23p58	≀		≀	≀							06 20					
Clapham Junction 10	d				≀					23p30		00∫02	≀												
Wandsworth Common	d				≀					23p33		00∫05	≀												
Balham 4 ⊖	d				≀					23p35		00∫07	≀												
Streatham Hill	d				≀					23p38		00∫10	≀												
West Norwood 4	d				≀					23p42		00∫14	00∫24												
Gipsy Hill	d				≀					23p45		00∫17	00∫27												
Crystal Palace 4	d	23p16			≀		23p43	23p46		23p51		00∫21	00a29				05 58							06 13	
Sydenham	d	23p19			23p36	23p39	23p46	23p49		23p54		00∫24		05 24	05 51		06 01					06 06		06 16	06 21
Forest Hill 4	d	23p22			23p38	23p41	23p49	23p52		23p57		00∫27		05 27	05 53		06 04					06 08		06 19	06 23
Honor Oak Park	d	23p24			23p41	23p44	23p51	23p54		23p59		00∫29		05 29	05 56		06 06					06 11		06 21	06 26
Brockley	d	23p27			23p43	23p46	23p54	23p57		00∫02		00∫32		05 32	05 58		06 09					06 13		06 24	06 28
New Cross Gate 4	a	23p29			23p46	23p49	23p56	23p59		00∫04		00∫34		05 34	06 01		06 11					06 16		06 26	06 31
	d	23p29			23p46	23p49	23p56	23p59		00∫04		00∫34		05 34	06 01		06 11					06 16		06 26	06 31
New Cross ELL	d		23p36	23p39	≀		≀			≀		≀				06 06							06 21		
Surrey Quays	d	23p33	23p40	23p43	23p49	23p52	23p59	00 02		≀		≀			06 05	06 10	06 15					06 19	06 25	06 30	06 35
Canada Water	d	23p35	23p42	23p45	23p51	23p54	00∫02	00 05		≀		≀			06 07	06 12	06 17					06 21	06 27	06 32	06 37
Rotherhithe	d	23p36	23p43	23p46	23p53	23p56	00∫03	00 06		≀		≀			06 08	06 13	06 18					06 23	06 28	06 33	06 38
Wapping	d	23p38	23p45	23p48	23p54	23p57	00∫05	00 08		≀		≀			06 10	06 15	06 20					06 24	06 30	06 35	06 40
Shadwell	d	23p40	23p47	23p50	23p56	23p59	00∫07	00 10		≀		≀			06 12	06 17	06 22					06 26	06 32	06 37	06 42
Whitechapel	d	23p42	23p49	23p52	23p59	00 02	00∫09	00 12		≀		≀			06 14	06 19	06 24					06 29	06 34	06 39	06 44
Shoreditch High Street	d	23p44	23p51	23p54	00∫01	00 04	00∫11	00 14		≀		≀			06 16	06 21	06 26					06 31	06 36	06 41	06 46
Hoxton	d	23p46	23p53	23p56	00∫03	00 06	00∫13	00 16		≀		≀			06 18	06 23	06 28					06 33	06 38	06 43	06 48
Haggerston	d	23p48	23p55	23p58	00∫05	00 08	00∫15	00 18		≀		≀			06 20	06 25	06 30					06 35	06 40	06 45	06 50
Dalston Junction Stn ELL	a	23p50	23p58	00 02	00∫07	00 10	00∫17	00 20		≀		≀			06 22	06 32	06 32					06 37	06 47	06 47	06 52
Canonbury	d	23p53	00∫01	00 05	00∫11	00 14	00∫20	00 23		≀		≀			06 27		06 35					06 42		06 50	06 57
Highbury & Islington	a	00 01	00∫10	00 14	00∫18	00 21	00∫28	00 31		≀		≀			06 35		06 43					06 49		06 59	07 05
	d									≀		≀													
London Bridge 4 ⊖	a								00 03	00∫11		00∫41		05 41						06 25					

		SN	LO	LO	LO	SN		LO	LO	SE	SE	SN	SN	LO	SN	SE		SN	SN	LO	SN	LO	LO	SN	LO
East Croydon ⇌	d	06 13																							
West Croydon 4 ⇌	d				06 22														06 31	06 39			06 52		
Norwood Junction 2	d	06 18			06 28	06 32														06 43	06 47		06 58	07 02	
Anerley	d	06 21			06 31	06 35														06 46			07 01	07 05	
Penge West	d	06 23			06 33	06 37														06 48			07 03	07 07	
London Victoria 15 ⊖	d									05 57	06 14	06 19						06 41							
Battersea Park 4	d											06 23						06 45							
Wandsworth Road	d																	06 47							
Clapham High Street ⊖	d																	06 49							
London Blackfriars 3 ⊖	d															06 42									
Denmark Hill 4	d									06a06	06 24					06 52		06 54							
Peckham Rye 4	d										06a28				06 42	06a55		06 56	06 59		07 08				
Queens Rd Peckham	d																	06 59	07 02		07 10				
South Bermondsey	d																	07 01	07 04		07 13				
Clapham Junction 10	d											06 27													
Wandsworth Common	d											06 30													
Balham 4 ⊖	d											06 32													
Streatham Hill	d											06 35	06 42												
West Norwood 4	d											06 39	06 45		06 53										
Gipsy Hill	d											06 42	06 48		06 56										
Crystal Palace 4	d			06 28					06 41			06 44	06 51	06 58	06a59										
Sydenham	d	06 25		06 31	06 36	06 39			06 44			06 48	06 54	07 01						06 51			07 06	07 09	
Forest Hill 4	d	06 28		06 34	06 38	06 42			06 47			06 50	06 57	07 04						06 53			07 08	07 12	
Honor Oak Park	d	06 30		06 36	06 41	06 44			06 49			06 53	06 59	07 06						06 56			07 11	07 14	
Brockley	d	06 33		06 39	06 43	06 47			06 52			06 55	07 02	07 09						06 58			07 13	07 17	
New Cross Gate 4	a	06 35		06 41	06 46	06 49			06 54			06 58	07 04	07 11						07 01			07 16	07 19	
	d	06 35		06 41	06 46	06 49			06 54			06 58	07 04	07 11						07 01			07 16	07 19	
New Cross ELL	d		06 36					06 51														07 06			07 21
Surrey Quays	d		06 40	06 45	06 49			06 55	07 00					07 15						07 05		07 10	07 19		07 25
Canada Water	d		06 42	06 47	06 51			06 57	07 02					07 17						07 07		07 12	07 21		07 27
Rotherhithe	d		06 43	06 48	06 53			06 58	07 03					07 18						07 08		07 13	07 23		07 28
Wapping	d		06 45	06 50	06 54			07 00	07 05					07 20						07 10		07 15	07 24		07 30
Shadwell	d		06 47	06 52	06 56			07 02	07 07					07 22						07 12		07 17	07 26		07 32
Whitechapel	d		06 49	06 54	06 59			07 04	07 09					07 24						07 14		07 19	07 29		07 34
Shoreditch High Street	d		06 51	06 56	07 01			07 06	07 11					07 26						07 16		07 21	07 31		07 36
Hoxton	d		06 53	06 58	07 03			07 08	07 13					07 28						07 18		07 23	07 33		07 38
Haggerston	d		06 55	07 00	07 05			07 10	07 15					07 30						07 20		07 25	07 35		07 40
Dalston Junction Stn ELL	a		07 02	07 02	07 07			07 17	07 17					07 32						07 23		07 32	07 37		07 47
Canonbury	d			07 05	07 12				07 20					07 35						07 27			07 42		
Highbury & Islington	a			07 13	07 19				07 28					07 43						07 35			07 49		
	d																								
London Bridge 4 ⊖	a	06 44				07 00						07 06	07 16					07 08	07 11		07 19			07 30	

A not 30 July, 6 August

East London Line and Croydon - London Victoria to London Bridge

Network Diagram - see first Page of Table 177

		LO		SN	SN	SN	SN	SN	LO	SN	SN	LO		LO	LO	SN	LO	LO	SN	SN	SN	SN		SE	SN
East Croydon	d																								
West Croydon 4	d							07 01	07 09	07 17					07 22										07 31
Norwood Junction 2	d								07 13	07 22					07 28	07 32									
Anerley	d								07 16						07 31	07 35									
Penge West	d								07 18						07 33	07 37									
London Victoria 15 ⊖	d			06 49			07 11												07 17			07 41		07 43	
Battersea Park 4	d			06 53			07 15												07 21			07 45			
Wandsworth Road	d						07 17															07 47			
Clapham High Street ⊖	d						07 19															07 49			
London Blackfriars 3 ⊖	d																								
Denmark Hill 4	d						07 24															07 54		07 53	
Peckham Rye 4	d					07 12	07 26	07 31			07 36										07 42	07 56		07a56	07 59
Queens Rd Peckham	d						07 29	07 34			07 39											07 59			08 02
South Bermondsey	d						07 31	07 36			07 41											08 01			08 04
Clapham Junction 10	d			06 57															07 25						
Wandsworth Common	d			07 00																					
Balham 4 ⊖	d			07 02															07 29						
Streatham Hill	d			07 05	07 12														07 32						
West Norwood 4	d			07 09	07 15	07 23													07 38		07 53				
Gipsy Hill	d			07 12	07 18	07 26													07 41		07 56				
Crystal Palace 4	d	07 11		07 14	07 21	07a29				07a26				07 28				07 41	07 44	07 52	07a59				
Sydenham	d	07 14		07 18	07 24				07 21					07 31	07 36	07 39		07 44	07 48	07 56					
Forest Hill 4	d	07 17		07 20	07 27				07 23					07 34	07 38	07 42		07 47	07 50	07 58					
Honor Oak Park	d	07 19		07 23	07 29				07 26					07 36	07 41	07 44		07 49	07 53	08 01					
Brockley	d	07 22		07 25	07 32				07 28					07 39	07 43	07 47		07 52	07 55	08 03					
New Cross Gate 4	a	07 24		07 28	07 34				07 31					07 41	07 46	07 49		07 54	07 58	08 06					
	d	07 24		07 28	07 34				07 31					07 41	07 46	07 49		07 54	07 58	08 06					
New Cross ELL	d											07 36					07 51								
Surrey Quays	d	07 30							07 35			07 40		07 45	07 49		07 55	08 00							
Canada Water	d	07 32							07 37			07 42		07 47	07 51		07 57	08 02							
Rotherhithe	d	07 33							07 38			07 43		07 48	07 53		07 58	08 03							
Wapping	d	07 35							07 40			07 45		07 50	07 54		08 00	08 05							
Shadwell	d	07 37							07 42			07 47		07 52	07 56		08 02	08 07							
Whitechapel	d	07 39							07 44			07 49		07 54	07 59		08 04	08 09							
Shoreditch High Street	d	07 41							07 46			07 51		07 56	08 01		08 06	08 11							
Hoxton	d	07 43							07 48			07 53		07 58	08 03		08 08	08 13							
Haggerston	d	07 45							07 50			07 55		08 00	08 05		08 10	08 15							
Dalston Junction Stn ELL	a	07 47							07 53			08 02		08 02	08 07		08 17	08 17							
Canonbury	d	07 50							07 57					08 05	08 12			08 20							
Highbury & Islington	a	07 58							08 05					08 13	08 19			08 28							
	d																								
London Bridge 4 ⊖	a			07 36	07 45		07 38	07 43			07 48					07 58			08 07	08 15		08 08			08 11

		LO	SN	SN	LO	LO	LO	SN		LO	LO	SN	SN	LO	SN	SE	SN	SN		LO	SN	SN	LO	LO	SN
East Croydon	d																								
West Croydon 4	d	07 39	07 47				07 52											08 01		08 09	08 19			08 23	
Norwood Junction 2	d	07 43	07 52				07 58	08 02												08 13	08 25			08 28	08 32
Anerley	d	07 46					08 01	08 05												08 16				08 31	08 35
Penge West	d	07 48					08 03	08 07												08 18				08 33	08 37
London Victoria 15 ⊖	d											07 52				08 09	08 11								
Battersea Park 4	d																08 15								
Wandsworth Road	d																08 17								
Clapham High Street ⊖	d																08 19								
London Blackfriars 3 ⊖	d																								
Denmark Hill 4	d															08 18	08 24								
Peckham Rye 4	d			08 06											08 12	08a21	08 26	08 29				08 36			
Queens Rd Peckham	d			08 09													08 29	08 32				08 38			
South Bermondsey	d			08 11													08 31	08 34				08 41			
Clapham Junction 10	d											07 58													
Wandsworth Common	d																								
Balham 4 ⊖	d											08 03													
Streatham Hill	d											08 06	08 15												
West Norwood 4	d											08 09	08 19		08 24										
Gipsy Hill	d											08 12	08 22		08 27										
Crystal Palace 4	d		07a56			07 58					08 11	08 15	08 24	08 28	08a29						08a29				
Sydenham	d	07 51				08 01	08 06	08 09			08 14	08 18	08 28	08 31						08 21				08 36	08 39
Forest Hill 4	d	07 53				08 04	08 08	08 12			08 17	08 21	08 30	08 34						08 23				08 38	08 42
Honor Oak Park	d	07 56				08 06	08 11	08 14			08 19	08 23	08 33	08 36						08 26				08 41	08 44
Brockley	d	07 58				08 09	08 13	08 17			08 22	08 26	08 35	08 39						08 28				08 43	08 47
New Cross Gate 4	a	08 01				08 11	08 16	08 19			08 24	08 28	08 38	08 41						08 31				08 46	08 49
	d	08 01				08 11	08 16	08 19			08 24	08 28	08 38	08 41						08 31				08 46	08 49
New Cross ELL	d				08 06					08 21													08 36		
Surrey Quays	d	08 05			08 10	08 15	08 21			08 25	08 30			08 45						08 37			08 40	08 49	
Canada Water	d	08 07			08 12	08 17	08 23			08 27	08 32			08 47						08 39			08 42	08 51	
Rotherhithe	d	08 08			08 13	08 18	08 25			08 28	08 33			08 48						08 40			08 43	08 53	
Wapping	d	08 10			08 15	08 20	08 26			08 30	08 35			08 50						08 42			08 45	08 54	
Shadwell	d	08 12			08 17	08 22	08 28			08 32	08 37			08 52						08 44			08 47	08 56	
Whitechapel	d	08 14			08 19	08 24	08 31			08 34	08 39			08 54						08 46			08 49	08 59	
Shoreditch High Street	d	08 16			08 21	08 26	08 33			08 36	08 41			08 56						08 48			08 51	09 01	
Hoxton	d	08 18			08 23	08 28	08 35			08 38	08 43			08 58						08 50			08 53	09 03	
Haggerston	d	08 20			08 25	08 30	08 37			08 40	08 45			09 00						08 52			08 55	09 05	
Dalston Junction Stn ELL	a	08 23			08 32	08 32	08 39			08 47	08 47			09 02						08 55			09 02	09 07	
Canonbury	d	08 27				08 35	08 42				08 50			09 05						08 57				09 12	
Highbury & Islington	a	08 35				08 43	08 49				08 58			09 13						09 05				09 19	
	d																								
London Bridge 4 ⊖	a			08 18				08 28				08 37	08 47				08 38	08 41				08 48			08 58

Table 178

Mondays to Fridays

30 July to 10 August

East London Line and Croydon - London Victoria to London Bridge

Network Diagram - see first Page of Table 177

Station		LO	LO	SN		SN	LO	SN	SE	SN	SN	LO	SN	LO		LO	SN	SN	LO	LO	SN	SN	LO	SN	
East Croydon	d																								
West Croydon 4	d										08 31	08 39	08 49			08 53									
Norwood Junction 2	d											08 43	08 54			08 58		09 02							
Anerley	d											08 46				09 01		09 05							
Penge West	d											08 48				09 03		09 07							
London Victoria 15 ⊖	d					08 22			08 39	08 41											08 49				
Battersea Park 4	d					08 26				08 45											08 53				
Wandsworth Road	d									08 47															
Clapham High Street ⊖	d									08 49															
London Blackfriars 3 ⊖	d																								
Denmark Hill 4	d								08 48	08 54															
Peckham Rye 4	d							08 42	08a51	08 56	09 02						09 07							09 12	
Queens Rd Peckham	d									08 59	09 05						09 09								
South Bermondsey	d									09 01	09 07						09 12								
Clapham Junction 10	d					08 30															08 57				
Wandsworth Common	d					08 33															09 00				
Balham 4 ⊖	d					08 35															09 02				
Streatham Hill	d			08 35		08 38															09 05				
West Norwood 4	d			08 38		08 42		08 53													09 09			09 23	
Gipsy Hill	d			08 41		08 45		08 56													09 12			09 26	
Crystal Palace 4	d		08 41	08 44		08 51	08 58	08a59					08a58							09 11	09 14	09 21	09 28	09a29	
Sydenham	d		08 44	08 47		08 54	09 01					08 51				09 06		09 09		09 14	09 18	09 24	09 31		
Forest Hill 4	d		08 47	08 50		08 57	09 04					08 53				09 08		09 12		09 17	09 20	09 27	09 34		
Honor Oak Park	d		08 49	08 52		08 59	09 06					08 56				09 11		09 14		09 19	09 23	09 29	09 36		
Brockley	d		08 52	08 55		09 02	09 09					08 58				09 13		09 17		09 22	09 25	09 32	09 39		
New Cross Gate 4	a		08 54	08 57		09 04	09 11					09 01				09 16		09 19		09 24	09 28	09 34	09 41		
	d		08 54	08 57		09 04	09 11					09 01				09 16		09 19		09 24	09 28	09 34	09 41		
New Cross ELL	d	08 51												09 06					09 21						
Surrey Quays	d	08 55	09 00				09 15					09 05		09 10		09 19			09 25	09 30			09 45		
Canada Water	d	08 57	09 02				09 17					09 07		09 12		09 21			09 27	09 32			09 47		
Rotherhithe	d	08 58	09 03				09 18					09 08		09 13		09 23			09 28	09 33			09 48		
Wapping	d	09 00	09 05				09 20					09 10		09 15		09 24			09 30	09 35			09 50		
Shadwell	d	09 02	09 07				09 22					09 12		09 17		09 26			09 32	09 37			09 52		
Whitechapel	d	09 04	09 09				09 24					09 14		09 19		09 29			09 34	09 39			09 54		
Shoreditch High Street	d	09 06	09 11				09 26					09 16		09 21		09 31			09 36	09 41			09 56		
Hoxton	d	09 08	09 13				09 28					09 18		09 23		09 33			09 38	09 43			09 58		
Haggerston	d	09 10	09 15				09 30					09 20		09 25		09 35			09 40	09 45			10 00		
Dalston Junction Stn ELL	a	09 17	09 17				09 32					09 23		09 32		09 37			09 47	09 47			10 02		
Canonbury	d		09 20				09 35					09 27				09 42				09 50			10 05		
Highbury & Islington	a		09 28				09 43					09 35				09 49				09 58			10 13		
	d																								
London Bridge 4 ⊖	a			09 06		09 14				09 08	09 14						09 19	09 29			09 37	09 43			

Station		SE	SN	SN	LO	SN	LO	LO	SN	SN		LO	LO	SN	LO	SN	SN	SE	SN	SN		LO	LO	LO	SN
East Croydon	d					09 20				09 30															10 00
West Croydon 4	d			09 01	09 09			09 22												09 31		09 39		09 52	
Norwood Junction 2	d				09 14	09 25		09 28		09 35												09 43		09 58	10 05
Anerley	d				09 17			09 31		09 38												09 46		10 01	10 08
Penge West	d				09 19			09 33		09 40												09 48		10 03	10 10
London Victoria 15 ⊖	d	09 09	09 11											09 19				09 39	09 41						
Battersea Park 4	d		09 15											09 23					09 45						
Wandsworth Road	d		09 17																09 47						
Clapham High Street ⊖	d		09 19																09 49						
London Blackfriars 3 ⊖	d																								
Denmark Hill 4	d	09 18	09 24															09 48	09 54						
Peckham Rye 4	d	09a21	09 26	09 33												09 42	09 47	09a51	09 56	10 01					
Queens Rd Peckham	d		09 29	09 36													09 49		09 59	10 04					
South Bermondsey	d		09 31	09 38													09 52		10 01	10 06					
Clapham Junction 10	d													09 27											
Wandsworth Common	d													09 30											
Balham 4 ⊖	d													09 32											
Streatham Hill	d													09 35											
West Norwood 4	d													09 40		09 53									
Gipsy Hill	d													09 43		09 56									
Crystal Palace 4	d								09 36				09 43	09 51	09 58	09a59									
Sydenham	d				09 21			09 36	09 39	09 42			09 46	09 54	10 01							09 51		10 06	10 12
Forest Hill 4	d				09 23			09 38	09 42	09 45			09 49	09 57	10 04							09 53		10 08	10 15
Honor Oak Park	d				09 26			09 41	09 44	09 47			09 51	09 59	10 06							09 56		10 11	10 17
Brockley	d				09 28			09 43	09 47	09 50			09 54	10 02	10 09							09 58		10 13	10 20
New Cross Gate 4	a				09 31	09 32		09 46	09 49	09 52			09 56	10 04	10 11							10 01		10 16	10 22
	d				09 31	09 33		09 46	09 49	09 52			09 56	10 04	10 11							10 01		10 16	10 22
New Cross ELL	d						09 36					09 51											10 06		
Surrey Quays	d				09 35		09 40	09 49				09 55	10 00		10 15							10 05	10 10	10 19	
Canada Water	d				09 37		09 42	09 51				09 57	10 02		10 17							10 07	10 12	10 21	
Rotherhithe	d				09 38		09 43	09 53				09 58	10 03		10 18							10 08	10 13	10 23	
Wapping	d				09 40		09 45	09 54				10 00	10 05		10 20							10 10	10 15	10 24	
Shadwell	d				09 42		09 47	09 56				10 02	10 07		10 22							10 12	10 17	10 26	
Whitechapel	d				09 44		09 49	09 59				10 04	10 09		10 24							10 14	10 19	10 29	
Shoreditch High Street	d				09 46		09 51	10 01				10 06	10 11		10 26							10 16	10 21	10 31	
Hoxton	d				09 48		09 53	10 03				10 08	10 13		10 28							10 18	10 23	10 33	
Haggerston	d				09 50		09 55	10 05				10 10	10 15		10 30							10 20	10 25	10 35	
Dalston Junction Stn ELL	a				09 53		10 02	10 07				10 17	10 17		10 32							10 22	10 32	10 37	
Canonbury	d				09 57			10 12					10 20		10 35							10 27		10 42	
Highbury & Islington	a				10 05			10 19					10 28		10 43							10 35		10 49	
	d																								
London Bridge 4 ⊖	a		09 38	09 44		09 41			09 59	10 00				10 11			09 58		10 06	10 11					10 29

East London Line and Croydon - London Victoria to London Bridge

Network Diagram - see first Page of Table 177

		LO	LO	SN	LO	SN		SN	SE	SN	SN	LO	LO	LO	SN	LO		LO	SN	LO	SN	SN	SE	SN	SN
East Croydon	d														10 30										
West Croydon 4	d										10 01	10 09		10 22											10 31
Norwood Junction 2	d											10 13		10 28	10 35										
Anerley	d											10 16		10 31	10 38										
Penge West	d											10 18		10 33	10 40										
London Victoria 15	d			09 49					10 09	10 11									10 19				10 39	10 41	
Battersea Park 4	d			09 53						10 15									10 23					10 45	
Wandsworth Road	d									10 17														10 47	
Clapham High Street	d									10 19														10 49	
London Blackfriars 3	d																								
Denmark Hill 4	d								10 18	10 24													10 48	10 54	
Peckham Rye 4	d					10 12		10 17	10a21	10 26	10 31										10 42	10 47	10a51	10 56	11 01
Queens Rd Peckham	d							10 19		10 29	10 34											10 49		10 59	11 04
South Bermondsey	d							10 22		10 31	10 36											10 52		11 01	11 06
Clapham Junction 10	d			09 57															10 27						
Wandsworth Common	d			10 00															10 30						
Balham 4	d			10 02															10 32						
Streatham Hill	d			10 05															10 35						
West Norwood 4	d			10 10		10 23													10 40		10 53				
Gipsy Hill	d			10 13		10 26													10 43		10 56				
Crystal Palace 4	d		10 13	10 21	10 28	10a29												10 43	10 51	10 58	10a59				
Sydenham	d		10 16	10 24	10 31							10 21		10 36	10 42			10 46	10 54	11 01					
Forest Hill 4	d		10 19	10 27	10 34							10 23		10 38	10 45			10 49	10 57	11 04					
Honor Oak Park	d		10 21	10 29	10 36							10 26		10 41	10 47			10 51	10 59	11 06					
Brockley	d		10 24	10 32	10 39							10 28		10 43	10 50			10 54	11 02	11 09					
New Cross Gate 4	a		10 26	10 34	10 41							10 31		10 46	10 52			10 56	11 04	11 11					
	d		10 26	10 34	10 41							10 31		10 46	10 52			10 56	11 04	11 11					
New Cross ELL	d	10 21											10 36			10 51									
Surrey Quays	d	10 25	10 30		10 45							10 35	10 40	10 49		10 55		11 00		11 15					
Canada Water	d	10 27	10 32		10 47							10 37	10 42	10 51		10 57		11 02		11 17					
Rotherhithe	d	10 28	10 33		10 48							10 38	10 43	10 53		10 58		11 03		11 18					
Wapping	d	10 30	10 35		10 50							10 40	10 45	10 54		11 00		11 05		11 20					
Shadwell	d	10 32	10 37		10 52							10 42	10 47	10 56		11 02		11 07		11 22					
Whitechapel	d	10 34	10 39		10 54							10 44	10 49	10 59		11 04		11 09		11 24					
Shoreditch High Street	d	10 36	10 41		10 56							10 46	10 51	11 01		11 06		11 11		11 26					
Hoxton	d	10 38	10 43		10 58							10 48	10 53	11 03		11 08		11 13		11 28					
Haggerston	d	10 40	10 45		11 00							10 50	10 55	11 05		11 10		11 15		11 30					
Dalston Junction Stn ELL	a	10 47	10 47		11 02							10 52	11 02	11 07		11 17		11 17		11 32					
Canonbury	d		10 50		11 05							10 57		11 12				11 20		11 35					
Highbury & Islington	a		10 58		11 13							11 05		11 19				11 28		11 43					
	d																								
London Bridge 4	a			10 41				10 26		10 36	10 41				10 59				11 11			10 56		11 06	11 11

		LO		LO	LO	SN	LO	LO	SN	LO	SN	SN		SE	SN	SN	LO	LO	LO	SN	LO	LO		SN	LO
East Croydon	d					11 00														11 30					
West Croydon 4	d	10 39			10 52											11 01	11 09		11 22						
Norwood Junction 2	d	10 43			10 58	11 05											11 13		11 28	11 35					
Anerley	d	10 46			11 01	11 08											11 16		11 31	11 38					
Penge West	d	10 48			11 03	11 10											11 18		11 33	11 40					
London Victoria 15	d								10 49					11 09	11 11									11 19	
Battersea Park 4	d								10 53						11 15									11 23	
Wandsworth Road	d														11 17										
Clapham High Street	d														11 19										
London Blackfriars 3	d																								
Denmark Hill 4	d													11 18	11 24										
Peckham Rye 4	d										11 12	11 17		11a21	11 26	11 31									
Queens Rd Peckham	d											11 19			11 29	11 34									
South Bermondsey	d											11 22			11 31	11 36									
Clapham Junction 10	d								10 57															11 27	
Wandsworth Common	d								11 00															11 30	
Balham 4	d								11 02															11 32	
Streatham Hill	d								11 05															11 35	
West Norwood 4	d								11 10		11 23													11 40	
Gipsy Hill	d								11 13		11 26													11 43	
Crystal Palace 4	d							11 13	11 21	11 28	11a29											11 43		11 51	11 58
Sydenham	d	10 51			11 06	11 12		11 16	11 24	11 31							11 21		11 36	11 42		11 46		11 54	12 01
Forest Hill 4	d	10 53			11 08	11 15		11 19	11 27	11 34							11 23		11 38	11 45		11 49		11 57	12 04
Honor Oak Park	d	10 56			11 11	11 17		11 21	11 29	11 36							11 26		11 41	11 47		11 51		11 59	12 06
Brockley	d	10 58			11 13	11 20		11 24	11 32	11 39							11 28		11 43	11 50		11 54		12 02	12 09
New Cross Gate 4	a	11 01			11 16	11 22		11 26	11 34	11 41							11 31		11 46	11 52		11 56		12 04	12 11
	d	11 01			11 16	11 22		11 26	11 34	11 41							11 31		11 46	11 52		11 56		12 04	12 11
New Cross ELL	d			11 06			11 21											11 36			11 51				
Surrey Quays	d	11 05		11 10	11 19		11 25	11 30		11 45							11 35	11 40	11 49		11 55	12 00			12 15
Canada Water	d	11 07		11 12	11 21		11 27	11 32		11 47							11 37	11 42	11 51		11 57	12 02			12 17
Rotherhithe	d	11 08		11 13	11 23		11 28	11 33		11 48							11 38	11 43	11 53		11 58	12 03			12 18
Wapping	d	11 10		11 15	11 24		11 30	11 35		11 50							11 40	11 45	11 54		12 00	12 05			12 20
Shadwell	d	11 12		11 17	11 26		11 32	11 37		11 52							11 42	11 47	11 56		12 02	12 07			12 22
Whitechapel	d	11 14		11 19	11 29		11 34	11 39		11 54							11 44	11 49	11 59		12 04	12 09			12 24
Shoreditch High Street	d	11 16		11 21	11 31		11 36	11 41		11 56							11 46	11 51	12 01		12 06	12 11			12 26
Hoxton	d	11 18		11 23	11 33		11 38	11 43		11 58							11 48	11 53	12 03		12 08	12 13			12 28
Haggerston	d	11 20		11 25	11 35		11 40	11 45		12 00							11 50	11 55	12 05		12 10	12 15			12 30
Dalston Junction Stn ELL	a	11 22		11 32	11 37		11 47	11 47		12 02							11 52	12 02	12 07		12 17	12 17			12 32
Canonbury	d	11 27			11 42			11 50		12 05							11 57		12 12			12 20			12 35
Highbury & Islington	a	11 35			11 49			11 58		12 13							12 05		12 19			12 28			12 43
	d																								
London Bridge 4	a					11 29			11 41			11 26			11 36	11 41				11 59				12 14	

Table 178

Mondays to Fridays

30 July to 10 August

East London Line and Croydon - London Victoria to London Bridge

Network Diagram - see first Page of Table 177

Station		SN	SN	SE	SN	SN	LO	LO		LO	SN	LO	LO	SN	LO	SN	SN	SE		SN	SN	LO	LO	LO	SN
East Croydon	d										12 00														12 30
West Croydon 4	d					11 31	11 39			11 52											12 01	12 09		12 22	
Norwood Junction 2	d						11 43			11 58	12 05											12 13		12 28	12 35
Anerley	d						11 46			12 01	12 08											12 16		12 31	12 38
Penge West	d						11 48			12 03	12 10											12 18		12 33	12 40
London Victoria 15 ⊖	d			11 39	11 41									11 49				12 09		12 11					
Battersea Park 4	d				11 45									11 53						12 15					
Wandsworth Road	d				11 47															12 17					
Clapham High Street ⊖	d				11 49															12 19					
London Blackfriars 3 ⊖	d																								
Denmark Hill 4	d			11 48	11 54													12 18		12 24					
Peckham Rye 4	d	11 42	11 47	11a51	11 56	12 01										12 12	12 17	12a21		12 26	12 31				
Queens Rd Peckham	d		11 49		11 59	12 04											12 19			12 29	12 34				
South Bermondsey	d		11 52		12 01	12 06											12 22			12 31	12 36				
Clapham Junction 10	d													11 57											
Wandsworth Common	d													12 00											
Balham 4 ⊖	d													12 02											
Streatham Hill	d													12 05											
West Norwood 4	d	11 53												12 10		12 23									
Gipsy Hill	d	11 56												12 13		12 26									
Crystal Palace 4	d	11a59											12 13	12 21	12 28	12a29									
Sydenham	d						11 51			12 06	12 12		12 16	12 24	12 31							12 21		12 36	12 42
Forest Hill 4	d						11 53			12 08	12 15		12 19	12 27	12 34							12 23		12 38	12 45
Honor Oak Park	d						11 56			12 11	12 17		12 21	12 29	12 36							12 26		12 41	12 47
Brockley	d						11 58			12 13	12 20		12 24	12 32	12 39							12 28		12 43	12 50
New Cross Gate 4	a						12 01			12 16	12 22		12 26	12 34	12 41							12 31		12 46	12 52
	d						12 01			12 16	12 22		12 26	12 34	12 41							12 31		12 46	12 52
New Cross ELL	d							12 06				12 21											12 36		
Surrey Quays	d						12 05	12 10		12 19		12 25	12 30		12 45							12 35	12 40	12 49	
Canada Water	d						12 07	12 12		12 21		12 27	12 32		12 47							12 37	12 42	12 51	
Rotherhithe	d						12 08	12 13		12 23		12 28	12 33		12 48							12 38	12 43	12 53	
Wapping	d						12 10	12 15		12 24		12 30	12 35		12 50							12 40	12 45	12 54	
Shadwell	d						12 12	12 17		12 26		12 32	12 37		12 52							12 42	12 47	12 56	
Whitechapel	d						12 14	12 19		12 29		12 34	12 39		12 54							12 44	12 49	12 59	
Shoreditch High Street	d						12 16	12 21		12 31		12 36	12 41		12 56							12 46	12 51	13 01	
Hoxton	d						12 18	12 23		12 33		12 38	12 43		12 58							12 48	12 53	13 03	
Haggerston	d						12 20	12 25		12 35		12 40	12 45		13 00							12 50	12 55	13 05	
Dalston Junction Stn ELL	a						12 22	12 32		12 37		12 47	12 47		13 02							12 52	13 02	13 07	
Canonbury	d						12 27			12 42			12 50		13 05							12 57		13 12	
Highbury & Islington	a						12 35			12 49			12 58		13 13							13 05		13 19	
	d																								
London Bridge 4 ⊖	a		11 56		12 06	12 11					12 29			12 41			12 26			12 36	12 41				12 59

Station		LO	LO	SN		LO	SN	SN	SE	SN	SN	LO	LO	LO		SN	LO	LO	SN	LO	SN	SN	SE	SN	
East Croydon	d															13 00									
West Croydon 4	d										12 31	12 39		12 52											
Norwood Junction 2	d											12 43		12 58		13 05									
Anerley	d											12 46		13 01		13 08									
Penge West	d											12 48		13 03		13 10									
London Victoria 15 ⊖	d			12 19					12 39	12 41									12 49				13 09	13 11	
Battersea Park 4	d			12 23						12 45									12 53					13 15	
Wandsworth Road	d									12 47														13 17	
Clapham High Street ⊖	d									12 49														13 19	
London Blackfriars 3 ⊖	d																								
Denmark Hill 4	d								12 48	12 54													13 18	13 24	
Peckham Rye 4	d						12 42	12 47	12a51	12 56	13 01										13 12	13 17	13a22	13 26	
Queens Rd Peckham	d							12 49		12 59	13 04											13 19		13 29	
South Bermondsey	d							12 52		13 01	13 06											13 22		13 31	
Clapham Junction 10	d			12 27															12 57						
Wandsworth Common	d			12 30															13 00						
Balham 4 ⊖	d			12 32															13 02						
Streatham Hill	d			12 35															13 05						
West Norwood 4	d			12 40			12 53												13 10		13 23				
Gipsy Hill	d			12 43			12 56												13 13		13 26				
Crystal Palace 4	d		12 43	12 51		12 58	12a59											13 13	13 21	13 28	13a29				
Sydenham	d		12 46	12 54		13 01						12 51		13 06		13 12		13 16	13 24	13 31					
Forest Hill 4	d		12 49	12 57		13 04						12 53		13 08		13 15		13 19	13 27	13 34					
Honor Oak Park	d		12 51	12 59		13 06						12 56		13 11		13 17		13 21	13 29	13 36					
Brockley	d		12 54	13 02		13 09						12 58		13 13		13 20		13 24	13 32	13 39					
New Cross Gate 4	a		12 56	13 04		13 11						13 01		13 16		13 22		13 26	13 34	13 41					
	d		12 56	13 04		13 11						13 01		13 16		13 22		13 26	13 34	13 41					
New Cross ELL	d	12 51											13 06				13 21								
Surrey Quays	d	12 55	13 00			13 15						13 05	13 10	13 19			13 25	13 30		13 45					
Canada Water	d	12 57	13 02			13 17						13 07	13 12	13 21			13 27	13 32		13 47					
Rotherhithe	d	12 58	13 03			13 18						13 08	13 13	13 23			13 28	13 33		13 48					
Wapping	d	13 00	13 05			13 20						13 10	13 15	13 24			13 30	13 35		13 50					
Shadwell	d	13 02	13 07			13 22						13 12	13 17	13 26			13 32	13 37		13 52					
Whitechapel	d	13 04	13 09			13 24						13 14	13 19	13 29			13 34	13 39		13 54					
Shoreditch High Street	d	13 06	13 11			13 26						13 16	13 21	13 31			13 36	13 41		13 56					
Hoxton	d	13 08	13 13			13 28						13 18	13 23	13 33			13 38	13 43		13 58					
Haggerston	d	13 10	13 15			13 30						13 20	13 25	13 35			13 40	13 45		14 00					
Dalston Junction Stn ELL	a	13 17	13 17			13 32						13 22	13 32	13 37			13 47	13 47		14 02					
Canonbury	d		13 20			13 35						13 27		13 42				13 50		14 05					
Highbury & Islington	a		13 28			13 43						13 35		13 49				13 58		14 13					
	d																								
London Bridge 4 ⊖	a			13 11				12 56		13 06	13 11					13 29			13 44			13 26		13 36	

East London Line and Croydon - London Victoria to London Bridge

Network Diagram - see first Page of Table 177

Station		SN	LO	LO	LO	SN	LO	LO	SN	LO		SN	SN	SE	SN	SN	LO	LO	LO	SN		LO	LO	SN	LO
East Croydon 🚋	d					13 30														14 00					
West Croydon [4] 🚋	d	13 01	13 09		13 22											13 31	13 39		13 52						
Norwood Junction [2]	d		13 13		13 28	13 35											13 43		13 58	14 05					
Anerley	d		13 16		13 31	13 38											13 46		14 01	14 08					
Penge West	d		13 18		13 33	13 40											13 48		14 03	14 10					
London Victoria [15] ⊖	d								13 19					13 39	13 41									13 49	
Battersea Park [4]	d								13 23						13 45									13 53	
Wandsworth Road	d														13 47										
Clapham High Street ⊖	d														13 49										
London Blackfriars [3] ⊖	d																								
Denmark Hill [4]	d													13 48	13 54										
Peckham Rye [4]	d	13 31										13 42	13 47	13a51	13 56	14 01									
Queens Rd Peckham	d	13 34											13 49		13 59	14 04									
South Bermondsey	d	13 36											13 52		14 01	14 06									
Clapham Junction [10]	d								13 27															13 57	
Wandsworth Common	d								13 30															14 00	
Balham [4] ⊖	d								13 32															14 02	
Streatham Hill	d								13 35															14 05	
West Norwood [4]	d								13 40			13 53												14 10	
Gipsy Hill	d								13 43			13 56												14 13	
Crystal Palace [4]	d							13 43	13 51	13 58		13a59											14 13	14 21	14 28
Sydenham	d		13 21		13 36	13 42		13 46	13 54	14 01							13 51		14 06	14 12			14 16	14 24	14 31
Forest Hill [4]	d		13 23		13 38	13 45		13 49	13 57	14 04							13 53		14 08	14 15			14 19	14 27	14 34
Honor Oak Park	d		13 26		13 41	13 47		13 51	13 59	14 06							13 56		14 11	14 17			14 21	14 29	14 36
Brockley	d		13 28		13 43	13 50		13 54	14 02	14 09							13 58		14 13	14 20			14 24	14 32	14 39
New Cross Gate [4]	a		13 31		13 46	13 52		13 56	14 04	14 11							14 01		14 16	14 22			14 26	14 34	14 41
	d		13 31		13 46	13 52		13 56	14 04	14 11							14 01		14 16	14 22			14 26	14 34	14 41
New Cross ELL	d			13 36			13 51											14 06				14 21			
Surrey Quays	d		13 35	13 40	13 49		13 55	14 00		14 15							14 05	14 10	14 19			14 25	14 30		14 45
Canada Water	d		13 37	13 42	13 51		13 57	14 02		14 17							14 07	14 12	14 21			14 27	14 32		14 47
Rotherhithe	d		13 38	13 43	13 53		13 58	14 03		14 18							14 08	14 13	14 23			14 28	14 33		14 48
Wapping	d		13 40	13 45	13 54		14 00	14 05		14 20							14 10	14 15	14 24			14 30	14 35		14 50
Shadwell	d		13 42	13 47	13 56		14 02	14 07		14 22							14 12	14 17	14 26			14 32	14 37		14 52
Whitechapel	d		13 44	13 49	13 59		14 04	14 09		14 24							14 14	14 19	14 29			14 34	14 39		14 54
Shoreditch High Street	d		13 46	13 51	14 01		14 06	14 11		14 26							14 16	14 21	14 31			14 36	14 41		14 56
Hoxton	d		13 48	13 53	14 03		14 08	14 13		14 28							14 18	14 23	14 33			14 38	14 43		14 58
Haggerston	d		13 50	13 55	14 05		14 10	14 15		14 30							14 20	14 25	14 35			14 40	14 45		15 00
Dalston Junction Stn ELL	a		13 52	14 02	14 07		14 17	14 17		14 32							14 22	14 32	14 37			14 47	14 47		15 02
Canonbury	d		13 57		14 12			14 20		14 35							14 27		14 42				14 50		15 05
Highbury & Islington	a		14 05		14 19			14 28		14 43							14 35		14 49				14 58		15 13
	d																								
London Bridge [4] ⊖	a	13 41				13 59			14 11				13 56		14 06	14 11				14 29				14 41	

Station		SN	SN	SE	SN	SN		LO	LO	LO	SN	LO	LO	SN	LO	SN		SN	SE	SN	SN	LO	LO	LO	SN
East Croydon 🚋	d										14 30														15 00
West Croydon [4] 🚋	d					14 01		14 09		14 22											14 31	14 39		14 52	
Norwood Junction [2]	d							14 13		14 28	14 35											14 43		14 58	15 05
Anerley	d							14 16		14 31	14 38											14 46		15 01	15 08
Penge West	d							14 18		14 33	14 40											14 48		15 03	15 10
London Victoria [15] ⊖	d			14 09	14 11									14 19					14 39	14 41					
Battersea Park [4]	d				14 15									14 23						14 45					
Wandsworth Road	d				14 17															14 47					
Clapham High Street ⊖	d				14 19															14 49					
London Blackfriars [3] ⊖	d																								
Denmark Hill [4]	d			14 18	14 24														14 48	14 54					
Peckham Rye [4]	d	14 12	14 17	14a21	14 26	14 31										14 42		14 47	14a51	14 56	15 01				
Queens Rd Peckham	d		14 19		14 29	14 34												14 49		14 59	15 04				
South Bermondsey	d		14 22		14 31	14 36												14 52		15 01	15 06				
Clapham Junction [10]	d													14 27											
Wandsworth Common	d													14 30											
Balham [4] ⊖	d													14 32											
Streatham Hill	d													14 35											
West Norwood [4]	d	14 23												14 40		14 53									
Gipsy Hill	d	14 26												14 43		14 56									
Crystal Palace [4]	d	14a29											14 43	14 51	14 58	14a59									
Sydenham	d							14 21		14 36	14 42		14 46	14 54	15 01							14 51		15 06	15 12
Forest Hill [4]	d							14 23		14 38	14 45		14 49	14 57	15 04							14 53		15 08	15 15
Honor Oak Park	d							14 26		14 41	14 47		14 51	14 59	15 06							14 56		15 11	15 17
Brockley	d							14 28		14 43	14 50		14 54	15 02	15 09							14 58		15 13	15 20
New Cross Gate [4]	a							14 31		14 46	14 52		14 56	15 04	15 11							15 01		15 16	15 22
	d							14 31		14 46	14 52		14 56	15 04	15 11							15 01		15 16	15 22
New Cross ELL	d								14 36			14 51											15 06		
Surrey Quays	d							14 35	14 40	14 49		14 55	15 00		15 15							15 05	15 10	15 19	
Canada Water	d							14 37	14 42	14 51		14 57	15 02		15 17							15 07	15 12	15 21	
Rotherhithe	d							14 38	14 43	14 53		14 58	15 03		15 18							15 08	15 13	15 23	
Wapping	d							14 40	14 45	14 54		15 00	15 05		15 20							15 10	15 15	15 24	
Shadwell	d							14 42	14 47	14 56		15 02	15 07		15 22							15 12	15 17	15 26	
Whitechapel	d							14 44	14 49	14 59		15 04	15 09		15 24							15 14	15 19	15 29	
Shoreditch High Street	d							14 46	14 51	15 01		15 06	15 11		15 26							15 16	15 21	15 31	
Hoxton	d							14 48	14 53	15 03		15 08	15 13		15 28							15 18	15 23	15 33	
Haggerston	d							14 50	14 55	15 05		15 10	15 15		15 30							15 20	15 25	15 35	
Dalston Junction Stn ELL	a							14 52	15 02	15 07		15 17	15 17		15 32							15 22	15 32	15 37	
Canonbury	d							14 57		15 12			15 20		15 35							15 27		15 42	
Highbury & Islington	a							15 05		15 19			15 28		15 43							15 35		15 49	
	d																								
London Bridge [4] ⊖	a		14 26		14 36	14 41					14 59			15 11				14 56		15 06	15 11				15 29

Table 178

Mondays to Fridays

30 July to 10 August

East London Line and Croydon - London Victoria to London Bridge

Network Diagram - see first Page of Table 177

		LO		LO	SN	LO	SN	SN	SE	SN	SN	LO		LO	LO	SN	LO	LO	SN	LO	SN	SN		SE	SN
East Croydon	d															15 30									
West Croydon 4	d										15 01	15 09			15 22										
Norwood Junction 2	d											15 13			15 28	15 35									
Anerley	d											15 16			15 31	15 38									
Penge West	d											15 18			15 33	15 40									
London Victoria 15	⊖ d				14 49				15 09	15 11									15 19					15 39	15 41
Battersea Park 4	d				14 53					15 15									15 23						15 45
Wandsworth Road	d									15 17															15 47
Clapham High Street	⊖ d									15 19															15 49
London Blackfriars 3	⊖ d																								
Denmark Hill 4	d								15 18	15 24														15 48	15 54
Peckham Rye 4	d						15 12	15 17	15a21	15 26	15 31										15 42	15 47		15a51	15 56
Queens Rd Peckham	d							15 19		15 29	15 34											15 49			15 59
South Bermondsey	d							15 22		15 31	15 36											15 52			16 01
Clapham Junction 10	d				14 57														15 27						
Wandsworth Common	d				15 00														15 30						
Balham 4	⊖ d				15 02														15 32						
Streatham Hill	d				15 05														15 35						
West Norwood 4	d				15 10		15 23												15 40		15 53				
Gipsy Hill	d				15 13		15 26												15 43		15 56				
Crystal Palace 4	d			15 13	15 21	15 28	15a29											15 43	15 51	15 58	15a59				
Sydenham	d			15 16	15 24	15 31						15 21			15 36	15 42		15 46	15 54	16 01					
Forest Hill 4	d			15 19	15 27	15 34						15 23			15 38	15 45		15 49	15 57	16 04					
Honor Oak Park	d			15 21	15 29	15 36						15 26			15 41	15 47		15 51	15 59	16 06					
Brockley	d			15 24	15 32	15 39						15 28			15 43	15 50		15 54	16 02	16 09					
New Cross Gate 4	a			15 26	15 34	15 41						15 31			15 46	15 52		15 56	16 04	16 11					
	d			15 26	15 34	15 41						15 31			15 46	15 52		15 56	16 04	16 11					
New Cross ELL	d	15 21												15 36			15 51								
Surrey Quays	d	15 25		15 30		15 45						15 35		15 40	15 49		15 55	16 00		16 15					
Canada Water	d	15 27		15 32		15 47						15 37		15 42	15 51		15 57	16 02		16 17					
Rotherhithe	d	15 28		15 33		15 48						15 38		15 43	15 53		15 58	16 03		16 18					
Wapping	d	15 30		15 35		15 50						15 40		15 45	15 54		16 00	16 05		16 20					
Shadwell	d	15 32		15 37		15 52						15 42		15 47	15 56		16 02	16 07		16 22					
Whitechapel	d	15 34		15 39		15 54						15 44		15 49	15 59		16 04	16 09		16 24					
Shoreditch High Street	d	15 36		15 41		15 56						15 46		15 51	16 01		16 06	16 11		16 26					
Hoxton	d	15 38		15 43		15 58						15 48		15 53	16 03		16 08	16 13		16 28					
Haggerston	d	15 40		15 45		16 00						15 50		15 55	16 05		16 10	16 15		16 30					
Dalston Junction Stn ELL	a	15 47		15 47		16 02						15 52		16 02	16 07		16 17	16 17		16 32					
Canonbury	d			15 50		16 05						15 57			16 12			16 20		16 35					
Highbury & Islington	a			15 58		16 13						16 05			16 19			16 28		16 43					
	d																								
London Bridge 4	⊖ a				15 41			15 26		15 36	15 41					15 59			16 11			15 56			16 06

		SN	LO	LO	LO	SN	SN	LO		LO	SN	LO	SN	SN	SE	SN	SN	LO		LO	LO	SN	LO	LO	SN
East Croydon	d						16 00															16 30			
West Croydon 4	d	15 31	15 39		15 52												16 01	16 09			16 22				
Norwood Junction 2	d		15 43		15 58		16 05											16 13			16 28	16 35			
Anerley	d		15 46		16 01		16 08											16 16			16 31	16 38			
Penge West	d		15 48		16 03		16 10											16 18			16 33	16 40			
London Victoria 15	⊖ d										15 49				16 09	16 11									16 19
Battersea Park 4	d										15 53					16 15									16 23
Wandsworth Road	d															16 17									
Clapham High Street	⊖ d															16 19									
London Blackfriars 3	⊖ d																								
Denmark Hill 4	d														16 18	16 24									
Peckham Rye 4	d	16 01				16 07							16 12	16 17	16a21	16 26	16 31								
Queens Rd Peckham	d	16 04				16 10								16 19		16 29	16 34								
South Bermondsey	d	16 06				16 12								16 22		16 31	16 36								
Clapham Junction 10	d										15 57														16 27
Wandsworth Common	d										16 00														16 30
Balham 4	⊖ d										16 02														16 32
Streatham Hill	d										16 05														16 35
West Norwood 4	d										16 10		16 23												16 39
Gipsy Hill	d										16 13		16 26												16 44
Crystal Palace 4	d									16 13	16 21	16 28	16a29											16 43	16 50
Sydenham	d		15 51		16 06		16 12			16 16	16 24	16 31						16 21			16 36	16 42		16 46	16 54
Forest Hill 4	d		15 53		16 08		16 15			16 19	16 27	16 34						16 23			16 38	16 45		16 49	16 56
Honor Oak Park	d		15 56		16 11		16 17			16 21	16 29	16 36						16 26			16 41	16 47		16 51	16 59
Brockley	d		15 58		16 13		16 20			16 24	16 32	16 39						16 28			16 43	16 50		16 54	17 01
New Cross Gate 4	a		16 01		16 16		16 22			16 26	16 34	16 41						16 31			16 46	16 52		16 56	17 04
	d		16 01		16 16		16 22			16 26	16 34	16 41						16 31			16 46	16 52		16 56	17 04
New Cross ELL	d			16 06				16 21												16 36			16 51		
Surrey Quays	d		16 05	16 10	16 19			16 25		16 30		16 45						16 35		16 40	16 49		16 55	17 00	
Canada Water	d		16 07	16 12	16 21			16 27		16 32		16 47						16 37		16 42	16 51		16 57	17 02	
Rotherhithe	d		16 08	16 13	16 23			16 28		16 33		16 48						16 38		16 43	16 53		16 58	17 03	
Wapping	d		16 10	16 15	16 24			16 30		16 35		16 50						16 40		16 45	16 54		17 00	17 05	
Shadwell	d		16 12	16 17	16 26			16 32		16 37		16 52						16 42		16 47	16 56		17 02	17 07	
Whitechapel	d		16 14	16 19	16 29			16 34		16 39		16 54						16 44		16 49	16 59		17 04	17 09	
Shoreditch High Street	d		16 16	16 21	16 31			16 36		16 41		16 56						16 46		16 51	17 01		17 06	17 11	
Hoxton	d		16 18	16 23	16 33			16 38		16 43		16 58						16 48		16 53	17 03		17 08	17 13	
Haggerston	d		16 20	16 25	16 35			16 40		16 45		17 00						16 50		16 55	17 05		17 10	17 15	
Dalston Junction Stn ELL	a		16 22	16 32	16 37			16 47		16 47		17 02						16 52		17 02	17 07		17 17	17 17	
Canonbury	d		16 27		16 42					16 50		17 05						16 57			17 12			17 20	
Highbury & Islington	a		16 35		16 49					16 58		17 13						17 05			17 19			17 28	
	d																								
London Bridge 4	⊖ a	16 11				16 17	16 29				16 41			16 26		16 38	16 41					17 02			17 12

30 July to 10 August

East London Line and Croydon - London Victoria to London Bridge

Network Diagram - see first Page of Table 177

		LO	SN	SN		SE	SN	SN	LO	LO	LO	SN	LO	LO		SN	SN	SE	SN	SN	SN	LO	SN	SN	
East Croydon	d											17 00													
West Croydon 4	d							16 31	16 39		16 52										17 01	17 09	17 12		
Norwood Junction 2	d								16 43		16 58	17 05										17 13			
Anerley	d								16 46		17 01	17 08										17 16			
Penge West	d								16 48		17 03	17 10										17 18			
London Victoria 15	d					16 39	16 41									16 49		17 04		17 11					
Battersea Park 4	d						16 45									16 53				17 15					
Wandsworth Road	d						16 47													17 17					
Clapham High Street	d						16 49													17 19					
London Blackfriars 3	d																								
Denmark Hill 4	d					16 48	16 54											17 13		17 24					
Peckham Rye 4	d		16 42	16 47		16a51	16 56	17 00									17 07	17a16	17 17	17 26	17 29			17 35	
Queens Rd Peckham	d			16 49			16 59	17 03											17 19	17 29	17 32			17 37	
South Bermondsey	d			16 52			17 01	17 05											17 22	17 31	17 34			17 40	
Clapham Junction 10	d															16 57									
Wandsworth Common	d															17 00									
Balham 4	d															17 03									
Streatham Hill	d															17 06									
West Norwood 4	d		16 53													17 09	17 20								
Gipsy Hill	d		16 56													17 12	17 23								
Crystal Palace 4	d	16 58	16a59											17 13		17 21	17a26								
Sydenham	d	17 01							16 51		17 06	17 12		17 16		17 24						17 21			
Forest Hill 4	d	17 04							16 53		17 08	17 15		17 19		17 27						17 23			
Honor Oak Park	d	17 06							16 56		17 11	17 17		17 21		17 29						17 26			
Brockley	d	17 09							16 58		17 13	17 20		17 24		17 32						17 28			
New Cross Gate 4	a	17 11							17 01		17 16	17 22		17 26		17 34						17 31			
	d	17 11							17 01		17 16	17 22		17 26		17 34						17 31			
New Cross ELL	d									17 06			17 21												
Surrey Quays	d	17 15							17 05	17 10	17 19		17 25	17 30								17 35			
Canada Water	d	17 17							17 07	17 12	17 21		17 27	17 32								17 37			
Rotherhithe	d	17 18							17 08	17 13	17 23		17 28	17 33								17 38			
Wapping	d	17 20							17 10	17 15	17 24		17 30	17 35								17 40			
Shadwell	d	17 22							17 12	17 17	17 26		17 32	17 37								17 42			
Whitechapel	d	17 24							17 14	17 19	17 29		17 34	17 39								17 44			
Shoreditch High Street	d	17 26							17 16	17 21	17 31		17 36	17 41								17 46			
Hoxton	d	17 28							17 18	17 23	17 33		17 38	17 43								17 48			
Haggerston	d	17 30							17 20	17 25	17 35		17 40	17 45								17 50			
Dalston Junction Stn ELL	a	17 32							17 22	17 32	17 37		17 47	17 47								17 52			
Canonbury	d	17 35							17 27		17 42			17 50								17 57			
Highbury & Islington	a	17 43							17 35		17 49			17 58								18 05			
	d																								
London Bridge 4	a			16 56			17 08	17 10				17 35				17 43			17 27	17 38	17 40		17 28	17 44	

		LO	LO	LO	LO	LO	SN	SN	SE	SN		SN	SN	SN	LO	SN	LO	LO	LO	SN		LO	LO	SN	SN
East Croydon	d											17 30													
West Croydon 4	d			17 22										17 31	17 39	17 42			17 52						
Norwood Junction 2	d			17 28						17 32		17 35			17 43				17 58	18 04					
Anerley	d			17 31								17 38			17 46				18 01	18 07					
Penge West	d			17 33								17 40			17 48				18 03	18 09					
London Victoria 15	d						17 22		17 34				17 41											17 52	
Battersea Park 4	d						17 26						17 45											17 56	
Wandsworth Road	d												17 47												
Clapham High Street	d												17 49												
London Blackfriars 3	d																								
Denmark Hill 4	d								17 43				17 54												
Peckham Rye 4	d							17 37	17a46	17 53			17 57	18 01											18 07
Queens Rd Peckham	d									17 55			17 59	18 04											
South Bermondsey	d									17 58			18 02	18 06											
Clapham Junction 10	d						17 30																	18 00	
Wandsworth Common	d						17 33																	18 03	
Balham 4	d						17 35																	18 05	
Streatham Hill	d						17 38																	18 08	
West Norwood 4	d						17 42	17 49																18 14	18 20
Gipsy Hill	d						17 45	17 52																18 17	18 23
Crystal Palace 4	d		17 28			17 43	17 48	17a54										17 58					18 13	18 20	18a26
Sydenham	d		17 31	17 36		17 46	17 54					17 42			17 51			18 01	18 06	18 11			18 16	18 24	
Forest Hill 4	d		17 34	17 38		17 49	17 57					17 45			17 53			18 04	18 08	18 14			18 19	18 27	
Honor Oak Park	d		17 36	17 41		17 51	17 59					17 47			17 56			18 06	18 11	18 16			18 21	18 29	
Brockley	d		17 39	17 43		17 54	18 02					17 50			17 58			18 09	18 13	18 19			18 24	18 32	
New Cross Gate 4	a		17 41	17 46		17 56	18 04					17 52			18 01			18 11	18 16	18 21			18 26	18 34	
	d		17 41	17 46		17 56	18 04					17 52			18 01			18 11	18 16	18 21			18 26	18 34	
New Cross ELL	d	17 36			17 51												18 06					18 21			
Surrey Quays	d	17 40	17 45	17 49	17 55	18 00									18 05		18 10	18 15	18 19			18 25	18 30		
Canada Water	d	17 42	17 47	17 51	17 57	18 02									18 07		18 12	18 17	18 21			18 27	18 32		
Rotherhithe	d	17 43	17 48	17 53	17 58	18 03									18 08		18 13	18 18	18 23			18 28	18 33		
Wapping	d	17 45	17 50	17 54	18 00	18 05									18 10		18 15	18 20	18 24			18 30	18 35		
Shadwell	d	17 47	17 52	17 56	18 02	18 07									18 12		18 17	18 22	18 26			18 32	18 37		
Whitechapel	d	17 49	17 54	17 59	18 04	18 09									18 14		18 19	18 24	18 29			18 34	18 39		
Shoreditch High Street	d	17 51	17 56	18 01	18 06	18 11									18 16		18 21	18 26	18 31			18 36	18 41		
Hoxton	d	17 53	17 58	18 03	18 08	18 13									18 18		18 23	18 28	18 33			18 38	18 43		
Haggerston	d	17 55	18 00	18 05	18 10	18 15									18 20		18 25	18 30	18 35			18 40	18 45		
Dalston Junction Stn ELL	a	18 02	18 02	18 07	18 17	18 17									18 23		18 32	18 32	18 37			18 47	18 47		
Canonbury	d		18 05	18 12		18 20									18 27			18 35	18 42				18 50		
Highbury & Islington	a		18 13	18 19		18 28									18 35			18 43	18 49				18 58		
	d																								
London Bridge 4	a						18 13			18 02		17 59	18 08	18 11		18 00				18 31				18 45	

Table 178

Mondays to Fridays

30 July to 10 August

East London Line and Croydon - London Victoria to London Bridge

Network Diagram - see first Page of Table 177

Station		SE	SN	SN	SN	LO		SN	LO	LO	LO	LO	SE	SN	SN	SN		LO	SN	SN	SE	SN	SN	LO	LO
East Croydon	d															18 30									
West Croydon 4	d				18 01	18 09		18 13			18 22												18 31	18 39	
Norwood Junction 2	d					18 13					18 28					18 35								18 43	
Anerley	d					18 16					18 31					18 38								18 46	
Penge West	d					18 18					18 33					18 40								18 48	
London Victoria 15 ⊖	d	17 56		18 11									18 18						18 22		18 39	18 41			
Battersea Park 4	d			18 15															18 26			18 45			
Wandsworth Road	d			18 17																		18 47			
Clapham High Street ⊖	d			18 19																		18 49			
London Blackfriars 3 ⊖	d																								
Denmark Hill 4	d	18 06		18 24									18 28								18 48	18 54			
Peckham Rye 4	d	18a08	18 12	18 26	18 29								18a31	18 32	18 36					18 37	18a51	18 57	19 01		
Queens Rd Peckham	d		18 15	18 29	18 32									18 35	18 38							19 00	19 04		
South Bermondsey	d		18 17	18 31	18 34									18 37	18 41							19 02	19 06		
Clapham Junction 10	d																		18 30						
Wandsworth Common	d																		18 33						
Balham 4 ⊖	d																		18 35						
Streatham Hill	d																		18 38						
West Norwood 4	d																		18 42	18 51					
Gipsy Hill	d																		18 45	18 54					
Crystal Palace 4	d									18 28								18 43	18 51	18a57					
Sydenham	d					18 21				18 31	18 36					18 42		18 46	18 54					18 51	
Forest Hill 4	d					18 23				18 34	18 38					18 45		18 49	18 57					18 53	
Honor Oak Park	d					18 26				18 36	18 41					18 47		18 51	18 59					18 56	
Brockley	d					18 28				18 39	18 43					18 50		18 54	19 02					18 58	
New Cross Gate 4	a					18 31				18 41	18 46					18 52		18 56	19 04					19 01	
	d					18 31				18 41	18 46					18 52		18 56	19 04					19 01	
New Cross ELL	d								18 36			18 51													19 06
Surrey Quays	d					18 35			18 40	18 45	18 49	18 55						19 00						19 05	19 10
Canada Water	d					18 37			18 42	18 47	18 51	18 57						19 02						19 07	19 12
Rotherhithe	d					18 38			18 43	18 48	18 53	18 58						19 03						19 08	19 13
Wapping	d					18 40			18 45	18 50	18 54	19 00						19 05						19 10	19 15
Shadwell	d					18 42			18 47	18 52	18 56	19 02						19 07						19 12	19 17
Whitechapel	d					18 44			18 49	18 54	18 59	19 04						19 09						19 14	19 19
Shoreditch High Street	d					18 46			18 51	18 56	19 01	19 06						19 11						19 16	19 21
Hoxton	d					18 48			18 53	18 58	19 03	19 08						19 13						19 18	19 23
Haggerston	d					18 50			18 55	19 00	19 05	19 10						19 15						19 20	19 25
Dalston Junction Stn ELL	a					18 52			19 02	19 02	19 07	19 17						19 17						19 22	19 32
Canonbury	d					18 57				19 05	19 12							19 20						19 27	
Highbury & Islington	a					19 05				19 13	19 19							19 28						19 35	
	d																								
London Bridge 4 ⊖	a		18 22	18 38	18 39			18 29						18 42	18 45	18 59			19 13			19 09	19 11		

Station		LO		LO	SN	LO	LO	SN	SN	SN	SN	LO		SN	SE	SN	SN	LO	LO	LO	SN	LO		LO	SN
East Croydon	d				19 00																19 30				
West Croydon 4	d			18 52													19 01	19 09		19 22					
Norwood Junction 2	d			18 58	19 05													19 13		19 28	19 35				
Anerley	d			19 01	19 08													19 16		19 31	19 38				
Penge West	d			19 03	19 10													19 18		19 33	19 40				
London Victoria 15 ⊖	d							18 52							19 09	19 11									19 22
Battersea Park 4	d							18 56								19 15									19 26
Wandsworth Road	d															19 17									
Clapham High Street ⊖	d															19 19									
London Blackfriars 3 ⊖	d																								
Denmark Hill 4	d														19 18	19 24									
Peckham Rye 4	d								19 06	19 07	19 14			19 17	19a21	19 26	19 29								
Queens Rd Peckham	d									19 10	19 17					19 29	19 32								
South Bermondsey	d									19 12	19 19					19 31	19 34								
Clapham Junction 10	d							19 00																	19 30
Wandsworth Common	d							19 03																	19 33
Balham 4 ⊖	d							19 05																	19 35
Streatham Hill	d							19 08																	19 38
West Norwood 4	d							19 12	19 17					19 30											19 42
Gipsy Hill	d							19 15	19 20					19 33											19 45
Crystal Palace 4	d	18 58					19 13	19 21	19a23			19 28		19a35										19 43	19 51
Sydenham	d	19 01		19 06	19 12		19 16	19 24				19 31						19 21		19 36	19 42			19 46	19 54
Forest Hill 4	d	19 04		19 08	19 15		19 19	19 27				19 34						19 23		19 38	19 45			19 49	19 57
Honor Oak Park	d	19 06		19 11	19 17		19 21	19 29				19 36						19 26		19 41	19 47			19 51	19 59
Brockley	d	19 09		19 13	19 20		19 24	19 32				19 39						19 28		19 43	19 50			19 54	20 02
New Cross Gate 4	a	19 11		19 16	19 22		19 26	19 34				19 41						19 31		19 46	19 52			19 56	20 04
	d	19 11		19 16	19 22		19 26	19 34				19 41						19 31		19 46	19 52			19 56	20 04
New Cross ELL	d					19 21													19 36			19 51			
Surrey Quays	d	19 15		19 19		19 25	19 30					19 45						19 35	19 40	19 49		19 55		20 00	
Canada Water	d	19 17		19 21		19 27	19 32					19 47						19 37	19 42	19 51		19 57		20 02	
Rotherhithe	d	19 18		19 23		19 28	19 33					19 48						19 38	19 43	19 53		19 58		20 03	
Wapping	d	19 20		19 24		19 30	19 35					19 50						19 40	19 45	19 54		20 00		20 05	
Shadwell	d	19 22		19 26		19 32	19 37					19 52						19 42	19 47	19 56		20 02		20 07	
Whitechapel	d	19 24		19 29		19 34	19 39					19 54						19 44	19 49	19 59		20 04		20 09	
Shoreditch High Street	d	19 26		19 31		19 36	19 41					19 56						19 46	19 51	20 01		20 06		20 11	
Hoxton	d	19 28		19 33		19 38	19 43					19 58						19 48	19 53	20 03		20 08		20 13	
Haggerston	d	19 30		19 35		19 40	19 45					20 00						19 50	19 55	20 05		20 10		20 15	
Dalston Junction Stn ELL	a	19 32		19 37		19 47	19 47					20 02						19 52	20 02	20 07		20 17		20 17	
Canonbury	d	19 35		19 42			19 50					20 05						19 57		20 12				20 20	
Highbury & Islington	a	19 43		19 49			19 58					20 13						20 05		20 19				20 28	
	d																								
London Bridge 4 ⊖	a				19 29			19 41		19 17	19 24					19 36	19 41				19 59				20 11

East London Line and Croydon - London Victoria to London Bridge

Network Diagram - see first Page of Table 177

		SN	SN	LO	SN	SN	SE	SN		SN	LO	LO	LO	SN	LO	LO	SN	LO		SN	SN	SN	SN	LO	LO
East Croydon	d													20 00											
West Croydon 4	d									19 31	19 39		19 52										20 01	20 09	
Norwood Junction 2	d										19 43		19 58	20 05										20 13	
Anerley	d										19 46		20 01	20 08										20 16	
Penge West	d										19 48		20 03	20 10										20 18	
London Victoria 15	d						19 39	19 41									19 52					20 11			
Battersea Park 4	d							19 45									19 56					20 15			
Wandsworth Road	d							19 47														20 17			
Clapham High Street	d							19 49														20 19			
London Blackfriars 3	d																								
Denmark Hill 4	d						19 48	19 54														20 24			
Peckham Rye 4	d	19 37	19 38		19 47	19 49	19a51	19 56		20 01										20 12	20 18	20 26	20 31		
Queens Rd Peckham	d		19 41			19 51		19 59		20 04											20 21	20 29	20 34		
South Bermondsey	d		19 43			19 54		20 01		20 06											20 23	20 31	20 36		
Clapham Junction 10	d																20 00								
Wandsworth Common	d																20 03								
Balham 4	d																20 05								
Streatham Hill	d																20 08								
West Norwood 4	d	19 49			20 00												20 12			20 24					
Gipsy Hill	d	19 52			20 03												20 15			20 27					
Crystal Palace 4	d	19a54		19 58	20a05											20 13	20 21	20 28		20a29					
Sydenham	d			20 01							19 51		20 06	20 12		20 16	20 24	20 31						20 21	
Forest Hill 4	d			20 04							19 53		20 08	20 15		20 19	20 27	20 34						20 23	
Honor Oak Park	d			20 06							19 56		20 11	20 17		20 21	20 29	20 36						20 26	
Brockley	d			20 09							19 58		20 13	20 20		20 24	20 32	20 39						20 28	
New Cross Gate 4	a			20 11							20 01		20 16	20 22		20 26	20 34	20 41						20 31	
	d			20 11							20 01		20 16	20 22		20 26	20 34	20 41						20 31	
New Cross ELL	d											20 06			20 21										20 36
Surrey Quays	d			20 15							20 05	20 10	20 19		20 25	20 30		20 45						20 35	20 40
Canada Water	d			20 17							20 07	20 12	20 21		20 27	20 32		20 47						20 37	20 42
Rotherhithe	d			20 18							20 08	20 13	20 23		20 28	20 33		20 48						20 38	20 43
Wapping	d			20 20							20 10	20 15	20 24		20 30	20 35		20 50						20 40	20 45
Shadwell	d			20 22							20 12	20 17	20 26		20 32	20 37		20 52						20 42	20 47
Whitechapel	d			20 24							20 14	20 19	20 29		20 34	20 39		20 54						20 44	20 49
Shoreditch High Street	d			20 26							20 16	20 21	20 31		20 36	20 41		20 56						20 46	20 51
Hoxton	d			20 28							20 18	20 23	20 33		20 38	20 43		20 58						20 48	20 53
Haggerston	d			20 30							20 20	20 25	20 35		20 40	20 45		21 00						20 50	20 55
Dalston Junction Stn ELL	a			20 32							20 22	20 32	20 37		20 47	20 47		21 02						20 52	21 02
Canonbury	d			20 35							20 27		20 42			20 50		21 05						20 57	
Highbury & Islington	a			20 43							20 35		20 49			20 58		21 13						21 05	
	d																								
London Bridge 4	a		19 51			19 58		20 06		20 14				20 29			20 41				20 28	20 36	20 41		

		LO	SN	LO		LO	SN	LO	SN	SN	SN	SN	LO	LO		LO	SN	LO	LO	SN	LO	SN	SN	SN	
East Croydon	d		20 31														21 00								
West Croydon 4	d	20 22										20 31	20 39			20 52									
Norwood Junction 2	d	20 28	20 35										20 43			20 58	21 05								
Anerley	d	20 31	20 38										20 46			21 01	21 08								
Penge West	d	20 33	20 40										20 48			21 03	21 10								
London Victoria 15	d						20 22				20 41									20 52				21 11	
Battersea Park 4	d						20 26				20 45									20 56				21 15	
Wandsworth Road	d										20 47													21 17	
Clapham High Street	d										20 49													21 19	
London Blackfriars 3	d																								
Denmark Hill 4	d										20 54													21 24	
Peckham Rye 4	d								20 42	20 48	20 56	21 01										21 12	21 17	21 26	
Queens Rd Peckham	d									20 50	20 59	21 04											21 19	21 29	
South Bermondsey	d									20 53	21 01	21 06											21 22	21 31	
Clapham Junction 10	d						20 30													21 00					
Wandsworth Common	d						20 33													21 03					
Balham 4	d						20 35													21 05					
Streatham Hill	d						20 38													21 08					
West Norwood 4	d						20 42		20 54											21 12		21 24			
Gipsy Hill	d						20 45		20 57											21 15		21 27			
Crystal Palace 4	d					20 43	20 51	20 58	20a59										21 13	21 21	21 28	21a29			
Sydenham	d	20 36	20 42			20 46	20 54	21 01					20 51			21 06	21 12		21 16	21 27	21 31				
Forest Hill 4	d	20 38	20 45			20 49	20 57	21 04					20 53			21 08	21 15		21 19	21 29	21 34				
Honor Oak Park	d	20 41	20 47			20 51	20 59	21 06					20 56			21 11	21 17		21 21	21 32	21 36				
Brockley	d	20 43	20 50			20 54	21 02	21 09					20 58			21 13	21 20		21 24	21 34	21 39				
New Cross Gate 4	a	20 46	20 52			20 56	21 04	21 11					21 01			21 16	21 22		21 26	21 37	21 41				
	d	20 46	20 52			20 56	21 04	21 11					21 01			21 16	21 22		21 26	21 37	21 41				
New Cross ELL	d			20 51										21 06				21 21							
Surrey Quays	d	20 49		20 55		21 00		21 15					21 05	21 10		21 19		21 25	21 30		21 45				
Canada Water	d	20 51		20 57		21 02		21 17					21 07	21 12		21 21		21 27	21 32		21 47				
Rotherhithe	d	20 53		20 58		21 03		21 18					21 08	21 13		21 23		21 28	21 33		21 48				
Wapping	d	20 54		21 00		21 05		21 20					21 10	21 15		21 24		21 30	21 35		21 50				
Shadwell	d	20 56		21 02		21 07		21 22					21 12	21 17		21 26		21 32	21 37		21 52				
Whitechapel	d	20 59		21 04		21 09		21 24					21 14	21 19		21 29		21 34	21 39		21 54				
Shoreditch High Street	d	21 01		21 06		21 11		21 26					21 16	21 21		21 31		21 36	21 41		21 56				
Hoxton	d	21 03		21 08		21 13		21 28					21 18	21 23		21 33		21 38	21 43		21 58				
Haggerston	d	21 05		21 10		21 15		21 30					21 20	21 25		21 35		21 40	21 45		22 00				
Dalston Junction Stn ELL	a	21 07		21 17		21 17		21 32					21 22	21 32		21 37		21 47	21 47		22 02				
Canonbury	d	21 12				21 20		21 35					21 27			21 42			21 50		22 05				
Highbury & Islington	a	21 19				21 28		21 43					21 35			21 49			21 58		22 13				
	d																								
London Bridge 4	a		20 59				21 11			20 57	21 06	21 11					21 29			21 43			21 26	21 36	

Table 178

Mondays to Fridays

30 July to 10 August

East London Line and Croydon - London Victoria to London Bridge

Network Diagram - see first Page of Table 177

Station		SN	LO	LO	LO	SN	LO	LO	SN	LO		SN	SN	SE	SN	SN	LO	LO	LO	SN		LO	SN	LO	SN
East Croydon	d					21 30														22 00					
West Croydon 4	d	21 01	21 09		21 22											21 31	21 39		21 52						
Norwood Junction 2	d		21 13		21 28	21 35											21 43		21 58	22 05					
Anerley	d		21 16		21 31	21 38											21 46		22 01	22 08					
Penge West	d		21 18		21 33	21 40											21 48		22 03	22 10					
London Victoria 15 ⊖	d								21 23						21 41								21 52		
Battersea Park 4	d								21 27						21 45								21 56		
Wandsworth Road	d														21 47										
Clapham High Street ⊖	d														21 49										
London Blackfriars 3 ⊖	d													21 42											
Denmark Hill 4	d													21 52	21 54										
Peckham Rye 4	d	21 31										21 42	21 47	21a55	21 56	22 01									22 12
Queens Rd Peckham	d	21 34											21 49		21 59	22 04									
South Bermondsey	d	21 36											21 52		22 01	22 06									
Clapham Junction 10	d								21 31														22 00		
Wandsworth Common	d								21 34														22 03		
Balham 4 ⊖	d								21 36														22 05		
Streatham Hill	d								21 39														22 08		
West Norwood 4	d								21 43			21 54											22 12		22 24
Gipsy Hill	d								21 46			21 57											22 15		22 27
Crystal Palace 4	d							21 43	21 51	21 58		21a59										22 13	22 21	22 28	22a29
Sydenham	d		21 21		21 36	21 42		21 46	21 54	22 01							21 51		22 06	22 12		22 16	22 24	22 31	
Forest Hill 4	d		21 23		21 38	21 45		21 49	21 57	22 04							21 53		22 08	22 15		22 19	22 27	22 34	
Honor Oak Park	d		21 26		21 41	21 47		21 51	21 59	22 06							21 56		22 11	22 17		22 21	22 29	22 36	
Brockley	d		21 28		21 43	21 50		21 54	22 02	22 09							21 58		22 13	22 20		22 24	22 32	22 39	
New Cross Gate 4	a		21 31		21 46	21 52		21 56	22 04	22 11							22 01		22 16	22 22		22 26	22 34	22 41	
	d		21 31		21 46	21 52		21 56	22 04	22 11							22 01		22 16	22 22		22 26	22 34	22 41	
New Cross ELL	d			21 36			21 51											22 06							
Surrey Quays	d		21 35	21 40	21 49		21 55	22 00		22 15							22 05	22 10	22 19			22 30		22 45	
Canada Water	d		21 37	21 42	21 51		21 57	22 02		22 17							22 07	22 12	22 21			22 32		22 47	
Rotherhithe	d		21 38	21 43	21 53		21 58	22 03		22 18							22 08	22 13	22 23			22 33		22 48	
Wapping	d		21 40	21 45	21 54		22 00	22 05		22 20							22 10	22 15	22 24			22 35		22 50	
Shadwell	d		21 42	21 47	21 56		22 02	22 07		22 22							22 12	22 17	22 26			22 37		22 52	
Whitechapel	d		21 44	21 49	21 59		22 04	22 09		22 24							22 14	22 19	22 29			22 39		22 54	
Shoreditch High Street	d		21 46	21 51	22 01		22 06	22 11		22 26							22 16	22 21	22 31			22 41		22 56	
Hoxton	d		21 48	21 53	22 03		22 08	22 13		22 28							22 18	22 23	22 33			22 43		22 58	
Haggerston	d		21 50	21 55	22 05		22 10	22 15		22 30							22 20	22 25	22 35			22 45		23 00	
Dalston Junction Stn ELL	a		21 52	22 02	22 07		22 17	22 17		22 32							22 22	22 33	22 37			22 47		23 02	
Canonbury	d		21 57		22 12			22 20		22 35							22 27		22 42			22 50		23 05	
Highbury & Islington	a		22 05		22 19			22 28		22 43							22 35		22 49			22 58		23 13	
	d																								
London Bridge 4 ⊖	a	21 41				21 59			22 13				21 56		22 06	22 11				22 29			22 45		

Station		SN	SE	SN	SN	LO		LO	LO	SN	LO	SN	SN	SN	SE	SN		SN	LO	LO	LO	SN	LO	SN	SN
East Croydon	d									22 30												23 01			
West Croydon 4	d				22 01	22 09			22 22									22 31	22 39		22 52				
Norwood Junction 2	d					22 13			22 28	22 35									22 43		22 58	23 06			
Anerley	d					22 16			22 31	22 38									22 46		23 01	23 09			
Penge West	d					22 18			22 33	22 40									22 48		23 03	23 11			
London Victoria 15 ⊖	d			22 11								22 22				22 41								22 52	
Battersea Park 4	d			22 15								22 26				22 45								22 56	
Wandsworth Road	d			22 17												22 47									
Clapham High Street ⊖	d			22 19												22 49									
London Blackfriars 3 ⊖	d		22 12												22 42										
Denmark Hill 4	d		22 22	22 24											22 52	22 54									
Peckham Rye 4	d	22 17	22a25	22 26	22 31								22 42	22 43	22a55	22 56		23 01							23 14
Queens Rd Peckham	d	22 19		22 29	22 34									22 45		22 59		23 04							
South Bermondsey	d	22 22		22 31	22 36									22 48		23 01		23 06							
Clapham Junction 10	d											22 30												23 00	
Wandsworth Common	d											22 33												23 03	
Balham 4 ⊖	d											22 35												23 05	
Streatham Hill	d											22 38												23 08	
West Norwood 4	d											22 42	22 54											23 12	23 26
Gipsy Hill	d											22 45	22 57											23 15	23 29
Crystal Palace 4	d										22 43	22 51	22a59										23 13	23 21	23a31
Sydenham	d					22 21			22 36	22 42	22 46	22 54							22 51		23 06	23 13	23 16	23 24	
Forest Hill 4	d					22 23			22 38	22 45	22 49	22 57							22 53		23 08	23 16	23 19	23 27	
Honor Oak Park	d					22 26			22 41	22 47	22 51	22 59							22 56		23 11	23 18	23 21	23 29	
Brockley	d					22 28			22 43	22 50	22 54	23 02							22 58		23 13	23 21	23 24	23 32	
New Cross Gate 4	a					22 31			22 46	22 52	22 56	23 04							23 01		23 16	23 23	23 26	23 34	
	d					22 31			22 46	22 52	22 56	23 04							23 01		23 16	23 23	23 26	23 34	
New Cross ELL	d							22 36												23 06					
Surrey Quays	d					22 35		22 40	22 49		23 00								23 05	23 10	23 19		23 30		
Canada Water	d					22 37		22 42	22 51		23 02								23 07	23 12	23 21		23 32		
Rotherhithe	d					22 38		22 43	22 53		23 03								23 08	23 13	23 23		23 33		
Wapping	d					22 40		22 45	22 54		23 05								23 10	23 15	23 24		23 35		
Shadwell	d					22 42		22 47	22 56		23 07								23 12	23 17	23 26		23 37		
Whitechapel	d					22 44		22 49	22 59		23 09								23 14	23 19	23 29		23 39		
Shoreditch High Street	d					22 46		22 51	23 01		23 11								23 16	23 21	23 31		23 41		
Hoxton	d					22 48		22 53	23 03		23 13								23 18	23 23	23 33		23 43		
Haggerston	d					22 50		22 55	23 05		23 15								23 20	23 25	23 35		23 45		
Dalston Junction Stn ELL	a					22 52		23 02	23 07		23 17								23 22	23 32	23 37		23 47		
Canonbury	d					22 57			23 12		23 20								23 27		23 44		23 50		
Highbury & Islington	a					23 05			23 19		23 28								23 35		23 51		23 58		
	d																								
London Bridge 4 ⊖	a	22 26		22 36	22 41					22 59		23 11		22 52		23 06		23 11				23 30		23 45	

30 July to 10 August

East London Line and Croydon - London Victoria to London Bridge

Network Diagram - see first Page of Table 177

		SN		SE	SN	SN	LO	LO	LO	SN	SN	SN		SE	SN
East Croydon	d														
West Croydon 4	d					23 01		23 22							
Norwood Junction 2	d							23 28							
Anerley	d							23 31							
Penge West	d							23 33							
London Victoria 15 ⊖	d				23 11					23 22					23 54
Battersea Park 4	d				23 15					23 26					23 58
Wandsworth Road	d				23 17										
Clapham High Street ⊖	d				23 19										
London Blackfriars 3 ⊖	d			23 12										23 42	
Denmark Hill 4	d			23 22	23 24									23 52	
Peckham Rye 4	d	23 17		23a25	23 26	23 31					23 42	23 47		23a55	
Queens Rd Peckham	d	23 19			23 29	23 34						23 49			
South Bermondsey	d	23 22			23 31	23 36						23 52			
Clapham Junction 10	d									23 30					00 02
Wandsworth Common	d									23 33					00 05
Balham 4 ⊖	d									23 35					00 07
Streatham Hill	d									23 38					00 10
West Norwood 4	d									23 42	23 54				00 14
Gipsy Hill	d									23 45	23 57				00 17
Crystal Palace 4	d								23 43	23 51	23a59				00 21
Sydenham	d							23 36	23 46	23 54					00 24
Forest Hill 4	d							23 38	23 49	23 57					00 27
Honor Oak Park	d							23 41	23 51	23 59					00 29
Brockley	d							23 43	23 54	00 02					00 32
New Cross Gate 4	a							23 46	23 56	00 04					00 34
	d							23 46	23 56	00 04					00 34
New Cross ELL	d						23 36								
Surrey Quays	d						23 40	23 49	23 59						
Canada Water	d						23 42	23 51	00 02						
Rotherhithe	d						23 43	23 53	00 03						
Wapping	d						23 45	23 54	00 05						
Shadwell	d						23 47	23 56	00 07						
Whitechapel	d						23 49	23 59	00 09						
Shoreditch High Street	d						23 51	00 01	00 11						
Hoxton	d						23 53	00 03	00 13						
Haggerston	d						23 55	00 05	00 15						
Dalston Junction Stn ELL	a						23 58	00 07	00 17						
Canonbury	d						00 01	00 11	00 20						
Highbury & Islington	a						00 10	00 18	00 28						
	d														
London Bridge 4 ⊖	a	23 26			23 36	23 41				00 11		23 56			00 41

Mondays to Fridays

13 August to 28 August

		LO A	LO MX	LO A	LO MX	LO A	LO MX	LO A	SN MO	SN MX		SN MX	SN MX	SN	LO	LO	LO	SE A	SE	SN		LO	LO	LO	LO
East Croydon	d													05 13						05 51					
West Croydon 4	d				23p22	23p25									05 39							05 52			06 09
Norwood Junction 2	d				23p28	23p31								05 17	05 43					05 55		05 58			06 13
Anerley	d				23p31	23p34								05 20	05 46							06 01			06 16
Penge West	d				23p33	23p36								05 22	05 48							06 03			06 18
London Victoria 15 ⊖	d									23p22		23p54						00 56							
Battersea Park 4	d									23p26		23p58													
Wandsworth Road	d																								
Clapham High Street ⊖	d																								
London Blackfriars 3 ⊖	d																		05 28						
Denmark Hill 4	d																	01s05	05 39						
Peckham Rye 4	d								23p53				00 12					01s08	05a41	06 15					
Queens Rd Peckham	d								23p56											06 18					
South Bermondsey	d								23p58											06 20					
Clapham Junction 10	d									23p30		00 02													
Wandsworth Common	d									23p33		00 05													
Balham 4 ⊖	d									23p35		00 07													
Streatham Hill	d									23p38		00 10													
West Norwood 4	d									23p42		00 14	00 24												
Gipsy Hill	d									23p45		00 17	00 27												
Crystal Palace 4	d	23p16					23p43	23p46		23p51		00 21	00a29				05 58							06 13	
Sydenham	d	23p19			23p36	23p39	23p46	23p49		23p54		00 24		05 24	05 51		06 01					06 06		06 16	06 21
Forest Hill 4	d	23p22			23p38	23p41	23p49	23p52		23p57		00 27		05 27	05 53		06 04					06 08		06 19	06 23
Honor Oak Park	d	23p24			23p41	23p44	23p51	23p54		23p59		00 29		05 29	05 56		06 06					06 11		06 21	06 26
Brockley	d	23p27			23p43	23p46	23p54	23p57		00 02		00 32		05 32	05 58		06 09					06 13		06 24	06 28
New Cross Gate 4	a	23p29			23p46	23p49	23p56	23p59		00 04		00 34		05 34	06 01		06 11					06 16		06 26	06 31
	d	23p29			23p46	23p49	23p56	23p59		00 04		00 34		05 34	06 01		06 11					06 16		06 26	06 31
New Cross ELL	d		23p36	23p39												06 06							06 21		
Surrey Quays	d	23p33	23p40	23p43	23p49	23p52	23p59	00 02							06 05	06 10	06 15					06 19	06 25	06 30	06 35
Canada Water	d	23p35	23p42	23p45	23p51	23p54	00 02	00 05							06 07	06 12	06 17					06 21	06 27	06 32	06 37
Rotherhithe	d	23p36	23p43	23p46	23p53	23p56	00 03	00 06							06 08	06 13	06 18					06 23	06 28	06 33	06 38
Wapping	d	23p38	23p45	23p48	23p54	23p57	00 05	00 08							06 10	06 15	06 20					06 24	06 30	06 35	06 40
Shadwell	d	23p40	23p47	23p50	23p56	23p59	00 07	00 10							06 12	06 17	06 22					06 26	06 32	06 37	06 42
Whitechapel	d	23p42	23p49	23p52	23p59	00 02	00 09	00 12							06 14	06 19	06 24					06 29	06 34	06 39	06 44
Shoreditch High Street	d	23p44	23p51	23p54	00 01	00 04	00 11	00 14							06 16	06 21	06 26					06 31	06 36	06 41	06 46
Hoxton	d	23p46	23p53	23p56	00 03	00 06	00 13	00 16							06 18	06 23	06 28					06 33	06 38	06 43	06 48
Haggerston	d	23p48	23p55	23p58	00 05	00 08	00 15	00 18							06 20	06 25	06 30					06 35	06 40	06 45	06 50
Dalston Junction Stn ELL	a	23p50	00 02	00 02	00 07	00 10	00 17	00 20							06 22	06 28	06 32					06 37	06 43	06 47	06 52
Canonbury	d	23p53		00 05	00 12	00 14	00 20	00 23							06 27		06 35					06 42		06 50	06 57
Highbury & Islington	a	00 01		00 14	00 19	00 21	00 28	00 31							06 32		06 40					06 46		06 56	07 02
	d																								
London Bridge 4 ⊖	a								00 03	00 11		00 41		05 41						06 25					

A 13 August

Table 178

Mondays to Fridays

13 August to 28 August

East London Line and Croydon - London Victoria to London Bridge

Network Diagram - see first Page of Table 177

Station		SN	LO	LO	LO	SN		LO	LO	SN	SN	LO	SN	SE	SN	SN		LO	SN	LO	LO	SN	LO	LO	SN
East Croydon	d	06 13																							
West Croydon 4	d				06 22											06 31		06 39			06 52				
Norwood Junction 2	d	06 18			06 28	06 32												06 43	06 47		06 58	07 02			
Anerley	d	06 21			06 31	06 35												06 46			07 01	07 05			
Penge West	d	06 23			06 33	06 37												06 48			07 03	07 07			
London Victoria 15 ⊖	d									06 19					06 41										06 49
Battersea Park 4	d									06 23					06 45										06 53
Wandsworth Road	d														06 47										
Clapham High Street ⊖	d														06 49										
London Blackfriars 3 ⊖	d													06 42											
Denmark Hill 4	d													06 52	06 54										
Peckham Rye 4	d												06 42	06a55	06 56	06 59			07 08						
Queens Rd Peckham	d														06 59	07 02			07 10						
South Bermondsey	d														07 01	07 04			07 13						
Clapham Junction 10	d									06 27															06 57
Wandsworth Common	d									06 30															07 00
Balham 4 ⊖	d									06 32															07 02
Streatham Hill	d									06 35	06 42														07 05
West Norwood 4	d									06 39	06 45		06 53												07 09
Gipsy Hill	d									06 42	06 48		06 56												07 12
Crystal Palace 4	d			06 28					06 41	06 44	06 51	06 58	06a59											07 11	07 14
Sydenham	d	06 25		06 31	06 36	06 39			06 44	06 48	06 54	07 01						06 51			07 06	07 09		07 14	07 18
Forest Hill 4	d	06 28		06 34	06 38	06 42			06 47	06 50	06 57	07 04						06 53			07 08	07 12		07 17	07 20
Honor Oak Park	d	06 30		06 36	06 41	06 44			06 49	06 53	06 59	07 06						06 56			07 11	07 14		07 19	07 23
Brockley	d	06 33		06 39	06 43	06 47			06 52	06 55	07 02	07 09						06 58			07 13	07 17		07 22	07 25
New Cross Gate 4	a	06 35		06 41	06 46	06 49			06 54	06 58	07 04	07 11						07 01			07 16	07 19		07 24	07 28
	d	06 35		06 41	06 46	06 49			06 54	06 58	07 04	07 11						07 01			07 16	07 19		07 24	07 28
New Cross ELL	d		06 36					06 51												07 06			07 21		
Surrey Quays	d		06 40	06 45	06 49			06 55	07 00			07 15						07 05		07 10	07 19		07 25	07 30	
Canada Water	d		06 42	06 47	06 51			06 57	07 02			07 17						07 07		07 12	07 21		07 27	07 32	
Rotherhithe	d		06 43	06 48	06 53			06 58	07 03			07 18						07 08		07 13	07 23		07 28	07 33	
Wapping	d		06 45	06 50	06 54			07 00	07 05			07 20						07 10		07 15	07 24		07 30	07 35	
Shadwell	d		06 47	06 52	06 56			07 02	07 07			07 22						07 12		07 17	07 26		07 32	07 37	
Whitechapel	d		06 49	06 54	06 59			07 04	07 09			07 24						07 14		07 19	07 29		07 34	07 39	
Shoreditch High Street	d		06 51	06 56	07 01			07 06	07 11			07 26						07 16		07 21	07 31		07 36	07 41	
Hoxton	d		06 53	06 58	07 03			07 08	07 13			07 28						07 18		07 23	07 33		07 38	07 43	
Haggerston	d		06 55	07 00	07 05			07 10	07 15			07 30						07 20		07 25	07 35		07 40	07 45	
Dalston Junction Stn ELL	a		06 58	07 02	07 07			07 13	07 17			07 32						07 23		07 28	07 37		07 43	07 47	
Canonbury	d			07 05	07 12				07 20			07 35						07 27			07 42			07 50	
Highbury & Islington	a			07 10	07 16				07 25			07 40						07 32			07 46			07 55	
	d																								
London Bridge 4 ⊖	a	06 44				07 00				07 06	07 16				07 08	07 11			07 19			07 30			07 36

Station		SN		SN	SN	SN	LO	SN	SN	LO	LO	LO		SN	LO	LO	SN	SN	SN	SN	SE	SN		LO	SN
East Croydon	d																								
West Croydon 4	d					07 01	07 09	07 17				07 22										07 31		07 39	07 47
Norwood Junction 2	d						07 13	07 22				07 28		07 32										07 43	07 52
Anerley	d						07 16					07 31		07 35										07 46	
Penge West	d						07 18					07 33		07 37										07 48	
London Victoria 15 ⊖	d				07 11												07 17			07 41	07 43				
Battersea Park 4	d				07 15												07 21			07 45					
Wandsworth Road	d				07 17															07 47					
Clapham High Street ⊖	d				07 19															07 49					
London Blackfriars 3 ⊖	d																								
Denmark Hill 4	d				07 24															07 54	07 53				
Peckham Rye 4	d			07 12	07 26	07 31			07 36										07 42	07 56	07a56	07 59			
Queens Rd Peckham	d				07 29	07 34			07 39											07 59		08 02			
South Bermondsey	d				07 31	07 36			07 41											08 01		08 04			
Clapham Junction 10	d																07 25								
Wandsworth Common	d																								
Balham 4 ⊖	d																07 29								
Streatham Hill	d	07 12															07 32								
West Norwood 4	d	07 15		07 23													07 38		07 53						
Gipsy Hill	d	07 18		07 26													07 41		07 56						
Crystal Palace 4	d	07 21		07a29				07a26			07 28					07 41	07 44	07 52	07a59						07a56
Sydenham	d	07 24					07 21				07 31	07 36		07 39		07 44	07 48	07 56						07 51	
Forest Hill 4	d	07 27					07 23				07 34	07 38		07 42		07 47	07 50	07 58						07 53	
Honor Oak Park	d	07 29					07 26				07 36	07 41		07 44		07 49	07 53	08 01						07 56	
Brockley	d	07 32					07 28				07 39	07 43		07 47		07 52	07 55	08 03						07 58	
New Cross Gate 4	a	07 34					07 31				07 41	07 46		07 49		07 54	07 58	08 06						08 01	
	d	07 34					07 31				07 41	07 46		07 49		07 54	07 58	08 06						08 01	
New Cross ELL	d									07 36					07 51										
Surrey Quays	d						07 35			07 40	07 45	07 49			07 55	08 00								08 05	
Canada Water	d						07 37			07 42	07 47	07 51			07 57	08 02								08 07	
Rotherhithe	d						07 38			07 43	07 48	07 53			07 58	08 03								08 08	
Wapping	d						07 40			07 45	07 50	07 54			08 00	08 05								08 10	
Shadwell	d						07 42			07 47	07 52	07 56			08 02	08 07								08 12	
Whitechapel	d						07 44			07 49	07 54	07 59			08 04	08 09								08 14	
Shoreditch High Street	d						07 46			07 51	07 56	08 01			08 06	08 11								08 16	
Hoxton	d						07 48			07 53	07 58	08 03			08 08	08 13								08 18	
Haggerston	d						07 50			07 55	08 00	08 05			08 10	08 15								08 20	
Dalston Junction Stn ELL	a						07 53			07 58	08 02	08 07			08 13	08 17								08 23	
Canonbury	d						07 57				08 05	08 12				08 20								08 27	
Highbury & Islington	a						08 02				08 10	08 16				08 25								08 32	
	d																								
London Bridge 4 ⊖	a	07 45			07 38	07 43			07 48					07 58			08 07	08 15		08 08		08 11			

Table 178

Mondays to Fridays

13 August to 28 August

East London Line and Croydon - London Victoria to London Bridge

Network Diagram - see first Page of Table 177

Station		SN	LO	LO	LO	LO	SN	LO		LO	SN	SN	LO	LO	SN	SE	SN	SN		LO	SN	SN	LO	LO	SN
East Croydon 🚊	d																								
West Croydon 4 🚊	d					07 52												08 01		08 09	08 19			08 23	
Norwood Junction 2	d					07 58	08 02													08 13	08 25			08 28	08 32
Anerley	d					08 01	08 05													08 16				08 31	08 35
Penge West	d					08 03	08 07													08 18				08 33	08 37
London Victoria 15 ⊖	d										07 52					08 09	08 11								
Battersea Park 4	d																08 15								
Wandsworth Road	d																08 17								
Clapham High Street ⊖	d																08 19								
London Blackfriars 3 ⊖	d																								
Denmark Hill 4	d															08 18	08 24								
Peckham Rye 4	d	08 06													08 12	08a21	08 26	08 29				08 36			
Queens Rd Peckham	d	08 09															08 29	08 32				08 38			
South Bermondsey	d	08 11															08 31	08 34				08 41			
Clapham Junction 10	d										07 58														
Wandsworth Common	d																								
Balham 4 ⊖	d										08 03														
Streatham Hill	d										08 06	08 15													
West Norwood 4	d										08 09	08 19			08 24										
Gipsy Hill	d										08 12	08 22			08 27										
Crystal Palace 4	d			07 58						08 11	08 15	08 24		08 28	08a29						08a29				
Sydenham	d			08 01		08 06	08 09			08 14	08 18	08 28		08 31						08 21				08 36	08 39
Forest Hill 4	d			08 04		08 08	08 12			08 17	08 21	08 30		08 34						08 23				08 38	08 42
Honor Oak Park	d			08 06		08 11	08 14			08 19	08 23	08 33		08 36						08 26				08 41	08 44
Brockley	d			08 09		08 13	08 17			08 22	08 26	08 35		08 39						08 28				08 43	08 47
New Cross Gate 4	a			08 11		08 16	08 19			08 24	08 28	08 38		08 41						08 31				08 46	08 49
	d			08 11		08 16	08 19			08 24	08 28	08 38		08 41						08 31				08 46	08 49
New Cross ELL	d		08 06					08 21															08 36		
Surrey Quays	d		08 10	08 15	08 19	08 21		08 25		08 30			08 34	08 45						08 37			08 40	08 49	
Canada Water	d		08 12	08 17	08 21	08 23		08 27		08 32			08 36	08 47						08 39			08 42	08 51	
Rotherhithe	d		08 13	08 18	08 22	08 25		08 28		08 33			08 37	08 48						08 40			08 43	08 53	
Wapping	d		08 15	08 20	08 24	08 26		08 30		08 35			08 39	08 50						08 42			08 45	08 54	
Shadwell	d		08 17	08 22	08 26	08 28		08 32		08 37			08 41	08 52						08 44			08 47	08 56	
Whitechapel	d		08 19	08 24	08 28	08 31		08 34		08 39			08 43	08 54						08 46			08 49	08 59	
Shoreditch High Street	d		08 21	08 26	08 30	08 33		08 36		08 41			08 45	08 56						08 48			08 51	09 01	
Hoxton	d		08 23	08 28	08 32	08 35		08 38		08 43			08 47	08 58						08 50			08 53	09 03	
Haggerston	d		08 25	08 30	08 34	08 37		08 40		08 45			08 49	09 00						08 52			08 55	09 05	
Dalston Junction Stn ELL	a		08 28	08 32	08 37	08 39		08 43		08 47			08 52	09 02						08 55			08 58	09 07	
Canonbury	d			08 35		08 42				08 50				09 05						08 57				09 12	
Highbury & Islington	a			08 40		08 46				08 55				09 10						09 02				09 16	
	d																								
London Bridge 4 ⊖	a	08 18					08 28				08 37	08 47					08 38	08 41				08 48			08 58

Station		LO	LO	SN		SN	LO	SN	SE	SN	SN	LO	SN	LO		LO	SN	SN	LO	LO	SN	SN	LO	SN	
East Croydon 🚊	d																								
West Croydon 4 🚊	d										08 31	08 39	08 49			08 53									
Norwood Junction 2	d											08 43	08 54			08 58		09 02							
Anerley	d											08 46				09 01		09 05							
Penge West	d											08 48				09 03		09 07							
London Victoria 15 ⊖	d					08 22			08 39	08 41											08 49				
Battersea Park 4	d					08 26				08 45											08 53				
Wandsworth Road	d									08 47															
Clapham High Street ⊖	d									08 49															
London Blackfriars 3 ⊖	d																								
Denmark Hill 4	d								08 48	08 54															
Peckham Rye 4	d							08 42	08a51	08 56	09 02						09 07							09 12	
Queens Rd Peckham	d									08 59	09 05						09 09								
South Bermondsey	d									09 01	09 07						09 12								
Clapham Junction 10	d					08 30															08 57				
Wandsworth Common	d					08 33															09 00				
Balham 4 ⊖	d					08 35															09 02				
Streatham Hill	d			08 35		08 38															09 05				
West Norwood 4	d			08 38		08 42		08 53													09 09			09 23	
Gipsy Hill	d			08 41		08 45		08 56													09 12			09 26	
Crystal Palace 4	d		08 41	08 44		08 51	08 58	08a59					08a58							09 11	09 14	09 21	09 28	09a29	
Sydenham	d		08 44	08 47		08 54	09 01					08 51				09 06		09 09		09 14	09 18	09 24	09 31		
Forest Hill 4	d		08 47	08 50		08 57	09 04					08 53				09 08		09 12		09 17	09 20	09 27	09 34		
Honor Oak Park	d		08 49	08 52		08 59	09 06					08 56				09 11		09 14		09 19	09 23	09 29	09 36		
Brockley	d		08 52	08 55		09 02	09 09					08 58				09 13		09 17		09 22	09 25	09 32	09 39		
New Cross Gate 4	a		08 54	08 57		09 04	09 11					09 01				09 16		09 19		09 24	09 28	09 34	09 41		
	d		08 54	08 57		09 04	09 11					09 01				09 16		09 19		09 24	09 28	09 34	09 41		
New Cross ELL	d	08 51												09 06					09 21						
Surrey Quays	d	08 55	09 00				09 15					09 05		09 10		09 19			09 25	09 30			09 45		
Canada Water	d	08 57	09 02				09 17					09 07		09 12		09 21			09 27	09 32			09 47		
Rotherhithe	d	08 58	09 03				09 18					09 08		09 13		09 23			09 28	09 33			09 48		
Wapping	d	09 00	09 05				09 20					09 10		09 15		09 24			09 30	09 35			09 50		
Shadwell	d	09 02	09 07				09 22					09 12		09 17		09 26			09 32	09 37			09 52		
Whitechapel	d	09 04	09 09				09 24					09 14		09 19		09 29			09 34	09 39			09 54		
Shoreditch High Street	d	09 06	09 11				09 26					09 16		09 21		09 31			09 36	09 41			09 56		
Hoxton	d	09 08	09 13				09 28					09 18		09 23		09 33			09 38	09 43			09 58		
Haggerston	d	09 10	09 15				09 30					09 20		09 25		09 35			09 40	09 45			10 00		
Dalston Junction Stn ELL	a	09 13	09 17				09 32					09 23		09 28		09 37			09 43	09 47			10 02		
Canonbury	d		09 20				09 35					09 27				09 42				09 50			10 05		
Highbury & Islington	a		09 25				09 40					09 32				09 46				09 55			10 10		
	d																								
London Bridge 4 ⊖	a			09 06		09 14				09 08	09 14						09 19	09 29			09 37	09 43			

Table 178

Mondays to Fridays

13 August to 28 August

East London Line and Croydon - London Victoria to London Bridge

Network Diagram - see first Page of Table 177

		SE	SN	SN	LO	SN	LO	LO	SN	SN		LO	LO	SN	LO	SN	SN	SE	SN	SN		LO	LO	LO	SN
East Croydon	d					09 20				09 30															10 00
West Croydon [4]	d			09 01	09 09			09 22												09 31		09 39		09 52	
Norwood Junction [2]	d				09 14	09 25		09 28		09 35												09 43		09 58	10 05
Anerley	d				09 17			09 31		09 38												09 46		10 01	10 08
Penge West	d				09 19			09 33		09 40												09 48		10 03	10 10
London Victoria [15]	d	09 09	09 11											09 19				09 39	09 41						
Battersea Park [4]	d		09 15											09 23					09 45						
Wandsworth Road	d		09 17																09 47						
Clapham High Street	d		09 19																09 49						
London Blackfriars [3]	d																								
Denmark Hill [4]	d	09 18	09 24															09 48	09 54						
Peckham Rye [4]	d	09a21	09 26	09 33												09 42	09 47	09a51	09 56	10 01					
Queens Rd Peckham	d		09 29	09 36													09 49		09 59	10 04					
South Bermondsey	d		09 31	09 38													09 52		10 01	10 06					
Clapham Junction [10]	d													09 27											
Wandsworth Common	d													09 30											
Balham [4]	d													09 32											
Streatham Hill	d													09 35											
West Norwood [4]	d													09 40		09 53									
Gipsy Hill	d													09 43		09 56									
Crystal Palace [4]	d								09 36				09 43	09 51	09 58	09a59									
Sydenham	d				09 21			09 36	09 39	09 42			09 46	09 54	10 01							09 51		10 06	10 12
Forest Hill [4]	d				09 23			09 38	09 42	09 45			09 49	09 57	10 04							09 53		10 08	10 15
Honor Oak Park	d				09 26			09 41	09 44	09 47			09 51	09 59	10 06							09 56		10 11	10 17
Brockley	d				09 28			09 43	09 47	09 50			09 54	10 02	10 09							09 58		10 13	10 20
New Cross Gate [4]	a				09 31	09 32		09 46	09 49	09 52			09 56	10 04	10 11							10 01		10 16	10 22
	d				09 31	09 33		09 46	09 49	09 52			09 56	10 04	10 11							10 01		10 16	10 22
New Cross ELL	d						09 36					09 51											10 06		
Surrey Quays	d				09 35		09 40	09 49				09 55	10 00		10 15							10 05	10 10	10 19	
Canada Water	d				09 37		09 42	09 51				09 57	10 02		10 17							10 07	10 12	10 21	
Rotherhithe	d				09 38		09 43	09 53				09 58	10 03		10 18							10 08	10 13	10 23	
Wapping	d				09 40		09 45	09 54				10 00	10 05		10 20							10 10	10 15	10 24	
Shadwell	d				09 42		09 47	09 56				10 02	10 07		10 22							10 12	10 17	10 26	
Whitechapel	d				09 44		09 49	09 59				10 04	10 09		10 24							10 14	10 19	10 29	
Shoreditch High Street	d				09 46		09 51	10 01				10 06	10 11		10 26							10 16	10 21	10 31	
Hoxton	d				09 48		09 53	10 03				10 08	10 13		10 28							10 18	10 23	10 33	
Haggerston	d				09 50		09 55	10 05				10 10	10 15		10 30							10 20	10 25	10 35	
Dalston Junction Stn ELL	a				09 53		09 58	10 07				10 13	10 17		10 32							10 22	10 28	10 37	
Canonbury	d				09 57			10 12					10 20		10 35							10 27		10 42	
Highbury & Islington	a				10 02			10 16					10 25		10 40							10 32		10 46	
	d																								
London Bridge [4]	a		09 38	09 44		09 41			09 59	10 00				10 11			09 58		10 06	10 11					10 29

		LO	LO	SN	LO	SN		SN	SE	SN	SN	LO	LO	LO	SN	LO		LO	SN	LO	SN	SN	SE	SN	SN
East Croydon	d														10 30										
West Croydon [4]	d										10 01	10 09		10 22											10 31
Norwood Junction [2]	d											10 13		10 28	10 35										
Anerley	d											10 16		10 31	10 38										
Penge West	d											10 18		10 33	10 40										
London Victoria [15]	d			09 49					10 09	10 11									10 19				10 39	10 41	
Battersea Park [4]	d			09 53						10 15									10 23					10 45	
Wandsworth Road	d									10 17														10 47	
Clapham High Street	d									10 19														10 49	
London Blackfriars [3]	d																								
Denmark Hill [4]	d								10 18	10 24													10 48	10 54	
Peckham Rye [4]	d					10 12		10 17	10a21	10 26	10 31										10 42	10 47	10a51	10 56	11 01
Queens Rd Peckham	d							10 19		10 29	10 34											10 49		10 59	11 04
South Bermondsey	d							10 22		10 31	10 36											10 52		11 01	11 06
Clapham Junction [10]	d			09 57															10 27						
Wandsworth Common	d			10 00															10 30						
Balham [4]	d			10 02															10 32						
Streatham Hill	d			10 05															10 35						
West Norwood [4]	d			10 10		10 23													10 40		10 53				
Gipsy Hill	d			10 13		10 26													10 43		10 56				
Crystal Palace [4]	d		10 13	10 21	10 28	10a29												10 43	10 51	10 58	10a59				
Sydenham	d		10 16	10 24	10 31							10 21		10 36	10 42			10 46	10 54	11 01					
Forest Hill [4]	d		10 19	10 27	10 34							10 23		10 38	10 45			10 49	10 57	11 04					
Honor Oak Park	d		10 21	10 29	10 36							10 26		10 41	10 47			10 51	10 59	11 06					
Brockley	d		10 24	10 32	10 39							10 28		10 43	10 50			10 54	11 02	11 09					
New Cross Gate [4]	a		10 26	10 34	10 41							10 31		10 46	10 52			10 56	11 04	11 11					
	d		10 26	10 34	10 41							10 31		10 46	10 52			10 56	11 04	11 11					
New Cross ELL	d	10 21											10 36			10 51									
Surrey Quays	d	10 25	10 30		10 45							10 35	10 40	10 49		10 55		11 00		11 15					
Canada Water	d	10 27	10 32		10 47							10 37	10 42	10 51		10 57		11 02		11 17					
Rotherhithe	d	10 28	10 33		10 48							10 38	10 43	10 53		10 58		11 03		11 18					
Wapping	d	10 30	10 35		10 50							10 40	10 45	10 54		11 00		11 05		11 20					
Shadwell	d	10 32	10 37		10 52							10 42	10 47	10 56		11 02		11 07		11 22					
Whitechapel	d	10 34	10 39		10 54							10 44	10 49	10 59		11 04		11 09		11 24					
Shoreditch High Street	d	10 36	10 41		10 56							10 46	10 51	11 01		11 06		11 11		11 26					
Hoxton	d	10 38	10 43		10 58							10 48	10 53	11 03		11 08		11 13		11 28					
Haggerston	d	10 40	10 45		11 00							10 50	10 55	11 05		11 10		11 15		11 30					
Dalston Junction Stn ELL	a	10 43	10 47		11 02							10 52	10 58	11 07		11 13		11 17		11 32					
Canonbury	d		10 50		11 05							10 57		11 12				11 20		11 35					
Highbury & Islington	a		10 55		11 10							11 02		11 16				11 25		11 40					
	d																								
London Bridge [4]	a			10 41				10 26		10 36	10 41				10 59				11 11			10 56		11 06	11 11

East London Line and Croydon - London Victoria to London Bridge

Network Diagram - see first Page of Table 177

		LO		LO	LO	SN	LO	LO	SN	LO	SN	SN		SE	SN	SN	LO	LO	LO	SN	LO	LO		SN	LO
East Croydon	d					11 00														11 30					
West Croydon 4	d	10 39			10 52											11 01	11 09		11 22						
Norwood Junction 2	d	10 43			10 58	11 05											11 13		11 28	11 35					
Anerley	d	10 46			11 01	11 08											11 16		11 31	11 38					
Penge West	d	10 48			11 03	11 10											11 18		11 33	11 40					
London Victoria 15 ⊖	d								10 49					11 09	11 11									11 19	
Battersea Park 4	d								10 53						11 15									11 23	
Wandsworth Road	d														11 17										
Clapham High Street ⊖	d														11 19										
London Blackfriars 3 ⊖	d																								
Denmark Hill 4	d													11 18	11 24										
Peckham Rye 4	d										11 12	11 17		11a21	11 26	11 31									
Queens Rd Peckham	d											11 19			11 29	11 34									
South Bermondsey	d											11 22			11 31	11 36									
Clapham Junction 10	d								10 57															11 27	
Wandsworth Common	d								11 00															11 30	
Balham 4 ⊖	d								11 02															11 32	
Streatham Hill	d								11 05															11 35	
West Norwood 4	d								11 10		11 23													11 40	
Gipsy Hill	d								11 13		11 26													11 43	
Crystal Palace 4	d							11 13	11 21	11 28	11a29											11 43		11 51	11 58
Sydenham	d	10 51			11 06	11 12		11 16	11 24	11 31							11 21		11 36	11 42		11 46		11 54	12 01
Forest Hill 4	d	10 53			11 08	11 15		11 19	11 27	11 34							11 23		11 38	11 45		11 49		11 57	12 04
Honor Oak Park	d	10 56			11 11	11 17		11 21	11 29	11 36							11 26		11 41	11 47		11 51		11 59	12 06
Brockley	d	10 58			11 13	11 20		11 24	11 32	11 39							11 28		11 43	11 50		11 54		12 02	12 09
New Cross Gate 4	a	11 01			11 16	11 22		11 26	11 34	11 41							11 31		11 46	11 52		11 56		12 04	12 11
	d	11 01			11 16	11 22		11 26	11 34	11 41							11 31		11 46	11 52		11 56		12 04	12 11
New Cross ELL	d			11 06			11 21											11 36			11 51				
Surrey Quays	d	11 05		11 10	11 19		11 25	11 30		11 45							11 35	11 40	11 49		11 55	12 00			12 15
Canada Water	d	11 07		11 12	11 21		11 27	11 32		11 47							11 37	11 42	11 51		11 57	12 02			12 17
Rotherhithe	d	11 08		11 13	11 23		11 28	11 33		11 48							11 38	11 43	11 53		11 58	12 03			12 18
Wapping	d	11 10		11 15	11 24		11 30	11 35		11 50							11 40	11 45	11 54		12 00	12 05			12 20
Shadwell	d	11 12		11 17	11 26		11 32	11 37		11 52							11 42	11 47	11 56		12 02	12 07			12 22
Whitechapel	d	11 14		11 19	11 29		11 34	11 39		11 54							11 44	11 49	11 59		12 04	12 09			12 24
Shoreditch High Street	d	11 16		11 21	11 31		11 36	11 41		11 56							11 46	11 51	12 01		12 06	12 11			12 26
Hoxton	d	11 18		11 23	11 33		11 38	11 43		11 58							11 48	11 53	12 03		12 08	12 13			12 28
Haggerston	d	11 20		11 25	11 35		11 40	11 45		12 00							11 50	11 55	12 05		12 10	12 15			12 30
Dalston Junction Stn ELL	a	11 22		11 28	11 37		11 43	11 47		12 02							11 52	11 58	12 07		12 13	12 17			12 32
Canonbury	d	11 27			11 42			11 50		12 05							11 57		12 12			12 20			12 35
Highbury & Islington	a	11 32			11 46			11 55		12 10							12 02		12 16			12 25			12 40
	d																								
London Bridge 4 ⊖	a					11 29			11 41			11 26			11 36	11 41				11 59				12 14	

		SN	SN	SE	SN	SN	LO	LO		LO	SN	LO	LO	SN	LO	SN	SN	SE		SN	SN	LO	LO	LO	SN
East Croydon	d										12 00														12 30
West Croydon 4	d					11 31	11 39			11 52											12 01	12 09		12 22	
Norwood Junction 2	d						11 43			11 58	12 05											12 13		12 28	12 35
Anerley	d						11 46			12 01	12 08											12 16		12 31	12 38
Penge West	d						11 48			12 03	12 10											12 18		12 33	12 40
London Victoria 15 ⊖	d			11 39	11 41									11 49				12 09		12 11					
Battersea Park 4	d				11 45									11 53						12 15					
Wandsworth Road	d				11 47															12 17					
Clapham High Street ⊖	d				11 49															12 19					
London Blackfriars 3 ⊖	d																								
Denmark Hill 4	d			11 48	11 54													12 18		12 24					
Peckham Rye 4	d	11 42	11 47	11a51	11 56	12 01										12 12	12 17	12a21		12 26	12 31				
Queens Rd Peckham	d		11 49		11 59	12 04											12 19			12 29	12 34				
South Bermondsey	d		11 52		12 01	12 06											12 22			12 31	12 36				
Clapham Junction 10	d													11 57											
Wandsworth Common	d													12 00											
Balham 4 ⊖	d													12 02											
Streatham Hill	d													12 05											
West Norwood 4	d	11 53												12 10		12 23									
Gipsy Hill	d	11 56												12 13		12 26									
Crystal Palace 4	d	11a59											12 13	12 21	12 28	12a29									
Sydenham	d						11 51			12 06	12 12		12 16	12 24	12 31							12 21		12 36	12 42
Forest Hill 4	d						11 53			12 08	12 15		12 19	12 27	12 34							12 23		12 38	12 45
Honor Oak Park	d						11 56			12 11	12 17		12 21	12 29	12 36							12 26		12 41	12 47
Brockley	d						11 58			12 13	12 20		12 24	12 32	12 39							12 28		12 43	12 50
New Cross Gate 4	a						12 01			12 16	12 22		12 26	12 34	12 41							12 31		12 46	12 52
	d						12 01			12 16	12 22		12 26	12 34	12 41							12 31		12 46	12 52
New Cross ELL	d							12 06				12 21											12 36		
Surrey Quays	d						12 05	12 10		12 19		12 25	12 30		12 45							12 35	12 40	12 49	
Canada Water	d						12 07	12 12		12 21		12 27	12 32		12 47							12 37	12 42	12 51	
Rotherhithe	d						12 08	12 13		12 23		12 28	12 33		12 48							12 38	12 43	12 53	
Wapping	d						12 10	12 15		12 24		12 30	12 35		12 50							12 40	12 45	12 54	
Shadwell	d						12 12	12 17		12 26		12 32	12 37		12 52							12 42	12 47	12 56	
Whitechapel	d						12 14	12 19		12 29		12 34	12 39		12 54							12 44	12 49	12 59	
Shoreditch High Street	d						12 16	12 21		12 31		12 36	12 41		12 56							12 46	12 51	13 01	
Hoxton	d						12 18	12 23		12 33		12 38	12 43		12 58							12 48	12 53	13 03	
Haggerston	d						12 20	12 25		12 35		12 40	12 45		13 00							12 50	12 55	13 05	
Dalston Junction Stn ELL	a						12 22	12 28		12 37		12 43	12 47		13 02							12 52	12 58	13 07	
Canonbury	d						12 27			12 42			12 50		13 05							12 57		13 12	
Highbury & Islington	a						12 32			12 46			12 55		13 10							13 02		13 16	
	d																								
London Bridge 4 ⊖	a		11 56		12 06	12 11					12 29			12 41			12 26			12 36	12 41				12 59

Table 178

Mondays to Fridays

13 August to 28 August

East London Line and Croydon - London Victoria to London Bridge

Network Diagram - see first Page of Table 177

		LO	LO	SN		LO	SN	SN	SE	SN	SN	LO	LO	LO		SN	LO	LO	SN	LO	SN	SN	SE	SN
East Croydon ⇌	d															13 00								
West Croydon 4 ⇌	d										12 31	12 39		12 52										
Norwood Junction 2	d											12 43		12 58		13 05								
Anerley	d											12 46		13 01		13 08								
Penge West	d											12 48		13 03		13 10								
London Victoria 15 ⊖	d			12 19					12 39	12 41									12 49				13 09	13 11
Battersea Park 4	d			12 23						12 45									12 53					13 15
Wandsworth Road	d									12 47														13 17
Clapham High Street ⊖	d									12 49														13 19
London Blackfriars 3 ⊖	d																							
Denmark Hill 4	d								12 48	12 54													13 18	13 24
Peckham Rye 4	d						12 42	12 47	12a51	12 56	13 01										13 12	13 17	13a21	13 26
Queens Rd Peckham	d							12 49		12 59	13 04											13 19		13 29
South Bermondsey	d							12 52		13 01	13 06											13 22		13 31
Clapham Junction 10	d			12 27															12 57					
Wandsworth Common	d			12 30															13 00					
Balham 4 ⊖	d			12 32															13 02					
Streatham Hill	d			12 35															13 05					
West Norwood 4	d			12 40			12 53												13 10		13 23			
Gipsy Hill	d			12 43			12 56												13 13		13 26			
Crystal Palace 4	d		12 43	12 51		12 58	12a59											13 13	13 21	13 28	13a29			
Sydenham	d		12 46	12 54		13 01						12 51		13 06		13 12		13 16	13 24	13 31				
Forest Hill 4	d		12 49	12 57		13 04						12 53		13 08		13 15		13 19	13 27	13 34				
Honor Oak Park	d		12 51	12 59		13 06						12 56		13 11		13 17		13 21	13 29	13 36				
Brockley	d		12 54	13 02		13 09						12 58		13 13		13 20		13 24	13 32	13 39				
New Cross Gate 4	a		12 56	13 04		13 11						13 01		13 16		13 22		13 26	13 34	13 41				
	d		12 56	13 04		13 11						13 01		13 16		13 22		13 26	13 34	13 41				
New Cross ELL	d	12 51											13 06				13 21							
Surrey Quays	d	12 55	13 00			13 15						13 05	13 10	13 19			13 25	13 30		13 45				
Canada Water	d	12 57	13 02			13 17						13 07	13 12	13 21			13 27	13 32		13 47				
Rotherhithe	d	12 58	13 03			13 18						13 08	13 13	13 23			13 28	13 33		13 48				
Wapping	d	13 00	13 05			13 20						13 10	13 15	13 24			13 30	13 35		13 50				
Shadwell	d	13 02	13 07			13 22						13 12	13 17	13 26			13 32	13 37		13 52				
Whitechapel	d	13 04	13 09			13 24						13 14	13 19	13 29			13 34	13 39		13 54				
Shoreditch High Street	d	13 06	13 11			13 26						13 16	13 21	13 31			13 36	13 41		13 56				
Hoxton	d	13 08	13 13			13 28						13 18	13 23	13 33			13 38	13 43		13 58				
Haggerston	d	13 10	13 15			13 30						13 20	13 25	13 35			13 40	13 45		14 00				
Dalston Junction Stn ELL	a	13 13	13 17			13 32						13 22	13 28	13 37			13 43	13 47		14 02				
Canonbury	d		13 20			13 35						13 27		13 42				13 50		14 05				
Highbury & Islington	a		13 25			13 40						13 32		13 46				13 55		14 10				
	d																							
London Bridge 4 ⊖	a			13 11				12 56		13 06	13 11					13 29			13 44			13 26		13 36

		SN	LO	LO	LO	SN	LO	LO	SN	LO		SN	SN	SE	SN	SN	LO	LO	LO	SN		LO	LO	SN	LO
East Croydon ⇌	d					13 30														14 00					
West Croydon 4 ⇌	d	13 01	13 09		13 22											13 31	13 39		13 52						
Norwood Junction 2	d		13 13		13 28	13 35											13 43		13 58	14 05					
Anerley	d		13 16		13 31	13 38											13 46		14 01	14 08					
Penge West	d		13 18		13 33	13 40											13 48		14 03	14 10					
London Victoria 15 ⊖	d								13 19					13 39	13 41									13 49	
Battersea Park 4	d								13 23						13 45									13 53	
Wandsworth Road	d														13 47										
Clapham High Street ⊖	d														13 49										
London Blackfriars 3 ⊖	d																								
Denmark Hill 4	d													13 48	13 54										
Peckham Rye 4	d	13 31										13 42	13 47	13a51	13 56	14 01									
Queens Rd Peckham	d	13 34											13 49		13 59	14 04									
South Bermondsey	d	13 36											13 52		14 01	14 06									
Clapham Junction 10	d								13 27															13 57	
Wandsworth Common	d								13 30															14 00	
Balham 4 ⊖	d								13 32															14 02	
Streatham Hill	d								13 35															14 05	
West Norwood 4	d								13 40			13 53												14 10	
Gipsy Hill	d								13 43			13 56												14 13	
Crystal Palace 4	d							13 43	13 51	13 58		13a59											14 13	14 21	14 28
Sydenham	d		13 21		13 36	13 42		13 46	13 54	14 01							13 51		14 06	14 12			14 16	14 24	14 31
Forest Hill 4	d		13 23		13 38	13 45		13 49	13 57	14 04							13 53		14 08	14 15			14 19	14 27	14 34
Honor Oak Park	d		13 26		13 41	13 47		13 51	13 59	14 06							13 56		14 11	14 17			14 21	14 29	14 36
Brockley	d		13 28		13 43	13 50		13 54	14 02	14 09							13 58		14 13	14 20			14 24	14 32	14 39
New Cross Gate 4	a		13 31		13 46	13 52		13 56	14 04	14 11							14 01		14 16	14 22			14 26	14 34	14 41
	d		13 31		13 46	13 52		13 56	14 04	14 11							14 01		14 16	14 22			14 26	14 34	14 41
New Cross ELL	d			13 36			13 51											14 06				14 21			
Surrey Quays	d		13 35	13 40	13 49		13 55	14 00		14 15							14 05	14 10	14 19			14 25	14 30		14 45
Canada Water	d		13 37	13 42	13 51		13 57	14 02		14 17							14 07	14 12	14 21			14 27	14 32		14 47
Rotherhithe	d		13 38	13 43	13 53		13 58	14 03		14 18							14 08	14 13	14 23			14 28	14 33		14 48
Wapping	d		13 40	13 45	13 54		14 00	14 05		14 20							14 10	14 15	14 24			14 30	14 35		14 50
Shadwell	d		13 42	13 47	13 56		14 02	14 07		14 22							14 12	14 17	14 26			14 32	14 37		14 52
Whitechapel	d		13 44	13 49	13 59		14 04	14 09		14 24							14 14	14 19	14 29			14 34	14 39		14 54
Shoreditch High Street	d		13 46	13 51	14 01		14 06	14 11		14 26							14 16	14 21	14 31			14 36	14 41		14 56
Hoxton	d		13 48	13 53	14 03		14 08	14 13		14 28							14 18	14 23	14 33			14 38	14 43		14 58
Haggerston	d		13 50	13 55	14 05		14 10	14 15		14 30							14 20	14 25	14 35			14 40	14 45		15 00
Dalston Junction Stn ELL	a		13 52	13 58	14 07		14 13	14 17		14 32							14 22	14 28	14 37			14 43	14 47		15 02
Canonbury	d		13 57		14 12			14 20		14 35							14 27		14 42				14 50		15 05
Highbury & Islington	a		14 02		14 16			14 25		14 40							14 32		14 46				14 55		15 10
	d																								
London Bridge 4 ⊖	a	13 41				13 59			14 11				13 56		14 06	14 11				14 29				14 41	

Table 178

Mondays to Fridays

13 August to 28 August

East London Line and Croydon - London Victoria to London Bridge

Network Diagram - see first Page of Table 177

		SN	SN	SE	SN	SN		LO	LO	LO	SN	LO	LO	SN	LO	SN		SN	SE	SN	SN	LO	LO	LO	SN
East Croydon	d										14 30														15 00
West Croydon 4	d					14 01		14 09		14 22											14 31	14 39		14 52	
Norwood Junction 2	d							14 13		14 28	14 35											14 43		14 58	15 05
Anerley	d							14 16		14 31	14 38											14 46		15 01	15 08
Penge West	d							14 18		14 33	14 40											14 48		15 03	15 10
London Victoria 15	d			14 09	14 11									14 19					14 39	14 41					
Battersea Park 4	d				14 15									14 23						14 45					
Wandsworth Road	d				14 17															14 47					
Clapham High Street	d				14 19															14 49					
London Blackfriars 3	d																								
Denmark Hill 4	d			14 18	14 24														14 48	14 54					
Peckham Rye 4	d	14 12	14 17	14a21	14 26	14 31										14 42		14 47	14a51	14 56	15 01				
Queens Rd Peckham	d		14 19		14 29	14 34												14 49		14 59	15 04				
South Bermondsey	d		14 22		14 31	14 36												14 52		15 01	15 06				
Clapham Junction 10	d													14 27											
Wandsworth Common	d													14 30											
Balham 4	d													14 32											
Streatham Hill	d													14 35											
West Norwood 4	d	14 23												14 40		14 53									
Gipsy Hill	d	14 26												14 43		14 56									
Crystal Palace 4	d	14a29											14 43	14 51	14 58	14a59									
Sydenham	d							14 21		14 36	14 42		14 46	14 54	15 01							14 51		15 06	15 12
Forest Hill 4	d							14 23		14 38	14 45		14 49	14 57	15 04							14 53		15 08	15 15
Honor Oak Park	d							14 26		14 41	14 47		14 51	14 59	15 06							14 56		15 11	15 17
Brockley	d							14 28		14 43	14 50		14 54	15 02	15 09							14 58		15 13	15 20
New Cross Gate 4	a							14 31		14 46	14 52		14 56	15 04	15 11							15 01		15 16	15 22
	d							14 31		14 46	14 52		14 56	15 04	15 11							15 01		15 16	15 22
New Cross ELL	d								14 36			14 51											15 06		
Surrey Quays	d							14 35	14 40	14 49		14 55	15 00		15 15							15 05	15 10	15 19	
Canada Water	d							14 37	14 42	14 51		14 57	15 02		15 17							15 07	15 12	15 21	
Rotherhithe	d							14 38	14 43	14 53		14 58	15 03		15 18							15 08	15 13	15 23	
Wapping	d							14 40	14 45	14 54		15 00	15 05		15 20							15 10	15 15	15 24	
Shadwell	d							14 42	14 47	14 56		15 02	15 07		15 22							15 12	15 17	15 26	
Whitechapel	d							14 44	14 49	14 59		15 04	15 09		15 24							15 14	15 19	15 29	
Shoreditch High Street	d							14 46	14 51	15 01		15 06	15 11		15 26							15 16	15 21	15 31	
Hoxton	d							14 48	14 53	15 03		15 08	15 13		15 28							15 18	15 23	15 33	
Haggerston	d							14 50	14 55	15 05		15 10	15 15		15 30							15 20	15 25	15 35	
Dalston Junction Stn ELL	a							14 52	14 58	15 07		15 13	15 17		15 32							15 22	15 28	15 37	
Canonbury	d							14 57		15 12			15 20		15 35							15 27		15 42	
Highbury & Islington	a							15 02		15 16			15 25		15 40							15 32		15 46	
	d																								
London Bridge 4	a		14 26		14 36	14 41					14 59			15 11				14 56		15 06	15 11				15 29

		LO		LO	SN	LO	SN	SN	SE	SN	SN	LO		LO	LO	SN	LO	LO	SN	LO	SN	SN		SE	SN
East Croydon	d															15 30									
West Croydon 4	d										15 01	15 09			15 22										
Norwood Junction 2	d											15 13			15 28	15 35									
Anerley	d											15 16			15 31	15 38									
Penge West	d											15 18			15 33	15 40									
London Victoria 15	d				14 49				15 09	15 11									15 19					15 39	15 41
Battersea Park 4	d				14 53					15 15									15 23						15 45
Wandsworth Road	d									15 17															15 47
Clapham High Street	d									15 19															15 49
London Blackfriars 3	d																								
Denmark Hill 4	d								15 18	15 24														15 48	15 54
Peckham Rye 4	d						15 12	15 17	15a21	15 26	15 31										15 42	15 47		15a51	15 56
Queens Rd Peckham	d							15 19		15 29	15 34											15 49			15 59
South Bermondsey	d							15 22		15 31	15 36											15 52			16 01
Clapham Junction 10	d				14 57														15 27						
Wandsworth Common	d				15 00														15 30						
Balham 4	d				15 02														15 32						
Streatham Hill	d				15 05														15 35						
West Norwood 4	d				15 10		15 23												15 40		15 53				
Gipsy Hill	d				15 13		15 26												15 43		15 56				
Crystal Palace 4	d			15 13	15 21	15 28	15a29											15 43	15 51	15 58	15a59				
Sydenham	d			15 16	15 24	15 31						15 21			15 36	15 42		15 46	15 54	16 01					
Forest Hill 4	d			15 19	15 27	15 34						15 23			15 38	15 45		15 49	15 57	16 04					
Honor Oak Park	d			15 21	15 29	15 36						15 26			15 41	15 47		15 51	15 59	16 06					
Brockley	d			15 24	15 32	15 39						15 28			15 43	15 50		15 54	16 02	16 09					
New Cross Gate 4	a			15 26	15 34	15 41						15 31			15 46	15 52		15 56	16 04	16 11					
	d			15 26	15 34	15 41						15 31			15 46	15 52		15 56	16 04	16 11					
New Cross ELL	d	15 21												15 36			15 51								
Surrey Quays	d	15 25		15 30		15 45						15 35		15 40	15 49		15 55	16 00		16 15					
Canada Water	d	15 27		15 32		15 47						15 37		15 42	15 51		15 57	16 02		16 17					
Rotherhithe	d	15 28		15 33		15 48						15 38		15 43	15 53		15 58	16 03		16 18					
Wapping	d	15 30		15 35		15 50						15 40		15 45	15 54		16 00	16 05		16 20					
Shadwell	d	15 32		15 37		15 52						15 42		15 47	15 56		16 02	16 07		16 22					
Whitechapel	d	15 34		15 39		15 54						15 44		15 49	15 59		16 04	16 09		16 24					
Shoreditch High Street	d	15 36		15 41		15 56						15 46		15 51	16 01		16 06	16 11		16 26					
Hoxton	d	15 38		15 43		15 58						15 48		15 53	16 03		16 08	16 13		16 28					
Haggerston	d	15 40		15 45		16 00						15 50		15 55	16 05		16 10	16 15		16 30					
Dalston Junction Stn ELL	a	15 43		15 47		16 02						15 52		15 58	16 07		16 13	16 17		16 32					
Canonbury	d			15 50		16 05						15 57			16 12			16 20		16 35					
Highbury & Islington	a			15 55		16 10						16 02			16 16			16 25		16 40					
	d																								
London Bridge 4	a				15 41			15 26		15 36	15 41					15 59			16 11			15 56			16 06

Table 178

Mondays to Fridays

13 August to 28 August

East London Line and Croydon - London Victoria to London Bridge

Network Diagram - see first Page of Table 177

		SN	LO	LO	LO	SN	SN	LO		LO	SN	LO	SN	SN	SE	SN	SN	LO		LO	LO	SN	LO	LO	SN
East Croydon	d						16 00															16 30			
West Croydon [4]	d	15 31	15 39		15 52												16 01	16 09			16 22				
Norwood Junction [2]	d		15 43		15 58		16 05											16 13			16 28	16 35			
Anerley	d		15 46		16 01		16 08											16 16			16 31	16 38			
Penge West	d		15 48		16 03		16 10											16 18			16 33	16 40			
London Victoria [15] ⊖	d										15 49				16 09	16 11									16 19
Battersea Park [4]	d										15 53					16 15									16 23
Wandsworth Road	d															16 17									
Clapham High Street ⊖	d															16 19									
London Blackfriars [3] ⊖	d																								
Denmark Hill [4]	d														16 18	16 24									
Peckham Rye [4]	d	16 01				16 07							16 12	16 17	16a21	16 26	16 31								
Queens Rd Peckham	d	16 04				16 10								16 19		16 29	16 34								
South Bermondsey	d	16 06				16 12								16 22		16 31	16 36								
Clapham Junction [10]	d										15 57														16 27
Wandsworth Common	d										16 00														16 30
Balham [4] ⊖	d										16 02														16 32
Streatham Hill	d										16 05														16 35
West Norwood [4]	d										16 10		16 23												16 39
Gipsy Hill	d										16 13		16 26												16 44
Crystal Palace [4]	d									16 13	16 21	16 28	16a29											16 43	16 50
Sydenham	d		15 51		16 06		16 12			16 16	16 24	16 31						16 21			16 36	16 42		16 46	16 54
Forest Hill [4]	d		15 53		16 08		16 15			16 19	16 27	16 34						16 23			16 38	16 45		16 49	16 56
Honor Oak Park	d		15 56		16 11		16 17			16 21	16 29	16 36						16 26			16 41	16 47		16 51	16 59
Brockley	d		15 58		16 13		16 20			16 24	16 32	16 39						16 28			16 43	16 50		16 54	17 01
New Cross Gate [4]	a		16 01		16 16		16 22			16 26	16 34	16 41						16 31			16 46	16 52		16 56	17 04
	d		16 01		16 16		16 22			16 26	16 34	16 41						16 31			16 46	16 52		16 56	17 04
New Cross ELL	d			16 06				16 21												16 36			16 51		
Surrey Quays	d		16 05	16 10	16 19			16 25		16 30		16 45						16 35		16 40	16 49		16 55	17 00	
Canada Water	d		16 07	16 12	16 21			16 27		16 32		16 47						16 37		16 42	16 51		16 57	17 02	
Rotherhithe	d		16 08	16 13	16 23			16 28		16 33		16 48						16 38		16 43	16 53		16 58	17 03	
Wapping	d		16 10	16 15	16 24			16 30		16 35		16 50						16 40		16 45	16 54		17 00	17 05	
Shadwell	d		16 12	16 17	16 26			16 32		16 37		16 52						16 42		16 47	16 56		17 02	17 07	
Whitechapel	d		16 14	16 19	16 29			16 34		16 39		16 54						16 44		16 49	16 59		17 04	17 09	
Shoreditch High Street	d		16 16	16 21	16 31			16 36		16 41		16 56						16 46		16 51	17 01		17 06	17 11	
Hoxton	d		16 18	16 23	16 33			16 38		16 43		16 58						16 48		16 53	17 03		17 08	17 13	
Haggerston	d		16 20	16 25	16 35			16 40		16 45		17 00						16 50		16 55	17 05		17 10	17 15	
Dalston Junction Stn ELL	a		16 22	16 28	16 37			16 43		16 47		17 02						16 52		16 58	17 07		17 13	17 17	
Canonbury	d		16 27		16 42					16 50		17 05						16 57			17 12			17 20	
Highbury & Islington	a		16 32		16 46					16 55		17 10						17 02			17 16			17 25	
	d																								
London Bridge [4] ⊖	a	16 11				16 17	16 29				16 41			16 26		16 38	16 41					17 02			17 12

		LO	SN	SN		SE	SN	SN	LO	LO	LO	SN	LO	LO		SN	SN	SE	SN	SN	SN	LO	SN	SN	
East Croydon	d											17 00													
West Croydon [4]	d							16 31	16 39		16 52										17 01	17 09	17 12		
Norwood Junction [2]	d								16 43		16 58	17 05										17 13			
Anerley	d								16 46		17 01	17 08										17 16			
Penge West	d								16 48		17 03	17 10										17 18			
London Victoria [15] ⊖	d					16 39	16 41									16 49		17 04		17 11					
Battersea Park [4]	d						16 45									16 53				17 15					
Wandsworth Road	d						16 47													17 17					
Clapham High Street ⊖	d						16 49													17 19					
London Blackfriars [3] ⊖	d																								
Denmark Hill [4]	d					16 48	16 54											17 13		17 24					
Peckham Rye [4]	d		16 42	16 47		16a51	16 56	17 00									17 07	17a16	17 17	17 26	17 29			17 35	
Queens Rd Peckham	d			16 49			16 59	17 03											17 19	17 29	17 32			17 37	
South Bermondsey	d			16 52			17 01	17 05											17 22	17 31	17 34			17 40	
Clapham Junction [10]	d															16 57									
Wandsworth Common	d															17 00									
Balham [4] ⊖	d															17 03									
Streatham Hill	d															17 06									
West Norwood [4]	d		16 53													17 09	17 20								
Gipsy Hill	d		16 56													17 12	17 23								
Crystal Palace [4]	d	16 58	16a59											17 13		17 21	17a26								
Sydenham	d	17 01							16 51		17 06	17 12		17 16		17 24						17 21			
Forest Hill [4]	d	17 04							16 53		17 08	17 15		17 19		17 27						17 23			
Honor Oak Park	d	17 06							16 56		17 11	17 17		17 21		17 29						17 26			
Brockley	d	17 09							16 58		17 13	17 20		17 24		17 32						17 28			
New Cross Gate [4]	a	17 11							17 01		17 16	17 22		17 26		17 34						17 31			
	d	17 11							17 01		17 16	17 22		17 26		17 34						17 31			
New Cross ELL	d									17 06			17 21												
Surrey Quays	d	17 15							17 05	17 10	17 19		17 25	17 30								17 35			
Canada Water	d	17 17							17 07	17 12	17 21		17 27	17 32								17 37			
Rotherhithe	d	17 18							17 08	17 13	17 23		17 28	17 33								17 38			
Wapping	d	17 20							17 10	17 15	17 24		17 30	17 35								17 40			
Shadwell	d	17 22							17 12	17 17	17 26		17 32	17 37								17 42			
Whitechapel	d	17 24							17 14	17 19	17 29		17 34	17 39								17 44			
Shoreditch High Street	d	17 26							17 16	17 21	17 31		17 36	17 41								17 46			
Hoxton	d	17 28							17 18	17 23	17 33		17 38	17 43								17 48			
Haggerston	d	17 30							17 20	17 25	17 35		17 40	17 45								17 50			
Dalston Junction Stn ELL	a	17 32							17 22	17 28	17 37		17 43	17 47								17 52			
Canonbury	d	17 35							17 27		17 42			17 50								17 57			
Highbury & Islington	a	17 40							17 32		17 46			17 55								18 02			
	d																								
London Bridge [4] ⊖	a			16 56			17 08	17 10				17 35				17 43			17 27	17 38	17 40		17 28	17 44	

13 August to 28 August

East London Line and Croydon - London Victoria to London Bridge

Network Diagram - see first Page of Table 177

		LO	LO	LO	LO	LO	SN	SN	SE	SN	SN	SN	SN	LO	SN	LO	LO	LO	SN	LO	LO	SN	SN
East Croydon	d										17 30												
West Croydon 4	d			17 22									17 31	17 39	17 42			17 52					
Norwood Junction 2	d			17 28						17 32	17 35			17 43				17 58	18 04				
Anerley	d			17 31							17 38			17 46				18 01	18 07				
Penge West	d			17 33							17 40			17 48				18 03	18 09				
London Victoria 15 ⊖	d						17 22		17 34			17 41										17 52	
Battersea Park 4	d						17 26					17 45										17 56	
Wandsworth Road	d											17 47											
Clapham High Street ⊖	d											17 49											
London Blackfriars 3 ⊖	d																						
Denmark Hill 4	d								17 43			17 54											
Peckham Rye 4	d							17 37	17a46	17 53		17 57	18 01										18 07
Queens Rd Peckham	d									17 55		17 59	18 04										
South Bermondsey	d									17 58		18 02	18 06										
Clapham Junction 10	d						17 30															18 00	
Wandsworth Common	d						17 33															18 03	
Balham 4 ⊖	d						17 35															18 05	
Streatham Hill	d						17 38															18 08	
West Norwood 4	d						17 42	17 49														18 14	18 20
Gipsy Hill	d						17 45	17 52														18 17	18 23
Crystal Palace 4	d		17 28			17 43	17 48	17a54									17 58				18 13	18 20	18a26
Sydenham	d		17 31	17 36		17 46	17 54				17 42			17 51			18 01	18 06	18 11		18 16	18 24	
Forest Hill 4	d		17 34	17 38		17 49	17 57				17 45			17 53			18 04	18 08	18 14		18 19	18 27	
Honor Oak Park	d		17 36	17 41		17 51	17 59				17 47			17 56			18 06	18 11	18 16		18 21	18 29	
Brockley	d		17 39	17 43		17 54	18 02				17 50			17 58			18 09	18 13	18 19		18 24	18 32	
New Cross Gate 4	a		17 41	17 46		17 56	18 04				17 52			18 01			18 11	18 16	18 21		18 26	18 34	
	d		17 41	17 46		17 56	18 04				17 52			18 01			18 11	18 16	18 21		18 26	18 34	
New Cross ELL	d	17 36			17 51											18 06				18 21			
Surrey Quays	d	17 40	17 45	17 49	17 55	18 00								18 05		18 10	18 15	18 19		18 25	18 30		
Canada Water	d	17 42	17 47	17 51	17 57	18 02								18 07		18 12	18 17	18 21		18 27	18 32		
Rotherhithe	d	17 43	17 48	17 53	17 58	18 03								18 08		18 13	18 18	18 23		18 28	18 33		
Wapping	d	17 45	17 50	17 54	18 00	18 05								18 10		18 15	18 20	18 24		18 30	18 35		
Shadwell	d	17 47	17 52	17 56	18 02	18 07								18 12		18 17	18 22	18 26		18 32	18 37		
Whitechapel	d	17 49	17 54	17 59	18 04	18 09								18 14		18 19	18 24	18 29		18 34	18 39		
Shoreditch High Street	d	17 51	17 56	18 01	18 06	18 11								18 16		18 21	18 26	18 31		18 36	18 41		
Hoxton	d	17 53	17 58	18 03	18 08	18 13								18 18		18 23	18 28	18 33		18 38	18 43		
Haggerston	d	17 55	18 00	18 05	18 10	18 15								18 20		18 25	18 30	18 35		18 40	18 45		
Dalston Junction Stn ELL	a	17 58	18 02	18 07	18 13	18 17								18 23		18 28	18 32	18 37		18 43	18 47		
Canonbury	d		18 05	18 12		18 20								18 27			18 35	18 42			18 50		
Highbury & Islington	a		18 10	18 16		18 25								18 32			18 40	18 46			18 55		
	d																						
London Bridge 4 ⊖	a						18 13			18 02	17 59	18 08	18 11		18 00				18 31			18 45	

		SE	SN	SN	SN	LO	SN	LO	LO	LO	LO	SE	SN	SN	SN	LO	SN	SN	SE	SN	SN	LO	LO
East Croydon	d														18 30								
West Croydon 4	d				18 01	18 09	18 13			18 22											18 31	18 39	
Norwood Junction 2	d					18 13				18 28					18 35							18 43	
Anerley	d					18 16				18 31					18 38							18 46	
Penge West	d					18 18				18 33					18 40							18 48	
London Victoria 15 ⊖	d	17 56		18 11								18 18					18 22		18 39	18 41			
Battersea Park 4	d			18 15													18 26			18 45			
Wandsworth Road	d			18 17																18 47			
Clapham High Street ⊖	d			18 19																18 49			
London Blackfriars 3 ⊖	d																						
Denmark Hill 4	d	18 06		18 24								18 28							18 48	18 54			
Peckham Rye 4	d	18a08	18 12	18 26	18 29							18a31	18 32	18 36				18 37	18a51	18 57	19 01		
Queens Rd Peckham	d		18 15	18 29	18 32								18 35	18 38						19 00	19 04		
South Bermondsey	d		18 17	18 31	18 34								18 37	18 41						19 02	19 06		
Clapham Junction 10	d																18 30						
Wandsworth Common	d																18 33						
Balham 4 ⊖	d																18 35						
Streatham Hill	d																18 38						
West Norwood 4	d																18 42	18 51					
Gipsy Hill	d																18 45	18 54					
Crystal Palace 4	d								18 28							18 43	18 51	18a57					
Sydenham	d					18 21			18 31	18 36					18 42	18 46	18 54					18 51	
Forest Hill 4	d					18 23			18 34	18 38					18 45	18 49	18 57					18 53	
Honor Oak Park	d					18 26			18 36	18 41					18 47	18 51	18 59					18 56	
Brockley	d					18 28			18 39	18 43					18 50	18 54	19 02					18 58	
New Cross Gate 4	a					18 31			18 41	18 46					18 52	18 56	19 04					19 01	
	d					18 31			18 41	18 46					18 52	18 56	19 04					19 01	
New Cross ELL	d							18 36			18 51												19 06
Surrey Quays	d					18 35		18 40	18 45	18 49	18 55					19 00						19 05	19 10
Canada Water	d					18 37		18 42	18 47	18 51	18 57					19 02						19 07	19 12
Rotherhithe	d					18 38		18 43	18 48	18 53	18 58					19 03						19 08	19 13
Wapping	d					18 40		18 45	18 50	18 54	19 00					19 05						19 10	19 15
Shadwell	d					18 42		18 47	18 52	18 56	19 02					19 07						19 12	19 17
Whitechapel	d					18 44		18 49	18 54	18 59	19 04					19 09						19 14	19 19
Shoreditch High Street	d					18 46		18 51	18 56	19 01	19 06					19 11						19 16	19 21
Hoxton	d					18 48		18 53	18 58	19 03	19 08					19 13						19 18	19 23
Haggerston	d					18 50		18 55	19 00	19 05	19 10					19 15						19 20	19 25
Dalston Junction Stn ELL	a					18 52		18 58	19 02	19 07	19 13					19 17						19 22	19 28
Canonbury	d					18 57			19 05	19 12						19 20						19 27	
Highbury & Islington	a					19 02			19 10	19 16						19 25						19 32	
	d																						
London Bridge 4 ⊖	a		18 22	18 38	18 39		18 29						18 42	18 45	18 59		19 13			19 09	19 11		

Table 178

Mondays to Fridays

13 August to 28 August

East London Line and Croydon - London Victoria to London Bridge

Network Diagram - see first Page of Table 177

		LO		LO	SN	LO	LO	SN	SN	SN	SN	LO	
East Croydon	d				19 00								
West Croydon 4	d			18 52									
Norwood Junction 2	d			18 58	19 05								
Anerley	d			19 01	19 08								
Penge West	d			19 03	19 10								
London Victoria 15 ⊖	d							18 52					
Battersea Park 4	d							18 56					
Wandsworth Road	d												
Clapham High Street ⊖	d												
London Blackfriars 3 ⊖	d												
Denmark Hill 4	d												
Peckham Rye 4	d								19 06	19 07	19 14		
Queens Rd Peckham	d									19 10	19 17		
South Bermondsey	d									19 12	19 19		
Clapham Junction 10	d							19 00					
Wandsworth Common	d							19 03					
Balham 4 ⊖	d							19 05					
Streatham Hill	d							19 08					
West Norwood 4	d							19 12	19 17				
Gipsy Hill	d							19 15	19 20				
Crystal Palace 4	d	18 58					19 13	19 21	19a23			19 28	
Sydenham	d	19 01		19 06	19 12		19 16	19 24				19 31	
Forest Hill 4	d	19 04		19 08	19 15		19 19	19 27				19 34	
Honor Oak Park	d	19 06		19 11	19 17		19 21	19 29				19 36	
Brockley	d	19 09		19 13	19 20		19 24	19 32				19 39	
New Cross Gate 4	a	19 11		19 16	19 22		19 26	19 34				19 41	
	d	19 11		19 16	19 22		19 26	19 34				19 41	
New Cross ELL	d					19 21							
Surrey Quays	d	19 15		19 19		19 25	19 30					19 45	
Canada Water	d	19 17		19 21		19 27	19 32					19 47	
Rotherhithe	d	19 18		19 23		19 28	19 33					19 48	
Wapping	d	19 20		19 24		19 30	19 35					19 50	
Shadwell	d	19 22		19 26		19 32	19 37					19 52	
Whitechapel	d	19 24		19 29		19 34	19 39					19 54	
Shoreditch High Street	d	19 26		19 31		19 36	19 41					19 56	
Hoxton	d	19 28		19 33		19 38	19 43					19 58	
Haggerston	d	19 30		19 35		19 40	19 45					20 00	
Dalston Junction Stn ELL	a	19 32		19 37		19 43	19 47					20 02	
Canonbury	d	19 35		19 42			19 50					20 05	
Highbury & Islington	a	19 40		19 46			19 55					20 10	
	d												
London Bridge 4 ⊖	a				19 29			19 41		19 17	19 24		

		SN	SE	SN	SN	LO	LO	LO	SN	LO		LO	SN
East Croydon	d								19 30				
West Croydon 4	d				19 01	19 09		19 22					
Norwood Junction 2	d					19 13		19 28	19 35				
Anerley	d					19 16		19 31	19 38				
Penge West	d					19 18		19 33	19 40				
London Victoria 15 ⊖	d		19 09	19 11									19 22
Battersea Park 4	d			19 15									19 26
Wandsworth Road	d			19 17									
Clapham High Street ⊖	d			19 19									
London Blackfriars 3 ⊖	d												
Denmark Hill 4	d		19 18	19 24									
Peckham Rye 4	d	19 17	19a21	19 26	19 29								
Queens Rd Peckham	d			19 29	19 32								
South Bermondsey	d			19 31	19 34								
Clapham Junction 10	d												19 30
Wandsworth Common	d												19 33
Balham 4 ⊖	d												19 35
Streatham Hill	d												19 38
West Norwood 4	d	19 30											19 42
Gipsy Hill	d	19 33											19 45
Crystal Palace 4	d	19a35										19 43	19 51
Sydenham	d					19 21		19 36	19 42			19 46	19 54
Forest Hill 4	d					19 23		19 38	19 45			19 49	19 57
Honor Oak Park	d					19 26		19 41	19 47			19 51	19 59
Brockley	d					19 28		19 43	19 50			19 54	20 02
New Cross Gate 4	a					19 31		19 46	19 52			19 56	20 04
	d					19 31		19 46	19 52			19 56	20 04
New Cross ELL	d						19 36			19 51			
Surrey Quays	d					19 35	19 40	19 49		19 55		20 00	
Canada Water	d					19 37	19 42	19 51		19 57		20 02	
Rotherhithe	d					19 38	19 43	19 53		19 58		20 03	
Wapping	d					19 40	19 45	19 54		20 00		20 05	
Shadwell	d					19 42	19 47	19 56		20 02		20 07	
Whitechapel	d					19 44	19 49	19 59		20 04		20 09	
Shoreditch High Street	d					19 46	19 51	20 01		20 06		20 11	
Hoxton	d					19 48	19 53	20 03		20 08		20 13	
Haggerston	d					19 50	19 55	20 05		20 10		20 15	
Dalston Junction Stn ELL	a					19 52	19 58	20 07		20 13		20 17	
Canonbury	d					19 57		20 12				20 20	
Highbury & Islington	a					20 02		20 16				20 25	
	d												
London Bridge 4 ⊖	a			19 36	19 41				19 59				20 11

		SN	SN	LO	SN	SN	SE	SN		SN	LO	LO	LO
East Croydon	d												
West Croydon 4	d									19 31	19 39		19 52
Norwood Junction 2	d										19 43		19 58
Anerley	d										19 46		20 01
Penge West	d										19 48		20 03
London Victoria 15 ⊖	d						19 39	19 41					
Battersea Park 4	d							19 45					
Wandsworth Road	d							19 47					
Clapham High Street ⊖	d							19 49					
London Blackfriars 3 ⊖	d												
Denmark Hill 4	d						19 48	19 54					
Peckham Rye 4	d	19 37	19 38		19 47	19 49	19a51	19 56		20 01			
Queens Rd Peckham	d		19 41			19 51		19 59		20 04			
South Bermondsey	d		19 43			19 54		20 01		20 06			
Clapham Junction 10	d												
Wandsworth Common	d												
Balham 4 ⊖	d												
Streatham Hill	d												
West Norwood 4	d	19 49			20 00								
Gipsy Hill	d	19 52			20 03								
Crystal Palace 4	d	19a54		19 58	20a05								
Sydenham	d			20 01							19 51		20 06
Forest Hill 4	d			20 04							19 53		20 08
Honor Oak Park	d			20 06							19 56		20 11
Brockley	d			20 09							19 58		20 13
New Cross Gate 4	a			20 11							20 01		20 16
	d			20 11							20 01		20 16
New Cross ELL	d											20 06	
Surrey Quays	d			20 15							20 05	20 10	20 19
Canada Water	d			20 17							20 07	20 12	20 21
Rotherhithe	d			20 18							20 08	20 13	20 23
Wapping	d			20 20							20 10	20 15	20 24
Shadwell	d			20 22							20 12	20 17	20 26
Whitechapel	d			20 24							20 14	20 19	20 29
Shoreditch High Street	d			20 26							20 16	20 21	20 31
Hoxton	d			20 28							20 18	20 23	20 33
Haggerston	d			20 30							20 20	20 25	20 35
Dalston Junction Stn ELL	a			20 32							20 22	20 28	20 37
Canonbury	d			20 35							20 27		20 42
Highbury & Islington	a			20 40							20 32		20 46
	d												
London Bridge 4 ⊖	a		19 51			19 58		20 06		20 14			

		SN	LO	LO	SN	LO		SN	SN	SN	SN	LO	LO
East Croydon	d	20 00											
West Croydon 4	d										20 01	20 09	
Norwood Junction 2	d	20 05										20 13	
Anerley	d	20 08										20 16	
Penge West	d	20 10										20 18	
London Victoria 15 ⊖	d				19 52					20 11			
Battersea Park 4	d				19 56					20 15			
Wandsworth Road	d									20 17			
Clapham High Street ⊖	d									20 19			
London Blackfriars 3 ⊖	d												
Denmark Hill 4	d									20 24			
Peckham Rye 4	d							20 12	20 18	20 26	20 31		
Queens Rd Peckham	d								20 21	20 29	20 34		
South Bermondsey	d								20 23	20 31	20 36		
Clapham Junction 10	d				20 00								
Wandsworth Common	d				20 03								
Balham 4 ⊖	d				20 05								
Streatham Hill	d				20 08								
West Norwood 4	d				20 12			20 24					
Gipsy Hill	d				20 15			20 27					
Crystal Palace 4	d			20 13	20 21	20 28		20a29					
Sydenham	d	20 12		20 16	20 24	20 31						20 21	
Forest Hill 4	d	20 15		20 19	20 27	20 34						20 23	
Honor Oak Park	d	20 17		20 21	20 29	20 36						20 26	
Brockley	d	20 20		20 24	20 32	20 39						20 28	
New Cross Gate 4	a	20 22		20 26	20 34	20 41						20 31	
	d	20 22		20 26	20 34	20 41						20 31	
New Cross ELL	d		20 21										20 36
Surrey Quays	d		20 25	20 30		20 45						20 35	20 40
Canada Water	d		20 27	20 32		20 47						20 37	20 42
Rotherhithe	d		20 28	20 33		20 48						20 38	20 43
Wapping	d		20 30	20 35		20 50						20 40	20 45
Shadwell	d		20 32	20 37		20 52						20 42	20 47
Whitechapel	d		20 34	20 39		20 54						20 44	20 49
Shoreditch High Street	d		20 36	20 41		20 56						20 46	20 51
Hoxton	d		20 38	20 43		20 58						20 48	20 53
Haggerston	d		20 40	20 45		21 00						20 50	20 55
Dalston Junction Stn ELL	a		20 43	20 47		21 02						20 52	20 58
Canonbury	d			20 50		21 05						20 57	
Highbury & Islington	a			20 55		21 10						21 02	
	d												
London Bridge 4 ⊖	a	20 29			20 41				20 28	20 36	20 41		

13 August to 28 August

East London Line and Croydon - London Victoria to London Bridge

Network Diagram - see first Page of Table 177

Station		LO	SN	LO		LO	SN	LO	SN	SN	SN	SN	LO	LO		LO	SN	LO	LO	SN	LO	SN	SN	SN	
East Croydon	d		20 31														21 00								
West Croydon 4	d	20 22										20 31	20 39			20 52									
Norwood Junction 2	d	20 28	20 35										20 43			20 58	21 05								
Anerley	d	20 31	20 38										20 46			21 01	21 08								
Penge West	d	20 33	20 40										20 48			21 03	21 10								
London Victoria 15 ⊖	d						20 22				20 41									20 52				21 11	
Battersea Park 4	d						20 26				20 45									20 56				21 15	
Wandsworth Road	d										20 47													21 17	
Clapham High Street ⊖	d										20 49													21 19	
London Blackfriars 3 ⊖	d																								
Denmark Hill 4	d										20 54													21 24	
Peckham Rye 4	d								20 42	20 48	20 56	21 01										21 12	21 17	21 26	
Queens Rd Peckham	d									20 50	20 59	21 04											21 19	21 29	
South Bermondsey	d									20 53	21 01	21 06											21 22	21 31	
Clapham Junction 10	d						20 30													21 00					
Wandsworth Common	d						20 33													21 03					
Balham 4 ⊖	d						20 35													21 05					
Streatham Hill	d						20 38													21 08					
West Norwood 4	d						20 42		20 54											21 12		21 24			
Gipsy Hill	d						20 45		20 57											21 15		21 27			
Crystal Palace 4	d					20 43	20 51	20 58	20a59										21 13	21 21	21 28	21a29			
Sydenham	d	20 36	20 42			20 46	20 54	21 01					20 51			21 06	21 12		21 16	21 27	21 31				
Forest Hill 4	d	20 38	20 45			20 49	20 57	21 04					20 53			21 08	21 15		21 19	21 29	21 34				
Honor Oak Park	d	20 41	20 47			20 51	20 59	21 06					20 56			21 11	21 17		21 21	21 32	21 36				
Brockley	d	20 43	20 50			20 54	21 02	21 09					20 58			21 13	21 20		21 24	21 34	21 39				
New Cross Gate 4	a	20 46	20 52			20 56	21 04	21 11					21 01			21 16	21 22		21 26	21 37	21 41				
	d	20 46	20 52			20 56	21 04	21 11					21 01			21 16	21 22		21 26	21 37	21 41				
New Cross ELL	d			20 51										21 06				21 21							
Surrey Quays	d	20 49		20 55		21 00		21 15					21 05	21 10		21 19		21 25	21 30		21 45				
Canada Water	d	20 51		20 57		21 02		21 17					21 07	21 12		21 21		21 27	21 32		21 47				
Rotherhithe	d	20 53		20 58		21 03		21 18					21 08	21 13		21 23		21 28	21 33		21 48				
Wapping	d	20 54		21 00		21 05		21 20					21 10	21 15		21 24		21 30	21 35		21 50				
Shadwell	d	20 56		21 02		21 07		21 22					21 12	21 17		21 26		21 32	21 37		21 52				
Whitechapel	d	20 59		21 04		21 09		21 24					21 14	21 19		21 29		21 34	21 39		21 54				
Shoreditch High Street	d	21 01		21 06		21 11		21 26					21 16	21 21		21 31		21 36	21 41		21 56				
Hoxton	d	21 03		21 08		21 13		21 28					21 18	21 23		21 33		21 38	21 43		21 58				
Haggerston	d	21 05		21 10		21 15		21 30					21 20	21 25		21 35		21 40	21 45		22 00				
Dalston Junction Stn ELL	a	21 07		21 13		21 17		21 32					21 22	21 28		21 37		21 43	21 47		22 02				
Canonbury	d	21 12				21 20		21 35					21 27			21 42			21 50		22 05				
Highbury & Islington	a	21 16				21 25		21 40					21 32			21 46			21 55		22 10				
	d																								
London Bridge 4 ⊖	a		20 59				21 11			20 57	21 06	21 11					21 29			21 43			21 26	21 36	

Station		SN	LO	LO	LO	SN	LO	LO	SN	LO		SN	SN	SE	SN	SN	LO	LO	LO	SN		LO	SN	LO	SN
East Croydon	d					21 30														22 00					
West Croydon 4	d	21 01	21 09		21 22											21 31	21 39		21 52						
Norwood Junction 2	d		21 13		21 28	21 35											21 43		21 58	22 05					
Anerley	d		21 16		21 31	21 38											21 46		22 01	22 08					
Penge West	d		21 18		21 33	21 40											21 48		22 03	22 10					
London Victoria 15 ⊖	d								21 23						21 41								21 52		
Battersea Park 4	d								21 27						21 45								21 56		
Wandsworth Road	d														21 47										
Clapham High Street ⊖	d														21 49										
London Blackfriars 3 ⊖	d													21 42											
Denmark Hill 4	d													21 52	21 54										
Peckham Rye 4	d	21 31										21 42	21 47	21a55	21 56	22 01									22 12
Queens Rd Peckham	d	21 34											21 49		21 59	22 04									
South Bermondsey	d	21 36											21 52		22 01	22 06									
Clapham Junction 10	d								21 31														22 00		
Wandsworth Common	d								21 34														22 03		
Balham 4 ⊖	d								21 36														22 05		
Streatham Hill	d								21 39														22 08		
West Norwood 4	d								21 43			21 54											22 12		22 24
Gipsy Hill	d								21 46			21 57											22 15		22 27
Crystal Palace 4	d							21 43	21 51	21 58		21a59										22 13	22 21	22 28	22a29
Sydenham	d		21 21		21 36	21 42		21 46	21 54	22 01							21 51		22 06	22 12		22 16	22 24	22 31	
Forest Hill 4	d		21 23		21 38	21 45		21 49	21 57	22 04							21 53		22 08	22 15		22 19	22 27	22 34	
Honor Oak Park	d		21 26		21 41	21 47		21 51	21 59	22 06							21 56		22 11	22 17		22 21	22 29	22 36	
Brockley	d		21 28		21 43	21 50		21 54	22 02	22 09							21 58		22 13	22 20		22 24	22 32	22 39	
New Cross Gate 4	a		21 31		21 46	21 52		21 56	22 04	22 11							22 01		22 16	22 22		22 26	22 34	22 41	
	d		21 31		21 46	21 52		21 56	22 04	22 11							22 01		22 16	22 22		22 26	22 34	22 41	
New Cross ELL	d			21 36			21 51											22 06							
Surrey Quays	d		21 35	21 40	21 49		21 55	22 00		22 15							22 05	22 10	22 19			22 30		22 45	
Canada Water	d		21 37	21 42	21 51		21 57	22 02		22 17							22 07	22 12	22 21			22 32		22 47	
Rotherhithe	d		21 38	21 43	21 53		21 58	22 03		22 18							22 08	22 13	22 23			22 33		22 48	
Wapping	d		21 40	21 45	21 54		22 00	22 05		22 20							22 10	22 15	22 24			22 35		22 50	
Shadwell	d		21 42	21 47	21 56		22 02	22 07		22 22							22 12	22 17	22 26			22 37		22 52	
Whitechapel	d		21 44	21 49	21 59		22 04	22 09		22 24							22 14	22 19	22 29			22 39		22 54	
Shoreditch High Street	d		21 46	21 51	22 01		22 06	22 11		22 26							22 16	22 21	22 31			22 41		22 56	
Hoxton	d		21 48	21 53	22 03		22 08	22 13		22 28							22 18	22 23	22 33			22 43		22 58	
Haggerston	d		21 50	21 55	22 05		22 10	22 15		22 30							22 20	22 25	22 35			22 45		23 00	
Dalston Junction Stn ELL	a		21 52	21 58	22 07		22 13	22 17		22 32							22 22	22 29	22 37			22 47		23 02	
Canonbury	d		21 57		22 12			22 20		22 35							22 27		22 42			22 50		23 05	
Highbury & Islington	a		22 02		22 16			22 25		22 40							22 32		22 46			22 55		23 10	
	d																								
London Bridge 4 ⊖	a	21 41				21 59			22 13				21 56		22 06	22 11				22 29			22 45		

East London Line and Croydon - London Victoria to London Bridge

Network Diagram - see first Page of Table 177

		SN	SE	SN	SN	LO		LO	LO	SN	LO	SN	SN	SN	SE	SN		SN	LO	LO	LO	SN	LO	SN	SN
East Croydon	d									22 30												23 01			
West Croydon 4	d				22 01	22 09			22 22									22 31	22 39		22 52				
Norwood Junction 2	d					22 13			22 28	22 35									22 43		22 58	23 06			
Anerley	d					22 16			22 31	22 38									22 46		23 01	23 09			
Penge West	d					22 18			22 33	22 40									22 48		23 03	23 11			
London Victoria 15 ⊖	d			22 11								22 22				22 41								22 52	
Battersea Park 4	d			22 15								22 26				22 45								22 56	
Wandsworth Road	d			22 17												22 47									
Clapham High Street ⊖	d			22 19												22 49									
London Blackfriars 3 ⊖	d		22 12												22 42										
Denmark Hill 4	d		22 22	22 24											22 52	22 54									
Peckham Rye 4	d	22 17	22a25	22 26	22 31								22 42	22 43	22a55	22 56		23 01							23 14
Queens Rd Peckham	d	22 19		22 29	22 34									22 45		22 59		23 04							
South Bermondsey	d	22 22		22 31	22 36									22 48		23 01		23 06							
Clapham Junction 10	d											22 30												23 00	
Wandsworth Common	d											22 33												23 03	
Balham 4 ⊖	d											22 35												23 05	
Streatham Hill	d											22 38												23 08	
West Norwood 4	d											22 42	22 54											23 12	23 26
Gipsy Hill	d											22 45	22 57											23 15	23 29
Crystal Palace 4	d										22 43	22 51	22a59										23 13	23 21	23a31
Sydenham	d					22 21			22 36	22 42	22 46	22 54							22 51		23 06	23 13	23 16	23 24	
Forest Hill 4	d					22 23			22 38	22 45	22 49	22 57							22 53		23 08	23 16	23 19	23 27	
Honor Oak Park	d					22 26			22 41	22 47	22 51	22 59							22 56		23 11	23 18	23 21	23 29	
Brockley	d					22 28			22 43	22 50	22 54	23 02							22 58		23 13	23 21	23 24	23 32	
New Cross Gate 4	a					22 31			22 46	22 52	22 56	23 04							23 01		23 16	23 23	23 26	23 34	
	d					22 31			22 46	22 52	22 56	23 04							23 01		23 16	23 23	23 26	23 34	
New Cross ELL	d							22 36												23 06					
Surrey Quays	d					22 35		22 40	22 49		23 00								23 05	23 10	23 19		23 30		
Canada Water	d					22 37		22 42	22 51		23 02								23 07	23 12	23 21		23 32		
Rotherhithe	d					22 38		22 43	22 53		23 03								23 08	23 13	23 23		23 33		
Wapping	d					22 40		22 45	22 54		23 05								23 10	23 15	23 24		23 35		
Shadwell	d					22 42		22 47	22 56		23 07								23 12	23 17	23 26		23 37		
Whitechapel	d					22 44		22 49	22 59		23 09								23 14	23 19	23 29		23 39		
Shoreditch High Street	d					22 46		22 51	23 01		23 11								23 16	23 21	23 31		23 41		
Hoxton	d					22 48		22 53	23 03		23 13								23 18	23 23	23 33		23 43		
Haggerston	d					22 50		22 55	23 05		23 15								23 20	23 25	23 35		23 45		
Dalston Junction Stn ELL	a					22 52		22 58	23 07		23 17								23 22	23 28	23 37		23 47		
Canonbury	d					22 57			23 12		23 20								23 27		23 42		23 50		
Highbury & Islington	a					23 02			23 16		23 25								23 32		23 46		23 55		
	d																								
London Bridge 4 ⊖	a	22 26		22 36	22 41					22 59		23 11		22 52		23 06		23 11				23 30		23 45	

		SN		SE	SN	SN	LO	LO	LO	SN	SN	SN		SE	SN
East Croydon	d														
West Croydon 4	d					23 01		23 22							
Norwood Junction 2	d							23 28							
Anerley	d							23 31							
Penge West	d							23 33							
London Victoria 15 ⊖	d				23 11					23 22					23 54
Battersea Park 4	d				23 15					23 26					23 58
Wandsworth Road	d				23 17										
Clapham High Street ⊖	d				23 19										
London Blackfriars 3 ⊖	d			23 12										23 42	
Denmark Hill 4	d			23 22	23 24									23 52	
Peckham Rye 4	d	23 17		23a25	23 26	23 31					23 42	23 47		23a55	
Queens Rd Peckham	d	23 19			23 29	23 34						23 49			
South Bermondsey	d	23 22			23 31	23 36						23 52			
Clapham Junction 10	d									23 30					00 02
Wandsworth Common	d									23 33					00 05
Balham 4 ⊖	d									23 35					00 07
Streatham Hill	d									23 38					00 10
West Norwood 4	d									23 42	23 54				00 14
Gipsy Hill	d									23 45	23 57				00 17
Crystal Palace 4	d								23 43	23 51	23a59				00 21
Sydenham	d							23 36	23 46	23 54					00 24
Forest Hill 4	d							23 38	23 49	23 57					00 27
Honor Oak Park	d							23 41	23 51	23 59					00 29
Brockley	d							23 43	23 54	00 02					00 32
New Cross Gate 4	a							23 46	23 56	00 04					00 34
	d							23 46	23 56	00 04					00 34
New Cross ELL	d						23 36								
Surrey Quays	d						23 40	23 49	23 59						
Canada Water	d						23 42	23 51	00 02						
Rotherhithe	d						23 43	23 53	00 03						
Wapping	d						23 45	23 54	00 05						
Shadwell	d						23 47	23 56	00 07						
Whitechapel	d						23 49	23 59	00 09						
Shoreditch High Street	d						23 51	00 01	00 11						
Hoxton	d						23 53	00 03	00 13						
Haggerston	d						23 55	00 05	00 15						
Dalston Junction Stn ELL	a						00 02	00 07	00 17						
Canonbury	d							00 12	00 20						
Highbury & Islington	a							00 19	00 28						
	d														
London Bridge 4 ⊖	a	23 26			23 36	23 41				00 11		23 56			00 41

29 August to 7 September

East London Line and Croydon - London Victoria to London Bridge

Network Diagram - see first Page of Table 177

		LO A	LO B	LO C	LO A	LO B	LO C	LO A	LO D	LO A		SN A	SN D	SN D	SN D	SN	LO	LO	LO	SE		SE	SN	LO	LO
East Croydon	d															05 13							05 51		
West Croydon 4	d					23p22	23p22	23p25									05 39							05 52	
Norwood Junction 2	d					23p28	23p28	23p31								05 17	05 43						05 55	05 58	
Anerley	d					23p31	23p31	23p34								05 20	05 46							06 01	
Penge West	d					23p33	23p33	23p36								05 22	05 48							06 03	
London Victoria 15 ⊖	d												23p22	23p54						00 56					
Battersea Park 4	d												23p26	23p58											
Wandsworth Road	d																								
Clapham High Street ⊖	d																								
London Blackfriars 3 ⊖	d																					05 28			
Denmark Hill 4	d																			01s05		05 39			
Peckham Rye 4	d											23p53			00 12					01s08		05a41	06 15		
Queens Rd Peckham	d											23p56											06 18		
South Bermondsey	d											23p58											06 20		
Clapham Junction 10	d												23p30	00 02											
Wandsworth Common	d												23p33	00 05											
Balham 4 ⊖	d												23p35	00 07											
Streatham Hill	d												23p38	00 10											
West Norwood 4	d												23p42	00 14	00 24										
Gipsy Hill	d												23p45	00 17	00 27										
Crystal Palace 4	d	23p16							23p43	23p46			23p51	00 21	00a29				05 58						
Sydenham	d	23p19				23p36	23p36	23p39	23p46	23p49			23p54	00 24		05 24	05 51		06 01					06 06	
Forest Hill 4	d	23p22				23p38	23p38	23p41	23p49	23p52			23p57	00 27		05 27	05 53		06 04					06 08	
Honor Oak Park	d	23p24				23p41	23p41	23p44	23p51	23p54			23p59	00 29		05 29	05 56		06 06					06 11	
Brockley	d	23p27				23p43	23p43	23p46	23p54	23p57			00 02	00 32		05 32	05 58		06 09					06 13	
New Cross Gate 4	a	23p29				23p46	23p46	23p49	23p56	23p59			00 04	00 34		05 34	06 01		06 11					06 16	
	d	23p29				23p46	23p46	23p49	23p56	23p59			00 04	00 34		05 34	06 01		06 11					06 16	
New Cross ELL	d		23p36	23p36	23p39													06 06							06 21
Surrey Quays	d	23p33	23p40	23p40	23p43	23p49	23p49	23p52	23p59	00 02							06 05	06 10	06 15					06 19	06 25
Canada Water	d	23p35	23p42	23p42	23p45	23p51	23p51	23p54	00 02	00 05							06 07	06 12	06 17					06 21	06 27
Rotherhithe	d	23p36	23p43	23p43	23p46	23p53	23p53	23p56	00 03	00 06							06 08	06 13	06 18					06 23	06 28
Wapping	d	23p38	23p45	23p45	23p48	23p54	23p54	23p57	00 05	00 08							06 10	06 15	06 20					06 24	06 30
Shadwell	d	23p40	23p47	23p47	23p50	23p56	23p56	23p59	00 07	00 10							06 12	06 17	06 22					06 26	06 32
Whitechapel	d	23p42	23p49	23p49	23p52	23p59	23p59	00 02	00 09	00 12							06 14	06 19	06 24					06 29	06 34
Shoreditch High Street	d	23p44	23p51	23p51	23p54	00 01	00 01	00 04	00 11	00 14							06 16	06 21	06 26					06 31	06 36
Hoxton	d	23p46	23p53	23p53	23p56	00 03	00 03	00 06	00 13	00 16							06 18	06 23	06 28					06 33	06 38
Haggerston	d	23p48	23p55	23p55	23p58	00 05	00 05	00 08	00 15	00 18							06 20	06 25	06 30					06 35	06 40
Dalston Junction Stn ELL	a	23p50	23p58	00 02	00 02	00 07	00 07	00 10	00 17	00 20							06 22	06 32	06 32					06 37	06 47
Canonbury	d	23p53	00 01		00 05	00 11	00 12	00 14	00 20	00 23							06 27		06 35					06 42	
Highbury & Islington	a	00 01	00 10		00 14	00 18	00 19	00 21	00 28	00 31							06 35		06 43					06 49	
	d																								
London Bridge 4 ⊖	a											00 03	00 11	00 41		05 41							06 25		

		LO	LO	SN	LO	LO		LO	SN	LO	LO	SN	SN	LO	SN	SE		SN	SN	LO	SN	LO	LO	SN	LO
East Croydon	d			06 13																					
West Croydon 4	d		06 09					06 22											06 31	06 39			06 52		
Norwood Junction 2	d		06 13	06 18				06 28	06 32											06 43	06 47		06 58	07 02	
Anerley	d		06 16	06 21				06 31	06 35											06 46			07 01	07 05	
Penge West	d		06 18	06 23				06 33	06 37											06 48			07 03	07 07	
London Victoria 15 ⊖	d											06 19						06 41							
Battersea Park 4	d											06 23						06 45							
Wandsworth Road	d																	06 47							
Clapham High Street ⊖	d																	06 49							
London Blackfriars 3 ⊖	d															06 42									
Denmark Hill 4	d															06 52		06 54							
Peckham Rye 4	d														06 42	06a55		06 56	06 59		07 08				
Queens Rd Peckham	d																	06 59	07 02		07 10				
South Bermondsey	d																	07 01	07 04		07 13				
Clapham Junction 10	d											06 27													
Wandsworth Common	d											06 30													
Balham 4 ⊖	d											06 32													
Streatham Hill	d											06 35	06 42												
West Norwood 4	d											06 39	06 45		06 53										
Gipsy Hill	d											06 42	06 48		06 56										
Crystal Palace 4	d	06 13				06 28					06 41	06 44	06 51	06 58	06a59										
Sydenham	d	06 16	06 21	06 25		06 31		06 36	06 39		06 44	06 48	06 54	07 01						06 51			07 06	07 09	
Forest Hill 4	d	06 19	06 23	06 28		06 34		06 38	06 42		06 47	06 50	06 57	07 04						06 53			07 08	07 12	
Honor Oak Park	d	06 21	06 26	06 30		06 36		06 41	06 44		06 49	06 53	06 59	07 06						06 56			07 11	07 14	
Brockley	d	06 24	06 28	06 33		06 39		06 43	06 47		06 52	06 55	07 02	07 09						06 58			07 13	07 17	
New Cross Gate 4	a	06 26	06 31	06 35		06 41		06 46	06 49		06 54	06 58	07 04	07 11						07 01			07 16	07 19	
	d	06 26	06 31	06 35		06 41		06 46	06 49		06 54	06 58	07 04	07 11						07 01			07 16	07 19	
New Cross ELL	d				06 36					06 51												07 06			07 21
Surrey Quays	d	06 30	06 35		06 40	06 45		06 49		06 55	07 00			07 15						07 05		07 10	07 19		07 25
Canada Water	d	06 32	06 37		06 42	06 47		06 51		06 57	07 02			07 17						07 07		07 12	07 21		07 27
Rotherhithe	d	06 33	06 38		06 43	06 48		06 53		06 58	07 03			07 18						07 08		07 13	07 23		07 28
Wapping	d	06 35	06 40		06 45	06 50		06 54		07 00	07 05			07 20						07 10		07 15	07 24		07 30
Shadwell	d	06 37	06 42		06 47	06 52		06 56		07 02	07 07			07 22						07 12		07 17	07 26		07 32
Whitechapel	d	06 39	06 44		06 49	06 54		06 59		07 04	07 09			07 24						07 14		07 19	07 29		07 34
Shoreditch High Street	d	06 41	06 46		06 51	06 56		07 01		07 06	07 11			07 26						07 16		07 21	07 31		07 36
Hoxton	d	06 43	06 48		06 53	06 58		07 03		07 08	07 13			07 28						07 18		07 23	07 33		07 38
Haggerston	d	06 45	06 50		06 55	07 00		07 05		07 10	07 15			07 30						07 20		07 25	07 35		07 40
Dalston Junction Stn ELL	a	06 47	06 52		07 02	07 02		07 07		07 17	07 17			07 32						07 23		07 32	07 37		07 47
Canonbury	d	06 50	06 57			07 05		07 12			07 20			07 35						07 27			07 42		
Highbury & Islington	a	06 59	07 05			07 13		07 19			07 28			07 43						07 35			07 49		
	d																								
London Bridge 4 ⊖	a			06 44					07 00			07 06	07 16					07 08	07 11		07 19			07 30	

A 3 September
B not 29 August, 3 September
C 29 August
D not 3 September

East London Line and Croydon - London Victoria to London Bridge

Network Diagram - see first Page of Table 177

		LO		SN	SN	SN	SN	SN	LO	SN	SN	LO		LO	LO	SN	LO	LO	SN	SN	SN	SN		SE	SN
East Croydon 🚊	d																								
West Croydon 4 🚊	d							07 01	07 09	07 17					07 22										07 31
Norwood Junction 2	d								07 13	07 22					07 28	07 32									
Anerley	d								07 16						07 31	07 35									
Penge West	d								07 18						07 33	07 37									
London Victoria 15 ⊖	d			06 49			07 11												07 17			07 41		07 43	
Battersea Park 4	d			06 53			07 15												07 21			07 45			
Wandsworth Road	d						07 17															07 47			
Clapham High Street ⊖	d						07 19															07 49			
London Blackfriars 3 ⊖	d																								
Denmark Hill 4	d						07 24															07 54		07 53	
Peckham Rye 4	d					07 12	07 26	07 31			07 36										07 42	07 56		07a56	07 59
Queens Rd Peckham	d						07 29	07 34			07 39											07 59			08 02
South Bermondsey	d						07 31	07 36			07 41											08 01			08 04
Clapham Junction 10	d			06 57															07 25						
Wandsworth Common	d			07 00																					
Balham 4 ⊖	d			07 02															07 29						
Streatham Hill	d			07 05	07 12														07 32						
West Norwood 4	d			07 09	07 15	07 23													07 38		07 53				
Gipsy Hill	d			07 12	07 18	07 26													07 41		07 56				
Crystal Palace 4	d	07 11		07 14	07 21	07a29				07a26				07 28				07 41	07 44	07 52	07a59				
Sydenham	d	07 14		07 18	07 24				07 21					07 31	07 36	07 39		07 44	07 48	07 56					
Forest Hill 4	d	07 17		07 20	07 27				07 23					07 34	07 38	07 42		07 47	07 50	07 58					
Honor Oak Park	d	07 19		07 23	07 29				07 26					07 36	07 41	07 44		07 49	07 53	08 01					
Brockley	d	07 22		07 25	07 32				07 28					07 39	07 43	07 47		07 52	07 55	08 03					
New Cross Gate 4	a	07 24		07 28	07 34				07 31					07 41	07 46	07 49		07 54	07 58	08 06					
	d	07 24		07 28	07 34				07 31					07 41	07 46	07 49		07 54	07 58	08 06					
New Cross ELL	d											07 36					07 51								
Surrey Quays	d	07 30							07 35			07 40		07 45	07 49		07 55	08 00							
Canada Water	d	07 32							07 37			07 42		07 47	07 51		07 57	08 02							
Rotherhithe	d	07 33							07 38			07 43		07 48	07 53		07 58	08 03							
Wapping	d	07 35							07 40			07 45		07 50	07 54		08 00	08 05							
Shadwell	d	07 37							07 42			07 47		07 52	07 56		08 02	08 07							
Whitechapel	d	07 39							07 44			07 49		07 54	07 59		08 04	08 09							
Shoreditch High Street	d	07 41							07 46			07 51		07 56	08 01		08 06	08 11							
Hoxton	d	07 43							07 48			07 53		07 58	08 03		08 08	08 13							
Haggerston	d	07 45							07 50			07 55		08 00	08 05		08 10	08 15							
Dalston Junction Stn ELL	a	07 47							07 53			08 02		08 02	08 07		08 17	08 17							
Canonbury	d	07 50							07 57					08 05	08 12			08 20							
Highbury & Islington	a	07 58							08 05					08 13	08 19			08 28							
	d																								
London Bridge 4 ⊖	a			07 36	07 45		07 38	07 43			07 48					07 58			08 07	08 15		08 08			08 11

		LO	SN	SN	LO	LO	LO	SN		LO	LO	SN	SN	LO	SN	SE	SN	SN		LO	SN	SN	LO	LO	SN
East Croydon 🚊	d																								
West Croydon 4 🚊	d	07 39	07 47				07 52											08 01		08 09	08 19			08 23	
Norwood Junction 2	d	07 43	07 52				07 58	08 02												08 13	08 25			08 28	08 32
Anerley	d	07 46					08 01	08 05												08 16				08 31	08 35
Penge West	d	07 48					08 03	08 07												08 18				08 33	08 37
London Victoria 15 ⊖	d											07 52				08 09	08 11								
Battersea Park 4	d																08 15								
Wandsworth Road	d																08 17								
Clapham High Street ⊖	d																08 19								
London Blackfriars 3 ⊖	d																								
Denmark Hill 4	d															08 18	08 24								
Peckham Rye 4	d			08 06											08 12	08a21	08 26	08 29				08 36			
Queens Rd Peckham	d			08 09													08 29	08 32				08 38			
South Bermondsey	d			08 11													08 31	08 34				08 41			
Clapham Junction 10	d											07 58													
Wandsworth Common	d																								
Balham 4 ⊖	d											08 03													
Streatham Hill	d											08 06	08 15												
West Norwood 4	d											08 09	08 19		08 24										
Gipsy Hill	d											08 12	08 22		08 27										
Crystal Palace 4	d		07a56			07 58					08 11	08 15	08 24	08 28	08a29						08a29				
Sydenham	d	07 51				08 01	08 06	08 09			08 14	08 18	08 28	08 31						08 21				08 36	08 39
Forest Hill 4	d	07 53				08 04	08 08	08 12			08 17	08 21	08 30	08 34						08 23				08 38	08 42
Honor Oak Park	d	07 56				08 06	08 11	08 14			08 19	08 23	08 33	08 36						08 26				08 41	08 44
Brockley	d	07 58				08 09	08 13	08 17			08 22	08 26	08 35	08 39						08 28				08 43	08 47
New Cross Gate 4	a	08 01				08 11	08 16	08 19			08 24	08 28	08 38	08 41						08 31				08 46	08 49
	d	08 01				08 11	08 16	08 19			08 24	08 28	08 38	08 41						08 31				08 46	08 49
New Cross ELL	d				08 06					08 21													08 36		
Surrey Quays	d	08 05			08 10	08 15	08 21			08 25	08 30			08 45						08 37			08 40	08 49	
Canada Water	d	08 07			08 12	08 17	08 23			08 27	08 32			08 47						08 39			08 42	08 51	
Rotherhithe	d	08 08			08 13	08 18	08 25			08 28	08 33			08 48						08 40			08 43	08 53	
Wapping	d	08 10			08 15	08 20	08 26			08 30	08 35			08 50						08 42			08 45	08 54	
Shadwell	d	08 12			08 17	08 22	08 28			08 32	08 37			08 52						08 44			08 47	08 56	
Whitechapel	d	08 14			08 19	08 24	08 31			08 34	08 39			08 54						08 46			08 49	08 59	
Shoreditch High Street	d	08 16			08 21	08 26	08 33			08 36	08 41			08 56						08 48			08 51	09 01	
Hoxton	d	08 18			08 23	08 28	08 35			08 38	08 43			08 58						08 50			08 53	09 03	
Haggerston	d	08 20			08 25	08 30	08 37			08 40	08 45			09 00						08 52			08 55	09 05	
Dalston Junction Stn ELL	a	08 23			08 32	08 32	08 39			08 47	08 47			09 02						08 55			09 02	09 07	
Canonbury	d	08 27				08 35	08 42				08 50			09 05						08 57				09 12	
Highbury & Islington	a	08 35				08 43	08 49				08 58			09 13						09 05				09 19	
	d																								
London Bridge 4 ⊖	a			08 18				08 28				08 37	08 47				08 38	08 41				08 48			08 58

East London Line and Croydon - London Victoria to London Bridge

Network Diagram - see first Page of Table 177

Station		LO	LO	SN		SN	LO	SN	SE	SN	SN	LO	SN	LO		LO	SN	SN	LO	LO	SN	SN	LO	SN
East Croydon	d																							
West Croydon 4	d										08 31	08 39	08 49			08 53								
Norwood Junction 2	d											08 43	08 54			08 58		09 02						
Anerley	d											08 46				09 01		09 05						
Penge West	d											08 48				09 03		09 07						
London Victoria 15 ⊖	d					08 22			08 39	08 41											08 49			
Battersea Park 4	d					08 26				08 45											08 53			
Wandsworth Road	d									08 47														
Clapham High Street ⊖	d									08 49														
London Blackfriars 3 ⊖	d																							
Denmark Hill 4	d								08 48	08 54														
Peckham Rye 4	d							08 42	08a51	08 56	09 02						09 07							09 12
Queens Rd Peckham	d									08 59	09 05						09 09							
South Bermondsey	d									09 01	09 07						09 12							
Clapham Junction 10	d					08 30															08 57			
Wandsworth Common	d					08 33															09 00			
Balham 4 ⊖	d					08 35															09 02			
Streatham Hill	d			08 35		08 38															09 05			
West Norwood 4	d			08 38		08 42		08 53													09 09			09 23
Gipsy Hill	d			08 41		08 45		08 56													09 12			09 26
Crystal Palace 4	d		08 41	08 44		08 51	08 58	08a59					08a58							09 11	09 14	09 21	09 28	09a29
Sydenham	d		08 44	08 47		08 54	09 01					08 51				09 06		09 09		09 14	09 18	09 24	09 31	
Forest Hill 4	d		08 47	08 50		08 57	09 04					08 53				09 08		09 12		09 17	09 20	09 27	09 34	
Honor Oak Park	d		08 49	08 52		08 59	09 06					08 56				09 11		09 14		09 19	09 23	09 29	09 36	
Brockley	d		08 52	08 55		09 02	09 09					08 58				09 13		09 17		09 22	09 25	09 32	09 39	
New Cross Gate 4	a		08 54	08 57		09 04	09 11					09 01				09 16		09 19		09 24	09 28	09 34	09 41	
	d		08 54	08 57		09 04	09 11					09 01				09 16		09 19		09 24	09 28	09 34	09 41	
New Cross ELL	d	08 51												09 06					09 21					
Surrey Quays	d	08 55	09 00				09 15					09 05		09 10		09 19			09 25	09 30			09 45	
Canada Water	d	08 57	09 02				09 17					09 07		09 12		09 21			09 27	09 32			09 47	
Rotherhithe	d	08 58	09 03				09 18					09 08		09 13		09 23			09 28	09 33			09 48	
Wapping	d	09 00	09 05				09 20					09 10		09 15		09 24			09 30	09 35			09 50	
Shadwell	d	09 02	09 07				09 22					09 12		09 17		09 26			09 32	09 37			09 52	
Whitechapel	d	09 04	09 09				09 24					09 14		09 19		09 29			09 34	09 39			09 54	
Shoreditch High Street	d	09 06	09 11				09 26					09 16		09 21		09 31			09 36	09 41			09 56	
Hoxton	d	09 08	09 13				09 28					09 18		09 23		09 33			09 38	09 43			09 58	
Haggerston	d	09 10	09 15				09 30					09 20		09 25		09 35			09 40	09 45			10 00	
Dalston Junction Stn ELL	a	09 17	09 17				09 32					09 23		09 32		09 37			09 47	09 47			10 02	
Canonbury	d		09 20				09 35					09 27				09 42				09 50			10 05	
Highbury & Islington	a		09 28				09 43					09 35				09 49				09 58			10 13	
	d																							
London Bridge 4 ⊖	a			09 06		09 14				09 08	09 14						09 19	09 29			09 37	09 43		

Station		SE	SN	SN	LO	SN	LO	LO	SN	SN		LO	LO	SN	LO	SN	SN	SE	SN	SN		LO	LO	LO	SN
East Croydon	d					09 20				09 30															10 00
West Croydon 4	d			09 01	09 09			09 22												09 31		09 39		09 52	
Norwood Junction 2	d				09 14	09 25		09 28		09 35												09 43		09 58	10 05
Anerley	d				09 17			09 31		09 38												09 46		10 01	10 08
Penge West	d				09 19			09 33		09 40												09 48		10 03	10 10
London Victoria 15 ⊖	d	09 09	09 11											09 19				09 39	09 41						
Battersea Park 4	d		09 15											09 23					09 45						
Wandsworth Road	d		09 17																09 47						
Clapham High Street ⊖	d		09 19																09 49						
London Blackfriars 3 ⊖	d																								
Denmark Hill 4	d	09 18	09 24															09 48	09 54						
Peckham Rye 4	d	09a21	09 26	09 33												09 42	09 47	09a51	09 56	10 01					
Queens Rd Peckham	d		09 29	09 36													09 49		09 59	10 04					
South Bermondsey	d		09 31	09 38													09 52		10 01	10 06					
Clapham Junction 10	d													09 27											
Wandsworth Common	d													09 30											
Balham 4 ⊖	d													09 32											
Streatham Hill	d													09 35											
West Norwood 4	d													09 40		09 53									
Gipsy Hill	d													09 43		09 56									
Crystal Palace 4	d								09 36				09 43	09 51	09 58	09a59									
Sydenham	d				09 21			09 36	09 39	09 42			09 46	09 54	10 01							09 51		10 06	10 12
Forest Hill 4	d				09 23			09 38	09 42	09 45			09 49	09 57	10 04							09 53		10 08	10 15
Honor Oak Park	d				09 26			09 41	09 44	09 47			09 51	09 59	10 06							09 56		10 11	10 17
Brockley	d				09 28			09 43	09 47	09 50			09 54	10 02	10 09							09 58		10 13	10 20
New Cross Gate 4	a				09 31	09 32		09 46	09 49	09 52			09 56	10 04	10 11							10 01		10 16	10 22
	d				09 31	09 33		09 46	09 49	09 52			09 56	10 04	10 11							10 01		10 16	10 22
New Cross ELL	d						09 36					09 51											10 06		
Surrey Quays	d				09 35		09 40	09 49				09 55	10 00		10 15							10 05	10 10	10 19	
Canada Water	d				09 37		09 42	09 51				09 57	10 02		10 17							10 07	10 12	10 21	
Rotherhithe	d				09 38		09 43	09 53				09 58	10 03		10 18							10 08	10 13	10 23	
Wapping	d				09 40		09 45	09 54				10 00	10 05		10 20							10 10	10 15	10 24	
Shadwell	d				09 42		09 47	09 56				10 02	10 07		10 22							10 12	10 17	10 26	
Whitechapel	d				09 44		09 49	09 59				10 04	10 09		10 24							10 14	10 19	10 29	
Shoreditch High Street	d				09 46		09 51	10 01				10 06	10 11		10 26							10 16	10 21	10 31	
Hoxton	d				09 48		09 53	10 03				10 08	10 13		10 28							10 18	10 23	10 33	
Haggerston	d				09 50		09 55	10 05				10 10	10 15		10 30							10 20	10 25	10 35	
Dalston Junction Stn ELL	a				09 53		10 02	10 07				10 17	10 17		10 32							10 22	10 32	10 37	
Canonbury	d				09 57			10 12					10 20		10 35							10 27		10 42	
Highbury & Islington	a				10 05			10 19					10 28		10 43							10 35		10 49	
	d																								
London Bridge 4 ⊖	a		09 38	09 44		09 41			09 59	10 00				10 11			09 58		10 06	10 11					10 29

Table 178

Mondays to Fridays

29 August to 7 September

East London Line and Croydon - London Victoria to London Bridge

Network Diagram - see first Page of Table 177

		LO	LO	SN	LO	SN		SN	SE	SN	SN	LO	LO	LO	SN	LO		LO	SN	LO	SN	SN	SE	SN	SN
East Croydon	d														10 30										
West Croydon 4	d										10 01	10 09		10 22											10 31
Norwood Junction 2	d											10 13		10 28	10 35										
Anerley	d											10 16		10 31	10 38										
Penge West	d											10 18		10 33	10 40										
London Victoria 15 ⊖	d			09 49					10 09	10 11									10 19				10 39	10 41	
Battersea Park 4	d			09 53						10 15									10 23					10 45	
Wandsworth Road	d									10 17														10 47	
Clapham High Street ⊖	d									10 19														10 49	
London Blackfriars 3 ⊖	d																								
Denmark Hill 4	d								10 18	10 24													10 48	10 54	
Peckham Rye 4	d					10 12		10 17	10a21	10 26	10 31										10 42	10 47	10a51	10 56	11 01
Queens Rd Peckham	d							10 19		10 29	10 34											10 49		10 59	11 04
South Bermondsey	d							10 22		10 31	10 36											10 52		11 01	11 06
Clapham Junction 10	d			09 57															10 27						
Wandsworth Common	d			10 00															10 30						
Balham 4 ⊖	d			10 02															10 32						
Streatham Hill	d			10 05															10 35						
West Norwood 4	d			10 10		10 23													10 40		10 53				
Gipsy Hill	d			10 13		10 26													10 43		10 56				
Crystal Palace 4	d		10 13	10 21	10 28	10a29												10 43	10 51	10 58	10a59				
Sydenham	d		10 16	10 24	10 31							10 21		10 36	10 42			10 46	10 54	11 01					
Forest Hill 4	d		10 19	10 27	10 34							10 23		10 38	10 45			10 49	10 57	11 04					
Honor Oak Park	d		10 21	10 29	10 36							10 26		10 41	10 47			10 51	10 59	11 06					
Brockley	d		10 24	10 32	10 39							10 28		10 43	10 50			10 54	11 02	11 09					
New Cross Gate 4	a		10 26	10 34	10 41							10 31		10 46	10 52			10 56	11 04	11 11					
	d		10 26	10 34	10 41							10 31		10 46	10 52			10 56	11 04	11 11					
New Cross ELL	d	10 21											10 36			10 51									
Surrey Quays	d	10 25	10 30		10 45							10 35	10 40	10 49		10 55		11 00		11 15					
Canada Water	d	10 27	10 32		10 47							10 37	10 42	10 51		10 57		11 02		11 17					
Rotherhithe	d	10 28	10 33		10 48							10 38	10 43	10 53		10 58		11 03		11 18					
Wapping	d	10 30	10 35		10 50							10 40	10 45	10 54		11 00		11 05		11 20					
Shadwell	d	10 32	10 37		10 52							10 42	10 47	10 56		11 02		11 07		11 22					
Whitechapel	d	10 34	10 39		10 54							10 44	10 49	10 59		11 04		11 09		11 24					
Shoreditch High Street	d	10 36	10 41		10 56							10 46	10 51	11 01		11 06		11 11		11 26					
Hoxton	d	10 38	10 43		10 58							10 48	10 53	11 03		11 08		11 13		11 28					
Haggerston	d	10 40	10 45		11 00							10 50	10 55	11 05		11 10		11 15		11 30					
Dalston Junction Stn ELL	a	10 47	10 47		11 02							10 52	11 02	11 07		11 17		11 17		11 32					
Canonbury	d		10 50		11 05							10 57		11 12				11 20		11 35					
Highbury & Islington	a		10 58		11 13							11 05		11 19				11 28		11 43					
	d																								
London Bridge 4 ⊖	a			10 41				10 26		10 36	10 41				10 59				11 11			10 56		11 06	11 11

		LO		LO	LO	SN	LO	LO	SN	LO	SN	SN		SE	SN	SN	LO	LO	LO	SN	LO	LO		SN	LO
East Croydon	d					11 00														11 30					
West Croydon 4	d	10 39			10 52											11 01	11 09		11 22						
Norwood Junction 2	d	10 43			10 58	11 05											11 13		11 28	11 35					
Anerley	d	10 46			11 01	11 08											11 16		11 31	11 38					
Penge West	d	10 48			11 03	11 10											11 18		11 33	11 40					
London Victoria 15 ⊖	d								10 49					11 09	11 11									11 19	
Battersea Park 4	d								10 53						11 15									11 23	
Wandsworth Road	d														11 17										
Clapham High Street ⊖	d														11 19										
London Blackfriars 3 ⊖	d																								
Denmark Hill 4	d													11 18	11 24										
Peckham Rye 4	d										11 12	11 17		11a21	11 26	11 31									
Queens Rd Peckham	d											11 19			11 29	11 34									
South Bermondsey	d											11 22			11 31	11 36									
Clapham Junction 10	d								10 57															11 27	
Wandsworth Common	d								11 00															11 30	
Balham 4 ⊖	d								11 02															11 32	
Streatham Hill	d								11 05															11 35	
West Norwood 4	d								11 10		11 23													11 40	
Gipsy Hill	d								11 13		11 26													11 43	
Crystal Palace 4	d							11 13	11 21	11 28	11a29											11 43		11 51	11 58
Sydenham	d	10 51			11 06	11 12		11 16	11 24	11 31							11 21		11 36	11 42		11 46		11 54	12 01
Forest Hill 4	d	10 53			11 08	11 15		11 19	11 27	11 34							11 23		11 38	11 45		11 49		11 57	12 04
Honor Oak Park	d	10 56			11 11	11 17		11 21	11 29	11 36							11 26		11 41	11 47		11 51		11 59	12 06
Brockley	d	10 58			11 13	11 20		11 24	11 32	11 39							11 28		11 43	11 50		11 54		12 02	12 09
New Cross Gate 4	a	11 01			11 16	11 22		11 26	11 34	11 41							11 31		11 46	11 52		11 56		12 04	12 11
	d	11 01			11 16	11 22		11 26	11 34	11 41							11 31		11 46	11 52		11 56		12 04	12 11
New Cross ELL	d			11 06			11 21											11 36			11 51				
Surrey Quays	d	11 05		11 10	11 19		11 25	11 30		11 45							11 35	11 40	11 49		11 55	12 00			12 15
Canada Water	d	11 07		11 12	11 21		11 27	11 32		11 47							11 37	11 42	11 51		11 57	12 02			12 17
Rotherhithe	d	11 08		11 13	11 23		11 28	11 33		11 48							11 38	11 43	11 53		11 58	12 03			12 18
Wapping	d	11 10		11 15	11 24		11 30	11 35		11 50							11 40	11 45	11 54		12 00	12 05			12 20
Shadwell	d	11 12		11 17	11 26		11 32	11 37		11 52							11 42	11 47	11 56		12 02	12 07			12 22
Whitechapel	d	11 14		11 19	11 29		11 34	11 39		11 54							11 44	11 49	11 59		12 04	12 09			12 24
Shoreditch High Street	d	11 16		11 21	11 31		11 36	11 41		11 56							11 46	11 51	12 01		12 06	12 11			12 26
Hoxton	d	11 18		11 23	11 33		11 38	11 43		11 58							11 48	11 53	12 03		12 08	12 13			12 28
Haggerston	d	11 20		11 25	11 35		11 40	11 45		12 00							11 50	11 55	12 05		12 10	12 15			12 30
Dalston Junction Stn ELL	a	11 22		11 32	11 37		11 47	11 47		12 02							11 52	12 02	12 07		12 17	12 17			12 32
Canonbury	d	11 27			11 42			11 50		12 05							11 57		12 12			12 20			12 35
Highbury & Islington	a	11 35			11 49			11 58		12 13							12 05		12 19			12 28			12 43
	d																								
London Bridge 4 ⊖	a					11 29			11 41			11 26			11 36	11 41				11 59				12 14	

East London Line and Croydon - London Victoria to London Bridge

Network Diagram - see first Page of Table 177

		SN	SN	SE	SN	SN	LO	LO	LO	SN	LO	LO	SN	LO	SN	SN	SE	SN	SN	LO	LO	LO	SN
East Croydon	d									12 00													12 30
West Croydon 4	d					11 31	11 39		11 52										12 01	12 09		12 22	
Norwood Junction 2	d						11 43		11 58	12 05										12 13		12 28	12 35
Anerley	d						11 46		12 01	12 08										12 16		12 31	12 38
Penge West	d						11 48		12 03	12 10										12 18		12 33	12 40
London Victoria 15 ⊖	d			11 39	11 41								11 49				12 09	12 11					
Battersea Park 4	d				11 45								11 53					12 15					
Wandsworth Road	d				11 47													12 17					
Clapham High Street ⊖	d				11 49													12 19					
London Blackfriars 3 ⊖	d																						
Denmark Hill 4	d			11 48	11 54												12 18	12 24					
Peckham Rye 4	d	11 42	11 47	11a51	11 56	12 01									12 12	12 17	12a21	12 26	12 31				
Queens Rd Peckham	d		11 49		11 59	12 04										12 19		12 29	12 34				
South Bermondsey	d		11 52		12 01	12 06										12 22		12 31	12 36				
Clapham Junction 10	d												11 57										
Wandsworth Common	d												12 00										
Balham 4 ⊖	d												12 02										
Streatham Hill	d												12 05										
West Norwood 4	d	11 53											12 10		12 23								
Gipsy Hill	d	11 56											12 13		12 26								
Crystal Palace 4	d	11a59										12 13	12 21	12 28	12a29								
Sydenham	d						11 51		12 06	12 12		12 16	12 24	12 31						12 21		12 36	12 42
Forest Hill 4	d						11 53		12 08	12 15		12 19	12 27	12 34						12 23		12 38	12 45
Honor Oak Park	d						11 56		12 11	12 17		12 21	12 29	12 36						12 26		12 41	12 47
Brockley	d						11 58		12 13	12 20		12 24	12 32	12 39						12 28		12 43	12 50
New Cross Gate 4	a						12 01		12 16	12 22		12 26	12 34	12 41						12 31		12 46	12 52
	d						12 01		12 16	12 22		12 26	12 34	12 41						12 31		12 46	12 52
New Cross ELL	d							12 06			12 21										12 36		
Surrey Quays	d						12 05	12 10	12 19		12 25	12 30		12 45						12 35	12 40	12 49	
Canada Water	d						12 07	12 12	12 21		12 27	12 32		12 47						12 37	12 42	12 51	
Rotherhithe	d						12 08	12 13	12 23		12 28	12 33		12 48						12 38	12 43	12 53	
Wapping	d						12 10	12 15	12 24		12 30	12 35		12 50						12 40	12 45	12 54	
Shadwell	d						12 12	12 17	12 26		12 32	12 37		12 52						12 42	12 47	12 56	
Whitechapel	d						12 14	12 19	12 29		12 34	12 39		12 54						12 44	12 49	12 59	
Shoreditch High Street	d						12 16	12 21	12 31		12 36	12 41		12 56						12 46	12 51	13 01	
Hoxton	d						12 18	12 23	12 33		12 38	12 43		12 58						12 48	12 53	13 03	
Haggerston	d						12 20	12 25	12 35		12 40	12 45		13 00						12 50	12 55	13 05	
Dalston Junction Stn ELL	a						12 22	12 32	12 37		12 47	12 47		13 02						12 52	13 02	13 07	
Canonbury	d						12 27		12 42			12 50		13 05						12 57		13 12	
Highbury & Islington	a						12 35		12 49			12 58		13 13						13 05		13 19	
	d																						
London Bridge 4 ⊖	a		11 56		12 06	12 11				12 29			12 41			12 26		12 36	12 41				12 59

		LO	LO	SN	LO	SN	SN	SE	SN	SN	LO	LO	LO	SN	LO	LO	SN	LO	SN	SN	SE	SN
East Croydon	d													13 00								
West Croydon 4	d									12 31	12 39		12 52									
Norwood Junction 2	d										12 43		12 58	13 05								
Anerley	d										12 46		13 01	13 08								
Penge West	d										12 48		13 03	13 10								
London Victoria 15 ⊖	d			12 19				12 39	12 41								12 49				13 09	13 11
Battersea Park 4	d			12 23					12 45								12 53					13 15
Wandsworth Road	d								12 47													13 17
Clapham High Street ⊖	d								12 49													13 19
London Blackfriars 3 ⊖	d																					
Denmark Hill 4	d							12 48	12 54												13 18	13 24
Peckham Rye 4	d					12 42	12 47	12a51	12 56	13 01									13 12	13 17	13a21	13 26
Queens Rd Peckham	d						12 49		12 59	13 04										13 19		13 29
South Bermondsey	d						12 52		13 01	13 06										13 22		13 31
Clapham Junction 10	d			12 27													12 57					
Wandsworth Common	d			12 30													13 00					
Balham 4 ⊖	d			12 32													13 02					
Streatham Hill	d			12 35													13 05					
West Norwood 4	d			12 40		12 53											13 10		13 23			
Gipsy Hill	d			12 43		12 56											13 13		13 26			
Crystal Palace 4	d		12 43	12 51	12 58	12a59										13 13	13 21	13 28	13a29			
Sydenham	d		12 46	12 54	13 01						12 51		13 06	13 12		13 16	13 24	13 31				
Forest Hill 4	d		12 49	12 57	13 04						12 53		13 08	13 15		13 19	13 27	13 34				
Honor Oak Park	d		12 51	12 59	13 06						12 56		13 11	13 17		13 21	13 29	13 36				
Brockley	d		12 54	13 02	13 09						12 58		13 13	13 20		13 24	13 32	13 39				
New Cross Gate 4	a		12 56	13 04	13 11						13 01		13 16	13 22		13 26	13 34	13 41				
	d		12 56	13 04	13 11						13 01		13 16	13 22		13 26	13 34	13 41				
New Cross ELL	d	12 51										13 06			13 21							
Surrey Quays	d	12 55	13 00		13 15						13 05	13 10	13 19		13 25	13 30		13 45				
Canada Water	d	12 57	13 02		13 17						13 07	13 12	13 21		13 27	13 32		13 47				
Rotherhithe	d	12 58	13 03		13 18						13 08	13 13	13 23		13 28	13 33		13 48				
Wapping	d	13 00	13 05		13 20						13 10	13 15	13 24		13 30	13 35		13 50				
Shadwell	d	13 02	13 07		13 22						13 12	13 17	13 26		13 32	13 37		13 52				
Whitechapel	d	13 04	13 09		13 24						13 14	13 19	13 29		13 34	13 39		13 54				
Shoreditch High Street	d	13 06	13 11		13 26						13 16	13 21	13 31		13 36	13 41		13 56				
Hoxton	d	13 08	13 13		13 28						13 18	13 23	13 33		13 38	13 43		13 58				
Haggerston	d	13 10	13 15		13 30						13 20	13 25	13 35		13 40	13 45		14 00				
Dalston Junction Stn ELL	a	13 17	13 17		13 32						13 22	13 32	13 37		13 47	13 47		14 02				
Canonbury	d		13 20		13 35						13 27		13 42			13 50		14 05				
Highbury & Islington	a		13 28		13 43						13 35		13 49			13 58		14 13				
	d																					
London Bridge 4 ⊖	a			13 11			12 56		13 06	13 11				13 29			13 44			13 26		13 36

Mondays to Fridays

29 August to 7 September

East London Line and Croydon - London Victoria to London Bridge

Network Diagram - see first Page of Table 177

		SN	LO	LO	LO	SN	LO	LO	SN	LO		SN	SN	SE	SN	SN	LO	LO	LO	SN		LO	LO	SN	LO
East Croydon	d					13 30														14 00					
West Croydon 4	d	13 01	13 09		13 22											13 31	13 39		13 52						
Norwood Junction 2	d		13 13		13 28	13 35											13 43		13 58	14 05					
Anerley	d		13 16		13 31	13 38											13 46		14 01	14 08					
Penge West	d		13 18		13 33	13 40											13 48		14 03	14 10					
London Victoria 15 ⊖	d								13 19					13 39	13 41									13 49	
Battersea Park 4	d								13 23						13 45									13 53	
Wandsworth Road	d														13 47										
Clapham High Street ⊖	d														13 49										
London Blackfriars 3 ⊖	d																								
Denmark Hill 4	d													13 48	13 54										
Peckham Rye 4	d	13 31										13 42	13 47	13a51	13 56	14 01									
Queens Rd Peckham	d	13 34											13 49		13 59	14 04									
South Bermondsey	d	13 36											13 52		14 01	14 06									
Clapham Junction 10	d								13 27															13 57	
Wandsworth Common	d								13 30															14 00	
Balham 4 ⊖	d								13 32															14 02	
Streatham Hill	d								13 35															14 05	
West Norwood 4	d								13 40			13 53												14 10	
Gipsy Hill	d								13 43			13 56												14 13	
Crystal Palace 4	d							13 43	13 51	13 58		13a59											14 13	14 21	14 28
Sydenham	d		13 21		13 36	13 42		13 46	13 54	14 01							13 51		14 06	14 12			14 16	14 24	14 31
Forest Hill 4	d		13 23		13 38	13 45		13 49	13 57	14 04							13 53		14 08	14 15			14 19	14 27	14 34
Honor Oak Park	d		13 26		13 41	13 47		13 51	13 59	14 06							13 56		14 11	14 17			14 21	14 29	14 36
Brockley	d		13 28		13 43	13 50		13 54	14 02	14 09							13 58		14 13	14 20			14 24	14 32	14 39
New Cross Gate 4	a		13 31		13 46	13 52		13 56	14 04	14 11							14 01		14 16	14 22			14 26	14 34	14 41
	d		13 31		13 46	13 52		13 56	14 04	14 11							14 01		14 16	14 22			14 26	14 34	14 41
New Cross ELL	d			13 36			13 51											14 06				14 21			
Surrey Quays	d		13 35	13 40	13 49		13 55	14 00		14 15							14 05	14 10	14 19			14 25	14 30		14 45
Canada Water	d		13 37	13 42	13 51		13 57	14 02		14 17							14 07	14 12	14 21			14 27	14 32		14 47
Rotherhithe	d		13 38	13 43	13 53		13 58	14 03		14 18							14 08	14 13	14 23			14 28	14 33		14 48
Wapping	d		13 40	13 45	13 54		14 00	14 05		14 20							14 10	14 15	14 24			14 30	14 35		14 50
Shadwell	d		13 42	13 47	13 56		14 02	14 07		14 22							14 12	14 17	14 26			14 32	14 37		14 52
Whitechapel	d		13 44	13 49	13 59		14 04	14 09		14 24							14 14	14 19	14 29			14 34	14 39		14 54
Shoreditch High Street	d		13 46	13 51	14 01		14 06	14 11		14 26							14 16	14 21	14 31			14 36	14 41		14 56
Hoxton	d		13 48	13 53	14 03		14 08	14 13		14 28							14 18	14 23	14 33			14 38	14 43		14 58
Haggerston	d		13 50	13 55	14 05		14 10	14 15		14 30							14 20	14 25	14 35			14 40	14 45		15 00
Dalston Junction Stn ELL	a		13 52	14 02	14 07		14 17	14 17		14 32							14 22	14 32	14 37			14 47	14 47		15 02
Canonbury	d		13 57		14 12			14 20		14 35							14 27		14 42				14 50		15 05
Highbury & Islington	a		14 05		14 19			14 28		14 43							14 35		14 49				14 58		15 13
	d																								
London Bridge 4 ⊖	a	13 41				13 59			14 11				13 56		14 06	14 11				14 29				14 41	

		SN	SN	SE	SN	SN		LO	LO	LO	SN	LO	LO	SN	LO	SN		SN	SE	SN	SN	LO	LO	LO	SN
East Croydon	d										14 30														15 00
West Croydon 4	d					14 01		14 09		14 22											14 31	14 39		14 52	
Norwood Junction 2	d							14 13		14 28	14 35											14 43		14 58	15 05
Anerley	d							14 16		14 31	14 38											14 46		15 01	15 08
Penge West	d							14 18		14 33	14 40											14 48		15 03	15 10
London Victoria 15 ⊖	d			14 09	14 11									14 19					14 39	14 41					
Battersea Park 4	d				14 15									14 23						14 45					
Wandsworth Road	d				14 17															14 47					
Clapham High Street ⊖	d				14 19															14 49					
London Blackfriars 3 ⊖	d																								
Denmark Hill 4	d			14 18	14 24														14 48	14 54					
Peckham Rye 4	d	14 12	14 17	14a21	14 26	14 31										14 42		14 47	14a51	14 56	15 01				
Queens Rd Peckham	d		14 19		14 29	14 34												14 49		14 59	15 04				
South Bermondsey	d		14 22		14 31	14 36												14 52		15 01	15 06				
Clapham Junction 10	d													14 27											
Wandsworth Common	d													14 30											
Balham 4 ⊖	d													14 32											
Streatham Hill	d													14 35											
West Norwood 4	d	14 23												14 40		14 53									
Gipsy Hill	d	14 26												14 43		14 56									
Crystal Palace 4	d	14a29											14 43	14 51	14 58	14a59									
Sydenham	d							14 21		14 36	14 42		14 46	14 54	15 01							14 51		15 06	15 12
Forest Hill 4	d							14 23		14 38	14 45		14 49	14 57	15 04							14 53		15 08	15 15
Honor Oak Park	d							14 26		14 41	14 47		14 51	14 59	15 06							14 56		15 11	15 17
Brockley	d							14 28		14 43	14 50		14 54	15 02	15 09							14 58		15 13	15 20
New Cross Gate 4	a							14 31		14 46	14 52		14 56	15 04	15 11							15 01		15 16	15 22
	d							14 31		14 46	14 52		14 56	15 04	15 11							15 01		15 16	15 22
New Cross ELL	d								14 36			14 51											15 06		
Surrey Quays	d							14 35	14 40	14 49		14 55	15 00		15 15							15 05	15 10	15 19	
Canada Water	d							14 37	14 42	14 51		14 57	15 02		15 17							15 07	15 12	15 21	
Rotherhithe	d							14 38	14 43	14 53		14 58	15 03		15 18							15 08	15 13	15 23	
Wapping	d							14 40	14 45	14 54		15 00	15 05		15 20							15 10	15 15	15 24	
Shadwell	d							14 42	14 47	14 56		15 02	15 07		15 22							15 12	15 17	15 26	
Whitechapel	d							14 44	14 49	14 59		15 04	15 09		15 24							15 14	15 19	15 29	
Shoreditch High Street	d							14 46	14 51	15 01		15 06	15 11		15 26							15 16	15 21	15 31	
Hoxton	d							14 48	14 53	15 03		15 08	15 13		15 28							15 18	15 23	15 33	
Haggerston	d							14 50	14 55	15 05		15 10	15 15		15 30							15 20	15 25	15 35	
Dalston Junction Stn ELL	a							14 52	15 02	15 07		15 17	15 17		15 32							15 22	15 32	15 37	
Canonbury	d							14 57		15 12			15 20		15 35							15 27		15 42	
Highbury & Islington	a							15 05		15 19			15 28		15 43							15 35		15 49	
	d																								
London Bridge 4 ⊖	a		14 26		14 36	14 41					14 59			15 11				14 56		15 06	15 11				15 29

East London Line and Croydon - London Victoria to London Bridge

Network Diagram - see first Page of Table 177

		LO		LO	SN	LO	SN	SN	SE	SN	SN	LO		LO	LO	SN	LO	LO	SN	LO	SN	SN		SE	SN
East Croydon	d															15 30									
West Croydon 4	d										15 01	15 09			15 22										
Norwood Junction 2	d											15 13			15 28	15 35									
Anerley	d											15 16			15 31	15 38									
Penge West	d											15 18			15 33	15 40									
London Victoria 15 ⊖	d				14 49				15 09	15 11									15 19					15 39	15 41
Battersea Park 4	d				14 53					15 15									15 23						15 45
Wandsworth Road	d									15 17															15 47
Clapham High Street ⊖	d									15 19															15 49
London Blackfriars 3 ⊖	d																								
Denmark Hill 4	d								15 18	15 24														15 48	15 54
Peckham Rye 4	d						15 12	15 17	15a21	15 26	15 31										15 42	15 47		15a51	15 56
Queens Rd Peckham	d							15 19		15 29	15 34											15 49			15 59
South Bermondsey	d							15 22		15 31	15 36											15 52			16 01
Clapham Junction 10	d				14 57														15 27						
Wandsworth Common	d				15 00														15 30						
Balham 4 ⊖	d				15 02														15 32						
Streatham Hill	d				15 05														15 35						
West Norwood 4	d				15 10		15 23												15 40		15 53				
Gipsy Hill	d				15 13		15 26												15 43		15 56				
Crystal Palace 4	d			15 13	15 21	15 28	15a29											15 43	15 51	15 58	15a59				
Sydenham	d			15 16	15 24	15 31						15 21			15 36	15 42		15 46	15 54	16 01					
Forest Hill 4	d			15 19	15 27	15 34						15 23			15 38	15 45		15 49	15 57	16 04					
Honor Oak Park	d			15 21	15 29	15 36						15 26			15 41	15 47		15 51	15 59	16 06					
Brockley	d			15 24	15 32	15 39						15 28			15 43	15 50		15 54	16 02	16 09					
New Cross Gate 4	a			15 26	15 34	15 41						15 31			15 46	15 52		15 56	16 04	16 11					
	d			15 26	15 34	15 41						15 31			15 46	15 52		15 56	16 04	16 11					
New Cross ELL	d	15 21												15 36			15 51								
Surrey Quays	d	15 25		15 30		15 45						15 35		15 40	15 49		15 55	16 00		16 15					
Canada Water	d	15 27		15 32		15 47						15 37		15 42	15 51		15 57	16 02		16 17					
Rotherhithe	d	15 28		15 33		15 48						15 38		15 43	15 53		15 58	16 03		16 18					
Wapping	d	15 30		15 35		15 50						15 40		15 45	15 54		16 00	16 05		16 20					
Shadwell	d	15 32		15 37		15 52						15 42		15 47	15 56		16 02	16 07		16 22					
Whitechapel	d	15 34		15 39		15 54						15 44		15 49	15 59		16 04	16 09		16 24					
Shoreditch High Street	d	15 36		15 41		15 56						15 46		15 51	16 01		16 06	16 11		16 26					
Hoxton	d	15 38		15 43		15 58						15 48		15 53	16 03		16 08	16 13		16 28					
Haggerston	d	15 40		15 45		16 00						15 50		15 55	16 05		16 10	16 15		16 30					
Dalston Junction Stn ELL	a	15 47		15 47		16 02						15 52		16 02	16 07		16 17	16 17		16 32					
Canonbury	d			15 50		16 05						15 57			16 12			16 20		16 35					
Highbury & Islington	a			15 58		16 13						16 05			16 19			16 28		16 43					
	d																								
London Bridge 4 ⊖	a				15 41			15 26		15 36	15 41					15 59			16 11			15 56			16 06

		SN	LO	LO	LO	SN	SN	LO		LO	SN	LO	SN	SN	SE	SN	SN	LO		LO	LO	SN	LO	LO	SN
East Croydon	d						16 00															16 30			
West Croydon 4	d	15 31	15 39		15 52												16 01	16 09			16 22				
Norwood Junction 2	d		15 43		15 58		16 05											16 13			16 28	16 35			
Anerley	d		15 46		16 01		16 08											16 16			16 31	16 38			
Penge West	d		15 48		16 03		16 10											16 18			16 33	16 40			
London Victoria 15 ⊖	d										15 49				16 09	16 11									16 19
Battersea Park 4	d										15 53					16 15									16 23
Wandsworth Road	d															16 17									
Clapham High Street ⊖	d															16 19									
London Blackfriars 3 ⊖	d																								
Denmark Hill 4	d														16 18	16 24									
Peckham Rye 4	d	16 01				16 07							16 12	16 17	16a21	16 26	16 31								
Queens Rd Peckham	d	16 04				16 10								16 19		16 29	16 34								
South Bermondsey	d	16 06				16 12								16 22		16 31	16 36								
Clapham Junction 10	d										15 57														16 27
Wandsworth Common	d										16 00														16 30
Balham 4 ⊖	d										16 02														16 32
Streatham Hill	d										16 05														16 35
West Norwood 4	d										16 10		16 23												16 39
Gipsy Hill	d										16 13		16 26												16 44
Crystal Palace 4	d									16 13	16 21	16 28	16a29											16 43	16 50
Sydenham	d		15 51		16 06		16 12			16 16	16 24	16 31						16 21			16 36	16 42		16 46	16 54
Forest Hill 4	d		15 53		16 08		16 15			16 19	16 27	16 34						16 23			16 38	16 45		16 49	16 56
Honor Oak Park	d		15 56		16 11		16 17			16 21	16 29	16 36						16 26			16 41	16 47		16 51	16 59
Brockley	d		15 58		16 13		16 20			16 24	16 32	16 39						16 28			16 43	16 50		16 54	17 01
New Cross Gate 4	a		16 01		16 16		16 22			16 26	16 34	16 41						16 31			16 46	16 52		16 56	17 04
	d		16 01		16 16		16 22			16 26	16 34	16 41						16 31			16 46	16 52		16 56	17 04
New Cross ELL	d			16 06				16 21												16 36			16 51		
Surrey Quays	d		16 05	16 10	16 19			16 25		16 30		16 45						16 35		16 40	16 49		16 55	17 00	
Canada Water	d		16 07	16 12	16 21			16 27		16 32		16 47						16 37		16 42	16 51		16 57	17 02	
Rotherhithe	d		16 08	16 13	16 23			16 28		16 33		16 48						16 38		16 43	16 53		16 58	17 03	
Wapping	d		16 10	16 15	16 24			16 30		16 35		16 50						16 40		16 45	16 54		17 00	17 05	
Shadwell	d		16 12	16 17	16 26			16 32		16 37		16 52						16 42		16 47	16 56		17 02	17 07	
Whitechapel	d		16 14	16 19	16 29			16 34		16 39		16 54						16 44		16 49	16 59		17 04	17 09	
Shoreditch High Street	d		16 16	16 21	16 31			16 36		16 41		16 56						16 46		16 51	17 01		17 06	17 11	
Hoxton	d		16 18	16 23	16 33			16 38		16 43		16 58						16 48		16 53	17 03		17 08	17 13	
Haggerston	d		16 20	16 25	16 35			16 40		16 45		17 00						16 50		16 55	17 05		17 10	17 15	
Dalston Junction Stn ELL	a		16 22	16 32	16 37			16 47		16 47		17 02						16 52		17 02	17 07		17 17	17 17	
Canonbury	d		16 27		16 42					16 50		17 05						16 57			17 12			17 20	
Highbury & Islington	a		16 35		16 49					16 58		17 13						17 05			17 19			17 28	
	d																								
London Bridge 4 ⊖	a	16 11				16 17	16 29				16 41			16 26		16 38	16 41					17 02			17 12

Table 178

Mondays to Fridays

29 August to 7 September

East London Line and Croydon - London Victoria to London Bridge

Network Diagram - see first Page of Table 177

		LO	SN	SN		SE	SN	SN	LO	LO	LO	SN	LO	LO		SN	SN	SE	SN	SN	SN	LO	SN	SN	
East Croydon	d											17 00													
West Croydon 4	d							16 31	16 39		16 52										17 01	17 09	17 12		
Norwood Junction 2	d								16 43		16 58	17 05										17 13			
Anerley	d								16 46		17 01	17 08										17 16			
Penge West	d								16 48		17 03	17 10										17 18			
London Victoria 15 ⊖	d					16 39	16 41									16 49		17 04		17 11					
Battersea Park 4	d						16 45									16 53				17 15					
Wandsworth Road	d						16 47													17 17					
Clapham High Street ⊖	d						16 49													17 19					
London Blackfriars 3 ⊖	d																								
Denmark Hill 4	d					16 48	16 54											17 13		17 24					
Peckham Rye 4	d		16 42	16 47		16a51	16 56	17 00									17 07	17a16	17 17	17 26	17 29			17 35	
Queens Rd Peckham	d			16 49			16 59	17 03											17 19	17 29	17 32			17 37	
South Bermondsey	d			16 52			17 01	17 05											17 22	17 31	17 34			17 40	
Clapham Junction 10	d															16 57									
Wandsworth Common	d															17 00									
Balham 4 ⊖	d															17 03									
Streatham Hill	d															17 06									
West Norwood 4	d		16 53													17 09	17 20								
Gipsy Hill	d		16 56													17 12	17 23								
Crystal Palace 4	d	16 58	16a59											17 13		17 21	17a26								
Sydenham	d	17 01							16 51		17 06	17 12		17 16		17 24						17 21			
Forest Hill 4	d	17 04							16 53		17 08	17 15		17 19		17 27						17 23			
Honor Oak Park	d	17 06							16 56		17 11	17 17		17 21		17 29						17 26			
Brockley	d	17 09							16 58		17 13	17 20		17 24		17 32						17 28			
New Cross Gate 4	a	17 11							17 01		17 16	17 22		17 26		17 34						17 31			
	d	17 11							17 01		17 16	17 22		17 26		17 34						17 31			
New Cross ELL	d									17 06			17 21												
Surrey Quays	d	17 15							17 05	17 10	17 19		17 25	17 30								17 35			
Canada Water	d	17 17							17 07	17 12	17 21		17 27	17 32								17 37			
Rotherhithe	d	17 18							17 08	17 13	17 23		17 28	17 33								17 38			
Wapping	d	17 20							17 10	17 15	17 24		17 30	17 35								17 40			
Shadwell	d	17 22							17 12	17 17	17 26		17 32	17 37								17 42			
Whitechapel	d	17 24							17 14	17 19	17 29		17 34	17 39								17 44			
Shoreditch High Street	d	17 26							17 16	17 21	17 31		17 36	17 41								17 46			
Hoxton	d	17 28							17 18	17 23	17 33		17 38	17 43								17 48			
Haggerston	d	17 30							17 20	17 25	17 35		17 40	17 45								17 50			
Dalston Junction Stn ELL	a	17 32							17 22	17 32	17 37		17 47	17 47								17 52			
Canonbury	d	17 35							17 27		17 42			17 50								17 57			
Highbury & Islington	a	17 43							17 35		17 49			17 58								18 05			
	d																								
London Bridge 4 ⊖	a			16 56			17 08	17 10				17 35				17 43			17 27	17 38	17 40		17 28	17 44	

		LO	LO	LO	LO	LO	SN	SN	SE	SN		SN	SN	SN	LO	SN	LO	LO	LO	SN		LO	LO	SN	SN
East Croydon	d											17 30													
West Croydon 4	d			17 22										17 31	17 39	17 42			17 52						
Norwood Junction 2	d			17 28						17 32		17 35			17 43				17 58	18 04					
Anerley	d			17 31								17 38			17 46				18 01	18 07					
Penge West	d			17 33								17 40			17 48				18 03	18 09					
London Victoria 15 ⊖	d						17 22		17 34				17 41											17 52	
Battersea Park 4	d						17 26						17 45											17 56	
Wandsworth Road	d												17 47												
Clapham High Street ⊖	d												17 49												
London Blackfriars 3 ⊖	d																								
Denmark Hill 4	d								17 43				17 54												
Peckham Rye 4	d							17 37	17a46	17 53			17 57	18 01											18 07
Queens Rd Peckham	d									17 55			17 59	18 04											
South Bermondsey	d									17 58			18 02	18 06											
Clapham Junction 10	d						17 30																	18 00	
Wandsworth Common	d						17 33																	18 03	
Balham 4 ⊖	d						17 35																	18 05	
Streatham Hill	d						17 38																	18 08	
West Norwood 4	d						17 42	17 49																18 14	18 20
Gipsy Hill	d						17 45	17 52																18 17	18 23
Crystal Palace 4	d		17 28			17 43	17 48	17a54										17 58					18 13	18 20	18a26
Sydenham	d		17 31	17 36		17 46	17 54					17 42			17 51			18 01	18 06	18 11			18 16	18 24	
Forest Hill 4	d		17 34	17 38		17 49	17 57					17 45			17 53			18 04	18 08	18 14			18 19	18 27	
Honor Oak Park	d		17 36	17 41		17 51	17 59					17 47			17 56			18 06	18 11	18 16			18 21	18 29	
Brockley	d		17 39	17 43		17 54	18 02					17 50			17 58			18 09	18 13	18 19			18 24	18 32	
New Cross Gate 4	a		17 41	17 46		17 56	18 04					17 52			18 01			18 11	18 16	18 21			18 26	18 34	
	d		17 41	17 46		17 56	18 04					17 52			18 01			18 11	18 16	18 21			18 26	18 34	
New Cross ELL	d	17 36			17 51												18 06					18 21			
Surrey Quays	d	17 40	17 45	17 49	17 55	18 00									18 05		18 10	18 15	18 19			18 25	18 30		
Canada Water	d	17 42	17 47	17 51	17 57	18 02									18 07		18 12	18 17	18 21			18 27	18 32		
Rotherhithe	d	17 43	17 48	17 53	17 58	18 03									18 08		18 13	18 18	18 23			18 28	18 33		
Wapping	d	17 45	17 50	17 54	18 00	18 05									18 10		18 15	18 20	18 24			18 30	18 35		
Shadwell	d	17 47	17 52	17 56	18 02	18 07									18 12		18 17	18 22	18 26			18 32	18 37		
Whitechapel	d	17 49	17 54	17 59	18 04	18 09									18 14		18 19	18 24	18 29			18 34	18 39		
Shoreditch High Street	d	17 51	17 56	18 01	18 06	18 11									18 16		18 21	18 26	18 31			18 36	18 41		
Hoxton	d	17 53	17 58	18 03	18 08	18 13									18 18		18 23	18 28	18 33			18 38	18 43		
Haggerston	d	17 55	18 00	18 05	18 10	18 15									18 20		18 25	18 30	18 35			18 40	18 45		
Dalston Junction Stn ELL	a	18 02	18 02	18 07	18 17	18 17									18 23		18 32	18 32	18 37			18 47	18 47		
Canonbury	d		18 05	18 12		18 20									18 27			18 35	18 42				18 50		
Highbury & Islington	a		18 13	18 19		18 28									18 35			18 43	18 49				18 58		
	d																								
London Bridge 4 ⊖	a						18 13			18 02		17 59	18 08	18 11		18 00				18 31				18 45	

East London Line and Croydon - London Victoria to London Bridge

Network Diagram - see first Page of Table 177

Station		SE	SN	SN	SN	LO		SN	LO	LO	LO	LO	SE	SN	SN	SN		LO	SN	SN	SE	SN	SN	LO	LO
East Croydon	d															18 30									
West Croydon 4	d				18 01	18 09		18 13			18 22												18 31	18 39	
Norwood Junction 2	d					18 13					18 28					18 35								18 43	
Anerley	d					18 16					18 31					18 38								18 46	
Penge West	d					18 18					18 33					18 40								18 48	
London Victoria 15 ⊖	d	17 56		18 11									18 18						18 22		18 39	18 41			
Battersea Park 4	d			18 15															18 26			18 45			
Wandsworth Road	d			18 17																		18 47			
Clapham High Street ⊖	d			18 19																		18 49			
London Blackfriars 3 ⊖	d																								
Denmark Hill 4	d	18 06		18 24									18 28								18 48	18 54			
Peckham Rye 4	d	18a08	18 12	18 26	18 29								18a31	18 32	18 36					18 37	18a51	18 57	19 01		
Queens Rd Peckham	d		18 15	18 29	18 32									18 35	18 38							19 00	19 04		
South Bermondsey	d		18 17	18 31	18 34									18 37	18 41							19 02	19 06		
Clapham Junction 10	d																		18 30						
Wandsworth Common	d																		18 33						
Balham 4 ⊖	d																		18 35						
Streatham Hill	d																		18 38						
West Norwood 4	d																		18 42	18 51					
Gipsy Hill	d																		18 45	18 54					
Crystal Palace 4	d									18 28								18 43	18 51	18a57					
Sydenham	d					18 21				18 31	18 36					18 42		18 46	18 54					18 51	
Forest Hill 4	d					18 23				18 34	18 38					18 45		18 49	18 57					18 53	
Honor Oak Park	d					18 26				18 36	18 41					18 47		18 51	18 59					18 56	
Brockley	d					18 28				18 39	18 43					18 50		18 54	19 02					18 58	
New Cross Gate 4	a					18 31				18 41	18 46					18 52		18 56	19 04					19 01	
	d					18 31				18 41	18 46					18 52		18 56	19 04					19 01	
New Cross ELL	d								18 36			18 51													19 06
Surrey Quays	d					18 35			18 40	18 45	18 49	18 55						19 00						19 05	19 10
Canada Water	d					18 37			18 42	18 47	18 51	18 57						19 02						19 07	19 12
Rotherhithe	d					18 38			18 43	18 48	18 53	18 58						19 03						19 08	19 13
Wapping	d					18 40			18 45	18 50	18 54	19 00						19 05						19 10	19 15
Shadwell	d					18 42			18 47	18 52	18 56	19 02						19 07						19 12	19 17
Whitechapel	d					18 44			18 49	18 54	18 59	19 04						19 09						19 14	19 19
Shoreditch High Street	d					18 46			18 51	18 56	19 01	19 06						19 11						19 16	19 21
Hoxton	d					18 48			18 53	18 58	19 03	19 08						19 13						19 18	19 23
Haggerston	d					18 50			18 55	19 00	19 05	19 10						19 15						19 20	19 25
Dalston Junction Stn ELL	a					18 52			19 02	19 02	19 07	19 17						19 17						19 22	19 32
Canonbury	d					18 57				19 05	19 12							19 20						19 27	
Highbury & Islington	a					19 05				19 13	19 19							19 28						19 35	
	d																								
London Bridge 4 ⊖	a		18 22	18 38	18 39			18 29						18 42	18 45	18 59			19 13			19 09	19 11		

Station		LO		LO	SN	LO	LO	SN	SN	SN	SN	LO		SN	SE	SN	SN	LO	LO	LO	SN	LO		LO	SN
East Croydon	d				19 00																19 30				
West Croydon 4	d			18 52													19 01	19 09		19 22					
Norwood Junction 2	d			18 58	19 05													19 13		19 28	19 35				
Anerley	d			19 01	19 08													19 16		19 31	19 38				
Penge West	d			19 03	19 10													19 18		19 33	19 40				
London Victoria 15 ⊖	d							18 52							19 09	19 11									19 22
Battersea Park 4	d							18 56								19 15									19 26
Wandsworth Road	d															19 17									
Clapham High Street ⊖	d															19 19									
London Blackfriars 3 ⊖	d																								
Denmark Hill 4	d														19 18	19 24									
Peckham Rye 4	d								19 06	19 07	19 14			19 17	19a21	19 26	19 29								
Queens Rd Peckham	d									19 10	19 17					19 29	19 32								
South Bermondsey	d									19 12	19 19					19 31	19 34								
Clapham Junction 10	d							19 00																	19 30
Wandsworth Common	d							19 03																	19 33
Balham 4 ⊖	d							19 05																	19 35
Streatham Hill	d							19 08																	19 38
West Norwood 4	d							19 12	19 17					19 30											19 42
Gipsy Hill	d							19 15	19 20					19 33											19 45
Crystal Palace 4	d	18 58					19 13	19 21	19a23			19 28		19a35										19 43	19 51
Sydenham	d	19 01		19 06	19 12		19 16	19 24				19 31						19 21		19 36	19 42			19 46	19 54
Forest Hill 4	d	19 04		19 08	19 15		19 19	19 27				19 34						19 23		19 38	19 45			19 49	19 57
Honor Oak Park	d	19 06		19 11	19 17		19 21	19 29				19 36						19 26		19 41	19 47			19 51	19 59
Brockley	d	19 09		19 13	19 20		19 24	19 32				19 39						19 28		19 43	19 50			19 54	20 02
New Cross Gate 4	a	19 11		19 16	19 22		19 26	19 34				19 41						19 31		19 46	19 52			19 56	20 04
	d	19 11		19 16	19 22		19 26	19 34				19 41						19 31		19 46	19 52			19 56	20 04
New Cross ELL	d					19 21													19 36			19 51			
Surrey Quays	d	19 15		19 19		19 25	19 30					19 45						19 35	19 40	19 49		19 55		20 00	
Canada Water	d	19 17		19 21		19 27	19 32					19 47						19 37	19 42	19 51		19 57		20 02	
Rotherhithe	d	19 18		19 23		19 28	19 33					19 48						19 38	19 43	19 53		19 58		20 03	
Wapping	d	19 20		19 24		19 30	19 35					19 50						19 40	19 45	19 54		20 00		20 05	
Shadwell	d	19 22		19 26		19 32	19 37					19 52						19 42	19 47	19 56		20 02		20 07	
Whitechapel	d	19 24		19 29		19 34	19 39					19 54						19 44	19 49	19 59		20 04		20 09	
Shoreditch High Street	d	19 26		19 31		19 36	19 41					19 56						19 46	19 51	20 01		20 06		20 11	
Hoxton	d	19 28		19 33		19 38	19 43					19 58						19 48	19 53	20 03		20 08		20 13	
Haggerston	d	19 30		19 35		19 40	19 45					20 00						19 50	19 55	20 05		20 10		20 15	
Dalston Junction Stn ELL	a	19 32		19 37		19 47	19 47					20 02						19 52	20 02	20 07		20 17		20 17	
Canonbury	d	19 35		19 42			19 50					20 05						19 57		20 12				20 20	
Highbury & Islington	a	19 43		19 49			19 58					20 13						20 05		20 19				20 28	
	d																								
London Bridge 4 ⊖	a				19 29			19 41		19 17	19 24					19 36	19 41				19 59				20 11

Table 178

East London Line and Croydon - London Victoria to London Bridge

Mondays to Fridays

29 August to 7 September

Network Diagram - see first Page of Table 177

Station		SN	SN	LO	SN	SN	SE	SN		SN	LO	LO	LO	SN	LO	LO	SN	LO		SN	SN	SN	SN	LO	LO
East Croydon	d													20 00											
West Croydon 4	d									19 31	19 39		19 52										20 01	20 09	
Norwood Junction 2	d										19 43		19 58	20 05										20 13	
Anerley	d										19 46		20 01	20 08										20 16	
Penge West	d										19 48		20 03	20 10										20 18	
London Victoria 15 ⊖	d						19 39	19 41									19 52					20 11			
Battersea Park 4	d							19 45									19 56					20 15			
Wandsworth Road	d							19 47														20 17			
Clapham High Street ⊖	d							19 49														20 19			
London Blackfriars 3 ⊖	d																								
Denmark Hill 4	d						19 48	19 54														20 24			
Peckham Rye 4	d	19 37	19 38		19 47	19 49	19a51	19 56		20 01										20 12	20 18	20 26	20 31		
Queens Rd Peckham	d		19 41			19 51		19 59		20 04											20 21	20 29	20 34		
South Bermondsey	d		19 43			19 54		20 01		20 06											20 23	20 31	20 36		
Clapham Junction 10	d																20 00								
Wandsworth Common	d																20 03								
Balham 4 ⊖	d																20 05								
Streatham Hill	d																20 08								
West Norwood 4	d	19 49			20 00												20 12			20 24					
Gipsy Hill	d	19 52			20 03												20 15			20 27					
Crystal Palace 4	d	19a54		19 58	20a05											20 13	20 21	20 28		20a29					
Sydenham	d			20 01							19 51		20 06	20 12		20 16	20 24	20 31						20 21	
Forest Hill 4	d			20 04							19 53		20 08	20 15		20 19	20 27	20 34						20 23	
Honor Oak Park	d			20 06							19 56		20 11	20 17		20 21	20 29	20 36						20 26	
Brockley	d			20 09							19 58		20 13	20 20		20 24	20 32	20 39						20 28	
New Cross Gate 4	a			20 11							20 01		20 16	20 22		20 26	20 34	20 41						20 31	
	d			20 11							20 01		20 16	20 22		20 26	20 34	20 41						20 31	
New Cross ELL	d											20 06			20 21										20 36
Surrey Quays	d			20 15							20 05	20 10	20 19		20 25	20 30		20 45						20 35	20 40
Canada Water	d			20 17							20 07	20 12	20 21		20 27	20 32		20 47						20 37	20 42
Rotherhithe	d			20 18							20 08	20 13	20 23		20 28	20 33		20 48						20 38	20 43
Wapping	d			20 20							20 10	20 15	20 24		20 30	20 35		20 50						20 40	20 45
Shadwell	d			20 22							20 12	20 17	20 26		20 32	20 37		20 52						20 42	20 47
Whitechapel	d			20 24							20 14	20 19	20 29		20 34	20 39		20 54						20 44	20 49
Shoreditch High Street	d			20 26							20 16	20 21	20 31		20 36	20 41		20 56						20 46	20 51
Hoxton	d			20 28							20 18	20 23	20 33		20 38	20 43		20 58						20 48	20 53
Haggerston	d			20 30							20 20	20 25	20 35		20 40	20 45		21 00						20 50	20 55
Dalston Junction Stn ELL	a			20 32							20 22	20 32	20 37		20 47	20 47		21 02						20 52	21 02
Canonbury	d			20 35							20 27		20 42			20 50		21 05						20 57	
Highbury & Islington	a			20 43							20 35		20 49			20 58		21 13						21 05	
	d																								
London Bridge 4 ⊖	a		19 51			19 58		20 06		20 14				20 29			20 41				20 28	20 36	20 41		

Station		LO	SN	LO		LO	SN	LO	SN	SN	SN	SN	LO	LO		LO	SN	LO	LO	SN	LO	SN	SN	SN
East Croydon	d		20 31														21 00							
West Croydon 4	d	20 22										20 31	20 39			20 52								
Norwood Junction 2	d	20 28	20 35										20 43			20 58	21 05							
Anerley	d	20 31	20 38										20 46			21 01	21 08							
Penge West	d	20 33	20 40										20 48			21 03	21 10							
London Victoria 15 ⊖	d						20 22				20 41									20 52				21 11
Battersea Park 4	d						20 26				20 45									20 56				21 15
Wandsworth Road	d										20 47													21 17
Clapham High Street ⊖	d										20 49													21 19
London Blackfriars 3 ⊖	d																							
Denmark Hill 4	d										20 54													21 24
Peckham Rye 4	d								20 42	20 48	20 56	21 01										21 12	21 17	21 26
Queens Rd Peckham	d									20 50	20 59	21 04											21 19	21 29
South Bermondsey	d									20 53	21 01	21 06											21 22	21 31
Clapham Junction 10	d						20 30													21 00				
Wandsworth Common	d						20 33													21 03				
Balham 4 ⊖	d						20 35													21 05				
Streatham Hill	d						20 38													21 08				
West Norwood 4	d						20 42		20 54											21 12		21 24		
Gipsy Hill	d						20 45		20 57											21 15		21 27		
Crystal Palace 4	d					20 43	20 51	20 58	20a59										21 13	21 21	21 28	21a29		
Sydenham	d	20 36	20 42			20 46	20 54	21 01					20 51			21 06	21 12		21 16	21 27	21 31			
Forest Hill 4	d	20 38	20 45			20 49	20 57	21 04					20 53			21 08	21 15		21 19	21 29	21 34			
Honor Oak Park	d	20 41	20 47			20 51	20 59	21 06					20 56			21 11	21 17		21 21	21 32	21 36			
Brockley	d	20 43	20 50			20 54	21 02	21 09					20 58			21 13	21 20		21 24	21 34	21 39			
New Cross Gate 4	a	20 46	20 52			20 56	21 04	21 11					21 01			21 16	21 22		21 26	21 37	21 41			
	d	20 46	20 52			20 56	21 04	21 11					21 01			21 16	21 22		21 26	21 37	21 41			
New Cross ELL	d			20 51										21 06				21 21						
Surrey Quays	d	20 49		20 55		21 00		21 15					21 05	21 10		21 19		21 25	21 30		21 45			
Canada Water	d	20 51		20 57		21 02		21 17					21 07	21 12		21 21		21 27	21 32		21 47			
Rotherhithe	d	20 53		20 58		21 03		21 18					21 08	21 13		21 23		21 28	21 33		21 48			
Wapping	d	20 54		21 00		21 05		21 20					21 10	21 15		21 24		21 30	21 35		21 50			
Shadwell	d	20 56		21 02		21 07		21 22					21 12	21 17		21 26		21 32	21 37		21 52			
Whitechapel	d	20 59		21 04		21 09		21 24					21 14	21 19		21 29		21 34	21 39		21 54			
Shoreditch High Street	d	21 01		21 06		21 11		21 26					21 16	21 21		21 31		21 36	21 41		21 56			
Hoxton	d	21 03		21 08		21 13		21 28					21 18	21 23		21 33		21 38	21 43		21 58			
Haggerston	d	21 05		21 10		21 15		21 30					21 20	21 25		21 35		21 40	21 45		22 00			
Dalston Junction Stn ELL	a	21 07		21 17		21 17		21 32					21 22	21 32		21 37		21 47	21 47		22 02			
Canonbury	d	21 12				21 20		21 35					21 27			21 42			21 50		22 05			
Highbury & Islington	a	21 19				21 28		21 43					21 35			21 49			21 58		22 13			
	d																							
London Bridge 4 ⊖	a		20 59				21 11			20 57	21 06	21 11					21 29			21 43			21 26	21 36

Table 178

Mondays to Fridays

29 August to 7 September

East London Line and Croydon - London Victoria to London Bridge

Network Diagram - see first Page of Table 177

Station		SN	LO	LO	LO	SN	LO	LO	SN	LO		SN	SN	SE	SN	SN	LO	LO	LO	SN		LO	SN	LO	SN
East Croydon ⇌	d					21 30														22 00					
West Croydon 4 ⇌	d	21 01	21 09		21 22											21 31	21 39		21 52						
Norwood Junction 2	d		21 13		21 28	21 35											21 43		21 58	22 05					
Anerley	d		21 16		21 31	21 38											21 46		22 01	22 08					
Penge West	d		21 18		21 33	21 40											21 48		22 03	22 10					
London Victoria 15 ⊖	d								21 23						21 41								21 52		
Battersea Park 4	d								21 27						21 45								21 56		
Wandsworth Road	d														21 47										
Clapham High Street ⊖	d														21 49										
London Blackfriars 3 ⊖	d													21 42											
Denmark Hill 4	d													21 52	21 54										
Peckham Rye 4	d	21 31										21 42	21 47	21a55	21 56	22 01									22 12
Queens Rd Peckham	d	21 34											21 49		21 59	22 04									
South Bermondsey	d	21 36											21 52		22 01	22 06									
Clapham Junction 10	d								21 31														22 00		
Wandsworth Common	d								21 34														22 03		
Balham 4 ⊖	d								21 36														22 05		
Streatham Hill	d								21 39														22 08		
West Norwood 4	d								21 43			21 54											22 12		22 24
Gipsy Hill	d								21 46			21 57											22 15		22 27
Crystal Palace 4	d							21 43	21 51	21 58		21a59										22 13	22 21	22 28	22a29
Sydenham	d		21 21		21 36	21 42		21 46	21 54	22 01							21 51		22 06	22 12		22 16	22 24	22 31	
Forest Hill 4	d		21 23		21 38	21 45		21 49	21 57	22 04							21 53		22 08	22 15		22 19	22 27	22 34	
Honor Oak Park	d		21 26		21 41	21 47		21 51	21 59	22 06							21 56		22 11	22 17		22 21	22 29	22 36	
Brockley	d		21 28		21 43	21 50		21 54	22 02	22 09							21 58		22 13	22 20		22 24	22 32	22 39	
New Cross Gate 4	a		21 31		21 46	21 52		21 56	22 04	22 11							22 01		22 16	22 22		22 26	22 34	22 41	
	d		21 31		21 46	21 52		21 56	22 04	22 11							22 01		22 16	22 22		22 26	22 34	22 41	
New Cross ELL	d			21 36			21 51											22 06							
Surrey Quays	d		21 35	21 40	21 49		21 55	22 00		22 15							22 05	22 10	22 19			22 30		22 45	
Canada Water	d		21 37	21 42	21 51		21 57	22 02		22 17							22 07	22 12	22 21			22 32		22 47	
Rotherhithe	d		21 38	21 43	21 53		21 58	22 03		22 18							22 08	22 13	22 23			22 33		22 48	
Wapping	d		21 40	21 45	21 54		22 00	22 05		22 20							22 10	22 15	22 24			22 35		22 50	
Shadwell	d		21 42	21 47	21 56		22 02	22 07		22 22							22 12	22 17	22 26			22 37		22 52	
Whitechapel	d		21 44	21 49	21 59		22 04	22 09		22 24							22 14	22 19	22 29			22 39		22 54	
Shoreditch High Street	d		21 46	21 51	22 01		22 06	22 11		22 26							22 16	22 21	22 31			22 41		22 56	
Hoxton	d		21 48	21 53	22 03		22 08	22 13		22 28							22 18	22 23	22 33			22 43		22 58	
Haggerston	d		21 50	21 55	22 05		22 10	22 15		22 30							22 20	22 25	22 35			22 45		23 00	
Dalston Junction Stn ELL	a		21 52	22 02	22 07		22 17	22 17		22 32							22 22	22 33	22 37			22 47		23 02	
Canonbury	d		21 57		22 12			22 20		22 35							22 27		22 42			22 50		23 05	
Highbury & Islington	a		22 05		22 19			22 28		22 43							22 35		22 49			22 58		23 13	
	d																								
London Bridge 4 ⊖	a	21 41				21 59			22 13				21 56		22 06	22 11				22 29			22 45		

Station		SN	SE	SN	SN	LO		LO	LO	SN	LO	SN	SN	SN	SE	SN		SN	LO	LO	LO	SN	LO	SN	SN
East Croydon ⇌	d									22 30												23 01			
West Croydon 4 ⇌	d				22 01	22 09			22 22									22 31	22 39		22 52				
Norwood Junction 2	d					22 13			22 28	22 35									22 43		22 58	23 06			
Anerley	d					22 16			22 31	22 38									22 46		23 01	23 09			
Penge West	d					22 18			22 33	22 40									22 48		23 03	23 11			
London Victoria 15 ⊖	d			22 11								22 22				22 41								22 52	
Battersea Park 4	d			22 15								22 26				22 45								22 56	
Wandsworth Road	d			22 17												22 47									
Clapham High Street ⊖	d			22 19												22 49									
London Blackfriars 3 ⊖	d		22 12												22 42										
Denmark Hill 4	d		22 22	22 24											22 52	22 54									
Peckham Rye 4	d	22 17	22a25	22 26	22 31								22 42	22 43	22a55	22 56		23 01							23 14
Queens Rd Peckham	d	22 19		22 29	22 34									22 45		22 59		23 04							
South Bermondsey	d	22 22		22 31	22 36									22 48		23 01		23 06							
Clapham Junction 10	d											22 30												23 00	
Wandsworth Common	d											22 33												23 03	
Balham 4 ⊖	d											22 35												23 05	
Streatham Hill	d											22 38												23 08	
West Norwood 4	d											22 42	22 54											23 12	23 26
Gipsy Hill	d											22 45	22 57											23 15	23 29
Crystal Palace 4	d										22 43	22 51	22a59										23 13	23 21	23a31
Sydenham	d					22 21			22 36	22 42	22 46	22 54							22 51		23 06	23 13	23 16	23 24	
Forest Hill 4	d					22 23			22 38	22 45	22 49	22 57							22 53		23 08	23 16	23 19	23 27	
Honor Oak Park	d					22 26			22 41	22 47	22 51	22 59							22 56		23 11	23 18	23 21	23 29	
Brockley	d					22 28			22 43	22 50	22 54	23 02							22 58		23 13	23 21	23 24	23 32	
New Cross Gate 4	a					22 31			22 46	22 52	22 56	23 04							23 01		23 16	23 23	23 26	23 34	
	d					22 31			22 46	22 52	22 56	23 04							23 01		23 16	23 23	23 26	23 34	
New Cross ELL	d							22 36												23 06					
Surrey Quays	d					22 35		22 40	22 49		23 00								23 05	23 10	23 19		23 30		
Canada Water	d					22 37		22 42	22 51		23 02								23 07	23 12	23 21		23 32		
Rotherhithe	d					22 38		22 43	22 53		23 03								23 08	23 13	23 23		23 33		
Wapping	d					22 40		22 45	22 54		23 05								23 10	23 15	23 24		23 35		
Shadwell	d					22 42		22 47	22 56		23 07								23 12	23 17	23 26		23 37		
Whitechapel	d					22 44		22 49	22 59		23 09								23 14	23 19	23 29		23 39		
Shoreditch High Street	d					22 46		22 51	23 01		23 11								23 16	23 21	23 31		23 41		
Hoxton	d					22 48		22 53	23 03		23 13								23 18	23 23	23 33		23 43		
Haggerston	d					22 50		22 55	23 05		23 15								23 20	23 25	23 35		23 45		
Dalston Junction Stn ELL	a					22 52		23 02	23 07		23 17								23 22	23 32	23 37		23 47		
Canonbury	d					22 57			23 12		23 20								23 27		23 44		23 50		
Highbury & Islington	a					23 05			23 19		23 28								23 35		23 51		23 58		
	d																								
London Bridge 4 ⊖	a	22 26		22 36	22 41					22 59		23 11		22 52		23 06		23 11				23 30		23 45	

Table 178

Mondays to Fridays

29 August to 7 September

East London Line and Croydon - London Victoria to London Bridge

Network Diagram - see first Page of Table 177

		SN		SE	SN	SN	LO	LO	LO	SN	SN	SN		SE	SN
East Croydon	d														
West Croydon 4	d					23 01		23 22							
Norwood Junction 2	d							23 28							
Anerley	d							23 31							
Penge West	d							23 33							
London Victoria 15 ⊖	d				23 11					23 22					23 54
Battersea Park 4	d				23 15					23 26					23 58
Wandsworth Road	d				23 17										
Clapham High Street ⊖	d				23 19										
London Blackfriars 3 ⊖	d			23 12										23 42	
Denmark Hill 4	d			23 22	23 24									23 52	
Peckham Rye 4	d	23 17		23a25	23 26	23 31					23 42	23 47		23a55	
Queens Rd Peckham	d	23 19			23 29	23 34						23 49			
South Bermondsey	d	23 22			23 31	23 36						23 52			
Clapham Junction 10	d									23 30					00 02
Wandsworth Common	d									23 33					00 05
Balham 4 ⊖	d									23 35					00 07
Streatham Hill	d									23 38					00 10
West Norwood 4	d									23 42	23 54				00 14
Gipsy Hill	d									23 45	23 57				00 17
Crystal Palace 4	d								23 43	23 51	23a59				00 21
Sydenham	d							23 36	23 46	23 54					00 24
Forest Hill 4	d							23 38	23 49	23 57					00 27
Honor Oak Park	d							23 41	23 51	23 59					00 29
Brockley	d							23 43	23 54	00 02					00 32
New Cross Gate 4	a							23 46	23 56	00 04					00 34
	d							23 46	23 56	00 04					00 34
New Cross ELL	d						23 36								
Surrey Quays	d						23 40	23 49	23 59						
Canada Water	d						23 42	23 51	00 02						
Rotherhithe	d						23 43	23 53	00 03						
Wapping	d						23 45	23 54	00 05						
Shadwell	d						23 47	23 56	00 07						
Whitechapel	d						23 49	23 59	00 09						
Shoreditch High Street	d						23 51	00 01	00 11						
Hoxton	d						23 53	00 03	00 13						
Haggerston	d						23 55	00 05	00 15						
Dalston Junction Stn ELL	a						23 58	00 07	00 17						
Canonbury	d						00 01	00 11	00 20						
Highbury & Islington	a						00 10	00 18	00 28						
	d														
London Bridge 4 ⊖	a	23 26			23 36	23 41				00 11		23 56			00 41

Mondays to Fridays

from 10 September

		LO A	LO A	LO MX	LO A	LO MX	LO A	SN MO	SN MX	SN MX		SN MX	SN	LO	LO	LO	SE A	SE	SN	LO		LO	LO	LO	SN
East Croydon	d												05 13						05 51						06 13
West Croydon 4	d			23p22	23p25									05 39						05 52				06 09	
Norwood Junction 2	d			23p28	23p31								05 17	05 43					05 55	05 58				06 13	06 18
Anerley	d			23p31	23p34								05 20	05 46						06 01				06 16	06 21
Penge West	d			23p33	23p36								05 22	05 48						06 03				06 18	06 23
London Victoria 15 ⊖	d								23p22	23p54							00 56								
Battersea Park 4	d								23p26	23p58															
Wandsworth Road	d																								
Clapham High Street ⊖	d																								
London Blackfriars 3 ⊖	d																	05 28							
Denmark Hill 4	d																01s05	05 39							
Peckham Rye 4	d							23p53				00 12					01s08	05a41	06 15						
Queens Rd Peckham	d							23p56											06 18						
South Bermondsey	d							23p58											06 20						
Clapham Junction 10	d								23p30	00 02															
Wandsworth Common	d								23p33	00 05															
Balham 4 ⊖	d								23p35	00 07															
Streatham Hill	d								23p38	00 10															
West Norwood 4	d								23p42	00 14		00 24													
Gipsy Hill	d								23p45	00 17		00 27													
Crystal Palace 4	d	23p16				23p43	23p46		23p51	00 21		00a29				05 58							06 13		
Sydenham	d	23p19		23p36	23p39	23p46	23p49		23p54	00 24			05 24	05 51		06 01				06 06			06 16	06 21	06 25
Forest Hill 4	d	23p22		23p38	23p41	23p49	23p52		23p57	00 27			05 27	05 53		06 04				06 08			06 19	06 23	06 28
Honor Oak Park	d	23p24		23p41	23p44	23p51	23p54		23p59	00 29			05 29	05 56		06 06				06 11			06 21	06 26	06 30
Brockley	d	23p27		23p43	23p46	23p54	23p57		00 02	00 32			05 32	05 58		06 09				06 13			06 24	06 28	06 33
New Cross Gate 4	a	23p29		23p46	23p49	23p56	23p59		00 04	00 34			05 34	06 01		06 11				06 16			06 26	06 31	06 35
	d	23p29		23p46	23p49	23p56	23p59		00 04	00 34			05 34	06 01		06 11				06 16			06 26	06 31	06 35
New Cross ELL	d		23p39												06 06							06 21			
Surrey Quays	d	23p33	23p43	23p49	23p52	23p59	00 02							06 05	06 10	06 15				06 19		06 25	06 30	06 35	
Canada Water	d	23p35	23p45	23p51	23p54	00 02	00 05							06 07	06 12	06 17				06 21		06 27	06 32	06 37	
Rotherhithe	d	23p36	23p46	23p53	23p56	00 03	00 06							06 08	06 13	06 18				06 23		06 28	06 33	06 38	
Wapping	d	23p38	23p48	23p54	23p57	00 05	00 08							06 10	06 15	06 20				06 24		06 30	06 35	06 40	
Shadwell	d	23p40	23p50	23p56	23p59	00 07	00 10							06 12	06 17	06 22				06 26		06 32	06 37	06 42	
Whitechapel	d	23p42	23p52	23p59	00 02	00 09	00 12							06 14	06 19	06 24				06 29		06 34	06 39	06 44	
Shoreditch High Street	d	23p44	23p54	00 01	00 04	00 11	00 14							06 16	06 21	06 26				06 31		06 36	06 41	06 46	
Hoxton	d	23p46	23p56	00 03	00 06	00 13	00 16							06 18	06 23	06 28				06 33		06 38	06 43	06 48	
Haggerston	d	23p48	23p58	00 05	00 08	00 15	00 18							06 20	06 25	06 30				06 35		06 40	06 45	06 50	
Dalston Junction Stn ELL	a	23p50	00 02	00 07	00 10	00 17	00 20							06 22	06 28	06 32				06 37		06 43	06 47	06 52	
Canonbury	d	23p53	00 05	00 12	00 14	00 20	00 23							06 27		06 35				06 42			06 50	06 57	
Highbury & Islington	a	00 01	00 14	00 16	00 21	00 25	00 31							06 32		06 40				06 46			06 56	07 02	
	d																								
London Bridge 4 ⊖	a							00 03	00 11	00 41			05 41						06 25						06 44

A 10 September

Table 178

Mondays to Fridays

from 10 September

East London Line and Croydon - London Victoria to London Bridge

Network Diagram - see first Page of Table 177

		LO	LO	LO	SN	LO		LO	SN	SN	LO	SN	SE	SN	SN	LO		SN	LO	LO	SN	LO	LO	SN	SN
East Croydon	d																								
West Croydon 4	d			06 22											06 31	06 39				06 52					
Norwood Junction 2	d			06 28	06 32											06 43		06 47		06 58	07 02				
Anerley	d			06 31	06 35											06 46				07 01	07 05				
Penge West	d			06 33	06 37											06 48				07 03	07 07				
London Victoria 15 ⊖	d								06 19					06 41										06 49	
Battersea Park 4	d								06 23					06 45										06 53	
Wandsworth Road	d													06 47											
Clapham High Street ⊖	d													06 49											
London Blackfriars 3 ⊖	d												06 42												
Denmark Hill 4	d												06 52	06 54											
Peckham Rye 4	d											06 42	06a55	06 56	06 59			07 08							
Queens Rd Peckham	d													06 59	07 02			07 10							
South Bermondsey	d													07 01	07 04			07 13							
Clapham Junction 10	d								06 27															06 57	
Wandsworth Common	d								06 30															07 00	
Balham 4 ⊖	d								06 32															07 02	
Streatham Hill	d								06 35	06 42														07 05	07 12
West Norwood 4	d								06 39	06 45		06 53												07 09	07 15
Gipsy Hill	d								06 42	06 48		06 56												07 12	07 18
Crystal Palace 4	d		06 28					06 41	06 44	06 51	06 58	06a59											07 11	07 14	07 21
Sydenham	d		06 31	06 36	06 39			06 44	06 48	06 54	07 01					06 51				07 06	07 09		07 14	07 18	07 24
Forest Hill 4	d		06 34	06 38	06 42			06 47	06 50	06 57	07 04					06 53				07 08	07 12		07 17	07 20	07 27
Honor Oak Park	d		06 36	06 41	06 44			06 49	06 53	06 59	07 06					06 56				07 11	07 14		07 19	07 23	07 29
Brockley	d		06 39	06 43	06 47			06 52	06 55	07 02	07 09					06 58				07 13	07 17		07 22	07 25	07 32
New Cross Gate 4	a		06 41	06 46	06 49			06 54	06 58	07 04	07 11					07 01				07 16	07 19		07 24	07 28	07 34
	d		06 41	06 46	06 49			06 54	06 58	07 04	07 11					07 01				07 16	07 19		07 24	07 28	07 34
New Cross ELL	d	06 36				06 51													07 06			07 21			
Surrey Quays	d	06 40	06 45	06 49		06 55		07 00			07 15					07 05			07 10	07 19		07 25	07 30		
Canada Water	d	06 42	06 47	06 51		06 57		07 02			07 17					07 07			07 12	07 21		07 27	07 32		
Rotherhithe	d	06 43	06 48	06 53		06 58		07 03			07 18					07 08			07 13	07 23		07 28	07 33		
Wapping	d	06 45	06 50	06 54		07 00		07 05			07 20					07 10			07 15	07 24		07 30	07 35		
Shadwell	d	06 47	06 52	06 56		07 02		07 07			07 22					07 12			07 17	07 26		07 32	07 37		
Whitechapel	d	06 49	06 54	06 59		07 04		07 09			07 24					07 14			07 19	07 29		07 34	07 39		
Shoreditch High Street	d	06 51	06 56	07 01		07 06		07 11			07 26					07 16			07 21	07 31		07 36	07 41		
Hoxton	d	06 53	06 58	07 03		07 08		07 13			07 28					07 18			07 23	07 33		07 38	07 43		
Haggerston	d	06 55	07 00	07 05		07 10		07 15			07 30					07 20			07 25	07 35		07 40	07 45		
Dalston Junction Stn ELL	a	06 58	07 02	07 07		07 13		07 17			07 32					07 23			07 28	07 37		07 43	07 47		
Canonbury	d		07 05	07 12				07 20			07 35					07 27				07 42			07 50		
Highbury & Islington	a		07 10	07 16				07 25			07 40					07 32				07 46			07 55		
	d																								
London Bridge 4 ⊖	a				07 00				07 06	07 16				07 08	07 11			07 19			07 30			07 36	07 45

		SN		SN	SN	LO	SN	SN	LO	LO	LO	SN		LO	LO	SN	SN	SN	SN	SE	SN	LO		SN	SN
East Croydon	d																								
West Croydon 4	d				07 01	07 09	07 17				07 22										07 31	07 39		07 47	
Norwood Junction 2	d					07 13	07 22				07 28	07 32										07 43		07 52	
Anerley	d					07 16					07 31	07 35										07 46			
Penge West	d					07 18					07 33	07 37										07 48			
London Victoria 15 ⊖	d			07 11												07 17			07 41	07 43					
Battersea Park 4	d			07 15												07 21			07 45						
Wandsworth Road	d			07 17															07 47						
Clapham High Street ⊖	d			07 19															07 49						
London Blackfriars 3 ⊖	d																								
Denmark Hill 4	d			07 24															07 54	07 53					
Peckham Rye 4	d	07 12		07 26	07 31			07 36										07 42	07 56	07a56	07 59				08 06
Queens Rd Peckham	d			07 29	07 34			07 39											07 59		08 02				08 09
South Bermondsey	d			07 31	07 36			07 41											08 01		08 04				08 11
Clapham Junction 10	d															07 25									
Wandsworth Common	d																								
Balham 4 ⊖	d															07 29									
Streatham Hill	d															07 32									
West Norwood 4	d	07 23														07 38		07 53							
Gipsy Hill	d	07 26														07 41		07 56							
Crystal Palace 4	d	07a29					07a26			07 28					07 41	07 44	07 52	07a59						07a56	
Sydenham	d					07 21				07 31	07 36	07 39			07 44	07 48	07 56					07 51			
Forest Hill 4	d					07 23				07 34	07 38	07 42			07 47	07 50	07 58					07 53			
Honor Oak Park	d					07 26				07 36	07 41	07 44			07 49	07 53	08 01					07 56			
Brockley	d					07 28				07 39	07 43	07 47			07 52	07 55	08 03					07 58			
New Cross Gate 4	a					07 31				07 41	07 46	07 49			07 54	07 58	08 06					08 01			
	d					07 31				07 41	07 46	07 49			07 54	07 58	08 06					08 01			
New Cross ELL	d								07 36					07 51											
Surrey Quays	d					07 35			07 40	07 45	07 49			07 55	08 00							08 05			
Canada Water	d					07 37			07 42	07 47	07 51			07 57	08 02							08 07			
Rotherhithe	d					07 38			07 43	07 48	07 53			07 58	08 03							08 08			
Wapping	d					07 40			07 45	07 50	07 54			08 00	08 05							08 10			
Shadwell	d					07 42			07 47	07 52	07 56			08 02	08 07							08 12			
Whitechapel	d					07 44			07 49	07 54	07 59			08 04	08 09							08 14			
Shoreditch High Street	d					07 46			07 51	07 56	08 01			08 06	08 11							08 16			
Hoxton	d					07 48			07 53	07 58	08 03			08 08	08 13							08 18			
Haggerston	d					07 50			07 55	08 00	08 05			08 10	08 15							08 20			
Dalston Junction Stn ELL	a					07 53			07 58	08 02	08 07			08 13	08 17							08 23			
Canonbury	d					07 57				08 05	08 12				08 20							08 27			
Highbury & Islington	a					08 02				08 10	08 16				08 25							08 32			
	d																								
London Bridge 4 ⊖	a			07 38	07 43			07 48				07 58				08 07	08 15		08 08		08 11				08 18

Table 178

Mondays to Fridays

from 10 September

East London Line and Croydon - London Victoria to London Bridge

Network Diagram - see first Page of Table 177

		LO	LO	LO	LO	SN	LO	LO		SN	SN	LO	LO	SN	SE	SN	SN	LO		SN	SN	LO	LO	SN	LO
East Croydon	d																								
West Croydon 4	d				07 52												08 01	08 09		08 19			08 23		
Norwood Junction 2	d				07 58	08 02												08 13		08 25			08 28	08 32	
Anerley	d				08 01	08 05												08 16					08 31	08 35	
Penge West	d				08 03	08 07												08 18					08 33	08 37	
London Victoria 15 ⊖	d									07 52					08 09	08 11									
Battersea Park 4	d															08 15									
Wandsworth Road	d															08 17									
Clapham High Street ⊖	d															08 19									
London Blackfriars 3 ⊖	d																								
Denmark Hill 4	d														08 18	08 24									
Peckham Rye 4	d													08 12	08a21	08 26	08 29				08 36				
Queens Rd Peckham	d															08 29	08 32				08 38				
South Bermondsey	d															08 31	08 34				08 41				
Clapham Junction 10	d									07 58															
Wandsworth Common	d																								
Balham 4 ⊖	d									08 03															
Streatham Hill	d									08 06	08 15														
West Norwood 4	d									08 09	08 19			08 24											
Gipsy Hill	d									08 12	08 22			08 27											
Crystal Palace 4	d		07 58					08 11		08 15	08 24		08 28	08a29						08a29					
Sydenham	d		08 01		08 06	08 09		08 14		08 18	08 28		08 31					08 21					08 36	08 39	
Forest Hill 4	d		08 04		08 08	08 12		08 17		08 21	08 30		08 34					08 23					08 38	08 42	
Honor Oak Park	d		08 06		08 11	08 14		08 19		08 23	08 33		08 36					08 26					08 41	08 44	
Brockley	d		08 09		08 13	08 17		08 22		08 26	08 35		08 39					08 28					08 43	08 47	
New Cross Gate 4	a		08 11		08 16	08 19		08 24		08 28	08 38		08 41					08 31					08 46	08 49	
	d		08 11		08 16	08 19		08 24		08 28	08 38		08 41					08 31					08 46	08 49	
New Cross ELL	d	08 06					08 21															08 36			08 51
Surrey Quays	d	08 10	08 15	08 19	08 21		08 25	08 30				08 34	08 45					08 37				08 40	08 49		08 55
Canada Water	d	08 12	08 17	08 21	08 23		08 27	08 32				08 36	08 47					08 39				08 42	08 51		08 57
Rotherhithe	d	08 13	08 18	08 22	08 25		08 28	08 33				08 37	08 48					08 40				08 43	08 53		08 58
Wapping	d	08 15	08 20	08 24	08 26		08 30	08 35				08 39	08 50					08 42				08 45	08 54		09 00
Shadwell	d	08 17	08 22	08 26	08 28		08 32	08 37				08 41	08 52					08 44				08 47	08 56		09 02
Whitechapel	d	08 19	08 24	08 28	08 31		08 34	08 39				08 43	08 54					08 46				08 49	08 59		09 04
Shoreditch High Street	d	08 21	08 26	08 30	08 33		08 36	08 41				08 45	08 56					08 48				08 51	09 01		09 06
Hoxton	d	08 23	08 28	08 32	08 35		08 38	08 43				08 47	08 58					08 50				08 53	09 03		09 08
Haggerston	d	08 25	08 30	08 34	08 37		08 40	08 45				08 49	09 00					08 52				08 55	09 05		09 10
Dalston Junction Stn ELL	a	08 28	08 32	08 37	08 39		08 43	08 47				08 52	09 02					08 55				08 58	09 07		09 13
Canonbury	d		08 35		08 42			08 50					09 05					08 57					09 12		
Highbury & Islington	a		08 40		08 46			08 55					09 10					09 02					09 16		
	d																								
London Bridge 4 ⊖	a					08 28				08 37	08 47					08 38	08 41				08 48			08 58	

		LO	SN	SN		LO	SN	SE	SN	SN	LO	SN	LO	LO		SN	SN	LO	LO	SN	SN	LO	SN	SE	
East Croydon	d																								
West Croydon 4	d									08 31	08 39	08 49		08 53											
Norwood Junction 2	d										08 43	08 54		08 58			09 02								
Anerley	d										08 46			09 01			09 05								
Penge West	d										08 48			09 03			09 07								
London Victoria 15 ⊖	d			08 22				08 39	08 41											08 49				09 09	
Battersea Park 4	d			08 26					08 45											08 53					
Wandsworth Road	d								08 47																
Clapham High Street ⊖	d								08 49																
London Blackfriars 3 ⊖	d																								
Denmark Hill 4	d							08 48	08 54															09 18	
Peckham Rye 4	d						08 42	08a51	08 56	09 02						09 07							09 12	09a21	
Queens Rd Peckham	d								08 59	09 05						09 09									
South Bermondsey	d								09 01	09 07						09 12									
Clapham Junction 10	d			08 30																08 57					
Wandsworth Common	d			08 33																09 00					
Balham 4 ⊖	d			08 35																09 02					
Streatham Hill	d		08 35	08 38																09 05					
West Norwood 4	d		08 38	08 42			08 53													09 09			09 23		
Gipsy Hill	d		08 41	08 45			08 56													09 12			09 26		
Crystal Palace 4	d	08 41	08 44	08 51		08 58	08a59					08a58							09 11	09 14	09 21	09 28	09a29		
Sydenham	d	08 44	08 47	08 54		09 01					08 51			09 06			09 09		09 14	09 18	09 24	09 31			
Forest Hill 4	d	08 47	08 50	08 57		09 04					08 53			09 08			09 12		09 17	09 20	09 27	09 34			
Honor Oak Park	d	08 49	08 52	08 59		09 06					08 56			09 11			09 14		09 19	09 23	09 29	09 36			
Brockley	d	08 52	08 55	09 02		09 09					08 58			09 13			09 17		09 22	09 25	09 32	09 39			
New Cross Gate 4	a	08 54	08 57	09 04		09 11					09 01			09 16			09 19		09 24	09 28	09 34	09 41			
	d	08 54	08 57	09 04		09 11					09 01			09 16			09 19		09 24	09 28	09 34	09 41			
New Cross ELL	d												09 06					09 21							
Surrey Quays	d	09 00				09 15					09 05		09 10	09 19				09 25	09 30			09 45			
Canada Water	d	09 02				09 17					09 07		09 12	09 21				09 27	09 32			09 47			
Rotherhithe	d	09 03				09 18					09 08		09 13	09 23				09 28	09 33			09 48			
Wapping	d	09 05				09 20					09 10		09 15	09 24				09 30	09 35			09 50			
Shadwell	d	09 07				09 22					09 12		09 17	09 26				09 32	09 37			09 52			
Whitechapel	d	09 09				09 24					09 14		09 19	09 29				09 34	09 39			09 54			
Shoreditch High Street	d	09 11				09 26					09 16		09 21	09 31				09 36	09 41			09 56			
Hoxton	d	09 13				09 28					09 18		09 23	09 33				09 38	09 43			09 58			
Haggerston	d	09 15				09 30					09 20		09 25	09 35				09 40	09 45			10 00			
Dalston Junction Stn ELL	a	09 17				09 32					09 23		09 28	09 37				09 43	09 47			10 02			
Canonbury	d	09 20				09 35					09 27			09 42					09 50			10 05			
Highbury & Islington	a	09 25				09 40					09 32			09 46					09 55			10 10			
	d																								
London Bridge 4 ⊖	a		09 06	09 14					09 08	09 14						09 19	09 29			09 37	09 43				

East London Line and Croydon - London Victoria to London Bridge

Network Diagram - see first Page of Table 177

Station		SN	SN	LO	SN	LO	LO	SN	SN	LO		LO	SN	LO	SN	SN	SE	SN	SN	LO		LO	LO	SN	LO
East Croydon (tram)	d				09 20				09 30															10 00	
West Croydon [4] (tram)	d		09 01	09 09			09 22												09 31	09 39			09 52		
Norwood Junction [2]	d			09 14	09 25		09 28		09 35											09 43			09 58	10 05	
Anerley	d			09 17			09 31		09 38											09 46			10 01	10 08	
Penge West	d			09 19			09 33		09 40											09 48			10 03	10 10	
London Victoria [15] ⊖	d	09 11											09 19				09 39	09 41							
Battersea Park [4]	d	09 15											09 23					09 45							
Wandsworth Road	d	09 17																09 47							
Clapham High Street ⊖	d	09 19																09 49							
London Blackfriars [3] ⊖	d																								
Denmark Hill [4]	d	09 24															09 48	09 54							
Peckham Rye [4]	d	09 26	09 33												09 42	09 47	09a51	09 56	10 01						
Queens Rd Peckham	d	09 29	09 36													09 49		09 59	10 04						
South Bermondsey	d	09 31	09 38													09 52		10 01	10 06						
Clapham Junction [10]	d												09 27												
Wandsworth Common	d												09 30												
Balham [4] ⊖	d												09 32												
Streatham Hill	d												09 35												
West Norwood [4]	d												09 40		09 53										
Gipsy Hill	d												09 43		09 56										
Crystal Palace [4]	d							09 36				09 43	09 51	09 58	09a59										
Sydenham	d			09 21			09 36	09 39	09 42			09 46	09 54	10 01						09 51			10 06	10 12	
Forest Hill [4]	d			09 23			09 38	09 42	09 45			09 49	09 57	10 04						09 53			10 08	10 15	
Honor Oak Park	d			09 26			09 41	09 44	09 47			09 51	09 59	10 06						09 56			10 11	10 17	
Brockley	d			09 28			09 43	09 47	09 50			09 54	10 02	10 09						09 58			10 13	10 20	
New Cross Gate [4]	a			09 31	09 32		09 46	09 49	09 52			09 56	10 04	10 11						10 01			10 16	10 22	
	d			09 31	09 33		09 46	09 49	09 52			09 56	10 04	10 11						10 01			10 16	10 22	
New Cross ELL	d					09 36				09 51												10 06			10 21
Surrey Quays	d			09 35		09 40	09 49			09 55		10 00		10 15						10 05		10 10	10 19		10 25
Canada Water	d			09 37		09 42	09 51			09 57		10 02		10 17						10 07		10 12	10 21		10 27
Rotherhithe	d			09 38		09 43	09 53			09 58		10 03		10 18						10 08		10 13	10 23		10 28
Wapping	d			09 40		09 45	09 54			10 00		10 05		10 20						10 10		10 15	10 24		10 30
Shadwell	d			09 42		09 47	09 56			10 02		10 07		10 22						10 12		10 17	10 26		10 32
Whitechapel	d			09 44		09 49	09 59			10 04		10 09		10 24						10 14		10 19	10 29		10 34
Shoreditch High Street	d			09 46		09 51	10 01			10 06		10 11		10 26						10 16		10 21	10 31		10 36
Hoxton	d			09 48		09 53	10 03			10 08		10 13		10 28						10 18		10 23	10 33		10 38
Haggerston	d			09 50		09 55	10 05			10 10		10 15		10 30						10 20		10 25	10 35		10 40
Dalston Junction Stn ELL	a			09 53		09 58	10 07			10 13		10 17		10 32						10 22		10 28	10 37		10 43
Canonbury	d			09 57			10 12					10 20		10 35						10 27			10 42		
Highbury & Islington	a			10 02			10 16					10 25		10 40						10 32			10 46		
	d																								
London Bridge [4] ⊖	a	09 38	09 44		09 41			09 59	10 00				10 11			09 58		10 06	10 11					10 29	

Station		LO	SN	LO	SN	SN		SE	SN	SN	LO	LO	LO	SN	LO	LO		SN	LO	SN	SN	SE	SN	SN	LO
East Croydon (tram)	d													10 30											
West Croydon [4] (tram)	d									10 01	10 09		10 22											10 31	10 39
Norwood Junction [2]	d										10 13		10 28	10 35											10 43
Anerley	d										10 16		10 31	10 38											10 46
Penge West	d										10 18		10 33	10 40											10 48
London Victoria [15] ⊖	d		09 49					10 09	10 11									10 19				10 39	10 41		
Battersea Park [4]	d		09 53						10 15									10 23					10 45		
Wandsworth Road	d								10 17														10 47		
Clapham High Street ⊖	d								10 19														10 49		
London Blackfriars [3] ⊖	d																								
Denmark Hill [4]	d							10 18	10 24													10 48	10 54		
Peckham Rye [4]	d				10 12	10 17		10a21	10 26	10 31										10 42	10 47	10a51	10 56	11 01	
Queens Rd Peckham	d					10 19			10 29	10 34											10 49		10 59	11 04	
South Bermondsey	d					10 22			10 31	10 36											10 52		11 01	11 06	
Clapham Junction [10]	d		09 57															10 27							
Wandsworth Common	d		10 00															10 30							
Balham [4] ⊖	d		10 02															10 32							
Streatham Hill	d		10 05															10 35							
West Norwood [4]	d		10 10		10 23													10 40		10 53					
Gipsy Hill	d		10 13		10 26													10 43		10 56					
Crystal Palace [4]	d	10 13	10 21	10 28	10a29											10 43		10 51	10 58	10a59					
Sydenham	d	10 16	10 24	10 31							10 21		10 36	10 42		10 46		10 54	11 01						10 51
Forest Hill [4]	d	10 19	10 27	10 34							10 23		10 38	10 45		10 49		10 57	11 04						10 53
Honor Oak Park	d	10 21	10 29	10 36							10 26		10 41	10 47		10 51		10 59	11 06						10 56
Brockley	d	10 24	10 32	10 39							10 28		10 43	10 50		10 54		11 02	11 09						10 58
New Cross Gate [4]	a	10 26	10 34	10 41							10 31		10 46	10 52		10 56		11 04	11 11						11 01
	d	10 26	10 34	10 41							10 31		10 46	10 52		10 56		11 04	11 11						11 01
New Cross ELL	d											10 36			10 51										
Surrey Quays	d	10 30		10 45							10 35	10 40	10 49		10 55	11 00			11 15						11 05
Canada Water	d	10 32		10 47							10 37	10 42	10 51		10 57	11 02			11 17						11 07
Rotherhithe	d	10 33		10 48							10 38	10 43	10 53		10 58	11 03			11 18						11 08
Wapping	d	10 35		10 50							10 40	10 45	10 54		11 00	11 05			11 20						11 10
Shadwell	d	10 37		10 52							10 42	10 47	10 56		11 02	11 07			11 22						11 12
Whitechapel	d	10 39		10 54							10 44	10 49	10 59		11 04	11 09			11 24						11 14
Shoreditch High Street	d	10 41		10 56							10 46	10 51	11 01		11 06	11 11			11 26						11 16
Hoxton	d	10 43		10 58							10 48	10 53	11 03		11 08	11 13			11 28						11 18
Haggerston	d	10 45		11 00							10 50	10 55	11 05		11 10	11 15			11 30						11 20
Dalston Junction Stn ELL	a	10 47		11 02							10 52	10 58	11 07		11 13	11 17			11 32						11 22
Canonbury	d	10 50		11 05							10 57		11 12			11 20			11 35						11 27
Highbury & Islington	a	10 55		11 10							11 02		11 16			11 25			11 40						11 32
	d																								
London Bridge [4] ⊖	a		10 41			10 26			10 36	10 41				10 59				11 11			10 56		11 06	11 11	

Table 178

Mondays to Fridays

from 10 September

East London Line and Croydon - London Victoria to London Bridge

Network Diagram - see first Page of Table 177

Station		LO		LO	SN	LO	LO	SN	LO	SN	SN	SE		SN	SN	LO	LO	LO	SN	LO	LO	SN		LO	SN
East Croydon	d				11 00														11 30						
West Croydon 4	d			10 52											11 01	11 09		11 22							
Norwood Junction 2	d			10 58	11 05											11 13		11 28	11 35						
Anerley	d			11 01	11 08											11 16		11 31	11 38						
Penge West	d			11 03	11 10											11 18		11 33	11 40						
London Victoria 15 ⊖	d							10 49				11 09		11 11								11 19			
Battersea Park 4	d							10 53						11 15								11 23			
Wandsworth Road	d													11 17											
Clapham High Street ⊖	d													11 19											
London Blackfriars 3 ⊖	d																								
Denmark Hill 4	d											11 18		11 24											
Peckham Rye 4	d									11 12	11 17	11a21		11 26	11 31										11 42
Queens Rd Peckham	d										11 19			11 29	11 34										
South Bermondsey	d										11 22			11 31	11 36										
Clapham Junction 10	d							10 57														11 27			
Wandsworth Common	d							11 00														11 30			
Balham 4 ⊖	d							11 02														11 32			
Streatham Hill	d							11 05														11 35			
West Norwood 4	d							11 10		11 23												11 40			11 53
Gipsy Hill	d							11 13		11 26												11 43			11 56
Crystal Palace 4	d						11 13	11 21	11 28	11a29											11 43	11 51		11 58	11a59
Sydenham	d			11 06	11 12		11 16	11 24	11 31							11 21		11 36	11 42		11 46	11 54		12 01	
Forest Hill 4	d			11 08	11 15		11 19	11 27	11 34							11 23		11 38	11 45		11 49	11 57		12 04	
Honor Oak Park	d			11 11	11 17		11 21	11 29	11 36							11 26		11 41	11 47		11 51	11 59		12 06	
Brockley	d			11 13	11 20		11 24	11 32	11 39							11 28		11 43	11 50		11 54	12 02		12 09	
New Cross Gate 4	a			11 16	11 22		11 26	11 34	11 41							11 31		11 46	11 52		11 56	12 04		12 11	
	d			11 16	11 22		11 26	11 34	11 41							11 31		11 46	11 52		11 56	12 04		12 11	
New Cross ELL	d	11 06				11 21											11 36			11 51					
Surrey Quays	d	11 10		11 19		11 25	11 30		11 45							11 35	11 40	11 49		11 55	12 00			12 15	
Canada Water	d	11 12		11 21		11 27	11 32		11 47							11 37	11 42	11 51		11 57	12 02			12 17	
Rotherhithe	d	11 13		11 23		11 28	11 33		11 48							11 38	11 43	11 53		11 58	12 03			12 18	
Wapping	d	11 15		11 24		11 30	11 35		11 50							11 40	11 45	11 54		12 00	12 05			12 20	
Shadwell	d	11 17		11 26		11 32	11 37		11 52							11 42	11 47	11 56		12 02	12 07			12 22	
Whitechapel	d	11 19		11 29		11 34	11 39		11 54							11 44	11 49	11 59		12 04	12 09			12 24	
Shoreditch High Street	d	11 21		11 31		11 36	11 41		11 56							11 46	11 51	12 01		12 06	12 11			12 26	
Hoxton	d	11 23		11 33		11 38	11 43		11 58							11 48	11 53	12 03		12 08	12 13			12 28	
Haggerston	d	11 25		11 35		11 40	11 45		12 00							11 50	11 55	12 05		12 10	12 15			12 30	
Dalston Junction Stn ELL	a	11 28		11 37		11 43	11 47		12 02							11 52	11 58	12 07		12 13	12 17			12 32	
Canonbury	d			11 42			11 50		12 05							11 57		12 12			12 20			12 35	
Highbury & Islington	a			11 46			11 55		12 10							12 02		12 16			12 25			12 40	
	d																								
London Bridge 4 ⊖	a				11 29			11 41			11 26			11 36	11 41				11 59			12 14			

Station		SN	SE	SN	SN	LO	LO	LO		SN	LO	LO	SN	LO	SN	SN	SE	SN		SN	LO	LO	LO	SN	LO
East Croydon	d									12 00														12 30	
West Croydon 4	d				11 31	11 39		11 52												12 01	12 09		12 22		
Norwood Junction 2	d					11 43		11 58		12 05											12 13		12 28	12 35	
Anerley	d					11 46		12 01		12 08											12 16		12 31	12 38	
Penge West	d					11 48		12 03		12 10											12 18		12 33	12 40	
London Victoria 15 ⊖	d		11 39	11 41									11 49				12 09	12 11							
Battersea Park 4	d			11 45									11 53					12 15							
Wandsworth Road	d			11 47														12 17							
Clapham High Street ⊖	d			11 49														12 19							
London Blackfriars 3 ⊖	d																								
Denmark Hill 4	d		11 48	11 54													12 18	12 24							
Peckham Rye 4	d	11 47	11a51	11 56	12 01										12 12	12 17	12a21	12 26		12 31					
Queens Rd Peckham	d	11 49		11 59	12 04											12 19		12 29		12 34					
South Bermondsey	d	11 52		12 01	12 06											12 22		12 31		12 36					
Clapham Junction 10	d												11 57												
Wandsworth Common	d												12 00												
Balham 4 ⊖	d												12 02												
Streatham Hill	d												12 05												
West Norwood 4	d												12 10		12 23										
Gipsy Hill	d												12 13		12 26										
Crystal Palace 4	d											12 13	12 21	12 28	12a29										
Sydenham	d					11 51		12 06		12 12		12 16	12 24	12 31							12 21		12 36	12 42	
Forest Hill 4	d					11 53		12 08		12 15		12 19	12 27	12 34							12 23		12 38	12 45	
Honor Oak Park	d					11 56		12 11		12 17		12 21	12 29	12 36							12 26		12 41	12 47	
Brockley	d					11 58		12 13		12 20		12 24	12 32	12 39							12 28		12 43	12 50	
New Cross Gate 4	a					12 01		12 16		12 22		12 26	12 34	12 41							12 31		12 46	12 52	
	d					12 01		12 16		12 22		12 26	12 34	12 41							12 31		12 46	12 52	
New Cross ELL	d						12 06				12 21											12 36			12 51
Surrey Quays	d					12 05	12 10	12 19			12 25	12 30		12 45							12 35	12 40	12 49		12 55
Canada Water	d					12 07	12 12	12 21			12 27	12 32		12 47							12 37	12 42	12 51		12 57
Rotherhithe	d					12 08	12 13	12 23			12 28	12 33		12 48							12 38	12 43	12 53		12 58
Wapping	d					12 10	12 15	12 24			12 30	12 35		12 50							12 40	12 45	12 54		13 00
Shadwell	d					12 12	12 17	12 26			12 32	12 37		12 52							12 42	12 47	12 56		13 02
Whitechapel	d					12 14	12 19	12 29			12 34	12 39		12 54							12 44	12 49	12 59		13 04
Shoreditch High Street	d					12 16	12 21	12 31			12 36	12 41		12 56							12 46	12 51	13 01		13 06
Hoxton	d					12 18	12 23	12 33			12 38	12 43		12 58							12 48	12 53	13 03		13 08
Haggerston	d					12 20	12 25	12 35			12 40	12 45		13 00							12 50	12 55	13 05		13 10
Dalston Junction Stn ELL	a					12 22	12 28	12 37			12 43	12 47		13 02							12 52	12 58	13 07		13 13
Canonbury	d					12 27		12 42				12 50		13 05							12 57		13 12		
Highbury & Islington	a					12 32		12 46				12 55		13 10							13 02		13 16		
	d																								
London Bridge 4 ⊖	a	11 56		12 06	12 11					12 29			12 41			12 26		12 36		12 41				12 59	

from 10 September

East London Line and Croydon - London Victoria to London Bridge

Network Diagram - see first Page of Table 177

Station		LO	SN	LO		SN	SN	SE	SN	SN	LO	LO	LO	SN		LO	LO	SN	LO	SN	SN	SE	SN	SN	
East Croydon (tram)	d													13 00											
West Croydon 4 (tram)	d									12 31	12 39		12 52											13 01	
Norwood Junction 2	d										12 43		12 58	13 05											
Anerley	d										12 46		13 01	13 08											
Penge West	d										12 48		13 03	13 10											
London Victoria 15 ⊖	d		12 19					12 39	12 41									12 49				13 09	13 11		
Battersea Park 4	d		12 23						12 45									12 53					13 15		
Wandsworth Road	d								12 47														13 17		
Clapham High Street ⊖	d								12 49														13 19		
London Blackfriars 3 ⊖	d																								
Denmark Hill 4	d							12 48	12 54													13 18	13 24		
Peckham Rye 4	d					12 42	12 47	12a51	12 56	13 01										13 12	13 17	13a21	13 26	13 31	
Queens Rd Peckham	d						12 49		12 59	13 04											13 19		13 29	13 34	
South Bermondsey	d						12 52		13 01	13 06											13 22		13 31	13 36	
Clapham Junction 10	d		12 27															12 57							
Wandsworth Common	d		12 30															13 00							
Balham 4 ⊖	d		12 32															13 02							
Streatham Hill	d		12 35															13 05							
West Norwood 4	d		12 40			12 53												13 10		13 23					
Gipsy Hill	d		12 43			12 56												13 13		13 26					
Crystal Palace 4	d	12 43	12 51	12 58		12a59											13 13	13 21	13 28	13a29					
Sydenham	d	12 46	12 54	13 01							12 51		13 06	13 12			13 16	13 24	13 31						
Forest Hill 4	d	12 49	12 57	13 04							12 53		13 08	13 15			13 19	13 27	13 34						
Honor Oak Park	d	12 51	12 59	13 06							12 56		13 11	13 17			13 21	13 29	13 36						
Brockley	d	12 54	13 02	13 09							12 58		13 13	13 20			13 24	13 32	13 39						
New Cross Gate 4	a	12 56	13 04	13 11							13 01		13 16	13 22			13 26	13 34	13 41						
	d	12 56	13 04	13 11							13 01		13 16	13 22			13 26	13 34	13 41						
New Cross ELL	d											13 06				13 21									
Surrey Quays	d	13 00		13 15							13 05	13 10	13 19			13 25	13 30		13 45						
Canada Water	d	13 02		13 17							13 07	13 12	13 21			13 27	13 32		13 47						
Rotherhithe	d	13 03		13 18							13 08	13 13	13 23			13 28	13 33		13 48						
Wapping	d	13 05		13 20							13 10	13 15	13 24			13 30	13 35		13 50						
Shadwell	d	13 07		13 22							13 12	13 17	13 26			13 32	13 37		13 52						
Whitechapel	d	13 09		13 24							13 14	13 19	13 29			13 34	13 39		13 54						
Shoreditch High Street	d	13 11		13 26							13 16	13 21	13 31			13 36	13 41		13 56						
Hoxton	d	13 13		13 28							13 18	13 23	13 33			13 38	13 43		13 58						
Haggerston	d	13 15		13 30							13 20	13 25	13 35			13 40	13 45		14 00						
Dalston Junction Stn ELL	a	13 17		13 32							13 22	13 28	13 37			13 43	13 47		14 02						
Canonbury	d	13 20		13 35							13 27		13 42				13 50		14 05						
Highbury & Islington	a	13 25		13 40							13 32		13 46				13 55		14 10						
	d																								
London Bridge 4 ⊖	a		13 11				12 56		13 06	13 11				13 29				13 44			13 26		13 36	13 41	

Station		LO	LO	LO	SN	LO	LO	SN	LO	SN		SN	SE	SN	SN	LO	LO	LO	SN	LO		LO	SN	LO	SN
East Croydon (tram)	d				13 30														14 00						
West Croydon 4 (tram)	d	13 09		13 22											13 31	13 39		13 52							
Norwood Junction 2	d	13 13		13 28	13 35											13 43		13 58	14 05						
Anerley	d	13 16		13 31	13 38											13 46		14 01	14 08						
Penge West	d	13 18		13 33	13 40											13 48		14 03	14 10						
London Victoria 15 ⊖	d							13 19					13 39	13 41									13 49		
Battersea Park 4	d							13 23						13 45									13 53		
Wandsworth Road	d													13 47											
Clapham High Street ⊖	d													13 49											
London Blackfriars 3 ⊖	d																								
Denmark Hill 4	d												13 48	13 54											
Peckham Rye 4	d									13 42		13 47	13a51	13 56	14 01										14 12
Queens Rd Peckham	d											13 49		13 59	14 04										
South Bermondsey	d											13 52		14 01	14 06										
Clapham Junction 10	d							13 27															13 57		
Wandsworth Common	d							13 30															14 00		
Balham 4 ⊖	d							13 32															14 02		
Streatham Hill	d							13 35															14 05		
West Norwood 4	d							13 40		13 53													14 10		14 23
Gipsy Hill	d							13 43		13 56													14 13		14 26
Crystal Palace 4	d						13 43	13 51	13 58	13a59												14 13	14 21	14 28	14a29
Sydenham	d	13 21		13 36	13 42		13 46	13 54	14 01							13 51		14 06	14 12			14 16	14 24	14 31	
Forest Hill 4	d	13 23		13 38	13 45		13 49	13 57	14 04							13 53		14 08	14 15			14 19	14 27	14 34	
Honor Oak Park	d	13 26		13 41	13 47		13 51	13 59	14 06							13 56		14 11	14 17			14 21	14 29	14 36	
Brockley	d	13 28		13 43	13 50		13 54	14 02	14 09							13 58		14 13	14 20			14 24	14 32	14 39	
New Cross Gate 4	a	13 31		13 46	13 52		13 56	14 04	14 11							14 01		14 16	14 22			14 26	14 34	14 41	
	d	13 31		13 46	13 52		13 56	14 04	14 11							14 01		14 16	14 22			14 26	14 34	14 41	
New Cross ELL	d		13 36			13 51											14 06			14 21					
Surrey Quays	d	13 35	13 40	13 49		13 55	14 00		14 15							14 05	14 10	14 19		14 25		14 30		14 45	
Canada Water	d	13 37	13 42	13 51		13 57	14 02		14 17							14 07	14 12	14 21		14 27		14 32		14 47	
Rotherhithe	d	13 38	13 43	13 53		13 58	14 03		14 18							14 08	14 13	14 23		14 28		14 33		14 48	
Wapping	d	13 40	13 45	13 54		14 00	14 05		14 20							14 10	14 15	14 24		14 30		14 35		14 50	
Shadwell	d	13 42	13 47	13 56		14 02	14 07		14 22							14 12	14 17	14 26		14 32		14 37		14 52	
Whitechapel	d	13 44	13 49	13 59		14 04	14 09		14 24							14 14	14 19	14 29		14 34		14 39		14 54	
Shoreditch High Street	d	13 46	13 51	14 01		14 06	14 11		14 26							14 16	14 21	14 31		14 36		14 41		14 56	
Hoxton	d	13 48	13 53	14 03		14 08	14 13		14 28							14 18	14 23	14 33		14 38		14 43		14 58	
Haggerston	d	13 50	13 55	14 05		14 10	14 15		14 30							14 20	14 25	14 35		14 40		14 45		15 00	
Dalston Junction Stn ELL	a	13 52	13 58	14 07		14 13	14 17		14 32							14 22	14 28	14 37		14 43		14 47		15 02	
Canonbury	d	13 57		14 12			14 20		14 35							14 27		14 42				14 50		15 05	
Highbury & Islington	a	14 02		14 16			14 25		14 40							14 32		14 46				14 55		15 10	
	d																								
London Bridge 4 ⊖	a				13 59			14 11				13 56		14 06	14 11				14 29				14 41		

Table 178

Mondays to Fridays

from 10 September

East London Line and Croydon - London Victoria to London Bridge

Network Diagram - see first Page of Table 177

		SN	SE	SN	SN	LO		LO	LO	SN	LO	LO	SN	LO	SN	SN		SE	SN	SN	LO	LO	LO	SN	LO
East Croydon 🚋	d									14 30														15 00	
West Croydon 4 🚋	d				14 01	14 09			14 22											14 31	14 39		14 52		
Norwood Junction 2	d					14 13			14 28	14 35											14 43		14 58	15 05	
Anerley	d					14 16			14 31	14 38											14 46		15 01	15 08	
Penge West	d					14 18			14 33	14 40											14 48		15 03	15 10	
London Victoria 15 ⊖	d		14 09	14 11									14 19					14 39	14 41						
Battersea Park 4	d			14 15									14 23						14 45						
Wandsworth Road	d			14 17															14 47						
Clapham High Street ⊖	d			14 19															14 49						
London Blackfriars 3 ⊖	d																								
Denmark Hill 4	d		14 18	14 24														14 48	14 54						
Peckham Rye 4	d	14 17	14a21	14 26	14 31										14 42	14 47		14a51	14 56	15 01					
Queens Rd Peckham	d	14 19		14 29	14 34											14 49			14 59	15 04					
South Bermondsey	d	14 22		14 31	14 36											14 52			15 01	15 06					
Clapham Junction 10	d												14 27												
Wandsworth Common	d												14 30												
Balham 4 ⊖	d												14 32												
Streatham Hill	d												14 35												
West Norwood 4	d												14 40		14 53										
Gipsy Hill	d												14 43		14 56										
Crystal Palace 4	d											14 43	14 51	14 58	14a59										
Sydenham	d					14 21			14 36	14 42		14 46	14 54	15 01							14 51		15 06	15 12	
Forest Hill 4	d					14 23			14 38	14 45		14 49	14 57	15 04							14 53		15 08	15 15	
Honor Oak Park	d					14 26			14 41	14 47		14 51	14 59	15 06							14 56		15 11	15 17	
Brockley	d					14 28			14 43	14 50		14 54	15 02	15 09							14 58		15 13	15 20	
New Cross Gate 4	a					14 31			14 46	14 52		14 56	15 04	15 11							15 01		15 16	15 22	
	d					14 31			14 46	14 52		14 56	15 04	15 11							15 01		15 16	15 22	
New Cross ELL	d							14 36			14 51											15 06			15 21
Surrey Quays	d					14 35		14 40	14 49		14 55	15 00		15 15							15 05	15 10	15 19		15 25
Canada Water	d					14 37		14 42	14 51		14 57	15 02		15 17							15 07	15 12	15 21		15 27
Rotherhithe	d					14 38		14 43	14 53		14 58	15 03		15 18							15 08	15 13	15 23		15 28
Wapping	d					14 40		14 45	14 54		15 00	15 05		15 20							15 10	15 15	15 24		15 30
Shadwell	d					14 42		14 47	14 56		15 02	15 07		15 22							15 12	15 17	15 26		15 32
Whitechapel	d					14 44		14 49	14 59		15 04	15 09		15 24							15 14	15 19	15 29		15 34
Shoreditch High Street	d					14 46		14 51	15 01		15 06	15 11		15 26							15 16	15 21	15 31		15 36
Hoxton	d					14 48		14 53	15 03		15 08	15 13		15 28							15 18	15 23	15 33		15 38
Haggerston	d					14 50		14 55	15 05		15 10	15 15		15 30							15 20	15 25	15 35		15 40
Dalston Junction Stn ELL	a					14 52		14 58	15 07		15 13	15 17		15 32							15 22	15 28	15 37		15 43
Canonbury	d					14 57			15 12			15 20		15 35							15 27		15 42		
Highbury & Islington	a					15 02			15 16			15 25		15 40							15 32		15 46		
	d																								
London Bridge 4 ⊖	a	14 26		14 36	14 41					14 59			15 11			14 56			15 06	15 11				15 29	

		LO		SN	LO	SN	SN	SE	SN	SN	LO	LO		LO	SN	LO	LO	SN	LO	SN	SN	SE		SN	SN
East Croydon 🚋	d														15 30										
West Croydon 4 🚋	d									15 01	15 09			15 22											15 31
Norwood Junction 2	d										15 13			15 28	15 35										
Anerley	d										15 16			15 31	15 38										
Penge West	d										15 18			15 33	15 40										
London Victoria 15 ⊖	d			14 49				15 09	15 11									15 19				15 39		15 41	
Battersea Park 4	d			14 53					15 15									15 23						15 45	
Wandsworth Road	d								15 17															15 47	
Clapham High Street ⊖	d								15 19															15 49	
London Blackfriars 3 ⊖	d																								
Denmark Hill 4	d							15 18	15 24													15 48		15 54	
Peckham Rye 4	d					15 12	15 17	15a21	15 26	15 31										15 42	15 47	15a51		15 56	16 01
Queens Rd Peckham	d						15 19		15 29	15 34											15 49			15 59	16 04
South Bermondsey	d						15 22		15 31	15 36											15 52			16 01	16 06
Clapham Junction 10	d			14 57														15 27							
Wandsworth Common	d			15 00														15 30							
Balham 4 ⊖	d			15 02														15 32							
Streatham Hill	d			15 05														15 35							
West Norwood 4	d			15 10		15 23												15 40		15 53					
Gipsy Hill	d			15 13		15 26												15 43		15 56					
Crystal Palace 4	d	15 13		15 21	15 28	15a29											15 43	15 51	15 58	15a59					
Sydenham	d	15 16		15 24	15 31						15 21			15 36	15 42		15 46	15 54	16 01						
Forest Hill 4	d	15 19		15 27	15 34						15 23			15 38	15 45		15 49	15 57	16 04						
Honor Oak Park	d	15 21		15 29	15 36						15 26			15 41	15 47		15 51	15 59	16 06						
Brockley	d	15 24		15 32	15 39						15 28			15 43	15 50		15 54	16 02	16 09						
New Cross Gate 4	a	15 26		15 34	15 41						15 31			15 46	15 52		15 56	16 04	16 11						
	d	15 26		15 34	15 41						15 31			15 46	15 52		15 56	16 04	16 11						
New Cross ELL	d											15 36				15 51									
Surrey Quays	d	15 30			15 45						15 35	15 40		15 49		15 55	16 00		16 15						
Canada Water	d	15 32			15 47						15 37	15 42		15 51		15 57	16 02		16 17						
Rotherhithe	d	15 33			15 48						15 38	15 43		15 53		15 58	16 03		16 18						
Wapping	d	15 35			15 50						15 40	15 45		15 54		16 00	16 05		16 20						
Shadwell	d	15 37			15 52						15 42	15 47		15 56		16 02	16 07		16 22						
Whitechapel	d	15 39			15 54						15 44	15 49		15 59		16 04	16 09		16 24						
Shoreditch High Street	d	15 41			15 56						15 46	15 51		16 01		16 06	16 11		16 26						
Hoxton	d	15 43			15 58						15 48	15 53		16 03		16 08	16 13		16 28						
Haggerston	d	15 45			16 00						15 50	15 55		16 05		16 10	16 15		16 30						
Dalston Junction Stn ELL	a	15 47			16 02						15 52	15 58		16 07		16 13	16 17		16 32						
Canonbury	d	15 50			16 05						15 57			16 12			16 20		16 35						
Highbury & Islington	a	15 55			16 10						16 02			16 16			16 25		16 40						
	d																								
London Bridge 4 ⊖	a			15 41			15 26		15 36	15 41					15 59			16 11			15 56			16 06	16 11

from 10 September

East London Line and Croydon - London Victoria to London Bridge

Network Diagram - see first Page of Table 177

Station		LO	LO	LO	SN	SN	LO	LO		SN	LO	SN	SN	SE	SN	SN	LO	LO		LO	SN	LO	LO	SN	LO
East Croydon	d					16 00															16 30				
West Croydon 4	d	15 39		15 52												16 01	16 09			16 22					
Norwood Junction 2	d	15 43		15 58		16 05											16 13			16 28	16 35				
Anerley	d	15 46		16 01		16 08											16 16			16 31	16 38				
Penge West	d	15 48		16 03		16 10											16 18			16 33	16 40				
London Victoria 15 ⊖	d									15 49				16 09	16 11									16 19	
Battersea Park 4	d									15 53					16 15									16 23	
Wandsworth Road	d														16 17										
Clapham High Street ⊖	d														16 19										
London Blackfriars 3 ⊖	d																								
Denmark Hill 4	d													16 18	16 24										
Peckham Rye 4	d				16 07							16 12	16 17	16a21	16 26	16 31									
Queens Rd Peckham	d				16 10								16 19		16 29	16 34									
South Bermondsey	d				16 12								16 22		16 31	16 36									
Clapham Junction 10	d									15 57														16 27	
Wandsworth Common	d									16 00														16 30	
Balham 4 ⊖	d									16 02														16 32	
Streatham Hill	d									16 05														16 35	
West Norwood 4	d									16 10		16 23												16 39	
Gipsy Hill	d									16 13		16 26												16 44	
Crystal Palace 4	d							16 13		16 21	16 28	16a29											16 43	16 50	16 58
Sydenham	d	15 51		16 06		16 12		16 16		16 24	16 31						16 21			16 36	16 42		16 46	16 54	17 01
Forest Hill 4	d	15 53		16 08		16 15		16 19		16 27	16 34						16 23			16 38	16 45		16 49	16 56	17 04
Honor Oak Park	d	15 56		16 11		16 17		16 21		16 29	16 36						16 26			16 41	16 47		16 51	16 59	17 06
Brockley	d	15 58		16 13		16 20		16 24		16 32	16 39						16 28			16 43	16 50		16 54	17 01	17 09
New Cross Gate 4	a	16 01		16 16		16 22		16 26		16 34	16 41						16 31			16 46	16 52		16 56	17 04	17 11
	d	16 01		16 16		16 22		16 26		16 34	16 41						16 31			16 46	16 52		16 56	17 04	17 11
New Cross ELL	d		16 06				16 21											16 36				16 51			
Surrey Quays	d	16 05	16 10	16 19			16 25	16 30			16 45						16 35	16 40		16 49		16 55	17 00		17 15
Canada Water	d	16 07	16 12	16 21			16 27	16 32			16 47						16 37	16 42		16 51		16 57	17 02		17 17
Rotherhithe	d	16 08	16 13	16 23			16 28	16 33			16 48						16 38	16 43		16 53		16 58	17 03		17 18
Wapping	d	16 10	16 15	16 24			16 30	16 35			16 50						16 40	16 45		16 54		17 00	17 05		17 20
Shadwell	d	16 12	16 17	16 26			16 32	16 37			16 52						16 42	16 47		16 56		17 02	17 07		17 22
Whitechapel	d	16 14	16 19	16 29			16 34	16 39			16 54						16 44	16 49		16 59		17 04	17 09		17 24
Shoreditch High Street	d	16 16	16 21	16 31			16 36	16 41			16 56						16 46	16 51		17 01		17 06	17 11		17 26
Hoxton	d	16 18	16 23	16 33			16 38	16 43			16 58						16 48	16 53		17 03		17 08	17 13		17 28
Haggerston	d	16 20	16 25	16 35			16 40	16 45			17 00						16 50	16 55		17 05		17 10	17 15		17 30
Dalston Junction Stn ELL	a	16 22	16 28	16 37			16 43	16 47			17 02						16 52	16 58		17 07		17 13	17 17		17 32
Canonbury	d	16 27		16 42				16 50			17 05						16 57			17 12			17 20		17 35
Highbury & Islington	a	16 32		16 46				16 55			17 10						17 02			17 16			17 25		17 40
	d																								
London Bridge 4 ⊖	a				16 17	16 29				16 41			16 26		16 38	16 41					17 02			17 12	

Station		SN	SN	SE		SN	SN	LO	LO	LO	SN	LO	LO	SN		SN	SE	SN	SN	SN	LO	SN	SN	LO	
East Croydon	d										17 00														
West Croydon 4	d						16 31	16 39		16 52										17 01	17 09	17 12			
Norwood Junction 2	d							16 43		16 58	17 05										17 13				
Anerley	d							16 46		17 01	17 08										17 16				
Penge West	d							16 48		17 03	17 10										17 18				
London Victoria 15 ⊖	d			16 39		16 41								16 49			17 04		17 11						
Battersea Park 4	d					16 45								16 53					17 15						
Wandsworth Road	d					16 47													17 17						
Clapham High Street ⊖	d					16 49													17 19						
London Blackfriars 3 ⊖	d																								
Denmark Hill 4	d			16 48		16 54											17 13		17 24						
Peckham Rye 4	d	16 42	16 47	16a51		16 56	17 00									17 07	17a16	17 17	17 26	17 29			17 35		
Queens Rd Peckham	d		16 49			16 59	17 03											17 19	17 29	17 32			17 37		
South Bermondsey	d		16 52			17 01	17 05											17 22	17 31	17 34			17 40		
Clapham Junction 10	d													16 57											
Wandsworth Common	d													17 00											
Balham 4 ⊖	d													17 03											
Streatham Hill	d													17 06											
West Norwood 4	d	16 53												17 09		17 20									
Gipsy Hill	d	16 56												17 12		17 23									
Crystal Palace 4	d	16a59											17 13	17 21		17a26									
Sydenham	d							16 51		17 06	17 12		17 16	17 24							17 21				
Forest Hill 4	d							16 53		17 08	17 15		17 19	17 27							17 23				
Honor Oak Park	d							16 56		17 11	17 17		17 21	17 29							17 26				
Brockley	d							16 58		17 13	17 20		17 24	17 32							17 28				
New Cross Gate 4	a							17 01		17 16	17 22		17 26	17 34							17 31				
	d							17 01		17 16	17 22		17 26	17 34							17 31				
New Cross ELL	d								17 06			17 21												17 36	
Surrey Quays	d							17 05	17 10	17 19		17 25	17 30								17 35			17 40	
Canada Water	d							17 07	17 12	17 21		17 27	17 32								17 37			17 42	
Rotherhithe	d							17 08	17 13	17 23		17 28	17 33								17 38			17 43	
Wapping	d							17 10	17 15	17 24		17 30	17 35								17 40			17 45	
Shadwell	d							17 12	17 17	17 26		17 32	17 37								17 42			17 47	
Whitechapel	d							17 14	17 19	17 29		17 34	17 39								17 44			17 49	
Shoreditch High Street	d							17 16	17 21	17 31		17 36	17 41								17 46			17 51	
Hoxton	d							17 18	17 23	17 33		17 38	17 43								17 48			17 53	
Haggerston	d							17 20	17 25	17 35		17 40	17 45								17 50			17 55	
Dalston Junction Stn ELL	a							17 22	17 28	17 37		17 43	17 47								17 52			17 58	
Canonbury	d							17 27		17 42			17 50								17 57				
Highbury & Islington	a							17 32		17 46			17 55								18 02				
	d																								
London Bridge 4 ⊖	a		16 56			17 08	17 10				17 35			17 43				17 27	17 38	17 40		17 28	17 44		

Table 178

Mondays to Fridays

from 10 September

East London Line and Croydon - London Victoria to London Bridge

Network Diagram - see first Page of Table 177

		LO	LO	LO	LO	SN	SN	SE	SN	SN		SN	SN	LO	SN	LO	LO	LO	SN	LO		LO	SN	SN	SE
East Croydon	d									17 30															
West Croydon 4	d		17 22										17 31	17 39	17 42			17 52							
Norwood Junction 2	d		17 28						17 32	17 35				17 43				17 58	18 04						
Anerley	d		17 31							17 38				17 46				18 01	18 07						
Penge West	d		17 33							17 40				17 48				18 03	18 09						
London Victoria 15	⊖ d					17 22		17 34				17 41											17 52		17 56
Battersea Park 4	d					17 26						17 45											17 56		
Wandsworth Road	d											17 47													
Clapham High Street	⊖ d											17 49													
London Blackfriars 3	⊖ d																								
Denmark Hill 4	d							17 43				17 54													18 06
Peckham Rye 4	d						17 37	17a46	17 53			17 57	18 01											18 07	18a08
Queens Rd Peckham	d								17 55			17 59	18 04												
South Bermondsey	d								17 58			18 02	18 06												
Clapham Junction 10	d					17 30																	18 00		
Wandsworth Common	d					17 33																	18 03		
Balham 4	⊖ d					17 35																	18 05		
Streatham Hill	d					17 38																	18 08		
West Norwood 4	d					17 42	17 49																18 14	18 20	
Gipsy Hill	d					17 45	17 52																18 17	18 23	
Crystal Palace 4	d	17 28			17 43	17 48	17a54										17 58					18 13	18 20	18a26	
Sydenham	d	17 31	17 36		17 46	17 54				17 42				17 51			18 01	18 06	18 11			18 16	18 24		
Forest Hill 4	d	17 34	17 38		17 49	17 57				17 45				17 53			18 04	18 08	18 14			18 19	18 27		
Honor Oak Park	d	17 36	17 41		17 51	17 59				17 47				17 56			18 06	18 11	18 16			18 21	18 29		
Brockley	d	17 39	17 43		17 54	18 02				17 50				17 58			18 09	18 13	18 19			18 24	18 32		
New Cross Gate 4	a	17 41	17 46		17 56	18 04				17 52				18 01			18 11	18 16	18 21			18 26	18 34		
	d	17 41	17 46		17 56	18 04				17 52				18 01			18 11	18 16	18 21			18 26	18 34		
New Cross ELL	d			17 51												18 06				18 21					
Surrey Quays	d	17 45	17 49	17 55	18 00									18 05		18 10	18 15	18 19		18 25		18 30			
Canada Water	d	17 47	17 51	17 57	18 02									18 07		18 12	18 17	18 21		18 27		18 32			
Rotherhithe	d	17 48	17 53	17 58	18 03									18 08		18 13	18 18	18 23		18 28		18 33			
Wapping	d	17 50	17 54	18 00	18 05									18 10		18 15	18 20	18 24		18 30		18 35			
Shadwell	d	17 52	17 56	18 02	18 07									18 12		18 17	18 22	18 26		18 32		18 37			
Whitechapel	d	17 54	17 59	18 04	18 09									18 14		18 19	18 24	18 29		18 34		18 39			
Shoreditch High Street	d	17 56	18 01	18 06	18 11									18 16		18 21	18 26	18 31		18 36		18 41			
Hoxton	d	17 58	18 03	18 08	18 13									18 18		18 23	18 28	18 33		18 38		18 43			
Haggerston	d	18 00	18 05	18 10	18 15									18 20		18 25	18 30	18 35		18 40		18 45			
Dalston Junction Stn ELL	a	18 02	18 07	18 13	18 17									18 23		18 28	18 32	18 37		18 43		18 47			
Canonbury	d	18 05	18 12		18 20									18 27			18 35	18 42				18 50			
Highbury & Islington	a	18 10	18 16		18 25									18 32			18 40	18 46				18 55			
	d																								
London Bridge 4	⊖ a					18 13			18 02	17 59		18 08	18 11		18 00				18 31				18 45		

		SN	SN	SN	LO	SN		LO	LO	LO	LO	SE	SN	SN	SN	LO		SN	SN	SE	SN	SN	LO	LO	LO
East Croydon	d														18 30										
West Croydon 4	d			18 01	18 09	18 13				18 22												18 31	18 39		
Norwood Junction 2	d				18 13					18 28					18 35								18 43		
Anerley	d				18 16					18 31					18 38								18 46		
Penge West	d				18 18					18 33					18 40								18 48		
London Victoria 15	⊖ d		18 11									18 18						18 22		18 39	18 41				
Battersea Park 4	d		18 15															18 26			18 45				
Wandsworth Road	d		18 17																		18 47				
Clapham High Street	⊖ d		18 19																		18 49				
London Blackfriars 3	⊖ d																								
Denmark Hill 4	d		18 24									18 28								18 48	18 54				
Peckham Rye 4	d	18 12	18 26	18 29								18a31	18 32	18 36					18 37	18a51	18 57	19 01			
Queens Rd Peckham	d	18 15	18 29	18 32									18 35	18 38							19 00	19 04			
South Bermondsey	d	18 17	18 31	18 34									18 37	18 41							19 02	19 06			
Clapham Junction 10	d																	18 30							
Wandsworth Common	d																	18 33							
Balham 4	⊖ d																	18 35							
Streatham Hill	d																	18 38							
West Norwood 4	d																	18 42	18 51						
Gipsy Hill	d																	18 45	18 54						
Crystal Palace 4	d								18 28							18 43		18 51	18a57						18 58
Sydenham	d				18 21				18 31	18 36					18 42	18 46		18 54					18 51		19 01
Forest Hill 4	d				18 23				18 34	18 38					18 45	18 49		18 57					18 53		19 04
Honor Oak Park	d				18 26				18 36	18 41					18 47	18 51		18 59					18 56		19 06
Brockley	d				18 28				18 39	18 43					18 50	18 54		19 02					18 58		19 09
New Cross Gate 4	a				18 31				18 41	18 46					18 52	18 56		19 04					19 01		19 11
	d				18 31				18 41	18 46					18 52	18 56		19 04					19 01		19 11
New Cross ELL	d							18 36			18 51													19 06	
Surrey Quays	d				18 35			18 40	18 45	18 49	18 55					19 00							19 05	19 10	19 15
Canada Water	d				18 37			18 42	18 47	18 51	18 57					19 02							19 07	19 12	19 17
Rotherhithe	d				18 38			18 43	18 48	18 53	18 58					19 03							19 08	19 13	19 18
Wapping	d				18 40			18 45	18 50	18 54	19 00					19 05							19 10	19 15	19 20
Shadwell	d				18 42			18 47	18 52	18 56	19 02					19 07							19 12	19 17	19 22
Whitechapel	d				18 44			18 49	18 54	18 59	19 04					19 09							19 14	19 19	19 24
Shoreditch High Street	d				18 46			18 51	18 56	19 01	19 06					19 11							19 16	19 21	19 26
Hoxton	d				18 48			18 53	18 58	19 03	19 08					19 13							19 18	19 23	19 28
Haggerston	d				18 50			18 55	19 00	19 05	19 10					19 15							19 20	19 25	19 30
Dalston Junction Stn ELL	a				18 52			18 58	19 02	19 07	19 13					19 17							19 22	19 28	19 32
Canonbury	d				18 57				19 05	19 12						19 20							19 27		19 35
Highbury & Islington	a				19 02				19 10	19 16						19 25							19 32		19 40
	d																								
London Bridge 4	⊖ a	18 22	18 38	18 39		18 29							18 42	18 45	18 59			19 13			19 09	19 11			

East London Line and Croydon - London Victoria to London Bridge

Network Diagram - see first Page of Table 177

		LO		SN	LO	LO	SN	SN	SN	SN	LO	SN		SE	SN	SN	LO	LO	LO	SN	LO	LO		SN	SN
East Croydon 🚋	d			19 00																19 30					
West Croydon [4] 🚋	d	18 52														19 01	19 09		19 22						
Norwood Junction [2]	d	18 58		19 05													19 13		19 28	19 35					
Anerley	d	19 01		19 08													19 16		19 31	19 38					
Penge West	d	19 03		19 10													19 18		19 33	19 40					
London Victoria [15] ⊖	d						18 52							19 09	19 11									19 22	
Battersea Park [4]	d						18 56								19 15									19 26	
Wandsworth Road	d														19 17										
Clapham High Street ⊖	d														19 19										
London Blackfriars [3] ⊖	d																								
Denmark Hill [4]	d													19 18	19 24										
Peckham Rye [4]	d							19 06	19 07	19 14		19 17		19a21	19 26	19 29									19 37
Queens Rd Peckham	d								19 10	19 17					19 29	19 32									
South Bermondsey	d								19 12	19 19					19 31	19 34									
Clapham Junction [10]	d						19 00																	19 30	
Wandsworth Common	d						19 03																	19 33	
Balham [4] ⊖	d						19 05																	19 35	
Streatham Hill	d						19 08																	19 38	
West Norwood [4]	d						19 12	19 17				19 30												19 42	19 49
Gipsy Hill	d						19 15	19 20				19 33												19 45	19 52
Crystal Palace [4]	d					19 13	19 21	19a23			19 28	19a35										19 43		19 51	19a54
Sydenham	d	19 06		19 12		19 16	19 24				19 31						19 21		19 36	19 42		19 46		19 54	
Forest Hill [4]	d	19 08		19 15		19 19	19 27				19 34						19 23		19 38	19 45		19 49		19 57	
Honor Oak Park	d	19 11		19 17		19 21	19 29				19 36						19 26		19 41	19 47		19 51		19 59	
Brockley	d	19 13		19 20		19 24	19 32				19 39						19 28		19 43	19 50		19 54		20 02	
New Cross Gate [4]	a	19 16		19 22		19 26	19 34				19 41						19 31		19 46	19 52		19 56		20 04	
	d	19 16		19 22		19 26	19 34				19 41						19 31		19 46	19 52		19 56		20 04	
New Cross ELL	d				19 21													19 36			19 51				
Surrey Quays	d	19 19			19 25	19 30					19 45						19 35	19 40	19 49		19 55	20 00			
Canada Water	d	19 21			19 27	19 32					19 47						19 37	19 42	19 51		19 57	20 02			
Rotherhithe	d	19 23			19 28	19 33					19 48						19 38	19 43	19 53		19 58	20 03			
Wapping	d	19 24			19 30	19 35					19 50						19 40	19 45	19 54		20 00	20 05			
Shadwell	d	19 26			19 32	19 37					19 52						19 42	19 47	19 56		20 02	20 07			
Whitechapel	d	19 29			19 34	19 39					19 54						19 44	19 49	19 59		20 04	20 09			
Shoreditch High Street	d	19 31			19 36	19 41					19 56						19 46	19 51	20 01		20 06	20 11			
Hoxton	d	19 33			19 38	19 43					19 58						19 48	19 53	20 03		20 08	20 13			
Haggerston	d	19 35			19 40	19 45					20 00						19 50	19 55	20 05		20 10	20 15			
Dalston Junction Stn ELL	a	19 37			19 43	19 47					20 02						19 52	19 58	20 07		20 13	20 17			
Canonbury	d	19 42				19 50					20 05						19 57		20 12			20 20			
Highbury & Islington	a	19 46				19 55					20 10						20 02		20 16			20 25			
	d																								
London Bridge [4] ⊖	a			19 29			19 41		19 17	19 24					19 36	19 41				19 59				20 11	

		SN	LO	SN	SN	SE	SN	SN		LO	LO	LO	SN	LO	LO	SN	LO	SN		SN	SN	SN	LO	LO	LO
East Croydon 🚋	d												20 00												
West Croydon [4] 🚋	d							19 31		19 39		19 52										20 01	20 09		20 22
Norwood Junction [2]	d									19 43		19 58	20 05										20 13		20 28
Anerley	d									19 46		20 01	20 08										20 16		20 31
Penge West	d									19 48		20 03	20 10										20 18		20 33
London Victoria [15] ⊖	d					19 39	19 41									19 52					20 11				
Battersea Park [4]	d						19 45									19 56					20 15				
Wandsworth Road	d						19 47														20 17				
Clapham High Street ⊖	d						19 49														20 19				
London Blackfriars [3] ⊖	d																								
Denmark Hill [4]	d					19 48	19 54														20 24				
Peckham Rye [4]	d	19 38		19 47	19 49	19a51	19 56	20 01										20 12		20 18	20 26	20 31			
Queens Rd Peckham	d	19 41			19 51		19 59	20 04												20 21	20 29	20 34			
South Bermondsey	d	19 43			19 54		20 01	20 06												20 23	20 31	20 36			
Clapham Junction [10]	d															20 00									
Wandsworth Common	d															20 03									
Balham [4] ⊖	d															20 05									
Streatham Hill	d															20 08									
West Norwood [4]	d			20 00												20 12		20 24							
Gipsy Hill	d			20 03												20 15		20 27							
Crystal Palace [4]	d		19 58	20a05											20 13	20 21	20 28	20a29							
Sydenham	d		20 01							19 51		20 06	20 12		20 16	20 24	20 31						20 21		20 36
Forest Hill [4]	d		20 04							19 53		20 08	20 15		20 19	20 27	20 34						20 23		20 38
Honor Oak Park	d		20 06							19 56		20 11	20 17		20 21	20 29	20 36						20 26		20 41
Brockley	d		20 09							19 58		20 13	20 20		20 24	20 32	20 39						20 28		20 43
New Cross Gate [4]	a		20 11							20 01		20 16	20 22		20 26	20 34	20 41						20 31		20 46
	d		20 11							20 01		20 16	20 22		20 26	20 34	20 41						20 31		20 46
New Cross ELL	d										20 06			20 21										20 36	
Surrey Quays	d		20 15							20 05	20 10	20 19		20 25	20 30		20 45						20 35	20 40	20 49
Canada Water	d		20 17							20 07	20 12	20 21		20 27	20 32		20 47						20 37	20 42	20 51
Rotherhithe	d		20 18							20 08	20 13	20 23		20 28	20 33		20 48						20 38	20 43	20 53
Wapping	d		20 20							20 10	20 15	20 24		20 30	20 35		20 50						20 40	20 45	20 54
Shadwell	d		20 22							20 12	20 17	20 26		20 32	20 37		20 52						20 42	20 47	20 56
Whitechapel	d		20 24							20 14	20 19	20 29		20 34	20 39		20 54						20 44	20 49	20 59
Shoreditch High Street	d		20 26							20 16	20 21	20 31		20 36	20 41		20 56						20 46	20 51	21 01
Hoxton	d		20 28							20 18	20 23	20 33		20 38	20 43		20 58						20 48	20 53	21 03
Haggerston	d		20 30							20 20	20 25	20 35		20 40	20 45		21 00						20 50	20 55	21 05
Dalston Junction Stn ELL	a		20 32							20 22	20 28	20 37		20 43	20 47		21 02						20 52	20 58	21 07
Canonbury	d		20 35							20 27		20 42			20 50		21 05						20 57		21 12
Highbury & Islington	a		20 40							20 32		20 46			20 55		21 10						21 02		21 16
	d																								
London Bridge [4] ⊖	a	19 51			19 58		20 06	20 14					20 29			20 41				20 28	20 36	20 41			

Table 178

Mondays to Fridays

from 10 September

East London Line and Croydon - London Victoria to London Bridge

Network Diagram - see first Page of Table 177

		SN	LO	LO		SN	LO	SN	SN	SN	SN	LO	LO	LO		SN	LO	LO	SN	LO	SN	SN	SN	SN
East Croydon	d	20 31														21 00								
West Croydon 4	d										20 31	20 39		20 52										21 01
Norwood Junction 2	d	20 35										20 43		20 58		21 05								
Anerley	d	20 38										20 46		21 01		21 08								
Penge West	d	20 40										20 48		21 03		21 10								
London Victoria 15	d					20 22				20 41									20 52				21 11	
Battersea Park 4	d					20 26				20 45									20 56				21 15	
Wandsworth Road	d									20 47													21 17	
Clapham High Street	d									20 49													21 19	
London Blackfriars 3	d																							
Denmark Hill 4	d									20 54													21 24	
Peckham Rye 4	d							20 42	20 48	20 56	21 01										21 12	21 17	21 26	21 31
Queens Rd Peckham	d								20 50	20 59	21 04											21 19	21 29	21 34
South Bermondsey	d								20 53	21 01	21 06											21 22	21 31	21 36
Clapham Junction 10	d					20 30													21 00					
Wandsworth Common	d					20 33													21 03					
Balham 4	d					20 35													21 05					
Streatham Hill	d					20 38													21 08					
West Norwood 4	d					20 42		20 54											21 12		21 24			
Gipsy Hill	d					20 45		20 57											21 15		21 27			
Crystal Palace 4	d			20 43		20 51	20 58	20a59										21 13	21 21	21 28	21a29			
Sydenham	d	20 42		20 46		20 54	21 01					20 51		21 06		21 12		21 16	21 27	21 31				
Forest Hill 4	d	20 45		20 49		20 57	21 04					20 53		21 08		21 15		21 19	21 29	21 34				
Honor Oak Park	d	20 47		20 51		20 59	21 06					20 56		21 11		21 17		21 21	21 32	21 36				
Brockley	d	20 50		20 54		21 02	21 09					20 58		21 13		21 20		21 24	21 34	21 39				
New Cross Gate 4	a	20 52		20 56		21 04	21 11					21 01		21 16		21 22		21 26	21 37	21 41				
	d	20 52		20 56		21 04	21 11					21 01		21 16		21 22		21 26	21 37	21 41				
New Cross ELL	d		20 51										21 06				21 21							
Surrey Quays	d		20 55	21 00			21 15					21 05	21 10	21 19			21 25	21 30		21 45				
Canada Water	d		20 57	21 02			21 17					21 07	21 12	21 21			21 27	21 32		21 47				
Rotherhithe	d		20 58	21 03			21 18					21 08	21 13	21 23			21 28	21 33		21 48				
Wapping	d		21 00	21 05			21 20					21 10	21 15	21 24			21 30	21 35		21 50				
Shadwell	d		21 02	21 07			21 22					21 12	21 17	21 26			21 32	21 37		21 52				
Whitechapel	d		21 04	21 09			21 24					21 14	21 19	21 29			21 34	21 39		21 54				
Shoreditch High Street	d		21 06	21 11			21 26					21 16	21 21	21 31			21 36	21 41		21 56				
Hoxton	d		21 08	21 13			21 28					21 18	21 23	21 33			21 38	21 43		21 58				
Haggerston	d		21 10	21 15			21 30					21 20	21 25	21 35			21 40	21 45		22 00				
Dalston Junction Stn ELL	a		21 13	21 17			21 32					21 22	21 28	21 37			21 43	21 47		22 02				
Canonbury	d			21 20			21 35					21 27		21 42				21 50		22 05				
Highbury & Islington	a			21 25			21 40					21 32		21 46				21 55		22 10				
	d																							
London Bridge 4	a	20 59				21 11			20 57	21 06	21 11					21 29			21 43			21 26	21 36	21 41

		LO	LO	LO	SN	LO	LO	SN	LO	SN		SN	SE	SN	SN	LO	LO	LO	SN	LO		SN	LO	SN	SN
East Croydon	d				21 30														22 00						
West Croydon 4	d	21 09		21 22											21 31	21 39		21 52							
Norwood Junction 2	d	21 13		21 28	21 35											21 43		21 58	22 05						
Anerley	d	21 16		21 31	21 38											21 46		22 01	22 08						
Penge West	d	21 18		21 33	21 40											21 48		22 03	22 10						
London Victoria 15	d							21 23						21 41								21 52			
Battersea Park 4	d							21 27						21 45								21 56			
Wandsworth Road	d													21 47											
Clapham High Street	d													21 49											
London Blackfriars 3	d												21 42												
Denmark Hill 4	d												21 52	21 54											
Peckham Rye 4	d									21 42		21 47	21a55	21 56	22 01									22 12	22 17
Queens Rd Peckham	d											21 49		21 59	22 04										22 19
South Bermondsey	d											21 52		22 01	22 06										22 22
Clapham Junction 10	d							21 31														22 00			
Wandsworth Common	d							21 34														22 03			
Balham 4	d							21 36														22 05			
Streatham Hill	d							21 39														22 08			
West Norwood 4	d							21 43		21 54												22 12		22 24	
Gipsy Hill	d							21 46		21 57												22 15		22 27	
Crystal Palace 4	d						21 43	21 51	21 58	21a59										22 13		22 21	22 28	22a29	
Sydenham	d	21 21		21 36	21 42		21 46	21 54	22 01							21 51		22 06	22 12	22 16		22 24	22 31		
Forest Hill 4	d	21 23		21 38	21 45		21 49	21 57	22 04							21 53		22 08	22 15	22 19		22 27	22 34		
Honor Oak Park	d	21 26		21 41	21 47		21 51	21 59	22 06							21 56		22 11	22 17	22 21		22 29	22 36		
Brockley	d	21 28		21 43	21 50		21 54	22 02	22 09							21 58		22 13	22 20	22 24		22 32	22 39		
New Cross Gate 4	a	21 31		21 46	21 52		21 56	22 04	22 11							22 01		22 16	22 22	22 26		22 34	22 41		
	d	21 31		21 46	21 52		21 56	22 04	22 11							22 01		22 16	22 22	22 26		22 34	22 41		
New Cross ELL	d		21 36			21 51											22 06								
Surrey Quays	d	21 35	21 40	21 49		21 55	22 00		22 15							22 05	22 10	22 19		22 30			22 45		
Canada Water	d	21 37	21 42	21 51		21 57	22 02		22 17							22 07	22 12	22 21		22 32			22 47		
Rotherhithe	d	21 38	21 43	21 53		21 58	22 03		22 18							22 08	22 13	22 23		22 33			22 48		
Wapping	d	21 40	21 45	21 54		22 00	22 05		22 20							22 10	22 15	22 24		22 35			22 50		
Shadwell	d	21 42	21 47	21 56		22 02	22 07		22 22							22 12	22 17	22 26		22 37			22 52		
Whitechapel	d	21 44	21 49	21 59		22 04	22 09		22 24							22 14	22 19	22 29		22 39			22 54		
Shoreditch High Street	d	21 46	21 51	22 01		22 06	22 11		22 26							22 16	22 21	22 31		22 41			22 56		
Hoxton	d	21 48	21 53	22 03		22 08	22 13		22 28							22 18	22 23	22 33		22 43			22 58		
Haggerston	d	21 50	21 55	22 05		22 10	22 15		22 30							22 20	22 25	22 35		22 45			23 00		
Dalston Junction Stn ELL	a	21 52	21 58	22 07		22 13	22 17		22 32							22 22	22 29	22 37		22 47			23 02		
Canonbury	d	21 57		22 12			22 20		22 35							22 27		22 42		22 50			23 05		
Highbury & Islington	a	22 02		22 16			22 25		22 40							22 32		22 46		22 55			23 10		
	d																								
London Bridge 4	a				21 59			22 13				21 56		22 06	22 11				22 29			22 45			22 26

East London Line and Croydon - London Victoria to London Bridge

Network Diagram - see first Page of Table 177

		SE	SN	SN	LO	LO		LO	SN	LO	SN	SN	SN	SE	SN	SN		LO	LO	LO	SN	LO	SN	SN	SN
East Croydon ⇌	d								22 30												23 01				
West Croydon 4 ⇌	d			22 01	22 09			22 22								22 31		22 39		22 52					
Norwood Junction 2	d				22 13			22 28	22 35									22 43		22 58	23 06				
Anerley	d				22 16			22 31	22 38									22 46		23 01	23 09				
Penge West	d				22 18			22 33	22 40									22 48		23 03	23 11				
London Victoria 15 ⊖	d		22 11								22 22				22 41								22 52		
Battersea Park 4	d		22 15								22 26				22 45								22 56		
Wandsworth Road	d		22 17												22 47										
Clapham High Street ⊖	d		22 19												22 49										
London Blackfriars 3 ⊖	d	22 12												22 42											
Denmark Hill 4	d	22 22	22 24											22 52	22 54										
Peckham Rye 4	d	22a25	22 26	22 31								22 42	22 43	22a55	22 56	23 01								23 14	23 17
Queens Rd Peckham	d		22 29	22 34									22 45		22 59	23 04									23 19
South Bermondsey	d		22 31	22 36									22 48		23 01	23 06									23 22
Clapham Junction 10	d										22 30												23 00		
Wandsworth Common	d										22 33												23 03		
Balham 4 ⊖	d										22 35												23 05		
Streatham Hill	d										22 38												23 08		
West Norwood 4	d										22 42	22 54											23 12	23 26	
Gipsy Hill	d										22 45	22 57											23 15	23 29	
Crystal Palace 4	d									22 43	22 51	22a59										23 13	23 21	23a31	
Sydenham	d				22 21			22 36	22 42	22 46	22 54							22 51		23 06	23 13	23 16	23 24		
Forest Hill 4	d				22 23			22 38	22 45	22 49	22 57							22 53		23 08	23 16	23 19	23 27		
Honor Oak Park	d				22 26			22 41	22 47	22 51	22 59							22 56		23 11	23 18	23 21	23 29		
Brockley	d				22 28			22 43	22 50	22 54	23 02							22 58		23 13	23 21	23 24	23 32		
New Cross Gate 4	a				22 31			22 46	22 52	22 56	23 04							23 01		23 16	23 23	23 26	23 34		
	d				22 31			22 46	22 52	22 56	23 04							23 01		23 16	23 23	23 26	23 34		
New Cross ELL	d					22 36													23 06						
Surrey Quays	d				22 35	22 40		22 49		23 00								23 05	23 10	23 19		23 30			
Canada Water	d				22 37	22 42		22 51		23 02								23 07	23 12	23 21		23 32			
Rotherhithe	d				22 38	22 43		22 53		23 03								23 08	23 13	23 23		23 33			
Wapping	d				22 40	22 45		22 54		23 05								23 10	23 15	23 24		23 35			
Shadwell	d				22 42	22 47		22 56		23 07								23 12	23 17	23 26		23 37			
Whitechapel	d				22 44	22 49		22 59		23 09								23 14	23 19	23 29		23 39			
Shoreditch High Street	d				22 46	22 51		23 01		23 11								23 16	23 21	23 31		23 41			
Hoxton	d				22 48	22 53		23 03		23 13								23 18	23 23	23 33		23 43			
Haggerston	d				22 50	22 55		23 05		23 15								23 20	23 25	23 35		23 45			
Dalston Junction Stn ELL	a				22 52	22 58		23 07		23 17								23 22	23 28	23 37		23 47			
Canonbury	d				22 57			23 12		23 20								23 27		23 42		23 50			
Highbury & Islington	a				23 02			23 16		23 25								23 32		23 46		23 55			
	d																								
London Bridge 4 ⊖	a		22 36	22 41					22 59		23 11		22 52		23 06	23 11					23 30		23 45		23 26

		SE		SN	SN	LO	LO	LO	SN	SN	SN	SE		SN
East Croydon ⇌	d													
West Croydon 4 ⇌	d				23 01		23 22							
Norwood Junction 2	d						23 28							
Anerley	d						23 31							
Penge West	d						23 33							
London Victoria 15 ⊖	d			23 11					23 22					23 54
Battersea Park 4	d			23 15					23 26					23 58
Wandsworth Road	d			23 17										
Clapham High Street ⊖	d			23 19										
London Blackfriars 3 ⊖	d	23 12										23 42		
Denmark Hill 4	d	23 22		23 24								23 52		
Peckham Rye 4	d	23a25		23 26	23 31					23 42	23 47	23a55		
Queens Rd Peckham	d			23 29	23 34						23 49			
South Bermondsey	d			23 31	23 36						23 52			
Clapham Junction 10	d								23 30					00 02
Wandsworth Common	d								23 33					00 05
Balham 4 ⊖	d								23 35					00 07
Streatham Hill	d								23 38					00 10
West Norwood 4	d								23 42	23 54				00 14
Gipsy Hill	d								23 45	23 57				00 17
Crystal Palace 4	d							23 43	23 51	23a59				00 21
Sydenham	d						23 36	23 46	23 54					00 24
Forest Hill 4	d						23 38	23 49	23 57					00 27
Honor Oak Park	d						23 41	23 51	23 59					00 29
Brockley	d						23 43	23 54	00 02					00 32
New Cross Gate 4	a						23 46	23 56	00 04					00 34
	d						23 46	23 56	00 04					00 34
New Cross ELL	d					23 36								
Surrey Quays	d					23 40	23 49	23 59						
Canada Water	d					23 42	23 51	00 02						
Rotherhithe	d					23 43	23 53	00 03						
Wapping	d					23 45	23 54	00 05						
Shadwell	d					23 47	23 56	00 07						
Whitechapel	d					23 49	23 59	00 09						
Shoreditch High Street	d					23 51	00 01	00 11						
Hoxton	d					23 53	00 03	00 13						
Haggerston	d					23 55	00 05	00 15						
Dalston Junction Stn ELL	a					23 58	00 07	00 17						
Canonbury	d						00 12	00 20						
Highbury & Islington	a						00 16	00 25						
	d													
London Bridge 4 ⊖	a			23 36	23 41				00 11		23 56			00 41

Table 178

Saturdays
until 21 July

East London Line and Croydon - London Victoria to London Bridge

Network Diagram - see first Page of Table 177

Station		LO	LO	LO	SN	SN	SN	SN	LO	LO		LO	LO	SE A	LO	LO	LO	SN	LO	LO		LO	SN	LO	LO
East Croydon ⇌	d																						06 30		
West Croydon 4 ⇌	d		23p22						05 39				05 52				06 09	06 18				06 22			
Norwood Junction 2	d		23p28						05 43				05 58				06 13	06 23				06 28	06 35		
Anerley	d		23p31						05 46				06 01				06 16					06 31	06 38		
Penge West	d		23p33						05 48				06 03				06 18					06 33	06 40		
London Victoria 15 ⊖	d				23p22	23p54																			
Battersea Park 4	d				23p26	23p58																			
Wandsworth Road	d																								
Clapham High Street ⊖	d																								
London Blackfriars 3 ⊖	d													06 12											
Denmark Hill 4	d													06 22											
Peckham Rye 4	d						00 12	00 42						06a25											
Queens Rd Peckham	d																								
South Bermondsey	d																								
Clapham Junction 10	d				23p30	00 02																			
Wandsworth Common	d				23p33	00 05																			
Balham 4 ⊖	d				23p35	00 07																			
Streatham Hill	d				23p38	00 10																			
West Norwood 4	d				23p42	00 14	00 24	00 54																	
Gipsy Hill	d				23p45	00 17	00 27	00 57																	
Crystal Palace 4	d			23p43	23p51	00 21	00a29	00a59				05 58				06 13		06a27		06 28					06 43
Sydenham	d		23p36	23p46	23p54	00 24			05 51			06 01	06 06			06 16	06 21			06 31		06 36	06 42		06 46
Forest Hill 4	d		23p38	23p49	23p57	00 27			05 53			06 04	06 08			06 19	06 23			06 34		06 38	06 45		06 49
Honor Oak Park	d		23p41	23p51	23p59	00 29			05 56			06 06	06 11			06 21	06 26			06 36		06 41	06 47		06 51
Brockley	d		23p43	23p54	00 02	00 32			05 58			06 09	06 13			06 24	06 28			06 39		06 43	06 50		06 54
New Cross Gate 4	a		23p46	23p56	00 04	00 34			06 01			06 11	06 16			06 26	06 31			06 41		06 46	06 52		06 56
	d		23p46	23p56	00 04	00 34			06 01			06 11	06 16			06 26	06 31			06 41		06 46	06 52		06 56
New Cross ELL	d	23p36								06 06					06 21				06 36					06 51	
Surrey Quays	d	23p40	23p49	23p59					06 05	06 10		06 15	06 19		06 25	06 30	06 35		06 40	06 45		06 49		06 55	07 00
Canada Water	d	23p42	23p51	00 02					06 07	06 12		06 17	06 21		06 27	06 32	06 37		06 42	06 47		06 51		06 57	07 02
Rotherhithe	d	23p43	23p53	00 03					06 08	06 13		06 18	06 23		06 28	06 33	06 38		06 43	06 48		06 53		06 58	07 03
Wapping	d	23p45	23p54	00 05					06 10	06 15		06 20	06 24		06 30	06 35	06 40		06 45	06 50		06 54		07 00	07 05
Shadwell	d	23p47	23p56	00 07					06 12	06 17		06 22	06 26		06 32	06 37	06 42		06 47	06 52		06 56		07 02	07 07
Whitechapel	d	23p49	23p59	00 09					06 14	06 19		06 24	06 29		06 34	06 39	06 44		06 49	06 54		06 59		07 04	07 09
Shoreditch High Street	d	23p51	00 01	00 11					06 16	06 21		06 26	06 31		06 36	06 41	06 46		06 51	06 56		07 01		07 06	07 11
Hoxton	d	23p53	00 03	00 13					06 18	06 23		06 28	06 33		06 38	06 43	06 48		06 53	06 58		07 03		07 08	07 13
Haggerston	d	23p55	00 05	00 15					06 20	06 25		06 30	06 35		06 40	06 45	06 50		06 55	07 00		07 05		07 10	07 15
Dalston Junction Stn ELL	a	00 02	00 07	00 17					06 22	06 28		06 32	06 37		06 43	06 47	06 52		06 58	07 02		07 07		07 13	07 17
Canonbury	d		00 12	00 20					06 27			06 35	06 42			06 50	06 57			07 05		07 12			07 20
Highbury & Islington	a		00 19	00 28					06 32			06 40	06 46			06 56	07 02			07 10		07 16			07 25
	d																								
London Bridge 4 ⊖	a				00 11	00 41																	06 59		

Station		SE B	SE A	SN	SE B	SN		LO	SN	SN	LO	LO	LO	SN	SE A	SN		LO	LO	SE B	SN	LO	LO	LO	LO
East Croydon ⇌	d								06 43					07 00											
West Croydon 4 ⇌	d							06 39		06 45			06 52								07 01	07 09			07 22
Norwood Junction 2	d					06 41		06 43	06 50	06 53			06 58	07 05								07 13			07 28
Anerley	d							06 46					07 01	07 08								07 16			07 31
Penge West	d							06 48					07 03	07 10								07 18			07 33
London Victoria 15 ⊖	d	06 13		06 41	06 43											07 11				07 13					
Battersea Park 4	d			06 45												07 15									
Wandsworth Road	d			06 47												07 17									
Clapham High Street ⊖	d			06 49												07 19									
London Blackfriars 3 ⊖	d		06 42												07 12										
Denmark Hill 4	d	06 22	06 52	06 54	06 52										07 22	07 24				07 22					
Peckham Rye 4	d	06a25	06a55	06 56	06a55	07 01									07a25	07 26				07a25	07 31				
Queens Rd Peckham	d			06 59		07 04										07 29					07 34				
South Bermondsey	d			07 01		07 06										07 31					07 36				
Clapham Junction 10	d																								
Wandsworth Common	d																								
Balham 4 ⊖	d																								
Streatham Hill	d																								
West Norwood 4	d																								
Gipsy Hill	d																								
Crystal Palace 4	d									06a57		06 58							07 13					07 28	
Sydenham	d							06 51	06 54			07 01	07 06	07 12					07 16			07 21		07 31	07 36
Forest Hill 4	d							06 53	06 57			07 04	07 08	07 15					07 19			07 23		07 34	07 38
Honor Oak Park	d							06 56	06 59			07 06	07 11	07 17					07 21			07 26		07 36	07 41
Brockley	d							06 58	07 02			07 09	07 13	07 20					07 24			07 28		07 39	07 43
New Cross Gate 4	a							07 01	07 04			07 11	07 16	07 22					07 26			07 31		07 41	07 46
	d							07 01	07 04			07 11	07 16	07 22					07 26			07 31		07 41	07 46
New Cross ELL	d										07 06							07 21					07 36		
Surrey Quays	d							07 05			07 10	07 15	07 19					07 25	07 30			07 35	07 40	07 45	07 49
Canada Water	d							07 07			07 12	07 17	07 21					07 27	07 32			07 37	07 42	07 47	07 51
Rotherhithe	d							07 08			07 13	07 18	07 23					07 28	07 33			07 38	07 43	07 48	07 53
Wapping	d							07 10			07 15	07 20	07 24					07 30	07 35			07 40	07 45	07 50	07 54
Shadwell	d							07 12			07 17	07 22	07 26					07 32	07 37			07 42	07 47	07 52	07 56
Whitechapel	d							07 14			07 19	07 24	07 29					07 34	07 39			07 44	07 49	07 54	07 59
Shoreditch High Street	d							07 16			07 21	07 26	07 31					07 36	07 41			07 46	07 51	07 56	08 01
Hoxton	d							07 18			07 23	07 28	07 33					07 38	07 43			07 48	07 53	07 58	08 03
Haggerston	d							07 20			07 25	07 30	07 35					07 40	07 45			07 50	07 55	08 00	08 05
Dalston Junction Stn ELL	a							07 22			07 28	07 32	07 37					07 43	07 47			07 52	07 58	08 02	08 07
Canonbury	d							07 27				07 35	07 42						07 50			07 57		08 05	08 12
Highbury & Islington	a							07 32				07 40	07 46						07 55			08 02		08 10	08 16
	d																								
London Bridge 4 ⊖	a			07 06		07 14			07 11					07 29		07 36					07 41				

A not 19 May

B 19 May

Table 178

Saturdays

until 21 July

East London Line and Croydon - London Victoria to London Bridge

Network Diagram - see first Page of Table 177

Station		SN		LO	LO	LO	SN	SE	SE A	SN	SE B	SN		LO	LO	LO	SN	LO	LO	SN	LO	SN		SE	SE A
East Croydon	d	07 30															08 00								
West Croydon 4	d											07 31		07 39		07 52									
Norwood Junction 2	d	07 35												07 43		07 58	08 05								
Anerley	d	07 38												07 46		08 01	08 08								
Penge West	d	07 40												07 48		08 03	08 10								
London Victoria 15 ⊖	d							07 39		07 41	07 43									07 49				08 09	
Battersea Park 4	d									07 45										07 53					
Wandsworth Road	d									07 47															
Clapham High Street ⊖	d									07 49															
London Blackfriars 3 ⊖	d								07 42																08 12
Denmark Hill 4	d							07 48	07 52	07 54	07 52													08 18	08 22
Peckham Rye 4	d						07 42	07a51	07a55	07 56	07a55	08 01										08 12		08a21	08a25
Queens Rd Peckham	d									07 59		08 04													
South Bermondsey	d									08 01		08 06													
Clapham Junction 10	d																			07 57					
Wandsworth Common	d																			08 00					
Balham 4 ⊖	d																			08 02					
Streatham Hill	d																			08 05					
West Norwood 4	d						07 53													08 10		08 23			
Gipsy Hill	d						07 56													08 13		08 26			
Crystal Palace 4	d				07 43	07 58	07a59												08 13	08 21	08 28	08a29			
Sydenham	d	07 42			07 46	08 01								07 51		08 06	08 12		08 16	08 24	08 31				
Forest Hill 4	d	07 45			07 49	08 04								07 53		08 08	08 15		08 19	08 27	08 34				
Honor Oak Park	d	07 47			07 51	08 06								07 56		08 11	08 17		08 21	08 29	08 36				
Brockley	d	07 50			07 54	08 09								07 58		08 13	08 20		08 24	08 32	08 39				
New Cross Gate 4	a	07 52			07 56	08 11								08 01		08 16	08 22		08 26	08 34	08 41				
	d	07 52			07 56	08 11								08 01		08 16	08 22		08 26	08 34	08 41				
New Cross ELL	d			07 51											08 06			08 21							
Surrey Quays	d			07 55	08 00	08 15								08 05	08 10	08 19		08 25	08 30		08 45				
Canada Water	d			07 57	08 02	08 17								08 07	08 12	08 21		08 27	08 32		08 47				
Rotherhithe	d			07 58	08 03	08 18								08 08	08 13	08 23		08 28	08 33		08 48				
Wapping	d			08 00	08 05	08 20								08 10	08 15	08 24		08 30	08 35		08 50				
Shadwell	d			08 02	08 07	08 22								08 12	08 17	08 26		08 32	08 37		08 52				
Whitechapel	d			08 04	08 09	08 24								08 14	08 19	08 29		08 34	08 39		08 54				
Shoreditch High Street	d			08 06	08 11	08 26								08 16	08 21	08 31		08 36	08 41		08 56				
Hoxton	d			08 08	08 13	08 28								08 18	08 23	08 33		08 38	08 43		08 58				
Haggerston	d			08 10	08 15	08 30								08 20	08 25	08 35		08 40	08 45		09 00				
Dalston Junction Stn ELL	a			08 13	08 17	08 32								08 22	08 28	08 37		08 43	08 47		09 02				
Canonbury	d				08 20	08 35								08 27		08 42			08 50		09 05				
Highbury & Islington	a				08 25	08 40								08 32		08 46			08 55		09 10				
	d																								
London Bridge 4 ⊖	a	07 59								08 06		08 11					08 29			08 41					

Station		SN	SE B	SN	LO	LO	LO	SN		LO	LO	SN	LO	SN	SN	SE	SE A	SN		SE B	SN	LO	LO	LO	SN
East Croydon	d							08 30																	09 00
West Croydon 4	d			08 01	08 09		08 22														08 31	08 39		08 52	
Norwood Junction 2	d				08 13		08 28	08 35														08 43		08 58	09 05
Anerley	d				08 16		08 31	08 38														08 46		09 01	09 08
Penge West	d				08 18		08 33	08 40														08 48		09 03	09 10
London Victoria 15 ⊖	d	08 11	08 13									08 19				08 39		08 41		08 43					
Battersea Park 4	d	08 15										08 23						08 45							
Wandsworth Road	d	08 17																08 47							
Clapham High Street ⊖	d	08 19																08 49							
London Blackfriars 3 ⊖	d																08 42								
Denmark Hill 4	d	08 24	08 22													08 48	08 52	08 54		08 52					
Peckham Rye 4	d	08 26	08a25	08 31										08 42	08 46	08a51	08a55	08 56		08a55	09 01				
Queens Rd Peckham	d	08 29		08 34											08 49			08 59			09 04				
South Bermondsey	d	08 31		08 36											08 51			09 01			09 06				
Clapham Junction 10	d											08 27													
Wandsworth Common	d											08 30													
Balham 4 ⊖	d											08 32													
Streatham Hill	d											08 35													
West Norwood 4	d											08 40		08 53											
Gipsy Hill	d											08 43		08 56											
Crystal Palace 4	d										08 43	08 51	08 58	08a59											
Sydenham	d				08 21		08 36	08 42			08 46	08 54	09 01									08 51		09 06	09 12
Forest Hill 4	d				08 23		08 38	08 45			08 49	08 57	09 04									08 53		09 08	09 15
Honor Oak Park	d				08 26		08 41	08 47			08 51	08 59	09 06									08 56		09 11	09 17
Brockley	d				08 28		08 43	08 50			08 54	09 02	09 09									08 58		09 13	09 20
New Cross Gate 4	a				08 31		08 46	08 52			08 56	09 04	09 11									09 01		09 16	09 22
	d				08 31		08 46	08 52			08 56	09 04	09 11									09 01		09 16	09 22
New Cross ELL	d					08 36				08 51													09 06		
Surrey Quays	d				08 35	08 40	08 49			08 55	09 00		09 15									09 05	09 10	09 19	
Canada Water	d				08 37	08 42	08 51			08 57	09 02		09 17									09 07	09 12	09 21	
Rotherhithe	d				08 38	08 43	08 53			08 58	09 03		09 18									09 08	09 13	09 23	
Wapping	d				08 40	08 45	08 54			09 00	09 05		09 20									09 10	09 15	09 24	
Shadwell	d				08 42	08 47	08 56			09 02	09 07		09 22									09 12	09 17	09 26	
Whitechapel	d				08 44	08 49	08 59			09 04	09 09		09 24									09 14	09 19	09 29	
Shoreditch High Street	d				08 46	08 51	09 01			09 06	09 11		09 26									09 16	09 21	09 31	
Hoxton	d				08 48	08 53	09 03			09 08	09 13		09 28									09 18	09 23	09 33	
Haggerston	d				08 50	08 55	09 05			09 10	09 15		09 30									09 20	09 25	09 35	
Dalston Junction Stn ELL	a				08 52	08 58	09 07			09 13	09 17		09 32									09 22	09 28	09 37	
Canonbury	d				08 57		09 12				09 20		09 35									09 27		09 42	
Highbury & Islington	a				09 02		09 16				09 25		09 40									09 32		09 46	
	d																								
London Bridge 4 ⊖	a	08 36		08 41				08 59				09 11			08 56			09 06			09 11				09 29

A not 19 May

B 19 May

Table 178

Saturdays
until 21 July

East London Line and Croydon - London Victoria to London Bridge

Network Diagram - see first Page of Table 177

		LO	LO	SN		LO	SN	SN	SE	SE A	SN	SE B	SN	LO		LO	LO	SN	LO	LO	SN	LO	SN	SN
East Croydon	d																	09 30						
West Croydon 4	d												09 01	09 09			09 22							
Norwood Junction 2	d													09 13			09 28	09 35						
Anerley	d													09 16			09 31	09 38						
Penge West	d													09 18			09 33	09 40						
London Victoria 15	⊖ d			08 49					09 09		09 11	09 13									09 19			
Battersea Park 4	d			08 53							09 15										09 23			
Wandsworth Road	d										09 17													
Clapham High Street	⊖ d										09 19													
London Blackfriars 3	⊖ d									09 12														
Denmark Hill 4	d								09 18	09 22	09 24	09 22												
Peckham Rye 4	d						09 12	09 16	09a21	09a25	09 26	09a25	09 31										09 42	09 46
Queens Rd Peckham	d							09 19			09 29		09 34											09 49
South Bermondsey	d							09 21			09 31		09 36											09 51
Clapham Junction 10	d			08 57																	09 27			
Wandsworth Common	d			09 00																	09 30			
Balham 4	⊖ d			09 02																	09 32			
Streatham Hill	d			09 05																	09 35			
West Norwood 4	d			09 10			09 23														09 40		09 53	
Gipsy Hill	d			09 13			09 26														09 43		09 56	
Crystal Palace 4	d		09 13	09 21		09 28	09a29													09 43	09 51	09 58	09a59	
Sydenham	d		09 16	09 24		09 31								09 21			09 36	09 42		09 46	09 54	10 01		
Forest Hill 4	d		09 19	09 27		09 34								09 23			09 38	09 45		09 49	09 57	10 04		
Honor Oak Park	d		09 21	09 29		09 36								09 26			09 41	09 47		09 51	09 59	10 06		
Brockley	d		09 24	09 32		09 39								09 28			09 43	09 50		09 54	10 02	10 09		
New Cross Gate 4	a		09 26	09 34		09 41								09 31			09 46	09 52		09 56	10 04	10 11		
	d		09 26	09 34		09 41								09 31			09 46	09 52		09 56	10 04	10 11		
New Cross ELL	d	09 21														09 36			09 51					
Surrey Quays	d	09 25	09 30			09 45								09 35		09 40	09 49		09 55	10 00		10 15		
Canada Water	d	09 27	09 32			09 47								09 37		09 42	09 51		09 57	10 02		10 17		
Rotherhithe	d	09 28	09 33			09 48								09 38		09 43	09 53		09 58	10 03		10 18		
Wapping	d	09 30	09 35			09 50								09 40		09 45	09 54		10 00	10 05		10 20		
Shadwell	d	09 32	09 37			09 52								09 42		09 47	09 56		10 02	10 07		10 22		
Whitechapel	d	09 34	09 39			09 54								09 44		09 49	09 59		10 04	10 09		10 24		
Shoreditch High Street	d	09 36	09 41			09 56								09 46		09 51	10 01		10 06	10 11		10 26		
Hoxton	d	09 38	09 43			09 58								09 48		09 53	10 03		10 08	10 13		10 28		
Haggerston	d	09 40	09 45			10 00								09 50		09 55	10 05		10 10	10 15		10 30		
Dalston Junction Stn ELL	a	09 43	09 47			10 02								09 52		09 58	10 07		10 13	10 17		10 32		
Canonbury	d		09 50			10 05								09 57			10 12			10 20		10 35		
Highbury & Islington	a		09 55			10 10								10 02			10 16			10 25		10 40		
	d																							
London Bridge 4	⊖ a			09 41				09 26			09 36		09 41					09 59			10 11			09 56

		SE	SE A	SN	SE B	SN	LO	LO	LO	SN		LO	LO	SN	LO	SN	SN	SE	SE A	SN		SE B	SN	LO	LO
East Croydon	d									10 00															
West Croydon 4	d					09 31	09 39		09 52														10 01	10 09	
Norwood Junction 2	d						09 43		09 58	10 05														10 13	
Anerley	d						09 46		10 01	10 08														10 16	
Penge West	d						09 48		10 03	10 10														10 18	
London Victoria 15	⊖ d	09 39		09 41	09 43									09 49				10 09		10 11		10 13			
Battersea Park 4	d			09 45										09 53						10 15					
Wandsworth Road	d			09 47																10 17					
Clapham High Street	⊖ d			09 49																10 19					
London Blackfriars 3	⊖ d		09 42																10 12						
Denmark Hill 4	d	09 48	09 52	09 54	09 52													10 18	10 22	10 24		10 22			
Peckham Rye 4	d	09a51	09a55	09 56	09a55	10 01										10 12	10 16	10a21	10a25	10 26		10a25	10 31		
Queens Rd Peckham	d			09 59		10 04											10 19			10 29			10 34		
South Bermondsey	d			10 01		10 06											10 21			10 31			10 36		
Clapham Junction 10	d													09 57											
Wandsworth Common	d													10 00											
Balham 4	⊖ d													10 02											
Streatham Hill	d													10 05											
West Norwood 4	d													10 10		10 23									
Gipsy Hill	d													10 13		10 26									
Crystal Palace 4	d												10 13	10 21	10 28	10a29									
Sydenham	d						09 51		10 06	10 12			10 16	10 24	10 31									10 21	
Forest Hill 4	d						09 53		10 08	10 15			10 19	10 27	10 34									10 23	
Honor Oak Park	d						09 56		10 11	10 17			10 21	10 29	10 36									10 26	
Brockley	d						09 58		10 13	10 20			10 24	10 32	10 39									10 28	
New Cross Gate 4	a						10 01		10 16	10 22			10 26	10 34	10 41									10 31	
	d						10 01		10 16	10 22			10 26	10 34	10 41									10 31	
New Cross ELL	d							10 06				10 21													10 36
Surrey Quays	d						10 05	10 10	10 19			10 25	10 30		10 45									10 35	10 40
Canada Water	d						10 07	10 12	10 21			10 27	10 32		10 47									10 37	10 42
Rotherhithe	d						10 08	10 13	10 23			10 28	10 33		10 48									10 38	10 43
Wapping	d						10 10	10 15	10 24			10 30	10 35		10 50									10 40	10 45
Shadwell	d						10 12	10 17	10 26			10 32	10 37		10 52									10 42	10 47
Whitechapel	d						10 14	10 19	10 29			10 34	10 39		10 54									10 44	10 49
Shoreditch High Street	d						10 16	10 21	10 31			10 36	10 41		10 56									10 46	10 51
Hoxton	d						10 18	10 23	10 33			10 38	10 43		10 58									10 48	10 53
Haggerston	d						10 20	10 25	10 35			10 40	10 45		11 00									10 50	10 55
Dalston Junction Stn ELL	a						10 22	10 28	10 37			10 43	10 47		11 02									10 52	10 58
Canonbury	d						10 27		10 42				10 50		11 05									10 57	
Highbury & Islington	a						10 32		10 46				10 55		11 10									11 02	
	d																								
London Bridge 4	⊖ a			10 06		10 11				10 29				10 41			10 26			10 36			10 41		

A not 19 May

B 19 May

Table 178

Saturdays

until 21 July

East London Line and Croydon - London Victoria to London Bridge

Network Diagram - see first Page of Table 177

		LO	SN	LO	LO	SN		LO	SN	SN	SE	SE	SN	SE	SN	LO		LO	LO	SN	LO	LO	SN	LO	SN
												A		B											
East Croydon	d		10 30																	11 00					
West Croydon 4	d	10 22													10 31	10 39			10 52						
Norwood Junction 2	d	10 28	10 35													10 43			10 58	11 05					
Anerley	d	10 31	10 38													10 46			11 01	11 08					
Penge West	d	10 33	10 40													10 48			11 03	11 10					
London Victoria 15 ⊖	d					10 19					10 39		10 41	10 43									10 49		
Battersea Park 4	d					10 23							10 45										10 53		
Wandsworth Road	d												10 47												
Clapham High Street ⊖	d												10 49												
London Blackfriars 3 ⊖	d											10 42													
Denmark Hill 4	d										10 48	10 52	10 54	10 52											
Peckham Rye 4	d								10 42	10 46	10a51	10a55	10 56	10a55	11 01										11 12
Queens Rd Peckham	d									10 49			10 59		11 04										
South Bermondsey	d									10 51			11 01		11 06										
Clapham Junction 10	d					10 27																	10 57		
Wandsworth Common	d					10 30																	11 00		
Balham 4 ⊖	d					10 32																	11 02		
Streatham Hill	d					10 35																	11 05		
West Norwood 4	d					10 40			10 53														11 10		11 23
Gipsy Hill	d					10 43			10 56														11 13		11 26
Crystal Palace 4	d				10 43	10 51		10 58	10a59													11 13	11 21	11 28	11a29
Sydenham	d	10 36	10 42		10 46	10 54		11 01								10 51			11 06	11 12		11 16	11 24	11 31	
Forest Hill 4	d	10 38	10 45		10 49	10 57		11 04								10 53			11 08	11 15		11 19	11 27	11 34	
Honor Oak Park	d	10 41	10 47		10 51	10 59		11 06								10 56			11 11	11 17		11 21	11 29	11 36	
Brockley	d	10 43	10 50		10 54	11 02		11 09								10 58			11 13	11 20		11 24	11 32	11 39	
New Cross Gate 4	a	10 46	10 52		10 56	11 04		11 11								11 01			11 16	11 22		11 26	11 34	11 41	
	d	10 46	10 52		10 56	11 04		11 11								11 01			11 16	11 22		11 26	11 34	11 41	
New Cross ELL	d			10 51														11 06			11 21				
Surrey Quays	d	10 49		10 55	11 00			11 15								11 05		11 10	11 19		11 25	11 30		11 45	
Canada Water	d	10 51		10 57	11 02			11 17								11 07		11 12	11 21		11 27	11 32		11 47	
Rotherhithe	d	10 53		10 58	11 03			11 18								11 08		11 13	11 23		11 28	11 33		11 48	
Wapping	d	10 54		11 00	11 05			11 20								11 10		11 15	11 24		11 30	11 35		11 50	
Shadwell	d	10 56		11 02	11 07			11 22								11 12		11 17	11 26		11 32	11 37		11 52	
Whitechapel	d	10 59		11 04	11 09			11 24								11 14		11 19	11 29		11 34	11 39		11 54	
Shoreditch High Street	d	11 01		11 06	11 11			11 26								11 16		11 21	11 31		11 36	11 41		11 56	
Hoxton	d	11 03		11 08	11 13			11 28								11 18		11 23	11 33		11 38	11 43		11 58	
Haggerston	d	11 05		11 10	11 15			11 30								11 20		11 25	11 35		11 40	11 45		12 00	
Dalston Junction Stn ELL	a	11 07		11 13	11 17			11 32								11 22		11 28	11 37		11 43	11 47		12 02	
Canonbury	d	11 12			11 20			11 35								11 27			11 42			11 50		12 05	
Highbury & Islington	a	11 16			11 25			11 40								11 32			11 46			11 55		12 10	
	d																								
London Bridge 4 ⊖	a		10 59			11 11				10 56			11 06		11 11					11 29			11 41		

		SN		SE	SE	SN	SE	SN	LO	LO	LO	SN		LO	LO	SN	LO	SN	SN	SE	SE	SN		SE	SN
					A		B														A			B	
East Croydon	d											11 30													
West Croydon 4	d							11 01	11 09		11 22														11 31
Norwood Junction 2	d								11 13		11 28	11 35													
Anerley	d								11 16		11 31	11 38													
Penge West	d								11 18		11 33	11 40													
London Victoria 15 ⊖	d			11 09		11 11	11 13									11 19				11 39		11 41		11 43	
Battersea Park 4	d					11 15										11 23						11 45			
Wandsworth Road	d					11 17																11 47			
Clapham High Street ⊖	d					11 19																11 49			
London Blackfriars 3 ⊖	d				11 12																11 42				
Denmark Hill 4	d			11 18	11 22	11 24	11 22													11 48	11 52	11 54		11 52	
Peckham Rye 4	d	11 16		11a21	11a25	11 26	11a25	11 31										11 42	11 46	11a51	11a55	11 56		11a55	12 01
Queens Rd Peckham	d	11 19				11 29		11 34											11 49			11 59			12 04
South Bermondsey	d	11 21				11 31		11 36											11 51			12 01			12 06
Clapham Junction 10	d															11 27									
Wandsworth Common	d															11 30									
Balham 4 ⊖	d															11 32									
Streatham Hill	d															11 35									
West Norwood 4	d															11 40		11 53							
Gipsy Hill	d															11 43		11 56							
Crystal Palace 4	d														11 43	11 51	11 58	11a59							
Sydenham	d								11 21		11 36	11 42			11 46	11 54	12 01								
Forest Hill 4	d								11 23		11 38	11 45			11 49	11 57	12 04								
Honor Oak Park	d								11 26		11 41	11 47			11 51	11 59	12 06								
Brockley	d								11 28		11 43	11 50			11 54	12 02	12 09								
New Cross Gate 4	a								11 31		11 46	11 52			11 56	12 04	12 11								
	d								11 31		11 46	11 52			11 56	12 04	12 11								
New Cross ELL	d									11 36				11 51											
Surrey Quays	d								11 35	11 40	11 49			11 55	12 00		12 15								
Canada Water	d								11 37	11 42	11 51			11 57	12 02		12 17								
Rotherhithe	d								11 38	11 43	11 53			11 58	12 03		12 18								
Wapping	d								11 40	11 45	11 54			12 00	12 05		12 20								
Shadwell	d								11 42	11 47	11 56			12 02	12 07		12 22								
Whitechapel	d								11 44	11 49	11 59			12 04	12 09		12 24								
Shoreditch High Street	d								11 46	11 51	12 01			12 06	12 11		12 26								
Hoxton	d								11 48	11 53	12 03			12 08	12 13		12 28								
Haggerston	d								11 50	11 55	12 05			12 10	12 15		12 30								
Dalston Junction Stn ELL	a								11 52	11 58	12 07			12 13	12 17		12 32								
Canonbury	d								11 57		12 12				12 20		12 35								
Highbury & Islington	a								12 02		12 16				12 25		12 40								
	d																								
London Bridge 4 ⊖	a	11 26				11 36		11 41				11 59				12 11			11 56			12 06			12 11

A not 19 May

B 19 May

Table 178

Saturdays
until 21 July

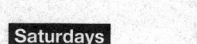

East London Line and Croydon - London Victoria to London Bridge

Network Diagram - see first Page of Table 177

		LO	LO	LO	SN	LO	LO	SN		LO	SN	SN	SE	SE A	SN	SE B	SN	LO		LO	LO	SN	LO	LO	SN
East Croydon	d				12 00																	12 30			
West Croydon 4	d	11 39		11 52													12 01	12 09			12 22				
Norwood Junction 2	d	11 43		11 58	12 05													12 13			12 28	12 35			
Anerley	d	11 46		12 01	12 08													12 16			12 31	12 38			
Penge West	d	11 48		12 03	12 10													12 18			12 33	12 40			
London Victoria 15	d							11 49					12 09		12 11	12 13									12 19
Battersea Park 4	d							11 53							12 15										12 23
Wandsworth Road	d														12 17										
Clapham High Street	d														12 19										
London Blackfriars 3	d													12 12											
Denmark Hill 4	d												12 18	12 22	12 24	12 22									
Peckham Rye 4	d										12 12	12 16	12a21	12a25	12 26	12a25	12 31								
Queens Rd Peckham	d											12 19			12 29		12 34								
South Bermondsey	d											12 21			12 31		12 36								
Clapham Junction 10	d							11 57																	12 27
Wandsworth Common	d							12 00																	12 30
Balham 4	d							12 02																	12 32
Streatham Hill	d							12 05																	12 35
West Norwood 4	d							12 10			12 23														12 40
Gipsy Hill	d							12 13			12 26														12 43
Crystal Palace 4	d						12 13	12 21		12 28	12a29													12 43	12 51
Sydenham	d	11 51		12 06	12 12		12 16	12 24		12 31								12 21			12 36	12 42		12 46	12 54
Forest Hill 4	d	11 53		12 08	12 15		12 19	12 27		12 34								12 23			12 38	12 45		12 49	12 57
Honor Oak Park	d	11 56		12 11	12 17		12 21	12 29		12 36								12 26			12 41	12 47		12 51	12 59
Brockley	d	11 58		12 13	12 20		12 24	12 32		12 39								12 28			12 43	12 50		12 54	13 02
New Cross Gate 4	a	12 01		12 16	12 22		12 26	12 34		12 41								12 31			12 46	12 52		12 56	13 04
	d	12 01		12 16	12 22		12 26	12 34		12 41								12 31			12 46	12 52		12 56	13 04
New Cross ELL	d		12 06			12 21														12 36			12 51		
Surrey Quays	d	12 05	12 10	12 19		12 25	12 30			12 45								12 35		12 40	12 49		12 55	13 00	
Canada Water	d	12 07	12 12	12 21		12 27	12 32			12 47								12 37		12 42	12 51		12 57	13 02	
Rotherhithe	d	12 08	12 13	12 23		12 28	12 33			12 48								12 38		12 43	12 53		12 58	13 03	
Wapping	d	12 10	12 15	12 24		12 30	12 35			12 50								12 40		12 45	12 54		13 00	13 05	
Shadwell	d	12 12	12 17	12 26		12 32	12 37			12 52								12 42		12 47	12 56		13 02	13 07	
Whitechapel	d	12 14	12 19	12 29		12 34	12 39			12 54								12 44		12 49	12 59		13 04	13 09	
Shoreditch High Street	d	12 16	12 21	12 31		12 36	12 41			12 56								12 46		12 51	13 01		13 06	13 11	
Hoxton	d	12 18	12 23	12 33		12 38	12 43			12 58								12 48		12 53	13 03		13 08	13 13	
Haggerston	d	12 20	12 25	12 35		12 40	12 45			13 00								12 50		12 55	13 05		13 10	13 15	
Dalston Junction Stn ELL	a	12 22	12 28	12 37		12 43	12 47			13 02								12 52		12 58	13 07		13 13	13 17	
Canonbury	d	12 27		12 42			12 50			13 05								12 57			13 12			13 20	
Highbury & Islington	a	12 32		12 46			12 55			13 10								13 02			13 16			13 25	
	d																								
London Bridge 4	a				12 29			12 44				12 26			12 36		12 41					12 59			13 11

		LO	SN	SN		SE	SE A	SN	SE B	SN	LO	LO	LO	SN		LO	LO	SN	LO	SN	SN	SE	SE A	SN
East Croydon	d													13 00										
West Croydon 4	d									12 31	12 39		12 52											
Norwood Junction 2	d										12 43		12 58	13 05										
Anerley	d										12 46		13 01	13 08										
Penge West	d										12 48		13 03	13 10										
London Victoria 15	d					12 39		12 41	12 43									12 49				13 09		13 11
Battersea Park 4	d							12 45										12 53						13 15
Wandsworth Road	d							12 47																13 17
Clapham High Street	d							12 49																13 19
London Blackfriars 3	d						12 42																13 12	
Denmark Hill 4	d					12 48	12 52	12 54	12 52													13 18	13 22	13 24
Peckham Rye 4	d		12 42	12 46		12a51	12a55	12 56	12a55	13 01										13 12	13 16	13a21	13a25	13 26
Queens Rd Peckham	d			12 49				12 59		13 04											13 19			13 29
South Bermondsey	d			12 51				13 01		13 06											13 21			13 31
Clapham Junction 10	d																	12 57						
Wandsworth Common	d																	13 00						
Balham 4	d																	13 02						
Streatham Hill	d																	13 05						
West Norwood 4	d		12 53															13 10		13 23				
Gipsy Hill	d		12 56															13 13		13 26				
Crystal Palace 4	d	12 58	12a59														13 13	13 21	13 28	13a29				
Sydenham	d	13 01									12 51		13 06	13 12			13 16	13 24	13 31					
Forest Hill 4	d	13 04									12 53		13 08	13 15			13 19	13 27	13 34					
Honor Oak Park	d	13 06									12 56		13 11	13 17			13 21	13 29	13 36					
Brockley	d	13 09									12 58		13 13	13 20			13 24	13 32	13 39					
New Cross Gate 4	a	13 11									13 01		13 16	13 22			13 26	13 34	13 41					
	d	13 11									13 01		13 16	13 22			13 26	13 34	13 41					
New Cross ELL	d											13 06				13 21								
Surrey Quays	d	13 15									13 05	13 10	13 19			13 25	13 30		13 45					
Canada Water	d	13 17									13 07	13 12	13 21			13 27	13 32		13 47					
Rotherhithe	d	13 18									13 08	13 13	13 23			13 28	13 33		13 48					
Wapping	d	13 20									13 10	13 15	13 24			13 30	13 35		13 50					
Shadwell	d	13 22									13 12	13 17	13 26			13 32	13 37		13 52					
Whitechapel	d	13 24									13 14	13 19	13 29			13 34	13 39		13 54					
Shoreditch High Street	d	13 26									13 16	13 21	13 31			13 36	13 41		13 56					
Hoxton	d	13 28									13 18	13 23	13 33			13 38	13 43		13 58					
Haggerston	d	13 30									13 20	13 25	13 35			13 40	13 45		14 00					
Dalston Junction Stn ELL	a	13 32									13 22	13 28	13 37			13 43	13 47		14 02					
Canonbury	d	13 35									13 27		13 42				13 50		14 05					
Highbury & Islington	a	13 40									13 32		13 46				13 55		14 10					
	d																							
London Bridge 4	a			12 56				13 06		13 11				13 29				13 44			13 26			13 36

A not 19 May

B 19 May

East London Line and Croydon - London Victoria to London Bridge

Network Diagram - see first Page of Table 177

		SE A	SN	LO	LO	LO	SN	LO	LO	SN		LO	SN	SN	SE	SE B	SN	SE A	SN	LO		LO	LO	SN	LO
East Croydon	d						13 30																	14 00	
West Croydon 4	d		13 01	13 09		13 22													13 31	13 39			13 52		
Norwood Junction 2	d			13 13		13 28	13 35													13 43			13 58	14 05	
Anerley	d			13 16		13 31	13 38													13 46			14 01	14 08	
Penge West	d			13 18		13 33	13 40													13 48			14 03	14 10	
London Victoria 15 ⊖	d	13 13								13 19					13 39		13 41	13 43							
Battersea Park 4	d									13 23							13 45								
Wandsworth Road	d																13 47								
Clapham High Street ⊖	d																13 49								
London Blackfriars 3 ⊖	d															13 42									
Denmark Hill 4	d	13 22													13 48	13 52	13 54	13 52							
Peckham Rye 4	d	13a25	13 31										13 42	13 46	13a51	13a55	13 56	13a55	14 01						
Queens Rd Peckham	d		13 34											13 49			13 59		14 04						
South Bermondsey	d		13 36											13 51			14 01		14 06						
Clapham Junction 10	d									13 27															
Wandsworth Common	d									13 30															
Balham 4 ⊖	d									13 32															
Streatham Hill	d									13 35															
West Norwood 4	d									13 40			13 53												
Gipsy Hill	d									13 43			13 56												
Crystal Palace 4	d								13 43	13 51		13 58	13a59												
Sydenham	d			13 21		13 36	13 42		13 46	13 54		14 01								13 51			14 06	14 12	
Forest Hill 4	d			13 23		13 38	13 45		13 49	13 57		14 04								13 53			14 08	14 15	
Honor Oak Park	d			13 26		13 41	13 47		13 51	13 59		14 06								13 56			14 11	14 17	
Brockley	d			13 28		13 43	13 50		13 54	14 02		14 09								13 58			14 13	14 20	
New Cross Gate 4	a			13 31		13 46	13 52		13 56	14 04		14 11								14 01			14 16	14 22	
	d			13 31		13 46	13 52		13 56	14 04		14 11								14 01			14 16	14 22	
New Cross ELL	d				13 36			13 51														14 06			14 21
Surrey Quays	d			13 35	13 40	13 49		13 55	14 00			14 15								14 05		14 10	14 19		14 25
Canada Water	d			13 37	13 42	13 51		13 57	14 02			14 17								14 07		14 12	14 21		14 27
Rotherhithe	d			13 38	13 43	13 53		13 58	14 03			14 18								14 08		14 13	14 23		14 28
Wapping	d			13 40	13 45	13 54		14 00	14 05			14 20								14 10		14 15	14 24		14 30
Shadwell	d			13 42	13 47	13 56		14 02	14 07			14 22								14 12		14 17	14 26		14 32
Whitechapel	d			13 44	13 49	13 59		14 04	14 09			14 24								14 14		14 19	14 29		14 34
Shoreditch High Street	d			13 46	13 51	14 01		14 06	14 11			14 26								14 16		14 21	14 31		14 36
Hoxton	d			13 48	13 53	14 03		14 08	14 13			14 28								14 18		14 23	14 33		14 38
Haggerston	d			13 50	13 55	14 05		14 10	14 15			14 30								14 20		14 25	14 35		14 40
Dalston Junction Stn ELL	a			13 52	13 58	14 07		14 13	14 17			14 32								14 22		14 28	14 37		14 43
Canonbury	d			13 57		14 12			14 20			14 35								14 27			14 42		
Highbury & Islington	a			14 02		14 16			14 25			14 40								14 32			14 46		
	d																								
London Bridge 4 ⊖	a		13 41				13 59			14 11				13 56			14 06		14 11					14 29	

		LO	SN	LO	SN	SN		SE	SE B	SN	SE A	SN	LO	LO	LO	SN		LO	LO	SN	LO	SN	SN	SE	SE B
East Croydon	d															14 30									
West Croydon 4	d											14 01	14 09		14 22										
Norwood Junction 2	d												14 13		14 28	14 35									
Anerley	d												14 16		14 31	14 38									
Penge West	d												14 18		14 33	14 40									
London Victoria 15 ⊖	d		13 49					14 09		14 11	14 13									14 19				14 39	
Battersea Park 4	d		13 53							14 15										14 23					
Wandsworth Road	d									14 17															
Clapham High Street ⊖	d									14 19															
London Blackfriars 3 ⊖	d								14 12																14 42
Denmark Hill 4	d							14 18	14 22	14 24	14 22													14 48	14 52
Peckham Rye 4	d				14 12	14 16		14a21	14a25	14 26	14a25	14 31										14 42	14 46	14a51	14a55
Queens Rd Peckham	d					14 19				14 29		14 34											14 49		
South Bermondsey	d					14 21				14 31		14 36											14 51		
Clapham Junction 10	d		13 57																	14 27					
Wandsworth Common	d		14 00																	14 30					
Balham 4 ⊖	d		14 02																	14 32					
Streatham Hill	d		14 05																	14 35					
West Norwood 4	d		14 10		14 23															14 40		14 53			
Gipsy Hill	d		14 13		14 26															14 43		14 56			
Crystal Palace 4	d	14 13	14 21	14 28	14a29														14 43	14 51	14 58	14a59			
Sydenham	d	14 16	14 24	14 31									14 21		14 36	14 42			14 46	14 54	15 01				
Forest Hill 4	d	14 19	14 27	14 34									14 23		14 38	14 45			14 49	14 57	15 04				
Honor Oak Park	d	14 21	14 29	14 36									14 26		14 41	14 47			14 51	14 59	15 06				
Brockley	d	14 24	14 32	14 39									14 28		14 43	14 50			14 54	15 02	15 09				
New Cross Gate 4	a	14 26	14 34	14 41									14 31		14 46	14 52			14 56	15 04	15 11				
	d	14 26	14 34	14 41									14 31		14 46	14 52			14 56	15 04	15 11				
New Cross ELL	d													14 36				14 51							
Surrey Quays	d	14 30		14 45									14 35	14 40	14 49			14 55	15 00		15 15				
Canada Water	d	14 32		14 47									14 37	14 42	14 51			14 57	15 02		15 17				
Rotherhithe	d	14 33		14 48									14 38	14 43	14 53			14 58	15 03		15 18				
Wapping	d	14 35		14 50									14 40	14 45	14 54			15 00	15 05		15 20				
Shadwell	d	14 37		14 52									14 42	14 47	14 56			15 02	15 07		15 22				
Whitechapel	d	14 39		14 54									14 44	14 49	14 59			15 04	15 09		15 24				
Shoreditch High Street	d	14 41		14 56									14 46	14 51	15 01			15 06	15 11		15 26				
Hoxton	d	14 43		14 58									14 48	14 53	15 03			15 08	15 13		15 28				
Haggerston	d	14 45		15 00									14 50	14 55	15 05			15 10	15 15		15 30				
Dalston Junction Stn ELL	a	14 47		15 02									14 52	14 58	15 07			15 13	15 17		15 32				
Canonbury	d	14 50		15 05									14 57		15 12				15 20		15 35				
Highbury & Islington	a	14 55		15 10									15 02		15 16				15 25		15 40				
	d																								
London Bridge 4 ⊖	a		14 44			14 26				14 36		14 41				14 59				15 11			14 56		

A 19 May

B not 19 May

Table 178

Saturdays
until 21 July

East London Line and Croydon - London Victoria to London Bridge

Network Diagram - see first Page of Table 177

		SN		SE A	SN	LO	LO	LO	SN	LO	LO	SN		LO	SN	SN	SE	SE B	SN	SE A	SN	LO		LO	LO
East Croydon	d								15 00																
West Croydon 4	d				14 31	14 39		14 52													15 01	15 09			15 22
Norwood Junction 2	d					14 43		14 58	15 05													15 13			15 28
Anerley	d					14 46		15 01	15 08													15 16			15 31
Penge West	d					14 48		15 03	15 10													15 18			15 33
London Victoria 15 ⊖	d	14 41		14 43								14 49					15 09		15 11	15 13					
Battersea Park 4	d	14 45										14 53							15 15						
Wandsworth Road	d	14 47																	15 17						
Clapham High Street ⊖	d	14 49																	15 19						
London Blackfriars 3 ⊖	d																	15 12							
Denmark Hill 4	d	14 54		14 52													15 18	15 22	15 24	15 22					
Peckham Rye 4	d	14 56		14a55	15 01										15 12	15 16	15a21	15a25	15 26	15a25	15 31				
Queens Rd Peckham	d	14 59			15 04											15 19			15 29		15 34				
South Bermondsey	d	15 01			15 06											15 21			15 31		15 36				
Clapham Junction 10	d											14 57													
Wandsworth Common	d											15 00													
Balham 4 ⊖	d											15 02													
Streatham Hill	d											15 05													
West Norwood 4	d											15 10			15 23										
Gipsy Hill	d											15 13			15 26										
Crystal Palace 4	d										15 13	15 21		15 28	15a29										
Sydenham	d					14 51		15 06	15 12		15 16	15 24		15 31								15 21			15 36
Forest Hill 4	d					14 53		15 08	15 15		15 19	15 27		15 34								15 23			15 38
Honor Oak Park	d					14 56		15 11	15 17		15 21	15 29		15 36								15 26			15 41
Brockley	d					14 58		15 13	15 20		15 24	15 32		15 39								15 28			15 43
New Cross Gate 4	a					15 01		15 16	15 22		15 26	15 34		15 41								15 31			15 46
	d					15 01		15 16	15 22		15 26	15 34		15 41								15 31			15 46
New Cross ELL	d						15 06			15 21														15 36	
Surrey Quays	d					15 05	15 10	15 19		15 25	15 30			15 45								15 35		15 40	15 49
Canada Water	d					15 07	15 12	15 21		15 27	15 32			15 47								15 37		15 42	15 51
Rotherhithe	d					15 08	15 13	15 23		15 28	15 33			15 48								15 38		15 43	15 53
Wapping	d					15 10	15 15	15 24		15 30	15 35			15 50								15 40		15 45	15 54
Shadwell	d					15 12	15 17	15 26		15 32	15 37			15 52								15 42		15 47	15 56
Whitechapel	d					15 14	15 19	15 29		15 34	15 39			15 54								15 44		15 49	15 59
Shoreditch High Street	d					15 16	15 21	15 31		15 36	15 41			15 56								15 46		15 51	16 01
Hoxton	d					15 18	15 23	15 33		15 38	15 43			15 58								15 48		15 53	16 03
Haggerston	d					15 20	15 25	15 35		15 40	15 45			16 00								15 50		15 55	16 05
Dalston Junction Stn ELL	a					15 22	15 28	15 37		15 43	15 47			16 02								15 52		15 58	16 07
Canonbury	d					15 27		15 42			15 50			16 05								15 57			16 12
Highbury & Islington	a					15 32		15 46			15 55			16 10								16 02			16 16
	d																								
London Bridge 4 ⊖	a	15 06			15 11				15 29			15 44				15 26			15 36		15 41				

		SN	LO	LO	SN	LO	SN	SN		SE	SE B	SN	SE A	SN	LO	LO	LO	SN		LO	LO	SN	LO	SN	SN
East Croydon	d	15 30																16 00							
West Croydon 4	d													15 31	15 39		15 52								
Norwood Junction 2	d	15 35													15 43		15 58	16 05							
Anerley	d	15 38													15 46		16 01	16 08							
Penge West	d	15 40													15 48		16 03	16 10							
London Victoria 15 ⊖	d				15 19					15 39		15 41	15 43									15 49			
Battersea Park 4	d				15 23							15 45										15 53			
Wandsworth Road	d											15 47													
Clapham High Street ⊖	d											15 49													
London Blackfriars 3 ⊖	d										15 42														
Denmark Hill 4	d									15 48	15 52	15 54	15 52												
Peckham Rye 4	d						15 42	15 46		15a51	15a55	15 56	15a55	16 01										16 12	16 16
Queens Rd Peckham	d							15 49				15 59		16 04											16 19
South Bermondsey	d							15 51				16 01		16 06											16 21
Clapham Junction 10	d				15 27																	15 57			
Wandsworth Common	d				15 30																	16 00			
Balham 4 ⊖	d				15 32																	16 02			
Streatham Hill	d				15 35																	16 05			
West Norwood 4	d				15 40		15 53															16 10		16 23	
Gipsy Hill	d				15 43		15 56															16 13		16 26	
Crystal Palace 4	d			15 43	15 51	15 58	15a59														16 13	16 21	16 28	16a29	
Sydenham	d	15 42		15 46	15 54	16 01									15 51		16 06	16 12			16 16	16 24	16 31		
Forest Hill 4	d	15 45		15 49	15 57	16 04									15 53		16 08	16 15			16 19	16 27	16 34		
Honor Oak Park	d	15 47		15 51	15 59	16 06									15 56		16 11	16 17			16 21	16 29	16 36		
Brockley	d	15 50		15 54	16 02	16 09									15 58		16 13	16 20			16 24	16 32	16 39		
New Cross Gate 4	a	15 52		15 56	16 04	16 11									16 01		16 16	16 22			16 26	16 34	16 41		
	d	15 52		15 56	16 04	16 11									16 01		16 16	16 22			16 26	16 34	16 41		
New Cross ELL	d		15 51													16 06				16 21					
Surrey Quays	d		15 55	16 00		16 15									16 05	16 10	16 19			16 25	16 30		16 45		
Canada Water	d		15 57	16 02		16 17									16 07	16 12	16 21			16 27	16 32		16 47		
Rotherhithe	d		15 58	16 03		16 18									16 08	16 13	16 23			16 28	16 33		16 48		
Wapping	d		16 00	16 05		16 20									16 10	16 15	16 24			16 30	16 35		16 50		
Shadwell	d		16 02	16 07		16 22									16 12	16 17	16 26			16 32	16 37		16 52		
Whitechapel	d		16 04	16 09		16 24									16 14	16 19	16 29			16 34	16 39		16 54		
Shoreditch High Street	d		16 06	16 11		16 26									16 16	16 21	16 31			16 36	16 41		16 56		
Hoxton	d		16 08	16 13		16 28									16 18	16 23	16 33			16 38	16 43		16 58		
Haggerston	d		16 10	16 15		16 30									16 20	16 25	16 35			16 40	16 45		17 00		
Dalston Junction Stn ELL	a		16 13	16 17		16 32									16 22	16 28	16 37			16 43	16 47		17 02		
Canonbury	d			16 20		16 35									16 27		16 42				16 50		17 05		
Highbury & Islington	a			16 25		16 40									16 32		16 46				16 55		17 10		
	d																								
London Bridge 4 ⊖	a	15 59			16 11			15 56				16 06		16 11				16 29				16 41			16 26

A 19 May

B not 19 May

Saturdays

until 21 July

East London Line and Croydon - London Victoria to London Bridge

Network Diagram - see first Page of Table 177

		SE	SE A	SN		SE B	SN	LO	LO	LO	SN	LO	LO	SN		LO	SN	SN	SE	SE A	SN	SE B	SN	LO
East Croydon	d										16 30													
West Croydon 4	d						16 01	16 09		16 22													16 31	16 39
Norwood Junction 2	d							16 13		16 28	16 35													16 43
Anerley	d							16 16		16 31	16 38													16 46
Penge West	d							16 18		16 33	16 40													16 48
London Victoria 15 ⊖	d	16 09		16 11		16 13								16 19					16 39		16 41	16 43		
Battersea Park 4	d			16 15										16 23							16 45			
Wandsworth Road	d			16 17																	16 47			
Clapham High Street ⊖	d			16 19																	16 49			
London Blackfriars 3 ⊖	d		16 12																	16 42				
Denmark Hill 4	d	16 18	16 22	16 24		16 22													16 48	16 52	16 54	16 52		
Peckham Rye 4	d	16a21	16a25	16 26		16a25	16 31										16 42	16 46	16a51	16a55	16 56	16a55	17 01	
Queens Rd Peckham	d			16 29			16 34											16 49			16 59		17 04	
South Bermondsey	d			16 31			16 36											16 51			17 01		17 06	
Clapham Junction 10	d													16 27										
Wandsworth Common	d													16 30										
Balham 4 ⊖	d													16 32										
Streatham Hill	d													16 35										
West Norwood 4	d													16 40			16 53							
Gipsy Hill	d													16 43			16 56							
Crystal Palace 4	d												16 43	16 51		16 58	16a59							
Sydenham	d							16 21		16 36	16 42		16 46	16 54		17 01								16 51
Forest Hill 4	d							16 23		16 38	16 45		16 49	16 57		17 04								16 53
Honor Oak Park	d							16 26		16 41	16 47		16 51	16 59		17 06								16 56
Brockley	d							16 28		16 43	16 50		16 54	17 02		17 09								16 58
New Cross Gate 4	a							16 31		16 46	16 52		16 56	17 04		17 11								17 01
	d							16 31		16 46	16 52		16 56	17 04		17 11								17 01
New Cross ELL	d								16 36			16 51												
Surrey Quays	d							16 35	16 40	16 49		16 55	17 00			17 15								17 05
Canada Water	d							16 37	16 42	16 51		16 57	17 02			17 17								17 07
Rotherhithe	d							16 38	16 43	16 53		16 58	17 03			17 18								17 08
Wapping	d							16 40	16 45	16 54		17 00	17 05			17 20								17 10
Shadwell	d							16 42	16 47	16 56		17 02	17 07			17 22								17 12
Whitechapel	d							16 44	16 49	16 59		17 04	17 09			17 24								17 14
Shoreditch High Street	d							16 46	16 51	17 01		17 06	17 11			17 26								17 16
Hoxton	d							16 48	16 53	17 03		17 08	17 13			17 28								17 18
Haggerston	d							16 50	16 55	17 05		17 10	17 15			17 30								17 20
Dalston Junction Stn ELL	a							16 52	16 58	17 07		17 13	17 17			17 32								17 22
Canonbury	d							16 57		17 12			17 20			17 35								17 27
Highbury & Islington	a							17 02		17 16			17 25			17 40								17 32
	d																							
London Bridge 4 ⊖	a			16 36			16 41				16 59			17 11				16 56			17 06		17 11	

		LO	LO	SN	LO	LO	SN	LO	SN	SN		SE	SE A	SN	SE B	SN	LO	LO	LO	SN		LO	LO	SN	LO
East Croydon	d			17 00																17 30					
West Croydon 4	d		16 52													17 01	17 09		17 22						
Norwood Junction 2	d		16 58	17 05													17 13		17 28	17 35					
Anerley	d		17 01	17 08													17 16		17 31	17 38					
Penge West	d		17 03	17 10													17 18		17 33	17 40					
London Victoria 15 ⊖	d						16 49					17 09		17 11	17 13									17 19	
Battersea Park 4	d						16 53							17 15										17 23	
Wandsworth Road	d													17 17											
Clapham High Street ⊖	d													17 19											
London Blackfriars 3 ⊖	d												17 12												
Denmark Hill 4	d											17 18	17 22	17 24	17 22										
Peckham Rye 4	d								17 12	17 16		17a21	17a25	17 26	17a25	17 31									
Queens Rd Peckham	d									17 19				17 29		17 34									
South Bermondsey	d									17 21				17 31		17 36									
Clapham Junction 10	d						16 57																	17 27	
Wandsworth Common	d						17 00																	17 30	
Balham 4 ⊖	d						17 02																	17 32	
Streatham Hill	d						17 05																	17 35	
West Norwood 4	d						17 10		17 23															17 40	
Gipsy Hill	d						17 13		17 26															17 43	
Crystal Palace 4	d					17 13	17 21	17 28	17a29														17 43	17 51	17 58
Sydenham	d		17 06	17 12		17 16	17 24	17 31									17 21		17 36	17 42			17 46	17 54	18 01
Forest Hill 4	d		17 08	17 15		17 19	17 27	17 34									17 23		17 38	17 45			17 49	17 57	18 04
Honor Oak Park	d		17 11	17 17		17 21	17 29	17 36									17 26		17 41	17 47			17 51	17 59	18 06
Brockley	d		17 13	17 20		17 24	17 32	17 39									17 28		17 43	17 50			17 54	18 02	18 09
New Cross Gate 4	a		17 16	17 22		17 26	17 34	17 41									17 31		17 46	17 52			17 56	18 04	18 11
	d		17 16	17 22		17 26	17 34	17 41									17 31		17 46	17 52			17 56	18 04	18 11
New Cross ELL	d	17 06			17 21													17 36				17 51			
Surrey Quays	d	17 10	17 19		17 25	17 30		17 45									17 35	17 40	17 49			17 55	18 00		18 15
Canada Water	d	17 12	17 21		17 27	17 32		17 47									17 37	17 42	17 51			17 57	18 02		18 17
Rotherhithe	d	17 13	17 23		17 28	17 33		17 48									17 38	17 43	17 53			17 58	18 03		18 18
Wapping	d	17 15	17 24		17 30	17 35		17 50									17 40	17 45	17 54			18 00	18 05		18 20
Shadwell	d	17 17	17 26		17 32	17 37		17 52									17 42	17 47	17 56			18 02	18 07		18 22
Whitechapel	d	17 19	17 29		17 34	17 39		17 54									17 44	17 49	17 59			18 04	18 09		18 24
Shoreditch High Street	d	17 21	17 31		17 36	17 41		17 56									17 46	17 51	18 01			18 06	18 11		18 26
Hoxton	d	17 23	17 33		17 38	17 43		17 58									17 48	17 53	18 03			18 08	18 13		18 28
Haggerston	d	17 25	17 35		17 40	17 45		18 00									17 50	17 55	18 05			18 10	18 15		18 30
Dalston Junction Stn ELL	a	17 28	17 37		17 43	17 47		18 02									17 52	17 58	18 07			18 13	18 17		18 32
Canonbury	d		17 42			17 50		18 05									17 57		18 12				18 20		18 35
Highbury & Islington	a		17 46			17 55		18 10									18 02		18 16				18 25		18 40
	d																								
London Bridge 4 ⊖	a			17 30			17 41			17 26				17 36		17 41				17 59				18 11	

A not 19 May

B 19 May

Table 178

Saturdays

until 21 July

East London Line and Croydon - London Victoria to London Bridge

Network Diagram - see first Page of Table 177

Station		SN	SN	SE	SE A	SN		SE B	SN	LO	LO	LO	SN	LO	LO	SN		LO	SN	SN	SE	SE A	SN	SE B	SN
East Croydon	d												18 00												
West Croydon 4	d								17 31	17 39		17 52													18 01
Norwood Junction 2	d									17 43		17 58	18 05												
Anerley	d									17 46		18 01	18 08												
Penge West	d									17 48		18 03	18 10												
London Victoria 15 ⊖	d			17 39		17 41		17 43								17 49					18 09		18 11	18 13	
Battersea Park 4	d					17 45										17 53							18 15		
Wandsworth Road	d					17 47																	18 17		
Clapham High Street ⊖	d					17 49																	18 19		
London Blackfriars 3 ⊖	d				17 42																	18 12			
Denmark Hill 4	d			17 48	17 52	17 54		17 52													18 18	18 22	18 24	18 22	
Peckham Rye 4	d	17 42	17 46	17a51	17a55	17 56		17a55	18 01										18 12	18 16	18a21	18a25	18 26	18a25	18 31
Queens Rd Peckham	d		17 49			17 59			18 04											18 19			18 29		18 34
South Bermondsey	d		17 51			18 01			18 06											18 21			18 31		18 36
Clapham Junction 10	d															17 57									
Wandsworth Common	d															18 00									
Balham 4 ⊖	d															18 02									
Streatham Hill	d															18 05									
West Norwood 4	d	17 53														18 10			18 23						
Gipsy Hill	d	17 56														18 13			18 26						
Crystal Palace 4	d	17a59													18 13	18 21		18 28	18a29						
Sydenham	d									17 51		18 06	18 12		18 16	18 24		18 31							
Forest Hill 4	d									17 53		18 08	18 15		18 19	18 27		18 34							
Honor Oak Park	d									17 56		18 11	18 17		18 21	18 29		18 36							
Brockley	d									17 58		18 13	18 20		18 24	18 32		18 39							
New Cross Gate 4	a									18 01		18 16	18 22		18 26	18 34		18 41							
	d									18 01		18 16	18 22		18 26	18 34		18 41							
New Cross ELL	d										18 06			18 21											
Surrey Quays	d									18 05	18 10	18 19		18 25	18 30			18 45							
Canada Water	d									18 07	18 12	18 21		18 27	18 32			18 47							
Rotherhithe	d									18 08	18 13	18 23		18 28	18 33			18 48							
Wapping	d									18 10	18 15	18 24		18 30	18 35			18 50							
Shadwell	d									18 12	18 17	18 26		18 32	18 37			18 52							
Whitechapel	d									18 14	18 19	18 29		18 34	18 39			18 54							
Shoreditch High Street	d									18 16	18 21	18 31		18 36	18 41			18 56							
Hoxton	d									18 18	18 23	18 33		18 38	18 43			18 58							
Haggerston	d									18 20	18 25	18 35		18 40	18 45			19 00							
Dalston Junction Stn ELL	a									18 22	18 28	18 37		18 43	18 47			19 02							
Canonbury	d									18 27		18 42			18 50			19 05							
Highbury & Islington	a									18 32		18 46			18 55			19 10							
	d																								
London Bridge 4 ⊖	a		17 56			18 06			18 11				18 29			18 41				18 26			18 36		18 41

Station		LO		LO	LO	SN	LO	LO	SN	LO	SN	SN		SE	SE A	SN	SE B	SN	LO	LO	LO	SN		LO	LO
East Croydon	d					18 30																19 00			
West Croydon 4	d	18 09			18 22													18 31	18 39		18 52				
Norwood Junction 2	d	18 13			18 28	18 35													18 43		18 58	19 05			
Anerley	d	18 16			18 31	18 38													18 46		19 01	19 08			
Penge West	d	18 18			18 33	18 40													18 48		19 03	19 10			
London Victoria 15 ⊖	d								18 19					18 39		18 41	18 43								
Battersea Park 4	d								18 23							18 45									
Wandsworth Road	d															18 47									
Clapham High Street ⊖	d															18 49									
London Blackfriars 3 ⊖	d														18 42										
Denmark Hill 4	d													18 48	18 52	18 54	18 52								
Peckham Rye 4	d										18 42	18 46		18a51	18a55	18 56	18a55	19 01							
Queens Rd Peckham	d											18 49				18 59		19 04							
South Bermondsey	d											18 51				19 01		19 06							
Clapham Junction 10	d								18 27																
Wandsworth Common	d								18 30																
Balham 4 ⊖	d								18 32																
Streatham Hill	d								18 35																
West Norwood 4	d								18 40		18 53														
Gipsy Hill	d								18 43		18 56														
Crystal Palace 4	d							18 43	18 51	18 58	18a59														19 13
Sydenham	d	18 21			18 36	18 42		18 46	18 54	19 01									18 51		19 06	19 12			19 16
Forest Hill 4	d	18 23			18 38	18 45		18 49	18 57	19 04									18 53		19 08	19 15			19 19
Honor Oak Park	d	18 26			18 41	18 47		18 51	18 59	19 06									18 56		19 11	19 17			19 21
Brockley	d	18 28			18 43	18 50		18 54	19 02	19 09									18 58		19 13	19 20			19 24
New Cross Gate 4	a	18 31			18 46	18 52		18 56	19 04	19 11									19 01		19 16	19 22			19 26
	d	18 31			18 46	18 52		18 56	19 04	19 11									19 01		19 16	19 22			19 26
New Cross ELL	d			18 36			18 51													19 06				19 21	
Surrey Quays	d	18 35		18 40	18 49		18 55	19 00		19 15									19 05	19 10	19 19			19 25	19 30
Canada Water	d	18 37		18 42	18 51		18 57	19 02		19 17									19 07	19 12	19 21			19 27	19 32
Rotherhithe	d	18 38		18 43	18 53		18 58	19 03		19 18									19 08	19 13	19 23			19 28	19 33
Wapping	d	18 40		18 45	18 54		19 00	19 05		19 20									19 10	19 15	19 24			19 30	19 35
Shadwell	d	18 42		18 47	18 56		19 02	19 07		19 22									19 12	19 17	19 26			19 32	19 37
Whitechapel	d	18 44		18 49	18 59		19 04	19 09		19 24									19 14	19 19	19 29			19 34	19 39
Shoreditch High Street	d	18 46		18 51	19 01		19 06	19 11		19 26									19 16	19 21	19 31			19 36	19 41
Hoxton	d	18 48		18 53	19 03		19 08	19 13		19 28									19 18	19 23	19 33			19 38	19 43
Haggerston	d	18 50		18 55	19 05		19 10	19 15		19 30									19 20	19 25	19 35			19 40	19 45
Dalston Junction Stn ELL	a	18 52		18 58	19 07		19 13	19 17		19 32									19 22	19 28	19 37			19 43	19 47
Canonbury	d	18 57			19 12			19 20		19 35									19 27		19 42				19 50
Highbury & Islington	a	19 02			19 16			19 25		19 40									19 32		19 46				19 55
	d																								
London Bridge 4 ⊖	a					18 59			19 11			18 56				19 06		19 11				19 29			

A not 19 May

B 19 May

Table 178

Saturdays
until 21 July

East London Line and Croydon - London Victoria to London Bridge

Network Diagram - see first Page of Table 177

Station		SN	LO	SN	SN	SE	SE A	SN		SE B	SN	LO	LO	LO	SN	LO	LO	SN		LO	SN	SN	SE	SE A	SN
East Croydon	d														19 30										
West Croydon 4	d										19 01	19 09		19 22											
Norwood Junction 2	d											19 13		19 28	19 35										
Anerley	d											19 16		19 31	19 38										
Penge West	d											19 18		19 33	19 40										
London Victoria 15 ⊖	d	18 49				19 09		19 11		19 13								19 19					19 39		19 41
Battersea Park 4	d	18 53						19 15										19 23							19 45
Wandsworth Road	d							19 17																	19 47
Clapham High Street ⊖	d							19 19																	19 49
London Blackfriars 3 ⊖	d						19 12																	19 42	
Denmark Hill 4	d					19 18	19 22	19 24		19 22													19 48	19 52	19 54
Peckham Rye 4	d			19 12	19 16	19a21	19a25	19 26		19a25	19 31										19 42	19 46	19a51	19a55	19 56
Queens Rd Peckham	d				19 19			19 29			19 34											19 49			19 59
South Bermondsey	d				19 21			19 31			19 36											19 51			20 01
Clapham Junction 10	d	18 57																19 27							
Wandsworth Common	d	19 00																19 30							
Balham 4 ⊖	d	19 02																19 32							
Streatham Hill	d	19 05																19 35							
West Norwood 4	d	19 10		19 23														19 40			19 53				
Gipsy Hill	d	19 13		19 26														19 43			19 56				
Crystal Palace 4	d	19 21	19 28	19a29													19 43	19 51		19 58	19a59				
Sydenham	d	19 24	19 31									19 21		19 36	19 42		19 46	19 54		20 01					
Forest Hill 4	d	19 27	19 34									19 23		19 38	19 45		19 49	19 57		20 04					
Honor Oak Park	d	19 29	19 36									19 26		19 41	19 47		19 51	19 59		20 06					
Brockley	d	19 32	19 39									19 28		19 43	19 50		19 54	20 02		20 09					
New Cross Gate 4	a	19 34	19 41									19 31		19 46	19 52		19 56	20 04		20 11					
	d	19 34	19 41									19 31		19 46	19 52		19 56	20 04		20 11					
New Cross ELL	d												19 36			19 51									
Surrey Quays	d		19 45									19 35	19 40	19 49		19 55	20 00			20 15					
Canada Water	d		19 47									19 37	19 42	19 51		19 57	20 02			20 17					
Rotherhithe	d		19 48									19 38	19 43	19 53		19 58	20 03			20 18					
Wapping	d		19 50									19 40	19 45	19 54		20 00	20 05			20 20					
Shadwell	d		19 52									19 42	19 47	19 56		20 02	20 07			20 22					
Whitechapel	d		19 54									19 44	19 49	19 59		20 04	20 09			20 24					
Shoreditch High Street	d		19 56									19 46	19 51	20 01		20 06	20 11			20 26					
Hoxton	d		19 58									19 48	19 53	20 03		20 08	20 13			20 28					
Haggerston	d		20 00									19 50	19 55	20 05		20 10	20 15			20 30					
Dalston Junction Stn ELL	a		20 02									19 52	19 58	20 07		20 13	20 17			20 32					
Canonbury	d		20 05									19 57		20 12			20 20			20 35					
Highbury & Islington	a		20 10									20 02		20 16			20 25			20 40					
	d																								
London Bridge 4 ⊖	a	19 41			19 26			19 36			19 41				19 59			20 11				19 56			20 06

Station		SE B	SN	LO		LO	LO	SN	LO	LO	SN	LO	SN	SN		SE A	SN	SE B	SN	LO	LO	LO	SN	LO	
East Croydon	d							20 00															20 30		
West Croydon 4	d		19 31	19 39			19 52												20 01	20 09		20 22			
Norwood Junction 2	d			19 43			19 58	20 05												20 13		20 28	20 35		
Anerley	d			19 46			20 01	20 08												20 16		20 31	20 38		
Penge West	d			19 48			20 03	20 10												20 18		20 33	20 40		
London Victoria 15 ⊖	d	19 43									19 49						20 11	20 13							
Battersea Park 4	d										19 53						20 15								
Wandsworth Road	d																20 17								
Clapham High Street ⊖	d																20 19								
London Blackfriars 3 ⊖	d															20 12									
Denmark Hill 4	d	19 52														20 22	20 24	20 22							
Peckham Rye 4	d	19a55	20 01										20 12	20 16		20a25	20 26	20a25	20 31						
Queens Rd Peckham	d		20 04											20 19			20 29		20 34						
South Bermondsey	d		20 06											20 21			20 31		20 36						
Clapham Junction 10	d										19 57														
Wandsworth Common	d										20 00														
Balham 4 ⊖	d										20 02														
Streatham Hill	d										20 05														
West Norwood 4	d										20 10		20 23												
Gipsy Hill	d										20 13		20 26												
Crystal Palace 4	d									20 13	20 21	20 28	20a29												
Sydenham	d			19 51			20 06	20 12		20 16	20 24	20 31								20 21		20 36	20 42		
Forest Hill 4	d			19 53			20 08	20 15		20 19	20 27	20 34								20 23		20 38	20 45		
Honor Oak Park	d			19 56			20 11	20 17		20 21	20 29	20 36								20 26		20 41	20 47		
Brockley	d			19 58			20 13	20 20		20 24	20 32	20 39								20 28		20 43	20 50		
New Cross Gate 4	a			20 01			20 16	20 22		20 26	20 34	20 41								20 31		20 46	20 52		
	d			20 01			20 16	20 22		20 26	20 34	20 41								20 31		20 46	20 52		
New Cross ELL	d					20 06			20 21												20 36			20 51	
Surrey Quays	d			20 05		20 10	20 19		20 25	20 30		20 45								20 35	20 40	20 49		20 55	
Canada Water	d			20 07		20 12	20 21		20 27	20 32		20 47								20 37	20 42	20 51		20 57	
Rotherhithe	d			20 08		20 13	20 23		20 28	20 33		20 48								20 38	20 43	20 53		20 58	
Wapping	d			20 10		20 15	20 24		20 30	20 35		20 50								20 40	20 45	20 54		21 00	
Shadwell	d			20 12		20 17	20 26		20 32	20 37		20 52								20 42	20 47	20 56		21 02	
Whitechapel	d			20 14		20 19	20 29		20 34	20 39		20 54								20 44	20 49	20 59		21 04	
Shoreditch High Street	d			20 16		20 21	20 31		20 36	20 41		20 56								20 46	20 51	21 01		21 06	
Hoxton	d			20 18		20 23	20 33		20 38	20 43		20 58								20 48	20 53	21 03		21 08	
Haggerston	d			20 20		20 25	20 35		20 40	20 45		21 00								20 50	20 55	21 05		21 10	
Dalston Junction Stn ELL	a			20 22		20 28	20 37		20 43	20 47		21 02								20 52	20 58	21 07		21 13	
Canonbury	d			20 27			20 42			20 50		21 05								20 57		21 12			
Highbury & Islington	a			20 32			20 46			20 55		21 10								21 02		21 16			
	d																								
London Bridge 4 ⊖	a		20 11					20 29			20 41			20 26			20 36		20 41				20 59		

A not 19 May

B 19 May

Table 178

Saturdays
until 21 July

East London Line and Croydon - London Victoria to London Bridge

Network Diagram - see first Page of Table 177

	LO	SN	LO	SN	SN	SE A	SN	SE B	SN		LO	LO	LO	SN	LO	LO	SN	LO	SN		SN	SE A	SN	SE B
East Croydon d														21 00										
West Croydon 4 d									20 31		20 39		20 52											
Norwood Junction 2 d											20 43		20 58	21 05										
Anerley d											20 46		21 01	21 08										
Penge West d											20 48		21 03	21 10										
London Victoria 15 ⊖ d		20 19					20 41	20 43									20 49						21 11	21 13
Battersea Park 4 d		20 23					20 45										20 53						21 15	
Wandsworth Road d							20 47																21 17	
Clapham High Street ⊖ d							20 49																21 19	
London Blackfriars 3 ⊖ d						20 42																21 12		
Denmark Hill 4 d						20 52	20 54	20 52														21 22	21 24	21 22
Peckham Rye 4 d				20 42	20 46	20a55	20 56	20a55	21 01										21 12		21 16	21a25	21 26	21a25
Queens Rd Peckham d					20 49		20 59		21 04												21 19		21 29	
South Bermondsey d					20 51		21 01		21 06												21 21		21 31	
Clapham Junction 10 d		20 27															20 57							
Wandsworth Common d		20 30															21 00							
Balham 4 ⊖ d		20 32															21 02							
Streatham Hill d		20 35															21 05							
West Norwood 4 d		20 40		20 53													21 10		21 23					
Gipsy Hill d		20 43		20 56													21 13		21 26					
Crystal Palace 4 d	20 43	20 51	20 58	20a59												21 13	21 21	21 28	21a29					
Sydenham d	20 46	20 54	21 01								20 51		21 06	21 12		21 16	21 24	21 31						
Forest Hill 4 d	20 49	20 57	21 04								20 53		21 08	21 15		21 19	21 27	21 34						
Honor Oak Park d	20 51	20 59	21 06								20 56		21 11	21 17		21 21	21 29	21 36						
Brockley d	20 54	21 02	21 09								20 58		21 13	21 20		21 24	21 32	21 39						
New Cross Gate 4 a	20 56	21 04	21 11								21 01		21 16	21 22		21 26	21 34	21 41						
d	20 56	21 04	21 11								21 01		21 16	21 22		21 26	21 34	21 41						
New Cross ELL d												21 06			21 21									
Surrey Quays d	21 00		21 15								21 05	21 10	21 19		21 25	21 30		21 45						
Canada Water d	21 02		21 17								21 07	21 12	21 21		21 27	21 32		21 47						
Rotherhithe d	21 03		21 18								21 08	21 13	21 23		21 28	21 33		21 48						
Wapping d	21 05		21 20								21 10	21 15	21 24		21 30	21 35		21 50						
Shadwell d	21 07		21 22								21 12	21 17	21 26		21 32	21 37		21 52						
Whitechapel d	21 09		21 24								21 14	21 19	21 29		21 34	21 39		21 54						
Shoreditch High Street d	21 11		21 26								21 16	21 21	21 31		21 36	21 41		21 56						
Hoxton d	21 13		21 28								21 18	21 23	21 33		21 38	21 43		21 58						
Haggerston d	21 15		21 30								21 20	21 25	21 35		21 40	21 45		22 00						
Dalston Junction Stn ELL a	21 17		21 32								21 22	21 28	21 37		21 43	21 47		22 02						
Canonbury d	21 20		21 35								21 27		21 42			21 50		22 05						
Highbury & Islington a	21 25		21 40								21 32		21 46			21 55		22 10						
d																								
London Bridge 4 ⊖ a		21 13			20 56		21 06		21 11					21 29			21 43				21 26		21 36	

	SN	LO	LO	LO	SN		LO	LO	SN	LO	SN	SN	SE A	SN	SE B		SN	LO	LO	LO	SN	LO	SN	LO
East Croydon d					21 30																22 00			
West Croydon 4 d	21 02	21 09		21 22													21 31	21 39		21 52				
Norwood Junction 2 d		21 13		21 28	21 35													21 43		21 58	22 05			
Anerley d		21 16		21 31	21 38													21 46		22 01	22 08			
Penge West d		21 18		21 33	21 40													21 48		22 03	22 10			
London Victoria 15 ⊖ d									21 19					21 41	21 43								21 49	
Battersea Park 4 d									21 23					21 45									21 53	
Wandsworth Road d														21 47										
Clapham High Street ⊖ d														21 49										
London Blackfriars 3 ⊖ d													21 42											
Denmark Hill 4 d													21 52	21 54	21 52									
Peckham Rye 4 d	21 31										21 42	21 46	21a55	21 56	21a55		22 01							
Queens Rd Peckham d	21 34											21 49		21 59			22 04							
South Bermondsey d	21 36											21 51		22 01			22 06							
Clapham Junction 10 d									21 27														21 57	
Wandsworth Common d									21 30														22 00	
Balham 4 ⊖ d									21 32														22 02	
Streatham Hill d									21 35														22 05	
West Norwood 4 d									21 40		21 53												22 10	
Gipsy Hill d									21 43		21 56												22 13	
Crystal Palace 4 d								21 43	21 51	21 58	21a59											22 13	22 21	22 28
Sydenham d		21 21		21 36	21 42			21 46	21 54	22 01								21 51		22 06	22 12	22 16	22 24	22 31
Forest Hill 4 d		21 23		21 38	21 45			21 49	21 57	22 04								21 53		22 08	22 15	22 19	22 27	22 34
Honor Oak Park d		21 26		21 41	21 47			21 51	21 59	22 06								21 56		22 11	22 17	22 21	22 29	22 36
Brockley d		21 28		21 43	21 50			21 54	22 02	22 09								21 58		22 13	22 20	22 24	22 32	22 39
New Cross Gate 4 a		21 31		21 46	21 52			21 56	22 04	22 11								22 01		22 16	22 22	22 26	22 34	22 41
d		21 31		21 46	21 52			21 56	22 04	22 11								22 01		22 16	22 22	22 26	22 34	22 41
New Cross ELL d			21 36				21 51												22 06					
Surrey Quays d		21 35	21 40	21 49			21 55	22 00		22 15								22 05	22 10	22 19		22 30		22 45
Canada Water d		21 37	21 42	21 51			21 57	22 02		22 17								22 07	22 12	22 21		22 32		22 47
Rotherhithe d		21 38	21 43	21 53			21 58	22 03		22 18								22 08	22 13	22 23		22 33		22 48
Wapping d		21 40	21 45	21 54			22 00	22 05		22 20								22 10	22 15	22 24		22 35		22 50
Shadwell d		21 42	21 47	21 56			22 02	22 07		22 22								22 12	22 17	22 26		22 37		22 52
Whitechapel d		21 44	21 49	21 59			22 04	22 09		22 24								22 14	22 19	22 29		22 39		22 54
Shoreditch High Street d		21 46	21 51	22 01			22 06	22 11		22 26								22 16	22 21	22 31		22 41		22 56
Hoxton d		21 48	21 53	22 03			22 08	22 13		22 28								22 18	22 23	22 33		22 43		22 58
Haggerston d		21 50	21 55	22 05			22 10	22 15		22 30								22 20	22 25	22 35		22 45		23 00
Dalston Junction Stn ELL a		21 52	21 58	22 07			22 13	22 17		22 32								22 22	22 28	22 37		22 47		23 02
Canonbury d		21 57		22 12				22 20		22 35								22 27		22 42		22 50		23 05
Highbury & Islington a		22 02		22 16				22 25		22 40								22 32		22 46		22 55		23 10
d																								
London Bridge 4 ⊖ a	21 41				21 59				22 13			21 56		22 06			22 11				22 29		22 43	

A not 19 May

B 19 May

East London Line and Croydon - London Victoria to London Bridge

Network Diagram - see first Page of Table 177

		SN		SN	SE A	SN	SE B	SN	LO	LO	LO	SN		LO	SN	SN	SN	SE A	SN	SE B	SN	LO		LO	LO
East Croydon	d											22 30													
West Croydon 4	d							22 01	22 09		22 22										22 31	22 39			22 52
Norwood Junction 2	d								22 13		22 28	22 35										22 43			22 58
Anerley	d								22 16		22 31	22 38										22 46			23 01
Penge West	d								22 18		22 33	22 40										22 48			23 03
London Victoria 15 ⊖	d					22 11	22 13								22 19				22 41	22 43					
Battersea Park 4	d					22 15									22 23				22 45						
Wandsworth Road	d					22 17													22 47						
Clapham High Street ⊖	d					22 19													22 49						
London Blackfriars 3 ⊖	d				22 12													22 42							
Denmark Hill 4	d				22 22	22 24	22 22											22 52	22 54	22 52					
Peckham Rye 4	d	22 12		22 16	22a25	22 26	22a25	22 31								22 42	22 46	22a55	22 56	22a55	23 01				
Queens Rd Peckham	d			22 19		22 29		22 34									22 49		22 59		23 04				
South Bermondsey	d			22 21		22 31		22 36									22 51		23 01		23 06				
Clapham Junction 10	d														22 27										
Wandsworth Common	d														22 30										
Balham 4 ⊖	d														22 32										
Streatham Hill	d														22 35										
West Norwood 4	d	22 23													22 40	22 53									
Gipsy Hill	d	22 26													22 43	22 56									
Crystal Palace 4	d	22a29												22 43	22 51	22a59									
Sydenham	d								22 21		22 36	22 42		22 46	22 54							22 51			23 06
Forest Hill 4	d								22 23		22 38	22 45		22 49	22 57							22 53			23 08
Honor Oak Park	d								22 26		22 41	22 47		22 51	22 59							22 56			23 11
Brockley	d								22 28		22 43	22 50		22 54	23 02							22 58			23 13
New Cross Gate 4	a								22 31		22 46	22 52		22 56	23 04							23 01			23 16
	d								22 31		22 46	22 52		22 56	23 04							23 01			23 16
New Cross ELL	d									22 36														23 06	
Surrey Quays	d								22 35	22 40	22 49			23 00								23 05		23 10	23 19
Canada Water	d								22 37	22 42	22 51			23 02								23 07		23 12	23 21
Rotherhithe	d								22 38	22 43	22 53			23 03								23 08		23 13	23 23
Wapping	d								22 40	22 45	22 54			23 05								23 10		23 15	23 24
Shadwell	d								22 42	22 47	22 56			23 07								23 12		23 17	23 26
Whitechapel	d								22 44	22 49	22 59			23 09								23 14		23 19	23 29
Shoreditch High Street	d								22 46	22 51	23 01			23 11								23 16		23 21	23 31
Hoxton	d								22 48	22 53	23 03			23 13								23 18		23 23	23 33
Haggerston	d								22 50	22 55	23 05			23 15								23 20		23 25	23 35
Dalston Junction Stn ELL	a								22 52	22 58	23 07			23 17								23 22		23 28	23 37
Canonbury	d								22 57		23 12			23 20								23 27			23 42
Highbury & Islington	a								23 02		23 16			23 25								23 32			23 46
	d																								
London Bridge 4 ⊖	a			22 26		22 36		22 41				22 59			23 13		22 56		23 06		23 11				

		SN	LO	SN	SN	SN	SE A	SN		LO	SE B	SN	LO	LO	SN	SN	SN	SE A		SE B	SN				
East Croydon	d	23 01																							
West Croydon 4	d											23 01	23 22												
Norwood Junction 2	d	23 06											23 28												
Anerley	d	23 09											23 31												
Penge West	d	23 11											23 33												
London Victoria 15 ⊖	d			22 49				23 11			23 13				23 19					23 43	23 54				
Battersea Park 4	d			22 53				23 15							23 23						23 58				
Wandsworth Road	d							23 17																	
Clapham High Street ⊖	d							23 19																	
London Blackfriars 3 ⊖	d						23 12											23 42							
Denmark Hill 4	d						23 22	23 24			23 22							23 52		23 52					
Peckham Rye 4	d				23 12	23 16	23a25	23 26			23a25	23 31				23 42	23 46	23a55		23a55					
Queens Rd Peckham	d					23 19		23 29				23 34					23 49								
South Bermondsey	d					23 21		23 31				23 36					23 51								
Clapham Junction 10	d			22 57											23 27						00 02				
Wandsworth Common	d			23 00											23 30						00 05				
Balham 4 ⊖	d			23 02											23 32						00 07				
Streatham Hill	d			23 05											23 35						00 10				
West Norwood 4	d			23 10	23 24										23 40	23 54					00 14				
Gipsy Hill	d			23 13	23 27										23 43	23 57					00 17				
Crystal Palace 4	d		23 13	23 21	23a29									23 43	23 51	23a59					00 21				
Sydenham	d	23 13	23 16	23 24									23 36	23 46	23 54						00 24				
Forest Hill 4	d	23 16	23 19	23 27									23 38	23 49	23 57						00 27				
Honor Oak Park	d	23 18	23 21	23 29									23 41	23 51	23 59						00 29				
Brockley	d	23 21	23 24	23 32									23 43	23 54	00 02						00 32				
New Cross Gate 4	a	23 23	23 26	23 34									23 46	23 56	00 04						00 35				
	d	23 23	23 26	23 34									23 46	23 56	00 04						00 35				
New Cross ELL	d									23 36															
Surrey Quays	d		23 30							23 40			23 49	23 59											
Canada Water	d		23 32							23 42			23 51	00 02											
Rotherhithe	d		23 33							23 43			23 53	00 03											
Wapping	d		23 35							23 45			23 54	00 05											
Shadwell	d		23 37							23 47			23 56	00 07											
Whitechapel	d		23 39							23 49			23 59	00 09											
Shoreditch High Street	d		23 41							23 51			00 01	00 11											
Hoxton	d		23 43							23 53			00 03	00 13											
Haggerston	d		23 45							23 55			00 05	00 15											
Dalston Junction Stn ELL	a		23 47							23 58			00 07	00 17											
Canonbury	d		23 50										00 12	00 20											
Highbury & Islington	a		23 55										00 16	00 25											
	d																								
London Bridge 4 ⊖	a	23 30		23 43		23 26		23 36				23 41			00 11		23 56				00 41				

A not 19 May

B 19 May

Table 178

Saturdays

28 July to 11 August

East London Line and Croydon - London Victoria to London Bridge

Network Diagram - see first Page of Table 177

Station		LO	LO	LO	SN	SN	SN	SN	LO	LO		LO	LO	LO	LO	LO	SN	LO	LO	LO		SN	LO	LO	SE
East Croydon	d																					06 30			
West Croydon 4	d		23p22						05 39				05 52			06 09	06 18			06 22					
Norwood Junction 2	d		23p28						05 43				05 58			06 13	06 23			06 28		06 35			
Anerley	d		23p31						05 46				06 01			06 16				06 31		06 38			
Penge West	d		23p33						05 48				06 03			06 18				06 33		06 40			
London Victoria 15 ⊖	d				23p22	23p54																			00 56
Battersea Park 4	d				23p26	23p58																			
Wandsworth Road	d																								
Clapham High Street ⊖	d																								
London Blackfriars 3 ⊖	d																								
Denmark Hill 4	d																								
Peckham Rye 4	d						00 12	00 42																	01 06
Queens Rd Peckham	d																								01a08
South Bermondsey	d																								
Clapham Junction 10	d				23p30	00 02																			
Wandsworth Common	d				23p33	00 05																			
Balham 4 ⊖	d				23p35	00 07																			
Streatham Hill	d				23p38	00 10																			
West Norwood 4	d				23p42	00 14	00 24	00 54																	
Gipsy Hill	d				23p45	00 17	00 27	00 57																	
Crystal Palace 4	d			23p43	23p51	00 21	00a29	00a59				05 58			06 13		06a27		06 28					06 41	
Sydenham	d		23p36	23p46	23p54	00 24			05 51			06 01	06 06		06 16	06 21			06 31	06 36		06 42		06 44	
Forest Hill 4	d		23p38	23p49	23p57	00 27			05 53			06 04	06 08		06 19	06 23			06 34	06 38		06 45		06 47	
Honor Oak Park	d		23p41	23p51	23p59	00 29			05 56			06 06	06 11		06 21	06 26			06 36	06 41		06 47		06 49	
Brockley	d		23p43	23p54	00 02	00 32			05 58			06 09	06 13		06 24	06 28			06 39	06 43		06 50		06 52	
New Cross Gate 4	a		23p46	23p56	00 04	00 34			06 01			06 11	06 16		06 26	06 31			06 41	06 46		06 52		06 54	
	d		23p46	23p56	00 04	00 34			06 01			06 11	06 16		06 26	06 31			06 41	06 46		06 52		06 54	
New Cross ELL	d	23p36								06 06				06 21				06 36					06 51		
Surrey Quays	d	23p40	23p49	23p59					06 05	06 10		06 15	06 19	06 25	06 30	06 35		06 40	06 45	06 49			06 55	07 00	
Canada Water	d	23p42	23p51	00 02					06 07	06 12		06 17	06 21	06 27	06 32	06 37		06 42	06 47	06 51			06 57	07 02	
Rotherhithe	d	23p43	23p53	00 03					06 08	06 13		06 18	06 23	06 28	06 33	06 38		06 43	06 48	06 53			06 58	07 03	
Wapping	d	23p45	23p54	00 05					06 10	06 15		06 20	06 24	06 30	06 35	06 40		06 45	06 50	06 54			07 00	07 05	
Shadwell	d	23p47	23p56	00 07					06 12	06 17		06 22	06 26	06 32	06 37	06 42		06 47	06 52	06 56			07 02	07 07	
Whitechapel	d	23p49	23p59	00 09					06 14	06 19		06 24	06 29	06 34	06 39	06 44		06 49	06 54	06 59			07 04	07 09	
Shoreditch High Street	d	23p51	00 01	00 11					06 16	06 21		06 26	06 31	06 36	06 41	06 46		06 51	06 56	07 01			07 06	07 11	
Hoxton	d	23p53	00 03	00 13					06 18	06 23		06 28	06 33	06 38	06 43	06 48		06 53	06 58	07 03			07 08	07 13	
Haggerston	d	23p55	00 05	00 15					06 20	06 25		06 30	06 35	06 40	06 45	06 50		06 55	07 00	07 05			07 10	07 15	
Dalston Junction Stn ELL	a	23p58	00 07	00 17					06 22	06 32		06 32	06 37	06 47	06 47	06 52		07 02	07 02	07 07			07 17	07 17	
Canonbury	d	00 01	00 11	00 20					06 27			06 35	06 42		06 50	06 57			07 05	07 12				07 20	
Highbury & Islington	a	00 10	00 18	00 28					06 35			06 43	06 49		06 59	07 05			07 13	07 19				07 28	
	d																								
London Bridge 4 ⊖	a				00 11	00 41																06 59			

Station		SE	SE	SN	SN	LO		SN	SN	LO	LO	LO	SN	SE	SN	SN		LO	LO	LO	LO	LO	LO	SN	LO
East Croydon	d							06 43					07 00											07 30	
West Croydon 4	d					06 39			06 45			06 52				07 01				07 09			07 22		
Norwood Junction 2	d				06 41	06 43		06 50	06 53			06 58	07 05							07 13			07 28	07 35	
Anerley	d					06 46						07 01	07 08							07 16			07 31	07 38	
Penge West	d					06 48						07 03	07 10							07 18			07 33	07 40	
London Victoria 15 ⊖	d			06 41											07 11										
Battersea Park 4	d			06 45											07 15										
Wandsworth Road	d			06 47											07 17										
Clapham High Street ⊖	d			06 49											07 19										
London Blackfriars 3 ⊖	d	06 12	06 42											07 12											
Denmark Hill 4	d	06 22	06 52	06 54										07 22	07 24										
Peckham Rye 4	d	06a25	06a55	06 56	07 01									07a25	07 26	07 31									
Queens Rd Peckham	d			06 59	07 04										07 29	07 34									
South Bermondsey	d			07 01	07 06										07 31	07 36									
Clapham Junction 10	d																								
Wandsworth Common	d																								
Balham 4 ⊖	d																								
Streatham Hill	d																								
West Norwood 4	d																								
Gipsy Hill	d																								
Crystal Palace 4	d								06a57		06 58								07 11			07 28			
Sydenham	d					06 51		06 54			07 01	07 06	07 12						07 14	07 21		07 31	07 36	07 42	
Forest Hill 4	d					06 53		06 57			07 04	07 08	07 15						07 17	07 23		07 34	07 38	07 45	
Honor Oak Park	d					06 56		06 59			07 06	07 11	07 17						07 19	07 26		07 36	07 41	07 47	
Brockley	d					06 58		07 02			07 09	07 13	07 20						07 22	07 28		07 39	07 43	07 50	
New Cross Gate 4	a					07 01		07 04			07 11	07 16	07 22						07 24	07 31		07 41	07 46	07 52	
	d					07 01		07 04			07 11	07 16	07 22						07 24	07 31		07 41	07 46	07 52	
New Cross ELL	d									07 06								07 21			07 36				07 51
Surrey Quays	d					07 05				07 10	07 15	07 19						07 25	07 30	07 35	07 40	07 45	07 49		07 55
Canada Water	d					07 07				07 12	07 17	07 21						07 27	07 32	07 37	07 42	07 47	07 51		07 57
Rotherhithe	d					07 08				07 13	07 18	07 23						07 28	07 33	07 38	07 43	07 48	07 53		07 58
Wapping	d					07 10				07 15	07 20	07 24						07 30	07 35	07 40	07 45	07 50	07 54		08 00
Shadwell	d					07 12				07 17	07 22	07 26						07 32	07 37	07 42	07 47	07 52	07 56		08 02
Whitechapel	d					07 14				07 19	07 24	07 29						07 34	07 39	07 44	07 49	07 54	07 59		08 04
Shoreditch High Street	d					07 16				07 21	07 26	07 31						07 36	07 41	07 46	07 51	07 56	08 01		08 06
Hoxton	d					07 18				07 23	07 28	07 33						07 38	07 43	07 48	07 53	07 58	08 03		08 08
Haggerston	d					07 20				07 25	07 30	07 35						07 40	07 45	07 50	07 55	08 00	08 05		08 10
Dalston Junction Stn ELL	a					07 23				07 32	07 32	07 37						07 47	07 47	07 53	08 02	08 02	08 07		08 17
Canonbury	d					07 27					07 35	07 42							07 50	07 57		08 05	08 12		
Highbury & Islington	a					07 35					07 43	07 49							07 58	08 05		08 13	08 19		
	d																								
London Bridge 4 ⊖	a			07 06	07 14			07 11					07 29		07 36	07 41								07 59	

Table 178

Saturdays

28 July to 11 August

East London Line and Croydon - London Victoria to London Bridge

Network Diagram - see first Page of Table 177

Station		LO		LO	SN	SE	SE	SN	SN	LO	LO	LO		SN	LO	LO	SN	LO	SN	SE	SE	SN		SN	LO
East Croydon	d													08 00											
West Croydon 4	d								07 31	07 39		07 52												08 01	08 09
Norwood Junction 2	d									07 43		07 58		08 05											08 13
Anerley	d									07 46		08 01		08 08											08 16
Penge West	d									07 48		08 03		08 10											08 18
London Victoria 15 ⊖	d					07 39		07 41									07 49			08 09		08 11			
Battersea Park 4	d							07 45									07 53					08 15			
Wandsworth Road	d							07 47														08 17			
Clapham High Street ⊖	d							07 49														08 19			
London Blackfriars 3 ⊖	d						07 42														08 12				
Denmark Hill 4	d					07 48	07 52	07 54												08 18	08 22	08 24			
Peckham Rye 4	d				07 42	07a51	07a55	07 56	08 01										08 12	08a21	08a25	08 26		08 31	
Queens Rd Peckham	d							07 59	08 04													08 29		08 34	
South Bermondsey	d							08 01	08 06													08 31		08 36	
Clapham Junction 10	d																07 57								
Wandsworth Common	d																08 00								
Balham 4 ⊖	d																08 02								
Streatham Hill	d																08 05								
West Norwood 4	d				07 53												08 10		08 23						
Gipsy Hill	d				07 56												08 13		08 26						
Crystal Palace 4	d	07 41		07 58	07a59											08 11	08 21	08 28	08a29						
Sydenham	d	07 44		08 01						07 51		08 06		08 12		08 14	08 24	08 31							08 21
Forest Hill 4	d	07 47		08 04						07 53		08 08		08 15		08 17	08 27	08 34							08 23
Honor Oak Park	d	07 49		08 06						07 56		08 11		08 17		08 19	08 29	08 36							08 26
Brockley	d	07 52		08 09						07 58		08 13		08 20		08 22	08 32	08 39							08 28
New Cross Gate 4	a	07 54		08 11						08 01		08 16		08 22		08 24	08 34	08 41							08 31
	d	07 54		08 11						08 01		08 16		08 22		08 24	08 34	08 41							08 31
New Cross ELL	d										08 06				08 21										
Surrey Quays	d	08 00		08 15						08 05	08 10	08 19			08 25	08 30		08 45							08 35
Canada Water	d	08 02		08 17						08 07	08 12	08 21			08 27	08 32		08 47							08 37
Rotherhithe	d	08 03		08 18						08 08	08 13	08 23			08 28	08 33		08 48							08 38
Wapping	d	08 05		08 20						08 10	08 15	08 24			08 30	08 35		08 50							08 40
Shadwell	d	08 07		08 22						08 12	08 17	08 26			08 32	08 37		08 52							08 42
Whitechapel	d	08 09		08 24						08 14	08 19	08 29			08 34	08 39		08 54							08 44
Shoreditch High Street	d	08 11		08 26						08 16	08 21	08 31			08 36	08 41		08 56							08 46
Hoxton	d	08 13		08 28						08 18	08 23	08 33			08 38	08 43		08 58							08 48
Haggerston	d	08 15		08 30						08 20	08 25	08 35			08 40	08 45		09 00							08 50
Dalston Junction Stn ELL	a	08 17		08 32						08 23	08 32	08 37			08 47	08 47		09 02							08 53
Canonbury	d	08 20		08 35						08 27		08 42				08 50		09 05							08 57
Highbury & Islington	a	08 28		08 43						08 35		08 49				08 58		09 13							09 05
	d																								
London Bridge 4 ⊖	a							08 06	08 11					08 29			08 41					08 36		08 41	

Station		LO	LO	SN	LO	LO	SN	LO		SN	SN	SE	SE	SN	SN	LO	LO	LO		SN	LO	LO	SN	LO	SN
East Croydon	d			08 30																09 00					
West Croydon 4	d		08 22												08 31	08 39		08 52							
Norwood Junction 2	d		08 28	08 35												08 43		08 58		09 05					
Anerley	d		08 31	08 38												08 46		09 01		09 08					
Penge West	d		08 33	08 40												08 48		09 03		09 10					
London Victoria 15 ⊖	d						08 19					08 39		08 41									08 49		
Battersea Park 4	d						08 23							08 45									08 53		
Wandsworth Road	d													08 47											
Clapham High Street ⊖	d													08 49											
London Blackfriars 3 ⊖	d												08 42												
Denmark Hill 4	d											08 48	08 52	08 54											
Peckham Rye 4	d									08 42	08 46	08a51	08a55	08 56	09 01										09 12
Queens Rd Peckham	d										08 49			08 59	09 04										
South Bermondsey	d										08 51			09 01	09 06										
Clapham Junction 10	d						08 27																08 57		
Wandsworth Common	d						08 30																09 00		
Balham 4 ⊖	d						08 32																09 02		
Streatham Hill	d						08 35																09 05		
West Norwood 4	d						08 40			08 53													09 10		09 23
Gipsy Hill	d						08 43			08 56													09 13		09 26
Crystal Palace 4	d					08 41	08 51	08 58		08a59												09 11	09 21	09 28	09a29
Sydenham	d		08 36	08 42		08 44	08 54	09 01								08 51		09 06		09 12		09 14	09 24	09 31	
Forest Hill 4	d		08 38	08 45		08 47	08 57	09 04								08 53		09 08		09 15		09 17	09 27	09 34	
Honor Oak Park	d		08 41	08 47		08 49	08 59	09 06								08 56		09 11		09 17		09 19	09 29	09 36	
Brockley	d		08 43	08 50		08 52	09 02	09 09								08 58		09 13		09 20		09 22	09 32	09 39	
New Cross Gate 4	a		08 46	08 52		08 54	09 04	09 11								09 01		09 16		09 22		09 24	09 34	09 41	
	d		08 46	08 52		08 54	09 04	09 11								09 01		09 16		09 22		09 24	09 34	09 41	
New Cross ELL	d	08 36			08 51												09 06				09 21				
Surrey Quays	d	08 40	08 49		08 55	09 00		09 15								09 05	09 10	09 19			09 25	09 30		09 45	
Canada Water	d	08 42	08 51		08 57	09 02		09 17								09 07	09 12	09 21			09 27	09 32		09 47	
Rotherhithe	d	08 43	08 53		08 58	09 03		09 18								09 08	09 13	09 23			09 28	09 33		09 48	
Wapping	d	08 45	08 54		09 00	09 05		09 20								09 10	09 15	09 24			09 30	09 35		09 50	
Shadwell	d	08 47	08 56		09 02	09 07		09 22								09 12	09 17	09 26			09 32	09 37		09 52	
Whitechapel	d	08 49	08 59		09 04	09 09		09 24								09 14	09 19	09 29			09 34	09 39		09 54	
Shoreditch High Street	d	08 51	09 01		09 06	09 11		09 26								09 16	09 21	09 31			09 36	09 41		09 56	
Hoxton	d	08 53	09 03		09 08	09 13		09 28								09 18	09 23	09 33			09 38	09 43		09 58	
Haggerston	d	08 55	09 05		09 10	09 15		09 30								09 20	09 25	09 35			09 40	09 45		10 00	
Dalston Junction Stn ELL	a	09 02	09 07		09 17	09 17		09 32								09 23	09 32	09 37			09 47	09 47		10 02	
Canonbury	d		09 12			09 20		09 35								09 27		09 42				09 50		10 05	
Highbury & Islington	a		09 19			09 28		09 43								09 35		09 49				09 58		10 13	
	d																								
London Bridge 4 ⊖	a			08 59			09 11				08 56			09 06	09 11					09 29			09 41		

Table 178

Saturdays

28 July to 11 August

East London Line and Croydon - London Victoria to London Bridge

Network Diagram - see first Page of Table 177

		SN	SE	SE		SN	SN	LO	LO	LO	SN	LO	LO	SN		LO	SN	SN	SE	SE	SN	SN	LO	LO
East Croydon	d										09 30													
West Croydon 4	d						09 01	09 09		09 22												09 31	09 39	
Norwood Junction 2	d							09 13		09 28	09 35												09 43	
Anerley	d							09 16		09 31	09 38												09 46	
Penge West	d							09 18		09 33	09 40												09 48	
London Victoria 15	⊖ d		09 09			09 11								09 19					09 39		09 41			
Battersea Park 4	d					09 15								09 23							09 45			
Wandsworth Road	d					09 17															09 47			
Clapham High Street	⊖ d					09 19															09 49			
London Blackfriars 3	⊖ d			09 12																09 42				
Denmark Hill 4	d		09 18	09 22		09 24													09 48	09 52	09 54			
Peckham Rye 4	d	09 16	09a21	09a25		09 26	09 31										09 42	09 46	09a51	09a55	09 56	10 01		
Queens Rd Peckham	d	09 19				09 29	09 34											09 49			09 59	10 04		
South Bermondsey	d	09 21				09 31	09 36											09 51			10 01	10 06		
Clapham Junction 10	d													09 27										
Wandsworth Common	d													09 30										
Balham 4	⊖ d													09 32										
Streatham Hill	d													09 35										
West Norwood 4	d													09 40			09 53							
Gipsy Hill	d													09 43			09 56							
Crystal Palace 4	d												09 43	09 51		09 58	09a59							
Sydenham	d							09 21		09 36	09 42		09 46	09 54		10 01							09 51	
Forest Hill 4	d							09 23		09 38	09 45		09 49	09 57		10 04							09 53	
Honor Oak Park	d							09 26		09 41	09 47		09 51	09 59		10 06							09 56	
Brockley	d							09 28		09 43	09 50		09 54	10 02		10 09							09 58	
New Cross Gate 4	a							09 31		09 46	09 52		09 56	10 04		10 11							10 01	
	d							09 31		09 46	09 52		09 56	10 04		10 11							10 01	
New Cross ELL	d								09 36			09 51												10 06
Surrey Quays	d							09 35	09 40	09 49		09 55	10 00			10 15							10 05	10 10
Canada Water	d							09 37	09 42	09 51		09 57	10 02			10 17							10 07	10 12
Rotherhithe	d							09 38	09 43	09 53		09 58	10 03			10 18							10 08	10 13
Wapping	d							09 40	09 45	09 54		10 00	10 05			10 20							10 10	10 15
Shadwell	d							09 42	09 47	09 56		10 02	10 07			10 22							10 12	10 17
Whitechapel	d							09 44	09 49	09 59		10 04	10 09			10 24							10 14	10 19
Shoreditch High Street	d							09 46	09 51	10 01		10 06	10 11			10 26							10 16	10 21
Hoxton	d							09 48	09 53	10 03		10 08	10 13			10 28							10 18	10 23
Haggerston	d							09 50	09 55	10 05		10 10	10 15			10 30							10 20	10 25
Dalston Junction Stn ELL	a							09 53	10 02	10 07		10 17	10 17			10 32							10 22	10 32
Canonbury	d							09 57		10 12			10 20			10 35							10 27	
Highbury & Islington	a							10 05		10 19			10 28			10 43							10 35	
	d																							
London Bridge 4	⊖ a	09 26				09 36	09 41				09 59			10 11				09 56			10 06	10 11		

		LO	SN	LO	LO	SN	LO	SN	SN	SE		SE	SN	SN	LO	LO	LO	SN	LO	LO		SN	LO	SN	SN
East Croydon	d		10 00															10 30							
West Croydon 4	d	09 52												10 01	10 09		10 22								
Norwood Junction 2	d	09 58	10 05												10 13		10 28	10 35							
Anerley	d	10 01	10 08												10 16		10 31	10 38							
Penge West	d	10 03	10 10												10 18		10 33	10 40							
London Victoria 15	⊖ d					09 49				10 09			10 11									10 19			
Battersea Park 4	d					09 53							10 15									10 23			
Wandsworth Road	d												10 17												
Clapham High Street	⊖ d												10 19												
London Blackfriars 3	⊖ d											10 12													
Denmark Hill 4	d									10 18		10 22	10 24												
Peckham Rye 4	d							10 12	10 16	10a21		10a25	10 26	10 31										10 42	10 46
Queens Rd Peckham	d								10 19				10 29	10 34											10 49
South Bermondsey	d								10 21				10 31	10 36											10 51
Clapham Junction 10	d					09 57																10 27			
Wandsworth Common	d					10 00																10 30			
Balham 4	⊖ d					10 02																10 32			
Streatham Hill	d					10 05																10 35			
West Norwood 4	d					10 10		10 23														10 40		10 53	
Gipsy Hill	d					10 13		10 26														10 43		10 56	
Crystal Palace 4	d				10 13	10 21	10 28	10a29												10 43		10 51	10 58	10a59	
Sydenham	d	10 06	10 12		10 16	10 24	10 31								10 21		10 36	10 42		10 46		10 54	11 01		
Forest Hill 4	d	10 08	10 15		10 19	10 27	10 34								10 23		10 38	10 45		10 49		10 57	11 04		
Honor Oak Park	d	10 11	10 17		10 21	10 29	10 36								10 26		10 41	10 47		10 51		10 59	11 06		
Brockley	d	10 13	10 20		10 24	10 32	10 39								10 28		10 43	10 50		10 54		11 02	11 09		
New Cross Gate 4	a	10 16	10 22		10 26	10 34	10 41								10 31		10 46	10 52		10 56		11 04	11 11		
	d	10 16	10 22		10 26	10 34	10 41								10 31		10 46	10 52		10 56		11 04	11 11		
New Cross ELL	d			10 21												10 36			10 51						
Surrey Quays	d	10 19		10 25	10 30		10 45								10 35	10 40	10 49		10 55	11 00			11 15		
Canada Water	d	10 21		10 27	10 32		10 47								10 37	10 42	10 51		10 57	11 02			11 17		
Rotherhithe	d	10 23		10 28	10 33		10 48								10 38	10 43	10 53		10 58	11 03			11 18		
Wapping	d	10 24		10 30	10 35		10 50								10 40	10 45	10 54		11 00	11 05			11 20		
Shadwell	d	10 26		10 32	10 37		10 52								10 42	10 47	10 56		11 02	11 07			11 22		
Whitechapel	d	10 29		10 34	10 39		10 54								10 44	10 49	10 59		11 04	11 09			11 24		
Shoreditch High Street	d	10 31		10 36	10 41		10 56								10 46	10 51	11 01		11 06	11 11			11 26		
Hoxton	d	10 33		10 38	10 43		10 58								10 48	10 53	11 03		11 08	11 13			11 28		
Haggerston	d	10 35		10 40	10 45		11 00								10 50	10 55	11 05		11 10	11 15			11 30		
Dalston Junction Stn ELL	a	10 37		10 47	10 47		11 02								10 52	11 02	11 07		11 17	11 17			11 32		
Canonbury	d	10 42			10 50		11 05								10 57		11 12			11 20			11 35		
Highbury & Islington	a	10 49			10 58		11 13								11 05		11 19			11 28			11 43		
	d																								
London Bridge 4	⊖ a		10 29			10 41			10 26				10 36	10 41				10 59				11 11			10 56

Table 178

Saturdays

28 July to 11 August

East London Line and Croydon - London Victoria to London Bridge

Network Diagram - see first Page of Table 177

		SE	SE	SN	SN	LO		LO	LO	SN	LO	LO	SN	LO	SN	SN		SE	SE	SN	SN	LO	LO	LO	SN
East Croydon	d									11 00															11 30
West Croydon 4	d				10 31	10 39			10 52												11 01	11 09		11 22	
Norwood Junction 2	d					10 43			10 58	11 05												11 13		11 28	11 35
Anerley	d					10 46			11 01	11 08												11 16		11 31	11 38
Penge West	d					10 48			11 03	11 10												11 18		11 33	11 40
London Victoria 15 ⊖	d	10 39		10 41									10 49					11 09		11 11					
Battersea Park 4	d			10 45									10 53							11 15					
Wandsworth Road	d			10 47																11 17					
Clapham High Street ⊖	d			10 49																11 19					
London Blackfriars 3 ⊖	d		10 42																11 12						
Denmark Hill 4	d	10 48	10 52	10 54														11 18	11 22	11 24					
Peckham Rye 4	d	10a51	10a55	10 56	11 01										11 12	11 16		11a21	11a25	11 26	11 31				
Queens Rd Peckham	d			10 59	11 04											11 19				11 29	11 34				
South Bermondsey	d			11 01	11 06											11 21				11 31	11 36				
Clapham Junction 10	d												10 57												
Wandsworth Common	d												11 00												
Balham 4 ⊖	d												11 02												
Streatham Hill	d												11 05												
West Norwood 4	d												11 10		11 23										
Gipsy Hill	d												11 13		11 26										
Crystal Palace 4	d											11 13	11 21	11 28	11a29										
Sydenham	d					10 51			11 06	11 12		11 16	11 24	11 31								11 21		11 36	11 42
Forest Hill 4	d					10 53			11 08	11 15		11 19	11 27	11 34								11 23		11 38	11 45
Honor Oak Park	d					10 56			11 11	11 17		11 21	11 29	11 36								11 26		11 41	11 47
Brockley	d					10 58			11 13	11 20		11 24	11 32	11 39								11 28		11 43	11 50
New Cross Gate 4	a					11 01			11 16	11 22		11 26	11 34	11 41								11 31		11 46	11 52
	d					11 01			11 16	11 22		11 26	11 34	11 41								11 31		11 46	11 52
New Cross ELL	d							11 06			11 21												11 36		
Surrey Quays	d					11 05		11 10	11 19		11 25	11 30		11 45								11 35	11 40	11 49	
Canada Water	d					11 07		11 12	11 21		11 27	11 32		11 47								11 37	11 42	11 51	
Rotherhithe	d					11 08		11 13	11 23		11 28	11 33		11 48								11 38	11 43	11 53	
Wapping	d					11 10		11 15	11 24		11 30	11 35		11 50								11 40	11 45	11 54	
Shadwell	d					11 12		11 17	11 26		11 32	11 37		11 52								11 42	11 47	11 56	
Whitechapel	d					11 14		11 19	11 29		11 34	11 39		11 54								11 44	11 49	11 59	
Shoreditch High Street	d					11 16		11 21	11 31		11 36	11 41		11 56								11 46	11 51	12 01	
Hoxton	d					11 18		11 23	11 33		11 38	11 43		11 58								11 48	11 53	12 03	
Haggerston	d					11 20		11 25	11 35		11 40	11 45		12 00								11 50	11 55	12 05	
Dalston Junction Stn ELL	a					11 22		11 32	11 37		11 47	11 47		12 02								11 52	12 02	12 07	
Canonbury	d					11 27			11 42			11 50		12 05								11 57		12 12	
Highbury & Islington	a					11 35			11 49			11 58		12 13								12 05		12 19	
	d																								
London Bridge 4 ⊖	a			11 06	11 11					11 29			11 41			11 26				11 36	11 41				11 59

		LO		LO	SN	LO	SN	SN	SE	SE	SN	SN		LO	LO	LO	SN	LO	LO	SN	LO	SN		SN	SE
East Croydon	d																12 00								
West Croydon 4	d											11 31		11 39		11 52									
Norwood Junction 2	d													11 43		11 58	12 05								
Anerley	d													11 46		12 01	12 08								
Penge West	d													11 48		12 03	12 10								
London Victoria 15 ⊖	d				11 19				11 39		11 41									11 49					12 09
Battersea Park 4	d				11 23						11 45									11 53					
Wandsworth Road	d										11 47														
Clapham High Street ⊖	d										11 49														
London Blackfriars 3 ⊖	d									11 42															
Denmark Hill 4	d								11 48	11 52	11 54														12 18
Peckham Rye 4	d						11 42	11 46	11a51	11a55	11 56	12 01										12 12		12 16	12a21
Queens Rd Peckham	d							11 49			11 59	12 04												12 19	
South Bermondsey	d							11 51			12 01	12 06												12 21	
Clapham Junction 10	d				11 27															11 57					
Wandsworth Common	d				11 30															12 00					
Balham 4 ⊖	d				11 32															12 02					
Streatham Hill	d				11 35															12 05					
West Norwood 4	d				11 40		11 53													12 10		12 23			
Gipsy Hill	d				11 43		11 56													12 13		12 26			
Crystal Palace 4	d			11 43	11 51	11 58	11a59												12 13	12 21	12 28	12a29			
Sydenham	d			11 46	11 54	12 01								11 51		12 06	12 12		12 16	12 24	12 31				
Forest Hill 4	d			11 49	11 57	12 04								11 53		12 08	12 15		12 19	12 27	12 34				
Honor Oak Park	d			11 51	11 59	12 06								11 56		12 11	12 17		12 21	12 29	12 36				
Brockley	d			11 54	12 02	12 09								11 58		12 13	12 20		12 24	12 32	12 39				
New Cross Gate 4	a			11 56	12 04	12 11								12 01		12 16	12 22		12 26	12 34	12 41				
	d			11 56	12 04	12 11								12 01		12 16	12 22		12 26	12 34	12 41				
New Cross ELL	d	11 51													12 06			12 21							
Surrey Quays	d	11 55		12 00		12 15								12 05	12 10	12 19		12 25	12 30		12 45				
Canada Water	d	11 57		12 02		12 17								12 07	12 12	12 21		12 27	12 32		12 47				
Rotherhithe	d	11 58		12 03		12 18								12 08	12 13	12 23		12 28	12 33		12 48				
Wapping	d	12 00		12 05		12 20								12 10	12 15	12 24		12 30	12 35		12 50				
Shadwell	d	12 02		12 07		12 22								12 12	12 17	12 26		12 32	12 37		12 52				
Whitechapel	d	12 04		12 09		12 24								12 14	12 19	12 29		12 34	12 39		12 54				
Shoreditch High Street	d	12 06		12 11		12 26								12 16	12 21	12 31		12 36	12 41		12 56				
Hoxton	d	12 08		12 13		12 28								12 18	12 23	12 33		12 38	12 43		12 58				
Haggerston	d	12 10		12 15		12 30								12 20	12 25	12 35		12 40	12 45		13 00				
Dalston Junction Stn ELL	a	12 17		12 17		12 32								12 22	12 32	12 37		12 47	12 47		13 02				
Canonbury	d			12 20		12 35								12 27		12 42			12 50		13 05				
Highbury & Islington	a			12 28		12 43								12 35		12 49			12 58		13 13				
	d																								
London Bridge 4 ⊖	a				12 11			11 56			12 06	12 11					12 29			12 44				12 26	

Table 178

Saturdays

28 July to 11 August

East London Line and Croydon - London Victoria to London Bridge

Network Diagram - see first Page of Table 177

		SE	SN	SN	LO	LO	LO	SN		LO	LO	SN	LO	SN	SN	SE	SE	SN		SN	LO	LO	LO	SN	LO
East Croydon	d							12 30																13 00	
West Croydon 4	d			12 01	12 09		12 22													12 31	12 39		12 52		
Norwood Junction 2	d				12 13		12 28	12 35													12 43		12 58	13 05	
Anerley	d				12 16		12 31	12 38													12 46		13 01	13 08	
Penge West	d				12 18		12 33	12 40													12 48		13 03	13 10	
London Victoria 15 ⊖	d		12 11									12 19				12 39		12 41							
Battersea Park 4	d		12 15									12 23						12 45							
Wandsworth Road	d		12 17															12 47							
Clapham High Street ⊖	d		12 19															12 49							
London Blackfriars 3 ⊖	d	12 12															12 42								
Denmark Hill 4	d	12 22	12 24													12 48	12 52	12 54							
Peckham Rye 4	d	12a25	12 26	12 31										12 42	12 46	12a51	12a55	12 56		13 01					
Queens Rd Peckham	d		12 29	12 34											12 49			12 59		13 04					
South Bermondsey	d		12 31	12 36											12 51			13 01		13 06					
Clapham Junction 10	d											12 27													
Wandsworth Common	d											12 30													
Balham 4 ⊖	d											12 32													
Streatham Hill	d											12 35													
West Norwood 4	d											12 40		12 53											
Gipsy Hill	d											12 43		12 56											
Crystal Palace 4	d										12 43	12 51	12 58	12a59											
Sydenham	d				12 21		12 36	12 42			12 46	12 54	13 01								12 51		13 06	13 12	
Forest Hill 4	d				12 23		12 38	12 45			12 49	12 57	13 04								12 53		13 08	13 15	
Honor Oak Park	d				12 26		12 41	12 47			12 51	12 59	13 06								12 56		13 11	13 17	
Brockley	d				12 28		12 43	12 50			12 54	13 02	13 09								12 58		13 13	13 20	
New Cross Gate 4	a				12 31		12 46	12 52			12 56	13 04	13 11								13 01		13 16	13 22	
	d				12 31		12 46	12 52			12 56	13 04	13 11								13 01		13 16	13 22	
New Cross ELL	d					12 36				12 51												13 06			13 21
Surrey Quays	d				12 35	12 40	12 49			12 55	13 00		13 15								13 05	13 10	13 19		13 25
Canada Water	d				12 37	12 42	12 51			12 57	13 02		13 17								13 07	13 12	13 21		13 27
Rotherhithe	d				12 38	12 43	12 53			12 58	13 03		13 18								13 08	13 13	13 23		13 28
Wapping	d				12 40	12 45	12 54			13 00	13 05		13 20								13 10	13 15	13 24		13 30
Shadwell	d				12 42	12 47	12 56			13 02	13 07		13 22								13 12	13 17	13 26		13 32
Whitechapel	d				12 44	12 49	12 59			13 04	13 09		13 24								13 14	13 19	13 29		13 34
Shoreditch High Street	d				12 46	12 51	13 01			13 06	13 11		13 26								13 16	13 21	13 31		13 36
Hoxton	d				12 48	12 53	13 03			13 08	13 13		13 28								13 18	13 23	13 33		13 38
Haggerston	d				12 50	12 55	13 05			13 10	13 15		13 30								13 20	13 25	13 35		13 40
Dalston Junction Stn ELL	a				12 52	13 02	13 07			13 17	13 17		13 32								13 22	13 32	13 37		13 47
Canonbury	d				12 57		13 12				13 20		13 35								13 27		13 42		
Highbury & Islington	a				13 05		13 19				13 28		13 43								13 35		13 49		
	d																								
London Bridge 4 ⊖	a		12 36	12 41				12 59				13 11			12 56			13 06		13 11				13 29	

		LO	SN	LO		SN	SN	SE	SE	SN	SN	LO	LO	LO		SN	LO	LO	SN	LO	SN	SN	SE	SE
East Croydon	d															13 30								
West Croydon 4	d										13 01	13 09		13 22										
Norwood Junction 2	d											13 13		13 28		13 35								
Anerley	d											13 16		13 31		13 38								
Penge West	d											13 18		13 33		13 40								
London Victoria 15 ⊖	d		12 49					13 09		13 11									13 19				13 39	
Battersea Park 4	d		12 53							13 15									13 23					
Wandsworth Road	d									13 17														
Clapham High Street ⊖	d									13 19														
London Blackfriars 3 ⊖	d								13 12															13 42
Denmark Hill 4	d							13 18	13 22	13 24													13 48	13 52
Peckham Rye 4	d					13 12	13 16	13a21	13a25	13 26	13 31										13 42	13 46	13a51	13a55
Queens Rd Peckham	d						13 19			13 29	13 34											13 49		
South Bermondsey	d						13 21			13 31	13 36											13 51		
Clapham Junction 10	d		12 57																13 27					
Wandsworth Common	d		13 00																13 30					
Balham 4 ⊖	d		13 02																13 32					
Streatham Hill	d		13 05																13 35					
West Norwood 4	d		13 10			13 23													13 40		13 53			
Gipsy Hill	d		13 13			13 26													13 43		13 56			
Crystal Palace 4	d	13 13	13 21	13 28		13a29												13 43	13 51	13 58	13a59			
Sydenham	d	13 16	13 24	13 31								13 21		13 36		13 42		13 46	13 54	14 01				
Forest Hill 4	d	13 19	13 27	13 34								13 23		13 38		13 45		13 49	13 57	14 04				
Honor Oak Park	d	13 21	13 29	13 36								13 26		13 41		13 47		13 51	13 59	14 06				
Brockley	d	13 24	13 32	13 39								13 28		13 43		13 50		13 54	14 02	14 09				
New Cross Gate 4	a	13 26	13 34	13 41								13 31		13 46		13 52		13 56	14 04	14 11				
	d	13 26	13 34	13 41								13 31		13 46		13 52		13 56	14 04	14 11				
New Cross ELL	d												13 36				13 51							
Surrey Quays	d	13 30		13 45								13 35	13 40	13 49			13 55	14 00		14 15				
Canada Water	d	13 32		13 47								13 37	13 42	13 51			13 57	14 02		14 17				
Rotherhithe	d	13 33		13 48								13 38	13 43	13 53			13 58	14 03		14 18				
Wapping	d	13 35		13 50								13 40	13 45	13 54			14 00	14 05		14 20				
Shadwell	d	13 37		13 52								13 42	13 47	13 56			14 02	14 07		14 22				
Whitechapel	d	13 39		13 54								13 44	13 49	13 59			14 04	14 09		14 24				
Shoreditch High Street	d	13 41		13 56								13 46	13 51	14 01			14 06	14 11		14 26				
Hoxton	d	13 43		13 58								13 48	13 53	14 03			14 08	14 13		14 28				
Haggerston	d	13 45		14 00								13 50	13 55	14 05			14 10	14 15		14 30				
Dalston Junction Stn ELL	a	13 47		14 02								13 52	14 02	14 07			14 17	14 17		14 32				
Canonbury	d	13 50		14 05								13 57		14 12				14 20		14 35				
Highbury & Islington	a	13 58		14 13								14 05		14 19				14 28		14 43				
	d																							
London Bridge 4 ⊖	a		13 44				13 26			13 36	13 41					13 59			14 11			13 56		

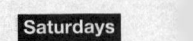

East London Line and Croydon - London Victoria to London Bridge

Network Diagram - see first Page of Table 177

		SN	SN	LO	LO	LO	SN	LO	LO	SN		LO	SN	SN	SE	SE	SN	SN	LO	LO		LO	SN	LO	LO
East Croydon	d						14 00																14 30		
West Croydon 4	d		13 31	13 39		13 52												14 01	14 09			14 22			
Norwood Junction 2	d			13 43		13 58	14 05												14 13			14 28	14 35		
Anerley	d			13 46		14 01	14 08												14 16			14 31	14 38		
Penge West	d			13 48		14 03	14 10												14 18			14 33	14 40		
London Victoria 15 ⊖	d	13 41								13 49					14 09		14 11								
Battersea Park 4	d	13 45								13 53							14 15								
Wandsworth Road	d	13 47															14 17								
Clapham High Street ⊖	d	13 49															14 19								
London Blackfriars 3 ⊖	d															14 12									
Denmark Hill 4	d	13 54													14 18	14 22	14 24								
Peckham Rye 4	d	13 56	14 01										14 12	14 16	14a21	14a25	14 26	14 31							
Queens Rd Peckham	d	13 59	14 04											14 19			14 29	14 34							
South Bermondsey	d	14 01	14 06											14 21			14 31	14 36							
Clapham Junction 10	d									13 57															
Wandsworth Common	d									14 00															
Balham 4 ⊖	d									14 02															
Streatham Hill	d									14 05															
West Norwood 4	d									14 10			14 23												
Gipsy Hill	d									14 13			14 26												
Crystal Palace 4	d								14 13	14 21		14 28	14a29												14 43
Sydenham	d			13 51		14 06	14 12		14 16	14 24		14 31							14 21			14 36	14 42		14 46
Forest Hill 4	d			13 53		14 08	14 15		14 19	14 27		14 34							14 23			14 38	14 45		14 49
Honor Oak Park	d			13 56		14 11	14 17		14 21	14 29		14 36							14 26			14 41	14 47		14 51
Brockley	d			13 58		14 13	14 20		14 24	14 32		14 39							14 28			14 43	14 50		14 54
New Cross Gate 4	a			14 01		14 16	14 22		14 26	14 34		14 41							14 31			14 46	14 52		14 56
	d			14 01		14 16	14 22		14 26	14 34		14 41							14 31			14 46	14 52		14 56
New Cross ELL	d				14 06			14 21												14 36				14 51	
Surrey Quays	d			14 05	14 10	14 19		14 25	14 30			14 45							14 35	14 40		14 49		14 55	15 00
Canada Water	d			14 07	14 12	14 21		14 27	14 32			14 47							14 37	14 42		14 51		14 57	15 02
Rotherhithe	d			14 08	14 13	14 23		14 28	14 33			14 48							14 38	14 43		14 53		14 58	15 03
Wapping	d			14 10	14 15	14 24		14 30	14 35			14 50							14 40	14 45		14 54		15 00	15 05
Shadwell	d			14 12	14 17	14 26		14 32	14 37			14 52							14 42	14 47		14 56		15 02	15 07
Whitechapel	d			14 14	14 19	14 29		14 34	14 39			14 54							14 44	14 49		14 59		15 04	15 09
Shoreditch High Street	d			14 16	14 21	14 31		14 36	14 41			14 56							14 46	14 51		15 01		15 06	15 11
Hoxton	d			14 18	14 23	14 33		14 38	14 43			14 58							14 48	14 53		15 03		15 08	15 13
Haggerston	d			14 20	14 25	14 35		14 40	14 45			15 00							14 50	14 55		15 05		15 10	15 15
Dalston Junction Stn ELL	a			14 22	14 32	14 37		14 47	14 47			15 02							14 52	15 02		15 07		15 17	15 17
Canonbury	d			14 27		14 42			14 50			15 05							14 57			15 12			15 20
Highbury & Islington	a			14 35		14 49			14 58			15 13							15 05			15 19			15 28
	d																								
London Bridge 4 ⊖	a	14 06	14 11				14 29			14 44				14 26			14 36	14 41					14 59		

		SN	LO	SN	SN	SE		SE	SN	SN	LO	LO	LO	SN	LO	LO		SN	LO	SN	SN	SE	SE	SN	SN
East Croydon	d													15 00											
West Croydon 4	d									14 31	14 39		14 52												15 01
Norwood Junction 2	d										14 43		14 58	15 05											
Anerley	d										14 46		15 01	15 08											
Penge West	d										14 48		15 03	15 10											
London Victoria 15 ⊖	d	14 19				14 39			14 41									14 49				15 09		15 11	
Battersea Park 4	d	14 23							14 45									14 53						15 15	
Wandsworth Road	d								14 47															15 17	
Clapham High Street ⊖	d								14 49															15 19	
London Blackfriars 3 ⊖	d							14 42															15 12		
Denmark Hill 4	d					14 48		14 52	14 54													15 18	15 22	15 24	
Peckham Rye 4	d			14 42	14 46	14a51		14a55	14 56	15 01										15 12	15 16	15a21	15a25	15 26	15 31
Queens Rd Peckham	d				14 49				14 59	15 04											15 19			15 29	15 34
South Bermondsey	d				14 51				15 01	15 06											15 21			15 31	15 36
Clapham Junction 10	d	14 27																14 57							
Wandsworth Common	d	14 30																15 00							
Balham 4 ⊖	d	14 32																15 02							
Streatham Hill	d	14 35																15 05							
West Norwood 4	d	14 40		14 53														15 10		15 23					
Gipsy Hill	d	14 43		14 56														15 13		15 26					
Crystal Palace 4	d	14 51	14 58	14a59												15 13		15 21	15 28	15a29					
Sydenham	d	14 54	15 01								14 51		15 06	15 12		15 16		15 24	15 31						
Forest Hill 4	d	14 57	15 04								14 53		15 08	15 15		15 19		15 27	15 34						
Honor Oak Park	d	14 59	15 06								14 56		15 11	15 17		15 21		15 29	15 36						
Brockley	d	15 02	15 09								14 58		15 13	15 20		15 24		15 32	15 39						
New Cross Gate 4	a	15 04	15 11								15 01		15 16	15 22		15 26		15 34	15 41						
	d	15 04	15 11								15 01		15 16	15 22		15 26		15 34	15 41						
New Cross ELL	d											15 06			15 21										
Surrey Quays	d		15 15								15 05	15 10	15 19		15 25	15 30			15 45						
Canada Water	d		15 17								15 07	15 12	15 21		15 27	15 32			15 47						
Rotherhithe	d		15 18								15 08	15 13	15 23		15 28	15 33			15 48						
Wapping	d		15 20								15 10	15 15	15 24		15 30	15 35			15 50						
Shadwell	d		15 22								15 12	15 17	15 26		15 32	15 37			15 52						
Whitechapel	d		15 24								15 14	15 19	15 29		15 34	15 39			15 54						
Shoreditch High Street	d		15 26								15 16	15 21	15 31		15 36	15 41			15 56						
Hoxton	d		15 28								15 18	15 23	15 33		15 38	15 43			15 58						
Haggerston	d		15 30								15 20	15 25	15 35		15 40	15 45			16 00						
Dalston Junction Stn ELL	a		15 32								15 22	15 32	15 37		15 47	15 47			16 02						
Canonbury	d		15 35								15 27		15 42			15 50			16 05						
Highbury & Islington	a		15 43								15 35		15 49			15 58			16 13						
	d																								
London Bridge 4 ⊖	a	15 11			14 56				15 06	15 11				15 29				15 44			15 26			15 36	15 41

Table 178

Saturdays

28 July to 11 August

East London Line and Croydon - London Victoria to London Bridge

Network Diagram - see first Page of Table 177

		LO		LO	LO	SN	LO	LO	SN	LO	SN	SN		SE	SE	SN	SN	LO	LO	LO	SN	LO		LO	SN
East Croydon 🚋	d					15 30															16 00				
West Croydon 4 🚋	d	15 09			15 22												15 31	15 39		15 52					
Norwood Junction 2	d	15 13			15 28	15 35												15 43		15 58	16 05				
Anerley	d	15 16			15 31	15 38												15 46		16 01	16 08				
Penge West	d	15 18			15 33	15 40												15 48		16 03	16 10				
London Victoria 15 ⊖	d								15 19					15 39		15 41									15 49
Battersea Park 4	d								15 23							15 45									15 53
Wandsworth Road	d															15 47									
Clapham High Street ⊖	d															15 49									
London Blackfriars 3 ⊖	d														15 42										
Denmark Hill 4	d													15 48	15 52	15 54									
Peckham Rye 4	d										15 42	15 46		15a51	15a55	15 56	16 01								
Queens Rd Peckham	d											15 49				15 59	16 04								
South Bermondsey	d											15 51				16 01	16 06								
Clapham Junction 10	d								15 27																15 57
Wandsworth Common	d								15 30																16 00
Balham 4 ⊖	d								15 32																16 02
Streatham Hill	d								15 35																16 05
West Norwood 4	d								15 40		15 53														16 10
Gipsy Hill	d								15 43		15 56														16 13
Crystal Palace 4	d							15 43	15 51	15 58	15a59													16 13	16 21
Sydenham	d	15 21			15 36	15 42		15 46	15 54	16 01								15 51		16 06	16 12			16 16	16 24
Forest Hill 4	d	15 23			15 38	15 45		15 49	15 57	16 04								15 53		16 08	16 15			16 19	16 27
Honor Oak Park	d	15 26			15 41	15 47		15 51	15 59	16 06								15 56		16 11	16 17			16 21	16 29
Brockley	d	15 28			15 43	15 50		15 54	16 02	16 09								15 58		16 13	16 20			16 24	16 32
New Cross Gate 4	a	15 31			15 46	15 52		15 56	16 04	16 11								16 01		16 16	16 22			16 26	16 34
	d	15 31			15 46	15 52		15 56	16 04	16 11								16 01		16 16	16 22			16 26	16 34
New Cross ELL	d			15 36			15 51												16 06			16 21			
Surrey Quays	d	15 35		15 40	15 49		15 55	16 00		16 15								16 05	16 10	16 19		16 25		16 30	
Canada Water	d	15 37		15 42	15 51		15 57	16 02		16 17								16 07	16 12	16 21		16 27		16 32	
Rotherhithe	d	15 38		15 43	15 53		15 58	16 03		16 18								16 08	16 13	16 23		16 28		16 33	
Wapping	d	15 40		15 45	15 54		16 00	16 05		16 20								16 10	16 15	16 24		16 30		16 35	
Shadwell	d	15 42		15 47	15 56		16 02	16 07		16 22								16 12	16 17	16 26		16 32		16 37	
Whitechapel	d	15 44		15 49	15 59		16 04	16 09		16 24								16 14	16 19	16 29		16 34		16 39	
Shoreditch High Street	d	15 46		15 51	16 01		16 06	16 11		16 26								16 16	16 21	16 31		16 36		16 41	
Hoxton	d	15 48		15 53	16 03		16 08	16 13		16 28								16 18	16 23	16 33		16 38		16 43	
Haggerston	d	15 50		15 55	16 05		16 10	16 15		16 30								16 20	16 25	16 35		16 40		16 45	
Dalston Junction Stn ELL	a	15 52		16 02	16 07		16 17	16 17		16 32								16 22	16 32	16 37		16 47		16 47	
Canonbury	d	15 57			16 12			16 20		16 35								16 27		16 42				16 50	
Highbury & Islington	a	16 05			16 19			16 28		16 43								16 35		16 49				16 58	
	d																								
London Bridge 4 ⊖	a					15 59			16 11			15 56				16 06	16 11				16 29				16 41

		LO	SN	SN	SE	SE	SN	SN		LO	LO	LO	SN	LO	LO	SN	LO	SN		SN	SE	SE	SN	SN	LO
East Croydon 🚋	d												16 30												
West Croydon 4 🚋	d							16 01		16 09		16 22												16 31	16 39
Norwood Junction 2	d									16 13		16 28	16 35												16 43
Anerley	d									16 16		16 31	16 38												16 46
Penge West	d									16 18		16 33	16 40												16 48
London Victoria 15 ⊖	d				16 09		16 11									16 19					16 39		16 41		
Battersea Park 4	d						16 15									16 23							16 45		
Wandsworth Road	d						16 17																16 47		
Clapham High Street ⊖	d						16 19																16 49		
London Blackfriars 3 ⊖	d					16 12																16 42			
Denmark Hill 4	d				16 18	16 22	16 24														16 48	16 52	16 54		
Peckham Rye 4	d		16 12	16 16	16a21	16a25	16 26	16 31										16 42		16 46	16a51	16a55	16 56	17 01	
Queens Rd Peckham	d			16 19			16 29	16 34												16 49			16 59	17 04	
South Bermondsey	d			16 21			16 31	16 36												16 51			17 01	17 06	
Clapham Junction 10	d															16 27									
Wandsworth Common	d															16 30									
Balham 4 ⊖	d															16 32									
Streatham Hill	d															16 35									
West Norwood 4	d		16 23													16 40		16 53							
Gipsy Hill	d		16 26													16 43		16 56							
Crystal Palace 4	d	16 28	16a29												16 43	16 51	16 58	16a59							
Sydenham	d	16 31								16 21		16 36	16 42		16 46	16 54	17 01								16 51
Forest Hill 4	d	16 34								16 23		16 38	16 45		16 49	16 57	17 04								16 53
Honor Oak Park	d	16 36								16 26		16 41	16 47		16 51	16 59	17 06								16 56
Brockley	d	16 39								16 28		16 43	16 50		16 54	17 02	17 09								16 58
New Cross Gate 4	a	16 41								16 31		16 46	16 52		16 56	17 04	17 11								17 01
	d	16 41								16 31		16 46	16 52		16 56	17 04	17 11								17 01
New Cross ELL	d										16 36			16 51											
Surrey Quays	d	16 45								16 35	16 40	16 49		16 55	17 00		17 15								17 05
Canada Water	d	16 47								16 37	16 42	16 51		16 57	17 02		17 17								17 07
Rotherhithe	d	16 48								16 38	16 43	16 53		16 58	17 03		17 18								17 08
Wapping	d	16 50								16 40	16 45	16 54		17 00	17 05		17 20								17 10
Shadwell	d	16 52								16 42	16 47	16 56		17 02	17 07		17 22								17 12
Whitechapel	d	16 54								16 44	16 49	16 59		17 04	17 09		17 24								17 14
Shoreditch High Street	d	16 56								16 46	16 51	17 01		17 06	17 11		17 26								17 16
Hoxton	d	16 58								16 48	16 53	17 03		17 08	17 13		17 28								17 18
Haggerston	d	17 00								16 50	16 55	17 05		17 10	17 15		17 30								17 20
Dalston Junction Stn ELL	a	17 02								16 52	17 02	17 07		17 17	17 17		17 32								17 22
Canonbury	d	17 05								16 57		17 12			17 20		17 35								17 27
Highbury & Islington	a	17 13								17 05		17 19			17 28		17 43								17 35
	d																								
London Bridge 4 ⊖	a			16 26			16 36	16 41					16 59			17 11				16 56			17 06	17 11	

Saturdays

28 July to 11 August

East London Line and Croydon - London Victoria to London Bridge

Network Diagram - see first Page of Table 177

		LO	LO	SN		LO	LO	SN	LO	SN	SN	SE	SE	SN		SN	LO	LO	LO	SN	LO	LO	SN	LO	
East Croydon	d			17 00																17 30					
West Croydon 4	d		16 52													17 01	17 09		17 22						
Norwood Junction 2	d		16 58	17 05													17 13		17 28	17 35					
Anerley	d		17 01	17 08													17 16		17 31	17 38					
Penge West	d		17 03	17 10													17 18		17 33	17 40					
London Victoria 15 ⊖	d							16 49				17 09		17 11									17 19		
Battersea Park 4	d							16 53						17 15									17 23		
Wandsworth Road	d													17 17											
Clapham High Street ⊖	d													17 19											
London Blackfriars 3 ⊖	d												17 12												
Denmark Hill 4	d											17 18	17 22	17 24											
Peckham Rye 4	d									17 12	17 16	17a21	17a25	17 26		17 31									
Queens Rd Peckham	d										17 19			17 29		17 34									
South Bermondsey	d										17 21			17 31		17 36									
Clapham Junction 10	d							16 57															17 27		
Wandsworth Common	d							17 00															17 30		
Balham 4 ⊖	d							17 02															17 32		
Streatham Hill	d							17 05															17 35		
West Norwood 4	d							17 10		17 23													17 40		
Gipsy Hill	d							17 13		17 26													17 43		
Crystal Palace 4	d						17 13	17 21	17 28	17a29												17 43	17 51	17 58	
Sydenham	d		17 06	17 12			17 16	17 24	17 31								17 21		17 36	17 42		17 46	17 54	18 01	
Forest Hill 4	d		17 08	17 15			17 19	17 27	17 34								17 23		17 38	17 45		17 49	17 57	18 04	
Honor Oak Park	d		17 11	17 17			17 21	17 29	17 36								17 26		17 41	17 47		17 51	17 59	18 06	
Brockley	d		17 13	17 20			17 24	17 32	17 39								17 28		17 43	17 50		17 54	18 02	18 09	
New Cross Gate 4	a		17 16	17 22			17 26	17 34	17 41								17 31		17 46	17 52		17 56	18 04	18 11	
	d		17 16	17 22			17 26	17 34	17 41								17 31		17 46	17 52		17 56	18 04	18 11	
New Cross ELL	d	17 06				17 21												17 36			17 51				
Surrey Quays	d	17 10	17 19			17 25	17 30		17 45								17 35	17 40	17 49		17 55	18 00		18 15	
Canada Water	d	17 12	17 21			17 27	17 32		17 47								17 37	17 42	17 51		17 57	18 02		18 17	
Rotherhithe	d	17 13	17 23			17 28	17 33		17 48								17 38	17 43	17 53		17 58	18 03		18 18	
Wapping	d	17 15	17 24			17 30	17 35		17 50								17 40	17 45	17 54		18 00	18 05		18 20	
Shadwell	d	17 17	17 26			17 32	17 37		17 52								17 42	17 47	17 56		18 02	18 07		18 22	
Whitechapel	d	17 19	17 29			17 34	17 39		17 54								17 44	17 49	17 59		18 04	18 09		18 24	
Shoreditch High Street	d	17 21	17 31			17 36	17 41		17 56								17 46	17 51	18 01		18 06	18 11		18 26	
Hoxton	d	17 23	17 33			17 38	17 43		17 58								17 48	17 53	18 03		18 08	18 13		18 28	
Haggerston	d	17 25	17 35			17 40	17 45		18 00								17 50	17 55	18 05		18 10	18 15		18 30	
Dalston Junction Stn ELL	a	17 32	17 37			17 47	17 47		18 02								17 52	18 02	18 07		18 17	18 17		18 32	
Canonbury	d		17 42				17 50		18 05								17 57		18 12			18 20		18 35	
Highbury & Islington	a		17 49				17 58		18 13								18 05		18 19			18 28		18 43	
	d																								
London Bridge 4 ⊖	a			17 30				17 41			17 26			17 36		17 41				17 59			18 11		

		SN	SN	SE	SE	SN	SN	LO	LO	LO		SN	LO	LO	SN	LO	SN	SN	SE	SE		SN	SN	LO	LO
East Croydon	d											18 00													
West Croydon 4	d						17 31	17 39		17 52													18 01	18 09	
Norwood Junction 2	d							17 43		17 58		18 05												18 13	
Anerley	d							17 46		18 01		18 08												18 16	
Penge West	d							17 48		18 03		18 10												18 18	
London Victoria 15 ⊖	d			17 39		17 41									17 49				18 09			18 11			
Battersea Park 4	d					17 45									17 53							18 15			
Wandsworth Road	d					17 47																18 17			
Clapham High Street ⊖	d					17 49																18 19			
London Blackfriars 3 ⊖	d				17 42															18 12					
Denmark Hill 4	d			17 48	17 52	17 54													18 18	18 22		18 24			
Peckham Rye 4	d	17 42	17 46	17a51	17a55	17 56	18 01										18 12	18 16	18a21	18a25		18 26	18 31		
Queens Rd Peckham	d		17 49			17 59	18 04											18 19				18 29	18 34		
South Bermondsey	d		17 51			18 01	18 06											18 21				18 31	18 36		
Clapham Junction 10	d														17 57										
Wandsworth Common	d														18 00										
Balham 4 ⊖	d														18 02										
Streatham Hill	d														18 05										
West Norwood 4	d	17 53													18 10		18 23								
Gipsy Hill	d	17 56													18 13		18 26								
Crystal Palace 4	d	17a59												18 13	18 21	18 28	18a29								
Sydenham	d							17 51		18 06		18 12		18 16	18 24	18 31								18 21	
Forest Hill 4	d							17 53		18 08		18 15		18 19	18 27	18 34								18 23	
Honor Oak Park	d							17 56		18 11		18 17		18 21	18 29	18 36								18 26	
Brockley	d							17 58		18 13		18 20		18 24	18 32	18 39								18 28	
New Cross Gate 4	a							18 01		18 16		18 22		18 26	18 34	18 41								18 31	
	d							18 01		18 16		18 22		18 26	18 34	18 41								18 31	
New Cross ELL	d								18 06				18 21												18 36
Surrey Quays	d							18 05	18 10	18 19			18 25	18 30		18 45								18 35	18 40
Canada Water	d							18 07	18 12	18 21			18 27	18 32		18 47								18 37	18 42
Rotherhithe	d							18 08	18 13	18 23			18 28	18 33		18 48								18 38	18 43
Wapping	d							18 10	18 15	18 24			18 30	18 35		18 50								18 40	18 45
Shadwell	d							18 12	18 17	18 26			18 32	18 37		18 52								18 42	18 47
Whitechapel	d							18 14	18 19	18 29			18 34	18 39		18 54								18 44	18 49
Shoreditch High Street	d							18 16	18 21	18 31			18 36	18 41		18 56								18 46	18 51
Hoxton	d							18 18	18 23	18 33			18 38	18 43		18 58								18 48	18 53
Haggerston	d							18 20	18 25	18 35			18 40	18 45		19 00								18 50	18 55
Dalston Junction Stn ELL	a							18 23	18 32	18 37			18 47	18 47		19 02								18 52	19 02
Canonbury	d							18 27		18 42				18 50		19 05								18 57	
Highbury & Islington	a							18 35		18 49				18 58		19 13								19 05	
	d																								
London Bridge 4 ⊖	a		17 56			18 06	18 11					18 29			18 41			18 26				18 36	18 41		

Table 178

Saturdays

28 July to 11 August

East London Line and Croydon - London Victoria to London Bridge

Network Diagram - see first Page of Table 177

		LO	SN	LO	LO	SN		LO	SN	SN	SE	SE	SN	SN	LO	LO		LO	SN	LO	LO	SN	LO	SN	SN
East Croydon	d		18 30																19 00						
West Croydon 4	d	18 22												18 31	18 39			18 52							
Norwood Junction 2	d	18 28	18 35												18 43			18 58	19 05						
Anerley	d	18 31	18 38												18 46			19 01	19 08						
Penge West	d	18 33	18 40												18 48			19 03	19 10						
London Victoria 15 ⊖	d					18 19					18 39		18 41									18 49			
Battersea Park 4	d					18 23							18 45									18 53			
Wandsworth Road	d												18 47												
Clapham High Street ⊖	d												18 49												
London Blackfriars 3 ⊖	d											18 42													
Denmark Hill 4	d										18 48	18 52	18 54												
Peckham Rye 4	d								18 42	18 46	18a51	18a55	18 56	19 01										19 12	19 16
Queens Rd Peckham	d									18 49			18 59	19 04											19 19
South Bermondsey	d									18 51			19 01	19 06											19 21
Clapham Junction 10	d					18 27																18 57			
Wandsworth Common	d					18 30																19 00			
Balham 4 ⊖	d					18 32																19 02			
Streatham Hill	d					18 35																19 05			
West Norwood 4	d					18 40			18 53													19 10		19 23	
Gipsy Hill	d					18 43			18 56													19 13		19 26	
Crystal Palace 4	d				18 43	18 51		18 58	18a59												19 13	19 21	19 28	19a29	
Sydenham	d	18 36	18 42		18 46	18 54		19 01							18 51			19 06	19 12		19 16	19 24	19 31		
Forest Hill 4	d	18 38	18 45		18 49	18 57		19 04							18 53			19 08	19 15		19 19	19 27	19 34		
Honor Oak Park	d	18 41	18 47		18 51	18 59		19 06							18 56			19 11	19 17		19 21	19 29	19 36		
Brockley	d	18 43	18 50		18 54	19 02		19 09							18 58			19 13	19 20		19 24	19 32	19 39		
New Cross Gate 4	a	18 46	18 52		18 56	19 04		19 11							19 01			19 16	19 22		19 26	19 34	19 41		
	d	18 46	18 52		18 56	19 04		19 11							19 01			19 16	19 22		19 26	19 34	19 41		
New Cross ELL	d			18 51												19 06				19 21					
Surrey Quays	d	18 49		18 55	19 00			19 15							19 05	19 10		19 19		19 25	19 30		19 45		
Canada Water	d	18 51		18 57	19 02			19 17							19 07	19 12		19 21		19 27	19 32		19 47		
Rotherhithe	d	18 53		18 58	19 03			19 18							19 08	19 13		19 23		19 28	19 33		19 48		
Wapping	d	18 54		19 00	19 05			19 20							19 10	19 15		19 24		19 30	19 35		19 50		
Shadwell	d	18 56		19 02	19 07			19 22							19 12	19 17		19 26		19 32	19 37		19 52		
Whitechapel	d	18 59		19 04	19 09			19 24							19 14	19 19		19 29		19 34	19 39		19 54		
Shoreditch High Street	d	19 01		19 06	19 11			19 26							19 16	19 21		19 31		19 36	19 41		19 56		
Hoxton	d	19 03		19 08	19 13			19 28							19 18	19 23		19 33		19 38	19 43		19 58		
Haggerston	d	19 05		19 10	19 15			19 30							19 20	19 25		19 35		19 40	19 45		20 00		
Dalston Junction Stn ELL	a	19 07		19 17	19 17			19 32							19 22	19 32		19 37		19 47	19 47		20 02		
Canonbury	d	19 12			19 20			19 35							19 27			19 42			19 50		20 05		
Highbury & Islington	a	19 19			19 28			19 43							19 35			19 49			19 58		20 13		
	d																								
London Bridge 4 ⊖	a		18 59			19 11				18 56			19 06	19 11					19 29			19 41			19 26

		SE		SE	SN	SN	LO	LO	LO	SN	LO	LO		SN	LO	SN	SN	SE	SE	SN	SN	LO		LO	LO
East Croydon	d									19 30															
West Croydon 4	d					19 01	19 09		19 22												19 31	19 39			19 52
Norwood Junction 2	d						19 13		19 28	19 35												19 43			19 58
Anerley	d						19 16		19 31	19 38												19 46			20 01
Penge West	d						19 18		19 33	19 40												19 48			20 03
London Victoria 15 ⊖	d	19 09			19 11									19 19				19 39		19 41					
Battersea Park 4	d				19 15									19 23						19 45					
Wandsworth Road	d				19 17															19 47					
Clapham High Street ⊖	d				19 19															19 49					
London Blackfriars 3 ⊖	d			19 12															19 42						
Denmark Hill 4	d	19 18		19 22	19 24													19 48	19 52	19 54					
Peckham Rye 4	d	19a21		19a25	19 26	19 31										19 42	19 46	19a51	19a55	19 56	20 01				
Queens Rd Peckham	d				19 29	19 34											19 49			19 59	20 04				
South Bermondsey	d				19 31	19 36											19 51			20 01	20 06				
Clapham Junction 10	d													19 27											
Wandsworth Common	d													19 30											
Balham 4 ⊖	d													19 32											
Streatham Hill	d													19 35											
West Norwood 4	d													19 40		19 53									
Gipsy Hill	d													19 43		19 56									
Crystal Palace 4	d											19 43		19 51	19 58	19a59									
Sydenham	d						19 21		19 36	19 42		19 46		19 54	20 01							19 51			20 06
Forest Hill 4	d						19 23		19 38	19 45		19 49		19 57	20 04							19 53			20 08
Honor Oak Park	d						19 26		19 41	19 47		19 51		19 59	20 06							19 56			20 11
Brockley	d						19 28		19 43	19 50		19 54		20 02	20 09							19 58			20 13
New Cross Gate 4	a						19 31		19 46	19 52		19 56		20 04	20 11							20 01			20 16
	d						19 31		19 46	19 52		19 56		20 04	20 11							20 01			20 16
New Cross ELL	d							19 36			19 51													20 06	
Surrey Quays	d						19 35	19 40	19 49		19 55	20 00			20 15							20 05		20 10	20 19
Canada Water	d						19 37	19 42	19 51		19 57	20 02			20 17							20 07		20 12	20 21
Rotherhithe	d						19 38	19 43	19 53		19 58	20 03			20 18							20 08		20 13	20 23
Wapping	d						19 40	19 45	19 54		20 00	20 05			20 20							20 10		20 15	20 24
Shadwell	d						19 42	19 47	19 56		20 02	20 07			20 22							20 12		20 17	20 26
Whitechapel	d						19 44	19 49	19 59		20 04	20 09			20 24							20 14		20 19	20 29
Shoreditch High Street	d						19 46	19 51	20 01		20 06	20 11			20 26							20 16		20 21	20 31
Hoxton	d						19 48	19 53	20 03		20 08	20 13			20 28							20 18		20 23	20 33
Haggerston	d						19 50	19 55	20 05		20 10	20 15			20 30							20 20		20 25	20 35
Dalston Junction Stn ELL	a						19 52	20 02	20 07		20 17	20 17			20 32							20 22		20 32	20 37
Canonbury	d						19 57		20 12			20 20			20 35							20 27			20 42
Highbury & Islington	a						20 05		20 19			20 28			20 43							20 35			20 49
	d																								
London Bridge 4 ⊖	a				19 36	19 41				19 59				20 11			19 56			20 06	20 11				

Table 178

Saturdays

28 July to 11 August

East London Line and Croydon - London Victoria to London Bridge

Network Diagram - see first Page of Table 177

Station		SN	LO	LO	SN	LO	SN	SN		SE	SN	SN	LO	LO	LO	SN	LO	LO		SN	LO	SN	SN	SE	SN
East Croydon	d	20 00														20 30									
West Croydon 4	d											20 01	20 09		20 22										
Norwood Junction 2	d	20 05											20 13		20 28	20 35									
Anerley	d	20 08											20 16		20 31	20 38									
Penge West	d	20 10											20 18		20 33	20 40									
London Victoria 15 ⊖	d				19 49						20 11									20 19					20 41
Battersea Park 4	d				19 53						20 15									20 23					20 45
Wandsworth Road	d										20 17														20 47
Clapham High Street ⊖	d										20 19														20 49
London Blackfriars 3 ⊖	d									20 12														20 42	
Denmark Hill 4	d									20 22	20 24													20 52	20 54
Peckham Rye 4	d						20 12	20 16		20a25	20 26	20 31										20 42	20 46	20a55	20 56
Queens Rd Peckham	d							20 19			20 29	20 34											20 49		20 59
South Bermondsey	d							20 21			20 31	20 36											20 51		21 01
Clapham Junction 10	d				19 57															20 27					
Wandsworth Common	d				20 00															20 30					
Balham 4 ⊖	d				20 02															20 32					
Streatham Hill	d				20 05															20 35					
West Norwood 4	d				20 10		20 23													20 40		20 53			
Gipsy Hill	d				20 13		20 26													20 43		20 56			
Crystal Palace 4	d			20 13	20 21	20 28	20a29											20 43		20 51	20 58	20a59			
Sydenham	d	20 12		20 16	20 24	20 31							20 21		20 36	20 42		20 46		20 54	21 01				
Forest Hill 4	d	20 15		20 19	20 27	20 34							20 23		20 38	20 45		20 49		20 57	21 04				
Honor Oak Park	d	20 17		20 21	20 29	20 36							20 26		20 41	20 47		20 51		20 59	21 06				
Brockley	d	20 20		20 24	20 32	20 39							20 28		20 43	20 50		20 54		21 02	21 09				
New Cross Gate 4	a	20 22		20 26	20 34	20 41							20 31		20 46	20 52		20 56		21 04	21 11				
	d	20 22		20 26	20 34	20 41							20 31		20 46	20 52		20 56		21 04	21 11				
New Cross ELL	d		20 21											20 36			20 51								
Surrey Quays	d		20 25	20 30		20 45							20 35	20 40	20 49		20 55	21 00			21 15				
Canada Water	d		20 27	20 32		20 47							20 37	20 42	20 51		20 57	21 02			21 17				
Rotherhithe	d		20 28	20 33		20 48							20 38	20 43	20 53		20 58	21 03			21 18				
Wapping	d		20 30	20 35		20 50							20 40	20 45	20 54		21 00	21 05			21 20				
Shadwell	d		20 32	20 37		20 52							20 42	20 47	20 56		21 02	21 07			21 22				
Whitechapel	d		20 34	20 39		20 54							20 44	20 49	20 59		21 04	21 09			21 24				
Shoreditch High Street	d		20 36	20 41		20 56							20 46	20 51	21 01		21 06	21 11			21 26				
Hoxton	d		20 38	20 43		20 58							20 48	20 53	21 03		21 08	21 13			21 28				
Haggerston	d		20 40	20 45		21 00							20 50	20 55	21 05		21 10	21 15			21 30				
Dalston Junction Stn ELL	a		20 47	20 47		21 02							20 52	21 02	21 07		21 17	21 17			21 32				
Canonbury	d			20 50		21 05							20 57		21 12			21 20			21 35				
Highbury & Islington	a			20 58		21 13							21 05		21 19			21 28			21 43				
	d																								
London Bridge 4 ⊖	a	20 29			20 41			20 26			20 36	20 41				20 59				21 13			20 56		21 06

Station		SN	LO	LO		LO	SN	LO	LO	SN	LO	SN	SN	SE		SN	SN	LO	LO	LO	SN	LO	LO	SN	
East Croydon	d						21 00														21 30				
West Croydon 4	d	20 31	20 39			20 52											21 02	21 09		21 22					
Norwood Junction 2	d		20 43			20 58	21 05											21 13		21 28	21 35				
Anerley	d		20 46			21 01	21 08											21 16		21 31	21 38				
Penge West	d		20 48			21 03	21 10											21 18		21 33	21 40				
London Victoria 15 ⊖	d									20 49						21 11								21 19	
Battersea Park 4	d									20 53						21 15								21 23	
Wandsworth Road	d															21 17									
Clapham High Street ⊖	d															21 19									
London Blackfriars 3 ⊖	d													21 12											
Denmark Hill 4	d													21 22		21 24									
Peckham Rye 4	d	21 01										21 12	21 16	21a25		21 26	21 31								
Queens Rd Peckham	d	21 04											21 19			21 29	21 34								
South Bermondsey	d	21 06											21 21			21 31	21 36								
Clapham Junction 10	d									20 57														21 27	
Wandsworth Common	d									21 00														21 30	
Balham 4 ⊖	d									21 02														21 32	
Streatham Hill	d									21 05														21 35	
West Norwood 4	d									21 10		21 23												21 40	
Gipsy Hill	d									21 13		21 26												21 43	
Crystal Palace 4	d								21 13	21 21	21 28	21a29											21 43	21 51	
Sydenham	d		20 51			21 06	21 12		21 16	21 24	21 31							21 21		21 36	21 42		21 46	21 54	
Forest Hill 4	d		20 53			21 08	21 15		21 19	21 27	21 34							21 23		21 38	21 45		21 49	21 57	
Honor Oak Park	d		20 56			21 11	21 17		21 21	21 29	21 36							21 26		21 41	21 47		21 51	21 59	
Brockley	d		20 58			21 13	21 20		21 24	21 32	21 39							21 28		21 43	21 50		21 54	22 02	
New Cross Gate 4	a		21 01			21 16	21 22		21 26	21 34	21 41							21 31		21 46	21 52		21 56	22 04	
	d		21 01			21 16	21 22		21 26	21 34	21 41							21 31		21 46	21 52		21 56	22 04	
New Cross ELL	d			21 06				21 21											21 36			21 51			
Surrey Quays	d		21 05	21 10		21 19		21 25	21 30		21 45							21 35	21 40	21 49		21 55	22 00		
Canada Water	d		21 07	21 12		21 21		21 27	21 32		21 47							21 37	21 42	21 51		21 57	22 02		
Rotherhithe	d		21 08	21 13		21 23		21 28	21 33		21 48							21 38	21 43	21 53		21 58	22 03		
Wapping	d		21 10	21 15		21 24		21 30	21 35		21 50							21 40	21 45	21 54		22 00	22 05		
Shadwell	d		21 12	21 17		21 26		21 32	21 37		21 52							21 42	21 47	21 56		22 02	22 07		
Whitechapel	d		21 14	21 19		21 29		21 34	21 39		21 54							21 44	21 49	21 59		22 04	22 09		
Shoreditch High Street	d		21 16	21 21		21 31		21 36	21 41		21 56							21 46	21 51	22 01		22 06	22 11		
Hoxton	d		21 18	21 23		21 33		21 38	21 43		21 58							21 48	21 53	22 03		22 08	22 13		
Haggerston	d		21 20	21 25		21 35		21 40	21 45		22 00							21 50	21 55	22 05		22 10	22 15		
Dalston Junction Stn ELL	a		21 22	21 32		21 37		21 47	21 47		22 02							21 52	22 02	22 07		22 17	22 17		
Canonbury	d		21 27			21 42			21 50		22 05							21 57		22 12			22 20		
Highbury & Islington	a		21 35			21 49			21 58		22 13							22 05		22 19			22 28		
	d																								
London Bridge 4 ⊖	a	21 11					21 29			21 43			21 26			21 36	21 41				21 59			22 13	

Table 178

Saturdays

28 July to 11 August

East London Line and Croydon - London Victoria to London Bridge

Network Diagram - see first Page of Table 177

		LO	SN	SN	SE	SN	SN	LO	LO	LO		SN	LO	SN	LO	SN	SN	SE	SN	SN		LO	LO	LO	SN
East Croydon	d											22 00													22 30
West Croydon 4	d						21 31	21 39		21 52										22 01		22 09		22 22	
Norwood Junction 2	d							21 43		21 58		22 05										22 13		22 28	22 35
Anerley	d							21 46		22 01		22 08										22 16		22 31	22 38
Penge West	d							21 48		22 03		22 10										22 18		22 33	22 40
London Victoria 15 ⊖	d					21 41								21 49					22 11						
Battersea Park 4	d					21 45								21 53					22 15						
Wandsworth Road	d					21 47													22 17						
Clapham High Street ⊖	d					21 49													22 19						
London Blackfriars 3 ⊖	d				21 42													22 12							
Denmark Hill 4	d				21 52	21 54												22 22	22 24						
Peckham Rye 4	d		21 42	21 46	21a55	21 56	22 01									22 12	22 16	22a25	22 26	22 31					
Queens Rd Peckham	d			21 49		21 59	22 04										22 19		22 29	22 34					
South Bermondsey	d			21 51		22 01	22 06										22 21		22 31	22 36					
Clapham Junction 10	d													21 57											
Wandsworth Common	d													22 00											
Balham 4 ⊖	d													22 02											
Streatham Hill	d													22 05											
West Norwood 4	d		21 53											22 10		22 23									
Gipsy Hill	d		21 56											22 13		22 26									
Crystal Palace 4	d	21 58	21a59										22 13	22 21	22 28	22a29									
Sydenham	d	22 01						21 51		22 06		22 12	22 16	22 24	22 31							22 21		22 36	22 42
Forest Hill 4	d	22 04						21 53		22 08		22 15	22 19	22 27	22 34							22 23		22 38	22 45
Honor Oak Park	d	22 06						21 56		22 11		22 17	22 21	22 29	22 36							22 26		22 41	22 47
Brockley	d	22 09						21 58		22 13		22 20	22 24	22 32	22 39							22 28		22 43	22 50
New Cross Gate 4	a	22 11						22 01		22 16		22 22	22 26	22 34	22 41							22 31		22 46	22 52
	d	22 11						22 01		22 16		22 22	22 26	22 34	22 41							22 31		22 46	22 52
New Cross ELL	d								22 06														22 36		
Surrey Quays	d	22 15						22 05	22 10	22 19			22 30		22 45							22 35	22 40	22 49	
Canada Water	d	22 17						22 07	22 12	22 21			22 32		22 47							22 37	22 42	22 51	
Rotherhithe	d	22 18						22 08	22 13	22 23			22 33		22 48							22 38	22 43	22 53	
Wapping	d	22 20						22 10	22 15	22 24			22 35		22 50							22 40	22 45	22 54	
Shadwell	d	22 22						22 12	22 17	22 26			22 37		22 52							22 42	22 47	22 56	
Whitechapel	d	22 24						22 14	22 19	22 29			22 39		22 54							22 44	22 49	22 59	
Shoreditch High Street	d	22 26						22 16	22 21	22 31			22 41		22 56							22 46	22 51	23 01	
Hoxton	d	22 28						22 18	22 23	22 33			22 43		22 58							22 48	22 53	23 03	
Haggerston	d	22 30						22 20	22 25	22 35			22 45		23 00							22 50	22 55	23 05	
Dalston Junction Stn ELL	a	22 32						22 22	22 33	22 37			22 47		23 02							22 52	23 02	23 07	
Canonbury	d	22 35						22 27		22 42			22 50		23 05							22 57		23 12	
Highbury & Islington	a	22 43						22 35		22 49			22 58		23 13							23 05		23 19	
	d																								
London Bridge 4 ⊖	a			21 56		22 06	22 11					22 29		22 43			22 26		22 36	22 41					22 59

		LO	SN	SN	SN	SE		SN	SN	LO	LO	LO	SN	LO	SN	SN		SN	SE	SN	SN	LO	LO	LO	SN
East Croydon	d												23 01												
West Croydon 4	d								22 31	22 39		22 52									23 01		23 22		
Norwood Junction 2	d									22 43		22 58	23 06										23 28		
Anerley	d									22 46		23 01	23 09										23 31		
Penge West	d									22 48		23 03	23 11										23 33		
London Victoria 15 ⊖	d		22 19					22 41							22 49					23 11					23 19
Battersea Park 4	d		22 23					22 45							22 53					23 15					23 23
Wandsworth Road	d							22 47												23 17					
Clapham High Street ⊖	d							22 49												23 19					
London Blackfriars 3 ⊖	d					22 42													23 12						
Denmark Hill 4	d					22 52		22 54											23 22	23 24					
Peckham Rye 4	d			22 42	22 46	22a55		22 56	23 01							23 12		23 16	23a25	23 26	23 31				
Queens Rd Peckham	d				22 49			22 59	23 04									23 19		23 29	23 34				
South Bermondsey	d				22 51			23 01	23 06									23 21		23 31	23 36				
Clapham Junction 10	d		22 27												22 57										23 27
Wandsworth Common	d		22 30												23 00										23 30
Balham 4 ⊖	d		22 32												23 02										23 32
Streatham Hill	d		22 35												23 05										23 35
West Norwood 4	d		22 40	22 53											23 10	23 24									23 40
Gipsy Hill	d		22 43	22 56											23 13	23 27									23 43
Crystal Palace 4	d	22 43	22 51	22a59										23 13	23 21	23a29								23 43	23 51
Sydenham	d	22 46	22 54							22 51		23 06	23 13	23 16	23 24								23 36	23 46	23 54
Forest Hill 4	d	22 49	22 57							22 53		23 08	23 16	23 19	23 27								23 38	23 49	23 57
Honor Oak Park	d	22 51	22 59							22 56		23 11	23 18	23 21	23 29								23 41	23 51	23 59
Brockley	d	22 54	23 02							22 58		23 13	23 21	23 24	23 32								23 43	23 54	00 02
New Cross Gate 4	a	22 56	23 04							23 01		23 16	23 23	23 26	23 34								23 46	23 56	00 04
	d	22 56	23 04							23 01		23 16	23 23	23 26	23 34								23 46	23 56	00 04
New Cross ELL	d										23 06											23 36			
Surrey Quays	d	23 00								23 05	23 10	23 19		23 30								23 40	23 49	23 59	
Canada Water	d	23 02								23 07	23 12	23 21		23 32								23 42	23 51	00 02	
Rotherhithe	d	23 03								23 08	23 13	23 23		23 33								23 43	23 53	00 03	
Wapping	d	23 05								23 10	23 15	23 24		23 35								23 45	23 54	00 05	
Shadwell	d	23 07								23 12	23 17	23 26		23 37								23 47	23 56	00 07	
Whitechapel	d	23 09								23 14	23 19	23 29		23 39								23 49	23 59	00 09	
Shoreditch High Street	d	23 11								23 16	23 21	23 31		23 41								23 51	00 01	00 11	
Hoxton	d	23 13								23 18	23 23	23 33		23 43								23 53	00 03	00 13	
Haggerston	d	23 15								23 20	23 25	23 35		23 45								23 55	00 05	00 15	
Dalston Junction Stn ELL	a	23 17								23 22	23 32	23 37		23 47								23 58	00 07	00 17	
Canonbury	d	23 20								23 27		23 42		23 50								00 01	00 11	00 20	
Highbury & Islington	a	23 28								23 35		23 51		23 58								00 10	00 18	00 28	
	d																								
London Bridge 4 ⊖	a		23 13		22 56			23 06	23 11				23 30		23 43			23 26		23 36	23 41				00 11

Table 178

Saturdays

28 July to 11 August

East London Line and Croydon - London Victoria to London Bridge

Network Diagram - see first Page of Table 177

		SN		SN	SE	SN
East Croydon	d					
West Croydon 4	d					
Norwood Junction 2	d					
Anerley	d					
Penge West	d					
London Victoria 15 ⊖	d					23 54
Battersea Park 4	d					23 58
Wandsworth Road	d					
Clapham High Street ⊖	d					
London Blackfriars 3 ⊖	d				23 42	
Denmark Hill 4	d				23 52	
Peckham Rye 4	d	23 42		23 46	23a55	
Queens Rd Peckham	d			23 49		
South Bermondsey	d			23 51		
Clapham Junction 10	d					00 02
Wandsworth Common	d					00 05
Balham 4 ⊖	d					00 07
Streatham Hill	d					00 10
West Norwood 4	d	23 54				00 14
Gipsy Hill	d	23 57				00 17
Crystal Palace 4	d	23a59				00 21
Sydenham	d					00 24
Forest Hill 4	d					00 27
Honor Oak Park	d					00 29
Brockley	d					00 32
New Cross Gate 4	a					00 35
	d					00 35
New Cross ELL	d					
Surrey Quays	d					
Canada Water	d					
Rotherhithe	d					
Wapping	d					
Shadwell	d					
Whitechapel	d					
Shoreditch High Street	d					
Hoxton	d					
Haggerston	d					
Dalston Junction Stn ELL	a					
Canonbury	d					
Highbury & Islington	a					
	d					
London Bridge 4 ⊖	a			23 56		00 41

Saturdays

18 August to 25 August

		LO	LO	LO	SN	SN	SN	SN	LO	LO		LO	LO	SE	LO	LO	LO	SN	LO	LO		LO	SN	SE	SN
East Croydon	d																						06 30		
West Croydon 4	d		23p22						05 39				05 52				06 09	06 18				06 22			
Norwood Junction 2	d		23p28						05 43				05 58				06 13	06 23				06 28	06 35		
Anerley	d		23p31						05 46				06 01				06 16					06 31	06 38		
Penge West	d		23p33						05 48				06 03				06 18					06 33	06 40		
London Victoria 15 ⊖	d				23p22	23p54																			06 41
Battersea Park 4	d				23p26	23p58																			06 45
Wandsworth Road	d																								06 47
Clapham High Street ⊖	d																								06 49
London Blackfriars 3 ⊖	d													06 12										06 42	
Denmark Hill 4	d													06 22										06 52	06 54
Peckham Rye 4	d						00 12	00 42						06a25										06a55	06 56
Queens Rd Peckham	d																								06 59
South Bermondsey	d																								07 01
Clapham Junction 10	d				23p30	00 02																			
Wandsworth Common	d				23p33	00 05																			
Balham 4 ⊖	d				23p35	00 07																			
Streatham Hill	d				23p38	00 10																			
West Norwood 4	d				23p42	00 14	00 24	00 54																	
Gipsy Hill	d				23p45	00 17	00 27	00 57																	
Crystal Palace 4	d			23p43	23p51	00 21	00a29	00a59				05 58				06 13		06a27		06 28					
Sydenham	d		23p36	23p46	23p54	00 24			05 51			06 01	06 06			06 16	06 21			06 31		06 36	06 42		
Forest Hill 4	d		23p38	23p49	23p57	00 27			05 53			06 04	06 08			06 19	06 23			06 34		06 38	06 45		
Honor Oak Park	d		23p41	23p51	23p59	00 29			05 56			06 06	06 11			06 21	06 26			06 36		06 41	06 47		
Brockley	d		23p43	23p54	00 02	00 32			05 58			06 09	06 13			06 24	06 28			06 39		06 43	06 50		
New Cross Gate 4	a		23p46	23p56	00 04	00 34			06 01			06 11	06 16			06 26	06 31			06 41		06 46	06 52		
	d		23p46	23p56	00 04	00 34			06 01			06 11	06 16			06 26	06 31			06 41		06 46	06 52		
New Cross ELL	d	23p36								06 06					06 21				06 36						
Surrey Quays	d	23p40	23p49	23p59					06 05	06 10		06 15	06 19		06 25	06 30	06 35		06 40	06 45		06 49			
Canada Water	d	23p42	23p51	00 02					06 07	06 12		06 17	06 21		06 27	06 32	06 37		06 42	06 47		06 51			
Rotherhithe	d	23p43	23p53	00 03					06 08	06 13		06 18	06 23		06 28	06 33	06 38		06 43	06 48		06 53			
Wapping	d	23p45	23p54	00 05					06 10	06 15		06 20	06 24		06 30	06 35	06 40		06 45	06 50		06 54			
Shadwell	d	23p47	23p56	00 07					06 12	06 17		06 22	06 26		06 32	06 37	06 42		06 47	06 52		06 56			
Whitechapel	d	23p49	23p59	00 09					06 14	06 19		06 24	06 29		06 34	06 39	06 44		06 49	06 54		06 59			
Shoreditch High Street	d	23p51	00 01	00 11					06 16	06 21		06 26	06 31		06 36	06 41	06 46		06 51	06 56		07 01			
Hoxton	d	23p53	00 03	00 13					06 18	06 23		06 28	06 33		06 38	06 43	06 48		06 53	06 58		07 03			
Haggerston	d	23p55	00 05	00 15					06 20	06 25		06 30	06 35		06 40	06 45	06 50		06 55	07 00		07 05			
Dalston Junction Stn ELL	a	00 02	00 07	00 17					06 22	06 28		06 32	06 37		06 43	06 47	06 52		06 58	07 02		07 07			
Canonbury	d		00 12	00 20					06 27			06 35	06 42			06 50	06 57			07 05		07 12			
Highbury & Islington	a		00 19	00 28					06 32			06 40	06 46			06 56	07 02			07 10		07 16			
	d																								
London Bridge 4 ⊖	a				00 11	00 41																	06 59		07 06

East London Line and Croydon - London Victoria to London Bridge

Network Diagram - see first Page of Table 177

		SN	LO	LO	LO	SN		SN	LO	LO	LO	SN	SE	SN	SN	LO		LO	LO	LO	LO	LO	SN	LO	LO
East Croydon	d					06 43						07 00											07 30		
West Croydon 4	d				06 39			06 45			06 52				07 01				07 09			07 22			
Norwood Junction 2	d	06 41			06 43	06 50		06 53			06 58	07 05							07 13			07 28	07 35		
Anerley	d				06 46						07 01	07 08							07 16			07 31	07 38		
Penge West	d				06 48						07 03	07 10							07 18			07 33	07 40		
London Victoria 15	d													07 11											
Battersea Park 4	d													07 15											
Wandsworth Road	d													07 17											
Clapham High Street	d													07 19											
London Blackfriars 3	d												07 12												
Denmark Hill 4	d												07 22	07 24											
Peckham Rye 4	d	07 01											07a25	07 26	07 31										
Queens Rd Peckham	d	07 04												07 29	07 34										
South Bermondsey	d	07 06												07 31	07 36										
Clapham Junction 10	d																								
Wandsworth Common	d																								
Balham 4	d																								
Streatham Hill	d																								
West Norwood 4	d																								
Gipsy Hill	d																								
Crystal Palace 4	d			06 43				06a57		06 58								07 13			07 28				07 43
Sydenham	d			06 46	06 51	06 54				07 01	07 06	07 12						07 16	07 21		07 31	07 36	07 42		07 46
Forest Hill 4	d			06 49	06 53	06 57				07 04	07 08	07 15						07 19	07 23		07 34	07 38	07 45		07 49
Honor Oak Park	d			06 51	06 56	06 59				07 06	07 11	07 17						07 21	07 26		07 36	07 41	07 47		07 51
Brockley	d			06 54	06 58	07 02				07 09	07 13	07 20						07 24	07 28		07 39	07 43	07 50		07 54
New Cross Gate 4	a			06 56	07 01	07 04				07 11	07 16	07 22						07 26	07 31		07 41	07 46	07 52		07 56
	d			06 56	07 01	07 04				07 11	07 16	07 22						07 26	07 31		07 41	07 46	07 52		07 56
New Cross ELL	d		06 51						07 06							07 21				07 36				07 51	
Surrey Quays	d		06 55	07 00	07 05				07 10	07 15	07 19					07 25		07 30	07 35	07 40	07 45	07 49		07 55	08 00
Canada Water	d		06 57	07 02	07 07				07 12	07 17	07 21					07 27		07 32	07 37	07 42	07 47	07 51		07 57	08 02
Rotherhithe	d		06 58	07 03	07 08				07 13	07 18	07 23					07 28		07 33	07 38	07 43	07 48	07 53		07 58	08 03
Wapping	d		07 00	07 05	07 10				07 15	07 20	07 24					07 30		07 35	07 40	07 45	07 50	07 54		08 00	08 05
Shadwell	d		07 02	07 07	07 12				07 17	07 22	07 26					07 32		07 37	07 42	07 47	07 52	07 56		08 02	08 07
Whitechapel	d		07 04	07 09	07 14				07 19	07 24	07 29					07 34		07 39	07 44	07 49	07 54	07 59		08 04	08 09
Shoreditch High Street	d		07 06	07 11	07 16				07 21	07 26	07 31					07 36		07 41	07 46	07 51	07 56	08 01		08 06	08 11
Hoxton	d		07 08	07 13	07 18				07 23	07 28	07 33					07 38		07 43	07 48	07 53	07 58	08 03		08 08	08 13
Haggerston	d		07 10	07 15	07 20				07 25	07 30	07 35					07 40		07 45	07 50	07 55	08 00	08 05		08 10	08 15
Dalston Junction Stn ELL	a		07 13	07 17	07 22				07 28	07 32	07 37					07 43		07 47	07 52	07 58	08 02	08 07		08 13	08 17
Canonbury	d			07 20	07 27					07 35	07 42							07 50	07 57		08 05	08 12			08 20
Highbury & Islington	a			07 25	07 32					07 40	07 46							07 55	08 02		08 10	08 16			08 25
	d																								
London Bridge 4	a	07 14				07 11						07 29		07 36	07 41								07 59		

		LO		SN	SE	SE	SN	SN	LO	LO	LO	SN		LO	LO	SN	LO	SN	SE	SE	SN	SN		LO	LO
East Croydon	d											08 00													
West Croydon 4	d							07 31	07 39		07 52											08 01		08 09	
Norwood Junction 2	d								07 43		07 58	08 05												08 13	
Anerley	d								07 46		08 01	08 08												08 16	
Penge West	d								07 48		08 03	08 10												08 18	
London Victoria 15	d				07 39		07 41									07 49			08 09		08 11				
Battersea Park 4	d						07 45									07 53					08 15				
Wandsworth Road	d						07 47														08 17				
Clapham High Street	d						07 49														08 19				
London Blackfriars 3	d					07 42														08 12					
Denmark Hill 4	d				07 48	07 52	07 54												08 18	08 22	08 24				
Peckham Rye 4	d			07 42	07a51	07a55	07 56	08 01										08 12	08a21	08a25	08 26	08 31			
Queens Rd Peckham	d						07 59	08 04													08 29	08 34			
South Bermondsey	d						08 01	08 06													08 31	08 36			
Clapham Junction 10	d															07 57									
Wandsworth Common	d															08 00									
Balham 4	d															08 02									
Streatham Hill	d															08 05									
West Norwood 4	d			07 53												08 10		08 23							
Gipsy Hill	d			07 56												08 13		08 26							
Crystal Palace 4	d	07 58		07a59											08 13	08 21	08 28	08a29							
Sydenham	d	08 01							07 51		08 06	08 12			08 16	08 24	08 31							08 21	
Forest Hill 4	d	08 04							07 53		08 08	08 15			08 19	08 27	08 34							08 23	
Honor Oak Park	d	08 06							07 56		08 11	08 17			08 21	08 29	08 36							08 26	
Brockley	d	08 09							07 58		08 13	08 20			08 24	08 32	08 39							08 28	
New Cross Gate 4	a	08 11							08 01		08 16	08 22			08 26	08 34	08 41							08 31	
	d	08 11							08 01		08 16	08 22			08 26	08 34	08 41							08 31	
New Cross ELL	d									08 06				08 21											08 36
Surrey Quays	d	08 15							08 05	08 10	08 19			08 25	08 30		08 45							08 35	08 40
Canada Water	d	08 17							08 07	08 12	08 21			08 27	08 32		08 47							08 37	08 42
Rotherhithe	d	08 18							08 08	08 13	08 23			08 28	08 33		08 48							08 38	08 43
Wapping	d	08 20							08 10	08 15	08 24			08 30	08 35		08 50							08 40	08 45
Shadwell	d	08 22							08 12	08 17	08 26			08 32	08 37		08 52							08 42	08 47
Whitechapel	d	08 24							08 14	08 19	08 29			08 34	08 39		08 54							08 44	08 49
Shoreditch High Street	d	08 26							08 16	08 21	08 31			08 36	08 41		08 56							08 46	08 51
Hoxton	d	08 28							08 18	08 23	08 33			08 38	08 43		08 58							08 48	08 53
Haggerston	d	08 30							08 20	08 25	08 35			08 40	08 45		09 00							08 50	08 55
Dalston Junction Stn ELL	a	08 32							08 22	08 28	08 37			08 43	08 47		09 02							08 52	08 58
Canonbury	d	08 35							08 27		08 42				08 50		09 05							08 57	
Highbury & Islington	a	08 40							08 32		08 46				08 55		09 10							09 02	
	d																								
London Bridge 4	a						08 06	08 11				08 29				08 41					08 36	08 41			

Table 178

Saturdays

18 August to 25 August

East London Line and Croydon - London Victoria to London Bridge

Network Diagram - see first Page of Table 177

		LO	SN	LO	LO	SN	LO	SN		SN	SE	SE	SN	SN	LO	LO	LO	SN		LO	LO	SN	LO	SN	SN
East Croydon ⇌	d		08 30															09 00							
West Croydon 4 ⇌	d	08 22												08 31	08 39		08 52								
Norwood Junction 2	d	08 28	08 35												08 43		08 58	09 05							
Anerley	d	08 31	08 38												08 46		09 01	09 08							
Penge West	d	08 33	08 40												08 48		09 03	09 10							
London Victoria 15 ⊖	d					08 19					08 39		08 41									08 49			
Battersea Park 4	d					08 23							08 45									08 53			
Wandsworth Road	d												08 47												
Clapham High Street ⊖	d												08 49												
London Blackfriars 3 ⊖	d											08 42													
Denmark Hill 4	d										08 48	08 52	08 54												
Peckham Rye 4	d							08 42		08 46	08a51	08a55	08 56	09 01										09 12	09 16
Queens Rd Peckham	d									08 49			08 59	09 04											09 19
South Bermondsey	d									08 51			09 01	09 06											09 21
Clapham Junction 10	d					08 27																08 57			
Wandsworth Common	d					08 30																09 00			
Balham 4 ⊖	d					08 32																09 02			
Streatham Hill	d					08 35																09 05			
West Norwood 4	d					08 40		08 53														09 10		09 23	
Gipsy Hill	d					08 43		08 56														09 13		09 26	
Crystal Palace 4	d				08 43	08 51	08 58	08a59													09 13	09 21	09 28	09a29	
Sydenham	d	08 36	08 42		08 46	08 54	09 01								08 51		09 06	09 12			09 16	09 24	09 31		
Forest Hill 4	d	08 38	08 45		08 49	08 57	09 04								08 53		09 08	09 15			09 19	09 27	09 34		
Honor Oak Park	d	08 41	08 47		08 51	08 59	09 06								08 56		09 11	09 17			09 21	09 29	09 36		
Brockley	d	08 43	08 50		08 54	09 02	09 09								08 58		09 13	09 20			09 24	09 32	09 39		
New Cross Gate 4	a	08 46	08 52		08 56	09 04	09 11								09 01		09 16	09 22			09 26	09 34	09 41		
	d	08 46	08 52		08 56	09 04	09 11								09 01		09 16	09 22			09 26	09 34	09 41		
New Cross ELL	d			08 51												09 06				09 21					
Surrey Quays	d	08 49		08 55	09 00		09 15								09 05	09 10	09 19			09 25	09 30		09 45		
Canada Water	d	08 51		08 57	09 02		09 17								09 07	09 12	09 21			09 27	09 32		09 47		
Rotherhithe	d	08 53		08 58	09 03		09 18								09 08	09 13	09 23			09 28	09 33		09 48		
Wapping	d	08 54		09 00	09 05		09 20								09 10	09 15	09 24			09 30	09 35		09 50		
Shadwell	d	08 56		09 02	09 07		09 22								09 12	09 17	09 26			09 32	09 37		09 52		
Whitechapel	d	08 59		09 04	09 09		09 24								09 14	09 19	09 29			09 34	09 39		09 54		
Shoreditch High Street	d	09 01		09 06	09 11		09 26								09 16	09 21	09 31			09 36	09 41		09 56		
Hoxton	d	09 03		09 08	09 13		09 28								09 18	09 23	09 33			09 38	09 43		09 58		
Haggerston	d	09 05		09 10	09 15		09 30								09 20	09 25	09 35			09 40	09 45		10 00		
Dalston Junction Stn ELL	a	09 07		09 13	09 17		09 32								09 22	09 28	09 37			09 43	09 47		10 02		
Canonbury	d	09 12			09 20		09 35								09 27		09 42				09 50		10 05		
Highbury & Islington	a	09 16			09 25		09 40								09 32		09 46				09 55		10 10		
	d																								
London Bridge 4 ⊖	a		08 59			09 11				08 56			09 06	09 11				09 29				09 41			09 26

		SE	SE	SN		SN	LO	LO	LO	SN	LO	LO	SN	LO		SN	SN	SE	SE	SN	SN	LO	LO	LO	
East Croydon ⇌	d									09 30															
West Croydon 4 ⇌	d					09 01	09 09		09 22												09 31	09 39		09 52	
Norwood Junction 2	d						09 13		09 28	09 35												09 43		09 58	
Anerley	d						09 16		09 31	09 38												09 46		10 01	
Penge West	d						09 18		09 33	09 40												09 48		10 03	
London Victoria 15 ⊖	d	09 09		09 11									09 19					09 39		09 41					
Battersea Park 4	d			09 15									09 23							09 45					
Wandsworth Road	d			09 17																09 47					
Clapham High Street ⊖	d			09 19																09 49					
London Blackfriars 3 ⊖	d		09 12																09 42						
Denmark Hill 4	d	09 18	09 22	09 24														09 48	09 52	09 54					
Peckham Rye 4	d	09a21	09a25	09 26		09 31										09 42	09 46	09a51	09a55	09 56	10 01				
Queens Rd Peckham	d			09 29		09 34											09 49			09 59	10 04				
South Bermondsey	d			09 31		09 36											09 51			10 01	10 06				
Clapham Junction 10	d												09 27												
Wandsworth Common	d												09 30												
Balham 4 ⊖	d												09 32												
Streatham Hill	d												09 35												
West Norwood 4	d												09 40			09 53									
Gipsy Hill	d												09 43			09 56									
Crystal Palace 4	d											09 43	09 51	09 58		09a59									
Sydenham	d						09 21		09 36	09 42		09 46	09 54	10 01								09 51		10 06	
Forest Hill 4	d						09 23		09 38	09 45		09 49	09 57	10 04								09 53		10 08	
Honor Oak Park	d						09 26		09 41	09 47		09 51	09 59	10 06								09 56		10 11	
Brockley	d						09 28		09 43	09 50		09 54	10 02	10 09								09 58		10 13	
New Cross Gate 4	a						09 31		09 46	09 52		09 56	10 04	10 11								10 01		10 16	
	d						09 31		09 46	09 52		09 56	10 04	10 11								10 01		10 16	
New Cross ELL	d							09 36			09 51												10 06		
Surrey Quays	d						09 35	09 40	09 49		09 55	10 00		10 15								10 05	10 10	10 19	
Canada Water	d						09 37	09 42	09 51		09 57	10 02		10 17								10 07	10 12	10 21	
Rotherhithe	d						09 38	09 43	09 53		09 58	10 03		10 18								10 08	10 13	10 23	
Wapping	d						09 40	09 45	09 54		10 00	10 05		10 20								10 10	10 15	10 24	
Shadwell	d						09 42	09 47	09 56		10 02	10 07		10 22								10 12	10 17	10 26	
Whitechapel	d						09 44	09 49	09 59		10 04	10 09		10 24								10 14	10 19	10 29	
Shoreditch High Street	d						09 46	09 51	10 01		10 06	10 11		10 26								10 16	10 21	10 31	
Hoxton	d						09 48	09 53	10 03		10 08	10 13		10 28								10 18	10 23	10 33	
Haggerston	d						09 50	09 55	10 05		10 10	10 15		10 30								10 20	10 25	10 35	
Dalston Junction Stn ELL	a						09 52	09 58	10 07		10 13	10 17		10 32								10 22	10 28	10 37	
Canonbury	d						09 57		10 12			10 20		10 35								10 27		10 42	
Highbury & Islington	a						10 02		10 16			10 25		10 40								10 32		10 46	
	d																								
London Bridge 4 ⊖	a			09 36		09 41				09 59			10 11				09 56			10 06	10 11				

Table 178

Saturdays

18 August to 25 August

East London Line and Croydon - London Victoria to London Bridge

Network Diagram - see first Page of Table 177

		SN	LO	LO	SN	LO	SN	SN	SE	SE		SN	SN	LO	LO	LO	SN	LO	LO	SN		LO	SN	SN	SE
East Croydon	d	10 00															10 30								
West Croydon 4	d												10 01	10 09		10 22									
Norwood Junction 2	d	10 05												10 13		10 28	10 35								
Anerley	d	10 08												10 16		10 31	10 38								
Penge West	d	10 10												10 18		10 33	10 40								
London Victoria 15 ⊖	d				09 49				10 09			10 11								10 19					10 39
Battersea Park 4	d				09 53							10 15								10 23					
Wandsworth Road	d											10 17													
Clapham High Street ⊖	d											10 19													
London Blackfriars 3 ⊖	d									10 12															
Denmark Hill 4	d								10 18	10 22		10 24													10 48
Peckham Rye 4	d						10 12	10 16	10a21	10a25		10 26	10 31										10 42	10 46	10a51
Queens Rd Peckham	d							10 19				10 29	10 34											10 49	
South Bermondsey	d							10 21				10 31	10 36											10 51	
Clapham Junction 10	d				09 57															10 27					
Wandsworth Common	d				10 00															10 30					
Balham 4 ⊖	d				10 02															10 32					
Streatham Hill	d				10 05															10 35					
West Norwood 4	d				10 10		10 23													10 40			10 53		
Gipsy Hill	d				10 13		10 26													10 43			10 56		
Crystal Palace 4	d			10 13	10 21	10 28	10a29												10 43	10 51		10 58	10a59		
Sydenham	d	10 12		10 16	10 24	10 31								10 21		10 36	10 42		10 46	10 54		11 01			
Forest Hill 4	d	10 15		10 19	10 27	10 34								10 23		10 38	10 45		10 49	10 57		11 04			
Honor Oak Park	d	10 17		10 21	10 29	10 36								10 26		10 41	10 47		10 51	10 59		11 06			
Brockley	d	10 20		10 24	10 32	10 39								10 28		10 43	10 50		10 54	11 02		11 09			
New Cross Gate 4	a	10 22		10 26	10 34	10 41								10 31		10 46	10 52		10 56	11 04		11 11			
	d	10 22		10 26	10 34	10 41								10 31		10 46	10 52		10 56	11 04		11 11			
New Cross ELL	d		10 21												10 36			10 51							
Surrey Quays	d		10 25	10 30		10 45								10 35	10 40	10 49		10 55	11 00			11 15			
Canada Water	d		10 27	10 32		10 47								10 37	10 42	10 51		10 57	11 02			11 17			
Rotherhithe	d		10 28	10 33		10 48								10 38	10 43	10 53		10 58	11 03			11 18			
Wapping	d		10 30	10 35		10 50								10 40	10 45	10 54		11 00	11 05			11 20			
Shadwell	d		10 32	10 37		10 52								10 42	10 47	10 56		11 02	11 07			11 22			
Whitechapel	d		10 34	10 39		10 54								10 44	10 49	10 59		11 04	11 09			11 24			
Shoreditch High Street	d		10 36	10 41		10 56								10 46	10 51	11 01		11 06	11 11			11 26			
Hoxton	d		10 38	10 43		10 58								10 48	10 53	11 03		11 08	11 13			11 28			
Haggerston	d		10 40	10 45		11 00								10 50	10 55	11 05		11 10	11 15			11 30			
Dalston Junction Stn ELL	a		10 43	10 47		11 02								10 52	10 58	11 07		11 13	11 17			11 32			
Canonbury	d			10 50		11 05								10 57		11 12			11 20			11 35			
Highbury & Islington	a			10 55		11 10								11 02		11 16			11 25			11 40			
	d																								
London Bridge 4 ⊖	a	10 29			10 41			10 26				10 36	10 41				10 59			11 11				10 56	

		SE	SN	SN	LO	LO		LO	SN	LO	LO	SN	LO	SN	SN	SE		SE	SN	SN	LO	LO	LO	SN	LO
East Croydon	d								11 00															11 30	
West Croydon 4	d			10 31	10 39			10 52												11 01	11 09		11 22		
Norwood Junction 2	d				10 43			10 58	11 05												11 13		11 28	11 35	
Anerley	d				10 46			11 01	11 08												11 16		11 31	11 38	
Penge West	d				10 48			11 03	11 10												11 18		11 33	11 40	
London Victoria 15 ⊖	d		10 41									10 49				11 09			11 11						
Battersea Park 4	d		10 45									10 53							11 15						
Wandsworth Road	d		10 47																11 17						
Clapham High Street ⊖	d		10 49																11 19						
London Blackfriars 3 ⊖	d	10 42																11 12							
Denmark Hill 4	d	10 52	10 54													11 18		11 22	11 24						
Peckham Rye 4	d	10a55	10 56	11 01										11 12	11 16	11a21		11a25	11 26	11 31					
Queens Rd Peckham	d		10 59	11 04											11 19				11 29	11 34					
South Bermondsey	d		11 01	11 06											11 21				11 31	11 36					
Clapham Junction 10	d											10 57													
Wandsworth Common	d											11 00													
Balham 4 ⊖	d											11 02													
Streatham Hill	d											11 05													
West Norwood 4	d											11 10		11 23											
Gipsy Hill	d											11 13		11 26											
Crystal Palace 4	d										11 13	11 21	11 28	11a29											
Sydenham	d				10 51			11 06	11 12		11 16	11 24	11 31								11 21		11 36	11 42	
Forest Hill 4	d				10 53			11 08	11 15		11 19	11 27	11 34								11 23		11 38	11 45	
Honor Oak Park	d				10 56			11 11	11 17		11 21	11 29	11 36								11 26		11 41	11 47	
Brockley	d				10 58			11 13	11 20		11 24	11 32	11 39								11 28		11 43	11 50	
New Cross Gate 4	a				11 01			11 16	11 22		11 26	11 34	11 41								11 31		11 46	11 52	
	d				11 01			11 16	11 22		11 26	11 34	11 41								11 31		11 46	11 52	
New Cross ELL	d					11 06				11 21												11 36			11 51
Surrey Quays	d				11 05	11 10		11 19		11 25	11 30		11 45								11 35	11 40	11 49		11 55
Canada Water	d				11 07	11 12		11 21		11 27	11 32		11 47								11 37	11 42	11 51		11 57
Rotherhithe	d				11 08	11 13		11 23		11 28	11 33		11 48								11 38	11 43	11 53		11 58
Wapping	d				11 10	11 15		11 24		11 30	11 35		11 50								11 40	11 45	11 54		12 00
Shadwell	d				11 12	11 17		11 26		11 32	11 37		11 52								11 42	11 47	11 56		12 02
Whitechapel	d				11 14	11 19		11 29		11 34	11 39		11 54								11 44	11 49	11 59		12 04
Shoreditch High Street	d				11 16	11 21		11 31		11 36	11 41		11 56								11 46	11 51	12 01		12 06
Hoxton	d				11 18	11 23		11 33		11 38	11 43		11 58								11 48	11 53	12 03		12 08
Haggerston	d				11 20	11 25		11 35		11 40	11 45		12 00								11 50	11 55	12 05		12 10
Dalston Junction Stn ELL	a				11 22	11 28		11 37		11 43	11 47		12 02								11 52	11 58	12 07		12 13
Canonbury	d				11 27			11 42			11 50		12 05								11 57		12 12		
Highbury & Islington	a				11 32			11 46			11 55		12 10								12 02		12 16		
	d																								
London Bridge 4 ⊖	a		11 06	11 11					11 29			11 41			11 26				11 36	11 41				11 59	

Table 178

Saturdays

18 August to 25 August

East London Line and Croydon - London Victoria to London Bridge

Network Diagram - see first Page of Table 177

Station		LO		SN	LO	SN	SN	SE	SE	SN	SN	LO		LO	LO	SN	LO	LO	SN	LO	SN	SN		SE	SE
East Croydon	d															12 00									
West Croydon 4	d										11 31	11 39			11 52										
Norwood Junction 2	d											11 43			11 58	12 05									
Anerley	d											11 46			12 01	12 08									
Penge West	d											11 48			12 03	12 10									
London Victoria 15 ⊖	d			11 19				11 39		11 41									11 49					12 09	
Battersea Park 4	d			11 23						11 45									11 53						
Wandsworth Road	d									11 47															
Clapham High Street ⊖	d									11 49															
London Blackfriars 3 ⊖	d								11 42																12 12
Denmark Hill 4	d							11 48	11 52	11 54														12 18	12 22
Peckham Rye 4	d					11 42	11 46	11a51	11a55	11 56	12 01										12 12	12 16		12a21	12a25
Queens Rd Peckham	d						11 49			11 59	12 04											12 19			
South Bermondsey	d						11 51			12 01	12 06											12 21			
Clapham Junction 10	d			11 27															11 57						
Wandsworth Common	d			11 30															12 00						
Balham 4 ⊖	d			11 32															12 02						
Streatham Hill	d			11 35															12 05						
West Norwood 4	d			11 40		11 53													12 10		12 23				
Gipsy Hill	d			11 43		11 56													12 13		12 26				
Crystal Palace 4	d	11 43		11 51	11 58	11a59												12 13	12 21	12 28	12a29				
Sydenham	d	11 46		11 54	12 01							11 51			12 06	12 12		12 16	12 24	12 31					
Forest Hill 4	d	11 49		11 57	12 04							11 53			12 08	12 15		12 19	12 27	12 34					
Honor Oak Park	d	11 51		11 59	12 06							11 56			12 11	12 17		12 21	12 29	12 36					
Brockley	d	11 54		12 02	12 09							11 58			12 13	12 20		12 24	12 32	12 39					
New Cross Gate 4	a	11 56		12 04	12 11							12 01			12 16	12 22		12 26	12 34	12 41					
	d	11 56		12 04	12 11							12 01			12 16	12 22		12 26	12 34	12 41					
New Cross ELL	d													12 06			12 21								
Surrey Quays	d	12 00			12 15							12 05		12 10	12 19		12 25	12 30		12 45					
Canada Water	d	12 02			12 17							12 07		12 12	12 21		12 27	12 32		12 47					
Rotherhithe	d	12 03			12 18							12 08		12 13	12 23		12 28	12 33		12 48					
Wapping	d	12 05			12 20							12 10		12 15	12 24		12 30	12 35		12 50					
Shadwell	d	12 07			12 22							12 12		12 17	12 26		12 32	12 37		12 52					
Whitechapel	d	12 09			12 24							12 14		12 19	12 29		12 34	12 39		12 54					
Shoreditch High Street	d	12 11			12 26							12 16		12 21	12 31		12 36	12 41		12 56					
Hoxton	d	12 13			12 28							12 18		12 23	12 33		12 38	12 43		12 58					
Haggerston	d	12 15			12 30							12 20		12 25	12 35		12 40	12 45		13 00					
Dalston Junction Stn ELL	a	12 17			12 32							12 22		12 28	12 37		12 43	12 47		13 02					
Canonbury	d	12 20			12 35							12 27			12 42			12 50		13 05					
Highbury & Islington	a	12 25			12 40							12 32			12 46			12 55		13 10					
	d																								
London Bridge 4 ⊖	a			12 11			11 56			12 06	12 11					12 29			12 44			12 26			

Station		SN	SN	LO	LO	LO	SN	LO		LO	SN	LO	SN	SN	SE	SE	SN	SN		LO	LO	LO	SN	LO	LO
East Croydon	d						12 30																13 00		
West Croydon 4	d		12 01	12 09		12 22												12 31		12 39		12 52			
Norwood Junction 2	d			12 13		12 28	12 35													12 43		12 58	13 05		
Anerley	d			12 16		12 31	12 38													12 46		13 01	13 08		
Penge West	d			12 18		12 33	12 40													12 48		13 03	13 10		
London Victoria 15 ⊖	d	12 11									12 19				12 39		12 41								
Battersea Park 4	d	12 15									12 23						12 45								
Wandsworth Road	d	12 17															12 47								
Clapham High Street ⊖	d	12 19															12 49								
London Blackfriars 3 ⊖	d															12 42									
Denmark Hill 4	d	12 24													12 48	12 52	12 54								
Peckham Rye 4	d	12 26	12 31										12 42	12 46	12a51	12a55	12 56	13 01							
Queens Rd Peckham	d	12 29	12 34											12 49			12 59	13 04							
South Bermondsey	d	12 31	12 36											12 51			13 01	13 06							
Clapham Junction 10	d										12 27														
Wandsworth Common	d										12 30														
Balham 4 ⊖	d										12 32														
Streatham Hill	d										12 35														
West Norwood 4	d										12 40		12 53												
Gipsy Hill	d										12 43		12 56												
Crystal Palace 4	d									12 43	12 51	12 58	12a59												13 13
Sydenham	d			12 21		12 36	12 42			12 46	12 54	13 01								12 51		13 06	13 12		13 16
Forest Hill 4	d			12 23		12 38	12 45			12 49	12 57	13 04								12 53		13 08	13 15		13 19
Honor Oak Park	d			12 26		12 41	12 47			12 51	12 59	13 06								12 56		13 11	13 17		13 21
Brockley	d			12 28		12 43	12 50			12 54	13 02	13 09								12 58		13 13	13 20		13 24
New Cross Gate 4	a			12 31		12 46	12 52			12 56	13 04	13 11								13 01		13 16	13 22		13 26
	d			12 31		12 46	12 52			12 56	13 04	13 11								13 01		13 16	13 22		13 26
New Cross ELL	d				12 36			12 51													13 06			13 21	
Surrey Quays	d			12 35	12 40	12 49		12 55		13 00		13 15								13 05	13 10	13 19		13 25	13 30
Canada Water	d			12 37	12 42	12 51		12 57		13 02		13 17								13 07	13 12	13 21		13 27	13 32
Rotherhithe	d			12 38	12 43	12 53		12 58		13 03		13 18								13 08	13 13	13 23		13 28	13 33
Wapping	d			12 40	12 45	12 54		13 00		13 05		13 20								13 10	13 15	13 24		13 30	13 35
Shadwell	d			12 42	12 47	12 56		13 02		13 07		13 22								13 12	13 17	13 26		13 32	13 37
Whitechapel	d			12 44	12 49	12 59		13 04		13 09		13 24								13 14	13 19	13 29		13 34	13 39
Shoreditch High Street	d			12 46	12 51	13 01		13 06		13 11		13 26								13 16	13 21	13 31		13 36	13 41
Hoxton	d			12 48	12 53	13 03		13 08		13 13		13 28								13 18	13 23	13 33		13 38	13 43
Haggerston	d			12 50	12 55	13 05		13 10		13 15		13 30								13 20	13 25	13 35		13 40	13 45
Dalston Junction Stn ELL	a			12 52	12 58	13 07		13 13		13 17		13 32								13 22	13 28	13 37		13 43	13 47
Canonbury	d			12 57		13 12				13 20		13 35								13 27		13 42			13 50
Highbury & Islington	a			13 02		13 16				13 25		13 40								13 32		13 46			13 55
	d																								
London Bridge 4 ⊖	a	12 36	12 41				12 59				13 11			12 56			13 06	13 11					13 29		

Table 178

Saturdays

18 August to 25 August

East London Line and Croydon - London Victoria to London Bridge

Network Diagram - see first Page of Table 177

		SN	LO	SN		SN	SE	SE	SN	SN	LO	LO	LO	SN		LO	LO	SN	LO	SN	SN	SE	SE	SN
East Croydon	d													13 30										
West Croydon 4	d									13 01	13 09		13 22											
Norwood Junction 2	d										13 13		13 28	13 35										
Anerley	d										13 16		13 31	13 38										
Penge West	d										13 18		13 33	13 40										
London Victoria 15 ⊖	d	12 49					13 09		13 11									13 19				13 39		13 41
Battersea Park 4	d	12 53							13 15									13 23						13 45
Wandsworth Road	d								13 17															13 47
Clapham High Street ⊖	d								13 19															13 49
London Blackfriars 3 ⊖	d							13 12															13 42	
Denmark Hill 4	d						13 18	13 22	13 24													13 48	13 52	13 54
Peckham Rye 4	d			13 12		13 16	13a21	13a25	13 26	13 31										13 42	13 46	13a51	13a55	13 56
Queens Rd Peckham	d					13 19			13 29	13 34											13 49			13 59
South Bermondsey	d					13 21			13 31	13 36											13 51			14 01
Clapham Junction 10	d	12 57																13 27						
Wandsworth Common	d	13 00																13 30						
Balham 4 ⊖	d	13 02																13 32						
Streatham Hill	d	13 05																13 35						
West Norwood 4	d	13 10		13 23														13 40		13 53				
Gipsy Hill	d	13 13		13 26														13 43		13 56				
Crystal Palace 4	d	13 21	13 28	13a29													13 43	13 51	13 58	13a59				
Sydenham	d	13 24	13 31								13 21		13 36	13 42			13 46	13 54	14 01					
Forest Hill 4	d	13 27	13 34								13 23		13 38	13 45			13 49	13 57	14 04					
Honor Oak Park	d	13 29	13 36								13 26		13 41	13 47			13 51	13 59	14 06					
Brockley	d	13 32	13 39								13 28		13 43	13 50			13 54	14 02	14 09					
New Cross Gate 4	a	13 34	13 41								13 31		13 46	13 52			13 56	14 04	14 11					
	d	13 34	13 41								13 31		13 46	13 52			13 56	14 04	14 11					
New Cross ELL	d											13 36				13 51								
Surrey Quays	d		13 45								13 35	13 40	13 49			13 55	14 00		14 15					
Canada Water	d		13 47								13 37	13 42	13 51			13 57	14 02		14 17					
Rotherhithe	d		13 48								13 38	13 43	13 53			13 58	14 03		14 18					
Wapping	d		13 50								13 40	13 45	13 54			14 00	14 05		14 20					
Shadwell	d		13 52								13 42	13 47	13 56			14 02	14 07		14 22					
Whitechapel	d		13 54								13 44	13 49	13 59			14 04	14 09		14 24					
Shoreditch High Street	d		13 56								13 46	13 51	14 01			14 06	14 11		14 26					
Hoxton	d		13 58								13 48	13 53	14 03			14 08	14 13		14 28					
Haggerston	d		14 00								13 50	13 55	14 05			14 10	14 15		14 30					
Dalston Junction Stn ELL	a		14 02								13 52	13 58	14 07			14 13	14 17		14 32					
Canonbury	d		14 05								13 57		14 12				14 20		14 35					
Highbury & Islington	a		14 10								14 02		14 16				14 25		14 40					
	d																							
London Bridge 4 ⊖	a	13 44				13 26			13 36	13 41				13 59				14 11			13 56			14 06

		SN	LO	LO	LO	SN	LO	LO	SN	LO		SN	SN	SE	SE	SN	SN	LO	LO	LO		SN	LO	LO	SN
East Croydon	d					14 00																14 30			
West Croydon 4	d	13 31	13 39		13 52												14 01	14 09		14 22					
Norwood Junction 2	d		13 43		13 58	14 05												14 13		14 28		14 35			
Anerley	d		13 46		14 01	14 08												14 16		14 31		14 38			
Penge West	d		13 48		14 03	14 10												14 18		14 33		14 40			
London Victoria 15 ⊖	d								13 49					14 09		14 11									14 19
Battersea Park 4	d								13 53							14 15									14 23
Wandsworth Road	d															14 17									
Clapham High Street ⊖	d															14 19									
London Blackfriars 3 ⊖	d														14 12										
Denmark Hill 4	d													14 18	14 22	14 24									
Peckham Rye 4	d	14 01										14 12	14 16	14a21	14a25	14 26	14 31								
Queens Rd Peckham	d	14 04											14 19			14 29	14 34								
South Bermondsey	d	14 06											14 21			14 31	14 36								
Clapham Junction 10	d								13 57																14 27
Wandsworth Common	d								14 00																14 30
Balham 4 ⊖	d								14 02																14 32
Streatham Hill	d								14 05																14 35
West Norwood 4	d								14 10			14 23													14 40
Gipsy Hill	d								14 13			14 26													14 43
Crystal Palace 4	d							14 13	14 21	14 28		14a29												14 43	14 51
Sydenham	d		13 51		14 06	14 12		14 16	14 24	14 31								14 21		14 36		14 42		14 46	14 54
Forest Hill 4	d		13 53		14 08	14 15		14 19	14 27	14 34								14 23		14 38		14 45		14 49	14 57
Honor Oak Park	d		13 56		14 11	14 17		14 21	14 29	14 36								14 26		14 41		14 47		14 51	14 59
Brockley	d		13 58		14 13	14 20		14 24	14 32	14 39								14 28		14 43		14 50		14 54	15 02
New Cross Gate 4	a		14 01		14 16	14 22		14 26	14 34	14 41								14 31		14 46		14 52		14 56	15 04
	d		14 01		14 16	14 22		14 26	14 34	14 41								14 31		14 46		14 52		14 56	15 04
New Cross ELL	d			14 06			14 21												14 36				14 51		
Surrey Quays	d		14 05	14 10	14 19		14 25	14 30		14 45								14 35	14 40	14 49			14 55	15 00	
Canada Water	d		14 07	14 12	14 21		14 27	14 32		14 47								14 37	14 42	14 51			14 57	15 02	
Rotherhithe	d		14 08	14 13	14 23		14 28	14 33		14 48								14 38	14 43	14 53			14 58	15 03	
Wapping	d		14 10	14 15	14 24		14 30	14 35		14 50								14 40	14 45	14 54			15 00	15 05	
Shadwell	d		14 12	14 17	14 26		14 32	14 37		14 52								14 42	14 47	14 56			15 02	15 07	
Whitechapel	d		14 14	14 19	14 29		14 34	14 39		14 54								14 44	14 49	14 59			15 04	15 09	
Shoreditch High Street	d		14 16	14 21	14 31		14 36	14 41		14 56								14 46	14 51	15 01			15 06	15 11	
Hoxton	d		14 18	14 23	14 33		14 38	14 43		14 58								14 48	14 53	15 03			15 08	15 13	
Haggerston	d		14 20	14 25	14 35		14 40	14 45		15 00								14 50	14 55	15 05			15 10	15 15	
Dalston Junction Stn ELL	a		14 22	14 28	14 37		14 43	14 47		15 02								14 52	14 58	15 07			15 13	15 17	
Canonbury	d		14 27		14 42			14 50		15 05								14 57		15 12				15 20	
Highbury & Islington	a		14 32		14 46			14 55		15 10								15 02		15 16				15 25	
	d																								
London Bridge 4 ⊖	a	14 11				14 29			14 44				14 26			14 36	14 41					14 59			15 11

East London Line and Croydon - London Victoria to London Bridge

Network Diagram - see first Page of Table 177

		LO	SN	SN	SE	SE		SN	SN	LO	LO	LO	SN	LO	LO	SN		LO	SN	SN	SE	SE	SN	SN	LO
East Croydon	d												15 00												
West Croydon 4	d								14 31	14 39		14 52												15 01	15 09
Norwood Junction 2	d									14 43		14 58	15 05												15 13
Anerley	d									14 46		15 01	15 08												15 16
Penge West	d									14 48		15 03	15 10												15 18
London Victoria 15 ⊖	d				14 39			14 41								14 49					15 09		15 11		
Battersea Park 4	d							14 45								14 53							15 15		
Wandsworth Road	d							14 47															15 17		
Clapham High Street ⊖	d							14 49															15 19		
London Blackfriars 3 ⊖	d					14 42																15 12			
Denmark Hill 4	d				14 48	14 52		14 54													15 18	15 22	15 24		
Peckham Rye 4	d		14 42	14 46	14a51	14a55		14 56	15 01										15 12	15 16	15a21	15a25	15 26	15 31	
Queens Rd Peckham	d			14 49				14 59	15 04											15 19			15 29	15 34	
South Bermondsey	d			14 51				15 01	15 06											15 21			15 31	15 36	
Clapham Junction 10	d															14 57									
Wandsworth Common	d															15 00									
Balham 4 ⊖	d															15 02									
Streatham Hill	d															15 05									
West Norwood 4	d		14 53													15 10			15 23						
Gipsy Hill	d		14 56													15 13			15 26						
Crystal Palace 4	d	14 58	14a59												15 13	15 21		15 28	15a29						
Sydenham	d	15 01								14 51		15 06	15 12		15 16	15 24		15 31							15 21
Forest Hill 4	d	15 04								14 53		15 08	15 15		15 19	15 27		15 34							15 23
Honor Oak Park	d	15 06								14 56		15 11	15 17		15 21	15 29		15 36							15 26
Brockley	d	15 09								14 58		15 13	15 20		15 24	15 32		15 39							15 28
New Cross Gate 4	a	15 11								15 01		15 16	15 22		15 26	15 34		15 41							15 31
	d	15 11								15 01		15 16	15 22		15 26	15 34		15 41							15 31
New Cross ELL	d										15 06			15 21											
Surrey Quays	d	15 15								15 05	15 10	15 19		15 25	15 30			15 45							15 35
Canada Water	d	15 17								15 07	15 12	15 21		15 27	15 32			15 47							15 37
Rotherhithe	d	15 18								15 08	15 13	15 23		15 28	15 33			15 48							15 38
Wapping	d	15 20								15 10	15 15	15 24		15 30	15 35			15 50							15 40
Shadwell	d	15 22								15 12	15 17	15 26		15 32	15 37			15 52							15 42
Whitechapel	d	15 24								15 14	15 19	15 29		15 34	15 39			15 54							15 44
Shoreditch High Street	d	15 26								15 16	15 21	15 31		15 36	15 41			15 56							15 46
Hoxton	d	15 28								15 18	15 23	15 33		15 38	15 43			15 58							15 48
Haggerston	d	15 30								15 20	15 25	15 35		15 40	15 45			16 00							15 50
Dalston Junction Stn ELL	a	15 32								15 22	15 28	15 37		15 43	15 47			16 02							15 52
Canonbury	d	15 35								15 27		15 42			15 50			16 05							15 57
Highbury & Islington	a	15 40								15 32		15 46			15 55			16 10							16 02
	d																								
London Bridge 4 ⊖	a			14 56				15 06	15 11				15 29			15 44				15 26			15 36	15 41	

		LO		LO	SN	LO	LO	SN	LO	SN	SN	SE		SE	SN	SN	LO	LO	LO	SN	LO	LO		SN	LO
East Croydon	d				15 30															16 00					
West Croydon 4	d			15 22												15 31	15 39		15 52						
Norwood Junction 2	d			15 28	15 35												15 43		15 58	16 05					
Anerley	d			15 31	15 38												15 46		16 01	16 08					
Penge West	d			15 33	15 40												15 48		16 03	16 10					
London Victoria 15 ⊖	d							15 19				15 39			15 41									15 49	
Battersea Park 4	d							15 23							15 45									15 53	
Wandsworth Road	d														15 47										
Clapham High Street ⊖	d														15 49										
London Blackfriars 3 ⊖	d													15 42											
Denmark Hill 4	d											15 48		15 52	15 54										
Peckham Rye 4	d									15 42	15 46	15a51		15a55	15 56	16 01									
Queens Rd Peckham	d										15 49				15 59	16 04									
South Bermondsey	d										15 51				16 01	16 06									
Clapham Junction 10	d							15 27																15 57	
Wandsworth Common	d							15 30																16 00	
Balham 4 ⊖	d							15 32																16 02	
Streatham Hill	d							15 35																16 05	
West Norwood 4	d							15 40		15 53														16 10	
Gipsy Hill	d							15 43		15 56														16 13	
Crystal Palace 4	d						15 43	15 51	15 58	15a59												16 13		16 21	16 28
Sydenham	d			15 36	15 42		15 46	15 54	16 01								15 51		16 06	16 12		16 16		16 24	16 31
Forest Hill 4	d			15 38	15 45		15 49	15 57	16 04								15 53		16 08	16 15		16 19		16 27	16 34
Honor Oak Park	d			15 41	15 47		15 51	15 59	16 06								15 56		16 11	16 17		16 21		16 29	16 36
Brockley	d			15 43	15 50		15 54	16 02	16 09								15 58		16 13	16 20		16 24		16 32	16 39
New Cross Gate 4	a			15 46	15 52		15 56	16 04	16 11								16 01		16 16	16 22		16 26		16 34	16 41
	d			15 46	15 52		15 56	16 04	16 11								16 01		16 16	16 22		16 26		16 34	16 41
New Cross ELL	d	15 36				15 51												16 06			16 21				
Surrey Quays	d	15 40		15 49		15 55	16 00		16 15								16 05	16 10	16 19		16 25	16 30			16 45
Canada Water	d	15 42		15 51		15 57	16 02		16 17								16 07	16 12	16 21		16 27	16 32			16 47
Rotherhithe	d	15 43		15 53		15 58	16 03		16 18								16 08	16 13	16 23		16 28	16 33			16 48
Wapping	d	15 45		15 54		16 00	16 05		16 20								16 10	16 15	16 24		16 30	16 35			16 50
Shadwell	d	15 47		15 56		16 02	16 07		16 22								16 12	16 17	16 26		16 32	16 37			16 52
Whitechapel	d	15 49		15 59		16 04	16 09		16 24								16 14	16 19	16 29		16 34	16 39			16 54
Shoreditch High Street	d	15 51		16 01		16 06	16 11		16 26								16 16	16 21	16 31		16 36	16 41			16 56
Hoxton	d	15 53		16 03		16 08	16 13		16 28								16 18	16 23	16 33		16 38	16 43			16 58
Haggerston	d	15 55		16 05		16 10	16 15		16 30								16 20	16 25	16 35		16 40	16 45			17 00
Dalston Junction Stn ELL	a	15 58		16 07		16 13	16 17		16 32								16 22	16 28	16 37		16 43	16 47			17 02
Canonbury	d			16 12			16 20		16 35								16 27		16 42			16 50			17 05
Highbury & Islington	a			16 16			16 25		16 40								16 32		16 46			16 55			17 10
	d																								
London Bridge 4 ⊖	a				15 59			16 11				15 56			16 06	16 11				16 29				16 41	

Table 178

Saturdays

18 August to 25 August

East London Line and Croydon - London Victoria to London Bridge

Network Diagram - see first Page of Table 177

Station		SN	SN	SE	SE	SN	SN	LO		LO	LO	SN	LO	LO	SN	LO	SN	SN		SE	SE	SN	SN	LO	LO
East Croydon	d											16 30													
West Croydon 4	d						16 01	16 09			16 22												16 31	16 39	
Norwood Junction 2	d							16 13			16 28	16 35												16 43	
Anerley	d							16 16			16 31	16 38												16 46	
Penge West	d							16 18			16 33	16 40												16 48	
London Victoria 15 ⊖	d			16 09		16 11									16 19					16 39		16 41			
Battersea Park 4	d					16 15									16 23							16 45			
Wandsworth Road	d					16 17																16 47			
Clapham High Street ⊖	d					16 19																16 49			
London Blackfriars 3 ⊖	d				16 12																16 42				
Denmark Hill 4	d			16 18	16 22	16 24														16 48	16 52	16 54			
Peckham Rye 4	d	16 12	16 16	16a21	16a25	16 26	16 31										16 42	16 46		16a51	16a55	16 56	17 01		
Queens Rd Peckham	d		16 19			16 29	16 34											16 49				16 59	17 04		
South Bermondsey	d		16 21			16 31	16 36											16 51				17 01	17 06		
Clapham Junction 10	d														16 27										
Wandsworth Common	d														16 30										
Balham 4 ⊖	d														16 32										
Streatham Hill	d														16 35										
West Norwood 4	d	16 23													16 40		16 53								
Gipsy Hill	d	16 26													16 43		16 56								
Crystal Palace 4	d	16a29												16 43	16 51	16 58	16a59								
Sydenham	d							16 21			16 36	16 42		16 46	16 54	17 01								16 51	
Forest Hill 4	d							16 23			16 38	16 45		16 49	16 57	17 04								16 53	
Honor Oak Park	d							16 26			16 41	16 47		16 51	16 59	17 06								16 56	
Brockley	d							16 28			16 43	16 50		16 54	17 02	17 09								16 58	
New Cross Gate 4	a							16 31			16 46	16 52		16 56	17 04	17 11								17 01	
	d							16 31			16 46	16 52		16 56	17 04	17 11								17 01	
New Cross ELL	d									16 36			16 51												17 06
Surrey Quays	d							16 35		16 40	16 49		16 55	17 00		17 15								17 05	17 10
Canada Water	d							16 37		16 42	16 51		16 57	17 02		17 17								17 07	17 12
Rotherhithe	d							16 38		16 43	16 53		16 58	17 03		17 18								17 08	17 13
Wapping	d							16 40		16 45	16 54		17 00	17 05		17 20								17 10	17 15
Shadwell	d							16 42		16 47	16 56		17 02	17 07		17 22								17 12	17 17
Whitechapel	d							16 44		16 49	16 59		17 04	17 09		17 24								17 14	17 19
Shoreditch High Street	d							16 46		16 51	17 01		17 06	17 11		17 26								17 16	17 21
Hoxton	d							16 48		16 53	17 03		17 08	17 13		17 28								17 18	17 23
Haggerston	d							16 50		16 55	17 05		17 10	17 15		17 30								17 20	17 25
Dalston Junction Stn ELL	a							16 52		16 58	17 07		17 13	17 17		17 32								17 22	17 28
Canonbury	d							16 57			17 12			17 20		17 35								17 27	
Highbury & Islington	a							17 02			17 16			17 25		17 40								17 32	
	d																								
London Bridge 4 ⊖	a		16 26			16 36	16 41					16 59			17 11			16 56				17 06	17 11		

Station		LO	SN	LO		LO	SN	LO	SN	SN	SE	SE	SN	SN		LO	LO	LO	SN	LO	LO	SN	LO	SN	
East Croydon	d		17 00																17 30						
West Croydon 4	d	16 52												17 01		17 09		17 22							
Norwood Junction 2	d	16 58	17 05													17 13		17 28	17 35						
Anerley	d	17 01	17 08													17 16		17 31	17 38						
Penge West	d	17 03	17 10													17 18		17 33	17 40						
London Victoria 15 ⊖	d						16 49				17 09		17 11									17 19			
Battersea Park 4	d						16 53						17 15									17 23			
Wandsworth Road	d												17 17												
Clapham High Street ⊖	d												17 19												
London Blackfriars 3 ⊖	d											17 12													
Denmark Hill 4	d										17 18	17 22	17 24												
Peckham Rye 4	d								17 12	17 16	17a21	17a25	17 26	17 31										17 42	
Queens Rd Peckham	d									17 19			17 29	17 34											
South Bermondsey	d									17 21			17 31	17 36											
Clapham Junction 10	d						16 57															17 27			
Wandsworth Common	d						17 00															17 30			
Balham 4 ⊖	d						17 02															17 32			
Streatham Hill	d						17 05															17 35			
West Norwood 4	d						17 10		17 23													17 40		17 53	
Gipsy Hill	d						17 13		17 26													17 43		17 56	
Crystal Palace 4	d					17 13	17 21	17 28	17a29												17 43	17 51	17 58	17a59	
Sydenham	d	17 06	17 12			17 16	17 24	17 31								17 21		17 36	17 42		17 46	17 54	18 01		
Forest Hill 4	d	17 08	17 15			17 19	17 27	17 34								17 23		17 38	17 45		17 49	17 57	18 04		
Honor Oak Park	d	17 11	17 17			17 21	17 29	17 36								17 26		17 41	17 47		17 51	17 59	18 06		
Brockley	d	17 13	17 20			17 24	17 32	17 39								17 28		17 43	17 50		17 54	18 02	18 09		
New Cross Gate 4	a	17 16	17 22			17 26	17 34	17 41								17 31		17 46	17 52		17 56	18 04	18 11		
	d	17 16	17 22			17 26	17 34	17 41								17 31		17 46	17 52		17 56	18 04	18 11		
New Cross ELL	d			17 21													17 36			17 51					
Surrey Quays	d	17 19		17 25		17 30		17 45								17 35	17 40	17 49		17 55	18 00		18 15		
Canada Water	d	17 21		17 27		17 32		17 47								17 37	17 42	17 51		17 57	18 02		18 17		
Rotherhithe	d	17 23		17 28		17 33		17 48								17 38	17 43	17 53		17 58	18 03		18 18		
Wapping	d	17 24		17 30		17 35		17 50								17 40	17 45	17 54		18 00	18 05		18 20		
Shadwell	d	17 26		17 32		17 37		17 52								17 42	17 47	17 56		18 02	18 07		18 22		
Whitechapel	d	17 29		17 34		17 39		17 54								17 44	17 49	17 59		18 04	18 09		18 24		
Shoreditch High Street	d	17 31		17 36		17 41		17 56								17 46	17 51	18 01		18 06	18 11		18 26		
Hoxton	d	17 33		17 38		17 43		17 58								17 48	17 53	18 03		18 08	18 13		18 28		
Haggerston	d	17 35		17 40		17 45		18 00								17 50	17 55	18 05		18 10	18 15		18 30		
Dalston Junction Stn ELL	a	17 37		17 43		17 47		18 02								17 52	17 58	18 07		18 13	18 17		18 32		
Canonbury	d	17 42				17 50		18 05								17 57		18 12			18 20		18 35		
Highbury & Islington	a	17 46				17 55		18 10								18 02		18 16			18 25		18 40		
	d																								
London Bridge 4 ⊖	a		17 30				17 41			17 26			17 36	17 41					17 59			18 11			

Table 178

Saturdays

18 August to 25 August

East London Line and Croydon - London Victoria to London Bridge

Network Diagram - see first Page of Table 177

Station		SN	SE	SE	SN	SN	LO	LO	LO	SN		LO	LO	SN	LO	SN	SN	SE	SE	SN		SN	LO	LO	LO
East Croydon 🚋	d									18 00															
West Croydon 4 🚋	d					17 31	17 39		17 52													18 01	18 09		18 22
Norwood Junction 2	d						17 43		17 58	18 05													18 13		18 28
Anerley	d						17 46		18 01	18 08													18 16		18 31
Penge West	d						17 48		18 03	18 10													18 18		18 33
London Victoria 15 ⊖	d		17 39		17 41									17 49				18 09		18 11					
Battersea Park 4	d				17 45									17 53						18 15					
Wandsworth Road	d				17 47															18 17					
Clapham High Street ⊖	d				17 49															18 19					
London Blackfriars 3 ⊖	d			17 42															18 12						
Denmark Hill 4	d		17 48	17 52	17 54													18 18	18 22	18 24					
Peckham Rye 4	d	17 46	17a51	17a55	17 56	18 01										18 12	18 16	18a21	18a25	18 26		18 31			
Queens Rd Peckham	d	17 49			17 59	18 04											18 19			18 29		18 34			
South Bermondsey	d	17 51			18 01	18 06											18 21			18 31		18 36			
Clapham Junction 10	d													17 57											
Wandsworth Common	d													18 00											
Balham 4 ⊖	d													18 02											
Streatham Hill	d													18 05											
West Norwood 4	d													18 10		18 23									
Gipsy Hill	d													18 13		18 26									
Crystal Palace 4	d												18 13	18 21	18 28	18a29									
Sydenham	d						17 51		18 06	18 12			18 16	18 24	18 31								18 21		18 36
Forest Hill 4	d						17 53		18 08	18 15			18 19	18 27	18 34								18 23		18 38
Honor Oak Park	d						17 56		18 11	18 17			18 21	18 29	18 36								18 26		18 41
Brockley	d						17 58		18 13	18 20			18 24	18 32	18 39								18 28		18 43
New Cross Gate 4	a						18 01		18 16	18 22			18 26	18 34	18 41								18 31		18 46
	d						18 01		18 16	18 22			18 26	18 34	18 41								18 31		18 46
New Cross ELL	d							18 06				18 21												18 36	
Surrey Quays	d						18 05	18 10	18 19			18 25	18 30		18 45								18 35	18 40	18 49
Canada Water	d						18 07	18 12	18 21			18 27	18 32		18 47								18 37	18 42	18 51
Rotherhithe	d						18 08	18 13	18 23			18 28	18 33		18 48								18 38	18 43	18 53
Wapping	d						18 10	18 15	18 24			18 30	18 35		18 50								18 40	18 45	18 54
Shadwell	d						18 12	18 17	18 26			18 32	18 37		18 52								18 42	18 47	18 56
Whitechapel	d						18 14	18 19	18 29			18 34	18 39		18 54								18 44	18 49	18 59
Shoreditch High Street	d						18 16	18 21	18 31			18 36	18 41		18 56								18 46	18 51	19 01
Hoxton	d						18 18	18 23	18 33			18 38	18 43		18 58								18 48	18 53	19 03
Haggerston	d						18 20	18 25	18 35			18 40	18 45		19 00								18 50	18 55	19 05
Dalston Junction Stn ELL	a						18 22	18 28	18 37			18 43	18 47		19 02								18 52	18 58	19 07
Canonbury	d						18 27		18 42				18 50		19 05								18 57		19 12
Highbury & Islington	a						18 32		18 46				18 55		19 10								19 02		19 16
	d																								
London Bridge 4 ⊖	a	17 56			18 06	18 11				18 29				18 41			18 26			18 36		18 41			

Station		SN	LO	LO	SN	LO		SN	SN	SE	SE	SN	SN	LO	LO	LO		SN	LO	LO	SN	LO	SN	SN	SE
East Croydon 🚋	d	18 30																19 00							
West Croydon 4 🚋	d												18 31	18 39		18 52									
Norwood Junction 2	d	18 35												18 43		18 58		19 05							
Anerley	d	18 38												18 46		19 01		19 08							
Penge West	d	18 40												18 48		19 03		19 10							
London Victoria 15 ⊖	d				18 19					18 39		18 41									18 49				19 09
Battersea Park 4	d				18 23							18 45									18 53				
Wandsworth Road	d											18 47													
Clapham High Street ⊖	d											18 49													
London Blackfriars 3 ⊖	d										18 42														
Denmark Hill 4	d									18 48	18 52	18 54													19 18
Peckham Rye 4	d							18 42	18 46	18a51	18a55	18 56	19 01										19 12	19 16	19a21
Queens Rd Peckham	d								18 49			18 59	19 04											19 19	
South Bermondsey	d								18 51			19 01	19 06											19 21	
Clapham Junction 10	d				18 27																18 57				
Wandsworth Common	d				18 30																19 00				
Balham 4 ⊖	d				18 32																19 02				
Streatham Hill	d				18 35																19 05				
West Norwood 4	d				18 40			18 53													19 10		19 23		
Gipsy Hill	d				18 43			18 56													19 13		19 26		
Crystal Palace 4	d			18 43	18 51	18 58		18a59												19 13	19 21	19 28	19a29		
Sydenham	d	18 42		18 46	18 54	19 01								18 51		19 06		19 12		19 16	19 24	19 31			
Forest Hill 4	d	18 45		18 49	18 57	19 04								18 53		19 08		19 15		19 19	19 27	19 34			
Honor Oak Park	d	18 47		18 51	18 59	19 06								18 56		19 11		19 17		19 21	19 29	19 36			
Brockley	d	18 50		18 54	19 02	19 09								18 58		19 13		19 20		19 24	19 32	19 39			
New Cross Gate 4	a	18 52		18 56	19 04	19 11								19 01		19 16		19 22		19 26	19 34	19 41			
	d	18 52		18 56	19 04	19 11								19 01		19 16		19 22		19 26	19 34	19 41			
New Cross ELL	d		18 51												19 06				19 21						
Surrey Quays	d		18 55	19 00		19 15								19 05	19 10	19 19			19 25	19 30		19 45			
Canada Water	d		18 57	19 02		19 17								19 07	19 12	19 21			19 27	19 32		19 47			
Rotherhithe	d		18 58	19 03		19 18								19 08	19 13	19 23			19 28	19 33		19 48			
Wapping	d		19 00	19 05		19 20								19 10	19 15	19 24			19 30	19 35		19 50			
Shadwell	d		19 02	19 07		19 22								19 12	19 17	19 26			19 32	19 37		19 52			
Whitechapel	d		19 04	19 09		19 24								19 14	19 19	19 29			19 34	19 39		19 54			
Shoreditch High Street	d		19 06	19 11		19 26								19 16	19 21	19 31			19 36	19 41		19 56			
Hoxton	d		19 08	19 13		19 28								19 18	19 23	19 33			19 38	19 43		19 58			
Haggerston	d		19 10	19 15		19 30								19 20	19 25	19 35			19 40	19 45		20 00			
Dalston Junction Stn ELL	a		19 13	19 17		19 32								19 22	19 28	19 37			19 43	19 47		20 02			
Canonbury	d			19 20		19 35								19 27		19 42				19 50		20 05			
Highbury & Islington	a			19 25		19 40								19 32		19 46				19 55		20 10			
	d																								
London Bridge 4 ⊖	a	18 59			19 11				18 56			19 06	19 11					19 29			19 41			19 26	

Table 178

Saturdays

18 August to 25 August

East London Line and Croydon - London Victoria to London Bridge

Network Diagram - see first Page of Table 177

		SE		SN	SN	LO	LO	LO	SN	LO	LO	SN		LO	SN	SN	SE	SE	SN	SN	LO	LO		LO	SN
East Croydon	d								19 30																20 00
West Croydon 4	d				19 01	19 09		19 22												19 31	19 39			19 52	
Norwood Junction 2	d					19 13		19 28	19 35												19 43			19 58	20 05
Anerley	d					19 16		19 31	19 38												19 46			20 01	20 08
Penge West	d					19 18		19 33	19 40												19 48			20 03	20 10
London Victoria 15 ⊖	d			19 11								19 19					19 39		19 41						
Battersea Park 4	d			19 15								19 23							19 45						
Wandsworth Road	d			19 17															19 47						
Clapham High Street ⊖	d			19 19															19 49						
London Blackfriars 3 ⊖	d	19 12																19 42							
Denmark Hill 4	d	19 22		19 24													19 48	19 52	19 54						
Peckham Rye 4	d	19a25		19 26	19 31										19 42	19 46	19a51	19a55	19 56	20 01					
Queens Rd Peckham	d			19 29	19 34											19 49			19 59	20 04					
South Bermondsey	d			19 31	19 36											19 51			20 01	20 06					
Clapham Junction 10	d											19 27													
Wandsworth Common	d											19 30													
Balham 4 ⊖	d											19 32													
Streatham Hill	d											19 35													
West Norwood 4	d											19 40			19 53										
Gipsy Hill	d											19 43			19 56										
Crystal Palace 4	d										19 43	19 51		19 58	19a59										
Sydenham	d					19 21		19 36	19 42		19 46	19 54		20 01							19 51			20 06	20 12
Forest Hill 4	d					19 23		19 38	19 45		19 49	19 57		20 04							19 53			20 08	20 15
Honor Oak Park	d					19 26		19 41	19 47		19 51	19 59		20 06							19 56			20 11	20 17
Brockley	d					19 28		19 43	19 50		19 54	20 02		20 09							19 58			20 13	20 20
New Cross Gate 4	a					19 31		19 46	19 52		19 56	20 04		20 11							20 01			20 16	20 22
	d					19 31		19 46	19 52		19 56	20 04		20 11							20 01			20 16	20 22
New Cross ELL	d						19 36			19 51												20 06			
Surrey Quays	d					19 35	19 40	19 49		19 55	20 00			20 15							20 05	20 10		20 19	
Canada Water	d					19 37	19 42	19 51		19 57	20 02			20 17							20 07	20 12		20 21	
Rotherhithe	d					19 38	19 43	19 53		19 58	20 03			20 18							20 08	20 13		20 23	
Wapping	d					19 40	19 45	19 54		20 00	20 05			20 20							20 10	20 15		20 24	
Shadwell	d					19 42	19 47	19 56		20 02	20 07			20 22							20 12	20 17		20 26	
Whitechapel	d					19 44	19 49	19 59		20 04	20 09			20 24							20 14	20 19		20 29	
Shoreditch High Street	d					19 46	19 51	20 01		20 06	20 11			20 26							20 16	20 21		20 31	
Hoxton	d					19 48	19 53	20 03		20 08	20 13			20 28							20 18	20 23		20 33	
Haggerston	d					19 50	19 55	20 05		20 10	20 15			20 30							20 20	20 25		20 35	
Dalston Junction Stn ELL	a					19 52	19 58	20 07		20 13	20 17			20 32							20 22	20 28		20 37	
Canonbury	d					19 57		20 12			20 20			20 35							20 27			20 42	
Highbury & Islington	a					20 02		20 16			20 25			20 40							20 32			20 46	
	d																								
London Bridge 4 ⊖	a			19 36	19 41				19 59			20 11				19 56			20 06	20 11					20 29

		LO	LO	SN	LO	SN	SN	SE		SN	SN	LO	LO	LO	SN	LO	LO	SN		LO	SN	SN	SE	SN	SN
East Croydon	d														20 30										
West Croydon 4	d										20 01	20 09		20 22											20 31
Norwood Junction 2	d											20 13		20 28	20 35										
Anerley	d											20 16		20 31	20 38										
Penge West	d											20 18		20 33	20 40										
London Victoria 15 ⊖	d			19 49						20 11								20 19						20 41	
Battersea Park 4	d			19 53						20 15								20 23						20 45	
Wandsworth Road	d									20 17														20 47	
Clapham High Street ⊖	d									20 19														20 49	
London Blackfriars 3 ⊖	d							20 12															20 42		
Denmark Hill 4	d							20 22		20 24													20 52	20 54	
Peckham Rye 4	d					20 12	20 16	20a25		20 26	20 31										20 42	20 46	20a55	20 56	21 01
Queens Rd Peckham	d						20 19			20 29	20 34											20 49		20 59	21 04
South Bermondsey	d						20 21			20 31	20 36											20 51		21 01	21 06
Clapham Junction 10	d			19 57														20 27							
Wandsworth Common	d			20 00														20 30							
Balham 4 ⊖	d			20 02														20 32							
Streatham Hill	d			20 05														20 35							
West Norwood 4	d			20 10		20 23												20 40			20 53				
Gipsy Hill	d			20 13		20 26												20 43			20 56				
Crystal Palace 4	d		20 13	20 21	20 28	20a29											20 43	20 51		20 58	20a59				
Sydenham	d		20 16	20 24	20 31							20 21		20 36	20 42		20 46	20 54		21 01					
Forest Hill 4	d		20 19	20 27	20 34							20 23		20 38	20 45		20 49	20 57		21 04					
Honor Oak Park	d		20 21	20 29	20 36							20 26		20 41	20 47		20 51	20 59		21 06					
Brockley	d		20 24	20 32	20 39							20 28		20 43	20 50		20 54	21 02		21 09					
New Cross Gate 4	a		20 26	20 34	20 41							20 31		20 46	20 52		20 56	21 04		21 11					
	d		20 26	20 34	20 41							20 31		20 46	20 52		20 56	21 04		21 11					
New Cross ELL	d	20 21											20 36			20 51									
Surrey Quays	d	20 25	20 30		20 45							20 35	20 40	20 49		20 55	21 00			21 15					
Canada Water	d	20 27	20 32		20 47							20 37	20 42	20 51		20 57	21 02			21 17					
Rotherhithe	d	20 28	20 33		20 48							20 38	20 43	20 53		20 58	21 03			21 18					
Wapping	d	20 30	20 35		20 50							20 40	20 45	20 54		21 00	21 05			21 20					
Shadwell	d	20 32	20 37		20 52							20 42	20 47	20 56		21 02	21 07			21 22					
Whitechapel	d	20 34	20 39		20 54							20 44	20 49	20 59		21 04	21 09			21 24					
Shoreditch High Street	d	20 36	20 41		20 56							20 46	20 51	21 01		21 06	21 11			21 26					
Hoxton	d	20 38	20 43		20 58							20 48	20 53	21 03		21 08	21 13			21 28					
Haggerston	d	20 40	20 45		21 00							20 50	20 55	21 05		21 10	21 15			21 30					
Dalston Junction Stn ELL	a	20 43	20 47		21 02							20 52	20 58	21 07		21 13	21 17			21 32					
Canonbury	d		20 50		21 05							20 57		21 12			21 20			21 35					
Highbury & Islington	a		20 55		21 10							21 02		21 16			21 25			21 40					
	d																								
London Bridge 4 ⊖	a			20 41			20 26			20 36	20 41				20 59			21 13				20 56		21 06	21 11

Table 178

Saturdays

18 August to 25 August

East London Line and Croydon - London Victoria to London Bridge

Network Diagram - see first Page of Table 177

		LO	LO	LO		SN	LO	LO	SN	LO	SN	SN	SE	SN		SN	LO	LO	LO	SN	LO	LO	SN	LO
East Croydon	d					21 00														21 30				
West Croydon 4	d	20 39		20 52												21 02	21 09		21 22					
Norwood Junction 2	d	20 43		20 58		21 05											21 13		21 28	21 35				
Anerley	d	20 46		21 01		21 08											21 16		21 31	21 38				
Penge West	d	20 48		21 03		21 10											21 18		21 33	21 40				
London Victoria 15 ⊖	d								20 49					21 11									21 19	
Battersea Park 4	d								20 53					21 15									21 23	
Wandsworth Road	d													21 17										
Clapham High Street ⊖	d													21 19										
London Blackfriars 3 ⊖	d												21 12											
Denmark Hill 4	d												21 22	21 24										
Peckham Rye 4	d										21 12	21 16	21a25	21 26		21 31								
Queens Rd Peckham	d											21 19		21 29		21 34								
South Bermondsey	d											21 21		21 31		21 36								
Clapham Junction 10	d								20 57														21 27	
Wandsworth Common	d								21 00														21 30	
Balham 4 ⊖	d								21 02														21 32	
Streatham Hill	d								21 05														21 35	
West Norwood 4	d								21 10		21 23												21 40	
Gipsy Hill	d								21 13		21 26												21 43	
Crystal Palace 4	d							21 13	21 21	21 28	21a29											21 43	21 51	21 58
Sydenham	d	20 51		21 06		21 12		21 16	21 24	21 31							21 21		21 36	21 42		21 46	21 54	22 01
Forest Hill 4	d	20 53		21 08		21 15		21 19	21 27	21 34							21 23		21 38	21 45		21 49	21 57	22 04
Honor Oak Park	d	20 56		21 11		21 17		21 21	21 29	21 36							21 26		21 41	21 47		21 51	21 59	22 06
Brockley	d	20 58		21 13		21 20		21 24	21 32	21 39							21 28		21 43	21 50		21 54	22 02	22 09
New Cross Gate 4	a	21 01		21 16		21 22		21 26	21 34	21 41							21 31		21 46	21 52		21 56	22 04	22 11
	d	21 01		21 16		21 22		21 26	21 34	21 41							21 31		21 46	21 52		21 56	22 04	22 11
New Cross ELL	d		21 06				21 21											21 36			21 51			
Surrey Quays	d	21 05	21 10	21 19			21 25	21 30		21 45							21 35	21 40	21 49		21 55	22 00		22 15
Canada Water	d	21 07	21 12	21 21			21 27	21 32		21 47							21 37	21 42	21 51		21 57	22 02		22 17
Rotherhithe	d	21 08	21 13	21 23			21 28	21 33		21 48							21 38	21 43	21 53		21 58	22 03		22 18
Wapping	d	21 10	21 15	21 24			21 30	21 35		21 50							21 40	21 45	21 54		22 00	22 05		22 20
Shadwell	d	21 12	21 17	21 26			21 32	21 37		21 52							21 42	21 47	21 56		22 02	22 07		22 22
Whitechapel	d	21 14	21 19	21 29			21 34	21 39		21 54							21 44	21 49	21 59		22 04	22 09		22 24
Shoreditch High Street	d	21 16	21 21	21 31			21 36	21 41		21 56							21 46	21 51	22 01		22 06	22 11		22 26
Hoxton	d	21 18	21 23	21 33			21 38	21 43		21 58							21 48	21 53	22 03		22 08	22 13		22 28
Haggerston	d	21 20	21 25	21 35			21 40	21 45		22 00							21 50	21 55	22 05		22 10	22 15		22 30
Dalston Junction Stn ELL	a	21 22	21 28	21 37			21 43	21 47		22 02							21 52	21 58	22 07		22 13	22 17		22 32
Canonbury	d	21 27		21 42				21 50		22 05							21 57		22 12			22 20		22 35
Highbury & Islington	a	21 32		21 46				21 55		22 10							22 02		22 16			22 25		22 40
	d																							
London Bridge 4 ⊖	a					21 29			21 43			21 26		21 36		21 41				21 59			22 13	

		SN	SN	SE	SN	SN	LO	LO	LO	SN		LO	SN	LO	SN	SN	SE	SN	SN	LO		LO	LO	SN	LO
East Croydon	d									22 00														22 30	
West Croydon 4	d					21 31	21 39		21 52										22 01	22 09			22 22		
Norwood Junction 2	d						21 43		21 58	22 05										22 13			22 28	22 35	
Anerley	d						21 46		22 01	22 08										22 16			22 31	22 38	
Penge West	d						21 48		22 03	22 10										22 18			22 33	22 40	
London Victoria 15 ⊖	d				21 41								21 49					22 11							
Battersea Park 4	d				21 45								21 53					22 15							
Wandsworth Road	d				21 47													22 17							
Clapham High Street ⊖	d				21 49													22 19							
London Blackfriars 3 ⊖	d			21 42													22 12								
Denmark Hill 4	d			21 52	21 54												22 22	22 24							
Peckham Rye 4	d	21 42	21 46	21a55	21 56	22 01									22 12	22 16	22a25	22 26	22 31						
Queens Rd Peckham	d		21 49		21 59	22 04										22 19		22 29	22 34						
South Bermondsey	d		21 51		22 01	22 06										22 21		22 31	22 36						
Clapham Junction 10	d												21 57												
Wandsworth Common	d												22 00												
Balham 4 ⊖	d												22 02												
Streatham Hill	d												22 05												
West Norwood 4	d	21 53											22 10		22 23										
Gipsy Hill	d	21 56											22 13		22 26										
Crystal Palace 4	d	21a59										22 13	22 21	22 28	22a29										22 43
Sydenham	d						21 51		22 06	22 12		22 16	22 24	22 31						22 21			22 36	22 42	22 46
Forest Hill 4	d						21 53		22 08	22 15		22 19	22 27	22 34						22 23			22 38	22 45	22 49
Honor Oak Park	d						21 56		22 11	22 17		22 21	22 29	22 36						22 26			22 41	22 47	22 51
Brockley	d						21 58		22 13	22 20		22 24	22 32	22 39						22 28			22 43	22 50	22 54
New Cross Gate 4	a						22 01		22 16	22 22		22 26	22 34	22 41						22 31			22 46	22 52	22 56
	d						22 01		22 16	22 22		22 26	22 34	22 41						22 31			22 46	22 52	22 56
New Cross ELL	d							22 06														22 36			
Surrey Quays	d						22 05	22 10	22 19			22 30		22 45						22 35		22 40	22 49		23 00
Canada Water	d						22 07	22 12	22 21			22 32		22 47						22 37		22 42	22 51		23 02
Rotherhithe	d						22 08	22 13	22 23			22 33		22 48						22 38		22 43	22 53		23 03
Wapping	d						22 10	22 15	22 24			22 35		22 50						22 40		22 45	22 54		23 05
Shadwell	d						22 12	22 17	22 26			22 37		22 52						22 42		22 47	22 56		23 07
Whitechapel	d						22 14	22 19	22 29			22 39		22 54						22 44		22 49	22 59		23 09
Shoreditch High Street	d						22 16	22 21	22 31			22 41		22 56						22 46		22 51	23 01		23 11
Hoxton	d						22 18	22 23	22 33			22 43		22 58						22 48		22 53	23 03		23 13
Haggerston	d						22 20	22 25	22 35			22 45		23 00						22 50		22 55	23 05		23 15
Dalston Junction Stn ELL	a						22 22	22 28	22 37			22 47		23 02						22 52		22 58	23 07		23 17
Canonbury	d						22 27		22 42			22 50		23 05						22 57			23 12		23 20
Highbury & Islington	a						22 32		22 46			22 55		23 10						23 02			23 16		23 25
	d																								
London Bridge 4 ⊖	a		21 56		22 06	22 11				22 29			22 43			22 26		22 36	22 41					22 59	

Table 178

Saturdays

18 August to 25 August

East London Line and Croydon - London Victoria to London Bridge

Network Diagram - see first Page of Table 177

		SN	SN	SN	SE	SN		SN	LO	LO	LO	SN	LO	SN	SN	SN		SE	SN	SN	LO	LO	LO	SN	SN
East Croydon 🚋	d											23 01													
West Croydon [4] 🚋	d							22 31	22 39		22 52									23 01		23 22			
Norwood Junction [2]	d								22 43		22 58	23 06										23 28			
Anerley	d								22 46		23 01	23 09										23 31			
Penge West	d								22 48		23 03	23 11										23 33			
London Victoria [15] ⊖	d	22 19				22 41								22 49					23 11					23 19	
Battersea Park [4]	d	22 23				22 45								22 53					23 15					23 23	
Wandsworth Road	d					22 47													23 17						
Clapham High Street ⊖	d					22 49													23 19						
London Blackfriars [3] ⊖	d				22 42													23 12							
Denmark Hill [4]	d				22 52	22 54												23 22	23 24						
Peckham Rye [4]	d		22 42	22 46	22a55	22 56		23 01							23 12	23 16		23a25	23 26	23 31					23 42
Queens Rd Peckham	d			22 49		22 59		23 04								23 19			23 29	23 34					
South Bermondsey	d			22 51		23 01		23 06								23 21			23 31	23 36					
Clapham Junction [10]	d	22 27												22 57										23 27	
Wandsworth Common	d	22 30												23 00										23 30	
Balham [4] ⊖	d	22 32												23 02										23 32	
Streatham Hill	d	22 35												23 05										23 35	
West Norwood [4]	d	22 40	22 53											23 10	23 24									23 40	23 54
Gipsy Hill	d	22 43	22 56											23 13	23 27									23 43	23 57
Crystal Palace [4]	d	22 51	22a59										23 13	23 21	23a29								23 43	23 51	23a59
Sydenham	d	22 54							22 51		23 06	23 13	23 16	23 24								23 36	23 46	23 54	
Forest Hill [4]	d	22 57							22 53		23 08	23 16	23 19	23 27								23 38	23 49	23 57	
Honor Oak Park	d	22 59							22 56		23 11	23 18	23 21	23 29								23 41	23 51	23 59	
Brockley	d	23 02							22 58		23 13	23 21	23 24	23 32								23 43	23 54	00 02	
New Cross Gate [4]	a	23 04							23 01		23 16	23 23	23 26	23 34								23 46	23 56	00 04	
	d	23 04							23 01		23 16	23 23	23 26	23 34								23 46	23 56	00 04	
New Cross ELL	d									23 06											23 36				
Surrey Quays	d								23 05	23 10	23 19		23 30								23 40	23 49	23 59		
Canada Water	d								23 07	23 12	23 21		23 32								23 42	23 51	00 02		
Rotherhithe	d								23 08	23 13	23 23		23 33								23 43	23 53	00 03		
Wapping	d								23 10	23 15	23 24		23 35								23 45	23 54	00 05		
Shadwell	d								23 12	23 17	23 26		23 37								23 47	23 56	00 07		
Whitechapel	d								23 14	23 19	23 29		23 39								23 49	23 59	00 09		
Shoreditch High Street	d								23 16	23 21	23 31		23 41								23 51	00 01	00 11		
Hoxton	d								23 18	23 23	23 33		23 43								23 53	00 03	00 13		
Haggerston	d								23 20	23 25	23 35		23 45								23 55	00 05	00 15		
Dalston Junction Stn ELL	a								23 22	23 28	23 37		23 47								23 58	00 07	00 17		
Canonbury	d								23 27		23 42		23 50									00 12	00 20		
Highbury & Islington	a								23 32		23 46		23 55									00 16	00 25		
	d																								
London Bridge [4] ⊖	a	23 13		22 56		23 06		23 11				23 30		23 43		23 26			23 36	23 41				00 11	

		SN		SE	SN
East Croydon 🚋	d				
West Croydon [4] 🚋	d				
Norwood Junction [2]	d				
Anerley	d				
Penge West	d				
London Victoria [15] ⊖	d				23 54
Battersea Park [4]	d				23 58
Wandsworth Road	d				
Clapham High Street ⊖	d				
London Blackfriars [3] ⊖	d			23 42	
Denmark Hill [4]	d			23 52	
Peckham Rye [4]	d	23 46		23a55	
Queens Rd Peckham	d	23 49			
South Bermondsey	d	23 51			
Clapham Junction [10]	d				00 02
Wandsworth Common	d				00 05
Balham [4] ⊖	d				00 07
Streatham Hill	d				00 10
West Norwood [4]	d				00 14
Gipsy Hill	d				00 17
Crystal Palace [4]	d				00 21
Sydenham	d				00 24
Forest Hill [4]	d				00 27
Honor Oak Park	d				00 29
Brockley	d				00 32
New Cross Gate [4]	a				00 35
	d				00 35
New Cross ELL	d				
Surrey Quays	d				
Canada Water	d				
Rotherhithe	d				
Wapping	d				
Shadwell	d				
Whitechapel	d				
Shoreditch High Street	d				
Hoxton	d				
Haggerston	d				
Dalston Junction Stn ELL	a				
Canonbury	d				
Highbury & Islington	a				
	d				
London Bridge [4] ⊖	a	23 56			00 41

Table 178

Saturdays

1 September to 8 September

East London Line and Croydon - London Victoria to London Bridge

Network Diagram - see first Page of Table 177

		LO	LO	LO	SN	SN	SN	SN	LO	LO		LO	LO	LO	LO	LO	SN	LO	LO	LO		SN	LO	LO	SE
East Croydon (tram)	d																					06 30			
West Croydon [4] (tram)	d		23p22						05 39				05 52			06 09	06 18			06 22					
Norwood Junction [2]	d		23p28						05 43				05 58			06 13	06 23			06 28		06 35			
Anerley	d		23p31						05 46				06 01			06 16				06 31		06 38			
Penge West	d		23p33						05 48				06 03			06 18				06 33		06 40			
London Victoria [15] ⊖	d				23p22	23p54																			00 56
Battersea Park [4]	d				23p26	23p58																			
Wandsworth Road	d																								
Clapham High Street ⊖	d																								
London Blackfriars [3] ⊖	d																								
Denmark Hill [4]	d																								01s05
Peckham Rye [4]	d						00 12	00 42																	01s08
Queens Rd Peckham	d																								
South Bermondsey	d																								
Clapham Junction [10]	d				23p30	00 02																			
Wandsworth Common	d				23p33	00 05																			
Balham [4] ⊖	d				23p35	00 07																			
Streatham Hill	d				23p38	00 10																			
West Norwood [4]	d				23p42	00 14	00 24	00 54																	
Gipsy Hill	d				23p45	00 17	00 27	00 57																	
Crystal Palace [4]	d			23p43	23p51	00 21	00a29	00a59				05 58			06 13		06a27		06 28					06 41	
Sydenham	d		23p36	23p46	23p54	00 24			05 51			06 01	06 06		06 16	06 21			06 31	06 36		06 42		06 44	
Forest Hill [4]	d		23p38	23p49	23p57	00 27			05 53			06 04	06 08		06 19	06 23			06 34	06 38		06 45		06 47	
Honor Oak Park	d		23p41	23p51	23p59	00 29			05 56			06 06	06 11		06 21	06 26			06 36	06 41		06 47		06 49	
Brockley	d		23p43	23p54	00 02	00 32			05 58			06 09	06 13		06 24	06 28			06 39	06 43		06 50		06 52	
New Cross Gate [4]	a		23p46	23p56	00 04	00 34			06 01			06 11	06 16		06 26	06 31			06 41	06 46		06 52		06 54	
	d		23p46	23p56	00 04	00 34			06 01			06 11	06 16		06 26	06 31			06 41	06 46		06 52		06 54	
New Cross ELL	d	23p36								06 06				06 21				06 36					06 51		
Surrey Quays	d	23p40	23p49	23p59					06 05	06 10		06 15	06 19	06 25	06 30	06 35		06 40	06 45	06 49			06 55	07 00	
Canada Water	d	23p42	23p51	00 02					06 07	06 12		06 17	06 21	06 27	06 32	06 37		06 42	06 47	06 51			06 57	07 02	
Rotherhithe	d	23p43	23p53	00 03					06 08	06 13		06 18	06 23	06 28	06 33	06 38		06 43	06 48	06 53			06 58	07 03	
Wapping	d	23p45	23p54	00 05					06 10	06 15		06 20	06 24	06 30	06 35	06 40		06 45	06 50	06 54			07 00	07 05	
Shadwell	d	23p47	23p56	00 07					06 12	06 17		06 22	06 26	06 32	06 37	06 42		06 47	06 52	06 56			07 02	07 07	
Whitechapel	d	23p49	23p59	00 09					06 14	06 19		06 24	06 29	06 34	06 39	06 44		06 49	06 54	06 59			07 04	07 09	
Shoreditch High Street	d	23p51	00 01	00 11					06 16	06 21		06 26	06 31	06 36	06 41	06 46		06 51	06 56	07 01			07 06	07 11	
Hoxton	d	23p53	00 03	00 13					06 18	06 23		06 28	06 33	06 38	06 43	06 48		06 53	06 58	07 03			07 08	07 13	
Haggerston	d	23p55	00 05	00 15					06 20	06 25		06 30	06 35	06 40	06 45	06 50		06 55	07 00	07 05			07 10	07 15	
Dalston Junction Stn ELL	a	23p58	00 07	00 17					06 22	06 32		06 32	06 37	06 47	06 47	06 52		07 02	07 02	07 07			07 17	07 17	
Canonbury	d	00 01	00 11	00 20					06 27			06 35	06 42		06 50	06 57			07 05	07 12				07 20	
Highbury & Islington	a	00 10	00 18	00 28					06 35			06 43	06 49		06 59	07 05			07 13	07 19				07 28	
	d																								
London Bridge [4] ⊖	a				00 11	00 41																06 59			

		SE	SE	SN	SN	LO		SN	SN	LO	LO	LO	SN	SE	SN	SN		LO	LO	LO	LO	LO	LO	SN	LO
East Croydon (tram)	d							06 43					07 00											07 30	
West Croydon [4] (tram)	d					06 39			06 45			06 52				07 01				07 09			07 22		
Norwood Junction [2]	d				06 41	06 43		06 50	06 53			06 58	07 05							07 13			07 28	07 35	
Anerley	d					06 46						07 01	07 08							07 16			07 31	07 38	
Penge West	d					06 48						07 03	07 10							07 18			07 33	07 40	
London Victoria [15] ⊖	d			06 41											07 11										
Battersea Park [4]	d			06 45											07 15										
Wandsworth Road	d			06 47											07 17										
Clapham High Street ⊖	d			06 49											07 19										
London Blackfriars [3] ⊖	d	06 12	06 42											07 12											
Denmark Hill [4]	d	06 22	06 52	06 54										07 22	07 24										
Peckham Rye [4]	d	06a25	06a55	06 56	07 01									07a25	07 26	07 31									
Queens Rd Peckham	d			06 59	07 04										07 29	07 34									
South Bermondsey	d			07 01	07 06										07 31	07 36									
Clapham Junction [10]	d																								
Wandsworth Common	d																								
Balham [4] ⊖	d																								
Streatham Hill	d																								
West Norwood [4]	d																								
Gipsy Hill	d																								
Crystal Palace [4]	d								06a57		06 58								07 11			07 28			
Sydenham	d					06 51		06 54			07 01	07 06	07 12						07 14	07 21		07 31	07 36	07 42	
Forest Hill [4]	d					06 53		06 57			07 04	07 08	07 15						07 17	07 23		07 34	07 38	07 45	
Honor Oak Park	d					06 56		06 59			07 06	07 11	07 17						07 19	07 26		07 36	07 41	07 47	
Brockley	d					06 58		07 02			07 09	07 13	07 20						07 22	07 28		07 39	07 43	07 50	
New Cross Gate [4]	a					07 01		07 04			07 11	07 16	07 22						07 24	07 31		07 41	07 46	07 52	
	d					07 01		07 04			07 11	07 16	07 22						07 24	07 31		07 41	07 46	07 52	
New Cross ELL	d									07 06								07 21			07 36				07 51
Surrey Quays	d					07 05				07 10	07 15	07 19						07 25	07 30	07 35	07 40	07 45	07 49		07 55
Canada Water	d					07 07				07 12	07 17	07 21						07 27	07 32	07 37	07 42	07 47	07 51		07 57
Rotherhithe	d					07 08				07 13	07 18	07 23						07 28	07 33	07 38	07 43	07 48	07 53		07 58
Wapping	d					07 10				07 15	07 20	07 24						07 30	07 35	07 40	07 45	07 50	07 54		08 00
Shadwell	d					07 12				07 17	07 22	07 26						07 32	07 37	07 42	07 47	07 52	07 56		08 02
Whitechapel	d					07 14				07 19	07 24	07 29						07 34	07 39	07 44	07 49	07 54	07 59		08 04
Shoreditch High Street	d					07 16				07 21	07 26	07 31						07 36	07 41	07 46	07 51	07 56	08 01		08 06
Hoxton	d					07 18				07 23	07 28	07 33						07 38	07 43	07 48	07 53	07 58	08 03		08 08
Haggerston	d					07 20				07 25	07 30	07 35						07 40	07 45	07 50	07 55	08 00	08 05		08 10
Dalston Junction Stn ELL	a					07 23				07 32	07 32	07 37						07 47	07 47	07 53	08 02	08 02	08 07		08 17
Canonbury	d					07 27					07 35	07 42							07 50	07 57		08 05	08 12		
Highbury & Islington	a					07 35					07 43	07 49							07 58	08 05		08 13	08 19		
	d																								
London Bridge [4] ⊖	a			07 06	07 14			07 11					07 29		07 36	07 41								07 59	

Table 178

Saturdays

1 September to 8 September

East London Line and Croydon - London Victoria to London Bridge

Network Diagram - see first Page of Table 177

		LO		LO	SN	SE	SE	SN	SN	LO	LO	LO		SN	LO	LO	SN	LO	SN	SE	SE	SN		SN	LO
East Croydon	d													08 00											
West Croydon 4	d								07 31	07 39		07 52												08 01	08 09
Norwood Junction 2	d									07 43		07 58		08 05											08 13
Anerley	d									07 46		08 01		08 08											08 16
Penge West	d									07 48		08 03		08 10											08 18
London Victoria 15 ⊖	d					07 39		07 41									07 49			08 09		08 11			
Battersea Park 4	d							07 45									07 53					08 15			
Wandsworth Road	d							07 47														08 17			
Clapham High Street ⊖	d							07 49														08 19			
London Blackfriars 3 ⊖	d						07 42														08 12				
Denmark Hill 4	d					07 48	07 52	07 54												08 18	08 22	08 24			
Peckham Rye 4	d				07 42	07a51	07a55	07 56	08 01										08 12	08a21	08a25	08 26		08 31	
Queens Rd Peckham	d							07 59	08 04													08 29		08 34	
South Bermondsey	d							08 01	08 06													08 31		08 36	
Clapham Junction 10	d																07 57								
Wandsworth Common	d																08 00								
Balham 4 ⊖	d																08 02								
Streatham Hill	d																08 05								
West Norwood 4	d				07 53												08 10		08 23						
Gipsy Hill	d				07 56												08 13		08 26						
Crystal Palace 4	d	07 41		07 58	07a59											08 11	08 21	08 28	08a29						
Sydenham	d	07 44		08 01						07 51		08 06		08 12		08 14	08 24	08 31							08 21
Forest Hill 4	d	07 47		08 04						07 53		08 08		08 15		08 17	08 27	08 34							08 23
Honor Oak Park	d	07 49		08 06						07 56		08 11		08 17		08 19	08 29	08 36							08 26
Brockley	d	07 52		08 09						07 58		08 13		08 20		08 22	08 32	08 39							08 28
New Cross Gate 4	a	07 54		08 11						08 01		08 16		08 22		08 24	08 34	08 41							08 31
	d	07 54		08 11						08 01		08 16		08 22		08 24	08 34	08 41							08 31
New Cross ELL	d										08 06				08 21										
Surrey Quays	d	08 00		08 15						08 05	08 10	08 19			08 25	08 30		08 45							08 35
Canada Water	d	08 02		08 17						08 07	08 12	08 21			08 27	08 32		08 47							08 37
Rotherhithe	d	08 03		08 18						08 08	08 13	08 23			08 28	08 33		08 48							08 38
Wapping	d	08 05		08 20						08 10	08 15	08 24			08 30	08 35		08 50							08 40
Shadwell	d	08 07		08 22						08 12	08 17	08 26			08 32	08 37		08 52							08 42
Whitechapel	d	08 09		08 24						08 14	08 19	08 29			08 34	08 39		08 54							08 44
Shoreditch High Street	d	08 11		08 26						08 16	08 21	08 31			08 36	08 41		08 56							08 46
Hoxton	d	08 13		08 28						08 18	08 23	08 33			08 38	08 43		08 58							08 48
Haggerston	d	08 15		08 30						08 20	08 25	08 35			08 40	08 45		09 00							08 50
Dalston Junction Stn ELL	a	08 17		08 32						08 23	08 32	08 37			08 47	08 47		09 02							08 53
Canonbury	d	08 20		08 35						08 27		08 42				08 50		09 05							08 57
Highbury & Islington	a	08 28		08 43						08 35		08 49				08 58		09 13							09 05
	d																								
London Bridge 4 ⊖	a							08 06	08 11					08 29			08 41					08 36		08 41	

		LO	LO	SN	LO	LO	SN	LO		SN	SN	SE	SE	SN	SN	LO	LO	LO		SN	LO	LO	SN	LO	SN
East Croydon	d			08 30																09 00					
West Croydon 4	d		08 22												08 31	08 39		08 52							
Norwood Junction 2	d		08 28	08 35												08 43		08 58		09 05					
Anerley	d		08 31	08 38												08 46		09 01		09 08					
Penge West	d		08 33	08 40												08 48		09 03		09 10					
London Victoria 15 ⊖	d						08 19					08 39		08 41									08 49		
Battersea Park 4	d						08 23							08 45									08 53		
Wandsworth Road	d													08 47											
Clapham High Street ⊖	d													08 49											
London Blackfriars 3 ⊖	d												08 42												
Denmark Hill 4	d											08 48	08 52	08 54											
Peckham Rye 4	d									08 42	08 46	08a51	08a55	08 56	09 01										09 12
Queens Rd Peckham	d										08 49			08 59	09 04										
South Bermondsey	d										08 51			09 01	09 06										
Clapham Junction 10	d						08 27																08 57		
Wandsworth Common	d						08 30																09 00		
Balham 4 ⊖	d						08 32																09 02		
Streatham Hill	d						08 35																09 05		
West Norwood 4	d						08 40			08 53													09 10		09 23
Gipsy Hill	d						08 43			08 56													09 13		09 26
Crystal Palace 4	d					08 41	08 51	08 58		08a59												09 11	09 21	09 28	09a29
Sydenham	d		08 36	08 42		08 44	08 54	09 01								08 51		09 06		09 12		09 14	09 24	09 31	
Forest Hill 4	d		08 38	08 45		08 47	08 57	09 04								08 53		09 08		09 15		09 17	09 27	09 34	
Honor Oak Park	d		08 41	08 47		08 49	08 59	09 06								08 56		09 11		09 17		09 19	09 29	09 36	
Brockley	d		08 43	08 50		08 52	09 02	09 09								08 58		09 13		09 20		09 22	09 32	09 39	
New Cross Gate 4	a		08 46	08 52		08 54	09 04	09 11								09 01		09 16		09 22		09 24	09 34	09 41	
	d		08 46	08 52		08 54	09 04	09 11								09 01		09 16		09 22		09 24	09 34	09 41	
New Cross ELL	d	08 36			08 51												09 06				09 21				
Surrey Quays	d	08 40	08 49		08 55	09 00		09 15								09 05	09 10	09 19			09 25	09 30		09 45	
Canada Water	d	08 42	08 51		08 57	09 02		09 17								09 07	09 12	09 21			09 27	09 32		09 47	
Rotherhithe	d	08 43	08 53		08 58	09 03		09 18								09 08	09 13	09 23			09 28	09 33		09 48	
Wapping	d	08 45	08 54		09 00	09 05		09 20								09 10	09 15	09 24			09 30	09 35		09 50	
Shadwell	d	08 47	08 56		09 02	09 07		09 22								09 12	09 17	09 26			09 32	09 37		09 52	
Whitechapel	d	08 49	08 59		09 04	09 09		09 24								09 14	09 19	09 29			09 34	09 39		09 54	
Shoreditch High Street	d	08 51	09 01		09 06	09 11		09 26								09 16	09 21	09 31			09 36	09 41		09 56	
Hoxton	d	08 53	09 03		09 08	09 13		09 28								09 18	09 23	09 33			09 38	09 43		09 58	
Haggerston	d	08 55	09 05		09 10	09 15		09 30								09 20	09 25	09 35			09 40	09 45		10 00	
Dalston Junction Stn ELL	a	09 02	09 07		09 17	09 17		09 32								09 23	09 32	09 37			09 47	09 47		10 02	
Canonbury	d		09 12			09 20		09 35								09 27		09 42				09 50		10 05	
Highbury & Islington	a		09 19			09 28		09 43								09 35		09 49				09 58		10 13	
	d																								
London Bridge 4 ⊖	a			08 59			09 11				08 56			09 06	09 11					09 29			09 41		

Table 178

Saturdays

1 September to 8 September

East London Line and Croydon - London Victoria to London Bridge

Network Diagram - see first Page of Table 177

Station		SN	SE	SE		SN	SN	LO	LO	LO	SN	LO	LO	SN		LO	SN	SN	SE	SE	SN	SN	LO	LO	
East Croydon (tram)	d										09 30														
West Croydon 4 (tram)	d						09 01	09 09		09 22												09 31	09 39		
Norwood Junction 2	d							09 13		09 28	09 35												09 43		
Anerley	d							09 16		09 31	09 38												09 46		
Penge West	d							09 18		09 33	09 40												09 48		
London Victoria 15 ⊖	d		09 09			09 11								09 19					09 39		09 41				
Battersea Park 4	d					09 15								09 23							09 45				
Wandsworth Road	d					09 17															09 47				
Clapham High Street ⊖	d					09 19															09 49				
London Blackfriars 3 ⊖	d			09 12																09 42					
Denmark Hill 4	d		09 18	09 22		09 24													09 48	09 52	09 54				
Peckham Rye 4	d	09 16	09a21	09a25		09 26	09 31										09 42	09 46	09a51	09a55	09 56	10 01			
Queens Rd Peckham	d	09 19				09 29	09 34											09 49			09 59	10 04			
South Bermondsey	d	09 21				09 31	09 36											09 51			10 01	10 06			
Clapham Junction 10	d													09 27											
Wandsworth Common	d													09 30											
Balham 4 ⊖	d													09 32											
Streatham Hill	d													09 35											
West Norwood 4	d													09 40			09 53								
Gipsy Hill	d													09 43			09 56								
Crystal Palace 4	d												09 43	09 51		09 58	09a59								
Sydenham	d							09 21		09 36	09 42		09 46	09 54		10 01							09 51		
Forest Hill 4	d							09 23		09 38	09 45		09 49	09 57		10 04							09 53		
Honor Oak Park	d							09 26		09 41	09 47		09 51	09 59		10 06							09 56		
Brockley	d							09 28		09 43	09 50		09 54	10 02		10 09							09 58		
New Cross Gate 4	a							09 31		09 46	09 52		09 56	10 04		10 11							10 01		
	d							09 31		09 46	09 52		09 56	10 04		10 11							10 01		
New Cross ELL	d								09 36			09 51												10 06	
Surrey Quays	d							09 35	09 40	09 49		09 55	10 00			10 15							10 05	10 10	
Canada Water	d							09 37	09 42	09 51		09 57	10 02			10 17							10 07	10 12	
Rotherhithe	d							09 38	09 43	09 53		09 58	10 03			10 18							10 08	10 13	
Wapping	d							09 40	09 45	09 54		10 00	10 05			10 20							10 10	10 15	
Shadwell	d							09 42	09 47	09 56		10 02	10 07			10 22							10 12	10 17	
Whitechapel	d							09 44	09 49	09 59		10 04	10 09			10 24							10 14	10 19	
Shoreditch High Street	d							09 46	09 51	10 01		10 06	10 11			10 26							10 16	10 21	
Hoxton	d							09 48	09 53	10 03		10 08	10 13			10 28							10 18	10 23	
Haggerston	d							09 50	09 55	10 05		10 10	10 15			10 30							10 20	10 25	
Dalston Junction Stn ELL	a							09 53	10 02	10 07		10 17	10 17			10 32							10 22	10 32	
Canonbury	d							09 57		10 12			10 20			10 35							10 27		
Highbury & Islington	a							10 05		10 19			10 28			10 43							10 35		
	d																								
London Bridge 4 ⊖	a	09 26				09 36	09 41				09 59			10 11				09 56			10 06	10 11			

Station		LO	SN	LO	LO	SN	LO	SN	SN	SE		SE	SN	SN	LO	LO	LO	SN	LO	LO		SN	LO	SN	SN
East Croydon (tram)	d		10 00															10 30							
West Croydon 4 (tram)	d	09 52												10 01	10 09		10 22								
Norwood Junction 2	d	09 58	10 05												10 13		10 28	10 35							
Anerley	d	10 01	10 08												10 16		10 31	10 38							
Penge West	d	10 03	10 10												10 18		10 33	10 40							
London Victoria 15 ⊖	d					09 49				10 09			10 11									10 19			
Battersea Park 4	d					09 53							10 15									10 23			
Wandsworth Road	d												10 17												
Clapham High Street ⊖	d												10 19												
London Blackfriars 3 ⊖	d											10 12													
Denmark Hill 4	d									10 18		10 22	10 24												
Peckham Rye 4	d							10 12	10 16	10a21		10a25	10 26	10 31										10 42	10 46
Queens Rd Peckham	d								10 19				10 29	10 34											10 49
South Bermondsey	d								10 21				10 31	10 36											10 51
Clapham Junction 10	d					09 57																10 27			
Wandsworth Common	d					10 00																10 30			
Balham 4 ⊖	d					10 02																10 32			
Streatham Hill	d					10 05																10 35			
West Norwood 4	d					10 10		10 23														10 40		10 53	
Gipsy Hill	d					10 13		10 26														10 43		10 56	
Crystal Palace 4	d				10 13	10 21	10 28	10a29												10 43		10 51	10 58	10a59	
Sydenham	d	10 06	10 12		10 16	10 24	10 31								10 21		10 36	10 42		10 46		10 54	11 01		
Forest Hill 4	d	10 08	10 15		10 19	10 27	10 34								10 23		10 38	10 45		10 49		10 57	11 04		
Honor Oak Park	d	10 11	10 17		10 21	10 29	10 36								10 26		10 41	10 47		10 51		10 59	11 06		
Brockley	d	10 13	10 20		10 24	10 32	10 39								10 28		10 43	10 50		10 54		11 02	11 09		
New Cross Gate 4	a	10 16	10 22		10 26	10 34	10 41								10 31		10 46	10 52		10 56		11 04	11 11		
	d	10 16	10 22		10 26	10 34	10 41								10 31		10 46	10 52		10 56		11 04	11 11		
New Cross ELL	d			10 21												10 36			10 51						
Surrey Quays	d	10 19		10 25	10 30		10 45								10 35	10 40	10 49		10 55	11 00			11 15		
Canada Water	d	10 21		10 27	10 32		10 47								10 37	10 42	10 51		10 57	11 02			11 17		
Rotherhithe	d	10 23		10 28	10 33		10 48								10 38	10 43	10 53		10 58	11 03			11 18		
Wapping	d	10 24		10 30	10 35		10 50								10 40	10 45	10 54		11 00	11 05			11 20		
Shadwell	d	10 26		10 32	10 37		10 52								10 42	10 47	10 56		11 02	11 07			11 22		
Whitechapel	d	10 29		10 34	10 39		10 54								10 44	10 49	10 59		11 04	11 09			11 24		
Shoreditch High Street	d	10 31		10 36	10 41		10 56								10 46	10 51	11 01		11 06	11 11			11 26		
Hoxton	d	10 33		10 38	10 43		10 58								10 48	10 53	11 03		11 08	11 13			11 28		
Haggerston	d	10 35		10 40	10 45		11 00								10 50	10 55	11 05		11 10	11 15			11 30		
Dalston Junction Stn ELL	a	10 37		10 47	10 47		11 02								10 52	11 02	11 07		11 17	11 17			11 32		
Canonbury	d	10 42			10 50		11 05								10 57		11 12			11 20			11 35		
Highbury & Islington	a	10 49			10 58		11 13								11 05		11 19			11 28			11 43		
	d																								
London Bridge 4 ⊖	a		10 29			10 41			10 26				10 36	10 41				10 59				11 11			10 56

Table 178

Saturdays

1 September to 8 September

East London Line and Croydon - London Victoria to London Bridge

Network Diagram - see first Page of Table 177

		SE	SE	SN	SN	LO		LO	LO	SN	LO	LO	SN	LO	SN	SN		SE	SE	SN	SN	LO	LO	LO	SN
East Croydon	d									11 00															11 30
West Croydon 4	d				10 31	10 39			10 52												11 01	11 09		11 22	
Norwood Junction 2	d					10 43			10 58	11 05												11 13		11 28	11 35
Anerley	d					10 46			11 01	11 08												11 16		11 31	11 38
Penge West	d					10 48			11 03	11 10												11 18		11 33	11 40
London Victoria 15 ⊖	d	10 39		10 41									10 49					11 09		11 11					
Battersea Park 4	d			10 45									10 53							11 15					
Wandsworth Road	d			10 47																11 17					
Clapham High Street ⊖	d			10 49																11 19					
London Blackfriars 3 ⊖	d		10 42																11 12						
Denmark Hill 4	d	10 48	10 52	10 54														11 18	11 22	11 24					
Peckham Rye 4	d	10a51	10a55	10 56	11 01										11 12	11 16		11a21	11a25	11 26	11 31				
Queens Rd Peckham	d			10 59	11 04											11 19				11 29	11 34				
South Bermondsey	d			11 01	11 06											11 21				11 31	11 36				
Clapham Junction 10	d												10 57												
Wandsworth Common	d												11 00												
Balham 4 ⊖	d												11 02												
Streatham Hill	d												11 05												
West Norwood 4	d												11 10		11 23										
Gipsy Hill	d												11 13		11 26										
Crystal Palace 4	d											11 13	11 21	11 28	11a29										
Sydenham	d					10 51			11 06	11 12		11 16	11 24	11 31								11 21		11 36	11 42
Forest Hill 4	d					10 53			11 08	11 15		11 19	11 27	11 34								11 23		11 38	11 45
Honor Oak Park	d					10 56			11 11	11 17		11 21	11 29	11 36								11 26		11 41	11 47
Brockley	d					10 58			11 13	11 20		11 24	11 32	11 39								11 28		11 43	11 50
New Cross Gate 4	a					11 01			11 16	11 22		11 26	11 34	11 41								11 31		11 46	11 52
	d					11 01			11 16	11 22		11 26	11 34	11 41								11 31		11 46	11 52
New Cross ELL	d							11 06			11 21												11 36		
Surrey Quays	d					11 05		11 10	11 19		11 25	11 30		11 45								11 35	11 40	11 49	
Canada Water	d					11 07		11 12	11 21		11 27	11 32		11 47								11 37	11 42	11 51	
Rotherhithe	d					11 08		11 13	11 23		11 28	11 33		11 48								11 38	11 43	11 53	
Wapping	d					11 10		11 15	11 24		11 30	11 35		11 50								11 40	11 45	11 54	
Shadwell	d					11 12		11 17	11 26		11 32	11 37		11 52								11 42	11 47	11 56	
Whitechapel	d					11 14		11 19	11 29		11 34	11 39		11 54								11 44	11 49	11 59	
Shoreditch High Street	d					11 16		11 21	11 31		11 36	11 41		11 56								11 46	11 51	12 01	
Hoxton	d					11 18		11 23	11 33		11 38	11 43		11 58								11 48	11 53	12 03	
Haggerston	d					11 20		11 25	11 35		11 40	11 45		12 00								11 50	11 55	12 05	
Dalston Junction Stn ELL	a					11 22		11 32	11 37		11 47	11 47		12 02								11 52	12 02	12 07	
Canonbury	d					11 27			11 42			11 50		12 05								11 57		12 12	
Highbury & Islington	a					11 35			11 49			11 58		12 13								12 05		12 19	
	d																								
London Bridge 4 ⊖	a			11 06	11 11					11 29			11 41			11 26				11 36	11 41				11 59

		LO		LO	SN	LO	SN	SN	SE	SE	SN	SN		LO	LO	LO	SN	LO	LO	SN	LO	SN		SN	SE
East Croydon	d																12 00								
West Croydon 4	d											11 31		11 39		11 52									
Norwood Junction 2	d													11 43		11 58	12 05								
Anerley	d													11 46		12 01	12 08								
Penge West	d													11 48		12 03	12 10								
London Victoria 15 ⊖	d				11 19				11 39		11 41									11 49					12 09
Battersea Park 4	d				11 23						11 45									11 53					
Wandsworth Road	d										11 47														
Clapham High Street ⊖	d										11 49														
London Blackfriars 3 ⊖	d									11 42															
Denmark Hill 4	d								11 48	11 52	11 54														12 18
Peckham Rye 4	d						11 42	11 46	11a51	11a55	11 56	12 01										12 12		12 16	12a21
Queens Rd Peckham	d							11 49			11 59	12 04												12 19	
South Bermondsey	d							11 51			12 01	12 06												12 21	
Clapham Junction 10	d				11 27															11 57					
Wandsworth Common	d				11 30															12 00					
Balham 4 ⊖	d				11 32															12 02					
Streatham Hill	d				11 35															12 05					
West Norwood 4	d				11 40		11 53													12 10		12 23			
Gipsy Hill	d				11 43		11 56													12 13		12 26			
Crystal Palace 4	d			11 43	11 51	11 58	11a59												12 13	12 21	12 28	12a29			
Sydenham	d			11 46	11 54	12 01								11 51		12 06	12 12		12 16	12 24	12 31				
Forest Hill 4	d			11 49	11 57	12 04								11 53		12 08	12 15		12 19	12 27	12 34				
Honor Oak Park	d			11 51	11 59	12 06								11 56		12 11	12 17		12 21	12 29	12 36				
Brockley	d			11 54	12 02	12 09								11 58		12 13	12 20		12 24	12 32	12 39				
New Cross Gate 4	a			11 56	12 04	12 11								12 01		12 16	12 22		12 26	12 34	12 41				
	d			11 56	12 04	12 11								12 01		12 16	12 22		12 26	12 34	12 41				
New Cross ELL	d	11 51													12 06			12 21							
Surrey Quays	d	11 55		12 00		12 15								12 05	12 10	12 19		12 25	12 30		12 45				
Canada Water	d	11 57		12 02		12 17								12 07	12 12	12 21		12 27	12 32		12 47				
Rotherhithe	d	11 58		12 03		12 18								12 08	12 13	12 23		12 28	12 33		12 48				
Wapping	d	12 00		12 05		12 20								12 10	12 15	12 24		12 30	12 35		12 50				
Shadwell	d	12 02		12 07		12 22								12 12	12 17	12 26		12 32	12 37		12 52				
Whitechapel	d	12 04		12 09		12 24								12 14	12 19	12 29		12 34	12 39		12 54				
Shoreditch High Street	d	12 06		12 11		12 26								12 16	12 21	12 31		12 36	12 41		12 56				
Hoxton	d	12 08		12 13		12 28								12 18	12 23	12 33		12 38	12 43		12 58				
Haggerston	d	12 10		12 15		12 30								12 20	12 25	12 35		12 40	12 45		13 00				
Dalston Junction Stn ELL	a	12 17		12 17		12 32								12 22	12 32	12 37		12 47	12 47		13 02				
Canonbury	d			12 20		12 35								12 27		12 42			12 50		13 05				
Highbury & Islington	a			12 28		12 43								12 35		12 49			12 58		13 13				
	d																								
London Bridge 4 ⊖	a				12 11			11 56			12 06	12 11					12 29			12 44				12 26	

Table 178

Saturdays

1 September to 8 September

East London Line and Croydon - London Victoria to London Bridge

Network Diagram - see first Page of Table 177

		SE	SN	SN	LO	LO	LO	SN		LO	LO	SN	LO	SN	SN	SE	SE	SN		SN	LO	LO	LO	SN	LO
East Croydon	d							12 30																13 00	
West Croydon [4]	d			12 01	12 09		12 22													12 31	12 39		12 52		
Norwood Junction [2]	d				12 13		12 28	12 35													12 43		12 58	13 05	
Anerley	d				12 16		12 31	12 38													12 46		13 01	13 08	
Penge West	d				12 18		12 33	12 40													12 48		13 03	13 10	
London Victoria [15] ⊖	d		12 11									12 19				12 39		12 41							
Battersea Park [4]	d		12 15									12 23						12 45							
Wandsworth Road	d		12 17															12 47							
Clapham High Street ⊖	d		12 19															12 49							
London Blackfriars [3] ⊖	d	12 12															12 42								
Denmark Hill [4]	d	12 22	12 24													12 48	12 52	12 54							
Peckham Rye [4]	d	12a25	12 26	12 31										12 42	12 46	12a51	12a55	12 56		13 01					
Queens Rd Peckham	d		12 29	12 34											12 49			12 59		13 04					
South Bermondsey	d		12 31	12 36											12 51			13 01		13 06					
Clapham Junction [10]	d											12 27													
Wandsworth Common	d											12 30													
Balham [4] ⊖	d											12 32													
Streatham Hill	d											12 35													
West Norwood [4]	d											12 40		12 53											
Gipsy Hill	d											12 43		12 56											
Crystal Palace [4]	d										12 43	12 51	12 58	12a59											
Sydenham	d				12 21		12 36	12 42			12 46	12 54	13 01								12 51		13 06	13 12	
Forest Hill [4]	d				12 23		12 38	12 45			12 49	12 57	13 04								12 53		13 08	13 15	
Honor Oak Park	d				12 26		12 41	12 47			12 51	12 59	13 06								12 56		13 11	13 17	
Brockley	d				12 28		12 43	12 50			12 54	13 02	13 09								12 58		13 13	13 20	
New Cross Gate [4]	a				12 31		12 46	12 52			12 56	13 04	13 11								13 01		13 16	13 22	
	d				12 31		12 46	12 52			12 56	13 04	13 11								13 01		13 16	13 22	
New Cross ELL	d					12 36				12 51												13 06			13 21
Surrey Quays	d				12 35	12 40	12 49			12 55	13 00		13 15								13 05	13 10	13 19		13 25
Canada Water	d				12 37	12 42	12 51			12 57	13 02		13 17								13 07	13 12	13 21		13 27
Rotherhithe	d				12 38	12 43	12 53			12 58	13 03		13 18								13 08	13 13	13 23		13 28
Wapping	d				12 40	12 45	12 54			13 00	13 05		13 20								13 10	13 15	13 24		13 30
Shadwell	d				12 42	12 47	12 56			13 02	13 07		13 22								13 12	13 17	13 26		13 32
Whitechapel	d				12 44	12 49	12 59			13 04	13 09		13 24								13 14	13 19	13 29		13 34
Shoreditch High Street	d				12 46	12 51	13 01			13 06	13 11		13 26								13 16	13 21	13 31		13 36
Hoxton	d				12 48	12 53	13 03			13 08	13 13		13 28								13 18	13 23	13 33		13 38
Haggerston	d				12 50	12 55	13 05			13 10	13 15		13 30								13 20	13 25	13 35		13 40
Dalston Junction Stn ELL	a				12 52	13 02	13 07			13 17	13 17		13 32								13 22	13 32	13 37		13 47
Canonbury	d				12 57		13 12				13 20		13 35								13 27		13 42		
Highbury & Islington	a				13 05		13 19				13 28		13 43								13 35		13 49		
	d																								
London Bridge [4] ⊖	a		12 36	12 41				12 59				13 11			12 56			13 06		13 11				13 29	

		LO	SN	LO		SN	SN	SE	SE	SN	SN	LO	LO	LO		SN	LO	LO	SN	LO	SN	SN	SE	SE	
East Croydon	d															13 30									
West Croydon [4]	d										13 01	13 09		13 22											
Norwood Junction [2]	d											13 13		13 28		13 35									
Anerley	d											13 16		13 31		13 38									
Penge West	d											13 18		13 33		13 40									
London Victoria [15] ⊖	d		12 49					13 09		13 11									13 19				13 39		
Battersea Park [4]	d		12 53							13 15									13 23						
Wandsworth Road	d									13 17															
Clapham High Street ⊖	d									13 19															
London Blackfriars [3] ⊖	d								13 12															13 42	
Denmark Hill [4]	d							13 18	13 22	13 24													13 48	13 52	
Peckham Rye [4]	d					13 12	13 16	13a21	13a25	13 26	13 31										13 42	13 46	13a51	13a55	
Queens Rd Peckham	d						13 19			13 29	13 34											13 49			
South Bermondsey	d						13 21			13 31	13 36											13 51			
Clapham Junction [10]	d		12 57																13 27						
Wandsworth Common	d		13 00																13 30						
Balham [4] ⊖	d		13 02																13 32						
Streatham Hill	d		13 05																13 35						
West Norwood [4]	d		13 10			13 23													13 40		13 53				
Gipsy Hill	d		13 13			13 26													13 43		13 56				
Crystal Palace [4]	d	13 13	13 21	13 28		13a29												13 43	13 51	13 58	13a59				
Sydenham	d	13 16	13 24	13 31								13 21		13 36		13 42		13 46	13 54	14 01					
Forest Hill [4]	d	13 19	13 27	13 34								13 23		13 38		13 45		13 49	13 57	14 04					
Honor Oak Park	d	13 21	13 29	13 36								13 26		13 41		13 47		13 51	13 59	14 06					
Brockley	d	13 24	13 32	13 39								13 28		13 43		13 50		13 54	14 02	14 09					
New Cross Gate [4]	a	13 26	13 34	13 41								13 31		13 46		13 52		13 56	14 04	14 11					
	d	13 26	13 34	13 41								13 31		13 46		13 52		13 56	14 04	14 11					
New Cross ELL	d												13 36				13 51								
Surrey Quays	d	13 30		13 45								13 35	13 40	13 49			13 55	14 00		14 15					
Canada Water	d	13 32		13 47								13 37	13 42	13 51			13 57	14 02		14 17					
Rotherhithe	d	13 33		13 48								13 38	13 43	13 53			13 58	14 03		14 18					
Wapping	d	13 35		13 50								13 40	13 45	13 54			14 00	14 05		14 20					
Shadwell	d	13 37		13 52								13 42	13 47	13 56			14 02	14 07		14 22					
Whitechapel	d	13 39		13 54								13 44	13 49	13 59			14 04	14 09		14 24					
Shoreditch High Street	d	13 41		13 56								13 46	13 51	14 01			14 06	14 11		14 26					
Hoxton	d	13 43		13 58								13 48	13 53	14 03			14 08	14 13		14 28					
Haggerston	d	13 45		14 00								13 50	13 55	14 05			14 10	14 15		14 30					
Dalston Junction Stn ELL	a	13 47		14 02								13 52	14 02	14 07			14 17	14 17		14 32					
Canonbury	d	13 50		14 05								13 57		14 12				14 20		14 35					
Highbury & Islington	a	13 58		14 13								14 05		14 19				14 28		14 43					
	d																								
London Bridge [4] ⊖	a		13 44				13 26			13 36	13 41					13 59			14 11			13 56			

Table 178

Saturdays

1 September to 8 September

East London Line and Croydon - London Victoria to London Bridge

Network Diagram - see first Page of Table 177

Station		SN	SN	LO	LO	LO	SN	LO	LO	SN		LO	SN	SN	SE	SE	SN	SN	LO	LO		LO	SN	LO	LO
East Croydon 🚋	d						14 00																14 30		
West Croydon 4 🚋	d		13 31	13 39		13 52												14 01	14 09			14 22			
Norwood Junction 2	d			13 43		13 58	14 05												14 13			14 28	14 35		
Anerley	d			13 46		14 01	14 08												14 16			14 31	14 38		
Penge West	d			13 48		14 03	14 10												14 18			14 33	14 40		
London Victoria 15 ⊖	d	13 41								13 49					14 09		14 11								
Battersea Park 4	d	13 45								13 53							14 15								
Wandsworth Road	d	13 47															14 17								
Clapham High Street ⊖	d	13 49															14 19								
London Blackfriars 3 ⊖	d															14 12									
Denmark Hill 4	d	13 54													14 18	14 22	14 24								
Peckham Rye 4	d	13 56	14 01										14 12	14 16	14a21	14a25	14 26	14 31							
Queens Rd Peckham	d	13 59	14 04											14 19			14 29	14 34							
South Bermondsey	d	14 01	14 06											14 21			14 31	14 36							
Clapham Junction 10	d									13 57															
Wandsworth Common	d									14 00															
Balham 4 ⊖	d									14 02															
Streatham Hill	d									14 05															
West Norwood 4	d									14 10			14 23												
Gipsy Hill	d									14 13			14 26												
Crystal Palace 4	d								14 13	14 21		14 28	14a29												14 43
Sydenham	d			13 51		14 06	14 12		14 16	14 24		14 31							14 21			14 36	14 42		14 46
Forest Hill 4	d			13 53		14 08	14 15		14 19	14 27		14 34							14 23			14 38	14 45		14 49
Honor Oak Park	d			13 56		14 11	14 17		14 21	14 29		14 36							14 26			14 41	14 47		14 51
Brockley	d			13 58		14 13	14 20		14 24	14 32		14 39							14 28			14 43	14 50		14 54
New Cross Gate 4	a			14 01		14 16	14 22		14 26	14 34		14 41							14 31			14 46	14 52		14 56
	d			14 01		14 16	14 22		14 26	14 34		14 41							14 31			14 46	14 52		14 56
New Cross ELL	d				14 06			14 21												14 36				14 51	
Surrey Quays	d			14 05	14 10	14 19		14 25	14 30			14 45							14 35	14 40		14 49		14 55	15 00
Canada Water	d			14 07	14 12	14 21		14 27	14 32			14 47							14 37	14 42		14 51		14 57	15 02
Rotherhithe	d			14 08	14 13	14 23		14 28	14 33			14 48							14 38	14 43		14 53		14 58	15 03
Wapping	d			14 10	14 15	14 24		14 30	14 35			14 50							14 40	14 45		14 54		15 00	15 05
Shadwell	d			14 12	14 17	14 26		14 32	14 37			14 52							14 42	14 47		14 56		15 02	15 07
Whitechapel	d			14 14	14 19	14 29		14 34	14 39			14 54							14 44	14 49		14 59		15 04	15 09
Shoreditch High Street	d			14 16	14 21	14 31		14 36	14 41			14 56							14 46	14 51		15 01		15 06	15 11
Hoxton	d			14 18	14 23	14 33		14 38	14 43			14 58							14 48	14 53		15 03		15 08	15 13
Haggerston	d			14 20	14 25	14 35		14 40	14 45			15 00							14 50	14 55		15 05		15 10	15 15
Dalston Junction Stn ELL	a			14 22	14 32	14 37		14 47	14 47			15 02							14 52	15 02		15 07		15 17	15 17
Canonbury	d			14 27		14 42			14 50			15 05							14 57			15 12			15 20
Highbury & Islington	a			14 35		14 49			14 58			15 13							15 05			15 19			15 28
	d																								
London Bridge 4 ⊖	a	14 06	14 11				14 29			14 44				14 26			14 36	14 41					14 59		

Station		SN	LO	SN	SN	SE		SE	SN	SN	LO	LO	LO	SN	LO	LO		SN	LO	SN	SN	SE	SE	SN	SN
East Croydon 🚋	d													15 00											
West Croydon 4 🚋	d									14 31	14 39		14 52												15 01
Norwood Junction 2	d										14 43		14 58	15 05											
Anerley	d										14 46		15 01	15 08											
Penge West	d										14 48		15 03	15 10											
London Victoria 15 ⊖	d	14 19				14 39			14 41									14 49				15 09		15 11	
Battersea Park 4	d	14 23							14 45									14 53						15 15	
Wandsworth Road	d								14 47															15 17	
Clapham High Street ⊖	d								14 49															15 19	
London Blackfriars 3 ⊖	d							14 42															15 12		
Denmark Hill 4	d					14 48		14 52	14 54													15 18	15 22	15 24	
Peckham Rye 4	d			14 42	14 46	14a51		14a55	14 56	15 01										15 12	15 16	15a21	15a25	15 26	15 31
Queens Rd Peckham	d				14 49				14 59	15 04											15 19			15 29	15 34
South Bermondsey	d				14 51				15 01	15 06											15 21			15 31	15 36
Clapham Junction 10	d	14 27																14 57							
Wandsworth Common	d	14 30																15 00							
Balham 4 ⊖	d	14 32																15 02							
Streatham Hill	d	14 35																15 05							
West Norwood 4	d	14 40		14 53														15 10		15 23					
Gipsy Hill	d	14 43		14 56														15 13		15 26					
Crystal Palace 4	d	14 51	14 58	14a59												15 13		15 21	15 28	15a29					
Sydenham	d	14 54	15 01								14 51		15 06	15 12		15 16		15 24	15 31						
Forest Hill 4	d	14 57	15 04								14 53		15 08	15 15		15 19		15 27	15 34						
Honor Oak Park	d	14 59	15 06								14 56		15 11	15 17		15 21		15 29	15 36						
Brockley	d	15 02	15 09								14 58		15 13	15 20		15 24		15 32	15 39						
New Cross Gate 4	a	15 04	15 11								15 01		15 16	15 22		15 26		15 34	15 41						
	d	15 04	15 11								15 01		15 16	15 22		15 26		15 34	15 41						
New Cross ELL	d											15 06			15 21										
Surrey Quays	d		15 15								15 05	15 10	15 19		15 25	15 30			15 45						
Canada Water	d		15 17								15 07	15 12	15 21		15 27	15 32			15 47						
Rotherhithe	d		15 18								15 08	15 13	15 23		15 28	15 33			15 48						
Wapping	d		15 20								15 10	15 15	15 24		15 30	15 35			15 50						
Shadwell	d		15 22								15 12	15 17	15 26		15 32	15 37			15 52						
Whitechapel	d		15 24								15 14	15 19	15 29		15 34	15 39			15 54						
Shoreditch High Street	d		15 26								15 16	15 21	15 31		15 36	15 41			15 56						
Hoxton	d		15 28								15 18	15 23	15 33		15 38	15 43			15 58						
Haggerston	d		15 30								15 20	15 25	15 35		15 40	15 45			16 00						
Dalston Junction Stn ELL	a		15 32								15 22	15 32	15 37		15 47	15 47			16 02						
Canonbury	d		15 35								15 27		15 42			15 50			16 05						
Highbury & Islington	a		15 43								15 35		15 49			15 58			16 13						
	d																								
London Bridge 4 ⊖	a	15 11			14 56				15 06	15 11				15 29				15 44			15 26			15 36	15 41

Table 178

Saturdays

1 September to 8 September

East London Line and Croydon - London Victoria to London Bridge

Network Diagram - see first Page of Table 177

		LO		LO	LO	SN	LO	LO	SN	LO	SN	SN		SE	SE	SN	SN	LO	LO	LO	SN	LO		LO	SN
East Croydon	d					15 30															16 00				
West Croydon 4	d	15 09			15 22												15 31	15 39		15 52					
Norwood Junction 2	d	15 13			15 28	15 35												15 43		15 58	16 05				
Anerley	d	15 16			15 31	15 38												15 46		16 01	16 08				
Penge West	d	15 18			15 33	15 40												15 48		16 03	16 10				
London Victoria 15	d								15 19					15 39		15 41									15 49
Battersea Park 4	d								15 23							15 45									15 53
Wandsworth Road	d															15 47									
Clapham High Street	d															15 49									
London Blackfriars 3	d														15 42										
Denmark Hill 4	d													15 48	15 52	15 54									
Peckham Rye 4	d										15 42	15 46		15a51	15a55	15 56	16 01								
Queens Rd Peckham	d											15 49				15 59	16 04								
South Bermondsey	d											15 51				16 01	16 06								
Clapham Junction 10	d								15 27																15 57
Wandsworth Common	d								15 30																16 00
Balham 4	d								15 32																16 02
Streatham Hill	d								15 35																16 05
West Norwood 4	d								15 40		15 53														16 10
Gipsy Hill	d								15 43		15 56														16 13
Crystal Palace 4	d							15 43	15 51	15 58	15a59													16 13	16 21
Sydenham	d	15 21			15 36	15 42		15 46	15 54	16 01								15 51		16 06	16 12			16 16	16 24
Forest Hill 4	d	15 23			15 38	15 45		15 49	15 57	16 04								15 53		16 08	16 15			16 19	16 27
Honor Oak Park	d	15 26			15 41	15 47		15 51	15 59	16 06								15 56		16 11	16 17			16 21	16 29
Brockley	d	15 28			15 43	15 50		15 54	16 02	16 09								15 58		16 13	16 20			16 24	16 32
New Cross Gate 4	a	15 31			15 46	15 52		15 56	16 04	16 11								16 01		16 16	16 22			16 26	16 34
	d	15 31			15 46	15 52		15 56	16 04	16 11								16 01		16 16	16 22			16 26	16 34
New Cross ELL	d			15 36			15 51												16 06			16 21			
Surrey Quays	d	15 35		15 40	15 49		15 55	16 00		16 15								16 05	16 10	16 19		16 25		16 30	
Canada Water	d	15 37		15 42	15 51		15 57	16 02		16 17								16 07	16 12	16 21		16 27		16 32	
Rotherhithe	d	15 38		15 43	15 53		15 58	16 03		16 18								16 08	16 13	16 23		16 28		16 33	
Wapping	d	15 40		15 45	15 54		16 00	16 05		16 20								16 10	16 15	16 24		16 30		16 35	
Shadwell	d	15 42		15 47	15 56		16 02	16 07		16 22								16 12	16 17	16 26		16 32		16 37	
Whitechapel	d	15 44		15 49	15 59		16 04	16 09		16 24								16 14	16 19	16 29		16 34		16 39	
Shoreditch High Street	d	15 46		15 51	16 01		16 06	16 11		16 26								16 16	16 21	16 31		16 36		16 41	
Hoxton	d	15 48		15 53	16 03		16 08	16 13		16 28								16 18	16 23	16 33		16 38		16 43	
Haggerston	d	15 50		15 55	16 05		16 10	16 15		16 30								16 20	16 25	16 35		16 40		16 45	
Dalston Junction Stn ELL	a	15 52		16 02	16 07		16 17	16 17		16 32								16 22	16 32	16 37		16 47		16 47	
Canonbury	d	15 57			16 12			16 20		16 35								16 27		16 42				16 50	
Highbury & Islington	a	16 05			16 19			16 28		16 43								16 35		16 49				16 58	
	d																								
London Bridge 4	a					15 59			16 11			15 56				16 06	16 11				16 29				16 41

		LO	SN	SN	SE	SE	SN	SN		LO	LO	LO	SN	LO	LO	SN	LO	SN		SN	SE	SE	SN	SN	LO
East Croydon	d												16 30												
West Croydon 4	d							16 01		16 09		16 22												16 31	16 39
Norwood Junction 2	d									16 13		16 28	16 35												16 43
Anerley	d									16 16		16 31	16 38												16 46
Penge West	d									16 18		16 33	16 40												16 48
London Victoria 15	d				16 09		16 11									16 19					16 39		16 41		
Battersea Park 4	d						16 15									16 23							16 45		
Wandsworth Road	d						16 17																16 47		
Clapham High Street	d						16 19																16 49		
London Blackfriars 3	d					16 12																16 42			
Denmark Hill 4	d				16 18	16 22	16 24														16 48	16 52	16 54		
Peckham Rye 4	d		16 12	16 16	16a21	16a25	16 26	16 31										16 42		16 46	16a51	16a55	16 56	17 01	
Queens Rd Peckham	d			16 19			16 29	16 34												16 49			16 59	17 04	
South Bermondsey	d			16 21			16 31	16 36												16 51			17 01	17 06	
Clapham Junction 10	d															16 27									
Wandsworth Common	d															16 30									
Balham 4	d															16 32									
Streatham Hill	d															16 35									
West Norwood 4	d		16 23													16 40		16 53							
Gipsy Hill	d		16 26													16 43		16 56							
Crystal Palace 4	d	16 28	16a29												16 43	16 51	16 58	16a59							
Sydenham	d	16 31								16 21		16 36	16 42		16 46	16 54	17 01								16 51
Forest Hill 4	d	16 34								16 23		16 38	16 45		16 49	16 57	17 04								16 53
Honor Oak Park	d	16 36								16 26		16 41	16 47		16 51	16 59	17 06								16 56
Brockley	d	16 39								16 28		16 43	16 50		16 54	17 02	17 09								16 58
New Cross Gate 4	a	16 41								16 31		16 46	16 52		16 56	17 04	17 11								17 01
	d	16 41								16 31		16 46	16 52		16 56	17 04	17 11								17 01
New Cross ELL	d										16 36			16 51											
Surrey Quays	d	16 45								16 35	16 40	16 49		16 55	17 00		17 15								17 05
Canada Water	d	16 47								16 37	16 42	16 51		16 57	17 02		17 17								17 07
Rotherhithe	d	16 48								16 38	16 43	16 53		16 58	17 03		17 18								17 08
Wapping	d	16 50								16 40	16 45	16 54		17 00	17 05		17 20								17 10
Shadwell	d	16 52								16 42	16 47	16 56		17 02	17 07		17 22								17 12
Whitechapel	d	16 54								16 44	16 49	16 59		17 04	17 09		17 24								17 14
Shoreditch High Street	d	16 56								16 46	16 51	17 01		17 06	17 11		17 26								17 16
Hoxton	d	16 58								16 48	16 53	17 03		17 08	17 13		17 28								17 18
Haggerston	d	17 00								16 50	16 55	17 05		17 10	17 15		17 30								17 20
Dalston Junction Stn ELL	a	17 02								16 52	17 02	17 07		17 17	17 17		17 32								17 22
Canonbury	d	17 05								16 57		17 12			17 20		17 35								17 27
Highbury & Islington	a	17 13								17 05		17 19			17 28		17 43								17 35
	d																								
London Bridge 4	a			16 26			16 36	16 41					16 59			17 11				16 56			17 06	17 11	

Table 178

Saturdays

1 September to 8 September

East London Line and Croydon - London Victoria to London Bridge

Network Diagram - see first Page of Table 177

Station		LO	LO	SN	LO	LO	SN	LO	SN	SN	SE	SE	SN	SN	LO	LO	LO	SN	LO	LO	SN	LO
East Croydon	d			17 00														17 30				
West Croydon 4	d		16 52											17 01	17 09		17 22					
Norwood Junction 2	d		16 58	17 05											17 13		17 28	17 35				
Anerley	d		17 01	17 08											17 16		17 31	17 38				
Penge West	d		17 03	17 10											17 18		17 33	17 40				
London Victoria 15	d						16 49				17 09		17 11								17 19	
Battersea Park 4	d						16 53						17 15								17 23	
Wandsworth Road	d												17 17									
Clapham High Street	d												17 19									
London Blackfriars 3	d											17 12										
Denmark Hill 4	d										17 18	17 22	17 24									
Peckham Rye 4	d								17 12	17 16	17a21	17a25	17 26	17 31								
Queens Rd Peckham	d									17 19			17 29	17 34								
South Bermondsey	d									17 21			17 31	17 36								
Clapham Junction 10	d						16 57														17 27	
Wandsworth Common	d						17 00														17 30	
Balham 4	d						17 02														17 32	
Streatham Hill	d						17 05														17 35	
West Norwood 4	d						17 10		17 23												17 40	
Gipsy Hill	d						17 13		17 26												17 43	
Crystal Palace 4	d					17 13	17 21	17 28	17a29											17 43	17 51	17 58
Sydenham	d		17 06	17 12		17 16	17 24	17 31							17 21		17 36	17 42		17 46	17 54	18 01
Forest Hill 4	d		17 08	17 15		17 19	17 27	17 34							17 23		17 38	17 45		17 49	17 57	18 04
Honor Oak Park	d		17 11	17 17		17 21	17 29	17 36							17 26		17 41	17 47		17 51	17 59	18 06
Brockley	d		17 13	17 20		17 24	17 32	17 39							17 28		17 43	17 50		17 54	18 02	18 09
New Cross Gate 4	a		17 16	17 22		17 26	17 34	17 41							17 31		17 46	17 52		17 56	18 04	18 11
	d		17 16	17 22		17 26	17 34	17 41							17 31		17 46	17 52		17 56	18 04	18 11
New Cross ELL	d	17 06			17 21											17 36			17 51			
Surrey Quays	d	17 10	17 19		17 25	17 30		17 45							17 35	17 40	17 49		17 55	18 00		18 15
Canada Water	d	17 12	17 21		17 27	17 32		17 47							17 37	17 42	17 51		17 57	18 02		18 17
Rotherhithe	d	17 13	17 23		17 28	17 33		17 48							17 38	17 43	17 53		17 58	18 03		18 18
Wapping	d	17 15	17 24		17 30	17 35		17 50							17 40	17 45	17 54		18 00	18 05		18 20
Shadwell	d	17 17	17 26		17 32	17 37		17 52							17 42	17 47	17 56		18 02	18 07		18 22
Whitechapel	d	17 19	17 29		17 34	17 39		17 54							17 44	17 49	17 59		18 04	18 09		18 24
Shoreditch High Street	d	17 21	17 31		17 36	17 41		17 56							17 46	17 51	18 01		18 06	18 11		18 26
Hoxton	d	17 23	17 33		17 38	17 43		17 58							17 48	17 53	18 03		18 08	18 13		18 28
Haggerston	d	17 25	17 35		17 40	17 45		18 00							17 50	17 55	18 05		18 10	18 15		18 30
Dalston Junction Stn ELL	a	17 32	17 37		17 47	17 47		18 02							17 52	18 02	18 07		18 17	18 17		18 32
Canonbury	d		17 42			17 50		18 05							17 57		18 12			18 20		18 35
Highbury & Islington	a		17 49			17 58		18 13							18 05		18 19			18 28		18 43
	d																					
London Bridge 4	a			17 30			17 41			17 26			17 36	17 41				17 59			18 11	

Station		SN	SN	SE	SE	SN	SN	LO	LO	LO	SN	LO	LO	SN	LO	SN	SN	SE	SE	SN	SN	LO	LO
East Croydon	d										18 00												
West Croydon 4	d						17 31	17 39		17 52											18 01	18 09	
Norwood Junction 2	d							17 43		17 58	18 05											18 13	
Anerley	d							17 46		18 01	18 08											18 16	
Penge West	d							17 48		18 03	18 10											18 18	
London Victoria 15	d			17 39		17 41								17 49				18 09		18 11			
Battersea Park 4	d					17 45								17 53						18 15			
Wandsworth Road	d					17 47														18 17			
Clapham High Street	d					17 49														18 19			
London Blackfriars 3	d				17 42														18 12				
Denmark Hill 4	d			17 48	17 52	17 54												18 18	18 22	18 24			
Peckham Rye 4	d	17 42	17 46	17a51	17a55	17 56	18 01									18 12	18 16	18a21	18a25	18 26	18 31		
Queens Rd Peckham	d		17 49			17 59	18 04										18 19			18 29	18 34		
South Bermondsey	d		17 51			18 01	18 06										18 21			18 31	18 36		
Clapham Junction 10	d													17 57									
Wandsworth Common	d													18 00									
Balham 4	d													18 02									
Streatham Hill	d													18 05									
West Norwood 4	d	17 53												18 10		18 23							
Gipsy Hill	d	17 56												18 13		18 26							
Crystal Palace 4	d	17a59											18 13	18 21	18 28	18a29							
Sydenham	d							17 51		18 06	18 12		18 16	18 24	18 31							18 21	
Forest Hill 4	d							17 53		18 08	18 15		18 19	18 27	18 34							18 23	
Honor Oak Park	d							17 56		18 11	18 17		18 21	18 29	18 36							18 26	
Brockley	d							17 58		18 13	18 20		18 24	18 32	18 39							18 28	
New Cross Gate 4	a							18 01		18 16	18 22		18 26	18 34	18 41							18 31	
	d							18 01		18 16	18 22		18 26	18 34	18 41							18 31	
New Cross ELL	d								18 06			18 21											18 36
Surrey Quays	d							18 05	18 10	18 19		18 25	18 30		18 45							18 35	18 40
Canada Water	d							18 07	18 12	18 21		18 27	18 32		18 47							18 37	18 42
Rotherhithe	d							18 08	18 13	18 23		18 28	18 33		18 48							18 38	18 43
Wapping	d							18 10	18 15	18 24		18 30	18 35		18 50							18 40	18 45
Shadwell	d							18 12	18 17	18 26		18 32	18 37		18 52							18 42	18 47
Whitechapel	d							18 14	18 19	18 29		18 34	18 39		18 54							18 44	18 49
Shoreditch High Street	d							18 16	18 21	18 31		18 36	18 41		18 56							18 46	18 51
Hoxton	d							18 18	18 23	18 33		18 38	18 43		18 58							18 48	18 53
Haggerston	d							18 20	18 25	18 35		18 40	18 45		19 00							18 50	18 55
Dalston Junction Stn ELL	a							18 23	18 32	18 37		18 47	18 47		19 02							18 52	19 02
Canonbury	d							18 27		18 42			18 50		19 05							18 57	
Highbury & Islington	a							18 35		18 49			18 58		19 13							19 05	
	d																						
London Bridge 4	a		17 56			18 06	18 11				18 29			18 41			18 26			18 36	18 41		

Table 178

Saturdays

1 September to 8 September

East London Line and Croydon - London Victoria to London Bridge

Network Diagram - see first Page of Table 177

		LO	SN	LO	LO	SN		LO	SN	SN	SE	SE	SN	SN	LO	LO		LO	SN	LO	LO	SN	LO	SN	SN
East Croydon 🚌	d		18 30																19 00						
West Croydon 4 🚌	d	18 22												18 31	18 39			18 52							
Norwood Junction 2	d	18 28	18 35												18 43			18 58	19 05						
Anerley	d	18 31	18 38												18 46			19 01	19 08						
Penge West	d	18 33	18 40												18 48			19 03	19 10						
London Victoria 15 ⊖	d					18 19					18 39		18 41									18 49			
Battersea Park 4	d					18 23							18 45									18 53			
Wandsworth Road	d												18 47												
Clapham High Street ⊖	d												18 49												
London Blackfriars 3 ⊖	d											18 42													
Denmark Hill 4	d										18 48	18 52	18 54												
Peckham Rye 4	d								18 42	18 46	18a51	18a55	18 56	19 01										19 12	19 16
Queens Rd Peckham	d									18 49			18 59	19 04											19 19
South Bermondsey	d									18 51			19 01	19 06											19 21
Clapham Junction 10	d					18 27																18 57			
Wandsworth Common	d					18 30																19 00			
Balham 4 ⊖	d					18 32																19 02			
Streatham Hill	d					18 35																19 05			
West Norwood 4	d					18 40			18 53													19 10		19 23	
Gipsy Hill	d					18 43			18 56													19 13		19 26	
Crystal Palace 4	d				18 43	18 51		18 58	18a59												19 13	19 21	19 28	19a29	
Sydenham	d	18 36	18 42		18 46	18 54		19 01							18 51			19 06	19 12		19 16	19 24	19 31		
Forest Hill 4	d	18 38	18 45		18 49	18 57		19 04							18 53			19 08	19 15		19 19	19 27	19 34		
Honor Oak Park	d	18 41	18 47		18 51	18 59		19 06							18 56			19 11	19 17		19 21	19 29	19 36		
Brockley	d	18 43	18 50		18 54	19 02		19 09							18 58			19 13	19 20		19 24	19 32	19 39		
New Cross Gate 4	a	18 46	18 52		18 56	19 04		19 11							19 01			19 16	19 22		19 26	19 34	19 41		
	d	18 46	18 52		18 56	19 04		19 11							19 01			19 16	19 22		19 26	19 34	19 41		
New Cross ELL	d			18 51												19 06				19 21					
Surrey Quays	d	18 49		18 55	19 00			19 15							19 05	19 10		19 19		19 25	19 30		19 45		
Canada Water	d	18 51		18 57	19 02			19 17							19 07	19 12		19 21		19 27	19 32		19 47		
Rotherhithe	d	18 53		18 58	19 03			19 18							19 08	19 13		19 23		19 28	19 33		19 48		
Wapping	d	18 54		19 00	19 05			19 20							19 10	19 15		19 24		19 30	19 35		19 50		
Shadwell	d	18 56		19 02	19 07			19 22							19 12	19 17		19 26		19 32	19 37		19 52		
Whitechapel	d	18 59		19 04	19 09			19 24							19 14	19 19		19 29		19 34	19 39		19 54		
Shoreditch High Street	d	19 01		19 06	19 11			19 26							19 16	19 21		19 31		19 36	19 41		19 56		
Hoxton	d	19 03		19 08	19 13			19 28							19 18	19 23		19 33		19 38	19 43		19 58		
Haggerston	d	19 05		19 10	19 15			19 30							19 20	19 25		19 35		19 40	19 45		20 00		
Dalston Junction Stn ELL	a	19 07		19 17	19 17			19 32							19 22	19 32		19 37		19 47	19 47		20 02		
Canonbury	d	19 12			19 20			19 35							19 27			19 42			19 50		20 05		
Highbury & Islington	a	19 19			19 28			19 43							19 35			19 49			19 58		20 13		
	d																								
London Bridge 4 ⊖	a		18 59			19 11				18 56			19 06	19 11					19 29			19 41			19 26

		SE		SE	SN	SN	LO	LO	LO	SN	LO	LO		SN	LO	SN	SN	SE	SE	SN	SN	LO		LO	LO
East Croydon 🚌	d									19 30															
West Croydon 4 🚌	d					19 01	19 09		19 22												19 31	19 39			19 52
Norwood Junction 2	d						19 13		19 28	19 35												19 43			19 58
Anerley	d						19 16		19 31	19 38												19 46			20 01
Penge West	d						19 18		19 33	19 40												19 48			20 03
London Victoria 15 ⊖	d	19 09			19 11									19 19				19 39		19 41					
Battersea Park 4	d				19 15									19 23						19 45					
Wandsworth Road	d				19 17															19 47					
Clapham High Street ⊖	d				19 19															19 49					
London Blackfriars 3 ⊖	d			19 12															19 42						
Denmark Hill 4	d	19 18		19 22	19 24													19 48	19 52	19 54					
Peckham Rye 4	d	19a21		19a25	19 26	19 31										19 42	19 46	19a51	19a55	19 56	20 01				
Queens Rd Peckham	d				19 29	19 34											19 49			19 59	20 04				
South Bermondsey	d				19 31	19 36											19 51			20 01	20 06				
Clapham Junction 10	d													19 27											
Wandsworth Common	d													19 30											
Balham 4 ⊖	d													19 32											
Streatham Hill	d													19 35											
West Norwood 4	d													19 40		19 53									
Gipsy Hill	d													19 43		19 56									
Crystal Palace 4	d											19 43		19 51	19 58	19a59									
Sydenham	d						19 21		19 36	19 42		19 46		19 54	20 01							19 51			20 06
Forest Hill 4	d						19 23		19 38	19 45		19 49		19 57	20 04							19 53			20 08
Honor Oak Park	d						19 26		19 41	19 47		19 51		19 59	20 06							19 56			20 11
Brockley	d						19 28		19 43	19 50		19 54		20 02	20 09							19 58			20 13
New Cross Gate 4	a						19 31		19 46	19 52		19 56		20 04	20 11							20 01			20 16
	d						19 31		19 46	19 52		19 56		20 04	20 11							20 01			20 16
New Cross ELL	d							19 36			19 51													20 06	
Surrey Quays	d						19 35	19 40	19 49		19 55	20 00			20 15							20 05		20 10	20 19
Canada Water	d						19 37	19 42	19 51		19 57	20 02			20 17							20 07		20 12	20 21
Rotherhithe	d						19 38	19 43	19 53		19 58	20 03			20 18							20 08		20 13	20 23
Wapping	d						19 40	19 45	19 54		20 00	20 05			20 20							20 10		20 15	20 24
Shadwell	d						19 42	19 47	19 56		20 02	20 07			20 22							20 12		20 17	20 26
Whitechapel	d						19 44	19 49	19 59		20 04	20 09			20 24							20 14		20 19	20 29
Shoreditch High Street	d						19 46	19 51	20 01		20 06	20 11			20 26							20 16		20 21	20 31
Hoxton	d						19 48	19 53	20 03		20 08	20 13			20 28							20 18		20 23	20 33
Haggerston	d						19 50	19 55	20 05		20 10	20 15			20 30							20 20		20 25	20 35
Dalston Junction Stn ELL	a						19 52	20 02	20 07		20 17	20 17			20 32							20 22		20 32	20 37
Canonbury	d						19 57		20 12			20 20			20 35							20 27			20 42
Highbury & Islington	a						20 05		20 19			20 28			20 43							20 35			20 49
	d																								
London Bridge 4 ⊖	a				19 36	19 41				19 59				20 11			19 56			20 06	20 11				

Saturdays

1 September to 8 September

East London Line and Croydon - London Victoria to London Bridge

Network Diagram - see first Page of Table 177

Station		SN	LO	LO	SN	LO	SN	SN		SE	SN	SN	LO	LO	LO	SN	LO	LO		SN	LO	SN	SN	SE	SN
East Croydon (tram)	d	20 00														20 30									
West Croydon 4 (tram)	d											20 01	20 09		20 22										
Norwood Junction 2	d	20 05											20 13		20 28	20 35									
Anerley	d	20 08											20 16		20 31	20 38									
Penge West	d	20 10											20 18		20 33	20 40									
London Victoria 15 ⊖	d				19 49						20 11									20 19					20 41
Battersea Park 4	d				19 53						20 15									20 23					20 45
Wandsworth Road	d										20 17														20 47
Clapham High Street ⊖	d										20 19														20 49
London Blackfriars 3 ⊖	d									20 12														20 42	
Denmark Hill 4	d									20 22	20 24													20 52	20 54
Peckham Rye 4	d						20 12	20 16		20a25	20 26	20 31										20 42	20 46	20a55	20 56
Queens Rd Peckham	d							20 19			20 29	20 34											20 49		20 59
South Bermondsey	d							20 21			20 31	20 36											20 51		21 01
Clapham Junction 10	d				19 57															20 27					
Wandsworth Common	d				20 00															20 30					
Balham 4 ⊖	d				20 02															20 32					
Streatham Hill	d				20 05															20 35					
West Norwood 4	d				20 10		20 23													20 40		20 53			
Gipsy Hill	d				20 13		20 26													20 43		20 56			
Crystal Palace 4	d			20 13	20 21	20 28	20a29											20 43		20 51	20 58	20a59			
Sydenham	d	20 12		20 16	20 24	20 31							20 21		20 36	20 42		20 46		20 54	21 01				
Forest Hill 4	d	20 15		20 19	20 27	20 34							20 23		20 38	20 45		20 49		20 57	21 04				
Honor Oak Park	d	20 17		20 21	20 29	20 36							20 26		20 41	20 47		20 51		20 59	21 06				
Brockley	d	20 20		20 24	20 32	20 39							20 28		20 43	20 50		20 54		21 02	21 09				
New Cross Gate 4	a	20 22		20 26	20 34	20 41							20 31		20 46	20 52		20 56		21 04	21 11				
	d	20 22		20 26	20 34	20 41							20 31		20 46	20 52		20 56		21 04	21 11				
New Cross ELL	d		20 21											20 36			20 51								
Surrey Quays	d		20 25	20 30		20 45							20 35	20 40	20 49		20 55	21 00			21 15				
Canada Water	d		20 27	20 32		20 47							20 37	20 42	20 51		20 57	21 02			21 17				
Rotherhithe	d		20 28	20 33		20 48							20 38	20 43	20 53		20 58	21 03			21 18				
Wapping	d		20 30	20 35		20 50							20 40	20 45	20 54		21 00	21 05			21 20				
Shadwell	d		20 32	20 37		20 52							20 42	20 47	20 56		21 02	21 07			21 22				
Whitechapel	d		20 34	20 39		20 54							20 44	20 49	20 59		21 04	21 09			21 24				
Shoreditch High Street	d		20 36	20 41		20 56							20 46	20 51	21 01		21 06	21 11			21 26				
Hoxton	d		20 38	20 43		20 58							20 48	20 53	21 03		21 08	21 13			21 28				
Haggerston	d		20 40	20 45		21 00							20 50	20 55	21 05		21 10	21 15			21 30				
Dalston Junction Stn ELL	a		20 47	20 47		21 02							20 52	21 02	21 07		21 17	21 17			21 32				
Canonbury	d			20 50		21 05							20 57		21 12			21 20			21 35				
Highbury & Islington	a			20 58		21 13							21 05		21 19			21 28			21 43				
	d																								
London Bridge 4 ⊖	a	20 29			20 41			20 26			20 36	20 41				20 59				21 13			20 56		21 06

Station		SN	LO	LO		LO	SN	LO	LO	SN	LO	SN	SN	SE		SN	SN	LO	LO	LO	SN	LO	LO	SN
East Croydon (tram)	d						21 00														21 30			
West Croydon 4 (tram)	d	20 31	20 39			20 52											21 02	21 09		21 22				
Norwood Junction 2	d		20 43			20 58	21 05											21 13		21 28	21 35			
Anerley	d		20 46			21 01	21 08											21 16		21 31	21 38			
Penge West	d		20 48			21 03	21 10											21 18		21 33	21 40			
London Victoria 15 ⊖	d									20 49						21 11								21 19
Battersea Park 4	d									20 53						21 15								21 23
Wandsworth Road	d															21 17								
Clapham High Street ⊖	d															21 19								
London Blackfriars 3 ⊖	d													21 12										
Denmark Hill 4	d													21 22		21 24								
Peckham Rye 4	d	21 01										21 12	21 16	21a25		21 26	21 31							
Queens Rd Peckham	d	21 04											21 19			21 29	21 34							
South Bermondsey	d	21 06											21 21			21 31	21 36							
Clapham Junction 10	d									20 57														21 27
Wandsworth Common	d									21 00														21 30
Balham 4 ⊖	d									21 02														21 32
Streatham Hill	d									21 05														21 35
West Norwood 4	d									21 10		21 23												21 40
Gipsy Hill	d									21 13		21 26												21 43
Crystal Palace 4	d								21 13	21 21	21 28	21a29											21 43	21 51
Sydenham	d		20 51			21 06	21 12		21 16	21 24	21 31							21 21		21 36	21 42		21 46	21 54
Forest Hill 4	d		20 53			21 08	21 15		21 19	21 27	21 34							21 23		21 38	21 45		21 49	21 57
Honor Oak Park	d		20 56			21 11	21 17		21 21	21 29	21 36							21 26		21 41	21 47		21 51	21 59
Brockley	d		20 58			21 13	21 20		21 24	21 32	21 39							21 28		21 43	21 50		21 54	22 02
New Cross Gate 4	a		21 01			21 16	21 22		21 26	21 34	21 41							21 31		21 46	21 52		21 56	22 04
	d		21 01			21 16	21 22		21 26	21 34	21 41							21 31		21 46	21 52		21 56	22 04
New Cross ELL	d			21 06				21 21											21 36			21 51		
Surrey Quays	d		21 05	21 10		21 19		21 25	21 30		21 45							21 35	21 40	21 49		21 55	22 00	
Canada Water	d		21 07	21 12		21 21		21 27	21 32		21 47							21 37	21 42	21 51		21 57	22 02	
Rotherhithe	d		21 08	21 13		21 23		21 28	21 33		21 48							21 38	21 43	21 53		21 58	22 03	
Wapping	d		21 10	21 15		21 24		21 30	21 35		21 50							21 40	21 45	21 54		22 00	22 05	
Shadwell	d		21 12	21 17		21 26		21 32	21 37		21 52							21 42	21 47	21 56		22 02	22 07	
Whitechapel	d		21 14	21 19		21 29		21 34	21 39		21 54							21 44	21 49	21 59		22 04	22 09	
Shoreditch High Street	d		21 16	21 21		21 31		21 36	21 41		21 56							21 46	21 51	22 01		22 06	22 11	
Hoxton	d		21 18	21 23		21 33		21 38	21 43		21 58							21 48	21 53	22 03		22 08	22 13	
Haggerston	d		21 20	21 25		21 35		21 40	21 45		22 00							21 50	21 55	22 05		22 10	22 15	
Dalston Junction Stn ELL	a		21 22	21 32		21 37		21 47	21 47		22 02							21 52	22 02	22 07		22 17	22 17	
Canonbury	d		21 27			21 42			21 50		22 05							21 57		22 12			22 20	
Highbury & Islington	a		21 35			21 49			21 58		22 13							22 05		22 19			22 28	
	d																							
London Bridge 4 ⊖	a	21 11					21 29			21 43			21 26			21 36	21 41				21 59			22 13

Table 178

Saturdays

1 September to 8 September

East London Line and Croydon - London Victoria to London Bridge

Network Diagram - see first Page of Table 177

		LO	SN	SN	SE	SN	SN	LO	LO	LO		SN	LO	SN	LO	SN	SN	SE	SN	SN		LO	LO	LO	SN
East Croydon ⇌	d											22 00													22 30
West Croydon 4 ⇌	d						21 31	21 39		21 52										22 01		22 09		22 22	
Norwood Junction 2	d							21 43		21 58		22 05										22 13		22 28	22 35
Anerley	d							21 46		22 01		22 08										22 16		22 31	22 38
Penge West	d							21 48		22 03		22 10										22 18		22 33	22 40
London Victoria 15 ⊖	d					21 41								21 49					22 11						
Battersea Park 4	d					21 45								21 53					22 15						
Wandsworth Road	d					21 47													22 17						
Clapham High Street ⊖	d					21 49													22 19						
London Blackfriars 3 ⊖	d				21 42													22 12							
Denmark Hill 4	d				21 52	21 54												22 22	22 24						
Peckham Rye 4	d		21 42	21 46	21a55	21 56	22 01									22 12	22 16	22a25	22 26	22 31					
Queens Rd Peckham	d			21 49		21 59	22 04										22 19		22 29	22 34					
South Bermondsey	d			21 51		22 01	22 06										22 21		22 31	22 36					
Clapham Junction 10	d													21 57											
Wandsworth Common	d													22 00											
Balham 4 ⊖	d													22 02											
Streatham Hill	d													22 05											
West Norwood 4	d		21 53											22 10		22 23									
Gipsy Hill	d		21 56											22 13		22 26									
Crystal Palace 4	d	21 58	21a59										22 13	22 21	22 28	22a29									
Sydenham	d	22 01						21 51		22 06		22 12	22 16	22 24	22 31							22 21		22 36	22 42
Forest Hill 4	d	22 04						21 53		22 08		22 15	22 19	22 27	22 34							22 23		22 38	22 45
Honor Oak Park	d	22 06						21 56		22 11		22 17	22 21	22 29	22 36							22 26		22 41	22 47
Brockley	d	22 09						21 58		22 13		22 20	22 24	22 32	22 39							22 28		22 43	22 50
New Cross Gate 4	a	22 11						22 01		22 16		22 22	22 26	22 34	22 41							22 31		22 46	22 52
	d	22 11						22 01		22 16		22 22	22 26	22 34	22 41							22 31		22 46	22 52
New Cross ELL	d								22 06														22 36		
Surrey Quays	d	22 15						22 05	22 10	22 19			22 30		22 45							22 35	22 40	22 49	
Canada Water	d	22 17						22 07	22 12	22 21			22 32		22 47							22 37	22 42	22 51	
Rotherhithe	d	22 18						22 08	22 13	22 23			22 33		22 48							22 38	22 43	22 53	
Wapping	d	22 20						22 10	22 15	22 24			22 35		22 50							22 40	22 45	22 54	
Shadwell	d	22 22						22 12	22 17	22 26			22 37		22 52							22 42	22 47	22 56	
Whitechapel	d	22 24						22 14	22 19	22 29			22 39		22 54							22 44	22 49	22 59	
Shoreditch High Street	d	22 26						22 16	22 21	22 31			22 41		22 56							22 46	22 51	23 01	
Hoxton	d	22 28						22 18	22 23	22 33			22 43		22 58							22 48	22 53	23 03	
Haggerston	d	22 30						22 20	22 25	22 35			22 45		23 00							22 50	22 55	23 05	
Dalston Junction Stn ELL	a	22 32						22 22	22 33	22 37			22 47		23 02							22 52	23 02	23 07	
Canonbury	d	22 35						22 27		22 42			22 50		23 05							22 57		23 12	
Highbury & Islington	a	22 43						22 35		22 49			22 58		23 13							23 05		23 19	
	d																								
London Bridge 4 ⊖	a			21 56		22 06	22 11					22 29		22 43			22 26		22 36	22 41					22 59

		LO	SN	SN	SN	SE		SN	SN	LO	LO	LO	SN	LO	SN	SN		SN	SE	SN	SN	LO	LO	LO	SN
East Croydon ⇌	d												23 01												
West Croydon 4 ⇌	d								22 31	22 39		22 52									23 01		23 22		
Norwood Junction 2	d									22 43		22 58	23 06										23 28		
Anerley	d									22 46		23 01	23 09										23 31		
Penge West	d									22 48		23 03	23 11										23 33		
London Victoria 15 ⊖	d		22 19					22 41							22 49					23 11					23 19
Battersea Park 4	d		22 23					22 45							22 53					23 15					23 23
Wandsworth Road	d							22 47												23 17					
Clapham High Street ⊖	d							22 49												23 19					
London Blackfriars 3 ⊖	d					22 42													23 12						
Denmark Hill 4	d					22 52		22 54											23 22	23 24					
Peckham Rye 4	d			22 42	22 46	22a55		22 56	23 01							23 12		23 16	23a25	23 26	23 31				
Queens Rd Peckham	d				22 49			22 59	23 04									23 19		23 29	23 34				
South Bermondsey	d				22 51			23 01	23 06									23 21		23 31	23 36				
Clapham Junction 10	d		22 27												22 57										23 27
Wandsworth Common	d		22 30												23 00										23 30
Balham 4 ⊖	d		22 32												23 02										23 32
Streatham Hill	d		22 35												23 05										23 35
West Norwood 4	d		22 40	22 53											23 10	23 24									23 40
Gipsy Hill	d		22 43	22 56											23 13	23 27									23 43
Crystal Palace 4	d	22 43	22 51	22a59										23 13	23 21	23a29								23 43	23 51
Sydenham	d	22 46	22 54							22 51		23 06	23 13	23 16	23 24								23 36	23 46	23 54
Forest Hill 4	d	22 49	22 57							22 53		23 08	23 16	23 19	23 27								23 38	23 49	23 57
Honor Oak Park	d	22 51	22 59							22 56		23 11	23 18	23 21	23 29								23 41	23 51	23 59
Brockley	d	22 54	23 02							22 58		23 13	23 21	23 24	23 32								23 43	23 54	00 02
New Cross Gate 4	a	22 56	23 04							23 01		23 16	23 23	23 26	23 34								23 46	23 56	00 04
	d	22 56	23 04							23 01		23 16	23 23	23 26	23 34								23 46	23 56	00 04
New Cross ELL	d										23 06											23 36			
Surrey Quays	d	23 00								23 05	23 10	23 19		23 30								23 40	23 49	23 59	
Canada Water	d	23 02								23 07	23 12	23 21		23 32								23 42	23 51	00 02	
Rotherhithe	d	23 03								23 08	23 13	23 23		23 33								23 43	23 53	00 03	
Wapping	d	23 05								23 10	23 15	23 24		23 35								23 45	23 54	00 05	
Shadwell	d	23 07								23 12	23 17	23 26		23 37								23 47	23 56	00 07	
Whitechapel	d	23 09								23 14	23 19	23 29		23 39								23 49	23 59	00 09	
Shoreditch High Street	d	23 11								23 16	23 21	23 31		23 41								23 51	00 01	00 11	
Hoxton	d	23 13								23 18	23 23	23 33		23 43								23 53	00 03	00 13	
Haggerston	d	23 15								23 20	23 25	23 35		23 45								23 55	00 05	00 15	
Dalston Junction Stn ELL	a	23 17								23 22	23 32	23 37		23 47								23 58	00 07	00 17	
Canonbury	d	23 20								23 27		23 42		23 50								00 01	00 11	00 20	
Highbury & Islington	a	23 28								23 35		23 51		23 58								00 10	00 18	00 28	
	d																								
London Bridge 4 ⊖	a		23 13		22 56			23 06	23 11				23 30		23 43			23 26		23 36	23 41				00 11

Table 178

Saturdays

1 September to 8 September

East London Line and Croydon - London Victoria to London Bridge

Network Diagram - see first Page of Table 177

		SN		SN	SE	SN
East Croydon	d					
West Croydon 4	d					
Norwood Junction 2	d					
Anerley	d					
Penge West	d					
London Victoria 15 ⊖	d					23 54
Battersea Park 4	d					23 58
Wandsworth Road	d					
Clapham High Street ⊖	d					
London Blackfriars 3 ⊖	d				23 42	
Denmark Hill 4	d				23 52	
Peckham Rye 4	d	23 42		23 46	23a55	
Queens Rd Peckham	d			23 49		
South Bermondsey	d			23 51		
Clapham Junction 10	d					00 02
Wandsworth Common	d					00 05
Balham 4 ⊖	d					00 07
Streatham Hill	d					00 10
West Norwood 4	d	23 54				00 14
Gipsy Hill	d	23 57				00 17
Crystal Palace 4	d	23a59				00 21
Sydenham	d					00 24
Forest Hill 4	d					00 27
Honor Oak Park	d					00 29
Brockley	d					00 32
New Cross Gate 4	a					00 35
	d					00 35
New Cross ELL	d					
Surrey Quays	d					
Canada Water	d					
Rotherhithe	d					
Wapping	d					
Shadwell	d					
Whitechapel	d					
Shoreditch High Street	d					
Hoxton	d					
Haggerston	d					
Dalston Junction Stn ELL	a					
Canonbury	d					
Highbury & Islington	a					
	d					
London Bridge 4 ⊖	a			23 56		00 41

Saturdays

from 15 September

		LO	LO	SN	SN	SN	SN	LO	LO	LO		LO	SE	LO	LO	LO	SN	LO	LO	LO		SN	SE	SN	SN
East Croydon	d																					06 30			
West Croydon 4	d	23p22						05 39				05 52				06 09	06 18			06 22					
Norwood Junction 2	d	23p28						05 43				05 58				06 13	06 23			06 28		06 35			06 41
Anerley	d	23p31						05 46				06 01				06 16				06 31		06 38			
Penge West	d	23p33						05 48				06 03				06 18				06 33		06 40			
London Victoria 15 ⊖	d			23p22	23p54																			06 41	
Battersea Park 4	d			23p26	23p58																			06 45	
Wandsworth Road	d																							06 47	
Clapham High Street ⊖	d																							06 49	
London Blackfriars 3 ⊖	d												06 12										06 42		
Denmark Hill 4	d												06 22										06 52	06 54	
Peckham Rye 4	d					00 12	00 42						06a25										06a55	06 56	07 01
Queens Rd Peckham	d																							06 59	07 04
South Bermondsey	d																							07 01	07 06
Clapham Junction 10	d			23p30	00 02																				
Wandsworth Common	d			23p33	00 05																				
Balham 4 ⊖	d			23p35	00 07																				
Streatham Hill	d			23p38	00 10																				
West Norwood 4	d			23p42	00 14	00 24	00 54																		
Gipsy Hill	d			23p45	00 17	00 27	00 57																		
Crystal Palace 4	d		23p43	23p51	00 21	00a29	00a59			05 58					06 13		06a27		06 28						
Sydenham	d	23p36	23p46	23p54	00 24			05 51		06 01		06 06			06 16	06 21			06 31	06 36		06 42			
Forest Hill 4	d	23p38	23p49	23p57	00 27			05 53		06 04		06 08			06 19	06 23			06 34	06 38		06 45			
Honor Oak Park	d	23p41	23p51	23p59	00 29			05 56		06 06		06 11			06 21	06 26			06 36	06 41		06 47			
Brockley	d	23p43	23p54	00 02	00 32			05 58		06 09		06 13			06 24	06 28			06 39	06 43		06 50			
New Cross Gate 4	a	23p46	23p56	00 04	00 34			06 01		06 11		06 16			06 26	06 31			06 41	06 46		06 52			
	d	23p46	23p56	00 04	00 34			06 01		06 11		06 16			06 26	06 31			06 41	06 46		06 52			
New Cross ELL	d								06 06					06 21				06 36							
Surrey Quays	d	23p49	23p59					06 05	06 10	06 15		06 19		06 25	06 30	06 35		06 40	06 45	06 49					
Canada Water	d	23p51	00 02					06 07	06 12	06 17		06 21		06 27	06 32	06 37		06 42	06 47	06 51					
Rotherhithe	d	23p53	00 03					06 08	06 13	06 18		06 23		06 28	06 33	06 38		06 43	06 48	06 53					
Wapping	d	23p54	00 05					06 10	06 15	06 20		06 24		06 30	06 35	06 40		06 45	06 50	06 54					
Shadwell	d	23p56	00 07					06 12	06 17	06 22		06 26		06 32	06 37	06 42		06 47	06 52	06 56					
Whitechapel	d	23p59	00 09					06 14	06 19	06 24		06 29		06 34	06 39	06 44		06 49	06 54	06 59					
Shoreditch High Street	d	00 01	00 11					06 16	06 21	06 26		06 31		06 36	06 41	06 46		06 51	06 56	07 01					
Hoxton	d	00 03	00 13					06 18	06 23	06 28		06 33		06 38	06 43	06 48		06 53	06 58	07 03					
Haggerston	d	00 05	00 15					06 20	06 25	06 30		06 35		06 40	06 45	06 50		06 55	07 00	07 05					
Dalston Junction Stn ELL	a	00 07	00 17					06 22	06 28	06 32		06 37		06 43	06 47	06 52		06 58	07 02	07 07					
Canonbury	d	00 12	00 20					06 27		06 35		06 42			06 50	06 57			07 05	07 12					
Highbury & Islington	a	00 16	00 25					06 32		06 40		06 46			06 56	07 02			07 10	07 16					
	d																								
London Bridge 4 ⊖	a			00 11	00 41																	06 59		07 06	07 14

East London Line and Croydon - London Victoria to London Bridge

Network Diagram - see first Page of Table 177

Station		LO	LO	LO	SN	SN		LO	LO	LO	SN	SE	SN	SN	LO	LO		LO	LO	LO	LO	SN	LO	LO	LO
East Croydon	d				06 43						07 00											07 30			
West Croydon 4	d			06 39		06 45				06 52				07 01				07 09			07 22				
Norwood Junction 2	d			06 43	06 50	06 53				06 58	07 05							07 13			07 28	07 35			
Anerley	d			06 46						07 01	07 08							07 16			07 31	07 38			
Penge West	d			06 48						07 03	07 10							07 18			07 33	07 40			
London Victoria 15 ⊖	d												07 11												
Battersea Park 4	d												07 15												
Wandsworth Road	d												07 17												
Clapham High Street ⊖	d												07 19												
London Blackfriars 3 ⊖	d											07 12													
Denmark Hill 4	d											07 22	07 24												
Peckham Rye 4	d											07a25	07 26	07 31											
Queens Rd Peckham	d												07 29	07 34											
South Bermondsey	d												07 31	07 36											
Clapham Junction 10	d																								
Wandsworth Common	d																								
Balham 4 ⊖	d																								
Streatham Hill	d																								
West Norwood 4	d																								
Gipsy Hill	d																								
Crystal Palace 4	d		06 43			06a57			06 58							07 13				07 28				07 43	07 58
Sydenham	d		06 46	06 51	06 54				07 01	07 06	07 12					07 16		07 21		07 31	07 36	07 42		07 46	08 01
Forest Hill 4	d		06 49	06 53	06 57				07 04	07 08	07 15					07 19		07 23		07 34	07 38	07 45		07 49	08 04
Honor Oak Park	d		06 51	06 56	06 59				07 06	07 11	07 17					07 21		07 26		07 36	07 41	07 47		07 51	08 06
Brockley	d		06 54	06 58	07 02				07 09	07 13	07 20					07 24		07 28		07 39	07 43	07 50		07 54	08 09
New Cross Gate 4	a		06 56	07 01	07 04				07 11	07 16	07 22					07 26		07 31		07 41	07 46	07 52		07 56	08 11
	d		06 56	07 01	07 04				07 11	07 16	07 22					07 26		07 31		07 41	07 46	07 52		07 56	08 11
New Cross ELL	d	06 51						07 06							07 21				07 36				07 51		
Surrey Quays	d	06 55	07 00	07 05				07 10	07 15	07 19					07 25	07 30		07 35	07 40	07 45	07 49		07 55	08 00	08 15
Canada Water	d	06 57	07 02	07 07				07 12	07 17	07 21					07 27	07 32		07 37	07 42	07 47	07 51		07 57	08 02	08 17
Rotherhithe	d	06 58	07 03	07 08				07 13	07 18	07 23					07 28	07 33		07 38	07 43	07 48	07 53		07 58	08 03	08 18
Wapping	d	07 00	07 05	07 10				07 15	07 20	07 24					07 30	07 35		07 40	07 45	07 50	07 54		08 00	08 05	08 20
Shadwell	d	07 02	07 07	07 12				07 17	07 22	07 26					07 32	07 37		07 42	07 47	07 52	07 56		08 02	08 07	08 22
Whitechapel	d	07 04	07 09	07 14				07 19	07 24	07 29					07 34	07 39		07 44	07 49	07 54	07 59		08 04	08 09	08 24
Shoreditch High Street	d	07 06	07 11	07 16				07 21	07 26	07 31					07 36	07 41		07 46	07 51	07 56	08 01		08 06	08 11	08 26
Hoxton	d	07 08	07 13	07 18				07 23	07 28	07 33					07 38	07 43		07 48	07 53	07 58	08 03		08 08	08 13	08 28
Haggerston	d	07 10	07 15	07 20				07 25	07 30	07 35					07 40	07 45		07 50	07 55	08 00	08 05		08 10	08 15	08 30
Dalston Junction Stn ELL	a	07 13	07 17	07 22				07 28	07 32	07 37					07 43	07 47		07 52	07 58	08 02	08 07		08 13	08 17	08 32
Canonbury	d		07 20	07 27					07 35	07 42						07 50		07 57		08 05	08 12			08 20	08 35
Highbury & Islington	a		07 25	07 32					07 40	07 46						07 55		08 02		08 10	08 16			08 25	08 40
	d																								
London Bridge 4 ⊖	a				07 11						07 29		07 36	07 41								07 59			

Station		SN		SE	SE	SN	SN	LO	LO	LO	SN	LO		LO	SN	LO	SN	SE	SE	SN	SN	LO		LO	LO
East Croydon	d										08 00														
West Croydon 4	d						07 31	07 39		07 52											08 01	08 09			08 22
Norwood Junction 2	d							07 43		07 58	08 05											08 13			08 28
Anerley	d							07 46		08 01	08 08											08 16			08 31
Penge West	d							07 48		08 03	08 10											08 18			08 33
London Victoria 15 ⊖	d			07 39		07 41									07 49			08 09		08 11					
Battersea Park 4	d					07 45									07 53					08 15					
Wandsworth Road	d					07 47														08 17					
Clapham High Street ⊖	d					07 49														08 19					
London Blackfriars 3 ⊖	d				07 42														08 12						
Denmark Hill 4	d			07 48	07 52	07 54												08 18	08 22	08 24					
Peckham Rye 4	d	07 42		07a51	07a55	07 56	08 01										08 12	08a21	08a25	08 26	08 31				
Queens Rd Peckham	d					07 59	08 04													08 29	08 34				
South Bermondsey	d					08 01	08 06													08 31	08 36				
Clapham Junction 10	d														07 57										
Wandsworth Common	d														08 00										
Balham 4 ⊖	d														08 02										
Streatham Hill	d														08 05										
West Norwood 4	d	07 53													08 10		08 23								
Gipsy Hill	d	07 56													08 13		08 26								
Crystal Palace 4	d	07a59												08 13	08 21	08 28	08a29								
Sydenham	d							07 51		08 06	08 12			08 16	08 24	08 31						08 21			08 36
Forest Hill 4	d							07 53		08 08	08 15			08 19	08 27	08 34						08 23			08 38
Honor Oak Park	d							07 56		08 11	08 17			08 21	08 29	08 36						08 26			08 41
Brockley	d							07 58		08 13	08 20			08 24	08 32	08 39						08 28			08 43
New Cross Gate 4	a							08 01		08 16	08 22			08 26	08 34	08 41						08 31			08 46
	d							08 01		08 16	08 22			08 26	08 34	08 41						08 31			08 46
New Cross ELL	d								08 06			08 21												08 36	
Surrey Quays	d							08 05	08 10	08 19		08 25		08 30		08 45						08 35		08 40	08 49
Canada Water	d							08 07	08 12	08 21		08 27		08 32		08 47						08 37		08 42	08 51
Rotherhithe	d							08 08	08 13	08 23		08 28		08 33		08 48						08 38		08 43	08 53
Wapping	d							08 10	08 15	08 24		08 30		08 35		08 50						08 40		08 45	08 54
Shadwell	d							08 12	08 17	08 26		08 32		08 37		08 52						08 42		08 47	08 56
Whitechapel	d							08 14	08 19	08 29		08 34		08 39		08 54						08 44		08 49	08 59
Shoreditch High Street	d							08 16	08 21	08 31		08 36		08 41		08 56						08 46		08 51	09 01
Hoxton	d							08 18	08 23	08 33		08 38		08 43		08 58						08 48		08 53	09 03
Haggerston	d							08 20	08 25	08 35		08 40		08 45		09 00						08 50		08 55	09 05
Dalston Junction Stn ELL	a							08 22	08 28	08 37		08 43		08 47		09 02						08 52		08 58	09 07
Canonbury	d							08 27		08 42				08 50		09 05						08 57			09 12
Highbury & Islington	a							08 32		08 46				08 55		09 10						09 02			09 16
	d																								
London Bridge 4 ⊖	a					08 06	08 11				08 29				08 41					08 36	08 41				

Saturdays

from 15 September

East London Line and Croydon - London Victoria to London Bridge

Network Diagram - see first Page of Table 177

		SN	LO	LO	SN	LO	SN	SN		SE	SE	SN	SN	LO	LO	LO	SN	LO		LO	SN	LO	SN	SN	SE
East Croydon 🚋	d	08 30															09 00								
West Croydon 4 🚋	d												08 31	08 39		08 52									
Norwood Junction 2	d	08 35												08 43		08 58	09 05								
Anerley	d	08 38												08 46		09 01	09 08								
Penge West	d	08 40												08 48		09 03	09 10								
London Victoria 15 ⊖	d				08 19					08 39		08 41									08 49				09 09
Battersea Park 4	d				08 23							08 45									08 53				
Wandsworth Road	d											08 47													
Clapham High Street ⊖	d											08 49													
London Blackfriars 3 ⊖	d										08 42														
Denmark Hill 4	d									08 48	08 52	08 54													09 18
Peckham Rye 4	d						08 42	08 46		08a51	08a55	08 56	09 01										09 12	09 16	09a21
Queens Rd Peckham	d							08 49				08 59	09 04											09 19	
South Bermondsey	d							08 51				09 01	09 06											09 21	
Clapham Junction 10	d				08 27																08 57				
Wandsworth Common	d				08 30																09 00				
Balham 4 ⊖	d				08 32																09 02				
Streatham Hill	d				08 35																09 05				
West Norwood 4	d				08 40		08 53														09 10		09 23		
Gipsy Hill	d				08 43		08 56														09 13		09 26		
Crystal Palace 4	d			08 43	08 51	08 58	08a59													09 13	09 21	09 28	09a29		
Sydenham	d	08 42		08 46	08 54	09 01								08 51		09 06	09 12			09 16	09 24	09 31			
Forest Hill 4	d	08 45		08 49	08 57	09 04								08 53		09 08	09 15			09 19	09 27	09 34			
Honor Oak Park	d	08 47		08 51	08 59	09 06								08 56		09 11	09 17			09 21	09 29	09 36			
Brockley	d	08 50		08 54	09 02	09 09								08 58		09 13	09 20			09 24	09 32	09 39			
New Cross Gate 4	a	08 52		08 56	09 04	09 11								09 01		09 16	09 22			09 26	09 34	09 41			
	d	08 52		08 56	09 04	09 11								09 01		09 16	09 22			09 26	09 34	09 41			
New Cross ELL	d		08 51												09 06			09 21							
Surrey Quays	d		08 55	09 00		09 15								09 05	09 10	09 19		09 25		09 30		09 45			
Canada Water	d		08 57	09 02		09 17								09 07	09 12	09 21		09 27		09 32		09 47			
Rotherhithe	d		08 58	09 03		09 18								09 08	09 13	09 23		09 28		09 33		09 48			
Wapping	d		09 00	09 05		09 20								09 10	09 15	09 24		09 30		09 35		09 50			
Shadwell	d		09 02	09 07		09 22								09 12	09 17	09 26		09 32		09 37		09 52			
Whitechapel	d		09 04	09 09		09 24								09 14	09 19	09 29		09 34		09 39		09 54			
Shoreditch High Street	d		09 06	09 11		09 26								09 16	09 21	09 31		09 36		09 41		09 56			
Hoxton	d		09 08	09 13		09 28								09 18	09 23	09 33		09 38		09 43		09 58			
Haggerston	d		09 10	09 15		09 30								09 20	09 25	09 35		09 40		09 45		10 00			
Dalston Junction Stn ELL	a		09 13	09 17		09 32								09 22	09 28	09 37		09 43		09 47		10 02			
Canonbury	d			09 20		09 35								09 27		09 42				09 50		10 05			
Highbury & Islington	a			09 25		09 40								09 32		09 46				09 55		10 10			
	d																								
London Bridge 4 ⊖	a	08 59			09 11			08 56				09 06	09 11				09 29				09 41			09 26	

		SE	SN	SN		LO	LO	LO	SN	LO	LO	SN	LO	SN		SN	SE	SE	SN	SN	LO	LO	LO	SN
East Croydon 🚋	d								09 30															10 00
West Croydon 4 🚋	d			09 01		09 09		09 22												09 31	09 39		09 52	
Norwood Junction 2	d					09 13		09 28	09 35												09 43		09 58	10 05
Anerley	d					09 16		09 31	09 38												09 46		10 01	10 08
Penge West	d					09 18		09 33	09 40												09 48		10 03	10 10
London Victoria 15 ⊖	d		09 11									09 19					09 39		09 41					
Battersea Park 4	d		09 15									09 23							09 45					
Wandsworth Road	d		09 17																09 47					
Clapham High Street ⊖	d		09 19																09 49					
London Blackfriars 3 ⊖	d	09 12																09 42						
Denmark Hill 4	d	09 22	09 24														09 48	09 52	09 54					
Peckham Rye 4	d	09a25	09 26	09 31										09 42		09 46	09a51	09a55	09 56	10 01				
Queens Rd Peckham	d		09 29	09 34												09 49			09 59	10 04				
South Bermondsey	d		09 31	09 36												09 51			10 01	10 06				
Clapham Junction 10	d											09 27												
Wandsworth Common	d											09 30												
Balham 4 ⊖	d											09 32												
Streatham Hill	d											09 35												
West Norwood 4	d											09 40		09 53										
Gipsy Hill	d											09 43		09 56										
Crystal Palace 4	d										09 43	09 51	09 58	09a59										
Sydenham	d					09 21		09 36	09 42		09 46	09 54	10 01								09 51		10 06	10 12
Forest Hill 4	d					09 23		09 38	09 45		09 49	09 57	10 04								09 53		10 08	10 15
Honor Oak Park	d					09 26		09 41	09 47		09 51	09 59	10 06								09 56		10 11	10 17
Brockley	d					09 28		09 43	09 50		09 54	10 02	10 09								09 58		10 13	10 20
New Cross Gate 4	a					09 31		09 46	09 52		09 56	10 04	10 11								10 01		10 16	10 22
	d					09 31		09 46	09 52		09 56	10 04	10 11								10 01		10 16	10 22
New Cross ELL	d						09 36			09 51												10 06		
Surrey Quays	d					09 35	09 40	09 49		09 55	10 00		10 15								10 05	10 10	10 19	
Canada Water	d					09 37	09 42	09 51		09 57	10 02		10 17								10 07	10 12	10 21	
Rotherhithe	d					09 38	09 43	09 53		09 58	10 03		10 18								10 08	10 13	10 23	
Wapping	d					09 40	09 45	09 54		10 00	10 05		10 20								10 10	10 15	10 24	
Shadwell	d					09 42	09 47	09 56		10 02	10 07		10 22								10 12	10 17	10 26	
Whitechapel	d					09 44	09 49	09 59		10 04	10 09		10 24								10 14	10 19	10 29	
Shoreditch High Street	d					09 46	09 51	10 01		10 06	10 11		10 26								10 16	10 21	10 31	
Hoxton	d					09 48	09 53	10 03		10 08	10 13		10 28								10 18	10 23	10 33	
Haggerston	d					09 50	09 55	10 05		10 10	10 15		10 30								10 20	10 25	10 35	
Dalston Junction Stn ELL	a					09 52	09 58	10 07		10 13	10 17		10 32								10 22	10 28	10 37	
Canonbury	d					09 57		10 12			10 20		10 35								10 27		10 42	
Highbury & Islington	a					10 02		10 16			10 25		10 40								10 32		10 46	
	d																							
London Bridge 4 ⊖	a		09 36	09 41					09 59			10 11				09 56			10 06	10 11				10 29

East London Line and Croydon - London Victoria to London Bridge

Network Diagram - see first Page of Table 177

		LO	LO	SN	LO	SN	SN	SE	SE	SN		SN	LO	LO	LO	SN	LO	LO	SN	LO		SN	SN	SE	SE
East Croydon	d															10 30									
West Croydon 4	d											10 01	10 09		10 22										
Norwood Junction 2	d												10 13		10 28	10 35									
Anerley	d												10 16		10 31	10 38									
Penge West	d												10 18		10 33	10 40									
London Victoria 15 ⊖	d			09 49				10 09		10 11									10 19					10 39	
Battersea Park 4	d			09 53						10 15									10 23						
Wandsworth Road	d									10 17															
Clapham High Street ⊖	d									10 19															
London Blackfriars 3 ⊖	d								10 12																10 42
Denmark Hill 4	d							10 18	10 22	10 24														10 48	10 52
Peckham Rye 4	d					10 12	10 16	10a21	10a25	10 26		10 31										10 42	10 46	10a51	10a55
Queens Rd Peckham	d						10 19			10 29		10 34											10 49		
South Bermondsey	d						10 21			10 31		10 36											10 51		
Clapham Junction 10	d			09 57															10 27						
Wandsworth Common	d			10 00															10 30						
Balham 4 ⊖	d			10 02															10 32						
Streatham Hill	d			10 05															10 35						
West Norwood 4	d			10 10		10 23													10 40			10 53			
Gipsy Hill	d			10 13		10 26													10 43			10 56			
Crystal Palace 4	d		10 13	10 21	10 28	10a29												10 43	10 51	10 58		10a59			
Sydenham	d		10 16	10 24	10 31								10 21		10 36	10 42		10 46	10 54	11 01					
Forest Hill 4	d		10 19	10 27	10 34								10 23		10 38	10 45		10 49	10 57	11 04					
Honor Oak Park	d		10 21	10 29	10 36								10 26		10 41	10 47		10 51	10 59	11 06					
Brockley	d		10 24	10 32	10 39								10 28		10 43	10 50		10 54	11 02	11 09					
New Cross Gate 4	a		10 26	10 34	10 41								10 31		10 46	10 52		10 56	11 04	11 11					
	d		10 26	10 34	10 41								10 31		10 46	10 52		10 56	11 04	11 11					
New Cross ELL	d	10 21												10 36			10 51								
Surrey Quays	d	10 25	10 30		10 45								10 35	10 40	10 49		10 55	11 00		11 15					
Canada Water	d	10 27	10 32		10 47								10 37	10 42	10 51		10 57	11 02		11 17					
Rotherhithe	d	10 28	10 33		10 48								10 38	10 43	10 53		10 58	11 03		11 18					
Wapping	d	10 30	10 35		10 50								10 40	10 45	10 54		11 00	11 05		11 20					
Shadwell	d	10 32	10 37		10 52								10 42	10 47	10 56		11 02	11 07		11 22					
Whitechapel	d	10 34	10 39		10 54								10 44	10 49	10 59		11 04	11 09		11 24					
Shoreditch High Street	d	10 36	10 41		10 56								10 46	10 51	11 01		11 06	11 11		11 26					
Hoxton	d	10 38	10 43		10 58								10 48	10 53	11 03		11 08	11 13		11 28					
Haggerston	d	10 40	10 45		11 00								10 50	10 55	11 05		11 10	11 15		11 30					
Dalston Junction Stn ELL	a	10 43	10 47		11 02								10 52	10 58	11 07		11 13	11 17		11 32					
Canonbury	d		10 50		11 05								10 57		11 12			11 20		11 35					
Highbury & Islington	a		10 55		11 10								11 02		11 16			11 25		11 40					
	d																								
London Bridge 4 ⊖	a			10 41			10 26			10 36		10 41				10 59			11 11				10 56		

		SN	SN	LO	LO	LO		SN	LO	LO	SN	LO	SN	SN	SE	SE		SN	SN	LO	LO	LO	SN	LO	LO
East Croydon	d							11 00															11 30		
West Croydon 4	d		10 31	10 39		10 52													11 01	11 09		11 22			
Norwood Junction 2	d			10 43		10 58		11 05												11 13		11 28	11 35		
Anerley	d			10 46		11 01		11 08												11 16		11 31	11 38		
Penge West	d			10 48		11 03		11 10												11 18		11 33	11 40		
London Victoria 15 ⊖	d	10 41									10 49				11 09			11 11							
Battersea Park 4	d	10 45									10 53							11 15							
Wandsworth Road	d	10 47																11 17							
Clapham High Street ⊖	d	10 49																11 19							
London Blackfriars 3 ⊖	d															11 12									
Denmark Hill 4	d	10 54													11 18	11 22		11 24							
Peckham Rye 4	d	10 56	11 01										11 12	11 16	11a21	11a25		11 26	11 31						
Queens Rd Peckham	d	10 59	11 04											11 19				11 29	11 34						
South Bermondsey	d	11 01	11 06											11 21				11 31	11 36						
Clapham Junction 10	d										10 57														
Wandsworth Common	d										11 00														
Balham 4 ⊖	d										11 02														
Streatham Hill	d										11 05														
West Norwood 4	d										11 10		11 23												
Gipsy Hill	d										11 13		11 26												
Crystal Palace 4	d									11 13	11 21	11 28	11a29												11 43
Sydenham	d			10 51		11 06		11 12		11 16	11 24	11 31								11 21		11 36	11 42		11 46
Forest Hill 4	d			10 53		11 08		11 15		11 19	11 27	11 34								11 23		11 38	11 45		11 49
Honor Oak Park	d			10 56		11 11		11 17		11 21	11 29	11 36								11 26		11 41	11 47		11 51
Brockley	d			10 58		11 13		11 20		11 24	11 32	11 39								11 28		11 43	11 50		11 54
New Cross Gate 4	a			11 01		11 16		11 22		11 26	11 34	11 41								11 31		11 46	11 52		11 56
	d			11 01		11 16		11 22		11 26	11 34	11 41								11 31		11 46	11 52		11 56
New Cross ELL	d				11 06				11 21												11 36			11 51	
Surrey Quays	d			11 05	11 10	11 19			11 25	11 30		11 45								11 35	11 40	11 49		11 55	12 00
Canada Water	d			11 07	11 12	11 21			11 27	11 32		11 47								11 37	11 42	11 51		11 57	12 02
Rotherhithe	d			11 08	11 13	11 23			11 28	11 33		11 48								11 38	11 43	11 53		11 58	12 03
Wapping	d			11 10	11 15	11 24			11 30	11 35		11 50								11 40	11 45	11 54		12 00	12 05
Shadwell	d			11 12	11 17	11 26			11 32	11 37		11 52								11 42	11 47	11 56		12 02	12 07
Whitechapel	d			11 14	11 19	11 29			11 34	11 39		11 54								11 44	11 49	11 59		12 04	12 09
Shoreditch High Street	d			11 16	11 21	11 31			11 36	11 41		11 56								11 46	11 51	12 01		12 06	12 11
Hoxton	d			11 18	11 23	11 33			11 38	11 43		11 58								11 48	11 53	12 03		12 08	12 13
Haggerston	d			11 20	11 25	11 35			11 40	11 45		12 00								11 50	11 55	12 05		12 10	12 15
Dalston Junction Stn ELL	a			11 22	11 28	11 37			11 43	11 47		12 02								11 52	11 58	12 07		12 13	12 17
Canonbury	d			11 27		11 42				11 50		12 05								11 57		12 12			12 20
Highbury & Islington	a			11 32		11 46				11 55		12 10								12 02		12 16			12 25
	d																								
London Bridge 4 ⊖	a	11 06	11 11					11 29			11 41			11 26				11 36	11 41				11 59		

Table 178

Saturdays

from 15 September

East London Line and Croydon - London Victoria to London Bridge

Network Diagram - see first Page of Table 177

		SN		LO	SN	SN	SE	SE	SN	SN	LO	LO		LO	SN	LO	LO	SN	LO	SN	SN	SE		SE	SN
East Croydon	d														12 00										
West Croydon 4	d									11 31	11 39			11 52											
Norwood Junction 2	d										11 43			11 58	12 05										
Anerley	d										11 46			12 01	12 08										
Penge West	d										11 48			12 03	12 10										
London Victoria 15 ⊖	d	11 19					11 39		11 41									11 49				12 09			12 11
Battersea Park 4	d	11 23							11 45									11 53							12 15
Wandsworth Road	d								11 47																12 17
Clapham High Street ⊖	d								11 49																12 19
London Blackfriars 3 ⊖	d							11 42																12 12	
Denmark Hill 4	d						11 48	11 52	11 54													12 18		12 22	12 24
Peckham Rye 4	d				11 42	11 46	11a51	11a55	11 56	12 01										12 12	12 16	12a21		12a25	12 26
Queens Rd Peckham	d					11 49			11 59	12 04											12 19				12 29
South Bermondsey	d					11 51			12 01	12 06											12 21				12 31
Clapham Junction 10	d	11 27																11 57							
Wandsworth Common	d	11 30																12 00							
Balham 4 ⊖	d	11 32																12 02							
Streatham Hill	d	11 35																12 05							
West Norwood 4	d	11 40			11 53													12 10		12 23					
Gipsy Hill	d	11 43			11 56													12 13		12 26					
Crystal Palace 4	d	11 51		11 58	11a59												12 13	12 21	12 28	12a29					
Sydenham	d	11 54		12 01							11 51			12 06	12 12		12 16	12 24	12 31						
Forest Hill 4	d	11 57		12 04							11 53			12 08	12 15		12 19	12 27	12 34						
Honor Oak Park	d	11 59		12 06							11 56			12 11	12 17		12 21	12 29	12 36						
Brockley	d	12 02		12 09							11 58			12 13	12 20		12 24	12 32	12 39						
New Cross Gate 4	a	12 04		12 11							12 01			12 16	12 22		12 26	12 34	12 41						
	d	12 04		12 11							12 01			12 16	12 22		12 26	12 34	12 41						
New Cross ELL	d											12 06				12 21									
Surrey Quays	d			12 15							12 05	12 10		12 19		12 25	12 30		12 45						
Canada Water	d			12 17							12 07	12 12		12 21		12 27	12 32		12 47						
Rotherhithe	d			12 18							12 08	12 13		12 23		12 28	12 33		12 48						
Wapping	d			12 20							12 10	12 15		12 24		12 30	12 35		12 50						
Shadwell	d			12 22							12 12	12 17		12 26		12 32	12 37		12 52						
Whitechapel	d			12 24							12 14	12 19		12 29		12 34	12 39		12 54						
Shoreditch High Street	d			12 26							12 16	12 21		12 31		12 36	12 41		12 56						
Hoxton	d			12 28							12 18	12 23		12 33		12 38	12 43		12 58						
Haggerston	d			12 30							12 20	12 25		12 35		12 40	12 45		13 00						
Dalston Junction Stn ELL	a			12 32							12 22	12 28		12 37		12 43	12 47		13 02						
Canonbury	d			12 35							12 27			12 42			12 50		13 05						
Highbury & Islington	a			12 40							12 32			12 46			12 55		13 10						
	d																								
London Bridge 4 ⊖	a	12 11				11 56			12 06	12 11					12 29			12 44			12 26				12 36

		SN	LO	LO	LO	SN	LO	LO		SN	LO	SN	SN	SE	SE	SN	SN	LO		LO	LO	SN	LO	LO	SN
East Croydon	d					12 30																13 00			
West Croydon 4	d	12 01	12 09		12 22												12 31	12 39			12 52				
Norwood Junction 2	d		12 13		12 28	12 35												12 43			12 58	13 05			
Anerley	d		12 16		12 31	12 38												12 46			13 01	13 08			
Penge West	d		12 18		12 33	12 40												12 48			13 03	13 10			
London Victoria 15 ⊖	d									12 19				12 39		12 41									12 49
Battersea Park 4	d									12 23						12 45									12 53
Wandsworth Road	d															12 47									
Clapham High Street ⊖	d															12 49									
London Blackfriars 3 ⊖	d														12 42										
Denmark Hill 4	d													12 48	12 52	12 54									
Peckham Rye 4	d	12 31										12 42	12 46	12a51	12a55	12 56	13 01								
Queens Rd Peckham	d	12 34											12 49			12 59	13 04								
South Bermondsey	d	12 36											12 51			13 01	13 06								
Clapham Junction 10	d									12 27															12 57
Wandsworth Common	d									12 30															13 00
Balham 4 ⊖	d									12 32															13 02
Streatham Hill	d									12 35															13 05
West Norwood 4	d									12 40		12 53													13 10
Gipsy Hill	d									12 43		12 56													13 13
Crystal Palace 4	d							12 43		12 51	12 58	12a59												13 13	13 21
Sydenham	d		12 21		12 36	12 42		12 46		12 54	13 01							12 51			13 06	13 12		13 16	13 24
Forest Hill 4	d		12 23		12 38	12 45		12 49		12 57	13 04							12 53			13 08	13 15		13 19	13 27
Honor Oak Park	d		12 26		12 41	12 47		12 51		12 59	13 06							12 56			13 11	13 17		13 21	13 29
Brockley	d		12 28		12 43	12 50		12 54		13 02	13 09							12 58			13 13	13 20		13 24	13 32
New Cross Gate 4	a		12 31		12 46	12 52		12 56		13 04	13 11							13 01			13 16	13 22		13 26	13 34
	d		12 31		12 46	12 52		12 56		13 04	13 11							13 01			13 16	13 22		13 26	13 34
New Cross ELL	d			12 36			12 51													13 06			13 21		
Surrey Quays	d		12 35	12 40	12 49		12 55	13 00			13 15							13 05		13 10	13 19		13 25	13 30	
Canada Water	d		12 37	12 42	12 51		12 57	13 02			13 17							13 07		13 12	13 21		13 27	13 32	
Rotherhithe	d		12 38	12 43	12 53		12 58	13 03			13 18							13 08		13 13	13 23		13 28	13 33	
Wapping	d		12 40	12 45	12 54		13 00	13 05			13 20							13 10		13 15	13 24		13 30	13 35	
Shadwell	d		12 42	12 47	12 56		13 02	13 07			13 22							13 12		13 17	13 26		13 32	13 37	
Whitechapel	d		12 44	12 49	12 59		13 04	13 09			13 24							13 14		13 19	13 29		13 34	13 39	
Shoreditch High Street	d		12 46	12 51	13 01		13 06	13 11			13 26							13 16		13 21	13 31		13 36	13 41	
Hoxton	d		12 48	12 53	13 03		13 08	13 13			13 28							13 18		13 23	13 33		13 38	13 43	
Haggerston	d		12 50	12 55	13 05		13 10	13 15			13 30							13 20		13 25	13 35		13 40	13 45	
Dalston Junction Stn ELL	a		12 52	12 58	13 07		13 13	13 17			13 32							13 22		13 28	13 37		13 43	13 47	
Canonbury	d		12 57		13 12			13 20			13 35							13 27			13 42			13 50	
Highbury & Islington	a		13 02		13 16			13 25			13 40							13 32			13 46			13 55	
	d																								
London Bridge 4 ⊖	a	12 41				12 59				13 11			12 56			13 06	13 11					13 29			13 44

Table 178

Saturdays

from 15 September

East London Line and Croydon - London Victoria to London Bridge

Network Diagram - see first Page of Table 177

		LO	SN	SN		SE	SE	SN	SN	LO	LO	LO	SN	LO		LO	SN	LO	SN	SN	SE	SE	SN	SN	
East Croydon	d												13 30												
West Croydon 4	d								13 01	13 09		13 22												13 31	
Norwood Junction 2	d									13 13		13 28	13 35												
Anerley	d									13 16		13 31	13 38												
Penge West	d									13 18		13 33	13 40												
London Victoria 15 ⊖	d					13 09		13 11									13 19				13 39		13 41		
Battersea Park 4	d							13 15									13 23						13 45		
Wandsworth Road	d							13 17															13 47		
Clapham High Street ⊖	d							13 19															13 49		
London Blackfriars 3 ⊖	d						13 12															13 42			
Denmark Hill 4	d					13 18	13 22	13 24													13 48	13 52	13 54		
Peckham Rye 4	d		13 12	13 16		13a21	13a25	13 26	13 31										13 42	13 46	13a51	13a55	13 56	14 01	
Queens Rd Peckham	d			13 19				13 29	13 34											13 49			13 59	14 04	
South Bermondsey	d			13 21				13 31	13 36											13 51			14 01	14 06	
Clapham Junction 10	d																13 27								
Wandsworth Common	d																13 30								
Balham 4 ⊖	d																13 32								
Streatham Hill	d																13 35								
West Norwood 4	d		13 23														13 40		13 53						
Gipsy Hill	d		13 26														13 43		13 56						
Crystal Palace 4	d	13 28	13a29													13 43	13 51	13 58	13a59						
Sydenham	d	13 31								13 21		13 36	13 42			13 46	13 54	14 01							
Forest Hill 4	d	13 34								13 23		13 38	13 45			13 49	13 57	14 04							
Honor Oak Park	d	13 36								13 26		13 41	13 47			13 51	13 59	14 06							
Brockley	d	13 39								13 28		13 43	13 50			13 54	14 02	14 09							
New Cross Gate 4	a	13 41								13 31		13 46	13 52			13 56	14 04	14 11							
	d	13 41								13 31		13 46	13 52			13 56	14 04	14 11							
New Cross ELL	d										13 36			13 51											
Surrey Quays	d	13 45								13 35	13 40	13 49		13 55		14 00		14 15							
Canada Water	d	13 47								13 37	13 42	13 51		13 57		14 02		14 17							
Rotherhithe	d	13 48								13 38	13 43	13 53		13 58		14 03		14 18							
Wapping	d	13 50								13 40	13 45	13 54		14 00		14 05		14 20							
Shadwell	d	13 52								13 42	13 47	13 56		14 02		14 07		14 22							
Whitechapel	d	13 54								13 44	13 49	13 59		14 04		14 09		14 24							
Shoreditch High Street	d	13 56								13 46	13 51	14 01		14 06		14 11		14 26							
Hoxton	d	13 58								13 48	13 53	14 03		14 08		14 13		14 28							
Haggerston	d	14 00								13 50	13 55	14 05		14 10		14 15		14 30							
Dalston Junction Stn ELL	a	14 02								13 52	13 58	14 07		14 13		14 17		14 32							
Canonbury	d	14 05								13 57		14 12				14 20		14 35							
Highbury & Islington	a	14 10								14 02		14 16				14 25		14 40							
	d																								
London Bridge 4 ⊖	a			13 26				13 36	13 41				13 59				14 11			13 56			14 06	14 11	

		LO	LO	LO	SN	LO	LO	SN	LO	SN		SN	SE	SE	SN	SN	LO	LO	LO	SN		LO	LO	SN	LO
East Croydon	d				14 00															14 30					
West Croydon 4	d	13 39		13 52												14 01	14 09		14 22						
Norwood Junction 2	d	13 43		13 58	14 05												14 13		14 28	14 35					
Anerley	d	13 46		14 01	14 08												14 16		14 31	14 38					
Penge West	d	13 48		14 03	14 10												14 18		14 33	14 40					
London Victoria 15 ⊖	d							13 49					14 09		14 11									14 19	
Battersea Park 4	d							13 53							14 15									14 23	
Wandsworth Road	d														14 17										
Clapham High Street ⊖	d														14 19										
London Blackfriars 3 ⊖	d													14 12											
Denmark Hill 4	d												14 18	14 22	14 24										
Peckham Rye 4	d									14 12		14 16	14a21	14a25	14 26	14 31									
Queens Rd Peckham	d											14 19			14 29	14 34									
South Bermondsey	d											14 21			14 31	14 36									
Clapham Junction 10	d							13 57																14 27	
Wandsworth Common	d							14 00																14 30	
Balham 4 ⊖	d							14 02																14 32	
Streatham Hill	d							14 05																14 35	
West Norwood 4	d							14 10		14 23														14 40	
Gipsy Hill	d							14 13		14 26														14 43	
Crystal Palace 4	d						14 13	14 21	14 28	14a29													14 43	14 51	14 58
Sydenham	d	13 51		14 06	14 12		14 16	14 24	14 31								14 21		14 36	14 42			14 46	14 54	15 01
Forest Hill 4	d	13 53		14 08	14 15		14 19	14 27	14 34								14 23		14 38	14 45			14 49	14 57	15 04
Honor Oak Park	d	13 56		14 11	14 17		14 21	14 29	14 36								14 26		14 41	14 47			14 51	14 59	15 06
Brockley	d	13 58		14 13	14 20		14 24	14 32	14 39								14 28		14 43	14 50			14 54	15 02	15 09
New Cross Gate 4	a	14 01		14 16	14 22		14 26	14 34	14 41								14 31		14 46	14 52			14 56	15 04	15 11
	d	14 01		14 16	14 22		14 26	14 34	14 41								14 31		14 46	14 52			14 56	15 04	15 11
New Cross ELL	d		14 06			14 21												14 36				14 51			
Surrey Quays	d	14 05	14 10	14 19		14 25	14 30		14 45								14 35	14 40	14 49			14 55	15 00		15 15
Canada Water	d	14 07	14 12	14 21		14 27	14 32		14 47								14 37	14 42	14 51			14 57	15 02		15 17
Rotherhithe	d	14 08	14 13	14 23		14 28	14 33		14 48								14 38	14 43	14 53			14 58	15 03		15 18
Wapping	d	14 10	14 15	14 24		14 30	14 35		14 50								14 40	14 45	14 54			15 00	15 05		15 20
Shadwell	d	14 12	14 17	14 26		14 32	14 37		14 52								14 42	14 47	14 56			15 02	15 07		15 22
Whitechapel	d	14 14	14 19	14 29		14 34	14 39		14 54								14 44	14 49	14 59			15 04	15 09		15 24
Shoreditch High Street	d	14 16	14 21	14 31		14 36	14 41		14 56								14 46	14 51	15 01			15 06	15 11		15 26
Hoxton	d	14 18	14 23	14 33		14 38	14 43		14 58								14 48	14 53	15 03			15 08	15 13		15 28
Haggerston	d	14 20	14 25	14 35		14 40	14 45		15 00								14 50	14 55	15 05			15 10	15 15		15 30
Dalston Junction Stn ELL	a	14 22	14 28	14 37		14 43	14 47		15 02								14 52	14 58	15 07			15 13	15 17		15 32
Canonbury	d	14 27		14 42			14 50		15 05								14 57		15 12				15 20		15 35
Highbury & Islington	a	14 32		14 46			14 55		15 10								15 02		15 16				15 25		15 40
	d																								
London Bridge 4 ⊖	a				14 29			14 44				14 26			14 36	14 41				14 59				15 11	

Table 178

Saturdays

from 15 September

East London Line and Croydon - London Victoria to London Bridge

Network Diagram - see first Page of Table 177

Station		SN	SN	SE	SE	SN		SN	LO	LO	LO	SN	LO
East Croydon	d											15 00	
West Croydon 4	d							14 31	14 39		14 52		
Norwood Junction 2	d								14 43		14 58	15 05	
Anerley	d								14 46		15 01	15 08	
Penge West	d								14 48		15 03	15 10	
London Victoria 15 ⊖	d			14 39		14 41							
Battersea Park 4	d					14 45							
Wandsworth Road	d					14 47							
Clapham High Street ⊖	d					14 49							
London Blackfriars 3 ⊖	d				14 42								
Denmark Hill 4	d			14 48	14 52	14 54							
Peckham Rye 4	d	14 42	14 46	14a51	14a55	14 56		15 01					
Queens Rd Peckham	d		14 49			14 59		15 04					
South Bermondsey	d		14 51			15 01		15 06					
Clapham Junction 10	d												
Wandsworth Common	d												
Balham 4 ⊖	d												
Streatham Hill	d												
West Norwood 4	d	14 53											
Gipsy Hill	d	14 56											
Crystal Palace 4	d	14a59											
Sydenham	d								14 51		15 06	15 12	
Forest Hill 4	d								14 53		15 08	15 15	
Honor Oak Park	d								14 56		15 11	15 17	
Brockley	d								14 58		15 13	15 20	
New Cross Gate 4	a								15 01		15 16	15 22	
	d								15 01		15 16	15 22	
New Cross ELL	d									15 06			15 21
Surrey Quays	d								15 05	15 10	15 19		15 25
Canada Water	d								15 07	15 12	15 21		15 27
Rotherhithe	d								15 08	15 13	15 23		15 28
Wapping	d								15 10	15 15	15 24		15 30
Shadwell	d								15 12	15 17	15 26		15 32
Whitechapel	d								15 14	15 19	15 29		15 34
Shoreditch High Street	d								15 16	15 21	15 31		15 36
Hoxton	d								15 18	15 23	15 33		15 38
Haggerston	d								15 20	15 25	15 35		15 40
Dalston Junction Stn ELL	a								15 22	15 28	15 37		15 43
Canonbury	d								15 27		15 42		
Highbury & Islington	a								15 32		15 46		
	d												
London Bridge 4 ⊖	a		14 56			15 06		15 11				15 29	

Station		LO	SN	LO		SN	SN	SE	SE	SN	SN	LO	LO
East Croydon	d												
West Croydon 4	d										15 01	15 09	
Norwood Junction 2	d											15 13	
Anerley	d											15 16	
Penge West	d											15 18	
London Victoria 15 ⊖	d		14 49					15 09		15 11			
Battersea Park 4	d		14 53							15 15			
Wandsworth Road	d									15 17			
Clapham High Street ⊖	d									15 19			
London Blackfriars 3 ⊖	d								15 12				
Denmark Hill 4	d							15 18	15 22	15 24			
Peckham Rye 4	d					15 12	15 16	15a21	15a25	15 26	15 31		
Queens Rd Peckham	d						15 19			15 29	15 34		
South Bermondsey	d						15 21			15 31	15 36		
Clapham Junction 10	d		14 57										
Wandsworth Common	d		15 00										
Balham 4 ⊖	d		15 02										
Streatham Hill	d		15 05										
West Norwood 4	d		15 10			15 23							
Gipsy Hill	d		15 13			15 26							
Crystal Palace 4	d	15 13	15 21	15 28		15a29							
Sydenham	d	15 16	15 24	15 31								15 21	
Forest Hill 4	d	15 19	15 27	15 34								15 23	
Honor Oak Park	d	15 21	15 29	15 36								15 26	
Brockley	d	15 24	15 32	15 39								15 28	
New Cross Gate 4	a	15 26	15 34	15 41								15 31	
	d	15 26	15 34	15 41								15 31	
New Cross ELL	d												15 36
Surrey Quays	d	15 30		15 45								15 35	15 40
Canada Water	d	15 32		15 47								15 37	15 42
Rotherhithe	d	15 33		15 48								15 38	15 43
Wapping	d	15 35		15 50								15 40	15 45
Shadwell	d	15 37		15 52								15 42	15 47
Whitechapel	d	15 39		15 54								15 44	15 49
Shoreditch High Street	d	15 41		15 56								15 46	15 51
Hoxton	d	15 43		15 58								15 48	15 53
Haggerston	d	15 45		16 00								15 50	15 55
Dalston Junction Stn ELL	a	15 47		16 02								15 52	15 58
Canonbury	d	15 50		16 05								15 57	
Highbury & Islington	a	15 55		16 10								16 02	
	d												
London Bridge 4 ⊖	a		15 44				15 26			15 36	15 41		

Station		LO		SN	LO	LO	SN	LO	SN	SN	SE	SE	
East Croydon	d			15 30									
West Croydon 4	d	15 22											
Norwood Junction 2	d	15 28		15 35									
Anerley	d	15 31		15 38									
Penge West	d	15 33		15 40									
London Victoria 15 ⊖	d						15 19				15 39		
Battersea Park 4	d						15 23						
Wandsworth Road	d												
Clapham High Street ⊖	d												
London Blackfriars 3 ⊖	d											15 42	
Denmark Hill 4	d										15 48	15 52	
Peckham Rye 4	d								15 42	15 46	15a51	15a55	
Queens Rd Peckham	d									15 49			
South Bermondsey	d									15 51			
Clapham Junction 10	d						15 27						
Wandsworth Common	d						15 30						
Balham 4 ⊖	d						15 32						
Streatham Hill	d						15 35						
West Norwood 4	d						15 40		15 53				
Gipsy Hill	d						15 43		15 56				
Crystal Palace 4	d					15 43	15 51	15 58	15a59				
Sydenham	d	15 36		15 42		15 46	15 54	16 01					
Forest Hill 4	d	15 38		15 45		15 49	15 57	16 04					
Honor Oak Park	d	15 41		15 47		15 51	15 59	16 06					
Brockley	d	15 43		15 50		15 54	16 02	16 09					
New Cross Gate 4	a	15 46		15 52		15 56	16 04	16 11					
	d	15 46		15 52		15 56	16 04	16 11					
New Cross ELL	d				15 51								
Surrey Quays	d	15 49			15 55	16 00		16 15					
Canada Water	d	15 51			15 57	16 02		16 17					
Rotherhithe	d	15 53			15 58	16 03		16 18					
Wapping	d	15 54			16 00	16 05		16 20					
Shadwell	d	15 56			16 02	16 07		16 22					
Whitechapel	d	15 59			16 04	16 09		16 24					
Shoreditch High Street	d	16 01			16 06	16 11		16 26					
Hoxton	d	16 03			16 08	16 13		16 28					
Haggerston	d	16 05			16 10	16 15		16 30					
Dalston Junction Stn ELL	a	16 07			16 13	16 17		16 32					
Canonbury	d	16 12				16 20		16 35					
Highbury & Islington	a	16 16				16 25		16 40					
	d												
London Bridge 4 ⊖	a			15 59			16 11			15 56			

Station		SN	SN	LO	LO	LO	SN	LO	LO	SN		LO	SN
East Croydon	d						16 00						
West Croydon 4	d		15 31	15 39		15 52							
Norwood Junction 2	d			15 43		15 58	16 05						
Anerley	d			15 46		16 01	16 08						
Penge West	d			15 48		16 03	16 10						
London Victoria 15 ⊖	d	15 41								15 49			
Battersea Park 4	d	15 45								15 53			
Wandsworth Road	d	15 47											
Clapham High Street ⊖	d	15 49											
London Blackfriars 3 ⊖	d												
Denmark Hill 4	d	15 54											
Peckham Rye 4	d	15 56	16 01										16 12
Queens Rd Peckham	d	15 59	16 04										
South Bermondsey	d	16 01	16 06										
Clapham Junction 10	d									15 57			
Wandsworth Common	d									16 00			
Balham 4 ⊖	d									16 02			
Streatham Hill	d									16 05			
West Norwood 4	d									16 10			16 23
Gipsy Hill	d									16 13			16 26
Crystal Palace 4	d								16 13	16 21		16 28	16a29
Sydenham	d			15 51		16 06	16 12		16 16	16 24		16 31	
Forest Hill 4	d			15 53		16 08	16 15		16 19	16 27		16 34	
Honor Oak Park	d			15 56		16 11	16 17		16 21	16 29		16 36	
Brockley	d			15 58		16 13	16 20		16 24	16 32		16 39	
New Cross Gate 4	a			16 01		16 16	16 22		16 26	16 34		16 41	
	d			16 01		16 16	16 22		16 26	16 34		16 41	
New Cross ELL	d				16 06			16 21					
Surrey Quays	d			16 05	16 10	16 19		16 25	16 30			16 45	
Canada Water	d			16 07	16 12	16 21		16 27	16 32			16 47	
Rotherhithe	d			16 08	16 13	16 23		16 28	16 33			16 48	
Wapping	d			16 10	16 15	16 24		16 30	16 35			16 50	
Shadwell	d			16 12	16 17	16 26		16 32	16 37			16 52	
Whitechapel	d			16 14	16 19	16 29		16 34	16 39			16 54	
Shoreditch High Street	d			16 16	16 21	16 31		16 36	16 41			16 56	
Hoxton	d			16 18	16 23	16 33		16 38	16 43			16 58	
Haggerston	d			16 20	16 25	16 35		16 40	16 45			17 00	
Dalston Junction Stn ELL	a			16 22	16 28	16 37		16 43	16 47			17 02	
Canonbury	d			16 27		16 42			16 50			17 05	
Highbury & Islington	a			16 32		16 46			16 55			17 10	
	d												
London Bridge 4 ⊖	a	16 06	16 11				16 29			16 41			

East London Line and Croydon - London Victoria to London Bridge

Network Diagram - see first Page of Table 177

		SN	SE	SE	SN	SN	LO	LO		LO	SN	LO	LO	SN	LO	SN	SN	SE		SE	SN	SN	LO	LO	LO
East Croydon	d										16 30														
West Croydon 4	d					16 01	16 09			16 22												16 31	16 39		16 52
Norwood Junction 2	d						16 13			16 28	16 35												16 43		16 58
Anerley	d						16 16			16 31	16 38												16 46		17 01
Penge West	d						16 18			16 33	16 40												16 48		17 03
London Victoria 15 ⊖	d		16 09		16 11									16 19				16 39			16 41				
Battersea Park 4	d				16 15									16 23							16 45				
Wandsworth Road	d				16 17																16 47				
Clapham High Street ⊖	d				16 19																16 49				
London Blackfriars 3 ⊖	d			16 12																16 42					
Denmark Hill 4	d		16 18	16 22	16 24													16 48		16 52	16 54				
Peckham Rye 4	d	16 16	16a21	16a25	16 26	16 31										16 42	16 46	16a51		16a55	16 56	17 01			
Queens Rd Peckham	d	16 19			16 29	16 34											16 49				16 59	17 04			
South Bermondsey	d	16 21			16 31	16 36											16 51				17 01	17 06			
Clapham Junction 10	d													16 27											
Wandsworth Common	d													16 30											
Balham 4 ⊖	d													16 32											
Streatham Hill	d													16 35											
West Norwood 4	d													16 40		16 53									
Gipsy Hill	d													16 43		16 56									
Crystal Palace 4	d												16 43	16 51	16 58	16a59									
Sydenham	d						16 21			16 36	16 42		16 46	16 54	17 01								16 51		17 06
Forest Hill 4	d						16 23			16 38	16 45		16 49	16 57	17 04								16 53		17 08
Honor Oak Park	d						16 26			16 41	16 47		16 51	16 59	17 06								16 56		17 11
Brockley	d						16 28			16 43	16 50		16 54	17 02	17 09								16 58		17 13
New Cross Gate 4	a						16 31			16 46	16 52		16 56	17 04	17 11								17 01		17 16
	d						16 31			16 46	16 52		16 56	17 04	17 11								17 01		17 16
New Cross ELL	d							16 36				16 51												17 06	
Surrey Quays	d						16 35	16 40		16 49		16 55	17 00		17 15								17 05	17 10	17 19
Canada Water	d						16 37	16 42		16 51		16 57	17 02		17 17								17 07	17 12	17 21
Rotherhithe	d						16 38	16 43		16 53		16 58	17 03		17 18								17 08	17 13	17 23
Wapping	d						16 40	16 45		16 54		17 00	17 05		17 20								17 10	17 15	17 24
Shadwell	d						16 42	16 47		16 56		17 02	17 07		17 22								17 12	17 17	17 26
Whitechapel	d						16 44	16 49		16 59		17 04	17 09		17 24								17 14	17 19	17 29
Shoreditch High Street	d						16 46	16 51		17 01		17 06	17 11		17 26								17 16	17 21	17 31
Hoxton	d						16 48	16 53		17 03		17 08	17 13		17 28								17 18	17 23	17 33
Haggerston	d						16 50	16 55		17 05		17 10	17 15		17 30								17 20	17 25	17 35
Dalston Junction Stn ELL	a						16 52	16 58		17 07		17 13	17 17		17 32								17 22	17 28	17 37
Canonbury	d						16 57			17 12			17 20		17 35								17 27		17 42
Highbury & Islington	a						17 02			17 16			17 25		17 40								17 32		17 46
	d																								
London Bridge 4 ⊖	a	16 26			16 36	16 41					16 59			17 11			16 56				17 06	17 11			

		SN	LO	LO		SN	LO	SN	SN	SE	SE	SN	SN	LO		LO	LO	SN	LO	LO	SN	LO	SN	SN	
East Croydon	d	17 00																17 30							
West Croydon 4	d												17 01	17 09			17 22								
Norwood Junction 2	d	17 05												17 13			17 28	17 35							
Anerley	d	17 08												17 16			17 31	17 38							
Penge West	d	17 10												17 18			17 33	17 40							
London Victoria 15 ⊖	d					16 49				17 09		17 11									17 19				
Battersea Park 4	d					16 53						17 15									17 23				
Wandsworth Road	d											17 17													
Clapham High Street ⊖	d											17 19													
London Blackfriars 3 ⊖	d										17 12														
Denmark Hill 4	d									17 18	17 22	17 24													
Peckham Rye 4	d							17 12	17 16	17a21	17a25	17 26	17 31										17 42	17 46	
Queens Rd Peckham	d								17 19			17 29	17 34											17 49	
South Bermondsey	d								17 21			17 31	17 36											17 51	
Clapham Junction 10	d					16 57															17 27				
Wandsworth Common	d					17 00															17 30				
Balham 4 ⊖	d					17 02															17 32				
Streatham Hill	d					17 05															17 35				
West Norwood 4	d					17 10		17 23													17 40		17 53		
Gipsy Hill	d					17 13		17 26													17 43		17 56		
Crystal Palace 4	d			17 13		17 21	17 28	17a29												17 43	17 51	17 58	17a59		
Sydenham	d	17 12		17 16		17 24	17 31							17 21			17 36	17 42		17 46	17 54	18 01			
Forest Hill 4	d	17 15		17 19		17 27	17 34							17 23			17 38	17 45		17 49	17 57	18 04			
Honor Oak Park	d	17 17		17 21		17 29	17 36							17 26			17 41	17 47		17 51	17 59	18 06			
Brockley	d	17 20		17 24		17 32	17 39							17 28			17 43	17 50		17 54	18 02	18 09			
New Cross Gate 4	a	17 22		17 26		17 34	17 41							17 31			17 46	17 52		17 56	18 04	18 11			
	d	17 22		17 26		17 34	17 41							17 31			17 46	17 52		17 56	18 04	18 11			
New Cross ELL	d		17 21													17 36			17 51						
Surrey Quays	d		17 25	17 30			17 45							17 35		17 40	17 49		17 55	18 00		18 15			
Canada Water	d		17 27	17 32			17 47							17 37		17 42	17 51		17 57	18 02		18 17			
Rotherhithe	d		17 28	17 33			17 48							17 38		17 43	17 53		17 58	18 03		18 18			
Wapping	d		17 30	17 35			17 50							17 40		17 45	17 54		18 00	18 05		18 20			
Shadwell	d		17 32	17 37			17 52							17 42		17 47	17 56		18 02	18 07		18 22			
Whitechapel	d		17 34	17 39			17 54							17 44		17 49	17 59		18 04	18 09		18 24			
Shoreditch High Street	d		17 36	17 41			17 56							17 46		17 51	18 01		18 06	18 11		18 26			
Hoxton	d		17 38	17 43			17 58							17 48		17 53	18 03		18 08	18 13		18 28			
Haggerston	d		17 40	17 45			18 00							17 50		17 55	18 05		18 10	18 15		18 30			
Dalston Junction Stn ELL	a		17 43	17 47			18 02							17 52		17 58	18 07		18 13	18 17		18 32			
Canonbury	d			17 50			18 05							17 57			18 12			18 20		18 35			
Highbury & Islington	a			17 55			18 10							18 02			18 16			18 25		18 40			
	d																								
London Bridge 4 ⊖	a	17 30				17 41			17 26			17 36	17 41					17 59			18 11			17 56	

Table 178

Saturdays
from 15 September

East London Line and Croydon - London Victoria to London Bridge

Network Diagram - see first Page of Table 177

		SE	SE	SN	SN	LO	LO	LO	SN	LO		LO	SN	LO	SN	SN	SE	SE	SN	SN		LO	LO	LO	SN
East Croydon	d								18 00																18 30
West Croydon 4	d				17 31	17 39		17 52												18 01		18 09		18 22	
Norwood Junction 2	d					17 43		17 58	18 05													18 13		18 28	18 35
Anerley	d					17 46		18 01	18 08													18 16		18 31	18 38
Penge West	d					17 48		18 03	18 10													18 18		18 33	18 40
London Victoria 15	d	17 39		17 41									17 49				18 09		18 11						
Battersea Park 4	d			17 45									17 53						18 15						
Wandsworth Road	d			17 47															18 17						
Clapham High Street	d			17 49															18 19						
London Blackfriars 3	d		17 42															18 12							
Denmark Hill 4	d	17 48	17 52	17 54													18 18	18 22	18 24						
Peckham Rye 4	d	17a51	17a55	17 56	18 01										18 12	18 16	18a21	18a25	18 26	18 31					
Queens Rd Peckham	d			17 59	18 04											18 19			18 29	18 34					
South Bermondsey	d			18 01	18 06											18 21			18 31	18 36					
Clapham Junction 10	d												17 57												
Wandsworth Common	d												18 00												
Balham 4	d												18 02												
Streatham Hill	d												18 05												
West Norwood 4	d												18 10		18 23										
Gipsy Hill	d												18 13		18 26										
Crystal Palace 4	d											18 13	18 21	18 28	18a29										
Sydenham	d					17 51		18 06	18 12			18 16	18 24	18 31								18 21		18 36	18 42
Forest Hill 4	d					17 53		18 08	18 15			18 19	18 27	18 34								18 23		18 38	18 45
Honor Oak Park	d					17 56		18 11	18 17			18 21	18 29	18 36								18 26		18 41	18 47
Brockley	d					17 58		18 13	18 20			18 24	18 32	18 39								18 28		18 43	18 50
New Cross Gate 4	a					18 01		18 16	18 22			18 26	18 34	18 41								18 31		18 46	18 52
	d					18 01		18 16	18 22			18 26	18 34	18 41								18 31		18 46	18 52
New Cross ELL	d						18 06			18 21													18 36		
Surrey Quays	d					18 05	18 10	18 19		18 25		18 30		18 45								18 35	18 40	18 49	
Canada Water	d					18 07	18 12	18 21		18 27		18 32		18 47								18 37	18 42	18 51	
Rotherhithe	d					18 08	18 13	18 23		18 28		18 33		18 48								18 38	18 43	18 53	
Wapping	d					18 10	18 15	18 24		18 30		18 35		18 50								18 40	18 45	18 54	
Shadwell	d					18 12	18 17	18 26		18 32		18 37		18 52								18 42	18 47	18 56	
Whitechapel	d					18 14	18 19	18 29		18 34		18 39		18 54								18 44	18 49	18 59	
Shoreditch High Street	d					18 16	18 21	18 31		18 36		18 41		18 56								18 46	18 51	19 01	
Hoxton	d					18 18	18 23	18 33		18 38		18 43		18 58								18 48	18 53	19 03	
Haggerston	d					18 20	18 25	18 35		18 40		18 45		19 00								18 50	18 55	19 05	
Dalston Junction Stn ELL	a					18 22	18 28	18 37		18 43		18 47		19 02								18 52	18 58	19 07	
Canonbury	d					18 27		18 42				18 50		19 05								18 57		19 12	
Highbury & Islington	a					18 32		18 46				18 55		19 10								19 02		19 16	
	d																								
London Bridge 4	a			18 06	18 11				18 29				18 41			18 26			18 36	18 41					18 59

		LO	LO	SN	LO	SN		SN	SE	SE	SN	SN	LO	LO	LO	SN		LO	LO	SN	LO	SN	SN	SE	SE
East Croydon	d															19 00									
West Croydon 4	d											18 31	18 39		18 52										
Norwood Junction 2	d												18 43		18 58	19 05									
Anerley	d												18 46		19 01	19 08									
Penge West	d												18 48		19 03	19 10									
London Victoria 15	d			18 19					18 39		18 41									18 49				19 09	
Battersea Park 4	d			18 23							18 45									18 53					
Wandsworth Road	d										18 47														
Clapham High Street	d										18 49														
London Blackfriars 3	d									18 42															19 12
Denmark Hill 4	d								18 48	18 52	18 54													19 18	19 22
Peckham Rye 4	d					18 42		18 46	18a51	18a55	18 56	19 01										19 12	19 16	19a21	19a25
Queens Rd Peckham	d							18 49			18 59	19 04											19 19		
South Bermondsey	d							18 51			19 01	19 06											19 21		
Clapham Junction 10	d			18 27																18 57					
Wandsworth Common	d			18 30																19 00					
Balham 4	d			18 32																19 02					
Streatham Hill	d			18 35																19 05					
West Norwood 4	d			18 40		18 53														19 10		19 23			
Gipsy Hill	d			18 43		18 56														19 13		19 26			
Crystal Palace 4	d		18 43	18 51	18 58	18a59													19 13	19 21	19 28	19a29			
Sydenham	d		18 46	18 54	19 01								18 51		19 06	19 12			19 16	19 24	19 31				
Forest Hill 4	d		18 49	18 57	19 04								18 53		19 08	19 15			19 19	19 27	19 34				
Honor Oak Park	d		18 51	18 59	19 06								18 56		19 11	19 17			19 21	19 29	19 36				
Brockley	d		18 54	19 02	19 09								18 58		19 13	19 20			19 24	19 32	19 39				
New Cross Gate 4	a		18 56	19 04	19 11								19 01		19 16	19 22			19 26	19 34	19 41				
	d		18 56	19 04	19 11								19 01		19 16	19 22			19 26	19 34	19 41				
New Cross ELL	d	18 51												19 06				19 21							
Surrey Quays	d	18 55	19 00		19 15								19 05	19 10	19 19			19 25	19 30		19 45				
Canada Water	d	18 57	19 02		19 17								19 07	19 12	19 21			19 27	19 32		19 47				
Rotherhithe	d	18 58	19 03		19 18								19 08	19 13	19 23			19 28	19 33		19 48				
Wapping	d	19 00	19 05		19 20								19 10	19 15	19 24			19 30	19 35		19 50				
Shadwell	d	19 02	19 07		19 22								19 12	19 17	19 26			19 32	19 37		19 52				
Whitechapel	d	19 04	19 09		19 24								19 14	19 19	19 29			19 34	19 39		19 54				
Shoreditch High Street	d	19 06	19 11		19 26								19 16	19 21	19 31			19 36	19 41		19 56				
Hoxton	d	19 08	19 13		19 28								19 18	19 23	19 33			19 38	19 43		19 58				
Haggerston	d	19 10	19 15		19 30								19 20	19 25	19 35			19 40	19 45		20 00				
Dalston Junction Stn ELL	a	19 13	19 17		19 32								19 22	19 28	19 37			19 43	19 47		20 02				
Canonbury	d		19 20		19 35								19 27		19 42				19 50		20 05				
Highbury & Islington	a		19 25		19 40								19 32		19 46				19 55		20 10				
	d																								
London Bridge 4	a			19 11				18 56			19 06	19 11				19 29				19 41			19 26		

Table 178

Saturdays

from 15 September

East London Line and Croydon - London Victoria to London Bridge

Network Diagram - see first Page of Table 177

		SN		SN	LO	LO	LO	SN	LO	LO	SN	LO		SN	SN	SE	SE	SN	SN	LO	LO	LO		SN	LO
East Croydon	d							19 30																20 00	
West Croydon [4]	d			19 01	19 09		19 22												19 31	19 39		19 52			
Norwood Junction [2]	d				19 13		19 28	19 35												19 43		19 58		20 05	
Anerley	d				19 16		19 31	19 38												19 46		20 01		20 08	
Penge West	d				19 18		19 33	19 40												19 48		20 03		20 10	
London Victoria [15] ⊖	d	19 11									19 19					19 39		19 41							
Battersea Park [4]	d	19 15									19 23							19 45							
Wandsworth Road	d	19 17																19 47							
Clapham High Street ⊖	d	19 19																19 49							
London Blackfriars [3] ⊖	d																19 42								
Denmark Hill [4]	d	19 24														19 48	19 52	19 54							
Peckham Rye [4]	d	19 26		19 31										19 42	19 46	19a51	19a55	19 56	20 01						
Queens Rd Peckham	d	19 29		19 34											19 49			19 59	20 04						
South Bermondsey	d	19 31		19 36											19 51			20 01	20 06						
Clapham Junction [10]	d										19 27														
Wandsworth Common	d										19 30														
Balham [4] ⊖	d										19 32														
Streatham Hill	d										19 35														
West Norwood [4]	d										19 40			19 53											
Gipsy Hill	d										19 43			19 56											
Crystal Palace [4]	d									19 43	19 51	19 58		19a59											
Sydenham	d				19 21		19 36	19 42		19 46	19 54	20 01								19 51		20 06		20 12	
Forest Hill [4]	d				19 23		19 38	19 45		19 49	19 57	20 04								19 53		20 08		20 15	
Honor Oak Park	d				19 26		19 41	19 47		19 51	19 59	20 06								19 56		20 11		20 17	
Brockley	d				19 28		19 43	19 50		19 54	20 02	20 09								19 58		20 13		20 20	
New Cross Gate [4]	a				19 31		19 46	19 52		19 56	20 04	20 11								20 01		20 16		20 22	
	d				19 31		19 46	19 52		19 56	20 04	20 11								20 01		20 16		20 22	
New Cross ELL	d					19 36			19 51												20 06				20 21
Surrey Quays	d				19 35	19 40	19 49		19 55	20 00		20 15								20 05	20 10	20 19			20 25
Canada Water	d				19 37	19 42	19 51		19 57	20 02		20 17								20 07	20 12	20 21			20 27
Rotherhithe	d				19 38	19 43	19 53		19 58	20 03		20 18								20 08	20 13	20 23			20 28
Wapping	d				19 40	19 45	19 54		20 00	20 05		20 20								20 10	20 15	20 24			20 30
Shadwell	d				19 42	19 47	19 56		20 02	20 07		20 22								20 12	20 17	20 26			20 32
Whitechapel	d				19 44	19 49	19 59		20 04	20 09		20 24								20 14	20 19	20 29			20 34
Shoreditch High Street	d				19 46	19 51	20 01		20 06	20 11		20 26								20 16	20 21	20 31			20 36
Hoxton	d				19 48	19 53	20 03		20 08	20 13		20 28								20 18	20 23	20 33			20 38
Haggerston	d				19 50	19 55	20 05		20 10	20 15		20 30								20 20	20 25	20 35			20 40
Dalston Junction Stn ELL	a				19 52	19 58	20 07		20 13	20 17		20 32								20 22	20 28	20 37			20 43
Canonbury	d				19 57		20 12			20 20		20 35								20 27		20 42			
Highbury & Islington	a				20 02		20 16			20 25		20 40								20 32		20 46			
	d																								
London Bridge [4] ⊖	a	19 36		19 41				19 59			20 11				19 56			20 06	20 11					20 29	

		LO	SN	LO	SN	SN	SE	SN		SN	LO	LO	LO	SN	LO	LO	SN	LO		SN	SN	SE	SN	SN	LO
East Croydon	d													20 30											
West Croydon [4]	d									20 01	20 09		20 22											20 31	20 39
Norwood Junction [2]	d										20 13		20 28	20 35											20 43
Anerley	d										20 16		20 31	20 38											20 46
Penge West	d										20 18		20 33	20 40											20 48
London Victoria [15] ⊖	d		19 49					20 11									20 19						20 41		
Battersea Park [4]	d		19 53					20 15									20 23						20 45		
Wandsworth Road	d							20 17															20 47		
Clapham High Street ⊖	d							20 19															20 49		
London Blackfriars [3] ⊖	d						20 12															20 42			
Denmark Hill [4]	d						20 22	20 24														20 52	20 54		
Peckham Rye [4]	d				20 12	20 16	20a25	20 26		20 31										20 42	20 46	20a55	20 56	21 01	
Queens Rd Peckham	d					20 19		20 29		20 34											20 49		20 59	21 04	
South Bermondsey	d					20 21		20 31		20 36											20 51		21 01	21 06	
Clapham Junction [10]	d		19 57														20 27								
Wandsworth Common	d		20 00														20 30								
Balham [4] ⊖	d		20 02														20 32								
Streatham Hill	d		20 05														20 35								
West Norwood [4]	d		20 10		20 23												20 40			20 53					
Gipsy Hill	d		20 13		20 26												20 43			20 56					
Crystal Palace [4]	d	20 13	20 21	20 28	20a29											20 43	20 51	20 58		20a59					
Sydenham	d	20 16	20 24	20 31							20 21		20 36	20 42		20 46	20 54	21 01							20 51
Forest Hill [4]	d	20 19	20 27	20 34							20 23		20 38	20 45		20 49	20 57	21 04							20 53
Honor Oak Park	d	20 21	20 29	20 36							20 26		20 41	20 47		20 51	20 59	21 06							20 56
Brockley	d	20 24	20 32	20 39							20 28		20 43	20 50		20 54	21 02	21 09							20 58
New Cross Gate [4]	a	20 26	20 34	20 41							20 31		20 46	20 52		20 56	21 04	21 11							21 01
	d	20 26	20 34	20 41							20 31		20 46	20 52		20 56	21 04	21 11							21 01
New Cross ELL	d											20 36			20 51										
Surrey Quays	d	20 30		20 45							20 35	20 40	20 49		20 55	21 00		21 15							21 05
Canada Water	d	20 32		20 47							20 37	20 42	20 51		20 57	21 02		21 17							21 07
Rotherhithe	d	20 33		20 48							20 38	20 43	20 53		20 58	21 03		21 18							21 08
Wapping	d	20 35		20 50							20 40	20 45	20 54		21 00	21 05		21 20							21 10
Shadwell	d	20 37		20 52							20 42	20 47	20 56		21 02	21 07		21 22							21 12
Whitechapel	d	20 39		20 54							20 44	20 49	20 59		21 04	21 09		21 24							21 14
Shoreditch High Street	d	20 41		20 56							20 46	20 51	21 01		21 06	21 11		21 26							21 16
Hoxton	d	20 43		20 58							20 48	20 53	21 03		21 08	21 13		21 28							21 18
Haggerston	d	20 45		21 00							20 50	20 55	21 05		21 10	21 15		21 30							21 20
Dalston Junction Stn ELL	a	20 47		21 02							20 52	20 58	21 07		21 13	21 17		21 32							21 22
Canonbury	d	20 50		21 05							20 57		21 12			21 20		21 35							21 27
Highbury & Islington	a	20 55		21 10							21 02		21 16			21 25		21 40							21 32
	d																								
London Bridge [4] ⊖	a		20 41			20 26		20 36		20 41				20 59			21 13				20 56		21 06	21 11	

Table 178

Saturdays

from 15 September

East London Line and Croydon - London Victoria to London Bridge

Network Diagram - see first Page of Table 177

		LO	LO	SN		LO	LO	SN	LO	SN	SN	SE	SN	SN		LO	LO	LO	SN	LO	LO	SN	LO	SN	
East Croydon	d			21 00															21 30						
West Croydon 4	d		20 52											21 02		21 09		21 22							
Norwood Junction 2	d		20 58	21 05												21 13		21 28	21 35						
Anerley	d		21 01	21 08												21 16		21 31	21 38						
Penge West	d		21 03	21 10												21 18		21 33	21 40						
London Victoria 15 ⊖	d							20 49					21 11									21 19			
Battersea Park 4	d							20 53					21 15									21 23			
Wandsworth Road	d												21 17												
Clapham High Street ⊖	d												21 19												
London Blackfriars 3 ⊖	d											21 12													
Denmark Hill 4	d											21 22	21 24												
Peckham Rye 4	d									21 12	21 16	21a25	21 26	21 31										21 42	
Queens Rd Peckham	d										21 19		21 29	21 34											
South Bermondsey	d										21 21		21 31	21 36											
Clapham Junction 10	d							20 57														21 27			
Wandsworth Common	d							21 00														21 30			
Balham 4 ⊖	d							21 02														21 32			
Streatham Hill	d							21 05														21 35			
West Norwood 4	d							21 10		21 23												21 40		21 53	
Gipsy Hill	d							21 13		21 26												21 43		21 56	
Crystal Palace 4	d						21 13	21 21	21 28	21a29											21 43	21 51	21 58	21a59	
Sydenham	d		21 06	21 12			21 16	21 24	21 31							21 21		21 36	21 42		21 46	21 54	22 01		
Forest Hill 4	d		21 08	21 15			21 19	21 27	21 34							21 23		21 38	21 45		21 49	21 57	22 04		
Honor Oak Park	d		21 11	21 17			21 21	21 29	21 36							21 26		21 41	21 47		21 51	21 59	22 06		
Brockley	d		21 13	21 20			21 24	21 32	21 39							21 28		21 43	21 50		21 54	22 02	22 09		
New Cross Gate 4	a		21 16	21 22			21 26	21 34	21 41							21 31		21 46	21 52		21 56	22 04	22 11		
	d		21 16	21 22			21 26	21 34	21 41							21 31		21 46	21 52		21 56	22 04	22 11		
New Cross ELL	d	21 06				21 21											21 36			21 51					
Surrey Quays	d	21 10	21 19			21 25	21 30		21 45							21 35	21 40	21 49		21 55	22 00		22 15		
Canada Water	d	21 12	21 21			21 27	21 32		21 47							21 37	21 42	21 51		21 57	22 02		22 17		
Rotherhithe	d	21 13	21 23			21 28	21 33		21 48							21 38	21 43	21 53		21 58	22 03		22 18		
Wapping	d	21 15	21 24			21 30	21 35		21 50							21 40	21 45	21 54		22 00	22 05		22 20		
Shadwell	d	21 17	21 26			21 32	21 37		21 52							21 42	21 47	21 56		22 02	22 07		22 22		
Whitechapel	d	21 19	21 29			21 34	21 39		21 54							21 44	21 49	21 59		22 04	22 09		22 24		
Shoreditch High Street	d	21 21	21 31			21 36	21 41		21 56							21 46	21 51	22 01		22 06	22 11		22 26		
Hoxton	d	21 23	21 33			21 38	21 43		21 58							21 48	21 53	22 03		22 08	22 13		22 28		
Haggerston	d	21 25	21 35			21 40	21 45		22 00							21 50	21 55	22 05		22 10	22 15		22 30		
Dalston Junction Stn ELL	a	21 28	21 37			21 43	21 47		22 02							21 52	21 58	22 07		22 13	22 17		22 32		
Canonbury	d		21 42				21 50		22 05							21 57		22 12			22 20		22 35		
Highbury & Islington	a		21 46				21 55		22 10							22 02		22 16			22 25		22 40		
	d																								
London Bridge 4 ⊖	a			21 29				21 43			21 26		21 36	21 41					21 59			22 13			

		SN	SE	SN	SN	LO	LO	LO	SN	LO		SN	LO	SN	SN	SE	SN	SN	LO	LO		LO	SN	LO	SN
East Croydon	d								22 00														22 30		
West Croydon 4	d				21 31	21 39		21 52										22 01	22 09			22 22			
Norwood Junction 2	d					21 43		21 58	22 05										22 13			22 28	22 35		
Anerley	d					21 46		22 01	22 08										22 16			22 31	22 38		
Penge West	d					21 48		22 03	22 10										22 18			22 33	22 40		
London Victoria 15 ⊖	d			21 41								21 49					22 11								22 19
Battersea Park 4	d			21 45								21 53					22 15								22 23
Wandsworth Road	d			21 47													22 17								
Clapham High Street ⊖	d			21 49													22 19								
London Blackfriars 3 ⊖	d		21 42													22 12									
Denmark Hill 4	d		21 52	21 54												22 22	22 24								
Peckham Rye 4	d	21 46	21a55	21 56	22 01									22 12	22 16	22a25	22 26	22 31							
Queens Rd Peckham	d	21 49		21 59	22 04										22 19		22 29	22 34							
South Bermondsey	d	21 51		22 01	22 06										22 21		22 31	22 36							
Clapham Junction 10	d											21 57													22 27
Wandsworth Common	d											22 00													22 30
Balham 4 ⊖	d											22 02													22 32
Streatham Hill	d											22 05													22 35
West Norwood 4	d											22 10		22 23											22 40
Gipsy Hill	d											22 13		22 26											22 43
Crystal Palace 4	d									22 13		22 21	22 28	22a29										22 43	22 51
Sydenham	d					21 51		22 06	22 12	22 16		22 24	22 31						22 21			22 36	22 42	22 46	22 54
Forest Hill 4	d					21 53		22 08	22 15	22 19		22 27	22 34						22 23			22 38	22 45	22 49	22 57
Honor Oak Park	d					21 56		22 11	22 17	22 21		22 29	22 36						22 26			22 41	22 47	22 51	22 59
Brockley	d					21 58		22 13	22 20	22 24		22 32	22 39						22 28			22 43	22 50	22 54	23 02
New Cross Gate 4	a					22 01		22 16	22 22	22 26		22 34	22 41						22 31			22 46	22 52	22 56	23 04
	d					22 01		22 16	22 22	22 26		22 34	22 41						22 31			22 46	22 52	22 56	23 04
New Cross ELL	d						22 06													22 36					
Surrey Quays	d					22 05	22 10	22 19		22 30			22 45						22 35	22 40		22 49		23 00	
Canada Water	d					22 07	22 12	22 21		22 32			22 47						22 37	22 42		22 51		23 02	
Rotherhithe	d					22 08	22 13	22 23		22 33			22 48						22 38	22 43		22 53		23 03	
Wapping	d					22 10	22 15	22 24		22 35			22 50						22 40	22 45		22 54		23 05	
Shadwell	d					22 12	22 17	22 26		22 37			22 52						22 42	22 47		22 56		23 07	
Whitechapel	d					22 14	22 19	22 29		22 39			22 54						22 44	22 49		22 59		23 09	
Shoreditch High Street	d					22 16	22 21	22 31		22 41			22 56						22 46	22 51		23 01		23 11	
Hoxton	d					22 18	22 23	22 33		22 43			22 58						22 48	22 53		23 03		23 13	
Haggerston	d					22 20	22 25	22 35		22 45			23 00						22 50	22 55		23 05		23 15	
Dalston Junction Stn ELL	a					22 22	22 28	22 37		22 47			23 02						22 52	22 58		23 07		23 17	
Canonbury	d					22 27		22 42		22 50			23 05						22 57			23 12		23 20	
Highbury & Islington	a					22 32		22 46		22 55			23 10						23 02			23 16		23 25	
	d																								
London Bridge 4 ⊖	a	21 56		22 06	22 11				22 29			22 43			22 26		22 36	22 41					22 59		23 13

Table 178

Saturdays

from 15 September

East London Line and Croydon - London Victoria to London Bridge

Network Diagram - see first Page of Table 177

		SN	SN	SE	SN	SN		LO	LO	LO	SN	LO	SN	SN	SN	SE		SN	SN	LO	LO	LO	SN	SN	SN
East Croydon	d										23 01														
West Croydon 4	d					22 31		22 39		22 52									23 01		23 22				
Norwood Junction 2	d							22 43		22 58	23 06										23 28				
Anerley	d							22 46		23 01	23 09										23 31				
Penge West	d							22 48		23 03	23 11										23 33				
London Victoria 15	d				22 41								22 49					23 11					23 19		
Battersea Park 4	d				22 45								22 53					23 15					23 23		
Wandsworth Road	d				22 47													23 17							
Clapham High Street	d				22 49													23 19							
London Blackfriars 3	d			22 42												23 12									
Denmark Hill 4	d			22 52	22 54											23 22		23 24							
Peckham Rye 4	d	22 42	22 46	22a55	22 56	23 01								23 12	23 16	23a25		23 26	23 31					23 42	23 46
Queens Rd Peckham	d		22 49		22 59	23 04									23 19			23 29	23 34						23 49
South Bermondsey	d		22 51		23 01	23 06									23 21			23 31	23 36						23 51
Clapham Junction 10	d												22 57										23 27		
Wandsworth Common	d												23 00										23 30		
Balham 4	d												23 02										23 32		
Streatham Hill	d												23 05										23 35		
West Norwood 4	d	22 53											23 10	23 24									23 40	23 54	
Gipsy Hill	d	22 56											23 13	23 27									23 43	23 57	
Crystal Palace 4	d	22a59										23 13	23 21	23a29								23 43	23 51	23a59	
Sydenham	d							22 51		23 06	23 13	23 16	23 24								23 36	23 46	23 54		
Forest Hill 4	d							22 53		23 08	23 16	23 19	23 27								23 38	23 49	23 57		
Honor Oak Park	d							22 56		23 11	23 18	23 21	23 29								23 41	23 51	23 59		
Brockley	d							22 58		23 13	23 21	23 24	23 32								23 43	23 54	00 02		
New Cross Gate 4	a							23 01		23 16	23 23	23 26	23 34								23 46	23 56	00 04		
	d							23 01		23 16	23 23	23 26	23 34								23 46	23 56	00 04		
New Cross ELL	d								23 06											23 36					
Surrey Quays	d							23 05	23 10	23 19		23 30								23 40	23 49	23 59			
Canada Water	d							23 07	23 12	23 21		23 32								23 42	23 51	00 02			
Rotherhithe	d							23 08	23 13	23 23		23 33								23 43	23 53	00 03			
Wapping	d							23 10	23 15	23 24		23 35								23 45	23 54	00 05			
Shadwell	d							23 12	23 17	23 26		23 37								23 47	23 56	00 07			
Whitechapel	d							23 14	23 19	23 29		23 39								23 49	23 59	00 09			
Shoreditch High Street	d							23 16	23 21	23 31		23 41								23 51	00 01	00 11			
Hoxton	d							23 18	23 23	23 33		23 43								23 53	00 03	00 13			
Haggerston	d							23 20	23 25	23 35		23 45								23 55	00 05	00 15			
Dalston Junction Stn ELL	a							23 22	23 28	23 37		23 47								23 58	00 07	00 17			
Canonbury	d							23 27		23 42		23 50									00 12	00 20			
Highbury & Islington	a							23 32		23 46		23 55									00 16	00 25			
	d																								
London Bridge 4	a		22 56		23 06	23 11					23 30		23 43		23 26			23 36	23 41				00 11		23 56

		SE		SN
East Croydon	d			
West Croydon 4	d			
Norwood Junction 2	d			
Anerley	d			
Penge West	d			
London Victoria 15	d			23 54
Battersea Park 4	d			23 58
Wandsworth Road	d			
Clapham High Street	d			
London Blackfriars 3	d	23 42		
Denmark Hill 4	d	23 52		
Peckham Rye 4	d	23a55		
Queens Rd Peckham	d			
South Bermondsey	d			
Clapham Junction 10	d			00 02
Wandsworth Common	d			00 05
Balham 4	d			00 07
Streatham Hill	d			00 10
West Norwood 4	d			00 14
Gipsy Hill	d			00 17
Crystal Palace 4	d			00 21
Sydenham	d			00 24
Forest Hill 4	d			00 27
Honor Oak Park	d			00 29
Brockley	d			00 32
New Cross Gate 4	a			00 35
	d			00 35
New Cross ELL	d			
Surrey Quays	d			
Canada Water	d			
Rotherhithe	d			
Wapping	d			
Shadwell	d			
Whitechapel	d			
Shoreditch High Street	d			
Hoxton	d			
Haggerston	d			
Dalston Junction Stn ELL	a			
Canonbury	d			
Highbury & Islington	a			
	d			
London Bridge 4	a			00 41

Table 178

Sundays

until 22 July

East London Line and Croydon - London Victoria to London Bridge

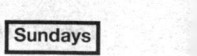

Network Diagram - see first Page of Table 177

		LO	LO	SN	SN	SN	SN	LO	SN	LO		SN	LO	SN	SN	SN	SN	LO	SN	LO		SN	SE	SN	SN
East Croydon	d								06 47						07 12	07 17									
West Croydon 4	d	23p22						06 42					07 12				07 22		07 34	07 42					
Norwood Junction 2	d	23p28						06 47	06 52				07 17			07 22	07 27		07 40	07 47					
Anerley	d	23p31						06 50	06 55				07 20			07 25				07 50					
Penge West	d	23p33						06 52	06 57				07 22			07 27				07 52					
London Victoria 15 ⊖	d			23p19	23p54																				07 41
Battersea Park 4	d			23p23	23p58																				07 45
Wandsworth Road	d																								07 47
Clapham High Street ⊖	d																								07 49
London Blackfriars 3 ⊖	d																						07 38		
Denmark Hill 4	d																						07 48		07 54
Peckham Rye 4	d					00 12	00 42					07 09		07 23	07 39							07 45	07a51	07 53	07 56
Queens Rd Peckham	d											07 12		07 26	07 42									07 56	07 59
South Bermondsey	d											07 14		07 28	07 44									07 58	08 01
Clapham Junction 10	d			23p27	00 02																				
Wandsworth Common	d			23p30	00 05																				
Balham 4 ⊖	d			23p32	00 07																				
Streatham Hill	d			23p35	00 10																				
West Norwood 4	d			23p40	00 14	00 24	00 54															07 57			
Gipsy Hill	d			23p43	00 17	00 27	00 57															08 00			
Crystal Palace 4	d		23p43	23p51	00 21	00a29	00a59			07 07							07a31	07 37				08a02			
Sydenham	d	23p36	23p46	23p54	00 24			06 55	06 59	07 10			07 25			07 29		07 40	07 44	07 55					
Forest Hill 4	d	23p38	23p49	23p57	00 27			06 57	07 02	07 13			07 27			07 32		07 43	07 47	07 57					
Honor Oak Park	d	23p41	23p51	23p59	00 29			07 00	07 04	07 15			07 30			07 34		07 45	07 49	08 00					
Brockley	d	23p43	23p54	00 02	00 32			07 02	07 07	07 18			07 32			07 37		07 48	07 52	08 02					
New Cross Gate 4	a	23p46	23p56	00 04	00 35			07 05	07 09	07 20			07 35			07 39		07 50	07 54	08 05					
	d	23p46	23p56	00 04	00 35			07 05	07 09	07 20			07 35			07 39		07 50	07 54	08 05					
New Cross ELL	d																								
Surrey Quays	d	23p49	23p59					07 09		07 24			07 39					07 54		08 09					
Canada Water	d	23p51	00 02					07 11		07 26			07 41					07 56		08 11					
Rotherhithe	d	23p53	00 03					07 12		07 27			07 42					07 57		08 12					
Wapping	d	23p54	00 05					07 14		07 29			07 44					07 59		08 14					
Shadwell	d	23p56	00 07					07 16		07 31			07 46					08 01		08 16					
Whitechapel	d	23p59	00 09					07 18		07 33			07 48					08 03		08 18					
Shoreditch High Street	d	00 01	00 11					07 20		07 35			07 50					08 05		08 20					
Hoxton	d	00 03	00 13					07 22		07 37			07 52					08 07		08 22					
Haggerston	d	00 05	00 15					07 24		07 39			07 54					08 09		08 24					
Dalston Junction Stn ELL	a	00 07	00 17					07 26		07 41			07 56					08 11		08 26					
Canonbury	d	00 12	00 20					07 31		07 44			08 01					08 14		08 31					
Highbury & Islington	a	00 16	00 25					07 36		07 49			08 06					08 21		08 36					
	d																								
London Bridge 4 ⊖	a			00 11	00 41				07 17			07 19		07 33	07 50	07 48			08 01					08 03	08 06

		SN	SN	SN	LO	SN		LO	SN	SE	SN	SN	SN	SN	LO	SN		SN	SE	SN	SN	SN	LO	LO	SN
East Croydon	d	07 42	07 47										08 12	08 17								08 42			08 47
West Croydon 4	d			07 52		08 04		08 12								08 34								08 42	
Norwood Junction 2	d		07 52	07 57		08 10		08 17						08 22		08 40								08 47	08 52
Anerley	d		07 55					08 20						08 25										08 50	08 55
Penge West	d		07 57					08 22						08 27										08 52	08 57
London Victoria 15 ⊖	d											08 11									08 41				
Battersea Park 4	d											08 15									08 45				
Wandsworth Road	d											08 17									08 47				
Clapham High Street ⊖	d											08 19									08 49				
London Blackfriars 3 ⊖	d									08 08									08 38						
Denmark Hill 4	d									08 18		08 24							08 48		08 54				
Peckham Rye 4	d	08 10							08 15	08a21	08 23	08 26	08 40					08 45	08a51	08 53	08 56	09 10			
Queens Rd Peckham	d	08 12									08 26	08 29	08 42							08 56	08 59	09 12			
South Bermondsey	d	08 15									08 28	08 31	08 45							08 58	09 01	09 15			
Clapham Junction 10	d																								
Wandsworth Common	d																								
Balham 4 ⊖	d																								
Streatham Hill	d																								
West Norwood 4	d								08 27									08 57							
Gipsy Hill	d								08 30									09 00							
Crystal Palace 4	d			08a01	08 07				08a32						08 37			09a02							
Sydenham	d		07 59		08 10	08 14		08 25						08 29	08 40	08 44								08 55	08 59
Forest Hill 4	d		08 02		08 13	08 17		08 27						08 32	08 43	08 47								08 57	09 02
Honor Oak Park	d		08 04		08 15	08 19		08 30						08 34	08 45	08 49								09 00	09 04
Brockley	d		08 07		08 18	08 22		08 32						08 37	08 48	08 52								09 02	09 07
New Cross Gate 4	a		08 09		08 20	08 24		08 35						08 39	08 50	08 54								09 05	09 09
	d		08 09		08 20	08 24		08 35						08 39	08 50	08 54								09 05	09 09
New Cross ELL	d																						08 54		
Surrey Quays	d				08 24			08 39							08 54								08 58	09 09	
Canada Water	d				08 26			08 41							08 56								09 00	09 11	
Rotherhithe	d				08 27			08 42							08 57								09 01	09 12	
Wapping	d				08 29			08 44							08 59								09 03	09 14	
Shadwell	d				08 31			08 46							09 01								09 05	09 16	
Whitechapel	d				08 33			08 48							09 03								09 07	09 18	
Shoreditch High Street	d				08 35			08 50							09 05								09 09	09 20	
Hoxton	d				08 37			08 52							09 07								09 11	09 22	
Haggerston	d				08 39			08 54							09 09								09 13	09 24	
Dalston Junction Stn ELL	a				08 41			08 56							09 11								09 15	09 26	
Canonbury	d				08 44			09 01							09 14								09 20	09 31	
Highbury & Islington	a				08 51			09 06							09 21								09 27	09 36	
	d																								
London Bridge 4 ⊖	a	08 19	08 17			08 31					08 33	08 36	08 49	08 48		09 01				09 03	09 06	09 19			09 18

Table 178

Sundays
until 22 July

East London Line and Croydon - London Victoria to London Bridge

Network Diagram - see first Page of Table 177

		LO		LO	SN	SN	SE	SN	SN	SN	LO	LO		SN	LO	LO	SN	SN	SE	SN	SN	SN		FC 1	LO
East Croydon	d									09 12				09 17								09 42		09 47	
West Croydon 4	d				09 04							09 12					09 34								
Norwood Junction 2	d				09 10							09 17		09 22			09 40								
Anerley	d											09 20		09 25											
Penge West	d											09 22		09 27											
London Victoria 15 ⊖	d								09 11												09 41				
Battersea Park 4	d								09 15												09 45				
Wandsworth Road	d								09 17												09 47				
Clapham High Street ⊖	d								09 19												09 49				
London Blackfriars 3 ⊖	d						09 08												09 38					10a07	
Denmark Hill 4	d						09 18		09 24										09 48		09 54				
Peckham Rye 4	d					09 15	09a21	09 23	09 26	09 40								09 45	09a51	09 53	09 56	10 10			
Queens Rd Peckham	d							09 26	09 29	09 42										09 56	09 59	10 12			
South Bermondsey	d							09 28	09 31	09 45										09 58	10 01	10 15			
Clapham Junction 10	d																								
Wandsworth Common	d																								
Balham 4 ⊖	d																								
Streatham Hill	d																								
West Norwood 4	d					09 27												09 57							
Gipsy Hill	d					09 30												10 00							
Crystal Palace 4	d			09 07		09a32										09 37		10a02							
Sydenham	d			09 10	09 14							09 25		09 29		09 40	09 44								
Forest Hill 4	d			09 13	09 17							09 27		09 32		09 43	09 47								
Honor Oak Park	d			09 15	09 19							09 30		09 34		09 45	09 49								
Brockley	d			09 18	09 22							09 32		09 37		09 48	09 52								
New Cross Gate 4	a			09 20	09 24							09 35		09 39		09 50	09 54								
	d			09 20	09 24							09 35		09 39		09 50	09 54								
New Cross ELL	d	09 09									09 24				09 39										09 54
Surrey Quays	d	09 13		09 24							09 28	09 39			09 43	09 54									09 58
Canada Water	d	09 15		09 26							09 30	09 41			09 45	09 56									10 00
Rotherhithe	d	09 16		09 27							09 31	09 42			09 46	09 57									10 01
Wapping	d	09 18		09 29							09 33	09 44			09 48	09 59									10 03
Shadwell	d	09 20		09 31							09 35	09 46			09 50	10 01									10 05
Whitechapel	d	09 22		09 33							09 37	09 48			09 52	10 03									10 07
Shoreditch High Street	d	09 24		09 35							09 39	09 50			09 54	10 05									10 09
Hoxton	d	09 26		09 37							09 41	09 52			09 56	10 07									10 11
Haggerston	d	09 28		09 39							09 43	09 54			09 58	10 09									10 13
Dalston Junction Stn ELL	a	09 31		09 41							09 45	09 56			10 01	10 11									10 15
Canonbury	d	09 36		09 44							09 50	10 01			10 06	10 14									10 20
Highbury & Islington	a	09 41		09 51							09 57	10 06			10 11	10 21									10 27
	d																								
London Bridge 4 ⊖	a				09 31			09 33	09 36	09 49				09 48			10 01			10 03	10 06	10 19			

		LO	SN	LO	LO	SN	SN	SE		SN	SN	SN	FC 1	LO	LO	SN	LO	LO		SN	SN	SE	SN	SN	SN
East Croydon	d		09 47									10 12	10 17			10 17									10 42
West Croydon 4	d	09 42				10 04									10 12					10 34					
Norwood Junction 2	d	09 47	09 52			10 10									10 17	10 22				10 40					
Anerley	d	09 50	09 55												10 20	10 25									
Penge West	d	09 52	09 57												10 22	10 27									
London Victoria 15 ⊖	d										10 11													10 41	
Battersea Park 4	d										10 15													10 45	
Wandsworth Road	d										10 17													10 47	
Clapham High Street ⊖	d										10 19													10 49	
London Blackfriars 3 ⊖	d							10 08					10a37									10 38			
Denmark Hill 4	d							10 18			10 24											10 48		10 54	
Peckham Rye 4	d						10 15	10a21		10 23	10 26	10 40									10 45	10a51	10 53	10 56	11 10
Queens Rd Peckham	d									10 26	10 29	10 42											10 56	10 59	11 12
South Bermondsey	d									10 28	10 31	10 45											10 58	11 01	11 15
Clapham Junction 10	d																								
Wandsworth Common	d																								
Balham 4 ⊖	d																								
Streatham Hill	d																								
West Norwood 4	d						10 27														10 57				
Gipsy Hill	d						10 30														11 00				
Crystal Palace 4	d				10 07		10a32											10 37			11a02				
Sydenham	d	09 55	09 59		10 10	10 14									10 25	10 29		10 40		10 44					
Forest Hill 4	d	09 57	10 02		10 13	10 17									10 27	10 32		10 43		10 47					
Honor Oak Park	d	10 00	10 04		10 15	10 19									10 30	10 34		10 45		10 49					
Brockley	d	10 02	10 07		10 18	10 22									10 32	10 37		10 48		10 52					
New Cross Gate 4	a	10 05	10 09		10 20	10 24									10 35	10 39		10 50		10 54					
	d	10 05	10 09		10 20	10 24									10 35	10 39		10 50		10 54					
New Cross ELL	d			10 09										10 24			10 39								
Surrey Quays	d	10 09		10 13	10 24									10 28	10 39		10 43	10 54							
Canada Water	d	10 11		10 15	10 26									10 30	10 41		10 45	10 56							
Rotherhithe	d	10 12		10 16	10 27									10 31	10 42		10 46	10 57							
Wapping	d	10 14		10 18	10 29									10 33	10 44		10 48	10 59							
Shadwell	d	10 16		10 20	10 31									10 35	10 46		10 50	11 01							
Whitechapel	d	10 18		10 22	10 33									10 37	10 48		10 52	11 03							
Shoreditch High Street	d	10 20		10 24	10 35									10 39	10 50		10 54	11 05							
Hoxton	d	10 22		10 26	10 37									10 41	10 52		10 56	11 07							
Haggerston	d	10 24		10 28	10 39									10 43	10 54		10 58	11 09							
Dalston Junction Stn ELL	a	10 26		10 31	10 41									10 45	10 56		11 01	11 11							
Canonbury	d	10 31		10 36	10 44									10 50	11 01		11 06	11 14							
Highbury & Islington	a	10 36		10 41	10 51									10 57	11 06		11 11	11 21							
	d																								
London Bridge 4 ⊖	a		10 18			10 31				10 33	10 36	10 49				10 48				11 01			11 03	11 06	11 19

Table 178

Sundays
until 22 July

East London Line and Croydon - London Victoria to London Bridge

Network Diagram - see first Page of Table 177

Station		FC 1	LO	LO		SN	LO	LO	SN	SN	SE	SN	SN	SN		FC 1	LO	LO	LO	SN	LO	LO	LO	SN	
East Croydon 🚋	d	10 47				10 47								11 12		11 17				11 17					
West Croydon 4 🚋	d			10 42					11 04										11 12					11 34	
Norwood Junction 2	d			10 47		10 52			11 10										11 17	11 22				11 40	
Anerley	d			10 50		10 55													11 20	11 25					
Penge West	d			10 52		10 57													11 22	11 27					
London Victoria 15 ⊖	d												11 11												
Battersea Park 4	d												11 15												
Wandsworth Road	d												11 17												
Clapham High Street ⊖	d												11 19												
London Blackfriars 3 ⊖	d	11a07									11 08					11a37									
Denmark Hill 4	d										11 18		11 24												
Peckham Rye 4	d									11 15	11a21	11 23	11 26	11 40											
Queens Rd Peckham	d											11 26	11 29	11 42											
South Bermondsey	d											11 28	11 31	11 45											
Clapham Junction 10	d																								
Wandsworth Common	d																								
Balham 4 ⊖	d																								
Streatham Hill	d																								
West Norwood 4	d									11 27															
Gipsy Hill	d									11 30															
Crystal Palace 4	d							11 07		11a32													11 37		
Sydenham	d			10 55		10 59		11 10	11 14										11 25	11 29			11 40	11 44	
Forest Hill 4	d			10 57		11 02		11 13	11 17										11 27	11 32			11 43	11 47	
Honor Oak Park	d			11 00		11 04		11 15	11 19										11 30	11 34			11 45	11 49	
Brockley	d			11 02		11 07		11 18	11 22										11 32	11 37			11 48	11 52	
New Cross Gate 4	a			11 05		11 09		11 20	11 24										11 35	11 39			11 50	11 54	
	d			11 05		11 09		11 20	11 24										11 35	11 39			11 50	11 54	
New Cross ELL	d		10 54				11 09										11 24				11 39				
Surrey Quays	d		10 58	11 09			11 13	11 24									11 28	11 35	11 39		11 43	11 51	11 54		
Canada Water	d		11 00	11 11			11 15	11 26									11 30	11 37	11 41		11 45	11 53	11 56		
Rotherhithe	d		11 01	11 12			11 16	11 27									11 31	11 38	11 42		11 46	11 54	11 57		
Wapping	d		11 03	11 14			11 18	11 29									11 33	11 40	11 44		11 48	11 56	11 59		
Shadwell	d		11 05	11 16			11 20	11 31									11 35	11 42	11 46		11 50	11 58	12 01		
Whitechapel	d		11 07	11 18			11 22	11 33									11 37	11 44	11 48		11 52	12 00	12 03		
Shoreditch High Street	d		11 09	11 20			11 24	11 35									11 39	11 46	11 50		11 54	12 02	12 05		
Hoxton	d		11 11	11 22			11 26	11 37									11 41	11 48	11 52		11 56	12 04	12 07		
Haggerston	d		11 13	11 24			11 28	11 39									11 43	11 50	11 54		11 58	12 06	12 09		
Dalston Junction Stn ELL	a		11 15	11 26			11 31	11 41									11 46	11 52	11 56		12 01	12 08	12 11		
Canonbury	d		11 20	11 31			11 36	11 44										11 55	12 01			12 11	12 14		
Highbury & Islington	a		11 27	11 36			11 41	11 49										12 00	12 06			12 16	12 19		
	d																								
London Bridge 4 ⊖	a					11 18			11 31			11 33	11 36	11 49						11 48				12 01	

Station		SN	SE	SN	SN	SN	FC 1	LO	LO	LO		SN	LO	LO	LO	SN	LO	LO	LO	LO		LO	SN	SE	SN
East Croydon 🚋	d					11 42	11 47					11 47													
West Croydon 4 🚋	d									11 42						12 04			12 12						
Norwood Junction 2	d									11 47		11 52				12 10			12 16						
Anerley	d									11 50		11 55							12 19						
Penge West	d									11 52		11 57							12 21						
London Victoria 15 ⊖	d				11 41																				
Battersea Park 4	d				11 45																				
Wandsworth Road	d				11 47																				
Clapham High Street ⊖	d				11 49																				
London Blackfriars 3 ⊖	d		11 38				12a07																	12 08	
Denmark Hill 4	d		11 48		11 54																			12 18	
Peckham Rye 4	d	11 45	11a51	11 53	11 56	12 10																	12 15	12a21	12 23
Queens Rd Peckham	d			11 56	11 59	12 12																			12 26
South Bermondsey	d			11 58	12 01	12 15																			12 28
Clapham Junction 10	d																								
Wandsworth Common	d																								
Balham 4 ⊖	d																								
Streatham Hill	d																								
West Norwood 4	d	11 57																					12 27		
Gipsy Hill	d	12 00																					12 30		
Crystal Palace 4	d	12a02													12 07							12 31	12a32		
Sydenham	d									11 55		11 59			12 10	12 14			12 24			12 34			
Forest Hill 4	d									11 57		12 02			12 13	12 17			12 26			12 37			
Honor Oak Park	d									12 00		12 04			12 15	12 19			12 29			12 39			
Brockley	d									12 02		12 07			12 18	12 22			12 31			12 42			
New Cross Gate 4	a									12 05		12 09			12 20	12 24			12 34			12 44			
	d									12 05		12 09			12 20	12 24			12 34			12 44			
New Cross ELL	d							11 54					12 09				12 24			12 39					
Surrey Quays	d							11 58	12 05	12 09			12 13	12 21	12 24		12 28	12 35	12 38	12 43		12 48			
Canada Water	d							12 00	12 07	12 11			12 15	12 23	12 26		12 30	12 37	12 40	12 45		12 50			
Rotherhithe	d							12 01	12 08	12 12			12 16	12 24	12 27		12 31	12 38	12 41	12 46		12 51			
Wapping	d							12 03	12 10	12 14			12 18	12 26	12 29		12 33	12 40	12 43	12 48		12 53			
Shadwell	d							12 05	12 12	12 16			12 20	12 28	12 31		12 35	12 42	12 45	12 50		12 55			
Whitechapel	d							12 07	12 14	12 18			12 22	12 30	12 33		12 37	12 44	12 47	12 52		12 57			
Shoreditch High Street	d							12 09	12 16	12 20			12 24	12 32	12 35		12 39	12 46	12 49	12 54		12 59			
Hoxton	d							12 11	12 18	12 22			12 26	12 34	12 37		12 41	12 48	12 51	12 56		13 01			
Haggerston	d							12 13	12 20	12 24			12 28	12 36	12 39		12 43	12 50	12 53	12 58		13 03			
Dalston Junction Stn ELL	a							12 16	12 22	12 26			12 31	12 38	12 41		12 46	12 52	12 55	13 01		13 05			
Canonbury	d								12 25	12 31				12 41	12 44			12 55	13 00			13 08			
Highbury & Islington	a								12 30	12 36				12 46	12 49			13 00	13 05			13 13			
	d																								
London Bridge 4 ⊖	a			12 03	12 06	12 19						12 18				12 31									12 33

Table 178

Sundays

until 22 July

East London Line and Croydon - London Victoria to London Bridge

Network Diagram - see first Page of Table 177

		SN	SN	SN	FC 1	SN		LO	LO	LO	LO	LO	LO	SN	SE	SN		SN	SN	SN	FC 1	LO	SN	LO	LO
East Croydon	d		12 12	12 17	12 17														12 42	12 47	12 47				
West Croydon 4	d					12 34					12 42											12 57	13 04		
Norwood Junction 2	d			12 22		12 40					12 46									12 52		13 01	13 10		
Anerley	d			12 25							12 49									12 55		13 04			
Penge West	d			12 27							12 51									12 57		13 06			
London Victoria 15	d	12 11																12 41							
Battersea Park 4	d	12 15																12 45							
Wandsworth Road	d	12 17																12 47							
Clapham High Street	d	12 19																12 49							
London Blackfriars 3	d				12a37										12 38						13a07				
Denmark Hill 4	d	12 24													12 48			12 54							
Peckham Rye 4	d	12 26	12 40											12 45	12a51	12 53		12 56	13 10						
Queens Rd Peckham	d	12 29	12 42													12 56		12 59	13 12						
South Bermondsey	d	12 31	12 45													12 58		13 01	13 15						
Clapham Junction 10	d																								
Wandsworth Common	d																								
Balham 4	d																								
Streatham Hill	d																								
West Norwood 4	d													12 57											
Gipsy Hill	d													13 00											
Crystal Palace 4	d									12 46			13 01	13a02											13 16
Sydenham	d			12 29		12 44				12 49	12 54		13 04							12 59		13 09	13 14		13 19
Forest Hill 4	d			12 32		12 47				12 52	12 56		13 07							13 02		13 11	13 17		13 22
Honor Oak Park	d			12 34		12 49				12 54	12 59		13 09							13 04		13 14	13 19		13 24
Brockley	d			12 37		12 52				12 57	13 01		13 12							13 07		13 16	13 22		13 27
New Cross Gate 4	a			12 39		12 54				12 59	13 04		13 14							13 09		13 19	13 24		13 29
	d			12 39		12 54				12 59	13 04		13 14							13 09		13 19	13 24		13 29
New Cross ELL	d								12 54			13 09												13 24	
Surrey Quays	d							12 53	12 58	13 03	13 08	13 13	13 18									13 23		13 28	13 33
Canada Water	d							12 55	13 00	13 05	13 10	13 15	13 20									13 25		13 30	13 35
Rotherhithe	d							12 56	13 01	13 06	13 11	13 16	13 21									13 26		13 31	13 36
Wapping	d							12 58	13 03	13 08	13 13	13 18	13 23									13 28		13 33	13 38
Shadwell	d							13 00	13 05	13 10	13 15	13 20	13 25									13 30		13 35	13 40
Whitechapel	d							13 02	13 07	13 12	13 17	13 22	13 27									13 32		13 37	13 42
Shoreditch High Street	d							13 04	13 09	13 14	13 19	13 24	13 29									13 34		13 39	13 44
Hoxton	d							13 06	13 11	13 16	13 21	13 26	13 31									13 36		13 41	13 46
Haggerston	d							13 08	13 13	13 18	13 23	13 28	13 33									13 38		13 43	13 48
Dalston Junction Stn ELL	a							13 10	13 16	13 20	13 25	13 31	13 35									13 40		13 46	13 50
Canonbury	d							13 15		13 23	13 30		13 38									13 45			13 53
Highbury & Islington	a							13 20		13 28	13 35		13 43									13 50			13 58
	d																								
London Bridge 4	a	12 36	12 49	12 48		13 01										13 03		13 06	13 19	13 18			13 31		

		LO		LO	LO	SN	SE	SN	SN	SN	SN	FC 1		LO	SN	LO	LO	LO	LO	LO	SN	SE		SN	SN
East Croydon	d									13 12	13 17	13 17													
West Croydon 4	d	13 12												13 27	13 34			13 42							
Norwood Junction 2	d	13 16									13 22			13 31	13 40			13 46							
Anerley	d	13 19									13 25			13 34				13 49							
Penge West	d	13 21									13 27			13 36				13 51							
London Victoria 15	d								13 11																13 41
Battersea Park 4	d								13 15																13 45
Wandsworth Road	d								13 17																13 47
Clapham High Street	d								13 19																13 49
London Blackfriars 3	d						13 08					13a37										13 38			
Denmark Hill 4	d						13 18		13 24													13 48			13 54
Peckham Rye 4	d					13 15	13a21	13 23	13 26	13 40											13 45	13a51		13 53	13 56
Queens Rd Peckham	d							13 26	13 29	13 42														13 56	13 59
South Bermondsey	d							13 28	13 31	13 45														13 58	14 01
Clapham Junction 10	d																								
Wandsworth Common	d																								
Balham 4	d																								
Streatham Hill	d																								
West Norwood 4	d					13 27															13 57				
Gipsy Hill	d					13 30															14 00				
Crystal Palace 4	d				13 31	13a32											13 46			14 01	14a02				
Sydenham	d	13 24			13 34						13 29			13 39	13 44		13 49	13 54		14 04					
Forest Hill 4	d	13 26			13 37						13 32			13 41	13 47		13 52	13 56		14 07					
Honor Oak Park	d	13 29			13 39						13 34			13 44	13 49		13 54	13 59		14 09					
Brockley	d	13 31			13 42						13 37			13 46	13 52		13 57	14 01		14 12					
New Cross Gate 4	a	13 34			13 44						13 39			13 49	13 54		13 59	14 04		14 14					
	d	13 34			13 44						13 39			13 49	13 54		13 59	14 04		14 14					
New Cross ELL	d			13 39												13 54			14 09						
Surrey Quays	d	13 38		13 43	13 48									13 53		13 58	14 03	14 08	14 13	14 18					
Canada Water	d	13 40		13 45	13 50									13 55		14 00	14 05	14 10	14 15	14 20					
Rotherhithe	d	13 41		13 46	13 51									13 56		14 01	14 06	14 11	14 16	14 21					
Wapping	d	13 43		13 48	13 53									13 58		14 03	14 08	14 13	14 18	14 23					
Shadwell	d	13 45		13 50	13 55									14 00		14 05	14 10	14 15	14 20	14 25					
Whitechapel	d	13 47		13 52	13 57									14 02		14 07	14 12	14 17	14 22	14 27					
Shoreditch High Street	d	13 49		13 54	13 59									14 04		14 09	14 14	14 19	14 24	14 29					
Hoxton	d	13 51		13 56	14 01									14 06		14 11	14 16	14 21	14 26	14 31					
Haggerston	d	13 53		13 58	14 03									14 08		14 13	14 18	14 23	14 28	14 33					
Dalston Junction Stn ELL	a	13 55		14 01	14 05									14 10		14 16	14 20	14 25	14 31	14 35					
Canonbury	d	14 00			14 08									14 15			14 23	14 30		14 38					
Highbury & Islington	a	14 05			14 13									14 20			14 28	14 35		14 43					
	d																								
London Bridge 4	a							13 33	13 36	13 49	13 48				14 01									14 03	14 06

Table 178

Sundays

until 22 July

East London Line and Croydon - London Victoria to London Bridge

Network Diagram - see first Page of Table 177

		SN	SN	FC 1	LO	SN	LO	LO		LO	LO	LO	SN	SE	SN	SN	SN	SN		FC 1	LO	SN	LO	LO	LO
East Croydon	d	13 42	13 47	13 47													14 12	14 17		14 17					
West Croydon 4	d				13 57	14 04				14 12											14 27	14 34			14 42
Norwood Junction 2	d		13 52		14 01	14 10				14 16								14 22			14 31	14 40			14 46
Anerley	d		13 55		14 04					14 19								14 25			14 34				14 49
Penge West	d		13 57		14 06					14 21								14 27			14 36				14 51
London Victoria 15 ⊖	d															14 11									
Battersea Park 4	d															14 15									
Wandsworth Road	d															14 17									
Clapham High Street ⊖	d															14 19									
London Blackfriars 3 ⊖	d			14a07										14 08						14a37					
Denmark Hill 4	d													14 18		14 24									
Peckham Rye 4	d	14 10											14 15	14a21	14 23	14 26	14 40								
Queens Rd Peckham	d	14 12													14 26	14 29	14 42								
South Bermondsey	d	14 15													14 28	14 31	14 45								
Clapham Junction 10	d																								
Wandsworth Common	d																								
Balham 4 ⊖	d																								
Streatham Hill	d																								
West Norwood 4	d												14 27												
Gipsy Hill	d												14 30												
Crystal Palace 4	d							14 16				14 31	14a32											14 46	
Sydenham	d		13 59		14 09	14 14		14 19		14 24		14 34						14 29			14 39	14 44		14 49	14 54
Forest Hill 4	d		14 02		14 11	14 17		14 22		14 26		14 37						14 32			14 41	14 47		14 52	14 56
Honor Oak Park	d		14 04		14 14	14 19		14 24		14 29		14 39						14 34			14 44	14 49		14 54	14 59
Brockley	d		14 07		14 16	14 22		14 27		14 31		14 42						14 37			14 46	14 52		14 57	15 01
New Cross Gate 4	a		14 09		14 19	14 24		14 29		14 34		14 44						14 39			14 49	14 54		14 59	15 04
	d		14 09		14 19	14 24		14 29		14 34		14 44						14 39			14 49	14 54		14 59	15 04
New Cross ELL	d						14 24				14 39												14 54		
Surrey Quays	d				14 23		14 28	14 33		14 38	14 43	14 48									14 53		14 58	15 03	15 08
Canada Water	d				14 25		14 30	14 35		14 40	14 45	14 50									14 55		15 00	15 05	15 10
Rotherhithe	d				14 26		14 31	14 36		14 41	14 46	14 51									14 56		15 01	15 06	15 11
Wapping	d				14 28		14 33	14 38		14 43	14 48	14 53									14 58		15 03	15 08	15 13
Shadwell	d				14 30		14 35	14 40		14 45	14 50	14 55									15 00		15 05	15 10	15 15
Whitechapel	d				14 32		14 37	14 42		14 47	14 52	14 57									15 02		15 07	15 12	15 17
Shoreditch High Street	d				14 34		14 39	14 44		14 49	14 54	14 59									15 04		15 09	15 14	15 19
Hoxton	d				14 36		14 41	14 46		14 51	14 56	15 01									15 06		15 11	15 16	15 21
Haggerston	d				14 38		14 43	14 48		14 53	14 58	15 03									15 08		15 13	15 18	15 23
Dalston Junction Stn ELL	a				14 40		14 46	14 50		14 55	15 01	15 05									15 10		15 16	15 20	15 25
Canonbury	d				14 45			14 53		15 00		15 08									15 15			15 23	15 30
Highbury & Islington	a				14 50			14 58		15 05		15 13									15 20			15 28	15 35
	d																								
London Bridge 4 ⊖	a	14 19	14 18			14 31									14 33	14 36	14 49	14 48				15 01			

		LO	LO	SN		SE	SN	SN	SN	SN	FC 1	LO	SN	LO		LO	LO	LO	LO	SN	SE	SN	SN	SN
East Croydon	d								14 42	14 47	14 47													15 12
West Croydon 4	d											14 57	15 04				15 12							
Norwood Junction 2	d									14 52		15 01	15 10				15 16							
Anerley	d									14 55		15 04					15 19							
Penge West	d									14 57		15 06					15 21							
London Victoria 15 ⊖	d							14 41															15 11	
Battersea Park 4	d							14 45															15 15	
Wandsworth Road	d							14 47															15 17	
Clapham High Street ⊖	d							14 49															15 19	
London Blackfriars 3 ⊖	d					14 38					15a07										15 08			
Denmark Hill 4	d					14 48		14 54													15 18		15 24	
Peckham Rye 4	d			14 45		14a51	14 53	14 56	15 10											15 15	15a21	15 23	15 26	15 40
Queens Rd Peckham	d						14 56	14 59	15 12													15 26	15 29	15 42
South Bermondsey	d						14 58	15 01	15 15													15 28	15 31	15 45
Clapham Junction 10	d																							
Wandsworth Common	d																							
Balham 4 ⊖	d																							
Streatham Hill	d																							
West Norwood 4	d			14 57																15 27				
Gipsy Hill	d			15 00																15 30				
Crystal Palace 4	d		15 01	15a02												15 16			15 31	15a32				
Sydenham	d		15 04							14 59		15 09	15 14			15 19	15 24		15 34					
Forest Hill 4	d		15 07							15 02		15 11	15 17			15 22	15 26		15 37					
Honor Oak Park	d		15 09							15 04		15 14	15 19			15 24	15 29		15 39					
Brockley	d		15 12							15 07		15 16	15 22			15 27	15 31		15 42					
New Cross Gate 4	a		15 14							15 09		15 19	15 24			15 29	15 34		15 44					
	d		15 14							15 09		15 19	15 24			15 29	15 34		15 44					
New Cross ELL	d	15 09												15 24				15 39						
Surrey Quays	d	15 13	15 18									15 23		15 28		15 33	15 38	15 43	15 48					
Canada Water	d	15 15	15 20									15 25		15 30		15 35	15 40	15 45	15 50					
Rotherhithe	d	15 16	15 21									15 26		15 31		15 36	15 41	15 46	15 51					
Wapping	d	15 18	15 23									15 28		15 33		15 38	15 43	15 48	15 53					
Shadwell	d	15 20	15 25									15 30		15 35		15 40	15 45	15 50	15 55					
Whitechapel	d	15 22	15 27									15 32		15 37		15 42	15 47	15 52	15 57					
Shoreditch High Street	d	15 24	15 29									15 34		15 39		15 44	15 49	15 54	15 59					
Hoxton	d	15 26	15 31									15 36		15 41		15 46	15 51	15 56	16 01					
Haggerston	d	15 28	15 33									15 38		15 43		15 48	15 53	15 58	16 03					
Dalston Junction Stn ELL	a	15 31	15 35									15 40		15 46		15 50	15 55	16 01	16 05					
Canonbury	d		15 38									15 45				15 53	16 00		16 08					
Highbury & Islington	a		15 43									15 50				15 58	16 05		16 13					
	d																							
London Bridge 4 ⊖	a						15 03	15 06	15 19	15 18			15 31									15 33	15 36	15 49

Table 178

Sundays
until 22 July

East London Line and Croydon - London Victoria to London Bridge

Network Diagram - see first Page of Table 177

		SN	FC 1	LO	SN	LO	LO	LO	LO	LO		SN	SE	SN	SN	SN	SN	FC 1	LO	SN		LO	LO	LO	LO
East Croydon 🚌	d	15 17	15 17													15 42	15 47	15 47							
West Croydon 4 🚌	d			15 27	15 34			15 42											15 57	16 04				16 12	
Norwood Junction 2	d	15 22		15 31	15 40			15 46									15 52		16 01	16 10				16 16	
Anerley	d	15 25		15 34				15 49									15 55		16 04					16 19	
Penge West	d	15 27		15 36				15 51									15 57		16 06					16 21	
London Victoria 15 ⊖	d														15 41										
Battersea Park 4	d														15 45										
Wandsworth Road	d														15 47										
Clapham High Street ⊖	d														15 49										
London Blackfriars 3 ⊖	d		15a37										15 38					16a07							
Denmark Hill 4	d												15 48		15 54										
Peckham Rye 4	d											15 45	15a51	15 53	15 56	16 10									
Queens Rd Peckham	d													15 56	15 59	16 12									
South Bermondsey	d													15 58	16 01	16 15									
Clapham Junction 10	d																								
Wandsworth Common	d																								
Balham 4 ⊖	d																								
Streatham Hill	d																								
West Norwood 4	d											15 57													
Gipsy Hill	d											16 00													
Crystal Palace 4	d						15 46			16 01		16a02											16 16		
Sydenham	d	15 29		15 39	15 44		15 49	15 54		16 04							15 59		16 09	16 14			16 19	16 24	
Forest Hill 4	d	15 32		15 41	15 47		15 52	15 56		16 07							16 02		16 11	16 17			16 22	16 26	
Honor Oak Park	d	15 34		15 44	15 49		15 54	15 59		16 09							16 04		16 14	16 19			16 24	16 29	
Brockley	d	15 37		15 46	15 52		15 57	16 01		16 12							16 07		16 16	16 22			16 27	16 31	
New Cross Gate 4	a	15 39		15 49	15 54		15 59	16 04		16 14							16 09		16 19	16 24			16 29	16 34	
	d	15 39		15 49	15 54		15 59	16 04		16 14							16 09		16 19	16 24			16 29	16 34	
New Cross ELL	d					15 54			16 09													16 24			16 39
Surrey Quays	d			15 53		15 58	16 03	16 08	16 13	16 18									16 23			16 28	16 33	16 38	16 43
Canada Water	d			15 55		16 00	16 05	16 10	16 15	16 20									16 25			16 30	16 35	16 40	16 45
Rotherhithe	d			15 56		16 01	16 06	16 11	16 16	16 21									16 26			16 31	16 36	16 41	16 46
Wapping	d			15 58		16 03	16 08	16 13	16 18	16 23									16 28			16 33	16 38	16 43	16 48
Shadwell	d			16 00		16 05	16 10	16 15	16 20	16 25									16 30			16 35	16 40	16 45	16 50
Whitechapel	d			16 02		16 07	16 12	16 17	16 22	16 27									16 32			16 37	16 42	16 47	16 52
Shoreditch High Street	d			16 04		16 09	16 14	16 19	16 24	16 29									16 34			16 39	16 44	16 49	16 54
Hoxton	d			16 06		16 11	16 16	16 21	16 26	16 31									16 36			16 41	16 46	16 51	16 56
Haggerston	d			16 08		16 13	16 18	16 23	16 28	16 33									16 38			16 43	16 48	16 53	16 58
Dalston Junction Stn ELL	a			16 10		16 16	16 20	16 25	16 31	16 35									16 40			16 46	16 50	16 55	17 01
Canonbury	d			16 15			16 23	16 30		16 38									16 45				16 53	17 00	
Highbury & Islington	a			16 20			16 28	16 35		16 43									16 50				16 58	17 05	
	d																								
London Bridge 4 ⊖	a	15 48			16 01									16 03	16 06	16 19	16 18			16 31					

		LO	SN	SE	SN	SN		SN	SN	FC 1	LO	SN	LO	LO	LO	LO		LO	SN	SE	SN	SN	SN	SN	FC 1
East Croydon 🚌	d							16 12	16 17	16 17													16 42	16 47	16 47
West Croydon 4 🚌	d										16 27	16 34			16 42										
Norwood Junction 2	d								16 22		16 31	16 40			16 46									16 52	
Anerley	d								16 25		16 34				16 49									16 55	
Penge West	d								16 27		16 36				16 51									16 57	
London Victoria 15 ⊖	d					16 11																16 41			
Battersea Park 4	d					16 15																16 45			
Wandsworth Road	d					16 17																16 47			
Clapham High Street ⊖	d					16 19																16 49			
London Blackfriars 3 ⊖	d			16 08						16a37										16 38					17a07
Denmark Hill 4	d			16 18		16 24														16 48		16 54			
Peckham Rye 4	d		16 15	16a21	16 23	16 26		16 40											16 45	16a51	16 53	16 56	17 10		
Queens Rd Peckham	d				16 26	16 29		16 42													16 56	16 59	17 12		
South Bermondsey	d				16 28	16 31		16 45													16 58	17 01	17 15		
Clapham Junction 10	d																								
Wandsworth Common	d																								
Balham 4 ⊖	d																								
Streatham Hill	d																								
West Norwood 4	d		16 27																16 57						
Gipsy Hill	d		16 30																17 00						
Crystal Palace 4	d	16 31	16a32											16 46				17 01	17a02						
Sydenham	d	16 34							16 29		16 39	16 44		16 49	16 54			17 04						16 59	
Forest Hill 4	d	16 37							16 32		16 41	16 47		16 52	16 56			17 07						17 02	
Honor Oak Park	d	16 39							16 34		16 44	16 49		16 54	16 59			17 09						17 04	
Brockley	d	16 42							16 37		16 46	16 52		16 57	17 01			17 12						17 07	
New Cross Gate 4	a	16 44							16 39		16 49	16 54		16 59	17 04			17 14						17 09	
	d	16 44							16 39		16 49	16 54		16 59	17 04			17 14						17 09	
New Cross ELL	d												16 54			17 09									
Surrey Quays	d	16 48									16 53		16 58	17 03	17 08	17 13		17 18							
Canada Water	d	16 50									16 55		17 00	17 05	17 10	17 15		17 20							
Rotherhithe	d	16 51									16 56		17 01	17 06	17 11	17 16		17 21							
Wapping	d	16 53									16 58		17 03	17 08	17 13	17 18		17 23							
Shadwell	d	16 55									17 00		17 05	17 10	17 15	17 20		17 25							
Whitechapel	d	16 57									17 02		17 07	17 12	17 17	17 22		17 27							
Shoreditch High Street	d	16 59									17 04		17 09	17 14	17 19	17 24		17 29							
Hoxton	d	17 01									17 06		17 11	17 16	17 21	17 26		17 31							
Haggerston	d	17 03									17 08		17 13	17 18	17 23	17 28		17 33							
Dalston Junction Stn ELL	a	17 05									17 10		17 16	17 20	17 25	17 31		17 35							
Canonbury	d	17 08									17 15			17 23	17 30			17 38							
Highbury & Islington	a	17 13									17 20			17 28	17 35			17 43							
	d																								
London Bridge 4 ⊖	a				16 33	16 36		16 49	16 48			17 01									17 03	17 06	17 19	17 18	

East London Line and Croydon - London Victoria to London Bridge

Sundays until 22 July

Network Diagram - see first Page of Table 177

		LO		SN	LO	LO	LO	LO	LO	SN	SE	SN		SN	SN	SN	FC 1	LO	SN	LO	LO	LO		LO	LO
East Croydon	d														17 12	17 17	17 17								
West Croydon 4	d	16 57		17 04			17 12											17 27	17 34			17 42			
Norwood Junction 2	d	17 01		17 10			17 16									17 22		17 31	17 40			17 46			
Anerley	d	17 04					17 19									17 25		17 34				17 49			
Penge West	d	17 06					17 21									17 27		17 36				17 51			
London Victoria 15	d													17 11											
Battersea Park 4	d													17 15											
Wandsworth Road	d													17 17											
Clapham High Street	d													17 19											
London Blackfriars 3	d										17 08						17a37								
Denmark Hill 4	d										17 18			17 24											
Peckham Rye 4	d									17 15	17a21	17 23		17 26	17 40										
Queens Rd Peckham	d											17 26		17 29	17 42										
South Bermondsey	d											17 28		17 31	17 45										
Clapham Junction 10	d																								
Wandsworth Common	d																								
Balham 4	d																								
Streatham Hill	d																								
West Norwood 4	d									17 27															
Gipsy Hill	d									17 30															
Crystal Palace 4	d					17 16			17 31	17a32											17 46				18 01
Sydenham	d	17 09		17 14		17 19	17 24		17 34							17 29		17 39	17 44		17 49	17 54			18 04
Forest Hill 4	d	17 11		17 17		17 22	17 26		17 37							17 32		17 41	17 47		17 52	17 56			18 07
Honor Oak Park	d	17 14		17 19		17 24	17 29		17 39							17 34		17 44	17 49		17 54	17 59			18 09
Brockley	d	17 16		17 22		17 27	17 31		17 42							17 37		17 46	17 52		17 57	18 01			18 12
New Cross Gate 4	a	17 19		17 24		17 29	17 34		17 44							17 39		17 49	17 54		17 59	18 04			18 14
	d	17 19		17 24		17 29	17 34		17 44							17 39		17 49	17 54		17 59	18 04			18 14
New Cross ELL	d				17 24			17 39												17 54				18 09	
Surrey Quays	d	17 23			17 28	17 33	17 38	17 43	17 48									17 53		17 58	18 03	18 08		18 13	18 18
Canada Water	d	17 25			17 30	17 35	17 40	17 45	17 50									17 55		18 00	18 05	18 10		18 15	18 20
Rotherhithe	d	17 26			17 31	17 36	17 41	17 46	17 51									17 56		18 01	18 06	18 11		18 16	18 21
Wapping	d	17 28			17 33	17 38	17 43	17 48	17 53									17 58		18 03	18 08	18 13		18 18	18 23
Shadwell	d	17 30			17 35	17 40	17 45	17 50	17 55									18 00		18 05	18 10	18 15		18 20	18 25
Whitechapel	d	17 32			17 37	17 42	17 47	17 52	17 57									18 02		18 07	18 12	18 17		18 22	18 27
Shoreditch High Street	d	17 34			17 39	17 44	17 49	17 54	17 59									18 04		18 09	18 14	18 19		18 24	18 29
Hoxton	d	17 36			17 41	17 46	17 51	17 56	18 01									18 06		18 11	18 16	18 21		18 26	18 31
Haggerston	d	17 38			17 43	17 48	17 53	17 58	18 03									18 08		18 13	18 18	18 23		18 28	18 33
Dalston Junction Stn ELL	a	17 40			17 46	17 50	17 55	18 01	18 05									18 10		18 16	18 20	18 25		18 31	18 35
Canonbury	d	17 45				17 53	18 00		18 08									18 15			18 23	18 30			18 38
Highbury & Islington	a	17 50				17 58	18 05		18 13									18 20			18 28	18 35			18 43
	d																								
London Bridge 4	a			17 31								17 33		17 36	17 49	17 48			18 01						

		SN	SE	SN	SN	SN	SN	FC 1		LO	SN	LO	LO	LO	LO	LO	SN	SE		SN	SN	SN	SN	FC 1	LO
East Croydon	d					17 42	17 47	17 47														18 12	18 17	18 17	
West Croydon 4	d									17 57	18 04			18 12											18 27
Norwood Junction 2	d						17 52			18 01	18 10			18 16									18 22		18 31
Anerley	d						17 55			18 04				18 19									18 25		18 34
Penge West	d						17 57			18 06				18 21									18 27		18 36
London Victoria 15	d				17 41																18 11				
Battersea Park 4	d				17 45																18 15				
Wandsworth Road	d				17 47																18 17				
Clapham High Street	d				17 49																18 19				
London Blackfriars 3	d		17 38					18a07										18 08						18a37	
Denmark Hill 4	d		17 48		17 54													18 18			18 24				
Peckham Rye 4	d	17 45	17a51	17 53	17 56	18 10											18 15	18a21		18 23	18 26	18 40			
Queens Rd Peckham	d			17 56	17 59	18 12														18 26	18 29	18 42			
South Bermondsey	d			17 58	18 01	18 15														18 28	18 31	18 45			
Clapham Junction 10	d																								
Wandsworth Common	d																								
Balham 4	d																								
Streatham Hill	d																								
West Norwood 4	d	17 57															18 27								
Gipsy Hill	d	18 00															18 30								
Crystal Palace 4	d	18a02											18 16			18 31	18a32								
Sydenham	d						17 59			18 09	18 14		18 19	18 24		18 34							18 29		18 39
Forest Hill 4	d						18 02			18 11	18 17		18 22	18 26		18 37							18 32		18 41
Honor Oak Park	d						18 04			18 14	18 19		18 24	18 29		18 39							18 34		18 44
Brockley	d						18 07			18 16	18 22		18 27	18 31		18 42							18 37		18 46
New Cross Gate 4	a						18 09			18 19	18 24		18 29	18 34		18 44							18 39		18 49
	d						18 09			18 19	18 24		18 29	18 34		18 44							18 40		18 49
New Cross ELL	d											18 24			18 39										
Surrey Quays	d									18 23		18 28	18 33	18 38	18 43	18 48									18 53
Canada Water	d									18 25		18 30	18 35	18 40	18 45	18 50									18 55
Rotherhithe	d									18 26		18 31	18 36	18 41	18 46	18 51									18 56
Wapping	d									18 28		18 33	18 38	18 43	18 48	18 53									18 58
Shadwell	d									18 30		18 35	18 40	18 45	18 50	18 55									19 00
Whitechapel	d									18 32		18 37	18 42	18 47	18 52	18 57									19 02
Shoreditch High Street	d									18 34		18 39	18 44	18 49	18 54	18 59									19 04
Hoxton	d									18 36		18 41	18 46	18 51	18 56	19 01									19 06
Haggerston	d									18 38		18 43	18 48	18 53	18 58	19 03									19 08
Dalston Junction Stn ELL	a									18 40		18 46	18 50	18 55	19 01	19 05									19 10
Canonbury	d									18 45			18 53	19 00		19 08									19 15
Highbury & Islington	a									18 50			18 58	19 05		19 13									19 20
	d																								
London Bridge 4	a			18 03	18 06	18 19	18 18				18 31									18 33	18 36	18 49	18 48		

Table 178

Sundays
until 22 July

East London Line and Croydon - London Victoria to London Bridge

Network Diagram - see first Page of Table 177

		SN	LO	LO		LO	LO	LO	SN	SE	SN	SN	SN	SN		FC 1	LO	SN	LO	LO	LO	LO	LO	SN
East Croydon ⇌	d												18 42	18 47		18 47								
West Croydon 4 ⇌	d	18 34				18 42											18 57	19 04			19 12			
Norwood Junction 2	d	18 40				18 46								18 52			19 01	19 10			19 16			
Anerley	d					18 49								18 55			19 04				19 19			
Penge West	d					18 51								18 57			19 06				19 21			
London Victoria 15 ⊖	d											18 41												
Battersea Park 4	d											18 45												
Wandsworth Road	d											18 47												
Clapham High Street ⊖	d											18 49												
London Blackfriars 3 ⊖	d									18 38						19a07								
Denmark Hill 4	d									18 48		18 54												
Peckham Rye 4	d								18 45	18a51	18 53	18 56	19 10											19 15
Queens Rd Peckham	d										18 56	18 59	19 12											
South Bermondsey	d										18 58	19 01	19 15											
Clapham Junction 10	d																							
Wandsworth Common	d																							
Balham 4 ⊖	d																							
Streatham Hill	d																							
West Norwood 4	d								18 57															19 27
Gipsy Hill	d								19 00															19 30
Crystal Palace 4	d			18 46				19 01	19a02											19 16			19 31	19a32
Sydenham	d	18 44		18 49		18 54		19 04						18 59			19 09	19 14		19 19	19 24		19 34	
Forest Hill 4	d	18 47		18 52		18 56		19 07						19 02			19 11	19 17		19 22	19 26		19 37	
Honor Oak Park	d	18 49		18 54		18 59		19 09						19 04			19 14	19 19		19 24	19 29		19 39	
Brockley	d	18 52		18 57		19 01		19 12						19 07			19 16	19 22		19 27	19 31		19 42	
New Cross Gate 4	a	18 54		18 59		19 04		19 14						19 09			19 19	19 24		19 29	19 34		19 44	
	d	18 54		18 59		19 04		19 14						19 09			19 19	19 24		19 29	19 34		19 44	
New Cross ELL	d		18 54				19 09												19 24			19 39		
Surrey Quays	d		18 58	19 03		19 08	19 13	19 18									19 23		19 28	19 33	19 38	19 43	19 48	
Canada Water	d		19 00	19 05		19 10	19 15	19 20									19 25		19 30	19 35	19 40	19 45	19 50	
Rotherhithe	d		19 01	19 06		19 11	19 16	19 21									19 26		19 31	19 36	19 41	19 46	19 51	
Wapping	d		19 03	19 08		19 13	19 18	19 23									19 28		19 33	19 38	19 43	19 48	19 53	
Shadwell	d		19 05	19 10		19 15	19 20	19 25									19 30		19 35	19 40	19 45	19 50	19 55	
Whitechapel	d		19 07	19 12		19 17	19 22	19 27									19 32		19 37	19 42	19 47	19 52	19 57	
Shoreditch High Street	d		19 09	19 14		19 19	19 24	19 29									19 34		19 39	19 44	19 49	19 54	19 59	
Hoxton	d		19 11	19 16		19 21	19 26	19 31									19 36		19 41	19 46	19 51	19 56	20 01	
Haggerston	d		19 13	19 18		19 23	19 28	19 33									19 38		19 43	19 48	19 53	19 58	20 03	
Dalston Junction Stn ELL	a		19 16	19 20		19 25	19 31	19 35									19 40		19 46	19 50	19 55	20 01	20 05	
Canonbury	d			19 23		19 30		19 38									19 45			19 53	20 00		20 08	
Highbury & Islington	a			19 28		19 35		19 43									19 50			19 58	20 05		20 13	
	d																							
London Bridge 4 ⊖	a	19 01									19 03	19 06	19 19	19 18				19 31						

		SE	SN	SN	SN	SN	FC 1	LO	SN	LO		LO	LO	LO	LO	SN	SE	SN	SN	SN		SN	LO	SN	LO
East Croydon ⇌	d				19 12	19 17	19 17													19 42		19 47			
West Croydon 4 ⇌	d							19 27	19 34				19 42										19 57	20 04	
Norwood Junction 2	d					19 22		19 31	19 40				19 46									19 52	20 01	20 10	
Anerley	d					19 25		19 34					19 49									19 55	20 04		
Penge West	d					19 27		19 36					19 51									19 57	20 06		
London Victoria 15 ⊖	d			19 11															19 41						
Battersea Park 4	d			19 15															19 45						
Wandsworth Road	d			19 17															19 47						
Clapham High Street ⊖	d			19 19															19 49						
London Blackfriars 3 ⊖	d	19 08					19a37										19 38								
Denmark Hill 4	d	19 18		19 24													19 48		19 54						
Peckham Rye 4	d	19a21	19 23	19 26	19 40											19 45	19a51	19 53	19 56	20 10					
Queens Rd Peckham	d		19 26	19 29	19 42													19 56	19 59	20 12					
South Bermondsey	d		19 28	19 31	19 45													19 58	20 01	20 15					
Clapham Junction 10	d																								
Wandsworth Common	d																								
Balham 4 ⊖	d																								
Streatham Hill	d																								
West Norwood 4	d															19 57									
Gipsy Hill	d															20 00									
Crystal Palace 4	d											19 46			20 01	20a02									
Sydenham	d					19 29		19 39	19 44			19 49	19 54		20 04							19 59	20 09	20 14	
Forest Hill 4	d					19 32		19 41	19 47			19 52	19 56		20 07							20 02	20 11	20 17	
Honor Oak Park	d					19 34		19 44	19 49			19 54	19 59		20 09							20 04	20 14	20 19	
Brockley	d					19 37		19 46	19 52			19 57	20 01		20 12							20 07	20 16	20 22	
New Cross Gate 4	a					19 39		19 49	19 54			19 59	20 04		20 14							20 09	20 19	20 24	
	d					19 39		19 49	19 54			19 59	20 04		20 14							20 09	20 19	20 24	
New Cross ELL	d									19 54				20 09											20 24
Surrey Quays	d							19 53		19 58		20 03	20 08	20 13	20 18								20 23		20 28
Canada Water	d							19 55		20 00		20 05	20 10	20 15	20 20								20 25		20 30
Rotherhithe	d							19 56		20 01		20 06	20 11	20 16	20 21								20 26		20 31
Wapping	d							19 58		20 03		20 08	20 13	20 18	20 23								20 28		20 33
Shadwell	d							20 00		20 05		20 10	20 15	20 20	20 25								20 30		20 35
Whitechapel	d							20 02		20 07		20 12	20 17	20 22	20 27								20 32		20 37
Shoreditch High Street	d							20 04		20 09		20 14	20 19	20 24	20 29								20 34		20 39
Hoxton	d							20 06		20 11		20 16	20 21	20 26	20 31								20 36		20 41
Haggerston	d							20 08		20 13		20 18	20 23	20 28	20 33								20 38		20 43
Dalston Junction Stn ELL	a							20 10		20 16		20 20	20 25	20 31	20 35								20 40		20 46
Canonbury	d							20 15				20 23	20 30		20 38								20 45		
Highbury & Islington	a							20 20				20 28	20 35		20 43								20 50		
	d																								
London Bridge 4 ⊖	a		19 33	19 36	19 49	19 48			20 01									20 03	20 06	20 19		20 18		20 31	

Table 178

Sundays
until 22 July

East London Line and Croydon - London Victoria to London Bridge

Network Diagram - see first Page of Table 177

		LO	LO	LO	LO	SN		SE	SN	SN	SN	SN	LO	SN	LO	LO		LO	LO	LO	SN	SE	SN	SN	SN
East Croydon	d										20 12	20 17													20 42
West Croydon 4	d		20 12										20 27	20 34				20 42							
Norwood Junction 2	d		20 16									20 22	20 31	20 40				20 46							
Anerley	d		20 19									20 25	20 34					20 49							
Penge West	d		20 21									20 27	20 36					20 51							
London Victoria 15	d									20 11														20 41	
Battersea Park 4	d									20 15														20 45	
Wandsworth Road	d									20 17														20 47	
Clapham High Street	d									20 19														20 49	
London Blackfriars 3	d							20 08														20 38			
Denmark Hill 4	d							20 18		20 24												20 48		20 54	
Peckham Rye 4	d					20 15		20a21	20 23	20 26	20 40										20 45	20a51	20 53	20 56	21 10
Queens Rd Peckham	d								20 26	20 29	20 42												20 56	20 59	21 12
South Bermondsey	d								20 28	20 31	20 45												20 58	21 01	21 15
Clapham Junction 10	d																								
Wandsworth Common	d																								
Balham 4	d																								
Streatham Hill	d																								
West Norwood 4	d					20 27															20 57				
Gipsy Hill	d					20 30															21 00				
Crystal Palace 4	d	20 16			20 31	20a32										20 46				21 01	21a02				
Sydenham	d	20 19	20 24		20 34							20 29	20 39	20 44		20 49		20 54		21 04					
Forest Hill 4	d	20 22	20 26		20 37							20 32	20 41	20 47		20 52		20 56		21 07					
Honor Oak Park	d	20 24	20 29		20 39							20 34	20 44	20 49		20 54		20 59		21 09					
Brockley	d	20 27	20 31		20 42							20 37	20 46	20 52		20 57		21 01		21 12					
New Cross Gate 4	a	20 29	20 34		20 44							20 39	20 49	20 54		20 59		21 04		21 14					
	d	20 29	20 34		20 44							20 39	20 49	20 54		20 59		21 04		21 14					
New Cross ELL	d			20 39											20 54				21 09						
Surrey Quays	d	20 33	20 38	20 43	20 48								20 53		20 58	21 03		21 08	21 13	21 18					
Canada Water	d	20 35	20 40	20 45	20 50								20 55		21 00	21 05		21 10	21 15	21 20					
Rotherhithe	d	20 36	20 41	20 46	20 51								20 56		21 01	21 06		21 11	21 16	21 21					
Wapping	d	20 38	20 43	20 48	20 53								20 58		21 03	21 08		21 13	21 18	21 23					
Shadwell	d	20 40	20 45	20 50	20 55								21 00		21 05	21 10		21 15	21 20	21 25					
Whitechapel	d	20 42	20 47	20 52	20 57								21 02		21 07	21 12		21 17	21 22	21 27					
Shoreditch High Street	d	20 44	20 49	20 54	20 59								21 04		21 09	21 14		21 19	21 24	21 29					
Hoxton	d	20 46	20 51	20 56	21 01								21 06		21 11	21 16		21 21	21 26	21 31					
Haggerston	d	20 48	20 53	20 58	21 03								21 08		21 13	21 18		21 23	21 28	21 33					
Dalston Junction Stn ELL	a	20 50	20 55	21 01	21 05								21 10		21 16	21 20		21 25	21 31	21 35					
Canonbury	d	20 53	21 00		21 08								21 15			21 23		21 30		21 38					
Highbury & Islington	a	20 58	21 05		21 13								21 20			21 28		21 35		21 43					
	d																								
London Bridge 4	a								20 33	20 36	20 49	20 48		21 01									21 03	21 06	21 19

		SN		LO	SN	LO	LO	LO	LO	LO	SN	SE		SN	SN	SN	SN	LO	SN	LO	LO	LO		LO	LO
East Croydon	d	20 47														21 12	21 17								
West Croydon 4	d			20 57	21 04			21 12										21 27	21 34			21 42			
Norwood Junction 2	d	20 52		21 01	21 10			21 16									21 22	21 31	21 40			21 46			
Anerley	d	20 55		21 04				21 19									21 25	21 34				21 49			
Penge West	d	20 57		21 06				21 21									21 27	21 36				21 51			
London Victoria 15	d														21 11										
Battersea Park 4	d														21 15										
Wandsworth Road	d														21 17										
Clapham High Street	d														21 19										
London Blackfriars 3	d											21 08													
Denmark Hill 4	d											21 18			21 24										
Peckham Rye 4	d										21 15	21a21		21 23	21 26	21 40									
Queens Rd Peckham	d													21 26	21 29	21 42									
South Bermondsey	d													21 28	21 31	21 45									
Clapham Junction 10	d																								
Wandsworth Common	d																								
Balham 4	d																								
Streatham Hill	d																								
West Norwood 4	d										21 27														
Gipsy Hill	d										21 30														
Crystal Palace 4	d						21 16			21 31	21a32										21 46				22 01
Sydenham	d	20 59		21 09	21 14		21 19	21 24		21 34							21 29	21 39	21 44		21 49	21 54			22 04
Forest Hill 4	d	21 02		21 11	21 17		21 22	21 26		21 37							21 32	21 41	21 47		21 52	21 56			22 07
Honor Oak Park	d	21 04		21 14	21 19		21 24	21 29		21 39							21 34	21 44	21 49		21 54	21 59			22 09
Brockley	d	21 07		21 16	21 22		21 27	21 31		21 42							21 37	21 46	21 52		21 57	22 01			22 12
New Cross Gate 4	a	21 09		21 19	21 24		21 29	21 34		21 44							21 39	21 49	21 54		21 59	22 04			22 14
	d	21 09		21 19	21 24		21 29	21 34		21 44							21 39	21 49	21 54		21 59	22 04			22 14
New Cross ELL	d					21 24			21 39											21 54				22 09	
Surrey Quays	d			21 23		21 28	21 33	21 38	21 43	21 48								21 53		21 58	22 03	22 08		22 13	22 18
Canada Water	d			21 25		21 30	21 35	21 40	21 45	21 50								21 55		22 00	22 05	22 10		22 15	22 20
Rotherhithe	d			21 26		21 31	21 36	21 41	21 46	21 51								21 56		22 01	22 06	22 11		22 16	22 21
Wapping	d			21 28		21 33	21 38	21 43	21 48	21 53								21 58		22 03	22 08	22 13		22 18	22 23
Shadwell	d			21 30		21 35	21 40	21 45	21 50	21 55								22 00		22 05	22 10	22 15		22 20	22 25
Whitechapel	d			21 32		21 37	21 42	21 47	21 52	21 57								22 02		22 07	22 12	22 17		22 22	22 27
Shoreditch High Street	d			21 34		21 39	21 44	21 49	21 54	21 59								22 04		22 09	22 14	22 19		22 24	22 29
Hoxton	d			21 36		21 41	21 46	21 51	21 56	22 01								22 06		22 11	22 16	22 21		22 26	22 31
Haggerston	d			21 38		21 43	21 48	21 53	21 58	22 03								22 08		22 13	22 18	22 23		22 28	22 33
Dalston Junction Stn ELL	a			21 40		21 46	21 50	21 55	22 01	22 05								22 10		22 16	22 20	22 25		22 31	22 35
Canonbury	d			21 45			21 53	22 00		22 08								22 15			22 23	22 30			22 38
Highbury & Islington	a			21 50			21 58	22 05		22 13								22 20			22 28	22 35			22 43
	d																								
London Bridge 4	a	21 18			21 31									21 33	21 36	21 49	21 48		22 01						

Table 178

Sundays

until 22 July

East London Line and Croydon - London Victoria to London Bridge

Network Diagram - see first Page of Table 177

		SN	SE	SN	SN	SN	SN	LO		SN	LO	LO	SN	SE	SN	SN	SN	SN		LO	LO	SN	LO	LO	SN
East Croydon	d					21 42	21 47										22 12	22 17							
West Croydon 4	d							21 57		22 04		22 12									22 27	22 34		22 42	
Norwood Junction 2	d						21 52	22 01		22 10		22 16						22 22			22 31	22 40		22 46	
Anerley	d						21 55	22 04				22 19						22 25			22 34			22 49	
Penge West	d						21 57	22 06				22 21						22 27			22 36			22 51	
London Victoria 15 ⊖	d				21 41											22 11									
Battersea Park 4	d				21 45											22 15									
Wandsworth Road	d				21 47											22 17									
Clapham High Street ⊖	d				21 49											22 19									
London Blackfriars 3 ⊖	d		21 38											22 08											
Denmark Hill 4	d		21 48		21 54									22 18		22 24									
Peckham Rye 4	d	21 45	21a51	21 53	21 56	22 10							22 15	22a21	22 23	22 26	22 40								22 45
Queens Rd Peckham	d			21 56	21 59	22 12									22 26	22 29	22 42								
South Bermondsey	d			21 58	22 01	22 15									22 28	22 31	22 45								
Clapham Junction 10	d																								
Wandsworth Common	d																								
Balham 4 ⊖	d																								
Streatham Hill	d																								
West Norwood 4	d	21 57											22 27												22 57
Gipsy Hill	d	22 00											22 30												23 00
Crystal Palace 4	d	22a02									22 16		22a32										22 46		23a02
Sydenham	d						21 59	22 09		22 14	22 19	22 24						22 29			22 39	22 44	22 49	22 54	
Forest Hill 4	d						22 02	22 11		22 17	22 22	22 26						22 32			22 41	22 47	22 52	22 56	
Honor Oak Park	d						22 04	22 14		22 19	22 24	22 29						22 34			22 44	22 49	22 54	22 59	
Brockley	d						22 07	22 16		22 22	22 27	22 31						22 37			22 46	22 52	22 57	23 01	
New Cross Gate 4	a						22 09	22 19		22 24	22 29	22 34						22 39			22 49	22 54	22 59	23 04	
	d						22 09	22 19		22 24	22 29	22 34						22 39			22 49	22 54	22 59	23 04	
New Cross ELL	d																			22 39					
Surrey Quays	d							22 23			22 33	22 38								22 43	22 53		23 03	23 08	
Canada Water	d							22 25			22 35	22 40								22 45	22 55		23 05	23 10	
Rotherhithe	d							22 26			22 36	22 41								22 46	22 56		23 06	23 11	
Wapping	d							22 28			22 38	22 43								22 48	22 58		23 08	23 13	
Shadwell	d							22 30			22 40	22 45								22 50	23 00		23 10	23 15	
Whitechapel	d							22 32			22 42	22 47								22 52	23 02		23 12	23 17	
Shoreditch High Street	d							22 34			22 44	22 49								22 54	23 04		23 14	23 19	
Hoxton	d							22 36			22 46	22 51								22 56	23 06		23 16	23 21	
Haggerston	d							22 38			22 48	22 53								22 58	23 08		23 18	23 23	
Dalston Junction Stn ELL	a							22 40			22 50	22 55								23 01	23 10		23 20	23 25	
Canonbury	d							22 45			22 53	23 00									23 15		23 23	23 30	
Highbury & Islington	a							22 50			22 58	23 05									23 20		23 28	23 35	
	d																								
London Bridge 4 ⊖	a			22 03	22 06	22 19	22 18			22 31					22 33	22 36	22 49	22 48				23 01			

		SE	SN	SN		SN	SN	LO	LO	LO	SN	SE	SN	SN		SE	SN
East Croydon	d					22 42	22 47										
West Croydon 4	d								22 57								
Norwood Junction 2	d						22 52		23 01								
Anerley	d						22 55		23 04								
Penge West	d						22 57		23 06								
London Victoria 15 ⊖	d			22 41										23 11			
Battersea Park 4	d			22 45										23 15			
Wandsworth Road	d			22 47										23 17			
Clapham High Street ⊖	d			22 49										23 19			
London Blackfriars 3 ⊖	d	22 38										23 08				23 38	
Denmark Hill 4	d	22 48		22 54								23 18		23 24		23 48	
Peckham Rye 4	d	22a51	22 53	22 56		23 10					23 15	23a21	23 23	23 26		23a51	23 53
Queens Rd Peckham	d		22 56	22 59		23 12							23 26	23 29			23 56
South Bermondsey	d		22 58	23 01		23 15							23 28	23 31			23 58
Clapham Junction 10	d																
Wandsworth Common	d																
Balham 4 ⊖	d																
Streatham Hill	d																
West Norwood 4	d										23 27						
Gipsy Hill	d										23 30						
Crystal Palace 4	d									23 16	23a32						
Sydenham	d						22 59		23 09	23 19							
Forest Hill 4	d						23 02		23 11	23 22							
Honor Oak Park	d						23 04		23 14	23 24							
Brockley	d						23 07		23 16	23 27							
New Cross Gate 4	a						23 09		23 19	23 29							
	d						23 09		23 19	23 29							
New Cross ELL	d							23 09									
Surrey Quays	d							23 13	23 23	23 33							
Canada Water	d							23 15	23 25	23 35							
Rotherhithe	d							23 16	23 26	23 36							
Wapping	d							23 18	23 28	23 38							
Shadwell	d							23 20	23 30	23 40							
Whitechapel	d							23 22	23 32	23 42							
Shoreditch High Street	d							23 24	23 34	23 44							
Hoxton	d							23 26	23 36	23 46							
Haggerston	d							23 28	23 38	23 48							
Dalston Junction Stn ELL	a							23 31	23 40	23 50							
Canonbury	d								23 45	23 53							
Highbury & Islington	a								23 50	23 58							
	d																
London Bridge 4 ⊖	a		23 03	23 06		23 19	23 18						23 33	23 36			00 03

Table 178

Sundays

29 July to 12 August

East London Line and Croydon - London Victoria to London Bridge

Network Diagram - see first Page of Table 177

		LO	LO	LO	SN	SN	SN	SN	LO	LO	LO	LO	LO	LO	LO	LO	LO	LO	LO	LO	LO	SN	LO
East Croydon	d																					06 47	
West Croydon 4	d		23p22						05 42			05 55			06 12			06 25			06 42		
Norwood Junction 2	d		23p28						05 46			06 01			06 16			06 31			06 46	06 52	
Anerley	d		23p31						05 49			06 04			06 19			06 34			06 49	06 55	
Penge West	d		23p33						05 51			06 06			06 21			06 36			06 51	06 57	
London Victoria 15 ⊖	d				23p19	23p54																	
Battersea Park 4	d				23p23	23p58																	
Wandsworth Road	d																						
Clapham High Street ⊖	d																						
London Blackfriars 3 ⊖	d																						
Denmark Hill 4	d																						
Peckham Rye 4	d						00 12	00 42															
Queens Rd Peckham	d																						
South Bermondsey	d																						
Clapham Junction 10	d				23p27	00 02																	
Wandsworth Common	d				23p30	00 05																	
Balham 4 ⊖	d				23p32	00 07																	
Streatham Hill	d				23p35	00 10																	
West Norwood 4	d				23p40	00 14	00 24	00 54															
Gipsy Hill	d				23p43	00 17	00 27	00 57															
Crystal Palace 4	d			23p43	23p51	00 21	00a29	00a59			06 01			06 16			06 31			06 44			
Sydenham	d		23p36	23p46	23p54	00 24			05 54		06 04	06 09		06 19	06 24		06 34	06 39		06 47	06 54	06 59	
Forest Hill 4	d		23p38	23p49	23p57	00 27			05 56		06 07	06 11		06 22	06 26		06 37	06 41		06 50	06 56	07 02	
Honor Oak Park	d		23p41	23p51	23p59	00 29			05 59		06 09	06 14		06 24	06 29		06 39	06 44		06 52	06 59	07 04	
Brockley	d		23p43	23p54	00 02	00 32			06 01		06 12	06 16		06 27	06 31		06 42	06 46		06 55	07 01	07 07	
New Cross Gate 4	a		23p46	23p56	00 04	00 35			06 04		06 14	06 19		06 29	06 34		06 44	06 49		06 57	07 04	07 09	
	d		23p46	23p56	00 04	00 35			06 04		06 14	06 19		06 29	06 34		06 44	06 49		06 57	07 04	07 09	
New Cross ELL	d	23p36								06 09			06 24			06 39			06 54				07 09
Surrey Quays	d	23p40	23p49	23p59					06 08	06 13	06 18	06 22	06 28	06 33	06 38	06 43	06 48	06 52	06 58	07 03	07 08		07 13
Canada Water	d	23p42	23p51	00 02					06 10	06 15	06 20	06 24	06 30	06 35	06 40	06 45	06 50	06 54	07 00	07 05	07 10		07 15
Rotherhithe	d	23p43	23p53	00 03					06 11	06 16	06 21	06 26	06 31	06 36	06 41	06 46	06 51	06 56	07 01	07 06	07 11		07 16
Wapping	d	23p45	23p54	00 05					06 13	06 18	06 23	06 27	06 33	06 38	06 43	06 48	06 53	06 57	07 03	07 08	07 13		07 18
Shadwell	d	23p47	23p56	00 07					06 15	06 20	06 25	06 29	06 35	06 40	06 45	06 50	06 55	06 59	07 05	07 10	07 15		07 20
Whitechapel	d	23p49	23p59	00 09					06 17	06 22	06 27	06 32	06 37	06 42	06 47	06 52	06 57	07 02	07 07	07 12	07 17		07 22
Shoreditch High Street	d	23p51	00 01	00 11					06 19	06 24	06 29	06 34	06 39	06 44	06 49	06 54	06 59	07 04	07 09	07 14	07 19		07 24
Hoxton	d	23p53	00 03	00 13					06 21	06 26	06 31	06 36	06 41	06 46	06 51	06 56	07 01	07 06	07 11	07 16	07 21		07 26
Haggerston	d	23p55	00 05	00 15					06 23	06 28	06 33	06 38	06 43	06 48	06 53	06 58	07 03	07 08	07 13	07 18	07 23		07 28
Dalston Junction Stn ELL	a	23p58	00 07	00 17					06 25	06 35	06 35	06 40	06 50	06 50	06 55	07 05	07 05	07 10	07 20	07 20	07 26		07 35
Canonbury	d	00 01	00 11	00 20					06 30		06 38	06 45		06 53	07 00		07 08	07 15		07 23	07 30		
Highbury & Islington	a	00 10	00 18	00 28					06 38		06 46	06 52		07 02	07 08		07 16	07 22		07 31	07 38		
	d																						
London Bridge 4 ⊖	a				00 11	00 41																07 17	

		LO	LO	LO	LO	LO	LO	SE	SE	SE	SN	SN	SE	SN	SN	SN	LO	LO	SN	LO	LO	LO	LO
East Croydon	d													07 12	07 17								
West Croydon 4	d		06 55			07 12										07 22		07 25	07 34			07 42	
Norwood Junction 2	d		07 01			07 16									07 22	07 27		07 31	07 40			07 46	
Anerley	d		07 04			07 19									07 25			07 34				07 49	
Penge West	d		07 06			07 21									07 27			07 36				07 51	
London Victoria 15 ⊖	d							00 56															
Battersea Park 4	d																						
Wandsworth Road	d																						
Clapham High Street ⊖	d																						
London Blackfriars 3 ⊖	d								06 12	06 42			07 12										
Denmark Hill 4	d							01 06	06 22	06 52			07 22										
Peckham Rye 4	d							01a08	06a25	06a55	07 09	07 23	07a25	07 39									
Queens Rd Peckham	d										07 12	07 26		07 42									
South Bermondsey	d										07 14	07 28		07 44									
Clapham Junction 10	d																						
Wandsworth Common	d																						
Balham 4 ⊖	d																						
Streatham Hill	d																						
West Norwood 4	d																						
Gipsy Hill	d																						
Crystal Palace 4	d	07 01			07 14											07a31	07 31				07 44		
Sydenham	d	07 04	07 09		07 17	07 24									07 29		07 34	07 39	07 44		07 47	07 54	
Forest Hill 4	d	07 07	07 11		07 20	07 26									07 32		07 37	07 41	07 47		07 50	07 56	
Honor Oak Park	d	07 09	07 14		07 22	07 29									07 34		07 39	07 44	07 49		07 52	07 59	
Brockley	d	07 12	07 16		07 25	07 31									07 37		07 42	07 46	07 52		07 55	08 01	
New Cross Gate 4	a	07 14	07 19		07 27	07 34									07 39		07 44	07 49	07 54		07 57	08 04	
	d	07 14	07 19		07 27	07 34									07 39		07 44	07 49	07 54		07 57	08 04	
New Cross ELL	d			07 24			07 39													07 54			08 09
Surrey Quays	d	07 18	07 22	07 28	07 33	07 38	07 43										07 48	07 52		07 58	08 03	08 08	08 13
Canada Water	d	07 20	07 24	07 30	07 35	07 40	07 45										07 50	07 54		08 00	08 05	08 10	08 15
Rotherhithe	d	07 21	07 26	07 31	07 36	07 41	07 46										07 51	07 56		08 01	08 06	08 11	08 16
Wapping	d	07 23	07 27	07 33	07 38	07 43	07 48										07 53	07 57		08 03	08 08	08 13	08 18
Shadwell	d	07 25	07 29	07 35	07 40	07 45	07 50										07 55	07 59		08 05	08 10	08 15	08 20
Whitechapel	d	07 27	07 32	07 37	07 42	07 47	07 52										07 57	08 02		08 07	08 12	08 17	08 22
Shoreditch High Street	d	07 29	07 34	07 39	07 44	07 49	07 54										07 59	08 04		08 09	08 14	08 19	08 24
Hoxton	d	07 31	07 36	07 41	07 46	07 51	07 56										08 01	08 06		08 11	08 16	08 21	08 26
Haggerston	d	07 33	07 38	07 43	07 48	07 53	07 58										08 03	08 08		08 13	08 18	08 23	08 28
Dalston Junction Stn ELL	a	07 35	07 40	07 50	07 50	07 56	08 05										08 05	08 10		08 20	08 20	08 26	08 35
Canonbury	d	07 38	07 45		07 53	08 00											08 08	08 15			08 23	08 30	
Highbury & Islington	a	07 46	07 52		08 01	08 08											08 16	08 22			08 31	08 38	
	d																						
London Bridge 4 ⊖	a										07 19	07 33		07 50	07 48				08 01				

Table 178

Sundays

29 July to 12 August

East London Line and Croydon - London Victoria to London Bridge

Network Diagram - see first Page of Table 177

		LO		SN	SE	SN	SE	SN	SN	SN	SN	LO		SN	LO	LO	LO	LO	LO	SN	SE	SN		SE	SN
East Croydon	d								07 42	07 47															
West Croydon 4	d										07 52	07 55		08 04			08 12								
Norwood Junction 2	d									07 52	07 57	08 01		08 10			08 16								
Anerley	d									07 55		08 04					08 19								
Penge West	d									07 57		08 06					08 21								
London Victoria 15	d				07 39			07 41													08 09				08 11
Battersea Park 4	d							07 45																	08 15
Wandsworth Road	d							07 47																	08 17
Clapham High Street	d							07 49																	08 19
London Blackfriars 3	d						07 42																	08 12	
Denmark Hill 4	d				07 48		07 52	07 54													08 18			08 22	08 24
Peckham Rye 4	d			07 45	07a51	07 53	07a55	07 56	08 10											08 15	08a21	08 23		08a25	08 26
Queens Rd Peckham	d					07 56		07 59	08 12													08 26			08 29
South Bermondsey	d					07 58		08 01	08 15													08 28			08 31
Clapham Junction 10	d																								
Wandsworth Common	d																								
Balham 4	d																								
Streatham Hill	d																								
West Norwood 4	d			07 57																08 27					
Gipsy Hill	d			08 00																08 30					
Crystal Palace 4	d	08 01		08a02							08a01					08 14			08 31	08a32					
Sydenham	d	08 04								07 59		08 09		08 14		08 17	08 24		08 34						
Forest Hill 4	d	08 07								08 02		08 11		08 17		08 20	08 26		08 37						
Honor Oak Park	d	08 09								08 04		08 14		08 19		08 22	08 29		08 39						
Brockley	d	08 12								08 07		08 16		08 22		08 25	08 31		08 42						
New Cross Gate 4	a	08 14								08 09		08 19		08 24		08 27	08 34		08 44						
	d	08 14								08 09		08 19		08 24		08 27	08 34		08 44						
New Cross ELL	d														08 24			08 39							
Surrey Quays	d	08 18										08 22			08 28	08 33	08 38	08 43	08 48						
Canada Water	d	08 20										08 24			08 30	08 35	08 40	08 45	08 50						
Rotherhithe	d	08 21										08 26			08 31	08 36	08 41	08 46	08 51						
Wapping	d	08 23										08 27			08 33	08 38	08 43	08 48	08 53						
Shadwell	d	08 25										08 29			08 35	08 40	08 45	08 50	08 55						
Whitechapel	d	08 27										08 32			08 37	08 42	08 47	08 52	08 57						
Shoreditch High Street	d	08 29										08 34			08 39	08 44	08 49	08 54	08 59						
Hoxton	d	08 31										08 36			08 41	08 46	08 51	08 56	09 01						
Haggerston	d	08 33										08 38			08 43	08 48	08 53	08 58	09 03						
Dalston Junction Stn ELL	a	08 35										08 40			08 50	08 50	08 56	09 05	09 05						
Canonbury	d	08 38										08 45				08 53	09 00		09 08						
Highbury & Islington	a	08 46										08 52				09 01	09 08		09 16						
	d																								
London Bridge 4	a					08 03		08 06	08 19	08 17				08 31								08 33			08 36

		SN	SN	LO	SN	LO	LO	LO		LO	LO	SN	SE	SN	SE	SN	SN	SN		LO	SN	LO	LO	LO	LO
East Croydon	d	08 12	08 17														08 42	08 47							
West Croydon 4	d			08 25	08 34			08 42												08 55	09 04			09 12	
Norwood Junction 2	d		08 22	08 31	08 40			08 46										08 52		09 01	09 10			09 16	
Anerley	d		08 25	08 34				08 49										08 55		09 04				09 19	
Penge West	d		08 27	08 36				08 51										08 57		09 06				09 21	
London Victoria 15	d												08 39			08 41									
Battersea Park 4	d															08 45									
Wandsworth Road	d															08 47									
Clapham High Street	d															08 49									
London Blackfriars 3	d														08 42										
Denmark Hill 4	d												08 48		08 52	08 54									
Peckham Rye 4	d	08 40										08 45	08a51	08 53	08a55	08 56	09 10								
Queens Rd Peckham	d	08 42												08 56		08 59	09 12								
South Bermondsey	d	08 45												08 58		09 01	09 15								
Clapham Junction 10	d																								
Wandsworth Common	d																								
Balham 4	d																								
Streatham Hill	d																								
West Norwood 4	d											08 57													
Gipsy Hill	d											09 00													
Crystal Palace 4	d						08 44				09 01	09a02											09 14		
Sydenham	d		08 29	08 39	08 44		08 47	08 54			09 04							08 59		09 09	09 14		09 17	09 24	
Forest Hill 4	d		08 32	08 41	08 47		08 50	08 56			09 07							09 02		09 11	09 17		09 20	09 26	
Honor Oak Park	d		08 34	08 44	08 49		08 52	08 59			09 09							09 04		09 14	09 19		09 22	09 29	
Brockley	d		08 37	08 46	08 52		08 55	09 01			09 12							09 07		09 16	09 22		09 25	09 31	
New Cross Gate 4	a		08 39	08 49	08 54		08 57	09 04			09 14							09 09		09 19	09 24		09 27	09 34	
	d		08 39	08 49	08 54		08 57	09 04			09 14							09 09		09 19	09 24		09 27	09 34	
New Cross ELL	d					08 54				09 09												09 24			09 39
Surrey Quays	d			08 52		08 58	09 03	09 08		09 13	09 18									09 22		09 28	09 33	09 38	09 43
Canada Water	d			08 54		09 00	09 05	09 10		09 15	09 20									09 24		09 30	09 35	09 40	09 45
Rotherhithe	d			08 56		09 01	09 06	09 11		09 16	09 21									09 26		09 31	09 36	09 41	09 46
Wapping	d			08 57		09 03	09 08	09 13		09 18	09 23									09 27		09 33	09 38	09 43	09 48
Shadwell	d			08 59		09 05	09 10	09 15		09 20	09 25									09 29		09 35	09 40	09 45	09 50
Whitechapel	d			09 02		09 07	09 12	09 17		09 22	09 27									09 32		09 37	09 42	09 47	09 52
Shoreditch High Street	d			09 04		09 09	09 14	09 19		09 24	09 29									09 34		09 39	09 44	09 49	09 54
Hoxton	d			09 06		09 11	09 16	09 21		09 26	09 31									09 36		09 41	09 46	09 51	09 56
Haggerston	d			09 08		09 13	09 18	09 23		09 28	09 33									09 38		09 43	09 48	09 53	09 58
Dalston Junction Stn ELL	a			09 10		09 20	09 20	09 26		09 35	09 35									09 40		09 50	09 50	09 56	10 05
Canonbury	d			09 15			09 23	09 30			09 38									09 45			09 53	10 00	
Highbury & Islington	a			09 22			09 31	09 38			09 46									09 52			10 01	10 08	
	d																								
London Bridge 4	a	08 49	08 48		09 01									09 03		09 06	09 19	09 18			09 31				

Table 178

Sundays

29 July to 12 August

East London Line and Croydon - London Victoria to London Bridge

Network Diagram - see first Page of Table 177

Station		LO	SN	SE		SN	SE	SN	SN	SN	LO	SN	LO	LO		LO	LO	LO	SN	SE	SN	SE	SN	SN	
East Croydon 🚌	d								09 12	09 17															
West Croydon 4 🚌	d										09 25	09 34				09 42								09 42	
Norwood Junction 2	d									09 22	09 31	09 40				09 46									
Anerley	d									09 25	09 34					09 49									
Penge West	d									09 27	09 36					09 51									
London Victoria 15 ⊖	d			09 09				09 11												09 39			09 41		
Battersea Park 4	d							09 15															09 45		
Wandsworth Road	d							09 17															09 47		
Clapham High Street ⊖	d							09 19															09 49		
London Blackfriars 3 ⊖	d						09 12															09 42			
Denmark Hill 4	d			09 18			09 22	09 24												09 47		09 52	09 54		
Peckham Rye 4	d		09 15	09a21		09 23	09a25	09 26	09 40										09 45	09a51	09 53	09a55	09 56	10 10	
Queens Rd Peckham	d					09 26		09 29	09 42												09 56		09 59	10 12	
South Bermondsey	d					09 28		09 31	09 45												09 58		10 01	10 15	
Clapham Junction 10	d																								
Wandsworth Common	d																								
Balham 4 ⊖	d																								
Streatham Hill	d																								
West Norwood 4	d		09 27																09 57						
Gipsy Hill	d		09 30																10 00						
Crystal Palace 4	d	09 31	09a32											09 46				10 01	10a02						
Sydenham	d	09 34								09 29	09 39	09 44		09 49		09 54		10 04							
Forest Hill 4	d	09 37								09 32	09 41	09 47		09 52		09 56		10 07							
Honor Oak Park	d	09 39								09 34	09 44	09 49		09 54		09 59		10 09							
Brockley	d	09 42								09 37	09 46	09 52		09 57		10 01		10 12							
New Cross Gate 4	a	09 44								09 39	09 49	09 54		09 59		10 04		10 14							
	d	09 44								09 39	09 49	09 54		09 59		10 04		10 14							
New Cross ELL	d												09 54				10 09								
Surrey Quays	d	09 48									09 52		09 58	10 03		10 08	10 13	10 18							
Canada Water	d	09 50									09 54		10 00	10 05		10 10	10 15	10 20							
Rotherhithe	d	09 51									09 56		10 01	10 06		10 11	10 16	10 21							
Wapping	d	09 53									09 57		10 03	10 08		10 13	10 18	10 23							
Shadwell	d	09 55									09 59		10 05	10 10		10 15	10 20	10 25							
Whitechapel	d	09 57									10 02		10 07	10 12		10 17	10 22	10 27							
Shoreditch High Street	d	09 59									10 04		10 09	10 14		10 19	10 24	10 29							
Hoxton	d	10 01									10 06		10 11	10 16		10 21	10 26	10 31							
Haggerston	d	10 03									10 08		10 13	10 18		10 23	10 28	10 33							
Dalston Junction Stn ELL	a	10 05									10 10		10 20	10 20		10 25	10 35	10 35							
Canonbury	d	10 08									10 15			10 23		10 30		10 38							
Highbury & Islington	a	10 16									10 22			10 31		10 38		10 46							
	d																								
London Bridge 4 ⊖	a					09 33		09 36	09 49	09 48		10 01									10 03		10 06	10 19	

Station		SN	FC 1	LO	SN	LO	LO	LO	LO	LO		SN	SE	SN	SE	SN	SN	SN	FC 1	LO		SN	LO	LO	LO
East Croydon 🚌	d	09 47	09 47														10 12	10 17	10 17						
West Croydon 4 🚌	d			09 55	10 04			10 12												10 25		10 34			10 42
Norwood Junction 2	d	09 52		10 01	10 10			10 16										10 22		10 31		10 40			10 46
Anerley	d	09 55		10 04				10 19										10 25		10 34					10 49
Penge West	d	09 57		10 06				10 21										10 27		10 36					10 51
London Victoria 15 ⊖	d												10 09			10 11									
Battersea Park 4	d															10 15									
Wandsworth Road	d															10 17									
Clapham High Street ⊖	d															10 19									
London Blackfriars 3 ⊖	d		10a07												10 12				10a37						
Denmark Hill 4	d												10 18		10 22	10 24									
Peckham Rye 4	d											10 15	10a21	10 23	10a25	10 26	10 40								
Queens Rd Peckham	d													10 26		10 29	10 42								
South Bermondsey	d													10 28		10 31	10 45								
Clapham Junction 10	d																								
Wandsworth Common	d																								
Balham 4 ⊖	d																								
Streatham Hill	d																								
West Norwood 4	d											10 27													
Gipsy Hill	d											10 30													
Crystal Palace 4	d						10 16			10 31		10a32												10 46	
Sydenham	d	09 59		10 09	10 14		10 19	10 24		10 34								10 29		10 39		10 44		10 49	10 54
Forest Hill 4	d	10 02		10 11	10 17		10 22	10 26		10 37								10 32		10 41		10 47		10 52	10 56
Honor Oak Park	d	10 04		10 14	10 19		10 24	10 29		10 39								10 34		10 44		10 49		10 54	10 59
Brockley	d	10 07		10 16	10 22		10 27	10 31		10 42								10 37		10 46		10 52		10 57	11 01
New Cross Gate 4	a	10 09		10 19	10 24		10 29	10 34		10 44								10 39		10 49		10 54		10 59	11 04
	d	10 09		10 19	10 24		10 29	10 34		10 44								10 39		10 49		10 54		10 59	11 04
New Cross ELL	d					10 24			10 39														10 54		
Surrey Quays	d			10 22		10 28	10 33	10 38	10 43	10 48										10 52			10 58	11 03	11 08
Canada Water	d			10 24		10 30	10 35	10 40	10 45	10 50										10 54			11 00	11 05	11 10
Rotherhithe	d			10 26		10 31	10 36	10 41	10 46	10 51										10 56			11 01	11 06	11 11
Wapping	d			10 27		10 33	10 38	10 43	10 48	10 53										10 57			11 03	11 08	11 13
Shadwell	d			10 29		10 35	10 40	10 45	10 50	10 55										10 59			11 05	11 10	11 15
Whitechapel	d			10 32		10 37	10 42	10 47	10 52	10 57										11 02			11 07	11 12	11 17
Shoreditch High Street	d			10 34		10 39	10 44	10 49	10 54	10 59										11 04			11 09	11 14	11 19
Hoxton	d			10 36		10 41	10 46	10 51	10 56	11 01										11 06			11 11	11 16	11 21
Haggerston	d			10 38		10 43	10 48	10 53	10 58	11 03										11 08			11 13	11 18	11 23
Dalston Junction Stn ELL	a			10 40		10 50	10 50	10 55	11 05	11 05										11 10			11 20	11 20	11 25
Canonbury	d			10 45			10 53	11 00		11 08										11 15				11 23	11 30
Highbury & Islington	a			10 52			11 01	11 08		11 16										11 22				11 31	11 38
	d																								
London Bridge 4 ⊖	a	10 18			10 31									10 33		10 36	10 49	10 48				11 01			

Table 178

Sundays
29 July to 12 August

East London Line and Croydon - London Victoria to London Bridge

Network Diagram - see first Page of Table 177

Station		LO	LO	SN	SE	SN		SE	SN	SN	SN	FC [1]	LO	SN	LO	LO		LO	LO	LO	SN	SE	SN	SE	SN
East Croydon	d									10 42	10 47	10 47													
West Croydon [4]	d												10 55	11 04				11 12							
Norwood Junction [2]	d										10 52		11 01	11 10				11 16							
Anerley	d										10 55		11 04					11 19							
Penge West	d										10 57		11 06					11 21							
London Victoria [15] ⊖	d				10 39				10 41													11 09			11 11
Battersea Park [4]	d								10 45																11 15
Wandsworth Road	d								10 47																11 17
Clapham High Street ⊖	d								10 49																11 19
London Blackfriars [3] ⊖	d							10 42				11a07												11 12	
Denmark Hill [4]	d				10 48			10 52	10 54													11 18		11 22	11 24
Peckham Rye [4]	d			10 45	10a51	10 53		10a55	10 56	11 10											11 15	11a21	11 23	11a25	11 26
Queens Rd Peckham	d					10 56			10 59	11 12													11 26		11 29
South Bermondsey	d					10 58			11 01	11 15													11 28		11 31
Clapham Junction [10]	d																								
Wandsworth Common	d																								
Balham [4] ⊖	d																								
Streatham Hill	d																								
West Norwood [4]	d			10 57																	11 27				
Gipsy Hill	d			11 00																	11 30				
Crystal Palace [4]	d		11 01	11a02												11 16				11 31	11a32				
Sydenham	d		11 04								10 59		11 09	11 14		11 19		11 24		11 34					
Forest Hill [4]	d		11 07								11 02		11 11	11 17		11 22		11 26		11 37					
Honor Oak Park	d		11 09								11 04		11 14	11 19		11 24		11 29		11 39					
Brockley	d		11 12								11 07		11 16	11 22		11 27		11 31		11 42					
New Cross Gate [4]	a		11 14								11 09		11 19	11 24		11 29		11 34		11 44					
	d		11 14								11 09		11 19	11 24		11 29		11 34		11 44					
New Cross ELL	d	11 09													11 24				11 39						
Surrey Quays	d	11 13	11 18										11 22		11 28	11 33		11 38	11 43	11 48					
Canada Water	d	11 15	11 20										11 24		11 30	11 35		11 40	11 45	11 50					
Rotherhithe	d	11 16	11 21										11 26		11 31	11 36		11 41	11 46	11 51					
Wapping	d	11 18	11 23										11 27		11 33	11 38		11 43	11 48	11 53					
Shadwell	d	11 20	11 25										11 29		11 35	11 40		11 45	11 50	11 55					
Whitechapel	d	11 22	11 27										11 32		11 37	11 42		11 47	11 52	11 57					
Shoreditch High Street	d	11 24	11 29										11 34		11 39	11 44		11 49	11 54	11 59					
Hoxton	d	11 26	11 31										11 36		11 41	11 46		11 51	11 56	12 01					
Haggerston	d	11 28	11 33										11 38		11 43	11 48		11 53	11 58	12 03					
Dalston Junction Stn ELL	a	11 35	11 35										11 40		11 50	11 50		11 55	12 05	12 05					
Canonbury	d		11 38										11 45			11 53		12 00		12 08					
Highbury & Islington	a		11 46										11 52			12 01		12 08		12 16					
	d																								
London Bridge [4] ⊖	a					11 03			11 06	11 19	11 18			11 31									11 33		11 36

Station		SN		SN	FC [1]	LO	SN	LO	LO	LO	LO	LO		SN	SE	SN	SE	SN	SN	SN	FC [1]	LO		SN	LO
East Croydon	d	11 12		11 17	11 17														11 42	11 47	11 47				
West Croydon [4]	d					11 25	11 34			11 42												11 55		12 04	
Norwood Junction [2]	d			11 22		11 31	11 40			11 46										11 52		12 01		12 10	
Anerley	d			11 25		11 34				11 49										11 55		12 04			
Penge West	d			11 27		11 36				11 51										11 57		12 06			
London Victoria [15] ⊖	d														11 39			11 41							
Battersea Park [4]	d																	11 45							
Wandsworth Road	d																	11 47							
Clapham High Street ⊖	d																	11 49							
London Blackfriars [3] ⊖	d				11a37												11 42				12a07				
Denmark Hill [4]	d														11 48		11 52	11 54							
Peckham Rye [4]	d	11 40												11 45	11a51	11 53	11a55	11 56	12 10						
Queens Rd Peckham	d	11 42														11 56		11 59	12 12						
South Bermondsey	d	11 45														11 58		12 01	12 15						
Clapham Junction [10]	d																								
Wandsworth Common	d																								
Balham [4] ⊖	d																								
Streatham Hill	d																								
West Norwood [4]	d													11 57											
Gipsy Hill	d													12 00											
Crystal Palace [4]	d								11 46			12 01		12a02											
Sydenham	d			11 29		11 39	11 44		11 49	11 54		12 04								11 59		12 09		12 14	
Forest Hill [4]	d			11 32		11 41	11 47		11 52	11 56		12 07								12 02		12 11		12 17	
Honor Oak Park	d			11 34		11 44	11 49		11 54	11 59		12 09								12 04		12 14		12 19	
Brockley	d			11 37		11 46	11 52		11 57	12 01		12 12								12 07		12 16		12 22	
New Cross Gate [4]	a			11 39		11 49	11 54		11 59	12 04		12 14								12 09		12 19		12 24	
	d			11 39		11 49	11 54		11 59	12 04		12 14								12 09		12 19		12 24	
New Cross ELL	d							11 54			12 09														12 24
Surrey Quays	d					11 52		11 58	12 03	12 08	12 13	12 18										12 22			12 28
Canada Water	d					11 54		12 00	12 05	12 10	12 15	12 20										12 24			12 30
Rotherhithe	d					11 56		12 01	12 06	12 11	12 16	12 21										12 26			12 31
Wapping	d					11 57		12 03	12 08	12 13	12 18	12 23										12 27			12 33
Shadwell	d					11 59		12 05	12 10	12 15	12 20	12 25										12 29			12 35
Whitechapel	d					12 02		12 07	12 12	12 17	12 22	12 27										12 32			12 37
Shoreditch High Street	d					12 04		12 09	12 14	12 19	12 24	12 29										12 34			12 39
Hoxton	d					12 06		12 11	12 16	12 21	12 26	12 31										12 36			12 41
Haggerston	d					12 08		12 13	12 18	12 23	12 28	12 33										12 38			12 43
Dalston Junction Stn ELL	a					12 10		12 20	12 20	12 25	12 35	12 35										12 40			12 50
Canonbury	d					12 15			12 23	12 30		12 38										12 45			
Highbury & Islington	a					12 22			12 31	12 38		12 46										12 52			
	d																								
London Bridge [4] ⊖	a	11 49		11 48			12 01									12 03		12 06	12 19	12 18				12 31	

Table 178

Sundays

29 July to 12 August

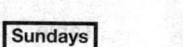

East London Line and Croydon - London Victoria to London Bridge

Network Diagram - see first Page of Table 177

Station		LO	LO	LO	LO	SN	SE	SN		SE	SN	SN	SN	FC 1	LO	SN	LO	LO		LO	LO	LO	SN	SE	SN
East Croydon	d											12 12	12 17	12 17											
West Croydon 4	d		12 12												12 25	12 34				12 42					
Norwood Junction 2	d		12 16										12 22		12 31	12 40				12 46					
Anerley	d		12 19										12 25		12 34					12 49					
Penge West	d		12 21										12 27		12 36					12 51					
London Victoria 15 ⊖	d						12 09				12 11													12 39	
Battersea Park 4	d										12 15														
Wandsworth Road	d										12 17														
Clapham High Street ⊖	d										12 19														
London Blackfriars 3 ⊖	d									12 12				12a37											
Denmark Hill 4	d						12 18			12 22	12 24													12 48	
Peckham Rye 4	d					12 15	12a21	12 23		12a25	12 26	12 40											12 45	12a51	12 53
Queens Rd Peckham	d							12 26			12 29	12 42													12 56
South Bermondsey	d							12 28			12 31	12 45													12 58
Clapham Junction 10	d																								
Wandsworth Common	d																								
Balham 4 ⊖	d																								
Streatham Hill	d																								
West Norwood 4	d					12 27																	12 57		
Gipsy Hill	d					12 30																	13 00		
Crystal Palace 4	d	12 16			12 31	12a32												12 46				13 01	13a02		
Sydenham	d	12 19	12 24		12 34								12 29		12 39	12 44		12 49		12 54		13 04			
Forest Hill 4	d	12 22	12 26		12 37								12 32		12 41	12 47		12 52		12 56		13 07			
Honor Oak Park	d	12 24	12 29		12 39								12 34		12 44	12 49		12 54		12 59		13 09			
Brockley	d	12 27	12 31		12 42								12 37		12 46	12 52		12 57		13 01		13 12			
New Cross Gate 4	a	12 29	12 34		12 44								12 39		12 49	12 54		12 59		13 04		13 14			
	d	12 29	12 34		12 44								12 39		12 49	12 54		12 59		13 04		13 14			
New Cross ELL	d			12 39													12 54				13 09				
Surrey Quays	d	12 33	12 38	12 43	12 48										12 52		12 58	13 03		13 08	13 13	13 18			
Canada Water	d	12 35	12 40	12 45	12 50										12 54		13 00	13 05		13 10	13 15	13 20			
Rotherhithe	d	12 36	12 41	12 46	12 51										12 56		13 01	13 06		13 11	13 16	13 21			
Wapping	d	12 38	12 43	12 48	12 53										12 57		13 03	13 08		13 13	13 18	13 23			
Shadwell	d	12 40	12 45	12 50	12 55										12 59		13 05	13 10		13 15	13 20	13 25			
Whitechapel	d	12 42	12 47	12 52	12 57										13 02		13 07	13 12		13 17	13 22	13 27			
Shoreditch High Street	d	12 44	12 49	12 54	12 59										13 04		13 09	13 14		13 19	13 24	13 29			
Hoxton	d	12 46	12 51	12 56	13 01										13 06		13 11	13 16		13 21	13 26	13 31			
Haggerston	d	12 48	12 53	12 58	13 03										13 08		13 13	13 18		13 23	13 28	13 33			
Dalston Junction Stn ELL	a	12 50	12 55	13 05	13 05										13 10		13 20	13 20		13 25	13 35	13 35			
Canonbury	d	12 53	13 00		13 08										13 15			13 23		13 30		13 38			
Highbury & Islington	a	13 01	13 08		13 16										13 22			13 31		13 38		13 46			
	d																								
London Bridge 4 ⊖	a							12 33			12 36	12 49	12 48			13 01									13 03

Station		SE	SN	SN		SN	FC 1	LO	SN	LO	LO	LO	LO	LO		SN	SE	SN	SE	SN	SN	SN	FC 1	LO	
East Croydon	d			12 42		12 47	12 47														13 12	13 17	13 17		
West Croydon 4	d							12 55	13 04			13 12												13 25	
Norwood Junction 2	d					12 52		13 01	13 10			13 16										13 22		13 31	
Anerley	d					12 55		13 04				13 19										13 25		13 34	
Penge West	d					12 57		13 06				13 21										13 27		13 36	
London Victoria 15 ⊖	d		12 41														13 09			13 11					
Battersea Park 4	d		12 45																	13 15					
Wandsworth Road	d		12 47																	13 17					
Clapham High Street ⊖	d		12 49																	13 19					
London Blackfriars 3 ⊖	d	12 42					13a07												13 12				13a37		
Denmark Hill 4	d	12 52	12 54														13 18		13 22	13 24					
Peckham Rye 4	d	12a55	12 56	13 10												13 15	13a21	13 23	13a25	13 26	13 40				
Queens Rd Peckham	d		12 59	13 12														13 26		13 29	13 42				
South Bermondsey	d		13 01	13 15														13 28		13 31	13 45				
Clapham Junction 10	d																								
Wandsworth Common	d																								
Balham 4 ⊖	d																								
Streatham Hill	d																								
West Norwood 4	d															13 27									
Gipsy Hill	d															13 30									
Crystal Palace 4	d										13 16			13 31		13a32									
Sydenham	d					12 59		13 09	13 14		13 19	13 24		13 34								13 29		13 39	
Forest Hill 4	d					13 02		13 11	13 17		13 22	13 26		13 37								13 32		13 41	
Honor Oak Park	d					13 04		13 14	13 19		13 24	13 29		13 39								13 34		13 44	
Brockley	d					13 07		13 16	13 22		13 27	13 31		13 42								13 37		13 46	
New Cross Gate 4	a					13 09		13 19	13 24		13 29	13 34		13 44								13 39		13 49	
	d					13 09		13 19	13 24		13 29	13 34		13 44								13 39		13 49	
New Cross ELL	d									13 24			13 39												
Surrey Quays	d							13 22		13 28	13 33	13 38	13 43	13 48										13 52	
Canada Water	d							13 24		13 30	13 35	13 40	13 45	13 50										13 54	
Rotherhithe	d							13 26		13 31	13 36	13 41	13 46	13 51										13 56	
Wapping	d							13 27		13 33	13 38	13 43	13 48	13 53										13 57	
Shadwell	d							13 29		13 35	13 40	13 45	13 50	13 55										13 59	
Whitechapel	d							13 32		13 37	13 42	13 47	13 52	13 57										14 02	
Shoreditch High Street	d							13 34		13 39	13 44	13 49	13 54	13 59										14 04	
Hoxton	d							13 36		13 41	13 46	13 51	13 56	14 01										14 06	
Haggerston	d							13 38		13 43	13 48	13 53	13 58	14 03										14 08	
Dalston Junction Stn ELL	a							13 40		13 50	13 50	13 55	14 05	14 05										14 10	
Canonbury	d							13 45			13 53	14 00		14 08										14 15	
Highbury & Islington	a							13 52			14 01	14 08		14 16										14 22	
	d																								
London Bridge 4 ⊖	a		13 06	13 19		13 18			13 31									13 33		13 36	13 49	13 48			

Table 178

Sundays

29 July to 12 August

East London Line and Croydon - London Victoria to London Bridge

Network Diagram - see first Page of Table 177

		SN	LO	LO	LO	LO	LO	SN	SE	SN		SE	SN	SN	SN	FC [1]	LO	SN	LO	LO		LO	LO	LO	SN
East Croydon	d													13 42	13 47	13 47									
West Croydon 4	d	13 34			13 42												13 55	14 04				14 12			
Norwood Junction 2	d	13 40			13 46										13 52		14 01	14 10				14 16			
Anerley	d				13 49										13 55		14 04					14 19			
Penge West	d				13 51										13 57		14 06					14 21			
London Victoria 15 ⊖	d								13 39				13 41												
Battersea Park 4	d												13 45												
Wandsworth Road	d												13 47												
Clapham High Street ⊖	d												13 49												
London Blackfriars 3 ⊖	d											13 42				14a07									
Denmark Hill 4	d								13 48			13 52	13 54												
Peckham Rye 4	d							13 45	13a51	13 53		13a55	13 56	14 10											14 15
Queens Rd Peckham	d									13 56			13 59	14 12											
South Bermondsey	d									13 58			14 01	14 15											
Clapham Junction 10	d																								
Wandsworth Common	d																								
Balham 4 ⊖	d																								
Streatham Hill	d																								
West Norwood 4	d							13 57																	14 27
Gipsy Hill	d							14 00																	14 30
Crystal Palace 4	d			13 46			14 01	14a02												14 16				14 31	14a32
Sydenham	d	13 44		13 49	13 54		14 04								13 59		14 09	14 14		14 19		14 24		14 34	
Forest Hill 4	d	13 47		13 52	13 56		14 07								14 02		14 11	14 17		14 22		14 26		14 37	
Honor Oak Park	d	13 49		13 54	13 59		14 09								14 04		14 14	14 19		14 24		14 29		14 39	
Brockley	d	13 52		13 57	14 01		14 12								14 07		14 16	14 22		14 27		14 31		14 42	
New Cross Gate 4	a	13 54		13 59	14 04		14 14								14 09		14 19	14 24		14 29		14 34		14 44	
	d	13 54		13 59	14 04		14 14								14 09		14 19	14 24		14 29		14 34		14 44	
New Cross ELL	d		13 54			14 09													14 24				14 39		
Surrey Quays	d		13 58	14 03	14 08	14 13	14 18										14 22		14 28	14 33		14 38	14 43	14 48	
Canada Water	d		14 00	14 05	14 10	14 15	14 20										14 24		14 30	14 35		14 40	14 45	14 50	
Rotherhithe	d		14 01	14 06	14 11	14 16	14 21										14 26		14 31	14 36		14 41	14 46	14 51	
Wapping	d		14 03	14 08	14 13	14 18	14 23										14 27		14 33	14 38		14 43	14 48	14 53	
Shadwell	d		14 05	14 10	14 15	14 20	14 25										14 29		14 35	14 40		14 45	14 50	14 55	
Whitechapel	d		14 07	14 12	14 17	14 22	14 27										14 32		14 37	14 42		14 47	14 52	14 57	
Shoreditch High Street	d		14 09	14 14	14 19	14 24	14 29										14 34		14 39	14 44		14 49	14 54	14 59	
Hoxton	d		14 11	14 16	14 21	14 26	14 31										14 36		14 41	14 46		14 51	14 56	15 01	
Haggerston	d		14 13	14 18	14 23	14 28	14 33										14 38		14 43	14 48		14 53	14 58	15 03	
Dalston Junction Stn ELL	a		14 20	14 20	14 25	14 35	14 35										14 40		14 50	14 50		14 55	15 05	15 05	
Canonbury	d			14 23	14 30		14 38										14 45			14 53		15 00		15 08	
Highbury & Islington	a			14 31	14 38		14 46										14 52			15 01		15 08		15 16	
	d																								
London Bridge 4 ⊖	a	14 01								14 03			14 06	14 19	14 18			14 31							

		SE	SN	SE	SN	SN		SN	FC [1]	LO	SN	LO	LO	LO	LO	LO		SN	SE	SN	SE	SN	SN	SN	FC [1]
East Croydon	d					14 12		14 17	14 17														14 42	14 47	14 47
West Croydon 4	d									14 25	14 34			14 42											
Norwood Junction 2	d							14 22		14 31	14 40			14 46										14 52	
Anerley	d							14 25		14 34				14 49										14 55	
Penge West	d							14 27		14 36				14 51										14 57	
London Victoria 15 ⊖	d	14 09			14 11														14 39			14 41			
Battersea Park 4	d				14 15																	14 45			
Wandsworth Road	d				14 17																	14 47			
Clapham High Street ⊖	d				14 19																	14 49			
London Blackfriars 3 ⊖	d			14 12					14a37												14 42				15a07
Denmark Hill 4	d	14 18		14 22	14 24														14 48		14 52	14 54			
Peckham Rye 4	d	14a21	14 23	14a25	14 26	14 40												14 45	14a51	14 53	14a55	14 56	15 10		
Queens Rd Peckham	d		14 26		14 29	14 42														14 56		14 59	15 12		
South Bermondsey	d		14 28		14 31	14 45														14 58		15 01	15 15		
Clapham Junction 10	d																								
Wandsworth Common	d																								
Balham 4 ⊖	d																								
Streatham Hill	d																								
West Norwood 4	d																	14 57							
Gipsy Hill	d																	15 00							
Crystal Palace 4	d												14 46			15 01		15a02							
Sydenham	d							14 29		14 39	14 44		14 49	14 54		15 04								14 59	
Forest Hill 4	d							14 32		14 41	14 47		14 52	14 56		15 07								15 02	
Honor Oak Park	d							14 34		14 44	14 49		14 54	14 59		15 09								15 04	
Brockley	d							14 37		14 46	14 52		14 57	15 01		15 12								15 07	
New Cross Gate 4	a							14 39		14 49	14 54		14 59	15 04		15 14								15 09	
	d							14 39		14 49	14 54		14 59	15 04		15 14								15 09	
New Cross ELL	d											14 54			15 09										
Surrey Quays	d									14 52		14 58	15 03	15 08	15 13	15 18									
Canada Water	d									14 54		15 00	15 05	15 10	15 15	15 20									
Rotherhithe	d									14 56		15 01	15 06	15 11	15 16	15 21									
Wapping	d									14 57		15 03	15 08	15 13	15 18	15 23									
Shadwell	d									14 59		15 05	15 10	15 15	15 20	15 25									
Whitechapel	d									15 02		15 07	15 12	15 17	15 22	15 27									
Shoreditch High Street	d									15 04		15 09	15 14	15 19	15 24	15 29									
Hoxton	d									15 06		15 11	15 16	15 21	15 26	15 31									
Haggerston	d									15 08		15 13	15 18	15 23	15 28	15 33									
Dalston Junction Stn ELL	a									15 10		15 20	15 20	15 25	15 35	15 35									
Canonbury	d									15 15			15 23	15 30		15 38									
Highbury & Islington	a									15 22			15 31	15 38		15 46									
	d																								
London Bridge 4 ⊖	a		14 33		14 36	14 49		14 48			15 01									15 03		15 06	15 19	15 18	

Table 178

Sundays

29 July to 12 August

East London Line and Croydon - London Victoria to London Bridge

Network Diagram - see first Page of Table 177

		LO		SN	LO	LO	LO	LO	LO	SN	SE	SN		SE	SN	SN	SN	FC 1	LO	SN	LO	LO		LO	LO
East Croydon (tram)	d															15 12	15 17	15 17							
West Croydon 4 (tram)	d	14 55		15 04			15 12												15 25	15 34				15 42	
Norwood Junction 2	d	15 01		15 10			15 16										15 22		15 31	15 40				15 46	
Anerley	d	15 04					15 19										15 25		15 34					15 49	
Penge West	d	15 06					15 21										15 27		15 36					15 51	
London Victoria 15 ⊖	d										15 09				15 11										
Battersea Park 4	d														15 15										
Wandsworth Road	d														15 17										
Clapham High Street ⊖	d														15 19										
London Blackfriars 3 ⊖	d													15 12				15a37							
Denmark Hill 4	d										15 18			15 22	15 24										
Peckham Rye 4	d									15 15	15a21	15 23		15a25	15 26	15 40									
Queens Rd Peckham	d											15 26			15 29	15 42									
South Bermondsey	d											15 28			15 31	15 45									
Clapham Junction 10	d																								
Wandsworth Common	d																								
Balham 4 ⊖	d																								
Streatham Hill	d																								
West Norwood 4	d									15 27															
Gipsy Hill	d									15 30															
Crystal Palace 4	d					15 16			15 31	15a32												15 46			
Sydenham	d	15 09		15 14		15 19	15 24		15 34								15 29		15 39	15 44		15 49		15 54	
Forest Hill 4	d	15 11		15 17		15 22	15 26		15 37								15 32		15 41	15 47		15 52		15 56	
Honor Oak Park	d	15 14		15 19		15 24	15 29		15 39								15 34		15 44	15 49		15 54		15 59	
Brockley	d	15 16		15 22		15 27	15 31		15 42								15 37		15 46	15 52		15 57		16 01	
New Cross Gate 4	a	15 19		15 24		15 29	15 34		15 44								15 39		15 49	15 54		15 59		16 04	
	d	15 19		15 24		15 29	15 34		15 44								15 39		15 49	15 54		15 59		16 04	
New Cross ELL	d				15 24			15 39													15 54				16 09
Surrey Quays	d	15 22			15 28	15 33	15 38	15 43	15 48										15 52		15 58	16 03		16 08	16 13
Canada Water	d	15 24			15 30	15 35	15 40	15 45	15 50										15 54		16 00	16 05		16 10	16 15
Rotherhithe	d	15 26			15 31	15 36	15 41	15 46	15 51										15 56		16 01	16 06		16 11	16 16
Wapping	d	15 27			15 33	15 38	15 43	15 48	15 53										15 57		16 03	16 08		16 13	16 18
Shadwell	d	15 29			15 35	15 40	15 45	15 50	15 55										15 59		16 05	16 10		16 15	16 20
Whitechapel	d	15 32			15 37	15 42	15 47	15 52	15 57										16 02		16 07	16 12		16 17	16 22
Shoreditch High Street	d	15 34			15 39	15 44	15 49	15 54	15 59										16 04		16 09	16 14		16 19	16 24
Hoxton	d	15 36			15 41	15 46	15 51	15 56	16 01										16 06		16 11	16 16		16 21	16 26
Haggerston	d	15 38			15 43	15 48	15 53	15 58	16 03										16 08		16 13	16 18		16 23	16 28
Dalston Junction Stn ELL	a	15 40			15 50	15 50	15 55	16 05	16 05										16 10		16 20	16 20		16 25	16 35
Canonbury	d	15 45				15 53	16 00		16 08										16 15			16 23		16 30	
Highbury & Islington	a	15 52				16 01	16 08		16 16										16 22			16 31		16 38	
	d																								
London Bridge 4 ⊖	a			15 31								15 33			15 36	15 49	15 48			16 01					

		LO	SN	SE	SN	SE	SN	SN		SN	FC 1	LO	SN	LO	LO	LO	LO	LO		SN	SE	SN	SE	SN	SN
East Croydon (tram)	d							15 42		15 47	15 47														16 12
West Croydon 4 (tram)	d											15 55	16 04			16 12									
Norwood Junction 2	d									15 52		16 01	16 10			16 16									
Anerley	d									15 55		16 04				16 19									
Penge West	d									15 57		16 06				16 21									
London Victoria 15 ⊖	d			15 39			15 41														16 09			16 11	
Battersea Park 4	d						15 45																	16 15	
Wandsworth Road	d						15 47																	16 17	
Clapham High Street ⊖	d						15 49																	16 19	
London Blackfriars 3 ⊖	d					15 42					16a07												16 12		
Denmark Hill 4	d			15 48		15 52	15 54														16 18		16 22	16 24	
Peckham Rye 4	d		15 45	15a51	15 53	15a55	15 56	16 10												16 15	16a21	16 23	16a25	16 26	16 40
Queens Rd Peckham	d				15 56		15 59	16 12														16 26		16 29	16 42
South Bermondsey	d				15 58		16 01	16 15														16 28		16 31	16 45
Clapham Junction 10	d																								
Wandsworth Common	d																								
Balham 4 ⊖	d																								
Streatham Hill	d																								
West Norwood 4	d		15 57																	16 27					
Gipsy Hill	d		16 00																	16 30					
Crystal Palace 4	d	16 01	16a02												16 16			16 31		16a32					
Sydenham	d	16 04								15 59		16 09	16 14		16 19	16 24		16 34							
Forest Hill 4	d	16 07								16 02		16 11	16 17		16 22	16 26		16 37							
Honor Oak Park	d	16 09								16 04		16 14	16 19		16 24	16 29		16 39							
Brockley	d	16 12								16 07		16 16	16 22		16 27	16 31		16 42							
New Cross Gate 4	a	16 14								16 09		16 19	16 24		16 29	16 34		16 44							
	d	16 14								16 09		16 19	16 24		16 29	16 34		16 44							
New Cross ELL	d													16 24			16 39								
Surrey Quays	d	16 18										16 22		16 28	16 33	16 38	16 43	16 48							
Canada Water	d	16 20										16 24		16 30	16 35	16 40	16 45	16 50							
Rotherhithe	d	16 21										16 26		16 31	16 36	16 41	16 46	16 51							
Wapping	d	16 23										16 27		16 33	16 38	16 43	16 48	16 53							
Shadwell	d	16 25										16 29		16 35	16 40	16 45	16 50	16 55							
Whitechapel	d	16 27										16 32		16 37	16 42	16 47	16 52	16 57							
Shoreditch High Street	d	16 29										16 34		16 39	16 44	16 49	16 54	16 59							
Hoxton	d	16 31										16 36		16 41	16 46	16 51	16 56	17 01							
Haggerston	d	16 33										16 38		16 43	16 48	16 53	16 58	17 03							
Dalston Junction Stn ELL	a	16 35										16 40		16 50	16 50	16 55	17 05	17 05							
Canonbury	d	16 38										16 45			16 53	17 00		17 08							
Highbury & Islington	a	16 46										16 52			17 01	17 08		17 16							
	d																								
London Bridge 4 ⊖	a				16 03		16 06	16 19		16 18			16 31									16 33		16 36	16 49

Table 178

Sundays

29 July to 12 August

East London Line and Croydon - London Victoria to London Bridge

Network Diagram - see first Page of Table 177

Station		SN	FC 1	LO		SN	LO	LO	LO	LO	LO	SN	SE	SN		SE	SN	SN	SN	FC 1	LO	SN	LO	LO	
East Croydon	d	16 17	16 17															16 42	16 47	16 47					
West Croydon 4	d			16 25		16 34			16 42												16 55	17 04			
Norwood Junction 2	d	16 22		16 31		16 40			16 46										16 52		17 01	17 10			
Anerley	d	16 25		16 34					16 49										16 55		17 04				
Penge West	d	16 27		16 36					16 51										16 57		17 06				
London Victoria 15 ⊖	d												16 39				16 41								
Battersea Park 4	d																16 45								
Wandsworth Road	d																16 47								
Clapham High Street ⊖	d																16 49								
London Blackfriars 3 ⊖	d		16a37													16 42				17a07					
Denmark Hill 4	d												16 48			16 52	16 54								
Peckham Rye 4	d											16 45	16a51	16 53		16a55	16 56	17 10							
Queens Rd Peckham	d													16 56			16 59	17 12							
South Bermondsey	d													16 58			17 01	17 15							
Clapham Junction 10	d																								
Wandsworth Common	d																								
Balham 4 ⊖	d																								
Streatham Hill	d																								
West Norwood 4	d											16 57													
Gipsy Hill	d											17 00													
Crystal Palace 4	d							16 46			17 01	17a02												17 16	
Sydenham	d	16 29		16 39		16 44		16 49	16 54		17 04								16 59		17 09	17 14		17 19	
Forest Hill 4	d	16 32		16 41		16 47		16 52	16 56		17 07								17 02		17 11	17 17		17 22	
Honor Oak Park	d	16 34		16 44		16 49		16 54	16 59		17 09								17 04		17 14	17 19		17 24	
Brockley	d	16 37		16 46		16 52		16 57	17 01		17 12								17 07		17 16	17 22		17 27	
New Cross Gate 4	a	16 39		16 49		16 54		16 59	17 04		17 14								17 09		17 19	17 24		17 29	
	d	16 39		16 49		16 54		16 59	17 04		17 14								17 09		17 19	17 24		17 29	
New Cross ELL	d						16 54			17 09													17 24		
Surrey Quays	d			16 52			16 58	17 03	17 08	17 13	17 18										17 22		17 28	17 33	
Canada Water	d			16 54			17 00	17 05	17 10	17 15	17 20										17 24		17 30	17 35	
Rotherhithe	d			16 56			17 01	17 06	17 11	17 16	17 21										17 26		17 31	17 36	
Wapping	d			16 57			17 03	17 08	17 13	17 18	17 23										17 27		17 33	17 38	
Shadwell	d			16 59			17 05	17 10	17 15	17 20	17 25										17 29		17 35	17 40	
Whitechapel	d			17 02			17 07	17 12	17 17	17 22	17 27										17 32		17 37	17 42	
Shoreditch High Street	d			17 04			17 09	17 14	17 19	17 24	17 29										17 34		17 39	17 44	
Hoxton	d			17 06			17 11	17 16	17 21	17 26	17 31										17 36		17 41	17 46	
Haggerston	d			17 08			17 13	17 18	17 23	17 28	17 33										17 38		17 43	17 48	
Dalston Junction Stn ELL	a			17 10			17 20	17 20	17 25	17 35	17 35										17 40		17 50	17 50	
Canonbury	d			17 15				17 23	17 30		17 38										17 45			17 53	
Highbury & Islington	a			17 22				17 31	17 38		17 46										17 52			18 01	
	d																								
London Bridge 4 ⊖	a	16 48				17 01								17 03			17 06	17 19	17 18			17 31			

Station		LO	LO	LO	SN	SE	SN	SE	SN	SN		SN	FC 1	LO	SN	LO	LO	LO	LO	LO		SN	SE	SN	SE
East Croydon	d									17 12		17 17	17 17												
West Croydon 4	d	17 12												17 25	17 34			17 42							
Norwood Junction 2	d	17 16										17 22		17 31	17 40			17 46							
Anerley	d	17 19										17 25		17 34				17 49							
Penge West	d	17 21										17 27		17 36				17 51							
London Victoria 15 ⊖	d					17 09			17 11														17 39		
Battersea Park 4	d								17 15																
Wandsworth Road	d								17 17																
Clapham High Street ⊖	d								17 19																
London Blackfriars 3 ⊖	d							17 12					17a37												17 42
Denmark Hill 4	d					17 18		17 22	17 24														17 48		17 52
Peckham Rye 4	d				17 15	17a21	17 23	17a25	17 26	17 40												17 45	17a51	17 53	17a55
Queens Rd Peckham	d						17 26		17 29	17 42														17 56	
South Bermondsey	d						17 28		17 31	17 45														17 58	
Clapham Junction 10	d																								
Wandsworth Common	d																								
Balham 4 ⊖	d																								
Streatham Hill	d																								
West Norwood 4	d				17 27																	17 57			
Gipsy Hill	d				17 30																	18 00			
Crystal Palace 4	d			17 31	17a32												17 46			18 01		18a02			
Sydenham	d	17 24		17 34								17 29		17 39	17 44		17 49	17 54		18 04					
Forest Hill 4	d	17 26		17 37								17 32		17 41	17 47		17 52	17 56		18 07					
Honor Oak Park	d	17 29		17 39								17 34		17 44	17 49		17 54	17 59		18 09					
Brockley	d	17 31		17 42								17 37		17 46	17 52		17 57	18 01		18 12					
New Cross Gate 4	a	17 34		17 44								17 39		17 49	17 54		17 59	18 04		18 14					
	d	17 34		17 44								17 39		17 49	17 54		17 59	18 04		18 14					
New Cross ELL	d		17 39													17 54			18 09						
Surrey Quays	d	17 38	17 43	17 48										17 52		17 58	18 03	18 08	18 13	18 18					
Canada Water	d	17 40	17 45	17 50										17 54		18 00	18 05	18 10	18 15	18 20					
Rotherhithe	d	17 41	17 46	17 51										17 56		18 01	18 06	18 11	18 16	18 21					
Wapping	d	17 43	17 48	17 53										17 57		18 03	18 08	18 13	18 18	18 23					
Shadwell	d	17 45	17 50	17 55										17 59		18 05	18 10	18 15	18 20	18 25					
Whitechapel	d	17 47	17 52	17 57										18 02		18 07	18 12	18 17	18 22	18 27					
Shoreditch High Street	d	17 49	17 54	17 59										18 04		18 09	18 14	18 19	18 24	18 29					
Hoxton	d	17 51	17 56	18 01										18 06		18 11	18 16	18 21	18 26	18 31					
Haggerston	d	17 53	17 58	18 03										18 08		18 13	18 18	18 23	18 28	18 33					
Dalston Junction Stn ELL	a	17 55	18 05	18 05										18 10		18 20	18 20	18 26	18 35	18 35					
Canonbury	d	18 00		18 08										18 15			18 23	18 30		18 38					
Highbury & Islington	a	18 08		18 16										18 22			18 31	18 38		18 46					
	d																								
London Bridge 4 ⊖	a						17 33		17 36	17 49		17 48			18 01									18 03	

Table 178

Sundays

29 July to 12 August

East London Line and Croydon - London Victoria to London Bridge

Network Diagram - see first Page of Table 177

		SN	SN	SN	FC 1	LO		SN	LO	LO	LO	LO	LO	SN	SE	SN		SE	SN	SN	SN	FC 1	LO	SN	LO
East Croydon	d		17 42	17 47	17 47															18 12	18 17	18 17			
West Croydon 4	d					17 55		18 04			18 12												18 25	18 34	
Norwood Junction 2	d			17 52		18 01		18 10			18 16										18 22		18 31	18 40	
Anerley	d			17 55		18 04					18 19										18 25		18 34		
Penge West	d			17 57		18 06					18 21										18 27		18 36		
London Victoria 15	d	17 41													18 09				18 11						
Battersea Park 4	d	17 45																	18 15						
Wandsworth Road	d	17 47																	18 17						
Clapham High Street	d	17 49																	18 19						
London Blackfriars 3	d				18a07													18 12				18a37			
Denmark Hill 4	d	17 54													18 18			18 22	18 24						
Peckham Rye 4	d	17 56	18 10											18 15	18a21	18 23		18a25	18 26	18 40					
Queens Rd Peckham	d	17 59	18 12													18 26			18 29	18 42					
South Bermondsey	d	18 01	18 15													18 28			18 31	18 45					
Clapham Junction 10	d																								
Wandsworth Common	d																								
Balham 4	d																								
Streatham Hill	d																								
West Norwood 4	d													18 27											
Gipsy Hill	d													18 30											
Crystal Palace 4	d									18 16			18 31	18a32											
Sydenham	d			17 59		18 09		18 14		18 19	18 24		18 34								18 29		18 39	18 44	
Forest Hill 4	d			18 02		18 11		18 17		18 22	18 26		18 37								18 32		18 41	18 47	
Honor Oak Park	d			18 04		18 14		18 19		18 24	18 29		18 39								18 34		18 44	18 49	
Brockley	d			18 07		18 16		18 22		18 27	18 31		18 42								18 37		18 46	18 52	
New Cross Gate 4	a			18 09		18 19		18 24		18 29	18 34		18 44								18 39		18 49	18 54	
	d			18 09		18 19		18 24		18 29	18 34		18 44								18 40		18 49	18 54	
New Cross ELL	d								18 24			18 39													18 54
Surrey Quays	d					18 22			18 28	18 33	18 38	18 43	18 48										18 52		18 58
Canada Water	d					18 24			18 30	18 35	18 40	18 45	18 50										18 54		19 00
Rotherhithe	d					18 26			18 31	18 36	18 41	18 46	18 51										18 56		19 01
Wapping	d					18 27			18 33	18 38	18 43	18 48	18 53										18 57		19 03
Shadwell	d					18 29			18 35	18 40	18 45	18 50	18 55										18 59		19 05
Whitechapel	d					18 32			18 37	18 42	18 47	18 52	18 57										19 02		19 07
Shoreditch High Street	d					18 34			18 39	18 44	18 49	18 54	18 59										19 04		19 09
Hoxton	d					18 36			18 41	18 46	18 51	18 56	19 01										19 06		19 11
Haggerston	d					18 38			18 43	18 48	18 53	18 58	19 03										19 08		19 13
Dalston Junction Stn ELL	a					18 40			18 50	18 50	18 55	19 05	19 05										19 10		19 20
Canonbury	d					18 45				18 53	19 00		19 08										19 15		
Highbury & Islington	a					18 52				19 01	19 08		19 16										19 22		
	d																								
London Bridge 4	a	18 06	18 19	18 18				18 31								18 33			18 36	18 49	18 48			19 01	

		LO		LO	LO	LO	SN	SE	SN	SE	SN	SN		SN	FC 1	LO	SN	LO	LO	LO	LO	LO		SN	SE
East Croydon	d											18 42		18 47	18 47										
West Croydon 4	d			18 42												18 55	19 04			19 12					
Norwood Junction 2	d			18 46										18 52		19 01	19 10			19 16					
Anerley	d			18 49										18 55		19 04				19 19					
Penge West	d			18 51										18 57		19 06				19 21					
London Victoria 15	d							18 39			18 41														19 09
Battersea Park 4	d										18 45														
Wandsworth Road	d										18 47														
Clapham High Street	d										18 49														
London Blackfriars 3	d									18 42					19a07										
Denmark Hill 4	d							18 48		18 52	18 54														19 18
Peckham Rye 4	d						18 45	18a51	18 53	18a55	18 56	19 10												19 15	19a21
Queens Rd Peckham	d								18 56		18 59	19 12													
South Bermondsey	d								18 58		19 01	19 15													
Clapham Junction 10	d																								
Wandsworth Common	d																								
Balham 4	d																								
Streatham Hill	d																								
West Norwood 4	d						18 57																	19 27	
Gipsy Hill	d						19 00																	19 30	
Crystal Palace 4	d	18 46				19 01	19a02												19 16			19 31		19a32	
Sydenham	d	18 49		18 54		19 04								18 59		19 09	19 14		19 19	19 24		19 34			
Forest Hill 4	d	18 52		18 56		19 07								19 02		19 11	19 17		19 22	19 26		19 37			
Honor Oak Park	d	18 54		18 59		19 09								19 04		19 14	19 19		19 24	19 29		19 39			
Brockley	d	18 57		19 01		19 12								19 07		19 16	19 22		19 27	19 31		19 42			
New Cross Gate 4	a	18 59		19 04		19 14								19 09		19 19	19 24		19 29	19 34		19 44			
	d	18 59		19 04		19 14								19 09		19 19	19 24		19 29	19 34		19 44			
New Cross ELL	d				19 09													19 24			19 39				
Surrey Quays	d	19 03		19 08	19 13	19 18										19 22		19 28	19 33	19 38	19 43	19 48			
Canada Water	d	19 05		19 10	19 15	19 20										19 24		19 30	19 35	19 40	19 45	19 50			
Rotherhithe	d	19 06		19 11	19 16	19 21										19 26		19 31	19 36	19 41	19 46	19 51			
Wapping	d	19 08		19 13	19 18	19 23										19 27		19 33	19 38	19 43	19 48	19 53			
Shadwell	d	19 10		19 15	19 20	19 25										19 29		19 35	19 40	19 45	19 50	19 55			
Whitechapel	d	19 12		19 17	19 22	19 27										19 32		19 37	19 42	19 47	19 52	19 57			
Shoreditch High Street	d	19 14		19 19	19 24	19 29										19 34		19 39	19 44	19 49	19 54	19 59			
Hoxton	d	19 16		19 21	19 26	19 31										19 36		19 41	19 46	19 51	19 56	20 01			
Haggerston	d	19 18		19 23	19 28	19 33										19 38		19 43	19 48	19 53	19 58	20 03			
Dalston Junction Stn ELL	a	19 20		19 25	19 35	19 35										19 40		19 50	19 50	19 55	20 05	20 05			
Canonbury	d	19 23		19 30		19 38										19 45			19 53	20 00		20 08			
Highbury & Islington	a	19 31		19 38		19 46										19 52			20 01	20 08		20 16			
	d																								
London Bridge 4	a								19 03		19 06	19 19		19 18			19 31								

Table 178

Sundays

29 July to 12 August

East London Line and Croydon - London Victoria to London Bridge

Network Diagram - see first Page of Table 177

		SN	SE	SN	SN	SN	FC 1	LO		SN	LO	LO	LO	LO	LO	SN	SE	SN		SE	SN	SN	SN	LO	SN
East Croydon	d				19 12	19 17	19 17															19 42	19 47		
West Croydon 4	d							19 25		19 34			19 42											19 55	20 04
Norwood Junction 2	d					19 22		19 31		19 40			19 46										19 52	20 01	20 10
Anerley	d					19 25		19 34					19 49										19 55	20 04	
Penge West	d					19 27		19 36					19 51										19 57	20 06	
London Victoria 15 ⊖	d			19 11													19 39				19 41				
Battersea Park 4	d			19 15																	19 45				
Wandsworth Road	d			19 17																	19 47				
Clapham High Street ⊖	d			19 19																	19 49				
London Blackfriars 3 ⊖	d		19 12				19a37													19 42					
Denmark Hill 4	d		19 22	19 24													19 48			19 52	19 54				
Peckham Rye 4	d	19 23	19a25	19 26	19 40											19 45	19a51	19 53		19a55	19 56	20 10			
Queens Rd Peckham	d	19 26		19 29	19 42													19 56			19 59	20 12			
South Bermondsey	d	19 28		19 31	19 45													19 58			20 01	20 15			
Clapham Junction 10	d																								
Wandsworth Common	d																								
Balham 4 ⊖	d																								
Streatham Hill	d																								
West Norwood 4	d															19 57									
Gipsy Hill	d															20 00									
Crystal Palace 4	d											19 46			20 01	20a02									
Sydenham	d					19 29		19 39		19 44		19 49	19 54		20 04								19 59	20 09	20 14
Forest Hill 4	d					19 32		19 41		19 47		19 52	19 56		20 07								20 02	20 11	20 17
Honor Oak Park	d					19 34		19 44		19 49		19 54	19 59		20 09								20 04	20 14	20 19
Brockley	d					19 37		19 46		19 52		19 57	20 01		20 12								20 07	20 16	20 22
New Cross Gate 4	a					19 39		19 49		19 54		19 59	20 04		20 14								20 09	20 19	20 24
	d					19 39		19 49		19 54		19 59	20 04		20 14								20 09	20 19	20 24
New Cross ELL	d										19 54			20 09											
Surrey Quays	d							19 52			19 58	20 03	20 08	20 13	20 18									20 22	
Canada Water	d							19 54			20 00	20 05	20 10	20 15	20 20									20 24	
Rotherhithe	d							19 56			20 01	20 06	20 11	20 16	20 21									20 26	
Wapping	d							19 57			20 03	20 08	20 13	20 18	20 23									20 27	
Shadwell	d							19 59			20 05	20 10	20 15	20 20	20 25									20 29	
Whitechapel	d							20 02			20 07	20 12	20 17	20 22	20 27									20 32	
Shoreditch High Street	d							20 04			20 09	20 14	20 19	20 24	20 29									20 34	
Hoxton	d							20 06			20 11	20 16	20 21	20 26	20 31									20 36	
Haggerston	d							20 08			20 13	20 18	20 23	20 28	20 33									20 38	
Dalston Junction Stn ELL	a							20 10			20 20	20 20	20 25	20 35	20 35									20 40	
Canonbury	d							20 15				20 23	20 30		20 38									20 45	
Highbury & Islington	a							20 22				20 31	20 38		20 46									20 52	
	d																								
London Bridge 4 ⊖	a	19 33		19 36	19 49	19 48				20 01								20 03			20 06	20 19	20 18		20 31

		LO	LO	LO		LO	LO	SN	SN	SE	SN	SN	SN	LO		SN	LO	LO	LO	LO	LO	SN	SN	SE	
East Croydon	d											20 12	20 17												
West Croydon 4	d			20 12										20 25		20 34			20 42						
Norwood Junction 2	d			20 16									20 22	20 31		20 40			20 46						
Anerley	d			20 19									20 25	20 34					20 49						
Penge West	d			20 21									20 27	20 36					20 51						
London Victoria 15 ⊖	d										20 11														
Battersea Park 4	d										20 15														
Wandsworth Road	d										20 17														
Clapham High Street ⊖	d										20 19														
London Blackfriars 3 ⊖	d									20 12														20 42	
Denmark Hill 4	d									20 22	20 24													20 52	
Peckham Rye 4	d							20 15	20 23	20a25	20 26	20 40										20 45	20 53	20a55	
Queens Rd Peckham	d								20 26		20 29	20 42											20 56		
South Bermondsey	d								20 28		20 31	20 45											20 58		
Clapham Junction 10	d																								
Wandsworth Common	d																								
Balham 4 ⊖	d																								
Streatham Hill	d																								
West Norwood 4	d							20 27														20 57			
Gipsy Hill	d							20 30														21 00			
Crystal Palace 4	d		20 16				20 31	20a32										20 46			21 01	21a02			
Sydenham	d		20 19	20 24			20 34						20 29	20 39		20 44		20 49	20 54		21 04				
Forest Hill 4	d		20 22	20 26			20 37						20 32	20 41		20 47		20 52	20 56		21 07				
Honor Oak Park	d		20 24	20 29			20 39						20 34	20 44		20 49		20 54	20 59		21 09				
Brockley	d		20 27	20 31			20 42						20 37	20 46		20 52		20 57	21 01		21 12				
New Cross Gate 4	a		20 29	20 34			20 44						20 39	20 49		20 54		20 59	21 04		21 14				
	d		20 29	20 34			20 44						20 39	20 49		20 54		20 59	21 04		21 14				
New Cross ELL	d	20 24				20 39											20 54			21 09					
Surrey Quays	d	20 28	20 33	20 38		20 43	20 48							20 52			20 58	21 03	21 08	21 13	21 18				
Canada Water	d	20 30	20 35	20 40		20 45	20 50							20 54			21 00	21 05	21 10	21 15	21 20				
Rotherhithe	d	20 31	20 36	20 41		20 46	20 51							20 56			21 01	21 06	21 11	21 16	21 21				
Wapping	d	20 33	20 38	20 43		20 48	20 53							20 57			21 03	21 08	21 13	21 18	21 23				
Shadwell	d	20 35	20 40	20 45		20 50	20 55							20 59			21 05	21 10	21 15	21 20	21 25				
Whitechapel	d	20 37	20 42	20 47		20 52	20 57							21 02			21 07	21 12	21 17	21 22	21 27				
Shoreditch High Street	d	20 39	20 44	20 49		20 54	20 59							21 04			21 09	21 14	21 19	21 24	21 29				
Hoxton	d	20 41	20 46	20 51		20 56	21 01							21 06			21 11	21 16	21 21	21 26	21 31				
Haggerston	d	20 43	20 48	20 53		20 58	21 03							21 08			21 13	21 18	21 23	21 28	21 33				
Dalston Junction Stn ELL	a	20 50	20 50	20 55		21 05	21 05							21 10			21 20	21 20	21 25	21 35	21 35				
Canonbury	d		20 53	21 00			21 08							21 15				21 23	21 30		21 38				
Highbury & Islington	a		21 01	21 08			21 16							21 22				21 31	21 38		21 46				
	d																								
London Bridge 4 ⊖	a								20 33		20 36	20 49	20 48			21 01							21 03		

Table 178

Sundays

29 July to 12 August

East London Line and Croydon - London Victoria to London Bridge

Network Diagram - see first Page of Table 177

		SN	SN	SN	LO	SN	LO	LO	LO	LO		LO	SN	SN	SE	SN	SN	SN	LO	SN		LO	LO	LO	LO
East Croydon (tram)	d		20 42	20 47													21 12	21 17							
West Croydon 4 (tram)	d				20 55	21 04			21 12										21 25	21 34				21 42	
Norwood Junction 2	d			20 52	21 01	21 10			21 16									21 22	21 31	21 40				21 46	
Anerley	d			20 55	21 04				21 19									21 25	21 34					21 49	
Penge West	d			20 57	21 06				21 21									21 27	21 36					21 51	
London Victoria 15 ⊖	d	20 41														21 11									
Battersea Park 4	d	20 45														21 15									
Wandsworth Road	d	20 47														21 17									
Clapham High Street ⊖	d	20 49														21 19									
London Blackfriars 3 ⊖	d														21 12										
Denmark Hill 4	d	20 54													21 22	21 24									
Peckham Rye 4	d	20 56	21 10										21 15	21 23	21a25	21 26	21 40								
Queens Rd Peckham	d	20 59	21 12											21 26		21 29	21 42								
South Bermondsey	d	21 01	21 15											21 28		21 31	21 45								
Clapham Junction 10	d																								
Wandsworth Common	d																								
Balham 4 ⊖	d																								
Streatham Hill	d																								
West Norwood 4	d												21 27												
Gipsy Hill	d												21 30												
Crystal Palace 4	d							21 16				21 31	21a32										21 46		
Sydenham	d			20 59	21 09	21 14		21 19	21 24			21 34						21 29	21 39	21 44			21 49	21 54	
Forest Hill 4	d			21 02	21 11	21 17		21 22	21 26			21 37						21 32	21 41	21 47			21 52	21 56	
Honor Oak Park	d			21 04	21 14	21 19		21 24	21 29			21 39						21 34	21 44	21 49			21 54	21 59	
Brockley	d			21 07	21 16	21 22		21 27	21 31			21 42						21 37	21 46	21 52			21 57	22 01	
New Cross Gate 4	a			21 09	21 19	21 24		21 29	21 34			21 44						21 39	21 49	21 54			21 59	22 04	
	d			21 09	21 19	21 24		21 29	21 34			21 44						21 39	21 49	21 54			21 59	22 04	
New Cross ELL	d						21 24			21 39												21 54			22 09
Surrey Quays	d				21 22		21 28	21 33	21 38	21 43		21 48							21 52			21 58	22 03	22 08	22 13
Canada Water	d				21 24		21 30	21 35	21 40	21 45		21 50							21 54			22 00	22 05	22 10	22 15
Rotherhithe	d				21 26		21 31	21 36	21 41	21 46		21 51							21 56			22 01	22 06	22 11	22 16
Wapping	d				21 27		21 33	21 38	21 43	21 48		21 53							21 57			22 03	22 08	22 13	22 18
Shadwell	d				21 29		21 35	21 40	21 45	21 50		21 55							21 59			22 05	22 10	22 15	22 20
Whitechapel	d				21 32		21 37	21 42	21 47	21 52		21 57							22 02			22 07	22 12	22 17	22 22
Shoreditch High Street	d				21 34		21 39	21 44	21 49	21 54		21 59							22 04			22 09	22 14	22 19	22 24
Hoxton	d				21 36		21 41	21 46	21 51	21 56		22 01							22 06			22 11	22 16	22 21	22 26
Haggerston	d				21 38		21 43	21 48	21 53	21 58		22 03							22 08			22 13	22 18	22 23	22 28
Dalston Junction Stn ELL	a				21 40		21 50	21 50	21 55	22 05		22 05							22 10			22 20	22 20	22 25	22 36
Canonbury	d				21 45			21 53	22 00			22 08							22 15				22 23	22 30	
Highbury & Islington	a				21 52			22 01	22 08			22 16							22 22				22 31	22 38	
	d																								
London Bridge 4 ⊖	a	21 06	21 19	21 18		21 31								21 33		21 36	21 49	21 48		22 01					

		LO	SN	SN	SE	SN		SN	SN	LO	SN	LO	LO	LO	LO	SN		SN	SE	SN	SN	SN	LO	SN	LO
East Croydon (tram)	d							21 42	21 47												22 12	22 17			
West Croydon 4 (tram)	d									21 55	22 04		22 12										22 25	22 34	
Norwood Junction 2	d								21 52	22 01	22 10		22 16									22 22	22 31	22 40	
Anerley	d								21 55	22 04			22 19									22 25	22 34		
Penge West	d								21 57	22 06			22 21									22 27	22 36		
London Victoria 15 ⊖	d					21 41														22 11					
Battersea Park 4	d					21 45														22 15					
Wandsworth Road	d					21 47														22 17					
Clapham High Street ⊖	d					21 49														22 19					
London Blackfriars 3 ⊖	d				21 42														22 12						
Denmark Hill 4	d				21 52	21 54													22 22	22 24					
Peckham Rye 4	d		21 45	21 53	21a55	21 56		22 10								22 15		22 23	22a25	22 26	22 40				
Queens Rd Peckham	d			21 56		21 59		22 12										22 26		22 29	22 42				
South Bermondsey	d			21 58		22 01		22 15										22 28		22 31	22 45				
Clapham Junction 10	d																								
Wandsworth Common	d																								
Balham 4 ⊖	d																								
Streatham Hill	d																								
West Norwood 4	d		21 57													22 27									
Gipsy Hill	d		22 00													22 30									
Crystal Palace 4	d	22 01	22a02									22 16			22 31	22a32									22 46
Sydenham	d	22 04							21 59	22 09	22 14	22 19	22 24		22 34							22 29	22 39	22 44	22 49
Forest Hill 4	d	22 07							22 02	22 11	22 17	22 22	22 26		22 37							22 32	22 41	22 47	22 52
Honor Oak Park	d	22 09							22 04	22 14	22 19	22 24	22 29		22 39							22 34	22 44	22 49	22 54
Brockley	d	22 12							22 07	22 16	22 22	22 27	22 31		22 42							22 37	22 46	22 52	22 57
New Cross Gate 4	a	22 14							22 09	22 19	22 24	22 29	22 34		22 44							22 39	22 49	22 54	22 59
	d	22 14							22 09	22 19	22 24	22 29	22 34		22 44							22 39	22 49	22 54	22 59
New Cross ELL	d													22 39											
Surrey Quays	d	22 18								22 22		22 33	22 38	22 43	22 48								22 52		23 03
Canada Water	d	22 20								22 24		22 35	22 40	22 45	22 50								22 54		23 05
Rotherhithe	d	22 21								22 26		22 36	22 41	22 46	22 51								22 56		23 06
Wapping	d	22 23								22 27		22 38	22 43	22 48	22 53								22 57		23 08
Shadwell	d	22 25								22 29		22 40	22 45	22 50	22 55								22 59		23 10
Whitechapel	d	22 27								22 32		22 42	22 47	22 52	22 57								23 02		23 12
Shoreditch High Street	d	22 29								22 34		22 44	22 49	22 54	22 59								23 04		23 14
Hoxton	d	22 31								22 36		22 46	22 51	22 56	23 01								23 06		23 16
Haggerston	d	22 33								22 38		22 48	22 53	22 58	23 03								23 08		23 18
Dalston Junction Stn ELL	a	22 35								22 40		22 50	22 55	23 05	23 05								23 10		23 20
Canonbury	d	22 38								22 45		22 53	23 00		23 08								23 15		23 23
Highbury & Islington	a	22 46								22 52		23 01	23 08		23 16								23 22		23 31
	d																								
London Bridge 4 ⊖	a			22 03		22 06		22 19	22 18		22 31							22 33		22 36	22 49	22 48		23 01	

Sundays

29 July to 12 August

East London Line and Croydon - London Victoria to London Bridge

Network Diagram - see first Page of Table 177

		LO		SN	SN	SE	SN	SN	SN	LO	LO	LO		SN	SN	SE	SN	LO	LO	LO	SN	SE			
East Croydon	d							22 42	22 47																
West Croydon 4	d	22 42									22 55								23 25						
Norwood Junction 2	d	22 46							22 52		23 01								23 31						
Anerley	d	22 49							22 55		23 04								23 34						
Penge West	d	22 51							22 57		23 06								23 36						
London Victoria 15 ⊖	d						22 41										23 11								
Battersea Park 4	d						22 45										23 15								
Wandsworth Road	d						22 47										23 17								
Clapham High Street ⊖	d						22 49										23 19								
London Blackfriars 3 ⊖	d					22 42										23 12						23 42			
Denmark Hill 4	d					22 52	22 54									23 22	23 24					23 52			
Peckham Rye 4	d			22 45	22 53	22a55	22 56	23 10						23 15	23 23	23a25	23 26				23 53	23a55			
Queens Rd Peckham	d				22 56		22 59	23 12							23 26		23 29				23 56				
South Bermondsey	d				22 58		23 01	23 15							23 28		23 31				23 58				
Clapham Junction 10	d																								
Wandsworth Common	d																								
Balham 4 ⊖	d																								
Streatham Hill	d																								
West Norwood 4	d			22 57										23 27											
Gipsy Hill	d			23 00										23 30											
Crystal Palace 4	d			23a02								23 16		23a32						23 46					
Sydenham	d	22 54							22 59		23 09	23 19							23 39	23 49					
Forest Hill 4	d	22 56							23 02		23 11	23 22							23 41	23 52					
Honor Oak Park	d	22 59							23 04		23 14	23 24							23 44	23 54					
Brockley	d	23 01							23 07		23 16	23 27							23 46	23 57					
New Cross Gate 4	a	23 04							23 09		23 19	23 29							23 49	23 59					
	d	23 04							23 09		23 19	23 29							23 49	23 59					
New Cross ELL	d									23 09								23 39							
Surrey Quays	d	23 08								23 13	23 22	23 33						23 43	23 52	00 02					
Canada Water	d	23 10								23 15	23 24	23 35						23 45	23 54	00 05					
Rotherhithe	d	23 11								23 16	23 26	23 36						23 46	23 56	00 06					
Wapping	d	23 13								23 18	23 27	23 38						23 48	23 57	00 08					
Shadwell	d	23 15								23 20	23 29	23 40						23 50	23 59	00 10					
Whitechapel	d	23 17								23 22	23 32	23 42						23 52	00 02	00 12					
Shoreditch High Street	d	23 19								23 24	23 34	23 44						23 54	00 04	00 14					
Hoxton	d	23 21								23 26	23 36	23 46						23 56	00 06	00 16					
Haggerston	d	23 23								23 28	23 38	23 48						23 58	00 08	00 18					
Dalston Junction Stn ELL	a	23 25								23 35	23 40	23 50						00 02	00 10	00 20					
Canonbury	d	23 30									23 45	23 53						00 05	00 14	00 23					
Highbury & Islington	a	23 38									23 54	00 01						00 14	00 21	00 31					
	d																								
London Bridge 4 ⊖	a				23 03		23 06	23 19	23 18						23 33		23 36				00 03				

Sundays

19 August to 26 August

		LO	LO	SN	SN	SN	SN	LO	SN	LO		SN	LO	SN	SN	SN	SN	LO	SN	LO		SN	SE	SN	SN
East Croydon	d								06 47						07 12	07 17									
West Croydon 4	d	23p22						06 42					07 12				07 22		07 34	07 42					
Norwood Junction 2	d	23p28						06 47	06 52				07 17			07 22	07 27		07 40	07 47					
Anerley	d	23p31						06 50	06 55				07 20			07 25				07 50					
Penge West	d	23p33						06 52	06 57				07 22			07 27				07 52					
London Victoria 15 ⊖	d			23p19	23p54																				07 41
Battersea Park 4	d			23p23	23p58																				07 45
Wandsworth Road	d																								07 47
Clapham High Street ⊖	d																								07 49
London Blackfriars 3 ⊖	d																						07 38		
Denmark Hill 4	d																						07 48		07 54
Peckham Rye 4	d					00 12	00 42					07 09		07 23	07 39							07 45	07a51	07 53	07 56
Queens Rd Peckham	d											07 12		07 26	07 42									07 56	07 59
South Bermondsey	d											07 14		07 28	07 44									07 58	08 01
Clapham Junction 10	d			23p27	00 02																				
Wandsworth Common	d			23p30	00 05																				
Balham 4 ⊖	d			23p32	00 07																				
Streatham Hill	d			23p35	00 10																				
West Norwood 4	d			23p40	00 14	00 24	00 54															07 57			
Gipsy Hill	d			23p43	00 17	00 27	00 57															08 00			
Crystal Palace 4	d		23p43	23p51	00 21	00a29	00a59			07 07							07a31	07 37				08a02			
Sydenham	d	23p36	23p46	23p54	00 24			06 55	06 59	07 10			07 25			07 29		07 40	07 44	07 55					
Forest Hill 4	d	23p38	23p49	23p57	00 27			06 57	07 02	07 13			07 27			07 32		07 43	07 47	07 57					
Honor Oak Park	d	23p41	23p51	23p59	00 29			07 00	07 04	07 15			07 30			07 34		07 45	07 49	08 00					
Brockley	d	23p43	23p54	00 02	00 32			07 02	07 07	07 18			07 32			07 37		07 48	07 52	08 02					
New Cross Gate 4	a	23p46	23p56	00 04	00 35			07 05	07 09	07 20			07 35			07 39		07 50	07 54	08 05					
	d	23p46	23p56	00 04	00 35			07 05	07 09	07 20			07 35			07 39		07 50	07 54	08 05					
New Cross ELL	d																								
Surrey Quays	d	23p49	23p59					07 09		07 24			07 39					07 54		08 09					
Canada Water	d	23p51	00 02					07 11		07 26			07 41					07 56		08 11					
Rotherhithe	d	23p53	00 03					07 12		07 27			07 42					07 57		08 12					
Wapping	d	23p54	00 05					07 14		07 29			07 44					07 59		08 14					
Shadwell	d	23p56	00 07					07 16		07 31			07 46					08 01		08 16					
Whitechapel	d	23p59	00 09					07 18		07 33			07 48					08 03		08 18					
Shoreditch High Street	d	00 01	00 11					07 20		07 35			07 50					08 05		08 20					
Hoxton	d	00 03	00 13					07 22		07 37			07 52					08 07		08 22					
Haggerston	d	00 05	00 15					07 24		07 39			07 54					08 09		08 24					
Dalston Junction Stn ELL	a	00 07	00 17					07 26		07 41			07 56					08 11		08 26					
Canonbury	d	00 12	00 20					07 31		07 44			08 01					08 14		08 31					
Highbury & Islington	a	00 16	00 25					07 36		07 49			08 06					08 21		08 36					
	d																								
London Bridge 4 ⊖	a			00 11	00 41				07 17			07 19		07 33	07 50	07 48			08 01					08 03	08 06

Table 178

Sundays

19 August to 26 August

East London Line and Croydon - London Victoria to London Bridge

Network Diagram - see first Page of Table 177

		SN	SN	SN	LO	SN		LO	SN	SE	SN	SN	SN	SN	LO	SN		SN	SE	SN	SN	SN	LO	LO	SN
East Croydon	d	07 42	07 47										08 12	08 17								08 42			08 47
West Croydon 4	d			07 52		08 04		08 12								08 34								08 42	
Norwood Junction 2	d		07 52	07 57		08 10		08 17						08 22		08 40								08 47	08 52
Anerley	d		07 55					08 20						08 25										08 50	08 55
Penge West	d		07 57					08 22						08 27										08 52	08 57
London Victoria 15 ⊖	d											08 11									08 41				
Battersea Park 4	d											08 15									08 45				
Wandsworth Road	d											08 17									08 47				
Clapham High Street ⊖	d											08 19									08 49				
London Blackfriars 3 ⊖	d									08 08									08 38						
Denmark Hill 4	d									08 18		08 24							08 48		08 54				
Peckham Rye 4	d	08 10							08 15	08a21	08 23	08 26	08 40					08 45	08a51	08 53	08 56	09 10			
Queens Rd Peckham	d	08 12									08 26	08 29	08 42							08 56	08 59	09 12			
South Bermondsey	d	08 15									08 28	08 31	08 45							08 58	09 01	09 15			
Clapham Junction 10	d																								
Wandsworth Common	d																								
Balham 4 ⊖	d																								
Streatham Hill	d																								
West Norwood 4	d								08 27									08 57							
Gipsy Hill	d								08 30									09 00							
Crystal Palace 4	d			08a01	08 07				08a32						08 37			09a02							
Sydenham	d		07 59		08 10	08 14		08 25						08 29	08 40	08 44								08 55	08 59
Forest Hill 4	d		08 02		08 13	08 17		08 27						08 32	08 43	08 47								08 57	09 02
Honor Oak Park	d		08 04		08 15	08 19		08 30						08 34	08 45	08 49								09 00	09 04
Brockley	d		08 07		08 18	08 22		08 32						08 37	08 48	08 52								09 02	09 07
New Cross Gate 4	a		08 09		08 20	08 24		08 35						08 39	08 50	08 54								09 05	09 09
	d		08 09		08 20	08 24		08 35						08 39	08 50	08 54								09 05	09 09
New Cross ELL	d																						08 54		
Surrey Quays	d				08 24			08 39							08 54								08 58	09 09	
Canada Water	d				08 26			08 41							08 56								09 00	09 11	
Rotherhithe	d				08 27			08 42							08 57								09 01	09 12	
Wapping	d				08 29			08 44							08 59								09 03	09 14	
Shadwell	d				08 31			08 46							09 01								09 05	09 16	
Whitechapel	d				08 33			08 48							09 03								09 07	09 18	
Shoreditch High Street	d				08 35			08 50							09 05								09 09	09 20	
Hoxton	d				08 37			08 52							09 07								09 11	09 22	
Haggerston	d				08 39			08 54							09 09								09 13	09 24	
Dalston Junction Stn ELL	a				08 41			08 56							09 11								09 15	09 26	
Canonbury	d				08 44			09 01							09 14								09 20	09 31	
Highbury & Islington	a				08 51			09 06							09 21								09 27	09 36	
	d																								
London Bridge 4 ⊖	a	08 19	08 17			08 31					08 33	08 36	08 49	08 48		09 01				09 03	09 06	09 19			09 18

		LO		LO	SN	SN	SE	SN	SN	SN	LO	LO		SN	LO	LO	SN	SN	SE	SN	SN	SN		FC 1	LO
East Croydon	d									09 12				09 17								09 42		09 47	
West Croydon 4	d				09 04							09 12					09 34								
Norwood Junction 2	d				09 10							09 17		09 22			09 40								
Anerley	d											09 20		09 25											
Penge West	d											09 22		09 27											
London Victoria 15 ⊖	d								09 11												09 41				
Battersea Park 4	d								09 15												09 45				
Wandsworth Road	d								09 17												09 47				
Clapham High Street ⊖	d								09 19												09 49				
London Blackfriars 3 ⊖	d						09 08												09 38					10a07	
Denmark Hill 4	d						09 18		09 24										09 48		09 54				
Peckham Rye 4	d					09 15	09a21	09 23	09 26	09 40								09 45	09a51	09 53	09 56	10 10			
Queens Rd Peckham	d							09 26	09 29	09 42										09 56	09 59	10 12			
South Bermondsey	d							09 28	09 31	09 45										09 58	10 01	10 15			
Clapham Junction 10	d																								
Wandsworth Common	d																								
Balham 4 ⊖	d																								
Streatham Hill	d																								
West Norwood 4	d					09 27												09 57							
Gipsy Hill	d					09 30												10 00							
Crystal Palace 4	d			09 07		09a32										09 37		10a02							
Sydenham	d			09 10	09 14							09 25		09 29		09 40	09 44								
Forest Hill 4	d			09 13	09 17							09 27		09 32		09 43	09 47								
Honor Oak Park	d			09 15	09 19							09 30		09 34		09 45	09 49								
Brockley	d			09 18	09 22							09 32		09 37		09 48	09 52								
New Cross Gate 4	a			09 20	09 24							09 35		09 39		09 50	09 54								
	d			09 20	09 24							09 35		09 39		09 50	09 54								
New Cross ELL	d	09 09									09 24				09 39										09 54
Surrey Quays	d	09 13		09 24							09 28	09 39			09 43	09 54									09 58
Canada Water	d	09 15		09 26							09 30	09 41			09 45	09 56									10 00
Rotherhithe	d	09 16		09 27							09 31	09 42			09 46	09 57									10 01
Wapping	d	09 18		09 29							09 33	09 44			09 48	09 59									10 03
Shadwell	d	09 20		09 31							09 35	09 46			09 50	10 01									10 05
Whitechapel	d	09 22		09 33							09 37	09 48			09 52	10 03									10 07
Shoreditch High Street	d	09 24		09 35							09 39	09 50			09 54	10 05									10 09
Hoxton	d	09 26		09 37							09 41	09 52			09 56	10 07									10 11
Haggerston	d	09 28		09 39							09 43	09 54			09 58	10 09									10 13
Dalston Junction Stn ELL	a	09 31		09 41							09 45	09 56			10 01	10 11									10 15
Canonbury	d	09 36		09 44							09 50	10 01			10 06	10 14									10 20
Highbury & Islington	a	09 41		09 51							09 57	10 06			10 11	10 21									10 27
	d																								
London Bridge 4 ⊖	a				09 31			09 33	09 36	09 49				09 48			10 01			10 03	10 06	10 19			

Table 178

Sundays

19 August to 26 August

East London Line and Croydon - London Victoria to London Bridge

Network Diagram - see first Page of Table 177

		LO	SN	LO	LO	SN	SN	SE		SN	SN	SN	FC 1	LO	LO	SN	LO	LO		SN	SN	SE	SN	SN	SN
East Croydon ⇌	d		09 47									10 12	10 17			10 17									10 42
West Croydon 4 ⇌	d	09 42				10 04									10 12					10 34					
Norwood Junction 2	d	09 47	09 52			10 10									10 17	10 22				10 40					
Anerley	d	09 50	09 55												10 20	10 25									
Penge West	d	09 52	09 57												10 22	10 27									
London Victoria 15 ⊖	d										10 11													10 41	
Battersea Park 4	d										10 15													10 45	
Wandsworth Road	d										10 17													10 47	
Clapham High Street ⊖	d										10 19													10 49	
London Blackfriars 3 ⊖	d							10 08					10a37									10 38			
Denmark Hill 4	d							10 18			10 24											10 48		10 54	
Peckham Rye 4	d						10 15	10a21		10 23	10 26	10 40									10 45	10a51	10 53	10 56	11 10
Queens Rd Peckham	d									10 26	10 29	10 42											10 56	10 59	11 12
South Bermondsey	d									10 28	10 31	10 45											10 58	11 01	11 15
Clapham Junction 10	d																								
Wandsworth Common	d																								
Balham 4 ⊖	d																								
Streatham Hill	d																								
West Norwood 4	d						10 27														10 57				
Gipsy Hill	d						10 30														11 00				
Crystal Palace 4	d				10 07		10a32											10 37			11a02				
Sydenham	d	09 55	09 59		10 10	10 14									10 25	10 29		10 40		10 44					
Forest Hill 4	d	09 57	10 02		10 13	10 17									10 27	10 32		10 43		10 47					
Honor Oak Park	d	10 00	10 04		10 15	10 19									10 30	10 34		10 45		10 49					
Brockley	d	10 02	10 07		10 18	10 22									10 32	10 37		10 48		10 52					
New Cross Gate 4	a	10 05	10 09		10 20	10 24									10 35	10 39		10 50		10 54					
	d	10 05	10 09		10 20	10 24									10 35	10 39		10 50		10 54					
New Cross ELL	d			10 09										10 24			10 39								
Surrey Quays	d	10 09		10 13	10 24									10 28	10 39		10 43	10 54							
Canada Water	d	10 11		10 15	10 26									10 30	10 41		10 45	10 56							
Rotherhithe	d	10 12		10 16	10 27									10 31	10 42		10 46	10 57							
Wapping	d	10 14		10 18	10 29									10 33	10 44		10 48	10 59							
Shadwell	d	10 16		10 20	10 31									10 35	10 46		10 50	11 01							
Whitechapel	d	10 18		10 22	10 33									10 37	10 48		10 52	11 03							
Shoreditch High Street	d	10 20		10 24	10 35									10 39	10 50		10 54	11 05							
Hoxton	d	10 22		10 26	10 37									10 41	10 52		10 56	11 07							
Haggerston	d	10 24		10 28	10 39									10 43	10 54		10 58	11 09							
Dalston Junction Stn ELL	a	10 26		10 31	10 41									10 45	10 56		11 01	11 11							
Canonbury	d	10 31		10 36	10 44									10 50	11 01		11 06	11 14							
Highbury & Islington	a	10 36		10 41	10 51									10 57	11 06		11 11	11 21							
	d																								
London Bridge 4 ⊖	a		10 18			10 31				10 33	10 36	10 49				10 48				11 01			11 03	11 06	11 19

		FC 1	LO	LO		SN	LO	LO	SN	SN	SE	SN	SN	SN		FC 1	LO	LO	LO	SN	LO	LO	LO	SN	
East Croydon ⇌	d	10 47				10 47								11 12		11 17				11 17					
West Croydon 4 ⇌	d			10 42					11 04										11 12					11 34	
Norwood Junction 2	d			10 47		10 52			11 10										11 17	11 22				11 40	
Anerley	d			10 50		10 55													11 20	11 25					
Penge West	d			10 52		10 57													11 22	11 27					
London Victoria 15 ⊖	d												11 11												
Battersea Park 4	d												11 15												
Wandsworth Road	d												11 17												
Clapham High Street ⊖	d												11 19												
London Blackfriars 3 ⊖	d	11a07									11 08					11a37									
Denmark Hill 4	d										11 18		11 24												
Peckham Rye 4	d									11 15	11a21	11 23	11 26	11 40											
Queens Rd Peckham	d											11 26	11 29	11 42											
South Bermondsey	d											11 28	11 31	11 45											
Clapham Junction 10	d																								
Wandsworth Common	d																								
Balham 4 ⊖	d																								
Streatham Hill	d																								
West Norwood 4	d									11 27															
Gipsy Hill	d									11 30															
Crystal Palace 4	d							11 07		11a32													11 37		
Sydenham	d			10 55		10 59		11 10	11 14										11 25	11 29			11 40	11 44	
Forest Hill 4	d			10 57		11 02		11 13	11 17										11 27	11 32			11 43	11 47	
Honor Oak Park	d			11 00		11 04		11 15	11 19										11 30	11 34			11 45	11 49	
Brockley	d			11 02		11 07		11 18	11 22										11 32	11 37			11 48	11 52	
New Cross Gate 4	a			11 05		11 09		11 20	11 24										11 35	11 39			11 50	11 54	
	d			11 05		11 09		11 20	11 24										11 35	11 39			11 50	11 54	
New Cross ELL	d		10 54				11 09										11 24				11 39				
Surrey Quays	d		10 58	11 09			11 13	11 24									11 28	11 35	11 39		11 43	11 51	11 54		
Canada Water	d		11 00	11 11			11 15	11 26									11 30	11 37	11 41		11 45	11 53	11 56		
Rotherhithe	d		11 01	11 12			11 16	11 27									11 31	11 38	11 42		11 46	11 54	11 57		
Wapping	d		11 03	11 14			11 18	11 29									11 33	11 40	11 44		11 48	11 56	11 59		
Shadwell	d		11 05	11 16			11 20	11 31									11 35	11 42	11 46		11 50	11 58	12 01		
Whitechapel	d		11 07	11 18			11 22	11 33									11 37	11 44	11 48		11 52	12 00	12 03		
Shoreditch High Street	d		11 09	11 20			11 24	11 35									11 39	11 46	11 50		11 54	12 02	12 05		
Hoxton	d		11 11	11 22			11 26	11 37									11 41	11 48	11 52		11 56	12 04	12 07		
Haggerston	d		11 13	11 24			11 28	11 39									11 43	11 50	11 54		11 58	12 06	12 09		
Dalston Junction Stn ELL	a		11 15	11 26			11 31	11 41									11 46	11 52	11 56		12 01	12 08	12 11		
Canonbury	d		11 20	11 31			11 36	11 44										11 55	12 01			12 11	12 14		
Highbury & Islington	a		11 27	11 36			11 41	11 49										12 00	12 06			12 16	12 19		
	d																								
London Bridge 4 ⊖	a					11 18			11 31			11 33	11 36	11 49						11 48				12 01	

Table 178

Sundays

19 August to 26 August

East London Line and Croydon - London Victoria to London Bridge

Network Diagram - see first Page of Table 177

		SN	SE	SN	SN	SN	FC 1	LO	LO	LO		SN	LO	LO	LO	SN	LO	LO	LO	LO		LO	SN	SE	SN
East Croydon	d					11 42	11 47					11 47													
West Croydon 4	d									11 42						12 04			12 12						
Norwood Junction 2	d									11 47		11 52				12 10			12 16						
Anerley	d									11 50		11 55							12 19						
Penge West	d									11 52		11 57							12 21						
London Victoria 15 ⊖	d				11 41																				
Battersea Park 4	d				11 45																				
Wandsworth Road	d				11 47																				
Clapham High Street ⊖	d				11 49																				
London Blackfriars 3 ⊖	d		11 38				12a07																	12 08	
Denmark Hill 4	d		11 48		11 54																			12 18	
Peckham Rye 4	d	11 45	11a51	11 53	11 56	12 10																	12 15	12a21	12 23
Queens Rd Peckham	d			11 56	11 59	12 12																			12 26
South Bermondsey	d			11 58	12 01	12 15																			12 28
Clapham Junction 10	d																								
Wandsworth Common	d																								
Balham 4 ⊖	d																								
Streatham Hill	d																								
West Norwood 4	d	11 57																					12 27		
Gipsy Hill	d	12 00																					12 30		
Crystal Palace 4	d	12a02													12 07							12 31	12a32		
Sydenham	d									11 55		11 59			12 10	12 14			12 24			12 34			
Forest Hill 4	d									11 57		12 02			12 13	12 17			12 26			12 37			
Honor Oak Park	d									12 00		12 04			12 15	12 19			12 29			12 39			
Brockley	d									12 02		12 07			12 18	12 22			12 31			12 42			
New Cross Gate 4	a									12 05		12 09			12 20	12 24			12 34			12 44			
	d									12 05		12 09			12 20	12 24			12 34			12 44			
New Cross ELL	d							11 54					12 09				12 24			12 39					
Surrey Quays	d							11 58	12 05	12 09			12 13	12 21	12 24		12 28	12 35	12 38	12 43		12 48			
Canada Water	d							12 00	12 07	12 11			12 15	12 23	12 26		12 30	12 37	12 40	12 45		12 50			
Rotherhithe	d							12 01	12 08	12 12			12 16	12 24	12 27		12 31	12 38	12 41	12 46		12 51			
Wapping	d							12 03	12 10	12 14			12 18	12 26	12 29		12 33	12 40	12 43	12 48		12 53			
Shadwell	d							12 05	12 12	12 16			12 20	12 28	12 31		12 35	12 42	12 45	12 50		12 55			
Whitechapel	d							12 07	12 14	12 18			12 22	12 30	12 33		12 37	12 44	12 47	12 52		12 57			
Shoreditch High Street	d							12 09	12 16	12 20			12 24	12 32	12 35		12 39	12 46	12 49	12 54		12 59			
Hoxton	d							12 11	12 18	12 22			12 26	12 34	12 37		12 41	12 48	12 51	12 56		13 01			
Haggerston	d							12 13	12 20	12 24			12 28	12 36	12 39		12 43	12 50	12 53	12 58		13 03			
Dalston Junction Stn ELL	a							12 16	12 22	12 26			12 31	12 38	12 41		12 46	12 52	12 55	13 01		13 05			
Canonbury	d								12 25	12 31				12 41	12 44			12 55	13 00			13 08			
Highbury & Islington	a								12 30	12 36				12 46	12 49			13 00	13 05			13 13			
	d																								
London Bridge 4 ⊖	a			12 03	12 06	12 19						12 18				12 31									12 33

		SN	SN	SN	FC 1	SN		LO	LO	LO	LO	LO	LO	SN	SE	SN		SN	SN	SN	FC 1	LO	SN	LO	LO
East Croydon	d		12 12	12 17	12 17														12 42	12 47	12 47				
West Croydon 4	d					12 34					12 42											12 57	13 04		
Norwood Junction 2	d			12 22		12 40					12 46									12 52		13 01	13 10		
Anerley	d			12 25							12 49									12 55		13 04			
Penge West	d			12 27							12 51									12 57		13 06			
London Victoria 15 ⊖	d	12 11																12 41							
Battersea Park 4	d	12 15																12 45							
Wandsworth Road	d	12 17																12 47							
Clapham High Street ⊖	d	12 19																12 49							
London Blackfriars 3 ⊖	d				12a37										12 38						13a07				
Denmark Hill 4	d	12 24													12 48			12 54							
Peckham Rye 4	d	12 26	12 40											12 45	12a51	12 53		12 56	13 10						
Queens Rd Peckham	d	12 29	12 42													12 56		12 59	13 12						
South Bermondsey	d	12 31	12 45													12 58		13 01	13 15						
Clapham Junction 10	d																								
Wandsworth Common	d																								
Balham 4 ⊖	d																								
Streatham Hill	d																								
West Norwood 4	d													12 57											
Gipsy Hill	d													13 00											
Crystal Palace 4	d									12 46			13 01	13a02											13 16
Sydenham	d			12 29		12 44				12 49	12 54		13 04							12 59		13 09	13 14		13 19
Forest Hill 4	d			12 32		12 47				12 52	12 56		13 07							13 02		13 11	13 17		13 22
Honor Oak Park	d			12 34		12 49				12 54	12 59		13 09							13 04		13 14	13 19		13 24
Brockley	d			12 37		12 52				12 57	13 01		13 12							13 07		13 16	13 22		13 27
New Cross Gate 4	a			12 39		12 54				12 59	13 04		13 14							13 09		13 19	13 24		13 29
	d			12 39		12 54				12 59	13 04		13 14							13 09		13 19	13 24		13 29
New Cross ELL	d								12 54			13 09												13 24	
Surrey Quays	d							12 53	12 58	13 03	13 08	13 13	13 18									13 23		13 28	13 33
Canada Water	d							12 55	13 00	13 05	13 10	13 15	13 20									13 25		13 30	13 35
Rotherhithe	d							12 56	13 01	13 06	13 11	13 16	13 21									13 26		13 31	13 36
Wapping	d							12 58	13 03	13 08	13 13	13 18	13 23									13 28		13 33	13 38
Shadwell	d							13 00	13 05	13 10	13 15	13 20	13 25									13 30		13 35	13 40
Whitechapel	d							13 02	13 07	13 12	13 17	13 22	13 27									13 32		13 37	13 42
Shoreditch High Street	d							13 04	13 09	13 14	13 19	13 24	13 29									13 34		13 39	13 44
Hoxton	d							13 06	13 11	13 16	13 21	13 26	13 31									13 36		13 41	13 46
Haggerston	d							13 08	13 13	13 18	13 23	13 28	13 33									13 38		13 43	13 48
Dalston Junction Stn ELL	a							13 10	13 16	13 20	13 25	13 31	13 35									13 40		13 46	13 50
Canonbury	d							13 15		13 23	13 30		13 38									13 45			13 53
Highbury & Islington	a							13 20		13 28	13 35		13 43									13 50			13 58
	d																								
London Bridge 4 ⊖	a	12 36	12 49	12 48		13 01										13 03		13 06	13 19	13 18			13 31		

East London Line and Croydon - London Victoria to London Bridge

Network Diagram - see first Page of Table 177

Station		LO		LO	LO	SN	SE	SN	SN	SN	SN	FC 1		LO	SN	LO	LO	LO	LO	LO	SN	SE		SN	SN
East Croydon ⇌	d									13 12	13 17	13 17													
West Croydon 4 ⇌	d	13 12												13 27	13 34			13 42							
Norwood Junction 2	d	13 16									13 22			13 31	13 40			13 46							
Anerley	d	13 19									13 25			13 34				13 49							
Penge West	d	13 21									13 27			13 36				13 51							
London Victoria 15 ⊖	d								13 11																13 41
Battersea Park 4	d								13 15																13 45
Wandsworth Road	d								13 17																13 47
Clapham High Street ⊖	d								13 19																13 49
London Blackfriars 3 ⊖	d						13 08					13a37										13 38			
Denmark Hill 4	d						13 18		13 24													13 48			13 54
Peckham Rye 4	d					13 15	13a21	13 23	13 26	13 40											13 45	13a51		13 53	13 56
Queens Rd Peckham	d							13 26	13 29	13 42														13 56	13 59
South Bermondsey	d							13 28	13 31	13 45														13 58	14 01
Clapham Junction 10	d																								
Wandsworth Common	d																								
Balham 4 ⊖	d																								
Streatham Hill	d																								
West Norwood 4	d					13 27															13 57				
Gipsy Hill	d					13 30															14 00				
Crystal Palace 4	d				13 31	13a32											13 46			14 01	14a02				
Sydenham	d	13 24			13 34						13 29			13 39	13 44		13 49	13 54		14 04					
Forest Hill 4	d	13 26			13 37						13 32			13 41	13 47		13 52	13 56		14 07					
Honor Oak Park	d	13 29			13 39						13 34			13 44	13 49		13 54	13 59		14 09					
Brockley	d	13 31			13 42						13 37			13 46	13 52		13 57	14 01		14 12					
New Cross Gate 4	a	13 34			13 44						13 39			13 49	13 54		13 59	14 04		14 14					
	d	13 34			13 44						13 39			13 49	13 54		13 59	14 04		14 14					
New Cross ELL	d			13 39												13 54			14 09						
Surrey Quays	d	13 38		13 43	13 48									13 53		13 58	14 03	14 08	14 13	14 18					
Canada Water	d	13 40		13 45	13 50									13 55		14 00	14 05	14 10	14 15	14 20					
Rotherhithe	d	13 41		13 46	13 51									13 56		14 01	14 06	14 11	14 16	14 21					
Wapping	d	13 43		13 48	13 53									13 58		14 03	14 08	14 13	14 18	14 23					
Shadwell	d	13 45		13 50	13 55									14 00		14 05	14 10	14 15	14 20	14 25					
Whitechapel	d	13 47		13 52	13 57									14 02		14 07	14 12	14 17	14 22	14 27					
Shoreditch High Street	d	13 49		13 54	13 59									14 04		14 09	14 14	14 19	14 24	14 29					
Hoxton	d	13 51		13 56	14 01									14 06		14 11	14 16	14 21	14 26	14 31					
Haggerston	d	13 53		13 58	14 03									14 08		14 13	14 18	14 23	14 28	14 33					
Dalston Junction Stn ELL	a	13 55		14 01	14 05									14 10		14 16	14 20	14 25	14 31	14 35					
Canonbury	d	14 00			14 08									14 15			14 23	14 30		14 38					
Highbury & Islington	a	14 05			14 13									14 20			14 28	14 35		14 43					
	d																								
London Bridge 4 ⊖	a							13 33	13 36	13 49	13 48				14 01									14 03	14 06

Station		SN	SN	FC 1	LO	SN	LO	LO		LO	LO	LO	SN	SE	SN	SN	SN	SN		FC 1	LO	SN	LO	LO	LO
East Croydon ⇌	d	13 42	13 47	13 47													14 12	14 17		14 17					
West Croydon 4 ⇌	d				13 57	14 04				14 12											14 27	14 34			14 42
Norwood Junction 2	d		13 52		14 01	14 10				14 16								14 22			14 31	14 40			14 46
Anerley	d		13 55		14 04					14 19								14 25			14 34				14 49
Penge West	d		13 57		14 06					14 21								14 27			14 36				14 51
London Victoria 15 ⊖	d															14 11									
Battersea Park 4	d															14 15									
Wandsworth Road	d															14 17									
Clapham High Street ⊖	d															14 19									
London Blackfriars 3 ⊖	d			14a07										14 08						14a37					
Denmark Hill 4	d													14 18		14 24									
Peckham Rye 4	d	14 10											14 15	14a21	14 23	14 26	14 40								
Queens Rd Peckham	d	14 12													14 26	14 29	14 42								
South Bermondsey	d	14 15													14 28	14 31	14 45								
Clapham Junction 10	d																								
Wandsworth Common	d																								
Balham 4 ⊖	d																								
Streatham Hill	d																								
West Norwood 4	d												14 27												
Gipsy Hill	d												14 30												
Crystal Palace 4	d							14 16				14 31	14a32											14 46	
Sydenham	d		13 59		14 09	14 14		14 19		14 24		14 34						14 29			14 39	14 44		14 49	14 54
Forest Hill 4	d		14 02		14 11	14 17		14 22		14 26		14 37						14 32			14 41	14 47		14 52	14 56
Honor Oak Park	d		14 04		14 14	14 19		14 24		14 29		14 39						14 34			14 44	14 49		14 54	14 59
Brockley	d		14 07		14 16	14 22		14 27		14 31		14 42						14 37			14 46	14 52		14 57	15 01
New Cross Gate 4	a		14 09		14 19	14 24		14 29		14 34		14 44						14 39			14 49	14 54		14 59	15 04
	d		14 09		14 19	14 24		14 29		14 34		14 44						14 39			14 49	14 54		14 59	15 04
New Cross ELL	d						14 24				14 39												14 54		
Surrey Quays	d				14 23		14 28	14 33		14 38	14 43	14 48									14 53		14 58	15 03	15 08
Canada Water	d				14 25		14 30	14 35		14 40	14 45	14 50									14 55		15 00	15 05	15 10
Rotherhithe	d				14 26		14 31	14 36		14 41	14 46	14 51									14 56		15 01	15 06	15 11
Wapping	d				14 28		14 33	14 38		14 43	14 48	14 53									14 58		15 03	15 08	15 13
Shadwell	d				14 30		14 35	14 40		14 45	14 50	14 55									15 00		15 05	15 10	15 15
Whitechapel	d				14 32		14 37	14 42		14 47	14 52	14 57									15 02		15 07	15 12	15 17
Shoreditch High Street	d				14 34		14 39	14 44		14 49	14 54	14 59									15 04		15 09	15 14	15 19
Hoxton	d				14 36		14 41	14 46		14 51	14 56	15 01									15 06		15 11	15 16	15 21
Haggerston	d				14 38		14 43	14 48		14 53	14 58	15 03									15 08		15 13	15 18	15 23
Dalston Junction Stn ELL	a				14 40		14 46	14 50		14 55	15 01	15 05									15 10		15 16	15 20	15 25
Canonbury	d				14 45			14 53		15 00		15 08									15 15			15 23	15 30
Highbury & Islington	a				14 50			14 58		15 05		15 13									15 20			15 28	15 35
	d																								
London Bridge 4 ⊖	a	14 19	14 18			14 31									14 33	14 36	14 49	14 48				15 01			

Table 178

Sundays

19 August to 26 August

East London Line and Croydon - London Victoria to London Bridge

Network Diagram - see first Page of Table 177

Station		LO	LO	SN		SE	SN	SN	SN	SN	FC 1	LO	SN	LO		LO	LO	LO	LO	SN	SE	SN	SN	SN	
East Croydon	d								14 42	14 47	14 47													15 12	
West Croydon 4	d											14 57	15 04				15 12								
Norwood Junction 2	d									14 52		15 01	15 10				15 16								
Anerley	d									14 55		15 04					15 19								
Penge West	d									14 57		15 06					15 21								
London Victoria 15 ⊖	d							14 41															15 11		
Battersea Park 4	d							14 45															15 15		
Wandsworth Road	d							14 47															15 17		
Clapham High Street ⊖	d							14 49															15 19		
London Blackfriars 3 ⊖	d					14 38					15a07										15 08				
Denmark Hill 4	d					14 48		14 54													15 18		15 24		
Peckham Rye 4	d			14 45		14a51	14 53	14 56	15 10											15 15	15a21	15 23	15 26	15 40	
Queens Rd Peckham	d						14 56	14 59	15 12													15 26	15 29	15 42	
South Bermondsey	d						14 58	15 01	15 15													15 28	15 31	15 45	
Clapham Junction 10	d																								
Wandsworth Common	d																								
Balham 4 ⊖	d																								
Streatham Hill	d																								
West Norwood 4	d			14 57																15 27					
Gipsy Hill	d			15 00																15 30					
Crystal Palace 4	d		15 01	15a02												15 16			15 31	15a32					
Sydenham	d		15 04							14 59		15 09	15 14			15 19	15 24		15 34						
Forest Hill 4	d		15 07							15 02		15 11	15 17			15 22	15 26		15 37						
Honor Oak Park	d		15 09							15 04		15 14	15 19			15 24	15 29		15 39						
Brockley	d		15 12							15 07		15 16	15 22			15 27	15 31		15 42						
New Cross Gate 4	a		15 14							15 09		15 19	15 24			15 29	15 34		15 44						
	d		15 14							15 09		15 19	15 24			15 29	15 34		15 44						
New Cross ELL	d	15 09												15 24				15 39							
Surrey Quays	d	15 13	15 18									15 23		15 28		15 33	15 38	15 43	15 48						
Canada Water	d	15 15	15 20									15 25		15 30		15 35	15 40	15 45	15 50						
Rotherhithe	d	15 16	15 21									15 26		15 31		15 36	15 41	15 46	15 51						
Wapping	d	15 18	15 23									15 28		15 33		15 38	15 43	15 48	15 53						
Shadwell	d	15 20	15 25									15 30		15 35		15 40	15 45	15 50	15 55						
Whitechapel	d	15 22	15 27									15 32		15 37		15 42	15 47	15 52	15 57						
Shoreditch High Street	d	15 24	15 29									15 34		15 39		15 44	15 49	15 54	15 59						
Hoxton	d	15 26	15 31									15 36		15 41		15 46	15 51	15 56	16 01						
Haggerston	d	15 28	15 33									15 38		15 43		15 48	15 53	15 58	16 03						
Dalston Junction Stn ELL	a	15 31	15 35									15 40		15 46		15 50	15 55	16 01	16 05						
Canonbury	d		15 38									15 45				15 53	16 00		16 08						
Highbury & Islington	a		15 43									15 50				15 58	16 05		16 13						
	d																								
London Bridge 4 ⊖	a						15 03	15 06	15 19	15 18			15 31									15 33	15 36	15 49	

Station		SN	FC 1	LO	SN	LO	LO	LO	LO	LO		SN	SE	SN	SN	SN	SN	FC 1	LO	SN		LO	LO	LO	LO
East Croydon	d	15 17	15 17													15 42	15 47	15 47							
West Croydon 4	d			15 27	15 34			15 42											15 57	16 04				16 12	
Norwood Junction 2	d	15 22		15 31	15 40			15 46									15 52		16 01	16 10				16 16	
Anerley	d	15 25		15 34				15 49									15 55		16 04					16 19	
Penge West	d	15 27		15 36				15 51									15 57		16 06					16 21	
London Victoria 15 ⊖	d														15 41										
Battersea Park 4	d														15 45										
Wandsworth Road	d														15 47										
Clapham High Street ⊖	d														15 49										
London Blackfriars 3 ⊖	d		15a37										15 38					16a07							
Denmark Hill 4	d												15 48		15 54										
Peckham Rye 4	d											15 45	15a51	15 53	15 56	16 10									
Queens Rd Peckham	d													15 56	15 59	16 12									
South Bermondsey	d													15 58	16 01	16 15									
Clapham Junction 10	d																								
Wandsworth Common	d																								
Balham 4 ⊖	d																								
Streatham Hill	d																								
West Norwood 4	d											15 57													
Gipsy Hill	d											16 00													
Crystal Palace 4	d						15 46			16 01		16a02											16 16		
Sydenham	d	15 29		15 39	15 44		15 49	15 54		16 04							15 59		16 09	16 14			16 19	16 24	
Forest Hill 4	d	15 32		15 41	15 47		15 52	15 56		16 07							16 02		16 11	16 17			16 22	16 26	
Honor Oak Park	d	15 34		15 44	15 49		15 54	15 59		16 09							16 04		16 14	16 19			16 24	16 29	
Brockley	d	15 37		15 46	15 52		15 57	16 01		16 12							16 07		16 16	16 22			16 27	16 31	
New Cross Gate 4	a	15 39		15 49	15 54		15 59	16 04		16 14							16 09		16 19	16 24			16 29	16 34	
	d	15 39		15 49	15 54		15 59	16 04		16 14							16 09		16 19	16 24			16 29	16 34	
New Cross ELL	d					15 54			16 09													16 24			16 39
Surrey Quays	d			15 53		15 58	16 03	16 08	16 13	16 18									16 23			16 28	16 33	16 38	16 43
Canada Water	d			15 55		16 00	16 05	16 10	16 15	16 20									16 25			16 30	16 35	16 40	16 45
Rotherhithe	d			15 56		16 01	16 06	16 11	16 16	16 21									16 26			16 31	16 36	16 41	16 46
Wapping	d			15 58		16 03	16 08	16 13	16 18	16 23									16 28			16 33	16 38	16 43	16 48
Shadwell	d			16 00		16 05	16 10	16 15	16 20	16 25									16 30			16 35	16 40	16 45	16 50
Whitechapel	d			16 02		16 07	16 12	16 17	16 22	16 27									16 32			16 37	16 42	16 47	16 52
Shoreditch High Street	d			16 04		16 09	16 14	16 19	16 24	16 29									16 34			16 39	16 44	16 49	16 54
Hoxton	d			16 06		16 11	16 16	16 21	16 26	16 31									16 36			16 41	16 46	16 51	16 56
Haggerston	d			16 08		16 13	16 18	16 23	16 28	16 33									16 38			16 43	16 48	16 53	16 58
Dalston Junction Stn ELL	a			16 10		16 16	16 20	16 25	16 31	16 35									16 40			16 46	16 50	16 55	17 01
Canonbury	d			16 15			16 23	16 30		16 38									16 45				16 53	17 00	
Highbury & Islington	a			16 20			16 28	16 35		16 43									16 50				16 58	17 05	
	d																								
London Bridge 4 ⊖	a	15 48			16 01									16 03	16 06	16 19	16 18			16 31					

Table 178

Sundays

19 August to 26 August

East London Line and Croydon - London Victoria to London Bridge

Network Diagram - see first Page of Table 177

		LO	SN	SE	SN	SN		SN	SN	FC 1	LO	SN	LO	LO	LO	LO		LO	SN	SE	SN	SN	SN	SN	FC 1
East Croydon	d							16 12	16 17	16 17													16 42	16 47	16 47
West Croydon 4	d										16 27	16 34			16 42										
Norwood Junction 2	d								16 22		16 31	16 40			16 46									16 52	
Anerley	d								16 25		16 34				16 49									16 55	
Penge West	d								16 27		16 36				16 51									16 57	
London Victoria 15 ⊖	d					16 11																16 41			
Battersea Park 4	d					16 15																16 45			
Wandsworth Road	d					16 17																16 47			
Clapham High Street ⊖	d					16 19																16 49			
London Blackfriars 3 ⊖	d			16 08						16a37										16 38					17a07
Denmark Hill 4	d			16 18		16 24														16 48		16 54			
Peckham Rye 4	d		16 15	16a21	16 23	16 26		16 40											16 45	16a51	16 53	16 56	17 10		
Queens Rd Peckham	d				16 26	16 29		16 42													16 56	16 59	17 12		
South Bermondsey	d				16 28	16 31		16 45													16 58	17 01	17 15		
Clapham Junction 10	d																								
Wandsworth Common	d																								
Balham 4 ⊖	d																								
Streatham Hill	d																								
West Norwood 4	d		16 27																16 57						
Gipsy Hill	d		16 30																17 00						
Crystal Palace 4	d	16 31	16a32											16 46				17 01	17a02						
Sydenham	d	16 34							16 29		16 39	16 44		16 49	16 54			17 04						16 59	
Forest Hill 4	d	16 37							16 32		16 41	16 47		16 52	16 56			17 07						17 02	
Honor Oak Park	d	16 39							16 34		16 44	16 49		16 54	16 59			17 09						17 04	
Brockley	d	16 42							16 37		16 46	16 52		16 57	17 01			17 12						17 07	
New Cross Gate 4	a	16 44							16 39		16 49	16 54		16 59	17 04			17 14						17 09	
	d	16 44							16 39		16 49	16 54		16 59	17 04			17 14						17 09	
New Cross ELL	d												16 54			17 09									
Surrey Quays	d	16 48									16 53		16 58	17 03	17 08	17 13		17 18							
Canada Water	d	16 50									16 55		17 00	17 05	17 10	17 15		17 20							
Rotherhithe	d	16 51									16 56		17 01	17 06	17 11	17 16		17 21							
Wapping	d	16 53									16 58		17 03	17 08	17 13	17 18		17 23							
Shadwell	d	16 55									17 00		17 05	17 10	17 15	17 20		17 25							
Whitechapel	d	16 57									17 02		17 07	17 12	17 17	17 22		17 27							
Shoreditch High Street	d	16 59									17 04		17 09	17 14	17 19	17 24		17 29							
Hoxton	d	17 01									17 06		17 11	17 16	17 21	17 26		17 31							
Haggerston	d	17 03									17 08		17 13	17 18	17 23	17 28		17 33							
Dalston Junction Stn ELL	a	17 05									17 10		17 16	17 20	17 25	17 31		17 35							
Canonbury	d	17 08									17 15			17 23	17 30			17 38							
Highbury & Islington	a	17 13									17 20			17 28	17 35			17 43							
	d																								
London Bridge 4 ⊖	a				16 33	16 36		16 49	16 48			17 01									17 03	17 06	17 19	17 18	

		LO		SN	LO	LO	LO	LO	LO	SN	SE	SN		SN	SN	SN	FC 1	LO	SN	LO	LO	LO		LO	LO
East Croydon	d														17 12	17 17	17 17								
West Croydon 4	d	16 57		17 04			17 12											17 27	17 34			17 42			
Norwood Junction 2	d	17 01		17 10			17 16									17 22		17 31	17 40			17 46			
Anerley	d	17 04					17 19									17 25		17 34				17 49			
Penge West	d	17 06					17 21									17 27		17 36				17 51			
London Victoria 15 ⊖	d													17 11											
Battersea Park 4	d													17 15											
Wandsworth Road	d													17 17											
Clapham High Street ⊖	d													17 19											
London Blackfriars 3 ⊖	d										17 08						17a37								
Denmark Hill 4	d										17 18			17 24											
Peckham Rye 4	d									17 15	17a21	17 23		17 26	17 40										
Queens Rd Peckham	d											17 26		17 29	17 42										
South Bermondsey	d											17 28		17 31	17 45										
Clapham Junction 10	d																								
Wandsworth Common	d																								
Balham 4 ⊖	d																								
Streatham Hill	d																								
West Norwood 4	d									17 27															
Gipsy Hill	d									17 30															
Crystal Palace 4	d					17 16			17 31	17a32											17 46				18 01
Sydenham	d	17 09		17 14		17 19	17 24		17 34							17 29		17 39	17 44		17 49	17 54			18 04
Forest Hill 4	d	17 11		17 17		17 22	17 26		17 37							17 32		17 41	17 47		17 52	17 56			18 07
Honor Oak Park	d	17 14		17 19		17 24	17 29		17 39							17 34		17 44	17 49		17 54	17 59			18 09
Brockley	d	17 16		17 22		17 27	17 31		17 42							17 37		17 46	17 52		17 57	18 01			18 12
New Cross Gate 4	a	17 19		17 24		17 29	17 34		17 44							17 39		17 49	17 54		17 59	18 04			18 14
	d	17 19		17 24		17 29	17 34		17 44							17 39		17 49	17 54		17 59	18 04			18 14
New Cross ELL	d				17 24			17 39												17 54				18 09	
Surrey Quays	d	17 23			17 28	17 33	17 38	17 43	17 48									17 53		17 58	18 03	18 08		18 13	18 18
Canada Water	d	17 25			17 30	17 35	17 40	17 45	17 50									17 55		18 00	18 05	18 10		18 15	18 20
Rotherhithe	d	17 26			17 31	17 36	17 41	17 46	17 51									17 56		18 01	18 06	18 11		18 16	18 21
Wapping	d	17 28			17 33	17 38	17 43	17 48	17 53									17 58		18 03	18 08	18 13		18 18	18 23
Shadwell	d	17 30			17 35	17 40	17 45	17 50	17 55									18 00		18 05	18 10	18 15		18 20	18 25
Whitechapel	d	17 32			17 37	17 42	17 47	17 52	17 57									18 02		18 07	18 12	18 17		18 22	18 27
Shoreditch High Street	d	17 34			17 39	17 44	17 49	17 54	17 59									18 04		18 09	18 14	18 19		18 24	18 29
Hoxton	d	17 36			17 41	17 46	17 51	17 56	18 01									18 06		18 11	18 16	18 21		18 26	18 31
Haggerston	d	17 38			17 43	17 48	17 53	17 58	18 03									18 08		18 13	18 18	18 23		18 28	18 33
Dalston Junction Stn ELL	a	17 40			17 46	17 50	17 55	18 01	18 05									18 10		18 16	18 20	18 25		18 31	18 35
Canonbury	d	17 45				17 53	18 00		18 08									18 15			18 23	18 30			18 38
Highbury & Islington	a	17 50				17 58	18 05		18 13									18 20			18 28	18 35			18 43
	d																								
London Bridge 4 ⊖	a			17 31								17 33		17 36	17 49	17 48			18 01						

Table 178

Sundays

19 August to 26 August

East London Line and Croydon - London Victoria to London Bridge

Network Diagram - see first Page of Table 177

		SN	SE	SN	SN	SN	SN	FC 1		LO	SN	LO	LO	LO	LO	LO	SN	SE		SN	SN	SN	SN	FC 1	LO
East Croydon	d					17 42	17 47	17 47														18 12	18 17	18 17	
West Croydon 4	d									17 57	18 04			18 12											18 27
Norwood Junction 2	d						17 52			18 01	18 10			18 16									18 22		18 31
Anerley	d						17 55			18 04				18 19									18 25		18 34
Penge West	d						17 57			18 06				18 21									18 27		18 36
London Victoria 15 ⊖	d				17 41																18 11				
Battersea Park 4	d				17 45																18 15				
Wandsworth Road	d				17 47																18 17				
Clapham High Street ⊖	d				17 49																18 19				
London Blackfriars 3 ⊖	d		17 38					18a07										18 08						18a37	
Denmark Hill 4	d		17 48		17 54													18 18			18 24				
Peckham Rye 4	d	17 45	17a51	17 53	17 56	18 10											18 15	18a21		18 23	18 26	18 40			
Queens Rd Peckham	d			17 56	17 59	18 12														18 26	18 29	18 42			
South Bermondsey	d			17 58	18 01	18 15														18 28	18 31	18 45			
Clapham Junction 10	d																								
Wandsworth Common	d																								
Balham 4 ⊖	d																								
Streatham Hill	d																								
West Norwood 4	d	17 57															18 27								
Gipsy Hill	d	18 00															18 30								
Crystal Palace 4	d	18a02											18 16			18 31	18a32								
Sydenham	d						17 59			18 09	18 14		18 19	18 24		18 34							18 29		18 39
Forest Hill 4	d						18 02			18 11	18 17		18 22	18 26		18 37							18 32		18 41
Honor Oak Park	d						18 04			18 14	18 19		18 24	18 29		18 39							18 34		18 44
Brockley	d						18 07			18 16	18 22		18 27	18 31		18 42							18 37		18 46
New Cross Gate 4	a						18 09			18 19	18 24		18 29	18 34		18 44							18 39		18 49
	d						18 09			18 19	18 24		18 29	18 34		18 44							18 40		18 49
New Cross ELL	d											18 24			18 39										
Surrey Quays	d									18 23		18 28	18 33	18 38	18 43	18 48									18 53
Canada Water	d									18 25		18 30	18 35	18 40	18 45	18 50									18 55
Rotherhithe	d									18 26		18 31	18 36	18 41	18 46	18 51									18 56
Wapping	d									18 28		18 33	18 38	18 43	18 48	18 53									18 58
Shadwell	d									18 30		18 35	18 40	18 45	18 50	18 55									19 00
Whitechapel	d									18 32		18 37	18 42	18 47	18 52	18 57									19 02
Shoreditch High Street	d									18 34		18 39	18 44	18 49	18 54	18 59									19 04
Hoxton	d									18 36		18 41	18 46	18 51	18 56	19 01									19 06
Haggerston	d									18 38		18 43	18 48	18 53	18 58	19 03									19 08
Dalston Junction Stn ELL	a									18 40		18 46	18 50	18 55	19 01	19 05									19 10
Canonbury	d									18 45			18 53	19 00		19 08									19 15
Highbury & Islington	a									18 50			18 58	19 05		19 13									19 20
	d																								
London Bridge 4 ⊖	a			18 03	18 06	18 19	18 18				18 31									18 33	18 36	18 49	18 48		

		SN	LO	LO		LO	LO	LO	SN	SE	SN	SN	SN	SN		FC 1	LO	SN	LO	LO	LO	LO	LO	SN	
East Croydon	d												18 42	18 47		18 47									
West Croydon 4	d	18 34				18 42											18 57	19 04			19 12				
Norwood Junction 2	d	18 40				18 46								18 52			19 01	19 10			19 16				
Anerley	d					18 49								18 55			19 04				19 19				
Penge West	d					18 51								18 57			19 06				19 21				
London Victoria 15 ⊖	d											18 41													
Battersea Park 4	d											18 45													
Wandsworth Road	d											18 47													
Clapham High Street ⊖	d											18 49													
London Blackfriars 3 ⊖	d									18 38						19a07									
Denmark Hill 4	d									18 48		18 54													
Peckham Rye 4	d								18 45	18a51	18 53	18 56	19 10											19 15	
Queens Rd Peckham	d										18 56	18 59	19 12												
South Bermondsey	d										18 58	19 01	19 15												
Clapham Junction 10	d																								
Wandsworth Common	d																								
Balham 4 ⊖	d																								
Streatham Hill	d																								
West Norwood 4	d								18 57															19 27	
Gipsy Hill	d								19 00															19 30	
Crystal Palace 4	d			18 46				19 01	19a02											19 16			19 31	19a32	
Sydenham	d	18 44		18 49		18 54		19 04						18 59			19 09	19 14		19 19	19 24		19 34		
Forest Hill 4	d	18 47		18 52		18 56		19 07						19 02			19 11	19 17		19 22	19 26		19 37		
Honor Oak Park	d	18 49		18 54		18 59		19 09						19 04			19 14	19 19		19 24	19 29		19 39		
Brockley	d	18 52		18 57		19 01		19 12						19 07			19 16	19 22		19 27	19 31		19 42		
New Cross Gate 4	a	18 54		18 59		19 04		19 14						19 09			19 19	19 24		19 29	19 34		19 44		
	d	18 54		18 59		19 04		19 14						19 09			19 19	19 24		19 29	19 34		19 44		
New Cross ELL	d		18 54				19 09												19 24			19 39			
Surrey Quays	d		18 58	19 03		19 08	19 13	19 18									19 23		19 28	19 33	19 38	19 43	19 48		
Canada Water	d		19 00	19 05		19 10	19 15	19 20									19 25		19 30	19 35	19 40	19 45	19 50		
Rotherhithe	d		19 01	19 06		19 11	19 16	19 21									19 26		19 31	19 36	19 41	19 46	19 51		
Wapping	d		19 03	19 08		19 13	19 18	19 23									19 28		19 33	19 38	19 43	19 48	19 53		
Shadwell	d		19 05	19 10		19 15	19 20	19 25									19 30		19 35	19 40	19 45	19 50	19 55		
Whitechapel	d		19 07	19 12		19 17	19 22	19 27									19 32		19 37	19 42	19 47	19 52	19 57		
Shoreditch High Street	d		19 09	19 14		19 19	19 24	19 29									19 34		19 39	19 44	19 49	19 54	19 59		
Hoxton	d		19 11	19 16		19 21	19 26	19 31									19 36		19 41	19 46	19 51	19 56	20 01		
Haggerston	d		19 13	19 18		19 23	19 28	19 33									19 38		19 43	19 48	19 53	19 58	20 03		
Dalston Junction Stn ELL	a		19 16	19 20		19 25	19 31	19 35									19 40		19 46	19 50	19 55	20 01	20 05		
Canonbury	d			19 23		19 30		19 38									19 45			19 53	20 00		20 08		
Highbury & Islington	a			19 28		19 35		19 43									19 50			19 58	20 05		20 13		
	d																								
London Bridge 4 ⊖	a	19 01									19 03	19 06	19 19	19 18				19 31							

Sundays

19 August to 26 August

East London Line and Croydon - London Victoria to London Bridge

Network Diagram - see first Page of Table 177

Station		SE	SN	SN	SN	SN	FC 1	LO	SN	LO		LO	LO	LO	LO	SN	SE	SN	SN	SN		SN	LO	SN	LO
East Croydon	d				19 12	19 17	19 17													19 42		19 47			
West Croydon 4	d							19 27	19 34				19 42										19 57	20 04	
Norwood Junction 2	d					19 22		19 31	19 40				19 46									19 52	20 01	20 10	
Anerley	d					19 25		19 34					19 49									19 55	20 04		
Penge West	d					19 27		19 36					19 51									19 57	20 06		
London Victoria 15 ⊖	d			19 11															19 41						
Battersea Park 4	d			19 15															19 45						
Wandsworth Road	d			19 17															19 47						
Clapham High Street ⊖	d			19 19															19 49						
London Blackfriars 3 ⊖	d	19 08					19a37										19 38								
Denmark Hill 4	d	19 18		19 24													19 48		19 54						
Peckham Rye 4	d	19a21	19 23	19 26	19 40											19 45	19a51	19 53	19 56	20 10					
Queens Rd Peckham	d		19 26	19 29	19 42													19 56	19 59	20 12					
South Bermondsey	d		19 28	19 31	19 45													19 58	20 01	20 15					
Clapham Junction 10	d																								
Wandsworth Common	d																								
Balham 4 ⊖	d																								
Streatham Hill	d																								
West Norwood 4	d															19 57									
Gipsy Hill	d															20 00									
Crystal Palace 4	d											19 46			20 01	20a02									
Sydenham	d					19 29		19 39	19 44			19 49	19 54		20 04							19 59	20 09	20 14	
Forest Hill 4	d					19 32		19 41	19 47			19 52	19 56		20 07							20 02	20 11	20 17	
Honor Oak Park	d					19 34		19 44	19 49			19 54	19 59		20 09							20 04	20 14	20 19	
Brockley	d					19 37		19 46	19 52			19 57	20 01		20 12							20 07	20 16	20 22	
New Cross Gate 4	a					19 39		19 49	19 54			19 59	20 04		20 14							20 09	20 19	20 24	
	d					19 39		19 49	19 54			19 59	20 04		20 14							20 09	20 19	20 24	
New Cross ELL	d									19 54				20 09											20 24
Surrey Quays	d							19 53		19 58		20 03	20 08	20 13	20 18								20 23		20 28
Canada Water	d							19 55		20 00		20 05	20 10	20 15	20 20								20 25		20 30
Rotherhithe	d							19 56		20 01		20 06	20 11	20 16	20 21								20 26		20 31
Wapping	d							19 58		20 03		20 08	20 13	20 18	20 23								20 28		20 33
Shadwell	d							20 00		20 05		20 10	20 15	20 20	20 25								20 30		20 35
Whitechapel	d							20 02		20 07		20 12	20 17	20 22	20 27								20 32		20 37
Shoreditch High Street	d							20 04		20 09		20 14	20 19	20 24	20 29								20 34		20 39
Hoxton	d							20 06		20 11		20 16	20 21	20 26	20 31								20 36		20 41
Haggerston	d							20 08		20 13		20 18	20 23	20 28	20 33								20 38		20 43
Dalston Junction Stn ELL	a							20 10		20 16		20 20	20 25	20 31	20 35								20 40		20 46
Canonbury	d							20 15				20 23	20 30		20 38								20 45		
Highbury & Islington	a							20 20				20 28	20 35		20 43								20 50		
	d																								
London Bridge 4 ⊖	a		19 33	19 36	19 49	19 48			20 01									20 03	20 06	20 19		20 18		20 31	

Station		LO	LO	LO	LO	SN		SE	SN	SN	SN	SN	LO	SN	LO	LO		LO	LO	LO	SN	SE	SN	SN	SN
East Croydon	d										20 12	20 17													20 42
West Croydon 4	d		20 12										20 27	20 34				20 42							
Norwood Junction 2	d		20 16									20 22	20 31	20 40				20 46							
Anerley	d		20 19									20 25	20 34					20 49							
Penge West	d		20 21									20 27	20 36					20 51							
London Victoria 15 ⊖	d									20 11														20 41	
Battersea Park 4	d									20 15														20 45	
Wandsworth Road	d									20 17														20 47	
Clapham High Street ⊖	d									20 19														20 49	
London Blackfriars 3 ⊖	d							20 08														20 38			
Denmark Hill 4	d							20 18		20 24												20 48		20 54	
Peckham Rye 4	d					20 15		20a21	20 23	20 26	20 40										20 45	20a51	20 53	20 56	21 10
Queens Rd Peckham	d								20 26	20 29	20 42												20 56	20 59	21 12
South Bermondsey	d								20 28	20 31	20 45												20 58	21 01	21 15
Clapham Junction 10	d																								
Wandsworth Common	d																								
Balham 4 ⊖	d																								
Streatham Hill	d																								
West Norwood 4	d					20 27															20 57				
Gipsy Hill	d					20 30															21 00				
Crystal Palace 4	d	20 16			20 31	20a32										20 46				21 01	21a02				
Sydenham	d	20 19	20 24		20 34							20 29	20 39	20 44		20 49		20 54		21 04					
Forest Hill 4	d	20 22	20 26		20 37							20 32	20 41	20 47		20 52		20 56		21 07					
Honor Oak Park	d	20 24	20 29		20 39							20 34	20 44	20 49		20 54		20 59		21 09					
Brockley	d	20 27	20 31		20 42							20 37	20 46	20 52		20 57		21 01		21 12					
New Cross Gate 4	a	20 29	20 34		20 44							20 39	20 49	20 54		20 59		21 04		21 14					
	d	20 29	20 34		20 44							20 39	20 49	20 54		20 59		21 04		21 14					
New Cross ELL	d			20 39											20 54				21 09						
Surrey Quays	d	20 33	20 38	20 43	20 48								20 53		20 58	21 03		21 08	21 13	21 18					
Canada Water	d	20 35	20 40	20 45	20 50								20 55		21 00	21 05		21 10	21 15	21 20					
Rotherhithe	d	20 36	20 41	20 46	20 51								20 56		21 01	21 06		21 11	21 16	21 21					
Wapping	d	20 38	20 43	20 48	20 53								20 58		21 03	21 08		21 13	21 18	21 23					
Shadwell	d	20 40	20 45	20 50	20 55								21 00		21 05	21 10		21 15	21 20	21 25					
Whitechapel	d	20 42	20 47	20 52	20 57								21 02		21 07	21 12		21 17	21 22	21 27					
Shoreditch High Street	d	20 44	20 49	20 54	20 59								21 04		21 09	21 14		21 19	21 24	21 29					
Hoxton	d	20 46	20 51	20 56	21 01								21 06		21 11	21 16		21 21	21 26	21 31					
Haggerston	d	20 48	20 53	20 58	21 03								21 08		21 13	21 18		21 23	21 28	21 33					
Dalston Junction Stn ELL	a	20 50	20 55	21 01	21 05								21 10		21 16	21 20		21 25	21 31	21 35					
Canonbury	d	20 53	21 00		21 08								21 15			21 23		21 30		21 38					
Highbury & Islington	a	20 58	21 05		21 13								21 20			21 28		21 35		21 43					
	d																								
London Bridge 4 ⊖	a								20 33	20 36	20 49	20 48		21 01									21 03	21 06	21 19

Table 178

Sundays

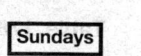

19 August to 26 August

East London Line and Croydon - London Victoria to London Bridge

Network Diagram - see first Page of Table 177

		SN		LO	SN	LO	LO	LO	LO	LO	SN	SE		SN	SN	SN	SN	LO	SN	LO	LO	LO		LO	LO
East Croydon	d	20 47														21 12	21 17								
West Croydon 4	d			20 57	21 04			21 12										21 27	21 34			21 42			
Norwood Junction 2	d	20 52		21 01	21 10			21 16									21 22	21 31	21 40			21 46			
Anerley	d	20 55		21 04				21 19									21 25	21 34				21 49			
Penge West	d	20 57		21 06				21 21									21 27	21 36				21 51			
London Victoria 15 ⊖	d														21 11										
Battersea Park 4	d														21 15										
Wandsworth Road	d														21 17										
Clapham High Street ⊖	d														21 19										
London Blackfriars 3 ⊖	d											21 08													
Denmark Hill 4	d											21 18			21 24										
Peckham Rye 4	d										21 15	21a21		21 23	21 26	21 40									
Queens Rd Peckham	d													21 26	21 29	21 42									
South Bermondsey	d													21 28	21 31	21 45									
Clapham Junction 10	d																								
Wandsworth Common	d																								
Balham 4 ⊖	d																								
Streatham Hill	d																								
West Norwood 4	d										21 27														
Gipsy Hill	d										21 30														
Crystal Palace 4	d						21 16			21 31	21a32										21 46				22 01
Sydenham	d	20 59		21 09	21 14		21 19	21 24		21 34							21 29	21 39	21 44		21 49	21 54			22 04
Forest Hill 4	d	21 02		21 11	21 17		21 22	21 26		21 37							21 32	21 41	21 47		21 52	21 56			22 07
Honor Oak Park	d	21 04		21 14	21 19		21 24	21 29		21 39							21 34	21 44	21 49		21 54	21 59			22 09
Brockley	d	21 07		21 16	21 22		21 27	21 31		21 42							21 37	21 46	21 52		21 57	22 01			22 12
New Cross Gate 4	a	21 09		21 19	21 24		21 29	21 34		21 44							21 39	21 49	21 54		21 59	22 04			22 14
	d	21 09		21 19	21 24		21 29	21 34		21 44							21 39	21 49	21 54		21 59	22 04			22 14
New Cross ELL	d					21 24			21 39											21 54				22 09	
Surrey Quays	d			21 23		21 28	21 33	21 38	21 43	21 48								21 53		21 58	22 03	22 08		22 13	22 18
Canada Water	d			21 25		21 30	21 35	21 40	21 45	21 50								21 55		22 00	22 05	22 10		22 15	22 20
Rotherhithe	d			21 26		21 31	21 36	21 41	21 46	21 51								21 56		22 01	22 06	22 11		22 16	22 21
Wapping	d			21 28		21 33	21 38	21 43	21 48	21 53								21 58		22 03	22 08	22 13		22 18	22 23
Shadwell	d			21 30		21 35	21 40	21 45	21 50	21 55								22 00		22 05	22 10	22 15		22 20	22 25
Whitechapel	d			21 32		21 37	21 42	21 47	21 52	21 57								22 02		22 07	22 12	22 17		22 22	22 27
Shoreditch High Street	d			21 34		21 39	21 44	21 49	21 54	21 59								22 04		22 09	22 14	22 19		22 24	22 29
Hoxton	d			21 36		21 41	21 46	21 51	21 56	22 01								22 06		22 11	22 16	22 21		22 26	22 31
Haggerston	d			21 38		21 43	21 48	21 53	21 58	22 03								22 08		22 13	22 18	22 23		22 28	22 33
Dalston Junction Stn ELL	a			21 40		21 46	21 50	21 55	22 01	22 05								22 10		22 16	22 20	22 25		22 31	22 35
Canonbury	d			21 45			21 53	22 00		22 08								22 15			22 23	22 30			22 38
Highbury & Islington	a			21 50			21 58	22 05		22 13								22 20			22 28	22 35			22 43
	d																								
London Bridge 4 ⊖	a	21 18			21 31									21 33	21 36	21 49	21 48		22 01						

		SN	SE	SN	SN	SN	SN	LO		SN	LO	LO	SN	SE	SN	SN	SN	SN		LO	LO	SN	LO	LO	SN
East Croydon	d					21 42	21 47										22 12	22 17							
West Croydon 4	d							21 57		22 04		22 12									22 27	22 34		22 42	
Norwood Junction 2	d						21 52	22 01		22 10		22 16						22 22			22 31	22 40		22 46	
Anerley	d						21 55	22 04				22 19						22 25			22 34			22 49	
Penge West	d						21 57	22 06				22 21						22 27			22 36			22 51	
London Victoria 15 ⊖	d				21 41											22 11									
Battersea Park 4	d				21 45											22 15									
Wandsworth Road	d				21 47											22 17									
Clapham High Street ⊖	d				21 49											22 19									
London Blackfriars 3 ⊖	d		21 38											22 08											
Denmark Hill 4	d		21 48		21 54									22 18		22 24									
Peckham Rye 4	d	21 45	21a51	21 53	21 56	22 10							22 15	22a21	22 23	22 26	22 40								22 45
Queens Rd Peckham	d			21 56	21 59	22 12									22 26	22 29	22 42								
South Bermondsey	d			21 58	22 01	22 15									22 28	22 31	22 45								
Clapham Junction 10	d																								
Wandsworth Common	d																								
Balham 4 ⊖	d																								
Streatham Hill	d																								
West Norwood 4	d	21 57											22 27												22 57
Gipsy Hill	d	22 00											22 30												23 00
Crystal Palace 4	d	22a02									22 16		22a32										22 46		23a02
Sydenham	d						21 59	22 09		22 14	22 19	22 24						22 29			22 39	22 44	22 49	22 54	
Forest Hill 4	d						22 02	22 11		22 17	22 22	22 26						22 32			22 41	22 47	22 52	22 56	
Honor Oak Park	d						22 04	22 14		22 19	22 24	22 29						22 34			22 44	22 49	22 54	22 59	
Brockley	d						22 07	22 16		22 22	22 27	22 31						22 37			22 46	22 52	22 57	23 01	
New Cross Gate 4	a						22 09	22 19		22 24	22 29	22 34						22 39			22 49	22 54	22 59	23 04	
	d						22 09	22 19		22 24	22 29	22 34						22 39			22 49	22 54	22 59	23 04	
New Cross ELL	d																			22 39					
Surrey Quays	d							22 23			22 33	22 38								22 43	22 53		23 03	23 08	
Canada Water	d							22 25			22 35	22 40								22 45	22 55		23 05	23 10	
Rotherhithe	d							22 26			22 36	22 41								22 46	22 56		23 06	23 11	
Wapping	d							22 28			22 38	22 43								22 48	22 58		23 08	23 13	
Shadwell	d							22 30			22 40	22 45								22 50	23 00		23 10	23 15	
Whitechapel	d							22 32			22 42	22 47								22 52	23 02		23 12	23 17	
Shoreditch High Street	d							22 34			22 44	22 49								22 54	23 04		23 14	23 19	
Hoxton	d							22 36			22 46	22 51								22 56	23 06		23 16	23 21	
Haggerston	d							22 38			22 48	22 53								22 58	23 08		23 18	23 23	
Dalston Junction Stn ELL	a							22 40			22 50	22 55								23 01	23 10		23 20	23 25	
Canonbury	d							22 45			22 53	23 00									23 15		23 23	23 30	
Highbury & Islington	a							22 50			22 58	23 05									23 20		23 28	23 35	
	d																								
London Bridge 4 ⊖	a			22 03	22 06	22 19	22 18			22 31					22 33	22 36	22 49	22 48				23 01			

Table 178

Sundays
19 August to 26 August

East London Line and Croydon - London Victoria to London Bridge

Network Diagram - see first Page of Table 177

		SE	SN	SN		SN	SN	LO	LO	LO	SN	SE	SN	SN		SE	SN
East Croydon	d					22 42	22 47										
West Croydon 4	d								22 57								
Norwood Junction 2	d						22 52		23 01								
Anerley	d						22 55		23 04								
Penge West	d						22 57		23 06								
London Victoria 15 ⊖	d			22 41										23 11			
Battersea Park 4	d			22 45										23 15			
Wandsworth Road	d			22 47										23 17			
Clapham High Street ⊖	d			22 49										23 19			
London Blackfriars 3 ⊖	d	22 38										23 08				23 38	
Denmark Hill 4	d	22 48		22 54								23 18		23 24		23 48	
Peckham Rye 4	d	22a51	22 53	22 56		23 10					23 15	23a21	23 23	23 26		23a51	23 53
Queens Rd Peckham	d		22 56	22 59		23 12							23 26	23 29			23 56
South Bermondsey	d		22 58	23 01		23 15							23 28	23 31			23 58
Clapham Junction 10	d																
Wandsworth Common	d																
Balham 4 ⊖	d																
Streatham Hill	d																
West Norwood 4	d										23 27						
Gipsy Hill	d										23 30						
Crystal Palace 4	d									23 16	23a32						
Sydenham	d						22 59		23 09	23 19							
Forest Hill 4	d						23 02		23 11	23 22							
Honor Oak Park	d						23 04		23 14	23 24							
Brockley	d						23 07		23 16	23 27							
New Cross Gate 4	a						23 09		23 19	23 29							
	d						23 09		23 19	23 29							
New Cross ELL	d							23 09									
Surrey Quays	d							23 13	23 23	23 33							
Canada Water	d							23 15	23 25	23 35							
Rotherhithe	d							23 16	23 26	23 36							
Wapping	d							23 18	23 28	23 38							
Shadwell	d							23 20	23 30	23 40							
Whitechapel	d							23 22	23 32	23 42							
Shoreditch High Street	d							23 24	23 34	23 44							
Hoxton	d							23 26	23 36	23 46							
Haggerston	d							23 28	23 38	23 48							
Dalston Junction Stn ELL	a							23 31	23 40	23 50							
Canonbury	d								23 45	23 53							
Highbury & Islington	a								23 50	23 58							
	d																
London Bridge 4 ⊖	a		23 03	23 06		23 19	23 18						23 33	23 36			00 03

Sundays
2 September to 9 September

		LO	LO	LO	SN	SN	SN	SN	LO	LO		LO	LO	LO	LO	LO	LO	LO	LO	LO		LO	LO	SN	LO
East Croydon	d																							06 47	
West Croydon 4	d		23p22						05 42				05 55			06 12			06 25				06 42		
Norwood Junction 2	d		23p28						05 46				06 01			06 16			06 31				06 46	06 52	
Anerley	d		23p31						05 49				06 04			06 19			06 34				06 49	06 55	
Penge West	d		23p33						05 51				06 06			06 21			06 36				06 51	06 57	
London Victoria 15 ⊖	d				23p19	23p54																			
Battersea Park 4	d				23p23	23p58																			
Wandsworth Road	d																								
Clapham High Street ⊖	d																								
London Blackfriars 3 ⊖	d																								
Denmark Hill 4	d																								
Peckham Rye 4	d						00 12	00 42																	
Queens Rd Peckham	d																								
South Bermondsey	d																								
Clapham Junction 10	d				23p27	00 02																			
Wandsworth Common	d				23p30	00 05																			
Balham 4 ⊖	d				23p32	00 07																			
Streatham Hill	d				23p35	00 10																			
West Norwood 4	d				23p40	00 14	00 24	00 54																	
Gipsy Hill	d				23p43	00 17	00 27	00 57																	
Crystal Palace 4	d			23p43	23p51	00 21	00a29	00a59				06 01			06 16			06 31				06 44			
Sydenham	d		23p36	23p46	23p54	00 24			05 54			06 04	06 09		06 19	06 24		06 34	06 39			06 47	06 54	06 59	
Forest Hill 4	d		23p38	23p49	23p57	00 27			05 56			06 07	06 11		06 22	06 26		06 37	06 41			06 50	06 56	07 02	
Honor Oak Park	d		23p41	23p51	23p59	00 29			05 59			06 09	06 14		06 24	06 29		06 39	06 44			06 52	06 59	07 04	
Brockley	d		23p43	23p54	00 02	00 32			06 01			06 12	06 16		06 27	06 31		06 42	06 46			06 55	07 01	07 07	
New Cross Gate 4	a		23p46	23p56	00 04	00 35			06 04			06 14	06 19		06 29	06 34		06 44	06 49			06 57	07 04	07 09	
	d		23p46	23p56	00 04	00 35			06 04			06 14	06 19		06 29	06 34		06 44	06 49			06 57	07 04	07 09	
New Cross ELL	d	23p36								06 09				06 24			06 39			06 54					07 09
Surrey Quays	d	23p40	23p49	23p59					06 08	06 13		06 18	06 22	06 28	06 33	06 38	06 43	06 48	06 52	06 58		07 03	07 08		07 13
Canada Water	d	23p42	23p51	00 02					06 10	06 15		06 20	06 24	06 30	06 35	06 40	06 45	06 50	06 54	07 00		07 05	07 10		07 15
Rotherhithe	d	23p43	23p53	00 03					06 11	06 16		06 21	06 26	06 31	06 36	06 41	06 46	06 51	06 56	07 01		07 06	07 11		07 16
Wapping	d	23p45	23p54	00 05					06 13	06 18		06 23	06 27	06 33	06 38	06 43	06 48	06 53	06 57	07 03		07 08	07 13		07 18
Shadwell	d	23p47	23p56	00 07					06 15	06 20		06 25	06 29	06 35	06 40	06 45	06 50	06 55	06 59	07 05		07 10	07 15		07 20
Whitechapel	d	23p49	23p59	00 09					06 17	06 22		06 27	06 32	06 37	06 42	06 47	06 52	06 57	07 02	07 07		07 12	07 17		07 22
Shoreditch High Street	d	23p51	00 01	00 11					06 19	06 24		06 29	06 34	06 39	06 44	06 49	06 54	06 59	07 04	07 09		07 14	07 19		07 24
Hoxton	d	23p53	00 03	00 13					06 21	06 26		06 31	06 36	06 41	06 46	06 51	06 56	07 01	07 06	07 11		07 16	07 21		07 26
Haggerston	d	23p55	00 05	00 15					06 23	06 28		06 33	06 38	06 43	06 48	06 53	06 58	07 03	07 08	07 13		07 18	07 23		07 28
Dalston Junction Stn ELL	a	23p58	00 07	00 17					06 25	06 35		06 35	06 40	06 50	06 50	06 55	07 05	07 05	07 10	07 20		07 20	07 26		07 35
Canonbury	d	00 01	00 11	00 20					06 30			06 38	06 45		06 53	07 00		07 08	07 15			07 23	07 30		
Highbury & Islington	a	00 10	00 18	00 28					06 38			06 46	06 52		07 02	07 08		07 16	07 22			07 31	07 38		
	d																								
London Bridge 4 ⊖	a				00 11	00 41																		07 17	

Table 178

Sundays

2 September to 9 September

East London Line and Croydon - London Victoria to London Bridge

Network Diagram - see first Page of Table 177

		LO	LO	LO	LO	LO		LO	SE	SN	SN	SN	SN	SN	LO	LO		SN	LO	LO	LO	LO	LO	SN	SE
East Croydon	d											07 12	07 17												
West Croydon 4	d		06 55			07 12								07 22		07 25		07 34			07 42				
Norwood Junction 2	d		07 01			07 16							07 22	07 27		07 31		07 40			07 46				
Anerley	d		07 04			07 19							07 25			07 34					07 49				
Penge West	d		07 06			07 21							07 27			07 36					07 51				
London Victoria 15	d								00 56																
Battersea Park 4	d																								
Wandsworth Road	d																								
Clapham High Street	d																								
London Blackfriars 3	d																								07 38
Denmark Hill 4	d								01s05																07 48
Peckham Rye 4	d								01s08	07 09	07 23	07 39												07 45	07a51
Queens Rd Peckham	d									07 12	07 26	07 42													
South Bermondsey	d									07 14	07 28	07 44													
Clapham Junction 10	d																								
Wandsworth Common	d																								
Balham 4	d																								
Streatham Hill	d																								
West Norwood 4	d																							07 57	
Gipsy Hill	d																							08 00	
Crystal Palace 4	d	07 01			07 14									07a31	07 31					07 44			08 01	08a02	
Sydenham	d	07 04	07 09		07 17	07 24							07 29		07 34	07 39		07 44		07 47	07 54		08 04		
Forest Hill 4	d	07 07	07 11		07 20	07 26							07 32		07 37	07 41		07 47		07 50	07 56		08 07		
Honor Oak Park	d	07 09	07 14		07 22	07 29							07 34		07 39	07 44		07 49		07 52	07 59		08 09		
Brockley	d	07 12	07 16		07 25	07 31							07 37		07 42	07 46		07 52		07 55	08 01		08 12		
New Cross Gate 4	a	07 14	07 19		07 27	07 34							07 39		07 44	07 49		07 54		07 57	08 04		08 14		
	d	07 14	07 19		07 27	07 34							07 39		07 44	07 49		07 54		07 57	08 04		08 14		
New Cross ELL	d			07 24				07 39											07 54			08 09			
Surrey Quays	d	07 18	07 22	07 28	07 33	07 38		07 43							07 48	07 52			07 58	08 03	08 08	08 13	08 18		
Canada Water	d	07 20	07 24	07 30	07 35	07 40		07 45							07 50	07 54			08 00	08 05	08 10	08 15	08 20		
Rotherhithe	d	07 21	07 26	07 31	07 36	07 41		07 46							07 51	07 56			08 01	08 06	08 11	08 16	08 21		
Wapping	d	07 23	07 27	07 33	07 38	07 43		07 48							07 53	07 57			08 03	08 08	08 13	08 18	08 23		
Shadwell	d	07 25	07 29	07 35	07 40	07 45		07 50							07 55	07 59			08 05	08 10	08 15	08 20	08 25		
Whitechapel	d	07 27	07 32	07 37	07 42	07 47		07 52							07 57	08 02			08 07	08 12	08 17	08 22	08 27		
Shoreditch High Street	d	07 29	07 34	07 39	07 44	07 49		07 54							07 59	08 04			08 09	08 14	08 19	08 24	08 29		
Hoxton	d	07 31	07 36	07 41	07 46	07 51		07 56							08 01	08 06			08 11	08 16	08 21	08 26	08 31		
Haggerston	d	07 33	07 38	07 43	07 48	07 53		07 58							08 03	08 08			08 13	08 18	08 23	08 28	08 33		
Dalston Junction Stn ELL	a	07 35	07 40	07 50	07 50	07 56		08 05							08 05	08 10			08 20	08 20	08 26	08 35	08 35		
Canonbury	d	07 38	07 45		07 53	08 00									08 08	08 15				08 23	08 30		08 38		
Highbury & Islington	a	07 46	07 52		08 01	08 08									08 16	08 22				08 31	08 38		08 46		
	d																								
London Bridge 4	a									07 19	07 33	07 50	07 48					08 01							

		SN		SN	SN	SN	SN	LO	SN	LO	LO	LO		LO	LO	SN	SE	SN	SN	SN	SN	LO		SN	LO
East Croydon	d				07 42	07 47														08 12	08 17				
West Croydon 4	d						07 52	07 55	08 04			08 12										08 25		08 34	
Norwood Junction 2	d					07 52	07 57	08 01	08 10			08 16									08 22	08 31		08 40	
Anerley	d					07 55		08 04				08 19									08 25	08 34			
Penge West	d					07 57		08 06				08 21									08 27	08 36			
London Victoria 15	d			07 41															08 11						
Battersea Park 4	d			07 45															08 15						
Wandsworth Road	d			07 47															08 17						
Clapham High Street	d			07 49															08 19						
London Blackfriars 3	d																08 08								
Denmark Hill 4	d			07 54													08 18		08 24						
Peckham Rye 4	d	07 53		07 56	08 10											08 15	08a21	08 23	08 26	08 40					
Queens Rd Peckham	d	07 56		07 59	08 12													08 26	08 29	08 42					
South Bermondsey	d	07 58		08 01	08 15													08 28	08 31	08 45					
Clapham Junction 10	d																								
Wandsworth Common	d																								
Balham 4	d																								
Streatham Hill	d																								
West Norwood 4	d															08 27									
Gipsy Hill	d															08 30									
Crystal Palace 4	d						08a01				08 14				08 31	08a32									
Sydenham	d					07 59		08 09	08 14		08 17	08 24			08 34						08 29	08 39		08 44	
Forest Hill 4	d					08 02		08 11	08 17		08 20	08 26			08 37						08 32	08 41		08 47	
Honor Oak Park	d					08 04		08 14	08 19		08 22	08 29			08 39						08 34	08 44		08 49	
Brockley	d					08 07		08 16	08 22		08 25	08 31			08 42						08 37	08 46		08 52	
New Cross Gate 4	a					08 09		08 19	08 24		08 27	08 34			08 44						08 39	08 49		08 54	
	d					08 09		08 19	08 24		08 27	08 34			08 44						08 39	08 49		08 54	
New Cross ELL	d									08 24				08 39											08 54
Surrey Quays	d							08 22		08 28	08 33	08 38		08 43	08 48							08 52			08 58
Canada Water	d							08 24		08 30	08 35	08 40		08 45	08 50							08 54			09 00
Rotherhithe	d							08 26		08 31	08 36	08 41		08 46	08 51							08 56			09 01
Wapping	d							08 27		08 33	08 38	08 43		08 48	08 53							08 57			09 03
Shadwell	d							08 29		08 35	08 40	08 45		08 50	08 55							08 59			09 05
Whitechapel	d							08 32		08 37	08 42	08 47		08 52	08 57							09 02			09 07
Shoreditch High Street	d							08 34		08 39	08 44	08 49		08 54	08 59							09 04			09 09
Hoxton	d							08 36		08 41	08 46	08 51		08 56	09 01							09 06			09 11
Haggerston	d							08 38		08 43	08 48	08 53		08 58	09 03							09 08			09 13
Dalston Junction Stn ELL	a							08 40		08 50	08 50	08 56		09 05	09 05							09 10			09 20
Canonbury	d							08 45			08 53	09 00			09 08							09 15			
Highbury & Islington	a							08 52			09 01	09 08			09 16							09 22			
	d																								
London Bridge 4	a	08 03		08 06	08 19	08 17			08 31									08 33	08 36	08 49	08 48			09 01	

Table 178

Sundays

2 September to 9 September

East London Line and Croydon - London Victoria to London Bridge

Network Diagram - see first Page of Table 177

		LO	LO	LO	LO	SN	SE	SN	SN	SN	SN	LO	SN	LO	LO	LO	LO	LO	SN	SE	SN	SN	SN
East Croydon 🚋	d									08 42	08 47												09 12
West Croydon [4] 🚋	d		08 42									08 55	09 04			09 12							
Norwood Junction [2]	d		08 46								08 52	09 01	09 10			09 16							
Anerley	d		08 49								08 55	09 04				09 19							
Penge West	d		08 51								08 57	09 06				09 21							
London Victoria [15] ⊖	d								08 41													09 11	
Battersea Park [4]	d								08 45													09 15	
Wandsworth Road	d								08 47													09 17	
Clapham High Street ⊖	d								08 49													09 19	
London Blackfriars [3] ⊖	d						08 38													09 08			
Denmark Hill [4]	d						08 48		08 54											09 18		09 24	
Peckham Rye [4]	d					08 45	08a51	08 53	08 56	09 10									09 15	09a21	09 23	09 26	09 40
Queens Rd Peckham	d							08 56	08 59	09 12											09 26	09 29	09 42
South Bermondsey	d							08 58	09 01	09 15											09 28	09 31	09 45
Clapham Junction [10]	d																						
Wandsworth Common	d																						
Balham [4] ⊖	d																						
Streatham Hill	d																						
West Norwood [4]	d					08 57													09 27				
Gipsy Hill	d					09 00													09 30				
Crystal Palace [4]	d	08 44			09 01	09a02									09 14			09 31	09a32				
Sydenham	d	08 47	08 54		09 04						08 59	09 09	09 14		09 17	09 24		09 34					
Forest Hill [4]	d	08 50	08 56		09 07						09 02	09 11	09 17		09 20	09 26		09 37					
Honor Oak Park	d	08 52	08 59		09 09						09 04	09 14	09 19		09 22	09 29		09 39					
Brockley	d	08 55	09 01		09 12						09 07	09 16	09 22		09 25	09 31		09 42					
New Cross Gate [4]	a	08 57	09 04		09 14						09 09	09 19	09 24		09 27	09 34		09 44					
	d	08 57	09 04		09 14						09 09	09 19	09 24		09 27	09 34		09 44					
New Cross ELL	d			09 09										09 24			09 39						
Surrey Quays	d	09 03	09 08	09 13	09 18							09 22		09 28	09 33	09 38	09 43	09 48					
Canada Water	d	09 05	09 10	09 15	09 20							09 24		09 30	09 35	09 40	09 45	09 50					
Rotherhithe	d	09 06	09 11	09 16	09 21							09 26		09 31	09 36	09 41	09 46	09 51					
Wapping	d	09 08	09 13	09 18	09 23							09 27		09 33	09 38	09 43	09 48	09 53					
Shadwell	d	09 10	09 15	09 20	09 25							09 29		09 35	09 40	09 45	09 50	09 55					
Whitechapel	d	09 12	09 17	09 22	09 27							09 32		09 37	09 42	09 47	09 52	09 57					
Shoreditch High Street	d	09 14	09 19	09 24	09 29							09 34		09 39	09 44	09 49	09 54	09 59					
Hoxton	d	09 16	09 21	09 26	09 31							09 36		09 41	09 46	09 51	09 56	10 01					
Haggerston	d	09 18	09 23	09 28	09 33							09 38		09 43	09 48	09 53	09 58	10 03					
Dalston Junction Stn ELL	a	09 20	09 26	09 35	09 35							09 40		09 50	09 50	09 56	10 05	10 05					
Canonbury	d	09 23	09 30		09 38							09 45			09 53	10 00		10 08					
Highbury & Islington	a	09 31	09 38		09 46							09 52			10 01	10 08		10 16					
	d																						
London Bridge [4] ⊖	a							09 03	09 06	09 19	09 18		09 31								09 33	09 36	09 49

		SN	LO	SN	LO	LO	LO	LO	LO	SN	SE	SN	SN	SN	SN	FC [1]	LO	SN	LO	LO	LO	LO
East Croydon 🚋	d	09 17												09 42	09 47	09 47						
West Croydon [4] 🚋	d		09 25	09 34			09 42										09 55	10 04			10 12	
Norwood Junction [2]	d	09 22	09 31	09 40			09 46								09 52		10 01	10 10			10 16	
Anerley	d	09 25	09 34				09 49								09 55		10 04				10 19	
Penge West	d	09 27	09 36				09 51								09 57		10 06				10 21	
London Victoria [15] ⊖	d												09 41									
Battersea Park [4]	d												09 45									
Wandsworth Road	d												09 47									
Clapham High Street ⊖	d												09 49									
London Blackfriars [3] ⊖	d										09 38					10a07						
Denmark Hill [4]	d										09 48		09 54									
Peckham Rye [4]	d									09 45	09a51	09 53	09 56	10 10								
Queens Rd Peckham	d											09 56	09 59	10 12								
South Bermondsey	d											09 58	10 01	10 15								
Clapham Junction [10]	d																					
Wandsworth Common	d																					
Balham [4] ⊖	d																					
Streatham Hill	d																					
West Norwood [4]	d									09 57												
Gipsy Hill	d									10 00												
Crystal Palace [4]	d					09 46			10 01	10a02										10 16		
Sydenham	d	09 29	09 39	09 44		09 49	09 54		10 04						09 59		10 09	10 14		10 19	10 24	
Forest Hill [4]	d	09 32	09 41	09 47		09 52	09 56		10 07						10 02		10 11	10 17		10 22	10 26	
Honor Oak Park	d	09 34	09 44	09 49		09 54	09 59		10 09						10 04		10 14	10 19		10 24	10 29	
Brockley	d	09 37	09 46	09 52		09 57	10 01		10 12						10 07		10 16	10 22		10 27	10 31	
New Cross Gate [4]	a	09 39	09 49	09 54		09 59	10 04		10 14						10 09		10 19	10 24		10 29	10 34	
	d	09 39	09 49	09 54		09 59	10 04		10 14						10 09		10 19	10 24		10 29	10 34	
New Cross ELL	d				09 54			10 09											10 24			10 39
Surrey Quays	d		09 52		09 58	10 03	10 08	10 13	10 18								10 22		10 28	10 33	10 38	10 43
Canada Water	d		09 54		10 00	10 05	10 10	10 15	10 20								10 24		10 30	10 35	10 40	10 45
Rotherhithe	d		09 56		10 01	10 06	10 11	10 16	10 21								10 26		10 31	10 36	10 41	10 46
Wapping	d		09 57		10 03	10 08	10 13	10 18	10 23								10 27		10 33	10 38	10 43	10 48
Shadwell	d		09 59		10 05	10 10	10 15	10 20	10 25								10 29		10 35	10 40	10 45	10 50
Whitechapel	d		10 02		10 07	10 12	10 17	10 22	10 27								10 32		10 37	10 42	10 47	10 52
Shoreditch High Street	d		10 04		10 09	10 14	10 19	10 24	10 29								10 34		10 39	10 44	10 49	10 54
Hoxton	d		10 06		10 11	10 16	10 21	10 26	10 31								10 36		10 41	10 46	10 51	10 56
Haggerston	d		10 08		10 13	10 18	10 23	10 28	10 33								10 38		10 43	10 48	10 53	10 58
Dalston Junction Stn ELL	a		10 10		10 20	10 20	10 25	10 35	10 35								10 40		10 50	10 50	10 55	11 05
Canonbury	d		10 15			10 23	10 30		10 38								10 45			10 53	11 00	
Highbury & Islington	a		10 22			10 31	10 38		10 46								10 52			11 01	11 08	
	d																					
London Bridge [4] ⊖	a	09 48		10 01								10 03	10 06	10 19	10 18			10 31				

Table 178

Sundays

2 September to 9 September

East London Line and Croydon - London Victoria to London Bridge

Network Diagram - see first Page of Table 177

		LO	SN	SE	SN	SN	SN	SN	FC 1	LO		SN	LO	LO	LO	LO	LO	SN	SE	SN		SN	SN	SN	FC 1
East Croydon	d						10 12	10 17	10 17														10 42	10 47	10 47
West Croydon 4	d									10 25		10 34			10 42										
Norwood Junction 2	d							10 22		10 31		10 40			10 46									10 52	
Anerley	d							10 25		10 34					10 49									10 55	
Penge West	d							10 27		10 36					10 51									10 57	
London Victoria 15 ⊖	d					10 11																10 41			
Battersea Park 4	d					10 15																10 45			
Wandsworth Road	d					10 17																10 47			
Clapham High Street ⊖	d					10 19																10 49			
London Blackfriars 3 ⊖	d			10 08					10a37										10 38						11a07
Denmark Hill 4	d			10 18		10 24													10 48			10 54			
Peckham Rye 4	d		10 15	10a21	10 23	10 26	10 40											10 45	10a51	10 53		10 56	11 10		
Queens Rd Peckham	d				10 26	10 29	10 42													10 56		10 59	11 12		
South Bermondsey	d				10 28	10 31	10 45													10 58		11 01	11 15		
Clapham Junction 10	d																								
Wandsworth Common	d																								
Balham 4 ⊖	d																								
Streatham Hill	d																								
West Norwood 4	d		10 27															10 57							
Gipsy Hill	d		10 30															11 00							
Crystal Palace 4	d	10 31	10a32											10 46			11 01	11a02							
Sydenham	d	10 34						10 29		10 39		10 44		10 49	10 54		11 04							10 59	
Forest Hill 4	d	10 37						10 32		10 41		10 47		10 52	10 56		11 07							11 02	
Honor Oak Park	d	10 39						10 34		10 44		10 49		10 54	10 59		11 09							11 04	
Brockley	d	10 42						10 37		10 46		10 52		10 57	11 01		11 12							11 07	
New Cross Gate 4	a	10 44						10 39		10 49		10 54		10 59	11 04		11 14							11 09	
	d	10 44						10 39		10 49		10 54		10 59	11 04		11 14							11 09	
New Cross ELL	d												10 54			11 09									
Surrey Quays	d	10 48								10 52			10 58	11 03	11 08	11 13	11 18								
Canada Water	d	10 50								10 54			11 00	11 05	11 10	11 15	11 20								
Rotherhithe	d	10 51								10 56			11 01	11 06	11 11	11 16	11 21								
Wapping	d	10 53								10 57			11 03	11 08	11 13	11 18	11 23								
Shadwell	d	10 55								10 59			11 05	11 10	11 15	11 20	11 25								
Whitechapel	d	10 57								11 02			11 07	11 12	11 17	11 22	11 27								
Shoreditch High Street	d	10 59								11 04			11 09	11 14	11 19	11 24	11 29								
Hoxton	d	11 01								11 06			11 11	11 16	11 21	11 26	11 31								
Haggerston	d	11 03								11 08			11 13	11 18	11 23	11 28	11 33								
Dalston Junction Stn ELL	a	11 05								11 10			11 20	11 20	11 25	11 35	11 35								
Canonbury	d	11 08								11 15				11 23	11 30		11 38								
Highbury & Islington	a	11 16								11 22				11 31	11 38		11 46								
	d																								
London Bridge 4 ⊖	a				10 33	10 36	10 49	10 48				11 01								11 03		11 06	11 19	11 18	

		LO	SN	LO	LO	LO		LO	LO	SN	SE	SN	SN	SN	SN	FC 1		LO	SN	LO	LO	LO	LO	LO	SN
East Croydon	d													11 12	11 17	11 17									
West Croydon 4	d	10 55	11 04			11 12												11 25	11 34			11 42			
Norwood Junction 2	d	11 01	11 10			11 16									11 22			11 31	11 40			11 46			
Anerley	d	11 04				11 19									11 25			11 34				11 49			
Penge West	d	11 06				11 21									11 27			11 36				11 51			
London Victoria 15 ⊖	d												11 11												
Battersea Park 4	d												11 15												
Wandsworth Road	d												11 17												
Clapham High Street ⊖	d												11 19												
London Blackfriars 3 ⊖	d										11 08					11a37									
Denmark Hill 4	d										11 18		11 24												
Peckham Rye 4	d									11 15	11a21	11 23	11 26	11 40											11 45
Queens Rd Peckham	d											11 26	11 29	11 42											
South Bermondsey	d											11 28	11 31	11 45											
Clapham Junction 10	d																								
Wandsworth Common	d																								
Balham 4 ⊖	d																								
Streatham Hill	d																								
West Norwood 4	d									11 27															11 57
Gipsy Hill	d									11 30															12 00
Crystal Palace 4	d				11 16				11 31	11a32											11 46			12 01	12a02
Sydenham	d	11 09	11 14		11 19	11 24			11 34						11 29			11 39	11 44		11 49	11 54		12 04	
Forest Hill 4	d	11 11	11 17		11 22	11 26			11 37						11 32			11 41	11 47		11 52	11 56		12 07	
Honor Oak Park	d	11 14	11 19		11 24	11 29			11 39						11 34			11 44	11 49		11 54	11 59		12 09	
Brockley	d	11 16	11 22		11 27	11 31			11 42						11 37			11 46	11 52		11 57	12 01		12 12	
New Cross Gate 4	a	11 19	11 24		11 29	11 34			11 44						11 39			11 49	11 54		11 59	12 04		12 14	
	d	11 19	11 24		11 29	11 34			11 44						11 39			11 49	11 54		11 59	12 04		12 14	
New Cross ELL	d			11 24				11 39												11 54			12 09		
Surrey Quays	d	11 22		11 28	11 33	11 38		11 43	11 48									11 52		11 58	12 03	12 08	12 13	12 18	
Canada Water	d	11 24		11 30	11 35	11 40		11 45	11 50									11 54		12 00	12 05	12 10	12 15	12 20	
Rotherhithe	d	11 26		11 31	11 36	11 41		11 46	11 51									11 56		12 01	12 06	12 11	12 16	12 21	
Wapping	d	11 27		11 33	11 38	11 43		11 48	11 53									11 57		12 03	12 08	12 13	12 18	12 23	
Shadwell	d	11 29		11 35	11 40	11 45		11 50	11 55									11 59		12 05	12 10	12 15	12 20	12 25	
Whitechapel	d	11 32		11 37	11 42	11 47		11 52	11 57									12 02		12 07	12 12	12 17	12 22	12 27	
Shoreditch High Street	d	11 34		11 39	11 44	11 49		11 54	11 59									12 04		12 09	12 14	12 19	12 24	12 29	
Hoxton	d	11 36		11 41	11 46	11 51		11 56	12 01									12 06		12 11	12 16	12 21	12 26	12 31	
Haggerston	d	11 38		11 43	11 48	11 53		11 58	12 03									12 08		12 13	12 18	12 23	12 28	12 33	
Dalston Junction Stn ELL	a	11 40		11 50	11 50	11 55		12 05	12 05									12 10		12 20	12 20	12 25	12 35	12 35	
Canonbury	d	11 45			11 53	12 00			12 08									12 15			12 23	12 30		12 38	
Highbury & Islington	a	11 52			12 01	12 08			12 16									12 22			12 31	12 38		12 46	
	d																								
London Bridge 4 ⊖	a		11 31									11 33	11 36	11 49	11 48				12 01						

Table 178

Sundays

2 September to 9 September

East London Line and Croydon - London Victoria to London Bridge

Network Diagram - see first Page of Table 177

Station		SE		SN	SN	SN	SN	FC 1	LO	SN	LO	LO		LO	LO	LO	SN	SE	SN	SN	SN	SN		FC 1	LO
East Croydon ⇌	d					11 42	11 47	11 47													12 12	12 17		12 17	
West Croydon 4 ⇌	d								11 55	12 04				12 12											12 25
Norwood Junction 2	d						11 52		12 01	12 10				12 16								12 22			12 31
Anerley	d						11 55		12 04					12 19								12 25			12 34
Penge West	d						11 57		12 06					12 21								12 27			12 36
London Victoria 15 ⊖	d				11 41															12 11					
Battersea Park 4	d				11 45															12 15					
Wandsworth Road	d				11 47															12 17					
Clapham High Street ⊖	d				11 49															12 19					
London Blackfriars 3 ⊖	d	11 38						12a07										12 08						12a37	
Denmark Hill 4	d	11 48			11 54													12 18		12 24					
Peckham Rye 4	d	11a51		11 53	11 56	12 10											12 15	12a21	12 23	12 26	12 40				
Queens Rd Peckham	d			11 56	11 59	12 12													12 26	12 29	12 42				
South Bermondsey	d			11 58	12 01	12 15													12 28	12 31	12 45				
Clapham Junction 10	d																								
Wandsworth Common	d																								
Balham 4 ⊖	d																								
Streatham Hill	d																								
West Norwood 4	d																12 27								
Gipsy Hill	d																12 30								
Crystal Palace 4	d											12 16				12 31	12a32								
Sydenham	d						11 59		12 09	12 14		12 19		12 24		12 34						12 29			12 39
Forest Hill 4	d						12 02		12 11	12 17		12 22		12 26		12 37						12 32			12 41
Honor Oak Park	d						12 04		12 14	12 19		12 24		12 29		12 39						12 34			12 44
Brockley	d						12 07		12 16	12 22		12 27		12 31		12 42						12 37			12 46
New Cross Gate 4	a						12 09		12 19	12 24		12 29		12 34		12 44						12 39			12 49
	d						12 09		12 19	12 24		12 29		12 34		12 44						12 39			12 49
New Cross ELL	d										12 24				12 39										
Surrey Quays	d								12 22		12 28	12 33		12 38	12 43	12 48									12 52
Canada Water	d								12 24		12 30	12 35		12 40	12 45	12 50									12 54
Rotherhithe	d								12 26		12 31	12 36		12 41	12 46	12 51									12 56
Wapping	d								12 27		12 33	12 38		12 43	12 48	12 53									12 57
Shadwell	d								12 29		12 35	12 40		12 45	12 50	12 55									12 59
Whitechapel	d								12 32		12 37	12 42		12 47	12 52	12 57									13 02
Shoreditch High Street	d								12 34		12 39	12 44		12 49	12 54	12 59									13 04
Hoxton	d								12 36		12 41	12 46		12 51	12 56	13 01									13 06
Haggerston	d								12 38		12 43	12 48		12 53	12 58	13 03									13 08
Dalston Junction Stn ELL	a								12 40		12 50	12 50		12 55	13 05	13 05									13 10
Canonbury	d								12 45			12 53		13 00		13 08									13 15
Highbury & Islington	a								12 52			13 01		13 08		13 16									13 22
	d																								
London Bridge 4 ⊖	a			12 03	12 06	12 19	12 18			12 31									12 33	12 36	12 49	12 48			

Station		SN	LO	LO	LO	LO	LO	SN		SE	SN	SN	SN	SN	FC 1	LO	SN	LO		LO	LO	LO	LO	SN	SE
East Croydon ⇌	d												12 42	12 47	12 47										
West Croydon 4 ⇌	d	12 34			12 42											12 55	13 04				13 12				
Norwood Junction 2	d	12 40			12 46									12 52		13 01	13 10				13 16				
Anerley	d				12 49									12 55		13 04					13 19				
Penge West	d				12 51									12 57		13 06					13 21				
London Victoria 15 ⊖	d											12 41													
Battersea Park 4	d											12 45													
Wandsworth Road	d											12 47													
Clapham High Street ⊖	d											12 49													
London Blackfriars 3 ⊖	d									12 38					13a07										13 08
Denmark Hill 4	d									12 48		12 54													13 18
Peckham Rye 4	d							12 45		12a51	12 53	12 56	13 10											13 15	13a21
Queens Rd Peckham	d										12 56	12 59	13 12												
South Bermondsey	d										12 58	13 01	13 15												
Clapham Junction 10	d																								
Wandsworth Common	d																								
Balham 4 ⊖	d																								
Streatham Hill	d																								
West Norwood 4	d							12 57																13 27	
Gipsy Hill	d							13 00																13 30	
Crystal Palace 4	d			12 46			13 01	13a02												13 16			13 31	13a32	
Sydenham	d	12 44		12 49	12 54		13 04							12 59		13 09	13 14			13 19	13 24		13 34		
Forest Hill 4	d	12 47		12 52	12 56		13 07							13 02		13 11	13 17			13 22	13 26		13 37		
Honor Oak Park	d	12 49		12 54	12 59		13 09							13 04		13 14	13 19			13 24	13 29		13 39		
Brockley	d	12 52		12 57	13 01		13 12							13 07		13 16	13 22			13 27	13 31		13 42		
New Cross Gate 4	a	12 54		12 59	13 04		13 14							13 09		13 19	13 24			13 29	13 34		13 44		
	d	12 54		12 59	13 04		13 14							13 09		13 19	13 24			13 29	13 34		13 44		
New Cross ELL	d		12 54			13 09												13 24				13 39			
Surrey Quays	d		12 58	13 03	13 08	13 13	13 18									13 22		13 28		13 33	13 38	13 43	13 48		
Canada Water	d		13 00	13 05	13 10	13 15	13 20									13 24		13 30		13 35	13 40	13 45	13 50		
Rotherhithe	d		13 01	13 06	13 11	13 16	13 21									13 26		13 31		13 36	13 41	13 46	13 51		
Wapping	d		13 03	13 08	13 13	13 18	13 23									13 27		13 33		13 38	13 43	13 48	13 53		
Shadwell	d		13 05	13 10	13 15	13 20	13 25									13 29		13 35		13 40	13 45	13 50	13 55		
Whitechapel	d		13 07	13 12	13 17	13 22	13 27									13 32		13 37		13 42	13 47	13 52	13 57		
Shoreditch High Street	d		13 09	13 14	13 19	13 24	13 29									13 34		13 39		13 44	13 49	13 54	13 59		
Hoxton	d		13 11	13 16	13 21	13 26	13 31									13 36		13 41		13 46	13 51	13 56	14 01		
Haggerston	d		13 13	13 18	13 23	13 28	13 33									13 38		13 43		13 48	13 53	13 58	14 03		
Dalston Junction Stn ELL	a		13 20	13 20	13 25	13 35	13 35									13 40		13 50		13 50	13 55	14 05	14 05		
Canonbury	d			13 23	13 30		13 38									13 45				13 53	14 00		14 08		
Highbury & Islington	a			13 31	13 38		13 46									13 52				14 01	14 08		14 16		
	d																								
London Bridge 4 ⊖	a	13 01									13 03	13 06	13 19	13 18			13 31								

Table 178

Sundays

2 September to 9 September

East London Line and Croydon - London Victoria to London Bridge

Network Diagram - see first Page of Table 177

Station		SN	SN	SN		SN	FC 1	LO	SN	LO	LO	LO	LO	LO		SN	SE	SN	SN	SN	SN	FC 1	LO	SN	
East Croydon	d			13 12		13 17	13 17													13 42	13 47	13 47			
West Croydon 4	d							13 25	13 34			13 42											13 55	14 04	
Norwood Junction 2	d					13 22		13 31	13 40			13 46									13 52		14 01	14 10	
Anerley	d					13 25		13 34				13 49									13 55		14 04		
Penge West	d					13 27		13 36				13 51									13 57		14 06		
London Victoria 15 ⊖	d		13 11																13 41						
Battersea Park 4	d		13 15																13 45						
Wandsworth Road	d		13 17																13 47						
Clapham High Street ⊖	d		13 19																13 49						
London Blackfriars 3 ⊖	d						13a37										13 38					14a07			
Denmark Hill 4	d		13 24														13 48		13 54						
Peckham Rye 4	d	13 23	13 26	13 40												13 45	13a51	13 53	13 56	14 10					
Queens Rd Peckham	d	13 26	13 29	13 42														13 56	13 59	14 12					
South Bermondsey	d	13 28	13 31	13 45														13 58	14 01	14 15					
Clapham Junction 10	d																								
Wandsworth Common	d																								
Balham 4 ⊖	d																								
Streatham Hill	d																								
West Norwood 4	d															13 57									
Gipsy Hill	d															14 00									
Crystal Palace 4	d										13 46			14 01		14a02									
Sydenham	d					13 29		13 39	13 44		13 49	13 54		14 04							13 59		14 09	14 14	
Forest Hill 4	d					13 32		13 41	13 47		13 52	13 56		14 07							14 02		14 11	14 17	
Honor Oak Park	d					13 34		13 44	13 49		13 54	13 59		14 09							14 04		14 14	14 19	
Brockley	d					13 37		13 46	13 52		13 57	14 01		14 12							14 07		14 16	14 22	
New Cross Gate 4	a					13 39		13 49	13 54		13 59	14 04		14 14							14 09		14 19	14 24	
	d					13 39		13 49	13 54		13 59	14 04		14 14							14 09		14 19	14 24	
New Cross ELL	d									13 54			14 09												
Surrey Quays	d							13 52		13 58	14 03	14 08	14 13	14 18									14 22		
Canada Water	d							13 54		14 00	14 05	14 10	14 15	14 20									14 24		
Rotherhithe	d							13 56		14 01	14 06	14 11	14 16	14 21									14 26		
Wapping	d							13 57		14 03	14 08	14 13	14 18	14 23									14 27		
Shadwell	d							13 59		14 05	14 10	14 15	14 20	14 25									14 29		
Whitechapel	d							14 02		14 07	14 12	14 17	14 22	14 27									14 32		
Shoreditch High Street	d							14 04		14 09	14 14	14 19	14 24	14 29									14 34		
Hoxton	d							14 06		14 11	14 16	14 21	14 26	14 31									14 36		
Haggerston	d							14 08		14 13	14 18	14 23	14 28	14 33									14 38		
Dalston Junction Stn ELL	a							14 10		14 20	14 20	14 25	14 35	14 35									14 40		
Canonbury	d							14 15			14 23	14 30		14 38									14 45		
Highbury & Islington	a							14 22			14 31	14 38		14 46									14 52		
	d																								
London Bridge 4 ⊖	a	13 33	13 36	13 49		13 48			14 01									14 03	14 06	14 19	14 18			14 31	

Station		LO	LO	LO	LO	LO	SN	SE	SN	SN		SN	SN	FC 1	LO	SN	LO	LO	LO	LO		LO	SN	SE	SN
East Croydon	d											14 12	14 17	14 17											
West Croydon 4	d			14 12											14 25	14 34			14 42						
Norwood Junction 2	d			14 16									14 22		14 31	14 40			14 46						
Anerley	d			14 19									14 25		14 34				14 49						
Penge West	d			14 21									14 27		14 36				14 51						
London Victoria 15 ⊖	d									14 11															
Battersea Park 4	d									14 15															
Wandsworth Road	d									14 17															
Clapham High Street ⊖	d									14 19															
London Blackfriars 3 ⊖	d							14 08						14a37										14 38	
Denmark Hill 4	d							14 18		14 24														14 48	
Peckham Rye 4	d						14 15	14a21	14 23	14 26		14 40											14 45	14a51	14 53
Queens Rd Peckham	d								14 26	14 29		14 42													14 56
South Bermondsey	d								14 28	14 31		14 45													14 58
Clapham Junction 10	d																								
Wandsworth Common	d																								
Balham 4 ⊖	d																								
Streatham Hill	d																								
West Norwood 4	d						14 27																14 57		
Gipsy Hill	d						14 30																15 00		
Crystal Palace 4	d		14 16			14 31	14a32											14 46				15 01	15a02		
Sydenham	d		14 19	14 24		14 34							14 29		14 39	14 44		14 49	14 54			15 04			
Forest Hill 4	d		14 22	14 26		14 37							14 32		14 41	14 47		14 52	14 56			15 07			
Honor Oak Park	d		14 24	14 29		14 39							14 34		14 44	14 49		14 54	14 59			15 09			
Brockley	d		14 27	14 31		14 42							14 37		14 46	14 52		14 57	15 01			15 12			
New Cross Gate 4	a		14 29	14 34		14 44							14 39		14 49	14 54		14 59	15 04			15 14			
	d		14 29	14 34		14 44							14 39		14 49	14 54		14 59	15 04			15 14			
New Cross ELL	d	14 24			14 39												14 54			15 09					
Surrey Quays	d	14 28	14 33	14 38	14 43	14 48									14 52		14 58	15 03	15 08	15 13		15 18			
Canada Water	d	14 30	14 35	14 40	14 45	14 50									14 54		15 00	15 05	15 10	15 15		15 20			
Rotherhithe	d	14 31	14 36	14 41	14 46	14 51									14 56		15 01	15 06	15 11	15 16		15 21			
Wapping	d	14 33	14 38	14 43	14 48	14 53									14 57		15 03	15 08	15 13	15 18		15 23			
Shadwell	d	14 35	14 40	14 45	14 50	14 55									14 59		15 05	15 10	15 15	15 20		15 25			
Whitechapel	d	14 37	14 42	14 47	14 52	14 57									15 02		15 07	15 12	15 17	15 22		15 27			
Shoreditch High Street	d	14 39	14 44	14 49	14 54	14 59									15 04		15 09	15 14	15 19	15 24		15 29			
Hoxton	d	14 41	14 46	14 51	14 56	15 01									15 06		15 11	15 16	15 21	15 26		15 31			
Haggerston	d	14 43	14 48	14 53	14 58	15 03									15 08		15 13	15 18	15 23	15 28		15 33			
Dalston Junction Stn ELL	a	14 50	14 50	14 55	15 05	15 05									15 10		15 20	15 20	15 25	15 35		15 35			
Canonbury	d		14 53	15 00		15 08									15 15			15 23	15 30			15 38			
Highbury & Islington	a		15 01	15 08		15 16									15 22			15 31	15 38			15 46			
	d																								
London Bridge 4 ⊖	a								14 33	14 36		14 49	14 48			15 01									15 03

Table 178

Sundays

2 September to 9 September

East London Line and Croydon - London Victoria to London Bridge

Network Diagram - see first Page of Table 177

		SN	SN	SN	FC 1	LO		SN	LO	LO	LO	LO	LO	SN	SE	SN		SN	SN	SN	FC 1	LO	SN	LO	LO
East Croydon	🚋 d		14 42	14 47	14 47														15 12	15 17	15 17				
West Croydon 4	🚋 d					14 55		15 04			15 12											15 25	15 34		
Norwood Junction 2	d			14 52		15 01		15 10			15 16									15 22		15 31	15 40		
Anerley	d			14 55		15 04					15 19									15 25		15 34			
Penge West	d			14 57		15 06					15 21									15 27		15 36			
London Victoria 15	⊖ d	14 41																15 11							
Battersea Park 4	d	14 45																15 15							
Wandsworth Road	d	14 47																15 17							
Clapham High Street	⊖ d	14 49																15 19							
London Blackfriars 3	⊖ d				15a07										15 08						15a37				
Denmark Hill 4	d	14 54													15 18			15 24							
Peckham Rye 4	d	14 56	15 10											15 15	15a21	15 23		15 26	15 40						
Queens Rd Peckham	d	14 59	15 12													15 26		15 29	15 42						
South Bermondsey	d	15 01	15 15													15 28		15 31	15 45						
Clapham Junction 10	d																								
Wandsworth Common	d																								
Balham 4	⊖ d																								
Streatham Hill	d																								
West Norwood 4	d													15 27											
Gipsy Hill	d													15 30											
Crystal Palace 4	d									15 16			15 31	15a32											15 46
Sydenham	d			14 59		15 09		15 14		15 19	15 24		15 34							15 29		15 39	15 44		15 49
Forest Hill 4	d			15 02		15 11		15 17		15 22	15 26		15 37							15 32		15 41	15 47		15 52
Honor Oak Park	d			15 04		15 14		15 19		15 24	15 29		15 39							15 34		15 44	15 49		15 54
Brockley	d			15 07		15 16		15 22		15 27	15 31		15 42							15 37		15 46	15 52		15 57
New Cross Gate 4	a			15 09		15 19		15 24		15 29	15 34		15 44							15 39		15 49	15 54		15 59
	d			15 09		15 19		15 24		15 29	15 34		15 44							15 39		15 49	15 54		15 59
New Cross ELL	d								15 24			15 39												15 54	
Surrey Quays	d					15 22			15 28	15 33	15 38	15 43	15 48									15 52		15 58	16 03
Canada Water	d					15 24			15 30	15 35	15 40	15 45	15 50									15 54		16 00	16 05
Rotherhithe	d					15 26			15 31	15 36	15 41	15 46	15 51									15 56		16 01	16 06
Wapping	d					15 27			15 33	15 38	15 43	15 48	15 53									15 57		16 03	16 08
Shadwell	d					15 29			15 35	15 40	15 45	15 50	15 55									15 59		16 05	16 10
Whitechapel	d					15 32			15 37	15 42	15 47	15 52	15 57									16 02		16 07	16 12
Shoreditch High Street	d					15 34			15 39	15 44	15 49	15 54	15 59									16 04		16 09	16 14
Hoxton	d					15 36			15 41	15 46	15 51	15 56	16 01									16 06		16 11	16 16
Haggerston	d					15 38			15 43	15 48	15 53	15 58	16 03									16 08		16 13	16 18
Dalston Junction Stn ELL	a					15 40			15 50	15 50	15 55	16 05	16 05									16 10		16 20	16 20
Canonbury	d					15 45				15 53	16 00		16 08									16 15			16 23
Highbury & Islington	a					15 52				16 01	16 08		16 16									16 22			16 31
	d																								
London Bridge 4	⊖ a	15 06	15 19	15 18				15 31								15 33		15 36	15 49	15 48			16 01		

		LO		LO	LO	SN	SE	SN	SN	SN	SN	FC 1		LO	SN	LO	LO	LO	LO	LO	SN	SE		SN	SN
East Croydon	🚋 d									15 42	15 47	15 47													
West Croydon 4	🚋 d	15 42												15 55	16 04			16 12							
Norwood Junction 2	d	15 46									15 52			16 01	16 10			16 16							
Anerley	d	15 49									15 55			16 04				16 19							
Penge West	d	15 51									15 57			16 06				16 21							
London Victoria 15	⊖ d								15 41																16 11
Battersea Park 4	d								15 45																16 15
Wandsworth Road	d								15 47																16 17
Clapham High Street	⊖ d								15 49																16 19
London Blackfriars 3	⊖ d						15 38					16a07										16 08			
Denmark Hill 4	d						15 48		15 54													16 18			16 24
Peckham Rye 4	d					15 45	15a51	15 53	15 56	16 10											16 15	16a21		16 23	16 26
Queens Rd Peckham	d							15 56	15 59	16 12														16 26	16 29
South Bermondsey	d							15 58	16 01	16 15														16 28	16 31
Clapham Junction 10	d																								
Wandsworth Common	d																								
Balham 4	⊖ d																								
Streatham Hill	d																								
West Norwood 4	d					15 57															16 27				
Gipsy Hill	d					16 00															16 30				
Crystal Palace 4	d				16 01	16a02											16 16			16 31	16a32				
Sydenham	d	15 54			16 04						15 59			16 09	16 14		16 19	16 24		16 34					
Forest Hill 4	d	15 56			16 07						16 02			16 11	16 17		16 22	16 26		16 37					
Honor Oak Park	d	15 59			16 09						16 04			16 14	16 19		16 24	16 29		16 39					
Brockley	d	16 01			16 12						16 07			16 16	16 22		16 27	16 31		16 42					
New Cross Gate 4	a	16 04			16 14						16 09			16 19	16 24		16 29	16 34		16 44					
	d	16 04			16 14						16 09			16 19	16 24		16 29	16 34		16 44					
New Cross ELL	d			16 09												16 24			16 39						
Surrey Quays	d	16 08		16 13	16 18									16 22		16 28	16 33	16 38	16 43	16 48					
Canada Water	d	16 10		16 15	16 20									16 24		16 30	16 35	16 40	16 45	16 50					
Rotherhithe	d	16 11		16 16	16 21									16 26		16 31	16 36	16 41	16 46	16 51					
Wapping	d	16 13		16 18	16 23									16 27		16 33	16 38	16 43	16 48	16 53					
Shadwell	d	16 15		16 20	16 25									16 29		16 35	16 40	16 45	16 50	16 55					
Whitechapel	d	16 17		16 22	16 27									16 32		16 37	16 42	16 47	16 52	16 57					
Shoreditch High Street	d	16 19		16 24	16 29									16 34		16 39	16 44	16 49	16 54	16 59					
Hoxton	d	16 21		16 26	16 31									16 36		16 41	16 46	16 51	16 56	17 01					
Haggerston	d	16 23		16 28	16 33									16 38		16 43	16 48	16 53	16 58	17 03					
Dalston Junction Stn ELL	a	16 25		16 35	16 35									16 40		16 50	16 50	16 55	17 05	17 05					
Canonbury	d	16 30			16 38									16 45			16 53	17 00		17 08					
Highbury & Islington	a	16 38			16 46									16 52			17 01	17 08		17 16					
	d																								
London Bridge 4	⊖ a							16 03	16 06	16 19	16 18				16 31									16 33	16 36

Sundays

2 September to 9 September

East London Line and Croydon - London Victoria to London Bridge

Network Diagram - see first Page of Table 177

Station		SN	SN	FC 1	LO	SN	LO	LO		LO	LO	LO	SN	SE	SN	SN	SN	SN		FC 1	LO	SN	LO	LO	LO
East Croydon	d	16 12	16 17	16 17													16 42	16 47		16 47					
West Croydon 4	d				16 25	16 34				16 42											16 55	17 04			17 12
Norwood Junction 2	d		16 22		16 31	16 40				16 46								16 52			17 01	17 10			17 16
Anerley	d		16 25		16 34					16 49								16 55			17 04				17 19
Penge West	d		16 27		16 36					16 51								16 57			17 06				17 21
London Victoria 15 ⊖	d															16 41									
Battersea Park 4	d															16 45									
Wandsworth Road	d															16 47									
Clapham High Street ⊖	d															16 49									
London Blackfriars 3 ⊖	d			16a37										16 38						17a07					
Denmark Hill 4	d													16 48		16 54									
Peckham Rye 4	d	16 40											16 45	16a51	16 53	16 56	17 10								
Queens Rd Peckham	d	16 42													16 56	16 59	17 12								
South Bermondsey	d	16 45													16 58	17 01	17 15								
Clapham Junction 10	d																								
Wandsworth Common	d																								
Balham 4 ⊖	d																								
Streatham Hill	d																								
West Norwood 4	d												16 57												
Gipsy Hill	d												17 00												
Crystal Palace 4	d							16 46				17 01	17a02											17 16	
Sydenham	d		16 29		16 39	16 44		16 49		16 54		17 04						16 59			17 09	17 14		17 19	17 24
Forest Hill 4	d		16 32		16 41	16 47		16 52		16 56		17 07						17 02			17 11	17 17		17 22	17 26
Honor Oak Park	d		16 34		16 44	16 49		16 54		16 59		17 09						17 04			17 14	17 19		17 24	17 29
Brockley	d		16 37		16 46	16 52		16 57		17 01		17 12						17 07			17 16	17 22		17 27	17 31
New Cross Gate 4	a		16 39		16 49	16 54		16 59		17 04		17 14						17 09			17 19	17 24		17 29	17 34
	d		16 39		16 49	16 54		16 59		17 04		17 14						17 09			17 19	17 24		17 29	17 34
New Cross ELL	d						16 54				17 09												17 24		
Surrey Quays	d				16 52		16 58	17 03		17 08	17 13	17 18									17 22		17 28	17 33	17 38
Canada Water	d				16 54		17 00	17 05		17 10	17 15	17 20									17 24		17 30	17 35	17 40
Rotherhithe	d				16 56		17 01	17 06		17 11	17 16	17 21									17 26		17 31	17 36	17 41
Wapping	d				16 57		17 03	17 08		17 13	17 18	17 23									17 27		17 33	17 38	17 43
Shadwell	d				16 59		17 05	17 10		17 15	17 20	17 25									17 29		17 35	17 40	17 45
Whitechapel	d				17 02		17 07	17 12		17 17	17 22	17 27									17 32		17 37	17 42	17 47
Shoreditch High Street	d				17 04		17 09	17 14		17 19	17 24	17 29									17 34		17 39	17 44	17 49
Hoxton	d				17 06		17 11	17 16		17 21	17 26	17 31									17 36		17 41	17 46	17 51
Haggerston	d				17 08		17 13	17 18		17 23	17 28	17 33									17 38		17 43	17 48	17 53
Dalston Junction Stn ELL	a				17 10		17 20	17 20		17 25	17 35	17 35									17 40		17 50	17 50	17 55
Canonbury	d				17 15			17 23		17 30		17 38									17 45			17 53	18 00
Highbury & Islington	a				17 22			17 31		17 38		17 46									17 52			18 01	18 08
	d																								
London Bridge 4 ⊖	a	16 49	16 48			17 01									17 03	17 06	17 19	17 18				17 31			

Station		LO	LO	SN		SE	SN	SN	SN	SN	FC 1	LO	SN	LO		LO	LO	LO	LO	SN	SE	SN	SN	SN	
East Croydon	d								17 12	17 17	17 17														
West Croydon 4	d											17 25	17 34				17 42							17 42	
Norwood Junction 2	d									17 22		17 31	17 40				17 46								
Anerley	d									17 25		17 34					17 49								
Penge West	d									17 27		17 36					17 51								
London Victoria 15 ⊖	d							17 11															17 41		
Battersea Park 4	d							17 15															17 45		
Wandsworth Road	d							17 17															17 47		
Clapham High Street ⊖	d							17 19															17 49		
London Blackfriars 3 ⊖	d					17 08					17a37										17 38				
Denmark Hill 4	d					17 18		17 24													17 48		17 54		
Peckham Rye 4	d			17 15		17a21	17 23	17 26	17 40											17 45	17a51	17 53	17 56	18 10	
Queens Rd Peckham	d						17 26	17 29	17 42													17 56	17 59	18 12	
South Bermondsey	d						17 28	17 31	17 45													17 58	18 01	18 15	
Clapham Junction 10	d																								
Wandsworth Common	d																								
Balham 4 ⊖	d																								
Streatham Hill	d																								
West Norwood 4	d			17 27																17 57					
Gipsy Hill	d			17 30																18 00					
Crystal Palace 4	d		17 31	17a32												17 46			18 01	18a02					
Sydenham	d		17 34							17 29		17 39	17 44			17 49	17 54		18 04						
Forest Hill 4	d		17 37							17 32		17 41	17 47			17 52	17 56		18 07						
Honor Oak Park	d		17 39							17 34		17 44	17 49			17 54	17 59		18 09						
Brockley	d		17 42							17 37		17 46	17 52			17 57	18 01		18 12						
New Cross Gate 4	a		17 44							17 39		17 49	17 54			17 59	18 04		18 14						
	d		17 44							17 39		17 49	17 54			17 59	18 04		18 14						
New Cross ELL	d	17 39												17 54				18 09							
Surrey Quays	d	17 43	17 48									17 52		17 58		18 03	18 08	18 13	18 18						
Canada Water	d	17 45	17 50									17 54		18 00		18 05	18 10	18 15	18 20						
Rotherhithe	d	17 46	17 51									17 56		18 01		18 06	18 11	18 16	18 21						
Wapping	d	17 48	17 53									17 57		18 03		18 08	18 13	18 18	18 23						
Shadwell	d	17 50	17 55									17 59		18 05		18 10	18 15	18 20	18 25						
Whitechapel	d	17 52	17 57									18 02		18 07		18 12	18 17	18 22	18 27						
Shoreditch High Street	d	17 54	17 59									18 04		18 09		18 14	18 19	18 24	18 29						
Hoxton	d	17 56	18 01									18 06		18 11		18 16	18 21	18 26	18 31						
Haggerston	d	17 58	18 03									18 08		18 13		18 18	18 23	18 28	18 33						
Dalston Junction Stn ELL	a	18 05	18 05									18 10		18 20		18 20	18 26	18 35	18 35						
Canonbury	d		18 08									18 15				18 23	18 30		18 38						
Highbury & Islington	a		18 16									18 22				18 31	18 38		18 46						
	d																								
London Bridge 4 ⊖	a						17 33	17 36	17 49	17 48			18 01									18 03	18 06	18 19	

Table 178

Sundays

2 September to 9 September

East London Line and Croydon - London Victoria to London Bridge

Network Diagram - see first Page of Table 177

		SN	FC 1	LO	SN	LO	LO	LO	LO	LO		SN	SE	SN	SN	SN	SN	FC 1	LO	SN		LO	LO	LO	LO
East Croydon	d	17 47	17 47													18 12	18 17	18 17							
West Croydon 4	d			17 55	18 04			18 12											18 25	18 34				18 42	
Norwood Junction 2	d	17 52		18 01	18 10			18 16									18 22		18 31	18 40				18 46	
Anerley	d	17 55		18 04				18 19									18 25		18 34					18 49	
Penge West	d	17 57		18 06				18 21									18 27		18 36					18 51	
London Victoria 15 ⊖	d														18 11										
Battersea Park 4	d														18 15										
Wandsworth Road	d														18 17										
Clapham High Street ⊖	d														18 19										
London Blackfriars 3 ⊖	d		18a07										18 08					18a37							
Denmark Hill 4	d												18 18		18 24										
Peckham Rye 4	d											18 15	18a21	18 23	18 26	18 40									
Queens Rd Peckham	d													18 26	18 29	18 42									
South Bermondsey	d													18 28	18 31	18 45									
Clapham Junction 10	d																								
Wandsworth Common	d																								
Balham 4 ⊖	d																								
Streatham Hill	d																								
West Norwood 4	d											18 27													
Gipsy Hill	d											18 30													
Crystal Palace 4	d						18 16			18 31		18a32											18 46		
Sydenham	d	17 59		18 09	18 14		18 19	18 24		18 34							18 29		18 39	18 44			18 49	18 54	
Forest Hill 4	d	18 02		18 11	18 17		18 22	18 26		18 37							18 32		18 41	18 47			18 52	18 56	
Honor Oak Park	d	18 04		18 14	18 19		18 24	18 29		18 39							18 34		18 44	18 49			18 54	18 59	
Brockley	d	18 07		18 16	18 22		18 27	18 31		18 42							18 37		18 46	18 52			18 57	19 01	
New Cross Gate 4	a	18 09		18 19	18 24		18 29	18 34		18 44							18 39		18 49	18 54			18 59	19 04	
	d	18 09		18 19	18 24		18 29	18 34		18 44							18 40		18 49	18 54			18 59	19 04	
New Cross ELL	d					18 24			18 39													18 54			19 09
Surrey Quays	d			18 22		18 28	18 33	18 38	18 43	18 48									18 52			18 58	19 03	19 08	19 13
Canada Water	d			18 24		18 30	18 35	18 40	18 45	18 50									18 54			19 00	19 05	19 10	19 15
Rotherhithe	d			18 26		18 31	18 36	18 41	18 46	18 51									18 56			19 01	19 06	19 11	19 16
Wapping	d			18 27		18 33	18 38	18 43	18 48	18 53									18 57			19 03	19 08	19 13	19 18
Shadwell	d			18 29		18 35	18 40	18 45	18 50	18 55									18 59			19 05	19 10	19 15	19 20
Whitechapel	d			18 32		18 37	18 42	18 47	18 52	18 57									19 02			19 07	19 12	19 17	19 22
Shoreditch High Street	d			18 34		18 39	18 44	18 49	18 54	18 59									19 04			19 09	19 14	19 19	19 24
Hoxton	d			18 36		18 41	18 46	18 51	18 56	19 01									19 06			19 11	19 16	19 21	19 26
Haggerston	d			18 38		18 43	18 48	18 53	18 58	19 03									19 08			19 13	19 18	19 23	19 28
Dalston Junction Stn ELL	a			18 40		18 50	18 50	18 55	19 05	19 05									19 10			19 20	19 20	19 25	19 35
Canonbury	d			18 45			18 53	19 00		19 08									19 15				19 23	19 30	
Highbury & Islington	a			18 52			19 01	19 08		19 16									19 22				19 31	19 38	
	d																								
London Bridge 4 ⊖	a	18 18			18 31									18 33	18 36	18 49	18 48			19 01					

		LO	SN	SE	SN	SN		SN	SN	FC 1	LO	SN	LO	LO	LO	LO		LO	SN	SE	SN	SN	SN	SN	FC 1
East Croydon	d							18 42	18 47	18 47													19 12	19 17	19 17
West Croydon 4	d										18 55	19 04			19 12										
Norwood Junction 2	d								18 52		19 01	19 10			19 16									19 22	
Anerley	d								18 55		19 04				19 19									19 25	
Penge West	d								18 57		19 06				19 21									19 27	
London Victoria 15 ⊖	d					18 41																19 11			
Battersea Park 4	d					18 45																19 15			
Wandsworth Road	d					18 47																19 17			
Clapham High Street ⊖	d					18 49																19 19			
London Blackfriars 3 ⊖	d			18 38						19a07										19 08					19a37
Denmark Hill 4	d			18 48		18 54														19 18		19 24			
Peckham Rye 4	d		18 45	18a51	18 53	18 56		19 10											19 15	19a21	19 23	19 26	19 40		
Queens Rd Peckham	d				18 56	18 59		19 12													19 26	19 29	19 42		
South Bermondsey	d				18 58	19 01		19 15													19 28	19 31	19 45		
Clapham Junction 10	d																								
Wandsworth Common	d																								
Balham 4 ⊖	d																								
Streatham Hill	d																								
West Norwood 4	d		18 57																19 27						
Gipsy Hill	d		19 00																19 30						
Crystal Palace 4	d	19 01	19a02											19 16				19 31	19a32						
Sydenham	d	19 04							18 59		19 09	19 14		19 19	19 24			19 34						19 29	
Forest Hill 4	d	19 07							19 02		19 11	19 17		19 22	19 26			19 37						19 32	
Honor Oak Park	d	19 09							19 04		19 14	19 19		19 24	19 29			19 39						19 34	
Brockley	d	19 12							19 07		19 16	19 22		19 27	19 31			19 42						19 37	
New Cross Gate 4	a	19 14							19 09		19 19	19 24		19 29	19 34			19 44						19 39	
	d	19 14							19 09		19 19	19 24		19 29	19 34			19 44						19 39	
New Cross ELL	d												19 24			19 39									
Surrey Quays	d	19 18									19 22		19 28	19 33	19 38	19 43		19 48							
Canada Water	d	19 20									19 24		19 30	19 35	19 40	19 45		19 50							
Rotherhithe	d	19 21									19 26		19 31	19 36	19 41	19 46		19 51							
Wapping	d	19 23									19 27		19 33	19 38	19 43	19 48		19 53							
Shadwell	d	19 25									19 29		19 35	19 40	19 45	19 50		19 55							
Whitechapel	d	19 27									19 32		19 37	19 42	19 47	19 52		19 57							
Shoreditch High Street	d	19 29									19 34		19 39	19 44	19 49	19 54		19 59							
Hoxton	d	19 31									19 36		19 41	19 46	19 51	19 56		20 01							
Haggerston	d	19 33									19 38		19 43	19 48	19 53	19 58		20 03							
Dalston Junction Stn ELL	a	19 35									19 40		19 50	19 50	19 55	20 05		20 05							
Canonbury	d	19 38									19 45			19 53	20 00			20 08							
Highbury & Islington	a	19 46									19 52			20 01	20 08			20 16							
	d																								
London Bridge 4 ⊖	a				19 03	19 06		19 19	19 18			19 31									19 33	19 36	19 49	19 48	

Table 178

Sundays

2 September to 9 September

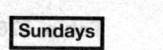

East London Line and Croydon - London Victoria to London Bridge

Network Diagram - see first Page of Table 177

		LO		SN	LO	LO	LO	LO	LO	SN	SE	SN		SN	SN	SN	LO	SN	LO	LO	LO	LO		LO	SN
East Croydon	d														19 42	19 47									
West Croydon 4	d	19 25		19 34			19 42										19 55	20 04			20 12				
Norwood Junction 2	d	19 31		19 40			19 46									19 52	20 01	20 10			20 16				
Anerley	d	19 34					19 49									19 55	20 04				20 19				
Penge West	d	19 36					19 51									19 57	20 06				20 21				
London Victoria 15 ⊖	d													19 41											
Battersea Park 4	d													19 45											
Wandsworth Road	d													19 47											
Clapham High Street ⊖	d													19 49											
London Blackfriars 3 ⊖	d										19 38														
Denmark Hill 4	d										19 48			19 54											
Peckham Rye 4	d									19 45	19a51	19 53		19 56	20 10										20 15
Queens Rd Peckham	d											19 56		19 59	20 12										
South Bermondsey	d											19 58		20 01	20 15										
Clapham Junction 10	d																								
Wandsworth Common	d																								
Balham 4 ⊖	d																								
Streatham Hill	d																								
West Norwood 4	d									19 57															20 27
Gipsy Hill	d									20 00															20 30
Crystal Palace 4	d					19 46			20 01	20a02										20 16				20 31	20a32
Sydenham	d	19 39		19 44		19 49	19 54		20 04							19 59	20 09	20 14		20 19	20 24			20 34	
Forest Hill 4	d	19 41		19 47		19 52	19 56		20 07							20 02	20 11	20 17		20 22	20 26			20 37	
Honor Oak Park	d	19 44		19 49		19 54	19 59		20 09							20 04	20 14	20 19		20 24	20 29			20 39	
Brockley	d	19 46		19 52		19 57	20 01		20 12							20 07	20 16	20 22		20 27	20 31			20 42	
New Cross Gate 4	a	19 49		19 54		19 59	20 04		20 14							20 09	20 19	20 24		20 29	20 34			20 44	
	d	19 49		19 54		19 59	20 04		20 14							20 09	20 19	20 24		20 29	20 34			20 44	
New Cross ELL	d				19 54			20 09											20 24			20 39			
Surrey Quays	d	19 52			19 58	20 03	20 08	20 13	20 18								20 22		20 28	20 33	20 38	20 43		20 48	
Canada Water	d	19 54			20 00	20 05	20 10	20 15	20 20								20 24		20 30	20 35	20 40	20 45		20 50	
Rotherhithe	d	19 56			20 01	20 06	20 11	20 16	20 21								20 26		20 31	20 36	20 41	20 46		20 51	
Wapping	d	19 57			20 03	20 08	20 13	20 18	20 23								20 27		20 33	20 38	20 43	20 48		20 53	
Shadwell	d	19 59			20 05	20 10	20 15	20 20	20 25								20 29		20 35	20 40	20 45	20 50		20 55	
Whitechapel	d	20 02			20 07	20 12	20 17	20 22	20 27								20 32		20 37	20 42	20 47	20 52		20 57	
Shoreditch High Street	d	20 04			20 09	20 14	20 19	20 24	20 29								20 34		20 39	20 44	20 49	20 54		20 59	
Hoxton	d	20 06			20 11	20 16	20 21	20 26	20 31								20 36		20 41	20 46	20 51	20 56		21 01	
Haggerston	d	20 08			20 13	20 18	20 23	20 28	20 33								20 38		20 43	20 48	20 53	20 58		21 03	
Dalston Junction Stn ELL	a	20 10			20 20	20 20	20 25	20 35	20 35								20 40		20 50	20 50	20 55	21 05		21 05	
Canonbury	d	20 15				20 23	20 30		20 38								20 45			20 53	21 00			21 08	
Highbury & Islington	a	20 22				20 31	20 38		20 46								20 52			21 01	21 08			21 16	
	d																								
London Bridge 4 ⊖	a			20 01								20 03		20 06	20 19	20 18		20 31							

		SE	SN	SN	SN	SN	LO	SN		LO	LO	LO	LO	LO	SN	SE	SN	SN		SN	SN	LO	SN	LO	LO
East Croydon	d				20 12	20 17														20 42	20 47				
West Croydon 4	d						20 25	20 34				20 42										20 55	21 04		
Norwood Junction 2	d					20 22	20 31	20 40				20 46									20 52	21 01	21 10		
Anerley	d					20 25	20 34					20 49									20 55	21 04			
Penge West	d					20 27	20 36					20 51									20 57	21 06			
London Victoria 15 ⊖	d			20 11														20 41							
Battersea Park 4	d			20 15														20 45							
Wandsworth Road	d			20 17														20 47							
Clapham High Street ⊖	d			20 19														20 49							
London Blackfriars 3 ⊖	d	20 08														20 38									
Denmark Hill 4	d	20 18		20 24												20 48		20 54							
Peckham Rye 4	d	20a21	20 23	20 26	20 40										20 45	20a51	20 53	20 56		21 10					
Queens Rd Peckham	d		20 26	20 29	20 42												20 56	20 59		21 12					
South Bermondsey	d		20 28	20 31	20 45												20 58	21 01		21 15					
Clapham Junction 10	d																								
Wandsworth Common	d																								
Balham 4 ⊖	d																								
Streatham Hill	d																								
West Norwood 4	d														20 57										
Gipsy Hill	d														21 00										
Crystal Palace 4	d										20 46			21 01	21a02										21 16
Sydenham	d					20 29	20 39	20 44			20 49	20 54		21 04							20 59	21 09	21 14		21 19
Forest Hill 4	d					20 32	20 41	20 47			20 52	20 56		21 07							21 02	21 11	21 17		21 22
Honor Oak Park	d					20 34	20 44	20 49			20 54	20 59		21 09							21 04	21 14	21 19		21 24
Brockley	d					20 37	20 46	20 52			20 57	21 01		21 12							21 07	21 16	21 22		21 27
New Cross Gate 4	a					20 39	20 49	20 54			20 59	21 04		21 14							21 09	21 19	21 24		21 29
	d					20 39	20 49	20 54			20 59	21 04		21 14							21 09	21 19	21 24		21 29
New Cross ELL	d									20 54			21 09											21 24	
Surrey Quays	d						20 52			20 58	21 03	21 08	21 13	21 18								21 22		21 28	21 33
Canada Water	d						20 54			21 00	21 05	21 10	21 15	21 20								21 24		21 30	21 35
Rotherhithe	d						20 56			21 01	21 06	21 11	21 16	21 21								21 26		21 31	21 36
Wapping	d						20 57			21 03	21 08	21 13	21 18	21 23								21 27		21 33	21 38
Shadwell	d						20 59			21 05	21 10	21 15	21 20	21 25								21 29		21 35	21 40
Whitechapel	d						21 02			21 07	21 12	21 17	21 22	21 27								21 32		21 37	21 42
Shoreditch High Street	d						21 04			21 09	21 14	21 19	21 24	21 29								21 34		21 39	21 44
Hoxton	d						21 06			21 11	21 16	21 21	21 26	21 31								21 36		21 41	21 46
Haggerston	d						21 08			21 13	21 18	21 23	21 28	21 33								21 38		21 43	21 48
Dalston Junction Stn ELL	a						21 10			21 20	21 20	21 25	21 35	21 35								21 40		21 50	21 50
Canonbury	d						21 15				21 23	21 30		21 38								21 45			21 53
Highbury & Islington	a						21 22				21 31	21 38		21 46								21 52			22 01
	d																								
London Bridge 4 ⊖	a		20 33	20 36	20 49	20 48		21 01									21 03	21 06		21 19	21 18		21 31		

East London Line and Croydon - London Victoria to London Bridge

Network Diagram - see first Page of Table 177

Station		LO	LO	LO		SN	SE	SN	SN	SN	SN	LO	SN
East Croydon 🚋	d									21 12	21 17		
West Croydon 4 🚋	d	21 12										21 25	21 34
Norwood Junction 2	d	21 16									21 22	21 31	21 40
Anerley	d	21 19									21 25	21 34	
Penge West	d	21 21									21 27	21 36	
London Victoria 15 ⊖	d								21 11				
Battersea Park 4	d								21 15				
Wandsworth Road	d								21 17				
Clapham High Street ⊖	d								21 19				
London Blackfriars 3 ⊖	d						21 08						
Denmark Hill 4	d						21 18		21 24				
Peckham Rye 4	d					21 15	21a21	21 23	21 26	21 40			
Queens Rd Peckham	d							21 26	21 29	21 42			
South Bermondsey	d							21 28	21 31	21 45			
Clapham Junction 10	d												
Wandsworth Common	d												
Balham 4 ⊖	d												
Streatham Hill	d												
West Norwood 4	d					21 27							
Gipsy Hill	d					21 30							
Crystal Palace 4	d			21 31		21a32							
Sydenham	d	21 24		21 34							21 29	21 39	21 44
Forest Hill 4	d	21 26		21 37							21 32	21 41	21 47
Honor Oak Park	d	21 29		21 39							21 34	21 44	21 49
Brockley	d	21 31		21 42							21 37	21 46	21 52
New Cross Gate 4	a	21 34		21 44							21 39	21 49	21 54
	d	21 34		21 44							21 39	21 49	21 54
New Cross ELL	d		21 39										
Surrey Quays	d	21 38	21 43	21 48								21 52	
Canada Water	d	21 40	21 45	21 50								21 54	
Rotherhithe	d	21 41	21 46	21 51								21 56	
Wapping	d	21 43	21 48	21 53								21 57	
Shadwell	d	21 45	21 50	21 55								21 59	
Whitechapel	d	21 47	21 52	21 57								22 02	
Shoreditch High Street	d	21 49	21 54	21 59								22 04	
Hoxton	d	21 51	21 56	22 01								22 06	
Haggerston	d	21 53	21 58	22 03								22 08	
Dalston Junction Stn ELL	a	21 55	22 05	22 05								22 10	
Canonbury	d	22 00		22 08								22 15	
Highbury & Islington	a	22 08		22 16								22 22	
	d												
London Bridge 4 ⊖	a							21 33	21 36	21 49	21 48		22 01

Station		LO		LO	LO	LO	LO	SN	SE	SN	SN	SN	
East Croydon 🚋	d											21 42	
West Croydon 4 🚋	d				21 42								
Norwood Junction 2	d				21 46								
Anerley	d				21 49								
Penge West	d				21 51								
London Victoria 15 ⊖	d										21 41		
Battersea Park 4	d										21 45		
Wandsworth Road	d										21 47		
Clapham High Street ⊖	d										21 49		
London Blackfriars 3 ⊖	d								21 38				
Denmark Hill 4	d								21 48		21 54		
Peckham Rye 4	d							21 45	21a51	21 53	21 56	22 10	
Queens Rd Peckham	d									21 56	21 59	22 12	
South Bermondsey	d									21 58	22 01	22 15	
Clapham Junction 10	d												
Wandsworth Common	d												
Balham 4 ⊖	d												
Streatham Hill	d												
West Norwood 4	d							21 57					
Gipsy Hill	d							22 00					
Crystal Palace 4	d			21 46			22 01	22a02					
Sydenham	d			21 49	21 54		22 04						
Forest Hill 4	d			21 52	21 56		22 07						
Honor Oak Park	d			21 54	21 59		22 09						
Brockley	d			21 57	22 01		22 12						
New Cross Gate 4	a			21 59	22 04		22 14						
	d			21 59	22 04		22 14						
New Cross ELL	d	21 54				22 09							
Surrey Quays	d	21 58		22 03	22 08	22 13	22 18						
Canada Water	d	22 00		22 05	22 10	22 15	22 20						
Rotherhithe	d	22 01		22 06	22 11	22 16	22 21						
Wapping	d	22 03		22 08	22 13	22 18	22 23						
Shadwell	d	22 05		22 10	22 15	22 20	22 25						
Whitechapel	d	22 07		22 12	22 17	22 22	22 27						
Shoreditch High Street	d	22 09		22 14	22 19	22 24	22 29						
Hoxton	d	22 11		22 16	22 21	22 26	22 31						
Haggerston	d	22 13		22 18	22 23	22 28	22 33						
Dalston Junction Stn ELL	a	22 20		22 20	22 25	22 36	22 35						
Canonbury	d			22 23	22 30		22 38						
Highbury & Islington	a			22 31	22 38		22 46						
	d												
London Bridge 4 ⊖	a									22 03	22 06	22 19	

Station		SN	LO	SN	LO	LO	LO	LO	SN	SE		SN	SN
East Croydon 🚋	d	21 47											
West Croydon 4 🚋	d		21 55	22 04		22 12							
Norwood Junction 2	d	21 52	22 01	22 10		22 16							
Anerley	d	21 55	22 04			22 19							
Penge West	d	21 57	22 06			22 21							
London Victoria 15 ⊖	d												22 11
Battersea Park 4	d												22 15
Wandsworth Road	d												22 17
Clapham High Street ⊖	d												22 19
London Blackfriars 3 ⊖	d									22 08			
Denmark Hill 4	d									22 18			22 24
Peckham Rye 4	d								22 15	22a21		22 23	22 26
Queens Rd Peckham	d											22 26	22 29
South Bermondsey	d											22 28	22 31
Clapham Junction 10	d												
Wandsworth Common	d												
Balham 4 ⊖	d												
Streatham Hill	d												
West Norwood 4	d								22 27				
Gipsy Hill	d								22 30				
Crystal Palace 4	d				22 16			22 31	22a32				
Sydenham	d	21 59	22 09	22 14	22 19	22 24		22 34					
Forest Hill 4	d	22 02	22 11	22 17	22 22	22 26		22 37					
Honor Oak Park	d	22 04	22 14	22 19	22 24	22 29		22 39					
Brockley	d	22 07	22 16	22 22	22 27	22 31		22 42					
New Cross Gate 4	a	22 09	22 19	22 24	22 29	22 34		22 44					
	d	22 09	22 19	22 24	22 29	22 34		22 44					
New Cross ELL	d						22 39						
Surrey Quays	d		22 22		22 33	22 38	22 43	22 48					
Canada Water	d		22 24		22 35	22 40	22 45	22 50					
Rotherhithe	d		22 26		22 36	22 41	22 46	22 51					
Wapping	d		22 27		22 38	22 43	22 48	22 53					
Shadwell	d		22 29		22 40	22 45	22 50	22 55					
Whitechapel	d		22 32		22 42	22 47	22 52	22 57					
Shoreditch High Street	d		22 34		22 44	22 49	22 54	22 59					
Hoxton	d		22 36		22 46	22 51	22 56	23 01					
Haggerston	d		22 38		22 48	22 53	22 58	23 03					
Dalston Junction Stn ELL	a		22 40		22 50	22 55	23 05	23 05					
Canonbury	d		22 45		22 53	23 00		23 08					
Highbury & Islington	a		22 52		23 01	23 08		23 16					
	d												
London Bridge 4 ⊖	a	22 18		22 31								22 33	22 36

Station		SN	SN	LO	SN	LO	LO	SN		SE	SN	SN	SN
East Croydon 🚋	d	22 12	22 17										22 42
West Croydon 4 🚋	d			22 25	22 34		22 42						
Norwood Junction 2	d		22 22	22 31	22 40		22 46						
Anerley	d		22 25	22 34			22 49						
Penge West	d		22 27	22 36			22 51						
London Victoria 15 ⊖	d											22 41	
Battersea Park 4	d											22 45	
Wandsworth Road	d											22 47	
Clapham High Street ⊖	d											22 49	
London Blackfriars 3 ⊖	d									22 38			
Denmark Hill 4	d									22 48		22 54	
Peckham Rye 4	d	22 40						22 45		22a51	22 53	22 56	23 10
Queens Rd Peckham	d	22 42									22 56	22 59	23 12
South Bermondsey	d	22 45									22 58	23 01	23 15
Clapham Junction 10	d												
Wandsworth Common	d												
Balham 4 ⊖	d												
Streatham Hill	d												
West Norwood 4	d							22 57					
Gipsy Hill	d							23 00					
Crystal Palace 4	d					22 46		23a02					
Sydenham	d		22 29	22 39	22 44	22 49	22 54						
Forest Hill 4	d		22 32	22 41	22 47	22 52	22 56						
Honor Oak Park	d		22 34	22 44	22 49	22 54	22 59						
Brockley	d		22 37	22 46	22 52	22 57	23 01						
New Cross Gate 4	a		22 39	22 49	22 54	22 59	23 04						
	d		22 39	22 49	22 54	22 59	23 04						
New Cross ELL	d												
Surrey Quays	d			22 52		23 03	23 08						
Canada Water	d			22 54		23 05	23 10						
Rotherhithe	d			22 56		23 06	23 11						
Wapping	d			22 57		23 08	23 13						
Shadwell	d			22 59		23 10	23 15						
Whitechapel	d			23 02		23 12	23 17						
Shoreditch High Street	d			23 04		23 14	23 19						
Hoxton	d			23 06		23 16	23 21						
Haggerston	d			23 08		23 18	23 23						
Dalston Junction Stn ELL	a			23 10		23 20	23 25						
Canonbury	d			23 15		23 23	23 30						
Highbury & Islington	a			23 22		23 31	23 38						
	d												
London Bridge 4 ⊖	a	22 49	22 48		23 01						23 03	23 06	23 19

Sundays

2 September to 9 September

East London Line and Croydon - London Victoria to London Bridge

Network Diagram - see first Page of Table 177

		SN	LO	LO	LO	SN		SE	SN	SN	SE	LO	LO	LO	SN
East Croydon	d	22 47													
West Croydon 4	d			22 55									23 25		
Norwood Junction 2	d	22 52		23 01									23 31		
Anerley	d	22 55		23 04									23 34		
Penge West	d	22 57		23 06									23 36		
London Victoria 15 ⊖	d									23 11					
Battersea Park 4	d									23 15					
Wandsworth Road	d									23 17					
Clapham High Street ⊖	d									23 19					
London Blackfriars 3 ⊖	d							23 08			23 38				
Denmark Hill 4	d							23 18		23 24	23 48				
Peckham Rye 4	d					23 15		23a21	23 23	23 26	23a51				23 53
Queens Rd Peckham	d								23 26	23 29					23 56
South Bermondsey	d								23 28	23 31					23 58
Clapham Junction 10	d														
Wandsworth Common	d														
Balham 4 ⊖	d														
Streatham Hill	d														
West Norwood 4	d					23 27									
Gipsy Hill	d					23 30									
Crystal Palace 4	d				23 16	23a32								23 46	
Sydenham	d	22 59		23 09	23 19								23 39	23 49	
Forest Hill 4	d	23 02		23 11	23 22								23 41	23 52	
Honor Oak Park	d	23 04		23 14	23 24								23 44	23 54	
Brockley	d	23 07		23 16	23 27								23 46	23 57	
New Cross Gate 4	a	23 09		23 19	23 29								23 49	23 59	
	d	23 09		23 19	23 29								23 49	23 59	
New Cross ELL	d		23 09									23 39			
Surrey Quays	d		23 13	23 22	23 33							23 43	23 52	00 02	
Canada Water	d		23 15	23 24	23 35							23 45	23 54	00 05	
Rotherhithe	d		23 16	23 26	23 36							23 46	23 56	00 06	
Wapping	d		23 18	23 27	23 38							23 48	23 57	00 08	
Shadwell	d		23 20	23 29	23 40							23 50	23 59	00 10	
Whitechapel	d		23 22	23 32	23 42							23 52	00 02	00 12	
Shoreditch High Street	d		23 24	23 34	23 44							23 54	00 04	00 14	
Hoxton	d		23 26	23 36	23 46							23 56	00 06	00 16	
Haggerston	d		23 28	23 38	23 48							23 58	00 08	00 18	
Dalston Junction Stn ELL	a		23 35	23 40	23 50							00 02	00 10	00 20	
Canonbury	d			23 45	23 53							00 05	00 14	00 23	
Highbury & Islington	a			23 54	00 01							00 14	00 21	00 31	
	d														
London Bridge 4 ⊖	a	23 18							23 33	23 36					00 03

Sundays

from 16 September

		LO	LO	SN	SN	SN	SN	LO	SN	LO		SN	LO	SN	SN	SN	SN	LO	SN	LO		SN	SE	SN	SN
East Croydon	d								06 47						07 12	07 17									
West Croydon 4	d	23p22						06 42					07 12				07 22		07 34	07 42					
Norwood Junction 2	d	23p28						06 47	06 52				07 17			07 22	07 27		07 40	07 47					
Anerley	d	23p31						06 50	06 55				07 20			07 25				07 50					
Penge West	d	23p33						06 52	06 57				07 22			07 27				07 52					
London Victoria 15 ⊖	d			23p19	23p54																				07 41
Battersea Park 4	d			23p23	23p58																				07 45
Wandsworth Road	d																								07 47
Clapham High Street ⊖	d																								07 49
London Blackfriars 3 ⊖	d																						07 38		
Denmark Hill 4	d																						07 48		07 54
Peckham Rye 4	d					00 12	00 42					07 09		07 23	07 39							07 45	07a51	07 53	07 56
Queens Rd Peckham	d											07 12		07 26	07 42									07 56	07 59
South Bermondsey	d											07 14		07 28	07 44									07 58	08 01
Clapham Junction 10	d			23p27	00 02																				
Wandsworth Common	d			23p30	00 05																				
Balham 4 ⊖	d			23p32	00 07																				
Streatham Hill	d			23p35	00 10																				
West Norwood 4	d			23p40	00 14	00 24	00 54															07 57			
Gipsy Hill	d			23p43	00 17	00 27	00 57															08 00			
Crystal Palace 4	d		23p43	23p51	00 21	00a29	00a59			07 07							07a31	07 37				08a02			
Sydenham	d	23p36	23p46	23p54	00 24			06 55	06 59	07 10			07 25			07 29		07 40	07 44	07 55					
Forest Hill 4	d	23p38	23p49	23p57	00 27			06 57	07 02	07 13			07 27			07 32		07 43	07 47	07 57					
Honor Oak Park	d	23p41	23p51	23p59	00 29			07 00	07 04	07 15			07 30			07 34		07 45	07 49	08 00					
Brockley	d	23p43	23p54	00 02	00 32			07 02	07 07	07 18			07 32			07 37		07 48	07 52	08 02					
New Cross Gate 4	a	23p46	23p56	00 04	00 35			07 05	07 09	07 20			07 35			07 39		07 50	07 54	08 05					
	d	23p46	23p56	00 04	00 35			07 05	07 09	07 20			07 35			07 39		07 50	07 54	08 05					
New Cross ELL	d																								
Surrey Quays	d	23p49	23p59					07 09		07 24			07 39					07 54		08 09					
Canada Water	d	23p51	00 02					07 11		07 26			07 41					07 56		08 11					
Rotherhithe	d	23p53	00 03					07 12		07 27			07 42					07 57		08 12					
Wapping	d	23p54	00 05					07 14		07 29			07 44					07 59		08 14					
Shadwell	d	23p56	00 07					07 16		07 31			07 46					08 01		08 16					
Whitechapel	d	23p59	00 09					07 18		07 33			07 48					08 03		08 18					
Shoreditch High Street	d	00 01	00 11					07 20		07 35			07 50					08 05		08 20					
Hoxton	d	00 03	00 13					07 22		07 37			07 52					08 07		08 22					
Haggerston	d	00 05	00 15					07 24		07 39			07 54					08 09		08 24					
Dalston Junction Stn ELL	a	00 07	00 17					07 26		07 41			07 56					08 11		08 26					
Canonbury	d	00 12	00 20					07 31		07 44			08 01					08 14		08 31					
Highbury & Islington	a	00 16	00 25					07 36		07 49			08 06					08 21		08 36					
	d																								
London Bridge 4 ⊖	a			00 11	00 41				07 17			07 19		07 33	07 50	07 48			08 01					08 03	08 06

Table 178

Sundays

from 16 September

East London Line and Croydon - London Victoria to London Bridge

Network Diagram - see first Page of Table 177

		SN	SN	SN	LO	SN		LO	SN	SE	SN	SN	SN	SN	LO	SN		SN	SE	SN	SN	SN	LO	LO	SN
East Croydon	d	07 42	07 47										08 12	08 17								08 42			08 47
West Croydon 4	d			07 52		08 04		08 12								08 34								08 42	
Norwood Junction 2	d		07 52	07 57		08 10		08 17						08 22		08 40								08 47	08 52
Anerley	d		07 55					08 20						08 25										08 50	08 55
Penge West	d		07 57					08 22						08 27										08 52	08 57
London Victoria 15	d											08 11									08 41				
Battersea Park 4	d											08 15									08 45				
Wandsworth Road	d											08 17									08 47				
Clapham High Street	d											08 19									08 49				
London Blackfriars 3	d									08 08									08 38						
Denmark Hill 4	d									08 18		08 24							08 48		08 54				
Peckham Rye 4	d	08 10							08 15	08a21	08 23	08 26	08 40					08 45	08a51	08 53	08 56	09 10			
Queens Rd Peckham	d	08 12									08 26	08 29	08 42							08 56	08 59	09 12			
South Bermondsey	d	08 15									08 28	08 31	08 45							08 58	09 01	09 15			
Clapham Junction 10	d																								
Wandsworth Common	d																								
Balham 4	d																								
Streatham Hill	d																								
West Norwood 4	d								08 27									08 57							
Gipsy Hill	d								08 30									09 00							
Crystal Palace 4	d			08a01	08 07				08a32						08 37			09a02							
Sydenham	d		07 59		08 10	08 14		08 25						08 29	08 40	08 44								08 55	08 59
Forest Hill 4	d		08 02		08 13	08 17		08 27						08 32	08 43	08 47								08 57	09 02
Honor Oak Park	d		08 04		08 15	08 19		08 30						08 34	08 45	08 49								09 00	09 04
Brockley	d		08 07		08 18	08 22		08 32						08 37	08 48	08 52								09 02	09 07
New Cross Gate 4	a		08 09		08 20	08 24		08 35						08 39	08 50	08 54								09 05	09 09
	d		08 09		08 20	08 24		08 35						08 39	08 50	08 54								09 05	09 09
New Cross ELL	d																						08 54		
Surrey Quays	d				08 24			08 39							08 54								08 58	09 09	
Canada Water	d				08 26			08 41							08 56								09 00	09 11	
Rotherhithe	d				08 27			08 42							08 57								09 01	09 12	
Wapping	d				08 29			08 44							08 59								09 03	09 14	
Shadwell	d				08 31			08 46							09 01								09 05	09 16	
Whitechapel	d				08 33			08 48							09 03								09 07	09 18	
Shoreditch High Street	d				08 35			08 50							09 05								09 09	09 20	
Hoxton	d				08 37			08 52							09 07								09 11	09 22	
Haggerston	d				08 39			08 54							09 09								09 13	09 24	
Dalston Junction Stn ELL	a				08 41			08 56							09 11								09 15	09 26	
Canonbury	d				08 44			09 01							09 14								09 20	09 31	
Highbury & Islington	a				08 51			09 06							09 21								09 27	09 36	
	d																								
London Bridge 4	a	08 19	08 17			08 31					08 33	08 36	08 49	08 48		09 01				09 03	09 06	09 19			09 18

		LO		LO	SN	SN	SE	SN	SN	SN	LO	LO		SN	LO	LO	SN	SN	SE	SN	SN	SN		LO	LO
East Croydon	d									09 12				09 17								09 42			
West Croydon 4	d				09 04							09 12					09 34								09 42
Norwood Junction 2	d				09 10							09 17		09 22			09 40								09 47
Anerley	d											09 20		09 25											09 50
Penge West	d											09 22		09 27											09 52
London Victoria 15	d								09 11												09 41				
Battersea Park 4	d								09 15												09 45				
Wandsworth Road	d								09 17												09 47				
Clapham High Street	d								09 19												09 49				
London Blackfriars 3	d						09 08												09 38						
Denmark Hill 4	d						09 18		09 24										09 48		09 54				
Peckham Rye 4	d					09 15	09a21	09 23	09 26	09 40								09 45	09a51	09 53	09 56	10 10			
Queens Rd Peckham	d							09 26	09 29	09 42										09 56	09 59	10 12			
South Bermondsey	d							09 28	09 31	09 45										09 58	10 01	10 15			
Clapham Junction 10	d																								
Wandsworth Common	d																								
Balham 4	d																								
Streatham Hill	d																								
West Norwood 4	d					09 27												09 57							
Gipsy Hill	d					09 30												10 00							
Crystal Palace 4	d			09 07		09a32										09 37		10a02							
Sydenham	d			09 10	09 14							09 25		09 29		09 40	09 44								09 55
Forest Hill 4	d			09 13	09 17							09 27		09 32		09 43	09 47								09 57
Honor Oak Park	d			09 15	09 19							09 30		09 34		09 45	09 49								10 00
Brockley	d			09 18	09 22							09 32		09 37		09 48	09 52								10 02
New Cross Gate 4	a			09 20	09 24							09 35		09 39		09 50	09 54								10 05
	d			09 20	09 24							09 35		09 39		09 50	09 54								10 05
New Cross ELL	d	09 09									09 24				09 39									09 54	
Surrey Quays	d	09 13		09 24							09 28	09 39			09 43	09 54								09 58	10 09
Canada Water	d	09 15		09 26							09 30	09 41			09 45	09 56								10 00	10 11
Rotherhithe	d	09 16		09 27							09 31	09 42			09 46	09 57								10 01	10 12
Wapping	d	09 18		09 29							09 33	09 44			09 48	09 59								10 03	10 14
Shadwell	d	09 20		09 31							09 35	09 46			09 50	10 01								10 05	10 16
Whitechapel	d	09 22		09 33							09 37	09 48			09 52	10 03								10 07	10 18
Shoreditch High Street	d	09 24		09 35							09 39	09 50			09 54	10 05								10 09	10 20
Hoxton	d	09 26		09 37							09 41	09 52			09 56	10 07								10 11	10 22
Haggerston	d	09 28		09 39							09 43	09 54			09 58	10 09								10 13	10 24
Dalston Junction Stn ELL	a	09 31		09 41							09 45	09 56			10 01	10 11								10 15	10 26
Canonbury	d	09 36		09 44							09 50	10 01			10 06	10 14								10 20	10 31
Highbury & Islington	a	09 41		09 51							09 57	10 06			10 11	10 21								10 27	10 36
	d																								
London Bridge 4	a				09 31			09 33	09 36	09 49				09 48			10 01			10 03	10 06	10 19			

Table 178

Sundays

from 16 September

East London Line and Croydon - London Victoria to London Bridge

Network Diagram - see first Page of Table 177

		SN	LO	LO	SN	SN	SE	SN		SN	SN	LO	LO	SN	LO	LO	SN	SN		SE	SN	SN	SN	FC 1	LO
East Croydon	d	09 47									10 12			10 17									10 42	10 47	
West Croydon 4	d				10 04								10 12				10 34								
Norwood Junction 2	d	09 52			10 10								10 17	10 22			10 40								
Anerley	d	09 55											10 20	10 25											
Penge West	d	09 57											10 22	10 27											
London Victoria 15 ⊖	d									10 11												10 41			
Battersea Park 4	d									10 15												10 45			
Wandsworth Road	d									10 17												10 47			
Clapham High Street ⊖	d									10 19												10 49			
London Blackfriars 3 ⊖	d						10 08													10 38				11a07	
Denmark Hill 4	d						10 18			10 24										10 48		10 54			
Peckham Rye 4	d					10 15	10a21	10 23		10 26	10 40							10 45		10a51	10 53	10 56	11 10		
Queens Rd Peckham	d							10 26		10 29	10 42										10 56	10 59	11 12		
South Bermondsey	d							10 28		10 31	10 45										10 58	11 01	11 15		
Clapham Junction 10	d																								
Wandsworth Common	d																								
Balham 4 ⊖	d																								
Streatham Hill	d																								
West Norwood 4	d					10 27												10 57							
Gipsy Hill	d					10 30												11 00							
Crystal Palace 4	d			10 07		10a32										10 37		11a02							
Sydenham	d	09 59		10 10	10 14								10 25	10 29		10 40	10 44								
Forest Hill 4	d	10 02		10 13	10 17								10 27	10 32		10 43	10 47								
Honor Oak Park	d	10 04		10 15	10 19								10 30	10 34		10 45	10 49								
Brockley	d	10 07		10 18	10 22								10 32	10 37		10 48	10 52								
New Cross Gate 4	a	10 09		10 20	10 24								10 35	10 39		10 50	10 54								
	d	10 09		10 20	10 24								10 35	10 39		10 50	10 54								
New Cross ELL	d		10 09									10 24			10 39										10 54
Surrey Quays	d		10 13	10 24								10 28	10 39		10 43	10 54									10 58
Canada Water	d		10 15	10 26								10 30	10 41		10 45	10 56									11 00
Rotherhithe	d		10 16	10 27								10 31	10 42		10 46	10 57									11 01
Wapping	d		10 18	10 29								10 33	10 44		10 48	10 59									11 03
Shadwell	d		10 20	10 31								10 35	10 46		10 50	11 01									11 05
Whitechapel	d		10 22	10 33								10 37	10 48		10 52	11 03									11 07
Shoreditch High Street	d		10 24	10 35								10 39	10 50		10 54	11 05									11 09
Hoxton	d		10 26	10 37								10 41	10 52		10 56	11 07									11 11
Haggerston	d		10 28	10 39								10 43	10 54		10 58	11 09									11 13
Dalston Junction Stn ELL	a		10 31	10 41								10 45	10 56		11 01	11 11									11 15
Canonbury	d		10 36	10 44								10 50	11 01		11 06	11 14									11 20
Highbury & Islington	a		10 41	10 51								10 57	11 06		11 11	11 21									11 27
	d																								
London Bridge 4 ⊖	a	10 18			10 31			10 33		10 36	10 49			10 48			11 01				11 03	11 06	11 19		

		LO	SN	LO		LO	SN	SN	SE	SN	SN	SN	FC 1	LO		LO	LO	SN	LO	LO	LO	SN	SN	SE
East Croydon	d		10 47									11 12	11 17					11 17						
West Croydon 4	d	10 42					11 04										11 12					11 34		
Norwood Junction 2	d	10 47	10 52				11 10										11 17	11 22				11 40		
Anerley	d	10 50	10 55														11 20	11 25						
Penge West	d	10 52	10 57														11 22	11 27						
London Victoria 15 ⊖	d										11 11													
Battersea Park 4	d										11 15													
Wandsworth Road	d										11 17													
Clapham High Street ⊖	d										11 19													
London Blackfriars 3 ⊖	d								11 08				11a37											11 38
Denmark Hill 4	d								11 18		11 24													11 48
Peckham Rye 4	d							11 15	11a21	11 23	11 26	11 40											11 45	11a51
Queens Rd Peckham	d									11 26	11 29	11 42												
South Bermondsey	d									11 28	11 31	11 45												
Clapham Junction 10	d																							
Wandsworth Common	d																							
Balham 4 ⊖	d																							
Streatham Hill	d																							
West Norwood 4	d							11 27															11 57	
Gipsy Hill	d							11 30															12 00	
Crystal Palace 4	d					11 07		11a32													11 37		12a02	
Sydenham	d	10 55	10 59			11 10	11 14										11 25	11 29			11 40	11 44		
Forest Hill 4	d	10 57	11 02			11 13	11 17										11 27	11 32			11 43	11 47		
Honor Oak Park	d	11 00	11 04			11 15	11 19										11 30	11 34			11 45	11 49		
Brockley	d	11 02	11 07			11 18	11 22										11 32	11 37			11 48	11 52		
New Cross Gate 4	a	11 05	11 09			11 20	11 24										11 35	11 39			11 50	11 54		
	d	11 05	11 09			11 20	11 24										11 35	11 39			11 50	11 54		
New Cross ELL	d			11 09										11 24					11 39					
Surrey Quays	d	11 09		11 13		11 24								11 28		11 35	11 39		11 43	11 51	11 54			
Canada Water	d	11 11		11 15		11 26								11 30		11 37	11 41		11 45	11 53	11 56			
Rotherhithe	d	11 12		11 16		11 27								11 31		11 38	11 42		11 46	11 54	11 57			
Wapping	d	11 14		11 18		11 29								11 33		11 40	11 44		11 48	11 56	11 59			
Shadwell	d	11 16		11 20		11 31								11 35		11 42	11 46		11 50	11 58	12 01			
Whitechapel	d	11 18		11 22		11 33								11 37		11 44	11 48		11 52	12 00	12 03			
Shoreditch High Street	d	11 20		11 24		11 35								11 39		11 46	11 50		11 54	12 02	12 05			
Hoxton	d	11 22		11 26		11 37								11 41		11 48	11 52		11 56	12 04	12 07			
Haggerston	d	11 24		11 28		11 39								11 43		11 50	11 54		11 58	12 06	12 09			
Dalston Junction Stn ELL	a	11 26		11 31		11 41								11 46		11 52	11 56		12 01	12 08	12 11			
Canonbury	d	11 31		11 36		11 44										11 55	12 01			12 11	12 14			
Highbury & Islington	a	11 36		11 41		11 49										12 00	12 06			12 16	12 19			
	d																							
London Bridge 4 ⊖	a		11 18				11 31			11 33	11 36	11 49						11 48				12 01		

Table 178

Sundays
from 16 September

East London Line and Croydon - London Victoria to London Bridge

Network Diagram - see first Page of Table 177

Station		SN	SN	SN	FC [1]	LO	LO	LO	SN	LO		LO	LO	SN	LO	LO	LO	LO	LO	SN		SE	SN	SN	SN
East Croydon	d			11 42	11 47				11 47																12 12
West Croydon [4]	d							11 42						12 04			12 12								
Norwood Junction [2]	d							11 47	11 52					12 10			12 16								
Anerley	d							11 50	11 55								12 19								
Penge West	d							11 52	11 57								12 21								
London Victoria [15] ⊖	d		11 41																					12 11	
Battersea Park [4]	d		11 45																					12 15	
Wandsworth Road	d		11 47																					12 17	
Clapham High Street ⊖	d		11 49																					12 19	
London Blackfriars [3] ⊖	d				12a07																	12 08			
Denmark Hill [4]	d		11 54																			12 18		12 24	
Peckham Rye [4]	d	11 53	11 56	12 10																12 15		12a21	12 23	12 26	12 40
Queens Rd Peckham	d	11 56	11 59	12 12																			12 26	12 29	12 42
South Bermondsey	d	11 58	12 01	12 15																			12 28	12 31	12 45
Clapham Junction [10]	d																								
Wandsworth Common	d																								
Balham [4] ⊖	d																								
Streatham Hill	d																								
West Norwood [4]	d																			12 27					
Gipsy Hill	d																			12 30					
Crystal Palace [4]	d												12 07						12 31	12a32					
Sydenham	d							11 55	11 59				12 10	12 14			12 24		12 34						
Forest Hill [4]	d							11 57	12 02				12 13	12 17			12 26		12 37						
Honor Oak Park	d							12 00	12 04				12 15	12 19			12 29		12 39						
Brockley	d							12 02	12 07				12 18	12 22			12 31		12 42						
New Cross Gate [4]	a							12 05	12 09				12 20	12 24			12 34		12 44						
	d							12 05	12 09				12 20	12 24			12 34		12 44						
New Cross ELL	d					11 54				12 09					12 24			12 39							
Surrey Quays	d					11 58	12 05	12 09		12 13		12 21	12 24		12 28	12 35	12 38	12 43	12 48						
Canada Water	d					12 00	12 07	12 11		12 15		12 23	12 26		12 30	12 37	12 40	12 45	12 50						
Rotherhithe	d					12 01	12 08	12 12		12 16		12 24	12 27		12 31	12 38	12 41	12 46	12 51						
Wapping	d					12 03	12 10	12 14		12 18		12 26	12 29		12 33	12 40	12 43	12 48	12 53						
Shadwell	d					12 05	12 12	12 16		12 20		12 28	12 31		12 35	12 42	12 45	12 50	12 55						
Whitechapel	d					12 07	12 14	12 18		12 22		12 30	12 33		12 37	12 44	12 47	12 52	12 57						
Shoreditch High Street	d					12 09	12 16	12 20		12 24		12 32	12 35		12 39	12 46	12 49	12 54	12 59						
Hoxton	d					12 11	12 18	12 22		12 26		12 34	12 37		12 41	12 48	12 51	12 56	13 01						
Haggerston	d					12 13	12 20	12 24		12 28		12 36	12 39		12 43	12 50	12 53	12 58	13 03						
Dalston Junction Stn ELL	a					12 16	12 22	12 26		12 31		12 38	12 41		12 46	12 52	12 55	13 01	13 05						
Canonbury	d						12 25	12 31				12 41	12 44			12 55	13 00		13 08						
Highbury & Islington	a						12 30	12 36				12 46	12 49			13 00	13 05		13 13						
	d																								
London Bridge [4] ⊖	a	12 03	12 06	12 19					12 18					12 31									12 33	12 36	12 49

Station		SN	FC [1]	SN	LO	LO		LO	LO	LO	LO	SN	SE	SN	SN	SN		SN	FC [1]	LO	SN	LO	LO	LO	LO
East Croydon	d	12 17	12 17													12 42		12 47	12 47						
West Croydon [4]	d			12 34					12 42											12 57	13 04			13 12	
Norwood Junction [2]	d	12 22		12 40					12 46									12 52		13 01	13 10			13 16	
Anerley	d	12 25							12 49									12 55		13 04				13 19	
Penge West	d	12 27							12 51									12 57		13 06				13 21	
London Victoria [15] ⊖	d														12 41										
Battersea Park [4]	d														12 45										
Wandsworth Road	d														12 47										
Clapham High Street ⊖	d														12 49										
London Blackfriars [3] ⊖	d		12a37										12 38						13a07						
Denmark Hill [4]	d												12 48		12 54										
Peckham Rye [4]	d											12 45	12a51	12 53	12 56	13 10									
Queens Rd Peckham	d													12 56	12 59	13 12									
South Bermondsey	d													12 58	13 01	13 15									
Clapham Junction [10]	d																								
Wandsworth Common	d																								
Balham [4] ⊖	d																								
Streatham Hill	d																								
West Norwood [4]	d											12 57													
Gipsy Hill	d											13 00													
Crystal Palace [4]	d							12 46			13 01	13a02											13 16		
Sydenham	d	12 29		12 44				12 49	12 54		13 04							12 59		13 09	13 14		13 19	13 24	
Forest Hill [4]	d	12 32		12 47				12 52	12 56		13 07							13 02		13 11	13 17		13 22	13 26	
Honor Oak Park	d	12 34		12 49				12 54	12 59		13 09							13 04		13 14	13 19		13 24	13 29	
Brockley	d	12 37		12 52				12 57	13 01		13 12							13 07		13 16	13 22		13 27	13 31	
New Cross Gate [4]	a	12 39		12 54				12 59	13 04		13 14							13 09		13 19	13 24		13 29	13 34	
	d	12 39		12 54				12 59	13 04		13 14							13 09		13 19	13 24		13 29	13 34	
New Cross ELL	d					12 54				13 09												13 24			13 39
Surrey Quays	d				12 53	12 58		13 03	13 08	13 13	13 18									13 23		13 28	13 33	13 38	13 43
Canada Water	d				12 55	13 00		13 05	13 10	13 15	13 20									13 25		13 30	13 35	13 40	13 45
Rotherhithe	d				12 56	13 01		13 06	13 11	13 16	13 21									13 26		13 31	13 36	13 41	13 46
Wapping	d				12 58	13 03		13 08	13 13	13 18	13 23									13 28		13 33	13 38	13 43	13 48
Shadwell	d				13 00	13 05		13 10	13 15	13 20	13 25									13 30		13 35	13 40	13 45	13 50
Whitechapel	d				13 02	13 07		13 12	13 17	13 22	13 27									13 32		13 37	13 42	13 47	13 52
Shoreditch High Street	d				13 04	13 09		13 14	13 19	13 24	13 29									13 34		13 39	13 44	13 49	13 54
Hoxton	d				13 06	13 11		13 16	13 21	13 26	13 31									13 36		13 41	13 46	13 51	13 56
Haggerston	d				13 08	13 13		13 18	13 23	13 28	13 33									13 38		13 43	13 48	13 53	13 58
Dalston Junction Stn ELL	a				13 10	13 16		13 20	13 25	13 31	13 35									13 40		13 46	13 50	13 55	14 01
Canonbury	d				13 15			13 23	13 30		13 38									13 45			13 53	14 00	
Highbury & Islington	a				13 20			13 28	13 35		13 43									13 50			13 58	14 05	
	d																								
London Bridge [4] ⊖	a	12 48		13 01										13 03	13 06	13 19		13 18			13 31				

Table 178

Sundays

from 16 September

East London Line and Croydon - London Victoria to London Bridge

Network Diagram - see first Page of Table 177

		LO		SN	SE	SN	SN	SN	SN	FC ■1	LO	SN		LO	LO	LO	LO	LO	SN	SE	SN	SN		SN	SN
East Croydon	d							13 12	13 17	13 17														13 42	13 47
West Croydon ■4	d										13 27	13 34				13 42									
Norwood Junction ■2	d								13 22		13 31	13 40				13 46									13 52
Anerley	d								13 25		13 34					13 49									13 55
Penge West	d								13 27		13 36					13 51									13 57
London Victoria ■15 ⊖	d						13 11															13 41			
Battersea Park ■4	d						13 15															13 45			
Wandsworth Road	d						13 17															13 47			
Clapham High Street ⊖	d						13 19															13 49			
London Blackfriars ■3 ⊖	d				13 08					13a37										13 38					
Denmark Hill ■4	d				13 18		13 24													13 48		13 54			
Peckham Rye ■4	d			13 15	13a21	13 23	13 26	13 40											13 45	13a51	13 53	13 56		14 10	
Queens Rd Peckham	d					13 26	13 29	13 42													13 56	13 59		14 12	
South Bermondsey	d					13 28	13 31	13 45													13 58	14 01		14 15	
Clapham Junction ■10	d																								
Wandsworth Common	d																								
Balham ■4 ⊖	d																								
Streatham Hill	d																								
West Norwood ■4	d			13 27															13 57						
Gipsy Hill	d			13 30															14 00						
Crystal Palace ■4	d	13 31		13a32											13 46			14 01	14a02						
Sydenham	d	13 34							13 29		13 39	13 44			13 49	13 54		14 04							13 59
Forest Hill ■4	d	13 37							13 32		13 41	13 47			13 52	13 56		14 07							14 02
Honor Oak Park	d	13 39							13 34		13 44	13 49			13 54	13 59		14 09							14 04
Brockley	d	13 42							13 37		13 46	13 52			13 57	14 01		14 12							14 07
New Cross Gate ■4	a	13 44							13 39		13 49	13 54			13 59	14 04		14 14							14 09
	d	13 44							13 39		13 49	13 54			13 59	14 04		14 14							14 09
New Cross ELL	d													13 54			14 09								
Surrey Quays	d	13 48									13 53			13 58	14 03	14 08	14 13	14 18							
Canada Water	d	13 50									13 55			14 00	14 05	14 10	14 15	14 20							
Rotherhithe	d	13 51									13 56			14 01	14 06	14 11	14 16	14 21							
Wapping	d	13 53									13 58			14 03	14 08	14 13	14 18	14 23							
Shadwell	d	13 55									14 00			14 05	14 10	14 15	14 20	14 25							
Whitechapel	d	13 57									14 02			14 07	14 12	14 17	14 22	14 27							
Shoreditch High Street	d	13 59									14 04			14 09	14 14	14 19	14 24	14 29							
Hoxton	d	14 01									14 06			14 11	14 16	14 21	14 26	14 31							
Haggerston	d	14 03									14 08			14 13	14 18	14 23	14 28	14 33							
Dalston Junction Stn ELL	a	14 05									14 10			14 16	14 20	14 25	14 31	14 35							
Canonbury	d	14 08									14 15				14 23	14 30		14 38							
Highbury & Islington	a	14 13									14 20				14 28	14 35		14 43							
	d																								
London Bridge ■4 ⊖	a					13 33	13 36	13 49	13 48			14 01									14 03	14 06		14 19	14 18

		FC ■1	LO	SN	LO	LO	LO	LO		LO	SN	SE	SN	SN	SN	SN	FC ■1	LO		SN	LO	LO	LO	LO	LO
East Croydon	d	13 47													14 12	14 17	14 17								
West Croydon ■4	d		13 57	14 04			14 12											14 27		14 34			14 42		
Norwood Junction ■2	d		14 01	14 10			14 16									14 22		14 31		14 40			14 46		
Anerley	d		14 04				14 19									14 25		14 34					14 49		
Penge West	d		14 06				14 21									14 27		14 36					14 51		
London Victoria ■15 ⊖	d													14 11											
Battersea Park ■4	d													14 15											
Wandsworth Road	d													14 17											
Clapham High Street ⊖	d													14 19											
London Blackfriars ■3 ⊖	d	14a07										14 08					14a37								
Denmark Hill ■4	d											14 18		14 24											
Peckham Rye ■4	d										14 15	14a21	14 23	14 26	14 40										
Queens Rd Peckham	d												14 26	14 29	14 42										
South Bermondsey	d												14 28	14 31	14 45										
Clapham Junction ■10	d																								
Wandsworth Common	d																								
Balham ■4 ⊖	d																								
Streatham Hill	d																								
West Norwood ■4	d										14 27														
Gipsy Hill	d										14 30														
Crystal Palace ■4	d					14 16				14 31	14a32											14 46			15 01
Sydenham	d		14 09	14 14		14 19	14 24			14 34						14 29		14 39		14 44		14 49	14 54		15 04
Forest Hill ■4	d		14 11	14 17		14 22	14 26			14 37						14 32		14 41		14 47		14 52	14 56		15 07
Honor Oak Park	d		14 14	14 19		14 24	14 29			14 39						14 34		14 44		14 49		14 54	14 59		15 09
Brockley	d		14 16	14 22		14 27	14 31			14 42						14 37		14 46		14 52		14 57	15 01		15 12
New Cross Gate ■4	a		14 19	14 24		14 29	14 34			14 44						14 39		14 49		14 54		14 59	15 04		15 14
	d		14 19	14 24		14 29	14 34			14 44						14 39		14 49		14 54		14 59	15 04		15 14
New Cross ELL	d				14 24			14 39													14 54			15 09	
Surrey Quays	d		14 23		14 28	14 33	14 38	14 43		14 48								14 53			14 58	15 03	15 08	15 13	15 18
Canada Water	d		14 25		14 30	14 35	14 40	14 45		14 50								14 55			15 00	15 05	15 10	15 15	15 20
Rotherhithe	d		14 26		14 31	14 36	14 41	14 46		14 51								14 56			15 01	15 06	15 11	15 16	15 21
Wapping	d		14 28		14 33	14 38	14 43	14 48		14 53								14 58			15 03	15 08	15 13	15 18	15 23
Shadwell	d		14 30		14 35	14 40	14 45	14 50		14 55								15 00			15 05	15 10	15 15	15 20	15 25
Whitechapel	d		14 32		14 37	14 42	14 47	14 52		14 57								15 02			15 07	15 12	15 17	15 22	15 27
Shoreditch High Street	d		14 34		14 39	14 44	14 49	14 54		14 59								15 04			15 09	15 14	15 19	15 24	15 29
Hoxton	d		14 36		14 41	14 46	14 51	14 56		15 01								15 06			15 11	15 16	15 21	15 26	15 31
Haggerston	d		14 38		14 43	14 48	14 53	14 58		15 03								15 08			15 13	15 18	15 23	15 28	15 33
Dalston Junction Stn ELL	a		14 40		14 46	14 50	14 55	15 01		15 05								15 10			15 16	15 20	15 25	15 31	15 35
Canonbury	d		14 45			14 53	15 00			15 08								15 15				15 23	15 30		15 38
Highbury & Islington	a		14 50			14 58	15 05			15 13								15 20				15 28	15 35		15 43
	d																								
London Bridge ■4 ⊖	a			14 31									14 33	14 36	14 49	14 48				15 01					

Table 178

Sundays
from 16 September

East London Line and Croydon - London Victoria to London Bridge

Network Diagram - see first Page of Table 177

		SN	SE	SN		SN	SN	SN	FC [1]	LO	SN	LO	LO	LO		LO	LO	SN	SE	SN	SN	SN	SN	FC [1]	
East Croydon	d						14 42	14 47	14 47													15 12	15 17	15 17	
West Croydon [4]	d									14 57	15 04			15 12											
Norwood Junction [2]	d							14 52		15 01	15 10			15 16									15 22		
Anerley	d							14 55		15 04				15 19									15 25		
Penge West	d							14 57		15 06				15 21									15 27		
London Victoria [15] ⊖	d					14 41															15 11				
Battersea Park [4]	d					14 45															15 15				
Wandsworth Road	d					14 47															15 17				
Clapham High Street ⊖	d					14 49															15 19				
London Blackfriars [3] ⊖	d		14 38						15a07										15 08					15a37	
Denmark Hill [4]	d		14 48			14 54													15 18		15 24				
Peckham Rye [4]	d	14 45	14a51	14 53		14 56	15 10											15 15	15a21	15 23	15 26	15 40			
Queens Rd Peckham	d			14 56		14 59	15 12													15 26	15 29	15 42			
South Bermondsey	d			14 58		15 01	15 15													15 28	15 31	15 45			
Clapham Junction [10]	d																								
Wandsworth Common	d																								
Balham [4] ⊖	d																								
Streatham Hill	d																								
West Norwood [4]	d	14 57																15 27							
Gipsy Hill	d	15 00																15 30							
Crystal Palace [4]	d	15a02											15 16				15 31	15a32							
Sydenham	d							14 59		15 09	15 14		15 19	15 24			15 34						15 29		
Forest Hill [4]	d							15 02		15 11	15 17		15 22	15 26			15 37						15 32		
Honor Oak Park	d							15 04		15 14	15 19		15 24	15 29			15 39						15 34		
Brockley	d							15 07		15 16	15 22		15 27	15 31			15 42						15 37		
New Cross Gate [4]	a							15 09		15 19	15 24		15 29	15 34			15 44						15 39		
	d							15 09		15 19	15 24		15 29	15 34			15 44						15 39		
New Cross ELL	d											15 24				15 39									
Surrey Quays	d									15 23		15 28	15 33	15 38		15 43	15 48								
Canada Water	d									15 25		15 30	15 35	15 40		15 45	15 50								
Rotherhithe	d									15 26		15 31	15 36	15 41		15 46	15 51								
Wapping	d									15 28		15 33	15 38	15 43		15 48	15 53								
Shadwell	d									15 30		15 35	15 40	15 45		15 50	15 55								
Whitechapel	d									15 32		15 37	15 42	15 47		15 52	15 57								
Shoreditch High Street	d									15 34		15 39	15 44	15 49		15 54	15 59								
Hoxton	d									15 36		15 41	15 46	15 51		15 56	16 01								
Haggerston	d									15 38		15 43	15 48	15 53		15 58	16 03								
Dalston Junction Stn ELL	a									15 40		15 46	15 50	15 55		16 01	16 05								
Canonbury	d									15 45			15 53	16 00			16 08								
Highbury & Islington	a									15 50			15 58	16 05			16 13								
	d																								
London Bridge [4] ⊖	a			15 03		15 06	15 19	15 18			15 31									15 33	15 36	15 49	15 48		

		LO	SN	LO	LO	LO	LO	LO	SN	SE		SN	SN	SN	SN	FC [1]	LO	SN	LO	LO		LO	LO	LO	SN
East Croydon	d													15 42	15 47	15 47									
West Croydon [4]	d	15 27	15 34			15 42											15 57	16 04				16 12			
Norwood Junction [2]	d	15 31	15 40			15 46									15 52		16 01	16 10				16 16			
Anerley	d	15 34				15 49									15 55		16 04					16 19			
Penge West	d	15 36				15 51									15 57		16 06					16 21			
London Victoria [15] ⊖	d												15 41												
Battersea Park [4]	d												15 45												
Wandsworth Road	d												15 47												
Clapham High Street ⊖	d												15 49												
London Blackfriars [3] ⊖	d									15 38						16a07									
Denmark Hill [4]	d									15 48			15 54												
Peckham Rye [4]	d								15 45	15a51		15 53	15 56	16 10											16 15
Queens Rd Peckham	d											15 56	15 59	16 12											
South Bermondsey	d											15 58	16 01	16 15											
Clapham Junction [10]	d																								
Wandsworth Common	d																								
Balham [4] ⊖	d																								
Streatham Hill	d																								
West Norwood [4]	d								15 57																16 27
Gipsy Hill	d								16 00																16 30
Crystal Palace [4]	d				15 46			16 01	16a02											16 16				16 31	16a32
Sydenham	d	15 39	15 44		15 49	15 54		16 04							15 59		16 09	16 14		16 19		16 24		16 34	
Forest Hill [4]	d	15 41	15 47		15 52	15 56		16 07							16 02		16 11	16 17		16 22		16 26		16 37	
Honor Oak Park	d	15 44	15 49		15 54	15 59		16 09							16 04		16 14	16 19		16 24		16 29		16 39	
Brockley	d	15 46	15 52		15 57	16 01		16 12							16 07		16 16	16 22		16 27		16 31		16 42	
New Cross Gate [4]	a	15 49	15 54		15 59	16 04		16 14							16 09		16 19	16 24		16 29		16 34		16 44	
	d	15 49	15 54		15 59	16 04		16 14							16 09		16 19	16 24		16 29		16 34		16 44	
New Cross ELL	d			15 54			16 09												16 24				16 39		
Surrey Quays	d	15 53		15 58	16 03	16 08	16 13	16 18									16 23		16 28	16 33		16 38	16 43	16 48	
Canada Water	d	15 55		16 00	16 05	16 10	16 15	16 20									16 25		16 30	16 35		16 40	16 45	16 50	
Rotherhithe	d	15 56		16 01	16 06	16 11	16 16	16 21									16 26		16 31	16 36		16 41	16 46	16 51	
Wapping	d	15 58		16 03	16 08	16 13	16 18	16 23									16 28		16 33	16 38		16 43	16 48	16 53	
Shadwell	d	16 00		16 05	16 10	16 15	16 20	16 25									16 30		16 35	16 40		16 45	16 50	16 55	
Whitechapel	d	16 02		16 07	16 12	16 17	16 22	16 27									16 32		16 37	16 42		16 47	16 52	16 57	
Shoreditch High Street	d	16 04		16 09	16 14	16 19	16 24	16 29									16 34		16 39	16 44		16 49	16 54	16 59	
Hoxton	d	16 06		16 11	16 16	16 21	16 26	16 31									16 36		16 41	16 46		16 51	16 56	17 01	
Haggerston	d	16 08		16 13	16 18	16 23	16 28	16 33									16 38		16 43	16 48		16 53	16 58	17 03	
Dalston Junction Stn ELL	a	16 10		16 16	16 20	16 25	16 31	16 35									16 40		16 46	16 50		16 55	17 01	17 05	
Canonbury	d	16 15			16 23	16 30		16 38									16 45			16 53		17 00		17 08	
Highbury & Islington	a	16 20			16 28	16 35		16 43									16 50			16 58		17 05		17 13	
	d																								
London Bridge [4] ⊖	a		16 01									16 03	16 06	16 19	16 18			16 31							

Table 178

Sundays

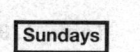

from 16 September

East London Line and Croydon - London Victoria to London Bridge

Network Diagram - see first Page of Table 177

		SE	SN	SN	SN	SN		FC 1	LO	SN	LO	LO	LO	LO	LO	SN		SE	SN	SN	SN	SN	FC 1	LO	SN
East Croydon	d				16 12	16 17		16 17													16 42	16 47	16 47		
West Croydon 4	d								16 27	16 34			16 42											16 57	17 04
Norwood Junction 2	d					16 22			16 31	16 40			16 46									16 52		17 01	17 10
Anerley	d					16 25			16 34				16 49									16 55		17 04	
Penge West	d					16 27			16 36				16 51									16 57		17 06	
London Victoria 15 ⊖	d			16 11																16 41					
Battersea Park 4	d			16 15																16 45					
Wandsworth Road	d			16 17																16 47					
Clapham High Street ⊖	d			16 19																16 49					
London Blackfriars 3 ⊖	d	16 08						16a37										16 38					17a07		
Denmark Hill 4	d	16 18		16 24														16 48		16 54					
Peckham Rye 4	d	16a21	16 23	16 26	16 40											16 45		16a51	16 53	16 56	17 10				
Queens Rd Peckham	d		16 26	16 29	16 42														16 56	16 59	17 12				
South Bermondsey	d		16 28	16 31	16 45														16 58	17 01	17 15				
Clapham Junction 10	d																								
Wandsworth Common	d																								
Balham 4 ⊖	d																								
Streatham Hill	d																								
West Norwood 4	d															16 57									
Gipsy Hill	d															17 00									
Crystal Palace 4	d											16 46			17 01	17a02									
Sydenham	d					16 29			16 39	16 44		16 49	16 54		17 04							16 59		17 09	17 14
Forest Hill 4	d					16 32			16 41	16 47		16 52	16 56		17 07							17 02		17 11	17 17
Honor Oak Park	d					16 34			16 44	16 49		16 54	16 59		17 09							17 04		17 14	17 19
Brockley	d					16 37			16 46	16 52		16 57	17 01		17 12							17 07		17 16	17 22
New Cross Gate 4	a					16 39			16 49	16 54		16 59	17 04		17 14							17 09		17 19	17 24
	d					16 39			16 49	16 54		16 59	17 04		17 14							17 09		17 19	17 24
New Cross ELL	d										16 54			17 09											
Surrey Quays	d								16 53		16 58	17 03	17 08	17 13	17 18									17 23	
Canada Water	d								16 55		17 00	17 05	17 10	17 15	17 20									17 25	
Rotherhithe	d								16 56		17 01	17 06	17 11	17 16	17 21									17 26	
Wapping	d								16 58		17 03	17 08	17 13	17 18	17 23									17 28	
Shadwell	d								17 00		17 05	17 10	17 15	17 20	17 25									17 30	
Whitechapel	d								17 02		17 07	17 12	17 17	17 22	17 27									17 32	
Shoreditch High Street	d								17 04		17 09	17 14	17 19	17 24	17 29									17 34	
Hoxton	d								17 06		17 11	17 16	17 21	17 26	17 31									17 36	
Haggerston	d								17 08		17 13	17 18	17 23	17 28	17 33									17 38	
Dalston Junction Stn ELL	a								17 10		17 16	17 20	17 25	17 31	17 35									17 40	
Canonbury	d								17 15			17 23	17 30		17 38									17 45	
Highbury & Islington	a								17 20			17 28	17 35		17 43									17 50	
	d																								
London Bridge 4 ⊖	a		16 33	16 36	16 49	16 48				17 01									17 03	17 06	17 19	17 18			17 31

		LO		LO	LO	LO	LO	SN	SE	SN	SN	SN		SN	FC 1	LO	SN	LO	LO	LO	LO	LO		SN	SE
East Croydon	d											17 12		17 17	17 17										
West Croydon 4	d				17 12											17 27	17 34			17 42					
Norwood Junction 2	d				17 16									17 22		17 31	17 40			17 46					
Anerley	d				17 19									17 25		17 34				17 49					
Penge West	d				17 21									17 27		17 36				17 51					
London Victoria 15 ⊖	d										17 11														
Battersea Park 4	d										17 15														
Wandsworth Road	d										17 17														
Clapham High Street ⊖	d										17 19														
London Blackfriars 3 ⊖	d								17 08						17a37										17 38
Denmark Hill 4	d								17 18		17 24														17 48
Peckham Rye 4	d							17 15	17a21	17 23	17 26	17 40												17 45	17a51
Queens Rd Peckham	d									17 26	17 29	17 42													
South Bermondsey	d									17 28	17 31	17 45													
Clapham Junction 10	d																								
Wandsworth Common	d																								
Balham 4 ⊖	d																								
Streatham Hill	d																								
West Norwood 4	d							17 27																17 57	
Gipsy Hill	d							17 30																18 00	
Crystal Palace 4	d			17 16			17 31	17a32											17 46			18 01		18a02	
Sydenham	d			17 19	17 24		17 34							17 29		17 39	17 44		17 49	17 54		18 04			
Forest Hill 4	d			17 22	17 26		17 37							17 32		17 41	17 47		17 52	17 56		18 07			
Honor Oak Park	d			17 24	17 29		17 39							17 34		17 44	17 49		17 54	17 59		18 09			
Brockley	d			17 27	17 31		17 42							17 37		17 46	17 52		17 57	18 01		18 12			
New Cross Gate 4	a			17 29	17 34		17 44							17 39		17 49	17 54		17 59	18 04		18 14			
	d			17 29	17 34		17 44							17 39		17 49	17 54		17 59	18 04		18 14			
New Cross ELL	d	17 24				17 39												17 54			18 09				
Surrey Quays	d	17 28		17 33	17 38	17 43	17 48									17 53		17 58	18 03	18 08	18 13	18 18			
Canada Water	d	17 30		17 35	17 40	17 45	17 50									17 55		18 00	18 05	18 10	18 15	18 20			
Rotherhithe	d	17 31		17 36	17 41	17 46	17 51									17 56		18 01	18 06	18 11	18 16	18 21			
Wapping	d	17 33		17 38	17 43	17 48	17 53									17 58		18 03	18 08	18 13	18 18	18 23			
Shadwell	d	17 35		17 40	17 45	17 50	17 55									18 00		18 05	18 10	18 15	18 20	18 25			
Whitechapel	d	17 37		17 42	17 47	17 52	17 57									18 02		18 07	18 12	18 17	18 22	18 27			
Shoreditch High Street	d	17 39		17 44	17 49	17 54	17 59									18 04		18 09	18 14	18 19	18 24	18 29			
Hoxton	d	17 41		17 46	17 51	17 56	18 01									18 06		18 11	18 16	18 21	18 26	18 31			
Haggerston	d	17 43		17 48	17 53	17 58	18 03									18 08		18 13	18 18	18 23	18 28	18 33			
Dalston Junction Stn ELL	a	17 46		17 50	17 55	18 01	18 05									18 10		18 16	18 20	18 25	18 31	18 35			
Canonbury	d			17 53	18 00		18 08									18 15			18 23	18 30		18 38			
Highbury & Islington	a			17 58	18 05		18 13									18 20			18 28	18 35		18 43			
	d																								
London Bridge 4 ⊖	a									17 33	17 36	17 49		17 48			18 01								

Table 178

Sundays

from 16 September

East London Line and Croydon - London Victoria to London Bridge

Network Diagram - see first Page of Table 177

		SN	SN	SN	SN	FC	LO	SN		LO	LO	LO	LO	LO	SN	SE	SN	SN		SN	SN	FC	LO	SN	LO
						1																1			
East Croydon	d			17 42	17 47	17 47														18 12	18 17	18 17			
West Croydon 4	d						17 57	18 04				18 12											18 27	18 34	
Norwood Junction 2	d				17 52		18 01	18 10				18 16									18 22		18 31	18 40	
Anerley	d				17 55		18 04					18 19									18 25		18 34		
Penge West	d				17 57		18 06					18 21									18 27		18 36		
London Victoria 15 ⊖	d		17 41															18 11							
Battersea Park 4	d		17 45															18 15							
Wandsworth Road	d		17 47															18 17							
Clapham High Street ⊖	d		17 49															18 19							
London Blackfriars 3 ⊖	d					18a07										18 08						18a37			
Denmark Hill 4	d		17 54													18 18		18 24							
Peckham Rye 4	d	17 53	17 56	18 10											18 15	18a21	18 23	18 26		18 40					
Queens Rd Peckham	d	17 56	17 59	18 12													18 26	18 29		18 42					
South Bermondsey	d	17 58	18 01	18 15													18 28	18 31		18 45					
Clapham Junction 10	d																								
Wandsworth Common	d																								
Balham 4 ⊖	d																								
Streatham Hill	d																								
West Norwood 4	d														18 27										
Gipsy Hill	d														18 30										
Crystal Palace 4	d										18 16			18 31	18a32										
Sydenham	d				17 59		18 09	18 14			18 19	18 24		18 34							18 29		18 39	18 44	
Forest Hill 4	d				18 02		18 11	18 17			18 22	18 26		18 37							18 32		18 41	18 47	
Honor Oak Park	d				18 04		18 14	18 19			18 24	18 29		18 39							18 34		18 44	18 49	
Brockley	d				18 07		18 16	18 22			18 27	18 31		18 42							18 37		18 46	18 52	
New Cross Gate 4	a				18 09		18 19	18 24			18 29	18 34		18 44							18 39		18 49	18 54	
	d				18 09		18 19	18 24			18 29	18 34		18 44							18 40		18 49	18 54	
New Cross ELL	d									18 24			18 39												18 54
Surrey Quays	d						18 23			18 28	18 33	18 38	18 43	18 48									18 53		18 58
Canada Water	d						18 25			18 30	18 35	18 40	18 45	18 50									18 55		19 00
Rotherhithe	d						18 26			18 31	18 36	18 41	18 46	18 51									18 56		19 01
Wapping	d						18 28			18 33	18 38	18 43	18 48	18 53									18 58		19 03
Shadwell	d						18 30			18 35	18 40	18 45	18 50	18 55									19 00		19 05
Whitechapel	d						18 32			18 37	18 42	18 47	18 52	18 57									19 02		19 07
Shoreditch High Street	d						18 34			18 39	18 44	18 49	18 54	18 59									19 04		19 09
Hoxton	d						18 36			18 41	18 46	18 51	18 56	19 01									19 06		19 11
Haggerston	d						18 38			18 43	18 48	18 53	18 58	19 03									19 08		19 13
Dalston Junction Stn ELL	a						18 40			18 46	18 50	18 55	19 01	19 05									19 10		19 16
Canonbury	d						18 45				18 53	19 00		19 08									19 15		
Highbury & Islington	a						18 50				18 58	19 05		19 13									19 20		
	d																								
London Bridge 4 ⊖	a	18 03	18 06	18 19	18 18			18 31									18 33	18 36		18 49	18 48			19 01	

		LO	LO	LO		LO	SN	SE	SN	SN	SN	SN	FC	LO		SN	LO	LO	LO	LO	LO	SN	SE	SN	
													1												
East Croydon	d										18 42	18 47	18 47												
West Croydon 4	d		18 42											18 57		19 04			19 12						
Norwood Junction 2	d		18 46									18 52		19 01		19 10			19 16						
Anerley	d		18 49									18 55		19 04					19 19						
Penge West	d		18 51									18 57		19 06					19 21						
London Victoria 15 ⊖	d									18 41															
Battersea Park 4	d									18 45															
Wandsworth Road	d									18 47															
Clapham High Street ⊖	d									18 49															
London Blackfriars 3 ⊖	d							18 38					19a07										19 08		
Denmark Hill 4	d							18 48		18 54													19 18		
Peckham Rye 4	d						18 45	18a51	18 53	18 56	19 10											19 15	19a21	19 23	
Queens Rd Peckham	d								18 56	18 59	19 12													19 26	
South Bermondsey	d								18 58	19 01	19 15													19 28	
Clapham Junction 10	d																								
Wandsworth Common	d																								
Balham 4 ⊖	d																								
Streatham Hill	d																								
West Norwood 4	d						18 57															19 27			
Gipsy Hill	d						19 00															19 30			
Crystal Palace 4	d	18 46				19 01	19a02											19 16			19 31	19a32			
Sydenham	d	18 49	18 54			19 04						18 59		19 09		19 14		19 19	19 24		19 34				
Forest Hill 4	d	18 52	18 56			19 07						19 02		19 11		19 17		19 22	19 26		19 37				
Honor Oak Park	d	18 54	18 59			19 09						19 04		19 14		19 19		19 24	19 29		19 39				
Brockley	d	18 57	19 01			19 12						19 07		19 16		19 22		19 27	19 31		19 42				
New Cross Gate 4	a	18 59	19 04			19 14						19 09		19 19		19 24		19 29	19 34		19 44				
	d	18 59	19 04			19 14						19 09		19 19		19 24		19 29	19 34		19 44				
New Cross ELL	d			19 09													19 24			19 39					
Surrey Quays	d	19 03	19 08	19 13		19 18								19 23			19 28	19 33	19 38	19 43	19 48				
Canada Water	d	19 05	19 10	19 15		19 20								19 25			19 30	19 35	19 40	19 45	19 50				
Rotherhithe	d	19 06	19 11	19 16		19 21								19 26			19 31	19 36	19 41	19 46	19 51				
Wapping	d	19 08	19 13	19 18		19 23								19 28			19 33	19 38	19 43	19 48	19 53				
Shadwell	d	19 10	19 15	19 20		19 25								19 30			19 35	19 40	19 45	19 50	19 55				
Whitechapel	d	19 12	19 17	19 22		19 27								19 32			19 37	19 42	19 47	19 52	19 57				
Shoreditch High Street	d	19 14	19 19	19 24		19 29								19 34			19 39	19 44	19 49	19 54	19 59				
Hoxton	d	19 16	19 21	19 26		19 31								19 36			19 41	19 46	19 51	19 56	20 01				
Haggerston	d	19 18	19 23	19 28		19 33								19 38			19 43	19 48	19 53	19 58	20 03				
Dalston Junction Stn ELL	a	19 20	19 25	19 31		19 35								19 40			19 46	19 50	19 55	20 01	20 05				
Canonbury	d	19 23	19 30			19 38								19 45				19 53	20 00		20 08				
Highbury & Islington	a	19 28	19 35			19 43								19 50				19 58	20 05		20 13				
	d																								
London Bridge 4 ⊖	a								19 03	19 06	19 19	19 18				19 31								19 33	

Table 178

Sundays
from 16 September

East London Line and Croydon - London Victoria to London Bridge

Network Diagram - see first Page of Table 177

		SN	SN	SN	FC 1	LO	SN	LO	LO	LO		LO	LO	SN	SE	SN	SN	SN	SN	LO		SN	LO	LO	LO
East Croydon	d		19 12	19 17	19 17													19 42	19 47						
West Croydon 4	d					19 27	19 34			19 42										19 57		20 04			20 12
Norwood Junction 2	d			19 22		19 31	19 40			19 46									19 52	20 01		20 10			20 16
Anerley	d			19 25		19 34				19 49									19 55	20 04					20 19
Penge West	d			19 27		19 36				19 51									19 57	20 06					20 21
London Victoria 15 ⊖	d	19 11															19 41								
Battersea Park 4	d	19 15															19 45								
Wandsworth Road	d	19 17															19 47								
Clapham High Street ⊖	d	19 19															19 49								
London Blackfriars 3 ⊖	d				19a37										19 38										
Denmark Hill 4	d	19 24													19 48		19 54								
Peckham Rye 4	d	19 26	19 40											19 45	19a51	19 53	19 56	20 10							
Queens Rd Peckham	d	19 29	19 42													19 56	19 59	20 12							
South Bermondsey	d	19 31	19 45													19 58	20 01	20 15							
Clapham Junction 10	d																								
Wandsworth Common	d																								
Balham 4 ⊖	d																								
Streatham Hill	d																								
West Norwood 4	d													19 57											
Gipsy Hill	d													20 00											
Crystal Palace 4	d								19 46				20 01	20a02										20 16	
Sydenham	d			19 29		19 39	19 44		19 49	19 54			20 04						19 59	20 09		20 14		20 19	20 24
Forest Hill 4	d			19 32		19 41	19 47		19 52	19 56			20 07						20 02	20 11		20 17		20 22	20 26
Honor Oak Park	d			19 34		19 44	19 49		19 54	19 59			20 09						20 04	20 14		20 19		20 24	20 29
Brockley	d			19 37		19 46	19 52		19 57	20 01			20 12						20 07	20 16		20 22		20 27	20 31
New Cross Gate 4	a			19 39		19 49	19 54		19 59	20 04			20 14						20 09	20 19		20 24		20 29	20 34
	d			19 39		19 49	19 54		19 59	20 04			20 14						20 09	20 19		20 24		20 29	20 34
New Cross ELL	d							19 54				20 09											20 24		
Surrey Quays	d					19 53		19 58	20 03	20 08		20 13	20 18							20 23			20 28	20 33	20 38
Canada Water	d					19 55		20 00	20 05	20 10		20 15	20 20							20 25			20 30	20 35	20 40
Rotherhithe	d					19 56		20 01	20 06	20 11		20 16	20 21							20 26			20 31	20 36	20 41
Wapping	d					19 58		20 03	20 08	20 13		20 18	20 23							20 28			20 33	20 38	20 43
Shadwell	d					20 00		20 05	20 10	20 15		20 20	20 25							20 30			20 35	20 40	20 45
Whitechapel	d					20 02		20 07	20 12	20 17		20 22	20 27							20 32			20 37	20 42	20 47
Shoreditch High Street	d					20 04		20 09	20 14	20 19		20 24	20 29							20 34			20 39	20 44	20 49
Hoxton	d					20 06		20 11	20 16	20 21		20 26	20 31							20 36			20 41	20 46	20 51
Haggerston	d					20 08		20 13	20 18	20 23		20 28	20 33							20 38			20 43	20 48	20 53
Dalston Junction Stn ELL	a					20 10		20 16	20 20	20 25		20 31	20 35							20 40			20 46	20 50	20 55
Canonbury	d					20 15			20 23	20 30			20 38							20 45				20 53	21 00
Highbury & Islington	a					20 20			20 28	20 35			20 43							20 50				20 58	21 05
	d																								
London Bridge 4 ⊖	a	19 36	19 49	19 48			20 01									20 03	20 06	20 19	20 18			20 31			

		LO	LO	SN	SE	SN		SN	SN	SN	LO	SN	LO	LO	LO	LO		LO	SN	SE	SN	SN	SN	SN	LO
East Croydon	d								20 12	20 17													20 42	20 47	
West Croydon 4	d										20 27	20 34			20 42										20 57
Norwood Junction 2	d									20 22	20 31	20 40			20 46									20 52	21 01
Anerley	d									20 25	20 34				20 49									20 55	21 04
Penge West	d									20 27	20 36				20 51									20 57	21 06
London Victoria 15 ⊖	d							20 11														20 41			
Battersea Park 4	d							20 15														20 45			
Wandsworth Road	d							20 17														20 47			
Clapham High Street ⊖	d							20 19														20 49			
London Blackfriars 3 ⊖	d				20 08															20 38					
Denmark Hill 4	d				20 18			20 24												20 48		20 54			
Peckham Rye 4	d			20 15	20a21	20 23		20 26	20 40										20 45	20a51	20 53	20 56	21 10		
Queens Rd Peckham	d					20 26		20 29	20 42												20 56	20 59	21 12		
South Bermondsey	d					20 28		20 31	20 45												20 58	21 01	21 15		
Clapham Junction 10	d																								
Wandsworth Common	d																								
Balham 4 ⊖	d																								
Streatham Hill	d																								
West Norwood 4	d			20 27															20 57						
Gipsy Hill	d			20 30															21 00						
Crystal Palace 4	d		20 31	20a32										20 46				21 01	21a02						
Sydenham	d		20 34							20 29	20 39	20 44		20 49	20 54			21 04						20 59	21 09
Forest Hill 4	d		20 37							20 32	20 41	20 47		20 52	20 56			21 07						21 02	21 11
Honor Oak Park	d		20 39							20 34	20 44	20 49		20 54	20 59			21 09						21 04	21 14
Brockley	d		20 42							20 37	20 46	20 52		20 57	21 01			21 12						21 07	21 16
New Cross Gate 4	a		20 44							20 39	20 49	20 54		20 59	21 04			21 14						21 09	21 19
	d		20 44							20 39	20 49	20 54		20 59	21 04			21 14						21 09	21 19
New Cross ELL	d	20 39											20 54			21 09									
Surrey Quays	d	20 43	20 48								20 53		20 58	21 03	21 08	21 13		21 18							21 23
Canada Water	d	20 45	20 50								20 55		21 00	21 05	21 10	21 15		21 20							21 25
Rotherhithe	d	20 46	20 51								20 56		21 01	21 06	21 11	21 16		21 21							21 26
Wapping	d	20 48	20 53								20 58		21 03	21 08	21 13	21 18		21 23							21 28
Shadwell	d	20 50	20 55								21 00		21 05	21 10	21 15	21 20		21 25							21 30
Whitechapel	d	20 52	20 57								21 02		21 07	21 12	21 17	21 22		21 27							21 32
Shoreditch High Street	d	20 54	20 59								21 04		21 09	21 14	21 19	21 24		21 29							21 34
Hoxton	d	20 56	21 01								21 06		21 11	21 16	21 21	21 26		21 31							21 36
Haggerston	d	20 58	21 03								21 08		21 13	21 18	21 23	21 28		21 33							21 38
Dalston Junction Stn ELL	a	21 01	21 05								21 10		21 16	21 20	21 25	21 31		21 35							21 40
Canonbury	d		21 08								21 15			21 23	21 30			21 38							21 45
Highbury & Islington	a		21 13								21 20			21 28	21 35			21 43							21 50
	d																								
London Bridge 4 ⊖	a					20 33		20 36	20 49	20 48		21 01									21 03	21 06	21 19	21 18	

Table 178

Sundays

from 16 September

East London Line and Croydon - London Victoria to London Bridge

Network Diagram - see first Page of Table 177

		SN		LO	LO	LO	LO	LO	SN	SE	SN	SN		SN	SN	LO	SN	LO	LO	LO	LO	LO		SN	SE
East Croydon	d													21 12	21 17										
West Croydon 4	d	21 04				21 12										21 27	21 34			21 42					
Norwood Junction 2	d	21 10				21 16									21 22	21 31	21 40			21 46					
Anerley	d					21 19									21 25	21 34				21 49					
Penge West	d					21 21									21 27	21 36				21 51					
London Victoria 15 ⊖	d											21 11													
Battersea Park 4	d											21 15													
Wandsworth Road	d											21 17													
Clapham High Street ⊖	d											21 19													
London Blackfriars 3 ⊖	d									21 08															21 38
Denmark Hill 4	d									21 18		21 24													21 48
Peckham Rye 4	d								21 15	21a21	21 23	21 26		21 40										21 45	21a51
Queens Rd Peckham	d										21 26	21 29		21 42											
South Bermondsey	d										21 28	21 31		21 45											
Clapham Junction 10	d																								
Wandsworth Common	d																								
Balham 4 ⊖	d																								
Streatham Hill	d																								
West Norwood 4	d								21 27															21 57	
Gipsy Hill	d								21 30															22 00	
Crystal Palace 4	d				21 16			21 31	21a32										21 46			22 01		22a02	
Sydenham	d	21 14			21 19	21 24		21 34							21 29	21 39	21 44		21 49	21 54		22 04			
Forest Hill 4	d	21 17			21 22	21 26		21 37							21 32	21 41	21 47		21 52	21 56		22 07			
Honor Oak Park	d	21 19			21 24	21 29		21 39							21 34	21 44	21 49		21 54	21 59		22 09			
Brockley	d	21 22			21 27	21 31		21 42							21 37	21 46	21 52		21 57	22 01		22 12			
New Cross Gate 4	a	21 24			21 29	21 34		21 44							21 39	21 49	21 54		21 59	22 04		22 14			
	d	21 24			21 29	21 34		21 44							21 39	21 49	21 54		21 59	22 04		22 14			
New Cross ELL	d			21 24			21 39											21 54			22 09				
Surrey Quays	d			21 28	21 33	21 38	21 43	21 48								21 53		21 58	22 03	22 08	22 13	22 18			
Canada Water	d			21 30	21 35	21 40	21 45	21 50								21 55		22 00	22 05	22 10	22 15	22 20			
Rotherhithe	d			21 31	21 36	21 41	21 46	21 51								21 56		22 01	22 06	22 11	22 16	22 21			
Wapping	d			21 33	21 38	21 43	21 48	21 53								21 58		22 03	22 08	22 13	22 18	22 23			
Shadwell	d			21 35	21 40	21 45	21 50	21 55								22 00		22 05	22 10	22 15	22 20	22 25			
Whitechapel	d			21 37	21 42	21 47	21 52	21 57								22 02		22 07	22 12	22 17	22 22	22 27			
Shoreditch High Street	d			21 39	21 44	21 49	21 54	21 59								22 04		22 09	22 14	22 19	22 24	22 29			
Hoxton	d			21 41	21 46	21 51	21 56	22 01								22 06		22 11	22 16	22 21	22 26	22 31			
Haggerston	d			21 43	21 48	21 53	21 58	22 03								22 08		22 13	22 18	22 23	22 28	22 33			
Dalston Junction Stn ELL	a			21 46	21 50	21 55	22 01	22 05								22 10		22 16	22 20	22 25	22 31	22 35			
Canonbury	d				21 53	22 00		22 08								22 15			22 23	22 30		22 38			
Highbury & Islington	a				21 58	22 05		22 13								22 20			22 28	22 35		22 43			
	d																								
London Bridge 4 ⊖	a	21 31									21 33	21 36		21 49	21 48		22 01								

		SN	SN	SN	SN	LO	SN	LO		LO	SN	SE	SN	SN	SN	SN	LO	LO		SN	LO	LO	SN	SE	SN
East Croydon	d			21 42	21 47										22 12	22 17									
West Croydon 4	d					21 57	22 04			22 12								22 27		22 34		22 42			
Norwood Junction 2	d				21 52	22 01	22 10			22 16						22 22		22 31		22 40		22 46			
Anerley	d				21 55	22 04				22 19						22 25		22 34				22 49			
Penge West	d				21 57	22 06				22 21						22 27		22 36				22 51			
London Victoria 15 ⊖	d		21 41											22 11											
Battersea Park 4	d		21 45											22 15											
Wandsworth Road	d		21 47											22 17											
Clapham High Street ⊖	d		21 49											22 19											
London Blackfriars 3 ⊖	d											22 08												22 38	
Denmark Hill 4	d		21 54									22 18		22 24										22 48	
Peckham Rye 4	d	21 53	21 56	22 10							22 15	22a21	22 23	22 26	22 40								22 45	22a51	22 53
Queens Rd Peckham	d	21 56	21 59	22 12									22 26	22 29	22 42										22 56
South Bermondsey	d	21 58	22 01	22 15									22 28	22 31	22 45										22 58
Clapham Junction 10	d																								
Wandsworth Common	d																								
Balham 4 ⊖	d																								
Streatham Hill	d																								
West Norwood 4	d										22 27												22 57		
Gipsy Hill	d										22 30												23 00		
Crystal Palace 4	d							22 16			22a32										22 46		23a02		
Sydenham	d				21 59	22 09	22 14	22 19		22 24						22 29		22 39		22 44	22 49	22 54			
Forest Hill 4	d				22 02	22 11	22 17	22 22		22 26						22 32		22 41		22 47	22 52	22 56			
Honor Oak Park	d				22 04	22 14	22 19	22 24		22 29						22 34		22 44		22 49	22 54	22 59			
Brockley	d				22 07	22 16	22 22	22 27		22 31						22 37		22 46		22 52	22 57	23 01			
New Cross Gate 4	a				22 09	22 19	22 24	22 29		22 34						22 39		22 49		22 54	22 59	23 04			
	d				22 09	22 19	22 24	22 29		22 34						22 39		22 49		22 54	22 59	23 04			
New Cross ELL	d																22 39								
Surrey Quays	d					22 23		22 33		22 38							22 43	22 53			23 03	23 08			
Canada Water	d					22 25		22 35		22 40							22 45	22 55			23 05	23 10			
Rotherhithe	d					22 26		22 36		22 41							22 46	22 56			23 06	23 11			
Wapping	d					22 28		22 38		22 43							22 48	22 58			23 08	23 13			
Shadwell	d					22 30		22 40		22 45							22 50	23 00			23 10	23 15			
Whitechapel	d					22 32		22 42		22 47							22 52	23 02			23 12	23 17			
Shoreditch High Street	d					22 34		22 44		22 49							22 54	23 04			23 14	23 19			
Hoxton	d					22 36		22 46		22 51							22 56	23 06			23 16	23 21			
Haggerston	d					22 38		22 48		22 53							22 58	23 08			23 18	23 23			
Dalston Junction Stn ELL	a					22 40		22 50		22 55							23 01	23 10			23 20	23 25			
Canonbury	d					22 45		22 53		23 00								23 15			23 23	23 30			
Highbury & Islington	a					22 50		22 58		23 05								23 20			23 28	23 35			
	d																								
London Bridge 4 ⊖	a	22 03	22 06	22 19	22 18		22 31						22 33	22 36	22 49	22 48				23 01					23 03

Table 178

Sundays

from 16 September

East London Line and Croydon - London Victoria to London Bridge

Network Diagram - see first Page of Table 177

		SN	SN	SN		LO	LO	LO	SN	SE	SN	SN	SE	SN
East Croydon	d		22 42	22 47										
West Croydon 4	d						22 57							
Norwood Junction 2	d			22 52			23 01							
Anerley	d			22 55			23 04							
Penge West	d			22 57			23 06							
London Victoria 15 ⊖	d	22 41										23 11		
Battersea Park 4	d	22 45										23 15		
Wandsworth Road	d	22 47										23 17		
Clapham High Street ⊖	d	22 49										23 19		
London Blackfriars 3 ⊖	d									23 08			23 38	
Denmark Hill 4	d	22 54								23 18		23 24	23 48	
Peckham Rye 4	d	22 56	23 10						23 15	23a21	23 23	23 26	23a51	23 53
Queens Rd Peckham	d	22 59	23 12								23 26	23 29		23 56
South Bermondsey	d	23 01	23 15								23 28	23 31		23 58
Clapham Junction 10	d													
Wandsworth Common	d													
Balham 4 ⊖	d													
Streatham Hill	d													
West Norwood 4	d								23 27					
Gipsy Hill	d								23 30					
Crystal Palace 4	d							23 16	23a32					
Sydenham	d			22 59			23 09	23 19						
Forest Hill 4	d			23 02			23 11	23 22						
Honor Oak Park	d			23 04			23 14	23 24						
Brockley	d			23 07			23 16	23 27						
New Cross Gate 4	a			23 09			23 19	23 29						
	d			23 09			23 19	23 29						
New Cross ELL	d					23 09								
Surrey Quays	d					23 13	23 23	23 33						
Canada Water	d					23 15	23 25	23 35						
Rotherhithe	d					23 16	23 26	23 36						
Wapping	d					23 18	23 28	23 38						
Shadwell	d					23 20	23 30	23 40						
Whitechapel	d					23 22	23 32	23 42						
Shoreditch High Street	d					23 24	23 34	23 44						
Hoxton	d					23 26	23 36	23 46						
Haggerston	d					23 28	23 38	23 48						
Dalston Junction Stn ELL	a					23 31	23 40	23 50						
Canonbury	d						23 45	23 53						
Highbury & Islington	a						23 50	23 58						
	d													
London Bridge 4 ⊖	a	23 06	23 19	23 18							23 33	23 36		00 03

Luton and London - Wimbledon and Sutton via Streatham

Network Diagram - see first Page of Table 177

Miles	Miles			FC MX A	FC MX B	FC MX A	FC MX B	SN	FC	SN	FC	FC	SN	FC	SN	FC	FC C	FC D	FC E	SN
—	—	Luton	d	22p20		22p46					05 08			05 48		06 06	06 32	06 34	06 39	
—	—	Luton Airport Parkway	d	22p22		22p49					05 10			05 50		06 08			06 41	
—	—	St Pancras International ⊖	d	23p06		23p36			05 36		05 54	06 12		06 34		06 52	07 04	07 04	07 16	
—	—	Farringdon ⊖	d	23p10		23p40			05 42		06 00	06 18		06 40		06 58	07 10	07 10	07 22	
—	0	City Thameslink	d						05 44		06 03	06 21		06 43		07 01	07 13	07 13	07 25	
—	0½	London Blackfriars ⊖	d	23p16		23p46			05 47		06 06	06 24		06 46		07 04	07 16	07 16	07 28	
—	1½	Elephant & Castle ⊖	d	23p19		23p49			05 50		06 09	06 27		06 49		07 07	07 19	07 19	07 33	
—	3½	Loughborough Jn	d	23b23							06 13	06 31		06 53		07 11	07 23	07 23	07 37	
—	4½	Herne Hill	d	23p27		23p57			05 57		06 17	06 35		06 57		07 15	07 27	07 27	07 41	
0	—	London Bridge ⊖	d		23p29		23p59			06 00			06 30		06 58					07 29
1¾	—	South Bermondsey	d							06 04			06 34		07 02					07 33
2¾	—	Queens Rd Peckham	d							06 06			06 36		07 04					07 35
3½	—	Peckham Rye	d							06 09			06 39		07 07					07 38
4½	—	East Dulwich	d							06 12			06 42		07 10					07 41
4¾	—	North Dulwich	d							06 14			06 44		07 12					07 43
6	5½	Tulse Hill	d	23p31	23p41	00 01	00 09		06 02	06 18	06 22	06 42	06 48	07 02	07 16	07 20	07 31	07 31	07 45	07 47
7½	7	Streatham	d	23p35	23p45	00 05	00 13		06 05	06 21	06 25	06 45	06 51	07 05	07 19	07 23	07 34	07 34	07 48	07 51
—	8	Mitcham Eastfields	d								06 29	06 49				07 27			07 52	
—	9	Mitcham Junction	d								06 32	06 52				07 30			07 55	
—	11	Hackbridge	d								06 35	06 55				07 33			07 58	
—	11¾	Carshalton	d								06 38	06 58				07 36			08 01	
9	—	Tooting	d	23p40	23p50	00 10	00 18		06 10	06 25			06 55	07 10	07 23		07 38	07 38		07 55
10¼	—	Haydons Road	d	23p43	23p53	00 13	00 21		06 13	06 28			06 58	07 13	07 26		07 41	07 41		07 58
11½	—	Wimbledon ⊖	a	23p46	23p56	00 16	00 24		06 15	06 31			07 01	07 16	07 30		07 44	07 44		08 01
—	—		d	23p49	23p57	00 19	00 25	05 56	06 16	06 32			07 02	07 16	07 31		07 47	07 47		08 02
12½	—	Wimbledon Chase	d	23p52	00 01	00 22	00 28	05 59	06 19	06 35			07 05	07 19	07 34		07 50	07 50		08 05
13	—	South Merton	d	23p54	00 03	00 24	00 30	06 01	06 21	06 37			07 07	07 21	07 36		07 52	07 52		08 07
13½	—	Morden South	d	23p56	00 05	00 26	00 32	06 03	06 23	06 39			07 09	07 23	07 38		07 54	07 54		08 09
14	—	St Helier	d	23p58	00 07	00 28	00 34	06 05	06 25	06 41			07 11	07 25	07 40		07 56	07 56		08 11
15	—	Sutton Common	d	00 01	00 09	00 30	00 36	06 07	06 27	06 43			07 13	07 27	07 42		07 58	07 58		08 13
16	—	West Sutton	d	00 04	00 12	00 33	00 39	06 10	06 30	06 46			07 16	07 30	07 45		08 01	08 01		08 16
17	13	Sutton (Surrey)	a	00 09	00 15	00 39	00 43	06 13	06 33	06 49	06 43	07 03	07 19	07 35	07 48	07 39	08 07	08 07	08 04	08 19

		FC	FC	SN	FC	SN	FC E	FC	FC	FC	FC	FC	FC	FC	FC	FC	FC	FC	FC	FC	FC
Luton	d	06 50	07 10		07 30			07 57	08 02			08 54		09 14		09 44		10 14		10 44	
Luton Airport Parkway	d	06 52	07 12		07 32			07 59	08 04			08 56		09 16		09 46		10 16		10 46	
St Pancras International ⊖	d	07 32	07 52		08 12		08 24	08 32	08 44	08 56	09 16	09 34	09 48	10 04	10 18	10 34	10 48	11 04	11 18	11 34	11 48
Farringdon ⊖	d	07 38	07 58		08 18		08 30	08 38	08 50	09 02	09 22	09 40	09 53	10 09	10 24	10 39	10 54	11 09	11 24	11 39	11 53
City Thameslink	d	07 41	08 01		08 21		08 33	08 41	08 53	09 05	09 25	09 43	09 57	10 13	10 27	10 43	10 57	11 13	11 27	11 43	11 57
London Blackfriars ⊖	d	07 44	08 04		08 24		08 36	08 44	08 56	09 08	09 28	09 46	10 00	10 16	10 30	10 46	11 00	11 16	11 30	11 46	12 00
Elephant & Castle ⊖	d	07 47	08 07		08 27			08 47	09 00	09 12	09 31	09 49	10 03	10 19	10 33	10 49	11 03	11 19	11 33	11 49	12 03
Loughborough Jn	d	07 51	08 11		08 31			08 51	09 04	09 16	09 35	09 53	10 07	10 23	10 37	10 53	11 07	11 23	11 37	11 53	12 07
Herne Hill	d	07 57	08 17		08 36		08 46	08 57	09 11	09 25	09 41	09 57	10 11	10 27	10 41	10 57	11 11	11 27	11 41	11 57	12 11
London Bridge ⊖	d			08 06		08 24															
South Bermondsey	d			08 11		08 28															
Queens Rd Peckham	d			08 13		08 30															
Peckham Rye	d			08 16		08 33															
East Dulwich	d			08 19		08 36															
North Dulwich	d			08 21		08 38															
Tulse Hill	d	08 05	08 21	08 25	08 40	08 47	08 50	09 01	09 16	09 31	09 46	10 01	10 16	10 31	10 46	11 01	11 16	11 31	11 46	12 01	12 16
Streatham	d	08 08	08 24	08 28	08 44	08 50	08 54	09 05	09 20	09 35	09 50	10 05	10 20	10 35	10 50	11 05	11 20	11 35	11 50	12 05	12 20
Mitcham Eastfields	d		08 28				08 58		09 24		09 54		10 24		10 54		11 24		11 54		12 24
Mitcham Junction	d		08 31				09 01		09 27		09 57		10 27		10 57		11 27		11 57		12 27
Hackbridge	d		08 34				09 04		09 30		10 00		10 30		11 00		11 30		12 00		12 30
Carshalton	d		08 37				09 07		09 33		10 03		10 33		11 03		11 33		12 03		12 33
Tooting	d	08 12		08 33	08 48			09 10		09 40		10 10		10 40		11 10		11 40		12 10	
Haydons Road	d	08 15		08 36	08 51			09 13		09 43		10 13		10 43		11 13		11 43		12 13	
Wimbledon ⊖	a	08 18		08 38	08 54			09 16		09 46		10 16		10 46		11 16		11 46		12 16	
	d	08 19		08 39	08 55			09 17		09 47		10 17		10 47		11 17		11 47		12 17	
Wimbledon Chase	d	08 22		08 42	08 58			09 20		09 50		10 20		10 50		11 20		11 50		12 20	
South Merton	d	08 24		08 44	09 00			09 22		09 52		10 22		10 52		11 22		11 52		12 22	
Morden South	d	08 26		08 46	09 02			09 24		09 54		10 24		10 54		11 24		11 54		12 24	
St Helier	d	08 28		08 48	09 04			09 26		09 56		10 26		10 56		11 26		11 56		12 26	
Sutton Common	d	08 30		08 50	09 06			09 28		09 58		10 28		10 58		11 28		11 58		12 28	
West Sutton	d	08 33		08 53	09 09			09 31		10 01		10 31		11 01		11 31		12 01		12 31	
Sutton (Surrey)	a	08 37	08 40	08 56	09 12	09 02	09 10	09 37	09 36	10 05	10 06	10 35	10 36	11 05	11 06	11 35	11 36	12 05	12 06	12 35	12 36

A from 22 May
B until 18 May
C from 8 October
D until 5 October
E ■ from London Blackfriars
b Previous night, stops to set down only

Table 179 Mondays to Fridays

Luton and London - Wimbledon and Sutton via Streatham

Network Diagram - see first Page of Table 177

		FC	FC		FC	FC	FC	FC	FC	FC	FC ■	FC	SN	FC	FC ■	FC	SN	FC	FC	FC	FC ■	SN
Luton	d	11 14				14 44		15 14		15 44	16 04			16 16	16 42			16 46	17 10		17 18	
Luton Airport Parkway	d	11 16				14 46		15 16		15 46	16 06			16 18	16 44			16 48	17 12		17 20	
St Pancras International ⊖	d	12 04	12 18		15 18	15 34	15 48	16 04	16 18	16 34	16 40	16 52		17 02	17 14	17 18		17 32	17 44	17 52	17 56	
Farringdon ⊖	d	12 09	12 23		15 23	15 39	15 53	16 09	16 23	16 39	16 45	16 57		17 07	17 19	17 23		17 37	17 49	17 57	18 01	
City Thameslink	d	12 13	12 27		15 27	15 43	15 57	16 13	16 27	16 43	16 49	17 01		17 11	17 23	17 27		17 41	17 53	18 01	18 05	
London Blackfriars ⊖	d	12 16	12 30		15 30	15 46	16 00	16 16	16 30	16 46	16 52	17 04		17 14	17 25	17 30		17 44	17 56	18 04	18 10	
Elephant & Castle ⊖	d	12 19	12 33		15 33	15 49	16 03	16 19	16 33	16 49	16 56	17 08		17 18	17 29	17 34		17 48	18 00	18 08	18 14	
Loughborough Jn	d	12 23	12 37		15 37	15 53	16 07	16 23	16 37	16 53	17 00	17 12		17 22		17 38		17 52		18 12		
Herne Hill	d	12 27	12 41		15 41	15 57	16 11	16 27	16 41	16 57	17a04	17 16		17 26	17a36	17 43		17 57	18a06	18 17	18a21	
London Bridge ⊖	d												17 06				17 37					18 08
South Bermondsey	d												17 10				17 41					18 12
Queens Rd Peckham	d			and at									17 12				17 43					18 14
Peckham Rye	d			the same									17 15				17 46					18 17
East Dulwich	d			minutes									17 18				17 49					18 20
North Dulwich	d			past									17 20				17 51					18 22
Tulse Hill	d	12 31	12 46	each	15 46	16 01	16 16	16 32	16 46	17 02		17 20	17 24	17 31		17 48	17 55	18 02		18 22		18 27
Streatham	d	12 35	12 50	hour until	15 50	16 05	16 20	16 36	16 50	17 06		17 24	17 28	17 36		17 52	17 58	18 06		18 26		18 30
Mitcham Eastfields	d		12 54		15 54		16 24		16 55			17 28	17 32			17 55	18 02			18 29		18 34
Mitcham Junction	d		12 57		15 57		16 27		16 58			17 31	17 35			17 58	18 05			18 32		18 37
Hackbridge	d		13 00		16 00		16 30		17 01			17 34	17 38			18 02	18 09			18 36		18 41
Carshalton	d		13 03		16 03		16 33		17 04			17 37	17 41			18 04	18 11			18 38		18 43
Tooting	d	12 40				16 10		16 40		17 10				17 40				18 10				
Haydons Road	d	12 43				16 13		16 43		17 13				17 43				18 13				
Wimbledon ⊖	a	12 46				16 16		16 46		17 16				17 46				18 16				
	d	12 47				16 17		16 47		17 19				17 49				18 19				
Wimbledon Chase	d	12 50				16 20		16 50		17 22				17 52				18 22				
South Merton	d	12 52				16 22		16 52		17 24				17 54				18 24				
Morden South	d	12 54				16 24		16 54		17 26				17 56				18 26				
St Helier	d	12 56				16 26		16 56		17 28				17 58				18 28				
Sutton Common	d	12 58				16 28		16 58		17 30				18 00				18 30				
West Sutton	d	13 01				16 31		17 01		17 33				18 03				18 33				
Sutton (Surrey)	a	13 05	13 06		16 06	16 35	16 36	17 05	17 08	17 37		17 40	17 44	18 07		18 08	18 15	18 37		18 42		18 47

		FC	FC	SN	FC	FC	FC	FC	FC	FC	FC	FC	FC	FC A	FC	FC	FC	FC A	FC B	FC A	FC B	FC A
Luton	d	17 22	17 38			18 06	18 22		18 54		19 24		19 46		20 20	20 50	21 20	21 50		22 20		22 46
Luton Airport Parkway	d	17 24	17 40			18 08	18 24		18 57		19 27		19 48		20 22	20 52	21 22	21 52		22 22		22 49
St Pancras International ⊖	d	18 04	18 24		18 38	18 48	19 04	19 18	19 34	19 48	20 04	20 18	20 34	20 48	21 06	21 36	22 06	22 36		23 06		23 36
Farringdon ⊖	d	18 09	18 29		18 43	18 53	19 09	19 23	19 39	19 53	20 09	20 23	20 39	20 53	21 10	21 40	22 10	22 40		23 10		23 40
City Thameslink	d	18 13	18 33		18 47	18 57	19 13	19 27	19 43	19 57	20 13	20 27	20 43	20 57	21 13	21 43	22 13	22 43				
London Blackfriars ⊖	d	18 16	18 36		18 50	19 00	19 16	19 30	19 46	20 00	20 16	20 30	20 46	21 00	21 16	21 46	22 16	22 46		23 16		23 46
Elephant & Castle ⊖	d	18 20	18 40		18 54	19 04	19 19	19 33	19 49	20 03	20 19	20 33	20 49	21 03	21 19	21 49	22 19	22 49		23 19		23 49
Loughborough Jn	d	18 24	18 44		18 58	19 08	19 23	19 37	19 53	20 07	20 23	20 37	20 53	21 07	21 23	21 53	22 23	22 53		23s23		
Herne Hill	d	18 28	18 48		19 02	19 12	19 27	19 41	19 57	20 11	20 27	20 41	20 57	21 11	21 27	21 57	22 27	22 57		23 27		23 57
London Bridge ⊖	d			18 38															23 01		23 29	
South Bermondsey	d			18 42																		
Queens Rd Peckham	d			18 44																		
Peckham Rye	d			18 47																		
East Dulwich	d			18 50																		
North Dulwich	d			18 52																		
Tulse Hill	d	18 32	18 52	18 56	19 09	19 16	19 31	19 46	20 01	20 16	20 31	20 50	21 01	21 20	21 31	22 01	22 31	23 01	23 11	23 31	23 41	00 01
Streatham	d	18 36	18 56	18 59	19 13	19 20	19 35	19 50	20 05	20 20	20 35	20 53	21 05	21 23	21 35	22 05	22 35	23 05	23 15	23 35	23 45	00 05
Mitcham Eastfields	d		18 59	19 03		19 24		19 54		20 24		20 57		21 27								
Mitcham Junction	d		19 02	19 06		19 27		19 57		20 27		21 00		21 30								
Hackbridge	d		19 06	19 10		19 30		20 00		20 30		21 03		21 33								
Carshalton	d		19 08	19 12		19 33		20 03		20 33		21 06		21 36								
Tooting	d	18 40			19 18		19 40		20 10		20 40		21 10		21 40	22 10	22 40	23 10	23 20	23 40	23 50	00 10
Haydons Road	d	18 43			19 21		19 43		20 13		20 43		21 13		21 43	22 13	22 43	23 13	23 23	23 43	23 53	00 13
Wimbledon ⊖	a	18 46			19 23		19 46		20 16		20 46		21 16		21 46	22 16	22 46	23 16	23 26	23 46	23 56	00 16
	d	18 49			19 24		19 49		20 19		20 49		21 19		21 49	22 19	22 49	23 17	23 27	23 49	23 57	00 19
Wimbledon Chase	d	18 52			19 27		19 52		20 22		20 52		21 22		21 52	22 22	22 52	23 20	23 30	23 52	00 01	00 22
South Merton	d	18 54			19 29		19 54		20 24		20 54		21 24		21 54	22 24	22 54	23 22	23 32	23 54	00 03	00 24
Morden South	d	18 56			19 31		19 56		20 26		20 56		21 26		21 56	22 26	22 56	23 24	23 34	23 56	00 05	00 26
St Helier	d	18 58			19 33		19 58		20 28		20 58		21 28		21 58	22 28	22 58	23 26	23 36	23 58	00 07	00 28
Sutton Common	d	19 00			19 35		20 00		20 30		21 00		21 30		22 00	22 30	23 00	23 28	23 38	00 01	00 09	00 30
West Sutton	d	19 03			19 38		20 03		20 33		21 03		21 33		22 03	22 33	23 03	23 31	23 41	00 04	00 12	00 33
Sutton (Surrey)	a	19 07	19 12	19 16	19 41	19 36	20 07	20 06	20 39	20 36	21 09	21 10	21 39	21 40	22 09	22 39	23 09	23 35	23 45	00 09	00 15	00 39

A from 21 May
B until 18 May

Luton and London - Wimbledon and Sutton via Streatham

Network Diagram - see first Page of Table 177

Station		FC A
Luton	d	
Luton Airport Parkway	d	
St Pancras International ⊖	d	
Farringdon ⊖	d	
City Thameslink	d	
London Blackfriars ⊖	d	
Elephant & Castle ⊖	d	
Loughborough Jn	d	
Herne Hill	d	
London Bridge ⊖	d	23 59
South Bermondsey	d	
Queens Rd Peckham	d	
Peckham Rye	d	
East Dulwich	d	
North Dulwich	d	
Tulse Hill	d	00 09
Streatham	d	00 13
Mitcham Eastfields	d	
Mitcham Junction	d	
Hackbridge	d	
Carshalton	d	
Tooting	d	00 18
Haydons Road	d	00 21
Wimbledon ⊖	a	00 24
	d	00 25
Wimbledon Chase	d	00 28
South Merton	d	00 30
Morden South	d	00 32
St Helier	d	00 34
Sutton Common	d	00 36
West Sutton	d	00 39
Sutton (Surrey)	a	00 43

Saturdays
until 23 June

Station		FC B	FC C	FC B	FC C	FC	FC	FC	FC	FC	FC	FC	FC	FC	FC	FC	FC	FC	FC	FC	FC
Luton	d	22p20		22p46				05 30		06 00		06 30		07 00	07 14	07 30	07 44	08 00	08 14		08 44
Luton Airport Parkway	d	22p22		22p49				05 32		06 02		06 32		07 02	07 16	07 32	07 46	08 02	08 16		08 46
St Pancras International ⊖	d	23p06		23p36		05 48		06 18	06 34	06 48	07 04	07 18	07 34	07 48	08 04	08 18	08 34	08 48	09 04	09 18	09 34
Farringdon ⊖	d	23p10		23p40		05 53		06 23	06 39	06 53	07 09	07 23	07 39	07 53	08 09	08 23	08 39	08 53	09 09	09 23	09 39
City Thameslink	d																		09 13	09 27	09 43
London Blackfriars ⊖	d	23p16		23p46		06 00	06 16	06 30	06 46	07 00	07 16	07 30	07 46	08 00	08 16	08 30	08 46	09 00	09 16	09 30	09 46
Elephant & Castle ⊖	d	23p19		23p49		06 03	06 19	06 33	06 49	07 03	07 19	07 33	07 49	08 03	08 19	08 33	08 49	09 03	09 19	09 33	09 49
Loughborough Jn	d	23b23							06 53	07 07	07 23	07 37	07 53	08 07	08 23	08 37	08 53	09 07	09 23	09 37	09 53
Herne Hill	d	23p27		23p57		06 11	06 27	06 41	06 57	07 11	07 27	07 41	07 57	08 11	08 27	08 41	08 57	09 11	09 27	09 41	09 57
London Bridge ⊖	d		23p29		23p59																
South Bermondsey	d																				
Queens Rd Peckham	d																				
Peckham Rye	d																				
East Dulwich	d																				
North Dulwich	d																				
Tulse Hill	d	23p31	23p41	00 01	00 09	06 16	06 31	06 46	07 01	07 16	07 31	07 46	08 01	08 16	08 31	08 46	09 01	09 16	09 31	09 46	10 01
Streatham	d	23p35	23p45	00 05	00 13	06 20	06 35	06 50	07 05	07 20	07 35	07 50	08 05	08 20	08 35	08 50	09 05	09 20	09 35	09 50	10 05
Mitcham Eastfields	d					06 24		06 54		07 24		07 54		08 24		08 54		09 24		09 54	
Mitcham Junction	d					06 27		06 57		07 27		07 57		08 27		08 57		09 27		09 57	
Hackbridge	d					06 30		07 00		07 30		08 00		08 30		09 00		09 30		10 00	
Carshalton	d					06 33		07 03		07 33		08 03		08 33		09 03		09 33		10 03	
Tooting	d	23p40	23p50	00 10	00 18		06 40		07 10		07 40		08 10		08 40		09 10		09 40		10 10
Haydons Road	d	23p43	23p53	00 13	00 21		06 43		07 13		07 43		08 13		08 43		09 13		09 43		10 13
Wimbledon ⊖	a	23p46	23p56	00 16	00 24		06 46		07 16		07 46		08 16		08 46		09 16		09 46		10 16
	d	23p49	23p57	00 19	00 25		06 47		07 17		07 47		08 17		08 47		09 17		09 47		10 17
Wimbledon Chase	d	23p52	00 01	00 22	00 28		06 50		07 20		07 50		08 20		08 50		09 20		09 50		10 20
South Merton	d	23p54	00 03	00 24	00 30		06 52		07 22		07 52		08 22		08 52		09 22		09 52		10 22
Morden South	d	23p56	00 05	00 26	00 32		06 54		07 24		07 54		08 24		08 54		09 24		09 54		10 24
St Helier	d	23p58	00 07	00 28	00 34		06 56		07 26		07 56		08 26		08 56		09 26		09 56		10 26
Sutton Common	d	00 01	00 09	00 30	00 36		06 58		07 28		07 58		08 28		08 58		09 28		09 58		10 28
West Sutton	d	00 04	00 12	00 33	00 39		07 01		07 31		08 01		08 31		09 01		09 31		10 01		10 31
Sutton (Surrey)	a	00 09	00 15	00 39	00 43	06 36	07 05	07 06	07 35	07 36	08 05	08 06	08 35	08 36	09 05	09 06	09 35	09 36	10 05	10 06	10 35

A until 18 May
B not 19 May
C 19 May
b Previous night, stops to set down only

Saturdays
until 23 June

Luton and London - Wimbledon and Sutton via Streatham

Network Diagram - see first Page of Table 177

Station		FC		FC	FC	FC	FC	FC	FC		FC	FC	FC
Luton	d				19 14		19 50		20 20		21 50		
Luton Airport Parkway	d				19 16		19 52		20 22		21 52		
St Pancras International ⊖	d	09 48		19 48	20 04	20 18	20 36	20 48	21 06		22 36	23 06	23 36
Farringdon ⊖	d	09 53		19 53	20 09	20 23	20 40	20 53	21 10		22 40	23 10	23 40
City Thameslink	d	09 57		19 57	20 13	20 27	20 43	20 57					
London Blackfriars ⊖	d	10 00		20 00	20 16	20 30	20 46	21 00	21 16		22 46	23 16	23 46
Elephant & Castle ⊖	d	10 03		20 03	20 19	20 33	20 49	21 03	21 19		22 49	23 19	23 49
Loughborough Jn	d	10 07		20 07	20 23	20 37	20 53	21 07	21 23		22 53	23 23	
Herne Hill	d	10 11		20 11	20 27	20 41	20 57	21 11	21 27		22 57	23 27	23 57
London Bridge ⊖	d												
South Bermondsey	d												
Queens Rd Peckham	d												
Peckham Rye	d		and at the same minutes past each hour until							and every 30 minutes until			
East Dulwich	d												
North Dulwich	d												
Tulse Hill	d	10 16		20 16	20 31	20 46	21 01	21 16	21 31		23 01	23 31	00 01
Streatham	d	10 20		20 20	20 35	20 50	21 05	21 20	21 35		23 05	23 35	00 05
Mitcham Eastfields	d	10 24		20 24		20 54		21 24					
Mitcham Junction	d	10 27		20 27		20 57		21 27					
Hackbridge	d	10 30		20 30		21 00		21 30					
Carshalton	d	10 33		20 33		21 03		21 33					
Tooting	d				20 40		21 10		21 40		23 10	23 40	00 10
Haydons Road	d				20 43		21 13		21 43		23 13	23 43	00 13
Wimbledon ⊖	a				20 46		21 16		21 46		23 16	23 46	00 16
	d				20 47		21 17		21 47		23 17	23 47	00 17
Wimbledon Chase	d				20 50		21 20		21 50		23 20	23 50	00 20
South Merton	d				20 52		21 22		21 52		23 22	23 52	00 22
Morden South	d				20 54		21 24		21 54		23 24	23 54	00 24
St Helier	d				20 56		21 26		21 56		23 26	23 56	00 26
Sutton Common	d				20 58		21 28		21 58		23 28	23 58	00 28
West Sutton	d				21 01		21 31		22 01		23 31	00 01	00 31
Sutton (Surrey)	a	10 36		20 36	21 05	21 06	21 35	21 42	22 05		23 35	00 05	00 35

Saturdays
30 June to 8 September

Station		FC	FC	FC	FC	FC	FC	FC	FC	FC	FC	FC	FC	FC	FC	FC	FC	FC	FC	FC		FC
Luton	d	22p20	22p46			05 30		06 00		06 30		07 00	07 14	07 30	07 44	08 00	08 14		08 44			
Luton Airport Parkway	d	22p22	22p49			05 32		06 02		06 32		07 02	07 16	07 32	07 46	08 02	08 16		08 46			
St Pancras International ⊖	d	23p06	23p36	05 48		06 18	06 34	06 48	07 04	07 18	07 34	07 48	08 04	08 18	08 34	08 48	09 04	09 18	09 34	09 48		19 48
Farringdon ⊖	d	23p10	23p40	05 53		06 23	06 39	06 53	07 09	07 23	07 39	07 53	08 09	08 23	08 39	08 53	09 09	09 23	09 39	09 53		19 53
City Thameslink	d																09 13	09 27	09 43	09 57		19 57
London Blackfriars ⊖	d	23p16	23p46	06 00	06 16	06 30	06 46	07 00	07 16	07 30	07 46	08 00	08 16	08 30	08 46	09 00	09 16	09 30	09 46	10 00		20 00
Elephant & Castle ⊖	d	23p19	23p49	06 03	06 19	06 33	06 49	07 03	07 19	07 33	07 49	08 03	08 19	08 33	08 49	09 03	09 19	09 33	09 49	10 03		20 03
Loughborough Jn	d	23b23					06 53	07 07	07 23	07 37	07 53	08 07	08 23	08 37	08 53	09 07	09 23	09 37	09 53	10 07		20 07
Herne Hill	d	23p27	23p57	06 11	06 27	06 41	06 57	07 11	07 27	07 41	07 57	08 11	08 27	08 41	08 57	09 11	09 27	09 41	09 57	10 11		20 11
London Bridge ⊖	d																					
South Bermondsey	d																					
Queens Rd Peckham	d																					
Peckham Rye	d																				and at the same minutes past each hour until	
East Dulwich	d																					
North Dulwich	d																					
Tulse Hill	d	23p31	00 01	06 16	06 31	06 46	07 01	07 16	07 31	07 46	08 01	08 16	08 31	08 46	09 01	09 16	09 31	09 46	10 01	10 16		20 16
Streatham	d	23p35	00 05	06 20	06 35	06 50	07 05	07 20	07 35	07 50	08 05	08 20	08 35	08 50	09 05	09 20	09 35	09 50	10 05	10 20		20 20
Mitcham Eastfields	d			06 24		06 54		07 24		07 54		08 24		08 54		09 24		09 54		10 24		20 24
Mitcham Junction	d			06 27		06 57		07 27		07 57		08 27		08 57		09 27		09 57		10 27		20 27
Hackbridge	d			06 30		07 00		07 30		08 00		08 30		09 00		09 30		10 00		10 30		20 30
Carshalton	d			06 33		07 03		07 33		08 03		08 33		09 03		09 33		10 03		10 33		20 33
Tooting	d	23p40	00 10		06 40		07 10		07 40		08 10		08 40		09 10		09 40		10 10			
Haydons Road	d	23p43	00 13		06 43		07 13		07 43		08 13		08 43		09 13		09 43		10 13			
Wimbledon ⊖	a	23p46	00 16		06 46		07 16		07 46		08 16		08 46		09 16		09 46		10 16			
	d	23p49	00 19		06 47		07 17		07 47		08 17		08 47		09 17		09 47		10 17			
Wimbledon Chase	d	23p52	00 22		06 50		07 20		07 50		08 20		08 50		09 20		09 50		10 20			
South Merton	d	23p54	00 24		06 52		07 22		07 52		08 22		08 52		09 22		09 52		10 22			
Morden South	d	23p56	00 26		06 54		07 24		07 54		08 24		08 54		09 24		09 54		10 24			
St Helier	d	23p58	00 28		06 56		07 26		07 56		08 26		08 56		09 26		09 56		10 26			
Sutton Common	d	00 01	00 30		06 58		07 28		07 58		08 28		08 58		09 28		09 58		10 28			
West Sutton	d	00 04	00 33		07 01		07 31		08 01		08 31		09 01		09 31		10 01		10 31			
Sutton (Surrey)	a	00 09	00 39	06 36	07 05	07 06	07 35	07 36	08 05	08 06	08 35	08 36	09 05	09 06	09 35	09 36	10 05	10 06	10 35	10 36		20 36

b Previous night, stops to set down only

Table 179

Saturdays
30 June to 8 September

Luton and London - Wimbledon and Sutton via Streatham

Network Diagram - see first Page of Table 177

		FC	FC	FC	FC	FC		FC	FC	FC
Luton	d	19 14		19 50		20 20		21 50	22 20	22 46
Luton Airport Parkway	d	19 16		19 52		20 22		21 52	22 22	22 49
St Pancras International ⊖	d	20 04	20 18	20 36	20 48	21 06		22 36	23 06	23 36
Farringdon ⊖	d	20 09	20 23	20 40	20 53	21 10		22 40	23 10	23 40
City Thameslink	d	20 13	20 27	20 43	20 57					
London Blackfriars ⊖	d	20 16	20 30	20 46	21 00	21 16		22 46	23 16	23 46
Elephant & Castle ⊖	d	20 19	20 33	20 49	21 03	21 19		22 49	23 19	23 49
Loughborough Jn	d	20 23	20 37	20 53	21 07	21 23		22 53	23 23	
Herne Hill	d	20 27	20 41	20 57	21 11	21 27		22 57	23 27	23 57
London Bridge ⊖	d									
South Bermondsey	d									
Queens Rd Peckham	d									
Peckham Rye	d									
East Dulwich	d									
North Dulwich	d									
Tulse Hill	d	20 31	20 46	21 01	21 16	21 31	and every 30 minutes until	23 01	23 31	00 01
Streatham	d	20 35	20 50	21 05	21 20	21 35		23 05	23 35	00 05
Mitcham Eastfields	d		20 54		21 24					
Mitcham Junction	d		20 57		21 27					
Hackbridge	d		21 00		21 30					
Carshalton	d		21 03		21 33					
Tooting	d	20 40		21 10		21 40		23 10	23 40	00 10
Haydons Road	d	20 43		21 13		21 43		23 13	23 43	00 13
Wimbledon ⊖	a	20 46		21 16		21 46		23 16	23 46	00 16
	d	20 47		21 17		21 47		23 17	23 47	00 17
Wimbledon Chase	d	20 50		21 20		21 50		23 20	23 50	00 20
South Merton	d	20 52		21 22		21 52		23 22	23 52	00 22
Morden South	d	20 54		21 24		21 54		23 24	23 54	00 24
St Helier	d	20 56		21 26		21 56		23 26	23 56	00 26
Sutton Common	d	20 58		21 28		21 58		23 28	23 58	00 28
West Sutton	d	21 01		21 31		22 01		23 31	00 01	00 31
Sutton (Surrey)	a	21 05	21 06	21 35	21 42	22 05		23 35	00 05	00 35

Saturdays
from 15 September

		FC	FC	FC	FC	FC	FC	FC	FC	FC	FC	FC	FC	FC	FC	FC	FC	FC	FC	FC		FC
Luton	d	22p20	22p46			05 30		06 00		06 30		07 00	07 14	07 30	07 44	08 00	08 14		08 44			
Luton Airport Parkway	d	22p22	22p49			05 32		06 02		06 32		07 02	07 16	07 32	07 46	08 02	08 16		08 46			
St Pancras International ⊖	d	23p06	23p36	05 48		06 18	06 34	06 48	07 04	07 18	07 34	07 48	08 04	08 18	08 34	08 48	09 04	09 18	09 34	09 48		19 48
Farringdon ⊖	d	23p10	23p40	05 53		06 23	06 39	06 53	07 09	07 23	07 39	07 53	08 09	08 23	08 39	08 53	09 09	09 23	09 39	09 53		19 53
City Thameslink	d																09 13	09 27	09 43	09 57		19 57
London Blackfriars ⊖	d	23p16	23p46	06 00	06 16	06 30	06 46	07 00	07 16	07 30	07 46	08 00	08 16	08 30	08 46	09 00	09 16	09 30	09 46	10 00		20 00
Elephant & Castle ⊖	d	23p19	23p49	06 03	06 19	06 33	06 49	07 03	07 19	07 33	07 49	08 03	08 19	08 33	08 49	09 03	09 19	09 33	09 49	10 03		20 03
Loughborough Jn	d	23b23					06 53	07 07	07 23	07 37	07 53	08 07	08 23	08 37	08 53	09 07	09 23	09 37	09 53	10 07		20 07
Herne Hill	d	23p27	23p57	06 11	06 27	06 41	06 57	07 11	07 27	07 41	07 57	08 11	08 27	08 41	08 57	09 11	09 27	09 41	09 57	10 11		20 11
London Bridge ⊖	d																					
South Bermondsey	d																					
Queens Rd Peckham	d																					
Peckham Rye	d																					
East Dulwich	d																					
North Dulwich	d																					
Tulse Hill	d	23p31	00 01	06 16	06 31	06 46	07 01	07 16	07 31	07 46	08 01	08 16	08 31	08 46	09 01	09 16	09 31	09 46	10 01	10 16	and at the same minutes past each hour until	20 16
Streatham	d	23p35	00 05	06 20	06 35	06 50	07 05	07 20	07 35	07 50	08 05	08 20	08 35	08 50	09 05	09 20	09 35	09 50	10 05	10 20		20 20
Mitcham Eastfields	d			06 24		06 54		07 24		07 54		08 24		08 54		09 24		09 54		10 24		20 24
Mitcham Junction	d			06 27		06 57		07 27		07 57		08 27		08 57		09 27		09 57		10 27		20 27
Hackbridge	d			06 30		07 00		07 30		08 00		08 30		09 00		09 30		10 00		10 30		20 30
Carshalton	d			06 33		07 03		07 33		08 03		08 33		09 03		09 33		10 03		10 33		20 33
Tooting	d	23p40	00 10		06 40		07 10		07 40		08 10		08 40		09 10		09 40		10 10			
Haydons Road	d	23p43	00 13		06 43		07 13		07 43		08 13		08 43		09 13		09 43		10 13			
Wimbledon ⊖	a	23p46	00 16		06 46		07 16		07 46		08 16		08 46		09 16		09 46		10 16			
	d	23p49	00 19		06 47		07 17		07 47		08 17		08 47		09 17		09 47		10 17			
Wimbledon Chase	d	23p52	00 22		06 50		07 20		07 50		08 20		08 50		09 20		09 50		10 20			
South Merton	d	23p54	00 24		06 52		07 22		07 52		08 22		08 52		09 22		09 52		10 22			
Morden South	d	23p56	00 26		06 54		07 24		07 54		08 24		08 54		09 24		09 54		10 24			
St Helier	d	23p58	00 28		06 56		07 26		07 56		08 26		08 56		09 26		09 56		10 26			
Sutton Common	d	00 01	00 30		06 58		07 28		07 58		08 28		08 58		09 28		09 58		10 28			
West Sutton	d	00 04	00 33		07 01		07 31		08 01		08 31		09 01		09 31		10 01		10 31			
Sutton (Surrey)	a	00 09	00 39	06 36	07 05	07 06	07 35	07 36	08 05	08 06	08 35	08 36	09 05	09 06	09 35	09 36	10 05	10 06	10 35	10 36		20 36

b Previous night, stops to set down only

Table 179

Saturdays
from 15 September

Luton and London - Wimbledon and Sutton via Streatham

Network Diagram - see first Page of Table 177

		FC	FC	FC	FC	FC		FC	FC	FC
Luton	d	19 14		19 50		20 20		21 50	22 20	22 46
Luton Airport Parkway	d	19 16		19 52		20 22		21 52	22 22	22 49
St Pancras International ⊖	d	20 04	20 18	20 36	20 48	21 06		22 36	23 06	23 36
Farringdon ⊖	d	20 09	20 23	20 40	20 53	21 10		22 40	23 10	23 40
City Thameslink	d	20 13	20 27	20 43	20 57					
London Blackfriars ⊖	d	20 16	20 30	20 46	21 00	21 16		22 46	23 16	23 46
Elephant & Castle ⊖	d	20 19	20 33	20 49	21 03	21 19		22 49	23 19	23 49
Loughborough Jn	d	20 23	20 37	20 53	21 07	21 23		22 53	23 23	
Herne Hill	d	20 27	20 41	20 57	21 11	21 27		22 57	23 27	23 57
London Bridge ⊖	d									
South Bermondsey	d									
Queens Rd Peckham	d									
Peckham Rye	d									
East Dulwich	d									
North Dulwich	d									
Tulse Hill	d	20 31	20 46	21 01	21 16	21 31	and every 30 minutes until	23 01	23 31	00 01
Streatham	d	20 35	20 50	21 05	21 20	21 35		23 05	23 35	00 05
Mitcham Eastfields	d		20 54		21 24					
Mitcham Junction	d		20 57		21 27					
Hackbridge	d		21 00		21 30					
Carshalton	d		21 03		21 33					
Tooting	d	20 40		21 10		21 40		23 10	23 40	00 10
Haydons Road	d	20 43		21 13		21 43		23 13	23 43	00 13
Wimbledon ⊖	a	20 46		21 16		21 46		23 16	23 46	00 16
	d	20 47		21 17		21 47		23 17	23 47	00 17
Wimbledon Chase	d	20 50		21 20		21 50		23 20	23 50	00 20
South Merton	d	20 52		21 22		21 52		23 22	23 52	00 22
Morden South	d	20 54		21 24		21 54		23 24	23 54	00 24
St Helier	d	20 56		21 26		21 56		23 26	23 56	00 26
Sutton Common	d	20 58		21 28		21 58		23 28	23 58	00 28
West Sutton	d	21 01		21 31		22 01		23 31	00 01	00 31
Sutton (Surrey)	a	21 05	21 06	21 35	21 42	22 05		23 35	00 05	00 35

Sundays
until 24 June

		FC	FC	FC	FC	FC	FC	FC	FC	FC	FC	FC	FC	FC	FC		FC	FC
Luton	d				08 18		08 48		09 18		09 48							
Luton Airport Parkway	d				08 21		08 51		09 21		09 51							
St Pancras International ⊖	d	23p06	23p36		09 05		09 35		10 05		10 35		11 05		11 35		20 35	21 05
Farringdon ⊖	d	23p10	23p40		09 10		09 40		10 10		10 40		11 10		11 40		20 40	21 10
City Thameslink	d																	
London Blackfriars ⊖	d	23p16	23p46	08 56	09 15	09 26	09 45	09 56	10 15	10 26	10 45	10 56	11 15	11 26	11 45		20 45	21 15
Elephant & Castle ⊖	d	23p19	23p49	09 00	09 18	09 30	09 48	10 00	10 18	10 30	10 48	11 00	11 18	11 30	11 48		20 48	21 18
Loughborough Jn	d	23p23		09 04	09 22	09 34	09 52	10 04	10 22	10 34	10 52	11 04	11 22	11 34	11 52		20 52	21 22
Herne Hill	d	23p27	23p57	09 08	09 26	09 38	09 56	10 08	10 26	10 38	10 56	11 08	11 26	11 38	11 56		20 56	21 26
London Bridge ⊖	d																	
South Bermondsey	d																	
Queens Rd Peckham	d																	
Peckham Rye	d																	
East Dulwich	d																	
North Dulwich	d																	
Tulse Hill	d	23p31	00 01	09 12	09 30	09 42	10 00	10 12	10 30	10 42	11 00	11 12	11 30	11 42	12 00	and at the same minutes past each hour until	21 00	21 30
Streatham	d	23p35	00 05	09 16	09 34	09 46	10 04	10 16	10 34	10 46	11 04	11 16	11 34	11 46	12 04		21 04	21 34
Mitcham Eastfields	d			09 20		09 50		10 20		10 50		11 20		11 50				
Mitcham Junction	d			09 23		09 53		10 23		10 53		11 23		11 53				
Hackbridge	d			09 26		09 56		10 26		10 56		11 26		11 56				
Carshalton	d			09 29		09 59		10 29		10 59		11 29		11 59				
Tooting	d	23p40	00 10		09 38		10 08		10 38		11 08		11 38		12 08		21 08	21 38
Haydons Road	d	23p43	00 13		09 41		10 11		10 41		11 11		11 41		12 11		21 11	21 41
Wimbledon ⊖	a	23p46	00 16		09 43		10 13		10 43		11 13		11 43		12 13		21 13	21 43
	d	23p47	00 17		09 44		10 14		10 44		11 14		11 44		12 14		21 14	21 44
Wimbledon Chase	d	23p50	00 20		09 47		10 17		10 47		11 17		11 47		12 17		21 17	21 47
South Merton	d	23p52	00 22		09 49		10 19		10 49		11 19		11 49		12 19		21 19	21 49
Morden South	d	23p54	00 24		09 51		10 21		10 51		11 21		11 51		12 21		21 21	21 51
St Helier	d	23p56	00 26		09 53		10 23		10 53		11 23		11 53		12 23		21 23	21 53
Sutton Common	d	23p58	00 28		09 55		10 25		10 55		11 25		11 55		12 25		21 25	21 55
West Sutton	d	00 01	00 31		09 58		10 28		10 58		11 28		11 58		12 28		21 28	21 58
Sutton (Surrey)	a	00 05	00 35	09 33	10 01	10 03	10 31	10 33	11 01	11 03	11 31	11 33	12 01	12 03	12 31		21 31	22 01

Luton and London - Wimbledon and Sutton via Streatham

Sundays
1 July to 9 September

Network Diagram - see first Page of Table 177

		FC	FC	FC	FC	FC	FC		FC	FC
Luton	d	22p20	22p46		08 18		08 48		19 48	20 18
Luton Airport Parkway	d	22p22	22p49		08 21		08 51		19 51	20 21
St Pancras International ⊖	d	23p06	23p36		09 05		09 35		20 35	21 05
Farringdon ⊖	d	23p10	23p40		09 10		09 40		20 40	21 10
City Thameslink	d									
London Blackfriars ⊖	d	23p16	23p46	08 56	09 15	09 26	09 45		20 45	21 15
Elephant & Castle ⊖	d	23p19	23p49	09 00	09 18	09 30	09 48		20 48	21 18
Loughborough Jn	d	23p23		09 04	09 22	09 34	09 52		20 52	21 22
Herne Hill	d	23p27	23p57	09 08	09 26	09 38	09 56		20 56	21 26
London Bridge ⊖	d									
South Bermondsey	d									
Queens Rd Peckham	d									
Peckham Rye	d							and at		
East Dulwich	d							the same		
North Dulwich	d							minutes		
Tulse Hill	d	23p31	00 01	09 12	09 30	09 42	10 00	past	21 00	21 30
Streatham	d	23p35	00 05	09 16	09 34	09 46	10 04	each	21 04	21 34
Mitcham Eastfields	d			09 20		09 50		hour until		
Mitcham Junction	d			09 23		09 53				
Hackbridge	d			09 26		09 56				
Carshalton	d			09 29		09 59				
Tooting	d	23p40	00 10		09 38		10 08		21 08	21 38
Haydons Road	d	23p43	00 13		09 41		10 11		21 11	21 41
Wimbledon ⊖	a	23p46	00 16		09 43		10 13		21 13	21 43
	d	23p47	00 17		09 44		10 14		21 14	21 44
Wimbledon Chase	d	23p50	00 20		09 47		10 17		21 17	21 47
South Merton	d	23p52	00 22		09 49		10 19		21 19	21 49
Morden South	d	23p54	00 24		09 51		10 21		21 21	21 51
St Helier	d	23p56	00 26		09 53		10 23		21 23	21 53
Sutton Common	d	23p58	00 28		09 55		10 25		21 25	21 55
West Sutton	d	00 01	00 31		09 58		10 28		21 28	21 58
Sutton (Surrey)	a	00 05	00 35	09 33	10 01	10 03	10 31		21 31	22 01

Sundays
from 16 September

		FC	FC	FC	FC	FC	FC		FC	FC
Luton	d	22p20	22p46		08 18		08 48		19 48	20 18
Luton Airport Parkway	d	22p22	22p49		08 21		08 51		19 51	20 21
St Pancras International ⊖	d	23p06	23p36		09 05		09 35		20 35	21 05
Farringdon ⊖	d	23p10	23p40		09 10		09 40		20 40	21 10
City Thameslink	d									
London Blackfriars ⊖	d	23p16	23p46	08 56	09 15	09 26	09 45		20 45	21 15
Elephant & Castle ⊖	d	23p19	23p49	09 00	09 18	09 30	09 48		20 48	21 18
Loughborough Jn	d	23p23		09 04	09 22	09 34	09 52		20 52	21 22
Herne Hill	d	23p27	23p57	09 08	09 26	09 38	09 56		20 56	21 26
London Bridge ⊖	d									
South Bermondsey	d									
Queens Rd Peckham	d									
Peckham Rye	d							and at		
East Dulwich	d							the same		
North Dulwich	d							minutes		
Tulse Hill	d	23p31	00 01	09 12	09 30	09 42	10 00	past	21 00	21 30
Streatham	d	23p35	00 05	09 16	09 34	09 46	10 04	each	21 04	21 34
Mitcham Eastfields	d			09 20		09 50		hour until		
Mitcham Junction	d			09 23		09 53				
Hackbridge	d			09 26		09 56				
Carshalton	d			09 29		09 59				
Tooting	d	23p40	00 10		09 38		10 08		21 08	21 38
Haydons Road	d	23p43	00 13		09 41		10 11		21 11	21 41
Wimbledon ⊖	a	23p46	00 16		09 43		10 13		21 13	21 43
	d	23p47	00 17		09 44		10 14		21 14	21 44
Wimbledon Chase	d	23p50	00 20		09 47		10 17		21 17	21 47
South Merton	d	23p52	00 22		09 49		10 19		21 19	21 49
Morden South	d	23p54	00 24		09 51		10 21		21 21	21 51
St Helier	d	23p56	00 26		09 53		10 23		21 23	21 53
Sutton Common	d	23p58	00 28		09 55		10 25		21 25	21 55
West Sutton	d	00 01	00 31		09 58		10 28		21 28	21 58
Sutton (Surrey)	a	00 05	00 35	09 33	10 01	10 03	10 31		21 31	22 01

Sutton and Wimbledon - London and Luton via Streatham

Mondays to Fridays

Network Diagram - see first Page of Table 177

Miles	Miles			FC MX A	FC MX A	SE	SN	SN	FC B	FC C	FC	SN		FC	SN	SE	FC	SE	FC	SN	SE	FC		FC	SN
0	0	**Sutton (Surrey)**	d	22p17	22p47		05 37	06 14	06 03	06 05	06 34	06 50		06 45	07 20		07 05		07 37	07 49		07 40		08 08	08 20
1	—	West Sutton	d	22p20	22p50				06 06	06 08				06 48			07 08					07 43			
2	—	Sutton Common	d	22p22	22p52				06 08	06 10				06 50			07 10					07 45			
3	—	St Helier	d	22p25	22p55				06 11	06 13				06 53			07 13					07 48			
3½	—	Morden South	d	22p27	22p57				06 13	06 15				06 55			07 15					07 50			
4	—	South Merton	d	22p29	22p59				06 15	06 17				06 57			07 17					07 52			
4½	—	Wimbledon Chase	d	22p31	23p01				06 17	06 19				06 59			07 19					07 54			
5½	—	Wimbledon ⊖	a	22p34	23p04				06 20	06 22				07 05			07 22					07 57			
—	—		d	22p38	23p08				06 26	06 28				07 06			07 26					07 58			
6¾	—	Haydons Road	d	22p40	23p10				06 28	06 30				07 08			07 28					08 00			
8	—	Tooting	d	22p43	23p13				06 33	06 33				07 11			07 31					08 03			
—	1¼	Carshalton	d				05 40	06 17			06 37	06 53			07 23				07 40	07 52				08 11	08 23
—	2	Hackbridge	d				05 42	06 19			06 39	06 55			07 25				07 42	07 54				08 13	08 25
—	4	Mitcham Junction	d				05 46	06 23			06 42	06 59			07 29				07 45	07 58				08 16	08 29
—	5	Mitcham Eastfields	d				05 49	06 26			06 45	07 02			07 32				07 48	08 01				08 19	08 32
9½	6	Streatham	d	22p49	23p19		05 53	06 30	06 38	06 38	06 49	07 05		07 16	07 35		07 38		07 52	08 05		08 09		08 23	08 36
11	7½	Tulse Hill	d	22p53	23p23		05 57	06 34	06 42	06 42	06 53	07 10		07 20	07 41		07 43		07 57	08 10		08 13		08 28	08 40
12¼	—	North Dulwich	d					06 37				07 13			07 44					08 13					08 43
12½	—	East Dulwich	d					06 39				07 15			07 46					08 15					08 45
13½	—	Peckham Rye	d				06 02	06 42				07 17			07 48					08 18					08 48
14¼	—	Queens Rd Peckham	d					06 44				07 20			07 51					08 20					08 50
15¼	—	South Bermondsey	d					06 47				07 22			07 53					08 23					08 53
17	—	**London Bridge** ⊖	a				06 08	06 51				07 28			07 59					08 28					08 57
—	8½	Herne Hill	d	22p57	23p27	05 23			06 46	06 46	06 57			07 24		07 31	07 47	07 57	08 01		08 13	08 20		08 32	
—	9½	Loughborough Jn	d	23p00					06 49	06 49	07 00			07 27		07 34	07 50	08 00	08 04		08 16	08 23		08 36	
—	11½	Elephant & Castle ⊖	d	23p04	23p34	05 29			06 54	06 54	07 06			07 32		07 38	07 54	08 05	08 09		08 21	08 28		08 40	
—	12½	**London Blackfriars** ⊖	a	23p07	23p37	05 32			06 57	06 57	07 09			07 35		07 42	07 58	08 08	08 12		08 25	08 32		08 45	
—	13	City Thameslink	a			05 35			07 00	07 00	07 14			07 38		07 44	08 00	08 11	08 15		08 27	08 35		08 48	
—	—	Farringdon ⊖	a	23p13	23p43	05 38			07 04	07 04	07 18			07 42		07 48	08 03	08 15	08 19		08 30	08 39		08 52	
—	—	St Pancras International ⊖	a	23p17	23p47	05 42			07 08	07 08	07 22			07 46		07 52	08 08	08 19	08 23		08 35	08 43		08 56	
—	—	Luton Airport Parkway	a	00 02	00 32				07 49	07 49				08 20				09 01			09 09	09 29			
—	—	**Luton**	a	00 05	00 35				07 53	07 53				08 23				09 04			09 12	09 34			

		FC	SE D	SE E	FC	FC	SN	FC		FC	FC	FC	FC	FC	FC	FC	FC	FC		FC	FC	FC	FC	FC	FC
Sutton (Surrey)	d	08 08			08 39	08 41	08 57	09 13		09 11	09 38	09 37	10 08	10 07	10 38	10 37	11 08	11 07		11 38	11 37	12 08	12 07	12 38	12 37
West Sutton	d	08 11				08 44				09 14		09 40		10 10		10 40		11 10			11 40		12 10		12 40
Sutton Common	d	08 13				08 46				09 16		09 42		10 12		10 42		11 12			11 42		12 12		12 42
St Helier	d	08 16				08 49				09 19		09 45		10 15		10 45		11 15			11 45		12 15		12 45
Morden South	d	08 18				08 51				09 21		09 47		10 17		10 47		11 17			11 47		12 17		12 47
South Merton	d	08 20				08 53				09 23		09 49		10 19		10 49		11 19			11 49		12 19		12 49
Wimbledon Chase	d	08 22				08 55				09 25		09 51		10 21		10 51		11 21			11 51		12 21		12 51
Wimbledon ⊖	a	08 25				08 58				09 28		09 54		10 24		10 54		11 24			11 54		12 24		12 54
	d	08 28				08 58				09 28		09 58		10 28		10 58		11 28			11 58		12 28		12 58
Haydons Road	d	08 30				09 00				09 30		10 00		10 30		11 00		11 30			12 00		12 30		13 00
Tooting	d	08 33				09 03				09 33		10 03		10 33		11 03		11 33			12 03		12 33		13 03
Carshalton	d				08 42		09 00	09 16			09 41		10 11		10 41		11 11			11 41		12 11		12 41	
Hackbridge	d				08 44		09 02	09 18			09 43		10 13		10 43		11 13			11 43		12 13		12 43	
Mitcham Junction	d				08 47		09 06	09 21			09 46		10 16		10 46		11 16			11 46		12 16		12 46	
Mitcham Eastfields	d				08 50		09 09	09 24			09 49		10 19		10 49		11 19			11 49		12 19		12 49	
Streatham	d	08 39			08 54	09 08	09 12	09 28		09 38	09 53	10 08	10 23	10 38	10 53	11 08	11 23	11 38		11 53	12 08	12 23	12 38	12 53	13 08
Tulse Hill	d	08 43			08 58	09 16	09 16	09 32		09 42	09 57	10 12	10 27	10 42	10 57	11 12	11 27	11 42		11 57	12 12	12 27	12 42	12 57	13 12
North Dulwich	d						09 19																		
East Dulwich	d						09 21																		
Peckham Rye	d						09 23																		
Queens Rd Peckham	d						09 26																		
South Bermondsey	d						09 28																		
London Bridge ⊖	a						09 35																		
Herne Hill	d	08 47	08 52	08 52	09 02	09 20		09 36		09 46	10 01	10 16	10 31	10 46	11 01	11 16	11 31	11 46		12 01	12 16	12 31	12 46	13 01	13 16
Loughborough Jn	d	08 50	08 57	08 55	09 05	09 23		09 40		09 50	10 04	10 19	10 34	10 49	11 04	11 19	11 34	11 49		12 04	12 19	12 34	12 49	13 04	13 19
Elephant & Castle ⊖	d	08 58	09 02	09 02	09 10	09 30		09 45		09 55	10 09	10 24	10 39	10 54	11 09	11 24	11 39	11 54		12 09	12 24	12 39	12 54	13 09	13 24
London Blackfriars ⊖	a	09 01	09 06	09 06	09 13	09 33		09 49		09 59	10 12	10 27	10 42	10 57	11 12	11 27	11 42	11 57		12 12	12 27	12 42	12 57	13 12	13 27
City Thameslink	a	09 04	09 08	09 08	09 16	09 36		09 52		10 02	10 16	10 32	10 46	11 02	11 16	11 32	11 46	12 02		12 16	12 32	12 46	13 02	13 16	13 32
Farringdon ⊖	a	09 08	09 12	09 12	09 20	09 40		09 56		10 06	10 19	10 35	10 49	11 06	11 19	11 36	11 49	12 06		12 19	12 36	12 49	13 06	13 19	13 36
St Pancras International ⊖	a	09 12	09 16	09 16	09 24	09 44		10 00		10 10	10 23	10 40	10 53	11 10	11 23	11 40	11 53	12 10		12 23	12 40	12 53	13 10	13 23	13 40
Luton Airport Parkway	a	09 58	09 43	09 43		10 29				10 58		11 27		11 55		12 25		12 55			13 25		13 55		14 25
Luton	a	10 03	09 46	09 46		10 33				11 03		11 31		11 59		12 29		12 57			13 29		13 59		14 29

A from 22 May
B from 8 October
C until 5 October
D from 21 May
E until 18 May

Sutton and Wimbledon - London and Luton via Streatham

Network Diagram - see first Page of Table 177

		FC	FC	FC	FC	FC	FC	FC	FC	FC	FC	FC	FC	FC	FC	FC	FC	FC	SE	FC	FC	FC
																A						
Sutton (Surrey)	d	13 08	13 07	13 38	13 37	14 08	14 07	14 38	14 37	15 08	15 07	15 38	15 37	16 08	16 07	16 38	16 37	17 08		17 11	17 42	17 41
West Sutton	d		13 10		13 40		14 10		14 40		15 10		15 40		16 10		16 40			17 14		17 44
Sutton Common	d		13 12		13 42		14 12		14 42		15 12		15 42		16 12		16 42			17 16		17 46
St Helier	d		13 15		13 45		14 15		14 45		15 15		15 45		16 15		16 45			17 19		17 49
Morden South	d		13 17		13 47		14 17		14 47		15 17		15 47		16 17		16 47			17 21		17 51
South Merton	d		13 19		13 49		14 19		14 49		15 19		15 49		16 19		16 49			17 23		17 53
Wimbledon Chase	d		13 21		13 51		14 21		14 51		15 21		15 51		16 21		16 51			17 25		17 55
Wimbledon	a		13 24		13 54		14 24		14 54		15 24		15 54		16 24		16 54			17 28		17 58
	d		13 28		13 58		14 28		14 58		15 28		15 58		16 30		17 00			17 30		18 00
Haydons Road	d		13 30		14 00		14 30		15 00		15 30		16 00		16 32		17 02			17 32		18 02
Tooting	d		13 33		14 03		14 33		15 03		15 33		16 03		16 35		17 05			17 35		18 05
Carshalton	d	13 11		13 41		14 11		14 41		15 11		15 41		16 11		16 41		17 11			17 45	
Hackbridge	d	13 13		13 43		14 13		14 43		15 13		15 43		16 13		16 43		17 13			17 47	
Mitcham Junction	d	13 16		13 46		14 16		14 46		15 16		15 46		16 16		16 46		17 16			17 50	
Mitcham Eastfields	d	13 19		13 49		14 19		14 49		15 19		15 49		16 19		16 49		17 19			17 53	
Streatham	d	13 23	13 38	13 53	14 08	14 23	14 38	14 53	15 08	15 23	15 38	15 53	16 08	16 23	16 40	16 53	17 10	17 23		17 40	17 57	18 10
Tulse Hill	d	13 27	13 42	13 57	14 12	14 27	14 42	14 57	15 12	15 27	15 42	15 57	16 12	16 27	16 46	16 57	17 16	17 27		17 44	18 01	18 16
North Dulwich	d																					
East Dulwich	d																					
Peckham Rye	d																					
Queens Rd Peckham	d																					
South Bermondsey	d																					
London Bridge	a																					
Herne Hill	d	13 31	13 46	14 01	14 16	14 31	14 46	15 01	15 16	15 31	15 46	16 01	16 16	16 31	16 50	17 01	17 21	17 31	17 44	17 48	18 06	18 20
Loughborough Jn	d	13 34	13 49	14 04	14 19	14 34	14 49	15 04	15 19	15 34	15 49	16 04	16 19	16 34	16 53		17 24	17 34	17 47	17 51	18 09	18 23
Elephant & Castle	d	13 39	13 54	14 09	14 24	14 39	14 54	15 09	15 24	15 39	15 54	16 09	16 24	16 39	17 00	17 08	17 28	17 39	17 52	17 56	18 14	18 28
London Blackfriars	a	13 42	13 57	14 12	14 27	14 42	14 57	15 12	15 27	15 42	15 57	16 12	16 29	16 42	17 03	17 11	17 31	17 43	17 55	17 59	18 17	18 31
City Thameslink	a	13 46	14 02	14 16	14 32	14 46	15 02	15 16	15 32	15 46	16 02	16 16	16 32	16 46	17 06	17 14	17 34	17 48	17 58	18 02	18 20	18 34
Farringdon	a	13 49	14 06	14 19	14 36	14 49	15 06	15 19	15 36	15 49	16 06	16 19	16 35	16 49	17 09	17 17	17 37	17 51	18 01	18 05	18 23	18 37
St Pancras International	a	13 53	14 10	14 23	14 40	14 53	15 10	15 23	15 40	15 53	16 10	16 23	16 39	16 53	17 13	17 21	17 41	17 55	18 05	18 09	18 27	18 41
Luton Airport Parkway	a		14 55		15 25		15 55		16 25		16 57		17 25			17 57	18 27		18 38	18 58		19 30
Luton	a		14 59		15 29		15 59		16 29		17 01		17 29			18 00	18 31		18 41	19 01		19 33

		SN	SN	FC	FC	SN	FC	SN	FC	SN	FC	SN	FC	FC	FC	FC	FC	FC	FC	FC	FC	FC	FC
																				B	C		B
Sutton (Surrey)	d	17 48		18 08	18 09	18 16	18 38		18 43	18 48	19 08		19 13	19 42	19 37	20 12	20 07	20 42	20 37	21 12	21 12	21 17	21 47
West Sutton	d	17 52			18 12	18 20			18 46	18 54			19 16		19 40		20 10		20 40			21 20	21 50
Sutton Common	d	17 54			18 14	18 22			18 48	18 56			19 18		19 42		20 12		20 42			21 22	21 52
St Helier	d	17 57			18 17	18 25			18 51	18 59			19 21		19 45		20 15		20 45			21 25	21 55
Morden South	d	17 59			18 19	18 27			18 53	19 01			19 23		19 47		20 17		20 47			21 27	21 57
South Merton	d	18 01			18 21	18 29			18 55	19 03			19 25		19 49		20 19		20 49			21 29	21 59
Wimbledon Chase	d	18 03			18 23	18 31			18 57	19 05			19 27		19 51		20 21		20 51			21 31	22 01
Wimbledon	a	18 06			18 26	18 34			19 00	19 08			19 30		19 54		20 24		20 54			21 34	22 04
	d		18 10		18 28			18 43	19 00			19 17	19 30		19 56		20 26		20 56			21 38	22 08
Haydons Road	d		18 12		18 30			18 45	19 02			19 19	19 32		19 58		20 28		20 58			21 40	22 10
Tooting	d		18 15		18 33			18 48	19 05			19 22	19 35		20 01		20 31		21 01			21 43	22 13
Carshalton	d			18 11			18 41				19 11			19 45		20 15		20 45		21 15	21 15		
Hackbridge	d			18 13			18 43				19 13			19 47		20 17		20 47		21 17	21 17		
Mitcham Junction	d			18 16			18 46				19 16			19 50		20 20		20 50		21 20	21 20		
Mitcham Eastfields	d			18 19			18 49				19 19			19 53		20 23		20 53		21 23	21 23		
Streatham	d		18 20	18 23	18 40		18 53	18 56	19 10		19 23	19 26	19 40	19 57	20 06	20 27	20 36	20 57	21 06	21 27	21 27	21 49	22 19
Tulse Hill	d		18 24	18 28	18 44		18 57	19 00	19 14		19 27	19 31	19 44	20 01	20 12	20 31	20 42	21 01	21 12	21 31	21 31	21 53	22 23
North Dulwich	d		18 27					19 03				19 34											
East Dulwich	d		18 29					19 05				19 36											
Peckham Rye	d		18 32					19 07				19 38											
Queens Rd Peckham	d		18 35					19 10				19 41											
South Bermondsey	d		18 37					19 12				19 43											
London Bridge	a		18 42					19 17				19 51											
Herne Hill	d			18 32	18 48		19 02		19 17		19 31		19 47	20 05	20 16	20 35	20 46	21 05	21 16	21 35	21 35	21 57	22 27
Loughborough Jn	d			18 35	18 51		19 05		19 20		19 34		19 50	20 08	20 19	20 38	20 49	21 08	21 19	21 38	21 38	22 00	22 30
Elephant & Castle	d			18 40	18 56		19 10		19 25		19 39		19 55	20 13	20 24	20 43	20 54	21 13	21 24	21 43	21 43	22 04	22 34
London Blackfriars	a			18 43	18 59		19 13		19 28		19 42		19 58	20 16	20 27	20 46	20 57	21 16	21 27	21 46	21 46	22 07	22 37
City Thameslink	a			18 46	19 02		19 20		19 32		19 48		20 02	20 20	20 32	20 50	21 02	21 20	21 32	21 50	21 50	22 10	22 40
Farringdon	a			18 49	19 05		19 23		19 36		19 51		20 06	20 23	20 36	20 53	21 06	21 23	21 36	21 53	21 53	22 13	22 43
St Pancras International	a			18 53	19 09		19 27		19 40		19 55		20 10	20 27	20 40	20 57	21 10	21 27	21 40	21 57	21 57	22 17	22 47
Luton Airport Parkway	a			19 33	19 54				20 25				20 55		21 25		21 55		22 25		22 41	23 01	23 32
Luton	a			19 36	19 57				20 29				20 59		21 29		21 59		22 29		22 44	23 04	23 35

A to Farringdon

B from 21 May

C until 18 May

Sutton and Wimbledon - London and Luton via Streatham

Network Diagram - see first Page of Table 177

		FC	FC	FC
		A	B	B
Sutton (Surrey)	d	22 12	22 17	22 47
West Sutton	d	22 15	22 20	22 50
Sutton Common	d	22 17	22 22	22 52
St Helier	d	22 20	22 25	22 55
Morden South	d	22 22	22 27	22 57
South Merton	d	22 24	22 29	22 59
Wimbledon Chase	d	22 26	22 31	23 01
Wimbledon	a	22 29	22 34	23 04
	d	22 30	22 38	23 08
Haydons Road	d	22 32	22 40	23 10
Tooting	d	22 35	22 43	23 13
Carshalton	d			
Hackbridge	d			
Mitcham Junction	d			
Mitcham Eastfields	d			
Streatham	d	22 40	22 49	23 19
Tulse Hill	d	22 44	22 53	23 23
North Dulwich	d			
East Dulwich	d			
Peckham Rye	d			
Queens Rd Peckham	d			
South Bermondsey	d			
London Bridge	a	22 55		
Herne Hill	d		22 57	23 27
Loughborough Jn	d		23 00	
Elephant & Castle	d		23 04	23 34
London Blackfriars	a		23 07	23 37
City Thameslink	a			
Farringdon	a		23 13	23 43
St Pancras International	a		23 17	23 47
Luton Airport Parkway	a		00 02	00 32
Luton	a		00 05	00 35

Saturdays
until 23 June

		FC	FC	FC	FC	FC	FC	FC	FC	FC	FC	FC	FC	FC	FC	FC	FC	FC	FC	FC	FC	FC
		C	C		D	D			D	D			D	D			D	D			D	D
Sutton (Surrey)	d	22p17	22p47	06 37		07 08	07 08	07 07	07 07	07 38	07 38	07 37	07 37	08 08	08 08	08 07	08 07	08 38	08 38	08 37	08 37	09 08
West Sutton	d	22p20	22p50	06 40				07 10	07 10			07 40	07 40			08 10	08 10			08 40	08 40	
Sutton Common	d	22p22	22p52	06 42				07 12	07 12			07 42	07 42			08 12	08 12			08 42	08 42	
St Helier	d	22p25	22p55	06 45				07 15	07 15			07 45	07 45			08 15	08 15			08 45	08 45	
Morden South	d	22p27	22p57	06 47				07 17	07 17			07 47	07 47			08 17	08 17			08 47	08 47	
South Merton	d	22p29	22p59	06 49				07 19	07 19			07 49	07 49			08 19	08 19			08 49	08 49	
Wimbledon Chase	d	22p31	23p01	06 51				07 21	07 21			07 51	07 51			08 21	08 21			08 51	08 51	
Wimbledon	a	22p34	23p04	06 54				07 24	07 25			07 54	07 55			08 24	08 25			08 54	08 55	
	d	22p38	23p08	06 58	07 00			07 28	07 30			07 58	08 00			08 28	08 30			08 58	09 00	
Haydons Road	d	22p40	23p10	07 00	07 02			07 30	07 32			08 00	08 02			08 30	08 32			09 00	09 02	
Tooting	d	22p43	23p13	07 03	07 05			07 33	07 35			08 03	08 05			08 33	08 35			09 03	09 05	
Carshalton	d					07 11	07 11			07 41	07 41			08 11	08 11			08 41	08 41			09 11
Hackbridge	d					07 13	07 13			07 43	07 43			08 13	08 13			08 43	08 43			09 13
Mitcham Junction	d					07 16	07 16			07 46	07 46			08 16	08 16			08 46	08 46			09 16
Mitcham Eastfields	d					07 19	07 19			07 49	07 49			08 19	08 19			08 49	08 49			09 19
Streatham	d	22p49	23p19	07 08	07 10	07 23	07 23	07 38	07 40	07 53	07 53	08 08	08 10	08 23	08 23	08 38	08 40	08 53	08 53	09 08	09 10	09 23
Tulse Hill	d	22p53	23p23	07 12	07 17	07 27	07 27	07 42	07 47	07 57	07 57	08 12	08 17	08 27	08 27	08 42	08 47	08 57	08 57	09 12	09 17	09 27
North Dulwich	d																					
East Dulwich	d																					
Peckham Rye	d																					
Queens Rd Peckham	d																					
South Bermondsey	d																					
London Bridge	a				07 30				08 00				08 30				09 00				09 30	
Herne Hill	d	22p57	23p27	07 16		07a31	07 31	07 46		08a01	08 01	08 16		08a31	08 31	08 46		09a01	09 01	09 16		09a31
Loughborough Jn	d	23p00		07 19			07 34	07 49			08 04	08 19			08 34	08 49			09 04	09 19		
Elephant & Castle	d	23p04	23p34	07 24			07 39	07 54			08 09	08 24			08 39	08 54			09 09	09 24		
London Blackfriars	a	23p07	23p37	07 27			07 42	07 57			08 12	08 27			08 42	08 57			09 12	09 27		
City Thameslink	a															09 02			09 16	09 32		
Farringdon	a	23p13	23p43	07 35			07 49	08 05			08 19	08 35			08 49	09 06			09 19	09 36		
St Pancras International	a	23p17	23p47	07 40			07 53	08 10			08 23	08 40			08 53	09 10			09 23	09 40		
Luton Airport Parkway	a	00 02	00 32	08 25				08 55				09 25				09 55				10 25		
Luton	a	00 05	00 35	08 29				08 59				09 29				09 59				10 29		

A until 18 May
B from 21 May
C not 19 May
D 19 May

Table 179

Saturdays
until 23 June

Sutton and Wimbledon - London and Luton via Streatham

Network Diagram - see first Page of Table 177

Station		FC		FC	FC	FC A	FC A	FC	FC	FC A	FC A	FC	FC	FC A	FC	FC	FC A	FC	FC	FC A	FC	FC
Sutton (Surrey) 4	d	09 08	and at the same minutes past each hour until	18 08	18 07	18 07	18 38	18 38	18 37	18 37	19 08	19 08	19 07	19 07	19 38	19 37	19 37	20 08	20 07	20 08	20 38	20 37
West Sutton	d				18 10	18 10			18 40	18 40			19 10	19 10		19 40	19 40		20 10	20 11		20 40
Sutton Common	d				18 12	18 12			18 42	18 42			19 12	19 12		19 42	19 42		20 12	20 13		20 42
St Helier	d				18 15	18 15			18 45	18 45			19 15	19 15		19 45	19 45		20 15	20 16		20 45
Morden South	d				18 17	18 17			18 47	18 47			19 17	19 17		19 47	19 47		20 17	20 18		20 47
South Merton	d				18 19	18 19			18 49	18 49			19 19	19 19		19 49	19 49		20 19	20 20		20 49
Wimbledon Chase	d				18 21	18 21			18 51	18 51			19 21	19 21		19 51	19 51		20 21	20 22		20 51
Wimbledon 6 ⊖	a				18 24	18 25			18 54	18 55			19 24	19 25		19 54	19 55		20 24	20 25		20 54
	d				18 28	18 30			18 58	19 00			19 28	19 30		19 58	20 00		20 28	20 30		20 58
Haydons Road	d				18 30	18 32			19 00	19 02			19 30	19 32		20 00	20 02		20 30	20 32		21 00
Tooting	d				18 33	18 35			19 03	19 05			19 33	19 35		20 03	20 05		20 33	20 35		21 03
Carshalton	d	09 11		18 11			18 41	18 41			19 11	19 11			19 41			20 11			20 41	
Hackbridge	d	09 13		18 13			18 43	18 43			19 13	19 13			19 43			20 13			20 43	
Mitcham Junction	d	09 16		18 16			18 46	18 46			19 16	19 16			19 46			20 16			20 46	
Mitcham Eastfields	d	09 19		18 19			18 49	18 49			19 19	19 19			19 49			20 19			20 49	
Streatham 4	d	09 23		18 23	18 38	18 40	18 53	18 53	19 08	19 10	19 23	19 23	19 38	19 40	19 53	20 08	20 10	20 23	20 38	20 40	20 53	21 08
Tulse Hill 3	d	09 27		18 27	18 42	18 47	18 57	18 57	19 12	19 17	19 27	19 27	19 42	19 47	19 57	20 12	20 17	20 27	20 42	20 47	20 57	21 12
North Dulwich	d																					
East Dulwich	d																					
Peckham Rye 4	d																					
Queens Rd Peckham	d																					
South Bermondsey	d																					
London Bridge 4 ⊖	a					19 00				19 30				20 00			20 30			21 00		
Herne Hill 4	d	09 31		18 31	18 46		19a01	19 01	19 16		19a31	19 31	19 46		20 01	20 16		20 31	20 46		21 01	21 16
Loughborough Jn.	d	09 34		18 34	18 49			19 04	19 19			19 34	19 49		20 04	20 19		20 34	20 49		21 04	21 19
Elephant & Castle ⊖	d	09 39		18 39	18 54			19 09	19 24			19 39	19 54		20 09	20 24		20 39	20 54		21 09	21 24
London Blackfriars 3 ⊖	a	09 42		18 42	18 57			19 12	19 27			19 42	19 57		20 12	20 27		20 42	20 57		21 12	21 27
City Thameslink 3	a	09 46		18 46	19 02			19 16	19 32			19 46	20 02		20 16	20 32		20 46				
Farringdon 3 ⊖	a	09 49		18 49	19 06			19 19	19 36			19 49	20 06		20 19	20 36		20 49	21 05		21 18	21 35
St Pancras International 15 ⊖	a	09 53		18 53	19 10			19 23	19 40			19 53	20 10		20 23	20 40		20 53	21 10		21 23	21 40
Luton Airport Parkway 7	a				19 55				20 25			20 41	20 55		21 11	21 25						
Luton 10	a				19 59				20 29			20 44	20 59		21 14	21 29						

Station		FC A	FC	FC A	FC	FC A	FC	FC A	FC	FC
Sutton (Surrey) 4	d	20 37	21 08	21 07	21 15	21 37	21 45	22 07	22 15	22 45
West Sutton	d	20 40		21 10	21 18	21 40	21 48	22 10	22 18	22 48
Sutton Common	d	20 42		21 12	21 20	21 42	21 50	22 12	22 20	22 50
St Helier	d	20 45		21 15	21 23	21 45	21 53	22 15	22 23	22 53
Morden South	d	20 47		21 17	21 25	21 47	21 55	22 17	22 25	22 55
South Merton	d	20 49		21 19	21 27	21 49	21 57	22 19	22 27	22 57
Wimbledon Chase	d	20 51		21 21	21 29	21 51	21 59	22 21	22 29	22 59
Wimbledon 6 ⊖	a	20 55		21 25	21 32	21 55	22 02	22 25	22 32	23 02
	d	21 00		21 30	21 38	22 00	22 08	22 30	22 38	23 08
Haydons Road	d	21 02		21 32	21 40	22 02	22 10	22 32	22 40	23 10
Tooting	d	21 05		21 35	21 43	22 05	22 13	22 35	22 43	23 13
Carshalton	d		21 11							
Hackbridge	d		21 13							
Mitcham Junction	d		21 16							
Mitcham Eastfields	d		21 19							
Streatham 4	d	21 10	21 23	21 40	21 49	22 10	22 19	22 40	22 49	23 19
Tulse Hill 3	d	21 17	21 27	21 47	21 53	22 17	22 23	22 47	22 53	23 23
North Dulwich	d									
East Dulwich	d									
Peckham Rye 4	d									
Queens Rd Peckham	d									
South Bermondsey	d									
London Bridge 4 ⊖	a	21 30		22 00		22 30		23 00		
Herne Hill 4	d		21 31		21 57		22 27		22 57	23 27
Loughborough Jn.	d		21 34		22 00		22 30		23 00	
Elephant & Castle ⊖	d		21 39		22 04		22 34		23 04	23 34
London Blackfriars 3 ⊖	a		21 42		22 07		22 37		23 07	23 37
City Thameslink 3	a									
Farringdon 3 ⊖	a		21 48		22 13		22 42		23 13	23 43
St Pancras International 15 ⊖	a		21 53		22 17		22 47		23 17	23 47
Luton Airport Parkway 7	a				23 02		23 32		00 02	00 32
Luton 10	a				23 05		23 35		00 05	00 35

A 19 May

Table 179

Saturdays
30 June to 8 September

Sutton and Wimbledon - London and Luton via Streatham

Network Diagram - see first Page of Table 177

Station		FC	FC	FC	FC	FC	FC	FC	FC	FC	FC	FC	FC		FC	FC	FC	FC	FC	FC	FC	FC
Sutton (Surrey) 4	d	22p17	22p47	06 37	07 08	07 07	07 38	07 37	08 08	08 07	08 38	08 37	09 08	and at the same minutes past each hour until	18 08	18 07	18 38	18 37	19 08	19 07	19 38	19 37
West Sutton	d	22p20	22p50	06 40		07 10		07 40		08 10		08 40				18 10		18 40		19 10		19 40
Sutton Common	d	22p22	22p52	06 42		07 12		07 42		08 12		08 42				18 12		18 42		19 12		19 42
St Helier	d	22p25	22p55	06 45		07 15		07 45		08 15		08 45				18 15		18 45		19 15		19 45
Morden South	d	22p27	22p57	06 47		07 17		07 47		08 17		08 47				18 17		18 47		19 17		19 47
South Merton	d	22p29	22p59	06 49		07 19		07 49		08 19		08 49				18 19		18 49		19 19		19 49
Wimbledon Chase	d	22p31	23p01	06 51		07 21		07 51		08 21		08 51				18 21		18 51		19 21		19 51
Wimbledon 6 ⊖	a	22p34	23p04	06 54		07 24		07 54		08 24		08 54				18 24		18 54		19 24		19 54
	d	22p38	23p08	06 58		07 28		07 58		08 28		08 58				18 28		18 58		19 28		19 58
Haydons Road	d	22p40	23p10	07 00		07 30		08 00		08 30		09 00				18 30		19 00		19 30		20 00
Tooting	d	22p43	23p13	07 03		07 33		08 03		08 33		09 03				18 33		19 03		19 33		20 03
Carshalton	d				07 11		07 41		08 11		08 41		09 11		18 11		18 41		19 11		19 41	
Hackbridge	d				07 13		07 43		08 13		08 43		09 13		18 13		18 43		19 13		19 43	
Mitcham Junction	d				07 16		07 46		08 16		08 46		09 16		18 16		18 46		19 16		19 46	
Mitcham Eastfields	d				07 19		07 49		08 19		08 49		09 19		18 19		18 49		19 19		19 49	
Streatham 4	d	22p49	23p19	07 08	07 23	07 38	07 53	08 08	08 23	08 38	08 53	09 08	09 23		18 23	18 38	18 53	19 08	19 23	19 38	19 53	20 08
Tulse Hill 3	d	22p53	23p23	07 12	07 27	07 42	07 57	08 12	08 27	08 42	08 57	09 12	09 27		18 27	18 42	18 57	19 12	19 27	19 42	19 57	20 12
North Dulwich	d																					
East Dulwich	d																					
Peckham Rye 4	d																					
Queens Rd Peckham	d																					
South Bermondsey	d																					
London Bridge 4 ⊖	a																					
Herne Hill 4	d	22p57	23p27	07 16	07 31	07 46	08 01	08 16	08 31	08 46	09 01	09 16	09 31		18 31	18 46	19 01	19 16	19 31	19 46	20 01	20 16
Loughborough Jn.	d	23p00		07 19	07 34	07 49	08 04	08 19	08 34	08 49	09 04	09 19	09 34		18 34	18 49	19 04	19 19	19 34	19 49	20 04	20 19
Elephant & Castle ⊖	d	23p04	23p34	07 24	07 39	07 54	08 09	08 24	08 39	08 54	09 09	09 24	09 39		18 39	18 54	19 09	19 24	19 39	19 54	20 09	20 24
London Blackfriars 3 ⊖	a	23p07	23p37	07 27	07 42	07 57	08 12	08 27	08 42	08 57	09 12	09 27	09 42		18 42	18 57	19 12	19 27	19 42	19 57	20 12	20 27
City Thameslink 3	a									09 02	09 16	09 32	09 46		18 46	19 02	19 16	19 32	19 46	20 02	20 16	20 32
Farringdon 3 ⊖	a	23p13	23p43	07 35	07 49	08 05	08 19	08 35	08 49	09 06	09 19	09 36	09 49		18 49	19 06	19 19	19 36	19 49	20 06	20 19	20 36
St Pancras International 15 ⊖	a	23p17	23p47	07 40	07 53	08 10	08 23	08 40	08 53	09 10	09 23	09 40	09 53		18 53	19 10	19 23	19 40	19 53	20 10	20 23	20 40
Luton Airport Parkway 7	a	00 02	00 32	08 25		08 55		09 25		09 55		10 25				19 55		20 25	20 41	20 55	21 11	21 25
Luton 10	a	00 05	00 35	08 29		08 59		09 29		09 59		10 29				19 59		20 29	20 44	20 59	21 14	21 29

Station		FC	FC	FC	FC	FC	FC	FC	FC	FC
Sutton (Surrey) 4	d	20 08	20 07	20 38	20 37	21 08	21 15	21 45	22 15	22 45
West Sutton	d		20 10		20 40		21 18	21 48	22 18	22 48
Sutton Common	d		20 12		20 42		21 20	21 50	22 20	22 50
St Helier	d		20 15		20 45		21 23	21 53	22 23	22 53
Morden South	d		20 17		20 47		21 25	21 55	22 25	22 55
South Merton	d		20 19		20 49		21 27	21 57	22 27	22 57
Wimbledon Chase	d		20 21		20 51		21 29	21 59	22 29	22 59
Wimbledon 6 ⊖	a		20 24		20 54		21 32	22 02	22 32	23 02
	d		20 28		20 58		21 38	22 08	22 38	23 08
Haydons Road	d		20 30		21 00		21 40	22 10	22 40	23 10
Tooting	d		20 33		21 03		21 43	22 13	22 43	23 13
Carshalton	d	20 11		20 41		21 11				
Hackbridge	d	20 13		20 43		21 13				
Mitcham Junction	d	20 16		20 46		21 16				
Mitcham Eastfields	d	20 19		20 49		21 19				
Streatham 4	d	20 23	20 38	20 53	21 08	21 23	21 49	22 19	22 49	23 19
Tulse Hill 3	d	20 27	20 42	20 57	21 12	21 27	21 53	22 23	22 53	23 23
North Dulwich	d									
East Dulwich	d									
Peckham Rye 4	d									
Queens Rd Peckham	d									
South Bermondsey	d									
London Bridge 4 ⊖	a									
Herne Hill 4	d	20 31	20 46	21 01	21 16	21 31	21 57	22 27	22 57	23 27
Loughborough Jn.	d	20 34	20 49	21 04	21 19	21 34	22 00	22 30	23 00	
Elephant & Castle ⊖	d	20 39	20 54	21 09	21 24	21 39	22 04	22 34	23 04	23 34
London Blackfriars 3 ⊖	a	20 42	20 57	21 12	21 27	21 42	22 07	22 37	23 07	23 37
City Thameslink 3	a	20 46								
Farringdon 3 ⊖	a	20 49	21 05	21 18	21 35	21 48	22 13	22 42	23 13	23 43
St Pancras International 15 ⊖	a	20 53	21 10	21 23	21 40	21 53	22 17	22 47	23 17	23 47
Luton Airport Parkway 7	a		21 55		22 25		23 01	23 32	00 02	00 32
Luton 10	a		21 59		22 29		23 04	23 35	00 05	00 35

Table 179

Sutton and Wimbledon - London and Luton via Streatham

Saturdays from 15 September

Network Diagram - see first Page of Table 177

Station		FC	FC	FC	FC	FC	FC	FC	FC	FC		FC	FC	FC		FC	FC	FC	FC		FC	FC	FC	FC
Sutton (Surrey)	d	22p17	22p47	06 37	07 08	07 07	07 38	07 37	08 08	08 07		08 38	08 37	09 08	and at the same minutes past each hour until	18 08	18 07	18 38	18 37		19 08	19 07	19 38	19 37
West Sutton	d	22p20	22p50	06 40		07 10		07 40		08 10			08 40				18 10		18 40			19 10		19 40
Sutton Common	d	22p22	22p52	06 42		07 12		07 42		08 12			08 42				18 12		18 42			19 12		19 42
St Helier	d	22p25	22p55	06 45		07 15		07 45		08 15			08 45				18 15		18 45			19 15		19 45
Morden South	d	22p27	22p57	06 47		07 17		07 47		08 17			08 47				18 17		18 47			19 17		19 47
South Merton	d	22p29	22p59	06 49		07 19		07 49		08 19			08 49				18 19		18 49			19 19		19 49
Wimbledon Chase	d	22p31	23p01	06 51		07 21		07 51		08 21			08 51				18 21		18 51			19 21		19 51
Wimbledon ⊖	a	22p34	23p04	06 54		07 24		07 54		08 24			08 54				18 24		18 54			19 24		19 54
	d	22p38	23p08	06 58		07 28		07 58		08 28			08 58				18 28		18 58			19 28		19 58
Haydons Road	d	22p40	23p10	07 00		07 30		08 00		08 30			09 00				18 30		19 00			19 30		20 00
Tooting	d	22p43	23p13	07 03		07 33		08 03		08 33			09 03				18 33		19 03			19 33		20 03
Carshalton	d				07 11		07 41		08 11			08 41		09 11		18 11		18 41			19 11		19 41	
Hackbridge	d				07 13		07 43		08 13			08 43		09 13		18 13		18 43			19 13		19 43	
Mitcham Junction	d				07 16		07 46		08 16			08 46		09 16		18 16		18 46			19 16		19 46	
Mitcham Eastfields	d				07 19		07 49		08 19			08 49		09 19		18 19		18 49			19 19		19 49	
Streatham	d	22p49	23p19	07 08	07 23	07 38	07 53	08 08	08 23	08 38		08 53	09 08	09 23		18 23	18 38	18 53	19 08		19 23	19 38	19 53	20 08
Tulse Hill	d	22p53	23p23	07 12	07 27	07 42	07 57	08 12	08 27	08 42		08 57	09 12	09 27		18 27	18 42	18 57	19 12		19 27	19 42	19 57	20 12
North Dulwich	d																							
East Dulwich	d																							
Peckham Rye	d																							
Queens Rd Peckham	d																							
South Bermondsey	d																							
London Bridge ⊖	a																							
Herne Hill	d	22p57	23p27	07 16	07 31	07 46	08 01	08 16	08 31	08 46		09 01	09 16	09 31		18 31	18 46	19 01	19 16		19 31	19 46	20 01	20 16
Loughborough Jn	d	23p00		07 19	07 34	07 49	08 04	08 19	08 34	08 49		09 04	09 19	09 34		18 34	18 49	19 04	19 19		19 34	19 49	20 04	20 19
Elephant & Castle ⊖	d	23p04	23p34	07 24	07 39	07 54	08 09	08 24	08 39	08 54		09 09	09 24	09 39		18 39	18 54	19 09	19 24		19 39	19 54	20 09	20 24
London Blackfriars ⊖	a	23p07	23p37	07 27	07 42	07 57	08 12	08 27	08 42	08 57		09 12	09 27	09 42		18 42	18 57	19 12	19 27		19 42	19 57	20 12	20 27
City Thameslink	a									09 02		09 16	09 32	09 46		18 46	19 02	19 16	19 32		19 46	20 02	20 16	20 32
Farringdon ⊖	a	23p13	23p43	07 35	07 49	08 05	08 19	08 35	08 49	09 06		09 19	09 36	09 49		18 49	19 06	19 19	19 36		19 49	20 06	20 19	20 36
St Pancras International ⊖	a	23p17	23p47	07 40	07 53	08 10	08 23	08 40	08 53	09 10		09 23	09 40	09 53		18 53	19 10	19 23	19 40		19 53	20 10	20 23	20 40
Luton Airport Parkway	a	00 02	00 32	08 25		08 55		09 25		09 55			10 25				19 55		20 25		20 41	20 55	21 11	21 25
Luton	a	00 05	00 35	08 29		08 59		09 29		09 59			10 29				19 59		20 29		20 44	20 59	21 14	21 29

Station		FC	FC	FC	FC	FC		FC	FC	FC	FC
Sutton (Surrey)	d	20 08	20 07	20 38	20 37	21 08		21 15	21 45	22 15	22 45
West Sutton	d		20 10		20 40			21 18	21 48	22 18	22 48
Sutton Common	d		20 12		20 42			21 20	21 50	22 20	22 50
St Helier	d		20 15		20 45			21 23	21 53	22 23	22 53
Morden South	d		20 17		20 47			21 25	21 55	22 25	22 55
South Merton	d		20 19		20 49			21 27	21 57	22 27	22 57
Wimbledon Chase	d		20 21		20 51			21 29	21 59	22 29	22 59
Wimbledon ⊖	a		20 24		20 54			21 32	22 02	22 32	23 02
	d		20 28		20 58			21 38	22 08	22 38	23 08
Haydons Road	d		20 30		21 00			21 40	22 10	22 40	23 10
Tooting	d		20 33		21 03			21 43	22 13	22 43	23 13
Carshalton	d	20 11		20 41		21 11					
Hackbridge	d	20 13		20 43		21 13					
Mitcham Junction	d	20 16		20 46		21 16					
Mitcham Eastfields	d	20 19		20 49		21 19					
Streatham	d	20 23	20 38	20 53	21 08	21 23		21 49	22 19	22 49	23 19
Tulse Hill	d	20 27	20 42	20 57	21 12	21 27		21 53	22 23	22 53	23 23
North Dulwich	d										
East Dulwich	d										
Peckham Rye	d										
Queens Rd Peckham	d										
South Bermondsey	d										
London Bridge ⊖	a										
Herne Hill	d	20 31	20 46	21 01	21 16	21 31		21 57	22 27	22 57	23 27
Loughborough Jn	d	20 34	20 49	21 04	21 19	21 34		22 00	22 30	23 00	
Elephant & Castle ⊖	d	20 39	20 54	21 09	21 24	21 39		22 04	22 34	23 04	23 34
London Blackfriars ⊖	a	20 42	20 57	21 12	21 27	21 42		22 07	22 37	23 07	23 37
City Thameslink	a	20 46									
Farringdon ⊖	a	20 49	21 05	21 18	21 35	21 48		22 13	22 42	23 13	23 43
St Pancras International ⊖	a	20 53	21 10	21 23	21 40	21 53		22 17	22 47	23 17	23 47
Luton Airport Parkway	a		21 55		22 25			23 01	23 32	00 02	00 32
Luton	a		21 59		22 29			23 04	23 35	00 05	00 35

Table 179

Sutton and Wimbledon - London and Luton via Streatham

Sundays until 24 June

Network Diagram - see first Page of Table 177

Station		FC	FC	FC	FC	FC	FC		FC		FC	FC	FC	FC	FC	FC	FC	FC	FC		FC	FC	FC	FC
Sutton (Surrey)	d	22p15	22p45	09 37	10 04	10 07	10 34	and at the same minutes past each hour until	18 34		18 37	19 04	19 07	19 34	19 37	20 04	20 07	20 34	20 37		21 04	21 07	21 34	22 04
West Sutton	d	22p18	22p48	09 40		10 10					18 40		19 10		19 40		20 10		20 40			21 10		
Sutton Common	d	22p20	22p50	09 42		10 12					18 42		19 12		19 42		20 12		20 42			21 12		
St Helier	d	22p23	22p53	09 45		10 15					18 45		19 15		19 45		20 15		20 45			21 15		
Morden South	d	22p25	22p55	09 47		10 17					18 47		19 17		19 47		20 17		20 47			21 17		
South Merton	d	22p27	22p57	09 49		10 19					18 49		19 19		19 49		20 19		20 49			21 19		
Wimbledon Chase	d	22p29	22p59	09 51		10 21					18 51		19 21		19 51		20 21		20 51			21 21		
Wimbledon ⊖	a	22p32	23p02	09 54		10 24					18 54		19 24		19 54		20 24		20 54			21 24		
	d	22p38	23p08	09 56		10 26					18 56		19 26		19 56		20 26		20 56			21 26		
Haydons Road	d	22p40	23p10	09 58		10 28					18 58		19 28		19 58		20 28		20 58			21 28		
Tooting	d	22p43	23p13	10 01		10 31					19 01		19 31		20 01		20 31		21 01			21 31		
Carshalton	d				10 07		10 37		18 37			19 07		19 37		20 07		20 37			21 07		21 37	22 07
Hackbridge	d				10 09		10 39		18 39			19 09		19 39		20 09		20 39			21 09		21 39	22 09
Mitcham Junction	d				10 12		10 42		18 42			19 12		19 42		20 12		20 42			21 12		21 42	22 12
Mitcham Eastfields	d				10 15		10 45		18 45			19 15		19 45		20 15		20 45			21 15		21 45	22 15
Streatham	d	22p49	23p19	10 06	10 19	10 36	10 49		18 49		19 06	19 19	19 36	19 49	20 06	20 19	20 36	20 49	21 06		21 19	21 36	21 49	22 19
Tulse Hill	d	22p53	23p23	10 10	10 23	10 40	10 53		18 53		19 10	19 23	19 40	19 53	20 10	20 23	20 40	20 53	21 10		21 23	21 40	21 53	22 23
North Dulwich	d																							
East Dulwich	d																							
Peckham Rye	d																							
Queens Rd Peckham	d																							
South Bermondsey	d																							
London Bridge ⊖	a																							
Herne Hill	d	22p57	23p27	10 14	10 27	10 44	10 57		18 57		19 14	19 27	19 44	19 57	20 14	20 27	20 44	20 57	21 14		21 27	21 44	21 57	22 27
Loughborough Jn	d	23p00		10 17	10 30	10 47	11 00		19 00		19 17	19 30	19 47	20 00	20 17	20 30	20 47	21 00	21 17		21 30	21 47	22 00	22 30
Elephant & Castle ⊖	d	23p04	23p34	10 22	10 34	10 52	11 04		19 04		19 22	19 34	19 52	20 04	20 22	20 34	20 52	21 04	21 22		21 34	21 52	22 04	22 34
London Blackfriars ⊖	a	23p07	23p37	10 25	10 37	10 55	11 07		19 07		19 25	19 37	19 55	20 07	20 25	20 37	20 55	21 07	21 25		21 37	21 55	22 07	22 37
City Thameslink	a																							
Farringdon ⊖	a	23p13	23p43	10 30		11 00					19 30		20 07		20 37		21 07		21 37			22 07		
St Pancras International ⊖	a	23p17	23p47	10 35		11 05					19 35		20 13		20 43		21 13		21 43			22 13		
Luton Airport Parkway	a	00 02	00 32										20 58		21 28		21 58		22 28			22 58		
Luton	a	00 05	00 35										21 01		21 31		22 01		22 31			23 01		

Sundays 1 July to 9 September

Station		FC	FC	FC	FC	FC	FC		FC		FC	FC	FC	FC	FC	FC	FC	FC	FC		FC	FC	FC	FC
Sutton (Surrey)	d	22p15	22p45	09 37	10 04	10 07	10 34	and at the same minutes past each hour until	18 34		18 37	19 04	19 07	19 34	19 37	20 04	20 07	20 34	20 37		21 04	21 07	21 34	22 04
West Sutton	d	22p18	22p48	09 40		10 10					18 40		19 10		19 40		20 10		20 40			21 10		
Sutton Common	d	22p20	22p50	09 42		10 12					18 42		19 12		19 42		20 12		20 42			21 12		
St Helier	d	22p23	22p53	09 45		10 15					18 45		19 15		19 45		20 15		20 45			21 15		
Morden South	d	22p25	22p55	09 47		10 17					18 47		19 17		19 47		20 17		20 47			21 17		
South Merton	d	22p27	22p57	09 49		10 19					18 49		19 19		19 49		20 19		20 49			21 19		
Wimbledon Chase	d	22p29	22p59	09 51		10 21					18 51		19 21		19 51		20 21		20 51			21 21		
Wimbledon ⊖	a	22p32	23p02	09 54		10 24					18 54		19 24		19 54		20 24		20 54			21 24		
	d	22p38	23p08	09 56		10 26					18 56		19 26		19 56		20 26		20 56			21 26		
Haydons Road	d	22p40	23p10	09 58		10 28					18 58		19 28		19 58		20 28		20 58			21 28		
Tooting	d	22p43	23p13	10 01		10 31					19 01		19 31		20 01		20 31		21 01			21 31		
Carshalton	d				10 07		10 37		18 37			19 07		19 37		20 07		20 37			21 07		21 37	22 07
Hackbridge	d				10 09		10 39		18 39			19 09		19 39		20 09		20 39			21 09		21 39	22 09
Mitcham Junction	d				10 12		10 42		18 42			19 12		19 42		20 12		20 42			21 12		21 42	22 12
Mitcham Eastfields	d				10 15		10 45		18 45			19 15		19 45		20 15		20 45			21 15		21 45	22 15
Streatham	d	22p49	23p19	10 06	10 19	10 36	10 49		18 49		19 06	19 19	19 36	19 49	20 06	20 19	20 36	20 49	21 06		21 19	21 36	21 49	22 19
Tulse Hill	d	22p53	23p23	10 10	10 23	10 40	10 53		18 53		19 10	19 23	19 40	19 53	20 10	20 23	20 40	20 53	21 10		21 23	21 40	21 53	22 23
North Dulwich	d																							
East Dulwich	d																							
Peckham Rye	d																							
Queens Rd Peckham	d																							
South Bermondsey	d																							
London Bridge ⊖	a																							
Herne Hill	d	22p57	23p27	10 14	10 27	10 44	10 57		18 57		19 14	19 27	19 44	19 57	20 14	20 27	20 44	20 57	21 14		21 27	21 44	21 57	22 27
Loughborough Jn	d	23p00		10 17	10 30	10 47	11 00		19 00		19 17	19 30	19 47	20 00	20 17	20 30	20 47	21 00	21 17		21 30	21 47	22 00	22 30
Elephant & Castle ⊖	d	23p04	23p34	10 22	10 34	10 52	11 04		19 04		19 22	19 34	19 52	20 04	20 22	20 34	20 52	21 04	21 22		21 34	21 52	22 04	22 34
London Blackfriars ⊖	a	23p07	23p37	10 25	10 37	10 55	11 07		19 07		19 25	19 37	19 55	20 07	20 25	20 37	20 55	21 07	21 25		21 37	21 55	22 07	22 37
City Thameslink	a																							
Farringdon ⊖	a	23p13	23p43	10 30		11 00					19 30		20 00		20 30		21 00		21 30			22 00		
St Pancras International ⊖	a	23p17	23p47	10 35		11 05					19 35		20 05		20 35		21 05		21 35			22 05		
Luton Airport Parkway	a	00 02	00 32	11 20		11 50					20 20		20 50		21 20		21 50		22 20			22 50		
Luton	a	00 05	00 35	11 24		11 54					20 23		20 53		21 23		21 53		22 23			22 53		

Table 179

Sundays
from 16 September

Sutton and Wimbledon - London and Luton via Streatham

Network Diagram - see first Page of Table 177

Station		FC	FC	FC	FC	FC	FC		FC	FC	FC	FC	FC	FC	FC	FC	FC	FC	FC	FC	FC	FC
Sutton (Surrey)	d	22p15	22p45	09 37	10 04	10 07	10 34	and at the same minutes past each hour until	18 34	18 37	19 04	19 07	19 34	19 37	20 04	20 07	20 34	20 37	21 04	21 07	21 34	22 04
West Sutton	d	22p18	22p48	09 40		10 10				18 40		19 10		19 40		20 10		20 40		21 10		
Sutton Common	d	22p20	22p50	09 42		10 12				18 42		19 12		19 42		20 12		20 42		21 12		
St Helier	d	22p23	22p53	09 45		10 15				18 45		19 15		19 45		20 15		20 45		21 15		
Morden South	d	22p25	22p55	09 47		10 17				18 47		19 17		19 47		20 17		20 47		21 17		
South Merton	d	22p27	22p57	09 49		10 19				18 49		19 19		19 49		20 19		20 49		21 19		
Wimbledon Chase	d	22p29	22p59	09 51		10 21				18 51		19 21		19 51		20 21		20 51		21 21		
Wimbledon	a	22p32	23p02	09 54		10 24				18 54		19 24		19 54		20 24		20 54		21 24		
	d	22p38	23p08	09 56		10 26				18 56		19 26		19 56		20 26		20 56		21 26		
Haydons Road	d	22p40	23p10	09 58		10 28				18 58		19 28		19 58		20 28		20 58		21 28		
Tooting	d	22p43	23p13	10 01		10 31				19 01		19 31		20 01		20 31		21 01		21 31		
Carshalton	d				10 07		10 37		18 37		19 07		19 37		20 07		20 37		21 07		21 37	22 07
Hackbridge	d				10 09		10 39		18 39		19 09		19 39		20 09		20 39		21 09		21 39	22 09
Mitcham Junction	d				10 12		10 42		18 42		19 12		19 42		20 12		20 42		21 12		21 42	22 12
Mitcham Eastfields	d				10 15		10 45		18 45		19 15		19 45		20 15		20 45		21 15		21 45	22 15
Streatham	d	22p49	23p19	10 06	10 19	10 36	10 49		18 49	19 06	19 19	19 36	19 49	20 06	20 19	20 36	20 49	21 06	21 19	21 36	21 49	22 19
Tulse Hill	d	22p53	23p23	10 10	10 23	10 40	10 53		18 53	19 10	19 23	19 40	19 53	20 10	20 23	20 40	20 53	21 10	21 23	21 40	21 53	22 23
North Dulwich	d																					
East Dulwich	d																					
Peckham Rye	d																					
Queens Rd Peckham	d																					
South Bermondsey	d																					
London Bridge	a																					
Herne Hill	d	22p57	23p27	10 14	10 27	10 44	10 57		18 57	19 14	19 27	19 44	19 57	20 14	20 27	20 44	20 57	21 14	21 27	21 44	21 57	22 27
Loughborough Jn.	d	23p00		10 17	10 30	10 47	11 00		19 00	19 17	19 30	19 47	20 00	20 17	20 30	20 47	21 00	21 17	21 30	21 47	22 00	22 30
Elephant & Castle	d	23p04	23p34	10 22	10 34	10 52	11 04		19 04	19 22	19 34	19 52	20 04	20 22	20 34	20 52	21 04	21 22	21 34	21 52	22 04	22 34
London Blackfriars	a	23p07	23p37	10 25	10 37	10 55	11 07		19 07	19 25	19 37	19 55	20 07	20 25	20 37	20 55	21 07	21 25	21 37	21 55	22 07	22 37
City Thameslink	a																					
Farringdon	a	23p13	23p43	10 30		11 00				19 30		20 00		20 30		21 00		21 30		22 00		
St Pancras International	a	23p17	23p47	10 35		11 05				19 35		20 05		20 35		21 05		21 35		22 05		
Luton Airport Parkway	a	00 02	00 32	11 20		11 50				20 20		20 50		21 20		21 50		22 20		22 50		
Luton	a	00 05	00 35	11 24		11 54				20 23		20 53		21 23		21 53		22 23		22 53		

Table 181

Mondays to Fridays

London and Croydon - Caterham and Tattenham Corner

Network Diagram - see first Page of Table 177

Miles	Miles	Station		SN MX	SN MX	SN MO A	SN MO A	SN MX	SN	SN	SN	SN		SN	SN	SN	SN		SN	SN	SN	SN	SN
0	—	**London Victoria**	d	23p15			23p50			06 13					07 23	07 20			07 45			08 15	
2¾	—	Clapham Junction	d	23p23			23p56			06 21					07 30	07 28			07 51			08 23	
—	0	**London Bridge**	d		23p36	23p39		00 06	06 06		06 36	06 54		07 06			07 36			08 14	08 06		08 47
—	2¾	New Cross Gate	d		23p41	23p44		00 11	06 11		06 41	06 59		07 11			07 41				08 11		
—	8¾	Norwood Junction	d		23p59	00 03		00 30	06 30		07 00	07 18		07 31			08 00			08 27	08 30		
10½	10	**East Croydon**	d	23p45	00 04	00 07	00 18	00 35	06 34	06 44	07 04	07 22		07 38	07 45	07 49	08 04		08 13	08 31	08 34	08 45	09 03
11½	11	South Croydon	d	23p47	00 06	00 09	00 20	00 37	06 37		07 06	07 25		07 40		07 52	08 06		08 15		08 36	08 47	
12½	12	Purley Oaks	d	23p50	00 09	00 12	00 23	00 40	06 40		07 09	07 28		07 43		07 55	08 09		08 18		08 39	08 50	
13½	13	Purley	a	23p54	00 12	00 15	00 26	00 43	06 43	06 51	07 12	07 31		07 46	07 52	07 58	08 12		08 21	08 38	08 42	08 54	09 09
—	—		d	23p55	00 15	00 16	00 27	00 46	06 45	06 54	07 13	07 34	07 36	07 49	07 53	07 58	08 16	08 18	08 24	08 39	08 45	08 54	09 11
—	14¼	Kenley	d		00 18	00 19	00 30	00 49	06 48		07 16	07 37		07 52	08 00		08 19		08 27		08 48	08 57	
—	15½	Whyteleafe	d		00 21	00 22	00 33	00 52	06 52		07 19	07 40		07 55	08 04		08 22		08 30		08 51	09 01	
—	16	Whyteleafe South	d		00 23	00 24	00 35	00 54	06 54		07 21	07 42		07 57	08 06		08 24		08 32		08 53	09 03	
—	17¾	**Caterham**	a		00 28	00 29	00 40	00 59	06 58		07 26	07 48		08 02	08 10		08 29		08 37		08 59	09 07	
14¼	—	Reedham	d	23p57						06 56			07 38			08 00		08 20		08 42			09 14
15	—	Coulsdon Town	d	23p59						06 59			07 41			08 03		08 23		08 44			09 16
15¾	—	Woodmansterne	d	00 03						07 02			07 44			08 06		08 26		08 47			09 19
16¾	—	Chipstead	d	00 06						07 05			07 47			08 09		08 29		08 50			09 22
19¼	—	Kingswood	d	00 11						07 10			07 52			08 14		08 34		08 56			09 28
20½	—	Tadworth	d	00 15						07 14			07 56			08 18		08 38		08 59			09 31
21¾	—	**Tattenham Corner**	a	00 18						07 18			07 59			08 21		08 41		09 03			09 36

Station		SN	SN	SN	SN	SN	SN	SN	SN	SN	SN		SN	SN	SN	SN	SN	SN	SN	SN	SN	SN
London Victoria	d		08 43			09 13				09 43		and at the same minutes past each hour until			14 13				14 43			15 13
Clapham Junction	d		08 51			09 21				09 51					14 21				14 51			15 21
London Bridge	d	08 36		09 06	09 20			09 36	09 50		10 06		14 06	14 20			14 36	14 50		15 06	15 20	
New Cross Gate	d	08 41		09 12				09 41			10 11		14 11				14 41			15 11		
Norwood Junction	d	09 00		09 30	09 33			10 00	10 03		10 30		14 30	14 33			15 00	15 03		15 30	15 33	
East Croydon	d	09 07	09 13	09 34	09 37	09 43		10 04	10 07	10 13	10 34		14 34	14 37	14 43		15 04	15 07	15 13	15 34	15 37	15 43
South Croydon	d	09 09	09 15	09 36		09 45		10 06		10 15	10 36		14 36		14 45		15 06		15 15	15 36		15 45
Purley Oaks	d	09 12	09 18	09 39		09 48		10 09		10 18	10 39		14 39		14 48		15 09		15 18	15 39		15 48
Purley	a	09 15	09 22	09 42	09 45	09 52		10 12	10 15	10 22	10 42		14 42	14 45	14 52		15 12	15 15	15 22	15 42	15 45	15 52
	d	09 18	09 26	09 43	09 46	09 52	10 02	10 13	10 16	10 22	10 43		14 43	14 46	14 54	15 02	15 13	15 16	15 22	15 43	15 46	15 52
Kenley	d	09 21	09 29	09 46		09 55		10 16		10 25	10 46		14 46		14 57		15 16		15 25	15 46		15 55
Whyteleafe	d	09 24	09 32	09 49		09 59		10 19		10 29	10 49		14 49		15 01		15 19		15 29	15 49		15 59
Whyteleafe South	d	09 26	09 34	09 51		10 01		10 21		10 31	10 51		14 51		15 03		15 21		15 31	15 51		16 01
Caterham	a	09 31	09 40	09 56		10 05		10 26		10 35	10 56		14 56		15 07		15 26		15 35	15 56		16 05
Reedham	d				09 48		10 04		10 18					14 48		15 04		15 18			15 48	
Coulsdon Town	d				09 51		10 07		10 21					14 51		15 07		15 21			15 51	
Woodmansterne	d				09 54		10 10		10 24					14 54		15 10		15 24			15 54	
Chipstead	d				09 57		10 13		10 27					14 57		15 13		15 27			15 57	
Kingswood	d				10 02		10 18		10 32					15 02		15 18		15 32			16 02	
Tadworth	d				10 06		10 22		10 36					15 06		15 22		15 36			16 06	
Tattenham Corner	a				10 09		10 25		10 39					15 09		15 25		15 39			16 09	

Station		SN	SN	SN	SN	SN	SN	SN	SN	SN		SN B	SN C	SN		SN		SN		SN	SN C	SN B
London Victoria	d				15 43			16 13	16 39			16 43	16 43	17 09				17 39				
Clapham Junction	d				15 51			16 21	16 45			16 51	16 51	17 15				17 45				
London Bridge	d		15 36	15 50		16 06	16 20			16 48						17 17				17 49	17 49	
New Cross Gate	d		15 41			16 11																
Norwood Junction	d		16 00	16 03		16 30	16 33			17 02						17 30				18 02	18 02	
East Croydon	d		16 04	16 07	16 13	16 34	16 37	16 43	16 56	17 06		17 16	17 17	17 27		17 35		17 56		18 06	18 06	
South Croydon	d		16 06		16 15	16 36		16 45	16 58	17 08		17 19	17 19	17 30		17 37		17 58		18 08	18 08	
Purley Oaks	d		16 09		16 18	16 39		16 48	17 01	17 11		17 22	17 22	17 33		17 40		18 01		18 11	18 11	
Purley	a		16 12	16 15	16 22	16 42	16 45	16 52	17 05	17 14		17 25	17 25	17 36		17 44		18 04		18 14	18 14	
	d	16 02	16 13	16 16	16 24	16 43	16 48	16 52	17 05	17 18	17 22	17 28	17 28	17 40	17 42	17 48	17 50	18 08	18 10	18 18	18 21	18 25
Kenley	d		16 16		16 27	16 46		16 55	17 08	17 21		17 31	17 31	17 43		17 51		18 11		18 21		
Whyteleafe	d		16 19		16 31	16 49		16 59	17 12	17 24		17 34	17 34	17 46		17 54		18 14		18 24		
Whyteleafe South	d		16 21		16 33	16 51		17 01	17 14	17 26		17 36	17 36	17 48		17 56		18 16		18 26		
Caterham	a		16 26		16 37	16 58		17 07	17 20	17 33		17 43	17 43	17 55		18 03		18 23		18 33		
Reedham	d	16 04		16 18			16 50				17 24				17 44		17 52		18 12		18 23	18 27
Coulsdon Town	d	16 07		16 21			16 53				17 27				17 47		17 55		18 15		18 26	18 30
Woodmansterne	d	16 10		16 24			16 56				17 30				17 50		17 58		18 18		18 29	18 33
Chipstead	d	16 13		16 27			16 59				17 33				17 53		18 01		18 21		18 32	18 36
Kingswood	d	16 18		16 32			17 04				17 38				17 58		18 06		18 26		18 37	18 41
Tadworth	d	16 22		16 36			17 08				17 42				18 02		18 10		18 30		18 41	18 45
Tattenham Corner	a	16 25		16 39			17 11				17 47				18 05		18 15		18 33		18 45	18 49

A from 21 May
B from 21 May
C until 18 May

London and Croydon - Caterham and Tattenham Corner

Network Diagram - see first Page of Table 177

		SN			SN		SN		SN		SN		SN		SN	SN	SN	SN	SN	SN	SN	SN		SN
London Victoria 15 ⊖	d	18 09					18 39				18 45				19 15		19 45		20 15		20 45		21 15		
Clapham Junction 10	d	18 15					18 45				18 53				19 23		19 53		20 23		20 53		21 23		
London Bridge 4 ⊖	d				18 18				18 49				19 06			19 36		20 06		20 36		21 06			21 36
New Cross Gate 4 ⊖	d												19 11			19 41		20 11		20 41		21 11			21 41
Norwood Junction 2	d				18 31				19 02				19 30			20 00		20 30		21 00		21 30			22 00
East Croydon	d	18 28			18 37		18 57		19 06		19 14		19 34		19 44	20 04	20 15	20 34	20 44	21 04	21 14	21 34	21 45		22 04
South Croydon 4	d	18 30			18 42		19 00		19 08		19 16		19 36		19 47	20 06	20 17	20 36	20 47	21 06	21 17	21 36	21 47		22 06
Purley Oaks	d	18 33			18 45		19 03		19 11		19 19		19 39		19 50	20 09	20 21	20 39	20 50	21 09	21 20	21 39	21 50		22 09
Purley 4	a	18 36			18 48		19 06		19 14		19 22		19 42		19 53	20 12	20 24	20 42	20 53	21 12	21 23	21 42	21 53		22 12
	d	18 40	18 42		18 51	18 54	19 10	19 12	19 18	19 20	19 26	19 28	19 45		19 53	20 15	20 24	20 45	20 53	21 15	21 23	21 45	21 54		22 15
Kenley	d	18 43			18 54		19 13		19 21		19 29		19 48			20 18		20 48		21 18		21 48			22 18
Whyteleafe	d	18 46			18 57		19 16		19 24		19 32		19 51			20 21		20 51		21 21		21 51			22 21
Whyteleafe South	d	18 48			18 59		19 18		19 26		19 34		19 53			20 23		20 53		21 23		21 53			22 23
Caterham	a	18 55			19 06		19 25		19 33		19 41		19 58			20 28		20 58		21 28		21 58			22 28
Reedham	d		18 44			18 56		19 14		19 22		19 31			19 56		20 27		20 56		21 26		21 56		
Coulsdon Town	d		18 47			18 59		19 17		19 25		19 34			19 58		20 29		20 58		21 28		21 59		
Woodmansterne	d		18 50			19 02		19 20		19 28		19 37			20 01		20 32		21 01		21 31		22 02		
Chipstead	d		18 53			19 05		19 23		19 31		19 40			20 04		20 35		21 04		21 34		22 05		
Kingswood	d		18 58			19 10		19 28		19 36		19 45			20 10		20 41		21 10		21 40		22 10		
Tadworth	d		19 02			19 14		19 32		19 40		19 49			20 13		20 44		21 13		21 43		22 14		
Tattenham Corner	a		19 05			19 17		19 35		19 45		19 52			20 17		20 48		21 17		21 47		22 17		

		SN	SN	SN	SN	SN	SN	SN	SN		SN FO
London Victoria 15 ⊖	d	21 45		22 15		22 45		23 15			23 45
Clapham Junction 10	d	21 53		22 23		22 53		23 23			23 53
London Bridge 4 ⊖	d		22 08		22 38		23 06		23 36		
New Cross Gate 4 ⊖	d		22 13		22 43		23 11		23 41		
Norwood Junction 2	d		22 32		23 02		23 30		23 59		
East Croydon	d	22 14	22 36	22 45	23 07	23 14	23 34	23 45	00 04		00 14
South Croydon 4	d	22 17	22 38	22 47	23 09	23 17	23 36	23 47	00 06		00 17
Purley Oaks	d	22 20	22 41	22 50	23 12	23 20	23 39	23 50	00 09		00 20
Purley 4	a	22 23	22 44	22 53	23 15	23 23	23 42	23 54	00 12		00 23
	d	22 23	22 47	22 54	23 15	23 24	23 45	23 55	00 15		00 23
Kenley	d		22 50		23 18		23 48		00 18		
Whyteleafe	d		22 53		23 22		23 51		00 21		
Whyteleafe South	d		22 55		23 24		23 53		00 23		
Caterham	a		23 00		23 28		23 58		00 28		
Reedham	d	22 26		22 56		23 26		23 57			00 26
Coulsdon Town	d	22 28		22 59		23 29		23 59			00 28
Woodmansterne	d	22 31		23 02		23 32		00 03			00 31
Chipstead	d	22 34		23 05		23 35		00 06			00 34
Kingswood	d	22 40		23 10		23 40		00 11			00 40
Tadworth	d	22 43		23 14		23 44		00 15			00 43
Tattenham Corner	a	22 47		23 17		23 47		00 18			00 47

Saturdays

		SN	SN	SN	SN	SN	SN	SN	SN	SN		SN	SN	SN	SN	SN	SN	SN	SN	SN		SN	SN	SN	SN
London Victoria 15 ⊖	d	23p15		23p45		00 16				06 43				07 13				07 43				08 13			
Clapham Junction 10	d	23p23		23p53		00 24				06 51				07 21				07 51				08 21			
London Bridge 4 ⊖	d		23p36		00 06			06 36	06 50			07 06	07 20			07 36	07 50		08 06	08 20				08 36	08 50
New Cross Gate 4 ⊖	d		23p41		00 11			06 41				07 11				07 41			08 11					08 41	
Norwood Junction 2	d		23p59		00 30		06 33	07 00	07 03			07 30	07 33			08 00	08 03		08 30	08 33				09 00	09 03
East Croydon	d	23p45	00 04	00 14	00 35	00 48	06 37	07 04	07 07	07 13		07 34	07 37	07 43		08 04	08 07	08 13	08 34	08 37		08 43		09 04	09 07
South Croydon 4	d	23p47	00 06	00 17	00 37	00 50		07 06		07 15		07 36		07 45		08 06		08 15	08 36			08 45		09 06	
Purley Oaks	d	23p50	00 09	00 20	00 40	00 53		07 09		07 18		07 39		07 48		08 09		08 18	08 39			08 48		09 09	
Purley 4	a	23p54	00 12	00 23	00 43	00 56	06 45	07 12	07 15	07 21		07 42	07 45	07 51		08 12	08 15	08 21	08 42	08 45		08 52		09 12	09 15
	d	23p55	00 15	00 23	00 46	00 57	06 46	07 13	07 16	07 22		07 43	07 46	07 52	08 02	08 13	08 16	08 22	08 43	08 46		08 52	09 02	09 13	09 16
Kenley	d		00 18		00 49			07 16		07 25		07 46		07 55		08 16		08 25	08 46			08 55		09 16	
Whyteleafe	d		00 21		00 52			07 19		07 28		07 49		07 58		08 19		08 28	08 49			08 59		09 19	
Whyteleafe South	d		00 23		00 54			07 21		07 30		07 51		08 00		08 21		08 30	08 51			09 01		09 21	
Caterham	a		00 28		00 59			07 26		07 35		07 56		08 05		08 26		08 35	08 56			09 05		09 26	
Reedham	d	23p57		00 26		00 59	06 48		07 18				07 48		08 04		08 18			08 48			09 04		09 18
Coulsdon Town	d	23p59		00 28		01 02	06 51		07 21				07 51		08 07		08 21			08 51			09 07		09 21
Woodmansterne	d	00 03		00 31		01 05	06 54		07 24				07 54		08 10		08 24			08 54			09 10		09 24
Chipstead	d	00 06		00 34		01 08	06 57		07 27				07 57		08 13		08 27			08 57			09 13		09 27
Kingswood	d	00 11		00 40		01 13	07 02		07 32				08 02		08 18		08 32			09 02			09 18		09 32
Tadworth	d	00 15		00 43		01 17	07 06		07 36				08 06		08 22		08 36			09 06			09 22		09 36
Tattenham Corner	a	00 18		00 47		01 20	07 09		07 39				08 09		08 25		08 39			09 09			09 25		09 39

London and Croydon - Caterham and Tattenham Corner

Network Diagram - see first Page of Table 177

		SN	SN	SN	SN		SN		SN	SN	SN	SN	SN	SN	SN	SN	SN		SN	SN	SN	SN
London Victoria 15 ⊖	d	08 43			09 13		13 13					13 43			14 13					14 43		
Clapham Junction 10	d	08 51			09 21		13 21					13 51			14 21					14 51		
London Bridge 4 ⊖	d		09 06	09 20						13 36	13 50		14 06	14 20			14 36		14 50		15 06	15 20
New Cross Gate 4 ⊖	d		09 11							13 41			14 11				14 41				15 11	
Norwood Junction 2	d		09 30	09 33						14 00	14 03		14 30	14 33			15 00		15 03		15 30	15 33
East Croydon	d	09 13	09 34	09 37	09 43		13 43			14 04	14 07	14 13	14 34	14 37	14 43		15 04		15 07	15 13	15 34	15 37
South Croydon 4	d	09 15	09 36		09 45	and at	13 45			14 06		14 15	14 36		14 45		15 06			15 15	15 36	
Purley Oaks	d	09 18	09 39		09 48	the same	13 48			14 09		14 18	14 39		14 48		15 09			15 18	15 39	
Purley 4	a	09 21	09 42	09 45	09 51	minutes	13 51			14 12	14 15	14 22	14 42	14 45	14 52		15 12		15 15	15 21	15 42	15 45
	d	09 22	09 43	09 46	09 52	past	13 52		14 02	14 13	14 16	14 22	14 43	14 46	14 52	15 02	15 13		15 16	15 22	15 43	15 46
Kenley	d	09 25	09 46		09 55	each	13 55			14 16		14 25	14 46		14 55		15 16			15 25	15 46	
Whyteleafe	d	09 28	09 49		09 58	hour until	13 58			14 19		14 29	14 49		14 59		15 19			15 28	15 49	
Whyteleafe South	d	09 30	09 51		10 00		14 00			14 21		14 31	14 51		15 01		15 21			15 30	15 51	
Caterham	a	09 35	09 56		10 05		14 05			14 26		14 35	14 56		15 05		15 26			15 35	15 56	
Reedham	d			09 48					14 04		14 18			14 48		15 04			15 18			15 48
Coulsdon Town	d			09 51					14 07		14 21			14 51		15 07			15 21			15 51
Woodmansterne	d			09 54					14 10		14 24			14 54		15 10			15 24			15 54
Chipstead	d			09 57					14 13		14 27			14 57		15 13			15 27			15 57
Kingswood	d			10 02					14 18		14 32			15 02		15 18			15 32			16 02
Tadworth	d			10 06					14 22		14 36			15 06		15 22			15 36			16 06
Tattenham Corner	a			10 09					14 25		14 39			15 09		15 25			15 39			16 09

		SN		SN	SN		SN	SN	SN	SN	SN	SN	SN	SN	SN		SN	SN	SN	SN	SN	SN	SN	SN
London Victoria 15 ⊖	d	15 13		20 13					20 43			21 13					21 43			22 13			22 43	
Clapham Junction 10	d	15 21		20 21					20 51			21 21					21 51			22 21			22 51	
London Bridge 4 ⊖	d						20 36	20 50		21 06	21 20			21 36	21 50			22 06	22 20		22 36	22 50		23 06
New Cross Gate 4 ⊖	d						20 41			21 11				21 41				22 11			22 41			23 11
Norwood Junction 2	d						21 00	21 03		21 30	21 33			22 00	22 03			22 30	22 33		23 00	23 03		23 30
East Croydon	d	15 43		20 43			21 04	21 07	21 13	21 34	21 37	21 43		22 05	22 07		22 13	22 36	22 38	22 43	23 04	23 07	23 14	23 34
South Croydon 4	d	15 45	and at	20 45			21 06		21 15	21 36		21 45		22 07			22 15	22 38		22 46	23 06		23 16	23 36
Purley Oaks	d	15 48	the same	20 48			21 09		21 18	21 39		21 48		22 10			22 18	22 41		22 49	23 09		23 19	23 39
Purley 4	a	15 51	minutes	20 51			21 12	21 15	21 21	21 42	21 45	21 51		22 13	22 16		22 21	22 44	22 47	22 52	23 12	23 15	23 22	23 42
	d	15 52	past	20 52	21 04		21 13	21 16	21 22	21 43	21 46	21 52	22 04	22 14	22 17		22 22	22 45	22 48	22 52	23 13	23 16	23 23	23 43
Kenley	d	15 55	each	20 55			21 16		21 25	21 46		21 55		22 17			22 25	22 48		22 55	23 16		23 26	23 46
Whyteleafe	d	15 58	hour until	20 58			21 19		21 28	21 49		21 58		22 20			22 28	22 51		22 59	23 19		23 29	23 49
Whyteleafe South	d	16 00		21 00			21 21		21 30	21 51		22 00		22 22			22 30	22 53		23 01	23 21		23 31	23 51
Caterham	a	16 05		21 05			21 26		21 35	21 56		22 05		22 27			22 36	22 58		23 06	23 26		23 36	23 56
Reedham	d				21 06			21 18			21 48		22 06		22 19				22 50			23 18		
Coulsdon Town	d				21 09			21 21			21 51		22 09		22 22				22 53			23 21		
Woodmansterne	d				21 12			21 24			21 54		22 12		22 25				22 56			23 24		
Chipstead	d				21 15			21 27			21 57		22 15		22 28				22 59			23 27		
Kingswood	d				21 20			21 32			22 02		22 20		22 33				23 04			23 32		
Tadworth	d				21 24			21 36			22 06		22 24		22 37				23 08			23 36		
Tattenham Corner	a				21 27			21 39			22 09		22 27		22 40				23 11			23 39		

		SN		SN	SN
London Victoria 15 ⊖	d	23 15			23 45
Clapham Junction 10	d	23 23			23 53
London Bridge 4 ⊖	d			23 36	
New Cross Gate 4 ⊖	d			23 41	
Norwood Junction 2	d			23 59	
East Croydon	d	23 44		00 04	00 14
South Croydon 4	d	23 47		00 06	00 17
Purley Oaks	d	23 50		00 09	00 20
Purley 4	a	23 53		00 13	00 23
	d	23 53		00 16	00 23
Kenley	d			00 19	
Whyteleafe	d			00 22	
Whyteleafe South	d			00 24	
Caterham	a			00 29	
Reedham	d	23 56			00 26
Coulsdon Town	d	23 58			00 28
Woodmansterne	d	00 01			00 31
Chipstead	d	00 04			00 34
Kingswood	d	00 10			00 40
Tadworth	d	00 13			00 43
Tattenham Corner	a	00 17			00 47

Sundays

		SN	SN	SN	SN	SN	SN	SN	SN	SN		SN	SN		SN	SN	SN	SN	SN		SN
London Victoria 15 ⊖	d	23p15		23p45		00 16	06 36	07 06	07 36			08 06				22 36		23 06			23 50
Clapham Junction 10	d	23p23		23p53		00 24	06 42	07 12	07 42			08 12				22 42		23 12			23 56
London Bridge 4 ⊖	d		23p36		00 06					07 39			08 09		22 09		22 39		23 39		
New Cross Gate 4 ⊖	d		23p41		00 11					07 44			08 14		22 14		22 44		23 44		
Norwood Junction 2	d		23p59		00 30					08 03			08 33		22 33		23 03		00 03		
East Croydon	d	23p44	00 04	00 14	00 35	00 48	07 04	07 34	08 04	08 08		08 34	08 38		22 38	23 04	23 08	23 35	00 07		00 18
South Croydon 4	d	23p47	00 06	00 17	00 37	00 50				08 10			08 40	and at	22 40		23 10	23 37	00 09		00 20
Purley Oaks	d	23p50	00 09	00 20	00 40	00 53				08 13			08 43	the same	22 43		23 13	23 40	00 12		00 23
Purley 4	a	23p53	00 13	00 23	00 43	00 56	07 10	07 40	08 10	08 16		08 40	08 46	minutes	22 46	23 10	23 16	23 43	00 15		00 26
	d	23p53	00 16	00 23	00 46	00 57	07 10	07 40	08 10	08 17		08 40	08 47	past	22 47	23 10	23 32	23 44	00 16		00 27
Kenley	d		00 19		00 49		07 13	07 43	08 13			08 43		each		23 13		23 47	00 19		00 30
Whyteleafe	d		00 22		00 52		07 17	07 47	08 17			08 47		hour until		23 17		23 50	00 22		00 33
Whyteleafe South	d		00 24		00 54		07 19	07 49	08 19			08 49				23 19		23 52	00 24		00 35
Caterham	a		00 29		00 59		07 23	07 53	08 23			08 53				23 23		23 57	00 29		00 40
Reedham	d	23p56		00 26		00 59				08 19			08 49		22 49		23 34				
Coulsdon Town	d	23p58		00 28		01 02				08 22			08 52		22 52		23 37				
Woodmansterne	d	00 01		00 31		01 05				08 25			08 55		22 55		23 40				
Chipstead	d	00 04		00 34		01 08				08 28			08 58		22 58		23 43				
Kingswood	d	00 10		00 40		01 13				08 33			09 03		23 03		23 48				
Tadworth	d	00 13		00 43		01 17				08 37			09 07		23 07		23 52				
Tattenham Corner	a	00 17		00 47		01 20				08 40			09 10		23 10		23 55				

Tattenham Corner and Caterham - Croydon and London

Network Diagram - see first Page of Table 177

Miles	Miles			SN	SN	SN	SN	SN	SN	SN	SN	SN	SN	SN	SN	SN	SN	SN	SN	SN	SN	SN
0	—	Tattenham Corner	d		05 56			06 32		06 48		07 02			07 18		07 32		07 48		08 04	
1¼	—	Tadworth	d		05 59			06 35		06 51		07 05			07 21		07 35		07 51		08 07	
2½	—	Kingswood	d		06 02			06 38		06 54		07 08			07 24		07 38		07 54		08 10	
5	—	Chipstead	d		06 08			06 44		07 00		07 14			07 30		07 44		08 00		08 16	
6	—	Woodmansterne	d		06 11			06 47		07 03		07 17			07 33		07 47		08 03		08 19	
6¾	—	Coulsdon Town	d		06 14			06 50		07 06		07 20		07 31	07 36		07 50		08 06		08 22	
7½	—	Reedham	d		06 16			06 52		07 08		07 22		07 34	07 38		07 52		08 08		08 24	
—	0	Caterham	d	05 52		06 15	06 35		06 45		07 01		07 15			07 31		07 45		08 01		08 17
—	1¾	Whyteleafe South	d	05 55		06 18	06 38		06 48		07 04		07 18			07 34		07 48		08 04		08 20
—	2¼	Whyteleafe	d	05 57		06 20	06 40		06 50		07 06		07 20			07 36		07 50		08 06		08 22
—	3½	Kenley	d	06 00		06 23	06 43		06 53		07 09		07 23			07 39		07 53		08 09		08 25
8¾	4¾	Purley	a	06 03	06 19	06 26	06 46	06 55	06 57	07 11	07 13	07 25	07 27	07 37	07 41	07 43	07 55	07 57	08 11	08 13	08 27	08 29
—	—		d	06 04	06 22	06 27	06 47	07 01		07 17		07 31		07 39	07 47		08 01		08 17		08 33	
9¼	5¾	Purley Oaks	d	06 07	06 25	06 30	06 50	07 04		07 20		07 34		07 42	07 50		08 04		08 20		08 36	
10¼	6¾	South Croydon	d	06 10	06 28	06 33	06 53	07 07		07 23		07 37		07 45	07 53		08 07		08 23		08 39	
11¼	7¾	East Croydon	d	06 13	06 31	06 36	06 57	07 10		07 26		07 40		07 48	07 56		08 10		08 26		08 42	
—	9	Norwood Junction	d	06 18	06 37	06 40		07 14				07 44					08 16				08 47	
—	15	New Cross Gate	a	06 35																		
—	17¾	London Bridge	a	06 44	06 49	06 52		07 28				07 58					08 28				09 01	
19	—	Clapham Junction	a				07 06			07 36				08 08	08 06				08 36			
21¾	—	London Victoria	a				07 15			07 46				08 19	08 15				08 45			

		SN	SN	SN	SN	SN	SN	SN	SN	SN	SN	SN	SN	SN	SN	SN	SN	SN	SN	SN	SN	SN	SN
Tattenham Corner	d	08 16		08 27			08 51			09 21		09 33		09 49			10 21		10 33		10 51		
Tadworth	d	08 19		08 30			08 54			09 24		09 36		09 52			10 24		10 36		10 54		
Kingswood	d	08 22		08 33			08 57			09 27		09 39		09 55			10 27		10 39		10 57		
Chipstead	d	08 28		08 39			09 03			09 33		09 45		10 01			10 33		10 45		11 03		
Woodmansterne	d	08 31		08 42			09 06			09 36		09 48		10 04			10 36		10 48		11 06		
Coulsdon Town	d	08 34		08 45			09 09			09 39		09 51		10 07			10 39		10 51		11 09		
Reedham	d	08 36		08 47			09 11			09 41		09 53		10 09			10 41		10 53		11 11		
Caterham	d		08 29		08 40	08 56		09 07	09 26		09 37		09 56		10 09	10 26		10 39		10 56		11 09	11 26
Whyteleafe South	d		08 32		08 43	08 59		09 10	09 29		09 40		09 59		10 12	10 29		10 42		10 59		11 12	11 29
Whyteleafe	d		08 34		08 45	09 01		09 12	09 31		09 42		10 01		10 14	10 31		10 44		11 01		11 14	11 31
Kenley	d		08 37		08 48	09 04		09 15	09 34		09 45		10 04		10 17	10 34		10 47		11 04		11 17	11 34
Purley	a	08 39	08 41	08 50	08 52	09 07	09 14	09 18	09 37	09 44	09 48	09 56	10 07	10 12	10 20	10 37	10 44	10 50	10 56	11 07	11 14	11 20	11 37
	d	08 45		08 56		09 08	09 14	09 21	09 38	09 45	09 51		10 08	10 15	10 21	10 38	10 45	10 51		11 08	11 15	11 21	11 38
Purley Oaks	d	08 48		08 59		09 11		09 24	09 41		09 54		10 11		10 24	10 41		10 54		11 11		11 24	11 41
South Croydon	d	08 51		09 02		09 14		09 27	09 44		09 57		10 14		10 27	10 44		10 57		11 14		11 27	11 44
East Croydon	d	08 54		09 05		09 17	09 20	09 30	09 47	09 51	10 00		10 17	10 21	10 30	10 47	10 51	11 00		11 17	11 21	11 30	11 47
Norwood Junction	d			09 09			09 25	09 35		09 55	10 05			10 25	10 35		10 55	11 05			11 25	11 35	
New Cross Gate	a						09 32	09 52			10 22				10 52			11 22				11 52	
London Bridge	a			09 23			09 41	10 00		10 09	10 29			10 39	10 59		11 09	11 29			11 39	11 59	
Clapham Junction	a	09 04				09 38			10 07				10 37			11 07				11 37			12 07
London Victoria	a	09 13				09 48			10 16				10 46			11 16				11 46			12 16

		SN	SN	SN	SN	SN	SN	SN	SN	SN	SN	SN	SN	SN	SN	SN	SN	SN	SN	SN	SN	SN	SN
Tattenham Corner	d	11 21		11 33		11 51			12 21		12 33		12 51			13 21		13 33		13 51			14 21
Tadworth	d	11 24		11 36		11 54			12 24		12 36		12 54			13 24		13 36		13 54			14 24
Kingswood	d	11 27		11 39		11 57			12 27		12 39		12 57			13 27		13 39		13 57			14 27
Chipstead	d	11 33		11 45		12 03			12 33		12 45		13 03			13 33		13 45		14 03			14 33
Woodmansterne	d	11 36		11 48		12 06			12 36		12 48		13 06			13 36		13 48		14 06			14 36
Coulsdon Town	d	11 39		11 51		12 09			12 39		12 51		13 09			13 39		13 51		14 09			14 39
Reedham	d	11 41		11 53		12 11			12 41		12 53		13 11			13 41		13 53		14 11			14 41
Caterham	d		11 39		11 56		12 09	12 26		12 39		12 56		13 09	13 26		13 39		13 56		14 09	14 26	
Whyteleafe South	d		11 42		11 59		12 12	12 29		12 42		12 59		13 12	13 29		13 42		13 59		14 12	14 29	
Whyteleafe	d		11 44		12 01		12 14	12 31		12 44		13 01		13 14	13 31		13 44		14 01		14 14	14 31	
Kenley	d		11 47		12 04		12 17	12 34		12 47		13 04		13 17	13 34		13 47		14 04		14 17	14 34	
Purley	a	11 44	11 50	11 56	12 07	12 14	12 20	12 37	12 44	12 50	12 56	13 07	13 14	13 20	13 37	13 44	13 50	13 56	14 07	14 14	14 20	14 37	14 44
	d	11 45	11 51		12 08	12 15	12 21	12 38	12 45	12 51		13 08	13 15	13 21	13 38	13 45	13 51		14 08	14 15	14 21	14 38	14 45
Purley Oaks	d		11 54		12 11		12 24	12 41		12 54		13 11		13 24	13 41		13 54		14 11		14 24	14 41	
South Croydon	d		11 57		12 14		12 27	12 44		12 57		13 14		13 27	13 44		13 57		14 14		14 27	14 44	
East Croydon	d	11 51	12 00		12 17	12 21	12 30	12 47	12 51	13 00		13 17	13 21	13 30	13 47	13 51	14 00		14 17	14 21	14 30	14 47	14 51
Norwood Junction	d	11 55	12 05			12 25	12 35		12 55	13 05			13 25	13 35		13 55	14 05			14 25	14 35		14 55
New Cross Gate	a		12 22				12 52			13 22				13 52			14 22				14 52		
London Bridge	a	12 09	12 29			12 39	12 59		13 09	13 29			13 39	13 59		14 09	14 29			14 39	14 59		15 09
Clapham Junction	a				12 37			13 07				13 37			14 07				14 37			15 07	
London Victoria	a				12 46			13 16				13 46			14 16				14 46			15 16	

		SN	SN	SN	SN	SN	SN	SN	SN	SN	SN	SN	SN	SN	SN	SN	SN	SN	SN	SN	SN	SN
Tattenham Corner	d		14 33		14 51			15 21		15 33		15 51			16 21		16 33		16 51			17 19
Tadworth	d		14 36		14 54			15 24		15 36		15 54			16 24		16 36		16 54			17 22
Kingswood	d		14 39		14 57			15 27		15 39		15 57			16 27		16 39		16 57			17 25
Chipstead	d		14 45		15 03			15 33		15 45		16 03			16 33		16 45		17 03			17 31
Woodmansterne	d		14 48		15 06			15 36		15 48		16 06			16 36		16 48		17 06			17 34
Coulsdon Town	d		14 51		15 09			15 39		15 51		16 09			16 39		16 51		17 09			17 37
Reedham	d		14 53		15 11			15 41		15 53		16 11			16 41		16 53		17 11			17 39
Caterham	d	14 39		14 56		15 09	15 24		15 39		15 56		16 09	16 26		16 39		16 52		17 09	17 26	
Whyteleafe South	d	14 42		14 59		15 12	15 27		15 42		15 59		16 12	16 29		16 42		16 55		17 12	17 29	
Whyteleafe	d	14 44		15 01		15 14	15 29		15 44		16 01		16 14	16 31		16 44		16 57		17 14	17 31	
Kenley	d	14 47		15 04		15 17	15 32		15 47		16 04		16 17	16 34		16 47		17 00		17 17	17 34	
Purley	a	14 50	14 56	15 07	15 14	15 20	15 35	15 44	15 50	15 56	16 07	16 14	16 20	16 37	16 44	16 50	16 56	17 04	17 14	17 20	17 37	17 42
	d	14 51		15 08	15 15	15 21	15 38	15 45	15 51		16 08	16 15	16 21	16 38	16 45	16 51	17 08		17 15	17 21	17 38	17 45
Purley Oaks	d	14 54		15 11		15 24	15 41		15 54		16 11		16 24	16 41		16 54	17 11			17 24	17 41	
South Croydon	d	14 57		15 14		15 27	15 44		15 57		16 14		16 27	16 44		16 57	17 14			17 27	17 44	
East Croydon	d	15 00		15 17	15 21	15 30	15 47	15 51	16 00		16 17	16 21	16 30	16 47	16 51	17 00	17 17		17 21	17 30	17 47	17 51
Norwood Junction	d	15 05			15 25	15 35		15 55	16 05			16 25	16 35		16 55	17 05			17 25	17 35		17 55
New Cross Gate	a	15 22				15 52			16 22				16 52			17 22				17 52		
London Bridge	a	15 29			15 39	15 59		16 09	16 29			16 39	17 02		17 08	17 35			17 37	17 59		18 09
Clapham Junction	a			15 37			16 07				16 37			17 07			17 37				18 07	
London Victoria	a			15 46			16 16				16 46			17 16			17 48				18 16	

		SN	SN	SN	SN	SN	SN	SN	SN	SN	SN	SN	SN	SN	SN	SN	SN	SN	SN	SN	SN	SN	SN
Tattenham Corner	d			17 51		18 12		18 42		19 14		19 42	19 53		20 12		20 42		21 12		21 42		22 12
Tadworth	d			17 54		18 15		18 45		19 17		19 45	19 56		20 15		20 45		21 15		21 45		22 15
Kingswood	d			17 57		18 18		18 48		19 20		19 48	19 59		20 18		20 48		21 18		21 48		22 18
Chipstead	d			18 03		18 24		18 54		19 26		19 54	20 05		20 24		20 54		21 24		21 54		22 24
Woodmansterne	d			18 06		18 27		18 57		19 29		19 57	20 08		20 27		20 57		21 27		21 57		22 27
Coulsdon Town	d			18 09		18 30		19 00		19 32		20 00	20 11		20 30		21 00		21 30		22 00		22 30
Reedham	d			18 11		18 32		19 02		19 34		20 02	20 13		20 32		21 02		21 32		22 02		22 32
Caterham	d	17 45	17 54		18 09		18 39		19 07		19 39			20 08		20 37		21 07		21 39		22 09	
Whyteleafe South	d	17 48	17 57		18 12		18 42		19 10		19 42			20 11		20 40		21 10		21 42		22 12	
Whyteleafe	d	17 50	17 59		18 14		18 44		19 12		19 44			20 13		20 42		21 12		21 44		22 14	
Kenley	d	17 53	18 02		18 17		18 47		19 15		19 47			20 16		20 45		21 15		21 47		22 17	
Purley	a	17 56	18 05	18 14	18 20	18 35	18 50	19 05	19 18	19 37	19 50	20 05	20 16	20 19	20 35	20 48	21 05	21 18	21 35	21 50	22 05	22 20	22 35
	d	17 59	18 08	18 15	18 21	18 37	18 51	19 08	19 21	19 38	19 51	20 08		20 22	20 38	20 51	21 08	21 21	21 38	21 51	22 08	22 21	22 38
Purley Oaks	d	18 02	18 11		18 24	18 40	18 54	19 11	19 24	19 41	19 54	20 11		20 25	20 41	20 54	21 11	21 24	21 41	21 54	22 11	22 24	22 41
South Croydon	d	18 05	18 14		18 27	18 44	18 57	19 14	19 27	19 44	19 57	20 14		20 28	20 44	20 57	21 14	21 27	21 44	21 57	22 14	22 27	22 44
East Croydon	d	18 08	18 17	18 21	18 30	18 47	19 00	19 17	19 30	19 47	20 00	20 17		20 31	20 47	21 00	21 17	21 30	21 47	22 00	22 17	22 30	22 47
Norwood Junction	d	18 12		18 29	18 35		19 05		19 35		20 05			20 35		21 05		21 35		22 05		22 35	
New Cross Gate	a				18 52		19 22		19 52		20 22			20 52		21 22		21 52		22 22		22 52	
London Bridge	a	18 26		18 41	18 59		19 29		19 59		20 29			20 59		21 29		21 59		22 29		22 59	
Clapham Junction	a		18 39			19 08		19 37		20 07		20 37			21 07		21 37		22 07		22 37		23 07
London Victoria	a		18 46			19 15		19 48		20 18		20 46			21 18		21 48		22 18		22 48		23 16

		SN	SN	SN
Tattenham Corner	d		22 42	
Tadworth	d		22 45	
Kingswood	d		22 48	
Chipstead	d		22 54	
Woodmansterne	d		22 57	
Coulsdon Town	d		23 00	
Reedham	d		23 02	
Caterham	d	22 38		23 20
Whyteleafe South	d	22 41		23 23
Whyteleafe	d	22 43		23 25
Kenley	d	22 46		23 28
Purley	a	22 49	23 05	23 31
	d	22 52	23 08	23 34
Purley Oaks	d	22 55	23 11	23 37
South Croydon	d	22 58	23 14	23 40
East Croydon	d	23 01	23 17	23 43
Norwood Junction	d	23 06		23a47
New Cross Gate	a	23 23		
London Bridge	a	23 30		
Clapham Junction	a		23 37	
London Victoria	a		23 48	

Saturdays

		SN	SN	SN	SN	SN	SN	SN	SN	SN	SN	SN	SN	SN	SN	SN	SN	SN	SN	SN	SN	SN
Tattenham Corner	d		06 12		06 42			07 21			07 51			08 21		08 35		08 51			09 21	
Tadworth	d		06 15		06 45			07 24			07 54			08 24		08 38		08 54			09 24	
Kingswood	d		06 18		06 48			07 27			07 57			08 27		08 41		08 57			09 27	
Chipstead	d		06 24		06 54			07 33			08 03			08 33		08 47		09 03			09 33	
Woodmansterne	d		06 27		06 57			07 36			08 06			08 36		08 50		09 06			09 36	
Coulsdon Town	d		06 30		07 00			07 39			08 09			08 39		08 53		09 09			09 39	
Reedham	d		06 32		07 02			07 41			08 11			08 41		08 55		09 11			09 41	
Caterham	d	06 07		06 39		07 09	07 26		07 39	07 56		08 09	08 26		08 39		08 56		09 09	09 26		09 39
Whyteleafe South	d	06 10		06 42		07 12	07 29		07 42	07 59		08 12	08 29		08 42		08 59		09 12	09 29		09 42
Whyteleafe	d	06 12		06 44		07 14	07 31		07 44	08 01		08 14	08 31		08 44		09 01		09 14	09 31		09 44
Kenley	d	06 15		06 47		07 17	07 34		07 47	08 04		08 17	08 34		08 47		09 04		09 17	09 34		09 47
Purley	a	06 18	06 35	06 50	07 05	07 20	07 37	07 44	07 50	08 07	08 14	08 20	08 37	08 44	08 50	08 58	09 07	09 14	09 20	09 37	09 44	09 50
	d	06 21	06 38	06 51	07 08	07 21	07 38	07 45	07 51	08 08	08 15	08 21	08 38	08 45	08 51		09 08	09 15	09 21	09 38	09 45	09 51
Purley Oaks	d	06 24	06 41	06 54	07 11	07 24	07 41		07 54	08 11		08 24	08 41		08 54		09 11		09 24	09 41		09 54
South Croydon	d	06 27	06 44	06 57	07 14	07 27	07 44		07 57	08 14		08 27	08 44		08 57		09 14		09 27	09 44		09 57
East Croydon	d	06 30	06 47	07 00	07 17	07 30	07 47	07 51	08 00	08 17	08 21	08 30	08 47	08 51	09 00		09 17	09 21	09 30	09 47	09 51	10 00
Norwood Junction	d	06 35		07 05		07 35		07 55	08 05		08 25	08 35		08 55	09 05			09 25	09 35		09 55	10 05
New Cross Gate	a	06 52		07 22		07 52			08 22			08 52			09 22				09 52			10 22
London Bridge	a	06 59		07 29		07 59		08 09	08 29		08 39	08 59		09 09	09 29			09 39	09 59		10 09	10 29
Clapham Junction	a		07 07		07 37		08 07			08 37			09 07				09 37			10 07		
London Victoria	a		07 16		07 46		08 16			08 46			09 16				09 46			10 16		

		SN		SN	SN	SN	SN	SN	SN	SN	SN	SN	SN	SN	SN	SN	SN	SN	SN		SN
Tattenham Corner	d	09 33	and at the same minutes past each hour until	15 33		15 51			16 21		16 33		16 51			17 21		17 33		and at the same minutes past each hour until	
Tadworth	d	09 36		15 36		15 54			16 24		16 36		16 54			17 24		17 36			
Kingswood	d	09 39		15 39		15 57			16 27		16 39		16 57			17 27		17 39			
Chipstead	d	09 45		15 45		16 03			16 33		16 45		17 03			17 33		17 45			
Woodmansterne	d	09 48		15 48		16 06			16 36		16 48		17 06			17 36		17 48			
Coulsdon Town	d	09 51		15 51		16 09			16 39		16 51		17 09			17 39		17 51			
Reedham	d	09 53		15 53		16 11			16 41		16 53		17 11			17 41		17 53			
Caterham	d				15 56		16 09	16 26		16 39		16 56		17 09	17 26		17 39		17 56		21 56
Whyteleafe South	d				15 59		16 12	16 29		16 42		16 59		17 12	17 29		17 42		17 59		21 59
Whyteleafe	d				16 01		16 14	16 31		16 44		17 01		17 14	17 31		17 44		18 01		22 01
Kenley	d				16 04		16 17	16 34		16 47		17 04		17 17	17 34		17 47		18 04		22 04
Purley	a	09 56		15 56	16 07	16 14	16 20	16 37	16 44	16 50	16 56	17 07	17 14	17 20	17 37	17 44	17 50	17 56	18 07		22 07
	d				16 08	16 15	16 21	16 38	16 45	16 51		17 08	17 15	17 21	17 38	17 45	17 51		18 08		22 08
Purley Oaks	d				16 11		16 24	16 41		16 54		17 11		17 24	17 41		17 54		18 11		22 11
South Croydon	d				16 14		16 27	16 44		16 57		17 14		17 27	17 44		17 57		18 14		22 14
East Croydon	d				16 17	16 21	16 30	16 47	16 51	17 00		17 17	17 21	17 30	17 47	17 51	18 00		18 17		22 17
Norwood Junction	d					16 25	16 35		16 55	17 05			17 25	17 35		17 55	18 05				
New Cross Gate	a						16 52			17 22				17 52			18 22				
London Bridge	a					16 39	16 59		17 09	17 30			17 39	17 59		18 09	18 29				
Clapham Junction	a				16 37			17 07				17 38			18 07				18 37		22 37
London Victoria	a				16 46			17 16				17 47			18 16				18 46		22 46

Table 181

Saturdays

Tattenham Corner and Caterham - Croydon and London

Network Diagram - see first Page of Table 177

		SN	SN	SN	SN	SN	SN	SN	SN	SN
Tattenham Corner	d	21 51			22 21		22 33		22 51	
Tadworth	d	21 54			22 24		22 36		22 54	
Kingswood	d	21 57			22 27		22 39		22 57	
Chipstead	d	22 03			22 33		22 45		23 03	
Woodmansterne	d	22 06			22 36		22 48		23 06	
Coulsdon Town	d	22 09			22 39		22 51		23 09	
Reedham	d	22 11			22 41		22 53		23 11	
Caterham	d		22 09	22 26		22 39		22 56		23 20
Whyteleafe South	d		22 12	22 29		22 42		22 59		23 23
Whyteleafe	d		22 14	22 31		22 44		23 01		23 25
Kenley	d		22 17	22 34		22 47		23 04		23 28
Purley	a	22 14	22 20	22 37	22 44	22 50	22 56	23 07	23 14	23 31
	d	22 15	22 21	22 38	22 45	22 52		23 08	23 15	23 34
Purley Oaks	d		22 24	22 41		22 55		23 11		23 37
South Croydon	d		22 27	22 44		22 58		23 14		23 40
East Croydon	d	22 21	22 30	22 47	22 51	23 01		23 17	23 21	23 43
Norwood Junction	d	22 25	22 35		22 55	23 06			23 25	23a47
New Cross Gate	a		22 52			23 23				
London Bridge	a	22 39	22 59		23 09	23 30			23 39	
Clapham Junction	a			23 07				23 37		
London Victoria	a			23 16				23 48		

Sundays

		SN	SN	SN	SN	SN		SN	SN	SN	SN	SN	SN	SN	SN
Tattenham Corner	d			07 45		08 15		21 15		21 45		22 15		22 45	
Tadworth	d			07 48		08 18		21 18		21 48		22 18		22 48	
Kingswood	d			07 51		08 21		21 21		21 51		22 21		22 51	
Chipstead	d			07 57		08 27		21 27		21 57		22 27		22 57	
Woodmansterne	d			08 00		08 30		21 30		22 00		22 30		23 00	
Coulsdon Town	d			08 03		08 33		21 33		22 03		22 33		23 03	
Reedham	d			08 05		08 35	and at	21 35		22 05		22 35		23 05	
Caterham	d	07 24	07 35		08 05		the same		21 35		22 05		22 35		23 05
Whyteleafe South	d	07 27	07 38		08 08		minutes		21 38		22 08		22 38		23 08
Whyteleafe	d	07 29	07 40		08 10		past		21 40		22 10		22 40		23 10
Kenley	d	07 32	07 43		08 13		each		21 43		22 13		22 43		23 13
Purley	a	07 35	07 46	08 08	08 16	08 38	hour until	21 38	21 46	22 08	22 16	22 38	22 46	23 08	23 16
	d	07 38	07 47	08 08	08 17	08 38		21 38	21 47	22 08	22 17	22 38	22 47	23 08	23 17
Purley Oaks	d	07 41		08 11		08 41		21 41		22 11		22 41		23 11	23 20
South Croydon	d	07 44		08 14		08 44		21 44		22 14		22 44		23 14	23 23
East Croydon	d	07 47	07 53	08 17	08 23	08 47		21 47	21 53	22 17	22 23	22 47	22 53	23 17	23a25
Norwood Junction	d	07 52		08 22		08 52		21 52		22 22		22 52		23a21	
New Cross Gate	a	08 09		08 39		09 09		22 09		22 39		23 09			
London Bridge	a	08 17		08 48		09 18		22 18		22 48		23 18			
Clapham Junction	a		08 12		08 42				22 12		22 42		23 12		
London Victoria	a		08 20		08 50				22 20		22 52		23 20		

Table 182

Mondays to Fridays

until 5 October

London - Sutton, Epsom, Guildford, Dorking and Horsham

Network Diagram - see first Page of Table 177

Miles	Miles	Miles			SN MO A	SN MO A	SN MX	SW MO A	FC MX B	FC MX C	SN MX	SW MX	SN MX	FC MX B	FC MX C	SW MX D	SW MX E	SW	SN	SN	SN	SN	FC
—	0	—	**London Victoria**	d	23p08	23p19	23p26				23p34		23p51									05 52	
—	—	—	**London Waterloo**	d				23p32				23p42				00 15	00 15	05 47					
—	2¾	—	Clapham Junction	d	23p16	23p27	23p34	23p41			23p42	23p51	23p59			00 25	00 25	05 56				05 58	
—	4¾	—	Balham	d	23p21	23p32	23p40				23p47		00 04									06 03	
—	—	—	**London Bridge**	d						23p29					23p59						05 36		
—	—	6	Tulse Hill	d					23p31	23p41				00 01	00 09								06 02
—	—	6	New Cross Gate	d																	05 42		
8¾	—	—	Norwood Junction	d																05 53	06 00		
10½	—	12	**West Croydon**	d		23p50					00 04		00 21						05 45	05 58	06 05		
11½	—	—	Waddon	d		23p52					00 06		00 24						05 47	06 00	06 08		
13	—	—	Wallington	d		23p56					00 10		00 27						05 51	06 04	06 11		
13¾	—	—	Carshalton Beeches	d		23p58					00 12		00 30						05 53	06 06	06 14		
—	8	—	Mitcham Eastfields	d	23p28		23p46															06 12	
—	9	—	Mitcham Junction	d	23p31		23p49															06 15	
—	9¾	—	Hackbridge	d	23p34		23p53															06 19	
—	10¾	—	Carshalton	d	23p37		23p55															06 21	
14¾	12	0	**Sutton (Surrey)**	a	23p40	00 02	23p59		00 09	00 15	00 16		00 33	00 39	00 43				05 57	06 10	06 17	06 25	06 33
—	—	—		d	23p41	00 04	00 01													06 11		06 25	
—	13	—	Belmont	d																06 14			
—	14½	—	Banstead	d																06 18			
—	16	—	**Epsom Downs**	a																06 21			
15¾	—	—	Cheam	d	23p43	00 06	00 03															06 28	
17¼	—	—	Ewell East	d	23p47	00 10	00 07															06 31	
18¾	—	—	**Epsom**	a	23p51	00 14	00 11	00 06				00 15				00 50	00 50	06 20				06 35	
—	—	—		d	23p51		00 11					00 19					00 51	06 21				06 36	
20½	—	—	Ashtead	d	23p55		00 15					00 23					00s55	06 25				06 40	
22½	—	0	Leatherhead	d	23p58		00 18					00 26					00s58	06 28				06 43	
25	—	—	Bookham	d								00 31					01s03	06 33					
26¾	—	—	Effingham Junction	d								00 36					01s07	06 37					
35	—	—	**Guildford**	a								00 53					01 24	06 50					
—	—	3¼	Box Hill & Westhumble	d	00 03		00 23															06 48	
—	—	4	**Dorking**	a	00 06		00 26															06 50	
—	—	—		d			00 26															06 51	
—	—	9	Holmwood	d			00s33															06 58	
—	—	11¼	Ockley	d			00s37															07 02	
—	—	15¾	Warnham	d			00s43															07 08	
—	—	17¾	**Horsham**	a			00 47															07 12	

		FC	SN	SN	SW	SN	SN	FC	SN	SW	SW	SN	FC	SW	FC	SN	SN	SW	SN	FC 1	FC 1	SN	SW
London Victoria	d		06 00			06 17	06 07		06 30			06 36				07 15	07 00		07 06			07 30	
London Waterloo	d				06 24					06 39	06 54			07 09				07 24					07 39
Clapham Junction	d		06 08		06 33	06 24	06 15		06 38	06 48	07 03	06 44		07 18		07 21	07 08	07 33	07 14			07 38	07 48
Balham	d		06 13			06 30	06 20		06 44			06 49				07 26	07 13		07 20			07 44	
London Bridge	d																						
Tulse Hill	d	06 22						06 42					07 02		07 20					07 31	07 45		
New Cross Gate	d																						
Norwood Junction	d						06 39					07 09							07 39				
West Croydon	d		06 32				06 46		07 03			07 14					07 32		07 46			08 04	
Waddon	d		06 34				06 48		07 05			07 16					07 35		07 48			08 06	
Wallington	d		06 38				06 52		07 09			07 20					07 38		07 52			08 10	
Carshalton Beeches	d		06 40				06 54		07 11			07 22					07 41		07 54			08 12	
Mitcham Eastfields	d	06 29				06 38		06 49							07 27						07 52		
Mitcham Junction	d	06 32				06 41		06 52							07 30	07 34					07 55		
Hackbridge	d	06 35				06 45		06 55							07 33	07 37					07 58		
Carshalton	d	06 38				06 47		06 58							07 36	07 40					08 01		
Sutton (Surrey)	a	06 43	06 44			06 51	06 58	07 03	07 15			07 26	07 35		07 39	07 43	07 44		07 58	08 07	08 04	08 16	
	d		06 48	06 39		06 52	07 00		07 18			07 26				07 44	07 45		07 59			08 16	
Belmont	d		06 51						07 21								07 48					08 20	
Banstead	d		06 55						07 25								07 52					08 23	
Epsom Downs	a		06 58						07 28								07 55					08 27	
Cheam	d			06 41		06 54	07 02					07 29				07 46			08 01				
Ewell East	d			06 45		06 58	07 06					07 32				07 50			08 05				
Epsom	a			06 49	06 57	07 02	07 10			07 11	07 27	07 36		07 42		07 54		07 58	08 09				08 13
	d			06 50	06 58	07 02				07 12	07 28	07 37				07 54		07 58					08 17
Ashtead	d				07 02	07 06				07 16	07 32	07 41				07 58		08 02					08 21
Leatherhead	d			06 56	07 05	07 09				07 19	07 35	07 44				08 01		08 05					08 24
Bookham	d			07 01						07 24		07 49											08 29
Effingham Junction	d			07 05						07a28		07 53											08 33
Guildford	a			07 17								08 06											08 50
Box Hill & Westhumble	d															08 06							
Dorking	a				07 11	07 15					07 41					08 09		08 12					
	d					07 16										08 09							
Holmwood	d					07 23										08 17							
Ockley	d					07 27										08 21							
Warnham	d					07 33										08 26							
Horsham	a					07 37										08 30							

A from 21 May until 1 October
B from 22 May until 5 October
C until 18 May
D not from 31 July until 10 August, from 30 August until 7 September
E from 31 July until 7 September, not from 14 August until 29 August

Table 182

Mondays to Fridays

until 5 October

London - Sutton, Epsom, Guildford, Dorking and Horsham

Network Diagram - see first Page of Table 177

		SN	SW	SN	SN	FC	FC	SN	SW	SW	SN	SN	FC	SN	SN	FC 1	SN	SW	SW	SN	SN	SN	FC 1
London Victoria 15 ⊖	d	07 47		07 55	07 36			08 03			08 19	08 07			08 26		08 31			08 47	08 36	09 01	
London Waterloo 15 ⊖	d		07 54						08 09	08 24								08 39	08 54				
Clapham Junction 10	d	07 55	08 03	08 02	07 44			08 11	08 18	08 33	08 26	08 16			08 33		08 40	08 48	09 03	08 54	08 44	09 08	
Balham 4 ⊖	d	08 00			07 50			08 16			08 31	08 21			08 38		08 46			09 00	08 50		
London Bridge 4 ⊖	d													08 24									
Tulse Hill 3	d					08 05	08 21						08 40	08 47		08 50							09 01
New Cross Gate 4 ⊖	d																						
Norwood Junction 2	d				08 09							08 39									09 09		
West Croydon 4	d				08 15			08 36				08 45			08 56		09 06				09 14		
Waddon	d				08 17			08 39				08 47			08 58		09 08				09 16		
Wallington	d				08 21			08 42				08 51			09 02		09 12				09 20		
Carshalton Beeches	d				08 23			08 45				08 53			09 04		09 14				09 22		
Mitcham Eastfields	d	08 07					08 28				08 37					08 58				09 06			
Mitcham Junction	d	08 10					08 31				08 40					09 01				09 09			
Hackbridge	d	08 13					08 34				08 44					09 04				09 13			
Carshalton	d	08 16					08 37				08 46					09 07				09 15			
Sutton (Surrey) 4	a	08 19		08 22	08 27	08 37	08 40	08 48			08 50	08 57	09 12	09 02	09 08	09 10	09 18			09 19	09 26	09 28	09 37
	d			08 23	08 27			08 53			08 50			09 02			09 19			09 19		09 29	
Belmont	d							08 56									09 22						
Banstead	d							09 00									09 26						
Epsom Downs	a							09 03									09 29						
Cheam	d			08 25	08 30						08 53			09 05						09 22		09 31	
Ewell East	d			08 29	08 33						08 56			09 08						09 25			
Epsom 3	a		08 27	08 33	08 37				08 42	08 57	09 00			09 12				09 16	09 27	09 29		09 37	
	d		08 28	08 33	08 38				08 47	08 58	09 01							09 17	09 28			09 37	
Ashtead	d		08 32	08 37	08 42				08 51	09 02	09 05							09 21	09 32			09 41	
Leatherhead	d		08 35	08 40	08 45				08 54	09 05	09 08							09 24	09 35			09 44	
Bookham	d								08 59									09 29					
Effingham Junction 6	d								09 03									09 33					
Guildford	a								09 20									09 50					
Box Hill & Westhumble	d				08 50						09 13											09 49	
Dorking 4	a		08 41	08 46	08 52					09 11	09 15								09 41			09 52	
	d			08 47							09 16												
Holmwood	d										09 23												
Ockley	d										09 27												
Warnham	d										09 33												
Horsham 4	a			09 03							09 37												

		SW	FC	SN	SN	SW	SN	SN	SN	FC	SN	FC	SN	SW	SW	SN	SN	SN	FC	SW	FC	SN
London Victoria 15 ⊖	d			08 52	09 03		09 17	09 05	09 31		09 22		09 33			09 47	09 35	10 01				09 53
London Waterloo 15 ⊖	d	09 09				09 24								09 39	09 54					10 09		
Clapham Junction 10	d	09 18		09 00	09 11	09 33	09 24	09 14	09 38		09 30		09 41	09 48	10 03	09 54	09 44	10 08		10 18		10 00
Balham 4 ⊖	d			09 05	09 16		09 30	09 20			09 35		09 46			10 00	09 50					10 05
London Bridge 4 ⊖	d																					
Tulse Hill 3	d		09 16							09 31		09 46							10 01		10 16	
New Cross Gate 4 ⊖	d																					
Norwood Junction 2	d							09 39									10 09					
West Croydon 4	d			09 24	09 34			09 44			09 54		10 04				10 14					10 24
Waddon	d			09 26	09 36			09 46			09 56		10 06				10 16					10 26
Wallington	d			09 30	09 40			09 50			10 00		10 10				10 20					10 30
Carshalton Beeches	d			09 32	09 42			09 52			10 02		10 12				10 22					10 32
Mitcham Eastfields	d		09 24				09 36					09 54				10 06					10 24	
Mitcham Junction	d		09 27				09 39					09 57				10 09					10 27	
Hackbridge	d		09 30				09 43					10 00				10 13					10 30	
Carshalton	d		09 33				09 45					10 03				10 15					10 33	
Sutton (Surrey) 4	a		09 36	09 39	09 46		09 49	09 56	09 58	10 05	10 06	10 06	10 16			10 19	10 26	10 28	10 35		10 36	10 39
	d			09 40			09 49		09 59		10 07					10 19		10 29				10 40
Belmont	d										10 10											
Banstead	d										10 14											
Epsom Downs	a										10 17											
Cheam	d			09 42			09 52		10 01							10 22		10 31				10 42
Ewell East	d			09 46			09 55		10 05							10 25						10 46
Epsom 3	a	09 42		09 50		09 57	09 59		10 09					10 16	10 27	10 29		10 37		10 46		10 52
	d	09 47				09 58			10 09					10 17	10 28			10 37		10 47		
Ashtead	d	09 51				10 02			10 13					10 21	10 32			10 41		10 51		
Leatherhead	d	09 54				10 05			10 16					10 24	10 35			10 44		10 54		
Bookham	d	09 59												10 29						10 59		
Effingham Junction 6	d	10 03												10 33						11 03		
Guildford	a	10 20												10 50						11 20		
Box Hill & Westhumble	d								10 21													
Dorking 4	a					10 11			10 24						10 41			10 50				
	d								10 24													
Holmwood	d								10 32													
Ockley	d								10 36													
Warnham	d								10 41													
Horsham 4	a								10 45													

Table 182

Mondays to Fridays

until 5 October

London - Sutton, Epsom, Guildford, Dorking and Horsham

Network Diagram - see first Page of Table 177

		SN	SW	SN	SN	SN	FC	SN	FC	SN	SW	SW	SN	SN	SN	FC	SW	FC	SN	SN	SW	SN	SN
London Victoria 15 ⊖	d	10 03		10 17	10 06	10 31		10 23		10 33			10 47	10 36	11 01				10 53	11 03		11 17	11 06
London Waterloo 15 ⊖	d		10 24								10 39	10 54					11 09				11 24		
Clapham Junction 10	d	10 11	10 33	10 24	10 14	10 38		10 30		10 41	10 48	11 03	10 54	10 44	11 08		11 18		11 00	11 11	11 33	11 24	11 14
Balham 4 ⊖	d	10 16		10 30	10 20			10 35		10 46			11 00	10 50					11 05	11 16		11 30	11 20
London Bridge 4 ⊖	d																						
Tulse Hill 3	d						10 31		10 46							11 01		11 16					
New Cross Gate 4 ⊖	d																						
Norwood Junction 2	d				10 39									11 09									11 39
West Croydon 4	d	10 34			10 44			10 54		11 04				11 14					11 24	11 34			11 44
Waddon	d	10 36			10 46			10 56		11 06				11 16					11 26	11 36			11 46
Wallington	d	10 40			10 50			11 00		11 10				11 20					11 30	11 40			11 50
Carshalton Beeches	d	10 42			10 52			11 02		11 12				11 22					11 32	11 42			11 52
Mitcham Eastfields	d			10 36					10 54				11 06					11 24				11 36	
Mitcham Junction	d			10 39					10 57				11 09					11 27				11 39	
Hackbridge	d			10 43					11 00				11 13					11 30				11 43	
Carshalton	d			10 45					11 03				11 15					11 33				11 45	
Sutton (Surrey) 4	a	10 46		10 49	10 56	10 58	11 05	11 06	11 06	11 16			11 19	11 26	11 28	11 35		11 36	11 39	11 46		11 49	11 56
	d			10 49		10 59		11 07					11 19		11 29				11 40			11 49	
Belmont	d							11 10															
Banstead	d							11 14															
Epsom Downs	a							11 17															
Cheam	d			10 52		11 01							11 22		11 31				11 42			11 52	
Ewell East	d			10 55		11 05							11 25						11 46			11 55	
Epsom 3	a		10 57	10 59		11 09					11 16	11 27	11 29		11 37		11 46		11 52		11 57	11 59	
	d		10 58			11 09					11 17	11 28			11 37		11 47				11 58		
Ashtead	d		11 02			11 13					11 21	11 32			11 41		11 51				12 02		
Leatherhead	d		11 05			11 16					11 24	11 35			11 44		11 54				12 05		
Bookham	d										11 29						11 59						
Effingham Junction 6	d										11 33						12 03						
Guildford	a										11 50						12 20						
Box Hill & Westhumble	d					11 21																	
Dorking 4	a		11 11			11 24						11 41			11 50						12 11		
	d					11 24																	
Holmwood	d					11 32																	
Ockley	d					11 36																	
Warnham	d					11 41																	
Horsham 4	a					11 45																	

		SN	FC	SN	FC	SN	SW	SW	SN	SN	SN	FC	SW	FC	SN	SN	SW	SN	SN	SN	FC	SN
London Victoria 15 ⊖	d	11 31		11 23		11 33			11 47	11 36	12 01				11 53	12 03		12 17	12 06	12 31		12 23
London Waterloo 15 ⊖	d						11 39	11 54					12 09				12 24					
Clapham Junction 10	d	11 38		11 30		11 41	11 48	12 03	11 54	11 44	12 08		12 18		12 00	12 11	12 33	12 24	12 14	12 38		12 30
Balham 4 ⊖	d			11 35		11 46			12 00	11 50					12 05	12 16		12 30	12 20			12 35
London Bridge 4 ⊖	d																					
Tulse Hill 3	d		11 31		11 46							12 01		12 16							12 31	
New Cross Gate 4 ⊖	d																					
Norwood Junction 2	d									12 09									12 39			
West Croydon 4	d			11 54		12 04				12 14					12 24	12 34			12 44			12 54
Waddon	d			11 56		12 06				12 16					12 26	12 36			12 46			12 56
Wallington	d			12 00		12 10				12 20					12 30	12 40			12 50			13 00
Carshalton Beeches	d			12 02		12 12				12 22					12 32	12 42			12 52			13 02
Mitcham Eastfields	d				11 54				12 06					12 24				12 36				
Mitcham Junction	d				11 57				12 09					12 27				12 39				
Hackbridge	d				12 00				12 13					12 30				12 43				
Carshalton	d				12 03				12 15					12 33				12 45				
Sutton (Surrey) 4	a	11 58	12 05	12 06	12 06	12 16			12 19	12 26	12 28	12 35		12 36	12 39	12 46		12 49	12 56	12 58	13 05	13 06
	d	11 59		12 07					12 19		12 29				12 40			12 49		12 59		13 07
Belmont	d			12 10																		13 10
Banstead	d			12 14																		13 14
Epsom Downs	a			12 17																		13 17
Cheam	d	12 01							12 22		12 31				12 42			12 52		13 01		
Ewell East	d	12 05							12 25						12 46			12 55		13 05		
Epsom 3	a	12 09					12 16	12 27	12 29		12 37		12 46		12 52		12 57	12 59		13 09		
	d	12 09					12 17	12 28			12 37		12 47				12 58			13 09		
Ashtead	d	12 13					12 21	12 32			12 41		12 51				13 02			13 13		
Leatherhead	d	12 16					12 24	12 35			12 44		12 54				13 05			13 16		
Bookham	d						12 29						12 59									
Effingham Junction 6	d						12 33						13 03									
Guildford	a						12 50						13 20									
Box Hill & Westhumble	d	12 21																		13 21		
Dorking 4	a	12 24						12 41			12 50						13 11			13 24		
	d	12 24																		13 24		
Holmwood	d	12 32																		13 32		
Ockley	d	12 36																		13 36		
Warnham	d	12 41																		13 41		
Horsham 4	a	12 45																		13 45		

Table 182

Mondays to Fridays

until 5 October

London - Sutton, Epsom, Guildford, Dorking and Horsham

Network Diagram - see first Page of Table 177

		FC	SN	SW	SW	SN	SN	SN	FC		SW	FC	SN	SN	SW	SN	SN	SN	FC		SN	FC	SN	SW	SW
London Victoria	⊖ d		12 33			12 47	12 36	13 01					12 53	13 03		13 17	13 06	13 31			13 23		13 33		
London Waterloo	⊖ d			12 39	12 54						13 09				13 24									13 39	13 54
Clapham Junction	d		12 41	12 48	13 03	12 54	12 44	13 08			13 18		13 00	13 11	13 33	13 24	13 14	13 38			13 30		13 41	13 48	14 03
Balham	⊖ d		12 46			13 00	12 50						13 05	13 16		13 30	13 20				13 35		13 46		
London Bridge	⊖ d																								
Tulse Hill	d	12 46							13 01			13 16							13 31			13 46			
New Cross Gate	⊖ d																								
Norwood Junction	d						13 09										13 39								
West Croydon	d		13 04				13 14						13 24	13 34			13 44				13 54		14 04		
Waddon	d		13 06				13 16						13 26	13 36			13 46				13 56		14 06		
Wallington	d		13 10				13 20						13 30	13 40			13 50				14 00		14 10		
Carshalton Beeches	d		13 12				13 22						13 32	13 42			13 52				14 02		14 12		
Mitcham Eastfields	d	12 54				13 06						13 24				13 36						13 54			
Mitcham Junction	d	12 57				13 09						13 27				13 39						13 57			
Hackbridge	d	13 00				13 13						13 30				13 43						14 00			
Carshalton	d	13 03				13 15						13 33				13 45						14 03			
Sutton (Surrey)	a	13 06	13 16			13 19	13 26	13 28	13 35			13 36	13 39	13 46		13 49	13 56	13 58	14 05		14 06	14 06	14 16		
	d					13 19		13 29					13 40			13 49		13 59			14 07				
Belmont	d																				14 10				
Banstead	d																				14 14				
Epsom Downs	a																				14 17				
Cheam	d					13 22		13 31					13 42			13 52		14 01							
Ewell East	d					13 25							13 46			13 55		14 05							
Epsom	a			13 16	13 27	13 29		13 37			13 46		13 52		13 57	13 59		14 09						14 16	14 27
	d			13 17	13 28			13 37			13 47				13 58			14 09						14 17	14 28
Ashtead	d			13 21	13 32			13 41			13 51				14 02			14 13						14 21	14 32
Leatherhead	d			13 24	13 35			13 44			13 54				14 05			14 16						14 24	14 35
Bookham	d			13 29							13 59													14 29	
Effingham Junction	d			13 33							14 03													14 33	
Guildford	a			13 50							14 20													14 50	
Box Hill & Westhumble	d																	14 21							
Dorking	a				13 41			13 50							14 11			14 24							14 41
	d																	14 24							
Holmwood	d																	14 32							
Ockley	d																	14 36							
Warnham	d																	14 41							
Horsham	a																	14 45							

		SN	SN	SN	FC		SW	FC	SN	SN	SW	SN	SN	SN	FC		SN	FC	SN	SW	SW	SN	SN	SN	FC
London Victoria	⊖ d	13 47	13 36	14 01					13 53	14 03		14 17	14 06	14 31			14 23		14 33			14 47	14 36	15 01	
London Waterloo	⊖ d						14 09				14 24									14 39	14 54				
Clapham Junction	d	13 54	13 44	14 08			14 18		14 00	14 11	14 33	14 24	14 14	14 38			14 30		14 41	14 48	15 03	14 54	14 44	15 08	
Balham	⊖ d	14 00	13 50						14 05	14 16		14 30	14 20				14 35		14 46			15 00	14 50		
London Bridge	⊖ d																								
Tulse Hill	d				14 01			14 16							14 31			14 46							15 01
New Cross Gate	⊖ d																								
Norwood Junction	d		14 09										14 39										15 09		
West Croydon	d		14 14						14 24	14 34			14 44				14 54		15 04				15 14		
Waddon	d		14 16						14 26	14 36			14 46				14 56		15 06				15 16		
Wallington	d		14 20						14 30	14 40			14 50				15 00		15 10				15 20		
Carshalton Beeches	d		14 22						14 32	14 42			14 52				15 02		15 12				15 22		
Mitcham Eastfields	d	14 06						14 24				14 36						14 54				15 06			
Mitcham Junction	d	14 09						14 27				14 39						14 57				15 09			
Hackbridge	d	14 13						14 30				14 43						15 00				15 13			
Carshalton	d	14 15						14 33				14 45						15 03				15 15			
Sutton (Surrey)	a	14 19	14 26	14 28	14 35			14 36	14 39	14 46		14 49	14 56	14 58	15 05		15 06	15 06	15 16			15 19	15 26	15 28	15 35
	d	14 19		14 29					14 40			14 49		14 59			15 07					15 19		15 29	
Belmont	d																15 10								
Banstead	d																15 14								
Epsom Downs	a																15 17								
Cheam	d	14 22		14 31					14 42			14 52		15 01								15 22		15 31	
Ewell East	d	14 25							14 46			14 55		15 05								15 25			
Epsom	a	14 29		14 37			14 46		14 52		14 57	14 59		15 09						15 16	15 27	15 29		15 37	
	d			14 37			14 47				14 58			15 09						15 17	15 28			15 37	
Ashtead	d			14 41			14 51				15 02			15 13						15 21	15 32			15 41	
Leatherhead	d			14 44			14 54				15 05			15 16						15 24	15 35			15 44	
Bookham	d						14 59													15 29					
Effingham Junction	d						15 03													15 33					
Guildford	a						15 20													15 50					
Box Hill & Westhumble	d													15 21											
Dorking	a			14 50							15 11			15 24							15 41			15 50	
	d													15 24											
Holmwood	d													15 32											
Ockley	d													15 36											
Warnham	d													15 41											
Horsham	a													15 45											

Table 182

Mondays to Fridays

until 5 October

London - Sutton, Epsom, Guildford, Dorking and Horsham

Network Diagram - see first Page of Table 177

			SW	FC	SN	SN	SW	SN	SN	SN	FC		SN	FC	SN	SW	SW	SN	SN	SN	FC		SN	FC	SN
London Victoria	⊖ d				14 53	15 03		15 17	15 06	15 31			15 23		15 33			15 47	15 36	16 01			15 53		16 03
London Waterloo	⊖ d		15 09				15 24									15 39	15 54								
Clapham Junction	d		15 18		15 00	15 11	15 33	15 24	15 14	15 38			15 30		15 41	15 48	16 03	15 54	15 44	16 08			16 00		16 11
Balham	⊖ d				15 05	15 16		15 30	15 20				15 35		15 46			16 00	15 50				16 05		16 16
London Bridge	⊖ d																								
Tulse Hill	d			15 16							15 31			15 46							16 01			16 16	
New Cross Gate	⊖ d																								
Norwood Junction	d								15 39										16 09						
West Croydon	d				15 24	15 34			15 44				15 54		16 04				16 14				16 24		16 34
Waddon	d				15 26	15 36			15 46				15 56		16 06				16 16				16 26		16 36
Wallington	d				15 30	15 40			15 50				16 00		16 10				16 20				16 30		16 40
Carshalton Beeches	d				15 32	15 42			15 52				16 02		16 12				16 22				16 32		16 42
Mitcham Eastfields	d			15 24				15 36						15 54				16 06						16 24	
Mitcham Junction	d			15 27				15 39						15 57				16 09		16 22				16 27	
Hackbridge	d			15 30				15 43						16 00				16 13						16 30	
Carshalton	d			15 33				15 45						16 03				16 15						16 33	
Sutton (Surrey)	a			15 36	15 39	15 46		15 49	15 56	15 58	16 05		16 06	16 06	16 16			16 19	16 26	16 29	16 35		16 36	16 36	16 47
	d				15 40			15 49		15 59			16 07					16 19		16 30			16 37		
Belmont	d												16 10										16 40		
Banstead	d												16 14										16 44		
Epsom Downs	a												16 17										16 47		
Cheam	d				15 42			15 52		16 01								16 22		16 32					
Ewell East	d				15 46			15 55		16 05								16 25		16 36					
Epsom	a		15 46		15 52		15 57	15 59		16 09						16 15	16 27	16 29		16 40					
	d		15 47				15 58			16 09						16 17	16 28			16 40					
Ashtead	d		15 51				16 02			16 13						16 21	16 32			16 44					
Leatherhead	d		15 54				16 05			16 16						16 24	16 35			16 47					
Bookham	d		15 59													16 29									
Effingham Junction	d		16 03													16 33									
Guildford	a		16 20													16 50									
Box Hill & Westhumble	d									16 21										16 52					
Dorking	a						16 11			16 24							16 41			16 57					
	d									16 24															
Holmwood	d									16 32															
Ockley	d									16 36															
Warnham	d									16 41															
Horsham	a									16 45															

		SW	SW	SN	SN	SW	SN		FC	FC	SN	SW	SN	SN	SW	SN	FC		FC	SN	SN	SW	SN	SN	SW
London Victoria	⊖ d			16 17	16 07		16 31				16 33		16 47	16 37							17 01		17 20	17 06	
London Waterloo	⊖ d	16 09	16 24			16 39						16 54			17 09							17 24			17 30
Clapham Junction	d	16 18	16 33	16 24	16 15	16 48	16 38				16 41	17 03	16 54	16 45	17 18						17 09	17 33	17 26	17 14	17 39
Balham	⊖ d			16 30	16 20						16 46		17 00	16 50							17 14		17 32	17 19	
London Bridge	⊖ d															17 03				17 06					
Tulse Hill	d								16 32	16 46							17 02		17 20	17 24					
New Cross Gate	⊖ d																								
Norwood Junction	d				16 39									17 09		17 16								17 38	
West Croydon	d				16 44						17 04			17 14		17 22					17 33			17 44	
Waddon	d				16 46						17 06			17 16		17 24					17 35			17 46	
Wallington	d				16 50						17 10			17 20		17 28					17 39			17 50	
Carshalton Beeches	d				16 52						17 12			17 22		17 30					17 41			17 52	
Mitcham Eastfields	d			16 36			16 51			16 55			17 07						17 28	17 32			17 38		
Mitcham Junction	d			16 39			16 54			16 58			17 10						17 31	17 35			17 41		
Hackbridge	d			16 43			16 57			17 01			17 13						17 34	17 38			17 45		
Carshalton	d			16 45			17 00			17 04			17 16						17 37	17 41			17 47		
Sutton (Surrey)	a			16 49	16 58		17 03		17 05	17 08	17 16		17 19	17 26		17 34	17 37		17 40	17 44	17 45		17 51	17 58	
	d			16 49			17 04				17 16		17 20	17 27		17 34					17 45		17 51		
Belmont	d										17 20										17 49				
Banstead	d										17 23										17 52				
Epsom Downs	a										17 28										17 58				
Cheam	d			16 52			17 06						17 22	17 29		17 37							17 54		
Ewell East	d			16 55			17 10						17 26	17 33		17 40							17 57		
Epsom	a	16 46	16 57	17 01		17 12	17 16					17 27	17 30	17 37	17 42	17 46						17 54	18 01		18 07
	d	16 47	16 58	17 02		17 17						17 28	17 31	17 37	17 47							17 54	18 02		
Ashtead	d	16 51	17 02	17 06		17 21						17 32	17 35	17 41	17 51							17 58	18 06		
Leatherhead	d	16 54	17 05	17 09		17 24						17 35	17 38	17 44	17 54							18 01	18 09		
Bookham	d	16 59				17 29								17 50	17 59										
Effingham Junction	d	17 03				17 33								17 53	18a05										
Guildford	a	17 22				17 52								18 13											
Box Hill & Westhumble	d		17 10	17 14								17 40	17 43									18 06	18 14		
Dorking	a		17 14	17 16								17 44	17 45									18 11	18 16		
	d			17 17									17 46										18 19		
Holmwood	d			17 24									17 53										18 26		
Ockley	d			17 28									17 57										18 30		
Warnham	d			17 34									18 03										18 36		
Horsham	a			17 40									18 09										18 42		

Table 182

Mondays to Fridays
until 5 October

London - Sutton, Epsom, Guildford, Dorking and Horsham

Network Diagram - see first Page of Table 177

		SN	SW	SN	FC	FC	SN	SN	SW	SN	SN	SW	SN	SW	SN	FC	FC	SN	SW	SN	SN	SN
London Victoria	d			17 31				17 33		17 50	17 37				18 01			18 03			18 20	18 07
London Waterloo	d		17 39						17 54			18 00		18 09					18 24			
Clapham Junction	d		17 48	17 37				17 41	18 03	17 56	17 45	18 09		18 18	18 08			18 11	18 33		18 26	18 15
Balham	d			17 42				17 46		18 02	17 50				18 12			18 16			18 32	18 20
London Bridge	d	17 29					17 37						18 02							18 08		
Tulse Hill	d				17 31	17 48	17 55									18 02	18 22			18 27		
New Cross Gate	d																					
Norwood Junction	d	17 43									18 09		18 16									18 39
West Croydon	d	17 48						18 04			18 15		18 21					18 35				18 45
Waddon	d	17 51						18 06			18 17		18 23					18 37				18 47
Wallington	d	17 54						18 10			18 21		18 27					18 41				18 51
Carshalton Beeches	d	17 57						18 12			18 23		18 29					18 43				18 53
Mitcham Eastfields	d			17 48		17 55	18 02			18 08					18 19		18 29			18 34	18 38	
Mitcham Junction	d			17 51		17 58	18 05			18 11					18 22		18 32			18 37	18 41	
Hackbridge	d			17 55		18 02	18 09			18 15					18 25		18 36			18 41	18 45	
Carshalton	d			17 57		18 04	18 11			18 17					18 28		18 38			18 43	18 47	
Sutton (Surrey)	a	18 00		18 03	18 07	18 08	18 15	18 18		18 21	18 29		18 33		18 36	18 37	18 42	18 47		18 47	18 51	18 58
	d	18 01		18 05				18 19		18 21			18 33		18 36			18 48			18 51	
Belmont	d							18 22										18 51				
Banstead	d							18 26										18 55				
Epsom Downs	a							18 31										19 00				
Cheam	d	18 03		18 07						18 24			18 36		18 39						18 54	
Ewell East	d	18 07		18 11						18 27			18 39		18 42						18 57	
Epsom	a	18 11	18 15	18 17					18 24	18 31		18 35	18 43	18 46	18 48				18 54		19 01	
	d	18 12	18 17						18 24	18 34			18 44	18 47					18 54		19 02	
Ashtead	d	18 16	18 21						18 28	18 38			18 48	18 51					18 58		19 06	
Leatherhead	d	18 19	18 24						18 31	18 41			18 51	18 54					19 01		19 09	
Bookham	d	18 24	18 29											18 59								
Effingham Junction	d	18 28	18a42											19 03								
Guildford	a	18 46												19 22								
Box Hill & Westhumble	d								18 36	18 46			18 56						19 06		19 14	
Dorking	a								18 41	18 48			19 00						19 11		19 16	
	d									18 49											19 19	
Holmwood	d									18 56											19 26	
Ockley	d									19 00											19 30	
Warnham	d									19 06											19 36	
Horsham	a									19 12											19 42	

		SW	SN	FC	FC	SN	SW	SW	SN	SN	SN	SW	FC	SW	FC	SN	SW	SN	SN	SN	FC	SW	FC
London Victoria	d					18 32				18 50	18 36					18 59		19 20	19 06				
London Waterloo	d	18 30					18 39	18 54				19 00		19 09			19 24					19 39	
Clapham Junction	d	18 39				18 40	18 48	19 03		18 56	18 44	19 09		19 18		19 08	19 33	19 26	19 14			19 48	
Balham	d					18 45				19 02	18 49					19 14		19 32	19 20				
London Bridge	d		18 32						18 38											19 31			
Tulse Hill	d			18 32	18 52				18 56				19 09		19 16						19 31		19 46
New Cross Gate	d																						
Norwood Junction	d		18 46								19 09								19 39	19 44			
West Croydon	d		18 51			19 04					19 15					19 32			19 45	19 49			
Waddon	d		18 53			19 07					19 17					19 35			19 47	19 52			
Wallington	d		18 57			19 10					19 21					19 38			19 51	19 55			
Carshalton Beeches	d		18 59			19 13					19 23					19 41			19 53	19 58			
Mitcham Eastfields	d				18 59				19 03	19 08					19 24			19 38					19 54
Mitcham Junction	d				19 02				19 06	19 11					19 27			19 41					19 57
Hackbridge	d				19 06				19 10	19 15					19 30			19 45					20 00
Carshalton	d				19 08				19 12	19 17					19 33			19 47					20 03
Sutton (Surrey)	a		19 03	19 07	19 12	19 16			19 16	19 21	19 28		19 41		19 36	19 44		19 51	19 57	20 01	20 07		20 06
	d		19 03			19 17			19 16	19 21						19 45		19 51	19 58	20 02			
Belmont	d					19 20													20 01				
Banstead	d					19 24													20 05				
Epsom Downs	a					19 29													20 08				
Cheam	d		19 06						19 19	19 24						19 47		19 54		20 04			
Ewell East	d		19 09						19 22	19 27						19 51		19 57		20 08			
Epsom	a	19 07	19 13				19 16	19 24	19 26	19 31		19 35		19 44		19 55	19 57	20 01		20 12		20 16	
	d		19 14				19 17	19 24		19 34				19 47			19 58	20 02		20 12		20 17	
Ashtead	d		19 18				19 21	19 28		19 38				19 51			20 02	20 06		20 16		20 21	
Leatherhead	d		19 21				19 24	19 31		19 41				19 54			20 05	20 09		20 19		20 24	
Bookham	d						19 29							19 59								20 29	
Effingham Junction	d						19 33							20 03								20 33	
Guildford	a						19 52							20 20								20 50	
Box Hill & Westhumble	d		19 26					19 36		19 46							20 10	20 14					
Dorking	a		19 30					19 41		19 50							20 14	20 16		20 25			
	d																	20 17					
Holmwood	d																	20 24					
Ockley	d																	20 28					
Warnham	d																	20 34					
Horsham	a																	20 38					

Table 182

Mondays to Fridays
until 5 October

London - Sutton, Epsom, Guildford, Dorking and Horsham

Network Diagram - see first Page of Table 177

		SN	SN	SW	SN	SN	FC	SW	FC	SN	SN	SW	SN	SN	SW	SN	FC	FC	SN	SW	SN	SN	SW
London Victoria	d	19 34	19 30		19 50	19 36				20 03	20 00		20 20	20 06		20 33			20 30		20 50	20 36	
London Waterloo	d			19 54				20 09				20 24			20 39					20 54			21 09
Clapham Junction	d	19 41	19 38	20 03	19 56	19 44		20 18		20 11	20 08	20 33	20 26	20 14	20 48	20 41			20 38	21 03	20 56	20 44	21 18
Balham	d	19 46	19 44		20 02	19 50				20 16	20 14		20 31	20 20		20 46			20 44		21 02	20 50	
London Bridge	d																						
Tulse Hill	d						20 01		20 16								20 31	20 50					
New Cross Gate	d																						
Norwood Junction	d					20 09								20 39								21 09	
West Croydon	d		20 02			20 14					20 32			20 44					21 02			21 14	
Waddon	d		20 05			20 16					20 35			20 46					21 05			21 16	
Wallington	d		20 08			20 20					20 38			20 50					21 08			21 20	
Carshalton Beeches	d		20 11			20 22					20 41			20 52					21 11			21 22	
Mitcham Eastfields	d	19 57			20 08				20 24	20 27			20 38			20 53		20 57			21 08		
Mitcham Junction	d	20 00			20 11				20 27	20 30			20 41			20 56		21 00			21 11		
Hackbridge	d	20 03			20 15				20 30	20 34			20 45			20 59		21 03			21 15		
Carshalton	d	20 06			20 17				20 33	20 36			20 47			21 02		21 06			21 17		
Sutton (Surrey)	a	20 09	20 14		20 21	20 26	20 39		20 36	20 40	20 44		20 51	20 56		21 05	21 09	21 10	21 14		21 21	21 26	
	d	20 10			20 21	20 27				20 40			20 51	20 57		21 06					21 21	21 27	
Belmont	d					20 30																21 30	
Banstead	d					20 34																21 34	
Epsom Downs	a					20 37																21 37	
Cheam	d	20 12			20 24					20 43			20 54	20 59		21 08					21 24		
Ewell East	d	20 16			20 27					20 46			20 57	21 03		21 12					21 27		
Epsom	a	20 20		20 27	20 31			20 42		20 50		20 57	21 01	21 07	21 12	21 16				21 27	21 31		21 42
	d				20 32			20 43					21 02		21 13						21 32		21 43
Ashtead	d				20 36			20 47					21 06		21 17						21 36		21 47
Leatherhead	d				20 39			20 50					21 09		21 20						21 39		21 50
Bookham	d														21 25								
Effingham Junction	d														21 29								
Guildford	a														21 46								
Box Hill & Westhumble	d				20 44			20 55					21 14								21 44		21 55
Dorking	a				20 46			20 57					21 16								21 46		21 57
	d																						
Holmwood	d																						
Ockley	d																						
Warnham	d																						
Horsham	a																						

		SN	FC	FC A	SN	SW	SN	SN	SW	SN	FC	SN	SW	SN	SN	SW	SN	FC	SN	SN	SN	SW
London Victoria	d	21 03			21 00		21 20	21 06		21 33		21 30		21 50	21 36		22 03		22 00	22 20	22 06	
London Waterloo	d					21 24			21 39				21 54			22 09						22 39
Clapham Junction	d	21 11			21 08	21 33	21 26	21 14	21 48	21 41		21 38	22 03	21 56	21 44	22 18	22 11		22 08	22 26	22 14	22 48
Balham	d	21 16			21 14		21 31	21 20		21 46		21 44		22 02	21 50		22 16		22 14	22 32	22 20	
London Bridge	d																					
Tulse Hill	d		21 01	21 20							21 31							22 01				
New Cross Gate	d																					
Norwood Junction	d							21 39							22 09						22 39	
West Croydon	d				21 32			21 44				22 02			22 14				22 32		22 44	
Waddon	d				21 35			21 46				22 05			22 16				22 35		22 46	
Wallington	d				21 38			21 50				22 08			22 20				22 38		22 50	
Carshalton Beeches	d				21 41			21 52				22 11			22 22				22 41		22 52	
Mitcham Eastfields	d	21 23		21 27			21 38			21 53				22 08			22 23			22 38		
Mitcham Junction	d	21 26		21 30			21 41			21 56				22 11			22 26			22 41		
Hackbridge	d	21 30		21 33			21 45			21 59				22 15			22 29			22 45		
Carshalton	d	21 32		21 36			21 47			22 02				22 17			22 32			22 47		
Sutton (Surrey)	a	21 36	21 39	21 40	21 44		21 51	21 56		22 05	22 09	22 14		22 21	22 26		22 35	22 39	22 44	22 51	22 56	
	d	21 36					21 51	21 57		22 06				22 21	22 27		22 36			22 51	22 57	
Belmont	d														22 30							
Banstead	d														22 34							
Epsom Downs	a														22 37							
Cheam	d	21 39					21 54	21 59		22 08				22 24			22 38			22 54	22 59	
Ewell East	d	21 42					21 57	22 03		22 12				22 27			22 42			22 57	23 03	
Epsom	a	21 46				21 57	22 01	22 07	22 12	22 16			22 27	22 31		22 42	22 46			23 01	23 07	23 12
	d						22 02		22 13					22 32		22 43				23 02		23 13
Ashtead	d						22 06		22 17					22 36		22 47				23 06		23 17
Leatherhead	d						22 09		22 20					22 39		22 50				23 09		23 20
Bookham	d								22 25													23 25
Effingham Junction	d								22 29													23 29
Guildford	a								22 46													23 46
Box Hill & Westhumble	d													22 44		22 55						
Dorking	a						22 15							22 46		22 57				23 15		
	d																					
Holmwood	d																					
Ockley	d																					
Warnham	d																					
Horsham	a																					

A from 21 May until 5 October

Table 182

London - Sutton, Epsom, Guildford, Dorking and Horsham

Mondays to Fridays

until 5 October

Network Diagram - see first Page of Table 177

		SN	FC	SN	SN	SN	FC	SW	SN	SN	FC	SN	SN	FC	FC	SN	SW	SN	SN	FC
							A				B			A	B			FX	FO	B
London Victoria 15 ⊖	d	22 33		22 30	22 50	22 36			23 03	23 00		23 06	23 26			23 34		23 51	23 59	
London Waterloo 15 ⊖	d							23 09									23 42			
Clapham Junction 10	d	22 41		22 38	22 56	22 46		23 18	23 11	23 08		23 14	23 34			23 42	23 51	23 59	00 07	
Balham 4 ⊖	d	22 46		22 44	23 01	22 52			23 16	23 14		23 20	23 40			23 47		00 04	00 12	
London Bridge 4 ⊖	d										23 01				23 29					23 59
Tulse Hill 3	d		22 31				23 01				23 11			23 31	23 41					00 09
New Cross Gate 4 ⊖	d																			
Norwood Junction 2	d					23 09						23 40								
West Croydon 4	d			23 02		23 14				23 32		23 45				00 04		00 21	00 31	
Waddon	d			23 05		23 16				23 35		23 47				00 06		00 24	00 33	
Wallington	d			23 08		23 20				23 38		23 51				00 10		00 27	00 37	
Carshalton Beeches	d			23 11		23 22				23 41		23 53				00 12		00 30	00 39	
Mitcham Eastfields	d	22 53			23 07				23 23				23 46							
Mitcham Junction	d	22 56			23 10				23 26				23 49							
Hackbridge	d	22 59			23 14				23 29				23 53							
Carshalton	d	23 02			23 16				23 32				23 55							
Sutton (Surrey) 4	a	23 05	23 09	23 14	23 20	23 26	23 35		23 35	23 44	23 45	23 57	23 59	00 09	00 15	00 16		00 33	00 43	00 43
	d	23 06			23 20	23 27			23 36	23 45			00 01							
Belmont	d					23 30														
Banstead	d					23 34														
Epsom Downs	a					23 37														
Cheam	d	23 08			23 23				23 38	23 47			00 03							
Ewell East	d	23 12			23 26				23 42	23 51			00 07							
Epsom 3	a	23 16			23 30			23 42	23 46	23 55			00 11				00 15			
	d				23 31			23 43					00 11				00 19			
Ashtead	d				23 35			23 47					00 15				00 23			
Leatherhead	d				23 38			23 50					00 18				00 26			
Bookham	d																00 31			
Effingham Junction 6	d																00 36			
Guildford	a																00 53			
Box Hill & Westhumble	d				23 43			23 55					00 23							
Dorking 4	a				23 45			23 57					00 26							
	d												00 26							
Holmwood	d												00s33							
Ockley	d												00s37							
Warnham	d												00s43							
Horsham 4	a												00 47							

Mondays to Fridays

from 8 October

		SN	SN	SN	SW	FC	SN	SW	SN	FC	SW	SN	SW	SN	SN	SN	FC	FC	SN	SN	SW	SN	SN
		MO	MO	MX	MO	MX	MX	MX	MX	MX	MX												
London Victoria 15 ⊖	d	23p08	23p19	23p26			23p34		23p51							05 52			06 00			06 17	06 07
London Waterloo 15 ⊖	d				23p32			23p42			00 15		05 47								06 24		
Clapham Junction 10	d	23p16	23p27	23p34	23p41		23p42	23p51	23p59		00 25		05 56			05 58			06 08		06 33	06 24	06 15
Balham 4 ⊖	d	23p21	23p32	23p40			23p47		00 04							06 03			06 13			06 30	06 20
London Bridge 4 ⊖	d														05 36								
Tulse Hill 3	d					23p31				00 01							06 02	06 22					
New Cross Gate 4 ⊖	d														05 42								
Norwood Junction 2	d													05 53	06 00								06 39
West Croydon 4	d		23p50				00 04		00 21			05 45		05 58	06 05				06 32				06 46
Waddon	d		23p52				00 06		00 24			05 47		06 00	06 08				06 34				06 48
Wallington	d		23p56				00 10		00 27			05 51		06 04	06 11				06 38				06 52
Carshalton Beeches	d		23p58				00 12		00 30			05 53		06 06	06 14				06 40				06 54
Mitcham Eastfields	d	23p28		23p46												06 12		06 29				06 38	
Mitcham Junction	d	23p31		23p49												06 15		06 32				06 41	
Hackbridge	d	23p34		23p53												06 19		06 35				06 45	
Carshalton	d	23p37		23p55												06 21		06 38				06 47	
Sutton (Surrey) 4	a	23p40	00 02	23p59		00 09	00 16		00 33	00 39		05 57		06 10	06 17	06 25	06 33	06 43	06 44			06 51	06 58
	d	23p41	00 04	00 01										06 11		06 25			06 48	06 39		06 52	07 00
Belmont	d													06 14					06 51				
Banstead	d													06 18					06 55				
Epsom Downs	a													06 21					06 58				
Cheam	d	23p43	00 06	00 03												06 28				06 41		06 54	07 02
Ewell East	d	23p47	00 10	00 07												06 31				06 45		06 58	07 06
Epsom 3	a	23p51	00 14	00 11	00 06			00 15			00 50		06 20			06 35				06 49	06 57	07 02	07 10
	d	23p51		00 11				00 19					06 21			06 36				06 50	06 58	07 02	
Ashtead	d	23p55		00 15				00 23					06 25			06 40					07 02	07 06	
Leatherhead	d	23p58		00 18				00 26					06 28			06 43				06 56	07 05	07 09	
Bookham	d							00 31					06 33							07 01			
Effingham Junction 6	d							00 36					06 37							07 05			
Guildford	a							00 56					06 53							07 17			
Box Hill & Westhumble	d	00 03		00 23												06 48							
Dorking 4	a	00 06		00 26												06 50					07 13	07 15	
	d			00 26												06 51						07 16	
Holmwood	d			00s33												06 58						07 23	
Ockley	d			00s37												07 02						07 27	
Warnham	d			00s43												07 08						07 33	
Horsham 4	a			00 47												07 12						07 37	

A from 21 May until 5 October

B until 18 May

Table 182

London - Sutton, Epsom, Guildford, Dorking and Horsham

Mondays to Fridays

from 8 October

Network Diagram - see first Page of Table 177

		FC	SN	SW	SW	SN	FC	SW	FC	SN	SN	SW	SN	FC	FC	SN	SW	SN	SW	SN	SN	FC	FC
														1	1								
London Victoria 15 ⊖	d		06 30			06 36				07 15	07 00		07 06			07 30		07 47		07 55	07 36		
London Waterloo 15 ⊖	d			06 39	06 54			07 09				07 24					07 39		07 54				
Clapham Junction 10	d		06 38	06 48	07 03	06 44		07 18		07 21	07 08	07 33	07 14			07 38	07 48	07 55	08 03	08 02	07 44		
Balham 4 ⊖	d		06 44			06 49				07 26	07 13		07 20			07 44		08 00			07 50		
London Bridge 4 ⊖	d																						
Tulse Hill 3	d	06 42					07 02		07 20					07 31	07 45							08 05	08 21
New Cross Gate 4 ⊖	d																						
Norwood Junction 2	d					07 09							07 39								08 09		
West Croydon 4	d		07 03			07 14					07 32		07 46			08 04					08 15		
Waddon	d		07 05			07 16					07 35		07 48			08 06					08 17		
Wallington	d		07 09			07 20					07 38		07 52			08 10					08 21		
Carshalton Beeches	d		07 11			07 22					07 41		07 54			08 12					08 23		
Mitcham Eastfields	d	06 49							07 27						07 52			08 07					08 28
Mitcham Junction	d	06 52							07 30	07 34					07 55			08 10					08 31
Hackbridge	d	06 55							07 33	07 37					07 58			08 13					08 34
Carshalton	d	06 58							07 36	07 40					08 01			08 16					08 37
Sutton (Surrey) 4	a	07 03	07 15			07 26	07 35		07 39	07 43	07 44		07 58	08 07	08 04	08 16		08 19		08 22	08 27	08 37	08 40
	d		07 18			07 26				07 44	07 45		07 59			08 16				08 23	08 27		
Belmont	d		07 21								07 48					08 20							
Banstead	d		07 25								07 52					08 23							
Epsom Downs	a		07 28								07 55					08 27							
Cheam	d					07 29				07 46			08 01							08 25	08 30		
Ewell East	d					07 32				07 50			08 05							08 29	08 33		
Epsom 3	a			07 11	07 27	07 36		07 42		07 54		07 58	08 09				08 13		08 27	08 33	08 37		
	d			07 12	07 28	07 37				07 54		07 58					08 17		08 28	08 33	08 38		
Ashtead	d			07 16	07 32	07 41				07 58		08 02					08 21		08 32	08 37	08 42		
Leatherhead	d			07 19	07 35	07 44				08 01		08 05					08 24		08 35	08 40	08 45		
Bookham	d			07 24		07 49											08 29						
Effingham Junction 6	d			07a28		07 53											08 33						
Guildford	a					08 06											08 53						
Box Hill & Westhumble	d									08 06											08 50		
Dorking 4	a				07 43					08 09		08 14							08 43	08 46	08 52		
	d									08 09										08 47			
Holmwood	d									08 17													
Ockley	d									08 21													
Warnham	d									08 26													
Horsham 4	a									08 30										09 03			

		SN	SW	SW	SN	SN	FC	SN	SN	FC	SN	SW	SW	SN	SN	SN	FC	SW	FC	SN	SN	SW
										1							1					
London Victoria 15 ⊖	d	08 03			08 19	08 07			08 26		08 31			08 47	08 36	09 01				08 52	09 03	
London Waterloo 15 ⊖	d		08 09	08 24								08 39	08 54					09 09				09 24
Clapham Junction 10	d	08 11	08 18	08 33	08 26	08 16			08 33		08 40	08 48	09 03	08 54	08 44	09 08		09 18		09 00	09 11	09 33
Balham 4 ⊖	d	08 16			08 31	08 21			08 38		08 46			09 00	08 50					09 05	09 16	
London Bridge 4 ⊖	d							08 24														
Tulse Hill 3	d						08 40	08 47		08 50							09 01		09 16			
New Cross Gate 4 ⊖	d																					
Norwood Junction 2	d					08 39									09 09							
West Croydon 4	d	08 36				08 45			08 56		09 06				09 14					09 24	09 34	
Waddon	d	08 39				08 47			08 58		09 08				09 16					09 26	09 36	
Wallington	d	08 42				08 51			09 02		09 12				09 20					09 30	09 40	
Carshalton Beeches	d	08 45				08 53			09 04		09 14				09 22					09 32	09 42	
Mitcham Eastfields	d				08 37					08 58				09 06					09 24			
Mitcham Junction	d				08 40					09 01				09 09					09 27			
Hackbridge	d				08 44					09 04				09 13					09 30			
Carshalton	d				08 46					09 07				09 15					09 33			
Sutton (Surrey) 4	a	08 48			08 50	08 57	09 12	09 02	09 08	09 10	09 18			09 19	09 26	09 28	09 37		09 36	09 39	09 46	
	d	08 53			08 50			09 02			09 19			09 19		09 29				09 40		
Belmont	d	08 56									09 22											
Banstead	d	09 00									09 26											
Epsom Downs	a	09 03									09 29											
Cheam	d				08 53			09 05						09 22		09 31				09 42		
Ewell East	d				08 56			09 08						09 25						09 46		
Epsom 3	a		08 42	08 57	09 00			09 12				09 16	09 27	09 29		09 37		09 42		09 50		09 57
	d		08 47	08 58	09 01							09 17	09 28			09 37		09 47				09 58
Ashtead	d		08 51	09 02	09 05							09 21	09 32			09 41		09 51				10 02
Leatherhead	d		08 54	09 05	09 08							09 24	09 35			09 44		09 54				10 05
Bookham	d		08 59									09 29						09 59				
Effingham Junction 6	d		09 03									09 33						10 03				
Guildford	a		09 23									09 53						10 23				
Box Hill & Westhumble	d				09 13											09 49						
Dorking 4	a			09 13	09 15								09 43			09 52						10 13
	d				09 16																	
Holmwood	d				09 23																	
Ockley	d				09 27																	
Warnham	d				09 33																	
Horsham 4	a				09 37																	

Table 182

London - Sutton, Epsom, Guildford, Dorking and Horsham

Mondays to Fridays
from 8 October

Network Diagram - see first Page of Table 177

Station		SN	SN	SN	FC	SN	FC	SN	SW	SW	SN	SN	SN	FC	SW	FC	SN	SN	SW	SN	SN	SN	FC
London Victoria	d	09 17	09 05	09 31		09 22		09 33			09 47	09 35	10 01				09 53	10 03		10 17	10 06	10 31	
London Waterloo	d								09 39	09 54					10 09				10 24				
Clapham Junction	d	09 24	09 14	09 38		09 30		09 41	09 48	10 03	09 54	09 44	10 08		10 18		10 00	10 11	10 33	10 24	10 14	10 38	
Balham	d	09 30	09 20			09 35		09 46			10 00	09 50					10 05	10 16		10 30	10 20		
London Bridge	d																						
Tulse Hill	d				09 31		09 46							10 01		10 16							10 31
New Cross Gate	d																						
Norwood Junction	d		09 39									10 09									10 39		
West Croydon	d		09 44			09 54		10 04				10 14					10 24	10 34			10 44		
Waddon	d		09 46			09 56		10 06				10 16					10 26	10 36			10 46		
Wallington	d		09 50			10 00		10 10				10 20					10 30	10 40			10 50		
Carshalton Beeches	d		09 52			10 02		10 12				10 22					10 32	10 42			10 52		
Mitcham Eastfields	d	09 36					09 54				10 06					10 24				10 36			
Mitcham Junction	d	09 39					09 57				10 09					10 27				10 39			
Hackbridge	d	09 43					10 00				10 13					10 30				10 43			
Carshalton	d	09 45					10 03				10 15					10 33				10 45			
Sutton (Surrey)	a	09 49	09 56	09 58	10 05	10 06	10 06	10 16			10 19	10 26	10 28	10 35		10 36	10 39	10 46		10 49	10 56	10 58	11 05
	d	09 49		09 59		10 07					10 19		10 29				10 40			10 49		10 59	
Belmont	d					10 10																	
Banstead	d					10 14																	
Epsom Downs	a					10 17																	
Cheam	d	09 52		10 01							10 22		10 31				10 42			10 52		11 01	
Ewell East	d	09 55		10 05							10 25						10 46			10 55		11 05	
Epsom	a	09 59		10 09					10 16	10 27	10 29		10 37		10 46		10 52		10 57	10 59		11 09	
	d			10 09					10 17	10 28			10 37		10 47				10 58			11 09	
Ashtead	d			10 13					10 21	10 32			10 41		10 51				11 02			11 13	
Leatherhead	d			10 16					10 24	10 35			10 44		10 54				11 05			11 16	
Bookham	d								10 29						10 59								
Effingham Junction	d								10 33						11 03								
Guildford	a								10 53						11 23								
Box Hill & Westhumble	d			10 21																		11 21	
Dorking	a			10 24						10 43			10 50						11 13			11 24	
	d			10 24																		11 24	
Holmwood	d			10 32																		11 32	
Ockley	d			10 36																		11 36	
Warnham	d			10 41																		11 41	
Horsham	a			10 45																		11 45	

Station		SN	FC	SN	SW	SW	SN	SN	SN	FC	SW	FC	SN	SN	SW	SN	SN	SN	FC	SN	FC	SN
London Victoria	d	10 23		10 33			10 47	10 36	11 01				10 53	11 03		11 17	11 06	11 31		11 23		11 33
London Waterloo	d				10 39	10 54					11 09				11 24							
Clapham Junction	d	10 30		10 41	10 48	11 03	10 54	10 44	11 08		11 18		11 00	11 11	11 33	11 24	11 14	11 38		11 30		11 41
Balham	d	10 35		10 46			11 00	10 50					11 05	11 16		11 30	11 20			11 35		11 46
London Bridge	d																					
Tulse Hill	d		10 46							11 01		11 16							11 31		11 46	
New Cross Gate	d																					
Norwood Junction	d							11 09									11 39					
West Croydon	d	10 54		11 04				11 14					11 24	11 34			11 44			11 54		12 04
Waddon	d	10 56		11 06				11 16					11 26	11 36			11 46			11 56		12 06
Wallington	d	11 00		11 10				11 20					11 30	11 40			11 50			12 00		12 10
Carshalton Beeches	d	11 02		11 12				11 22					11 32	11 42			11 52			12 02		12 12
Mitcham Eastfields	d		10 54				11 06					11 24				11 36					11 54	
Mitcham Junction	d		10 57				11 09					11 27				11 39					11 57	
Hackbridge	d		11 00				11 13					11 30				11 43					12 00	
Carshalton	d		11 03				11 15					11 33				11 45					12 03	
Sutton (Surrey)	a	11 06	11 06	11 16			11 19	11 26	11 28	11 35		11 36	11 39	11 46		11 49	11 56	11 58	12 05	12 06	12 06	12 16
	d	11 07					11 19		11 29				11 40			11 49		11 59		12 07		
Belmont	d	11 10																		12 10		
Banstead	d	11 14																		12 14		
Epsom Downs	a	11 17																		12 17		
Cheam	d						11 22		11 31				11 42			11 52		12 01				
Ewell East	d						11 25						11 46			11 55		12 05				
Epsom	a				11 16	11 27	11 29		11 37		11 46		11 52		11 57	11 59		12 09				
	d				11 17	11 28			11 37		11 47				11 58			12 09				
Ashtead	d				11 21	11 32			11 41		11 51				12 02			12 13				
Leatherhead	d				11 24	11 35			11 44		11 54				12 05			12 16				
Bookham	d				11 29						11 59											
Effingham Junction	d				11 33						12 03											
Guildford	a				11 53						12 23											
Box Hill & Westhumble	d																	12 21				
Dorking	a					11 43			11 50						12 13			12 24				
	d																	12 24				
Holmwood	d																	12 32				
Ockley	d																	12 36				
Warnham	d																	12 41				
Horsham	a																	12 45				

Table 182

London - Sutton, Epsom, Guildford, Dorking and Horsham

Mondays to Fridays
from 8 October

Network Diagram - see first Page of Table 177

Station		SW	SW	SN	SN	SN	FC	SW	FC	SN	SN	SW	SN	SN	SN	FC	SN	FC	SN	SW	SW	SN	SN
London Victoria	d			11 47	11 36	12 01				11 53	12 03		12 17	12 06	12 31		12 23		12 33			12 47	12 36
London Waterloo	d	11 39	11 54					12 09				12 24								12 39	12 54		
Clapham Junction	d	11 48	12 03	11 54	11 44	12 08		12 18		12 00	12 11	12 33	12 24	12 14	12 38		12 30		12 41	12 48	13 03	12 54	12 44
Balham	d			12 00	11 50					12 05	12 16		12 30	12 20			12 35		12 46			13 00	12 50
London Bridge	d																						
Tulse Hill	d						12 01		12 16							12 31		12 46					
New Cross Gate	d																						
Norwood Junction	d				12 09									12 39									13 09
West Croydon	d				12 14					12 24	12 34			12 44			12 54		13 04				13 14
Waddon	d				12 16					12 26	12 36			12 46			12 56		13 06				13 16
Wallington	d				12 20					12 30	12 40			12 50			13 00		13 10				13 20
Carshalton Beeches	d				12 22					12 32	12 42			12 52			13 02		13 12				13 22
Mitcham Eastfields	d			12 06					12 24				12 36					12 54				13 06	
Mitcham Junction	d			12 09					12 27				12 39					12 57				13 09	
Hackbridge	d			12 13					12 30				12 43					13 00				13 13	
Carshalton	d			12 15					12 33				12 45					13 03				13 15	
Sutton (Surrey)	a			12 19	12 26	12 28	12 35		12 36	12 39	12 46		12 49	12 56	12 58	13 05	13 06	13 06	13 16			13 19	13 26
	d			12 19		12 29				12 40			12 49		12 59		13 07					13 19	
Belmont	d																13 10						
Banstead	d																13 14						
Epsom Downs	a																13 17						
Cheam	d			12 22		12 31				12 42			12 52		13 01							13 22	
Ewell East	d			12 25						12 46			12 55		13 05							13 25	
Epsom	a	12 16	12 27	12 29		12 37		12 46		12 52		12 57	12 59		13 09					13 16	13 27	13 29	
	d	12 17	12 28			12 37		12 47				12 58			13 09					13 17	13 28		
Ashtead	d	12 21	12 32			12 41		12 51				13 02			13 13					13 21	13 32		
Leatherhead	d	12 24	12 35			12 44		12 54				13 05			13 16					13 24	13 35		
Bookham	d	12 29						12 59												13 29			
Effingham Junction	d	12 33						13 03												13 33			
Guildford	a	12 53						13 23												13 53			
Box Hill & Westhumble	d														13 21								
Dorking	a		12 43			12 50						13 13			13 24						13 43		
	d														13 24								
Holmwood	d														13 32								
Ockley	d														13 36								
Warnham	d														13 41								
Horsham	a														13 45								

Station		SN	FC	SW	FC	SN	SN	SW	SN	SN	SN	FC	SN	FC	SN	SW	SW	SN	SN	SN	FC	SW	FC
London Victoria	d	13 01				12 53	13 03		13 17	13 06	13 31		13 23		13 33			13 47	13 36	14 01			
London Waterloo	d			13 09				13 24								13 39	13 54					14 09	
Clapham Junction	d	13 08		13 18		13 00	13 11	13 33	13 24	13 14	13 38		13 30		13 41	13 48	14 03	13 54	13 44	14 08		14 18	
Balham	d					13 05	13 16		13 30	13 20			13 35		13 46			14 00	13 50				
London Bridge	d																						
Tulse Hill	d		13 01		13 16							13 31		13 46							14 01		14 16
New Cross Gate	d																						
Norwood Junction	d									13 39									14 09				
West Croydon	d					13 24	13 34			13 44			13 54		14 04				14 14				
Waddon	d					13 26	13 36			13 46			13 56		14 06				14 16				
Wallington	d					13 30	13 40			13 50			14 00		14 10				14 20				
Carshalton Beeches	d					13 32	13 42			13 52			14 02		14 12				14 22				
Mitcham Eastfields	d				13 24				13 36					13 54				14 06					14 24
Mitcham Junction	d				13 27				13 39					13 57				14 09					14 27
Hackbridge	d				13 30				13 43					14 00				14 13					14 30
Carshalton	d				13 33				13 45					14 03				14 15					14 33
Sutton (Surrey)	a	13 28	13 35		13 36	13 39	13 46		13 49	13 56	13 58	14 05	14 06	14 06	14 16			14 19	14 26	14 28	14 35		14 36
	d	13 29				13 40			13 49		13 59		14 07					14 19		14 29			
Belmont	d												14 10										
Banstead	d												14 14										
Epsom Downs	a												14 17										
Cheam	d	13 31				13 42			13 52		14 01							14 22		14 31			
Ewell East	d					13 46			13 55		14 05							14 25					
Epsom	a	13 37		13 46		13 52		13 57	13 59		14 09					14 16	14 27	14 29		14 37		14 46	
	d	13 37		13 47				13 58			14 09					14 17	14 28			14 37		14 47	
Ashtead	d	13 41		13 51				14 02			14 13					14 21	14 32			14 41		14 51	
Leatherhead	d	13 44		13 54				14 05			14 16					14 24	14 35			14 44		14 54	
Bookham	d			13 59												14 29						14 59	
Effingham Junction	d			14 03												14 33						15 03	
Guildford	a			14 23												14 53						15 23	
Box Hill & Westhumble	d										14 21												
Dorking	a	13 50						14 13			14 24						14 43			14 50			
	d										14 24												
Holmwood	d										14 32												
Ockley	d										14 36												
Warnham	d										14 41												
Horsham	a										14 45												

Table 182

Mondays to Fridays
from 8 October

London - Sutton, Epsom, Guildford, Dorking and Horsham

Network Diagram - see first Page of Table 177

		SN		SN	SW	SN	SN	SN	FC	SN	FC	SN		SW	SW	SN	SN	SN	FC	SW	FC	SN		SN	SW
London Victoria	⊖ d	13 53		14 03		14 17	14 06	14 31		14 23		14 33				14 47	14 36	15 01				14 53		15 03	
London Waterloo	⊖ d				14 24									14 39	14 54					15 09					15 24
Clapham Junction	d	14 00		14 11	14 33	14 24	14 14	14 38		14 30		14 41		14 48	15 03	14 54	14 44	15 08		15 18		15 00		15 11	15 33
Balham	⊖ d	14 05		14 16		14 30	14 20			14 35		14 46				15 00	14 50					15 05		15 16	
London Bridge	⊖ d																								
Tulse Hill	d								14 31		14 46								15 01		15 16				
New Cross Gate	⊖ d																								
Norwood Junction	d						14 39										15 09								
West Croydon	d	14 24		14 34			14 44			14 54		15 04					15 14					15 24		15 34	
Waddon	d	14 26		14 36			14 46			14 56		15 06					15 16					15 26		15 36	
Wallington	d	14 30		14 40			14 50			15 00		15 10					15 20					15 30		15 40	
Carshalton Beeches	d	14 32		14 42			14 52			15 02		15 12					15 22					15 32		15 42	
Mitcham Eastfields	d					14 36					14 54					15 06					15 24				
Mitcham Junction	d					14 39					14 57					15 09					15 27				
Hackbridge	d					14 43					15 00					15 13					15 30				
Carshalton	d					14 45					15 03					15 15					15 33				
Sutton (Surrey)	a	14 39		14 46		14 49	14 56	14 58	15 05	15 06	15 06	15 16				15 19	15 26	15 28	15 35		15 36	15 39		15 46	
	d	14 40				14 49		14 59		15 07						15 19		15 29				15 40			
Belmont	d									15 10															
Banstead	d									15 14															
Epsom Downs	a									15 17															
Cheam	d	14 42				14 52		15 01								15 22		15 31				15 42			
Ewell East	d	14 46				14 55		15 05								15 25						15 46			
Epsom	a	14 52			14 57	14 59		15 09						15 16	15 27	15 29		15 37		15 46		15 52			15 57
	d				14 58			15 09						15 17	15 28			15 37		15 47					15 58
Ashtead	d				15 02			15 13						15 21	15 32			15 41		15 51					16 02
Leatherhead	d				15 05			15 16						15 24	15 35			15 44		15 54					16 05
Bookham	d													15 29						15 59					
Effingham Junction	d													15 33						16 03					
Guildford	a													15 53						16 23					
Box Hill & Westhumble	d							15 21																	
Dorking	a				15 13			15 24							15 43			15 50							16 13
	d							15 24																	
Holmwood	d							15 32																	
Ockley	d							15 36																	
Warnham	d							15 41																	
Horsham	a							15 45																	

		SN	SN	SN	FC	SN	FC	SN		SW	SW	SN	SN	SN	FC	SN	FC	SN		SW	SW	SN	SN	SW	SN
London Victoria	⊖ d	15 17	15 06	15 31		15 23		15 33				15 47	15 36	16 01		15 53		16 03				16 17	16 07		16 31
London Waterloo	⊖ d									15 39	15 54									16 09	16 24			16 39	
Clapham Junction	d	15 24	15 14	15 38		15 30		15 41		15 48	16 03	15 54	15 44	16 08		16 00		16 11		16 18	16 33	16 24	16 15	16 48	16 38
Balham	⊖ d	15 30	15 20			15 35		15 46				16 00	15 50			16 05		16 16				16 30	16 20		
London Bridge	⊖ d																								
Tulse Hill	d				15 31		15 46								16 01		16 16								
New Cross Gate	⊖ d																								
Norwood Junction	d		15 39										16 09										16 39		
West Croydon	d		15 44			15 54		16 04					16 14			16 24		16 34					16 44		
Waddon	d		15 46			15 56		16 06					16 16			16 26		16 36					16 46		
Wallington	d		15 50			16 00		16 10					16 20			16 30		16 40					16 50		
Carshalton Beeches	d		15 52			16 02		16 12					16 22			16 32		16 42					16 52		
Mitcham Eastfields	d	15 36					15 54					16 06					16 24					16 36			16 51
Mitcham Junction	d	15 39					15 57					16 09		16 22			16 27					16 39			16 54
Hackbridge	d	15 43					16 00					16 13					16 30					16 43			16 57
Carshalton	d	15 45					16 03					16 15					16 33					16 45			17 00
Sutton (Surrey)	a	15 49	15 56	15 58	16 05	16 06	16 06	16 16				16 19	16 26	16 29	16 35	16 36	16 36	16 47				16 49	16 58		17 03
	d	15 49		15 59		16 07						16 19		16 30		16 37						16 49			17 04
Belmont	d					16 10										16 40									
Banstead	d					16 14										16 44									
Epsom Downs	a					16 17										16 47									
Cheam	d	15 52		16 01								16 22		16 32								16 52			17 06
Ewell East	d	15 55		16 05								16 25		16 36								16 55			17 10
Epsom	a	15 59		16 09						16 15	16 27	16 29		16 40						16 46	16 57	17 01		17 12	17 16
	d			16 09						16 17	16 28			16 40						16 47	16 58	17 02		17 17	
Ashtead	d			16 13						16 21	16 32			16 44						16 51	17 02	17 06		17 21	
Leatherhead	d			16 16						16 24	16 35			16 47						16 54	17 05	17 09		17 24	
Bookham	d									16 29										16 59				17 29	
Effingham Junction	d									16 33										17 03				17 33	
Guildford	a									16 53										17 25				17 55	
Box Hill & Westhumble	d			16 21										16 52							17 10	17 14			
Dorking	a			16 24							16 43			16 57							17 16	17 16			
	d			16 24																		17 17			
Holmwood	d			16 32																		17 24			
Ockley	d			16 36																		17 28			
Warnham	d			16 41																		17 34			
Horsham	a			16 45																		17 40			

Table 182

Mondays to Fridays
from 8 October

London - Sutton, Epsom, Guildford, Dorking and Horsham

Network Diagram - see first Page of Table 177

		FC	FC	SN		SW	SN	SN	SW	SN	FC	FC	SN	SN		SW	SN	SN	SW	SN	SW	SN	FC	FC	
London Victoria	⊖ d			16 33			16 47	16 37						17 01			17 20	17 06				17 31			
London Waterloo	⊖ d					16 54			17 09							17 24			17 30		17 39				
Clapham Junction	d			16 41		17 03	16 54	16 45	17 18					17 09		17 33	17 26	17 14	17 39		17 48	17 37			
Balham	⊖ d			16 46			17 00	16 50						17 14			17 32	17 19				17 42			
London Bridge	⊖ d									17 03			17 06							17 29					
Tulse Hill	d	16 32	16 46								17 02	17 20	17 24										17 31	17 48	
New Cross Gate	⊖ d																								
Norwood Junction	d							17 09		17 16								17 38		17 43					
West Croydon	d			17 04				17 14		17 22				17 33				17 44		17 48					
Waddon	d			17 06				17 16		17 24				17 35				17 46		17 51					
Wallington	d			17 10				17 20		17 28				17 39				17 50		17 54					
Carshalton Beeches	d			17 12				17 22		17 30				17 41				17 52		17 57					
Mitcham Eastfields	d		16 55				17 07					17 28	17 32				17 38					17 48		17 55	
Mitcham Junction	d		16 58				17 10					17 31	17 35				17 41					17 51		17 58	
Hackbridge	d		17 01				17 13					17 34	17 38				17 45					17 55		18 02	
Carshalton	d		17 04				17 16					17 37	17 41				17 47					17 57		18 04	
Sutton (Surrey)	a	17 05	17 08	17 16			17 19	17 26		17 34	17 37	17 40	17 44	17 45			17 51	17 58		18 00		18 03	18 07	18 08	
	d			17 16			17 20	17 27		17 34				17 45			17 51			18 01		18 05			
Belmont	d			17 20										17 49											
Banstead	d			17 23										17 52											
Epsom Downs	a			17 28										17 58											
Cheam	d						17 22	17 29		17 37							17 54			18 03		18 07			
Ewell East	d						17 26	17 33		17 40							17 57			18 07		18 11			
Epsom	a					17 27	17 30	17 37	17 42	17 46						17 54	18 01		18 07	18 11	18 15	18 17			
	d					17 28	17 31	17 37	17 47							17 54	18 02			18 12	18 17				
Ashtead	d					17 32	17 35	17 41	17 51							17 58	18 06			18 16	18 21				
Leatherhead	d					17 35	17 38	17 44	17 54							18 01	18 09			18 19	18 24				
Bookham	d							17 50	17 59											18 24	18 29				
Effingham Junction	d							17 53	18a05											18 28	18a42				
Guildford	a							18 13												18 46					
Box Hill & Westhumble	d					17 40	17 43									18 06	18 14								
Dorking	a					17 46	17 45									18 13	18 16								
	d						17 46										18 19								
Holmwood	d						17 53										18 26								
Ockley	d						17 57										18 30								
Warnham	d						18 03										18 36								
Horsham	a						18 09										18 42								

		SN	SN	SW	SN	SN	SW	SN	SW	SN		FC	FC	SN	SW	SN	SN	SN	SW	SN		FC	FC	SN	SW
London Victoria	⊖ d		17 33		17 50	17 37				18 01				18 03			18 20	18 07						18 32	
London Waterloo	⊖ d			17 54			18 00		18 09						18 24				18 30						18 39
Clapham Junction	d		17 41	18 03	17 56	17 45	18 09		18 18	18 08				18 11	18 33		18 26	18 15	18 39					18 40	18 48
Balham	⊖ d		17 46		18 02	17 50				18 12				18 16			18 32	18 20						18 45	
London Bridge	⊖ d	17 37						18 02								18 08				18 32					
Tulse Hill	d	17 55										18 02	18 22			18 27						18 32	18 52		
New Cross Gate	⊖ d																								
Norwood Junction	d					18 09		18 16										18 39		18 46					
West Croydon	d		18 04			18 15		18 21						18 35				18 45		18 51				19 04	
Waddon	d		18 06			18 17		18 23						18 37				18 47		18 53				19 07	
Wallington	d		18 10			18 21		18 27						18 41				18 51		18 57				19 10	
Carshalton Beeches	d		18 12			18 23		18 29						18 43				18 53		18 59				19 13	
Mitcham Eastfields	d	18 02			18 08					18 19			18 29			18 34	18 38						18 59		
Mitcham Junction	d	18 05			18 11					18 22			18 32			18 37	18 41						19 02		
Hackbridge	d	18 09			18 15					18 25			18 36			18 41	18 45						19 06		
Carshalton	d	18 11			18 17					18 28			18 38			18 43	18 47						19 08		
Sutton (Surrey)	a	18 15	18 18		18 21	18 29		18 33		18 36		18 37	18 42	18 47		18 47	18 51	18 58		19 03		19 07	19 12	19 16	
	d		18 19		18 21			18 33		18 36				18 48			18 51			19 03				19 17	
Belmont	d		18 22											18 51										19 20	
Banstead	d		18 26											18 55										19 24	
Epsom Downs	a		18 31											19 00										19 29	
Cheam	d				18 24			18 36		18 39							18 54			19 06					
Ewell East	d				18 27			18 39		18 42							18 57			19 09					
Epsom	a			18 24	18 31		18 35	18 43	18 46	18 48					18 54		19 01		19 07	19 13					19 16
	d			18 24	18 34			18 44	18 47						18 54		19 02			19 14					19 17
Ashtead	d			18 28	18 38			18 48	18 51						18 58		19 06			19 18					19 21
Leatherhead	d			18 31	18 41			18 51	18 54						19 01		19 09			19 21					19 24
Bookham	d								18 59																19 29
Effingham Junction	d								19 03																19 33
Guildford	a								19 25																19 55
Box Hill & Westhumble	d			18 36	18 46			18 56							19 06		19 14			19 26					
Dorking	a			18 43	18 48			19 00							19 13		19 16			19 30					
	d				18 49												19 19								
Holmwood	d				18 56												19 26								
Ockley	d				19 00												19 30								
Warnham	d				19 06												19 36								
Horsham	a				19 12												19 42								

Table 182

London - Sutton, Epsom, Guildford, Dorking and Horsham

Mondays to Fridays
from 8 October

Network Diagram - see first Page of Table 177

		SW	SN	SN	SN	SW		FC	SW	FC	SN	SW	SN	SN	SN	FC		SW	FC	SN	SN	SW	SN	SN	FC
London Victoria 15 ⊖	d			18 50	18 36						18 59		19 20	19 06						19 34	19 30		19 50	19 36	
London Waterloo 15 ⊖	d	18 54				19 00			19 09			19 24						19 39				19 54			
Clapham Junction 10	d	19 03		18 56	18 44	19 09			19 18		19 08	19 33	19 26	19 14				19 48		19 41	19 38	20 03	19 56	19 44	
Balham 4 ⊖	d			19 02	18 49						19 14		19 32	19 20						19 46	19 44		20 02	19 50	
London Bridge 4 ⊖	d		18 38												19 31										
Tulse Hill 3	d		18 56					19 09		19 16						19 31			19 46						20 01
New Cross Gate 4 ⊖	d																								
Norwood Junction 2	d				19 09									19 39	19 44									20 09	
West Croydon 4	d				19 15						19 32			19 45	19 49						20 02			20 14	
Waddon	d				19 17						19 35			19 47	19 52						20 05			20 16	
Wallington	d				19 21						19 38			19 51	19 55						20 08			20 20	
Carshalton Beeches	d				19 23						19 41			19 53	19 58						20 11			20 22	
Mitcham Eastfields	d		19 03	19 08						19 24			19 38						19 54	19 57			20 08		
Mitcham Junction	d		19 06	19 11						19 27			19 41						19 57	20 00			20 11		
Hackbridge	d		19 10	19 15						19 30			19 45						20 00	20 03			20 15		
Carshalton	d		19 12	19 17						19 33			19 47						20 03	20 06			20 17		
Sutton (Surrey) 4	a		19 16	19 21	19 28			19 41		19 36	19 44		19 51	19 57	20 01	20 07			20 06	20 09	20 14		20 21	20 26	20 39
	d		19 16	19 21							19 45		19 51	19 58	20 02					20 10			20 21	20 27	
Belmont	d													20 01										20 30	
Banstead	d													20 05										20 34	
Epsom Downs	a													20 08										20 37	
Cheam	d		19 19	19 24							19 47		19 54		20 04					20 12			20 24		
Ewell East	d		19 22	19 27							19 51		19 57		20 08					20 16			20 27		
Epsom 3	a	19 24	19 26	19 31		19 35			19 44		19 55	19 57	20 01		20 12			20 16		20 20		20 27	20 31		
	d	19 24		19 34					19 47			19 58	20 02		20 12			20 17					20 32		
Ashtead	d	19 28		19 38					19 51			20 02	20 06		20 16			20 21					20 36		
Leatherhead	d	19 31		19 41					19 54			20 05	20 09		20 19			20 24					20 39		
Bookham	d								19 59									20 29							
Effingham Junction 6	d								20 03									20 33							
Guildford	a								20 23									20 53							
Box Hill & Westhumble	d	19 36		19 46								20 10	20 14										20 44		
Dorking 4	a	19 43		19 50								20 14	20 16		20 25								20 46		
	d												20 17												
Holmwood	d												20 24												
Ockley	d												20 28												
Warnham	d												20 34												
Horsham 4	a												20 38												

		SW		FC	SN	SN	SW	SN	SN	SW	SN	FC		FC	SN	SW	SN	SN	SW	SN	FC	FC		SN	SW
London Victoria 15 ⊖	d				20 03	20 00		20 20	20 06		20 33				20 30		20 50	20 36		21 03				21 00	
London Waterloo 15 ⊖	d	20 09					20 24			20 39						20 54			21 09						21 24
Clapham Junction 10	d	20 18			20 11	20 08	20 33	20 26	20 14	20 48	20 41				20 38	21 03	20 56	20 44	21 18	21 11				21 08	21 33
Balham 4 ⊖	d				20 16	20 14		20 31	20 20		20 46				20 44		21 02	20 50		21 16				21 14	
London Bridge 4 ⊖	d																								
Tulse Hill 3	d			20 16								20 31		20 50							21 01	21 20			
New Cross Gate 4 ⊖	d																								
Norwood Junction 2	d								20 39									21 09							
West Croydon 4	d					20 32			20 44						21 02			21 14						21 32	
Waddon	d					20 35			20 46						21 05			21 16						21 35	
Wallington	d					20 38			20 50						21 08			21 20						21 38	
Carshalton Beeches	d					20 41			20 52						21 11			21 22						21 41	
Mitcham Eastfields	d			20 24	20 27			20 38			20 53			20 57			21 08			21 23		21 27			
Mitcham Junction	d			20 27	20 30			20 41			20 56			21 00			21 11			21 26		21 30			
Hackbridge	d			20 30	20 34			20 45			20 59			21 03			21 15			21 30		21 33			
Carshalton	d			20 33	20 36			20 47			21 02			21 06			21 17			21 32		21 36			
Sutton (Surrey) 4	a			20 36	20 40	20 44		20 51	20 56		21 05	21 09		21 10	21 14		21 21	21 26		21 36	21 39	21 40		21 44	
	d				20 40			20 51	20 57		21 06						21 21	21 27		21 36					
Belmont	d																	21 30							
Banstead	d																	21 34							
Epsom Downs	a																	21 37							
Cheam	d				20 43			20 54	20 59		21 08						21 24			21 39					
Ewell East	d				20 46			20 57	21 03		21 12						21 27			21 42					
Epsom 3	a	20 42			20 50		20 57	21 01	21 07	21 12	21 16					21 27	21 31		21 42	21 46					21 57
	d	20 43						21 02		21 13							21 32		21 43						
Ashtead	d	20 47						21 06		21 17							21 36		21 47						
Leatherhead	d	20 50						21 09		21 20							21 39		21 50						
Bookham	d									21 25															
Effingham Junction 6	d									21 29															
Guildford	a									21 49															
Box Hill & Westhumble	d	20 55						21 14									21 44		21 55						
Dorking 4	a	20 59						21 16									21 46		21 59						
	d																								
Holmwood	d																								
Ockley	d																								
Warnham	d																								
Horsham 4	a																								

Table 182

London - Sutton, Epsom, Guildford, Dorking and Horsham

Mondays to Fridays
from 8 October

Network Diagram - see first Page of Table 177

		SN	SN	SW	SN	FC	SN	SW		SN	SN	SW	SN	FC	SN	SN	SN	SW		SN	FC	SN	SN	SN	FC
London Victoria 15 ⊖	d	21 20	21 06		21 33		21 30			21 50	21 36		22 03		22 00	22 20	22 06			22 33		22 30	22 50	22 36	
London Waterloo 15 ⊖	d			21 39				21 54				22 09						22 39							
Clapham Junction 10	d	21 26	21 14	21 48	21 41		21 38	22 03		21 56	21 44	22 18	22 11		22 08	22 26	22 14	22 48		22 41		22 38	22 56	22 46	
Balham 4 ⊖	d	21 31	21 20		21 46		21 44			22 02	21 50		22 16		22 14	22 32	22 20			22 46		22 44	23 01	22 52	
London Bridge 4 ⊖	d																								
Tulse Hill 3	d					21 31								22 01							22 31				23 01
New Cross Gate 4 ⊖	d																								
Norwood Junction 2	d		21 39								22 09						22 39							23 09	
West Croydon 4	d		21 44				22 02				22 14				22 32		22 44					23 02		23 14	
Waddon	d		21 46				22 05				22 16				22 35		22 46					23 05		23 16	
Wallington	d		21 50				22 08				22 20				22 38		22 50					23 08		23 20	
Carshalton Beeches	d		21 52				22 11				22 22				22 41		22 52					23 11		23 22	
Mitcham Eastfields	d	21 38			21 53					22 08			22 23			22 38				22 53			23 07		
Mitcham Junction	d	21 41			21 56					22 11			22 26			22 41				22 56			23 10		
Hackbridge	d	21 45			21 59					22 15			22 29			22 45				22 59			23 14		
Carshalton	d	21 47			22 02					22 17			22 32			22 47				23 02			23 16		
Sutton (Surrey) 4	a	21 51	21 56		22 05	22 09	22 14			22 21	22 26		22 35	22 39	22 44	22 51	22 56			23 05	23 09	23 14	23 20	23 26	23 35
	d	21 51	21 57		22 06					22 21	22 27		22 36			22 51	22 57			23 06			23 20	23 27	
Belmont	d										22 30													23 30	
Banstead	d										22 34													23 34	
Epsom Downs	a										22 37													23 37	
Cheam	d	21 54	21 59		22 08					22 24			22 38			22 54	22 59			23 08			23 23		
Ewell East	d	21 57	22 03		22 12					22 27			22 42			22 57	23 03			23 12			23 26		
Epsom 3	a	22 01	22 07	22 12	22 16			22 27		22 31		22 42	22 46			23 01	23 07	23 12		23 16			23 30		
	d	22 02		22 13						22 32		22 43				23 02		23 13					23 31		
Ashtead	d	22 06		22 17						22 36		22 47				23 06		23 17					23 35		
Leatherhead	d	22 09		22 20						22 39		22 50				23 09		23 20					23 38		
Bookham	d			22 25														23 25							
Effingham Junction 6	d			22 29														23 29							
Guildford	a			22 49														23 49							
Box Hill & Westhumble	d									22 44		22 55											23 43		
Dorking 4	a	22 15								22 46		22 59				23 15							23 45		
	d																								
Holmwood	d																								
Ockley	d																								
Warnham	d																								
Horsham 4	a																								

		SW	SN	SN		SN	SN	FC	SN	SW	SN FX	SN FO
London Victoria 15 ⊖	d		23 03	23 00		23 06	23 26		23 34		23 51	23 59
London Waterloo 15 ⊖	d	23 09								23 42		
Clapham Junction 10	d	23 18	23 11	23 08		23 14	23 34		23 42	23 51	23 59	00 07
Balham 4 ⊖	d		23 16	23 14		23 20	23 40		23 47		00 04	00 12
London Bridge 4 ⊖	d											
Tulse Hill 3	d							23 31				
New Cross Gate 4 ⊖	d											
Norwood Junction 2	d					23 40						
West Croydon 4	d			23 32		23 45			00 04		00 21	00 31
Waddon	d			23 35		23 47			00 06		00 24	00 33
Wallington	d			23 38		23 51			00 10		00 27	00 37
Carshalton Beeches	d			23 41		23 53			00 12		00 30	00 39
Mitcham Eastfields	d		23 23				23 46					
Mitcham Junction	d		23 26				23 49					
Hackbridge	d		23 29				23 53					
Carshalton	d		23 32				23 55					
Sutton (Surrey) 4	a		23 35	23 44		23 57	23 59	00 09	00 16		00 33	00 43
	d		23 36	23 45			00 01					
Belmont	d											
Banstead	d											
Epsom Downs	a											
Cheam	d		23 38	23 47			00 03					
Ewell East	d		23 42	23 51			00 07					
Epsom 3	a	23 42	23 46	23 55			00 11			00 15		
	d	23 43					00 11			00 19		
Ashtead	d	23 47					00 15			00 23		
Leatherhead	d	23 50					00 18			00 26		
Bookham	d									00 31		
Effingham Junction 6	d									00 36		
Guildford	a									00 56		
Box Hill & Westhumble	d	23 55					00 23					
Dorking 4	a	23 59					00 26					
	d						00 26					
Holmwood	d						00s33					
Ockley	d						00s37					
Warnham	d						00s43					
Horsham 4	a						00 47					

London - Sutton, Epsom, Guildford, Dorking and Horsham

Network Diagram - see first Page of Table 177

		SN	FC A	FC B	SN	SW	FC A	SN	SW C	SW D		FC B	SN	SN	FC	SN	FC	SN	SW	FC		SN	SN	FC	SW
London Victoria ⊖	d	23p26			23p34			23p59					00 20	00 34				06 23				06 47			
London Waterloo ⊖	d					23p42			00 15	00 15									06 39						07 09
Clapham Junction	d	23p34			23p42	23p51		00 07	00 25	00 25			00 27	00 42				06 30	06 48			06 54			07 18
Balham ⊖	d	23p40			23p47			00 12					00 32	00 47				06 35				07 00			
London Bridge ⊖	d			23p29								23p59													
Tulse Hill	d		23p31	23p41			00 01					00 09			06 16		06 31			06 46				07 01	
New Cross Gate ⊖	d																						07 09		
Norwood Junction	d																						07 15		
West Croydon	d				00 04			00 31						01 04		06 45		06 54					07 17		
Waddon	d				00 06			00 33						01 07		06 47		06 56					07 21		
Wallington	d				00 10			00 37						01 10		06 51		07 00					07 23		
Carshalton Beeches	d				00 12			00 39						01 13		06 53		07 02							
Mitcham Eastfields	d	23p46											00 38		06 24					06 54		07 06			
Mitcham Junction	d	23p49											00 41		06 27					06 57		07 09			
Hackbridge	d	23p53											00 45		06 30					07 00		07 13			
Carshalton	d	23p55											00 47		06 33					07 03		07 15			
Sutton (Surrey)	a	23p59	00 09	00 15	00 16		00 39	00 43				00 43	00 51	01 16	06 36	06 57	07 05	07 06		07 06		07 19	07 27	07 35	
	d	00 01														06 57		07 07				07 19			
Belmont	d																	07 10							
Banstead	d																	07 14							
Epsom Downs	a																	07 17							
Cheam	d	00 03														07 00						07 22			
Ewell East	d	00 07														07 03						07 25			
Epsom	a	00 11				00 15			00 50	00 50						07 07			07 16			07 29			07 46
	d	00 11				00 19				00 51						07 08			07 17			07 30			07 47
Ashtead	d	00 15				00 23				00s55						07 12			07 21			07 34			07 51
Leatherhead	d	00 18				00 26				00s58						07 15			07 24			07 37			07 54
Bookham	d					00 31				01s03									07 29						07 59
Effingham Junction	d					00 36				01s07									07 33						08 03
Guildford	a					00 53				01 24									07 50						08 20
Box Hill & Westhumble	d	00 23																				07 42			
Dorking	a	00 26														07 21						07 44			
	d	00 26																							
Holmwood	d	00s33																							
Ockley	d	00s37																							
Warnham	d	00s43																							
Horsham	a	00 47																							

		FC	SN	SW	SN	SN		SN	FC	SN	FC	SN	SW	SW	SN	SN		SN	FC	SW	FC	SN	SN	SW	SN
London Victoria ⊖	d		06 53		07 17	07 06		07 31		07 23		07 33			07 47	07 36		08 01				07 53	08 03		08 17
London Waterloo ⊖	d			07 24									07 39	07 54						08 09				08 24	
Clapham Junction	d		07 00	07 33	07 24	07 14		07 38		07 30		07 41	07 48	08 03	07 54	07 44		08 08		08 18		08 00	08 11	08 33	08 24
Balham ⊖	d		07 05		07 30	07 20				07 35		07 46			08 00	07 50						08 05	08 16		08 30
London Bridge ⊖	d																								
Tulse Hill	d	07 16							07 31		07 46								08 01		08 16				
New Cross Gate ⊖	d																								
Norwood Junction	d					07 39										08 09									
West Croydon	d		07 24			07 44				07 54		08 04				08 14						08 24	08 34		
Waddon	d		07 26			07 46				07 56		08 06				08 16						08 26	08 36		
Wallington	d		07 30			07 50				08 00		08 10				08 20						08 30	08 40		
Carshalton Beeches	d		07 32			07 52				08 02		08 12				08 22						08 32	08 42		
Mitcham Eastfields	d	07 24			07 36						07 54				08 06						08 24				08 36
Mitcham Junction	d	07 27			07 39						07 57				08 09						08 27				08 39
Hackbridge	d	07 30			07 43						08 00				08 13						08 30				08 43
Carshalton	d	07 33			07 45						08 03				08 15						08 33				08 45
Sutton (Surrey)	a	07 36	07 39		07 49	07 56		07 58	08 05	08 06	08 06	08 16			08 19	08 26		08 28	08 35		08 36	08 39	08 46		08 49
	d		07 40		07 49			07 59		08 07					08 19			08 29				08 40			08 49
Belmont	d									08 10															
Banstead	d									08 14															
Epsom Downs	a									08 17															
Cheam	d		07 42		07 52			08 01							08 22			08 31				08 42			08 52
Ewell East	d		07 46		07 55			08 05							08 25							08 46			08 55
Epsom	a		07 52	07 57	07 59			08 09					08 16	08 27	08 29			08 37		08 46		08 52		08 57	08 59
	d			07 58				08 09					08 17	08 28				08 37		08 47				08 58	
Ashtead	d			08 02				08 13					08 21	08 32				08 41		08 51				09 02	
Leatherhead	d			08 05				08 16					08 24	08 35				08 44		08 54				09 05	
Bookham	d												08 29							08 59					
Effingham Junction	d												08 33							09 03					
Guildford	a												08 50							09 20					
Box Hill & Westhumble	d							08 21																	
Dorking	a			08 11				08 24						08 41				08 50						09 11	
	d							08 24																	
Holmwood	d							08 32																	
Ockley	d							08 36																	
Warnham	d							08 41																	
Horsham	a							08 45																	

A not 19 May
B 19 May
C until 21 July, 18 August, 25 August, 15 September, 22 September, 29 September, 6 October
D 28 July, 4 August, 11 August, 1 September, 8 September

London - Sutton, Epsom, Guildford, Dorking and Horsham

Network Diagram - see first Page of Table 177

		SN		SN	FC	SN	FC	SN	SW	SW	SN	SN		SN	FC	SW	FC	SN	SN	SW	SN	SN		SN	FC
London Victoria ⊖	d	08 06		08 31		08 23		08 33			08 47	08 36		09 01				08 53	09 03		09 17	09 06		09 31	
London Waterloo ⊖	d								08 39	08 54						09 09				09 24					
Clapham Junction	d	08 14		08 38		08 30		08 41	08 48	09 03	08 54	08 44		09 08		09 18		09 00	09 11	09 33	09 24	09 14		09 38	
Balham ⊖	d	08 20				08 35		08 46			09 00	08 50						09 05	09 16		09 30	09 20			
London Bridge ⊖	d																								
Tulse Hill	d				08 31		08 46								09 01		09 16								09 31
New Cross Gate ⊖	d																								
Norwood Junction	d	08 39										09 09										09 39			
West Croydon	d	08 44				08 54		09 04				09 14						09 24	09 34			09 44			
Waddon	d	08 46				08 56		09 06				09 16						09 26	09 36			09 46			
Wallington	d	08 50				09 00		09 10				09 20						09 30	09 40			09 50			
Carshalton Beeches	d	08 52				09 02		09 12				09 22						09 32	09 42			09 52			
Mitcham Eastfields	d						08 54				09 06						09 24				09 36				
Mitcham Junction	d						08 57				09 09						09 27				09 39				
Hackbridge	d						09 00				09 13						09 30				09 43				
Carshalton	d						09 03				09 15						09 33				09 45				
Sutton (Surrey)	a	08 56		08 58	09 05	09 06	09 06	09 16			09 19	09 26		09 28	09 35		09 36	09 39	09 46		09 49	09 56		09 58	10 05
	d			08 59		09 07					09 19			09 29				09 40			09 49			09 59	
Belmont	d					09 10																			
Banstead	d					09 14																			
Epsom Downs	a					09 17																			
Cheam	d			09 01							09 22			09 31				09 42			09 52			10 01	
Ewell East	d			09 05							09 25							09 46			09 55			10 05	
Epsom	a			09 09					09 16	09 27	09 29			09 37		09 46		09 52		09 57	09 59			10 09	
	d			09 09					09 17	09 28				09 37		09 47				09 58				10 09	
Ashtead	d			09 13					09 21	09 32				09 41		09 51				10 02				10 13	
Leatherhead	d			09 16					09 24	09 35				09 44		09 54				10 05				10 16	
Bookham	d								09 29							09 59									
Effingham Junction	d								09 33							10 03									
Guildford	a								09 50							10 20									
Box Hill & Westhumble	d			09 21																				10 21	
Dorking	a			09 24						09 41				09 50						10 11				10 24	
	d			09 24																				10 24	
Holmwood	d			09 32																				10 32	
Ockley	d			09 36																				10 36	
Warnham	d			09 41																				10 41	
Horsham	a			09 45																				10 45	

		SN	FC	SN	SW	SW	SN	SN		SN	FC	SW	FC	SN	SN	SW	SN	SN		SN	FC	SN	FC	SN	SW
London Victoria ⊖	d	09 23		09 33			09 47	09 36		10 01				09 53	10 03		10 17	10 06		10 31		10 23		10 33	
London Waterloo ⊖	d				09 39	09 54						10 09				10 24									10 39
Clapham Junction	d	09 30		09 41	09 48	10 03	09 54	09 44		10 08		10 18		10 00	10 11	10 33	10 24	10 14		10 38		10 30		10 41	10 48
Balham ⊖	d	09 35		09 46			10 00	09 50						10 05	10 16		10 30	10 20				10 35		10 46	
London Bridge ⊖	d																								
Tulse Hill	d		09 46								10 01		10 16								10 31		10 46		
New Cross Gate ⊖	d																								
Norwood Junction	d							10 09										10 39							
West Croydon	d	09 54		10 04				10 14						10 24	10 34			10 44				10 54		11 04	
Waddon	d	09 56		10 06				10 16						10 26	10 36			10 46				10 56		11 06	
Wallington	d	10 00		10 10				10 20						10 30	10 40			10 50				11 00		11 10	
Carshalton Beeches	d	10 02		10 12				10 22						10 32	10 42			10 52				11 02		11 12	
Mitcham Eastfields	d		09 54				10 06						10 24				10 36						10 54		
Mitcham Junction	d		09 57				10 09						10 27				10 39						10 57		
Hackbridge	d		10 00				10 13						10 30				10 43						11 00		
Carshalton	d		10 03				10 15						10 33				10 45						11 03		
Sutton (Surrey)	a	10 06	10 06	10 16			10 19	10 26		10 28	10 35		10 36	10 39	10 46		10 49	10 56		10 58	11 05	11 06	11 06	11 16	
	d	10 07					10 19			10 29				10 40			10 49			10 59		11 07			
Belmont	d	10 10																				11 10			
Banstead	d	10 14																				11 14			
Epsom Downs	a	10 17																				11 17			
Cheam	d						10 22			10 31				10 42			10 52			11 01					
Ewell East	d						10 25							10 46			10 55			11 05					
Epsom	a				10 16	10 27	10 29			10 37		10 46		10 52		10 57	10 59			11 09					11 16
	d				10 17	10 28				10 37		10 47				10 58				11 09					11 17
Ashtead	d				10 21	10 32				10 41		10 51				11 02				11 13					11 21
Leatherhead	d				10 24	10 35				10 44		10 54				11 05				11 16					11 24
Bookham	d				10 29							10 59													11 29
Effingham Junction	d				10 33							11 03													11 33
Guildford	a				10 50							11 20													11 50
Box Hill & Westhumble	d																			11 21					
Dorking	a					10 41				10 50						11 11				11 24					
	d																			11 24					
Holmwood	d																			11 32					
Ockley	d																			11 36					
Warnham	d																			11 41					
Horsham	a																			11 45					

London - Sutton, Epsom, Guildford, Dorking and Horsham

Saturdays until 6 October

Network Diagram - see first Page of Table 177

Station	SW	SN	SN	SN	FC	SW	FC	SN	SN	SW	SN	SN	SN	FC	SN	FC	SN	SW	SW	SN	SN
London Victoria ⊖ d		10 47	10 36	11 01				10 53	11 03		11 17	11 06	11 31		11 23		11 33			11 47	11 36
London Waterloo ⊖ d	10 54					11 09				11 24								11 39	11 54		
Clapham Junction d	11 03	10 54	10 44	11 08		11 18		11 00	11 11	11 33	11 24	11 14	11 38		11 30		11 41	11 48	12 03	11 54	11 44
Balham ⊖ d		11 00	10 50					11 05	11 16		11 30	11 20			11 35		11 46			12 00	11 50
London Bridge ⊖ d																					
Tulse Hill d					11 01		11 16							11 31		11 46					
New Cross Gate ⊖ d																					
Norwood Junction d			11 09									11 39									12 09
West Croydon d			11 14					11 24	11 34			11 44			11 54		12 04				12 14
Waddon d			11 16					11 26	11 36			11 46			11 56		12 06				12 16
Wallington d			11 20					11 30	11 40			11 50			12 00		12 10				12 20
Carshalton Beeches d			11 22					11 32	11 42			11 52			12 02		12 12				12 22
Mitcham Eastfields d		11 06					11 24				11 36					11 54				12 06	
Mitcham Junction d		11 09					11 27				11 39					11 57				12 09	
Hackbridge d		11 13					11 30				11 43					12 00				12 13	
Carshalton d		11 15					11 33				11 45					12 03				12 15	
Sutton (Surrey) a		11 19	11 26	11 28	11 35		11 36	11 39	11 46		11 49	11 56	11 58	12 05	12 06	12 06	12 16			12 19	12 26
Sutton (Surrey) d		11 19		11 29				11 40			11 49		11 59		12 07					12 19	
Belmont d															12 10						
Banstead d															12 14						
Epsom Downs a															12 17						
Cheam d		11 22		11 31				11 42			11 52		12 01							12 22	
Ewell East d		11 25						11 46			11 55		12 05							12 25	
Epsom a	11 27	11 29		11 37		11 46		11 52		11 57	11 59		12 09					12 16	12 27	12 29	
Epsom d	11 28			11 37		11 47				11 58			12 09					12 17	12 28		
Ashtead d	11 32			11 41		11 51				12 02			12 13					12 21	12 32		
Leatherhead d	11 35			11 44		11 54				12 05			12 16					12 24	12 35		
Bookham d						11 59												12 29			
Effingham Junction d						12 03												12 33			
Guildford a						12 20												12 50			
Box Hill & Westhumble d													12 21								
Dorking a	11 41			11 50						12 11			12 24						12 41		
Dorking d													12 24								
Holmwood d													12 32								
Ockley d													12 36								
Warnham d													12 41								
Horsham a													12 45								

Station	SN	FC	SW	FC	SN	SN	SW	SN	SN	SN	FC	SN	FC	SN	SW	SW	SN	SN	SN	FC	SW	FC
London Victoria ⊖ d	12 01				11 53	12 03		12 17	12 06	12 31		12 23		12 33			12 47	12 36	13 01			
London Waterloo ⊖ d			12 09				12 24								12 39	12 54					13 09	
Clapham Junction d	12 08		12 18		12 00	12 11	12 33	12 24	12 14	12 38		12 30		12 41	12 48	13 03	12 54	12 44	13 08		13 18	
Balham ⊖ d					12 05	12 16		12 30	12 20			12 35		12 46			13 00	12 50				
London Bridge ⊖ d																						
Tulse Hill d		12 01		12 16							12 31		12 46							13 01		13 16
New Cross Gate ⊖ d																						
Norwood Junction d									12 39									13 09				
West Croydon d					12 24	12 34			12 44			12 54		13 04				13 14				
Waddon d					12 26	12 36			12 46			12 56		13 06				13 16				
Wallington d					12 30	12 40			12 50			13 00		13 10				13 20				
Carshalton Beeches d					12 32	12 42			12 52			13 02		13 12				13 22				
Mitcham Eastfields d				12 24				12 36					12 54				13 06					13 24
Mitcham Junction d				12 27				12 39					12 57				13 09					13 27
Hackbridge d				12 30				12 43					13 00				13 13					13 30
Carshalton d				12 33				12 45					13 03				13 15					13 33
Sutton (Surrey) a	12 28	12 35		12 36	12 39	12 46		12 49	12 56	12 58	13 05	13 06	13 06	13 16			13 19	13 26	13 28	13 35		13 36
Sutton (Surrey) d	12 29				12 40			12 49		12 59		13 07					13 19		13 29			
Belmont d												13 10										
Banstead d												13 14										
Epsom Downs a												13 17										
Cheam d	12 31				12 42			12 52		13 01							13 22		13 31			
Ewell East d					12 46			12 55		13 05							13 25					
Epsom a	12 37		12 46		12 52		12 57	12 59		13 09					13 16	13 27	13 29		13 37		13 46	
Epsom d	12 37		12 47				12 58			13 09					13 17	13 28			13 37		13 47	
Ashtead d	12 41		12 51				13 02			13 13					13 21	13 32			13 41		13 51	
Leatherhead d	12 44		12 54				13 05			13 16					13 24	13 35			13 44		13 54	
Bookham d			12 59												13 29						13 59	
Effingham Junction d			13 03												13 33						14 03	
Guildford a			13 20												13 50						14 20	
Box Hill & Westhumble d										13 21												
Dorking a	12 50						13 11			13 24						13 41			13 50			
Dorking d										13 24												
Holmwood d										13 32												
Ockley d										13 36												
Warnham d										13 41												
Horsham a										13 45												

London - Sutton, Epsom, Guildford, Dorking and Horsham

Saturdays until 6 October

Network Diagram - see first Page of Table 177

Station	SN	SN	SW	SN	SN	SN	FC	SN	FC	SN	SW	SW	SN	SN	SN	FC	SW	FC	SN	SN	SW	SN
London Victoria ⊖ d	12 53	13 03		13 17	13 06	13 31		13 23		13 33			13 47	13 36	14 01				13 53	14 03		14 17
London Waterloo ⊖ d			13 24								13 39	13 54					14 09				14 24	
Clapham Junction d	13 00	13 11	13 33	13 24	13 14	13 38		13 30		13 41	13 48	14 03	13 54	13 44	14 08		14 18		14 00	14 11	14 33	14 24
Balham ⊖ d	13 05	13 16		13 30	13 20			13 35		13 46			14 00	13 50					14 05	14 16		14 30
London Bridge ⊖ d																						
Tulse Hill d							13 31		13 46							14 01		14 16				
New Cross Gate ⊖ d																						
Norwood Junction d					13 39									14 09								
West Croydon d	13 24	13 34			13 44			13 54		14 04				14 14					14 24	14 34		
Waddon d	13 26	13 36			13 46			13 56		14 06				14 16					14 26	14 36		
Wallington d	13 30	13 40			13 50			14 00		14 10				14 20					14 30	14 40		
Carshalton Beeches d	13 32	13 42			13 52			14 02		14 12				14 22					14 32	14 42		
Mitcham Eastfields d				13 36					13 54				14 06					14 24				14 36
Mitcham Junction d				13 39					13 57				14 09					14 27				14 39
Hackbridge d				13 43					14 00				14 13					14 30				14 43
Carshalton d				13 45					14 03				14 15					14 33				14 45
Sutton (Surrey) a	13 39	13 46		13 49	13 56	13 58	14 05	14 06	14 06	14 16			14 19	14 26	14 28	14 35		14 36	14 39	14 46		14 49
Sutton (Surrey) d	13 40			13 49		13 59		14 07					14 19		14 29				14 40			14 49
Belmont d								14 10														
Banstead d								14 14														
Epsom Downs a								14 17														
Cheam d	13 42			13 52		14 01							14 22		14 31				14 42			14 52
Ewell East d	13 46			13 55		14 05							14 25						14 46			14 55
Epsom a	13 52		13 57	13 59		14 09					14 16	14 27	14 29		14 37		14 46		14 52		14 57	14 59
Epsom d			13 58			14 09					14 17	14 28			14 37		14 47				14 58	
Ashtead d			14 02			14 13					14 21	14 32			14 41		14 51				15 02	
Leatherhead d			14 05			14 16					14 24	14 35			14 44		14 54				15 05	
Bookham d											14 29						14 59					
Effingham Junction d											14 33						15 03					
Guildford a											14 50						15 20					
Box Hill & Westhumble d						14 21																
Dorking a			14 11			14 24						14 41			14 50						15 11	
Dorking d						14 24																
Holmwood d						14 32																
Ockley d						14 36																
Warnham d						14 41																
Horsham a						14 45																

Station	SN	SN	FC	SN	FC	SN	SW	SW	SN	SN	SN	FC	SW	FC	SN	SN	SW	SN	SN	SN	FC
London Victoria ⊖ d	14 06	14 31		14 23		14 33			14 47	14 36	15 01				14 53	15 03		15 17	15 06	15 31	
London Waterloo ⊖ d							14 39	14 54					15 09				15 24				
Clapham Junction d	14 14	14 38		14 30		14 41	14 48	15 03	14 54	14 44	15 08		15 18		15 00	15 11	15 33	15 24	15 14	15 38	
Balham ⊖ d	14 20			14 35		14 46			15 00	14 50					15 05	15 16		15 30	15 20		
London Bridge ⊖ d																					
Tulse Hill d			14 31		14 46							15 01		15 16							15 31
New Cross Gate ⊖ d																					
Norwood Junction d	14 39									15 09									15 39		
West Croydon d	14 44			14 54		15 04				15 14					15 24	15 34			15 44		
Waddon d	14 46			14 56		15 06				15 16					15 26	15 36			15 46		
Wallington d	14 50			15 00		15 10				15 20					15 30	15 40			15 50		
Carshalton Beeches d	14 52			15 02		15 12				15 22					15 32	15 42			15 52		
Mitcham Eastfields d					14 54				15 06					15 24				15 36			
Mitcham Junction d					14 57				15 09					15 27				15 39			
Hackbridge d					15 00				15 13					15 30				15 43			
Carshalton d					15 03				15 15					15 33				15 45			
Sutton (Surrey) a	14 56	14 58	15 05	15 06	15 06	15 16			15 19	15 26	15 28	15 35		15 36	15 39	15 46		15 49	15 56	15 58	16 05
Sutton (Surrey) d		14 59		15 07					15 19		15 29				15 40			15 49		15 59	
Belmont d				15 10																	
Banstead d				15 14																	
Epsom Downs a				15 17																	
Cheam d		15 01							15 22		15 31				15 42			15 52		16 01	
Ewell East d		15 05							15 25						15 46			15 55		16 05	
Epsom a		15 09					15 16	15 27	15 29		15 37		15 46		15 52		15 57	15 59		16 09	
Epsom d		15 09					15 17	15 28			15 37		15 47				15 58			16 09	
Ashtead d		15 13					15 21	15 32			15 41		15 51				16 02			16 13	
Leatherhead d		15 16					15 24	15 35			15 44		15 54				16 05			16 16	
Bookham d							15 29						15 59								
Effingham Junction d							15 33						16 03								
Guildford a							15 50						16 20								
Box Hill & Westhumble d		15 21																		16 21	
Dorking a		15 24						15 41			15 50						16 11			16 24	
Dorking d		15 24																		16 24	
Holmwood d		15 32																		16 32	
Ockley d		15 36																		16 36	
Warnham d		15 41																		16 41	
Horsham a		15 45																		16 45	

London - Sutton, Epsom, Guildford, Dorking and Horsham

Network Diagram - see first Page of Table 177

Station		SN	FC	SN	SW	SW	SN	SN	SN	FC	SW	FC	SN	SN	SW	SN	SN	SN	FC	SN	FC	SN	SW
London Victoria ⊖	d	15 23		15 33			15 47	15 36	16 01				15 53	16 03		16 17	16 06	16 31		16 23		16 33	
London Waterloo ⊖	d				15 39	15 54					16 09				16 24								16 39
Clapham Junction	d	15 30		15 41	15 48	16 03	15 54	15 44	16 08		16 18		16 00	16 11	16 33	16 24	16 14	16 38		16 30		16 41	16 48
Balham ⊖	d	15 35		15 46			16 00	15 50					16 05	16 16		16 30	16 20			16 35		16 46	
London Bridge ⊖	d																						
Tulse Hill	d		15 46							16 01		16 16							16 31		16 46		
New Cross Gate ⊖	d																						
Norwood Junction	d							16 09									16 39						
West Croydon	d	15 54		16 04				16 14					16 24	16 34			16 44			16 54		17 04	
Waddon	d	15 56		16 06				16 16					16 26	16 36			16 46			16 56		17 06	
Wallington	d	16 00		16 10				16 20					16 30	16 40			16 50			17 00		17 10	
Carshalton Beeches	d	16 02		16 12				16 22					16 32	16 42			16 52			17 02		17 12	
Mitcham Eastfields	d		15 54				16 06					16 24				16 36					16 54		
Mitcham Junction	d		15 57				16 09					16 27				16 39					16 57		
Hackbridge	d		16 00				16 13					16 30				16 43					17 00		
Carshalton	d		16 03				16 15					16 33				16 45					17 03		
Sutton (Surrey)	a	16 06	16 06	16 16			16 19	16 26	16 28	16 35		16 36	16 39	16 46		16 49	16 56	16 58	17 05	17 06	17 06	17 16	
	d	16 07					16 19		16 29				16 40			16 49		16 59		17 07			
Belmont	d	16 10																		17 10			
Banstead	d	16 14																		17 14			
Epsom Downs	a	16 17																		17 17			
Cheam	d						16 22		16 31				16 42			16 52		17 01					
Ewell East	d						16 25						16 46			16 55		17 05					
Epsom	a				16 16	16 27	16 29		16 37		16 46		16 52		16 57	16 59		17 09					17 16
	d				16 17	16 28			16 37		16 47				16 58			17 09					17 17
Ashtead	d				16 21	16 32			16 41		16 51				17 02			17 13					17 21
Leatherhead	d				16 24	16 35			16 44		16 54				17 05			17 16					17 24
Bookham	d				16 29						16 59												17 29
Effingham Junction	d				16 33						17 03												17 33
Guildford	a				16 50						17 20												17 50
Box Hill & Westhumble	d																	17 21					
Dorking	a					16 41			16 50						17 11			17 24					
	d																	17 24					
Holmwood	d																	17 32					
Ockley	d																	17 36					
Warnham	d																	17 41					
Horsham	a																	17 45					

Station		SW	SN	SN	SN	FC	SW	FC	SN	SN	SW	SN	SN	SN	FC	SN	FC	SN	SW	SW	SN	SN
London Victoria ⊖	d		16 47	16 36	17 01				16 53	17 03		17 17	17 06	17 31		17 23		17 33			17 47	17 36
London Waterloo ⊖	d	16 54					17 09				17 24								17 39	17 54		
Clapham Junction	d	17 03	16 54	16 44	17 08		17 18		17 00	17 11	17 33	17 24	17 14	17 38		17 30		17 41	17 48	18 03	17 54	17 44
Balham ⊖	d		17 00	16 50					17 05	17 16		17 30	17 20			17 35		17 46			18 00	17 50
London Bridge ⊖	d																					
Tulse Hill	d					17 01		17 16							17 31		17 46					
New Cross Gate ⊖	d																					
Norwood Junction	d			17 09									17 39									18 09
West Croydon	d			17 14					17 24	17 34			17 44			17 54		18 04				18 14
Waddon	d			17 16					17 26	17 36			17 46			17 56		18 06				18 16
Wallington	d			17 20					17 30	17 40			17 50			18 00		18 10				18 20
Carshalton Beeches	d			17 22					17 32	17 42			17 52			18 02		18 12				18 22
Mitcham Eastfields	d		17 06					17 24				17 36					17 54				18 06	
Mitcham Junction	d		17 09					17 27				17 39					17 57				18 09	
Hackbridge	d		17 13					17 30				17 43					18 00				18 13	
Carshalton	d		17 15					17 33				17 45					18 03				18 15	
Sutton (Surrey)	a		17 19	17 26	17 28	17 35		17 36	17 39	17 46		17 49	17 56	17 58	18 05	18 06	18 06	18 16			18 19	18 26
	d		17 19		17 29				17 40			17 49		17 59		18 07					18 19	
Belmont	d															18 10						
Banstead	d															18 14						
Epsom Downs	a															18 17						
Cheam	d		17 22		17 31				17 42			17 52		18 01							18 22	
Ewell East	d		17 25						17 46			17 55		18 05							18 25	
Epsom	a	17 27	17 29		17 37		17 46		17 52		17 57	17 59		18 09					18 16	18 27	18 29	
	d	17 28			17 37		17 47				17 58			18 09					18 17	18 28		
Ashtead	d	17 32			17 41		17 51				18 02			18 13					18 21	18 32		
Leatherhead	d	17 35			17 44		17 54				18 05			18 16					18 24	18 35		
Bookham	d						17 59												18 29			
Effingham Junction	d						18 03												18 33			
Guildford	a						18 20												18 50			
Box Hill & Westhumble	d													18 21								
Dorking	a	17 41			17 50						18 11			18 24						18 41		
	d													18 24								
Holmwood	d													18 32								
Ockley	d													18 36								
Warnham	d													18 41								
Horsham	a													18 45								

London - Sutton, Epsom, Guildford, Dorking and Horsham

Network Diagram - see first Page of Table 177

Station		SN	FC	SW	FC	SN	SN	SW	SN	SN	SN	FC	SN	FC	SN	SW	SW	SN	SN	SN	FC	SW	FC
London Victoria ⊖	d	18 01				17 53	18 03		18 17	18 06	18 31		18 23		18 33			18 47	18 36	19 01			
London Waterloo ⊖	d			18 09				18 24								18 39	18 54					19 09	
Clapham Junction	d	18 08		18 18		18 00	18 11	18 33	18 24	18 14	18 38		18 30		18 41	18 48	19 03	18 54	18 44	19 08		19 18	
Balham ⊖	d					18 05	18 16		18 30	18 20			18 35		18 46			19 00	18 50				
London Bridge ⊖	d																						
Tulse Hill	d		18 01		18 16							18 31		18 46							19 01		19 16
New Cross Gate ⊖	d																						
Norwood Junction	d									18 39									19 09				
West Croydon	d					18 24	18 34			18 44			18 54		19 04				19 14				
Waddon	d					18 26	18 36			18 46			18 56		19 06				19 16				
Wallington	d					18 30	18 40			18 50			19 00		19 10				19 20				
Carshalton Beeches	d					18 32	18 42			18 52			19 02		19 12				19 22				
Mitcham Eastfields	d				18 24				18 36					18 54				19 06					19 24
Mitcham Junction	d				18 27				18 39					18 57				19 09					19 27
Hackbridge	d				18 30				18 43					19 00				19 13					19 30
Carshalton	d				18 33				18 45					19 03				19 15					19 33
Sutton (Surrey)	a	18 28	18 35		18 36	18 39	18 46		18 49	18 56	18 58	19 05	19 06	19 06	19 16			19 19	19 26	19 28	19 35		19 36
	d	18 29				18 40			18 49		18 59		19 07					19 19		19 29			
Belmont	d												19 10										
Banstead	d												19 14										
Epsom Downs	a												19 17										
Cheam	d	18 31				18 42			18 52		19 01							19 22		19 31			
Ewell East	d					18 46			18 55		19 05							19 25					
Epsom	a	18 37		18 46		18 52		18 57	18 59		19 09					19 16	19 27	19 29		19 37		19 46	
	d	18 37		18 47				18 58			19 09					19 17	19 28			19 37		19 47	
Ashtead	d	18 41		18 51				19 02			19 13					19 21	19 32			19 41		19 51	
Leatherhead	d	18 44		18 54				19 05			19 16					19 24	19 35			19 44		19 54	
Bookham	d			18 59												19 29						19 59	
Effingham Junction	d			19 03												19 33						20 03	
Guildford	a			19 20												19 50						20 20	
Box Hill & Westhumble	d	18 49																		19 49			
Dorking	a	18 52						19 11			19 22						19 41			19 52			
	d																						
Holmwood	d																						
Ockley	d																						
Warnham	d																						
Horsham	a																						

Station		SN	SN	SW	SN	SN	SN	FC	SN	FC	SN	SW	SW	SN	SN	SN	FC	SW	FC	SN	SN	SW	SN
London Victoria ⊖	d	18 53	19 03		19 17	19 06	19 31		19 23		19 33			19 47	19 36	20 01				19 53	20 03		20 17
London Waterloo ⊖	d			19 24								19 39	19 54					20 09				20 24	
Clapham Junction	d	19 00	19 11	19 33	19 24	19 14	19 38		19 30		19 41	19 48	20 03	19 54	19 44	20 08		20 18		20 00	20 11	20 33	20 24
Balham ⊖	d	19 05	19 16		19 30	19 20			19 35		19 46			20 00	19 50					20 05	20 16		20 30
London Bridge ⊖	d																						
Tulse Hill	d							19 31		19 46							20 01		20 16				
New Cross Gate ⊖	d																						
Norwood Junction	d					19 39									20 09								
West Croydon	d	19 24	19 34			19 44			19 54		20 04				20 15					20 25	20 34		
Waddon	d	19 26	19 36			19 46			19 56		20 06				20 17					20 27	20 36		
Wallington	d	19 30	19 40			19 50			20 00		20 10				20 21					20 31	20 40		
Carshalton Beeches	d	19 32	19 42			19 52			20 02		20 12				20 23					20 33	20 42		
Mitcham Eastfields	d				19 36					19 54				20 06					20 24				20 36
Mitcham Junction	d				19 39					19 57				20 09					20 27				20 39
Hackbridge	d				19 43					20 00				20 13					20 30				20 43
Carshalton	d				19 45					20 03				20 15					20 33				20 45
Sutton (Surrey)	a	19 39	19 46		19 49	19 56	19 58	20 05	20 06	20 06	20 16			20 19	20 27	20 28	20 35		20 36	20 39	20 46		20 49
	d	19 40			19 49		19 59		20 07					20 19		20 29				20 40			20 49
Belmont	d								20 10														
Banstead	d								20 14														
Epsom Downs	a								20 17														
Cheam	d	19 42			19 52		20 01							20 22		20 31				20 42			20 52
Ewell East	d	19 46			19 55		20 05							20 25						20 46			20 55
Epsom	a	19 52		19 57	19 59		20 09					20 16	20 27	20 29		20 37		20 46		20 52		20 57	20 59
	d			19 58			20 09					20 17				20 37		20 47					
Ashtead	d			20 02			20 13					20 21				20 41		20 51					
Leatherhead	d			20 05			20 16					20 24				20 44		20 54					
Bookham	d											20 29											
Effingham Junction	d											20 33											
Guildford	a											20 50											
Box Hill & Westhumble	d															20 49							
Dorking	a			20 11			20 22									20 52		21 00					
	d																						
Holmwood	d																						
Ockley	d																						
Warnham	d																						
Horsham	a																						

Table 182

Saturdays until 6 October

London - Sutton, Epsom, Guildford, Dorking and Horsham

Network Diagram - see first Page of Table 177

Station		SN		SN	FC	FC	SN	SN	SW	SW	SN	SN		SN	FC	SW	SN	FC	SN	SW	SN	SN		SN	FC
London Victoria ⊖	d	20 06		20 31			20 23	20 33			20 47	20 36		21 01			20 53		21 03		21 17	21 06		21 31	
London Waterloo ⊖	d								20 39	20 54						21 09				21 24					
Clapham Junction	d	20 14		20 38			20 30	20 41	20 48	21 03	20 54	20 44		21 08		21 18	21 00		21 11	21 33	21 24	21 14		21 38	
Balham ⊖	d	20 20					20 35	20 46			21 00	20 50					21 05		21 16		21 30	21 20			
London Bridge ⊖	d																								
Tulse Hill	d				20 31	20 46									21 01			21 16							21 31
New Cross Gate ⊖	d																								
Norwood Junction	d	20 39										21 09										21 39			
West Croydon	d	20 45					20 55	21 04				21 15					21 25		21 34			21 45			
Waddon	d	20 47					20 57	21 06				21 17					21 27		21 36			21 47			
Wallington	d	20 51					21 01	21 10				21 21					21 31		21 40			21 51			
Carshalton Beeches	d	20 53					21 03	21 12				21 23					21 33		21 42			21 53			
Mitcham Eastfields	d					20 54					21 06							21 24			21 36				
Mitcham Junction	d					20 57					21 09							21 27			21 39				
Hackbridge	d					21 00					21 13							21 30			21 43				
Carshalton	d					21 03					21 15							21 33			21 45				
Sutton (Surrey)	a	20 57		20 58	21 05	21 06	21 07	21 16			21 19	21 27		21 28	21 35		21 39	21 42	21 46		21 49	21 57		21 58	22 05
	d			20 59			21 08				21 19			21 29			21 40				21 49			21 59	
Belmont	d						21 11																		
Banstead	d						21 15																		
Epsom Downs	a						21 18																		
Cheam	d			21 01							21 22			21 31			21 42				21 52			22 01	
Ewell East	d			21 05							21 25						21 46				21 55			22 05	
Epsom	a			21 09					21 16	21 27	21 29			21 37		21 46	21 52			21 57	21 59			22 09	
	d			21 09					21 17					21 37		21 47								22 09	
Ashtead	d			21 13					21 21					21 41		21 51								22 13	
Leatherhead	d			21 16					21 24					21 44		21 54								22 16	
Bookham	d								21 29																
Effingham Junction	d								21 33																
Guildford	a								21 50																
Box Hill & Westhumble	d													21 49											
Dorking	a			21 22										21 52		22 00								22 22	
	d																								
Holmwood	d																								
Ockley	d																								
Warnham	d																								
Horsham	a																								

Station		SN	SN	SW	SW	SN	SN	SN		FC	SW	SN	SN	SN	SN	SN	FC	SN		SN	SW	SN	SN	SN	FC
London Victoria ⊖	d	21 23	21 33			21 47	21 36	22 01				21 53	22 03	22 17	22 06	22 31		22 23		22 33		22 47	22 36	23 01	
London Waterloo ⊖	d			21 39	21 54						22 09										22 39				
Clapham Junction	d	21 30	21 41	21 48	22 03	21 54	21 44	22 08			22 18	22 00	22 11	22 24	22 14	22 38		22 30		22 41	22 48	22 54	22 44	23 08	
Balham ⊖	d	21 35	21 46			22 00	21 50					22 05	22 16	22 30	22 20			22 35		22 46		23 00	22 50		
London Bridge ⊖	d																								
Tulse Hill	d									22 01							22 31								23 01
New Cross Gate ⊖	d																								
Norwood Junction	d						22 09								22 39								23 09		
West Croydon	d	21 55	22 04				22 14					22 24	22 34		22 44			22 54		23 04			23 14		
Waddon	d	21 57	22 06				22 16					22 26	22 36		22 46			22 56		23 06			23 16		
Wallington	d	22 01	22 10				22 20					22 30	22 40		22 50			23 00		23 10			23 20		
Carshalton Beeches	d	22 03	22 12				22 22					22 32	22 42		22 52			23 02		23 12			23 22		
Mitcham Eastfields	d					22 06								22 36								23 06			
Mitcham Junction	d					22 09								22 39								23 09			
Hackbridge	d					22 13								22 43								23 13			
Carshalton	d					22 15								22 45								23 15			
Sutton (Surrey)	a	22 07	22 16			22 19	22 26	22 28		22 35		22 39	22 46	22 49	22 56	22 58	23 05	23 06		23 16		23 19	23 26	23 28	23 35
	d	22 08				22 19		22 29				22 40		22 49		22 59		23 07				23 19	23 33	23 29	
Belmont	d	22 11																23 10					23 36		
Banstead	d	22 15																23 14					23 40		
Epsom Downs	a	22 18																23 17					23 43		
Cheam	d					22 22		22 31				22 42		22 52		23 01						23 22		23 31	
Ewell East	d					22 25						22 46		22 55		23 05						23 25			
Epsom	a			22 16	22 27	22 29		22 37			22 46	22 52		22 59		23 09					23 12	23 29		23 37	
	d			22 17				22 37			22 47					23 09					23 17			23 37	
Ashtead	d			22 21				22 41			22 51					23 13					23 21			23 41	
Leatherhead	d			22 24				22 44			22 54					23 16					23 24			23 44	
Bookham	d			22 29																	23 29				
Effingham Junction	d			22 33																	23 33				
Guildford	a			22 50																	23 50				
Box Hill & Westhumble	d							22 49								23 21									
Dorking	a							22 52			23 00					23 24								23 50	
	d																								
Holmwood	d																								
Ockley	d																								
Warnham	d																								
Horsham	a																								

Table 182

Saturdays until 6 October

London - Sutton, Epsom, Guildford, Dorking and Horsham

Network Diagram - see first Page of Table 177

Station		SW	SN	SN		SN	SN	FC	SN	SW	SN
London Victoria ⊖	d		22 53	23 03		23 06	23 26		23 34		23 59
London Waterloo ⊖	d	23 09								23 42	
Clapham Junction	d	23 18	23 00	23 11		23 14	23 32		23 42	23 51	00 07
Balham ⊖	d		23 05	23 16		23 20	23 37		23 47		00 12
London Bridge ⊖	d										
Tulse Hill	d							23 31			
New Cross Gate ⊖	d										
Norwood Junction	d					23 39					
West Croydon	d		23 24	23 34		23 44			00 04		00 31
Waddon	d		23 26	23 36		23 46			00 06		00 33
Wallington	d		23 30	23 40		23 50			00 10		00 37
Carshalton Beeches	d		23 32	23 42		23 52			00 12		00 39
Mitcham Eastfields	d						23 43				
Mitcham Junction	d						23 46				
Hackbridge	d						23 50				
Carshalton	d						23 52				
Sutton (Surrey)	a		23 39	23 46		23 56	23 59	00 05	00 16		00 43
	d		23 40				00 01				
Belmont	d										
Banstead	d										
Epsom Downs	a										
Cheam	d		23 42				00 03				
Ewell East	d		23 46				00 07				
Epsom	a	23 42	23 52				00 11			00 15	
	d	23 47					00 11			00 19	
Ashtead	d	23 51					00 15			00 23	
Leatherhead	d	23 54					00 18			00 26	
Bookham	d									00 31	
Effingham Junction	d									00 36	
Guildford	a									00 53	
Box Hill & Westhumble	d						00 23				
Dorking	a	00 01					00 26				
	d										
Holmwood	d										
Ockley	d										
Warnham	d										
Horsham	a										

Saturdays from 13 October

Station		SN	FC	SN	SW	FC	SN	SW	SN	SN		FC	SN	FC	SN	SW	FC	SN	SN	FC		SW	FC	SN	SW
London Victoria ⊖	d	23p26		23p34			23p59		00 20	00 34					06 23			06 47						06 53	
London Waterloo ⊖	d				23p42			00 15								06 39						07 09			07 24
Clapham Junction	d	23p34		23p42	23p51		00 07	00 25	00 27	00 42					06 30	06 48		06 54				07 18		07 00	07 33
Balham ⊖	d	23p40		23p47			00 12		00 32	00 47					06 35			07 00						07 05	
London Bridge ⊖	d																								
Tulse Hill	d		23p31			00 01						06 16		06 31			06 46			07 01			07 16		
New Cross Gate ⊖	d																								
Norwood Junction	d																		07 09						
West Croydon	d			00 04			00 31			01 04			06 45		06 54				07 15					07 24	
Waddon	d			00 06			00 33			01 07			06 47		06 56				07 17					07 26	
Wallington	d			00 10			00 37			01 10			06 51		07 00				07 21					07 30	
Carshalton Beeches	d			00 12			00 39			01 13			06 53		07 02				07 23					07 32	
Mitcham Eastfields	d	23p46							00 38			06 24					06 54	07 06					07 24		
Mitcham Junction	d	23p49							00 41			06 27					06 57	07 09					07 27		
Hackbridge	d	23p53							00 45			06 30					07 00	07 13					07 30		
Carshalton	d	23p55							00 47			06 33					07 03	07 15					07 33		
Sutton (Surrey)	a	23p59	00 09	00 16		00 39	00 43		00 51	01 16		06 36	06 57	07 05	07 06		07 06	07 19	07 27	07 35			07 36	07 39	
	d	00 01											06 57		07 07			07 19						07 40	
Belmont	d														07 10										
Banstead	d														07 14										
Epsom Downs	a														07 17										
Cheam	d	00 03											07 00					07 22						07 42	
Ewell East	d	00 07											07 03					07 25						07 46	
Epsom	a	00 11			00 15			00 50					07 07			07 16		07 29				07 46		07 52	07 57
	d	00 11			00 19								07 08			07 17		07 30				07 47			07 58
Ashtead	d	00 15			00 23								07 12			07 21		07 34				07 51			08 02
Leatherhead	d	00 18			00 26								07 15			07 24		07 37				07 54			08 05
Bookham	d				00 31											07 29						07 59			
Effingham Junction	d				00 36											07 33						08 03			
Guildford	a				00 56											07 53						08 23			
Box Hill & Westhumble	d	00 23																07 42							
Dorking	a	00 26											07 21					07 44							08 13
	d	00 26																							
Holmwood	d	00s33																							
Ockley	d	00s37																							
Warnham	d	00s43																							
Horsham	a	00 47																							

Table 182

Saturdays
from 13 October

London - Sutton, Epsom, Guildford, Dorking and Horsham

Network Diagram - see first Page of Table 177

		SN	SN	SN	FC	SN		FC	SN	SW	SW	SN	SN	SN	FC	SW		FC	SN	SN	SW	SN	SN	SN	FC
London Victoria	⊖ d	07 17	07 06	07 31		07 23			07 33			07 47	07 36	08 01					07 53	08 03		08 17	08 06	08 31	
London Waterloo	⊖ d									07 39	07 54					08 09					08 24				
Clapham Junction	d	07 24	07 14	07 38		07 30			07 41	07 48	08 03	07 54	07 44	08 08		08 18			08 00	08 11	08 33	08 24	08 14	08 38	
Balham	⊖ d	07 30	07 20			07 35			07 46			08 00	07 50						08 05	08 16		08 30	08 20		
London Bridge	⊖ d																								
Tulse Hill	d				07 31			07 46							08 01			08 16							08 31
New Cross Gate	⊖ d																								
Norwood Junction	d		07 39										08 09										08 39		
West Croydon	d		07 44			07 54			08 04				08 14						08 24	08 34			08 44		
Waddon	d		07 46			07 56			08 06				08 16						08 26	08 36			08 46		
Wallington	d		07 50			08 00			08 10				08 20						08 30	08 40			08 50		
Carshalton Beeches	d		07 52			08 02			08 12				08 22						08 32	08 42			08 52		
Mitcham Eastfields	d	07 36						07 54				08 06						08 24				08 36			
Mitcham Junction	d	07 39						07 57				08 09						08 27				08 39			
Hackbridge	d	07 43						08 00				08 13						08 30				08 43			
Carshalton	d	07 45						08 03				08 15						08 33				08 45			
Sutton (Surrey)	a	07 49	07 56	07 58	08 05	08 06		08 06	08 16			08 19	08 26	08 28	08 35			08 36	08 39	08 46		08 49	08 56	08 58	09 05
	d	07 49		07 59		08 07						08 19		08 29					08 40			08 49		08 59	
Belmont	d					08 10																			
Banstead	d					08 14																			
Epsom Downs	a					08 17																			
Cheam	d	07 52		08 01								08 22		08 31					08 42			08 52		09 01	
Ewell East	d	07 55		08 05								08 25							08 46			08 55		09 05	
Epsom	a	07 59		08 09						08 16	08 27	08 29		08 37		08 46			08 52		08 57	08 59		09 09	
	d			08 09						08 17	08 28			08 37		08 47					08 58			09 09	
Ashtead	d			08 13						08 21	08 32			08 41		08 51					09 02			09 13	
Leatherhead	d			08 16						08 24	08 35			08 44		08 54					09 05			09 16	
Bookham	d									08 29						08 59									
Effingham Junction	d									08 33						09 03									
Guildford	a									08 53						09 23									
Box Hill & Westhumble	d			08 21																				09 21	
Dorking	a			08 24							08 43			08 50							09 13			09 24	
	d			08 24																				09 24	
Holmwood	d			08 32																				09 32	
Ockley	d			08 36																				09 36	
Warnham	d			08 41																				09 41	
Horsham	a			08 45																				09 45	

		SN		FC	SN	SW	SW	SN	SN	SN	FC	SW		FC	SN	SN	SW	SN	SN	SN	FC	SN		FC	SN
London Victoria	⊖ d	08 23			08 33			08 47	08 36	09 01					08 53	09 03		09 17	09 06	09 31		09 23			09 33
London Waterloo	⊖ d					08 39	08 54					09 09					09 24								
Clapham Junction	d	08 30			08 41	08 48	09 03	08 54	08 44	09 08		09 18			09 00	09 11	09 33	09 24	09 14	09 38		09 30			09 41
Balham	⊖ d	08 35			08 46			09 00	08 50						09 05	09 16		09 30	09 20			09 35			09 46
London Bridge	⊖ d																								
Tulse Hill	d			08 46							09 01			09 16							09 31			09 46	
New Cross Gate	⊖ d																								
Norwood Junction	d								09 09										09 39						
West Croydon	d	08 54			09 04				09 14						09 24	09 34			09 44			09 54			10 04
Waddon	d	08 56			09 06				09 16						09 26	09 36			09 46			09 56			10 06
Wallington	d	09 00			09 10				09 20						09 30	09 40			09 50			10 00			10 10
Carshalton Beeches	d	09 02			09 12				09 22						09 32	09 42			09 52			10 02			10 12
Mitcham Eastfields	d			08 54				09 06						09 24				09 36						09 54	
Mitcham Junction	d			08 57				09 09						09 27				09 39						09 57	
Hackbridge	d			09 00				09 13						09 30				09 43						10 00	
Carshalton	d			09 03				09 15						09 33				09 45						10 03	
Sutton (Surrey)	a	09 06		09 06	09 16			09 19	09 26	09 28	09 35			09 36	09 39	09 46		09 49	09 56	09 58	10 05	10 06		10 06	10 16
	d	09 07						09 19		09 29					09 40			09 49		09 59		10 07			
Belmont	d	09 10																				10 10			
Banstead	d	09 14																				10 14			
Epsom Downs	a	09 17																				10 17			
Cheam	d							09 22		09 31					09 42			09 52		10 01					
Ewell East	d							09 25							09 46			09 55		10 05					
Epsom	a					09 16	09 27	09 29		09 37		09 46			09 52		09 57	09 59		10 09					
	d					09 17	09 28			09 37		09 47					09 58			10 09					
Ashtead	d					09 21	09 32			09 41		09 51					10 02			10 13					
Leatherhead	d					09 24	09 35			09 44		09 54					10 05			10 16					
Bookham	d					09 29						09 59													
Effingham Junction	d					09 33						10 03													
Guildford	a					09 53						10 23													
Box Hill & Westhumble	d																			10 21					
Dorking	a						09 43			09 50							10 13			10 24					
	d																			10 24					
Holmwood	d																			10 32					
Ockley	d																			10 36					
Warnham	d																			10 41					
Horsham	a																			10 45					

Table 182

Saturdays
from 13 October

London - Sutton, Epsom, Guildford, Dorking and Horsham

Network Diagram - see first Page of Table 177

		SW	SW	SN	SN	SN	FC	SW		FC	SN	SN	SW	SN	SN	SN	FC	SN		FC	SN	SW	SW	SN	SN
London Victoria	⊖ d			09 47	09 36	10 01					09 53	10 03		10 17	10 06	10 31		10 23			10 33			10 47	10 36
London Waterloo	⊖ d	09 39	09 54					10 09					10 24									10 39	10 54		
Clapham Junction	d	09 48	10 03	09 54	09 44	10 08		10 18			10 00	10 11	10 33	10 24	10 14	10 38		10 30			10 41	10 48	11 03	10 54	10 44
Balham	⊖ d			10 00	09 50						10 05	10 16		10 30	10 20			10 35			10 46			11 00	10 50
London Bridge	⊖ d																								
Tulse Hill	d						10 01			10 16							10 31			10 46					
New Cross Gate	⊖ d																								
Norwood Junction	d				10 09										10 39										11 09
West Croydon	d				10 14						10 24	10 34			10 44			10 54			11 04				11 14
Waddon	d				10 16						10 26	10 36			10 46			10 56			11 06				11 16
Wallington	d				10 20						10 30	10 40			10 50			11 00			11 10				11 20
Carshalton Beeches	d				10 22						10 32	10 42			10 52			11 02			11 12				11 22
Mitcham Eastfields	d			10 06						10 24				10 36						10 54				11 06	
Mitcham Junction	d			10 09						10 27				10 39						10 57				11 09	
Hackbridge	d			10 13						10 30				10 43						11 00				11 13	
Carshalton	d			10 15						10 33				10 45						11 03				11 15	
Sutton (Surrey)	a			10 19	10 26	10 28	10 35			10 36	10 39	10 46		10 49	10 56	10 58	11 05	11 06		11 06	11 16			11 19	11 26
	d			10 19		10 29					10 40			10 49		10 59		11 07						11 19	
Belmont	d																	11 10							
Banstead	d																	11 14							
Epsom Downs	a																	11 17							
Cheam	d			10 22		10 31					10 42			10 52		11 01								11 22	
Ewell East	d			10 25							10 46			10 55		11 05								11 25	
Epsom	a	10 16	10 27	10 29		10 37		10 46			10 52		10 57	10 59		11 09						11 16	11 27	11 29	
	d	10 17	10 28			10 37		10 47					10 58			11 09						11 17	11 28		
Ashtead	d	10 21	10 32			10 41		10 51					11 02			11 13						11 21	11 32		
Leatherhead	d	10 24	10 35			10 44		10 54					11 05			11 16						11 24	11 35		
Bookham	d	10 29						10 59														11 29			
Effingham Junction	d	10 33						11 03														11 33			
Guildford	a	10 53						11 23														11 53			
Box Hill & Westhumble	d															11 21									
Dorking	a		10 43			10 50							11 13			11 24							11 43		
	d															11 24									
Holmwood	d															11 32									
Ockley	d															11 36									
Warnham	d															11 41									
Horsham	a															11 45									

		SN	FC	SW		FC	SN	SN	SW	SN	SN	SN	FC	SN		FC	SN	SW	SW	SN	SN	SN	FC	SW	
London Victoria	⊖ d	11 01					10 53	11 03		11 17	11 06	11 31		11 23			11 33			11 47	11 36	12 01			
London Waterloo	⊖ d			11 09					11 24									11 39	11 54					12 09	
Clapham Junction	d	11 08		11 18			11 00	11 11	11 33	11 24	11 14	11 38		11 30			11 41	11 48	12 03	11 54	11 44	12 08		12 18	
Balham	⊖ d						11 05	11 16		11 30	11 20			11 35			11 46			12 00	11 50				
London Bridge	⊖ d																								
Tulse Hill	d		11 01			11 16							11 31			11 46							12 01		
New Cross Gate	⊖ d																								
Norwood Junction	d										11 39										12 09				
West Croydon	d						11 24	11 34			11 44			11 54			12 04				12 14				
Waddon	d						11 26	11 36			11 46			11 56			12 06				12 16				
Wallington	d						11 30	11 40			11 50			12 00			12 10				12 20				
Carshalton Beeches	d						11 32	11 42			11 52			12 02			12 12				12 22				
Mitcham Eastfields	d					11 24				11 36						11 54				12 06					
Mitcham Junction	d					11 27				11 39						11 57				12 09					
Hackbridge	d					11 30				11 43						12 00				12 13					
Carshalton	d					11 33				11 45						12 03				12 15					
Sutton (Surrey)	a	11 28	11 35			11 36	11 39	11 46		11 49	11 56	11 58	12 05	12 06		12 06	12 16			12 19	12 26	12 28	12 35		
	d	11 29					11 40			11 49		11 59		12 07						12 19		12 29			
Belmont	d													12 10											
Banstead	d													12 14											
Epsom Downs	a													12 17											
Cheam	d	11 31					11 42			11 52		12 01								12 22		12 31			
Ewell East	d						11 46			11 55		12 05								12 25					
Epsom	a	11 37		11 46			11 52		11 57	11 59		12 09						12 16	12 27	12 29		12 37		12 46	
	d	11 37		11 47					11 58			12 09						12 17	12 28			12 37		12 47	
Ashtead	d	11 41		11 51					12 02			12 13						12 21	12 32			12 41		12 51	
Leatherhead	d	11 44		11 54					12 05			12 16						12 24	12 35			12 44		12 54	
Bookham	d			11 59														12 29						12 59	
Effingham Junction	d			12 03														12 33						13 03	
Guildford	a			12 23														12 53						13 23	
Box Hill & Westhumble	d											12 21													
Dorking	a	11 50							12 13			12 24							12 43			12 50			
	d											12 24													
Holmwood	d											12 32													
Ockley	d											12 36													
Warnham	d											12 41													
Horsham	a											12 45													

Table 182

London - Sutton, Epsom, Guildford, Dorking and Horsham

Saturdays from 13 October

Network Diagram - see first Page of Table 177

Station		FC	SN	SN	SW	SN	SN	SN	FC	SN	FC	SN	SW	SW	SN	SN	SN	FC	SW	FC	SN	SN	SW
London Victoria 15 ⊖	d		11 53	12 03		12 17	12 06	12 31		12 23		12 33			12 47	12 36	13 01				12 53	13 03	
London Waterloo 15 ⊖	d				12 24								12 39	12 54					13 09				13 24
Clapham Junction 10	d		12 00	12 11	12 33	12 24	12 14	12 38		12 30		12 41	12 48	13 03	12 54	12 44	13 08		13 18		13 00	13 11	13 33
Balham 4 ⊖	d		12 05	12 16		12 30	12 20			12 35		12 46			13 00	12 50					13 05	13 16	
London Bridge 4 ⊖	d																						
Tulse Hill 3	d	12 16							12 31		12 46							13 01		13 16			
New Cross Gate 4 ⊖	d																						
Norwood Junction 2	d						12 39									13 09							
West Croydon 4	d		12 24	12 34			12 44			12 54		13 04				13 14					13 24	13 34	
Waddon	d		12 26	12 36			12 46			12 56		13 06				13 16					13 26	13 36	
Wallington	d		12 30	12 40			12 50			13 00		13 10				13 20					13 30	13 40	
Carshalton Beeches	d		12 32	12 42			12 52			13 02		13 12				13 22					13 32	13 42	
Mitcham Eastfields	d	12 24				12 36					12 54				13 06					13 24			
Mitcham Junction	d	12 27				12 39					12 57				13 09					13 27			
Hackbridge	d	12 30				12 43					13 00				13 13					13 30			
Carshalton	d	12 33				12 45					13 03				13 15					13 33			
Sutton (Surrey) 4	a	12 36	12 39	12 46		12 49	12 56	12 58	13 05	13 06	13 06	13 16			13 19	13 26	13 28	13 35		13 36	13 39	13 46	
	d		12 40			12 49		12 59		13 07					13 19		13 29				13 40		
Belmont	d									13 10													
Banstead	d									13 14													
Epsom Downs	a									13 17													
Cheam	d		12 42			12 52		13 01							13 22		13 31				13 42		
Ewell East	d		12 46			12 55		13 05							13 25						13 46		
Epsom 3	a		12 52		12 57	12 59		13 09					13 16	13 27	13 29		13 37		13 46		13 52		13 57
	d				12 58			13 09					13 17	13 28			13 37		13 47				13 58
Ashtead	d				13 02			13 13					13 21	13 32			13 41		13 51				14 02
Leatherhead	d				13 05			13 16					13 24	13 35			13 44		13 54				14 05
Bookham	d												13 29						13 59				
Effingham Junction 6	d												13 33						14 03				
Guildford	a												13 53						14 23				
Box Hill & Westhumble	d							13 21															
Dorking 4	a				13 13			13 24						13 43			13 50						14 13
	d							13 24															
Holmwood	d							13 32															
Ockley	d							13 36															
Warnham	d							13 41															
Horsham 4	a							13 45															

Station		SN	SN	SN	FC	SN	FC	SN	SW	SW	SN	SN	SN	FC	SW	FC	SN	SN	SW	SN	SN	SN	FC
London Victoria 15 ⊖	d	13 17	13 06	13 31		13 23		13 33			13 47	13 36	14 01				13 53	14 03		14 17	14 06	14 31	
London Waterloo 15 ⊖	d								13 39	13 54					14 09				14 24				
Clapham Junction 10	d	13 24	13 14	13 38		13 30		13 41	13 48	14 03	13 54	13 44	14 08		14 18		14 00	14 11	14 33	14 24	14 14	14 38	
Balham 4 ⊖	d	13 30	13 20			13 35		13 46			14 00	13 50					14 05	14 16		14 30	14 20		
London Bridge 4 ⊖	d																						
Tulse Hill 3	d				13 31		13 46							14 01		14 16							14 31
New Cross Gate 4 ⊖	d																						
Norwood Junction 2	d		13 39									14 09									14 39		
West Croydon 4	d		13 44			13 54		14 04				14 14					14 24	14 34			14 44		
Waddon	d		13 46			13 56		14 06				14 16					14 26	14 36			14 46		
Wallington	d		13 50			14 00		14 10				14 20					14 30	14 40			14 50		
Carshalton Beeches	d		13 52			14 02		14 12				14 22					14 32	14 42			14 52		
Mitcham Eastfields	d	13 36					13 54				14 06					14 24				14 36			
Mitcham Junction	d	13 39					13 57				14 09					14 27				14 39			
Hackbridge	d	13 43					14 00				14 13					14 30				14 43			
Carshalton	d	13 45					14 03				14 15					14 33				14 45			
Sutton (Surrey) 4	a	13 49	13 56	13 58	14 05	14 06	14 06	14 16			14 19	14 26	14 28	14 35		14 36	14 39	14 46		14 49	14 56	14 58	15 05
	d	13 49		13 59		14 07					14 19		14 29				14 40			14 49		14 59	
Belmont	d					14 10																	
Banstead	d					14 14																	
Epsom Downs	a					14 17																	
Cheam	d	13 52		14 01							14 22		14 31				14 42			14 52		15 01	
Ewell East	d	13 55		14 05							14 25						14 46			14 55		15 05	
Epsom 3	a	13 59		14 09					14 16	14 27	14 29		14 37		14 46		14 52		14 57	14 59		15 09	
	d			14 09					14 17	14 28			14 37		14 47				14 58			15 09	
Ashtead	d			14 13					14 21	14 32			14 41		14 51				15 02			15 13	
Leatherhead	d			14 16					14 24	14 35			14 44		14 54				15 05			15 16	
Bookham	d								14 29						14 59								
Effingham Junction 6	d								14 33						15 03								
Guildford	a								14 53						15 23								
Box Hill & Westhumble	d			14 21																		15 21	
Dorking 4	a			14 24						14 43			14 50						15 13			15 24	
	d			14 24																		15 24	
Holmwood	d			14 32																		15 32	
Ockley	d			14 36																		15 36	
Warnham	d			14 41																		15 41	
Horsham 4	a			14 45																		15 45	

Table 182

London - Sutton, Epsom, Guildford, Dorking and Horsham

Saturdays from 13 October

Network Diagram - see first Page of Table 177

Station		SN	FC	SN	SW	SW	SN	SN	SN	FC	SW	FC	SN	SN	SW	SN	SN	SN	FC	SN	FC	SN
London Victoria 15 ⊖	d	14 23		14 33			14 47	14 36	15 01				14 53	15 03		15 17	15 06	15 31		15 23		15 33
London Waterloo 15 ⊖	d				14 39	14 54					15 09				15 24							
Clapham Junction 10	d	14 30		14 41	14 48	15 03	14 54	14 44	15 08		15 18		15 00	15 11	15 33	15 24	15 14	15 38		15 30		15 41
Balham 4 ⊖	d	14 35		14 46			15 00	14 50					15 05	15 16		15 30	15 20			15 35		15 46
London Bridge 4 ⊖	d																					
Tulse Hill 3	d		14 46							15 01		15 16							15 31		15 46	
New Cross Gate 4 ⊖	d																					
Norwood Junction 2	d							15 09									15 39					
West Croydon 4	d	14 54		15 04				15 14					15 24	15 34			15 44			15 54		16 04
Waddon	d	14 56		15 06				15 16					15 26	15 36			15 46			15 56		16 06
Wallington	d	15 00		15 10				15 20					15 30	15 40			15 50			16 00		16 10
Carshalton Beeches	d	15 02		15 12				15 22					15 32	15 42			15 52			16 02		16 12
Mitcham Eastfields	d		14 54				15 06					15 24				15 36					15 54	
Mitcham Junction	d		14 57				15 09					15 27				15 39					15 57	
Hackbridge	d		15 00				15 13					15 30				15 43					16 00	
Carshalton	d		15 03				15 15					15 33				15 45					16 03	
Sutton (Surrey) 4	a	15 06	15 06	15 16			15 19	15 26	15 28	15 35		15 36	15 39	15 46		15 49	15 56	15 58	16 05	16 06	16 06	16 16
	d	15 07					15 19		15 29				15 40			15 49		15 59		16 07		
Belmont	d	15 10																		16 10		
Banstead	d	15 14																		16 14		
Epsom Downs	a	15 17																		16 17		
Cheam	d						15 22		15 31				15 42			15 52		16 01				
Ewell East	d						15 25						15 46			15 55		16 05				
Epsom 3	a				15 16	15 27	15 29		15 37		15 46		15 52		15 57	15 59		16 09				
	d				15 17	15 28			15 37		15 47				15 58			16 09				
Ashtead	d				15 21	15 32			15 41		15 51				16 02			16 13				
Leatherhead	d				15 24	15 35			15 44		15 54				16 05			16 16				
Bookham	d				15 29						15 59											
Effingham Junction 6	d				15 33						16 03											
Guildford	a				15 53						16 23											
Box Hill & Westhumble	d																	16 21				
Dorking 4	a					15 43			15 50						16 13			16 24				
	d																	16 24				
Holmwood	d																	16 32				
Ockley	d																	16 36				
Warnham	d																	16 41				
Horsham 4	a																	16 45				

Station		SW	SW	SN	SN	SN	FC	SW	FC	SN	SN	SW	SN	SN	SN	FC	SN	FC	SN	SW	SW	SN	SN
London Victoria 15 ⊖	d			15 47	15 36	16 01				15 53	16 03		16 17	16 06	16 31		16 23		16 33			16 47	16 36
London Waterloo 15 ⊖	d	15 39	15 54					16 09				16 24								16 39	16 54		
Clapham Junction 10	d	15 48	16 03	15 54	15 44	16 08		16 18		16 00	16 11	16 33	16 24	16 14	16 38		16 30		16 41	16 48	17 03	16 54	16 44
Balham 4 ⊖	d			16 00	15 50					16 05	16 16		16 30	16 20			16 35		16 46			17 00	16 50
London Bridge 4 ⊖	d																						
Tulse Hill 3	d						16 01		16 16							16 31		16 46					
New Cross Gate 4 ⊖	d																						
Norwood Junction 2	d				16 09									16 39									17 09
West Croydon 4	d				16 14					16 24	16 34			16 44			16 54		17 04				17 14
Waddon	d				16 16					16 26	16 36			16 46			16 56		17 06				17 16
Wallington	d				16 20					16 30	16 40			16 50			17 00		17 10				17 20
Carshalton Beeches	d				16 22					16 32	16 42			16 52			17 02		17 12				17 22
Mitcham Eastfields	d			16 06					16 24				16 36					16 54				17 06	
Mitcham Junction	d			16 09					16 27				16 39					16 57				17 09	
Hackbridge	d			16 13					16 30				16 43					17 00				17 13	
Carshalton	d			16 15					16 33				16 45					17 03				17 15	
Sutton (Surrey) 4	a			16 19	16 26	16 28	16 35		16 36	16 39	16 46		16 49	16 56	16 58	17 05	17 06	17 06	17 16			17 19	17 26
	d			16 19		16 29				16 40			16 49		16 59		17 07					17 19	
Belmont	d																17 10						
Banstead	d																17 14						
Epsom Downs	a																17 17						
Cheam	d			16 22		16 31				16 42			16 52		17 01							17 22	
Ewell East	d			16 25						16 46			16 55		17 05							17 25	
Epsom 3	a	16 16	16 27	16 29		16 37		16 46		16 52		16 57	16 59		17 09					17 16	17 27	17 29	
	d	16 17	16 28			16 37		16 47				16 58			17 09					17 17	17 28		
Ashtead	d	16 21	16 32			16 41		16 51				17 02			17 13					17 21	17 32		
Leatherhead	d	16 24	16 35			16 44		16 54				17 05			17 16					17 24	17 35		
Bookham	d	16 29						16 59												17 29			
Effingham Junction 6	d	16 33						17 03												17 33			
Guildford	a	16 53						17 23												17 53			
Box Hill & Westhumble	d														17 21								
Dorking 4	a		16 43			16 50						17 13			17 24						17 43		
	d														17 24								
Holmwood	d														17 32								
Ockley	d														17 36								
Warnham	d														17 41								
Horsham 4	a														17 45								

Table 182

London - Sutton, Epsom, Guildford, Dorking and Horsham

Saturdays from 13 October

Network Diagram - see first Page of Table 177

		SN	FC	SW	FC	SN	SN	SW	SN	SN	SN	FC	SN	FC	SN	SW	SW	SN	SN	SN	FC	SW
London Victoria ⊖	d	17 01				16 53	17 03		17 17	17 06	17 31		17 23		17 33			17 47	17 36	18 01		
London Waterloo ⊖	d			17 09				17 24								17 39	17 54					18 09
Clapham Junction	d	17 08		17 18		17 00	17 11	17 33	17 24	17 14	17 38		17 30		17 41	17 48	18 03	17 54	17 44	18 08		18 18
Balham ⊖	d					17 05	17 16		17 30	17 20			17 35		17 46			18 00	17 50			
London Bridge ⊖	d																					
Tulse Hill	d		17 01		17 16							17 31		17 46							18 01	
New Cross Gate ⊖	d																					
Norwood Junction	d									17 39									18 09			
West Croydon	d					17 24	17 34			17 44			17 54		18 04				18 14			
Waddon	d					17 26	17 36			17 46			17 56		18 06				18 16			
Wallington	d					17 30	17 40			17 50			18 00		18 10				18 20			
Carshalton Beeches	d					17 32	17 42			17 52			18 02		18 12				18 22			
Mitcham Eastfields	d				17 24				17 36					17 54				18 06				
Mitcham Junction	d				17 27				17 39					17 57				18 09				
Hackbridge	d				17 30				17 43					18 00				18 13				
Carshalton	d				17 33				17 45					18 03				18 15				
Sutton (Surrey)	a	17 28	17 35		17 36	17 39	17 46		17 49	17 56	17 58	18 05	18 06	18 06	18 16			18 19	18 26	18 28	18 35	
	d	17 29				17 40			17 49		17 59		18 07					18 19		18 29		
Belmont	d												18 10									
Banstead	d												18 14									
Epsom Downs	a												18 17									
Cheam	d	17 31				17 42			17 52		18 01							18 22		18 31		
Ewell East	d					17 46			17 55		18 05							18 25				
Epsom	a	17 37		17 46		17 52		17 57	17 59		18 09					18 16	18 27	18 29		18 37		18 46
	d	17 37		17 47				17 58			18 09					18 17	18 28			18 37		18 47
Ashtead	d	17 41		17 51				18 02			18 13					18 21	18 32			18 41		18 51
Leatherhead	d	17 44		17 54				18 05			18 16					18 24	18 35			18 44		18 54
Bookham	d			17 59												18 29						18 59
Effingham Junction	d			18 03												18 33						19 03
Guildford	a			18 23												18 53						19 23
Box Hill & Westhumble	d										18 21									18 49		
Dorking	a	17 50						18 13			18 24						18 43			18 52		
	d										18 24											
Holmwood	d										18 32											
Ockley	d										18 36											
Warnham	d										18 41											
Horsham	a										18 45											

		FC	SN	SN	SW	SN	SN	SN	FC	SN	FC	SN	SW	SW	SN	SN	SN	FC	SW	FC	SN	SN	SW
London Victoria ⊖	d		17 53	18 03		18 17	18 06	18 31		18 23		18 33			18 47	18 36	19 01				18 53	19 03	
London Waterloo ⊖	d				18 24								18 39	18 54					19 09				19 24
Clapham Junction	d		18 00	18 11	18 33	18 24	18 14	18 38		18 30		18 41	18 48	19 03	18 54	18 44	19 08		19 18		19 00	19 11	19 33
Balham ⊖	d		18 05	18 16		18 30	18 20			18 35		18 46			19 00	18 50					19 05	19 16	
London Bridge ⊖	d																						
Tulse Hill	d	18 16							18 31		18 46							19 01		19 16			
New Cross Gate ⊖	d																						
Norwood Junction	d						18 39									19 09							
West Croydon	d		18 24	18 34			18 44			18 54		19 04				19 14					19 24	19 34	
Waddon	d		18 26	18 36			18 46			18 56		19 06				19 16					19 26	19 36	
Wallington	d		18 30	18 40			18 50			19 00		19 10				19 20					19 30	19 40	
Carshalton Beeches	d		18 32	18 42			18 52			19 02		19 12				19 22					19 32	19 42	
Mitcham Eastfields	d	18 24				18 36					18 54				19 06					19 24			
Mitcham Junction	d	18 27				18 39					18 57				19 09					19 27			
Hackbridge	d	18 30				18 43					19 00				19 13					19 30			
Carshalton	d	18 33				18 45					19 03				19 15					19 33			
Sutton (Surrey)	a	18 36	18 39	18 46		18 49	18 56	18 58	19 05	19 06	19 06	19 16			19 19	19 26	19 28	19 35		19 36	19 39	19 46	
	d		18 40			18 49		18 59		19 07					19 19		19 29				19 40		
Belmont	d									19 10													
Banstead	d									19 14													
Epsom Downs	a									19 17													
Cheam	d		18 42			18 52		19 01							19 22		19 31				19 42		
Ewell East	d		18 46			18 55		19 05							19 25						19 46		
Epsom	a		18 52		18 57	18 59		19 09					19 16	19 27	19 29		19 37		19 46		19 52		19 57
	d				18 58			19 09					19 17	19 28			19 37		19 47				19 58
Ashtead	d				19 02			19 13					19 21	19 32			19 41		19 51				20 02
Leatherhead	d				19 05			19 16					19 24	19 35			19 44		19 54				20 05
Bookham	d												19 29						19 59				
Effingham Junction	d												19 33						20 03				
Guildford	a												19 53						20 23				
Box Hill & Westhumble	d																19 49						
Dorking	a				19 13			19 22						19 43			19 52						20 13
	d																						
Holmwood	d																						
Ockley	d																						
Warnham	d																						
Horsham	a																						

Table 182

London - Sutton, Epsom, Guildford, Dorking and Horsham

Saturdays from 13 October

Network Diagram - see first Page of Table 177

		SN	SN	SN	FC	SN	FC	SN	SW	SW	SN	SN	SN	FC	SW	FC	SN	SN	SW	SN	SN	SN	FC
London Victoria ⊖	d	19 17	19 06	19 31		19 23		19 33			19 47	19 36	20 01				19 53	20 03		20 17	20 06	20 31	
London Waterloo ⊖	d								19 39	19 54					20 09				20 24				
Clapham Junction	d	19 24	19 14	19 38		19 30		19 41	19 48	20 03	19 54	19 44	20 08		20 18		20 00	20 11	20 33	20 24	20 14	20 38	
Balham ⊖	d	19 30	19 20			19 35		19 46			20 00	19 50					20 05	20 16		20 30	20 20		
London Bridge ⊖	d																						
Tulse Hill	d				19 31		19 46							20 01		20 16							20 31
New Cross Gate ⊖	d																						
Norwood Junction	d		19 39									20 09									20 39		
West Croydon	d		19 44			19 54		20 04				20 15					20 25	20 34			20 45		
Waddon	d		19 46			19 56		20 06				20 17					20 27	20 36			20 47		
Wallington	d		19 50			20 00		20 10				20 21					20 31	20 40			20 51		
Carshalton Beeches	d		19 52			20 02		20 12				20 23					20 33	20 42			20 53		
Mitcham Eastfields	d	19 36					19 54				20 06					20 24				20 36			
Mitcham Junction	d	19 39					19 57				20 09					20 27				20 39			
Hackbridge	d	19 43					20 00				20 13					20 30				20 43			
Carshalton	d	19 45					20 03				20 15					20 33				20 45			
Sutton (Surrey)	a	19 49	19 56	19 58	20 05	20 06	20 06	20 16			20 19	20 27	20 28	20 35		20 36	20 39	20 46		20 49	20 57	20 58	21 05
	d	19 49		19 59		20 07					20 19		20 29				20 40			20 49		20 59	
Belmont	d					20 10																	
Banstead	d					20 14																	
Epsom Downs	a					20 17																	
Cheam	d	19 52		20 01							20 22		20 31				20 42			20 52		21 01	
Ewell East	d	19 55		20 05							20 25						20 46			20 55		21 05	
Epsom	a	19 59		20 09					20 16	20 27	20 29		20 37		20 46		20 52		20 57	20 59		21 09	
	d			20 09					20 17				20 37		20 47							21 09	
Ashtead	d			20 13					20 21				20 41		20 51							21 13	
Leatherhead	d			20 16					20 24				20 44		20 54							21 16	
Bookham	d								20 29														
Effingham Junction	d								20 33														
Guildford	a								20 53														
Box Hill & Westhumble	d												20 49										
Dorking	a			20 22									20 52		21 02							21 22	
	d																						
Holmwood	d																						
Ockley	d																						
Warnham	d																						
Horsham	a																						

		FC	SN	SN	SW	SW	SN	SN	SN	FC	SW	SN	FC	SN	SW	SN	SN	SN	FC	SN	SN	SW
London Victoria ⊖	d		20 23	20 33			20 47	20 36	21 01			20 53		21 03		21 17	21 06	21 31		21 23	21 33	
London Waterloo ⊖	d				20 39	20 54					21 09				21 24							21 39
Clapham Junction	d		20 30	20 41	20 48	21 03	20 54	20 44	21 08		21 18	21 00		21 11	21 33	21 24	21 14	21 38		21 30	21 41	21 48
Balham ⊖	d		20 35	20 46			21 00	20 50				21 05		21 16		21 30	21 20			21 35	21 46	
London Bridge ⊖	d																					
Tulse Hill	d	20 46								21 01			21 16						21 31			
New Cross Gate ⊖	d																					
Norwood Junction	d							21 09									21 39					
West Croydon	d		20 55	21 04				21 15				21 25		21 34			21 45			21 55	22 04	
Waddon	d		20 57	21 06				21 17				21 27		21 36			21 47			21 57	22 06	
Wallington	d		21 01	21 10				21 21				21 31		21 40			21 51			22 01	22 10	
Carshalton Beeches	d		21 03	21 12				21 23				21 33		21 42			21 53			22 03	22 12	
Mitcham Eastfields	d	20 54					21 06						21 24			21 36						
Mitcham Junction	d	20 57					21 09						21 27			21 39						
Hackbridge	d	21 00					21 13						21 30			21 43						
Carshalton	d	21 03					21 15						21 33			21 45						
Sutton (Surrey)	a	21 06	21 07	21 16			21 19	21 27	21 28	21 35		21 39	21 42	21 46		21 49	21 57	21 58	22 05	22 07	22 16	
	d		21 08				21 19		21 29			21 40				21 49		21 59		22 08		
Belmont	d		21 11																	22 11		
Banstead	d		21 15																	22 15		
Epsom Downs	a		21 18																	22 18		
Cheam	d						21 22		21 31			21 42				21 52		22 01				
Ewell East	d						21 25					21 46				21 55		22 05				
Epsom	a				21 16	21 27	21 29		21 37		21 46	21 52			21 57	21 59		22 09				22 16
	d				21 17				21 37		21 47							22 09				22 17
Ashtead	d				21 21				21 41		21 51							22 13				22 21
Leatherhead	d				21 24				21 44		21 54							22 16				22 24
Bookham	d				21 29																	22 29
Effingham Junction	d				21 33																	22 33
Guildford	a				21 53																	22 53
Box Hill & Westhumble	d								21 49													
Dorking	a								21 52		22 02							22 22				
	d																					
Holmwood	d																					
Ockley	d																					
Warnham	d																					
Horsham	a																					

Table 182

London - Sutton, Epsom, Guildford, Dorking and Horsham

Saturdays from 13 October

Network Diagram - see first Page of Table 177

		SW	SN	SN	SN	FC	SW	SN		SN	SN	SN	SN	FC	SN	SN	SW	SN		SN	SN	FC	SW	SN	SN
London Victoria ⊖	d		21 47	21 36	22 01			21 53		22 03	22 17	22 06	22 31		22 23	22 33		22 47		22 36	23 01			22 53	23 03
London Waterloo ⊖	d	21 54					22 09										22 39						23 09		
Clapham Junction	d	22 03	21 54	21 44	22 08		22 18	22 00		22 11	22 24	22 14	22 38		22 30	22 41	22 48	22 54		22 44	23 08		23 18	23 00	23 11
Balham ⊖	d		22 00	21 50				22 05		22 16	22 30	22 20			22 35	22 46		23 00		22 50				23 05	23 16
London Bridge ⊖	d																								
Tulse Hill	d					22 01								22 31								23 01			
New Cross Gate ⊖	d																								
Norwood Junction	d			22 09								22 39								23 09					
West Croydon	d			22 14				22 24		22 34		22 44			22 54	23 04				23 14				23 24	23 34
Waddon	d			22 16				22 26		22 36		22 46			22 56	23 06				23 16				23 26	23 36
Wallington	d			22 20				22 30		22 40		22 50			23 00	23 10				23 20				23 30	23 40
Carshalton Beeches	d			22 22				22 32		22 42		22 52			23 02	23 12				23 22				23 32	23 42
Mitcham Eastfields	d		22 06								22 36							23 06							
Mitcham Junction	d		22 09								22 39							23 09							
Hackbridge	d		22 13								22 43							23 13							
Carshalton	d		22 15								22 45							23 15							
Sutton (Surrey)	a		22 19	22 26	22 28	22 35		22 39		22 46	22 49	22 56	22 58	23 05	23 06	23 16		23 19		23 26	23 28	23 35		23 39	23 46
	d		22 19		22 29			22 40			22 49		22 59		23 07			23 19		23 33	23 29			23 40	
Belmont	d														23 10					23 36					
Banstead	d														23 14					23 40					
Epsom Downs	a														23 17					23 43					
Cheam	d		22 22		22 31			22 42			22 52		23 01					23 22			23 31			23 42	
Ewell East	d		22 25					22 46			22 55		23 05					23 25						23 46	
Epsom	a	22 27	22 29		22 37		22 46	22 52			22 59		23 09				23 12	23 29			23 37		23 42	23 52	
	d				22 37		22 47						23 09				23 17				23 37		23 47		
Ashtead	d				22 41		22 51						23 13				23 21				23 41		23 51		
Leatherhead	d				22 44		22 54						23 16				23 24				23 44		23 54		
Bookham	d																23 29								
Effingham Junction	d																23 33								
Guildford	a																23 53								
Box Hill & Westhumble	d				22 49								23 21												
Dorking	a				22 52		23 02						23 24								23 50		00 03		
	d																								
Holmwood	d																								
Ockley	d																								
Warnham	d																								
Horsham	a																								

		SN	SN	FC		SN	SW	SN
London Victoria ⊖	d	23 06	23 26			23 34		23 59
London Waterloo ⊖	d						23 42	
Clapham Junction	d	23 14	23 32			23 42	23 51	00 07
Balham ⊖	d	23 20	23 37			23 47		00 12
London Bridge ⊖	d							
Tulse Hill	d			23 31				
New Cross Gate ⊖	d							
Norwood Junction	d	23 39						
West Croydon	d	23 44				00 04		00 31
Waddon	d	23 46				00 06		00 33
Wallington	d	23 50				00 10		00 37
Carshalton Beeches	d	23 52				00 12		00 39
Mitcham Eastfields	d		23 43					
Mitcham Junction	d		23 46					
Hackbridge	d		23 50					
Carshalton	d		23 52					
Sutton (Surrey)	a	23 56	23 59	00 05		00 16		00 43
	d		00 01					
Belmont	d							
Banstead	d							
Epsom Downs	a							
Cheam	d		00 03					
Ewell East	d		00 07					
Epsom	a		00 11				00 15	
	d		00 11				00 19	
Ashtead	d		00 15				00 23	
Leatherhead	d		00 18				00 26	
Bookham	d						00 31	
Effingham Junction	d						00 36	
Guildford	a						00 56	
Box Hill & Westhumble	d		00 23					
Dorking	a		00 26					
	d							
Holmwood	d							
Ockley	d							
Warnham	d							
Horsham	a							

Table 182

London - Sutton, Epsom, Guildford, Dorking and Horsham

Sundays until 30 September

Network Diagram - see first Page of Table 177

		SW	SN	FC	SN	SW	FC	SN	SW A	SW B		SN	SN	SN	SW	SN	SN	SN	SN	SW		SN	SN	SN	SN
London Victoria ⊖	d		23p26		23p34			23p59				00 34	06 49	07 22		07 19	07 24	07 52	07 49			08 08	07 54	08 22	08 19
London Waterloo ⊖	d	23p09				23p42			00 15	00 15										08 02					
Clapham Junction	d	23p18	23p32		23p42	23p51		00 07	00 25	00 25		00 42	06 57	07 29		07 26	07 32	07 59	07 56	08 11		08 16	08 02	08 29	08 26
Balham ⊖	d		23p37		23p47			00 12				00 47	07 02	07 33		07 30	07 37	08 03	08 00			08 22	08 07	08 33	08 30
London Bridge ⊖	d																								
Tulse Hill	d			23p31			00 01																		
New Cross Gate ⊖	d																								
Norwood Junction	d																07 57						08 27		
West Croydon	d				00 04			00 31				01 04	07 21			07 49	08 04		08 19				08 34		08 49
Waddon	d				00 06			00 33				01 07	07 23			07 51	08 06		08 21				08 36		08 51
Wallington	d				00 10			00 37				01 10	07 27			07 55	08 10		08 25				08 40		08 55
Carshalton Beeches	d				00 12			00 39				01 13	07 29			07 57	08 12		08 27				08 42		08 57
Mitcham Eastfields	d		23p43											07 40				08 10				08 28		08 40	
Mitcham Junction	d		23p46											07 43				08 13				08 31		08 43	
Hackbridge	d		23p50											07 46				08 16				08 35		08 46	
Carshalton	d		23p52											07 49				08 19				08 37		08 49	
Sutton (Surrey)	a		23p59	00 05	00 16		00 35	00 43				01 16	07 33	07 52		08 01	08 16	08 22	08 31			08 41	08 46	08 52	09 01
	d		00 01										07 41	07 53		08 11		08 23				08 41		08 53	
Belmont	d																								
Banstead	d																								
Epsom Downs	a																								
Cheam	d		00 03										07 43	07 55		08 13		08 25				08 44		08 55	
Ewell East	d		00 07										07 47	07 59		08 17		08 29				08 47		08 59	
Epsom	a	23p42	00 11			00 15			00 50	00 50			07 52	08 03		08 22		08 33		08 36		08 51		09 03	
	d	23p47	00 11			00 19				00 51			07 53		08 08	08 23				08 38		08 52			
Ashtead	d	23p51	00 15			00 23				00 55			07 57		08 12	08 27				08 42		08 56			
Leatherhead	d	23p54	00 18			00 26				00 58			08 00		08 15	08 30				08 45		08 59			
Bookham	d					00 31				01 03					08 21										
Effingham Junction	d					00 36				01 07					08 25										
Guildford	a					00 53				01 24					08 41										
Box Hill & Westhumble	d		00 23										08 05			08 35						09 04			
Dorking	a	00 01	00 26										08 07			08 37				08 51		09 06			
	d																								
Holmwood	d																								
Ockley	d																								
Warnham	d																								
Horsham	a																								

		SW	SN	SN	SN	SN		SW	FC	SN	SN	SN	SN	FC	SW	FC		SN	SN	SN	SN	FC	SW	FC	SN
London Victoria ⊖	d		08 38	08 24	08 52	08 49				09 08	08 54	09 22	09 19					09 38	09 24	09 52	09 49				10 08
London Waterloo ⊖	d	08 32						09 02							09 32								10 02		
Clapham Junction	d	08 41	08 46	08 32	08 59	08 56		09 11		09 16	09 02	09 29	09 26		09 41			09 46	09 32	09 59	09 56		10 11		10 16
Balham ⊖	d		08 51	08 37	09 03	09 00				09 21	09 07	09 33	09 30					09 51	09 37	10 03	10 00				10 21
London Bridge ⊖	d																								
Tulse Hill	d								09 12					09 30		09 42						10 00		10 12	
New Cross Gate ⊖	d																								
Norwood Junction	d			08 57							09 27								09 57						
West Croydon	d			09 04		09 19					09 34		09 49						10 04		10 19				
Waddon	d			09 06		09 21					09 36		09 51						10 06		10 21				
Wallington	d			09 10		09 25					09 40		09 55						10 10		10 25				
Carshalton Beeches	d			09 12		09 27					09 42		09 57						10 12		10 27				
Mitcham Eastfields	d		08 58		09 10				09 20	09 28		09 40				09 50		09 58		10 10				10 20	10 28
Mitcham Junction	d		09 01		09 13				09 23	09 31		09 43				09 53		10 01		10 13				10 23	10 31
Hackbridge	d		09 04		09 16				09 26	09 34		09 46				09 56		10 04		10 16				10 26	10 34
Carshalton	d		09 07		09 19				09 29	09 37		09 49				09 59		10 07		10 19				10 29	10 37
Sutton (Surrey)	a		09 10	09 16	09 22	09 31			09 33	09 40	09 46	09 52	10 01	10 01		10 03		10 10	10 16	10 22	10 31	10 31		10 33	10 40
	d		09 11		09 23					09 41		09 53						10 11		10 23					10 41
Belmont	d																								
Banstead	d																								
Epsom Downs	a																								
Cheam	d		09 13		09 25					09 43		09 55						10 13		10 25					10 43
Ewell East	d		09 17		09 29					09 47		09 59						10 17		10 29					10 47
Epsom	a	09 06	09 21		09 33			09 36		09 51		10 03			10 06			10 21		10 33			10 36		10 51
	d	09 08	09 21					09 38		09 51					10 08			10 21					10 38		10 51
Ashtead	d	09 12	09 25					09 42		09 55					10 12			10 25					10 42		10 55
Leatherhead	d	09 15	09 28					09 45		09 58					10 15			10 28					10 45		10 58
Bookham	d	09 21													10 21										
Effingham Junction	d	09 25													10 25										
Guildford	a	09 41													10 41										
Box Hill & Westhumble	d		09 33							10 03								10 33							11 03
Dorking	a		09 36					09 51		10 06								10 36					10 51		11 06
	d																								
Holmwood	d																								
Ockley	d																								
Warnham	d																								
Horsham	a																								

A until 22 July, 19 August, 26 August, 16 September, 23 September, 30 September

B 29 July, 5 August, 12 August, 2 September, 9 September

Table 182

Sundays until 30 September

London - Sutton, Epsom, Guildford, Dorking and Horsham

Network Diagram - see first Page of Table 177

Station		SN	SN	SN	FC	SW	FC	SN	SN	SN	SN	FC	SW	FC	SN	SN	SN	SN	FC	SW	FC	SN
London Victoria	⊖ d	09 54	10 22	10 19				10 38	10 24	10 52	10 49				11 08	10 54	11 22	11 19				11 38
London Waterloo	⊖ d					10 32							11 02							11 32		
Clapham Junction	d	10 02	10 29	10 26		10 41		10 46	10 32	10 59	10 56		11 11		11 16	11 02	11 29	11 26		11 41		11 46
Balham	⊖ d	10 07	10 33	10 30				10 51	10 37	11 03	11 00				11 21	11 07	11 33	11 30				11 51
London Bridge	⊖ d																					
Tulse Hill	d				10 30		10 42					11 00		11 12					11 30		11 42	
New Cross Gate	⊖ d																					
Norwood Junction	d	10 27							10 57							11 27						
West Croydon	d	10 34		10 49					11 04		11 19					11 34		11 49				
Waddon	d	10 36		10 51					11 06		11 21					11 36		11 51				
Wallington	d	10 40		10 55					11 10		11 25					11 40		11 55				
Carshalton Beeches	d	10 42		10 57					11 12		11 27					11 42		11 57				
Mitcham Eastfields	d		10 40				10 50	10 58		11 10				11 20	11 28		11 40				11 50	11 58
Mitcham Junction	d		10 43				10 53	11 01		11 13				11 23	11 31		11 43				11 53	12 01
Hackbridge	d		10 46				10 56	11 04		11 16				11 26	11 34		11 46				11 56	12 04
Carshalton	d		10 49				10 59	11 07		11 19				11 29	11 37		11 49				11 59	12 07
Sutton (Surrey)	a	10 46	10 52	11 01	11 01		11 03	11 10	11 16	11 22	11 31	11 31		11 33	11 40	11 46	11 52	12 01	12 01		12 03	12 10
	d		10 53					11 11		11 23					11 41		11 53					12 11
Belmont	d																					
Banstead	d																					
Epsom Downs	a																					
Cheam	d		10 55					11 13		11 25					11 43		11 55					12 13
Ewell East	d		10 59					11 17		11 29					11 47		11 59					12 17
Epsom	a		11 03			11 06		11 21		11 33			11 36		11 51		12 03			12 06		12 21
	d					11 08		11 21					11 38		11 51					12 08		12 21
Ashtead	d					11 12		11 25					11 42		11 55					12 12		12 25
Leatherhead	d					11 15		11 28					11 45		11 58					12 15		12 28
Bookham	d					11 21														12 21		
Effingham Junction	d					11 25														12 25		
Guildford	a					11 41														12 41		
Box Hill & Westhumble	d							11 33							12 03							12 33
Dorking	a							11 36					11 51		12 06							12 36
	d																					
Holmwood	d																					
Ockley	d																					
Warnham	d																					
Horsham	a																					

Station		SN	SN	SN	FC	SW	FC	SN	SN	SN	SN	FC	SW	FC	SN	SN	SN	SN	FC	SW	FC	SN	SN
London Victoria	⊖ d	11 24	11 52	11 49				12 08	11 54	12 22	12 19				12 38	12 24	12 52	12 49				13 08	12 54
London Waterloo	⊖ d					12 02							12 32							13 02			
Clapham Junction	d	11 32	11 59	11 56		12 11		12 16	12 02	12 29	12 26		12 41		12 46	12 32	12 59	12 56		13 11		13 16	13 02
Balham	⊖ d	11 37	12 03	12 00				12 21	12 07	12 33	12 30				12 51	12 37	13 03	13 00				13 21	13 07
London Bridge	⊖ d																						
Tulse Hill	d				12 00		12 12					12 30		12 42					13 00		13 12		
New Cross Gate	⊖ d																						
Norwood Junction	d	11 57							12 27							12 57							13 27
West Croydon	d	12 04		12 19					12 34		12 49					13 04		13 19					13 34
Waddon	d	12 06		12 21					12 36		12 51					13 06		13 21					13 36
Wallington	d	12 10		12 25					12 40		12 55					13 10		13 25					13 40
Carshalton Beeches	d	12 12		12 27					12 42		12 57					13 12		13 27					13 42
Mitcham Eastfields	d		12 10				12 20	12 28		12 40				12 50	12 58		13 10				13 20	13 28	
Mitcham Junction	d		12 13				12 23	12 31		12 43				12 53	13 01		13 13				13 23	13 31	
Hackbridge	d		12 16				12 26	12 34		12 46				12 56	13 04		13 16				13 26	13 34	
Carshalton	d		12 19				12 29	12 37		12 49				12 59	13 07		13 19				13 29	13 37	
Sutton (Surrey)	a	12 16	12 22	12 31	12 31		12 33	12 40	12 46	12 52	13 01	13 01		13 03	13 10	13 16	13 22	13 31	13 31		13 33	13 40	13 46
	d		12 23					12 41		12 53					13 11		13 23					13 41	
Belmont	d																						
Banstead	d																						
Epsom Downs	a																						
Cheam	d		12 25					12 43		12 55					13 13		13 25					13 43	
Ewell East	d		12 29					12 47		12 59					13 17		13 29					13 47	
Epsom	a		12 33			12 36		12 51		13 05			13 06		13 21		13 33			13 36		13 51	
	d					12 38		12 51					13 08		13 21					13 38		13 51	
Ashtead	d					12 42		12 55					13 12		13 25					13 42		13 55	
Leatherhead	d					12 45		12 58					13 15		13 28					13 45		13 58	
Bookham	d												13 21										
Effingham Junction	d												13 25										
Guildford	a												13 41										
Box Hill & Westhumble	d							13 03							13 33							14 03	
Dorking	a					12 51		13 06							13 36					13 51		14 06	
	d																						
Holmwood	d																						
Ockley	d																						
Warnham	d																						
Horsham	a																						

Table 182

Sundays until 30 September

London - Sutton, Epsom, Guildford, Dorking and Horsham

Network Diagram - see first Page of Table 177

Station		SN	SN	FC	SW	FC	SN	SN	SN	SN	FC	SW	FC	SN	SN	SN	SN	FC	SW	FC	SN	SN
London Victoria	⊖ d	13 22	13 19				13 38	13 24	13 52	13 49				14 08	13 54	14 22	14 19				14 38	14 24
London Waterloo	⊖ d				13 32							14 02							14 32			
Clapham Junction	d	13 29	13 26		13 41		13 46	13 32	13 59	13 56		14 11		14 16	14 02	14 29	14 26		14 41		14 46	14 32
Balham	⊖ d	13 33	13 30				13 51	13 37	14 03	14 00				14 21	14 07	14 33	14 30				14 51	14 37
London Bridge	⊖ d																					
Tulse Hill	d			13 30		13 42					14 00		14 12					14 30		14 42		
New Cross Gate	⊖ d																					
Norwood Junction	d							13 57							14 27							14 57
West Croydon	d		13 49					14 04		14 19					14 34		14 49					15 04
Waddon	d		13 51					14 06		14 21					14 36		14 51					15 06
Wallington	d		13 55					14 10		14 25					14 40		14 55					15 10
Carshalton Beeches	d		13 57					14 12		14 27					14 42		14 57					15 12
Mitcham Eastfields	d	13 40				13 50	13 58		14 10				14 20	14 28		14 40				14 50	14 58	
Mitcham Junction	d	13 43				13 53	14 01		14 13				14 23	14 31		14 43				14 53	15 01	
Hackbridge	d	13 46				13 56	14 04		14 16				14 26	14 34		14 46				14 56	15 04	
Carshalton	d	13 49				13 59	14 07		14 19				14 29	14 37		14 49				14 59	15 07	
Sutton (Surrey)	a	13 52	14 01	14 01		14 03	14 10	14 16	14 22	14 31	14 31		14 33	14 40	14 46	14 52	15 01	15 01		15 03	15 10	15 16
	d	13 53					14 11		14 23					14 41		14 53					15 11	
Belmont	d																					
Banstead	d																					
Epsom Downs	a																					
Cheam	d	13 55					14 13		14 25					14 43		14 55					15 13	
Ewell East	d	13 59					14 17		14 29					14 47		14 59					15 17	
Epsom	a	14 03			14 06		14 21		14 33			14 36		14 51		15 03			15 06		15 21	
	d				14 08		14 21					14 38		14 51					15 08		15 21	
Ashtead	d				14 12		14 25					14 42		14 55					15 12		15 25	
Leatherhead	d				14 15		14 28					14 45		14 58					15 15		15 28	
Bookham	d				14 21														15 21			
Effingham Junction	d				14 25														15 25			
Guildford	a				14 41														15 41			
Box Hill & Westhumble	d						14 33							15 03							15 33	
Dorking	a						14 36					14 51		15 06							15 36	
	d																					
Holmwood	d																					
Ockley	d																					
Warnham	d																					
Horsham	a																					

Station		SN	SN	FC	SW	FC	SN	SN	SN	SN	FC	SW	FC	SN	SN	SN	SN	FC	SW	FC	SN	SN	SN
London Victoria	⊖ d	14 52	14 49				15 08	14 54	15 22	15 19				15 38	15 24	15 52	15 49				16 08	15 54	16 22
London Waterloo	⊖ d				15 02							15 32							16 02				
Clapham Junction	d	14 59	14 56		15 11		15 16	15 02	15 29	15 26		15 41		15 46	15 32	15 59	15 56		16 11		16 16	16 02	16 29
Balham	⊖ d	15 03	15 00				15 21	15 07	15 33	15 30				15 51	15 37	16 03	16 00				16 21	16 07	16 33
London Bridge	⊖ d																						
Tulse Hill	d			15 00		15 12					15 30		15 42					16 00		16 12			
New Cross Gate	⊖ d																						
Norwood Junction	d							15 27							15 57							16 27	
West Croydon	d		15 19					15 34		15 49					16 04		16 19					16 34	
Waddon	d		15 21					15 36		15 51					16 06		16 21					16 36	
Wallington	d		15 25					15 40		15 55					16 10		16 25					16 40	
Carshalton Beeches	d		15 27					15 42		15 57					16 12		16 27					16 42	
Mitcham Eastfields	d	15 10				15 20	15 28		15 40				15 50	15 58		16 10				16 20	16 28		16 40
Mitcham Junction	d	15 13				15 23	15 31		15 43				15 53	16 01		16 13				16 23	16 31		16 43
Hackbridge	d	15 16				15 26	15 34		15 46				15 56	16 04		16 16				16 26	16 34		16 46
Carshalton	d	15 19				15 29	15 37		15 49				15 59	16 07		16 19				16 29	16 37		16 49
Sutton (Surrey)	a	15 22	15 31	15 31		15 33	15 40	15 46	15 52	16 01	16 01		16 03	16 10	16 16	16 22	16 31	16 31		16 33	16 40	16 46	16 52
	d	15 23					15 41		15 53					16 11		16 23					16 41		16 53
Belmont	d																						
Banstead	d																						
Epsom Downs	a																						
Cheam	d	15 25					15 43		15 55					16 13		16 25					16 43		16 55
Ewell East	d	15 29					15 47		15 59					16 17		16 29					16 47		16 59
Epsom	a	15 33			15 36		15 51		16 03			16 06		16 21		16 33			16 36		16 51		17 03
	d				15 38		15 51					16 08		16 21					16 38		16 51		
Ashtead	d				15 42		15 55					16 12		16 25					16 42		16 55		
Leatherhead	d				15 45		15 58					16 15		16 28					16 45		16 58		
Bookham	d											16 21											
Effingham Junction	d											16 25											
Guildford	a											16 41											
Box Hill & Westhumble	d						16 03							16 33							17 03		
Dorking	a				15 51		16 06							16 36					16 51		17 06		
	d																						
Holmwood	d																						
Ockley	d																						
Warnham	d																						
Horsham	a																						

Table 182

London - Sutton, Epsom, Guildford, Dorking and Horsham

Sundays
until 30 September

Network Diagram - see first Page of Table 177

		SN	FC	SW	FC	SN	SN	SN	SN	FC	SW	FC	SN	SN	SN	SN	FC	SW	FC	SN	SN	SN	SN
London Victoria [15] ⊖	d	16 19				16 38	16 24	16 52	16 49				17 08	16 54	17 22	17 19				17 38	17 24	17 52	17 49
London Waterloo [15] ⊖	d			16 32							17 02							17 32					
Clapham Junction [10]	d	16 26		16 41		16 46	16 32	16 59	16 56		17 11		17 16	17 02	17 29	17 26		17 41		17 46	17 32	17 59	17 56
Balham [4] ⊖	d	16 30				16 51	16 37	17 03	17 00				17 21	17 07	17 33	17 30				17 51	17 37	18 03	18 00
London Bridge [4] ⊖	d																						
Tulse Hill [3]	d		16 30		16 42					17 00		17 12					17 30		17 42				
New Cross Gate [4] ⊖	d																						
Norwood Junction [2]	d						16 57							17 27							17 57		
West Croydon [4]	d	16 49					17 04		17 19					17 34		17 49					18 04		18 19
Waddon	d	16 51					17 06		17 21					17 36		17 51					18 06		18 21
Wallington	d	16 55					17 10		17 25					17 40		17 55					18 10		18 25
Carshalton Beeches	d	16 57					17 12		17 27					17 42		17 57					18 12		18 27
Mitcham Eastfields	d				16 50	16 58		17 10				17 20	17 28		17 40				17 50	17 58		18 10	
Mitcham Junction	d				16 53	17 01		17 13				17 23	17 31		17 43				17 53	18 01		18 13	
Hackbridge	d				16 56	17 04		17 16				17 26	17 34		17 46				17 56	18 04		18 16	
Carshalton	d				16 59	17 07		17 19				17 29	17 37		17 49				17 59	18 07		18 19	
Sutton (Surrey) [4]	a	17 01	17 01		17 03	17 10	17 16	17 22	17 31	17 31		17 33	17 40	17 46	17 52	18 01	18 01		18 03	18 10	18 16	18 22	18 31
	d					17 11		17 23					17 41		17 53					18 11		18 23	
Belmont	d																						
Banstead	d																						
Epsom Downs	a																						
Cheam	d					17 13		17 25					17 43		17 55					18 13		18 25	
Ewell East	d					17 17		17 29					17 47		17 59					18 17		18 29	
Epsom [3]	a			17 06		17 21		17 33			17 36		17 51		18 03			18 06		18 21		18 33	
	d			17 08		17 21					17 38		17 51					18 08		18 21			
Ashtead	d			17 12		17 25					17 42		17 55					18 12		18 25			
Leatherhead	d			17 15		17 28					17 45		17 58					18 15		18 28			
Bookham	d			17 21														18 21					
Effingham Junction [6]	d			17 25														18 25					
Guildford	a			17 41														18 41					
Box Hill & Westhumble	d					17 33							18 03							18 33			
Dorking [4]	a					17 36					17 51		18 06							18 36			
	d																						
Holmwood	d																						
Ockley	d																						
Warnham	d																						
Horsham [4]	a																						

		FC	SW	FC	SN	SN	SN	FC	SW	FC	SN	SN	SN	FC	SW	FC	SN	SN	SN	FC	SW	FC
London Victoria [15] ⊖	d				18 08	17 54	18 19				18 38	18 24	18 49				19 08	18 54	19 19			
London Waterloo [15] ⊖	d		18 02						18 32						19 02						19 32	
Clapham Junction [10]	d		18 11		18 16	18 02	18 26		18 41		18 46	18 32	18 56		19 11		19 16	19 02	19 26		19 41	
Balham [4] ⊖	d				18 21	18 07	18 30				18 51	18 37	19 00				19 21	19 07	19 30			
London Bridge [4] ⊖	d																					
Tulse Hill [3]	d	18 00		18 12				18 30		18 42				19 00		19 12				19 30		19 42
New Cross Gate [4] ⊖	d																					
Norwood Junction [2]	d					18 27						18 57						19 27				
West Croydon [4]	d					18 34	18 49					19 04	19 19					19 34	19 49			
Waddon	d					18 36	18 51					19 06	19 21					19 36	19 51			
Wallington	d					18 40	18 55					19 10	19 25					19 40	19 55			
Carshalton Beeches	d					18 42	18 57					19 12	19 27					19 42	19 57			
Mitcham Eastfields	d			18 20	18 28					18 50	18 58					19 20	19 28					19 50
Mitcham Junction	d			18 23	18 31					18 53	19 01					19 23	19 31					19 53
Hackbridge	d			18 26	18 34					18 56	19 04					19 26	19 34					19 56
Carshalton	d			18 29	18 37					18 59	19 07					19 29	19 37					19 59
Sutton (Surrey) [4]	a	18 31		18 33	18 40	18 46	19 01	19 01		19 03	19 10	19 16	19 31	19 31		19 33	19 40	19 46	20 01	20 01		20 03
	d				18 41						19 11						19 41					
Belmont	d																					
Banstead	d																					
Epsom Downs	a																					
Cheam	d				18 43						19 13						19 43					
Ewell East	d				18 47						19 17						19 47					
Epsom [3]	a		18 36		18 51				19 06		19 21				19 36		19 51				20 06	
	d		18 38		18 51				19 08		19 21				19 38		19 51				20 08	
Ashtead	d		18 42		18 55				19 12		19 25				19 42		19 55				20 12	
Leatherhead	d		18 45		18 58				19 15		19 28				19 45		19 58				20 15	
Bookham	d								19 21												20 21	
Effingham Junction [6]	d								19 25												20 25	
Guildford	a								19 41												20 41	
Box Hill & Westhumble	d				19 03						19 33						20 03					
Dorking [4]	a		18 51		19 06						19 36				19 51		20 06					
	d																					
Holmwood	d																					
Ockley	d																					
Warnham	d																					
Horsham [4]	a																					

Table 182

London - Sutton, Epsom, Guildford, Dorking and Horsham

Sundays
until 30 September

Network Diagram - see first Page of Table 177

		SN	SN	SN	FC	SW	FC	SN	SN	SN	FC	SW	FC	SN	SN	SN	FC	SW	SN	SN	SN	FC	SW
London Victoria [15] ⊖	d	19 38	19 24	19 49				20 08	19 54	20 19				20 38	20 24	20 49			21 08	20 54	21 19		
London Waterloo [15] ⊖	d					20 02						20 32						21 02					21 32
Clapham Junction [10]	d	19 46	19 32	19 56		20 11		20 16	20 02	20 26		20 41		20 46	20 32	20 56		21 11	21 16	21 02	21 26		21 41
Balham [4] ⊖	d	19 51	19 37	20 00				20 21	20 07	20 30				20 51	20 37	21 00			21 21	21 07	21 30		
London Bridge [4] ⊖	d																						
Tulse Hill [3]	d				20 00		20 12				20 30		20 42				21 00					21 30	
New Cross Gate [4] ⊖	d																						
Norwood Junction [2]	d		19 57						20 27						20 57					21 27			
West Croydon [4]	d		20 04	20 19					20 34	20 49					21 04	21 19				21 34	21 49		
Waddon	d		20 06	20 21					20 36	20 51					21 06	21 21				21 36	21 51		
Wallington	d		20 10	20 25					20 40	20 55					21 10	21 25				21 40	21 55		
Carshalton Beeches	d		20 12	20 27					20 42	20 57					21 12	21 27				21 42	21 57		
Mitcham Eastfields	d	19 58					20 20	20 28					20 50	20 58					21 28				
Mitcham Junction	d	20 01					20 23	20 31					20 53	21 01					21 31				
Hackbridge	d	20 04					20 26	20 34					20 56	21 04					21 34				
Carshalton	d	20 07					20 29	20 37					20 59	21 07					21 37				
Sutton (Surrey) [4]	a	20 10	20 16	20 31	20 31		20 33	20 40	20 46	21 01	21 01		21 03	21 10	21 16	21 31	21 31		21 40	21 46	22 01	22 01	
	d	20 11						20 41						21 11					21 41				
Belmont	d																						
Banstead	d																						
Epsom Downs	a																						
Cheam	d	20 13						20 43						21 13					21 43				
Ewell East	d	20 17						20 47						21 17					21 47				
Epsom [3]	a	20 21				20 36		20 51				21 06		21 21				21 36	21 51				22 06
	d	20 21				20 38		20 51				21 08		21 21				21 38	21 51				22 08
Ashtead	d	20 25				20 42		20 55				21 12		21 25				21 42	21 55				22 12
Leatherhead	d	20 28				20 45		20 58				21 15		21 28				21 45	21 58				22 15
Bookham	d											21 21											22 21
Effingham Junction [6]	d											21 25											22 25
Guildford	a											21 41											22 41
Box Hill & Westhumble	d	20 33						21 03						21 33					22 03				
Dorking [4]	a	20 36				20 51		21 06						21 36				21 51	22 06				
	d																						
Holmwood	d																						
Ockley	d																						
Warnham	d																						
Horsham [4]	a																						

		SN	SN	SN	SW	SN	SN	SN	SW	SN	SN	SN	SW	SN	SN	SW	SN
London Victoria [15] ⊖	d	21 38	21 24	21 49		22 08	21 54	22 19		22 38	22 24	22 49		23 08	22 54		23 19
London Waterloo [15] ⊖	d				22 02				22 32				23 02			23 32	
Clapham Junction [10]	d	21 46	21 32	21 56	22 11	22 16	22 02	22 26	22 41	22 46	22 32	22 56	23 11	23 16	23 02	23 41	23 27
Balham [4] ⊖	d	21 51	21 38	22 00		22 21	22 07	22 30		22 51	22 38	23 00		23 21	23 07		23 32
London Bridge [4] ⊖	d																
Tulse Hill [3]	d																
New Cross Gate [4] ⊖	d																
Norwood Junction [2]	d		21 57				22 27				22 57				23 27		
West Croydon [4]	d		22 04	22 19			22 34	22 49			23 04	23 19			23 34		23 50
Waddon	d		22 06	22 21			22 36	22 51			23 06	23 21			23 36		23 52
Wallington	d		22 10	22 25			22 40	22 55			23 10	23 25			23 40		23 56
Carshalton Beeches	d		22 12	22 27			22 42	22 57			23 12	23 27			23 42		23 58
Mitcham Eastfields	d	21 58				22 28				22 58				23 28			
Mitcham Junction	d	22 01				22 31				23 01				23 31			
Hackbridge	d	22 04				22 34				23 04				23 34			
Carshalton	d	22 07				22 37				23 07				23 37			
Sutton (Surrey) [4]	a	22 10	22 16	22 31		22 40	22 46	23 01		23 10	23 16	23 31		23 40	23 46		00 02
	d	22 11				22 41				23 11				23 41			00 04
Belmont	d																
Banstead	d																
Epsom Downs	a																
Cheam	d	22 13				22 43				23 13				23 43			00 06
Ewell East	d	22 17				22 47				23 17				23 47			00 10
Epsom [3]	a	22 21			22 36	22 51			23 06	23 21			23 36	23 51		00 06	00 14
	d	22 21			22 38	22 51			23 08	23 21				23 51			
Ashtead	d	22 25			22 42	22 55			23 12	23 25				23 55			
Leatherhead	d	22 28			22 45	22 58			23 15	23 28				23 58			
Bookham	d								23 21								
Effingham Junction [6]	d								23 25								
Guildford	a								23 41								
Box Hill & Westhumble	d	22 33				23 03				23 33				00 03			
Dorking [4]	a	22 36			22 51	23 06				23 36				00 06			
	d																
Holmwood	d																
Ockley	d																
Warnham	d																
Horsham [4]	a																

Table 182

Sundays from 7 October

London - Sutton, Epsom, Guildford, Dorking and Horsham

Network Diagram - see first Page of Table 177

Station		SW A	SW B	SN	FC	SN	SW A	SW B	FC	SN		SW	SN	SN	SN	SW	SN	SN	SN	SN		SW	SN	SN	SN
London Victoria ⊖	d			23p26		23p34				23p59			00 34	06 49	07 22		07 19	07 24	07 52	07 49			08 08	07 54	08 22
London Waterloo ⊖	d	23p09	23p09				23p42	23p42				00 15										08 02			
Clapham Junction	d	23p18	23p18	23p32		23p42	23p51	23p51		00 07		00 25	00 42	06 57	07 29		07 26	07 32	07 59	07 56		08 11	08 16	08 02	08 29
Balham ⊖	d			23p37		23p47				00 12			00 47	07 02	07 33		07 30	07 37	08 03	08 00			08 22	08 07	08 33
London Bridge ⊖	d																								
Tulse Hill	d				23p31				00 01																
New Cross Gate ⊖	d																								
Norwood Junction	d																	07 57						08 27	
West Croydon	d					00 04				00 31			01 04	07 21			07 49	08 04		08 19				08 34	
Waddon	d					00 06				00 33			01 07	07 23			07 51	08 06		08 21				08 36	
Wallington	d					00 10				00 37			01 10	07 27			07 55	08 10		08 25				08 40	
Carshalton Beeches	d					00 12				00 39			01 13	07 29			07 57	08 12		08 27				08 42	
Mitcham Eastfields	d			23p43											07 40				08 10				08 28		08 40
Mitcham Junction	d			23p46											07 43				08 13				08 31		08 43
Hackbridge	d			23p50											07 46				08 16				08 35		08 46
Carshalton	d			23p52											07 49				08 19				08 37		08 49
Sutton (Surrey)	a			23p59	00 05	00 16			00 35	00 43			01 16	07 33	07 52		08 01	08 16	08 22	08 31			08 41	08 46	08 52
	d			00 01										07 41	07 53		08 11		08 23				08 41		08 53
Belmont	d																								
Banstead	d																								
Epsom Downs	a																								
Cheam	d			00 03										07 43	07 55		08 13		08 25				08 44		08 55
Ewell East	d			00 07										07 47	07 59		08 17		08 29				08 47		08 59
Epsom	a	23p42	23p42	00 11			00 15	00 15				00 50		07 52	08 03		08 22		08 33			08 36	08 51		09 03
	d	23p47	23p47	00 11			00 19	00 19						07 53		08 08	08 23					08 38	08 52		
Ashtead	d	23p51	23p51	00 15			00 23	00 23						07 57		08 12	08 27					08 42	08 56		
Leatherhead	d	23p54	23p54	00 18			00 26	00 26						08 00		08 15	08 30					08 45	08 59		
Bookham	d						00 31	00 31								08 21									
Effingham Junction	d						00 36	00 36								08 25									
Guildford	a						00 53	00 56								08 44									
Box Hill & Westhumble	d			00 23										08 05			08 35						09 04		
Dorking	a	00 01	00 03	00 26										08 07			08 37					08 53	09 06		
	d																								
Holmwood	d																								
Ockley	d																								
Warnham	d																								
Horsham	a																								

Station		SN	SW	SN	SN	SN		SN	SW	FC	SN	SN	SN	SN	FC	SW		FC	SN	SN	SN	SN	FC	SW	FC
London Victoria ⊖	d	08 19		08 38	08 24	08 52		08 49			09 08	08 54	09 22	09 19					09 38	09 24	09 52	09 49			
London Waterloo ⊖	d		08 32						09 02							09 32								10 02	
Clapham Junction	d	08 26	08 41	08 46	08 32	08 59		08 56	09 11		09 16	09 02	09 29	09 26		09 41			09 46	09 32	09 59	09 56		10 11	
Balham ⊖	d	08 30		08 51	08 37	09 03		09 00			09 21	09 07	09 33	09 30					09 51	09 37	10 03	10 00			
London Bridge ⊖	d																								
Tulse Hill	d									09 12					09 30			09 42					10 00		10 12
New Cross Gate ⊖	d																								
Norwood Junction	d				08 57							09 27								09 57					
West Croydon	d	08 49			09 04			09 19				09 34		09 49						10 04		10 19			
Waddon	d	08 51			09 06			09 21				09 36		09 51						10 06		10 21			
Wallington	d	08 55			09 10			09 25				09 40		09 55						10 10		10 25			
Carshalton Beeches	d	08 57			09 12			09 27				09 42		09 57						10 12		10 27			
Mitcham Eastfields	d			08 58		09 10				09 20	09 28		09 40					09 50	09 58		10 10				10 20
Mitcham Junction	d			09 01		09 13				09 23	09 31		09 43					09 53	10 01		10 13				10 23
Hackbridge	d			09 04		09 16				09 26	09 34		09 46					09 56	10 04		10 16				10 26
Carshalton	d			09 07		09 19				09 29	09 37		09 49					09 59	10 07		10 19				10 29
Sutton (Surrey)	a	09 01		09 10	09 16	09 22		09 31		09 33	09 40	09 46	09 52	10 01	10 01			10 03	10 10	10 16	10 22	10 31	10 31		10 33
	d			09 11		09 23					09 41		09 53						10 11		10 23				
Belmont	d																								
Banstead	d																								
Epsom Downs	a																								
Cheam	d			09 13		09 25					09 43		09 55						10 13		10 25				
Ewell East	d			09 17		09 29					09 47		09 59						10 17		10 29				
Epsom	a		09 06	09 21		09 33			09 36		09 51		10 03			10 06			10 21		10 33			10 36	
	d		09 08	09 21					09 38		09 51					10 08			10 21					10 38	
Ashtead	d		09 12	09 25					09 42		09 55					10 12			10 25					10 42	
Leatherhead	d		09 15	09 28					09 45		09 58					10 15			10 28					10 45	
Bookham	d		09 21													10 21									
Effingham Junction	d		09 25													10 25									
Guildford	a		09 44													10 44									
Box Hill & Westhumble	d			09 33							10 03								10 33						
Dorking	a			09 36					09 53		10 06								10 36					10 53	
	d																								
Holmwood	d																								
Ockley	d																								
Warnham	d																								
Horsham	a																								

A 7 October

B not 7 October

Table 182

Sundays from 7 October

London - Sutton, Epsom, Guildford, Dorking and Horsham

Network Diagram - see first Page of Table 177

Station		SN		SN	SN	SN	FC	SW	FC	SN	SN	SN		SN	FC	SW	FC	SN	SN	SN	SN	FC		SW	FC
London Victoria ⊖	d	10 08		09 54	10 22	10 19				10 38	10 24	10 52		10 49				11 08	10 54	11 22	11 19				
London Waterloo ⊖	d							10 32								11 02								11 32	
Clapham Junction	d	10 16		10 02	10 29	10 26		10 41		10 46	10 32	10 59		10 56		11 11		11 16	11 02	11 29	11 26			11 41	
Balham ⊖	d	10 21		10 07	10 33	10 30				10 51	10 37	11 03		11 00				11 21	11 07	11 33	11 30				
London Bridge ⊖	d																								
Tulse Hill	d						10 30		10 42						11 00		11 12					11 30			11 42
New Cross Gate ⊖	d																								
Norwood Junction	d			10 27							10 57								11 27						
West Croydon	d			10 34		10 49					11 04			11 19					11 34		11 49				
Waddon	d			10 36		10 51					11 06			11 21					11 36		11 51				
Wallington	d			10 40		10 55					11 10			11 25					11 40		11 55				
Carshalton Beeches	d			10 42		10 57					11 12			11 27					11 42		11 57				
Mitcham Eastfields	d	10 28			10 40				10 50	10 58		11 10					11 20	11 28		11 40					11 50
Mitcham Junction	d	10 31			10 43				10 53	11 01		11 13					11 23	11 31		11 43					11 53
Hackbridge	d	10 34			10 46				10 56	11 04		11 16					11 26	11 34		11 46					11 56
Carshalton	d	10 37			10 49				10 59	11 07		11 19					11 29	11 37		11 49					11 59
Sutton (Surrey)	a	10 40		10 46	10 52	11 01	11 01		11 03	11 10	11 16	11 22		11 31	11 31		11 33	11 40	11 46	11 52	12 01	12 01			12 03
	d	10 41			10 53					11 11		11 23						11 41		11 53					
Belmont	d																								
Banstead	d																								
Epsom Downs	a																								
Cheam	d	10 43			10 55					11 13		11 25						11 43		11 55					
Ewell East	d	10 47			10 59					11 17		11 29						11 47		11 59					
Epsom	a	10 51			11 03			11 06		11 21		11 33				11 36		11 51		12 03				12 06	
	d	10 51						11 08		11 21						11 38		11 51						12 08	
Ashtead	d	10 55						11 12		11 25						11 42		11 55						12 12	
Leatherhead	d	10 58						11 15		11 28						11 45		11 58						12 15	
Bookham	d							11 21																12 21	
Effingham Junction	d							11 25																12 25	
Guildford	a							11 44																12 44	
Box Hill & Westhumble	d	11 03								11 33								12 03							
Dorking	a	11 06								11 36						11 53		12 06							
	d																								
Holmwood	d																								
Ockley	d																								
Warnham	d																								
Horsham	a																								

Station		SN	SN	SN	SN	FC	SW	FC		SN	SN	SN	SN	FC	SW	FC	SN	SN		SN	SN	FC	SW	FC	SN
London Victoria ⊖	d	11 38	11 24	11 52	11 49					12 08	11 54	12 22	12 19				12 38	12 24		12 52	12 49				13 08
London Waterloo ⊖	d						12 02								12 32								13 02		
Clapham Junction	d	11 46	11 32	11 59	11 56		12 11			12 16	12 02	12 29	12 26		12 41		12 46	12 32		12 59	12 56		13 11		13 16
Balham ⊖	d	11 51	11 37	12 03	12 00					12 21	12 07	12 33	12 30				12 51	12 37		13 03	13 00				13 21
London Bridge ⊖	d																								
Tulse Hill	d					12 00		12 12						12 30		12 42						13 00		13 12	
New Cross Gate ⊖	d																								
Norwood Junction	d		11 57								12 27							12 57							
West Croydon	d		12 04		12 19						12 34		12 49					13 04			13 19				
Waddon	d		12 06		12 21						12 36		12 51					13 06			13 21				
Wallington	d		12 10		12 25						12 40		12 55					13 10			13 25				
Carshalton Beeches	d		12 12		12 27						12 42		12 57					13 12			13 27				
Mitcham Eastfields	d	11 58		12 10				12 20		12 28		12 40				12 50	12 58			13 10				13 20	13 28
Mitcham Junction	d	12 01		12 13				12 23		12 31		12 43				12 53	13 01			13 13				13 23	13 31
Hackbridge	d	12 04		12 16				12 26		12 34		12 46				12 56	13 04			13 16				13 26	13 34
Carshalton	d	12 07		12 19				12 29		12 37		12 49				12 59	13 07			13 19				13 29	13 37
Sutton (Surrey)	a	12 10	12 16	12 22	12 31	12 31		12 33		12 40	12 46	12 52	13 01	13 01		13 03	13 10	13 16		13 22	13 31	13 31		13 33	13 40
	d	12 11		12 23						12 41		12 53					13 11			13 23					13 41
Belmont	d																								
Banstead	d																								
Epsom Downs	a																								
Cheam	d	12 13		12 25						12 43		12 55					13 13			13 25					13 43
Ewell East	d	12 17		12 29						12 47		12 59					13 17			13 29					13 47
Epsom	a	12 21		12 33			12 36			12 51		13 05			13 06		13 21			13 33			13 36		13 51
	d	12 21					12 38			12 51					13 08		13 21						13 38		13 51
Ashtead	d	12 25					12 42			12 55					13 12		13 25						13 42		13 55
Leatherhead	d	12 28					12 45			12 58					13 15		13 28						13 45		13 58
Bookham	d														13 21										
Effingham Junction	d														13 25										
Guildford	a														13 44										
Box Hill & Westhumble	d	12 33								13 03							13 33								14 03
Dorking	a	12 36					12 53			13 06							13 36						13 53		14 06
	d																								
Holmwood	d																								
Ockley	d																								
Warnham	d																								
Horsham	a																								

Table 182

Sundays from 7 October

London - Sutton, Epsom, Guildford, Dorking and Horsham

Network Diagram - see first Page of Table 177

		SN	SN	SN		FC	SW	FC	SN	SN	SN	SN	FC	SW		FC	SN	SN	SN	SN	FC	SW	FC	SN	
London Victoria 15 ⊖	d	12 54	13 22	13 19					13 38	13 24	13 52	13 49					14 08	13 54	14 22	14 19				14 38	
London Waterloo 15 ⊖	d						13 32							14 02								14 32			
Clapham Junction 10	d	13 02	13 29	13 26			13 41		13 46	13 32	13 59	13 56		14 11			14 16	14 02	14 29	14 26		14 41		14 46	
Balham 4 ⊖	d	13 07	13 33	13 30					13 51	13 37	14 03	14 00					14 21	14 07	14 33	14 30				14 51	
London Bridge 4 ⊖	d																								
Tulse Hill 3	d					13 30		13 42					14 00			14 12					14 30		14 42		
New Cross Gate 4 ⊖	d																								
Norwood Junction 2	d	13 27								13 57								14 27							
West Croydon 4	d	13 34		13 49						14 04		14 19						14 34		14 49					
Waddon	d	13 36		13 51						14 06		14 21						14 36		14 51					
Wallington	d	13 40		13 55						14 10		14 25						14 40		14 55					
Carshalton Beeches	d	13 42		13 57						14 12		14 27						14 42		14 57					
Mitcham Eastfields	d		13 40					13 50	13 58		14 10					14 20	14 28		14 40				14 50	14 58	
Mitcham Junction	d		13 43					13 53	14 01		14 13					14 23	14 31		14 43				14 53	15 01	
Hackbridge	d		13 46					13 56	14 04		14 16					14 26	14 34		14 46				14 56	15 04	
Carshalton	d		13 49					13 59	14 07		14 19					14 29	14 37		14 49				14 59	15 07	
Sutton (Surrey) 4	a	13 46	13 52	14 01		14 01		14 03	14 10	14 16	14 22	14 31	14 31			14 33	14 40	14 46	14 52	15 01	15 01		15 03	15 10	
	d		13 53						14 11		14 23						14 41		14 53					15 11	
Belmont	d																								
Banstead	d																								
Epsom Downs	a																								
Cheam	d		13 55						14 13		14 25						14 43		14 55					15 13	
Ewell East	d		13 59						14 17		14 29						14 47		14 59					15 17	
Epsom 3	a		14 03				14 06		14 21		14 33			14 36			14 51		15 03			15 06		15 21	
	d						14 08		14 21					14 38			14 51					15 08		15 21	
Ashtead	d						14 12		14 25					14 42			14 55					15 12		15 25	
Leatherhead	d						14 15		14 28					14 45			14 58					15 15		15 28	
Bookham	d						14 21															15 21			
Effingham Junction 6	d						14 25															15 25			
Guildford	a						14 44															15 44			
Box Hill & Westhumble	d								14 33								15 03							15 33	
Dorking 4	a								14 36					14 53			15 06							15 36	
	d																								
Holmwood	d																								
Ockley	d																								
Warnham	d																								
Horsham 4	a																								

		SN	SN	SN	FC	SW	FC	SN	SN	SN		SN	FC	SW	FC	SN	SN	SN	SN	FC		SW	FC	SN	SN
London Victoria 15 ⊖	d	14 24	14 52	14 49				15 08	14 54	15 22		15 19				15 38	15 24	15 52	15 49					16 08	15 54
London Waterloo 15 ⊖	d					15 02								15 32								16 02			
Clapham Junction 10	d	14 32	14 59	14 56		15 11		15 16	15 02	15 29		15 26		15 41		15 46	15 32	15 59	15 56			16 11		16 16	16 02
Balham 4 ⊖	d	14 37	15 03	15 00				15 21	15 07	15 33		15 30				15 51	15 37	16 03	16 00					16 21	16 07
London Bridge 4 ⊖	d																								
Tulse Hill 3	d				15 00		15 12						15 30		15 42					16 00			16 12		
New Cross Gate 4 ⊖	d																								
Norwood Junction 2	d	14 57							15 27								15 57								16 27
West Croydon 4	d	15 04		15 19					15 34			15 49					16 04		16 19						16 34
Waddon	d	15 06		15 21					15 36			15 51					16 06		16 21						16 36
Wallington	d	15 10		15 25					15 40			15 55					16 10		16 25						16 40
Carshalton Beeches	d	15 12		15 27					15 42			15 57					16 12		16 27						16 42
Mitcham Eastfields	d		15 10				15 20	15 28		15 40					15 50	15 58		16 10					16 20	16 28	
Mitcham Junction	d		15 13				15 23	15 31		15 43					15 53	16 01		16 13					16 23	16 31	
Hackbridge	d		15 16				15 26	15 34		15 46					15 56	16 04		16 16					16 26	16 34	
Carshalton	d		15 19				15 29	15 37		15 49					15 59	16 07		16 19					16 29	16 37	
Sutton (Surrey) 4	a	15 16	15 22	15 31	15 31		15 33	15 40	15 46	15 52		16 01	16 01		16 03	16 10	16 16	16 22	16 31	16 31			16 33	16 40	16 46
	d		15 23					15 41		15 53						16 11		16 23						16 41	
Belmont	d																								
Banstead	d																								
Epsom Downs	a																								
Cheam	d		15 25					15 43		15 55						16 13		16 25						16 43	
Ewell East	d		15 29					15 47		15 59						16 17		16 29						16 47	
Epsom 3	a		15 33			15 36		15 51		16 03				16 06		16 21		16 33				16 36		16 51	
	d					15 38		15 51						16 08		16 21						16 38		16 51	
Ashtead	d					15 42		15 55						16 12		16 25						16 42		16 55	
Leatherhead	d					15 45		15 58						16 15		16 28						16 45		16 58	
Bookham	d													16 21											
Effingham Junction 6	d													16 25											
Guildford	a													16 44											
Box Hill & Westhumble	d							16 03								16 33								17 03	
Dorking 4	a					15 53		16 06								16 36						16 53		17 06	
	d																								
Holmwood	d																								
Ockley	d																								
Warnham	d																								
Horsham 4	a																								

Table 182

Sundays from 7 October

London - Sutton, Epsom, Guildford, Dorking and Horsham

Network Diagram - see first Page of Table 177

		SN	SN	FC	SW	FC		SN	SN	SN	SN	FC	SW	FC	SN	SN		SN	SN	FC	SW	FC	SN	SN	SN
London Victoria 15 ⊖	d	16 22	16 19					16 38	16 24	16 52	16 49				17 08	16 54		17 22	17 19				17 38	17 24	17 52
London Waterloo 15 ⊖	d				16 32								17 02								17 32				
Clapham Junction 10	d	16 29	16 26		16 41			16 46	16 32	16 59	16 56		17 11		17 16	17 02		17 29	17 26		17 41		17 46	17 32	17 59
Balham 4 ⊖	d	16 33	16 30					16 51	16 37	17 03	17 00				17 21	17 07		17 33	17 30				17 51	17 37	18 03
London Bridge 4 ⊖	d																								
Tulse Hill 3	d			16 30		16 42						17 00		17 12						17 30		17 42			
New Cross Gate 4 ⊖	d																								
Norwood Junction 2	d								16 57							17 27								17 57	
West Croydon 4	d		16 49						17 04		17 19					17 34			17 49					18 04	
Waddon	d		16 51						17 06		17 21					17 36			17 51					18 06	
Wallington	d		16 55						17 10		17 25					17 40			17 55					18 10	
Carshalton Beeches	d		16 57						17 12		17 27					17 42			17 57					18 12	
Mitcham Eastfields	d	16 40				16 50		16 58		17 10				17 20	17 28			17 40				17 50	17 58		18 10
Mitcham Junction	d	16 43				16 53		17 01		17 13				17 23	17 31			17 43				17 53	18 01		18 13
Hackbridge	d	16 46				16 56		17 04		17 16				17 26	17 34			17 46				17 56	18 04		18 16
Carshalton	d	16 49				16 59		17 07		17 19				17 29	17 37			17 49				17 59	18 07		18 19
Sutton (Surrey) 4	a	16 52	17 01	17 01		17 03		17 10	17 16	17 22	17 31	17 31		17 33	17 40	17 46		17 52	18 01	18 01		18 03	18 10	18 16	18 22
	d	16 53						17 11		17 23					17 41			17 53					18 11		18 23
Belmont	d																								
Banstead	d																								
Epsom Downs	a																								
Cheam	d	16 55						17 13		17 25					17 43			17 55					18 13		18 25
Ewell East	d	16 59						17 17		17 29					17 47			17 59					18 17		18 29
Epsom 3	a	17 03			17 06			17 21		17 33			17 36		17 51			18 03			18 06		18 21		18 33
	d				17 08			17 21					17 38		17 51						18 08		18 21		
Ashtead	d				17 12			17 25					17 42		17 55						18 12		18 25		
Leatherhead	d				17 15			17 28					17 45		17 58						18 15		18 28		
Bookham	d				17 21																18 21				
Effingham Junction 6	d				17 25																18 25				
Guildford	a				17 44																18 44				
Box Hill & Westhumble	d							17 33							18 03								18 33		
Dorking 4	a							17 36					17 53		18 06								18 36		
	d																								
Holmwood	d																								
Ockley	d																								
Warnham	d																								
Horsham 4	a																								

		SN		FC	SW	FC	SN	SN	SN	FC	SW	FC		SN	SN	SN	FC	SW	FC	SN	SN	SN		FC	SW
London Victoria 15 ⊖	d	17 49					18 08	17 54	18 19					18 38	18 24	18 49				19 08	18 54	19 19			
London Waterloo 15 ⊖	d				18 02						18 32							19 02							19 32
Clapham Junction 10	d	17 56			18 11		18 16	18 02	18 26		18 41			18 46	18 32	18 56		19 11		19 16	19 02	19 26			19 41
Balham 4 ⊖	d	18 00					18 21	18 07	18 30					18 51	18 37	19 00				19 21	19 07	19 30			
London Bridge 4 ⊖	d																								
Tulse Hill 3	d			18 00		18 12				18 30		18 42					19 00		19 12					19 30	
New Cross Gate 4 ⊖	d																								
Norwood Junction 2	d							18 27							18 57						19 27				
West Croydon 4	d	18 19						18 34	18 49						19 04	19 19					19 34	19 49			
Waddon	d	18 21						18 36	18 51						19 06	19 21					19 36	19 51			
Wallington	d	18 25						18 40	18 55						19 10	19 25					19 40	19 55			
Carshalton Beeches	d	18 27						18 42	18 57						19 12	19 27					19 42	19 57			
Mitcham Eastfields	d					18 20	18 28					18 50		18 58					19 20	19 28					
Mitcham Junction	d					18 23	18 31					18 53		19 01					19 23	19 31					
Hackbridge	d					18 26	18 34					18 56		19 04					19 26	19 34					
Carshalton	d					18 29	18 37					18 59		19 07					19 29	19 37					
Sutton (Surrey) 4	a	18 31		18 31		18 33	18 40	18 46	19 01	19 01		19 03		19 10	19 16	19 31	19 31		19 33	19 40	19 46	20 01		20 01	
	d						18 41							19 11						19 41					
Belmont	d																								
Banstead	d																								
Epsom Downs	a																								
Cheam	d						18 43							19 13						19 43					
Ewell East	d						18 47							19 17						19 47					
Epsom 3	a				18 36		18 51				19 06			19 21				19 36		19 51					20 06
	d				18 38		18 51				19 08			19 21				19 38		19 51					20 08
Ashtead	d				18 42		18 55				19 12			19 25				19 42		19 55					20 12
Leatherhead	d				18 45		18 58				19 15			19 28				19 45		19 58					20 15
Bookham	d										19 21														20 21
Effingham Junction 6	d										19 25														20 25
Guildford	a										19 44														20 44
Box Hill & Westhumble	d						19 03							19 33						20 03					
Dorking 4	a				18 53		19 06							19 36				19 53		20 06					
	d																								
Holmwood	d																								
Ockley	d																								
Warnham	d																								
Horsham 4	a																								

Table 182

London - Sutton, Epsom, Guildford, Dorking and Horsham

Sundays from 7 October

Network Diagram - see first Page of Table 177

		FC	SN	SN	SN	FC	SW	FC		SN	SN	SN	FC	SW	FC	SN	SN	SN		FC	SW	SN	SN	SN	FC
London Victoria ⊖	d		19 38	19 24	19 49					20 08	19 54	20 19				20 38	20 24	20 49				21 08	20 54	21 19	
London Waterloo ⊖	d						20 02							20 32							21 02				
Clapham Junction	d		19 46	19 32	19 56		20 11			20 16	20 02	20 26		20 41		20 46	20 32	20 56			21 11	21 16	21 02	21 26	
Balham ⊖	d		19 51	19 37	20 00					20 21	20 07	20 30				20 51	20 37	21 00				21 21	21 07	21 30	
London Bridge ⊖	d																								
Tulse Hill	d	19 42				20 00		20 12					20 30		20 42					21 00					21 30
New Cross Gate ⊖	d																								
Norwood Junction	d			19 57							20 27						20 57						21 27		
West Croydon	d			20 04	20 19						20 34	20 49					21 04	21 19					21 34	21 49	
Waddon	d			20 06	20 21						20 36	20 51					21 06	21 21					21 36	21 51	
Wallington	d			20 10	20 25						20 40	20 55					21 10	21 25					21 40	21 55	
Carshalton Beeches	d			20 12	20 27						20 42	20 57					21 12	21 27					21 42	21 57	
Mitcham Eastfields	d	19 50	19 58					20 20		20 28					20 50	20 58						21 28			
Mitcham Junction	d	19 53	20 01					20 23		20 31					20 53	21 01						21 31			
Hackbridge	d	19 56	20 04					20 26		20 34					20 56	21 04						21 34			
Carshalton	d	19 59	20 07					20 29		20 37					20 59	21 07						21 37			
Sutton (Surrey)	a	20 03	20 10	20 16	20 31	20 31		20 33		20 40	20 46	21 01	21 01		21 03	21 10	21 16	21 31		21 31		21 40	21 46	22 01	22 01
	d		20 11							20 41						21 11						21 41			
Belmont	d																								
Banstead	d																								
Epsom Downs	a																								
Cheam	d		20 13							20 43						21 13						21 43			
Ewell East	d		20 17							20 47						21 17						21 47			
Epsom	a		20 21				20 36			20 51				21 06		21 21					21 36	21 51			
	d		20 21				20 38			20 51				21 08		21 21					21 38	21 51			
Ashtead	d		20 25				20 42			20 55				21 12		21 25					21 42	21 55			
Leatherhead	d		20 28				20 45			20 58				21 15		21 28					21 45	21 58			
Bookham	d													21 21											
Effingham Junction	d													21 25											
Guildford	a													21 44											
Box Hill & Westhumble	d		20 33							21 03						21 33						22 03			
Dorking	a		20 36				20 53			21 06						21 36					21 53	22 06			
	d																								
Holmwood	d																								
Ockley	d																								
Warnham	d																								
Horsham	a																								

		SW	SN	SN		SN	SW	SN	SN	SN	SW	SN	SN	SN		SW	SN	SN	SW	SN
London Victoria ⊖	d		21 38	21 24		21 49		22 08	21 54	22 19		22 38	22 24	22 49			23 08	22 54		23 19
London Waterloo ⊖	d	21 32					22 02				22 32					23 02			23 32	
Clapham Junction	d	21 41	21 46	21 32		21 56	22 11	22 16	22 02	22 26	22 41	22 46	22 32	22 56		23 11	23 16	23 02	23 41	23 27
Balham ⊖	d		21 51	21 38		22 00		22 21	22 07	22 30		22 51	22 38	23 00			23 21	23 07		23 32
London Bridge ⊖	d																			
Tulse Hill	d																			
New Cross Gate ⊖	d																			
Norwood Junction	d			21 57					22 27				22 57					23 27		
West Croydon	d			22 04		22 19			22 34	22 49			23 04	23 19				23 34		23 50
Waddon	d			22 06		22 21			22 36	22 51			23 06	23 21				23 36		23 52
Wallington	d			22 10		22 25			22 40	22 55			23 10	23 25				23 40		23 56
Carshalton Beeches	d			22 12		22 27			22 42	22 57			23 12	23 27				23 42		23 58
Mitcham Eastfields	d		21 58					22 28				22 58					23 28			
Mitcham Junction	d		22 01					22 31				23 01					23 31			
Hackbridge	d		22 04					22 34				23 04					23 34			
Carshalton	d		22 07					22 37				23 07					23 37			
Sutton (Surrey)	a		22 10	22 16		22 31		22 40	22 46	23 01		23 10	23 16	23 31			23 40	23 46		00 02
	d		22 11					22 41				23 11					23 41			00 04
Belmont	d																			
Banstead	d																			
Epsom Downs	a																			
Cheam	d		22 13					22 43				23 13					23 43			00 06
Ewell East	d		22 17					22 47				23 17					23 47			00 10
Epsom	a	22 06	22 21				22 36	22 51			23 06	23 21				23 36	23 51		00 06	00 14
	d	22 08	22 21				22 38	22 51			23 08	23 21					23 51			
Ashtead	d	22 12	22 25				22 42	22 55			23 12	23 25					23 55			
Leatherhead	d	22 15	22 28				22 45	22 58			23 15	23 28					23 58			
Bookham	d	22 21									23 21									
Effingham Junction	d	22 25									23 25									
Guildford	a	22 44									23 44									
Box Hill & Westhumble	d		22 33					23 03				23 33					00 03			
Dorking	a		22 36				22 53	23 06				23 36					00 06			
	d																			
Holmwood	d																			
Ockley	d																			
Warnham	d																			
Horsham	a																			

Table 182

Horsham, Dorking, Guildford, Epsom and Sutton - London

Mondays to Fridays until 5 October

Network Diagram - see first Page of Table 177

Miles	Miles	Miles			SN MO A	SN MO A	SN MO A	SN MX	SN	SW	SN	SN	SN		FC	SN	SW	SN	SW	SN	SN	FC	SN		SW
—	—	0	Horsham	d																			05 49		
—	—	2	Warnham	d																			05 53		
—	—	6½	Ockley	d																			06 00		
—	—	8¾	Holmwood	d																			06 04		
—	—	13¾	Dorking	a																			06 10		
—	—	—		d			23p16										05 48						06 11		
—	—	14½	Box Hill & Westhumble	d			23p18										05 50						06 13		
0	—	—	Guildford	d						04 58															05 58
8¼	—	—	Effingham Junction	d						05 16															06 16
10	—	—	Bookham	d						05 19															06 19
12½	—	17¾	Leatherhead	d			23p23			05 24							05 56						06 18		06 24
14½	—	—	Ashtead	d			23p27			05 28							05 59						06 22		06 28
16¼	—	—	Epsom	a			23p31			05 32							06 04						06 26		06 32
—	—	—		d			23p32		05 23	05 34		05 39				05 57	06 04		06 18				06 27		06 34
17¾	—	—	Ewell East	d			23p36		05 27			05 43				06 01							06 31		
19¼	—	—	Cheam	d			23p39		05 30			05 46				06 04							06 34		
—	0	—	Epsom Downs	d				23p43																	
—	1½	—	Banstead	d				23p46																	
—	3	—	Belmont	d				23p49																	
20¼	4	5½	Sutton (Surrey)	a			23p42	23p52	05 33			05 49				06 07							06 37		
—	—	—		d	23p25	23p40	23p43	23p53	05 33		05 37	05 49	06 03		06 05	06 08		06 14		06 14	06 33	06 34	06 37		
—	5¼	—	Carshalton	d			23p46				05 40					06 11		06 17				06 37	06 40		
—	6¼	—	Hackbridge	d			23p48				05 42					06 13		06 19				06 39	06 43		
—	7	—	Mitcham Junction	d			23p52				05 46					06 17		06 23				06 42	06 46		
—	8	—	Mitcham Eastfields	d			23p55				05 49					06 20		06 26				06 45	06 49		
21¼	—	—	Carshalton Beeches	d	23p28	23p43		23p56	05 36			05 52	06 06							06 17	06 36				
22	—	—	Wallington	d	23p30	23p45		23p58	05 39			05 55	06 08							06 20	06 38				
23½	—	—	Waddon	d	23p33	23p48		00 01	05 42			05 58	06 11							06 23	06 41				
24½	—	0	West Croydon	d	23p37	23p52		00a04	05 45			06 01	06 15							06 26	06 45				
26¼	—	—	Norwood Junction	d					05 50				06 20								06 50				
32¼	—	—	New Cross Gate ⊖	d					06 08																
—	—	6	Tulse Hill	a							05 57				06 42			06 34				06 53			
—	—	—		d							05 57							06 34							
35	—	12	London Bridge ⊖	a					06 14		06 08		06 33					06 51			07 04				
—	11¼	—	Balham ⊖	d	23p53	00 08	00 01					06 17				06 27				06 42			06 57		
—	13¼	—	Clapham Junction	a	23p57	00 12	00 06			06 00		06 23				06 31	06 30		06 45	06 48			07 01		07 00
—	—	—	London Waterloo ⊖	a						06 11							06 40		06 55						07 12
—	16	—	London Victoria ⊖	a	00 04	00 19	00 15					06 31				06 38				06 58			07 08		

		SW	SN	FC	SN	SN	FC	SN	SW		SN	SN	SN	SN	SW	SN	SW	FC	SN		SW	SW	FC	SN	SN
Horsham	d							06 20											06 55						
Warnham	d							06 24											06 59						
Ockley	d							06 31											07 06						
Holmwood	d							06 35											07 10						
Dorking	a							06 41											07 16						
	d	06 32						06 44						06 59	07 02				07 17			07 32			
Box Hill & Westhumble	d	06 34						06 46						07 01	07 04							07 34			
Guildford	d								06 28												06 58				
Effingham Junction	d								06 48												07 16				
Bookham	d								06 51												07 19				
Leatherhead	d	06 39						06 51	06 56					07 06	07 09				07 23		07 26	07 39			
Ashtead	d	06 43						06 55	06 59					07 10	07 13				07 26		07 29	07 43			
Epsom	a	06 47						06 59	07 04					07 14	07 17				07 31		07 34	07 47			
	d	06 48				06 49		07 00	07 04					07 15	07 18	07 21	07 22		07 31		07 34	07 48			
Ewell East	d					06 53		07 04						07 19		07 25									
Cheam	d					06 56		07 07						07 22		07 28			07 37						
Epsom Downs	d		06 34								07 05													07 34	
Banstead	d		06 37								07 08													07 37	
Belmont	d		06 40								07 11													07 40	
Sutton (Surrey)	a		06 43			06 59		07 10			07 14			07 25		07 31			07 40					07 43	
	d		06 44	06 45	06 50	07 00	07 05	07 10			07 15	07 20	07 22	07 26		07 32		07 37	07 42				07 40	07 45	07 49
Carshalton	d				06 53			07 13				07 23		07 29				07 40	07 45						07 52
Hackbridge	d				06 55			07 16				07 25		07 31				07 42							07 54
Mitcham Junction	d				06 59			07 19				07 29		07 35				07 45	07 49						07 58
Mitcham Eastfields	d				07 02			07 22				07 32		07 38				07 48	07 52						08 01
Carshalton Beeches	d		06 47			07 03					07 18		07 25			07 35								07 48	
Wallington	d		06 50			07 05					07 20		07 27			07 37								07 50	
Waddon	d		06 53			07 08					07 23		07 30			07 40								07 53	
West Croydon	d		06 58			07 13					07 28		07 34			07 44								07 58	
Norwood Junction	d					07 18										07 49									
New Cross Gate ⊖	d																								
Tulse Hill	a			07 20	07 09		07 43					07 39						07 56					08 13		08 09
	d				07 10							07 41													08 10
London Bridge ⊖	a				07 28	07 32						07 59				08 05									08 28
Balham ⊖	d		07 14					07 29			07 44		07 50	07 47					07 59					08 14	
Clapham Junction	a	07 15	07 19					07 34	07 30		07 49		07 55	07 51	07 42		07 48		08 04		08 01	08 12		08 19	
London Waterloo ⊖	a	07 27							07 42						07 54		08 00				08 13	08 24			
London Victoria ⊖	a		07 30					07 41			08 00		08 06	08 00					08 11					08 30	

A from 21 May until 1 October

Horsham, Dorking, Guildford, Epsom and Sutton - London

Network Diagram - see first Page of Table 177

		SN	SN	SW	SN		FC	FC	SN	SW	SW	SW	SN	SN	SN		SN	SW	FC	FC	SN	SN	SW	SN	SN
Horsham 4	d								07 21													07 56			
Warnham	d								07 25													08 00			
Ockley	d								07 32													08 07			
Holmwood	d								07 36													08 11			
Dorking 4	a								07 42													08 17			
	d								07 46		08 02											08 22	08 31		
Box Hill & Westhumble	d										08 04											08 24	08 33		
Guildford	d				07 25													07 58							08 16
Effingham Junction 6	d				07 37					07 46								08 16							08 32
Bookham	d				07 40					07 49								08 19							08 35
Leatherhead	d				07 45				07 52	07 56	08 09							08 25				08 29	08 38		08 41
Ashtead	d				07 49				07 55	07 59	08 13							08 28				08 33	08 42		08 45
Epsom 3	a				07 53				08 00	08 04	08 17							08 33				08 37	08 46		08 49
	d		07 49	07 52	07 54				08 02	08 04	08 18	08 22					08 22	08 34				08 38	08 48		08 50
Ewell East	d		07 53		07 58				08 06								08 26					08 42			08 54
Cheam	d		07 56		08 01				08 09								08 29					08 45			08 57
Epsom Downs	d												08 04								08 34				
Banstead	d												08 07								08 37				
Belmont	d												08 10								08 40				
Sutton (Surrey) 4	a		07 59		08 04				08 12				08 13				08 32				08 43	08 48			09 00
	d	07 53	07 59		08 05		08 08	08 08	08 12				08 14	08 20	08 29		08 32		08 39	08 41	08 45	08 48		08 57	09 00
Carshalton	d		08 02				08 11		08 15					08 23	08 32				08 42			08 51		09 00	09 03
Hackbridge	d		08 05				08 13		08 18					08 25	08 34				08 44			08 54		09 02	09 06
Mitcham Junction	d		08 08				08 16		08 21					08 29	08 38				08 47			08 57		09 06	09 09
Mitcham Eastfields	d		08 11				08 19		08 24					08 32	08 41				08 50			09 00		09 09	09 12
Carshalton Beeches	d	07 56			08 08								08 17				08 35				08 48				
Wallington	d	07 58			08 10								08 19				08 38				08 50				
Waddon	d	08 01											08 22				08 41				08 53				
West Croydon 4	d	08 05			08 15								08 26				08 44				08 57				
Norwood Junction 2	d				08 20												08 49								
New Cross Gate 4 ⊖	d																								
Tulse Hill 3	a						08 27	08 43						08 40					08 58	09 12				09 16	
	d													08 40										09 16	
London Bridge 4 ⊖	a				08 35									08 57			09 04							09 35	
Balham 4 ⊖	d	08 21	08 18										08 43		08 49						09 13	09 07			09 18
Clapham Junction 10	a	08 25	08 22	08 18					08 32	08 31	08 42	08 48	08 49		08 54			09 00			09 18	09 11	09 15		09 22
London Waterloo 15 ⊖	a			08 30						08 43	08 54	09 00						09 12					09 27		
London Victoria 15 ⊖	a	08 36	08 30						08 39				09 00		09 04						09 31	09 20			09 33

			SW	SN	FC	FC	SN	SN	SW	SN	SN		SW	SN	FC	FC	SN	SN	SN	SN	SW		SW	SN	FC
Horsham 4	d																			09 09					
Warnham	d																			09 13					
Ockley	d																			09 20					
Holmwood	d																			09 24					
Dorking 4	a																			09 30					
	d							08 57	09 02											09 31	09 35				
Box Hill & Westhumble	d							08 59	09 04											09 33					
Guildford	d												08 58										09 28		
Effingham Junction 6	d		08 48										09 16										09 46		
Bookham	d		08 51										09 19										09 49		
Leatherhead	d		08 56					09 04	09 09				09 24							09 38	09 41		09 54		
Ashtead	d		08 59					09 08	09 13				09 28							09 42	09 45		09 58		
Epsom 3	a		09 04					09 12	09 17				09 32							09 46	09 49		10 02		
	d		09 04					09 13	09 18		09 19		09 35					09 42		09 49	09 50		10 05		
Ewell East	d							09 17			09 23							09 46		09 53					
Cheam	d							09 20			09 26							09 49		09 56					
Epsom Downs	d									09 09							09 35								
Banstead	d									09 12							09 38								
Belmont	d									09 15							09 41								
Sutton (Surrey) 4	a							09 23		09 18	09 29						09 44	09 52		09 59					
	d			09 03	09 11	09 13	09 15	09 23		09 23	09 29			09 33	09 37	09 38	09 45	09 52	09 52	09 59				10 03	10 07
Carshalton	d					09 16					09 32					09 41				10 02					
Hackbridge	d					09 18					09 35					09 43				10 05					
Mitcham Junction	d					09 21					09 38					09 46				10 08					
Mitcham Eastfields	d					09 24		09 32			09 41					09 49				10 11					
Carshalton Beeches	d			09 06			09 18			09 26				09 36			09 48		09 55					10 06	
Wallington	d			09 08			09 20			09 28				09 38			09 50		09 57					10 08	
Waddon	d			09 11			09 23			09 31				09 41			09 53		10 00					10 11	
West Croydon 4	d			09 15			09 28			09 35				09 45			09 58		10 04					10 15	
Norwood Junction 2	d			09 22										09 52										10 22	
New Cross Gate 4 ⊖	d																								
Tulse Hill 3	a				09 42	09 32									10 12	09 57									10 42
	d																								
London Bridge 4 ⊖	a																								
Balham 4 ⊖	d			09 41			09 44			09 52	09 49			10 09			10 14		10 21	10 18				10 39	
Clapham Junction 10	a		09 30	09 46			09 49	09 42	09 45	09 57	09 53		10 00	10 15			10 19	10 10	10 26	10 22	10 15		10 30	10 45	
London Waterloo 15 ⊖	a		09 42						09 57				10 10								10 25		10 40		
London Victoria 15 ⊖	a			09 58			09 58	09 52		10 05	10 00			10 24			10 28	10 20	10 34	10 31				10 53	

Table 182

Horsham, Dorking, Guildford, Epsom and Sutton - London

Mondays to Fridays

until 5 October

Network Diagram - see first Page of Table 177

		FC	SN	SN	SN	SW	SN		SW	SN	FC	FC	SN	SN	SW	SN	SN		SW	SN	FC	FC	SN	SN	SW
Horsham 4	d													10 04											
Warnham	d													10 08											
Ockley	d													10 15											
Holmwood	d													10 19											
Dorking 4	a													10 25											
	d				09 57	10 05								10 26	10 35									10 58	11 05
Box Hill & Westhumble	d				09 59									10 28											
Guildford	d								09 58										10 28						
Effingham Junction 6	d								10 16										10 46						
Bookham	d								10 19										10 49						
Leatherhead	d				10 04	10 11			10 24					10 33	10 41				10 54					11 04	11 11
Ashtead	d				10 08	10 14			10 28					10 37	10 44				10 58					11 07	11 14
Epsom 3	a				10 12	10 19			10 32					10 41	10 49				11 02					11 12	11 19
	d		10 04		10 13	10 20	10 19		10 35					10 42	10 50		10 49		11 05				11 04	11 13	11 20
Ewell East	d		10 08		10 17		10 23							10 46			10 53						11 08		
Cheam	d		10 11		10 20		10 26							10 49			10 56						11 11	11 18	
Epsom Downs	d												10 35												
Banstead	d												10 38												
Belmont	d												10 41												
Sutton (Surrey) 4	a		10 14		10 23		10 29						10 44	10 52			10 59						11 14	11 21	
	d	10 08	10 15	10 22	10 23		10 29			10 33	10 37	10 38	10 45	10 52		10 52	10 59			11 03	11 07	11 08	11 15	11 22	
Carshalton	d	10 11					10 32					10 41					11 02					11 11			
Hackbridge	d	10 13					10 35					10 43					11 05					11 13			
Mitcham Junction	d	10 16					10 38					10 46					11 08					11 16			
Mitcham Eastfields	d	10 19					10 41					10 49					11 11					11 19			
Carshalton Beeches	d		10 18	10 25						10 36			10 48			10 55				11 06			11 18		
Wallington	d		10 20	10 27						10 38			10 50			10 57				11 08			11 20		
Waddon	d		10 23	10 30						10 41			10 53			11 00				11 11			11 23		
West Croydon 4	d		10 28	10 34						10 45			10 58			11 04				11 15			11 28		
Norwood Junction 2	d									10 52										11 22					
New Cross Gate 4 ⊖	d																								
Tulse Hill 3	a	10 27									11 12	10 57									11 42	11 27			
	d																								
London Bridge 4 ⊖	a																								
Balham 4 ⊖	d		10 44	10 51			10 48			11 09			11 14			11 21	11 18			11 40			11 44		
Clapham Junction 10	a		10 49	10 56	10 40	10 45	10 52		11 00	11 14			11 19	11 10	11 15	11 26	11 22		11 30	11 45			11 49	11 40	11 45
London Waterloo 15 ⊖	a					10 55			11 10						11 25				11 40						11 55
London Victoria 15 ⊖	a		10 58	11 04	10 48		11 00			11 23			11 28	11 20		11 34	11 30			11 54			11 58	11 50	

		SN	SN		SW	SN	FC	FC	SN	SN	SW	SN	SN		SW	SN	FC	FC	SN	SN	SW	SN	SN		SW
Horsham 4	d									11 04															
Warnham	d									11 08															
Ockley	d									11 15															
Holmwood	d									11 19															
Dorking 4	a									11 25															
	d									11 26	11 35									11 58	12 05				
Box Hill & Westhumble	d									11 28															
Guildford	d				10 58										11 28										11 58
Effingham Junction 6	d				11 16										11 46										12 16
Bookham	d				11 19										11 49										12 19
Leatherhead	d				11 24					11 33	11 41				11 54					12 04	12 11				12 24
Ashtead	d				11 28					11 37	11 44				11 58					12 07	12 14				12 28
Epsom 3	a				11 32					11 41	11 49				12 02					12 12	12 19				12 32
	d		11 19		11 35					11 42	11 50		11 49		12 05				12 04	12 13	12 20		12 19		12 35
Ewell East	d		11 23							11 46			11 53						12 08				12 23		
Cheam	d		11 26							11 49			11 56						12 11	12 18			12 26		
Epsom Downs	d								11 35																
Banstead	d								11 38																
Belmont	d								11 41																
Sutton (Surrey) 4	a		11 29						11 44	11 52			11 59						12 14	12 21			12 29		
	d	11 22	11 29			11 33	11 37	11 38	11 45	11 52		11 52	11 59			12 03	12 07	12 08	12 15	12 22		12 22	12 29		
Carshalton	d		11 32					11 41					12 02					12 11					12 32		
Hackbridge	d		11 35					11 43					12 05					12 13					12 35		
Mitcham Junction	d		11 38					11 46					12 08					12 16					12 38		
Mitcham Eastfields	d		11 41					11 49					12 11					12 19					12 41		
Carshalton Beeches	d	11 25				11 36			11 48			11 55				12 06			12 18			12 25			
Wallington	d	11 27				11 38			11 50			11 57				12 08			12 20			12 27			
Waddon	d	11 30				11 41			11 53			12 00				12 11			12 23			12 30			
West Croydon 4	d	11 34				11 45			11 58			12 04				12 15			12 28			12 34			
Norwood Junction 2	d					11 52										12 22									
New Cross Gate 4 ⊖	d																								
Tulse Hill 3	a						12 12	11 57									12 42	12 27							
	d																								
London Bridge 4 ⊖	a																								
Balham 4 ⊖	d	11 51	11 48			12 09			12 14			12 21	12 18			12 39			12 44			12 51	12 48		
Clapham Junction 10	a	11 56	11 52		12 00	12 14			12 19	12 10	12 15	12 26	12 22		12 30	12 44			12 49	12 40	12 45	12 56	12 52		13 00
London Waterloo 15 ⊖	a				12 10						12 25				12 40						12 55				13 10
London Victoria 15 ⊖	a	12 04	12 00			12 23			12 28	12 18		12 34	12 30			12 53			12 58	12 48		13 04	13 00		

Table 182

Mondays to Fridays

until 5 October

Horsham, Dorking, Guildford, Epsom and Sutton - London

Network Diagram - see first Page of Table 177

		SN	FC	FC	SN	SN	SW	SN	SN		SW	SN	FC	FC	SN	SN	SW	SN	SN		SW	SN	FC	FC	SN
Horsham ■	d					12 04																			
Warnham	d					12 08																			
Ockley	d					12 15																			
Holmwood	d					12 19																			
Dorking ■	a					12 25																			
	d					12 26	12 35									12 58	13 05								
Box Hill & Westhumble	d					12 28																			
Guildford	d										12 28										12 58				
Effingham Junction ■	d										12 46										13 16				
Bookham	d										12 49										13 19				
Leatherhead	d					12 33	12 41				12 54					13 04	13 11				13 24				
Ashtead	d					12 37	12 44				12 58					13 07	13 14				13 28				
Epsom ■	a					12 41	12 49				13 02					13 12	13 19				13 32				
	d					12 42	12 50		12 49		13 05				13 04	13 13	13 20		13 19		13 35				
Ewell East	d					12 46			12 53						13 08				13 23						
Cheam	d					12 49			12 56						13 11	13 18			13 26						
Epsom Downs	d				12 35																				13 35
Banstead	d				12 38																				13 38
Belmont	d				12 41																				13 41
Sutton (Surrey) ■	a				12 44	12 52			12 59						13 14	13 21			13 29						13 44
	d	12 33	12 37	12 38	12 45	12 52		12 52	12 59			13 03	13 07	13 08	13 15	13 22		13 22	13 29			13 33	13 37	13 38	13 45
Carshalton	d			12 41					13 02					13 11					13 32					13 41	
Hackbridge	d			12 43					13 05					13 13					13 35					13 43	
Mitcham Junction	d			12 46					13 08					13 16					13 38					13 46	
Mitcham Eastfields	d			12 49					13 11					13 19					13 41					13 49	
Carshalton Beeches	d	12 36			12 48			12 55				13 06			13 18			13 25				13 36			13 48
Wallington	d	12 38			12 50			12 57				13 08			13 20			13 27				13 38			13 50
Waddon	d	12 41			12 53			13 00				13 11			13 23			13 30				13 41			13 53
West Croydon ■	d	12 45			12 58			13 04				13 15			13 28			13 34				13 45			13 58
Norwood Junction ■	d	12 52										13 22										13 52			
New Cross Gate ■ ⊖	d																								
Tulse Hill ■	a		13 12	12 57									13 42	13 27									14 12	13 57	
	d																								
London Bridge ■ ⊖	a																								
Balham ■ ⊖	d	13 09			13 14			13 21	13 18			13 39			13 44			13 51	13 48			14 09			14 14
Clapham Junction ■	a	13 14			13 19	13 10	13 15	13 26	13 22		13 30	13 44			13 49	13 40	13 45	13 56	13 52		14 00	14 14			14 19
London Waterloo ■ ⊖	a						13 25				13 40						13 55				14 10				
London Victoria ■ ⊖	a	13 23			13 28	13 18		13 34	13 30			13 53			13 58	13 48		14 04	14 00			14 23			14 28

		SN	SW	SN	SN		SW	SN	FC	FC	SN	SN	SW	SN	SN		SW	SN	FC	FC	SN	SN	SW	SN	SN
Horsham ■	d	13 04																				14 04			
Warnham	d	13 08																				14 08			
Ockley	d	13 15																				14 15			
Holmwood	d	13 19																				14 19			
Dorking ■	a	13 25																				14 25			
	d	13 26	13 35									13 58	14 05									14 26	14 35		
Box Hill & Westhumble	d	13 28																				14 28			
Guildford	d						13 28										13 58								
Effingham Junction ■	d						13 46										14 16								
Bookham	d						13 49										14 19								
Leatherhead	d	13 33	13 41				13 54					14 04	14 11				14 24					14 33	14 41		
Ashtead	d	13 37	13 44				13 58					14 07	14 14				14 28					14 37	14 44		
Epsom ■	a	13 41	13 49				14 02					14 12	14 19				14 32					14 41	14 49		
	d	13 42	13 50		13 49		14 05				14 04	14 13	14 20		14 19		14 35					14 42	14 50		14 49
Ewell East	d	13 46			13 53						14 08				14 23							14 46			14 53
Cheam	d	13 49			13 56						14 11	14 18			14 26							14 49			14 56
Epsom Downs	d																				14 35				
Banstead	d																				14 38				
Belmont	d																				14 41				
Sutton (Surrey) ■	a	13 52			13 59						14 14	14 21			14 29						14 44	14 52			14 59
	d	13 52		13 52	13 59			14 03	14 07	14 08	14 15	14 22		14 22	14 29			14 33	14 37	14 38	14 45	14 52		14 52	14 59
Carshalton	d				14 02					14 11					14 32					14 41					15 02
Hackbridge	d				14 05					14 13					14 35					14 43					15 05
Mitcham Junction	d				14 08					14 16					14 38					14 46					15 08
Mitcham Eastfields	d				14 11					14 19					14 41					14 49					15 11
Carshalton Beeches	d			13 55				14 06			14 18			14 25				14 36			14 48			14 55	
Wallington	d			13 57				14 08			14 20			14 27				14 38			14 50			14 57	
Waddon	d			14 00				14 11			14 23			14 30				14 41			14 53			15 00	
West Croydon ■	d			14 04				14 15			14 28			14 34				14 45			14 58			15 04	
Norwood Junction ■	d							14 22										14 52							
New Cross Gate ■ ⊖	d																								
Tulse Hill ■	a								14 42	14 27									15 12	14 57					
	d																								
London Bridge ■ ⊖	a																								
Balham ■ ⊖	d			14 21	14 18			14 39			14 44			14 51	14 48			15 09			15 14			15 21	15 18
Clapham Junction ■	a	14 10	14 15	14 26	14 22		14 30	14 44			14 49	14 40	14 45	14 56	14 52		15 00	15 14			15 19	15 10	15 15	15 26	15 22
London Waterloo ■ ⊖	a		14 25				14 40						14 55				15 10						15 25		
London Victoria ■ ⊖	a	14 18		14 34	14 30			14 53			14 58	14 48		15 04	15 00			15 24			15 28	15 22		15 34	15 30

Table 182

Mondays to Fridays

until 5 October

Horsham, Dorking, Guildford, Epsom and Sutton - London

Network Diagram - see first Page of Table 177

			SW	SN	FC	FC	SN	SN	SW	SN	SN		SW	SN	FC	FC	SN	SN	SW	SN	SN		SW	SN	FC
Horsham ■	d																	15 04							
Warnham	d																	15 08							
Ockley	d																	15 15							
Holmwood	d																	15 19							
Dorking ■	a																	15 25							
	d							14 58	15 05									15 26	15 35						
Box Hill & Westhumble	d																	15 28							
Guildford	d		14 28										14 58										15 28		
Effingham Junction ■	d		14 46										15 16										15 46		
Bookham	d		14 49										15 19										15 49		
Leatherhead	d		14 54					15 04	15 11				15 24					15 33	15 41				15 54		
Ashtead	d		14 58					15 07	15 14				15 28					15 37	15 44				15 58		
Epsom ■	a		15 02					15 12	15 19				15 32					15 41	15 49				16 02		
	d		15 05				15 04	15 13	15 20		15 19		15 35					15 42	15 50		15 49		16 05		
Ewell East	d						15 08				15 23							15 46			15 53				
Cheam	d						15 11	15 18			15 26							15 49			15 56				
Epsom Downs	d																15 35								
Banstead	d																15 38								
Belmont	d																15 41								
Sutton (Surrey) ■	a						15 14	15 21			15 29						15 44	15 52			15 59				
	d			15 03	15 07	15 08	15 15	15 22		15 22	15 29			15 33	15 37	15 38	15 45	15 52		15 52	15 59			16 03	16 07
Carshalton	d					15 11					15 32					15 41					16 02				
Hackbridge	d					15 13					15 35					15 43					16 05				
Mitcham Junction	d					15 16					15 38					15 46					16 08				
Mitcham Eastfields	d					15 19					15 41					15 49					16 11				
Carshalton Beeches	d			15 06			15 18			15 25				15 36			15 48			15 55				16 06	
Wallington	d			15 08			15 20			15 27				15 38			15 50			15 57				16 08	
Waddon	d			15 11			15 23			15 30				15 41			15 53			16 00				16 11	
West Croydon ■	d			15 15			15 28			15 34				15 45			15 58			16 04				16 15	
Norwood Junction ■	d			15 22										15 52										16 22	
New Cross Gate ■ ⊖	d																								
Tulse Hill ■	a				15 42	15 27									16 12	15 57									16 46
	d																								
London Bridge ■ ⊖	a																								
Balham ■ ⊖	d			15 39			15 44			15 51	15 48			16 09			16 14			16 21	16 18			16 39	
Clapham Junction ■	a		15 30	15 44			15 49	15 40	15 45	15 56	15 52		16 00	16 14			16 19	16 10	16 15	16 26	16 23		16 30	16 45	
London Waterloo ■ ⊖	a		15 40						15 55				16 10						16 25				16 40		
London Victoria ■ ⊖	a			15 54			15 58	15 52		16 04	16 00			16 23			16 28	16 18		16 34	16 30			16 55	

		FC	SN	SN	SW	SN	SN		SW	SN	SN	FC	FC ■	SN	SW	SN	SN		SW	SN	FC	SN	FC	SN	SW
Horsham ■	d													16 04											
Warnham	d													16 08											
Ockley	d													16 15											
Holmwood	d													16 19											
Dorking ■	a													16 25											
	d			15 56	16 05									16 26	16 35									17 00	17 05
Box Hill & Westhumble	d			15 58										16 28										17 02	
Guildford	d								15 58										16 28						
Effingham Junction ■	d								16 16										16 46						
Bookham	d								16 19										16 49						
Leatherhead	d			16 03	16 11				16 24					16 33	16 41				16 54					17 07	17 11
Ashtead	d			16 07	16 14				16 28					16 37	16 44				16 58					17 11	17 14
Epsom ■	a			16 11	16 19				16 32					16 41	16 49				17 02					17 15	17 19
	d		16 04	16 12	16 20		16 19		16 35					16 42	16 50		16 49		17 05					17 19	17 20
Ewell East	d		16 08	16 16			16 23							16 46			16 53							17 23	
Cheam	d		16 11	16 19			16 26							16 49			16 56							17 26	
Epsom Downs	d										16 26											17 02			
Banstead	d										16 29											17 05			
Belmont	d										16 32											17 08			
Sutton (Surrey) ■	a		16 14	16 22			16 29				16 35			16 52			16 59					17 11		17 29	
	d	16 08	16 15	16 22		16 22	16 29			16 33	16 45	16 37	16 38	16 52		16 52	16 59			17 03	17 08	17 15	17 11	17 29	
Carshalton	d	16 11					16 32						16 41				17 02				17 11			17 32	
Hackbridge	d	16 13					16 35						16 43				17 05				17 13			17 35	
Mitcham Junction	d	16 16					16 38						16 46				17 08				17 16			17 38	
Mitcham Eastfields	d	16 19					16 41						16 49				17 11				17 19			17 41	
Carshalton Beeches	d		16 18			16 25				16 36	16 48					16 55				17 06		17 18			
Wallington	d		16 20			16 27				16 38	16 50					16 57				17 08		17 20			
Waddon	d		16 23			16 30				16 41	16 53					17 00				17 11		17 23			
West Croydon ■	d		16 28			16 34				16 45	16 58					17 04				17 18		17 28			
Norwood Junction ■	d									16 52										17 23					
New Cross Gate ■ ⊖	d																								
Tulse Hill ■	a	16 27										17 15	16 57								17 27		17 44		
	d																								
London Bridge ■ ⊖	a																								
Balham ■ ⊖	d		16 44			16 51	16 48			17 09	17 14					17 21	17 18			17 39		17 44		17 48	
Clapham Junction ■	a		16 49	16 40	16 45	16 56	16 53		17 00	17 14	17 19			17 10	17 15	17 26	17 23		17 30	17 44		17 49		17 52	17 45
London Waterloo ■ ⊖	a				16 55				17 10						17 25				17 40						17 55
London Victoria ■ ⊖	a		16 58	16 48		17 04	17 00			17 23	17 28			17 18		17 34	17 30			17 55		17 58		18 00	

Table 182

Mondays to Fridays

until 5 October

Horsham, Dorking, Guildford, Epsom and Sutton - London

Network Diagram - see first Page of Table 177

		SN	SW		FC	FC	SN	SN	SW	SN	SW	FC	FC		SN	SN	SW	SN	SW	FC	FC	SN	SN		SW
Horsham	d							17 07								17 34							18 04		
Warnham	d							17 11								17 38							18 08		
Ockley	d							17 18								17 45							18 15		
Holmwood	d							17 22								17 49							18 19		
Dorking	a							17 28								17 55							18 25		
	d							17 31	17 35							17 56	18 05						18 26		18 35
Box Hill & Westhumble	d							17 33								17 58							18 28		
Guildford	d		16 58								17 28								17 58						
Effingham Junction	d		17 16								17 46								18 16						
Bookham	d		17 19								17 49								18 19						
Leatherhead	d		17 24					17 38	17 41		17 54					18 03	18 11		18 24				18 33		18 41
Ashtead	d		17 28					17 42	17 45		17 58					18 07	18 14		18 28				18 37		18 45
Epsom	a		17 32					17 46	17 49		18 02					18 14	18 19		18 32				18 43		18 49
	d	17 23	17 35					17 49	17 50	17 52	18 05					18 17	18 20	18 22	18 35				18 49		18 50
Ewell East	d	17 27						17 53		17 56						18 23		18 26					18 53		
Cheam	d	17 30						17 56		17 59						18 26		18 29					18 56		
Epsom Downs	d						17 35								18 02							18 35			
Banstead	d						17 38								18 05							18 38			
Belmont	d						17 41								18 08							18 41			
Sutton (Surrey)	a	17 33					17 44	17 59		18 02					18 11	18 29		18 32				18 44	18 59		
	d	17 33			17 41	17 42	17 45	17 59		18 04		18 08	18 09		18 12	18 29		18 33		18 38	18 43	18 45	18 59		
Carshalton	d					17 45		18 02				18 11				18 32				18 41			19 02		
Hackbridge	d					17 47		18 05				18 13				18 35				18 43			19 05		
Mitcham Junction	d					17 50		18 08				18 16				18 38				18 46			19 08		
Mitcham Eastfields	d					17 53		18 11				18 19				18 41				18 49			19 11		
Carshalton Beeches	d	17 36					17 48			18 07					18 15			18 36				18 48			
Wallington	d	17 39					17 50			18 09					18 17			18 38				18 50			
Waddon	d	17 42					17 53			18 12					18 20			18 41				18 53			
West Croydon	d	17 48					17 58			18 18					18 28			18 47				18 58			
Norwood Junction	d	17 55								18 24								18 52							
New Cross Gate	d																								
Tulse Hill	a				18 15	18 01						18 28	18 44							18 57	19 14				
	d																								
London Bridge	a																								
Balham	d	18 11					18 14	18 18		18 40					18 44	18 48		19 09				19 14	19 18		
Clapham Junction	a	18 16	18 00				18 19	18 22	18 15	18 45	18 30				18 49	18 52	18 45	19 14	19 00			19 19	19 22		19 16
London Waterloo	a		18 10						18 25		18 40						18 55		19 10						19 27
London Victoria	a	18 25					18 28	18 33		18 54					18 57	19 01		19 25				19 28	19 30		

		SN	SW	FC	FC	SN	SN	SW	SN		SW	FC	FC	SN	SN	SN	SW	SN	SW		FC	FC	SN	SN	SW
Horsham	d						18 34									19 04									
Warnham	d						18 38									19 08									
Ockley	d						18 45									19 15									
Holmwood	d						18 49									19 19									
Dorking	a						18 55									19 25									
	d		18 50				18 56		19 05							19 28	19 33	19 37						19 57	20 05
Box Hill & Westhumble	d						18 58									19 30								19 59	
Guildford	d	18 22													19 04				19 28						
Effingham Junction	d	18 39						18 59							19 20				19 46						
Bookham	d	18 42						19 02							19 23				19 49						
Leatherhead	d	18 47	18 56				19 03	19 08	19 11						19 28	19 35	19 39	19 43	19 54					20 04	20 11
Ashtead	d	18 51	18 59				19 07	19 12	19 15						19 32	19 39	19 42	19 46	19 58					20 08	20 14
Epsom	a	18 57	19 04				19 11	19 16	19 19						19 36	19 43	19 47	19 51	20 02					20 12	20 19
	d	18 57	19 05				19 12	19 20	19 20		19 35				19 37	19 46	19 50	19 52	20 05					20 13	20 20
Ewell East	d						19 16		19 24						19 41	19 50		19 56						20 17	
Cheam	d						19 19		19 27						19 44	19 53		19 59						20 20	
Epsom Downs	d					19 06								19 36									20 13		
Banstead	d					19 09								19 39									20 16		
Belmont	d					19 12								19 42									20 19		
Sutton (Surrey)	a	19 04				19 15	19 22		19 30					19 45	19 47	19 56		20 02					20 22	20 23	
	d	19 05		19 08	19 13	19 16	19 22		19 33			19 37	19 42	19 46		19 56		20 03			20 07	20 12	20 23	20 25	
Carshalton	d			19 11			19 25						19 45			19 59						20 15		20 28	
Hackbridge	d			19 13			19 28						19 47			20 02						20 17		20 31	
Mitcham Junction	d			19 16			19 31						19 50			20 05						20 20		20 34	
Mitcham Eastfields	d			19 19			19 34						19 53			20 08						20 23		20 37	
Carshalton Beeches	d	19 08				19 19			19 36					19 49				20 06					20 26		
Wallington	d	19 10				19 21			19 38					19 51				20 08					20 28		
Waddon	d	19 13				19 24			19 41					19 54				20 11					20 31		
West Croydon	d	19 17				19 28			19 47					19 58				20 18					20 35		
Norwood Junction	d	19 22							19 52									20 23							
New Cross Gate	d																								
Tulse Hill	a			19 27	19 44							20 10	20 01								20 40	20 31			
	d																								
London Bridge	a																								
Balham	d	19 39				19 45	19 42		20 08					20 14		20 17		20 39					20 51	20 44	
Clapham Junction	a	19 44	19 30			19 50	19 47	19 45	20 14		20 00			20 19		20 22	20 15	20 44	20 30				20 56	20 48	20 45
London Waterloo	a		19 41					19 55			20 10						20 25		20 41						20 55
London Victoria	a	19 54				19 59	19 56		20 22					20 28		20 30		20 53					21 04	20 56	

Table 182

Mondays to Fridays

until 5 October

Horsham, Dorking, Guildford, Epsom and Sutton - London

Network Diagram - see first Page of Table 177

		SN	SN	SW	FC		FC	SN	SN	SW	SN	SW	SN	FC	FC		SN	SN	SW	SN	SN	SW	FC A	SN	SN
Horsham	d								20 06																
Warnham	d								20 10																
Ockley	d								20 17																
Holmwood	d								20 21																
Dorking	a								20 27																
	d								20 30	20 35								20 59							21 30
Box Hill & Westhumble	d																	21 01							
Guildford	d			19 58															20 46						
Effingham Junction	d			20 16															21 03						
Bookham	d			20 19															21 06						
Leatherhead	d			20 24					20 36	20 41								21 06	21 11						21 36
Ashtead	d			20 28					20 39	20 44								21 10	21 14						21 40
Epsom	a			20 32					20 44	20 49								21 14	21 19						21 44
	d	20 22	20 25	20 35					20 45	20 50	20 55	21 05						21 15	21 20	21 21	21 25	21 35			21 45
Ewell East	d	20 26	20 29						20 49		20 59							21 19		21 25	21 29				21 49
Cheam	d	20 29	20 32						20 52		21 02							21 22		21 28	21 32				21 52
Epsom Downs	d												20 54												
Banstead	d												20 57												
Belmont	d												21 00												
Sutton (Surrey)	a	20 32	20 35						20 55		21 05		21 03					21 25		21 31	21 35				21 55
	d	20 33	20 36		20 37		20 42	20 52	20 55		21 06		21 06	21 12	21 17		21 22	21 25		21 32	21 36		21 47	21 52	21 55
Carshalton	d		20 39				20 45		20 58		21 09			21 15				21 28			21 39				21 58
Hackbridge	d		20 41				20 47		21 01		21 11			21 17				21 31			21 41				22 01
Mitcham Junction	d		20 45				20 50		21 04		21 15			21 20				21 34			21 45				22 04
Mitcham Eastfields	d		20 48				20 53		21 07		21 18			21 23				21 37			21 48				22 07
Carshalton Beeches	d	20 36						20 55					21 09				21 25			21 35				21 55	
Wallington	d	20 38						20 57					21 11				21 27			21 37				21 57	
Waddon	d	20 41						21 00					21 14				21 30			21 40				22 00	
West Croydon	d	20 45						21 04					21 18				21 34			21 48				22 04	
Norwood Junction	d	20 52											21 23							21 53					
New Cross Gate	d																								
Tulse Hill	a				21 10		21 01							21 31	21 53								22 23		
	d																								
London Bridge	a																								
Balham	d	21 08	20 54					21 21	21 14		21 24		21 39				21 51	21 44		22 09	21 54			22 21	22 14
Clapham Junction	a	21 14	20 59	21 00				21 26	21 18	21 15	21 29	21 30	21 44				21 56	21 49	21 45	22 14	21 59	22 00		22 26	22 19
London Waterloo	a			21 10						21 25		21 40							21 55			22 10			
London Victoria	a	21 22	21 09					21 34	21 26		21 39		21 53				22 04	21 58		22 23	22 09			22 34	22 27

			SW	SN	SN	FC B	FC A	SN	SN	SW	SN		SN	FC A	SN	SN	SW	SN	SN	SN	SN		SW	SN	SN
Horsham	d																								
Warnham	d																								
Ockley	d																								
Holmwood	d																								
Dorking	a																								
	d		21 35						21 59							22 30	22 35				23 00				23 30
Box Hill & Westhumble	d								22 01												23 02				
Guildford	d									21 46													22 46		
Effingham Junction	d									22 03													23 03		
Bookham	d									22 06													23 06		
Leatherhead	d		21 41						22 06	22 11						22 36	22 41				23 07		23 11		23 36
Ashtead	d		21 44						22 10	22 14						22 40	22 44				23 11		23 14		23 39
Epsom	a		21 49						22 14	22 19						22 44	22 49				23 15		23 19		23 45
	d		21 50	21 55					22 15	22 20	22 21		22 25			22 45	22 50	22 55			23 16		23 20	23 27	
Ewell East	d			21 59					22 19		22 25		22 29			22 49		22 59			23 20			23 31	
Cheam	d			22 02					22 22		22 28		22 32			22 52		23 02			23 23			23 35	
Epsom Downs	d				21 54														22 54						
Banstead	d				21 57														22 57						
Belmont	d				22 00														23 00						
Sutton (Surrey)	a			22 05	22 03				22 25		22 31		22 35			22 55		23 05	23 03		23 26			23 40	
	d			22 06	22 06	22 12	22 17	22 22	22 25		22 32		22 36	22 47	22 52	22 55		23 06	23 06	23 20	23 30			23 41	
Carshalton	d			22 09					22 28				22 39			22 58		23 09							
Hackbridge	d			22 11					22 31				22 41			23 01		23 11							
Mitcham Junction	d			22 15					22 34				22 45			23 04		23 15							
Mitcham Eastfields	d			22 18					22 37				22 48			23 07		23 18							
Carshalton Beeches	d				22 09			22 25			22 35				22 55				23 09	23 23	23 33			23 44	
Wallington	d				22 11			22 27			22 37				22 57				23 11	23 25	23 35			23 46	
Waddon	d				22 14			22 30			22 40				23 00				23 14	23 28	23 38			23 49	
West Croydon	d				22 18			22 34			22 48				23 04				23 18	23a31	23a41			23a52	
Norwood Junction	d				22 23						22 53								23 23						
New Cross Gate	d																								
Tulse Hill	a					22 44	22 53							23 23											
	d					22 44																			
London Bridge	a					22 55																			
Balham	d			22 24	22 39			22 51	22 44		23 09		22 54		23 21	23 14		23 24	23 40						
Clapham Junction	a		22 15	22 29	22 44			22 56	22 48	22 45	23 15		22 59		23 26	23 18	23 15	23 29	23 45				23 48		
London Waterloo	a		22 25							22 55							23 27						23 58		
London Victoria	a			22 39	22 53			23 04	22 56		23 25		23 09		23 34	23 27		23 39	23 54						

A from 21 May until 5 October

B until 18 May

Table 182

Mondays to Fridays
until 5 October

Horsham, Dorking, Guildford, Epsom and Sutton - London

Network Diagram - see first Page of Table 177

		SN
Horsham	d	
Warnham	d	
Ockley	d	
Holmwood	d	
Dorking	a	
	d	
Box Hill & Westhumble	d	
Guildford	d	
Effingham Junction	d	
Bookham	d	
Leatherhead	d	
Ashtead	d	
Epsom	a	
	d	
Ewell East	d	
Cheam	d	
Epsom Downs	d	23 43
Banstead	d	23 46
Belmont	d	23 49
Sutton (Surrey)	a	23 52
	d	23 53
Carshalton	d	
Hackbridge	d	
Mitcham Junction	d	
Mitcham Eastfields	d	
Carshalton Beeches	d	23 56
Wallington	d	23 58
Waddon	d	00 01
West Croydon	d	00a04
Norwood Junction	d	
New Cross Gate ⊖	d	
Tulse Hill	a	
	d	
London Bridge ⊖	a	
Balham ⊖	d	
Clapham Junction	a	
London Waterloo ⊖	a	
London Victoria ⊖	a	

Mondays to Fridays
from 8 October

		SN MO	SN MO	SN MO	SN MX	SN	SW	SN	SN	SN		FC	SN	SW	SN	SW	SN	SN	FC	SN		SW	SW	SN	FC
Horsham	d																			05 49					
Warnham	d																			05 53					
Ockley	d																			06 00					
Holmwood	d																			06 04					
Dorking	a																			06 10					
	d			23p16										05 48						06 11			06 32		
Box Hill & Westhumble	d			23p18										05 50						06 13			06 34		
Guildford	d						04 58															05 58			
Effingham Junction	d						05 16															06 16			
Bookham	d						05 19															06 19			
Leatherhead	d			23p23			05 24							05 56						06 18		06 24	06 39		
Ashtead	d			23p27			05 28							05 59						06 22		06 28	06 43		
Epsom	a			23p31			05 32							06 04						06 26		06 32	06 47		
	d			23p32		05 23	05 34		05 39				05 57	06 04		06 18				06 27		06 34	06 48		
Ewell East	d			23p36		05 27			05 43				06 01							06 31					
Cheam	d			23p39		05 30			05 46				06 04							06 34					
Epsom Downs	d				23p43																			06 34	
Banstead	d				23p46																			06 37	
Belmont	d				23p49																			06 40	
Sutton (Surrey)	a			23p42	23p52	05 33			05 49				06 07							06 37				06 43	
	d	23p25	23p40	23p43	23p53	05 33		05 37	05 49	06 03		06 03	06 08		06 14		06 14	06 33	06 34	06 37				06 44	06 45
Carshalton	d			23p46				05 40					06 11		06 17				06 37	06 40					
Hackbridge	d			23p48				05 42					06 13		06 19				06 39	06 43					
Mitcham Junction	d			23p52				05 46					06 17		06 23				06 42	06 46					
Mitcham Eastfields	d			23p55				05 49					06 20		06 26				06 45	06 49					
Carshalton Beeches	d	23p28	23p43		23p56	05 36			05 52	06 06							06 17	06 36						06 47	
Wallington	d	23p30	23p45		23p58	05 39			05 55	06 08							06 20	06 38						06 50	
Waddon	d	23p33	23p48		00 01	05 42			05 58	06 11							06 23	06 41						06 53	
West Croydon	d	23p37	23p52		00a04	05 45			06 01	06 15							06 26	06 45						06 58	
Norwood Junction	d					05 50				06 20								06 50							
New Cross Gate ⊖	d					06 08																			
Tulse Hill	a							05 57				06 42			06 34				06 53						07 20
	d							05 57							06 34										
London Bridge ⊖	a					06 14		06 08		06 33					06 51			07 04							
Balham ⊖	d	23p53	00 08	00 01					06 17				06 27				06 42			06 57				07 14	
Clapham Junction	a	23p57	00 12	00 06			06 00		06 23				06 31	06 30		06 45	06 48			07 01		07 00	07 15	07 19	
London Waterloo ⊖	a						06 11							06 40		06 55						07 12	07 27		
London Victoria ⊖	a	00 04	00 19	00 15					06 31				06 38				06 58			07 08				07 30	

Table 182

Mondays to Fridays
from 8 October

Horsham, Dorking, Guildford, Epsom and Sutton - London

Network Diagram - see first Page of Table 177

		SN	SN	FC	SN	SW		SN	SN	SN	SN	SW	SN	SW	FC	SN		SW	SW	FC	SN	SN	SN	SN	SW
Horsham	d				06 20											06 55									
Warnham	d				06 24											06 59									
Ockley	d				06 31											07 06									
Holmwood	d				06 35											07 10									
Dorking	a				06 41											07 16									
	d				06 44						06 59	07 02				07 17			07 32						
Box Hill & Westhumble	d				06 46						07 01	07 04							07 34						
Guildford	d					06 28												06 58							
Effingham Junction	d					06 48												07 16							
Bookham	d					06 51												07 19							
Leatherhead	d				06 51	06 56					07 06	07 09				07 23		07 26	07 39						
Ashtead	d				06 55	06 59					07 10	07 13				07 26		07 29	07 43						
Epsom	a				06 59	07 04					07 14	07 17				07 31		07 34	07 47						
	d		06 49		07 00	07 04					07 15	07 18	07 21	07 22		07 31		07 34	07 48					07 49	07 52
Ewell East	d		06 53		07 04						07 19		07 25											07 53	
Cheam	d		06 56		07 07						07 22		07 28			07 37								07 56	
Epsom Downs	d							07 05													07 34				
Banstead	d							07 08													07 37				
Belmont	d							07 11													07 40				
Sutton (Surrey)	a		06 59		07 10			07 14			07 25		07 31			07 40					07 43			07 59	
	d	06 50	07 00	07 05	07 10			07 15	07 20	07 22	07 26		07 32		07 37	07 42				07 40	07 45	07 49	07 53	07 59	
Carshalton	d	06 53			07 13				07 23		07 29				07 40	07 45						07 52		08 02	
Hackbridge	d	06 55			07 16				07 25		07 31				07 42							07 54		08 05	
Mitcham Junction	d	06 59			07 19				07 29		07 35				07 45	07 49						07 58		08 08	
Mitcham Eastfields	d	07 02			07 22				07 32		07 38				07 48	07 52						08 01		08 11	
Carshalton Beeches	d		07 03					07 18		07 25			07 35								07 48		07 56		
Wallington	d		07 05					07 20		07 27			07 37								07 50		07 58		
Waddon	d		07 08					07 23		07 30			07 40								07 53		08 01		
West Croydon	d		07 13					07 28		07 34			07 44								07 58		08 05		
Norwood Junction	d		07 18										07 49												
New Cross Gate ⊖	d																								
Tulse Hill	a	07 09		07 43					07 39						07 56					08 13		08 09			
	d	07 10							07 41													08 10			
London Bridge ⊖	a	07 28	07 32						07 59				08 05									08 28			
Balham ⊖	d				07 29			07 44		07 50	07 47					07 59					08 14		08 21	08 18	
Clapham Junction	a				07 34	07 30		07 49		07 55	07 51	07 42		07 48		08 04		08 01	08 12		08 19		08 25	08 22	08 18
London Waterloo ⊖	a					07 42						07 54		08 00				08 13	08 24						08 30
London Victoria ⊖	a				07 41			08 00		08 06	08 00					08 11					08 30		08 36	08 30	

		SN		FC	FC	SN	SW	SW	SW	SN	SN	SN		SN	SW	FC	FC	SN	SN	SW	SN	SN		SW	SN
Horsham	d					07 21													07 56						
Warnham	d					07 25													08 00						
Ockley	d					07 32													08 07						
Holmwood	d					07 36													08 11						
Dorking	a					07 42													08 17						
	d					07 46		08 02											08 22	08 31					
Box Hill & Westhumble	d							08 04											08 24	08 33					
Guildford	d	07 25													07 58							08 16			
Effingham Junction	d	07 37					07 46								08 16							08 32		08 48	
Bookham	d	07 40					07 49								08 19							08 35		08 51	
Leatherhead	d	07 45				07 52	07 56	08 09							08 25				08 29	08 38		08 41		08 56	
Ashtead	d	07 49				07 55	07 59	08 13							08 28				08 33	08 42		08 45		08 59	
Epsom	a	07 53				08 00	08 04	08 17							08 33				08 37	08 46		08 49		09 04	
	d	07 54				08 02	08 04	08 18	08 22					08 22	08 34				08 38	08 48		08 50		09 04	
Ewell East	d	07 58				08 06								08 26					08 42			08 54			
Cheam	d	08 01				08 09								08 29					08 45			08 57			
Epsom Downs	d									08 04								08 34							
Banstead	d									08 07								08 37							
Belmont	d									08 10								08 40							
Sutton (Surrey)	a	08 04				08 12				08 13				08 32				08 43	08 48			09 00			
	d	08 05		08 08	08 08	08 12				08 14	08 20	08 29		08 32		08 39	08 41	08 45	08 48		08 57	09 00			09 03
Carshalton	d			08 11		08 15					08 23	08 32				08 42			08 51		09 00	09 03			
Hackbridge	d			08 13		08 18					08 25	08 34				08 44			08 54		09 02	09 06			
Mitcham Junction	d			08 16		08 21					08 29	08 38				08 47			08 57		09 06	09 09			
Mitcham Eastfields	d			08 19		08 24					08 32	08 41				08 50			09 00		09 09	09 12			
Carshalton Beeches	d	08 08								08 17				08 35				08 48							09 06
Wallington	d	08 10								08 19				08 38				08 50							09 08
Waddon	d									08 22				08 41				08 53							09 11
West Croydon	d	08 15								08 26				08 44				08 57							09 15
Norwood Junction	d	08 20												08 49											09 22
New Cross Gate ⊖	d																								
Tulse Hill	a			08 27	08 43						08 40					08 58	09 12				09 16				
	d										08 40										09 16				
London Bridge ⊖	a	08 35									08 57			09 04							09 35				
Balham ⊖	d									08 43		08 49						09 13	09 07			09 18			09 41
Clapham Junction	a					08 32	08 31	08 42	08 48	08 49		08 54			09 00			09 18	09 11	09 15		09 22		09 30	09 46
London Waterloo ⊖	a						08 43	08 54	09 00						09 12					09 27				09 42	
London Victoria ⊖	a					08 39				09 00		09 04						09 31	09 20			09 33			09 58

Table 182

Mondays to Fridays

from 8 October

Horsham, Dorking, Guildford, Epsom and Sutton - London

Network Diagram - see first Page of Table 177

		FC	FC	SN	SN	SW	SN	SN	SW	SN	FC	FC	SN	SN	SN	SN	SW	SW	SN	FC	FC	SN	SN
Horsham	d														09 09							
Warnham	d														09 13							
Ockley	d														09 20							
Holmwood	d														09 24							
Dorking	a														09 30							
	d				08 57	09 02									09 31	09 35						
Box Hill & Westhumble	d				08 59	09 04									09 33							
Guildford	d								08 58								09 28					
Effingham Junction	d								09 16								09 46					
Bookham	d								09 19								09 49					
Leatherhead	d				09 04	09 09			09 24						09 38	09 41	09 54					
Ashtead	d				09 08	09 13			09 28						09 42	09 45	09 58					
Epsom	a				09 12	09 17			09 32						09 46	09 49	10 02					
	d				09 13	09 18		09 19	09 35					09 42		09 49	09 50	10 05				10 04	
Ewell East	d				09 17			09 23						09 46		09 53						10 08	
Cheam	d				09 20			09 26						09 49		09 56						10 11	
Epsom Downs	d						09 09						09 35										
Banstead	d						09 12						09 38										
Belmont	d						09 15						09 41										
Sutton (Surrey)	a				09 23		09 18	09 29					09 44	09 52		09 59						10 14	
	d	09 11	09 13	09 15	09 23		09 23	09 29		09 33	09 37	09 38	09 45	09 52	09 52	09 59			10 03	10 07	10 08	10 15	10 22
Carshalton	d		09 16					09 32				09 41				10 02					10 11		
Hackbridge	d		09 18					09 35				09 43				10 05					10 13		
Mitcham Junction	d		09 21					09 38				09 46				10 08					10 16		
Mitcham Eastfields	d		09 24		09 32			09 41				09 49				10 11					10 19		
Carshalton Beeches	d			09 18			09 26			09 36			09 48		09 55				10 06			10 18	10 25
Wallington	d			09 20			09 28			09 38			09 50		09 57				10 08			10 20	10 27
Waddon	d			09 23			09 31			09 41			09 53		10 00				10 11			10 23	10 30
West Croydon	d			09 28			09 35			09 45			09 58		10 04				10 15			10 28	10 34
Norwood Junction	d									09 52									10 22				
New Cross Gate	d																						
Tulse Hill	a	09 42	09 32								10 12	09 57								10 42	10 27		
	d																						
London Bridge	a																						
Balham	d			09 44			09 52	09 49		10 09			10 14		10 21	10 18			10 39			10 44	10 51
Clapham Junction	a			09 49	09 42	09 45	09 57	09 53	10 00	10 15			10 19	10 10	10 26	10 22	10 15	10 30	10 45			10 49	10 56
London Waterloo	a					09 57			10 10								10 25	10 40					
London Victoria	a			09 58	09 52		10 05	10 00		10 24			10 28	10 20	10 34	10 31			10 53			10 58	11 04

		SN	SW	SN	SW	SN	FC	FC	SN	SN	SW	SN	SN	SW	SN	FC	FC	SN	SN	SW	SN	SN
Horsham	d									10 04												
Warnham	d									10 08												
Ockley	d									10 15												
Holmwood	d									10 19												
Dorking	a									10 25												
	d	09 57	10 05							10 26	10 35								10 58	11 05		
Box Hill & Westhumble	d	09 59								10 28												
Guildford	d				09 58									10 28								
Effingham Junction	d				10 16									10 46								
Bookham	d				10 19									10 49								
Leatherhead	d	10 04	10 11		10 24					10 33	10 41			10 54					11 04	11 11		
Ashtead	d	10 08	10 14		10 28					10 37	10 44			10 58					11 07	11 14		
Epsom	a	10 12	10 19		10 32					10 41	10 49			11 02					11 12	11 19		
	d	10 13	10 20	10 19	10 35					10 42	10 50		10 49	11 05				11 04	11 13	11 20		11 19
Ewell East	d	10 17		10 23						10 46			10 53					11 08				11 23
Cheam	d	10 20		10 26						10 49			10 56					11 11	11 18			11 26
Epsom Downs	d								10 35													
Banstead	d								10 38													
Belmont	d								10 41													
Sutton (Surrey)	a	10 23		10 29					10 44	10 52			10 59					11 14	11 21			11 29
	d	10 23		10 29		10 33	10 37	10 38	10 45	10 52		10 52	10 59		11 03	11 07	11 08	11 15	11 22		11 22	11 29
Carshalton	d			10 32				10 41					11 02				11 11					11 32
Hackbridge	d			10 35				10 43					11 05				11 13					11 35
Mitcham Junction	d			10 38				10 46					11 08				11 16					11 38
Mitcham Eastfields	d			10 41				10 49					11 11				11 19					11 41
Carshalton Beeches	d					10 36			10 48			10 55			11 06			11 18			11 25	
Wallington	d					10 38			10 50			10 57			11 08			11 20			11 27	
Waddon	d					10 41			10 53			11 00			11 11			11 23			11 30	
West Croydon	d					10 45			10 58			11 04			11 15			11 28			11 34	
Norwood Junction	d					10 52									11 22							
New Cross Gate	d																					
Tulse Hill	a						11 12	10 57								11 42	11 27					
	d																					
London Bridge	a																					
Balham	d			10 48		11 09			11 14			11 21	11 18		11 40			11 44			11 51	11 48
Clapham Junction	a	10 40	10 45	10 52	11 00	11 14			11 19	11 10	11 15	11 26	11 22	11 30	11 45			11 49	11 40	11 45	11 56	11 52
London Waterloo	a		10 55		11 10						11 25			11 40						11 55		
London Victoria	a	10 48		11 00		11 23			11 28	11 20		11 34	11 30		11 54			11 58	11 50		12 04	12 00

Table 182

Mondays to Fridays

from 8 October

Horsham, Dorking, Guildford, Epsom and Sutton - London

Network Diagram - see first Page of Table 177

		SW	SN	FC	FC	SN	SN	SW	SN	SN	SW	SN	FC	FC	SN	SN	SW	SN	SN	SW	SN	FC	FC
Horsham	d						11 04																
Warnham	d						11 08																
Ockley	d						11 15																
Holmwood	d						11 19																
Dorking	a						11 25																
	d						11 26	11 35								11 58	12 05						
Box Hill & Westhumble	d						11 28																
Guildford	d	10 58									11 28									11 58			
Effingham Junction	d	11 16									11 46									12 16			
Bookham	d	11 19									11 49									12 19			
Leatherhead	d	11 24					11 33	11 41			11 54					12 04	12 11			12 24			
Ashtead	d	11 28					11 37	11 44			11 58					12 07	12 14			12 28			
Epsom	a	11 32					11 41	11 49			12 02					12 12	12 19			12 32			
	d	11 35					11 42	11 50		11 49	12 05				12 04	12 13	12 20		12 19	12 35			
Ewell East	d						11 46			11 53					12 08				12 23				
Cheam	d						11 49			11 56					12 11	12 18			12 26				
Epsom Downs	d					11 35																	
Banstead	d					11 38																	
Belmont	d					11 41																	
Sutton (Surrey)	a					11 44	11 52			11 59					12 14	12 21			12 29				
	d		11 33	11 37	11 38	11 45	11 52		11 52	11 59		12 03	12 07	12 08	12 15	12 22		12 22	12 29		12 33	12 37	12 38
Carshalton	d				11 41					12 02				12 11					12 32				12 41
Hackbridge	d				11 43					12 05				12 13					12 35				12 43
Mitcham Junction	d				11 46					12 08				12 16					12 38				12 46
Mitcham Eastfields	d				11 49					12 11				12 19					12 41				12 49
Carshalton Beeches	d		11 36			11 48			11 55			12 06			12 18			12 25			12 36		
Wallington	d		11 38			11 50			11 57			12 08			12 20			12 27			12 38		
Waddon	d		11 41			11 53			12 00			12 11			12 23			12 30			12 41		
West Croydon	d		11 45			11 58			12 04			12 15			12 28			12 34			12 45		
Norwood Junction	d		11 52									12 22									12 52		
New Cross Gate	d																						
Tulse Hill	a			12 12	11 57								12 42	12 27								13 12	12 57
	d																						
London Bridge	a																						
Balham	d		12 09			12 14			12 21	12 18		12 39			12 44			12 51	12 48		13 09		
Clapham Junction	a	12 00	12 14			12 19	12 10	12 15	12 26	12 22	12 30	12 44			12 49	12 40	12 45	12 56	12 52	13 00	13 14		
London Waterloo	a	12 10						12 25			12 40						12 55			13 10			
London Victoria	a		12 23			12 28	12 18		12 34	12 30		12 53			12 58	12 48		13 04	13 00		13 23		

		SN	SN	SW	SN	SN	SW	SN	FC	FC	SN	SN	SW	SN	SN	SW	SN	FC	FC	SN	SN	SW	SN
Horsham	d		12 04																		13 04		
Warnham	d		12 08																		13 08		
Ockley	d		12 15																		13 15		
Holmwood	d		12 19																		13 19		
Dorking	a		12 25																		13 25		
	d		12 26	12 35								12 58	13 05								13 26	13 35	
Box Hill & Westhumble	d		12 28																		13 28		
Guildford	d						12 28									12 58							
Effingham Junction	d						12 46									13 16							
Bookham	d						12 49									13 19							
Leatherhead	d		12 33	12 41			12 54					13 04	13 11			13 24					13 33	13 41	
Ashtead	d		12 37	12 44			12 58					13 07	13 14			13 28					13 37	13 44	
Epsom	a		12 41	12 49			13 02					13 12	13 19			13 32					13 41	13 49	
	d		12 42	12 50		12 49	13 05				13 04	13 13	13 20		13 19	13 35					13 42	13 50	
Ewell East	d		12 46			12 53					13 08				13 23						13 46		
Cheam	d		12 49			12 56					13 11	13 18			13 26						13 49		
Epsom Downs	d	12 35																		13 35			
Banstead	d	12 38																		13 38			
Belmont	d	12 41																		13 41			
Sutton (Surrey)	a	12 44	12 52			12 59					13 14	13 21			13 29					13 44	13 52		
	d	12 45	12 52		12 52	12 59		13 03	13 07	13 08	13 15	13 22		13 22	13 29		13 33	13 37	13 38	13 45	13 52		13 52
Carshalton	d					13 02				13 11					13 32				13 41				
Hackbridge	d					13 05				13 13					13 35				13 43				
Mitcham Junction	d					13 08				13 16					13 38				13 46				
Mitcham Eastfields	d					13 11				13 19					13 41				13 49				
Carshalton Beeches	d	12 48			12 55			13 06			13 18			13 25			13 36			13 48			13 55
Wallington	d	12 50			12 57			13 08			13 20			13 27			13 38			13 50			13 57
Waddon	d	12 53			13 00			13 11			13 23			13 30			13 41			13 53			14 00
West Croydon	d	12 58			13 04			13 15			13 28			13 34			13 45			13 58			14 04
Norwood Junction	d							13 22									13 52						
New Cross Gate	d																						
Tulse Hill	a								13 42	13 27								14 12	13 57				
	d																						
London Bridge	a																						
Balham	d	13 14			13 21	13 18		13 39			13 44			13 51	13 48		14 09			14 14			14 21
Clapham Junction	a	13 19	13 10	13 15	13 26	13 22	13 30	13 44			13 49	13 40	13 45	13 56	13 52	14 00	14 14			14 19	14 10	14 15	14 26
London Waterloo	a			13 25			13 40						13 55			14 10						14 25	
London Victoria	a	13 28	13 18		13 34	13 30		13 53			13 58	13 48		14 04	14 00		14 23			14 28	14 18		14 34

Horsham, Dorking, Guildford, Epsom and Sutton - London

Network Diagram - see first Page of Table 177

		SN		SW	SN	FC	FC	SN	SN	SW	SN	SN		SW	SN	FC	FC	SN	SN	SW	SN	SN		SW	SN
Horsham [4]	d																		14 04						
Warnham	d																		14 08						
Ockley	d																		14 15						
Holmwood	d																		14 19						
Dorking [4]	a																		14 25						
	d								13 58	14 05									14 26	14 35					
Box Hill & Westhumble	d																		14 28						
Guildford	d			13 28										13 58										14 28	
Effingham Junction [6]	d			13 46										14 16										14 46	
Bookham	d			13 49										14 19										14 49	
Leatherhead	d			13 54					14 04	14 11				14 24					14 33	14 41				14 54	
Ashtead	d			13 58					14 07	14 14				14 28					14 37	14 44				14 58	
Epsom [3]	a			14 02					14 12	14 19				14 32					14 41	14 49				15 02	
	d	13 49		14 05				14 04	14 13	14 20		14 19		14 35					14 42	14 50		14 49		15 05	
Ewell East	d	13 53						14 08				14 23							14 46			14 53			
Cheam	d	13 56						14 11	14 18			14 26							14 49			14 56			
Epsom Downs	d																	14 35							
Banstead	d																	14 38							
Belmont	d																	14 41							
Sutton (Surrey) [4]	a	13 59						14 14	14 21			14 29						14 44	14 52			14 59			
	d	13 59			14 03	14 07	14 08	14 15	14 22		14 22	14 29			14 33	14 37	14 38	14 45	14 52		14 52	14 59			15 03
Carshalton	d	14 02					14 11					14 32					14 41					15 02			
Hackbridge	d	14 05					14 13					14 35					14 43					15 05			
Mitcham Junction	d	14 08					14 16					14 38					14 46					15 08			
Mitcham Eastfields	d	14 11					14 19					14 41					14 49					15 11			
Carshalton Beeches	d				14 06			14 18			14 25				14 36			14 48			14 55				15 06
Wallington	d				14 08			14 20			14 27				14 38			14 50			14 57				15 08
Waddon	d				14 11			14 23			14 30				14 41			14 53			15 00				15 11
West Croydon [4]	d				14 15			14 28			14 34				14 45			14 58			15 04				15 15
Norwood Junction [2]	d				14 22										14 52										15 22
New Cross Gate [4] ⊖	d																								
Tulse Hill [3]	a					14 42	14 27									15 12	14 57								
	d																								
London Bridge [4] ⊖	a																								
Balham [4] ⊖	d	14 18			14 39			14 44			14 51	14 48			15 09			15 14			15 21	15 18			15 39
Clapham Junction [10]	a	14 22		14 30	14 44			14 49	14 40	14 45	14 56	14 52		15 00	15 14			15 19	15 10	15 15	15 26	15 22		15 30	15 44
London Waterloo [15] ⊖	a			14 40						14 55				15 10						15 25				15 40	
London Victoria [15] ⊖	a	14 30			14 53			14 58	14 48		15 04	15 00			15 24			15 28	15 22		15 34	15 30			15 54

		FC	FC	SN	SN	SW	SN	SN		SW	SN	FC	FC	SN	SN	SW	SN	SN		SW	SN	FC	FC	SN	SN
Horsham [4]	d														15 04										
Warnham	d														15 08										
Ockley	d														15 15										
Holmwood	d														15 19										
Dorking [4]	a														15 25										15 56
	d				14 58	15 05									15 26	15 35									15 58
Box Hill & Westhumble	d														15 28										
Guildford	d									14 58										15 28					
Effingham Junction [6]	d									15 16										15 46					
Bookham	d									15 19										15 49					
Leatherhead	d				15 04	15 11				15 24					15 33	15 41				15 54					16 03
Ashtead	d				15 07	15 14				15 28					15 37	15 44				15 58					16 07
Epsom [3]	a				15 12	15 19				15 32					15 41	15 49				16 02					16 11
	d			15 04	15 13	15 20		15 19		15 35					15 42	15 50		15 49		16 05				16 04	16 12
Ewell East	d			15 08				15 23							15 46			15 53						16 08	16 16
Cheam	d			15 11	15 18			15 26							15 49			15 56						16 11	16 19
Epsom Downs	d													15 35											
Banstead	d													15 38											
Belmont	d													15 41											
Sutton (Surrey) [4]	a			15 14	15 21			15 29						15 44	15 52			15 59						16 14	16 22
	d	15 07	15 08	15 15	15 22		15 22	15 29			15 33	15 37	15 38	15 45	15 52		15 52	15 59			16 03	16 07	16 08	16 15	16 22
Carshalton	d		15 11					15 32					15 41					16 02					16 11		
Hackbridge	d		15 13					15 35					15 43					16 05					16 13		
Mitcham Junction	d		15 16					15 38					15 46					16 08					16 16		
Mitcham Eastfields	d		15 19					15 41					15 49					16 11					16 19		
Carshalton Beeches	d			15 18			15 25				15 36			15 48			15 55				16 06			16 18	
Wallington	d			15 20			15 27				15 38			15 50			15 57				16 08			16 20	
Waddon	d			15 23			15 30				15 41			15 53			16 00				16 11			16 23	
West Croydon [4]	d			15 28			15 34				15 45			15 58			16 04				16 15			16 28	
Norwood Junction [2]	d										15 52										16 22				
New Cross Gate [4] ⊖	d																								
Tulse Hill [3]	a	15 42	15 27									16 12	15 57									16 46	16 27		
	d																								
London Bridge [4] ⊖	a																								
Balham [4] ⊖	d			15 44			15 51	15 48			16 09			16 14			16 21	16 18			16 39			16 44	
Clapham Junction [10]	a			15 49	15 40	15 45	15 56	15 52		16 00	16 14			16 19	16 10	16 15	16 26	16 23		16 30	16 45			16 49	16 40
London Waterloo [15] ⊖	a					15 55				16 10						16 25				16 40					
London Victoria [15] ⊖	a			15 58	15 52		16 04	16 00			16 23			16 28	16 18		16 34	16 30			16 55			16 58	16 48

Table 182

Mondays to Fridays
from 8 October

Horsham, Dorking, Guildford, Epsom and Sutton - London

Network Diagram - see first Page of Table 177

		SW	SN	SN		SW	SN	SN	FC	FC [1]	SN	SW	SN	SN		SW	SN	FC	SN	FC	SN	SW	SN	SW	
Horsham [4]	d										16 04														
Warnham	d										16 08														
Ockley	d										16 15														
Holmwood	d										16 19														
Dorking [4]	a										16 25														
	d	16 05									16 26	16 35									17 00	17 05			
Box Hill & Westhumble	d										16 28										17 02				
Guildford	d					15 58										16 28								16 58	
Effingham Junction [6]	d					16 16										16 46								17 16	
Bookham	d					16 19										16 49								17 19	
Leatherhead	d	16 11				16 24					16 33	16 41				16 54					17 07	17 11		17 24	
Ashtead	d	16 14				16 28					16 37	16 44				16 58					17 11	17 14		17 28	
Epsom [3]	a	16 19				16 32					16 41	16 49				17 02					17 15	17 19		17 32	
	d	16 20		16 19		16 35					16 42	16 50		16 49		17 05					17 19	17 20	17 23	17 35	
Ewell East	d			16 23							16 46			16 53							17 23		17 27		
Cheam	d			16 26							16 49			16 56							17 26		17 30		
Epsom Downs	d							16 26											17 02						
Banstead	d							16 29											17 05						
Belmont	d							16 32											17 08						
Sutton (Surrey) [4]	a			16 29				16 35			16 52			16 59					17 11		17 29		17 33		
	d		16 22	16 29			16 33	16 45	16 37	16 38	16 52		16 52	16 59			17 03	17 08	17 15	17 11	17 29		17 33		
Carshalton	d			16 32						16 41				17 02				17 11			17 32				
Hackbridge	d			16 35						16 43				17 05				17 13			17 35				
Mitcham Junction	d			16 38						16 46				17 08				17 16			17 38				
Mitcham Eastfields	d			16 41						16 49				17 11				17 19			17 41				
Carshalton Beeches	d		16 25				16 36	16 48					16 55				17 06		17 18				17 36		
Wallington	d		16 27				16 38	16 50					16 57				17 08		17 20				17 39		
Waddon	d		16 30				16 41	16 53					17 00				17 11		17 23				17 42		
West Croydon [4]	d		16 34				16 45	16 58					17 04				17 18		17 28				17 48		
Norwood Junction [2]	d						16 52										17 23						17 55		
New Cross Gate [4] ⊖	d																								
Tulse Hill [3]	a								17 15	16 57								17 27		17 44					
	d																								
London Bridge [4] ⊖	a																								
Balham [4] ⊖	d		16 51	16 48			17 09	17 14					17 21	17 18			17 39		17 44		17 48		18 11		
Clapham Junction [10]	a	16 45	16 56	16 53		17 00	17 14	17 19			17 10	17 15	17 26	17 23		17 30	17 44		17 49		17 52	17 45	18 16	18 00	
London Waterloo [15] ⊖	a	16 55				17 10						17 25				17 40						17 55		18 10	
London Victoria [15] ⊖	a		17 04	17 00			17 23	17 28			17 18		17 34	17 30			17 55		17 58		18 00		18 25		

		FC	FC	SN	SN	SW	SN	SW	FC	FC		SN	SN	SW	SN	SW	FC	FC	SN	SN		SW	SN	SW	FC
Horsham [4]	d				17 07								17 34							18 04					
Warnham	d				17 11								17 38							18 08					
Ockley	d				17 18								17 45							18 15					
Holmwood	d				17 22								17 49							18 19					
Dorking [4]	a				17 28								17 55							18 25					
	d				17 31	17 35							17 56	18 05						18 26		18 35		18 50	
Box Hill & Westhumble	d				17 33								17 58							18 28					
Guildford	d							17 28								17 58							18 22		
Effingham Junction [6]	d							17 46								18 16							18 39		
Bookham	d							17 49								18 19							18 42		
Leatherhead	d				17 38	17 41		17 54					18 03	18 11		18 24				18 33		18 41	18 47	18 56	
Ashtead	d				17 42	17 45		17 58					18 07	18 14		18 28				18 37		18 45	18 51	18 59	
Epsom [3]	a				17 46	17 49		18 02					18 14	18 19		18 32				18 43		18 49	18 57	19 04	
	d				17 49	17 50	17 52	18 05					18 17	18 20	18 22	18 35				18 49		18 50	18 57	19 05	
Ewell East	d				17 53		17 56						18 23		18 26					18 53					
Cheam	d				17 56		17 59						18 26		18 29					18 56					
Epsom Downs	d			17 35								18 02							18 35						
Banstead	d			17 38								18 05							18 38						
Belmont	d			17 41								18 08							18 41						
Sutton (Surrey) [4]	a			17 44	17 59		18 02					18 11	18 29		18 32				18 44	18 59			19 04		
	d	17 41	17 42	17 45	17 59		18 04		18 08	18 09		18 12	18 29		18 33		18 38	18 43	18 45	18 59			19 05		19 08
Carshalton	d		17 45		18 02				18 11				18 32				18 41			19 02					19 11
Hackbridge	d		17 47		18 05				18 13				18 35				18 43			19 05					19 13
Mitcham Junction	d		17 50		18 08				18 16				18 38				18 46			19 08					19 16
Mitcham Eastfields	d		17 53		18 11				18 19				18 41				18 49			19 11					19 19
Carshalton Beeches	d			17 48			18 07					18 15			18 36				18 48				19 08		
Wallington	d			17 50			18 09					18 17			18 38				18 50				19 10		
Waddon	d			17 53			18 12					18 20			18 41				18 53				19 13		
West Croydon [4]	d			17 58			18 18					18 28			18 47				18 58				19 17		
Norwood Junction [2]	d						18 24								18 52								19 22		
New Cross Gate [4] ⊖	d																								
Tulse Hill [3]	a	18 15	18 01						18 28	18 44							18 57	19 14							19 27
	d																								
London Bridge [4] ⊖	a																								
Balham [4] ⊖	d			18 14	18 18		18 40					18 44	18 48		19 09				19 14	19 18			19 39		
Clapham Junction [10]	a			18 19	18 22	18 15	18 45	18 30				18 49	18 52	18 45	19 14	19 00			19 19	19 22		19 16	19 44	19 30	
London Waterloo [15] ⊖	a					18 25		18 40						18 55		19 10						19 27		19 41	
London Victoria [15] ⊖	a			18 28	18 33		18 54					18 57	19 01		19 25				19 28	19 30			19 54		

Table 182

Horsham, Dorking, Guildford, Epsom and Sutton - London

Mondays to Fridays
from 8 October

Network Diagram - see first Page of Table 177

		FC	SN	SN	SW	SN		SW	FC	FC	SN	SN	SN	SW	SN	SW		FC	FC	SN	SN	SW	SN	SN	SW
Horsham	d			18 34									19 04												
Warnham	d			18 38									19 08												
Ockley	d			18 45									19 15												
Holmwood	d			18 49									19 19												
Dorking	a			18 55									19 25												
	d			18 56		19 05							19 28	19 33	19 37						19 57	20 05			
Box Hill & Westhumble	d			18 58									19 30								19 59				
Guildford	d											19 04				19 28									19 58
Effingham Junction	d				18 59							19 20				19 46									20 16
Bookham	d				19 02							19 23				19 49									20 19
Leatherhead	d			19 03	19 08	19 11						19 28	19 35	19 39	19 43	19 54					20 04	20 11			20 24
Ashtead	d			19 07	19 12	19 15						19 32	19 39	19 42	19 46	19 58					20 08	20 14			20 28
Epsom	a			19 11	19 16	19 19						19 36	19 43	19 47	19 51	20 02					20 12	20 19			20 32
	d			19 12	19 20	19 20		19 35				19 37	19 46	19 50	19 52	20 05					20 13	20 20	20 22	20 25	20 35
Ewell East	d			19 16		19 24						19 41	19 50		19 56						20 17		20 26	20 29	
Cheam	d			19 19		19 27						19 44	19 53		19 59						20 20		20 29	20 32	
Epsom Downs	d		19 06								19 36									20 13					
Banstead	d		19 09								19 39									20 16					
Belmont	d		19 12								19 42									20 19					
Sutton (Surrey)	a		19 15	19 22		19 30					19 45	19 47	19 56		20 02					20 22	20 23		20 32	20 35	
	d	19 13	19 16	19 22		19 33			19 37	19 42	19 46		19 56		20 03			20 07	20 12	20 23	20 25		20 33	20 36	
Carshalton	d			19 25						19 45			19 59						20 15		20 28			20 39	
Hackbridge	d			19 28						19 47			20 02						20 17		20 31			20 41	
Mitcham Junction	d			19 31						19 50			20 05						20 20		20 34			20 45	
Mitcham Eastfields	d			19 34						19 53			20 08						20 23		20 37			20 48	
Carshalton Beeches	d		19 19			19 36					19 49				20 06					20 26			20 36		
Wallington	d		19 21			19 38					19 51				20 08					20 28			20 38		
Waddon	d		19 24			19 41					19 54				20 11					20 31			20 41		
West Croydon	d		19 28			19 47					19 58				20 18					20 35			20 45		
Norwood Junction	d					19 52									20 23								20 52		
New Cross Gate	d																								
Tulse Hill	a	19 44							20 10	20 01								20 40	20 31						
	d																								
London Bridge	a																								
Balham	d		19 45	19 42		20 08					20 14		20 17		20 39					20 51	20 44		21 08	20 54	
Clapham Junction	a		19 50	19 47	19 45	20 14		20 00			20 19		20 22	20 15	20 44	20 30				20 56	20 48	20 45	21 14	20 59	21 00
London Waterloo	a				19 55			20 10						20 25		20 41						20 55			21 10
London Victoria	a		19 59	19 56		20 22					20 28		20 30		20 53					21 04	20 56		21 22	21 09	

		FC		FC	SN	SN	SW	SN	SW	SN	FC	FC		SN	SN	SW	SN	SN	SW	FC	SN	SN		SW	SN
Horsham	d					20 06																			
Warnham	d					20 10																			
Ockley	d					20 17																			
Holmwood	d					20 21																			
Dorking	a					20 27																			
	d					20 30	20 35								20 59							21 30		21 35	
Box Hill & Westhumble	d														21 01										
Guildford	d															20 46									
Effingham Junction	d															21 03									
Bookham	d															21 06									
Leatherhead	d					20 36	20 41								21 06	21 11						21 36		21 41	
Ashtead	d					20 39	20 44								21 10	21 14						21 40		21 44	
Epsom	a					20 44	20 49								21 14	21 19						21 44		21 49	
	d					20 45	20 50	20 55	21 05						21 15	21 20	21 21	21 25	21 35			21 45		21 50	21 55
Ewell East	d					20 49		20 59							21 19		21 25	21 29				21 49			21 59
Cheam	d					20 52		21 02							21 22		21 28	21 32				21 52			22 02
Epsom Downs	d									20 54															
Banstead	d									20 57															
Belmont	d									21 00															
Sutton (Surrey)	a					20 55		21 05		21 03					21 25		21 31	21 35				21 55			22 05
	d	20 37		20 42	20 52	20 55		21 06		21 06	21 12	21 17		21 22	21 25		21 32	21 36		21 47	21 52	21 55			22 06
Carshalton	d			20 45		20 58		21 09			21 15				21 28			21 39				21 58			22 09
Hackbridge	d			20 47		21 01		21 11			21 17				21 31			21 41				22 01			22 11
Mitcham Junction	d			20 50		21 04		21 15			21 20				21 34			21 45				22 04			22 15
Mitcham Eastfields	d			20 53		21 07		21 18			21 23				21 37			21 48				22 07			22 18
Carshalton Beeches	d				20 55					21 09				21 25			21 35				21 55				
Wallington	d				20 57					21 11				21 27			21 37				21 57				
Waddon	d				21 00					21 14				21 30			21 40				22 00				
West Croydon	d				21 04					21 18				21 34			21 48				22 04				
Norwood Junction	d									21 23							21 53								
New Cross Gate	d																								
Tulse Hill	a	21 10		21 01							21 31	21 53								22 23					
	d																								
London Bridge	a																								
Balham	d				21 21	21 14		21 24		21 39				21 51	21 44		22 09	21 54			22 21	22 14			22 24
Clapham Junction	a				21 26	21 18	21 15	21 29	21 30	21 44				21 56	21 49	21 45	22 14	21 59	22 00		22 26	22 19		22 15	22 29
London Waterloo	a						21 25		21 40							21 55			22 10					22 25	
London Victoria	a				21 34	21 26		21 39		21 53				22 04	21 58		22 23	22 09			22 34	22 27			22 39

Table 182

Horsham, Dorking, Guildford, Epsom and Sutton - London

Mondays to Fridays
from 8 October

Network Diagram - see first Page of Table 177

		SN	FC	SN	SN	SW	SN	SN		FC	SN	SN	SW	SN	SN	SN	SN	SW		SN	SN	SN
Horsham	d																					
Warnham	d																					
Ockley	d																					
Holmwood	d																					
Dorking	a																					
	d				21 59							22 30	22 35				23 00				23 30	
Box Hill & Westhumble	d				22 01												23 02					
Guildford	d					21 46												22 46				
Effingham Junction	d					22 03												23 03				
Bookham	d					22 06												23 06				
Leatherhead	d				22 06	22 11						22 36	22 41				23 07	23 11			23 36	
Ashtead	d				22 10	22 14						22 40	22 44				23 11	23 14			23 39	
Epsom	a				22 14	22 19						22 44	22 49				23 15	23 19			23 45	
	d				22 15	22 20	22 21	22 25				22 45	22 50	22 55			23 16	23 20		23 27		
Ewell East	d				22 19		22 25	22 29				22 49		22 59			23 20			23 31		
Cheam	d				22 22		22 28	22 32				22 52		23 02			23 23			23 35		
Epsom Downs	d	21 54													22 54							23 43
Banstead	d	21 57													22 57							23 46
Belmont	d	22 00													23 00							23 49
Sutton (Surrey)	a	22 03			22 25		22 31	22 35				22 55		23 05	23 03		23 26			23 40		23 52
	d	22 06	22 17	22 22	22 25		22 32	22 36		22 47	22 52	22 55		23 06	23 06	23 20	23 30			23 41		23 53
Carshalton	d				22 28			22 39				22 58		23 09								
Hackbridge	d				22 31			22 41				23 01		23 11								
Mitcham Junction	d				22 34			22 45				23 04		23 15								
Mitcham Eastfields	d				22 37			22 48				23 07		23 18								
Carshalton Beeches	d	22 09		22 25			22 35				22 55				23 09	23 23	23 33			23 44		23 56
Wallington	d	22 11		22 27			22 37				22 57				23 11	23 25	23 35			23 46		23 58
Waddon	d	22 14		22 30			22 40				23 00				23 14	23 28	23 38			23 49		00 01
West Croydon	d	22 18		22 34			22 48				23 04				23 18	23a31	23a41			23a52		00a04
Norwood Junction	d	22 23					22 53								23 23							
New Cross Gate	d																					
Tulse Hill	a		22 53							23 23												
	d																					
London Bridge	a																					
Balham	d	22 39		22 51	22 44		23 09	22 54			23 21	23 14		23 24	23 40							
Clapham Junction	a	22 44		22 56	22 48	22 45	23 15	22 59			23 26	23 18	23 15	23 29	23 45			23 48				
London Waterloo	a					22 55							23 27					23 58				
London Victoria	a	22 53		23 04	22 56		23 25	23 09			23 34	23 27		23 39	23 54							

Saturdays
until 6 October

		SN	SW	SW	SW	FC	SN	SN	SN	SW		SN	FC	FC A	FC	SN	SN	SN	SW	SN		FC	FC A	FC	SN
Horsham	d																								
Warnham	d																								
Ockley	d																								
Holmwood	d																								
Dorking	a																								
	d							06 28									06 57								
Box Hill & Westhumble	d																06 59								
Guildford	d									06 28									06 58						
Effingham Junction	d									06 46									07 16						
Bookham	d									06 49									07 19						
Leatherhead	d							06 34		06 54							07 04		07 24						
Ashtead	d							06 37		06 58							07 08		07 28						
Epsom	a							06 42		07 02							07 12		07 32						
	d		05 35	06 05	06 35			06 42	06 49	07 05						07 04	07 13	07 19	07 35						
Ewell East	d							06 46	06 53							07 08		07 23							
Cheam	d							06 49	06 56							07 11	07 18	07 26							
Epsom Downs	d	23p43																							07 35
Banstead	d	23p46																							07 38
Belmont	d	23p49																							07 41
Sutton (Surrey)	a	23p52						06 52	06 59							07 14	07 22	07 29							07 44
	d	23p53				06 37	06 45	06 53	06 59			07 03	07 07	07 07	07 08	07 15	07 22	07 29		07 33		07 37	07 37	07 38	07 45
Carshalton	d								07 02						07 11			07 32						07 41	
Hackbridge	d								07 05						07 13			07 35						07 43	
Mitcham Junction	d								07 08						07 16			07 38						07 46	
Mitcham Eastfields	d								07 11						07 19			07 41						07 49	
Carshalton Beeches	d	23p56					06 48					07 06				07 18				07 36					07 48
Wallington	d	23p58					06 50					07 08				07 20				07 38					07 50
Waddon	d	00 01					06 53					07 11				07 23				07 41					07 53
West Croydon	d	00a04					06 58					07 15				07 28				07 45					07 58
Norwood Junction	d											07 20								07 50					
New Cross Gate	d											07 34								08 04					
Tulse Hill	a					07 12							07 42	07 44	07 27							08 12	08 14	07 57	
	d													07 47									08 17		
London Bridge	a											07 41		08 00						08 11			08 30		
Balham	d						07 14		07 18							07 44		07 48							
Clapham Junction	a		06 01	06 30	07 00		07 19	07 10	07 22	07 30						07 49	07 40	07 52	08 00						08 14
London Waterloo	a		06 11	06 40	07 10					07 40									08 10						08 19
London Victoria	a						07 28	07 18	07 30							07 58	07 48	08 00							08 28

A 19 May

Table 182

Saturdays
until 6 October

Horsham, Dorking, Guildford, Epsom and Sutton - London

Network Diagram - see first Page of Table 177

		SN	SN	SW	SN	FC		FC A	FC	SN	SN	SW	SN	SN	SW	SN		FC	FC A	FC	SN	SN	SW	SN	SN
Horsham	d																					08 04			
Warnham	d																					08 08			
Ockley	d																					08 15			
Holmwood	d																					08 19			
Dorking	a																					08 25			
	d	07 26									07 58	08 05										08 26	08 35		
Box Hill & Westhumble	d	07 28																				08 28			
Guildford	d			07 28											07 58										
Effingham Junction	d			07 46											08 16										
Bookham	d			07 49											08 19										
Leatherhead	d	07 33		07 54							08 04	08 11			08 24							08 33	08 41		
Ashtead	d	07 37		07 58							08 07	08 14			08 28							08 37	08 44		
Epsom	a	07 41		08 02							08 12	08 19			08 32							08 41	08 49		
	d	07 42	07 49	08 05						08 04	08 13	08 20		08 19	08 35							08 42	08 50		08 49
Ewell East	d	07 46	07 53							08 08				08 23								08 46			08 53
Cheam	d	07 49	07 56							08 11	08 18			08 26								08 49			08 56
Epsom Downs	d																				08 35				
Banstead	d																				08 38				
Belmont	d																				08 41				
Sutton (Surrey)	a	07 52	07 59							08 14	08 21			08 29							08 44	08 52			08 59
	d	07 52	07 59		08 03	08 07		08 07	08 08	08 15	08 22		08 22	08 29		08 33		08 37	08 37	08 38	08 45	08 52		08 52	08 59
Carshalton	d		08 02						08 11					08 32						08 41					09 02
Hackbridge	d		08 05						08 13					08 35						08 43					09 05
Mitcham Junction	d		08 08						08 16					08 38						08 46					09 08
Mitcham Eastfields	d		08 11						08 19					08 41						08 49					09 11
Carshalton Beeches	d				08 06					08 18			08 25			08 36					08 48			08 55	
Wallington	d				08 08					08 20			08 27			08 38					08 50			08 57	
Waddon	d				08 11					08 23			08 30			08 41					08 53			09 00	
West Croydon	d				08 15					08 28			08 34			08 45					08 58			09 04	
Norwood Junction	d				08 22											08 52									
New Cross Gate	⊖ d																								
Tulse Hill	a					08 42		08 44	08 27									09 12	09 14	08 57					
	d							08 47											09 17						
London Bridge	⊖ a							09 00											09 30						
Balham	⊖ d		08 18		08 39					08 44			08 51	08 48		09 09					09 14			09 21	09 18
Clapham Junction	a	08 10	08 22	08 30	08 44					08 49	08 40	08 45	08 56	08 52	09 00	09 14					09 19	09 10	09 15	09 26	09 22
London Waterloo	⊖ a			08 40								08 55			09 10								09 25		
London Victoria	⊖ a	08 18	08 30		08 53					08 58	08 48		09 04	09 00		09 23					09 28	09 18		09 34	09 30

		SW		SN	FC	FC A	FC	SN	SN	SW	SN	SN		SW	SN	FC	FC A	FC	SN	SN	SW	SN		SN	SW
Horsham	d																			09 04					
Warnham	d																			09 08					
Ockley	d																			09 15					
Holmwood	d																			09 19					
Dorking	a																			09 25					
	d								08 58	09 05										09 26	09 35				
Box Hill & Westhumble	d																			09 28					
Guildford	d	08 28												08 58											09 28
Effingham Junction	d	08 46												09 16											09 46
Bookham	d	08 49												09 19											09 49
Leatherhead	d	08 54							09 04	09 11				09 24						09 33	09 41				09 54
Ashtead	d	08 58							09 07	09 14				09 28						09 37	09 44				09 58
Epsom	a	09 02							09 12	09 19				09 32						09 41	09 49				10 02
	d	09 05						09 04	09 13	09 20		09 19		09 35						09 42	09 50			09 49	10 05
Ewell East	d							09 08				09 23								09 46				09 53	
Cheam	d							09 11	09 18			09 26								09 49				09 56	
Epsom Downs	d																		09 35						
Banstead	d																		09 38						
Belmont	d																		09 41						
Sutton (Surrey)	a							09 14	09 21			09 29							09 44	09 52				09 59	
	d			09 03	09 07	09 07	09 08	09 15	09 22		09 22	09 29			09 33	09 37	09 37	09 38	09 45	09 52		09 52		09 59	
Carshalton	d						09 11					09 32						09 41						10 02	
Hackbridge	d						09 13					09 35						09 43						10 05	
Mitcham Junction	d						09 16					09 38						09 46						10 08	
Mitcham Eastfields	d						09 19					09 41						09 49						10 11	
Carshalton Beeches	d			09 06				09 18			09 25				09 36				09 48			09 55			
Wallington	d			09 08				09 20			09 27				09 38				09 50			09 57			
Waddon	d			09 11				09 23			09 30				09 41				09 53			10 00			
West Croydon	d			09 15				09 28			09 34				09 45				09 58			10 04			
Norwood Junction	d			09 22											09 52										
New Cross Gate	⊖ d																								
Tulse Hill	a				09 42	09 44	09 27									10 12	10 14	09 57							
	d					09 47											10 17								
London Bridge	⊖ a					10 00											10 30								
Balham	⊖ d			09 39				09 44			09 51	09 48			10 09				10 14			10 21		10 18	
Clapham Junction	a	09 30		09 44				09 49	09 40	09 45	09 56	09 52		10 00	10 14				10 19	10 10	10 15	10 26		10 22	10 30
London Waterloo	⊖ a	09 40								09 55				10 10							10 25				10 40
London Victoria	⊖ a			09 53				09 58	09 48		10 04	10 00			10 23				10 28	10 18		10 34		10 30	

A 19 May

Table 182

Saturdays
until 6 October

Horsham, Dorking, Guildford, Epsom and Sutton - London

Network Diagram - see first Page of Table 177

		SN	FC	FC A	FC	SN	SN	SW		SN	SN	SW	SN	FC	FC A	FC	SN	SN		SW	SN	SN	SW	SN	FC
Horsham	d																	10 04							
Warnham	d																	10 08							
Ockley	d																	10 15							
Holmwood	d																	10 19							
Dorking	a																	10 25							
	d						09 58	10 05										10 26		10 35					
Box Hill & Westhumble	d																	10 28							
Guildford	d											09 58											10 28		
Effingham Junction	d											10 16											10 46		
Bookham	d											10 19											10 49		
Leatherhead	d						10 04	10 11				10 24						10 33		10 41			10 54		
Ashtead	d						10 07	10 14				10 28						10 37		10 44			10 58		
Epsom	a						10 12	10 19				10 32						10 41		10 49			11 02		
	d					10 04	10 13	10 20			10 19	10 35						10 42		10 50		10 49	11 05		
Ewell East	d					10 08					10 23							10 46				10 53			
Cheam	d					10 11	10 18				10 26							10 49				10 56			
Epsom Downs	d																10 35								
Banstead	d																10 38								
Belmont	d																10 41								
Sutton (Surrey)	a					10 14	10 21				10 29						10 44	10 52				10 59			
	d	10 03	10 07	10 07	10 08	10 15	10 22			10 22	10 29		10 33	10 37	10 37	10 38	10 45	10 53			10 52	10 59		11 03	11 07
Carshalton	d				10 11						10 32					10 41						11 02			
Hackbridge	d				10 13						10 35					10 43						11 05			
Mitcham Junction	d				10 16						10 38					10 46						11 08			
Mitcham Eastfields	d				10 19						10 41					10 49						11 11			
Carshalton Beeches	d	10 06				10 18				10 25			10 36				10 48				10 55			11 06	
Wallington	d	10 08				10 20				10 27			10 38				10 50				10 57			11 08	
Waddon	d	10 11				10 23				10 30			10 41				10 53				11 00			11 11	
West Croydon	d	10 15				10 28				10 34			10 45				10 58				11 04			11 15	
Norwood Junction	d	10 22											10 52											11 22	
New Cross Gate	⊖ d																								
Tulse Hill	a		10 42	10 44	10 27									11 12	11 14	10 57									11 42
	d			10 47											11 17										
London Bridge	⊖ a			11 00											11 30										
Balham	⊖ d	10 39				10 44				10 51	10 48		11 09				11 14				11 21	11 18		11 39	
Clapham Junction	a	10 44				10 49	10 40	10 45		10 56	10 52	11 00	11 14				11 19	11 10		11 15	11 26	11 22	11 30	11 44	
London Waterloo	⊖ a							10 55				11 10								11 25			11 40		
London Victoria	⊖ a	10 53				10 58	10 48			11 04	11 00		11 23				11 28	11 18			11 34	11 30		11 53	

		FC A	FC	SN		SN	SW	SN	SN	SW	SN	FC	FC A	FC		SN	SN	SW	SN	SN	SW	SN	FC	FC A	
Horsham	d																11 04								
Warnham	d																11 08								
Ockley	d																11 15								
Holmwood	d																11 19								
Dorking	a																11 25								
	d					10 58	11 05										11 26	11 35							
Box Hill & Westhumble	d																11 28								
Guildford	d									10 58											11 28				
Effingham Junction	d									11 16											11 46				
Bookham	d									11 19											11 49				
Leatherhead	d					11 04	11 11			11 24							11 33	11 41			11 54				
Ashtead	d					11 07	11 14			11 28							11 37	11 44			11 58				
Epsom	a					11 12	11 19			11 32							11 41	11 49			12 02				
	d			11 04		11 13	11 20		11 19	11 35							11 42	11 50		11 49	12 05				
Ewell East	d			11 08					11 23								11 46			11 53					
Cheam	d			11 11		11 18			11 26								11 49			11 56					
Epsom Downs	d															11 35									
Banstead	d															11 38									
Belmont	d															11 41									
Sutton (Surrey)	a			11 14		11 21			11 29							11 44	11 52			11 59					
	d	11 07	11 08	11 15		11 22		11 22	11 29		11 33	11 37	11 37	11 38		11 45	11 52		11 52	11 59		12 03	12 07	12 07	
Carshalton	d		11 11						11 32					11 41						12 02					
Hackbridge	d		11 13						11 35					11 43						12 05					
Mitcham Junction	d		11 16						11 38					11 46						12 08					
Mitcham Eastfields	d		11 19						11 41					11 49						12 11					
Carshalton Beeches	d			11 18				11 25			11 36					11 48			11 55			12 06			
Wallington	d			11 20				11 27			11 38					11 50			11 57			12 08			
Waddon	d			11 23				11 30			11 41					11 53			12 00			12 11			
West Croydon	d			11 28				11 34			11 45					11 58			12 04			12 15			
Norwood Junction	d										11 52											12 22			
New Cross Gate	⊖ d																								
Tulse Hill	a	11 44	11 27									12 12	12 14	11 57									12 42	12 44	
	d	11 47											12 17											12 47	
London Bridge	⊖ a	12 00											12 30											13 00	
Balham	⊖ d			11 44				11 51	11 48		12 09					12 14			12 21	12 18		12 39			
Clapham Junction	a			11 49		11 40	11 45	11 56	11 52	12 00	12 14					12 19	12 10	12 15	12 26	12 22	12 30	12 44			
London Waterloo	⊖ a						11 55			12 10								12 25			12 40				
London Victoria	⊖ a			11 58		11 48		12 04	12 00		12 23					12 28	12 18		12 34	12 30		12 53			

A 19 May

Table 182

Saturdays until 6 October

Horsham, Dorking, Guildford, Epsom and Sutton - London

Network Diagram - see first Page of Table 177

		FC	SN	SN	SW	SN	SN	SW	SN	FC		FC A	FC	SN	SN	SW	SN	SN	SW	SN		FC	FC A	FC	SN
Horsham	d														12 04										
Warnham	d														12 08										
Ockley	d														12 15										
Holmwood	d														12 19										
Dorking	a														12 25										
	d			11 58	12 05										12 26	12 35									
Box Hill & Westhumble	d														12 28										
Guildford	d							11 58											12 28						
Effingham Junction	d							12 16											12 46						
Bookham	d							12 19											12 49						
Leatherhead	d			12 04	12 11			12 24							12 33	12 41			12 54						
Ashtead	d			12 07	12 14			12 28							12 37	12 44			12 58						
Epsom	a			12 12	12 19			12 32							12 41	12 49			13 02						
	d		12 04	12 13	12 20		12 19	12 35							12 42	12 50		12 49	13 05						13 04
Ewell East	d		12 08				12 23								12 46			12 53							13 08
Cheam	d		12 11	12 18			12 26								12 49			12 56							13 11
Epsom Downs	d													12 35											
Banstead	d													12 38											
Belmont	d													12 41											
Sutton (Surrey)	a		12 14	12 21			12 29							12 44	12 52			12 59							13 14
	d	12 08	12 15	12 22		12 22	12 29		12 33	12 37		12 37	12 38	12 45	12 52		12 52	12 59		13 03		13 07	13 07	13 08	13 15
Carshalton	d	12 11					12 32						12 41					13 02						13 11	
Hackbridge	d	12 13					12 35						12 43					13 05						13 13	
Mitcham Junction	d	12 16					12 38						12 46					13 08						13 16	
Mitcham Eastfields	d	12 19					12 41						12 49					13 11						13 19	
Carshalton Beeches	d		12 18			12 25			12 36					12 48			12 55			13 06					13 18
Wallington	d		12 20			12 27			12 38					12 50			12 57			13 08					13 20
Waddon	d		12 23			12 30			12 41					12 53			13 00			13 11					13 23
West Croydon	d		12 28			12 34			12 45					12 58			13 04			13 15					13 28
Norwood Junction	d								12 52											13 22					
New Cross Gate	d																								
Tulse Hill	a	12 27								13 12		13 14	12 57									13 42	13 44	13 27	
	d											13 17											13 47		
London Bridge	a											13 30											14 00		
Balham	d		12 44			12 51	12 48		13 09					13 14			13 21	13 18		13 39					13 44
Clapham Junction	a		12 49	12 40	12 45	12 56	12 52	13 00	13 14					13 19	13 10	13 15	13 26	13 22	13 30	13 44					13 49
London Waterloo	a				12 55			13 10								13 25			13 40						
London Victoria	a		12 58	12 48		13 04	13 00		13 23					13 28	13 18		13 34	13 30		13 53					13 58

		SN	SW	SN	SN	SW		SN	FC	FC A	FC	SN	SN	SW	SN	SN		SW	SN	FC	FC A	FC	SN	SN	SW
Horsham	d												13 04												
Warnham	d												13 08												
Ockley	d												13 15												
Holmwood	d												13 19												
Dorking	a												13 25												
	d	12 58	13 05										13 26	13 35										13 58	14 05
Box Hill & Westhumble	d												13 28												
Guildford	d					12 58												13 28							
Effingham Junction	d					13 16												13 46							
Bookham	d					13 19												13 49							
Leatherhead	d	13 04	13 11			13 24							13 33	13 41				13 54						14 04	14 11
Ashtead	d	13 07	13 14			13 28							13 37	13 44				13 58						14 07	14 14
Epsom	a	13 12	13 19			13 32							13 41	13 49				14 02						14 12	14 19
	d	13 13	13 20		13 19	13 35							13 42	13 50		13 49		14 05					14 04	14 13	14 20
Ewell East	d				13 23								13 46			13 53							14 08		
Cheam	d	13 18			13 26								13 49			13 56							14 11	14 18	
Epsom Downs	d											13 35													
Banstead	d											13 38													
Belmont	d											13 41													
Sutton (Surrey)	a	13 21			13 29							13 44	13 52			13 59							14 14	14 21	
	d	13 22		13 22	13 29			13 33	13 37	13 37	13 38	13 45	13 52		13 52	13 59			14 03	14 07	14 07	14 08	14 15	14 22	
Carshalton	d				13 32						13 41					14 02						14 11			
Hackbridge	d				13 35						13 43					14 05						14 13			
Mitcham Junction	d				13 38						13 46					14 08						14 16			
Mitcham Eastfields	d				13 41						13 49					14 11						14 19			
Carshalton Beeches	d			13 25				13 36				13 48			13 55				14 06				14 18		
Wallington	d			13 27				13 38				13 50			13 57				14 08				14 20		
Waddon	d			13 30				13 41				13 53			14 00				14 11				14 23		
West Croydon	d			13 34				13 45				13 58			14 04				14 15				14 28		
Norwood Junction	d							13 52											14 22						
New Cross Gate	d																								
Tulse Hill	a								14 12	14 14	13 57									14 42	14 44	14 27			
	d									14 17											14 47				
London Bridge	a									14 30											15 00				
Balham	d			13 51	13 48			14 09				14 14			14 21	14 18			14 39				14 44		
Clapham Junction	a	13 40	13 45	13 56	13 52	14 00		14 14				14 19	14 10	14 15	14 26	14 22		14 30	14 44				14 49	14 40	14 45
London Waterloo	a		13 55			14 10								14 25				14 40							14 55
London Victoria	a	13 48		14 04	14 00			14 23				14 28	14 18		14 34	14 30			14 53				14 58	14 48	

A 19 May

Table 182

Saturdays until 6 October

Horsham, Dorking, Guildford, Epsom and Sutton - London

Network Diagram - see first Page of Table 177

		SN		SN	SW	SN	FC	FC A	FC	SN	SN	SW		SN	SN	SW	SN	FC	FC A	FC	SN	SN		SW	SN
Horsham	d										14 04														
Warnham	d										14 08														
Ockley	d										14 15														
Holmwood	d										14 19														
Dorking	a										14 25														
	d										14 26	14 35										14 58		15 05	
Box Hill & Westhumble	d										14 28														
Guildford	d				13 58											14 28									
Effingham Junction	d				14 16											14 46									
Bookham	d				14 19											14 49									
Leatherhead	d				14 24						14 33	14 41				14 54						15 04		15 11	
Ashtead	d				14 28						14 37	14 44				14 58						15 07		15 14	
Epsom	a				14 32						14 41	14 49				15 02						15 12		15 19	
	d			14 19	14 35						14 42	14 50			14 49	15 05					15 04	15 13		15 20	
Ewell East	d			14 23							14 46				14 53						15 08				
Cheam	d			14 26							14 49				14 56						15 11	15 18			
Epsom Downs	d									14 35															
Banstead	d									14 38															
Belmont	d									14 41															
Sutton (Surrey)	a			14 29						14 44	14 52				14 59						15 14	15 21			
	d	14 22		14 29		14 33	14 37	14 37	14 38	14 45	14 52			14 52	14 59		15 03	15 07	15 07	15 08	15 15	15 22			15 22
Carshalton	d			14 32					14 41						15 02					15 11					
Hackbridge	d			14 35					14 43						15 05					15 13					
Mitcham Junction	d			14 38					14 46						15 08					15 16					
Mitcham Eastfields	d			14 41					14 49						15 11					15 19					
Carshalton Beeches	d	14 25				14 36				14 48				14 55			15 06				15 18				15 25
Wallington	d	14 27				14 38				14 50				14 57			15 08				15 20				15 27
Waddon	d	14 30				14 41				14 53				15 00			15 11				15 23				15 30
West Croydon	d	14 34				14 45				14 58				15 04			15 15				15 28				15 34
Norwood Junction	d					14 52											15 22								
New Cross Gate	d																								
Tulse Hill	a						15 12	15 14	14 57									15 42	15 44	15 27					
	d							15 17											15 47						
London Bridge	a							15 30											16 00						
Balham	d	14 51		14 48		15 09				15 14				15 21	15 18		15 39				15 44				15 51
Clapham Junction	a	14 56		14 52	15 00	15 14				15 19	15 10	15 15		15 26	15 22	15 30	15 44				15 49	15 40		15 45	15 56
London Waterloo	a				15 10							15 25				15 40								15 55	
London Victoria	a	15 04		15 00		15 23				15 28	15 18			15 34	15 30		15 53				15 58	15 48			16 04

		SN	SW	SN	FC	FC A	FC	SN		SN	SW	SN	SN	SW	SN	FC	FC A	FC		SN	SN	SW	SN	SN	SW
Horsham	d									15 04															
Warnham	d									15 08															
Ockley	d									15 15															
Holmwood	d									15 19															
Dorking	a									15 25															
	d									15 26	15 35										15 58	16 05			
Box Hill & Westhumble	d									15 28															
Guildford	d		14 58											15 28											15 58
Effingham Junction	d		15 16											15 46											16 16
Bookham	d		15 19											15 49											16 19
Leatherhead	d		15 24							15 33	15 41			15 54							16 04	16 11			16 24
Ashtead	d		15 28							15 37	15 44			15 58							16 07	16 14			16 28
Epsom	a		15 32							15 41	15 49			16 02							16 12	16 19			16 32
	d	15 19	15 35							15 42	15 50		15 49	16 05						16 04	16 13	16 20		16 19	16 35
Ewell East	d	15 23								15 46			15 53							16 08				16 23	
Cheam	d	15 26								15 49			15 56							16 11	16 18			16 26	
Epsom Downs	d							15 35																	
Banstead	d							15 38																	
Belmont	d							15 41																	
Sutton (Surrey)	a	15 29						15 44		15 52			15 59							16 14	16 21			16 29	
	d	15 29		15 33	15 37	15 37	15 38	15 45		15 52		15 52	15 59		16 03	16 07	16 07	16 08		16 15	16 22		16 22	16 29	
Carshalton	d	15 32					15 41						16 02					16 11						16 32	
Hackbridge	d	15 35					15 43						16 05					16 13						16 35	
Mitcham Junction	d	15 38					15 46						16 08					16 16						16 38	
Mitcham Eastfields	d	15 41					15 49						16 11					16 19						16 41	
Carshalton Beeches	d			15 36				15 48				15 55			16 06					16 18			16 25		
Wallington	d			15 38				15 50				15 57			16 08					16 20			16 27		
Waddon	d			15 41				15 53				16 00			16 11					16 23			16 30		
West Croydon	d			15 45				15 58				16 04			16 15					16 28			16 34		
Norwood Junction	d			15 52											16 22										
New Cross Gate	d																								
Tulse Hill	a				16 12	16 14	15 57									16 42	16 44	16 27							
	d					16 17											16 47								
London Bridge	a					16 30											17 00								
Balham	d	15 48		16 09				16 14				16 21	16 18		16 39					16 44			16 51	16 48	
Clapham Junction	a	15 52	16 00	16 14				16 19		16 10	16 15	16 26	16 22	16 30	16 44					16 49	16 40	16 45	16 56	16 52	17 00
London Waterloo	a		16 10								16 25			16 40								16 55			17 10
London Victoria	a	16 00		16 23				16 28		16 18		16 34	16 30		16 53					16 58	16 48		17 04	17 00	

A 19 May

Horsham, Dorking, Guildford, Epsom and Sutton - London

Saturdays until 6 October

Network Diagram - see first Page of Table 177

		SN	FC	FC A	FC	SN	SN	SW	SN	SN	SW	SN	FC	FC A	FC	SN	SN	SW	SN	SN	SW	SN
Horsham	d						16 04															
Warnham	d						16 08															
Ockley	d						16 15															
Holmwood	d						16 19															
Dorking	a						16 25															
	d						16 26	16 35									16 58	17 05				
Box Hill & Westhumble	d						16 28															
Guildford	d										16 28										16 58	
Effingham Junction	d										16 46										17 16	
Bookham	d										16 49										17 19	
Leatherhead	d						16 33	16 41			16 54						17 04	17 11			17 24	
Ashtead	d						16 37	16 44			16 58						17 07	17 14			17 28	
Epsom	a						16 41	16 49			17 02						17 12	17 19			17 32	
	d						16 42	16 50		16 49	17 05					17 04	17 13	17 20		17 19	17 35	
Ewell East	d						16 46			16 53						17 08				17 23		
Cheam	d						16 49			16 56						17 11	17 18			17 26		
Epsom Downs	d					16 35																
Banstead	d					16 38																
Belmont	d					16 41																
Sutton (Surrey)	a					16 44	16 52			16 59						17 14	17 21			17 29		
	d	16 33	16 37	16 37	16 38	16 45	16 52		16 52	16 59		17 03	17 07	17 07	17 08	17 15	17 22		17 22	17 29		17 33
Carshalton	d				16 41					17 02					17 11					17 32		
Hackbridge	d				16 43					17 05					17 13					17 35		
Mitcham Junction	d				16 46					17 08					17 16					17 38		
Mitcham Eastfields	d				16 49					17 11					17 19					17 41		
Carshalton Beeches	d	16 36				16 48			16 55			17 06				17 18			17 25			17 36
Wallington	d	16 38				16 50			16 57			17 08				17 20			17 27			17 38
Waddon	d	16 41				16 53			17 00			17 11				17 23			17 30			17 41
West Croydon	d	16 45				16 58			17 04			17 15				17 28			17 34			17 45
Norwood Junction	d	16 52										17 22										17 52
New Cross Gate	d																					
Tulse Hill	a		17 12	17 14	16 57								17 42	17 44	17 27							
	d			17 17										17 47								
London Bridge	a			17 30										18 00								
Balham	d	17 09				17 14			17 21	17 18		17 39				17 44			17 51	17 48		18 09
Clapham Junction	a	17 14				17 19	17 10	17 15	17 26	17 22	17 30	17 44				17 49	17 41	17 45	17 56	17 52	18 00	18 14
London Waterloo	a							17 25			17 40							17 55			18 10	
London Victoria	a	17 23				17 28	17 18		17 34	17 30		17 53				17 58	17 49		18 04	18 00		18 23

		FC	FC A	FC	SN	SN	SW	SN	SN	SW	SN	FC	FC A	FC	SN	SN	SW	SN	SN	SW	SN	FC	FC A
Horsham	d					17 04																	
Warnham	d					17 08																	
Ockley	d					17 15																	
Holmwood	d					17 19																	
Dorking	a					17 25																	
	d					17 26	17 35									17 58	18 05						
Box Hill & Westhumble	d					17 28																	
Guildford	d									17 28										17 58			
Effingham Junction	d									17 46										18 16			
Bookham	d									17 49										18 19			
Leatherhead	d					17 33	17 41			17 54						18 04	18 11			18 24			
Ashtead	d					17 37	17 44			17 58						18 07	18 14			18 28			
Epsom	a					17 41	17 49			18 02						18 12	18 19			18 32			
	d					17 42	17 50		17 49	18 05					18 04	18 13	18 20		18 19	18 35			
Ewell East	d					17 46			17 53						18 08				18 23				
Cheam	d					17 49			17 56						18 11	18 18			18 26				
Epsom Downs	d				17 35																		
Banstead	d				17 38																		
Belmont	d				17 41																		
Sutton (Surrey)	a				17 44	17 52			17 59						18 14	18 21			18 29				
	d	17 37	17 37	17 38	17 45	17 52		17 52	17 59		18 03	18 07	18 07	18 08	18 15	18 22		18 22	18 29		18 33	18 37	18 37
Carshalton	d			17 41					18 02					18 11					18 32				
Hackbridge	d			17 43					18 05					18 13					18 35				
Mitcham Junction	d			17 46					18 08					18 16					18 38				
Mitcham Eastfields	d			17 49					18 11					18 19					18 41				
Carshalton Beeches	d				17 48			17 55			18 06				18 18			18 25			18 36		
Wallington	d				17 50			17 57			18 08				18 20			18 27			18 38		
Waddon	d				17 53			18 00			18 11				18 23			18 30			18 41		
West Croydon	d				17 58			18 04			18 15				18 28			18 34			18 45		
Norwood Junction	d										18 22										18 52		
New Cross Gate	d																						
Tulse Hill	a	18 12	18 14	17 57								18 42	18 44	18 27								19 12	19 14
	d		18 17										18 47										19 17
London Bridge	a		18 30										19 00										19 30
Balham	d				18 14			18 21	18 18		18 39				18 44			18 51	18 48		19 09		
Clapham Junction	a				18 19	18 10	18 15	18 26	18 22	18 30	18 44				18 49	18 40	18 45	18 56	18 52	19 00	19 14		
London Waterloo	a						18 25			18 40							18 55			19 10			
London Victoria	a				18 28	18 18		18 34	18 30		18 53				18 58	18 48		19 04	19 00		19 23		

A 19 May

Table 182

Horsham, Dorking, Guildford, Epsom and Sutton - London

Saturdays until 6 October

Network Diagram - see first Page of Table 177

		FC	SN	SN	SW	SN	SN	SW	SN	FC	FC A	FC	SN	SN	SW	SN	SN	SW	SN	FC	FC A	FC	SN
Horsham	d			18 04																			
Warnham	d			18 08																			
Ockley	d			18 15																			
Holmwood	d			18 19																			
Dorking	a			18 25																			
	d			18 26	18 35									18 58	19 05								
Box Hill & Westhumble	d			18 28										19 00									
Guildford	d							18 28										18 58					
Effingham Junction	d							18 46										19 16					
Bookham	d							18 49										19 19					
Leatherhead	d			18 33	18 41			18 54						19 05	19 11			19 24					
Ashtead	d			18 37	18 44			18 58						19 09	19 14			19 28					
Epsom	a			18 41	18 49			19 02						19 13	19 19			19 32					
	d			18 42	18 50		18 49	19 05					19 04	19 14	19 20		19 19	19 35					
Ewell East	d			18 46			18 53						19 08				19 23						
Cheam	d			18 49			18 56						19 11	19 19			19 26						
Epsom Downs	d		18 35																				19 35
Banstead	d		18 38																				19 38
Belmont	d		18 41																				19 41
Sutton (Surrey)	a		18 44	18 52			18 59						19 14	19 22			19 29						19 44
	d	18 38	18 45	18 52		18 52	18 59		19 03	19 07	19 07	19 08	19 15	19 23		19 22	19 29		19 33	19 37	19 37	19 38	19 45
Carshalton	d	18 41					19 02					19 11					19 32					19 41	
Hackbridge	d	18 43					19 05					19 13					19 35					19 43	
Mitcham Junction	d	18 46					19 08					19 16					19 38					19 46	
Mitcham Eastfields	d	18 49					19 11					19 19					19 41					19 49	
Carshalton Beeches	d		18 48			18 55			19 06				19 18			19 25			19 36				19 48
Wallington	d		18 50			18 57			19 08				19 20			19 27			19 38				19 50
Waddon	d		18 53			19 00			19 11				19 23			19 30			19 41				19 53
West Croydon	d		18 58			19 04			19 15				19 28			19 34			19 45				19 58
Norwood Junction	d								19 22										19 52				
New Cross Gate	d																						
Tulse Hill	a	18 57								19 42	19 44	19 27								20 12	20 14	19 57	
	d										19 47										20 17		
London Bridge	a										20 00										20 30		
Balham	d		19 14			19 21	19 18		19 39				19 44			19 51	19 48		20 09				20 14
Clapham Junction	a		19 19	19 10	19 15	19 26	19 22	19 30	19 44				19 49	19 40	19 45	19 56	19 52	20 00	20 14				20 19
London Waterloo	a				19 25			19 40							19 55			20 10					
London Victoria	a		19 28	19 18		19 34	19 30		19 53				19 58	19 48		20 04	20 00		20 23				20 28

		SN	SW	SN	SN	SW	SN	FC	FC	FC A	SN	SN	SW	SN	SN	SW	SN	FC	FC A	FC	SN	SN
Horsham	d																					
Warnham	d																					
Ockley	d																					
Holmwood	d																					
Dorking	a																					
	d	19 28	19 35									19 58	20 05									20 28
Box Hill & Westhumble	d											20 00										
Guildford	d					19 28										19 58						
Effingham Junction	d					19 46										20 16						
Bookham	d					19 49										20 19						
Leatherhead	d	19 34	19 41			19 54						20 05	20 11			20 24						20 34
Ashtead	d	19 37	19 44			19 58						20 09	20 14			20 28						20 37
Epsom	a	19 42	19 49			20 02						20 13	20 19			20 32						20 42
	d	19 42	19 50		19 49	20 05					20 04	20 14	20 20		20 19	20 35						20 42
Ewell East	d	19 46			19 53						20 08				20 23							20 46
Cheam	d	19 49			19 56						20 11	20 19			20 26							20 49
Epsom Downs	d																				20 35	
Banstead	d																				20 38	
Belmont	d																				20 41	
Sutton (Surrey)	a	19 52			19 59						20 14	20 22			20 29						20 44	20 52
	d	19 53		19 52	19 59		20 03	20 07	20 08	20 08	20 15	20 23		20 22	20 29		20 33	20 37	20 37	20 38	20 45	20 53
Carshalton	d				20 02				20 11						20 32					20 41		
Hackbridge	d				20 05				20 13						20 35					20 43		
Mitcham Junction	d				20 08				20 16						20 38					20 46		
Mitcham Eastfields	d				20 11				20 19						20 41					20 49		
Carshalton Beeches	d			19 55			20 06				20 18			20 25			20 36				20 48	
Wallington	d			19 57			20 08				20 20			20 27			20 38				20 50	
Waddon	d			20 00			20 11				20 23			20 30			20 41				20 53	
West Croydon	d			20 04			20 15				20 28			20 34			20 45				20 58	
Norwood Junction	d						20 22										20 52					
New Cross Gate	d																					
Tulse Hill	a							20 42	20 27	20 44								21 12	21 14	20 57		
	d									20 47									21 17			
London Bridge	a									21 00									21 30			
Balham	d			20 21	20 18		20 39				20 44			20 51	20 48		21 09				21 14	
Clapham Junction	a	20 10	20 15	20 26	20 22	20 30	20 44				20 49	20 40	20 45	20 56	20 52	21 00	21 14				21 19	21 10
London Waterloo	a		20 25			20 40							20 55			21 10						
London Victoria	a	20 18		20 34	20 30		20 53				20 58	20 48		21 04	21 00		21 23				21 28	21 18

A 19 May

Table 182

Horsham, Dorking, Guildford, Epsom and Sutton - London

Saturdays until 6 October

Network Diagram - see first Page of Table 177

		SW	SN	SN	SN	FC A	FC	SN	SW	FC	SN	SW	SN	SN	SW	SN	FC A	SN	FC	SN	SW	SN	SN
Horsham	d																						
Warnham	d																						
Ockley	d																						
Holmwood	d																						
Dorking	a																						
	d	20 35									20 58									21 28	21 35		
Box Hill & Westhumble	d										21 00												
Guildford	d											20 46											
Effingham Junction	d											21 03											
Bookham	d											21 06											
Leatherhead	d	20 41									21 05	21 11								21 34	21 41		
Ashtead	d	20 44									21 09	21 14								21 37	21 44		
Epsom	a	20 49									21 13	21 19								21 42	21 49		
	d	20 50		20 49				21 03	21 05		21 14	21 20		21 19	21 35					21 42	21 50		21 49
Ewell East	d			20 53				21 08						21 23						21 46			21 53
Cheam	d			20 56				21 11			21 19			21 26						21 49			21 56
Epsom Downs	d																	21 35					
Banstead	d																	21 38					
Belmont	d																	21 41					
Sutton (Surrey)	a			20 59				21 14			21 22			21 29				21 44		21 52			21 59
	d		20 52	20 59	21 03	21 07	21 08	21 15		21 15	21 23		21 22	21 29		21 33	21 37	21 45	21 45	21 53		21 52	21 59
Carshalton	d			21 02			21 11							21 32									22 02
Hackbridge	d			21 05			21 13							21 35									22 05
Mitcham Junction	d			21 08			21 16							21 38									22 08
Mitcham Eastfields	d			21 11			21 19							21 41									22 11
Carshalton Beeches	d		20 55		21 06			21 18					21 25			21 36		21 48				21 55	
Wallington	d		20 57		21 08			21 20					21 27			21 38		21 50				21 57	
Waddon	d		21 00		21 11			21 23					21 30			21 41		21 53				22 00	
West Croydon	d		21 04		21 15			21 28					21 34			21 45		21 58				22 04	
Norwood Junction	d				21 22																		
New Cross Gate ⊖	d															21 52							
Tulse Hill	a					21 44	21 27			21 53							22 14		22 23				
	d					21 47											22 17						
London Bridge ⊖	a					22 00											22 30						
Balham ⊖	d		21 21	21 18	21 39			21 44					21 51	21 48		22 09		22 14				22 22	22 18
Clapham Junction	a	21 15	21 26	21 22	21 44			21 49	21 30		21 40	21 45	21 56	21 52	22 00	22 14		22 19		22 10	22 15	22 27	22 22
London Waterloo ⊖	a	21 25							21 40			21 55			22 10						22 25		
London Victoria ⊖	a		21 34	21 30	21 53			21 58			21 48		22 04	22 00		22 23		22 28		22 18		22 34	22 30

		SN	FC A	SN	FC	SN	SW	SN	SN	SN	SN	FC	SN	SW	SN	SN	SN	SN	SN	SN	SW	SN
Horsham	d																					
Warnham	d																					
Ockley	d																					
Holmwood	d																					
Dorking	a																					
	d					21 58							22 28	22 35						23 00		
Box Hill & Westhumble	d					22 00														23 02		
Guildford	d						21 46														22 46	
Effingham Junction	d						22 03														23 03	
Bookham	d						22 06														23 06	
Leatherhead	d					22 05	22 11						22 34	22 41						23 07	23 11	
Ashtead	d					22 09	22 14						22 37	22 44						23 11	23 14	
Epsom	a					22 13	22 19						22 42	22 49						23 15	23 19	
	d			22 04		22 14	22 20		22 19				22 42	22 50		22 49		23 04		23 16	23 20	
Ewell East	d			22 08					22 23				22 46			22 53		23 08		23 20		
Cheam	d			22 11		22 19			22 26				22 49			22 56		23 11		23 23		
Epsom Downs	d										22 35											23 23
Banstead	d										22 38											23 26
Belmont	d										22 41											23 29
Sutton (Surrey)	a			22 14		22 22			22 29		22 44		22 52			22 59		23 14		23 26		23 32
	d	22 03	22 07	22 15	22 15	22 23		22 22	22 29	22 33	22 45	22 45	22 53		22 52	22 59	23 03	23 15	23 22	23 30		23 34
Carshalton	d								22 32							23 02						
Hackbridge	d								22 35							23 05						
Mitcham Junction	d								22 38							23 08						
Mitcham Eastfields	d								22 41							23 11						
Carshalton Beeches	d	22 06		22 18				22 25		22 36	22 48				22 55		23 06	23 18	23 25	23 33		23 37
Wallington	d	22 08		22 20				22 27		22 38	22 51				22 57		23 08	23 20	23 27	23 35		23 39
Waddon	d	22 11		22 23				22 30		22 41	22 54				23 00		23 11	23 23	23 30	23 38		23 42
West Croydon	d	22 15		22 28				22 34		22 45	22 58				23 04		23 15	23 28	23 34	23a41		23a45
Norwood Junction	d	22 22								22 52												
New Cross Gate ⊖	d																23 22					
Tulse Hill	a		22 44		22 53							23 23										
	d		22 47																			
London Bridge ⊖	a		23 00																			
Balham ⊖	d	22 39		22 44				22 51	22 48	23 09	23 14				23 21	23 18	23 39	23 44	23 50			
Clapham Junction	a	22 44		22 49		22 40	22 45	22 56	22 52	23 14	23 19		23 10	23 15	23 26	23 22	23 45	23 49	23 56		23 48	
London Waterloo ⊖	a						22 55							23 25							23 58	
London Victoria ⊖	a	22 53		22 58		22 48		23 04	23 00	23 24	23 29		23 22		23 34	23 31	23 53	23 58	00 04			

A 19 May

Table 182

Horsham, Dorking, Guildford, Epsom and Sutton - London

Saturdays until 6 October

Network Diagram - see first Page of Table 177

		SN	SN	SN
Horsham	d			
Warnham	d			
Ockley	d			
Holmwood	d			
Dorking	a			
	d		23 30	
Box Hill & Westhumble	d			
Guildford	d			
Effingham Junction	d			
Bookham	d			
Leatherhead	d		23 36	
Ashtead	d		23 39	
Epsom	a		23 45	
	d	23 35		
Ewell East	d	23 39		
Cheam	d	23 42		
Epsom Downs	d			23 50
Banstead	d			23 53
Belmont	d			23 56
Sutton (Surrey)	a	23 45		23 59
	d	23 46		00 01
Carshalton	d			
Hackbridge	d			
Mitcham Junction	d			
Mitcham Eastfields	d			
Carshalton Beeches	d	23 49		00 04
Wallington	d	23 51		00 06
Waddon	d	23 54		00 09
West Croydon	d	23a57		00a12
Norwood Junction	d			
New Cross Gate ⊖	d			
Tulse Hill	a			
	d			
London Bridge ⊖	a			
Balham ⊖	d			
Clapham Junction	a			
London Waterloo ⊖	a			
London Victoria ⊖	a			

Saturdays from 13 October

		SN	SW	SW	SW	FC	SN	SN	SN	SW	SN	FC	FC	SN	SN	SN	SW	SN	FC	FC	SN	SN	SN
Horsham	d																						
Warnham	d																						
Ockley	d																						
Holmwood	d																						
Dorking	a																						
	d							06 28							06 57							07 26	
Box Hill & Westhumble	d														06 59							07 28	
Guildford	d									06 28							06 58						
Effingham Junction	d									06 46							07 16						
Bookham	d									06 49							07 19						
Leatherhead	d							06 34		06 54					07 04		07 24					07 33	
Ashtead	d							06 37		06 58					07 08		07 28					07 37	
Epsom	a							06 42		07 02					07 12		07 32					07 41	
	d		05 35	06 05	06 35			06 42	06 49	07 05				07 04	07 13	07 19	07 35					07 42	07 49
Ewell East	d							06 46	06 53					07 08		07 23						07 46	07 53
Cheam	d							06 49	06 56					07 11	07 18	07 26						07 49	07 56
Epsom Downs	d	23p43																			07 35		
Banstead	d	23p46																			07 38		
Belmont	d	23p49																			07 41		
Sutton (Surrey)	a	23p52						06 52	06 59					07 14	07 22	07 29					07 44	07 52	07 59
	d	23p53				06 37	06 45	06 53	06 59		07 03	07 07	07 08	07 15	07 22	07 29		07 33	07 37	07 38	07 45	07 52	07 59
Carshalton	d								07 02				07 11			07 32				07 41			08 02
Hackbridge	d								07 05				07 13			07 35				07 43			08 05
Mitcham Junction	d								07 08				07 16			07 38				07 46			08 08
Mitcham Eastfields	d								07 11				07 19			07 41				07 49			08 11
Carshalton Beeches	d	23p56					06 48				07 06			07 18				07 36			07 48		
Wallington	d	23p58					06 50				07 08			07 20				07 38			07 50		
Waddon	d	00 01					06 53				07 11			07 23				07 41			07 53		
West Croydon	d	00a04					06 58				07 15			07 28				07 45			07 58		
Norwood Junction	d										07 20							07 50					
New Cross Gate ⊖	d										07 34							08 04					
Tulse Hill	a					07 12						07 42	07 27						08 12	07 57			
	d																						
London Bridge ⊖	a										07 41							08 11					
Balham ⊖	d						07 14		07 18					07 44		07 48					08 14		08 18
Clapham Junction	a		06 01	06 30	07 00		07 19	07 10	07 22	07 30				07 49	07 40	07 52	08 00				08 19	08 10	08 22
London Waterloo ⊖	a		06 11	06 40	07 10					07 40							08 10						
London Victoria ⊖	a						07 28	07 18	07 30					07 58	07 48	08 00					08 28	08 18	08 30

Horsham, Dorking, Guildford, Epsom and Sutton - London

Network Diagram - see first Page of Table 177

		SW	SN	FC	FC	SN		SN	SW	SN	SN	SW	SN	FC	FC	SN		SN	SW	SN	SN	SW	SN	FC	FC
Horsham	d																	08 04							
Warnham	d																	08 08							
Ockley	d																	08 15							
Holmwood	d																	08 19							
Dorking	a																	08 25							
	d							07 58	08 05									08 26	08 35						
Box Hill & Westhumble	d																	08 28							
Guildford	d	07 28										07 58										08 28			
Effingham Junction	d	07 46										08 16										08 46			
Bookham	d	07 49										08 19										08 49			
Leatherhead	d	07 54						08 04	08 11			08 24						08 33	08 41			08 54			
Ashtead	d	07 58						08 07	08 14			08 28						08 37	08 44			08 58			
Epsom	a	08 02						08 12	08 19			08 32						08 41	08 49			09 02			
	d	08 05				08 04		08 13	08 20		08 19	08 35						08 42	08 50		08 49	09 05			
Ewell East	d					08 08					08 23							08 46			08 53				
Cheam	d					08 11		08 18			08 26							08 49			08 56				
Epsom Downs	d															08 35									
Banstead	d															08 38									
Belmont	d															08 41									
Sutton (Surrey)	a					08 14		08 21			08 29					08 44		08 52			08 59				
	d		08 03	08 07	08 08	08 15		08 22		08 22	08 29		08 33	08 37	08 38	08 45		08 52		08 52	08 59		09 03	09 07	09 08
Carshalton	d				08 11						08 32				08 41						09 02				09 11
Hackbridge	d				08 13						08 35				08 43						09 05				09 13
Mitcham Junction	d				08 16						08 38				08 46						09 08				09 16
Mitcham Eastfields	d				08 19						08 41				08 49						09 11				09 19
Carshalton Beeches	d		08 06			08 18				08 25			08 36			08 48				08 55			09 06		
Wallington	d		08 08			08 20				08 27			08 38			08 50				08 57			09 08		
Waddon	d		08 11			08 23				08 30			08 41			08 53				09 00			09 11		
West Croydon	d		08 15			08 28				08 34			08 45			08 58				09 04			09 15		
Norwood Junction	d		08 22										08 52										09 22		
New Cross Gate ⊖	d																								
Tulse Hill	a			08 42	08 27									09 12	08 57									09 42	09 27
	d																								
London Bridge ⊖	a																								
Balham ⊖	d		08 39			08 44				08 51	08 48		09 09			09 14				09 21	09 18		09 39		
Clapham Junction	a	08 30	08 44			08 49		08 40	08 45	08 56	08 52	09 00	09 14			09 19		09 10	09 15	09 26	09 22	09 30	09 44		
London Waterloo ⊖	a	08 40							08 55			09 10							09 25			09 40			
London Victoria ⊖	a		08 53			08 58		08 48		09 04	09 00		09 23			09 28		09 18		09 34	09 30		09 53		

		SN		SN	SW	SN	SN	SW	SN	FC	FC	SN		SN	SW	SN	SN	SW	SN	FC	FC	SN		SN	SW
Horsham	d													09 04											
Warnham	d													09 08											
Ockley	d													09 15											
Holmwood	d													09 19											
Dorking	a													09 25											
	d			08 58	09 05									09 26	09 35									09 58	10 05
Box Hill & Westhumble	d													09 28											
Guildford	d							08 58										09 28							
Effingham Junction	d							09 16										09 46							
Bookham	d							09 19										09 49							
Leatherhead	d			09 04	09 11			09 24						09 33	09 41			09 54						10 04	10 11
Ashtead	d			09 07	09 14			09 28						09 37	09 44			09 58						10 07	10 14
Epsom	a			09 12	09 19			09 32						09 41	09 49			10 02						10 12	10 19
	d	09 04		09 13	09 20		09 19	09 35						09 42	09 50		09 49	10 05				10 04		10 13	10 20
Ewell East	d	09 08					09 23							09 46			09 53					10 08			
Cheam	d	09 11		09 18			09 26							09 49			09 56					10 11		10 18	
Epsom Downs	d											09 35													
Banstead	d											09 38													
Belmont	d											09 41													
Sutton (Surrey)	a	09 14		09 21			09 29					09 44		09 52			09 59					10 14		10 21	
	d	09 15		09 22		09 22	09 29		09 33	09 37	09 38	09 45		09 52		09 52	09 59		10 03	10 07	10 08	10 15		10 22	
Carshalton	d						09 32				09 41						10 02				10 11				
Hackbridge	d						09 35				09 43						10 05				10 13				
Mitcham Junction	d						09 38				09 46						10 08				10 16				
Mitcham Eastfields	d						09 41				09 49						10 11				10 19				
Carshalton Beeches	d	09 18				09 25			09 36			09 48				09 55			10 06			10 18			
Wallington	d	09 20				09 27			09 38			09 50				09 57			10 08			10 20			
Waddon	d	09 23				09 30			09 41			09 53				10 00			10 11			10 23			
West Croydon	d	09 28				09 34			09 45			09 58				10 04			10 15			10 28			
Norwood Junction	d								09 52										10 22						
New Cross Gate ⊖	d																								
Tulse Hill	a									10 12	09 57									10 42	10 27				
	d																								
London Bridge ⊖	a																								
Balham ⊖	d	09 44				09 51	09 48		10 09			10 14				10 21	10 18		10 39			10 44			
Clapham Junction	a	09 49		09 40	09 45	09 56	09 52	10 00	10 14			10 19		10 10	10 15	10 26	10 22	10 30	10 44			10 49		10 40	10 45
London Waterloo ⊖	a				09 55			10 10							10 25			10 40							10 55
London Victoria ⊖	a	09 58		09 48		10 04	10 00		10 23			10 28		10 18		10 34	10 30		10 53			10 58		10 48	

Table 182

Saturdays
from 13 October

Horsham, Dorking, Guildford, Epsom and Sutton - London

Network Diagram - see first Page of Table 177

		SN	SN	SW	SN	FC	FC	SN		SN	SW	SN	SN	SW	SN	FC	FC	SN		SN	SW	SN	SN	SW	SN
Horsham	d									10 04															
Warnham	d									10 08															
Ockley	d									10 15															
Holmwood	d									10 19															
Dorking	a									10 25															
	d									10 26	10 35									10 58	11 05				
Box Hill & Westhumble	d									10 28															
Guildford	d			09 58										10 28										10 58	
Effingham Junction	d			10 16										10 46										11 16	
Bookham	d			10 19										10 49										11 19	
Leatherhead	d			10 24						10 33	10 41			10 54						11 04	11 11			11 24	
Ashtead	d			10 28						10 37	10 44			10 58						11 07	11 14			11 28	
Epsom	a			10 32						10 41	10 49			11 02						11 12	11 19			11 32	
	d		10 19	10 35						10 42	10 50		10 49	11 05				11 04		11 13	11 20		11 19	11 35	
Ewell East	d		10 23							10 46			10 53					11 08					11 23		
Cheam	d		10 26							10 49			10 56					11 11		11 18			11 26		
Epsom Downs	d							10 35																	
Banstead	d							10 38																	
Belmont	d							10 41																	
Sutton (Surrey)	a		10 29					10 44		10 52			10 59					11 14		11 21			11 29		
	d	10 22	10 29		10 33	10 37	10 38	10 45		10 53		10 52	10 59		11 03	11 07	11 08	11 15		11 22		11 22	11 29		11 33
Carshalton	d		10 32				10 41						11 02				11 11						11 32		
Hackbridge	d		10 35				10 43						11 05				11 13						11 35		
Mitcham Junction	d		10 38				10 46						11 08				11 16						11 38		
Mitcham Eastfields	d		10 41				10 49						11 11				11 19						11 41		
Carshalton Beeches	d	10 25			10 36			10 48				10 55			11 06			11 18				11 25			11 36
Wallington	d	10 27			10 38			10 50				10 57			11 08			11 20				11 27			11 38
Waddon	d	10 30			10 41			10 53				11 00			11 11			11 23				11 30			11 41
West Croydon	d	10 34			10 45			10 58				11 04			11 15			11 28				11 34			11 45
Norwood Junction	d				10 52										11 22										11 52
New Cross Gate ⊖	d																								
Tulse Hill	a					11 12	10 57									11 42	11 27								
	d																								
London Bridge ⊖	a																								
Balham ⊖	d	10 51	10 48		11 09			11 14				11 21	11 18		11 39			11 44				11 51	11 48		12 09
Clapham Junction	a	10 56	10 52	11 00	11 14			11 19		11 10	11 15	11 26	11 22	11 30	11 44			11 49		11 40	11 45	11 56	11 52	12 00	12 14
London Waterloo ⊖	a			11 10							11 25			11 40							11 55			12 10	
London Victoria ⊖	a	11 04	11 00		11 23			11 28		11 18		11 34	11 30		11 53			11 58		11 48		12 04	12 00		12 23

		FC	FC	SN		SN	SW	SN	SN	SW	SN	FC	FC	SN		SN	SW	SN	SN	SW	SN	FC	FC	SN
Horsham	d					11 04																		
Warnham	d					11 08																		
Ockley	d					11 15																		
Holmwood	d					11 19																		
Dorking	a					11 25																		
	d					11 26	11 35									11 58	12 05							
Box Hill & Westhumble	d					11 28																		
Guildford	d									11 28										11 58				
Effingham Junction	d									11 46										12 16				
Bookham	d									11 49										12 19				
Leatherhead	d					11 33	11 41			11 54						12 04	12 11			12 24				
Ashtead	d					11 37	11 44			11 58						12 07	12 14			12 28				
Epsom	a					11 41	11 49			12 02						12 12	12 19			12 32				
	d					11 42	11 50		11 49	12 05				12 04		12 13	12 20		12 19	12 35				
Ewell East	d					11 46			11 53					12 08					12 23					
Cheam	d					11 49			11 56					12 11		12 18			12 26					
Epsom Downs	d			11 35																				12 35
Banstead	d			11 38																				12 38
Belmont	d			11 41																				12 41
Sutton (Surrey)	a			11 44		11 52			11 59					12 14		12 21			12 29					12 44
	d	11 37	11 38	11 45		11 52		11 52	11 59		12 03	12 07	12 08	12 15		12 22		12 22	12 29		12 33	12 37	12 38	12 45
Carshalton	d		11 41						12 02				12 11						12 32				12 41	
Hackbridge	d		11 43						12 05				12 13						12 35				12 43	
Mitcham Junction	d		11 46						12 08				12 16						12 38				12 46	
Mitcham Eastfields	d		11 49						12 11				12 19						12 41				12 49	
Carshalton Beeches	d			11 48				11 55			12 06			12 18				12 25			12 36			12 48
Wallington	d			11 50				11 57			12 08			12 20				12 27			12 38			12 50
Waddon	d			11 53				12 00			12 11			12 23				12 30			12 41			12 53
West Croydon	d			11 58				12 04			12 15			12 28				12 34			12 45			12 58
Norwood Junction	d										12 22										12 52			
New Cross Gate ⊖	d																							
Tulse Hill	a	12 12	11 57									12 42	12 27									13 12	12 57	
	d																							
London Bridge ⊖	a																							
Balham ⊖	d			12 14				12 21	12 18		12 39			12 44				12 51	12 48		13 09			13 14
Clapham Junction	a			12 19		12 10	12 15	12 26	12 22	12 30	12 44			12 49		12 40	12 45	12 56	12 52	13 00	13 14			13 19
London Waterloo ⊖	a						12 25			12 40							12 55			13 10				
London Victoria ⊖	a			12 28		12 18		12 34	12 30		12 53			12 58		12 48		13 04	13 00		13 23			13 28

Table 182

Saturdays from 13 October

Horsham, Dorking, Guildford, Epsom and Sutton - London

Network Diagram - see first Page of Table 177

		SN	SW	SN	SN	SW	SN	FC	FC	SN		SN	SW	SN	SN	SW	SN	FC	FC	SN		SN	SW	SN	SN
Horsham 4	d	12 04																				13 04			
Warnham	d	12 08																				13 08			
Ockley	d	12 15																				13 15			
Holmwood	d	12 19																				13 19			
Dorking 4	a	12 25																				13 25			
	d	12 26	12 35									12 58	13 05									13 26	13 35		
Box Hill & Westhumble	d	12 28																				13 28			
Guildford	d					12 28										12 58									
Effingham Junction 6	d					12 46										13 16									
Bookham	d					12 49										13 19									
Leatherhead	d	12 33	12 41			12 54						13 04	13 11			13 24						13 33	13 41		
Ashtead	d	12 37	12 44			12 58						13 07	13 14			13 28						13 37	13 44		
Epsom 3	a	12 41	12 49			13 02						13 12	13 19			13 32						13 41	13 49		
	d	12 42	12 50		12 49	13 05				13 04		13 13	13 20		13 19	13 35						13 42	13 50		13 49
Ewell East	d	12 46			12 53					13 08					13 23							13 46			13 53
Cheam	d	12 49			12 56					13 11		13 18			13 26							13 49			13 56
Epsom Downs	d																			13 35					
Banstead	d																			13 38					
Belmont	d																			13 41					
Sutton (Surrey) 4	a	12 52			12 59					13 14		13 21			13 29					13 44		13 52			13 59
	d	12 52		12 52	12 59		13 03	13 07	13 08	13 15		13 22		13 22	13 29		13 33	13 37	13 38	13 45		13 52		13 52	13 59
Carshalton	d				13 02				13 11						13 32				13 41						14 02
Hackbridge	d				13 05				13 13						13 35				13 43						14 05
Mitcham Junction	d				13 08				13 16						13 38				13 46						14 08
Mitcham Eastfields	d				13 11				13 19						13 41				13 49						14 11
Carshalton Beeches	d			12 55			13 06			13 18				13 25			13 36			13 48				13 55	
Wallington	d			12 57			13 08			13 20				13 27			13 38			13 50				13 57	
Waddon	d			13 00			13 11			13 23				13 30			13 41			13 53				14 00	
West Croydon 4	d			13 04			13 15			13 28				13 34			13 45			13 58				14 04	
Norwood Junction 2	d						13 22										13 52								
New Cross Gate 4 ⊖	d																								
Tulse Hill 3	a							13 42	13 27									14 12	13 57						
	d																								
London Bridge 4 ⊖	a																								
Balham 4 ⊖	d			13 21	13 18		13 39			13 44				13 51	13 48		14 09			14 14				14 21	14 18
Clapham Junction 10	a	13 10	13 15	13 26	13 22	13 30	13 44			13 49		13 40	13 45	13 56	13 52	14 00	14 14			14 19		14 10	14 15	14 26	14 22
London Waterloo 15 ⊖	a		13 25			13 40							13 55			14 10							14 25		
London Victoria 15 ⊖	a	13 18		13 34	13 30		13 53			13 58		13 48		14 04	14 00		14 23			14 28		14 18		14 34	14 30

		SW	SN	FC	FC	SN		SN	SW	SN	SN	SW	SN	FC	FC	SN		SN	SW	SN	SN	SW	SN	FC	FC
Horsham 4	d																	14 04							
Warnham	d																	14 08							
Ockley	d																	14 15							
Holmwood	d																	14 19							
Dorking 4	a																	14 25							
	d							13 58	14 05									14 26	14 35						
Box Hill & Westhumble	d																	14 28							
Guildford	d	13 28										13 58										14 28			
Effingham Junction 6	d	13 46										14 16										14 46			
Bookham	d	13 49										14 19										14 49			
Leatherhead	d	13 54						14 04	14 11			14 24						14 33	14 41			14 54			
Ashtead	d	13 58						14 07	14 14			14 28						14 37	14 44			14 58			
Epsom 3	a	14 02						14 12	14 19			14 32						14 41	14 49			15 02			
	d	14 05				14 04		14 13	14 20		14 19	14 35						14 42	14 50		14 49	15 05			
Ewell East	d					14 08					14 23							14 46			14 53				
Cheam	d					14 11		14 18			14 26							14 49			14 56				
Epsom Downs	d															14 35									
Banstead	d															14 38									
Belmont	d															14 41									
Sutton (Surrey) 4	a					14 14		14 21			14 29					14 44		14 52			14 59				
	d		14 03	14 07	14 08	14 15		14 22		14 22	14 29		14 33	14 37	14 38	14 45		14 52		14 52	14 59		15 03	15 07	15 08
Carshalton	d				14 11						14 32				14 41						15 02				15 11
Hackbridge	d				14 13						14 35				14 43						15 05				15 13
Mitcham Junction	d				14 16						14 38				14 46						15 08				15 16
Mitcham Eastfields	d				14 19						14 41				14 49						15 11				15 19
Carshalton Beeches	d		14 06			14 18				14 25			14 36			14 48				14 55			15 06		
Wallington	d		14 08			14 20				14 27			14 38			14 50				14 57			15 08		
Waddon	d		14 11			14 23				14 30			14 41			14 53				15 00			15 11		
West Croydon 4	d		14 15			14 28				14 34			14 45			14 58				15 04			15 15		
Norwood Junction 2	d		14 22										14 52										15 22		
New Cross Gate 4 ⊖	d																								
Tulse Hill 3	a			14 42	14 27									15 12	14 57									15 42	15 27
	d																								
London Bridge 4 ⊖	a																								
Balham 4 ⊖	d		14 39			14 44				14 51	14 48		15 09			15 14				15 21	15 18		15 39		
Clapham Junction 10	a	14 30	14 44			14 49		14 40	14 45	14 56	14 52	15 00	15 14			15 19		15 10	15 15	15 26	15 22	15 30	15 44		
London Waterloo 15 ⊖	a	14 40							14 55			15 10							15 25			15 40			
London Victoria 15 ⊖	a		14 53			14 58		14 48		15 04	15 00		15 23			15 28		15 18		15 34	15 30		15 53		

Table 182

Saturdays from 13 October

Horsham, Dorking, Guildford, Epsom and Sutton - London

Network Diagram - see first Page of Table 177

		SN		SN	SW	SN	SN	SW	SN	FC	FC	SN		SN	SW	SN	SN	SW	SN	FC	FC	SN		SN	SW
Horsham 4	d													15 04											
Warnham	d													15 08											
Ockley	d													15 15											
Holmwood	d													15 19											
Dorking 4	a													15 25											
	d			14 58	15 05									15 26	15 35									15 58	16 05
Box Hill & Westhumble	d													15 28											
Guildford	d							14 58										15 28							
Effingham Junction 6	d							15 16										15 46							
Bookham	d							15 19										15 49							
Leatherhead	d			15 04	15 11			15 24						15 33	15 41			15 54						16 04	16 11
Ashtead	d			15 07	15 14			15 28						15 37	15 44			15 58						16 07	16 14
Epsom 3	a			15 12	15 19			15 32						15 41	15 49			16 02						16 12	16 19
	d	15 04		15 13	15 20		15 19	15 35						15 42	15 50		15 49	16 05				16 04		16 13	16 20
Ewell East	d	15 08					15 23							15 46			15 53					16 08			
Cheam	d	15 11		15 18			15 26							15 49			15 56					16 11		16 18	
Epsom Downs	d											15 35													
Banstead	d											15 38													
Belmont	d											15 41													
Sutton (Surrey) 4	a	15 14		15 21			15 29					15 44		15 52			15 59					16 14		16 21	
	d	15 15		15 22		15 22	15 29		15 33	15 37	15 38	15 45		15 52		15 52	15 59		16 03	16 07	16 08	16 15		16 22	
Carshalton	d						15 32				15 41						16 02				16 11				
Hackbridge	d						15 35				15 43						16 05				16 13				
Mitcham Junction	d						15 38				15 46						16 08				16 16				
Mitcham Eastfields	d						15 41				15 49						16 11				16 19				
Carshalton Beeches	d	15 18				15 25			15 36			15 48				15 55			16 06			16 18			
Wallington	d	15 20				15 27			15 38			15 50				15 57			16 08			16 20			
Waddon	d	15 23				15 30			15 41			15 53				16 00			16 11			16 23			
West Croydon 4	d	15 28				15 34			15 45			15 58				16 04			16 15			16 28			
Norwood Junction 2	d								15 52										16 22						
New Cross Gate 4 ⊖	d																								
Tulse Hill 3	a									16 12	15 57									16 42	16 27				
	d																								
London Bridge 4 ⊖	a																								
Balham 4 ⊖	d	15 44				15 51	15 48		16 09			16 14				16 21	16 18		16 39			16 44			
Clapham Junction 10	a	15 49		15 40	15 45	15 56	15 52	16 00	16 14			16 19		16 10	16 15	16 26	16 22	16 30	16 44			16 49		16 40	16 45
London Waterloo 15 ⊖	a				15 55			16 10							16 25			16 40							16 55
London Victoria 15 ⊖	a	15 58		15 48		16 04	16 00		16 23			16 28		16 18		16 34	16 30		16 53			16 58		16 48	

		SN	SN	SW	SN	FC	FC	SN		SN	SW	SN	SN	SW	SN	FC	FC	SN		SN	SW	SN	SN	SW	SN
Horsham 4	d									16 04															
Warnham	d									16 08															
Ockley	d									16 15															
Holmwood	d									16 19															
Dorking 4	a									16 25															
	d									16 26	16 35									16 58	17 05				
Box Hill & Westhumble	d									16 28															
Guildford	d			15 58										16 28										16 58	
Effingham Junction 6	d			16 16										16 46										17 16	
Bookham	d			16 19										16 49										17 19	
Leatherhead	d			16 24						16 33	16 41			16 54						17 04	17 11			17 24	
Ashtead	d			16 28						16 37	16 44			16 58						17 07	17 14			17 28	
Epsom 3	a			16 32						16 41	16 49			17 02						17 12	17 19			17 32	
	d		16 19	16 35						16 42	16 50		16 49	17 05				17 04		17 13	17 20		17 19	17 35	
Ewell East	d		16 23							16 46			16 53					17 08					17 23		
Cheam	d		16 26							16 49			16 56					17 11		17 18			17 26		
Epsom Downs	d							16 35																	
Banstead	d							16 38																	
Belmont	d							16 41																	
Sutton (Surrey) 4	a		16 29					16 44		16 52			16 59					17 14		17 21			17 29		
	d	16 22	16 29		16 33	16 37	16 38	16 45		16 52		16 52	16 59		17 03	17 07	17 08	17 15		17 22		17 22	17 29		17 33
Carshalton	d		16 32				16 41						17 02				17 11						17 32		
Hackbridge	d		16 35				16 43						17 05				17 13						17 35		
Mitcham Junction	d		16 38				16 46						17 08				17 16						17 38		
Mitcham Eastfields	d		16 41				16 49						17 11				17 19						17 41		
Carshalton Beeches	d	16 25			16 36			16 48				16 55			17 06			17 18				17 25			17 36
Wallington	d	16 27			16 38			16 50				16 57			17 08			17 20				17 27			17 38
Waddon	d	16 30			16 41			16 53				17 00			17 11			17 23				17 30			17 41
West Croydon 4	d	16 34			16 45			16 58				17 04			17 15			17 28				17 34			17 45
Norwood Junction 2	d				16 52										17 22										17 52
New Cross Gate 4 ⊖	d																								
Tulse Hill 3	a					17 12	16 57									17 42	17 27								
	d																								
London Bridge 4 ⊖	a																								
Balham 4 ⊖	d	16 51	16 48		17 09			17 14				17 21	17 18		17 39			17 44				17 51	17 48		18 09
Clapham Junction 10	a	16 56	16 52	17 00	17 14			17 19		17 10	17 15	17 26	17 22	17 30	17 44			17 49		17 41	17 45	17 56	17 52	18 00	18 14
London Waterloo 15 ⊖	a			17 10							17 25			17 40							17 55			18 10	
London Victoria 15 ⊖	a	17 04	17 00		17 23			17 28		17 18		17 34	17 30		17 53			17 58		17 49		18 04	18 00		18 23

Table 182

Saturdays from 13 October

Horsham, Dorking, Guildford, Epsom and Sutton - London

Network Diagram - see first Page of Table 177

		FC	FC	SN		SN	SW	SN	SN	SW	SN	FC	FC	SN		SN	SW	SN	SN	SW	SN	FC	FC	SN	
Horsham	d					17 04																			
Warnham	d					17 08																			
Ockley	d					17 15																			
Holmwood	d					17 19																			
Dorking	a					17 25																			
	d					17 26	17 35									17 58	18 05								
Box Hill & Westhumble	d					17 28																			
Guildford	d									17 28										17 58					
Effingham Junction	d									17 46										18 16					
Bookham	d									17 49										18 19					
Leatherhead	d					17 33	17 41			17 54						18 04	18 11			18 24					
Ashtead	d					17 37	17 44			17 58						18 07	18 14			18 28					
Epsom	a					17 41	17 49			18 02						18 12	18 19			18 32					
	d					17 42	17 50		17 49	18 05				18 04		18 13	18 20		18 19	18 35					
Ewell East	d					17 46			17 53					18 08					18 23						
Cheam	d					17 49			17 56					18 11		18 18			18 26						
Epsom Downs	d			17 35																				18 35	
Banstead	d			17 38																				18 38	
Belmont	d			17 41																				18 41	
Sutton (Surrey)	a			17 44		17 52			17 59					18 14		18 21			18 29					18 44	
	d	17 37	17 38	17 45		17 52		17 52	17 59		18 03	18 07	18 08	18 15		18 22		18 22	18 29		18 33	18 37	18 38	18 45	
Carshalton	d		17 41						18 02				18 11						18 32				18 41		
Hackbridge	d		17 43						18 05				18 13						18 35				18 43		
Mitcham Junction	d		17 46						18 08				18 16						18 38				18 46		
Mitcham Eastfields	d		17 49						18 11				18 19						18 41				18 49		
Carshalton Beeches	d			17 48				17 55			18 06			18 18				18 25			18 36			18 48	
Wallington	d			17 50				17 57			18 08			18 20				18 27			18 38			18 50	
Waddon	d			17 53				18 00			18 11			18 23				18 30			18 41			18 53	
West Croydon	d			17 58				18 04			18 15			18 28				18 34			18 45			18 58	
Norwood Junction	d										18 22										18 52				
New Cross Gate	d																								
Tulse Hill	a	18 12	17 57									18 42	18 27									19 12	18 57		
	d																								
London Bridge	a																								
Balham	d			18 14				18 21	18 18		18 39			18 44				18 51	18 48		19 09			19 14	
Clapham Junction	a			18 19		18 10	18 15	18 26	18 22	18 30	18 44			18 49		18 40	18 45	18 56	18 52	19 00	19 14			19 19	
London Waterloo	a						18 25			18 40							18 55			19 10					
London Victoria	a			18 28		18 18		18 34	18 30		18 53			18 58		18 48		19 04	19 00		19 23			19 28	

		SN	SW	SN	SN	SW	SN	FC	FC	SN		SN	SW	SN	SN	SW	SN	FC	FC	SN		SN	SW	SN	SN
Horsham	d	18 04																							
Warnham	d	18 08																							
Ockley	d	18 15																							
Holmwood	d	18 19																							
Dorking	a	18 25																							
	d	18 26	18 35									18 58	19 05									19 28	19 35		
Box Hill & Westhumble	d	18 28										19 00													
Guildford	d					18 28										18 58									
Effingham Junction	d					18 46										19 16									
Bookham	d					18 49										19 19									
Leatherhead	d	18 33	18 41			18 54						19 05	19 11			19 24						19 34	19 41		
Ashtead	d	18 37	18 44			18 58						19 09	19 14			19 28						19 37	19 44		
Epsom	a	18 41	18 49			19 02						19 13	19 19			19 32						19 42	19 49		
	d	18 42	18 50		18 49	19 05				19 04		19 14	19 20		19 19	19 35						19 42	19 50		19 49
Ewell East	d	18 46			18 53					19 08					19 23							19 46			19 53
Cheam	d	18 49			18 56					19 11		19 19			19 26							19 49			19 56
Epsom Downs	d																			19 35					
Banstead	d																			19 38					
Belmont	d																			19 41					
Sutton (Surrey)	a	18 52			18 59					19 14		19 22			19 29					19 44		19 52			19 59
	d	18 52		18 52	18 59		19 03	19 07	19 08	19 15		19 23		19 22	19 29		19 33	19 37	19 38	19 45		19 53		19 52	19 59
Carshalton	d				19 02				19 11						19 32				19 41						20 02
Hackbridge	d				19 05				19 13						19 35				19 43						20 05
Mitcham Junction	d				19 08				19 16						19 38				19 46						20 08
Mitcham Eastfields	d				19 11				19 19						19 41				19 49						20 11
Carshalton Beeches	d			18 55			19 06			19 18				19 25			19 36			19 48				19 55	
Wallington	d			18 57			19 08			19 20				19 27			19 38			19 50				19 57	
Waddon	d			19 00			19 11			19 23				19 30			19 41			19 53				20 00	
West Croydon	d			19 04			19 15			19 28				19 34			19 45			19 58				20 04	
Norwood Junction	d						19 22										19 52								
New Cross Gate	d																								
Tulse Hill	a							19 42	19 27									20 12	19 57						
	d																								
London Bridge	a																								
Balham	d			19 21	19 18		19 39			19 44				19 51	19 48		20 09			20 14				20 21	20 18
Clapham Junction	a	19 10	19 15	19 26	19 22	19 30	19 44			19 49		19 40	19 45	19 56	19 52	20 00	20 14			20 19		20 10	20 15	20 26	20 22
London Waterloo	a		19 25			19 40							19 55			20 10							20 25		
London Victoria	a	19 18		19 34	19 30		19 53			19 58		19 48		20 04	20 00		20 23			20 28		20 18		20 34	20 30

Table 182

Saturdays from 13 October

Horsham, Dorking, Guildford, Epsom and Sutton - London

Network Diagram - see first Page of Table 177

		SW	SN	FC	FC	SN		SN	SW	SN	SN	SW	SN	FC	FC	SN		SN	SW	SN	SN	SN	FC	SN	SW
Horsham	d																								
Warnham	d																								
Ockley	d																								
Holmwood	d																								
Dorking	a																								
	d							19 58	20 05									20 28	20 35						
Box Hill & Westhumble	d							20 00																	
Guildford	d	19 28										19 58													
Effingham Junction	d	19 46										20 16													
Bookham	d	19 49										20 19													
Leatherhead	d	19 54						20 05	20 11			20 24						20 34	20 41						
Ashtead	d	19 58						20 09	20 14			20 28						20 37	20 44						
Epsom	a	20 02						20 13	20 19			20 32						20 42	20 49						
	d	20 05				20 04		20 14	20 20		20 19	20 35						20 42	20 50		20 49			21 03	21 05
Ewell East	d					20 08					20 23							20 46			20 53			21 08	
Cheam	d					20 11		20 19			20 26							20 49			20 56			21 11	
Epsom Downs	d															20 35									
Banstead	d															20 38									
Belmont	d															20 41									
Sutton (Surrey)	a					20 14		20 22			20 29					20 44		20 52			20 59			21 14	
	d		20 03	20 07	20 08	20 15		20 23		20 22	20 29		20 33	20 37	20 38	20 45		20 53		20 52	20 59	21 03	21 08	21 15	
Carshalton	d				20 11						20 32				20 41						21 02		21 11		
Hackbridge	d				20 13						20 35				20 43						21 05		21 13		
Mitcham Junction	d				20 16						20 38				20 46						21 08		21 16		
Mitcham Eastfields	d				20 19						20 41				20 49						21 11		21 19		
Carshalton Beeches	d		20 06			20 18				20 25			20 36			20 48				20 55		21 06		21 18	
Wallington	d		20 08			20 20				20 27			20 38			20 50				20 57		21 08		21 20	
Waddon	d		20 11			20 23				20 30			20 41			20 53				21 00		21 11		21 23	
West Croydon	d		20 15			20 28				20 34			20 45			20 58				21 04		21 15		21 28	
Norwood Junction	d		20 22										20 52									21 22			
New Cross Gate	d																								
Tulse Hill	a			20 42	20 27									21 12	20 57								21 27		
	d																								
London Bridge	a																								
Balham	d		20 39			20 44				20 51	20 48		21 09			21 14				21 21	21 18	21 39		21 44	
Clapham Junction	a	20 30	20 44			20 49		20 40	20 45	20 56	20 52	21 00	21 14			21 19		21 10	21 15	21 26	21 22	21 44		21 49	21 30
London Waterloo	a	20 40							20 55			21 10							21 25						21 40
London Victoria	a		20 53			20 58		20 48		21 04	21 00		21 23			21 28		21 18		21 34	21 30	21 53		21 58	

		FC		SN	SW	SN	SN	SW	SN	SN	FC	SN		SW	SN	SN	SN	SN	FC	SN	SW	SN		SN	SN
Horsham	d																								
Warnham	d																								
Ockley	d																								
Holmwood	d																								
Dorking	a																								
	d			20 58								21 28		21 35						21 58					
Box Hill & Westhumble	d			21 00																22 00					
Guildford	d				20 46																21 46				
Effingham Junction	d				21 03																22 03				
Bookham	d				21 06																22 06				
Leatherhead	d			21 05	21 11							21 34		21 41						22 05	22 11				
Ashtead	d			21 09	21 14							21 37		21 44						22 09	22 14				
Epsom	a			21 13	21 19							21 42		21 49						22 13	22 19				
	d			21 14	21 20		21 19	21 35				21 42		21 50		21 49		22 04		22 14	22 20			22 19	
Ewell East	d						21 23					21 46				21 53		22 08						22 23	
Cheam	d			21 19			21 26					21 49				21 56		22 11		22 19				22 26	
Epsom Downs	d									21 35															
Banstead	d									21 38															
Belmont	d									21 41															
Sutton (Surrey)	a			21 22			21 29			21 44		21 52				21 59		22 14		22 22				22 29	
	d	21 15		21 23		21 22	21 29		21 33	21 45	21 45	21 53			21 52	21 59	22 03	22 15	22 15	22 23		22 22		22 29	22 33
Carshalton	d						21 32									22 02								22 32	
Hackbridge	d						21 35									22 05								22 35	
Mitcham Junction	d						21 38									22 08								22 38	
Mitcham Eastfields	d						21 41									22 11								22 41	
Carshalton Beeches	d					21 25			21 36	21 48					21 55		22 06	22 18				22 25			22 36
Wallington	d					21 27			21 38	21 50					21 57		22 08	22 20				22 27			22 38
Waddon	d					21 30			21 41	21 53					22 00		22 11	22 23				22 30			22 41
West Croydon	d					21 34			21 45	21 58					22 04		22 15	22 28				22 34			22 45
Norwood Junction	d								21 52								22 22								22 52
New Cross Gate	d																								
Tulse Hill	a	21 53									22 23								22 53						
	d																								
London Bridge	a																								
Balham	d					21 51	21 48		22 09	22 14					22 22	22 18	22 39	22 44				22 51		22 48	23 09
Clapham Junction	a			21 40	21 45	21 56	21 52	22 00	22 14	22 19		22 10		22 15	22 27	22 22	22 44	22 49		22 40	22 45	22 56		22 52	23 14
London Waterloo	a				21 55			22 10						22 25							22 55				
London Victoria	a			21 48		22 04	22 00		22 23	22 28		22 18			22 34	22 30	22 53	22 58		22 48		23 04		23 00	23 24

Table 182

Horsham, Dorking, Guildford, Epsom and Sutton - London

Saturdays from 13 October

Network Diagram - see first Page of Table 177

		SN	FC	SN	SW	SN	SN	SN	SN	SN	SN	SW	SN	SN	SN	SN
Horsham 4	d															
Warnham	d															
Ockley	d															
Holmwood	d															
Dorking 4	a															
	d			22 28	22 35						23 00				23 30	
Box Hill & Westhumble	d										23 02					
Guildford	d											22 46				
Effingham Junction 6	d											23 03				
Bookham	d											23 06				
Leatherhead	d			22 34	22 41						23 07	23 11			23 36	
Ashtead	d			22 37	22 44						23 11	23 14			23 39	
Epsom 3	a			22 42	22 49						23 15	23 19			23 45	
	d			22 42	22 50		22 49		23 04		23 16	23 20		23 35		
Ewell East	d			22 46			22 53		23 08		23 20			23 39		
Cheam	d			22 49			22 56		23 11		23 23			23 42		
Epsom Downs	d	22 35											23 23			23 50
Banstead	d	22 38											23 26			23 53
Belmont	d	22 41											23 29			23 56
Sutton (Surrey) 4	a	22 44		22 52			22 59		23 14		23 26		23 32	23 45		23 59
	d	22 45	22 45	22 53		22 52	22 59	23 03	23 15	23 22	23 30		23 34	23 46		00 01
Carshalton	d						23 02									
Hackbridge	d						23 05									
Mitcham Junction	d						23 08									
Mitcham Eastfields	d						23 11									
Carshalton Beeches	d	22 48				22 55		23 06	23 18	23 25	23 33		23 37	23 49		00 04
Wallington	d	22 51				22 57		23 08	23 20	23 27	23 35		23 39	23 51		00 06
Waddon	d	22 54				23 00		23 11	23 23	23 30	23 38		23 42	23 54		00 09
West Croydon 4	d	22 58				23 04		23 15	23 28	23 34	23a41		23a45	23a57		00a12
Norwood Junction 2	d							23 22								
New Cross Gate 4 ⊖	d															
Tulse Hill 3	a		23 23													
	d															
London Bridge 4 ⊖	a															
Balham 4 ⊖	d	23 14				23 21	23 18	23 39	23 44	23 50						
Clapham Junction 10	a	23 19		23 10	23 15	23 26	23 22	23 45	23 49	23 56		23 48				
London Waterloo 15 ⊖	a				23 25							23 58				
London Victoria 15 ⊖	a	23 29		23 22		23 34	23 31	23 53	23 58	00 04						

Sundays until 30 September

		SN	SN	SN	SN	SN	SW	SN	SN	SN	SW	SN	SN	SN	SN	SW	SN	SN	SN	SN	SW	SN	SN
Horsham 4	d																						
Warnham	d																						
Ockley	d																						
Holmwood	d																						
Dorking 4	a																						
	d							07 16					07 46					08 16					08 46
Box Hill & Westhumble	d							07 18					07 48					08 18					08 48
Guildford	d																				08 20		
Effingham Junction 6	d																				08 36		
Bookham	d																				08 39		
Leatherhead	d							07 23					07 53					08 23			08 45		08 53
Ashtead	d							07 27					07 57					08 27			08 48		08 57
Epsom 3	a							07 31					08 01					08 31			08 53		09 01
	d			06 44		07 17	07 24	07 32		07 47	07 54		08 02		08 17	08 24		08 32		08 47	08 54		09 02
Ewell East	d			06 48		07 21		07 36		07 51			08 06		08 21			08 36		08 51			09 06
Cheam	d			06 51		07 24		07 39		07 54			08 09		08 24			08 39		08 54			09 09
Epsom Downs	d		23p50																				
Banstead	d		23p53																				
Belmont	d		23p56																				
Sutton (Surrey) 4	a		23p59	06 54		07 27		07 42		07 57			08 12		08 27			08 42		08 57			09 12
	d	23p22	00 01	06 55	07 25	07 28		07 43	07 55	07 58		08 10	08 13	08 25	08 28		08 40	08 43	08 55	08 58		09 10	09 13
Carshalton	d					07 31		07 46		08 01			08 16		08 31			08 46		09 01			09 16
Hackbridge	d					07 33		07 48		08 03			08 18		08 33			08 48		09 03			09 18
Mitcham Junction	d					07 37		07 52		08 07			08 22		08 37			08 52		09 07			09 22
Mitcham Eastfields	d					07 40		07 55		08 10			08 25		08 40			08 55		09 10			09 25
Carshalton Beeches	d	23p25	00 04	06 58	07 28				07 58			08 13		08 28			08 43		08 58			09 13	
Wallington	d	23p27	00 06	07 00	07 30				08 00			08 15		08 30			08 45		09 00			09 15	
Waddon	d	23p30	00 09	07 03	07 33				08 03			08 18		08 33			08 48		09 03			09 18	
West Croydon 4	d	23p34	00a12	07 07	07 37				08 07			08 22		08 37			08 52		09 07			09 22	
Norwood Junction 2	d											08 27					08 57					09 27	
New Cross Gate 4 ⊖	d																						
Tulse Hill 3	a																						
	d																						
London Bridge 4 ⊖	a																						
Balham 4 ⊖	d	23p50		07 23	07 53	07 48		08 01	08 23	08 18		08 43	08 31	08 53	08 48		09 13	09 01	09 23	09 18		09 43	09 31
Clapham Junction 10	a	23p56		07 27	07 57	07 52	07 49	08 06	08 27	08 22	08 19	08 48	08 36	08 57	08 52	08 49	09 19	09 06	09 27	09 22	09 19	09 49	09 36
London Waterloo 15 ⊖	a						08 04				08 34					09 04					09 34		
London Victoria 15 ⊖	a	00 04		07 34	08 04	07 59		08 15	08 34	08 29		08 57	08 45	09 04	08 59		09 27	09 15	09 34	09 29		09 57	09 45

Table 182

Sundays until 30 September

Horsham, Dorking, Guildford, Epsom and Sutton - London

Network Diagram - see first Page of Table 177

		SN	SN	SW	FC	SN	SN	SN	SN	SW	FC	FC	SN	SN	SN	SN	SW	FC	FC	SN	SN	SN	SN
Horsham 4	d																						
Warnham	d																						
Ockley	d																						
Holmwood	d																						
Dorking 4	a																						
	d			09 08			09 16							09 46			10 08				10 16		
Box Hill & Westhumble	d						09 18							09 48							10 18		
Guildford	d									09 20													
Effingham Junction 6	d									09 36													
Bookham	d									09 39													
Leatherhead	d			09 15			09 23			09 45				09 53			10 15				10 23		
Ashtead	d			09 18			09 27			09 48				09 57			10 18				10 27		
Epsom 3	a			09 23			09 31			09 53				10 01			10 23				10 31		
	d		09 17	09 24			09 32		09 47	09 54				10 02		10 17	10 24				10 32		10 47
Ewell East	d		09 21				09 36		09 51					10 06		10 21					10 36		10 51
Cheam	d		09 24				09 39		09 54					10 09		10 24					10 39		10 54
Epsom Downs	d																						
Banstead	d																						
Belmont	d																						
Sutton (Surrey) 4	a		09 27				09 42		09 57					10 12		10 27					10 42		10 57
	d	09 25	09 28		09 37	09 40	09 43	09 55	09 58		10 04	10 07	10 10	10 13	10 25	10 28		10 34	10 37	10 40	10 43	10 55	10 58
Carshalton	d		09 31				09 46		10 01		10 07			10 16		10 31		10 37			10 46		11 01
Hackbridge	d		09 33				09 48		10 03		10 09			10 18		10 33		10 39			10 48		11 03
Mitcham Junction	d		09 37				09 52		10 07		10 12			10 22		10 37		10 42			10 52		11 07
Mitcham Eastfields	d		09 40				09 55		10 10		10 15			10 25		10 40		10 45			10 55		11 10
Carshalton Beeches	d	09 28				09 43		09 58					10 13		10 28					10 43		10 58	
Wallington	d	09 30				09 45		10 00					10 15		10 30					10 45		11 00	
Waddon	d	09 33				09 48		10 03					10 18		10 33					10 48		11 03	
West Croydon 4	d	09 37				09 52		10 07					10 22		10 37					10 52		11 07	
Norwood Junction 2	d					09 57							10 27							10 57			
New Cross Gate 4 ⊖	d																						
Tulse Hill 3	a				10 10						10 23	10 40						10 53	11 10				
	d																						
London Bridge 4 ⊖	a																						
Balham 4 ⊖	d	09 53	09 48			10 13	10 01	10 23	10 18				10 43	10 31	10 53	10 48				11 13	11 01	11 23	11 18
Clapham Junction 10	a	09 57	09 52	09 49		10 18	10 06	10 27	10 22	10 19			10 48	10 36	10 57	10 52	10 49			11 18	11 06	11 27	11 22
London Waterloo 15 ⊖	a			10 04						10 34							11 04						
London Victoria 15 ⊖	a	10 04	09 59			10 27	10 15	10 34	10 29				10 57	10 45	11 04	10 59				11 27	11 15	11 34	11 29

		SW	FC	FC	SN	SN	SN	SN	SW	FC	FC	SN	SN	SN	SN	SW	FC	FC	SN	SN	SN	SN
Horsham 4	d																					
Warnham	d																					
Ockley	d																					
Holmwood	d																					
Dorking 4	a																					
	d					10 46			11 08				11 16							11 46		
Box Hill & Westhumble	d					10 48							11 18							11 48		
Guildford	d	10 20														11 20						
Effingham Junction 6	d	10 36														11 36						
Bookham	d	10 39														11 39						
Leatherhead	d	10 45				10 53			11 15				11 23			11 45				11 53		
Ashtead	d	10 48				10 57			11 18				11 27			11 48				11 57		
Epsom 3	a	10 53				11 01			11 23				11 31			11 53				12 01		
	d	10 54				11 02		11 17	11 24				11 32		11 47	11 54				12 02		12 17
Ewell East	d					11 06		11 21					11 36		11 51					12 06		12 21
Cheam	d					11 09		11 24					11 39		11 54					12 09		12 24
Epsom Downs	d																					
Banstead	d																					
Belmont	d																					
Sutton (Surrey) 4	a					11 12		11 27					11 42		11 57					12 12		12 27
	d		11 04	11 07	11 10	11 13	11 25	11 28		11 34	11 37	11 40	11 43	11 55	11 58		12 04	12 07	12 10	12 13	12 25	12 28
Carshalton	d		11 07			11 16		11 31		11 37			11 46		12 01		12 07			12 16		12 31
Hackbridge	d		11 09			11 18		11 33		11 39			11 48		12 03		12 09			12 18		12 33
Mitcham Junction	d		11 12			11 22		11 37		11 42			11 52		12 07		12 12			12 22		12 37
Mitcham Eastfields	d		11 15			11 25		11 40		11 45			11 55		12 10		12 15			12 25		12 40
Carshalton Beeches	d				11 13		11 28					11 43		11 58					12 13		12 28	
Wallington	d				11 15		11 30					11 45		12 00					12 15		12 30	
Waddon	d				11 18		11 33					11 48		12 03					12 18		12 33	
West Croydon 4	d				11 22		11 37					11 52		12 07					12 22		12 37	
Norwood Junction 2	d				11 27							11 57							12 27			
New Cross Gate 4 ⊖	d																					
Tulse Hill 3	a		11 23	11 40						11 53	12 10						12 23	12 40				
	d																					
London Bridge 4 ⊖	a																					
Balham 4 ⊖	d				11 43	11 31	11 53	11 48				12 13	12 01	12 23	12 18				12 43	12 31	12 53	12 48
Clapham Junction 10	a	11 19			11 48	11 36	11 57	11 52	11 49			12 18	12 06	12 27	12 22	12 19			12 48	12 36	12 57	12 52
London Waterloo 15 ⊖	a	11 34							12 04							12 34						
London Victoria 15 ⊖	a				11 57	11 45	12 04	11 59				12 27	12 15	12 34	12 29				12 57	12 45	13 04	12 59

Table 182

Sundays
until 30 September

Horsham, Dorking, Guildford, Epsom and Sutton - London

Network Diagram - see first Page of Table 177

	SW	FC	FC	SN	SN	SN	SN		SW	FC	FC	SN	SN	SN	SN	SW	FC		FC	SN	SN	SN	SN	SW
Horsham d																								
Warnham d																								
Ockley d																								
Holmwood d																								
Dorking a																								
Dorking d	12 08				12 16								12 46			13 08					13 16			
Box Hill & Westhumble d					12 18								12 48								13 18			
Guildford d									12 20															13 20
Effingham Junction d									12 36															13 36
Bookham d									12 39															13 39
Leatherhead d	12 15				12 23				12 45				12 53			13 15					13 23			13 45
Ashtead d	12 18				12 27				12 48				12 57			13 18					13 27			13 48
Epsom a	12 23				12 31				12 53				13 01			13 23					13 31			13 53
Epsom d	12 24				12 32		12 47		12 54				13 02		13 17	13 24					13 32		13 47	13 54
Ewell East d					12 36		12 51						13 06		13 21						13 36		13 51	
Cheam d					12 39		12 54						13 09		13 24						13 39		13 54	
Epsom Downs d																								
Banstead d																								
Belmont d																								
Sutton (Surrey) a					12 42		12 57						13 12		13 27						13 42		13 57	
Sutton (Surrey) d		12 34	12 37	12 40	12 43	12 55	12 58			13 04	13 07	13 10	13 13	13 25	13 28		13 34		13 37	13 40	13 43	13 55	13 58	
Carshalton d		12 37			12 46		13 01			13 07			13 16		13 31		13 37				13 46		14 01	
Hackbridge d		12 39			12 48		13 03			13 09			13 18		13 33		13 39				13 48		14 03	
Mitcham Junction d		12 42			12 52		13 07			13 12			13 22		13 37		13 42				13 52		14 07	
Mitcham Eastfields d		12 45			12 55		13 10			13 15			13 25		13 40		13 45				13 55		14 10	
Carshalton Beeches d				12 43		12 58						13 13		13 28						13 43		13 58		
Wallington d				12 45		13 00						13 15		13 30						13 45		14 00		
Waddon d				12 48		13 03						13 18		13 33						13 48		14 03		
West Croydon d				12 52		13 07						13 22		13 37						13 52		14 07		
Norwood Junction d				12 57								13 27								13 57				
New Cross Gate ⊖ d																								
Tulse Hill a		12 53	13 10							13 23	13 40						13 53		14 10					
Tulse Hill d																								
London Bridge ⊖ a																								
Balham ⊖ d				13 13	13 01	13 23	13 18					13 43	13 31	13 53	13 48					14 13	14 01	14 23	14 18	
Clapham Junction a	12 49			13 19	13 06	13 27	13 22		13 19			13 48	13 36	13 57	13 52	13 49				14 19	14 06	14 27	14 22	14 19
London Waterloo ⊖ a	13 04								13 34							14 04								14 34
London Victoria ⊖ a				13 27	13 15	13 34	13 29					13 57	13 45	14 04	13 59					14 27	14 15	14 34	14 29	

	FC	FC	SN		SN	SN	SN	SW	FC	FC	SN	SN	SN		SN	SW	FC	FC	SN	SN	SN	SN	SW
Horsham d																							
Warnham d																							
Ockley d																							
Holmwood d																							
Dorking a																							
Dorking d					13 46			14 08				14 16								14 46			15 08
Box Hill & Westhumble d					13 48							14 18								14 48			
Guildford d																14 20							
Effingham Junction d																14 36							
Bookham d																14 39							
Leatherhead d					13 53			14 15				14 23				14 45				14 53			15 15
Ashtead d					13 57			14 18				14 27				14 48				14 57			15 18
Epsom a					14 01			14 23				14 31				14 53				15 01			15 23
Epsom d					14 02		14 17	14 24				14 32			14 47	14 54				15 02		15 17	15 24
Ewell East d					14 06		14 21					14 36			14 51					15 06		15 21	
Cheam d					14 09		14 24					14 39			14 54					15 09		15 24	
Epsom Downs d																							
Banstead d																							
Belmont d																							
Sutton (Surrey) a					14 12		14 27					14 42			14 57					15 12		15 27	
Sutton (Surrey) d	14 04	14 07	14 10		14 13	14 25	14 28		14 34	14 37	14 40	14 43	14 55		14 58		15 04	15 07	15 10	15 13	15 25	15 28	
Carshalton d	14 07				14 16		14 31		14 37			14 46			15 01		15 07			15 16		15 31	
Hackbridge d	14 09				14 18		14 33		14 39			14 48			15 03		15 09			15 18		15 33	
Mitcham Junction d	14 12				14 22		14 37		14 42			14 52			15 07		15 12			15 22		15 37	
Mitcham Eastfields d	14 15				14 25		14 40		14 45			14 55			15 10		15 15			15 25		15 40	
Carshalton Beeches d			14 13			14 28					14 43		14 58						15 13		15 28		
Wallington d			14 15			14 30					14 45		15 00						15 15		15 30		
Waddon d			14 18			14 33					14 48		15 03						15 18		15 33		
West Croydon d			14 22			14 37					14 52		15 07						15 22		15 37		
Norwood Junction d			14 27								14 57								15 27				
New Cross Gate ⊖ d																							
Tulse Hill a	14 23	14 40							14 53	15 10							15 23	15 40					
Tulse Hill d																							
London Bridge ⊖ a																							
Balham ⊖ d			14 43		14 31	14 53	14 48				15 13	15 01	15 23		15 18				15 43	15 31	15 53	15 48	
Clapham Junction a			14 48		14 36	14 57	14 52	14 49			15 19	15 06	15 27		15 22	15 19			15 48	15 36	15 57	15 52	15 49
London Waterloo ⊖ a								14 59								15 29							15 59
London Victoria ⊖ a			14 57		14 45	15 04	14 59				15 27	15 15	15 34		15 29				15 57	15 45	16 04	15 59	

Table 182

Sundays
until 30 September

Horsham, Dorking, Guildford, Epsom and Sutton - London

Network Diagram - see first Page of Table 177

	FC	FC	SN	SN	SN	SN	SW	FC	FC		SN	SN	SN	SN	SW	FC	FC	SN	SN		SN	SN	SW	FC
Horsham d																								
Warnham d																								
Ockley d																								
Holmwood d																								
Dorking a																								
Dorking d				15 16								15 46			16 08				16 16					
Box Hill & Westhumble d				15 18								15 48							16 18					
Guildford d							15 20																16 20	
Effingham Junction d							15 36																16 36	
Bookham d							15 39																16 39	
Leatherhead d				15 23			15 45					15 53			16 15				16 23				16 45	
Ashtead d				15 27			15 48					15 57			16 18				16 27				16 48	
Epsom a				15 31			15 53					16 01			16 23				16 31				16 53	
Epsom d				15 32		15 47	15 54					16 02		16 17	16 24				16 32			16 47	16 54	
Ewell East d				15 36		15 51						16 06		16 21					16 36			16 51		
Cheam d				15 39		15 54						16 09		16 24					16 39			16 54		
Epsom Downs d																								
Banstead d																								
Belmont d																								
Sutton (Surrey) a				15 42		15 57						16 12		16 27					16 42			16 57		
Sutton (Surrey) d	15 34	15 37	15 40	15 43	15 55	15 58		16 04	16 07		16 10	16 13	16 25	16 28		16 34	16 37	16 40	16 43		16 55	16 58		17 04
Carshalton d	15 37			15 46		16 01		16 07				16 16		16 31		16 37			16 46			17 01		17 07
Hackbridge d	15 39			15 48		16 03		16 09				16 18		16 33		16 39			16 48			17 03		17 09
Mitcham Junction d	15 42			15 52		16 07		16 12				16 22		16 37		16 42			16 52			17 07		17 12
Mitcham Eastfields d	15 45			15 55		16 10		16 15				16 25		16 40		16 45			16 55			17 10		17 15
Carshalton Beeches d			15 43		15 58						16 13		16 28					16 43			16 58			
Wallington d			15 45		16 00						16 15		16 30					16 45			17 00			
Waddon d			15 48		16 03						16 18		16 33					16 48			17 03			
West Croydon d			15 52		16 07						16 22		16 37					16 52			17 07			
Norwood Junction d			15 57								16 27							16 57						
New Cross Gate ⊖ d																								
Tulse Hill a	15 53	16 10						16 23	16 40							16 53	17 10							17 23
Tulse Hill d																								
London Bridge ⊖ a																								
Balham ⊖ d			16 13	16 01	16 23	16 18					16 43	16 31	16 53	16 48				17 13	17 01		17 23	17 18		
Clapham Junction a			16 19	16 06	16 27	16 22	16 19				16 48	16 36	16 57	16 52	16 49			17 19	17 06		17 27	17 22	17 19	
London Waterloo ⊖ a							16 29								16 59								17 29	
London Victoria ⊖ a			16 27	16 15	16 34	16 29					16 57	16 45	17 04	16 59				17 27	17 15		17 34	17 29		

	FC	SN	SN	SN	SN		SW	FC	FC	SN	SN	SN	SN	SW	FC		FC	SN	SN	SN	SN	SW	FC	FC
Horsham d																								
Warnham d																								
Ockley d																								
Holmwood d																								
Dorking a																								
Dorking d			16 46				17 08				17 16								17 46			18 08		
Box Hill & Westhumble d			16 48								17 18								17 48					
Guildford d														17 20										
Effingham Junction d														17 36										
Bookham d														17 39										
Leatherhead d			16 53				17 15				17 23			17 45					17 53			18 15		
Ashtead d			16 57				17 18				17 27			17 48					17 57			18 18		
Epsom a			17 01				17 23				17 31			17 53					18 01			18 23		
Epsom d			17 02		17 17		17 24				17 32		17 47	17 54					18 02		18 17	18 24		
Ewell East d			17 06		17 21						17 36		17 51						18 06		18 21			
Cheam d			17 09		17 24						17 39		17 54						18 09		18 24			
Epsom Downs d																								
Banstead d																								
Belmont d																								
Sutton (Surrey) a			17 12		17 27						17 42		17 57						18 12		18 27			
Sutton (Surrey) d	17 07	17 10	17 13	17 25	17 28			17 34	17 37	17 40	17 43	17 55	17 58		18 04		18 07	18 10	18 13	18 25	18 28		18 34	18 37
Carshalton d			17 16		17 31			17 37			17 46		18 01		18 07				18 16		18 31		18 37	
Hackbridge d			17 18		17 33			17 39			17 48		18 03		18 09				18 18		18 33		18 39	
Mitcham Junction d			17 22		17 37			17 42			17 52		18 07		18 12				18 22		18 37		18 42	
Mitcham Eastfields d			17 25		17 40			17 45			17 55		18 10		18 15				18 25		18 40		18 45	
Carshalton Beeches d		17 13		17 28						17 43		17 58						18 13		18 28				
Wallington d		17 15		17 30						17 45		18 00						18 15		18 30				
Waddon d		17 18		17 33						17 48		18 03						18 18		18 33				
West Croydon d		17 22		17 37						17 52		18 07						18 22		18 37				
Norwood Junction d		17 27								17 57								18 27						
New Cross Gate ⊖ d																								
Tulse Hill a	17 40							17 53	18 10						18 23		18 40						18 53	19 10
Tulse Hill d																								
London Bridge ⊖ a																								
Balham ⊖ d		17 43	17 31	17 53	17 48					18 13	18 01	18 23	18 18					18 43	18 31	18 53	18 48			
Clapham Junction a		17 48	17 36	17 57	17 52		17 49			18 19	18 06	18 27	18 22	18 19				18 48	18 36	18 57	18 52	18 49		
London Waterloo ⊖ a							17 59							18 29								18 59		
London Victoria ⊖ a		17 57	17 45	18 04	17 59					18 27	18 15	18 34	18 29					18 57	18 45	19 04	18 59			

Table 182

Horsham, Dorking, Guildford, Epsom and Sutton - London

Sundays until 30 September

Network Diagram - see first Page of Table 177

Station		SN	SN	SN	SN	SW	FC	FC	SN	SN	SW	SN	FC	FC	SN	SN	SW	SN	FC	FC	SN	SN
Horsham	d																					
Warnham	d																					
Ockley	d																					
Holmwood	d																					
Dorking	a																					
	d		18 16							18 46	19 08					19 16						19 46
Box Hill & Westhumble	d		18 18							18 48						19 18						19 48
Guildford	d					18 20											19 20					
Effingham Junction	d					18 36											19 36					
Bookham	d					18 39											19 39					
Leatherhead	d		18 23			18 45				18 53	19 15					19 23	19 45					19 53
Ashtead	d		18 27			18 48				18 57	19 18					19 27	19 48					19 57
Epsom	a		18 31			18 53				19 01	19 23					19 31	19 53					20 01
	d		18 32		18 47	18 54				19 02	19 24					19 32	19 54					20 02
Ewell East	d		18 36		18 51					19 06						19 36						20 06
Cheam	d		18 39		18 54					19 09						19 39						20 09
Epsom Downs	d																					
Banstead	d																					
Belmont	d																					
Sutton (Surrey)	a		18 42		18 57					19 12						19 42						20 12
	d	18 40	18 43	18 55	18 58		19 04	19 07	19 10	19 13		19 25	19 34	19 37	19 40	19 43		19 55	20 04	20 07	20 10	20 13
Carshalton	d		18 46		19 01		19 07			19 16			19 37			19 46			20 07			20 16
Hackbridge	d		18 48		19 03		19 09			19 18			19 39			19 48			20 09			20 18
Mitcham Junction	d		18 52		19 07		19 12			19 22			19 42			19 52			20 12			20 22
Mitcham Eastfields	d		18 55		19 10		19 15			19 25			19 45			19 55			20 15			20 25
Carshalton Beeches	d	18 43		18 58					19 13			19 28			19 43			19 58			20 13	
Wallington	d	18 45		19 00					19 15			19 30			19 45			20 00			20 15	
Waddon	d	18 48		19 03					19 18			19 33			19 48			20 03			20 18	
West Croydon	d	18 52		19 07					19 22			19 37			19 52			20 07			20 22	
Norwood Junction	d	18 57							19 27						19 57						20 27	
New Cross Gate	d																					
Tulse Hill	a						19 23	19 40					19 53	20 10					20 23	20 40		
	d																					
London Bridge	a																					
Balham	d	19 13	19 01	19 23	19 18				19 43	19 31		19 53			20 13	20 01		20 23			20 43	20 31
Clapham Junction	a	19 19	19 06	19 27	19 22	19 19			19 48	19 36	19 49	19 57			20 18	20 06	20 19	20 27			20 48	20 36
London Waterloo	a					19 29					19 59						20 29					
London Victoria	a	19 27	19 15	19 34	19 29				19 57	19 45		20 04			20 27	20 15		20 34			20 57	20 45

Station		SW	SN	FC	FC	SN	SN	SW	SN	FC	FC	SN	SN	SW	SN	FC	SN	SN	SW	SN	FC	SN	SN
Horsham	d																						
Warnham	d																						
Ockley	d																						
Holmwood	d																						
Dorking	a																						
	d	20 08					20 16						20 46	21 08				21 16					21 46
Box Hill & Westhumble	d						20 18						20 48					21 18					21 48
Guildford	d							20 20											21 20				
Effingham Junction	d							20 36											21 36				
Bookham	d							20 39											21 39				
Leatherhead	d	20 15					20 23	20 45					20 53	21 15				21 23	21 45				21 53
Ashtead	d	20 18					20 27	20 48					20 57	21 18				21 27	21 48				21 57
Epsom	a	20 23					20 31	20 53					21 01	21 23				21 31	21 53				22 01
	d	20 24					20 32	20 54					21 02	21 24				21 32	21 54				22 02
Ewell East	d						20 36						21 06					21 36					22 06
Cheam	d						20 39						21 09					21 39					22 09
Epsom Downs	d																						
Banstead	d																						
Belmont	d																						
Sutton (Surrey)	a						20 42						21 12					21 42					22 12
	d		20 25	20 34	20 37	20 40	20 43		20 55	21 04	21 07	21 10	21 13		21 25	21 34	21 40	21 43		21 55	22 04	22 10	22 13
Carshalton	d			20 37			20 46			21 07			21 16			21 37		21 46			22 07		22 16
Hackbridge	d			20 39			20 48			21 09			21 18			21 39		21 48			22 09		22 18
Mitcham Junction	d			20 42			20 52			21 12			21 22			21 42		21 52			22 12		22 22
Mitcham Eastfields	d			20 45			20 55			21 15			21 25			21 45		21 55			22 15		22 25
Carshalton Beeches	d		20 28			20 43			20 58			21 13			21 28		21 43			21 58		22 13	
Wallington	d		20 30			20 45			21 00			21 15			21 30		21 45			22 00		22 15	
Waddon	d		20 33			20 48			21 03			21 18			21 33		21 48			22 03		22 18	
West Croydon	d		20 37			20 52			21 07			21 22			21 37		21 52			22 07		22 22	
Norwood Junction	d					20 57						21 27					21 57					22 27	
New Cross Gate	d																						
Tulse Hill	a			20 53	21 10					21 23	21 40					21 53					22 23		
	d																						
London Bridge	a																						
Balham	d		20 53			21 13	21 01		21 23			21 43	21 31		21 53		22 13	22 01		22 23		22 43	22 31
Clapham Junction	a	20 49	20 57			21 19	21 06	21 19	21 27			21 49	21 36	21 49	21 57		22 19	22 06	22 19	22 27		22 49	22 36
London Waterloo	a	21 00						21 29						22 00					22 29				
London Victoria	a		21 04			21 27	21 15		21 34			21 57	21 45		22 04		22 27	22 15		22 34		22 57	22 45

Table 182

Horsham, Dorking, Guildford, Epsom and Sutton - London

Sundays until 30 September

Network Diagram - see first Page of Table 177

Station		SW	SN	SN	SN	SW	SN	SN	SN	SW	SN	SN	SN
Horsham	d												
Warnham	d												
Ockley	d												
Holmwood	d												
Dorking	a												
	d	22 08			22 16				22 46	23 08			23 16
Box Hill & Westhumble	d				22 18				22 48				23 18
Guildford	d					22 20							
Effingham Junction	d					22 36							
Bookham	d					22 39							
Leatherhead	d	22 15			22 23	22 45			22 53	23 15			23 23
Ashtead	d	22 18			22 27	22 48			22 57	23 18			23 27
Epsom	a	22 23			22 31	22 53			23 01	23 23			23 31
	d	22 24			22 32	22 54			23 02	23 24			23 32
Ewell East	d				22 36				23 06				23 36
Cheam	d				22 39				23 09				23 39
Epsom Downs	d												
Banstead	d												
Belmont	d												
Sutton (Surrey)	a				22 42				23 12				23 42
	d		22 25	22 40	22 43		22 55	23 10	23 13		23 25	23 40	23 43
Carshalton	d				22 46				23 16				23 46
Hackbridge	d				22 48				23 18				23 48
Mitcham Junction	d				22 52				23 22				23 52
Mitcham Eastfields	d				22 55				23 25				23 55
Carshalton Beeches	d		22 28	22 43			22 58	23 13			23 28	23 43	
Wallington	d		22 30	22 45			23 00	23 15			23 30	23 45	
Waddon	d		22 33	22 48			23 03	23 18			23 33	23 48	
West Croydon	d		22 37	22 52			23 07	23 22			23 37	23 52	
Norwood Junction	d			22 57				23 27					
New Cross Gate	d												
Tulse Hill	a												
	d												
London Bridge	a												
Balham	d		22 53	23 13	23 01		23 23	23 43	23 31		23 53	00 08	00 01
Clapham Junction	a	22 49	22 57	23 19	23 06	23 19	23 27	23 49	23 36	23 49	23 57	00 12	00 06
London Waterloo	a	23 00				23 29				23 59			
London Victoria	a		23 04	23 27	23 15		23 34	23 57	23 45		00 04	00 19	00 15

Sundays from 7 October

Station		SN	SN	SN	SN	SN	SW	SN	SN	SN	SW	SN	SN	SN	SN	SW	SN	SN	SN	SN	SW	SN	SN
Horsham	d																						
Warnham	d																						
Ockley	d																						
Holmwood	d																						
Dorking	a																						
	d							07 16					07 46					08 16					08 46
Box Hill & Westhumble	d							07 18					07 48					08 18					08 48
Guildford	d																				08 18		
Effingham Junction	d																				08 34		
Bookham	d																				08 37		
Leatherhead	d							07 23					07 53					08 23			08 45		08 53
Ashtead	d							07 27					07 57					08 27			08 48		08 57
Epsom	a							07 31					08 01					08 31			08 53		09 01
	d			06 44		07 17	07 24	07 32		07 47	07 54		08 02		08 17	08 24		08 32		08 47	08 54		09 02
Ewell East	d			06 48		07 21		07 36		07 51			08 06		08 21			08 36		08 51			09 06
Cheam	d			06 51		07 24		07 39		07 54			08 09		08 24			08 39		08 54			09 09
Epsom Downs	d		23p50																				
Banstead	d		23p53																				
Belmont	d		23p56																				
Sutton (Surrey)	a		23p59	06 54		07 27		07 42		07 57			08 12		08 27			08 42		08 57			09 12
	d	23p22	00 01	06 55	07 25	07 28		07 43	07 55	07 58		08 10	08 13	08 25	08 28		08 40	08 43	08 55	08 58		09 10	09 13
Carshalton	d					07 31		07 46		08 01			08 16		08 31			08 46		09 01			09 16
Hackbridge	d					07 33		07 48		08 03			08 18		08 33			08 48		09 03			09 18
Mitcham Junction	d					07 37		07 52		08 07			08 22		08 37			08 52		09 07			09 22
Mitcham Eastfields	d					07 40		07 55		08 10			08 25		08 40			08 55		09 10			09 25
Carshalton Beeches	d	23p25	00 04	06 58	07 28				07 58			08 13		08 28			08 43		08 58			09 13	
Wallington	d	23p27	00 06	07 00	07 30				08 00			08 15		08 30			08 45		09 00			09 15	
Waddon	d	23p30	00 09	07 03	07 33				08 03			08 18		08 33			08 48		09 03			09 18	
West Croydon	d	23p34	00a12	07 07	07 37				08 07			08 22		08 37			08 52		09 07			09 22	
Norwood Junction	d											08 27					08 57					09 27	
New Cross Gate	d																						
Tulse Hill	a																						
	d																						
London Bridge	a																						
Balham	d	23p50		07 23	07 53	07 48		08 01	08 23	08 18		08 43	08 31	08 53	08 48		09 13	09 01	09 23	09 18		09 43	09 31
Clapham Junction	a	23p56		07 27	07 57	07 52	07 49	08 06	08 27	08 22	08 19	08 48	08 36	08 57	08 52	08 49	09 19	09 06	09 27	09 22	09 19	09 49	09 36
London Waterloo	a						08 04				08 34					09 04					09 34		
London Victoria	a	00 04		07 34	08 04	07 59		08 15	08 34	08 29		08 57	08 45	09 04	08 59		09 27	09 15	09 34	09 29		09 57	09 45

Table 182

Sundays from 7 October

Horsham, Dorking, Guildford, Epsom and Sutton - London

Network Diagram - see first Page of Table 177

		SN	SN	SW	FC	SN		SN	SN	SN	SW	FC	FC	SN	SN	SN		SN	SW	FC	FC	SN	SN	SN	SN
Horsham 4	d																								
Warnham	d																								
Ockley	d																								
Holmwood	d																								
Dorking 4	a																								
	d			09 08				09 16							09 46				10 08				10 16		
Box Hill & Westhumble	d							09 18							09 48								10 18		
Guildford	d										09 18														
Effingham Junction 6	d										09 34														
Bookham	d										09 37														
Leatherhead	d			09 15				09 23			09 45				09 53				10 15				10 23		
Ashtead	d			09 18				09 27			09 48				09 57				10 18				10 27		
Epsom 3	a			09 23				09 31			09 53				10 01				10 23				10 31		
	d		09 17	09 24				09 32		09 47	09 54				10 02			10 17	10 24				10 32		10 47
Ewell East	d		09 21					09 36		09 51					10 06			10 21					10 36		10 51
Cheam	d		09 24					09 39		09 54					10 09			10 24					10 39		10 54
Epsom Downs	d																								
Banstead	d																								
Belmont	d																								
Sutton (Surrey) 4	a		09 27					09 42		09 57					10 12			10 27					10 42		10 57
	d	09 25	09 28		09 37	09 40		09 43	09 55	09 58		10 04	10 07	10 10	10 13	10 25		10 28		10 34	10 37	10 40	10 43	10 55	10 58
Carshalton	d		09 31					09 46		10 01		10 07			10 16			10 31		10 37			10 46		11 01
Hackbridge	d		09 33					09 48		10 03		10 09			10 18			10 33		10 39			10 48		11 03
Mitcham Junction	d		09 37					09 52		10 07		10 12			10 22			10 37		10 42			10 52		11 07
Mitcham Eastfields	d		09 40					09 55		10 10		10 15			10 25			10 40		10 45			10 55		11 10
Carshalton Beeches	d	09 28				09 43			09 58					10 13		10 28						10 43		10 58	
Wallington	d	09 30				09 45			10 00					10 15		10 30						10 45		11 00	
Waddon	d	09 33				09 48			10 03					10 18		10 33						10 48		11 03	
West Croydon 4	d	09 37				09 52			10 07					10 22		10 37						10 52		11 07	
Norwood Junction 2	d					09 57								10 27								10 57			
New Cross Gate 4 ⊖	d																								
Tulse Hill 3	a				10 10							10 23	10 40							10 53	11 10				
	d																								
London Bridge 4 ⊖	a																								
Balham 4 ⊖	d	09 53	09 48			10 13		10 01	10 23	10 18				10 43	10 31	10 53		10 48				11 13	11 01	11 23	11 18
Clapham Junction 10	a	09 57	09 52	09 49		10 18		10 06	10 27	10 22	10 19			10 48	10 36	10 57		10 52	10 49			11 18	11 06	11 27	11 22
London Waterloo 15 ⊖	a			10 04							10 34								11 04						
London Victoria 15 ⊖	a	10 04	09 59			10 27		10 15	10 34	10 29				10 57	10 45	11 04		10 59				11 27	11 15	11 34	11 29

		SW		FC	FC	SN	SN	SN	SN	SW	FC	FC		SN	SN	SN	SN	SW	FC	FC	SN	SN		SN	SN
Horsham 4	d																								
Warnham	d																								
Ockley	d																								
Holmwood	d																								
Dorking 4	a																								
	d						10 46			11 08					11 16							11 46			
Box Hill & Westhumble	d						10 48								11 18							11 48			
Guildford	d	10 18																11 18							
Effingham Junction 6	d	10 34																11 34							
Bookham	d	10 37																11 37							
Leatherhead	d	10 45					10 53			11 15					11 23			11 45				11 53			
Ashtead	d	10 48					10 57			11 18					11 27			11 48				11 57			
Epsom 3	a	10 53					11 01			11 23					11 31			11 53				12 01			
	d	10 54					11 02		11 17	11 24					11 32		11 47	11 54				12 02			12 17
Ewell East	d						11 06		11 21						11 36		11 51					12 06			12 21
Cheam	d						11 09		11 24						11 39		11 54					12 09			12 24
Epsom Downs	d																								
Banstead	d																								
Belmont	d																								
Sutton (Surrey) 4	a						11 12		11 27						11 42		11 57					12 12			12 27
	d			11 04	11 07	11 10	11 13	11 25	11 28		11 34	11 37		11 40	11 43	11 55	11 58		12 04	12 07	12 10	12 13		12 25	12 28
Carshalton	d			11 07			11 16		11 31		11 37				11 46		12 01		12 07			12 16			12 31
Hackbridge	d			11 09			11 18		11 33		11 39				11 48		12 03		12 09			12 18			12 33
Mitcham Junction	d			11 12			11 22		11 37		11 42				11 52		12 07		12 12			12 22			12 37
Mitcham Eastfields	d			11 15			11 25		11 40		11 45				11 55		12 10		12 15			12 25			12 40
Carshalton Beeches	d					11 13		11 28						11 43		11 58					12 13			12 28	
Wallington	d					11 15		11 30						11 45		12 00					12 15			12 30	
Waddon	d					11 18		11 33						11 48		12 03					12 18			12 33	
West Croydon 4	d					11 22		11 37						11 52		12 07					12 22			12 37	
Norwood Junction 2	d					11 27								11 57							12 27				
New Cross Gate 4 ⊖	d																								
Tulse Hill 3	a			11 23	11 40						11 53	12 10							12 23	12 40					
	d																								
London Bridge 4 ⊖	a																								
Balham 4 ⊖	d					11 43	11 31	11 53	11 48					12 13	12 01	12 23	12 18				12 43	12 31		12 53	12 48
Clapham Junction 10	a	11 19				11 48	11 36	11 57	11 52	11 49				12 18	12 06	12 27	12 22	12 19			12 48	12 36		12 57	12 52
London Waterloo 15 ⊖	a	11 34								12 04								12 34							
London Victoria 15 ⊖	a					11 57	11 45	12 04	11 59					12 27	12 15	12 34	12 29				12 57	12 45		13 04	12 59

Table 182

Sundays from 7 October

Horsham, Dorking, Guildford, Epsom and Sutton - London

Network Diagram - see first Page of Table 177

		SW	FC	FC	SN	SN	SN	SN		SW	FC	FC	SN	SN	SN	SN	SW	FC		FC	SN	SN	SN	SN	SW
Horsham 4	d																								
Warnham	d																								
Ockley	d																								
Holmwood	d																								
Dorking 4	a																								
	d	12 08				12 16								12 46			13 08					13 16			
Box Hill & Westhumble	d					12 18								12 48								13 18			
Guildford	d									12 18															13 18
Effingham Junction 6	d									12 34															13 34
Bookham	d									12 37															13 37
Leatherhead	d	12 15				12 23				12 45				12 53			13 15					13 23			13 45
Ashtead	d	12 18				12 27				12 48				12 57			13 18					13 27			13 48
Epsom 3	a	12 23				12 31				12 53				13 01			13 23					13 31			13 53
	d	12 24				12 32		12 47		12 54				13 02		13 17	13 24					13 32		13 47	13 54
Ewell East	d					12 36		12 51						13 06		13 21						13 36		13 51	
Cheam	d					12 39		12 54						13 09		13 24						13 39		13 54	
Epsom Downs	d																								
Banstead	d																								
Belmont	d																								
Sutton (Surrey) 4	a					12 42		12 57						13 12		13 27						13 42		13 57	
	d		12 34	12 37	12 40	12 43	12 55	12 58			13 04	13 07	13 10	13 13	13 25	13 28		13 34		13 37	13 40	13 43	13 55	13 58	
Carshalton	d		12 37			12 46		13 01			13 07			13 16		13 31		13 37				13 46		14 01	
Hackbridge	d		12 39			12 48		13 03			13 09			13 18		13 33		13 39				13 48		14 03	
Mitcham Junction	d		12 42			12 52		13 07			13 12			13 22		13 37		13 42				13 52		14 07	
Mitcham Eastfields	d		12 45			12 55		13 10			13 15			13 25		13 40		13 45				13 55		14 10	
Carshalton Beeches	d				12 43		12 58						13 13		13 28						13 43		13 58		
Wallington	d				12 45		13 00						13 15		13 30						13 45		14 00		
Waddon	d				12 48		13 03						13 18		13 33						13 48		14 03		
West Croydon 4	d				12 52		13 07						13 22		13 37						13 52		14 07		
Norwood Junction 2	d				12 57								13 27								13 57				
New Cross Gate 4 ⊖	d																								
Tulse Hill 3	a		12 53	13 10							13 23	13 40						13 53		14 10					
	d																								
London Bridge 4 ⊖	a																								
Balham 4 ⊖	d				13 13	13 01	13 23	13 18					13 43	13 31	13 53	13 48					14 13	14 01	14 23	14 18	
Clapham Junction 10	a	12 49			13 19	13 06	13 27	13 22		13 19			13 48	13 36	13 57	13 52	13 49				14 19	14 06	14 27	14 22	14 19
London Waterloo 15 ⊖	a	13 04								13 34							14 04								14 34
London Victoria 15 ⊖	a				13 27	13 15	13 34	13 29					13 57	13 45	14 04	13 59					14 27	14 15	14 34	14 29	

		FC	FC	SN		SN	SN	SN	SW	FC	FC	SN	SN	SN		SN	SW	FC	FC	SN	SN	SN	SN	SW	
Horsham 4	d																								
Warnham	d																								
Ockley	d																								
Holmwood	d																								
Dorking 4	a																								
	d					13 46			14 08				14 16								14 46			15 08	
Box Hill & Westhumble	d					13 48							14 18								14 48				
Guildford	d																14 18								
Effingham Junction 6	d																14 34								
Bookham	d																14 37								
Leatherhead	d					13 53			14 15				14 23				14 45				14 53			15 15	
Ashtead	d					13 57			14 18				14 27				14 48				14 57			15 18	
Epsom 3	a					14 01			14 23				14 31				14 53				15 01			15 23	
	d					14 02		14 17	14 24				14 32			14 47	14 54				15 02		15 17	15 24	
Ewell East	d					14 06		14 21					14 36			14 51					15 06		15 21		
Cheam	d					14 09		14 24					14 39			14 54					15 09		15 24		
Epsom Downs	d																								
Banstead	d																								
Belmont	d																								
Sutton (Surrey) 4	a					14 12		14 27					14 42			14 57					15 12		15 27		
	d	14 04	14 07	14 10		14 13	14 25	14 28		14 34	14 37	14 40	14 43	14 55		14 58		15 04	15 07	15 10	15 13	15 25	15 28		
Carshalton	d	14 07				14 16		14 31		14 37			14 46			15 01		15 07			15 16		15 31		
Hackbridge	d	14 09				14 18		14 33		14 39			14 48			15 03		15 09			15 18		15 33		
Mitcham Junction	d	14 12				14 22		14 37		14 42			14 52			15 07		15 12			15 22		15 37		
Mitcham Eastfields	d	14 15				14 25		14 40		14 45			14 55			15 10		15 15			15 25		15 40		
Carshalton Beeches	d			14 13			14 28					14 43		14 58						15 13		15 28			
Wallington	d			14 15			14 30					14 45		15 00						15 15		15 30			
Waddon	d			14 18			14 33					14 48		15 03						15 18		15 33			
West Croydon 4	d			14 22			14 37					14 52		15 07						15 22		15 37			
Norwood Junction 2	d			14 27								14 57								15 27					
New Cross Gate 4 ⊖	d																								
Tulse Hill 3	a	14 23	14 40							14 53	15 10							15 23	15 40						
	d																								
London Bridge 4 ⊖	a																								
Balham 4 ⊖	d			14 43		14 31	14 53	14 48				15 13	15 01	15 23		15 18				15 43	15 31	15 53	15 48		
Clapham Junction 10	a			14 48		14 36	14 57	14 52	14 49			15 19	15 06	15 27		15 22	15 19			15 48	15 36	15 57	15 52	15 49	
London Waterloo 15 ⊖	a								14 59								15 29							15 59	
London Victoria 15 ⊖	a			14 57		14 45	15 04	14 59				15 27	15 15	15 34		15 29				15 57	15 45	16 04	15 59		

Table 182

Horsham, Dorking, Guildford, Epsom and Sutton - London

Sundays from 7 October

Network Diagram - see first Page of Table 177

		FC	FC	SN	SN	SN	SN	SW	FC	FC	SN	SN	SN	SN	SW	FC	FC	SN	SN	SN	SN	SW	FC
Horsham	d																						
Warnham	d																						
Ockley	d																						
Holmwood	d																						
Dorking	a																						
	d				15 16							15 46			16 08				16 16				
Box Hill & Westhumble	d				15 18							15 48							16 18				
Guildford	d							15 18														16 18	
Effingham Junction	d							15 34														16 34	
Bookham	d							15 37														16 37	
Leatherhead	d				15 23			15 45				15 53			16 15				16 23			16 45	
Ashtead	d				15 27			15 48				15 57			16 18				16 27			16 48	
Epsom	a				15 31			15 53				16 01			16 23				16 31			16 53	
	d				15 32		15 47	15 54				16 02		16 17	16 24				16 32		16 47	16 54	
Ewell East	d				15 36		15 51					16 06		16 21					16 36		16 51		
Cheam	d				15 39		15 54					16 09		16 24					16 39		16 54		
Epsom Downs	d																						
Banstead	d																						
Belmont	d																						
Sutton (Surrey)	a				15 42		15 57					16 12		16 27					16 42		16 57		
	d	15 34	15 37	15 40	15 43	15 55	15 58		16 04	16 07	16 10	16 13	16 25	16 28		16 34	16 37	16 40	16 43	16 55	16 58		17 04
Carshalton	d	15 37			15 46		16 01		16 07			16 16		16 31		16 37			16 46		17 01		17 07
Hackbridge	d	15 39			15 48		16 03		16 09			16 18		16 33		16 39			16 48		17 03		17 09
Mitcham Junction	d	15 42			15 52		16 07		16 12			16 22		16 37		16 42			16 52		17 07		17 12
Mitcham Eastfields	d	15 45			15 55		16 10		16 15			16 25		16 40		16 45			16 55		17 10		17 15
Carshalton Beeches	d			15 43		15 58					16 13		16 28					16 43		16 58			
Wallington	d			15 45		16 00					16 15		16 30					16 45		17 00			
Waddon	d			15 48		16 03					16 18		16 33					16 48		17 03			
West Croydon	d			15 52		16 07					16 22		16 37					16 52		17 07			
Norwood Junction	d			15 57							16 27							16 57					
New Cross Gate	d																						
Tulse Hill	a	15 53	16 10						16 23	16 40						16 53	17 10						17 23
	d																						
London Bridge	a																						
Balham	d			16 13	16 01	16 23	16 18				16 43	16 31	16 53	16 48				17 13	17 01	17 23	17 18		
Clapham Junction	a			16 19	16 06	16 27	16 22	16 19			16 48	16 36	16 57	16 52	16 49			17 19	17 06	17 27	17 22	17 19	
London Waterloo	a							16 29							16 59							17 29	
London Victoria	a			16 27	16 15	16 34	16 29				16 57	16 45	17 04	16 59				17 27	17 15	17 34	17 29		

		FC	SN	SN	SN	SN	SW	FC	FC	SN	SN	SN	SN	SW	FC	FC	SN	SN	SN	SN	SW	FC	FC
Horsham	d																						
Warnham	d																						
Ockley	d																						
Holmwood	d																						
Dorking	a																						
	d			16 46			17 08				17 16							17 46			18 08		
Box Hill & Westhumble	d			16 48							17 18							17 48					
Guildford	d													17 18									
Effingham Junction	d													17 34									
Bookham	d													17 37									
Leatherhead	d			16 53			17 15				17 23			17 45				17 53			18 15		
Ashtead	d			16 57			17 18				17 27			17 48				17 57			18 18		
Epsom	a			17 01			17 23				17 31			17 53				18 01			18 23		
	d			17 02		17 17	17 24				17 32		17 47	17 54				18 02		18 17	18 24		
Ewell East	d			17 06		17 21					17 36		17 51					18 06		18 21			
Cheam	d			17 09		17 24					17 39		17 54					18 09		18 24			
Epsom Downs	d																						
Banstead	d																						
Belmont	d																						
Sutton (Surrey)	a			17 12		17 27					17 42		17 57					18 12		18 27			
	d	17 07	17 10	17 13	17 25	17 28		17 34	17 37	17 40	17 43	17 55	17 58		18 04	18 07	18 10	18 13	18 25	18 28		18 34	18 37
Carshalton	d			17 16		17 31		17 37			17 46		18 01		18 07			18 16		18 31		18 37	
Hackbridge	d			17 18		17 33		17 39			17 48		18 03		18 09			18 18		18 33		18 39	
Mitcham Junction	d			17 22		17 37		17 42			17 52		18 07		18 12			18 22		18 37		18 42	
Mitcham Eastfields	d			17 25		17 40		17 45			17 55		18 10		18 15			18 25		18 40		18 45	
Carshalton Beeches	d		17 13		17 28					17 43		17 58					18 13		18 28				
Wallington	d		17 15		17 30					17 45		18 00					18 15		18 30				
Waddon	d		17 18		17 33					17 48		18 03					18 18		18 33				
West Croydon	d		17 22		17 37					17 52		18 07					18 22		18 37				
Norwood Junction	d		17 27							17 57							18 27						
New Cross Gate	d																						
Tulse Hill	a	17 40						17 53	18 10						18 23	18 40						18 53	19 10
	d																						
London Bridge	a																						
Balham	d		17 43	17 31	17 53	17 48				18 13	18 01	18 23	18 18				18 43	18 31	18 53	18 48			
Clapham Junction	a		17 48	17 36	17 57	17 52	17 49			18 19	18 06	18 27	18 22	18 19			18 48	18 36	18 57	18 52	18 49		
London Waterloo	a						17 59							18 29							18 59		
London Victoria	a		17 57	17 45	18 04	17 59				18 27	18 15	18 34	18 29				18 57	18 45	19 04	18 59			

Table 182

Horsham, Dorking, Guildford, Epsom and Sutton - London

Sundays from 7 October

Network Diagram - see first Page of Table 177

		SN	SN	SN	SN	SW	FC	FC	SN	SN	SW	SN	FC	FC	SN	SN	SW	SN	FC	FC	SN	SN
Horsham	d																					
Warnham	d																					
Ockley	d																					
Holmwood	d																					
Dorking	a																					
	d		18 16							18 46	19 08					19 16						19 46
Box Hill & Westhumble	d		18 18							18 48						19 18						19 48
Guildford	d					18 18											19 18					
Effingham Junction	d					18 34											19 34					
Bookham	d					18 37											19 37					
Leatherhead	d		18 23			18 45				18 53	19 15					19 23	19 45					19 53
Ashtead	d		18 27			18 48				18 57	19 18					19 27	19 48					19 57
Epsom	a		18 31			18 53				19 01	19 23					19 31	19 53					20 01
	d		18 32		18 47	18 54				19 02	19 24					19 32	19 54					20 02
Ewell East	d		18 36		18 51					19 06						19 36						20 06
Cheam	d		18 39		18 54					19 09						19 39						20 09
Epsom Downs	d																					
Banstead	d																					
Belmont	d																					
Sutton (Surrey)	a		18 42		18 57					19 12						19 42						20 12
	d	18 40	18 43	18 55	18 58		19 04	19 07	19 10	19 13		19 25	19 34	19 37	19 40	19 43		19 55	20 04	20 07	20 10	20 13
Carshalton	d		18 46		19 01		19 07			19 16			19 37			19 46			20 07			20 16
Hackbridge	d		18 48		19 03		19 09			19 18			19 39			19 48			20 09			20 18
Mitcham Junction	d		18 52		19 07		19 12			19 22			19 42			19 52			20 12			20 22
Mitcham Eastfields	d		18 55		19 10		19 15			19 25			19 45			19 55			20 15			20 25
Carshalton Beeches	d	18 43		18 58					19 13			19 28			19 43			19 58			20 13	
Wallington	d	18 45		19 00					19 15			19 30			19 45			20 00			20 15	
Waddon	d	18 48		19 03					19 18			19 33			19 48			20 03			20 18	
West Croydon	d	18 52		19 07					19 22			19 37			19 52			20 07			20 22	
Norwood Junction	d	18 57							19 27						19 57						20 27	
New Cross Gate	d																					
Tulse Hill	a						19 23	19 40					19 53	20 10					20 23	20 40		
	d																					
London Bridge	a																					
Balham	d	19 13	19 01	19 23	19 18				19 43	19 31		19 53			20 13	20 01		20 23			20 43	20 31
Clapham Junction	a	19 19	19 06	19 27	19 22	19 19			19 48	19 36	19 49	19 57			20 18	20 06	20 19	20 27			20 48	20 36
London Waterloo	a					19 29					19 59						20 29					
London Victoria	a	19 27	19 15	19 34	19 29				19 57	19 45		20 04			20 27	20 15		20 34			20 57	20 45

		SW	SN	FC	FC	SN	SN	SW	SN	FC	FC	SN	SN	SW	SN	FC	SN	SN	SW	SN	FC	SN	SN
Horsham	d																						
Warnham	d																						
Ockley	d																						
Holmwood	d																						
Dorking	a																						
	d	20 08					20 16						20 46	21 08				21 16					21 46
Box Hill & Westhumble	d						20 18						20 48					21 18					21 48
Guildford	d							20 18											21 18				
Effingham Junction	d							20 34											21 34				
Bookham	d							20 37											21 37				
Leatherhead	d	20 15					20 23	20 45					20 53	21 15				21 23	21 45				21 53
Ashtead	d	20 18					20 27	20 48					20 57	21 18				21 27	21 48				21 57
Epsom	a	20 23					20 31	20 53					21 01	21 23				21 31	21 53				22 01
	d	20 24					20 32	20 54					21 02	21 24				21 32	21 54				22 02
Ewell East	d						20 36						21 06					21 36					22 06
Cheam	d						20 39						21 09					21 39					22 09
Epsom Downs	d																						
Banstead	d																						
Belmont	d																						
Sutton (Surrey)	a						20 42						21 12					21 42					22 12
	d		20 25	20 34	20 37	20 40	20 43		20 55	21 04	21 07	21 10	21 13		21 25	21 34	21 40	21 43		21 55	22 04	22 10	22 13
Carshalton	d			20 37			20 46			21 07			21 16			21 37		21 46			22 07		22 16
Hackbridge	d			20 39			20 48			21 09			21 18			21 39		21 48			22 09		22 18
Mitcham Junction	d			20 42			20 52			21 12			21 22			21 42		21 52			22 12		22 22
Mitcham Eastfields	d			20 45			20 55			21 15			21 25			21 45		21 55			22 15		22 25
Carshalton Beeches	d		20 28			20 43			20 58			21 13			21 28		21 43			21 58		22 13	
Wallington	d		20 30			20 45			21 00			21 15			21 30		21 45			22 00		22 15	
Waddon	d		20 33			20 48			21 03			21 18			21 33		21 48			22 03		22 18	
West Croydon	d		20 37			20 52			21 07			21 22			21 37		21 52			22 07		22 22	
Norwood Junction	d					20 57						21 27					21 57					22 27	
New Cross Gate	d																						
Tulse Hill	a			20 53	21 10					21 23	21 40					21 53					22 23		
	d																						
London Bridge	a																						
Balham	d		20 53			21 13	21 01		21 23			21 43	21 31		21 53		22 13	22 01		22 23		22 43	22 31
Clapham Junction	a	20 49	20 57			21 19	21 06	21 19	21 27			21 49	21 36	21 49	21 57		22 19	22 06	22 19	22 27		22 49	22 36
London Waterloo	a	21 00						21 29						22 00					22 29				
London Victoria	a		21 04			21 27	21 15		21 34			21 57	21 45		22 04		22 27	22 15		22 34		22 57	22 45

Table 182

Sundays
from 7 October

Horsham, Dorking, Guildford, Epsom and Sutton - London

Network Diagram - see first Page of Table 177

		SW	SN	SN	SN	SW	SN	SN	SN	SW	SN	SN	SN
Horsham	d												
Warnham	d												
Ockley	d												
Holmwood	d												
Dorking	a												
	d	22 08			22 16				22 46	23 08			23 16
Box Hill & Westhumble	d				22 18				22 48				23 18
Guildford	d					22 20							
Effingham Junction	d					22 36							
Bookham	d					22 39							
Leatherhead	d	22 15			22 23	22 45			22 53	23 15			23 23
Ashtead	d	22 18			22 27	22 48			22 57	23 18			23 27
Epsom	a	22 23			22 31	22 53			23 01	23 23			23 31
	d	22 24			22 32	22 54			23 02	23 24			23 32
Ewell East	d				22 36				23 06				23 36
Cheam	d				22 39				23 09				23 39
Epsom Downs	d												
Banstead	d												
Belmont	d												
Sutton (Surrey)	a				22 42				23 12				23 42
	d		22 25	22 40	22 43		22 55	23 10	23 13		23 25	23 40	23 43
Carshalton	d				22 46				23 16				23 46
Hackbridge	d				22 48				23 18				23 48
Mitcham Junction	d				22 52				23 22				23 52
Mitcham Eastfields	d				22 55				23 25				23 55
Carshalton Beeches	d		22 28	22 43			22 58	23 13			23 28	23 43	
Wallington	d		22 30	22 45			23 00	23 15			23 30	23 45	
Waddon	d		22 33	22 48			23 03	23 18			23 33	23 48	
West Croydon	d		22 37	22 52			23 07	23 22			23 37	23 52	
Norwood Junction	d			22 57				23 27					
New Cross Gate ⊖	d												
Tulse Hill	a												
	d												
London Bridge ⊖	a												
Balham ⊖	d		22 53	23 13	23 01		23 23	23 43	23 31		23 53	00 08	00 01
Clapham Junction	a	22 49	22 57	23 19	23 06	23 19	23 27	23 49	23 36	23 49	23 57	00 12	00 06
London Waterloo ⊖	a	23 00				23 29				23 59			
London Victoria ⊖	a		23 04	23 27	23 15		23 34	23 57	23 45		00 04	00 19	00 15

Network Diagram for Tables 184, 189

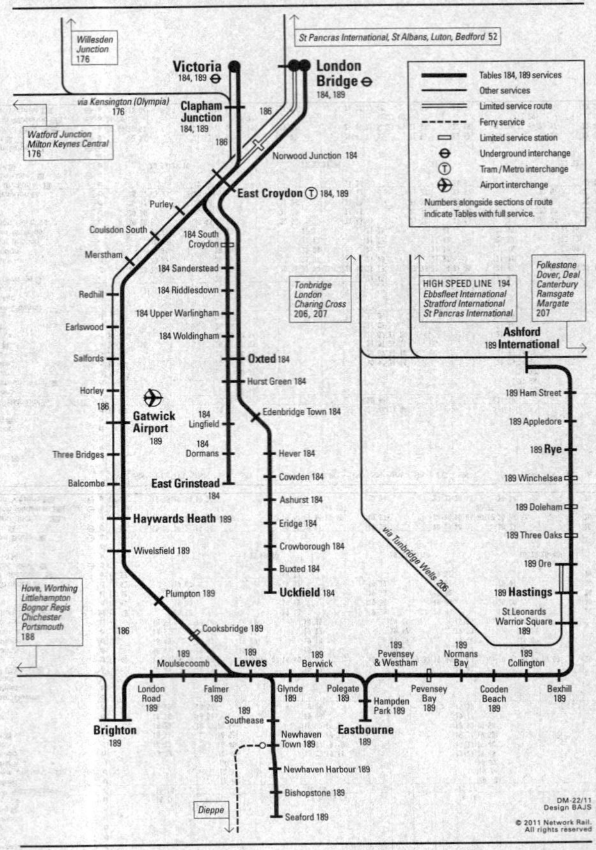

London - Oxted, East Grinstead and Uckfield

Network Diagram - see first Page of Table 184

Miles	Miles			SN MX	SN MX	SN MX	SN	SN	SN	SN	SN	SN	SN	SN	SN	SN	SN	SN	SN	SN	SN	SN
0	—	London Victoria ⊖175,177	d		23p24	23p49		05 25	05 53		06 24		06 54		07 10		07 32		08 10		08 53		09 23
2¾	—	Clapham Junction 175,177	d		23p30	23p56		05 33	05 59		06 30		07 00		07 16		07 38		08 16		08 59		09 29
—	0	London Bridge ⊖175,177	d	23p04						06 08		06 38		07 03		07 19		08 02		08 25		09 08	
—	8¾	Norwood Junction 175,177	d	23p15				05 50								07 30				08 36			
10½	10¼	East Croydon 175,177 ⇌	d	23p19	23p41	00 10	05 26	05 55	06 10	06 22	06 41	06 53	07 11	07 17	07 27	07 34	07 52	08 16	08 27	08 41	09 10	09 23	09 40
11½	—	South Croydon 175	d					05 57															
12½	—	Sanderstead	d	23p24	23p46	00s14			06 14		06 45		07 15	07 21	07 31	07 38	07 57	08 20	08 31	08 45	09 14		09 44
13¾	—	Riddlesdown	d		23p49	00s17			06 17		06 48			07 24		07 41	08 00	08 23		08 48	09 17		09 47
15½	—	Upper Warlingham	d	23p29	23p53	00s21			06 21		06 52			07 28		07 45	08 04	08 27		08 52	09 21		09 51
17¼	—	Woldingham	d		23p57	00s25			06 25		06 56			07 32		07 49	08 08	08 31		08 56	09 25		09 55
20½	—	Oxted	a	23p36	00 02	00 30	05 41	06 09	06 30	06 36	07 01	07 06	07 26	07 37	07 43	07 54	08 13	08 36	08 42	09 01	09 30	09 36	10 00
—	—		d	23p37	00 02		05 41	06 09	06 31	06 36	07 02	07 07	07 26	07 38	07 43	07 55	08 13	08 37	08 42	09 02	09 31	09 37	10 00
21½	0	Hurst Green	d	23p39	00 05		05 44	06 11	06 33	06 39	07 04	07 09	07 29	07 40	07 46	07 57	08 16	08 39	08 46	09 04	09 33	09 39	10 03
26¼	—	Lingfield	d		00 11			06 17	06 39		07 10		07 35		07 52	08 03	08 22		08 52	09 10	09 39		10 09
28	—	Dormans	d		00 14			06 21	06 43		07 14		07 38		07 55	08 07	08 25		08 55	09 14	09 43		10 12
30¼	—	East Grinstead	a		00 19			06 25	06 47		07 18		07 43		08 00	08 12	08 30		09 00	09 18	09 47		10 17
—	4¼	Edenbridge Town	d	23b45			05 50			06 45		07 15		07 46				08 45				09 45	
—	6	Hever	d							06 48		07 19		07 50				08 49				09 49	
—	8	Cowden	d							06 52		07 23		07 54				08 53				09 53	
—	10¾	Ashurst	d							06 57		07 27		07 58				08 57				09 57	
—	14½	Eridge	d	23b58			06 11			07 02		07 35		08 04				09 03				10 03	
—	17¾	Crowborough	d	00s04			06 17			07 14		07 41		08 10				09 09				10 09	
—	22½	Buxted	d	00s10			06 23			07 20		07 47		08 16				09 15				10 15	
—	25	Uckfield	a	00 16			06 29			07 26		07 53		08 22				09 21				10 21	

		SN	SN	SN	SN	SN	SN	SN	SN	SN	SN	SN	SN	SN	SN	SN	SN	SN	SN	SN	SN	SN	SN
London Victoria ⊖175,177	d	09 53		10 23	10 53		11 23	11 53		12 23	12 53		13 23	13 53		14 23	14 53		15 23		15 53		16 23
Clapham Junction 175,177	d	09 59		10 29	10 59		11 29	11 59		12 29	12 59		13 29	13 59		14 29	14 59		15 29		15 59		16 29
London Bridge ⊖175,177	d		10 08			11 08			12 08			13 08			14 08			15 08		15 38		16 08	
Norwood Junction 175,177	d																						
East Croydon 175,177 ⇌	d	10 10	10 23	10 40	11 10	11 24	11 40	12 10	12 23	12 40	13 10	13 24	13 40	14 10	14 23	14 40	15 10	15 23	15 40	15 53	16 10	16 23	16 40
South Croydon 175	d																		15 43		16 12		16 42
Sanderstead	d	10 14		10 44	11 14		11 44	12 14		12 44	13 14		13 44	14 14		14 45	15 14		15 46		16 15		16 45
Riddlesdown	d	10 17		10 47	11 17		11 47	12 17		12 47	13 17		13 47	14 17		14 48	15 17		15 49		16 18		16 48
Upper Warlingham	d	10 21		10 51	11 21		11 51	12 21		12 51	13 21		13 51	14 21		14 52	15 21		15 53		16 22		16 52
Woldingham	d	10 25		10 55	11 25		11 55	12 25		12 55	13 25		13 55	14 25		14 56	15 25		15 57		16 26		16 56
Oxted	a	10 30	10 36	11 00	11 30	11 36	12 00	12 30	12 36	13 00	13 30	13 36	14 00	14 30	14 36	15 01	15 30	15 36	16 02	16 06	16 31	16 36	17 01
	d	10 30	10 37	11 00	11 30	11 37	12 00	12 30	12 37	13 00	13 30	13 37	14 00	14 30	14 37	15 01	15 30	15 37	16 02	16 07	16 31	16 37	17 02
Hurst Green	d	10 33	10 39	11 03	11 33	11 39	12 03	12 33	12 39	13 03	13 33	13 39	14 03	14 33	14 39	15 03	15 33	15 39	16 04	16 09	16 34	16 39	17 04
Lingfield	d	10 39		11 09	11 39		12 09	12 39		13 09	13 39		14 09	14 39		15 09	15 39		16 10		16 40		17 10
Dormans	d	10 42		11 12	11 42		12 12	12 42		13 12	13 42		14 12	14 42		15 13	15 42		16 14		16 43		17 14
East Grinstead	a	10 47		11 17	11 47		12 17	12 47		13 17	13 47		14 17	14 47		15 17	15 47		16 18		16 48		17 20
Edenbridge Town	d		10 45			11 45			12 45			13 45			14 45			15 45		16 15		16 45	
Hever	d		10 49			11 49			12 49			13 49			14 49			15 49		16 19		16 49	
Cowden	d		10 53			11 53			12 53			13 53			14 53			15 53		16 23		16 53	
Ashurst	d		10 57			11 57			12 57			13 57			14 57			15 57		16 27		16 57	
Eridge	d		11 03			12 03			13 03			14 03			15 03			16 03		16 33		17 03	
Crowborough	d		11 09			12 09			13 09			14 09			15 09			16 09		16 39		17 09	
Buxted	d		11 15			12 15			13 15			14 15			15 15			16 15		16 45		17 15	
Uckfield	a		11 21			12 21			13 21			14 21			15 21			16 21		16 51		17 21	

		SN	SN	SN	SN	SN	SN	SN	SN	SN	SN	SN	SN	SN	SN	SN	SN	SN	SN	SN	SN	SN
London Victoria ⊖175,177	d		16 53			17 23			17 53			18 23			18 53		19 23	19 53		20 23	20 53	
Clapham Junction 175,177	d		16 59			17 30			18 00			18 30			19 00		19 29	19 59		20 29	20 59	
London Bridge ⊖175,177	d	16 38		17 09	17 15			17 44		18 08	18 16			18 47		19 08			20 04			21 04
Norwood Junction 175,177	d																		20 16			21 15
East Croydon 175,177 ⇌	d	16 53	17 10	17 23	17 30	17 41		17 58	18 11	18 22	18 31	18 41		19 01	19 11	19 23	19 40	20 10	20 20	20 40	21 10	21 19
South Croydon 175	d		17 12		17 32			18 01			18 33			19 03								
Sanderstead	d		17 15		17 35	17 45		18 04	18 15		18 36	18 46		19 06	19 15		19 44	20 14	20 24	20 44	21 14	21 24
Riddlesdown	d		17 18		17 38	17 48		18 07	18 18		18 39	18 49		19 09	19 18		19 47	20 17		20 47	21 17	
Upper Warlingham	d		17 22		17 42	17 52		18 11	18 22		18 43	18 53		19 13	19 22		19 51	20 21	20 30	20 51	21 21	21 29
Woldingham	d		17 26		17 46	17 56		18 15	18 26		18 47	18 57		19 17	19 26		19 55	20 25		20 55	21 25	
Oxted	a	17 06	17 31	17 36	17 51	18 01		18 20	18 31	18 36	18 52	19 02		19 22	19 31	19 36	20 00	20 30	20 37	21 00	21 30	21 36
	d	17 07	17 32	17 37	17 52	18 02	18 07	18 20	18 32	18 37	18 53	19 03	19 07	19 23	19 32	19 37	20 00	20 30	20 37	21 00	21 30	21 37
Hurst Green	d	17 09	17 34	17 40	17 54	18 04	18 09	18 23	18 34	18 39	18 55	19 05	19 09	19 25	19 34	19 39	20 03	20 33	20 40	21 03	21 33	21 39
Lingfield	d		17 40		18 00	18 10		18 29	18 40		19 01	19 11		19 31	19 40		20 09	20 39		21 09	21 39	
Dormans	d		17 44		18 04	18 14		18 32	18 44		19 05	19 15		19 35	19 44		20 12	20 42		21 12	21 42	
East Grinstead	a		17 50		18 12	18 22		18 40	18 52		19 12	19 22		19 42	19 52		20 17	20 47		21 17	21 47	
Edenbridge Town	d	17 15		17 46			18 15			18 45			19 15			19 45			20 46			21 45
Hever	d	17 19					18 19						19 19			19 49			20 49			21 49
Cowden	d	17 23					18 23			18 51			19 23			19 53			20 53			21 53
Ashurst	d	17 27					18 27						19 27			19 57			20 58			21 57
Eridge	d	17 33		17 58			18 33			18 59			19 33			20 03			21 03			22 03
Crowborough	d	17 39		18 04			18 39			19 05			19 39			20 09			21 09			22 09
Buxted	d	17 45		18 10			18 45			19 11			19 45			20 15			21 15			22 15
Uckfield	a	17 51		18 18			18 51			19 19			19 51			20 21			21 21			22 21

b Previous night, stops to set down only

London - Oxted, East Grinstead and Uckfield

Network Diagram - see first Page of Table 184

		SN	SN	SN	SN	SN	SN	SN	SN
London Victoria ⊖175,177	d	21 23	21 53		22 23	22 53		23 24	23 49
Clapham Junction 175,177	d	21 29	21 59		22 29	22 59		23 30	23 56
London Bridge ⊖175,177	d			22 04			23 04		
Norwood Junction 175,177	d			22 15			23 15		
East Croydon 175,177 ⇌	d	21 40	22 10	22 19	22 40	23 10	23 19	23 41	00 10
South Croydon 175	d								
Sanderstead	d	21 44	22 14	22 24	22 44	23 14	23 24	23 46	00s14
Riddlesdown	d	21 47	22 17		22 47	23 17		23 49	00s17
Upper Warlingham	d	21 51	22 21	22 29	22 51	23 21	23 29	23 53	00s21
Woldingham	d	21 55	22 25		22 55	23 25		23 57	00s25
Oxted	a	22 00	22 30	22 36	23 00	23 30	23 36	00 02	00 30
	d	22 00	22 30	22 37	23 00	23 30	23 37	00 02	
Hurst Green	d	22 03	22 33	22 39	23 03	23 33	23 39	00 05	
Lingfield	d	22 09	22 39		23 09	23 39		00 11	
Dormans	d	22 12	22 42		23 12	23 42		00 14	
East Grinstead	a	22 17	22 47		23 17	23 47		00 19	
Edenbridge Town	d			22 45			23s45		
Hever	d			22s49					
Cowden	d			22s53					
Ashurst	d			22s57					
Eridge	d			23 03			23s58		
Crowborough	d			23 09			00s04		
Buxted	d			23 15			00s10		
Uckfield	a			23 21			00 16		

Saturdays

		SN	SN	SN	SN	SN	SN	SN		SN	SN	SN	SN	SN	SN	SN	SN	SN	SN	SN	SN	SN
London Victoria ⊖175,177	d		23p24	23p49	05 23		06 23	06 53		19 53		20 23	20 53		21 23	21 53		22 23	22 53		23 24	23 49
Clapham Junction 175,177	d		23p30	23p56	05 29		06 29	06 59		19 59		20 29	20 59		21 29	21 59		22 29	22 59		23 30	23 56
London Bridge ⊖175,177	d	23p04				06 08					20 08			21 08			22 08			23 04		
Norwood Junction 175,177	d	23p15			05 46						20 19			21 19			22 19			23 15		
East Croydon 175,177 ⇌	d	23p19	23p41	00 10	05 50	06 23	06 40	07 10		20 10	20 23	20 40	21 10	21 23	21 40	22 10	22 23	22 40	23 10	23 19	23 41	00 10
South Croydon 175	d				05 52																	
Sanderstead	d	23p24	23p46	00s14			06 44	07 14		20 14		20 44	21 14		21 44	22 14		22 44	23 14	23 24	23 46	00s14
Riddlesdown	d		23p49	00s17			06 47	07 17	and at the same minutes past each hour until	20 17		20 47	21 17		21 47	22 17		22 47	23 17		23 49	00s17
Upper Warlingham	d	23p29	23p53	00s21			06 51	07 21		20 21		20 51	21 21		21 51	22 21		22 51	23 21	23 29	23 53	00s21
Woldingham	d		23p57	00s25			06 55	07 25		20 25		20 55	21 25		21 55	22 25		22 55	23 25		23 57	00s25
Oxted	a	23p36	00 02	00 30	06 04	06 36	07 00	07 30		20 30	20 36	21 00	21 30	21 36	22 00	22 30	22 36	23 00	23 30	23 36	00 02	00 30
	d	23p37	00 02		06 04	06 37	07 01	07 31		20 31	20 37	21 01	21 31	21 37	22 01	22 31	22 37	23 01	23 31	23 37	00 02	
Hurst Green	d	23p39	00 05		06 07	06 39	07 03	07 33		20 33	20 39	21 03	21 33	21 39	22 03	22 33	22 39	23 03	23 33	23 39	00 05	
Lingfield	d		00 11		06 13		07 09	07 39		20 39		21 09	21 39		22 09	22 39		23 09	23 39		00 11	
Dormans	d		00 14		06 16		07 13	07 43		20 43		21 13	21 43		22 13	22 43		23 13	23 43		00 14	
East Grinstead	a		00 19		06 21		07 17	07 47		20 47		21 17	21 47		22 17	22 47		23 17	23 47		00 19	
Edenbridge Town	d	23b45				06 45					20 45			21 45			22 45			23s45		
Hever	d					06 49					20 49			21 49			22s49					
Cowden	d					06 53					20 53			21 53			22s53					
Ashurst	d					06 57					20 57			21 57			22s57					
Eridge	d	23b58				07 03					21 03			22 03			23 03			23s58		
Crowborough	d	00s04				07 09					21 09			22 09			23 09			00s04		
Buxted	d	00s10				07 15					21 15			22 15			23 15			00s10		
Uckfield	a	00 16				07 21					21 21			22 21			23 21			00 16		

Sundays

until 9 September

		SN	SN	SN	SN	SN	SN	SN	SN	SN	SN		SN	SN
London Victoria ⊖175,177	d		23p24	23p49	07 40	08 40		09 40		10 40				22 40
Clapham Junction 175,177	d		23p30	23p56	07 45	08 45		09 45		10 45				22 45
London Bridge ⊖175,177	d	23p04												
Norwood Junction 175,177	d	23p15												
East Croydon 175,177 ⇌	d	23p19	23p41	00 10	07 58	08 58	09 15	09 58	10 15	10 58				22 58
South Croydon 175	d													
Sanderstead	d	23p24	23p46	00s14	08 02	09 02	09 19	10 02	10 19	11 02				23 02
Riddlesdown	d		23p49	00s17	08 05	09 05		10 05		11 05		and at the same minutes past each hour until		23 05
Upper Warlingham	d	23p29	23p53	00s21	08 09	09 09	09 25	10 09	10 25	11 09				23 09
Woldingham	d		23p57	00s25	08 13	09 13		10 13		11 13				23 13
Oxted	a	23p36	00 02	00 30	08 18	09 18	09 32	10 18	10 32	11 18				23 18
	d	23p37	00 02		08 18	09 18	09 33	10 18	10 33	11 18	11 33		22 33	23 18
Hurst Green	d	23p39	00 05		08 21	09 21	09 36	10 21	10 36	11 21	11 36		22 36	23 21
Lingfield	d		00 11		08 27	09 27		10 27		11 27				23 27
Dormans	d		00 14		08 30	09 30		10 30		11 30				23 30
East Grinstead	a		00 19		08 35	09 35		10 35		11 35				23 35
Edenbridge Town	d	23b45					09 42		10 42		11 42		22 42	
Hever	d						09 46		10 46		11 46		22 46	
Cowden	d						09 50		10 50		11 50		22 50	
Ashurst	d						09 54		10 54		11 54		22 54	
Eridge	d	23b58					10 00		11 00		12 00		23 00	
Crowborough	d	00s04					10 06		11 06		12 06		23 06	
Buxted	d	00s10					10 12		11 12		12 12		23 12	
Uckfield	a	00 16					10 18		11 18		12 18		23 18	

b Previous night, stops to set down only

Sundays from 16 September

London - Oxted, East Grinstead and Uckfield

Network Diagram - see first Page of Table 184

		SN ■	SN ■	SN ■	SN ■	SN ■	SN ■	SN ■	SN ■	SN ■	SN ■		SN ■	SN ■
London Victoria ■ ⊖175,177	d		23p24	23p49	07 34	08 34		09 34		10 34				22 34
Clapham Junction ■ 175,177	d		23p30	23p56	07 40	08 40		09 40		10 40				22 40
London Bridge ■ ⊖175,177	d	23p04												
Norwood Junction ■ 175,177	d	23p15												
East Croydon 175,177 ⇌	d	23p19	23p41	00 10	07 58	08 58	09 15	09 58	10 15	10 58				22 58
South Croydon ■ 175	d													
Sanderstead	d	23p24	23p46	00s14	08 02	09 02	09 19	10 02	10 19	11 02				23 02
Riddlesdown	d		23p49	00s17	08 05	09 05		10 05		11 05		and at		23 05
Upper Warlingham	d	23p29	23p53	00s21	08 09	09 09	09 25	10 09	10 25	11 09		the same		23 09
Woldingham	d		23p57	00s25	08 13	09 13		10 13		11 13		minutes		23 13
Oxted ■	a	23p36	00 02	00 30	08 18	09 18	09 32	10 18	10 32	11 18		past		23 18
	d	23p37	00 02		08 19	09 19	09 33	10 19	10 33	11 19	11 33	each	22 33	23 19
Hurst Green	d	23p39	00 05		08 21	09 21	09 36	10 21	10 36	11 21	11 36	hour until	22 36	23 21
Lingfield	d		00 11		08 27	09 27		10 27		11 27				23 27
Dormans	d		00 14		08 31	09 31		10 31		11 31				23 31
East Grinstead	a		00 19		08 35	09 35		10 35		11 35				23 35
Edenbridge Town	d	23b45					09 42		10 42		11 42		22 42	
Hever	d						09 46		10 46		11 46		22 46	
Cowden	d						09 50		10 50		11 50		22 50	
Ashurst	d						09 54		10 54		11 54		22 54	
Eridge	d	23b58					10 00		11 00		12 00		23 00	
Crowborough	d	00s04					10 06		11 06		12 06		23 06	
Buxted	d	00s10					10 12		11 12		12 12		23 12	
Uckfield	a	00 16					10 18		11 18		12 18		23 18	

b Previous night, stops to set down only

Mondays to Fridays

Uckfield, East Grinstead and Oxted - London

Network Diagram - see first Page of Table 184

Miles	Miles			SN MO ■ A	SN ■	SN ■	SN ■	SN ■	SN ■	SN ■	SN ■	SN ■	SN ■	SN ■	SN ■	SN ■	SN ■	SN ■	SN ■	SN ■	SN ■	SN ■	SN ■
—	0	Uckfield	d				05 45				06 34			07 08			07 34			08 04		08 34	
—	2½	Buxted	d				05 50				06 39			07 14			07 39			08 09		08 39	
—	7¼	Crowborough	d				05 57				06 46			07 21			07 46			08 16		08 46	
—	10½	Eridge	d				06 02				06 51			07 27			07 51			08 21		08 51	
—	14¼	Ashurst	d								06 56						07 56			08 26		08 56	
—	17	Cowden	d				06 10				07 01						08 01			08 31		09 01	
—	19	Hever	d								07 05						08 05			08 35		09 05	
—	20¾	Edenbridge Town	d				06 15				07 09			07 39			08 09			08 39		09 08	
0	—	East Grinstead	d	23p12		05 58		06 14	06 37	06 49		07 07	07 19		07 37	07 49		08 07	08 17		08 37		09 07
2¼	—	Dormans	d	23p16		06 02		06 18	06 41	06 53		07 11	07 23		07 41	07 53		08 11	08 21		08 41		09 11
4	—	Lingfield	d	23p19		06 05		06 21	06 44	06 56		07 14	07 26		07 44	07 56		08 14	08 24		08 44		09 14
8¾	—	Hurst Green	d	23p26	06 00	06 12	06 22	06 28	06 51	07 03	07 17	07 21	07 33	07 47	07 51	08 03	08 16	08 21	08 31	08 46	08 51	09 15	09 21
9¾	25	Oxted ■	a	23p28	06 02	06 14	06 24	06 30	06 53	07 05	07 19	07 23	07 35	07 49	07 53	08 05	08 19	08 23	08 33	08 48	08 53	09 18	09 23
—	—		d	23p28	06 03	06 15	06 25	06 30	06 54	07 06	07 20	07 24	07 36	07 50	07 54	08 06	08 20	08 24	08 34	08 49	08 53	09 19	09 23
13	—	Woldingham	d	23p34	06 08			06 36	06 59	07 11		07 29	07 41		07 59	08 11		08 29	08 39		08 59		09 29
14¾	—	Upper Warlingham	d	23p37	06 12			06 39	07 03	07 15		07 33	07 45		08 03	08 15		08 33	08 43		09 02		09 32
16½	—	Riddlesdown	d	23p41	06 15			06 43	07 06	07 18		07 36	07 48		08 06	08 18		08 36	08 46		09 06		09 36
17¾	—	Sanderstead	d	23p44	06 18			06 46	07 10	07 22		07 40	07 51		08 10	08 22		08 39	08 49		09 09		09 39
18¾	—	South Croydon ■ 175	d					06 50		07 25			07 54			08 26		08 42	08 52				
19¾	0	East Croydon 175,177 ⇌	a	23p49	06 23	06 27	06 38	06 53	07 15	07 27	07 31	07 44	07 58	08 04	08 14	08 29	08 32	08 45	08 55	09 01	09 13	09 32	09 43
—	1½	Norwood Junction ■ 175,177	a																				
—	10¼	London Bridge ■ ⊖175,177	a		06 39		06 55	07 11		07 47	07 49		08 16	08 23		08 47	08 52		09 13	09 20		09 51	
27½	—	Clapham Junction ■ 175,177	a	00 01		06 38			07 27			07 55			08 26			08 55			09 26		09 55
30¼	—	London Victoria ■ ⊖175,177	a	00 08		06 45			07 36			08 04			08 35			09 04			09 35		10 05

		SN ■	SN ■	SN ■	SN ■	SN ■	SN ■	SN ■	SN ■	SN ■	SN ■	SN ■	SN ■	SN ■	SN ■	SN ■	SN ■	SN ■	SN ■	SN ■	SN ■	SN ■	SN ■
Uckfield	d		09 34			10 34			11 34			12 34			13 34			14 34			15 34		
Buxted	d		09 39			10 39			11 39			12 39			13 39			14 39			15 39		
Crowborough	d		09 46			10 46			11 46			12 46			13 46			14 46			15 46		
Eridge	d		09 51			10 51			11 51			12 51			13 51			14 51			15 51		
Ashurst	d		09 56			10 56			11 56			12 56			13 56			14 56			15 56		
Cowden	d		10 01			11 01			12 01			13 01			14 01			15 01			16 01		
Hever	d		10 05			11 05			12 05			13 05			14 05			15 05			16 05		
Edenbridge Town	d		10 08			11 08			12 08			13 08			14 08			15 08			16 08		
East Grinstead	d	09 37		10 07	10 37		11 07	11 37		12 07	12 37		13 07	13 37		14 07	14 37		15 07	15 37		16 07	16 37
Dormans	d	09 41		10 11	10 41		11 11	11 41		12 11	12 41		13 11	13 41		14 11	14 41		15 11	15 41		16 11	16 41
Lingfield	d	09 44		10 14	10 44		11 14	11 44		12 14	12 44		13 14	13 44		14 14	14 44		15 14	15 44		16 14	16 44
Hurst Green	d	09 51	10 15	10 21	10 51	11 15	11 21	11 51	12 15	12 21	12 51	13 15	13 21	13 51	14 15	14 21	14 51	15 15	15 21	15 51	16 15	16 21	16 51
Oxted ■	a	09 53	10 17	10 23	10 53	11 17	11 23	11 53	12 17	12 23	12 53	13 17	13 23	13 53	14 17	14 23	14 53	15 17	15 23	15 53	16 17	16 23	16 53
	d	09 53	10 18	10 23	10 53	11 18	11 23	11 53	12 18	12 23	12 53	13 18	13 23	13 53	14 18	14 23	14 53	15 18	15 23	15 53	16 18	16 23	16 53
Woldingham	d	09 59		10 29	10 59		11 29	11 59		12 29	12 59		13 29	13 59		14 29	14 59		15 29	15 59		16 29	16 59
Upper Warlingham	d	10 02		10 32	11 02		11 32	12 02		12 32	13 02		13 32	14 02		14 32	15 02		15 32	16 02		16 32	17 02
Riddlesdown	d	10 06		10 36	11 06		11 36	12 06		12 36	13 06		13 36	14 06		14 36	15 06		15 36	16 06		16 36	17 06
Sanderstead	d	10 09		10 39	11 09		11 39	12 09		12 39	13 09		13 39	14 09		14 39	15 09		15 39	16 09		16 39	17 09
South Croydon ■ 175	d																						
East Croydon 175,177 ⇌	a	10 13	10 32	10 43	11 13	11 32	11 43	12 13	12 32	12 43	13 13	13 32	13 43	14 13	14 32	14 43	15 13	15 32	15 43	16 13	16 32	16 43	17 13
Norwood Junction ■ 175,177	a																						
London Bridge ■ ⊖175,177	a		10 49			11 49			12 49			13 49			14 49			15 49			16 47		
Clapham Junction ■ 175,177	a	10 25		10 55	11 25		11 55	12 25		12 55	13 25		13 55	14 25		14 55	15 25		15 55	16 25		16 55	17 25
London Victoria ■ ⊖175,177	a	10 35		11 05	11 32		12 02	12 32		13 02	13 32		14 03	14 32		15 02	15 35		16 05	16 35		17 05	17 35

		SN ■	SN ■	SN ■	SN ■	SN ■	SN ■	SN ■	SN ■	SN ■	SN ■	SN ■	SN ■	SN ■	SN ■	SN ■	SN ■	SN ■	SN ■	SN ■	SN ■	SN ■
Uckfield	d	16 33		17 03		17 32			17 58			18 32			18 57			19 33		20 04		20 34
Buxted	d	16 38		17 08		17 37			18 03			18 37			19 02			19 38		20 09		20 39
Crowborough	d	16 46		17 16		17 44			18 16			18 45			19 16			19 46		20 16		20 46
Eridge	d	16 51		17 21		17 49			18 21			18 50			19 21			19 51		20 21		20 51
Ashurst	d	16 56				17 54						18 55			19 26			19 56				20 56
Cowden	d	17 01				17 59						18 59			19 31			20 01				21 01
Hever	d	17 05				18 03						19 03			19 35			20 05				21 05
Edenbridge Town	d	17 08		17 34		18 06			18 34			19 07			19 38			20 08		20 33		21 08
East Grinstead	d		17 07		17 37		18 07	18 17		18 37	18 47		19 07	19 17		19 37	19 47		20 07		20 37	
Dormans	d		17 11		17 41		18 11	18 21		18 41	18 51		19 11	19 21		19 41	19 51		20 11		20 41	
Lingfield	d		17 14		17 44		18 14	18 24		18 44	18 54		19 14	19 24		19 44	19 54		20 14		20 44	
Hurst Green	d	17 15	17 21	17 40	17 51	18 13	18 21	18 31	18 40	18 51	19 01	19 13	19 21	19 31	19 45	19 51	20 01	20 15	20 21	20 39	20 51	21 15
Oxted ■	a	17 17	17 23	17 43	17 53	18 15	18 23	18 33	18 43	18 53	19 03	19 16	19 23	19 33	19 47	19 53	20 03	20 17	20 23	20 42	20 53	21 17
	d	17 18	17 23		17 53	18 18	18 23	18 34		18 53	19 04	19 18	19 23	19 34	19 48	19 53	20 04	20 18	20 23	20 42	20 53	21 18
Woldingham	d		17 29		17 59		18 29	18 39		18 59	19 09		19 29	19 39		19 59	20 09		20 29		20 59	
Upper Warlingham	d		17 32		18 02		18 32	18 43		19 02	19 13		19 32	19 43		20 02	20 13		20 32		21 02	
Riddlesdown	d		17 36		18 06		18 36	18 46		19 06	19 16		19 36	19 46		20 06	20 16		20 36		21 06	
Sanderstead	d		17 39		18 09		18 39	18 49		19 09	19 19		19 39	19 49		20 09	20 19		20 39		21 09	
South Croydon ■ 175	d																					
East Croydon 175,177 ⇌	a	17 35	17 43		18 13	18 35	18 43	18 56		19 13	19 25	19 33	19 43	19 57	20 06	20 13	20 25	20 33	20 43	20 54	21 13	21 30
Norwood Junction ■ 175,177	a							19 01														
London Bridge ■ ⊖175,177	a	17 52				18 50		19 15				19 49			20 21			20 48		21 09		21 49
Clapham Junction ■ 175,177	a		17 55		18 25		18 55			19 25			19 55			20 25			20 55		21 25	
London Victoria ■ ⊖175,177	a		18 05		18 35		19 05			19 35			20 05			20 32			21 03		21 32	

A from 21 May

Table 184

Mondays to Fridays

Uckfield, East Grinstead and Oxted - London

Network Diagram - see first Page of Table 184

		SN	SN	SN	SN	SN	SN	SN
Uckfield	d			21 34				22 34
Buxted	d			21 39				22 39
Crowborough	d			21 46				22 46
Eridge	d			21 51				22 51
Ashurst	d			21 56				
Cowden	d			22 01				
Hever	d			22 05				
Edenbridge Town	d			22 08				23 04
East Grinstead	d	21 07	21 37		22 07	22 37	22 54	
Dormans	d	21 11	21 41		22 11	22 41		
Lingfield	d	21 14	21 44		22 14	22 44		
Hurst Green	d	21 21	21 51	22 15	22 21	22 51		23 10
Oxted	a	21 23	21 53	22 17	22 23	22 53	23 06	23 13
	d	21 23	21 53	22 18	22 23	22 53	23 07	23 13
Woldingham	d	21 29	21 59		22 29	22 59		
Upper Warlingham	d	21 32	22 02		22 32	23 02		
Riddlesdown	d	21 36	22 06		22 36	23 06		
Sanderstead	d	21 39	22 09		22 39	23 09		
South Croydon 175	d							
East Croydon 175,177	a	21 43	22 13	22 33	22 43	23 13	23 19	23 28
Norwood Junction 175,177	a							
London Bridge ⊖175,177	a			22 49				
Clapham Junction 175,177	a	21 55	22 25		22 55	23 25	23 32	
London Victoria ⊖175,177	a	22 05	22 35		23 05	23 35	23 40	

Saturdays

		SN	SN	SN	SN	SN	SN	SN	SN		SN	SN	SN	SN	SN	SN	SN	SN	SN	SN	SN	SN
Uckfield	d		06 34			07 34			08 34		18 34			19 34			20 34			21 34		
Buxted	d		06 39			07 39			08 39		18 39			19 39			20 39			21 39		
Crowborough	d		06 46			07 46			08 46		18 46			19 46			20 46			21 46		
Eridge	d		06 51			07 51			08 51		18 51			19 51			20 51			21 51		
Ashurst	d		06 56			07 56			08 56		18 56			19 56			20 56			21 56		
Cowden	d		07 01			08 01			09 01		19 01			20 01			21 01			22 01		
Hever	d		07 05			08 05			09 05		19 05			20 05			21 05			22 05		
Edenbridge Town	d		07 08			08 08			09 08	and at the same minutes past each hour until	19 08			20 08			21 08			22 08		
East Grinstead	d	06 37		07 07	07 37		08 07	08 37				19 07	19 37		20 07	20 37		21 07	21 37		22 07	22 37
Dormans	d	06 41		07 11	07 41		08 11	08 41				19 11	19 41		20 11	20 41		21 11	21 41		22 11	22 41
Lingfield	d	06 44		07 14	07 44		08 14	08 44				19 14	19 44		20 14	20 44		21 14	21 44		22 14	22 44
Hurst Green	d	06 51	07 15	07 21	07 51	08 15	08 21	08 51	09 15		19 15	19 21	19 51	20 15	20 21	20 51	21 15	21 21	21 51	22 15	22 21	22 51
Oxted	a	06 53	07 18	07 23	07 53	08 18	08 23	08 53	09 17		19 17	19 23	19 53	20 17	20 23	20 53	21 17	21 23	21 53	22 17	22 23	22 53
	d	06 53	07 19	07 23	07 53	08 19	08 23	08 53	09 18		19 18	19 23	19 53	20 18	20 23	20 53	21 18	21 23	21 53	22 18	22 23	22 53
Woldingham	d	06 59		07 29	07 59		08 29	08 59				19 29	19 59		20 29	20 59		21 29	21 59		22 29	22 59
Upper Warlingham	d	07 02		07 32	08 02		08 32	09 02				19 32	20 02		20 32	21 02		21 32	22 02		22 32	23 02
Riddlesdown	d	07 06		07 36	08 06		08 36	09 06				19 36	20 06		20 36	21 06		21 36	22 06		22 36	23 06
Sanderstead	d	07 09		07 39	08 09		08 39	09 09				19 39	20 09		20 39	21 09		21 39	22 09		22 39	23 09
South Croydon 175	d																					
East Croydon 175,177	a	07 13	07 33	07 43	08 13	08 32	08 43	09 13	09 32		19 32	19 43	20 13	20 32	20 43	21 13	21 32	21 43	22 13	22 32	22 43	23 13
Norwood Junction 175,177	a																					
London Bridge ⊖175,177	a		07 49			08 49			09 49		19 49			20 49			21 49			22 49		
Clapham Junction 175,177	a	07 25		07 55	08 25		08 55	09 25				19 55	20 25		20 55	21 25		21 55	22 25		22 55	23 25
London Victoria ⊖175,177	a	07 32		08 02	08 32		09 02	09 32				20 05	20 32		21 02	21 32		22 02	22 35		23 05	23 35

		SN
Uckfield	d	22 34
Buxted	d	22 39
Crowborough	d	22 46
Eridge	d	22 51
Ashurst	d	
Cowden	d	
Hever	d	
Edenbridge Town	d	23 04
East Grinstead	d	
Dormans	d	
Lingfield	d	
Hurst Green	d	23 10
Oxted	a	23 13
	d	23 13
Woldingham	d	
Upper Warlingham	d	
Riddlesdown	d	
Sanderstead	d	
South Croydon 175	d	
East Croydon 175,177	a	23 26
Norwood Junction 175,177	a	
London Bridge ⊖175,177	a	
Clapham Junction 175,177	a	
London Victoria ⊖175,177	a	

Table 184

Sundays
until 9 September

Uckfield, East Grinstead and Oxted - London

Network Diagram - see first Page of Table 184

		SN	SN	SN	SN		SN	SN	SN	SN
Uckfield	d				10 32		21 32		22 32	
Buxted	d				10 37		21 37		22 37	
Crowborough	d				10 44		21 44		22 44	
Eridge	d				10 49		21 49		22 49	
Ashurst	d				10 54		21 54		22 54	
Cowden	d				10 59		21 59		22 59	
Hever	d				11 03		22 03		23 03	
Edenbridge Town	d				11 06	and at the same minutes past each hour until	22 06		23 06	
East Grinstead	d	08 12	09 12	10 12				22 12		23 12
Dormans	d	08 16	09 16	10 16				22 16		23 16
Lingfield	d	08 19	09 19	10 19				22 19		23 19
Hurst Green	d	08 26	09 26	10 26	11 13		22 13	22 26	23 13	23 26
Oxted	a	08 28	09 28	10 28	11 16		22 16	22 28	23 16	23 28
	d	08 28	09 28	10 28				22 28	23 17	23 28
Woldingham	d	08 34	09 34	10 34				22 34		23 34
Upper Warlingham	d	08 37	09 37	10 37				22 37		23 37
Riddlesdown	d	08 41	09 41	10 41				22 41		23 41
Sanderstead	d	08 44	09 44	10 44				22 44		23 44
South Croydon 175	d									
East Croydon 175,177	a	08 49	09 49	10 49				22 49	23 29	23 49
Norwood Junction 175,177	a									
London Bridge ⊖175,177	a									
Clapham Junction 175,177	a	09 02	10 02	11 02				23 02		00 01
London Victoria ⊖175,177	a	09 09	10 09	11 09				23 09		00 08

Sundays
from 16 September

		SN	SN	SN	SN		SN	SN	SN	SN
Uckfield	d				10 32		21 32		22 32	
Buxted	d				10 37		21 37		22 37	
Crowborough	d				10 44		21 44		22 44	
Eridge	d				10 49		21 49		22 49	
Ashurst	d				10 54		21 54		22 54	
Cowden	d				10 59		21 59		22 59	
Hever	d				11 03		22 03		23 03	
Edenbridge Town	d				11 06	and at the same minutes past each hour until	22 06		23 06	
East Grinstead	d	08 12	09 12	10 12				22 12		23 12
Dormans	d	08 16	09 16	10 16				22 16		23 16
Lingfield	d	08 19	09 19	10 19				22 19		23 19
Hurst Green	d	08 26	09 26	10 26	11 13		22 13	22 26	23 13	23 26
Oxted	a	08 28	09 28	10 28	11 16		22 16	22 28	23 16	23 28
	d	08 28	09 28	10 28				22 28	23 17	23 28
Woldingham	d	08 34	09 34	10 34				22 34		23 34
Upper Warlingham	d	08 37	09 37	10 37				22 37		23 37
Riddlesdown	d	08 41	09 41	10 41				22 41		23 41
Sanderstead	d	08 44	09 44	10 44				22 44		23 44
South Croydon 175	d									
East Croydon 175,177	a	08 49	09 49	10 49				22 49	23 29	23 49
Norwood Junction 175,177	a									
London Bridge ⊖175,177	a									
Clapham Junction 175,177	a	09 01	10 01	11 01				23 01		00 01
London Victoria ⊖175,177	a	09 08	10 08	11 08				23 08		00 08

Network Diagram for Tables 186, 188

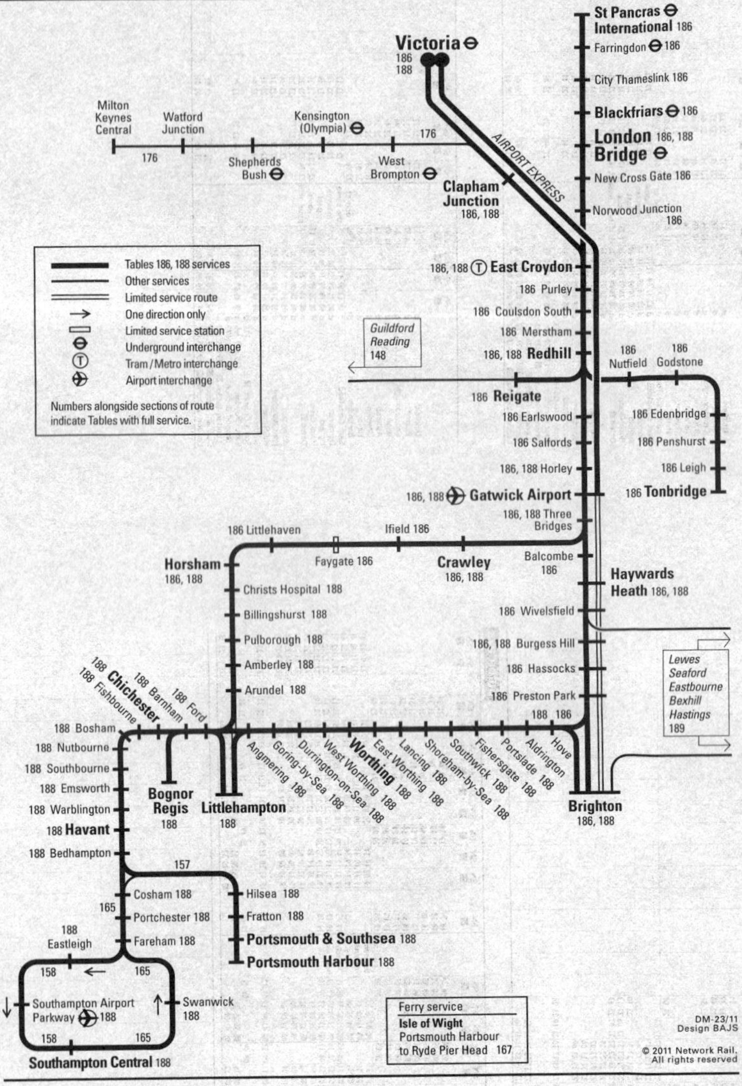

DM-23/11
Design BAJS

Table 186

Mondays to Fridays

until 18 May

Bedford and London - Brighton

Network Diagram - see first Page of Table 186

Miles	Miles	Miles	Station		SN	SN	FC	SN	SN	SN	SN	SN	GW	SN	FC	SN	SN	SN	SN	SN	FC	SN
					◇1	◇1	1	1	◇1	1	1	1	1	◇1	1	1	1	1	1	◇1		1
					A	A	A	A	A	A	A	A	A	A	A	A	A	A		A		
0	—	—	**London Victoria** 15 ⊖	d	23p02	23p06		23p10	23p17		23p30			23p32		23p45	23p47	23p49	00 02	00 05		00 14
2¾	50¾	6¼	Clapham Junction 10	d	23p08	23p12		23p16	23p23					23p38			23p53	23p56		00 11		00 20
—	—	—	**Bedford**	d																		
—	—	—	Luton 10	d																		
—	—	—	Luton Airport Parkway 7 ✈	d																		
—	—	—	St Albans City	d																		
—	—	—	St Pancras International 15 ⊖	d																		
—	—	—	Farringdon 3 ⊖	d																		
—	—	—	City Thameslink 3	d																		
—	—	—	**London Blackfriars** 3 ⊖	d																		
—	0	—	**London Bridge** 4 ⊖	d			23p12								23p42						00 12	
—	—	—	New Cross Gate	d																		
—	9	—	Norwood Junction 2	d																		
10½	10¼	—	**East Croydon**	a	23p19	23p22	23p24	23p27	23p33					23p51	23p56		00 05	00 09		00 26	00 26	00 31
—	—	—		d	23p20	23p23	23p25	23p28	23p33					23p52	23p57		00 06			00 27	00 27	00 32
13½	—	—	Purley 4	d				23p33									00 12					00 37
15½	—	—	Coulsdon South	d				23p37									00 15					00 41
19	—	—	Merstham	d				23p42									00 21					00 47
21	0	0	**Redhill**	a	23p31			23p46						00 03			00 24					00 50
—	—	—		d	23p31			23p46				23p55	00 01	00 05			00 25					00 51
—	1¾	—	**Reigate**	a																		
—	—	2	Nutfield	d																		
—	—	5¾	Godstone	d																		
—	—	10½	Edenbridge	d								00 06										
—	—	15½	Penshurst	d																		
—	—	17¼	Leigh (Kent)	d																		
—	—	19¾	**Tonbridge** 4	a								00 15										
21¾	—	—	Earlswood (Surrey)	d				23p49														
23¾	—	—	Salfords	d				23p52														
26	—	—	Horley 4	d				23p56		←							00 31					00 57
26¾	—	—	**Gatwick Airport** 10 ✈	a	23p38		23p40	23p58	23p50	23p58	00 05		00 11	00 14	00 18	00 20	00 33		00 37	00 43	00 48	00 59
—	—	—		d	23p39		23p41	23p59	23p51	23p59				00 15	00 19		00 34			00 44	00 49	
29½	0	—	Three Bridges 15	a	23p44		23p47	→	23p55	00 04				00 20	00 24		00 39			00 48	00 54	
—	—	—		d	23p44		23p47		23p56	00 04				00 20			00 39			00 49		
—	1½	—	Crawley	d						00 07							00 43					
—	2¾	—	Ifield	d						00 10							00 46					
—	5¼	—	Faygate	d																		
—	7½	—	Littlehaven	d						00 16							00 52					
—	8½	—	**Horsham** 4	a						00 19							00 55					
34	—	—	Balcombe	d			23p53							00 26								
38	—	—	**Haywards Heath**	a	23p53	23p46	23p58		00 05					00 31						00 58		
—	—	—		d	23p53	23p46	23p59		00 05					00 31						01 02 / 01 06		
41	0	—	Wivelsfield	d	23p57		00 03							00 35								
—	9¼	—	Lewes 4	a																01 20		
41¾	—	—	Burgess Hill 4	d	23p59		00 05		00 11					00 37								
43¾	—	—	Hassocks 4	d	00 03		00 08							00 41								
49½	0	—	Preston Park	d	00 09		00 15							00 48								
—	1½	—	Hove 2	a					00 21													
51	—	—	Brighton 10	a	00 15	00 01	00 19							00 52						01s16		

A not 14 May

Table 186

Bedford and London - Brighton

Mondays to Fridays

until 18 May

Network Diagram - see first Page of Table 186

		GW 1 A	SN 1		FC	SN ◇1	FC 1	FC 1	SN 1	FC 1	SN 1		FC	SN 1	FC 1	SN ◇1	FC 1	SN 1	FC 1		SN 1	SN 1	SN ◇1	SN 1	GW 1
London Victoria 15 ⊖	d		00 30			01 00			02 00		03 00			03 30		04 00		04 30			05 00		05 02	05 15	
Clapham unction 10	d					01 08			02 08		03 08					04 08							05 08		
Bedford	d																								
Lton 10	d																								
Lton Airport Parkway 7 ✈	d																								
St Albans City	d																								
St Pancras hternational 15 ⊖	d																								
Farringdon 3 ⊖	d																								
City Thameslink 3	d																								
London Blackfriars 3 ⊖	d																								
London Bridge 4 ⊖	d				00 42		01 08	01 35		02 05			03 05		03 35		04 05		04 35						
Nw Cross Gate	d																								
Nrwood unction 2	d																								
East Croydon	a				00 56	01 23	01 31	02 01	02 23	02 31	03 23		03 31		04 01	04 23	04 31		05 01				05 20		
	d				00 57	01 24	01 32	02 02	02 24	02 32	03 24		03 32		04 02	04 24	04 32		05 02				05 20		
Purley 4	d					01 29			02 29		03 29					04 29							05 25		
Coulsdon South	d																						05 28		
Merstham	d																						05 34		
Redhill	a																						05 37		
	d	00 54																				05 35	05 38		05 43
Reigate	a																								05 48
Ntfield	d																					05 39			
Godstone	d																					05 45			
Eenbridge	d																					05 50			
Penshurst	d																					05 57			
Ligh (Kent)	d																					06 00			
Tonbridge 4	a																					06 05			
Erlswood (Surrey)	d																								
Salfords	d																								
Horley 4	d					01 44			02 44		03 44					04 44							05 44		
Gatwick Airport 10 ✈	a	01 03	01 05		01 18	01 46	01 51	02 21	02 46	02 51	03 46		03 51	04 05	04 24	04 46	04 51	05 05	05 21		05 35		05 46	05 50	
	d				01 22	01 48	01 52	02 22	02 48	02 52	03 48		03 52		04 24	04 48	04 52		05 21				05 47		
Three Bridges 15	a				01 28	01 52	01 58	02 28	02 53	02 58	03 53		03 58		04 30	04 52	04 58		05 26				05 52		
	d					01 53										04 53	05 00		05 27				05 52		
Crawley	d																								
field	d																								
Faygate	d																								
Ittlehaven	d																								
Horsham 4	a																								
Balcombe	d																						05 58		
Haywards Heath	a					02 05										05 02	05 10		05 36				06 03		
	d					02 06										05 02	05 11		05 36				06 04		
Wivelsfield	d																		05 40				06 08		
Lewes 4	a																								
Burgess Hill 4	d																		05 43				06 10		
Hassocks 4	d																		05 46				06 13		
Preston Park	d																		05 53				06 20		
Hove 2	a																								
Brighton 10	a					02 23										05 18	05 29		05 57				06 26		

A not 14 May

Table 186

Mondays to Fridays

until 18 May

Bedford and London - Brighton

Network Diagram - see first Page of Table 186

		GW	SN	SN	FC	SN	SN	FC	SN	SN	FC	SN	GW	GW	GW	SN	SN		SN	FC	SN	SN
		1	1		1	1	1	1	◇1	1	1	1	1	1	1	1	◇1		1	1	◇1	1
												🛒							A 🛒			
London Victoria 15 ⊖	d						05 30		05 32	05 45		06 00					06 02		06 15			
Clapham Junction 10	d								05 38								06 08					
Bedford	d				03 42			04 08			04 20									05 00		
Luton 10	d				04 06			04 33			04 45									05 24		
Luton Airport Parkway 7 ✈	d				04 09			04 35			04 47									05 27		
St Albans City	d				04 21			04 47			04 59									05 39		
St Pancras International 15 ⊖	d				04 54			05 12			05 32									06 02		
Farringdon 3 ⊖	d				04 59			05 18			05 38									06 08		
City Thameslink 3	d							05 21			05 41									06 11		
London Blackfriars 3 ⊖	d				05 04			05 24			05 44									06 14		
London Bridge 4 ⊖	d							05 30			05 50									06 20		
New Cross Gate	d																					
Norwood Junction 2	d																					
East Croydon	a				05 29			05 47	05 48		06 05						06 17			06 33		
	d				05 32			05 47	05 49		06 05						06 18			06 35		
Purley 4	d								05 53								06 23					
Coulsdon South	d								05 57								06 26					
Merstham	d								06 02								06 32					
Redhill	a								06 06								06 35					
	d	05 44	05 56						06 06				06 13	06 24	06 33	06 39	06 39	06 41				
Reigate	a												06 18	06 28		06 43						
Nutfield	d		06 00															06 45				
Godstone	d		06 06															06 51				
Edenbridge	d		06 11															06 56				
Penshurst	d		06 18															07 03				
Leigh (Kent)	d		06 21															07 06				
Tonbridge 4	a		06 26															07 11				
Earlswood (Surrey)	d								06 09								06 41					
Salfords	d								06 12								06 45					
Horley 4	d								06 16								06 48				←	
Gatwick Airport 10 ✈	a	05 54			05 53		06 00	06 02	06 18	06 15	06 21	06 30			06 40		06 54		06 45	06 51	06 54	
	d				05 54	05 56		06 04	06 20		06 22						06 55		06 48	06 52	06 55	
Three Bridges 15	a				05 59	06 00		06 08	06 24		06 26						→			06 56	06 59	
	d				06 00	06 01		06 08	06 25		06 26									06 56	07 00	07 05
Crawley	d					06 05															07 03	07 08
Ifield	d					06 07																07 11
Faygate	d																					07 15
Littlehaven	d					06 14																07 19
Horsham 4	a					06 17															07 11	07 22
Balcombe	d							06 14			06 33											
Haywards Heath	a				06 09			06 19	06 34		06 39								06 58	07 05		
	d			06 07	06 11			06 19	06 34		06 39								07 00	07 06		
Wivelsfield	d			06 11				06 23	06 38		06 43									07 10		
Lewes 4	a			06 22					06 50													
Burgess Hill 4	d				06 16			06 25			06 45									07 12		
Hassocks 4	d				06 20			06 29			06 49									07 16		
Preston Park	d				06 27			06 35			06 55									07 22		
Hove 2	a																					
Brighton 10	a				06 31			06 40			06 59								07 13	07 27		

A 1 from Gatwick Airport 🛒 to Gatwick Airport

Table 186

Mondays to Fridays

until 18 May

Bedford and London - Brighton

Network Diagram - see first Page of Table 186

		SN	SN	SN	SN	SN	GW	SN		FC	GW	SN	SN	SN	SN	SN		FC	SN	SN	GW	SN
		1	◇1	1	◇1	1	1	◇1		1	1	1	◇1	◇1	1	1		1	1	1	1	1
				A 🚌								🚌							🚌			
London Victoria 15 ⊖	d		06 21	06 30				06 32				06 45	06 47			06 51			07 00			07 02
Clapham Junction 10	d		06 27					06 38					06 53			06 57						07 08
Bedford	d									05 20								05 40				
Luton 10	d									05 44								06 04				
Luton Airport Parkway 7 ✈	d									05 46								06 06				
St Albans City	d									05 58								06 18				
St Pancras International 15 ⊖	d									06 22								06 38				
Farringdon 3 ⊖	d									06 28								06 44				
City Thameslink 3	d									06 31								06 47				
London Blackfriars 3 ⊖	d									06 34								06 50				
London Bridge 4 ⊖	d									06 42								07 00				
New Cross Gate	d																					
Norwood Junction 2	d																					
East Croydon	a		06 38					06 48		06 54			07 03			07 06		07 14				07 17
	d		06 38					06 49		06 55			07 04			07 07		07 15				07 18
Purley 4	d		06 43					06 55														07 23
Coulsdon South	d		06 47					06 58								07 13						07 26
Merstham	d		06 52					07 04								07 19						07 32
Redhill	a		06 56					07 08								07 23						07 35
	d		06 57			07 00	07 10	07 12	07 14		07 28					07 28	07 30				07 41	07 44
Reigate	a					07 04	07 15				07 32											07 48
Nutfield	d								07 18								07 34					
Godstone	d								07 24								07 40					
Edenbridge	d								07 29								07 45					
Penshurst	d								07 36								07 52					
Leigh (Kent)	d								07 39								07 55					
Tonbridge 4	a								07 44								08 02					
Earlswood (Surrey)	d							07 14								07 30						
Salfords	d							07 18								07 34						
Horley 4	d		07 03		←			07 21						←	←	07 37				←		
Gatwick Airport 10 ✈	a		07 05	06 59	07 05			07 24		07 10		07 16	07 19	07 24	07 16	07 40		07 30	07 31	07 40	07 50	
	d		07 06	07 04	07 06			07 25		07 11		07 25	07 20	07 25	07 25	07 41		07 31		07 41		
Three Bridges 15	a		→		07 11			→		07 15		→	07 24	07 29		→		07 35		07 45		
	d				07 11					07 15			07 24	07 30				07 35		07 46		
Crawley	d													07 34						07 50		
Ifield	d													07 36						07 53		
Faygate	d																					
Littlehaven	d													07 43						07 59		
Horsham 4	a													07 46						08 02		
Balcombe	d									07 21												
Haywards Heath	a			07 14	07 20					07 26			07 33					07 44				
	d	07 10		07 16	07 21					07 26			07 33					07 46				
Wivelsfield	d	07 14			07 25								07 37					07 50				
Lewes 4	a	07 29											07 52									
Burgess Hill 4	d				07 27					07 31								07 52				
Hassocks 4	d				07 30					07 35								07 55				
Preston Park	d				07 37													08 02				
Hove 2	a																					
Brighton 10	a			07 35	07 41					07 44					07 53			08 06				

A 🚌 to Gatwick Airport

Table 186

Mondays to Fridays

until 18 May

Bedford and London - Brighton

Network Diagram - see first Page of Table 186

		SN 1	FC 1	SN ◇1		SN 1	SN 1	SN 1	SN 1	GW 1	SN 1	FC 1		SN 1	SN ◇1	SN 1	SN 1	SN 1		SN ◇1		SN 1	SN 1	SN ◇1	GW 1
London Victoria 15 ⊖	d	07 15		07 17		07 30					07 36			07 45	07 47					07 52			08 00	08 02	
Clapham unction 10	d			07 23							07 42				07 53					07 58				08 08	
Bedford	d		05 58									06 22													
Luton 10	d		06 22									06 46													
Luton Airport Parkway 7 ✈	d		06 24									06 48													
St Albans City	d		06 36									07 00													
St Pancras hternational 15 ⊖	d		06 58									07 20													
Farringdon 3 ⊖	d		07 04									07 26													
City Thameslink 3	d		07 07									07 29													
London Blackfriars 3 ⊖	d		07 09									07 32													
London Bridge 4 ⊖	d		07 16					07 30	07 33			07 42						07 53							
New Cross Gate	d								07 38																
Norwood unction 2	d							07 42																	
East Croydon	a		07 30	07 33				07 45	07 48		07 51	07 54			08 02			08 05		08 09				08 18	
	d		07 31	07 34				07 46	07 49		07 52	07 55			08 03			08 06		08 09				08 18	
Purley 4	d										07 57														
Coulsdon South	d							07 52			08 01														
Merstham	d							07 58			08 07														
Redhill	a			07 47				08 01			08 10							08 18						08 30	
	d			07 47			08 00	08 02		08 08	08 11						08 17	08 22	08 24					08 30	08 33
Reigate	a						08 04			08 13							08 21								08 37
Oxted	d							08 06											08 28						
Godstone	d							08 12											08 34						
Edenbridge	d							08 17											08 39						
Penshurst	d							08 24											08 46						
Leigh (Kent)	d							08 27											08 49						
Tonbridge 4	a							08 32											08 54						
Earlswood (Surrey)	d			07 50							08 13														
Salfords	d			07 53							08 17														
Horley 4	d			07 57							08 21					←						←			
Gatwick Airport 10 ✈	a	07 45	07 46	07 59		08 02			08 03		08 23	08 11		08 15	08 18	08 23		08 29		08 24		08 29	08 31	08 37	
	d		07 47	08 00					08 05		08 24	08 12			08 20	08 24		08 30		08 26		08 30		08 40	
Three Bridges 15	a		07 51	08 05					08 09		→	08 16				08 29		→				08 34		08 44	
	d		07 51	08 05					08 09			08 16				08 30						08 35		08 45	
Crawley	d			08 09												08 34								08 48	
field	d			08 11												08 36									
Faygate	d			08 15												08 40									
Littlehaven	d			08 19												08 44									
Horsham 4	a			08 22												08 48									
Balcombe	d		07 57									08 22												08 56	
Haywards Heath	a		08 02						08 18			08 27			08 30					08 36		08 44			
	d		08 02						08 19			08 27			08 31					08 37		08 44			
Wivelsfield	d		08 06									08 31			08 35							08 48			
Lewes 4	a														08 50										
Burgess Hill 4	d		08 08						08 24			08 33										08 50			
Hassocks 4	d		08 12									08 37										08 54			
Preston Park	d		08 18									08 43										09 00			
Hove 2	a																			08 53					
Brighton 10	a		08 23						08 36			08 48										09 05			

Table 186

Mondays to Fridays

until 18 May

Bedford and London - Brighton

Network Diagram - see first Page of Table 186

		SN	SN	FC	SN	SN		FC	SN	GW	SN		SN	SN	SN	SN	SN	FC	SN	SN	SN	
		1	◇1	1	1	◇1		1	1	1	1		◇1	1	◇1	1	◇1	1	1	1	◇1	
					⚲									⚲	⚲		⚲		⚲		⚲	
London Victoria 15 ⊖	d		08 07		08 15	08 17							08 21	08 30	08 32		08 36		08 45		08 47	
Clapham Junction 10	d		08 13			08 23							08 27		08 38		08 43				08 53	
Bedford	d			06 54				06 58										07 30				
Luton 10	d			07 14				07 22										07 50				
Luton Airport Parkway 7 ✈	d							07 25														
St Albans City	d			07 26				07 38										08 02				
St Pancras International 15 ⊖	d			07 44				07 56										08 20				
Farringdon 3 ⊖	d			07 50				08 02										08 26				
City Thameslink 3	d			07 53				08 05										08 29				
London Blackfriars 3 ⊖	d			07 56				08 08										08 32				
London Bridge 4 ⊖	d	08 00						08 18			08 23					08 30				08 45		
New Cross Gate	d	08 08														08 36						
Norwood Junction 2	d	08 16														08 44				08 56		
East Croydon 🚋	a	08 20	08 22	08 26		08 34		08 37			08 37		08 40		08 48	08 48	08 52	08 57		08 59	09 03	
	d	08 20	08 23	08 26		08 34		08 37			08 38		08 40		08 48	08 51	08 53	08 58		09 00	09 04	
Purley 4	d	08 26														08 59				09 06		
Coulsdon South	d	08 29									08 47					09 02				09 09		
Merstham	d	08 35														09 08						
Redhill	a	08 38									08 54				09 02	09 12				09 17		
	d	08 41								08 50	08 58	09 00			09 03	09 12				09 17		
Reigate	a											09 04										
Nutfield	d										09 02									09 22		
Godstone	d										09 08									09 27		
Edenbridge	d										09 13									09 33		
Penshurst	d										09 20									09 39		
Leigh (Kent)	d										09 23									09 43		
Tonbridge 4	a										09 28									09 48		
Earlswood (Surrey)	d	08 43														09 15						
Salfords	d	08 47														09 18						
Horley 4	d	08 50							←							09 22						
Gatwick Airport 10 ✈	a	08 53		08 41	08 45	08 49		08 52	08 53	08 59			08 56	09 00	09 10	09 24		09 12	09 15		09 18	
	d	08 54		08 42		08 50		08 53	08 54				08 57		09 11	09 25		09 13			09 20	
Three Bridges 15	a	↦	08 41	08 46				08 57	08 59				09 01		09 16	↦		09 17				
	d		08 42	08 46				08 58	08 59				09 01		09 16			09 17				
Crawley	d								09 03						09 19							
Ifield	d								09 06													
Faygate	d								09 10													
Littlehaven	d								09 14													
Horsham 4	a								09 17						09 27							
Balcombe	d			08 52																		
Haywards Heath	a		08 51	08 57		09 00		09 07					09 12					09 26			09 30	
	d		08 51	08 58		09 04	09 10	09 08					09 21					09 27			09 35	09 37
Wivelsfield	d			09 02			09 14						09 25									
Lewes 4	a						09 25														09 53	
Burgess Hill 4	d			09 04		09 09		09 13					09 27					09 32				
Hassocks 4	d			09 07									09 30					09 35				
Preston Park	d			09 14		09 18							09 37					09 42				
Hove 2	a					09 21																09 53
Brighton 10	a		09 08	09 18				09 25					09 41				09 28	09 46				

Bedford and London - Brighton

Network Diagram - see first Page of Table 186

		SN	SN	SN	SN	GW	SN	GW	SN	SN	FC	SN	GW	SN	SN		SN	FC	SN	SN	SN	SN
		◇1	1	1		1	◇1	1	1	◇1	1	1	1	1	◇1		1	1	1	◇1	1	◇1
															A							
				🛒			🛒			🛒		🛒			🛒				🛒	🛒		
London Victoria 15 ⊖	d	08 51		09 00	09 01		09 02			09 06		09 15			09 17				09 30	09 32		09 36
Clapham Junction 10	d				09 08		09 08			09 12					09 23					09 38		09 42
Bedford	d										07 48							08 04				
Luton 10	d										08 12							08 28				
Luton Airport Parkway 7 ✈	d										08 15							08 30				
St Albans City	d										08 27							08 44				
St Pancras International 15 ⊖	d										08 48							09 04				
Farringdon 3 ⊖	d										08 54							09 10				
City Thameslink 3	d										08 57							09 13				
London Blackfriars 3 ⊖	d										09 00							09 16				
London Bridge 4 ⊖	d								09 03		09 12			09 15				09 27			09 32	
New Cross Gate	d								09 08												09 37	
Norwood Junction 2	d								09 16					09 26							09 45	
East Croydon	a	09 07					09 18		09 20	09 22	09 24			09 29	09 32			09 39		09 48	09 49	09 52
	d	09 08					09 19		09 21	09 23	09 25			09 30	09 33			09 41		09 48	09 51	09 53
Purley 4	d								09 27					09 36							09 57	
Coulsdon South	d								09 30					09 39							10 00	
Merstham	d								09 36					09 45							10 06	
Redhill	a						09 30		09 39					09 49						10 00	10 09	
	d					09 23	09 30	09 34	09 40				09 51	09 53						10 00	10 10	
Reigate	a					09 28		09 38						09 57								
Nutfield	d																					
Godstone	d																					
Edenbridge	d																					
Penshurst	d																					
Leigh (Kent)	d																					
Tonbridge 4	a																					
Earlswood (Surrey)	d								09 42												10 12	
Salfords	d								09 46												10 16	
Horley 4	d		←				09 36		09 50								←				10 19	
Gatwick Airport 10 ✈	a	09 22	09 24	09 30			09 39		09 53		09 40	09 45	09 59		09 48		09 53	09 56	10 00	10 08	10 23	
	d	09 23	09 25				09 40		09 54		09 41				09 50		09 54	09 57		10 09	10 24	
Three Bridges 15	a		09 30				09 44		→		09 45						09 59	10 01		10 14	→	
	d		09 30				09 45				09 45						10 00	10 02		10 14		
Crawley	d		09 34				09 48										10 03			10 18		
Ifield	d		09 36														10 06					
Faygate	d																					
Littlehaven	d		09 43														10 12					
Horsham 4	a		09 46				09 56										10 15			10 26		
Balcombe	d										09 51											
Haywards Heath	a										09 56				10 00			10 11				
	d										09 56				10 05	10 07		10 11				
Wivelsfield	d										10 00					10 11						
Lewes 4	a															10 22						
Burgess Hill 4	d	09 38									10 02				10 10							
Hassocks 4	d	09 41									10 06											
Preston Park	d										10 12				10 18							
Hove 2	a														10 22							
Brighton 10	a	09 52								09 58	10 17							10 25				10 28

A 🛒 to Haywards Heath

Table 186

Mondays to Fridays

until 18 May

Bedford and London - Brighton

Network Diagram - see first Page of Table 186

		FC	SN	GW	SN		SN		SN	SN	FC	SN	SN		SN	GW	GW	SN	SN	FC	SN		SN	SN	
		1	1	1	1		◇1		◇1	1	1	1			◇1	1	1	1	◇1	1	1		1	◇1	
																								A	
			trolley				trolley					trolley			trolley				trolley		trolley			trolley	
London Victoria 15 ⊖	d		09 45				09 47		09 51			10 00	10 01		10 02				10 06		10 15			10 17	
Clapham Junction 10	d						09 53						10 08		10 08				10 12					10 23	
Bedford	d	08 24									08 40									08 54					
Luton 10	d	08 48									09 04									09 18					
Luton Airport Parkway 7 ✈	d	08 50									09 06									09 20					
St Albans City	d	09 02									09 18									09 32					
St Pancras International 15 ⊖	d	09 22									09 40									09 54					
Farringdon 3 ⊖	d	09 28									09 45									09 59					
City Thameslink 3	d	09 31									09 48									10 03					
London Blackfriars 3 ⊖	d	09 34									09 50									10 05					
London Bridge 4 ⊖	d	09 42			09 45						09 57							10 03		10 12			10 15		
New Cross Gate	d																	10 08							
Norwood Junction 2	d				09 56													10 16					10 26		
East Croydon 🚌	a	09 54			09 59		10 02		10 07		10 09				10 17			10 20	10 22	10 24			10 29	10 32	
	d	09 55			10 00		10 03		10 08		10 11				10 18			10 21	10 23	10 25			10 30	10 33	
Purley 4	d				10 06													10 26					10 36		
Coulsdon South	d				10 09													10 30					10 39		
Merstham	d																	10 35					10 45		
Redhill	a				10 17										10 30			10 39					10 49		
	d			10 13	10 17										10 30	10 34	10 41	10 45					10 52		
Reigate	a			10 18												10 38							10 56		
Nutfield	d				10 22																				
Godstone	d				10 27																				
Edenbridge	d				10 33																				
Penshurst	d				10 39																				
Leigh (Kent)	d				10 43																				
Tonbridge 4	a				10 48																				
Earlswood (Surrey)	d																								
Salfords	d																								
Horley 4	d									←					10 36			10 53							
Gatwick Airport 10 ✈	a	10 10	10 15				10 18		10 22	10 23	10 26	10 30			10 39		10 50	10 55		10 40	10 45			10 48	
	d	10 11					10 20		10 23	10 24	10 27				10 40			10 56		10 41				10 50	
Three Bridges 15	a	10 15								10 29	10 31				10 44			→		10 45					
	d	10 15								10 30	10 32				10 45					10 45					
Crawley	d									10 33					10 48										
Ifield	d									10 36															
Faygate	d																								
Littlehaven	d									10 42															
Horsham 4	a									10 47					10 56										
Balcombe	d	10 21																							
Haywards Heath	a	10 26					10 30				10 41									10 54				11 00	
	d	10 27					10 35	10 37			10 41									10 55				11 04	11 07
Wivelsfield	d	10 31																		10 59					11 11
Lewes 4	a						10 52																		11 22
Burgess Hill 4	d	10 33							10 38											11 01				11 09	
Hassocks 4	d	10 36							10 41											11 04					
Preston Park	d	10 43																		11 11				11 18	
Hove 2	a							10 53																11 22	
Brighton 10	a	10 47							10 52		10 55								10 58	11 15					

A trolley to Haywards Heath

Table 186

Bedford and London - Brighton

Mondays to Fridays

until 18 May

Network Diagram - see first Page of Table 186

		SN	FC	SN	SN		SN	SN	FC	SN	GW	SN	SN			SN	SN	FC	SN	SN	SN	GW		GW	SN
		1	1	1	◇1		1	◇1	1	1	1	1	◇1			◇1	1	1	1		◇1	1		1	1
				✠	✠					✠			✠						✠						
London Victoria 15 ⊖	d			10 30	10 32			10 36		10 45			10 47			10 51			11 00	11 01	11 02				
Clapham Junction 10	d				10 38			10 42					10 53							11 08	11 08				
Bedford	d		09 10						09 24									09 40							
Luton 10	d		09 34						09 48									10 04							
Luton Airport Parkway 7 ✈	d		09 36						09 50									10 06							
St Albans City	d		09 48						10 02									10 18							
St Pancras International 15 ⊖	d		10 09						10 24									10 39							
Farringdon 3 ⊖	d		10 14						10 29									10 44							
City Thameslink 3	d		10 18						10 33									10 48							
London Blackfriars 3 ⊖	d		10 20						10 35									10 50							
London Bridge 4 ⊖	d		10 27				10 33		10 42			10 45						10 57							11 03
New Cross Gate	d						10 38																		11 08
Norwood Junction 2	d						10 46					10 56													11 16
East Croydon 🚋	a		10 39		10 48		10 50	10 52	10 54			10 59	11 02			11 07		11 09			11 17				11 20
	d		10 41		10 48		10 51	10 53	10 55			11 00	11 03			11 08		11 11			11 18				11 21
Purley 4	d						10 57					11 07													11 27
Coulsdon South	d						11 00					11 10													11 30
Merstham	d						11 06																		11 36
Redhill	a				11 00		11 09					11 18									11 30				11 39
	d				11 00		11 10				11 13	11 18									11 30	11 34		11 41	11 45
Reigate	a										11 18											11 38			
Nutfield	d											11 23													
Godstone	d											11 28													
Edenbridge	d											11 34													
Penshurst	d											11 40													
Leigh (Kent)	d											11 44													
Tonbridge 4	a											11 48													
Earlswood (Surrey)	d						11 12																		
Salfords	d						11 16																		
Horley 4	d	←					11 19										←				11 36				11 53
Gatwick Airport 10 ✈	a	10 55	10 56	11 00	11 08		11 23		11 10	11 15			11 18			11 22	11 23	11 26	11 30		11 39			11 50	11 55
	d	10 56	10 57		11 09		11 24		11 11				11 20			11 23	11 24	11 27			11 40				11 56
Three Bridges 15	a	11 01	11 01		11 14		→		11 15								11 29	11 31			11 44				→
	d	11 01	11 02		11 14				11 15								11 30	11 32			11 45				
Crawley	d	11 05			11 18												11 33				11 48				
Ifield	d	11 07															11 36								
Faygate	d																								
Littlehaven	d	11 14															11 42								
Horsham 4	a	11 17			11 26												11 45				11 56				
Balcombe	d								11 21																
Haywards Heath	a		11 11						11 26				11 30					11 41							
	d		11 11						11 27				11 35	11 37				11 41							
Wivelsfield	d								11 31																
Lewes 4	a												11 52												
Burgess Hill 4	d								11 33							11 38									
Hassocks 4	d								11 36							11 41									
Preston Park	d								11 43																
Hove 2	a													11 53											
Brighton 10	a		11 25					11 28	11 47							11 52		11 55							

Table 186

Mondays to Fridays

until 18 May

Bedford and London - Brighton

Network Diagram - see first Page of Table 186

		SN	FC	SN	SN	SN			SN	FC	SN	SN	SN	SN	FC		SN	GW	SN	SN		SN	SN		FC
		◇1	1	1	1	◇1			1	1	1	◇1	1	◇1	1		1	1	1	◇1		◇1	1		1
				🚲							🚲			🚲			🚲								
London Victoria [15] ⊖	d	11 06		11 15		11 17					11 30	11 32		11 36			11 45			11 47		11 51			
Clapham Junction [10]	d	11 12				11 23						11 38		11 42						11 53					
Bedford	d		09 54							10 10					10 25										10 40
Luton [10]	d		10 18							10 34					10 49										11 04
Luton Airport Parkway [7] ✈	d		10 20							10 36					10 51										11 06
St Albans City	d		10 32							10 48					11 03										11 18
St Pancras International [15] ⊖	d		10 54							11 09					11 24										11 39
Farringdon [3] ⊖	d		10 59							11 14					11 29										11 44
City Thameslink [3]	d		11 03							11 18					11 33										11 48
London Blackfriars [3] ⊖	d		11 05							11 20					11 35										11 50
London Bridge [4] ⊖	d		11 12		11 15					11 27			11 33		11 42				11 45						11 57
New Cross Gate	d												11 38												
Norwood Junction [2]	d				11 26								11 46						11 56						
East Croydon ⇌	a	11 22	11 24		11 29	11 32				11 39		11 48	11 50	11 52	11 54				11 59	12 02		12 07			12 09
	d	11 23	11 25		11 30	11 33				11 41		11 48	11 51	11 53	11 55				12 00	12 03		12 08			12 11
Purley [4]	d				11 36								11 57						12 06						
Coulsdon South	d				11 39								12 00						12 09						
Merstham	d				11 45								12 06												
Redhill	a				11 49							12 00	12 09						12 17						
	d				11 52							12 00	12 10					12 13	12 17						
Reigate	a				11 56													12 18							
Nutfield	d																		12 22						
Godstone	d																		12 27						
Edenbridge	d																		12 33						
Penshurst	d																		12 39						
Leigh (Kent)	d																		12 43						
Tonbridge [4]	a																		12 48						
Earlswood (Surrey)	d												12 12												
Salfords	d												12 16												
Horley [4]	d								←				12 19										←		
Gatwick Airport [10] ✈	a		11 40	11 45		11 48			11 55	11 56	12 00	12 08	12 23		12 10		12 15			12 18		12 22	12 23		12 26
	d		11 41			11 50			11 56	11 57		12 09	12 24		12 11					12 20		12 23	12 24		12 27
Three Bridges [15]	a		11 45						12 01	12 01		12 14	→		12 15								12 29		12 31
	d		11 45						12 01	12 02		12 14			12 15								12 30		12 32
Crawley	d								12 05			12 18											12 33		
Ifield	d								12 07														12 36		
Faygate	d								12 11																
Littlehaven	d								12 15														12 42		
Horsham [4]	a								12 18			12 26											12 45		
Balcombe	d														12 21										
Haywards Heath	a		11 54			12 00				12 11					12 26					12 30					12 41
	d		11 55			12 04	12 07			12 11					12 27					12 35	12 37				12 41
Wivelsfield	d		11 59				12 11								12 31										
Lewes [4]	a						12 22													12 52					
Burgess Hill [4]	d		12 01			12 09									12 33							12 38			
Hassocks [4]	d		12 04												12 36							12 41			
Preston Park	d		12 11			12 18									12 43										
Hove [2]	a					12 22															12 53				
Brighton [10]	a	11 58	12 15							12 25				12 28	12 47							12 52			12 55

Table 186

Mondays to Fridays

until 18 May

Bedford and London - Brighton

Network Diagram - see first Page of Table 186

		SN 1 🚲	SN	SN ◇1	GW 1	GW 1	SN 1		SN ◇1 🚲	FC 1	SN 1 🚲	SN 1	SN ◇1		SN 1		FC 1	SN 1 🚲	SN ◇1	SN 1	SN ◇1 🚲	FC 1	SN 1 🚲		GW 1
London Victoria 15 ⊖	d	12 00	12 01	12 02					12 06		12 15		12 17					12 30	12 32		12 36		12 45		
Clapham Junction 10	d		12 08	12 08					12 12				12 23						12 38		12 42				
Bedford	d									10 54							11 10					11 24			
Luton 10	d									11 18							11 34					11 48			
Luton Airport Parkway 7 ✈	d									11 20							11 36					11 50			
St Albans City	d									11 32							11 48					12 02			
St Pancras International 15 ⊖	d									11 54							12 09					12 24			
Farringdon 3 ⊖	d									11 59							12 14					12 29			
City Thameslink 3	d									12 03							12 18					12 33			
London Blackfriars 3 ⊖	d									12 05							12 20					12 35			
London Bridge 4 ⊖	d						12 03			12 12		12 15					12 27			12 33		12 42			
New Cross Gate	d						12 08													12 38					
Norwood Junction 2	d						12 16					12 26								12 46					
East Croydon 🚌	a			12 17			12 20		12 22	12 24		12 29	12 32				12 39		12 48	12 50	12 52	12 54			
	d			12 18			12 21		12 23	12 25		12 30	12 33				12 41		12 48	12 51	12 53	12 55			
Purley 4	d						12 27					12 36								12 58					
Coulsdon South	d						12 30					12 39								13 01					
Merstham	d						12 36					12 45								13 07					
Redhill	a			12 30			12 39					12 49							13 00	13 10					
	d			12 30	12 34	12 41	12 45					12 52							13 00	13 11					13 13
Reigate	a				12 38							12 56													13 18
Nutfield	d																								
Godstone	d																								
Edenbridge	d																								
Penshurst	d																								
Leigh (Kent)	d																								
Tonbridge 4	a																								
Earlswood (Surrey)	d																			13 13					
Salfords	d																			13 17					
Horley 4	d			12 36			12 53								←					13 20					
Gatwick Airport 10 ✈	a	12 30		12 39		12 50	12 55			12 40	12 45		12 48		12 55		12 56	13 00	13 08	13 23		13 10	13 15		
	d			12 40			12 56			12 41			12 50		12 56		12 57		13 09	13 24		13 11			
Three Bridges 15	a			12 44			→			12 45					13 01		13 01		13 14	→		13 15			
	d			12 45						12 45					13 01		13 02		13 14			13 15			
Crawley	d			12 48											13 05				13 18						
Ifield	d														13 07										
Faygate	d																								
Littlehaven	d														13 14										
Horsham 4	a			12 56											13 17				13 26						
Balcombe	d																					13 21			
Haywards Heath	a									12 54			13 00				13 11					13 26			
	d									12 55			13 04	13 07			13 11					13 27			
Wivelsfield	d									12 59				13 11								13 31			
Lewes 4	a													13 22											
Burgess Hill 4	d									13 01			13 09									13 33			
Hassocks 4	d									13 04												13 36			
Preston Park	d									13 11			13 18									13 43			
Hove 2	a												13 22												
Brighton 10	a								12 58	13 15							13 25				13 28	13 47			

Bedford and London - Brighton

Network Diagram - see first Page of Table 186

Station		SN	SN		SN	SN	FC	SN	SN	SN	GW	GW	SN	SN	FC	SN	SN	SN		SN	FC	SN
		■1	◇■1		◇■1	■1	■1	■1	■1	◇■1	■1	■1	■1	◇■1	■1	■1	■1	◇■1		■1	■1	■1
								🚲						🚲		🚲						🚲
London Victoria ■15 ⊖	d		12 47		12 51			13 00	13 01	13 02				13 06		13 15		13 17				13 30
Clapham Junction ■10	d		12 53						13 08	13 08				13 12				13 23				
Bedford	d						11 40								11 54						12 10	
Luton ■10	d						12 04								12 18						12 34	
Luton Airport Parkway ■7 ✈	d						12 06								12 20						12 36	
St Albans City	d						12 18								12 32						12 48	
St Pancras International ■15 ⊖	d						12 39								12 54						13 09	
Farringdon ■3 ⊖	d						12 44								12 59						13 14	
City Thameslink ■3	d						12 48								13 03						13 18	
London Blackfriars ■3 ⊖	d						12 50								13 05						13 20	
London Bridge ■4 ⊖	d	12 45					12 57						13 03		13 12		13 15				13 27	
New Cross Gate	d												13 08									
Norwood Junction ■2	d	12 56											13 16				13 26					
East Croydon	a	12 59	13 02		13 07		13 09			13 17			13 20	13 22	13 24		13 29	13 32			13 39	
	d	13 00	13 03		13 08		13 11			13 18			13 21	13 23	13 25		13 30	13 33			13 41	
Purley ■4	d	13 06											13 27				13 36					
Coulsdon South	d	13 09											13 30				13 39					
Merstham	d												13 36				13 45					
Redhill	a	13 17								13 30			13 39				13 49					
	d	13 17								13 30	13 34	13 41	13 45				13 52					
Reigate	a										13 38						13 56					
Nutfield	d	13 22																				
Godstone	d	13 27																				
Penbridge	d	13 33																				
Penshurst	d	13 39																				
Leigh (Kent)	d	13 43																				
Tonbridge ■4	a	13 48																				
Earlswood (Surrey)	d																					
Salfords	d																					
Horley ■4	d					←				13 36			13 53							←		
Gatwick Airport ■10 ✈	a		13 18		13 22	13 23	13 26	13 30		13 39		13 50	13 55		13 40	13 45		13 48		13 55	13 56	14 00
	d		13 20		13 23	13 24	13 27			13 40			13 56		13 41			13 50		13 56	13 57	
Three Bridges ■15	a					13 29	13 31			13 44			→		13 45					14 01	14 01	
	d					13 30	13 32			13 45					13 45					14 01	14 02	
Crawley	d					13 33				13 48										14 05		
Ifield	d					13 36														14 07		
Faygate	d																					
Littlehaven	d					13 42														14 14		
Horsham ■4	a					13 45				13 56										14 17		
Balcombe	d																					
Haywards Heath	a		13 30				13 41								13 54			14 00			14 11	
	d		13 35	13 37			13 41								13 55			14 04	14 07		14 11	
Wivelsfield	d														13 59				14 11			
Lewes ■4	a		13 52																14 22			
Burgess Hill ■4	d				13 38										14 01			14 09				
Hassocks ■4	d				13 41										14 04							
Preston Park	d														14 11			14 18				
Hove ■2	a			13 53														14 22				
Brighton ■10	a				13 52		13 55							13 58	14 15						14 25	

Table 186

Mondays to Fridays

until 18 May

Bedford and London - Brighton

Network Diagram - see first Page of Table 186

		SN ◇1 🚲	SN 1	SN ◇1 🚲	FC 1	SN 1 🚲	GW 1		SN 1	SN ◇1		SN ◇1	SN 1	FC 1	SN 1 🚲		SN	SN ◇1	GW 1	GW 1	SN 1	SN ◇1 🚲	FC 1		SN 1 🚲
London Victoria 15 ⊖	d	13 32		13 36		13 45				13 47		13 51			14 00		14 01	14 02				14 06			14 15
Clapham Junction 10	d	13 38		13 42						13 53							14 08	14 08				14 12			
Bedford	d				12 24									12 40									12 54		
Luton 10	d				12 48									13 04									13 18		
Luton Airport Parkway 7 ✈	d				12 50									13 06									13 20		
St Albans City	d				13 02									13 18									13 32		
St Pancras International 15 ⊖	d				13 24									13 39									13 54		
Farringdon 3 ⊖	d				13 29									13 44									13 59		
City Thameslink 3	d				13 33									13 48									14 03		
London Blackfriars 3 ⊖	d				13 35									13 50									14 05		
London Bridge 4 ⊖	d		13 33		13 42				13 45					13 57							14 03		14 12		
New Cross Gate	d		13 38																		14 08				
Norwood Junction 2	d		13 46						13 56												14 16				
East Croydon ⇌	a	13 48	13 50	13 52	13 54				13 59	14 02		14 07		14 09				14 17			14 20	14 22	14 25		
	d	13 48	13 51	13 53	13 55				14 00	14 03		14 08		14 11				14 18			14 21	14 23	14 25		
Purley 4	d		13 57						14 06												14 27				
Coulsdon South	d		14 00						14 09												14 30				
Merstham	d		14 06																		14 36				
Redhill	a	14 00	14 09						14 17									14 30			14 39				
	d	14 00	14 10				14 13		14 17									14 30	14 34	14 41	14 45				
Reigate	a						14 18												14 38						
Nutfield	d								14 22																
Godstone	d								14 27																
Edenbridge	d								14 33																
Penshurst	d								14 39																
Leigh (Kent)	d								14 43																
Tonbridge 4	a								14 48																
Earlswood (Surrey)	d		14 12																						
Salfords	d		14 16																						
Horley 4	d		14 19										←					14 36			14 53				
Gatwick Airport 10 ✈	a	14 08	14 23		14 10	14 15				14 18		14 22	14 23	14 26	14 30			14 39		14 50	14 55		14 40		14 45
	d	14 09	14 24		14 11					14 20		14 23	14 24	14 27				14 40			14 56		14 41		
Three Bridges 15	a	14 14	→		14 15								14 29	14 31				14 44			→		14 45		
	d	14 14			14 15								14 30	14 32				14 45					14 45		
Crawley	d	14 18											14 33					14 48							
Ifield	d												14 36												
Faygate	d																								
Littlehaven	d												14 42												
Horsham 4	a	14 26											14 45					14 56							
Balcombe	d				14 21																				
Haywards Heath	a				14 26					14 30				14 41									14 54		
	d				14 27					14 35	14 37			14 41									14 55		
Wivelsfield	d				14 31																		14 59		
Lewes 4	a									14 52															
Burgess Hill 4	d				14 33							14 38											15 01		
Hassocks 4	d				14 36							14 41											15 04		
Preston Park	d				14 43																		15 11		
Hove 2	a										14 53														
Brighton 10	a			14 28	14 47							14 52		14 55								14 58	15 15		

until 18 May

Bedford and London - Brighton

Network Diagram - see first Page of Table 186

		SN	SN		SN	FC	SN		SN	SN	SN	FC	SN	GW	SN		SN		SN	SN	FC	SN	SN		GW
		1	◇1		1	1	1		◇1	1	◇1	1	1	1	1		◇1		◇1	1	1	1			1
							⚲		⚲		⚲		⚲									⚲			
London Victoria 15 ⊖	d		14 17				14 30		14 32		14 36		14 45				14 47		14 51			15 00	15 01		
Clapham Junction 10	d		14 23						14 38		14 42						14 53						15 08		
Bedford	d					13 10						13 24									13 40				
Luton 10	d					13 34						13 48									14 04				
Luton Airport Parkway 7 ✈	d					13 36						13 50									14 06				
St Albans City	d					13 48						14 02									14 18				
St Pancras International 15 ⊖	d					14 09						14 24									14 39				
Farringdon 3 ⊖	d					14 14						14 29									14 44				
City Thameslink 3	d					14 18						14 33									14 48				
London Blackfriars 3 ⊖	d					14 20						14 35									14 50				
London Bridge 4 ⊖	d	14 15				14 27				14 33		14 42			14 45						14 57				
New Cross Gate	d									14 38															
Norwood Junction 2	d	14 26								14 46					14 56										
East Croydon	a	14 29	14 32			14 39			14 48	14 50	14 52	14 54			14 59		15 02		15 07		15 09				
	d	14 30	14 33			14 41			14 48	14 51	14 53	14 55			15 00		15 03		15 08		15 11				
Purley 4	d	14 36								14 57					15 06										
Coulsdon South	d	14 39								15 00					15 09										
Merstham	d	14 45								15 06															
Redhill	a	14 49							15 00	15 09					15 17										
	d	14 52							15 00	15 10				15 13	15 17										15 29
Reigate	a	14 56												15 18											15 33
Nutfield	d														15 22										
Godstone	d														15 27										
Edenbridge	d														15 33										
Penshurst	d														15 39										
Leigh (Kent)	d														15 43										
Tonbridge 4	a														15 48										
Earlswood (Surrey)	d									15 12															
Salfords	d									15 16															
Horley 4	d				←					15 19										←					
Gatwick Airport 10 ✈	a		14 48		14 55	14 56	15 00		15 08	15 23		15 10	15 15				15 18		15 22	15 23	15 26	15 30			
	d		14 50		14 56	14 57			15 09	15 24		15 11					15 20		15 23	15 24	15 27				
Three Bridges 15	a				15 01	15 01			15 14	→		15 15								15 29	15 31				
	d				15 01	15 02			15 14			15 15								15 30	15 32				
Crawley	d				15 05				15 18											15 33					
Ifield	d				15 07															15 36					
Faygate	d																								
Littlehaven	d				15 14															15 42					
Horsham 4	a				15 17				15 26											15 48					
Balcombe	d											15 21													
Haywards Heath	a		15 00			15 11						15 26					15 30				15 41				
	d		15 04	15 07		15 11						15 27					15 35	15 37			15 41				
Wivelsfield	d			15 11								15 31					15 39								
Lewes 4	a			15 22													15 52								
Burgess Hill 4	d		15 09									15 33							15 38						
Hassocks 4	d											15 36							15 41						
Preston Park	d		15 18									15 43													
Hove 2	a		15 22															15 53							
Brighton 10	a					15 25					15 28	15 47							15 52		15 55				

Table 186

Mondays to Fridays

until 18 May

Bedford and London - Brighton

Network Diagram - see first Page of Table 186

		SN ◇[1]	GW [1]	SN [1]	SN ◇[1] 🚲	FC [1]	SN [1] 🚲		SN [1]	SN ◇[1]		FC [1]	SN [1]	SN [1] 🚲	SN ◇[1]		SN [1]	SN ◇[1] 🚲	FC [1]	SN [1] 🚲	GW [1]	SN [1]	SN ◇[1]		
London Victoria [15] ⊖	d	15 02			15 06		15 15			15 17				15 30	15 32			15 36		15 45			15 47		
Clapham Junction [10]	d	15 08			15 12					15 23					15 38			15 42					15 53		
Bedford	d					13 54						14 10							14 24						
Luton [10]	d					14 18						14 34							14 48						
Luton Airport Parkway [7] ✈	d					14 20						14 36							14 50						
St Albans City	d					14 32						14 48							15 02						
St Pancras International [15] ⊖	d					14 54						15 09							15 24						
Farringdon [3] ⊖	d					14 59						15 14							15 29						
City Thameslink [3]	d					15 03						15 18							15 33						
London Blackfriars [3] ⊖	d					15 05						15 20							15 35						
London Bridge [4] ⊖	d			15 03		15 12			15 15			15 27					15 33		15 42			15 45			
New Cross Gate	d			15 08													15 38								
Norwood Junction [2]	d			15 16					15 26								15 46					15 56			
East Croydon	a	15 17		15 20	15 22	15 24			15 29	15 32		15 39			15 47		15 50	15 52	15 54			15 59	16 02		
	d	15 18		15 21	15 23	15 25			15 30	15 33		15 41			15 48		15 51	15 53	15 55			16 00	16 03		
Purley [4]	d			15 27					15 36								15 57					16 06			
Coulsdon South	d			15 30					15 39								16 00					16 09			
Merstham	d			15 36					15 45								16 06					16 15			
Redhill	a	15 30		15 39					15 49						16 00		16 09					16 19			
	d	15 30	15 41	15 45					15 52						16 00		16 10				16 13	16 20			
Reigate	a								15 56												16 18				
Nutfield	d																					16 24			
Godstone	d																					16 30			
Edenbridge	d																					16 35			
Penshurst	d																					16 42			
Leigh (Kent)	d																					16 45			
Tonbridge [4]	a																					16 52			
Earlswood (Surrey)	d			15 48													16 12								
Salfords	d			15 51													16 16								
Horley [4]	d	15 36		15 55									←				16 19								
Gatwick Airport [10] ✈	a	15 39	15 50	15 57		15 40	15 45			15 48		15 56	15 57	16 00	16 08		16 23		16 10	16 15			16 18		
	d	15 40		15 58		15 41				15 50		15 57	15 58		16 09		16 24		16 11				16 20		
Three Bridges [15]	a	15 44		→		15 45						16 01	16 03		16 14		→		16 15						
	d	15 45				15 45						16 02	16 03		16 14				16 15						
Crawley	d	15 48											16 07		16 18										
Ifield	d												16 10												
Faygate	d												16 14												
Littlehaven	d												16 18												
Horsham [4]	a	15 56											16 21		16 26										
Balcombe	d																		16 21						
Haywards Heath	a					15 54				16 00		16 11							16 26				16 30		
	d					15 55				16 04	16 07	16 11							16 27				16 35	16 37	
Wivelsfield	d					15 59					16 11								16 31				16 39		
Lewes [4]	a										16 22												16 54		
Burgess Hill [4]	d					16 01				16 09									16 33						
Hassocks [4]	d					16 04													16 36						
Preston Park	d					16 11				16 18									16 43						
Hove [2]	a									16 22														16 53	
Brighton [10]	a				15 58	16 15						16 25						16 28	16 47						

Bedford and London - Brighton

Network Diagram - see first Page of Table 186

		SN	SN	FC	SN	SN	SN	GW		SN		SN	FC	SN	GW	SN		SN		SN	SN	FC	SN	SN	
		◇1	1	1	1	1	◇1	1		1		1	1	1	1	1		◇1		1	1	1	1		
																		A							
					🛒							🛒						🛒					🛒		
London Victoria 15 ⊖	d	15 51			16 00	16 01	16 02					16 06		16 15				16 17		16 19			16 30	16 31	
Clapham Junction 10	d					16 08	16 08					16 12						16 23		16 26				16a37	
Bedford	d			14 40									14 54									15 10			
Luton 10	d			15 04									15 18									15 34			
Luton Airport Parkway 7 ✈	d			15 06									15 20									15 36			
St Albans City	d			15 18									15 32									15 48			
St Pancras International 15 ⊖	d			15 39									15 54									16 09			
Farringdon 3 ⊖	d			15 44									15 59									16 14			
City Thameslink 3	d			15 48									16 03									16 18			
London Blackfriars 3 ⊖	d			15 50									16 05									16 20			
London Bridge 4 ⊖	d			15 57						16 03			16 12			16 15						16 27			
New Cross Gate	d									16 08															
Norwood Junction 2	d									16 16						16 26									
East Croydon 🚌	a	16 07		16 09			16 17			16 20		16 22	16 24			16 29		16 33		16 36		16 39			
	d	16 08		16 11			16 18			16 21		16 23	16 25			16 30		16 33		16 36		16 41			
Purley 4	d									16 27						16 36									
Coulsdon South	d									16 30						16 39									
Merstham	d									16 36						16 45									
Redhill	a						16 30			16 39						16 49									
	d						16 30	16 32		16 43	16 45				16 51	16 53									
Reigate	a							16 36								16 59									
Nutfield	d										16 49														
Godstone	d										16 55														
Edenbridge	d										17 00														
Penshurst	d										17 07														
Leigh (Kent)	d										17 10														
Tonbridge 4	a										17 15														
Earlswood (Surrey)	d									16 45															
Salfords	d									16 49															
Horley 4	d		←				16 36			16 52											←				
Gatwick Airport 10 ✈	a	16 22	16 23	16 26	16 30		16 39			16 55			16 40	16 45	16 59			16 48		16 52	16 55	16 56	17 00		
	d	16 23	16 24	16 27			16 40			16 56			16 41					16 49		16 53	16 56	16 57			
Three Bridges 15	a		16 29	16 31			16 44			→			16 45							16 57	17 00	17 01			
	d		16 30	16 32			16 45						16 45							16 58	17 02	17 02			
Crawley	d		16 34				16 48													17 02	17 06				
Ifield	d		16 36																		17 08				
Faygate	d		16 40																		17 12				
Littlehaven	d		16 44																		17 16				
Horsham 4	a		16 47				16 56													17 12	17 19				
Balcombe	d																								
Haywards Heath	a			16 41									16 54					17 00				17 11			
	d			16 41									16 55					17 04	17 06			17 11			
Wivelsfield	d												16 59						17 10						
Lewes 4	a																		17 21						
Burgess Hill 4	d	16 38											17 01					17 09				17 17			
Hassocks 4	d	16 41											17 04									17 21			
Preston Park	d												17 11												
Hove 2	a																	17 20							
Brighton 10	a	16 52		16 55								17 00	17 15									17 30			

A 🛒 to Haywards Heath

Table 186

Mondays to Fridays

until 18 May

Bedford and London - Brighton

Network Diagram - see first Page of Table 186

		SN		SN	SN		FC	SN	SN	GW	SN	SN	SN		SN	SN	SN		SN	SN	FC	SN
		◇1		1	1		1	1	1	1	◇1	1	1		1	1	1		◇1	1	1	1
		A																				
		[trolley]			[trolley]			[trolley]			[trolley]					[trolley]			[trolley]			[trolley]
London Victoria 15 ⊖	d	16 32			16 36			16 45			16 47		16 49			17 00			17 02	17 06		17 15
Clapham Junction 10	d	16 38			16 42						16 53		16 56						17 08	17 12		
Bedford	d						15 24														15 52	
Luton 10	d						15 48														16 14	
Luton Airport Parkway 7 ✈	d						15 50														16 17	
St Albans City	d						16 02														16 25	
St Pancras International 15 ⊖	d						16 22														16 46	
Farringdon 3 ⊖	d						16 27														16 51	
City Thameslink 3	d						16 31														16 55	
London Blackfriars 3 ⊖	d						16 36														16 58	
London Bridge 4 ⊖	d			16 33			16 43								16 57		16 59					
New Cross Gate	d																					
Norwood Junction 2	d			16 44													17 10					
East Croydon	a	16 47		16 48	16 52		16 59				17 03		17 06		17 09		17 14		17 17	17 22	17 26	
	d	16 48		16 49	16 52		17 00				17 03		17 07		17 10		17 15		17 18	17 23	17 26	
Purley 4	d			16 55													17 21					
Coulsdon South	d			16 59									17 13				17 24					
Merstham	d			17 04									17 19				17 30					
Redhill	a	16 59		17 08									17 22				17 33					
	d	17 00		17 08					17 12	17 13			17 27	17 29			17 37	17 39				
Reigate	a									17 18				17 35								
Nutfield	d								17 16									17 43				
Godstone	d								17 22									17 49				
Edenbridge	d								17 27									17 54				
Penshurst	d								17 34									18 01				
Leigh (Kent)	d								17 37									18 04				
Tonbridge 4	a								17 42									18 09				
Earlswood (Surrey)	d			17 11									17 29				17 39					
Salfords	d			17 14									17 33				17 43					
Horley 4	d	17 06		17 18								←	17 36				17 46					
Gatwick Airport 10 ✈	a	17 08		17 20			17 15	17 15			17 19	17 20	17 39			17 30	17 49				17 41	17 45
	d	17 09		17 21			17 16				17 20	17 21	17 40				17 50				17 42	
Three Bridges 15	a	17 14		→	17 09		17 20				17 24	17 26	17 46		17 29		→		17 36		17 46	
	d	17 18	17 22		17 10		17 21				17 25	17 26			17 29				17 37		17 46	
Crawley	d	17 22	17 26									17 30							17 41			
Ifield	d		17 28									17 33										
Faygate	d											17 37										
Littlehaven	d		17 35									17 41										
Horsham 4	a	17 30	17 38									17 44							17 49			
Balcombe	d						17 27														17 52	
Haywards Heath	a				17 19		17 32				17 35				17 38					17 46	17 57	
	d				17 23	17 26	17 32				17 36				17 39					17 47	17 58	
Wivelsfield	d					17 30	17 37				17 41									17 52		
Lewes 4	a										17 56											
Burgess Hill 4	d					17 32	17 39								17 46					17 55	18 03	
Hassocks 4	d					17 35	17 43								17 49					17 59	18 07	
Preston Park	d					17 42	17 50								17 56					18 06	18 14	
Hove 2	a														18 00							
Brighton 10	a				17 39	17 46	17 54													18 12	18 18	

A [trolley] to Three Bridges

Table 186

Bedford and London - Brighton

Mondays to Fridays

until 18 May

Network Diagram - see first Page of Table 186

		SN	SN	SN	GW	GW	SN			SN	FC	SN	SN		SN	SN		SN	FC	SN	SN	SN	SN	GW
		◇[1]	[1]	[1]	[1]	[1]	[1]			[1]	[1]	◇[1]	[1]		◇[1]	[1]		[1]	[1]	[1]	[1]	◇[1]	[1]	[1]
										🛒					🛒					🛒				
London Victoria [15] ⊖	d	17 17					17 21			17 30		17 32			17 35					17 45		17 47		
Clapham Junction [10]	d	17 23					17 27					17 38			17 42							17 53		
Bedford	d										16 10													
Luton [10]	d										16 34													
Luton Airport Parkway [7] ✈	d										16 36													
St Albans City	d										16 48													
St Pancras International [15] ⊖	d										17 10													
Farringdon [3] ⊖	d										17 15													
City Thameslink [3]	d										17 19													
London Blackfriars [3] ⊖	d										17 22													
London Bridge [4] ⊖	d			17 23									17 32					17 42			17 47			
New Cross Gate	d																							
Norwood Junction [2]	d												17 44											
East Croydon	a	17 32		17 35			17 36				17 47	17 48	17 49		17 51			17 54			17 58	18 02		
	d	17 33		17 36			17 38				17 47	17 49	17 49		17 52			17 55			18 00	18 03		
Purley [4]	d												17 55											
Coulsdon South	d						17 44						17 58											
Merstham	d						17 50						18 04											
Redhill	a						17 53				18 02		18 07											
	d				17 41	17 43	17 57	17 59			18 03		18 11	18 13										18 13
Reigate	a					17 48		18 05																18 18
Nutfield	d													18 17										
Godstone	d													18 23										
Edenbridge	d													18 28										
Penshurst	d													18 35										
Leigh (Kent)	d													18 38										
Tonbridge [4]	a													18 45										
Earlswood (Surrey)	d						17 59						18 13											
Salfords	d						18 03						18 17											
Horley [4]	d		←	17 50			18 06						18 20			←			←			18 18	←	
Gatwick Airport [10] ✈	a	17 47	17 49		17 54		18 09			17 57	18 13		18 23		18 06	18 09			18 13	18 12		18 20	18 23	
	d	17 48	17 50				18 10			18 00	18 14		18 24		18 07	18 10			18 14	18 15		18 21	18 24	
Three Bridges [15]	a		17 54	17 55			→				→	18 06	→			18 16			18 18		18 21		18 28	
	d		17 55	17 56								18 07							18 19		18 22		18 29	
Crawley	d		17 59									18 11									18 26		18 33	
Ifield	d		18 01																		18 28		18 35	
Faygate	d																						18 39	
Littlehaven	d		18 08									18 19									18 35		18 43	
Horsham [4]	a		18 11									18 22									18 38		18 48	
Balcombe	d																		18 25					
Haywards Heath	a	18 00		18 05						18 10					18 18			18 22	18 30	18 25		18 33		
	d	18 01		18 05						18 11					18 18			18 22	18 31	18 26		18 34		
Wivelsfield	d			18 10											18 23									
Lewes [4]	a			18 21											18 38									
Burgess Hill [4]	d	18 07								18 17								18 28	18 36			18 41		
Hassocks [4]	d	18 11								18 22								18 32	18 40			18 45		
Preston Park	d																	18 39	18 47	18 43		18 53		
Hove [2]	a	18 21																18 43				18 57		
Brighton [10]	a									18 34									18 53	18 49				

Table 186

Mondays to Fridays

until 18 May

Bedford and London - Brighton

Network Diagram - see first Page of Table 186

		SN		FC	SN	SN	SN	SN		SN	SN	SN	SN	SN	SN	FC		SN	SN	GW	GW	SN	SN		
		1		1	1	1	1	1		1	◇1	◇1	1	1	1	1		◇1	1	1	1	1	1		
London Victoria 15 ⊖	d	17 49				18 00					18 02	18 06		18 15				18 17					18 19		
Clapham Junction 10	d	17 56									18 08	18 12						18 23					18 26		
Bedford	d			16 26																					
Luton 10	d			16 50																					
Luton Airport Parkway 7 ✈	d			16 52																					
St Albans City	d			17 04																					
St Pancras International 15 ⊖	d			17 28												17 40									
Farringdon 3 ⊖	d			17 33												17 45									
City Thameslink 3	d			17 37												17 49									
London Blackfriars 3 ⊖	d			17 40												17 51									
London Bridge 4 ⊖	d				17 57					17 59			18 12						18 23						
New Cross Gate	d																								
Norwood Junction 2	d									18 11															
East Croydon	a	18 05		18 07	18 11					18 15	18 17	18 22	18 24			18 24		18 33	18 36				18 37		
	d	18 06		18 09	18 15					18 15	18 19	18 22	18 25			18 25		18 33	18 37				18 38		
Purley 4	d									18 21													18 43		
Coulsdon South	d	18 12								18 24													18 46		
Merstham	d	18 18								18 30													18 52		
Redhill	a	18 21								18 33						18 37							18 55		
	d	18 25	18 27					18 32		18 34						18 38				18 43	18 51	18 54	18 59	19 01	
Reigate	a		18 33																	18 47		18 58			
Nutfield	d							18 36																19 05	
Godstone	d							18 42																19 11	
Edenbridge	d							18 47																19 16	
Penshurst	d							18 54																19 23	
Leigh (Kent)	d							18 57																19 26	
Tonbridge 4	a							19 02																19 34	
Earlswood (Surrey)	d	18 27								18 36													19 01		
Salfords	d	18 31								18 40													19 05		
Horley 4	d	18 34					←			18 43					←			18 48					19 08		
Gatwick Airport 10 ✈	a	18 37		18 24		18 28	18 37			18 46		18 37		18 44	18 46	18 49					19 00		19 13		
	d	18 38		18 25		18 35	18 38			18 47		18 38		18 46	18 47	18 50							19 14		
Three Bridges 15	a	↪		18 29	18 34		18 42			↪	18 37		18 44		18 51	18 56			18 56				↪		
	d			18 30	18 35						18 38		18 45		18 52				18 57						
Crawley	d										18 42				18 56										
Ifield	d														18 58										
Faygate	d																								
Littlehaven	d														19 05										
Horsham 4	a										18 50				19 08										
Balcombe	d																	18 57							
Haywards Heath	a			18 39	18 43	18 46						18 49	18 54	18 57				19 02	19 05						
	d			18 39	18 44	18 47						18 50	18 54	18 58				19 03	19 06						
Wivelsfield	d			18 44								18 54							19 11						
Lewes 4	a											19 09							19 27						
Burgess Hill 4	d			18 46	18 50	18 54							19 00					19 09							
Hassocks 4	d			18 50	18 54	18 59							19 04					19 13							
Preston Park	d			18 57	19 01								19 11	19 15											
Hove 2	a												19 17					19 22							
Brighton 10	a			19 02	19 07	19 10								19 22											

Table 186

Mondays to Fridays

until 18 May

Bedford and London - Brighton

Network Diagram - see first Page of Table 186

		FC 1	SN 1	SN 1		SN ◇1	SN 1	SN 1	SN 1	FC 1	SN 1	SN ◇1		SN 1	FC 1	SN 1	SN 1	GW 1	SN ◇1	SN 1	SN 1	SN
London Victoria 15 ⊖	d		18 30			18 32		18 36	18 45			18 47		18 51		19 00			19 02			19 06
Clapham Junction 10	d					18 38		18 42				18 53		18 57					19 08			19 12
Bedford	d	17 06								17 22					17 36							
Luton 10	d	17 30								17 46					18 00							
Luton Airport Parkway 7 ✈	d	17 33								17 48					18 02							
St Albans City	d	17 45								18 00					18 14							
St Pancras International 15 ⊖	d	18 08								18 20					18 34							
Farringdon 3 ⊖	d	18 13								18 25					18 40							
City Thameslink 3	d	18 17								18 29					18 43							
London Blackfriars 3 ⊖	d	18 20								18 32					18 46							
London Bridge 4 ⊖	d	18 27		18 30											18 57						18 59	
New Cross Gate	d																				19 06	
Norwood Junction 2	d			18 42																	19 14	
East Croydon	a	18 41		18 45		18 48		18 52		19 00		19 03		19 07	19 10				19 18		19 17	19 22
	d	18 41		18 46		18 48		18 53		19 01		19 04		19 08	19 11				19 18		19 19	19 23
Purley 4	d			18 51																	19 24	
Coulsdon South	d			18 54										19 14							19 28	
Merstham	d			19 00										19 20							19 33	
Redhill	a			19 03										19 23					19 30		19 37	
	d			19 07	19 09									19 24				19 26	19 31	19 36	19 37	
Reigate	a				19 15													19 30		19 40		
Nutfield	d																					
Godstone	d																					
Edenbridge	d																					
Penshurst	d																					
Leigh (Kent)	d																					
Tonbridge 4	a																					
Earlswood (Surrey)	d			19 09										19 26							19 40	
Salfords	d			19 13										19 30							19 43	
Horley 4	d			19 16			←				←			19 33			←				19 47	
Gatwick Airport 10 ✈	a	18 56	19 00	19 19			19 13		19 12	19 16	19 19	19 20		19 36	19 25	19 30	19 36		19 39		19 49	
	d	18 57	19 05	19 20			19 14		19 15	19 18	19 20	19 21		19 37	19 26		19 37		19 40		19 50	
Three Bridges 15	a	19 01		→		19 06	19 19				19 24			→	19 30		19 41		19 45		→	
	d	19 02				19 07	19 19				19 25				19 31				19 45			
Crawley	d					19 11	19 23				19 29								19 49			
Ifield	d						19 26				19 31											
Faygate	d										19 35											
Littlehaven	d					19 19	19 32				19 39											
Horsham 4	a					19 22	19 37				19 43								19 57			
Balcombe	d	19 08													19 37							
Haywards Heath	a	19 13	19 16					19 19	19 25	19 29		19 32			19 42							19 46
	d	19 14	19 17					19 21	19 26	19 30		19 35	19 38		19 42							19 47
Wivelsfield	d							19 25				19 39										
Lewes 4	a											19 54										
Burgess Hill 4	d	19 19	19 23							19 35			19 43		19 48							
Hassocks 4	d	19 23	19 27							19 39			19 47		19 51							
Preston Park	d								19 41	19 46												
Hove 2	a												19 57									
Brighton 10	a	19 33	19 39					19 42	19 47	19 52					20 01							20 03

Table 186

Bedford and London - Brighton

Mondays to Fridays

until 18 May

Network Diagram - see first Page of Table 186

		FC	GW	SN	SN	SN		SN	FC	SN	SN	SN	SN	SN	SN	SN	FC	GW	SN	SN	SN	SN	
		1	1	1	1	◇1		1	1	1	1	1	◇1	1	1		1	1	1	1	1	◇1	
					🚲	A 🚲					🚲		🚲							🚲		A 🚲	
London Victoria 15 ⊖	d			19 10	19 15	19 17					19 30		19 32			19 36			19 40	19 45		19 47	
Clapham Junction 10	d			19 16		19 23							19 38			19 42			19 46			19 53	
Bedford	d	17 54							18 10								18 24						
Luton 10	d	18 18							18 34								18 48						
Luton Airport Parkway 7 ✈	d	18 20							18 36								18 50						
St Albans City	d	18 32							18 48								19 02						
St Pancras International 15 ⊖	d	18 54							19 09								19 24						
Farringdon 3 ⊖	d	18 59							19 14								19 29						
City Thameslink 3	d	19 03							19 18								19 33						
London Blackfriars 3 ⊖	d	19 05							19 20								19 35						
London Bridge 4 ⊖	d	19 12							19 27						19 33		19 42						
New Cross Gate	d														19 39								
Norwood Junction 2	d														19 47								
East Croydon	a	19 24		19 27		19 33			19 39				19 48		19 50	19 52	19 54		19 57			20 03	
	d	19 25		19 28		19 33			19 41				19 48		19 51	19 53	19 55		19 58			20 03	
Purley 4	d			19 33											19 57				20 03				
Coulsdon South	d			19 36											20 00				20 06				
Merstham	d			19 42											20 06				20 12				
Redhill	a			19 45									20 00		20 09				20 15				
	d		19 43	19 46								19 51	20 00	20 05	20 10			20 13	20 16				
Reigate	a													20 10				20 18					
Nutfield	d											19 55											
Godstone	d											20 01											
Edenbridge	d											20 06											
Penshurst	d											20 13											
Leigh (Kent)	d											20 16											
Tonbridge 4	a											20 21											
Earlswood (Surrey)	d			19 48															20 18				
Salfords	d			19 52															20 22				
Horley 4	d			19 55				←		←					20 16				20 25		←		
Gatwick Airport 10 ✈	a	19 40	19 55	19 58	19 45	19 48		19 49	19 55	19 58	20 00		20 08		20 18		20 10		20 28	20 15	20 18	20 18	
	d	19 41		19 59		19 49		19 50	19 57	19 59			20 09		20 19		20 11		20 29		20 19	20 19	
Three Bridges 15	a	19 45		→				19 55	20 01	20 03			20 14		→		20 15		→		20 24		
	d	19 45						19 55	20 02	20 04			20 14				20 15				20 24		
Crawley	d							19 59		20 08			20 18								20 28		
Ifield	d							20 02		20 10											20 31		
Faygate	d									20 14													
Littlehaven	d							20 08		20 18											20 37		
Horsham 4	a							20 11		20 21			20 26								20 40		
Balcombe	d	19 51																					
Haywards Heath	a	19 56				20 00			20 11							20 16	20 24					20 30	
	d	19 57				20 04	20 07		20 11							20 17	20 25					20 34	20 36
Wivelsfield	d	20 01					20 11										20 29						20 40
Lewes 4	a						20 22																20 55
Burgess Hill 4	d	20 03				20 09			20 16								20 31					20 39	
Hassocks 4	d	20 06							20 20								20 34					20 42	
Preston Park	d	20 13															20 41					20 49	
Hove 2	a					20 21																20 53	
Brighton 10	a	20 17							20 29							20 33	20 45						

A 🚲 to Haywards Heath

until 18 May

Bedford and London - Brighton

Network Diagram - see first Page of Table 186

		SN 1	FC 1	SN 1	SN 1	SN ◇1	SN ◇1	FC 1	GW 1	GW 1	SN 1	SN 1	SN ◇1		SN 1	SN 1	SN 1	SN 1	SN ◇1	SN ◇1	FC 1	SN 1
London Victoria 15 ⊖	d				20 00	20 02	20 06				20 10	20 15	20 17				20 30		20 32	20 36		
Clapham Junction 10	d					20 08	20 12				20 16		20 23						20 38	20 42		
Bedford	d		18 40					18 54													19 26	
Luton 10	d		19 04					19 18													19 50	
Luton Airport Parkway 7 ✈	d		19 06					19 20													19 52	
St Albans City	d		19 18					19 32													20 04	
St Pancras International 15 ⊖	d		19 39					19 54													20 24	
Farringdon 3 ⊖	d		19 44					19 59													20 29	
City Thameslink 3	d		19 48					20 03													20 33	
London Blackfriars 3 ⊖	d		19 50					20 05													20 35	
London Bridge 4 ⊖	d	19 52	19 57					20 12							20 28						20 42	
New Cross Gate	d																					
Norwood Junction 2	d	20 03																				
East Croydon	a	20 06	20 09			20 19	20 22	20 24			20 27		20 33		20 40				20 48	20 52	20 54	
	d	20 07	20 11			20 19	20 23	20 25			20 28		20 33		20 41				20 48	20 53	20 55	
Purley 4	d	20 12									20 33											
Coulsdon South	d	20 15									20 36											
Merstham	d	20 21									20 42											
Redhill	a	20 24				20 30					20 45								21 00			
	d	20 25				20 31			20 34	20 41	20 46							20 51	21 00			21 05
Reigate	a	20 30							20 38													21 09
Nutfield	d																	20 55				
Godstone	d																	21 01				
Edenbridge	d																	21 06				
Penshurst	d																	21 13				
Leigh (Kent)	d																	21 16				
Tonbridge 4	a																	21 21				
Earlswood (Surrey)	d										20 48											
Salfords	d																					
Horley 4	d			←							20 54					←						
Gatwick Airport 10 ✈	a		20 25	20 28	20 30	20 38		20 40		20 50	20 56	20 45	20 48		20 55	20 56	21 00		21 08		21 10	
	d		20 27	20 29		20 39		20 41			20 57		20 49		20 56	20 57			21 09		21 11	
Three Bridges 15	a		20 31	20 33		20 44		20 45			→				21 00	21 02			21 14		21 15	
	d		20 32	20 34		20 44		20 45							21 01	21 03			21 14		21 15	
Crawley	d			20 37		20 48										21 06			21 18			
Ifield	d			20 40												21 09						
Faygate	d																					
Littlehaven	d			20 46												21 15						
Horsham 4	a			20 49		20 56										21 18			21 26			
Balcombe	d							20 51														
Haywards Heath	a		20 41				20 47	20 56					21 00		21 10					21 16	21 24	
	d		20 41				20 47	20 57					21 04	21 07	21 11					21 16	21 25	
Wivelsfield	d							21 01						21 11							21 29	
Lewes 4	a													21 22								
Burgess Hill 4	d		20 46					21 03					21 09								21 31	
Hassocks 4	d							21 06													21 34	
Preston Park	d							21 13													21 41	
Hove 2	a												21 21									
Brighton 10	a		20 57				21 01	21 17							21 26					21 30	21 45	

Table 186

Mondays to Fridays

until 18 May

Bedford and London - Brighton

Network Diagram - see first Page of Table 186

		GW 1	SN 1	SN 1	SN ◇1		SN 1	SN 1	SN 1	SN 1	SN 1	SN ◇1	FC 1	GW 1	SN 1	SN 1	SN ◇1		SN 1	SN 1	GW 1	SN 1
London Victoria 15 ⊖	d		20 40	20 45	20 47				21 00		21 02	21 06			21 10	21 15	21 17			21 30		
Clapham Junction 10	d		20 46		20 53						21 08	21 12			21 16		21 23					
Bedford	d												19 52									
Luton 10	d												20 16									
Luton Airport Parkway 7 ✈	d												20 18									
St Albans City	d												20 30									
St Pancras International 15 ⊖	d												20 54									
Farringdon 3 ⊖	d												20 59									
City Thameslink 3	d												21 03									
London Blackfriars 3 ⊖	d												21 05									
London Bridge 4 ⊖	d						20 58						21 12									
New Cross Gate	d																					
Norwood Junction 2	d																					
East Croydon	a		20 57		21 03		21 10				21 18	21 22	21 24		21 27		21 33					
	d		20 58		21 04		21 11				21 18	21 23	21 25		21 28		21 33					
Purley 4	d		21 03												21 33							
Coulsdon South	d		21 06												21 36							
Merstham	d		21 12												21 42							
Redhill	a		21 15								21 30				21 45							
	d	21 13	21 16							21 22	21 31			21 35	21 46						21 53	21 55
Reigate	a	21 18								21 26				21 39								
Nutfield	d																					21 59
Godstone	d																					22 05
Edenbridge	d																					22 10
Penshurst	d																					22 17
Leigh (Kent)	d																					22 20
Tonbridge 4	a																					22 28
Earlswood (Surrey)	d		21 18												21 48							
Salfords	d		21 22																			
Horley 4	d		21 25					←							21 54				←			
Gatwick Airport 10 ✈	a		21 28	21 15	21 18		21 26	21 28	21 30		21 38		21 40		21 56	21 45	21 48		21 56	22 00	22 06	
	d		21 29		21 19		21 27	21 29			21 39		21 41		21 57		21 49		21 57			
Three Bridges 15	a		→				21 31	21 33			21 44		21 45		→		21 53		22 02			
	d						21 31	21 34			21 44		21 45				21 53		22 03			
Crawley	d							21 37											22 06			
Ifield	d							21 40											22 09			
Faygate	d																					
Littlehaven	d							21 46											22 15			
Horsham 4	a							21 49											22 18			
Balcombe	d												21 53									
Haywards Heath	a				21 30		21 40				21 53	21 46	21 58				22 02					
	d				21 34	21 37	21 41				21 53	21 46	21 59				22 06	22 08				
Wivelsfield	d					21 41					21 57		22 03					22 12				
Lewes 4	a					21 54												22 23				
Burgess Hill 4	d				21 39						21 59		22 05				22 11					
Hassocks 4	d				21 42						22 03		22 08									
Preston Park	d				21 49						22 09		22 15									
Hove 2	a				21 53												22 22					
Brighton 10	a						21 56				22 15	22 00	22 19									

Table 186

Mondays to Fridays

until 18 May

Bedford and London - Brighton

Network Diagram - see first Page of Table 186

		SN	SN	FC	SN	SN	SN	SN			SN	SN	SN	SN	SN	FC	GW		SN	SN	SN	SN	SN	GW
		1	◇1	1	1	1	1	◇1			1	1	1	◇1	◇1	1	1		1	1	◇1	1	1	1
London Victoria 15 ⊖	d	21 32	21 36			21 40	21 45	21 47				22 00		22 02	22 06				22 10	22 15	22 17		22 30	
Clapham Junction 10	d	21 38	21 42			21 46		21 53						22 08	22 12				22 16		22 23			
Bedford	d			20 22												20 52								
Luton 10	d			20 46												21 16								
Luton Airport Parkway 7 ✈	d			20 48												21 18								
St Albans City	d			21 00												21 30								
St Pancras International 15 ⊖	d			21 24												21 54								
Farringdon 3 ⊖	d			21 29												21 59								
City Thameslink 3	d			21 33												22 03								
London Blackfriars 3 ⊖	d			21 35												22 05								
London Bridge 4 ⊖	d			21 42												22 12								
New Cross Gate	d																							
Norwood Junction 2	d																							
East Croydon	a	21 48	21 52	21 54		21 57		22 03						22 18	22 22	22 24			22 26		22 33			
	d	21 48	21 53	21 55		21 58		22 03						22 18	22 23	22 25			22 28		22 34			
Purley 4	d					22 03													22 33					
Coulsdon South	d					22 06													22 36					
Merstham	d					22 12													22 42					
Redhill	a	21 59				22 15								22 30					22 45					
	d	22 00			22 05	22 16							22 22	22 31			22 33		22 46					22 52
Reigate	a				22 09								22 26				22 38							
Nutfield	d																							
Godstone	d																							
Edenbridge	d																							
Penshurst	d																							
Leigh (Kent)	d																							
Tonbridge 4	a																							
Earlswood (Surrey)	d					22 18													22 48					
Salfords	d					22 22																		
Horley 4	d					22 25					←								22 54			←		
Gatwick Airport 10 ✈	a	22 08		22 10		22 28	22 15	22 18			22 28	22 30		22 38		22 40			22 56	22 45	22 48	22 56	23 00	23 06
	d	22 09		22 11		22 29		22 19			22 29			22 39		22 41			22 57		22 49	22 57		
Three Bridges 15	a	22 14		22 15		→					22 33			22 44		22 45			→		22 53	23 02		
	d	22 14		22 15							22 36			22 44		22 45					22 53	23 03		
Crawley	d	22 18									22 39											23 06		
Ifield	d										22 42											23 09		
Faygate	d																							
Littlehaven	d										22 48											23 15		
Horsham 4	a	22 26									22 51											23 18		
Balcombe	d															22 53								
Haywards Heath	a		22 16	22 24				22 30						22 53	22 46	22 58					23 02			
	d		22 16	22 25				22 34	22 37					22 53	22 46	22 59					23 03			
Wivelsfield	d			22 29				22 38						22 57		23 03								
Lewes 4	a							22 53																
Burgess Hill 4	d			22 31										22 59		23 05					23 08			
Hassocks 4	d			22 34										23 03		23 08								
Preston Park	d			22 41										23 09		23 15								
Hove 2	a								22 51												23 21			
Brighton 10	a		22 30	22 45										23 15	23 00	23 19								

Table 186

Bedford and London - Brighton

Mondays to Fridays

until 18 May

Network Diagram - see first Page of Table 186

		SN 1		SN 1	SN	FC 1	SN 1	SN 1	SN 1	SN ◇1			SN 1	SN 1	GW 1	SN ◇1	SN ◇1	FC 1	SN 1		SN 1	SN ◇1	SN 1	SN 1	SN 1
London Victoria 15 ⊖	d			22 32	22 36			22 40	22 45	22 47				23 00		23 02	23 06		23 10		23 15	23 17		23 30	
Clapham Junction 10	d			22 38	22 42			22 46		22 53						23 08	23 12		23 16			23 23			
Bedford	d																								
Luton 10	d																								
Luton Airport Parkway 7 ✈	d																								
St Albans City	d																								
St Pancras International 15 ⊖	d																								
Farringdon 3 ⊖	d																								
City Thameslink 3	d																								
London Blackfriars 3 ⊖	d																								
London Bridge 4 ⊖	d					22 42												23 12							
New Cross Gate	d																								
Norwood Junction 2	d																								
East Croydon	a			22 48	22 52	22 54		22 57		23 03						23 19	23 22	23 24	23 27			23 33			
	d			22 48	22 53	22 55		22 58		23 03						23 20	23 23	23 25	23 28			23 33			
Purley 4	d							23 03											23 33						
Coulsdon South	d							23 06											23 37						
Merstham	d							23 12											23 42						
Redhill	a			23 00				23 15								23 31			23 46						
	d	22 55		23 01			23 05	23 16							23 28	23 31			23 46						23 55
Reigate	a						23 09								23 33										
Nutfield	d	22 59																							
Godstone	d	23 05																							
Edenbridge	d	23 10																							
Penshurst	d	23 17																							00 06
Leigh (Kent)	d	23 20																							
Tonbridge 4	a	23 25																							00 15
Earlswood (Surrey)	d							23 18											23 49						
Salfords	d							23 22											23 52						
Horley 4	d							23 25					←						23 56				←		
Gatwick Airport 10 ✈	a			23 08		23 10		23 28	23 15	23 18			23 28	23 30		23 38		23 40	23 58		23 45	23 50	23 58	00 05	
	d			23 09		23 11		23 29		23 19			23 29			23 39		23 41	23 59			23 51	23 59		
Three Bridges 15	a			23 15		23 15		→					23 33			23 44		23 47	→			23 55	00 04		
	d			23 16		23 15							23 38			23 44		23 47				23 56	00 04		
Crawley	d			23 19									23 41										00 07		
Ifield	d												23 44										00 10		
Faygate	d																								
Littlehaven	d												23 50										00 16		
Horsham 4	a			23 27									23 53										00 19		
Balcombe	d																	23 53							
Haywards Heath	a				23 16	23 24				23 30						23 53	23 46	23 58				00 05			
	d				23 16	23 25				23 34	23 37					23 53	23 46	23 59				00 05			
Wivelsfield	d					23 29				23 38						23 57		00 03							
Lewes 4	a									23 51															
Burgess Hill 4	d					23 31										23 59		00 05				00 11			
Hassocks 4	d					23 34										00 03		00 08							
Preston Park	d					23 41										00 09		00 15							
Hove 2	a										23 51											00 21			
Brighton 10	a				23 30	23 45										00 15	00 01	00 19							

Table 186

Mondays to Fridays

until 18 May

Bedford and London - Brighton

Network Diagram - see first Page of Table 186

		SN ◇1	FC 1		SN 1	SN 1	SN 1
London Victoria 15 ⊖	d	23 32			23 45	23 47	23 49
Clapham Junction 10	d	23 38				23 53	23 56
Bedford	d						
Luton 10	d						
Luton Airport Parkway 7 ✈	d						
St Albans City	d						
St Pancras International 15 ⊖	d						
Farringdon 3 ⊖	d						
City Thameslink 3	d						
London Blackfriars 3 ⊖	d						
London Bridge 4 ⊖	d		23 42				
New Cross Gate	d						
Norwood Junction 2	d						
East Croydon	a	23 51	23 56			00 05	00 09
	d	23 52	23 57			00 06	
Purley 4	d					00 12	
Coulsdon South	d					00 15	
Merstham	d					00 21	
Redhill	a	00 03				00 24	
	d	00 05				00 25	
Reigate	a						
Nutfield	d						
Godstone	d						
Edenbridge	d						
Penshurst	d						
Leigh (Kent)	d						
Tonbridge 4	a						
Earlswood (Surrey)	d						
Salfords	d						
Horley 4	d					00 31	
Gatwick Airport 10 ✈	a	00 14	00 18		00 20	00 33	
	d	00 15	00 19			00 34	
Three Bridges 15	a	00 20	00 24			00 39	
	d	00 20				00 39	
Crawley	d					00 43	
Ifield	d					00 46	
Faygate	d						
Littlehaven	d					00 52	
Horsham 4	a					00 55	
Balcombe	d	00 26					
Haywards Heath	a	00 31					
	d	00 31					
Wivelsfield	d	00 35					
Lewes 4	a						
Burgess Hill 4	d	00 37					
Hassocks 4	d	00 41					
Preston Park	d	00 48					
Hove 2	a						
Brighton 10	a	00 52					

Table 186

Mondays to Fridays

from 21 May

Bedford and London - Brighton

Network Diagram - see first Page of Table 186

		SN	SN	SN	FC	FC	FC	FC		SN	SN	SN	SN	SN	SN	SN		GW	SN	SN	FC	FC	FC	SN	
		MX	MO	MX	MX	MO	MO	MO		MX	MX	MO	MX	MO		MX		MX	MX	MO	MO	MO	MX		
		◇1	1	◇1	1	1	1	1		1	◇1	1	1	◇1	1	1		1	◇1	◇1	1	1	1	1	
						A	B	C													A	D			
London Victoria 15 ⊖	d	23p02	23p04	23p06						23p10	23p17			23p17	23p30				23p32	23p32				23p45	
Clapham Junction 10	d	23p08	23p10	23p12						23p16	23p23			23p23					23p38	23p38					
Bedford	d				21p52	21p40	21p42	21p42													22p10	22p12	22p16		
Luton 10	d				22p16	22p07	22p06	22p06													22p37	22p36	22p40		
Luton Airport Parkway 7 ✈	d				22p18	22p09	22p09	22p09													22p39	22p39	22p42		
St Albans City	d				22p30	22p21	22p21	22p21													22p51	22p51	22p54		
St Pancras International 15 ⊖	d				22p54	22p54	22p54	22p54													23p24	23p24	23p24		
Farringdon 3 ⊖	d				22p59	22p59	22p59	22p59													23p29	23p29	23p29		
City Thameslink 3	d				23p03																				
London Blackfriars 3 ⊖	d				23p05	23p04	23p04	23p04													23p34	23p34	23p35		
London Bridge 4 ⊖	d				23p12	23p11	23p11	23p11													23p41	23p41	23p42		
New Cross Gate	d																								
Norwood Junction 2	d																								
East Croydon	a	23p19	23p22	23p22	23p24	23p25	23p25	23p26		23p27	23p33			23p37					23p51	23p52	23p56	23p56	23p56		
	d	23p20	23p22	23p23	23p25	23p25	23p25	23p27		23p28	23p33			23p38					23p52	23p53	23p57	23p57	23p57		
Purley 4	d		23p29							23p33															
Coulsdon South	d		23p33							23p37															
Merstham	d		23p38							23p42															
Redhill	a	23p31	23p42							23p46									00 03	00 05					
	d	23p31	23p42							23p46						23p55		00 01	00 05	00 05					
Reigate	a																								
Nutfield	d																								
Godstone	d																								
Edenbridge	d															00 06									
Penshurst	d																								
Leigh (Kent)	d																								
Tonbridge 4	a															00 15									
Earlswood (Surrey)	d									23p49															
Salfords	d									23p52															
Horley 4	d		23p50							23p56		←	←												
Gatwick Airport 10 ✈	a	23p38	23p54		23p40	23p41	23p41	23p48		23p58	23p50	23p54	23p58	23p59	00 05			00 11	00 14	00 14	00 18	00 18	00 18	00 20	
	d	23p39	23p55		23p41	23p42	23p42	23p50		23p59	23p51	23p55	23p59	00 01					00 15	00 15	00 20	00 20	00 19		
Three Bridges 15	a	23p44	→		23p47	23p46	23p46	23p54		→	23p55	00 01	00 04	00 05					00 20	00 19	00 25	00 25	00 24		
	d	23p44			23p47	23p47	23p47	23p54			23p56	00 01	00 04	00 06					00 20	00 20					
Crawley	d											00 05	00 07												
Ifield	d											00 07	00 10												
Faygate	d																								
Littlehaven	d											00 14	00 16												
Horsham 4	a											00 17	00 19												
Balcombe	d				23p53														00 26	00 26					
Haywards Heath	a	23p53		23p46	23p58	23p56	23p56	00 03			00 05			00 15					00 31	00 31					
	d	23p53		23p46	23p59	23p56	23p56	00 04			00 05			00 15					00 31	00 31					
Wivelsfield	d	23p57			00 03														00 35	00 35					
Lewes 4	a																								
Burgess Hill 4	d	23p59			00 05	00 02	00 02	00 09			00 11			00 20					00 37	00 37					
Hassocks 4	d	00 03			00 08	00 06	00 06	00 12											00 41	00 41					
Preston Park	d	00 09			00 15														00 48	00 48					
Hove 2	a										00 21			00 31											
Brighton 10	a	00 15		00 01	00 19	00 16	00 16	00 22											00 52	00 52					

A from 21 May until 25 June
B from 2 July until 10 September
C from 17 September
D from 2 July

Table 186

Bedford and London - Brighton

Mondays to Fridays

from 21 May

Network Diagram - see first Page of Table 186

Station		SN MO	SN MX 1	SN MX 1	SN 1	GW MO 1 A	SN MX ◇1	FC MO 1 B	FC MO 1 C	FC MX 1	SN 1	GW MX 1	SN ◇1 D	SN 1	SN ◇1 D	FC MO 1 B	FC MX 1 E	SN ◇1 D	SN ◇1	FC MO 1 B	FC MO 1 C
London Victoria 15 ⊖	d	23p47	23p47	23p49	00 02		00 05				00 14		00 25	00 30	00 40				01 00		
Clapham Junction 10	d	23p53	23p53	23p56			00 11				00 20		00 31		00 46				01 08		
Bedford	d							22p40	22p42	22p42						23p10	23p12			23p40	23p42
Luton 10	d							23p07	23p06	23p06						23p37	23p36			00 07	00 06
Luton Airport Parkway 7 ✈	d							23p09	23p09	23p09						23p39	23p39			00 09	00 09
St Albans City	d							23p21	23p21	23p21						23p51	23p51			00 21	00 21
St Pancras International 15 ⊖	d							23p54	23p54	23p54						00 24	00 24			00 54	00 54
Farringdon 3 ⊖	d							23p59	23p59	23p59						00 29	00 29				
City Thameslink 3	d																				
London Blackfriars 3 ⊖	d							00 05	00 05	00 05						00 35	00 35			01 05	01 05
London Bridge 4 ⊖	d							00 12	00 12	00 12						00 42	00 42				
New Cross Gate	d																				
Norwood Junction 2	d																				
East Croydon	a	00 06	00 05	00 09			00 26	00 26	00 26	00 26	00 31		00 40		00 55	00 56	00 56		01 23	01 31	01 31
	d		00 06				00 27	00 26	00 26	00 27	00 32		00 41		00 56	00 57	00 57		01 24	01 32	01 32
Purley 4	d		00 12								00 37		00 46						01 29		
Coulsdon South	d		00 15								00 41										
Merstham	d		00 21								00 47										
Redhill	a		00 24								00 50		00 55								
	d		00 25			00 34					00 51	00 54	00 55								
Reigate	a																				
Nutfield	d																				
Godstone	d																				
Edenbridge	d																				
Penshurst	d																				
Leigh (Kent)	d																				
Tonbridge 4	a																				
Earlswood (Surrey)	d																				
Salfords	d																				
Horley 4	d		00 31								00 57		01 02						01 44		
Gatwick Airport 10 ✈	a		00 33		00 37	00 41	00 43	00 48	00 48	00 48	00 59	01 03	01 04	01 05	01 13	01 18	01 18		01 46	01 51	01 51
	d		00 34				00 44	00 49	00 49	00 49			01 06		01 14	01 22	01 22		01 48	01 52	01 52
Three Bridges 15	a		00 39				00 48	00 54	00 54	00 54			01 10		01 18	01 28	01 28		01 52	01 58	01 58
	d		00 39				00 49								01 18				01 53		
Crawley	d		00 43																		
Ifield	d		00 46																		
Faygate	d																				
Littlehaven	d		00 52																		
Horsham 4	a		00 55																		
Balcombe	d																				
Haywards Heath	a						00 58								01 27				02 05		
	d						01 02 / 01 06								01 32			01 35	02 06		
Wivelsfield	d																				
Lewes 4	a						01 20											01s49			
Burgess Hill 4	d																				
Hassocks 4	d																				
Preston Park	d																				
Hove 2	a																				
Brighton 10	a						01s16								01s46				02 23		

A from 21 May until 10 September
B from 21 May until 25 June
C from 2 July
D from 30 July until 7 September, not from 13 August until 29 August
E from 22 May until 22 June, from 26 June

Bedford and London - Brighton

from 21 May

Network Diagram - see first Page of Table 186

		FC	SN	SN	FC	FC	SN	FC	FC	SN	FC	SN	FC	FC	SN	FC	SN	SN	SN	SN	GW	GW
		MX			MO	MX			MX				MO	MX								
			◇									◇							◇			
			A		B	C		B	C			A	B	C								
London Victoria	d		01 30	02 00			03 00			03 30		04 00			04 30		05 00		05 02	05 15		
Clapham Junction	d		01 36	02 08			03 08					04 08							05 08			
Bedford	d	23p42			00 40	00 42		01 40	01 42				02 40	02 42								
Luton	d	00 06			01 06	01 06		02 06	02 06				03 06	03 06								
Luton Airport Parkway	d	00 09			01 09	01 09		02 09	02 09				03 09	03 09								
St Albans City	d	00 21			01 21	01 21		02 21	02 21				03 21	03 21								
St Pancras International	d	00 54			01 54	01 54		02 54	02 54		03 28		03 54	03 54		04 24						
Farringdon	d	00 59																				
City Thameslink	d																					
London Blackfriars	d	01 05			02 05	02 05		03 05	03 05		03 39		04 05	04 05		04 35						
London Bridge	d																					
New Cross Gate	d																					
Norwood Junction	d																					
East Croydon	a	01 31	01 45	02 23	02 31	02 31	03 23	03 31	03 31		04 03	04 23	04 31	04 31		05 01			05 20			
	d	01 32	01 46	02 24	02 32	02 32	03 24	03 32	03 32		04 04	04 24	04 32	04 32		05 02			05 20			
Purley	d		01 51	02 29			03 29					04 29							05 25			
Coulsdon South	d																		05 28			
Merstham	d																		05 34			
Redhill	a		02 00																05 37			
	d		02 00															05 35	05 38		05 43	05 44
Reigate	a																				05 48	
Nutfield	d																	05 39				
Godstone	d																	05 45				
Edenbridge	d																	05 50				
Penshurst	d																	05 57				
Leigh (Kent)	d																	06 00				
Tonbridge	a																	06 05				
Earlswood (Surrey)	d																					
Salfords	d																					
Horley	d		02 07	02 44			03 44					04 44							05 44			
Gatwick Airport	a	01 51	02 09	02 46	02 51	02 51	03 46	03 51	03 51	04 05	04 24	04 46	04 51	04 51	05 05	05 21	05 35		05 46	05 50		05 54
	d	01 52	02 11	02 48	02 52	02 52	03 48	03 52	03 52		04 24	04 48	04 52	04 52		05 22			05 47			
Three Bridges	a	01 58	02 15	02 53	02 58	02 58	03 53	03 58	03 58		04 30	04 52	04 58	04 58		05 26			05 52			
	d		02 16									04 53	05 00	05 00		05 27			05 52			
Crawley	d																					
Ifield	d																					
Faygate	d																					
Littlehaven	d																					
Horsham	a																					
Balcombe	d																		05 58			
Haywards Heath	a		02 25									05 02	05 10	05 10		05 36			06 03			
	d		02 25									05 02	05 11	05 11		05 36			06 04			
Wivelsfield	d															05 40			06 08			
Lewes	a																					
Burgess Hill	d															05 43			06 10			
Hassocks	d															05 46			06 13			
Preston Park	d															05 53			06 20			
Hove	a																					
Brighton	a		02 40									05 18	05 29	05 29		05 57			06 26			

A from 30 July until 7 September, not from 13 August until 29 August

B from 21 May until 25 June

C from 22 May until 22 June, from 26 June

Table 186

Mondays to Fridays

from 21 May

Bedford and London - Brighton

Network Diagram - see first Page of Table 186

		SN	SN	FC MO	FC MX	SN	SN	FC MO	FC MX	SN	SN	FC MO	FC MX	SN	GW	GW	GW	SN	SN	SN	SN	FC
		1		1	1	1	1	1	1	◇1	1	1	1	1	1	1	1	1	◇1	◇1	1	1
				A	B			A	B			A	B	🚌							C 🚌	
London Victoria 15 ⊖	d						05 30			05 32	05 45			06 00					06 02		06 15	
Clapham Junction 10	d									05 38									06 08			
Bedford	d			03 40	03 42			04 06	04 08			04 18	04 20									05 00
Luton 10	d			04 06	04 06			04 32	04 32			04 44	04 44									05 24
Luton Airport Parkway 7 ✈	d			04 09	04 09			04 35	04 35			04 47	04 47									05 27
St Albans City	d			04 21	04 21			04 47	04 47			04 59	04 59									05 39
St Pancras International 15 ⊖	d			04 54	04 54			05 12	05 12			05 32	05 32									06 02
Farringdon 3 ⊖	d			04 59	04 59			05 18	05 18			05 38	05 38									06 08
City Thameslink 3	d							05 21	05 21			05 41	05 41									06 11
London Blackfriars 3 ⊖	d			05 04	05 04			05 24	05 24			05 44	05 44									06 14
London Bridge 4 ⊖	d							05 30	05 30			05 50	05 50									06 20
New Cross Gate	d																					
Norwood Junction 2	d																					
East Croydon	a			05 29	05 29			05 47	05 47	05 48		06 05	06 05						06 17			06 33
	d			05 32	05 32			05 47	05 47	05 49		06 05	06 05						06 18			06 35
Purley 4	d									05 53									06 23			
Coulsdon South	d									05 57									06 26			
Merstham	d									06 02									06 32			
Redhill	a									06 06									06 35			
	d	05 56								06 06					06 13	06 24	06 33	06 39	06 39	06 41		
Reigate	a														06 18	06 28		06 43				
Nutfield	d	06 00																		06 45		
Godstone	d	06 06																		06 51		
Edenbridge	d	06 11																		06 56		
Penshurst	d	06 18																		07 03		
Leigh (Kent)	d	06 21																		07 06		
Tonbridge 4	a	06 26																		07 11		
Earlswood (Surrey)	d									06 09									06 41			
Salfords	d									06 12									06 45			
Horley 4	d									06 16									06 48			
Gatwick Airport 10 ✈	a			05 53	05 53		06 00	06 02	06 02	06 18	06 15	06 21	06 21	06 30			06 40		06 54		06 45	06 51
	d			05 54	05 54	05 56		06 04	06 04	06 20		06 22	06 22						06 55		06 48	06 52
Three Bridges 15	a			05 59	05 59	06 00		06 08	06 08	06 24		06 26	06 26						↔			06 56
	d			06 00	06 00	06 01		06 08	06 08	06 25		06 26	06 26									06 56
Crawley	d					06 05																
Ifield	d					06 07																
Faygate	d																					
Littlehaven	d					06 14																
Horsham 4	a					06 17																
Balcombe	d							06 14	06 14			06 33	06 33									
Haywards Heath	a			06 09	06 09			06 19	06 19	06 34		06 39	06 39								06 58	07 05
	d		06 07	06 11	06 11			06 19	06 19	06 34		06 39	06 39								07 00	07 06
Wivelsfield	d		06 11					06 23	06 23	06 38		06 43	06 43									07 10
Lewes 4	a		06 22							06 50												
Burgess Hill 4	d			06 16	06 16			06 25	06 25			06 45	06 45									07 12
Hassocks 4	d			06 20	06 20			06 29	06 29			06 49	06 49									07 16
Preston Park	d			06 27	06 27			06 35	06 35			06 55	06 55									07 22
Hove 2	a																					
Brighton 10	a			06 31	06 31			06 40	06 40			06 59	06 59								07 13	07 27

A from 21 May until 25 June
B from 22 May until 22 June, from 26 June
C 1 from Gatwick Airport 🚌 to Gatwick Airport

Table 186

Bedford and London - Brighton

Mondays to Fridays

from 21 May

Network Diagram - see first Page of Table 186

		SN ◇[1]	SN [1]	SN [1]	SN ◇[1]	SN [1] A 🚌	SN ◇[1]	SN [1]		GW [1]	SN ◇[1]		FC [1]	GW [1]	SN [1] 🚌	SN ◇[1]		SN ◇[1]	SN [1]	SN [1]		FC [1]	SN [1] 🚌	SN [1]
London Victoria [15] ⊖	d				06 21	06 30					06 32				06 45	06 47				06 51			07 00	
Clapham Junction [10]	d				06 27						06 38					06 53				06 57				
Bedford	d												05 20									05 40		
Luton [10]	d												05 44									06 04		
Luton Airport Parkway [7] ✈	d												05 46									06 06		
St Albans City	d												05 58									06 18		
St Pancras International [15] ⊖	d												06 22									06 38		
Farringdon [3] ⊖	d												06 28									06 44		
City Thameslink [3]	d												06 31									06 47		
London Blackfriars [3] ⊖	d												06 34									06 50		
London Bridge [4] ⊖	d												06 42									07 00		
New Cross Gate	d																							
Norwood Junction [2]	d																							
East Croydon 🚋	a				06 38						06 48		06 54			07 03				07 06		07 14		
	d				06 38						06 49		06 55			07 04				07 07		07 15		
Purley [4]	d				06 43						06 55													
Coulsdon South	d				06 47						06 58									07 13				
Merstham	d				06 52						07 04									07 19				
Redhill	a				06 56						07 08									07 23				
	d				06 57			07 00		07 10	07 12	07 14		07 28						07 28	07 30			
Reigate	a							07 04		07 15				07 32										
Nutfield	d											07 18									07 34			
Godstone	d											07 24									07 40			
Edenbridge	d											07 29									07 45			
Penshurst	d											07 36									07 52			
Leigh (Kent)	d											07 39									07 55			
Tonbridge [4]	a											07 44									08 02			
Earlswood (Surrey)	d										07 14									07 30				
Salfords	d										07 18									07 34				
Horley [4]	d	←			07 03		←				07 21							←	←	07 37				←
Gatwick Airport [10] ✈	a	06 54			07 05	06 59	07 05				07 24		07 10		07 16	07 19		07 24	07 16	07 40		07 30	07 31	07 40
	d	06 55			07 06	07 04	07 06				07 25		07 11		07 25	07 20		07 25	07 25	07 41		07 31		07 41
Three Bridges [15]	a	06 59			→		07 11				→		07 15		→	07 24		07 29		→		07 35		07 45
	d	07 00	07 05				07 11						07 15			07 24		07 30				07 35		07 46
Crawley	d	07 03	07 08															07 34						07 50
Ifield	d		07 11															07 36						07 53
Faygate	d		07 15																					
Littlehaven	d		07 19															07 43						07 59
Horsham [4]	a	07 11	07 22															07 46						08 02
Balcombe	d												07 21											
Haywards Heath	a					07 14	07 20						07 26			07 33						07 44		
	d			07 10		07 16	07 21						07 26			07 33						07 46		
Wivelsfield	d			07 14			07 25									07 37						07 50		
Lewes [4]	a			07 29												07 52								
Burgess Hill [4]	d						07 27						07 31									07 52		
Hassocks [4]	d						07 30						07 35									07 55		
Preston Park	d						07 37															08 02		
Hove [2]	a																							
Brighton [10]	a					07 35	07 41						07 44						07 53			08 06		

A 🚌 to Gatwick Airport

Bedford and London - Brighton

Network Diagram - see first Page of Table 186

		GW	SN	SN	FC	FC	SN	SN		SN	SN	SN	GW	SN	FC	SN		SN	SN	SN	SN	SN	SN	SN	
		1	1	1	1	1	◇1	1		1	1	1	1	1	1	1		◇1	1	1	1	1a	◇1	1	
					A	B																			
				🚲				🚲								🚲									
London Victoria 15 ⊖	d		07 02	07 15			07 17	07 30						07 36		07 45		07 47					07 52		
Clapham Junction 10	d		07 08				07 23							07 42				07 53					07 58		
Bedford	d				05 56	05 58									06 22										
Luton 10	d				06 22	06 22									06 46										
Luton Airport Parkway 7 ✈	d				06 24	06 24									06 48										
St Albans City	d				06 36	06 36									07 00										
St Pancras International 15 ⊖	d				06 58	06 58									07 20										
Farringdon 3 ⊖	d				07 04	07 04									07 26										
City Thameslink 3	d				07 07	07 07									07 29										
London Blackfriars 3 ⊖	d				07 09	07 09									07 32										
London Bridge 4 ⊖	d				07 16	07 16					07 30	07 33			07 42						07 51				
New Cross Gate	d											07 38													
Norwood Junction 2	d										07 42										08 02				
East Croydon	a		07 17		07 30	07 30	07 33				07 45	07 48		07 51	07 54			08 02			08 05		08 09		
	d		07 18		07 31	07 31	07 34				07 46	07 49		07 52	07 55			08 03			08 06		08 09		
Purley 4	d		07 23											07 57											
Coulsdon South	d		07 26								07 52			08 01											
Merstham	d		07 32								07 58			08 07											
Redhill	a		07 35				07 47				08 01			08 10							08 18				
	d	07 41	07 44				07 47			08 00	08 02		08 08	08 11						08 17	08 22	08 24			
Reigate	a		07 48							08 04			08 13							08 21					
Nutfield	d										08 06											08 28			
Godstone	d										08 12											08 34			
Edenbridge	d										08 17											08 39			
Penshurst	d										08 24											08 46			
Leigh (Kent)	d										08 27											08 49			
Tonbridge 4	a										08 32											08 54			
Earlswood (Surrey)	d						07 50							08 13											
Salfords	d						07 53							08 17											
Horley 4	d						07 57							08 21					←					←	
Gatwick Airport 10 ✈	a	07 50		07 45	07 46	07 46	07 59	08 02				08 03		08 23	08 11	08 15		08 18	08 23		08 29		08 24	08 29	
	d				07 47	07 47	08 00					08 05		08 24	08 12			08 20	08 24		08 30		08 26	08 30	
Three Bridges 15	a				07 51	07 51	08 05					08 09		→	08 16				08 29		→			08 34	
	d				07 51	07 51	08 05					08 09			08 16				08 30					08 35	
Crawley	d						08 09												08 34						
Ifield	d						08 11												08 36						
Faygate	d						08 15												08 40						
Littlehaven	d						08 19												08 44						
Horsham 4	a						08 22												08 48						
Balcombe	d				07 57	07 57									08 22										
Haywards Heath	a				08 02	08 02						08 18			08 27			08 30					08 36	08 44	
	d				08 02	08 02						08 19			08 27			08 31					08 37	08 44	
Wivelsfield	d				08 06	08 06									08 31			08 35						08 48	
Lewes 4	a																	08 50							
Burgess Hill 4	d				08 08	08 08						08 24			08 33									08 50	
Hassocks 4	d				08 12	08 12									08 37									08 54	
Preston Park	d				08 18	08 18									08 43									09 00	
Hove 2	a																						08 53		
Brighton 10	a				08 23	08 23						08 36			08 48									09 05	

A from 8 October

B from 21 May until 5 October

Table 186

Mondays to Fridays

Bedford and London - Brighton

from 21 May

Network Diagram - see first Page of Table 186

		SN	SN	GW	SN	SN	FC	SN		SN		FC	SN	GW	SN			SN	SN	SN	SN	SN	FC	SN
		1 🛒	◇1	1	1	◇1	1	1 🛒		◇1		1	1	1	1			◇1	1 🛒	◇1 🛒	1	◇1 🛒	1	1 🛒
London Victoria 15 ⊖	d	08 00	08 02			08 07		08 15		08 17								08 21	08 30	08 32		08 36		08 45
Clapham unction 10	d		08 08			08 13				08 23								08 27		08 38		08 43		
Bedford	d						06 54					06 58											07 30	
Lton 10	d						07 14					07 22											07 50	
Lton Airport Parkway 7 ✈	d											07 25												
St Albans City	d						07 26					07 38											08 02	
St Pancras hternational 15 ⊖	d						07 44					07 56											08 20	
Farringdon 3 ⊖	d						07 50					08 02											08 26	
City Thameslink 3	d						07 53					08 05											08 29	
London Blackfriars 3 ⊖	d						07 56					08 08											08 32	
London Bridge 4 ⊖	d				08 00							08 18			08 23						08 30			
Nw Cross Gate	d				08 08																08 36			
Nrwood unction 2	d				08 16																08 44			
East Croydon	a		08 18		08 20	08 22	08 26			08 34		08 37			08 37			08 40		08 48	08 48	08 52	08 57	
	d		08 18		08 20	08 23	08 26			08 34		08 37			08 38			08 40		08 48	08 51	08 53	08 58	
Purley 4	d				08 26																08 59			
Coulsdon South	d				08 29										08 47						09 02			
Merstham	d				08 35																09 08			
Redhill	a		08 30		08 38										08 54					09 02	09 12			
	d		08 30	08 33	08 41									08 50	08 58	09 00				09 03	09 12			
Reigate	a			08 37												09 04								
Ntfield	d														09 02									
Godstone	d														09 08									
Eenbridge	d														09 13									
Penshurst	d														09 20									
Lεigh (Kent)	d														09 23									
Tonbridge 4	a														09 28									
Erlswood (Surrey)	d				08 43																09 15			
Salfords	d				08 47																09 18			
Horley 4	d				08 50								←								09 22			
Gatwick Airport 10 ✈	a	08 31	08 37		08 53		08 41	08 45		08 49		08 52	08 53	08 59				08 56	09 00	09 10	09 24		09 12	09 15
	d		08 40		08 54		08 42			08 50		08 53	08 54					08 57		09 11	09 25		09 13	
Three Bridges 15	a		08 44		→	08 41	08 46					08 57	08 59					09 01		09 16	→		09 17	
	d		08 45			08 42	08 46					08 58	08 59					09 01		09 16			09 17	
Crawley	d		08 48										09 03							09 19				
field	d												09 06											
Faygate	d												09 10											
Ittlehaven	d												09 14											
Horsham 4	a		08 56										09 17							09 27				
Balcombe	d						08 52																	
Haywards Heath	a					08 51	08 57			09 00		09 07						09 12					09 26	
	d					08 51	08 58			09 04	09 10	09 08						09 21					09 27	
Welsfield	d						09 02				09 14							09 25						
Lewes 4	a										09 25													
Burgess Hill 4	d						09 04			09 09		09 13						09 27					09 32	
Hassocks 4	d						09 07											09 30					09 35	
Preston Park	d						09 14			09 18								09 37					09 42	
Hove 2	a									09 21														
Brighton 10	a					09 08	09 18					09 25						09 41				09 28	09 46	

Bedford and London - Brighton

Network Diagram - see first Page of Table 186

		SN	SN		SN	SN	SN	SN	GW	SN	GW	SN	SN	FC	SN	GW	SN	SN		SN	FC	SN
		1	◇1		◇1	1	1		1	◇1	1	1	◇1	1	1	1	1	◇1		1	1	1
																		A				
			trolley				trolley			trolley			trolley		trolley			trolley				trolley
London Victoria 15 ⊖	d		08 47		08 51		09 00	09 01		09 02			09 06		09 15			09 17				09 30
Clapham Junction 10	d		08 53					09 08		09 08			09 12					09 23				
Bedford	d													07 48							08 04	
Luton 10	d													08 12							08 28	
Luton Airport Parkway 7 ✈	d													08 15							08 30	
St Albans City	d													08 27							08 44	
St Pancras International 15 ⊖	d													08 48							09 04	
Farringdon 3 ⊖	d													08 54							09 10	
City Thameslink 3	d													08 57							09 13	
London Blackfriars 3 ⊖	d													09 00							09 16	
London Bridge 4 ⊖	d	08 45										09 03		09 12			09 15				09 27	
New Cross Gate	d											09 08										
Norwood Junction 2	d	08 56										09 16					09 26					
East Croydon	a	08 59	09 03		09 07					09 18		09 20	09 22	09 24			09 29	09 32			09 39	
	d	09 00	09 04		09 08					09 19		09 21	09 23	09 25			09 30	09 33			09 41	
Purley 4	d	09 06										09 27					09 36					
Coulsdon South	d	09 09										09 30					09 39					
Merstham	d											09 36					09 45					
Redhill	a	09 17								09 30		09 39					09 49					
	d	09 17							09 23	09 30	09 34	09 40				09 51	09 53					
Reigate	a								09 28		09 38						09 57					
Nutfield	d	09 22																				
Godstone	d	09 27																				
Edenbridge	d	09 33																				
Penshurst	d	09 39																				
Leigh (Kent)	d	09 43																				
Tonbridge 4	a	09 48																				
Earlswood (Surrey)	d											09 42										
Salfords	d											09 46										
Horley 4	d					←				09 36		09 50								←		
Gatwick Airport 10 ✈	a		09 18		09 22	09 24	09 30			09 39		09 53		09 40	09 45	09 59		09 48		09 53	09 56	10 00
	d		09 20		09 23	09 25				09 40		09 54		09 41				09 50		09 54	09 57	
Three Bridges 15	a					09 30				09 44		→		09 45						09 59	10 01	
	d					09 30				09 45				09 45						10 00	10 02	
Crawley	d					09 34				09 48										10 03		
Ifield	d					09 36														10 06		
Faygate	d																					
Littlehaven	d					09 43														10 12		
Horsham 4	a					09 46				09 56										10 15		
Balcombe	d													09 51								
Haywards Heath	a		09 30											09 56				10 00			10 11	
	d		09 35	09 37										09 56				10 05	10 07		10 11	
Wivelsfield	d													10 00					10 11			
Lewes 4	a		09 53																10 22			
Burgess Hill 4	d				09 38									10 02				10 10				
Hassocks 4	d				09 41									10 06								
Preston Park	d													10 12				10 18				
Hove 2	a			09 53														10 22				
Brighton 10	a				09 52								09 58	10 17							10 25	

A trolley to Haywards Heath

Table 186

Bedford and London - Brighton

Mondays to Fridays

from 21 May

Network Diagram - see first Page of Table 186

		SN	SN	SN	FC	SN	GW	SN		SN		SN	SN	FC	SN	SN		SN	GW	GW	SN	SN	FC	SN	
		◇1	1	◇1	1	1	1	1		◇1		◇1	1	1	1			◇1	1	1	1	◇1	1	1	
		🛒				🛒				🛒					🛒			🛒				🛒		🛒	
London Victoria 15 ⊖	d	09 32		09 36		09 45				09 47		09 51			10 00	10 01		10 02				10 06		10 15	
Clapham Junction 10	d	09 38		09 42						09 53						10 08		10 08				10 12			
Bedford	d				08 24									08 40									08 54		
Luton 10	d				08 48									09 04									09 18		
Luton Airport Parkway 7 ✈	d				08 50									09 06									09 20		
St Albans City	d				09 02									09 18									09 32		
St Pancras International 15 ⊖	d				09 22									09 40									09 54		
Farringdon 3 ⊖	d				09 28									09 45									09 59		
City Thameslink 3	d				09 31									09 48									10 03		
London Blackfriars 3 ⊖	d				09 34									09 50									10 05		
London Bridge 4 ⊖	d		09 32		09 42			09 45						09 57							10 03		10 12		
New Cross Gate	d		09 37																		10 08				
Norwood Junction 2	d		09 45					09 56													10 16				
East Croydon 🚌	a	09 48	09 49	09 52	09 54			09 59		10 02		10 07		10 09				10 17			10 20	10 22	10 24		
	d	09 48	09 51	09 53	09 55			10 00		10 03		10 08		10 11				10 18			10 21	10 23	10 25		
Purley 4	d		09 57					10 06													10 26				
Coulsdon South	d		10 00					10 09													10 30				
Merstham	d		10 06																		10 35				
Redhill	a	10 00	10 09					10 17										10 30			10 39				
	d	10 00	10 10				10 13	10 17										10 30	10 34	10 41	10 45				
Reigate	a						10 18												10 38						
Nutfield	d							10 22																	
Godstone	d							10 27																	
Edenbridge	d							10 33																	
Penshurst	d							10 39																	
Leigh (Kent)	d							10 43																	
Tonbridge 4	a							10 48																	
Earlswood (Surrey)	d		10 12																						
Salfords	d		10 16																						
Horley 4	d		10 19										←					10 36			10 53				
Gatwick Airport 10 ✈	a	10 08	10 23		10 10	10 15				10 18		10 22	10 23	10 26	10 30			10 39		10 50	10 55		10 40	10 45	
	d	10 09	10 24		10 11					10 20		10 23	10 24	10 27				10 40			10 56		10 41		
Three Bridges 15	a	10 14	→		10 15								10 29	10 31				10 44			→		10 45		
	d	10 14			10 15								10 30	10 32				10 45					10 45		
Crawley	d	10 18											10 33					10 48							
Ifield	d												10 36												
Faygate	d																								
Littlehaven	d												10 42												
Horsham 4	a	10 26											10 47					10 56							
Balcombe	d				10 21																				
Haywards Heath	a				10 26					10 30				10 41									10 54		
	d				10 27					10 35	10 37			10 41									10 55		
Wivelsfield	d				10 31																		10 59		
Lewes 4	a									10 52															
Burgess Hill 4	d				10 33							10 38											11 01		
Hassocks 4	d				10 36							10 41											11 04		
Preston Park	d				10 43																		11 11		
Hove 2	a										10 53														
Brighton 10	a			10 28	10 47							10 52		10 55								10 58	11 15		

Table 186

Mondays to Fridays

from 21 May

Bedford and London - Brighton

Network Diagram - see first Page of Table 186

		SN	SN		SN	FC	SN	SN		SN	SN	FC	SN	GW	SN	SN			SN	SN	FC	SN	SN	SN	GW
		[1]	◇[1]		[1]	[1]	[1]	◇[1]		[1]	◇[1]	[1]	[1]	[1]	[1]	◇[1]			◇[1]	[1]	[1]	[1]		◇[1]	[1]
			A																						
			🍴				🍴	🍴					🍴			🍴						🍴			
London Victoria [15] ⊖	d		10 17				10 30	10 32			10 36		10 45			10 47			10 51			11 00	11 01	11 02	
Clapham Junction [10]	d		10 23					10 38			10 42					10 53							11 08	11 08	
Bedford	d					09 10						09 24									09 40				
Luton [10]	d					09 34						09 48									10 04				
Luton Airport Parkway [7] ✈	d					09 36						09 50									10 06				
St Albans City	d					09 48						10 02									10 18				
St Pancras International [15] ⊖	d					10 09						10 24									10 39				
Farringdon [3] ⊖	d					10 14						10 29									10 44				
City Thameslink [3]	d					10 18						10 33									10 48				
London Blackfriars [3] ⊖	d					10 20						10 35									10 50				
London Bridge [4] ⊖	d	10 15				10 27				10 33		10 42			10 45						10 57				
New Cross Gate	d									10 38															
Norwood Junction [2]	d	10 26								10 46					10 56										
East Croydon 🚊	a	10 29	10 32			10 39		10 48		10 50	10 52	10 54			10 59	11 02			11 07		11 09			11 17	
	d	10 30	10 33			10 41		10 48		10 51	10 53	10 55			11 00	11 03			11 08		11 11			11 18	
Purley [4]	d	10 36								10 57					11 07										
Coulsdon South	d	10 39								11 00					11 10										
Merstham	d	10 45								11 06															
Redhill	a	10 49						11 00		11 09					11 18									11 30	
	d	10 52						11 00		11 10				11 13	11 18									11 30	11 34
Reigate	a	10 56												11 18											11 38
Nutfield	d														11 23										
Godstone	d														11 28										
Edenbridge	d														11 34										
Penshurst	d														11 40										
Leigh (Kent)	d														11 44										
Tonbridge [4]	a														11 48										
Earlswood (Surrey)	d									11 12															
Salfords	d									11 16															
Horley [4]	d				←					11 19										←				11 36	
Gatwick Airport [10] ✈	a		10 48		10 55	10 56	11 00	11 08		11 23		11 10	11 15			11 18			11 22	11 23	11 26	11 30		11 39	
	d		10 50		10 56	10 57		11 09		11 24		11 11				11 20			11 23	11 24	11 27			11 40	
Three Bridges [15]	a				11 01	11 01		11 14		→		11 15								11 29	11 31			11 44	
	d				11 01	11 02		11 14				11 15								11 30	11 32			11 45	
Crawley	d				11 05			11 18												11 33				11 48	
Ifield	d				11 07															11 36					
Faygate	d																								
Littlehaven	d				11 14															11 42					
Horsham [4]	a				11 17			11 26												11 45				11 56	
Balcombe	d											11 21													
Haywards Heath	a		11 00			11 11						11 26				11 30					11 41				
	d		11 04	11 07		11 11						11 27				11 35	11 37				11 41				
Wivelsfield	d			11 11								11 31													
Lewes [4]	a			11 22												11 52									
Burgess Hill [4]	d		11 09									11 33							11 38						
Hassocks [4]	d											11 36							11 41						
Preston Park	d		11 18									11 43													
Hove [2]	a		11 22														11 53								
Brighton [10]	a					11 25					11 28	11 47							11 52		11 55				

A 🍴 to Haywards Heath

Table 186

Mondays to Fridays

from 21 May

Bedford and London - Brighton

Network Diagram - see first Page of Table 186

		GW	SN	SN	FC	SN	SN	SN		SN	FC	SN	SN	SN	SN	FC	SN	GW	SN	SN		SN
		1	1	◇1	1	1	1	◇1		1	1	1	◇1	1	◇1	1	1	1	1	◇1		◇1
						[trolley]						[trolley]			[trolley]		[trolley]					
London Victoria 15 ⊖	d			11 06		11 15		11 17				11 30	11 32		11 36		11 45			11 47		11 51
Clapham Junction 10	d			11 12				11 23					11 38		11 42					11 53		
Bedford	d				09 54						10 10					10 25						
Luton 10	d				10 18						10 34					10 49						
Luton Airport Parkway 7 ✈	d				10 20						10 36					10 51						
St Albans City	d				10 32						10 48					11 03						
St Pancras International 15 ⊖	d				10 54						11 09					11 24						
Farringdon 3 ⊖	d				10 59						11 14					11 29						
City Thameslink 3	d				11 03						11 18					11 33						
London Blackfriars 3 ⊖	d				11 05						11 20					11 35						
London Bridge 4 ⊖	d		11 03		11 12		11 15				11 27			11 33		11 42			11 45			
New Cross Gate	d		11 08											11 38								
Norwood Junction 2	d		11 16				11 26							11 46					11 56			
East Croydon	a		11 20	11 22	11 24		11 29	11 32			11 39		11 48	11 50	11 52	11 54			11 59	12 02		12 07
	d		11 21	11 23	11 25		11 30	11 33			11 41		11 48	11 51	11 53	11 55			12 00	12 03		12 08
Purley 4	d		11 27				11 36							11 57					12 06			
Coulsdon South	d		11 30				11 39							12 00					12 09			
Merstham	d		11 36				11 45							12 06								
Redhill	a		11 39				11 49						12 00	12 09					12 17			
	d	11 41	11 45				11 52						12 00	12 10				12 13	12 17			
Reigate	a						11 56											12 18				
Nutfield	d																		12 22			
Godstone	d																		12 27			
Edenbridge	d																		12 33			
Penshurst	d																		12 39			
Leigh (Kent)	d																		12 43			
Tonbridge 4	a																		12 48			
Earlswood (Surrey)	d													12 12								
Salfords	d													12 16								
Horley 4	d		11 53							←				12 19								
Gatwick Airport 10 ✈	a	11 50	11 55		11 40	11 45		11 48		11 55	11 56	12 00	12 08	12 23		12 10	12 15			12 18		12 22
	d		11 56		11 41			11 50		11 56	11 57		12 09	12 24		12 11				12 20		12 23
Three Bridges 15	a		→		11 45					12 01	12 01		12 14	→		12 15						
	d				11 45					12 01	12 02		12 14			12 15						
Crawley	d									12 05			12 18									
Ifield	d									12 07												
Faygate	d									12 11												
Littlehaven	d									12 15												
Horsham 4	a									12 18			12 26									
Balcombe	d															12 21						
Haywards Heath	a				11 54			12 00			12 11					12 26				12 30		
	d				11 55			12 04	12 07		12 11					12 27				12 35	12 37	
Wivelsfield	d				11 59				12 11							12 31						
Lewes 4	a								12 22											12 52		
Burgess Hill 4	d				12 01			12 09								12 33						12 38
Hassocks 4	d				12 04											12 36						12 41
Preston Park	d				12 11			12 18								12 43						
Hove 2	a							12 22													12 53	
Brighton 10	a			11 58	12 15						12 25				12 28	12 47						12 52

Table 186

Mondays to Fridays

from 21 May

Bedford and London - Brighton

Network Diagram - see first Page of Table 186

		SN		FC	SN	SN	SN	GW	GW	SN		SN	FC	SN	SN	SN		SN		FC	SN	SN	SN	SN	FC
		1		1	1		◇1	1	1	1		◇1	1	1	1	◇1		1		1	1	◇1	1	◇1	1
					🛒							🛒		🛒							🛒			🛒	
London Victoria 15 ⊖	d				12 00	12 01	12 02					12 06		12 15		12 17					12 30	12 32		12 36	
Clapham Junction 10	d					12 08	12 08					12 12				12 23						12 38		12 42	
Bedford	d			10 40									10 54							11 10					11 24
Luton 10	d			11 04									11 18							11 34					11 48
Luton Airport Parkway 7 ✈	d			11 06									11 20							11 36					11 50
St Albans City	d			11 18									11 32							11 48					12 02
St Pancras International 15 ⊖	d			11 39									11 54							12 09					12 24
Farringdon 3 ⊖	d			11 44									11 59							12 14					12 29
City Thameslink 3	d			11 48									12 03							12 18					12 33
London Blackfriars 3 ⊖	d			11 50									12 05							12 20					12 35
London Bridge 4 ⊖	d			11 57						12 03			12 12		12 15					12 27			12 33		12 42
New Cross Gate	d									12 08													12 38		
Norwood Junction 2	d									12 16					12 26								12 46		
East Croydon	a			12 09			12 17			12 20		12 22	12 24		12 29	12 32				12 39		12 48	12 50	12 52	12 54
	d			12 11			12 18			12 21		12 23	12 25		12 30	12 33				12 41		12 48	12 51	12 53	12 55
Purley 4	d									12 27					12 36								12 58		
Coulsdon South	d									12 30					12 39								13 01		
Merstham	d									12 36					12 45								13 07		
Redhill	a						12 30			12 39					12 49							13 00	13 10		
	d						12 30	12 34	12 41	12 45					12 52							13 00	13 11		
Reigate	a							12 38							12 56										
Nutfield	d																								
Godstone	d																								
Edenbridge	d																								
Penshurst	d																								
Leigh (Kent)	d																								
Tonbridge 4	a																								
Earlswood (Surrey)	d																						13 13		
Salfords	d																						13 17		
Horley 4	d	←					12 36			12 53								←					13 20		
Gatwick Airport 10 ✈	a	12 23		12 26	12 30		12 39		12 50	12 55			12 40	12 45		12 48		12 55		12 56	13 00	13 08	13 23		13 10
	d	12 24		12 27			12 40			12 56			12 41			12 50		12 56		12 57		13 09	13 24		13 11
Three Bridges 15	a	12 29		12 31			12 44			→			12 45					13 01		13 01		13 14	→		13 15
	d	12 30		12 32			12 45						12 45					13 01		13 02		13 14			13 15
Crawley	d	12 33					12 48											13 05				13 18			
Ifield	d	12 36																13 07							
Faygate	d																								
Littlehaven	d	12 42																13 14							
Horsham 4	a	12 45					12 56											13 17				13 26			
Balcombe	d																								13 21
Haywards Heath	a			12 41									12 54			13 00				13 11					13 26
	d			12 41									12 55			13 04	13 07			13 11					13 27
Wivelsfield	d												12 59				13 11								13 31
Lewes 4	a																13 22								
Burgess Hill 4	d												13 01			13 09									13 33
Hassocks 4	d												13 04												13 36
Preston Park	d												13 11			13 18									13 43
Hove 2	a															13 22									
Brighton 10	a			12 55								12 58	13 15							13 25				13 28	13 47

Table 186

Bedford and London - Brighton

Mondays to Fridays

from 21 May

Network Diagram - see first Page of Table 186

		SN	GW	SN	SN		SN	SN	FC	SN	SN	SN	GW	GW	SN	SN	FC	SN	SN	SN		SN
		1	1	1	◇1		◇1	1	1	1		◇1	1	1	1	◇1	1	1	1	◇1		1
		bike								bike						bike		bike				
London Victoria 15 ⊖	d	12 45			12 47		12 51			13 00	13 01	13 02				13 06		13 15		13 17		
Clapham Junction 10	d				12 53						13 08	13 08				13 12				13 23		
Bedford	d								11 40								11 54					
Luton 10	d								12 04								12 18					
Luton Airport Parkway 7 ✈	d								12 06								12 20					
St Albans City	d								12 18								12 32					
St Pancras International 15 ⊖	d								12 39								12 54					
Farringdon 3 ⊖	d								12 44								12 59					
City Thameslink 3	d								12 48								13 03					
London Blackfriars 3 ⊖	d								12 50								13 05					
London Bridge 4 ⊖	d			12 45					12 57						13 03		13 12		13 15			
New Cross Gate	d														13 08							
Norwood Junction 2	d			12 56											13 16				13 26			
East Croydon	a			12 59	13 02		13 07		13 09			13 17			13 20	13 22	13 24		13 29	13 32		
	d			13 00	13 03		13 08		13 11			13 18			13 21	13 23	13 25		13 30	13 33		
Purley 4	d			13 06											13 27				13 36			
Coulsdon South	d			13 09											13 30				13 39			
Merstham	d														13 36				13 45			
Redhill	a			13 17								13 30			13 39				13 49			
	d		13 13	13 17								13 30	13 34	13 41	13 45				13 52			
Reigate	a		13 18										13 38						13 56			
Nutfield	d			13 22																		
Godstone	d			13 27																		
Edenbridge	d			13 33																		
Penshurst	d			13 39																		
Leigh (Kent)	d			13 43																		
Tonbridge 4	a			13 48																		
Earlswood (Surrey)	d																					
Salfords	d																					
Horley 4	d							←				13 36			13 53							←
Gatwick Airport 10 ✈	a	13 15			13 18		13 22	13 23	13 26	13 30		13 39		13 50	13 55		13 40	13 45		13 48		13 55
	d				13 20		13 23	13 24	13 27			13 40			13 56		13 41			13 50		13 56
Three Bridges 15	a							13 29	13 31			13 44			→		13 45					14 01
	d							13 30	13 32			13 45					13 45					14 01
Crawley	d							13 33				13 48										14 05
Ifield	d							13 36														14 07
Faygate	d																					
Littlehaven	d							13 42														14 14
Horsham 4	a							13 45				13 56										14 17
Balcombe	d																					
Haywards Heath	a				13 30				13 41								13 54			14 00		
	d				13 35	13 37			13 41								13 55			14 04	14 07	
Wivelsfield	d																13 59				14 11	
Lewes 4	a				13 52																14 22	
Burgess Hill 4	d						13 38										14 01			14 09		
Hassocks 4	d						13 41										14 04					
Preston Park	d																14 11			14 18		
Hove 2	a					13 53														14 22		
Brighton 10	a						13 52		13 55							13 58	14 15					

Table 186

Bedford and London - Brighton

Mondays to Fridays

from 21 May

Network Diagram - see first Page of Table 186

		FC		SN	SN	SN	SN	FC	SN	GW		SN	SN	SN	SN	FC	SN		SN	SN	GW	GW	SN	SN
		1		1	◇1	1	◇1	1	1	1		1	◇1	◇1	1	1	1			◇1	1	1	1	◇1
				🛒	🛒		🛒		🛒								🛒							🛒
London Victoria 15 ⊖	d			13 30	13 32		13 36		13 45				13 47	13 51			14 00		14 01	14 02				14 06
Clapham Junction 10	d				13 38		13 42						13 53						14 08	14 08				14 12
Bedford	d	12 10						12 24								12 40								
Luton 10	d	12 34						12 48								13 04								
Luton Airport Parkway 7 ✈	d	12 36						12 50								13 06								
St Albans City	d	12 48						13 02								13 18								
St Pancras International 15 ⊖	d	13 09						13 24								13 39								
Farringdon 3 ⊖	d	13 14						13 29								13 44								
City Thameslink 3	d	13 18						13 33								13 48								
London Blackfriars 3 ⊖	d	13 20						13 35								13 50								
London Bridge 4 ⊖	d	13 27				13 33		13 42				13 45				13 57							14 03	
New Cross Gate	d					13 38																	14 08	
Norwood Junction 2	d					13 46						13 56											14 16	
East Croydon 🚌	a	13 39			13 48	13 50	13 52	13 54				13 59	14 02	14 07		14 09				14 17			14 20	14 22
	d	13 41			13 48	13 51	13 53	13 55				14 00	14 03	14 08		14 11				14 18			14 21	14 23
Purley 4	d					13 57						14 06											14 27	
Coulsdon South	d					14 00						14 09											14 30	
Merstham	d					14 06																	14 36	
Redhill	a				14 00	14 09						14 17								14 30			14 39	
	d				14 00	14 10				14 13		14 17								14 30	14 34	14 41	14 45	
Reigate	a									14 18											14 38			
Nutfield	d											14 22												
Godstone	d											14 27												
Edenbridge	d											14 33												
Penshurst	d											14 39												
Leigh (Kent)	d											14 43												
Tonbridge 4	a											14 48												
Earlswood (Surrey)	d					14 12																		
Salfords	d					14 16																		
Horley 4	d					14 19									←					14 36			14 53	
Gatwick Airport 10 ✈	a	13 56		14 00	14 08	14 23		14 10	14 15				14 18	14 22	14 23	14 26	14 30			14 39		14 50	14 55	
	d	13 57			14 09	14 24		14 11					14 20	14 23	14 24	14 27				14 40			14 56	
Three Bridges 15	a	14 01			14 14	→		14 15							14 29	14 31				14 44			→	
	d	14 02			14 14			14 15							14 30	14 32				14 45				
Crawley	d				14 18										14 33					14 48				
Ifield	d														14 36									
Faygate	d																							
Littlehaven	d														14 42									
Horsham 4	a				14 26										14 45					14 56				
Balcombe	d							14 21																
Haywards Heath	a	14 11						14 26					14 30			14 41								
	d	14 11						14 27					14 35 / 14 37			14 41								
Wivelsfield	d							14 31																
Lewes 4	a												14 52											
Burgess Hill 4	d							14 33						14 38										
Hassocks 4	d							14 36						14 41										
Preston Park	d							14 43																
Hove 2	a												14 53											
Brighton 10	a	14 25					14 28	14 47						14 52		14 55								14 58

Table 186

Bedford and London - Brighton

Mondays to Fridays

from 21 May

Network Diagram - see first Page of Table 186

		FC 1		SN 1 🛒	SN 1	SN ◇1		SN 1	FC 1	SN 1 🛒		SN ◇1 🛒	SN 1	SN ◇1 🛒	FC 1	SN 1 🛒	GW 1	SN 1		SN ◇1		SN ◇1	SN 1	FC 1	SN 1 🛒
London Victoria 15 ⊖	d			14 15		14 17				14 30		14 32		14 36		14 45				14 47		14 51			15 00
Clapham unction 10	d					14 23						14 38		14 42						14 53					
Bedford	d	12 54							13 10						13 24									13 40	
uton 10	d	13 18							13 34						13 48									14 04	
uton Airport Parkway 7 ✈	d	13 20							13 36						13 50									14 06	
St Albans City	d	13 32							13 48						14 02									14 18	
St Pancras hternational 15 ⊖	d	13 54							14 09						14 24									14 39	
Farringdon 3 ⊖	d	13 59							14 14						14 29									14 44	
City Thameslink 3	d	14 03							14 18						14 33									14 48	
London Blackfriars 3 ⊖	d	14 05							14 20						14 35									14 50	
London Bridge 4 ⊖	d	14 12			14 15				14 27				14 33		14 42			14 45						14 57	
New Cross Gate	d												14 38												
Norwood Junction 2	d				14 26								14 46					14 56							
East Croydon	a	14 25			14 29	14 32			14 39			14 48	14 50	14 52	14 54			14 59		15 02		15 07		15 09	
	d	14 25			14 30	14 33			14 41			14 48	14 51	14 53	14 55			15 00		15 03		15 08		15 11	
Purley 4	d				14 36								14 57					15 06							
Coulsdon South	d				14 39								15 00					15 09							
Merstham	d				14 45								15 06												
Redhill	a				14 49							15 00	15 09					15 17							
	d				14 52							15 00	15 10				15 13	15 17							
Reigate	a				14 56												15 18								
Nutfield	d																	15 22							
Godstone	d																	15 27							
Edenbridge	d																	15 33							
Penshurst	d																	15 39							
Leigh (Kent)	d																	15 43							
Tonbridge 4	a																	15 48							
Earlswood (Surrey)	d												15 12												
Salfords	d												15 16												
Horley 4	d							←					15 19										←		
Gatwick Airport 10 ✈	a	14 40		14 45		14 48		14 55	14 56	15 00		15 08	15 23		15 10	15 15				15 18		15 22	15 23	15 26	15 30
	d	14 41				14 50		14 56	14 57			15 09	15 24		15 11					15 20		15 23	15 24	15 27	
Three Bridges 15	a	14 45						15 01	15 01			15 14	→		15 15								15 29	15 31	
	d	14 45						15 01	15 02			15 14			15 15								15 30	15 32	
Crawley	d							15 05				15 18											15 33		
field	d							15 07															15 36		
Faygate	d																								
Littlehaven	d							15 14															15 42		
Horsham 4	a							15 17				15 26											15 48		
Balcombe	d														15 21										
Haywards Heath	a	14 54				15 00			15 11						15 26					15 30				15 41	
	d	14 55				15 04	15 07		15 11						15 27					15 35	15 37			15 41	
Wivelsfield	d	14 59					15 11								15 31					15 39					
Lewes 4	a						15 22													15 52					
Burgess Hill 4	d	15 01				15 09									15 33							15 38			
Hassocks 4	d	15 04													15 36							15 41			
Preston Park	d	15 11				15 18									15 43										
Hove 2	a					15 22															15 53				
Brighton 10	a	15 15							15 25					15 28	15 47							15 52		15 55	

Table 186

Mondays to Fridays

from 21 May

Bedford and London - Brighton

Network Diagram - see first Page of Table 186

		SN		GW	SN	GW	SN	SN	FC	SN		SN	SN		FC	SN	SN	SN		SN	SN	FC	SN	GW	SN
				1	◇1	1	1	◇1 🚲	1	1 🚲		1	◇1		1	1	1 🚲	◇1		1	◇1 🚲	1	1 🚲	1	1
London Victoria 15 ⊖	d	15 01			15 02			15 06		15 15			15 17				15 30	15 32			15 36		15 45		
Clapham Junction 10	d	15 08			15 08			15 12					15 23					15 38			15 42				
Bedford	d								13 54						14 10							14 24			
Luton 10	d								14 18						14 34							14 48			
Luton Airport Parkway 7 ✈	d								14 20						14 36							14 50			
St Albans City	d								14 32						14 48							15 02			
St Pancras International 15 ⊖	d								14 54						15 09							15 24			
Farringdon 3 ⊖	d								14 59						15 14							15 29			
City Thameslink 3	d								15 03						15 18							15 33			
London Blackfriars 3 ⊖	d								15 05						15 20							15 35			
London Bridge 4 ⊖	d						15 03		15 12			15 15			15 27					15 33		15 42			15 45
New Cross Gate	d						15 08													15 38					
Norwood Junction 2	d						15 16					15 26								15 46					15 56
East Croydon	a				15 17		15 20	15 22	15 24			15 29	15 32		15 39			15 47		15 50	15 52	15 54			15 59
	d				15 18		15 21	15 23	15 25			15 30	15 33		15 41			15 48		15 51	15 53	15 55			16 00
Purley 4	d						15 27					15 36								15 57					16 06
Coulsdon South	d						15 30					15 39								16 00					16 09
Merstham	d						15 36					15 45								16 06					16 15
Redhill	a				15 30		15 39					15 49						16 00		16 09					16 19
	d			15 29	15 30	15 41	15 45					15 52						16 00		16 10				16 13	16 20
Reigate	a			15 33								15 56												16 18	
Nutfield	d																								16 24
Godstone	d																								16 30
Edenbridge	d																								16 35
Penshurst	d																								16 42
Leigh (Kent)	d																								16 45
Tonbridge 4	a																								16 52
Earlswood (Surrey)	d						15 48													16 12					
Salfords	d						15 51													16 16					
Horley 4	d				15 36		15 55									←				16 19					
Gatwick Airport 10 ✈	a				15 39	15 50	15 57		15 40	15 45			15 48		15 56	15 57	16 00	16 08		16 23		16 10	16 15		
	d				15 40		15 58		15 41				15 50		15 57	15 58		16 09		16 24		16 11			
Three Bridges 15	a				15 44		→		15 45						16 01	16 03		16 14		→		16 15			
	d				15 45				15 45						16 02	16 03		16 14				16 15			
Crawley	d				15 48											16 07		16 18							
Ifield	d															16 10									
Faygate	d															16 14									
Littlehaven	d															16 18									
Horsham 4	a				15 56											16 21		16 26							
Balcombe	d																					16 21			
Haywards Heath	a								15 54				16 00		16 11							16 26			
	d								15 55				16 04	16 07	16 11							16 27			
Wivelsfield	d								15 59					16 11								16 31			
Lewes 4	a													16 22											
Burgess Hill 4	d								16 01				16 09									16 33			
Hassocks 4	d								16 04													16 36			
Preston Park	d								16 11				16 18									16 43			
Hove 2	a												16 22												
Brighton 10	a							15 58	16 15						16 25						16 28	16 47			

Table 186

Bedford and London - Brighton

Mondays to Fridays

from 21 May

Network Diagram - see first Page of Table 186

		SN			SN	SN	FC	SN	SN	SN	GW		SN		SN	FC	SN	GW	SN		SN		SN	SN	FC
		◇1			◇1	1	1	1		◇1	1		1		1	1	1	1	1		◇1		1	1	1
								[trolley]							[trolley]						A [trolley]				
London Victoria 15 ⊖	d	15 47			15 51			16 00	16 01	16 02					16 06		16 15				16 17		16 19		
Clapham Junction 10	d	15 53							16 08	16 08					16 12						16 23		16 26		
Bedford	d						14 40									14 54									15 10
Luton 10	d						15 04									15 18									15 34
Luton Airport Parkway 7 ✈	d						15 06									15 20									15 36
St Albans City	d						15 18									15 32									15 48
St Pancras International 15 ⊖	d						15 39									15 54									16 09
Farringdon 3 ⊖	d						15 44									15 59									16 14
City Thameslink 3	d						15 48									16 03									16 18
London Blackfriars 3 ⊖	d						15 50									16 05									16 20
London Bridge 4 ⊖	d						15 57						16 03			16 12			16 15						16 27
New Cross Gate	d												16 08												
Norwood Junction 2	d												16 16						16 26						
East Croydon	a	16 02			16 07		16 09			16 17			16 20		16 22	16 24			16 29		16 33		16 36		16 39
	d	16 03			16 08		16 11			16 18			16 21		16 23	16 25			16 30		16 33		16 36		16 41
Purley 4	d												16 27						16 36						
Coulsdon South	d												16 30						16 39						
Merstham	d												16 36						16 45						
Redhill	a									16 30			16 39						16 49						
	d									16 30	16 32		16 43	16 45				16 51	16 53						
Reigate	a										16 36								16 59						
Nutfield	d													16 49											
Godstone	d													16 55											
Edenbridge	d													17 00											
Penshurst	d													17 07											
Leigh (Kent)	d													17 10											
Tonbridge 4	a													17 15											
Earlswood (Surrey)	d												16 45												
Salfords	d												16 49												
Horley 4	d					←				16 36			16 52											←	
Gatwick Airport 10 ✈	a	16 18			16 22	16 23	16 26	16 30		16 39			16 55			16 40	16 45	16 59			16 48		16 52	16 55	16 56
	d	16 20			16 23	16 24	16 27			16 40			16 56			16 41					16 49		16 53	16 56	16 57
Three Bridges 15	a					16 29	16 31			16 44			→			16 45							16 57	17 00	17 01
	d					16 30	16 32			16 45						16 45							16 58	17 02	17 02
Crawley	d					16 34				16 48													17 02	17 06	
Ifield	d					16 36																		17 08	
Faygate	d					16 40																		17 12	
Littlehaven	d					16 44																		17 16	
Horsham 4	a					16 47				16 56													17 12	17 19	
Balcombe	d																								
Haywards Heath	a	16 30					16 41									16 54					17 00				17 11
	d	16 35	16 37				16 41									16 55					17 04	17 06			17 11
Wivelsfield	d	16 39														16 59						17 10			
Lewes 4	a	16 54																				17 21			
Burgess Hill 4	d				16 38											17 01					17 09				17 17
Hassocks 4	d				16 41											17 04									17 21
Preston Park	d															17 11									
Hove 2	a		16 53																		17 20				
Brighton 10	a				16 52		16 55								17 00	17 15									17 30

A [trolley] to Haywards Heath

Table 186

Mondays to Fridays

from 21 May

Bedford and London - Brighton

Network Diagram - see first Page of Table 186

		SN	SN		SN		SN	SN		FC	SN		SN	GW	SN	SN	SN		SN		SN	SN		SN	SN
		1			◇1		1	1		1	1		1	1	◇1	1	1		1		1	1		◇1	1
					A																				
		[trolley]			[trolley]			[trolley]			[trolley]				[trolley]						[trolley]			[trolley]	
London Victoria [15] ⊖	d	16 30	16 31		16 32			16 36			16 45				16 47		16 49				17 00			17 02	17 06
Clapham Junction [10]	d		16a37		16 38			16 42							16 53		16 56							17 08	17 12
Bedford	d									15 24															
Luton [10]	d									15 48															
Luton Airport Parkway [7] ✈	d									15 50															
St Albans City	d									16 02															
St Pancras International [15] ⊖	d									16 22															
Farringdon [3] ⊖	d									16 27															
City Thameslink [3]	d									16 31															
London Blackfriars [3] ⊖	d									16 36															
London Bridge [4] ⊖	d						16 33			16 43									16 57			16 59			
New Cross Gate	d																								
Norwood Junction [2]	d						16 44															17 10			
East Croydon 🚊	a				16 47		16 48	16 52		16 59					17 03		17 06		17 09			17 14		17 17	17 22
	d				16 48		16 49	16 52		17 00					17 03		17 07		17 10			17 15		17 18	17 23
Purley [4]	d						16 55															17 21			
Coulsdon South	d						16 59										17 13					17 24			
Merstham	d						17 04										17 19					17 30			
Redhill	a				16 59		17 08										17 22					17 33			
	d				17 00		17 08						17 12	17 13			17 27	17 29				17 37	17 39		
Reigate	a													17 18				17 35							
Nutfield	d												17 16										17 43		
Godstone	d												17 22										17 49		
Edenbridge	d												17 27										17 54		
Penshurst	d												17 34										18 01		
Leigh (Kent)	d												17 37										18 04		
Tonbridge [4]	a												17 42										18 09		
Earlswood (Surrey)	d						17 11										17 29					17 39			
Salfords	d						17 14										17 33					17 43			
Horley [4]	d				17 06		17 18									←	17 36					17 46			
Gatwick Airport [10] ✈	a	17 00			17 08		17 20			17 15	17 15				17 19	17 20	17 39				17 30	17 49			
	d				17 09		17 21			17 16					17 20	17 21	17 40					17 50			
Three Bridges [15]	a				17 14		→	17 09		17 20					17 24	17 26	17 46		17 29			→		17 36	
	d				17 18	17 22		17 10		17 21					17 25	17 26			17 29					17 37	
Crawley	d				17 22	17 26										17 30								17 41	
Ifield	d					17 28										17 33									
Faygate	d															17 37									
Littlehaven	d					17 35										17 41									
Horsham [4]	a				17 30	17 38										17 44								17 49	
Balcombe	d									17 27															
Haywards Heath	a							17 19		17 32					17 35				17 38						17 46
	d							17 23	17 26	17 32					17 36				17 39						17 47
Wivelsfield	d								17 30	17 37					17 41										17 52
Lewes [4]	a														17 56										
Burgess Hill [4]	d								17 32	17 39									17 46						17 55
Hassocks [4]	d								17 35	17 43									17 49						17 59
Preston Park	d								17 42	17 50									17 56						18 06
Hove [2]	a																		18 00						
Brighton [10]	a							17 39	17 46	17 54															18 12

A [trolley] to Three Bridges

Table 186

Mondays to Fridays

from 21 May

Bedford and London - Brighton

Network Diagram - see first Page of Table 186

		FC	SN		SN	SN	SN	GW	GW	SN			SN	FC	SN	SN		SN	SN		SN	FC	SN	SN	SN
		1	1		◇1	1	1	1	1	1			1	1	◇1	1		◇1	1		1	1	1	1	◇1
			🛒										🛒					🛒					🛒		
London Victoria 15 ⊖	d		17 15		17 17					17 21			17 30		17 32			17 35					17 45		17 47
Clapham unction 10	d				17 23					17 27					17 38			17 42							17 53
Bedford	d	15 52												16 10											
uton 10	d	16 14												16 34											
uton Airport Parkway 7 ✈	d	16 17												16 36											
St Albans City	d	16 25												16 48											
St Pancras hternational 15 ⊖	d	16 46												17 10											
Farringdon 3 ⊖	d	16 51												17 15											
City Thameslink 3	d	16 55												17 19											
London Blackfriars 3 ⊖	d	16 58												17 22											
London Bridge 4 ⊖	d						17 23									17 32					17 42			17 47	
New Cross Gate	d																								
Norwood unction 2	d															17 44									
East Croydon	a	17 26			17 32		17 35			17 36				17 47	17 48	17 49		17 51			17 54			17 58	18 02
	d	17 26			17 33		17 36			17 38				17 47	17 49	17 49		17 52			17 55			18 00	18 03
Purley 4	d															17 55									
Coulsdon South	d									17 44						17 58									
Merstham	d									17 50						18 04									
Redhill	a									17 53				18 02		18 07									
	d							17 41	17 43	17 57	17 59			18 03		18 11	18 13								
Reigate	a								17 48		18 05														
Nutfield	d																18 17								
Godstone	d																18 23								
Edenbridge	d																18 28								
Penshurst	d																18 35								
Leigh (Kent)	d																18 38								
Tonbridge 4	a																18 45								
Earlswood (Surrey)	d									17 59						18 13									
Salfords	d									18 03						18 17									
Horley 4	d					←	17 50			18 06						18 20			←			←			18 18
Gatwick Airport 10 ✈	a	17 41	17 45		17 47	17 49		17 54		18 09			17 57	18 13		18 23		18 06	18 09			18 13	18 12		18 20
	d	17 42			17 48	17 50				18 10			18 00	18 14		18 24		18 07	18 10			18 14	18 15		18 21
Three Bridges 15	a	17 46				17 54	17 55			→				→	18 06	→			18 16			18 18		18 21	
	d	17 46				17 55	17 56								18 07							18 19		18 22	
Crawley	d					17 59									18 11									18 26	
field	d					18 01																		18 28	
Faygate	d																								
ttlehaven	d					18 08									18 19									18 35	
Horsham 4	a					18 11									18 22									18 38	
Balcombe	d	17 52																				18 25			
Haywards Heath	a	17 57			18 00		18 05						18 10					18 18			18 22	18 30	18 25		18 33
	d	17 58			18 01		18 05						18 11					18 18			18 22	18 31	18 26		18 34
Wivelsfield	d						18 10											18 23							
Lewes 4	a						18 21											18 38							
Burgess Hill 4	d	18 03			18 07								18 17								18 28	18 36			18 41
Hassocks 4	d	18 07			18 11								18 22								18 32	18 40			18 45
Preston Park	d	18 14																			18 39	18 47	18 43		18 53
Hove 2	a				18 21																18 43				18 57
Brighton 10	a	18 18											18 34									18 53	18 49		

Table 186

Mondays to Fridays

from 21 May

Bedford and London - Brighton

Network Diagram - see first Page of Table 186

		SN 1	GW 1		SN 1		FC 1	SN 1	SN 1	SN 1	SN 1 🛒		SN 1	SN ◇1	SN ◇1 🛒	SN 1	SN 1 🛒	SN 1	FC 1		SN ◇1	SN 1	GW 1	GW 1	SN 1
London Victoria 15 ⊖	d				17 49						18 00			18 02	18 06		18 15				18 17				
Clapham Junction 10	d				17 56									18 08	18 12						18 23				
Bedford	d						16 26																		
Luton 10	d						16 50																		
Luton Airport Parkway 7 ✈	d						16 52																		
St Albans City	d						17 04																		
St Pancras International 15 ⊖	d						17 28												17 40						
Farringdon 3 ⊖	d						17 33												17 45						
City Thameslink 3	d						17 37												17 49						
London Blackfriars 3 ⊖	d						17 40												17 51						
London Bridge 4 ⊖	d								17 57	17 59						18 12						18 23			
New Cross Gate	d																								
Norwood Junction 2	d								18 08																
East Croydon 🚌	a				18 05		18 07		18 13	18 14				18 17	18 22	18 24			18 24		18 33	18 36			
	d				18 06		18 09		18 14	18 15				18 19	18 22	18 25			18 25		18 33	18 37			
Purley 4	d								18 20																
Coulsdon South	d				18 12				18 23																
Merstham	d				18 18				18 29																
Redhill	a				18 21				18 33										18 37						
	d		18 13		18 25	18 27		18 32	18 34										18 38				18 43	18 51	18 54
Reigate	a		18 18			18 33																	18 47		18 58
Nutfield	d							18 36																	
Godstone	d							18 42																	
Edenbridge	d							18 47																	
Penshurst	d							18 54																	
Leigh (Kent)	d							18 57																	
Tonbridge 4	a							19 02																	
Earlswood (Surrey)	d				18 27				18 36																
Salfords	d				18 31				18 40																
Horley 4	d	←			18 34				18 43				←					←			18 48				
Gatwick Airport 10 ✈	a	18 23			18 37		18 24		18 46		18 28		18 37		18 37		18 44	18 46	18 49					19 00	
	d	18 24			18 38		18 25		18 47		18 35		18 38		18 38		18 46	18 47	18 50						
Three Bridges 15	a	18 28			→		18 29		→	18 34			18 42	18 37		18 44		18 51	18 56			18 56			
	d	18 29					18 30			18 35				18 38		18 45		18 52				18 57			
Crawley	d	18 33												18 42				18 56							
Ifield	d	18 35																18 58							
Faygate	d	18 39																							
Littlehaven	d	18 43																19 05							
Horsham 4	a	18 48												18 50				19 08							
Balcombe	d																				18 57				
Haywards Heath	a						18 39			18 43	18 46				18 49	18 54	18 57				19 02	19 05			
	d						18 39			18 44	18 47				18 50	18 54	18 58				19 03	19 06			
Wivelsfield	d						18 44								18 54							19 11			
Lewes 4	a														19 09							19 27			
Burgess Hill 4	d						18 46			18 50	18 54					19 00					19 09				
Hassocks 4	d						18 50			18 54	18 59					19 04					19 13				
Preston Park	d						18 57			19 01						19 11	19 15								
Hove 2	a															19 17					19 22				
Brighton 10	a						19 02			19 08	19 10						19 22								

Table 186

Mondays to Fridays

from 21 May

Bedford and London - Brighton

Network Diagram - see first Page of Table 186

		SN			FC	SN	SN		SN	SN	SN		SN	FC	SN	SN		SN	FC		SN	SN	GW	SN	SN
		1			1	1	1		◇1	1	1		1	1	1	◇1		1	1		1	1	1	◇1	1
						(trolley)							(trolley)			(trolley)					(trolley)			(trolley)	
London Victoria 15 ⊖	d	18 19				18 30			18 32		18 36		18 45			18 47		18 51			19 00			19 02	
Clapham Junction 10	d	18 26							18 38		18 42					18 53		18 57						19 08	
Bedford	d				17 06									17 22					17 36						
Luton 10	d				17 30									17 46					18 00						
Luton Airport Parkway 7 ✈	d				17 33									17 48					18 02						
St Albans City	d				17 45									18 00					18 14						
St Pancras International 15 ⊖	d				18 08									18 20					18 34						
Farringdon 3 ⊖	d				18 13									18 25					18 40						
City Thameslink 3	d				18 17									18 29					18 43						
London Blackfriars 3 ⊖	d				18 20									18 32					18 46						
London Bridge 4 ⊖	d				18 27		18 30												18 57						
New Cross Gate	d																								
Norwood Junction 2	d						18 42																		
East Croydon	a	18 37			18 41		18 45		18 48		18 52			19 00		19 03		19 07	19 10					19 18	
	d	18 38			18 41		18 46		18 48		18 53			19 01		19 04		19 08	19 11					19 18	
Purley 4	d	18 43					18 51																		
Coulsdon South	d	18 46					18 54											19 14							
Merstham	d	18 52					19 00											19 20							
Redhill	a	18 55					19 03											19 23						19 30	
	d	18 59	19 01				19 07	19 09										19 24					19 26	19 31	19 36
Reigate	a							19 15															19 30		19 40
Nutfield	d		19 05																						
Godstone	d		19 11																						
Edenbridge	d		19 16																						
Penshurst	d		19 23																						
Leigh (Kent)	d		19 26																						
Tonbridge 4	a		19 34																						
Earlswood (Surrey)	d	19 01					19 09											19 26							
Salfords	d	19 05					19 13											19 30							
Horley 4	d	19 08					19 16			←					←			19 33				←			
Gatwick Airport 10 ✈	a	19 13			18 56	19 00	19 19			19 13			19 12	19 16	19 19	19 20		19 36	19 25		19 30	19 36		19 39	
	d	19 14			18 57	19 05	19 20			19 14			19 15	19 18	19 20	19 21		19 37	19 26			19 37		19 40	
Three Bridges 15	a	→			19 01		→		19 06	19 19					19 24			→	19 30			19 41		19 45	
	d				19 02				19 07	19 19					19 25				19 31					19 45	
Crawley	d								19 11	19 23					19 29									19 49	
Ifield	d									19 26					19 31										
Faygate	d														19 35										
Littlehaven	d								19 19	19 32					19 39										
Horsham 4	a								19 22	19 37					19 43									19 57	
Balcombe	d				19 08														19 37						
Haywards Heath	a				19 13	19 16					19 19		19 25	19 29		19 32			19 42						
	d				19 14	19 17					19 21		19 26	19 30		19 35	19 38		19 42						
Wivelsfield	d										19 25					19 39									
Lewes 4	a															19 54									
Burgess Hill 4	d				19 19	19 23								19 35			19 43		19 48						
Hassocks 4	d				19 23	19 27								19 39			19 47		19 51						
Preston Park	d												19 41	19 46											
Hove 2	a																19 57								
Brighton 10	a				19 33	19 39					19 42		19 47	19 52					20 01						

from 21 May

Bedford and London - Brighton

Network Diagram - see first Page of Table 186

		SN	SN	FC	GW	SN	SN	SN		SN	FC	SN	SN	SN	SN	SN	SN	SN	FC	GW	SN	SN
		1		1	1	1	1	◇1		1	1	1	1	1	◇1	1	1		1	1	1	1
								A														
			🛒				🛒	🛒					🛒		🛒							🛒
London Victoria 15 ⊖	d		19 06			19 10	19 15	19 17					19 30		19 32			19 36			19 40	19 45
Clapham unction 10	d		19 12			19 16		19 23							19 38			19 42			19 46	
Bedford	d			17 54							18 10								18 24			
Lton 10	d			18 18							18 34								18 48			
Lton Airport Parkway 7 ✈	d			18 20							18 36								18 50			
St Albans City	d			18 32							18 48								19 02			
St Pancras hternational 15 ⊖	d			18 54							19 09								19 24			
Farringdon 3 ⊖	d			18 59							19 14								19 29			
City Thameslink 3	d			19 03							19 18								19 33			
London Blackfriars 3 ⊖	d			19 05							19 20								19 35			
London Bridge 4 ⊖	d	18 59		19 12							19 27						19 33		19 42			
Nw Cross Gate	d	19 06															19 39					
Nrwood unction 2	d	19 14															19 47					
East Croydon (tram)	a	19 17	19 22	19 24		19 27		19 33			19 39				19 48		19 50	19 52	19 54		19 57	
	d	19 19	19 23	19 25		19 28		19 33			19 41				19 48		19 51	19 53	19 55		19 58	
Purley 4	d	19 24				19 33											19 57				20 03	
Coulsdon South	d	19 28				19 36											20 00				20 06	
Merstham	d	19 33				19 42											20 06				20 12	
Redhill	a	19 37				19 45									20 00		20 09				20 15	
	d	19 37			19 43	19 46								19 51	20 00	20 05	20 10			20 13	20 16	
Reigate	a															20 10				20 18		
Ntfield	d													19 55								
Godstone	d													20 01								
Eenbridge	d													20 06								
Penshurst	d													20 13								
Ligh (Kent)	d													20 16								
Tonbridge 4	a													20 21								
Erlswood (Surrey)	d	19 40				19 48															20 18	
Salfords	d	19 43				19 52															20 22	
Horley 4	d	19 47				19 55				←		←					20 16				20 25	
Gatwick Airport 10 ✈	a	19 49		19 40	19 55	19 58	19 45	19 48		19 49	19 55	19 58	20 00		20 08		20 18		20 10		20 28	20 15
	d	19 50		19 41		19 59		19 49		19 50	19 57	19 59			20 09		20 19		20 11		20 29	
Three Bridges 15	a	→		19 45		→				19 55	20 01	20 03			20 14		→		20 15		→	
	d			19 45						19 55	20 02	20 04			20 14				20 15			
Crawley	d									19 59		20 08			20 18							
field	d									20 02		20 10										
Faygate	d											20 14										
Ittlehaven	d									20 08		20 18										
Horsham 4	a									20 11		20 21			20 26							
Balcombe	d			19 51																		
Haywards Heath	a		19 46	19 56				20 00			20 11							20 16	20 24			
	d		19 47	19 57				20 04	20 07		20 11							20 17	20 25			
Welsfield	d			20 01					20 11										20 29			
Lwes 4	a								20 22													
Burgess Hill 4	d			20 03				20 09			20 16								20 31			
Hassocks 4	d			20 06							20 20								20 34			
Preston Park	d			20 13															20 41			
Hove 2	a							20 21														
Brighton 10	a		20 03	20 17							20 29							20 33	20 45			

A 🛒 to Haywards Heath

from 21 May

Bedford and London - Brighton

Network Diagram - see first Page of Table 186

		SN 1	SN ◇1 A 🚲		SN 1	FC 1	SN 1	SN 1 🚲	SN ◇1 🚲	SN ◇1	FC 1	GW 1	GW 1	SN 1	SN 1	SN ◇1		SN 1	SN 1	SN 1	SN 1	SN ◇1
London Victoria 15 ⊖	d		19 47					20 00	20 02	20 06				20 10	20 15	20 17				20 30		20 32
Clapham Junction 10	d		19 53						20 08	20 12				20 16		20 23						20 38
Bedford	d					18 40					18 54											
Luton 10	d					19 04					19 18											
Luton Airport Parkway 7 ✈	d					19 06					19 20											
St Albans City	d					19 18					19 32											
St Pancras International 15 ⊖	d					19 39					19 54											
Farringdon 3 ⊖	d					19 44					19 59											
City Thameslink 3	d					19 48					20 03											
London Blackfriars 3 ⊖	d					19 50					20 05											
London Bridge 4 ⊖	d				19 52	19 57					20 12							20 28				
New Cross Gate	d																					
Norwood Junction 2	d				20 03																	
East Croydon 🚋	a		20 03		20 06	20 09			20 19	20 22	20 24			20 27		20 33		20 40				20 48
	d		20 03		20 07	20 11			20 19	20 23	20 25			20 28		20 33		20 41				20 48
Purley 4	d				20 12									20 33								
Coulsdon South	d				20 15									20 36								
Merstham	d				20 21									20 42								
Redhill	a				20 24				20 30					20 45								21 00
	d				20 25				20 31			20 34	20 41	20 46							20 51	21 00
Reigate	a				20 30							20 38										
Nutfield	d																				20 55	
Godstone	d																				21 01	
Edenbridge	d																				21 06	
Penshurst	d																				21 13	
Leigh (Kent)	d																				21 16	
Tonbridge 4	a																				21 21	
Earlswood (Surrey)	d													20 48								
Salfords	d																					
Horley 4	d	←					←							20 54					←			
Gatwick Airport 10 ✈	a	20 18	20 18			20 25	20 28	20 30	20 38		20 40		20 50	20 56	20 45	20 48		20 55	20 56	21 00		21 08
	d	20 19	20 19			20 27	20 29		20 39		20 41			20 57		20 49		20 56	20 57			21 09
Three Bridges 15	a	20 24				20 31	20 33		20 44		20 45			→				21 00	21 02			21 14
	d	20 24				20 32	20 34		20 44		20 45							21 01	21 03			21 14
Crawley	d	20 28					20 37		20 48										21 06			21 18
Ifield	d	20 31					20 40												21 09			
Faygate	d																					
Littlehaven	d	20 37					20 46												21 15			
Horsham 4	a	20 40					20 49		20 56										21 18			21 26
Balcombe	d										20 51											
Haywards Heath	a		20 30			20 41				20 47	20 56					21 00		21 10				
	d		20 34	20 36		20 41				20 47	20 57					21 04	21 07	21 11				
Wivelsfield	d			20 40							21 01						21 11					
Lewes 4	a			20 55													21 22					
Burgess Hill 4	d		20 39			20 46					21 03					21 09						
Hassocks 4	d		20 42								21 06											
Preston Park	d		20 49								21 13											
Hove 2	a		20 53													21 21						
Brighton 10	a					20 57				21 01	21 17							21 26				

A 🚲 to Haywards Heath

from 21 May

Bedford and London - Brighton

Network Diagram - see first Page of Table 186

		SN ◇1	FC 1	SN 1		GW 1	SN 1	SN 1	SN ◇1		SN 1	SN 1		SN 1	SN 1	SN 1	SN ◇1	FC 1	GW 1	SN 1		SN 1	SN ◇1		SN 1
London Victoria 15 ⊖	d	20 36					20 40	20 45	20 47					21 00		21 02	21 06			21 10		21 15	21 17		
Clapham Junction 10	d	20 42					20 46		20 53							21 08	21 12			21 16			21 23		
Bedford	d		19 26															19 52							
Luton 10	d		19 50															20 16							
Luton Airport Parkway 7 ✈	d		19 52															20 18							
St Albans City	d		20 04															20 30							
St Pancras International 15 ⊖	d		20 24															20 54							
Farringdon 3 ⊖	d		20 29															20 59							
City Thameslink 3	d		20 33															21 03							
London Blackfriars 3 ⊖	d		20 35															21 05							
London Bridge 4 ⊖	d		20 42								20 58							21 12							
New Cross Gate	d																								
Norwood Junction 2	d																								
East Croydon	a	20 52	20 54				20 57		21 03		21 10					21 18	21 22	21 24		21 27			21 33		
	d	20 53	20 55				20 58		21 04		21 11					21 18	21 23	21 25		21 28			21 33		
Purley 4	d						21 03													21 33					
Coulsdon South	d						21 06													21 36					
Merstham	d						21 12													21 42					
Redhill	a						21 15									21 30				21 45					
	d			21 05		21 13	21 16								21 22	21 31			21 35	21 46					
Reigate	a			21 09		21 18									21 26				21 39						
Nutfield	d																								
Godstone	d																								
Edenbridge	d																								
Penshurst	d																								
Leigh (Kent)	d																								
Tonbridge 4	a																								
Earlswood (Surrey)	d						21 18													21 48					
Salfords	d						21 22																		
Horley 4	d						21 25					←								21 54					←
Gatwick Airport 10 ✈	a		21 10				21 28	21 15	21 18		21 26	21 28		21 30		21 38		21 40		21 56		21 45	21 48		21 56
	d		21 11				21 29		21 19		21 27	21 29				21 39		21 41		21 57			21 49		21 57
Three Bridges 15	a		21 15				→				21 31	21 33				21 44		21 45		→			21 53		22 02
	d		21 15								21 31	21 34				21 44		21 45					21 53		22 03
Crawley	d											21 37													22 06
Ifield	d											21 40													22 09
Faygate	d																								
Littlehaven	d											21 46													22 15
Horsham 4	a											21 49													22 18
Balcombe	d																	21 53							
Haywards Heath	a	21 16	21 24						21 30		21 40					21 53	21 46	21 58					22 02		
	d	21 16	21 25						21 34	21 37	21 41					21 53	21 46	21 59					22 06	22 08	
Wivelsfield	d		21 29							21 41						21 57		22 03						22 12	
Lewes 4	a									21 54														22 23	
Burgess Hill 4	d		21 31						21 39							21 59		22 05					22 11		
Hassocks 4	d		21 34						21 42							22 03		22 08							
Preston Park	d		21 41						21 49							22 09		22 15							
Hove 2	a								21 53														22 22		
Brighton 10	a	21 30	21 45								21 56					22 15	22 00	22 19							

Table 186

Mondays to Fridays

from 21 May

Bedford and London - Brighton

Network Diagram - see first Page of Table 186

		SN	GW	SN		SN	SN	FC	SN	SN	SN	SN			SN	SN	SN	SN	SN	FC	GW		SN	SN	SN
		1	1	1		1	◇1	1	1	1	1	◇1			1	1	1	◇1	◇1	1	1		1	1	◇1
London Victoria 15 ⊖	d	21 30				21 32	21 36			21 40	21 45	21 47				22 00		22 02	22 06				22 10	22 15	22 17
Clapham Junction 10	d					21 38	21 42			21 46		21 53						22 08	22 12				22 16		22 23
Bedford	d							20 22												20 52					
Luton 10	d							20 46												21 16					
Luton Airport Parkway 7 ✈	d							20 48												21 18					
St Albans City	d							21 00												21 30					
St Pancras International 15 ⊖	d							21 24												21 54					
Farringdon 3 ⊖	d							21 29												21 59					
City Thameslink 3	d							21 33												22 03					
London Blackfriars 3 ⊖	d							21 35												22 05					
London Bridge 4 ⊖	d							21 42												22 12					
New Cross Gate	d																								
Norwood Junction 2	d																								
East Croydon	a					21 48	21 52	21 54		21 57		22 03						22 18	22 22	22 24			22 26		22 33
	d					21 48	21 53	21 55		21 58		22 03						22 18	22 23	22 25			22 28		22 34
Purley 4	d									22 03													22 33		
Coulsdon South	d									22 06													22 36		
Merstham	d									22 12													22 42		
Redhill	a					21 59				22 15								22 30					22 45		
	d		21 53	21 55		22 00			22 05	22 16							22 22	22 31			22 33		22 46		
Reigate	a								22 09								22 26				22 38				
Nutfield	d			21 59																					
Godstone	d			22 05																					
Edenbridge	d			22 10																					
Penshurst	d			22 17																					
Leigh (Kent)	d			22 20																					
Tonbridge 4	a			22 28																					
Earlswood (Surrey)	d									22 18													22 48		
Salfords	d									22 22															
Horley 4	d									22 25					←								22 54		
Gatwick Airport 10 ✈	a	22 00	22 06			22 08		22 10		22 28	22 15	22 18			22 28	22 30		22 38		22 40			22 56	22 45	22 48
	d					22 09		22 11		22 29		22 19			22 29			22 39		22 41			22 57		22 49
Three Bridges 15	a					22 14		22 15		↦					22 33			22 44		22 45			↦		22 53
	d					22 14		22 15							22 36			22 44		22 45					22 53
Crawley	d					22 18									22 39										
Ifield	d														22 42										
Faygate	d																								
Littlehaven	d														22 48										
Horsham 4	a					22 26									22 51										
Balcombe	d																			22 53					
Haywards Heath	a						22 16	22 24				22 30						22 53	22 46	22 58					23 02
	d						22 16	22 25				22 34	22 37					22 53	22 46	22 59					23 03
Wivelsfield	d							22 29				22 38						22 57		23 03					
Lewes 4	a											22 53													
Burgess Hill 4	d							22 31										22 59		23 05					23 08
Hassocks 4	d							22 34										23 03		23 08					
Preston Park	d							22 41										23 09		23 15					
Hove 2	a												22 51												23 21
Brighton 10	a						22 30	22 45										23 15	23 00	23 19					

from 21 May

Bedford and London - Brighton

Network Diagram - see first Page of Table 186

		SN 1	SN 1	GW 1	SN 1		SN 1	SN	FC 1	SN 1	SN 1	SN 1	SN ◇1			SN 1	SN 1	GW 1	SN ◇1	SN ◇1	FC 1	SN 1		SN 1	SN ◇1
London Victoria 15 ⊖	d		22 30				22 32	22 36			22 40	22 45	22 47				23 00		23 02	23 06		23 10		23 15	23 17
Clapham Junction 10	d						22 38	22 42			22 46		22 53						23 08	23 12		23 16			23 23
Bedford	d								21 22												21 52				
Luton 10	d								21 46												22 16				
Luton Airport Parkway 7 ✈	d								21 48												22 18				
St Albans City	d								22 00												22 30				
St Pancras International 15 ⊖	d								22 24												22 54				
Farringdon 3 ⊖	d								22 29												22 59				
City Thameslink 3	d								22 33												23 03				
London Blackfriars 3 ⊖	d								22 35												23 05				
London Bridge 4 ⊖	d								22 42												23 12				
New Cross Gate	d																								
Norwood Junction 2	d																								
East Croydon	a						22 48	22 52	22 54		22 57		23 03						23 19	23 22	23 24	23 27			23 33
	d						22 48	22 53	22 55		22 58		23 03						23 20	23 23	23 25	23 28			23 33
Purley 4	d										23 03											23 33			
Coulsdon South	d										23 06											23 37			
Merstham	d										23 12											23 42			
Redhill	a						23 00				23 15								23 31			23 46			
	d			22 52	22 55		23 01			23 05	23 16							23 28	23 31			23 46			
Reigate	a									23 09								23 33							
Nutfield	d				22 59																				
Godstone	d				23 05																				
Edenbridge	d				23 10																				
Penshurst	d				23 17																				
Leigh (Kent)	d				23 20																				
Tonbridge 4	a				23 25																				
Earlswood (Surrey)	d										23 18											23 49			
Salfords	d										23 22											23 52			
Horley 4	d	←									23 25					←						23 56			
Gatwick Airport 10 ✈	a	22 56	23 00	23 06			23 08		23 10		23 28	23 15	23 18			23 28	23 30		23 38		23 40	23 58		23 45	23 50
	d	22 57					23 09		23 11		23 29		23 19			23 29			23 39		23 41	23 59			23 51
Three Bridges 15	a	23 02					23 15		23 15		→					23 33			23 44		23 47	→			23 55
	d	23 03					23 16		23 15							23 38			23 44		23 47				23 56
Crawley	d	23 06					23 19									23 41									
Ifield	d	23 09														23 44									
Faygate	d																								
Littlehaven	d	23 15														23 50									
Horsham 4	a	23 18					23 27									23 53									
Balcombe	d																				23 53				
Haywards Heath	a							23 16	23 24				23 30						23 53	23 46	23 58				00 05
	d							23 16	23 25				23 34	23 37					23 53	23 46	23 59				00 05
Wivelsfield	d								23 29				23 38						23 57		00 03				
Lewes 4	a												23 51												
Burgess Hill 4	d								23 31										23 59		00 05				00 11
Hassocks 4	d								23 34										00 03		00 08				
Preston Park	d								23 41										00 09		00 15				
Hove 2	a													23 51											00 21
Brighton 10	a							23 30	23 45										00 15	00 01	00 19				

Table 186

Mondays to Fridays

from 21 May

Bedford and London - Brighton

Network Diagram - see first Page of Table 186

		SN 1	SN 1	SN 1	SN ◇1	FC 1		SN 1	SN 1	SN 1	FC 1	FC 1	FC 1
London Victoria 15 ⊖	d		23 30		23 32			23 45	23 47	23 49			
Clapham Junction 10	d				23 38				23 53	23 56			
Bedford	d					22 16					22 42	23 12	23 42
Luton 10	d					22 40					23 06	23 36	00 06
Luton Airport Parkway 7 ✈	d					22 42					23 09	23 39	00 09
St Albans City	d					22 54					23 21	23 51	00 21
St Pancras International 15 ⊖	d					23 24					23 54	00 24	00 54
Farringdon 3 ⊖	d					23 29					23 59	00 29	00 59
City Thameslink 3	d												
London Blackfriars 3 ⊖	d					23 35					00 05	00 35	01 05
London Bridge 4 ⊖	d					23 42					00 12	00 42	
New Cross Gate	d												
Norwood Junction 2	d												
East Croydon 🚋	a				23 51	23 56			00 05	00 09	00 26	00 56	01 31
	d				23 52	23 57			00 06		00 27	00 57	01 32
Purley 4	d								00 12				
Coulsdon South	d								00 15				
Merstham	d								00 21				
Redhill	a				00 03				00 24				
	d			23 55	00 05				00 25				
Reigate	a												
Nutfield	d												
Godstone	d												
Edenbridge	d			00 06									
Penshurst	d												
Leigh (Kent)	d												
Tonbridge 4	a			00 15									
Earlswood (Surrey)	d												
Salfords	d												
Horley 4	d	←							00 31				
Gatwick Airport 10 ✈	a	23 58	00 05		00 14	00 18		00 20	00 33		00 48	01 18	01 51
	d	23 59			00 15	00 19			00 34		00 49	01 22	01 52
Three Bridges 15	a	00 04			00 20	00 24			00 39		00 54	01 28	01 58
	d	00 04			00 20				00 39				
Crawley	d	00 07							00 43				
Ifield	d	00 10							00 46				
Faygate	d												
Littlehaven	d	00 16							00 52				
Horsham 4	a	00 19							00 55				
Balcombe	d				00 26								
Haywards Heath	a				00 31								
	d				00 31								
Wivelsfield	d				00 35								
Lewes 4	a												
Burgess Hill 4	d				00 37								
Hassocks 4	d				00 41								
Preston Park	d				00 48								
Hove 2	a												
Brighton 10	a				00 52								

Table 186

Saturdays

until 23 June

Bedford and London - Brighton

Network Diagram - see first Page of Table 186

		SN	SN	FC	FC	SN	SN	SN	SN	SN	GW	SN	FC	FC	SN	SN	SN	SN	SN	FC	FC
		◇[1]	◇[1]	[1]	[1]	[1]	◇[1]	[1]	[1]	[1]	[1]	◇[1]	[1]	[1]	[1]	[1]	[1]	[1]	◇[1]	[1]	
				A	B								A	B						A	B
London Victoria [15] ⊖	d	23p02	23p06			23p10	23p17		23p30			23p32			23p45	23p47	23p49	00 02	00 05		
Clapham Junction [10]	d	23p08	23p12			23p16	23p23					23p38				23p53	23p56		00 11		
Bedford	d			21p52									22p16							22p42	
Luton [10]	d			22p16									22p40							23p06	
Luton Airport Parkway [7] ✈	d			22p18									22p42							23p09	
St Albans City	d			22p30									22p54							23p21	
St Pancras International [15] ⊖	d			22p54									23p24							23p54	
Farringdon [3] ⊖	d			22p59									23p29							23p59	
City Thameslink [3]	d			23p03																	
London Blackfriars [3] ⊖	d			23p05									23p35							00 05	
London Bridge [4] ⊖	d			23p12	23p12								23p42	23p42						00 12	00 12
New Cross Gate	d																				
Norwood Junction [2]	d																				
East Croydon	a	23p19	23p22	23p24	23p24	23p27	23p33					23p51	23p56	23p56		00 05	00 09		00 24	00 26	00 26
	d	23p20	23p23	23p25	23p25	23p28	23p33					23p52	23p57	23p57		00 06			00 24	00 27	00 27
Purley [4]	d					23p33										00 12					
Coulsdon South	d					23p37										00 15					
Merstham	d					23p42										00 21					
Redhill	a	23p31				23p46						00 03				00 24					
	d	23p31				23p46				23p55	00 01	00 05				00 25					
Reigate	a																				
Nutfield	d																				
Godstone	d																				
Edenbridge	d									00 06											
Penshurst	d																				
Leigh (Kent)	d																				
Tonbridge [4]	a									00 15											
Earlswood (Surrey)	d					23p49															
Salfords	d					23p52															
Horley [4]	d					23p56		←								00 31					
Gatwick Airport [10] ✈	a	23p38		23p40	23p40	23p58	23p50	23p58	00 05		00 11	00 14	00 18	00 18	00 20	00 33		00 37	00 41	00 48	00 49
	d	23p39		23p41	23p41	23p59	23p51	23p59				00 15	00 19	00 19		00 34			00 42	00 49	00 50
Three Bridges [15]	a	23p44		23p47	23p47	→	23p55	00 04				00 20	00 24	00 24		00 39			00 47	00 54	00 55
	d	23p44		23p47	23p47		23p56	00 04				00 20				00 39			00 47		
Crawley	d							00 07								00 43					
Ifield	d							00 10								00 46					
Faygate	d																				
Littlehaven	d							00 16								00 52					
Horsham [4]	a							00 19								00 55					
Balcombe	d			23p53	23p53							00 26									
Haywards Heath	a	23p53	23p46	23p58	23p58		00 05					00 31							00 58		
	d	23p53	23p46	23p59	23p59		00 05					00 31							01 02 / 01 06		
Wivelsfield	d	23p57		00 03	00 03							00 35									
Lewes [4]	a																		01 20		
Burgess Hill [4]	d	23p59		00 05	00 05		00 11					00 37									
Hassocks [4]	d	00 03		00 08	00 08							00 41									
Preston Park	d	00 09		00 15	00 15							00 48									
Hove [2]	a						00 21														
Brighton [10]	a	00 15	00 01	00 19	00 19							00 52							01s16		

A not 19 May

B 19 May

Table 186

Saturdays

until 23 June

Bedford and London - Brighton

Network Diagram - see first Page of Table 186

		SN 1	GW 1	FC 1 A	SN 1	FC B	SN ◇1	FC 1 A	FC 1 B	FC 1 B	SN 1	FC 1 A	FC 1 B	SN 1	FC 1 A	FC 1 B	SN 1	FC 1 B	FC 1	SN ◇1	FC 1 B	FC 1 A
London Victoria 15 ⊖	d	00 14			00 30		01 00				02 00			03 00			03 30			04 00		
Clapham Junction 10	d	00 20					01 08				02 08			03 08						04 08		
Bedford	d			23p12				23p42				00 42			01 42							02 42
Luton 10	d			23p36				00 06				01 06			02 06							03 06
Luton Airport Parkway 7 ✈	d			23p39				00 09				01 09			02 09							03 09
St Albans City	d			23p51				00 21				01 21			02 21							03 21
St Pancras International 15 ⊖	d			00 24				00 54				01 54			02 54				03 28			03 54
Farringdon 3 ⊖	d			00 29				00 59														
City Thameslink 3	d																					
London Blackfriars 3 ⊖	d			00 35				01 05				02 05			03 05				03 39			04 05
London Bridge 4 ⊖	d			00 42		00 42			01 05	01 35			02 05			03 05		03 35			04 05	
New Cross Gate	d																					
Norwood Junction 2	d																					
East Croydon	a	00 31		00 56		00 56	01 21	01 31	01 31	02 02	02 21	02 31	02 31	03 21	03 31	03 31		04 01	04 03	04 21	04 31	04 31
	d	00 32		00 57		00 57	01 22	01 32	01 31	02 02	02 22	02 32	02 32	03 22	03 32	03 32		04 02	04 04	04 22	04 31	04 32
Purley 4	d	00 37					01 27				02 27			03 27						04 27		
Coulsdon South	d	00 41																				
Merstham	d	00 47																				
Redhill	a	00 50																				
	d	00 51	00 54																			
Reigate	a																					
Nutfield	d																					
Godstone	d																					
Edenbridge	d																					
Penshurst	d																					
Leigh (Kent)	d																					
Tonbridge 4	a																					
Earlswood (Surrey)	d																					
Salfords	d																					
Horley 4	d	00 57					01 43				02 42			03 42						04 44		
Gatwick Airport 10 ✈	a	00 59	01 03	01 18	01 20	01 18	01 46	01 51	01 51	02 21	02 44	02 51	02 51	03 44	03 51	03 51	04 05	04 24	04 24	04 46	04 50	04 51
	d			01 22		01 22	01 48	01 52	01 52	02 22	02 46	02 52	02 52	03 46	03 52	03 52		04 24	04 24	04 47	04 51	04 52
Three Bridges 15	a			01 28		01 28	01 52	01 58	01 58	02 28	02 50	02 58	02 58	03 50	03 58	03 58		04 30	04 30	04 51	04 58	04 58
	d						01 53													04 52		
Crawley	d																					
Ifield	d																					
Faygate	d																					
Littlehaven	d																					
Horsham 4	a																					
Balcombe	d																					
Haywards Heath	a						02 06													05 01		
	d						02 06													05 01		
Wivelsfield	d																					
Lewes 4	a																					
Burgess Hill 4	d																					
Hassocks 4	d																					
Preston Park	d																					
Hove 2	a																					
Brighton 10	a						02 23													05 16		

A not 19 May

B 19 May

Table 186

Saturdays

until 23 June

Bedford and London - Brighton

Network Diagram - see first Page of Table 186

		FC	SN	FC	FC	SN	SN	SN		FC	FC	GW	GW	SN	SN	SN		SN	SN	SN	FC	FC	SN		
		1	1	1	1	1	◇1	1		1	1	1	1	1	1	1		◇1	◇1	1	1	1	◇1		
		A		B	A						A											A			
London Victoria [15] ⊖	d		04 30			05 00	05 02	05 15							05 30			05 32	05 32	05 45					
Clapham Junction [10]	d						05 08											05 38	05 38						
Bedford	d			03 12						03 42											04 22				
Luton [10]	d			03 36						04 06											04 46				
Luton Airport Parkway [7] ✈	d			03 39						04 09											04 49				
St Albans City	d			03 51						04 21											05 01				
St Pancras International [15] ⊖	d			04 24						04 54											05 34				
Farringdon [3] ⊖	d									04 59											05 39				
City Thameslink [3]	d																								
London Blackfriars [3] ⊖	d			04 35						05 04											05 45				
London Bridge [4] ⊖	d	04 05			04 35						05 05										05 52	05 52			
New Cross Gate	d																								
Norwood Junction [2]	d																								
East Croydon	a	04 31		05 01	05 01		05 21			05 31	05 31							05 47	05 47		06 04	06 04			
	d	04 32		05 02	05 02		05 22			05 32	05 32							05 48	05 48		06 05	06 05			
Purley [4]	d						05 26											05 53	05 53						
Coulsdon South	d						05 30											05 57	05 57						
Merstham	d						05 35											06 03	06 03						
Redhill	a						05 39											06 07	06 07						
	d						05 40					05 41	05 49					06 07	06 07						
Reigate	a											05 47													
Nutfield	d																								
Godstone	d																								
Edenbridge	d																								
Penshurst	d																								
Leigh (Kent)	d																								
Tonbridge [4]	a																								
Earlswood (Surrey)	d																	06 11	06 11						
Salfords	d																	06 15	06 15						
Horley [4]	d						05 46											06 18	06 18				←		
Gatwick Airport [10] ✈	a	04 51	05 05	05 21	05 21	05 35	05 48	05 50		05 53	05 53		05 58		06 00			06 21	06 21	06 15	06 19	06 19	06 21		
	d	04 52		05 22	05 22		05 49			05 54	05 54			05 58		06 11		06 22	06 22		06 20	06 20	06 22		
Three Bridges [15]	a	04 58		05 26	05 26		05 54			05 59	05 59			06 02		06 15		→	→		06 24	06 24	06 26		
	d			05 27	05 27		05 54			06 00	06 00			06 03		06 16					06 25	06 25	06 30	06 34	
Crawley	d													06 06										06 37	
Ifield	d													06 09										06 40	
Faygate	d																								
Littlehaven	d													06 15										06 46	
Horsham [4]	a													06 18										06 49	
Balcombe	d			05 33	05 33					06 06	06 06										06 31	06 31	06 36		
Haywards Heath	a			05 38	05 38		06 03			06 11	06 11					06 26					06 36	06 36	06 41		
	d			05 39	05 39		06 04			06 11	06 11					06 26					06 37	06 37	06 41		
Wivelsfield	d			05 43	05 43		06 08			06 15	06 15					06 30					06 41	06 41	06 45		
Lewes [4]	a															06 41									
Burgess Hill [4]	d			05 45	05 45		06 10			06 17	06 17										06 43	06 43	06 47		
Hassocks [4]	d			05 48	05 48		06 13			06 21	06 21										06 46	06 46	06 51		
Preston Park	d			05 55	05 55		06 20			06 27	06 27										06 53	06 53	06 57		
Hove [2]	a																								
Brighton [10]	a			05 59	05 59		06 24			06 31	06 31										06 57	06 57	07 03		

A 19 May

B not 19 May

Table 186

Saturdays

until 23 June

Bedford and London - Brighton

Network Diagram - see first Page of Table 186

		SN	GW	SN	GW	GW	SN			FC	SN	FC	SN	SN	SN			GW	FC	FC	SN	SN	SN	GW
		1	1	1	1	1	1			1	1	1	1	1	1			1	1	1	1	1	1	1
												A								A				
		🛒									🛒			🛒							🛒			
London Victoria 15 ⊖	d	06 00					06 02				06 15			06 30	06 32						06 45			
Clapham Junction 10	d						06 08								06 38									
Bedford	d									04 52									05 22					
Luton 10	d									05 16									05 46					
Luton Airport Parkway 7 ✈	d									05 19									05 49					
St Albans City	d									05 31									06 01					
St Pancras International 15 ⊖	d									05 54									06 24					
Farringdon 3 ⊖	d									05 59									06 29					
City Thameslink 3	d																							
London Blackfriars 3 ⊖	d									06 05									06 35					
London Bridge 4 ⊖	d									06 12		06 27							06 42	06 42				
New Cross Gate	d																							
Norwood Junction 2	d																							
East Croydon	a						06 17			06 24		06 39			06 47				06 54	06 54				
	d						06 18			06 25		06 41			06 48				06 55	06 55				
Purley 4	d						06 23								06 53									
Coulsdon South	d						06 27								06 57									
Merstham	d						06 32								07 02									
Redhill	a						06 36								07 06									
	d		06 13	06 22	06 34	06 41	06 46	06 52							07 10	07 22		07 13						07 34
Reigate	a		06 18		06 38			06 56										07 18						07 38
Nutfield	d			06 26												07 26								
Godstone	d			06 32												07 32								
Edenbridge	d			06 37												07 37								
Penshurst	d			06 44												07 44								
Leigh (Kent)	d			06 47												07 47								
Tonbridge 4	a			06 52												07 52								
Earlswood (Surrey)	d						06 48								07 12									
Salfords	d						06 52								07 16									
Horley 4	d						06 55						←		07 19							←		
Gatwick Airport 10 ✈	a	06 30				06 50	06 58			06 40	06 45	06 56	06 58	07 00	07 23				07 10	07 10	07 15	07 23		
	d						06 59			06 41		06 57	06 59		07 24				07 11	07 11		07 24		
Three Bridges 15	a						→			06 45		07 01	07 03		→				07 15	07 15		07 29		
	d									06 45		07 02	07 04						07 15	07 15		07 30		
Crawley	d												07 07									07 33		
Ifield	d												07 10									07 36		
Faygate	d																							
Littlehaven	d												07 16									07 42		
Horsham 4	a												07 19									07 45		
Balcombe	d																		07 21	07 21				
Haywards Heath	a									06 54		07 11							07 26	07 26				
	d									06 55		07 11							07 27	07 27			07 33	
Wivelsfield	d									06 59									07 31	07 31			07 37	
Lewes 4	a																						07 48	
Burgess Hill 4	d									07 01									07 33	07 33				
Hassocks 4	d									07 04									07 36	07 36				
Preston Park	d									07 11									07 43	07 43				
Hove 2	a																							
Brighton 10	a									07 15		07 25							07 47	07 47				

A 19 May

Table 186

Saturdays
until 23 June

Bedford and London - Brighton

Network Diagram - see first Page of Table 186

		SN	FC	FC	SN	GW	SN		SN	FC	SN	SN	FC	FC	SN	SN	SN	SN	FC	SN	GW	SN
		◇1	1	1	1	1	1		◇1	1	1	1	1	1	1	◇1	1	◇1	1	1	1	1
				A										A								
					trolley						trolley				trolley					trolley		
London Victoria 15 ⊖	d				07 00				07 06		07 15				07 30	07 32		07 36		07 45		
Clapham Junction 10	d								07 12							07 38		07 42				
Bedford	d		05 40							05 54			06 10						06 24			
Luton 10	d		06 04							06 18			06 34						06 48			
Luton Airport Parkway 7 ✈	d		06 06							06 20			06 36						06 50			
St Albans City	d		06 18							06 32			06 48						07 02			
St Pancras International 15 ⊖	d		06 39							06 54			07 09						07 24			
Farringdon 3 ⊖	d		06 44							06 59			07 14						07 29			
City Thameslink 3	d																					
London Blackfriars 3 ⊖	d		06 50							07 05			07 20						07 35			
London Bridge 4 ⊖	d		06 57	06 57			07 03			07 12			07 27	07 27			07 33		07 42			07 45
New Cross Gate	d						07 08										07 38					
Norwood Junction 2	d						07 16										07 46					07 56
East Croydon	a		07 09	07 09			07 20		07 22	07 24			07 39	07 39		07 47	07 50	07 52	07 54			07 59
	d		07 11	07 11			07 21		07 23	07 25			07 41	07 41		07 48	07 51	07 53	07 55			08 00
Purley 4	d						07 26										07 56					08 06
Coulsdon South	d						07 30										08 00					08 09
Merstham	d						07 35										08 05					
Redhill	a						07 39									08 00	08 09					08 17
	d					07 41	07 44	07 52								08 00	08 10				08 13	08 17
Reigate	a							07 56													08 18	
Nutfield	d																					08 22
Godstone	d																					08 27
Edenbridge	d																					08 33
Penshurst	d																					08 39
Leigh (Kent)	d																					08 43
Tonbridge 4	a																					08 48
Earlswood (Surrey)	d																08 12					
Salfords	d																08 16					
Horley 4	d						07 51					←					08 19					
Gatwick Airport 10 ✈	a		07 26	07 26	07 30	07 50	07 55			07 40	07 45	07 55	07 56	07 56	08 00	08 08	08 23		08 10	08 15		
	d		07 27	07 27			07 56			07 41		07 56	07 57	07 57		08 09	08 24		08 11			
Three Bridges 15	a		07 31	07 31			→			07 45		08 01	08 01	08 01		08 14	→		08 15			
	d		07 32	07 32						07 45		08 01	08 02	08 02		08 14			08 15			
Crawley	d											08 05				08 18						
Ifield	d											08 07										
Faygate	d																					
Littlehaven	d											08 14										
Horsham 4	a											08 17				08 26						
Balcombe	d																		08 21			
Haywards Heath	a		07 41	07 41						07 54			08 11	08 11					08 26			
	d	07 37	07 41	07 41						07 55			08 11	08 11					08 27			
Wivelsfield	d									07 59									08 31			
Lewes 4	a																					
Burgess Hill 4	d									08 01									08 33			
Hassocks 4	d									08 04									08 36			
Preston Park	d									08 11									08 43			
Hove 2	a	07 51																				
Brighton 10	a		07 55	07 55					07 57	08 15			08 25	08 25				08 27	08 47			

A 19 May

Table 186

Saturdays

until 23 June

Bedford and London - Brighton

Network Diagram - see first Page of Table 186

		SN		SN	SN	FC	FC	SN	SN	SN	GW	GW	SN	SN	FC	SN	SN	SN		SN	FC	FC
		◇1		◇1	1	1	1	1		◇1	1	1	1	◇1	1	1	1	◇1		1	1	1
							A	🚲								🚲						A
London Victoria 15 ⊖	d	07 47		07 51				08 00	08 01	08 02				08 06		08 15		08 17				
Clapham Junction 10	d	07 53							08 08	08 08				08 12				08 23				
Bedford	d					06 40									06 54						07 10	
Luton 10	d					07 04									07 18						07 34	
Luton Airport Parkway 7 ✈	d					07 06									07 20						07 36	
St Albans City	d					07 18									07 32						07 48	
St Pancras International 15 ⊖	d					07 39									07 54						08 09	
Farringdon 3 ⊖	d					07 44									07 59						08 14	
City Thameslink 3	d																					
London Blackfriars 3 ⊖	d					07 50									08 05						08 20	
London Bridge 4 ⊖	d					07 57	07 57						08 03		08 12		08 15				08 27	08 27
New Cross Gate	d												08 08									
Norwood Junction 2	d												08 16				08 26					
East Croydon 🚊	a	08 02		08 07		08 09	08 09			08 17			08 20	08 22	08 24		08 29	08 32			08 39	08 39
	d	08 03		08 08		08 11	08 11			08 18			08 21	08 23	08 25		08 30	08 33			08 41	08 40
Purley 4	d												08 26				08 36					
Coulsdon South	d												08 30				08 39					
Merstham	d												08 35				08 45					
Redhill	a									08 30			08 39				08 49					
	d									08 30	08 34	08 41	08 44				08 52					
Reigate	a										08 38						08 56					
Nutfield	d																					
Godstone	d																					
Edenbridge	d																					
Penshurst	d																					
Leigh (Kent)	d																					
Tonbridge 4	a																					
Earlswood (Surrey)	d																					
Salfords	d																					
Horley 4	d				←					08 36			08 51							←		
Gatwick Airport 10 ✈	a	08 18		08 22	08 23	08 26	08 26	08 30		08 39		08 50	08 55		08 40	08 45		08 48		08 55	08 56	08 56
	d	08 20		08 23	08 24	08 27	08 27			08 40			08 56		08 41			08 50		08 56	08 57	08 57
Three Bridges 15	a				08 29	08 31	08 31			08 44			→		08 45					09 01	09 01	09 01
	d				08 30	08 32	08 32			08 45					08 45					09 01	09 02	09 02
Crawley	d				08 33					08 48										09 05		
Ifield	d				08 36															09 07		
Faygate	d																					
Littlehaven	d				08 42															09 14		
Horsham 4	a				08 45					08 56										09 17		
Balcombe	d																					
Haywards Heath	a	08 30				08 41	08 41								08 54			09 00			09 11	09 11
	d	08 35	08 37			08 41	08 41								08 55			09 05	09 07		09 11	09 11
Wivelsfield	d														08 59				09 11			
Lewes 4	a	08 49																	09 22			
Burgess Hill 4	d			08 38											09 01			09 10				
Hassocks 4	d			08 41											09 04							
Preston Park	d														09 11			09 18				
Hove 2	a		08 53															09 22				
Brighton 10	a			08 52		08 55	08 55							08 57	09 15						09 25	09 25

A 19 May

Table 186

Saturdays
until 23 June

Bedford and London - Brighton

Network Diagram - see first Page of Table 186

		SN	SN	SN	SN	FC	SN	GW		SN	SN	SN	SN	FC	FC		SN	SN	SN	GW	GW	SN	SN
		1	◇1	1	◇1	1	1	1		1	◇1	◇1	1	1	1		1		◇1	1	1	1	◇1
															A								
		🍴					🍴										🍴						🍴
London Victoria 15 ⊖	d	08 30	08 32		08 36		08 45				08 47	08 51					09 00	09 01	09 02				09 06
Clapham Junction 10	d		08 38		08 42						08 53							09 08	09 08				09 12
Bedford	d					07 24								07 40									
Luton 10	d					07 48								08 04									
Luton Airport Parkway 7 ✈	d					07 50								08 06									
St Albans City	d					08 02								08 18									
St Pancras International 15 ⊖	d					08 24								08 39									
Farringdon 3 ⊖	d					08 29								08 44									
City Thameslink 3	d																						
London Blackfriars 3 ⊖	d					08 35								08 50									
London Bridge 4 ⊖	d			08 33		08 42				08 45				08 57	08 57							09 03	
New Cross Gate	d			08 38																		09 08	
Norwood Junction 2	d			08 46						08 56												09 16	
East Croydon 🚋	a		08 47	08 50	08 52	08 54				08 59	09 02	09 07		09 09	09 09				09 17			09 20	09 22
	d		08 48	08 51	08 53	08 55				09 00	09 03	09 08		09 11	09 11				09 18			09 21	09 23
Purley 4	d			08 56						09 06												09 26	
Coulsdon South	d			09 00						09 09												09 30	
Merstham	d			09 05																		09 35	
Redhill	a		09 00	09 09						09 17									09 30			09 39	
	d		09 00	09 10				09 13		09 17									09 30	09 34	09 41	09 44	
Reigate	a							09 18												09 38			
Nutfield	d									09 22													
Godstone	d									09 27													
Edenbridge	d									09 33													
Penshurst	d									09 39													
Leigh (Kent)	d									09 43													
Tonbridge 4	a									09 48													
Earlswood (Surrey)	d			09 12																			
Salfords	d			09 16																			
Horley 4	d			09 19									←						09 36			09 51	
Gatwick Airport 10 ✈	a	09 00	09 08	09 23		09 10	09 15				09 18	09 22	09 23	09 26	09 26		09 30		09 39		09 50	09 55	
	d		09 09	09 24		09 11					09 20	09 23	09 24	09 27	09 27				09 40			09 56	
Three Bridges 15	a		09 14	↦		09 15							09 29	09 31	09 31				09 44			↦	
	d		09 14			09 15							09 30	09 32	09 32				09 45				
Crawley	d		09 18										09 33						09 48				
Ifield	d												09 36										
Faygate	d																						
Littlehaven	d												09 42										
Horsham 4	a		09 26										09 45						09 56				
Balcombe	d					09 21																	
Haywards Heath	a					09 26					09 30			09 41	09 41								
	d					09 27					09 35 / 09 37			09 41	09 41								
Wivelsfield	d					09 31																	
Lewes 4	a										09 52												
Burgess Hill 4	d					09 33						09 38											
Hassocks 4	d					09 36						09 41											
Preston Park	d					09 43																	
Hove 2	a										09 53												
Brighton 10	a				09 27	09 47						09 52		09 55	09 55								09 57

A 19 May

Table 186

Saturdays

until 23 June

Bedford and London - Brighton

Network Diagram - see first Page of Table 186

		FC 1	SN 1	SN 1	SN ◇1		SN 1	FC 1	FC 1 A	SN 1	SN ◇1	SN 1	SN ◇1	FC 1	SN 1	GW 1	SN 1	SN ◇1		SN ◇1	SN 1	FC 1
London Victoria [15] ⊖	d		09 15		09 17					09 30	09 32		09 36		09 45			09 47		09 51		
Clapham Junction [10]	d				09 23						09 38		09 42					09 53				
Bedford	d	07 54						08 10						08 24								08 40
Luton [10]	d	08 18						08 34						08 48								09 04
Luton Airport Parkway [7] ✈	d	08 20						08 36						08 50								09 06
St Albans City	d	08 32						08 48						09 02								09 18
St Pancras International [15] ⊖	d	08 54						09 09						09 24								09 39
Farringdon [3] ⊖	d	08 59						09 14						09 29								09 44
City Thameslink [3]	d	09 03						09 18						09 33								09 48
London Blackfriars [3] ⊖	d	09 05						09 20						09 35								09 50
London Bridge [4] ⊖	d	09 12		09 15				09 27	09 27			09 33		09 42			09 45					09 57
New Cross Gate	d											09 38										
Norwood Junction [2]	d			09 26								09 46					09 56					
East Croydon	a	09 24		09 29	09 32			09 39	09 39		09 47	09 50	09 52	09 54			09 59	10 02		10 07		10 09
	d	09 25		09 30	09 33			09 41	09 41		09 48	09 51	09 53	09 55			10 00	10 03		10 08		10 11
Purley [4]	d			09 36								09 56					10 06					
Coulsdon South	d			09 39								10 00					10 09					
Merstham	d			09 45								10 05										
Redhill	a			09 49							10 00	10 09					10 17					
	d			09 52							10 00	10 10				10 13	10 17					
Reigate	a			09 56												10 18						
Nutfield	d																10 22					
Godstone	d																10 27					
Edenbridge	d																10 33					
Penshurst	d																10 39					
Leigh (Kent)	d																10 43					
Tonbridge [4]	a																10 48					
Earlswood (Surrey)	d											10 12										
Salfords	d											10 16										
Horley [4]	d											10 19										
Gatwick Airport [10] ✈	a	09 40	09 45		09 48		← 09 55	09 56	09 56	10 00	10 08	10 23		10 10	10 15			10 18		10 22	← 10 23	10 26
	d	09 41			09 50		09 56	09 57	09 57		10 09	10 24		10 11				10 20		10 23	10 24	10 27
Three Bridges [15]	a	09 45					10 01	10 01	10 01		10 14	→		10 15							10 29	10 31
	d	09 45					10 01	10 02	10 02		10 14			10 15							10 30	10 32
Crawley	d						10 05				10 18										10 33	
Ifield	d						10 07														10 36	
Faygate	d																					
Littlehaven	d						10 14														10 42	
Horsham [4]	a						10 17				10 26										10 45	
Balcombe	d													10 21								
Haywards Heath	a	09 54			10 00			10 11	10 11					10 26				10 30				10 41
	d	09 55			10 04	10 07		10 11	10 11					10 27				10 35	10 37			10 41
Wivelsfield	d	09 59				10 11								10 31								
Lewes [4]	a					10 22												10 52				
Burgess Hill [4]	d	10 01			10 09									10 33						10 38		
Hassocks [4]	d	10 04												10 36						10 41		
Preston Park	d	10 11			10 18									10 43								
Hove [2]	a				10 22														10 53			
Brighton [10]	a	10 15						10 25	10 25				10 27	10 47						10 52		10 55

A 19 May

Table 186

Saturdays

until 23 June

Bedford and London - Brighton

Network Diagram - see first Page of Table 186

		FC	SN	SN	SN	GW	GW	SN	SN	FC	SN	SN	SN		SN	FC	FC	SN	SN	SN	SN	FC
		1	1		◇1	1	1	1	◇1	1	1	1	◇1		1	1	1	1	◇1	1	◇1	1
		A															A					
			🛒		🛒				🛒		🛒							🛒			🛒	
London Victoria 15 ⊖	d		10 00	10 01	10 02				10 06		10 15		10 17					10 30	10 32		10 36	
Clapham Junction 10	d			10 08	10 08				10 12				10 23						10 38		10 42	
Bedford	d									08 54						09 10						09 24
Luton 10	d									09 18						09 34						09 48
Luton Airport Parkway 7 ✈	d									09 20						09 36						09 50
St Albans City	d									09 32						09 48						10 02
St Pancras International 15 ⊖	d									09 54						10 09						10 24
Farringdon 3 ⊖	d									09 59						10 14						10 29
City Thameslink 3	d									10 03						10 18						10 33
London Blackfriars 3 ⊖	d									10 05						10 20						10 35
London Bridge 4 ⊖	d	09 57						10 03		10 12		10 15				10 27	10 27			10 33		10 42
New Cross Gate	d							10 08												10 38		
Norwood Junction 2	d							10 16				10 26								10 46		
East Croydon	a	10 09			10 17			10 20	10 22	10 24		10 29	10 32			10 39	10 39		10 47	10 50	10 52	10 54
	d	10 11			10 18			10 21	10 23	10 25		10 30	10 33			10 41	10 41		10 48	10 51	10 53	10 55
Purley 4	d							10 26				10 36								10 56		
Coulsdon South	d							10 30				10 39								11 00		
Merstham	d							10 35				10 45								11 05		
Redhill	a				10 30			10 39				10 49							11 00	11 09		
	d				10 30	10 34	10 41	10 44				10 52							11 00	11 10		
Reigate	a					10 38						10 56										
Nutfield	d																					
Godstone	d																					
Edenbridge	d																					
Penshurst	d																					
Leigh (Kent)	d																					
Tonbridge 4	a																					
Earlswood (Surrey)	d																			11 12		
Salfords	d																			11 16		
Horley 4	d				10 36			10 51							←					11 19		
Gatwick Airport 10 ✈	a	10 26	10 30		10 39		10 50	10 55		10 40	10 45		10 48		10 55	10 56	10 56	11 00	11 08	11 23		11 10
	d	10 27			10 40			10 56		10 41			10 50		10 56	10 57	10 57		11 09	11 24		11 11
Three Bridges 15	a	10 31			10 44			→		10 45					11 01	11 01	11 01		11 14	→		11 15
	d	10 32			10 45					10 45					11 01	11 02	11 02		11 14			11 15
Crawley	d				10 48										11 05				11 18			
Ifield	d														11 07							
Faygate	d																					
Littlehaven	d														11 14							
Horsham 4	a				10 56										11 17				11 26			
Balcombe	d																					11 21
Haywards Heath	a	10 41								10 54			11 00			11 11	11 11					11 26
	d	10 41								10 55			11 04	11 07		11 11	11 11					11 27
Wivelsfield	d									10 59				11 11								11 31
Lewes 4	a													11 22								
Burgess Hill 4	d									11 01			11 09									11 33
Hassocks 4	d									11 04												11 36
Preston Park	d									11 11			11 18									11 43
Hove 2	a												11 22									
Brighton 10	a	10 55							10 57	11 15						11 25	11 25				11 27	11 47

A 19 May

Table 186

Saturdays

until 23 June

Bedford and London - Brighton

Network Diagram - see first Page of Table 186

		SN 1	GW 1	SN 1	SN ◇1		SN ◇1	SN 1	FC 1	FC 1 A	SN 1	SN	SN ◇1	GW 1	GW 1	SN 1	SN ◇1	FC 1	SN 1	SN 1	SN ◇1	
London Victoria 15 ⊖	d	10 45			10 47		10 51				11 00	11 01	11 02				11 06		11 15		11 17	
Clapham unction 10	d				10 53							11 08	11 08				11 12				11 23	
Bedford	d								09 40									09 54				
Lton 10	d								10 04									10 18				
Lton Airport Parkway 7 ✈	d								10 06									10 20				
St Albans City	d								10 18									10 32				
St Pancras hternational 15 ⊖	d								10 39									10 54				
Farringdon 3 ⊖	d								10 44									10 59				
City Thameslink 3	d								10 48									11 03				
London Blackfriars 3 ⊖	d								10 50									11 05				
London Bridge 4 ⊖	d			10 45					10 57	10 57						11 03		11 12		11 15		
Nw Cross Gate	d															11 08						
Nrwood unction 2	d			10 56												11 16				11 26		
East Croydon	a			10 59	11 02		11 07		11 09	11 09			11 17			11 20	11 22	11 24		11 29	11 32	
	d			11 00	11 03		11 08		11 11	11 11			11 18			11 21	11 23	11 25		11 30	11 33	
Purley 4	d			11 06												11 26				11 36		
Coulsdon South	d			11 09												11 30				11 39		
Merstham	d															11 35				11 45		
Redhill	a			11 17									11 30			11 39				11 49		
	d		11 13	11 17									11 30	11 34	11 41	11 44				11 52		
Reigate	a		11 18											11 38						11 56		
Ntfield	d			11 22																		
Godstone	d			11 27																		
Eenbridge	d			11 33																		
Penshurst	d			11 39																		
Lgh (Kent)	d			11 43																		
Tonbridge 4	a			11 48																		
Erlswood (Surrey)	d																					
Salfords	d																					
Horley 4	d							←					11 36			11 51						
Gatwick Airport 10 ✈	a	11 15			11 18		11 22	11 23	11 26	11 26	11 30		11 39		11 50	11 55		11 40	11 45		11 48	
	d				11 20		11 23	11 24	11 27	11 27			11 40			11 56		11 41			11 50	
Three Bridges 15	a							11 29	11 31	11 31			11 44			→		11 45				
	d							11 30	11 32	11 32			11 45					11 45				
Crawley	d							11 33					11 48									
field	d							11 36														
Faygate	d																					
Lttlehaven	d							11 42														
Horsham 4	a							11 45					11 56									
Balcombe	d																					
Haywards Heath	a				11 30				11 41	11 41								11 54			12 00	
	d				11 35	11 37			11 41	11 41								11 55			12 04	12 07
Wvelsfield	d																	11 59				12 11
Lwes 4	a				11 52																	12 22
Burgess Hill 4	d						11 38											12 01			12 09	
Hassocks 4	d						11 41											12 04				
Preston Park	d																	12 11			12 18	
Hove 2	a					11 53															12 22	
Brighton 10	a						11 52		11 55	11 55							11 57	12 15				

A 19 May

Table 186

Saturdays
until 23 June

Bedford and London - Brighton

Network Diagram - see first Page of Table 186

		SN	FC	FC	SN	SN	SN	SN		FC	SN	GW	SN	SN	SN		SN	FC	FC	SN	SN	SN	GW
		1	1	1	1	◇1	1	◇1		1	1	1	1	◇1	◇1		1	1	1	1		◇1	1
				A															A				
					🚲			🚲			🚲									🚲		🚲	
London Victoria 15 ⊖	d				11 30	11 32		11 36			11 45			11 47	11 51					12 00	12 01	12 02	
Clapham Junction 10	d					11 38		11 42						11 53							12 08	12 08	
Bedford	d		10 10							10 24								10 40					
Luton 10	d		10 34							10 48								11 04					
Luton Airport Parkway 7 ✈	d		10 36							10 50								11 06					
St Albans City	d		10 48							11 02								11 18					
St Pancras International 15 ⊖	d		11 09							11 24								11 39					
Farringdon 3 ⊖	d		11 14							11 29								11 44					
City Thameslink 3	d		11 18							11 33								11 48					
London Blackfriars 3 ⊖	d		11 20							11 35								11 50					
London Bridge 4 ⊖	d		11 27	11 27			11 33			11 42			11 45					11 57	11 57				
New Cross Gate	d						11 38																
Norwood Junction 2	d						11 46						11 56										
East Croydon	a		11 39	11 39		11 47	11 50	11 52		11 54			11 59	12 02	12 07			12 09	12 09			12 17	
	d		11 41	11 41		11 48	11 51	11 53		11 55			12 00	12 03	12 08			12 11	12 11			12 18	
Purley 4	d						11 56						12 06										
Coulsdon South	d						12 00						12 09										
Merstham	d						12 05																
Redhill	a					12 00	12 09						12 17									12 30	
	d					12 00	12 10					12 13	12 17									12 30	12 34
Reigate	a											12 18											12 38
Nutfield	d												12 22										
Godstone	d												12 27										
Edenbridge	d												12 33										
Penshurst	d												12 39										
Leigh (Kent)	d												12 43										
Tonbridge 4	a												12 48										
Earlswood (Surrey)	d						12 12																
Salfords	d						12 16																
Horley 4	d	←					12 19										←					12 36	
Gatwick Airport 10 ✈	a	11 55	11 56	11 56	12 00	12 08	12 23			12 10	12 15			12 18	12 22		12 23	12 26	12 26	12 30		12 39	
	d	11 56	11 57	11 57		12 09	12 24			12 11				12 20	12 23		12 24	12 27	12 27			12 40	
Three Bridges 15	a	12 01	12 01	12 01		12 14	→			12 15							12 29	12 31	12 31			12 44	
	d	12 01	12 02	12 02		12 14				12 15							12 30	12 32	12 32			12 45	
Crawley	d	12 05				12 18											12 33					12 48	
Ifield	d	12 07															12 36						
Faygate	d																						
Littlehaven	d	12 14															12 42						
Horsham 4	a	12 17				12 26											12 45					12 56	
Balcombe	d									12 21													
Haywards Heath	a		12 11	12 11						12 26				12 30				12 41	12 41				
	d		12 11	12 11						12 27				12 35 / 12 37				12 41	12 41				
Wivelsfield	d									12 31													
Lewes 4	a													12 52									
Burgess Hill 4	d									12 33					12 38								
Hassocks 4	d									12 36					12 41								
Preston Park	d									12 43													
Hove 2	a													12 53									
Brighton 10	a		12 25	12 25				12 27		12 47					12 52			12 55	12 55				

A 19 May

Table 186

Saturdays

until 23 June

Bedford and London - Brighton

Network Diagram - see first Page of Table 186

		GW	SN	SN	FC	SN	SN	SN		SN	FC	FC	SN	SN	SN	SN	FC	SN	GW	SN	SN		SN
		1	1	◇1	1	1	1	◇1		1	1	1	1	◇1	1	◇1	1	1	1	1	◇1		◇1
												A											
				(trolley)		(trolley)							(trolley)			(trolley)		(trolley)					
London Victoria 15 ⊖	d			12 06		12 15		12 17					12 30	12 32		12 36		12 45			12 47		12 51
Clapham Junction 10	d			12 12				12 23						12 38		12 42					12 53		
Bedford	d				10 54						11 10						11 24						
Luton 10	d				11 18						11 34						11 48						
Luton Airport Parkway 7 ✈	d				11 20						11 36						11 50						
St Albans City	d				11 32						11 48						12 02						
St Pancras International 15 ⊖	d				11 54						12 09						12 24						
Farringdon 3 ⊖	d				11 59						12 14						12 29						
City Thameslink 3	d				12 03						12 18						12 33						
London Blackfriars 3 ⊖	d				12 05						12 20						12 35						
London Bridge 4 ⊖	d		12 03		12 12		12 15				12 27	12 27			12 33		12 42			12 45			
New Cross Gate	d		12 08												12 38								
Norwood Junction 2	d		12 16				12 26								12 46					12 56			
East Croydon	a		12 20	12 22	12 24		12 29	12 32			12 39	12 39		12 47	12 50	12 52	12 54			12 59	13 02		13 07
	d		12 21	12 23	12 25		12 30	12 33			12 41	12 41		12 48	12 51	12 53	12 55			13 00	13 03		13 08
Purley 4	d		12 26				12 36								12 56					13 06			
Coulsdon South	d		12 30				12 39								13 00					13 09			
Merstham	d		12 35				12 45								13 05								
Redhill	a		12 39				12 49							13 00	13 09					13 17			
	d	12 41	12 44				12 52							13 00	13 10				13 13	13 17			
Reigate	a						12 56												13 18				
Nutfield	d																			13 22			
Godstone	d																			13 27			
Edenbridge	d																			13 33			
Penshurst	d																			13 39			
Leigh (Kent)	d																			13 43			
Tonbridge 4	a																			13 48			
Earlswood (Surrey)	d														13 12								
Salfords	d														13 16								
Horley 4	d		12 51							←					13 19								
Gatwick Airport 10 ✈	a	12 50	12 55		12 40	12 45		12 48		12 55	12 56	12 56	13 00	13 08	13 23		13 10	13 15			13 18		13 22
	d		12 56		12 41			12 50		12 56	12 57	12 57		13 09	13 24		13 11				13 20		13 23
Three Bridges 15	a		→		12 45					13 01	13 01	13 01		13 14	→		13 15						
	d				12 45					13 01	13 02	13 02		13 14			13 15						
Crawley	d									13 05				13 18									
Ifield	d									13 07													
Faygate	d																						
Littlehaven	d									13 14													
Horsham 4	a									13 17				13 26									
Balcombe	d																13 21						
Haywards Heath	a				12 54			13 00			13 11	13 11					13 26				13 30		
	d				12 55			13 04	13 07		13 11	13 11					13 27				13 35	13 37	
Wivelsfield	d				12 59				13 11								13 31						
Lewes 4	a								13 22												13 52		
Burgess Hill 4	d				13 01			13 09									13 33						13 38
Hassocks 4	d				13 04												13 36						13 41
Preston Park	d				13 11			13 18									13 43						
Hove 2	a							13 22														13 53	
Brighton 10	a			12 57	13 15						13 25	13 25				13 27	13 47						13 52

A 19 May

Table 186

Saturdays
until 23 June

Bedford and London - Brighton

Network Diagram - see first Page of Table 186

		SN	FC	FC	SN	SN	SN	GW	GW	SN	SN	FC	SN	SN	SN		SN	FC	FC	SN	SN	SN
		1	1	1	1		◇1	1	1	1	◇1	1	1	1	◇1		1	1	1	1	◇1	1
				A															A			
					ᴛ		ᴛ				ᴛ		ᴛ							ᴛ		
London Victoria 15 ⊖	d				13 00	13 01	13 02				13 06		13 15		13 17					13 30	13 32	
Clapham Junction 10	d					13 08	13 08				13 12				13 23						13 38	
Bedford	d		11 40									11 54						12 10				
Luton 10	d		12 04									12 18						12 34				
Luton Airport Parkway 7 ✈	d		12 06									12 20						12 36				
St Albans City	d		12 18									12 32						12 48				
St Pancras International 15 ⊖	d		12 39									12 54						13 09				
Farringdon 3 ⊖	d		12 44									12 59						13 14				
City Thameslink 3	d		12 48									13 03						13 18				
London Blackfriars 3 ⊖	d		12 50									13 05						13 20				
London Bridge 4 ⊖	d		12 57	12 57						13 03		13 12		13 15				13 27	13 27			13 33
New Cross Gate	d									13 08												13 38
Norwood Junction 2	d									13 16				13 26								13 46
East Croydon	a		13 09	13 09			13 17			13 20	13 22	13 24		13 29	13 32			13 39	13 39		13 47	13 50
	d		13 11	13 11			13 18			13 21	13 23	13 25		13 30	13 33			13 41	13 41		13 48	13 51
Purley 4	d									13 26				13 36								13 56
Coulsdon South	d									13 30				13 39								14 00
Merstham	d									13 35				13 45								14 05
Redhill	a						13 30			13 39				13 49							14 00	14 09
	d						13 30	13 34	13 41	13 44				13 52							14 00	14 10
Reigate	a							13 38						13 56								
Nutfield	d																					
Godstone	d																					
Edenbridge	d																					
Penshurst	d																					
Leigh (Kent)	d																					
Tonbridge 4	a																					
Earlswood (Surrey)	d																					14 12
Salfords	d																					14 16
Horley 4	d	←					13 36			13 51							←					14 19
Gatwick Airport 10 ✈	a	13 23	13 26	13 26	13 30		13 39		13 50	13 55		13 40	13 45		13 48		13 55	13 56	13 56	14 00	14 08	14 23
	d	13 24	13 27	13 27			13 40			13 56		13 41			13 50		13 56	13 57	13 57		14 09	14 24
Three Bridges 15	a	13 29	13 31	13 31			13 44			→		13 45					14 01	14 01	14 01		14 14	→
	d	13 30	13 32	13 32			13 45					13 45					14 01	14 02	14 02		14 14	
Crawley	d	13 33					13 48										14 05				14 18	
Ifield	d	13 36															14 07					
Faygate	d																					
Littlehaven	d	13 42															14 14					
Horsham 4	a	13 45					13 56										14 17				14 26	
Balcombe	d																					
Haywards Heath	a		13 41	13 41								13 54			14 00			14 11	14 11			
	d		13 41	13 41								13 55			14 04	14 07		14 11	14 11			
Wivelsfield	d											13 59				14 11						
Lewes 4	a															14 22						
Burgess Hill 4	d											14 01			14 09							
Hassocks 4	d											14 04										
Preston Park	d											14 11			14 18							
Hove 2	a														14 22							
Brighton 10	a		13 55	13 55							13 57	14 15						14 25	14 25			

A 19 May

Table 186

Saturdays

until 23 June

Bedford and London - Brighton

Network Diagram - see first Page of Table 186

		SN	FC	SN	GW	SN	SN		SN	SN	FC	FC	SN	SN	SN	GW	GW	SN	SN	FC	SN	SN
		◇1	1	1	1	1	◇1		◇1	1	1	1	1		◇1	1	1	1	◇1	1	1	1
												A										
		🛒		🛒									🛒		🛒				🛒		🛒	
London Victoria 15 ⊖	d	13 36		13 45			13 47		13 51				14 00	14 01	14 02				14 06		14 15	
Clapham Junction 10	d	13 42					13 53							14 08	14 08				14 12			
Bedford	d		12 24								12 40									12 54		
Luton 10	d		12 48								13 04									13 18		
Luton Airport Parkway 7 ✈	d		12 50								13 06									13 20		
St Albans City	d		13 02								13 18									13 32		
St Pancras International 15 ⊖	d		13 24								13 39									13 54		
Farringdon 3 ⊖	d		13 29								13 44									13 59		
City Thameslink 3	d		13 33								13 48									14 03		
London Blackfriars 3 ⊖	d		13 35								13 50									14 05		
London Bridge 4 ⊖	d		13 42			13 45					13 57	13 57						14 03		14 12		14 15
New Cross Gate	d																	14 08				
Norwood Junction 2	d					13 56												14 16				14 26
East Croydon	a	13 52	13 54			13 59	14 02		14 07		14 09	14 09			14 17			14 20	14 22	14 24		14 29
	d	13 53	13 55			14 00	14 03		14 08		14 11	14 11			14 18			14 21	14 23	14 25		14 30
Purley 4	d					14 06												14 26				14 36
Coulsdon South	d					14 09												14 30				14 39
Merstham	d																	14 35				14 45
Redhill	a					14 17									14 30			14 39				14 49
	d				14 13	14 17									14 30	14 34	14 41	14 44				14 52
Reigate	a				14 18											14 38						14 56
Nutfield	d					14 22																
Godstone	d					14 27																
Edenbridge	d					14 33																
Penshurst	d					14 39																
Leigh (Kent)	d					14 43																
Tonbridge 4	a					14 48																
Earlswood (Surrey)	d																					
Salfords	d																					
Horley 4	d									←					14 36			14 51				
Gatwick Airport 10 ✈	a		14 10	14 15			14 18		14 22	14 23	14 26	14 26	14 30		14 39		14 50	14 55		14 40	14 45	
	d		14 11				14 20		14 23	14 24	14 27	14 27			14 40			14 56		14 41		
Three Bridges 15	a		14 15							14 29	14 31	14 31			14 44			→		14 45		
	d		14 15							14 30	14 32	14 32			14 45					14 45		
Crawley	d									14 33					14 48							
Ifield	d									14 36												
Faygate	d																					
Littlehaven	d									14 42												
Horsham 4	a									14 45					14 56							
Balcombe	d		14 21																			
Haywards Heath	a		14 26				14 30				14 41	14 41								14 54		
	d		14 27				14 35	14 37			14 41	14 41								14 55		
Wivelsfield	d		14 31																	14 59		
Lewes 4	a						14 52															
Burgess Hill 4	d		14 33						14 38											15 01		
Hassocks 4	d		14 36						14 41											15 04		
Preston Park	d		14 43																	15 11		
Hove 2	a							14 53														
Brighton 10	a	14 27	14 47						14 52		14 55	14 55							14 57	15 15		

A 19 May

Table 186

Saturdays

until 23 June

Bedford and London - Brighton

Network Diagram - see first Page of Table 186

		SN ◇1			SN 1	FC 1	FC 1 A	SN 1 🚲	SN ◇1	SN 1	SN ◇1 🚲		FC 1	SN 1 🚲	GW 1	SN 1	SN ◇1		SN ◇1		SN 1	FC 1	FC 1 A	SN 1 🚲	SN
London Victoria 15 ⊖	d	14 17						14 30	14 32		14 36			14 45			14 47		14 51					15 00	15 01
Clapham Junction 10	d	14 23							14 38		14 42						14 53								15 08
Bedford	d					13 10							13 24									13 40			
Luton 10	d					13 34							13 48									14 04			
Luton Airport Parkway 7 ✈	d					13 36							13 50									14 06			
St Albans City	d					13 48							14 02									14 18			
St Pancras International 15 ⊖	d					14 09							14 24									14 39			
Farringdon 3 ⊖	d					14 14							14 29									14 44			
City Thameslink 3	d					14 18							14 33									14 48			
London Blackfriars 3 ⊖	d					14 20							14 35									14 50			
London Bridge 4 ⊖	d					14 27	14 27			14 33			14 42			14 45						14 57	14 57		
New Cross Gate	d									14 38															
Norwood Junction 2	d									14 46						14 56									
East Croydon 🚊	a	14 32				14 39	14 39		14 47	14 50	14 52		14 54			14 59	15 02		15 07			15 09	15 09		
	d	14 33				14 41	14 41		14 48	14 51	14 53		14 55			15 00	15 03		15 08			15 11	15 11		
Purley 4	d									14 56						15 06									
Coulsdon South	d									15 00						15 09									
Merstham	d									15 05															
Redhill	a								15 00	15 09						15 17									
	d								15 00	15 10					15 13	15 17									
Reigate	a														15 18										
Nutfield	d															15 22									
Godstone	d															15 27									
Edenbridge	d															15 33									
Penshurst	d															15 39									
Leigh (Kent)	d															15 43									
Tonbridge 4	a															15 48									
Earlswood (Surrey)	d									15 12															
Salfords	d									15 16															
Horley 4	d				←					15 19											←				
Gatwick Airport 10 ✈	a	14 48			14 55	14 56	14 56	15 00	15 08	15 23			15 10	15 15			15 18		15 22		15 23	15 26	15 26	15 30	
	d	14 50			14 56	14 57	14 57		15 09	15 24			15 11				15 20		15 23		15 24	15 27	15 27		
Three Bridges 15	a				15 01	15 01	15 01		15 14	→			15 15								15 29	15 31	15 31		
	d				15 01	15 02	15 02		15 14				15 15								15 30	15 32	15 32		
Crawley	d				15 05				15 18												15 33				
Ifield	d				15 07																15 36				
Faygate	d																								
Littlehaven	d				15 14																15 42				
Horsham 4	a				15 17				15 26												15 45				
Balcombe	d												15 21												
Haywards Heath	a	15 00				15 11	15 11						15 26				15 30					15 41	15 41		
	d	15 04	15 07			15 11	15 11						15 27				15 35	15 37				15 41	15 41		
Wivelsfield	d		15 11										15 31												
Lewes 4	a		15 22														15 52								
Burgess Hill 4	d	15 09											15 33						15 38						
Hassocks 4	d												15 36						15 41						
Preston Park	d	15 18											15 43												
Hove 2	a	15 22																15 53							
Brighton 10	a					15 25	15 25				15 27		15 47						15 52			15 55	15 55		

A 19 May

Table 186

Saturdays

until 23 June

Bedford and London - Brighton

Network Diagram - see first Page of Table 186

		SN	GW		GW	SN	SN	FC	SN	SN	SN			SN	FC	FC	SN	SN	SN	SN		FC	SN	GW	SN
		◇1	1		1	1	◇1	1	1	1	◇1			1	1	1	1	◇1	1	◇1		1	1	1	1
																A									
		🛒					🛒		🛒								🛒			🛒			🛒		
London Victoria 15 ⊖	d	15 02					15 06		15 15		15 17						15 30	15 32		15 36			15 45		
Clapham Junction 10	d	15 08					15 12				15 23							15 38		15 42					
Bedford	d							13 54							14 10							14 24			
Luton 10	d							14 18							14 34							14 48			
Luton Airport Parkway 7 ✈	d							14 20							14 36							14 50			
St Albans City	d							14 32							14 48							15 02			
St Pancras International 15 ⊖	d							14 54							15 09							15 24			
Farringdon 3 ⊖	d							14 59							15 14							15 29			
City Thameslink 3	d							15 03							15 18							15 33			
London Blackfriars 3 ⊖	d							15 05							15 20							15 35			
London Bridge 4 ⊖	d					15 03		15 12		15 15					15 27	15 27			15 33			15 42			15 45
New Cross Gate	d					15 08													15 38						
Norwood Junction 2	d					15 16				15 26									15 46						15 56
East Croydon	a	15 17				15 20	15 22	15 24		15 29	15 32				15 39	15 39		15 47	15 50	15 52		15 54			15 59
	d	15 18				15 21	15 23	15 25		15 30	15 33				15 41	15 41		15 48	15 51	15 53		15 55			16 00
Purley 4	d					15 26				15 36									15 56						16 06
Coulsdon South	d					15 30				15 39									16 00						16 09
Merstham	d					15 35				15 45									16 05						
Redhill	a	15 30				15 39				15 49								16 00	16 09						16 17
	d	15 30	15 34		15 41	15 44				15 52								16 00	16 10					16 13	16 17
Reigate	a		15 38							15 56														16 18	
Nutfield	d																								16 22
Godstone	d																								16 27
Edenbridge	d																								16 33
Penshurst	d																								16 39
Leigh (Kent)	d																								16 43
Tonbridge 4	a																								16 48
Earlswood (Surrey)	d																		16 12						
Salfords	d																		16 16						
Horley 4	d	15 36				15 51								←					16 19						
Gatwick Airport 10 ✈	a	15 39			15 50	15 55		15 40	15 45		15 48			15 55	15 56	15 56	16 00	16 08	16 23			16 10	16 15		
	d	15 40				15 56		15 41			15 50			15 56	15 57	15 57		16 09	16 24			16 11			
Three Bridges 15	a	15 44				→		15 45						16 01	16 01	16 01		16 14	→			16 15			
	d	15 45						15 45						16 01	16 02	16 02		16 14				16 15			
Crawley	d	15 48												16 05				16 18							
Ifield	d													16 07											
Faygate	d																								
Littlehaven	d													16 14											
Horsham 4	a	15 56												16 17				16 26							
Balcombe	d																					16 21			
Haywards Heath	a							15 54			16 00				16 11	16 11						16 26			
	d							15 55			16 04	16 07			16 11	16 11						16 27			
Wivelsfield	d							15 59				16 11										16 31			
Lewes 4	a											16 22													
Burgess Hill 4	d							16 01			16 09											16 33			
Hassocks 4	d							16 04														16 36			
Preston Park	d							16 11			16 18											16 43			
Hove 2	a										16 22														
Brighton 10	a						15 57	16 15							16 25	16 25				16 27		16 47			

A 19 May

Table 186

Saturdays

until 23 June

Bedford and London - Brighton

Network Diagram - see first Page of Table 186

		SN		SN		SN	FC	FC	SN	SN	SN	GW		GW	SN	SN	FC	SN	SN	SN			SN	FC	FC
		◇1		◇1		1	1	1	1		◇1	1		1	1	◇1	1	1	1	◇1			1	1	1
								A																	A
									🛒		🛒					🛒		🛒							
London Victoria 15 ⊖	d	15 47		15 51					16 00	16 01	16 02					16 06		16 15		16 17					
Clapham Junction 10	d	15 53								16 08	16 08					16 12				16 23					
Bedford	d						14 40										14 54							15 10	
Luton 10	d						15 04										15 18							15 34	
Luton Airport Parkway 7 ✈	d						15 06										15 20							15 36	
St Albans City	d						15 18										15 32							15 48	
St Pancras International 15 ⊖	d						15 39										15 54							16 09	
Farringdon 3 ⊖	d						15 44										15 59							16 14	
City Thameslink 3	d						15 48										16 03							16 18	
London Blackfriars 3 ⊖	d						15 50										16 05							16 20	
London Bridge 4 ⊖	d						15 57	15 57							16 03		16 12		16 15					16 27	16 27
New Cross Gate	d														16 08										
Norwood Junction 2	d														16 16				16 26						
East Croydon	a	16 02		16 07			16 09	16 09			16 17				16 20	16 22	16 24		16 29	16 32				16 39	16 39
	d	16 03		16 08			16 11	16 11			16 18				16 21	16 23	16 25		16 30	16 33				16 41	16 41
Purley 4	d														16 26				16 36						
Coulsdon South	d														16 30				16 39						
Merstham	d														16 35				16 45						
Redhill	a										16 30				16 39				16 49						
	d										16 30	16 34		16 41	16 44				16 52						
Reigate	a											16 38							16 56						
Nutfield	d																								
Godstone	d																								
Edenbridge	d																								
Penshurst	d																								
Leigh (Kent)	d																								
Tonbridge 4	a																								
Earlswood (Surrey)	d																								
Salfords	d																								
Horley 4	d					←					16 36				16 51								←		
Gatwick Airport 10 ✈	a	16 18		16 22		16 23	16 26	16 26	16 30		16 39			16 50	16 55		16 40	16 45		16 48			16 55	16 56	16 56
	d	16 20		16 23		16 24	16 27	16 27			16 40				16 56		16 41			16 50			16 56	16 57	16 57
Three Bridges 15	a					16 29	16 31	16 31			16 44				→		16 45						17 01	17 01	17 01
	d					16 30	16 32	16 32			16 45						16 45						17 01	17 02	17 02
Crawley	d					16 33					16 48												17 05		
Ifield	d					16 36																	17 07		
Faygate	d																								
Littlehaven	d					16 42																	17 14		
Horsham 4	a					16 45					16 56												17 17		
Balcombe	d																								
Haywards Heath	a	16 30					16 41	16 41									16 54			17 00				17 11	17 11
	d	16 35	16 37				16 41	16 41									16 55			17 04	17 07			17 11	17 11
Wivelsfield	d																16 59				17 11				
Lewes 4	a	16 52																			17 22				
Burgess Hill 4	d			16 38													17 01			17 09					
Hassocks 4	d			16 41													17 04								
Preston Park	d																17 11			17 18					
Hove 2	a		16 53																	17 22					
Brighton 10	a			16 52			16 55	16 55								16 57	17 15							17 25	17 25

A 19 May

Table 186

Saturdays

until 23 June

Bedford and London - Brighton

Network Diagram - see first Page of Table 186

		SN	SN	SN	SN		FC	SN	GW	SN	SN	SN		SN	FC	FC	SN	SN	SN	GW		GW	SN	SN
		1	◇1	1	◇1		1	1	1	1	◇1	◇1		1	1	1	1		◇1	1		1	1	◇1
																A								
London Victoria 15 ⊖	d	16 30	16 32		16 36			16 45			16 47	16 51					17 00	17 01	17 02					17 06
Clapham Junction 10	d		16 38		16 42						16 53							17 08	17 08					17 12
Bedford	d						15 24								15 40									
Luton 10	d						15 48								16 04									
Luton Airport Parkway 7 ✈	d						15 50								16 06									
St Albans City	d						16 02								16 18									
St Pancras International 15 ⊖	d						16 24								16 39									
Farringdon 3 ⊖	d						16 29								16 44									
City Thameslink 3	d						16 33								16 48									
London Blackfriars 3 ⊖	d						16 35								16 50									
London Bridge 4 ⊖	d			16 33			16 42			16 45					16 57	16 57							17 03	
New Cross Gate	d			16 38																			17 08	
Norwood Junction 2	d			16 46						16 56													17 16	
East Croydon	a		16 47	16 50	16 52		16 54			16 59	17 02	17 07			17 09	17 09			17 17				17 20	17 22
	d		16 48	16 51	16 53		16 55			17 00	17 03	17 08			17 11	17 11			17 18				17 21	17 23
Purley 4	d			16 56						17 06													17 26	
Coulsdon South	d			17 00						17 09													17 30	
Merstham	d			17 05																			17 35	
Redhill	a		17 00	17 09						17 17									17 30				17 39	
	d		17 00	17 10					17 13	17 17									17 30	17 34		17 41	17 44	
Reigate	a								17 18											17 38				
Nutfield	d									17 22														
Godstone	d									17 27														
Edenbridge	d									17 33														
Penshurst	d									17 39														
Leigh (Kent)	d									17 43														
Tonbridge 4	a									17 48														
Earlswood (Surrey)	d			17 12																				
Salfords	d			17 16																				
Horley 4	d			17 19										←					17 36				17 51	
Gatwick Airport 10 ✈	a	17 00	17 08	17 23			17 10	17 15			17 18	17 22		17 23	17 26	17 26	17 30		17 39			17 50	17 55	
	d		17 09	17 24			17 11				17 20	17 23		17 24	17 27	17 27			17 40				17 56	
Three Bridges 15	a		17 14	→			17 15							17 29	17 31	17 31			17 44				→	
	d		17 14				17 15							17 30	17 32	17 32			17 45					
Crawley	d		17 18											17 33					17 48					
Ifield	d													17 36										
Faygate	d																							
Littlehaven	d													17 42										
Horsham 4	a		17 26											17 45					17 56					
Balcombe	d						17 21																	
Haywards Heath	a						17 26				17 30				17 41	17 41								
	d						17 27				17 35 17 37				17 41	17 41								
Wivelsfield	d						17 31																	
Lewes 4	a										17 52													
Burgess Hill 4	d						17 33					17 38												
Hassocks 4	d						17 36					17 41												
Preston Park	d						17 43																	
Hove 2	a										17 53													
Brighton 10	a				17 27		17 47					17 52			17 55	17 55								17 57

A 19 May

Table 186

Saturdays

until 23 June

Bedford and London - Brighton

Network Diagram - see first Page of Table 186

		FC	SN	SN	SN	SN	SN	FC	FC	SN	SN	SN	SN	FC	SN	GW	SN	SN		SN	SN	FC
		1	1	1	◇1	1	◇1	1	1	1	◇1	1	◇1	1	1	1	1	◇1		◇1	1	1
									A													
			🚲							🚲			🚲		🚲							
London Victoria 15 ⊖	d		17 15		17 17					17 30	17 32		17 36		17 45			17 47		17 51		
Clapham Junction 10	d				17 23						17 38		17 42					17 53				
Bedford	d	15 54						16 10						16 24								16 40
Luton 10	d	16 18						16 34						16 48								17 04
Luton Airport Parkway 7 ✈	d	16 20						16 36						16 50								17 06
St Albans City	d	16 32						16 48						17 02								17 18
St Pancras International 15 ⊖	d	16 54						17 09						17 24								17 39
Farringdon 3 ⊖	d	16 59						17 14						17 29								17 44
City Thameslink 3	d	17 03						17 18						17 33								17 48
London Blackfriars 3 ⊖	d	17 05						17 20						17 35								17 50
London Bridge 4 ⊖	d	17 12		17 15				17 27	17 27			17 33		17 42			17 45					17 57
New Cross Gate	d											17 38										
Norwood Junction 2	d			17 26								17 46					17 56					
East Croydon	a	17 24		17 29	17 32			17 39	17 39		17 47	17 50	17 52	17 54			18 00	18 02		18 07		18 09
	d	17 25		17 30	17 33			17 41	17 41		17 48	17 51	17 53	17 55			18 00	18 03		18 08		18 11
Purley 4	d			17 36								17 56					18 06					
Coulsdon South	d			17 39								18 00					18 09					
Merstham	d			17 45								18 05										
Redhill	a			17 49							18 00	18 09					18 17					
	d			17 52							18 00	18 10				18 13	18 17					
Reigate	a			17 56												18 18						
Oxted	d																18 22					
Godstone	d																18 27					
Edenbridge	d																18 33					
Penshurst	d																18 39					
Leigh (Kent)	d																18 43					
Tonbridge 4	a																18 48					
Earlswood (Surrey)	d											18 12										
Salfords	d											18 16										
Horley 4	d					←						18 19									←	
Gatwick Airport 10 ✈	a	17 40	17 45		17 48	17 55		17 56	17 56	18 00	18 08	18 23		18 10	18 15			18 18		18 22	18 23	18 26
	d	17 41			17 50	17 56		17 57	17 57		18 09	18 24		18 11				18 20		18 23	18 24	18 27
Three Bridges 15	a	17 45				18 01		18 01	18 01		18 14	→		18 15							18 29	18 31
	d	17 45				18 01		18 02	18 02		18 14			18 15							18 30	18 32
Crawley	d					18 05					18 18										18 33	
Ifield	d					18 07															18 36	
Faygate	d																					
Littlehaven	d					18 14															18 42	
Horsham 4	a					18 17					18 26										18 47	
Balcombe	d													18 21								
Haywards Heath	a	17 54			18 00			18 11	18 11					18 26				18 30				18 41
	d	17 55			18 04		18 07	18 11	18 11					18 27				18 35	18 37			18 41
Wivelsfield	d	17 59					18 11							18 31								
Lewes 4	a						18 22											18 52				
Burgess Hill 4	d	18 01			18 09									18 33						18 38		
Hassocks 4	d	18 04												18 36						18 41		
Preston Park	d	18 11			18 18									18 43								
Hove 2	a				18 22														18 53			
Brighton 10	a	18 15						18 25	18 25				18 27	18 47						18 52		18 55

A 19 May

Table 186

Saturdays

until 23 June

Bedford and London - Brighton

Network Diagram - see first Page of Table 186

		FC	SN	SN	SN		GW	GW	SN	SN	FC	SN	SN		SN		SN	FC	FC	SN	SN		SN	SN	SN
		1	1		◇1		1	1	1	◇1	1	1	1		◇1		1	1	1	1			◇1	1	◇1
		A																	A						
			🚲		🚲					🚲		🚲								🚲					🚲
London Victoria 15 ⊖	d		18 00	18 01	18 02					18 06		18 15			18 17					18 30	18 31		18 32		18 36
Clapham Junction 10	d			18 08	18 08					18 12					18 23						18 38		18 38		18 42
Bedford	d										16 54							17 10							
Luton 10	d										17 18							17 34							
Luton Airport Parkway 7 ✈	d										17 20							17 36							
St Albans City	d										17 32							17 48							
St Pancras International 15 ⊖	d										17 54							18 09							
Farringdon 3 ⊖	d										17 59							18 14							
City Thameslink 3	d										18 03							18 18							
London Blackfriars 3 ⊖	d										18 05							18 20							
London Bridge 4 ⊖	d	17 57							18 03		18 12		18 15					18 27	18 27					18 33	
New Cross Gate	d								18 08															18 38	
Norwood Junction 2	d								18 16				18 26											18 46	
East Croydon	a	18 09			18 17				18 20	18 22	18 24		18 29		18 32			18 39	18 39				18 47	18 50	18 52
	d	18 11			18 18				18 21	18 23	18 25		18 30		18 33			18 41	18 41				18 48	18 51	18 53
Purley 4	d								18 26				18 36											18 56	
Coulsdon South	d								18 30				18 39											19 00	
Merstham	d								18 35				18 45											19 05	
Redhill	a				18 30				18 39				18 49										19 00	19 09	
	d				18 30		18 34	18 41	18 44				18 52										19 00	19 10	
Reigate	a						18 38						18 56												
Nutfield	d																								
Godstone	d																								
Edenbridge	d																								
Penshurst	d																								
Leigh (Kent)	d																								
Tonbridge 4	a																								
Earlswood (Surrey)	d																							19 12	
Salfords	d																							19 16	
Horley 4	d				18 36				18 51								←							19 19	
Gatwick Airport 10 ✈	a	18 26	18 30		18 39			18 50	18 55		18 40	18 45			18 48		18 55	18 56	18 56	19 00			19 08	19 23	
	d	18 27			18 40				18 56		18 41				18 50		18 56	18 57	18 57				19 09	19 24	
Three Bridges 15	a	18 31			18 44				→		18 45						19 01	19 01	19 01				19 14	→	
	d	18 32			18 45						18 45						19 01	19 02	19 02				19 14		
Crawley	d				18 48												19 05						19 18		
Ifield	d																19 07								
Faygate	d																								
Littlehaven	d																19 14								
Horsham 4	a				18 56												19 17						19 26		
Balcombe	d																								
Haywards Heath	a	18 41									18 54				19 00			19 11	19 11						
	d	18 41									18 55				19 04	19 07		19 11	19 11						
Wivelsfield	d										18 59					19 11									
Lewes 4	a															19 22									
Burgess Hill 4	d										19 01				19 09										
Hassocks 4	d										19 04														
Preston Park	d										19 11				19 18										
Hove 2	a														19 22										
Brighton 10	a	18 55								18 57	19 15							19 25	19 25						19 27

A 19 May

Table 186

Saturdays

until 23 June

Bedford and London - Brighton

Network Diagram - see first Page of Table 186

		FC	SN	GW	SN		SN		SN	SN	FC	FC	SN		SN	SN	GW	GW	SN	SN	FC		SN	SN	
		1	1	1	1		◇1		◇1	1	1	1	1			◇1	1	1	1	◇1	1		1	◇1	
												A													
			🛒										🛒			🛒				🛒			🛒		
London Victoria 15 ⊖	d		18 45				18 47		18 51				19 00		19 01	19 02				19 06			19 15	19 17	
Clapham Junction 10	d						18 53								19 08	19 08				19 12				19 23	
Bedford	d	17 24									17 40										17 54				
Luton 10	d	17 48									18 04										18 18				
Luton Airport Parkway 7 ✈	d	17 50									18 06										18 20				
St Albans City	d	18 02									18 18										18 32				
St Pancras International 15 ⊖	d	18 24									18 39										18 54				
Farringdon 3 ⊖	d	18 29									18 44										18 59				
City Thameslink 3	d	18 33									18 48										19 03				
London Blackfriars 3 ⊖	d	18 35									18 50										19 05				
London Bridge 4 ⊖	d	18 42			18 45						18 57	18 57							19 03		19 12				
New Cross Gate	d																		19 08						
Norwood Junction 2	d				18 56														19 16						
East Croydon	a	18 54			18 59		19 02		19 07		19 09	19 09				19 17			19 20	19 22	19 24			19 33	
	d	18 55			19 00		19 03		19 08		19 11	19 11				19 18			19 21	19 23	19 25			19 33	
Purley 4	d				19 06														19 26						
Coulsdon South	d				19 09														19 30						
Merstham	d																		19 35						
Redhill	a				19 17											19 30			19 39						
	d			19 13	19 17											19 30	19 34	19 41	19 46						
Reigate	a			19 18													19 38								
Nutfield	d				19 22																				
Godstone	d				19 27																				
Edenbridge	d				19 33																				
Penshurst	d				19 39																				
Leigh (Kent)	d				19 43																				
Tonbridge 4	a				19 48																				
Earlswood (Surrey)	d																								
Salfords	d																								
Horley 4	d									←						19 36			19 52						
Gatwick Airport 10 ✈	a	19 10	19 15				19 18		19 22	19 23	19 26	19 26	19 30			19 39		19 50	19 55		19 40		19 45	19 48	
	d	19 11					19 20		19 23	19 24	19 27	19 27				19 40			19 56		19 41			19 50	
Three Bridges 15	a	19 15								19 28	19 31	19 31				19 44			→		19 45				
	d	19 15								19 30	19 32	19 32				19 45					19 45				
Crawley	d									19 33						19 48									
Ifield	d									19 36															
Faygate	d																								
Littlehaven	d									19 42															
Horsham 4	a									19 45						19 56									
Balcombe	d	19 21																							
Haywards Heath	a	19 26					19 30				19 41	19 41									19 54			20 00	
	d	19 27					19 35	19 37			19 41	19 41									19 55			20 04	20 07
Wivelsfield	d	19 31																			19 59				20 11
Lewes 4	a						19 52																		20 22
Burgess Hill 4	d	19 33							19 38												20 01			20 09	
Hassocks 4	d	19 36							19 41												20 04				
Preston Park	d	19 43																			20 11			20 18	
Hove 2	a							19 52																20 22	
Brighton 10	a	19 47							19 52		19 55	19 55								19 57	20 15				

A 19 May

Table 186

Saturdays

until 23 June

Bedford and London - Brighton

Network Diagram - see first Page of Table 186

		SN	FC	FC	SN		SN	SN	SN	SN	SN	FC	SN		SN		SN	SN	FC	FC	SN		SN	GW	SN
		1	1	1	1			1	◇1	1	◇1	1	1		◇1		◇1	1	1	1	1			1	◇1
				A																A					
					bus								bus								bus				
London Victoria 15 ⊖	d				19 30		19 31		19 32		19 36		19 45		19 47		19 51				20 00		20 01		20 02
Clapham Junction 10	d						19 38		19 38		19 42				19 53								20 08		20 08
Bedford	d		18 10									18 24							18 40						
Luton 10	d		18 34									18 48							19 04						
Luton Airport Parkway 7 ✈	d		18 36									18 50							19 06						
St Albans City	d		18 48									19 02							19 18						
St Pancras International 15 ⊖	d		19 09									19 24							19 39						
Farringdon 3 ⊖	d		19 14									19 29							19 44						
City Thameslink 3	d		19 18									19 33							19 48						
London Blackfriars 3 ⊖	d		19 20									19 35							19 50						
London Bridge 4 ⊖	d		19 27	19 27						19 33		19 42							19 57	19 57					
New Cross Gate	d									19 38															
Norwood Junction 2	d									19 46															
East Croydon	a		19 39	19 39					19 47	19 50	19 52	19 54			20 02		20 07		20 09	20 09					20 17
	d		19 41	19 41					19 48	19 51	19 53	19 55			20 03		20 08		20 11	20 11					20 18
Purley 4	d									19 56															
Coulsdon South	d									20 00															
Merstham	d									20 05															
Redhill	a								20 00	20 09															20 30
	d							19 51	20 00	20 10														20 13	20 30
Reigate	a																							20 18	
Nutfield	d							19 55																	
Godstone	d							20 01																	
Edenbridge	d							20 06																	
Penshurst	d							20 13																	
Leigh (Kent)	d							20 16																	
Tonbridge 4	a							20 21																	
Earlswood (Surrey)	d									20 12															
Salfords	d									20 16															
Horley 4	d	←								20 19								←							
Gatwick Airport 10 ✈	a	19 55	19 56	19 56	20 00				20 08	20 23		20 10	20 15		20 18		20 22	20 23	20 26	20 26	20 30				20 38
	d	19 56	19 57	19 57					20 09	20 24		20 11			20 20		20 23	20 24	20 27	20 27					20 40
Three Bridges 15	a	20 01	20 01	20 01					20 14	→		20 15						20 29	20 31	20 31					20 44
	d	20 01	20 02	20 02					20 14			20 15						20 33	20 32	20 32					20 45
Crawley	d	20 05							20 18									20 36							20 48
Ifield	d	20 07																20 39							
Faygate	d																								
Littlehaven	d	20 14																20 45							
Horsham 4	a	20 17							20 26									20 48							20 56
Balcombe	d											20 21													
Haywards Heath	a		20 11	20 11								20 26			20 30				20 41	20 41					
	d		20 11	20 11								20 27			20 35	20 37			20 41	20 41					
Wivelsfield	d											20 31			20 39										
Lewes 4	a														20 52										
Burgess Hill 4	d											20 33					20 38								
Hassocks 4	d											20 36					20 41								
Preston Park	d											20 43													
Hove 2	a															20 53									
Brighton 10	a		20 25	20 25							20 27	20 47					20 52		20 55	20 55					

A 19 May

Table 186

Saturdays

until 23 June

Bedford and London - Brighton

Network Diagram - see first Page of Table 186

		SN	FC	GW	GW		SN	SN	SN		SN	SN	SN		SN	SN	SN	SN	FC	GW	SN		SN	SN	
		◇1	1	1	1		1	1	◇1		◇1	1	1			1	◇1	◇1	1	1	1		1	◇1	
London Victoria 15 ⊖	d	20 06					20 10	20 15	20 17		20 21		20 30		20 31		20 32	20 36			20 40		20 45	20 47	
Clapham Junction 10	d	20 12					20 16		20 23						20 38		20 38	20 42			20 46			20 53	
Bedford	d		18 54																19 22						
Luton 10	d		19 18																19 46						
Luton Airport Parkway 7 ✈	d		19 20																19 48						
St Albans City	d		19 32																20 00						
St Pancras International 15 ⊖	d		19 54																20 24						
Farringdon 3 ⊖	d		19 59																20 29						
City Thameslink 3	d		20 03																20 33						
London Blackfriars 3 ⊖	d		20 05																20 35						
London Bridge 4 ⊖	d		20 12																20 42						
New Cross Gate	d																								
Norwood Junction 2	d																								
East Croydon	a	20 22	20 24				20 29		20 32		20 37						20 47	20 52	20 54		20 57			21 02	
	d	20 23	20 25				20 29		20 33		20 38						20 48	20 53	20 55		20 58			21 03	
Purley 4	d						20 34														21 03				
Coulsdon South	d						20 38														21 06				
Merstham	d						20 44														21 12				
Redhill	a						20 47										21 00				21 15				
	d			20 34	20 41		20 48									20 51	21 00			21 13	21 16				
Reigate	a			20 38																21 18					
Nutfield	d															20 55									
Godstone	d															21 01									
Edenbridge	d															21 06									
Penshurst	d															21 13									
Leigh (Kent)	d															21 16									
Tonbridge 4	a															21 21									
Earlswood (Surrey)	d																				21 18				
Salfords	d																				21 22				
Horley 4	d						20 54					←									21 25				
Gatwick Airport 10 ✈	a		20 40		20 50		20 58	20 45	20 48		20 52	20 58	21 00				21 08		21 10		21 28		21 15	21 18	
	d		20 41				20 59		20 50		20 53	20 59					21 09		21 11		21 29			21 20	
Three Bridges 15	a		20 45				→					21 03					21 14		21 15		→				
	d		20 45									21 04					21 14		21 15						
Crawley	d											21 07					21 18								
Ifield	d											21 10													
Faygate	d																								
Littlehaven	d											21 16													
Horsham 4	a											21 19					21 26								
Balcombe	d		20 51																						
Haywards Heath	a		20 56						21 00										21 24					21 30	
	d		20 57						21 05	21 07									21 25					21 34	21 37
Wivelsfield	d		21 01							21 11									21 29					21 38	
Lewes 4	a									21 22														21 51	
Burgess Hill 4	d		21 03						21 10										21 31						
Hassocks 4	d		21 06								21 10								21 34						
Preston Park	d		21 13						21 19										21 41						
Hove 2	a								21 22																21 51
Brighton 10	a	20 57	21 17								21 22							21 27	21 45						

Table 186

Saturdays

until 23 June

Bedford and London - Brighton

Network Diagram - see first Page of Table 186

		SN	SN	SN	SN		SN	FC	GW	SN	SN	SN			SN	GW	SN	SN	SN	SN	SN		FC	SN	SN
		1	1		◇1		◇1	1	1	1	1	◇1			1	1	1		1		◇1		1	1	1
London Victoria 15 ⊖	d		21 00	21 01	21 02		21 06			21 10	21 15	21 17					21 30	21 31		21 32	21 36			21 40	21 45
Clapham Junction 10	d			21 08	21 08		21 12			21 16		21 23						21 38		21 38	21 42			21 46	
Bedford	d							19 52															20 22		
Luton 10	d							20 16															20 46		
Luton Airport Parkway 7 ✈	d							20 18															20 48		
St Albans City	d							20 30															21 00		
St Pancras International 15 ⊖	d							20 54															21 24		
Farringdon 3 ⊖	d							20 59															21 29		
City Thameslink 3	d							21 03																	
London Blackfriars 3 ⊖	d							21 05															21 35		
London Bridge 4 ⊖	d							21 12															21 42		
New Cross Gate	d																								
Norwood Junction 2	d																								
East Croydon	a				21 17		21 22	21 24		21 27		21 33								21 47	21 52		21 54	21 57	
	d				21 18		21 23	21 25		21 28		21 33								21 48	21 53		21 55	21 58	
Purley 4	d									21 33														22 03	
Coulsdon South	d									21 37														22 06	
Merstham	d									21 42														22 12	
Redhill	a				21 30					21 46										22 00				22 15	
	d				21 31				21 36	21 46						21 49			21 51	22 00				22 16	
Reigate	a								21 40																
Nutfield	d																		21 55						
Godstone	d																		22 01						
Edenbridge	d																		22 06						
Penshurst	d																		22 13						
Leigh (Kent)	d																		22 16						
Tonbridge 4	a																		22 21						
Earlswood (Surrey)	d																							22 18	
Salfords	d																							22 22	
Horley 4	d	←								21 52					←									22 25	
Gatwick Airport 10 ✈	a	21 28	21 30		21 38			21 40		21 55	21 45	21 48			21 55	21 59	22 00			22 08			22 10	22 28	22 15
	d	21 29			21 39			21 41		21 56		21 49			21 56					22 09			22 11	22 29	
Three Bridges 15	a	21 33			21 44			21 45		→		21 53			22 00					22 14			22 15	→	
	d	21 36			21 44			21 45				21 53			22 01					22 14			22 15		
Crawley	d	21 39													22 04					22 18					
Ifield	d	21 42													22 07										
Faygate	d																								
Littlehaven	d	21 48													22 13										
Horsham 4	a	21 52													22 16					22 26					
Balcombe	d							21 53																	
Haywards Heath	a				21 53		21 46	21 58				22 02									22 16		22 24		
	d				21 53		21 46	21 59				22 06	22 08								22 16		22 25		
Wivelsfield	d				21 57			22 03					22 12										22 29		
Lewes 4	a												22 23												
Burgess Hill 4	d				21 59			22 05				22 11											22 31		
Hassocks 4	d				22 03			22 08															22 34		
Preston Park	d				22 09			22 15															22 41		
Hove 2	a											22 22													
Brighton 10	a				22 15		22 00	22 19													22 30		22 45		

Table 186

Saturdays

until 23 June

Bedford and London - Brighton

Network Diagram - see first Page of Table 186

		SN ◇1	SN 1	SN 1	SN	SN ◇1	SN ◇1	FC 1	GW 1	SN 1	SN 1	SN ◇1	SN 1	SN 1	SN	SN 1	GW 1	SN 1	SN ◇1	FC 1	SN 1
London Victoria 15 ⊖	d	21 47		22 00	22 01	22 02	22 06			22 10	22 15	22 17		22 30	22 31			22 32	22 36		22 40
Clapham Junction 10	d	21 53			22 08	22 08	22 12			22 16		22 23			22 38			22 38	22 42		22 46
Bedford	d							20 52												21 22	
Luton 10	d							21 16												21 46	
Luton Airport Parkway 7 ✈	d							21 18												21 48	
St Albans City	d							21 30												22 00	
St Pancras International 15 ⊖	d							21 54												22 24	
Farringdon 3 ⊖	d							21 59												22 29	
City Thameslink 3	d																				
London Blackfriars 3 ⊖	d							22 05												22 35	
London Bridge 4 ⊖	d							22 12												22 42	
New Cross Gate	d																				
Norwood Junction 2	d																				
East Croydon	a	22 03				22 17	22 22	22 24		22 27		22 33						22 47	22 52	22 54	22 57
	d	22 03				22 18	22 23	22 25		22 28		22 33						22 48	22 53	22 55	22 58
Purley 4	d									22 33											23 03
Coulsdon South	d									22 37											23 07
Merstham	d									22 42											23 12
Redhill	a					22 30				22 46								23 00			23 16
	d					22 31			22 33	22 46						22 55	22 56	23 00			23 16
Reigate	a								22 38												
Nutfield	d															22 59					
Godstone	d															23 05					
Edenbridge	d															23 10					
Penshurst	d															23 17					
Leigh (Kent)	d															23 20					
Tonbridge 4	a															23 25					
Earlswood (Surrey)	d																				23 19
Salfords	d																				23 22
Horley 4	d		←							22 52			←								23 26
Gatwick Airport 10 ✈	a	22 18	22 28	22 30		22 38		22 40		22 55	22 45	22 48	22 55	23 00			23 05	23 08		23 10	23 28
	d	22 20	22 29			22 39		22 41		22 56		22 50	22 56					23 09		23 11	23 29
Three Bridges 15	a		22 33			22 44		22 45		→		22 54	23 00					23 14		23 15	→
	d		22 36			22 44		22 45				22 54	23 01					23 15		23 15	
Crawley	d		22 39										23 04					23 18			
Ifield	d		22 42										23 07								
Faygate	d																				
Littlehaven	d		22 48										23 13								
Horsham 4	a		22 52										23 16					23 26			
Balcombe	d							22 53													
Haywards Heath	a	22 30				22 53	22 46	22 58				23 03							23 16	23 24	
	d	22 34 / 22 37				22 53	22 46	22 59				23 03							23 16	23 25	
Wivelsfield	d	22 38				22 57		23 03												23 29	
Lewes 4	a	22 51																			
Burgess Hill 4	d					22 59		23 05				23 09								23 31	
Hassocks 4	d					23 03		23 08												23 34	
Preston Park	d					23 09		23 15												23 41	
Hove 2	a	22 51										23 21									
Brighton 10	a					23 15	23 00	23 19											23 30	23 45	

Table 186

Bedford and London - Brighton

Saturdays

until 23 June

Network Diagram - see first Page of Table 186

		SN 1	SN ◇1		SN 1		SN 1	SN	GW 1	SN ◇1	SN ◇1	FC 1	SN 1		SN 1	SN ◇1	SN 1	SN 1	SN 1	SN 1	FC 1		SN 1	SN 1	SN 1
London Victoria 15 ⊖	d	22 45	22 47				23 00	23 01		23 02	23 06		23 10		23 15	23 17		23 30		23 32			23 45	23 47	23 49
Clapham Junction 10	d		22 53					23 08		23 08	23 12		23 16			23 23				23 38				23 53	23 56
Bedford	d											21 50									22 16				
Luton 10	d											22 15									22 42				
Luton Airport Parkway 7 ✈	d											22 18									22 45				
St Albans City	d											22 30									22 57				
St Pancras International 15 ⊖	d											22 54									23 24				
Farringdon 3 ⊖	d											22 59									23 29				
City Thameslink 3	d																								
London Blackfriars 3 ⊖	d											23 05									23 35				
London Bridge 4 ⊖	d											23 12									23 42				
New Cross Gate	d																								
Norwood Junction 2	d																								
East Croydon	a		23 03							23 17	23 22	23 24	23 27			23 32				23 52	23 56			00 05	00 09
	d		23 03							23 18	23 23	23 25	23 28			23 33				23 52	23 57			00 06	
Purley 4	d												23 33											00 12	
Coulsdon South	d												23 37											00 15	
Merstham	d												23 42											00 21	
Redhill	a									23 30			23 46							00 03				00 24	
	d								23 28	23 31			23 46						23 55	00 05				00 25	
Reigate	a								23 33																
Nutfield	d																								
Godstone	d																								
Edenbridge	d																								
Penshurst	d																		00 06						
Leigh (Kent)	d																								
Tonbridge 4	a																		00 15						
Earlswood (Surrey)	d												23 49												
Salfords	d												23 52												
Horley 4	d				←								23 56				←							00 31	
Gatwick Airport 10 ✈	a	23 15	23 18		23 28		23 30			23 38		23 40	23 58		23 45	23 49	23 58	00 05		00 14	00 18		00 20	00 33	
	d		23 20		23 29					23 39		23 41	23 59			23 50	23 59			00 15	00 19			00 34	
Three Bridges 15	a				23 34					23 44		23 47	→			23 54	00 04			00 20	00 24			00 39	
	d				23 38					23 44		23 47				23 55	00 04			00 20				00 39	
Crawley	d				23 41												00 07							00 43	
Ifield	d				23 44												00 10							00 46	
Faygate	d																								
Littlehaven	d				23 50												00 16							00 52	
Horsham 4	a				23 53												00 19							00 55	
Balcombe	d											23 53								00 28					
Haywards Heath	a		23 30							23 53	23 46	23 58				00 04				00 34					
	d		23 34	23 37						23 53	23 46	23 59				00 05				00 35					
Wivelsfield	d		23 38							23 57		00 03								00 39					
Lewes 4	a		23 51																						
Burgess Hill 4	d									23 59		00 05				00 10				00 41					
Hassocks 4	d									00 03		00 08								00 44					
Preston Park	d									00 09		00 15								00 51					
Hove 2	a			23 51												00 23									
Brighton 10	a									00 15	00 01	00 19								00 55					

Table 186

Saturdays
until 23 June

Bedford and London - Brighton

Network Diagram - see first Page of Table 186

Station		FC 1	FC 1	FC 1
London Victoria 15 ⊖	d			
Clapham unction 10	d			
Bedford	d	22 40	23 10	23 40
uton 10	d	23 06	23 36	00 06
uton Airport Parkway 7 ✈	d	23 09	23 39	00 09
St Albans City	d	23 21	23 51	00 21
St Pancras hternational 15 ⊖	d	23 54	00 24	00 54
Farringdon 3 ⊖	d	23 59	00 29	
City Thameslink 3	d			
London Blackfriars 3 ⊖	d	00 05	00 35	01 05
London Bridge 4 ⊖	d	00 12	00 42	
New Cross Gate	d			
Norwood unction 2	d			
East Croydon	a	00 26	00 56	01 31
	d	00 27	00 57	01 32
Purley 4	d			
Coulsdon South	d			
Merstham	d			
Redhill	a			
	d			
Reigate	a			
Nutfield	d			
Godstone	d			
Edenbridge	d			
Penshurst	d			
Leigh (Kent)	d			
Tonbridge 4	a			
Earlswood (Surrey)	d			
Salfords	d			
Horley 4	d			
Gatwick Airport 10 ✈	a	00 49	01 18	01 51
	d	00 50	01 22	01 52
Three Bridges 15	a	00 55	01 28	01 58
	d			
Crawley	d			
field	d			
Faygate	d			
Littlehaven	d			
Horsham 4	a			
Balcombe	d			
Haywards Heath	a			
	d			
Wivelsfield	d			
Lewes 4	a			
Burgess Hill 4	d			
Hassocks 4	d			
Preston Park	d			
Hove 2	a			
Brighton 10	a			

Table 186

Saturdays

from 30 June

Bedford and London - Brighton

Network Diagram - see first Page of Table 186

		SN	SN	FC	SN	SN	SN	SN	SN	GW	SN	FC	SN	SN	SN	SN	SN	FC	SN	GW	SN
		◇1	◇1	1	1	◇1	1	1	1	1	◇1	1	1	1	1	1	◇1	1	1	1	◇1
																					A
London Victoria 15 ⊖	d	23p02	23p06		23p10	23p17		23p30			23p32		23p45	23p47	23p49	00 02	00 05		00 14		00 25
Clapham Junction 10	d	23p08	23p12		23p16	23p23					23p38			23p53	23p56		00 11		00 20		00 31
Bedford	d			21p52								22p16						22p42			
Luton 10	d			22p16								22p40						23p06			
Luton Airport Parkway 7 ✈	d			22p18								22p42						23p09			
St Albans City	d			22p30								22p54						23p21			
St Pancras International 15 ⊖	d			22p54								23p24						23p54			
Farringdon 3 ⊖	d			22p59								23p29						23p59			
City Thameslink 3	d			23p03																	
London Blackfriars 3 ⊖	d			23p05								23p35						00 05			
London Bridge 4 ⊖	d			23p12								23p42						00 12			
New Cross Gate	d																				
Norwood Junction 2	d																				
East Croydon	a	23p19	23p22	23p24	23p27	23p33					23p51	23p56		00 05	00 09		00 24	00 26	00 31		00 40
	d	23p20	23p23	23p25	23p28	23p33					23p52	23p57		00 06			00 24	00 27	00 32		00 41
Purley 4	d				23p33									00 12					00 37		00 46
Coulsdon South	d				23p37									00 15					00 41		
Merstham	d				23p42									00 21					00 47		
Redhill	a	23p31			23p46						00 03			00 24					00 50		00 55
	d	23p31			23p46				23p55	00 01	00 05			00 25					00 51	00 54	00 59
Reigate	a																				
Nutfield	d																				
Godstone	d																				
Edenbridge	d								00 06												
Penshurst	d																				
Leigh (Kent)	d																				
Tonbridge 4	a								00 15												
Earlswood (Surrey)	d				23p49																
Salfords	d				23p52																
Horley 4	d				23p56		←							00 31					00 57		01 06
Gatwick Airport 10 ✈	a	23p38		23p40	23p58	23p50	23p58	00 05		00 11	00 14	00 18	00 20	00 33		00 37	00 41	00 48	00 59	01 03	01 08
	d	23p39		23p41	23p59	23p51	23p59				00 15	00 19		00 34			00 42	00 49			01 10
Three Bridges 15	a	23p44		23p47	→	23p55	00 04				00 20	00 24		00 39			00 47	00 54			01 14
	d	23p44		23p47		23p56	00 04				00 20			00 39			00 47				
Crawley	d						00 07							00 43							
Ifield	d						00 10							00 46							
Faygate	d																				
Littlehaven	d						00 16							00 52							
Horsham 4	a						00 19							00 55							
Balcombe	d			23p53							00 26										
Haywards Heath	a	23p53	23p46	23p58		00 05					00 31						00 58				
	d	23p53	23p46	23p59		00 05					00 31										
Wivelsfield	d	23p57		00 03							00 35						01 02 / 01 06				
Lewes 4	a																01 20				
Burgess Hill 4	d	23p59		00 05		00 11					00 37										
Hassocks 4	d	00 03		00 08							00 41										
Preston Park	d	00 09		00 15							00 48										
Hove 2	a					00 21															
Brighton 10	a	00 15	00 01	00 19							00 52						01s16				

A 28 July, 4 August, 11 August, 1 September, 8 September

Table 186

Saturdays
from 30 June

Bedford and London - Brighton

Network Diagram - see first Page of Table 186

		SN	SN	FC	SN	SN	FC	SN		SN	FC	SN	FC	SN	FC	SN		FC	SN	FC	SN	SN	SN	FC
		1	◇1	1	◇1	◇1	1	◇1		1	1	1	1	1	1	◇1		1	1	1	1	◇1	1	1
			A		A			A																
London Victoria 15 ⊖	d	00 30	00 40			01 00		01 30		02 00		03 00		03 30		04 00			04 30		05 00	05 02	05 15	
Clapham Junction 10	d		00 46			01 08		01 36		02 08		03 08				04 08						05 08		
Bedford	d			23p12			23p42				00 42		01 42					02 42		03 12				03 42
Luton 10	d			23p36			00 06				01 06		02 06					03 06		03 36				04 06
Luton Airport Parkway 7 ✈	d			23p39			00 09				01 09		02 09					03 09		03 39				04 09
St Albans City	d			23p51			00 21				01 21		02 21					03 21		03 51				04 21
St Pancras International 15 ⊖	d			00 24			00 54				01 54		02 54		03 28			03 54		04 24				04 54
Farringdon 3 ⊖	d			00 29			00 59																	04 59
City Thameslink 3	d																							
London Blackfriars 3 ⊖	d			00 35			01 05				02 05		03 05		03 39			04 05		04 35				05 04
London Bridge 4 ⊖	d			00 42																				
New Cross Gate	d																							
Norwood Junction 2	d																							
East Croydon	a		00 55	00 56		01 21	01 31	01 45		02 21	02 31	03 21	03 31		04 03	04 21		04 31		05 01		05 21		05 31
	d		00 56	00 57		01 22	01 32	01 45		02 22	02 32	03 22	03 32		04 04	04 22		04 32		05 02		05 22		05 32
Purley 4	d					01 27		01 51		02 27		03 27				04 27						05 26		
Coulsdon South	d																					05 30		
Merstham	d																					05 35		
Redhill	a							02 00														05 39		
	d							02 00														05 40		
Reigate	a																							
Nutfield	d																							
Godstone	d																							
Edenbridge	d																							
Penshurst	d																							
Leigh (Kent)	d																							
Tonbridge 4	a																							
Earlswood (Surrey)	d																							
Salfords	d																							
Horley 4	d					01 43		02 07		02 42		03 42				04 44						05 46		
Gatwick Airport 10 ✈	a	01 20	01 12	01 18		01 46	01 51	02 09		02 44	02 51	03 44	03 51	04 05	04 24	04 46		04 51	05 05	05 21	05 35	05 48	05 50	05 53
	d		01 14	01 22		01 48	01 52	02 11		02 46	02 52	03 46	03 52		04 24	04 47		04 52		05 22		05 49		05 54
Three Bridges 15	a		01 18	01 28		01 52	01 58	02 15		02 50	02 58	03 50	03 58		04 30	04 51		04 58		05 26		05 54		05 59
	d		01 18			01 53		02 16								04 52				05 27		05 54		06 00
Crawley	d																							
Ifield	d																							
Faygate	d																							
Littlehaven	d																							
Horsham 4	a																							
Balcombe	d																			05 33				06 06
Haywards Heath	a		01 27			02 06		02 25								05 01				05 38		06 03		06 11
	d		01 32		01 35	02 06		02 25								05 01				05 39		06 04		06 11
Wivelsfield	d																			05 43		06 08		06 15
Lewes 4	a				01s49																			
Burgess Hill 4	d																			05 45		06 10		06 17
Hassocks 4	d																			05 48		06 13		06 21
Preston Park	d																			05 55		06 20		06 27
Hove 2	a																							
Brighton 10	a		01s46			02 23		02 40								05 16				05 59		06 24		06 31

A 28 July, 4 August, 11 August, 1 September, 8 September

Table 186

Saturdays

from 30 June

Bedford and London - Brighton

Network Diagram - see first Page of Table 186

		GW 1	GW 1	SN 1	SN 1	SN 1	SN ◇1	SN ◇1		SN 1	FC 1	SN ◇1		SN 1	GW 1	SN 1		GW 1	GW 1	SN 1		FC 1	SN 1	SN 1
London Victoria 15 ⊖	d				05 30		05 32	05 32		05 45				06 00						06 02			06 15	
Clapham Junction 10	d						05 38	05 38												06 08				
Bedford	d										04 22											04 52		
Luton 10	d										04 46											05 16		
Luton Airport Parkway 7 ✈	d										04 49											05 19		
St Albans City	d										05 01											05 31		
St Pancras International 15 ⊖	d										05 34											05 54		
Farringdon 3 ⊖	d										05 39											05 59		
City Thameslink 3	d																							
London Blackfriars 3 ⊖	d										05 45											06 05		
London Bridge 4 ⊖	d										05 52											06 12		
New Cross Gate	d																							
Norwood Junction 2	d																							
East Croydon	a						05 47	05 47			06 04									06 17		06 24		
	d						05 48	05 48			06 05									06 18		06 25		
Purley 4	d						05 53	05 53												06 23				
Coulsdon South	d						05 57	05 57												06 27				
Merstham	d						06 03	06 03												06 32				
Redhill	a						06 07	06 07												06 36				
	d	05 41	05 49				06 07	06 07							06 13	06 22		06 34	06 41	06 46	06 52			
Reigate	a	05 47													06 18			06 38			06 56			
Nutfield	d															06 26								
Godstone	d															06 32								
Edenbridge	d															06 37								
Penshurst	d															06 44								
Leigh (Kent)	d															06 47								
Tonbridge 4	a															06 52								
Earlswood (Surrey)	d						06 11	06 11												06 48				
Salfords	d						06 15	06 15												06 52				
Horley 4	d						06 18	06 18				←								06 55				←
Gatwick Airport 10 ✈	a		05 58		06 00		06 21	06 21		06 15	06 19	06 21		06 30					06 50	06 58		06 40	06 45	06 58
	d			05 58		06 11	06 22	06 22			06 20	06 22								06 59		06 41		06 59
Three Bridges 15	a			06 02		06 15	→	→			06 24	06 26								→		06 45		07 03
	d			06 03		06 16					06 25	06 30	06 34									06 45		07 04
Crawley	d			06 06									06 37											07 07
Ifield	d			06 09									06 40											07 10
Faygate	d																							
Littlehaven	d			06 15									06 46											07 16
Horsham 4	a			06 18									06 49											07 19
Balcombe	d										06 31	06 36												
Haywards Heath	a					06 26					06 36	06 41										06 54		
	d					06 26					06 37	06 41										06 55		
Wivelsfield	d					06 30					06 41	06 45										06 59		
Lewes 4	a					06 41																		
Burgess Hill 4	d										06 43	06 47										07 01		
Hassocks 4	d										06 46	06 51										07 04		
Preston Park	d										06 53	06 57										07 11		
Hove 2	a																							
Brighton 10	a										06 57	07 03										07 15		

Table 186

Saturdays

from 30 June

Bedford and London - Brighton

Network Diagram - see first Page of Table 186

		SN	SN		GW	FC	SN	SN		SN	GW	SN	FC	SN	GW	SN			SN	FC	SN	SN	FC	SN	SN
		1	1		1	1	1	1		1	1	◇1	1	1	1	1			◇1	1	1	1	1	1	◇1
London Victoria 15 ⊖	d	06 30	06 32				06 45							07 00					07 06		07 15			07 30	07 32
Clapham Junction 10	d		06 38																07 12						07 38
Bedford	d					05 22							05 40							05 54			06 10		
Luton 10	d					05 46							06 04							06 18			06 34		
Luton Airport Parkway 7 ✈	d					05 49							06 06							06 20			06 36		
St Albans City	d					06 01							06 18							06 32			06 48		
St Pancras International 15 ⊖	d					06 24							06 39							06 54			07 09		
Farringdon 3 ⊖	d					06 29							06 44							06 59			07 14		
City Thameslink 3	d																								
London Blackfriars 3 ⊖	d					06 35							06 50							07 05			07 20		
London Bridge 4 ⊖	d					06 42							06 57			07 03				07 12			07 27		
New Cross Gate	d															07 08									
Norwood Junction 2	d															07 16									
East Croydon	a		06 47			06 54							07 09			07 20			07 22	07 24			07 39		07 47
	d		06 48			06 55							07 11			07 21			07 23	07 25			07 41		07 48
Purley 4	d		06 53													07 26									
Coulsdon South	d		06 57													07 30									
Merstham	d		07 02													07 35									
Redhill	a		07 06													07 39									08 00
	d		07 10	07 22	07 13						07 34				07 41	07 44	07 52								08 00
Reigate	a				07 18						07 38						07 56								
Nutfield	d			07 26																					
Godstone	d			07 32																					
Edenbridge	d			07 37																					
Penshurst	d			07 44																					
Leigh (Kent)	d			07 47																					
Tonbridge 4	a			07 52																					
Earlswood (Surrey)	d		07 12																						
Salfords	d		07 16																						
Horley 4	d		07 19					←								07 51						←			
Gatwick Airport 10 ✈	a	07 00	07 23			07 10	07 15	07 23					07 26	07 30	07 50	07 55				07 40	07 45	07 55	07 56	08 00	08 08
	d		07 24			07 11		07 24					07 27			07 56				07 41		07 56	07 57		08 09
Three Bridges 15	a		→			07 15		07 29					07 31			→				07 45		08 01	08 01		08 14
	d					07 15		07 30					07 32							07 45		08 01	08 02		08 14
Crawley	d							07 33														08 05			08 18
Ifield	d							07 36														08 07			
Faygate	d																								
Littlehaven	d							07 42														08 14			
Horsham 4	a							07 45														08 17			08 26
Balcombe	d					07 21																			
Haywards Heath	a					07 26							07 41							07 54			08 11		
	d					07 27				07 33		07 37	07 41							07 55			08 11		
Wivelsfield	d					07 31				07 37										07 59					
Lewes 4	a									07 48															
Burgess Hill 4	d					07 33														08 01					
Hassocks 4	d					07 36														08 04					
Preston Park	d					07 43														08 11					
Hove 2	a											07 51													
Brighton 10	a					07 47							07 55						07 57	08 15			08 25		

Table 186

Saturdays

from 30 June

Bedford and London - Brighton

Network Diagram - see first Page of Table 186

		SN 1	SN ◇1	FC 1	SN 1	GW 1	SN 1	SN ◇1	SN ◇1	SN 1	FC 1	SN 1	SN	SN ◇1	GW 1	GW 1	SN 1	SN ◇1	FC 1	SN 1	SN 1
London Victoria 15 ⊖	d		07 36		07 45			07 47	07 51			08 00	08 01	08 02				08 06		08 15	
Clapham Junction 10	d		07 42					07 53					08 08	08 08				08 12			
Bedford	d			06 24							06 40								06 54		
Luton 10	d			06 48							07 04								07 18		
Luton Airport Parkway 7 ✈	d			06 50							07 06								07 20		
St Albans City	d			07 02							07 18								07 32		
St Pancras International 15 ⊖	d			07 24							07 39								07 54		
Farringdon 3 ⊖	d			07 29							07 44								07 59		
City Thameslink 3	d																				
London Blackfriars 3 ⊖	d			07 35							07 50								08 05		
London Bridge 4 ⊖	d	07 33		07 42			07 45				07 57						08 03		08 12		08 15
New Cross Gate	d	07 38															08 08				
Norwood Junction 2	d	07 46					07 56										08 16				08 26
East Croydon	a	07 50	07 52	07 54			07 59	08 02	08 07		08 09			08 17			08 20	08 22	08 24		08 29
	d	07 51	07 53	07 55			08 00	08 03	08 08		08 11			08 18			08 21	08 23	08 25		08 30
Purley 4	d	07 56					08 06										08 26				08 36
Coulsdon South	d	08 00					08 09										08 30				08 39
Merstham	d	08 05															08 35				08 45
Redhill	a	08 09					08 17							08 30			08 39				08 49
	d	08 10				08 13	08 17							08 30	08 34	08 41	08 44				08 52
Reigate	a					08 18									08 38						08 56
Oxted	d						08 22														
Godstone	d						08 27														
Edenbridge	d						08 33														
Penshurst	d						08 39														
Leigh (Kent)	d						08 43														
Tonbridge 4	a						08 48														
Earlswood (Surrey)	d	08 12																			
Salfords	d	08 16																			
Horley 4	d	08 19												08 36			08 51				
Gatwick Airport 10 ✈	a	08 23		08 10	08 15			08 18	08 22	← 08 23	08 26	08 30		08 39		08 50	08 55		08 40	08 45	
	d	08 24		08 11				08 20	08 23	08 24	08 27			08 40			08 56		08 41		
Three Bridges 15	a	→		08 15						08 29	08 31			08 44			→		08 45		
	d			08 15						08 30	08 32			08 45					08 45		
Crawley	d									08 33				08 48							
Ifield	d									08 36											
Faygate	d																				
Littlehaven	d									08 42											
Horsham 4	a									08 45				08 56							
Balcombe	d			08 21																	
Haywards Heath	a			08 26				08 30			08 41								08 54		
	d			08 27				08 35 / 08 37			08 41								08 55		
Wivelsfield	d			08 31															08 59		
Lewes 4	a							08 49													
Burgess Hill 4	d			08 33					08 38										09 01		
Hassocks 4	d			08 36					08 41										09 04		
Preston Park	d			08 43															09 11		
Hove 2	a							08 53													
Brighton 10	a		08 27	08 47					08 52		08 55							08 57	09 15		

Table 186

Saturdays

from 30 June

Bedford and London - Brighton

Network Diagram - see first Page of Table 186

		SN			SN	FC	SN	SN	SN	SN	FC		SN	GW	SN	SN		SN	SN		FC	SN	SN	SN	GW
		◇1			1	1	1	◇1	1	◇1	1		1	1	1	◇1		◇1	1		1	1		◇1	1
							🛒						🛒									🛒			
London Victoria 15 ⊖	d	08 17					08 30	08 32		08 36			08 45			08 47		08 51				09 00	09 01	09 02	
Clapham Junction 10	d	08 23						08 38		08 42						08 53							09 08	09 08	
Bedford	d					07 10					07 24										07 40				
Luton 10	d					07 34					07 48										08 04				
Luton Airport Parkway 7 ✈	d					07 36					07 50										08 06				
St Albans City	d					07 48					08 02										08 18				
St Pancras International 15 ⊖	d					08 09					08 24										08 39				
Farringdon 3 ⊖	d					08 14					08 29										08 44				
City Thameslink 3	d																								
London Blackfriars 3 ⊖	d					08 20					08 35										08 50				
London Bridge 4 ⊖	d					08 27			08 33		08 42				08 45						08 57				
New Cross Gate	d								08 38																
Norwood Junction 2	d								08 46						08 56										
East Croydon	a	08 32				08 39		08 47	08 50	08 52	08 54				08 59	09 02		09 07			09 09			09 17	
	d	08 33				08 41		08 48	08 51	08 53	08 55				09 00	09 03		09 08			09 11			09 18	
Purley 4	d								08 56						09 06										
Coulsdon South	d								09 00						09 09										
Merstham	d								09 05																
Redhill	a							09 00	09 09						09 17									09 30	
	d							09 00	09 10					09 13	09 17									09 30	09 34
Reigate	a													09 18											09 38
Nutfield	d														09 22										
Godstone	d														09 27										
Edenbridge	d														09 33										
Penshurst	d														09 39										
Leigh (Kent)	d														09 43										
Tonbridge 4	a														09 48										
Earlswood (Surrey)	d								09 12																
Salfords	d								09 16																
Horley 4	d				←				09 19										←					09 36	
Gatwick Airport 10 ✈	a	08 48			08 55	08 56	09 00	09 08	09 23		09 10		09 15			09 18		09 22	09 23		09 26	09 30		09 39	
	d	08 50			08 56	08 57		09 09	09 24		09 11					09 20		09 23	09 24		09 27			09 40	
Three Bridges 15	a				09 01	09 01		09 14	→		09 15								09 29		09 31			09 44	
	d				09 01	09 02		09 14			09 15								09 30		09 32			09 45	
Crawley	d				09 05			09 18											09 33					09 48	
Ifield	d				09 07														09 36						
Faygate	d																								
Littlehaven	d				09 14														09 42						
Horsham 4	a				09 17			09 26											09 45					09 56	
Balcombe	d										09 21														
Haywards Heath	a	09 00				09 11					09 26					09 30					09 41				
	d	09 05	09 07			09 11					09 27					09 35	09 37				09 41				
Wivelsfield	d		09 11								09 31														
Lewes 4	a		09 22													09 52									
Burgess Hill 4	d	09 10									09 33							09 38							
Hassocks 4	d										09 36							09 41							
Preston Park	d	09 18									09 43														
Hove 2	a	09 22															09 53								
Brighton 10	a					09 25				09 27	09 47							09 52			09 55				

Table 186

Saturdays from 30 June

Bedford and London - Brighton

Network Diagram - see first Page of Table 186

		GW	SN	SN	FC	SN	SN	SN (a)	SN (b)	SN	FC	SN	SN	SN	SN	FC	SN	GW	SN	SN (a)	SN (b)	SN
		1	1	◇1 🚲	1	1 🚲	1	◇1		1	1	1 🚲	◇1	1	◇1 🚲	1	1 🚲	1	1	◇1		◇1
London Victoria 15 ⊖	d			09 06		09 15		09 17				09 30	09 32		09 36		09 45			09 47		09 51
Clapham Junction 10	d			09 12				09 23					09 38		09 42					09 53		
Bedford	d				07 54						08 10					08 24						
Luton 10	d				08 18						08 34					08 48						
Luton Airport Parkway 7 ✈	d				08 20						08 36					08 50						
St Albans City	d				08 32						08 48					09 02						
St Pancras International 15 ⊖	d				08 54						09 09					09 24						
Farringdon 3 ⊖	d				08 59						09 14					09 29						
City Thameslink 3	d				09 03						09 18					09 33						
London Blackfriars 3 ⊖	d				09 05						09 20					09 35						
London Bridge 4 ⊖	d		09 03		09 12		09 15				09 27			09 33		09 42			09 45			
New Cross Gate	d		09 08											09 38								
Norwood Junction 2	d		09 16				09 26							09 46					09 56			
East Croydon	a		09 20	09 22	09 24		09 29	09 32			09 39		09 47	09 50	09 52	09 54			09 59	10 02		10 07
	d		09 21	09 23	09 25		09 30	09 33			09 41		09 48	09 51	09 53	09 55			10 00	10 03		10 08
Purley 4	d		09 26				09 36							09 56					10 06			
Coulsdon South	d		09 30				09 39							10 00					10 09			
Merstham	d		09 35				09 45							10 05								
Redhill	a		09 39				09 49						10 00	10 09					10 17			
	d	09 41	09 44				09 52						10 00	10 10				10 13	10 17			
Reigate	a						09 56											10 18				
Nutfield	d																		10 22			
Godstone	d																		10 27			
Edenbridge	d																		10 33			
Penshurst	d																		10 39			
Leigh (Kent)	d																		10 43			
Tonbridge 4	a																		10 48			
Earlswood (Surrey)	d													10 12								
Salfords	d													10 16								
Horley 4	d		09 51							←				10 19								
Gatwick Airport 10 ✈	a	09 50	09 55		09 40	09 45		09 48		09 55	09 56	10 00	10 08	10 23		10 10	10 15			10 18		10 22
	d		09 56		09 41			09 50		09 56	09 57		10 09	10 24		10 11				10 20		10 23
Three Bridges 15	a		→		09 45					10 01	10 01		10 14	→		10 15						
	d				09 45					10 01	10 02		10 14			10 15						
Crawley	d									10 05			10 18									
Ifield	d									10 07												
Faygate	d																					
Littlehaven	d									10 14												
Horsham 4	a									10 17			10 26									
Balcombe	d															10 21						
Haywards Heath	a				09 54			10 00			10 11					10 26				10 30		
	d				09 55			10 04	10 07		10 11					10 27				10 35	10 37	
Wivelsfield	d				09 59				10 11							10 31						
Lewes 4	a								10 22											10 52		
Burgess Hill 4	d				10 01			10 09								10 33						10 38
Hassocks 4	d				10 04											10 36						10 41
Preston Park	d				10 11			10 18								10 43						
Hove 2	a							10 22													10 53	
Brighton 10	a			09 57	10 15						10 25				10 27	10 47						10 52

Table 186

Saturdays

from 30 June

Bedford and London - Brighton

Network Diagram - see first Page of Table 186

		SN	FC		SN	SN	SN	GW	GW	SN	SN		FC	SN	SN	SN		SN	FC		SN	SN	SN	SN	FC
		1	1		1 ⊥		◇1 ⊥	1	1	1	◇1 ⊥		1	1 ⊥	1	◇1		1	1		1 ⊥	◇1	1	◇1 ⊥	1
London Victoria 15 ⊖	d				10 00	10 01	10 02				10 06			10 15		10 17					10 30	10 32		10 36	
Clapham Junction 10	d					10 08	10 08				10 12					10 23						10 38		10 42	
Bedford	d		08 40										08 54						09 10						09 24
Luton 10	d		09 04										09 18						09 34						09 48
Luton Airport Parkway 7 ✈	d		09 06										09 20						09 36						09 50
St Albans City	d		09 18										09 32						09 48						10 02
St Pancras International 15 ⊖	d		09 39										09 54						10 09						10 24
Farringdon 3 ⊖	d		09 44										09 59						10 14						10 29
City Thameslink 3	d		09 48										10 03						10 18						10 33
London Blackfriars 3 ⊖	d		09 50										10 05						10 20						10 35
London Bridge 4 ⊖	d		09 57							10 03			10 12		10 15				10 27				10 33		10 42
New Cross Gate	d									10 08													10 38		
Norwood Junction 2	d									10 16					10 26								10 46		
East Croydon	a		10 09				10 17			10 20	10 22		10 24		10 29	10 32			10 39			10 47	10 50	10 52	10 54
	d		10 11				10 18			10 21	10 23		10 25		10 30	10 33			10 41			10 48	10 51	10 53	10 55
Purley 4	d									10 26					10 36								10 56		
Coulsdon South	d									10 30					10 39								11 00		
Merstham	d									10 35					10 45								11 05		
Redhill	a						10 30			10 39					10 49							11 00	11 09		
	d						10 30	10 34	10 41	10 44					10 52							11 00	11 10		
Reigate	a							10 38							10 56										
Nutfield	d																								
Godstone	d																								
Edenbridge	d																								
Penshurst	d																								
Leigh (Kent)	d																								
Tonbridge 4	a																								
Earlswood (Surrey)	d																						11 12		
Salfords	d																						11 16		
Horley 4	d	←					10 36			10 51								←					11 19		
Gatwick Airport 10 ✈	a	10 23	10 26		10 30		10 39		10 50	10 55			10 40	10 45		10 48		10 55	10 56		11 00	11 08	11 23		11 10
	d	10 24	10 27				10 40			10 56			10 41			10 50		10 56	10 57			11 09	11 24		11 11
Three Bridges 15	a	10 29	10 31				10 44			→			10 45					11 01	11 01			11 14	→		11 15
	d	10 30	10 32				10 45						10 45					11 01	11 02			11 14			11 15
Crawley	d	10 33					10 48											11 05				11 18			
Ifield	d	10 36																11 07							
Faygate	d																								
Littlehaven	d	10 42																11 14							
Horsham 4	a	10 45					10 56											11 17				11 26			
Balcombe	d																								11 21
Haywards Heath	a		10 41										10 54			11 00			11 11						11 26
	d		10 41										10 55			11 04	11 07		11 11						11 27
Wivelsfield	d												10 59				11 11								11 31
Lewes 4	a																11 22								
Burgess Hill 4	d												11 01			11 09									11 33
Hassocks 4	d												11 04												11 36
Preston Park	d												11 11			11 18									11 43
Hove 2	a															11 22									
Brighton 10	a		10 55								10 57		11 15						11 25					11 27	11 47

Table 186

Bedford and London - Brighton

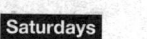

Network Diagram - see first Page of Table 186

		SN	GW		SN	SN		SN	SN	FC	SN		SN	SN	GW	GW	SN	SN	FC		SN	SN	SN		SN
		1	1		1	◇1		◇1	1	1	1		1	◇1	1	1	1	◇1	1		1	1	◇1		1
London Victoria 15 ⊖	d	10 45				10 47		10 51			11 00		11 01	11 02				11 06			11 15		11 17		
Clapham Junction 10	d					10 53							11 08	11 08				11 12					11 23		
Bedford	d									09 40									09 54						
Luton 10	d									10 04									10 18						
Luton Airport Parkway 7 ✈	d									10 06									10 20						
St Albans City	d									10 18									10 32						
St Pancras International 15 ⊖	d									10 39									10 54						
Farringdon 3 ⊖	d									10 44									10 59						
City Thameslink 3	d									10 48									11 03						
London Blackfriars 3 ⊖	d									10 50									11 05						
London Bridge 4 ⊖	d				10 45					10 57							11 03		11 12			11 15			
New Cross Gate	d																11 08								
Norwood Junction 2	d				10 56												11 16					11 26			
East Croydon	a				10 59	11 02		11 07		11 09				11 17			11 20	11 22	11 24			11 29	11 32		
	d				11 00	11 03		11 08		11 11				11 18			11 21	11 23	11 25			11 30	11 33		
Purley 4	d				11 06												11 26					11 36			
Coulsdon South	d				11 09												11 30					11 39			
Merstham	d																11 35					11 45			
Redhill	a				11 17									11 30			11 39					11 49			
	d		11 13		11 17									11 30	11 34	11 41	11 44					11 52			
Reigate	a		11 18												11 38							11 56			
Nutfield	d				11 22																				
Godstone	d				11 27																				
Edenbridge	d				11 33																				
Penshurst	d				11 39																				
Leigh (Kent)	d				11 43																				
Tonbridge 4	a				11 48																				
Earlswood (Surrey)	d																								
Salfords	d																								
Horley 4	d								←					11 36			11 51								←
Gatwick Airport 10 ✈	a	11 15				11 18		11 22	11 23	11 26	11 30			11 39		11 50	11 55		11 40		11 45		11 48		11 55
	d					11 20		11 23	11 24	11 27				11 40			11 56		11 41				11 50		11 56
Three Bridges 15	a								11 29	11 31				11 44			→		11 45						12 01
	d								11 30	11 32				11 45					11 45						12 01
Crawley	d								11 33					11 48											12 05
Ifield	d								11 36																12 07
Faygate	d																								
Littlehaven	d								11 42																12 14
Horsham 4	a								11 45					11 56											12 17
Balcombe	d																								
Haywards Heath	a					11 30				11 41									11 54				12 00		
	d					11 35	11 37			11 41									11 55				12 04	12 07	
Wivelsfield	d																		11 59					12 11	
Lewes 4	a					11 52																		12 22	
Burgess Hill 4	d							11 38											12 01				12 09		
Hassocks 4	d							11 41											12 04						
Preston Park	d																		12 11				12 18		
Hove 2	a						11 53																12 22		
Brighton 10	a							11 52		11 55								11 57	12 15						

Bedford and London - Brighton

Network Diagram - see first Page of Table 186

		FC	SN		SN	SN	SN	FC	SN	GW	SN		SN		SN	SN	FC	SN	SN		SN	GW	GW	SN	SN
		1	1 ⊼		◇1	1	◇1 ⊼	1	1 ⊼	1	1		◇1		◇1	1	1	1 ⊼			◇1 ⊼	1	1	1	◇1 ⊼
London Victoria 15 ⊖	d		11 30		11 32		11 36		11 45				11 47		11 51			12 00	12 01		12 02				12 06
Clapham Junction 10	d				11 38		11 42						11 53						12 08		12 08				12 12
Bedford	d	10 10						10 24									10 40								
Luton 10	d	10 34						10 48									11 04								
Luton Airport Parkway 7 ✈	d	10 36						10 50									11 06								
St Albans City	d	10 48						11 02									11 18								
St Pancras International 15 ⊖	d	11 09						11 24									11 39								
Farringdon 3 ⊖	d	11 14						11 29									11 44								
City Thameslink 3	d	11 18						11 33									11 48								
London Blackfriars 3 ⊖	d	11 20						11 35									11 50								
London Bridge 4 ⊖	d	11 27				11 33		11 42			11 45						11 57							12 03	
New Cross Gate	d					11 38																		12 08	
Norwood Junction 2	d					11 46					11 56													12 16	
East Croydon	a	11 39			11 47	11 50	11 52	11 54			11 59		12 02		12 07		12 09				12 17			12 20	12 22
	d	11 41			11 48	11 51	11 53	11 55			12 00		12 03		12 08		12 11				12 18			12 21	12 23
Purley 4	d					11 56					12 06													12 26	
Coulsdon South	d					12 00					12 09													12 30	
Merstham	d					12 05																		12 35	
Redhill	a				12 00	12 09					12 17										12 30			12 39	
	d				12 00	12 10				12 13	12 17										12 30	12 34	12 41	12 44	
Reigate	a									12 18												12 38			
Nutfield	d										12 22														
Godstone	d										12 27														
Edenbridge	d										12 33														
Penshurst	d										12 39														
Leigh (Kent)	d										12 43														
Tonbridge 4	a										12 48														
Earlswood (Surrey)	d					12 12																			
Salfords	d					12 16																			
Horley 4	d					12 19										←					12 36			12 51	
Gatwick Airport 10 ✈	a	11 56	12 00		12 08	12 23		12 10	12 15				12 18		12 22	12 23	12 26	12 30			12 39		12 50	12 55	
	d	11 57			12 09	12 24		12 11					12 20		12 23	12 24	12 27				12 40			12 56	
Three Bridges 15	a	12 01			12 14	→		12 15								12 29	12 31				12 44			→	
	d	12 02			12 14			12 15								12 30	12 32				12 45				
Crawley	d				12 18											12 33					12 48				
Ifield	d															12 36									
Faygate	d																								
Littlehaven	d															12 42									
Horsham 4	a				12 26											12 45					12 56				
Balcombe	d							12 21																	
Haywards Heath	a	12 11						12 26					12 30				12 41								
	d	12 11						12 27					12 35	12 37			12 41								
Wivelsfield	d							12 31																	
Lewes 4	a												12 52												
Burgess Hill 4	d							12 33							12 38										
Hassocks 4	d							12 36							12 41										
Preston Park	d							12 43																	
Hove 2	a													12 53											
Brighton 10	a	12 25					12 27	12 47							12 52		12 55								12 57

Table 186

Saturdays

from 30 June

Bedford and London - Brighton

Network Diagram - see first Page of Table 186

		FC	SN		SN	SN		SN	FC	SN	SN		SN	SN	FC	SN	GW	SN	SN			SN	SN	FC	SN
		1	1		1	◇1		1	1	1	◇1		1	◇1	1	1	1	1	◇1			◇1	1	1	1
			🚲							🚲				🚲		🚲									🚲
London Victoria 15 ⊖	d		12 15			12 17				12 30	12 32			12 36		12 45			12 47			12 51			13 00
Clapham Junction 10	d					12 23					12 38			12 42					12 53						
Bedford	d	10 54							11 10						11 24									11 40	
Luton 10	d	11 18							11 34						11 48									12 04	
Luton Airport Parkway 7 ✈	d	11 20							11 36						11 50									12 06	
St Albans City	d	11 32							11 48						12 02									12 18	
St Pancras International 15 ⊖	d	11 54							12 09						12 24									12 39	
Farringdon 3 ⊖	d	11 59							12 14						12 29									12 44	
City Thameslink 3	d	12 03							12 18						12 33									12 48	
London Blackfriars 3 ⊖	d	12 05							12 20						12 35									12 50	
London Bridge 4 ⊖	d	12 12			12 15				12 27				12 33		12 42			12 45						12 57	
New Cross Gate	d												12 38												
Norwood Junction 2	d				12 26								12 46					12 56							
East Croydon	a	12 24			12 29	12 32			12 39		12 47		12 50	12 52	12 54			12 59	13 02			13 07		13 09	
	d	12 25			12 30	12 33			12 41		12 48		12 51	12 53	12 55			13 00	13 03			13 08		13 11	
Purley 4	d				12 36								12 56					13 06							
Coulsdon South	d				12 39								13 00					13 09							
Merstham	d				12 45								13 05												
Redhill	a				12 49						13 00		13 09					13 17							
	d				12 52						13 00		13 10				13 13	13 17							
Reigate	a				12 56												13 18								
Lingfield	d																	13 22							
Godstone	d																	13 27							
Edenbridge	d																	13 33							
Penshurst	d																	13 39							
Leigh (Kent)	d																	13 43							
Tonbridge 4	a																	13 48							
Earlswood (Surrey)	d												13 12												
Salfords	d												13 16												
Horley 4	d							←					13 19										←		
Gatwick Airport 10 ✈	a	12 40	12 45			12 48		12 55	12 56	13 00	13 08		13 23		13 10	13 15			13 18			13 22	13 23	13 26	13 30
	d	12 41				12 50		12 56	12 57		13 09		13 24		13 11				13 20			13 23	13 24	13 27	
Three Bridges 15	a	12 45						13 01	13 01		13 14		↦		13 15								13 29	13 31	
	d	12 45						13 01	13 02		13 14				13 15								13 30	13 32	
Crawley	d							13 05			13 18												13 33		
Ifield	d							13 07															13 36		
Faygate	d																								
Littlehaven	d							13 14															13 42		
Horsham 4	a							13 17			13 26												13 45		
Balcombe	d														13 21										
Haywards Heath	a	12 54				13 00			13 11						13 26				13 30					13 41	
	d	12 55				13 04	13 07		13 11						13 27				13 35	13 37				13 41	
Wivelsfield	d	12 59					13 11								13 31										
Lewes 4	a						13 22												13 52						
Burgess Hill 4	d	13 01				13 09									13 33							13 38			
Hassocks 4	d	13 04													13 36							13 41			
Preston Park	d	13 11				13 18									13 43										
Hove 2	a					13 22														13 53					
Brighton 10	a	13 15							13 25					13 27	13 47							13 52		13 55	

Table 186

Bedford and London - Brighton

Saturdays
from 30 June

Network Diagram - see first Page of Table 186

		SN	SN	GW		GW	SN	SN	FC	SN	SN	SN			SN	FC	SN	SN	SN	SN	FC		SN	GW	SN
			◇1 🚲	1		1	1	◇1 🚲	1	1 🚲	1	◇1			1	1	1 🚲	◇1	1	◇1 🚲	1		1 🚲	1	1
London Victoria 15 ⊖	d	13 01	13 02					13 06		13 15		13 17					13 30	13 32		13 36			13 45		
Clapham Junction 10	d	13 08	13 08					13 12				13 23						13 38		13 42					
Bedford	d								11 54							12 10					12 24				
Luton 10	d								12 18							12 34					12 48				
Luton Airport Parkway 7 ✈	d								12 20							12 36					12 50				
St Albans City	d								12 32							12 48					13 02				
St Pancras International 15 ⊖	d								12 54							13 09					13 24				
Farringdon 3 ⊖	d								12 59							13 14					13 29				
City Thameslink 3	d								13 03							13 18					13 33				
London Blackfriars 3 ⊖	d								13 05							13 20					13 35				
London Bridge 4 ⊖	d						13 03		13 12		13 15					13 27			13 33		13 42				13 45
New Cross Gate	d						13 08												13 38						
Norwood Junction 2	d						13 16				13 26								13 46						13 56
East Croydon	a		13 17				13 20	13 22	13 24		13 29	13 32				13 39		13 47	13 50	13 52	13 54				13 59
	d		13 18				13 21	13 23	13 25		13 30	13 33				13 41		13 48	13 51	13 53	13 55				14 00
Purley 4	d						13 26				13 36								13 56						14 06
Coulsdon South	d						13 30				13 39								14 00						14 09
Merstham	d						13 35				13 45								14 05						
Redhill	a		13 30				13 39				13 49							14 00	14 09						14 17
	d		13 30	13 34		13 41	13 44				13 52							14 00	14 10					14 13	14 17
Reigate	a			13 38							13 56													14 18	
Nutfield	d																								14 22
Godstone	d																								14 27
Edenbridge	d																								14 33
Penshurst	d																								14 39
Leigh (Kent)	d																								14 43
Tonbridge 4	a																								14 48
Earlswood (Surrey)	d																		14 12						
Salfords	d																		14 16						
Horley 4	d		13 36				13 51								←				14 19						
Gatwick Airport 10 ✈	a		13 39			13 50	13 55		13 40	13 45		13 48			13 55	13 56	14 00	14 08	14 23		14 10		14 15		
	d		13 40				13 56		13 41			13 50			13 56	13 57		14 09	14 24		14 11				
Three Bridges 15	a		13 44				→		13 45						14 01	14 01		14 14	→		14 15				
	d		13 45						13 45						14 01	14 02		14 14			14 15				
Crawley	d		13 48												14 05			14 18							
Ifield	d														14 07										
Faygate	d																								
Littlehaven	d														14 14										
Horsham 4	a		13 56												14 17			14 26							
Balcombe	d																				14 21				
Haywards Heath	a								13 54			14 00				14 11					14 26				
	d								13 55			14 04	14 07			14 11					14 27				
Wivelsfield	d								13 59				14 11								14 31				
Lewes 4	a												14 22												
Burgess Hill 4	d								14 01			14 09									14 33				
Hassocks 4	d								14 04												14 36				
Preston Park	d								14 11			14 18									14 43				
Hove 2	a											14 22													
Brighton 10	a							13 57	14 15							14 25				14 27	14 47				

Table 186

Saturdays

from 30 June

Bedford and London - Brighton

Network Diagram - see first Page of Table 186

		SN		SN	SN		FC	SN	SN	SN	GW	GW	SN		SN	FC	SN	SN	SN		SN		FC	SN	SN
		◇1		◇1	1		1	1		◇1	1	1	1		◇1	1	1	1	◇1		1		1	1	◇1
								🛒		🛒					🛒		🛒							🛒	
London Victoria 15 ⊖	d	13 47		13 51				14 00	14 01	14 02					14 06		14 15		14 17					14 30	14 32
Clapham Junction 10	d	13 53							14 08	14 08					14 12				14 23						14 38
Bedford	d						12 40									12 54							13 10		
Luton 10	d						13 04									13 18							13 34		
Luton Airport Parkway 7 ✈	d						13 06									13 20							13 36		
St Albans City	d						13 18									13 32							13 48		
St Pancras International 15 ⊖	d						13 39									13 54							14 09		
Farringdon 3 ⊖	d						13 44									13 59							14 14		
City Thameslink 3	d						13 48									14 03							14 18		
London Blackfriars 3 ⊖	d						13 50									14 05							14 20		
London Bridge 4 ⊖	d						13 57						14 03			14 12		14 15					14 27		
New Cross Gate	d												14 08												
Norwood Junction 2	d												14 16					14 26							
East Croydon	a	14 02		14 07			14 09			14 17			14 20		14 22	14 24		14 29	14 32				14 39		14 47
	d	14 03		14 08			14 11			14 18			14 21		14 23	14 25		14 30	14 33				14 41		14 48
Purley 4	d												14 26					14 36							
Coulsdon South	d												14 30					14 39							
Merstham	d												14 35					14 45							
Redhill	a									14 30			14 39					14 49							15 00
	d									14 30	14 34	14 41	14 44					14 52							15 00
Reigate	a										14 38							14 56							
Nutfield	d																								
Godstone	d																								
Edenbridge	d																								
Penshurst	d																								
Leigh (Kent)	d																								
Tonbridge 4	a																								
Earlswood (Surrey)	d																								
Salfords	d																								
Horley 4	d				←					14 36			14 51								←				
Gatwick Airport 10 ✈	a	14 18		14 22	14 23		14 26	14 30		14 39		14 50	14 55			14 40	14 45		14 48		14 55		14 56	15 00	15 08
	d	14 20		14 23	14 24		14 27			14 40			14 56			14 41			14 50		14 56		14 57		15 09
Three Bridges 15	a				14 29		14 31			14 44			→			14 45					15 01		15 01		15 14
	d				14 30		14 32			14 45						14 45					15 01		15 02		15 14
Crawley	d				14 33					14 48											15 05				15 18
Ifield	d				14 36																15 07				
Faygate	d																								
Littlehaven	d				14 42																15 14				
Horsham 4	a				14 45					14 56											15 17				15 26
Balcombe	d																								
Haywards Heath	a	14 30					14 41									14 54			15 00				15 11		
	d	14 35	14 37				14 41									14 55			15 04	15 07			15 11		
Wivelsfield	d															14 59				15 11					
Lewes 4	a	14 52																		15 22					
Burgess Hill 4	d			14 38												15 01			15 09						
Hassocks 4	d			14 41												15 04									
Preston Park	d															15 11			15 18						
Hove 2	a		14 53																15 22						
Brighton 10	a			14 52			14 55								14 57	15 15							15 25		

Table 186

Saturdays
from 30 June

Bedford and London - Brighton

Network Diagram - see first Page of Table 186

		SN	SN	FC	SN		GW	SN	SN		SN	SN	FC		SN	SN	SN	GW	GW	SN	SN		FC	SN	SN
		1	◇1	1	1		1	1	◇1		◇1	1	1		1		◇1	1	1	1	◇1		1	1	1
			🛒		🛒										🛒		🛒				🛒			🛒	
London Victoria 15 ⊖	d		14 36		14 45				14 47		14 51				15 00	15 01	15 02				15 06			15 15	
Clapham Junction 10	d		14 42						14 53							15 08	15 08				15 12				
Bedford	d			13 24									13 40										13 54		
Luton 10	d			13 48									14 04										14 18		
Luton Airport Parkway 7 ✈	d			13 50									14 06										14 20		
St Albans City	d			14 02									14 18										14 32		
St Pancras International 15 ⊖	d			14 24									14 39										14 54		
Farringdon 3 ⊖	d			14 29									14 44										14 59		
City Thameslink 3	d			14 33									14 48										15 03		
London Blackfriars 3 ⊖	d			14 35									14 50										15 05		
London Bridge 4 ⊖	d	14 33		14 42				14 45					14 57							15 03			15 12		15 15
New Cross Gate	d	14 38																		15 08					
Norwood Junction 2	d	14 46						14 56												15 16					15 26
East Croydon	a	14 50	14 52	14 54				14 59	15 02		15 07		15 09				15 17			15 20	15 22		15 24		15 29
	d	14 51	14 53	14 55				15 00	15 03		15 08		15 11				15 18			15 21	15 23		15 25		15 30
Purley 4	d	14 56						15 06												15 26					15 36
Coulsdon South	d	15 00						15 09												15 30					15 39
Merstham	d	15 05																		15 35					15 45
Redhill	a	15 09						15 17									15 30			15 39					15 49
	d	15 10					15 13	15 17									15 30	15 34	15 41	15 44					15 52
Reigate	a						15 18											15 38							15 56
Nutfield	d							15 22																	
Godstone	d							15 27																	
Edenbridge	d							15 33																	
Penshurst	d							15 39																	
Leigh (Kent)	d							15 43																	
Tonbridge 4	a							15 48																	
Earlswood (Surrey)	d	15 12																							
Salfords	d	15 16																							
Horley 4	d	15 19										←					15 36			15 51					
Gatwick Airport 10 ✈	a	15 23		15 10	15 15				15 18		15 22	15 23	15 26		15 30		15 39		15 50	15 55			15 40	15 45	
	d	15 24		15 11					15 20		15 23	15 24	15 27				15 40			15 56			15 41		
Three Bridges 15	a	↦		15 15								15 29	15 31				15 44			↦			15 45		
	d			15 15								15 30	15 32				15 45						15 45		
Crawley	d											15 33					15 48								
Ifield	d											15 36													
Faygate	d																								
Littlehaven	d											15 42													
Horsham 4	a											15 45					15 56								
Balcombe	d			15 21																					
Haywards Heath	a			15 26					15 30				15 41										15 54		
	d			15 27					15 35	15 37			15 41										15 55		
Wivelsfield	d			15 31																			15 59		
Lewes 4	a								15 52																
Burgess Hill 4	d			15 33							15 38												16 01		
Hassocks 4	d			15 36							15 41												16 04		
Preston Park	d			15 43																			16 11		
Hove 2	a									15 53															
Brighton 10	a		15 27	15 47							15 52		15 55								15 57		16 15		

Table 186

Saturdays

from 30 June

Bedford and London - Brighton

Network Diagram - see first Page of Table 186

		SN		SN	FC	SN	SN	SN	SN	FC	SN	GW	SN	SN		SN	SN	FC	SN	SN	SN	GW
		◇1		1	1	1	◇1	1	◇1	1	1	1	1	◇1		◇1	1	1	1		◇1	1
						🛒			🛒		🛒								🛒		🛒	
London Victoria 15 ⊖	d	15 17				15 30	15 32		15 36		15 45			15 47		15 51			16 00	16 01	16 02	
Clapham Junction 10	d	15 23					15 38		15 42					15 53						16 08	16 08	
Bedford	d				14 10					14 24								14 40				
Luton 10	d				14 34					14 48								15 04				
Luton Airport Parkway 7 ✈	d				14 36					14 50								15 06				
St Albans City	d				14 48					15 02								15 18				
St Pancras International 15 ⊖	d				15 09					15 24								15 39				
Farringdon 3 ⊖	d				15 14					15 29								15 44				
City Thameslink 3	d				15 18					15 33								15 48				
London Blackfriars 3 ⊖	d				15 20					15 35								15 50				
London Bridge 4 ⊖	d				15 27			15 33		15 42			15 45					15 57				
New Cross Gate	d							15 38														
Norwood Junction 2	d							15 46					15 56									
East Croydon	a	15 32			15 39		15 47	15 50	15 52	15 54			15 59	16 02		16 07		16 09			16 17	
	d	15 33			15 41		15 48	15 51	15 53	15 55			16 00	16 03		16 08		16 11			16 18	
Purley 4	d							15 56					16 06									
Coulsdon South	d							16 00					16 09									
Merstham	d							16 05														
Redhill	a						16 00	16 09					16 17								16 30	
	d						16 00	16 10				16 13	16 17								16 30	16 34
Reigate	a											16 18										16 38
Nutfield	d												16 22									
Godstone	d												16 27									
Edenbridge	d												16 33									
Penshurst	d												16 39									
Leigh (Kent)	d												16 43									
Tonbridge 4	a												16 48									
Earlswood (Surrey)	d							16 12														
Salfords	d							16 16														
Horley 4	d			←				16 19									←				16 36	
Gatwick Airport 10 ✈	a	15 48		15 55	15 56	16 00	16 08	16 23		16 10	16 15			16 18		16 22	16 23	16 26	16 30		16 39	
	d	15 50		15 56	15 57		16 09	16 24		16 11				16 20		16 23	16 24	16 27			16 40	
Three Bridges 15	a			16 01	16 01		16 14	→		16 15							16 29	16 31			16 44	
	d			16 01	16 02		16 14			16 15							16 30	16 32			16 45	
Crawley	d			16 05			16 18										16 33				16 48	
Ifield	d			16 07													16 36					
Faygate	d																					
Littlehaven	d			16 14													16 42					
Horsham 4	a			16 17			16 26										16 45				16 56	
Balcombe	d									16 21												
Haywards Heath	a	16 00			16 11					16 26				16 30				16 41				
	d	16 04	16 07		16 11					16 27				16 35	16 37			16 41				
Wivelsfield	d		16 11							16 31												
Lewes 4	a		16 22											16 52								
Burgess Hill 4	d	16 09								16 33						16 38						
Hassocks 4	d									16 36						16 41						
Preston Park	d	16 18								16 43												
Hove 2	a	16 22													16 53							
Brighton 10	a				16 25				16 27	16 47						16 52		16 55				

Table 186

Saturdays

from 30 June

Bedford and London - Brighton

Network Diagram - see first Page of Table 186

		GW	SN	SN	FC	SN	SN	SN		SN	FC	SN	SN	SN	SN	FC	SN	GW	SN	SN		SN
		1	1	◇1	1	1	1	◇1		1	1	1	◇1	1	◇1	1	1	1	1	◇1		◇1
				🛒		🛒						🛒			🛒		🛒					
London Victoria 15 ⊖	d			16 06		16 15		16 17				16 30	16 32		16 36		16 45			16 47		16 51
Clapham Junction 10	d			16 12				16 23					16 38		16 42					16 53		
Bedford	d				14 54						15 10					15 24						
Luton 10	d				15 18						15 34					15 48						
Luton Airport Parkway 7 ✈	d				15 20						15 36					15 50						
St Albans City	d				15 32						15 48					16 02						
St Pancras International 15 ⊖	d				15 54						16 09					16 24						
Farringdon 3 ⊖	d				15 59						16 14					16 29						
City Thameslink 3	d				16 03						16 18					16 33						
London Blackfriars 3 ⊖	d				16 05						16 20					16 35						
London Bridge 4 ⊖	d		16 03		16 12		16 15				16 27			16 33		16 42			16 45			
New Cross Gate	d		16 08											16 38								
Norwood Junction 2	d		16 16				16 26							16 46					16 56			
East Croydon	a		16 20	16 22	16 24		16 29	16 32			16 39		16 47	16 50	16 52	16 54			16 59	17 02		17 07
	d		16 21	16 23	16 25		16 30	16 33			16 41		16 48	16 51	16 53	16 55			17 00	17 03		17 08
Purley 4	d		16 26				16 36							16 56					17 06			
Coulsdon South	d		16 30				16 39							17 00					17 09			
Merstham	d		16 35				16 45							17 05								
Redhill	a		16 39				16 49						17 00	17 09					17 17			
	d	16 41	16 44				16 52						17 00	17 10				17 13	17 17			
Reigate	a						16 56											17 18				
Nutfield	d																		17 22			
Godstone	d																		17 27			
Edenbridge	d																		17 33			
Penshurst	d																		17 39			
Leigh (Kent)	d																		17 43			
Tonbridge 4	a																		17 48			
Earlswood (Surrey)	d													17 12								
Salfords	d													17 16								
Horley 4	d		16 51							←				17 19								
Gatwick Airport 10 ✈	a	16 50	16 55		16 40	16 45		16 48		16 55	16 56	17 00	17 08	17 23		17 10	17 15			17 18		17 22
	d		16 56		16 41			16 50		16 56	16 57		17 09	17 24		17 11				17 20		17 23
Three Bridges 15	a		→		16 45					17 01	17 01		17 14	→		17 15						
	d				16 45					17 01	17 02		17 14			17 15						
Crawley	d									17 05			17 18									
Ifield	d									17 07												
Faygate	d																					
Littlehaven	d									17 14												
Horsham 4	a									17 17			17 26									
Balcombe	d															17 21						
Haywards Heath	a				16 54			17 00			17 11					17 26				17 30		
	d				16 55			17 04	17 07		17 11					17 27				17 35	17 37	
Wivelsfield	d				16 59				17 11							17 31						
Lewes 4	a								17 22											17 52		
Burgess Hill 4	d				17 01			17 09								17 33						17 38
Hassocks 4	d				17 04											17 36						17 41
Preston Park	d				17 11			17 18								17 43					17 53	
Hove 2	a							17 22														
Brighton 10	a			16 57	17 15						17 25				17 27	17 47						17 52

Table 186

Bedford and London - Brighton

Saturdays

from 30 June

Network Diagram - see first Page of Table 186

		SN	FC	SN	SN		SN	GW	GW	SN	SN	FC	SN		SN	SN	SN	SN	FC	SN	SN		SN	SN	FC
		1	1	1			◇1	1	1	1	◇1	1	1		1	◇1	1	◇1	1	1	◇1		1	◇1	1
London Victoria 15 ⊖	d			17 00	17 01		17 02				17 06		17 15			17 17				17 30	17 32			17 36	
Clapham Junction 10	d				17 08		17 08				17 12					17 23					17 38			17 42	
Bedford	d		15 40									15 54							16 10						16 24
Luton 10	d		16 04									16 18							16 34						16 48
Luton Airport Parkway 7 ✈	d		16 06									16 20							16 36						16 50
St Albans City	d		16 18									16 32							16 48						17 02
St Pancras International 15 ⊖	d		16 39									16 54							17 09						17 24
Farringdon 3 ⊖	d		16 44									16 59							17 14						17 29
City Thameslink 3	d		16 48									17 03							17 18						17 33
London Blackfriars 3 ⊖	d		16 50									17 05							17 20						17 35
London Bridge 4 ⊖	d		16 57							17 03		17 12			17 15				17 27				17 33		17 42
New Cross Gate	d									17 08													17 38		
Norwood Junction 2	d									17 16					17 26								17 46		
East Croydon	a		17 09				17 17			17 20	17 22	17 24			17 29	17 32			17 39		17 47		17 50	17 52	17 54
	d		17 11				17 18			17 21	17 23	17 25			17 30	17 33			17 41		17 48		17 51	17 53	17 55
Purley 4	d									17 26					17 36								17 56		
Coulsdon South	d									17 30					17 39								18 00		
Merstham	d									17 35					17 45								18 05		
Redhill	a						17 30			17 39					17 49						18 00		18 09		
	d						17 30	17 34	17 41	17 44					17 52						18 00		18 10		
Reigate	a							17 38							17 56										
Nutfield	d																								
Godstone	d																								
Edenbridge	d																								
Penshurst	d																								
Leigh (Kent)	d																								
Tonbridge 4	a																								
Earlswood (Surrey)	d																						18 12		
Salfords	d																						18 16		
Horley 4	d	←					17 36			17 51							←						18 19		
Gatwick Airport 10 ✈	a	17 23	17 26	17 30			17 39		17 50	17 55		17 40	17 45			17 48	17 55		17 56	18 00	18 08		18 23		18 10
	d	17 24	17 27				17 40			17 56		17 41				17 50	17 56		17 57		18 09		18 24		18 11
Three Bridges 15	a	17 29	17 31				17 44			→		17 45					18 01		18 01		18 14		→		18 15
	d	17 30	17 32				17 45					17 45					18 01		18 02		18 14				18 15
Crawley	d	17 33					17 48										18 05				18 18				
Ifield	d	17 36															18 07								
Faygate	d																								
Littlehaven	d	17 42															18 14								
Horsham 4	a	17 45					17 56										18 17				18 26				
Balcombe	d																								18 21
Haywards Heath	a		17 41									17 54				18 00			18 11						18 26
	d		17 41									17 55				18 04		18 07	18 11						18 27
Wivelsfield	d											17 59						18 11							18 31
Lewes 4	a																	18 22							
Burgess Hill 4	d											18 01				18 09									18 33
Hassocks 4	d											18 04													18 36
Preston Park	d											18 11				18 18									18 43
Hove 2	a															18 22									
Brighton 10	a		17 55								17 57	18 15							18 25					18 27	18 47

Table 186

Saturdays

from 30 June

Bedford and London - Brighton

Network Diagram - see first Page of Table 186

		SN	GW	SN	SN			SN	SN	FC	SN	SN	SN	GW		GW	SN	SN	FC	SN	SN	SN			SN
		1	1	1	◇1			◇1	1	1	1		◇1	1		1	1	◇1	1	1	1	◇1			1
		⚯									⚯		⚯					⚯		⚯					
London Victoria 15 ⊖	d	17 45			17 47			17 51			18 00	18 01	18 02					18 06		18 15		18 17			
Clapham Junction 10	d				17 53							18 08	18 08					18 12				18 23			
Bedford	d									16 40									16 54						
Luton 10	d									17 04									17 18						
Luton Airport Parkway 7 ✈	d									17 06									17 20						
St Albans City	d									17 18									17 32						
St Pancras International 15 ⊖	d									17 39									17 54						
Farringdon 3 ⊖	d									17 44									17 59						
City Thameslink 3	d									17 48									18 03						
London Blackfriars 3 ⊖	d									17 50									18 05						
London Bridge 4 ⊖	d			17 45						17 57							18 03		18 12		18 15				
New Cross Gate	d																18 08								
Norwood Junction 2	d			17 56													18 16				18 26				
East Croydon	a			18 00	18 02			18 07		18 09			18 17				18 20	18 22	18 24		18 29	18 32			
	d			18 00	18 03			18 08		18 11			18 18				18 21	18 23	18 25		18 30	18 33			
Purley 4	d			18 06													18 26				18 36				
Coulsdon South	d			18 09													18 30				18 39				
Merstham	d																18 35				18 45				
Redhill	a			18 17									18 30				18 39				18 49				
	d		18 13	18 17									18 30	18 34		18 41	18 44				18 52				
Reigate	a		18 18											18 38							18 56				
Nutfield	d			18 22																					
Godstone	d			18 27																					
Edenbridge	d			18 33																					
Penshurst	d			18 39																					
Leigh (Kent)	d			18 43																					
Tonbridge 4	a			18 48																					
Earlswood (Surrey)	d																								
Salfords	d																								
Horley 4	d								←				18 36				18 51								↔
Gatwick Airport 10 ✈	a	18 15			18 18			18 22	18 23	18 26	18 30		18 39			18 50	18 55		18 40	18 45		18 48			18 55
	d				18 20			18 23	18 24	18 27			18 40				18 56		18 41			18 50			18 56
Three Bridges 15	a								18 29	18 31			18 44				→		18 45						19 01
	d								18 30	18 32			18 45						18 45						19 01
Crawley	d								18 33				18 48												19 05
Ifield	d								18 36																19 07
Faygate	d																								
Littlehaven	d								18 42																19 14
Horsham 4	a								18 47				18 56												19 17
Balcombe	d																								
Haywards Heath	a				18 30					18 41									18 54			19 00			
	d				18 35	18 37				18 41									18 55			19 04	19 07		
Wivelsfield	d																		18 59				19 11		
Lewes 4	a				18 52																		19 22		
Burgess Hill 4	d							18 38											19 01			19 09			
Hassocks 4	d							18 41											19 04						
Preston Park	d																		19 11			19 18			
Hove 2	a					18 53																19 22			
Brighton 10	a							18 52		18 55								18 57	19 15						

Table 186

Saturdays

from 30 June

Bedford and London - Brighton

Network Diagram - see first Page of Table 186

Station		FC	SN	SN	SN	SN	SN	FC	SN	GW	SN	SN		SN	SN	FC	SN	SN	SN	GW	GW	SN
		1	1		◇1	1	◇1	1	1	1	1	◇1		◇1	1	1	1		◇1	1	1	1
			🚲				🚲		🚲								🚲		🚲			
London Victoria [15] ⊖	d		18 30	18 31	18 32		18 36		18 45			18 47		18 51			19 00	19 01	19 02			
Clapham Junction [10]	d			18 38	18 38		18 42					18 53						19 08	19 08			
Bedford	d	17 10						17 24								17 40						
Luton [10]	d	17 34						17 48								18 04						
Luton Airport Parkway [7] ✈	d	17 36						17 50								18 06						
St Albans City	d	17 48						18 02								18 18						
St Pancras International [15] ⊖	d	18 09						18 24								18 39						
Farringdon [3] ⊖	d	18 14						18 29								18 44						
City Thameslink [3]	d	18 18						18 33								18 48						
London Blackfriars [3] ⊖	d	18 20						18 35								18 50						
London Bridge [4] ⊖	d	18 27				18 33		18 42			18 45					18 57						19 03
New Cross Gate	d					18 38																19 08
Norwood Junction [2]	d					18 46					18 56											19 16
East Croydon	a	18 39			18 47	18 50	18 52	18 54			18 59	19 02		19 07		19 09			19 17			19 20
	d	18 41			18 48	18 51	18 53	18 55			19 00	19 03		19 08		19 11			19 18			19 21
Purley [4]	d					18 56					19 06											19 26
Coulsdon South	d					19 00					19 09											19 30
Merstham	d					19 05																19 35
Redhill	a				19 00	19 09					19 17								19 30			19 39
	d				19 00	19 10				19 13	19 17								19 30	19 34	19 41	19 46
Reigate	a									19 18										19 38		
Nutfield	d										19 22											
Godstone	d										19 27											
Edenbridge	d										19 33											
Penshurst	d										19 39											
Leigh (Kent)	d										19 43											
Tonbridge [4]	a										19 48											
Earlswood (Surrey)	d					19 12																
Salfords	d					19 16																
Horley [4]	d					19 19									←				19 36			19 52
Gatwick Airport [10] ✈	a	18 56	19 00		19 08	19 23		19 10	19 15			19 18		19 22	19 23	19 26	19 30		19 39		19 50	19 55
	d	18 57			19 09	19 24		19 11				19 20		19 23	19 24	19 27			19 40			19 56
Three Bridges [15]	a	19 01			19 14	→		19 15							19 28	19 31			19 44			→
	d	19 02			19 14			19 15							19 30	19 32			19 45			
Crawley	d				19 18										19 33				19 48			
Ifield	d														19 36							
Faygate	d																					
Littlehaven	d														19 42							
Horsham [4]	a				19 26										19 45				19 56			
Balcombe	d							19 21														
Haywards Heath	a	19 11						19 26				19 30				19 41						
	d	19 11						19 27				19 35	19 37			19 41						
Wivelsfield	d							19 31														
Lewes [4]	a											19 52										
Burgess Hill [4]	d							19 33						19 38								
Hassocks [4]	d							19 36						19 41								
Preston Park	d							19 43														
Hove [2]	a												19 52									
Brighton [10]	a	19 25					19 27	19 47						19 52		19 55						

Table 186

Saturdays
from 30 June

Bedford and London - Brighton

Network Diagram - see first Page of Table 186

		SN ◇1 🚲	FC 1	SN 1 🚲	SN ◇1		SN 1		FC 1	SN 1 🚲	SN	SN 1	SN ◇1	SN 1	SN ◇1		FC 1	SN 1 🚲	SN ◇1		SN ◇1	SN 1	FC 1		SN 1 🚲
London Victoria 15 ⊖	d	19 06		19 15	19 17					19 30	19 31		19 32		19 36			19 45	19 47		19 51				20 00
Clapham unction 10	d	19 12			19 23						19 38		19 38		19 42				19 53						
Bedford	d		17 54						18 10								18 24						18 40		
uton 10	d		18 18						18 34								18 48						19 04		
uton Airport Parkway 7 ✈	d		18 20						18 36								18 50						19 06		
St Albans City	d		18 32						18 48								19 02						19 18		
St Pancras hternational 15 ⊖	d		18 54						19 09								19 24						19 39		
Farringdon 3 ⊖	d		18 59						19 14								19 29						19 44		
City Thameslink 3	d		19 03						19 18								19 33						19 48		
London Blackfriars 3 ⊖	d		19 05						19 20								19 35						19 50		
London Bridge 4 ⊖	d		19 12						19 27					19 33			19 42						19 57		
Nw Cross Gate	d													19 38											
Nrwood unction 2	d													19 46											
East Croydon	a	19 22	19 24		19 33				19 39				19 47	19 50	19 52		19 54		20 02		20 07		20 09		
	d	19 23	19 25		19 33				19 41				19 48	19 51	19 53		19 55		20 03		20 08		20 11		
Purley 4	d													19 56											
Coulsdon South	d													20 00											
Merstham	d													20 05											
Redhill	a												20 00	20 09											
	d											19 51	20 00	20 10											
Reigate	a																								
Nfield	d											19 55													
Godstone	d											20 01													
Eenbridge	d											20 06													
Penshurst	d											20 13													
eigh (Kent)	d											20 16													
Tonbridge 4	a											20 21													
Erlswood (Surrey)	d													20 12											
Salfords	d													20 16											
Horley 4	d						←							20 19								←			
Gatwick Airport 10 ✈	a		19 40	19 45	19 48		19 55		19 56	20 00			20 08	20 23			20 10	20 15	20 18		20 22	20 23	20 26		20 30
	d		19 41		19 50		19 56		19 57				20 09	20 24			20 11		20 20		20 23	20 24	20 27		
Three Bridges 15	a		19 45				20 01		20 01				20 14	→			20 15					20 29	20 31		
	d		19 45				20 01		20 02				20 14				20 15					20 33	20 32		
Crawley	d						20 05						20 18									20 36			
field	d						20 07															20 39			
Faygate	d																								
ittlehaven	d						20 14															20 45			
Horsham 4	a						20 17						20 26									20 48			
Balcombe	d																20 21								
Haywards Heath	a		19 54		20 00				20 11								20 26		20 30				20 41		
	d		19 55		20 04	20 07			20 11								20 27		20 35	20 37			20 41		
Welsfield	d		19 59			20 11											20 31		20 39						
ewes 4	a					20 22													20 52						
Burgess Hill 4	d		20 01		20 09												20 33				20 38				
Hassocks 4	d		20 04														20 36				20 41				
Preston Park	d		20 11		20 18												20 43								
Hove 2	a				20 22															20 53					
Brighton 10	a	19 57	20 15						20 25						20 27		20 47				20 52		20 55		

Table 186

Saturdays

from 30 June

Bedford and London - Brighton

Network Diagram - see first Page of Table 186

		SN	GW 1	SN ◇1	SN ◇1	FC 1	GW 1		GW 1	SN 1	SN 1	SN ◇1		SN ◇1	SN 1		SN 1	SN	SN 1	SN ◇1	SN ◇1	FC 1	GW 1		SN 1
London Victoria 15 ⊖	d	20 01		20 02	20 06					20 10	20 15	20 17		20 21			20 30	20 31		20 32	20 36				20 40
Clapham Junction 10	d	20 08		20 08	20 12					20 16		20 23						20 38		20 38	20 42				20 46
Bedford	d					18 54																19 22			
Luton 10	d					19 18																19 46			
Luton Airport Parkway 7 ✈	d					19 20																19 48			
St Albans City	d					19 32																20 00			
St Pancras International 15 ⊖	d					19 54																20 24			
Farringdon 3 ⊖	d					19 59																20 29			
City Thameslink 3	d					20 03																20 33			
London Blackfriars 3 ⊖	d					20 05																20 35			
London Bridge 4 ⊖	d					20 12																20 42			
New Cross Gate	d																								
Norwood Junction 2	d																								
East Croydon 🚌	a			20 17	20 22	20 24				20 29		20 32		20 37						20 47	20 52	20 54			20 57
	d			20 18	20 23	20 25				20 29		20 33		20 38						20 48	20 53	20 55			20 58
Purley 4	d									20 34															21 03
Coulsdon South	d									20 38															21 06
Merstham	d									20 44															21 12
Redhill	a			20 30						20 47										21 00					21 15
	d		20 13	20 30			20 34		20 41	20 48									20 51	21 00			21 13		21 16
Reigate	a		20 18				20 38																21 18		
Nutfield	d																		20 55						
Godstone	d																		21 01						
Edenbridge	d																		21 06						
Penshurst	d																		21 13						
Leigh (Kent)	d																		21 16						
Tonbridge 4	a																		21 21						
Earlswood (Surrey)	d																								21 18
Salfords	d																								21 22
Horley 4	d									20 54					←										21 25
Gatwick Airport 10 ✈	a			20 38		20 40			20 50	20 58	20 45	20 48		20 52	20 58		21 00			21 08		21 10			21 28
	d			20 40		20 41				20 59		20 50		20 53	20 59					21 09		21 11			21 29
Three Bridges 15	a			20 44		20 45				→					21 03					21 14		21 15			→
	d			20 45		20 45									21 04					21 14		21 15			
Crawley	d			20 48											21 07					21 18					
Ifield	d														21 10										
Faygate	d																								
Littlehaven	d														21 16										
Horsham 4	a			20 56											21 19					21 26					
Balcombe	d					20 51																			
Haywards Heath	a					20 56						21 00										21 24			
	d					20 57						21 05	21 07									21 25			
Wivelsfield	d					21 01							21 11									21 29			
Lewes 4	a												21 22												
Burgess Hill 4	d					21 03						21 10										21 31			
Hassocks 4	d					21 06								21 10								21 34			
Preston Park	d					21 13						21 19										21 41			
Hove 2	a											21 22													
Brighton 10	a				20 57	21 17								21 22							21 27	21 45			

Table 186

Saturdays
from 30 June

Bedford and London - Brighton

Network Diagram - see first Page of Table 186

		SN	SN		SN	SN	SN	SN	SN	FC	GW	SN	SN	SN		SN	GW	SN	SN	SN	SN	SN
		1	◇1		1	1		◇1	◇1	1	1	1	1	◇1		1	1	1		1		◇1
London Victoria 15 ⊖	d	20 45	20 47			21 00	21 01	21 02	21 06			21 10	21 15	21 17				21 30	21 31		21 32	21 36
Clapham Junction 10	d		20 53				21 08	21 08	21 12			21 16		21 23					21 38		21 38	21 42
Bedford	d									19 52												
Luton 10	d									20 16												
Luton Airport Parkway 7 ✈	d									20 18												
St Albans City	d									20 30												
St Pancras International 15 ⊖	d									20 54												
Farringdon 3 ⊖	d									20 59												
City Thameslink 3	d									21 03												
London Blackfriars 3 ⊖	d									21 05												
London Bridge 4 ⊖	d									21 12												
New Cross Gate	d																					
Norwood Junction 2	d																					
East Croydon	a		21 02					21 17	21 22	21 24		21 27		21 33							21 47	21 52
	d		21 03					21 18	21 23	21 25		21 28		21 33							21 48	21 53
Purley 4	d											21 33										
Coulsdon South	d											21 37										
Merstham	d											21 42										
Redhill	a							21 30				21 46									22 00	
	d							21 31			21 36	21 46					21 49			21 51	22 00	
Reigate	a										21 40											
Nutfield	d																			21 55		
Godstone	d																			22 01		
Edenbridge	d																			22 06		
Penshurst	d																			22 13		
Leigh (Kent)	d																			22 16		
Tonbridge 4	a																			22 21		
Earlswood (Surrey)	d																					
Salfords	d																					
Horley 4	d				←							21 52				←						
Gatwick Airport 10 ✈	a	21 15	21 18		21 28	21 30		21 38		21 40		21 55	21 45	21 48		21 55	21 59	22 00			22 08	
	d		21 20		21 29			21 39		21 41		21 56		21 49		21 56					22 09	
Three Bridges 15	a				21 33			21 44		21 45		→		21 53		22 00					22 14	
	d				21 36			21 44		21 45				21 53		22 01					22 14	
Crawley	d				21 39											22 04					22 18	
Ifield	d				21 42											22 07						
Faygate	d																					
Littlehaven	d				21 48											22 13						
Horsham 4	a				21 52											22 16					22 26	
Balcombe	d									21 53												
Haywards Heath	a		21 30					21 53	21 46	21 58				22 02								22 16
	d		21 34	21 37				21 53	21 46	21 59				22 06	22 08							22 16
Wivelsfield	d		21 38					21 57		22 03					22 12							
Lewes 4	a		21 51												22 23							
Burgess Hill 4	d							21 59		22 05				22 11								
Hassocks 4	d							22 03		22 08												
Preston Park	d							22 09		22 15												
Hove 2	a			21 51										22 22								
Brighton 10	a							22 15	22 00	22 19												22 30

Table 186

Saturdays

from 30 June

Bedford and London - Brighton

Network Diagram - see first Page of Table 186

		FC	SN	SN	SN		SN	SN	SN	SN	SN	FC	GW	SN	SN	SN	SN	SN	SN	SN	GW	SN
		1	1	1	◇1		1	1		◇1	◇1	1	1	1	1	◇1	1	1		1	1	1
London Victoria 15 ⊖	d		21 40	21 45	21 47			22 00	22 01	22 02	22 06			22 10	22 15	22 17		22 30	22 31			22 32
Clapham Junction 10	d		21 46		21 53				22 08	22 08	22 12			22 16		22 23			22 38			22 38
Bedford	d	20 22										20 52										
Luton 10	d	20 46										21 16										
Luton Airport Parkway 7 ✈	d	20 48										21 18										
St Albans City	d	21 00										21 30										
St Pancras International 15 ⊖	d	21 24										21 54										
Farringdon 3 ⊖	d	21 29										21 59										
City Thameslink 3	d																					
London Blackfriars 3 ⊖	d	21 35										22 05										
London Bridge 4 ⊖	d	21 42										22 12										
New Cross Gate	d																					
Norwood Junction 2	d																					
East Croydon	a	21 54	21 57		22 03					22 17	22 22	22 24		22 27		22 33						22 47
	d	21 55	21 58		22 03					22 18	22 23	22 25		22 28		22 33						22 48
Purley 4	d		22 03											22 33								
Coulsdon South	d		22 06											22 37								
Merstham	d		22 12											22 42								
Redhill	a		22 15							22 30				22 46								23 00
	d		22 16							22 31			22 33	22 46						22 55	22 56	23 00
Reigate	a												22 38									
Nutfield	d																			22 59		
Godstone	d																			23 05		
Edenbridge	d																			23 10		
Penshurst	d																			23 17		
Leigh (Kent)	d																			23 20		
Tonbridge 4	a																			23 25		
Earlswood (Surrey)	d		22 18																			
Salfords	d		22 22																			
Horley 4	d		22 25				←							22 52			←					
Gatwick Airport 10 ✈	a	22 10	22 28	22 15	22 18		22 28	22 30		22 38		22 40		22 55	22 45	22 48	22 55	23 00			23 05	23 08
	d	22 11	22 29		22 20		22 29			22 39		22 41		22 56		22 50	22 56					23 09
Three Bridges 15	a	22 15	→				22 33			22 44		22 45		→		22 54	23 00					23 14
	d	22 15					22 36			22 44		22 45				22 54	23 01					23 15
Crawley	d						22 39										23 04					23 18
Ifield	d						22 42										23 07					
Faygate	d																					
Littlehaven	d						22 48										23 13					
Horsham 4	a						22 52										23 16					23 26
Balcombe	d											22 53										
Haywards Heath	a	22 24			22 30					22 53	22 46	22 58				23 03						
	d	22 25			22 34	22 37				22 53	22 46	22 59				23 03						
Wivelsfield	d	22 29			22 38					22 57		23 03										
Lewes 4	a				22 51																	
Burgess Hill 4	d	22 31								22 59		23 05				23 09						
Hassocks 4	d	22 34								23 03		23 08										
Preston Park	d	22 41								23 09		23 15										
Hove 2	a					22 51										23 21						
Brighton 10	a	22 45								23 15	23 00	23 19										

Table 186

Saturdays

from 30 June

Bedford and London - Brighton

Network Diagram - see first Page of Table 186

		SN ◇1	FC 1	SN 1	SN 1	SN ◇1		SN 1		SN 1	SN	GW 1	SN ◇1	SN ◇1	FC 1	SN 1		SN 1	SN ◇1	SN 1	SN 1	SN 1	SN 1	FC 1
London Victoria 15 ⊖	d	22 36		22 40	22 45	22 47				23 00	23 01		23 02	23 06		23 10		23 15	23 17		23 30		23 32	
Clapham Junction 10	d	22 42		22 46		22 53					23 08		23 08	23 12		23 16			23 23				23 38	
Bedford	d		21 22												21 52									22 16
Luton 10	d		21 46												22 16									22 40
Luton Airport Parkway 7 ✈	d		21 48												22 18									22 42
St Albans City	d		22 00												22 30									22 54
St Pancras International 15 ⊖	d		22 24												22 54									23 24
Farringdon 3 ⊖	d		22 29												22 59									23 29
City Thameslink 3	d																							
London Blackfriars 3 ⊖	d		22 35												23 05									23 35
London Bridge 4 ⊖	d		22 42												23 12									23 42
New Cross Gate	d																							
Norwood Junction 2	d																							
East Croydon	a	22 52	22 54	22 57		23 03							23 17	23 22	23 24	23 27			23 32				23 52	23 56
	d	22 53	22 55	22 58		23 03							23 18	23 23	23 25	23 28			23 33				23 52	23 57
Purley 4	d			23 03												23 33								
Coulsdon South	d			23 07												23 37								
Merstham	d			23 12												23 42								
Redhill	a			23 16									23 30			23 46							00 03	
	d			23 16								23 28	23 31			23 46						23 55	00 05	
Reigate	a											23 33												
Nutfield	d																							
Godstone	d																					00 06		
Edenbridge	d																							
Penshurst	d																							
Leigh (Kent)	d																					00 15		
Tonbridge 4	a																							
Earlswood (Surrey)	d			23 19												23 49								
Salfords	d			23 22												23 52								
Horley 4	d			23 26				←								23 56				←				
Gatwick Airport 10 ✈	a		23 10	23 28	23 15	23 18		23 28		23 30			23 38		23 40	23 58		23 45	23 49	23 58	00 05		00 14	00 18
	d		23 11	23 29		23 20		23 29					23 39		23 41	23 59			23 50	23 59			00 15	00 19
Three Bridges 15	a		23 15	→				23 34					23 44		23 47	→			23 54	00 04			00 20	00 24
	d		23 15					23 38					23 44		23 47				23 55	00 04			00 20	
Crawley	d							23 41												00 07				
Ifield	d							23 44												00 10				
Faygate	d																							
Littlehaven	d							23 50												00 16				
Horsham 4	a							23 53												00 19				
Balcombe	d														23 53								00 28	
Haywards Heath	a	23 16	23 24			23 30							23 53	23 46	23 58				00 04				00 34	
	d	23 16	23 25			23 34	23 37						23 53	23 46	23 59				00 05				00 35	
Wivelsfield	d		23 29			23 38							23 57		00 03								00 39	
Lewes 4	a					23 51																		
Burgess Hill 4	d		23 31										23 59		00 05				00 10				00 41	
Hassocks 4	d		23 34										00 03		00 08								00 44	
Preston Park	d		23 41										00 09		00 15								00 51	
Hove 2	a						23 51												00 23					
Brighton 10	a	23 30	23 45										00 15	00 01	00 19								00 55	

Table 186

Saturdays
from 30 June

Bedford and London - Brighton

Network Diagram - see first Page of Table 186

Station		SN 1	SN 1	SN 1	FC 1	FC 1	FC 1
London Victoria 15 ⊖	d	23 45	23 47	23 49			
Clapham Junction 10	d		23 53	23 56			
Bedford	d				22 42	23 12	23 42
Luton 10	d				23 06	23 36	00 06
Luton Airport Parkway 7 ✈	d				23 09	23 39	00 09
St Albans City	d				23 21	23 51	00 21
St Pancras International 15 ⊖	d				23 54	00 24	00 54
Farringdon 3 ⊖	d				23 59	00 29	
City Thameslink 3	d						
London Blackfriars 3 ⊖	d				00 05	00 35	01 05
London Bridge 4 ⊖	d				00 12	00 42	
New Cross Gate	d						
Norwood Junction 2	d						
East Croydon	a		00 05	00 09	00 26	00 56	01 31
	d		00 06		00 27	00 57	01 32
Purley 4	d		00 12				
Coulsdon South	d		00 15				
Merstham	d		00 21				
Redhill	a		00 24				
	d		00 25				
Reigate	a						
Nutfield	d						
Godstone	d						
Edenbridge	d						
Penshurst	d						
Leigh (Kent)	d						
Tonbridge 4	a						
Earlswood (Surrey)	d						
Salfords	d						
Horley 4	d		00 31				
Gatwick Airport 10 ✈	a	00 20	00 33		00 48	01 18	01 51
	d		00 34		00 49	01 22	01 52
Three Bridges 15	a		00 39		00 54	01 28	01 58
	d		00 39				
Crawley	d		00 43				
Ifield	d		00 46				
Faygate	d						
Littlehaven	d		00 52				
Horsham 4	a		00 55				
Balcombe	d						
Haywards Heath	a						
	d						
Wivelsfield	d						
Lewes 4	a						
Burgess Hill 4	d						
Hassocks 4	d						
Preston Park	d						
Hove 2	a						
Brighton 10	a						

Table 186

Sundays
until 24 June

Bedford and London - Brighton

Network Diagram - see first Page of Table 186

		SN	SN	FC	SN	SN	SN	SN	SN	GW	SN	FC	SN	SN	SN	SN	SN	FC	SN	GW	SN
		◇1	◇1	1	1	◇1	1	1	1	1	1	1	1	1	1	1	◇1	1	1	1	1
London Victoria 15 ⊖	d	23p02	23p06		23p10	23p17		23p30			23p32		23p45	23p47	23p49	00 02	00 05		00 14		00 30
Clapham Junction 10	d	23p08	23p12		23p16	23p23					23p38			23p53	23p56		00 11		00 20		
Bedford	d			21p50								22p16						22p40			
Luton 10	d			22p15								22p42						23p06			
Luton Airport Parkway 7 ✈	d			22p18								22p45						23p09			
St Albans City	d			22p30								22p57						23p21			
St Pancras International 15 ⊖	d			22p54								23p24						23p54			
Farringdon 3 ⊖	d			22p59								23p29						23p59			
City Thameslink 3	d																				
London Blackfriars 3 ⊖	d			23p05								23p35						00 05			
London Bridge 4 ⊖	d			23p12								23p42						00 12			
New Cross Gate	d																				
Norwood Junction 2	d																				
East Croydon	a	23p17	23p22	23p24	23p27	23p32					23p52	23p56		00 05	00 09		00 24	00 26	00 31		
	d	23p18	23p23	23p25	23p28	23p33					23p52	23p57		00 06			00 24	00 27	00 32		
Purley 4	d				23p33									00 12					00 37		
Coulsdon South	d				23p37									00 15					00 41		
Merstham	d				23p42									00 21					00 47		
Redhill	a	23p30			23p46						00 03			00 24					00 50		
	d	23p31			23p46				23p55	00 03	00 05			00 25					00 51	00 54	
Reigate	a																				
Nutfield	d																				
Godstone	d																				
Edenbridge	d								00 06												
Penshurst	d																				
Leigh (Kent)	d																				
Tonbridge 4	a								00 15												
Earlswood (Surrey)	d				23p49																
Salfords	d				23p52																
Horley 4	d				23p56		←							00 31					00 57		
Gatwick Airport 10 ✈	a	23p38		23p40	23p58	23p49	23p58	00 05		00 10	00 14	00 18	00 20	00 33		00 38	00 42	00 49	00 59	01 02	01 05
	d	23p39		23p41	23p59	23p50	23p59				00 15	00 19		00 34			00 43	00 50	01 00		
Three Bridges 15	a	23p44		23p47	→	23p54	00 04				00 20	00 24		00 39			00 48	00 55	01 05		
	d	23p44		23p47		23p55	00 04				00 20			00 39			00 48				
Crawley	d						00 07							00 43							
Ifield	d						00 10							00 46							
Faygate	d																				
Littlehaven	d						00 16							00 52							
Horsham 4	a						00 19							00 55							
Balcombe	d			23p53							00 28										
Haywards Heath	a	23p53	23p46	23p58		00 04					00 34						00 58				
	d	23p53	23p46	23p59		00 05					00 35						01 02 / 01 06				
Wivelsfield	d	23p57		00 03							00 39										
Lewes 4	a																01 20				
Burgess Hill 4	d	23p59		00 05		00 10					00 41										
Hassocks 4	d	00 03		00 08							00 44										
Preston Park	d	00 09		00 15							00 51										
Hove 2	a					00 23											01s16				
Brighton 10	a	00 15	00 01	00 19							00 55										

Table 186

Bedford and London - Brighton

Sundays

until 24 June

Network Diagram - see first Page of Table 186

Station		FC	SN	FC	SN	SN	SN	SN		SN	SN	SN	SN	SN	SN	SN		SN	SN	SN	GW	SN	SN	SN
		1	1	1	1	1	1	1		1	1	1	1	1	1	1		◇1	1 ⊼	1 ⊼	1	1 ⊼	◇1	1 ⊼
London Victoria 15 ⊖	d		01 00		02 00	03 00	03 30	04 00		04 30	05 00	05 02	05 15	05 30	05 45			05 47	06 00	06 15		06 30	06 32	06 45
Clapham Junction 10	d		01 08		02 08	03 08		04 08				05 08						05 53					06 38	
Bedford	d	23p10		23p40																				
Luton 10	d	23p36		00 06																				
Luton Airport Parkway 7 ✈	d	23p39		00 09																				
St Albans City	d	23p51		00 21																				
St Pancras International 15 ⊖	d	00 24		00 54																				
Farringdon 3 ⊖	d	00 29																						
City Thameslink 3	d																							
London Blackfriars 3 ⊖	d	00 35		01 05																				
London Bridge 4 ⊖	d	00 42																						
New Cross Gate	d																							
Norwood Junction 2	d																							
East Croydon	a	00 56	01 21	01 31	02 21	03 21		04 21				05 21						06 05					06 51	
	d	00 57	01 22	01 32	02 22	03 22		04 21				05 23						06 06					06 52	
Purley 4	d		01 27		02 27	03 27		04 26				05 28											06 56	
Coulsdon South	d																						07 00	
Merstham	d																						07 05	
Redhill	a																	06 18					07 09	
	d																	06 19			06 20		07 09	
Reigate	a																				06 24			
Nutfield	d																							
Godstone	d																							
Edenbridge	d																							
Penshurst	d																							
Leigh (Kent)	d																							
Tonbridge 4	a																							
Earlswood (Surrey)	d																							
Salfords	d																							
Horley 4	d		01 43		02 42	03 42		04 42										06 25					07 15	
Gatwick Airport 10 ✈	a	01 18	01 46	01 51	02 44	03 44	04 05	04 45		05 05	05 35	05 44	05 50	06 05	06 20			06 31	06 35	06 47		07 05	07 18	07 15
	d	01 22	01 48	01 52	02 46	03 46		04 46				05 45				06 29		06 32					07 19	
Three Bridges 15	a	01 28	01 52	01 58	03 00	04 00		04 54				05 50				06 33		06 36					07 23	
	d		01 53					04 54				05 50				06 40		06 36					07 24	
Crawley	d															06 43								
Ifield	d															06 46								
Faygate	d																							
Littlehaven	d															06 52								
Horsham 4	a															06 56								
Balcombe	d																						07 30	
Haywards Heath	a		02 06					05 06				05 59						06 47					07 35	
	d		02 06					05 07				06 00						06 47					07 36	
Wivelsfield	d																	06 51					07 40	
Lewes 4	a																							
Burgess Hill 4	d																	06 53					07 42	
Hassocks 4	d																	06 57					07 45	
Preston Park	d																	07 03					07 52	
Hove 2	a																							
Brighton 10	a		02 23					05 21				06 18						07 08					07 58	

Table 186

Sundays
until 24 June

Bedford and London - Brighton

Network Diagram - see first Page of Table 186

		GW	SN	GW	SN	SN	FC	SN	SN	SN	SN	FC	SN	SN	SN	GW	GW	SN	SN	FC	SN	SN
		■1	■1	■1	◇■1	■1	■1	◇■1	■1	◇■1	■1	■1	■1	■1	■1	■1	■1	◇■1	■1	■1	■1	◇■1
			🛒						🛒		🛒		🛒		🛒						🛒	
London Victoria ■15 ⊖	d		07 00		07 02				07 15	07 27	07 30		07 45		08 00			08 02			08 15	08 17
Clapham unction ■10	d				07 08					07 33								08 08				08 23
Bedford	d											06 10								06 40		
Lton ■10	d											06 37								07 07		
Lton Airport Parkway ■7 ✈	d											06 39								07 09		
St Albans City	d											06 51								07 21		
St Pancras hternational ■15 ⊖	d											07 24								07 54		
Farringdon ■3 ⊖	d											07 29								07 59		
City Thameslink ■3	d																					
London Blackfriars ■3 ⊖	d						06 55					07 34								08 04		
London Bridge ■4 ⊖	d					07 05						07 41		07 37					08 05	08 11		
Nw Cross Gate	d																					
Nrwood unction ■2	d					07 17								07 48					08 16			
East Croydon	a				07 19	07 21	07 24			07 42		07 55		07 54				08 17	08 20	08 25		08 32
	d				07 20	07 22	07 25			07 43		07 55		07 55				08 18	08 21	08 25		08 33
Purley ■4	d				07 25	07 28								08 00				08 23	08 27			
Coulsdon South	d					07 31								08 04					08 30			
Merstham	d					07 37								08 09					08 36			
Redhill	a				07 33	07 40				07 57				08 13				08 31	08 39			
	d	07 15		07 20	07 34	07 41				07 57				08 13		08 19	08 21	08 32	08 40			
Reigate	a			07 24												08 23						
Ntfield	d					07 45													08 44			
Godstone	d					07 51													08 50			
Eenbridge	d					07 56													08 55			
Penshurst	d					08 03													09 02			
Ligh (Kent)	d					08 06													09 05			
Tonbridge ■4	a					08 11													09 10			
Erlswood (Surrey)	d													08 18								
Salfords	d													08 22								
Horley ■4	d				07 40			←						08 25				08 38				
Gatwick Airport ■10 ✈	a	07 27	07 30		07 42		07 41	07 42	07 45	08 04	08 00	08 11	08 15	08 28	08 30		08 33	08 40		08 41	08 45	08 48
	d				07 43		07 42	07 43		08 05		08 12		08 29				08 41		08 42		08 49
Three Bridges ■15	a				→		07 46	07 48		08 10		08 16		08 33				08 46		08 46		
	d						07 47	07 48		08 10		08 17		08 34				08 46		08 47		
Crawley	d							07 52						08 37				08 50				
field	d							07 54						08 40								
Faygate	d																					
Ittlehaven	d							08 01						08 46								
Horsham ■4	a							08 04						08 49				08 58				
Balcombe	d									08 16												
Haywards Heath	a						07 56			08 21		08 26								08 56		09 00
	d						07 56			08 22		08 26								08 56		09 00
Wlsfield	d									08 26												
Lwes ■4	a																					
Burgess Hill ■4	d						08 01			08 28		08 31								09 01		09 06
Hassocks ■4	d						08 05			08 31		08 35								09 05		
Preston Park	d									08 38												
Hove ■2	a																					09 18
Brighton ■10	a						08 14			08 43		08 45								09 15		

Table 186

Sundays

until 24 June

Bedford and London - Brighton

Network Diagram - see first Page of Table 186

		SN ◇1	SN 1 🚲	SN 1	FC 1	SN 1 🚲	SN ◇1 🚲	SN 1		SN 1 🚲	GW 1	GW 1	SN ◇1	SN 1	SN ◇1	SN ◇1		FC 1	SN 1 🚲	SN ◇1	SN ◇1	SN 1 🚲	SN ◇1	SN 1
London Victoria 15 ⊖	d	08 27	08 30			08 45	08 47			09 00			09 02		09 06				09 15	09 17	09 27	09 30	09 36	
Clapham Junction 10	d	08 33					08 53						09 08		09 12					09 23	09 33		09 42	
Bedford	d				07 10													07 49						
Luton 10	d				07 37													08 14						
Luton Airport Parkway 7 ✈	d				07 39													08 17						
St Albans City	d				07 51													08 29						
St Pancras International 15 ⊖	d				08 24													08 54						
Farringdon 3 ⊖	d				08 29													08 58						
City Thameslink 3	d																							
London Blackfriars 3 ⊖	d				08 34													09 04						
London Bridge 4 ⊖	d			08 37	08 41									09 05				09 11						09 37
New Cross Gate	d																							
Norwood Junction 2	d			08 48										09 16										09 48
East Croydon	a	08 42		08 54	08 55		09 02						09 17	09 20	09 22			09 25		09 32	09 42		09 52	09 54
	d	08 43		08 55	08 55		09 03						09 18	09 21	09 23			09 25		09 33	09 43		09 53	09 55
Purley 4	d			09 00									09 23	09 27										10 00
Coulsdon South	d			09 04										09 30										10 04
Merstham	d			09 09										09 36										10 09
Redhill	a	08 57		09 13									09 31	09 39							09 57			10 13
	d	08 57		09 13							09 20	09 21	09 32	09 40							09 57			10 13
Reigate	a										09 24													
Nutfield	d													09 44										
Godstone	d													09 50										
Edenbridge	d													09 55										
Penshurst	d													10 02										
Leigh (Kent)	d													10 05										
Tonbridge 4	a													10 10										
Earlswood (Surrey)	d			09 18																				10 18
Salfords	d			09 22																				10 22
Horley 4	d			09 25				←					09 38			←								10 25
Gatwick Airport 10 ✈	a	09 04	09 00	09 28	09 11	09 15	09 18	09 28		09 30		09 33	09 40		09 37	09 40		09 41	09 45	09 48	10 04	10 00		10 28
	d	09 05		09 29	09 12		09 19	09 29					09 41		09 39	09 41		09 42		09 49	10 05			10 29
Three Bridges 15	a	09 10		→	09 16			09 33					→			09 46		09 46			10 10			→
	d	09 10			09 17			09 34								09 46		09 47			10 10			
Crawley	d							09 37								09 50								
Ifield	d							09 40																
Faygate	d																							
Littlehaven	d							09 46																
Horsham 4	a							09 49								09 58								
Balcombe	d	09 16																			10 16			
Haywards Heath	a	09 21			09 26		09 30											09 56		10 00	10 21			
	d	09 22			09 26		09 30											09 56		10 00	10 22			
Wivelsfield	d	09 26					09 34														10 26			
Lewes 4	a						09 48																	
Burgess Hill 4	d	09 28			09 31													10 01		10 06	10 28			
Hassocks 4	d	09 31			09 35													10 05			10 31			
Preston Park	d	09 38																			10 38			
Hove 2	a																			10 18				
Brighton 10	a	09 43			09 45										10 03			10 15			10 43		10 27	

Table 186

Sundays
until 24 June

Bedford and London - Brighton

Network Diagram - see first Page of Table 186

		FC	SN	SN	SN	SN	GW	GW		SN	SN	SN	SN	FC	SN	SN		SN	SN	SN	SN	FC	SN	SN
		1	1	◇1	1	1	1	1		◇1	1	◇1	◇1	1	1	◇1		◇1	1	◇1	1	1	1	◇1
			🛒	🛒		🛒						🛒			🛒				🛒	🛒			🛒	🛒
London Victoria 15 ⊖	d		09 45	09 47		10 00				10 02		10 06			10 15	10 17		10 27	10 30	10 36			10 45	10 47
Clapham Junction 10	d			09 53						10 08		10 12				10 23		10 33		10 42				10 53
Bedford	d	08 19												08 49								09 19		
Luton 10	d	08 44												09 14								09 44		
Luton Airport Parkway 7 ✈	d	08 47												09 17								09 47		
St Albans City	d	08 59												09 29								09 59		
St Pancras International 15 ⊖	d	09 24												09 54								10 24		
Farringdon 3 ⊖	d	09 29												09 59								10 29		
City Thameslink 3	d																							
London Blackfriars 3 ⊖	d	09 34												10 04								10 34		
London Bridge 4 ⊖	d	09 41									10 05			10 11							10 37	10 41		
New Cross Gate	d																							
Norwood Junction 2	d										10 16										10 48			
East Croydon 🚋	a	09 55		10 02						10 17	10 20	10 22		10 25		10 32		10 42		10 52	10 54	10 55		11 02
	d	09 55		10 03						10 18	10 21	10 23		10 26		10 33		10 43		10 53	10 55	10 55		11 03
Purley 4	d									10 23	10 27										11 00			
Coulsdon South	d										10 30										11 04			
Merstham	d										10 36										11 09			
Redhill	a									10 31	10 39							10 57			11 13			
	d						10 19	10 21		10 32	10 40							10 57			11 13			
Reigate	a						10 23																	
Nutfield	d										10 44													
Godstone	d										10 50													
Edenbridge	d										10 55													
Penshurst	d										11 02													
Leigh (Kent)	d										11 05													
Tonbridge 4	a										11 10													
Earlswood (Surrey)	d																				11 18			
Salfords	d																				11 22			
Horley 4	d				←					10 38			←								11 25			
Gatwick Airport 10 ✈	a	10 11	10 15	10 18	10 28	10 30		10 33		10 40		10 37	10 40	10 41	10 45	10 48		11 04	11 00		11 28	11 11	11 15	11 18
	d	10 12		10 19	10 29					10 41		10 39	10 41	10 42		10 49		11 05			11 29	11 12		11 19
Three Bridges 15	a	10 16			10 33					→			10 46	10 46				11 10			→	11 16		
	d	10 17			10 34								10 46	10 47				11 10				11 17		
Crawley	d				10 37								10 50											
Ifield	d				10 40																			
Faygate	d																							
Littlehaven	d				10 46																			
Horsham 4	a				10 49								10 58											
Balcombe	d																	11 16						
Haywards Heath	a	10 26		10 30										10 56		11 00		11 21				11 26		11 30
	d	10 26		10 30										10 56		11 00		11 22				11 26		11 30
Wivelsfield	d			10 34														11 26						11 34
Lewes 4	a			10 48																				11 48
Burgess Hill 4	d	10 31												11 01		11 06		11 28				11 31		
Hassocks 4	d	10 35												11 05				11 31				11 35		
Preston Park	d																	11 38						
Hove 2	a															11 18								
Brighton 10	a	10 45										11 03		11 15				11 43		11 27		11 45		

Table 186

Sundays
until 24 June

Bedford and London - Brighton

Network Diagram - see first Page of Table 186

		SN	SN	GW	GW	SN	SN	SN	SN	FC	SN	SN	SN	SN	SN	SN	FC	SN	SN	SN	SN	GW
		1	1	1	1	◇1	1	◇1	◇1	1	1	◇1	◇1	1	◇1	1	1	1	◇1	1	1	1
			🛒			🛒		🛒	🛒		🛒			🛒	🛒			🛒	🛒		🛒	
London Victoria 15 ⊖	d		11 00			11 02		11 06			11 15	11 17	11 27	11 30	11 36			11 45	11 47		12 00	
Clapham Junction 10	d					11 08		11 12				11 23	11 33		11 42				11 53			
Bedford	d									09 49							10 19					
Luton 10	d									10 14							10 44					
Luton Airport Parkway 7 ✈	d									10 17							10 47					
St Albans City	d									10 29							10 59					
St Pancras International 15 ⊖	d									10 54							11 24					
Farringdon 3 ⊖	d									10 58							11 29					
City Thameslink 3	d																					
London Blackfriars 3 ⊖	d									11 04							11 34					
London Bridge 4 ⊖	d						11 05			11 11						11 37	11 41					
New Cross Gate	d																					
Norwood Junction 2	d						11 16									11 48						
East Croydon	a					11 17	11 20	11 22		11 25		11 32	11 42		11 52	11 54	11 55		12 02			
	d					11 18	11 21	11 23		11 25		11 33	11 43		11 53	11 55	11 55		12 03			
Purley 4	d					11 23	11 27									12 00						
Coulsdon South	d						11 30									12 04						
Merstham	d						11 36									12 09						
Redhill	a					11 31	11 39						11 57			12 13						
	d			11 20	11 21	11 32	11 40						11 57			12 13						12 19
Reigate	a			11 24																		12 23
Nutfield	d						11 44															
Godstone	d						11 50															
Edenbridge	d						11 55															
Penshurst	d						12 02															
Leigh (Kent)	d						12 05															
Tonbridge 4	a						12 10															
Earlswood (Surrey)	d															12 18						
Salfords	d															12 22						
Horley 4	d	←				11 38			←							12 25				←		
Gatwick Airport 10 ✈	a	11 28	11 30		11 33	11 40		11 37	11 40	11 41	11 45	11 48	12 04	12 00		12 28	12 11	12 15	12 18	12 28	12 30	
	d	11 29				11 41		11 39	11 41	11 42		11 49	12 05			12 29	12 12		12 19	12 29		
Three Bridges 15	a	11 33				→			11 46	11 46			12 10			→	12 16			12 33		
	d	11 34							11 46	11 47			12 10				12 17			12 34		
Crawley	d	11 37							11 50											12 37		
Ifield	d	11 40																		12 40		
Faygate	d																					
Littlehaven	d	11 46																		12 46		
Horsham 4	a	11 49							11 58											12 49		
Balcombe	d												12 16									
Haywards Heath	a									11 56		12 00	12 21				12 26		12 30			
	d									11 56		12 00	12 22				12 26		12 30			
Wivelsfield	d												12 26						12 34			
Lewes 4	a																		12 48			
Burgess Hill 4	d									12 01		12 06	12 28				12 31					
Hassocks 4	d									12 05			12 31				12 35					
Preston Park	d												12 38									
Hove 2	a											12 18										
Brighton 10	a							12 03		12 15			12 43		12 27		12 45					

Table 186

Sundays

until 24 June

Bedford and London - Brighton

Network Diagram - see first Page of Table 186

		GW	SN	SN	SN	SN	FC	SN		SN	SN	SN	SN	SN	FC	SN		SN	SN	SN	GW	GW	SN	SN	
		1	◇1	1	◇1	◇1	1	1		◇1	◇1	1	◇1	1	1	1		◇1	1	1	1	1	◇1	1	
					🛒			🛒				🛒	🛒			🛒		🛒		🛒					
London Victoria 15 ⊖	d		12 02		12 06			12 15		12 17	12 27	12 30	12 36			12 45		12 47		13 00			13 02		
Clapham Junction 10	d		12 08		12 12					12 23	12 33		12 42					12 53					13 08		
Bedford	d						10 49								11 19										
Luton 10	d						11 14								11 44										
Luton Airport Parkway 7 ✈	d						11 17								11 47										
St Albans City	d						11 29								11 59										
St Pancras International 15 ⊖	d						11 54								12 24										
Farringdon 3 ⊖	d						11 58								12 29										
City Thameslink 3	d																								
London Blackfriars 3 ⊖	d						12 04								12 34										
London Bridge 4 ⊖	d			12 05			12 11							12 37	12 41									13 05	
New Cross Gate	d																								
Norwood Junction 2	d			12 16										12 48										13 16	
East Croydon	a		12 17	12 20	12 22		12 25			12 32	12 42		12 52	12 54	12 55			13 02					13 17	13 20	
	d		12 18	12 21	12 23		12 25			12 33	12 43		12 53	12 55	12 55			13 03					13 18	13 21	
Purley 4	d		12 23	12 27										13 00									13 23	13 27	
Coulsdon South	d			12 30										13 04										13 30	
Merstham	d			12 36										13 09										13 36	
Redhill	a		12 31	12 39							12 57			13 13									13 31	13 39	
	d	12 21	12 32	12 40							12 57			13 13							13 20	13 21	13 32	13 40	
Reigate	a																				13 24				
Nutfield	d			12 44																				13 44	
Godstone	d			12 50																				13 50	
Edenbridge	d			12 55																				13 55	
Penshurst	d			13 02																				14 02	
Leigh (Kent)	d			13 05																				14 05	
Tonbridge 4	a			13 10																				14 10	
Earlswood (Surrey)	d													13 18											
Salfords	d													13 22											
Horley 4	d		12 38			←								13 25					←				13 38		
Gatwick Airport 10 ✈	a	12 33	12 40		12 37	12 40	12 41	12 45		12 48	13 04	13 00		13 28	13 11	13 15		13 18	13 28	13 30		13 33	13 40		
	d		12 41		12 39	12 41	12 42			12 49	13 05			13 29	13 12			13 19	13 29				13 41		
Three Bridges 15	a		→			12 46	12 46				13 10			→	13 16				13 33				→		
	d					12 46	12 47				13 10				13 17				13 34						
Crawley	d					12 50													13 37						
Ifield	d																		13 40						
Faygate	d																								
Littlehaven	d																		13 46						
Horsham 4	a					12 58													13 49						
Balcombe	d										13 16														
Haywards Heath	a						12 56			13 00	13 21				13 26			13 30							
	d						12 56			13 00	13 22				13 26			13 30							
Wivelsfield	d										13 26							13 34							
Lewes 4	a																	13 48							
Burgess Hill 4	d						13 01			13 06	13 28				13 31										
Hassocks 4	d						13 05				13 31				13 35										
Preston Park	d										13 38														
Hove 2	a									13 18															
Brighton 10	a				13 03		13 15				13 43		13 27		13 45										

Table 186

Bedford and London - Brighton

Sundays

until 24 June

Network Diagram - see first Page of Table 186

		SN	SN	FC	SN	SN	SN	SN		SN	SN	FC	SN	SN	SN	SN		GW	GW	SN	SN	SN	SN	FC
		◇**1** trolley	◇**1**	**1**	**1** trolley	◇**1**	◇**1**	**1** trolley		◇**1** trolley	**1**	**1**	**1** trolley	◇**1** trolley	**1**	**1** trolley		**1**	**1**	◇**1**	**1**	◇**1** trolley	◇**1**	**1**
London Victoria 15 ⊖	d	13 06			13 15	13 17	13 27	13 30		13 36			13 45	13 47		14 00				14 02		14 06		
Clapham Junction 10	d	13 12				13 23	13 33			13 42				13 53						14 08		14 12		
Bedford	d			11 49								12 19												12 49
Luton 10	d			12 14								12 44												13 14
Luton Airport Parkway 7 ✈	d			12 17								12 47												13 17
St Albans City	d			12 29								12 59												13 29
St Pancras International 15 ⊖	d			12 54								13 24												13 54
Farringdon 3 ⊖	d			12 58								13 29												13 58
City Thameslink 3	d																							
London Blackfriars 3 ⊖	d			13 04								13 34												14 04
London Bridge 4 ⊖	d			13 11							13 37	13 41									14 05			14 11
New Cross Gate	d																							
Norwood Junction 2	d										13 48										14 16			
East Croydon	a	13 22		13 25		13 32	13 42			13 52	13 54	13 55		14 02						14 17	14 20	14 22		14 25
	d	13 23		13 25		13 33	13 43			13 53	13 55	13 55		14 03						14 18	14 21	14 23		14 25
Purley 4	d										14 00									14 23	14 27			
Coulsdon South	d										14 04										14 30			
Merstham	d										14 09										14 36			
Redhill	a						13 57				14 13									14 31	14 39			
	d						13 57				14 13							14 19	14 21	14 32	14 40			
Reigate	a																	14 23						
Nutfield	d																				14 44			
Godstone	d																				14 50			
Edenbridge	d																				14 55			
Penshurst	d																				15 02			
Leigh (Kent)	d																				15 05			
Tonbridge 4	a																				15 10			
Earlswood (Surrey)	d										14 18													
Salfords	d										14 22													
Horley 4	d		←								14 25				←					14 38			←	
Gatwick Airport 10 ✈	a	13 37	13 40	13 41	13 45	13 48	14 04	14 00			14 28	14 11	14 15	14 18	14 28	14 30			14 33	14 40		14 37	14 40	14 41
	d	13 39	13 41	13 42		13 49	14 05				14 29	14 12		14 19	14 29					14 41		14 39	14 41	14 42
Three Bridges 15	a		13 46	13 46			14 10				→	14 16			14 33					→			14 46	14 46
	d		13 46	13 47			14 10					14 17			14 34								14 46	14 47
Crawley	d		13 50												14 37								14 50	
Ifield	d														14 40									
Faygate	d																							
Littlehaven	d														14 46									
Horsham 4	a		13 58												14 49								14 58	
Balcombe	d						14 16																	
Haywards Heath	a			13 56		14 00	14 21					14 26		14 30										14 56
	d			13 56		14 00	14 22					14 26		14 30										14 56
Wivelsfield	d						14 26							14 34										
Lewes 4	a													14 48										
Burgess Hill 4	d			14 01		14 06	14 28					14 31												15 01
Hassocks 4	d			14 05			14 31					14 35												15 05
Preston Park	d						14 38																	
Hove 2	a					14 18																		
Brighton 10	a	14 03		14 15			14 43			14 27		14 45										15 03		15 15

Table 186

Sundays
until 24 June

Bedford and London - Brighton

Network Diagram - see first Page of Table 186

		SN	SN	SN	SN	SN	SN	FC		SN	SN	SN	SN	GW	GW	SN		SN	SN	SN	FC	SN	SN	SN
		1	◇1	◇1	1	◇1	1	1		1	◇1	1	1	1	1	◇1		1	◇1	◇1	1	1	◇1	◇1
		🛒			🛒	🛒				🛒	🛒		🛒						🛒			🛒		
London Victoria 15 ⊖	d	14 15	14 17	14 27	14 30	14 36				14 45	14 47		15 00			15 02			15 06			15 15	15 17	15 27
Clapham Junction 10	d		14 23	14 33		14 42					14 53					15 08			15 12				15 23	15 33
Bedford	d							13 19													13 49			
Luton 10	d							13 44													14 14			
Luton Airport Parkway 7 ✈	d							13 47													14 17			
St Albans City	d							13 59													14 29			
St Pancras International 15 ⊖	d							14 24													14 54			
Farringdon 3 ⊖	d							14 29													14 58			
City Thameslink 3	d																							
London Blackfriars 3 ⊖	d							14 34													15 04			
London Bridge 4 ⊖	d						14 37	14 41										15 05			15 11			
New Cross Gate	d																							
Norwood Junction 2	d						14 48											15 16						
East Croydon 🚌	a		14 32	14 42		14 52	14 54	14 55			15 02					15 17		15 20	15 22		15 25		15 32	15 42
	d		14 33	14 43		14 53	14 55	14 55			15 03					15 18		15 21	15 23		15 25		15 32	15 43
Purley 4	d						15 00									15 23		15 27						
Coulsdon South	d						15 04											15 30						
Merstham	d						15 09											15 36						
Redhill	a			14 57			15 13									15 31		15 39						15 57
	d			14 57			15 13							15 20	15 21	15 32		15 40						15 57
Reigate	a													15 24										
Nutfield	d																	15 44						
Godstone	d																	15 50						
Edenbridge	d																	15 55						
Penshurst	d																	16 02						
Leigh (Kent)	d																	16 05						
Tonbridge 4	a																	16 10						
Earlswood (Surrey)	d						15 18																	
Salfords	d						15 22																	
Horley 4	d						15 25					←				15 38				←				
Gatwick Airport 10 ✈	a	14 45	14 48	15 04	15 00		15 28	15 11		15 15	15 18	15 28	15 30		15 33	15 40			15 37	15 40	15 41	15 45	15 48	16 04
	d		14 49	15 05			15 29	15 12			15 19	15 29				15 41			15 39	15 41	15 42		15 49	16 05
Three Bridges 15	a			15 10			→	15 16				15 33				→				15 46	15 46			16 10
	d			15 10				15 17				15 34								15 46	15 47			16 10
Crawley	d											15 37								15 50				
Ifield	d											15 40												
Faygate	d																							
Littlehaven	d											15 46												
Horsham 4	a											15 49								15 58				
Balcombe	d			15 16																				16 16
Haywards Heath	a		15 00	15 21				15 26			15 30										15 56		16 00	16 21
	d		15 00	15 22				15 26			15 30										15 56		16 00	16 22
Wivelsfield	d			15 26							15 34													16 26
Lewes 4	a										15 48													
Burgess Hill 4	d		15 06	15 28				15 31													16 01		16 06	16 28
Hassocks 4	d			15 31				15 35													16 05			16 31
Preston Park	d			15 38																				16 38
Hove 2	a		15 18																				16 18	
Brighton 10	a			15 43		15 27		15 45											16 03		16 15			16 43

Table 186

Sundays

until 24 June

Bedford and London - Brighton

Network Diagram - see first Page of Table 186

		SN 1	SN ◇1	SN 1	FC 1	SN 1	SN ◇1	SN 1	SN 1	GW 1	GW 1	SN ◇1	SN 1	SN ◇1	SN ◇1	FC 1	SN 1	SN ◇1	SN ◇1	SN 1	SN ◇1	SN 1
London Victoria 15 ⊖	d	15 30	15 36			15 45	15 47		16 00			16 02		16 06			16 15	16 17	16 27	16 30	16 36	
Clapham Junction 10	d		15 42				15 53					16 08		16 12				16 23	16 33		16 42	
Bedford	d				14 19											14 49						
Luton 10	d				14 44											15 14						
Luton Airport Parkway 7 ✈	d				14 47											15 17						
St Albans City	d				14 59											15 29						
St Pancras International 15 ⊖	d				15 24											15 54						
Farringdon 3 ⊖	d				15 29											15 58						
City Thameslink 3	d																					
London Blackfriars 3 ⊖	d				15 34											16 04						
London Bridge 4 ⊖	d			15 37	15 41								16 05			16 11						16 37
New Cross Gate	d																					
Norwood Junction 2	d			15 48									16 16									16 48
East Croydon	a		15 52	15 54	15 55		16 02					16 17	16 20	16 22		16 25		16 32	16 42		16 52	16 54
	d		15 53	15 55	15 55		16 03					16 18	16 21	16 23		16 25		16 33	16 43		16 53	16 55
Purley 4	d			16 00								16 23	16 27									17 00
Coulsdon South	d			16 04									16 30									17 04
Merstham	d			16 09									16 36									17 09
Redhill	a			16 13								16 31	16 39						16 57			17 13
	d			16 13						16 19	16 21	16 32	16 40						16 57			17 13
Reigate	a									16 23												
Nutfield	d												16 44									
Godstone	d												16 50									
Edenbridge	d												16 55									
Penshurst	d												17 02									
Leigh (Kent)	d												17 05									
Tonbridge 4	a												17 10									
Earlswood (Surrey)	d			16 18																		17 18
Salfords	d			16 22																		17 22
Horley 4	d			16 25								16 38										17 25
Gatwick Airport 10 ✈	a	16 00		16 28	16 11	16 15	16 18	← 16 28	16 30		16 33	16 40		16 37	← 16 40	16 41	16 45	16 48	17 04	17 00		17 28
	d			16 29	16 12		16 19	16 29				16 41		16 39	16 41	16 42		16 49	17 05			17 29
Three Bridges 15	a			→	16 16			16 33				→			16 46	16 46			17 10			→
	d				16 17			16 34							16 46	16 47			17 10			
Crawley	d							16 37							16 50							
Ifield	d							16 40														
Faygate	d																					
Littlehaven	d							16 46														
Horsham 4	a							16 49							16 58							
Balcombe	d																		17 16			
Haywards Heath	a				16 26		16 30									16 56		17 00	17 21			
	d				16 26		16 30									16 56		17 00	17 22			
Wivelsfield	d						16 34												17 26			
Lewes 4	a						16 48															
Burgess Hill 4	d				16 31											17 01		17 06	17 28			
Hassocks 4	d				16 35											17 05			17 31			
Preston Park	d																		17 38			
Hove 2	a																	17 18				
Brighton 10	a		16 27		16 45									17 03		17 15			17 43	17 27		

Table 186

Sundays

until 24 June

Bedford and London - Brighton

Network Diagram - see first Page of Table 186

		FC	SN	SN	SN	SN	GW	GW		SN	SN	SN	SN	FC	SN	SN		SN	SN	SN	SN	FC	SN	SN
		1	1	◇1	1	1	1	1		◇1	1	◇1	◇1	1	1	◇1		◇1	1	◇1	1	1	1	◇1
			🛒	🛒		🛒						🛒			🛒				🛒	🛒			🛒	🛒
London Victoria 15 ⊖	d		16 45	16 47		17 00				17 02		17 06			17 15	17 17		17 27	17 30	17 36			17 45	17 47
Clapham Junction 10	d			16 53						17 08		17 12				17 23		17 33		17 42				17 53
Bedford	d	15 19												15 49								16 19		
Luton 10	d	15 44												16 14								16 44		
Luton Airport Parkway 7 ✈	d	15 47												16 17								16 47		
St Albans City	d	15 59												16 29								16 59		
St Pancras International 15 ⊖	d	16 24												16 54								17 24		
Farringdon 3 ⊖	d	16 29												16 58								17 29		
City Thameslink 3	d																							
London Blackfriars 3 ⊖	d	16 34												17 04								17 34		
London Bridge 4 ⊖	d	16 41									17 05			17 11							17 37	17 41		
New Cross Gate	d																							
Norwood Junction 2	d										17 16										17 48			
East Croydon	a	16 55		17 02						17 17	17 20	17 22		17 25		17 32		17 42		17 52	17 54	17 55		18 02
	d	16 55		17 03						17 18	17 21	17 23		17 25		17 33		17 43		17 53	17 55	17 55		18 03
Purley 4	d									17 23	17 27										18 00			
Coulsdon South	d										17 30										18 04			
Merstham	d										17 36										18 09			
Redhill	a									17 31	17 39							17 57			18 13			
	d						17 20	17 21		17 32	17 40							17 57			18 13			
Reigate	a						17 24																	
Nutfield	d										17 44													
Godstone	d										17 50													
Edenbridge	d										17 55													
Penshurst	d										18 02													
Leigh (Kent)	d										18 05													
Tonbridge 4	a										18 10													
Earlswood (Surrey)	d																				18 18			
Salfords	d																				18 22			
Horley 4	d				←					17 38			←								18 25			
Gatwick Airport 10 ✈	a	17 11	17 15	17 18	17 28	17 30		17 33		17 40		17 37	17 40	17 41	17 45	17 48		18 04	18 00		18 28	18 11	18 15	18 18
	d	17 12		17 19	17 29					17 41		17 39	17 41	17 42		17 49		18 05			18 29	18 12		18 19
Three Bridges 15	a	17 16			17 33					→			17 46	17 46				18 10			→	18 16		
	d	17 17			17 34								17 46	17 47				18 10				18 17		
Crawley	d				17 37								17 50											
Ifield	d				17 40																			
Faygate	d																							
Littlehaven	d				17 46																			
Horsham 4	a				17 49								17 58											
Balcombe	d																	18 16						
Haywards Heath	a	17 26		17 30										17 56		18 00		18 21				18 26		18 30
	d	17 26		17 30										17 56		18 00		18 22				18 26		18 30
Wivelsfield	d			17 34														18 26						18 34
Lewes 4	a			17 48																				18 48
Burgess Hill 4	d	17 31												18 01		18 06		18 28				18 31		
Hassocks 4	d	17 35												18 05				18 31				18 35		
Preston Park	d																	18 38						
Hove 2	a															18 18								
Brighton 10	a	17 45										18 03		18 15				18 43		18 27		18 45		

Table 186

Sundays

until 24 June

Bedford and London - Brighton

Network Diagram - see first Page of Table 186

		SN	SN	GW	GW	SN	SN	SN	SN	FC	SN	SN	SN	SN	SN	SN	FC	SN	SN	SN	SN	GW
		1	1	1	1	◇1	1	◇1	◇1	1	1	◇1	◇1	1	◇1	1	1	1	◇1	1	1	1
			🛒					🛒			🛒			🛒	🛒			🛒	🛒		🛒	
London Victoria 15 ⊖	d		18 00			18 02		18 06			18 15	18 17	18 27	18 30	18 36			18 45	18 47		19 00	
Clapham Junction 10	d					18 08		18 12				18 23	18 33		18 42				18 53			
Bedford	d									16 49							17 19					
Luton 10	d									17 14							17 44					
Luton Airport Parkway 7 ✈	d									17 17							17 47					
St Albans City	d									17 29							17 59					
St Pancras International 15 ⊖	d									17 54							18 24					
Farringdon 3 ⊖	d									17 58							18 29					
City Thameslink 3	d																					
London Blackfriars 3 ⊖	d									18 04							18 34					
London Bridge 4 ⊖	d						18 05			18 11						18 37	18 41					
New Cross Gate	d																					
Norwood Junction 2	d						18 16									18 48						
East Croydon	a					18 17	18 20	18 22		18 25		18 32	18 42		18 52	18 54	18 55		19 02			
	d					18 18	18 21	18 23		18 25		18 33	18 43		18 53	18 55	18 55		19 03			
Purley 4	d					18 23	18 27									19 00						
Coulsdon South	d						18 30									19 04						
Merstham	d						18 36									19 09						
Redhill	a					18 31	18 39						18 57			19 13						
	d			18 19	18 21	18 32	18 40						18 57			19 13						19 20
Reigate	a			18 23																		19 24
Nutfield	d						18 44															
Godstone	d						18 50															
Edenbridge	d						18 55															
Penshurst	d						19 02															
Leigh (Kent)	d						19 05															
Tonbridge 4	a						19 10															
Earlswood (Surrey)	d															19 18						
Salfords	d															19 22						
Horley 4	d	←				18 38			←							19 25				←		
Gatwick Airport 10 ✈	a	18 28	18 30		18 34	18 40		18 37	18 40	18 41	18 45	18 48	19 04	19 00		19 28	19 11	19 15	19 18	19 28	19 30	
	d	18 29				18 41		18 39	18 41	18 42		18 49	19 05			19 29	19 12		19 19	19 29		
Three Bridges 15	a	18 33				→			18 46	18 46			19 10			→	19 16			19 33		
	d	18 34							18 46	18 47			19 10				19 17			19 34		
Crawley	d	18 37							18 50											19 37		
Ifield	d	18 40																		19 40		
Faygate	d																					
Littlehaven	d	18 46																		19 46		
Horsham 4	a	18 49							18 58											19 49		
Balcombe	d												19 16									
Haywards Heath	a									18 56		19 00	19 21				19 26		19 30			
	d									18 56		19 00	19 22				19 26		19 30			
Wivelsfield	d												19 26						19 34			
Lewes 4	a																		19 48			
Burgess Hill 4	d									19 01		19 06	19 28				19 31					
Hassocks 4	d									19 05			19 31				19 35					
Preston Park	d												19 38									
Hove 2	a											19 18										
Brighton 10	a							19 03		19 15			19 43		19 27		19 45					

Table 186

Sundays

until 24 June

Bedford and London - Brighton

Network Diagram - see first Page of Table 186

		GW	SN	SN	SN	SN	FC	SN		SN	SN	SN	SN	SN	FC	SN		SN	SN	SN	GW	GW	SN	SN
		1	◇1	1	◇1	◇1	1	1		◇1	◇1	1	◇1	1	1	1		◇1	1	1	1	1	◇1	1
					🛒													🛒						
London Victoria 15 ⊖	d		19 02		19 06			19 15		19 17	19 27	19 30	19 36			19 45		19 47		20 00			20 02	
Clapham Junction 10	d		19 08		19 12					19 23	19 33		19 42					19 53					20 08	
Bedford	d						17 49								18 19									
Luton 10	d						18 14								18 44									
Luton Airport Parkway 7 ✈	d						18 17								18 47									
St Albans City	d						18 29								18 59									
St Pancras International 15 ⊖	d						18 54								19 24									
Farringdon 3 ⊖	d						18 58								19 29									
City Thameslink 3	d																							
London Blackfriars 3 ⊖	d						19 04								19 34									
London Bridge 4 ⊖	d			19 05			19 11							19 37	19 41									20 05
New Cross Gate	d																							
Norwood Junction 2	d			19 16										19 48										20 16
East Croydon 🚋	a		19 17	19 20	19 22		19 25			19 32	19 42		19 52	19 54	19 55			20 02					20 17	20 20
	d		19 18	19 21	19 23		19 25			19 33	19 43		19 53	19 55	19 55			20 03					20 18	20 21
Purley 4	d		19 23	19 27										20 00									20 23	20 27
Coulsdon South	d			19 30										20 04										20 30
Merstham	d			19 36										20 09										20 36
Redhill	a		19 31	19 39							19 57			20 13									20 31	20 39
	d	19 21	19 32	19 40							19 57			20 13							20 19	20 21	20 32	20 40
Reigate	a																				20 23			
Nutfield	d			19 44																				20 44
Godstone	d			19 50																				20 50
Edenbridge	d			19 55																				20 55
Penshurst	d			20 02																				21 02
Leigh (Kent)	d			20 05																				21 05
Tonbridge 4	a			20 10																				21 10
Earlswood (Surrey)	d													20 18										
Salfords	d													20 22										
Horley 4	d		19 38			←								20 25					←				20 38	
Gatwick Airport 10 ✈	a	19 34	19 40		19 37	19 40	19 41	19 45		19 48	20 04	20 00		20 28	20 11	20 15		20 18	20 28	20 30		20 34	20 40	
	d		19 41		19 39	19 41	19 42			19 49	20 05			20 29	20 12			20 19	20 29				20 41	
Three Bridges 15	a		→			19 46	19 46				20 10			→	20 16				20 33				→	
	d					19 46	19 47				20 10				20 17				20 34					
Crawley	d					19 50													20 37					
Ifield	d																		20 40					
Faygate	d																							
Littlehaven	d																		20 46					
Horsham 4	a					19 58													20 49					
Balcombe	d										20 16													
Haywards Heath	a						19 56			20 00	20 21				20 26			20 30						
	d						19 56			20 00	20 22				20 26			20 30						
Wivelsfield	d										20 26							20 34						
Lewes 4	a																	20 48						
Burgess Hill 4	d						20 01			20 06	20 28				20 31									
Hassocks 4	d						20 05				20 31				20 35									
Preston Park	d										20 38													
Hove 2	a									20 18														
Brighton 10	a				20 03		20 15				20 43		20 27		20 45									

Table 186

Sundays
until 24 June

Bedford and London - Brighton

Network Diagram - see first Page of Table 186

		SN ◇1	SN ◇1	FC 1	SN 1	SN ◇1	SN ◇1	SN 1	SN ◇1	SN 1	FC 1	SN 1	SN ◇1	SN 1	SN 1	GW 1	GW 1	SN ◇1	SN 1	SN ◇1	SN ◇1	FC 1
London Victoria 15 ⊖	d	20 06			20 15	20 17	20 27	20 30	20 36			20 45	20 47		21 00			21 02		21 06		
Clapham Junction 10	d	20 12				20 23	20 33		20 42				20 53					21 08		21 12		
Bedford	d			18 49							19 19											19 49
Luton 10	d			19 14							19 44											20 14
Luton Airport Parkway 7 ✈	d			19 17							19 47											20 17
St Albans City	d			19 29							19 59											20 29
St Pancras International 15 ⊖	d			19 54							20 24											20 54
Farringdon 3 ⊖	d			19 58							20 29											20 58
City Thameslink 3	d																					
London Blackfriars 3 ⊖	d			20 04							20 34											21 04
London Bridge 4 ⊖	d			20 11						20 37	20 41								21 05			21 11
New Cross Gate	d																					
Norwood Junction 2	d									20 48									21 16			
East Croydon	a	20 22		20 25		20 32	20 42		20 52	20 54	20 55		21 02					21 17	21 20	21 22		21 25
	d	20 23		20 25		20 33	20 43		20 53	20 55	20 55		21 03					21 18	21 21	21 23		21 25
Purley 4	d									21 00								21 23	21 27			
Coulsdon South	d									21 04									21 30			
Merstham	d									21 09									21 36			
Redhill	a						20 57			21 13								21 31	21 39			
	d						20 57			21 13						21 20	21 21	21 32	21 40			
Reigate	a															21 24						
Nutfield	d																		21 44			
Godstone	d																		21 50			
Edenbridge	d																		21 55			
Penshurst	d																		22 02			
Leigh (Kent)	d																		22 05			
Tonbridge 4	a																		22 10			
Earlswood (Surrey)	d									21 18												
Salfords	d									21 22												
Horley 4	d		←							21 25				←				21 38			←	
Gatwick Airport 10 ✈	a	20 37	20 40	20 41	20 45	20 48	21 04	21 00		21 28	21 11	21 15	21 18	21 28	21 30		21 34	21 40		21 37	21 40	21 41
	d	20 39	20 41	20 42		20 49	21 05			21 29	21 12		21 19	21 29				21 41		21 39	21 41	21 42
Three Bridges 15	a		20 46	20 46			21 10			→	21 16			21 33				→			21 46	21 46
	d		20 46	20 47			21 10				21 17			21 34							21 46	21 47
Crawley	d		20 50											21 37							21 50	
Ifield	d													21 40								
Faygate	d																					
Littlehaven	d													21 46								
Horsham 4	a		20 58											21 49							21 58	
Balcombe	d						21 16															
Haywards Heath	a			20 56		21 00	21 21				21 26		21 30									21 56
	d			20 56		21 00	21 22				21 26		21 30									21 56
Wivelsfield	d						21 26						21 34									
Lewes 4	a												21 48									
Burgess Hill 4	d			21 01		21 06	21 28				21 31											22 01
Hassocks 4	d			21 05			21 31				21 35											22 05
Preston Park	d						21 38															
Hove 2	a					21 18																
Brighton 10	a	21 03		21 15			21 43		21 27		21 45									22 03		22 15

Table 186

Sundays

until 24 June

Bedford and London - Brighton

Network Diagram - see first Page of Table 186

		SN	SN	SN	SN	SN	FC	SN		SN	SN	SN	GW	GW	SN	SN		FC	SN	SN	SN	SN	SN	SN
		1	◇1	◇1	1	1	1	1		◇1	1	1	1	1	◇1	1		1	1	◇1	◇1	1	1	1
London Victoria 15 ⊖	d	21 15	21 17	21 27	21 30			21 45		21 47		22 00			22 02				22 15	22 17	22 27	22 30		
Clapham Junction 10	d		21 23	21 33						21 53					22 08					22 23	22 33			
Bedford	d						20 10											20 40						
Luton 10	d						20 37											21 07						
Luton Airport Parkway 7 ✈	d						20 39											21 09						
St Albans City	d						20 51											21 21						
St Pancras International 15 ⊖	d						21 24											21 54						
Farringdon 3 ⊖	d						21 29											21 59						
City Thameslink 3	d																							
London Blackfriars 3 ⊖	d						21 34											22 04						
London Bridge 4 ⊖	d					21 37	21 41									22 05		22 11						22 37
New Cross Gate	d																							
Norwood Junction 2	d					21 48										22 16								22 48
East Croydon	a		21 32	21 42		21 54	21 55			22 02					22 17	22 20		22 25		22 32	22 42			22 54
	d		21 33	21 43		21 55	21 55			22 03					22 18	22 21		22 25		22 33	22 43			22 55
Purley 4	d					22 00									22 23	22 27								23 00
Coulsdon South	d					22 04										22 30								23 04
Merstham	d					22 09										22 36								23 09
Redhill	a			21 57		22 13									22 31	22 39					22 57			23 13
	d			21 57		22 13							22 19	22 21	22 32	22 40					22 57		23 10	23 13
Reigate	a												22 23											
Nutfield	d															22 44							23 14	
Godstone	d															22 50							23 20	
Edenbridge	d															22 55							23 25	
Penshurst	d															23 02							23 32	
Leigh (Kent)	d															23 05							23 35	
Tonbridge 4	a															23 10							23 40	
Earlswood (Surrey)	d					22 18																		23 18
Salfords	d					22 22																		23 22
Horley 4	d					22 25					←				22 38									23 25
Gatwick Airport 10 ✈	a	21 45	21 48	22 04	22 00	22 28	22 11	22 15		22 18	22 28	22 30		22 33	22 40			22 41	22 45	22 48	23 04	23 00		23 28
	d		21 49	22 05		22 29	22 12			22 19	22 29				22 41			22 42		22 49	23 05			23 29
Three Bridges 15	a			22 10		→	22 16				22 33				22 46			22 46			23 10			→
	d			22 10			22 17				22 34				22 46			22 47			23 10			
Crawley	d										22 37				22 50									
Ifield	d										22 40													
Faygate	d																							
Littlehaven	d										22 46													
Horsham 4	a										22 49				22 58									
Balcombe	d			22 16																	23 16			
Haywards Heath	a		22 00	22 21			22 26			22 30								22 56		23 00	23 21			
	d		22 00	22 22			22 26			22 30								22 56		23 00	23 22			
Wivelsfield	d			22 26						22 34											23 26			
Lewes 4	a									22 48														
Burgess Hill 4	d		22 06	22 28			22 31											23 01		23 06	23 28			
Hassocks 4	d			22 31			22 35											23 05			23 31			
Preston Park	d			22 38																	23 38			
Hove 2	a		22 18																	23 21				
Brighton 10	a			22 43			22 45											23 15			23 42			

Table 186

Bedford and London - Brighton

Sundays

until 24 June

Network Diagram - see first Page of Table 186

		FC 1	SN 1	SN ◇1	SN 1	SN 1	GW 1	GW 1		SN 1	FC 1	SN 1	SN 1	SN ◇1	SN 1	SN ◇1		FC 1	SN 1	SN	FC 1	FC 1	FC 1
London Victoria 15 ⊖	d		22 45	22 47		23 00				23 04		23 15		23 17	23 30	23 32			23 45	23 47			
Clapham Junction 10	d			22 53						23 10				23 23		23 38				23 53			
Bedford	d	21 10									21 40							22 10			22 40	23 10	23 40
Luton 10	d	21 37									22 07							22 37			23 07	23 37	00 07
Luton Airport Parkway 7 ✈	d	21 39									22 09							22 39			23 09	23 39	00 09
St Albans City	d	21 51									22 21							22 51			23 21	23 51	00 21
St Pancras International 15 ⊖	d	22 24									22 54							23 24			23 54	00 24	00 54
Farringdon 3 ⊖	d	22 29									22 59							23 29			23 59	00 29	
City Thameslink 3	d																						
London Blackfriars 3 ⊖	d	22 34									23 04							23 34			00 05	00 35	01 05
London Bridge 4 ⊖	d	22 41									23 11							23 41			00 12	00 42	
New Cross Gate	d																						
Norwood Junction 2	d																						
East Croydon	a	22 55		23 03						23 22	23 25			23 37		23 52		23 56		00 06	00 26	00 56	01 31
	d	22 55		23 03						23 22	23 25			23 38		23 53		23 57			00 26	00 57	01 32
Purley 4	d									23 29													
Coulsdon South	d									23 33													
Merstham	d									23 38													
Redhill	a									23 42						00 05							
	d						23 20	23 21		23 42						00 05							
Reigate	a						23 24																
Nutfield	d																						
Godstone	d																						
Edenbridge	d																						
Penshurst	d																						
Leigh (Kent)	d																						
Tonbridge 4	a																						
Earlswood (Surrey)	d																						
Salfords	d																						
Horley 4	d				←					23 50			←										
Gatwick Airport 10 ✈	a	23 11	23 15	23 18	23 28	23 30		23 34		23 54	23 41	23 50	23 54	23 59	00 05	00 14		00 18	00 20		00 48	01 18	01 51
	d	23 12		23 19	23 29					23 55	23 42		23 55	00 01		00 15		00 20			00 49	01 22	01 52
Three Bridges 15	a	23 16			23 33					→	23 46		00 01	00 05		00 19		00 25			00 54	01 28	01 58
	d	23 17			23 34						23 47		00 01	00 06		00 20							
Crawley	d				23 37								00 05										
Ifield	d				23 40								00 07										
Faygate	d																						
Littlehaven	d				23 46								00 14										
Horsham 4	a				23 49								00 17										
Balcombe	d															00 26							
Haywards Heath	a	23 26		23 30							23 56			00 15		00 31							
	d	23 26		23 30							23 56			00 15		00 31							
Wivelsfield	d			23 34												00 35							
Lewes 4	a			23 48																			
Burgess Hill 4	d	23 31									00 02			00 20		00 37							
Hassocks 4	d	23 35									00 06					00 41							
Preston Park	d															00 48							
Hove 2	a													00 31									
Brighton 10	a	23 45									00 16					00 52							

Table 186

Sundays

1 July to 9 September

Bedford and London - Brighton

Network Diagram - see first Page of Table 186

		SN	SN	FC	SN	SN	SN	SN		SN	GW	SN	FC	SN	SN	SN		SN	SN	FC	SN	GW	SN
		◇1	◇1	1	1	◇1	1	1		1	1	1	1	1	1	1		1	◇1	1	1	1	◇1
																							A
London Victoria 15 ⊖	d	23p02	23p06		23p10	23p17		23p30				23p32		23p45	23p47	23p49		00 02	00 05		00 14		00 25
Clapham Junction 10	d	23p08	23p12		23p16	23p23						23p38			23p53	23p56			00 11		00 20		00 31
Bedford	d			21p52									22p16							22p42			
Luton 10	d			22p16									22p40							23p06			
Luton Airport Parkway 7 ✈	d			22p18									22p42							23p09			
St Albans City	d			22p30									22p54							23p21			
St Pancras International 15 ⊖	d			22p54									23p24							23p54			
Farringdon 3 ⊖	d			22p59									23p29							23p59			
City Thameslink 3	d																						
London Blackfriars 3 ⊖	d			23p05									23p35							00 05			
London Bridge 4 ⊖	d			23p12									23p42							00 12			
New Cross Gate	d																						
Norwood Junction 2	d																						
East Croydon	a	23p17	23p22	23p24	23p27	23p32						23p52	23p56		00 05	00 09			00 24	00 26	00 31		00 40
	d	23p18	23p23	23p25	23p28	23p33						23p52	23p57		00 06				00 24	00 27	00 32		00 41
Purley 4	d				23p33										00 12						00 37		00 51
Coulsdon South	d				23p37										00 15						00 41		
Merstham	d				23p42										00 21						00 47		
Redhill	a	23p30			23p46							00 03			00 24						00 50		01 00
	d	23p31			23p46					23p55	00 03	00 05			00 25						00 51	00 54	01 00
Reigate	a																						
Nutfield	d																						
Godstone	d																						
Edenbridge	d									00 06													
Penshurst	d																						
Leigh (Kent)	d																						
Tonbridge 4	a									00 15													
Earlswood (Surrey)	d				23p49																		
Salfords	d				23p52																		
Horley 4	d				23p56		←								00 31						00 57		01 07
Gatwick Airport 10 ✈	a	23p38		23p40	23p58	23p49	23p58	00 05			00 10	00 14	00 18	00 20	00 33			00 38	00 42	00 48	00 59	01 02	01 09
	d	23p39		23p41	23p59	23p50	23p59					00 15	00 19		00 34				00 43	00 49	01 00		01 11
Three Bridges 15	a	23p44		23p47	→	23p54	00 04					00 20	00 24		00 39				00 48	00 54	01 05		01 15
	d	23p44		23p47		23p55	00 04					00 20			00 39				00 48				
Crawley	d						00 07								00 43								
Ifield	d						00 10								00 46								
Faygate	d																						
Littlehaven	d						00 16								00 52								
Horsham 4	a						00 19								00 55								
Balcombe	d			23p53								00 28											
Haywards Heath	a	23p53	23p46	23p58		00 04						00 34							00 58				
	d	23p53	23p46	23p59		00 05						00 35							01 02 / 01 06				
Wivelsfield	d	23p57		00 03								00 39											
Lewes 4	a																		01 20				
Burgess Hill 4	d	23p59		00 05		00 10						00 41											
Hassocks 4	d	00 03		00 08								00 44											
Preston Park	d	00 09		00 15								00 51											
Hove 2	a					00 23																	
Brighton 10	a	00 15	00 01	00 19								00 55							01s16				

A 29 July, 5 August, 12 August, 2 September, 9 September

Table 186

Bedford and London - Brighton

Sundays

1 July to 9 September

Network Diagram - see first Page of Table 186

			SN	SN	FC	SN	SN	FC	SN	SN	SN	SN	SN	SN	SN	SN	SN	SN	SN	SN	SN	SN	SN
			1	◇1	1	◇1	1	1	◇1	1	1	1	1	1	1	1	1	1	1	1	◇1	1	1
				A		A			A														
																						🚲	🚲
London Victoria 15	⊖	d	00 30	00 40			01 00		01 30	02 00	03 00	03 30	04 00	04 30	05 00	05 02	05 15	05 30	05 45		05 47	06 00	06 15
Clapham Junction 10		d		00 46			01 08		01 36	02 08	03 08		04 08			05 08					05 53		
Bedford		d			23p12			23p42															
Luton 10		d			23p36			00 06															
Luton Airport Parkway 7	✈	d			23p39			00 09															
St Albans City		d			23p51			00 21															
St Pancras International 15	⊖	d			00 24			00 54															
Farringdon 3	⊖	d			00 29																		
City Thameslink 3		d																					
London Blackfriars 3	⊖	d			00 35			01 05															
London Bridge 4	⊖	d			00 42																		
New Cross Gate		d																					
Norwood Junction 2		d																					
East Croydon	🚋	a		00 55	00 56		01 21	01 31	01 45	02 21	03 21		04 21			05 21					06 05		
		d		00 55	00 57		01 22	01 32	01 46	02 22	03 22		04 21			05 23					06 06		
Purley 4		d					01 27		01 51	02 27	03 27		04 26			05 28							
Coulsdon South		d																					
Merstham		d																					
Redhill		a							02 00												06 18		
		d							02 00												06 19		
Reigate		a																					
Nutfield		d																					
Godstone		d																					
Edenbridge		d																					
Penshurst		d																					
Leigh (Kent)		d																					
Tonbridge 4		a																					
Earlswood (Surrey)		d																					
Salfords		d																					
Horley 4		d					01 43		02 07	02 42	03 42		04 42								06 25		
Gatwick Airport 10	✈	a	01 05	01 12	01 18		01 46	01 51	02 09	02 44	03 44	04 05	04 45	05 05	05 35	05 44	05 50	06 05	06 20		06 31	06 35	06 47
		d		01 13	01 22		01 48	01 52	02 11	02 46	03 46		04 46			05 45				06 29	06 32		
Three Bridges 15		a		01 17	01 28		01 52	01 58	02 15	03 00	04 00		04 54			05 50				06 33	06 36		
		d		01 17			01 53		02 16				04 54			05 50				06 40	06 36		
Crawley		d																		06 43			
Ifield		d																		06 46			
Faygate		d																					
Littlehaven		d																		06 52			
Horsham 4		a																		06 56			
Balcombe		d																					
Haywards Heath		a		01 26			02 06		02 25				05 06			05 59					06 47		
		d		01 31		01 35	02 06		02 25				05 07			06 00					06 47		
Wivelsfield		d																			06 51		
Lewes 4		a				01s49																	
Burgess Hill 4		d																			06 53		
Hassocks 4		d																			06 57		
Preston Park		d																			07 03		
Hove 2		a																					
Brighton 10		a		01s45			02 23		02 40				05 21			06 18					07 08		

A 29 July, 5 August, 12 August, 2 September, 9 September

Table 186

Sundays

1 July to 9 September

Bedford and London - Brighton

Network Diagram - see first Page of Table 186

		GW 1	SN 1	SN ◇1	SN 1	GW 1	SN 1	GW 1	SN ◇1	SN 1	FC 1 A	SN ◇1	SN 1	SN ◇1	SN 1	FC 1	SN 1	SN 1	SN 1	GW 1	GW 1	SN ◇1
London Victoria 15 ⊖	d		06 30	06 32	06 45		07 00		07 02				07 15	07 27	07 30		07 45		08 00			08 02
Clapham Junction 10	d			06 38					07 08					07 33								08 08
Bedford	d															06 12						
Luton 10	d															06 36						
Luton Airport Parkway 7 ✈	d															06 39						
St Albans City	d															06 51						
St Pancras International 15 ⊖	d															07 24						
Farringdon 3 ⊖	d															07 29						
City Thameslink 3	d															07 34						
London Blackfriars 3 ⊖	d										06 55											
London Bridge 4 ⊖	d									07 05						07 41		07 37				
New Cross Gate	d																					
Norwood Junction 2	d									07 17								07 48				
East Croydon ⇌	a			06 51					07 19	07 21	07 25			07 42		07 55		07 54				08 17
	d			06 52					07 20	07 22	07 25			07 43		07 55		07 55				08 18
Purley 4	d			06 56					07 25	07 28								08 00				08 23
Coulsdon South	d			07 00						07 31								08 04				
Merstham	d			07 05						07 37								08 09				
Redhill	a			07 09					07 33	07 40				07 57				08 13				08 31
	d	06 20		07 09		07 15		07 20	07 34	07 41				07 57				08 13		08 19	08 21	08 32
Reigate	a	06 24						07 24												08 23		
Nutfield	d									07 45												
Godstone	d									07 51												
Edenbridge	d									07 56												
Penshurst	d									08 03												
Leigh (Kent)	d									08 06												
Tonbridge 4	a									08 11												
Earlswood (Surrey)	d																	08 18				
Salfords	d																	08 22				
Horley 4	d			07 15					07 40			←						08 25				08 38
Gatwick Airport 10 ✈	a		07 05	07 18	07 15	07 27	07 30		07 42		07 41	07 42	07 45	08 04	08 00	08 11	08 15	08 28	08 30		08 33	08 40
	d			07 19					07 43		07 42	07 43		08 05		08 12		08 29				08 41
Three Bridges 15	a			07 23					⟶		07 46	07 48		08 10		08 16		08 33				08 46
	d			07 24							07 47	07 48		08 10		08 17		08 34				08 46
Crawley	d											07 52						08 37				08 50
Ifield	d											07 54						08 40				
Faygate	d																					
Littlehaven	d											08 01						08 46				
Horsham 4	a											08 04						08 49				08 58
Balcombe	d			07 30										08 16								
Haywards Heath	a			07 35							07 56			08 21		08 26						
	d			07 36							07 56			08 22		08 26						
Wivelsfield	d			07 40										08 26								
Lewes 4	a																					
Burgess Hill 4	d			07 42							08 01			08 28		08 31						
Hassocks 4	d			07 45							08 05			08 31		08 35						
Preston Park	d			07 52										08 38								
Hove 2	a																					
Brighton 10	a			07 58							08 15			08 43		08 45						

A from 1 July until 22 July, from 19 August until 9 September

Table 186

Sundays

1 July to 9 September

Bedford and London - Brighton

Network Diagram - see first Page of Table 186

Station		SN	FC	SN	SN	SN	SN	SN	FC	SN	SN	SN	SN	GW	GW	SN	SN	SN	SN	FC	SN	SN
		1	1	1 🚲	◇1	◇1	1 🚲	1	1	1 🚲	◇1 🚲	1	1 🚲	1	1	◇1	1	◇1	◇1	1	1 🚲	◇1
London Victoria 15 ⊖	d			08 15	08 17	08 27	08 30			08 45	08 47		09 00			09 02		09 06			09 15	09 17
Clapham Junction 10	d				08 23	08 33					08 53					09 08		09 12				09 23
Bedford	d		06 42						07 12											07 50		
Luton 10	d		07 06						07 36											08 14		
Luton Airport Parkway 7 ✈	d		07 09						07 39											08 17		
St Albans City	d		07 21						07 51											08 29		
St Pancras International 15 ⊖	d		07 54						08 24											08 54		
Farringdon 3 ⊖	d		07 59						08 29											08 58		
City Thameslink 3	d																					
London Blackfriars 3 ⊖	d		08 04						08 34											09 04		
London Bridge 4 ⊖	d	08 05	08 11					08 37	08 41								09 05			09 11		
New Cross Gate	d																					
Norwood Junction 2	d	08 16						08 48									09 16					
East Croydon	a	08 20	08 25		08 32	08 42		08 54	08 55		09 02					09 17	09 20	09 22		09 25		09 32
	d	08 21	08 25		08 33	08 43		08 55	08 55		09 03					09 18	09 21	09 23		09 25		09 33
Purley 4	d	08 27						09 00								09 23	09 27					
Coulsdon South	d	08 30						09 04									09 30					
Merstham	d	08 36						09 09									09 36					
Redhill	a	08 39				08 57		09 13								09 31	09 39					
	d	08 40				08 57		09 13						09 20	09 21	09 32	09 40					
Reigate	a													09 24								
Nutfield	d	08 44															09 44					
Godstone	d	08 50															09 50					
Edenbridge	d	08 55															09 55					
Penshurst	d	09 02															10 02					
Leigh (Kent)	d	09 05															10 05					
Tonbridge 4	a	09 10															10 10					
Earlswood (Surrey)	d							09 18														
Salfords	d							09 22														
Horley 4	d							09 25				←				09 38			←			
Gatwick Airport 10 ✈	a		08 41	08 45	08 48	09 04	09 00	09 28	09 11	09 15	09 18	09 28	09 30		09 33	09 40		09 37	09 40	09 41	09 45	09 48
	d		08 42		08 49	09 05		09 29	09 12		09 19	09 29				09 41		09 39	09 41	09 42		09 49
Three Bridges 15	a		08 46			09 10		→	09 16			09 33				→			09 46	09 46		
	d		08 47			09 10			09 17			09 34							09 46	09 47		
Crawley	d											09 37							09 50			
Ifield	d											09 40										
Faygate	d																					
Littlehaven	d											09 46										
Horsham 4	a											09 49							09 58			
Balcombe	d					09 16																
Haywards Heath	a		08 56		09 00	09 21			09 26		09 30									09 56		10 00
	d		08 56		09 00	09 22			09 26		09 30									09 56		10 00
Wivelsfield	d					09 26					09 34											
Lewes 4	a										09 48											
Burgess Hill 4	d		09 01		09 06	09 28			09 31											10 01		10 06
Hassocks 4	d		09 05			09 31			09 35											10 05		
Preston Park	d					09 38																
Hove 2	a				09 18																	10 18
Brighton 10	a		09 15			09 43			09 45									10 03		10 15		

Table 186

Sundays

1 July to 9 September

Bedford and London - Brighton

Network Diagram - see first Page of Table 186

		SN	SN	SN	SN	FC	SN	SN		SN	SN	GW	GW	SN	SN	SN		SN	FC	SN	SN	SN	SN	SN
		◇1	1	◇1	1	1	1	◇1		1	1	1	1	◇1	1	◇1		◇1	1	1	◇1	◇1	1	◇1
			⚲				⚲	⚲			⚲					⚲				⚲			⚲	⚲
London Victoria 15 ⊖	d	09 27	09 30	09 36			09 45	09 47			10 00			10 02		10 06				10 15	10 17	10 27	10 30	10 36
Clapham Junction 10	d	09 33		09 42				09 53						10 08		10 12					10 23	10 33		10 42
Bedford	d					08 20													08 50					
Luton 10	d					08 44													09 14					
Luton Airport Parkway 7 ✈	d					08 47													09 17					
St Albans City	d					08 59													09 29					
St Pancras International 15 ⊖	d					09 24													09 54					
Farringdon 3 ⊖	d					09 29													09 58					
City Thameslink 3	d																							
London Blackfriars 3 ⊖	d					09 34													10 04					
London Bridge 4 ⊖	d				09 37	09 41									10 05				10 11					
New Cross Gate	d																							
Norwood Junction 2	d				09 48										10 16									
East Croydon	a	09 42		09 52	09 54	09 55		10 02						10 17	10 20	10 22			10 25		10 32	10 42		10 52
	d	09 43		09 53	09 55	09 55		10 03						10 18	10 21	10 23			10 26		10 33	10 43		10 53
Purley 4	d				10 00									10 23	10 27									
Coulsdon South	d				10 04										10 30									
Merstham	d				10 09										10 36									
Redhill	a	09 57			10 13									10 31	10 39							10 57		
	d	09 57			10 13							10 19	10 21	10 32	10 40							10 57		
Reigate	a											10 23												
Nutfield	d														10 44									
Godstone	d														10 50									
Edenbridge	d														10 55									
Penshurst	d														11 02									
Leigh (Kent)	d														11 05									
Tonbridge 4	a														11 10									
Earlswood (Surrey)	d				10 18																			
Salfords	d				10 22																			
Horley 4	d				10 25					←				10 38				←						
Gatwick Airport 10 ✈	a	10 04	10 00		10 28	10 11	10 15	10 18		10 28	10 30		10 33	10 40		10 37		10 40	10 41	10 45	10 48	11 04	11 00	
	d	10 05			10 29	10 12		10 19		10 29				10 41		10 39		10 41	10 42		10 49	11 05		
Three Bridges 15	a	10 10			→	10 16				10 33				→				10 46	10 46			11 10		
	d	10 10				10 17				10 34								10 46	10 47			11 10		
Crawley	d									10 37								10 50						
Ifield	d									10 40														
Faygate	d																							
Littlehaven	d									10 46														
Horsham 4	a									10 49								10 58						
Balcombe	d	10 16																				11 16		
Haywards Heath	a	10 21				10 26		10 30											10 56		11 00	11 21		
	d	10 22				10 26		10 30											10 56		11 00	11 22		
Wivelsfield	d	10 26						10 34														11 26		
Lewes 4	a							10 48																
Burgess Hill 4	d	10 28				10 31													11 01		11 06	11 28		
Hassocks 4	d	10 31				10 35													11 05			11 31		
Preston Park	d	10 38																				11 38		
Hove 2	a																				11 18			
Brighton 10	a	10 43		10 27		10 45										11 03			11 15			11 43		11 27

Table 186

Sundays

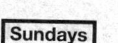

1 July to 9 September

Bedford and London - Brighton

Network Diagram - see first Page of Table 186

		SN	FC	SN	SN	SN	SN	GW		GW	SN	SN	SN	SN	FC	SN		SN	SN	SN	SN	SN	FC	SN
		1	1	1	◇1	1	1	1		1	◇1	1	◇1	◇1	1	1		◇1	◇1	1	◇1	1	1	1
				🛒	🛒		🛒				🛒		🛒	🛒		🛒				🛒	🛒			🛒
London Victoria 15 ⊖	d			10 45	10 47		11 00				11 02		11 06			11 15		11 17	11 27	11 30	11 36			11 45
Clapham Junction 10	d				10 53						11 08		11 12					11 23	11 33		11 42			
Bedford	d		09 20												09 50								10 20	
Luton 10	d		09 44												10 14								10 44	
Luton Airport Parkway 7 ✈	d		09 47												10 17								10 47	
St Albans City	d		09 59												10 29								10 59	
St Pancras International 15 ⊖	d		10 24												10 54								11 24	
Farringdon 3 ⊖	d		10 29												10 58								11 29	
City Thameslink 3	d																							
London Blackfriars 3 ⊖	d		10 34												11 04								11 34	
London Bridge 4 ⊖	d	10 37	10 41									11 05			11 11							11 37	11 41	
New Cross Gate	d																							
Norwood Junction 2	d	10 48										11 16										11 48		
East Croydon 🚊	a	10 54	10 55		11 02						11 17	11 20	11 22		11 25			11 32	11 42		11 52	11 54	11 55	
	d	10 55	10 55		11 03						11 18	11 21	11 23		11 25			11 33	11 43		11 53	11 55	11 55	
Purley 4	d	11 00									11 23	11 27										12 00		
Coulsdon South	d	11 04										11 30										12 04		
Merstham	d	11 09										11 36										12 09		
Redhill	a	11 13									11 31	11 39							11 57			12 13		
	d	11 13						11 20		11 21	11 32	11 40							11 57			12 13		
Reigate	a							11 24																
Nutfield	d											11 44												
Godstone	d											11 50												
Edenbridge	d											11 55												
Penshurst	d											12 02												
Leigh (Kent)	d											12 05												
Tonbridge 4	a											12 10												
Earlswood (Surrey)	d	11 18																				12 18		
Salfords	d	11 22																				12 22		
Horley 4	d	11 25									11 38											12 25		
Gatwick Airport 10 ✈	a	11 28	11 11	11 15	11 18	← 11 28	11 30			11 33	11 40		11 37	← 11 40	11 41	11 45		11 48	12 04	12 00		12 28	12 11	12 15
	d	11 29	11 12		11 19	11 29					11 41		11 39	11 41	11 42			11 49	12 05			12 29	12 12	
Three Bridges 15	a	→	11 16			11 33					→			11 46	11 46				12 10			→	12 16	
	d		11 17			11 34								11 46	11 47				12 10				12 17	
Crawley	d					11 37								11 50										
Ifield	d					11 40																		
Faygate	d																							
Littlehaven	d					11 46																		
Horsham 4	a					11 49								11 58										
Balcombe	d																		12 16					
Haywards Heath	a		11 26		11 30										11 56			12 00	12 21				12 26	
	d		11 26		11 30										11 56			12 00	12 22				12 26	
Wivelsfield	d				11 34														12 26					
Lewes 4	a				11 48																			
Burgess Hill 4	d		11 31												12 01			12 06	12 28				12 31	
Hassocks 4	d		11 35												12 05				12 31				12 35	
Preston Park	d																		12 38					
Hove 2	a																	12 18						
Brighton 10	a		11 45										12 03		12 15				12 43		12 27		12 45	

Table 186

Sundays

1 July to 9 September

Bedford and London - Brighton

Network Diagram - see first Page of Table 186

		SN	SN	SN	GW	GW	SN	SN		SN	SN	FC	SN	SN	SN	SN		SN	SN	FC	SN	SN	SN	SN	
		◇1 ⊼	1	1 ⊼	1	1	◇1	1		◇1 ⊼	◇1	1	1 ⊼	◇1	◇1	1 ⊼		◇1 ⊼	1	1	1 ⊼	◇1 ⊼	1	1 ⊼	
London Victoria 15 ⊖	d	11 47		12 00			12 02			12 06			12 15	12 17	12 27	12 30		12 36			12 45	12 47		13 00	
Clapham Junction 10	d	11 53					12 08			12 12				12 23	12 33			12 42				12 53			
Bedford	d											10 50								11 20					
Luton 10	d											11 14								11 44					
Luton Airport Parkway 7 ✈	d											11 17								11 47					
St Albans City	d											11 29								11 59					
St Pancras International 15 ⊖	d											11 54								12 24					
Farringdon 3 ⊖	d											11 58								12 29					
City Thameslink 3	d																								
London Blackfriars 3 ⊖	d											12 04								12 34					
London Bridge 4 ⊖	d							12 05				12 11							12 37	12 41					
New Cross Gate	d																								
Norwood Junction 2	d							12 16											12 48						
East Croydon	a	12 02					12 17	12 20		12 22		12 25		12 32	12 42			12 52	12 54	12 55		13 02			
	d	12 03					12 18	12 21		12 23		12 25		12 33	12 43			12 53	12 55	12 55		13 03			
Purley 4	d						12 23	12 27											13 00						
Coulsdon South	d							12 30											13 04						
Merstham	d							12 36											13 09						
Redhill	a						12 31	12 39							12 57				13 13						
	d				12 19	12 21	12 32	12 40							12 57				13 13						
Reigate	a				12 23																				
Nutfield	d							12 44																	
Godstone	d							12 50																	
Edenbridge	d							12 55																	
Penshurst	d							13 02																	
Leigh (Kent)	d							13 05																	
Tonbridge 4	a							13 10																	
Earlswood (Surrey)	d																		13 18						
Salfords	d																		13 22						
Horley 4	d		←				12 38				←								13 25				←		
Gatwick Airport 10 ✈	a	12 18	12 28	12 30		12 33	12 40			12 37	12 40	12 41	12 45	12 48	13 04	13 00			13 28	13 11	13 15	13 18	13 28	13 30	
	d	12 19	12 29				12 41			12 39	12 41	12 42		12 49	13 05				13 29	13 12		13 19	13 29		
Three Bridges 15	a		12 33				→				12 46	12 46			13 10				→	13 16			13 33		
	d		12 34								12 46	12 47			13 10					13 17			13 34		
Crawley	d		12 37								12 50												13 37		
Ifield	d		12 40																				13 40		
Faygate	d																								
Littlehaven	d		12 46																				13 46		
Horsham 4	a		12 49								12 58												13 49		
Balcombe	d														13 16										
Haywards Heath	a	12 30										12 56		13 00	13 21					13 26		13 30			
	d	12 30										12 56		13 00	13 22					13 26		13 30			
Wivelsfield	d	12 34													13 26							13 34			
Lewes 4	a	12 48																				13 48			
Burgess Hill 4	d											13 01		13 06	13 28					13 31					
Hassocks 4	d											13 05			13 31					13 35					
Preston Park	d														13 38										
Hove 2	a													13 18											
Brighton 10	a									13 03		13 15			13 43			13 27		13 45					

Table 186

Sundays

1 July to 9 September

Bedford and London - Brighton

Network Diagram - see first Page of Table 186

		GW	GW	SN	SN	SN	SN	FC		SN	SN	SN	SN	SN	SN	FC		SN	SN	SN	SN	GW	GW	SN
		1	1	◇1	1	◇1	◇1	1		1	◇1	◇1	1	◇1	1	1		1	◇1	1	1	1	1	◇1
						🛒				🛒			🛒	🛒				🛒	🛒		🛒			
London Victoria 15 ⊖	d			13 02		13 06				13 15	13 17	13 27	13 30	13 36				13 45	13 47		14 00			14 02
Clapham Junction 10	d			13 08		13 12					13 23	13 33		13 42					13 53					14 08
Bedford	d							11 50								12 20								
Luton 10	d							12 14								12 44								
Luton Airport Parkway 7 ✈	d							12 17								12 47								
St Albans City	d							12 29								12 59								
St Pancras International 15 ⊖	d							12 54								13 24								
Farringdon 3 ⊖	d							12 58								13 29								
City Thameslink 3	d																							
London Blackfriars 3 ⊖	d							13 04								13 34								
London Bridge 4 ⊖	d				13 05			13 11							13 37	13 41								
New Cross Gate	d																							
Norwood Junction 2	d				13 16										13 48									
East Croydon	a			13 17	13 20	13 22		13 25			13 32	13 42		13 52	13 54	13 55			14 02					14 17
	d			13 18	13 21	13 23		13 25			13 33	13 43		13 53	13 55	13 55			14 03					14 18
Purley 4	d			13 23	13 27										14 00									14 23
Coulsdon South	d				13 30										14 04									
Merstham	d				13 36										14 09									
Redhill	a			13 31	13 39							13 57			14 13									14 31
	d	13 20	13 21	13 32	13 40							13 57			14 13							14 19	14 21	14 32
Reigate	a	13 24																				14 23		
Nutfield	d				13 44																			
Godstone	d				13 50																			
Edenbridge	d				13 55																			
Penshurst	d				14 02																			
Leigh (Kent)	d				14 05																			
Tonbridge 4	a				14 10																			
Earlswood (Surrey)	d														14 18									
Salfords	d														14 22									
Horley 4	d			13 38			←								14 25					←				14 38
Gatwick Airport 10 ✈	a		13 33	13 40		13 37	13 40	13 41		13 45	13 48	14 04	14 00		14 28	14 11		14 15	14 18	14 28	14 30		14 33	14 40
	d			13 41		13 39	13 41	13 42			13 49	14 05			14 29	14 12			14 19	14 29				14 41
Three Bridges 15	a			→			13 46	13 46				14 10			→	14 16				14 33				→
	d						13 46	13 47				14 10				14 17				14 34				
Crawley	d						13 50													14 37				
Ifield	d																			14 40				
Faygate	d																							
Littlehaven	d																			14 46				
Horsham 4	a						13 58													14 49				
Balcombe	d											14 16												
Haywards Heath	a							13 56			14 00	14 21				14 26			14 30					
	d							13 56			14 00	14 22				14 26			14 30					
Wivelsfield	d											14 26							14 34					
Lewes 4	a																		14 48					
Burgess Hill 4	d							14 01			14 06	14 28				14 31								
Hassocks 4	d							14 05				14 31				14 35								
Preston Park	d											14 38												
Hove 2	a										14 18													
Brighton 10	a					14 03		14 15				14 43		14 27		14 45								

Table 186

Sundays

1 July to 9 September

Bedford and London - Brighton

Network Diagram - see first Page of Table 186

		SN	SN	SN	FC	SN	SN	SN		SN	SN	SN	FC	SN	SN	SN		SN	GW	GW	SN	SN	SN	SN	
		1	◇1	◇1	1	1	◇1	◇1		1	◇1	1	1	1	◇1	1		1	1	1	◇1	1	◇1	◇1	
			trolley			trolley				trolley	trolley			trolley	trolley			trolley					trolley		
London Victoria 15 ⊖	d		14 06			14 15	14 17	14 27		14 30	14 36			14 45	14 47			15 00			15 02		15 06		
Clapham Junction 10	d		14 12				14 23	14 33			14 42				14 53						15 08		15 12		
Bedford	d				12 50								13 20												
Luton 10	d				13 14								13 44												
Luton Airport Parkway 7 ✈	d				13 17								13 47												
St Albans City	d				13 29								13 59												
St Pancras International 15 ⊖	d				13 54								14 24												
Farringdon 3 ⊖	d				13 58								14 29												
City Thameslink 3	d																								
London Blackfriars 3 ⊖	d				14 04								14 34												
London Bridge 4 ⊖	d	14 05			14 11							14 37	14 41									15 05			
New Cross Gate	d																					15 16			
Norwood Junction 2	d	14 16										14 48													
East Croydon	a	14 20	14 22		14 25		14 32	14 42			14 52	14 54	14 55		15 02						15 17	15 20	15 22		
	d	14 21	14 23		14 25		14 33	14 43			14 53	14 55	14 55		15 03						15 18	15 21	15 23		
Purley 4	d	14 27										15 00									15 23	15 27			
Coulsdon South	d	14 30										15 04										15 30			
Merstham	d	14 36										15 09										15 36			
Redhill	a	14 39						14 57				15 13									15 31	15 39			
	d	14 40						14 57				15 13							15 20	15 21	15 32	15 40			
Reigate	a																		15 24						
Nutfield	d	14 44																				15 44			
Godstone	d	14 50																				15 50			
Edenbridge	d	14 55																				15 55			
Penshurst	d	15 02																				16 02			
Leigh (Kent)	d	15 05																				16 05			
Tonbridge 4	a	15 10																				16 10			
Earlswood (Surrey)	d											15 18													
Salfords	d											15 22													
Horley 4	d			←								15 25				←					15 38			←	
Gatwick Airport 10 ✈	a		14 37	14 40	14 41	14 45	14 48	15 04		15 00		15 28	15 11	15 15	15 18	15 28		15 30		15 33	15 40		15 37	15 40	
	d		14 39	14 41	14 42		14 49	15 05				15 29	15 12		15 19	15 29					15 41		15 39	15 41	
Three Bridges 15	a			14 46	14 46			15 10				→	15 16			15 33					→			15 46	
	d			14 46	14 47			15 10					15 17			15 34								15 46	
Crawley	d			14 50												15 37								15 50	
Ifield	d															15 40									
Faygate	d																								
Littlehaven	d															15 46									
Horsham 4	a			14 58												15 49								15 58	
Balcombe	d							15 16																	
Haywards Heath	a				14 56		15 00	15 21					15 26		15 30										
	d				14 56		15 00	15 22					15 26		15 30										
Wivelsfield	d							15 26							15 34										
Lewes 4	a														15 48										
Burgess Hill 4	d				15 01		15 06	15 28					15 31												
Hassocks 4	d				15 05			15 31					15 35												
Preston Park	d							15 38																	
Hove 2	a						15 18																		
Brighton 10	a		15 03		15 15			15 43			15 27		15 45										16 03		

Table 186

Sundays

1 July to 9 September

Bedford and London - Brighton

Network Diagram - see first Page of Table 186

		FC	SN	SN	SN	SN	SN	SN	FC	SN	SN	SN
		[1]	[1] ⊤	◇[1]	◇[1]	[1] ⊤	◇[1] ⊤	[1]	[1]	[1] ⊤	◇[1] ⊤	[1]
London Victoria [15] ⊖	d		15 15	15 17	15 27	15 30	15 36			15 45	15 47	
Clapham Junction [10]	d			15 23	15 33		15 42				15 53	
Bedford	d	13 50							14 20			
Luton [10]	d	14 14							14 44			
Luton Airport Parkway [7] ✈	d	14 17							14 47			
St Albans City	d	14 29							14 59			
St Pancras International [15] ⊖	d	14 54							15 24			
Farringdon [3] ⊖	d	14 58							15 29			
City Thameslink [3]	d											
London Blackfriars [3] ⊖	d	15 04							15 34			
London Bridge [4] ⊖	d	15 11						15 37	15 41			
New Cross Gate	d											
Norwood Junction [2]	d							15 48				
East Croydon	a	15 25		15 32	15 42		15 52	15 54	15 55		16 02	
	d	15 25		15 32	15 43		15 53	15 55	15 55		16 03	
Purley [4]	d							16 00				
Coulsdon South	d							16 04				
Merstham	d							16 09				
Redhill	a				15 57			16 13				
	d				15 57			16 13				
Reigate	a											
Nutfield	d											
Godstone	d											
Edenbridge	d											
Penshurst	d											
Leigh (Kent)	d											
Tonbridge [4]	a											
Earlswood (Surrey)	d							16 18				
Salfords	d							16 22				
Horley [4]	d							16 25				←
Gatwick Airport [10] ✈	a	15 41	15 45	15 48	16 04	16 00		16 28	16 11	16 15	16 18	16 28
	d	15 42		15 49	16 05			16 29	16 12		16 19	16 29
Three Bridges [15]	a	15 46			16 10			→	16 16			16 33
	d	15 47			16 10				16 17			16 34
Crawley	d											16 37
Ifield	d											16 40
Faygate	d											
Littlehaven	d											16 46
Horsham [4]	a											16 49
Balcombe	d				16 16							
Haywards Heath	a	15 56		16 00	16 21				16 26		16 30	
	d	15 56		16 00	16 22				16 26		16 30	
Wivelsfield	d				16 26						16 34	
Lewes [4]	a										16 48	
Burgess Hill [4]	d	16 01		16 06	16 28				16 31			
Hassocks [4]	d	16 05			16 31				16 35			
Preston Park	d				16 38							
Hove [2]	a			16 18								
Brighton [10]	a	16 15			16 43		16 27		16 45			

		SN	GW	GW	SN	SN	SN	SN	FC	SN	SN
		[1] ⊤	[1]	[1]	◇[1]	[1]	◇[1] ⊤	◇[1]	[1]	[1] ⊤	◇[1]
London Victoria [15] ⊖	d	16 00			16 02		16 06			16 15	16 17
Clapham Junction [10]	d				16 08		16 12				16 23
Bedford	d								14 50		
Luton [10]	d								15 14		
Luton Airport Parkway [7] ✈	d								15 17		
St Albans City	d								15 29		
St Pancras International [15] ⊖	d								15 54		
Farringdon [3] ⊖	d								15 58		
City Thameslink [3]	d										
London Blackfriars [3] ⊖	d								16 04		
London Bridge [4] ⊖	d					16 05			16 11		
New Cross Gate	d										
Norwood Junction [2]	d					16 16					
East Croydon	a				16 17	16 20	16 22		16 25		16 32
	d				16 18	16 21	16 23		16 25		16 33
Purley [4]	d				16 23	16 27					
Coulsdon South	d					16 30					
Merstham	d					16 36					
Redhill	a				16 31	16 39					
	d		16 19	16 21	16 32	16 40					
Reigate	a		16 23								
Nutfield	d					16 44					
Godstone	d					16 50					
Edenbridge	d					16 55					
Penshurst	d					17 02					
Leigh (Kent)	d					17 05					
Tonbridge [4]	a					17 10					
Earlswood (Surrey)	d										
Salfords	d										
Horley [4]	d				16 38			←			
Gatwick Airport [10] ✈	a	16 30		16 33	16 40		16 37	16 40	16 41	16 45	16 48
	d				16 41		16 39	16 41	16 42		16 49
Three Bridges [15]	a				→			16 46	16 46		
	d							16 46	16 47		
Crawley	d							16 50			
Ifield	d										
Faygate	d										
Littlehaven	d										
Horsham [4]	a							16 58			
Balcombe	d										
Haywards Heath	a								16 56		17 00
	d								16 56		17 00
Wivelsfield	d										
Lewes [4]	a										
Burgess Hill [4]	d								17 01		17 06
Hassocks [4]	d								17 05		
Preston Park	d										
Hove [2]	a										17 18
Brighton [10]	a						17 03		17 15		

Table 186

Sundays

1 July to 9 September

Bedford and London - Brighton

Network Diagram - see first Page of Table 186

		SN	SN	SN	SN	FC	SN	SN		SN	SN	GW	GW	SN	SN	SN		SN	FC	SN	SN	SN	SN	SN
		◇1	1	◇1	1	1	1	◇1		1	1	1	1	◇1	1	◇1		◇1	1	1	◇1	◇1	1	◇1
			🚲	🚲			🚲	🚲			🚲					🚲				🚲			🚲	🚲
London Victoria 15 ⊖	d	16 27	16 30	16 36			16 45	16 47			17 00			17 02		17 06				17 15	17 17	17 27	17 30	17 36
Clapham Junction 10	d	16 33		16 42				16 53						17 08		17 12					17 23	17 33		17 42
Bedford	d					15 20													15 50					
Luton 10	d					15 44													16 14					
Luton Airport Parkway 7 ✈	d					15 47													16 17					
St Albans City	d					15 59													16 29					
St Pancras International 15 ⊖	d					16 24													16 54					
Farringdon 3 ⊖	d					16 29													16 58					
City Thameslink 3	d																							
London Blackfriars 3 ⊖	d					16 34													17 04					
London Bridge 4 ⊖	d				16 37	16 41									17 05				17 11					
New Cross Gate	d																							
Norwood Junction 2	d				16 48										17 16									
East Croydon	a	16 42		16 52	16 54	16 55		17 02						17 17	17 20	17 22			17 25		17 32	17 42		17 52
	d	16 43		16 53	16 55	16 55		17 03						17 18	17 21	17 23			17 25		17 33	17 43		17 53
Purley 4	d				17 00									17 23	17 27									
Coulsdon South	d				17 04										17 30									
Merstham	d				17 09										17 36									
Redhill	a	16 57			17 13									17 31	17 39							17 57		
	d	16 57			17 13							17 20	17 21	17 32	17 40							17 57		
Reigate	a											17 24												
Nutfield	d														17 44									
Godstone	d														17 50									
Edenbridge	d														17 55									
Penshurst	d														18 02									
Leigh (Kent)	d														18 05									
Tonbridge 4	a														18 10									
Earlswood (Surrey)	d				17 18																			
Salfords	d				17 22																			
Horley 4	d				17 25					←				17 38				←						
Gatwick Airport 10 ✈	a	17 04	17 00		17 28	17 11	17 15	17 18		17 28	17 30		17 33	17 40		17 37		17 40	17 41	17 45	17 48	18 04	18 00	
	d	17 05			17 29	17 12		17 19		17 29				17 41		17 39		17 41	17 42		17 49	18 05		
Three Bridges 15	a	17 10			→	17 16				17 33				→				17 46	17 46			18 10		
	d	17 10				17 17				17 34								17 46	17 47			18 10		
Crawley	d									17 37								17 50						
Ifield	d									17 40														
Faygate	d																							
Littlehaven	d									17 46														
Horsham 4	a									17 49								17 58						
Balcombe	d	17 16																				18 16		
Haywards Heath	a	17 21				17 26		17 30											17 56		18 00	18 21		
	d	17 22				17 26		17 30											17 56		18 00	18 22		
Wivelsfield	d	17 26						17 34														18 26		
Lewes 4	a							17 48																
Burgess Hill 4	d	17 28				17 31													18 01		18 06	18 28		
Hassocks 4	d	17 31				17 35													18 05			18 31		
Preston Park	d	17 38																				18 38		
Hove 2	a																				18 18			
Brighton 10	a	17 43		17 27		17 45										18 03			18 15			18 43		18 27

Table 186

Sundays

1 July to 9 September

Bedford and London - Brighton

Network Diagram - see first Page of Table 186

		SN	FC	SN	SN	SN	SN	GW		GW	SN	SN	SN	SN	FC	SN		SN	SN	SN	SN	SN	FC	SN
		1	1	1	◇1	1	1	1		1	◇1	1	◇1	◇1	1	1		◇1	◇1	1	◇1	1	1	1
				🛒	🛒		🛒						🛒			🛒				🛒	🛒			🛒
London Victoria 15 ⊖	d			17 45	17 47		18 00				18 02		18 06			18 15		18 17	18 27	18 30	18 36			18 45
Clapham Junction 10	d				17 53						18 08		18 12					18 23	18 33		18 42			
Bedford	d		16 20												16 50								17 20	
Luton 10	d		16 44												17 14								17 44	
Luton Airport Parkway 7 ✈	d		16 47												17 17								17 47	
St Albans City	d		16 59												17 29								17 59	
St Pancras International 15 ⊖	d		17 24												17 54								18 24	
Farringdon 3 ⊖	d		17 29												17 58								18 29	
City Thameslink 3	d																							
London Blackfriars 3 ⊖	d		17 34												18 04								18 34	
London Bridge 4 ⊖	d	17 37	17 41									18 05			18 11							18 37	18 41	
New Cross Gate	d																							
Norwood Junction 2	d	17 48										18 16										18 48		
East Croydon 🚌	a	17 54	17 55		18 02						18 17	18 20	18 22		18 25			18 32	18 42		18 52	18 54	18 55	
	d	17 55	17 55		18 03						18 18	18 21	18 23		18 25			18 33	18 43		18 53	18 55	18 55	
Purley 4	d	18 00									18 23	18 27										19 00		
Coulsdon South	d	18 04										18 30										19 04		
Merstham	d	18 09										18 36										19 09		
Redhill	a	18 13									18 31	18 39							18 57			19 13		
	d	18 13						18 19		18 21	18 32	18 40							18 57			19 13		
Reigate	a							18 23																
Nutfield	d											18 44												
Godstone	d											18 50												
Edenbridge	d											18 55												
Penshurst	d											19 02												
Leigh (Kent)	d											19 05												
Tonbridge 4	a											19 10												
Earlswood (Surrey)	d	18 18																				19 18		
Salfords	d	18 22																				19 22		
Horley 4	d	18 25				←					18 38			←								19 25		
Gatwick Airport 10 ✈	a	18 28	18 11	18 15	18 18	18 28	18 30			18 34	18 40		18 37	18 40	18 41	18 45		18 48	19 04	19 00		19 28	19 11	19 15
	d	18 29	18 12		18 19	18 29					18 41		18 39	18 41	18 42			18 49	19 05			19 29	19 12	
Three Bridges 15	a	→	18 16			18 33					→			18 46	18 46				19 10			→	19 16	
	d		18 17			18 34								18 46	18 47				19 10				19 17	
Crawley	d					18 37								18 50										
Ifield	d					18 40																		
Faygate	d																							
Littlehaven	d					18 46																		
Horsham 4	a					18 49								18 58										
Balcombe	d																		19 16					
Haywards Heath	a		18 26		18 30										18 56			19 00	19 21				19 26	
	d		18 26		18 30										18 56			19 00	19 22				19 26	
Wivelsfield	d				18 34														19 26					
Lewes 4	a				18 48																			
Burgess Hill 4	d		18 31												19 01			19 06	19 28				19 31	
Hassocks 4	d		18 35												19 05				19 31				19 35	
Preston Park	d																		19 38					
Hove 2	a																	19 18						
Brighton 10	a		18 45										19 03		19 15				19 43		19 27		19 45	

Table 186

Sundays

1 July to 9 September

Bedford and London - Brighton

Network Diagram - see first Page of Table 186

		SN	SN	SN	GW	GW	SN	SN	SN	SN	FC	SN	SN	SN	SN	SN	SN	FC	SN	SN	SN	SN
		◇1 ⚲	1	1 ⚲	1	1	◇1	1	◇1 ⚲	◇1	1	1	◇1	◇1	1	◇1	1	1	1	◇1 ⚲	1	1
London Victoria 15 ⊖	d	18 47		19 00			19 02		19 06			19 15	19 17	19 27	19 30	19 36			19 45	19 47		20 00
Clapham Junction 10	d	18 53					19 08		19 12				19 23	19 33		19 42				19 53		
Bedford	d										17 50							18 20				
Luton 10	d										18 14							18 44				
Luton Airport Parkway 7 ✈	d										18 17							18 47				
St Albans City	d										18 29							18 59				
St Pancras International 15 ⊖	d										18 54							19 24				
Farringdon 3 ⊖	d										18 58							19 29				
City Thameslink 3	d																					
London Blackfriars 3 ⊖	d										19 04							19 34				
London Bridge 4 ⊖	d							19 05			19 11						19 37	19 41				
New Cross Gate	d																					
Norwood Junction 2	d							19 16									19 48					
East Croydon 🚌	a	19 02					19 17	19 20	19 22		19 25		19 32	19 42		19 52	19 54	19 55		20 02		
	d	19 03					19 18	19 21	19 23		19 25		19 33	19 43		19 53	19 55	19 55		20 03		
Purley 4	d						19 23	19 27									20 00					
Coulsdon South	d							19 30									20 04					
Merstham	d							19 36									20 09					
Redhill	a						19 31	19 39						19 57			20 13					
	d				19 20	19 21	19 32	19 40						19 57			20 13					
Reigate	a				19 24																	
Nutfield	d							19 44														
Godstone	d							19 50														
Edenbridge	d							19 55														
Penshurst	d							20 02														
Leigh (Kent)	d							20 05														
Tonbridge 4	a							20 10														
Earlswood (Surrey)	d																20 18					
Salfords	d																20 22					
Horley 4	d		←				19 38			←							20 25				←	
Gatwick Airport 10 ✈	a	19 18	19 28	19 30		19 34	19 40		19 37	19 40	19 41	19 45	19 48	20 04	20 00		20 28	20 11	20 15	20 18	20 28	20 30
	d	19 19	19 29				19 41		19 39	19 41	19 42		19 49	20 05			20 29	20 12		20 19	20 29	
Three Bridges 15	a		19 33				→			19 46	19 46			20 10			→	20 16			20 33	
	d		19 34							19 46	19 47			20 10				20 17			20 34	
Crawley	d		19 37							19 50											20 37	
Ifield	d		19 40																		20 40	
Faygate	d																					
Littlehaven	d		19 46																		20 46	
Horsham 4	a		19 49							19 58											20 49	
Balcombe	d													20 16								
Haywards Heath	a	19 30									19 56		20 00	20 21				20 26		20 30		
	d	19 30									19 56		20 00	20 22				20 26		20 30		
Wivelsfield	d	19 34												20 26						20 34		
Lewes 4	a	19 48																		20 48		
Burgess Hill 4	d										20 01		20 06	20 28				20 31				
Hassocks 4	d										20 05			20 31				20 35				
Preston Park	d													20 38								
Hove 2	a												20 18									
Brighton 10	a								20 03		20 15			20 43		20 27		20 45				

Table 186

Bedford and London - Brighton

Sundays

1 July to 9 September

Network Diagram - see first Page of Table 186

		GW	GW	SN	SN	SN	SN	FC		SN	SN	SN	SN	SN	SN	FC		SN	SN	SN	SN	GW	GW	SN
		1	1	◇1	1	◇1	◇1	1		1	◇1	◇1	1	◇1	1	1		1	◇1	1	1	1	1	◇1
London Victoria 15 ⊖	d			20 02		20 06				20 15	20 17	20 27	20 30	20 36				20 45	20 47		21 00			21 02
Clapham Junction 10	d			20 08		20 12					20 23	20 33		20 42					20 53					21 08
Bedford	d							18 50								19 20								
Luton 10	d							19 14								19 44								
Luton Airport Parkway 7 ✈	d							19 17								19 47								
St Albans City	d							19 29								19 59								
St Pancras International 15 ⊖	d							19 54								20 24								
Farringdon 3 ⊖	d							19 58								20 29								
City Thameslink 3	d																							
London Blackfriars 3 ⊖	d							20 04								20 34								
London Bridge 4 ⊖	d				20 05			20 11							20 37	20 41								
New Cross Gate	d																							
Norwood Junction 2	d				20 16										20 48									
East Croydon	a			20 17	20 20	20 22		20 25			20 32	20 42		20 52	20 54	20 55			21 02					21 17
	d			20 18	20 21	20 23		20 25			20 33	20 43		20 53	20 55	20 55			21 03					21 18
Purley 4	d			20 23	20 27										21 00									21 23
Coulsdon South	d				20 30										21 04									
Merstham	d				20 36										21 09									
Redhill	a			20 31	20 39							20 57			21 13									21 31
	d	20 19	20 21	20 32	20 40							20 57			21 13							21 20	21 21	21 32
Reigate	a	20 23																				21 24		
Nutfield	d				20 44																			
Godstone	d				20 50																			
Edenbridge	d				20 55																			
Penshurst	d				21 02																			
Leigh (Kent)	d				21 05																			
Tonbridge 4	a				21 10																			
Earlswood (Surrey)	d														21 18									
Salfords	d														21 22									
Horley 4	d			20 38			←								21 25					←				21 38
Gatwick Airport 10 ✈	a		20 34	20 40		20 37	20 40	20 41		20 45	20 48	21 04	21 00		21 28	21 11		21 15	21 18	21 28	21 30		21 34	21 40
	d			20 41		20 39	20 41	20 42			20 49	21 05			21 29	21 12			21 19	21 29				21 41
Three Bridges 15	a			→			20 46	20 46				21 10			→	21 16				21 33				→
	d						20 46	20 47				21 10				21 17				21 34				
Crawley	d						20 50													21 37				
Ifield	d																			21 40				
Faygate	d																							
Littlehaven	d																			21 46				
Horsham 4	a						20 58													21 49				
Balcombe	d											21 16												
Haywards Heath	a							20 56			21 00	21 21				21 26			21 30					
	d							20 56			21 00	21 22				21 26			21 30					
Wivelsfield	d											21 26							21 34					
Lewes 4	a																		21 48					
Burgess Hill 4	d							21 01			21 06	21 28				21 31								
Hassocks 4	d							21 05				21 31				21 35								
Preston Park	d											21 38												
Hove 2	a										21 18													
Brighton 10	a					21 03		21 15				21 43		21 27		21 45								

Table 186

Sundays

1 July to 9 September

Bedford and London - Brighton

Network Diagram - see first Page of Table 186

		SN	SN	SN	FC	SN	SN	SN	SN	SN	FC	SN	SN	SN	SN	GW	GW	SN	SN	FC	SN	SN
		1	◇1	◇1	1	1	◇1	◇1	1	1	1	1	◇1	1	1	1	1	◇1	1	1	1	◇1
London Victoria 15 ⊖	d		21 06			21 15	21 17	21 27	21 30			21 45	21 47		22 00			22 02			22 15	22 17
Clapham Junction 10	d		21 12				21 23	21 33					21 53					22 08				22 23
Bedford	d				19 50						20 12									20 42		
Luton 10	d				20 14						20 36									21 06		
Luton Airport Parkway 7 ✈	d				20 17						20 39									21 09		
St Albans City	d				20 29						20 51									21 21		
St Pancras International 15 ⊖	d				20 54						21 24									21 54		
Farringdon 3 ⊖	d				20 58						21 29									21 59		
City Thameslink 3	d																					
London Blackfriars 3 ⊖	d				21 04						21 34									22 04		
London Bridge 4 ⊖	d	21 05			21 11					21 37	21 41								22 05	22 11		
New Cross Gate	d																					
Norwood Junction 2	d	21 16								21 48									22 16			
East Croydon	a	21 20	21 22		21 25		21 32	21 42		21 54	21 55		22 02					22 17	22 20	22 25		22 32
	d	21 21	21 23		21 25		21 33	21 43		21 55	21 55		22 03					22 18	22 21	22 25		22 33
Purley 4	d	21 27								22 00								22 23	22 27			
Coulsdon South	d	21 30								22 04									22 30			
Merstham	d	21 36								22 09									22 36			
Redhill	a	21 39						21 57		22 13								22 31	22 39			
	d	21 40						21 57		22 13						22 19	22 21	22 32	22 40			
Reigate	a															22 23						
Nutfield	d	21 44																	22 44			
Godstone	d	21 50																	22 50			
Edenbridge	d	21 55																	22 55			
Penshurst	d	22 02																	23 02			
Leigh (Kent)	d	22 05																	23 05			
Tonbridge 4	a	22 10																	23 10			
Earlswood (Surrey)	d									22 18												
Salfords	d									22 22												
Horley 4	d			←						22 25				←				22 38				
Gatwick Airport 10 ✈	a		21 37	21 40	21 41	21 45	21 48	22 04	22 00	22 28	22 11	22 15	22 18	22 28	22 30		22 33	22 40		22 41	22 45	22 48
	d		21 39	21 41	21 42		21 49	22 05		22 29	22 12		22 19	22 29				22 41		22 42		22 49
Three Bridges 15	a			21 46	21 46			22 10		→	22 16			22 33				22 46		22 46		
	d			21 46	21 47			22 10			22 17			22 34				22 46		22 47		
Crawley	d			21 50										22 37				22 50				
Ifield	d													22 40								
Faygate	d																					
Littlehaven	d													22 46								
Horsham 4	a			21 58										22 49				22 58				
Balcombe	d							22 16														
Haywards Heath	a				21 56		22 00	22 21			22 26		22 30							22 56		23 00
	d				21 56		22 00	22 22			22 26		22 30							22 56		23 00
Wivelsfield	d							22 26					22 34									
Lewes 4	a												22 48									
Burgess Hill 4	d				22 01		22 06	22 28			22 31									23 01		23 06
Hassocks 4	d				22 05			22 31			22 35									23 05		
Preston Park	d							22 38														
Hove 2	a						22 18															23 21
Brighton 10	a		22 03		22 15			22 43			22 45									23 15		

Table 186

Sundays

Bedford and London - Brighton

1 July to 9 September

Network Diagram - see first Page of Table 186

		SN	SN	SN	SN	FC	SN	SN		SN	SN	GW	GW	SN	FC	SN		SN	SN	SN	SN	FC	SN	SN
		◇1	1	1	1	1	1	◇1		1	1	1	1	1	1	1		1	◇1	1	◇1	1	1	
London Victoria 15 ⊖	d	22 27	22 30				22 45	22 47			23 00			23 04		23 15			23 17	23 30	23 32		23 45	23 47
Clapham Junction 10	d	22 33						22 53						23 10					23 23		23 38			23 53
Bedford	d					21 12									21 42							22 12		
Luton 10	d					21 36									22 06							22 36		
Luton Airport Parkway 7 ✈	d					21 39									22 09							22 39		
St Albans City	d					21 51									22 21							22 51		
St Pancras International 15 ⊖	d					22 24									22 54							23 24		
Farringdon 3 ⊖	d					22 29									22 59							23 29		
City Thameslink 3	d																							
London Blackfriars 3 ⊖	d					22 34									23 04							23 34		
London Bridge 4 ⊖	d				22 37	22 41									23 11							23 41		
New Cross Gate	d																							
Norwood Junction 2	d				22 48																			
East Croydon	a	22 42			22 54	22 55		23 03						23 22	23 25				23 37		23 52	23 56		00 06
	d	22 43			22 55	22 55		23 03						23 22	23 25				23 38		23 53	23 57		
Purley 4	d				23 00									23 29										
Coulsdon South	d				23 04									23 33										
Merstham	d				23 09									23 38										
Redhill	a	22 57			23 13									23 42							00 05			
	d	22 57		23 10	23 13							23 20	23 21	23 42							00 05			
Reigate	a											23 24												
Nutfield	d			23 14																				
Godstone	d			23 20																				
Edenbridge	d			23 25																				
Penshurst	d			23 32																				
Leigh (Kent)	d			23 35																				
Tonbridge 4	a			23 40																				
Earlswood (Surrey)	d				23 18																			
Salfords	d				23 22																			
Horley 4	d				23 25					←				23 50				←						
Gatwick Airport 10 ✈	a	23 04	23 00		23 28	23 11	23 15	23 18		23 28	23 30		23 34	23 54	23 41	23 50		23 54	23 59	00 05	00 14	00 18	00 20	
	d	23 05			23 29	23 12		23 19		23 29				23 55	23 42			23 55	00 01		00 15	00 20		
Three Bridges 15	a	23 10			→	23 16				23 33				→	23 46			00 01	00 05		00 19	00 25		
	d	23 10				23 17				23 34					23 47			00 01	00 06		00 20			
Crawley	d									23 37								00 05						
Ifield	d									23 40								00 07						
Faygate	d																							
Littlehaven	d									23 46								00 14						
Horsham 4	a									23 49								00 17						
Balcombe	d	23 16																			00 26			
Haywards Heath	a	23 21				23 26		23 30							23 56				00 15		00 31			
	d	23 22				23 26		23 30							23 56				00 15		00 31			
Wivelsfield	d	23 26						23 34													00 35			
Lewes 4	a							23 48																
Burgess Hill 4	d	23 28				23 31									00 02				00 20		00 37			
Hassocks 4	d	23 31				23 35									00 06						00 41			
Preston Park	d	23 38																			00 48			
Hove 2	a																		00 31					
Brighton 10	a	23 42				23 45									00 16						00 52			

Table 186

Sundays

1 July to 9 September

Bedford and London - Brighton

Network Diagram - see first Page of Table 186

			FC 1	FC 1	FC 1
London Victoria 15	⊖	d			
Clapham Junction 10		d			
Bedford		d	22 42	23 12	23 42
Luton 10		d	23 06	23 36	00 06
Luton Airport Parkway 7	✈	d	23 09	23 39	00 09
St Albans City		d	23 21	23 51	00 21
St Pancras International 15	⊖	d	23 54	00 24	00 54
Farringdon 3	⊖	d	23 59	00 29	
City Thameslink 3		d			
London Blackfriars 3	⊖	d	00 05	00 35	01 05
London Bridge 4	⊖	d	00 12	00 42	
New Cross Gate		d			
Norwood Junction 2		d			
East Croydon	🚌	a	00 26	00 56	01 31
		d	00 26	00 57	01 32
Purley 4		d			
Coulsdon South		d			
Merstham		d			
Redhill		a			
		d			
Reigate		a			
Nutfield		d			
Godstone		d			
Edenbridge		d			
Penshurst		d			
Leigh (Kent)		d			
Tonbridge 4		a			
Earlswood (Surrey)		d			
Salfords		d			
Horley 4		d			
Gatwick Airport 10	✈	a	00 48	01 18	01 51
		d	00 49	01 22	01 52
Three Bridges 15		a	00 54	01 28	01 58
		d			
Crawley		d			
Ifield		d			
Faygate		d			
Littlehaven		d			
Horsham 4		a			
Balcombe		d			
Haywards Heath		a			
		d			
Wivelsfield		d			
Lewes 4		a			
Burgess Hill 4		d			
Hassocks 4		d			
Preston Park		d			
Hove 2		a			
Brighton 10		a			

Table 186

Sundays

from 16 September

Bedford and London - Brighton

Network Diagram - see first Page of Table 186

		SN	SN	FC	SN	SN	SN	SN		SN	GW	SN	FC	SN	SN	SN		SN	SN		FC	SN	GW	SN	
		◇1	◇1	1	1	◇1	1	1		1	1	1	1	1	1	1		1	◇1		1	1	1	1	
London Victoria 15 ⊖	d	23p02	23p06		23p10	23p17		23p30				23p32		23p45	23p47	23p49		00 02	00 05			00 14		00 30	
Clapham unction 10	d	23p08	23p12		23p16	23p23						23p38			23p53	23p56			00 11			00 20			
Bedford	d			21p52									22p16								22p42				
uton 10	d			22p16									22p40								23p06				
uton Airport Parkway 7 ✈	d			22p18									22p42								23p09				
St Albans City	d			22p30									22p54								23p21				
St Pancras hternational 15 ⊖	d			22p54									23p24								23p54				
Farringdon 3 ⊖	d			22p59									23p29								23p59				
City Thameslink 3	d																								
London Blackfriars 3 ⊖	d			23p05									23p35								00 05				
London Bridge 4 ⊖	d			23p12									23p42								00 12				
bw Cross Gate	d																								
brwood unction 2	d																								
East Croydon	a	23p17	23p22	23p24	23p27	23p32						23p52	23p56		00 05	00 09			00 24		00 26	00 31			
	d	23p18	23p23	23p25	23p28	23p33						23p52	23p57		00 06				00 24		00 27	00 32			
Purley 4	d				23p33										00 12							00 37			
Coulsdon South	d				23p37										00 15							00 41			
Merstham	d				23p42										00 21							00 47			
Redhill	a	23p30			23p46							00 03			00 24							00 50			
	d	23p31			23p46					23p55	00 03	00 05			00 25							00 51	00 54		
Reigate	a																								
btfield	d																								
Godstone	d																								
Eenbridge	d									00 06															
Penshurst	d																								
eigh (Kent)	d																								
Tonbridge 4	a									00 15															
Erlswood (Surrey)	d				23p49																				
Salfords	d				23p52																				
Horley 4	d				23p56		←								00 31							00 57			
Gatwick Airport 10 ✈	a	23p38		23p40	23p58	23p49	23p58	00 05			00 10	00 14	00 18	00 20	00 33			00 38	00 42		00 48	00 59	01 02	01 05	
	d	23p39		23p41	23p59	23p50	23p59					00 15	00 19		00 34				00 43		00 49	01 00			
Three Bridges 15	a	23p44		23p47	→	23p54	00 04					00 20	00 24		00 39				00 48		00 54	01 05			
	d	23p44		23p47		23p55	00 04					00 20			00 39				00 48						
Crawley	d						00 07								00 43										
field	d						00 10								00 46										
Faygate	d																								
ttlehaven	d						00 16								00 52										
Horsham 4	a						00 19								00 55										
Balcombe	d			23p53								00 28													
Haywards Heath	a	23p53	23p46	23p58		00 04						00 34							00 58						
	d	23p53	23p46	23p59		00 05						00 35							01 02	01 06					
Welsfield	d	23p57		00 03								00 39													
ewes 4	a																			01 20					
Burgess Hill 4	d	23p59		00 05		00 10						00 41													
Hassocks 4	d	00 03		00 08								00 44													
Preston Park	d	00 09		00 15								00 51													
Hove 2	a					00 23																			
Brighton 10	a	00 15	00 01	00 19								00 55							01s16						

Table 186

Sundays

from 16 September

Bedford and London - Brighton

Network Diagram - see first Page of Table 186

		FC	SN	FC	SN	SN	SN	SN		SN	SN	SN	SN	SN	SN	SN		SN	SN	SN	GW	SN	SN	SN
		1	1	1	1	1	1	1		1	1	1	1	1	1	1		◇1	1	1	1	1	◇1	1
																			ᚗ	ᚗ		ᚗ		ᚗ
London Victoria 15 ⊖	d		01 00		02 00	03 00	03 30	04 00		04 30	05 00	05 02	05 15	05 30	05 45			05 47	06 00	06 15		06 30	06 32	06 45
Clapham Junction 10	d		01 08		02 08	03 08		04 08				05 08						05 53					06 38	
Bedford	d	23p12		23p42																				
Luton 10	d	23p36		00 06																				
Luton Airport Parkway 7 ✈	d	23p39		00 09																				
St Albans City	d	23p51		00 21																				
St Pancras International 15 ⊖	d	00 24		00 54																				
Farringdon 3 ⊖	d	00 29																						
City Thameslink 3	d																							
London Blackfriars 3 ⊖	d	00 35		01 05																				
London Bridge 4 ⊖	d	00 42																						
New Cross Gate	d																							
Norwood Junction 2	d																							
East Croydon	a	00 56	01 21	01 31	02 21	03 21		04 21				05 21						06 05					06 51	
	d	00 57	01 22	01 32	02 22	03 22		04 21				05 23						06 06					06 52	
Purley 4	d		01 27		02 27	03 27		04 26				05 28											06 56	
Coulsdon South	d																						07 00	
Merstham	d																						07 05	
Redhill	a																	06 18					07 09	
	d																	06 19			06 20		07 09	
Reigate	a																				06 24			
Nutfield	d																							
Godstone	d																							
Edenbridge	d																							
Penshurst	d																							
Leigh (Kent)	d																							
Tonbridge 4	a																							
Earlswood (Surrey)	d																							
Salfords	d																							
Horley 4	d		01 43		02 42	03 42		04 42										06 25					07 15	
Gatwick Airport 10 ✈	a	01 18	01 46	01 51	02 44	03 44	04 05	04 45		05 05	05 35	05 44	05 50	06 05	06 20			06 31	06 35	06 47		07 05	07 18	07 20
	d	01 22	01 48	01 52	02 46	03 46		04 46				05 45				06 29		06 32					07 19	
Three Bridges 15	a	01 28	01 52	01 58	03 00	04 00		04 54				05 50				06 33		06 36					07 23	
	d		01 53					04 54				05 50				06 40		06 36					07 24	
Crawley	d															06 43								
Ifield	d															06 46								
Faygate	d																							
Littlehaven	d															06 52								
Horsham 4	a															06 56								
Balcombe	d																						07 30	
Haywards Heath	a		02 06					05 06				05 59						06 47					07 35	
	d		02 06					05 07				06 00						06 47					07 36	
Wivelsfield	d																	06 51					07 40	
Lewes 4	a																							
Burgess Hill 4	d																	06 53					07 42	
Hassocks 4	d																	06 57					07 45	
Preston Park	d																	07 03					07 52	
Hove 2	a																							
Brighton 10	a		02 23					05 21				06 18						07 08					07 58	

Table 186

Sundays

from 16 September

Bedford and London - Brighton

Network Diagram - see first Page of Table 186

		GW	SN	GW	SN	FC	SN	SN		SN	SN	SN	SN	SN	FC	SN		GW	GW	SN	SN	FC	SN	SN
		1	1	1	◇1	1	◇1	1		1	◇1	1	1	1	1	1		1	1	1	◇1	1	1	◇1
			T					T		T		T								T			T	
London Victoria 15 ⊖	d		07 00		07 02			07 15		07 30	07 32	07 45								08 00	08 04		08 15	08 17
Clapham Junction 10	d				07 08						07 38										08 10			08 23
Bedford	d														06 12							06 42		
Luton 10	d														06 36							07 06		
Luton Airport Parkway 7 ✈	d														06 39							07 09		
St Albans City	d														06 51							07 21		
St Pancras International 15 ⊖	d														07 24							07 54		
Farringdon 3 ⊖	d														07 29							07 59		
City Thameslink 3	d																							
London Blackfriars 3 ⊖	d					06 55									07 34							08 04		
London Bridge 4 ⊖	d													07 37	07 41							08 11		
New Cross Gate	d																							
Norwood Junction 2	d													07 48										
East Croydon	a				07 23	07 25					07 50			07 54	07 56						08 23	08 27		08 36
	d				07 23	07 25					07 51			07 55	07 57						08 24	08 28		08 37
Purley 4	d				07 29									08 00							08 30			
Coulsdon South	d													08 04										
Merstham	d													08 09										
Redhill	a				07 37						08 03			08 13							08 38			
	d	07 15		07 20	07 37						08 04		08 10	08 13				08 19	08 21		08 39			
Reigate	a			07 24														08 23						
Nutfield	d												08 14											
Godstone	d												08 20											
Edenbridge	d												08 25											
Penshurst	d												08 32											
Leigh (Kent)	d												08 35											
Tonbridge 4	a												08 40											
Earlswood (Surrey)	d																							
Salfords	d																							
Horley 4	d				07 43		←							08 22		←					08 45			
Gatwick Airport 10 ✈	a	07 27	07 35		07 46	07 41	07 46	07 50		08 05	08 11	08 20		08 24	08 18	08 24			08 31	08 35	08 47	08 48	08 50	08 54
	d				07 47	07 42	07 47				08 12			08 25	08 20	08 25					08 48	08 50		08 56
Three Bridges 15	a				→	07 46	07 51				08 16			→	08 24	08 30					08 53	08 54		
	d					07 47	07 52				08 17				08 24	08 33					08 53	08 54		
Crawley	d						07 55									08 36					08 56			
Ifield	d						07 58									08 39								
Faygate	d																							
Littlehaven	d						08 04									08 45								
Horsham 4	a						08 07									08 49					09 04			
Balcombe	d										08 23													
Haywards Heath	a					07 56					08 28				08 33							09 03		09 06
	d					07 56					08 28				08 34							09 04		09 07
Wivelsfield	d										08 32													
Lewes 4	a																							
Burgess Hill 4	d					08 01					08 34				08 39							09 09		09 12
Hassocks 4	d					08 05					08 38				08 42							09 12		
Preston Park	d										08 44													
Hove 2	a																							09 24
Brighton 10	a					08 15					08 48				08 52							09 22		

Table 186

Sundays

from 16 September

Bedford and London - Brighton

Network Diagram - see first Page of Table 186

		SN 1 🚲	SN ◇1	SN 1 🚲	SN 1	SN 1	FC 1	SN 1		SN ◇1 🚲	GW 1	GW 1	SN 1 🚲	SN ◇1	SN ◇1	FC 1		SN 1 🚲	SN ◇1	SN 1 🚲	SN ◇1	SN 1 🚲	SN 1	SN 1
London Victoria 15 ⊖	d	08 30	08 32	08 45						08 47			09 00	09 02	09 04			09 15	09 17	09 30	09 32	09 45		
Clapham Junction 10	d		08 38							08 53				09 08	09 10				09 23		09 38			
Bedford	d						07 12									07 50								
Luton 10	d						07 36									08 14								
Luton Airport Parkway 7 ✈	d						07 39									08 17								
St Albans City	d						07 51									08 29								
St Pancras International 15 ⊖	d						08 24									08 54								
Farringdon 3 ⊖	d						08 29									08 58								
City Thameslink 3	d																							
London Blackfriars 3 ⊖	d						08 34									09 04								
London Bridge 4 ⊖	d					08 37	08 41									09 11								09 37
New Cross Gate	d																							
Norwood Junction 2	d					08 48																		09 48
East Croydon	a		08 50			08 54	08 56			09 06				09 21	09 23	09 27			09 36		09 52			09 54
	d		08 51			08 55	08 57			09 07				09 22	09 24	09 28			09 37		09 53			09 55
Purley 4	d					09 00									09 30									10 00
Coulsdon South	d					09 04																		10 04
Merstham	d					09 09																		10 09
Redhill	a		09 03			09 13									09 38						10 05			10 13
	d		09 04		09 10	09 16					09 20	09 21			09 39						10 06		10 10	10 16
Reigate	a										09 24													
Nutfield	d				09 14																		10 14	
Godstone	d				09 20																		10 20	
Edenbridge	d				09 25																		10 25	
Penshurst	d				09 32																		10 32	
Leigh (Kent)	d				09 35																		10 35	
Tonbridge 4	a				09 40																		10 40	
Earlswood (Surrey)	d																							
Salfords	d																							
Horley 4	d					09 22		←							09 45									10 22
Gatwick Airport 10 ✈	a	09 05	09 11	09 20		09 24	09 18	09 24		09 27		09 33	09 35	09 39	09 47	09 49		09 50	09 54	10 05	10 13	10 20		10 24
	d		09 12			09 25	09 20	09 25		09 29				09 40	09 48	09 50			09 56		10 14			10 25
Three Bridges 15	a		09 16			→	09 24	09 30							09 53	09 54					10 18			→
	d		09 17				09 24	09 33							09 53	09 54					10 19			
Crawley	d							09 37							09 56									
Ifield	d							09 39																
Faygate	d																							
Littlehaven	d							09 46																
Horsham 4	a							09 49							10 04									
Balcombe	d		09 23																		10 25			
Haywards Heath	a		09 28				09 33			09 40						10 03			10 06		10 30			
	d		09 28				09 34			09 41						10 04			10 07		10 30			
Wivelsfield	d		09 32							09 45											10 34			
Lewes 4	a									09 58														
Burgess Hill 4	d		09 34				09 39									10 09			10 12		10 36			
Hassocks 4	d		09 38				09 42									10 12					10 40			
Preston Park	d		09 44																		10 46			
Hove 2	a																		10 24					
Brighton 10	a		09 48				09 52							10 03		10 22					10 50			

Table 186

Sundays

from 16 September

Bedford and London - Brighton

Network Diagram - see first Page of Table 186

		FC 1	SN 1	SN ◇1 🛒	GW 1	GW 1	SN 1 🛒	SN ◇1 🛒		SN ◇1 🛒	FC 1	SN 1 🛒	SN ◇1	SN 1 🛒	SN ◇1	SN 1 🛒		SN 1	SN 1	FC 1	SN 1	SN ◇1 🛒	GW 1	GW 1	
London Victoria 15 ⊖	d			09 47			10 00	10 02		10 04		10 15	10 17	10 30	10 32	10 45						10 47			
Clapham Junction 10	d			09 53				10 08		10 10			10 23		10 38							10 53			
Bedford	d	08 20									08 50									09 20					
Luton 10	d	08 44									09 14									09 44					
Luton Airport Parkway 7 ✈	d	08 47									09 17									09 47					
St Albans City	d	08 59									09 29									09 59					
St Pancras International 15 ⊖	d	09 24									09 54									10 24					
Farringdon 3 ⊖	d	09 29									09 58									10 29					
City Thameslink 3	d																								
London Blackfriars 3 ⊖	d	09 34									10 04									10 34					
London Bridge 4 ⊖	d	09 41									10 11								10 37	10 41					
New Cross Gate	d																								
Norwood Junction 2	d																		10 48						
East Croydon 🚊	a	09 56		10 06				10 21		10 23	10 27		10 36		10 52				10 54	10 56		11 06			
	d	09 57		10 07				10 22		10 24	10 28		10 37		10 53				10 55	10 57		11 07			
Purley 4	d									10 30									11 00						
Coulsdon South	d																		11 04						
Merstham	d																		11 09						
Redhill	a									10 38					11 05				11 13						
	d				10 19	10 21				10 39					11 06			11 10	11 16				11 20	11 21	
Reigate	a				10 23																		11 24		
Nutfield	d																	11 14							
Godstone	d																	11 20							
Edenbridge	d																	11 25							
Penshurst	d																	11 32							
Leigh (Kent)	d																	11 35							
Tonbridge 4	a																	11 40							
Earlswood (Surrey)	d																								
Salfords	d																								
Horley 4	d		←							10 45									11 22		←				
Gatwick Airport 10 ✈	a	10 18	10 24	10 27		10 30	10 35	10 39		10 47	10 49	10 50	10 54	11 05	11 13	11 20			11 24	11 18	11 24	11 27		11 30	
	d	10 20	10 25	10 29				10 40		10 48	10 50		10 56		11 14				11 25	11 20	11 25	11 29			
Three Bridges 15	a	10 24	10 30							10 53	10 54				11 18				→	11 24	11 30				
	d	10 24	10 33							10 53	10 54				11 19					11 24	11 33				
Crawley	d		10 37							10 56											11 37				
Ifield	d		10 39																		11 39				
Faygate	d																								
Littlehaven	d		10 46																		11 46				
Horsham 4	a		10 49							11 04											11 49				
Balcombe	d														11 25										
Haywards Heath	a	10 35		10 40							11 03		11 06		11 30					11 35		11 40			
	d	10 36		10 41							11 04		11 07		11 30					11 36		11 41			
Wivelsfield	d			10 45											11 34							11 45			
Lewes 4	a			10 58																		11 58			
Burgess Hill 4	d	10 41									11 09		11 12		11 36					11 41					
Hassocks 4	d	10 44									11 12				11 40					11 44					
Preston Park	d														11 46										
Hove 2	a												11 24												
Brighton 10	a	10 54						11 03			11 22				11 50					11 54					

Table 186

Sundays

from 16 September

Bedford and London - Brighton

Network Diagram - see first Page of Table 186

		SN	SN	SN	FC	SN	SN	SN		SN	SN	SN	SN	FC	SN	SN		GW	GW	SN	SN	SN	FC	SN	
		1	◇1	◇1	1	1	◇1	1		◇1	1	1	1	1	1	◇1		1	1	1	◇1	◇1	1	1	
		[trolley]	[trolley]	[trolley]		[trolley]		[trolley]			[trolley]					[trolley]				[trolley]	[trolley]	[trolley]		[trolley]	
London Victoria 15 ⊖	d	11 00	11 02	11 04		11 15	11 17	11 30		11 32	11 45					11 47				12 00	12 02	12 04		12 15	
Clapham Junction 10	d		11 08	11 10			11 23			11 38						11 53					12 08	12 10			
Bedford	d				09 50									10 20									10 50		
Luton 10	d				10 14									10 44									11 14		
Luton Airport Parkway 7 ✈	d				10 17									10 47									11 17		
St Albans City	d				10 29									10 59									11 29		
St Pancras International 15 ⊖	d				10 54									11 24									11 54		
Farringdon 3 ⊖	d				10 58									11 29									11 58		
City Thameslink 3	d																								
London Blackfriars 3 ⊖	d				11 04									11 34									12 04		
London Bridge 4 ⊖	d				11 11								11 37	11 41									12 11		
New Cross Gate	d																								
Norwood Junction 2	d												11 48												
East Croydon	a		11 21	11 23	11 27		11 36			11 52			11 54	11 56		12 06					12 21	12 23	12 27		
	d		11 22	11 24	11 28		11 37			11 53			11 55	11 57		12 07					12 22	12 24	12 28		
Purley 4	d			11 30									12 00									12 30			
Coulsdon South	d												12 04												
Merstham	d												12 09												
Redhill	a			11 38						12 05			12 13									12 38			
	d			11 39						12 06		12 10	12 16					12 19	12 21			12 39			
Reigate	a																	12 23							
Nutfield	d											12 14													
Godstone	d											12 20													
Edenbridge	d											12 25													
Penshurst	d											12 32													
Leigh (Kent)	d											12 35													
Tonbridge 4	a											12 40													
Earlswood (Surrey)	d																								
Salfords	d																								
Horley 4	d			11 45									12 22		←							12 45			
Gatwick Airport 10 ✈	a	11 35	11 39	11 47	11 49	11 50	11 54	12 05		12 13	12 20		12 24	12 18	12 24	12 27			12 30	12 35	12 39	12 47	12 49	12 50	
	d		11 40	11 48	11 50		11 56			12 14			12 25	12 20	12 25	12 29					12 40	12 48	12 50		
Three Bridges 15	a			11 53	11 54					12 18			→	12 24	12 30							12 53	12 54		
	d			11 53	11 54					12 19				12 24	12 33							12 53	12 54		
Crawley	d			11 56											12 37							12 56			
Ifield	d														12 39										
Faygate	d																								
Littlehaven	d														12 46										
Horsham 4	a			12 04											12 49							13 04			
Balcombe	d									12 25															
Haywards Heath	a				12 03		12 06			12 30				12 35		12 40							13 03		
	d				12 04		12 07			12 30				12 36		12 41							13 04		
Wivelsfield	d									12 34						12 45									
Lewes 4	a															12 58									
Burgess Hill 4	d				12 09		12 12			12 36				12 41									13 09		
Hassocks 4	d				12 12					12 40				12 44									13 12		
Preston Park	d									12 46															
Hove 2	a						12 24																		
Brighton 10	a		12 03		12 22					12 50				12 54							13 03		13 22		

Table 186

Sundays

from 16 September

Bedford and London - Brighton

Network Diagram - see first Page of Table 186

		SN	FC	SN	SN	SN	SN	SN		FC	SN	SN	GW	GW	FC	SN		SN	SN	FC	SN	SN	SN	SN
		◇1	1	1	◇1	1	1	1		1	1	◇1	1	1	1	1		◇1	◇1	1	1	◇1	1	◇1
				🚲		🚲						🚲				🚲		🚲	🚲		🚲		🚲	
London Victoria 15 ⊖	d	12 17		12 30	12 32	12 45						12 47				13 00		13 02	13 04		13 15	13 17	13 30	13 32
Clapham Junction 10	d	12 23			12 38							12 53						13 08	13 10			13 23		13 38
Bedford	d		11 06							11 20					11 36					11 50				
Luton 10	d		11 30							11 44					12 00					12 14				
Luton Airport Parkway 7 ✈	d		11 33							11 47					12 03					12 17				
St Albans City	d		11 45							11 59					12 15					12 29				
St Pancras International 15 ⊖	d		12 09							12 24					12 39					12 54				
Farringdon 3 ⊖	d		12 14							12 29					12 44					12 58				
City Thameslink 3	d																							
London Blackfriars 3 ⊖	d		12 19							12 34					12 49					13 04				
London Bridge 4 ⊖	d		12 26					12 37		12 41					12 56					13 11				
New Cross Gate	d																							
Norwood Junction 2	d							12 48																
East Croydon 🚊	a	12 36	12 42		12 52			12 54		12 56		13 06			13 12			13 21	13 23	13 27		13 36		13 52
	d	12 37	12 43		12 53			12 55		12 57		13 07			13 13			13 22	13 24	13 28		13 37		13 53
Purley 4	d							13 00											13 30					
Coulsdon South	d							13 04																
Merstham	d							13 09																
Redhill	a				13 05			13 13											13 38					14 05
	d				13 06		13 10	13 16					13 20	13 21					13 39					14 06
Reigate	a												13 24											
Nutfield	d						13 14																	
Godstone	d						13 20																	
Edenbridge	d						13 25																	
Penshurst	d						13 32																	
Leigh (Kent)	d						13 35																	
Tonbridge 4	a						13 40																	
Earlswood (Surrey)	d																							
Salfords	d																							
Horley 4	d							13 22			←								13 45					
Gatwick Airport 10 ✈	a	12 54	13 00	13 05	13 13	13 20		13 24		13 18	13 24	13 27		13 30	13 33	13 35		13 39	13 47	13 49	13 50	13 54	14 05	14 13
	d	12 56	13 01		13 14			13 25		13 20	13 25	13 29			13 33			13 40	13 48	13 50		13 56		14 14
Three Bridges 15	a		13 05		13 18			→		13 24	13 30				13 38				13 53	13 54				14 18
	d				13 19					13 24	13 33								13 53	13 54				14 19
Crawley	d										13 37								13 56					
Ifield	d										13 39													
Faygate	d																							
Littlehaven	d										13 46													
Horsham 4	a										13 49								14 04					
Balcombe	d				13 25																			14 25
Haywards Heath	a	13 06			13 30					13 35		13 40								14 03		14 06		14 30
	d	13 07			13 30					13 36		13 41								14 04		14 07		14 30
Wivelsfield	d				13 34							13 45												14 34
Lewes 4	a											13 56												
Burgess Hill 4	d	13 12			13 36					13 41										14 09		14 12		14 36
Hassocks 4	d				13 40					13 44										14 12				14 40
Preston Park	d				13 46																			14 46
Hove 2	a	13 24																				14 24		
Brighton 10	a				13 50					13 54								14 03		14 22				14 50

Table 186

Sundays

from 16 September

Bedford and London - Brighton

Network Diagram - see first Page of Table 186

		SN	SN	SN	FC	SN	SN	GW		GW	FC	SN	SN	SN	FC	SN		SN	SN	SN	SN	SN	SN	FC
		1	1	1	1	1	◇1	1		1	1	1	◇1	◇1	1	1		◇1	1	◇1	1	1	1	1
		🛒					🛒					🛒	🛒	🛒		🛒			🛒		🛒			
London Victoria 15 ⊖	d	13 45					13 47					14 00	14 02	14 04		14 15		14 17	14 30	14 32	14 45			
Clapham Junction 10	d						13 53						14 08	14 10				14 23		14 38				
Bedford	d				12 20						12 36				12 50									13 20
Luton 10	d				12 44						13 00				13 14									13 44
Luton Airport Parkway 7 ✈	d				12 47						13 03				13 17									13 47
St Albans City	d				12 59						13 15				13 29									13 59
St Pancras International 15 ⊖	d				13 24						13 39				13 54									14 24
Farringdon 3 ⊖	d				13 29						13 44				13 58									14 29
City Thameslink 3	d																							
London Blackfriars 3 ⊖	d				13 34						13 49				14 04									14 34
London Bridge 4 ⊖	d			13 37	13 41						13 56				14 11								14 37	14 41
New Cross Gate	d																							
Norwood Junction 2	d			13 48																			14 48	
East Croydon	a			13 54	13 56		14 06				14 12		14 21	14 23	14 27			14 36		14 52			14 54	14 56
	d			13 55	13 57		14 07				14 13		14 22	14 24	14 28			14 37		14 53			14 55	14 57
Purley 4	d			14 00										14 30									15 00	
Coulsdon South	d			14 04																			15 04	
Merstham	d			14 09																			15 09	
Redhill	a			14 13										14 38						15 05			15 13	
	d		14 10	14 16				14 19		14 21				14 39						15 06		15 10	15 16	
Reigate	a							14 23																
Nutfield	d		14 14																			15 14		
Godstone	d		14 20																			15 20		
Edenbridge	d		14 25																			15 25		
Penshurst	d		14 32																			15 32		
Leigh (Kent)	d		14 35																			15 35		
Tonbridge 4	a		14 40																			15 40		
Earlswood (Surrey)	d																							
Salfords	d																							
Horley 4	d			14 22		←								14 45									15 22	
Gatwick Airport 10 ✈	a	14 20		14 24	14 18	14 24	14 27			14 30	14 33	14 35	14 39	14 47	14 49	14 50		14 54	15 05	15 13	15 20		15 24	15 18
	d			14 25	14 20	14 25	14 29				14 33		14 40	14 48	14 50			14 56		15 14			15 25	15 20
Three Bridges 15	a			→	14 24	14 30					14 38			14 53	14 54					15 18			→	15 24
	d				14 24	14 33								14 53	14 54					15 19				15 24
Crawley	d					14 37								14 56										
Ifield	d					14 39																		
Faygate	d																							
Littlehaven	d					14 46																		
Horsham 4	a					14 49								15 04										
Balcombe	d																			15 25				
Haywards Heath	a				14 35		14 40								15 03			15 06		15 30				15 35
	d				14 36		14 41								15 04			15 07		15 30				15 36
Wivelsfield	d						14 45													15 34				
Lewes 4	a						14 56																	
Burgess Hill 4	d				14 41										15 09			15 12		15 36				15 41
Hassocks 4	d				14 44										15 12					15 40				15 44
Preston Park	d																			15 46				
Hove 2	a																	15 24						
Brighton 10	a				14 54								15 03		15 22					15 50				15 54

Table 186

Sundays

from 16 September

Bedford and London - Brighton

Network Diagram - see first Page of Table 186

		SN	SN	GW	GW	SN	SN	SN		FC	SN	SN	SN	SN	SN	SN		SN	FC	SN	SN	GW	GW	SN
		[1]	◇[1]	[1]	[1]	[1]	◇[1]	◇[1]		[1]	[1]	◇[1]	[1]	◇[1]	[1]	[1]		[1]	[1]	[1]	◇[1]	[1]	[1]	[1]
			🛒			🛒	🛒	🛒			🛒		🛒		🛒						🛒			🛒
London Victoria [15] ⊖	d		14 47			15 00	15 02	15 04			15 15	15 17	15 30	15 32	15 45						15 47			16 00
Clapham Junction [10]	d		14 53				15 08	15 10				15 23		15 38							15 53			
Bedford	d									13 50									14 20					
Luton [10]	d									14 14									14 44					
Luton Airport Parkway [7] ✈	d									14 17									14 47					
St Albans City	d									14 29									14 59					
St Pancras International [15] ⊖	d									14 54									15 24					
Farringdon [3] ⊖	d									14 58									15 29					
City Thameslink [3]	d																							
London Blackfriars [3] ⊖	d									15 04									15 34					
London Bridge [4] ⊖	d									15 11								15 37	15 41					
New Cross Gate	d																							
Norwood Junction [2]	d																	15 48						
East Croydon 🚋	a		15 06				15 21	15 23		15 27		15 36		15 52				15 54	15 56		16 06			
	d		15 07				15 22	15 24		15 28		15 37		15 53				15 55	15 57		16 07			
Purley [4]	d							15 30										16 00						
Coulsdon South	d																	16 04						
Merstham	d																	16 09						
Redhill	a							15 38						16 05				16 13						
	d			15 20	15 21			15 39						16 06		16 10		16 16				16 19	16 21	
Reigate	a			15 24																		16 23		
Nutfield	d															16 14								
Godstone	d															16 20								
Edenbridge	d															16 25								
Penshurst	d															16 32								
Leigh (Kent)	d															16 35								
Tonbridge [4]	a															16 40								
Earlswood (Surrey)	d																							
Salfords	d																							
Horley [4]	d	←						15 45										16 22		←				
Gatwick Airport [10] ✈	a	15 24	15 27		15 30	15 35	15 39	15 47		15 49	15 50	15 54	16 05	16 13	16 20			16 24	16 18	16 24	16 27		16 30	16 35
	d	15 25	15 29				15 40	15 48		15 50		15 56		16 14				16 25	16 20	16 25	16 29			
Three Bridges [15]	a	15 30						15 53		15 54				16 18				→	16 24	16 30				
	d	15 33						15 53		15 54				16 19					16 24	16 33				
Crawley	d	15 37						15 56												16 37				
Ifield	d	15 39																		16 39				
Faygate	d																							
Littlehaven	d	15 46																		16 46				
Horsham [4]	a	15 49						16 04												16 49				
Balcombe	d													16 25										
Haywards Heath	a		15 40							16 03		16 06		16 30					16 35		16 40			
	d		15 41							16 04		16 07		16 30					16 36		16 41			
Wivelsfield	d		15 45											16 34							16 45			
Lewes [4]	a		15 56																		16 58			
Burgess Hill [4]	d									16 09		16 12		16 36					16 41					
Hassocks [4]	d									16 12				16 40					16 44					
Preston Park	d													16 46										
Hove [2]	a											16 24												
Brighton [10]	a						16 03			16 22				16 50					16 54					

Table 186

Sundays

from 16 September

Bedford and London - Brighton

Network Diagram - see first Page of Table 186

		SN	SN	FC	SN	SN	SN	SN		SN	SN	SN	FC	SN	SN	GW		GW	SN	SN	SN	FC	SN	SN	
		◇1	◇1	1	1	◇1	1	◇1		1	1	1	1	1	◇1	1		1	1	◇1	◇1	1	1	◇1	
		🛒	🛒		🛒		🛒			🛒					🛒				🛒	🛒	🛒		🛒		
London Victoria 15 ⊖	d	16 02	16 04		16 15	16 17	16 30	16 32		16 45					16 47				17 00	17 02	17 04		17 15	17 17	
Clapham Junction 10	d	16 08	16 10			16 23		16 38							16 53					17 08	17 10			17 23	
Bedford	d			14 50									15 20									15 50			
Luton 10	d			15 14									15 44									16 14			
Luton Airport Parkway 7 ✈	d			15 17									15 47									16 17			
St Albans City	d			15 29									15 59									16 29			
St Pancras International 15 ⊖	d			15 54									16 24									16 54			
Farringdon 3 ⊖	d			15 58									16 29									16 58			
City Thameslink 3	d																								
London Blackfriars 3 ⊖	d			16 04									16 34									17 04			
London Bridge 4 ⊖	d			16 11								16 37	16 41									17 11			
New Cross Gate	d																								
Norwood Junction 2	d											16 48													
East Croydon	a	16 21	16 23	16 27		16 36		16 52				16 54	16 56		17 06					17 21	17 23	17 27		17 36	
	d	16 22	16 24	16 28		16 37		16 53				16 55	16 57		17 07					17 22	17 24	17 28		17 37	
Purley 4	d		16 30									17 00									17 30				
Coulsdon South	d											17 04													
Merstham	d											17 09													
Redhill	a		16 38					17 05				17 13									17 38				
	d		16 39					17 06			17 10	17 16				17 20		17 21			17 39				
Reigate	a															17 24									
Nutfield	d										17 14														
Godstone	d										17 20														
Edenbridge	d										17 25														
Penshurst	d										17 32														
Leigh (Kent)	d										17 35														
Tonbridge 4	a										17 40														
Earlswood (Surrey)	d																								
Salfords	d																								
Horley 4	d		16 45									17 22		←							17 45				
Gatwick Airport 10 ✈	a	16 39	16 47	16 49	16 50	16 54	17 05	17 13		17 20		17 24	17 18	17 24	17 27			17 30	17 35	17 39	17 47	17 49	17 50	17 54	
	d	16 40	16 48	16 50		16 56		17 14				17 25	17 20	17 25	17 29					17 40	17 48	17 50		17 56	
Three Bridges 15	a		16 53	16 54				17 18				→	17 24	17 30							17 53	17 54			
	d		16 53	16 54				17 19					17 24	17 33							17 53	17 54			
Crawley	d		16 56											17 37							17 56				
Ifield	d													17 39											
Faygate	d																								
Littlehaven	d													17 46											
Horsham 4	a		17 04											17 49							18 04				
Balcombe	d							17 25																	
Haywards Heath	a			17 03		17 06		17 30					17 35		17 40							18 03		18 06	
	d			17 04		17 07		17 30					17 36		17 41							18 04		18 07	
Wivelsfield	d							17 34							17 45										
Lewes 4	a														17 58										
Burgess Hill 4	d			17 09		17 12		17 36					17 41									18 09		18 12	
Hassocks 4	d			17 12				17 40					17 44									18 12			
Preston Park	d							17 46																	
Hove 2	a					17 24																		18 24	
Brighton 10	a	17 03		17 22				17 50					17 54							18 03		18 22			

Table 186

Sundays

from 16 September

Bedford and London - Brighton

Network Diagram - see first Page of Table 186

		SN	SN	SN	SN	SN	FC	SN	SN	GW	GW	SN	SN	SN	FC	SN	SN	FC	SN	SN	SN	SN
		1	◇1	1	1	1	1	1	◇1	1	1	1	◇1	◇1	1	1	◇1	1	1	◇1	1	1
		🛒		🛒					🛒			🛒	🛒	🛒		🛒			🛒		🛒	
London Victoria 15 ⊖	d	17 30	17 32	17 45					17 47			18 00	18 02	18 04		18 15	18 17		18 30	18 32	18 45	
Clapham Junction 10	d		17 38						17 53				18 08	18 10			18 23			18 38		
Bedford	d						16 20								16 50			17 06				
Luton 10	d						16 44								17 14			17 30				
Luton Airport Parkway 7 ✈	d						16 47								17 17			17 33				
St Albans City	d						16 59								17 29			17 45				
St Pancras International 15 ⊖	d						17 24								17 54			18 09				
Farringdon 3 ⊖	d						17 29								17 58			18 14				
City Thameslink 3	d																					
London Blackfriars 3 ⊖	d						17 34								18 04			18 19				
London Bridge 4 ⊖	d					17 37	17 41								18 11			18 26				
New Cross Gate	d																					
Norwood Junction 2	d					17 48																
East Croydon	a		17 52			17 54	17 56		18 06				18 21	18 23	18 27		18 36	18 38		18 52		
	d		17 53			17 55	17 57		18 07				18 22	18 24	18 28		18 37	18 39		18 53		
Purley 4	d					18 00								18 30								
Coulsdon South	d					18 04																
Merstham	d					18 09																
Redhill	a		18 05			18 13								18 38						19 05		
	d		18 06		18 10	18 16				18 19	18 21			18 39						19 06		19 10
Reigate	a									18 23												
Nutfield	d				18 14																	19 14
Godstone	d				18 20																	19 20
Edenbridge	d				18 25																	19 25
Penshurst	d				18 32																	19 32
Leigh (Kent)	d				18 35																	19 35
Tonbridge 4	a				18 40																	19 40
Earlswood (Surrey)	d																					
Salfords	d																					
Horley 4	d					18 22		←						18 45								
Gatwick Airport 10 ✈	a	18 05	18 13	18 20		18 24	18 18	18 24	18 27		18 30	18 35	18 39	18 47	18 49	18 50	18 54	18 54	19 05	19 13	19 20	
	d		18 14			18 25	18 20	18 25	18 29				18 40	18 48	18 50		18 56	18 55		19 14		
Three Bridges 15	a		18 18			→	18 24	18 30						18 53	18 54			18 59		19 18		
	d		18 19				18 24	18 33						18 53	18 54			18 59		19 19		
Crawley	d							18 37						18 56								
Ifield	d							18 39														
Faygate	d																					
Littlehaven	d							18 46														
Horsham 4	a							18 49						19 04								
Balcombe	d		18 25																	19 25		
Haywards Heath	a		18 30				18 35		18 40						19 03		19 06	19 08		19 30		
	d		18 30				18 36		18 41						19 04		19 07	19 09		19 30		
Wivelsfield	d		18 34						18 45									19 13		19 34		
Lewes 4	a								18 58													
Burgess Hill 4	d		18 36				18 41								19 09		19 12	19 15		19 36		
Hassocks 4	d		18 40				18 44								19 12			19 18		19 40		
Preston Park	d		18 46															19 25		19 46		
Hove 2	a																19 24					
Brighton 10	a		18 50				18 54						19 03		19 22			19 29		19 50		

Table 186

Sundays

from 16 September

Bedford and London - Brighton

Network Diagram - see first Page of Table 186

Station		SN	FC	GW	SN	FC	SN	SN		GW	SN	SN	SN	FC	SN	SN		SN	SN	SN	SN	SN	FC	SN
		1	1	1	◇1 🛒	1	1	◇1 🛒		1	1 🛒	◇1 🛒	◇1 🛒	1	1	◇1		1	◇1	1	1	1	1	1
London Victoria 15 ⊖	d				18 47						19 00	19 02	19 04		19 15	19 17		19 30	19 32	19 45				
Clapham Junction 10	d				18 53							19 08	19 10			19 23			19 38					
Bedford	d		17 20			17 36								17 50									18 20	
Luton 10	d		17 44			18 00								18 14									18 44	
Luton Airport Parkway 7 ✈	d		17 47			18 03								18 17									18 47	
St Albans City	d		17 59			18 15								18 29									18 59	
St Pancras International 15 ⊖	d		18 24			18 39								18 54									19 24	
Farringdon 3 ⊖	d		18 29			18 44								18 58									19 29	
City Thameslink 3	d																							
London Blackfriars 3 ⊖	d		18 34			18 49								19 04									19 34	
London Bridge 4 ⊖	d	18 37	18 41			18 56								19 11								19 37	19 41	
New Cross Gate	d																							
Norwood Junction 2	d	18 48																				19 48		
East Croydon 🚌	a	18 54	18 56		19 06	19 08						19 21	19 23	19 27		19 36			19 50			19 54	19 56	
	d	18 55	18 57		19 07	19 09						19 22	19 24	19 28		19 37			19 51			19 55	19 57	
Purley 4	d	19 00											19 30									20 00		
Coulsdon South	d	19 04																				20 04		
Merstham	d	19 09																				20 09		
Redhill	a	19 13											19 38						20 03			20 13		
	d	19 16		19 20						19 21			19 39						20 04		20 10	20 16		
Reigate	a			19 24																				
Nutfield	d																				20 14			
Godstone	d																				20 20			
Edenbridge	d																				20 25			
Penshurst	d																				20 32			
Leigh (Kent)	d																				20 35			
Tonbridge 4	a																				20 40			
Earlswood (Surrey)	d																							
Salfords	d																							
Horley 4	d	19 22					←	←					19 45									20 22		←
Gatwick Airport 10 ✈	a	19 24	19 18		19 27	19 24	19 24	19 27		19 30	19 35	19 39	19 47	19 49	19 50	19 54		20 05	20 11	20 20		20 24	20 18	20 24
	d	19 25	19 20		19 29	19 25	19 25	19 29				19 40	19 48	19 50		19 56			20 12			20 25	20 20	20 25
Three Bridges 15	a	→	19 24		→	19 29	19 30						19 53	19 54					20 16			→	20 24	20 30
	d		19 24			19 29	19 33						19 53	19 54					20 17				20 24	20 33
Crawley	d						19 37						19 56											20 37
Ifield	d						19 39																	20 39
Faygate	d																							
Littlehaven	d						19 46																	20 46
Horsham 4	a						19 49						20 04											20 49
Balcombe	d																		20 23					
Haywards Heath	a		19 35			19 38		19 40						20 03		20 06			20 28				20 33	
	d		19 36			19 39		19 41						20 04		20 07			20 28				20 34	
Wivelsfield	d					19 43		19 45											20 32					
Lewes 4	a							19 58																
Burgess Hill 4	d		19 41			19 45								20 09		20 12			20 34				20 39	
Hassocks 4	d		19 44			19 48								20 12					20 38				20 42	
Preston Park	d					19 55													20 44					
Hove 2	a															20 24								
Brighton 10	a		19 54			19 59						20 03		20 22					20 48				20 52	

Table 186

Sundays

from 16 September

Bedford and London - Brighton

Network Diagram - see first Page of Table 186

		SN	GW	GW	SN	SN	SN	FC	SN	SN	SN	SN	SN	SN	SN	FC	SN	SN	GW	GW	SN	SN
		◇1	1	1	1	◇1	◇1	1	1	◇1	1	◇1	1	1	1	1	1	◇1	1	1	1	◇1
London Victoria 15 ⊖	d	19 47			20 00	20 02	20 04		20 15	20 17	20 30	20 32	20 45					20 47			21 00	21 02
Clapham Junction 10	d	19 53				20 08	20 10			20 23		20 38						20 53				21 08
Bedford	d							18 50								19 20						
Luton 10	d							19 14								19 44						
Luton Airport Parkway 7 ✈	d							19 17								19 47						
St Albans City	d							19 29								19 59						
St Pancras International 15 ⊖	d							19 54								20 24						
Farringdon 3 ⊖	d							19 58								20 29						
City Thameslink 3	d																					
London Blackfriars 3 ⊖	d							20 04								20 34						
London Bridge 4 ⊖	d							20 11							20 37	20 41						
New Cross Gate	d																					
Norwood Junction 2	d														20 48							
East Croydon	a	20 06				20 21	20 23	20 27		20 36		20 50			20 54	20 56		21 06				21 21
	d	20 07				20 22	20 24	20 28		20 37		20 51			20 55	20 57		21 07				21 22
Purley 4	d						20 30								21 00							
Coulsdon South	d														21 04							
Merstham	d														21 09							
Redhill	a						20 38					21 03			21 13							
	d		20 19	20 21			20 39					21 03		21 10	21 16				21 20	21 21		
Reigate	a		20 23																21 24			
Nutfield	d													21 14								
Godstone	d													21 20								
Edenbridge	d													21 25								
Penshurst	d													21 32								
Leigh (Kent)	d													21 35								
Tonbridge 4	a													21 40								
Earlswood (Surrey)	d																					
Salfords	d																					
Horley 4	d						20 45								21 22		←					
Gatwick Airport 10 ✈	a	20 27		20 30	20 35	20 39	20 47	20 49	20 50	20 54	21 05	21 10	21 20		21 24	21 18	21 24	21 27		21 30	21 35	21 39
	d	20 29				20 40	20 48	20 50		20 56		21 11			21 25	21 20	21 25	21 29				21 40
Three Bridges 15	a						20 53	20 54				21 16			→	21 24	21 30					
	d						20 53	20 54				21 16				21 24	21 33					
Crawley	d						20 56										21 37					
Ifield	d																21 39					
Faygate	d																					
Littlehaven	d																21 46					
Horsham 4	a						21 04										21 49					
Balcombe	d											21 22										
Haywards Heath	a	20 40						21 03		21 06		21 27				21 33		21 40				
	d	20 41						21 04		21 07		21 28				21 34		21 41				
Wivelsfield	d	20 45										21 32						21 45				
Lewes 4	a	20 58																21 58				
Burgess Hill 4	d							21 09		21 12		21 34				21 39						
Hassocks 4	d							21 12				21 37				21 42						
Preston Park	d											21 44										
Hove 2	a									21 24												
Brighton 10	a					21 03		21 22				21 49				21 52						22 03

Table 186

Sundays

from 16 September

Bedford and London - Brighton

Network Diagram - see first Page of Table 186

		SN	FC	SN	SN	SN	SN	SN	SN	SN	FC	SN	SN	GW	GW	SN	SN	FC	SN	SN	SN	SN
		◇1	1	1	◇1	1	◇1	1	1	1	1	1	◇1	1	1	1	◇1	1	1	◇1	1	◇1
London Victoria 15 ⊖	d	21 04		21 15	21 17	21 30	21 32	21 45					21 47			22 00	22 04		22 15	22 17	22 30	22 32
Clapham Junction 10	d	21 10			21 23		21 38						21 53				22 10			22 23		22 38
Bedford	d		19 50								20 12							20 42				
Luton 10	d		20 14								20 36							21 06				
Luton Airport Parkway 7 ✈	d		20 17								20 39							21 09				
St Albans City	d		20 29								20 51							21 21				
St Pancras International 15 ⊖	d		20 54								21 24							21 54				
Farringdon 3 ⊖	d		20 58								21 29							21 59				
City Thameslink 3	d																					
London Blackfriars 3 ⊖	d		21 04								21 34							22 04				
London Bridge 4 ⊖	d		21 11							21 37	21 41							22 11				
New Cross Gate	d																					
Norwood Junction 2	d									21 48												
East Croydon	a	21 23	21 27		21 36		21 50			21 54	21 56		22 06				22 23	22 27		22 36		22 50
	d	21 24	21 28		21 37		21 51			21 55	21 57		22 07				22 24	22 28		22 37		22 51
Purley 4	d	21 30								22 00							22 30					
Coulsdon South	d									22 04												
Merstham	d									22 09												
Redhill	a	21 38					22 03			22 13							22 38					23 03
	d	21 39					22 04		22 10	22 16				22 19	22 21		22 39					23 04
Reigate	a													22 23								
Nutfield	d								22 14													
Godstone	d								22 20													
Edenbridge	d								22 25													
Penshurst	d								22 32													
Leigh (Kent)	d								22 35													
Tonbridge 4	a								22 40													
Earlswood (Surrey)	d																					
Salfords	d																					
Horley 4	d	21 45								22 22		←					22 45					
Gatwick Airport 10 ✈	a	21 47	21 49	21 50	21 55	22 05	22 12	22 20		22 24	22 18	22 24	22 27		22 30	22 35	22 47	22 48	22 50	22 54	23 05	23 11
	d	21 48	21 50		21 56		22 13			22 25	22 20	22 25	22 29				22 48	22 50		22 56		23 12
Three Bridges 15	a	21 53	21 54				22 18			→	22 24	22 30					22 53	22 54				23 16
	d	21 53	21 54				22 18				22 24	22 33					22 53	22 54				23 17
Crawley	d	21 56										22 37					22 56					
Ifield	d											22 39										
Faygate	d																					
Littlehaven	d											22 46										
Horsham 4	a	22 04										22 49					23 04					
Balcombe	d						22 24															23 23
Haywards Heath	a		22 03		22 06		22 29				22 33		22 40					23 03		23 06		23 28
	d		22 04		22 07		22 30				22 34		22 41					23 04		23 07		23 28
Wivelsfield	d						22 34						22 45									23 32
Lewes 4	a												22 58									
Burgess Hill 4	d		22 09		22 12		22 36				22 39							23 09		23 12		23 34
Hassocks 4	d		22 12				22 39				22 42							23 12				23 38
Preston Park	d						22 46															23 44
Hove 2	a				22 24															23 24		
Brighton 10	a		22 22				22 50				22 52							23 22				23 48

Table 186

Sundays

from 16 September

Bedford and London - Brighton

Network Diagram - see first Page of Table 186

		SN 1	SN 1	SN 1	FC 1	SN 1	SN ◇1	GW 1		GW 1	SN 1	SN 1	FC 1	SN 1	SN 1	SN ◇1		SN 1	SN ◇1	FC 1	SN 1	SN	FC 1	FC 1
London Victoria 15 ⊖	d	22 45					22 47				23 00	23 04		23 15		23 17		23 30	23 32		23 45	23 47		
Clapham Junction 10	d						22 53					23 10				23 23			23 38			23 53		
Bedford	d				21 12								21 42							22 12			22 42	23 12
Luton 10	d				21 36								22 06							22 36			23 06	23 36
Luton Airport Parkway 7 ✈	d				21 39								22 09							22 39			23 09	23 39
St Albans City	d				21 51								22 21							22 51			23 21	23 51
St Pancras International 15 ⊖	d				22 24								22 54							23 24			23 54	00 24
Farringdon 3 ⊖	d				22 29								22 59							23 29			23 59	00 29
City Thameslink 3	d																							
London Blackfriars 3 ⊖	d				22 34								23 04							23 34			00 05	00 35
London Bridge 4 ⊖	d			22 37	22 41								23 11							23 41			00 12	00 42
New Cross Gate	d																							
Norwood Junction 2	d			22 48																				
East Croydon 🚌	a			22 54	22 56		23 06					23 22	23 26			23 37			23 52	23 56		00 06	00 26	00 56
	d			22 55	22 57		23 07					23 22	23 27			23 38			23 53	23 57			00 26	00 57
Purley 4	d			23 00								23 29												
Coulsdon South	d			23 04								23 33												
Merstham	d			23 09								23 38												
Redhill	a			23 13								23 42							00 05					
	d		23 10	23 16				23 20		23 21		23 42							00 05					
Reigate	a							23 24																
Nutfield	d		23 14																					
Godstone	d		23 20																					
Edenbridge	d		23 25																					
Penshurst	d		23 32																					
Leigh (Kent)	d		23 35																					
Tonbridge 4	a		23 40																					
Earlswood (Surrey)	d																							
Salfords	d																							
Horley 4	d			23 22		←						23 50			←									
Gatwick Airport 10 ✈	a	23 20		23 24	23 18	23 24	23 27			23 31	23 35	23 54	23 48	23 50	23 54	23 59		00 05	00 14	00 18	00 20		00 48	01 18
	d			23 25	23 20	23 25	23 29					23 55	23 50		23 55	00 01			00 15	00 20			00 49	01 22
Three Bridges 15	a			↪	23 24	23 30						↪	23 54		00 01	00 05			00 19	00 25			00 54	01 28
	d				23 24	23 33							23 54		00 01	00 06			00 20					
Crawley	d					23 37									00 05									
Ifield	d					23 39									00 07									
Faygate	d																							
Littlehaven	d					23 46									00 14									
Horsham 4	a					23 49									00 17									
Balcombe	d																		00 26					
Haywards Heath	a				23 33		23 40						00 03			00 15			00 31					
	d				23 34		23 41						00 04			00 15			00 31					
Wivelsfield	d						23 45												00 35					
Lewes 4	a						23 58																	
Burgess Hill 4	d				23 39								00 09			00 20			00 37					
Hassocks 4	d				23 42								00 12						00 41					
Preston Park	d																		00 48					
Hove 2	a															00 31								
Brighton 10	a				23 52								00 22						00 52					

Table 186

Sundays

from 16 September

Bedford and London - Brighton

Network Diagram - see first Page of Table 186

		FC 1
London Victoria 15 ⊖	d	
Clapham Junction 10	d	
Bedford	d	23 42
Luton 10	d	00 06
Luton Airport Parkway 7 ✈	d	00 09
St Albans City	d	00 21
St Pancras International 15 ⊖	d	00 54
Farringdon 3 ⊖	d	
City Thameslink 3	d	
London Blackfriars 3 ⊖	d	01 05
London Bridge 4 ⊖	d	
New Cross Gate	d	
Norwood Junction 2	d	
East Croydon 🚌	a	01 31
	d	01 32
Purley 4	d	
Coulsdon South	d	
Merstham	d	
Redhill	a	
	d	
Reigate	a	
Nutfield	d	
Godstone	d	
Edenbridge	d	
Penshurst	d	
Leigh (Kent)	d	
Tonbridge 4	a	
Earlswood (Surrey)	d	
Salfords	d	
Horley 4	d	
Gatwick Airport 10 ✈	a	01 51
	d	01 52
Three Bridges 15	a	01 58
	d	
Crawley	d	
Ifield	d	
Faygate	d	
Littlehaven	d	
Horsham 4	a	
Balcombe	d	
Haywards Heath	a	
	d	
Wivelsfield	d	
Lewes 4	a	
Burgess Hill 4	d	
Hassocks 4	d	
Preston Park	d	
Hove 2	a	
Brighton 10	a	

Brighton - London and Bedford

Network Diagram - see first Page of Table 186

Miles	Miles	Miles			SN	SN	SN	FC	SN	SN	SN	FC	SN		GW	SN	SN	SN	SN	FC	SN	SN	FC		SN
					1	1	◇1	1	1	◇1	1	1	1		1		1	1	1	1	1	1	1		1
					A	A	A	A	A	A		A			A										
0	—	—	**Brighton** 10	d			23p02	23p11				23p37													
—	0	—	Hove 2	d																					
1½	1½	—	Preston Park	d			23p06					23p41													
7¼	—	—	Hassocks 4	d			23p12	23p20				23p47													
9¾	—	—	Burgess Hill 4	d			23p16	23p23				23p51													
—	—	—	Lewes 4	d																					
10	9¾	—	Wivelsfield 4	d			23p19					23p53													
13	—	—	**Haywards Heath** 3	a			23p23	23p28				23p58													
—	—	—		d			23p24	23p29				23p59													
17	—	—	Balcombe	d								00 04													
—	0	—	**Horsham** 4	d	23p02																				
—	1	—	Littlehaven	d	23p05																				
—	3¼	—	Faygate	d																					
—	5¾	—	Ifield	d	23p11																				
—	7	—	Crawley	d	23p14					←															
21½	8½	—	Three Bridges 4	a	23p18		23p33	23p38		23p33		00 10													
—	—	—		d	23p18		23p47	23p38		23p47		00 10								01 25		01 59	02 25		02 59
24¼	—	—	**Gatwick Airport** 10 ✈	a	23p22		→	23p42		23p52		00 14								01 29		02 03	02 29		03 03
—	—	—		d	23p23	23p35		23p43	23p50	23p53	00 05	00 15	00 20				00 36	00 50	01 05	01 30	01 35	02 05	02 30		03 05
25	—	—	Horley 4	d	23p26					23p56									01 07			02 07			03 07
27¼	—	—	Salfords	d	23p30																				
29¼	—	—	Earlswood (Surrey)	d	23p33																				
—	—	0	**Tonbridge** 4	d																					
—	—	2½	Leigh (Kent)	d																					
—	—	4¼	Penshurst	d																					
—	—	9¼	Edenbridge	d																					
—	—	14	Godstone	d																					
—	—	17¾	Nutfield	d																					
—	0	—	**Reigate**	d											00 45										
30	1¾	19¾	**Redhill** 5	a	23p36					00 03		00 22			00 49										
—	—	—		d	23p37					00 03		00 23													
32	—	—	Merstham	d	23p41																				
35½	—	—	Coulsdon South	d	23p46																				
37½	—	—	Purley 4	d	23p49					00 11									01 22			02 22			03 22
40½	0	—	**East Croydon** 🚋	a	23p54			00 01		00 16		00 35							01 27	01 49		02 27	02 47		03 27
—	—	—		d	23p58			00 04		00 17		00 36				00 49			01 28	01 49		02 28	02 47		03 28
—	1¾	—	Norwood Junction 2	a																					
—	—	—	New Cross Gate	d																					
—	10¼	—	**London Bridge** 4 ⊖	a				00 19				00 52								02 14			03 12		
—	—	—	**London Blackfriars** 3 ⊖	a																					
—	—	—	City Thameslink 3	a																					
—	—	—	Farringdon 3 ⊖	a																					
—	—	—	St Pancras International 15 ⊖	a																					
—	—	—	St Albans City	a																					
—	—	—	Luton Airport Parkway 4 ✈	a																					
—	—	—	Luton 7	a																					
—	—	—	**Bedford** 10	a																					
48¼	0	0	Clapham Junction 10	a	00 11					00 29						01 01			01 40			02 40			03 40
51	—	—	**London Victoria** 15 ⊖	a	00 18	00 10			00 25	00 37	00 40		00 55			01 09	01 11	01 25	01 49		02 10	02 49			03 49

A not 14 May

Table 186

Mondays to Fridays

until 18 May

Brighton - London and Bedford

Network Diagram - see first Page of Table 186

		FC	SN	FC	SN	FC	SN	SN	FC		GW	GW	SN	FC	SN	SN	SN	GW	SN		SN	SN	SN	FC	SN
		1	1		1	1	1	1	1		1	1	1	1	1	1		1	◇1		1	1	1	1	1
																							✠		✠
Brighton 10	d													05 10			05 23							05 40	
Hove 2	d																								
Preston Park	d													05 14										05 44	
Hassocks 4	d													05 20										05 50	
Burgess Hill 4	d													05 24			05 33							05 54	
Lewes 4	d																		05 29						
Wivelsfield 4	d													05 26										05 56	
Haywards Heath 3	a													05 30			05 38		05 46					06 00	
	d													05 31			05 39		05 47					06 01	
Balcombe	d													05 36			05 44							06 06	
Horsham 4	d												05 17									05 38			
Littlehaven	d												05 20									05 41			
Faygate	d																								
Ifield	d												05 26									05 47			
Crawley	d												05 29									05 50			
Three Bridges 4	a												05 33	05 42			05 50					05 54		06 12	
	d	03 25	03 59	04 25		04 55							05 33	05 42			05 50					05 54		06 12	
Gatwick Airport 10 ✈	a	03 29	04 03	04 29		04 59							05 37	05 46			05 54		05 58			05 58		06 16	
	d	03 30	04 04	04 30	04 35	05 00		05 20	05 27			05 31	05 38	05 47		05 50	05 55	05 56	05 59			05 59	06 06	06 17	06 20
Horley 4	d		04 07										05 40									06 02			
Salfords	d																					06 06			
Earlswood (Surrey)	d																					06 09			
Tonbridge 4	d						04 59								05 20										
Leigh (Kent)	d						05 03								05 24										
Penshurst	d						05 07								05 28										
Edenbridge	d						05 13								05 34										
Godstone	d						05 20								05 41										
Nutfield	d						05 25								05 46										
Reigate	d										05 34														
Redhill 5	a						05 30		05 34		05 39	05 41	05 47		05 51			06 07				06 12			
	d								05 35				05 48									06 13			
Merstham	d												05 52									06 17			
Coulsdon South	d												05 57									06 22			
Purley 4	d		04 26										06 00									06 25			
East Croydon 🚌	a	03 47	04 31	04 47		05 17			05 47				06 06	06 01			06 10		06 14			06 30		06 32	
	d	03 47	04 32	04 47		05 17			05 47				06 06	06 02			06 11		06 15		06 27	06 31		06 32	
Norwood Junction 2	a																								
New Cross Gate	d																								
London Bridge 4 ⊖	a	04 12				05 34			06 02					06 15										06 46	
London Blackfriars 3 ⊖	a			05 13		05 41			06 10					06 23										06 52	
City Thameslink 3	a			05 16		05 44			06 14					06 26										06 54	
Farringdon 3 ⊖	a			05 20		05 47			06 18					06 30										06 58	
St Pancras International 15 ⊖	a			05 24		05 52			06 22					06 34										07 02	
St Albans City	a			05 57		06 23			06 43					06 57										07 22	
Luton Airport Parkway 4 ✈	a			06 09		06 35			06 55					07 09										07 34	
Luton 7	a			06 12		06 38			06 58					07 12										07 37	
Bedford 10	a			06 39		07 04			07 24					07 40										08 03	
Clapham Junction 10	a		04 51										06 18				06 21		06 25		06 38	06 41			
London Victoria 15 ⊖	a		04 58		05 12			05 55					06 25			06 20	06 28		06 32		06 45	06 48	06 35		06 50

Table 186

Brighton - London and Bedford

Mondays to Fridays

until 18 May

Network Diagram - see first Page of Table 186

		GW 1	FC 1	SN 1	SN 1		SN 1	SN 1	SN 1	SN 1	SN 1	FC 1	SN 1	SN ◇1 A	SN ◇1		GW 1	FC 1	SN 1	SN 1	SN 1	SN 1	SN 1	SN 1	SN ◇1
Brighton 10	d		05 50						06 01			06 08		06 17				06 24				06 30			
Hove 2	d			05 57																				06 31	
Preston Park	d		05 54									06 12						06 28							
Hassocks 4	d		06 00						06 09			06 19		06 26				06 35						06 43	
Burgess Hill 4	d		06 04						06 13			06 23		06 30				06 39				06 43		06 47	
Lewes 4	d									06 05															
Wivelsfield 4	d		06 06						06 15			06 25										06 46			
Haywards Heath 3	a		06 10	06 12					06 19	06 23		06 30		06 35				06 44				06 50		06 53	
	d		06 11	06 13					06 27			06 30		06 36				06 45				06 51		07 00	
Balcombe	d											06 36						06 51							
Horsham 4	d						06 10								06 24				06 38						06 50
Littlehaven	d						06 13								06 27				06 41						06 53
Faygate	d																		06 45						
Ifield	d						06 19								06 33				06 49						07 00
Crawley	d						06 23								06 37				06 52						07 04
Three Bridges 4	a		06 19	06 21			06 26		06 36			06 41		06 45	06 40			06 56	06 56						07 07
	d		06 20	06 22			06 27		06 37			06 42		06 48				06 57	06 56				07 04		07 08
Gatwick Airport 10 ✈	a		06 24	06 26			06 31		06 41			06 46		06 52				07 01	07 01			07 04	07 08	07 11	07 12
	d		06 25	06 27			06 32	06 35	06 42			06 47	06 50	06 53			06 58	07 02	07 02			07 06	07 09	07 12	07 14
Horley 4	d						06 35							06 56					07 04				07 12		07 16
Salfords	d						06 39												07 08				07 16		
Earlswood (Surrey)	d						06 42												07 12				07 19		
Tonbridge 4	d				06 10															06 47					
Leigh (Kent)	d				06 14															06 51					
Penshurst	d				06 18															06 55					
Edenbridge	d				06 24															07 01					
Godstone	d				06 31															07 08					
Nutfield	d				06 36															07 13					
Reigate	d	06 24									06 49														
Redhill 5	a	06 29	06 32		06 42		06 46				06 53	06 54		07 02			07 07	07 10	07 15	07 18			07 22		
	d		06 33		06 43		06 46					06 56		07 03				07 11	07 15				07 23		
Merstham	d						06 50												07 19				07 27		
Coulsdon South	d				06 50		06 55												07 25				07 33		
Purley 4	d				06 54		06 59												07 29				07 37		
East Croydon	a		06 44	06 41	06 59		07 04		06 58			07 08		07 14				07 22	07 34				07 41	07 26	07 31
	d		06 44	06 42	07 00		07 05		06 59			07 09		07 15				07 23	07 35		07 15		07 42	07 28	07 31
Norwood Junction 2	a																								
New Cross Gate	d																								
London Bridge 4 ⊖	a		06 58		07 16				07 14			07 23							07 51					07 43	
London Blackfriars 3 ⊖	a		07 04									07 30						07 51							
City Thameslink 3	a		07 08									07 32						07 56							
Farringdon 3 ⊖	a		07 12									07 36						08 00							
St Pancras International 15 ⊖	a		07 16									07 40						08 04							
St Albans City	a		07 41															08 24							
Luton Airport Parkway 4 ✈	a		07 53									08 06						08 37							
Luton 7	a		07 57									08 10						08 40							
Bedford 10	a		08 23															09 05							
Clapham Junction 10	a			06 51			07 16							07 24							07 27		07 51		07 40
London Victoria 15 ⊖	a			07 00			07 25	07 05					07 20	07 33							07 36	07 37	08 00		07 49

A ◇ from Three Bridges

Table 186

Mondays to Fridays

until 18 May

Brighton - London and Bedford

Network Diagram - see first Page of Table 186

		SN	GW	SN	SN	SN	SN	SN	GW	SN	SN	SN	FC	SN	SN	SN	SN	SN	SN	SN	SN
		1	1	◇1	◇1	1	1	1	1	1	1	1	1	1	1	1	◇1	1	1	◇1	◇1
					A																
		🛒		🛒	🛒							🛒					🛒		🛒		🛒
Brighton 10	d	06 40		06 51								06 56	07 02						07 14		
Hove 2	d													07 11						07 21	
Preston Park	d	06 44										07 00	07 06						07 19		
Hassocks 4	d	06 52											07 13	07 20						07 30	
Burgess Hill 4	d	06 56		07 01								07 10	07 17						07 28		
Lewes 4	d					06 51															07 22
Wivelsfield 4	d					07 08						07 14	07 20	07 25						07 35	07 39
Haywards Heath 3	a	07 01		07 06		07 12						07 18	07 24	07 30					07 34	07 40	07 44
	d	07 03		07 07		07 13						07 20	07 25	07 31					07 35	07 40	07 44
Balcombe	d					07 19															
Horsham 4	d				07 04					07 09						07 17	07 25				
Littlehaven	d									07 12						07 20	07 29				
Faygate	d									07 16											
Ifield	d									07 20						07 27					
Crawley	d				07 13					07 23						07 31	07 37				
Three Bridges 4	a			07 16	07 18	07 24				07 27			07 33			07 34	07 40				
	d			07 22		07 25	07 14			07 28			07 34			07 35	07 41				
Gatwick Airport 10 ✈	a	07 15				07 29	07 21			07 32		07 32	07 38			07 39			07 47		
	d	07 20				07 30	07 22			07 33		07 35	07 39			07 40			07 50		07 58
Horley 4	d						07 25			07 36						07 43					
Salfords	d						07 29			07 40						07 47					
Earlswood (Surrey)	d						07 32			07 43						07 50					
Tonbridge 4	d																				
Leigh (Kent)	d																				
Penshurst	d																				
Edenbridge	d																				
Godstone	d																				
Nutfield	d																				
Reigate	d		07 18					07 27	07 34						07 40			07 52			
Redhill 5	a		07 24				07 36	07 31	07 38	07 47					07 45	07 53		07 56			
	d						07 40								07 51	07 54					
Merstham	d						07 44									07 59					
Coulsdon South	d						07 50									08 04					
Purley 4	d						07 55														
East Croydon 🚌	a			07 38		07 45	08 01						07 53	07 56	08 02	08 11	07 59			08 08	08 13
	d			07 39		07 46	08 02				07 45		07 54	07 57	08 03	08 11	08 01			08 08	08 13
Norwood Junction 2	a																				
New Cross Gate	d																				
London Bridge 4 ⊖	a					08 01	08 19							08 13	08 21						
London Blackfriars 3 ⊖	a												08 20								
City Thameslink 3	a												08 23								
Farringdon 3 ⊖	a												08 27								
St Pancras International 15 ⊖	a												08 31								
St Albans City	a												08 51								
Luton Airport Parkway 4 ✈	a												09 00								
Luton 7	a												09 04								
Bedford 10	a												09 26								
Clapham Junction 10	a			07 48							07 55					08 20	08 10			08 17	08 23
London Victoria 15 ⊖	a	07 50		07 57							08 04	08 06				08 29	08 19		08 20	08 26	08 32

A 🛒 from Three Bridges

Table 186

Mondays to Fridays

Brighton - London and Bedford

until 18 May

Network Diagram - see first Page of Table 186

		SN 1	SN 1	GW 1	FC 1	SN 1	SN 1	SN 1		SN 1	SN 1	SN 1	SN ◇1	SN 1	SN 1	SN 1	SN 1	FC 1		SN ◇1	GW 1	SN 1	SN ◇1	SN 1	SN 1
Brighton 10	d				07 24	07 29						07 32					07 44	07 50							
Hove 2	d												07 41												
Preston Park	d				07 28							07 37					07 48	07 54							
Hassocks 4	d				07 35	07 39											07 56	08 01							
Burgess Hill 4	d				07 39							07 47	07 52				08 00								
Lewes 4	d													07 42									07 55		
Wivelsfield 4	d					07 46						07 49											08 11		
Haywards Heath 3	a				07 46	07 50						07 54	07 58	08 03			08 05	08 09					08 16		
	d				07 47	07 51						07 55	07 59	08 04			08 06	08 09					08 16		
Balcombe	d											08 01						08 15					08 22		
Horsham 4	d									07 40	07 46				07 51					08 09					
Littlehaven	d									07 43	07 49				07 54										
Faygate	d														07 58										
Ifield	d									07 50	07 56				08 02										
Crawley	d									07 53	08 00				08 06					08 18					
Three Bridges 4	a				07 55					07 57	08 05	08 06			08 09					08 22			08 28		
	d				07 56					07 58	08 06	08 07			08 10					08 22			08 28		
Gatwick Airport 10 ✈	a				08 00	08 02				08 04			08 13		08 14		08 18	08 23							
	d	07 44		07 58	08 01	08 05				08 05			08 14		08 15	08 18	08 20	08 24				08 35			
Horley 4	d	07 47								08 07					08 18					08 28					
Salfords	d	07 51								08 11					08 22										
Earlswood (Surrey)	d	07 54								08 15					08 25										
Tonbridge 4	d		07 25																					07 59	
Leigh (Kent)	d		07 29																					08 03	
Penshurst	d		07 33																					08 07	
Edenbridge	d		07 39																					08 13	
Godstone	d		07 46																					08 20	
Nutfield	d		07 51																					08 25	
Reigate	d						08 09														08 24				08 27
Redhill 5	a	07 58	07 56	08 05	08 08		08 13			08 18					08 28						08 30			08 34	08 32
	d	08 02			08 09					08 18					08 29									08 38	
Merstham	d	08 06								08 22														08 43	
Coulsdon South	d	08 11								08 27					08 36									08 48	
Purley 4	d	08 15								08 31														08 52	
East Croydon	a	08 20			08 22					08 36	08 26	08 24	08 29	08 31	08 50			08 38		08 43			08 46	08 58	
	d	08 21			08 23			08 15		08 37	08 27	08 25	08 30	08 33	08 51			08 39		08 43			08 50	08 59	
Norwood Junction 2	a																								
New Cross Gate	d																								
London Bridge 4 ⊖	a	08 37									08 45	08 41		08 52	09 06									09 15	
London Blackfriars 3 ⊖	a				08 53													09 09							
City Thameslink 3	a				08 56													09 12							
Farringdon 3 ⊖	a				09 00													09 16							
St Pancras International 15 ⊖	a				09 04													09 20							
St Albans City	a				09 25													09 40							
Luton Airport Parkway 4 ✈	a				09 37													09 51							
Luton 7	a				09 40													09 54							
Bedford 10	a				10 08													10 20							
Clapham Junction 10	a							08 26		08 48			08 39							08 52			09 00		
London Victoria 15 ⊖	a					08 35		08 35		08 56			08 48			08 50	08 52			09 01		09 05	09 09		

Brighton - London and Bedford

Network Diagram - see first Page of Table 186

Station		GW [1]	FC [1]	SN ◇[1]		SN ◇[1] 🚲	FC [1]	SN [1]	SN [1]	SN ◇[1] 🚲	SN [1] 🚲	SN [1]	SN ◇[1] 🚲	SN ◇[1]	SN ◇[1]		GW [1]	FC [1]	SN [1]	FC [1]	SN [1]	SN [1] 🚲	SN ◇[1] 🚲	GW [1]	SN [1]
Brighton [10]	d		08 02			08 13	08 16											08 34	08 45						
Hove [2]	d			08 08																					
Preston Park	d		08 06	08 12			08 20											08 38							
Hassocks [4]	d		08 13	08 19			08 27											08 44							
Burgess Hill [4]	d		08 17	08 23			08 31											08 48							
Lewes [4]	d									08 23													08 48		
Wivelsfield [4]	d		08 20				08 34			08 39								08 50		←			09 01		
Haywards Heath [3]	a		08 24	08 28			08 38			08 44								08 55	08 58	08 55			09 05		
	d		08 25	08 29			08 39			08 44								09 00	08 58	09 00			09 08		
Balcombe	d																	→		09 06					
Horsham [4]	d							08 12					08 49	08 35											09 00
Littlehaven	d							08 15						08 38											09 03
Faygate	d							08 19																	
Ifield	d							08 23						08 44											09 09
Crawley	d							08 26					08 58	08 47											09 13
Three Bridges [4]	a		08 33	08 38			08 47	08 29					09 01	08 51						09 11			09 17		09 16
	d		08 34	08 39			08 48	08 30					09 02	08 51						09 12			09 17		09 18
Gatwick Airport [10] ✈	a		08 38			08 46	08 52	08 34		08 56			09 06	08 55					09 09	09 16			09 22		09 22
	d		08 39			08 50	08 53	08 35		08 57	09 05		09 07	08 56			09 07		09 10	09 17		09 20	09 23		09 23
Horley [4]	d							08 38		08 59				08 59											09 26
Salfords	d							08 42						09 03											09 30
Earlswood (Surrey)	d							08 45						09 06											09 33
Tonbridge [4]	d								08 16						08 37										
Leigh (Kent)	d								08 20						08 41										
Penshurst	d								08 24						08 45										
Edenbridge	d								08 30						08 51										
Godstone	d								08 37						08 58										
Nutfield	d								08 42						09 03										
Reigate	d	08 42																			09 14			09 24	
Redhill [5]	a	08 46						08 49	08 47					09 10	09 08		09 15				09 18			09 30	09 36
	d							08 53						09 14							09 19				09 37
Merstham	d							08 57						09 18							09 23				09 41
Coulsdon South	d							09 02						09 23							09 28				09 46
Purley [4]	d							09 05													09 32				09 49
East Croydon ⇌	a		08 53	08 57			09 08	09 10		09 14			09 22	09 30					09 25	09 32	09 37		09 38		09 54
	d		08 54	08 58			09 09	09 11		09 14		09 14	09 23	09 31					09 26	09 32	09 37		09 39		09 55
Norwood Junction [2]	a																				09 41				09 59
New Cross Gate	d																								10 07
London Bridge [4] ⊖	a		09 08																	09 46	09 55				10 13
London Blackfriars [3] ⊖	a		09 21				09 37													09 53					
City Thameslink [3]	a		09 24				09 40													09 56					
Farringdon [3] ⊖	a		09 27				09 44													10 00					
St Pancras International [15] ⊖	a		09 32				09 48													10 04					
St Albans City	a		09 51				10 10													10 23					
Luton Airport Parkway [4] ✈	a		10 00				10 21													10 37					
Luton [7]	a		10 03				10 24													10 40					
Bedford [10]	a		10 24				10 50													11 05					
Clapham Junction [10]	a			09 07				09 20		09 23		09 26	09 32	09 41					09 36				09 48		
London Victoria [15] ⊖	a			09 16		09 20		09 27		09 32	09 35	09 35	09 42	09 50					09 43			09 50	09 58		

Table 186

Mondays to Fridays

until 18 May

Brighton - London and Bedford

Network Diagram - see first Page of Table 186

		SN	FC	SN	GW	SN	SN	FC	SN	SN	SN	SN	SN	SN	SN	FC	GW	SN	SN	SN	FC	SN
		◇1	1	1	1	1	◇1	1	◇1	1	1	◇1	1	◇1	◇1	1	1	1	1	◇1	1	◇1
				🛒			🛒		🛒		🛒			🛒	A 🛒			🛒				🛒
Brighton 10	d		09 00					09 07	09 19			09 25				09 34					09 37	09 49
Hove 2	d	08 52													09 22							
Preston Park	d	08 57						09 11													09 41	
Hassocks 4	d	09 04	09 09					09 17				09 34			09 31						09 47	
Burgess Hill 4	d	09 08	09 12					09 21				09 38									09 51	
Lewes 4	d													09 18								
Wivelsfield 4	d							09 23						09 34							09 53	
Haywards Heath 3	a	09 13	09 17					09 28						09 38	09 40	09 47					09 58	
	d	09 14	09 18					09 32						09 44		09 48					10 02	
Balcombe	d							09 37														
Horsham 4	d						09 20						09 30							09 51		
Littlehaven	d												09 33									
Faygate	d												09 37									
Ifield	d												09 41									
Crawley	d						09 29						09 44							10 00		
Three Bridges 4	a		09 26				09 32	09 43					09 48			09 56				10 03	10 11	
	d		09 27				09 33	09 43					09 48			09 57				10 04	10 12	
Gatwick Airport 10 ✈	a	09 26	09 31				09 37	09 47				09 51	09 53	09 56		10 01				10 08	10 16	
	d	09 27	09 32	09 35			09 38	09 47			09 50	09 53	09 54	09 57		10 02	10 03	10 05		10 09	10 17	
Horley 4	d						09 41						09 56									
Salfords	d																					
Earlswood (Surrey)	d																					
Tonbridge 4	d									09 19												
Leigh (Kent)	d									09 23												
Penshurst	d									09 27												
Edenbridge	d									09 33												
Godstone	d									09 40												
Nutfield	d									09 45												
Reigate	d				09 37																	
Redhill 5	a				09 42		09 47			09 50			10 03				10 10			10 16		
	d						09 48			09 51			10 07							10 17		
Merstham	d												10 11									
Coulsdon South	d									09 58			10 16									
Purley 4	d									10 02			10 19									
East Croydon	a	09 42	09 46				09 59	10 02	09 52	10 07		10 08	10 24	10 11		10 16				10 28	10 31	10 22
	d	09 43	09 47			09 44	10 00	10 02	09 53	10 07		10 08	10 25	10 12		10 17			10 14	10 28	10 32	10 23
Norwood Junction 2	a									10 12			10 29									
New Cross Gate	d												10 37									
London Bridge 4 ⊖	a		10 00					10 15		10 25			10 43			10 30					10 45	
London Blackfriars 3 ⊖	a		10 08					10 23								10 37					10 52	
City Thameslink 3	a		10 10					10 26								10 40					10 56	
Farringdon 3 ⊖	a		10 14					10 30								10 44					11 00	
St Pancras International 15 ⊖	a		10 18					10 34								10 48					11 04	
St Albans City	a		10 38					10 54								11 10					11 23	
Luton Airport Parkway 4 ✈	a		10 50					11 06								11 21					11 37	
Luton 7	a		10 53					11 09								11 24					11 40	
Bedford 10	a		11 19					11 35								11 50					12 05	
Clapham Junction 10	a	09 52				09 55	10 09		10 02			10 17		10 21					10 25	10 37		10 32
London Victoria 15 ⊖	a	09 59		10 05		10 05	10 16		10 11		10 20	10 26		10 28				10 35	10 35	10 45		10 41

A 🛒 from Haywards Heath

Table 186

Mondays to Fridays

until 18 May

Brighton - London and Bedford

Network Diagram - see first Page of Table 186

		SN	GW	SN	SN	SN	SN	FC	GW	SN	SN	SN	FC	SN	SN	SN	SN	SN	SN	SN	FC	GW	SN
		1	1	1	1	◇1	◇1	1	1	1	1	◇1	1	◇1	1	1	◇1	1	◇1	◇1	1	1	1
							A																
				🚲		🚲	🚲			🚲				🚲		🚲							
Brighton 10	d							10 04					10 07	10 19			10 25				10 34		
Hove 2	d						09 51													10 21			
Preston Park	d						09 55						10 11										
Hassocks 4	d												10 17				10 34						
Burgess Hill 4	d						10 04						10 21				10 38						
Lewes 4	d					09 48													10 19				
Wivelsfield 4	d												10 23						10 35				
Haywards Heath 3	a					10 07	10 10	10 17					10 28						10 40	10 35	10 47		
	d					10 14		10 18					10 32						10 44		10 48		
Balcombe	d												10 37										
Horsham 4	d				10 00							10 20						10 30					
Littlehaven	d				10 03													10 33					
Faygate	d																						
Ifield	d				10 09													10 39					
Crawley	d				10 13							10 29						10 43					
Three Bridges 4	a				10 16			10 26				10 32	10 43					10 46			10 56		
	d				10 18			10 27				10 33	10 43					10 48			10 57		
Gatwick Airport 10 ✈	a				10 22	10 25		10 31				10 37	10 47				10 51	10 52	10 55		11 01		
	d			10 20	10 23	10 26		10 32		10 35		10 38	10 47			10 50	10 53	10 53	10 56		11 02	11 03	
Horley 4	d				10 26							10 41						10 56					
Salfords	d				10 30																		
Earlswood (Surrey)	d				10 33																		
Tonbridge 4	d														10 19								
Leigh (Kent)	d														10 23								
Penshurst	d														10 27								
Edenbridge	d														10 33								
Godstone	d														10 40								
Nutfield	d														10 45								
Reigate	d	10 14	10 19						10 34														
Redhill 5	a	10 18	10 25		10 36				10 38			10 47			10 50			11 02				11 10	
	d	10 20			10 37							10 48			10 51			11 07					
Merstham	d	10 24			10 41													11 11					
Coulsdon South	d	10 29			10 46										10 58			11 16					
Purley 4	d	10 33			10 49										11 01			11 19					
East Croydon	a	10 38			10 54	10 41		10 46				10 59	11 02	10 52	11 06		11 08	11 24	11 11		11 16		
	d	10 38			10 55	10 42		10 47			10 44	11 00	11 02	10 53	11 07		11 08	11 25	11 12		11 17		11 14
Norwood Junction 2	a	10 42			10 59										11 12			11 29					
New Cross Gate	d				11 07													11 37					
London Bridge 4 ⊖	a	10 55			11 13			11 00					11 15		11 25			11 43			11 30		
London Blackfriars 3 ⊖	a							11 07					11 22								11 37		
City Thameslink 3	a							11 10					11 26								11 40		
Farringdon 3 ⊖	a							11 14					11 30								11 44		
St Pancras International 15 ⊖	a							11 18					11 34								11 48		
St Albans City	a							11 38					11 53								12 08		
Luton Airport Parkway 4 ✈	a							11 50					12 07								12 20		
Luton 7	a							11 53					12 10								12 23		
Bedford 10	a							12 19					12 35								12 49		
Clapham Junction 10	a					10 51					10 55	11 09		11 02			11 17		11 21				11 25
London Victoria 15 ⊖	a			10 50		10 58				11 05	11 05	11 16		11 10		11 20	11 24		11 28				11 32

A 🚲 from Haywards Heath

Table 186

Mondays to Fridays

until 18 May

Brighton - London and Bedford

Network Diagram - see first Page of Table 186

		SN 1 🚲	SN ◇1		FC 1	SN ◇1 🚲	SN 1	GW 1	SN 1 🚲	SN 1	SN ◇1	SN ◇1	FC 1		GW 1	SN 1	SN 1 🚲	SN ◇1	FC 1	SN ◇1 🚲	SN 1	SN 1 🚲	SN ◇1		SN 1
Brighton 10	d				10 37	10 49							11 04						11 07	11 19			11 25		
Hove 2	d											10 51													
Preston Park	d				10 41							10 55							11 11						
Hassocks 4	d				10 47														11 17				11 34		
Burgess Hill 4	d				10 51							11 04							11 21				11 38		
Lewes 4	d										10 50														
Wivelsfield 4	d				10 53														11 23						
Haywards Heath 3	a				10 58						11 05	11 09	11 17						11 28						
	d				11 02						11 13		11 18						11 32						
Balcombe	d																		11 37						
Horsham 4	d		10 50							11 00								11 20							11 30
Littlehaven	d									11 03															11 33
Faygate	d																								
Ifield	d									11 09															11 39
Crawley	d		10 59							11 13								11 29							11 43
Three Bridges 4	a		11 02		11 11					11 16			11 26					11 32	11 43						11 46
	d		11 03		11 12					11 18			11 27					11 33	11 43						11 48
Gatwick Airport 10 ✈	a		11 07		11 16					11 22	11 24		11 31					11 37	11 47				11 51		11 52
	d	11 05	11 08		11 17				11 20	11 23	11 25		11 32				11 35	11 38	11 47			11 50	11 53		11 53
Horley 4	d									11 26								11 41							11 56
Salfords	d									11 30															
Earlswood (Surrey)	d									11 33															
Tonbridge 4	d																				11 19				
Leigh (Kent)	d																				11 23				
Penshurst	d																				11 27				
Edenbridge	d																				11 33				
Godstone	d																				11 40				
Nutfield	d																				11 45				
Reigate	d						11 14	11 19							11 34										
Redhill 5	a		11 15				11 18	11 25		11 36					11 38			11 47			11 50				12 02
	d		11 16				11 19			11 37								11 48			11 51				12 07
Merstham	d						11 23			11 41															12 11
Coulsdon South	d						11 28			11 46											11 58				12 16
Purley 4	d						11 32			11 49											12 02				12 19
East Croydon 🚋	a		11 27		11 31	11 22	11 37			11 54	11 40		11 46					11 59	12 02	11 52	12 07		12 08		12 24
	d		11 28		11 32	11 23	11 37			11 55	11 41		11 47			11 44		12 00	12 02	11 53	12 07		12 08		12 25
Norwood Junction 2	a						11 42			11 59											12 12				12 29
New Cross Gate	d									12 07															12 37
London Bridge 4 ⊖	a				11 45		11 55			12 13			12 00						12 15		12 25				12 43
London Blackfriars 3 ⊖	a				11 52								12 07						12 22						
City Thameslink 3	a				11 56								12 10						12 26						
Farringdon 3 ⊖	a				12 00								12 14						12 30						
St Pancras International 15 ⊖	a				12 04								12 18						12 34						
St Albans City	a				12 24								12 38						12 53						
Luton Airport Parkway 4 ✈	a				12 37								12 50						13 06						
Luton 7	a				12 40								12 53						13 09						
Bedford 10	a				13 05								13 19						13 35						
Clapham Junction 10	a		11 37			11 32					11 50					11 55		12 09		12 02			12 17		
London Victoria 15 ⊖	a	11 35	11 44			11 40			11 50		11 57					12 02	12 05	12 18		12 10		12 20	12 24		

Table 186

Mondays to Fridays

until 18 May

Brighton - London and Bedford

Network Diagram - see first Page of Table 186

		SN	SN	FC	GW	SN	SN	SN	FC		SN	SN	GW	SN	SN	SN	SN	FC	GW		SN	SN	SN	FC	SN
		◇1	◇1	1	1	1	1	◇1	1		◇1	1	1	1	1	◇1	◇1	1	1		1	1	◇1	1	◇1
							🚲				🚲			🚲								🚲			🚲
Brighton 10	d			11 34					11 37		11 49							12 04						12 07	12 19
Hove 2	d		11 21														11 51								
Preston Park	d								11 41								11 55							12 11	
Hassocks 4	d								11 47															12 17	
Burgess Hill 4	d								11 51								12 04							12 21	
Lewes 4	d	11 20														11 50									
Wivelsfield 4	d	11 35							11 53															12 23	
Haywards Heath 3	a	11 40	11 35	11 47					11 58							12 05	12 09	12 17						12 28	
	d		11 44	11 48					12 02								12 13	12 18						12 32	
Balcombe	d																							12 37	
Horsham 4	d							11 50							12 00								12 20		
Littlehaven	d														12 03										
Faygate	d																								
Ifield	d														12 09										
Crawley	d							11 59							12 13								12 29		
Three Bridges 4	a			11 56				12 02	12 11						12 16			12 26					12 32	12 43	
	d			11 57				12 03	12 12						12 18			12 27					12 33	12 43	
Gatwick Airport 10 ✈	a		11 55	12 01				12 07	12 16						12 22		12 24	12 31					12 37	12 47	
	d		11 56	12 02	12 03		12 05	12 08	12 17					12 20	12 23		12 25	12 32				12 35	12 38	12 47	
Horley 4	d														12 26								12 41		
Salfords	d														12 30										
Earlswood (Surrey)	d														12 33										
Tonbridge 4	d																								
Leigh (Kent)	d																								
Penshurst	d																								
Edenbridge	d																								
Godstone	d																								
Nutfield	d																								
Reigate	d											12 14	12 19						12 34						
Redhill 5	a				12 10			12 15				12 18	12 25		12 36				12 38				12 47		
	d							12 16				12 19			12 37								12 48		
Merstham	d											12 23			12 41										
Coulsdon South	d											12 28			12 46										
Purley 4	d											12 32			12 49										
East Croydon	a		12 11	12 16				12 27	12 31		12 22	12 37			12 54		12 40	12 46					12 59	13 02	12 52
	d		12 12	12 17		12 14		12 28	12 32		12 23	12 37			12 55		12 41	12 47			12 44		13 00	13 02	12 53
Norwood Junction 2	a											12 42			12 59										
New Cross Gate	d														13 07										
London Bridge 4 ⊖	a			12 30					12 45			12 55			13 13			13 00						13 15	
London Blackfriars 3 ⊖	a			12 37					12 52									13 07						13 22	
City Thameslink 3	a			12 40					12 56									13 10						13 26	
Farringdon 3 ⊖	a			12 44					13 00									13 14						13 30	
St Pancras International 15 ⊖	a			12 48					13 04									13 18						13 34	
St Albans City	a			13 08					13 24									13 38						13 53	
Luton Airport Parkway 4 ✈	a			13 20					13 37									13 50						14 07	
Luton 7	a			13 23					13 40									13 53						14 10	
Bedford 10	a			13 49					14 05									14 19						14 35	
Clapham Junction 10	a		12 21			12 25		12 37			12 32						12 50				12 55		13 09		13 02
London Victoria 15 ⊖	a		12 28			12 32	12 35	12 44			12 40			12 50			12 57				13 02	13 05	13 16		13 10

Brighton - London and Bedford

Network Diagram - see first Page of Table 186

		SN	SN	SN	SN		SN	SN	FC	GW	SN	SN	SN	FC	SN		SN	GW	SN	SN	SN	SN	FC	GW	SN
		1	1 trolley	◇1	1		◇1	◇1	1	1	1	1 trolley	◇1	1	◇1 trolley		1	1	1 trolley	1	◇1	◇1	1	1	1
Brighton [10]	d			12 25					12 34					12 37	12 49								13 04		
Hove [2]	d							12 21														12 51			
Preston Park	d													12 41								12 55			
Hassocks [4]	d			12 34										12 47											
Burgess Hill [4]	d			12 38										12 51								13 04			
Lewes [4]	d						12 20														12 50				
Wivelsfield [4]	d						12 35							12 53											
Haywards Heath [3]	a						12 40	12 35	12 47					12 58							13 05	13 09	13 17		
	d						12 44		12 48					13 02							13 13		13 18		
Balcombe	d																								
Horsham [4]	d				12 30								12 50							13 00					
Littlehaven	d				12 33															13 03					
Faygate	d				12 37																				
Ifield	d				12 41															13 09					
Crawley	d				12 44								12 59							13 13					
Three Bridges [4]	a				12 47				12 56				13 02	13 11						13 16			13 26		
	d				12 48				12 57				13 03	13 12						13 18			13 27		
Gatwick Airport [10] ✈	a			12 51	12 52		12 55		13 01				13 07	13 16						13 22	13 24		13 31		
	d		12 50	12 53	12 53		12 56		13 02	13 03		13 05	13 08	13 17					13 20	13 23	13 25		13 32		
Horley [4]	d				12 56															13 26					
Salfords	d																			13 30					
Earlswood (Surrey)	d																			13 33					
Tonbridge [4]	d	12 19																							
Leigh (Kent)	d	12 23																							
Penshurst	d	12 27																							
Edenbridge	d	12 33																							
Godstone	d	12 40																							
Nutfield	d	12 45																							
Reigate	d																13 14	13 19						13 34	
Redhill [5]	a	12 50			13 02					13 10			13 15				13 18	13 25		13 36				13 38	
	d	12 51			13 07								13 16				13 19			13 37					
Merstham	d				13 11												13 23			13 41					
Coulsdon South	d	12 58			13 16												13 28			13 46					
Purley [4]	d	13 02			13 19												13 32			13 49					
East Croydon 🚊	a	13 07		13 08	13 24		13 11		13 16				13 27	13 31	13 22		13 37			13 54	13 40		13 46		
	d	13 07		13 08	13 25		13 12		13 17		13 14		13 28	13 32	13 23		13 37			13 55	13 41		13 47		13 44
Norwood Junction [2]	a	13 12			13 29												13 42			13 59					
New Cross Gate	d				13 37															14 07					
London Bridge [4] ⊖	a	13 25			13 43				13 30					13 45			13 55			14 13			14 00		
London Blackfriars [3] ⊖	a								13 37					13 52									14 07		
City Thameslink [3]	a								13 40					13 56									14 10		
Farringdon [3] ⊖	a								13 44					14 00									14 14		
St Pancras International [15] ⊖	a								13 48					14 04									14 18		
St Albans City	a								14 08					14 23									14 38		
Luton Airport Parkway [4] ✈	a								14 20					14 37									14 50		
Luton [7]	a								14 23					14 40									14 53		
Bedford [10]	a								14 49					15 05									15 19		
Clapham Junction [10]	a			13 17			13 21				13 25		13 37		13 32						13 50				13 55
London Victoria [15] ⊖	a		13 20	13 24			13 28				13 32	13 35	13 44		13 40				13 50		13 57				14 03

Table 186 | **Mondays to Fridays**

until 18 May

Brighton - London and Bedford

Network Diagram - see first Page of Table 186

		SN	SN	FC	SN	SN	SN	SN	SN	SN	SN	FC	GW	SN	SN	SN	FC	SN	SN	GW	SN	SN
		1 ⚲	◇1	1	◇1 ⚲	1	1 ⚲	◇1	1	◇1	◇1	1	1	1	1 ⚲	◇1	1	◇1 ⚲	1	1	1 ⚲	1
Brighton 10	d			13 07	13 19			13 25				13 34					13 37	13 49				
Hove 2	d										13 21											
Preston Park	d			13 11													13 41					
Hassocks 4	d			13 17				13 34									13 47					
Burgess Hill 4	d			13 21				13 38									13 51					
ewes 4	d									13 20												
Welsfield 4	d			13 23						13 35							13 53					
Haywards Heath 3	a			13 28						13 40	13 35	13 47					13 58					
	d			13 32						13 44		13 48					14 02					
Balcombe	d			13 37																		
Horsham 4	d		13 20						13 30							13 50						14 00
ittlehaven	d								13 33													14 03
Faygate	d																					
field	d								13 39													14 09
Crawley	d		13 29						13 43							13 59						14 13
Three Bridges 4	a		13 32	13 43					13 46			13 56				14 02	14 11					14 16
	d		13 33	13 43					13 48			13 57				14 03	14 12					14 18
Gatwick Airport 10 ✈	a		13 37	13 47				13 51	13 52	13 55		14 01				14 07	14 16					14 22
	d	13 35	13 38	13 47			13 50	13 53	13 53	13 56		14 02	14 03		14 05	14 08	14 17				14 20	14 23
Horley 4	d		13 41						13 56													14 26
Salfords	d																					14 30
Erlswood (Surrey)	d																					14 33
Tonbridge 4	d					13 19																
eigh (Kent)	d					13 23																
Penshurst	d					13 27																
Eenbridge	d					13 33																
Godstone	d					13 40																
Nfield	d					13 45																
Reigate	d																		14 14	14 19		
Redhill 5	a		13 47			13 50			14 02				14 10			14 15			14 18	14 25		14 36
	d		13 48			13 51			14 07							14 16			14 19			14 37
Merstham	d								14 11										14 23			14 41
Coulsdon South	d					13 58			14 16										14 28			14 46
Purley 4	d					14 02			14 19										14 32			14 49
East Croydon ⇌	a		13 59	14 02	13 52	14 07		14 08	14 24	14 11		14 16				14 27	14 31	14 22	14 37			14 54
	d		14 00	14 02	13 53	14 08		14 08	14 25	14 12		14 17		14 14		14 28	14 32	14 23	14 37			14 55
Nrwood unction 2	a					14 12			14 29										14 42			14 59
Nw Cross Gate	d								14 37													15 07
London Bridge 4 ⊖	a			14 15		14 25			14 43			14 30					14 45		14 55			15 13
London Blackfriars 3 ⊖	a			14 22								14 37					14 52					
City Thameslink 3	a			14 26								14 40					14 56					
Farringdon 3 ⊖	a			14 29								14 44					15 00					
St Pancras hternational 15 ⊖	a			14 34								14 48					15 04					
St Albans City	a			14 54								15 08					15 24					
uton Airport Parkway 4 ✈	a			15 07								15 20					15 37					
uton 7	a			15 10								15 23					15 40					
Bedford 10	a			15 35								15 49					16 05					
Clapham unction 10	a		14 09		14 02			14 17		14 21				14 25		14 37		14 32				
London Victoria 15 ⊖	a	14 05	14 16		14 10		14 20	14 24		14 28				14 32	14 35	14 44		14 40			14 50	

Brighton - London and Bedford

until 18 May

Network Diagram - see first Page of Table 186

		SN	SN	FC	GW	SN	SN	SN		FC	SN	SN	SN	SN	SN	SN	SN	FC		GW	SN	SN	SN	FC	SN
		◇1	◇1	1	1	1	1	◇1		1	◇1	1	1	◇1	1	◇1	◇1	1		1	1	1	◇1	1	◇1
							🚲				🚲		🚲								🚲				🚲
Brighton 10	d			14 04						14 07	14 19			14 25				14 34						14 37	14 49
Hove 2	d		13 51														14 21								
Preston Park	d		13 55							14 11														14 41	
Hassocks 4	d									14 17				14 34										14 47	
Burgess Hill 4	d		14 04							14 21				14 38										14 51	
Lewes 4	d	13 50														14 20									
Wivelsfield 4	d									14 23						14 35								14 53	
Haywards Heath 3	a	14 05	14 09	14 17						14 28						14 40	14 35	14 47						14 58	
	d	14 13		14 18						14 32						14 44		14 48						15 02	
Balcombe	d									14 37															
Horsham 4	d							14 20							14 30								14 50		
Littlehaven	d														14 33										
Faygate	d																								
Ifield	d														14 39										
Crawley	d							14 29							14 43								14 59		
Three Bridges 4	a			14 26				14 32		14 43					14 46			14 56					15 02	15 11	
	d			14 27				14 33		14 43					14 48			14 57					15 03	15 12	
Gatwick Airport 10 ✈	a	14 24		14 31				14 37		14 47				14 51	14 52	14 55		15 01					15 07	15 16	
	d	14 25		14 32			14 35	14 38		14 47			14 50	14 53	14 53	14 56		15 02		15 03	15 05		15 08	15 17	
Horley 4	d							14 41							14 56										
Salfords	d																								
Earlswood (Surrey)	d																								
Tonbridge 4	d											14 19													
Leigh (Kent)	d											14 23													
Penshurst	d											14 27													
Edenbridge	d											14 33													
Godstone	d											14 40													
Nutfield	d											14 45													
Reigate	d				14 34																				
Redhill 5	a				14 38			14 47				14 50			15 02					15 10			15 16		
	d							14 48				14 51			15 07								15 17		
Merstham	d														15 11										
Coulsdon South	d											14 58			15 16										
Purley 4	d											15 02			15 19										
East Croydon	a	14 40		14 46				14 59		15 02	14 52	15 07		15 08	15 24	15 11		15 16					15 28	15 31	15 22
	d	14 41		14 47		14 44		15 00		15 02	14 53	15 07		15 08	15 25	15 12		15 17				15 14	15 28	15 32	15 23
Norwood Junction 2	a											15 12			15 29										
New Cross Gate	d														15 37										
London Bridge 4 ⊖	a			15 00						15 15		15 25			15 43			15 30						15 45	
London Blackfriars 3 ⊖	a			15 07						15 22								15 37						15 52	
City Thameslink 3	a			15 10						15 26								15 40						15 56	
Farringdon 3 ⊖	a			15 14						15 29								15 44						15 59	
St Pancras International 15 ⊖	a			15 18						15 34								15 48						16 04	
St Albans City	a			15 38						15 52								16 08						16 24	
Luton Airport Parkway 4 ✈	a			15 50						16 04								16 20						16 37	
Luton 7	a			15 53						16 07								16 23						16 40	
Bedford 10	a			16 19						16 33								16 49						17 05	
Clapham Junction 10	a	14 50				14 55		15 09			15 02			15 17		15 21						15 25	15 37		15 32
London Victoria 15 ⊖	a	14 57				15 02	15 05	15 20			15 10		15 20	15 24		15 28					15 35	15 35	15 46		15 40

Table 186

Mondays to Fridays

until 18 May

Brighton - London and Bedford

Network Diagram - see first Page of Table 186

		SN	GW	SN		SN	SN	SN	FC	GW	SN	SN	SN	FC		SN	SN	SN	SN	SN	SN	SN	FC	GW	
		1	1	1		1	◇1	◇1	1	1	1	1	◇1	1		◇1	1	1	◇1	1	◇1	◇1	1	1	
								A														A			
				🚲			🚲	🚲			🚲		🚲			🚲		🚲			🚲	🚲			
Brighton 10	d								15 04					15 07		15 19			15 25				15 34		
Hove 2	d							14 51														15 21			
Preston Park	d							14 55						15 11											
Hassocks 4	d													15 17					15 34						
Burgess Hill 4	d							15 04						15 21					15 38						
Lewes 4	d						14 50														15 19				
Wivelsfield 4	d													15 23							15 35				
Haywards Heath 3	a						15 05	15 09	15 17					15 28							15 40	15 35	15 47		
	d						15 13		15 18					15 32							15 44		15 48		
Balcombe	d													15 37											
Horsham 4	d					15 00							15 20							15 30					
Littlehaven	d					15 03														15 33					
Faygate	d																								
Ifield	d					15 09														15 39					
Crawley	d					15 13							15 29							15 43					
Three Bridges 4	a					15 16			15 26				15 32	15 43						15 46			15 56		
	d					15 18			15 27				15 33	15 43						15 48			15 57		
Gatwick Airport 10 ✈	a					15 22	15 24		15 31				15 37	15 47					15 51	15 52	15 55		16 01		
	d			15 20		15 23	15 25		15 32		15 35		15 38	15 47				15 50	15 53	15 53	15 56		16 02	16 03	
Horley 4	d					15 26							15 41							15 56					
Salfords	d					15 30																			
Earlswood (Surrey)	d					15 33																			
Tonbridge 4	d																15 19								
Leigh (Kent)	d																15 23								
Penshurst	d																15 27								
Edenbridge	d																15 33								
Godstone	d																15 40								
Nutfield	d																15 45								
Reigate	d	15 14	15 19							15 34															
Redhill 5	a	15 18	15 25			15 36				15 38			15 47				15 50			16 02				16 10	
	d	15 19				15 37							15 48				15 51			16 06					
Merstham	d	15 23				15 41														16 10					
Coulsdon South	d	15 28				15 46											15 58			16 15					
Purley 4	d	15 32				15 49											16 02			16 18					
East Croydon	a	15 37				15 54	15 40		15 46				15 59	16 02		15 52	16 07		16 08	16 23	16 11		16 16		
	d	15 37				15 55	15 41		15 47			15 44	16 00	16 02		15 53	16 07		16 08	16 24	16 12		16 17		
Norwood Junction 2	a	15 42				15 59											16 12			16 28					
New Cross Gate	d					16 07														16 36					
London Bridge 4 ⊖	a	15 55				16 13			16 00					16 15			16 25			16 43					
London Blackfriars 3 ⊖	a								16 07					16 25									16 47		
City Thameslink 3	a								16 10					16 28									16 54		
Farringdon 3 ⊖	a								16 13					16 31									16 57		
St Pancras International 15 ⊖	a								16 17					16 35									17 01		
St Albans City	a								16 38					16 55									17 19		
Luton Airport Parkway 4 ✈	a								16 51					17 08											
Luton 7	a								16 54					17 11									17 32		
Bedford 10	a								17 19					17 36									17 53		
Clapham Junction 10	a						15 50					15 55	16 09			16 02			16 17		16 21				
London Victoria 15 ⊖	a			15 50			15 57				16 05	16 05	16 16			16 10		16 22	16 24		16 28				

A 🚲 from Haywards Heath

Table 186

Mondays to Fridays

until 18 May

Brighton - London and Bedford

Network Diagram - see first Page of Table 186

		SN	SN	SN	FC	SN	SN	SN	SN	GW	SN	SN	SN	FC	SN	GW	SN	SN	FC	SN	SN	SN	FC
		1	1	◇1	1	◇1	1	◇1	1	1	1	◇1	◇1	1	1	1	1	◇1	1	1	1	1	1
													A										
		🛒		🛒		🛒	🛒					🛒	🛒		🛒					🛒		🛒	
Brighton 10	d				15 37	15 49		15 55						16 04					16 07	16 19			16 24
Hove 2	d												15 52										
Preston Park	d				15 41								15 56						16 11				
Hassocks 4	d				15 47			16 06											16 17				
Burgess Hill 4	d				15 51								16 05						16 21				
Lewes 4	d											15 50											
Wivelsfield 4	d				15 53																		
Haywards Heath 3	a				15 57							16 05	16 10	16 17					16 26				16 38
	d				15 58							16 14		16 18					16 26				16 38
Balcombe	d																		16 32				
Horsham 4	d			15 50							16 00							16 20					
Littlehaven	d										16 03												
Faygate	d																						
Ifield	d										16 09												
Crawley	d			15 59							16 13							16 29					
Three Bridges 4	a			16 02	16 06						16 16			16 26				16 32	16 37				16 47
	d			16 03	16 07						16 18			16 27				16 33	16 37				16 47
Gatwick Airport 10 ✈	a			16 07	16 11			16 21			16 22	16 25		16 31				16 37	16 41				16 52
	d	16 05		16 08	16 12		16 20	16 23			16 23	16 26		16 32	16 35			16 38	16 42			16 50	16 53
Horley 4	d										16 26												
Salfords	d										16 30												
Earlswood (Surrey)	d										16 33												
Tonbridge 4	d																				16 19		
Leigh (Kent)	d																				16 23		
Penshurst	d																				16 27		
Edenbridge	d																				16 33		
Godstone	d																				16 40		
Nutfield	d																				16 45		
Reigate	d								16 14	16 21						16 38							
Redhill 5	a			16 17					16 18	16 27	16 36					16 42		16 46			16 50		
	d			16 18					16 21		16 37							16 47			16 51		
Merstham	d								16 25		16 41												
Coulsdon South	d								16 30		16 46										16 58		
Purley 4	d								16 34		16 49										17 02		
East Croydon 🚋	a			16 30	16 27	16 24		16 38	16 39		16 54	16 40		16 46				17 01	16 57	16 54	17 07		17 07
	d		16 14	16 30	16 28	16 24		16 38	16 40		16 55	16 41		16 47			16 44	17 01	16 58	16 54	17 07		17 09
Norwood Junction 2	a								16 44		16 59										17 11		
New Cross Gate	d										17 06												
London Bridge 4 ⊖	a								17 00		17 14										17 26		17 27
London Blackfriars 3 ⊖	a				16 55									17 19					17 25				17 35
City Thameslink 3	a				16 58									17 24					17 28				17 38
Farringdon 3 ⊖	a				17 01									17 27					17 31				17 41
St Pancras International 15 ⊖	a				17 05									17 31					17 35				17 45
St Albans City	a				17 25									17 49					17 55				18 06
Luton Airport Parkway 4 ✈	a				17 38														18 08				18 20
Luton 7	a				17 41									18 02					18 11				18 23
Bedford 10	a				18 06									18 23					18 36				18 48
Clapham Junction 10	a		16 25	16 39		16 33		16 47				16 50					16 55	17 10		17 03			
London Victoria 15 ⊖	a	16 35	16 35	16 46		16 42	16 52	16 56				16 58			17 05		17 05	17 17		17 10		17 20	

A 🛒 from Haywards Heath

Brighton - London and Bedford

Network Diagram - see first Page of Table 186

		SN	SN	SN	SN	GW		SN	SN	FC	SN	SN	SN	SN	SN	GW		SN	SN	SN	GW	SN	SN	FC	SN
		1	◇1	◇1	1	1		1	1	1	1	◇1	1	1	1	1		1	◇1	◇1	1	1	1	1	1
				A																A					
			🛒	🛒					🛒		🛒	🛒	🛒						🛒	🛒					🛒
Brighton [10]	d									16 30	16 49												16 55	17 02	
Hove [2]	d			16 21																16 51					
Preston Park	d									16 34													16 58		
Hassocks [4]	d									16 40													17 05		
Burgess Hill [4]	d									16 44										17 02			17 08	17 13	
Lewes [4]	d		16 20																16 50						
Wivelsfield [4]	d		16 38							16 46													17 11		
Haywards Heath [3]	a		16 42	16 35						16 50									17 06	17 09			17 15	17 18	
	d		16 46							16 51									17 14				17 21 →	17 18	
Balcombe	d									16 56															
Horsham [4]	d	16 30										16 52						17 00							
Littlehaven	d	16 33																17 03							
Faygate	d	16 37																17 07							
Ifield	d	16 41																17 11							
Crawley	d	16 44										17 01						17 14							
Three Bridges [4]	a	16 47								17 02		17 04						17 17						17 27	
	d	16 48								17 02		17 05						17 18						17 27	
Gatwick Airport [10] ✈	a	16 52	16 57							17 07		17 09						17 22	17 25					17 31	
	d	16 53	16 58			17 03			17 05	17 08		17 10	17 20					17 23	17 26					17 32	17 35
Horley [4]	d	16 56																17 26							
Salfords	d	17 00																17 30							
Earlswood (Surrey)	d	17 03																17 33							
Tonbridge [4]	d													16 49	17 03										
Leigh (Kent)	d													16 53											
Penshurst	d													16 57											
Edenbridge	d													17 03	17 13										
Godstone	d													17 10											
Nutfield	d													17 15											
Reigate	d				17 03											17 26					17 34				
Redhill [5]	a	17 06			17 07	17 10						17 17		17 20	17 25	17 32		17 36			17 38				
	d	17 07										17 18		17 21	17 28			17 37							
Merstham	d	17 11												17 25				17 41							
Coulsdon South	d	17 16												17 30				17 46							
Purley [4]	d	17 19																17 49							
East Croydon 🚊	a	17 24	17 13							17 22	17 26	17 30		17 38	17 40			17 54	17 41					17 46	
	d	17 25	17 13					17 14		17 23	17 26	17 30		17 38	17 41			17 55	17 41			17 44		17 47	
Norwood Junction [2]	a	17 30													17 45			17 59							
New Cross Gate	d	17 38																18 07							
London Bridge [4] ⊖	a	17 45													17 58			18 16						18 13	
London Blackfriars [3] ⊖	a									17 49														18 21	
City Thameslink [3]	a									17 54														18 24	
Farringdon [3] ⊖	a									17 57														18 27	
St Pancras International [15] ⊖	a									18 01														18 31	
St Albans City	a									18 19														18 49	
Luton Airport Parkway [4] ✈	a																								
Luton [7]	a									18 32														19 02	
Bedford [10]	a									18 55														19 23	
Clapham Junction [10]	a		17 22					17 25			17 35	17 39		17 47					17 50			17 55			
London Victoria [15] ⊖	a		17 29					17 35	17 38		17 42	17 46	17 52	17 54					17 58			18 05			18 05

A 🛒 from Haywards Heath

Table 186

Mondays to Fridays

until 18 May

Brighton - London and Bedford

Network Diagram - see first Page of Table 186

		SN		FC	SN	SN	SN	SN	SN	SN	SN	SN		FC	GW	SN	SN	SN	FC	SN	SN	SN		SN	GW
		[1]		[1]	[1]	◇[1]	[1]	[1]	[1]	[1]	◇[1]	◇[1]		[1]	[1]	[1]	[1]	◇[1]	[1]	[1]	[1]	[1]		[1]	[1]
												A													
					🛒	🛒	🛒				🛒	🛒				🛒		🛒			🛒	🛒			
Brighton [10]	d			17 07	17 19									17 24					17 37		17 49				
Hove [2]	d											17 21													
Preston Park	d			17 11										17 28					17 41						
Hassocks [4]	d			17 17										17 34					17 47						
Burgess Hill [4]	d			17 21										17 38					17 51						
Lewes [4]	d										17 19														
Wivelsfield [4]	d	←									17 35			17 40					17 53						
Haywards Heath [3]	a	17 15		17 26							17 39	17 35		17 45					17 58						
	d	17 21		17 26							17 43			17 46					18 02						
Balcombe	d	17 26																	18 07						
Horsham [4]	d					17 22				17 30								17 52							
Littlehaven	d									17 33															
Faygate	d									17 37															
Ifield	d									17 41															
Crawley	d					17 31				17 44								18 01							
Three Bridges [4]	a	17 32				17 34				17 47				17 54				18 04	18 13						
	d	17 32				17 36				17 48				17 55				18 05	18 13						
Gatwick Airport [10] ✈	a	17 36		17 38		17 41				17 52	17 54			17 59				18 09	18 17						
	d	17 38		17 39		17 42	17 50			17 53	17 55			18 00	18 03	18 05		18 10	18 17			18 20			
Horley [4]	d									17 56															
Salfords	d									18 00															
Earlswood (Surrey)	d									18 03															
Tonbridge [4]	d							17 21												17 49					
Leigh (Kent)	d							17 25												17 53					
Penshurst	d							17 29												17 57					
Edenbridge	d							17 35												18 03					
Godstone	d							17 42												18 10					
Nutfield	d							17 47												18 15					
Reigate	d								17 44																
Redhill [5]	a					17 49		17 53	17 48	18 06					18 10			18 17		18 21				18 14	18 26
	d					17 49		17 57		18 07								18 18						18 19	18 32
Merstham	d									18 11														18 24	
Coulsdon South	d									18 16														18 28	
Purley [4]	d									18 19														18 33	
East Croydon	a	17 53		17 57	17 56	18 01		18 08		18 24	18 11			18 15				18 29	18 32		18 25			18 40	
	d	17 53		17 58	17 57	18 02		18 09		18 27	18 12			18 16			18 14	18 30	18 32		18 26			18 40	
Norwood Junction [2]	a																								
New Cross Gate	d																								
London Bridge [4] ⊖	a																		18 46						
London Blackfriars [3] ⊖	a			18 25										18 51					18 55						
City Thameslink [3]	a			18 28										18 54					18 58						
Farringdon [3] ⊖	a			18 31										18 57					19 01						
St Pancras International [15] ⊖	a			18 35										19 01					19 05						
St Albans City	a			18 57										19 19					19 25						
Luton Airport Parkway [4] ✈	a			19 09															19 38						
Luton [7]	a			19 12										19 32					19 41						
Bedford [10]	a			19 38										19 55					20 06						
Clapham Junction [10]	a	18 02			18 06	18 13		18 18		18 38	18 21						18 25	18 41			18 35			18 49	
London Victoria [15] ⊖	a	18 09			18 14	18 20	18 22	18 26		18 45	18 29					18 35	18 35	18 48			18 42	18 50		18 56	

A 🛒 from Haywards Heath

until 18 May

Brighton - London and Bedford

Network Diagram - see first Page of Table 186

Station		SN 1	SN ◇1 [trolley]	SN ◇1 A [trolley]	SN 1	GW 1	SN 1	SN 1		FC 1	SN 1 [trolley]	SN 1	SN ◇1	FC 1	SN 1	SN 1	SN 1 [trolley]	SN 1		SN ◇1 [trolley]	SN ◇1 A [trolley]	FC 1	SN 1	SN 1 [trolley]	SN 1
Brighton 10	d							17 55		18 02				18 07	18 19							18 34			
Hove 2	d			17 51																	18 21				
Preston Park	d							17 59						18 11											
Hassocks 4	d							18 05						18 17											
Burgess Hill 4	d			18 04				18 09		18 13				18 21							18 34				
Lewes 4	d		17 50																	18 18					
Wivelsfield 4	d							18 11				←		18 23						18 34					
Haywards Heath 3	a		18 07	18 11				18 16		18 18		18 16		18 28						18 38	18 41	18 47			
	d		18 15					18 22		18 18		18 22		18 32						18 45		18 48			
Balcombe	d							→						18 37											
Horsham 4	d	18 00											18 22					18 30							
Littlehaven	d	18 03																18 33							
Faygate	d	18 07																18 37							
Ifield	d	18 11																18 41							
Crawley	d	18 14											18 31					18 44							
Three Bridges 4	a	18 17								18 27		18 31	18 34	18 43				18 47				18 56			
	d	18 18								18 27		18 31	18 35	18 43				18 48				18 57			
Gatwick Airport 10 ✈	a	18 22	18 26							18 31		18 36	18 39	18 47				18 52		18 56		19 01			
	d	18 23	18 27							18 32	18 35	18 38	18 40	18 47			18 50	18 53		18 57		19 02		19 05	
Horley 4	d	18 26																18 56							
Salfords	d	18 30																19 00							
Earlswood (Surrey)	d	18 33																19 03							
Tonbridge 4	d															18 23									
Leigh (Kent)	d															18 27									
Penshurst	d															18 31									
Edenbridge	d															18 37									
Godstone	d															18 44									
Nutfield	d															18 49									
Reigate	d				18 38	18 42																	19 02		
Redhill 5	a	18 36			18 42	18 47							18 47			18 54		19 06					19 06		
	d	18 37											18 48			18 57		19 07							
Merstham	d	18 41																19 11							
Coulsdon South	d	18 46																19 16							
Purley 4	d	18 49																19 19							
East Croydon	a	18 54	18 42							18 47		18 53	18 59	19 02	18 56	19 09		19 24		19 12		19 16			
	d	18 55	18 43				18 44			18 47		18 53	19 00	19 02	18 57	19 10		19 25		19 12		19 17			19 14
Norwood Junction 2	a															19 13									
New Cross Gate	d																								
London Bridge 4 ⊖	a									19 00				19 15		19 25						19 30			
London Blackfriars 3 ⊖	a									19 09				19 22								19 37			
City Thameslink 3	a									19 12				19 26								19 40			
Farringdon 3 ⊖	a									19 15				19 30								19 44			
St Pancras International 15 ⊖	a									19 19				19 34								19 48			
St Albans City	a									19 45				19 55								20 08			
Luton Airport Parkway 4 ✈	a									19 57				20 06								20 20			
Luton 7	a									20 00				20 09								20 23			
Bedford 10	a									20 26				20 35								20 49			
Clapham Junction 10	a	19 05	18 52				18 55					19 02	19 11		19 08			19 37		19 21					19 25
London Victoria 15 ⊖	a	19 13	18 59				19 05				19 05	19 09	19 18		19 15		19 20	19 44		19 29				19 35	19 35

A [trolley] from Haywards Heath

Table 186

Mondays to Fridays

until 18 May

Brighton - London and Bedford

Network Diagram - see first Page of Table 186

		SN	FC	SN		GW	SN	SN	SN	GW	SN	SN	SN	FC		SN	GW	SN	SN	SN	SN	FC	SN	SN	
		◇1	1	◇1		1	1	1	1	1	1	◇1	◇1	1		1	1	1	1	◇1	1	1	◇1	1	
																				A					
							bus									bus								bus	
Brighton 10	d		18 37	18 49																18 59		19 07	19 19		
Hove 2	d												18 52												
Preston Park	d		18 41																	19 03		19 11			
Hassocks 4	d		18 47																	19 09		19 17			
Burgess Hill 4	d		18 51																	19 13		19 21			
Lewes 4	d											18 50													
Wivelsfield 4	d		18 53									19 06								19 15		19 23			
Haywards Heath 3	a		18 58									19 10	19 07							19 20		19 28			
	d		19 02									19 14								19 21		19 32			
Balcombe	d																					19 37			
Horsham 4	d	18 52									19 02										19 17				
Littlehaven	d										19 05														
Faygate	d																								
Ifield	d										19 11														
Crawley	d	19 01									19 14										19 26				
Three Bridges 4	a	19 04	19 11								19 18									19 31	19 29	19 43			
	d	19 05	19 12								19 18			19 27						19 35		19 43			
Gatwick Airport 10 ✈	a	19 09	19 16								19 22	19 25		19 31						19 39		19 47			
	d	19 10	19 17			19 16	19 20				19 23	19 26		19 32		19 35				19 40		19 47		19 50	
Horley 4	d										19 26														
Salfords	d										19 30														
Earlswood (Surrey)	d										19 33														
Tonbridge 4	d							18 50										19 10							
Leigh (Kent)	d							18 54										19 14							
Penshurst	d							18 58										19 18							
Edenbridge	d							19 04										19 24							
Godstone	d							19 11										19 31							
Nutfield	d							19 16										19 36							
Reigate	d								19 21	19 30							19 36								
Redhill 5	a	19 17				19 23		19 21	19 25	19 35	19 38						19 40	19 41		19 47					
	d	19 18						19 23			19 39									19 48					
Merstham	d							19 27			19 43														
Coulsdon South	d							19 32			19 48														
Purley 4	d										19 53														
East Croydon	a	19 29	19 31	19 23				19 40			19 58	19 43		19 46						20 00		20 02	19 53		
	d	19 29	19 32	19 24				19 40			19 59	19 43		19 47					19 44	20 01		20 02	19 54		
Norwood Junction 2	a																								
New Cross Gate	d																								
London Bridge 4 ⊖	a		19 45											20 00								20 15			
London Blackfriars 3 ⊖	a		19 52											20 07								20 22			
City Thameslink 3	a		19 56											20 10								20 26			
Farringdon 3 ⊖	a		20 00											20 14								20 30			
St Pancras International 15 ⊖	a		20 04											20 18								20 34			
St Albans City	a		20 25											20 38								20 55			
Luton Airport Parkway 4 ✈	a		20 37											20 50								21 07			
Luton 7	a		20 40											20 53								21 10			
Bedford 10	a		21 05											21 19								21 35			
Clapham Junction 10	a	19 40		19 33				19 49			20 08	19 52							19 55	20 11			20 03		
London Victoria 15 ⊖	a	19 47		19 41			19 50	19 56			20 15	19 59				20 05			20 05	20 20			20 10	20 20	

A ◇ to Three Bridges

Table 186

Mondays to Fridays

until 18 May

Brighton - London and Bedford

Network Diagram - see first Page of Table 186

		SN	SN	SN	SN	SN	FC	GW	SN	SN		FC	SN	SN	SN	SN	SN	SN	GW	SN		SN	SN	FC	SN
		◇1	◇1	1	1	1	1	1	1	◇1		1	◇1	1	1	1	◇1	◇1	1	1		1	◇1	1	1
Brighton [10]	d						19 34					19 37	19 49										19 55	20 02	
Hove [2]	d		19 22															19 52							
Preston Park	d											19 41											19 58		
Hassocks [4]	d											19 47											20 05		
Burgess Hill [4]	d		19 32									19 51											20 08	20 13	
Lewes [4]	d	19 21															19 50								
Wivelsfield [4]	d											19 53					20 05						20 11		
Haywards Heath [3]	a	19 40	19 37				19 47					19 58					20 10	20 05					20 15	20 18	
	d		19 44				19 48					20 02					20 14						20 22 ↦	20 19	
Balcombe	d																								
Horsham [4]	d					19 32				19 52						20 02									
Littlehaven	d					19 35										20 05									
Faygate	d																								
Ifield	d					19 41										20 11									
Crawley	d					19 45				20 01						20 14									
Three Bridges [4]	a					19 49	19 56			20 04		20 11				20 18								20 27	
	d					19 51	19 57			20 05		20 12				20 18								20 27	
Gatwick Airport [10] ✈	a		19 55			19 55	20 01			20 10		20 16				20 22	20 25							20 31	
	d		19 56			19 56	20 02	20 03	20 05	20 11		20 17			20 20	20 23	20 26							20 32	20 35
Horley [4]	d					19 59										20 26									
Salfords	d															20 30									
Earlswood (Surrey)	d															20 33									
Tonbridge [4]	d																			20 10					
Leigh (Kent)	d																			20 14					
Penshurst	d																			20 18					
Edenbridge	d																			20 24					
Godstone	d																			20 31					
Nutfield	d																			20 36					
Reigate	d			19 51										20 14					20 34						
Redhill [5]	a			19 55		20 05		20 11		20 18				20 18		20 36			20 38	20 45					
	d					20 06				20 18						20 37									
Merstham	d					20 10										20 41									
Coulsdon South	d					20 15										20 46									
Purley [4]	d					20 18										20 49									
East Croydon	a		20 11			20 23	20 16			20 30		20 32	20 23			20 57	20 41							20 47	
	d		20 11		20 14	20 26	20 17			20 30		20 32	20 24			20 57	20 41					20 44		20 47	
Norwood Junction [2]	a																								
New Cross Gate	d																								
London Bridge [4] ⊖	a						20 30					20 45												21 00	
London Blackfriars [3] ⊖	a						20 37					20 52												21 07	
City Thameslink [3]	a						20 40					20 56												21 10	
Farringdon [3] ⊖	a						20 44					21 00												21 14	
St Pancras International [15] ⊖	a						20 48					21 04												21 18	
St Albans City	a						21 08					21 25												21 38	
Luton Airport Parkway [4] ✈	a						21 20					21 37												21 50	
Luton [7]	a						21 23					21 40												21 53	
Bedford [10]	a						21 49					22 05												22 19	
Clapham Junction [10]	a		20 20		20 25	20 37				20 40			20 33			21 07	20 50					20 55			
London Victoria [15] ⊖	a		20 28		20 32	20 44			20 35	20 50			20 40		20 50	21 15	20 59					21 03			21 05

Table 186

Brighton - London and Bedford

Mondays to Fridays

until 18 May

Network Diagram - see first Page of Table 186

		SN ◇1	FC 1	SN ◇1	SN 1	SN 1		SN ◇1	SN 1	SN 1	FC 1	GW 1	SN 1	SN 1	SN ◇1	FC 1		SN ◇1	SN 1	GW 1	SN 1	SN ◇1	SN ◇1	SN 1	SN 1
Brighton 10	d		20 07	20 19							20 34					20 37		20 49							
Hove 2	d							20 22																	
Preston Park	d		20 11													20 41							20 52		
Hassocks 4	d		20 17													20 47									
Burgess Hill 4	d		20 21					20 33								20 51									
Lewes 4	d																								
Wivelsfield 4	d	←	20 23													20 53						20 50			
Haywards Heath 3	a	20 15	20 28					20 38			20 47					20 58						21 05 21 09	21 05		
	d	20 22	20 32					20 38			20 48					21 02						21 13			
Balcombe	d		20 37																						
Horsham 4	d									20 32					20 52						21 02				
Littlehaven	d									20 35											21 05				
Faygate	d																								
Ifield	d									20 41											21 11				
Crawley	d									20 45					21 01						21 14				
Three Bridges 4	a	20 32	20 43					20 47		20 48	20 56				21 05	21 11					21 18				
	d	20 32	20 43					20 47		20 51	20 57				21 05	21 12					21 18				
Gatwick Airport 10 ✈	a	20 37	20 47					20 51		20 56	21 01				21 10	21 16					21 22	21 25			
	d	20 38	20 47			20 50		20 53		20 57	21 02	21 03	21 05		21 11	21 17			21 20		21 23	21 26			21 35
Horley 4	d									20 59											21 26				
Salfords	d																				21 30				
Earlswood (Surrey)	d																				21 33				
Tonbridge 4	d																							21 10	
Leigh (Kent)	d																							21 14	
Penshurst	d																							21 18	
Edenbridge	d																							21 24	
Godstone	d																							21 31	
Nutfield	d																							21 36	
Reigate	d				20 50									21 13						21 24					
Redhill 5	a	20 47			20 54					21 06		21 10		21 17	21 18					21 30	21 36			21 42	
	d	20 48								21 07					21 18						21 37				
Merstham	d									21 11											21 41				
Coulsdon South	d									21 16											21 46				
Purley 4	d									21 19											21 49				
East Croydon	a	20 59	21 02	20 53				21 08		21 25	21 16				21 30	21 32		21 23			21 54	21 41			
	d	21 00	21 02	20 54				21 09	21 14	21 26	21 17				21 30	21 32		21 24			21 57	21 42			
Norwood Junction 2	a																								
New Cross Gate	d																								
London Bridge 4 ⊖	a		21 15								21 30					21 45									
London Blackfriars 3 ⊖	a		21 22								21 37					21 52									
City Thameslink 3	a		21 26								21 40					21 56									
Farringdon 3 ⊖	a		21 30								21 44					22 00									
St Pancras International 15 ⊖	a		21 34								21 48					22 04									
St Albans City	a		21 55								22 08					22 25									
Luton Airport Parkway 4 ✈	a		22 07								22 20					22 37									
Luton 7	a		22 10								22 23					22 40									
Bedford 10	a		22 35								22 49					23 05									
Clapham Junction 10	a	21 11		21 03				21 18	21 25	21 37					21 40			21 33			22 07	21 51			
London Victoria 15 ⊖	a	21 18		21 10		21 20		21 28	21 32	21 45			21 35		21 47			21 40	21 50		22 14	21 58			22 05

Table 186

Mondays to Fridays

until 18 May

Brighton - London and Bedford

Network Diagram - see first Page of Table 186

		SN		SN	FC	SN	GW	SN	SN	SN	SN	SN		SN	SN	SN	SN	FC	SN	SN	GW	SN		SN	SN
		1		◇1	1	◇1	1	1	◇1	1	1	1		1	1	1	◇1	1	◇1	1	1	1		◇1	◇1
																									A
																								🛒	🛒
Brighton 10	d			21 02	21 11	21 19								21 34				21 37	21 49						
Hove 2	d								21 22																21 52
Preston Park	d			21 06														21 41							
Hassocks 4	d			21 12	21 20													21 47							
Burgess Hill 4	d			21 16	21 23				21 33									21 51							22 04
Lewes 4	d																							21 50	
Wivelsfield 4	d			21 18														21 53						22 02	
Haywards Heath 3	a			21 23	21 28				21 38					21 47				21 58						22 06	22 10
	d			21 23	21 32				21 38					21 47				22 02						22 14	
Balcombe	d				21 37																				
Horsham 4	d											21 32					21 52					22 02			
Littlehaven	d											21 35										22 05			
Faygate	d																								
Ifield	d											21 41										22 11			
Crawley	d											21 45					22 01					22 14			
Three Bridges 4	a			21 32	21 43				21 47			21 48		21 56			22 05	22 11				22 18			
	d			21 33	21 43				21 47			21 51		21 56			22 05	22 12				22 19			
Gatwick Airport 10 ✈	a			21 37	21 47				21 51			21 55		22 00			22 10	22 16				22 23			22 25
	d			21 38	21 47			21 50	21 53			21 56		22 02	22 05		22 11	22 17		22 20	22 22	22 24			22 26
Horley 4	d											21 59										22 27			
Salfords	d																					22 31			
Earlswood (Surrey)	d																					22 34			
Tonbridge 4	d																								
Leigh (Kent)	d																								
Penshurst	d																								
Edenbridge	d																								
Godstone	d																								
Nutfield	d																								
Reigate	d						21 45			21 52						22 13									
Redhill 5	a			21 45			21 49			21 57		22 05				22 17	22 18				22 30	22 37			
	d			21 46								22 06					22 18					22 38			
Merstham	d											22 10										22 42			
Coulsdon South	d											22 15										22 47			
Purley 4	d											22 19										22 50			
East Croydon 🚌	a			21 59	22 02	21 53			22 08			22 24		22 17			22 30	22 32	22 23			22 55			22 41
	d	21 44		22 00	22 02	21 54			22 09		22 14	22 25		22 18			22 30	22 32	22 24			22 56			22 41
Norwood Junction 2	a																								
New Cross Gate	d																								
London Bridge 4 ⊖	a				22 17									22 33				22 47							
London Blackfriars 3 ⊖	a																								
City Thameslink 3	a																								
Farringdon 3 ⊖	a																								
St Pancras International 15 ⊖	a																								
St Albans City	a																								
Luton Airport Parkway 4 ✈	a																								
Luton 7	a																								
Bedford 10	a																								
Clapham Junction 10	a	21 55		22 10		22 03			22 18		22 25	22 37					22 40		22 33			23 06			22 50
London Victoria 15 ⊖	a	22 05		22 20		22 11		22 20	22 26		22 35	22 44			22 35		22 50		22 41	22 50		23 15			22 57

A 🛒 from Haywards Heath

Table 186

Brighton - London and Bedford

Mondays to Fridays

until 18 May

Network Diagram - see first Page of Table 186

		SN 1	SN 1	SN 1	SN 1	SN ◇1	FC 1	SN ◇1		GW 1	SN 1	SN 1	SN 1	SN 1	FC 1	SN ◇1	FC 1	GW 1		SN 1	SN 1	SN 1	SN 1	GW 1	SN ◇1
Brighton 10	d					22 03	22 07	22 19							22 33										23 02
Hove 2	d																								
Preston Park	d					22 06	22 11								22 37										23 06
Hassocks 4	d					22 13	22 17								22 43										23 12
Burgess Hill 4	d					22 16	22 21								22 47										23 16
Lewes 4	d															22 40									
Wivelsfield 4	d					22 18	22 23								22 49	22 54									23 19
Haywards Heath 3	a					22 23	22 28								22 53	22 58									23 23
	d					22 23	22 32								22 54	22 59									23 24
Balcombe	d						22 37								22 59										
Horsham 4	d																				23 02				
Littlehaven	d																				23 05				
Faygate	d																								
Ifield	d																				23 11				
Crawley	d																←				23 14				
Three Bridges 4	a					22 32	22 43								23 05	23 08	23 05				23 18				23 33
	d					22 33	22 43								23 12	23 08	23 12				23 18				23 47
Gatwick Airport 10 ✈	a					22 37	22 47								↦	23 12	23 16				23 22				→
	d			22 35		22 38	22 47				22 50	23 05				23 13	23 17	23 18		23 20	23 23		23 35		
Horley 4	d																				23 26				
Salfords	d																				23 30				
Earlswood (Surrey)	d																				23 33				
Tonbridge 4	d		22 10																			23 17			
Leigh (Kent)	d		22 14																			23 21			
Penshurst	d		22 18																			23 25			
Edenbridge	d		22 24																			23 31			
Godstone	d		22 31																			23 38			
Nutfield	d		22 36																			23 43			
Reigate	d	22 33								22 44														23 54	
Redhill 5	a	22 37	22 42			22 45				22 48								23 25			23 36	23 49		23 58	
	d					22 46															23 37				
Merstham	d																				23 41				
Coulsdon South	d																				23 46				
Purley 4	d																				23 49				
East Croydon	a					22 59	23 02	22 53								23 30	23 32				23 54				
	d				22 44	23 00	23 02	22 54					23 14	23 20		23 30	23 32				23 58				
Norwood Junction 2	a																								
New Cross Gate	d																								
London Bridge 4 ⊖	a						23 17										23 47								
London Blackfriars 3 ⊖	a																								
City Thameslink 3	a																								
Farringdon 3 ⊖	a																								
St Pancras International 15 ⊖	a																								
St Albans City	a																								
Luton Airport Parkway 4 ✈	a																								
Luton 7	a																								
Bedford 10	a																								
Clapham Junction 10	a				22 55	23 10		23 03					23 25	23 32		23 42					00 11				
London Victoria 15 ⊖	a			23 05	23 05	23 20		23 13			23 20	23 35	23 35	23 40		23 52				23 55	00 18		00 10		

Table 186

Mondays to Fridays

until 18 May

Brighton - London and Bedford

Network Diagram - see first Page of Table 186

		FC 1	SN 1	SN ◇1		FC 1
Brighton 10	d	23 11				23 37
Hove 2	d					
Preston Park	d					23 41
Hassocks 4	d	23 20				23 47
Burgess Hill 4	d	23 23				23 51
Lewes 4	d					
Wivelsfield 4	d					23 53
Haywards Heath 3	a	23 28				23 58
	d	23 29				23 59
Balcombe	d					00 04
Horsham 4	d					
Littlehaven	d					
Faygate	d					
Ifield	d					
Crawley	d			⟵		
Three Bridges 4	a	23 38		23 33		00 10
	d	23 38		23 47		00 10
Gatwick Airport 10 ✈	a	23 42		23 52		00 14
	d	23 43	23 50	23 53		00 15
Horley 4	d			23 56		
Salfords	d					
Earlswood (Surrey)	d					
Tonbridge 4	d					
Leigh (Kent)	d					
Penshurst	d					
Edenbridge	d					
Godstone	d					
Nutfield	d					
Reigate	d					
Redhill 5	a			00 03		00 22
	d			00 03		00 23
Merstham	d					
Coulsdon South	d					
Purley 4	d			00 11		
East Croydon	a	00 01		00 16		00 35
	d	00 04		00 17		00 36
Norwood Junction 2	a					
New Cross Gate	d					
London Bridge 4 ⊖	a	00 19				00 52
London Blackfriars 3 ⊖	a					
City Thameslink 3	a					
Farringdon 3 ⊖	a					
St Pancras International 15 ⊖	a					
St Albans City	a					
Luton Airport Parkway 4 ✈	a					
Luton 7	a					
Bedford 10	a					
Clapham Junction 10	a			00 29		
London Victoria 15 ⊖	a		00 25	00 37		

Table 186

Brighton - London and Bedford

Mondays to Fridays

from 21 May

Network Diagram - see first Page of Table 186

		SN MO ■	FC MX ■	FC MO ■ A	FC MO ■ B	FC MO ■ C	FC MX ■	FC MX ■	FC MO ■ A	FC MO ■ B	FC MO ■ C	FC MX ■	FC MX ■	FC MO ■ A	FC MO ■ B	FC MO ■ C	FC MX ■	SN MX ■	SN MO ■	SN ■	SN MX ■	SN MO ◇■	SN MX ◇■
Brighton ■	d		21p37	21p44	21p45	21p45		22p07	22p14	22p15	22p15		22p33	22p44	22p45	22p45						23p02	23p02
Hove ■	d																						
Preston Park	d		21p41					22p11					22p37									23p06	23p06
Hassocks ■	d		21p47	21p53	21p54	21p54		22p17	22p23	22p24	22p24		22p43	22p53	22p54	22p54						23p12	23p12
Burgess Hill ■	d		21p51	21p56	21p57	21p57		22p21	22p26	22p27	22p27		22p47	22p56	22p57	22p57						23p16	23p16
Lewes ■	d																						
Wivelsfield ■	d		21p53					22p23					22p49									23p18	23p19
Haywards Heath ■	a		21p58	22p01	22p02	22p02		22p28	22p31	22p32	22p32		22p53	23p01	23p02	23p02						23p23	23p23
	d		22p02	22p02	22p03	22p03		22p32	22p32	22p33	22p33		22p54	23p02	23p03	23p03						23p23	23p24
Balcombe	d							22p37					22p59									23p29	
Horsham ■	d																	23p02	23p03				
Littlehaven	d																	23p05	23p06				
Faygate	d																						
Ifield	d																	23p11	23p12				
Crawley	d						←					←					←	23p14	23p16				
Three Bridges ■	a		22p11	22p10	22p11	22p11	22p11	22p43	22p40	22p41	22p41	22p43	23p05	23p10	23p11	23p11	23p05	23p18	23p19			23p36	23p33
	d		22p12	22p11	22p12	22p12	22p12	22p43	22p41	22p42	22p42	22p43	23p12	23p11	23p12	23p12	23p12	23p18	23p20			23p41	23p47
Gatwick Airport ■ ✈	a		→	22p15	22p16	22p16	22p16	→	22p45	22p46	22p46	22p47	→	23p15	23p16	23p16	23p16	23p22	23p24			→	→
	d			22p16	22p17	22p17	22p17		22p46	22p47	22p47	22p47		23p16	23p17	23p17	23p17	23p23	23p25	23p35			
Horley ■	d																	23p26	23p28				
Salfords	d																	23p30					
Earlswood (Surrey)	d																	23p33					
Tonbridge ■	d																						
Leigh (Kent)	d																						
Penshurst	d																						
Edenbridge	d																						
Godstone	d																						
Nutfield	d																						
Reigate	d																				←		
Redhill ■	a																	23p36	23p34		23p36		
	d																	23p37	23p35		23p37		
Merstham	d																	→	23p39		23p41		
Coulsdon South	d																		23p44		23p46		
Purley ■	d																		23p50		23p49		
East Croydon	a			22p31	22p31	22p31	22p32		23p01	23p02	23p02	23p02		23p31	23p31	23p31	23p32		23p55		23p54		
	d	23p50		22p32	22p32	22p32	22p32		23p01	23p02	23p02	23p02		23p32	23p32	23p32	23p32		23p56		23p58		
Norwood Junction ■	a																						
New Cross Gate	d																						
London Bridge ■ ⊖	a			22p45	22p45	22p45	22p45		23p15	23p15	23p15	23p15		23p45	23p45	23p45	23p45						
London Blackfriars ■ ⊖	a			22p52	22p52	22p52	22p52		23p22	23p22	23p22	23p22		23p52	23p52	23p52	23p52						
City Thameslink ■	a						22p53																
Farringdon ■ ⊖	a			22p56	22p56	22p56	22p58		23p26	23p26	23p26	23p28		23p56	23p56	23p56	23p58						
St Pancras International ■ ⊖	a			23p01	23p01	23p01	23p02		23p31	23p31	23p31	23p32		00 01	00 01	00 01	00 02						
St Albans City	a			23p35	23p35	23p35	23p26		00 05	00 05	00 05	23p56		00 35	00 35	00 35	00 26						
Luton Airport Parkway ■ ✈	a			23p47	23p48	23p47	23p38		00 17	00 18	00 17	00 08		00 47	00 48	00 47	00 38						
Luton ■	a			23p50	23p51	23p50	23p41		00 20	00 21	00 20	00 11		00 50	00 51	00 50	00 41						
Bedford ■	a			00 17	00 17	00 17	00 08		00 47	00 47	00 47	00 38		01 17	01 17	01 17	01 08						
Clapham Junction ■	a	00 01																	00 11		00 11		
London Victoria ■ ⊖	a	00 08																	00 19	00 10	00 18		

A from 17 September

B from 21 May until 25 June

C from 2 July until 10 September

Brighton - London and Bedford

Network Diagram - see first Page of Table 186

		FC	FC	SN	FC	FC		SN	SN	SN	FC	FC	FC	SN	GW	GW		SN	SN	SN	SN	FC	FC	SN	SN
		MX	MO	MO	MO	MO			MX		MX	MO	MO		MO	MX						MX	MO		
		1	1	◇1	1	1		1	◇1	1	1	1	1	1	1	1			1	1	1			1	1
			A		B	C						D	A		D							E	C		
Brighton 10	d	23p11	23p14		23p15	23p15					23p37	23p45	23p45												
Hove 2	d																								
Preston Park	d										23p41														
Hassocks 4	d	23p20	23p23		23p24	23p24					23p47	23p54	23p54												
Burgess Hill 4	d	23p23	23p26		23p27	23p27					23p51	23p57	23p57												
Lewes 4	d																								
Wivelsfield 4	d										23p53														
Haywards Heath 3	a	23p28	23p31		23p32	23p32					23p58	00 02	00 02												
	d	23p29	23p32		23p33	23p33					23p59	00 03	00 03												
Balcombe	d										00 04														
Horsham 4	d																								
Littlehaven	d																								
Faygate	d																								
Ifield	d																								
Crawley	d			←					←																
Three Bridges 4	a	23p38	23p40	23p36	23p41	23p41			23p33		00 10	00 11	00 11												
	d	23p38	23p41	23p41	23p42	23p42			23p47		00 10	00 12	00 12									01 25	01 25		01 59
Gatwick Airport 10 ✈	a	23p42	23p45	23p45	23p46	23p46			23p52		00 14	00 16	00 16									01 29	01 29		02 03
	d	23p43	23p46	23p46	23p47	23p47		23p50	23p53	00 05	00 15	00 17	00 17	00 20					00 36	00 50	01 05	01 30	01 30	01 35	02 05
Horley 4	d			23p49					23p56												01 07				02 07
Salfords	d																								
Earlswood (Surrey)	d																								
Tonbridge 4	d																								
Leigh (Kent)	d																								
Penshurst	d																								
Edenbridge	d																								
Godstone	d																								
Nutfield	d																								
Reigate	d														00 26	00 45									
Redhill 5	a			23p57					00 03		00 22	00 24	00 24		00 30	00 49									
	d			00 01					00 03		00 23	00 24	00 24												
Merstham	d																								
Coulsdon South	d																								
Purley 4	d			00 11					00 11												01 22				02 22
East Croydon	a	00 01	00 02	00 16	00 02	00 02			00 16		00 35	00 36	00 36								01 27	01 47	01 47		02 27
	d	00 04	00 03	00 16	00 04	00 04			00 17		00 36	00 36	00 37					00 49			01 28	01 47	01 47		02 28
Norwood Junction 2	a																								
New Cross Gate	d																								
London Bridge 4 ⊖	a	00 21	00 21		00 21	00 21					00 51	00 50	00 50												
London Blackfriars 3 ⊖	a	00 28	00 27		00 27	00 27					00 58	00 57	00 57									02 13	02 13		
City Thameslink 3	a																								
Farringdon 3 ⊖	a	00 33	00 33		00 33	00 33																			
St Pancras International 15 ⊖	a	00 37	00 37		00 37	00 37					01 07	01 07	01 07									02 23	02 23		
St Albans City	a	01 10	01 10		01 10	01 10					01 40	01 40	01 40									02 57	02 57		
Luton Airport Parkway 4 ✈	a	01 22	01 22		01 22	01 25					01 52	01 52	01 52									03 09	03 10		
Luton 7	a	01 25	01 25		01 25	01 28					01 55	01 55	01 55									03 12	03 13		
Bedford 10	a	01 52	01 52		01 52	01 55					02 22	02 22	02 22									03 39	03 39		
Clapham Junction 10	a			00 29					00 29									01 01			01 40				02 40
London Victoria 15 ⊖	a			00 37				00 25	00 37	00 40				00 55				01 09	01 11	01 25	01 49			02 10	02 49

A from 17 September
B from 2 July until 10 September
C from 21 May until 25 June
D from 21 May until 10 September
E from 22 May until 22 June, from 26 June

Table 186

Mondays to Fridays

from 21 May

Brighton - London and Bedford

Network Diagram - see first Page of Table 186

		FC		FC	SN	FC	SN	FC	SN	FC	SN	SN		FC	GW	GW	SN	FC	FC	SN	SN	SN		GW	SN
		MX		MO																					
					1		1		1	1	1	1		1	1	1	1	1	1	1	1			1	◇1
		A		B														C	D						
Brighton 10	d																	05 07	05 10			05 23			
Hove 2	d																								
Preston Park	d																	05 11	05 14						
Hassocks 4	d																	05 19	05 20						
Burgess Hill 4	d																	05 23	05 24			05 33			
Lewes 4	d																								05 29
Wivelsfield 4	d																	05 25	05 26						
Haywards Heath 3	a																	05 29	05 30			05 38			05 46
	d																	05 30	05 31			05 39			05 47
Balcombe	d																	05 35	05 36			05 44			
Horsham 4	d																05 17								
Littlehaven	d																05 20								
Faygate	d																								
Ifield	d																05 26								
Crawley	d																05 29								
Three Bridges 4	a																05 33	05 41	05 42			05 50			
	d	02 25		02 25	02 59	03 25	03 59	04 25		04 55							05 33	05 41	05 42			05 50			
Gatwick Airport 10 ✈	a	02 29		02 29	03 03	03 29	04 03	04 29		04 59							05 37	05 45	05 46			05 54			05 58
	d	02 30		02 30	03 05	03 30	04 04	04 30	04 35	05 00		05 20		05 27		05 31	05 38	05 46	05 47		05 50	05 55		05 56	05 59
Horley 4	d				03 07		04 07										05 40								
Salfords	d																								
Earlswood (Surrey)	d																								
Tonbridge 4	d										04 59									05 20					
Leigh (Kent)	d										05 03									05 24					
Penshurst	d										05 07									05 28					
Edenbridge	d										05 13									05 34					
Godstone	d										05 20									05 41					
Nutfield	d										05 25									05 46					
Reigate	d														05 34										
Redhill 5	a										05 30			05 34	05 39	05 41	05 47			05 51				06 07	
	d													05 35			05 48								
Merstham	d																05 52								
Coulsdon South	d																05 57								
Purley 4	d				03 22		04 26										06 00								
East Croydon 🚊	a	02 47		02 47	03 27	03 47	04 31	04 47		05 17				05 47			06 06	06 01	06 01			06 10			06 14
	d	02 47		02 47	03 28	03 47	04 32	04 47		05 17				05 47			06 06	06 02	06 02			06 11			06 15
Norwood Junction 2	a																								
New Cross Gate	d																								
London Bridge 4 ⊖	a									05 34				06 02				06 15	06 15						
London Blackfriars 3 ⊖	a	03 13		03 13		04 13		05 13		05 41				06 10				06 23	06 23						
City Thameslink 3	a							05 16		05 44				06 14				06 26	06 26						
Farringdon 3 ⊖	a							05 20		05 47				06 18				06 30	06 30						
St Pancras International 15 ⊖	a	03 23		03 23		04 22		05 24		05 52				06 22				06 34	06 34						
St Albans City	a	03 57		03 57		04 57		05 57		06 23				06 43				06 57	06 57						
Luton Airport Parkway 4 ✈	a	04 09		04 10		05 09		06 09		06 35				06 55				07 09	07 09						
Luton 7	a	04 12		04 13		05 12		06 12		06 38				06 58				07 12	07 12						
Bedford 10	a	04 39		04 40		05 39		06 39		07 04				07 24				07 40	07 40						
Clapham Junction 10	a				03 40		04 51										06 18					06 21			06 25
London Victoria 15 ⊖	a				03 49		04 58		05 12			05 55					06 25				06 20	06 28			06 32

A from 22 May until 22 June, from 26 June

B from 21 May until 25 June

C from 8 October

D from 21 May until 5 October

Table 186

Mondays to Fridays

from 21 May

Brighton - London and Bedford

Network Diagram - see first Page of Table 186

Station		SN 1	SN 1	SN 1 ⊥	FC 1 A	FC 1 B	SN 1 ⊥	GW 1		FC 1 A	FC 1 B	SN 1	SN 1	SN 1	SN 1 ⊥	SN 1	SN 1	SN 1		FC 1	SN 1 ⊥	SN ◇1 C	SN ◇1	GW 1	FC 1
Brighton 10	d				05 37	05 40				05 48	05 50					06 01				06 08		06 17			06 24
Hove 2	d											05 57													
Preston Park	d				05 41	05 44				05 52	05 54									06 12					06 28
Hassocks 4	d				05 47	05 50				05 58	06 00					06 09				06 19		06 26			06 35
Burgess Hill 4	d				05 51	05 54				06 02	06 04					06 13				06 23		06 30			06 39
Lewes 4	d																06 05								
Wivelsfield 4	d				05 54	05 56				06 04	06 06					06 15				06 25					
Haywards Heath 3	a				05 58	06 00				06 08	06 10	06 12				06 19	06 23			06 30		06 35			06 44
	d				05 59	06 01				06 09	06 11	06 13				06 27				06 30		06 36			06 45
Balcombe	d				06 04	06 06														06 36					06 51
Horsham 4	d		05 38											06 10									06 24		
Littlehaven	d		05 41											06 13									06 27		
Faygate	d																								
Ifield	d		05 47											06 19									06 33		
Crawley	d		05 50											06 23									06 37		
Three Bridges 4	a		05 54		06 11	06 12				06 18	06 19	06 21		06 26		06 36				06 41		06 45	06 40		06 56
	d		05 54		06 11	06 12				06 19	06 20	06 22		06 27		06 37				06 42		06 48			06 57
Gatwick Airport 10 ✈	a		05 58		06 16	06 16				06 24	06 24	06 26		06 31		06 41				06 46		06 52			07 01
	d		05 59	06 06	06 17	06 17	06 20			06 25	06 25	06 27		06 32	06 35	06 42				06 47	06 50	06 53		06 58	07 02
Horley 4	d		06 02											06 35								06 56			
Salfords	d		06 06											06 39											
Earlswood (Surrey)	d		06 09											06 42											
Tonbridge 4	d												06 10												
Leigh (Kent)	d												06 14												
Penshurst	d												06 18												
Edenbridge	d												06 24												
Godstone	d												06 31												
Nutfield	d												06 36												
Reigate	d							06 24										06 49							
Redhill 5	a		06 12					06 29		06 32	06 32		06 42	06 46				06 53		06 54		07 02		07 07	07 10
	d		06 13							06 33	06 33		06 43	06 46						06 56		07 03			07 11
Merstham	d		06 17											06 50											
Coulsdon South	d		06 22										06 50	06 55											
Purley 4	d		06 25										06 54	06 59											
East Croydon	a		06 30		06 32	06 32				06 44	06 44	06 41	06 59	07 04		06 58				07 08		07 14			07 22
	d	06 27	06 31		06 32	06 32				06 44	06 44	06 42	07 00	07 05		06 59				07 09		07 15			07 23
Norwood Junction 2	a																								
New Cross Gate	d																								
London Bridge 4 ⊖	a				06 46	06 46				06 58	06 58		07 16			07 14				07 23					
London Blackfriars 3 ⊖	a				06 52	06 52				07 04	07 04									07 30					07 51
City Thameslink 3	a				06 54	06 54				07 08	07 08									07 32					07 56
Farringdon 3 ⊖	a				06 58	06 58				07 12	07 12									07 36					08 00
St Pancras International 15 ⊖	a				07 02	07 02				07 16	07 16									07 40					08 04
St Albans City	a				07 22	07 22				07 41	07 41														08 24
Luton Airport Parkway 4 ✈	a				07 34	07 34				07 53	07 53									08 06					08 37
Luton 7	a				07 37	07 37				07 57	07 57									08 10					08 40
Bedford 10	a				08 03	08 03				08 23	08 23														09 05
Clapham Junction 10	a	06 38	06 41									06 51		07 16								07 24			
London Victoria 15 ⊖	a	06 45	06 48	06 35			06 50					07 00		07 25	07 05						07 20	07 33			

A from 8 October

B from 21 May until 5 October

C ◇ from Three Bridges

Table 186

Brighton - London and Bedford

Mondays to Fridays

from 21 May

Network Diagram - see first Page of Table 186

Station		SN 1	SN 1	SN 1	SN 1 [trolley]	SN 1	SN 1	SN ◇1 [trolley]	SN 1 [trolley]	GW 1	SN ◇1 [trolley]	SN ◇1 A [trolley]	SN 1	SN 1	SN 1	GW 1	SN 1	SN 1	SN 1 [trolley]	FC 1	SN 1	SN 1
Brighton 10	d				06 30				06 40		06 51								06 56	07 02		
Hove 2	d						06 31														07 11	
Preston Park	d								06 44										07 00	07 06		
Hassocks 4	d						06 43		06 52											07 13	07 20	
Burgess Hill 4	d				06 43		06 47		06 56		07 01								07 10	07 17		
Lewes 4	d												06 51									
Wivelsfield 4	d				06 46								07 08						07 14	07 20	07 25	
Haywards Heath 3	a				06 50		06 53		07 01		07 06		07 12						07 18	07 24	07 30	
	d				06 51		07 00		07 03		07 07		07 13						07 20	07 25	07 31	
Balcombe	d												07 19									
Horsham 4	d	06 38						06 50				07 04					07 09					
Littlehaven	d	06 41						06 53									07 12					
Faygate	d	06 45															07 16					
Ifield	d	06 49						07 00									07 20					
Crawley	d	06 52						07 04				07 13					07 23					
Three Bridges 4	a	06 56						07 07			07 16	07 18	07 24				07 27			07 33		
	d	06 56				07 04		07 08			07 22		07 25	07 14			07 28			07 34		
Gatwick Airport 10 ✈	a	07 01			07 04	07 08	07 11	07 12	07 15				07 29	07 21			07 32		07 32	07 38		
	d	07 02			07 06	07 09	07 12	07 14	07 20				07 30	07 22			07 33		07 35	07 39		
Horley 4	d	07 04				07 12		07 16						07 25			07 36					
Salfords	d	07 08				07 16								07 29			07 40					
Earlswood (Surrey)	d	07 12				07 19								07 32			07 43					
Tonbridge 4	d		06 47																			
Leigh (Kent)	d		06 51																			
Penshurst	d		06 55																			
Edenbridge	d		07 01																			
Godstone	d		07 08																			
Nutfield	d		07 13																			
Reigate	d									07 18					07 27	07 34						07 40
Redhill 5	a	07 15	07 18			07 22				07 24				07 36	07 31	07 38	07 47					07 45
	d	07 15				07 23								07 40								07 51
Merstham	d	07 19				07 27								07 44								
Coulsdon South	d	07 25				07 33								07 50								
Purley 4	d	07 29				07 37								07 55								
East Croydon	a	07 34				07 41	07 26	07 31			07 38		07 45	08 01						07 53	07 56	08 02
	d	07 35		07 15		07 42	07 28	07 31			07 39		07 46	08 02				07 45		07 54	07 57	08 03
Norwood Junction 2	a																					
New Cross Gate	d																					
London Bridge 4 ⊖	a	07 51					07 43						08 01	08 19							08 13	08 21
London Blackfriars 3 ⊖	a																			08 20		
City Thameslink 3	a																			08 23		
Farringdon 3 ⊖	a																			08 27		
St Pancras International 15 ⊖	a																			08 31		
St Albans City	a																			08 51		
Luton Airport Parkway 4 ✈	a																			09 00		
Luton 7	a																			09 04		
Bedford 10	a																			09 26		
Clapham Junction 10	a			07 27		07 51		07 40			07 48							07 55				
London Victoria 15 ⊖	a			07 36	07 37	08 00		07 49	07 50		07 57							08 04	08 06			

A [trolley] from Three Bridges

from 21 May

Brighton - London and Bedford

Network Diagram - see first Page of Table 186

		SN	SN	SN	SN	SN	SN	SN	SN	GW		FC	SN	SN	SN	SN	SN	SN	SN	SN		SN	SN	SN	FC
		1	◇1	1	1	◇1	◇1	1	1	1		1	1	1	1	1	1	1	◇1	1		1	1	1	1
			✕		✕		✕						✕										✕	✕	
Brighton 10	d				07 14							07 24	07 29					07 32						07 44	07 50
Hove 2	d					07 21													07 41						
Preston Park	d				07 19							07 28						07 37						07 48	07 54
Hassocks 4	d					07 30						07 35	07 39											07 56	08 01
Burgess Hill 4	d				07 28							07 39						07 47	07 52					08 00	
Lewes 4	d						07 22													07 42					
Wivelsfield 4	d					07 35	07 39						07 46					07 49							
Haywards Heath 3	a				07 34	07 40	07 44					07 46	07 50					07 54	07 58	08 03				08 05	08 09
	d				07 35	07 40	07 44					07 47	07 51					07 55	07 59	08 04				08 06	08 09
Balcombe	d																	08 01							08 15
Horsham 4	d	07 17	07 25													07 40	07 46					07 51			
Littlehaven	d	07 20	07 29													07 43	07 49					07 54			
Faygate	d																					07 58			
Ifield	d	07 27														07 50	07 56					08 02			
Crawley	d	07 31	07 37													07 53	08 00					08 06			
Three Bridges 4	a	07 34	07 40									07 55				07 57	08 05	08 06				08 09			
	d	07 35	07 41									07 56				07 58	08 06	08 07				08 10			
Gatwick Airport 10 ✈	a	07 39			07 47							08 00	08 02			08 04			08 13			08 14		08 18	08 23
	d	07 40			07 50			07 44		07 58		08 01	08 05			08 05			08 14			08 15	08 18	08 20	08 24
Horley 4	d	07 43					07 58	07 47								08 07						08 18			
Salfords	d	07 47						07 51								08 11						08 22			
Earlswood (Surrey)	d	07 50						07 54								08 15						08 25			
Tonbridge 4	d								07 25																
Leigh (Kent)	d								07 29																
Penshurst	d								07 33																
Edenbridge	d								07 39																
Godstone	d								07 46																
Nutfield	d								07 51																
Reigate	d			07 52										08 09											
Redhill 5	a	07 53		07 56				07 58	07 56	08 05		08 08		08 13		08 18						08 28			
	d	07 54							08 02			08 09				08 18						08 29			
Merstham	d	07 59							08 06							08 22									
Coulsdon South	d	08 04							08 11							08 27						08 36			
Purley 4	d								08 15							08 31									
East Croydon	a	08 11	07 59			08 08	08 13		08 20			08 22				08 36	08 26	08 24	08 29	08 31		08 50			08 38
	d	08 11	08 01			08 08	08 13		08 21			08 23			08 15	08 37	08 27	08 25	08 30	08 33		08 51			08 39
Norwood Junction 2	a																								
New Cross Gate	d																								
London Bridge 4 ⊖	a								08 37								08 45	08 41		08 52		09 06			09 09
London Blackfriars 3 ⊖	a											08 53													09 12
City Thameslink 3	a											08 56													09 16
Farringdon 3 ⊖	a											09 00													09 20
St Pancras International 15 ⊖	a											09 04													09 40
St Albans City	a											09 25													09 51
Luton Airport Parkway 4 ✈	a											09 37													09 54
Luton 7	a											09 40													10 20
Bedford 10	a											10 08													
Clapham Junction 10	a	08 20	08 10			08 17	08 23								08 26	08 48			08 39						
London Victoria 15 ⊖	a	08 29	08 19		08 20	08 26	08 32						08 35		08 35	08 56			08 48				08 50	08 52	

Table 186

Brighton - London and Bedford

Mondays to Fridays

from 21 May

Network Diagram - see first Page of Table 186

Station		SN ◇1 🛒	GW 1	SN 1 🛒	SN ◇1 🛒	SN 1	SN 1		GW 1	FC 1	SN ◇1	SN ◇1 🛒	FC 1	SN 1	SN 1	SN ◇1 🛒	SN 1 🛒		SN 1	SN ◇1 🛒	SN ◇1	SN ◇1	GW 1	FC 1	SN 1
Brighton 10	d									08 02		08 13	08 16											08 34	08 45
Hove 2	d										08 08														
Preston Park	d									08 06	08 12		08 20											08 38	
Hassocks 4	d									08 13	08 19		08 27											08 44	
Burgess Hill 4	d									08 17	08 23		08 31											08 48	
Lewes 4	d				07 55											08 23									
Wivelsfield 4	d				08 11					08 20			08 34			08 39								08 50	
Haywards Heath 3	a				08 16					08 24	08 28		08 38			08 44								08 55	08 58
	d				08 16					08 25	08 29		08 39			08 44								09 00	08 58
Balcombe	d				08 22																			↳	
Horsham 4	d	08 09												08 12						08 49	08 35				
Littlehaven	d													08 15							08 38				
Faygate	d													08 19											
Ifield	d													08 23							08 44				
Crawley	d	08 18												08 26						08 58	08 47				
Three Bridges 4	a	08 22			08 28					08 33	08 38		08 47	08 29						09 01	08 51				
	d	08 22			08 28					08 34	08 39		08 48	08 30						09 02	08 51				
Gatwick Airport 10 ✈	a									08 38		08 46	08 52	08 34		08 56				09 06	08 55				09 09
	d			08 35						08 39		08 50	08 53	08 35		08 57	09 05			09 07	08 56		09 07		09 10
Horley 4	d	08 28												08 38		08 59					08 59				
Salfords	d													08 42							09 03				
Earlswood (Surrey)	d													08 45							09 06				
Tonbridge 4	d					07 59									08 16							08 37			
Leigh (Kent)	d					08 03									08 20							08 41			
Penshurst	d					08 07									08 24							08 45			
Edenbridge	d					08 13									08 30							08 51			
Godstone	d					08 20									08 37							08 58			
Nutfield	d					08 25									08 42							09 03			
Reigate	d		08 24				08 27		08 42																
Redhill 5	a		08 30			08 34	08 32		08 46					08 49	08 47						09 10	09 08	09 15		
	d					08 38								08 53							09 14				
Merstham	d					08 43								08 57							09 18				
Coulsdon South	d					08 48								09 02							09 23				
Purley 4	d					08 52								09 05											
East Croydon	a	08 43			08 46	08 58				08 53	08 57		09 08	09 10		09 14				09 22	09 30				09 25
	d	08 43			08 50	08 59				08 54	08 58		09 09	09 11		09 14			09 14	09 23	09 31				09 26
Norwood Junction 2	a																								
New Cross Gate	d																								
London Bridge 4 ⊖	a					09 15				09 08															
London Blackfriars 3 ⊖	a									09 21			09 37												
City Thameslink 3	a									09 24			09 40												
Farringdon 3 ⊖	a									09 27			09 44												
St Pancras International 15 ⊖	a									09 32			09 48												
St Albans City	a									09 51			10 10												
Luton Airport Parkway 4 ✈	a									10 00			10 21												
Luton 7	a									10 03			10 24												
Bedford 10	a									10 24			10 50												
Clapham Junction 10	a	08 52			09 00						09 07			09 20		09 23			09 26	09 32	09 41				09 36
London Victoria 15 ⊖	a	09 01		09 05	09 09						09 16	09 20		09 27		09 32	09 35		09 35	09 42	09 50				09 43

Brighton - London and Bedford

Network Diagram - see first Page of Table 186

		FC	SN		SN	SN	GW	SN	SN	FC	SN	GW	SN		SN	FC	SN	SN	SN	SN	SN	SN	SN		FC
		1	1		1	◇1	1	1	◇1	1	1	1	1		◇1	1	◇1	1	1	◇1	1	◇1	◇1		1
																							A		
					🛒	🛒					🛒				🛒		🛒		🛒			🛒	🛒		
Brighton 10	d									09 00						09 07	09 19			09 25					09 34
Hove 2	d								08 52														09 22		
Preston Park	d								08 57							09 11									
Hassocks 4	d								09 04	09 09						09 17				09 34			09 31		
Burgess Hill 4	d								09 08	09 12						09 21				09 38					
Lewes 4	d					08 48																09 18			
Wivelsfield 4	d	←				09 01										09 23						09 34			
Haywards Heath 3	a	08 55				09 05			09 13	09 17						09 28						09 38	09 40		09 47
	d	09 00				09 08			09 14	09 18						09 32						09 44			09 48
Balcombe	d	09 06														09 37									
Horsham 4	d							09 00							09 20						09 30				
Littlehaven	d							09 03													09 33				
Faygate	d																				09 37				
Ifield	d							09 09													09 41				
Crawley	d							09 13							09 29						09 44				
Three Bridges 4	a	09 11				09 17		09 16		09 26					09 32	09 43					09 48				09 56
	d	09 12				09 17		09 18		09 27					09 33	09 43					09 48				09 57
Gatwick Airport 10 ✈	a	09 16				09 22		09 22	09 26	09 31					09 37	09 47				09 51	09 53	09 56			10 01
	d	09 17			09 20	09 23		09 23	09 27	09 32	09 35				09 38	09 47			09 50	09 53	09 54	09 57			10 02
Horley 4	d							09 26							09 41						09 56				
Salfords	d							09 30																	
Earlswood (Surrey)	d							09 33																	
Tonbridge 4	d																	09 19							
Leigh (Kent)	d																	09 23							
Penshurst	d																	09 27							
Edenbridge	d																	09 33							
Godstone	d																	09 40							
Nutfield	d																	09 45							
Reigate	d		09 14				09 24					09 37													
Redhill 5	a		09 18				09 30	09 36				09 42			09 47			09 50			10 03				
	d		09 19					09 37							09 48			09 51			10 07				
Merstham	d		09 23					09 41													10 11				
Coulsdon South	d		09 28					09 46										09 58			10 16				
Purley 4	d		09 32					09 49										10 02			10 19				
East Croydon	a	09 32	09 37			09 38		09 54	09 42	09 46					09 59	10 02	09 52	10 07		10 08	10 24	10 11			10 16
	d	09 32	09 37			09 39		09 55	09 43	09 47			09 44		10 00	10 02	09 53	10 07		10 08	10 25	10 12			10 17
Norwood Junction 2	a		09 41					09 59										10 12			10 29				
New Cross Gate	d							10 07													10 37				
London Bridge 4 ⊖	a	09 46	09 55					10 13		10 00						10 15		10 25			10 43				10 30
London Blackfriars 3 ⊖	a	09 53								10 08						10 23									10 37
City Thameslink 3	a	09 56								10 10						10 26									10 40
Farringdon 3 ⊖	a	10 00								10 14						10 30									10 44
St Pancras International 15 ⊖	a	10 04								10 18						10 34									10 48
St Albans City	a	10 23								10 38						10 54									11 10
Luton Airport Parkway 4 ✈	a	10 37								10 50						11 06									11 21
Luton 7	a	10 40								10 53						11 09									11 24
Bedford 10	a	11 05								11 19						11 35									11 50
Clapham Junction 10	a					09 48			09 52				09 55		10 09		10 02			10 17		10 21			
London Victoria 15 ⊖	a				09 50	09 58			09 59		10 05		10 05		10 16		10 11		10 20	10 26		10 28			

A 🛒 from Haywards Heath

Table 186

Brighton - London and Bedford

Mondays to Fridays

from 21 May

Network Diagram - see first Page of Table 186

		GW	SN	SN	SN	FC	SN	SN	GW		SN	SN	SN	SN	FC	GW	SN	SN	SN		FC	SN	SN	SN	SN
		1	1	1	◇1	1	◇1	1	1		1	1	◇1	◇1	1	1	1	1	◇1		1	◇1	1	1	◇1
														A											
			T				T				T		T	T			T					T		T	
Brighton 10	d					09 37	09 49								10 04						10 07	10 19			10 25
Hove 2	d													09 51											
Preston Park	d					09 41								09 55							10 11				
Hassocks 4	d					09 47															10 17				10 34
Burgess Hill 4	d					09 51								10 04							10 21				10 38
Lewes 4	d												09 48												
Wivelsfield 4	d					09 53															10 23				
Haywards Heath 3	a					09 58							10 07	10 10	10 17						10 28				
	d					10 02							10 14		10 18						10 32				
Balcombe	d																				10 37				
Horsham 4	d				09 51							10 00							10 20						
Littlehaven	d											10 03													
Faygate	d																								
Ifield	d											10 09													
Crawley	d				10 00							10 13							10 29						
Three Bridges 4	a				10 03	10 11						10 16			10 26				10 32		10 43				
	d				10 04	10 12						10 18			10 27				10 33		10 43				
Gatwick Airport 10 ✈	a				10 08	10 16						10 22	10 25		10 31				10 37		10 47				10 51
	d	10 03	10 05		10 09	10 17					10 20	10 23	10 26		10 32		10 35		10 38		10 47			10 50	10 53
Horley 4	d											10 26							10 41						
Salfords	d											10 30													
Earlswood (Surrey)	d											10 33													
Tonbridge 4	d																						10 19		
Leigh (Kent)	d																						10 23		
Penshurst	d																						10 27		
Edenbridge	d																						10 33		
Godstone	d																						10 40		
Nutfield	d																						10 45		
Reigate	d							10 14	10 19							10 34									
Redhill 5	a	10 10			10 16			10 18	10 25			10 36				10 38			10 47				10 50		
	d				10 17			10 20				10 37							10 48				10 51		
Merstham	d							10 24				10 41													
Coulsdon South	d							10 29				10 46											10 58		
Purley 4	d							10 33				10 49											11 01		
East Croydon	a				10 28	10 31	10 22	10 38				10 54	10 41		10 46				10 59		11 02	10 52	11 06		11 08
	d			10 14	10 28	10 32	10 23	10 38				10 55	10 42		10 47			10 44	11 00		11 02	10 53	11 07		11 08
Norwood Junction 2	a							10 42				10 59											11 12		
New Cross Gate	d											11 07													
London Bridge 4 ⊖	a					10 45		10 55				11 13			11 00						11 15		11 25		
London Blackfriars 3 ⊖	a					10 52									11 07						11 22				
City Thameslink 3	a					10 56									11 10						11 26				
Farringdon 3 ⊖	a					11 00									11 14						11 30				
St Pancras International 15 ⊖	a					11 04									11 18						11 34				
St Albans City	a					11 23									11 38						11 53				
Luton Airport Parkway 4 ✈	a					11 37									11 50						12 07				
Luton 7	a					11 40									11 53						12 10				
Bedford 10	a					12 05									12 19						12 35				
Clapham Junction 10	a			10 25	10 37		10 32						10 51					10 55	11 09			11 02			11 17
London Victoria 15 ⊖	a		10 35	10 35	10 45		10 41				10 50		10 58				11 05	11 05	11 16			11 10		11 20	11 24

A T from Haywards Heath

Table 186

Mondays to Fridays

from 21 May

Brighton - London and Bedford

Network Diagram - see first Page of Table 186

Station		SN 1	SN ◇1	SN ◇1	FC 1	GW 1	SN 1	SN 1	SN ◇1	FC 1	SN ◇1	SN 1	GW 1	SN 1	SN 1	SN ◇1	SN ◇1	FC 1	GW 1	SN 1	SN 1	SN ◇1	FC 1
Brighton 10	d				10 34					10 37	10 49							11 04					11 07
Hove 2	d			10 21													10 51						
Preston Park	d									10 41							10 55						11 11
Hassocks 4	d									10 47													11 17
Burgess Hill 4	d									10 51							11 04						11 21
Lewes 4	d		10 19													10 50							
Wivelsfield 4	d		10 35							10 53													11 23
Haywards Heath 3	a		10 40	10 35	10 47					10 58						11 05	11 09	11 17					11 28
	d		10 44		10 48					11 02						11 13		11 18					11 32
Balcombe	d																						11 37
Horsham 4	d	10 30							10 50						11 00							11 20	
Littlehaven	d	10 33													11 03								
Faygate	d																						
Ifield	d	10 39													11 09								
Crawley	d	10 43							10 59						11 13							11 29	
Three Bridges 4	a	10 46			10 56				11 02	11 11					11 16			11 26				11 32	11 43
	d	10 48			10 57				11 03	11 12					11 18			11 27				11 33	11 43
Gatwick Airport 10 ✈	a	10 52	10 55		11 01				11 07	11 16					11 22	11 24		11 31				11 37	11 47
	d	10 53	10 56		11 02	11 03		11 05	11 08	11 17				11 20	11 23	11 25		11 32			11 35	11 38	11 47
Horley 4	d	10 56													11 26							11 41	
Salfords	d														11 30								
Earlswood (Surrey)	d														11 33								
Tonbridge 4	d																						
Leigh (Kent)	d																						
Penshurst	d																						
Edenbridge	d																						
Godstone	d																						
Nutfield	d																						
Reigate	d											11 14	11 19						11 34				
Redhill 5	a	11 02				11 10			11 15			11 18	11 25		11 36				11 38			11 47	
	d	11 07							11 16			11 19			11 37							11 48	
Merstham	d	11 11										11 23			11 41								
Coulsdon South	d	11 16										11 28			11 46								
Purley 4	d	11 19										11 32			11 49								
East Croydon	a	11 24	11 11		11 16				11 27	11 31	11 22	11 37			11 54	11 40		11 46				11 59	12 02
	d	11 25	11 12		11 17		11 14		11 28	11 32	11 23	11 37			11 55	11 41		11 47		11 44		12 00	12 02
Norwood Junction 2	a	11 29										11 42			11 59								
New Cross Gate	d	11 37													12 07								
London Bridge 4 ⊖	a	11 43			11 30					11 45		11 55			12 13			12 00					12 15
London Blackfriars 3 ⊖	a				11 37					11 52								12 07					12 22
City Thameslink 3	a				11 40					11 56								12 10					12 26
Farringdon 3 ⊖	a				11 44					12 00								12 14					12 30
St Pancras International 15 ⊖	a				11 48					12 04								12 18					12 34
St Albans City	a				12 08					12 24								12 38					12 53
Luton Airport Parkway 4 ✈	a				12 20					12 37								12 50					13 06
Luton 7	a				12 23					12 40								12 53					13 09
Bedford 10	a				12 49					13 05								13 19					13 35
Clapham Junction 10	a		11 21				11 25		11 37		11 32					11 50				11 55		12 09	
London Victoria 15 ⊖	a		11 28				11 32	11 35	11 44		11 40			11 50		11 57				12 02	12 05	12 18	

Table 186

Mondays to Fridays

from 21 May

Brighton - London and Bedford

Network Diagram - see first Page of Table 186

Station		SN	SN	SN	SN	SN	SN	SN	FC	GW	SN	SN	SN	FC	SN	SN	GW	SN	SN	SN	SN	FC
		◇1	1	1	◇1	1	◇1	◇1	1	1	1	1	◇1	1	◇1	1	1	1	1	◇1	◇1	1
Brighton 10	d	11 19			11 25				11 34					11 37	11 49							12 04
Hove 2	d							11 21													11 51	
Preston Park	d													11 41							11 55	
Hassocks 4	d				11 34									11 47								
Burgess Hill 4	d				11 38									11 51							12 04	
Lewes 4	d						11 20													11 50		
Wivelsfield 4	d						11 35							11 53								
Haywards Heath 3	a						11 40	11 35	11 47					11 58						12 05	12 09	12 17
	d						11 44		11 48					12 02						12 13		12 18
Balcombe	d																					
Horsham 4	d					11 30							11 50						12 00			
Littlehaven	d					11 33													12 03			
Faygate	d																					
Ifield	d					11 39													12 09			
Crawley	d					11 43							11 59						12 13			
Three Bridges 4	a					11 46			11 56				12 02	12 11					12 16			12 26
	d					11 48			11 57				12 03	12 12					12 18			12 27
Gatwick Airport 10	a				11 51	11 52	11 55		12 01				12 07	12 16					12 22	12 24		12 31
	d			11 50	11 53	11 53	11 56		12 02	12 03		12 05	12 08	12 17				12 20	12 23	12 25		12 32
Horley 4	d					11 56													12 26			
Salfords	d																		12 30			
Earlswood (Surrey)	d																		12 33			
Tonbridge 4	d		11 19																			
Leigh (Kent)	d		11 23																			
Penshurst	d		11 27																			
Edenbridge	d		11 33																			
Godstone	d		11 40																			
Nutfield	d		11 45																			
Reigate	d															12 14	12 19					
Redhill 5	a		11 50			12 02				12 10			12 15			12 18	12 25		12 36			
	d		11 51			12 07							12 16			12 19			12 37			
Merstham	d					12 11										12 23			12 41			
Coulsdon South	d		11 58			12 16										12 28			12 46			
Purley 4	d		12 02			12 19										12 32			12 49			
East Croydon	a	11 52	12 07		12 08	12 24	12 11		12 16				12 27	12 31	12 22	12 37			12 54	12 40		12 46
	d	11 53	12 07		12 08	12 25	12 12		12 17		12 14		12 28	12 32	12 23	12 37			12 55	12 41		12 47
Norwood Junction 2	a		12 12			12 29										12 42			12 59			
New Cross Gate	d					12 37													13 07			
London Bridge 4 ⊖	a		12 25			12 43			12 30					12 45		12 55			13 13			13 00
London Blackfriars 3 ⊖	a								12 37					12 52								13 07
City Thameslink 3	a								12 40					12 56								13 10
Farringdon 3 ⊖	a								12 44					13 00								13 14
St Pancras International 15 ⊖	a								12 48					13 04								13 18
St Albans City	a								13 08					13 24								13 38
Luton Airport Parkway 4	a								13 20					13 37								13 50
Luton 7	a								13 23					13 40								13 53
Bedford 10	a								13 49					14 05								14 19
Clapham Junction 10	a	12 02			12 17		12 21				12 25		12 37		12 32					12 50		
London Victoria 15 ⊖	a	12 10		12 20	12 24		12 28				12 32	12 35	12 44		12 40			12 50		12 57		

Table 186

Mondays to Fridays

from 21 May

Brighton - London and Bedford

Network Diagram - see first Page of Table 186

		GW	SN	SN	SN	FC	SN	SN	SN	SN	SN	SN	SN	FC	GW	SN	SN	SN	FC	SN	SN	GW	SN
		1	1	1	◇1	1	◇1	1	1	◇1	1	◇1	◇1	1	1	1	1	◇1	1	◇1	1	1	1
				🛒			🛒		🛒								🛒			🛒			🛒
Brighton 10	d					12 07	12 19			12 25				12 34					12 37	12 49			
Hove 2	d												12 21										
Preston Park	d					12 11													12 41				
Hassocks 4	d					12 17				12 34									12 47				
Burgess Hill 4	d					12 21				12 38									12 51				
Lewes 4	d											12 20											
Wivelsfield 4	d					12 23						12 35							12 53				
Haywards Heath 3	a					12 28						12 40	12 35	12 47					12 58				
	d					12 32							12 44	12 48					13 02				
Balcombe	d					12 37																	
Horsham 4	d				12 20						12 30							12 50					
Littlehaven	d										12 33												
Faygate	d										12 37												
Ifield	d										12 41												
Crawley	d				12 29						12 44							12 59					
Three Bridges 4	a				12 32	12 43					12 47			12 56				13 02	13 11				
	d				12 33	12 43					12 48			12 57				13 03	13 12				
Gatwick Airport 10 ✈	a				12 37	12 47				12 51	12 52		12 55	13 01				13 07	13 16				
	d			12 35	12 38	12 47			12 50	12 53	12 53		12 56	13 02	13 03		13 05	13 08	13 17				13 20
Horley 4	d				12 41						12 56												
Salfords	d																						
Earlswood (Surrey)	d																						
Tonbridge 4	d							12 19															
Leigh (Kent)	d							12 23															
Penshurst	d							12 27															
Edenbridge	d							12 33															
Godstone	d							12 40															
Nutfield	d							12 45															
Reigate	d	12 34																			13 14	13 19	
Redhill 5	a	12 38			12 47			12 50			13 02				13 10			13 15			13 18	13 25	
	d				12 48			12 51			13 07							13 16			13 19		
Merstham	d										13 11										13 23		
Coulsdon South	d							12 58			13 16										13 28		
Purley 4	d							13 02			13 19										13 32		
East Croydon 🚌	a				12 59	13 02	12 52	13 07		13 08	13 24		13 11	13 16				13 27	13 31	13 22	13 37		
	d		12 44		13 00	13 02	12 53	13 07		13 08	13 25		13 12	13 17		13 14		13 28	13 32	13 23	13 37		
Norwood Junction 2	a							13 12			13 29										13 42		
New Cross Gate	d										13 37												
London Bridge 4 ⊖	a					13 15		13 25			13 43			13 30					13 45		13 55		
London Blackfriars 3 ⊖	a					13 22								13 37					13 52				
City Thameslink 3	a					13 26								13 40					13 56				
Farringdon 3 ⊖	a					13 30								13 44					14 00				
St Pancras International 15 ⊖	a					13 34								13 48					14 04				
St Albans City	a					13 53								14 08					14 23				
Luton Airport Parkway 4 ✈	a					14 07								14 20					14 37				
Luton 7	a					14 10								14 23					14 40				
Bedford 10	a					14 35								14 49					15 05				
Clapham Junction 10	a		12 55		13 09		13 02			13 17			13 21			13 25		13 37		13 32			
London Victoria 15 ⊖	a		13 02	13 05	13 16		13 10		13 20	13 24			13 28			13 32	13 35	13 44		13 40			13 50

Table 186

Brighton - London and Bedford

Mondays to Fridays

from 21 May

Network Diagram - see first Page of Table 186

		SN 1	SN ◇1	SN ◇1	FC 1	GW 1	SN 1	SN 1 🚲	SN ◇1	FC 1	SN ◇1 🚲	SN 1	SN 1 🚲	SN ◇1	SN 1	SN ◇1	SN ◇1	FC 1	GW 1	SN 1	SN 1 🚲	SN ◇1
Brighton 10	d				13 04					13 07	13 19			13 25				13 34				
Hove 2	d			12 51													13 21					
Preston Park	d			12 55						13 11												
Hassocks 4	d									13 17				13 34								
Burgess Hill 4	d			13 04						13 21				13 38								
Lewes 4	d		12 50													13 20						
Wivelsfield 4	d									13 23						13 35						
Haywards Heath 3	a		13 05	13 09	13 17					13 28						13 40	13 35	13 47				
	d		13 13		13 18					13 32						13 44		13 48				
Balcombe	d									13 37												
Horsham 4	d	13 00							13 20						13 30							13 50
Littlehaven	d	13 03													13 33							
Faygate	d																					
Ifield	d	13 09													13 39							
Crawley	d	13 13							13 29						13 43							13 59
Three Bridges 4	a	13 16			13 26				13 32	13 43					13 46			13 56				14 02
	d	13 18			13 27				13 33	13 43					13 48			13 57				14 03
Gatwick Airport 10 ✈	a	13 22	13 24		13 31				13 37	13 47				13 51	13 52	13 55		14 01				14 07
	d	13 23	13 25		13 32			13 35	13 38	13 47			13 50	13 53	13 53	13 56		14 02	14 03		14 05	14 08
Horley 4	d	13 26							13 41						13 56							
Salfords	d	13 30																				
Earlswood (Surrey)	d	13 33																				
Tonbridge 4	d											13 19										
Leigh (Kent)	d											13 23										
Penshurst	d											13 27										
Edenbridge	d											13 33										
Godstone	d											13 40										
Nutfield	d											13 45										
Reigate	d					13 34																
Redhill 5	a	13 36				13 38			13 47			13 50			14 02				14 10			14 15
	d	13 37							13 48			13 51			14 07							14 16
Merstham	d	13 41													14 11							
Coulsdon South	d	13 46										13 58			14 16							
Purley 4	d	13 49										14 02			14 19							
East Croydon 🚋	a	13 54	13 40		13 46				13 59	14 02	13 52	14 07		14 08	14 24	14 11		14 16				14 27
	d	13 55	13 41		13 47		13 44		14 00	14 02	13 53	14 08		14 08	14 25	14 12		14 17		14 14		14 28
Norwood Junction 2	a	13 59										14 12			14 29							
New Cross Gate	d	14 07													14 37							
London Bridge 4 ⊖	a	14 13			14 00					14 15		14 25			14 43			14 30				
London Blackfriars 3 ⊖	a				14 07					14 22								14 37				
City Thameslink 3	a				14 10					14 26								14 40				
Farringdon 3 ⊖	a				14 14					14 29								14 44				
St Pancras International 15 ⊖	a				14 18					14 34								14 48				
St Albans City	a				14 38					14 54								15 08				
Luton Airport Parkway 4 ✈	a				14 50					15 07								15 20				
Luton 7	a				14 53					15 10								15 23				
Bedford 10	a				15 19					15 35								15 49				
Clapham Junction 10	a		13 50				13 55		14 09		14 02			14 17		14 21				14 25		14 37
London Victoria 15 ⊖	a		13 57				14 03	14 05	14 16		14 10		14 20	14 24		14 28				14 32	14 35	14 44

from 21 May

Brighton - London and Bedford

Network Diagram - see first Page of Table 186

		FC	SN	SN	GW	SN	SN	SN	SN	FC		GW	SN	SN	SN	FC	SN	SN	SN	SN		SN	SN	SN	FC
		1	◇1 ⓣ	1	1	1 ⓣ	1	◇1	◇1	1		1	1	1 ⓣ	◇1	1	◇1 ⓣ	1	1 ⓣ	◇1		1	◇1	◇1	1
Brighton 10	d	13 37	13 49							14 04						14 07	14 19			14 25					14 34
Hove 2	d								13 51															14 21	
Preston Park	d	13 41							13 55							14 11									
Hassocks 4	d	13 47														14 17				14 34					
Burgess Hill 4	d	13 51							14 04							14 21				14 38					
Lewes 4	d							13 50															14 20		
Wivelsfield 4	d	13 53														14 23							14 35		
Haywards Heath 3	a	13 58						14 05	14 09	14 17						14 28							14 40	14 35	14 47
	d	14 02						14 13		14 18						14 32							14 44		14 48
Balcombe	d															14 37									
Horsham 4	d						14 00								14 20							14 30			
Littlehaven	d						14 03															14 33			
Faygate	d																								
Ifield	d						14 09															14 39			
Crawley	d						14 13								14 29							14 43			
Three Bridges 4	a	14 11					14 16			14 26					14 32	14 43						14 46			14 56
	d	14 12					14 18			14 27					14 33	14 43						14 48			14 57
Gatwick Airport 10 ✈	a	14 16					14 22	14 24		14 31					14 37	14 47				14 51		14 52	14 55		15 01
	d	14 17				14 20	14 23	14 25		14 32				14 35	14 38	14 47			14 50	14 53		14 53	14 56		15 02
Horley 4	d						14 26								14 41							14 56			
Salfords	d						14 30																		
Earlswood (Surrey)	d						14 33																		
Tonbridge 4	d																	14 19							
Leigh (Kent)	d																	14 23							
Penshurst	d																	14 27							
Edenbridge	d																	14 33							
Godstone	d																	14 40							
Nutfield	d																	14 45							
Reigate	d			14 14	14 19							14 34													
Redhill 5	a			14 18	14 25		14 36					14 38			14 47			14 50				15 02			
	d			14 19			14 37								14 48			14 51				15 07			
Merstham	d			14 23			14 41															15 11			
Coulsdon South	d			14 28			14 46											14 58				15 16			
Purley 4	d			14 32			14 49											15 02				15 19			
East Croydon	a	14 31	14 22	14 37			14 54	14 40		14 46					14 59	15 02	14 52	15 07		15 08		15 24	15 11		15 16
	d	14 32	14 23	14 37			14 55	14 41		14 47			14 44		15 00	15 02	14 53	15 07		15 08		15 25	15 12		15 17
Norwood Junction 2	a			14 42			14 59											15 12				15 29			
New Cross Gate	d						15 07															15 37			
London Bridge 4 ⊖	a	14 45		14 55			15 13			15 00						15 15		15 25				15 43			15 30
London Blackfriars 3 ⊖	a	14 52								15 07						15 22									15 37
City Thameslink 3	a	14 56								15 10						15 26									15 40
Farringdon 3 ⊖	a	15 00								15 14						15 29									15 44
St Pancras International 15 ⊖	a	15 04								15 18						15 34									15 48
St Albans City	a	15 24								15 38						15 52									16 08
Luton Airport Parkway 4 ✈	a	15 37								15 50						16 04									16 20
Luton 7	a	15 40								15 53						16 07									16 23
Bedford 10	a	16 05								16 19						16 33									16 49
Clapham Junction 10	a		14 32					14 50					14 55		15 09		15 02			15 17			15 21		
London Victoria 15 ⊖	a		14 40			14 50		14 57					15 02	15 05	15 20		15 10		15 20	15 24			15 28		

Table 186

Mondays to Fridays

from 21 May

Brighton - London and Bedford

Network Diagram - see first Page of Table 186

		GW	SN	SN	SN	FC		SN	SN	GW	SN	SN	SN	SN	FC	GW		SN	SN	SN	FC	SN	SN	SN	SN
		1	1	1	◇1	1		◇1	1	1	1	1	◇1	◇1	1	1		1	1	◇1	1	◇1	1	1	◇1
														A											
			🚲					🚲			🚲		🚲	🚲				🚲		🚲		🚲		🚲	
Brighton 10	d					14 37		14 49							15 04						15 07	15 19			15 25
Hove 2	d													14 51											
Preston Park	d					14 41								14 55							15 11				
Hassocks 4	d					14 47															15 17				15 34
Burgess Hill 4	d					14 51								15 04							15 21				15 38
Lewes 4	d												14 50												
Wivelsfield 4	d					14 53															15 23				
Haywards Heath 3	a					14 58							15 05	15 09	15 17						15 28				
	d					15 02							15 13		15 18						15 32				
Balcombe	d																				15 37				
Horsham 4	d				14 50							15 00								15 20					
Littlehaven	d											15 03													
Faygate	d																								
Ifield	d											15 09													
Crawley	d				14 59							15 13								15 29					
Three Bridges 4	a				15 02	15 11						15 16			15 26					15 32	15 43				
	d				15 03	15 12						15 18			15 27					15 33	15 43				
Gatwick Airport 10 ✈	a				15 07	15 16						15 22	15 24		15 31					15 37	15 47				15 51
	d	15 03	15 05		15 08	15 17					15 20	15 23	15 25		15 32			15 35		15 38	15 47			15 50	15 53
Horley 4	d											15 26								15 41					
Salfords	d											15 30													
Earlswood (Surrey)	d											15 33													
Tonbridge 4	d																						15 19		
Leigh (Kent)	d																						15 23		
Penshurst	d																						15 27		
Edenbridge	d																						15 33		
Godstone	d																						15 40		
Nutfield	d																						15 45		
Reigate	d								15 14	15 19						15 34									
Redhill 5	a	15 10			15 16				15 18	15 25		15 36				15 38				15 47			15 50		
	d				15 17				15 19			15 37								15 48			15 51		
Merstham	d								15 23			15 41													
Coulsdon South	d								15 28			15 46											15 58		
Purley 4	d								15 32			15 49											16 02		
East Croydon	a				15 28	15 31		15 22	15 37			15 54	15 40		15 46					15 59	16 02	15 52	16 07		16 08
	d			15 14	15 28	15 32		15 23	15 37			15 55	15 41		15 47				15 44	16 00	16 02	15 53	16 07		16 08
Norwood Junction 2	a								15 42			15 59											16 12		
New Cross Gate	d											16 07													
London Bridge 4 ⊖	a					15 45			15 55			16 13			16 00						16 15		16 25		
London Blackfriars 3 ⊖	a					15 52									16 07						16 25				
City Thameslink 3	a					15 56									16 10						16 28				
Farringdon 3 ⊖	a					15 59									16 13						16 31				
St Pancras International 15 ⊖	a					16 04									16 17						16 35				
St Albans City	a					16 24									16 38						16 55				
Luton Airport Parkway 4 ✈	a					16 37									16 51						17 08				
Luton 7	a					16 40									16 54						17 11				
Bedford 10	a					17 05									17 19						17 36				
Clapham Junction 10	a			15 25	15 37			15 32					15 50						15 55	16 09		16 02			16 17
London Victoria 15 ⊖	a		15 35	15 35	15 46			15 40			15 50		15 57					16 05	16 05	16 16		16 10		16 22	16 24

A 🚲 from Haywards Heath

Table 186

Mondays to Fridays

from 21 May

Brighton - London and Bedford

Network Diagram - see first Page of Table 186

		SN		SN	SN	FC	GW	SN	SN	SN	FC	SN		SN	SN	SN	GW	SN	SN	SN	FC	SN		GW	SN
		1		◇1	◇1	1	1	1	1	◇1	1	◇1		1	◇1	1	1	1	◇1	◇1	1	1		1	1
					A															A					
				🛒	🛒			🛒		🛒		🛒		🛒					🛒	🛒		🛒			
Brighton 10	d					15 34					15 37	15 49			15 55						16 04				
Hove 2	d				15 21															15 52					
Preston Park	d										15 41									15 56					
Hassocks 4	d										15 47				16 06										
Burgess Hill 4	d										15 51									16 05					
Lewes 4	d			15 19															15 50						
Wivelsfield 4	d			15 35							15 53														
Haywards Heath 3	a			15 40	15 35	15 47					15 57								16 05	16 10	16 17				
	d			15 44		15 48					15 58								16 14		16 18				
Balcombe	d																								
Horsham 4	d	15 30								15 50								16 00							
Littlehaven	d	15 33																16 03							
Faygate	d																								
Ifield	d	15 39																16 09							
Crawley	d	15 43								15 59								16 13							
Three Bridges 4	a	15 46				15 56				16 02	16 06							16 16			16 26				
	d	15 48				15 57				16 03	16 07							16 18			16 27				
Gatwick Airport 10 ✈	a	15 52			15 55	16 01				16 07	16 11				16 21			16 22	16 25		16 31				
	d	15 53			15 56	16 02	16 03	16 05		16 08	16 12			16 20	16 23			16 23	16 26		16 32	16 35			
Horley 4	d	15 56																16 26							
Salfords	d																	16 30							
Earlswood (Surrey)	d																	16 33							
Tonbridge 4	d																								
Leigh (Kent)	d																								
Penshurst	d																								
Edenbridge	d																								
Godstone	d																								
Nutfield	d																								
Reigate	d															16 14	16 21							16 38	
Redhill 5	a	16 02					16 10			16 17						16 18	16 27	16 36						16 42	
	d	16 06								16 18						16 21		16 37							
Merstham	d	16 10														16 25		16 41							
Coulsdon South	d	16 15														16 30		16 46							
Purley 4	d	16 18														16 34		16 49							
East Croydon 🚌	a	16 23			16 11	16 16				16 30	16 27	16 24			16 38	16 39		16 54	16 40		16 46				16 44
	d	16 24			16 12	16 17			16 14	16 30	16 28	16 24			16 38	16 40		16 55	16 41		16 47				
Norwood Junction 2	a	16 28														16 44		16 59							
New Cross Gate	d	16 36																17 06							
London Bridge 4 ⊖	a	16 43														17 00		17 14							
London Blackfriars 3 ⊖	a					16 47					16 55										17 19				
City Thameslink 3	a					16 54					16 58										17 24				
Farringdon 3 ⊖	a					16 57					17 01										17 27				
St Pancras International 15 ⊖	a					17 01					17 05										17 31				
St Albans City	a					17 19					17 25										17 49				
Luton Airport Parkway 4 ✈	a										17 38														
Luton 7	a					17 32					17 41										18 02				
Bedford 10	a					17 53					18 06										18 23				
Clapham Junction 10	a				16 21				16 25	16 39		16 33			16 47				16 50						16 55
London Victoria 15 ⊖	a				16 28			16 35	16 35	16 46		16 42		16 52	16 56				16 58			17 05			17 05

A 🛒 from Haywards Heath

Table 186

Brighton - London and Bedford

Mondays to Fridays

from 21 May

Network Diagram - see first Page of Table 186

		SN	FC	SN	SN	SN	FC	SN	SN	SN	SN	GW	SN	SN	FC	SN	SN	SN	SN	SN	GW	SN
		◇1	1	1	1	1	1	1	◇1	◇1	1	1	1	1	1	1	◇1	1	1	1	1	1
										A												
				[trolley]		[trolley]			[trolley]	[trolley]				[trolley]		[trolley]	[trolley]	[trolley]				
Brighton 10	d		16 07	16 19			16 24								16 30	16 49						
Hove 2	d									16 21												
Preston Park	d		16 11												16 34							
Hassocks 4	d		16 17												16 40							
Burgess Hill 4	d		16 21												16 44							
Lewes 4	d								16 20													
Wivelsfield 4	d								16 38						16 46							
Haywards Heath 3	a		16 26				16 38		16 42	16 35					16 50							
	d		16 26				16 38		16 46						16 51							
Balcombe	d		16 32												16 56							
Horsham 4	d	16 20						16 30									16 52					17 00
Littlehaven	d							16 33														17 03
Faygate	d							16 37														17 07
Ifield	d							16 41														17 11
Crawley	d	16 29						16 44									17 01					17 14
Three Bridges 4	a	16 32	16 37				16 47	16 47							17 02		17 04					17 17
	d	16 33	16 37				16 47	16 48							17 02		17 05					17 18
Gatwick Airport 10 ✈	a	16 37	16 41				16 52	16 52	16 57						17 07		17 09					17 22
	d	16 38	16 42			16 50	16 53	16 53	16 58			17 03		17 05	17 08		17 10	17 20				17 23
Horley 4	d							16 56														17 26
Salfords	d							17 00														17 30
Earlswood (Surrey)	d							17 03														17 33
Tonbridge 4	d				16 19														16 49	17 03		
Leigh (Kent)	d				16 23														16 53			
Penshurst	d				16 27														16 57			
Edenbridge	d				16 33														17 03	17 13		
Godstone	d				16 40														17 10			
Nutfield	d				16 45														17 15			
Reigate	d										17 03										17 26	
Redhill 5	a	16 46			16 50			17 06			17 07	17 10					17 17		17 20	17 25	17 32	17 36
	d	16 47			16 51			17 07									17 18		17 21	17 28		17 37
Merstham	d							17 11											17 25			17 41
Coulsdon South	d				16 58			17 16											17 30			17 46
Purley 4	d				17 02			17 19														17 49
East Croydon ⇌	a	17 01	16 57	16 54	17 07		17 07	17 24	17 13						17 22	17 26	17 30		17 38	17 40		17 54
	d	17 01	16 58	16 54	17 07		17 09	17 25	17 13				17 14		17 23	17 26	17 30		17 38	17 41		17 55
Norwood Junction 2	a				17 11			17 30												17 45		17 59
New Cross Gate	d							17 38														18 07
London Bridge 4 ⊖	a				17 26		17 27	17 45												17 58		18 16
London Blackfriars 3 ⊖	a		17 25				17 35								17 49							
City Thameslink 3	a		17 28				17 38								17 54							
Farringdon 3 ⊖	a		17 31				17 41								17 57							
St Pancras International 15 ⊖	a		17 35				17 45								18 01							
St Albans City	a		17 55				18 06								18 19							
Luton Airport Parkway 4 ✈	a		18 08				18 20															
Luton 7	a		18 11				18 23								18 32							
Bedford 10	a		18 36				18 48								18 55							
Clapham Junction 10	a	17 10		17 03					17 22				17 25			17 35	17 39		17 47			
London Victoria 15 ⊖	a	17 17		17 10		17 20			17 29				17 35	17 38		17 42	17 46	17 52	17 54			

A [trolley] from Haywards Heath

Table 186

Mondays to Fridays

from 21 May

Brighton - London and Bedford

Network Diagram - see first Page of Table 186

		SN	SN	GW	SN		SN	FC	SN	SN	FC	SN	SN	SN	SN	SN		SN	SN	SN	FC	GW	SN	SN	SN
		◇1	◇1	1	1		1	1	1	1	1	1	◇1	1	1	1		1	◇1	◇1	1	1	1	1	◇1
			A																	A					
		🚌	🚌						🚌			🚌	🚌	🚌					🚌	🚌			🚌		🚌
Brighton 10	d						16 55	17 02			17 07	17 19									17 24				
Hove 2	d		16 51																	17 21					
Preston Park	d						16 58				17 11										17 28				
Hassocks 4	d						17 05				17 17										17 34				
Burgess Hill 4	d		17 02				17 08	17 13			17 21										17 38				
Lewes 4	d	16 50																	17 19						
Wivelsfield 4	d						17 11			←									17 35		17 40				
Haywards Heath 3	a	17 06	17 09				17 15	17 18		17 15	17 26								17 39	17 35	17 45				
	d	17 14					17 21	17 18		17 21	17 26								17 43		17 46				
Balcombe	d						→			17 26															
Horsham 4	d												17 22					17 30							17 52
Littlehaven	d																	17 33							
Faygate	d																	17 37							
Ifield	d																	17 41							
Crawley	d												17 31					17 44							18 01
Three Bridges 4	a							17 27		17 32			17 34					17 47			17 54				18 04
	d							17 27		17 32			17 36					17 48			17 55				18 05
Gatwick Airport 10 ✈	a	17 25						17 31		17 36	17 38		17 41					17 52	17 54		17 59				18 09
	d	17 26						17 32	17 35	17 38	17 39		17 42	17 50				17 53	17 55		18 00	18 03	18 05		18 10
Horley 4	d																	17 56							
Salfords	d																	18 00							
Earlswood (Surrey)	d																	18 03							
Tonbridge 4	d														17 21										
Leigh (Kent)	d														17 25										
Penshurst	d														17 29										
Edenbridge	d														17 35										
Godstone	d														17 42										
Nutfield	d														17 47										
Reigate	d			17 34												17 44									
Redhill 5	a			17 38									17 49		17 53	17 48		18 06				18 10			18 17
	d												17 49		17 57			18 07							18 18
Merstham	d																	18 11							
Coulsdon South	d																	18 16							
Purley 4	d																	18 19							
East Croydon 🚋	a	17 41						17 46		17 53	17 57	17 56	18 01		18 08			18 24	18 11		18 15				18 29
	d	17 41			17 44			17 47		17 53	17 58	17 57	18 02		18 09			18 27	18 12		18 16			18 14	18 30
Norwood Junction 2	a																								
New Cross Gate	d																								
London Bridge 4 ⊖	a							18 13																	
London Blackfriars 3 ⊖	a							18 21			18 25										18 51				
City Thameslink 3	a							18 24			18 28										18 54				
Farringdon 3 ⊖	a							18 27			18 31										18 57				
St Pancras International 15 ⊖	a							18 31			18 35										19 01				
St Albans City	a							18 49			18 57										19 19				
Luton Airport Parkway 4 ✈	a										19 09														
Luton 7	a							19 02			19 12										19 32				
Bedford 10	a							19 23			19 38										19 55				
Clapham Junction 10	a	17 50			17 55					18 02		18 06	18 13		18 18			18 38	18 21					18 25	18 41
London Victoria 15 ⊖	a	17 58			18 05				18 05	18 09		18 14	18 20	18 22	18 26			18 45	18 29				18 35	18 35	18 48

A 🚌 from Haywards Heath

Table 186

Mondays to Fridays

from 21 May

Brighton - London and Bedford

Network Diagram - see first Page of Table 186

		FC	SN	SN	SN	SN	GW	SN	SN	SN	SN	GW	SN	SN	FC	SN	SN	SN	FC	SN	SN	SN
		1	1	1	1	1	1	1	◇1	◇1	1	1	1	1	1	1	1	◇1	1	1	1	1
										A												
				[trolley]	[trolley]				[trolley]	[trolley]						[trolley]						[trolley]
Brighton 10	d	17 37		17 49										17 55	18 02				18 07	18 19		
Hove 2	d									17 51												
Preston Park	d	17 41												17 59					18 11			
Hassocks 4	d	17 47												18 05					18 17			
Burgess Hill 4	d	17 51								18 04				18 09	18 13				18 21			
Lewes 4	d								17 50													
Wivelsfield 4	d	17 53												18 11			←		18 23			
Haywards Heath 3	a	17 58							18 07	18 11				18 16	18 18		18 16		18 28			
	d	18 02							18 15					18 22	18 18		18 22		18 32			
Balcombe	d	18 07												→					18 37			
Horsham 4	d							18 00										18 22				
Littlehaven	d							18 03														
Faygate	d							18 07														
Ifield	d							18 11														
Crawley	d							18 14										18 31				
Three Bridges 4	a	18 13						18 17							18 27		18 31	18 34	18 43			
	d	18 13						18 18							18 27		18 31	18 35	18 43			
Gatwick Airport 10 ✈	a	18 17						18 22	18 26						18 31		18 36	18 39	18 47			
	d	18 17			18 20			18 23	18 27						18 32	18 35	18 38	18 40	18 47			18 50
Horley 4	d							18 26														
Salfords	d							18 30														
Earlswood (Surrey)	d							18 33														
Tonbridge 4	d		17 49																		18 23	
Leigh (Kent)	d		17 53																		18 27	
Penshurst	d		17 57																		18 31	
Edenbridge	d		18 03																		18 37	
Godstone	d		18 10																		18 44	
Nutfield	d		18 15																		18 49	
Reigate	d					18 14	18 26				18 38	18 42										
Redhill 5	a		18 21			18 19	18 32	18 36			18 42	18 47						18 47			18 54	
	d					18 24		18 37										18 48			18 57	
Merstham	d					18 28		18 41														
Coulsdon South	d					18 33		18 46														
Purley 4	d							18 49														
East Croydon	a	18 32		18 25		18 40		18 54	18 42						18 47		18 53	18 59	19 02	18 56	19 09	
	d	18 32		18 26		18 40		18 55	18 43				18 44		18 47		18 53	19 00	19 02	18 57	19 10	
Norwood Junction 2	a																				19 13	
New Cross Gate	d																					
London Bridge 4 ⊖	a	18 46													19 00				19 15		19 25	
London Blackfriars 3 ⊖	a	18 55													19 09				19 22			
City Thameslink 3	a	18 58													19 12				19 26			
Farringdon 3 ⊖	a	19 01													19 15				19 30			
St Pancras International 15 ⊖	a	19 05													19 19				19 34			
St Albans City	a	19 25													19 45				19 55			
Luton Airport Parkway 4 ✈	a	19 38													19 57				20 06			
Luton 7	a	19 41													20 00				20 09			
Bedford 10	a	20 06													20 26				20 35			
Clapham Junction 10	a			18 35		18 49		19 05	18 52				18 55				19 02	19 11		19 08		
London Victoria 15 ⊖	a			18 42	18 50	18 56		19 13	18 59				19 05			19 05	19 09	19 18		19 15		19 20

A [trolley] from Haywards Heath

Brighton - London and Bedford

Network Diagram - see first Page of Table 186

		SN	SN	SN	FC	SN	SN	SN		SN	FC	SN	GW	SN	SN	SN	GW	SN		SN	SN	FC	SN	GW	SN
		[1]	◇[1]	◇[1]	[1]	[1]	[1]	[1]		◇[1]	[1]	◇[1]	[1]	[1]	[1]	[1]	[1]	[1]		◇[1]	◇[1]	[1]	[1]	[1]	[1]
				A																					
			🚲	🚲			🚲							🚲									🚲		
Brighton [10]	d				18 34						18 37	18 49													
Hove [2]	d			18 21																	18 52				
Preston Park	d										18 41														
Hassocks [4]	d										18 47														
Burgess Hill [4]	d			18 34							18 51														
Lewes [4]	d		18 18																	18 50					
Wivelsfield [4]	d		18 34								18 53									19 06					
Haywards Heath [3]	a		18 38	18 41	18 47						18 58									19 10	19 07				
	d			18 45	18 48						19 02										19 14				
Balcombe	d																								
Horsham [4]	d	18 30								18 52								19 02							
Littlehaven	d	18 33																19 05							
Faygate	d	18 37																							
Ifield	d	18 41																19 11							
Crawley	d	18 44								19 01								19 14							
Three Bridges [4]	a	18 47			18 56					19 04	19 11							19 18							
	d	18 48			18 57					19 05	19 12							19 18				19 27			
Gatwick Airport [10] ✈	a	18 52		18 56	19 01					19 09	19 16							19 22			19 25	19 31			
	d	18 53		18 57	19 02		19 05			19 10	19 17		19 16	19 20				19 23			19 26	19 32	19 35		
Horley [4]	d	18 56																19 26							
Salfords	d	19 00																19 30							
Earlswood (Surrey)	d	19 03																19 33							
Tonbridge [4]	d														18 50										19 10
Leigh (Kent)	d														18 54										19 14
Penshurst	d														18 58										19 18
Edenbridge	d														19 04										19 24
Godstone	d														19 11										19 31
Nutfield	d														19 16										19 36
Reigate	d					19 02										19 21	19 30							19 36	
Redhill [5]	a	19 06				19 06				19 17			19 23		19 21	19 25	19 35	19 38						19 40	19 41
	d	19 07								19 18					19 23			19 39							
Merstham	d	19 11													19 27			19 43							
Coulsdon South	d	19 16													19 32			19 48							
Purley [4]	d	19 19																19 53							
East Croydon 🚋	a	19 24		19 12	19 16					19 29	19 31	19 23			19 40			19 58			19 43	19 46			
	d	19 25		19 12	19 17			19 14		19 29	19 32	19 24			19 40			19 59			19 43	19 47			
Norwood Junction [2]	a																								
New Cross Gate	d																								
London Bridge [4] ⊖	a				19 30						19 45											20 00			
London Blackfriars [3] ⊖	a				19 37						19 52											20 07			
City Thameslink [3]	a				19 40						19 56											20 10			
Farringdon [3] ⊖	a				19 44						20 00											20 14			
St Pancras International [15] ⊖	a				19 48						20 04											20 18			
St Albans City	a				20 08						20 25											20 38			
Luton Airport Parkway [4] ✈	a				20 20						20 37											20 50			
Luton [7]	a				20 23						20 40											20 53			
Bedford [10]	a				20 49						21 05											21 19			
Clapham Junction [10]	a	19 37		19 21				19 25		19 40		19 33			19 49			20 08			19 52				
London Victoria [15] ⊖	a	19 44		19 29			19 35	19 35		19 47		19 41		19 50	19 56			20 15			19 59		20 05		

A 🚲 from Haywards Heath

Mondays to Fridays

from 21 May

Brighton - London and Bedford

Network Diagram - see first Page of Table 186

		SN	SN	SN		FC	SN	SN	SN	SN	SN	SN	SN	FC		GW	SN	SN	FC	SN	SN	SN	SN	SN	SN
		1	◇1	1		1	◇1	1	◇1	◇1	1	1	1	1		1	1	◇1	1	◇1	1	1	1	◇1	◇1
			A					🚲																	
Brighton 10	d		18 59			19 07	19 19							19 34					19 37	19 49					
Hove 2	d									19 22															19 52
Preston Park	d		19 03			19 11													19 41						
Hassocks 4	d		19 09			19 17													19 47						
Burgess Hill 4	d		19 13			19 21				19 32									19 51						
Lewes 4	d								19 21															19 50	
Wivelsfield 4	d		19 15			19 23													19 53					20 05	
Haywards Heath 3	a		19 20			19 28			19 40	19 37				19 47					19 58					20 10	20 05
	d		19 21			19 32			19 44					19 48					20 02					20 14	
Balcombe	d					19 37																			
Horsham 4	d			19 17									19 32					19 52					20 02		
Littlehaven	d												19 35										20 05		
Faygate	d																								
Ifield	d												19 41										20 11		
Crawley	d			19 26									19 45					20 01					20 14		
Three Bridges 4	a		19 31	19 29		19 43							19 49	19 56				20 04	20 11				20 18		
	d		19 35			19 43							19 51	19 57				20 05	20 12				20 18		
Gatwick Airport 10 ✈	a		19 39			19 47			19 55				19 55	20 01				20 10	20 16				20 22	20 25	
	d		19 40			19 47		19 50	19 56				19 56	20 02		20 03	20 05	20 11	20 17			20 20	20 23	20 26	
Horley 4	d												19 59										20 26		
Salfords	d																						20 30		
Earlswood (Surrey)	d																						20 33		
Tonbridge 4	d																								
Leigh (Kent)	d																								
Penshurst	d																								
Edenbridge	d																								
Godstone	d																								
Nutfield	d																								
Reigate	d										19 51										20 14				
Redhill 5	a		19 47								19 55		20 05			20 11		20 18			20 18		20 36		
	d		19 48										20 06					20 18					20 37		
Merstham	d												20 10										20 41		
Coulsdon South	d												20 15										20 46		
Purley 4	d												20 18										20 49		
East Croydon	a		20 00			20 02	19 53		20 11				20 23	20 16				20 30	20 32	20 23			20 57	20 41	
	d	19 44	20 01			20 02	19 54		20 11			20 14	20 26	20 17				20 30	20 32	20 24			20 57	20 41	
Norwood Junction 2	a																								
New Cross Gate	d																								
London Bridge 4 ⊖	a					20 15								20 30					20 45						
London Blackfriars 3 ⊖	a					20 22								20 37					20 52						
City Thameslink 3	a					20 26								20 40					20 56						
Farringdon 3 ⊖	a					20 30								20 44					21 00						
St Pancras International 15 ⊖	a					20 34								20 48					21 04						
St Albans City	a					20 55								21 08					21 25						
Luton Airport Parkway 4 ✈	a					21 07								21 20					21 37						
Luton 7	a					21 10								21 23					21 40						
Bedford 10	a					21 35								21 49					22 05						
Clapham Junction 10	a	19 55	20 11				20 03		20 20			20 25	20 37					20 40		20 33			21 07	20 50	
London Victoria 15 ⊖	a	20 05	20 20				20 10	20 20	20 28			20 32	20 44				20 35	20 50		20 40		20 50	21 15	20 59	

A ◇ to Three Bridges

Brighton - London and Bedford

Network Diagram - see first Page of Table 186

		GW 1	SN 1	SN 1	SN ◇1	FC 1	SN 1	SN ◇1	FC 1	SN ◇1	SN 1	SN 1	SN ◇1	SN 1	SN 1	FC 1	GW 1	SN 1	SN 1	SN ◇1	FC 1	SN ◇1
Brighton 10	d				19 55	20 02			20 07	20 19						20 34					20 37	20 49
Hove 2	d												20 22									
Preston Park	d				19 58				20 11												20 41	
Hassocks 4	d				20 05				20 17												20 47	
Burgess Hill 4	d				20 08	20 13			20 21				20 33								20 51	
Lewes 4	d																					
Wivelsfield 4	d				20 11			←	20 23												20 53	
Haywards Heath 3	a				20 15	20 18		20 15	20 28				20 38			20 47					20 58	
	d				20 22	20 19		20 22	20 32				20 38			20 48					21 02	
Balcombe	d				→				20 37													
Horsham 4	d														20 32					20 52		
Littlehaven	d														20 35							
Faygate	d																					
Ifield	d														20 41					21 01		
Crawley	d														20 45							
Three Bridges 4	a					20 27		20 32	20 43				20 47		20 48	20 56				21 05	21 11	
	d					20 27		20 32	20 43				20 47		20 51	20 57				21 05	21 12	
Gatwick Airport 10 ✈	a					20 31		20 37	20 47				20 51		20 56	21 01				21 10	21 16	
	d					20 32	20 35	20 38	20 47			20 50	20 53		20 57	21 02	21 03	21 05		21 11	21 17	
Horley 4	d														20 59							
Salfords	d																					
Earlswood (Surrey)	d																					
Tonbridge 4	d		20 10																			
Leigh (Kent)	d		20 14																			
Penshurst	d		20 18																			
Edenbridge	d		20 24																			
Godstone	d		20 31																			
Nutfield	d		20 36																			
Reigate	d	20 34									20 50								21 13			
Redhill 5	a	20 38	20 45					20 47			20 54				21 06		21 10		21 17	21 18		
	d							20 48							21 07					21 18		
Merstham	d														21 11							
Coulsdon South	d														21 16							
Purley 4	d														21 19							
East Croydon	a					20 47		20 59	21 02	20 53			21 08		21 25	21 16				21 30	21 32	21 23
	d			20 44		20 47		21 00	21 02	20 54			21 09	21 14	21 26	21 17				21 30	21 32	21 24
Norwood Junction 2	a																					
New Cross Gate	d																					
London Bridge 4 ⊖	a					21 00			21 15							21 30					21 45	
London Blackfriars 3 ⊖	a					21 07			21 22							21 37					21 52	
City Thameslink 3	a					21 10			21 26							21 40					21 56	
Farringdon 3 ⊖	a					21 14			21 30							21 44					22 00	
St Pancras International 15 ⊖	a					21 18			21 34							21 48					22 04	
St Albans City	a					21 38			21 55							22 08					22 25	
Luton Airport Parkway 4 ✈	a					21 50			22 07							22 20					22 37	
Luton 7	a					21 53			22 10							22 23					22 40	
Bedford 10	a					22 19			22 35							22 49					23 05	
Clapham Junction 10	a			20 55				21 11		21 03			21 18	21 25	21 37					21 40		21 33
London Victoria 15 ⊖	a			21 03			21 05	21 18		21 10		21 20	21 28	21 32	21 45			21 35		21 47		21 40

Table 186

Mondays to Fridays

from 21 May

Brighton - London and Bedford

Network Diagram - see first Page of Table 186

		SN	GW	SN	SN	SN	SN		SN	SN	SN	FC	SN	GW	SN	SN	SN		SN	SN	SN	SN	SN	SN	FC
		1	1	1	◇1	◇1	1		1	1	◇1	1	◇1	1	1	◇1	1		1	1	1	1	1	◇1	1
Brighton 10	d										21 02	21 11	21 19								21 34				21 37
Hove 2	d					20 52										21 22									
Preston Park	d										21 06														21 41
Hassocks 4	d										21 12	21 20													21 47
Burgess Hill 4	d										21 16	21 23				21 33									21 51
Lewes 4	d				20 50																				
Wivelsfield 4	d				21 05						21 18														21 53
Haywards Heath 3	a				21 09	21 05					21 23	21 28				21 38					21 47				21 58
	d				21 13						21 23	21 32				21 38					21 47				22 02
Balcombe	d											21 37													
Horsham 4	d			21 02																21 32				21 52	
Littlehaven	d			21 05																21 35					
Faygate	d																								
Ifield	d			21 11																21 41					
Crawley	d			21 14																21 45				22 01	
Three Bridges 4	a			21 18							21 32	21 43				21 47				21 48	21 56			22 05	22 11
	d			21 18							21 33	21 43				21 47				21 51	21 56			22 05	22 12
Gatwick Airport 10 ✈	a			21 22	21 25						21 37	21 47				21 51				21 55	22 00			22 10	22 16
	d	21 20		21 23	21 26				21 35		21 38	21 47			21 50	21 53				21 56	22 02	22 05		22 11	22 17
Horley 4	d			21 26																21 59					
Salfords	d			21 30																					
Earlswood (Surrey)	d			21 33																					
Tonbridge 4	d						21 10																		
Leigh (Kent)	d						21 14																		
Penshurst	d						21 18																		
Edenbridge	d						21 24																		
Godstone	d						21 31																		
Nutfield	d						21 36																		
Reigate	d		21 24											21 45			21 52						22 13		
Redhill 5	a		21 30	21 36			21 42				21 45			21 49			21 57			22 05			22 17	22 18	
	d			21 37							21 46									22 06				22 18	
Merstham	d			21 41																22 10					
Coulsdon South	d			21 46																22 15					
Purley 4	d			21 49																22 19					
East Croydon 🚋	a			21 54	21 41						21 59	22 02	21 53			22 08				22 24	22 17			22 30	22 32
	d			21 57	21 42					21 44	22 00	22 02	21 54			22 09			22 14	22 25	22 18			22 30	22 32
Norwood Junction 2	a																								
New Cross Gate	d																								
London Bridge 4 ⊖	a											22 15									22 33				22 45
London Blackfriars 3 ⊖	a											22 22													22 52
City Thameslink 3	a											22 23													22 53
Farringdon 3 ⊖	a											22 28													22 58
St Pancras International 15 ⊖	a											22 32													23 02
St Albans City	a											22 56													23 26
Luton Airport Parkway 4 ✈	a											23 08													23 38
Luton 7	a											23 11													23 41
Bedford 10	a											23 38													00 08
Clapham Junction 10	a			22 07	21 51					21 55	22 10		22 03			22 18			22 25	22 37				22 40	
London Victoria 15 ⊖	a	21 50		22 14	21 58				22 05	22 05	22 20		22 11		22 20	22 26			22 35	22 44		22 35		22 50	

Table 186

Mondays to Fridays

from 21 May

Brighton - London and Bedford

Network Diagram - see first Page of Table 186

		SN	SN		GW	SN	SN	SN	SN	SN	SN	SN	SN		FC	SN	GW	SN	SN	SN	SN	FC	SN		FC
		◇1	1		1	1	◇1	◇1	1	1	1	1	◇1		1	◇1	1	1	1	1	1	1	◇1		1
							(trolley)	A (trolley)																	
Brighton 10	d	21 49											22 03		22 07	22 19						22 33			
Hove 2	d							21 52																	
Preston Park	d												22 06		22 11							22 37			
Hassocks 4	d												22 13		22 17							22 43			
Burgess Hill 4	d							22 04					22 16		22 21							22 47			
Lewes 4	d						21 50																22 40		
Wivelsfield 4	d						22 02						22 18		22 23							22 49	22 54		
Haywards Heath 3	a						22 06	22 10					22 23		22 28							22 53	22 58		
	d							22 14					22 23		22 32							22 54	22 59		
Balcombe	d														22 37							22 59			
Horsham 4	d					22 02																			
Littlehaven	d					22 05																			
Faygate	d																								
Ifield	d					22 11																			
Crawley	d					22 14																			←
Three Bridges 4	a					22 18							22 32		22 43							23 05	23 08		23 05
	d					22 19							22 33		22 43							23 12	23 08		23 12
Gatwick Airport 10 ✈	a					22 23		22 25					22 37		22 47							→	23 12		23 16
	d		22 20		22 22	22 24		22 26			22 35		22 38		22 47			22 50	23 05				23 13		23 17
Horley 4	d					22 27																			
Salfords	d					22 31																			
Earlswood (Surrey)	d					22 34																			
Tonbridge 4	d									22 10															
Leigh (Kent)	d									22 14															
Penshurst	d									22 18															
Edenbridge	d									22 24															
Godstone	d									22 31															
Nutfield	d									22 36															
Reigate	d								22 33								22 44								
Redhill 5	a				22 30	22 37			22 37	22 42			22 45				22 48								
	d					22 38							22 46												
Merstham	d					22 42																			
Coulsdon South	d					22 47																			
Purley 4	d					22 50																			
East Croydon	a	22 23				22 55		22 41					22 59		23 02	22 53							23 30		23 32
	d	22 24				22 56		22 41				22 44	23 00		23 02	22 54				23 14	23 20		23 30		23 32
Norwood Junction 2	a																								
New Cross Gate	d																								
London Bridge 4 ⊖	a														23 15										23 45
London Blackfriars 3 ⊖	a														23 22										23 52
City Thameslink 3	a																								
Farringdon 3 ⊖	a														23 28										23 58
St Pancras International 15 ⊖	a														23 32										00 02
St Albans City	a														23 56										00 26
Luton Airport Parkway 4 ✈	a														00 08										00 38
Luton 7	a														00 11										00 41
Bedford 10	a														00 38										01 08
Clapham Junction 10	a	22 33				23 06		22 50				22 55	23 10			23 03				23 25	23 32		23 42		
London Victoria 15 ⊖	a	22 41	22 50			23 15		22 57			23 05	23 05	23 20			23 13		23 20	23 35	23 35	23 40		23 52		

A (trolley) from Haywards Heath

Table 186

Mondays to Fridays

from 21 May

Brighton - London and Bedford

Network Diagram - see first Page of Table 186

		GW	SN	SN	SN	SN	GW	SN	FC		SN	SN	FC
		1	1	1	1	1	1	◇1	1		1	◇1	1
Brighton 10	d							23 02	23 11				23 37
Hove 2	d												
Preston Park	d							23 06					23 41
Hassocks 4	d							23 12	23 20				23 47
Burgess Hill 4	d							23 16	23 23				23 51
Lewes 4	d												
Wivelsfield 4	d							23 19					23 53
Haywards Heath 3	a							23 23	23 28				23 58
	d							23 24	23 29				23 59
Balcombe	d												00 04
Horsham 4	d			23 02									
Littlehaven	d			23 05									
Faygate	d												
Ifield	d			23 11									
Crawley	d			23 14								↩	
Three Bridges 4	a			23 18				23 33	23 38			23 33	00 10
	d			23 18				23 47	23 38			23 47	00 10
Gatwick Airport 10 ✈	a			23 22				↪	23 42			23 52	00 14
	d	23 18	23 20	23 23		23 35			23 43		23 50	23 53	00 15
Horley 4	d			23 26								23 56	
Salfords	d			23 30									
Earlswood (Surrey)	d			23 33									
Tonbridge 4	d				23 17								
Leigh (Kent)	d				23 21								
Penshurst	d				23 25								
Edenbridge	d				23 31								
Godstone	d				23 38								
Nutfield	d				23 43								
Reigate	d						23 54						
Redhill 5	a	23 25		23 36	23 49		23 58					00 03	00 22
	d			23 37								00 03	00 23
Merstham	d			23 41									
Coulsdon South	d			23 46									
Purley 4	d			23 49								00 11	
East Croydon	a			23 54					00 01			00 16	00 35
	d			23 58					00 04			00 17	00 36
Norwood Junction 2	a												
New Cross Gate	d												
London Bridge 4 ⊖	a								00 21				00 51
London Blackfriars 3 ⊖	a								00 28				00 58
City Thameslink 3	a												
Farringdon 3 ⊖	a								00 33				
St Pancras International 15 ⊖	a								00 37				01 07
St Albans City	a								01 10				01 40
Luton Airport Parkway 4 ✈	a								01 22				01 52
Luton 7	a								01 25				01 55
Bedford 10	a								01 52				02 22
Clapham Junction 10	a			00 11								00 29	
London Victoria 15 ⊖	a		23 55	00 18		00 10					00 25	00 37	

Table 186

Saturdays

until 23 June

Brighton - London and Bedford

Network Diagram - see first Page of Table 186

		FC	FC	FC	SN	SN	SN	FC	FC	SN		SN	SN	FC	FC	SN	GW	SN	SN	SN		SN	FC	FC	SN
		1	1	1	1	1	◇1	1	1	1		◇1	1	1	1	1	1		1	1		1	1		1
		A	A	A				B	A					B	A								B		
Brighton 10	d	21p37	22p07	22p33			23p02	23p11	23p11					23p37	23p37										
Hove 2	d																								
Preston Park	d	21p41	22p11	22p37			23p06							23p41	23p41										
Hassocks 4	d	21p47	22p17	22p43			23p12	23p20	23p20					23p47	23p47										
Burgess Hill 4	d	21p51	22p21	22p47			23p16	23p23	23p23					23p51	23p51										
Lewes 4	d																								
Wivelsfield 4	d	21p53	22p23	22p49			23p19							23p53	23p53										
Haywards Heath 3	a	21p58	22p28	22p53			23p23	23p28	23p28					23p58	23p58										
	d	22p02	22p32	22p54			23p24	23p29	23p29					23p59	23p59										
Balcombe	d		22p37	22p59										00 04	00 04										
Horsham 4	d				23p02																				
Littlehaven	d				23p05																				
Faygate	d																								
Ifield	d				23p11																				
Crawley	d				23p14							←													
Three Bridges 4	a	22p11	22p43	23p05	23p18		23p33	23p38	23p38			23p33		00 10	00 10										
	d	22p12	22p43	23p12	23p18		23p47	23p38	23p38			23p47		00 10	00 10								01 25	01 25	
Gatwick Airport 10 ✈	a	22p16	22p47	23p16	23p22		→	23p42	23p42			23p52		00 14	00 14								01 29	01 29	
	d	22p17	22p47	23p17	23p23	23p35		23p43	23p43	23p50		23p53	00 05	00 15	00 15	00 20			00 35	00 50		01 05	01 30	01 30	01 35
Horley 4	d				23p26							23p56										01 07			
Salfords	d				23p30																				
Earlswood (Surrey)	d				23p33																				
Tonbridge 4	d																								
Leigh (Kent)	d																								
Penshurst	d																								
Edenbridge	d																								
Godstone	d																								
Nutfield	d																								
Reigate	d																00 45								
Redhill 5	a				23p36							00 03		00 22	00 22		00 49								
	d				23p37							00 03		00 23	00 23										
Merstham	d				23p41																				
Coulsdon South	d				23p46																				
Purley 4	d				23p49							00 11										01 22			
East Croydon	a	22p32	23p02	23p32	23p54			00 01	00 01			00 16		00 35	00 35							01 27	01 49	01 49	
	d	22p32	23p02	23p32	23p58			00 04	00 04			00 17		00 36	00 36			00 49				01 28	01 50	01 50	
Norwood Junction 2	a																								
New Cross Gate	d																								
London Bridge 4 ⊖	a	22p45	23p15	23p45				00 19	00 21					00 52	00 51								02 14		
London Blackfriars 3 ⊖	a	22p52	23p22	23p52					00 28						00 58									02 13	
City Thameslink 3	a	22p53																							
Farringdon 3 ⊖	a	22p58	23p28	23p58					00 33																
St Pancras International 15 ⊖	a	23p02	23p32	00 02					00 37						01 07									02 24	
St Albans City	a	23p26	23p56	00 26					01 10						01 40									02 57	
Luton Airport Parkway 4 ✈	a	23p38	00 08	00 38					01 22						01 52									03 09	
Luton 7	a	23p41	00 11	00 41					01 25						01 55									03 12	
Bedford 10	a	00 08	00 38	01 08					01 52						02 22									03 39	
Clapham Junction 10	a				00 11							00 29						01 01				01 41			
London Victoria 15 ⊖	a				00 18	00 10				00 25		00 37	00 40			00 55		01 09	01 11	01 25		01 49			02 10

A not 19 May

B 19 May

Table 186

Saturdays

until 23 June

Brighton - London and Bedford

Network Diagram - see first Page of Table 186

		SN	FC	FC	SN	FC		FC	SN	FC	FC	SN	FC	FC	SN	SN		FC	FC	GW	GW	SN	SN	SN	SN
		1	1		1	1			1	1		1	1		1	1		1		1	1	◇1	1	1	◇1
			A			A				A			A					A							
Brighton 10	d														03 50										05 21
Hove 2	d																								
Preston Park	d																								
Hassocks 4	d																								
Burgess Hill 4	d																								
Lewes 4	d																								05 31
Wivelsfield 4	d																								
Haywards Heath 3	a														04 24										05 36
	d														04 25										05 37
Balcombe	d																								
Horsham 4	d																								
Littlehaven	d																								
Faygate	d																								
Ifield	d																								
Crawley	d																								
Three Bridges 4	a														04 45										05 46
	d	01 59	02 25	02 25	02 55	03 25		03 25	03 55	04 25	04 25		04 55	04 55	05 00			05 21	05 21			05 33			05 46
Gatwick Airport 10 ✈	a	02 03	02 29	02 29	02 59	03 29		03 29	03 59	04 29	04 29		04 59	04 59	05 04			05 25	05 25			05 37			05 50
	d	02 05	02 30	02 30	03 05	03 30		03 30	04 05	04 30	04 30	04 35	05 00	05 00	05 05	05 20		05 27	05 27	05 31		05 38		05 50	05 53
Horley 4	d	02 07			03 07				04 07						05 07							05 40			
Salfords	d																								
Earlswood (Surrey)	d																								
Tonbridge 4	d																						05 24		
Leigh (Kent)	d																						05 28		
Penshurst	d																						05 32		
Edenbridge	d																						05 38		
Godstone	d																						05 45		
Nutfield	d																						05 50		
Reigate	d																				05 34				
Redhill 5	a																	05 34	05 34	05 38	05 39	05 47	05 55		
	d																	05 35	05 35			05 48			
Merstham	d																								
Coulsdon South	d																								
Purley 4	d	02 22			03 22				04 22						05 24							05 58			
East Croydon	a	02 27	02 47	02 47	03 27	03 47		03 47	04 27	04 47	04 47		05 17	05 17	05 29			05 47	05 47			06 02			06 10
	d	02 28	02 47	02 47	03 28	03 47		03 47	04 28	04 47	04 47		05 17	05 17	05 29			05 47	05 47			06 07			06 11
Norwood Junction 2	a																								
New Cross Gate	d																								
London Bridge 4 ⊖	a		03 12			04 12				05 12			05 42					06 01	06 02						
London Blackfriars 3 ⊖	a			03 13				04 13			05 13			05 43					06 08						
City Thameslink 3	a																								
Farringdon 3 ⊖	a										05 19			05 49					06 12						
St Pancras International 15 ⊖	a			03 23				04 22			05 24			05 54					06 16						
St Albans City	a			03 57				04 57			05 57			06 25					06 38						
Luton Airport Parkway 4 ✈	a			04 09				05 09			06 09			06 37					06 50						
Luton 7	a			04 12				05 12			06 12			06 40					06 53						
Bedford 10	a			04 39				05 39			06 39			07 05					07 19						
Clapham Junction 10	a	02 41			03 41				04 41						05 49							06 18			06 21
London Victoria 15 ⊖	a	02 49			03 49				04 50			05 10			05 58	05 55						06 26		06 20	06 30

A 19 May

Table 186

Saturdays

until 23 June

Brighton - London and Bedford

Network Diagram - see first Page of Table 186

		SN		FC	FC	SN	GW	SN	SN	SN	SN	SN		GW	SN	FC	FC	SN	SN	SN	SN	SN		SN	SN
		1		1	1	1	1	1	1	1	◇1	◇1		1	◇1	1	1	1	◇1	1	1	1		◇1	◇1
					A												A								
								🚲	🚲									🚲			🚲				
Brighton 10	d			05 25	05 25						05 50				05 56	06 02	06 02							06 11	
Hove 2	d											05 54													06 21
Preston Park	d			05 29	05 29										06 00									06 15	
Hassocks 4	d			05 35	05 35										06 06									06 21	
Burgess Hill 4	d			05 39	05 39											06 12	06 12							06 25	
Lewes 4	d					05 26																			
Wivelsfield 4	d			05 41	05 41										06 11									06 27	
Haywards Heath 3	a			05 45	05 45	05 41					06 03	06 08			06 15	06 17	06 17							06 31	06 35
	d			05 46	05 46	05 49					06 12				06 16	06 18	06 17							06 40	
Balcombe	d			05 51	05 51																				
Horsham 4	d	05 30								06 00												06 30			
Littlehaven	d	05 33								06 03												06 33			
Faygate	d																								
Ifield	d	05 39								06 09												06 39			
Crawley	d	05 43								06 13									←			06 43			
Three Bridges 4	a	05 46		05 57	05 57	05 59				06 16	06 20				06 24	06 26	06 26		06 24			06 46		06 48	
	d	05 48		05 57	05 57	05 59				06 18	06 21				06 31	06 27	06 27		06 31			06 48		06 49	
Gatwick Airport 10 ✈	a	05 52		06 01	06 01	06 03				06 22	06 25				→	06 31	06 31		06 37			06 52		06 53	
	d	05 53		06 02	06 02		06 03	06 05	06 20	06 23	06 26					06 32	06 32	06 35	06 38		06 50	06 53		06 55	
Horley 4	d	05 56								06 26												06 56			
Salfords	d	06 00								06 30															
Earlswood (Surrey)	d	06 03								06 33															
Tonbridge 4	d																			06 19					
Leigh (Kent)	d																			06 23					
Penshurst	d																			06 27					
Edenbridge	d																			06 33					
Godstone	d																			06 40					
Nutfield	d																			06 45					
Reigate	d													06 34											
Redhill 5	a	06 06					06 12			06 36				06 39						06 50		07 02			
	d	06 07								06 37										06 51		07 07			
Merstham	d	06 11								06 41												07 11			
Coulsdon South	d	06 16								06 46										06 58		07 16			
Purley 4	d	06 19								06 49										07 02		07 19			
East Croydon 🚋	a	06 24		06 16	06 16					06 54	06 40					06 46	06 46		06 53	07 07		07 24		07 09	
	d	06 25		06 17	06 17					06 55	06 41					06 47	06 47		06 53	07 07		07 25		07 10	
Norwood Junction 2	a	06 29								06 59										07 12		07 29			
New Cross Gate	d	06 37								07 07												07 37			
London Bridge 4 ⊖	a	06 43		06 30	06 32					07 13						07 00	07 02			07 25		07 43			
London Blackfriars 3 ⊖	a			06 37												07 07									
City Thameslink 3	a																								
Farringdon 3 ⊖	a			06 42												07 12									
St Pancras International 15 ⊖	a			06 46												07 16									
St Albans City	a			07 08												07 38									
Luton Airport Parkway 4 ✈	a			07 20												07 50									
Luton 7	a			07 23												07 53									
Bedford 10	a			07 49												08 19									
Clapham Junction 10	a										06 50								07 02					07 19	
London Victoria 15 ⊖	a							06 35	06 50		06 57							07 05	07 09		07 20			07 27	

A 19 May

Table 186

Brighton - London and Bedford

Saturdays

until 23 June

Network Diagram - see first Page of Table 186

		FC	FC	GW	SN	SN	SN	FC	FC	SN	SN	GW	SN	SN	SN	SN	FC	FC	GW	SN	SN	SN	FC
		1	1	1	1	1	◇1	1	1	◇1	1	1	1	1	◇1	◇1	1	1	1	1	1	◇1	1
			A						A									A					A
						bus							bus								bus		
Brighton 10	d	06 25	06 25					06 37	06 37	06 49							07 04	07 04					07 07
Hove 2	d															06 51							
Preston Park	d	06 29	06 29					06 41	06 41							06 55							07 11
Hassocks 4	d	06 35	06 35					06 47	06 47														07 17
Burgess Hill 4	d	06 39	06 39					06 51	06 51							07 04							07 21
Lewes 4	d														06 50								
Wivelsfield 4	d	06 41	06 41					06 53	06 53														07 23
Haywards Heath 3	a	06 45	06 45					06 58	06 58						07 05	07 09	07 17	07 17					07 28
	d	06 46	06 46					07 02	07 02						07 14		07 18	07 18					07 32
Balcombe	d	06 51	06 51																				07 37
Horsham 4	d						06 52							07 00								07 20	
Littlehaven	d													07 03									
Faygate	d																						
Ifield	d													07 09									
Crawley	d						07 01							07 13								07 29	
Three Bridges 4	a	06 57	06 57				07 04	07 11	07 11					07 16			07 26	07 26				07 32	07 42
	d	06 57	06 57				07 05	07 12	07 12					07 18			07 27	07 27				07 33	07 42
Gatwick Airport 10 ✈	a	07 01	07 01				07 09	07 16	07 16					07 22	07 25		07 31	07 31				07 37	07 46
	d	07 02	07 02	07 03		07 05	07 10	07 17	07 16				07 20	07 23	07 26		07 32	07 32			07 35	07 38	07 46
Horley 4	d													07 26								07 41	
Salfords	d													07 30									
Earlswood (Surrey)	d													07 33									
Tonbridge 4	d																						
Leigh (Kent)	d																						
Penshurst	d																						
Edenbridge	d																						
Godstone	d																						
Nutfield	d																						
Reigate	d										07 14	07 18							07 34				
Redhill 5	a			07 10			07 17				07 18	07 25		07 36					07 39			07 47	
	d						07 18				07 21			07 37								07 48	
Merstham	d										07 25			07 41									
Coulsdon South	d										07 30			07 46									
Purley 4	d										07 34			07 49									
East Croydon	a	07 16	07 16				07 29	07 31	07 31	07 22	07 39			07 54	07 41		07 46	07 46				07 59	08 01
	d	07 17	07 17		07 14		07 30	07 32	07 32	07 23	07 39			07 55	07 42		07 47	07 47		07 44		08 00	08 01
Norwood Junction 2	a										07 44			07 59									
New Cross Gate	d													08 07									
London Bridge 4 ⊖	a	07 30	07 32					07 45	07 47		07 57			08 13			08 00	08 02					08 17
London Blackfriars 3 ⊖	a	07 37						07 52									08 07						
City Thameslink 3	a																						
Farringdon 3 ⊖	a	07 43						07 59									08 13						
St Pancras International 15 ⊖	a	07 48						08 04									08 18						
St Albans City	a	08 08						08 24									08 38						
Luton Airport Parkway 4 ✈	a	08 20						08 37									08 50						
Luton 7	a	08 23						08 40									08 53						
Bedford 10	a	08 49						09 05									09 19						
Clapham Junction 10	a				07 25		07 39			07 32					07 51					07 55		08 09	
London Victoria 15 ⊖	a				07 32	07 35	07 46			07 40			07 50		07 58					08 02	08 05	08 16	

A 19 May

Table 186

Saturdays

until 23 June

Brighton - London and Bedford

Network Diagram - see first Page of Table 186

		FC	SN	SN		SN	SN	SN	SN	SN	FC	FC	GW	SN		SN	SN	FC	FC	SN	SN	GW	SN	SN
		1	◇1	1		1	◇1	1	◇1	◇1	1	1	1	1		1	◇1	1	1	◇1	1	1	1	1
												A							A					
						🚲										🚲				🚲			🚲	
Brighton 10	d	07 07	07 19				07 26				07 34	07 34						07 37	07 37	07 49				
Hove 2	d									07 22														
Preston Park	d	07 11																07 41	07 41					
Hassocks 4	d	07 17					07 34											07 47	07 47					
Burgess Hill 4	d	07 21					07 38											07 51	07 51					
Lewes 4	d								07 20															
Wivelsfield 4	d	07 23							07 35									07 53	07 53					
Haywards Heath 3	a	07 28							07 40	07 35	07 47	07 47						07 58	07 58					
	d	07 32							07 44		07 48	07 48						08 02	08 02					
Balcombe	d	07 37																						
Horsham 4	d							07 30									07 50							08 00
Littlehaven	d							07 33																08 03
Faygate	d																							
Ifield	d							07 39																08 09
Crawley	d							07 43									07 59							08 13
Three Bridges 4	a	07 42						07 46			07 56	07 56					08 02	08 11	08 11					08 16
	d	07 42						07 48			07 57	07 57					08 03	08 12	08 12					08 18
Gatwick Airport 10 ✈	a	07 47					07 51	07 52	07 55		08 01	08 01					08 07	08 16	08 16					08 22
	d	07 47				07 50	07 53	07 53	07 56		08 02	08 02	08 03			08 05	08 08	08 17	08 16				08 20	08 23
Horley 4	d							07 56																08 26
Salfords	d																							08 30
Earlswood (Surrey)	d																							08 33
Tonbridge 4	d			07 19																				
Leigh (Kent)	d			07 23																				
Penshurst	d			07 27																				
Edenbridge	d			07 33																				
Godstone	d			07 40																				
Nutfield	d			07 45																				
Reigate	d																				08 14	08 19		
Redhill 5	a			07 50				08 02					08 10				08 15				08 18	08 25		08 36
	d			07 51				08 07									08 16				08 19			08 37
Merstham	d							08 11													08 23			08 41
Coulsdon South	d			07 58				08 16													08 28			08 46
Purley 4	d			08 02				08 19													08 32			08 49
East Croydon	a	08 02	07 52	08 07			08 08	08 24	08 11		08 16	08 16					08 27	08 31	08 31	08 22	08 37			08 54
	d	08 02	07 53	08 07			08 08	08 25	08 12		08 17	08 17		08 14			08 28	08 32	08 32	08 23	08 37			08 55
Norwood Junction 2	a			08 12				08 29													08 42			08 59
New Cross Gate	d							08 37																09 07
London Bridge 4 ⊖	a	08 15		08 25				08 43			08 30	08 32						08 45	08 47		08 55			09 13
London Blackfriars 3 ⊖	a	08 22									08 37							08 52						
City Thameslink 3	a																							
Farringdon 3 ⊖	a	08 29									08 43							08 59						
St Pancras International 15 ⊖	a	08 34									08 48							09 04						
St Albans City	a	08 54									09 08							09 24						
Luton Airport Parkway 4 ✈	a	09 07									09 20							09 37						
Luton 7	a	09 10									09 23							09 40						
Bedford 10	a	09 35									09 49							10 05						
Clapham Junction 10	a		08 02				08 17		08 21					08 25			08 37			08 32				
London Victoria 15 ⊖	a		08 10			08 20	08 24		08 28					08 32		08 35	08 44			08 40			08 50	

A 19 May

Table 186

Brighton - London and Bedford

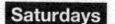

Network Diagram - see first Page of Table 186

		SN	SN	FC	FC	GW	SN	SN	SN	FC		FC	SN	SN	SN	SN	SN	SN	SN	FC		FC	GW	SN	SN
		◇1	◇1	1	1	1	1	1	◇1	1		1	◇1	1	1	◇1	1	◇1	◇1	1		1	1	1	1
					A					A												A			
								🚲					🚲		🚲										🚲
Brighton 10	d			08 04	08 04					08 07		08 07	08 19			08 24				08 34		08 34			
Hove 2	d		07 51																08 21						
Preston Park	d		07 55							08 11		08 11													
Hassocks 4	d									08 17		08 17				08 34									
Burgess Hill 4	d		08 04							08 21		08 21				08 38									
Lewes 4	d	07 50																08 20							
Wivelsfield 4	d									08 23		08 23						08 35							
Haywards Heath 3	a	08 05	08 09	08 17	08 17					08 28		08 28						08 40	08 35	08 47		08 47			
	d	08 13		08 18	08 18					08 32		08 32						08 44		08 48		08 48			
Balcombe	d									08 37		08 37													
Horsham 4	d								08 20								08 30								
Littlehaven	d																08 33								
Faygate	d																								
Ifield	d																08 39								
Crawley	d								08 29								08 43								
Three Bridges 4	a			08 26	08 26				08 32	08 42		08 42					08 46			08 56		08 56			
	d			08 27	08 27				08 33	08 42		08 42					08 48			08 57		08 57			
Gatwick Airport 10 ✈	a	08 24		08 31	08 31				08 37	08 46		08 47				08 51	08 52	08 55		09 01		09 01			
	d	08 25		08 32	08 32			08 35	08 38	08 46		08 47			08 50	08 53	08 53	08 56		09 02		09 02	09 03		09 05
Horley 4	d								08 41								08 56								
Salfords	d																								
Earlswood (Surrey)	d																								
Tonbridge 4	d													08 19											
Leigh (Kent)	d													08 23											
Penshurst	d													08 27											
Edenbridge	d													08 33											
Godstone	d													08 40											
Nutfield	d													08 45											
Reigate	d					08 34																			
Redhill 5	a					08 38			08 47					08 50			09 02						09 10		
	d								08 48					08 51			09 07								
Merstham	d																09 11								
Coulsdon South	d													08 58			09 16								
Purley 4	d													09 02			09 19								
East Croydon 🚋	a	08 40		08 46	08 46				08 59	09 01		09 02	08 52	09 07		09 08	09 24	09 11		09 16		09 16			
	d	08 40		08 47	08 47		08 44		09 00	09 01		09 02	08 53	09 07		09 08	09 25	09 12		09 17		09 17		09 14	
Norwood Junction 2	a													09 12			09 29								
New Cross Gate	d																09 37								
London Bridge 4 ⊖	a			09 00	09 02					09 17		09 15		09 25			09 43			09 30		09 32			
London Blackfriars 3 ⊖	a			09 07								09 22								09 37					
City Thameslink 3	a			09 10								09 26								09 40					
Farringdon 3 ⊖	a			09 14								09 30								09 44					
St Pancras International 15 ⊖	a			09 18								09 34								09 48					
St Albans City	a			09 38								09 54								10 08					
Luton Airport Parkway 4 ✈	a			09 50								10 07								10 20					
Luton 7	a			09 53								10 10								10 23					
Bedford 10	a			10 19								10 35								10 49					
Clapham Junction 10	a	08 50					08 55		09 09				09 02			09 17		09 21						09 25	
London Victoria 15 ⊖	a	08 57					09 02	09 05	09 16				09 10		09 20	09 24		09 28						09 32	09 35

A 19 May

Table 186

Saturdays

until 23 June

Brighton - London and Bedford

Network Diagram - see first Page of Table 186

		SN	FC	FC	SN	SN		GW	SN	SN	SN	FC	FC	GW	SN	SN		SN	FC	FC	SN	SN	SN	SN	SN
		◇1	1	1	◇1	1		1	1	1	◇1	1	1	1	1	1		◇1	1	1	◇1	1	1	◇1	1
				A									A						A						
Brighton 10	d		08 37	08 37	08 49							09 04	09 04						09 07	09 07	09 19			09 24	
Hove 2	d																								
Preston Park	d		08 41	08 41															09 11	09 11					
Hassocks 4	d		08 47	08 47															09 17	09 17				09 34	
Burgess Hill 4	d		08 51	08 51															09 21	09 21				09 38	
Lewes 4	d										08 50														
Wivelsfield 4	d		08 53	08 53															09 23	09 23					
Haywards Heath 3	a		08 58	08 58							09 05	09 17	09 17						09 28	09 28					
	d		09 02	09 02							09 13	09 18	09 18						09 32	09 32					
Balcombe	d																		09 37	09 37					
Horsham 4	d	08 50								09 00								09 20							09 30
Littlehaven	d									09 03															09 33
Faygate	d																								
Ifield	d									09 09															09 39
Crawley	d	08 59								09 13								09 29							09 43
Three Bridges 4	a	09 02	09 11	09 11						09 16		09 26	09 26					09 32	09 42	09 42					09 46
	d	09 03	09 12	09 12						09 18		09 27	09 27					09 33	09 42	09 42					09 48
Gatwick Airport 10 ✈	a	09 07	09 16	09 16						09 22	09 24	09 31	09 31					09 37	09 46	09 47				09 51	09 52
	d	09 08	09 17	09 16					09 20	09 23	09 25	09 32	09 32			09 35		09 38	09 46	09 47			09 50	09 53	09 53
Horley 4	d									09 26								09 41							09 56
Salfords	d									09 30															
Earlswood (Surrey)	d									09 33															
Tonbridge 4	d																					09 19			
Leigh (Kent)	d																					09 23			
Penshurst	d																					09 27			
Edenbridge	d																					09 33			
Godstone	d																					09 40			
Nutfield	d																					09 45			
Reigate	d					09 14		09 18						09 34											
Redhill 5	a	09 15				09 18		09 25		09 36				09 38				09 47				09 50			10 02
	d	09 16				09 19				09 37								09 48				09 51			10 07
Merstham	d					09 23				09 41															10 11
Coulsdon South	d					09 28				09 46												09 58			10 16
Purley 4	d					09 32				09 49												10 02			10 19
East Croydon	a	09 27	09 31	09 31	09 22	09 37				09 54	09 40	09 46	09 46					09 59	10 01	10 02	09 52	10 07		10 08	10 24
	d	09 28	09 32	09 32	09 23	09 37				09 55	09 40	09 47	09 47		09 44			10 00	10 01	10 02	09 53	10 07		10 08	10 25
Norwood Junction 2	a					09 42				09 59												10 12			10 29
New Cross Gate	d									10 07															10 37
London Bridge 4 ⊖	a		09 45	09 47		09 55				10 13		10 00	10 02						10 17	10 15		10 25			10 43
London Blackfriars 3 ⊖	a		09 52									10 07								10 22					
City Thameslink 3	a		09 56									10 10								10 26					
Farringdon 3 ⊖	a		10 00									10 14								10 30					
St Pancras International 15 ⊖	a		10 04									10 18								10 34					
St Albans City	a		10 24									10 38								10 54					
Luton Airport Parkway 4 ✈	a		10 37									10 50								11 07					
Luton 7	a		10 40									10 53								11 10					
Bedford 10	a		11 05									11 19								11 35					
Clapham Junction 10	a	09 37			09 32						09 50				09 55			10 09			10 02			10 17	
London Victoria 15 ⊖	a	09 44			09 40				09 50		09 57				10 02	10 05		10 16			10 10		10 20	10 24	

A 19 May

Table 186

Saturdays

until 23 June

Brighton - London and Bedford

Network Diagram - see first Page of Table 186

		SN	SN	FC	FC	GW	SN	SN	SN	FC	FC	SN	SN	GW	SN	SN	SN	SN	FC	FC	GW	SN
		◇1	◇1	1	1	1	1	1	◇1	1	1	◇1	1	1	1	1	◇1	◇1	1	1	1	1
					A						A									A		
								⊥	⊥			⊥			⊥							
Brighton 10	d			09 34	09 34					09 37	09 37	09 49							10 04	10 04		
Hove 2	d		09 21															09 51				
Preston Park	d									09 41	09 41							09 55				
Hassocks 4	d									09 47	09 47											
Burgess Hill 4	d									09 51	09 51							10 04				
Lewes 4	d	09 20															09 50					
Wivelsfield 4	d	09 35								09 53	09 53											
Haywards Heath 3	a	09 40	09 35	09 47	09 47					09 58	09 58						10 05	10 09	10 17	10 17		
	d	09 44		09 48	09 48					10 02	10 02						10 13		10 18	10 18		
Balcombe	d																					
Horsham 4	d								09 50							10 00						
Littlehaven	d															10 03						
Faygate	d																					
Ifield	d															10 09						
Crawley	d								09 59							10 13						
Three Bridges 4	a			09 56	09 56				10 02	10 11	10 11					10 16			10 26	10 26		
	d			09 57	09 57				10 03	10 12	10 12					10 18			10 27	10 27		
Gatwick Airport 10 ✈	a	09 55		10 01	10 01				10 07	10 16	10 16					10 22	10 24		10 31	10 31		
	d	09 56		10 02	10 02	10 03		10 05	10 08	10 17	10 16				10 20	10 23	10 25		10 32	10 32		
Horley 4	d															10 26						
Salfords	d															10 30						
Earlswood (Surrey)	d															10 33						
Tonbridge 4	d																					
Leigh (Kent)	d																					
Penshurst	d																					
Edenbridge	d																					
Godstone	d																					
Lingfield	d																					
Reigate	d												10 14	10 19							10 34	
Redhill 5	a					10 10			10 15				10 18	10 25		10 36					10 38	
	d								10 16				10 19			10 37						
Merstham	d												10 23			10 41						
Coulsdon South	d												10 28			10 46						
Purley 4	d												10 32			10 49						
East Croydon	a	10 11		10 16	10 16				10 27	10 31	10 31	10 22	10 37			10 54	10 40		10 46	10 46		
	d	10 12		10 17	10 17		10 14		10 28	10 32	10 32	10 23	10 37			10 55	10 40		10 47	10 47		10 44
Norwood Junction 2	a												10 42			10 59						
New Cross Gate	d															11 07						
London Bridge 4 ⊖	a			10 30	10 32					10 45	10 47		10 55			11 13			11 00	11 02		
London Blackfriars 3 ⊖	a			10 37						10 52									11 07			
City Thameslink 3	a			10 40						10 56									11 10			
Farringdon 3 ⊖	a			10 44						11 00									11 14			
St Pancras International 15 ⊖	a			10 48						11 04									11 18			
St Albans City	a			11 08						11 24									11 38			
Luton Airport Parkway 4 ✈	a			11 20						11 37									11 50			
Luton 7	a			11 23						11 40									11 53			
Bedford 10	a			11 49						12 05									12 19			
Clapham Junction 10	a	10 21					10 25		10 37			10 32					10 50					10 55
London Victoria 15 ⊖	a	10 28					10 32	10 35	10 44			10 40			10 50		10 57					11 02

A 19 May

Table 186

Saturdays
until 23 June

Brighton - London and Bedford

Network Diagram - see first Page of Table 186

		SN	SN	FC	FC	SN	SN	SN	SN		SN	SN	SN	FC	FC	GW	SN	SN	SN		FC	FC	SN	SN	GW
		1	◇1	1	1	◇1	1	1	◇1		1	◇1	◇1	1	1	1	1	1	◇1		1	1	◇1	1	1
				A											A							A			
		🚲				🚲		🚲										🚲	🚲				🚲		
Brighton 10	d			10 07	10 07	10 19			10 24					10 34	10 34						10 37	10 37	10 49		
Hove 2	d												10 21												
Preston Park	d			10 11	10 11																10 41	10 41			
Hassocks 4	d			10 17	10 17				10 34												10 47	10 47			
Burgess Hill 4	d			10 21	10 21				10 38												10 51	10 51			
Lewes 4	d											10 20													
Wivelsfield 4	d			10 23	10 23							10 35									10 53	10 53			
Haywards Heath 3	a			10 28	10 28							10 40	10 35	10 47	10 47						10 58	10 58			
	d			10 32	10 32								10 44	10 48	10 48						11 02	11 02			
Balcombe	d			10 37	10 37																				
Horsham 4	d		10 20								10 30								10 50						
Littlehaven	d										10 33														
Faygate	d																								
Ifield	d										10 39														
Crawley	d		10 29								10 43								10 59						
Three Bridges 4	a		10 32	10 42	10 42						10 46			10 56	10 56				11 02		11 11	11 11			
	d		10 33	10 42	10 42						10 48			10 57	10 57				11 03		11 12	11 12			
Gatwick Airport 10 ✈	a		10 37	10 46	10 47				10 51		10 52		10 55	11 01	11 01				11 07		11 16	11 16			
	d	10 35	10 38	10 46	10 47			10 50	10 53		10 53		10 56	11 02	11 02	11 03		11 05	11 08		11 17	11 16			
Horley 4	d		10 41								10 56														
Salfords	d																								
Earlswood (Surrey)	d																								
Tonbridge 4	d						10 19																		
Leigh (Kent)	d						10 23																		
Penshurst	d						10 27																		
Edenbridge	d						10 33																		
Godstone	d						10 40																		
Nutfield	d						10 45																		
Reigate	d																							11 14	11 18
Redhill 5	a		10 47				10 50				11 02					11 10			11 15					11 18	11 25
	d		10 48				10 51				11 07								11 16					11 19	
Merstham	d										11 11													11 23	
Coulsdon South	d						10 58				11 16													11 28	
Purley 4	d						11 02				11 19													11 32	
East Croydon	a		10 59	11 01	11 02	10 52	11 07		11 08		11 24		11 11	11 16	11 16				11 27		11 31	11 31	11 22	11 37	
	d		11 00	11 01	11 02	10 53	11 07		11 08		11 25		11 12	11 17	11 17		11 14		11 28		11 32	11 32	11 23	11 37	
Norwood Junction 2	a						11 12				11 29													11 42	
New Cross Gate	d										11 37														
London Bridge 4 ⊖	a			11 17	11 15		11 25				11 43			11 30	11 32						11 45	11 47		11 55	
London Blackfriars 3 ⊖	a				11 22									11 37							11 52				
City Thameslink 3	a				11 26									11 40							11 56				
Farringdon 3 ⊖	a				11 30									11 44							12 00				
St Pancras International 15 ⊖	a				11 34									11 48							12 04				
St Albans City	a				11 54									12 08							12 24				
Luton Airport Parkway 4 ✈	a				12 07									12 20							12 37				
Luton 7	a				12 10									12 23							12 40				
Bedford 10	a				12 35									12 49							13 05				
Clapham Junction 10	a		11 09			11 02			11 17				11 21				11 25		11 37				11 32		
London Victoria 15 ⊖	a	11 05	11 16			11 10		11 20	11 24				11 28				11 32	11 35	11 44				11 40		

A 19 May

Table 186

Brighton - London and Bedford

Saturdays

until 23 June

Network Diagram - see first Page of Table 186

Station		SN 1	SN 1	SN ◇1	SN ◇1		FC 1	FC 1 A	GW 1	SN 1	SN 1	SN ◇1	FC 1 A	FC 1	SN ◇1		SN 1	SN 1	SN ◇1	SN 1	SN ◇1	SN ◇1	FC 1	FC 1 A	GW 1
Brighton 10	d						11 04	11 04					11 07	11 07	11 19				11 24				11 34	11 34	
Hove 2	d				10 51																	11 21			
Preston Park	d				10 55								11 11	11 11											
Hassocks 4	d												11 17	11 17					11 34						
Burgess Hill 4	d				11 04								11 21	11 21					11 38						
Lewes 4	d			10 50																	11 20				
Wivelsfield 4	d												11 23	11 23							11 35				
Haywards Heath 3	a			11 05	11 09		11 17	11 17					11 28	11 28							11 40	11 35	11 47	11 47	
	d			11 13			11 18	11 18					11 32	11 32							11 44		11 48	11 48	
Balcombe	d												11 37	11 37											
Horsham 4	d		11 00									11 20								11 30					
Littlehaven	d		11 03																	11 33					
Faygate	d																								
field	d		11 09																	11 39					
Crawley	d		11 13									11 29								11 43					
Three Bridges 4	a		11 16				11 26	11 26				11 32	11 42	11 42						11 46			11 56	11 56	
	d		11 18				11 27	11 27				11 33	11 42	11 42						11 48			11 57	11 57	
Gatwick Airport 10 ✈	a		11 22	11 24			11 31	11 31				11 37	11 46	11 47					11 51	11 52	11 55		12 01	12 01	
	d	11 20	11 23	11 25			11 32	11 32			11 35	11 38	11 46	11 47				11 50	11 53	11 53	11 56		12 02	12 02	12 03
Horley 4	d		11 26									11 41								11 56					
Salfords	d		11 30																						
Earlswood (Surrey)	d		11 33																						
Tonbridge 4	d																11 19								
Leigh (Kent)	d																11 23								
Penshurst	d																11 27								
Edenbridge	d																11 33								
Godstone	d																11 40								
Nutfield	d																11 45								
Reigate	d								11 34																
Redhill 5	a		11 36						11 38			11 47					11 50			12 02					12 10
	d		11 37									11 48					11 51			12 07					
Merstham	d		11 41																	12 11					
Coulsdon South	d		11 46														11 58			12 16					
Purley 4	d		11 49														12 02			12 19					
East Croydon	a		11 54	11 40			11 46	11 46				11 59	12 01	12 02	11 52		12 07		12 08	12 24	12 11		12 16	12 16	
	d		11 55	11 40			11 47	11 47		11 44		12 00	12 01	12 02	11 53		12 07		12 08	12 25	12 12		12 17	12 17	
Norwood Junction 2	a		11 59														12 12			12 29					
New Cross Gate	d		12 07																	12 37					
London Bridge 4 ⊖	a		12 13				12 00	12 02					12 17	12 15			12 25			12 43			12 30	12 32	
London Blackfriars 3 ⊖	a						12 07							12 22									12 37		
City Thameslink 3	a						12 10							12 26									12 40		
Farringdon 3 ⊖	a						12 14							12 30									12 44		
St Pancras hternational 15 ⊖	a						12 18							12 34									12 48		
St Albans City	a						12 38							12 54									13 08		
Luton Airport Parkway 4 ✈	a						12 50							13 07									13 20		
Luton 7	a						12 53							13 10									13 23		
Bedford 10	a						13 19							13 35									13 49		
Clapham Junction 10	a			11 50						11 55		12 09			12 02				12 17		12 21				
London Victoria 15 ⊖	a	11 50		11 57						12 02	12 05	12 16			12 10			12 20	12 24		12 28				

A 19 May

Table 186

Saturdays

until 23 June

Brighton - London and Bedford

Network Diagram - see first Page of Table 186

		SN	SN	SN	FC	FC	SN	SN	GW	SN	SN	SN	SN	FC	FC	GW	SN	SN	SN	FC	FC	SN
		1	1	◇1	1	1	◇1	1	1	1	1	◇1	◇1	1	1	1	1	1	◇1	1	1	◇1
						A									A					A		
			⚲	⚲			⚲			⚲								⚲				⚲
Brighton 10	d				11 37	11 37	11 49							12 04	12 04					12 07	12 07	12 19
Hove 2	d												11 51									
Preston Park	d				11 41	11 41							11 55							12 11	12 11	
Hassocks 4	d				11 47	11 47														12 17	12 17	
Burgess Hill 4	d				11 51	11 51							12 04							12 21	12 21	
Lewes 4	d											11 50										
Wivelsfield 4	d				11 53	11 53														12 23	12 23	
Haywards Heath 3	a				11 58	11 58						12 05	12 09	12 17	12 17					12 28	12 28	
	d				12 02	12 02						12 13		12 18	12 18					12 32	12 32	
Balcombe	d																			12 37	12 37	
Horsham 4	d			11 50							12 00								12 20			
Littlehaven	d										12 03											
Faygate	d																					
Ifield	d										12 09											
Crawley	d			11 59							12 13								12 29			
Three Bridges 4	a			12 02	12 11	12 11					12 16			12 26	12 26				12 32	12 42	12 42	
	d			12 03	12 12	12 12					12 18			12 27	12 27				12 33	12 42	12 42	
Gatwick Airport 10 ✈	a			12 07	12 16	12 16					12 22	12 24		12 31	12 31				12 37	12 46	12 47	
	d		12 05	12 08	12 17	12 16				12 20	12 23	12 25		12 32	12 32			12 35	12 38	12 46	12 47	
Horley 4	d										12 26								12 41			
Salfords	d										12 30											
Earlswood (Surrey)	d										12 33											
Tonbridge 4	d																					
Leigh (Kent)	d																					
Penshurst	d																					
Edenbridge	d																					
Godstone	d																					
Nutfield	d																					
Reigate	d							12 14	12 19							12 34						
Redhill 5	a			12 15				12 18	12 25		12 36					12 38			12 47			
	d			12 16				12 19			12 37								12 48			
Merstham	d							12 23			12 41											
Coulsdon South	d							12 28			12 46											
Purley 4	d							12 32			12 49											
East Croydon 🚋	a			12 27	12 31	12 31	12 22	12 37			12 54	12 40		12 46	12 46				12 59	13 01	13 02	12 52
	d	12 14		12 28	12 32	12 32	12 23	12 38			12 55	12 40		12 47	12 47		12 44		13 00	13 01	13 02	12 53
Norwood Junction 2	a							12 42			12 59											
New Cross Gate	d										13 07											
London Bridge 4 ⊖	a				12 45	12 47		12 55			13 13			13 00	13 02					13 17	13 15	
London Blackfriars 3 ⊖	a				12 52									13 07							13 22	
City Thameslink 3	a				12 56									13 10							13 26	
Farringdon 3 ⊖	a				13 00									13 14							13 30	
St Pancras International 15 ⊖	a				13 04									13 18							13 34	
St Albans City	a				13 24									13 38							13 54	
Luton Airport Parkway 4 ✈	a				13 37									13 50							14 07	
Luton 7	a				13 40									13 53							14 10	
Bedford 10	a				14 05									14 19							14 35	
Clapham Junction 10	a	12 25		12 37			12 32					12 50					12 55		13 09			13 02
London Victoria 15 ⊖	a	12 32	12 35	12 44			12 40			12 50		12 57					13 02	13 05	13 16			13 10

A 19 May

Table 186

Saturdays

until 23 June

Brighton - London and Bedford

Network Diagram - see first Page of Table 186

		SN	SN	SN	SN	SN	SN		FC	FC	GW	SN	SN	SN	FC	FC	SN		SN	GW	SN	SN	SN	SN	FC
		1	1	◇1	1	◇1	◇1		1	1	1	1	1	◇1	1	1	◇1		1	1	1	1	◇1	◇1	1
										A						A									
			trolley										trolley	trolley			trolley				trolley				
Brighton [10]	d			12 24					12 34	12 34					12 37	12 37	12 49								13 04
Hove [2]	d						12 21																	12 51	
Preston Park	d														12 41	12 41								12 55	
Hassocks [4]	d			12 34											12 47	12 47									
Burgess Hill [4]	d			12 38											12 51	12 51								13 04	
Lewes [4]	d					12 20																	12 50		
Wivelsfield [4]	d					12 35									12 53	12 53									
Haywards Heath [3]	a					12 40	12 35		12 47	12 47					12 58	12 58							13 05	13 09	13 17
	d					12 44			12 48	12 48					13 02	13 02							13 13		13 18
Balcombe	d																								
Horsham [4]	d				12 30									12 50								13 00			
Littlehaven	d				12 33																	13 03			
Faygate	d																								
Ifield	d				12 39																	13 09			
Crawley	d				12 43									12 59								13 13			
Three Bridges [4]	a				12 46				12 56	12 56				13 02	13 11	13 11						13 16			13 26
	d				12 48				12 57	12 57				13 03	13 12	13 12						13 18			13 27
Gatwick Airport [10] ✈	a			12 51	12 52	12 55			13 01	13 01				13 07	13 16	13 16						13 22	13 24		13 31
	d		12 50	12 53	12 53	12 56			13 02	13 02	13 03		13 05	13 08	13 17	13 16					13 20	13 23	13 25		13 32
Horley [4]	d				12 56																	13 26			
Salfords	d																					13 30			
Earlswood (Surrey)	d																					13 33			
Tonbridge [4]	d	12 19																							
Leigh (Kent)	d	12 23																							
Penshurst	d	12 27																							
Edenbridge	d	12 33																							
Godstone	d	12 40																							
Nutfield	d	12 45																							
Reigate	d																		13 14	13 18					
Redhill [5]	a	12 50			13 02						13 10			13 15					13 18	13 25		13 36			
	d	12 51			13 07									13 16					13 19			13 37			
Merstham	d				13 11														13 23			13 41			
Coulsdon South	d	12 58			13 16														13 28			13 46			
Purley [4]	d	13 02			13 19														13 32			13 49			
East Croydon	a	13 07		13 08	13 24	13 11			13 16	13 16				13 27	13 31	13 31	13 22		13 37			13 54	13 40		13 46
	d	13 07		13 08	13 25	13 12			13 17	13 17		13 14		13 28	13 32	13 32	13 23		13 37			13 55	13 40		13 47
Norwood Junction [2]	a	13 12			13 29														13 42			13 59			
New Cross Gate	d				13 37																	14 07			
London Bridge [4] ⊖	a	13 25			13 43				13 30	13 32					13 45	13 47			13 55			14 13			14 00
London Blackfriars [3] ⊖	a								13 37						13 52										14 07
City Thameslink [3]	a								13 40						13 56										14 10
Farringdon [3] ⊖	a								13 44						14 00										14 14
St Pancras International [15] ⊖	a								13 48						14 04										14 18
St Albans City	a								14 08						14 24										14 38
Luton Airport Parkway [4] ✈	a								14 20						14 37										14 50
Luton [7]	a								14 23						14 40										14 53
Bedford [10]	a								14 49						15 05										15 19
Clapham Junction [10]	a			13 17		13 21						13 25		13 37			13 32						13 50		
London Victoria [15] ⊖	a		13 20	13 24		13 28						13 32	13 35	13 44			13 40				13 50		13 57		

A 19 May

Table 186

Saturdays

until 23 June

Brighton - London and Bedford

Network Diagram - see first Page of Table 186

		FC	GW		SN	SN	SN	FC	FC	SN	SN	SN	SN		SN	SN	SN	FC	FC	GW	SN	SN	SN		FC
		1	1		1	1	◇1	1	1	◇1	1	1	◇1		1	◇1	◇1	1	1	1	1	1	◇1		1
		A						A											A						
						🛒				🛒		🛒										🛒	🛒		
Brighton 10	d	13 04						13 07	13 07	13 19			13 24					13 34	13 34						13 37
Hove 2	d																13 21								
Preston Park	d							13 11	13 11																13 41
Hassocks 4	d							13 17	13 17				13 34												13 47
Burgess Hill 4	d							13 21	13 21				13 38												13 51
Lewes 4	d															13 20									
Wivelsfield 4	d							13 23	13 23							13 35									13 53
Haywards Heath 3	a	13 17						13 28	13 28							13 40	13 35	13 47	13 47						13 58
	d	13 18						13 32	13 32							13 44	13 44	13 48	13 48						14 02
Balcombe	d							13 37	13 37																
Horsham 4	d						13 20								13 30								13 50		
Littlehaven	d														13 33										
Faygate	d																								
Ifield	d														13 39										
Crawley	d						13 29								13 43								13 59		
Three Bridges 4	a	13 26					13 32	13 42	13 42						13 46			13 56	13 56				14 02		14 11
	d	13 27					13 33	13 42	13 42						13 48			13 57	13 57				14 03		14 12
Gatwick Airport 10 ✈	a	13 31					13 37	13 46	13 47				13 51		13 52	13 55		14 01	14 01				14 07		14 16
	d	13 32				13 35	13 38	13 46	13 47			13 50	13 53		13 53	13 56		14 02	14 02	14 03		14 05	14 08		14 17
Horley 4	d						13 41								13 56										
Salfords	d																								
Earlswood (Surrey)	d																								
Tonbridge 4	d										13 19														
Leigh (Kent)	d										13 23														
Penshurst	d										13 27														
Edenbridge	d										13 33														
Godstone	d										13 40														
Nutfield	d										13 45														
Reigate	d		13 34																						
Redhill 5	a		13 38				13 47				13 50				14 02					14 10			14 15		
	d						13 48				13 51				14 07								14 16		
Merstham	d														14 11										
Coulsdon South	d										13 58				14 16										
Purley 4	d										14 02				14 19										
East Croydon 🚋	a	13 46					13 59	14 01	14 02	13 52	14 07		14 08		14 24	14 11		14 16	14 16				14 27		14 31
	d	13 47			13 44		14 00	14 01	14 02	13 53	14 07		14 08		14 25	14 12		14 17	14 17		14 14		14 28		14 32
Norwood Junction 2	a										14 12				14 29										
New Cross Gate	d														14 37										
London Bridge 4 ⊖	a	14 02						14 17	14 15		14 25				14 43			14 30	14 32						14 45
London Blackfriars 3 ⊖	a								14 22									14 37							14 52
City Thameslink 3	a								14 26									14 40							14 56
Farringdon 3 ⊖	a								14 30									14 44							15 00
St Pancras International 15 ⊖	a								14 34									14 48							15 04
St Albans City	a								14 54									15 08							15 24
Luton Airport Parkway 4 ✈	a								15 07									15 20							15 37
Luton 7	a								15 10									15 23							15 40
Bedford 10	a								15 35									15 49							16 05
Clapham Junction 10	a				13 55		14 09			14 02			14 17			14 21					14 25		14 37		
London Victoria 15 ⊖	a				14 02	14 05	14 16			14 10		14 20	14 24			14 28					14 32	14 35	14 44		

A 19 May

Table 186

Saturdays

until 23 June

Brighton - London and Bedford

Network Diagram - see first Page of Table 186

Station		FC 1 A	SN ◇1 🛒	SN 1	GW 1	SN 1 🛒	SN 1	SN ◇1	SN ◇1	FC 1	FC 1 A	GW 1	SN 1	SN 1 🛒	SN ◇1	FC 1 A	FC 1	SN ◇1 🛒	SN 1	SN 1 🛒	SN ◇1	SN 1
Brighton 10	d	13 37	13 49							14 04	14 04					14 07	14 07	14 19			14 24	
Hove 2	d								13 51													
Preston Park	d	13 41							13 55							14 11	14 11					
Hassocks 4	d	13 47														14 17	14 17				14 34	
Burgess Hill 4	d	13 51							14 04							14 21	14 21				14 38	
Lewes 4	d							13 50														
Wivelsfield 4	d	13 53														14 23	14 23					
Haywards Heath 3	a	13 58						14 05	14 09	14 17	14 17					14 28	14 28					
	d	14 02						14 13		14 18	14 18					14 32	14 32					
Balcombe	d															14 37	14 37					
Horsham 4	d						14 00								14 20							14 30
Littlehaven	d						14 03															14 33
Faygate	d																					
Ifield	d						14 09															14 39
Crawley	d						14 13								14 29							14 43
Three Bridges 4	a	14 11					14 16			14 26	14 26				14 32	14 42	14 42					14 46
	d	14 12					14 18			14 27	14 27				14 33	14 42	14 42					14 48
Gatwick Airport 10 ✈	a	14 16					14 22	14 24		14 31	14 31				14 37	14 46	14 47				14 51	14 52
	d	14 16				14 20	14 23	14 25		14 32	14 32			14 35	14 38	14 46	14 47			14 50	14 53	14 53
Horley 4	d						14 26								14 41							14 56
Salfords	d						14 30															
Earlswood (Surrey)	d						14 33															
Tonbridge 4	d																		14 19			
Leigh (Kent)	d																		14 23			
Penshurst	d																		14 27			
Edenbridge	d																		14 33			
Godstone	d																		14 40			
Nutfield	d																		14 45			
Reigate	d			14 14	14 19							14 34										
Redhill 5	a			14 18	14 25		14 36					14 38			14 47				14 50			15 02
	d			14 19			14 37								14 48				14 51			15 07
Merstham	d			14 23			14 41															15 11
Coulsdon South	d			14 28			14 46												14 58			15 16
Purley 4	d			14 32			14 49												15 02			15 19
East Croydon	a	14 31	14 22	14 37			14 54	14 40		14 46	14 46				14 59	15 01	15 02	14 52	15 07		15 08	15 24
	d	14 32	14 23	14 37			14 55	14 40		14 47	14 47		14 44		15 00	15 01	15 02	14 53	15 07		15 08	15 25
Norwood Junction 2	a			14 42			14 59												15 12			15 29
New Cross Gate	d						15 07															15 37
London Bridge 4 ⊖	a	14 47		14 55			15 13			15 00	15 02					15 17	15 15		15 25			15 43
London Blackfriars 3 ⊖	a									15 07							15 22					
City Thameslink 3	a									15 10							15 26					
Farringdon 3 ⊖	a									15 14							15 30					
St Pancras International 15 ⊖	a									15 18							15 34					
St Albans City	a									15 38							15 54					
Luton Airport Parkway 4 ✈	a									15 50							16 07					
Luton 7	a									15 53							16 10					
Bedford 10	a									16 19							16 35					
Clapham Junction 10	a		14 32					14 50					14 55		15 09			15 02			15 17	
London Victoria 15 ⊖	a		14 40			14 50		14 57					15 02	15 05	15 16			15 10		15 20	15 24	

A 19 May

Brighton - London and Bedford

Network Diagram - see first Page of Table 186

		SN	SN	FC	FC	GW		SN	SN	SN	FC	FC	SN	SN	GW	SN		SN	SN	SN	FC	FC	GW	SN	SN
		◇1	◇1	1	1	1		1	1	◇1	1	1	◇1	1	1	1		1	◇1	◇1	1	1	1	1	1
					A							A										A			
									🚲	🚲			🚲			🚲									🚲
Brighton 10	d			14 34	14 34						14 37	14 37	14 49								15 04	15 04			
Hove 2	d		14 21																	14 51					
Preston Park	d										14 41	14 41								14 55					
Hassocks 4	d										14 47	14 47													
Burgess Hill 4	d										14 51	14 51								15 04					
Lewes 4	d	14 20																	14 50						
Wivelsfield 4	d	14 35									14 53	14 53													
Haywards Heath 3	a	14 40	14 35	14 47	14 47						14 58	14 58							15 05	15 09	15 17	15 17			
	d		14 44	14 48	14 48						15 02	15 02								15 13	15 18	15 18			
Balcombe	d																								
Horsham 4	d									14 50								15 00							
Littlehaven	d																	15 03							
Faygate	d																								
Ifield	d																	15 09							
Crawley	d									14 59								15 13							
Three Bridges 4	a			14 56	14 56					15 02	15 11	15 11						15 16			15 26	15 26			
	d			14 57	14 57					15 03	15 12	15 12						15 18			15 27	15 27			
Gatwick Airport 10 ✈	a		14 55	15 01	15 01					15 07	15 16	15 16						15 22		15 24	15 31	15 31			
	d		14 56	15 02	15 02	15 03			15 05	15 08	15 17	15 16				15 20		15 23		15 25	15 32	15 32			15 35
Horley 4	d																	15 26							
Salfords	d																	15 30							
Earlswood (Surrey)	d																	15 33							
Tonbridge 4	d																								
Leigh (Kent)	d																								
Penshurst	d																								
Edenbridge	d																								
Godstone	d																								
Nutfield	d																								
Reigate	d													15 14	15 18								15 34		
Redhill 5	a					15 10				15 15				15 18	15 25			15 36					15 38		
	d									15 16				15 19				15 37							
Merstham	d													15 23				15 41							
Coulsdon South	d													15 28				15 46							
Purley 4	d													15 32				15 49							
East Croydon 🚌	a		15 11	15 16	15 16					15 27	15 31	15 31	15 22	15 37				15 54		15 40	15 46	15 46			
	d		15 12	15 17	15 17			15 14		15 28	15 32	15 32	15 23	15 37				15 55		15 40	15 47	15 47		15 44	
Norwood Junction 2	a													15 42				15 59							
New Cross Gate	d																	16 07							
London Bridge 4 ⊖	a			15 30	15 32						15 45	15 47		15 55				16 13			16 00	16 02			
London Blackfriars 3 ⊖	a			15 37							15 52										16 07				
City Thameslink 3	a			15 40							15 56										16 10				
Farringdon 3 ⊖	a			15 44							16 00										16 14				
St Pancras International 15 ⊖	a			15 48							16 04										16 18				
St Albans City	a			16 08							16 24										16 38				
Luton Airport Parkway 4 ✈	a			16 20							16 37										16 50				
Luton 7	a			16 23							16 40										16 53				
Bedford 10	a			16 49							17 05										17 19				
Clapham Junction 10	a		15 21					15 25		15 37			15 32							15 50				15 55	
London Victoria 15 ⊖	a		15 28					15 32	15 35	15 44			15 40			15 50				15 57				16 02	16 05

A 19 May

Table 186

Saturdays

until 23 June

Brighton - London and Bedford

Network Diagram - see first Page of Table 186

		SN		FC	FC	SN	SN	SN	SN	SN	SN	SN		FC	FC	GW	SN	SN	SN	FC	FC	SN		SN	GW
		◇1		1	1	◇1	1	1	◇1	1	◇1	◇1		1	1	1	1	1	◇1	1	1	◇1		1	1
				A											A						A				
						🚲		🚲										🚲	🚲			🚲			
Brighton 10	d			15 07	15 07	15 19			15 24					15 34	15 34					15 37	15 37	15 49			
Hove 2	d											15 21													
Preston Park	d			15 11	15 11															15 41	15 41				
Hassocks 4	d			15 17	15 17				15 34											15 47	15 47				
Burgess Hill 4	d			15 21	15 21				15 38											15 51	15 51				
Lewes 4	d										15 20														
Wivelsfield 4	d			15 23	15 23						15 35									15 53	15 53				
Haywards Heath 3	a			15 28	15 28						15 40	15 35		15 47	15 47					15 58	15 58				
	d			15 32	15 32						15 44			15 48	15 48					16 02	16 02				
Balcombe	d			15 37	15 37																				
Horsham 4	d	15 20								15 30									15 50						
Littlehaven	d									15 33															
Faygate	d																								
Ifield	d									15 39															
Crawley	d	15 29								15 43									15 59						
Three Bridges 4	a	15 32		15 42	15 42					15 46				15 56	15 56				16 02	16 11	16 11				
	d	15 33		15 42	15 42					15 48				15 57	15 57				16 03	16 12	16 12				
Gatwick Airport 10 ✈	a	15 37		15 46	15 47				15 51	15 52	15 55			16 01	16 01				16 07	16 16	16 16				
	d	15 38		15 46	15 47			15 50	15 53	15 53	15 56			16 02	16 02	16 03		16 05	16 08	16 17	16 16				
Horley 4	d	15 41								15 56															
Salfords	d																								
Earlswood (Surrey)	d																								
Tonbridge 4	d						15 19																		
Leigh (Kent)	d						15 23																		
Penshurst	d						15 27																		
Edenbridge	d						15 33																		
Godstone	d						15 40																		
Nutfield	d						15 45																		
Reigate	d																							16 14	16 19
Redhill 5	a	15 47					15 50			16 02						16 10			16 15					16 18	16 25
	d	15 48					15 51			16 07									16 16					16 19	
Merstham	d									16 11														16 23	
Coulsdon South	d						15 58			16 16														16 28	
Purley 4	d						16 02			16 19														16 32	
East Croydon 🚌	a	15 59		16 01	16 02	15 52	16 07		16 08	16 24	16 11			16 16	16 16				16 27	16 31	16 31	16 22		16 37	
	d	16 00		16 01	16 02	15 53	16 07		16 08	16 25	16 12			16 17	16 17		16 14		16 28	16 32	16 32	16 23		16 37	
Norwood Junction 2	a						16 12			16 29														16 42	
New Cross Gate	d									16 37															
London Bridge 4 ⊖	a			16 17	16 15		16 25			16 43				16 30	16 32					16 45	16 47			16 55	
London Blackfriars 3 ⊖	a				16 22									16 37						16 52					
City Thameslink 3	a				16 26									16 40						16 56					
Farringdon 3 ⊖	a				16 30									16 44						17 00					
St Pancras International 15 ⊖	a				16 34									16 48						17 04					
St Albans City	a				16 54									17 08						17 24					
Luton Airport Parkway 4 ✈	a				17 07									17 20						17 37					
Luton 7	a				17 10									17 23						17 40					
Bedford 10	a				17 35									17 49						18 05					
Clapham Junction 10	a	16 09				16 02			16 17		16 21						16 25		16 37			16 32			
London Victoria 15 ⊖	a	16 16				16 10		16 20	16 24		16 28						16 32	16 35	16 44			16 40			

A 19 May

Table 186

Saturdays
until 23 June

Brighton - London and Bedford

Network Diagram - see first Page of Table 186

		SN	SN	SN	FC	FC	GW	SN		SN	SN	FC	FC	SN	SN	SN	SN	SN		SN	SN	FC	FC	GW	SN
		1	1	◇1	1	1	1	1		1	◇1	1	1	◇1	1	1	◇1	1		◇1	◇1	1	1	1	1
						A						A											A		
Brighton 10	d				16 04	16 04						16 07	16 07	16 19			16 24					16 34	16 34		
Hove 2	d																				16 21				
Preston Park	d											16 11	16 11												
Hassocks 4	d											16 17	16 17				16 34								
Burgess Hill 4	d											16 21	16 21				16 38								
Lewes 4	d			15 50																16 20					
Wivelsfield 4	d											16 23	16 23							16 35					
Haywards Heath 3	a			16 05	16 17	16 17						16 28	16 28							16 40	16 35	16 47	16 47		
	d			16 13	16 18	16 18						16 32	16 32							16 44		16 48	16 48		
Balcombe	d											16 37	16 37												
Horsham 4	d		16 00								16 20							16 30							
Littlehaven	d		16 03															16 33							
Faygate	d																								
Ifield	d		16 09															16 39							
Crawley	d		16 13								16 29							16 43							
Three Bridges 4	a		16 16		16 26	16 26					16 32	16 42	16 42					16 46				16 56	16 56		
	d		16 18		16 27	16 27					16 33	16 42	16 42					16 48				16 57	16 57		
Gatwick Airport 10 ✈	a		16 22	16 24	16 31	16 31					16 37	16 46	16 47				16 51	16 52		16 55		17 01	17 01		
	d	16 20	16 23	16 25	16 32	16 32				16 35	16 38	16 46	16 47			16 50	16 53	16 53		16 56		17 02	17 02	17 03	
Horley 4	d		16 26								16 41							16 56							
Salfords	d		16 30																						
Earlswood (Surrey)	d		16 33																						
Tonbridge 4	d														16 19										
Leigh (Kent)	d														16 23										
Penshurst	d														16 27										
Edenbridge	d														16 33										
Godstone	d														16 40										
Nutfield	d														16 45										
Reigate	d						16 34																		
Redhill 5	a		16 36				16 38				16 47				16 50			17 02						17 10	
	d		16 37								16 48				16 51			17 07							
Merstham	d		16 41															17 11							
Coulsdon South	d		16 46												16 58			17 16							
Purley 4	d		16 49												17 02			17 19							
East Croydon	a		16 54	16 40	16 46	16 46					16 59	17 01	17 02	16 52	17 07		17 08	17 24		17 11		17 16	17 16		
	d		16 55	16 40	16 47	16 47		16 44			17 00	17 01	17 02	16 53	17 07		17 08	17 25		17 12		17 17	17 17		17 14
Norwood Junction 2	a		16 59												17 12			17 29							
New Cross Gate	d		17 07															17 37							
London Bridge 4 ⊖	a		17 13		17 00	17 02						17 17	17 15		17 25			17 43				17 30	17 32		
London Blackfriars 3 ⊖	a				17 07								17 22									17 37			
City Thameslink 3	a				17 10								17 26									17 40			
Farringdon 3 ⊖	a				17 14								17 30									17 44			
St Pancras International 15 ⊖	a				17 18								17 34									17 48			
St Albans City	a				17 38								17 54									18 08			
Luton Airport Parkway 4 ✈	a				17 50								18 07									18 20			
Luton 7	a				17 53								18 10									18 23			
Bedford 10	a				18 19								18 35									18 49			
Clapham Junction 10	a			16 50				16 55			17 09			17 02			17 17			17 21					17 25
London Victoria 15 ⊖	a	16 50		16 57				17 02		17 05	17 16			17 10		17 20	17 24			17 28					17 32

A 19 May

Table 186

Saturdays

until 23 June

Brighton - London and Bedford

Network Diagram - see first Page of Table 186

		SN	SN	FC		FC	FC	SN	SN	GW	SN	SN	SN	SN		FC	FC	GW	SN	SN	SN	FC	FC	SN
		1	◇1	1		1	1	◇1	1	1	1	1	◇1	◇1		1	1	1	1	1	◇1	1	1	◇1
				A		B	B										B					B		
		🚲	🚲					🚲			🚲									🚲				🚲
Brighton 10	d			16 37		16 37	16 37	16 49								17 04	17 04					17 07	17 07	17 19
Hove 2	d													16 51										
Preston Park	d			16 41		16 41	16 41							16 55								17 11	17 11	
Hassocks 4	d			16 47		16 47	16 47															17 17	17 17	
Burgess Hill 4	d			16 51		16 51	16 51							17 04								17 21	17 21	
Lewes 4	d												16 50											
Wivelsfield 4	d			16 53		16 53	16 53															17 23	17 23	
Haywards Heath 3	a			16 58		16 58	16 58						17 05	17 09		17 17	17 17					17 28	17 28	
	d			17 02		17 02	17 02						17 13			17 18	17 18					17 32	17 32	
Balcombe	d																					17 37	17 37	
Horsham 4	d		16 50									17 00									17 20			
Littlehaven	d											17 03												
Faygate	d																							
Ifield	d											17 09												
Crawley	d		16 59									17 13									17 29			
Three Bridges 4	a		17 02	17 11		17 11	17 11					17 16				17 26	17 26				17 32	17 42	17 42	
	d		17 03	17 11		17 12	17 12					17 18				17 27	17 27				17 33	17 42	17 42	
Gatwick Airport 10 ✈	a		17 07	17 15		17 16	17 16					17 22	17 24			17 31	17 31				17 37	17 46	17 47	
	d	17 05	17 08	17 16		17 17	17 16				17 20	17 23	17 25			17 32	17 32			17 35	17 38	17 46	17 47	
Horley 4	d											17 26									17 41			
Salfords	d											17 30												
Earlswood (Surrey)	d											17 33												
Tonbridge 4	d																							
Leigh (Kent)	d																							
Penshurst	d																							
Edenbridge	d																							
Godstone	d																							
Nutfield	d																							
Reigate	d								17 14	17 18								17 34						
Redhill 5	a		17 15						17 18	17 25		17 36						17 38			17 47			
	d		17 16						17 19			17 37									17 48			
Merstham	d								17 23			17 41												
Coulsdon South	d								17 28			17 46												
Purley 4	d								17 32			17 49												
East Croydon	a		17 27	17 31		17 31	17 31	17 22	17 37			17 54	17 40			17 46	17 46				17 59	18 01	18 02	17 52
	d		17 28	17 31		17 32	17 32	17 23	17 37			17 55	17 40			17 47	17 47		17 44		18 00	18 01	18 02	17 53
Norwood Junction 2	a								17 42			17 59												
New Cross Gate	d											18 07												
London Bridge 4 ⊖	a			17 45		17 45	17 47		17 55			18 13				18 00	18 02					18 17	18 15	
London Blackfriars 3 ⊖	a			17 52		17 52										18 07							18 22	
City Thameslink 3	a			17 56		17 56										18 10							18 26	
Farringdon 3 ⊖	a			18 00		18 00										18 14							18 30	
St Pancras International 15 ⊖	a			18 04		18 04										18 18							18 34	
St Albans City	a			18 24		18 24										18 38							18 54	
Luton Airport Parkway 4 ✈	a			18 37		18 37										18 50							19 07	
Luton 7	a			18 40		18 40										18 53							19 10	
Bedford 10	a			19 05		19 05										19 19							19 35	
Clapham Junction 10	a		17 37					17 32					17 50						17 55		18 09			18 02
London Victoria 15 ⊖	a	17 35	17 44					17 40			17 50		17 57						18 02	18 05	18 16			18 10

A not 19 May

B 19 May

Table 186

Saturdays

until 23 June

Brighton - London and Bedford

Network Diagram - see first Page of Table 186

		SN	SN	SN	SN	SN	SN	FC	FC	GW	SN	SN	SN	FC	FC	SN	SN	GW	SN	SN	SN	SN	FC
		1	1	◇1	1	◇1	◇1	1	1	1	1	1	◇1	1	1	◇1	1	1	1	1	◇1	◇1	1
									A						A								
			⚲									⚲	⚲			⚲			⚲				
Brighton 10	d			17 24				17 34	17 34					17 37	17 37	17 49							18 04
Hove 2	d						17 21															17 51	
Preston Park	d													17 41	17 41							17 55	
Hassocks 4	d			17 34										17 47	17 47								
Burgess Hill 4	d			17 38										17 51	17 51							18 04	
Lewes 4	d					17 20															17 50		
Wivelsfield 4	d					17 35								17 53	17 53								
Haywards Heath 3	a					17 40	17 35	17 47	17 47					17 58	17 58						18 05	18 09	18 17
	d						17 44	17 48	17 48					18 02	18 02							18 13	18 18
Balcombe	d																						
Horsham 4	d				17 30								17 50							18 00			
Littlehaven	d				17 33															18 03			
Faygate	d																						
Ifield	d				17 39															18 09			
Crawley	d				17 43								17 59							18 13			
Three Bridges 4	a				17 46			17 56	17 56				18 02	18 11	18 11					18 16			18 26
	d				17 48			17 57	17 57				18 03	18 12	18 12					18 18			18 27
Gatwick Airport 10 ✈	a			17 51	17 52		17 55	18 01	18 01				18 07	18 16	18 16					18 22		18 24	18 31
	d		17 50	17 53	17 53		17 56	18 02	18 02	18 03		18 05	18 08	18 17	18 16				18 20	18 23		18 25	18 32
Horley 4	d				17 56															18 26			
Salfords	d																			18 30			
Earlswood (Surrey)	d																			18 33			
Tonbridge 4	d	17 19																					
Leigh (Kent)	d	17 23																					
Penshurst	d	17 27																					
Edenbridge	d	17 33																					
Godstone	d	17 40																					
Nutfield	d	17 45																					
Reigate	d																18 14	18 19					
Redhill 5	a	17 50			18 02					18 10			18 15				18 18	18 25		18 36			
	d	17 51			18 07								18 16				18 19			18 37			
Merstham	d				18 11												18 23			18 41			
Coulsdon South	d	17 58			18 16												18 28			18 46			
Purley 4	d	18 02			18 19												18 32			18 49			
East Croydon	a	18 07		18 08	18 24		18 11	18 16	18 16				18 27	18 31	18 31	18 22	18 37			18 54		18 40	18 46
	d	18 07		18 08	18 25		18 12	18 17	18 17		18 14		18 28	18 32	18 32	18 23	18 37			18 55		18 40	18 47
Norwood Junction 2	a	18 12			18 29												18 42			18 59			
New Cross Gate	d				18 37															19 07			
London Bridge 4 ⊖	a	18 25			18 43			18 30	18 32					18 45	18 47		18 55			19 13			19 00
London Blackfriars 3 ⊖	a							18 37						18 52									19 07
City Thameslink 3	a							18 40						18 56									19 10
Farringdon 3 ⊖	a							18 44						19 00									19 14
St Pancras International 15 ⊖	a							18 48						19 04									19 18
St Albans City	a							19 08						19 24									19 38
Luton Airport Parkway 4 ✈	a							19 20						19 37									19 50
Luton 7	a							19 23						19 40									19 53
Bedford 10	a							19 49						20 05									20 19
Clapham Junction 10	a			18 17			18 21				18 25		18 37			18 32						18 50	
London Victoria 15 ⊖	a		18 20	18 24			18 28				18 32	18 35	18 44			18 40			18 50			18 57	

A 19 May

Table 186

Saturdays

until 23 June

Brighton - London and Bedford

Network Diagram - see first Page of Table 186

Station		FC 1 A	GW 1	SN 1	SN 1 bus	SN ◇1	FC 1 A	FC 1	SN ◇1	SN 1	SN 1 bus	SN ◇1	SN 1	SN ◇1	SN ◇1	FC 1	FC 1 A	GW 1	SN 1	SN 1 bus	SN ◇1	FC 1	FC 1 A
Brighton 10	d	18 04					18 07	18 07	18 19			18 24				18 34	18 34					18 37	18 37
Hove 2	d														18 21								
Preston Park	d						18 11	18 11														18 41	18 41
Hassocks 4	d						18 17	18 17				18 34										18 47	18 47
Burgess Hill 4	d						18 21	18 21				18 38										18 51	18 51
Lewes 4	d													18 20									
Wivelsfield 4	d						18 23	18 23						18 35								18 53	18 53
Haywards Heath 3	a	18 17					18 28	18 28						18 40	18 35	18 47	18 47					18 58	18 58
	d	18 18					18 32	18 32						18 44		18 48	18 48					19 02	19 02
Balcombe	d						18 37	18 37															
Horsham 4	d					18 20							18 32								18 50		
Littlehaven	d												18 35										
Faygate	d																						
Ifield	d												18 41										
Crawley	d					18 29							18 45								18 59		
Three Bridges 4	a	18 26				18 32	18 42	18 42					18 48			18 56	18 56				19 02	19 11	19 11
	d	18 27				18 33	18 42	18 42					18 50			18 57	18 57				19 03	19 12	19 12
Gatwick Airport 10 ✈	a	18 31				18 37	18 46	18 47				18 51	18 54	18 55		19 01	19 01				19 07	19 16	19 16
	d	18 32			18 35	18 38	18 46	18 47			18 50	18 53	18 55	18 56		19 02	19 02	19 03		19 05	19 08	19 17	19 16
Horley 4	d					18 41							18 58								19 11		
Salfords	d																						
Earlswood (Surrey)	d																						
Tonbridge 4	d									18 19													
Leigh (Kent)	d									18 23													
Penshurst	d									18 27													
Edenbridge	d									18 33													
Godstone	d									18 40													
Nutfield	d									18 45													
Reigate	d		18 34																				
Redhill 5	a		18 38			18 47				18 50			19 04					19 10			19 17		
	d					18 48				18 51			19 07								19 18		
Merstham	d												19 11										
Coulsdon South	d									18 58			19 16										
Purley 4	d									19 02			19 19										
East Croydon	a	18 46				18 59	19 01	19 02	18 52	19 07		19 08	19 24	19 11		19 16	19 16				19 29	19 31	19 31
	d	18 47		18 44		19 00	19 01	19 02	18 53	19 07		19 08	19 25	19 12		19 17	19 17		19 14		19 29	19 32	19 32
Norwood Junction 2	a									19 12													
New Cross Gate	d																						
London Bridge 4 ⊖	a	19 02					19 17	19 15		19 25						19 30	19 32					19 45	19 47
London Blackfriars 3 ⊖	a							19 22								19 37						19 52	
City Thameslink 3	a							19 26								19 40						19 56	
Farringdon 3 ⊖	a							19 30								19 44						20 00	
St Pancras International 15 ⊖	a							19 34								19 48						20 04	
St Albans City	a							19 54								20 08						20 24	
Luton Airport Parkway 4 ✈	a							20 07								20 20						20 37	
Luton 7	a							20 10								20 23						20 40	
Bedford 10	a							20 35								20 49						21 05	
Clapham Junction 10	a			18 55		19 09			19 02			19 17	19 37	19 21					19 25		19 40		
London Victoria 15 ⊖	a			19 02	19 05	19 16			19 10		19 20	19 24	19 44	19 28					19 32	19 35	19 50		

A 19 May

Table 186

Saturdays

until 23 June

Brighton - London and Bedford

Network Diagram - see first Page of Table 186

		SN		SN	GW	SN	SN	SN	SN	SN	FC	FC		GW	SN	SN	SN	SN	FC	FC	SN	SN		SN
		◇1			1	1	◇1	1	◇1	◇1	1	1		1	1	1	1	1	1	1	◇1	1		1
												A							A					
						🛒										🛒						🛒		
Brighton 10	d	18 49					18 54				19 04	19 04							19 07	19 07	19 19			
Hove 2	d									18 51														
Preston Park	d									18 55									19 11	19 11				
Hassocks 4	d						19 06												19 17	19 17				
Burgess Hill 4	d									19 04									19 21	19 21				
Lewes 4	d								18 50															
Wivelsfield 4	d																		19 23	19 23				
Haywards Heath 3	a								19 05	19 09	19 17	19 17							19 28	19 28				
	d								19 14		19 18	19 18							19 32	19 32				
Balcombe	d																		19 37	19 37				
Horsham 4	d							19 02										19 21						19 32
Littlehaven	d							19 05																19 35
Faygate	d																							
Ifield	d							19 11																19 41
Crawley	d							19 14										19 30						19 45
Three Bridges 4	a							19 18			19 26	19 26						19 33	19 42	19 42				19 48
	d							19 18			19 27	19 27						19 34	19 42	19 42				19 50
Gatwick Airport 10 ✈	a						19 21	19 22	19 25		19 31	19 31						19 38	19 46	19 47				19 54
	d					19 20	19 23	19 23	19 26		19 32	19 32				19 35		19 39	19 46	19 47		19 50		19 55
Horley 4	d							19 26																19 58
Salfords	d							19 30																
Earlswood (Surrey)	d							19 33																
Tonbridge 4	d														19 10									
Leigh (Kent)	d														19 14									
Penshurst	d														19 18									
Edenbridge	d														19 24									
Godstone	d														19 31									
Nutfield	d														19 36									
Reigate	d			19 14	19 18									19 34										
Redhill 5	a			19 18	19 25			19 36						19 38	19 45			19 47						20 04
	d							19 37										19 48						20 07
Merstham	d							19 41																20 11
Coulsdon South	d							19 46																20 16
Purley 4	d							19 49																20 19
East Croydon	a	19 22					19 38	19 54	19 41		19 46	19 46						20 00	20 01	20 02	19 52			20 24
	d	19 23					19 38	19 57	19 42		19 47	19 47					19 44	20 00	20 01	20 02	19 53			20 26
Norwood Junction 2	a																							
New Cross Gate	d																							
London Bridge 4 ⊖	a										20 00	20 02							20 17	20 15				
London Blackfriars 3 ⊖	a										20 07									20 22				
City Thameslink 3	a										20 10									20 26				
Farringdon 3 ⊖	a										20 14									20 30				
St Pancras International 15 ⊖	a										20 18									20 34				
St Albans City	a										20 38									20 54				
Luton Airport Parkway 4 ✈	a										20 50									21 07				
Luton 7	a										20 53									21 10				
Bedford 10	a										21 19									21 35				
Clapham Junction 10	a	19 32					19 47	20 08	19 51								19 55	20 11			20 02			20 37
London Victoria 15 ⊖	a	19 40				19 50	19 54	20 15	19 58							20 05	20 05	20 20			20 10	20 20		20 44

A 19 May

Table 186

Brighton - London and Bedford

Saturdays

until 23 June

Network Diagram - see first Page of Table 186

		SN	SN	FC	FC	GW	SN	SN	SN		FC	FC	SN	GW	SN	SN	SN	SN	GW		SN	SN	SN	FC	FC
		◇1	◇1	1	1	1	1	1	◇1		1	1	◇1	1	1	1	◇1	◇1	1		1	1	◇1	1	1
					A							A													A
Brighton 10	d			19 34	19 34						19 37	19 37	19 49										19 54	20 04	20 04
Hove 2	d		19 21															19 52							
Preston Park	d										19 41	19 41											19 58		
Hassocks 4	d										19 47	19 47											20 04		
Burgess Hill 4	d										19 51	19 51						20 02					20 08		
Lewes 4	d	19 20															19 50								
Wivelsfield 4	d	19 35									19 53	19 53					20 02						20 10		
Haywards Heath 3	a	19 40	19 35	19 47	19 47						19 58	19 58					20 07	20 10					20 14	20 17	20 17
	d	19 44		19 48	19 48						20 02	20 02					20 14						20 22 ↪	20 18	20 18
Balcombe	d																								
Horsham 4	d								19 52							20 02									
Littlehaven	d															20 05									
Faygate	d																								
Ifield	d															20 11									
Crawley	d								20 01							20 14									
Three Bridges 4	a			19 56	19 56				20 05		20 11	20 11				20 18								20 26	20 26
	d			19 57	19 57				20 05		20 12	20 12				20 18								20 27	20 28
Gatwick Airport 10 ✈	a	19 55		20 01	20 01				20 10		20 16	20 16				20 22	20 25							20 31	20 31
	d	19 56		20 02	20 02	20 03		20 05	20 11		20 17	20 16			20 20	20 23	20 26							20 32	20 31
Horley 4	d															20 26									
Salfords	d															20 30									
Earlswood (Surrey)	d															20 33									
Tonbridge 4	d																				20 10				
Leigh (Kent)	d																				20 14				
Penshurst	d																				20 18				
Edenbridge	d																				20 24				
Godstone	d																				20 31				
Nutfield	d																				20 36				
Reigate	d													20 19					20 34						
Redhill 5	a					20 10			20 18					20 25		20 36			20 38		20 45				
	d								20 18							20 37									
Merstham	d															20 41									
Coulsdon South	d															20 46									
Purley 4	d															20 49									
East Croydon	a	20 11		20 16	20 16				20 29		20 31	20 31	20 22			20 54	20 41							20 46	20 46
	d	20 12		20 17	20 17		20 14		20 30		20 32	20 32	20 23			20 56	20 42					20 44		20 47	20 47
Norwood Junction 2	a																								
New Cross Gate	d																								
London Bridge 4 ⊖	a			20 30	20 32						20 45	20 47												21 00	21 02
London Blackfriars 3 ⊖	a			20 37							20 52													21 07	
City Thameslink 3	a			20 40							20 56														
Farringdon 3 ⊖	a			20 44							21 00													21 13	
St Pancras International 15 ⊖	a			20 48							21 04													21 18	
St Albans City	a			21 08							21 24													21 38	
Luton Airport Parkway 4 ✈	a			21 20							21 37													21 50	
Luton 7	a			21 23							21 40													21 53	
Bedford 10	a			21 49							22 05													22 20	
Clapham Junction 10	a	20 21					20 25		20 40				20 32			21 07	20 51					20 55			
London Victoria 15 ⊖	a	20 28					20 32	20 35	20 50				20 40		20 50	21 14	20 58					21 02			

A 19 May

Table 186

Saturdays
until 23 June

Brighton - London and Bedford

Network Diagram - see first Page of Table 186

		SN 1	SN ◇1	FC 1 A	FC 1	SN ◇1	SN 1	SN ◇1	SN 1	SN 1	FC 1	FC 1 A	GW 1	SN 1	SN ◇1	FC 1	FC 1 A	SN ◇1	GW 1	SN 1	SN 1	SN ◇1	SN ◇1
Brighton 10	d			20 07	20 07	20 19					20 34	20 34				20 37	20 37	20 49					20 52
Hove 2	d							20 22															
Preston Park	d			20 11	20 11											20 41	20 41						
Hassocks 4	d			20 17	20 17											20 47	20 47						21 04
Burgess Hill 4	d			20 21	20 21											20 51	20 51						
Lewes 4	d																					20 50	
Wivelsfield 4	d		←	20 23	20 23											20 53	20 53					21 04	
Haywards Heath 3	a		20 14	20 28	20 28			20 36			20 47	20 47				20 58	20 58					21 09	21 11
	d		20 22	20 32	20 32			20 39			20 48	20 48				21 02	21 02					21 15	
Balcombe	d			20 37	20 37																		
Horsham 4	d									20 32					20 52						21 02		
Littlehaven	d									20 35											21 05		
Faygate	d																						
Ifield	d									20 41											21 11		
Crawley	d									20 45					21 01						21 14		
Three Bridges 4	a		20 32	20 42	20 42			20 47		20 48	20 56	20 56			21 05	21 11	21 11				21 18		
	d		20 32	20 42	20 42			20 48		20 51	20 57	20 57			21 05	21 12	21 12				21 18		
Gatwick Airport 10 ✈	a		20 37	20 46	20 47			20 52		20 56	21 01	21 01			21 10	21 16	21 16				21 22		21 26
	d	20 35	20 38	20 46	20 47		20 50	20 53		20 57	21 02	21 02	21 03	21 05	21 11	21 17	21 16			21 20	21 23		21 27
Horley 4	d									20 59											21 26		
Salfords	d																				21 30		
Earlswood (Surrey)	d																				21 33		
Tonbridge 4	d																						
Leigh (Kent)	d																						
Penshurst	d																						
Edenbridge	d																						
Godstone	d																						
Nutfield	d																		21 18				
Reigate	d																		21 25				
Redhill 5	a		20 47							21 06			21 10		21 18						21 36		
	d		20 48							21 07					21 18						21 37		
Merstham	d									21 11											21 41		
Coulsdon South	d									21 16											21 46		
Purley 4	d									21 19											21 49		
East Croydon 🚋	a		20 59	21 01	21 02	20 52		21 08		21 24	21 16	21 16			21 30	21 31	21 31	21 22			21 54		21 41
	d		21 00	21 01	21 02	20 53		21 09	21 14	21 26	21 17	21 17			21 31	21 32	21 32	21 23			21 56		21 42
Norwood Junction 2	a																						
New Cross Gate	d																						
London Bridge 4 ⊖	a			21 17	21 15						21 30	21 32				21 45	21 47						
London Blackfriars 3 ⊖	a				21 22						21 37					21 52							
City Thameslink 3	a																						
Farringdon 3 ⊖	a				21 29						21 43					21 59							
St Pancras International 15 ⊖	a				21 34						21 48					22 04							
St Albans City	a				21 54						22 08					22 24							
Luton Airport Parkway 4 ✈	a				22 07						22 28					22 37							
Luton 7	a				22 10						22 31					22 40							
Bedford 10	a				22 37						22 56					23 07							
Clapham Junction 10	a		21 10			21 02		21 18	21 25	21 37					21 40			21 32				22 07	21 51
London Victoria 15 ⊖	a	21 05	21 17			21 10	21 20	21 26	21 32	21 44				21 35	21 50			21 40		21 50		22 15	21 58

A 19 May

Table 186

Saturdays

until 23 June

Brighton - London and Bedford

Network Diagram - see first Page of Table 186

			SN 1	GW 1	SN 1	SN 1	SN ◇1	FC 1	FC 1	SN ◇1	SN 1		SN ◇1	SN 1	SN 1	SN 1	SN ◇1	FC 1	SN ◇1	SN 1	GW 1		SN 1	SN ◇1	SN ◇1
								A																⊼	B ⊼
Brighton 10	d						21 00	21 07	21 07	21 19								21 37	21 49						
Hove 2	d												21 22												21 52
Preston Park	d						21 04	21 11	21 11									21 41							
Hassocks 4	d						21 10	21 17	21 17									21 47							
Burgess Hill 4	d						21 14	21 21	21 21									21 51							22 04
Lewes 4	d																							21 50	
Wivelsfield 4	d						21 16	21 23	21 23									21 53						22 02	
Haywards Heath 3	a						21 21	21 28	21 28				21 36					21 58						22 06	22 09
	d						21 22	21 32	21 32				21 39					22 02						22 13	
Balcombe	d							21 37	21 37																
Horsham 4	d														21 32		21 52						22 02		
Littlehaven	d														21 35								22 05		
Faygate	d																								
Ifield	d														21 41								22 11		
Crawley	d														21 45		22 01						22 14		
Three Bridges 4	a						21 31	21 42	21 42				21 47		21 48		22 05	22 11					22 18		
	d						21 32	21 42	21 42				21 48		21 52		22 05	22 12					22 19		
Gatwick Airport 10 ✈	a						21 37	21 46	21 47				21 52		21 56		22 10	22 16					22 23	22 24	
	d					21 35	21 38	21 46	21 47		21 50		21 53		21 57	22 05	22 11	22 17		22 20	22 22		22 24	22 25	
Horley 4	d														22 00								22 27		
Salfords	d																						22 31		
Earlswood (Surrey)	d																						22 34		
Tonbridge 4	d		21 10																						
Leigh (Kent)	d		21 14																						
Penshurst	d		21 18																						
Edenbridge	d		21 24																						
Godstone	d		21 31																						
Nutfield	d		21 36																						
Reigate	d			21 40																					
Redhill 5	a		21 41	21 44			21 47								22 06		22 18				22 30		22 37		
	d						21 47								22 07		22 18						22 38		
Merstham	d														22 11								22 42		
Coulsdon South	d														22 16								22 47		
Purley 4	d														22 19								22 50		
East Croydon 🚊	a						21 59	22 01	22 02	21 52			22 08		22 24		22 30	22 32	22 22				22 55	22 40	
	d				21 44		22 00	22 01	22 02	21 53			22 09	22 14	22 26		22 31	22 32	22 23				22 56	22 40	
Norwood Junction 2	a																								
New Cross Gate	d																								
London Bridge 4 ⊖	a							22 17	22 15									22 45							
London Blackfriars 3 ⊖	a								22 22									22 52							
City Thameslink 3	a																								
Farringdon 3 ⊖	a								22 27									22 57							
St Pancras International 15 ⊖	a								22 32									23 02							
St Albans City	a								22 56									23 26							
Luton Airport Parkway 4 ✈	a								23 09									23 39							
Luton 7	a								23 12									23 42							
Bedford 10	a								23 39									00 09							
Clapham Junction 10	a				21 55		22 10			22 02			22 18	22 25	22 37		22 40		22 32				23 06	22 49	
London Victoria 15 ⊖	a				22 02	22 05	22 20			22 13	22 20		22 26	22 35	22 44	22 35	22 50		22 40	22 50			23 14	22 57	

A 19 May

B ⊼ from Haywards Heath

Table 186

Saturdays

until 23 June

Brighton - London and Bedford

Network Diagram - see first Page of Table 186

		SN	SN	SN	SN	FC	FC		GW	SN	SN	SN	FC	FC	SN	FC	FC		GW	SN	SN	SN	SN	GW	SN
		1	1	1	◇1	1	1		1	1	1	1	1	1	◇1	1	1		1	1	1	1	1	1	◇1
						A								A			A								
Brighton 10	d				22 00	22 07	22 07						22 33	22 33											23 02
Hove 2	d																								
Preston Park	d				22 04	22 11	22 11						22 37	22 37											23 06
Hassocks 4	d				22 10	22 17	22 17						22 43	22 43											23 12
Burgess Hill 4	d				22 14	22 21	22 21						22 47	22 47											23 16
Lewes 4	d														22 40										
Wivelsfield 4	d				22 16	22 23	22 23						22 49	22 49	22 54										23 19
Haywards Heath 3	a				22 21	22 28	22 28						22 53	22 53	22 58										23 23
	d				22 22	22 32	22 32						22 54	22 54	22 59										23 24
Balcombe	d					22 37	22 37						22 59	22 59											
Horsham 4	d																				23 02				
Littlehaven	d																				23 05				
Faygate	d																								
Ifield	d																				23 11				
Crawley	d															←	←				23 14				
Three Bridges 4	a				22 31	22 42	22 43						23 05	23 05	23 08	23 05	23 05				23 18				23 32
	d				22 32	22 42	22 43						23 12	23 12	23 08	23 12	23 12				23 18				23 47
Gatwick Airport 10 ✈	a				22 37	22 46	22 47						→	→	23 12	23 16	23 16				23 22				→
	d		22 35		22 38	22 46	22 47			22 50	23 05				23 13	23 17	23 16		23 18	23 20	23 23		23 35		
Horley 4	d																				23 26				
Salfords	d																				23 30				
Earlswood (Surrey)	d																				23 33				
Tonbridge 4	d	22 10																				23 17			
Leigh (Kent)	d	22 14																				23 21			
Penshurst	d	22 18																				23 25			
Edenbridge	d	22 24																				23 31			
Godstone	d	22 31																				23 38			
Nutfield	d	22 36																				23 43			
Reigate	d								22 48															23 54	
Redhill 5	a	22 42			22 46				22 52										23 25		23 36	23 49		23 58	
	d				22 46																23 37				
Merstham	d																				23 41				
Coulsdon South	d																				23 46				
Purley 4	d																				23 49				
East Croydon	a				22 59	23 01	23 02								23 29	23 32	23 32				23 55				
	d			22 44	23 00	23 01	23 02					23 14			23 30	23 32	23 32				23 56				
Norwood Junction 2	a																								
New Cross Gate	d																								
London Bridge 4 ⊖	a					23 17	23 15									23 46	23 47								
London Blackfriars 3 ⊖	a						23 22									23 52									
City Thameslink 3	a																								
Farringdon 3 ⊖	a						23 28									23 58									
St Pancras International 15 ⊖	a						23 32									00 02									
St Albans City	a						23 56									00 26									
Luton Airport Parkway 4 ✈	a						00 09									00 39									
Luton 7	a						00 12									00 42									
Bedford 10	a						00 39									01 09									
Clapham Junction 10	a			22 55	23 10							23 25			23 41						00 11				
London Victoria 15 ⊖	a		23 05	23 05	23 20					23 20	23 35	23 35			23 52					23 55	00 18		00 10		

A 19 May

Table 186

Saturdays
until 23 June

Brighton - London and Bedford

Network Diagram - see first Page of Table 186

		FC 1 A	FC 1		SN 1	SN ◇1	FC 1 A	FC 1
Brighton 10	d	23 11	23 11				23 37	23 37
Hove 2	d							
Preston Park	d						23 41	23 41
Hassocks 4	d	23 20	23 20				23 47	23 47
Burgess Hill 4	d	23 23	23 23				23 51	23 51
ewes 4	d							
Welsfield 4	d						23 53	23 53
Haywards Heath 3	a	23 28	23 28				23 58	23 58
	d	23 29	23 29				23 59	23 59
Balcombe	d						00 04	00 04
Horsham 4	d							
Ittlehaven	d							
Faygate	d							
field	d							
Crawley	d					←		
Three Bridges 4	a	23 37	23 37			23 32	00 10	00 10
	d	23 38	23 38			23 47	00 10	00 10
Gatwick Airport 10 ✈	a	23 42	23 42			23 52	00 14	00 14
	d	23 43	23 43		23 50	23 53	00 15	00 15
Horley 4	d					23 56		
Salfords	d							
Erlswood (Surrey)	d							
Tonbridge 4	d							
eigh (Kent)	d							
Penshurst	d							
Eenbridge	d							
Godstone	d							
Ntfield	d							
Reigate	d							
Redhill 5	a					00 03	00 22	00 22
	d					00 03	00 23	00 23
Merstham	d							
Coulsdon South	d							
Purley 4	d					00 11		
East Croydon	a	00 01	00 01			00 16	00 35	00 35
	d	00 04	00 04			00 17	00 36	00 36
Nrwood unction 2	a							
Nw Cross Gate	d							
London Bridge 4 ⊖	a	00 19	00 21				00 52	00 51
London Blackfriars 3 ⊖	a		00 28					00 58
City Thameslink 3	a							
Farringdon 3 ⊖	a		00 33					
St Pancras hternational 15 ⊖	a		00 37					01 07
St Albans City	a		01 10					01 40
Lton Airport Parkway 4 ✈	a		01 22					01 52
Lton 7	a		01 25					01 55
Bedford 10	a		01 52					02 22
Clapham unction 10	a					00 29		
London Victoria 15 ⊖	a				00 20	00 37		

A 19 May

Table 186

Saturdays

from 30 June

Brighton - London and Bedford

Network Diagram - see first Page of Table 186

		FC 1	FC 1	FC 1	SN 1	SN 1	SN ◇1	FC 1	SN 1	SN ◇1		SN 1	FC 1	SN 1	GW 1	SN	SN 1	SN 1	SN 1	FC		SN 1	SN 1	FC	SN 1
Brighton 10	d	21p37	22p07	22p33			23p02	23p11					23p37												
Hove 2	d																								
Preston Park	d	21p41	22p11	22p37			23p06						23p41												
Hassocks 4	d	21p47	22p17	22p43			23p12	23p20					23p47												
Burgess Hill 4	d	21p51	22p21	22p47			23p16	23p23					23p51												
Lewes 4	d																								
Wivelsfield 4	d	21p53	22p23	22p49			23p19						23p53												
Haywards Heath 3	a	21p58	22p28	22p53			23p23	23p28					23p58												
	d	22p02	22p32	22p54			23p24	23p29					23p59												
Balcombe	d		22p37	22p59									00 04												
Horsham 4	d				23p02																				
Littlehaven	d				23p05																				
Faygate	d																								
Ifield	d				23p11																				
Crawley	d				23p14					←															
Three Bridges 4	a	22p11	22p43	23p05	23p18		23p33	23p38		23p33			00 10												
	d	22p12	22p43	23p12	23p18		23p47	23p38		23p47			00 10							01 25			01 59	02 25	02 55
Gatwick Airport 10 ✈	a	22p16	22p47	23p16	23p22		→	23p42		23p52			00 14							01 29			02 03	02 29	02 59
	d	22p17	22p47	23p17	23p23	23p35		23p43	23p50	23p53		00 05	00 15	00 20			00 35	00 50	01 05	01 30		01 35	02 05	02 30	03 05
Horley 4	d				23p26					23p56									01 07				02 07		03 07
Salfords	d				23p30																				
Earlswood (Surrey)	d				23p33																				
Tonbridge 4	d																								
Leigh (Kent)	d																								
Penshurst	d																								
Edenbridge	d																								
Godstone	d																								
Nutfield	d																								
Reigate	d														00 45										
Redhill 5	a				23p36					00 03			00 22		00 49										
	d				23p37					00 03			00 23												
Merstham	d				23p41																				
Coulsdon South	d				23p46																				
Purley 4	d				23p49					00 11									01 22				02 22		03 22
East Croydon	a	22p32	23p02	23p32	23p54			00 01		00 16			00 35						01 27	01 49			02 27	02 47	03 27
	d	22p32	23p02	23p32	23p58			00 04		00 17			00 36			00 49			01 28	01 50			02 28	02 47	03 28
Norwood Junction 2	a																								
New Cross Gate	d																								
London Bridge 4 ⊖	a	22p45	23p15	23p45				00 21					00 51												
London Blackfriars 3 ⊖	a	22p52	23p22	23p52				00 28					00 58							02 13				03 13	
City Thameslink 3	a	22p53																							
Farringdon 3 ⊖	a	22p58	23p28	23p58				00 33																	
St Pancras International 15 ⊖	a	23p02	23p32	00 02				00 37					01 07							02 24				03 23	
St Albans City	a	23p26	23p56	00 26				01 10					01 40							02 57				03 57	
Luton Airport Parkway 4 ✈	a	23p38	00 08	00 38				01 22					01 52							03 09				04 09	
Luton 7	a	23p41	00 11	00 41				01 25					01 55							03 12				04 12	
Bedford 10	a	00 08	00 38	01 08				01 52					02 22							03 39				04 39	
Clapham Junction 10	a				00 11					00 29						01 01			01 41				02 41		03 41
London Victoria 15 ⊖	a				00 18	00 10			00 25	00 37		00 40		00 55		01 09	01 11	01 25	01 49			02 10	02 49		03 49

Table 186

Saturdays

from 30 June

Brighton - London and Bedford

Network Diagram - see first Page of Table 186

		FC	SN [1]	FC	SN [1]	FC	SN [1]	SN [1]	FC	GW [1]	GW [1]	SN ◇[1]	SN [1]	SN [1]	SN ◇[1]	SN [1]	FC [1]	SN [1]	GW [1]	SN [1] 🚲	SN [1] 🚲	SN [1]
Brighton [10]	d						03 50								05 21		05 25					
Hove [2]	d																					
Preston Park	d																05 29					
Hassocks [4]	d																05 35					
Burgess Hill [4]	d														05 31		05 39					
Lewes [4]	d																	05 26				
Wivelsfield [4]	d																05 41					
Haywards Heath [3]	a						04 24								05 36		05 45	05 41				
	d						04 25								05 37		05 46	05 49				
Balcombe	d																05 51					
Horsham [4]	d															05 30						06 00
Littlehaven	d															05 33						06 03
Faygate	d																					
Ifield	d															05 39						06 09
Crawley	d															05 43						06 13
Three Bridges [4]	a						04 45								05 46	05 46	05 57	05 59				06 16
	d	03 25	03 55	04 25		04 55	05 00		05 21			05 33			05 46	05 48	05 57	05 59				06 18
Gatwick Airport [10] ✈	a	03 29	03 59	04 29		04 59	05 04		05 25			05 37			05 50	05 52	06 01	06 03				06 22
	d	03 30	04 05	04 30	04 35	05 00	05 05	05 20	05 27	05 31		05 38		05 50	05 53	05 53	06 02		06 03	06 05	06 20	06 23
Horley [4]	d		04 07				05 07					05 40				05 56						06 26
Salfords	d															06 00						06 30
Earlswood (Surrey)	d															06 03						06 33
Tonbridge [4]	d												05 24									
Leigh (Kent)	d												05 28									
Penshurst	d												05 32									
Edenbridge	d												05 38									
Godstone	d												05 45									
Nutfield	d												05 50									
Reigate	d										05 34											
Redhill [5]	a								05 34	05 38	05 39	05 47	05 55			06 06			06 12			06 36
	d								05 35			05 48				06 07						06 37
Merstham	d															06 11						06 41
Coulsdon South	d															06 16						06 46
Purley [4]	d		04 22				05 24					05 58				06 19						06 49
East Croydon 🚌	a	03 47	04 27	04 47		05 17	05 29		05 47			06 02			06 10	06 24	06 16					06 54
	d	03 47	04 28	04 47		05 17	05 29		05 47			06 07			06 11	06 25	06 17					06 55
Norwood Junction [2]	a															06 29						06 59
New Cross Gate	d															06 37						07 07
London Bridge [4] ⊖	a								06 02							06 43	06 30					07 13
London Blackfriars [3] ⊖	a	04 13		05 13		05 43			06 08								06 37					
City Thameslink [3]	a																					
Farringdon [3] ⊖	a			05 19		05 49			06 12								06 42					
St Pancras International [15] ⊖	a	04 22		05 24		05 54			06 16								06 46					
St Albans City	a	04 57		05 57		06 25			06 38								07 08					
Luton Airport Parkway [4] ✈	a	05 09		06 09		06 37			06 50								07 20					
Luton [7]	a	05 12		06 12		06 40			06 53								07 23					
Bedford [10]	a	05 39		06 39		07 05			07 19								07 49					
Clapham Junction [10]	a		04 41				05 49					06 18			06 21							
London Victoria [15] ⊖	a		04 50		05 10		05 58	05 55				06 26		06 20	06 30					06 35	06 50	

Table 186

Saturdays

from 30 June

Brighton - London and Bedford

Network Diagram - see first Page of Table 186

		SN	SN	GW	SN	FC	SN	SN	SN	SN	SN	SN	SN	FC	GW	SN	SN	SN	FC	SN	SN	GW
		◇1	◇1	1	◇1	1	1	◇1	1	1	1	◇1	◇1	1	1	1	1	◇1	1	◇1	1	1
Brighton 10	d	05 50			05 56	06 02						06 11		06 25					06 37	06 49		
Hove 2	d		05 54										06 21									
Preston Park	d				06 00							06 15		06 29					06 41			
Hassocks 4	d				06 06							06 21		06 35					06 47			
Burgess Hill 4	d					06 12						06 25		06 39					06 51			
Lewes 4	d																					
Wivelsfield 4	d				06 11							06 27		06 41					06 53			
Haywards Heath 3	a	06 03	06 08		06 15	06 17						06 31	06 35	06 45					06 58			
	d		06 12		06 16	06 18						06 40		06 46					07 02			
Balcombe	d													06 51								
Horsham 4	d										06 30							06 52				
Littlehaven	d										06 33											
Faygate	d																					
Ifield	d										06 39											
Crawley	d							←			06 43							07 01				
Three Bridges 4	a		06 20		06 24	06 26		06 24			06 46	06 48		06 57				07 04	07 11			
	d		06 21		06 31	06 27		06 31			06 48	06 49		06 57				07 05	07 12			
Gatwick Airport 10 ✈	a		06 25		→	06 31		06 37			06 52	06 53		07 01				07 09	07 16			
	d		06 26			06 32	06 35	06 38		06 50	06 53	06 55		07 02	07 03		07 05	07 10	07 17			
Horley 4	d										06 56											
Salfords	d																					
Earlswood (Surrey)	d																					
Tonbridge 4	d								06 19													
Leigh (Kent)	d								06 23													
Penshurst	d								06 27													
Edenbridge	d								06 33													
Godstone	d								06 40													
Nutfield	d								06 45													
Reigate	d			06 34																	07 14	07 18
Redhill 5	a			06 39					06 50		07 02				07 10			07 17			07 18	07 25
	d								06 51		07 07							07 18			07 21	
Merstham	d										07 11										07 25	
Coulsdon South	d								06 58		07 16										07 30	
Purley 4	d								07 02		07 19										07 34	
East Croydon	a		06 40			06 46		06 53	07 07		07 24	07 09		07 16				07 29	07 31	07 22	07 39	
	d		06 41			06 47		06 53	07 07		07 25	07 10		07 17		07 14		07 30	07 32	07 23	07 39	
Norwood Junction 2	a								07 12		07 29										07 44	
New Cross Gate	d										07 37											
London Bridge 4 ⊖	a					07 00			07 25		07 43			07 30					07 45		07 57	
London Blackfriars 3 ⊖	a					07 07								07 37					07 52			
City Thameslink 3	a																					
Farringdon 3 ⊖	a					07 12								07 43					07 59			
St Pancras International 15 ⊖	a					07 16								07 48					08 04			
St Albans City	a					07 38								08 08					08 24			
Luton Airport Parkway 4 ✈	a					07 50								08 20					08 37			
Luton 7	a					07 53								08 23					08 40			
Bedford 10	a					08 19								08 49					09 05			
Clapham Junction 10	a		06 50					07 02				07 19				07 25		07 39		07 32		
London Victoria 15 ⊖	a		06 57				07 05	07 09		07 20		07 27				07 32	07 35	07 46		07 40		

Table 186

Saturdays

from 30 June

Brighton - London and Bedford

Network Diagram - see first Page of Table 186

		SN 1 🚲	SN 1	SN ◇1	SN ◇1	FC 1	GW 1	SN 1	SN 1 🚲	SN ◇1		FC 1	SN ◇1	SN 1	SN 1 🚲	SN ◇1	SN 1	SN ◇1	SN ◇1	FC 1		GW 1	SN 1	SN 1 🚲	SN ◇1
Brighton 10	d					07 04						07 07	07 19			07 26				07 34					
Hove 2	d				06 51														07 22						
Preston Park	d				06 55							07 11													
Hassocks 4	d											07 17				07 34									
Burgess Hill 4	d				07 04							07 21				07 38									
ewes 4	d			06 50														07 20							
Welsfield 4	d											07 23						07 35							
Haywards Heath 3	a			07 05	07 09	07 17						07 28						07 40	07 35	07 47					
	d			07 14		07 18						07 32						07 44		07 48					
Balcombe	d											07 37													
Horsham 4	d		07 00							07 20							07 30								07 50
ittlehaven	d		07 03														07 33								
Faygate	d																								
field	d		07 09														07 39								
Crawley	d		07 13							07 29							07 43								07 59
Three Bridges 4	a		07 16			07 26				07 32		07 42					07 46			07 56					08 02
	d		07 18			07 27				07 33		07 42					07 48			07 57					08 03
Gatwick Airport 10 ✈	a		07 22	07 25		07 31				07 37		07 47				07 51	07 52	07 55		08 01					08 07
	d	07 20	07 23	07 26		07 32			07 35	07 38		07 47			07 50	07 53	07 53	07 56		08 02		08 03		08 05	08 08
Horley 4	d		07 26							07 41							07 56								
Salfords	d		07 30																						
Erlswood (Surrey)	d		07 33																						
Tonbridge 4	d													07 19											
eigh (Kent)	d													07 23											
Penshurst	d													07 27											
Eenbridge	d													07 33											
Godstone	d													07 40											
Ntfield	d													07 45											
Reigate	d						07 34																		
Redhill 5	a		07 36				07 39			07 47				07 50			08 02					08 10			08 15
	d		07 37							07 48				07 51			08 07								08 16
Merstham	d		07 41														08 11								
Coulsdon South	d		07 46											07 58			08 16								
Purley 4	d		07 49											08 02			08 19								
East Croydon 🚋	a		07 54	07 41		07 46				07 59		08 02	07 52	08 07		08 08	08 24	08 11		08 16					08 27
	d		07 55	07 42		07 47		07 44		08 00		08 02	07 53	08 07		08 08	08 25	08 12		08 17			08 14		08 28
Nrwood unction 2	a		07 59											08 12			08 29								
Nw Cross Gate	d		08 07														08 37								
London Bridge 4 ⊖	a		08 13			08 00						08 15		08 25			08 43			08 30					
London Blackfriars 3 ⊖	a					08 07						08 22								08 37					
City Thameslink 3	a																								
Farringdon 3 ⊖	a					08 13						08 29								08 43					
St Pancras hternational 15 ⊖	a					08 18						08 34								08 48					
St Albans City	a					08 38						08 54								09 08					
uton Airport Parkway 4 ✈	a					08 50						09 07								09 20					
uton 7	a					08 53						09 10								09 23					
Bedford 10	a					09 19						09 35								09 49					
Clapham unction 10	a			07 51				07 55		08 09			08 02			08 17		08 21					08 25		08 37
London Victoria 15 ⊖	a	07 50		07 58				08 02	08 05	08 16			08 10		08 20	08 24		08 28					08 32	08 35	08 44

Table 186

Saturdays

from 30 June

Brighton - London and Bedford

Network Diagram - see first Page of Table 186

		FC 1	SN ◇1 🚲	SN 1	GW 1	SN 1 🚲		SN 1	SN ◇1	SN ◇1	FC 1	GW 1	SN 1	SN 1 🚲	SN ◇1	FC 1		SN ◇1 🚲	SN 1	SN 1 🚲	SN ◇1	SN 1	SN ◇1	SN ◇1	FC 1
Brighton 10	d	07 37	07 49								08 04					08 07		08 19			08 24				08 34
Hove 2	d									07 51														08 21	
Preston Park	d	07 41								07 55						08 11									
Hassocks 4	d	07 47														08 17					08 34				
Burgess Hill 4	d	07 51								08 04						08 21					08 38				
Lewes 4	d								07 50														08 20		
Wivelsfield 4	d	07 53														08 23							08 35		
Haywards Heath 3	a	07 58							08 05	08 09	08 17					08 28							08 40	08 35	08 47
	d	08 02							08 13		08 18					08 32							08 44		08 48
Balcombe	d															08 37									
Horsham 4	d							08 00							08 20							08 30			
Littlehaven	d							08 03														08 33			
Faygate	d																								
Ifield	d							08 09														08 39			
Crawley	d							08 13							08 29							08 43			
Three Bridges 4	a	08 11						08 16			08 26				08 32	08 42						08 46			08 56
	d	08 12						08 18			08 27				08 33	08 42						08 48			08 57
Gatwick Airport 10 ✈	a	08 16						08 22	08 24		08 31				08 37	08 47					08 51	08 52	08 55		09 01
	d	08 17				08 20		08 23	08 25		08 32			08 35	08 38	08 47				08 50	08 53	08 53	08 56		09 02
Horley 4	d							08 26							08 41							08 56			
Salfords	d							08 30																	
Earlswood (Surrey)	d							08 33																	
Tonbridge 4	d																		08 19						
Leigh (Kent)	d																		08 23						
Penshurst	d																		08 27						
Edenbridge	d																		08 33						
Godstone	d																		08 40						
Nutfield	d																		08 45						
Reigate	d			08 14	08 19							08 34													
Redhill 5	a			08 18	08 25			08 36				08 38			08 47				08 50			09 02			
	d			08 19				08 37							08 48				08 51			09 07			
Merstham	d			08 23				08 41														09 11			
Coulsdon South	d			08 28				08 46											08 58			09 16			
Purley 4	d			08 32				08 49											09 02			09 19			
East Croydon	a	08 31	08 22	08 37				08 54	08 40		08 46				08 59	09 02		08 52	09 07		09 08	09 24	09 11		09 16
	d	08 32	08 23	08 37				08 55	08 40		08 47		08 44		09 00	09 02		08 53	09 07		09 08	09 25	09 12		09 17
Norwood Junction 2	a			08 42				08 59											09 12			09 29			
New Cross Gate	d							09 07														09 37			
London Bridge 4 ⊖	a	08 45		08 55				09 13			09 00					09 15			09 25			09 43			09 30
London Blackfriars 3 ⊖	a	08 52									09 07					09 22									09 37
City Thameslink 3	a										09 10					09 26									09 40
Farringdon 3 ⊖	a	08 59									09 14					09 30									09 44
St Pancras International 15 ⊖	a	09 04									09 18					09 34									09 48
St Albans City	a	09 24									09 38					09 54									10 08
Luton Airport Parkway 4 ✈	a	09 37									09 50					10 07									10 20
Luton 7	a	09 40									09 53					10 10									10 23
Bedford 10	a	10 05									10 19					10 35									10 49
Clapham Junction 10	a		08 32						08 50				08 55		09 09			09 02			09 17		09 21		
London Victoria 15 ⊖	a		08 40			08 50			08 57				09 02	09 05	09 16			09 10		09 20	09 24		09 28		

Table 186

Saturdays

from 30 June

Brighton - London and Bedford

Network Diagram - see first Page of Table 186

		GW		SN	SN	SN	FC	SN	SN	GW	SN	SN		SN	FC	GW	SN	SN	SN	FC	SN	SN		SN	SN
		1		1	1 🚲	◇1 🚲	1	◇1 🚲	1	1	1 🚲	1		◇1	1	1	1	1 🚲	◇1	1	◇1 🚲	1		1 🚲	◇1
Brighton 10	d						08 37	08 49							09 04					09 07	09 19				09 24
Hove 2	d																								
Preston Park	d						08 41													09 11					
Hassocks 4	d						08 47													09 17					09 34
Burgess Hill 4	d						08 51													09 21					09 38
Lewes 4	d													08 50											
Wivelsfield 4	d						08 53													09 23					
Haywards Heath 3	a						08 58							09 05	09 17					09 28					
	d						09 02							09 13	09 18					09 32					
Balcombe	d																			09 37					
Horsham 4	d					08 50						09 00							09 20						
Littlehaven	d											09 03													
Faygate	d																								
Ifield	d											09 09													
Crawley	d					08 59						09 13							09 29						
Three Bridges 4	a					09 02	09 11					09 16			09 26				09 32	09 42					
	d					09 03	09 12					09 18			09 27				09 33	09 42					
Gatwick Airport 10 ✈	a					09 07	09 16					09 22		09 24	09 31				09 37	09 47					09 51
	d	09 03			09 05	09 08	09 17				09 20	09 23		09 25	09 32			09 35	09 38	09 47				09 50	09 53
Horley 4	d											09 26							09 41						
Salfords	d											09 30													
Earlswood (Surrey)	d											09 33													
Tonbridge 4	d																					09 19			
Leigh (Kent)	d																					09 23			
Penshurst	d																					09 27			
Edenbridge	d																					09 33			
Godstone	d																					09 40			
Nutfield	d																					09 45			
Reigate	d								09 14	09 18						09 34									
Redhill 5	a	09 10				09 15			09 18	09 25		09 36				09 38			09 47			09 50			
	d					09 16			09 19			09 37							09 48			09 51			
Merstham	d								09 23			09 41													
Coulsdon South	d								09 28			09 46										09 58			
Purley 4	d								09 32			09 49										10 02			
East Croydon 🚋	a					09 27	09 31	09 22	09 37			09 54		09 40	09 46				09 59	10 02	09 52	10 07			10 08
	d			09 14		09 28	09 32	09 23	09 37			09 55		09 40	09 47		09 44		10 00	10 02	09 53	10 07			10 08
Norwood Junction 2	a								09 42			09 59										10 12			
New Cross Gate	d											10 07													
London Bridge 4 ⊖	a						09 45		09 55			10 13			10 00					10 15		10 25			
London Blackfriars 3 ⊖	a						09 52								10 07					10 22					
City Thameslink 3	a						09 56								10 10					10 26					
Farringdon 3 ⊖	a						10 00								10 14					10 30					
St Pancras International 15 ⊖	a						10 04								10 18					10 34					
St Albans City	a						10 24								10 38					10 54					
Luton Airport Parkway 4 ✈	a						10 37								10 50					11 07					
Luton 7	a						10 40								10 53					11 10					
Bedford 10	a						11 05								11 19					11 35					
Clapham Junction 10	a			09 25		09 37		09 32						09 50			09 55		10 09		10 02				10 17
London Victoria 15 ⊖	a			09 32	09 35	09 44		09 40			09 50			09 57			10 02	10 05	10 16		10 10			10 20	10 24

Table 186

Saturdays

from 30 June

Brighton - London and Bedford

Network Diagram - see first Page of Table 186

		SN	SN	SN	FC	GW	SN	SN		SN	FC	SN	SN	GW	SN	SN	SN	SN		FC	GW	SN	SN	SN	FC
		1	◇1	◇1	1	1	1	1 🚲		◇1 🚲	1	◇1 🚲	1	1	1 🚲	1	◇1	◇1		1	1	1	1 🚲	◇1	1
Brighton 10	d				09 34						09 37	09 49								10 04					10 07
Hove 2	d			09 21														09 51							
Preston Park	d										09 41							09 55							10 11
Hassocks 4	d										09 47														10 17
Burgess Hill 4	d										09 51							10 04							10 21
Lewes 4	d		09 20														09 50								
Wivelsfield 4	d		09 35								09 53														10 23
Haywards Heath 3	a		09 40	09 35	09 47						09 58						10 05	10 09		10 17					10 28
	d		09 44		09 48						10 02						10 13			10 18					10 32
Balcombe	d																								10 37
Horsham 4	d	09 30								09 50						10 00								10 20	
Littlehaven	d	09 33														10 03									
Faygate	d																								
Ifield	d	09 39														10 09									
Crawley	d	09 43								09 59						10 13								10 29	
Three Bridges 4	a	09 46			09 56					10 02	10 11					10 16				10 26				10 32	10 42
	d	09 48			09 57					10 03	10 12					10 18				10 27				10 33	10 42
Gatwick Airport 10 ✈	a	09 52	09 55		10 01					10 07	10 16					10 22	10 24			10 31				10 37	10 47
	d	09 53	09 56		10 02	10 03		10 05		10 08	10 17				10 20	10 23	10 25			10 32			10 35	10 38	10 47
Horley 4	d	09 56														10 26								10 41	
Salfords	d															10 30									
Earlswood (Surrey)	d															10 33									
Tonbridge 4	d																								
Leigh (Kent)	d																								
Penshurst	d																								
Edenbridge	d																								
Godstone	d																								
Nutfield	d																								
Reigate	d												10 14	10 19							10 34				
Redhill 5	a	10 02				10 10				10 15			10 18	10 25		10 36					10 38			10 47	
	d	10 07								10 16			10 19			10 37								10 48	
Merstham	d	10 11											10 23			10 41									
Coulsdon South	d	10 16											10 28			10 46									
Purley 4	d	10 19											10 32			10 49									
East Croydon	a	10 24	10 11		10 16					10 27	10 31	10 22	10 37			10 54	10 40			10 46				10 59	11 02
	d	10 25	10 12		10 17		10 14			10 28	10 32	10 23	10 37			10 55	10 40			10 47		10 44		11 00	11 02
Norwood Junction 2	a	10 29											10 42			10 59									
New Cross Gate	d	10 37														11 07									
London Bridge 4 ⊖	a	10 43			10 30						10 45		10 55			11 13				11 00					11 15
London Blackfriars 3 ⊖	a				10 37						10 52									11 07					11 22
City Thameslink 3	a				10 40						10 56									11 10					11 26
Farringdon 3 ⊖	a				10 44						11 00									11 14					11 30
St Pancras International 15 ⊖	a				10 48						11 04									11 18					11 34
St Albans City	a				11 08						11 24									11 38					11 54
Luton Airport Parkway 4 ✈	a				11 20						11 37									11 50					12 07
Luton 7	a				11 23						11 40									11 53					12 10
Bedford 10	a				11 49						12 05									12 19					12 35
Clapham Junction 10	a		10 21				10 25			10 37		10 32					10 50					10 55		11 09	
London Victoria 15 ⊖	a		10 28				10 32	10 35		10 44		10 40			10 50		10 57					11 02	11 05	11 16	

Table 186

Saturdays
from 30 June

Brighton - London and Bedford

Network Diagram - see first Page of Table 186

Station		SN	SN	SN	SN	SN	SN	SN	FC	GW	SN	SN	SN	FC	SN	SN	GW	SN	SN	SN	SN	FC
		◇1	1	1	◇1	1	◇1	◇1	1	1	1	1	◇1	1	◇1	1	1	1	1	◇1	◇1	1
		🍴		🍴								🍴	🍴		🍴			🍴				
Brighton 10	d	10 19			10 24				10 34					10 37	10 49							11 04
Hove 2	d							10 21													10 51	
Preston Park	d													10 41							10 55	
Hassocks 4	d				10 34									10 47								
Burgess Hill 4	d				10 38									10 51							11 04	
Lewes 4	d						10 20													10 50		
Wivelsfield 4	d						10 35							10 53								
Haywards Heath 3	a						10 40	10 35	10 47					10 58						11 05	11 09	11 17
	d						10 44		10 48					11 02						11 13		11 18
Balcombe	d																					
Horsham 4	d					10 30							10 50						11 00			
Littlehaven	d					10 33													11 03			
Faygate	d																					
Ifield	d					10 39													11 09			
Crawley	d					10 43							10 59						11 13			
Three Bridges 4	a					10 46			10 56				11 02	11 11					11 16			11 26
	d					10 48			10 57				11 03	11 12					11 18			11 27
Gatwick Airport 10 ✈	a				10 51	10 52	10 55		11 01				11 07	11 16					11 22	11 24		11 31
	d			10 50	10 53	10 53	10 56		11 02	11 03		11 05	11 08	11 17				11 20	11 23	11 25		11 32
Horley 4	d					10 56													11 26			
Salfords	d																		11 30			
Earlswood (Surrey)	d																		11 33			
Tonbridge 4	d		10 19																			
Leigh (Kent)	d		10 23																			
Penshurst	d		10 27																			
Edenbridge	d		10 33																			
Godstone	d		10 40																			
Nutfield	d		10 45																			
Reigate	d															11 14	11 18					
Redhill 5	a		10 50			11 02				11 10			11 15			11 18	11 25		11 36			
	d		10 51			11 07							11 16			11 19			11 37			
Merstham	d					11 11										11 23			11 41			
Coulsdon South	d		10 58			11 16										11 28			11 46			
Purley 4	d		11 02			11 19										11 32			11 49			
East Croydon 🚋	a	10 52	11 07		11 08	11 24	11 11		11 16				11 27	11 31	11 22	11 37			11 54	11 40		11 46
	d	10 53	11 07		11 08	11 25	11 12		11 17		11 14		11 28	11 32	11 23	11 37			11 55	11 40		11 47
Norwood Junction 2	a		11 12			11 29										11 42			11 59			
New Cross Gate	d					11 37													12 07			
London Bridge 4 ⊖	a		11 25			11 43			11 30					11 45		11 55			12 13			12 00
London Blackfriars 3 ⊖	a								11 37					11 52								12 07
City Thameslink 3	a								11 40					11 56								12 10
Farringdon 3 ⊖	a								11 44					12 00								12 14
St Pancras International 15 ⊖	a								11 48					12 04								12 18
St Albans City	a								12 08					12 24								12 38
Luton Airport Parkway 4 ✈	a								12 20					12 37								12 50
Luton 7	a								12 23					12 40								12 53
Bedford 10	a								12 49					13 05								13 19
Clapham Junction 10	a	11 02			11 17		11 21				11 25		11 37		11 32					11 50		
London Victoria 15 ⊖	a	11 10		11 20	11 24		11 28				11 32	11 35	11 44		11 40			11 50		11 57		

Table 186

Saturdays

from 30 June

Brighton - London and Bedford

Network Diagram - see first Page of Table 186

		GW	SN	SN	SN	FC	SN	SN	SN	SN		SN	SN	SN	FC	GW	SN	SN	SN	FC		SN	SN	GW	SN
		1	1	1	◇1	1	◇1	1	1	◇1		1	◇1	◇1	1	1	1	1	◇1	1		◇1	1	1	1
				⚲			⚲		⚲									⚲	⚲			⚲			⚲
Brighton 10	d					11 07	11 19			11 24					11 34					11 37		11 49			
Hove 2	d													11 21											
Preston Park	d					11 11														11 41					
Hassocks 4	d					11 17				11 34										11 47					
Burgess Hill 4	d					11 21				11 38										11 51					
Lewes 4	d												11 20												
Wivelsfield 4	d					11 23							11 35							11 53					
Haywards Heath 3	a					11 28							11 40	11 35	11 47					11 58					
	d					11 32							11 44		11 48					12 02					
Balcombe	d					11 37																			
Horsham 4	d				11 20							11 30							11 50						
Littlehaven	d											11 33													
Faygate	d																								
Ifield	d											11 39													
Crawley	d				11 29							11 43							11 59						
Three Bridges 4	a				11 32	11 42						11 46			11 56				12 02	12 11					
	d				11 33	11 42						11 48			11 57				12 03	12 12					
Gatwick Airport 10 ✈	a				11 37	11 47				11 51		11 52	11 55		12 01				12 07	12 16					
	d			11 35	11 38	11 47			11 50	11 53		11 53	11 56		12 02	12 03		12 05	12 08	12 17					12 20
Horley 4	d				11 41							11 56													
Salfords	d																								
Earlswood (Surrey)	d																								
Tonbridge 4	d							11 19																	
Leigh (Kent)	d							11 23																	
Penshurst	d							11 27																	
Edenbridge	d							11 33																	
Godstone	d							11 40																	
Nutfield	d							11 45																	
Reigate	d	11 34																					12 14	12 19	
Redhill 5	a	11 38			11 47			11 50				12 02				12 10			12 15				12 18	12 25	
	d				11 48			11 51				12 07							12 16				12 19		
Merstham	d											12 11											12 23		
Coulsdon South	d							11 58				12 16											12 28		
Purley 4	d							12 02				12 19											12 32		
East Croydon	a				11 59	12 02	11 52	12 07		12 08		12 24	12 11		12 16				12 27	12 31		12 22	12 37		
	d		11 44		12 00	12 02	11 53	12 07		12 08		12 25	12 12		12 17		12 14		12 28	12 32		12 23	12 38		
Norwood Junction 2	a							12 12				12 29											12 42		
New Cross Gate	d											12 37													
London Bridge 4 ⊖	a					12 15		12 25				12 43			12 30					12 45			12 55		
London Blackfriars 3 ⊖	a					12 22									12 37					12 52					
City Thameslink 3	a					12 26									12 40					12 56					
Farringdon 3 ⊖	a					12 30									12 44					13 00					
St Pancras International 15 ⊖	a					12 34									12 48					13 04					
St Albans City	a					12 54									13 08					13 24					
Luton Airport Parkway 4 ✈	a					13 07									13 20					13 37					
Luton 7	a					13 10									13 23					13 40					
Bedford 10	a					13 35									13 49					14 05					
Clapham Junction 10	a		11 55		12 09		12 02			12 17			12 21				12 25		12 37			12 32			
London Victoria 15 ⊖	a		12 02	12 05	12 16		12 10		12 20	12 24			12 28				12 32	12 35	12 44			12 40			12 50

Table 186

Saturdays
from 30 June

Brighton - London and Bedford

Network Diagram - see first Page of Table 186

		SN	SN	SN	FC	GW		SN	SN	SN	FC	SN	SN	SN	SN	SN		SN	SN	FC	GW	SN	SN	SN	FC
		1	◇1	◇1	1	1		1	1 🛒	◇1	1	◇1 🛒	1	1 🛒	◇1	1		◇1	◇1	1	1	1	1 🛒	◇1 🛒	1
Brighton 10	d				12 04						12 07	12 19			12 24					12 34					12 37
Hove 2	d			11 51															12 21						
Preston Park	d			11 55							12 11														12 41
Hassocks 4	d										12 17				12 34										12 47
Burgess Hill 4	d			12 04							12 21				12 38										12 51
Lewes 4	d		11 50															12 20							
Wivelsfield 4	d										12 23							12 35							12 53
Haywards Heath 3	a		12 05	12 09	12 17						12 28							12 40	12 35	12 47					12 58
	d		12 13		12 18						12 32							12 44		12 48					13 02
Balcombe	d										12 37														
Horsham 4	d	12 00								12 20						12 30								12 50	
Littlehaven	d	12 03														12 33									
Faygate	d																								
Ifield	d	12 09														12 39									
Crawley	d	12 13								12 29						12 43								12 59	
Three Bridges 4	a	12 16			12 26					12 32	12 42					12 46				12 56				13 02	13 11
	d	12 18			12 27					12 33	12 42					12 48				12 57				13 03	13 12
Gatwick Airport 10 ✈	a	12 22	12 24		12 31					12 37	12 47				12 51	12 52		12 55		13 01				13 07	13 16
	d	12 23	12 25		12 32				12 35	12 38	12 47			12 50	12 53	12 53		12 56		13 02	13 03		13 05	13 08	13 17
Horley 4	d	12 26								12 41						12 56									
Salfords	d	12 30																							
Earlswood (Surrey)	d	12 33																							
Tonbridge 4	d												12 19												
Leigh (Kent)	d												12 23												
Penshurst	d												12 27												
Edenbridge	d												12 33												
Godstone	d												12 40												
Nutfield	d												12 45												
Reigate	d					12 34																			
Redhill 5	a	12 36				12 38				12 47			12 50			13 02					13 10			13 15	
	d	12 37								12 48			12 51			13 07								13 16	
Merstham	d	12 41														13 11									
Coulsdon South	d	12 46											12 58			13 16									
Purley 4	d	12 49											13 02			13 19									
East Croydon 🚋	a	12 54	12 40		12 46					12 59	13 02	12 52	13 07		13 08	13 24		13 11		13 16				13 27	13 31
	d	12 55	12 40		12 47			12 44		13 00	13 02	12 53	13 07		13 08	13 25		13 12		13 17		13 14		13 28	13 32
Norwood Junction 2	a	12 59											13 12			13 29									
New Cross Gate	d	13 07														13 37									
London Bridge 4 ⊖	a	13 13			13 00						13 15		13 25			13 43				13 30					13 45
London Blackfriars 3 ⊖	a				13 07						13 22									13 37					13 52
City Thameslink 3	a				13 10						13 26									13 40					13 56
Farringdon 3 ⊖	a				13 14						13 30									13 44					14 00
St Pancras International 15 ⊖	a				13 18						13 34									13 48					14 04
St Albans City	a				13 38						13 54									14 08					14 24
Luton Airport Parkway 4 ✈	a				13 50						14 07									14 20					14 37
Luton 7	a				13 53						14 10									14 23					14 40
Bedford 10	a				14 19						14 35									14 49					15 05
Clapham Junction 10	a		12 50					12 55		13 09		13 02			13 17			13 21				13 25		13 37	
London Victoria 15 ⊖	a		12 57					13 02	13 05	13 16		13 10		13 20	13 24			13 28				13 32	13 35	13 44	

Table 186

Saturdays

from 30 June

Brighton - London and Bedford

Network Diagram - see first Page of Table 186

		SN ◇1 (trolley)		SN 1	GW 1	SN 1 (trolley)	SN 1	SN ◇1	SN ◇1	FC 1	GW 1	SN 1		SN 1 (trolley)	SN ◇1	FC 1	SN ◇1 (trolley)	SN 1	SN 1 (trolley)	SN ◇1	SN 1	SN ◇1	SN ◇1		FC 1
Brighton 10	d	12 49								13 04						13 07	13 19			13 24					13 34
Hove 2	d								12 51														13 21		
Preston Park	d								12 55							13 11									
Hassocks 4	d															13 17				13 34					
Burgess Hill 4	d								13 04							13 21				13 38					
Lewes 4	d							12 50														13 20			
Wivelsfield 4	d															13 23						13 35			
Haywards Heath 3	a							13 05	13 09	13 17						13 28						13 40	13 35		13 47
	d							13 13		13 18						13 32						13 44			13 48
Balcombe	d															13 37									
Horsham 4	d						13 00								13 20						13 30				
Littlehaven	d						13 03														13 33				
Faygate	d																								
Ifield	d						13 09														13 39				
Crawley	d						13 13								13 29						13 43				
Three Bridges 4	a						13 16			13 26					13 32	13 42					13 46				13 56
	d						13 18			13 27					13 33	13 42					13 48				13 57
Gatwick Airport 10 ✈	a						13 22	13 24		13 31					13 37	13 47				13 51	13 52	13 55			14 01
	d					13 20	13 23	13 25		13 32				13 35	13 38	13 47			13 50	13 53	13 53	13 56			14 02
Horley 4	d						13 26								13 41						13 56				
Salfords	d						13 30																		
Earlswood (Surrey)	d						13 33																		
Tonbridge 4	d																	13 19							
Leigh (Kent)	d																	13 23							
Penshurst	d																	13 27							
Edenbridge	d																	13 33							
Godstone	d																	13 40							
Nutfield	d																	13 45							
Reigate	d			13 14	13 18						13 34														
Redhill 5	a			13 18	13 25		13 36				13 38				13 47			13 50			14 02				
	d			13 19			13 37								13 48			13 51			14 07				
Merstham	d			13 23			13 41														14 11				
Coulsdon South	d			13 28			13 46											13 58			14 16				
Purley 4	d			13 32			13 49											14 02			14 19				
East Croydon	a	13 22		13 37			13 54	13 40		13 46					13 59	14 02	13 52	14 07		14 08	14 24	14 11			14 16
	d	13 23		13 37			13 55	13 40		13 47		13 44			14 00	14 02	13 53	14 07		14 08	14 25	14 12			14 17
Norwood Junction 2	a			13 42			13 59											14 12			14 29				
New Cross Gate	d						14 07														14 37				
London Bridge 4 ⊖	a			13 55			14 13			14 00						14 15		14 25			14 43				14 30
London Blackfriars 3 ⊖	a									14 07						14 22									14 37
City Thameslink 3	a									14 10						14 26									14 40
Farringdon 3 ⊖	a									14 14						14 30									14 44
St Pancras International 15 ⊖	a									14 18						14 34									14 48
St Albans City	a									14 38						14 54									15 08
Luton Airport Parkway 4 ✈	a									14 50						15 07									15 20
Luton 7	a									14 53						15 10									15 23
Bedford 10	a									15 19						15 35									15 49
Clapham Junction 10	a	13 32						13 50				13 55			14 09		14 02			14 17		14 21			
London Victoria 15 ⊖	a	13 40				13 50		13 57				14 02		14 05	14 16		14 10		14 20	14 24		14 28			

Table 186

Saturdays
from 30 June

Brighton - London and Bedford

Network Diagram - see first Page of Table 186

Station		GW	SN	SN	SN	FC	SN	SN	GW	SN	SN	SN	SN	FC	GW	SN	SN	SN	FC	SN	SN	SN	SN
		1	1	1	◇1	1	◇1	1	1	1	1	◇1	◇1	1	1	1	1	◇1	1	◇1	1	1	◇1
				⚯	⚯		⚯			⚯							⚯			⚯		⚯	
Brighton 10	d					13 37	13 49							14 04					14 07	14 19			14 24
Hove 2	d												13 51										
Preston Park	d					13 41							13 55						14 11				
Hassocks 4	d					13 47													14 17				14 34
Burgess Hill 4	d					13 51							14 04						14 21				14 38
Lewes 4	d											13 50											
Wivelsfield 4	d					13 53													14 23				
Haywards Heath 3	a					13 58						14 05	14 09	14 17					14 28				
	d					14 02						14 13		14 18					14 32				
Balcombe	d																		14 37				
Horsham 4	d				13 50						14 00							14 20					
Littlehaven	d										14 03												
Faygate	d																						
Ifield	d										14 09												
Crawley	d				13 59						14 13							14 29					
Three Bridges 4	a				14 02	14 11					14 16			14 26				14 32	14 42				
	d				14 03	14 12					14 18			14 27				14 33	14 42				
Gatwick Airport 10 ✈	a				14 07	14 16					14 22	14 24		14 31				14 37	14 47				14 51
	d	14 03		14 05	14 08	14 17				14 20	14 23	14 25		14 32			14 35	14 38	14 47			14 50	14 53
Horley 4	d										14 26							14 41					
Salfords	d										14 30												
Earlswood (Surrey)	d										14 33												
Tonbridge 4	d																				14 19		
Leigh (Kent)	d																				14 23		
Penshurst	d																				14 27		
Edenbridge	d																				14 33		
Godstone	d																				14 40		
Nutfield	d																				14 45		
Reigate	d							14 14	14 19						14 34								
Redhill 5	a	14 10			14 15			14 18	14 25		14 36				14 38			14 47			14 50		
	d				14 16			14 19			14 37							14 48			14 51		
Merstham	d							14 23			14 41												
Coulsdon South	d							14 28			14 46										14 58		
Purley 4	d							14 32			14 49										15 02		
East Croydon	a				14 27	14 31	14 22	14 37			14 54	14 40		14 46				14 59	15 02	14 52	15 07		15 08
	d		14 14		14 28	14 32	14 23	14 37			14 55	14 40		14 47		14 44		15 00	15 02	14 53	15 07		15 08
Norwood Junction 2	a							14 42			14 59										15 12		
New Cross Gate	d										15 07												
London Bridge 4 ⊖	a					14 45		14 55			15 13			15 00					15 15		15 25		
London Blackfriars 3 ⊖	a					14 52								15 07					15 22				
City Thameslink 3	a					14 56								15 10					15 26				
Farringdon 3 ⊖	a					15 00								15 14					15 30				
St Pancras International 15 ⊖	a					15 04								15 18					15 34				
St Albans City	a					15 24								15 38					15 54				
Luton Airport Parkway 4 ✈	a					15 37								15 50					16 07				
Luton 7	a					15 40								15 53					16 10				
Bedford 10	a					16 05								16 19					16 35				
Clapham Junction 10	a		14 25		14 37		14 32					14 50				14 55		15 09		15 02			15 17
London Victoria 15 ⊖	a		14 32	14 35	14 44		14 40			14 50		14 57				15 02	15 05	15 16		15 10		15 20	15 24

Saturdays

from 30 June

Brighton - London and Bedford

Network Diagram - see first Page of Table 186

		SN	SN	SN	FC	GW	SN	SN	SN	FC	SN	SN	GW	SN	SN	SN	SN	FC	GW	SN	SN	SN	FC
		1	◇1	◇1	1	1	1	1	◇1	1	◇1	1	1	1	1	◇1	◇1	1	1	1	1	◇1	1
								⚲	⚲		⚲			⚲							⚲		
Brighton 10	d				14 34					14 37	14 49							15 04					15 07
Hove 2	d			14 21													14 51						
Preston Park	d									14 41							14 55						15 11
Hassocks 4	d									14 47													15 17
Burgess Hill 4	d									14 51							15 04						15 21
Lewes 4	d		14 20													14 50							
Wivelsfield 4	d		14 35							14 53													15 23
Haywards Heath 3	a		14 40	14 35	14 47					14 58						15 05	15 09	15 17					15 28
	d		14 44		14 48					15 02						15 13		15 18					15 32
Balcombe	d																						15 37
Horsham 4	d	14 30							14 50						15 00							15 20	
Littlehaven	d	14 33													15 03								
Faygate	d																						
Ifield	d	14 39													15 09								
Crawley	d	14 43							14 59						15 13							15 29	
Three Bridges 4	a	14 46			14 56				15 02	15 11					15 16			15 26				15 32	15 42
	d	14 48			14 57				15 03	15 12					15 18			15 27				15 33	15 42
Gatwick Airport 10 ✈	a	14 52	14 55		15 01				15 07	15 16					15 22	15 24		15 31				15 37	15 47
	d	14 53	14 56		15 02	15 03		15 05	15 08	15 17				15 20	15 23	15 25		15 32			15 35	15 38	15 47
Horley 4	d	14 56													15 26							15 41	
Salfords	d														15 30								
Earlswood (Surrey)	d														15 33								
Tonbridge 4	d																						
Leigh (Kent)	d																						
Penshurst	d																						
Edenbridge	d																						
Godstone	d																						
Nutfield	d																						
Reigate	d											15 14	15 18						15 34				
Redhill 5	a	15 02				15 10			15 15			15 18	15 25		15 36				15 38			15 47	
	d	15 07							15 16			15 19			15 37							15 48	
Merstham	d	15 11										15 23			15 41								
Coulsdon South	d	15 16										15 28			15 46								
Purley 4	d	15 19										15 32			15 49								
East Croydon 🚌	a	15 24	15 11		15 16				15 27	15 31	15 22	15 37			15 54	15 40		15 46				15 59	16 02
	d	15 25	15 12		15 17		15 14		15 28	15 32	15 23	15 37			15 55	15 40		15 47		15 44		16 00	16 02
Norwood Junction 2	a	15 29										15 42			15 59								
New Cross Gate	d	15 37													16 07								
London Bridge 4 ⊖	a	15 43			15 30					15 45		15 55			16 13			16 00					16 15
London Blackfriars 3 ⊖	a				15 37					15 52								16 07					16 22
City Thameslink 3	a				15 40					15 56								16 10					16 26
Farringdon 3 ⊖	a				15 44					16 00								16 14					16 30
St Pancras International 15 ⊖	a				15 48					16 04								16 18					16 34
St Albans City	a				16 08					16 24								16 38					16 54
Luton Airport Parkway 4 ✈	a				16 20					16 37								16 50					17 07
Luton 7	a				16 23					16 40								16 53					17 10
Bedford 10	a				16 49					17 05								17 19					17 35
Clapham Junction 10	a		15 21				15 25		15 37		15 32					15 50				15 55		16 09	
London Victoria 15 ⊖	a		15 28				15 32	15 35	15 44		15 40			15 50		15 57				16 02	16 05	16 16	

Table 186

Saturdays

from 30 June

Brighton - London and Bedford

Network Diagram - see first Page of Table 186

		SN	SN	SN	SN	SN	SN	SN	FC	GW	SN	SN	SN	FC	SN	SN	GW	SN	SN	SN	FC	GW
		◇1 🛒	1	1 🛒	◇1	1	◇1	◇1	1	1	1	1 🛒	◇1 🛒	1	◇1 🛒	1	1	1 🛒	1	◇1	1	1
Brighton 10	d	15 19			15 24				15 34					15 37	15 49						16 04	
Hove 2	d							15 21														
Preston Park	d													15 41								
Hassocks 4	d				15 34									15 47								
Burgess Hill 4	d				15 38									15 51								
Lewes 4	d						15 20													15 50		
Wivelsfield 4	d						15 35							15 53								
Haywards Heath 3	a						15 40	15 35	15 47					15 58						16 05	16 17	
	d						15 44		15 48					16 02						16 13	16 18	
Balcombe	d																					
Horsham 4	d					15 30							15 50						16 00			
Littlehaven	d					15 33													16 03			
Faygate	d																					
Ifield	d					15 39													16 09			
Crawley	d					15 43							15 59						16 13			
Three Bridges 4	a					15 46			15 56				16 02	16 11					16 16		16 26	
	d					15 48			15 57				16 03	16 12					16 18		16 27	
Gatwick Airport 10 ✈	a				15 51	15 52	15 55		16 01				16 07	16 16					16 22	16 24	16 31	
	d			15 50	15 53	15 53	15 56		16 02	16 03		16 05	16 08	16 17				16 20	16 23	16 25	16 32	
Horley 4	d					15 56													16 26			
Salfords	d																		16 30			
Earlswood (Surrey)	d																		16 33			
Tonbridge 4	d		15 19																			
Leigh (Kent)	d		15 23																			
Penshurst	d		15 27																			
Edenbridge	d		15 33																			
Godstone	d		15 40																			
Oxted	d		15 45																			
Reigate	d															16 14	16 19					16 34
Redhill 5	a		15 50			16 02				16 10			16 15			16 18	16 25		16 36			16 38
	d		15 51			16 07							16 16			16 19			16 37			
Merstham	d					16 11										16 23			16 41			
Coulsdon South	d		15 58			16 16										16 28			16 46			
Purley 4	d		16 02			16 19										16 32			16 49			
East Croydon 🚋	a	15 52	16 07		16 08	16 24	16 11		16 16				16 27	16 31	16 22	16 37			16 54	16 40	16 46	
	d	15 53	16 07		16 08	16 25	16 12		16 17		16 14		16 28	16 32	16 23	16 37			16 55	16 40	16 47	
Norwood Junction 2	a		16 12			16 29										16 42			16 59			
New Cross Gate	d					16 37													17 07			
London Bridge 4 ⊖	a		16 25			16 43			16 30					16 45		16 55			17 13		17 00	
London Blackfriars 3 ⊖	a								16 37					16 52							17 07	
City Thameslink 3	a								16 40					16 56							17 10	
Farringdon 3 ⊖	a								16 44					17 00							17 14	
St Pancras International 15 ⊖	a								16 48					17 04							17 18	
St Albans City	a								17 08					17 24							17 38	
Luton Airport Parkway 4 ✈	a								17 20					17 37							17 50	
Luton 7	a								17 23					17 40							17 53	
Bedford 10	a								17 49					18 05							18 19	
Clapham Junction 10	a	16 02			16 17		16 21				16 25		16 37		16 32					16 50		
London Victoria 15 ⊖	a	16 10		16 20	16 24		16 28				16 32	16 35	16 44		16 40			16 50		16 57		

Table 186

Saturdays

from 30 June

Brighton - London and Bedford

Network Diagram - see first Page of Table 186

		SN	SN	SN	FC	SN	SN		SN	SN	SN	SN	SN	FC	GW	SN	SN		SN	FC	SN	SN	GW	SN	SN
		1	1	◇1	1	◇1	1		1	◇1	1	◇1	◇1	1	1	1	1		◇1	1	◇1	1	1	1	1
			🚲			🚲			🚲								🚲		🚲		🚲			🚲	
Brighton 10	d				16 07	16 19				16 24				16 34						16 37	16 49				
Hove 2	d												16 21												
Preston Park	d				16 11															16 41					
Hassocks 4	d				16 17					16 34										16 47					
Burgess Hill 4	d				16 21					16 38										16 51					
Lewes 4	d											16 20													
Wivelsfield 4	d				16 23							16 35								16 53					
Haywards Heath 3	a				16 28							16 40	16 35	16 47						16 58					
	d				16 32							16 44		16 48						17 02					
Balcombe	d				16 37																				
Horsham 4	d			16 20							16 30								16 50						17 00
Littlehaven	d										16 33														17 03
Faygate	d																								
Ifield	d										16 39														17 09
Crawley	d			16 29							16 43								16 59						17 13
Three Bridges 4	a			16 32	16 42						16 46			16 56					17 02	17 11					17 16
	d			16 33	16 42						16 48			16 57					17 03	17 11					17 18
Gatwick Airport 10 ✈	a			16 37	16 47					16 51	16 52	16 55		17 01					17 07	17 15					17 22
	d		16 35	16 38	16 47				16 50	16 53	16 53	16 56		17 02	17 03		17 05		17 08	17 16				17 20	17 23
Horley 4	d			16 41							16 56														17 26
Salfords	d																								17 30
Earlswood (Surrey)	d																								17 33
Tonbridge 4	d						16 19																		
Leigh (Kent)	d						16 23																		
Penshurst	d						16 27																		
Edenbridge	d						16 33																		
Godstone	d						16 40																		
Nutfield	d						16 45																		
Reigate	d																					17 14	17 18		
Redhill 5	a			16 47			16 50				17 02				17 10				17 15			17 18	17 25		17 36
	d			16 48			16 51				17 07								17 16			17 19			17 37
Merstham	d										17 11											17 23			17 41
Coulsdon South	d						16 58				17 16											17 28			17 46
Purley 4	d						17 02				17 19											17 32			17 49
East Croydon 🚋	a			16 59	17 02	16 52	17 07			17 08	17 24	17 11		17 16					17 27	17 31	17 22	17 37			17 54
	d	16 44		17 00	17 02	16 53	17 07			17 08	17 25	17 12		17 17		17 14			17 28	17 31	17 23	17 37			17 55
Norwood Junction 2	a						17 12				17 29											17 42			17 59
New Cross Gate	d										17 37														18 07
London Bridge 4 ⊖	a				17 15		17 25				17 43			17 30						17 45		17 55			18 13
London Blackfriars 3 ⊖	a				17 22									17 37						17 52					
City Thameslink 3	a				17 26									17 40						17 56					
Farringdon 3 ⊖	a				17 30									17 44						18 00					
St Pancras International 15 ⊖	a				17 34									17 48						18 04					
St Albans City	a				17 54									18 08						18 24					
Luton Airport Parkway 4 ✈	a				18 07									18 20						18 37					
Luton 7	a				18 10									18 23						18 40					
Bedford 10	a				18 35									18 49						19 05					
Clapham Junction 10	a	16 55		17 09		17 02				17 17		17 21				17 25			17 37		17 32				
London Victoria 15 ⊖	a	17 02	17 05	17 16		17 10			17 20	17 24		17 28				17 32	17 35		17 44		17 40			17 50	

Table 186

Brighton - London and Bedford

Network Diagram - see first Page of Table 186

Station		SN ◇1	SN ◇1		FC 1	GW 1	SN 1	SN 1 🚲	SN ◇1	FC 1	SN ◇1 🚲	SN 1	SN 1 🚲		SN ◇1	SN 1	SN ◇1	SN ◇1	FC 1	GW 1	SN 1	SN 1 🚲	SN ◇1 🚲		FC 1
Brighton 10	d				17 04					17 07	17 19				17 24				17 34						17 37
Hove 2	d		16 51															17 21							
Preston Park	d		16 55							17 11															17 41
Hassocks 4	d									17 17					17 34										17 47
Burgess Hill 4	d		17 04							17 21					17 38										17 51
Lewes 4	d	16 50															17 20								
Wivelsfield 4	d									17 23							17 35								17 53
Haywards Heath 3	a	17 05	17 09		17 17					17 28							17 40	17 35	17 47						17 58
	d	17 13			17 18					17 32							17 44		17 48						18 02
Balcombe	d									17 37															
Horsham 4	d								17 20							17 30							17 50		
Littlehaven	d															17 33									
Faygate	d																								
Ifield	d															17 39									
Crawley	d								17 29							17 43							17 59		
Three Bridges 4	a				17 26				17 32	17 42						17 46			17 56				18 02		18 11
	d				17 27				17 33	17 42						17 48			17 57				18 03		18 12
Gatwick Airport 10 ✈	a	17 24			17 31				17 37	17 47					17 51	17 52	17 55		18 01				18 07		18 16
	d	17 25			17 32			17 35	17 38	17 47			17 50		17 53	17 53	17 56		18 02	18 03		18 05	18 08		18 17
Horley 4	d								17 41							17 56									
Salfords	d																								
Earlswood (Surrey)	d																								
Tonbridge 4	d											17 19													
Leigh (Kent)	d											17 23													
Penshurst	d											17 27													
Edenbridge	d											17 33													
Godstone	d											17 40													
Nutfield	d											17 45													
Reigate	d					17 34																			
Redhill 5	a					17 38			17 47			17 50				18 02				18 10			18 15		
	d								17 48			17 51				18 07							18 16		
Merstham	d															18 11									
Coulsdon South	d											17 58				18 16									
Purley 4	d											18 02				18 19									
East Croydon	a	17 40			17 46				17 59	18 02	17 52	18 07			18 08	18 24	18 11		18 16				18 27		18 31
	d	17 40			17 47		17 44		18 00	18 02	17 53	18 07			18 08	18 25	18 12		18 17		18 14		18 28		18 32
Norwood Junction 2	a											18 12				18 29									
New Cross Gate	d															18 37									
London Bridge 4 ⊖	a				18 00					18 15		18 25				18 43			18 30						18 45
London Blackfriars 3 ⊖	a				18 07					18 22									18 37						18 52
City Thameslink 3	a				18 10					18 26									18 40						18 56
Farringdon 3 ⊖	a				18 14					18 30									18 44						19 00
St Pancras International 15 ⊖	a				18 18					18 34									18 48						19 04
St Albans City	a				18 38					18 54									19 08						19 24
Luton Airport Parkway 4 ✈	a				18 50					19 07									19 20						19 37
Luton 7	a				18 53					19 10									19 23						19 40
Bedford 10	a				19 19					19 35									19 49						20 05
Clapham Junction 10	a	17 50					17 55		18 09		18 02				18 17		18 21				18 25		18 37		
London Victoria 15 ⊖	a	17 57					18 02	18 05	18 16		18 10		18 20		18 24		18 28				18 32	18 35	18 44		

Table 186

Saturdays

from 30 June

Brighton - London and Bedford

Network Diagram - see first Page of Table 186

		SN	SN	GW	SN	SN	SN	SN	FC		GW	SN	SN	SN	FC	SN	SN	SN	SN		SN	SN	SN	FC	GW
		◇1 🛒	1	1	1 🛒	1	◇1	◇1	1		1	1	1 🛒	◇1	1	◇1	1	1 🛒	◇1		1	◇1	◇1	1	1
Brighton 10	d	17 49							18 04						18 07	18 19			18 24					18 34	
Hove 2	d							17 51															18 21		
Preston Park	d							17 55							18 11										
Hassocks 4	d														18 17				18 34						
Burgess Hill 4	d							18 04							18 21				18 38						
Lewes 4	d						17 50															18 20			
Wivelsfield 4	d														18 23							18 35			
Haywards Heath 3	a						18 05	18 09	18 17						18 28							18 40	18 35	18 47	
	d						18 13		18 18						18 32							18 44		18 48	
Balcombe	d														18 37										
Horsham 4	d					18 00								18 20							18 32				
Littlehaven	d					18 03															18 35				
Faygate	d																								
Ifield	d					18 09															18 41				
Crawley	d					18 13								18 29							18 45				
Three Bridges 4	a					18 16			18 26					18 32	18 42						18 48			18 56	
	d					18 18			18 27					18 33	18 42						18 50			18 57	
Gatwick Airport 10 ✈	a					18 22	18 24		18 31					18 37	18 47				18 51		18 54	18 55		19 01	
	d				18 20	18 23	18 25		18 32				18 35	18 38	18 47			18 50	18 53		18 55	18 56		19 02	19 03
Horley 4	d					18 26								18 41							18 58				
Salfords	d					18 30																			
Earlswood (Surrey)	d					18 33																			
Tonbridge 4	d																18 19								
Leigh (Kent)	d																18 23								
Penshurst	d																18 27								
Edenbridge	d																18 33								
Godstone	d																18 40								
Nutfield	d																18 45								
Reigate	d		18 14	18 19							18 34														
Redhill 5	a		18 18	18 25		18 36					18 38			18 47			18 50				19 04				19 10
	d		18 19			18 37								18 48			18 51				19 07				
Merstham	d		18 23			18 41															19 11				
Coulsdon South	d		18 28			18 46											18 58				19 16				
Purley 4	d		18 32			18 49											19 02				19 19				
East Croydon	a	18 22	18 37			18 54	18 40		18 46					18 59	19 02	18 52	19 07		19 08		19 24	19 11		19 16	
	d	18 23	18 37			18 55	18 40		18 47			18 44		19 00	19 02	18 53	19 07		19 08		19 25	19 12		19 17	
Norwood Junction 2	a		18 42			18 59											19 12								
New Cross Gate	d					19 07																			
London Bridge 4 ⊖	a		18 55			19 13			19 00						19 15		19 25							19 30	
London Blackfriars 3 ⊖	a								19 07						19 22									19 37	
City Thameslink 3	a								19 10						19 26									19 40	
Farringdon 3 ⊖	a								19 14						19 30									19 44	
St Pancras International 15 ⊖	a								19 18						19 34									19 48	
St Albans City	a								19 38						19 54									20 08	
Luton Airport Parkway 4 ✈	a								19 50						20 07									20 20	
Luton 7	a								19 53						20 10									20 23	
Bedford 10	a								20 19						20 35									20 49	
Clapham Junction 10	a	18 32					18 50					18 55		19 09		19 02			19 17		19 37	19 21			
London Victoria 15 ⊖	a	18 40			18 50		18 57					19 02	19 05	19 16		19 10		19 20	19 24		19 44	19 28			

Table 186

Brighton - London and Bedford

Saturdays

from 30 June

Network Diagram - see first Page of Table 186

		SN 1	SN 1	SN ◇1	FC 1		SN ◇1	SN	GW 1	SN 1	SN ◇1	SN 1	SN ◇1	SN ◇1	FC 1		GW 1	SN 1	SN 1	SN 1	SN 1	FC 1	SN ◇1	SN 1	SN 1
Brighton 10	d				18 37		18 49				18 54				19 04							19 07	19 19		
Hove 2	d													18 51											
Preston Park	d				18 41									18 55								19 11			
Hassocks 4	d				18 47						19 06											19 17			
Burgess Hill 4	d				18 51									19 04								19 21			
Lewes 4	d												18 50												
Wivelsfield 4	d				18 53																	19 23			
Haywards Heath 3	a				18 58								19 05	19 09	19 17							19 28			
	d				19 02								19 14		19 18							19 32			
Balcombe	d																					19 37			
Horsham 4	d			18 50								19 02									19 21				19 32
Littlehaven	d											19 05													19 35
Faygate	d																								
Ifield	d											19 11													19 41
Crawley	d			18 59								19 14									19 30				19 45
Three Bridges 4	a			19 02	19 11							19 18			19 26						19 33	19 42			19 48
	d			19 03	19 12							19 18			19 27						19 34	19 42			19 50
Gatwick Airport 10 ✈	a			19 07	19 16						19 21	19 22	19 25		19 31						19 38	19 47			19 54
	d		19 05	19 08	19 17					19 20	19 23	19 23	19 26		19 32				19 35		19 39	19 47		19 50	19 55
Horley 4	d			19 11								19 26													19 58
Salfords	d											19 30													
Earlswood (Surrey)	d											19 33													
Tonbridge 4	d																	19 10							
Leigh (Kent)	d																	19 14							
Penshurst	d																	19 18							
Edenbridge	d																	19 24							
Godstone	d																	19 31							
Nutfield	d																	19 36							
Reigate	d							19 14	19 18								19 34								
Redhill 5	a			19 17				19 18	19 25			19 36					19 38	19 45			19 47				20 04
	d			19 18								19 37									19 48				20 07
Merstham	d											19 41													20 11
Coulsdon South	d											19 46													20 16
Purley 4	d											19 49													20 19
East Croydon	a			19 29	19 31		19 22				19 38	19 54	19 41		19 46						20 00	20 02	19 52		20 24
	d	19 14		19 29	19 32		19 23				19 38	19 57	19 42		19 47					19 44	20 00	20 02	19 53		20 26
Norwood Junction 2	a																								
New Cross Gate	d																								
London Bridge 4 ⊖	a				19 45										20 00							20 15			
London Blackfriars 3 ⊖	a				19 52										20 07							20 22			
City Thameslink 3	a				19 56										20 10							20 26			
Farringdon 3 ⊖	a				20 00										20 14							20 30			
St Pancras International 15 ⊖	a				20 04										20 18							20 34			
St Albans City	a				20 24										20 38							20 54			
Luton Airport Parkway 4 ✈	a				20 37										20 50							21 07			
Luton 7	a				20 40										20 53							21 10			
Bedford 10	a				21 05										21 19							21 35			
Clapham Junction 10	a	19 25		19 40			19 32				19 47	20 08	19 51							19 55	20 11		20 02		20 37
London Victoria 15 ⊖	a	19 32	19 35	19 50			19 40			19 50	19 54	20 15	19 58						20 05	20 05	20 20		20 10	20 20	20 44

Table 186

Saturdays

from 30 June

Brighton - London and Bedford

Network Diagram - see first Page of Table 186

		SN	SN	FC	GW	SN	SN	SN	FC	SN		GW	SN	SN	SN	SN	GW	SN	SN	SN		FC	SN	SN
		◇1	◇1	1	1	1	1	◇1	1	◇1		1	1	1	◇1	◇1	1	1	1	◇1		1	1	◇1
Brighton 10	d			19 34					19 37	19 49										19 54		20 04		
Hove 2	d		19 21													19 52								
Preston Park	d								19 41											19 58				
Hassocks 4	d								19 47											20 04				
Burgess Hill 4	d								19 51							20 02				20 08				
Lewes 4	d	19 20													19 50									
Wivelsfield 4	d	19 35							19 53						20 02					20 10				←
Haywards Heath 3	a	19 40	19 35	19 47					19 58						20 07	20 10				20 14		20 17		20 14
	d	19 44		19 48					20 02						20 14					20 22		20 18		20 22
Balcombe	d																			→				
Horsham 4	d							19 52						20 02										
Littlehaven	d													20 05										
Faygate	d																							
Ifield	d													20 11										
Crawley	d							20 01						20 14										
Three Bridges 4	a			19 56				20 05	20 11					20 18								20 26		20 32
	d			19 57				20 05	20 12					20 18								20 27		20 32
Gatwick Airport 10 ✈	a		19 55	20 01				20 10	20 16					20 22	20 25							20 31		20 37
	d		19 56	20 02	20 03		20 05	20 11	20 17				20 20	20 23	20 26							20 32	20 35	20 38
Horley 4	d													20 26										
Salfords	d													20 30										
Earlswood (Surrey)	d													20 33										
Tonbridge 4	d																	20 10						
Leigh (Kent)	d																	20 14						
Penshurst	d																	20 18						
Edenbridge	d																	20 24						
Godstone	d																	20 31						
Nutfield	d																	20 36						
Reigate	d											20 19					20 34							
Redhill 5	a				20 10			20 18				20 25		20 36			20 38	20 45						20 47
	d							20 18						20 37										20 48
Merstham	d													20 41										
Coulsdon South	d													20 46										
Purley 4	d													20 49										
East Croydon	a		20 11	20 16				20 29	20 31	20 22				20 54	20 41							20 46		20 59
	d		20 12	20 17		20 14		20 30	20 32	20 23				20 56	20 42				20 44			20 47		21 00
Norwood Junction 2	a																							
New Cross Gate	d																							
London Bridge 4 ⊖	a			20 30					20 45													21 00		
London Blackfriars 3 ⊖	a			20 37					20 52													21 07		
City Thameslink 3	a			20 40					20 56															
Farringdon 3 ⊖	a			20 44					21 00													21 13		
St Pancras International 15 ⊖	a			20 48					21 04													21 18		
St Albans City	a			21 08					21 24													21 38		
Luton Airport Parkway 4 ✈	a			21 20					21 37													21 50		
Luton 7	a			21 23					21 40													21 53		
Bedford 10	a			21 49					22 05													22 19		
Clapham Junction 10	a		20 21			20 25		20 40		20 32				21 07	20 51				20 55					21 10
London Victoria 15 ⊖	a		20 28			20 32	20 35	20 50		20 40			20 50	21 14	20 58				21 02				21 05	21 17

Table 186

Saturdays

from 30 June

Brighton - London and Bedford

Network Diagram - see first Page of Table 186

		FC	SN	SN	SN	SN	SN	FC	GW	SN	SN	FC	SN	GW	SN	SN	SN	SN	SN	GW	SN	SN	SN
		1	◇1	1	◇1	1	1	1	1	1	◇1	1	◇1	1	1	1	◇1	◇1	1	1	1	1	◇1
Brighton 10	d	20 07	20 19					20 34				20 37	20 49										21 00
Hove 2	d				20 22													20 52					
Preston Park	d	20 11										20 41											21 04
Hassocks 4	d	20 17										20 47											21 10
Burgess Hill 4	d	20 21										20 51						21 04					21 14
Lewes 4	d																20 50						
Wivelsfield 4	d	20 23										20 53					21 04						21 16
Haywards Heath 3	a	20 28			20 36			20 47				20 58					21 09	21 11					21 21
	d	20 32			20 39			20 48				21 02					21 15						21 22
Balcombe	d	20 37																					
Horsham 4	d						20 32				20 52					21 02							
Littlehaven	d						20 35									21 05							
Faygate	d																						
Ifield	d						20 41									21 11							
Crawley	d						20 45				21 01					21 14							
Three Bridges 4	a	20 42			20 47		20 48	20 56			21 05	21 11				21 18							21 31
	d	20 42			20 48		20 51	20 57			21 05	21 12				21 18							21 32
Gatwick Airport 10 ✈	a	20 47			20 52		20 56	21 01			21 10	21 16				21 22	21 26						21 37
	d	20 47		20 50	20 53		20 57	21 02	21 03	21 05	21 11	21 17			21 20	21 23	21 27					21 35	21 38
Horley 4	d						20 59									21 26							
Salfords	d															21 30							
Earlswood (Surrey)	d															21 33							
Tonbridge 4	d																		21 10				
Leigh (Kent)	d																		21 14				
Penshurst	d																		21 18				
Edenbridge	d																		21 24				
Godstone	d																		21 31				
Nutfield	d																		21 36				
Reigate	d													21 18						21 40			
Redhill 5	a						21 06		21 10		21 18			21 25		21 36			21 41	21 44			21 47
	d						21 07				21 18					21 37							21 47
Merstham	d						21 11									21 41							
Coulsdon South	d						21 16									21 46							
Purley 4	d						21 19									21 49							
East Croydon ⇌	a	21 02	20 52		21 08		21 24	21 16			21 30	21 31	21 22			21 54	21 41						21 59
	d	21 02	20 53		21 09	21 14	21 26	21 17			21 31	21 32	21 23			21 56	21 42				21 44		22 00
Norwood Junction 2	a																						
New Cross Gate	d																						
London Bridge 4 ⊖	a	21 15						21 30				21 45											
London Blackfriars 3 ⊖	a	21 22						21 37				21 52											
City Thameslink 3	a																						
Farringdon 3 ⊖	a	21 29						21 43				21 59											
St Pancras International 15 ⊖	a	21 34						21 48				22 04											
St Albans City	a	21 54						22 08				22 24											
Luton Airport Parkway 4 ✈	a	22 07						22 20				22 37											
Luton 7	a	22 10						22 23				22 40											
Bedford 10	a	22 35						22 49				23 05											
Clapham Junction 10	a		21 02		21 18	21 25	21 37				21 40		21 32			22 07	21 51				21 55		22 10
London Victoria 15 ⊖	a		21 10	21 20	21 26	21 32	21 44			21 35	21 50		21 40		21 50	22 15	21 58				22 02	22 05	22 20

Table 186

Saturdays
from 30 June

Brighton - London and Bedford

Network Diagram - see first Page of Table 186

		FC	SN		SN	SN	SN	SN	SN	SN	FC	SN	SN		GW	SN	SN	SN	SN	SN	SN	SN	FC		GW
		1	◇1		1	◇1	1	1	1	◇1	1	◇1	1		1	1	◇1	◇1	1	1	1	◇1	1		1
																		A							
Brighton 10	d	21 07	21 19								21 37	21 49										22 00	22 07		
Hove 2	d					21 22												21 52							
Preston Park	d	21 11									21 41											22 04	22 11		
Hassocks 4	d	21 17									21 47											22 10	22 17		
Burgess Hill 4	d	21 21									21 51							22 04				22 14	22 21		
Lewes 4	d																21 50								
Wivelsfield 4	d	21 23									21 53						22 02					22 16	22 23		
Haywards Heath 3	a	21 28				21 36					21 58						22 06	22 09				22 21	22 28		
	d	21 32				21 39					22 02						22 13					22 22	22 32		
Balcombe	d	21 37																					22 37		
Horsham 4	d							21 32		21 52						22 02									
Littlehaven	d							21 35								22 05									
Faygate	d																								
Ifield	d							21 41								22 11									
Crawley	d							21 45		22 01						22 14									
Three Bridges 4	a	21 42				21 47		21 48		22 05	22 11					22 18						22 31	22 43		
	d	21 42				21 48		21 52		22 05	22 12					22 19						22 32	22 43		
Gatwick Airport 10 ✈	a	21 47				21 52		21 56		22 10	22 16					22 23	22 24					22 37	22 47		
	d	21 47			21 50	21 53		21 57	22 05	22 11	22 17		22 20		22 22	22 24	22 25			22 35		22 38	22 47		
Horley 4	d							22 00								22 27									
Salfords	d															22 31									
Earlswood (Surrey)	d															22 34									
Tonbridge 4	d																		22 10						
Leigh (Kent)	d																		22 14						
Penshurst	d																		22 18						
Edenbridge	d																		22 24						
Godstone	d																		22 31						
Nutfield	d																		22 36						
Reigate	d																								22 48
Redhill 5	a							22 06		22 18					22 30	22 37			22 42			22 46			22 52
	d							22 07		22 18						22 38						22 46			
Merstham	d							22 11								22 42									
Coulsdon South	d							22 16								22 47									
Purley 4	d							22 19								22 50									
East Croydon	a	22 02	21 52			22 08		22 24		22 30	22 32	22 22				22 55	22 40					22 59	23 02		
	d	22 02	21 53			22 09	22 14	22 26		22 31	22 32	22 23				22 56	22 40				22 44	23 00	23 02		
Norwood Junction 2	a																								
New Cross Gate	d																								
London Bridge 4 ⊖	a	22 15									22 45												23 15		
London Blackfriars 3 ⊖	a	22 22									22 52												23 22		
City Thameslink 3	a																								
Farringdon 3 ⊖	a	22 27									22 57												23 28		
St Pancras International 15 ⊖	a	22 32									23 02												23 32		
St Albans City	a	22 56									23 26												23 56		
Luton Airport Parkway 4 ✈	a	23 08									23 38												00 08		
Luton 7	a	23 11									23 41												00 11		
Bedford 10	a	23 38									00 08												00 38		
Clapham Junction 10	a		22 02			22 18	22 25	22 37		22 40		22 32				23 06	22 49				22 55	23 10			
London Victoria 15 ⊖	a		22 13		22 20	22 26	22 35	22 44	22 35	22 50		22 40	22 50			23 14	22 57			23 05	23 05	23 20			

A (symbol) from Haywards Heath

Table 186

Saturdays

from 30 June

Brighton - London and Bedford

Network Diagram - see first Page of Table 186

Station		SN 1	SN 1	SN 1	FC 1	SN ◇1	FC 1	GW 1	SN 1		SN 1	SN 1	SN 1	GW 1	SN ◇1	FC 1	SN 1	SN ◇1	FC 1
Brighton 10	d				22 33										23 02	23 11			23 37
Hove 2	d																		
Preston Park	d				22 37										23 06				23 41
Hassocks 4	d				22 43										23 12	23 20			23 47
Burgess Hill 4	d				22 47										23 16	23 23			23 51
Lewes 4	d					22 40													
Wivelsfield 4	d				22 49	22 54									23 19				23 53
Haywards Heath 3	a				22 53	22 58									23 23	23 28			23 58
	d				22 54	22 59									23 24	23 29			23 59
Balcombe	d				22 59														00 04
Horsham 4	d										23 02								
Littlehaven	d										23 05								
Faygate	d																		
Ifield	d										23 11								
Crawley	d						←				23 14							←	
Three Bridges 4	a				23 05	23 08	23 05				23 18				23 32	23 37		23 32	00 10
	d				23 12	23 08	23 12				23 18				23 47	23 38		23 47	00 10
Gatwick Airport 10 ✈	a				→	23 12	23 16				23 22				→	23 42		23 52	00 14
	d	22 50	23 05			23 13	23 17	23 18	23 20		23 23		23 35			23 43	23 50	23 53	00 15
Horley 4	d										23 26							23 56	
Salfords	d										23 30								
Earlswood (Surrey)	d										23 33								
Tonbridge 4	d											23 17							
Leigh (Kent)	d											23 21							
Penshurst	d											23 25							
Edenbridge	d											23 31							
Godstone	d											23 38							
Nutfield	d											23 43							
Reigate	d													23 54					
Redhill 5	a							23 25			23 36	23 49		23 58				00 03	00 22
	d										23 37							00 03	00 23
Merstham	d										23 41								
Coulsdon South	d										23 46								
Purley 4	d										23 49							00 11	
East Croydon 🚋	a					23 29	23 32				23 55							00 16	00 35
	d			23 14		23 30	23 32				23 56					00 01		00 17	00 36
Norwood Junction 2	a															00 04			
New Cross Gate	d																		
London Bridge 4 ⊖	a						23 44									00 21			00 51
London Blackfriars 3 ⊖	a						23 52									00 28			00 58
City Thameslink 3	a																		
Farringdon 3 ⊖	a						23 58									00 33			
St Pancras International 15 ⊖	a						00 02									00 37			01 07
St Albans City	a						00 26									01 10			01 40
Luton Airport Parkway 4 ✈	a						00 38									01 22			01 52
Luton 7	a						00 41									01 25			01 55
Bedford 10	a						01 08									01 52			02 22
Clapham Junction 10	a			23 25		23 41					00 11							00 29	
London Victoria 15 ⊖	a	23 20	23 35	23 35		23 52			23 55		00 18		00 10				00 20	00 37	

Table 186

Sundays

until 24 June

Brighton - London and Bedford

Network Diagram - see first Page of Table 186

		FC	FC	FC	SN	SN	SN	FC	FC	SN	SN	SN	FC	FC	SN	GW	SN	SN	SN	SN	SN	SN	SN
		1	1	1	1	1	◇1	1	1	1	◇1	1	1	1	1	1		1	1	1	1	1	1
								A					A										
Brighton 10	d	21p37	22p07	22p33			23p02	23p11	23p11				23p37	23p37									
Hove 2	d																						
Preston Park	d	21p41	22p11	22p37			23p06						23p41	23p41									
Hassocks 4	d	21p47	22p17	22p43			23p12	23p20	23p20				23p47	23p47									
Burgess Hill 4	d	21p51	22p21	22p47			23p16	23p23	23p23				23p51	23p51									
Lewes 4	d																						
Wivelsfield 4	d	21p53	22p23	22p49			23p19						23p53	23p53									
Haywards Heath 3	a	21p58	22p28	22p53			23p23	23p28	23p28				23p58	23p58									
	d	22p02	22p32	22p54			23p24	23p29	23p29				23p59	23p59									
Balcombe	d		22p37	22p59									00 04	00 04									
Horsham 4	d				23p02																		
Littlehaven	d				23p05																		
Faygate	d																						
Ifield	d				23p11																		
Crawley	d				23p14						←												
Three Bridges 4	a	22p11	22p43	23p05	23p18		23p32	23p37	23p37		23p32		00 10	00 10									
	d	22p12	22p43	23p12	23p18		23p47	23p38	23p38		23p47		00 10	00 10						01 10		02 10	03 10
Gatwick Airport 10 ✈	a	22p16	22p47	23p16	23p22		→	23p42	23p42		23p52		00 14	00 14						01 19		02 14	03 14
	d	22p17	22p47	23p17	23p23	23p35		23p43	23p43	23p50	23p53	00 07	00 15	00 15	00 20			00 35	00 50	01 20	01 35	02 15	03 15
Horley 4	d				23p26						23p56									01 22		02 18	03 18
Salfords	d				23p30																		
Earlswood (Surrey)	d				23p33																		
Tonbridge 4	d																						
Leigh (Kent)	d																						
Penshurst	d																						
Edenbridge	d																						
Godstone	d																						
Nutfield	d																						
Reigate	d															00 45							
Redhill 5	a				23p36						00 03		00 22	00 22		00 49							
	d				23p37						00 03		00 23	00 23									
Merstham	d				23p41																		
Coulsdon South	d				23p46																		
Purley 4	d				23p49						00 11									01 37		02 33	03 33
East Croydon	a	22p32	23p02	23p32	23p55			00 01	00 01		00 16		00 35	00 35						01 42		02 39	03 39
	d	22p32	23p02	23p32	23p56			00 04	00 04		00 17		00 36	00 36			00 49			01 43		02 40	03 40
Norwood Junction 2	a																						
New Cross Gate	d																						
London Bridge 4 ⊖	a	22p45	23p15	23p46				00 19	00 21				00 52	00 51									
London Blackfriars 3 ⊖	a	22p52	23p22	23p52					00 28					00 58									
City Thameslink 3	a																						
Farringdon 3 ⊖	a	22p57	23p28	23p58					00 33														
St Pancras International 15 ⊖	a	23p02	23p32	00 02					00 37					01 07									
St Albans City	a	23p26	23p56	00 26					01 10					01 40									
Luton Airport Parkway 4 ✈	a	23p39	00 09	00 39					01 22					01 52									
Luton 7	a	23p42	00 12	00 42					01 25					01 55									
Bedford 10	a	00 09	00 39	01 09					01 52					02 22									
Clapham Junction 10	a				00 11						00 29						01 03			01 54		02 53	03 53
London Victoria 15 ⊖	a				00 18	00 10				00 20	00 37	00 42			00 55		01 10	01 11	01 25	02 05	02 10	03 05	04 05

A 20 May

Table 186

Sundays

until 24 June

Brighton - London and Bedford

Network Diagram - see first Page of Table 186

		SN	SN	FC	SN	SN	SN	SN	GW	FC	SN	SN	SN	FC	SN	SN	GW	SN	GW	FC	SN	SN	SN
		1	1		1	1	1	1	1		1	1	1	1	1	◇1	1	1	1	1	1	1	1
								🛒			🛒		🛒		🛒			🛒			🛒		🛒
Brighton 10	d									05 45				06 15		06 19				06 45			
Hove 2	d																						
Preston Park	d															06 22							
Hassocks 4	d									05 54				06 24		06 29				06 54			
Burgess Hill 4	d									05 57				06 27		06 32				06 57			
Lewes 4	d																						
Wivelsfield 4	d															06 34							
Haywards Heath 3	a									06 02				06 32		06 39				07 02			
	d									06 03				06 33		06 39				07 03			
Balcombe	d																						
Horsham 4	d											06 04										07 00	
Littlehaven	d											06 07										07 03	
Faygate	d																						
Ifield	d											06 13										07 09	
Crawley	d											06 17										07 13	
Three Bridges 4	a									06 11		06 20		06 41		06 48				07 11		07 16	
	d	04 10		05 12		05 30				06 12		06 21		06 42		06 48				07 12		07 18	
Gatwick Airport 10 ✈	a	04 14		05 16		05 34				06 16		06 25		06 46		06 52				07 16		07 22	
	d	04 15	04 35	05 17	05 20	05 36	05 50	06 05	06 08	06 17	06 20		06 35	06 47	06 50	06 53		07 05	07 08	07 17	07 20	07 23	07 35
Horley 4	d	04 18				05 38																07 26	
Salfords	d																					07 30	
Earlswood (Surrey)	d																					07 33	
Tonbridge 4	d																						
Leigh (Kent)	d																						
Penshurst	d																						
Edenbridge	d																						
Godstone	d																						
Nutfield	d																						
Reigate	d																07 05						
Redhill 5	a					05 46			06 17								07 09		07 16			07 36	
	d					05 46																07 37	
Merstham	d																					07 41	
Coulsdon South	d																					07 46	
Purley 4	d	04 33				05 56																07 50	
East Croydon	a	04 39		05 32		06 01				06 32				07 01		07 10				07 31		07 56	
	d	04 40		05 32		06 02				06 32				07 02		07 10				07 32		07 56	
Norwood Junction 2	a																					08 00	
New Cross Gate	d																						
London Bridge 4 ⊖	a													07 15						07 45		08 12	
London Blackfriars 3 ⊖	a			05 59						06 59				07 22						07 52			
City Thameslink 3	a																						
Farringdon 3 ⊖	a													07 27						07 57			
St Pancras International 15 ⊖	a													07 32						08 02			
St Albans City	a													08 07						08 37			
Luton Airport Parkway 4 ✈	a													08 20						08 50			
Luton 7	a													08 23						08 53			
Bedford 10	a													08 50						09 20			
Clapham Junction 10	a	04 53				06 14										07 24							
London Victoria 15 ⊖	a	05 05	05 10		05 58	06 22	06 25	06 40			06 55		07 10		07 20	07 31		07 35			07 50		08 05

Table 186

Sundays

until 24 June

Brighton - London and Bedford

Network Diagram - see first Page of Table 186

		SN ◇1		FC 1	SN 1 🚲	SN ◇1 🚲	SN ◇1	SN 1	SN 1 🚲	GW 1	FC 1	GW 1		SN 1 🚲	SN ◇1	SN 1	SN 1 🚲	SN ◇1	SN ◇1 🚲	FC 1	SN 1	SN 1 🚲		SN ◇1 🚲	SN ◇1
Brighton 10	d	07 04		07 15							07 45							08 00	08 10	08 15					
Hove 2	d														07 54										
Preston Park	d	07 07																08 03							
Hassocks 4	d	07 14		07 24							07 54							08 10		08 24					
Burgess Hill 4	d	07 17		07 27							07 57				08 04			08 13		08 27					
Lewes 4	d					07 22																		08 22	
Wivelsfield 4	d	07 19				07 36												08 15						08 36	
Haywards Heath 3	a	07 24		07 32		07 40					08 02				08 09			08 20		08 32				08 40	
	d	07 25		07 33		07 41					08 03				08 11			08 25		08 33				08 41	
Balcombe	d	07 30																08 30							
Horsham 4	d						07 37									08 00									08 37
Littlehaven	d															08 03									
Faygate	d																								
Ifield	d															08 09									
Crawley	d						07 46									08 13									08 46
Three Bridges 4	a	07 36		07 41			07 50				08 11					08 16		08 36		08 41					08 50
	d	07 36		07 42			07 50				08 12					08 18		08 36		08 42					08 50
Gatwick Airport 10 ✈	a	07 40		07 46		07 52	07 55				08 16				08 22	08 22		08 40		08 46				08 52	08 55
	d	07 41		07 47	07 50	07 53	07 56		08 05	08 08	08 17			08 20	08 23	08 23	08 35	08 41		08 47		08 50		08 53	08 56
Horley 4	d						07 58									08 26									08 58
Salfords	d															08 30									
Earlswood (Surrey)	d															08 33									
Tonbridge 4	d							07 41																	
Leigh (Kent)	d							07 45																	
Penshurst	d							07 49																	
Edenbridge	d							07 55																	
Godstone	d							08 02																	
Nutfield	d							08 07																	
Reigate	d											08 13													
Redhill 5	a	07 48					08 05	08 12		08 16		08 18				08 36		08 48							09 05
	d	07 49					08 05	08 13								08 37		08 49							09 05
Merstham	d							08 17								08 41									
Coulsdon South	d							08 22								08 46									
Purley 4	d						08 14	08 27								08 50									09 14
East Croydon 🚋	a	08 00		08 02		08 09	08 19	08 32			08 31				08 38	08 56		09 00	08 45	09 02				09 09	09 19
	d	08 00		08 02		08 09	08 20	08 34			08 32				08 39	08 56		09 00	08 46	09 02	08 50			09 09	09 20
Norwood Junction 2	a							08 38								09 00									
New Cross Gate	d																								
London Bridge 4 ⊖	a			08 15				08 51			08 45					09 12				09 15					
London Blackfriars 3 ⊖	a			08 22							08 52									09 22					
City Thameslink 3	a																								
Farringdon 3 ⊖	a			08 27							08 57									09 27					
St Pancras International 15 ⊖	a			08 32							09 02									09 32					
St Albans City	a			09 07							09 38									10 07					
Luton Airport Parkway 4 ✈	a			09 20							09 50									10 20					
Luton 7	a			09 23							09 53									10 23					
Bedford 10	a			09 50							10 20									10 50					
Clapham Junction 10	a	08 09				08 18	08 32								08 48			09 09	08 55		09 02			09 18	09 32
London Victoria 15 ⊖	a	08 16			08 20	08 25	08 39		08 35					08 50	08 55		09 05	09 17	09 03		09 09	09 20		09 25	09 39

Table 186

Sundays

until 24 June

Brighton - London and Bedford

Network Diagram - see first Page of Table 186

		SN	SN	SN	GW	FC	GW	SN		SN	SN	SN	SN	SN	FC	SN	SN	SN		SN	SN	SN	SN	GW	FC
		◇1	1	1	1	1	1	1		◇1	1	1	◇1	◇1	1	1	1	◇1		◇1	◇1	1	1	1	1
						A																			
		[trolley]		[trolley]				[trolley]				[trolley]		[trolley]			[trolley]	[trolley]			[trolley]		[trolley]		
Brighton 10	d	08 40				08 45							09 00	09 10	09 15						09 40				09 45
Hove 2	d									08 54															
Preston Park	d												09 03												
Hassocks 4	d					08 54							09 10		09 24										09 54
Burgess Hill 4	d					08 57				09 04			09 13		09 27										09 57
Lewes 4	d																	09 22							
Wivelsfield 4	d												09 15					09 36							
Haywards Heath 3	a					09 02				09 09			09 20		09 32			09 40							10 02
	d					09 03				09 11			09 25		09 33			09 41							10 03
Balcombe	d												09 30												
Horsham 4	d										09 00									09 37					
Littlehaven	d										09 03														
Faygate	d																								
Ifield	d										09 09														
Crawley	d										09 13									09 46					
Three Bridges 4	a					09 11					09 16		09 36		09 41					09 50					10 11
	d					09 12					09 18		09 36		09 42					09 50					10 12
Gatwick Airport 10 ✈	a	09 01				09 16				09 22	09 22		09 40		09 46			09 52		09 55	10 01				10 16
	d	09 02		09 05	09 08	09 17		09 20		09 23	09 23	09 35	09 41		09 47		09 50	09 53		09 56	10 02		10 05	10 08	10 17
Horley 4	d										09 26									09 58					
Salfords	d										09 30														
Earlswood (Surrey)	d										09 33														
Tonbridge 4	d		08 41																			09 41			
Leigh (Kent)	d		08 45																			09 45			
Penshurst	d		08 49																			09 49			
Edenbridge	d		08 55																			09 55			
Godstone	d		09 02																			10 02			
Nutfield	d		09 07																			10 07			
Reigate	d						09 13																		
Redhill 5	a		09 12		09 16		09 18				09 36		09 48							10 05		10 12		10 16	
	d		09 13								09 37		09 49							10 05		10 13			
Merstham	d		09 17								09 41											10 17			
Coulsdon South	d		09 22								09 46											10 22			
Purley 4	d		09 27								09 50									10 14		10 27			
East Croydon	a	09 16	09 32			09 31				09 38	09 56		10 00	09 45	10 02			10 09		10 19	10 16	10 32			10 31
	d	09 17	09 34			09 32				09 39	09 56		10 00	09 46	10 02	09 50		10 09		10 20	10 17	10 34			10 32
Norwood Junction 2	a		09 38								10 00											10 38			
New Cross Gate	d																								
London Bridge 4 ⊖	a		09 51			09 45					10 12				10 15							10 51			10 45
London Blackfriars 3 ⊖	a					09 52									10 22										10 52
City Thameslink 3	a																								
Farringdon 3 ⊖	a					09 56									10 26										10 56
St Pancras International 15 ⊖	a					10 01									10 31										11 01
St Albans City	a					10 33									10 56										11 25
Luton Airport Parkway 4 ✈	a					10 46									11 08										11 38
Luton 7	a					10 49									11 11										11 41
Bedford 10	a					11 15									11 37										12 07
Clapham Junction 10	a	09 26								09 48			10 09	09 55		10 02		10 18		10 32	10 26				
London Victoria 15 ⊖	a	09 33		09 35				09 50		09 55		10 05	10 17	10 03		10 09	10 20	10 25		10 39	10 33		10 35		

A not 20 May

Table 186

Sundays
until 24 June

Brighton - London and Bedford

Network Diagram - see first Page of Table 186

		GW	SN	SN		SN	SN	SN	SN	FC	SN	SN	SN	SN		SN	SN	SN	GW	FC	GW	SN	SN	SN	
		1	1	◇1		1	1	◇1	◇1	1	1	1	◇1	◇1		◇1	1	1	1	1	1	1	◇1	1	
			🚲				🚲		🚲			🚲	🚲	🚲		🚲		🚲				🚲			
Brighton 10	d							10 00	10 10	10 15						10 40				10 45					
Hove 2	d			09 54																			10 54		
Preston Park	d							10 03																	
Hassocks 4	d							10 10		10 24										10 54					
Burgess Hill 4	d			10 04				10 13		10 27										10 57			11 04		
Lewes 4	d												10 22												
Wivelsfield 4	d							10 15					10 36												
Haywards Heath 3	a			10 09				10 20		10 32			10 40							11 02			11 09		
	d			10 11				10 25		10 33			10 41							11 03			11 11		
Balcombe	d							10 30																	
Horsham 4	d					10 00								10 37										11 00	
Littlehaven	d					10 03																		11 03	
Faygate	d																								
Ifield	d					10 09																		11 09	
Crawley	d					10 13								10 46										11 13	
Three Bridges 4	a					10 16		10 36		10 41				10 50						11 11				11 16	
	d					10 18		10 36		10 42				10 50						11 12				11 18	
Gatwick Airport 10 ✈	a			10 22		10 22		10 40		10 46			10 52	10 55		11 01				11 16			11 22	11 22	
	d		10 20	10 23		10 23	10 35	10 41		10 47		10 50	10 53	10 56		11 02		11 05	11 08	11 17		11 20	11 23	11 23	
Horley 4	d					10 26								10 58										11 26	
Salfords	d					10 30																		11 30	
Earlswood (Surrey)	d					10 33																		11 33	
Tonbridge 4	d																10 41								
Leigh (Kent)	d																10 45								
Penshurst	d																10 49								
Edenbridge	d																10 55								
Godstone	d																11 02								
Nutfield	d																11 07								
Reigate	d	10 13																			11 13				
Redhill 5	a	10 18				10 36		10 48						11 05			11 12		11 16		11 18			11 36	
	d					10 37		10 49						11 05			11 13							11 37	
Merstham	d					10 41											11 17							11 41	
Coulsdon South	d					10 46											11 22							11 46	
Purley 4	d					10 50								11 14			11 27							11 50	
East Croydon	a			10 39		10 56		11 00	10 45	11 02			11 09	11 19		11 16	11 32			11 31			11 38	11 56	
	d			10 39		10 56		11 00	10 46	11 02	10 50		11 09	11 20		11 17	11 34			11 32			11 39	11 56	
Norwood Junction 2	a					11 00											11 38							12 00	
New Cross Gate	d																								
London Bridge 4 ⊖	a					11 12				11 15							11 51			11 45				12 12	
London Blackfriars 3 ⊖	a									11 22										11 52					
City Thameslink 3	a																								
Farringdon 3 ⊖	a									11 26										11 56					
St Pancras International 15 ⊖	a									11 31										12 01					
St Albans City	a									11 56										12 25					
Luton Airport Parkway 4 ✈	a									12 08										12 38					
Luton 7	a									12 11										12 41					
Bedford 10	a									12 37										13 07					
Clapham Junction 10	a			10 48				11 09	10 55		11 02		11 18	11 32		11 26							11 48		
London Victoria 15 ⊖	a		10 50	10 55			11 05	11 18	11 03		11 09	11 20	11 25	11 39		11 33		11 35				11 50	11 55		

Table 186

Sundays

until 24 June

Brighton - London and Bedford

Network Diagram - see first Page of Table 186

Station		SN 1 (trolley)	SN ◇1	SN ◇1 (trolley)	FC 1	SN 1	SN 1 (trolley)	SN ◇1 (trolley)	SN ◇1 (trolley)	SN ◇1 (trolley)		SN 1	SN 1 (trolley)	GW 1	FC 1	GW 1	SN 1 (trolley)	SN ◇1	SN 1	SN 1 (trolley)		SN ◇1	SN ◇1 (trolley)	FC 1	SN 1
Brighton 10	d		11 00	11 10	11 15					11 40					11 45							12 00	12 10	12 15	
Hove 2	d																	11 54							
Preston Park	d		11 03																			12 03			
Hassocks 4	d		11 10		11 24										11 54							12 10		12 24	
Burgess Hill 4	d		11 13		11 27										11 57			12 04				12 13		12 27	
Lewes 4	d							11 22																	
Wivelsfield 4	d		11 15					11 36														12 15			
Haywards Heath 3	a		11 20		11 32			11 40							12 02			12 09				12 20		12 32	
	d		11 25		11 33			11 41							12 03			12 11				12 25		12 33	
Balcombe	d		11 30																			12 30			
Horsham 4	d								11 37										12 00						
Littlehaven	d																		12 03						
Faygate	d																								
Ifield	d																		12 09						
Crawley	d								11 46										12 13						
Three Bridges 4	a		11 36		11 41				11 50						12 11				12 16			12 36		12 41	
	d		11 36		11 42				11 50						12 12				12 18			12 36		12 42	
Gatwick Airport 10 ✈	a		11 40		11 46			11 52	11 55	12 01					12 16			12 22	12 22			12 40		12 46	
	d	11 35	11 41		11 47		11 50	11 53	11 56	12 02			12 05	12 08	12 17		12 20	12 23	12 23	12 35		12 41		12 47	
Horley 4	d								11 58										12 26						
Salfords	d																		12 30						
Earlswood (Surrey)	d																		12 33						
Tonbridge 4	d											11 41													
Leigh (Kent)	d											11 45													
Penshurst	d											11 49													
Edenbridge	d											11 55													
Godstone	d											12 02													
Nutfield	d											12 07													
Reigate	d															12 13									
Redhill 5	a		11 48						12 05			12 12		12 16		12 18			12 36			12 48			
	d		11 49						12 05			12 13							12 37			12 49			
Merstham	d											12 17							12 41						
Coulsdon South	d											12 22							12 46						
Purley 4	d								12 14			12 27							12 50						
East Croydon	a		12 00	11 45	12 02			12 09	12 19	12 16		12 32			12 31			12 38	12 56			13 00	12 45	13 02	
	d		12 00	11 46	12 02	11 50		12 09	12 20	12 17		12 34			12 32			12 39	12 56			13 00	12 46	13 02	12 50
Norwood Junction 2	a											12 38							13 00						
New Cross Gate	d																								
London Bridge 4 ⊖	a				12 15							12 51			12 45				13 12					13 15	
London Blackfriars 3 ⊖	a				12 22										12 52									13 22	
City Thameslink 3	a																								
Farringdon 3 ⊖	a				12 26										12 56									13 26	
St Pancras International 15 ⊖	a				12 31										13 01									13 31	
St Albans City	a				12 56										13 25									13 56	
Luton Airport Parkway 4 ✈	a				13 08										13 38									14 08	
Luton 7	a				13 11										13 41									14 11	
Bedford 10	a				13 37										14 07									14 37	
Clapham Junction 10	a		12 09	11 55		12 02		12 18	12 32	12 26								12 48				13 09	12 55		13 02
London Victoria 15 ⊖	a	12 05	12 17	12 03		12 09	12 20	12 25	12 39	12 33			12 35				12 50	12 55		13 05		13 17	13 03		13 09

Table 186

Sundays
until 24 June

Brighton - London and Bedford

Network Diagram - see first Page of Table 186

		SN	SN	SN	SN	SN		SN	GW	FC	GW	SN	SN	SN	SN	SN		SN	FC	SN	SN	SN	SN	SN	SN
		1	◇1	◇1	◇1	1		1	1	1	1	1	◇1	1	1	◇1		◇1	1	1	1	◇1	◇1	◇1	1
Brighton 10	d				12 40					12 45						13 00		13 10	13 15					13 40	
Hove 2	d												12 54												
Preston Park	d															13 03									
Hassocks 4	d									12 54						13 10			13 24						
Burgess Hill 4	d									12 57			13 04			13 13			13 27						
Lewes 4	d		12 22																			13 22			
Wivelsfield 4	d		12 36													13 15						13 36			
Haywards Heath 3	a		12 40							13 02			13 09			13 20			13 32			13 40			
	d		12 41							13 03			13 11			13 25			13 33			13 41			
Balcombe	d															13 30									
Horsham 4	d			12 37										13 00									13 37		
Littlehaven	d													13 03											
Faygate	d																								
Ifield	d													13 09											
Crawley	d			12 46										13 13									13 46		
Three Bridges 4	a			12 50						13 11				13 16		13 36			13 41				13 50		
	d			12 50						13 12				13 18		13 36			13 42				13 50		
Gatwick Airport 10 ✈	a		12 52	12 55	13 01					13 16			13 22	13 22		13 40			13 46			13 52	13 55	14 01	
	d	12 50	12 53	12 56	13 02			13 05	13 08	13 17		13 20	13 23	13 23	13 35	13 41			13 47		13 50	13 53	13 56	14 02	
Horley 4	d			12 58										13 26									13 58		
Salfords	d													13 30											
Earlswood (Surrey)	d													13 33											
Tonbridge 4	d					12 41																			13 41
Leigh (Kent)	d					12 45																			13 45
Penshurst	d					12 49																			13 49
Edenbridge	d					12 55																			13 55
Godstone	d					13 02																			14 02
Nutfield	d					13 07																			14 07
Reigate	d										13 13														
Redhill 5	a			13 05		13 12			13 16		13 18			13 36		13 48							14 05		14 12
	d			13 05		13 13								13 37		13 49							14 05		14 13
Merstham	d					13 17								13 41											14 17
Coulsdon South	d					13 22								13 46											14 22
Purley 4	d			13 14		13 27								13 50									14 14		14 27
East Croydon	a		13 09	13 19	13 16	13 32				13 31			13 38	13 56		14 00		13 45	14 02			14 09	14 19	14 16	14 32
	d		13 09	13 20	13 17	13 34				13 32			13 39	13 56		14 00		13 46	14 02	13 50		14 09	14 20	14 17	14 34
Norwood Junction 2	a					13 38								14 00											14 38
New Cross Gate	d																								
London Bridge 4 ⊖	a					13 51				13 45				14 12					14 15						14 51
London Blackfriars 3 ⊖	a									13 52									14 22						
City Thameslink 3	a																								
Farringdon 3 ⊖	a									13 56									14 26						
St Pancras International 15 ⊖	a									14 01									14 31						
St Albans City	a									14 25									14 56						
Luton Airport Parkway 4 ✈	a									14 38									15 08						
Luton 7	a									14 41									15 11						
Bedford 10	a									15 07									15 37						
Clapham Junction 10	a		13 18	13 32	13 26								13 48			14 09		13 55		14 02		14 18	14 32	14 26	
London Victoria 15 ⊖	a	13 20	13 25	13 39	13 33			13 35				13 50	13 55		14 05	14 17		14 03		14 09	14 20	14 25	14 39	14 33	

Table 186

Sundays

until 24 June

Brighton - London and Bedford

Network Diagram - see first Page of Table 186

		SN [1] 🚲		GW [1]	FC [1]	GW [1]	SN [1] 🚲	SN ◇[1]	SN [1]	SN [1] 🚲	SN ◇[1]	SN ◇[1] 🚲		FC [1]	SN [1]	SN [1] 🚲	SN ◇[1] 🚲	SN ◇[1] 🚲	SN ◇[1] 🚲	SN [1]	SN [1] 🚲	GW [1]		FC [1]	GW [1]
Brighton [10]	d				13 45						14 00	14 10		14 15					14 40					14 45	
Hove [2]	d							13 54																	
Preston Park	d										14 03														
Hassocks [4]	d				13 54						14 10			14 24										14 54	
Burgess Hill [4]	d				13 57			14 04			14 13			14 27										14 57	
Lewes [4]	d																14 22								
Wivelsfield [4]	d										14 15						14 36								
Haywards Heath [3]	a				14 02			14 09			14 20			14 32			14 40							15 02	
	d				14 03			14 11			14 25			14 33			14 41							15 03	
Balcombe	d										14 30														
Horsham [4]	d								14 00									14 37							
Littlehaven	d								14 03																
Faygate	d																								
Ifield	d								14 09																
Crawley	d								14 13									14 46							
Three Bridges [4]	a				14 11				14 16		14 36			14 41				14 50						15 11	
	d				14 12				14 18		14 36			14 42				14 50						15 12	
Gatwick Airport [10] ✈	a				14 16			14 22	14 22		14 40			14 46			14 52	14 55	15 01					15 16	
	d	14 05		14 08	14 17		14 20	14 23	14 23	14 35	14 41			14 47		14 50	14 53	14 56	15 02		15 05	15 08		15 17	
Horley [4]	d								14 26									14 58							
Salfords	d								14 30																
Earlswood (Surrey)	d								14 33																
Tonbridge [4]	d																			14 41					
Leigh (Kent)	d																			14 45					
Penshurst	d																			14 49					
Edenbridge	d																			14 55					
Godstone	d																			15 02					
Nutfield	d																			15 07					
Reigate	d					14 13																			15 13
Redhill [5]	a			14 16		14 18			14 36		14 48							15 05		15 12		15 16			15 18
	d								14 37		14 49							15 05		15 13					
Merstham	d								14 41											15 17					
Coulsdon South	d								14 46											15 22					
Purley [4]	d								14 50									15 14		15 27					
East Croydon	a				14 31			14 38	14 56		15 00	14 45		15 02			15 09	15 19	15 16	15 32				15 31	
	d				14 32			14 39	14 56		15 00	14 46		15 02	14 50		15 09	15 20	15 17	15 34				15 32	
Norwood Junction [2]	a								15 00											15 38					
New Cross Gate	d																								
London Bridge [4] ⊖	a				14 45				15 12					15 15						15 51				15 45	
London Blackfriars [3] ⊖	a				14 52									15 22										15 52	
City Thameslink [3]	a																								
Farringdon [3] ⊖	a				14 56									15 26										15 56	
St Pancras International [15] ⊖	a				15 01									15 31										16 01	
St Albans City	a				15 25									15 56										16 25	
Luton Airport Parkway [4] ✈	a				15 38									16 08										16 38	
Luton [7]	a				15 41									16 11										16 41	
Bedford [10]	a				16 07									16 37										17 07	
Clapham Junction [10]	a							14 48			15 09	14 55			15 02		15 18	15 32	15 26						
London Victoria [15] ⊖	a	14 35					14 50	14 55		15 05	15 17	15 03			15 09	15 20	15 25	15 39	15 33		15 35				

Table 186

Sundays
until 24 June

Brighton - London and Bedford

Network Diagram - see first Page of Table 186

		SN	SN	SN	SN	SN	SN	FC		SN	SN	SN	SN	SN	SN	SN	GW	FC		GW	SN	SN	SN	SN	SN
		1	◇1	1	1	◇1	◇1	1		1	1	◇1	◇1	◇1	1	1	1	1		1	1	◇1	1	1	◇1
		trolley			trolley		trolley				trolley	trolley	trolley	trolley		trolley					trolley			trolley	
Brighton 10	d					15 00	15 10	15 15						15 40				15 45							16 00
Hove 2	d		14 54																			15 54			
Preston Park	d					15 03																			16 03
Hassocks 4	d					15 10		15 24										15 54							16 10
Burgess Hill 4	d		15 04			15 13		15 27										15 57				16 04			16 13
Lewes 4	d											15 22													
Wivelsfield 4	d					15 15						15 36													16 15
Haywards Heath 3	a		15 09			15 20		15 32				15 40						16 02				16 09			16 20
	d		15 11			15 25		15 33				15 41						16 03				16 11			16 25
Balcombe	d					15 30																			16 30
Horsham 4	d			15 00									15 37										16 00		
Littlehaven	d			15 03																			16 03		
Faygate	d																								
Ifield	d			15 09																			16 09		
Crawley	d			15 13									15 46										16 13		
Three Bridges 4	a			15 16		15 36		15 41					15 50					16 11					16 16		16 36
	d			15 18		15 36		15 42					15 50					16 12					16 18		16 36
Gatwick Airport 10 ✈	a		15 22	15 22		15 40		15 46				15 52	15 55	16 01				16 16				16 22	16 22		16 40
	d	15 20	15 23	15 23	15 35	15 41		15 47			15 50	15 53	15 56	16 02		16 05	16 08	16 17			16 20	16 23	16 23	16 35	16 41
Horley 4	d			15 26									15 58										16 26		
Salfords	d			15 30																			16 30		
Earlswood (Surrey)	d			15 33																			16 33		
Tonbridge 4	d														15 41										
Leigh (Kent)	d														15 45										
Penshurst	d														15 49										
Edenbridge	d														15 55										
Godstone	d														16 02										
Nutfield	d														16 07										
Reigate	d																			16 13					
Redhill 5	a			15 36		15 48							16 05		16 12		16 16			16 18			16 36		16 48
	d			15 37		15 49							16 05		16 13								16 37		16 49
Merstham	d			15 41											16 17								16 41		
Coulsdon South	d			15 46											16 22								16 46		
Purley 4	d			15 50									16 14		16 27								16 50		
East Croydon	a		15 39	15 56		16 00	15 45	16 02				16 09	16 19	16 16	16 32			16 31				16 38	16 56		17 00
	d		15 39	15 56		16 00	15 46	16 02		15 50		16 09	16 20	16 17	16 34			16 32				16 39	16 56		17 00
Norwood Junction 2	a			16 00											16 38								17 00		
New Cross Gate	d																								
London Bridge 4 ⊖	a			16 12				16 15							16 51			16 45					17 12		
London Blackfriars 3 ⊖	a							16 22										16 52							
City Thameslink 3	a																								
Farringdon 3 ⊖	a							16 26										16 56							
St Pancras International 15 ⊖	a							16 31										17 01							
St Albans City	a							16 56										17 24							
Luton Airport Parkway 4 ✈	a							17 08										17 37							
Luton 7	a							17 11										17 40							
Bedford 10	a							17 37										18 07							
Clapham Junction 10	a		15 48			16 09	15 55			16 02		16 18	16 32	16 26								16 48			17 09
London Victoria 15 ⊖	a	15 50	15 55		16 05	16 17	16 03			16 09	16 20	16 25	16 39	16 33		16 35					16 50	16 55		17 05	17 17

Table 186

Sundays

until 24 June

Brighton - London and Bedford

Network Diagram - see first Page of Table 186

		SN	FC	SN		SN	SN	SN	SN	SN	SN	GW	FC	GW		SN	SN	SN	SN	SN	SN	FC	SN	SN	
		◇1	1	1		1	◇1	◇1	◇1	1	1	1	1	1		1	◇1	1	1	◇1	◇1	1	1	1	
		🚲				🚲	🚲	🚲	🚲		🚲					🚲			🚲		🚲			🚲	
Brighton 10	d	16 10	16 15						16 40				16 45							17 00	17 10	17 15			
Hove 2	d																16 54								
Preston Park	d																			17 03					
Hassocks 4	d		16 24										16 54							17 10		17 24			
Burgess Hill 4	d		16 27										16 57				17 04			17 13		17 27			
Lewes 4	d						16 22																		
Wivelsfield 4	d						16 36													17 15					
Haywards Heath 3	a		16 32				16 40						17 02				17 09			17 20		17 32			
	d		16 33				16 41						17 03				17 11			17 25		17 33			
Balcombe	d																			17 30					
Horsham 4	d							16 37										17 00							
Littlehaven	d																	17 03							
Faygate	d																								
Ifield	d																	17 09							
Crawley	d							16 46										17 13							
Three Bridges 4	a		16 41					16 50					17 11					17 16		17 36		17 41			
	d		16 42					16 50					17 12					17 18		17 36		17 42			
Gatwick Airport 10 ✈	a		16 46				16 52	16 55	17 01				17 16				17 22	17 22		17 40		17 46			
	d		16 47			16 50	16 53	16 56	17 02		17 05	17 08	17 17			17 20	17 23	17 23	17 35	17 41		17 47		17 50	
Horley 4	d							16 58										17 26							
Salfords	d																	17 30							
Earlswood (Surrey)	d																	17 33							
Tonbridge 4	d									16 41															
Leigh (Kent)	d									16 45															
Penshurst	d									16 49															
Edenbridge	d									16 55															
Godstone	d									17 02															
Nutfield	d									17 07															
Reigate	d													17 13											
Redhill 5	a							17 05		17 12		17 16		17 18				17 36		17 48					
	d							17 05		17 13								17 37		17 49					
Merstham	d									17 17								17 41							
Coulsdon South	d									17 22								17 46							
Purley 4	d							17 14		17 27								17 50							
East Croydon 🚋	a	16 45	17 02				17 09	17 19	17 16	17 32			17 31				17 38	17 56		18 00	17 45	18 02			
	d	16 46	17 02	16 50			17 09	17 20	17 17	17 34			17 32				17 39	17 56		18 00	17 46	18 02	17 50		
Norwood Junction 2	a									17 38								18 00							
New Cross Gate	d																								
London Bridge 4 ⊖	a		17 15							17 51			17 45					18 12				18 15			
London Blackfriars 3 ⊖	a		17 22										17 52									18 22			
City Thameslink 3	a																								
Farringdon 3 ⊖	a		17 26										17 56									18 26			
St Pancras International 15 ⊖	a		17 31										18 01									18 31			
St Albans City	a		17 56										18 25									18 56			
Luton Airport Parkway 4 ✈	a		18 08										18 37									19 08			
Luton 7	a		18 11										18 40									19 11			
Bedford 10	a		18 37										19 07									19 37			
Clapham Junction 10	a	16 55		17 02			17 18	17 32	17 26								17 48			18 09	17 55		18 02		
London Victoria 15 ⊖	a	17 03		17 09		17 20	17 25	17 39	17 33		17 35					17 50	17 55		18 05	18 17	18 03		18 09	18 20	

Table 186

Sundays
until 24 June

Brighton - London and Bedford

Network Diagram - see first Page of Table 186

		SN	SN	SN	SN	SN	GW	FC	GW	SN	SN	SN	SN	SN	SN	FC	SN	SN	SN	SN	SN	SN	SN
		◇1	◇1	◇1	1	1	1	1	1	1	◇1	1	1	◇1	◇1	1	1	1	◇1	◇1	◇1	1	1
		🚲	🚲	🚲		🚲				🚲			🚲					🚲	🚲				
Brighton 10	d			17 40				17 45						18 00	18 10	18 15					18 40		
Hove 2	d										17 54												
Preston Park	d													18 03									
Hassocks 4	d							17 54						18 10		18 24							
Burgess Hill 4	d							17 57			18 04			18 13		18 27							
Lewes 4	d	17 22																	18 22				
Wivelsfield 4	d	17 36												18 15					18 36				
Haywards Heath 3	a	17 40						18 02			18 09			18 20		18 32			18 40				
	d	17 41						18 03			18 11			18 25		18 33			18 41				
Balcombe	d													18 30									
Horsham 4	d		17 37									18 00								18 37			
Littlehaven	d											18 03											
Faygate	d																						
Ifield	d											18 09											
Crawley	d		17 46									18 13								18 46			
Three Bridges 4	a		17 50					18 11				18 16		18 36		18 41				18 50			
	d		17 50					18 12				18 18		18 36		18 42				18 50			
Gatwick Airport 10 ✈	a	17 52	17 55	18 01				18 16			18 22	18 22		18 40		18 46			18 52	18 55	19 01		
	d	17 53	17 56	18 02		18 05	18 08	18 17		18 20	18 23	18 23	18 35	18 41		18 47		18 50	18 53	18 56	19 02		19 05
Horley 4	d		17 58									18 26								18 58			
Salfords	d											18 30											
Earlswood (Surrey)	d											18 33											
Tonbridge 4	d				17 41																	18 41	
Leigh (Kent)	d				17 45																	18 45	
Penshurst	d				17 49																	18 49	
Edenbridge	d				17 55																	18 55	
Godstone	d				18 02																	19 02	
Nutfield	d				18 07																	19 07	
Reigate	d								18 13														
Redhill 5	a		18 05		18 12		18 16		18 18			18 36		18 48						19 05		19 12	
	d		18 05		18 13							18 37		18 49						19 05		19 13	
Merstham	d				18 17							18 41										19 17	
Coulsdon South	d				18 22							18 46										19 22	
Purley 4	d		18 14		18 27							18 50								19 14		19 27	
East Croydon	a	18 09	18 19	18 16	18 32			18 31			18 38	18 56		19 00	18 45	19 02			19 09	19 19	19 16	19 32	
	d	18 09	18 20	18 17	18 34			18 32			18 39	18 56		19 00	18 46	19 02	18 50		19 09	19 20	19 17	19 34	
Norwood Junction 2	a				18 38							19 00										19 38	
New Cross Gate	d																						
London Bridge 4 ⊖	a				18 51			18 45				19 12				19 15						19 51	
London Blackfriars 3 ⊖	a							18 52								19 22							
City Thameslink 3	a																						
Farringdon 3 ⊖	a							18 56								19 26							
St Pancras International 15 ⊖	a							19 01								19 31							
St Albans City	a							19 25								19 56							
Luton Airport Parkway 4 ✈	a							19 37								20 08							
Luton 7	a							19 40								20 11							
Bedford 10	a							20 07								20 37							
Clapham Junction 10	a	18 18	18 32	18 26							18 48			19 09	18 55		19 02		19 18	19 32	19 26		
London Victoria 15 ⊖	a	18 25	18 39	18 33		18 35				18 50	18 55		19 05	19 17	19 03		19 09	19 20	19 25	19 39	19 33		19 35

Table 186

Sundays
until 24 June

Brighton - London and Bedford

Network Diagram - see first Page of Table 186

Station		GW 1	FC 1	GW 1	SN 1	SN ◇1	SN 1	SN 1	SN ◇1	SN ◇1	FC 1	SN 1	SN 1	SN ◇1	SN ◇1	SN ◇1	SN 1	SN 1	GW 1	FC 1	GW 1	SN 1	SN ◇1
Brighton 10	d		18 45						19 00	19 10	19 15					19 40				19 45			
Hove 2	d					18 54																	19 54
Preston Park	d								19 03														
Hassocks 4	d		18 54						19 10		19 24									19 54			
Burgess Hill 4	d		18 57			19 04			19 13		19 27									19 57			20 04
Lewes 4	d													19 22									
Wivelsfield 4	d								19 15					19 36									
Haywards Heath 3	a		19 02			19 09			19 20		19 32			19 40						20 02			20 09
	d		19 03			19 11			19 25		19 33			19 41						20 03			20 11
Balcombe	d								19 30														
Horsham 4	d						19 00								19 37								
Littlehaven	d						19 03																
Faygate	d																						
Ifield	d						19 09																
Crawley	d						19 13								19 46								
Three Bridges 4	a		19 11				19 16		19 36		19 41				19 50					20 11			
	d		19 12				19 18		19 36		19 42				19 50					20 12			
Gatwick Airport 10 ✈	a		19 16			19 22	19 22		19 40		19 46			19 52	19 55	20 01				20 16			20 22
	d	19 08	19 17		19 20	19 23	19 23	19 35	19 41		19 47		19 50	19 53	19 56	20 02		20 05	20 08	20 17		20 20	20 23
Horley 4	d						19 26								19 58								
Salfords	d						19 30																
Earlswood (Surrey)	d						19 33																
Tonbridge 4	d																19 41						
Leigh (Kent)	d																19 45						
Penshurst	d																19 49						
Edenbridge	d																19 55						
Godstone	d																20 02						
Nutfield	d																20 07						
Reigate	d			19 13																	20 13		
Redhill 5	a	19 16		19 18			19 36		19 48						20 05		20 12		20 16		20 18		
	d						19 37		19 49						20 05		20 13						
Merstham	d						19 41										20 17						
Coulsdon South	d						19 46										20 22						
Purley 4	d						19 50								20 14		20 27						
East Croydon	a		19 31			19 38	19 56		20 00	19 45	20 02			20 09	20 19	20 16	20 32			20 31			20 38
	d		19 32			19 39	19 56		20 00	19 46	20 02	19 50		20 09	20 20	20 17	20 34			20 32			20 39
Norwood Junction 2	a						20 00										20 38						
New Cross Gate	d																						
London Bridge 4 ⊖	a		19 45				20 12				20 15						20 51			20 45			
London Blackfriars 3 ⊖	a		19 52								20 22									20 52			
City Thameslink 3	a																						
Farringdon 3 ⊖	a		19 56								20 26									20 56			
St Pancras International 15 ⊖	a		20 01								20 31									21 01			
St Albans City	a		20 25								20 56									21 25			
Luton Airport Parkway 4 ✈	a		20 38								21 08									21 38			
Luton 7	a		20 41								21 11									21 41			
Bedford 10	a		21 07								21 37									22 07			
Clapham Junction 10	a					19 48			20 09	19 55		20 02		20 18	20 32	20 26							20 48
London Victoria 15 ⊖	a				19 50	19 55		20 05	20 17	20 03		20 09	20 20	20 25	20 39	20 33		20 35				20 50	20 55

Table 186

Sundays

until 24 June

Brighton - London and Bedford

Network Diagram - see first Page of Table 186

		SN 1	SN 1	SN ◇1	SN ◇1	FC 1	SN 1	SN 1	SN ◇1	SN ◇1	SN ◇1	SN 1	SN 1	GW 1	FC 1	GW 1	SN 1	SN ◇1	SN 1	SN 1	SN 1	SN ◇1
Brighton 10	d			20 00	20 10	20 15					20 40				20 45							21 04
Hove 2	d																	20 54				
Preston Park	d			20 03																		21 07
Hassocks 4	d			20 10		20 24									20 54							21 14
Burgess Hill 4	d			20 13		20 27									20 57			21 04				21 17
Lewes 4	d								20 22													
Wivelsfield 4	d			20 15					20 36													21 19
Haywards Heath 3	a			20 20		20 32			20 40						21 02			21 09				21 24
	d			20 25		20 33			20 41						21 03			21 11				21 25
Balcombe	d			20 30																		21 30
Horsham 4	d	20 00								20 37									21 00			
Littlehaven	d	20 03																	21 03			
Faygate	d																					
Ifield	d	20 09																	21 09			
Crawley	d	20 13								20 46									21 13			
Three Bridges 4	a	20 16		20 36		20 41				20 50					21 11				21 16			21 36
	d	20 18		20 36		20 42				20 50					21 12				21 18			21 36
Gatwick Airport 10 ✈	a	20 22		20 40		20 46			20 52	20 55	21 01				21 16			21 22	21 22			21 40
	d	20 23	20 35	20 41		20 47		20 50	20 53	20 56	21 02		21 05	21 08	21 17		21 20	21 23	21 23	21 35		21 41
Horley 4	d	20 26								20 58									21 26			
Salfords	d	20 30																	21 30			
Earlswood (Surrey)	d	20 33																	21 33			
Tonbridge 4	d											20 41										
Leigh (Kent)	d											20 45										
Penshurst	d											20 49										
Edenbridge	d											20 55										
Godstone	d											21 02										
Nutfield	d											21 07										
Reigate	d															21 13						
Redhill 5	a	20 36		20 48						21 05		21 12		21 16		21 18			21 36			21 48
	d	20 37		20 49						21 05		21 13							21 37			21 49
Merstham	d	20 41										21 17							21 41			
Coulsdon South	d	20 46										21 22							21 46			
Purley 4	d	20 50								21 14		21 27							21 50			
East Croydon	a	20 56		21 00	20 45	21 02			21 09	21 19	21 16	21 32			21 31			21 38	21 56			22 00
	d	20 56		21 00	20 46	21 02	20 50		21 09	21 20	21 17	21 34			21 32			21 39	21 56		21 50	22 00
Norwood Junction 2	a	21 00										21 38							22 00			
New Cross Gate	d																					
London Bridge 4 ⊖	a	21 12				21 15						21 51			21 45				22 12			
London Blackfriars 3 ⊖	a					21 22									21 52							
City Thameslink 3	a																					
Farringdon 3 ⊖	a					21 26									21 56							
St Pancras International 15 ⊖	a					21 31									22 01							
St Albans City	a					21 56									22 26							
Luton Airport Parkway 4 ✈	a					22 08									22 38							
Luton 7	a					22 11									22 41							
Bedford 10	a					22 37									23 07							
Clapham Junction 10	a			21 09	20 55		21 02		21 18	21 32	21 26							21 48			22 02	22 09
London Victoria 15 ⊖	a		21 05	21 17	21 03		21 09	21 20	21 25	21 39	21 33		21 35				21 50	21 55		22 05	22 09	22 17

Table 186

Brighton - London and Bedford

Sundays

until 24 June

Network Diagram - see first Page of Table 186

		FC 1	SN 1	SN ◇1	SN ◇1	SN 1	SN 1	GW 1		FC 1	GW 1	SN 1	SN 1	SN 1	SN 1	SN ◇1	FC 1	SN 1		SN 1	SN ◇1	SN 1	GW 1	FC 1	GW 1
Brighton 10	d	21 15								21 45						22 04	22 15							22 45	
Hove 2	d																								
Preston Park	d															22 07									
Hassocks 4	d	21 24								21 54						22 14	22 24							22 54	
Burgess Hill 4	d	21 27								21 57						22 17	22 27							22 57	
Lewes 4	d			21 22																					
Wivelsfield 4	d			21 36												22 19									
Haywards Heath 3	a	21 32		21 40						22 02						22 24	22 32							23 02	
	d	21 33		21 41						22 03						22 25	22 33							23 03	
Balcombe	d															22 30									
Horsham 4	d				21 37									22 00							22 37				
Littlehaven	d													22 03											
Faygate	d																								
Ifield	d													22 09											
Crawley	d				21 46									22 13							22 46				
Three Bridges 4	a	21 41			21 50					22 11				22 16		22 36	22 41				22 50			23 11	
	d	21 42			21 50					22 12				22 18		22 36	22 42				22 50			23 12	
Gatwick Airport 10 ✈	a	21 46		21 52	21 55					22 16				22 22		22 40	22 46				22 55			23 16	
	d	21 47	21 50	21 53	21 56		22 05	22 08		22 17		22 20		22 23	22 35	22 41	22 47			22 50	22 56	23 05	23 08	23 17	
Horley 4	d				21 58									22 26							22 58				
Salfords	d													22 30											
Earlswood (Surrey)	d													22 33											
Tonbridge 4	d					21 41												22 29							
Leigh (Kent)	d					21 45												22 33							
Penshurst	d					21 49												22 37							
Edenbridge	d					21 55												22 43							
Godstone	d					22 02												22 50							
Nutfield	d					22 07												22 55							
Reigate	d										22 13														23 13
Redhill 5	a				22 05	22 12		22 16			22 18			22 36		22 48		23 00			23 05		23 16		23 18
	d				22 05	22 13								22 37		22 49					23 05				
Merstham	d					22 17								22 41											
Coulsdon South	d					22 22								22 46											
Purley 4	d				22 14	22 27								22 50							23 14				
East Croydon 🚋	a	22 02		22 09	22 19	22 32				22 31				22 55		23 00	23 02				23 20			23 31	
	d	22 02		22 09	22 20	22 34				22 32			22 50	22 56		23 00	23 02				23 21			23 32	
Norwood Junction 2	a					22 38																			
New Cross Gate	d																								
London Bridge 4 ⊖	a	22 15				22 51				22 45							23 15							23 45	
London Blackfriars 3 ⊖	a	22 22								22 52							23 22							23 52	
City Thameslink 3	a																								
Farringdon 3 ⊖	a	22 26								22 56							23 26							23 56	
St Pancras International 15 ⊖	a	22 31								23 01							23 31							00 01	
St Albans City	a	23 05								23 35							00 05							00 35	
Luton Airport Parkway 4 ✈	a	23 18								23 48							00 18							00 48	
Luton 7	a	23 21								23 51							00 21							00 51	
Bedford 10	a	23 47								00 17							00 47							01 17	
Clapham Junction 10	a			22 18	22 32								23 02	23 07		23 10					23 31				
London Victoria 15 ⊖	a		22 20	22 25	22 39		22 35					22 50	23 09	23 14	23 05	23 20				23 25	23 38	23 35			

Table 186

Sundays
until 24 June

Brighton - London and Bedford

Network Diagram - see first Page of Table 186

		SN 1	SN 1	SN 1		SN 1	SN ◇1	FC 1	SN 1	FC 1
Brighton 10	d						23 02	23 15		23 45
Hove 2	d									
Preston Park	d						23 06			
Hassocks 4	d						23 12	23 24		23 54
Burgess Hill 4	d						23 16	23 27		23 57
Lewes 4	d									
Wivelsfield 4	d						23 18			
Haywards Heath 3	a						23 23	23 32		00 02
	d						23 23	23 33		00 03
Balcombe	d						23 29			
Horsham 4	d			23 03						
Littlehaven	d			23 06						
Faygate	d									
Ifield	d			23 12						
Crawley	d			23 16						
Three Bridges 4	a			23 19			23 36	23 41		00 11
	d			23 20			23 41	23 42		00 12
Gatwick Airport 10 ✈	a			23 24			23 45	23 46		00 16
	d	23 20		23 25		23 35	23 46	23 47	23 50	00 17
Horley 4	d			23 28			23 49			
Salfords	d									
Earlswood (Surrey)	d									
Tonbridge 4	d									
Leigh (Kent)	d									
Penshurst	d									
Edenbridge	d									
Godstone	d									
Nutfield	d									
Reigate	d									
Redhill 5	a			23 34			23 57			00 24
	d			23 35			00 01			00 24
Merstham	d			23 39						
Coulsdon South	d			23 44						
Purley 4	d			23 50			00 11			
East Croydon	a			23 55			00 16	00 02		00 36
	d		23 50	23 56			00 16	00 04		00 36
Norwood Junction 2	a									
New Cross Gate	d									
London Bridge 4 ⊖	a							00 21		00 50
London Blackfriars 3 ⊖	a							00 27		00 57
City Thameslink 3	a									
Farringdon 3 ⊖	a							00 33		
St Pancras International 15 ⊖	a							00 37		01 07
St Albans City	a							01 10		01 40
Luton Airport Parkway 4 ✈	a							01 25		01 52
Luton 7	a							01 28		01 55
Bedford 10	a							01 55		02 22
Clapham Junction 10	a		00 01	00 11			00 29			
London Victoria 15 ⊖	a	23 55	00 08	00 19		00 10	00 37		00 25	

Table 186

Brighton - London and Bedford

1 July to 9 September

Network Diagram - see first Page of Table 186

		FC 1	FC 1	FC 1	SN 1	SN 1	SN ◇1	FC 1	SN 1	SN ◇1		SN 1	FC 1	SN 1	GW 1	SN	SN 1	SN 1	SN 1	SN 1		SN 1	SN 1	SN 1	SN 1
Brighton 10	d	21p37	22p07	22p33			23p02	23p11					23p37												
Hove 2	d																								
Preston Park	d	21p41	22p11	22p37			23p06						23p41												
Hassocks 4	d	21p47	22p17	22p43			23p12	23p20					23p47												
Burgess Hill 4	d	21p51	22p21	22p47			23p16	23p23					23p51												
Lewes 4	d																								
Wivelsfield 4	d	21p53	22p23	22p49			23p19						23p53												
Haywards Heath 3	a	21p58	22p28	22p53			23p23	23p28					23p58												
	d	22p02	22p32	22p54			23p24	23p29					23p59												
Balcombe	d		22p37	22p59									00 04												
Horsham 4	d				23p02																				
Littlehaven	d				23p05																				
Faygate	d																								
Ifield	d				23p11																				
Crawley	d				23p14					←															
Three Bridges 4	a	22p11	22p43	23p05	23p18		23p32	23p37		23p32			00 10												
	d	22p12	22p43	23p12	23p18		23p47	23p38		23p47			00 10						01 10			02 10	03 10	04 10	
Gatwick Airport 10 ✈	a	22p16	22p47	23p16	23p22		→	23p42		23p52			00 14						01 19			02 14	03 14	04 14	
	d	22p17	22p47	23p17	23p23	23p35		23p43	23p50	23p53		00 07	00 15	00 20			00 35	00 50	01 20	01 35		02 15	03 15	04 15	04 35
Horley 4	d				23p26					23p56									01 22			02 18	03 18	04 18	
Salfords	d				23p30																				
Earlswood (Surrey)	d				23p33																				
Tonbridge 4	d																								
Leigh (Kent)	d																								
Penshurst	d																								
Edenbridge	d																								
Godstone	d																								
Nutfield	d																								
Reigate	d														00 45										
Redhill 5	a				23p36					00 03			00 22		00 49										
	d				23p37					00 03			00 23												
Merstham	d				23p41																				
Coulsdon South	d				23p46																				
Purley 4	d				23p49					00 11									01 37			02 33	03 33	04 33	
East Croydon	a	22p32	23p02	23p32	23p55			00 01		00 16			00 35						01 42			02 39	03 39	04 39	
	d	22p32	23p02	23p32	23p56			00 04		00 17			00 36			00 49			01 43			02 40	03 40	04 40	
Norwood Junction 2	a																								
New Cross Gate	d																								
London Bridge 4 ⊖	a	22p45	23p15	23p44				00 21					00 51												
London Blackfriars 3 ⊖	a	22p52	23p22	23p52				00 28					00 58												
City Thameslink 3	a																								
Farringdon 3 ⊖	a	22p57	23p28	23p58				00 33																	
St Pancras International 15 ⊖	a	23p02	23p32	00 02				00 37					01 07												
St Albans City	a	23p26	23p56	00 26				01 10					01 40												
Luton Airport Parkway 4 ✈	a	23p38	00 08	00 38				01 22					01 52												
Luton 7	a	23p41	00 11	00 41				01 25					01 55												
Bedford 10	a	00 08	00 38	01 08				01 52					02 22												
Clapham Junction 10	a				00 11					00 29						01 03			01 54			02 53	03 53	04 53	
London Victoria 15 ⊖	a				00 18	00 10			00 20	00 37		00 42		00 55		01 10	01 11	01 25	02 05	02 10		03 05	04 05	05 05	05 10

Table 186

Sundays

1 July to 9 September

Brighton - London and Bedford

Network Diagram - see first Page of Table 186

		FC	FC	SN	SN	SN		SN	GW	FC	FC	SN	SN	SN	FC	SN		SN	GW	SN	GW	FC	SN	SN	SN
				1	1	1		1	1			1	1	1	1	1		◇1	1	1	1	1	1	1	1
		A	B							A	B														
								Bus				Bus		Bus		Bus				Bus			Bus		Bus
Brighton 10	d									05 45	05 45				06 15			06 19				06 45			
Hove 2	d																								
Preston Park	d																	06 22							
Hassocks 4	d									05 54	05 54				06 24			06 29				06 54			
Burgess Hill 4	d									05 57	05 57				06 27			06 32				06 57			
Lewes 4	d																								
Wivelsfield 4	d																	06 34							
Haywards Heath 3	a									06 02	06 02				06 32			06 39				07 02			
	d									06 03	06 03				06 33			06 39				07 03			
Balcombe	d																								
Horsham 4	d												06 04											07 00	
Littlehaven	d												06 07											07 03	
Faygate	d																								
Ifield	d												06 13											07 09	
Crawley	d												06 17											07 13	
Three Bridges 4	a									06 11	06 11		06 20		06 41			06 48				07 11		07 16	
	d	05 12	05 12		05 30					06 12	06 12		06 21		06 42			06 48				07 12		07 18	
Gatwick Airport 10 ✈	a	05 16	05 16		05 34					06 16	06 16		06 25		06 46			06 52				07 16		07 22	
	d	05 17	05 17	05 20	05 36	05 50		06 05	06 08	06 17	06 17	06 20		06 35	06 47	06 50		06 53		07 05	07 08	07 17	07 20	07 23	07 35
Horley 4	d				05 38																			07 26	
Salfords	d																							07 30	
Earlswood (Surrey)	d																							07 33	
Tonbridge 4	d																								
Leigh (Kent)	d																								
Penshurst	d																								
Edenbridge	d																								
Godstone	d																								
Nutfield	d																								
Reigate	d																		07 05						
Redhill 5	a				05 46				06 17										07 09		07 16			07 36	
	d				05 46																			07 37	
Merstham	d																							07 41	
Coulsdon South	d																							07 46	
Purley 4	d				05 56																			07 50	
East Croydon	a	05 32	05 32		06 01					06 32	06 32				07 01			07 10				07 31		07 56	
	d	05 32	05 32		06 02					06 32	06 32				07 02			07 10				07 32		07 56	
Norwood Junction 2	a																							08 00	
New Cross Gate	d																								
London Bridge 4 ⊖	a														07 15							07 45		08 12	
London Blackfriars 3 ⊖	a	05 59	05 59							06 59	06 59				07 22							07 52			
City Thameslink 3	a										07 01														
Farringdon 3 ⊖	a		06 03												07 26							07 56			
St Pancras International 15 ⊖	a		06 07								07 09				07 31							08 01			
St Albans City	a		06 41								07 41				08 05							08 35			
Luton Airport Parkway 4 ✈	a		06 53								07 53				08 17							08 47			
Luton 7	a		06 56								07 56				08 20							08 50			
Bedford 10	a		07 23								08 23				08 47							09 17			
Clapham Junction 10	a				06 14													07 24							
London Victoria 15 ⊖	a			05 58	06 22	06 25		06 40				06 55		07 10		07 20		07 31		07 35			07 50		08 05

A from 1 July until 22 July, from 19 August until 9 September

B 29 July, 5 August, 12 August

Table 186

Sundays

Brighton - London and Bedford

1 July to 9 September

Network Diagram - see first Page of Table 186

		SN		FC	SN	SN	SN	SN	SN	GW	FC	GW		SN	SN	SN	SN	SN	SN	FC	SN	SN		SN	SN
		◇1		1	1	◇1	◇1	1	1	1	1	1		1	◇1	1	1	◇1	◇1	1	1	1		◇1	◇1
					🛒	🛒			🛒					🛒			🛒		🛒			🛒		🛒	
Brighton 10	d	07 04		07 15							07 45							08 00	08 10	08 15					
Hove 2	d														07 54										
Preston Park	d	07 07																08 03							
Hassocks 4	d	07 14		07 24							07 54							08 10		08 24					
Burgess Hill 4	d	07 17		07 27							07 57				08 04			08 13		08 27					
Lewes 4	d					07 22																		08 22	
Wivelsfield 4	d	07 19				07 36												08 15						08 36	
Haywards Heath 3	a	07 24		07 32		07 40					08 02				08 09			08 20		08 32				08 40	
	d	07 25		07 33		07 41					08 03				08 11			08 25		08 33				08 41	
Balcombe	d	07 30																08 30							
Horsham 4	d						07 37									08 00									08 37
Littlehaven	d															08 03									
Faygate	d																								
Ifield	d															08 09									
Crawley	d						07 46									08 13									08 46
Three Bridges 4	a	07 36		07 41			07 50				08 11					08 16		08 36		08 41					08 50
	d	07 36		07 42			07 50				08 12					08 18		08 36		08 42					08 50
Gatwick Airport 10 ✈	a	07 40		07 46		07 52	07 55				08 16				08 22	08 22		08 40		08 46				08 52	08 55
	d	07 41		07 47	07 50	07 53	07 56		08 05	08 08	08 17			08 20	08 23	08 23	08 35	08 41		08 47		08 50		08 53	08 56
Horley 4	d						07 58									08 26									08 58
Salfords	d															08 30									
Earlswood (Surrey)	d															08 33									
Tonbridge 4	d							07 41																	
Leigh (Kent)	d							07 45																	
Penshurst	d							07 49																	
Edenbridge	d							07 55																	
Godstone	d							08 02																	
Nutfield	d							08 07																	
Reigate	d											08 13													
Redhill 5	a	07 48					08 05	08 12		08 16		08 18				08 36		08 48							09 05
	d	07 49					08 05	08 13								08 37		08 49							09 05
Merstham	d							08 17								08 41									
Coulsdon South	d							08 22								08 46									
Purley 4	d						08 14	08 27								08 50									09 14
East Croydon 🚌	a	08 00		08 02		08 09	08 19	08 32			08 31				08 38	08 56		09 00	08 45	09 02				09 09	09 19
	d	08 00		08 02		08 09	08 20	08 34			08 32				08 39	08 56		09 00	08 46	09 02	08 50			09 09	09 20
Norwood Junction 2	a							08 38								09 00									
New Cross Gate	d																								
London Bridge 4 ⊖	a			08 15				08 51			08 45					09 12				09 15					
London Blackfriars 3 ⊖	a			08 22							08 52									09 22					
City Thameslink 3	a																								
Farringdon 3 ⊖	a			08 26							08 56									09 26					
St Pancras International 15 ⊖	a			08 31							09 01									09 31					
St Albans City	a			09 05							09 35									10 05					
Luton Airport Parkway 4 ✈	a			09 17							09 47									10 17					
Luton 7	a			09 20							09 50									10 20					
Bedford 10	a			09 47							10 17									10 47					
Clapham Junction 10	a	08 09				08 18	08 32								08 48			09 09	08 55		09 02			09 18	09 32
London Victoria 15 ⊖	a	08 16			08 20	08 25	08 39		08 35					08 50	08 55		09 05	09 17	09 03		09 09	09 20		09 25	09 39

Table 186 — **Sundays**

1 July to 9 September

Brighton - London and Bedford

Network Diagram - see first Page of Table 186

		SN	SN	SN	GW	FC	GW	SN		SN	SN	SN	SN	SN	FC	SN	SN	SN		SN	SN	SN	SN	GW	FC
		◇1	1	1	1	1	1	1		◇1	1	1	◇1	◇1	1	1	1	◇1		◇1	◇1	1	1	1	1
		(trolley)		(trolley)				(trolley)				(trolley)		(trolley)			(trolley)	(trolley)			(trolley)		(trolley)		
Brighton 10	d	08 40				08 45							09 00	09 10	09 15						09 40				09 45
Hove 2	d									08 54															
Preston Park	d												09 03												
Hassocks 4	d					08 54							09 10		09 24										09 54
Burgess Hill 4	d					08 57				09 04			09 13		09 27										09 57
Lewes 4	d																	09 22							
Wivelsfield 4	d												09 15					09 36							
Haywards Heath 3	a					09 02				09 09			09 20		09 32			09 40							10 02
	d					09 03				09 11			09 25		09 33			09 41							10 03
Balcombe	d												09 30												
Horsham 4	d										09 00									09 37					
Littlehaven	d										09 03														
Faygate	d																								
Ifield	d										09 09														
Crawley	d										09 13									09 46					
Three Bridges 4	a					09 11					09 16		09 36		09 41					09 50					10 11
	d					09 12					09 18		09 36		09 42					09 50					10 12
Gatwick Airport 10 ✈	a	09 01				09 16				09 22	09 22		09 40		09 46			09 52		09 55	10 01				10 16
	d	09 02		09 05	09 08	09 17		09 20		09 23	09 23	09 35	09 41		09 47		09 50	09 53		09 56	10 02		10 05	10 08	10 17
Horley 4	d										09 26									09 58					
Salfords	d										09 30														
Earlswood (Surrey)	d										09 33														
Tonbridge 4	d		08 41																			09 41			
Leigh (Kent)	d		08 45																			09 45			
Penshurst	d		08 49																			09 49			
Edenbridge	d		08 55																			09 55			
Godstone	d		09 02																			10 02			
Nutfield	d		09 07																			10 07			
Reigate	d						09 13																		
Redhill 5	a		09 12		09 16		09 18				09 36		09 48							10 05		10 12		10 16	
	d		09 13								09 37		09 49							10 05		10 13			
Merstham	d		09 17								09 41											10 17			
Coulsdon South	d		09 22								09 46											10 22			
Purley 4	d		09 27								09 50									10 14		10 27			
East Croydon 🚊	a	09 16	09 32			09 31				09 38	09 56		10 00	09 45	10 02			10 09		10 19	10 16	10 32			10 31
	d	09 17	09 34			09 32				09 39	09 56		10 00	09 46	10 02	09 50		10 09		10 20	10 17	10 34			10 32
Norwood Junction 2	a		09 38								10 00											10 38			
New Cross Gate	d																								
London Bridge 4 ⊖	a		09 51			09 45					10 12				10 15							10 51			10 45
London Blackfriars 3 ⊖	a					09 52									10 22										10 52
City Thameslink 3	a																								
Farringdon 3 ⊖	a					09 56									10 26										10 56
St Pancras International 15 ⊖	a					10 01									10 31										11 01
St Albans City	a					10 26									10 56										11 26
Luton Airport Parkway 4 ✈	a					10 38									11 08										11 38
Luton 7	a					10 41									11 11										11 41
Bedford 10	a					11 08									11 38										12 08
Clapham Junction 10	a	09 26								09 48			10 09	09 55		10 02		10 18		10 32	10 26				
London Victoria 15 ⊖	a	09 33		09 35				09 50		09 55		10 05	10 17	10 03		10 09	10 20	10 25		10 39	10 33		10 35		

Table 186

Sundays

1 July to 9 September

Brighton - London and Bedford

Network Diagram - see first Page of Table 186

		GW	SN	SN		SN	SN	SN	SN	FC	SN	SN	SN	SN		SN	SN	SN	GW	FC	GW	SN	SN	SN
		1	1	◇1		1	1	◇1	◇1	1	1	1	◇1	◇1		◇1	1	1	1	1	1	1	◇1	1
			⊥				⊥		⊥			⊥	⊥	⊥		⊥		⊥				⊥		
Brighton 10	d							10 00	10 10	10 15						10 40				10 45				
Hove 2	d			09 54																			10 54	
Preston Park	d							10 03																
Hassocks 4	d							10 10		10 24										10 54				
Burgess Hill 4	d			10 04				10 13		10 27										10 57			11 04	
Lewes 4	d												10 22											
Wivelsfield 4	d							10 15					10 36											
Haywards Heath 3	a			10 09				10 20		10 32			10 40							11 02			11 09	
	d			10 11				10 25		10 33			10 41							11 03			11 11	
Balcombe	d							10 30																
Horsham 4	d					10 00								10 37										11 00
Littlehaven	d					10 03																		11 03
Faygate	d																							
Ifield	d					10 09																		11 09
Crawley	d					10 13								10 46										11 13
Three Bridges 4	a					10 16		10 36		10 41				10 50						11 11				11 16
	d					10 18		10 36		10 42				10 50						11 12				11 18
Gatwick Airport 10 ✈	a			10 22		10 22		10 40		10 46			10 52	10 55		11 01				11 16			11 22	11 22
	d		10 20	10 23		10 23	10 35	10 41		10 47		10 50	10 53	10 56		11 02		11 05	11 08	11 17		11 20	11 23	11 23
Horley 4	d					10 26								10 58										11 26
Salfords	d					10 30																		11 30
Earlswood (Surrey)	d					10 33																		11 33
Tonbridge 4	d																10 41							
Leigh (Kent)	d																10 45							
Penshurst	d																10 49							
Edenbridge	d																10 55							
Godstone	d																11 02							
Nutfield	d																11 07							
Reigate	d	10 13																			11 13			
Redhill 5	a	10 18				10 36		10 48						11 05			11 12		11 16		11 18			11 36
	d					10 37		10 49						11 05			11 13							11 37
Merstham	d					10 41											11 17							11 41
Coulsdon South	d					10 46											11 22							11 46
Purley 4	d					10 50								11 14			11 27							11 50
East Croydon	a			10 39		10 56		11 00	10 45	11 02			11 09	11 19		11 16	11 32			11 31			11 38	11 56
	d			10 39		10 56		11 00	10 46	11 02	10 50		11 09	11 20		11 17	11 34			11 32			11 39	11 56
Norwood Junction 2	a					11 00											11 38							12 00
New Cross Gate	d																							
London Bridge 4 ⊖	a					11 12				11 15							11 51			11 45				12 12
London Blackfriars 3 ⊖	a									11 22										11 52				
City Thameslink 3	a																							
Farringdon 3 ⊖	a									11 26										11 56				
St Pancras International 15 ⊖	a									11 31										12 01				
St Albans City	a									11 56										12 26				
Luton Airport Parkway 4 ✈	a									12 08										12 38				
Luton 7	a									12 11										12 41				
Bedford 10	a									12 38										13 08				
Clapham Junction 10	a			10 48				11 09	10 55		11 02		11 18	11 32		11 26							11 48	
London Victoria 15 ⊖	a		10 50	10 55			11 05	11 18	11 03		11 09	11 20	11 25	11 39		11 33		11 35				11 50	11 55	

Table 186

Sundays

1 July to 9 September

Brighton - London and Bedford

Network Diagram - see first Page of Table 186

		SN 1 🛒	SN ◇1	SN ◇1 🛒	FC 1	SN 1	SN 1 🛒	SN ◇1 🛒	SN ◇1 🛒	SN ◇1 🛒	SN 1	SN 1 🛒	GW 1	FC 1	GW 1	SN 1 🛒	SN ◇1	SN 1	SN 1 🛒	SN ◇1	SN ◇1 🛒	FC 1	SN 1
Brighton 10	d		11 00	11 10	11 15					11 40				11 45						12 00	12 10	12 15	
Hove 2	d																11 54						
Preston Park	d		11 03																	12 03			
Hassocks 4	d		11 10		11 24									11 54						12 10		12 24	
Burgess Hill 4	d		11 13		11 27									11 57			12 04			12 13		12 27	
Lewes 4	d							11 22															
Wivelsfield 4	d		11 15					11 36												12 15			
Haywards Heath 3	a		11 20		11 32			11 40						12 02			12 09			12 20		12 32	
	d		11 25		11 33			11 41						12 03			12 11			12 25		12 33	
Balcombe	d		11 30																	12 30			
Horsham 4	d								11 37									12 00					
Littlehaven	d																	12 03					
Faygate	d																						
Ifield	d																	12 09					
Crawley	d								11 46									12 13					
Three Bridges 4	a		11 36		11 41				11 50					12 11				12 16		12 36		12 41	
	d		11 36		11 42				11 50					12 12				12 18		12 36		12 42	
Gatwick Airport 10 ✈	a		11 40		11 46			11 52	11 55	12 01				12 16			12 22	12 22		12 40		12 46	
	d	11 35	11 41		11 47		11 50	11 53	11 56	12 02		12 05	12 08	12 17		12 20	12 23	12 23	12 35	12 41		12 47	
Horley 4	d								11 58									12 26					
Salfords	d																	12 30					
Earlswood (Surrey)	d																	12 33					
Tonbridge 4	d										11 41												
Leigh (Kent)	d										11 45												
Penshurst	d										11 49												
Edenbridge	d										11 55												
Godstone	d										12 02												
Nutfield	d										12 07												
Reigate	d														12 13								
Redhill 5	a		11 48						12 05		12 12		12 16		12 18			12 36		12 48			
	d		11 49						12 05		12 13							12 37		12 49			
Merstham	d										12 17							12 41					
Coulsdon South	d										12 22							12 46					
Purley 4	d								12 14		12 27							12 50					
East Croydon	a		12 00	11 45	12 02			12 09	12 19	12 16	12 32			12 31			12 38	12 56		13 00	12 45	13 02	
	d		12 00	11 46	12 02	11 50		12 09	12 20	12 17	12 34			12 32			12 39	12 56		13 00	12 46	13 02	12 50
Norwood Junction 2	a										12 38							13 00					
New Cross Gate	d																						
London Bridge 4 ⊖	a				12 15						12 51			12 45				13 12				13 15	
London Blackfriars 3 ⊖	a				12 22									12 52								13 22	
City Thameslink 3	a																						
Farringdon 3 ⊖	a				12 26									12 56								13 26	
St Pancras International 15 ⊖	a				12 31									13 01								13 31	
St Albans City	a				12 56									13 26								13 56	
Luton Airport Parkway 4 ✈	a				13 08									13 38								14 08	
Luton 7	a				13 11									13 41								14 11	
Bedford 10	a				13 38									14 08								14 38	
Clapham Junction 10	a		12 09	11 55		12 02		12 18	12 32	12 26							12 48			13 09	12 55		13 02
London Victoria 15 ⊖	a	12 05	12 17	12 03		12 09	12 20	12 25	12 39	12 33		12 35				12 50	12 55		13 05	13 17	13 03		13 09

Table 186

Sundays

1 July to 9 September

Brighton - London and Bedford

Network Diagram - see first Page of Table 186

		SN 1 🚲	SN ◇1 🚲	SN ◇1 🚲	SN ◇1 🚲	SN 1		SN 1 🚲	GW 1	FC 1	GW 1	SN 1 🚲	SN ◇1	SN 1	SN 1 🚲	SN ◇1		SN ◇1 🚲	FC 1	SN 1	SN 1 🚲	SN ◇1 🚲	SN ◇1 🚲	SN ◇1 🚲	SN 1
Brighton 10	d				12 40					12 45						13 00		13 10	13 15					13 40	
Hove 2	d												12 54												
Preston Park	d															13 03									
Hassocks 4	d									12 54						13 10			13 24						
Burgess Hill 4	d									12 57			13 04			13 13			13 27						
Lewes 4	d		12 22																			13 22			
Wivelsfield 4	d		12 36													13 15						13 36			
Haywards Heath 3	a		12 40							13 02			13 09			13 20			13 32			13 40			
	d		12 41							13 03			13 11			13 25			13 33			13 41			
Balcombe	d															13 30									
Horsham 4	d			12 37										13 00									13 37		
Littlehaven	d													13 03											
Faygate	d																								
Ifield	d													13 09											
Crawley	d			12 46										13 13									13 46		
Three Bridges 4	a			12 50						13 11				13 16		13 36			13 41				13 50		
	d			12 50						13 12				13 18		13 36			13 42				13 50		
Gatwick Airport 10 ✈	a		12 52	12 55	13 01					13 16			13 22	13 22		13 40			13 46			13 52	13 55	14 01	
	d	12 50	12 53	12 56	13 02			13 05	13 08	13 17		13 20	13 23	13 23	13 35	13 41			13 47		13 50	13 53	13 56	14 02	
Horley 4	d			12 58										13 26									13 58		
Salfords	d													13 30											
Earlswood (Surrey)	d													13 33											
Tonbridge 4	d					12 41																			13 41
Leigh (Kent)	d					12 45																			13 45
Penshurst	d					12 49																			13 49
Edenbridge	d					12 55																			13 55
Godstone	d					13 02																			14 02
Nutfield	d					13 07																			14 07
Reigate	d										13 13														
Redhill 5	a			13 05		13 12			13 16		13 18			13 36		13 48							14 05		14 12
	d			13 05		13 13								13 37		13 49							14 05		14 13
Merstham	d					13 17								13 41											14 17
Coulsdon South	d					13 22								13 46											14 22
Purley 4	d			13 14		13 27								13 50									14 14		14 27
East Croydon 🚋	a		13 09	13 19	13 16	13 32				13 31			13 38	13 56		14 00		13 45	14 02			14 09	14 19	14 16	14 32
	d		13 09	13 20	13 17	13 34				13 32			13 39	13 56		14 00		13 46	14 02	13 50		14 09	14 20	14 17	14 34
Norwood Junction 2	a					13 38								14 00											14 38
New Cross Gate	d																								
London Bridge 4 ⊖	a					13 51				13 45				14 12					14 15						14 51
London Blackfriars 3 ⊖	a									13 52									14 22						
City Thameslink 3	a																								
Farringdon 3 ⊖	a									13 56									14 26						
St Pancras International 15 ⊖	a									14 01									14 31						
St Albans City	a									14 26									14 56						
Luton Airport Parkway 4 ✈	a									14 38									15 08						
Luton 7	a									14 41									15 11						
Bedford 10	a									15 08									15 38						
Clapham Junction 10	a		13 18	13 32	13 26								13 48			14 09		13 55		14 02		14 18	14 32	14 26	
London Victoria 15 ⊖	a	13 20	13 25	13 39	13 33			13 35				13 50	13 55		14 05	14 17		14 03		14 09	14 20	14 25	14 39	14 33	

Table 186

Sundays

1 July to 9 September

Brighton - London and Bedford

Network Diagram - see first Page of Table 186

		SN		GW	FC	GW	SN	SN	SN	SN	SN	SN		FC	SN	SN	SN	SN	SN	SN	SN	GW		FC	GW
		1		1	1	1	1	◇1	1	1	◇1	◇1		1	1	1	◇1	◇1	◇1	1	1	1		1	1
		🍴					🍴			🍴		🍴				🍴	🍴	🍴	🍴		🍴				
Brighton 10	d				13 45						14 00	14 10		14 15					14 40					14 45	
Hove 2	d							13 54																	
Preston Park	d										14 03														
Hassocks 4	d				13 54						14 10			14 24										14 54	
Burgess Hill 4	d				13 57			14 04			14 13			14 27										14 57	
Lewes 4	d																14 22								
Wivelsfield 4	d										14 15						14 36								
Haywards Heath 3	a				14 02			14 09			14 20			14 32			14 40							15 02	
	d				14 03			14 11			14 25			14 33			14 41							15 03	
Balcombe	d										14 30														
Horsham 4	d								14 00									14 37							
Littlehaven	d								14 03																
Faygate	d																								
Ifield	d								14 09																
Crawley	d								14 13									14 46							
Three Bridges 4	a				14 11				14 16		14 36			14 41				14 50						15 11	
	d				14 12				14 18		14 36			14 42				14 50						15 12	
Gatwick Airport 10 ✈	a				14 16			14 22	14 22		14 40			14 46			14 52	14 55	15 01					15 16	
	d	14 05		14 08	14 17		14 20	14 23	14 23	14 35	14 41			14 47		14 50	14 53	14 56	15 02		15 05	15 08		15 17	
Horley 4	d								14 26									14 58							
Salfords	d								14 30																
Earlswood (Surrey)	d								14 33																
Tonbridge 4	d																			14 41					
Leigh (Kent)	d																			14 45					
Penshurst	d																			14 49					
Edenbridge	d																			14 55					
Godstone	d																			15 02					
Nutfield	d																			15 07					
Reigate	d					14 13																			15 13
Redhill 5	a			14 16		14 18			14 36		14 48							15 05		15 12		15 16			15 18
	d								14 37		14 49							15 05		15 13					
Merstham	d								14 41											15 17					
Coulsdon South	d								14 46											15 22					
Purley 4	d								14 50									15 14		15 27					
East Croydon	a				14 31			14 38	14 56		15 00	14 45		15 02			15 09	15 19	15 16	15 32				15 31	
	d				14 32			14 39	14 56		15 00	14 46		15 02	14 50		15 09	15 20	15 17	15 34				15 32	
Norwood Junction 2	a								15 00											15 38					
New Cross Gate	d																								
London Bridge 4 ⊖	a				14 45				15 12					15 15						15 51				15 45	
London Blackfriars 3 ⊖	a				14 52									15 22										15 52	
City Thameslink 3	a																								
Farringdon 3 ⊖	a				14 56									15 26										15 56	
St Pancras International 15 ⊖	a				15 01									15 31										16 01	
St Albans City	a				15 26									15 56										16 26	
Luton Airport Parkway 4 ✈	a				15 38									16 08										16 38	
Luton 7	a				15 41									16 11										16 41	
Bedford 10	a				16 08									16 38										17 08	
Clapham Junction 10	a							14 48			15 09	14 55			15 02		15 18	15 32	15 26						
London Victoria 15 ⊖	a	14 35					14 50	14 55		15 05	15 17	15 03			15 09	15 20	15 25	15 39	15 33		15 35				

Table 186

Sundays

Brighton - London and Bedford

1 July to 9 September

Network Diagram - see first Page of Table 186

		SN	SN	SN	SN	SN	SN	FC		SN	SN	SN	SN	SN	SN	SN	GW	FC		GW	SN	SN	SN	SN	SN
		■1	◇■1	■1	■1	◇■1	◇■1	■1		■1	■1	◇■1	◇■1	◇■1	■1	■1	■1	■1		■1	■1	◇■1	■1	■1	◇■1
		🛒			🛒		🛒				🛒	🛒	🛒	🛒		🛒					🛒			🛒	
Brighton ■10	d					15 00	15 10	15 15						15 40				15 45							16 00
Hove ■2	d		14 54																			15 54			
Preston Park	d					15 03																			16 03
Hassocks ■4	d					15 10		15 24										15 54							16 10
Burgess Hill ■4	d		15 04			15 13		15 27										15 57				16 04			16 13
Lewes ■4	d											15 22													
Wivelsfield ■4	d					15 15						15 36													16 15
Haywards Heath ■3	a		15 09			15 20		15 32				15 40						16 02				16 09			16 20
	d		15 11			15 25		15 33				15 41						16 03				16 11			16 25
Balcombe	d					15 30																			16 30
Horsham ■4	d			15 00									15 37										16 00		
Littlehaven	d			15 03																			16 03		
Faygate	d																								
Ifield	d			15 09																			16 09		
Crawley	d			15 13									15 46										16 13		
Three Bridges ■4	a			15 16		15 36		15 41					15 50					16 11					16 16		16 36
	d			15 18		15 36		15 42					15 50					16 12					16 18		16 36
Gatwick Airport ■10 ✈	a		15 22	15 22		15 40		15 46				15 52	15 55	16 01				16 16				16 22	16 22		16 40
	d	15 20	15 23	15 23	15 35	15 41		15 47			15 50	15 53	15 56	16 02		16 05	16 08	16 17			16 20	16 23	16 23	16 35	16 41
Horley ■4	d			15 26									15 58										16 26		
Salfords	d			15 30																			16 30		
Earlswood (Surrey)	d			15 33																			16 33		
Tonbridge ■4	d														15 41										
Leigh (Kent)	d														15 45										
Penshurst	d														15 49										
Edenbridge	d														15 55										
Godstone	d														16 02										
Nutfield	d														16 07										
Reigate	d																			16 13					
Redhill ■5	a			15 36		15 48							16 05		16 12		16 16			16 18			16 36		16 48
	d			15 37		15 49							16 05		16 13								16 37		16 49
Merstham	d			15 41											16 17								16 41		
Coulsdon South	d			15 46											16 22								16 46		
Purley ■4	d			15 50									16 14		16 27								16 50		
East Croydon	a		15 39	15 56		16 00	15 45	16 02				16 09	16 19	16 16	16 32			16 31				16 38	16 56		17 00
	d		15 39	15 56		16 00	15 46	16 02		15 50		16 09	16 20	16 17	16 34			16 32				16 39	16 56		17 00
Norwood Junction ■2	a			16 00											16 38								17 00		
New Cross Gate	d																								
London Bridge ■4 ⊖	a			16 12				16 15							16 51			16 45					17 12		
London Blackfriars ■3 ⊖	a							16 22										16 52							
City Thameslink ■3	a																								
Farringdon ■3 ⊖	a							16 26										16 56							
St Pancras International ■15 ⊖	a							16 31										17 01							
St Albans City	a							16 56										17 26							
Luton Airport Parkway ■4 ✈	a							17 08										17 38							
Luton ■7	a							17 11										17 41							
Bedford ■10	a							17 38										18 08							
Clapham Junction ■10	a		15 48			16 09	15 55			16 02		16 18	16 32	16 26								16 48			17 09
London Victoria ■15 ⊖	a	15 50	15 55		16 05	16 17	16 03			16 09	16 20	16 25	16 39	16 33		16 35					16 50	16 55		17 05	17 17

Table 186

Sundays

1 July to 9 September

Brighton - London and Bedford

Network Diagram - see first Page of Table 186

		SN	FC	SN		SN	SN	SN	SN	SN	SN	GW	FC	GW		SN	SN	SN	SN	SN	SN	FC	SN	SN
		◇1	1	1		1	◇1	◇1	◇1	1	1	1	1	1		1	◇1	1	1	◇1	◇1	1	1	1
Brighton 10	d	16 10	16 15						16 40				16 45							17 00	17 10	17 15		
Hove 2	d																16 54							
Preston Park	d																			17 03				
Hassocks 4	d		16 24										16 54							17 10		17 24		
Burgess Hill 4	d		16 27										16 57				17 04			17 13		17 27		
Lewes 4	d						16 22																	
Wivelsfield 4	d						16 36													17 15				
Haywards Heath 3	a		16 32				16 40						17 02				17 09			17 20		17 32		
	d		16 33				16 41						17 03				17 11			17 25		17 33		
Balcombe	d																			17 30				
Horsham 4	d							16 37										17 00						
Littlehaven	d																	17 03						
Faygate	d																							
Ifield	d																	17 09						
Crawley	d							16 46										17 13						
Three Bridges 4	a		16 41					16 50					17 11					17 16		17 36		17 41		
	d		16 42					16 50					17 12					17 18		17 36		17 42		
Gatwick Airport 10 ✈	a		16 46				16 52	16 55	17 01				17 16				17 22	17 22		17 40		17 46		
	d		16 47			16 50	16 53	16 56	17 02		17 05	17 08	17 17			17 20	17 23	17 23	17 35	17 41		17 47		17 50
Horley 4	d							16 58										17 26						
Salfords	d																	17 30						
Earlswood (Surrey)	d																	17 33						
Tonbridge 4	d									16 41														
Leigh (Kent)	d									16 45														
Penshurst	d									16 49														
Edenbridge	d									16 55														
Godstone	d									17 02														
Nutfield	d									17 07														
Reigate	d													17 13										
Redhill 5	a							17 05		17 12		17 16		17 18				17 36		17 48				
	d							17 05		17 13								17 37		17 49				
Merstham	d									17 17								17 41						
Coulsdon South	d									17 22								17 46						
Purley 4	d							17 14		17 27								17 50						
East Croydon	a	16 45	17 02				17 09	17 19	17 16	17 32			17 31				17 38	17 56		18 00	17 45	18 02		
	d	16 46	17 02	16 50			17 09	17 20	17 17	17 34			17 32				17 39	17 56		18 00	17 46	18 02	17 50	
Norwood Junction 2	a									17 38								18 00						
New Cross Gate	d																							
London Bridge 4 ⊖	a		17 15							17 51			17 45					18 12				18 15		
London Blackfriars 3 ⊖	a		17 22										17 52									18 22		
City Thameslink 3	a																							
Farringdon 3 ⊖	a		17 26										17 56									18 26		
St Pancras International 15 ⊖	a		17 31										18 01									18 31		
St Albans City	a		17 56										18 26									18 56		
Luton Airport Parkway 4 ✈	a		18 08										18 38									19 08		
Luton 7	a		18 11										18 41									19 11		
Bedford 10	a		18 38										19 08									19 38		
Clapham Junction 10	a	16 55		17 02			17 18	17 32	17 26								17 48			18 09	17 55		18 02	
London Victoria 15 ⊖	a	17 03		17 09		17 20	17 25	17 39	17 33		17 35					17 50	17 55		18 05	18 17	18 03		18 09	18 20

Table 186

Brighton - London and Bedford

Sundays

1 July to 9 September

Network Diagram - see first Page of Table 186

		SN	SN	SN	SN	SN	GW	FC	GW	SN		SN	SN
		◇1	◇1	◇1	1	1	1	1	1	1		◇1	1
		🚲	🚲	🚲		🚲				🚲			
Brighton 10	d			17 40				17 45					
Hove 2	d											17 54	
Preston Park	d												
Hassocks 4	d							17 54					
Burgess Hill 4	d							17 57				18 04	
Lewes 4	d	17 22											
Wivelsfield 4	d	17 36											
Haywards Heath 3	a	17 40						18 02				18 09	
	d	17 41						18 03				18 11	
Balcombe	d												
Horsham 4	d		17 37										18 00
Littlehaven	d												18 03
Faygate	d												
Ifield	d												18 09
Crawley	d		17 46										18 13
Three Bridges 4	a		17 50					18 11					18 16
	d		17 50					18 12					18 18
Gatwick Airport 10 ✈	a	17 52	17 55	18 01				18 16				18 22	18 22
	d	17 53	17 56	18 02		18 05	18 08	18 17		18 20		18 23	18 23
Horley 4	d		17 58										18 26
Salfords	d												18 30
Earlswood (Surrey)	d												18 33
Tonbridge 4	d				17 41								
Leigh (Kent)	d				17 45								
Penshurst	d				17 49								
Edenbridge	d				17 55								
Godstone	d				18 02								
Nutfield	d				18 07								
Reigate	d								18 13				
Redhill 5	a		18 05		18 12		18 16		18 18				18 36
	d		18 05		18 13								18 37
Merstham	d				18 17								18 41
Coulsdon South	d				18 22								18 46
Purley 4	d		18 14		18 27								18 50
East Croydon 🚊	a	18 09	18 19	18 16	18 32			18 31				18 38	18 56
	d	18 09	18 20	18 17	18 34			18 32				18 39	18 56
Norwood Junction 2	a				18 38								19 00
New Cross Gate	d												
London Bridge 4 ⊖	a				18 51			18 45					19 12
London Blackfriars 3 ⊖	a							18 52					
City Thameslink 3	a												
Farringdon 3 ⊖	a							18 56					
St Pancras International 15 ⊖	a							19 01					
St Albans City	a							19 26					
Luton Airport Parkway 4 ✈	a							19 38					
Luton 7	a							19 41					
Bedford 10	a							20 08					
Clapham Junction 10	a	18 18	18 32	18 26								18 48	
London Victoria 15 ⊖	a	18 25	18 39	18 33		18 35				18 50		18 55	

		SN	SN	SN	FC	SN	SN	SN		SN	SN	SN	SN
		1	◇1	◇1	1	1	1	◇1		◇1	◇1	1	1
		🚲					🚲	🚲					
Brighton 10	d		18 00	18 10	18 15						18 40		
Hove 2	d												
Preston Park	d		18 03										
Hassocks 4	d		18 10		18 24								
Burgess Hill 4	d		18 13		18 27								
Lewes 4	d							18 22					
Wivelsfield 4	d		18 15					18 36					
Haywards Heath 3	a		18 20		18 32			18 40					
	d		18 25		18 33			18 41					
Balcombe	d		18 30										
Horsham 4	d									18 37			
Littlehaven	d												
Faygate	d												
Ifield	d												
Crawley	d									18 46			
Three Bridges 4	a		18 36		18 41					18 50			
	d		18 36		18 42					18 50			
Gatwick Airport 10 ✈	a		18 40		18 46			18 52		18 55	19 01		
	d	18 35	18 41		18 47		18 50	18 53		18 56	19 02		19 05
Horley 4	d									18 58			
Salfords	d												
Earlswood (Surrey)	d												
Tonbridge 4	d											18 41	
Leigh (Kent)	d											18 45	
Penshurst	d											18 49	
Edenbridge	d											18 55	
Godstone	d											19 02	
Nutfield	d											19 07	
Reigate	d												
Redhill 5	a		18 48							19 05		19 12	
	d		18 49							19 05		19 13	
Merstham	d											19 17	
Coulsdon South	d											19 22	
Purley 4	d									19 14		19 27	
East Croydon 🚊	a		19 00	18 45	19 02			19 09		19 19	19 16	19 32	
	d		19 00	18 46	19 02	18 50		19 09		19 20	19 17	19 34	
Norwood Junction 2	a											19 38	
New Cross Gate	d												
London Bridge 4 ⊖	a				19 15							19 51	
London Blackfriars 3 ⊖	a				19 22								
City Thameslink 3	a												
Farringdon 3 ⊖	a				19 26								
St Pancras International 15 ⊖	a				19 31								
St Albans City	a				19 56								
Luton Airport Parkway 4 ✈	a				20 08								
Luton 7	a				20 11								
Bedford 10	a				20 38								
Clapham Junction 10	a		19 09	18 55		19 02		19 18		19 32	19 26		
London Victoria 15 ⊖	a	19 05	19 17	19 03		19 09	19 20	19 25		19 39	19 33		19 35

Table 186

Sundays

1 July to 9 September

Brighton - London and Bedford

Network Diagram - see first Page of Table 186

		GW 1	FC 1	GW 1	SN 1	SN ◇1	SN 1	SN 1	SN ◇1	SN ◇1	FC 1	SN 1	SN 1	SN ◇1	SN ◇1	SN ◇1	SN 1	SN 1	GW 1	FC 1	GW 1	SN 1	SN ◇1
Brighton 10	d		18 45						19 00	19 10	19 15					19 40				19 45			
Hove 2	d					18 54																	19 54
Preston Park	d								19 03														
Hassocks 4	d		18 54						19 10		19 24									19 54			
Burgess Hill 4	d		18 57			19 04			19 13		19 27									19 57			20 04
Lewes 4	d													19 22									
Wivelsfield 4	d								19 15					19 36									20 09
Haywards Heath 3	a		19 02			19 09			19 20		19 32			19 40						20 02			20 11
	d		19 03			19 11			19 25		19 33			19 41						20 03			
Balcombe	d								19 30														
Horsham 4	d						19 00								19 37								
Littlehaven	d						19 03																
Faygate	d																						
Ifield	d						19 09																
Crawley	d						19 13								19 46								
Three Bridges 4	a		19 11				19 16		19 36		19 41				19 50					20 11			
	d		19 12				19 18		19 36		19 42				19 50					20 12			
Gatwick Airport 10 ✈	a		19 16			19 22	19 22		19 40		19 46			19 52	19 55	20 01				20 16			20 22
	d	19 08	19 17		19 20	19 23	19 23	19 35	19 41		19 47		19 50	19 53	19 56	20 02		20 05	20 08	20 17		20 20	20 23
Horley 4	d						19 26								19 58								
Salfords	d						19 30																
Earlswood (Surrey)	d						19 33																
Tonbridge 4	d																19 41						
Leigh (Kent)	d																19 45						
Penshurst	d																19 49						
Edenbridge	d																19 55						
Godstone	d																20 02						
Nutfield	d																20 07						
Reigate	d			19 13																	20 13		
Redhill 5	a	19 16		19 18			19 36		19 48						20 05		20 12		20 16		20 18		
	d						19 37		19 49						20 05		20 13						
Merstham	d						19 41										20 17						
Coulsdon South	d						19 46										20 22						
Purley 4	d						19 50								20 14		20 27						
East Croydon 🚌	a		19 31			19 38	19 56		20 00	19 45	20 02			20 09	20 19	20 16	20 32			20 31			20 38
	d		19 32			19 39	19 56		20 00	19 46	20 02	19 50		20 09	20 20	20 17	20 34			20 32			20 39
Norwood Junction 2	a						20 00										20 38						
New Cross Gate	d																						
London Bridge 4 ⊖	a		19 45				20 12				20 15						20 51			20 45			
London Blackfriars 3 ⊖	a		19 52								20 22									20 52			
City Thameslink 3	a																						
Farringdon 3 ⊖	a		19 56								20 26									20 56			
St Pancras International 15 ⊖	a		20 01								20 31									21 01			
St Albans City	a		20 26								20 56									21 26			
Luton Airport Parkway 4 ✈	a		20 38								21 08									21 38			
Luton 7	a		20 41								21 11									21 41			
Bedford 10	a		21 08								21 38									22 08			
Clapham Junction 10	a					19 48			20 09	19 55		20 02		20 18	20 32	20 26							20 48
London Victoria 15 ⊖	a				19 50	19 55		20 05	20 17	20 03		20 09	20 20	20 25	20 39	20 33		20 35				20 50	20 55

Table 186

Brighton - London and Bedford

Sundays

1 July to 9 September

Network Diagram - see first Page of Table 186

		SN		SN	SN	SN	FC	SN	SN	SN	SN	SN		SN	SN	GW	FC	GW	SN	SN	SN	SN		SN	SN
		1		1	◇1	◇1	1	1	1	◇1	◇1	◇1		1	1	1	1	1	1	◇1	1	1		1	◇1
Brighton 10	d				20 00	20 10	20 15					20 40					20 45								21 04
Hove 2	d																			20 54					
Preston Park	d				20 03																				21 07
Hassocks 4	d				20 10		20 24										20 54								21 14
Burgess Hill 4	d				20 13		20 27										20 57			21 04					21 17
Lewes 4	d									20 22															
Wivelsfield 4	d				20 15					20 36															21 19
Haywards Heath 3	a				20 20		20 32			20 40							21 02			21 09					21 24
	d				20 25		20 33			20 41							21 03			21 11					21 25
Balcombe	d				20 30																				21 30
Horsham 4	d	20 00									20 37										21 00				
Littlehaven	d	20 03																			21 03				
Faygate	d																								
Ifield	d	20 09																			21 09				
Crawley	d	20 13									20 46										21 13				
Three Bridges 4	a	20 16			20 36		20 41				20 50						21 11				21 16				21 36
	d	20 18			20 36		20 42				20 50						21 12				21 18				21 36
Gatwick Airport 10 ✈	a	20 22			20 40		20 46			20 52	20 55	21 01					21 16			21 22	21 22				21 40
	d	20 23		20 35	20 41		20 47		20 50	20 53	20 56	21 02			21 05	21 08	21 17		21 20	21 23	21 23	21 35			21 41
Horley 4	d	20 26									20 58										21 26				
Salfords	d	20 30																			21 30				
Earlswood (Surrey)	d	20 33																			21 33				
Tonbridge 4	d													20 41											
Leigh (Kent)	d													20 45											
Penshurst	d													20 49											
Edenbridge	d													20 55											
Godstone	d													21 02											
Nutfield	d													21 07											
Reigate	d																	21 13							
Redhill 5	a	20 36			20 48						21 05			21 12		21 16		21 18			21 36				21 48
	d	20 37			20 49						21 05			21 13							21 37				21 49
Merstham	d	20 41												21 17							21 41				
Coulsdon South	d	20 46												21 22							21 46				
Purley 4	d	20 50									21 14			21 27							21 50				
East Croydon 🚋	a	20 56			21 00	20 45	21 02			21 09	21 19	21 16		21 32			21 31			21 38	21 56				22 00
	d	20 56			21 00	20 46	21 02	20 50		21 09	21 20	21 17		21 34			21 32			21 39	21 56			21 50	22 00
Norwood Junction 2	a	21 00												21 38							22 00				
New Cross Gate	d																								
London Bridge 4 ⊖	a	21 12					21 15							21 51			21 45				22 12				
London Blackfriars 3 ⊖	a						21 22										21 52								
City Thameslink 3	a																								
Farringdon 3 ⊖	a						21 26										21 56								
St Pancras International 15 ⊖	a						21 31										22 01								
St Albans City	a						21 56										22 26								
Luton Airport Parkway 4 ✈	a						22 08										22 38								
Luton 7	a						22 11										22 41								
Bedford 10	a						22 38										23 08								
Clapham Junction 10	a				21 09	20 55		21 02		21 18	21 32	21 26								21 48				22 02	22 09
London Victoria 15 ⊖	a			21 05	21 17	21 03		21 09	21 20	21 25	21 39	21 33			21 35				21 50	21 55		22 05		22 09	22 17

Table 186

Sundays

1 July to 9 September

Brighton - London and Bedford

Network Diagram - see first Page of Table 186

		FC 1	SN 1	SN ◇1	SN ◇1	SN 1	SN 1	GW 1		FC 1	GW 1	SN 1	SN 1	SN 1	SN 1	SN ◇1	FC 1	SN 1		SN 1	SN ◇1	SN 1	GW 1	FC 1	GW 1
Brighton 10	d	21 15								21 45						22 04	22 15							22 45	
Hove 2	d																								
Preston Park	d															22 07									
Hassocks 4	d	21 24								21 54						22 14	22 24							22 54	
Burgess Hill 4	d	21 27								21 57						22 17	22 27							22 57	
Lewes 4	d			21 22																					
Wivelsfield 4	d			21 36												22 19									
Haywards Heath 3	a	21 32		21 40						22 02						22 24	22 32							23 02	
	d	21 33		21 41						22 03						22 25	22 33							23 03	
Balcombe	d															22 30									
Horsham 4	d				21 37									22 00							22 37				
Littlehaven	d													22 03											
Faygate	d																								
Ifield	d													22 09											
Crawley	d				21 46									22 13							22 46				
Three Bridges 4	a	21 41			21 50					22 11				22 16		22 36	22 41				22 50			23 11	
	d	21 42			21 50					22 12				22 18		22 36	22 42				22 50			23 12	
Gatwick Airport 10 ✈	a	21 46		21 52	21 55					22 16				22 22		22 40	22 46				22 55			23 16	
	d	21 47	21 50	21 53	21 56		22 05	22 08		22 17		22 20		22 23	22 35	22 41	22 47			22 50	22 56	23 05	23 08	23 17	
Horley 4	d				21 58									22 26							22 58				
Salfords	d													22 30											
Earlswood (Surrey)	d													22 33											
Tonbridge 4	d					21 41												22 29							
Leigh (Kent)	d					21 45												22 33							
Penshurst	d					21 49												22 37							
Edenbridge	d					21 55												22 43							
Godstone	d					22 02												22 50							
Nutfield	d					22 07												22 55							
Reigate	d										22 13														23 13
Redhill 5	a				22 05	22 12		22 16			22 18			22 36		22 48		23 00			23 05		23 16		23 18
	d				22 05	22 13								22 37		22 49					23 05				
Merstham	d					22 17								22 41											
Coulsdon South	d					22 22								22 46											
Purley 4	d				22 14	22 27								22 50							23 14				
East Croydon	a	22 02		22 09	22 19	22 32				22 31				22 55		23 00	23 02				23 20			23 31	
	d	22 02		22 09	22 20	22 34				22 32			22 50	22 56		23 00	23 02				23 21			23 32	
Norwood Junction 2	a					22 38																			
New Cross Gate	d																								
London Bridge 4 ⊖	a	22 15				22 51				22 45							23 15							23 45	
London Blackfriars 3 ⊖	a	22 22								22 52							23 22							23 52	
City Thameslink 3	a																								
Farringdon 3 ⊖	a	22 26								22 56							23 26							23 56	
St Pancras International 15 ⊖	a	22 31								23 01							23 31							00 01	
St Albans City	a	23 05								23 35							00 05							00 35	
Luton Airport Parkway 4 ✈	a	23 17								23 47							00 17							00 47	
Luton 7	a	23 20								23 50							00 20							00 50	
Bedford 10	a	23 47								00 17							00 47							01 17	
Clapham Junction 10	a			22 18	22 32								23 02	23 07		23 10					23 31				
London Victoria 15 ⊖	a		22 20	22 25	22 39		22 35					22 50	23 09	23 14	23 05	23 20				23 25	23 38	23 35			

Table 186

Sundays

Brighton - London and Bedford

1 July to 9 September

Network Diagram - see first Page of Table 186

Station		SN 1	SN 1	SN 1		SN 1	SN ◇1	FC 1	SN 1	FC 1
Brighton 10	d						23 02	23 15		23 45
Hove 2	d									
Preston Park	d						23 06			
Hassocks 4	d						23 12	23 24		23 54
Burgess Hill 4	d						23 16	23 27		23 57
ewes 4	d									
Welsfield 4	d						23 18			
Haywards Heath 3	a						23 23	23 32		00 02
	d						23 23	23 33		00 03
Balcombe	d						23 29			
Horsham 4	d			23 03						
ttlehaven	d			23 06						
Faygate	d									
field	d			23 12						
Crawley	d			23 16						
Three Bridges 4	a			23 19			23 36	23 41		00 11
	d			23 20			23 41	23 42		00 12
Gatwick Airport 10 ✈	a			23 24			23 45	23 46		00 16
	d	23 20		23 25		23 35	23 46	23 47	23 50	00 17
Horley 4	d			23 28			23 49			
Salfords	d									
Erlswood (Surrey)	d									
Tonbridge 4	d									
eigh (Kent)	d									
Penshurst	d									
Eenbridge	d									
Godstone	d									
Ntfield	d									
Reigate	d									
Redhill 5	a			23 34			23 57			00 24
	d			23 35			00 01			00 24
Merstham	d			23 39						
Coulsdon South	d			23 44						
Purley 4	d			23 50			00 11			
East Croydon	a			23 55			00 16	00 02		00 36
	d		23 50	23 56			00 16	00 04		00 36
Nrwood unction 2	a									
Nw Cross Gate	d									
London Bridge 4 ⊖	a							00 21		00 50
London Blackfriars 3 ⊖	a							00 27		00 57
City Thameslink 3	a									
Farringdon 3 ⊖	a							00 33		
St Pancras hternational 15 ⊖	a							00 37		01 07
St Albans City	a							01 10		01 40
Lton Airport Parkway 4 ✈	a							01 22		01 52
Lton 7	a							01 25		01 55
Bedford 10	a							01 52		02 22
Clapham unction 10	a		00 01	00 11			00 29			
London Victoria 15 ⊖	a	23 55	00 08	00 19		00 10	00 37		00 25	

Table 186

Sundays

from 16 September

Brighton - London and Bedford

Network Diagram - see first Page of Table 186

		FC	FC	FC	SN	SN	SN	FC	SN	SN		SN	FC	SN	GW	SN	SN	SN	SN	SN		SN	SN	SN	SN
		1	1	1	1	1	◇1	1	1	◇1		1	1	1	1		1	1	1	1		1	1	1	1
Brighton 10	d	21p37	22p07	22p33			23p02	23p11					23p37												
Hove 2	d																								
Preston Park	d	21p41	22p11	22p37			23p06						23p41												
Hassocks 4	d	21p47	22p17	22p43			23p12	23p20					23p47												
Burgess Hill 4	d	21p51	22p21	22p47			23p16	23p23					23p51												
Lewes 4	d																								
Wivelsfield 4	d	21p53	22p23	22p49			23p19						23p53												
Haywards Heath 3	a	21p58	22p28	22p53			23p23	23p28					23p58												
	d	22p02	22p32	22p54			23p24	23p29					23p59												
Balcombe	d		22p37	22p59									00 04												
Horsham 4	d				23p02																				
Littlehaven	d				23p05																				
Faygate	d																								
Ifield	d				23p11																				
Crawley	d				23p14					←															
Three Bridges 4	a	22p11	22p43	23p05	23p18		23p32	23p37		23p32			00 10												
	d	22p12	22p43	23p12	23p18		23p47	23p38		23p47			00 10						01 10			02 10	03 10	04 10	
Gatwick Airport 10 ✈	a	22p16	22p47	23p16	23p22		→	23p42		23p52			00 14						01 19			02 14	03 14	04 14	
	d	22p17	22p47	23p17	23p23	23p35		23p43	23p50	23p53		00 07	00 15	00 20			00 35	00 50	01 20	01 35		02 15	03 15	04 15	04 35
Horley 4	d				23p26					23p56									01 22			02 18	03 18	04 18	
Salfords	d				23p30																				
Earlswood (Surrey)	d				23p33																				
Tonbridge 4	d																								
Leigh (Kent)	d																								
Penshurst	d																								
Edenbridge	d																								
Godstone	d																								
Nutfield	d																								
Reigate	d														00 45										
Redhill 5	a				23p36					00 03			00 22		00 49										
	d				23p37					00 03			00 23												
Merstham	d				23p41																				
Coulsdon South	d				23p46																				
Purley 4	d				23p49					00 11									01 37			02 33	03 33	04 33	
East Croydon 🚋	a	22p32	23p02	23p32	23p55			00 01		00 16			00 35						01 42			02 39	03 39	04 39	
	d	22p32	23p02	23p32	23p56			00 04		00 17			00 36			00 49			01 43			02 40	03 40	04 40	
Norwood Junction 2	a																								
New Cross Gate	d																								
London Bridge 4 ⊖	a	22p45	23p15	23p44				00 21					00 51												
London Blackfriars 3 ⊖	a	22p52	23p22	23p52				00 28					00 58												
City Thameslink 3	a																								
Farringdon 3 ⊖	a	22p57	23p28	23p58				00 33																	
St Pancras International 15 ⊖	a	23p02	23p32	00 02				00 37					01 07												
St Albans City	a	23p26	23p56	00 26				01 10					01 40												
Luton Airport Parkway 4 ✈	a	23p38	00 08	00 38				01 22					01 52												
Luton 7	a	23p41	00 11	00 41				01 25					01 55												
Bedford 10	a	00 08	00 38	01 08				01 52					02 22												
Clapham Junction 10	a				00 11					00 29						01 03			01 54			02 53	03 53	04 53	
London Victoria 15 ⊖	a				00 18	00 10			00 20	00 37		00 42		00 55		01 10	01 11	01 25	02 05	02 10		03 05	04 05	05 05	05 10

Table 186

Sundays

from 16 September

Brighton - London and Bedford

Network Diagram - see first Page of Table 186

Station		FC	SN	SN	SN	SN		GW	SN	SN	SN	FC	SN	SN	GW	SN		GW	FC	SN	SN	SN	SN	FC	SN
			1	1	1	1 🛒		1	1 🛒	1	1 🛒	1	1 🛒	◇1	1	1 🛒		1	1	1 🛒	1	1 🛒	◇1	1	1
Brighton 10	d											06 11		06 19					06 44				07 00	07 14	
Hove 2	d																								
Preston Park	d													06 22									07 03		
Hassocks 4	d											06 20		06 29					06 53				07 10	07 23	
Burgess Hill 4	d											06 26		06 32					06 56				07 13	07 26	
Lewes 4	d																								
Wivelsfield 4	d													06 34									07 15		
Haywards Heath 3	a											06 31		06 39					07 01				07 20	07 31	
	d											06 32		06 39					07 02				07 20	07 32	
Balcombe	d																						07 26		
Horsham 4	d									06 04											07 03				
Littlehaven	d									06 07											07 06				
Faygate	d																								
Ifield	d									06 13											07 12				
Crawley	d									06 17											07 16				
Three Bridges 4	a									06 20		06 40		06 48					07 10		07 19		07 31	07 40	
	d	05 12		05 30						06 21		06 41		06 48					07 11		07 20		07 32	07 41	
Gatwick Airport 10 ✈	a	05 16		05 34						06 25		06 45		06 52					07 15		07 24		07 37	07 45	
	d	05 17	05 20	05 36	05 50	06 05		06 08	06 20		06 35	06 46	06 50	06 53		07 05		07 08	07 16	07 20	07 25	07 35	07 38	07 46	
Horley 4	d			05 38																	07 28				
Salfords	d																								
Earlswood (Surrey)	d																								
Tonbridge 4	d																								07 29
Leigh (Kent)	d																								07 33
Penshurst	d																								07 37
Edenbridge	d																								07 43
Godstone	d																								07 50
Nutfield	d																								07 55
Reigate	d														07 05										
Redhill 5	a			05 46				06 17							07 09			07 16			07 34		07 45		08 00
	d			05 46																	07 35		07 46		
Merstham	d																				07 39				
Coulsdon South	d																				07 44				
Purley 4	d			05 56																	07 50				
East Croydon	a	05 32		06 01								07 01		07 10					07 31		07 56		07 58	08 01	
	d	05 32		06 02								07 02		07 10					07 32		07 56		08 00	08 01	
Norwood Junction 2	a																				08 00				
New Cross Gate	d																								
London Bridge 4 ⊖	a											07 15							07 45		08 12			08 15	
London Blackfriars 3 ⊖	a	05 59										07 22							07 52					08 22	
City Thameslink 3	a																								
Farringdon 3 ⊖	a											07 26							07 56					08 26	
St Pancras International 15 ⊖	a	06 07										07 31							08 01					08 31	
St Albans City	a	06 41										08 05							08 37					09 05	
Luton Airport Parkway 4 ✈	a	06 53										08 17							08 49					09 17	
Luton 7	a	06 56										08 20							08 52					09 20	
Bedford 10	a	07 24										08 47							09 19					09 47	
Clapham Junction 10	a			06 14										07 24									08 11		
London Victoria 15 ⊖	a		05 58	06 22	06 25	06 40			06 55		07 10		07 25	07 31		07 40				07 55		08 10	08 18		

Table 186

Sundays
from 16 September

Brighton - London and Bedford

Network Diagram - see first Page of Table 186

		SN 1 🚲		SN ◇1 🚲	SN ◇1	SN 1 🚲	GW 1	FC 1	GW 1	SN 1 🚲	SN ◇1	SN 1		SN 1	SN 1 🚲	SN ◇1	FC 1	SN 1	SN 1 🚲	SN ◇1 🚲	SN ◇1 🚲	SN ◇1 🚲		SN 1 🚲	GW 1
Brighton 10	d							07 44								08 00	08 14				08 34				
Hove 2	d										07 54														
Preston Park	d															08 03									
Hassocks 4	d							07 53								08 10	08 23								
Burgess Hill 4	d							07 56			08 04					08 13	08 26								
Lewes 4	d			07 20																08 16					
Wivelsfield 4	d			07 32												08 15				08 31					
Haywards Heath 3	a			07 36				08 01			08 09					08 20	08 31			08 36					
	d			07 39				08 02			08 10					08 20	08 32			08 39					
Balcombe	d															08 26									
Horsham 4	d				07 42							08 03										08 42			
Littlehaven	d											08 06													
Faygate	d																								
Ifield	d											08 12													
Crawley	d				07 51							08 16										08 51			
Three Bridges 4	a				07 54			08 10				08 19				08 31	08 40					08 54			
	d				07 55			08 11				08 20				08 32	08 41					08 55			
Gatwick Airport 10 ✈	a			07 51	07 59			08 15			08 22	08 24				08 37	08 45			08 51	08 56	08 59			
	d	07 50		07 53	08 00	08 05	08 08	08 16		08 20	08 23	08 25			08 35	08 38	08 46		08 50	08 53	08 57	09 00		09 05	09 08
Horley 4	d				08 02							08 28										09 02			
Salfords	d																								
Earlswood (Surrey)	d																								
Tonbridge 4	d																	08 29							
Leigh (Kent)	d																	08 33							
Penshurst	d																	08 37							
Edenbridge	d																	08 43							
Godstone	d																	08 50							
Nutfield	d																	08 55							
Reigate	d								08 13																09 16
Redhill 5	a				08 09		08 16		08 18			08 34				08 45		09 00				09 09			
	d				08 09							08 35				08 46						09 10			
Merstham	d											08 39													
Coulsdon South	d											08 44													
Purley 4	d				08 20							08 50										09 20			
East Croydon 🚋	a			08 08	08 26			08 31			08 39	08 56				08 58	09 01			09 09	09 12	09 26			
	d			08 09	08 26			08 32			08 40	08 56		08 50		09 00	09 01			09 10	09 13	09 26			
Norwood Junction 2	a											09 00													
New Cross Gate	d																								
London Bridge 4 ⊖	a							08 45				09 12					09 15								
London Blackfriars 3 ⊖	a							08 52									09 22								
City Thameslink 3	a																								
Farringdon 3 ⊖	a							08 56									09 26								
St Pancras International 15 ⊖	a							09 01									09 31								
St Albans City	a							09 37									10 05								
Luton Airport Parkway 4 ✈	a							09 49									10 17								
Luton 7	a							09 52									10 20								
Bedford 10	a							10 19									10 47								
Clapham Junction 10	a			08 23	08 37						08 54			09 01		09 11				09 24	09 27	09 37			
London Victoria 15 ⊖	a	08 25		08 30	08 46	08 40				08 55	09 01			09 08	09 10	09 18			09 25	09 31	09 35	09 46		09 40	

Table 186

Brighton - London and Bedford

Sundays

from 16 September

Network Diagram - see first Page of Table 186

		FC	GW	SN	SN	SN	SN	SN		SN	FC	SN	SN	SN	SN	SN	SN	GW		FC	GW	SN	SN	SN	SN
		1	1	1	◇1	1	1	1		◇1	1	1	1	◇1	◇1	◇1	1	1		1	1	1	◇1	1	1
				🚲				🚲					🚲	🚲	🚲	🚲	🚲					🚲			
Brighton 10	d	08 44								09 00	09 14				09 34					09 44					
Hove 2	d				08 54																		09 54		
Preston Park	d									09 03															
Hassocks 4	d	08 53								09 10	09 23									09 53					
Burgess Hill 4	d	08 56			09 05					09 13	09 26									09 56			10 05		
Lewes 4	d													09 16											
Wivelsfield 4	d									09 15				09 31											
Haywards Heath 3	a	09 01			09 10					09 20	09 31			09 35						10 01			10 10		
	d	09 02			09 10					09 20	09 32			09 39						10 02			10 10		
Balcombe	d									09 26															
Horsham 4	d					09 03										09 42								10 03	
Littlehaven	d					09 06																		10 06	
Faygate	d																								
Ifield	d					09 12																		10 12	
Crawley	d					09 16										09 51								10 16	
Three Bridges 4	a	09 10				09 19				09 31	09 40					09 54				10 10				10 19	
	d	09 11				09 20				09 32	09 41					09 55				10 11				10 20	
Gatwick Airport 10 ✈	a	09 15			09 21	09 24				09 37	09 45			09 51	09 56	09 59				10 15			10 21	10 24	
	d	09 16		09 20	09 23	09 25		09 35		09 38	09 46		09 50	09 53	09 57	10 00	10 05	10 08		10 16		10 20	10 23	10 25	
Horley 4	d					09 28										10 02								10 28	
Salfords	d																								
Earlswood (Surrey)	d																								
Tonbridge 4	d											09 29													
Leigh (Kent)	d											09 33													
Penshurst	d											09 37													
Edenbridge	d											09 43													
Godstone	d											09 50													
Nutfield	d											09 55													
Reigate	d		09 13																		10 13				
Redhill 5	a		09 18			09 34				09 45		10 00				10 09		10 16			10 18			10 34	
	d					09 35				09 46						10 10								10 35	
Merstham	d					09 39																		10 39	
Coulsdon South	d					09 44																		10 44	
Purley 4	d					09 50										10 20								10 50	
East Croydon 🚋	a	09 31			09 39	09 56				09 58	10 01			10 09	10 12	10 26				10 31			10 39	10 56	
	d	09 32			09 40	09 56	09 50			10 00	10 01			10 10	10 13	10 26				10 32			10 40	10 56	10 50
Norwood Junction 2	a					10 00																		11 00	
New Cross Gate	d																								
London Bridge 4 ⊖	a	09 45				10 12					10 15									10 45				11 12	
London Blackfriars 3 ⊖	a	09 52									10 22									10 52					
City Thameslink 3	a																								
Farringdon 3 ⊖	a	09 56									10 26									10 56					
St Pancras International 15 ⊖	a	10 01									10 31									11 01					
St Albans City	a	10 26									10 56									11 26					
Luton Airport Parkway 4 ✈	a	10 38									11 08									11 38					
Luton 7	a	10 41									11 11									11 41					
Bedford 10	a	11 08									11 38									12 08					
Clapham Junction 10	a				09 54		10 01			10 11				10 24	10 27	10 37							10 54		11 01
London Victoria 15 ⊖	a			09 55	10 01		10 08	10 10		10 18			10 25	10 31	10 35	10 46	10 40					10 55	11 01		11 08

Table 186

Sundays

from 16 September

Brighton - London and Bedford

Network Diagram - see first Page of Table 186

		SN	SN	FC		SN	SN	SN	SN	SN	SN	GW	FC	GW		SN	SN	SN	SN	SN	SN	FC	SN	SN
		1	◇1	1		1	1	◇1	◇1	◇1	1	1	1	1		1	◇1	1	1	1	◇1	1	1	1
		🚲					🚲	🚲	🚲	🚲	🚲					🚲				🚲				🚲
Brighton 10	d		10 00	10 14					10 34				10 44								11 00	11 14		
Hove 2	d																10 54							
Preston Park	d		10 03																		11 03			
Hassocks 4	d		10 10	10 23									10 53								11 10	11 23		
Burgess Hill 4	d		10 13	10 26									10 56				11 05				11 13	11 26		
Lewes 4	d							10 16																
Wivelsfield 4	d		10 15					10 31													11 15			
Haywards Heath 3	a		10 20	10 31				10 35					11 01				11 10				11 20	11 31		
	d		10 20	10 32				10 39					11 02				11 10				11 20	11 32		
Balcombe	d		10 26																		11 26			
Horsham 4	d									10 42								11 03						
Littlehaven	d																	11 06						
Faygate	d																							
Ifield	d																	11 12						
Crawley	d									10 51								11 16						
Three Bridges 4	a		10 31	10 40						10 54			11 10					11 19			11 31	11 40		
	d		10 32	10 41						10 55			11 11					11 20			11 32	11 41		
Gatwick Airport 10 ✈	a		10 37	10 45				10 51	10 56	10 59			11 15				11 21	11 24			11 37	11 45		
	d	10 35	10 38	10 46			10 50	10 53	10 57	11 00	11 05	11 08	11 16			11 20	11 23	11 25		11 35	11 38	11 46		11 50
Horley 4	d									11 02								11 28						
Salfords	d																							
Earlswood (Surrey)	d																							
Tonbridge 4	d					10 29																	11 29	
Leigh (Kent)	d					10 33																	11 33	
Penshurst	d					10 37																	11 37	
Edenbridge	d					10 43																	11 43	
Godstone	d					10 50																	11 50	
Nutfield	d					10 55																	11 55	
Reigate	d													11 13										
Redhill 5	a		10 45			11 00				11 09		11 16		11 18				11 34			11 45		12 00	
	d		10 46							11 10								11 35			11 46			
Merstham	d																	11 39						
Coulsdon South	d																	11 44						
Purley 4	d									11 20								11 50						
East Croydon 🚋	a		10 58	11 01				11 09	11 12	11 26			11 31				11 39	11 56			11 58	12 01		
	d		11 00	11 01				11 10	11 13	11 26			11 32				11 40	11 56	11 50		12 00	12 01		
Norwood Junction 2	a																	12 00						
New Cross Gate	d																							
London Bridge 4 ⊖	a			11 15									11 45					12 12				12 15		
London Blackfriars 3 ⊖	a			11 22									11 52									12 22		
City Thameslink 3	a																							
Farringdon 3 ⊖	a			11 26									11 56									12 26		
St Pancras International 15 ⊖	a			11 31									12 01									12 31		
St Albans City	a			11 56									12 26									12 56		
Luton Airport Parkway 4 ✈	a			12 08									12 38									13 08		
Luton 7	a			12 11									12 41									13 11		
Bedford 10	a			12 38									13 08									13 38		
Clapham Junction 10	a		11 11					11 24	11 27	11 37							11 54		12 01		12 11			
London Victoria 15 ⊖	a	11 10	11 18				11 25	11 31	11 35	11 46	11 40					11 55	12 01		12 08	12 10	12 18			12 25

Table 186

Sundays

from 16 September

Brighton - London and Bedford

Network Diagram - see first Page of Table 186

		SN ◇1 🚲	SN ◇1 🚲	SN ◇1 🚲	SN 1 🚲	GW 1	FC 1	GW 1	SN 1 🚲	SN ◇1		SN 1	SN 1	SN 1 🚲	SN ◇1	FC 1	SN 1	SN 1 🚲	SN ◇1 🚲	SN ◇1 🚲		SN ◇1 🚲	SN 1 🚲	GW 1	FC 1
Brighton 10	d		11 34				11 44								12 00	12 14				12 34					12 44
Hove 2	d									11 54															
Preston Park	d														12 03										
Hassocks 4	d						11 53								12 10	12 23									12 53
Burgess Hill 4	d						11 56			12 05					12 13	12 26									12 56
Lewes 4	d	11 16																	12 16						
Wivelsfield 4	d	11 31													12 15				12 31						
Haywards Heath 3	a	11 35					12 01			12 10					12 20	12 31			12 35						13 01
	d	11 39					12 02			12 10					12 20	12 32			12 39						13 02
Balcombe	d														12 26										
Horsham 4	d			11 42								12 03										12 42			
Littlehaven	d											12 06													
Faygate	d																								
Ifield	d											12 12													
Crawley	d			11 51								12 16										12 51			
Three Bridges 4	a			11 54			12 10					12 19			12 31	12 40						12 54			13 10
	d			11 55			12 11					12 20			12 32	12 41						12 55			13 11
Gatwick Airport 10 ✈	a	11 51	11 56	11 59			12 15			12 22		12 24			12 37	12 45			12 52	12 56		12 59			13 15
	d	11 53	11 57	12 00	12 05	12 08	12 16		12 20	12 23		12 25		12 35	12 38	12 46		12 50	12 53	12 57		13 00	13 05	13 08	13 16
Horley 4	d			12 02								12 28										13 02			
Salfords	d																								
Earlswood (Surrey)	d																								
Tonbridge 4	d																12 29								
Leigh (Kent)	d																12 33								
Penshurst	d																12 37								
Edenbridge	d																12 43								
Godstone	d																12 50								
Nutfield	d																12 55								
Reigate	d							12 13																	
Redhill 5	a			12 09		12 16		12 18				12 34			12 45		13 00					13 09		13 16	
	d			12 10								12 35			12 46							13 10			
Merstham	d											12 39													
Coulsdon South	d											12 44													
Purley 4	d			12 20								12 50										13 19			
East Croydon	a	12 09	12 12	12 26			12 31			12 39		12 56			12 58	13 01			13 09	13 12		13 26			13 31
	d	12 10	12 13	12 26			12 32			12 40		12 56	12 50		13 00	13 01			13 10	13 13		13 26			13 32
Norwood Junction 2	a											13 00													
New Cross Gate	d																								
London Bridge 4 ⊖	a						12 45					13 12				13 15									13 45
London Blackfriars 3 ⊖	a						12 52									13 22									13 52
City Thameslink 3	a																								
Farringdon 3 ⊖	a						12 56									13 26									13 56
St Pancras International 15 ⊖	a						13 01									13 31									14 01
St Albans City	a						13 26									13 56									14 26
Luton Airport Parkway 4 ✈	a						13 38									14 08									14 38
Luton 7	a						13 41									14 11									14 41
Bedford 10	a						14 08									14 38									15 08
Clapham Junction 10	a	12 24	12 27	12 37						12 54			13 01		13 11				13 24	13 27		13 37			
London Victoria 15 ⊖	a	12 31	12 35	12 46	12 40				12 55	13 01			13 08	13 10	13 18			13 25	13 31	13 35		13 46	13 40		

Table 186

Sundays from 16 September

Brighton - London and Bedford

Network Diagram - see first Page of Table 186

		GW	SN	SN	SN	SN		SN	SN	FC	SN	SN	SN	SN	SN	SN		GW	FC	GW	SN	SN	SN	SN	SN
		1	1	◇1	1	1		1	◇1	1	1	1	◇1	◇1	◇1	1		1	1	1	1	◇1	1	1	1
Brighton 10	d								13 00	13 14				13 34					13 44						
Hove 2	d			12 54																		13 54			
Preston Park	d								13 03																
Hassocks 4	d								13 10	13 23									13 53						
Burgess Hill 4	d			13 05					13 13	13 26									13 56			14 05			
Lewes 4	d												13 16												
Wivelsfield 4	d								13 15				13 31												
Haywards Heath 3	a			13 10					13 20	13 31			13 35						14 01			14 10			
	d			13 10					13 20	13 32			13 39						14 02			14 10			
Balcombe	d								13 26																
Horsham 4	d				13 03										13 42								14 03		
Littlehaven	d				13 06																		14 06		
Faygate	d																								
Ifield	d				13 12																		14 12		
Crawley	d				13 16										13 51								14 16		
Three Bridges 4	a				13 19				13 31	13 40					13 54				14 10				14 19		
	d				13 20				13 32	13 41					13 55				14 11				14 20		
Gatwick Airport 10 ✈	a			13 22	13 24				13 37	13 45			13 52	13 56	13 59				14 15			14 22	14 24		
	d		13 20	13 23	13 25			13 35	13 38	13 46		13 50	13 53	13 57	14 00	14 05		14 08	14 16		14 20	14 23	14 25		14 35
Horley 4	d				13 28										14 02								14 28		
Salfords	d																								
Earlswood (Surrey)	d																								
Tonbridge 4	d										13 29														
Leigh (Kent)	d										13 33														
Penshurst	d										13 37														
Edenbridge	d										13 43														
Godstone	d										13 50														
Nutfield	d										13 55														
Reigate	d	13 13																		14 13					
Redhill 5	a	13 18			13 34				13 45		14 00				14 09			14 16		14 18			14 34		
	d				13 35				13 46						14 10								14 35		
Merstham	d				13 39																		14 39		
Coulsdon South	d				13 44																		14 44		
Purley 4	d				13 50										14 20								14 50		
East Croydon	a			13 39	13 56				13 58	14 01			14 09	14 12	14 26				14 31			14 39	14 56		
	d			13 40	13 56	13 50			14 00	14 01			14 10	14 13	14 26				14 32			14 40	14 56	14 50	
Norwood Junction 2	a				14 00																		15 00		
New Cross Gate	d																								
London Bridge 4 ⊖	a				14 12					14 15									14 45				15 12		
London Blackfriars 3 ⊖	a									14 22									14 52						
City Thameslink 3	a																								
Farringdon 3 ⊖	a									14 26									14 56						
St Pancras International 15 ⊖	a									14 31									15 01						
St Albans City	a									14 56									15 26						
Luton Airport Parkway 4 ✈	a									15 08									15 38						
Luton 7	a									15 11									15 41						
Bedford 10	a									15 38									16 08						
Clapham Junction 10	a			13 54		14 01			14 11				14 24	14 27	14 37							14 54		15 01	
London Victoria 15 ⊖	a		13 55	14 01		14 08		14 10	14 18			14 25	14 31	14 35	14 46	14 40					14 55	15 01		15 08	15 10

Table 186

Sundays

from 16 September

Brighton - London and Bedford

Network Diagram - see first Page of Table 186

		SN		FC	SN	SN	SN	SN	SN	SN	GW	FC		GW	SN	SN	SN	SN	SN	SN	FC	SN		SN	SN
		◇1		1	1	1 ⚲	◇1 ⚲	◇1 ⚲	◇1 ⚲	1 ⚲	1	1		1	1 ⚲	◇1	1	1	1 ⚲	◇1	1	1		1 ⚲	◇1 ⚲
Brighton 10	d	14 00		14 14				14 34				14 44								15 00	15 14				
Hove 2	d															14 54									
Preston Park	d	14 03																		15 03					
Hassocks 4	d	14 10		14 23								14 53								15 10	15 23				
Burgess Hill 4	d	14 13		14 26								14 56				15 05				15 13	15 26				
Lewes 4	d						14 16																		15 16
Wivelsfield 4	d	14 15					14 31													15 15					15 31
Haywards Heath 3	a	14 20		14 31			14 35					15 01				15 10				15 20	15 31				15 35
	d	14 20		14 32			14 39					15 02				15 10				15 20	15 32				15 39
Balcombe	d	14 26																		15 26					
Horsham 4	d								14 42								15 03								
Littlehaven	d																15 06								
Faygate	d																								
Ifield	d																15 12								
Crawley	d								14 51								15 16								
Three Bridges 4	a	14 31		14 40					14 54			15 10					15 19			15 31	15 40				
	d	14 32		14 41					14 55			15 11					15 20			15 32	15 41				
Gatwick Airport 10 ✈	a	14 37		14 45			14 52	14 56	14 59			15 15				15 22	15 24			15 37	15 45				15 52
	d	14 38		14 46		14 50	14 53	14 57	15 00	15 05	15 08	15 16			15 20	15 23	15 25		15 35	15 38	15 46			15 50	15 53
Horley 4	d								15 02								15 28								
Salfords	d																								
Earlswood (Surrey)	d																								
Tonbridge 4	d				14 29																	15 29			
Leigh (Kent)	d				14 33																	15 33			
Penshurst	d				14 37																	15 37			
Edenbridge	d				14 43																	15 43			
Godstone	d				14 50																	15 50			
Nutfield	d				14 55																	15 55			
Reigate	d													15 13											
Redhill 5	a	14 45			15 00				15 09		15 16			15 18			15 34			15 45		16 00			
	d	14 46							15 10								15 35			15 46					
Merstham	d																15 39								
Coulsdon South	d																15 44								
Purley 4	d								15 20								15 50								
East Croydon 🚌	a	14 58		15 01			15 09	15 12	15 26			15 31				15 39	15 56			15 58	16 01				16 09
	d	15 00		15 01			15 10	15 13	15 26			15 32				15 40	15 56	15 50		16 00	16 01				16 10
Norwood Junction 2	a																16 00								
New Cross Gate	d																								
London Bridge 4 ⊖	a			15 15								15 45					16 12				16 15				
London Blackfriars 3 ⊖	a			15 22								15 52									16 22				
City Thameslink 3	a																								
Farringdon 3 ⊖	a			15 26								15 56									16 26				
St Pancras International 15 ⊖	a			15 31								16 01									16 31				
St Albans City	a			15 56								16 26									16 56				
Luton Airport Parkway 4 ✈	a			16 08								16 38									17 08				
Luton 7	a			16 11								16 41									17 11				
Bedford 10	a			16 38								17 08									17 38				
Clapham Junction 10	a	15 11					15 24	15 27	15 37							15 54		16 01		16 11					16 24
London Victoria 15 ⊖	a	15 18				15 25	15 31	15 35	15 46	15 40					15 55	16 01		16 08	16 10	16 18				16 25	16 31

Table 186

Sundays

from 16 September

Brighton - London and Bedford

Network Diagram - see first Page of Table 186

		SN	SN	SN	GW	FC	GW	SN		SN	SN	SN	SN	SN	FC	SN	SN	SN		SN	SN	SN	GW	FC	GW
		◇1	◇1	1	1	1	1	1		◇1	1	1	1	◇1	1	1	1	◇1		◇1	◇1	1	1	1	1
		🛒	🛒	🛒				🛒					🛒				🛒	🛒		🛒	🛒	🛒			
Brighton 10	d	15 34				15 44								16 00	16 14					16 34				16 44	
Hove 2	d									15 54															
Preston Park	d													16 03											
Hassocks 4	d					15 53								16 10	16 23									16 53	
Burgess Hill 4	d					15 56				16 05				16 13	16 26									16 56	
Lewes 4	d																	16 16							
Wivelsfield 4	d													16 15				16 31							
Haywards Heath 3	a					16 01				16 10				16 20	16 31			16 35						17 01	
	d					16 02				16 10				16 20	16 32			16 39						17 02	
Balcombe	d													16 26											
Horsham 4	d		15 42								16 03										16 42				
Littlehaven	d										16 06														
Faygate	d																								
Ifield	d										16 12														
Crawley	d		15 51								16 16										16 51				
Three Bridges 4	a		15 54			16 10					16 19			16 31	16 40						16 54			17 10	
	d		15 55			16 11					16 20			16 32	16 41						16 55			17 11	
Gatwick Airport 10 ✈	a	15 56	15 59			16 15				16 22	16 24			16 37	16 45			16 52		16 56	16 59			17 15	
	d	15 57	16 00	16 05	16 08	16 16		16 20		16 23	16 25		16 35	16 38	16 46		16 50	16 53		16 57	17 00	17 05	17 08	17 16	
Horley 4	d		16 02								16 28										17 02				
Salfords	d																								
Earlswood (Surrey)	d																								
Tonbridge 4	d															16 29									
Leigh (Kent)	d															16 33									
Penshurst	d															16 37									
Edenbridge	d															16 43									
Godstone	d															16 50									
Nutfield	d															16 55									
Reigate	d						16 13																		17 13
Redhill 5	a		16 09		16 16		16 18				16 34			16 45		17 00					17 09		17 16		17 18
	d		16 10								16 35			16 46							17 10				
Merstham	d										16 39														
Coulsdon South	d										16 44														
Purley 4	d		16 20								16 50										17 20				
East Croydon 🚋	a	16 12	16 26			16 31				16 39	16 56			16 58	17 01			17 09		17 12	17 26			17 31	
	d	16 13	16 26			16 32				16 40	16 56	16 50		17 00	17 01			17 10		17 13	17 26			17 32	
Norwood Junction 2	a										17 00														
New Cross Gate	d																								
London Bridge 4 ⊖	a					16 45					17 12				17 15									17 45	
London Blackfriars 3 ⊖	a					16 52									17 22									17 52	
City Thameslink 3	a																								
Farringdon 3 ⊖	a					16 56									17 26									17 56	
St Pancras International 15 ⊖	a					17 01									17 31									18 01	
St Albans City	a					17 26									17 56									18 26	
Luton Airport Parkway 4 ✈	a					17 38									18 08									18 38	
Luton 7	a					17 41									18 11									18 41	
Bedford 10	a					18 08									18 38									19 08	
Clapham Junction 10	a	16 27	16 37							16 54		17 01		17 11				17 24		17 27	17 37				
London Victoria 15 ⊖	a	16 35	16 46	16 40				16 55		17 01		17 08	17 10	17 18			17 25	17 31		17 35	17 46	17 40			

Table 186

Sundays from 16 September

Brighton - London and Bedford

Network Diagram - see first Page of Table 186

		SN	SN	SN		SN	SN	SN	FC	SN	SN	SN	SN	SN		SN	GW	FC	GW	SN	SN	SN	SN	SN
		1	◇1	1		1	1	◇1	1	1	1	◇1	◇1	◇1		1	1	1	1	1	◇1	1	1	1
		🚲					🚲				🚲	🚲	🚲	🚲		🚲				🚲				🚲
Brighton 10	d							17 00	17 14				17 34					17 44						
Hove 2	d		16 54																		17 54			
Preston Park	d							17 03																
Hassocks 4	d							17 10	17 23									17 53						
Burgess Hill 4	d		17 05					17 13	17 26									17 56			18 05			
Lewes 4	d											17 16												
Wivelsfield 4	d							17 15				17 31												
Haywards Heath 3	a		17 10					17 20	17 31			17 35						18 01			18 10			
	d		17 10					17 20	17 32			17 39						18 02			18 10			
Balcombe	d							17 26																
Horsham 4	d			17 03										17 42								18 03		
Littlehaven	d			17 06																		18 06		
Faygate	d																							
Ifield	d			17 12																		18 12		
Crawley	d			17 16										17 51								18 16		
Three Bridges 4	a			17 19				17 31	17 40					17 54				18 10				18 19		
	d			17 20				17 32	17 41					17 55				18 11				18 20		
Gatwick Airport 10 ✈	a		17 22	17 24				17 37	17 45			17 52	17 56	17 59				18 15			18 22	18 24		
	d	17 20	17 23	17 25			17 35	17 38	17 46		17 50	17 53	17 57	18 00		18 05	18 08	18 16		18 20	18 23	18 25		18 35
Horley 4	d			17 28										18 02								18 28		
Salfords	d																							
Earlswood (Surrey)	d																							
Tonbridge 4	d									17 29														
Leigh (Kent)	d									17 33														
Penshurst	d									17 37														
Edenbridge	d									17 43														
Godstone	d									17 50														
Nutfield	d									17 55														
Reigate	d																		18 13					
Redhill 5	a			17 34				17 45		18 00				18 09			18 16		18 18			18 34		
	d			17 35				17 46						18 10								18 35		
Merstham	d			17 39																		18 39		
Coulsdon South	d			17 44																		18 44		
Purley 4	d			17 50										18 20								18 50		
East Croydon	a		17 39	17 56				17 58	18 01			18 09	18 12	18 26				18 31			18 39	18 56		
	d		17 40	17 56		17 50		18 00	18 01			18 10	18 13	18 26				18 32			18 40	18 56	18 50	
Norwood Junction 2	a			18 00																		19 00		
New Cross Gate	d																							
London Bridge 4 ⊖	a			18 12					18 15									18 45				19 12		
London Blackfriars 3 ⊖	a								18 22									18 52						
City Thameslink 3	a																							
Farringdon 3 ⊖	a								18 26									18 56						
St Pancras International 15 ⊖	a								18 31									19 01						
St Albans City	a								18 56									19 26						
Luton Airport Parkway 4 ✈	a								19 08									19 38						
Luton 7	a								19 11									19 41						
Bedford 10	a								19 38									20 08						
Clapham Junction 10	a		17 54			18 01		18 11				18 24	18 27	18 37							18 54		19 01	
London Victoria 15 ⊖	a	17 55	18 01			18 08	18 10	18 18			18 25	18 31	18 35	18 46		18 40				18 55	19 01		19 08	19 10

Table 186

Sundays

from 16 September

Brighton - London and Bedford

Network Diagram - see first Page of Table 186

		SN	FC	SN	SN	SN	SN	SN	SN	GW		FC	GW	SN	SN	SN	SN	SN	SN	FC		SN	SN	SN	SN
		◇[1]	[1]	[1]	[1]	◇[1]	◇[1]	◇[1]	[1]	[1]		[1]	[1]	[1]	◇[1]	[1]	[1]	[1]	◇[1]	[1]		[1]	[1]	◇[1]	◇[1]
					trolley	trolley			trolley					trolley				trolley					trolley		
Brighton [10]	d	18 00	18 14				18 34					18 44							19 00	19 14					19 34
Hove [2]	d														18 54										
Preston Park	d	18 03																	19 03						
Hassocks [4]	d	18 10	18 23									18 53							19 10	19 23					
Burgess Hill [4]	d	18 13	18 26									18 56			19 05				19 13	19 26					
Lewes [4]	d					18 16																		19 16	
Wivelsfield [4]	d	18 15				18 31													19 15					19 31	
Haywards Heath [3]	a	18 20	18 31			18 35						19 01			19 10				19 20	19 31				19 35	
	d	18 20	18 32			18 39						19 02			19 10				19 20	19 32				19 39	
Balcombe	d	18 26																	19 26						
Horsham [4]	d							18 42								19 03									
Littlehaven	d															19 06									
Faygate	d																								
Ifield	d															19 12									
Crawley	d							18 51								19 16									
Three Bridges [4]	a	18 31	18 40					18 54				19 10				19 19			19 31	19 40					
	d	18 32	18 41					18 55				19 11				19 20			19 32	19 41					
Gatwick Airport [10] ✈	a	18 37	18 45			18 52	18 56	18 59				19 15			19 22	19 24			19 37	19 45				19 52	19 56
	d	18 38	18 46		18 50	18 53	18 57	19 00	19 05	19 08		19 16		19 20	19 23	19 25		19 35	19 38	19 46			19 50	19 53	19 57
Horley [4]	d							19 02								19 28									
Salfords	d																								
Earlswood (Surrey)	d																								
Tonbridge [4]	d			18 29																		19 29			
Leigh (Kent)	d			18 33																		19 33			
Penshurst	d			18 37																		19 37			
Edenbridge	d			18 43																		19 43			
Godstone	d			18 50																		19 50			
Nutfield	d			18 55																		19 55			
Reigate	d												19 13												
Redhill [5]	a	18 45		19 00				19 09		19 16			19 18			19 34			19 45			20 00			
	d	18 46						19 10								19 35			19 46						
Merstham	d															19 39									
Coulsdon South	d															19 44									
Purley [4]	d							19 20								19 50									
East Croydon 🚋	a	18 58	19 01			19 09	19 12	19 26				19 31			19 39	19 56			19 58	20 01				20 09	20 12
	d	19 00	19 01			19 10	19 13	19 26				19 32			19 40	19 56	19 50		20 00	20 01				20 10	20 13
Norwood Junction [2]	a															20 00									
New Cross Gate	d																								
London Bridge [4] ⊖	a		19 15									19 45				20 12				20 15					
London Blackfriars [3] ⊖	a		19 22									19 52								20 22					
City Thameslink [3]	a																								
Farringdon [3] ⊖	a		19 26									19 56								20 26					
St Pancras International [15] ⊖	a		19 31									20 01								20 31					
St Albans City	a		19 56									20 26								20 56					
Luton Airport Parkway [4] ✈	a		20 08									20 38								21 08					
Luton [7]	a		20 11									20 41								21 11					
Bedford [10]	a		20 38									21 08								21 38					
Clapham Junction [10]	a	19 11				19 24	19 27	19 37							19 54		20 01		20 11					20 24	20 27
London Victoria [15] ⊖	a	19 18			19 25	19 31	19 35	19 46	19 40					19 55	20 01		20 08	20 10	20 18				20 25	20 31	20 35

Table 186

Sundays

from 16 September

Brighton - London and Bedford

Network Diagram - see first Page of Table 186

		SN	SN	GW	FC	GW		SN	SN	SN	SN	SN	SN	FC	SN	SN		SN	SN	SN	SN	GW	FC	GW	SN
		◇1	1	1	1	1		1	◇1	1	1	1	◇1	1	1	1		◇1	◇1	◇1	1	1	1	1	1
			🚲					🚲				🚲				🚲					🚲				🚲
Brighton 10	d				19 44								20 00	20 14					20 34				20 44		
Hove 2	d								19 54																
Preston Park	d												20 03												
Hassocks 4	d				19 53								20 10	20 23									20 53		
Burgess Hill 4	d				19 56				20 05				20 13	20 26									20 56		
Lewes 4	d																	20 16							
Wivelsfield 4	d												20 15					20 31							
Haywards Heath 3	a				20 01				20 10				20 20	20 31				20 35					21 01		
	d				20 02				20 10				20 20	20 32				20 39					21 02		
Balcombe	d												20 26												
Horsham 4	d	19 42								20 03										20 42					
Littlehaven	d									20 06															
Faygate	d																								
Ifield	d									20 12															
Crawley	d	19 51								20 16										20 51					
Three Bridges 4	a	19 54			20 10					20 19			20 31	20 40						20 54			21 10		
	d	19 55			20 11					20 20			20 32	20 41						20 55			21 11		
Gatwick Airport 10 ✈	a	19 59			20 15				20 22	20 24			20 37	20 45				20 52	20 56	20 59			21 15		
	d	20 00	20 05	20 08	20 16			20 20	20 23	20 25		20 35	20 38	20 46		20 50		20 53	20 57	21 00	21 05	21 08	21 16		21 20
Horley 4	d	20 02								20 28										21 02					
Salfords	d																								
Earlswood (Surrey)	d																								
Tonbridge 4	d														20 29										
Leigh (Kent)	d														20 33										
Penshurst	d														20 37										
Edenbridge	d														20 43										
Godstone	d														20 50										
Nutfield	d														20 55										
Reigate	d					20 13																		21 13	
Redhill 5	a	20 09		20 16		20 18				20 34			20 45		21 00					21 09		21 16		21 18	
	d	20 10								20 35			20 46							21 10					
Merstham	d									20 39															
Coulsdon South	d									20 44															
Purley 4	d	20 20								20 50										21 20					
East Croydon	a	20 26			20 31				20 39	20 56			20 59	21 01				21 09	21 12	21 26			21 31		
	d	20 26			20 32				20 40	20 56	20 50		21 00	21 01				21 10	21 13	21 26			21 32		
Norwood Junction 2	a									21 00															
New Cross Gate	d																								
London Bridge 4 ⊖	a				20 45					21 12				21 15									21 45		
London Blackfriars 3 ⊖	a				20 52									21 22									21 52		
City Thameslink 3	a																								
Farringdon 3 ⊖	a				20 56									21 26									21 56		
St Pancras International 15 ⊖	a				21 01									21 31									22 01		
St Albans City	a				21 26									21 56									22 26		
Luton Airport Parkway 4 ✈	a				21 38									22 08									22 38		
Luton 7	a				21 41									22 11									22 41		
Bedford 10	a				22 08									22 38									23 08		
Clapham Junction 10	a	20 37							20 54		21 01		21 11					21 24	21 27	21 37					
London Victoria 15 ⊖	a	20 46	20 40					20 55	21 01		21 08	21 10	21 18			21 25		21 31	21 35	21 46	21 40				21 55

Table 186

Sundays
from 16 September

Brighton - London and Bedford

Network Diagram - see first Page of Table 186

		SN		SN	SN	SN	SN	FC	SN	SN	SN	SN		SN	GW	FC	GW	SN	SN	SN	SN	SN		FC	SN
		◇1		1	1	1	◇1	1	1	1	◇1	◇1		1	1	1	1	1	1	1	1	◇1		1	1
						🚲				🚲				🚲				🚲			🚲				
Brighton 10	d						21 00	21 14								21 44						22 00		22 14	
Hove 2	d	20 54																							
Preston Park	d						21 03															22 03			
Hassocks 4	d						21 10	21 23								21 53						22 10		22 23	
Burgess Hill 4	d	21 05					21 13	21 26								21 56						22 13		22 26	
Lewes 4	d										21 16														
Wivelsfield 4	d						21 15				21 31											22 15			
Haywards Heath 3	a	21 10					21 20	21 31			21 35					22 01						22 20		22 31	
	d	21 10					21 20	21 32			21 39					22 02						22 20		22 32	
Balcombe	d						21 26															22 26			
Horsham 4	d			21 03								21 42								22 03					
Littlehaven	d			21 06																22 06					
Faygate	d																								
Ifield	d			21 12																22 12					
Crawley	d			21 16								21 51								22 16					
Three Bridges 4	a			21 19			21 31	21 40				21 54				22 10				22 19		22 31		22 40	
	d			21 20			21 32	21 41				21 55				22 11				22 20		22 32		22 41	
Gatwick Airport 10 ✈	a	21 22		21 24			21 37	21 45			21 52	21 59				22 15				22 24		22 37		22 45	
	d	21 23		21 25		21 35	21 38	21 46		21 50	21 53	22 00		22 05	22 08	22 16		22 20		22 25	22 35	22 38		22 46	
Horley 4	d			21 28								22 02								22 28					
Salfords	d																								
Earlswood (Surrey)	d																								
Tonbridge 4	d								21 29																22 29
Leigh (Kent)	d								21 33																22 33
Penshurst	d								21 37																22 37
Edenbridge	d								21 43																22 43
Godstone	d								21 50																22 50
Nutfield	d								21 55																22 55
Reigate	d																22 13								
Redhill 5	a			21 34			21 45		22 00			22 09			22 16		22 18			22 34		22 45			23 00
	d			21 35			21 46					22 10								22 35		22 46			
Merstham	d			21 39																22 39					
Coulsdon South	d			21 44																22 44					
Purley 4	d			21 50								22 20								22 50					
East Croydon	a	21 39		21 56			21 58	22 01			22 09	22 26				22 31				22 55		22 58		23 01	
	d	21 40		21 56	21 50		22 00	22 01			22 10	22 26				22 32			22 50	22 56		23 00		23 01	
Norwood Junction 2	a			22 00																					
New Cross Gate	d																								
London Bridge 4 ⊖	a			22 12				22 15								22 45								23 15	
London Blackfriars 3 ⊖	a							22 22								22 52								23 22	
City Thameslink 3	a																								
Farringdon 3 ⊖	a							22 26								22 56								23 26	
St Pancras International 15 ⊖	a							22 31								23 01								23 31	
St Albans City	a							23 05								23 35								00 05	
Luton Airport Parkway 4 ✈	a							23 17								23 47								00 17	
Luton 7	a							23 20								23 50								00 20	
Bedford 10	a							23 47								00 17								00 47	
Clapham Junction 10	a	21 54			22 01		22 11				22 24	22 37							23 01	23 07		23 12			
London Victoria 15 ⊖	a	22 01			22 08	22 10	22 18			22 25	22 31	22 46		22 40				22 55	23 08	23 14	23 10	23 20			

Table 186

Sundays

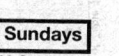

from 16 September

Brighton - London and Bedford

Network Diagram - see first Page of Table 186

		SN	SN	SN	GW	FC	GW	SN		SN	SN	SN	SN	FC	SN	FC
		1	◇1	1	1	1	1	1		1	1	1	◇1	1	1	1
		🚲		🚲												
Brighton 10	d					22 44							23 02	23 14		23 45
Hove 2	d															
Preston Park	d												23 06			
Hassocks 4	d					22 53							23 12	23 23		23 54
Burgess Hill 4	d					22 56							23 16	23 26		23 57
Lewes 4	d															
Wivelsfield 4	d												23 18			
Haywards Heath 3	a					23 01							23 23	23 31		00 02
	d					23 02							23 23	23 32		00 03
Balcombe	d												23 29			
Horsham 4	d		22 42								23 03					
Littlehaven	d										23 06					
Faygate	d															
Ifield	d										23 12					
Crawley	d		22 51								23 16					
Three Bridges 4	a		22 54			23 10					23 19		23 36	23 40		00 11
	d		22 55			23 11					23 20		23 41	23 41		00 12
Gatwick Airport 10 ✈	a		22 59			23 15					23 24		23 45	23 45		00 16
	d	22 50	23 00	23 05	23 08	23 16		23 20			23 25	23 35	23 46	23 46	23 50	00 17
Horley 4	d		23 02								23 28		23 49			
Salfords	d															
Earlswood (Surrey)	d															
Tonbridge 4	d															
Leigh (Kent)	d															
Penshurst	d															
Edenbridge	d															
Godstone	d															
Nutfield	d															
Reigate	d						23 13									
Redhill 5	a		23 09		23 16		23 18				23 34		23 57			00 24
	d		23 10								23 35		00 01			00 24
Merstham	d										23 39					
Coulsdon South	d										23 44					
Purley 4	d		23 20								23 50		00 11			
East Croydon 🚋	a		23 26			23 31					23 55		00 16	00 02		00 36
	d		23 27			23 32				23 50	23 56		00 16	00 03		00 37
Norwood Junction 2	a															
New Cross Gate	d															
London Bridge 4 ⊖	a					23 45								00 21		00 50
London Blackfriars 3 ⊖	a					23 52								00 27		00 57
City Thameslink 3	a															
Farringdon 3 ⊖	a					23 56								00 33		
St Pancras International 15 ⊖	a					00 01								00 37		01 07
St Albans City	a					00 35								01 10		01 40
Luton Airport Parkway 4 ✈	a					00 47								01 22		01 52
Luton 7	a					00 50								01 25		01 55
Bedford 10	a					01 17								01 52		02 22
Clapham Junction 10	a		23 38							00 01	00 11		00 29			
London Victoria 15 ⊖	a	23 25	23 46	23 40				23 55		00 08	00 19	00 10	00 37		00 25	

London, Gatwick Airport, Brighton - Sussex Coast, Portsmouth and Southampton

Network Diagram - see first Page of Table 186

Miles	Miles	Miles			SN MX ◇1	SN MX 1	SN MX ◇1	SN MX ◇1	SN MX	SN	SN MX ◇1	SN MO 1 A	SN MX 1	SN MO ◇1 A	SN MX 1	SN MX ◇1	SN ◇1 B	SN 1	SN	SN	SN	SN	SN 1
0	—	0	London Victoria	d	22p17	22p32		22p47			23p17	23p04	23p10	23p17	23p47	00 05	00 40						
2¾	—	—	Clapham Junction	d	22p23	22p38		22p53			23p23	23p10	23p16	23p23	23p53	00 11	00 46						
—	0	—	London Bridge	d																			
10½	10¼	—	East Croydon	d	22p34	22p48		23p03			23p33	23p22	23p28	23p38	00 06	00 27	00 56						
21	—	—	Redhill	d		23p01						23p42	23p46		00 25								
26	—	—	Horley	d								23p50	23p56		00 31								
26¾	—	—	Gatwick Airport	d	22p49	23p09		23p19			23p51	23p55	23p59	00 01	00 34	00 44	01 14						
29½	—	29½	Three Bridges	a	22p53	23p15					23p55	00 01	00 04	00 05	00 39	00 48	01 18						
—	—	—		d	22p53	23p16					23p56	00 01	00 04	00 06	00 39	00 49	01 18						
—	—	31	Crawley	d		23p19						00 05	00 07		00 43								
—	—	38	Horsham	a		23p27						00 17	00 19		00 55								
—	—	—		d		23p28																	
—	—	40½	Christs Hospital	d		23p31																	
—	—	45¼	Billingshurst	d		23p37																	
—	—	50¼	Pulborough	d		23p44																	
—	—	55	Amberley	d		23p50																	
—	—	58¾	Arundel	d		23p55																	
38	—	—	Haywards Heath	d	23p03			23p37			00 05			00 15		01 02	01 32						
41¾	—	—	Burgess Hill	d	23p08						00 11			00 20									
—	—	—	Preston Park	d																			
—	0	—	Brighton	d					00 04	00 10						01s16	01s46						
51	1½	—	Hove	a	23p21			23p51	00 07	00 14	00 21			00 31		01s24	01s55						
—	—	—		d	23p22			23p52	00 08		00 22			00 31									
—	2	—	Aldrington	d					00 10														
—	3	—	Portslade	d	23p25			23p55	00 12		00s25			00s34		01s27	01s59						
—	3½	—	Fishersgate	d					00 14														
—	4½	—	Southwick	d	23p28			23p58	00 16		00s28			00s37		01s30	02s02						
—	5½	—	Shoreham-by-Sea	d	23p31			00 01	00 19		00s31			00s40		01s33	02s05						
—	8¼	—	Lancing	d	23p35			00 05	00 23		00s35			00s44		01s37	02s09						
—	9¾	—	East Worthing	d					00 26														
—	10½	—	Worthing	a	23p39			00 09	00 29		00 39			00 48		01 42	02 13						
—	—	—		d	23p39				00 29														
—	11½	—	West Worthing	d	23p41				00a31														
—	12¼	—	Durrington-on-Sea	d	23p44																		
—	13	—	Goring-by-Sea	d	23p46																		
0	15½	—	Angmering	d	23p50																		
6	—	—	Littlehampton	a																			
—	—	—		d																			
8	19¾	61	Ford	d	23p56	00 01																	
—	—	—	Bognor Regis	d			←													05 13			05 35
0	22½	—	Barnham	a	00 01	00 06	00 01													05 19			05 41
—	—	—		d	00 09	00 06	00 09											04 58	05 02		05 21	05 36	
3½	—	—	Bognor Regis	a	→		00 15															05 43	
—	28¾	—	Chichester	a		00 14												05 05	05 09		05 28		
—	—	—		d														05 06	05 10		05 29		
—	30¼	—	Fishbourne (Sussex)	d																			
—	31¼	—	Bosham	d																			
—	33¼	—	Nutbourne	d																			
—	34¼	—	Southbourne	d																			
—	35¾	—	Emsworth	d																			
—	37	—	Warblington	d																			
0	37½	—	Havant	d														05 17	05 21		05 40		
—	38¼	—	Bedhampton	a																			
—	41¼	—	Hilsea	a																			
—	44	—	Fratton	a															05 29		05 48		
—	44¾	—	Portsmouth & Southsea	a															05 33		05 52		
—	45½	—	Portsmouth Harbour	a															05 37		05 56		
4	—	—	Cosham	a														05 23					
6½	—	—	Portchester	a														05 28					
9¾	—	—	Fareham	a														05 33					
13½	—	—	Swanwick	a														05 40					
—	—	—	Eastleigh	a																			
—	—	—	Southampton Airport Parkway	a																			
24¼	—	—	Southampton Central	a														05 59					

A from 21 May

B from 30 July until 7 September, not from 13 August until 29 August

London, Gatwick Airport, Brighton - Sussex Coast, Portsmouth and Southampton

Network Diagram - see first Page of Table 186

		SN 1	SN	SN 1	SN	SN	SN ◇1	SN 1	SN	SN	SN	SN	SN	SN	SN	SN	SN ◇1	SN	SN 1	SN 1	SN 1	SN
London Victoria	d																					
Clapham Junction	d																					
London Bridge	d																					
East Croydon	d																					
Redhill	d																					
Horley	d																					
Gatwick Airport	d																				05 56	
Three Bridges	a																				06 00	
	d																				06 01	
Crawley	d																				06 05	
Horsham	a																				06 17	
	d																				06 17	
Christs Hospital	d																				06 21	
Billingshurst	d																				06 27	
Pulborough	d																				06 34	
Amberley	d																				06 40	
Arundel	d																				06 46	
Haywards Heath	d																					
Burgess Hill	d																					
Preston Park	d																					
Brighton	d			05 14				05 30	05 44		05 53				05 57	06 14				06 27		
Hove	a			05 17				05 33	05 48		05 56				06 00	06 17				06 30		
	d			05 18				05 34			05 57				06 01	06 18				06 31		
Aldrington	d			05 20				05 36							06 03	06 20						
Portslade	d			05 22				05 38							06 05	06 22						
Fishersgate	d			05 24				05 40							06 07	06 24						
Southwick	d			05 26				05 42							06 09	06 26						
Shoreham-by-Sea	d			05 29				05 45			06 03				06 12	06 29				06 37		
Lancing	d			05 33				05 49							06 16	06 33						
East Worthing	d			05 36				05 52							06 19	06 36						
Worthing	a			05 39				05 55			06 09				06 22	06 39				06 43		
	d			05 39				05 55			06 09				06 22	06 39				06 43		
West Worthing	d			05 41				05 57							06 24	06a41				06 45		
Durrington-on-Sea	d			05 44				06 00							06 27					06 48		
Goring-by-Sea	d			05 46				06 02							06 29					06 50		
Angmering	d			05 50				06 06							06 33					06 54		
Littlehampton	a														06 42							
	d	05 35				06 04								06 35								06 58
Ford	d	05 39		05 56		06 08		06 13						06 39							06 51	07 04
Bognor Regis	d		05 49		05 55		06 06			06 13			06 22				06 41	06 50	06 57			
Barnham	a	05 43	05 55	06 01	06 02	06 12	06 12	06 17		06 19	06 24		06 28	06 43			06 47	06 56	07 03	07 04	06 55	07 08
	d	05 44		06 01		06 13		06 18			06 24	06 27		06 48						07 05	07 00 / 07 13	07 09
Bognor Regis	a					06 20						06 34		06 55							→	
Chichester	a	05 51		06 09				06 25			06 32									07 12	07 07	07 16
	d	05 52		06 09				06 26			06 32									07 13	07 08	07 17
Fishbourne (Sussex)	d	05 55									06 35											07 20
Bosham	d	05 58									06 38									07 17		
Nutbourne	d	06 01									06 42											07 25
Southbourne	d	06 04						06 33			06 44									07 22		07 27
Emsworth	d	06 07						06 36			06 47									07 25		07 30
Warblington	d	06 10									06 50									07 28		
Havant	d	06 13		06 20				06 40			06 53									07 31	07 19	07 35
Bedhampton	a	06 15									06 56											07 37
Hilsea	a	06 20									07 01											07 42
Fratton	a	06 24									07 05											07 46
Portsmouth & Southsea	a	06 28									07 08											07 50
Portsmouth Harbour	a	06 32									07 12											
Cosham	a			06 27				06 49												07 38	07 25	
Portchester	a							06 54													07 30	
Fareham	a			06 36				06 59												07 46	07 35	
Swanwick	a			06 43				07 06												07 53	07 42	
Eastleigh	a																					
Southampton Airport Parkway	a																					
Southampton Central	a			07 02				07 25												08 13	08 01	

London, Gatwick Airport, Brighton - Sussex Coast, Portsmouth and Southampton

Network Diagram - see first Page of Table 186

		SN	SN 1	SN ◇1	SN	SN	SN	SN	SN	SN 1	SN ◇1	SN 1	SN	SN	SN ◇1	SN	SN	SN 1	SN	SN 1	SN	SN ◇1	SN ◇1
London Victoria	d										06 02												06 32
Clapham Junction	d										06 08												06 38
London Bridge	d																						
East Croydon	d										06 18												06 49
Redhill	d										06 39												07 12
Horley	d										06 48												07 21
Gatwick Airport	d										06 55												07 25
Three Bridges	a										06 59												07 29
	d										07 00	07 05											07 30
Crawley	d										07 03	07 08											07 34
Horsham	a										07 11	07 22											07 46
	d										07 12												07 46
Christs Hospital	d										07 15												07 50
Billingshurst	d										07 21												07 56
Pulborough	d										07 28												08 03
Amberley	d										07 34												08 09
Arundel	d										07 39												08 14
Haywards Heath	d																						
Burgess Hill	d																						
Preston Park	d																						
Brighton	d		06 35						06 53	07 06			07 15				07 20	07 30		07 37	07 46		
Hove	a		06 38						06 56	07 09			07 18				07 23	07 33		07 40	07 49		
	d		06 39						06 57	07 10			07 19				07 24	07 34		07 41	07 50		
Aldrington	d								06 59								07 26						
Portslade	d		06 42						07 01				07 22				07 28	07 37		07 44	07 53		
Fishersgate	d								07 03								07 30						
Southwick	d		06 45						07 05				07 25				07 32	07 40		07 47	07 56		
Shoreham-by-Sea	d		06 48						07 09	07 16			07 28				07 35	07 43		07 50	08 00		
Lancing	d		06 52						07 13				07 32				07 39	07 47		07 54	08 04		
East Worthing	d								07 16								07 42						
Worthing	a		06 56						07 18	07 22			07 36				07 45	07 51		07 58	08 08		
	d		06 56						07 19	07 23			07 36				07 45	07 52		07 59	08 08		
West Worthing	d		06 58						07 21	07 25							07 47	07 54		08 01			
Durrington-on-Sea	d		07 01						07 23	07 27							07 50	07 56		08 03	08 12		
Goring-by-Sea	d		07 03						07 26	07 30							07 52	07 59		08 06			
Angmering	d		07 07						07 30	07 34							07 56	08 03		08 10	08 17		
Littlehampton	a								07 38								08 05						08 21
	d				07 18				07 48					←		07 56							08 26
Ford	d		07 13		07 22				07 52		07 44		07 48	07 52		08 00		08 09		08 17			08 30
Bognor Regis	d	←		07 17		07 27		07 36	→						07 55				08 13			08 26	
Barnham	a	06 55	07 18	07 23	07 26	07 33		07 42		07 43	07 49		07 53	07 56	08 01	08 04		08 13	08 19	08 21	08 27	08 32	08 34
	d	07 13	07 18		07 27		07 39			07 44	07 50		07 53	07 57		08 05		08 14		08 22	08 28		08 35
Bognor Regis	a	07 20					07 46				07 58					08 12					08 36		
Chichester	a		07 26		07 34					07 51			08 01	08 05				08 21		08 29			08 42
	d		07 28		07 35					07 52			08 01					08 22		08 30			
Fishbourne (Sussex)	d				07 38								08 04										
Bosham	d				07 41								08 07										
Nutbourne	d				07 44								08 11										
Southbourne	d				07 47								08 13					08 29		08 37			
Emsworth	d				07 50								08 16					08 32		08 40			
Warblington	d				07 53								08 19										
Havant	d		07 41		07 58					08 03			08 22					08 37		08 44			
Bedhampton	a				08 00								08 25										
Hilsea	a				08 05								08 30										
Fratton	a		07 49		08 09								08 34							08 53			
Portsmouth & Southsea	a		07 53		08 15								08 37							08 56			
Portsmouth Harbour	a		07 58		08 20								08 41							09 02			
Cosham	a									08 09								08 45					
Portchester	a									08 13								08 49					
Fareham	a									08 18								08 54					
Swanwick	a									08 26								09 01					
Eastleigh	a																						
Southampton Airport Parkway	a																						
Southampton Central	a									08 52								09 19					

London, Gatwick Airport, Brighton - Sussex Coast, Portsmouth and Southampton

Network Diagram - see first Page of Table 186

		SN 1	SN	SN	SN	SN	SN	SN	SN	SN	SN ◇1	SN 1	SN ◇1	SN	SN	SN	SN 1	SN	SN ◇1	SN	SN	SN ◇1
London Victoria	d	06 51									07 17	07 36							07 52			
Clapham Junction	d	06 57									07 23	07 42							07 58			
London Bridge	d																					
East Croydon	d	07 07									07 34	07 52							08 09			
Redhill	d	07 28									07 47	08 11										
Horley	d	07 37									07 57	08 21										
Gatwick Airport	d	07 41									08 00	08 24							08 26			
Three Bridges	a	07 45									08 05	08 29										
	d	07 46									08 05	08 30										
Crawley	d	07 50									08 09	08 34										
Horsham	a	08 02									08 22	08 48										
	d										08 23											
Christs Hospital	d										08 26											
Billingshurst	d										08 32											
Pulborough	d										08 39											
Amberley	d										08 45											
Arundel	d										08 50											
Haywards Heath	d																		08 37			
Burgess Hill	d																					
Preston Park	d																					
Brighton	d		07 50		08 03		08 07	08 14	08 23								08 33	08 44		08 53		
Hove	a		07 53		08 06		08 10	08 18	08 26								08 36	08 48	08 53	08 56		
	d		07 54		08 07		08 11		08 27								08 37		08 53	08 57		
Aldrington	d		07 56						08 29											08 59		
Portslade	d		07 58				08 14		08 31								08 40			09 01		
Fishersgate	d		08 00						08 33											09 03		
Southwick	d		08 02				08 17		08 35								08 43			09 05		
Shoreham-by-Sea	d		08 06		08 13		08 20		08 39								08 46		08 59	09 08		
Lancing	d		08 10				08 24		08 43								08 50		09 04	09 12		
East Worthing	d		08 13						08 46											09 15		
Worthing	a		08 15		08 19		08 28		08 48								08 54		09 08	09 18		
	d		08 16		08 20		08 28		08 49								08 55		09 08	09 18		
West Worthing	d		08 18		08 22		08 30		08a51								08 57		09 10	09a20		
Durrington-on-Sea	d		08 20		08 24		08 33										08 59		09 13			
Goring-by-Sea	d		08 23		08 27		08 35										09 02		09 15			
Angmering	d		08 27		08 31		08 39										09 06		09 19			
Littlehampton	a		08 35																09 28			
	d													08 54								
Ford	d				08 37		08 45				08 55			08 59								
Bognor Regis	d			08 32						08 48			08 56			09 06						09 30
Barnham	a			08 38	08 41		08 50			08 55	08 59		09 02	09 03		09 12	09 16					09 36
	d				08 42	08 45	08 52				09 00			09 04	09 11		09 17				09 19	
Bognor Regis	a					08 52	08 58								09 18						09 26	
Chichester	a				08 49						09 07			09 11			09 24					
	d				08 50						09 08			09 12			09 25					
Fishbourne (Sussex)	d													09 15								
Bosham	d													09 18								
Nutbourne	d													09 21								
Southbourne	d										09 15			09 24			09 32					
Emsworth	d										09 18			09 27			09 35					
Warblington	d													09 30								
Havant	d				09 01						09 23			09 33			09 39					
Bedhampton	a													09 36								
Hilsea	a													09 42								
Fratton	a				09 11									09 46								
Portsmouth & Southsea	a				09 17									09 50								
Portsmouth Harbour	a				09 21																	
Cosham	a										09 29						09 45					
Portchester	a																					
Fareham	a										09 37						09 53					
Swanwick	a										09 44						10 00					
Eastleigh	a																					
Southampton Airport Parkway	a																					
Southampton Central	a										10 01						10 20					

Table 188

Mondays to Fridays

London, Gatwick Airport, Brighton - Sussex Coast, Portsmouth and Southampton

Network Diagram - see first Page of Table 186

Station		GW	SN		SN	SN	SN		SN	SN	SN	SN	SN	SN		SN	SN		SN	SN	SN	SN	SN	SN	
		◇ ⌶	◇1				◇1						◇1	◇1 A ⌶							◇1 B ⌶		◇1	◇1 A ⌶	
London Victoria 15 ⊖	d		08 02				08 17							08 32							08 47			09 02	
Clapham Junction 10	d		08 08				08 23							08 38							08 53			09 08	
London Bridge 4 ⊖	d																								
East Croydon ⇌	d		08 18				08 34							08 48							09 04			09 19	
Redhill 5	d		08 30											09 03										09 30	
Horley	d																							09 36	
Gatwick Airport 10 ✈	d		08 40				08 50							09 11							09 20			09 40	
Three Bridges 4	a		08 44											09 16										09 44	
	d		08 45											09 16										09 45	
Crawley	d		08 48											09 19										09 48	
Horsham 4	a		08 56											09 27										09 56	
	d		09 00	09 05										09 31	09 36									10 00	10 05
Christs Hospital	d			09 08											09 39										
Billingshurst	d			09 14											09 45										10 14
Pulborough	d			09 21											09 52										10 20
Amberley	d			09 27											09 58										
Arundel	d			09 32											10 03										10 29
Haywards Heath 5	d						09 04														09 37				
Burgess Hill	d						09 09																		
Preston Park	d						09 18																		
Brighton 10	d	08 59			09 03	09 14			09 23								09 33		09 44			09 53			
Hove 2	a	09 02			09 07	09 18	09 21		09 26								09 36		09 48		09 53	09 56			
	d	09 03			09 08		09 22		09 27								09 37				09 53	09 57			
Aldrington	d								09 29													09 59			
Portslade	d				09 11		09 25		09 31								09 40					10 01			
Fishersgate	d								09 33													10 03			
Southwick	d				09 14				09 35								09 43					10 05			
Shoreham-by-Sea	d	09 13			09 18		09 30		09 39								09 46				10 00	10 09			
Lancing	d				09 22				09 43								09 50				10 04	10 13			
East Worthing	d								09 46													10 16			
Worthing 4	a	09 21			09 26		09 36		09 48								09 54				10 08	10 18			
	d	09 22			09 26		09 37		09 49								09 55				10 08	10 19			
West Worthing	d						09 39		09a51								09 57				10 10	10a21			
Durrington-on-Sea	d						09 41										09 59				10 13				
Goring-by-Sea	d						09 44										10 02				10 15				
Angmering 3	d				09 34		09 48										10 06				10 19				
Littlehampton 4	a						09 58														10 28				
	d											09 54								10 11					
Ford 4	d			09 37								09 58			10 08		10 12			10 16					10 34
Bognor Regis 4	d									09 39			09 56			10 07							10 30		
Barnham	a	09 37	09 26	09 41	09 44					09 45		10 02	10 02	09 57	10 12	10 13	10 16			10 20			10 36	10 26	10 39
	d	09 38	09 27	09 42	09 45						09 52	10 03		09 58	10 13		10 17			10 22				10 27	10 39
Bognor Regis	a			09 48							09 59				10 19					10 29					10 46
Chichester 4	a	09 45	09 34		09 52							10 10		10 05			10 24							10 34	
	d	09 47	09 35		09 53							10 11		10 06			10 25							10 35	
Fishbourne (Sussex)	d											10 14													
Bosham	d											10 17													
Nutbourne	d											10 20													
Southbourne	d				10 00							10 23		10 13											
Emsworth	d				10 03							10 26		10 16			10 33								
Warblington	d											10 29													
Havant	d	09 59	09 46		10 07							10 32		10 20			10 37							10 46	
Bedhampton	a											10 34													
Hilsea	a											10 42													
Fratton	a		09 54		10 16							10 46												10 54	
Portsmouth & Southsea	a		09 58		10 19							10 50												10 58	
Portsmouth Harbour ⛴	a		10 02		10 23																			11 02	
Cosham	a	10 05												10 28			10 45								
Portchester	a													10 32											
Fareham	a	10 14												10 37			10 53								
Swanwick	a													10 44			11 00								
Eastleigh	a																								
Southampton Airport Parkway	a																								
Southampton Central ⛴	a	10 40												11 01			11 19								

A ⌶ to Horsham

B ⌶ to Haywards Heath

Table 188

Mondays to Fridays

London, Gatwick Airport, Brighton - Sussex Coast, Portsmouth and Southampton

Network Diagram - see first Page of Table 186

Station		SN	SN		SN	SN	SN	SN	SN	SN	SN		SN		SN	SN	SN	SN	SN	SN	SN		SN		SN
					◇1 A ⌶					◇1	◇1 B ⌶							◇1 A ⌶		◇1	◇1 B ⌶				
London Victoria 15 ⊖	d				09 17						09 32							09 47			10 02				
Clapham Junction 10	d				09 23						09 38							09 53			10 08				
London Bridge 4 ⊖	d																								
East Croydon ⇌	d				09 33						09 48							10 03			10 18				
Redhill 5	d										10 00										10 30				
Horley	d																				10 36				
Gatwick Airport 10 ✈	d				09 50						10 09							10 20			10 40				
Three Bridges 4	a										10 14										10 44				
	d										10 14										10 45				
Crawley	d										10 18										10 48				
Horsham 4	a										10 26										10 56				
	d										10 30	10 35									11 00	11 05			
Christs Hospital	d											10 38													
Billingshurst	d											10 44										11 14			
Pulborough	d											10 51										11 20			
Amberley	d											10 57													
Arundel	d											11 02										11 29			
Haywards Heath 5	d				10 05													10 37							
Burgess Hill	d				10 10																				
Preston Park	d				10 18																				
Brighton 10	d	10 03	10 14			10 23									10 33	10 44			10 53				11 03		11 14
Hove 2	a	10 06	10 18		10 22	10 26									10 36	10 48		10 53	10 56				11 06		11 18
	d	10 07			10 23	10 27									10 37			10 53	10 57				11 07		
Aldrington	d					10 29													10 59						
Portslade	d	10 10			10 26	10 31									10 40				11 01				11 10		
Fishersgate	d					10 33													11 03						
Southwick	d	10 13				10 35									10 43				11 05				11 13		
Shoreham-by-Sea	d	10 16			10 31	10 39									10 46			11 00	11 09				11 16		
Lancing	d	10 20				10 43									10 50			11 04	11 13				11 20		
East Worthing	d					10 46													11 16						
Worthing 4	a	10 24			10 37	10 48									10 54			11 08	11 18				11 24		
	d	10 25			10 37	10 49									10 55			11 08	11 19				11 25		
West Worthing	d				10 39	10a51									10 57			11 10	11a21						
Durrington-on-Sea	d				10 42										10 59			11 13							
Goring-by-Sea	d				10 44										11 02			11 15							
Angmering 3	d	10 31			10 48										11 06			11 19					11 31		
Littlehampton 4	a				10 57													11 28							
	d								10 54								11 11								
Ford 4	d								10 58			11 07			11 12		11 16					11 34			
Bognor Regis 4	d						10 39			10 56			11 07							11 30					
Barnham	a	10 42					10 45		11 02	11 02	10 56	11 11	11 13		11 16		11 20			11 36	11 26	11 39	11 42		
	d	10 42						10 52	11 03		10 57	11 12			11 17		11 22				11 27	11 39	11 42		
Bognor Regis	a							10 59				11 18					11 29					11 46			
Chichester 4	a	10 50							11 10		11 04				11 24						11 34		11 50		
	d	10 50							11 11		11 05				11 25						11 35		11 50		
Fishbourne (Sussex)	d								11 14																
Bosham	d								11 17																
Nutbourne	d								11 20																
Southbourne	d	10 57							11 23		11 12												11 57		
Emsworth	d	11 00							11 26		11 15				11 33								12 00		
Warblington	d								11 29																
Havant	d	11 05							11 32		11 19				11 37						11 46		12 05		
Bedhampton	a								11 34																
Hilsea	a								11 42																
Fratton	a	11 13							11 46												11 54		12 13		
Portsmouth & Southsea	a	11 17							11 50												11 58		12 17		
Portsmouth Harbour ⛴	a	11 21																			12 02		12 21		
Cosham	a										11 26				11 45										
Portchester	a										11 30														
Fareham	a										11 35				11 53										
Swanwick	a										11 42				12 00										
Eastleigh	a																								
Southampton Airport Parkway	a																								
Southampton Central ⛴	a										12 01				12 19										

A ⌶ to Haywards Heath

B ⌶ to Horsham

London, Gatwick Airport, Brighton - Sussex Coast, Portsmouth and Southampton

Network Diagram - see first Page of Table 186

Station		SN ◇1 A	SN	SN	SN	SN	SN ◇1	SN ◇1 B		SN	SN	SN	SN	SN ◇1 A	SN	SN ◇1	SN ◇1		SN	SN	SN ◇1	SN	SN
London Victoria 15	d	10 17						10 32						10 47			11 02				11 17		
Clapham Junction 10	d	10 23						10 38						10 53			11 08				11 23		
London Bridge 4	d																						
East Croydon	d	10 33						10 48						11 03			11 18				11 33		
Redhill 5	d							11 00									11 30						
Horley	d																11 36						
Gatwick Airport 10	d	10 50						11 09						11 20			11 40				11 50		
Three Bridges 4	a							11 14									11 44						
	d							11 14									11 45						
Crawley	d							11 18									11 48						
Horsham 4	a							11 26									11 56						
	d							11 30	11 35								12 00	12 05					
Christs Hospital	d								11 38														
Billingshurst	d								11 44									12 14					
Pulborough	d								11 51									12 20					
Amberley	d								11 57														
Arundel	d								12 02									12 29					
Haywards Heath 3	d	11 04												11 37							12 04		
Burgess Hill	d	11 09																			12 09		
Preston Park	d	11 18																			12 18		
Brighton 10	d		11 23								11 33	11 44			11 53				12 03	12 14		12 23	
Hove 2	a	11 22	11 26								11 36	11 48		11 53	11 56				12 06	12 18	12 22	12 26	
	d	11 22	11 27								11 37			11 53	11 57				12 07		12 22	12 27	
Aldrington	d		11 29												11 59							12 29	
Portslade	d	11 25	11 31								11 40				12 01				12 10		12 25	12 31	
Fishersgate	d		11 33												12 03							12 33	
Southwick	d		11 35								11 43				12 05				12 13			12 35	
Shoreham-by-Sea	d	11 30	11 39								11 46			12 00	12 09				12 16		12 30	12 39	
Lancing	d		11 43								11 50			12 04	12 13				12 20			12 43	
East Worthing	d		11 46												12 16							12 46	
Worthing 4	a	11 36	11 48								11 54			12 08	12 18				12 24		12 36	12 48	
	d	11 37	11 49								11 55			12 08	12 19				12 25		12 37	12 49	
West Worthing	d	11 39	11a51								11 57			12 10	12a21						12 39	12a51	
Durrington-on-Sea	d	11 41									11 59			12 13							12 41		
Goring-by-Sea	d	11 44									12 02			12 15							12 44		
Angmering 3	d	11 48									12 06			12 19					12 31		12 48		
Littlehampton 4	a	11 57												12 28							12 57		
	d					11 54							12 11										
Ford 4	d					11 58			12 07		12 12		12 16					12 34					
Bognor Regis 4	d			11 39			11 56			12 07						12 30							12 39
Barnham	a			11 45		12 02	12 02	11 56	12 11	12 13	12 16		12 20			12 36	12 26	12 39	12 42				12 45
	d				11 52	12 03		11 57	12 12		12 17		12 22				12 27	12 39	12 42				
Bognor Regis	a				11 59				12 18				12 29					12 46					
Chichester 4	a					12 10		12 04			12 24						12 34		12 50				
	d					12 11		12 05			12 25						12 35		12 50				
Fishbourne (Sussex)	d					12 14																	
Bosham	d					12 17																	
Nutbourne	d					12 20																	
Southbourne	d					12 23		12 12											12 57				
Emsworth	d					12 26		12 15			12 33								13 00				
Warblington	d					12 29																	
Havant	d					12 32		12 19			12 37						12 46		13 05				
Bedhampton	a					12 34																	
Hilsea	a					12 42																	
Fratton	a					12 46											12 54		13 13				
Portsmouth & Southsea	a					12 50											12 58		13 17				
Portsmouth Harbour	a																13 02		13 21				
Cosham	a							12 26			12 45												
Portchester	a							12 30															
Fareham	a							12 35			12 53												
Swanwick	a							12 42			13 00												
Eastleigh	a																						
Southampton Airport Parkway	a																						
Southampton Central	a							12 59			13 19												

A to Haywards Heath

B to Horsham

London, Gatwick Airport, Brighton - Sussex Coast, Portsmouth and Southampton

Network Diagram - see first Page of Table 186

Station		SN	SN	SN ◇1	SN ◇1		SN	SN 1	SN	SN	SN ◇1	SN	SN ◇1	SN ◇1		SN	SN	SN ◇1	SN	SN	SN	SN	SN ◇1
London Victoria 15	d				11 32						11 47			12 02				12 17					
Clapham Junction 10	d				11 38						11 53			12 08				12 23					
London Bridge 4	d																						
East Croydon	d				11 48						12 03			12 18				12 33					
Redhill 5	d				12 00									12 30									
Horley	d													12 36									
Gatwick Airport 10	d				12 09						12 20			12 40				12 50					
Three Bridges 4	a				12 14									12 44									
	d				12 14									12 45									
Crawley	d				12 18									12 48									
Horsham 4	a				12 26									12 56									
	d				12 30	12 35								13 00	13 05								
Christs Hospital	d					12 38																	
Billingshurst	d					12 44									13 14								
Pulborough	d					12 51									13 20								
Amberley	d					12 57																	
Arundel	d					13 02									13 29								
Haywards Heath 3	d										12 37							13 04					
Burgess Hill	d																	13 09					
Preston Park	d																	13 18					
Brighton 10	d							12 33	12 44			12 53				13 03	13 14		13 23				
Hove 2	a							12 36	12 48		12 53	12 56				13 06	13 19	13 22	13 26				
	d							12 37			12 53	12 57				13 07		13 22	13 27				
Aldrington	d											12 59							13 29				
Portslade	d							12 40				13 01				13 10		13 25	13 31				
Fishersgate	d											13 03							13 33				
Southwick	d							12 43				13 05				13 13			13 35				
Shoreham-by-Sea	d							12 46			13 00	13 09				13 16		13 30	13 39				
Lancing	d							12 50			13 04	13 13				13 20			13 43				
East Worthing	d											13 16							13 46				
Worthing 4	a							12 54			13 08	13 18				13 24		13 36	13 48				
	d							12 55			13 08	13 19				13 25		13 37	13 49				
West Worthing	d							12 57			13 10	13a21						13 39	13a51				
Durrington-on-Sea	d							12 59			13 13							13 41					
Goring-by-Sea	d							13 02			13 15							13 44					
Angmering 3	d							13 06			13 19					13 31		13 48					
Littlehampton 4	a										13 28							13 57					
	d		12 54							13 11												13 54	
Ford 4	d		12 58			13 07		13 12		13 16					13 34							13 58	
Bognor Regis 4	d			12 56			13 07						13 30							13 39			13 56
Barnham	a		13 02	13 02	12 56	13 11	13 13	13 16		13 20			13 36	13 26	13 39	13 42				13 45		14 02	14 02
	d	12 52	13 03		12 57	13 12		13 17		13 22				13 27	13 39	13 42					13 52	14 03	
Bognor Regis	a	12 59				13 18				13 29					13 46						13 59		
Chichester 4	a		13 10		13 04			13 24						13 34		13 50						14 10	
	d		13 11		13 05			13 25						13 35		13 50						14 11	
Fishbourne (Sussex)	d		13 14																			14 14	
Bosham	d		13 17																			14 17	
Nutbourne	d		13 20																			14 20	
Southbourne	d		13 23		13 12											13 57						14 23	
Emsworth	d		13 26		13 15			13 33								14 00						14 26	
Warblington	d		13 29																			14 29	
Havant	d		13 32		13 19			13 37						13 46		14 05						14 32	
Bedhampton	a		13 34																			14 34	
Hilsea	a		13 42																			14 42	
Fratton	a		13 46											13 54		14 13						14 46	
Portsmouth & Southsea	a		13 50											13 58		14 17						14 50	
Portsmouth Harbour	a													14 02		14 21							
Cosham	a				13 26			13 45															
Portchester	a				13 30																		
Fareham	a				13 35			13 53															
Swanwick	a				13 42			14 02															
Eastleigh	a							14n37															
Southampton Airport Parkway	a							14n33															
Southampton Central	a				13 59			14 19															

n will stop at these stations after Southampton Central

London, Gatwick Airport, Brighton - Sussex Coast, Portsmouth and Southampton

Network Diagram - see first Page of Table 186

Station		SN ◇■		SN	SN	SN	SN	SN ◇■	SN	SN ◇■ H	SN ◇■		SN	SN	SN ◇■	SN	SN	SN	SN	SN ◇■ H	SN ◇■ A H	
London Victoria ■ ⊖	d	12 32						12 47			13 02				13 17						13 32	
Clapham Junction ■	d	12 38						12 53			13 08				13 23						13 38	
London Bridge ■ ⊖	d																					
East Croydon ⇌	d	12 48						13 03			13 18				13 33						13 48	
Redhill ■	d	13 00									13 30										14 00	
Horley	d										13 36											
Gatwick Airport ■ ✈	d	13 09						13 20			13 40				13 50						14 09	
Three Bridges ■	a	13 14									13 44										14 14	
	d	13 14									13 45										14 14	
Crawley	d	13 18									13 48										14 18	
Horsham ■	a	13 26									13 56										14 26	
	d	13 30	13 35								14 00	14 05									14 30	14 35
Christs Hospital	d		13 38																			14 38
Billingshurst	d		13 44									14 14										14 44
Pulborough	d		13 51									14 20										14 51
Amberley	d		13 57																			14 57
Arundel	d		14 02									14 29										15 02
Haywards Heath ■	d							13 37							14 04							
Burgess Hill	d														14 09							
Preston Park	d														14 18							
Brighton ■	d				13 33	13 44			13 53				14 03	14 14		14 23						
Hove ■	a				13 36	13 48		13 53	13 56				14 06	14 18	14 22	14 26						
	d				13 37			13 53	13 57				14 07		14 22	14 27						
Aldrington	d								13 59							14 29						
Portslade	d				13 40				14 01				14 10		14 25	14 31						
Fishersgate	d								14 03							14 33						
Southwick	d				13 43				14 05				14 13			14 35						
Shoreham-by-Sea	d				13 46			14 00	14 09				14 16		14 30	14 39						
Lancing	d				13 50			14 04	14 13				14 20			14 43						
East Worthing	d								14 16							14 46						
Worthing ■	a				13 54			14 08	14 18				14 24		14 36	14 48						
	d				13 55			14 08	14 19				14 25		14 37	14 49						
West Worthing	d				13 57			14 10	14a21						14 39	14a51						
Durrington-on-Sea	d				13 59			14 13							14 41							
Goring-by-Sea	d				14 02			14 15							14 44							
Angmering ■	d				14 06			14 19					14 31		14 48							
Littlehampton ■	a							14 28							14 57							
	d						14 11												14 54			
Ford ■	d		14 07		14 12		14 16					14 34							14 58			15 07
Bognor Regis ■	d			14 07						14 30							14 39			14 56		
Barnham	a	13 56	14 11	14 13	14 16		14 20			14 36	14 26	14 39	14 42				14 45		15 02	15 02	14 56	15 11
	d	13 57	14 12		14 17		14 22				14 27	14 39	14 42					14 52	15 03		14 57	15 12
Bognor Regis	a		14 18				14 29					14 46						14 59				15 18
Chichester ■	a	14 04			14 24						14 34		14 50						15 10		15 04	
	d	14 05			14 25						14 35		14 50						15 11		15 05	
Fishbourne (Sussex)	d																		15 14			
Bosham	d																		15 17			
Nutbourne	d																		15 20			
Southbourne	d	14 12											14 57						15 23		15 12	
Emsworth	d	14 15			14 33								15 00						15 26		15 15	
Warblington	d																		15 29			
Havant	d	14 19			14 37						14 46		15 05						15 32		15 19	
Bedhampton	a																		15 34			
Hilsea	a																		15 42			
Fratton	a										14 54		15 13						15 46			
Portsmouth & Southsea	a										14 58		15 17						15 50			
Portsmouth Harbour ⛴	a										15 02		15 21									
Cosham	a	14 26			14 45																15 26	
Portchester	a	14 30																			15 30	
Fareham	a	14 35			14 53																15 35	
Swanwick	a	14 42			15 00																15 42	
Eastleigh	a																					
Southampton Airport Parkway	a																					
Southampton Central ⛴	a	14 59			15 19																15 59	

A H to Horsham

London, Gatwick Airport, Brighton - Sussex Coast, Portsmouth and Southampton

Network Diagram - see first Page of Table 186

Station		SN	SN	SN	SN	SN ◇■	SN	SN	SN ◇■	SN ◇■		SN	SN	SN	SN ◇■	SN	SN	SN ■	SN ◇■ H	SN ◇■ A H		SN	SN ■
London Victoria ■ ⊖	d					13 47				14 02					14 17					14 32			
Clapham Junction ■	d					13 53				14 08					14 23					14 38			
London Bridge ■ ⊖	d																						
East Croydon ⇌	d					14 03				14 18					14 33					14 48			
Redhill ■	d									14 30										15 00			
Horley	d									14 36													
Gatwick Airport ■ ✈	d					14 20				14 40					14 50					15 09			
Three Bridges ■	a									14 44										15 14			
	d									14 45										15 14			
Crawley	d									14 48										15 18			
Horsham ■	a									14 56										15 26			
	d									15 00	15 05									15 30	15 35		
Christs Hospital	d										15 08										15 38		
Billingshurst	d										15 14										15 44		
Pulborough	d										15 21										15 51		
Amberley	d																				15 57		
Arundel	d										15 30										16 02		
Haywards Heath ■	d					14 37									15 04								
Burgess Hill	d														15 09								
Preston Park	d														15 18								
Brighton ■	d		14 33	14 44			14 53						15 03	15 14				15 23					15 33
Hove ■	a		14 36	14 48		14 53	14 56						15 06	15 18	15 22			15 26					15 36
	d		14 37			14 53	14 57						15 07		15 22			15 27					15 37
Aldrington	d						14 59											15 29					
Portslade	d		14 40				15 01						15 10		15 25			15 31					15 40
Fishersgate	d						15 03											15 33					
Southwick	d		14 43				15 05						15 13					15 35					15 43
Shoreham-by-Sea	d		14 46			15 00	15 09						15 16		15 30			15 39					15 46
Lancing	d		14 50			15 04	15 13						15 20					15 43					15 50
East Worthing	d						15 16								15 35			15 46					
Worthing ■	a		14 54			15 08	15 18						15 24		15 38			15 48					15 54
	d		14 55			15 08	15 19						15 25		15 38			15 49					15 55
West Worthing	d		14 57			15 10	15a21						15 27		15 40			15 51					15 57
Durrington-on-Sea	d		14 59			15 13							15 29		15 43			15 53					15 59
Goring-by-Sea	d		15 02			15 15							15 32		15 45			15 56					16 02
Angmering ■	d		15 06			15 19							15 36		15 49			16 00					16 06
Littlehampton ■	a					15 30									15 58			16 11					
	d				15 11			15 23									15 54						
Ford ■	d		15 12		15 16			15 27			15 35		15 42				15 58				16 07		16 13
Bognor Regis ■	d	15 07							15 27			15 39							15 56			16 09	
Barnham	a	15 13	15 16		15 20			15 31	15 33	15 26	15 39	15 45	15 46				16 02		16 02	15 56	16 11	16 15	16 17
	d		15 17		15 22			15 33		15 27	15 40		15 47			15 53	16 03			15 57	16 12		16 18
Bognor Regis	a				15 29						15 46					16 00					16 18		
Chichester ■	a		15 24					15 40		15 34			15 54				16 10			16 04			16 25
	d		15 25					15 41		15 35			15 55				16 11			16 05			16 26
Fishbourne (Sussex)	d							15 44									16 14						
Bosham	d							15 47									16 17						
Nutbourne	d							15 50									16 20						
Southbourne	d							15 53					16 02				16 23			16 12			
Emsworth	d		15 33					15 56					16 05				16 26			16 15			16 34
Warblington	d							15 59									16 29						
Havant	d		15 37					16 02		15 46			16 09				16 32			16 19			16 38
Bedhampton	a							16 04									16 34						
Hilsea	a																16 42						
Fratton	a							16 12		15 54			16 18				16 46						
Portsmouth & Southsea	a							16 15		15 58			16 21				16 50						
Portsmouth Harbour ⛴	a							16 21		16 02			16 26										
Cosham	a		15 45																	16 26			16 45
Portchester	a																			16 30			
Fareham	a		15 53																	16 35			16 53
Swanwick	a		16 00																	16 42			
Eastleigh	a																						17 11
Southampton Airport Parkway	a																						17 20
Southampton Central ⛴	a		16 20																	17 01			17 28

A H to Horsham

London, Gatwick Airport, Brighton - Sussex Coast, Portsmouth and Southampton

Network Diagram - see first Page of Table 186

		SN	SN	SN	SN	SN	SN	SN		SN	SN	SN	SN	SN	SN	SN	SN	SN		SN	SN	SN	SN
			◇1				◇1 🚲	◇1					◇1			1	◇1 🚲	◇1		1			◇1
London Victoria ⊖	d		14 47					15 02					15 17					15 32					15 47
Clapham Junction	d		14 53					15 08					15 23					15 38					15 53
London Bridge ⊖	d																						
East Croydon	d		15 03					15 18					15 33					15 48					16 03
Redhill	d							15 30										16 00					
Horley	d							15 36															
Gatwick Airport ✈	d		15 20					15 40					15 50					16 09					16 20
Three Bridges	a							15 44										16 14					
	d							15 45										16 14					
Crawley	d							15 48										16 18					
Horsham	a							15 56										16 26					
	d							16 00	16 05									16 30	16 35				
Christs Hospital	d								16 08										16 38				
Billingshurst	d								16 14										16 44				
Pulborough	d								16 21										16 51				
Amberley	d																		16 57				
Arundel	d								16 30										17 02				
Haywards Heath	d		15 37										16 04										16 37
Burgess Hill	d												16 09										
Preston Park	d												16 18										
Brighton	d	15 44		15 53							16 03	16 14		16 24						16 33	16 44		
Hove	a	15 48	15 53	15 56							16 06	16 18	16 22	16 27						16 36	16 48		16 53
	d		15 53	15 57							16 07		16 22	16 28						16 37			16 53
Aldrington	d			15 59										16 30									
Portslade	d			16 01							16 10		16 25	16 32						16 40			16 56
Fishersgate	d			16 03										16 34									
Southwick	d			16 05							16 13			16 36						16 43			
Shoreham-by-Sea	d		16 00	16 09							16 16		16 30	16 40						16 46			17 01
Lancing	d		16 04	16 13							16 20			16 44						16 50			17 05
East Worthing	d			16 16										16 47									
Worthing	a		16 08	16 18							16 24		16 36	16 49						16 54			17 09
	d		16 08	16 19							16 25		16 37	16 50						16 55			17 10
West Worthing	d		16 10	16a21							16 27		16 39	16a52						16 57			17 12
Durrington-on-Sea	d		16 13								16 29		16 41							16 59			17 14
Goring-by-Sea	d		16 15								16 32		16 44							17 02			17 17
Angmering	d		16 19								16 36		16 48							17 06			17 21
Littlehampton	a		16 28										16 57										17 29
	d					16 22										16 54						17 11	
Ford	d					16 26			16 35		16 42					16 58			17 07	17 12		17 16	
Bognor Regis	d						16 30			16 39							16 56						
Barnham	a					16 30	16 36	16 26	16 39	16 45	16 46					17 02	17 02	16 56	17 11	17 16		17 20	
	d				16 24	16 31		16 27	16 40		16 47				16 54	17 03		16 57	17 12	17 17		17 24	
Bognor Regis	a				16 31				16 46						17 01				17 18			17 31	
Chichester	a					16 38		16 34			16 54					17 10		17 04		17 24			
	d					16 39		16 35			16 55					17 11		17 05		17 25			
Fishbourne (Sussex)	d					16 42										17 14							
Bosham	d					16 45										17 17							
Nutbourne	d					16 48										17 20							
Southbourne	d					16 51					17 02					17 23		17 12					
Emsworth	d					16 54					17 05					17 26		17 15		17 33			
Warblington	d					16 57										17 29							
Havant	d					17 00		16 46			17 09					17 32		17 19		17 37			
Bedhampton	a					17 02										17 34							
Hilsea	a					17 07										17 42							
Fratton	a					17 11		16 54			17 18					17 46							
Portsmouth & Southsea	a					17 16		16 58			17 22					17 50							
Portsmouth Harbour ⛴	a					17 20		17 02															
Cosham	a																	17 26		17 45			
Portchester	a																	17 31					
Fareham	a																	17 36		17 53			
Swanwick	a																	17 43		18 00			
Eastleigh	a																						
Southampton Airport Parkway	a																						
Southampton Central ⛴	a																	18 03		18 20			

London, Gatwick Airport, Brighton - Sussex Coast, Portsmouth and Southampton

Network Diagram - see first Page of Table 186

		SN	SN	SN	GW	SN		SN	SN	SN	SN	SN	SN	SN	SN	SN	SN	SN		SN	SN	SN	SN
			◇1		◇ 🚲	◇1					◇1 A 🚲	1				◇1		◇1 B 🚲		1	1		
London Victoria ⊖	d					16 02					16 17	16 19						16 32					
Clapham Junction	d					16 08					16 23	16 26						16 38					
London Bridge ⊖	d																			16 33			
East Croydon	d					16 18					16 33	16 36						16 48		16 49			
Redhill	d					16 30												17 00		17 08			
Horley	d					16 36												17 06		17 18			
Gatwick Airport ✈	d					16 40					16 49	16 53						17 09		17 21			
Three Bridges	a					16 44						16 57						17 14		17 26			
	d					16 45						16 58						17 18	17 22	17 26			
Crawley	d					16 48						17 02						17 22	17 26	17 30			
Horsham	a					16 56						17 12						17 30	17 38	17 44			
	d					17 00	17 05											17 30	17 38				
Christs Hospital	d						17 08												17 42				
Billingshurst	d						17 15												17 48				
Pulborough	d						17 21												17 54				
Amberley	d						17 27																
Arundel	d						17 32												18 03				
Haywards Heath	d										17 04												
Burgess Hill	d										17 09												
Preston Park	d																						
Brighton	d			16 53	16 59			17 03		17 14					17 23						17 33	17 45	17 53
Hove	a			16 56	17 02			17 06		17 18	17 20				17 26						17 36	17 48	17 57
	d			16 57	17 03			17 07			17 21				17 27						17 37	17 49	
Aldrington	d			16 59											17 29							17 51	
Portslade	d			17 01				17 10			17 24				17 31						17 40	17 53	
Fishersgate	d			17 03											17 33							17 55	
Southwick	d			17 05				17 13							17 35						17 43	17 57	
Shoreham-by-Sea	d			17 08	17 13			17 16			17 29				17 39						17 46	18 01	
Lancing	d			17 12				17 20			17 33				17 43						17 50	18 05	
East Worthing	d			17 15											17 46							18 08	
Worthing	a			17 18	17 21			17 24			17 37				17 48						17 54	18 10	
	d			17 18	17 22			17 25			17 38				17 49						17 55	18 11	
West Worthing	d			17 20				17 27			17 40				17 51						17 57	18 13	
Durrington-on-Sea	d							17 29			17 42				17 53						17 59	18 15	
Goring-by-Sea	d							17 32			17 45				17 56						18 02	18 18	
Angmering	d							17 36			17 49				18 00						18 06	18 22	
Littlehampton	a			17 33					←		18 00				18 08							18 30	
	d			17 41										17 54									
Ford	d			17 46			17 37	17 42	17 46					17 58					18 08		18 12		
Bognor Regis	d	17 18	17 30	→									17 51			17 57							
Barnham	a	17 24	17 36		17 38	17 26	17 42	17 46	17 50				17 57	18 02		18 03		17 57	18 13		18 16		
	d				17 39	17 27	17 42	17 47	17 54					18 04			18 08	17 57	18 14		18 17		
Bognor Regis	a						17 49		18 01								18 15		18 22				
Chichester	a				17 46	17 34		17 54						18 11				18 05			18 24		
	d				17 47	17 35		17 55						18 12				18 05			18 25		
Fishbourne (Sussex)	d					17 38								18 15									
Bosham	d					17 41								18 18				18 10					
Nutbourne	d													18 21									
Southbourne	d					17 45		18 04						18 24				18 14					
Emsworth	d					17 48		18 07						18 27				18 17			18 33		
Warblington	d							18 10						18 30									
Havant	d				17 58	17 54		18 13						18 34				18 23			18 37		
Bedhampton	a					17 56								18 36									
Hilsea	a					18 01								18 42									
Fratton	a					18 05		18 22						18 46									
Portsmouth & Southsea	a					18 09		18 25						18 49									
Portsmouth Harbour ⛴	a					18 15		18 31															
Cosham	a				18 04													18 29			18 44		
Portchester	a																	18 34					
Fareham	a				18 12													18 39			18 52		
Swanwick	a																	18 46			18 59		
Eastleigh	a																						
Southampton Airport Parkway	a																						
Southampton Central ⛴	a				18 40													19 05			19 20		

A 🚲 to Haywards Heath

B 🚲 to Three Bridges

London, Gatwick Airport, Brighton - Sussex Coast, Portsmouth and Southampton

Network Diagram - see first Page of Table 186

Station		SN ■	SN	SN	SN ◇■ A		SN ◇■	SN	SN	SN ◇■	SN ■	SN	SN	SN	SN ◇■		SN	SN	SN ■	SN ■	SN	SN
London Victoria	d				17 02					17 17					17 32							
Clapham Junction	d				17 08					17 23					17 38							
London Bridge	d	16 57									16 59								17 42	17 47		
East Croydon	d	17 10			17 18					17 33	17 15				17 49				17 55	18 00		
Redhill	d										17 37											
Horley	d										17 46											
Gatwick Airport	d									17 48	17 50											
Three Bridges	a	17 29			17 36						17 54				18 06					18 21		
Three Bridges	d	17 29			17 37						17 55				18 07					18 22		
Crawley	d				17 41						17 59				18 11					18 26		
Horsham	a				17 49						18 11				18 22					18 38		
Horsham	d				17 53	17 58									18 26	18 31				18 39		
Christs Hospital	d					18 01										18 35				18 42		
Billingshurst	d					18 07										18 41				18 49		
Pulborough	d					18 14										18 48				18 56		
Amberley	d					18 20														19 02		
Arundel	d					18 25										18 57				19 07		
Haywards Heath	d	17 39								18 01									18 22			
Burgess Hill	d	17 46								18 07									18 28			
Preston Park	d	17 56																	18 39			
Brighton	d							18 00	18 14									18 28			18 48	
Hove	a	18 00						18 03	18 18	18 21								18 31	18 43		18 53	
Hove	d	18 01						18 04		18 22								18 32	18 44			
Aldrington	d							18 06										18 34				
Portslade	d	18 04						18 08		18 25								18 36	18 47			
Fishersgate	d							18 10										18 38				
Southwick	d							18 12										18 40				
Shoreham-by-Sea	d	18 09						18 16		18 30								18 44	18 52			
Lancing	d	18 13						18 20		18 34								18 48	18 56			
East Worthing	d							18 23										18 51				
Worthing	a	18 17						18 25		18 38								18 53	19 00			
Worthing	d	18 17						18 27		18 38								18 54	19 00			
West Worthing	d	18 19						18 29		18 40									19 02			
Durrington-on-Sea	d	18 22						18 31		18 43									19 05			
Goring-by-Sea	d	18 24						18 34		18 45									19 07			
Angmering	d	18 28						18 38		18 49								19 00	19 11			
Littlehampton	a	18 39								19 00									19 24			
Littlehampton	d			18 18										18 48								19 11
Ford	d			18 22		18 30		18 44						18 53		19 02		19 07				19 15
Bognor Regis	d		18 19				18 33					18 46					19 03					
Barnham	a		18 25	18 26	18 20	18 34	18 39	18 48				18 52		18 57	18 53	19 06	19 09	19 11		19 15		19 19
Barnham	d			18 27	18 21	18 35		18 49					18 55	19 00	18 54	19 07		19 12		19 16		19 24
Bognor Regis	a			18 34		18 41							19 02			19 13				19 24		19 31
Chichester	a				18 28			18 56						19 07	19 01			19 19				
Chichester	d				18 29			18 57						19 11	19 02			19 20				
Fishbourne (Sussex)	d				18 32									19 14	19 05							
Bosham	d				18 35									19 17	19 08							
Nutbourne	d				18 38									19 20								
Southbourne	d				18 41									19 23	19 12							
Emsworth	d				18 44									19 26	19 15			19 30				
Warblington	d				18 47									19 29								
Havant	d				18 54			19 08						19 33	19 20			19 37				
Bedhampton	a				18 57									19 35								
Hilsea	a				19 02									19 43								
Fratton	a				19 06			19 17						19 47								
Portsmouth & Southsea	a				19 09			19 21						19 50								
Portsmouth Harbour	a							19 26														
Cosham	a														19 29			19 46				
Portchester	a														19 33							
Fareham	a														19 38			19 54				
Swanwick	a														19 45			20 01				
Eastleigh	a																					
Southampton Airport Parkway	a																					
Southampton Central	a														20 03			20 18				

A ⌶ to Horsham

Table 188
Mondays to Fridays

London, Gatwick Airport, Brighton - Sussex Coast, Portsmouth and Southampton

Network Diagram - see first Page of Table 186

Station		SN ◇■	SN ■	SN ◇■		SN ■ A	SN ■ B	SN ◇■	SN	SN	SN ■	SN	SN ◇■	SN	SN ◇■		SN ■	SN ■	SN	SN	SN ■	SN	SN
London Victoria	d	17 47		18 02									18 17		18 32		18 19						
Clapham Junction	d	17 53		18 08									18 23		18 38		18 26						
London Bridge	d		17 32			17 57	17 59				18 12							18 30					
East Croydon	d	18 03	17 49	18 19		18 14	18 15				18 25		18 33		18 48		18 38	18 46					
Redhill	d		18 11			18 34	18 34										18 59	19 07					
Horley	d	18 18	18 20			18 43	18 43						18 48				19 08	19 16					
Gatwick Airport	d	18 21	18 24			18 47	18 47										19 14	19 20					
Three Bridges	a		18 28	18 37		18 51	18 51				18 44				19 06		19 19	19 24					
Three Bridges	d		18 29	18 38		18 52	18 52				18 45				19 07		19 19	19 25					
Crawley	d		18 33	18 42		18 56	18 56								19 11		19 23	19 29					
Horsham	a		18 48	18 50		19 08	19 08								19 22		19 37	19 43					
Horsham	d			18 54	18 58										19 26	19 31							
Christs Hospital	d				19 01											19 34							
Billingshurst	d				19 07											19 41							
Pulborough	d				19 14											19 48							
Amberley	d															19 54							
Arundel	d				19 23											19 59							
Haywards Heath	d	18 34									18 54		19 03										
Burgess Hill	d	18 41									19 00		19 09										
Preston Park	d	18 53									19 11												
Brighton	d									19 00		19 15									19 30		19 44
Hove	a	18 57								19 03	19 17	19 19	19 22								19 33		19 48
Hove	d	18 58								19 04	19 18		19 23								19 34		
Aldrington	d									19 06											19 36		
Portslade	d	19 01								19 08	19 21		19 26								19 38		
Fishersgate	d									19 10											19 40		
Southwick	d									19 12											19 42		
Shoreham-by-Sea	d	19 06								19 16	19 26		19 31								19 46		
Lancing	d	19 10								19 20	19 30		19 36								19 50		
East Worthing	d									19 23											19 53		
Worthing	a	19 14								19 25	19 34		19 40								19 55		
Worthing	d	19 14								19 26	19 35		19 40								19 56		
West Worthing	d	19 16								19 28	19 37		19 42								19 58		
Durrington-on-Sea	d	19 19								19 30	19 39		19 45								20 00		
Goring-by-Sea	d	19 21								19 33	19 42		19 47								20 03		
Angmering	d	19 25								19 37	19 46		19 51								20 07		
Littlehampton	a	19 36									19 57		20 03										
Littlehampton	d								19 35											20 06			
Ford	d				19 28				19 39	19 43										20 10	20 13		
Bognor Regis	d							19 36						←					20 05			←	
Barnham	a			19 23	19 32			19 42	19 43	19 47				19 43	19 52	20 07			20 11	20 14	20 18	20 14	
Barnham	d			19 24	19 33				19 55	19 48				19 55	19 53	20 08				20 22	20 18	20 22	
Bognor Regis	a				19 39				→					20 01		20 14				→		20 28	
Chichester	a			19 31						19 55					20 00						20 26		
Chichester	d			19 32						19 56					20 01						20 26		
Fishbourne (Sussex)	d														20 04								
Bosham	d														20 07								
Nutbourne	d														20 10								
Southbourne	d			19 39											20 13								
Emsworth	d			19 42											20 16								
Warblington	d														20 19								
Havant	d			19 46						20 07					20 22						20 37		
Bedhampton	a																						
Hilsea	a																						
Fratton	a			19 56						20 15													
Portsmouth & Southsea	a			20 01						20 19													
Portsmouth Harbour	a			20 07																			
Cosham	a														20 28						20 44		
Portchester	a																				20 49		
Fareham	a														20 36						20 54		
Swanwick	a														20 43						21 01		
Eastleigh	a																						
Southampton Airport Parkway	a																						
Southampton Central	a														21 01						21 19		

A from 21 May

B until 18 May

London, Gatwick Airport, Brighton - Sussex Coast, Portsmouth and Southampton

Network Diagram - see first Page of Table 186

		SN	SN	SN		SN	SN	SN	SN	SN	SN	SN	SN		SN	SN	SN	SN	SN	SN	SN		SN
		◇■	◇■	◇■			■			◇■	■		◇■			■			◇■	■	◇■		
		A		B						A			B						A				
		🍴		🍴						🍴			🍴						🍴		🍴		
London Victoria 15 ⊖	d	18 47			19 02					19 17	19 10			19 32					19 47	19 40		20 02	
Clapham Junction 10	d	18 53			19 08					19 23	19 16			19 38					19 53	19 46		20 08	
London Bridge 4 ⊖	d																						
East Croydon	d	19 04			19 18					19 33	19 28			19 48					20 03	19 58		20 19	
Redhill 5	d				19 31						19 46			20 00						20 16		20 31	
Horley	d										19 55									20 25			
Gatwick Airport 10 ✈	d	19 21			19 40					19 49	19 59			20 09					20 19	20 29		20 39	
Three Bridges 4	a				19 45						20 03			20 14						20 33		20 44	
	d				19 45						20 04			20 14						20 34		20 44	
Crawley	d				19 49						20 08			20 18						20 37		20 48	
Horsham 4	a				19 57						20 21			20 26						20 49		20 56	
	d			20 01	20 06								20 30	20 35							21 00	21 05	
Christs Hospital	d				20 09									20 38								21 08	
Billingshurst	d				20 15									20 44								21 14	
Pulborough	d				20 22									20 51								21 21	
Amberley	d				20 28									20 57								21 27	
Arundel	d				20 33									21 02								21 32	
Haywards Heath 3	d	19 38								20 04									20 34				
Burgess Hill	d	19 43								20 09									20 39				
Preston Park	d																		20 49				
Brighton 10	d						20 03		20 14							20 30		20 47					
Hove 2	a	19 57					20 06		20 18	20 21						20 33		20 51	20 53				
	d	19 57					20 07			20 22						20 34			20 54				
Aldrington	d						20 09									20 36							
Portslade	d	20 00					20 11			20 25						20 38			20 57				
Fishersgate	d						20 13									20 40							
Southwick	d						20 15									20 42							
Shoreham-by-Sea	d	20 05					20 19			20 30						20 46			21 01				
Lancing	d	20 09					20 23			20 34						20 50			21 05				
East Worthing	d						20 26									20 53							
Worthing 4	a	20 13					20 28			20 38						20 55			21 09				
	d	20 13					20 29			20 38						20 56			21 10				
West Worthing	d	20 15					20 31			20 40						20 58			21 12				
Durrington-on-Sea	d	20 18					20 33			20 43						21 00			21 14				
Goring-by-Sea	d	20 20					20 36			20 45						21 03			21 17				
Angmering 3	d	20 24					20 40			20 49						21 07			21 21				
Littlehampton 4	a	20 35								20 58									21 29				
	d					20 37									21 06								
Ford 4	d				20 38	20 42	20 46							21 07	21 10	21 13						21 37	
Bognor Regis 4	d		20 33					←				21 04					←						21 39
Barnham	a		20 39	20 27	20 42	20 46	20 50	20 46				21 10	20 56	21 11	21 14	21 17	21 14				21 26	21 41	21 45
	d			20 28	20 43	20 52	20 51	20 52					20 57	21 12	21 22	21 18	21 22				21 27	21 42	
Bognor Regis	a				20 49	→		20 59						21 18	→		21 28					21 48	
Chichester 4	a			20 35			20 58						21 04			21 25					21 34		
	d			20 36			20 59						21 05			21 26					21 35		
Fishbourne (Sussex)	d												21 08										
Bosham	d												21 11										
Nutbourne	d												21 14										
Southbourne	d			20 43									21 17								21 42		
Emsworth	d			20 46									21 20								21 45		
Warblington	d												21 23										
Havant	d			20 52			21 10						21 26			21 37					21 49		
Bedhampton	a																						
Hilsea	a																						
Fratton	a			21 01			21 18														21 58		
Portsmouth & Southsea	a			21 06			21 23														22 01		
Portsmouth Harbour ⛴	a						21 27														22 05		
Cosham	a												21 33			21 43							
Portchester	a												21 38										
Fareham	a												21 43			21 51							
Swanwick	a												21 49			21 58							
Eastleigh	a																						
Southampton Airport Parkway	a																						
Southampton Central ⛴	a												22 07			22 16							

A 🍴 to Haywards Heath

B 🍴 to Horsham

London, Gatwick Airport, Brighton - Sussex Coast, Portsmouth and Southampton

Network Diagram - see first Page of Table 186

		SN	SN	SN	SN	SN	SN	SN		SN	SN	SN	SN	SN	SN	SN	SN	SN	SN	SN	SN	SN
				◇■	■			◇■		■			◇■	■							◇■	■
London Victoria 15 ⊖	d			20 17	20 10				20 32				20 47	20 40							21 17	21 10
Clapham Junction 10	d			20 23	20 16				20 38				20 53	20 46							21 23	21 16
London Bridge 4 ⊖	d																					
East Croydon	d			20 33	20 28				20 48				21 04	20 58							21 33	21 28
Redhill 5	d				20 46				21 00					21 16								21 46
Horley	d				20 54									21 25								21 54
Gatwick Airport 10 ✈	d			20 49	20 57				21 09				21 19	21 29							21 49	21 57
Three Bridges 4	a				21 02				21 14					21 33							21 53	22 02
	d				21 03				21 14					21 34							21 53	22 03
Crawley	d				21 06				21 18					21 37								22 06
Horsham 4	a				21 18				21 26					21 49								22 18
	d							21 30	21 35													
Christs Hospital	d								21 38													
Billingshurst	d								21 44													
Pulborough	d								21 51													
Amberley	d								21 57													
Arundel	d								22 02													
Haywards Heath 3	d			21 04									21 34								22 06	
Burgess Hill	d			21 09									21 39								22 11	
Preston Park	d												21 49									
Brighton 10	d	21 03	21 14								21 33	21 44						22 03		22 14		
Hove 2	a	21 06	21 18	21 21							21 36	21 48	21 53					22 06		22 18	22 22	
	d	21 07		21 22							21 37		21 54					22 07			22 23	
Aldrington	d	21 09									21 39							22 09				
Portslade	d	21 11		21 25							21 41		21 57					22 11			22 26	
Fishersgate	d	21 13									21 43							22 13				
Southwick	d	21 15									21 45							22 15				
Shoreham-by-Sea	d	21 19		21 30							21 49		22 01					22 19			22 31	
Lancing	d	21 23		21 34							21 53		22 05					22 23			22 35	
East Worthing	d	21 26									21 56							22 26				
Worthing 4	a	21 28		21 38							21 58		22 09					22 28			22 39	
	d	21 29		21 38							21 59		22 10					22 29			22 39	
West Worthing	d	21 31		21 40							22 01		22 12					22 31			22 41	
Durrington-on-Sea	d	21 33		21 43							22 03		22 14					22 33			22 44	
Goring-by-Sea	d	21 36		21 45							22 06		22 17					22 36			22 46	
Angmering 3	d	21 40		21 49							22 10		22 21					22 40			22 50	
Littlehampton 4	a			21 58									22 30									
	d									22 08							22 38					
Ford 4	d	21 46							22 07	22 12	22 16						22 42	22 46			22 56	
Bognor Regis 4	d						22 00									22 30			←			
Barnham	a	21 50					22 06	21 56	22 11	22 16	22 20					22 36	22 46	22 50	22 46		23 01	
	d	21 51				21 52		21 57	22 12	22 17	22 21				22 22		22 52	22 51	22 52		23 06	
Bognor Regis	a					21 59			22 18						22 29		→		22 59		→	
Chichester 4	a	21 58						22 04		22 24	22 28							22 58				
	d	21 59						22 05			22 29							22 59				
Fishbourne (Sussex)	d							22 08														
Bosham	d							22 11														
Nutbourne	d							22 14														
Southbourne	d							22 17			22 36											
Emsworth	d							22 20			22 39											
Warblington	d							22 23														
Havant	d	22 10						22 26			22 43							23 11				
Bedhampton	a																					
Hilsea	a																					
Fratton	a	22 18									22 52							23 20				
Portsmouth & Southsea	a	22 22									22 55							23 23				
Portsmouth Harbour ⛴	a	22 26									22 59							23 27				
Cosham	a							22 33														
Portchester	a																					
Fareham	a							22 42														
Swanwick	a							22 49														
Eastleigh	a																					
Southampton Airport Parkway	a																					
Southampton Central ⛴	a							23 07														

Table 188

Mondays to Fridays

London, Gatwick Airport, Brighton - Sussex Coast, Portsmouth and Southampton

Network Diagram - see first Page of Table 186

		SN 1	SN ◇1	SN	SN	SN	SN ◇1	SN 1	SN	SN	SN	SN ◇1	SN 1	SN 1	SN ◇1	SN	SN ◇1	SN 1	SN ◇1	SN 1	SN 1
London Victoria 15 ⊖	d	21 32					21 47	21 40				22 17	22 10	22 32			22 47	22 40	23 17	23 10	23 47
Clapham Junction 10	d	21 38					21 53	21 46				22 23	22 16	22 38			22 53	22 46	23 23	23 16	23 53
London Bridge 4 ⊖	d																				
East Croydon ⇌	d	21 48					22 03	21 58				22 34	22 28	22 48			23 03	22 58	23 33	23 28	00 06
Redhill 5	d	22 00						22 16					22 46	23 01				23 16		23 46	00 25
Horley	d							22 25					22 54					23 25		23 56	00 31
Gatwick Airport 10 ✈	d	22 09					22 19	22 29				22 49	22 57	23 09			23 19	23 29	23 51	23 59	00 34
Three Bridges 4	a	22 14						22 33				22 53	23 02	23 15				23 33	23 55	00 04	00 39
	d	22 14						22 36				22 53	23 03	23 16				23 38	23 56	00 04	00 39
Crawley	d	22 18						22 39					23 06	23 19				23 41		00 07	00 43
Horsham 4	a	22 26						22 51					23 18	23 27				23 53		00 19	00 55
	d	22 27												23 28							
Christs Hospital	d	22 30												23 31							
Billingshurst	d	22 36												23 37							
Pulborough	d	22 43												23 44							
Amberley	d	22 49												23 50							
Arundel	d	22 54												23 55							
Haywards Heath 3	d						22 37					23 03					23 37		00 05		
Burgess Hill	d											23 08							00 11		
Preston Park	d																				
Brighton 10	d				22 33	22 44			23 04	23 14						23 44					
Hove 2	a				22 36	22 48	22 51		23 07	23 18		23 21				23 48	23 51		00 21		
	d				22 37		22 52		23 08			23 22					23 52		00 22		
Aldrington	d				22 39				23 10												
Portslade	d				22 41		22 55		23 12			23 25					23 55		00s25		
Fishersgate	d				22 43				23 14												
Southwick	d				22 45				23 16			23 28					23 58		00s28		
Shoreham-by-Sea	d				22 49		23 00		23 19			23 31					00 01		00s31		
Lancing	d				22 53		23 04		23 23			23 35					00 05		00s35		
East Worthing	d				22 56				23 26												
Worthing 4	a				22 58		23 08		23 29			23 39					00 09		00 39		
	d				22 59		23 08		23 29			23 39									
West Worthing	d				23 01		23 10		23a31			23 41									
Durrington-on-Sea	d				23 03		23 13					23 44									
Goring-by-Sea	d				23 06		23 15					23 46									
Angmering 3	d				23 10		23 19					23 50									
Littlehampton 4	a				23 18		23 28														
	d				23 23																
Ford 4	d	23 00			23 27							23 56		00 01							
Bognor Regis 4	d		←	23 15											←						
Barnham	a	23 04	23 01	23 21	23 31							00 01		00 06	00 01						
	d	23 05	23 06		23 32						23 36	00 09		00 06	00 09						
Bognor Regis	a		23 12								23 43	→			00 15						
Chichester 4	a	23 12			23 39									00 14							
	d	23 13																			
Fishbourne (Sussex)	d	23 16																			
Bosham	d	23 19																			
Nutbourne	d	23 22																			
Southbourne	d	23 25																			
Emsworth	d	23 28																			
Warblington	d	23 31																			
Havant	d	23 34																			
Bedhampton	a																				
Hilsea	a																				
Fratton	a	23 47																			
Portsmouth & Southsea	a	23 54																			
Portsmouth Harbour ⛴	a																				
Cosham	a																				
Portchester	a																				
Fareham	a																				
Swanwick	a																				
Eastleigh	a																				
Southampton Airport Parkway	a																				
Southampton Central ⛴	a																				

Table 188

Saturdays

London, Gatwick Airport, Brighton - Sussex Coast, Portsmouth and Southampton

Network Diagram - see first Page of Table 186

		SN ◇1	SN 1	SN ◇1	SN ◇1	SN	SN	SN ◇1	SN 1	SN 1	SN ◇1	SN ◇1 A	SN 1	SN ◇	SN	SN 1	SN 1	SN 1	SN	SN 1	SN	SN	SN 1
London Victoria 15 ⊖	d	22p17	22p32		22p47			23p17	23p10	23p47	00 05	00 40											
Clapham Junction 10	d	22p23	22p38		22p53			23p23	23p16	23p53	00 11	00 46											
London Bridge 4 ⊖	d																						
East Croydon ⇌	d	22p34	22p48		23p03			23p33	23p28	00 06	00 24	00 56											
Redhill 5	d		23p01						23p46	00 25													
Horley	d								23p56	00 31													
Gatwick Airport 10 ✈	d	22p49	23p09		23p19			23p51	23p59	00 34	00 42	01 14											
Three Bridges 4	a	22p53	23p15					23p55	00 04	00 39	00 47	01 18											
	d	22p53	23p16					23p56	00 04	00 39	00 47	01 18											
Crawley	d		23p19						00 07	00 43													
Horsham 4	a		23p27						00 19	00 55													
	d		23p28																				
Christs Hospital	d		23p31																				
Billingshurst	d		23p37																				
Pulborough	d		23p44																				
Amberley	d		23p50																				
Arundel	d		23p55																				
Haywards Heath 3	d	23p03			23p37			00 05			01 02	01 32											
Burgess Hill	d	23p08						00 11															
Preston Park	d																						
Brighton 10	d					00 04	00 10				01s16	01s46								05 15			05 27
Hove 2	a	23p21			23p51	00 07	00 14	00 21			01s24	01s55								05 18			05 30
	d	23p22			23p52	00 08		00 22												05 20			05 31
Aldrington	d					00 10																	05 33
Portslade	d	23p25			23p55	00 12		00s25			01s27	01s59								05 23			05 35
Fishersgate	d					00 14																	05 37
Southwick	d	23p28			23p58	00 16		00s28			01s30	02s02											05 39
Shoreham-by-Sea	d	23p31			00 01	00 19		00s31			01s33	02s05								05 27			05 43
Lancing	d	23p35			00 05	00 23		00s35			01s37	02s09								05 31			05 47
East Worthing	d					00 26																	05 50
Worthing 4	a	23p39			00 09	00 29		00 39			01 41	02 13								05 35			05 52
	d	23p39				00 29														05 36			05 53
West Worthing	d	23p41				00a31														05 38			05 55
Durrington-on-Sea	d	23p44																		05 40			05 57
Goring-by-Sea	d	23p46																		05 43			06 00
Angmering 3	d	23p50																		05 47			06 04
Littlehampton 4	a																						
	d																				05 54		
Ford 4	d	23p56	00 01																	05 53	05 58		06 10
Bognor Regis 4	d			←											05 13				05 43			06 04	
Barnham	a	00 01	00 06	00 01											05 19				05 49	05 57	06 02	06 10	06 14
	d	00 09	00 06	00 09									04 57	05 15		05 20	05 30	05 38		05 58	06 03		06 15
Bognor Regis	a	→		00 15																			
Chichester 4	a		00 14										05 04	05 22		05 27	05 37	05 45		06 05	06 10		06 22
	d												05 05	05 23		05 28	05 38	05 46		06 06	06 11		06 23
Fishbourne (Sussex)	d																				06 14		
Bosham	d																			06 10	06 17		
Nutbourne	d																				06 20		
Southbourne	d																			06 15	06 23		06 30
Emsworth	d																			06 18	06 26		06 33
Warblington	d																			06 21	06 29		
Havant	d												05 16	05 34		05 39	05 49	05 57		06 24	06 32		06 37
Bedhampton	a																				06 34		
Hilsea	a																				06 42		
Fratton	a													05 42			05 57	06 05			06 46		
Portsmouth & Southsea	a													05 46			06 01	06 09			06 50		
Portsmouth Harbour ⛴	a																06 05	06 16					
Cosham	a												05 22			05 49				06 30			06 45
Portchester	a												05 27							06 34			
Fareham	a												05 32			05 57				06 39			06 53
Swanwick	a												05 39			06 04				06 46			
Eastleigh	a																						07 10
Southampton Airport Parkway	a																						07 17
Southampton Central ⛴	a												05 58			06 24				07 05			07 28

A 28 July, 4 August, 11 August, 1 September, 8 September

Table 188

Saturdays

London, Gatwick Airport, Brighton - Sussex Coast, Portsmouth and Southampton

Network Diagram - see first Page of Table 186

		SN	SN	SN	SN	SN		SN ◇1	SN 1	SN	SN	SN	SN	SN ◇1	SN 1			SN	SN	SN	SN 1	SN	SN	SN ◇1 A	SN
London Victoria 15 ⊖	d																							05 32	
Clapham Junction 10	d																							05 38	
London Bridge 4 ⊖	d																								
East Croydon ⇌	d																							05 48	
Redhill 5	d																							06 07	
Horley	d																							06 18	
Gatwick Airport 10 ✈	d														05 58									06 22	
Three Bridges 4	a														06 02									06 26	
	d														06 03									06 34	
Crawley	d														06 06									06 37	
Horsham 4	a														06 18									06 49	
	d														06 19									06 50	
Christs Hospital	d														06 22									06 53	
Billingshurst	d														06 28									06 59	
Pulborough	d														06 35									07 06	
Amberley	d														06 41									07 12	
Arundel	d														06 46									07 17	
Haywards Heath 3	d																								
Burgess Hill	d																								
Preston Park	d																								
Brighton 10	d	05 44	05 53						06 01	06 14	06 23										06 33	06 44			06 48
Hove 2	a	05 48	05 56						06 04	06 18	06 26										06 36	06 48			06 51
	d		05 57						06 05		06 27										06 37				06 52
Aldrington	d		05 59								06 29														
Portslade	d		06 01						06 08		06 31										06 40				06 55
Fishersgate	d		06 03								06 33														
Southwick	d		06 05						06 11		06 35										06 43				
Shoreham-by-Sea	d		06 09						06 14		06 39										06 46				06 59
Lancing	d		06 13						06 18		06 43										06 50				07 03
East Worthing	d		06 16								06 46														
Worthing 4	a		06 18						06 22		06 48										06 54				07 07
	d		06 19						06 23		06 49										06 55				07 08
West Worthing	d		06a21						06 25		06a51										06 57				07 10
Durrington-on-Sea	d								06 27												06 59				07 12
Goring-by-Sea	d								06 30												07 02				07 15
Angmering 3	d								06 34												07 06				07 19
Littlehampton 4	a																								07 27
	d					06 19												06 54					07 11		
Ford 4	d								06 40						06 51			06 58			07 12		07 16	07 22	
Bognor Regis 4	d			06 13				06 30				06 39		06 56					←	07 07					
Barnham	a			06 19		06 26		06 36	06 44			06 45		07 02	06 55			07 02	06 55	07 13	07 16		07 20	07 27	
	d				06 22	06 27			06 45				06 52		06 59	07 05		07 03	07 05		07 17		07 22	07 27	
Bognor Regis	a				06 29								06 59			→			07 12				07 29		
Chichester 4	a					06 34			06 52						07 06			07 10			07 24			07 35	
	d					06 35			06 53						07 07			07 11			07 25			07 35	
Fishbourne (Sussex)	d																	07 14							
Bosham	d																	07 17							
Nutbourne	d																	07 20							
Southbourne	d														07 14			07 23							
Emsworth	d														07 17			07 26			07 33				
Warblington	d																	07 29							
Havant	d					06 46			07 04						07 23			07 32			07 37			07 46	
Bedhampton	a																	07 34							
Hilsea	a																	07 42							
Fratton	a					06 54			07 12									07 46						07 55	
Portsmouth & Southsea	a					06 58			07 16									07 50						07 58	
Portsmouth Harbour ⛴	a					07 02			07 20															08 02	
Cosham	a														07 29						07 45				
Portchester	a														07 34										
Fareham	a														07 39						07 53				
Swanwick	a														07 45										
Eastleigh	a																				08 10				
Southampton Airport Parkway	a																				08 17				
Southampton Central ⛴	a														08 03						08 28				

A 1 to Three Bridges ◇ to Three Bridges

Table 188

Saturdays

London, Gatwick Airport, Brighton - Sussex Coast, Portsmouth and Southampton

Network Diagram - see first Page of Table 186

		SN		SN ◇1	SN	SN	SN	SN	SN	SN 1	SN	SN ◇1		SN	SN	SN	SN	SN 1	SN ◇1	SN	SN ◇1	SN		SN	SN
London Victoria 15 ⊖	d									06 02								06 32							
Clapham Junction 10	d									06 08								06 38							
London Bridge 4 ⊖	d																								
East Croydon ⇌	d									06 18								06 48							
Redhill 5	d									06 46								07 10							
Horley	d									06 55								07 19							
Gatwick Airport 10 ✈	d									06 59								07 24							
Three Bridges 4	a									07 03								07 29							
	d									07 04								07 30							
Crawley	d									07 07								07 33							
Horsham 4	a									07 19								07 45							
	d									07 20								07 50							
Christs Hospital	d									07 23								07 53							
Billingshurst	d									07 29								07 59							
Pulborough	d									07 36								08 06							
Amberley	d									07 42								08 12							
Arundel	d									07 47								08 17							
Haywards Heath 3	d																		07 37						
Burgess Hill	d																								
Preston Park	d																								
Brighton 10	d	06 53			07 03	07 14	07 23								07 33	07 44				07 53		08 03		08 14	08 23
Hove 2	a	06 56			07 06	07 18	07 26								07 36	07 48			07 51	07 56		08 06		08 18	08 26
	d	06 57			07 07		07 27								07 37				07 52	07 57		08 07			08 27
Aldrington	d	06 59					07 29													07 59					08 29
Portslade	d	07 01			07 10		07 31								07 40					08 01		08 10			08 31
Fishersgate	d	07 03					07 33													08 03					08 33
Southwick	d	07 05			07 13		07 35								07 43					08 05		08 13			08 35
Shoreham-by-Sea	d	07 09			07 16		07 39								07 46				07 58	08 09		08 16			08 39
Lancing	d	07 13			07 20		07 43								07 50				08 02	08 13		08 20			08 43
East Worthing	d	07 16					07 46													08 16					08 46
Worthing 4	a	07 18			07 24		07 48								07 54				08 06	08 18		08 24			08 48
	d	07 19			07 25		07 49								07 55				08 07	08 19		08 25			08 49
West Worthing	d	07a21					07a51								07 57				08 09	08a21					08a51
Durrington-on-Sea	d														07 59				08 11						
Goring-by-Sea	d														08 02				08 14						
Angmering 3	d				07 31										08 06				08 18			08 31			
Littlehampton 4	a																		08 27						
	d										07 54						08 11								
Ford 4	d									07 52	07 58				08 12		08 16	08 22							
Bognor Regis 4	d			07 30				07 39				07 56		08 07							08 30				
Barnham	a			07 36	07 41			07 45		07 57	08 02	08 02		08 13	08 16		08 20	08 27			08 36	08 41			
	d				07 41				07 52	07 57	08 03				08 17		08 22	08 27				08 41			
Bognor Regis	a								07 59								08 29								
Chichester 4	a				07 49					08 05	08 10				08 24			08 35				08 49			
	d				07 49					08 05	08 11				08 25			08 35				08 49			
Fishbourne (Sussex)	d										08 14														
Bosham	d										08 17														
Nutbourne	d										08 20														
Southbourne	d				07 56					08 12	08 23											08 56			
Emsworth	d				07 59					08 15	08 26				08 33							08 59			
Warblington	d										08 29														
Havant	d				08 04					08 20	08 32				08 37			08 46				09 04			
Bedhampton	a										08 34														
Hilsea	a										08 42														
Fratton	a				08 12						08 46							08 55				09 12			
Portsmouth & Southsea	a				08 16						08 50							08 58				09 16			
Portsmouth Harbour ⛴	a				08 20													09 02				09 20			
Cosham	a									08 28					08 45										
Portchester	a									08 32															
Fareham	a									08 37					08 53										
Swanwick	a									08 44					09 00										
Eastleigh	a																								
Southampton Airport Parkway	a																								
Southampton Central ⛴	a									09 01					09 19										

London, Gatwick Airport, Brighton - Sussex Coast, Portsmouth and Southampton

Network Diagram - see first Page of Table 186

		SN	SN	SN	SN	SN		SN		SN	SN	SN	SN	SN	SN	SN		GW		SN	SN	SN	SN	SN	SN
					◇■ H	◇■				■			◇■		◇■	◇■		◇				◇■			
London Victoria ■ ⊖	d					07 32							07 47			08 02						08 17			
Clapham Junction ■	d					07 38							07 53			08 08						08 23			
London Bridge ■ ⊖	d																								
East Croydon	d					07 48							08 03			08 18						08 33			
Redhill ■	d					08 00										08 30									
Horley	d															08 36									
Gatwick Airport ■ ✈	d					08 09							08 20			08 40						08 50			
Three Bridges ■	a					08 14										08 44									
	d					08 14										08 45									
Crawley	d					08 18										08 48									
Horsham ■	a					08 26										08 56									
	d					08 30	08 35									09 00	09 05								
Christs Hospital	d						08 38																		
Billingshurst	d						08 44										09 13								
Pulborough	d						08 51										09 19								
Amberley	d						08 57																		
Arundel	d						09 02										09 28								
Haywards Heath ■	d												08 37									09 05			
Burgess Hill	d																					09 10			
Preston Park	d																					09 18			
Brighton ■	d									08 33	08 44			08 53				09 00		09 03	09 14		09 23		
Hove ■	a									08 36	08 48		08 53	08 56				09 03		09 06	09 18	09 22	09 26		
	d									08 37			08 53	08 57				09 04		09 07		09 22	09 27		
Aldrington	d													08 59									09 29		
Portslade	d									08 40				09 01						09 10		09 25	09 31		
Fishersgate	d													09 03									09 33		
Southwick	d									08 43				09 05						09 13			09 35		
Shoreham-by-Sea	d									08 46			09 00	09 09				09 13		09 17		09 30	09 39		
Lancing	d									08 50			09 04	09 13						09 21			09 43		
East Worthing	d													09 16									09 46		
Worthing ■	a									08 54			09 08	09 18				09 22		09 26		09 36	09 48		
	d									08 55			09 08	09 19				09 22		09 26		09 37	09 49		
West Worthing	d									08 57			09 10	09a21								09 39	09a51		
Durrington-on-Sea	d									08 59			09 13									09 41			
Goring-by-Sea	d									09 02			09 15									09 44			
Angmering ■	d									09 06			09 19							09 34		09 48			
Littlehampton ■	a												09 28									09 57			
	d			08 54								09 11													
Ford ■	d			08 58			09 07			09 12		09 16					09 33								
Bognor Regis ■	d	08 39			08 56			09 07							09 30									09 39	
Barnham	a	08 45		09 02	09 02	08 56	09 11	09 13		09 16		09 20			09 36	09 26	09 38	09 40		09 44				09 45	
	d		08 52	09 03		08 57	09 12			09 17		09 22				09 27	09 38	09 41		09 45					09 52
Bognor Regis	a		08 59				09 18					09 29					09 45								09 59
Chichester ■	a			09 10		09 04				09 24						09 34		09 48		09 52					
	d			09 11		09 05				09 25						09 35		09 49		09 53					
Fishbourne (Sussex)	d			09 14																					
Bosham	d			09 17																					
Nutbourne	d			09 20																					
Southbourne	d			09 23		09 12														10 00					
Emsworth	d			09 26		09 15				09 33										10 03					
Warblington	d			09 29																					
Havant	d			09 32		09 19				09 37						09 46		10 00		10 07					
Bedhampton	a			09 34																					
Hilsea	a			09 42																					
Fratton	a			09 46												09 54				10 16					
Portsmouth & Southsea	a			09 50												09 58				10 19					
Portsmouth Harbour ⛴	a															10 02				10 23					
Cosham	a					09 26				09 45								10 06							
Portchester	a					09 30																			
Fareham	a					09 35				09 53								10 15							
Swanwick	a					09 42																			
Eastleigh	a									10 10															
Southampton Airport Parkway	a									10 17															
Southampton Central ⛴	a					09 59				10 28								10 40							

London, Gatwick Airport, Brighton - Sussex Coast, Portsmouth and Southampton

Network Diagram - see first Page of Table 186

		SN	SN	SN			SN	SN	SN	SN	SN	SN	SN	SN			SN	SN	SN	SN	SN	SN	SN	SN	
			◇■ H	◇■							◇■		◇■	◇■					◇■					◇■ H	
London Victoria ■ ⊖	d			08 32							08 47			09 02					09 17						
Clapham Junction ■	d			08 38							08 53			09 08					09 23						
London Bridge ■ ⊖	d																								
East Croydon	d			08 48							09 03			09 18					09 33						
Redhill ■	d			09 00										09 30											
Horley	d													09 36											
Gatwick Airport ■ ✈	d			09 09							09 20			09 40					09 50						
Three Bridges ■	a			09 14										09 44											
	d			09 14										09 45											
Crawley	d			09 18										09 48											
Horsham ■	a			09 26										09 56											
	d			09 30	09 35									10 00	10 05										
Christs Hospital	d				09 38																				
Billingshurst	d				09 44										10 14										
Pulborough	d				09 51										10 20										
Amberley	d				09 57																				
Arundel	d				10 02										10 29										
Haywards Heath ■	d										09 37								10 04						
Burgess Hill	d																		10 09						
Preston Park	d																		10 18						
Brighton ■	d							09 33	09 44			09 53					10 03	10 14		10 23					
Hove ■	a							09 36	09 48		09 53	09 56					10 06	10 18	10 22	10 26					
	d							09 37			09 53	09 57					10 07		10 22	10 27					
Aldrington	d											09 59								10 29					
Portslade	d							09 40				10 01					10 10		10 25	10 31					
Fishersgate	d											10 03								10 33					
Southwick	d							09 43				10 05					10 13			10 35					
Shoreham-by-Sea	d							09 46			10 00	10 09					10 16		10 30	10 39					
Lancing	d							09 50			10 04	10 13					10 20			10 43					
East Worthing	d											10 16								10 46					
Worthing ■	a							09 54			10 08	10 18					10 24		10 36	10 48					
	d							09 55			10 08	10 19					10 25		10 37	10 49					
West Worthing	d							09 57			10 10	10a21							10 39	10a51					
Durrington-on-Sea	d							09 59			10 13								10 41						
Goring-by-Sea	d							10 02			10 15								10 44						
Angmering ■	d							10 06			10 19						10 31		10 48						
Littlehampton ■	a										10 28								10 57						
	d	09 54								10 11													10 54		
Ford ■	d	09 58			10 07			10 12		10 16					10 34								10 58		
Bognor Regis ■	d		09 56				10 07						10 30								10 39			10 56	
Barnham	a	10 02	10 02	09 56	10 11		10 13	10 16		10 20			10 36	10 26	10 39		10 42				10 45		11 02	11 02	
	d	10 03		09 57	10 12			10 17		10 22				10 27	10 39		10 42					10 52	11 03		
Bognor Regis	a				10 18					10 29					10 46							10 59			
Chichester ■	a	10 10		10 04				10 24						10 34			10 50						11 10		
	d	10 11		10 05				10 25						10 35			10 50						11 11		
Fishbourne (Sussex)	d	10 14																					11 14		
Bosham	d	10 17																					11 17		
Nutbourne	d	10 20																					11 20		
Southbourne	d	10 23		10 12													10 57						11 23		
Emsworth	d	10 26		10 15				10 33									11 00						11 26		
Warblington	d	10 29																					11 29		
Havant	d	10 32		10 19				10 37						10 46			11 05						11 32		
Bedhampton	a	10 34																					11 34		
Hilsea	a	10 43																					11 42		
Fratton	a	10 47												10 54			11 13						11 46		
Portsmouth & Southsea	a	10 50												10 58			11 17						11 50		
Portsmouth Harbour ⛴	a													11 02			11 21								
Cosham	a			10 26				10 45																	
Portchester	a			10 30																					
Fareham	a			10 35				10 53																	
Swanwick	a			10 42				11 00																	
Eastleigh	a																								
Southampton Airport Parkway	a																								
Southampton Central ⛴	a			10 59				11 19																	

Table 188

Saturdays

London, Gatwick Airport, Brighton - Sussex Coast, Portsmouth and Southampton

Network Diagram - see first Page of Table 186

		SN ◇■			SN	SN ■	SN	SN	SN ◇■	SN	SN ◇■	SN ◇■ A 🛒			SN	SN	SN ◇■	SN	SN	SN	SN	SN ◇■ 🛒	SN ◇■		
London Victoria ⊖	d	09 32							09 47			10 02					10 17						10 32		
Clapham Junction	d	09 38							09 53			10 08					10 23						10 38		
London Bridge ⊖	d																								
East Croydon	d	09 48							10 03			10 18					10 33						10 48		
Redhill	d	10 00										10 30											11 00		
Horley	d											10 36													
Gatwick Airport ✈	d	10 09							10 20			10 40					10 50						11 09		
Three Bridges	a	10 14										10 44											11 14		
	d	10 14										10 45											11 14		
Crawley	d	10 18										10 48											11 18		
Horsham	a	10 26										10 56											11 26		
	d	10 30	10 35									11 00	11 05										11 30	11 35	
Christs Hospital	d		10 38																					11 38	
Billingshurst	d		10 44										11 14											11 44	
Pulborough	d		10 51										11 20											11 51	
Amberley	d		10 57																					11 57	
Arundel	d		11 02										11 29											12 02	
Haywards Heath	d								10 37								11 04								
Burgess Hill	d																11 09								
Preston Park	d																11 18								
Brighton	d					10 33	10 44			10 53					11 03	11 14		11 23							
Hove	a					10 36	10 48		10 53	10 56					11 06	11 18	11 22	11 26							
	d					10 37			10 53	10 57					11 07		11 22	11 27							
Aldrington	d									10 59								11 29							
Portslade	d					10 40				11 01					11 10		11 25	11 31							
Fishersgate	d									11 03								11 33							
Southwick	d					10 43				11 05					11 13			11 35							
Shoreham-by-Sea	d					10 46			11 00	11 09					11 16		11 30	11 39							
Lancing	d					10 50			11 04	11 13					11 20			11 43							
East Worthing	d									11 16								11 46							
Worthing	a					10 54			11 08	11 18					11 24		11 36	11 48							
	d					10 55			11 08	11 19					11 25		11 37	11 49							
West Worthing	d					10 57			11 10	11a21							11 39	11a51							
Durrington-on-Sea	d					10 59			11 13								11 41								
Goring-by-Sea	d					11 02			11 15								11 44								
Angmering	d					11 06			11 19						11 31		11 48								
Littlehampton	a								11 28								11 57								
	d							11 11													11 54				
Ford	d		11 07			11 12		11 16					11 34								11 58			12 07	
Bognor Regis	d				11 07						11 30								11 39			11 56			
Barnham	a	10 56	11 11		11 13	11 16		11 20			11 36	11 26	11 39		11 42				11 45		12 02	12 02	11 56	12 11	
	d	10 57	11 12			11 17		11 22				11 27	11 39		11 42					11 52	12 03		11 57	12 12	
Bognor Regis	a		11 18					11 29					11 46							11 59				12 18	
Chichester	a	11 04				11 24						11 34			11 50						12 10		12 04		
	d	11 05				11 25						11 35			11 50						12 11		12 05		
Fishbourne (Sussex)	d																				12 14				
Bosham	d																				12 17				
Nutbourne	d																				12 20				
Southbourne	d	11 12													11 57						12 23		12 12		
Emsworth	d	11 15				11 33									12 00						12 26		12 15		
Warblington	d																				12 29				
Havant	d	11 19				11 37						11 46			12 05						12 32		12 19		
Bedhampton	a																				12 34				
Hilsea	a																				12 42				
Fratton	a											11 54			12 13						12 46				
Portsmouth & Southsea	a											11 58			12 17						12 50				
Portsmouth Harbour ⛴	a											12 02			12 21										
Cosham	a	11 26				11 45																	12 26		
Portchester	a	11 30																					12 30		
Fareham	a	11 35				11 53																	12 35		
Swanwick	a	11 42																					12 42		
Eastleigh	a					12 10																			
Southampton Airport Parkway	a					12 18																			
Southampton Central ⛴	a	11 59				12 28																	12 59		

A 🛒 to Horsham

Table 188

Saturdays

London, Gatwick Airport, Brighton - Sussex Coast, Portsmouth and Southampton

Network Diagram - see first Page of Table 186

		SN	SN	SN	SN	SN ◇■	SN	SN ◇■	SN ◇■ A 🛒			SN	SN	SN ◇■	SN	SN	SN	SN	SN ◇■ 🛒	SN ◇■			SN	SN ■	SN
London Victoria ⊖	d					10 47			11 02					11 17						11 32					
Clapham Junction	d					10 53			11 08					11 23						11 38					
London Bridge ⊖	d																								
East Croydon	d					11 03			11 18					11 33						11 48					
Redhill	d								11 30											12 00					
Horley	d								11 36																
Gatwick Airport ✈	d					11 20			11 40					11 50						12 09					
Three Bridges	a								11 44											12 14					
	d								11 45											12 14					
Crawley	d								11 48											12 18					
Horsham	a								11 56											12 26					
	d								12 00	12 05										12 30	12 35				
Christs Hospital	d																				12 38				
Billingshurst	d									12 14											12 44				
Pulborough	d									12 20											12 51				
Amberley	d																				12 57				
Arundel	d									12 29											13 02				
Haywards Heath	d					11 37								12 04											
Burgess Hill	d													12 09											
Preston Park	d													12 18											
Brighton	d		11 33	11 44			11 53					12 03	12 14		12 23									12 33	12 44
Hove	a		11 36	11 48		11 53	11 56					12 06	12 18	12 22	12 26									12 36	12 48
	d		11 37			11 53	11 57					12 07		12 22	12 27									12 37	
Aldrington	d						11 59								12 29										
Portslade	d		11 40				12 01					12 10		12 25	12 31									12 40	
Fishersgate	d						12 03								12 33										
Southwick	d		11 43				12 05					12 13			12 35									12 43	
Shoreham-by-Sea	d		11 46			12 00	12 09					12 16		12 30	12 39									12 46	
Lancing	d		11 50			12 04	12 13					12 20			12 43									12 50	
East Worthing	d						12 16								12 46										
Worthing	a		11 54			12 08	12 18					12 24		12 36	12 48									12 54	
	d		11 55			12 08	12 19					12 25		12 37	12 49									12 55	
West Worthing	d		11 57			12 10	12a21							12 39	12a51									12 57	
Durrington-on-Sea	d		11 59			12 13								12 41										12 59	
Goring-by-Sea	d		12 02			12 15								12 44										13 02	
Angmering	d		12 06			12 19						12 31		12 48										13 06	
Littlehampton	a					12 28								12 57											
	d				12 11													12 54							
Ford	d		12 12		12 16					12 34								12 58			13 07			13 12	
Bognor Regis	d	12 07						12 30								12 39			12 56				13 07		
Barnham	a	12 13	12 16		12 20			12 36	12 26	12 39		12 42				12 45		13 02	13 02	12 56	13 11		13 13	13 16	
	d		12 17		12 22				12 27	12 39		12 42					12 52	13 03		12 57	13 12			13 17	
Bognor Regis	a				12 29					12 46							12 59				13 18				
Chichester	a		12 24						12 34			12 50						13 10		13 04				13 24	
	d		12 25						12 35			12 50						13 11		13 05				13 25	
Fishbourne (Sussex)	d																	13 14							
Bosham	d																	13 17							
Nutbourne	d																	13 20							
Southbourne	d											12 57						13 23		13 12					
Emsworth	d		12 33									13 00						13 26		13 15				13 33	
Warblington	d																	13 29							
Havant	d		12 37						12 46			13 05						13 32		13 19				13 37	
Bedhampton	a																	13 34							
Hilsea	a																	13 42							
Fratton	a								12 54			13 13						13 46							
Portsmouth & Southsea	a								12 58			13 17						13 50							
Portsmouth Harbour ⛴	a								13 02			13 21													
Cosham	a		12 45																	13 26				13 45	
Portchester	a																			13 30					
Fareham	a		12 53																	13 35				13 53	
Swanwick	a		13 00																	13 42				14 02	
Eastleigh	a																							14n37	
Southampton Airport Parkway	a																							14n33	
Southampton Central ⛴	a		13 19																	13 59				14 19	

A 🛒 to Horsham

n Stops at these stations after Southampton Central

London, Gatwick Airport, Brighton - Sussex Coast, Portsmouth and Southampton

Network Diagram - see first Page of Table 186

		SN	SN	SN	SN	SN		SN	SN	SN	SN	SN	SN	SN	SN	SN		SN	SN	SN	SN	SN	SN
			◇1		◇1	◇1				◇1					◇1	◇1						◇1	
						A ⌶									⌶								
London Victoria 15 ⊖	d		11 47			12 02				12 17						12 32						12 47	
Clapham Junction 10	d		11 53			12 08				12 23						12 38						12 53	
London Bridge 4 ⊖	d																					13 03	
East Croydon	d		12 03			12 18				12 33						12 48							
Redhill 5	d					12 30										13 00							
Horley	d					12 36																	
Gatwick Airport 10 ✈	d		12 20			12 40				12 50						13 09						13 20	
Three Bridges 4	a					12 44										13 14							
	d					12 45										13 14							
Crawley	d					12 48										13 18							
Horsham 4	a					12 56										13 26							
	d					13 00	13 05									13 30	13 35						
Christs Hospital	d																13 38						
Billingshurst	d						13 14										13 44						
Pulborough	d						13 20										13 51						
Amberley	d																13 57						
Arundel	d						13 29										14 02					13 37	
Haywards Heath 3	d		12 37							13 04													
Burgess Hill	d									13 09													
Preston Park	d									13 18													
Brighton 10	d			12 53				13 03	13 14		13 23								13 33	13 44			13 53
Hove 2	a		12 53	12 56				13 06	13 18	13 22	13 26								13 36	13 48		13 53	13 56
	d		12 53	12 57				13 07		13 22	13 27								13 37			13 53	13 57
Aldrington	d			12 59							13 29												13 59
Portslade	d			13 01				13 10		13 25	13 31								13 40				14 01
Fishersgate	d			13 03							13 33												14 03
Southwick	d			13 05				13 13			13 35								13 43				14 05
Shoreham-by-Sea	d		13 00	13 09				13 16		13 30	13 39								13 46			14 00	14 09
Lancing	d		13 04	13 13				13 20			13 43								13 50			14 04	14 13
East Worthing	d			13 16							13 46												14 16
Worthing 4	a		13 08	13 18				13 24		13 36	13 48								13 54			14 08	14 18
	d		13 08	13 19				13 25		13 37	13 49								13 55			14 08	14 19
West Worthing	d		13 10	13a21						13 39	13a51								13 57			14 10	14a21
Durrington-on-Sea	d		13 13							13 41									13 59			14 13	
Goring-by-Sea	d		13 15							13 44									14 02			14 15	
Angmering 3	d		13 19					13 31		13 48									14 06			14 19	
Littlehampton 4	a		13 28							13 57												14 28	
	d	13 11												13 54							14 11		
Ford 4	d	13 16					13 34							13 58			14 07		14 12		14 16		
Bognor Regis 4	d				13 30							13 39			13 56			14 07					
Barnham	a	13 20			13 36	13 26	13 39	13 42				13 45		14 02	14 02	13 56	14 11	14 13	14 16		14 20		
	d	13 22				13 27	13 39	13 42					13 52	14 03		13 57	14 12		14 17		14 22		
Bognor Regis	a	13 29					13 46						13 59				14 18				14 29		
Chichester 4	a					13 34		13 50						14 10		14 04			14 24				
	d					13 35		13 50						14 11		14 05			14 25				
Fishbourne (Sussex)	d													14 14									
Bosham	d													14 17									
Nutbourne	d													14 20									
Southbourne	d							13 57						14 23		14 12							
Emsworth	d							14 00						14 26		14 15			14 33				
Warblington	d													14 29									
Havant	d					13 46		14 05						14 32		14 19			14 37				
Bedhampton	a													14 34									
Hilsea	a													14 42									
Fratton	a					13 54		14 13						14 46									
Portsmouth & Southsea	a					13 58		14 17						14 50									
Portsmouth Harbour ⛴	a					14 02		14 21															
Cosham	a															14 26			14 45				
Portchester	a															14 30							
Fareham	a															14 35			14 53				
Swanwick	a															14 42			15 00				
Eastleigh	a																						
Southampton Airport Parkway	a																						
Southampton Central ⛴	a															14 59			15 19				

A ⌶ to Horsham

London, Gatwick Airport, Brighton - Sussex Coast, Portsmouth and Southampton

Network Diagram - see first Page of Table 186

		SN	SN		SN	SN	SN	SN	SN	SN	SN	SN	SN		SN	SN	SN	SN	SN	SN	SN	SN	
		◇1	◇1				◇1					◇1	◇1			1			◇1		◇1	◇1	
			A ⌶									⌶										A ⌶	
London Victoria 15 ⊖	d		13 02				13 17						13 32						13 47			14 02	
Clapham Junction 10	d		13 08				13 23						13 38						13 53			14 08	
London Bridge 4 ⊖	d																						
East Croydon	d		13 18				13 33						13 48						14 03			14 18	
Redhill 5	d		13 30										14 00									14 30	
Horley	d		13 36																			14 36	
Gatwick Airport 10 ✈	d		13 40				13 50						14 09						14 20			14 40	
Three Bridges 4	a		13 44										14 14									14 44	
	d		13 45										14 14									14 45	
Crawley	d		13 48										14 18									14 48	
Horsham 4	a		13 56										14 26									14 56	
	d		14 00	14 05									14 30	14 35								15 00	15 05
Christs Hospital	d													14 38									
Billingshurst	d			14 14										14 44									15 14
Pulborough	d			14 20										14 51									15 20
Amberley	d													14 57									
Arundel	d			14 29										15 02									15 29
Haywards Heath 3	d						14 04												14 37				
Burgess Hill	d						14 09																
Preston Park	d						14 18																
Brighton 10	d				14 03	14 14		14 23								14 33	14 44			14 53			
Hove 2	a				14 06	14 18	14 22	14 26								14 36	14 48		14 53	14 56			
	d				14 07		14 22	14 27								14 37			14 53	14 57			
Aldrington	d							14 29												14 59			
Portslade	d				14 10		14 25	14 31								14 40				15 01			
Fishersgate	d							14 33												15 03			
Southwick	d				14 13			14 35								14 43				15 05			
Shoreham-by-Sea	d				14 16		14 30	14 39								14 46			15 00	15 09			
Lancing	d				14 20			14 43								14 50			15 04	15 13			
East Worthing	d							14 46												15 16			
Worthing 4	a				14 24		14 36	14 48								14 54			15 08	15 18			
	d				14 25		14 37	14 49								14 55			15 08	15 19			
West Worthing	d						14 39	14a51								14 57			15 10	15a21			
Durrington-on-Sea	d						14 41									14 59			15 13				
Goring-by-Sea	d						14 44									15 02			15 15				
Angmering 3	d				14 31		14 48									15 06			15 19				
Littlehampton 4	a						14 57												15 28				
	d										14 54							15 11					
Ford 4	d			14 34							14 58			15 07		15 12		15 16					15 34
Bognor Regis 4	d	14 30							14 39			14 56			15 07						15 30		
Barnham	a	14 36	14 26	14 39	14 42				14 45		15 02	15 02	14 56	15 11	15 13	15 16		15 20			15 36	15 26	15 39
	d		14 27	14 39	14 42					14 52	15 03		14 57	15 12		15 17		15 22				15 27	15 39
Bognor Regis	a			14 46						14 59				15 18				15 29					15 46
Chichester 4	a		14 34		14 50						15 10		15 04			15 24						15 34	
	d		14 35		14 50						15 11		15 05			15 25						15 35	
Fishbourne (Sussex)	d										15 14												
Bosham	d										15 17												
Nutbourne	d										15 20												
Southbourne	d				14 57						15 23		15 12										
Emsworth	d				15 00						15 26		15 15			15 33							
Warblington	d										15 29												
Havant	d		14 46		15 05						15 32		15 19			15 37						15 46	
Bedhampton	a										15 34												
Hilsea	a										15 42												
Fratton	a		14 54		15 13						15 46											15 54	
Portsmouth & Southsea	a		14 58		15 17						15 50											15 58	
Portsmouth Harbour ⛴	a		15 02		15 21																	16 02	
Cosham	a												15 26			15 45							
Portchester	a												15 30										
Fareham	a												15 35			15 53							
Swanwick	a												15 42										
Eastleigh	a															16 10							
Southampton Airport Parkway	a															16 17							
Southampton Central ⛴	a												15 59			16 28							

A ⌶ to Horsham

Table 188

London, Gatwick Airport, Brighton - Sussex Coast, Portsmouth and Southampton

Network Diagram - see first Page of Table 186

		SN	SN	SN ◇1	SN	SN	SN	SN	SN ◇1 ⌶	SN ◇1		SN	SN	SN	SN	SN ◇1	SN	SN ◇1	SN ◇1 A ⌶		SN	SN
London Victoria 15 ⊖	d			14 17						14 32						14 47			15 02			
Clapham Junction 10	d			14 23						14 38						14 53			15 08			
London Bridge 4 ⊖	d																					
East Croydon	d			14 33						14 48						15 03			15 18			
Redhill 5	d									15 00									15 30			
Horley	d																		15 36			
Gatwick Airport 10 ✈	d			14 50						15 09						15 20			15 40			
Three Bridges 4	a									15 14									15 44			
	d									15 14									15 45			
Crawley	d									15 18									15 48			
Horsham 4	a									15 26									15 56			
	d									15 30	15 35								16 00	16 05		
Christs Hospital	d										15 38											
Billingshurst	d										15 44									16 14		
Pulborough	d										15 51									16 20		
Amberley	d										15 57											
Arundel	d										16 02									16 29		
Haywards Heath 3	d			15 04												15 37						
Burgess Hill	d			15 09																		
Preston Park	d			15 18																		
Brighton 10	d	15 03	15 14		15 23								15 33	15 44			15 53				16 03	16 14
Hove 2	a	15 06	15 18	15 22	15 26								15 36	15 48		15 53	15 56				16 06	16 18
	d	15 07		15 22	15 27								15 37			15 53	15 57				16 07	
Aldrington	d				15 29												15 59					
Portslade	d	15 10		15 25	15 31								15 40				16 01				16 10	
Fishersgate	d				15 33												16 03					
Southwick	d	15 13			15 35								15 43				16 05				16 13	
Shoreham-by-Sea	d	15 16		15 30	15 39								15 46			16 00	16 09				16 16	
Lancing	d	15 20			15 43								15 50			16 04	16 13				16 20	
East Worthing	d				15 46												16 16					
Worthing 4	a	15 24		15 36	15 48								15 54			16 08	16 18				16 24	
	d	15 25		15 37	15 49								15 55			16 08	16 19				16 25	
West Worthing	d			15 39	15a51								15 57			16 10	16a21					
Durrington-on-Sea	d			15 41									15 59			16 13						
Goring-by-Sea	d			15 44									16 02			16 15						
Angmering 3	d	15 31		15 48									16 06			16 19					16 31	
Littlehampton 4	a			15 58												16 28						
	d							15 54							16 11							
Ford 4	d							15 58			16 07		16 12		16 16					16 34		
Bognor Regis 4	d					15 39			15 56			16 07						16 30				
Barnham	a	15 42				15 45		16 02	16 02	15 56	16 11	16 13	16 16		16 20			16 36	16 26	16 39	16 42	
	d	15 42					15 52	16 03		15 57	16 12		16 17		16 22				16 27	16 39	16 42	
Bognor Regis	a						15 59				16 18				16 29					16 46		
Chichester 4	a	15 50						16 10		16 04			16 24						16 34		16 50	
	d	15 50						16 11		16 05			16 25						16 35		16 50	
Fishbourne (Sussex)	d							16 14														
Bosham	d							16 17														
Nutbourne	d							16 20														
Southbourne	d	15 57						16 23		16 12											16 57	
Emsworth	d	16 00						16 26		16 15			16 33								17 00	
Warblington	d							16 29														
Havant	d	16 05						16 32		16 19			16 37						16 46		17 05	
Bedhampton	a							16 34														
Hilsea	a							16 42														
Fratton	a	16 13						16 46											16 54		17 13	
Portsmouth & Southsea	a	16 17						16 50											16 58		17 17	
Portsmouth Harbour ⛴	a	16 21																	17 02		17 21	
Cosham	a									16 26			16 45									
Portchester	a									16 30												
Fareham	a									16 35			16 53									
Swanwick	a									16 42			17 00									
Eastleigh	a																					
Southampton Airport Parkway	a																					
Southampton Central ⛴	a									16 59			17 19									

A ⌶ to Horsham

Table 188

London, Gatwick Airport, Brighton - Sussex Coast, Portsmouth and Southampton

Network Diagram - see first Page of Table 186

		SN ◇1	SN	SN	SN	SN	SN ◇1 ⌶	SN ◇1		SN	SN 1	SN	SN	SN ◇1	SN	SN ◇1	GW ◇	SN ◇1 A ⌶		SN	SN	SN ◇1	SN
London Victoria 15 ⊖	d	15 17						15 32						15 47				16 02				16 17	
Clapham Junction 10	d	15 23						15 38						15 53				16 08				16 23	
London Bridge 4 ⊖	d																						
East Croydon	d	15 33						15 48						16 03				16 18				16 33	
Redhill 5	d							16 00										16 30					
Horley	d																	16 36					
Gatwick Airport 10 ✈	d	15 50						16 09						16 20				16 40				16 50	
Three Bridges 4	a							16 14										16 44					
	d							16 14										16 45					
Crawley	d							16 18										16 48					
Horsham 4	a							16 26										16 56					
	d							16 30	16 35									17 00	17 05				
Christs Hospital	d								16 38														
Billingshurst	d								16 44										17 14				
Pulborough	d								16 51										17 20				
Amberley	d								16 57														
Arundel	d								17 02										17 29				
Haywards Heath 3	d	16 04												16 37								17 04	
Burgess Hill	d	16 09																				17 09	
Preston Park	d	16 18																				17 18	
Brighton 10	d		16 23								16 33	16 44			16 53		17 00			17 03	17 14		17 23
Hove 2	a	16 22	16 26								16 36	16 48		16 53	16 56		17 03			17 06	17 18	17 22	17 26
	d	16 22	16 27								16 37			16 53	16 57		17 04			17 07		17 22	17 27
Aldrington	d		16 29												16 59								17 29
Portslade	d	16 25	16 31								16 40				17 01					17 10		17 25	17 31
Fishersgate	d		16 33												17 03								17 33
Southwick	d		16 35								16 43				17 05					17 13			17 35
Shoreham-by-Sea	d	16 30	16 39								16 46			17 00	17 09		17 13			17 17		17 30	17 39
Lancing	d		16 43								16 50			17 04	17 13					17 21			17 43
East Worthing	d		16 46												17 16								17 46
Worthing 4	a	16 36	16 48								16 54			17 08	17 18		17 22			17 25		17 36	17 48
	d	16 37	16 49								16 55			17 08	17 19		17 22			17 25		17 37	17 49
West Worthing	d	16 39	16a51								16 57			17 10	17a21							17 39	17a51
Durrington-on-Sea	d	16 41									16 59			17 13								17 41	
Goring-by-Sea	d	16 44									17 02			17 15								17 44	
Angmering 3	d	16 48									17 06			17 19						17 34		17 48	
Littlehampton 4	a	16 57												17 28								17 57	
	d					16 54							17 11										
Ford 4	d					16 58			17 07		17 12		17 16						17 36				
Bognor Regis 4	d			16 39			16 56			17 07						17 30							
Barnham	a			16 45		17 02	17 02	16 56	17 11	17 13	17 16		17 20			17 36	17 37	17 26	17 40	17 43			
	d				16 52	17 03		16 57	17 12		17 17		17 22				17 38	17 27	17 41	17 44			
Bognor Regis	a				16 59				17 18				17 29						17 47				
Chichester 4	a					17 10		17 04			17 24						17 45	17 34		17 51			
	d					17 11		17 05			17 25						17 46	17 35		17 52			
Fishbourne (Sussex)	d					17 14																	
Bosham	d					17 17																	
Nutbourne	d					17 20																	
Southbourne	d					17 23		17 12												17 59			
Emsworth	d					17 26		17 15			17 33									18 02			
Warblington	d					17 29																	
Havant	d					17 32		17 19			17 37						18 00	17 46		18 06			
Bedhampton	a					17 34																	
Hilsea	a					17 42																	
Fratton	a					17 46												17 54		18 15			
Portsmouth & Southsea	a					17 50												17 58		18 18			
Portsmouth Harbour ⛴	a																	18 02		18 22			
Cosham	a							17 26			17 45						18 06						
Portchester	a							17 30															
Fareham	a							17 35			17 53						18 14						
Swanwick	a							17 42															
Eastleigh	a										18 10												
Southampton Airport Parkway	a										18 17												
Southampton Central ⛴	a							17 59			18 28						18 43						

A ⌶ to Horsham

Table 188

Saturdays

London, Gatwick Airport, Brighton - Sussex Coast, Portsmouth and Southampton

Network Diagram - see first Page of Table 186

Station		SN	SN	SN	SN ◇1	SN ◇1		SN	SN	SN	SN	SN ◇1	SN ◇1 A		SN	SN ◇1	SN	SN	SN ◇1	SN	SN	SN	SN
London Victoria ⊖	d					16 32						16 47	17 02						17 17				
Clapham Junction	d					16 38						16 53	17 08						17 23				
London Bridge ⊖	d																						
East Croydon	d					16 48						17 03	17 18						17 33				
Redhill	d					17 00							17 30										
Horley	d												17 36										
Gatwick Airport ✈	d					17 09						17 20	17 40						17 50				
Three Bridges	a					17 14							17 44										
	d					17 14							17 45										
Crawley	d					17 18							17 48										
Horsham	a					17 26							17 56										
	d					17 30	17 35						18 00	18 05									
Christs Hospital	d						17 38																
Billingshurst	d						17 44							18 14									
Pulborough	d						17 51							18 20									
Amberley	d						17 57																
Arundel	d						18 02							18 29									
Haywards Heath	d											17 37							18 04				
Burgess Hill	d																		18 09				
Preston Park	d																		18 18				
Brighton	d								17 33	17 44					17 53		18 03	18 14					18 23
Hove	a								17 36	17 48		17 53			17 56		18 06	18 18	18 22				18 26
	d								17 37			17 53			17 57		18 07		18 22				18 27
Aldrington	d														17 59								18 29
Portslade	d								17 40						18 01		18 10		18 25				18 31
Fishersgate	d														18 03								18 33
Southwick	d								17 43						18 05		18 13						18 35
Shoreham-by-Sea	d								17 46			18 00			18 09		18 16		18 30				18 39
Lancing	d								17 50			18 04			18 13		18 20						18 43
East Worthing	d														18 16								18 46
Worthing	a								17 54			18 08			18 18		18 24		18 36				18 48
	d								17 55			18 08			18 19		18 25		18 37				18 49
West Worthing	d								17 57			18 10			18a21				18 39				18 51
Durrington-on-Sea	d								17 59			18 13							18 41				18 53
Goring-by-Sea	d								18 02			18 15							18 44				18 56
Angmering	d								18 06			18 19					18 31		18 48				19 00
Littlehampton	a											18 28							18 57				19 11
	d			17 54							18 11											18 54	
Ford	d			17 58			18 07		18 12		18 16			18 34								18 58	
Bognor Regis	d	17 39			17 56			18 07								18 33				18 39			
Barnham	a	17 45		18 02	18 02	17 56	18 11	18 13	18 16		18 20		18 26	18 39		18 40	18 42			18 46		19 02	
	d		17 52	18 03		17 57	18 12		18 17		18 22		18 27	18 39			18 42				18 52	19 03	
Bognor Regis	a		17 59				18 18				18 29			18 46							18 59		
Chichester	a			18 10		18 04			18 24				18 34				18 50					19 10	
	d			18 11		18 05			18 25				18 35				18 50					19 11	
Fishbourne (Sussex)	d			18 14																		19 14	
Bosham	d			18 17																		19 17	
Nutbourne	d			18 20																		19 20	
Southbourne	d			18 23		18 12											18 57					19 23	
Emsworth	d			18 26		18 15			18 33								19 00					19 26	
Warblington	d			18 29																		19 29	
Havant	d			18 32		18 19			18 37				18 46				19 05					19 32	
Bedhampton	a			18 34																		19 34	
Hilsea	a			18 42																		19 42	
Fratton	a			18 46									18 54				19 13					19 46	
Portsmouth & Southsea	a			18 50									18 58				19 17					19 50	
Portsmouth Harbour ⛴	a												19 02				19 21						
Cosham	a					18 26			18 45														
Portchester	a					18 30																	
Fareham	a					18 35			18 53														
Swanwick	a					18 42			19 00														
Eastleigh	a																						
Southampton Airport Parkway	a																						
Southampton Central ⛴	a					18 59			19 19														

A ⚏ to Horsham

Table 188

Saturdays

London, Gatwick Airport, Brighton - Sussex Coast, Portsmouth and Southampton

Network Diagram - see first Page of Table 186

Station		SN	SN ◇1		SN 1	SN	SN	SN ◇1	SN ◇1 A		SN ◇1	SN	SN 1	SN	SN ◇1	SN	SN	SN ◇1		SN 1	SN	SN
London Victoria ⊖	d		17 32					17 47	18 02						18 17			18 32				
Clapham Junction	d		17 38					17 53	18 08						18 23			18 38				
London Bridge ⊖	d																					
East Croydon	d		17 48					18 03	18 18						18 33			18 48				
Redhill	d		18 00						18 30									19 00				
Horley	d								18 36													
Gatwick Airport ✈	d		18 09					18 20	18 40						18 50			19 09				
Three Bridges	a		18 14						18 44									19 14				
	d		18 14						18 45									19 14				
Crawley	d		18 18						18 48									19 18				
Horsham	a		18 26						18 56									19 26				
	d		18 30	18 35					19 00	19 05								19 30	19 35			
Christs Hospital	d			18 38															19 38			
Billingshurst	d			18 44						19 14									19 44			
Pulborough	d			18 51						19 20									19 51			
Amberley	d			18 57															19 57			
Arundel	d			19 02						19 29									20 02			
Haywards Heath	d							18 37							19 04							
Burgess Hill	d														19 09							
Preston Park	d														19 18							
Brighton	d				18 33	18 44							19 03	19 14						19 29	19 44	
Hove	a				18 36	18 48		18 53					19 06	19 18	19 22					19 32	19 48	
	d				18 37			18 53					19 07		19 22					19 33		
Aldrington	d												19 09							19 35		
Portslade	d				18 40			18 56					19 11		19 25					19 37		
Fishersgate	d												19 13							19 39		
Southwick	d				18 43								19 15							19 41		
Shoreham-by-Sea	d				18 46			19 01					19 19		19 30					19 45		
Lancing	d				18 50			19 05					19 23		19 34					19 49		
East Worthing	d												19 26							19 52		
Worthing	a				18 54			19 09					19 28		19 38					19 54		
	d				18 55			19 10					19 29		19 39					19 55		
West Worthing	d				18 57			19 12					19 31		19 41					19 57		
Durrington-on-Sea	d				18 59			19 14					19 33		19 43					19 59		
Goring-by-Sea	d				19 02			19 17					19 36		19 46					20 02		
Angmering	d				19 06			19 21					19 40		19 50					20 06		
Littlehampton	a							19 29							19 58							
	d						19 11															20 11
Ford	d			19 07	19 12		19 16			19 34			19 46						20 07	20 12		20 16
Bognor Regis	d	19 03									19 33	19 39					20 04					
Barnham	a	19 09	18 56	19 11	19 16		19 20		19 26	19 39	19 40	19 46	19 50				20 10	19 56	20 11	20 16		20 20
	d		18 57	19 12	19 17		19 22		19 27	19 39			19 51			19 52		19 57	20 12	20 17		20 22
Bognor Regis	a			19 18			19 29			19 46						19 59			20 18			20 29
Chichester	a		19 04		19 24				19 34				19 58					20 04		20 24		
	d		19 05		19 25				19 35				19 59					20 05		20 25		
Fishbourne (Sussex)	d																	20 08				
Bosham	d																	20 11				
Nutbourne	d																	20 14				
Southbourne	d		19 12															20 17				
Emsworth	d		19 15		19 33													20 20		20 33		
Warblington	d																	20 23				
Havant	d		19 19		19 37				19 46				20 10					20 26		20 37		
Bedhampton	a																					
Hilsea	a																					
Fratton	a								19 54				20 18									
Portsmouth & Southsea	a								19 58				20 22									
Portsmouth Harbour ⛴	a								20 02				20 26									
Cosham	a		19 26		19 45													20 32		20 45		
Portchester	a		19 30															20 36				
Fareham	a		19 35		19 53													20 41		20 53		
Swanwick	a		19 42															20 48		21 00		
Eastleigh	a				20 10																	
Southampton Airport Parkway	a				20 17																	
Southampton Central ⛴	a		19 59		20 26													21 05		21 19		

A ⚏ to Horsham

Table 188

Saturdays

London, Gatwick Airport, Brighton - Sussex Coast, Portsmouth and Southampton

Network Diagram - see first Page of Table 186

Station		SN ◇■	SN ◇■ A 🚌		SN ◇■	SN ■	SN	SN ◇■	SN	SN		SN	SN ◇■		SN	SN ■	SN	SN	SN ◇■	SN ◇■			SN	SN	SN
London Victoria ⊖	d	18 47	19 02					19 17					19 32						19 47	20 02					
Clapham Junction	d	18 53	19 08					19 23					19 38						19 53	20 08					
London Bridge ⊖	d																								
East Croydon	d	19 03	19 18					19 33					19 48						20 03	20 18					
Redhill	d		19 30										20 00							20 30					
Horley	d		19 36																						
Gatwick Airport ✈	d	19 20	19 40					19 50					20 09						20 20	20 40					
Three Bridges	a		19 44										20 14							20 44					
	d		19 45										20 14							20 45					
Crawley	d		19 48										20 18							20 48					
Horsham	a		19 56										20 26							20 56					
	d		20 00	20 05									20 30	20 35						21 00	21 05				
Christs Hospital	d													20 38							21 08				
Billingshurst	d			20 14										20 44							21 14				
Pulborough	d			20 20										20 51							21 21				
Amberley	d													20 57							21 27				
Arundel	d			20 29										21 02							21 32				
Haywards Heath	d	19 37						20 04											20 37						
Burgess Hill	d							20 09																	
Preston Park	d							20 18																	
Brighton	d					19 56	20 14									20 30		20 44						21 03	21 14
Hove	a	19 52				19 59	20 18	20 22								20 33		20 48	20 53					21 06	21 18
	d	19 53				20 00		20 22								20 34			20 53					21 07	
Aldrington	d					20 02										20 36								21 09	
Portslade	d	19 56				20 04		20 25								20 38			20 56					21 11	
Fishersgate	d					20 06										20 40								21 13	
Southwick	d					20 08										20 42								21 15	
Shoreham-by-Sea	d	20 01				20 12		20 30								20 46			21 01					21 19	
Lancing	d	20 05				20 16		20 34								20 50			21 05					21 23	
East Worthing	d					20 19										20 53								21 26	
Worthing	a	20 09				20 21		20 38								20 55			21 09					21 28	
	d	20 09				20 22		20 39								20 56			21 10					21 29	
West Worthing	d	20 11				20 24		20 41								20 58			21 12					21 31	
Durrington-on-Sea	d	20 14				20 26		20 43								21 00			21 14					21 33	
Goring-by-Sea	d	20 16				20 29		20 46								21 03			21 17					21 36	
Angmering	d	20 20				20 33		20 50								21 07			21 21					21 40	
Littlehampton	a	20 29						20 58											21 29						
	d														21 07										
Ford	d			20 34		20 39								21 07	21 11	21 15					21 37			21 46	
Bognor Regis	d				20 33				20 39			21 04					←						21 39		
Barnham	a		20 26	20 39	20 39	20 43			20 45			21 10	20 56	21 11	21 15	21 19	21 15			21 26	21 41		21 45	21 50	
	d		20 27	20 39		20 44				20 52			20 57	21 12	21 22	21 20	21 22			21 27	21 42			21 51	
Bognor Regis	a			20 46						20 59				21 18	→		21 29				21 48				
Chichester	a		20 34			20 51							21 04			21 27				21 34				21 58	
	d		20 35			20 52							21 05			21 28				21 35				21 59	
Fishbourne (Sussex)	d					20 55																			
Bosham	d												21 09												
Nutbourne	d					21 00																			
Southbourne	d					21 02							21 14							21 42					
Emsworth	d					21 05							21 17			21 36				21 45					
Warblington	d												21 20												
Havant	d		20 46			21 10							21 23			21 40				21 49				22 10	
Bedhampton	a																								
Hilsea	a																								
Fratton	a		20 54			21 18														21 59				22 18	
Portsmouth & Southsea	a		20 58			21 22														22 02				22 22	
Portsmouth Harbour ⛴	a		21 02			21 26														22 06				22 26	
Cosham	a												21 29			21 46									
Portchester	a												21 33												
Fareham	a												21 38			21 54									
Swanwick	a												21 45			22 01									
Eastleigh	a																								
Southampton Airport Parkway	a																								
Southampton Central ⛴	a												22 02			22 20									

A 🚌 to Horsham

Table 188

Saturdays

London, Gatwick Airport, Brighton - Sussex Coast, Portsmouth and Southampton

Network Diagram - see first Page of Table 186

Station		SN ◇■	SN ■	SN	SN	SN ◇■			SN ■	SN	SN	SN ◇■	SN ■	SN ◇	SN	SN	SN		SN	SN	SN ◇■	SN ■	SN	SN ◇■	SN
London Victoria ⊖	d	20 17	20 10			20 32						20 47	20 40								21 17	21 10	21 32		
Clapham Junction	d	20 23	20 16			20 38						20 53	20 46								21 23	21 16	21 38		
London Bridge ⊖	d																								
East Croydon	d	20 33	20 29			20 48						21 03	20 58								21 33	21 28	21 48		
Redhill	d		20 48			21 00							21 16									21 46	22 00		
Horley	d		20 54										21 25									21 52			
Gatwick Airport ✈	d	20 50	20 59			21 09						21 20	21 29								21 49	21 56	22 09		
Three Bridges	a		21 03			21 14							21 33								21 53	22 00	22 14		
	d		21 04			21 14							21 36								21 53	22 01	22 14		
Crawley	d		21 07			21 18							21 39									22 04	22 18		
Horsham	a		21 19			21 26							21 52									22 16	22 26		
	d					21 30	21 35																22 27		
Christs Hospital	d						21 38																22 30		
Billingshurst	d						21 44																22 36		
Pulborough	d						21 51																22 43		
Amberley	d						21 57																22 49		
Arundel	d						22 02																22 54		
Haywards Heath	d	21 05										21 37									22 06				
Burgess Hill	d	21 10																			22 11				
Preston Park	d	21 19																							
Brighton	d									21 33	21 44						22 03			22 14					
Hove	a	21 22								21 36	21 48	21 51					22 06			22 18	22 22				
	d	21 23								21 37		21 52					22 07				22 23				
Aldrington	d									21 39							22 09								
Portslade	d	21 26								21 41		21 55					22 11				22 26				
Fishersgate	d									21 43							22 13								
Southwick	d									21 45							22 15								
Shoreham-by-Sea	d	21 31								21 49		22 00					22 19				22 31				
Lancing	d	21 35								21 53		22 04					22 23				22 35				
East Worthing	d									21 56							22 26								
Worthing	a	21 39								21 58		22 08					22 28				22 39				
	d	21 39								21 59		22 08					22 29				22 39				
West Worthing	d	21 41								22 01		22 10					22 31				22 41				
Durrington-on-Sea	d	21 44								22 03		22 13					22 33				22 44				
Goring-by-Sea	d	21 46								22 06		22 15					22 36				22 46				
Angmering	d	21 50								22 10		22 19					22 40				22 50				
Littlehampton	a	21 59										22 28													
	d								22 08							22 38									
Ford	d						22 07		22 12	22 16						22 42	22 46				22 56		23 00		
Bognor Regis	d				22 00										22 30				←					←	23 15
Barnham	a				22 06	21 56	22 11		22 16	22 20					22 36	22 46	22 50		22 46		23 01		23 04	23 01	23 21
	d			21 52		21 57	22 12		22 17	22 21				22 22		22 52	22 51		22 52		23 06		23 05	23 06	
Bognor Regis	a			21 59			22 18							22 29		→			22 59		→			23 12	
Chichester	a					22 04			22 24	22 28							22 58						23 12		
	d					22 05				22 29							22 59						23 13		
Fishbourne (Sussex)	d					22 08																	23 16		
Bosham	d					22 11																	23 19		
Nutbourne	d					22 14																	23 22		
Southbourne	d					22 17				22 36													23 25		
Emsworth	d					22 20				22 39													23 28		
Warblington	d					22 23																	23 31		
Havant	d					22 26				22 43							23 10						23 36		
Bedhampton	a																								
Hilsea	a																								
Fratton	a									22 52							23 18						23 48		
Portsmouth & Southsea	a									22 55							23 22						23 51		
Portsmouth Harbour ⛴	a									22 59							23 26								
Cosham	a					22 33																			
Portchester	a																								
Fareham	a					22 41																			
Swanwick	a					22 48																			
Eastleigh	a																								
Southampton Airport Parkway	a																								
Southampton Central ⛴	a					23 05																			

Table 188

Saturdays

London, Gatwick Airport, Brighton - Sussex Coast, Portsmouth and Southampton

Network Diagram - see first Page of Table 186

Station		SN	SN		SN ◇1	SN 1	SN	SN	SN ◇	SN ◇1	SN 1	SN 1	SN ◇1		SN	SN ◇1	SN 1	SN ◇1	SN 1	SN 1
London Victoria 15 ⊖	d				21 47	21 40				22 17	22 10	22 32				22 47	22 40	23 17	23 10	23 47
Clapham Junction 10	d				21 53	21 46				22 23	22 16	22 38				22 53	22 46	23 23	23 16	23 53
London Bridge 4 ⊖	d																			
East Croydon ⇌	d				22 03	21 58				22 33	22 28	22 48				23 03	22 58	23 33	23 28	00 06
Redhill 5	d					22 16					22 46	23 00					23 16		23 46	00 25
Horley	d					22 25					22 52						23 26		23 56	00 31
Gatwick Airport 10 ✈	d				22 20	22 29				22 50	22 56	23 09				23 20	23 29	23 50	23 59	00 34
Three Bridges 4	a					22 33				22 54	23 00	23 14					23 34	23 54	00 04	00 39
	d					22 36				22 54	23 01	23 15					23 38	23 55	00 04	00 39
Crawley	d					22 39					23 04	23 18					23 41		00 07	00 43
Horsham 4	a					22 52					23 16	23 26					23 53		00 19	00 55
	d											23 27								
Christs Hospital	d											23 30								
Billingshurst	d											23 36								
Pulborough	d											23 43								
Amberley	d											23 49								
Arundel	d											23 54								
Haywards Heath 3	d				22 37					23 03						23 37		00 05		
Burgess Hill	d									23 09								00 10		
Preston Park	d																			
Brighton 10	d	22 33	22 44				23 04	23 14							23 44					
Hove 2	a	22 36	22 48		22 51		23 07	23 18		23 21					23 48	23 51		00 23		
	d	22 37			22 52		23 08			23 22						23 52		00 23		
Aldrington	d	22 39					23 10													
Portslade	d	22 41			22 55		23 12			23 25						23 55		00s26		
Fishersgate	d	22 43					23 14													
Southwick	d	22 45					23 16			23 28						23 58		00s29		
Shoreham-by-Sea	d	22 49			23 00		23 19			23 31						00 01		00s32		
Lancing	d	22 53			23 04		23 23			23 35						00 05		00s36		
East Worthing	d	22 56					23 26													
Worthing 4	a	22 58			23 08		23 29			23 39						00 09		00s40		
	d	22 59			23 08		23 29			23 39										
West Worthing	d	23 01			23 10		23a31			23 41								00s43		
Durrington-on-Sea	d	23 03			23 13					23 44								00s45		
Goring-by-Sea	d	23 06			23 15					23 46								00s48		
Angmering 3	d	23 10			23 19					23 50								00s52		
Littlehampton 4	a	23 18			23 28															
	d	23 23																		
Ford 4	d	23 27								23 56		23 59						00s58		
Bognor Regis 4	d												←							
Barnham	a	23 31								00 01		00 04	00 01					01s02		
	d	23 32							23 36	00 09		00 05	00 09							
Bognor Regis	a								23 43	→			00 15							
Chichester 4	a	23 39										00 12						01 10		
	d																			
Fishbourne (Sussex)	d																			
Bosham	d																			
Nutbourne	d																			
Southbourne	d																			
Emsworth	d																			
Warblington	d																			
Havant	d																			
Bedhampton	a																			
Hilsea	a																			
Fratton	a																			
Portsmouth & Southsea	a																			
Portsmouth Harbour ⛴	a																			
Cosham	a																			
Portchester	a																			
Fareham	a																			
Swanwick	a																			
Eastleigh	a																			
Southampton Airport Parkway	a																			
Southampton Central ⛴	a																			

Table 188

Sundays
until 9 September

London, Gatwick Airport, Brighton - Sussex Coast, Portsmouth and Southampton

Network Diagram - see first Page of Table 186

Station		SN ◇1	SN 1	SN ◇1	SN ◇1	SN	SN	SN ◇1	SN 1	SN 1		SN ◇1	SN ◇1 A	SN 1	SN	SN 1	SN ◇1	SN 1	SN ◇1	SN 1		SN 1	SN ◇1	SN 1	SN 1
London Victoria 15 ⊖	d	22p17	22p32		22p47			23p17	23p10	23p47		00 05	00 40												
Clapham Junction 10	d	22p23	22p38		22p53			23p23	23p16	23p53		00 11	00 46												
London Bridge 4 ⊖	d																								
East Croydon ⇌	d	22p33	22p48		23p03			23p33	23p28	00 06		00 24	00 55												
Redhill 5	d		23p00						23p46	00 25															
Horley	d								23p56	00 31															
Gatwick Airport 10 ✈	d	22p50	23p09		23p20			23p50	23p59	00 34		00 43	01 13	06 29											
Three Bridges 4	a	22p54	23p14					23p54	00 04	00 39		00 48	01 17	06 33											
	d	22p54	23p15					23p55	00 04	00 39		00 48	01 17	06 40											
Crawley	d		23p18						00 07	00 43				06 43											
Horsham 4	a		23p26						00 19	00 55				06 56											
	d		23p27																						
Christs Hospital	d		23p30																						
Billingshurst	d		23p36																						
Pulborough	d		23p43																						
Amberley	d		23p49																						
Arundel	d		23p54																						
Haywards Heath 3	d	23p03			23p37			00 05				01 02	01 31												
Burgess Hill	d	23p09						00 10																	
Preston Park	d																								
Brighton 10	d					00 04	00 10					01s16	01s45									07 14			07 18
Hove 2	a	23p21			23p51	00 07	00 14	00 23				01s24	01s54									07 17			07 21
	d	23p22			23p52	00 08		00 23														07 18			07 22
Aldrington	d					00 10																			07 24
Portslade	d	23p25			23p55	00 12		00s26				01s27	01s58												07 26
Fishersgate	d					00 14																			07 28
Southwick	d	23p28			23p58	00 16		00s29				01s30	02s01												07 30
Shoreham-by-Sea	d	23p31			00 01	00 19		00s32				01s33	02s04									07 24			07 33
Lancing	d	23p35			00 05	00 23		00s36				01s37	02s08												07 37
East Worthing	d					00 26																			07 40
Worthing 4	a	23p39			00 09	00 29		00s40				01 41	02 12									07 30			07 43
	d	23p39				00 29																07 30			07 43
West Worthing	d	23p41				00a31		00s43																	07 45
Durrington-on-Sea	d	23p44						00s45																	07 48
Goring-by-Sea	d	23p46						00s48																	07 50
Angmering 3	d	23p50						00s52														07 37			07 54
Littlehampton 4	a																								
	d															06 42		07 19	07 29					07 54	
Ford 4	d	23p56	23p59					00s58								06 46		07 23				07 43		07 58	08 01
Bognor Regis 4	d			←													06 52			07 34			07 52		
Barnham	a	00 01	00 04	00 01				01s02								06 50	06 58	07 27	07 37	07 40		07 48	07 58	08 02	08 05
	d	00 09	00 05	00 09											06 45	06 51		07 28	07 37			07 48		08 09	08 06
Bognor Regis	a	→		00 15											06 51			07 34						→	
Chichester 4	a		00 12					01 10								06 58			07 45			07 56			08 13
	d															06 59			07 45			07 56			08 14
Fishbourne (Sussex)	d																								08 17
Bosham	d																								08 20
Nutbourne	d																								08 23
Southbourne	d																					08 03			08 26
Emsworth	d																		07 53			08 06			08 29
Warblington	d																								08 32
Havant	d															07 10			07 58			08 11			08 35
Bedhampton	a																								08 37
Hilsea	a																								
Fratton	a															07 18						08 19			08 45
Portsmouth & Southsea	a															07 22						08 23			08 48
Portsmouth Harbour ⛴	a															07 26						08 27			08 52
Cosham	a																		08 05						
Portchester	a																								
Fareham	a																		08 13						
Swanwick	a																		08 20						
Eastleigh	a																								
Southampton Airport Parkway	a																								
Southampton Central ⛴	a																		08 44						

A 29 July, 5 August, 12 August, 2 September, 9 September

Table 188

London, Gatwick Airport, Brighton - Sussex Coast, Portsmouth and Southampton

Sundays until 9 September

Network Diagram - see first Page of Table 186

		SN 1	SN ◇1	SN ◇1	SN 1	SN 1		SN 1	SN ◇1	SN 1	SN 1	SN 1	SN ◇1	SN ◇1	SN 1	SN ◇1 ⌶		SN 1	SN ◇1		SN 1	SN 1	SN 1	SN ◇1	SN ◇1
London Victoria 15 ⊖	d			07 02										08 02					08 17						09 02
Clapham Junction 10	d			07 08										08 08					08 23						09 08
London Bridge 4 ⊖	d				07 37																08 37				
East Croydon	d			07 20	07 55									08 18					08 33		08 55				09 18
Redhill 5	d			07 34	08 13									08 32							09 13				09 32
Horley	d			07 40	08 25									08 38							09 25				09 38
Gatwick Airport 10 ✈	d			07 43	08 29									08 41					08 49		09 29				09 41
Three Bridges 4	a			07 48	08 33									08 46							09 33				09 46
	d			07 48	08 34									08 46							09 34				09 46
Crawley	d			07 52	08 37									08 50							09 37				09 50
Horsham 4	a			08 04	08 49									08 58							09 49				09 58
	d			08 04										08 59											09 59
Christs Hospital	d													09 02											10 02
Billingshurst	d			08 13										09 09											10 09
Pulborough	d			08 19										09 15											10 15
Amberley	d													09 21											10 21
Arundel	d			08 29										09 27											10 27
Haywards Heath 3	d																		09 00						
Burgess Hill	d																		09 06						
Preston Park	d																								
Brighton 10	d		07 48					08 14			08 18		08 48									09 12		09 48	
Hove 2	a		07 51					08 17			08 21		08 51						09 18			09 15		09 51	
	d		07 52					08 18			08 22		08 52						09 19			09 22		09 52	
Aldrington	d		07 54								08 24		08 54									09 24		09 54	
Portslade	d		07 56								08 26		08 56									09 26		09 56	
Fishersgate	d		07 58								08 28		08 58									09 28		09 58	
Southwick	d		08 00								08 30		09 00									09 30		10 00	
Shoreham-by-Sea	d		08 03					08 24			08 33		09 03						09 25			09 33		10 03	
Lancing	d		08 07								08 37		09 07									09 37		10 07	
East Worthing	d		08 10								08 40		09 10									09 40		10 10	
Worthing 4	a		08 13					08 30			08 43		09 13						09 31			09 43		10 13	
	d		08 13					08 30			08 43		09 13						09 35	09 37		09 43		10 13	
West Worthing	d		08 15								08 45		09 15							09 39		09 45		10 15	
Durrington-on-Sea	d		08 18								08 48		09 18							09 41		09 48		10 18	
Goring-by-Sea	d		08 20								08 50		09 20							09 44		09 50		10 20	
Angmering 3	d		08 24					08 37			08 54		09 24							09 48		09 54		10 24	
Littlehampton 4	a																			09 57					
	d									08 54								09 54							
Ford 4	d		08 31	08 35				08 43		08 58	09 01		09 31	09 35				09 58				10 01		10 31	10 35
Bognor Regis 4	d	←				08 34			08 52			←			09 34	09 52							←		
Barnham	a	08 02	08 35	08 39		08 40		08 48	08 58	09 02	09 05	09 02	09 35	09 39	09 40	09 58		10 02	09 51			10 05	10 02	10 35	10 39
	d	08 09	08 36	08 40				08 48		09 09	09 06	09 09	09 36	09 40				10 09	09 52			10 06	10 09	10 36	10 40
Bognor Regis	a	08 15		08 46						→		09 15		09 46				→					10 15		10 46
Chichester 4	a		08 43					08 56			09 13		09 43						09 59			10 13		10 43	
	d		08 44					08 56			09 14		09 44						10 00			10 14		10 44	
Fishbourne (Sussex)	d										09 17											10 17			
Bosham	d										09 20											10 20			
Nutbourne	d										09 23											10 23			
Southbourne	d							09 03			09 26								10 07			10 26			
Emsworth	d		08 52					09 06			09 29		09 52						10 10			10 29		10 52	
Warblington	d										09 32											10 32			
Havant	d		08 58					09 11			09 35		09 58						10 14			10 35		10 58	
Bedhampton	a										09 37											10 37			
Hilsea	a																								
Fratton	a							09 19			09 45								10 23			10 45			
Portsmouth & Southsea	a							09 23			09 48								10 26			10 50			
Portsmouth Harbour ⛴	a							09 27			09 52								10 30			10 54			
Cosham	a		09 05										10 06											11 06	
Portchester	a																								
Fareham	a		09 13										10 14											11 14	
Swanwick	a		09 20										10 21											11 21	
Eastleigh	a																								
Southampton Airport Parkway	a																								
Southampton Central ⛴	a		09 44										10 44											11 45	

Table 188

London, Gatwick Airport, Brighton - Sussex Coast, Portsmouth and Southampton

Sundays until 9 September

Network Diagram - see first Page of Table 186

		SN 1		SN ◇1 ⌶	SN 1	SN ◇1		SN 1	SN 1	SN 1	SN ◇1	SN ◇1		SN 1	GW ◇	SN ◇1 ⌶	SN 1	SN ◇1		SN 1	SN 1	SN 1		SN ◇1	SN ◇1 ⌶
London Victoria 15 ⊖	d					09 17						10 02						10 17							11 02
Clapham Junction 10	d					09 23						10 08						10 23							11 08
London Bridge 4 ⊖	d							09 37												10 37					
East Croydon	d					09 33		09 55				10 18						10 33		10 55					11 18
Redhill 5	d							10 13				10 32								11 13					11 32
Horley	d							10 25				10 38								11 25					11 38
Gatwick Airport 10 ✈	d					09 49		10 29				10 41						10 49		11 29					11 41
Three Bridges 4	a							10 33				10 46								11 33					11 46
	d							10 34				10 46								11 34					11 46
Crawley	d							10 37				10 50								11 37					11 50
Horsham 4	a							10 49				10 58								11 49					11 58
	d											10 59													11 59
Christs Hospital	d											11 02													12 02
Billingshurst	d											11 09													12 09
Pulborough	d											11 15													12 15
Amberley	d											11 21													12 21
Arundel	d											11 27													12 27
Haywards Heath 3	d					10 00												11 00							
Burgess Hill	d					10 06												11 06							
Preston Park	d																								
Brighton 10	d								10 13		10 48				11 10						11 13			11 48	
Hove 2	a					10 18			10 16		10 51				11 13			11 18			11 16			11 51	
	d					10 19			10 22		10 52				11 14			11 19			11 22			11 52	
Aldrington	d								10 24		10 54										11 24			11 54	
Portslade	d								10 26		10 56										11 26			11 56	
Fishersgate	d								10 28		10 58										11 28			11 58	
Southwick	d								10 30		11 00										11 30			12 00	
Shoreham-by-Sea	d					10 25			10 33		11 03				11 20			11 25			11 33			12 03	
Lancing	d								10 37		11 07										11 37			12 07	
East Worthing	d								10 40		11 10										11 40			12 10	
Worthing 4	a					10 31			10 43		11 13				11 26			11 31			11 43			12 13	
	d					10 35	10 37		10 43		11 13				11 29			11 35	11 37		11 43			12 13	
West Worthing	d						10 39		10 45		11 15								11 39		11 45			12 15	
Durrington-on-Sea	d						10 41		10 48		11 18								11 41		11 48			12 18	
Goring-by-Sea	d						10 44		10 50		11 20								11 44		11 50			12 20	
Angmering 3	d						10 48		10 54		11 24								11 48		11 54			12 24	
Littlehampton 4	a						10 57												11 57						
	d				10 54												11 54								
Ford 4	d				10 58				11 01		11 31	11 35					11 58				12 01			12 31	12 35
Bognor Regis 4	d	10 34		10 52						←				11 34		11 52						←			
Barnham	a	10 40		10 58	11 02	10 51			11 05	11 02	11 35	11 39		11 40	11 45	11 58	12 02	11 51			12 05	12 02		12 35	12 39
	d				11 09	10 52			11 06	11 09	11 36	11 40			11 46		12 09	11 52			12 06	12 09		12 36	12 40
Bognor Regis	a				→					11 15		11 46					→					12 15			12 46
Chichester 4	a					10 59			11 13		11 43				11 53			11 59			12 13			12 43	
	d					11 00			11 14		11 44				11 54			12 00			12 14			12 44	
Fishbourne (Sussex)	d								11 17												12 17				
Bosham	d								11 20												12 20				
Nutbourne	d								11 23												12 23				
Southbourne	d					11 07			11 26									12 07			12 26				
Emsworth	d					11 10			11 29		11 52							12 10			12 29			12 52	
Warblington	d								11 32												12 32				
Havant	d					11 14			11 35		11 58				12 10			12 14			12 35			12 58	
Bedhampton	a								11 37												12 37				
Hilsea	a																								
Fratton	a					11 23			11 45									12 23			12 46				
Portsmouth & Southsea	a					11 26			11 49									12 26			12 57				
Portsmouth Harbour ⛴	a					11 30			11 53									12 30			13 01				
Cosham	a										12 05				12 16									13 05	
Portchester	a																								
Fareham	a										12 13				12 31									13 13	
Swanwick	a										12 20													13 20	
Eastleigh	a																								
Southampton Airport Parkway	a																								
Southampton Central ⛴	a										12 44				12 53									13 44	

Table 188

Sundays until 9 September

London, Gatwick Airport, Brighton - Sussex Coast, Portsmouth and Southampton

Network Diagram - see first Page of Table 186

		SN ■	SN ◇■ ✠	SN ■	SN ◇■		SN ■	SN ■	SN ■	SN ◇■	SN ◇■	SN ■	SN ◇■ ✠	SN ■	SN ◇■		SN ■	SN ■	SN ■	SN ◇■	SN ◇■	SN ■	SN ◇■ ✠
London Victoria ⊖	d				11 17						12 02				12 17						13 02		
Clapham Junction	d				11 23						12 08				12 23						13 08		
London Bridge ⊖	d						11 37										12 37						
East Croydon	d				11 33		11 55				12 18				12 33		12 55				13 18		
Redhill	d						12 13				12 32						13 13				13 32		
Horley	d						12 25				12 38						13 25				13 38		
Gatwick Airport ✈	d				11 49		12 29				12 41				12 49		13 29				13 41		
Three Bridges	a						12 33				12 46						13 33				13 46		
	d						12 34				12 46						13 34				13 46		
Crawley	d						12 37				12 50						13 37				13 50		
Horsham	a						12 49				12 58						13 49				13 58		
	d										12 59										13 59		
Christs Hospital	d										13 02										14 02		
Billingshurst	d										13 09										14 09		
Pulborough	d										13 15										14 15		
Amberley	d										13 21										14 21		
Arundel	d										13 27										14 27		
Haywards Heath	d				12 00										13 00								
Burgess Hill	d				12 06										13 06								
Preston Park	d																						
Brighton	d							12 12		12 48								13 12		13 48			
Hove	a				12 18			12 15		12 51					13 18			13 15		13 51			
	d				12 19			12 22		12 52					13 19			13 22		13 52			
Aldrington	d							12 24		12 54								13 24		13 54			
Portslade	d							12 26		12 56								13 26		13 56			
Fishersgate	d							12 28		12 58								13 28		13 58			
Southwick	d							12 30		13 00								13 30		14 00			
Shoreham-by-Sea	d				12 25			12 33		13 03					13 25			13 33		14 03			
Lancing	d							12 37		13 07								13 37		14 07			
East Worthing	d							12 40		13 10								13 40		14 10			
Worthing	a				12 31			12 43		13 13					13 31			13 43		14 13			
	d				12 35	12 37		12 43		13 13					13 35	13 37		13 43		14 13			
West Worthing	d					12 39		12 45		13 15						13 39		13 45		14 15			
Durrington-on-Sea	d					12 41		12 48		13 18						13 41		13 48		14 18			
Goring-by-Sea	d					12 44		12 50		13 20						13 44		13 50		14 20			
Angmering	d					12 48		12 54		13 24						13 48		13 54		14 24			
Littlehampton	a					12 57										13 57							
	d			12 54										13 54									
Ford	d			12 58				13 01		13 31	13 35			13 58				14 01		14 31	14 36		
Bognor Regis	d	12 34	12 52						←			13 34	13 52						←			14 34	14 52
Barnham	a	12 40	12 58	13 02	12 51			13 05	13 02	13 35	13 39	13 40	13 58	14 02	13 51			14 05	14 02	14 35	14 40	14 40	14 58
	d			13 09	12 52			13 06	13 09	13 36	13 40			14 09	13 52			14 06	14 09	14 36	14 41		
Bognor Regis	a			→					13 15		13 46			→					14 15		14 47		
Chichester	a				12 59			13 13		13 43					13 59			14 13		14 43			
	d				13 00			13 14		13 44					14 00			14 14		14 44			
Fishbourne (Sussex)	d							13 17										14 17					
Bosham	d							13 20										14 20					
Nutbourne	d							13 23										14 23					
Southbourne	d				13 07			13 26							14 07			14 26					
Emsworth	d				13 10			13 29		13 52					14 10			14 29		14 52			
Warblington	d							13 32										14 32					
Havant	d				13 14			13 35		13 58					14 14			14 35		14 58			
Bedhampton	a							13 37										14 37					
Hilsea	a																						
Fratton	a				13 23			13 45							14 23			14 45					
Portsmouth & Southsea	a				13 26			13 48							14 26			14 48					
Portsmouth Harbour ⛴	a				13 30			13 52							14 30			14 53					
Cosham	a									14 05										15 05			
Portchester	a																						
Fareham	a									14 13										15 13			
Swanwick	a									14 20										15 20			
Eastleigh	a																						
Southampton Airport Parkway	a																						
Southampton Central ⛴	a									14 44										15 44			

Table 188

Sundays until 9 September

London, Gatwick Airport, Brighton - Sussex Coast, Portsmouth and Southampton

Network Diagram - see first Page of Table 186

		SN ■	SN ◇■		SN ■	SN ■	SN ■	SN ◇■	SN ◇■	SN ■	SN ◇■ ✠	SN ■	SN ◇■		SN ■	SN ■	SN ■	GW ◇	SN ◇■	SN ◇■	SN ■	SN ◇■ ✠	SN ■
London Victoria ⊖	d		13 17						14 02				14 17							15 02			
Clapham Junction	d		13 23						14 08				14 23							15 08			
London Bridge ⊖	d				13 37										14 37								
East Croydon	d		13 33		13 55				14 18				14 33		14 55					15 18			
Redhill	d				14 13				14 32						15 13					15 32			
Horley	d				14 25				14 38						15 25					15 38			
Gatwick Airport ✈	d		13 49		14 29				14 41				14 49		15 29					15 41			
Three Bridges	a				14 33				14 46						15 33					15 46			
	d				14 34				14 46						15 34					15 46			
Crawley	d				14 37				14 50						15 37					15 50			
Horsham	a				14 49				14 58						15 49					15 58			
	d								14 59											15 59			
Christs Hospital	d								15 02											16 02			
Billingshurst	d								15 09											16 09			
Pulborough	d								15 15											16 15			
Amberley	d								15 21											16 21			
Arundel	d								15 27											16 27			
Haywards Heath	d		14 00										15 00										
Burgess Hill	d		14 06										15 06										
Preston Park	d																						
Brighton	d					14 12		14 48								15 13		15 46	15 50				
Hove	a		14 18			14 15		14 51					15 18			15 16		15 49	15 53				
	d		14 19			14 22		14 52					15 19			15 22		15 50	15 54				
Aldrington	d					14 24		14 54								15 24			15 56				
Portslade	d					14 26		14 56								15 26			15 58				
Fishersgate	d					14 28		14 58								15 28			16 00				
Southwick	d					14 30		15 00								15 30			16 02				
Shoreham-by-Sea	d		14 25			14 33		15 03					15 25			15 33		15 56	16 05				
Lancing	d					14 37		15 07								15 37			16 09				
East Worthing	d					14 40		15 10								15 40			16 12				
Worthing	a		14 31			14 43		15 13					15 31			15 43		16 03	16 15				
	d		14 35	14 37		14 43		15 13					15 35	15 37		15 43		16 08	16 15				
West Worthing	d			14 39		14 45		15 15						15 39		15 45			16 17				
Durrington-on-Sea	d			14 41		14 48		15 18						15 41		15 48			16 20				
Goring-by-Sea	d			14 44		14 50		15 20						15 44		15 50			16 22				
Angmering	d			14 48		14 54		15 24						15 48		15 54			16 26				
Littlehampton	a			14 57										15 57									
	d	14 54										15 54											16 54
Ford	d	14 58				15 01		15 31	15 35			15 58				16 01			16 32	16 36			16 58
Bognor Regis	d						←			15 34	15 52						←				16 34	16 52	
Barnham	a	15 02	14 51			15 05	15 02	15 35	15 39	15 40	15 58	16 02	15 51			16 05	16 02	16 25	16 37	16 40	16 40	16 58	17 02
	d	15 09	14 52			15 06	15 09	15 36	15 40			16 09	15 52			16 06	16 09	16 25	16 37	16 41			17 09
Bognor Regis	a	→					15 15		15 46			→					16 15			16 47			→
Chichester	a		14 59			15 13		15 43					15 59			16 13		16 33	16 45				
	d		15 00			15 14		15 44					16 00			16 14		16 34	16 45				
Fishbourne (Sussex)	d					15 17										16 17							
Bosham	d					15 20										16 20							
Nutbourne	d					15 23										16 23							
Southbourne	d		15 07			15 26							16 07			16 26							
Emsworth	d		15 10			15 29		15 52					16 10			16 29			16 53				
Warblington	d					15 32										16 32							
Havant	d		15 14			15 35		15 56					16 14			16 35		16 48	16 59				
Bedhampton	a					15 37										16 37							
Hilsea	a																						
Fratton	a		15 23			15 45							16 23			16 46							
Portsmouth & Southsea	a		15 26			15 48							16 26			16 57							
Portsmouth Harbour ⛴	a		15 30			15 52							16 30			17 01							
Cosham	a							16 04										16 54	17 06				
Portchester	a																						
Fareham	a							16 12										17 02	17 15				
Swanwick	a							16 19											17 23				
Eastleigh	a																						
Southampton Airport Parkway	a																						
Southampton Central ⛴	a							16 44										17 24	17 49				

Table 188

Sundays until 9 September

London, Gatwick Airport, Brighton - Sussex Coast, Portsmouth and Southampton

Network Diagram - see first Page of Table 186

		SN ◇1		SN 1	SN 1	SN 1	SN ◇1	SN ◇1	SN 1	SN ◇1	SN 1	SN ◇1		SN 1	SN 1	SN 1	GW ◇	SN ◇1	SN ◇1	SN 1	SN ◇1	SN 1
London Victoria 15 ⊖	d	15 17						16 02				16 17							17 02			
Clapham Junction 10	d	15 23						16 08				16 23							17 08			
London Bridge 4 ⊖	d			15 37										16 37								
East Croydon	d	15 32		15 55				16 18				16 33		16 55					17 18			
Redhill 5	d			16 13				16 32						17 13					17 32			
Horley	d			16 25				16 38						17 25					17 38			
Gatwick Airport 10 ✈	d	15 49		16 29				16 41				16 49		17 29					17 41			
Three Bridges 4	a			16 33				16 46						17 33					17 46			
	d			16 34				16 46						17 34					17 46			
Crawley	d			16 37				16 50						17 37					17 50			
Horsham 4	a			16 49				16 58						17 49					17 58			
	d							16 59											17 59			
Christs Hospital	d							17 02											18 02			
Billingshurst	d							17 09											18 09			
Pulborough	d							17 15											18 15			
Amberley	d							17 21											18 21			
Arundel	d							17 27											18 27			
Haywards Heath 3	d	16 00										17 00										
Burgess Hill	d	16 06										17 06										
Preston Park	d																					
Brighton 10	d				16 12		16 48								17 13		17 46	17 50				
Hove 2	a	16 18			16 15		16 51					17 18			17 16		17 49	17 53				
	d	16 19			16 22		16 52					17 19			17 22		17 50	17 54				
Aldrington	d				16 24		16 54								17 24			17 56				
Portslade	d				16 26		16 56								17 26			17 58				
Fishersgate	d				16 28		16 58								17 28			18 00				
Southwick	d				16 30		17 00								17 30			18 02				
Shoreham-by-Sea	d	16 25			16 33		17 03					17 25			17 33		17 56	18 05				
Lancing	d				16 37		17 07								17 37			18 09				
East Worthing	d				16 40		17 10								17 40			18 12				
Worthing 4	a	16 31			16 43		17 13					17 31			17 43		18 03	18 15				
	d	16 35	16 37		16 43		17 13					17 35	17 37		17 43		18 08	18 15				
West Worthing	d		16 39		16 45		17 15						17 39		17 45			18 17				
Durrington-on-Sea	d		16 41		16 48		17 18						17 41		17 48			18 20				
Goring-by-Sea	d		16 44		16 50		17 20						17 44		17 50			18 22				
Angmering 3	d		16 48		16 54		17 24						17 48		17 54			18 26				
Littlehampton 4	a		16 57										17 57									
	d										17 54											18 54
Ford 4	d				17 01		17 31	17 35			17 58				18 01			18 32	18 36			18 58
Bognor Regis 4	d					←			17 34	17 52						←				18 34	18 52	
Barnham	a	16 51			17 05	17 02	17 35	17 39	17 40	17 58	18 02	17 51			18 05	18 02	18 25	18 37	18 40	18 40	18 58	19 02
	d	16 52			17 06	17 09	17 36	17 40			18 09	17 52			18 06	18 09	18 25	18 37	18 41			19 09
Bognor Regis	a					17 15		17 46			→					18 15			18 47			→
Chichester 4	a	16 59			17 13		17 43					17 59			18 13		18 33	18 45				
	d	17 00			17 14		17 44					18 00			18 14		18 34	18 45				
Fishbourne (Sussex)	d				17 17										18 17							
Bosham	d				17 20										18 20							
Nutbourne	d				17 23										18 23							
Southbourne	d	17 07			17 26							18 07			18 26							
Emsworth	d	17 10			17 29		17 52					18 10			18 29			18 53				
Warblington	d				17 32										18 32							
Havant	d	17 14			17 35		17 58					18 14			18 35		18 48	18 58				
Bedhampton	a				17 37										18 37							
Hilsea	a																					
Fratton	a	17 23			17 46							18 23			18 46							
Portsmouth & Southsea	a	17 26			17 57							18 26			18 57							
Portsmouth Harbour ⛴	a	17 30			18 01							18 30			19 01							
Cosham	a						18 05										18 54	19 05				
Portchester	a																					
Fareham	a						18 13										19 02	19 13				
Swanwick	a						18 20											19 22				
Eastleigh	a																					
Southampton Airport Parkway	a																					
Southampton Central ⛴	a						18 42										19 24	19 48				

Table 188

Sundays until 9 September

London, Gatwick Airport, Brighton - Sussex Coast, Portsmouth and Southampton

Network Diagram - see first Page of Table 186

		SN ◇1		SN 1	SN 1	SN 1	SN ◇1	SN ◇1	SN 1	SN ◇1	SN 1	SN ◇1		SN 1	SN 1	SN 1	SN ◇1	SN ◇1	SN 1	SN ◇1	SN 1	SN ◇1	
London Victoria 15 ⊖	d	17 17						18 02				18 17						19 02				19 17	
Clapham Junction 10	d	17 23						18 08				18 23						19 08				19 23	
London Bridge 4 ⊖	d			17 37										18 37									
East Croydon	d	17 33		17 55				18 18				18 33		18 55				19 18				19 33	
Redhill 5	d			18 13				18 32						19 13				19 32					
Horley	d			18 25				18 38						19 25				19 38					
Gatwick Airport 10 ✈	d	17 49		18 29				18 41				18 49		19 29				19 41				19 49	
Three Bridges 4	a			18 33				18 46						19 33				19 46					
	d			18 34				18 46						19 34				19 46					
Crawley	d			18 37				18 50						19 37				19 50					
Horsham 4	a			18 49				18 58						19 49				19 58					
	d							18 59										19 59					
Christs Hospital	d							19 02										20 02					
Billingshurst	d							19 09										20 09					
Pulborough	d							19 15										20 15					
Amberley	d							19 21										20 21					
Arundel	d							19 27										20 27					
Haywards Heath 3	d	18 00										19 00										20 00	
Burgess Hill	d	18 06										19 06										20 06	
Preston Park	d																						
Brighton 10	d				18 12		18 48								19 12		19 48						
Hove 2	a	18 18			18 15		18 51					19 18			19 15		19 51					20 18	
	d	18 19			18 22		18 52					19 19			19 22		19 52					20 19	
Aldrington	d				18 24		18 54								19 24		19 54						
Portslade	d				18 26		18 56								19 26		19 56						
Fishersgate	d				18 28		18 58								19 28		19 58						
Southwick	d				18 30		19 00								19 30		20 00						
Shoreham-by-Sea	d	18 25			18 33		19 03					19 25			19 33		20 03					20 25	
Lancing	d				18 37		19 07								19 37		20 07						
East Worthing	d				18 40		19 10								19 40		20 10						
Worthing 4	a	18 31			18 43		19 13					19 31			19 43		20 13					20 31	
	d	18 35	18 37		18 43		19 13					19 35	19 37		19 43		20 13					20 35	20 37
West Worthing	d		18 39		18 45		19 15						19 39		19 45		20 15						20 39
Durrington-on-Sea	d		18 41		18 48		19 18						19 41		19 48		20 18						20 41
Goring-by-Sea	d		18 44		18 50		19 20						19 44		19 50		20 20						20 44
Angmering 3	d		18 48		18 54		19 24						19 48		19 54		20 24						20 48
Littlehampton 4	a		18 57										19 57										20 57
	d										19 54										20 55		
Ford 4	d				19 01		19 31	19 35			19 58				20 01		20 31	20 35			20 59		
Bognor Regis 4	d					←			19 34	19 52						←			20 34	20 52			
Barnham	a	18 51			19 05	19 02	19 35	19 39	19 40	19 58	20 02	19 51			20 05	20 02	20 35	20 39	20 41	20 58	21 03	20 52	
	d	18 52			19 06	19 09	19 36	19 40			20 09	19 52			20 06	20 09	20 36	20 40			21 10	20 53	
Bognor Regis	a					19 15		19 46			→					20 15		20 46			→		
Chichester 4	a	18 59			19 13		19 43					19 59			20 13		20 43					21 00	
	d	19 00			19 14		19 44					20 00			20 14		20 44					21 01	
Fishbourne (Sussex)	d				19 17										20 17								
Bosham	d				19 20										20 20								
Nutbourne	d				19 23										20 23								
Southbourne	d	19 07			19 26							20 07			20 26							21 08	
Emsworth	d	19 10			19 29		19 52					20 10			20 29		20 52					21 11	
Warblington	d				19 32										20 32								
Havant	d	19 14			19 35		19 58					20 14			20 35		20 58					21 15	
Bedhampton	a				19 37										20 37								
Hilsea	a																						
Fratton	a	19 23			19 46							20 23			20 45							21 24	
Portsmouth & Southsea	a	19 26			19 57							20 26			20 48							21 27	
Portsmouth Harbour ⛴	a	19 30			20 01							20 30			20 52							21 31	
Cosham	a						20 05										21 07						
Portchester	a																						
Fareham	a						20 13										21 15						
Swanwick	a						20 20										21 22						
Eastleigh	a																						
Southampton Airport Parkway	a																						
Southampton Central ⛴	a						20 46										21 45						

Sundays
until 9 September

London, Gatwick Airport, Brighton - Sussex Coast, Portsmouth and Southampton

Network Diagram - see first Page of Table 186

		SN ■	SN ■		SN ■	SN ◇■	SN ◇■	SN ■	SN ◇■	SN ■	SN ◇■		SN ■		SN ■	SN ■	GW	SN ■	SN	SN	SN ◇■	SN ◇■			SN ■
London Victoria	d						20 02				20 17										21 02	21 17			
Clapham Junction	d						20 08				20 23										21 08	21 23			
London Bridge	d	19 37											20 37												21 37
East Croydon	d	19 55					20 18				20 33		20 55								21 18	21 33			21 55
Redhill	d	20 13					20 32						21 13								21 32				22 13
Horley	d	20 25					20 38						21 25								21 38				22 25
Gatwick Airport	d	20 29					20 41				20 49		21 29								21 41	21 49			22 29
Three Bridges	a	20 33					20 46						21 33								21 46				22 33
	d	20 34					20 46						21 34								21 46				22 34
Crawley	d	20 37					20 50						21 37								21 50				22 37
Horsham	a	20 49					20 58						21 49								21 58				22 49
	d						20 59														21 59				
Christs Hospital	d						21 02														22 02				
Billingshurst	d						21 09														22 09				
Pulborough	d						21 15														22 15				
Amberley	d						21 21														22 21				
Arundel	d						21 27														22 27				
Haywards Heath	d										21 00											22 00			
Burgess Hill	d										21 06											22 06			
Preston Park	d																								
Brighton	d		20 12			20 48									21 12		21 46	21 50	22 12						
Hove	a		20 15			20 51					21 18				21 15		21 49	21 53	22 15			22 18			
	d		20 22			20 52					21 19				21 22		21 50	21 54				22 19			
Aldrington	d		20 24			20 54									21 24			21 56							
Portslade	d		20 26			20 56									21 26			21 58							
Fishersgate	d		20 28			20 58									21 28			22 00							
Southwick	d		20 30			21 00									21 30			22 02							
Shoreham-by-Sea	d		20 33			21 03					21 25				21 33		21 56	22 05				22 25			
Lancing	d		20 37			21 07									21 37			22 09							
East Worthing	d		20 40			21 10									21 40			22 12							
Worthing	a		20 43			21 13					21 31				21 43		22 02	22 15				22 31			
	d		20 43			21 13					21 35	21 37			21 43		22 03	22 15				22 35	22 37		
West Worthing	d		20 45			21 15						21 39			21 45			22 17					22 39		
Durrington-on-Sea	d		20 48			21 18						21 41			21 48			22 20					22 41		
Goring-by-Sea	d		20 50			21 20						21 44			21 50			22 22					22 44		
Angmering	d		20 54			21 24						21 48			21 54			22 26					22 48		
Littlehampton	a											21 57						22 36					22 57		
	d									21 54															
Ford	d		21 01			21 31	21 35			21 58					22 01						22 32				
Bognor Regis	d				←			21 34	21 52							←				22 12					
Barnham	a		21 06		21 03	21 35	21 39	21 40	21 58	22 02	21 51				22 05	22 02	22 17			22 18	22 36	22 49			
	d		21 06		21 10	21 36	21 40			22 09	21 52				22 06	22 09	22 18				22 37	22 56			
Bognor Regis	a				21 16		21 46			→						22 15					22 43				
Chichester	a		21 14			21 43					21 59				22 13		22 25					23 03			
	d		21 14			21 44					22 00				22 14		22 26					23 04			
Fishbourne (Sussex)	d		21 17												22 17										
Bosham	d		21 20												22 20							23 08			
Nutbourne	d		21 24												22 23							23 12			
Southbourne	d		21 26								22 07				22 26							23 14			
Emsworth	d		21 29			21 52					22 10				22 29							23 17			
Warblington	d		21 32												22 32										
Havant	d		21 35			21 58					22 14				22 35		22 47					23 22			
Bedhampton	a		21 38												22 37										
Hilsea	a																								
Fratton	a		21 45								22 23				22 45		22 57					23 32			
Portsmouth & Southsea	a		21 49								22 26				22 48		23 00					23 35			
Portsmouth Harbour	a		21 53								22 30				22 52		23 04					23 39			
Cosham	a					22 05																			
Portchester	a																								
Fareham	a					22 13																			
Swanwick	a					22 20																			
Eastleigh	a																								
Southampton Airport Parkway	a																								
Southampton Central	a					22 44																			

Sundays
until 9 September

London, Gatwick Airport, Brighton - Sussex Coast, Portsmouth and Southampton

Network Diagram - see first Page of Table 186

		SN	SN ■	SN ◇■	SN ■	SN	SN ◇■	SN ■	SN ■		SN ◇■
London Victoria	d			22 02			22 17		23 04		23 17
Clapham Junction	d			22 08			22 23		23 10		23 23
London Bridge	d							22 37			
East Croydon	d			22 18			22 33	22 55	23 22		23 38
Redhill	d			22 32				23 13	23 42		
Horley	d			22 38				23 25	23 50		
Gatwick Airport	d			22 41			22 49	23 29	23 55		00 01
Three Bridges	a			22 46				23 33	00 01		00 05
	d			22 46				23 34	00 01		00 06
Crawley	d			22 50				23 37	00 05		
Horsham	a			22 58				23 49	00 17		
	d			22 59							
Christs Hospital	d			23 02							
Billingshurst	d			23 09							
Pulborough	d			23 15							
Amberley	d			23 21							
Arundel	d			23 27							
Haywards Heath	d						23 00				00 15
Burgess Hill	d						23 06				00 20
Preston Park	d										
Brighton	d				22 40	23 15					
Hove	a				22 43	23 18	23 21				00 31
	d				22 44		23 25				00 31
Aldrington	d				22 46						
Portslade	d				22 48		23 28				00s34
Fishersgate	d				22 50						
Southwick	d				22 52		23 31				00s37
Shoreham-by-Sea	d				22 55		23 34				00s40
Lancing	d				22 59		23 38				00s44
East Worthing	d				23 02						
Worthing	a				23 05		23 42				00 48
	d				23 05						
West Worthing	d				23 07						
Durrington-on-Sea	d				23 09						
Goring-by-Sea	d				23 12						
Angmering	d				23 16						
Littlehampton	a				23 24						
	d		23 06		23 29						
Ford	d		23 10	23 32	23 36						
Bognor Regis	d										
Barnham	a		23 14	23 36	23 40						
	d	22 52	23 15	23 42	23 45						
Bognor Regis	a	22 59	23 21	23 48							
Chichester	a				23 52						
	d										
Fishbourne (Sussex)	d										
Bosham	d										
Nutbourne	d										
Southbourne	d										
Emsworth	d										
Warblington	d										
Havant	d										
Bedhampton	a										
Hilsea	a										
Fratton	a										
Portsmouth & Southsea	a										
Portsmouth Harbour	a										
Cosham	a										
Portchester	a										
Fareham	a										
Swanwick	a										
Eastleigh	a										
Southampton Airport Parkway	a										
Southampton Central	a										

London, Gatwick Airport, Brighton - Sussex Coast, Portsmouth and Southampton

Sundays from 16 September

Network Diagram - see first Page of Table 186

		SN ◇■	SN ■	SN ◇■	SN ◇■	SN	SN	SN ◇■	SN ■	SN ■		SN ◇■	SN ■	SN	SN ■	SN ◇■	SN ■	SN ◇■	SN ■	SN ■		SN ◇■ ⌶	SN ■	SN ■	SN ■
London Victoria ■ ⊖	d	22p17	22p32		22p47			23p17	23p10	23p47		00 05													
Clapham Junction ■	d	22p23	22p38		22p53			23p23	23p16	23p53		00 11													
London Bridge ■ ⊖	d																								
East Croydon ⇌	d	22p33	22p48		23p03			23p33	23p28	00 06		00 24													
Redhill ■	d		23p00						23p46	00 25															
Horley	d								23p56	00 31															
Gatwick Airport ■ ✈	d	22p50	23p09		23p20			23p50	23p59	00 34		00 43	06 29												
Three Bridges ■	a	22p54	23p14					23p54	00 04	00 39		00 48	06 33												
	d	22p54	23p15					23p55	00 04	00 39		00 48	06 40												
Crawley	d		23p18						00 07	00 43			06 43												
Horsham ■	a		23p26						00 19	00 55			06 56												
	d		23p27																						
Christs Hospital	d		23p30																						
Billingshurst	d		23p36																						
Pulborough	d		23p43																						
Amberley	d		23p49																						
Arundel	d		23p54																						
Haywards Heath ■	d	23p03			23p37			00 05				01 02													
Burgess Hill	d	23p09						00 10																	
Preston Park	d																								
Brighton ■	d					00 04	00 10					01s16								07 14				07 22	
Hove ■	a	23p21			23p51	00 07	00 14	00 23				01s24								07 17				07 25	
	d	23p22			23p52	00 08		00 23												07 18				07 26	
Aldrington	d					00 10																		07 28	
Portslade	d	23p25			23p55	00 12		00s26				01s27												07 30	
Fishersgate	d					00 14																		07 32	
Southwick	d	23p28			23p58	00 16		00s29				01s30												07 34	
Shoreham-by-Sea	d	23p31			00 01	00 19		00s32				01s33								07 24				07 37	
Lancing	d	23p35			00 05	00 23		00s36				01s37												07 41	
East Worthing	d					00 26																		07 44	
Worthing ■	a	23p39			00 09	00 29		00s40				01 41								07 30				07 47	
	d	23p39				00 29														07 30				07 47	
West Worthing	d	23p41				00a31		00s43																07 49	
Durrington-on-Sea	d	23p44						00s45																07 51	
Goring-by-Sea	d	23p46						00s48																07 54	
Angmering ■	d	23p50						00s52												07 37				07 58	
Littlehampton ■	a																							08 06	
	d														06 42		07 19	07 29					07 57	08 11	
Ford ■	d	23p56	23p59					00s58							06 46		07 23			07 43			08 01	08 15	
Bognor Regis ■	d			←												06 58			07 34			07 58			←
Barnham	a	00 01	00 04	00 01				01s02							06 50	07 04	07 27	07 37	07 40	07 48		08 04	08 08	08 19	08 08
	d	00 09	00 05	00 09										06 45	06 51		07 28	07 37		07 48			08 26	08 20	08 26
Bognor Regis	a	→		00 15										06 51			07 34						→		08 32
Chichester ■	a		00 12					01 10							06 58			07 45		07 56				08 27	
	d														06 59			07 45		07 56				08 28	
Fishbourne (Sussex)	d																							08 31	
Bosham	d																							08 34	
Nutbourne	d																							08 37	
Southbourne	d																			08 03				08 40	
Emsworth	d																	07 53		08 06				08 43	
Warblington	d																							08 46	
Havant	d														07 10			07 58		08 11				08 49	
Bedhampton	a																							08 51	
Hilsea	a																								
Fratton	a														07 18					08 19				08 59	
Portsmouth & Southsea	a														07 22					08 23				09 03	
Portsmouth Harbour ⛴	a														07 26					08 27				09 07	
Cosham	a																	08 05							
Portchester	a																								
Fareham	a																	08 13							
Swanwick	a																	08 20							
Eastleigh	a																								
Southampton Airport Parkway	a																								
Southampton Central ⛴	a																	08 44							

Table 188

London, Gatwick Airport, Brighton - Sussex Coast, Portsmouth and Southampton

Sundays from 16 September

Network Diagram - see first Page of Table 186

		SN ◇■	SN ◇■	SN ■	SN ■	SN ■		SN ◇■ ⌶	SN ■	SN ■	SN ■	SN ◇■	SN ■	SN ◇■	SN ◇■ ⌶	SN ■		SN ◇■		SN ■	SN ■	SN ■	SN ◇■	SN ■	SN ◇■
London Victoria ■ ⊖	d		07 02											08 04				08 17							09 04
Clapham Junction ■	d		07 08											08 10				08 23							09 10
London Bridge ■ ⊖	d			07 37																08 37					
East Croydon ⇌	d		07 23	07 55										08 24				08 37		08 55					09 24
Redhill ■	d		07 37	08 13										08 39						09 16					09 39
Horley	d		07 43	08 22										08 45						09 22					09 45
Gatwick Airport ■ ✈	d		07 47	08 25										08 48				08 56		09 25					09 48
Three Bridges ■	a		07 51	08 30										08 53						09 30					09 53
	d		07 52	08 33										08 53						09 33					09 53
Crawley	d		07 55	08 36										08 56						09 37					09 56
Horsham ■	a		08 07	08 49										09 04						09 49					10 04
	d		08 08											09 05											10 05
Christs Hospital	d													09 08											10 08
Billingshurst	d		08 16											09 15											10 15
Pulborough	d		08 23											09 21											10 21
Amberley	d													09 27											10 27
Arundel	d		08 33											09 33											10 33
Haywards Heath ■	d																	09 07							
Burgess Hill	d																	09 12							
Preston Park	d																								
Brighton ■	d	07 50				08 14				08 22		08 50									09 17		09 50		
Hove ■	a	07 53				08 17				08 25		08 53						09 24			09 20		09 53		
	d	07 54				08 18				08 26		08 54						09 24			09 27		09 54		
Aldrington	d	07 56								08 28		08 56									09 29		09 56		
Portslade	d	07 58								08 30		08 58									09 32		09 58		
Fishersgate	d	08 00								08 32		09 00									09 34		10 00		
Southwick	d	08 02								08 34		09 02									09 36		10 02		
Shoreham-by-Sea	d	08 05				08 24				08 37		09 05						09 30			09 39		10 05		
Lancing	d	08 09								08 41		09 09									09 43		10 09		
East Worthing	d	08 12								08 44		09 12									09 46		10 12		
Worthing ■	a	08 15				08 30				08 47		09 15						09 36			09 48		10 15		
	d	08 15				08 30				08 47		09 15						09 40	09 42		09 49		10 15		
West Worthing	d	08 17								08 49		09 17							09 44		09 51		10 17		
Durrington-on-Sea	d	08 20								08 51		09 20							09 46		09 53		10 20		
Goring-by-Sea	d	08 22								08 54		09 22							09 49		09 56		10 22		
Angmering ■	d	08 26				08 37				08 58		09 26							09 53		10 00		10 26		
Littlehampton ■	a									09 06									10 02						
	d								08 57	09 11						09 57									
Ford ■	d	08 32	08 38			08 43			09 01	09 15		09 32		09 39		10 01					10 06		10 32		10 38
Bognor Regis ■	d				08 36			08 58			←		09 36		09 58							←		10 34	
Barnham	a	08 37	08 42		08 42	08 48		09 04	09 08	09 19	09 08	09 37	09 42	09 43	10 04	10 08		09 54			10 11	10 08	10 37	10 40	10 42
	d	08 37	08 43			08 48			09 26	09 20	09 26	09 37		09 44		10 15		09 55			10 12	10 15	10 37		10 43
Bognor Regis	a		08 49						→		09 32			09 50		→						10 21			10 49
Chichester ■	a	08 45				08 56				09 27		09 45						10 02			10 19		10 45		
	d	08 45				08 56				09 28		09 45						10 03			10 20		10 45		
Fishbourne (Sussex)	d									09 31											10 23				
Bosham	d									09 34											10 26				
Nutbourne	d									09 37											10 29				
Southbourne	d					09 03				09 40								10 10			10 32				
Emsworth	d	08 53				09 06				09 43		09 53						10 13			10 35		10 53		
Warblington	d									09 46											10 38				
Havant	d	08 58				09 11				09 49		09 58						10 17			10 41		10 58		
Bedhampton	a									09 51											10 43				
Hilsea	a																								
Fratton	a					09 19				09 59								10 26			10 51				
Portsmouth & Southsea	a					09 23				10 03								10 29			10 54				
Portsmouth Harbour ⛴	a					09 27				10 07								10 35			10 58				
Cosham	a	09 05										10 06											11 06		
Portchester	a																								
Fareham	a	09 13										10 14											11 14		
Swanwick	a	09 20										10 21											11 21		
Eastleigh	a																								
Southampton Airport Parkway	a																								
Southampton Central ⛴	a	09 44										10 44											11 45		

Table 188

Sundays from 16 September

London, Gatwick Airport, Brighton - Sussex Coast, Portsmouth and Southampton

Network Diagram - see first Page of Table 186

Station		SN ◇1 ⊼		SN 1	SN ◇1		SN 1	SN 1	SN 1	SN ◇1	SN 1	SN ◇1 ⊼	
London Victoria 15 ⊖	d				09 17							10 04	
Clapham Junction 10	d				09 23							10 10	
London Bridge 4 ⊖	d						09 37						
East Croydon	d				09 37		09 55					10 24	
Redhill 5	d						10 16					10 39	
Horley	d						10 22					10 45	
Gatwick Airport 10 ✈	d				09 56		10 25					10 48	
Three Bridges 4	a						10 30					10 53	
	d						10 33					10 53	
Crawley	d						10 37					10 56	
Horsham 4	a						10 49					11 04	
	d											11 05	
Christs Hospital	d											11 08	
Billingshurst	d											11 15	
Pulborough	d											11 21	
Amberley	d											11 27	
Arundel	d											11 33	
Haywards Heath 3	d				10 07								
Burgess Hill	d				10 12								
Preston Park	d												
Brighton 10	d							10 17		10 50			
Hove 2	a				10 24			10 20		10 53			
	d				10 24			10 27		10 54			
Aldrington	d							10 29		10 56			
Portslade	d							10 32		10 58			
Fishersgate	d							10 34		11 00			
Southwick	d							10 36		11 02			
Shoreham-by-Sea	d				10 30			10 39		11 05			
Lancing	d							10 43		11 09			
East Worthing	d							10 46		11 12			
Worthing 4	a				10 36			10 48		11 15			
	d				10 40	10 42		10 49		11 15			
West Worthing	d					10 44		10 51		11 17			
Durrington-on-Sea	d					10 46		10 53		11 20			
Goring-by-Sea	d					10 49		10 56		11 22			
Angmering 3	d					10 53		11 00		11 26			
Littlehampton 4	a					11 02							
	d			10 57									
Ford 4	d			11 01				11 06		11 32		11 38	
Bognor Regis 4	d	10 58							←		11 34		
Barnham	a	11 04		11 08	10 54			11 11	11 08	11 37	11 40	11 42	
	d			11 15	10 55			11 12	11 15	11 37		11 43	
Bognor Regis	a			→					11 21			11 49	
Chichester 4	a				11 02			11 19		11 45			
	d				11 03			11 20		11 45			
Fishbourne (Sussex)	d							11 23					
Bosham	d							11 26					
Nutbourne	d							11 29					
Southbourne	d				11 10			11 32					
Emsworth	d				11 13			11 35		11 53			
Warblington	d							11 38					
Havant	d				11 17			11 44		11 58			
Bedhampton	a							11 46					
Hilsea	a												
Fratton	a				11 26			11 54					
Portsmouth & Southsea	a				11 29			11 57					
Portsmouth Harbour ⛴	a				11 35			12 01					
Cosham	a									12 05			
Portchester	a												
Fareham	a									12 13			
Swanwick	a									12 20			
Eastleigh	a												
Southampton Airport Parkway	a												
Southampton Central ⛴	a									12 44			

Station		GW ◇	SN ◇1 ⊼	SN 1	SN ◇1		SN 1	SN 1	SN 1	SN ◇1		SN 1	SN ◇1 ⊼
London Victoria 15 ⊖	d				10 17								11 04
Clapham Junction 10	d				10 23								11 10
London Bridge 4 ⊖	d						10 37						
East Croydon	d				10 37		10 55						11 24
Redhill 5	d						11 16						11 39
Horley	d						11 22						11 45
Gatwick Airport 10 ✈	d				10 56		11 25						11 48
Three Bridges 4	a						11 30						11 53
	d						11 33						11 53
Crawley	d						11 37						11 56
Horsham 4	a						11 49						12 04
	d												12 05
Christs Hospital	d												12 08
Billingshurst	d												12 15
Pulborough	d												12 21
Amberley	d												12 27
Arundel	d												12 33
Haywards Heath 3	d				11 07								
Burgess Hill	d				11 12								
Preston Park	d												
Brighton 10	d	11 10						11 17		11 50			
Hove 2	a	11 13			11 24			11 20		11 53			
	d	11 14			11 24			11 27		11 54			
Aldrington	d							11 29		11 56			
Portslade	d							11 32		11 58			
Fishersgate	d							11 34		12 00			
Southwick	d							11 36		12 02			
Shoreham-by-Sea	d	11 20			11 30			11 39		12 05			
Lancing	d							11 43		12 09			
East Worthing	d							11 46		12 12			
Worthing 4	a	11 26			11 36			11 48		12 15			
	d	11 29			11 40	11 42		11 49		12 15			
West Worthing	d					11 44		11 51		12 17			
Durrington-on-Sea	d					11 46		11 53		12 20			
Goring-by-Sea	d					11 49		11 56		12 22			
Angmering 3	d					11 53		12 00		12 26			
Littlehampton 4	a					12 02							
	d			11 57									
Ford 4	d			12 01				12 06		12 32			12 38
Bognor Regis 4	d		11 58						←			12 34	
Barnham	a	11 45	12 04	12 08	11 54			12 11	12 08	12 37		12 40	12 42
	d	11 46		12 15	11 55			12 12	12 15	12 37			12 43
Bognor Regis	a			→					12 21				12 49
Chichester 4	a	11 53			12 02			12 19		12 45			
	d	11 54			12 03			12 20		12 45			
Fishbourne (Sussex)	d							12 23					
Bosham	d							12 26					
Nutbourne	d							12 29					
Southbourne	d				12 10			12 32					
Emsworth	d				12 13			12 35		12 53			
Warblington	d							12 38					
Havant	d	12 10			12 17			12 44		12 58			
Bedhampton	a							12 46					
Hilsea	a												
Fratton	a				12 26			12 54					
Portsmouth & Southsea	a				12 29			12 57					
Portsmouth Harbour ⛴	a				12 35			13 01					
Cosham	a	12 16								13 05			
Portchester	a												
Fareham	a	12 31								13 13			
Swanwick	a									13 20			
Eastleigh	a												
Southampton Airport Parkway	a												
Southampton Central ⛴	a	12 53								13 44			

Table 188

Sundays from 16 September

London, Gatwick Airport, Brighton - Sussex Coast, Portsmouth and Southampton

Network Diagram - see first Page of Table 186

Station		SN ◇1 ⊼	SN 1	SN ◇1		SN 1	SN 1	SN 1		SN ◇1	SN 1	SN ◇1 ⊼	SN ◇1 ⊼
London Victoria 15 ⊖	d			11 17								12 04	
Clapham Junction 10	d			11 23								12 10	
London Bridge 4 ⊖	d					11 37							
East Croydon	d			11 37		11 55						12 24	
Redhill 5	d					12 16						12 39	
Horley	d					12 22						12 45	
Gatwick Airport 10 ✈	d			11 56		12 25						12 48	
Three Bridges 4	a					12 30						12 53	
	d					12 33						12 53	
Crawley	d					12 37						12 56	
Horsham 4	a					12 49						13 04	
	d											13 05	
Christs Hospital	d											13 08	
Billingshurst	d											13 15	
Pulborough	d											13 21	
Amberley	d											13 27	
Arundel	d											13 33	
Haywards Heath 3	d			12 07									
Burgess Hill	d			12 12									
Preston Park	d												
Brighton 10	d						12 17			12 50			
Hove 2	a			12 24			12 20			12 53			
	d			12 24			12 27			12 54			
Aldrington	d						12 29			12 56			
Portslade	d						12 32			12 58			
Fishersgate	d						12 34			13 00			
Southwick	d						12 36			13 02			
Shoreham-by-Sea	d			12 30			12 39			13 05			
Lancing	d						12 43			13 09			
East Worthing	d						12 46			13 12			
Worthing 4	a			12 36			12 48			13 15			
	d			12 40	12 42		12 49			13 15			
West Worthing	d				12 44		12 51			13 17			
Durrington-on-Sea	d				12 46		12 53			13 20			
Goring-by-Sea	d				12 49		12 56			13 22			
Angmering 3	d				12 53		13 00			13 26			
Littlehampton 4	a				13 02								
	d		12 57										
Ford 4	d		13 01				13 06			13 32		13 38	
Bognor Regis 4	d	12 58						←			13 34		13 58
Barnham	a	13 04	13 08	12 54			13 11	13 08		13 37	13 40	13 42	14 04
	d		13 15	12 55			13 12	13 15		13 37		13 43	
Bognor Regis	a		→					13 21				13 49	
Chichester 4	a			13 02			13 19			13 45			
	d			13 03			13 20			13 45			
Fishbourne (Sussex)	d						13 23						
Bosham	d						13 26						
Nutbourne	d						13 29						
Southbourne	d			13 10			13 32						
Emsworth	d			13 13			13 35			13 53			
Warblington	d						13 38						
Havant	d			13 17			13 44			13 58			
Bedhampton	a						13 46						
Hilsea	a												
Fratton	a			13 26			13 54						
Portsmouth & Southsea	a			13 29			13 57						
Portsmouth Harbour ⛴	a			13 35			14 01						
Cosham	a									14 05			
Portchester	a												
Fareham	a									14 13			
Swanwick	a									14 20			
Eastleigh	a												
Southampton Airport Parkway	a												
Southampton Central ⛴	a									14 44			

Station		SN 1	SN ◇1		SN 1	SN 1		SN 1	SN ◇1	SN 1	SN ◇1 ⊼	SN ◇1 ⊼	SN 1
London Victoria 15 ⊖	d		12 17								13 04		
Clapham Junction 10	d		12 23								13 10		
London Bridge 4 ⊖	d				12 37								
East Croydon	d		12 37		12 55						13 24		
Redhill 5	d				13 16						13 39		
Horley	d				13 22						13 45		
Gatwick Airport 10 ✈	d		12 56		13 25						13 48		
Three Bridges 4	a				13 30						13 53		
	d				13 33						13 53		
Crawley	d				13 37						13 56		
Horsham 4	a				13 49						14 04		
	d										14 05		
Christs Hospital	d										14 08		
Billingshurst	d										14 15		
Pulborough	d										14 21		
Amberley	d										14 27		
Arundel	d										14 33		
Haywards Heath 3	d		13 07										
Burgess Hill	d		13 12										
Preston Park	d												
Brighton 10	d					13 17			13 50				
Hove 2	a		13 24			13 20			13 53				
	d		13 24			13 27			13 54				
Aldrington	d					13 29			13 56				
Portslade	d					13 32			13 58				
Fishersgate	d					13 34			14 00				
Southwick	d					13 36			14 02				
Shoreham-by-Sea	d		13 30			13 39			14 05				
Lancing	d					13 43			14 09				
East Worthing	d					13 46			14 12				
Worthing 4	a		13 36			13 48			14 15				
	d		13 40	13 42		13 49			14 15				
West Worthing	d			13 44		13 51			14 17				
Durrington-on-Sea	d			13 46		13 53			14 20				
Goring-by-Sea	d			13 49		13 56			14 22				
Angmering 3	d			13 53		14 00			14 26				
Littlehampton 4	a			14 02									
	d	13 57											14 57
Ford 4	d	14 01				14 06			14 32		14 38		15 01
Bognor Regis 4	d							←		14 34		14 58	
Barnham	a	14 08	13 54			14 11		14 08	14 37	14 40	14 42	15 04	15 08
	d	14 15	13 55			14 12		14 15	14 37		14 43		15 15
Bognor Regis	a	→						14 21			14 49		→
Chichester 4	a		14 02			14 19			14 45				
	d		14 03			14 20			14 45				
Fishbourne (Sussex)	d					14 23							
Bosham	d					14 26							
Nutbourne	d					14 29							
Southbourne	d		14 10			14 32							
Emsworth	d		14 13			14 35			14 53				
Warblington	d					14 38							
Havant	d		14 17			14 44			14 58				
Bedhampton	a					14 46							
Hilsea	a												
Fratton	a		14 26			14 54							
Portsmouth & Southsea	a		14 29			14 57							
Portsmouth Harbour ⛴	a		14 35			15 01							
Cosham	a								15 05				
Portchester	a												
Fareham	a								15 13				
Swanwick	a								15 20				
Eastleigh	a												
Southampton Airport Parkway	a												
Southampton Central ⛴	a								15 44				

London, Gatwick Airport, Brighton - Sussex Coast, Portsmouth and Southampton

Sundays from 16 September

Network Diagram - see first Page of Table 186

		SN ◇1		SN 1	SN 1	SN 1	SN ◇1	SN 1	SN ◇1 🚌	SN ◇1 🚌	SN 1	SN ◇1		SN 1	SN 1	SN 1	GW ◇	SN ◇1	SN 1	SN ◇1 🚌	SN ◇1 🚌	SN 1
London Victoria 15 ⊖	d	13 17							14 04			14 17								15 04		
Clapham Junction 10	d	13 23							14 10			14 23								15 10		
London Bridge 4 ⊖	d			13 37										14 37								
East Croydon	d	13 37		13 55					14 24			14 37		14 55						15 24		
Redhill 5	d			14 16					14 39					15 16						15 39		
Horley	d			14 22					14 45					15 22						15 45		
Gatwick Airport 10 ✈	d	13 56		14 25					14 48			14 56		15 25						15 48		
Three Bridges 4	a			14 30					14 53					15 30						15 53		
	d			14 33					14 53					15 33						15 53		
Crawley	d			14 37					14 56					15 37						15 56		
Horsham 4	a			14 49					15 04					15 49						16 04		
	d								15 05											16 05		
Christs Hospital	d								15 08											16 08		
Billingshurst	d								15 15											16 15		
Pulborough	d								15 21											16 21		
Amberley	d								15 27											16 27		
Arundel	d								15 33											16 33		
Haywards Heath 3	d	14 07										15 07										
Burgess Hill	d	14 12										15 12										
Preston Park	d																					
Brighton 10	d				14 17		14 50								15 17		15 46	15 50				
Hove 2	a	14 24			14 20		14 53					15 24			15 20		15 49	15 53				
	d	14 24			14 27		14 54					15 24			15 27		15 50	15 54				
Aldrington	d				14 29		14 56								15 29			15 56				
Portslade	d				14 32		14 58								15 32			15 58				
Fishersgate	d				14 34		15 00								15 34			16 00				
Southwick	d				14 36		15 02								15 36			16 02				
Shoreham-by-Sea	d	14 30			14 39		15 05					15 30			15 39		15 56	16 05				
Lancing	d				14 43		15 09								15 43			16 09				
East Worthing	d				14 46		15 12								15 46			16 12				
Worthing 4	a	14 36			14 48		15 15					15 36			15 48		16 03	16 15				
	d	14 40	14 42		14 49		15 15					15 40	15 42		15 49		16 08	16 15				
West Worthing	d		14 44		14 51		15 17						15 44		15 51			16 17				
Durrington-on-Sea	d		14 46		14 53		15 20						15 46		15 53			16 20				
Goring-by-Sea	d		14 49		14 56		15 22						15 49		15 56			16 22				
Angmering 3	d		14 53		15 00		15 26						15 53		16 00			16 26				
Littlehampton 4	a		15 02										16 02									
	d										15 57											16 57
Ford 4	d				15 06		15 32		15 38		16 01				16 06			16 32		16 39		17 01
Bognor Regis 4	d					←		15 34		15 58						←			16 34		16 58	
Barnham	a	14 54			15 11	15 08	15 37	15 40	15 42	16 04	16 08	15 54			16 11	16 08	16 25	16 37	16 40	16 43	17 04	17 08
	d	14 55			15 12	15 15	15 37		15 43		16 15	15 55			16 12	16 15	16 25	16 37		16 44		17 15
Bognor Regis	a					15 21			15 49		→					16 21				16 50		→
Chichester 4	a	15 02			15 19		15 45					16 02			16 19		16 33	16 45				
	d	15 03			15 20		15 45					16 03			16 20		16 34	16 45				
Fishbourne (Sussex)	d				15 23										16 23							
Bosham	d				15 26										16 26							
Nutbourne	d				15 29										16 29							
Southbourne	d	15 10			15 32							16 10			16 32							
Emsworth	d	15 13			15 35		15 53					16 13			16 35			16 53				
Warblington	d				15 38										16 38							
Havant	d	15 17			15 44		15 58					16 17			16 44		16 48	16 58				
Bedhampton	a				15 46										16 46							
Hilsea	a																					
Fratton	a	15 26			15 54							16 26			16 54							
Portsmouth & Southsea	a	15 29			15 57							16 29			16 57							
Portsmouth Harbour ⛴	a	15 35			16 01							16 35			17 01							
Cosham	a						16 05										16 54	17 05				
Portchester	a																					
Fareham	a						16 13										17 02	17 14				
Swanwick	a						16 20											17 22				
Eastleigh	a																					
Southampton Airport Parkway	a																					
Southampton Central ⛴	a						16 44										17 24	17 48				

London, Gatwick Airport, Brighton - Sussex Coast, Portsmouth and Southampton

Sundays from 16 September

Network Diagram - see first Page of Table 186

		SN ◇1		SN 1	SN 1	SN 1	SN ◇1	SN 1	SN ◇1 🚌	SN ◇1	SN 1	SN ◇1		SN 1	SN 1	SN 1	GW ◇	SN ◇1	SN 1	SN ◇1 🚌	SN ◇1	SN 1
London Victoria 15 ⊖	d	15 17							16 04			16 17								17 04		
Clapham Junction 10	d	15 23							16 10			16 23								17 10		
London Bridge 4 ⊖	d			15 37										16 37								
East Croydon	d	15 37		15 55					16 24			16 37		16 55						17 24		
Redhill 5	d			16 16					16 39					17 16						17 39		
Horley	d			16 22					16 45					17 22						17 45		
Gatwick Airport 10 ✈	d	15 56		16 25					16 48			16 56		17 25						17 48		
Three Bridges 4	a			16 30					16 53					17 30						17 53		
	d			16 33					16 53					17 33						17 53		
Crawley	d			16 37					16 56					17 37						17 56		
Horsham 4	a			16 49					17 04					17 49						18 04		
	d								17 05											18 05		
Christs Hospital	d								17 08											18 08		
Billingshurst	d								17 15											18 15		
Pulborough	d								17 21											18 21		
Amberley	d								17 27											18 27		
Arundel	d								17 33											18 33		
Haywards Heath 3	d	16 07										17 07										
Burgess Hill	d	16 12										17 12										
Preston Park	d																					
Brighton 10	d				16 17		16 50								17 17		17 46	17 50				
Hove 2	a	16 24			16 20		16 53					17 24			17 20		17 49	17 53				
	d	16 24			16 27		16 54					17 24			17 27		17 50	17 54				
Aldrington	d				16 29		16 56								17 29			17 56				
Portslade	d				16 32		16 58								17 32			17 58				
Fishersgate	d				16 34		17 00								17 34			18 00				
Southwick	d				16 36		17 02								17 36			18 02				
Shoreham-by-Sea	d	16 30			16 39		17 05					17 30			17 39		17 56	18 05				
Lancing	d				16 43		17 09								17 43			18 09				
East Worthing	d				16 46		17 12								17 46			18 12				
Worthing 4	a	16 36			16 48		17 15					17 36			17 48		18 03	18 15				
	d	16 40	16 42		16 49		17 15					17 40	17 42		17 49		18 08	18 15				
West Worthing	d		16 44		16 51		17 17						17 44		17 51			18 17				
Durrington-on-Sea	d		16 46		16 53		17 20						17 46		17 53			18 20				
Goring-by-Sea	d		16 49		16 56		17 22						17 49		17 56			18 22				
Angmering 3	d		16 53		17 00		17 26						17 53		18 00			18 26				
Littlehampton 4	a		17 02										18 02									
	d										17 57											18 57
Ford 4	d				17 06		17 32		17 38		18 01				18 06			18 32		18 38		19 01
Bognor Regis 4	d					←		17 34		17 58						←			18 34		18 58	
Barnham	a	16 54			17 11	17 08	17 37	17 40	17 42	18 04	18 08	17 54			18 11	18 08	18 25	18 37	18 40	18 42	19 04	19 08
	d	16 55			17 12	17 15	17 37		17 43		18 15	17 55			18 12	18 15	18 25	18 37		18 43		19 15
Bognor Regis	a					17 21			17 49		→					18 21				18 49		→
Chichester 4	a	17 02			17 19		17 45					18 02			18 19		18 33	18 45				
	d	17 03			17 20		17 45					18 03			18 20		18 34	18 45				
Fishbourne (Sussex)	d				17 23										18 23							
Bosham	d				17 26										18 26							
Nutbourne	d				17 29										18 29							
Southbourne	d	17 10			17 32							18 10			18 32							
Emsworth	d	17 13			17 35		17 53					18 13			18 35			18 53				
Warblington	d				17 38										18 38							
Havant	d	17 17			17 44		17 58					18 17			18 44		18 48	18 58				
Bedhampton	a				17 46										18 46							
Hilsea	a																					
Fratton	a	17 26			17 54							18 26			18 54							
Portsmouth & Southsea	a	17 29			17 57							18 29			18 57							
Portsmouth Harbour ⛴	a	17 35			18 01							18 35			19 01							
Cosham	a						18 05										18 54	19 05				
Portchester	a																					
Fareham	a						18 13										19 02	19 13				
Swanwick	a						18 20											19 22				
Eastleigh	a																					
Southampton Airport Parkway	a																					
Southampton Central ⛴	a						18 42										19 24	19 48				

Sundays from 16 September

London, Gatwick Airport, Brighton - Sussex Coast, Portsmouth and Southampton

Network Diagram - see first Page of Table 186

		SN ◇■		SN ■	SN ■	SN ■	SN ◇■	SN ■	SN ◇■ ⚒	SN ◇■	SN ■	SN ◇■		SN ■	SN ■	SN ■	SN ◇■	SN ■	SN ◇■ ⚒	SN ◇■	SN ■	SN ◇■	
London Victoria ■ ⊖	d	17 17							18 04			18 17							19 04			19 17	
Clapham Junction ■	d	17 23							18 10			18 23							19 10			19 23	
London Bridge ■ ⊖	d			17 37										18 37									
East Croydon	d	17 37		17 55					18 24			18 37		18 55					19 24			19 37	
Redhill ■	d			18 16					18 39					19 16					19 39				
Horley	d			18 22					18 45					19 22					19 45				
Gatwick Airport ■ ✈	d	17 56		18 25					18 48			18 56		19 25					19 48			19 56	
Three Bridges ■	a			18 30					18 53					19 30					19 53				
	d			18 33					18 53					19 33					19 53				
Crawley	d			18 37					18 56					19 37					19 56				
Horsham ■	a			18 49					19 04					19 49					20 04				
	d								19 05										20 05				
Christs Hospital	d								19 08										20 08				
Billingshurst	d								19 15										20 15				
Pulborough	d								19 21										20 21				
Amberley	d								19 27										20 27				
Arundel	d								19 33										20 33				
Haywards Heath ■	d	18 07										19 07										20 07	
Burgess Hill	d	18 12										19 12										20 12	
Preston Park	d																						
Brighton ■	d				18 17		18 50								19 17		19 50						
Hove ■	a	18 24			18 20		18 53					19 24			19 20		19 53					20 24	
	d	18 24			18 27		18 54					19 24			19 27		19 54					20 24	
Aldrington	d				18 29		18 56								19 29		19 56						
Portslade	d				18 32		18 58								19 32		19 58						
Fishersgate	d				18 34		19 00								19 34		20 00						
Southwick	d				18 36		19 02								19 36		20 02						
Shoreham-by-Sea	d	18 30			18 39		19 05					19 30			19 39		20 05					20 30	
Lancing	d				18 43		19 09								19 43		20 09						
East Worthing	d				18 46		19 12								19 46		20 12						
Worthing ■	a	18 36			18 48		19 15					19 36			19 48		20 15					20 36	
	d	18 40	18 42		18 49		19 15					19 40	19 42		19 49		20 15					20 40	20 42
West Worthing	d		18 44		18 51		19 17						19 44		19 51		20 17						20 44
Durrington-on-Sea	d		18 46		18 53		19 20						19 46		19 53		20 20						20 46
Goring-by-Sea	d		18 49		18 56		19 22						19 49		19 56		20 22						20 49
Angmering ■	d		18 53		19 00		19 26						19 53		20 00		20 26						20 53
Littlehampton ■	a		19 02										20 02										21 02
	d										19 57										20 57		
Ford ■	d				19 06		19 32		19 38		20 01				20 06		20 32		20 38		21 01		
Bognor Regis ■	d					←		19 34		19 58						←		20 34		20 58			
Barnham	a	18 54			19 11	19 08	19 37	19 40	19 42	20 04	20 08	19 54			20 11	20 08	20 37	20 41	20 42	21 04	21 08	20 54	
	d	18 55			19 12	19 15	19 37		19 43		20 15	19 55			20 12	20 15	20 37		20 43		21 15	20 55	
Bognor Regis	a					19 21			19 49		→					20 21			20 49		→		
Chichester ■	a	19 02			19 19		19 45					20 02			20 19		20 45					21 02	
	d	19 03			19 20		19 45					20 03			20 20		20 45					21 03	
Fishbourne (Sussex)	d				19 23										20 23								
Bosham	d				19 26										20 26								
Nutbourne	d				19 29										20 29								
Southbourne	d	19 10			19 32							20 10			20 32							21 10	
Emsworth	d	19 13			19 35		19 53					20 13			20 35		20 53					21 13	
Warblington	d				19 38										20 38								
Havant	d	19 17			19 44		19 58					20 17			20 44		20 58					21 17	
Bedhampton	a				19 46										20 46								
Hilsea	a																						
Fratton	a	19 26			19 54							20 26			20 54							21 26	
Portsmouth & Southsea	a	19 29			19 57							20 29			20 57							21 29	
Portsmouth Harbour ⛴	a	19 35			20 01							20 35			21 01							21 35	
Cosham	a						20 05										21 07						
Portchester	a																						
Fareham	a						20 13										21 15						
Swanwick	a						20 20										21 22						
Eastleigh	a																						
Southampton Airport Parkway	a																						
Southampton Central ⛴	a						20 46										21 45						

Sundays from 16 September

London, Gatwick Airport, Brighton - Sussex Coast, Portsmouth and Southampton

Network Diagram - see first Page of Table 186

		SN ■	SN ■	SN ■	SN ◇■	SN ■	SN ◇■	SN ◇■	SN ■	SN ◇■		SN ■	SN ■	SN ■	GW	SN ■	SN	SN	SN ◇■	SN ◇■		SN ■
London Victoria ■ ⊖	d						20 04			20 17									21 04	21 17		
Clapham Junction ■	d						20 10			20 23									21 10	21 23		
London Bridge ■ ⊖	d	19 37										20 37										21 37
East Croydon	d	19 55					20 24			20 37		20 55							21 24	21 37		21 55
Redhill ■	d	20 16					20 39					21 16							21 39			22 16
Horley	d	20 22					20 45					21 22							21 45			22 22
Gatwick Airport ■ ✈	d	20 25					20 48			20 56		21 25							21 48	21 56		22 25
Three Bridges ■	a	20 30					20 53					21 30							21 53			22 30
	d	20 33					20 53					21 33							21 53			22 33
Crawley	d	20 37					20 56					21 37							21 56			22 37
Horsham ■	a	20 49					21 04					21 49							22 04			22 49
	d						21 05												22 05			
Christs Hospital	d						21 08												22 08			
Billingshurst	d						21 15												22 15			
Pulborough	d						21 21												22 21			
Amberley	d						21 27												22 27			
Arundel	d						21 33												22 33			
Haywards Heath ■	d									21 07										22 07		
Burgess Hill	d									21 12										22 12		
Preston Park	d																					
Brighton ■	d		20 17		20 50								21 17		21 46	21 50	22 12					
Hove ■	a		20 20		20 53					21 24			21 20		21 49	21 53	22 15			22 24		
	d		20 27		20 54					21 24			21 27		21 50	21 54				22 25		
Aldrington	d		20 29		20 56								21 29			21 56						
Portslade	d		20 32		20 58								21 32			21 58						
Fishersgate	d		20 34		21 00								21 34			22 00						
Southwick	d		20 36		21 02								21 36			22 02						
Shoreham-by-Sea	d		20 39		21 05					21 30			21 39		21 56	22 05				22 31		
Lancing	d		20 43		21 09								21 43			22 09						
East Worthing	d		20 46		21 12								21 46			22 12						
Worthing ■	a		20 48		21 15					21 36			21 48		22 02	22 15				22 37		
	d		20 49		21 15					21 40	21 42		21 49		22 03	22 15				22 41	22 43	
West Worthing	d		20 51		21 17						21 44		21 51			22 17					22 45	
Durrington-on-Sea	d		20 53		21 20						21 46		21 53			22 20					22 47	
Goring-by-Sea	d		20 56		21 22						21 49		21 56			22 22					22 50	
Angmering ■	d		21 00		21 26						21 53		22 00			22 26					22 54	
Littlehampton ■	a										22 02					22 36					23 02	
	d								21 57													
Ford ■	d		21 06		21 32		21 38		22 01				22 06						22 38			
Bognor Regis ■	d			←		21 34		21 58						←				22 12				
Barnham	a		21 11	21 08	21 37	21 40	21 42	22 04	22 08	21 54			22 11	22 08	22 17			22 18	22 42	22 55		
	d		21 12	21 15	21 37		21 43		22 15	21 55			22 12	22 15	22 18				22 43	22 56		
Bognor Regis	a			21 21			21 49		→					22 21					22 49			
Chichester ■	a		21 19		21 45					22 02			22 19		22 25					23 03		
	d		21 20		21 45					22 03			22 20		22 26					23 04		
Fishbourne (Sussex)	d		21 23										22 23									
Bosham	d		21 26										22 26							23 08		
Nutbourne	d		21 29										22 29							23 12		
Southbourne	d		21 32							22 10			22 32							23 14		
Emsworth	d		21 35		21 53					22 13			22 35							23 17		
Warblington	d		21 38										22 38									
Havant	d		21 44		21 58					22 17			22 44		22 47					23 22		
Bedhampton	a		21 46										22 46									
Hilsea	a																					
Fratton	a		21 54							22 26			22 54		22 57					23 32		
Portsmouth & Southsea	a		21 57							22 29			22 57		23 00					23 35		
Portsmouth Harbour ⛴	a		22 01							22 35			23 01		23 04					23 39		
Cosham	a				22 05																	
Portchester	a																					
Fareham	a				22 13																	
Swanwick	a				22 20																	
Eastleigh	a																					
Southampton Airport Parkway	a																					
Southampton Central ⛴	a				22 44																	

Table 188

Sundays from 16 September

London, Gatwick Airport, Brighton - Sussex Coast, Portsmouth and Southampton

Network Diagram - see first Page of Table 186

		SN	SN ■	SN ■	SN ◇■	SN ■	SN	SN ◇■	SN ■	SN ■	SN ◇■
London Victoria 15 ⊖	d				22 04			22 17		23 04	23 17
Clapham Junction 10	d				22 10			22 23		23 10	23 23
London Bridge 4 ⊖	d								22 37		
East Croydon	d				22 24			22 37	22 55	23 22	23 38
Redhill 5	d				22 39				23 16	23 42	
Horley	d				22 45				23 22	23 50	
Gatwick Airport 10 ✈	d				22 48			22 56	23 25	23 55	00 01
Three Bridges 4	a				22 53				23 30	00 01	00 05
	d				22 53				23 33	00 01	00 06
Crawley	d				22 56				23 37	00 05	
Horsham 4	a				23 04				23 49	00 17	
	d				23 05						
Christs Hospital	d				23 08						
Billingshurst	d				23 15						
Pulborough	d				23 21						
Amberley	d				23 27						
Arundel	d				23 33						
Haywards Heath 3	d							23 07			00 15
Burgess Hill	d							23 12			00 20
Preston Park	d										
Brighton 10	d			22 40			23 15				
Hove 2	a			22 43			23 18	23 24			00 31
	d			22 44				23 25			00 31
Aldrington	d			22 46							
Portslade	d			22 48				23 28			00s34
Fishersgate	d			22 50							
Southwick	d			22 52				23 31			00s37
Shoreham-by-Sea	d			22 55				23 34			00s40
Lancing	d			22 59				23 38			00s44
East Worthing	d			23 02							
Worthing 4	a			23 05				23 42			00 48
	d			23 05							
West Worthing	d			23 07							
Durrington-on-Sea	d			23 09							
Goring-by-Sea	d			23 12							
Angmering 3	d			23 16							
Littlehampton 4	a			23 24							
	d		23 06	23 29							
Ford 4	d		23 10	23 33	23 38						
Bognor Regis 4	d					←					
Barnham	a		23 14	23 37	23 42	23 37					
	d	22 57	23 15	23 45	23 43	23 45					
Bognor Regis	a	23 04	23 21	→	23 49						
Chichester 4	a					23 52					
	d										
Fishbourne (Sussex)	d										
Bosham	d										
Nutbourne	d										
Southbourne	d										
Emsworth	d										
Warblington	d										
Havant	d										
Bedhampton	a										
Hilsea	a										
Fratton	a										
Portsmouth &Southsea	a										
Portsmouth Harbour ⛴	a										
Cosham	a										
Portchester	a										
Fareham	a										
Swanwick	a										
Eastleigh	a										
Southampton Airport Parkway	a										
Southampton Central ⛴	a										

Table 188

Mondays to Fridays

Southampton, Portsmouth and Sussex Coast - Brighton, Gatwick Airport and London

Network Diagram - see first Page of Table 186

Miles	Miles	Miles			SN MX	SN MO ■ A	SN MX ■	SN MO ■ A	SN MX ◇	SN MX	SN MX ◇■	SN ■	SN ■	SN ■
—	—	—	Eastleigh	d										
—	—	—	Southampton Airport Parkway	d										
0	—	—	Southampton Central ⛴	d		22p52								
10¾	—	—	Swanwick	d		23p11								
14½	—	—	Fareham	d		23p17								
17¾	—	—	Portchester	d										
20¼	—	—	Cosham	d		23p26								
—	0	—	Portsmouth Harbour ⛴	d	22p44					23p15				
—	0¾	—	Portsmouth &Southsea	d	22p48					23p19				
—	1½	—	Fratton	d	22p52					23p23				
—	4¼	—	Hilsea	d	22p56					23p27				
—	7¼	—	Bedhampton	d	23p01					23p33				
24¼	8	—	Havant	d	23p05	23p32				23p36				
—	8½	—	Warblington	d						23p38				
—	9¾	—	Emsworth	d		23p36				23p41				
—	11¼	—	Southbourne	d						23p44				
—	12¼	—	Nutbourne	d						23p47				
—	14	—	Bosham	d						23p50				
—	15¼	—	Fishbourne (Sussex)	d						23p53				
—	16¾	—	Chichester 4	a	23p16	23p44				23p57				
—	—	—		d	23p17	23p45			23p52	23p57				
0	—	—	Bognor Regis 4	d										
3½	23	—	Barnham	a	23p24	23p52			23p59	00 05				
—	—	—		d	23p25	23p53			00 01	00 06	00 09	04 48		
—	—	—	Bognor Regis	a							00 15			
0	25¾	0	Ford 4	d	23p29				00 05	00 10		04 52		
2	—	2	Littlehampton 4	a	23p34	00 01			00 10	00 15		04 57		
—	—	—		d	23p39							05 02		
8	30	—	Angmering 3	d	23p47							05 10		
—	32½	—	Goring-by-Sea	d	23p51							05 14		
—	33¼	—	Durrington-on-Sea	d	23p53							05 17		
—	34	—	West Worthing	d	23p55							05 19		
—	35	—	Worthing 4	a	23p58							05 21		
—	—	—		d	23p59							05 22		
—	35¾	—	East Worthing	d	00 01							05 24		
—	37¼	—	Lancing	d	00 04							05 27		
—	40	—	Shoreham-by-Sea	d	00 08							05 32		
—	41	—	Southwick	d	00 11							05 35		
—	42	—	Fishersgate	d	00 13							05 37		
—	42½	—	Portslade	d	00 15							05 39		
—	43½	—	Aldrington	d	00 18							05 41		
0	44	—	Hove 2	a	00 21							05 43		
—	—	—		d	00 21							05 44		
—	45½	—	Brighton 10	a	00 25							05 48		
—	—	—	Preston Park	d										
9¼	—	—	Burgess Hill	a										
13	—	—	Haywards Heath 3	a										
—	—	2¼	Arundel	d										
—	—	6	Amberley	d										
—	—	10¾	Pulborough	d										
—	—	15¾	Billingshurst	d										
—	—	20½	Christs Hospital	d										
—	—	23	Horsham 4	a										
—	—	—		d			23p02	23p03					05 17	05 38
—	—	30	Crawley	d			23p14	23p16					05 29	05 50
21½	—	31½	Three Bridges 4	a			23p18	23p19					05 33	05 54
24¼	—	—	Gatwick Airport 10 ✈	a			23p22	23p24					05 37	05 58
—	—	—		d			23p23	23p25					05 38	05 59
25	—	—	Horley	a			23p26	23p28					05 40	06 02
30	—	—	Redhill 5	a			23p36	23p34					05 47	06 12
40½	0	—	East Croydon	a			23p54	23p55					06 06	06 30
—	10¼	—	London Bridge 4 ⊖	a										
48¼	—	—	Clapham Junction 10	a			00 11	00 11					06 18	06 41
51	—	61	London Victoria 15 ⊖	a			00 18	00 19					06 25	06 48

A from 21 May

Table 188

Southampton, Portsmouth and Sussex Coast - Brighton, Gatwick Airport and London

Network Diagram - see first Page of Table 186

		SN ■	SN	SN	SN	SN ■		SN ■	SN ◇■		SN ■	SN		SN	SN	SN	SN ■	SN ◇■ 🚌	SN		SN ■	SN	SN	SN ◇■ A 🚌	SN ■
Eastleigh	d																								
Southampton Airport Parkway	d																								
Southampton Central	d																								
Swanwick	d																								
Fareham	d																								
Portchester	d																								
Cosham	d																								
Portsmouth Harbour	d																				05 33			05 47	
Portsmouth & Southsea	d																				05 37			05 51	
Fratton	d																				05 41			05 55	
Hilsea	d																				05 45			05 59	
Bedhampton	d																				05 50			06 04	
Havant	d	05 01							05 30												05 53			06 07	
Warblington	d																				05 55				
Emsworth	d																				05 58			06 11	
Southbourne	d																				06 01			06 14	
Nutbourne	d																				06 03				
Bosham	d																				06 07			06 18	
Fishbourne (Sussex)	d																				06 10			06 21	
Chichester ■	a	05 14							05 40												06 13			06 25	
	d	05 15							05 41												06 14			06 29	
Bognor Regis ■	d		05 13			05 35						05 49			05 55			06 06	06 13				06 22		
Barnham	a	05 22	05 19			05 41			05 48			05 55			06 02			06 12	06 19		06 21		06 28	06 36	
	d	05 23	05 27	05 36		05 42			05 49			05 56			06 02	06 13		06 13			06 22	06 27	06 29	06 37	
Bognor Regis	a			05 43												06 20						06 34			
Ford ■	d		05 31			05 46						06 00			06 07						06 26		06 33		
Littlehampton ■	a		05 38									06 05											06 38		
	d										05 53														06 31
Angmering ■	d	05 33				05 53					06 02				06 13						06 32				06 40
Goring-by-Sea	d					05 57					06 06				06 17						06 36				06 44
Durrington-on-Sea	d					05 59					06 09				06 19						06 39				06 47
West Worthing	d					06 01					06 11				06 21						06 41				06 49
Worthing ■	a	05 40				06 04					06 13				06 24						06 43				06 52
	d	05 41				06 04					06 14				06 24						06 44				06 52
East Worthing	d					06 07									06 27						06 46				
Lancing	d	05 45				06 10					06 18				06 30						06 49				06 57
Shoreham-by-Sea	d	05 49				06 14					06 22				06 34						06 53				07 01
Southwick	d					06 17									06 37						06 56				
Fishersgate	d					06 19									06 39						06 58				
Portslade	d	05 53				06 21					06 27				06 41						07 00				07 06
Aldrington	d					06 23									06 43						07 03				
Hove ■	a	05 57				06 25					06 30				06 45						07 05				07 10
	d	05 57			05 59	06 26					06 31			06 38	06 46						07 05				07 11
Brighton ■	a				06 03	06 30								06 42	06 50						07 09				
Preston Park	d																								
Burgess Hill	a										06 46														
Haywards Heath ■	a	06 12									06 53														07 30
Arundel	d								05 57									06 21							
Amberley	d																	06 26							
Pulborough	d								06 06									06 32							
Billingshurst	d								06 13									06 39							
Christs Hospital	d								06 19									06 45							
Horsham ■	a								06 23									06 49						07 03	
	d							06 10	06 24								06 38	06 50						07 04	
Crawley	d							06 23	06 37								06 52	07 04						07 13	
Three Bridges ■	a	06 21						06 26	06 40								06 56	07 07						07 18	
Gatwick Airport ■ ✈	a	06 26						06 31	06 52		07 11						07 01	07 12							
	d	06 27						06 32	06 53		07 12						07 02	07 14							
Horley	a							06 35	06 56								07 04	07 16							
Redhill ■	a							06 46	07 02								07 15								
East Croydon	a	06 41						07 04	07 14		07 26						07 34	07 31						07 38	07 56
London Bridge ■ ⊖	a										07 43						07 51								08 13
Clapham Junction ■	a	06 51						07 16	07 24									07 40						07 48	
London Victoria ■ ⊖	a	07 00						07 25	07 33									07 49						07 57	

A 🚌 from Three Bridges

Table 188

Southampton, Portsmouth and Sussex Coast - Brighton, Gatwick Airport and London

Network Diagram - see first Page of Table 186

		SN ■	SN	SN ◇■	SN	SN	SN	SN ■	SN ◇■ 🚌	SN	SN ■	SN ■	SN ■	SN ◇■	SN	SN	SN ■	SN	SN ■	SN	SN ◇■ 🚌	SN ◇■ A 🚌			SN ◇■
Eastleigh	d																								
Southampton Airport Parkway	d																								
Southampton Central	d											05 48					06 10								
Swanwick	d											06 06					06 27								
Fareham	d											06 13					06 34								
Portchester	d											06 18					06 40								
Cosham	d											06 23					06 44								
Portsmouth Harbour	d				06 04																	06 46			
Portsmouth & Southsea	d				06 08																	06 50			
Fratton	d				06 12																	06 54			
Hilsea	d																					06 58			
Bedhampton	d											06 34										07 03			
Havant	d				06 20							06 37					06 53					07 06			
Warblington	d											06 39										07 08			
Emsworth	d				06 24							06 42					06 57					07 11			
Southbourne	d				06 27							06 45					07 00					07 14			
Nutbourne	d											06 48										07 16			
Bosham	d											06 51										07 20			
Fishbourne (Sussex)	d											06 54										07 23			
Chichester ■	a				06 34							06 58					07 07					07 26			
	d				06 35							06 59					07 08					07 28			
Bognor Regis ■	d								06 41	06 50			06 57							07 27	07 17				
Barnham	a				06 42				06 47	06 56		07 07	07 03				07 15			07 33	07 23	07 35			
	d				06 43	06 48			06 48	06 57		07 11			07 13		07 16				07 24	07 36			
Bognor Regis	a					06 55									07 20										
Ford ■	d				06 47				06 52	07 01							07 20								
Littlehampton ■	a									07 06															
	d			06 41										07 02				07 22							07 29
Angmering ■	d			06 50	06 56									07 11			07 26	07 30							07 38
Goring-by-Sea	d			06 54	07 00									07 15			07 30	07 34							07 42
Durrington-on-Sea	d			06 57	07 03									07 17			07 33	07 37							07 45
West Worthing	d			07 00	07 05		07 12							07 20			07 35	07 39							07 47
Worthing ■	a			07 02	07 07		07 14							07 22			07 37	07 41							07 50
	d			07 03	07 08		07 15							07 23			07 38	07 42							07 50
East Worthing	d						07 17											07 44							
Lancing	d			07 07	07 12		07 20							07 27			07 42	07 47							07 54
Shoreham-by-Sea	d			07 12	07 16		07 25							07 31			07 46	07 52							07 59
Southwick	d				07 19		07 28										07 49	07 55							
Fishersgate	d						07 30											07 57							
Portslade	d			07 17	07 22		07 32							07 36			07 52	07 59							08 04
Aldrington	d						07 34											08 01							
Hove ■	a			07 20	07 25		07 36							07 40			07 55	08 03							08 07
	d		07 17	07 21	07 26		07 37							07 41		07 49	07 56	08 04							08 08
Brighton ■	a		07 21		07 30		07 41									07 54	08 01	08 08							
Preston Park	d																								08 12
Burgess Hill	a													07 51											08 23
Haywards Heath ■	a			07 40										07 58											08 28
Arundel	d								06 58			07 18									07 31				
Amberley	d																				07 36				
Pulborough	d								07 07			07 28									07 42				
Billingshurst	d								07 14			07 35									07 49				
Christs Hospital	d								07 20			07 41									07 55				
Horsham ■	a								07 24			07 45									07 59	08 05			
	d	07 09						07 17	07 25		07 40	07 46							07 51		08 09				
Crawley	d	07 23						07 31	07 37		07 53	08 00							08 06		08 18				
Three Bridges ■	a	07 27						07 34	07 40		07 57	08 05							08 09		08 22				08 38
Gatwick Airport ■ ✈	a	07 32						07 39			08 04			08 13					08 14						
	d	07 33						07 40			08 05			08 14					08 15						
Horley	a	07 36						07 42			08 07								08 18		08 28				
Redhill ■	a	07 47						07 53			08 18								08 28						
East Croydon	a			08 08				08 11	07 59		08 36	08 26		08 29					08 50		08 43				08 57
London Bridge ■ ⊖	a											08 45							09 06						
Clapham Junction ■	a			08 17				08 20	08 10		08 48			08 39							08 52				09 07
London Victoria ■ ⊖	a			08 26				08 29	08 19		08 56			08 48							09 01				09 16

A 🚌 from Horsham

Table 188

Mondays to Fridays

Southampton, Portsmouth and Sussex Coast - Brighton, Gatwick Airport and London

Network Diagram - see first Page of Table 186

		GW ⚒	SN	SN ■	SN	SN	SN	SN ◇■	SN	SN	SN ◇■	SN ◇■ ⚒	SN ◇■ A ⚒	SN	SN ◇■	SN	SN	SN ◇	SN	SN ■
Eastleigh	d																			
Southampton Airport Parkway	d																			
Southampton Central	d												07 06							07 33
Swanwick	d												07 24							07 51
Fareham	d												07 31							07 58
Portchester	d												07 36							
Cosham	d												07 40							08 07
Portsmouth Harbour	d	07 01							07 20											
Portsmouth & Southsea	d	07 05							07 24											
Fratton	d	07 10							07 28											
Hilsea	d																			
Bedhampton	d																			
Havant	d	07 20							07 36				07 47							08 13
Warblington	d												07 49							
Emsworth	d												07 52							
Southbourne	d												07 55							
Nutbourne	d												07 58							
Bosham	d												08 01							08 21
Fishbourne (Sussex)	d												08 04							08 24
Chichester ■	a	07 31							07 47				08 08							08 27
	d	07 32							07 47				08 08					08 21		08 28
Bognor Regis ■	d						07 36					07 55					08 13			
Barnham	a	07 39					07 42		07 55			08 01	08 16				08 19	08 28		08 35
	d	07 40	07 39				07 45	07 50	07 55			08 02	08 16	08 05			08 20	08 29	08 28	08 36
Bognor Regis	a		07 46					07 58						08 12					08 36	
Ford ■	d						07 50		08 00			08 06					08 24	08 33		08 40
Littlehampton ■	a						07 54											08 38		
	d					07 45				08 01					08 15					
Angmering ■	d					07 53			08 06	08 10					08 23		08 30			08 46
Goring-by-Sea	d					07 57				08 14					08 27		08 34			
Durrington-on-Sea	d					08 00			08 12	08 17					08 30		08 37			08 52
West Worthing	d					08 02				08 19					08 32		08 39			
Worthing ■	a	07 56				08 04			08 16	08 21					08 34		08 41			08 56
	d	08 00				08 05			08 16	08 22					08 35		08 42			08 56
East Worthing	d					08 07				08 24							08 44			
Lancing	d					08 10			08 20	08 27					08 39		08 47			09 00
Shoreham-by-Sea	d	08 06				08 15			08 24	08 32					08 43		08 52			09 04
Southwick	d					08 18			08 27	08 35							08 55			09 07
Fishersgate	d					08 20				08 37							08 57			
Portslade	d					08 22			08 31	08 39					08 48		08 59			09 11
Aldrington	d					08 24				08 41							09 01			
Hove ■	a	08 14				08 26			08 34	08 43					08 51		09 03			09 14
	d	08 14			08 22	08 27			08 34	08 44					08 52	08 54	09 04			09 14
Brighton ■	a	08 20			08 26	08 31			08 38	08 48						08 58	09 08			09 18
Preston Park	d														08 57					
Burgess Hill	a														09 07					
Haywards Heath ■	a														09 13					
Arundel	d											08 11								
Amberley	d											08 16								
Pulborough	d											08 22								
Billingshurst	d											08 29								
Christs Hospital	d											08 35								
Horsham ■	a											08 39	08 45							
	d			08 12							08 35	08 49								
Crawley	d			08 26							08 47	08 58								
Three Bridges ■	a			08 29							08 51	09 01								
Gatwick Airport ■	a			08 34							08 55	09 06			09 26					
	d			08 35							08 56	09 07			09 27					
Horley	a			08 38							08 59									
Redhill ■	a			08 49							09 10									
East Croydon	a			09 10							09 30	09 22			09 42					
London Bridge ■	a																			
Clapham Junction ■	a			09 20							09 41	09 32			09 52					
London Victoria ■	a			09 27							09 50	09 42			09 59					

A ⚒ from Horsham

Table 188

Mondays to Fridays

Southampton, Portsmouth and Sussex Coast - Brighton, Gatwick Airport and London

Network Diagram - see first Page of Table 186

		SN	SN	SN	SN ◇■ ⚒	SN ◇■ A ⚒	SN ◇■ B ⚒	SN	SN	SN	SN	SN	SN	SN ◇	SN	SN ◇■	SN ◇■	SN ◇■ B ⚒	SN	SN	SN
Eastleigh	d																				
Southampton Airport Parkway	d																				
Southampton Central	d																08 10				
Swanwick	d																08 28				
Fareham	d																08 35				
Portchester	d																08 40				
Cosham	d																08 44				
Portsmouth Harbour	d					08 10						08 29									
Portsmouth & Southsea	d		08 03			08 14						08 33									
Fratton	d		08 07			08 18						08 37									
Hilsea	d		08 11																		
Bedhampton	d		08 16																		
Havant	d		08 19			08 27						08 46					08 51				
Warblington	d		08 21														08 53				
Emsworth	d		08 24			08 31						08 50					08 56				
Southbourne	d		08 27									08 53					08 59				
Nutbourne	d		08 29														09 01				
Bosham	d																09 05				
Fishbourne (Sussex)	d																09 08				
Chichester ■	a		08 35			08 40						09 00					09 11				
	d		08 36			08 41						09 00		09 06			09 12				
Bognor Regis ■	d	08 32			08 26				08 48						09 06	08 56					
Barnham	a	08 38	08 43		08 32	08 48			08 55			09 08		09 14	09 12	09 02	09 19				
	d		08 44	08 45	08 33	08 49		08 52				09 08	09 11		09 15	09 03	09 20		09 19		
Bognor Regis	a			08 52				08 58					09 18						09 26		
Ford ■	d		08 48		08 37										09 19	09 07					
Littlehampton ■	a		08 53												09 24						
	d						08 45											09 15			
Angmering ■	d						08 53					09 17						09 23			
Goring-by-Sea	d						08 57											09 27			
Durrington-on-Sea	d						09 00											09 30			
West Worthing	d						09 02				09 09							09 32			09 39
Worthing ■	a						09 04				09 11	09 24						09 34			09 41
	d						09 05				09 12	09 26						09 36			09 42
East Worthing	d										09 14										09 44
Lancing	d						09 09				09 17	09 30									09 47
Shoreham-by-Sea	d						09 13				09 22	09 34						09 42			09 52
Southwick	d										09 25	09 37									09 55
Fishersgate	d										09 27										09 57
Portslade	d						09 18				09 29	09 40						09 47			09 59
Aldrington	d										09 31										10 01
Hove ■	a						09 21				09 33	09 43						09 50			10 03
	d						09 22			09 24	09 34	09 44						09 51		09 54	10 04
Brighton ■	a									09 28	09 38	09 48								09 58	10 08
Preston Park	d																	09 55			
Burgess Hill	a																	10 04			
Haywards Heath ■	a						09 40											10 10			
Arundel	d				08 42											09 12					
Amberley	d				08 47											09 17					
Pulborough	d				08 53											09 23					
Billingshurst	d				09 00											09 29					
Christs Hospital	d				09 06											09 36					
Horsham ■	a				09 11	09 16										09 40	09 47				
	d				09 20											09 51					
Crawley	d				09 29											10 00					
Three Bridges ■	a				09 32											10 03					
Gatwick Airport ■	a				09 37		09 56									10 08		10 25			
	d				09 38		09 57									10 09		10 26			
Horley	a				09 41																
Redhill ■	a				09 47											10 16					
East Croydon	a				09 59		10 11									10 28		10 41			
London Bridge ■	a																				
Clapham Junction ■	a				10 09		10 21									10 37		10 51			
London Victoria ■	a				10 16		10 28									10 45		10 58			

A ⚒ from Horsham

B ⚒ from Haywards Heath

Southampton, Portsmouth and Sussex Coast - Brighton, Gatwick Airport and London

Network Diagram - see first Page of Table 186

		SN ■	SN ◇■	SN	SN	SN ◇■	SN ◇■	SN ◇■	SN	SN	SN	SN	SN	SN ◇■ H	SN ◇■	SN ◇■
Eastleigh	d															
Southampton Airport Parkway	d															
Southampton Central	d	08 33														09 10
Swanwick	d	08 50														09 28
Fareham	d	08 57														09 37
Portchester	d															09 42
Cosham	d	09 05														09 46
Portsmouth Harbour	d			08 51			09 12					09 29				
Portsmouth &Southsea	d			08 55			09 16					09 33				
Fratton	d			08 59			09 20					09 37				
Hilsea	d			09 04												
Bedhampton	d			09 13												
Havant	d	09 12		09 16			09 30					09 46				09 54
Warblington	d			09 18												
Emsworth	d	09 16		09 21								09 50				10 00
Southbourne	d			09 24								09 53				10 03
Nutbourne	d			09 26												
Bosham	d			09 30												
Fishbourne (Sussex)	d			09 33												
Chichester	a	09 24		09 36			09 40					10 00				10 10
	d	09 25		09 37			09 41					10 00				10 11
Bognor Regis	d				09 39	09 30							10 07		09 56	
Barnham	a	09 32		09 44	09 45	09 36	09 48					10 08	10 13		10 02	10 18
	d	09 33	09 42	09 45		09 37	09 49		09 52			10 08	10 15	10 13	10 03	10 19
Bognor Regis	a		09 48						09 59					10 19		
Ford	d	09 37		09 49		09 41							10 19		10 07	
Littlehampton	a			09 54									10 24			
	d							09 45								
Angmering	d	09 43						09 54				10 17				
Goring-by-Sea	d	09 47						09 58								
Durrington-on-Sea	d	09 50						10 00								
West Worthing	d	09 52						10 02			10 09					
Worthing	a	09 54						10 05			10 11	10 24				
	d	09 56						10 06			10 12	10 26				
East Worthing	d										10 14					
Lancing	d	10 00						10 10			10 17	10 30				
Shoreham-by-Sea	d	10 04						10 14			10 22	10 34				
Southwick	d	10 07									10 25	10 37				
Fishersgate	d										10 27					
Portslade	d	10 10									10 29	10 40				
Aldrington	d										10 31					
Hove	a	10 13						10 20			10 33	10 43				
	d	10 14						10 21		10 24	10 34	10 44				
Brighton	a	10 18								10 28	10 38	10 48				
Preston Park	d															
Burgess Hill	a															
Haywards Heath	a							10 35								
Arundel	d					09 46									10 12	
Amberley	d														10 17	
Pulborough	d					09 55									10 23	
Billingshurst	d					10 01									10 29	
Christs Hospital	d														10 36	
Horsham	a					10 10	10 16								10 40	10 46
	d						10 20									10 50
Crawley	d						10 29									10 59
Three Bridges	a						10 32									11 02
Gatwick Airport	a						10 37	10 55								11 07
	d						10 38	10 56								11 08
Horley	a						10 41									
Redhill	a						10 47									11 15
East Croydon	a						10 59	11 11								11 27
London Bridge	a															
Clapham Junction	a						11 09	11 21								11 37
London Victoria	a						11 16	11 28								11 44

Southampton, Portsmouth and Sussex Coast - Brighton, Gatwick Airport and London

Network Diagram - see first Page of Table 186

		SN ◇■	SN	SN	SN	SN ■	SN ◇■ H	SN	SN	SN ◇■	SN ◇■	SN ◇■	SN	SN	SN	SN	SN ◇■ H	SN
Eastleigh	d																	
Southampton Airport Parkway	d																	
Southampton Central	d					09 33												
Swanwick	d					09 50												
Fareham	d					09 56												
Portchester	d																	
Cosham	d					10 05												
Portsmouth Harbour	d										10 12					10 29		
Portsmouth &Southsea	d							09 59			10 16					10 33		
Fratton	d							10 04			10 20					10 37		
Hilsea	d							10 08										
Bedhampton	d							10 13										
Havant	d					10 11		10 16			10 30					10 46		
Warblington	d							10 18										
Emsworth	d					10 15		10 21								10 50		
Southbourne	d							10 24								10 53		
Nutbourne	d							10 26										
Bosham	d							10 30										
Fishbourne (Sussex)	d							10 33										
Chichester	a					10 23		10 36			10 40					11 00		
	d					10 25		10 37			10 41					11 00		
Bognor Regis	d								10 39	10 30								11 07
Barnham	a					10 32		10 44	10 45	10 36	10 48					11 08		11 13
	d		10 22			10 33	10 39	10 45		10 37	10 49		10 52			11 08	11 12	11 15
Bognor Regis	a		10 29				10 46						10 59				11 18	
Ford	d					10 37		10 49		10 41								11 19
Littlehampton	a							10 54										11 24
	d	10 15										10 45						
Angmering	d	10 23				10 43						10 53				11 17		
Goring-by-Sea	d	10 27				10 47						10 57						
Durrington-on-Sea	d	10 30				10 50						11 00						
West Worthing	d	10 32			10 39	10 52						11 02			11 09			
Worthing	a	10 34			10 41	10 54						11 04			11 11	11 24		
	d	10 36			10 42	10 56						11 06			11 12	11 26		
East Worthing	d				10 44										11 14			
Lancing	d				10 47	11 00						11 10			11 17	11 30		
Shoreham-by-Sea	d	10 42			10 52	11 04						11 14			11 22	11 34		
Southwick	d				10 55	11 07									11 25	11 37		
Fishersgate	d				10 57										11 27			
Portslade	d	10 47			10 59	11 10									11 29	11 40		
Aldrington	d				11 01										11 31			
Hove	a	10 50			11 03	11 13						11 20			11 33	11 43		
	d	10 51		10 54	11 04	11 14						11 21		11 24	11 34	11 44		
Brighton	a			10 58	11 08	11 18								11 28	11 38	11 48		
Preston Park	d	10 55																
Burgess Hill	a	11 03																
Haywards Heath	a	11 09										11 35						
Arundel	d									10 46								
Amberley	d																	
Pulborough	d									10 55								
Billingshurst	d									11 01								
Christs Hospital	d																	
Horsham	a									11 10	11 16							
	d										11 20							
Crawley	d										11 29							
Three Bridges	a										11 32							
Gatwick Airport	a	11 24									11 37	11 55						
	d	11 25									11 38	11 56						
Horley	a										11 41							
Redhill	a										11 47							
East Croydon	a	11 40									11 59	12 11						
London Bridge	a																	
Clapham Junction	a	11 50									12 09	12 21						
London Victoria	a	11 57									12 18	12 28						

Table 188

Mondays to Fridays

Southampton, Portsmouth and Sussex Coast - Brighton, Gatwick Airport and London

Network Diagram - see first Page of Table 186

		SN ◇1	SN ◇1	SN ◇1	SN	SN	SN	SN 1	SN ◇1	SN	SN	SN ◇1	SN ◇1	SN ◇1	SN	SN
Eastleigh	d															
Southampton Airport Parkway	d															
Southampton Central	d		10 13					10 33								
Swanwick	d		10 32					10 50								
Fareham	d		10 39					10 57								
Portchester	d		10 44													
Cosham	d		10 48					11 05								
Portsmouth Harbour	d												11 12			
Portsmouth & Southsea	d									10 59			11 16			
Fratton	d									11 04			11 20			
Hilsea	d									11 08						
Bedhampton	d									11 13						
Havant	d		10 56					11 12		11 16			11 30			
Warblington	d									11 18						
Emsworth	d		11 00					11 16		11 21						
Southbourne	d		11 03							11 24						
Nutbourne	d									11 26						
Bosham	d									11 30						
Fishbourne (Sussex)	d									11 33						
Chichester 4	a		11 10					11 24		11 36			11 40			
	d		11 11					11 25		11 37			11 41			
Bognor Regis 4	d	10 56									11 39	11 30				
Barnham	a	11 02	11 18					11 32		11 44	11 45	11 36	11 48			
	d	11 03	11 19		11 22			11 33	11 39	11 45		11 37	11 49		11 52	
Bognor Regis	a				11 29				11 46						11 59	
Ford 4	d	11 07						11 37		11 49		11 41				
Littlehampton 4	a									11 54						
	d			11 15										11 45		
Angmering 3	d			11 23				11 43						11 53		
Goring-by-Sea	d			11 27				11 47						11 57		
Durrington-on-Sea	d			11 30				11 50						12 00		
West Worthing	d			11 32			11 39	11 52						12 02		
Worthing 4	a			11 34			11 41	11 54						12 04		
	d			11 36			11 42	11 56						12 06		
East Worthing	d						11 44									
Lancing	d						11 47	12 00						12 10		
Shoreham-by-Sea	d			11 42			11 52	12 04						12 14		
Southwick	d						11 55	12 07								
Fishersgate	d						11 57									
Portslade	d			11 47			11 59	12 10								
Aldrington	d						12 01									
Hove 2	a			11 50			12 03	12 13						12 20		
	d			11 51		11 54	12 04	12 14						12 21		12 24
Brighton 10	a					11 58	12 08	12 18								12 28
Preston Park	d			11 55												
Burgess Hill	a			12 03												
Haywards Heath 3	a			12 09										12 35		
Arundel	d	11 12										11 46				
Amberley	d	11 17														
Pulborough	d	11 23										11 55				
Billingshurst	d	11 29										12 01				
Christs Hospital	d	11 36														
Horsham 4	a	11 40	11 46									12 10	12 16			
	d	11 50										12 20				
Crawley	d	11 59										12 29				
Three Bridges 4	a	12 02										12 32				
Gatwick Airport 10	a	12 07		12 24								12 37		12 55		
	d	12 08		12 25								12 38		12 56		
Horley	a											12 41				
Redhill 5	a	12 15										12 47				
East Croydon	a	12 27		12 40								12 59		13 11		
London Bridge 4	a															
Clapham Junction 10	a	12 37		12 50								13 09		13 21		
London Victoria 15	a	12 44		12 57								13 16		13 28		

Table 188

Mondays to Fridays

Southampton, Portsmouth and Sussex Coast - Brighton, Gatwick Airport and London

Network Diagram - see first Page of Table 186

		SN	SN	SN ◇1	SN	SN ◇1	SN ◇1	SN ◇1	SN	SN	SN	SN 1	SN ◇1	SN	SN
Eastleigh	d														
Southampton Airport Parkway	d														
Southampton Central	d						11 13					11 33			
Swanwick	d						11 33					11 50			
Fareham	d						11 40					11 57			
Portchester	d						11 45								
Cosham	d						11 49					12 05			
Portsmouth Harbour	d		11 29												
Portsmouth & Southsea	d		11 33											11 59	
Fratton	d		11 37											12 04	
Hilsea	d													12 08	
Bedhampton	d													12 13	
Havant	d		11 46				11 56					12 12		12 16	
Warblington	d													12 18	
Emsworth	d		11 50				12 00					12 16		12 21	
Southbourne	d		11 53				12 03							12 24	
Nutbourne	d													12 26	
Bosham	d													12 30	
Fishbourne (Sussex)	d													12 33	
Chichester 4	a		12 00				12 10					12 24		12 36	
	d		12 00				12 11					12 25		12 37	
Bognor Regis 4	d				12 07	11 56									12 39
Barnham	a		12 08		12 13	12 02	12 18					12 32		12 44	12 45
	d		12 08	12 12	12 15	12 03	12 19		12 22			12 33	12 39	12 45	
Bognor Regis	a			12 18					12 29				12 46		
Ford 4	d				12 19	12 07						12 37		12 49	
Littlehampton 4	a				12 24									12 54	
	d							12 15							
Angmering 3	d		12 17					12 23				12 43			
Goring-by-Sea	d							12 27				12 47			
Durrington-on-Sea	d							12 30				12 50			
West Worthing	d	12 09						12 32			12 39	12 52			
Worthing 4	a	12 11	12 24					12 34			12 41	12 54			
	d	12 12	12 26					12 36			12 42	12 56			
East Worthing	d	12 14									12 44				
Lancing	d	12 17	12 30								12 47	13 00			
Shoreham-by-Sea	d	12 22	12 34					12 42			12 52	13 04			
Southwick	d	12 25	12 37								12 55	13 07			
Fishersgate	d	12 27									12 57				
Portslade	d	12 29	12 40					12 47			12 59	13 10			
Aldrington	d	12 31									13 01				
Hove 2	a	12 33	12 43					12 50			13 03	13 13			
	d	12 34	12 44					12 51		12 54	13 04	13 14			
Brighton 10	a	12 38	12 48							12 58	13 08	13 18			
Preston Park	d							12 55							
Burgess Hill	a							13 03							
Haywards Heath 3	a							13 09							
Arundel	d					12 12									
Amberley	d					12 17									
Pulborough	d					12 23									
Billingshurst	d					12 29									
Christs Hospital	d					12 36									
Horsham 4	a					12 40	12 46								
	d					12 50									
Crawley	d					12 59									
Three Bridges 4	a					13 02									
Gatwick Airport 10	a					13 07		13 24							
	d					13 08		13 25							
Horley	a														
Redhill 5	a					13 15									
East Croydon	a					13 27		13 40							
London Bridge 4	a														
Clapham Junction 10	a					13 37		13 50							
London Victoria 15	a					13 44		13 57							

Southampton, Portsmouth and Sussex Coast - Brighton, Gatwick Airport and London

Network Diagram - see first Page of Table 186

		SN ◇1	SN ◇1	SN ◇1	SN	SN	SN	SN	SN ◇1	SN	SN ◇1	SN ◇1	SN ◇1	SN	SN	SN	SN 1
Eastleigh	d																
Southampton Airport Parkway	d																
Southampton Central	d											12 13					12 33
Swanwick	d											12 33					12 50
Fareham	d											12 40					12 56
Portchester	d											12 45					
Cosham	d											12 49					13 05
Portsmouth Harbour	d		12 12					12 29									
Portsmouth &Southsea	d		12 16					12 33									
Fratton	d		12 20					12 37									
Hilsea	d																
Bedhampton	d																
Havant	d		12 30					12 46				12 56					13 11
Warblington	d																
Emsworth	d							12 50				13 00					13 15
Southbourne	d							12 53				13 03					
Nutbourne	d																
Bosham	d																
Fishbourne (Sussex)	d																
Chichester 4	a		12 40					13 00				13 10					13 23
	d		12 41					13 00				13 11					13 25
Bognor Regis 4	d	12 30								13 07	12 56						
Barnham	a	12 36	12 48					13 08		13 13	13 02	13 18					13 32
	d	12 37	12 49		12 52			13 08	13 12	13 15	13 03	13 19		13 22			13 33
Bognor Regis	a				12 59				13 18					13 29			
Ford 4	d	12 41								13 19	13 07						13 37
Littlehampton 4	a									13 24							
	d			12 45									13 15				
Angmering 4	d			12 53				13 17					13 23				13 43
Goring-by-Sea	d			12 57									13 27				13 47
Durrington-on-Sea	d			13 00									13 30				13 50
West Worthing	d			13 02			13 09						13 32			13 39	13 52
Worthing 4	a			13 04			13 11	13 24					13 34			13 41	13 54
	d			13 06			13 12	13 26					13 36			13 42	13 56
East Worthing	d						13 14									13 44	
Lancing	d			13 10			13 17	13 30								13 47	14 00
Shoreham-by-Sea	d			13 14			13 22	13 34					13 42			13 52	14 04
Southwick	d						13 25	13 37								13 55	14 07
Fishersgate	d						13 27									13 57	
Portslade	d						13 29	13 40					13 47			13 59	14 10
Aldrington	d						13 31									14 01	
Hove 2	a			13 20			13 33	13 43					13 50			14 03	14 13
	d			13 21		13 24	13 34	13 44					13 51		13 54	14 04	14 14
Brighton 10	a					13 28	13 38	13 48							13 58	14 08	14 18
Preston Park	d												13 55				
Burgess Hill	a												14 03				
Haywards Heath 3	a			13 35									14 09				
Arundel	d	12 46									13 12						
Amberley	d										13 17						
Pulborough	d	12 55									13 23						
Billingshurst	d	13 01									13 29						
Christs Hospital	d										13 36						
Horsham 4	a	13 10	13 16								13 40	13 46					
	d	13 20									13 50						
Crawley	d	13 29									13 59						
Three Bridges 4	a	13 32									14 02						
Gatwick Airport 10	a	13 37		13 55							14 07		14 24				
	d	13 38		13 56							14 08		14 25				
Horley	a	13 41															
Redhill 5	a	13 47									14 15						
East Croydon	a	13 59		14 11							14 27		14 40				
London Bridge 4	a																
Clapham Junction 10	a	14 09		14 21							14 37		14 50				
London Victoria 15	a	14 16		14 28							14 44		14 57				

Southampton, Portsmouth and Sussex Coast - Brighton, Gatwick Airport and London

Network Diagram - see first Page of Table 186

		SN ◇1	SN	SN	SN ◇1	SN ◇1	SN ◇1	SN	SN	SN	SN	SN ◇1	SN	SN ◇1	SN ◇1	SN ◇1 A ⊼	SN	SN	SN
Eastleigh	d																		
Southampton Airport Parkway	d																		
Southampton Central	d														13 13				
Swanwick	d														13 33				
Fareham	d														13 40				
Portchester	d														13 45				
Cosham	d														13 49				
Portsmouth Harbour	d					13 12					13 29								
Portsmouth &Southsea	d		12 59			13 16					13 33								
Fratton	d		13 04			13 20					13 37								
Hilsea	d		13 08																
Bedhampton	d		13 13																
Havant	d		13 16			13 30					13 46				13 56				
Warblington	d		13 18																
Emsworth	d		13 21								13 50				14 00				
Southbourne	d		13 24								13 53				14 03				
Nutbourne	d		13 26																
Bosham	d		13 30																
Fishbourne (Sussex)	d		13 33																
Chichester 4	a		13 36			13 40					14 00				14 10				
	d		13 37			13 41					14 00				14 11				
Bognor Regis 4	d			13 39	13 30								14 07	13 56					
Barnham	a		13 44	13 45	13 36	13 48					14 08		14 13	14 02	14 18				
	d	13 39	13 45		13 37	13 49		13 52			14 08	14 12	14 15	14 03	14 19		14 22		
Bognor Regis	a	13 46						13 59				14 18					14 29		
Ford 4	d		13 49		13 41								14 19	14 07					
Littlehampton 4	a		13 54										14 24						
	d						13 45									14 15			
Angmering 4	d						13 53				14 17					14 23			
Goring-by-Sea	d						13 57									14 27			
Durrington-on-Sea	d						14 00									14 30			
West Worthing	d						14 02			14 09						14 32			14 39
Worthing 4	a						14 04			14 11	14 24					14 34			14 41
	d						14 06			14 12	14 26					14 36			14 42
East Worthing	d									14 14									14 44
Lancing	d						14 10			14 17	14 30								14 47
Shoreham-by-Sea	d						14 14			14 22	14 34					14 42			14 52
Southwick	d									14 25	14 37								14 55
Fishersgate	d									14 27									14 57
Portslade	d									14 29	14 40					14 47			14 59
Aldrington	d									14 31									15 01
Hove 2	a						14 20			14 33	14 43					14 50			15 03
	d						14 21		14 24	14 34	14 44					14 51		14 54	15 04
Brighton 10	a								14 28	14 38	14 48							14 58	15 08
Preston Park	d															14 55			
Burgess Hill	a															15 03			
Haywards Heath 3	a						14 35									15 09			
Arundel	d				13 46									14 12					
Amberley	d													14 17					
Pulborough	d				13 55									14 23					
Billingshurst	d				14 01									14 29					
Christs Hospital	d													14 36					
Horsham 4	a				14 10	14 16								14 40	14 46				
	d				14 20									14 50					
Crawley	d				14 29									14 59					
Three Bridges 4	a				14 32									15 02					
Gatwick Airport 10	a				14 37		14 55							15 07		15 24			
	d				14 38		14 56							15 08		15 25			
Horley	a				14 41														
Redhill 5	a				14 47									15 16					
East Croydon	a				14 59		15 11							15 28		15 40			
London Bridge 4	a																		
Clapham Junction 10	a				15 09		15 21							15 37		15 50			
London Victoria 15	a				15 20		15 28							15 46		15 57			

A ⊼ from Haywards Heath

Southampton, Portsmouth and Sussex Coast - Brighton, Gatwick Airport and London

Network Diagram - see first Page of Table 186

		SN	SN	SN	SN	SN	SN	SN	SN	SN	SN	SN	SN	SN	SN	SN	SN
		■1	◇■1			◇■1	◇■1	◇■1					◇■1		◇■1	◇■1	◇■1
							A	B								A	B
						⊼	⊼	⊼							⊼	⊼	⊼
Eastleigh	d																
Southampton Airport Parkway	d																
Southampton Central	d	13 33														14 13	
Swanwick	d	13 50														14 33	
Fareham	d	13 56														14 40	
Portchester	d															14 45	
Cosham	d	14 05														14 49	
Portsmouth Harbour	d						14 12					14 29					
Portsmouth & Southsea	d			13 59			14 16					14 33					
Fratton	d			14 04			14 20					14 37					
Hilsea	d			14 08													
Bedhampton	d			14 13													
Havant	d	14 11		14 16			14 30					14 46				14 56	
Warblington	d			14 18													
Emsworth	d	14 15		14 21													
Southbourne	d			14 24								14 50				15 00	
Nutbourne	d			14 26								14 53				15 03	
Bosham	d			14 30													
Fishbourne (Sussex)	d			14 33													
Chichester ■4	a	14 23		14 36			14 40					15 00				15 10	
	d	14 25		14 37			14 41					15 00				15 11	
Bognor Regis ■4	d				14 39	14 30								15 07	14 56		
Barnham	a	14 32		14 44	14 45	14 36	14 48					15 08		15 13	15 02	15 18	
	d	14 33	14 39	14 45		14 37	14 49		14 52			15 08	15 12	15 15	15 03	15 19	
Bognor Regis	a		14 46						14 59				15 18				
Ford ■4	d	14 37		14 49		14 41								15 19	15 07		
Littlehampton ■4	a			14 54										15 26			
	d							14 45									15 15
Angmering ■3	d	14 43						14 53				15 17					15 23
Goring-by-Sea	d	14 47						14 57									15 27
Durrington-on-Sea	d	14 50						15 00									15 30
West Worthing	d	14 52						15 02			15 09						15 32
Worthing ■4	a	14 54						15 04			15 11	15 24					15 34
	d	14 56						15 06			15 12	15 26					15 35
East Worthing	d										15 14						15 37
Lancing	d	15 00						15 10			15 17	15 30					
Shoreham-by-Sea	d	15 04						15 14			15 22	15 34					15 43
Southwick	d	15 07									15 25	15 37					
Fishersgate	d										15 27						
Portslade	d	15 10									15 29	15 40					15 48
Aldrington	d										15 31						
Hove ■2	a	15 13						15 20			15 33	15 43					15 51
	d	15 14						15 21		15 24	15 34	15 44					15 52
Brighton ■10	a	15 18								15 28	15 38	15 48					
Preston Park	d																15 56
Burgess Hill	a																16 04
Haywards Heath ■3	a							15 35									16 10
Arundel	d					14 46									15 12		
Amberley	d														15 17		
Pulborough	d					14 55									15 23		
Billingshurst	d					15 01									15 29		
Christs Hospital	d														15 36		
Horsham ■4	a					15 10	15 16								15 40	15 46	
	d					15 20									15 50		
Crawley	d					15 29									15 59		
Three Bridges ■4	a					15 32									16 02		
Gatwick Airport ■10	a					15 37		15 55							16 07		16 25
	d					15 38		15 56							16 08		16 26
Horley	a					15 41											
Redhill ■5	a					15 47									16 17		
East Croydon	a					15 59		16 11							16 30		16 40
London Bridge ■4	a																
Clapham Junction ■10	a					16 09		16 21							16 39		16 50
London Victoria ■15	a					16 16		16 28							16 46		16 58

A ⊼ from Horsham

B ⊼ from Haywards Heath

Southampton, Portsmouth and Sussex Coast - Brighton, Gatwick Airport and London

Network Diagram - see first Page of Table 186

		SN	SN	SN	GW	SN	SN	SN	SN	SN	SN	SN	SN	SN	SN	SN	SN	SN
					■	■1	◇■1			◇■1	◇■1	◇■1					◇■1	
												A						
					⊼							⊼						
Eastleigh	d					14 41												
Southampton Airport Parkway	d					14n34												
Southampton Central	d				14 34	14n26												
Swanwick	d																	
Fareham	d				14 56	15 00												
Portchester	d																	
Cosham	d				15 04													
Portsmouth Harbour	d										15 12					15 29		
Portsmouth & Southsea	d							14 59			15 16					15 33		
Fratton	d							15 04			15 20					15 37		
Hilsea	d							15 08										
Bedhampton	d							15 14										
Havant	d				15 11	15 15		15 17			15 30					15 46		
Warblington	d							15 19										
Emsworth	d							15 22										
Southbourne	d							15 25								15 50		
Nutbourne	d							15 28								15 53		
Bosham	d							15 31										
Fishbourne (Sussex)	d							15 34										
Chichester ■4	a				15 21	15 25		15 37			15 41					16 00		
	d				15 22	15 29		15 38			15 42					16 00		
Bognor Regis ■4	d								15 39	15 27								16 09
Barnham	a				15 29	15 36		15 45	15 45	15 33	15 49					16 08		16 15
	d	15 22			15 30	15 37	15 40	15 46		15 34	15 50		15 53			16 08	16 12	
Bognor Regis	a	15 29					15 46						16 00				16 18	
Ford ■4	d					15 41		15 50		15 38								
Littlehampton ■4	a							15 55										
	d											15 45			15 50			
Angmering ■3	d					15 47						15 53			16 00	16 17		
Goring-by-Sea	d					15 51						15 57			16 04			
Durrington-on-Sea	d					15 54						16 00			16 07			
West Worthing	d			15 39		15 56						16 02			16 09			
Worthing ■4	a			15 41	15 45	15 58						16 04			16 11	16 24		
	d			15 42	15 50	15 59						16 06			16 12	16 26		
East Worthing	d			15 44											16 14			
Lancing	d			15 47		16 03						16 10			16 17	16 30		
Shoreham-by-Sea	d			15 52	15 57	16 07						16 14			16 22	16 34		
Southwick	d			15 55		16 10									16 25	16 37		
Fishersgate	d			15 57											16 27			
Portslade	d			15 59		16 13									16 29	16 40		
Aldrington	d			16 01											16 31			
Hove ■2	a			16 03	16 07	16 16						16 20			16 33	16 43		
	d		15 54	16 04	16 08	16 17						16 21		16 24	16 34	16 44		
Brighton ■10	a		15 58	16 08	16 14	16 21								16 28	16 38	16 48		
Preston Park	d																	
Burgess Hill	a																	
Haywards Heath ■3	a											16 35						
Arundel	d									15 43								
Amberley	d																	
Pulborough	d									15 52								
Billingshurst	d									15 58								
Christs Hospital	d									16 05								
Horsham ■4	a									16 10	16 16							
	d									16 20								
Crawley	d									16 29								
Three Bridges ■4	a									16 32								
Gatwick Airport ■10	a									16 37		16 57						
	d									16 38		16 58						
Horley	a																	
Redhill ■5	a									16 46								
East Croydon	a									17 01		17 13						
London Bridge ■4	a																	
Clapham Junction ■10	a									17 10		17 22						
London Victoria ■15	a									17 17		17 29						

A ⊼ from Haywards Heath

n Stops at these stations before Eastleigh

Southampton, Portsmouth and Sussex Coast - Brighton, Gatwick Airport and London

Network Diagram - see first Page of Table 186

		SN ◇■ ✠	SN ◇■ A ✠	SN ◇■ B ✠	SN	SN	SN	SN ■	SN ◇■	SN	SN	SN ◇■ ✠	SN ◇■ A ✠	SN ◇■ B ✠	SN	SN
Eastleigh	d															
Southampton Airport Parkway	d															
Southampton Central	d		15 13					15 33								
Swanwick	d		15 33					15 50								
Fareham	d		15 40					15 57								
Portchester	d		15 45													
Cosham	d		15 49					16 05								
Portsmouth Harbour	d												16 12			
Portsmouth & Southsea	d									15 59			16 16			
Fratton	d									16 04			16 20			
Hilsea	d									16 08						
Bedhampton	d									16 13						
Havant	d		15 58					16 12		16 16			16 30			
Warblington	d									16 18						
Emsworth	d		16 02					16 16		16 21			16 34			
Southbourne	d		16 05							16 24						
Nutbourne	d									16 26						
Bosham	d									16 30						
Fishbourne (Sussex)	d									16 33						
Chichester	a		16 12					16 24		16 36			16 42			
	d		16 13					16 25		16 37			16 43			
Bognor Regis	d	15 56									16 39	16 30				
Barnham	a	16 02	16 20					16 32		16 44	16 45	16 36	16 50			
	d	16 03	16 21		16 24			16 33	16 40	16 45		16 37	16 51		16 54	
Bognor Regis	a				16 31				16 46						17 01	
Ford	d	16 07						16 37		16 49		16 41				
Littlehampton	a									16 54						
	d			16 15										16 45		
Angmering	d			16 23				16 43						16 53		
Goring-by-Sea	d			16 27				16 47						16 57		
Durrington-on-Sea	d			16 30				16 50						17 00		
West Worthing	d			16 32			16 39	16 52						17 02		
Worthing	a			16 34			16 41	16 54						17 04		
	d			16 36			16 42	16 56						17 06		
East Worthing	d						16 44									
Lancing	d						16 47	17 00						17 10		
Shoreham-by-Sea	d			16 42			16 52	17 04						17 14		
Southwick	d						16 55	17 07								
Fishersgate	d						16 57									
Portslade	d			16 47			16 59	17 10								
Aldrington	d						17 01									
Hove	a			16 50			17 03	17 13						17 20		
	d			16 51		16 54	17 04	17 14						17 21		17 24
Brighton	a					16 58	17 08	17 18								17 28
Preston Park	d															
Burgess Hill	a			17 01												
Haywards Heath	a			17 09										17 35		
Arundel	d	16 12										16 46				
Amberley	d	16 17														
Pulborough	d	16 23										16 55				
Billingshurst	d	16 29										17 01				
Christs Hospital	d	16 36										17 08				
Horsham	a	16 40	16 48									17 12	17 18			
	d		16 52										17 22			
Crawley	d		17 01										17 31			
Three Bridges	a		17 04										17 34			
Gatwick Airport	a		17 09	17 25									17 41	17 54		
	d		17 10	17 26									17 42	17 55		
Horley	a															
Redhill	a		17 17										17 49			
East Croydon	a		17 30	17 41									18 01	18 11		
London Bridge	a															
Clapham Junction	a		17 39	17 50									18 13	18 21		
London Victoria	a		17 46	17 58									18 20	18 29		

A ✠ from Horsham

B ✠ from Haywards Heath

Table 188

Mondays to Fridays

Southampton, Portsmouth and Sussex Coast - Brighton, Gatwick Airport and London

Network Diagram - see first Page of Table 186

		SN	SN ■	SN	SN ◇■	SN ◇■ ✠	SN ◇■ A ✠	SN ◇■ B ✠	SN	SN	SN ■	SN	SN	SN ■	SN ◇■	SN
Eastleigh	d															
Southampton Airport Parkway	d															
Southampton Central	d						16 12							16 33		
Swanwick	d						16 29							16 50		
Fareham	d						16 36							16 57		
Portchester	d						16 41									
Cosham	d						16 45							17 05		
Portsmouth Harbour	d			16 29									16 40			
Portsmouth & Southsea	d			16 33									16 46			17 00
Fratton	d			16 37									16 50			17 04
Hilsea	d												16 54			17 08
Bedhampton	d															17 14
Havant	d			16 46			16 52						17 00	17 12		17 17
Warblington	d												17 02			17 19
Emsworth	d			16 50			16 56						17 05	17 17		17 22
Southbourne	d			16 53			16 59						17 08			17 25
Nutbourne	d												17 10			17 28
Bosham	d						17 03						17 14			17 31
Fishbourne (Sussex)	d												17 17			17 34
Chichester	a			17 00			17 08						17 20	17 25		17 37
	d			17 00			17 13						17 21	17 25		17 38
Bognor Regis	d					16 56			17 18							
Barnham	a			17 08		17 02	17 20		17 24				17 28	17 33		17 45
	d			17 08	17 12	17 03	17 21		17 25	17 24			17 29	17 33	17 42	17 46
Bognor Regis	a				17 18					17 31					17 49	
Ford	d					17 07			17 29					17 38		17 50
Littlehampton	a								17 37							17 55
	d							17 15								
Angmering	d			17 17				17 23						17 44		
Goring-by-Sea	d							17 27						17 48		
Durrington-on-Sea	d							17 30						17 50		
West Worthing	d	17 09						17 32						17 52		
Worthing	a	17 11		17 24				17 34					17 43	17 55		
	d	17 12		17 26				17 36					17 43	17 56		
East Worthing	d	17 14											17 46			
Lancing	d	17 17		17 30									17 49	18 00		
Shoreham-by-Sea	d	17 22		17 34				17 42					17 53	18 04		
Southwick	d	17 25		17 37									17 56	18 07		
Fishersgate	d	17 27											17 58			
Portslade	d	17 29		17 40				17 47					18 00	18 10		
Aldrington	d	17 31											18 02			
Hove	a	17 33		17 43				17 50					18 04	18 13		
	d	17 34		17 44				17 51				18 01	18 05	18 14		
Brighton	a	17 38		17 48								18 05	18 09	18 18		
Preston Park	d															
Burgess Hill	a							18 03								
Haywards Heath	a							18 11								
Arundel	d					17 12										
Amberley	d					17 17										
Pulborough	d					17 23										
Billingshurst	d					17 29										
Christs Hospital	d					17 36										
Horsham	a					17 40	17 48									
	d		17 30				17 52				18 00					
Crawley	d		17 44				18 01				18 14					
Three Bridges	a		17 47				18 04				18 17					
Gatwick Airport	a		17 52				18 09	18 26			18 22					
	d		17 53				18 10	18 27			18 23					
Horley	a		17 56								18 26					
Redhill	a		18 06				18 17				18 36					
East Croydon	a		18 24				18 29	18 42			18 54					
London Bridge	a															
Clapham Junction	a		18 38				18 41	18 52			19 05					
London Victoria	a		18 45				18 48	18 59			19 13					

A ✠ from Horsham

B ✠ from Haywards Heath

Southampton, Portsmouth and Sussex Coast - Brighton, Gatwick Airport and London

Network Diagram - see first Page of Table 186

		SN ◇■	SN ◇■	SN ◇■ A ⌶	SN	SN	SN	SN ■	SN	SN	SN ◇■ ⌶	SN ◇■	SN ◇■	SN ■	SN ◇■	SN	SN	SN	SN
Eastleigh	d													17 16					
Southampton Airport Parkway	d													17 20					
Southampton Central	d												17 13	17 33					
Swanwick	d												17 33	17 50					
Fareham	d												17 40	17 56					
Portchester	d												17 45						
Cosham	d												17 49	18 05					
Portsmouth Harbour	d		17 12						17 29										
Portsmouth &Southsea	d		17 16						17 33									17 46	
Fratton	d		17 20						17 37									17 50	
Hilsea	d																	17 54	
Bedhampton	d																		
Havant	d		17 30						17 46				17 56	18 11				18 00	
Warblington	d																	18 02	
Emsworth	d								17 50				18 00	18 15				18 05	
Southbourne	d								17 53				18 03					18 08	
Nutbourne	d																	18 10	
Bosham	d																	18 14	
Fishbourne (Sussex)	d																	18 17	
Chichester ■	a		17 42						18 00				18 10	18 24				18 20	
	d		17 43						18 00				18 13	18 25				18 21	
Bognor Regis ■	d	17 30				17 51						17 57				18 19			
Barnham	a	17 36	17 50			17 57			18 08			18 03	18 20	18 32		18 25		18 28	
	d	17 37	17 51		17 54				18 08	18 08	18 14	18 04	18 21	18 33			18 27	18 29	
Bognor Regis	a				18 01					18 15	18 22						18 34		
Ford ■	d	17 41										18 08						18 33	
Littlehampton ■	a																	18 40	
	d			17 45											18 15				
Angmering ■	d			17 53					18 18					18 42	18 23				
Goring-by-Sea	d			17 57											18 27				
Durrington-on-Sea	d			18 00										18 48	18 30				
West Worthing	d			18 02											18 32				
Worthing ■	a			18 04					18 25					18 52	18 34				
	d			18 06					18 25					18 52	18 35				
East Worthing	d								18 28					18 55					
Lancing	d			18 10					18 31					18 58	18 39				
Shoreham-by-Sea	d			18 14					18 35					19 02	18 43				
Southwick	d								18 38					19 05					
Fishersgate	d								18 40					19 07					
Portslade	d								18 42					19 09	18 48				
Aldrington	d								18 44					19 11					
Hove ■	a			18 20					18 46					19 13	18 51				
	d			18 21			18 24		18 47					19 14	18 52				19 00
Brighton ■	a						18 28		18 51					19 18					19 04
Preston Park	d																		
Burgess Hill	a			18 33															
Haywards Heath ■	a			18 41											19 07				
Arundel	d	17 46										18 13							
Amberley	d											18 18							
Pulborough	d	17 55										18 24							
Billingshurst	d	18 01										18 30							
Christs Hospital	d	18 08										18 37							
Horsham ■	a	18 12	18 18									18 42	18 48						
	d	18 22						18 30				18 52							
Crawley	d	18 31						18 44				19 01							
Three Bridges ■	a	18 34						18 47				19 04							
Gatwick Airport ■ ✈	a	18 39		18 56				18 52				19 09			19 25				
	d	18 40		18 57				18 53				19 10			19 26				
Horley	a							18 56											
Redhill ■	a	18 47						19 06				19 17							
East Croydon	a	18 59		19 12				19 24				19 29			19 43				
London Bridge ■ ⊖	a																		
Clapham Junction ■	a	19 11		19 21				19 37				19 40			19 52				
London Victoria ■ ⊖	a	19 18		19 29				19 44				19 47			19 59				

A ⌶ from Haywards Heath

Southampton, Portsmouth and Sussex Coast - Brighton, Gatwick Airport and London

Network Diagram - see first Page of Table 186

		SN ◇■ ⌶	SN ■	SN ◇■	SN ■	SN	SN	SN	SN	SN ■	SN ◇■	SN	SN ■	SN ◇■	SN ◇■
Eastleigh	d														
Southampton Airport Parkway	d														
Southampton Central	d													18 11	
Swanwick	d													18 28	
Fareham	d													18 35	
Portchester	d													18 40	
Cosham	d													18 44	
Portsmouth Harbour	d									18 28					
Portsmouth &Southsea	d				17 59					18 32					
Fratton	d				18 04					18 36					
Hilsea	d				18 08										
Bedhampton	d				18 13										
Havant	d				18 16					18 44				18 51	
Warblington	d				18 18										
Emsworth	d				18 21					18 48				18 55	
Southbourne	d				18 24					18 51				18 58	
Nutbourne	d				18 26										
Bosham	d				18 30										
Fishbourne (Sussex)	d				18 33										
Chichester ■	a				18 36					18 58				19 05	
	d				18 37					18 59				19 06	
Bognor Regis ■	d			18 33				18 46				19 03			
Barnham	a			18 39	18 44			18 52		19 06		19 09		19 13	
	d	18 35		18 40	18 45			18 53	18 55	19 07	19 07	19 10		19 14	
Bognor Regis	a	18 41							19 02		19 13				
Ford ■	d			18 44				18 57				19 14		19 18	
Littlehampton ■	a							19 02				19 19			
	d						18 52								19 15
Angmering ■	d			18 53			19 00			19 16					19 23
Goring-by-Sea	d			18 57			19 04								19 27
Durrington-on-Sea	d			19 00			19 07								19 30
West Worthing	d			19 02			19 09								19 32
Worthing ■	a			19 04			19 11			19 23					19 34
	d			19 05			19 12			19 24					19 35
East Worthing	d						19 14			19 26					
Lancing	d			19 09			19 17			19 29					19 39
Shoreham-by-Sea	d			19 13			19 22			19 33					19 43
Southwick	d						19 25			19 36					
Fishersgate	d						19 27			19 38					
Portslade	d			19 18			19 29			19 40					19 48
Aldrington	d						19 31			19 43					
Hove ■	a			19 21			19 33			19 45					19 51
	d			19 22		19 24	19 34			19 45					19 52
Brighton ■	a					19 28	19 38			19 49					
Preston Park	d														
Burgess Hill	a			19 32											
Haywards Heath ■	a			19 37											20 05
Arundel	d				18 52									19 23	
Amberley	d													19 28	
Pulborough	d				19 01									19 34	
Billingshurst	d				19 08									19 41	
Christs Hospital	d													19 47	
Horsham ■	a				19 16									19 51	
	d		19 02		19 17								19 32	19 52	
Crawley	d		19 14		19 26								19 45	20 01	
Three Bridges ■	a		19 18		19 29								19 49	20 04	
Gatwick Airport ■ ✈	a		19 22	19 55	19 39								19 55	20 10	20 25
	d		19 23	19 56	19 40								19 56	20 11	20 26
Horley	a		19 26										19 59		
Redhill ■	a		19 38		19 47								20 05	20 18	
East Croydon	a		19 58	20 11	20 00								20 23	20 30	20 41
London Bridge ■ ⊖	a														
Clapham Junction ■	a		20 08	20 20	20 11								20 37	20 40	20 50
London Victoria ■ ⊖	a		20 15	20 28	20 20								20 44	20 50	20 59

Southampton, Portsmouth and Sussex Coast - Brighton, Gatwick Airport and London

Network Diagram - see first Page of Table 186

		SN	SN	SN	SN	SN	SN	SN	SN	SN	SN	SN	SN	SN	SN	SN	SN	SN
		1				1	◇1	1	◇1					1	◇1		1	◇1
Eastleigh	d																	
Southampton Airport Parkway	d																	
Southampton Central	d					18 33												19 12
Swanwick	d					18 50												19 29
Fareham	d					18 56												19 36
Portchester	d																	19 41
Cosham	d					19 05												19 46
Portsmouth Harbour	d			18 37														
Portsmouth & Southsea	d			18 42								18 59		19 32				
Fratton	d			18 46								19 04		19 36				
Hilsea	d			18 50								19 08						
Bedhampton	d											19 13						
Havant	d			18 56		19 11						19 16		19 46				19 52
Warblington	d			18 58								19 18						
Emsworth	d			19 01								19 21		19 50				19 56
Southbourne	d			19 04								19 24		19 53				19 59
Nutbourne	d			19 07								19 27						
Bosham	d			19 10								19 30						
Fishbourne (Sussex)	d			19 13								19 33						
Chichester 4	a			19 17		19 22						19 36		20 00				20 06
	d			19 17		19 22						19 40		20 01				20 07
Bognor Regis 4	d								19 36							20 05		
Barnham	a			19 25		19 30			19 42			19 47		20 08		20 11		20 14
	d	19 16	19 24	19 25		19 30	19 33		19 43			19 48	19 55	20 09	20 08	20 12		20 15
Bognor Regis	a	19 24	19 31				19 39						20 01		20 14			
Ford 4	d			19 30					19 47			19 52				20 16		20 19
Littlehampton 4	a			19 38								19 58				20 21		
	d										19 52							
Angmering 3	d					19 40			19 53		20 00			20 18				
Goring-by-Sea	d					19 44			19 57		20 04							
Durrington-on-Sea	d					19 46			20 00		20 07							
West Worthing	d					19 48			20 02		20 09							
Worthing 4	a					19 51			20 04		20 11			20 25				
	d					19 52			20 05		20 12			20 25				
East Worthing	d					19 55					20 14			20 28				
Lancing	d					19 58			20 09		20 17			20 31				
Shoreham-by-Sea	d					20 02			20 13		20 22			20 35				
Southwick	d					20 05					20 25			20 38				
Fishersgate	d					20 07					20 27			20 40				
Portslade	d					20 09			20 18		20 29			20 42				
Aldrington	d					20 11					20 31			20 44				
Hove 2	a					20 13			20 21		20 33			20 46				
	d				19 54	20 14			20 22	20 24	20 34			20 47				
Brighton 10	a				19 58	20 18				20 28	20 38			20 51				
Preston Park	d																	
Burgess Hill	a								20 32									
Haywards Heath 3	a								20 38									
Arundel	d																	20 24
Amberley	d																	20 29
Pulborough	d																	20 35
Billingshurst	d																	20 41
Christs Hospital	d																	20 48
Horsham 4	a																	20 52
	d							20 02									20 32	20 52
Crawley	d							20 14									20 45	21 01
Three Bridges 4	a							20 18	20 47								20 48	21 05
Gatwick Airport 10 ✈	a							20 22	20 51								20 56	21 10
	d							20 23	20 53								20 57	21 11
Horley	a							20 26									20 59	
Redhill 5	a							20 36									21 06	21 18
East Croydon	a							20 57	21 08								21 25	21 30
London Bridge 4 ⊖	a																	
Clapham Junction 10	a							21 07	21 18								21 37	21 40
London Victoria 15 ⊖	a							21 15	21 28								21 45	21 47

Southampton, Portsmouth and Sussex Coast - Brighton, Gatwick Airport and London

Network Diagram - see first Page of Table 186

		SN	SN	SN	SN	SN	SN	SN	SN	SN	SN	SN	SN	SN
		◇1		1		1	1	◇1	◇1 ⊼					
Eastleigh	d													
Southampton Airport Parkway	d													
Southampton Central	d					19 33								
Swanwick	d					19 51								
Fareham	d					19 57								
Portchester	d													
Cosham	d					20 06								
Portsmouth Harbour	d			19 40										
Portsmouth & Southsea	d			19 44								19 59		20 32
Fratton	d			19 48								20 04		20 36
Hilsea	d											20 08		
Bedhampton	d											20 14		
Havant	d			19 57		20 12						20 17		20 45
Warblington	d			19 59								20 19		
Emsworth	d			20 02		20 16						20 22		20 49
Southbourne	d			20 05								20 25		20 52
Nutbourne	d			20 07								20 27		
Bosham	d			20 11								20 31		
Fishbourne (Sussex)	d			20 14								20 34		
Chichester 4	a			20 17		20 24						20 37		20 59
	d			20 18		20 25						20 38		20 59
Bognor Regis 4	d							20 33						
Barnham	a			20 25		20 32		20 39				20 45		21 07
	d		20 22	20 27		20 33		20 40	20 43			20 46	20 52	21 07
Bognor Regis	a		20 28						20 49				20 59	
Ford 4	d			20 31				20 44				20 50		
Littlehampton 4	a			20 36								20 55		
	d	20 15									20 52			
Angmering 3	d	20 23				20 42		20 53			21 00			21 16
Goring-by-Sea	d	20 27						20 57			21 04			
Durrington-on-Sea	d	20 30				20 48		21 00			21 07			
West Worthing	d	20 32						21 02			21 09			
Worthing 4	a	20 34				20 52		21 04			21 11			21 23
	d	20 35				20 52		21 05			21 12			21 24
East Worthing	d					20 55					21 14			21 26
Lancing	d	20 39				20 58		21 09			21 17			21 29
Shoreham-by-Sea	d	20 43				21 02		21 13			21 22			21 33
Southwick	d					21 05					21 25			21 36
Fishersgate	d					21 07					21 27			21 38
Portslade	d	20 48				21 09		21 18			21 29			21 40
Aldrington	d					21 11					21 31			21 43
Hove 2	a	20 51				21 13		21 21			21 33			21 45
	d	20 52			20 55	21 14		21 22		21 24	21 34			21 45
Brighton 10	a				20 59	21 18				21 28	21 38			21 49
Preston Park	d													
Burgess Hill	a							21 32						
Haywards Heath 3	a	21 05						21 38						
Arundel	d													
Amberley	d													
Pulborough	d													
Billingshurst	d													
Christs Hospital	d													
Horsham 4	a													
	d						21 02							
Crawley	d						21 14							
Three Bridges 4	a						21 18	21 47						
Gatwick Airport 10 ✈	a	21 25					21 22	21 51						
	d	21 26					21 23	21 53						
Horley	a						21 26							
Redhill 5	a						21 36							
East Croydon	a	21 41					21 54	22 08						
London Bridge 4 ⊖	a													
Clapham Junction 10	a	21 51					22 07	22 18						
London Victoria 15 ⊖	a	21 58					22 14	22 26						

Table 188

Mondays to Fridays

Southampton, Portsmouth and Sussex Coast - Brighton, Gatwick Airport and London

Network Diagram - see first Page of Table 186

		SN	SN ◇1 🛒	SN 1	SN ◇1	SN ◇1 A 🛒	SN	SN 1	SN	SN 1	SN ◇1 🛒	SN	SN	SN 1	SN	SN
Eastleigh	d															
Southampton Airport Parkway	d															
Southampton Central	d				20 11					20 33						
Swanwick	d				20 28					20 50						
Fareham	d				20 35					20 57						
Portchester	d				20 40											
Cosham	d				20 44					21 06						
Portsmouth Harbour	d							20 40								
Portsmouth & Southsea	d							20 44								
Fratton	d							20 48								
Hilsea	d															
Bedhampton	d															
Havant	d				20 51			20 57		21 12						
Warblington	d							20 59								
Emsworth	d				20 55			21 02		21 16						
Southbourne	d				20 58			21 05								
Nutbourne	d							21 07								
Bosham	d							21 11								
Fishbourne (Sussex)	d							21 14								
Chichester 4	a				21 05			21 17		21 24						
	d				21 07			21 18		21 25						
Bognor Regis 4	d	21 04										21 39				
Barnham	a	21 10			21 14			21 25		21 32		21 45				
	d	21 11	21 12		21 15		21 22	21 26		21 33	21 42		21 52			
Bognor Regis	a		21 18				21 28				21 48		21 59			
Ford 4	d	21 15			21 19			21 30		21 37						
Littlehampton 4	a	21 20						21 35								
	d					21 15										21 52
Angmering 3	d					21 23				21 43						22 00
Goring-by-Sea	d					21 27				21 47						22 04
Durrington-on-Sea	d					21 30				21 50						22 07
West Worthing	d					21 32				21 52						22 09
Worthing 4	a					21 34				21 54						22 11
	d					21 35				21 55						22 12
East Worthing	d									21 57						22 14
Lancing	d					21 39				22 00						22 17
Shoreham-by-Sea	d					21 43				22 04						22 22
Southwick	d									22 07						22 25
Fishersgate	d									22 09						22 27
Portslade	d					21 48				22 11						22 29
Aldrington	d									22 14						22 31
Hove 2	a					21 51				22 16						22 33
	d					21 52			21 54	22 16					22 24	22 34
Brighton 10	a								21 58	22 21					22 28	22 38
Preston Park	d															
Burgess Hill	a					22 03										
Haywards Heath 3	a					22 10										
Arundel	d				21 24											
Amberley	d				21 29											
Pulborough	d				21 35											
Billingshurst	d				21 41											
Christs Hospital	d				21 48											
Horsham 4	a				21 52											
	d			21 32	21 52									22 02		
Crawley	d			21 45	22 01									22 14		
Three Bridges 4	a			21 48	22 05									22 18		
Gatwick Airport 10	a			21 55	22 10	22 25								22 23		
	d			21 56	22 11	22 26								22 24		
Horley	a			21 59										22 27		
Redhill 5	a			22 05	22 18									22 37		
East Croydon	a			22 24	22 30	22 41								22 55		
London Bridge 4	a															
Clapham Junction 10	a			22 37	22 40	22 50								23 06		
London Victoria 15	a			22 44	22 50	22 57								23 15		

A 🛒 from Haywards Heath

Table 188

Mondays to Fridays

Southampton, Portsmouth and Sussex Coast - Brighton, Gatwick Airport and London

Network Diagram - see first Page of Table 186

		SN 1	SN	SN ◇1	SN	SN 1	SN 1	SN	SN	SN 1	SN 1	SN 1	SN	SN	SN	SN ◇1	SN 1
Eastleigh	d																
Southampton Airport Parkway	d																
Southampton Central	d					21 13				21 33							22 13
Swanwick	d					21 33				21 51							22 30
Fareham	d					21 40				21 58							22 37
Portchester	d					21 45				22 03							22 42
Cosham	d					21 49				22 07							22 47
Portsmouth Harbour	d						21 40								22 15		
Portsmouth & Southsea	d	21 15					21 44								22 19		
Fratton	d	21 19					21 48								22 23		
Hilsea	d	21 23					21 52								22 27		
Bedhampton	d	21 28					21 57								22 32		
Havant	d	21 31				21 56	22 00			22 14					22 35		22 57
Warblington	d	21 33								22 16							
Emsworth	d	21 36								22 19					22 39		23 01
Southbourne	d	21 39								22 22					22 42		23 04
Nutbourne	d	21 41								22 24							
Bosham	d	21 45								22 28							
Fishbourne (Sussex)	d	21 48								22 31							
Chichester 4	a	21 51				22 06	22 10			22 34					22 49		23 11
	d	21 52				22 07	22 11			22 34		22 40			22 52		23 12
Bognor Regis 4	d		22 00						22 30								
Barnham	a	21 59	22 06			22 14	22 18		22 36	22 42		22 47			22 59		23 19
	d	22 00		22 12		22 15	22 19	22 22	22 37			22 48	22 52		23 00	23 06	23 20
Bognor Regis	a			22 18				22 29					22 59			23 12	
Ford 4	d	22 04				22 19	22 23		22 41			22 52			23 04		
Littlehampton 4	a					22 24			22 46								23 31
	d					22 33											
Angmering 3	d	22 11				22 41									23 11		
Goring-by-Sea	d	22 15				22 45									23 15		
Durrington-on-Sea	d	22 18				22 47									23 17		
West Worthing	d	22 20				22 49									23 19		
Worthing 4	a	22 22				22 52									23 22		
	d	22 23				22 52									23 22		
East Worthing	d	22 25				22 55									23 25		
Lancing	d	22 28				22 58									23 28		
Shoreham-by-Sea	d	22 32				23 02									23 32		
Southwick	d	22 35				23 05									23 35		
Fishersgate	d	22 37				23 07									23 37		
Portslade	d	22 39				23 09									23 39		
Aldrington	d	22 42				23 11									23 41		
Hove 2	a	22 44				23 13									23 43		
	d	22 44			22 54	23 14								23 24	23 44		
Brighton 10	a	22 48			22 58	23 18								23 28	23 48		
Preston Park	d																
Burgess Hill	a																
Haywards Heath 3	a																
Arundel	d						22 28					22 57					
Amberley	d											23 02					
Pulborough	d						22 37					23 08					
Billingshurst	d						22 43					23 14					
Christs Hospital	d						22 50					23 21					
Horsham 4	a						22 54					23 25					
	d						22 55				23 02	23 25					
Crawley	d						23 03				23 14	23 38					
Three Bridges 4	a						23 07				23 18	23 42					
Gatwick Airport 10	a										23 22						
	d										23 23						
Horley	a										23 26						
Redhill 5	a										23 36						
East Croydon	a										23 54						
London Bridge 4	a																
Clapham Junction 10	a										00 11						
London Victoria 15	a										00 18						

Table 188

Mondays to Fridays

Southampton, Portsmouth and Sussex Coast - Brighton, Gatwick Airport and London

Network Diagram - see first Page of Table 186

		GW	SN	SN	SN	SN ■	GW ◇	SN	SN ◇	SN
Eastleigh	d	22 11					22 24			
Southampton Airport Parkway	d									
Southampton Central	d	22a21				22 33				
Swanwick	d					22 50				
Fareham	d					22 57	22 42			
Portchester	d									
Cosham	d					23 05				
Portsmouth Harbour	d				22 44					23 15
Portsmouth & Southsea	d				22 48					23 19
Fratton	d				22 52		22a56			23 23
Hilsea	d				22 56					23 27
Bedhampton	d				23 01					23 33
Havant	d				23 05	23 12				23 36
Warblington	d									23 38
Emsworth	d									23 41
Southbourne	d									23 44
Nutbourne	d									23 47
Bosham	d									23 50
Fishbourne (Sussex)	d									23 53
Chichester	a				23 16	23 22				23 57
	d				23 17	23 23			23 52	23 57
Bognor Regis	d		23 15							
Barnham	a		23 21		23 24	23 30			23 59	00 05
	d				23 25	23 31		23 36	00 01	00 06
Bognor Regis	a							23 43		
Ford	d				23 29				00 05	00 10
Littlehampton	a				23 34	23 42			00 10	00 15
	d				23 39					
Angmering	d				23 47					
Goring-by-Sea	d				23 51					
Durrington-on-Sea	d				23 53					
West Worthing	d				23 55					
Worthing	a				23 58					
	d				23 59					
East Worthing	d				00 01					
Lancing	d				00 04					
Shoreham-by-Sea	d				00 08					
Southwick	d				00 11					
Fishersgate	d				00 13					
Portslade	d				00 15					
Aldrington	d				00 18					
Hove	a				00 21					
	d			23 54	00 21					
Brighton	a			23 58	00 25					
Preston Park	d									
Burgess Hill	a									
Haywards Heath	a									
Arundel	d									
Amberley	d									
Pulborough	d									
Billingshurst	d									
Christs Hospital	d									
Horsham	a									
	d									
Crawley	d									
Three Bridges	a									
Gatwick Airport	a									
	d									
Horley	a									
Redhill	a									
East Croydon	a									
London Bridge	a									
Clapham Junction	a									
London Victoria	a									

Table 188

Saturdays

Southampton, Portsmouth and Sussex Coast - Brighton, Gatwick Airport and London

Network Diagram - see first Page of Table 186

		SN	SN ■	SN ◇	SN	SN ◇■	SN ■	SN ◇■	SN	SN	SN ◇■	SN	SN	SN	SN ◇■	SN ◇■	SN
Eastleigh	d																
Southampton Airport Parkway	d																
Southampton Central	d																
Swanwick	d																
Fareham	d																
Portchester	d																
Cosham	d																
Portsmouth Harbour	d	22p44			23p15			04 56									
Portsmouth & Southsea	d	22p48			23p19			05 00									
Fratton	d	22p52			23p23												
Hilsea	d	22p56			23p27												
Bedhampton	d	23p01			23p33												
Havant	d	23p05			23p36			05 08							05 52		
Warblington	d				23p38												
Emsworth	d				23p41										05 56		
Southbourne	d				23p44										05 59		
Nutbourne	d				23p47												
Bosham	d				23p50												
Fishbourne (Sussex)	d				23p53												
Chichester	a	23p16			23p57			05 19							06 06		
	d	23p17		23p52	23p57			05 19							06 06		
Bognor Regis	d								05 13				05 43	06 04			06 13
Barnham	a	23p24		23p59	00 05			05 27	05 19				05 49	06 10	06 14		06 19
	d	23p25		00 01	00 06	00 09	04 48	05 27	05 31				05 50		06 14		06 20
Bognor Regis	a					00 15											
Ford	d	23p29		00 05	00 10		04 52		05 35				05 54		06 19		06 24
Littlehampton	a	23p34		00 10	00 15		04 57		05 40								06 29
	d	23p39					05 02				05 45					06 15	
Angmering	d	23p47					05 10				05 53		06 00			06 23	
Goring-by-Sea	d	23p51					05 14				05 57		06 04			06 27	
Durrington-on-Sea	d	23p53					05 17				06 00		06 07			06 30	
West Worthing	d	23p55					05 19				06 02		06 09			06 32	
Worthing	a	23p58					05 21	05 41			06 04		06 11			06 34	
	d	23p59					05 22	05 42			06 05		06 12			06 35	
East Worthing	d	00 01					05 24						06 14				
Lancing	d	00 04					05 27				06 09		06 17			06 39	
Shoreham-by-Sea	d	00 08					05 32	05 48			06 13		06 22			06 43	
Southwick	d	00 11					05 35						06 25				
Fishersgate	d	00 13					05 37						06 27				
Portslade	d	00 15					05 39				06 17		06 29			06 47	
Aldrington	d	00 18					05 41						06 31				
Hove	a	00 21					05 43	05 54			06 21		06 33			06 51	
	d	00 21					05 44	05 54		05 56	06 21	06 24	06 34			06 51	
Brighton	a	00 25					05 48			06 00		06 28	06 38				
Preston Park	d															06 55	
Burgess Hill	a															07 04	
Haywards Heath	a							06 08			06 35					07 09	
Arundel	d														06 23		
Amberley	d														06 28		
Pulborough	d														06 34		
Billingshurst	d														06 41		
Christs Hospital	d														06 47		
Horsham	a														06 51		
	d		23p02												06 52		
Crawley	d		23p14												07 01		
Three Bridges	a		23p18					06 20			06 48				07 04		
Gatwick Airport	a		23p22					06 25			06 53				07 09	07 25	
	d		23p23					06 26			06 55				07 10	07 26	
Horley	a		23p26														
Redhill	a		23p36												07 17		
East Croydon	a		23p54					06 40			07 09				07 29	07 41	
London Bridge	a																
Clapham Junction	a		00 11					06 50			07 19				07 39	07 51	
London Victoria	a		00 18					06 57			07 27				07 46	07 58	

Southampton, Portsmouth and Sussex Coast - Brighton, Gatwick Airport and London

Network Diagram - see first Page of Table 186

		SN	SN	SN	SN ◇■	SN		SN	SN ◇■	SN ◇■	SN ◇■	SN	SN	SN	SN	SN ■		SN	SN ◇■	SN ◇■		SN ◇■	SN	SN	SN
Eastleigh	d																								
Southampton Airport Parkway	d																								
Southampton Central	d																			06 13					
Swanwick	d																			06 33					
Fareham	d																			06 40					
Portchester	d																			06 45					
Cosham	d																			06 49					
Portsmouth Harbour	d									06 12						06 29									
Portsmouth & Southsea	d					05 59				06 16						06 33									
Fratton	d					06 04				06 20						06 37									
Hilsea	d					06 08																			
Bedhampton	d					06 13																			
Havant	d					06 16				06 30						06 46				06 56					
Warblington	d					06 18																			
Emsworth	d					06 21										06 50				07 00					
Southbourne	d					06 24										06 53				07 03					
Nutbourne	d					06 26																			
Bosham	d					06 30																			
Fishbourne (Sussex)	d					06 33																			
Chichester ■	a					06 36				06 40						07 00				07 10					
	d				06 25	06 37				06 41						07 00				07 11					
Bognor Regis ■	d							06 39	06 30									07 07	06 56						
Barnham	a				06 32	06 44		06 45	06 36	06 48						07 08		07 13	07 02	07 18					
	d	06 22			06 33	06 45			06 37	06 49		06 52	07 05			07 08		07 15	07 03	07 19			07 22		
Bognor Regis	a	06 29										06 59	07 12										07 29		
Ford ■	d				06 37	06 49			06 41									07 19	07 07						
Littlehampton ■	a					06 54												07 24							
	d										06 45											07 15			
Angmering ■	d				06 43						06 55					07 17						07 23			
Goring-by-Sea	d				06 47						06 59											07 27			
Durrington-on-Sea	d				06 50						07 02											07 30			
West Worthing	d			06 39	06 52						07 04				07 09							07 32			07 39
Worthing ■	a			06 41	06 54						07 06				07 11	07 24						07 34			07 41
	d			06 42	06 56						07 07				07 12	07 26						07 36			07 42
East Worthing	d			06 44											07 14										07 44
Lancing	d			06 47	07 00						07 11				07 17	07 30									07 47
Shoreham-by-Sea	d			06 52	07 04						07 15				07 22	07 34						07 42			07 52
Southwick	d			06 55	07 07										07 25	07 37									07 55
Fishersgate	d			06 57											07 27										07 57
Portslade	d			06 59	07 10										07 29	07 40						07 47			07 59
Aldrington	d			07 01											07 31										08 01
Hove ■	a			07 03	07 13						07 21				07 33	07 43						07 50			08 03
	d		06 54	07 04	07 14						07 22			07 24	07 34	07 44						07 51		07 54	08 04
Brighton ■	a		06 58	07 08	07 18									07 28	07 38	07 48								07 58	08 08
Preston Park	d																					07 55			
Burgess Hill	a																					08 03			
Haywards Heath ■	a										07 35											08 09			
Arundel	d								06 46										07 12						
Amberley	d																		07 17						
Pulborough	d								06 55										07 23						
Billingshurst	d								07 01										07 29						
Christs Hospital	d																		07 36						
Horsham ■	a								07 10	07 16									07 40	07 46					
	d								07 20										07 50						
Crawley	d								07 29										07 59						
Three Bridges ■	a								07 32										08 02						
Gatwick Airport ■ ✈	a								07 37		07 55								08 07			08 24			
	d								07 38		07 56								08 08			08 25			
Horley	a								07 41																
Redhill ■	a								07 47										08 15						
East Croydon	a								07 59		08 11								08 27			08 40			
London Bridge ■ ⊖	a																								
Clapham Junction ■	a								08 09		08 21								08 37			08 50			
London Victoria ■ ⊖	a								08 16		08 28								08 44			08 57			

Southampton, Portsmouth and Sussex Coast - Brighton, Gatwick Airport and London

Network Diagram - see first Page of Table 186

		GW		SN ■		SN	SN	SN ◇■	SN ◇■	SN ◇■	SN	SN		SN	SN	SN ◇■	SN	SN ◇■ ⌶	SN ◇■ A ⌶	SN ■	SN	SN		SN
Eastleigh	d																			07 14				
Southampton Airport Parkway	d																			07 18				
Southampton Central	d			06 33															07 13	07 33				
Swanwick	d			06 50															07 33	07 50				
Fareham	d			06 56															07 40	07 56				
Portchester	d																		07 45					
Cosham	d			07 05															07 49	08 05				
Portsmouth Harbour	d	06 48							07 12						07 29									
Portsmouth & Southsea	d	06 54				06 56			07 16						07 33									
Fratton	d	06 58				07 01			07 20						07 37									
Hilsea	d					07 05																		
Bedhampton	d					07 13																		
Havant	d	07 08		07 11		07 16			07 30						07 46				07 56	08 11				
Warblington	d					07 18																		
Emsworth	d			07 15		07 21									07 50				08 00	08 15				
Southbourne	d					07 24									07 53				08 03					
Nutbourne	d					07 26																		
Bosham	d					07 30																		
Fishbourne (Sussex)	d					07 33																		
Chichester ■	a	07 19		07 23		07 36			07 40						08 00				08 10	08 23				
	d	07 20		07 25		07 37			07 41						08 00				08 11	08 25				
Bognor Regis ■	d						07 39	07 30									08 07	07 56						
Barnham	a	07 27		07 32		07 44	07 45	07 36	07 48						08 08		08 13	08 02	08 18	08 32				
	d	07 28		07 33		07 45		07 37	07 49		07 52				08 08		08 15	08 03	08 19	08 33	08 22			
Bognor Regis	a										07 59										08 29			
Ford ■	d			07 37		07 49		07 41									08 19	08 07		08 37				
Littlehampton ■	a					07 54											08 24							
	d									07 45						08 15								
Angmering ■	d			07 43						07 53					08 17	08 23				08 43				
Goring-by-Sea	d			07 47						07 57						08 27				08 47				
Durrington-on-Sea	d			07 50						08 00						08 30				08 50				
West Worthing	d			07 52						08 02				08 09		08 32				08 52				08 39
Worthing ■	a	07 45		07 54						08 04				08 11	08 24	08 34				08 54				08 41
	d	07 50		07 56						08 06				08 12	08 26	08 36				08 56				08 42
East Worthing	d													08 14										08 44
Lancing	d			08 00						08 10				08 17	08 30					09 00				08 47
Shoreham-by-Sea	d	07 57		08 04						08 14				08 22	08 34	08 42				09 04				08 52
Southwick	d			08 07										08 25	08 37					09 07				08 55
Fishersgate	d													08 27										08 57
Portslade	d			08 10										08 29	08 40	08 47				09 10				08 59
Aldrington	d													08 31										09 01
Hove ■	a	08 07		08 13						08 20				08 33	08 43	08 50				09 13				09 03
	d	08 08		08 14						08 21		08 24		08 34	08 44	08 51				09 14		08 54		09 04
Brighton ■	a	08 15		08 18								08 28		08 38	08 48					09 18		08 58		09 08
Preston Park	d															08 55								
Burgess Hill	a															09 03								
Haywards Heath ■	a									08 35						09 09								
Arundel	d							07 46										08 12						
Amberley	d																	08 17						
Pulborough	d							07 55										08 23						
Billingshurst	d							08 01										08 29						
Christs Hospital	d																	08 36						
Horsham ■	a							08 10	08 16									08 40	08 46					
	d							08 20										08 50						
Crawley	d							08 29										08 59						
Three Bridges ■	a							08 32										09 02						
Gatwick Airport ■ ✈	a							08 37		08 55								09 07						
	d							08 38		08 56								09 08						
Horley	a							08 41																
Redhill ■	a							08 47										09 15						
East Croydon	a							08 59		09 11								09 27						
London Bridge ■ ⊖	a																							
Clapham Junction ■	a							09 09		09 21								09 37						
London Victoria ■ ⊖	a							09 16		09 28								09 44						

A ⌶ from Horsham

Table 188

Southampton, Portsmouth and Sussex Coast - Brighton, Gatwick Airport and London

Network Diagram - see first Page of Table 186

		SN	SN	SN ◇■	SN ◇■	SN ◇■	SN	SN	SN	SN	SN ◇■	SN	SN ◇■ 🛒	SN ◇■ A 🛒	SN ■	SN ◇■	SN	SN	SN
Eastleigh	d														08 14				
Southampton Airport Parkway	d														08 18				
Southampton Central	d													08 13	08 33				
Swanwick	d													08 33	08 50				
Fareham	d													08 40	08 56				
Portchester	d													08 45					
Cosham	d													08 49	09 05				
Portsmouth Harbour	d				08 12					08 29									
Portsmouth &Southsea	d	07 59			08 16					08 33									
Fratton	d	08 04			08 20					08 37									
Hilsea	d	08 08																	
Bedhampton	d	08 13																	
Havant	d	08 16			08 30					08 46				08 56	09 11				
Warblington	d	08 18																	
Emsworth	d	08 21								08 50				09 00	09 15				
Southbourne	d	08 24								08 53				09 03					
Nutbourne	d	08 27																	
Bosham	d	08 30																	
Fishbourne (Sussex)	d	08 33																	
Chichester ■	a	08 36			08 40					09 00				09 10	09 23				
	d	08 37			08 41					09 00				09 11	09 25				
Bognor Regis ■	d		08 39	08 30								09 07	08 56						
Barnham	a	08 44	08 45	08 36	08 48					09 08		09 13	09 02	09 18	09 32				
	d	08 45		08 37	08 49		08 52			09 08	09 12	09 15	09 03	09 19	09 33		09 22		
Bognor Regis	a						08 59				09 18						09 29		
Ford ■	d	08 49		08 41								09 19	09 07		09 37				
Littlehampton ■	a	08 54										09 24							
	d					08 45										09 15			
Angmering ■	d					08 53				09 17					09 43	09 23			
Goring-by-Sea	d					08 57									09 47	09 27			
Durrington-on-Sea	d					09 00									09 50	09 30			
West Worthing	d					09 02			09 09						09 52	09 32			09 39
Worthing ■	a					09 04			09 11	09 24					09 54	09 34			09 41
	d					09 06			09 12	09 26					09 56	09 36			09 42
East Worthing	d								09 14										09 44
Lancing	d					09 10			09 17	09 30					10 00				09 47
Shoreham-by-Sea	d					09 14			09 22	09 34					10 04	09 42			09 52
Southwick	d								09 25	09 37					10 07				09 55
Fishersgate	d								09 27										09 57
Portslade	d								09 29	09 40					10 10	09 47			09 59
Aldrington	d								09 31										10 01
Hove ■	a					09 20			09 33	09 43					10 13	09 50			10 03
	d					09 21		09 24	09 34	09 44					10 14	09 51		09 54	10 04
Brighton ■	a							09 28	09 38	09 48					10 18			09 58	10 08
Preston Park	d															09 55			
Burgess Hill	a															10 03			
Haywards Heath ■	a					09 35										10 09			
Arundel	d			08 46									09 12						
Amberley	d												09 17						
Pulborough	d			08 55									09 23						
Billingshurst	d			09 01									09 29						
Christs Hospital	d												09 36						
Horsham ■	a			09 10	09 16								09 40	09 46					
	d			09 20									09 50						
Crawley	d			09 29									09 59						
Three Bridges ■	a			09 32									10 02						
Gatwick Airport ■	a			09 37		09 55							10 07			10 24			
	d			09 38		09 56							10 08			10 25			
Horley	a			09 41															
Redhill ■	a			09 47									10 15						
East Croydon	a			09 59		10 11							10 27			10 40			
London Bridge ■	a																		
Clapham Junction ■	a			10 09		10 21							10 37			10 50			
London Victoria ■	a			10 16		10 28							10 44			10 57			

A 🛒 from Horsham

Table 188

Southampton, Portsmouth and Sussex Coast - Brighton, Gatwick Airport and London

Network Diagram - see first Page of Table 186

		SN ◇■	SN	SN	SN ◇■	SN ◇■	SN ◇■	SN	SN	SN	SN	SN ◇■	SN	SN ◇■ 🛒	SN ◇■ A 🛒
Eastleigh	d														
Southampton Airport Parkway	d														
Southampton Central	d														09 13
Swanwick	d														09 33
Fareham	d														09 40
Portchester	d														09 45
Cosham	d														09 49
Portsmouth Harbour	d					09 12					09 29				
Portsmouth &Southsea	d		08 59			09 16					09 33				
Fratton	d		09 04			09 20					09 37				
Hilsea	d		09 08												
Bedhampton	d		09 13												
Havant	d		09 16			09 30					09 46				09 56
Warblington	d		09 18												
Emsworth	d		09 21								09 50				10 00
Southbourne	d		09 24								09 53				10 03
Nutbourne	d		09 26												
Bosham	d		09 30												
Fishbourne (Sussex)	d		09 33												
Chichester ■	a		09 36			09 40					10 00				10 10
	d		09 37			09 41					10 00				10 11
Bognor Regis ■	d			09 39	09 30								10 07	09 56	
Barnham	a		09 44	09 45	09 36	09 48					10 08		10 13	10 02	10 18
	d	09 38	09 45		09 37	09 49		09 52			10 08	10 12	10 15	10 03	10 19
Bognor Regis	a	09 45						09 59				10 18			
Ford ■	d		09 49		09 41								10 19	10 07	
Littlehampton ■	a		09 54										10 24		
	d						09 45								
Angmering ■	d						09 53				10 17				
Goring-by-Sea	d						09 57								
Durrington-on-Sea	d						10 00								
West Worthing	d						10 02			10 09					
Worthing ■	a						10 04			10 11	10 24				
	d						10 06			10 12	10 26				
East Worthing	d									10 14					
Lancing	d						10 10			10 17	10 30				
Shoreham-by-Sea	d						10 14			10 22	10 34				
Southwick	d									10 25	10 37				
Fishersgate	d									10 27					
Portslade	d									10 29	10 40				
Aldrington	d									10 31					
Hove ■	a						10 20			10 33	10 43				
	d						10 21		10 24	10 34	10 44				
Brighton ■	a								10 28	10 38	10 48				
Preston Park	d														
Burgess Hill	a														
Haywards Heath ■	a						10 35								
Arundel	d				09 46									10 12	
Amberley	d													10 17	
Pulborough	d				09 55									10 23	
Billingshurst	d				10 01									10 29	
Christs Hospital	d													10 36	
Horsham ■	a				10 10	10 16								10 40	10 46
	d				10 20									10 50	
Crawley	d				10 29									10 59	
Three Bridges ■	a				10 32									11 02	
Gatwick Airport ■	a				10 37		10 55							11 07	
	d				10 38		10 56							11 08	
Horley	a				10 41										
Redhill ■	a				10 47									11 15	
East Croydon	a				10 59		11 11							11 27	
London Bridge ■	a														
Clapham Junction ■	a				11 09		11 21							11 37	
London Victoria ■	a				11 16		11 28							11 44	

A 🛒 from Horsham

Table 188

Saturdays

Southampton, Portsmouth and Sussex Coast - Brighton, Gatwick Airport and London

Network Diagram - see first Page of Table 186

		SN	SN	SN	SN	SN	SN	SN	SN	SN	SN	SN	SN	SN	SN	SN	SN	SN
		◇1				1	◇1			◇1	◇1	◇1					◇1	
Eastleigh	d																	
Southampton Airport Parkway	d																	
Southampton Central ⛴	d					09 33												
Swanwick	d					09 50												
Fareham	d					09 56												
Portchester	d																	
Cosham	d					10 05												
Portsmouth Harbour ⛴	d										10 12					10 29		
Portsmouth & Southsea	d							09 59			10 16					10 33		
Fratton	d							10 04			10 20					10 37		
Hilsea	d							10 08										
Bedhampton	d							10 13										
Havant	d					10 11		10 16			10 30					10 46		
Warblington	d							10 18										
Emsworth	d					10 15		10 21								10 50		
Southbourne	d							10 24								10 53		
Nutbourne	d							10 26										
Bosham	d							10 30										
Fishbourne (Sussex)	d							10 33										
Chichester 4	a					10 23		10 36			10 40					11 00		
	d					10 25		10 37			10 41					11 00		
Bognor Regis 4	d								10 39	10 30								11 07
Barnham	a					10 32		10 44	10 45	10 36	10 48					11 08		11 13
	d		10 22			10 33	10 39	10 45		10 37	10 49		10 52			11 08	11 12	11 15
Bognor Regis	a		10 29				10 46						10 59				11 18	
Ford 4	d					10 37		10 49		10 41								11 19
Littlehampton 4	a							10 54										11 24
	d	10 15										10 45						
Angmering 3	d	10 23				10 43						10 53				11 17		
Goring-by-Sea	d	10 27				10 47						10 57						
Durrington-on-Sea	d	10 30				10 50						11 00						
West Worthing	d	10 32			10 39	10 52						11 02			11 09			
Worthing 4	a	10 34			10 41	10 54						11 04			11 11	11 24		
	d	10 36			10 42	10 56						11 06			11 12	11 26		
East Worthing	d				10 44										11 14			
Lancing	d				10 47	11 00						11 10			11 17	11 30		
Shoreham-by-Sea	d	10 42			10 52	11 04						11 14			11 22	11 34		
Southwick	d				10 55	11 07									11 25	11 37		
Fishersgate	d				10 57										11 27			
Portslade	d	10 47			10 59	11 10									11 29	11 40		
Aldrington	d				11 01										11 31			
Hove 2	a	10 50			11 03	11 13						11 20			11 33	11 43		
	d	10 51		10 54	11 04	11 14						11 21		11 24	11 34	11 44		
Brighton 10	a			10 58	11 08	11 18								11 28	11 38	11 48		
Preston Park	d	10 55																
Burgess Hill	a	11 03																
Haywards Heath 3	a	11 09										11 35						
Arundel	d									10 46								
Amberley	d																	
Pulborough	d									10 55								
Billingshurst	d									11 01								
Christs Hospital	d																	
Horsham 4	a									11 10	11 16							
	d									11 20								
Crawley	d									11 29								
Three Bridges 4	a									11 32								
Gatwick Airport 10 ✈	a	11 24								11 37		11 55						
	d	11 25								11 38		11 56						
Horley	a									11 41								
Redhill 5	a									11 47								
East Croydon	a	11 40								11 59		12 11						
London Bridge 4 ⊖	a																	
Clapham Junction 10	a	11 50								12 09		12 21						
London Victoria 15 ⊖	a	11 57								12 16		12 28						

Table 188

Saturdays

Southampton, Portsmouth and Sussex Coast - Brighton, Gatwick Airport and London

Network Diagram - see first Page of Table 186

		SN	SN	SN	SN	SN	SN	SN	SN	SN	SN	SN	SN	SN	SN	SN
		◇1	◇1	1	◇1				◇1			◇1	◇1	◇1		
			A													
		🚌	🚌						🚌							
Eastleigh	d			10 14												
Southampton Airport Parkway	d			10 18												
Southampton Central ⛴	d		10 13	10 33												
Swanwick	d		10 33	10 50												
Fareham	d		10 40	10 56												
Portchester	d		10 45													
Cosham	d		10 49	11 05												
Portsmouth Harbour ⛴	d												11 12			
Portsmouth & Southsea	d									10 59			11 16			
Fratton	d									11 04			11 20			
Hilsea	d									11 08						
Bedhampton	d									11 13						
Havant	d		10 56	11 11						11 16			11 30			
Warblington	d									11 18						
Emsworth	d		11 00	11 15						11 21						
Southbourne	d		11 03							11 24						
Nutbourne	d									11 26						
Bosham	d									11 30						
Fishbourne (Sussex)	d									11 33						
Chichester 4	a		11 10	11 23						11 36			11 40			
	d		11 11	11 25						11 37			11 41			
Bognor Regis 4	d	10 56									11 39	11 30				
Barnham	a	11 02	11 18	11 32						11 44	11 45	11 36	11 48			
	d	11 03	11 19	11 33		11 22			11 39	11 45		11 37	11 49		11 52	
Bognor Regis	a					11 29			11 46						11 59	
Ford 4	d	11 07		11 37						11 49		11 41				
Littlehampton 4	a									11 54						
	d				11 15									11 45		
Angmering 3	d			11 43	11 23									11 53		
Goring-by-Sea	d			11 47	11 27									11 57		
Durrington-on-Sea	d			11 50	11 30									12 00		
West Worthing	d			11 52	11 32			11 39						12 02		
Worthing 4	a			11 54	11 34			11 41						12 04		
	d			11 56	11 36			11 42						12 06		
East Worthing	d							11 44								
Lancing	d			12 00				11 47						12 10		
Shoreham-by-Sea	d			12 04	11 42			11 52						12 14		
Southwick	d			12 07				11 55								
Fishersgate	d							11 57								
Portslade	d			12 10	11 47			11 59								
Aldrington	d							12 01								
Hove 2	a			12 13	11 50			12 03						12 20		
	d			12 14	11 51		11 54	12 04						12 21		12 24
Brighton 10	a			12 18			11 58	12 08								12 28
Preston Park	d				11 55											
Burgess Hill	a				12 03											
Haywards Heath 3	a				12 09									12 35		
Arundel	d	11 12										11 46				
Amberley	d	11 17														
Pulborough	d	11 23										11 55				
Billingshurst	d	11 29										12 01				
Christs Hospital	d	11 36														
Horsham 4	a	11 40	11 46									12 10	12 16			
	d	11 50										12 20				
Crawley	d	11 59										12 29				
Three Bridges 4	a	12 02										12 32				
Gatwick Airport 10 ✈	a	12 07			12 24							12 37		12 55		
	d	12 08			12 25							12 38		12 56		
Horley	a											12 41				
Redhill 5	a	12 15										12 47				
East Croydon	a	12 27			12 40							12 59		13 11		
London Bridge 4 ⊖	a															
Clapham Junction 10	a	12 37			12 50							13 09		13 21		
London Victoria 15 ⊖	a	12 44			12 57							13 16		13 28		

A 🚌 from Horsham

Southampton, Portsmouth and Sussex Coast - Brighton, Gatwick Airport and London

Network Diagram - see first Page of Table 186

Station		SN	SN	SN ◇■	SN	SN ◇■ H	SN ◇■ A H	SN ◇■	SN	SN	SN	SN ■	SN ◇■ H	SN	SN
Eastleigh	d														
Southampton Airport Parkway	d														
Southampton Central	d						11 13					11 33			
Swanwick	d						11 33					11 50			
Fareham	d						11 40					11 56			
Portchester	d						11 45								
Cosham	d						11 49					12 05			
Portsmouth Harbour	d		11 29												
Portsmouth &Southsea	d		11 33											11 59	
Fratton	d		11 37											12 04	
Hilsea	d													12 08	
Bedhampton	d													12 13	
Havant	d		11 46				11 56					12 11		12 16	
Warblington	d													12 18	
Emsworth	d		11 50				12 00					12 15		12 21	
Southbourne	d		11 53				12 03							12 24	
Nutbourne	d													12 26	
Bosham	d													12 30	
Fishbourne (Sussex)	d													12 33	
Chichester ■	a		12 00				12 10					12 23		12 36	
	d		12 00				12 11					12 25		12 37	
Bognor Regis ■	d				12 07	11 56									12 39
Barnham	a		12 08		12 13	12 02	12 18					12 32		12 44	12 45
	d		12 08	12 12	12 15	12 03	12 19		12 22			12 33	12 39	12 45	
Bognor Regis	a			12 18					12 29				12 46		
Ford ■	d				12 19	12 07						12 37		12 49	
Littlehampton ■	a				12 24									12 54	
	d							12 15							
Angmering ■	d		12 17					12 23				12 43			
Goring-by-Sea	d							12 27				12 47			
Durrington-on-Sea	d							12 30				12 50			
West Worthing	d	12 09						12 32			12 39	12 52			
Worthing ■	a	12 11	12 24					12 34			12 41	12 54			
	d	12 12	12 26					12 36			12 42	12 56			
East Worthing	d	12 14									12 44				
Lancing	d	12 17	12 30								12 47	13 00			
Shoreham-by-Sea	d	12 22	12 34					12 42			12 52	13 04			
Southwick	d	12 25	12 37								12 55	13 07			
Fishersgate	d	12 27									12 57				
Portslade	d	12 29	12 40					12 47			12 59	13 10			
Aldrington	d	12 31									13 01				
Hove ■	a	12 33	12 43					12 50			13 03	13 13			
	d	12 34	12 44					12 51		12 54	13 04	13 14			
Brighton ■	a	12 38	12 48							12 58	13 08	13 18			
Preston Park	d							12 55							
Burgess Hill	a							13 03							
Haywards Heath ■	a							13 09							
Arundel	d					12 12									
Amberley	d					12 17									
Pulborough	d					12 23									
Billingshurst	d					12 29									
Christs Hospital	d					12 36									
Horsham ■	a					12 40	12 46								
	d						12 50								
Crawley	d						12 59								
Three Bridges ■	a						13 02								
Gatwick Airport ■	a						13 07	13 24							
	d						13 08	13 25							
Horley	a														
Redhill ■	a						13 15								
East Croydon	a						13 27	13 40							
London Bridge ■	a														
Clapham Junction ■	a						13 37	13 50							
London Victoria ■	a						13 44	13 57							

A H from Horsham

Southampton, Portsmouth and Sussex Coast - Brighton, Gatwick Airport and London

Network Diagram - see first Page of Table 186

Station		SN ◇■	SN ◇■	SN ◇■	SN	SN	SN	SN	SN ◇■	SN	SN ◇■ H	SN ◇■ A H	SN ■	SN ◇■	SN	SN	SN
Eastleigh	d												12 14				
Southampton Airport Parkway	d												12 19				
Southampton Central	d											12 13	12 33				
Swanwick	d											12 33	12 50				
Fareham	d											12 40	12 56				
Portchester	d											12 45					
Cosham	d											12 49	13 05				
Portsmouth Harbour	d		12 12					12 29									
Portsmouth &Southsea	d		12 16					12 33									
Fratton	d		12 20					12 37									
Hilsea	d																
Bedhampton	d																
Havant	d		12 30					12 46				12 56	13 11				
Warblington	d																
Emsworth	d							12 50				13 00	13 15				
Southbourne	d							12 53				13 03					
Nutbourne	d																
Bosham	d																
Fishbourne (Sussex)	d																
Chichester ■	a		12 40					13 00				13 10	13 23				
	d		12 41					13 00				13 11	13 25				
Bognor Regis ■	d	12 30								13 07	12 56						
Barnham	a	12 36	12 48					13 08		13 13	13 02	13 18	13 32				
	d	12 37	12 49		12 52			13 08	13 12	13 15	13 03	13 19	13 33		13 22		
Bognor Regis	a				12 59				13 18						13 29		
Ford ■	d	12 41								13 19	13 07		13 37				
Littlehampton ■	a									13 24							
	d			12 45										13 15			
Angmering ■	d			12 53				13 17					13 43	13 23			
Goring-by-Sea	d			12 57									13 47	13 27			
Durrington-on-Sea	d			13 00									13 50	13 30			
West Worthing	d			13 02			13 09						13 52	13 32			13 39
Worthing ■	a			13 04			13 11	13 24					13 54	13 34			13 41
	d			13 06			13 12	13 26					13 56	13 36			13 42
East Worthing	d						13 14										13 44
Lancing	d			13 10			13 17	13 30					14 00				13 47
Shoreham-by-Sea	d			13 14			13 22	13 34					14 04	13 42			13 52
Southwick	d						13 25	13 37					14 07				13 55
Fishersgate	d						13 27										13 57
Portslade	d						13 29	13 40					14 10	13 47			13 59
Aldrington	d						13 31										14 01
Hove ■	a			13 20			13 33	13 43					14 13	13 50			14 03
	d			13 21		13 24	13 34	13 44					14 14	13 51		13 54	14 04
Brighton ■	a					13 28	13 38	13 48					14 18			13 58	14 08
Preston Park	d													13 55			
Burgess Hill	a													14 03			
Haywards Heath ■	a			13 35										14 09			
Arundel	d	12 46									13 12						
Amberley	d										13 17						
Pulborough	d	12 55									13 23						
Billingshurst	d	13 01									13 29						
Christs Hospital	d										13 36						
Horsham ■	a	13 10	13 16								13 40	13 46					
	d		13 20									13 50					
Crawley	d		13 29									13 59					
Three Bridges ■	a		13 32									14 02					
Gatwick Airport ■	a		13 37	13 55								14 07		14 24			
	d		13 38	13 56								14 08		14 25			
Horley	a		13 41														
Redhill ■	a		13 47									14 15					
East Croydon	a		13 59	14 11								14 27		14 40			
London Bridge ■	a																
Clapham Junction ■	a		14 09	14 21								14 37		14 50			
London Victoria ■	a		14 16	14 28								14 44		14 57			

A H from Horsham

Southampton, Portsmouth and Sussex Coast - Brighton, Gatwick Airport and London

Network Diagram - see first Page of Table 186

		SN ◇1 [trolley]	SN	SN	SN ◇1	SN ◇1	SN ◇1	SN	SN	SN	SN	SN ◇1	SN	SN ◇1 [trolley]	SN ◇1 A [trolley]	SN ◇1	SN	SN	SN
Eastleigh	d																		
Southampton Airport Parkway	d																		
Southampton Central	d														13 13				
Swanwick	d														13 33				
Fareham	d														13 40				
Portchester	d														13 45				
Cosham	d														13 49				
Portsmouth Harbour	d					13 12					13 29								
Portsmouth & Southsea	d		12 59			13 16					13 33								
Fratton	d		13 04			13 20					13 37								
Hilsea	d		13 08																
Bedhampton	d		13 13																
Havant	d		13 16			13 30					13 46				13 56				
Warblington	d		13 18																
Emsworth	d		13 21								13 50				14 00				
Southbourne	d		13 24								13 53				14 03				
Nutbourne	d		13 26																
Bosham	d		13 30																
Fishbourne (Sussex)	d		13 33																
Chichester	a		13 36			13 40					14 00				14 10				
	d		13 37			13 41					14 00				14 11				
Bognor Regis	d			13 39	13 30								14 07	13 56					
Barnham	a		13 44	13 45	13 36	13 48					14 08		14 13	14 02	14 18				
	d	13 39	13 45		13 37	13 49		13 52			14 08	14 12	14 15	14 03	14 19		14 22		
Bognor Regis	a	13 46						13 59				14 18					14 29		
Ford	d		13 49		13 41								14 19	14 07					
Littlehampton	a		13 54										14 24						
	d						13 45									14 15			
Angmering	d						13 53				14 17					14 23			
Goring-by-Sea	d						13 57									14 27			
Durrington-on-Sea	d						14 00									14 30			
West Worthing	d						14 02			14 09						14 32			14 39
Worthing	a						14 04			14 11	14 24					14 34			14 41
	d						14 06			14 12	14 26					14 36			14 42
East Worthing	d									14 14									14 44
Lancing	d						14 10			14 17	14 30								14 47
Shoreham-by-Sea	d						14 14			14 22	14 34					14 42			14 52
Southwick	d									14 25	14 37								14 55
Fishersgate	d									14 27									14 57
Portslade	d									14 29	14 40					14 47			14 59
Aldrington	d									14 31									15 01
Hove	a						14 20			14 33	14 43					14 50			15 03
	d						14 21		14 24	14 34	14 44					14 51		14 54	15 04
Brighton	a								14 28	14 38	14 48							14 58	15 08
Preston Park	d															14 55			
Burgess Hill	a															15 03			
Haywards Heath	a						14 35									15 09			
Arundel	d				13 46									14 12					
Amberley	d													14 17					
Pulborough	d				13 55									14 23					
Billingshurst	d				14 01									14 29					
Christs Hospital	d													14 36					
Horsham	a				14 10	14 16								14 40	14 46				
	d				14 20									14 50					
Crawley	d				14 29									14 59					
Three Bridges	a				14 32									15 02					
Gatwick Airport	a				14 37		14 55							15 07		15 24			
	d				14 38		14 56							15 08		15 25			
Horley	a				14 41														
Redhill	a				14 47									15 15					
East Croydon	a				14 59		15 11							15 27		15 40			
London Bridge	a																		
Clapham Junction	a				15 09		15 21							15 37		15 50			
London Victoria	a				15 16		15 28							15 44		15 57			

A [trolley] from Horsham

Southampton, Portsmouth and Sussex Coast - Brighton, Gatwick Airport and London

Network Diagram - see first Page of Table 186

		SN 1	SN ◇1 [trolley]	SN	SN	SN ◇1	SN ◇1	SN ◇1	SN	SN	SN	SN	SN ◇1	SN ◇1	SN	SN ◇1 [trolley]	SN ◇1 A [trolley]
Eastleigh	d																
Southampton Airport Parkway	d																
Southampton Central	d	13 33															14 13
Swanwick	d	13 50															14 33
Fareham	d	13 56															14 40
Portchester	d																14 45
Cosham	d	14 05															14 49
Portsmouth Harbour	d						14 12					14 29					
Portsmouth & Southsea	d			13 59			14 16					14 33					
Fratton	d			14 04			14 20					14 37					
Hilsea	d			14 08													
Bedhampton	d			14 13													
Havant	d	14 11		14 16			14 30					14 46					14 56
Warblington	d			14 18													
Emsworth	d	14 15		14 21								14 50					15 00
Southbourne	d			14 24								14 53					15 03
Nutbourne	d			14 26													
Bosham	d			14 30													
Fishbourne (Sussex)	d			14 33													
Chichester	a	14 23		14 36			14 40					15 00					15 10
	d	14 25		14 37			14 41					15 00					15 11
Bognor Regis	d				14 39	14 30									15 07	14 56	
Barnham	a	14 32		14 44	14 45	14 36	14 48					15 08			15 13	15 02	15 18
	d	14 33	14 39	14 45		14 37	14 49		14 52			15 08	15 12		15 15	15 03	15 19
Bognor Regis	a		14 46						14 59				15 18				
Ford	d	14 37		14 49		14 41									15 19	15 07	
Littlehampton	a			14 54											15 24		
	d							14 45						15 15			
Angmering	d	14 43						14 53				15 17		15 23			
Goring-by-Sea	d	14 47						14 57						15 27			
Durrington-on-Sea	d	14 50						15 00						15 30			
West Worthing	d	14 52						15 02			15 09			15 32			
Worthing	a	14 54						15 04			15 11	15 24		15 34			
	d	14 56						15 06			15 12	15 26		15 36			
East Worthing	d										15 14						
Lancing	d	15 00						15 10			15 17	15 30					
Shoreham-by-Sea	d	15 04						15 14			15 22	15 34		15 42			
Southwick	d	15 07									15 25	15 37					
Fishersgate	d										15 27						
Portslade	d	15 10									15 29	15 40		15 47			
Aldrington	d										15 31						
Hove	a	15 13						15 20			15 33	15 43		15 50			
	d	15 14						15 21		15 24	15 34	15 44		15 51			
Brighton	a	15 18								15 28	15 38	15 48					
Preston Park	d													15 55			
Burgess Hill	a													16 03			
Haywards Heath	a							15 35						16 09			
Arundel	d					14 46										15 12	
Amberley	d															15 17	
Pulborough	d					14 55										15 23	
Billingshurst	d					15 01										15 29	
Christs Hospital	d															15 36	
Horsham	a					15 10	15 16									15 40	15 46
	d					15 20										15 50	
Crawley	d					15 29										15 59	
Three Bridges	a					15 32										16 02	
Gatwick Airport	a					15 37		15 55								16 07	
	d					15 38		15 56								16 08	
Horley	a					15 41											
Redhill	a					15 47										16 15	
East Croydon	a					15 59		16 11								16 27	
London Bridge	a																
Clapham Junction	a					16 09		16 21								16 37	
London Victoria	a					16 16		16 28								16 44	

A [trolley] from Horsham

Southampton, Portsmouth and Sussex Coast - Brighton, Gatwick Airport and London

Network Diagram - see first Page of Table 186

		SN	SN	SN	GW ◇	SN 1	SN ◇1 🍴	SN	SN	SN ◇1	SN ◇1	SN ◇1	SN	SN	SN	SN	SN ◇1	SN
Eastleigh	d					14 41												
Southampton Airport Parkway	d					14n34												
Southampton Central	d				14 34	14n26												
Swanwick	d																	
Fareham	d				14 55	15 00												
Portchester	d																	
Cosham	d				15 03													
Portsmouth Harbour	d										15 12					15 29		
Portsmouth & Southsea	d							14 59			15 16					15 33		
Fratton	d							15 04			15 20					15 37		
Hilsea	d							15 08										
Bedhampton	d							15 14										
Havant	d				15 10	15 14		15 17			15 30					15 46		
Warblington	d							15 19								15 50		
Emsworth	d							15 22								15 53		
Southbourne	d							15 25										
Nutbourne	d							15 28										
Bosham	d							15 31										
Fishbourne (Sussex)	d							15 34										
Chichester 4	a				15 21	15 25		15 37			15 41					16 00		
	d				15 21	15 25		15 38			15 42					16 00		
Bognor Regis 4	d								15 39	15 30								16 07
Barnham	a				15 29	15 33		15 45	15 45	15 36	15 49					16 08		16 13
	d	15 22			15 29	15 33	15 39	15 46		15 37	15 50		15 52			16 08	16 12	16 15
Bognor Regis	a	15 29					15 46						15 59				16 18	
Ford 4	d					15 38		15 50		15 41								16 19
Littlehampton 4	a							15 55										16 24
	d											15 45						
Angmering 3	d					15 44						15 53				16 17		
Goring-by-Sea	d					15 48						15 57						
Durrington-on-Sea	d					15 50						16 00						
West Worthing	d			15 39		15 52						16 02			16 09			
Worthing 4	a			15 41	15 44	15 55						16 04			16 11	16 24		
	d			15 42	15 48	15 56						16 06			16 12	16 26		
East Worthing	d			15 44											16 14			
Lancing	d			15 47		16 00						16 10			16 17	16 30		
Shoreham-by-Sea	d			15 52	15 56	16 04						16 14			16 22	16 34		
Southwick	d			15 55		16 07									16 25	16 37		
Fishersgate	d			15 57											16 27			
Portslade	d			15 59		16 10									16 29	16 40		
Aldrington	d			16 01											16 31			
Hove 2	a			16 03	16 07	16 13						16 20			16 33	16 43		
	d		15 54	16 04	16 08	16 14						16 21		16 24	16 34	16 44		
Brighton 10	a		15 58	16 08	16 14	16 18								16 28	16 38	16 48		
Preston Park	d																	
Burgess Hill	a																	
Haywards Heath 3	a											16 35						
Arundel	d									15 46								
Amberley	d																	
Pulborough	d									15 55								
Billingshurst	d									16 01								
Christs Hospital	d																	
Horsham 4	a									16 10	16 16							
	d										16 20							
Crawley	d										16 29							
Three Bridges 4	a										16 32							
Gatwick Airport 10	a										16 37	16 55						
	d										16 38	16 56						
Horley	a										16 41							
Redhill 5	a										16 47							
East Croydon	a										16 59	17 11						
London Bridge 4	a																	
Clapham Junction 10	a										17 09	17 21						
London Victoria 15	a										17 16	17 28						

n Stops at these stations before Eastleigh

Southampton, Portsmouth and Sussex Coast - Brighton, Gatwick Airport and London

Network Diagram - see first Page of Table 186

		SN ◇1 🍴	SN ◇1 A 🍴	SN ◇1	SN	SN	SN	SN 1	SN ◇1 🍴	SN	SN	SN ◇1	SN ◇1	SN ◇1	SN
Eastleigh	d														
Southampton Airport Parkway	d														
Southampton Central	d		15 13					15 33							
Swanwick	d		15 33					15 50							
Fareham	d		15 40					15 56							
Portchester	d		15 45												
Cosham	d		15 49					16 05							
Portsmouth Harbour	d												16 12		
Portsmouth & Southsea	d									15 59			16 16		
Fratton	d									16 04			16 20		
Hilsea	d									16 08					
Bedhampton	d									16 13					
Havant	d		15 56					16 11		16 16			16 30		
Warblington	d									16 18					
Emsworth	d		16 00					16 15		16 21					
Southbourne	d		16 03							16 24					
Nutbourne	d									16 26					
Bosham	d									16 30					
Fishbourne (Sussex)	d									16 33					
Chichester 4	a		16 10					16 23		16 36			16 40		
	d		16 11					16 25		16 37			16 41		
Bognor Regis 4	d	15 56									16 39	16 30			
Barnham	a	16 02	16 18					16 32		16 44	16 45	16 36	16 48		
	d	16 03	16 19		16 22			16 33	16 39	16 45		16 37	16 49		16 52
Bognor Regis	a				16 29				16 46						16 59
Ford 4	d	16 07						16 37		16 49		16 41			
Littlehampton 4	a									16 54					
	d			16 15										16 45	
Angmering 3	d			16 23				16 43						16 53	
Goring-by-Sea	d			16 27				16 47						16 57	
Durrington-on-Sea	d			16 30				16 50						17 00	
West Worthing	d			16 32			16 39	16 52						17 02	
Worthing 4	a			16 34			16 41	16 54						17 04	
	d			16 36			16 42	16 56						17 06	
East Worthing	d						16 44								
Lancing	d						16 47	17 00						17 10	
Shoreham-by-Sea	d			16 42			16 52	17 04						17 14	
Southwick	d						16 55	17 07							
Fishersgate	d						16 57								
Portslade	d			16 47			16 59	17 10							
Aldrington	d						17 01								
Hove 2	a			16 50			17 03	17 13						17 20	
	d			16 51		16 54	17 04	17 14						17 21	
Brighton 10	a					16 58	17 08	17 18							
Preston Park	d			16 55											
Burgess Hill	a			17 03											
Haywards Heath 3	a			17 09										17 35	
Arundel	d	16 12										16 46			
Amberley	d	16 17													
Pulborough	d	16 23										16 55			
Billingshurst	d	16 29										17 01			
Christs Hospital	d	16 36													
Horsham 4	a	16 40	16 46									17 10	17 16		
	d		16 50										17 20		
Crawley	d		16 59										17 29		
Three Bridges 4	a		17 02										17 32		
Gatwick Airport 10	a		17 07	17 24									17 37	17 55	
	d		17 08	17 25									17 38	17 56	
Horley	a												17 41		
Redhill 5	a		17 15										17 47		
East Croydon	a		17 27	17 40									17 59	18 11	
London Bridge 4	a														
Clapham Junction 10	a		17 37	17 50									18 09	18 21	
London Victoria 15	a		17 44	17 57									18 16	18 28	

A 🍴 from Horsham

Table 188

Saturdays

Southampton, Portsmouth and Sussex Coast - Brighton, Gatwick Airport and London

Network Diagram - see first Page of Table 186

		SN	SN	SN	SN ◇■	SN	SN ◇■ 🚌	SN ◇■ A 🚌	SN ■	SN ◇■	SN	SN	SN	SN ◇■ 🚌	SN	SN
Eastleigh	d								16 14							
Southampton Airport Parkway	d								16 18							
Southampton Central	d							16 13	16 33							
Swanwick	d							16 33	16 50							
Fareham	d							16 40	16 56							
Portchester	d							16 45								
Cosham	d							16 49	17 05							
Portsmouth Harbour	d			16 29												
Portsmouth & Southsea	d			16 33											16 59	
Fratton	d			16 37											17 04	
Hilsea	d														17 08	
Bedhampton	d														17 13	
Havant	d			16 46				16 56	17 11						17 16	
Warblington	d														17 18	
Emsworth	d			16 50				17 00	17 15						17 21	
Southbourne	d			16 53				17 03							17 24	
Nutbourne	d														17 26	
Bosham	d														17 30	
Fishbourne (Sussex)	d														17 33	
Chichester	a			17 00				17 10	17 23						17 36	
	d			17 00				17 11	17 25						17 37	
Bognor Regis	d					17 07	16 56									17 39
Barnham	a			17 08		17 13	17 02	17 18	17 32						17 44	17 45
	d			17 08	17 12	17 15	17 03	17 19	17 33		17 22			17 41	17 45	
Bognor Regis	a				17 18						17 29			17 47		
Ford	d					17 19	17 07		17 37						17 49	
Littlehampton	a					17 24									17 54	
	d									17 15						
Angmering	d			17 17					17 43	17 23						
Goring-by-Sea	d								17 47	17 27						
Durrington-on-Sea	d								17 50	17 30						
West Worthing	d		17 09						17 52	17 32			17 39			
Worthing	a		17 11	17 24					17 54	17 34			17 41			
	d		17 12	17 26					17 56	17 36			17 42			
East Worthing	d		17 14										17 44			
Lancing	d		17 17	17 30					18 00				17 47			
Shoreham-by-Sea	d		17 22	17 34					18 04	17 42			17 52			
Southwick	d		17 25	17 37					18 07				17 55			
Fishersgate	d		17 27										17 57			
Portslade	d		17 29	17 40					18 10	17 47			17 59			
Aldrington	d		17 31										18 01			
Hove	a		17 33	17 43					18 13	17 50			18 03			
	d	17 24	17 34	17 44					18 14	17 51		17 54	18 04			
Brighton	a	17 28	17 38	17 48					18 18			17 58	18 08			
Preston Park	d									17 55						
Burgess Hill	a									18 03						
Haywards Heath	a									18 09						
Arundel	d						17 12									
Amberley	d						17 17									
Pulborough	d						17 23									
Billingshurst	d						17 29									
Christs Hospital	d						17 36									
Horsham	a						17 40	17 46								
	d						17 50									
Crawley	d						17 59									
Three Bridges	a						18 02									
Gatwick Airport	a						18 07			18 24						
	d						18 08			18 25						
Horley	a															
Redhill	a						18 15									
East Croydon	a						18 27			18 40						
London Bridge	a															
Clapham Junction	a						18 37			18 50						
London Victoria	a						18 44			18 57						

A 🚌 from Horsham

Table 188

Saturdays

Southampton, Portsmouth and Sussex Coast - Brighton, Gatwick Airport and London

Network Diagram - see first Page of Table 186

		SN ◇■	SN ◇■	SN ◇■	SN	SN	SN	SN ■	SN	SN ◇■	SN	SN ◇■	SN ◇■	SN ◇■	SN	SN	SN	SN ■
Eastleigh	d																	
Southampton Airport Parkway	d																	
Southampton Central	d												17 13					17 33
Swanwick	d												17 33					17 50
Fareham	d												17 40					17 56
Portchester	d												17 45					
Cosham	d												17 49					18 05
Portsmouth Harbour	d		17 12						17 29									
Portsmouth & Southsea	d		17 16						17 33									
Fratton	d		17 20						17 37									
Hilsea	d																	
Bedhampton	d																	
Havant	d		17 30						17 46				17 56					18 11
Warblington	d																	
Emsworth	d								17 50				18 00					18 15
Southbourne	d								17 53				18 03					
Nutbourne	d																	
Bosham	d																	
Fishbourne (Sussex)	d																	
Chichester	a		17 40						18 00				18 10					18 23
	d		17 41						18 00				18 11					18 25
Bognor Regis	d	17 30									18 07	17 56						
Barnham	a	17 36	17 48						18 08		18 13	18 02	18 18					18 32
	d	17 37	17 49		17 52				18 08	18 12	18 15	18 03	18 19		18 22			18 33
Bognor Regis	a				17 59					18 18					18 29			
Ford	d	17 41									18 19	18 07						18 37
Littlehampton	a										18 24							
	d			17 45										18 15				
Angmering	d			17 53					18 17					18 23				18 43
Goring-by-Sea	d			17 57										18 27				18 47
Durrington-on-Sea	d			18 00										18 30				18 50
West Worthing	d			18 02			18 09							18 32			18 39	18 52
Worthing	a			18 04			18 11		18 24					18 34			18 41	18 54
	d			18 06			18 12		18 26					18 36			18 42	18 56
East Worthing	d						18 14										18 44	
Lancing	d			18 10			18 17		18 30								18 47	19 00
Shoreham-by-Sea	d			18 14			18 22		18 34					18 42			18 52	19 04
Southwick	d						18 25		18 37								18 55	19 07
Fishersgate	d						18 27										18 57	
Portslade	d						18 29		18 40					18 47			18 59	19 10
Aldrington	d						18 31										19 01	
Hove	a			18 20			18 33		18 43					18 50			19 03	19 13
	d			18 21		18 24	18 34		18 44					18 51		18 54	19 04	19 14
Brighton	a					18 28	18 38		18 48							18 58	19 08	19 18
Preston Park	d													18 55				
Burgess Hill	a													19 03				
Haywards Heath	a			18 35										19 09				
Arundel	d	17 46										18 12						
Amberley	d											18 17						
Pulborough	d	17 55										18 23						
Billingshurst	d	18 01										18 29						
Christs Hospital	d											18 36						
Horsham	a	18 10	18 16									18 40	18 46					
	d	18 20						18 32				18 50						
Crawley	d	18 29						18 45				18 59						
Three Bridges	a	18 32						18 48				19 02						
Gatwick Airport	a	18 37		18 55				18 54				19 07		19 25				
	d	18 38		18 56				18 55				19 08		19 26				
Horley	a	18 41						18 58				19 11						
Redhill	a	18 47						19 04				19 17						
East Croydon	a	18 59		19 11				19 24				19 29		19 41				
London Bridge	a																	
Clapham Junction	a	19 09		19 21				19 37				19 40		19 51				
London Victoria	a	19 16		19 28				19 44				19 50		19 58				

Table 188

Southampton, Portsmouth and Sussex Coast - Brighton, Gatwick Airport and London

Network Diagram - see first Page of Table 186

		SN	SN	SN	SN	SN	SN	SN	SN	SN	SN	SN	SN	SN	SN	SN	SN	SN
		◇1 ✠	1	◇1	1							◇1	1	◇1	1	◇1		
Eastleigh	d														18 14			
Southampton Airport Parkway	d														18 18			
Southampton Central ⛴	d													18 11	18 33			
Swanwick	d													18 28	18 50			
Fareham	d													18 35	18 56			
Portchester	d													18 40				
Cosham	d													18 44	19 05			
Portsmouth Harbour ⛴	d									18 12	18 29							
Portsmouth &Southsea	d				17 59					18 16	18 33							
Fratton	d				18 04					18 20	18 37							
Hilsea	d				18 08													
Bedhampton	d				18 13													
Havant	d				18 16					18 30	18 46			18 51	19 11			
Warblington	d				18 18													
Emsworth	d				18 21					18 34	18 50			18 55	19 15			
Southbourne	d				18 24					18 37	18 53			18 58				
Nutbourne	d				18 26													
Bosham	d				18 30													
Fishbourne (Sussex)	d				18 33													
Chichester 4	a				18 36					18 44	19 00			19 05	19 23			
	d				18 37					18 45	19 00			19 07	19 25			
Bognor Regis 4	d			18 33		18 39											19 03	
Barnham	a			18 40	18 44	18 46				18 52	19 08			19 14	19 32		19 09	
	d	18 39		18 41	18 45		18 52			18 53	19 08	19 12		19 15	19 33		19 22	19 22
Bognor Regis	a	18 46					18 59					19 18						19 29
Ford 4	d			18 45	18 49					18 57				19 19	19 37		19 26	
Littlehampton 4	a									19 02							19 32	
	d								18 51							19 15		
Angmering 3	d			18 53					19 00		19 17				19 43	19 23		
Goring-by-Sea	d			18 57					19 04							19 27		
Durrington-on-Sea	d			19 00					19 07						19 49	19 30		
West Worthing	d			19 02					19 09							19 32		
Worthing 4	a			19 04					19 11		19 24				19 53	19 34		
	d			19 06					19 12		19 26				19 53	19 35		
East Worthing	d								19 14						19 56			
Lancing	d			19 10					19 17		19 30				19 59	19 39		
Shoreham-by-Sea	d			19 14					19 22		19 34				20 03	19 43		
Southwick	d								19 25		19 37				20 06			
Fishersgate	d								19 27						20 08			
Portslade	d								19 29		19 40				20 10	19 48		
Aldrington	d								19 31						20 12			
Hove 2	a			19 20					19 33		19 43				20 14	19 51		
	d			19 21				19 24	19 34		19 44				20 15	19 52		
Brighton 10	a							19 28	19 38		19 50				20 19			
Preston Park	d																	
Burgess Hill	a															20 02		
Haywards Heath 3	a			19 35												20 10		
Arundel	d				18 54									19 24				
Amberley	d				18 59									19 29				
Pulborough	d				19 05									19 35				
Billingshurst	d				19 11									19 41				
Christs Hospital	d													19 48				
Horsham 4	a				19 20									19 52				
	d		19 02		19 21								19 32	19 52				
Crawley	d		19 14		19 30								19 45	20 01				
Three Bridges 4	a		19 18		19 33								19 48	20 05				
Gatwick Airport 10 ✈	a		19 22	19 55	19 38								19 54	20 10		20 25		
	d		19 23	19 56	19 39								19 55	20 11		20 26		
Horley	a		19 26										19 58					
Redhill 5	a		19 36		19 47								20 04	20 18				
East Croydon	a		19 54	20 11	20 00								20 24	20 29		20 41		
London Bridge 4 ⊖	a																	
Clapham Junction 10	a		20 08	20 21	20 11								20 37	20 40		20 51		
London Victoria 15 ⊖	a		20 15	20 28	20 20								20 44	20 50		20 58		

Table 188

Southampton, Portsmouth and Sussex Coast - Brighton, Gatwick Airport and London

Network Diagram - see first Page of Table 186

		SN	SN	SN	SN	SN	SN	SN	SN	SN	SN	SN	SN	SN	SN	SN
			◇1 ✠	1	◇1					1				◇1	1	◇1
Eastleigh	d															
Southampton Airport Parkway	d															
Southampton Central ⛴	d															19 09
Swanwick	d															19 28
Fareham	d															19 35
Portchester	d															19 40
Cosham	d															19 44
Portsmouth Harbour ⛴	d									19 12		19 29				
Portsmouth &Southsea	d							18 59		19 16		19 33				
Fratton	d							19 04		19 20		19 37				
Hilsea	d							19 08								
Bedhampton	d							19 13								
Havant	d							19 16		19 30		19 46				19 52
Warblington	d							19 18								
Emsworth	d							19 21		19 34						19 56
Southbourne	d							19 24		19 37						19 59
Nutbourne	d							19 26								
Bosham	d							19 30								
Fishbourne (Sussex)	d							19 33								
Chichester 4	a							19 36		19 44		19 57				20 06
	d							19 37		19 45		19 59				20 07
Bognor Regis 4	d				19 33				19 39				20 04			
Barnham	a				19 40			19 44	19 46	19 52		20 06	20 10			20 14
	d		19 39		19 41			19 45		19 53	19 52	20 07	20 11	20 12		20 15
Bognor Regis	a		19 46								19 59			20 18		
Ford 4	d				19 45			19 49		19 57			20 15			20 19
Littlehampton 4	a							19 55		20 02			20 20			
	d						19 52									
Angmering 3	d				19 53		20 00					20 16				
Goring-by-Sea	d				19 57		20 04									
Durrington-on-Sea	d				20 00		20 07									
West Worthing	d				20 02		20 09									
Worthing 4	a				20 04		20 11					20 23				
	d				20 05		20 12					20 23				
East Worthing	d						20 14					20 26				
Lancing	d				20 09		20 17					20 29				
Shoreham-by-Sea	d				20 13		20 22					20 33				
Southwick	d						20 25					20 36				
Fishersgate	d						20 27					20 38				
Portslade	d				20 17		20 29					20 40				
Aldrington	d						20 31					20 42				
Hove 2	a				20 21		20 33					20 44				
	d	19 54			20 22	20 24	20 34					20 45				
Brighton 10	a	19 59				20 28	20 38					20 49				
Preston Park	d															
Burgess Hill	a															
Haywards Heath 3	a				20 36											
Arundel	d															20 24
Amberley	d															20 29
Pulborough	d															20 35
Billingshurst	d															20 41
Christs Hospital	d															20 48
Horsham 4	a															20 52
	d			20 02											20 32	20 52
Crawley	d			20 14											20 45	21 01
Three Bridges 4	a			20 18	20 47										20 48	21 05
Gatwick Airport 10 ✈	a			20 22	20 52										20 56	21 10
	d			20 23	20 53										20 57	21 11
Horley	a			20 26											20 59	
Redhill 5	a			20 36											21 06	21 18
East Croydon	a			20 54	21 08										21 24	21 30
London Bridge 4 ⊖	a															
Clapham Junction 10	a			21 07	21 18										21 37	21 40
London Victoria 15 ⊖	a			21 14	21 26										21 44	21 50

Table 188

Saturdays

Southampton, Portsmouth and Sussex Coast - Brighton, Gatwick Airport and London

Network Diagram - see first Page of Table 186

		SN ◇1	SN	SN	SN 1	SN ◇1 ⊥	SN 1	SN ◇1	SN	SN	SN	SN	SN	SN 1	SN	SN ◇1	SN 1
Eastleigh	d																
Southampton Airport Parkway	d																
Southampton Central	d				19 33												
Swanwick	d				19 50												
Fareham	d				19 56												
Portchester	d																
Cosham	d				20 05												
Portsmouth Harbour	d													20 28			
Portsmouth & Southsea	d											19 59		20 32			
Fratton	d											20 04		20 36			
Hilsea	d											20 08					
Bedhampton	d											20 13					
Havant	d				20 11							20 16		20 44			
Warblington	d											20 18					
Emsworth	d				20 15							20 21		20 48			
Southbourne	d											20 24		20 51			
Nutbourne	d											20 26					
Bosham	d											20 30					
Fishbourne (Sussex)	d											20 33					
Chichester 4	a				20 23							20 36		20 58			
	d				20 25							20 37		20 59			
Bognor Regis 4	d							20 33	20 39						21 04		
Barnham	a				20 32			20 39	20 45			20 44		21 06	21 10		
	d		20 22		20 33	20 39		20 40				20 45	20 52	21 07	21 11	21 12	
Bognor Regis	a		20 29			20 46							20 59			21 18	
Ford 4	d							20 44				20 49			21 15		
Littlehampton 4	a											20 55			21 20		
	d	20 15									20 52						
Angmering 3	d	20 23			20 42			20 53			21 00			21 16			
Goring-by-Sea	d	20 27						20 57			21 04						
Durrington-on-Sea	d	20 30			20 48			21 00			21 07						
West Worthing	d	20 32						21 02			21 09						
Worthing 4	a	20 34			20 52			21 04			21 11			21 23			
	d	20 35			20 52			21 05			21 12			21 23			
East Worthing	d				20 55						21 14			21 26			
Lancing	d	20 39			20 58			21 09			21 17			21 29			
Shoreham-by-Sea	d	20 43			21 02			21 13			21 22			21 33			
Southwick	d				21 05						21 25			21 36			
Fishersgate	d				21 07						21 27			21 38			
Portslade	d	20 48			21 09			21 18			21 29			21 40			
Aldrington	d				21 11						21 31			21 42			
Hove 2	a	20 51			21 13			21 21			21 33			21 44			
	d	20 52		20 54	21 14			21 22		21 24	21 34			21 45			
Brighton 10	a			20 58	21 18					21 28	21 38			21 49			
Preston Park	d																
Burgess Hill	a	21 03															
Haywards Heath 3	a	21 11						21 36									
Arundel	d																
Amberley	d																
Pulborough	d																
Billingshurst	d																
Christs Hospital	d																
Horsham 4	a																
	d						21 02										21 32
Crawley	d						21 14										21 45
Three Bridges 4	a						21 18	21 47									21 48
Gatwick Airport 10	a	21 26					21 22	21 52									21 56
	d	21 27					21 23	21 53									21 57
Horley	a						21 26										22 00
Redhill 5	a						21 36										22 06
East Croydon	a	21 41					21 54	22 08									22 24
London Bridge 4	a																
Clapham Junction 10	a	21 51					22 07	22 18									22 37
London Victoria 15	a	21 58					22 15	22 26									22 44

Table 188

Saturdays

Southampton, Portsmouth and Sussex Coast - Brighton, Gatwick Airport and London

Network Diagram - see first Page of Table 186

		SN ◇1	SN 1	SN ◇1 A ⊥	SN	SN	SN	SN ◇1	SN	SN	SN 1	SN	SN	SN 1	SN
Eastleigh	d		20 14												
Southampton Airport Parkway	d		20 18												
Southampton Central	d	20 11	20 33												
Swanwick	d	20 28	20 50												
Fareham	d	20 35	20 56												
Portchester	d	20 40													
Cosham	d	20 44	21 05												
Portsmouth Harbour	d					20 40								21 11	
Portsmouth & Southsea	d					20 44								21 15	
Fratton	d					20 48								21 19	
Hilsea	d					20 52								21 23	
Bedhampton	d													21 28	
Havant	d	20 51	21 11			20 58								21 31	
Warblington	d					21 00								21 33	
Emsworth	d	20 55	21 15			21 03								21 36	
Southbourne	d	20 58				21 06								21 39	
Nutbourne	d					21 09								21 41	
Bosham	d					21 12								21 45	
Fishbourne (Sussex)	d					21 15								21 48	
Chichester 4	a	21 05	21 23			21 18								21 51	
	d	21 07	21 25			21 19								21 52	
Bognor Regis 4	d								21 39						22 00
Barnham	a	21 14	21 32			21 26			21 45					21 59	22 06
	d	21 15	21 33		21 22	21 27		21 42		21 52				22 00	
Bognor Regis	a				21 29			21 48		21 59					
Ford 4	d	21 19	21 37			21 31								22 04	
Littlehampton 4	a					21 36									
	d			21 15									21 52		
Angmering 3	d		21 43	21 23									22 00	22 11	
Goring-by-Sea	d		21 47	21 27									22 04	22 15	
Durrington-on-Sea	d		21 50	21 30									22 07	22 18	
West Worthing	d		21 52	21 32									22 09	22 20	
Worthing 4	a		21 54	21 34									22 11	22 22	
	d		21 55	21 35									22 12	22 23	
East Worthing	d		21 57										22 14	22 25	
Lancing	d		22 00	21 39									22 17	22 28	
Shoreham-by-Sea	d		22 04	21 43									22 22	22 32	
Southwick	d		22 07										22 25	22 35	
Fishersgate	d		22 09										22 27	22 37	
Portslade	d		22 11	21 48									22 29	22 39	
Aldrington	d		22 14										22 31	22 42	
Hove 2	a		22 16	21 51									22 33	22 44	
	d		22 16	21 52			21 54					22 24	22 34	22 44	
Brighton 10	a		22 21				21 58					22 28	22 38	22 48	
Preston Park	d														
Burgess Hill	a			22 03											
Haywards Heath 3	a			22 09											
Arundel	d	21 24													
Amberley	d	21 29													
Pulborough	d	21 35													
Billingshurst	d	21 41													
Christs Hospital	d	21 48													
Horsham 4	a	21 52													
	d	21 52									22 02				
Crawley	d	22 01									22 14				
Three Bridges 4	a	22 05									22 18				
Gatwick Airport 10	a	22 10		22 24							22 23				
	d	22 11		22 25							22 24				
Horley	a										22 27				
Redhill 5	a	22 18									22 37				
East Croydon	a	22 30		22 40							22 55				
London Bridge 4	a														
Clapham Junction 10	a	22 40		22 49							23 06				
London Victoria 15	a	22 50		22 57							23 14				

A ⊥ from Haywards Heath

Southampton, Portsmouth and Sussex Coast - Brighton, Gatwick Airport and London

Network Diagram - see first Page of Table 186

		SN ◇■	SN	SN ■	SN ■	SN ◇	SN	SN ■	SN ■	SN ■	SN	SN	SN ■	SN ◇■	SN ■	SN
Eastleigh	d															
Southampton Airport Parkway	d															
Southampton Central	d			21 13				21 33							22 13	
Swanwick	d			21 33				21 50							22 31	
Fareham	d			21 40				21 57							22 39	
Portchester	d			21 45				22 02							22 44	
Cosham	d			21 49				22 06							22 48	
Portsmouth Harbour	d				21 40								22 15			
Portsmouth & Southsea	d				21 44								22 19			
Fratton	d				21 48								22 23			
Hilsea	d				21 52								22 27			
Bedhampton	d				21 57								22 32			
Havant	d			21 56	22 00			22 13					22 35		22 55	
Warblington	d							22 15								
Emsworth	d							22 18					22 39		22 59	
Southbourne	d							22 21					22 42		23 02	
Nutbourne	d							22 23								
Bosham	d							22 27								
Fishbourne (Sussex)	d							22 30								
Chichester	a			22 06	22 10			22 33					22 49		23 09	
	d			22 07	22 11			22 34		22 40			22 52		23 09	
Bognor Regis	d						22 30									23 15
Barnham	a			22 14	22 18		22 36	22 41		22 47			22 59		23 17	23 21
	d	22 12		22 15	22 19	22 22	22 37			22 48	22 52		23 00	23 06	23 17	
Bognor Regis	a	22 18				22 29					22 59			23 12		
Ford	d			22 19	22 23		22 41			22 52			23 04			
Littlehampton	a			22 24			22 46								23 25	
	d			22 33												
Angmering	d			22 41									23 11			
Goring-by-Sea	d			22 45									23 15			
Durrington-on-Sea	d			22 47									23 17			
West Worthing	d			22 49									23 19			
Worthing	a			22 52									23 22			
	d			22 52									23 22			
East Worthing	d			22 55									23 25			
Lancing	d			22 58									23 28			
Shoreham-by-Sea	d			23 02									23 32			
Southwick	d			23 05									23 35			
Fishersgate	d			23 07									23 37			
Portslade	d			23 09									23 39			
Aldrington	d			23 11									23 41			
Hove	a			23 13									23 43			
	d		22 54	23 14								23 24	23 44			
Brighton	a		22 58	23 18								23 28	23 48			
Preston Park	d															
Burgess Hill	a															
Haywards Heath	a															
Arundel	d				22 28					22 57						
Amberley	d									23 02						
Pulborough	d				22 37					23 08						
Billingshurst	d				22 43					23 14						
Christs Hospital	d				22 50					23 21						
Horsham	a				22 54					23 25						
	d				22 55				23 02	23 25						
Crawley	d				23 03				23 14	23 38						
Three Bridges	a				23 07				23 18	23 42						
Gatwick Airport	a								23 22							
	d								23 23							
Horley	a								23 26							
Redhill	a								23 36							
East Croydon	a								23 55							
London Bridge	a															
Clapham Junction	a								00 11							
London Victoria	a								00 18							

Southampton, Portsmouth and Sussex Coast - Brighton, Gatwick Airport and London

Network Diagram - see first Page of Table 186

		SN	SN	SN ■	SN ◇	SN ◇	SN
Eastleigh	d						
Southampton Airport Parkway	d						
Southampton Central	d			22 33			
Swanwick	d			22 50			
Fareham	d			23 00			
Portchester	d						
Cosham	d			23 08			
Portsmouth Harbour	d		22 44				23 15
Portsmouth & Southsea	d		22 48				23 19
Fratton	d		22 52				23 23
Hilsea	d		22 56				23 27
Bedhampton	d		23 01				23 33
Havant	d		23 05	23 15			23 36
Warblington	d						23 38
Emsworth	d						23 41
Southbourne	d						23 44
Nutbourne	d						23 47
Bosham	d						23 50
Fishbourne (Sussex)	d						23 53
Chichester	a		23 16	23 25			23 57
	d		23 18	23 26		23 52	23 57
Bognor Regis	d						
Barnham	a		23 26	23 33		23 59	00 05
	d		23 26	23 34	23 36	00 01	00 06
Bognor Regis	a				23 43		
Ford	d		23 31			00 05	00 10
Littlehampton	a		23 35	23 42		00 10	00 15
	d		23 40				
Angmering	d		23 48				
Goring-by-Sea	d		23 52				
Durrington-on-Sea	d		23 54				
West Worthing	d		23 56				
Worthing	a		23 59				
	d		23 59				
East Worthing	d		00 02				
Lancing	d		00 05				
Shoreham-by-Sea	d		00 09				
Southwick	d		00 12				
Fishersgate	d		00 14				
Portslade	d		00 16				
Aldrington	d		00 18				
Hove	a		00 20				
	d	23 54	00 21				
Brighton	a	23 58	00 25				
Preston Park	d						
Burgess Hill	a						
Haywards Heath	a						
Arundel	d						
Amberley	d						
Pulborough	d						
Billingshurst	d						
Christs Hospital	d						
Horsham	a						
	d						
Crawley	d						
Three Bridges	a						
Gatwick Airport	a						
	d						
Horley	a						
Redhill	a						
East Croydon	a						
London Bridge	a						
Clapham Junction	a						
London Victoria	a						

Table 188

Sundays until 9 September

Southampton, Portsmouth and Sussex Coast - Brighton, Gatwick Airport and London

Network Diagram - see first Page of Table 186

Station		SN	SN ■	SN ◇	SN	SN ◇■	SN ■	SN ■	SN ■	SN	SN ■	SN ◇■	SN ◇■	SN ■	SN	SN	SN ■
Eastleigh	d																
Southampton Airport Parkway	d																
Southampton Central ⛴	d																
Swanwick	d																
Fareham	d																
Portchester	d																
Cosham	d																
Portsmouth Harbour ⛴	d	22p44			23p15												
Portsmouth & Southsea	d	22p48			23p19												
Fratton	d	22p52			23p23												
Hilsea	d	22p56			23p27												
Bedhampton	d	23p01			23p33												
Havant	d	23p05			23p36												
Warblington	d				23p38												
Emsworth	d				23p41												
Southbourne	d				23p44												
Nutbourne	d				23p47												
Bosham	d				23p50												
Fishbourne (Sussex)	d				23p53												
Chichester ■	a	23p16			23p57												
	d	23p18		23p52	23p57												
Bognor Regis ■	d											06 52					07 34
Barnham	a	23p26		23p59	00 05							06 58					07 40
	d	23p26		00 01	00 06	00 09		06 06		06 45		06 59		07 28			07 41
Bognor Regis	a					00 15				06 51				07 34			
Ford ■	d	23p31		00 05	00 10							07 03					07 45
Littlehampton ■	a	23p35		00 10	00 15			06 13									07 50
	d	23p40						06 20					07 14			07 40	
Angmering ■	d	23p48											07 22			07 48	
Goring-by-Sea	d	23p52											07 26			07 52	
Durrington-on-Sea	d	23p54											07 29			07 55	
West Worthing	d	23p56											07 31			07 57	
Worthing ■	a	23p59						06 33					07 33			07 59	
	d	23p59						06 33					07 35			08 00	
East Worthing	d	00 02														08 02	
Lancing	d	00 05						06 37					07 39			08 05	
Shoreham-by-Sea	d	00 09						06 41					07 43			08 09	
Southwick	d	00 12						06 44					07 46			08 12	
Fishersgate	d	00 14														08 14	
Portslade	d	00 16						06 48					07 49			08 16	
Aldrington	d	00 18														08 19	
Hove ■	a	00 20						06 51					07 53			08 21	
	d	00 21						06 51					07 54		07 56	08 21	
Brighton ■	a	00 25						06 55							08 00	08 25	
Preston Park	d																
Burgess Hill	a												08 04				
Haywards Heath ■	a												08 09				
Arundel	d											07 08					
Amberley	d											07 13					
Pulborough	d											07 19					
Billingshurst	d											07 26					
Christs Hospital	d											07 32					
Horsham ■	a											07 37					
	d		23p02				06 04		06 34		07 00	07 37					
Crawley	d		23p14				06 17		06 47		07 13	07 46					
Three Bridges ■	a		23p18				06 20		06 51		07 16	07 50					
Gatwick Airport ■ ✈	a		23p22				06 25		06 57		07 22	07 55	08 22				
	d		23p23						06 58		07 23	07 56	08 23				
Horley	a		23p26						07 00		07 26	07 58					
Redhill ■	a		23p36						07 07		07 36	08 05					
East Croydon	a		23p55						07 26		07 56	08 19	08 38				
London Bridge ■ ⊖	a										08 12						
Clapham Junction ■	a		00 11						07 41			08 32	08 48				
London Victoria ■ ⊖	a		00 18						07 48			08 39	08 55				

Table 188

Sundays until 9 September

Southampton, Portsmouth and Sussex Coast - Brighton, Gatwick Airport and London

Network Diagram - see first Page of Table 186

Station		SN ■	SN ◇■	SN ■	SN ■	SN ◇■	SN ◇■	SN ■	SN ■	SN ◇■	SN ■	SN ◇■	SN ◇■	SN ■	SN ■	SN ◇■	SN ◇■	GW	SN ■	SN ■
Eastleigh	d																			
Southampton Airport Parkway	d																			
Southampton Central ⛴	d									07 29								08 31		
Swanwick	d									07 46										
Fareham	d									07 53								08 52		
Portchester	d																			
Cosham	d									08 02								09 00		
Portsmouth Harbour ⛴	d			07 05			07 43							08 05			08 43			
Portsmouth & Southsea	d			07 09			07 47							08 09			08 47			
Fratton	d			07 13			07 51							08 13			08 51			
Hilsea	d																			
Bedhampton	d			07 21										08 20						
Havant	d			07 27			08 00			08 11				08 27			09 00	09 11		
Warblington	d			07 29										08 29						
Emsworth	d			07 32			08 04			08 15				08 32			09 04			
Southbourne	d			07 35			08 07							08 35			09 07			
Nutbourne	d			07 38										08 38						
Bosham	d			07 41										08 41						
Fishbourne (Sussex)	d			07 44										08 44						
Chichester ■	a			07 47			08 14			08 23				08 47			09 14	09 22		
	d			07 48			08 14			08 23				08 48			09 14	09 22		
Bognor Regis ■	d		07 52								08 34		08 52							
Barnham	a		07 58	07 55			08 22			08 31	08 40		08 58	08 55			09 22	09 30		
	d		07 59	08 02	08 09		08 22			08 32	08 41	08 40	08 59	09 02	09 09		09 22	09 30		
Bognor Regis	a				08 15							08 46			09 15					
Ford ■	d		08 03	08 06						08 36	08 45		09 03	09 06						
Littlehampton ■	a										08 50									
	d					08 14										09 14				
Angmering ■	d			08 12		08 22				08 42				09 12		09 22				
Goring-by-Sea	d			08 16		08 26				08 46				09 16		09 26				
Durrington-on-Sea	d			08 19		08 29				08 49				09 19		09 29				
West Worthing	d			08 21		08 31				08 51				09 21		09 31				
Worthing ■	a			08 23		08 33	08 37			08 53				09 23		09 33	09 37	09 45		
	d			08 24		08 41				08 54				09 24		09 41		09 45		
East Worthing	d			08 26						08 56				09 26						
Lancing	d			08 29						08 59				09 29						
Shoreham-by-Sea	d			08 33		08 47				09 03				09 33		09 47		09 52		
Southwick	d			08 36						09 06				09 36						
Fishersgate	d			08 38						09 08				09 38						
Portslade	d			08 40						09 10				09 40						
Aldrington	d			08 43						09 13				09 43						
Hove ■	a			08 45		08 53				09 15				09 45		09 53		09 59		
	d			08 45		08 54			09 01	09 15				09 45		09 54		09 59		10 03
Brighton ■	a			08 49					09 05	09 19				09 49				10 05		10 07
Preston Park	d																			
Burgess Hill	a					09 04										10 04				
Haywards Heath ■	a					09 09										10 09				
Arundel	d		08 08										09 08							
Amberley	d		08 13										09 13							
Pulborough	d		08 19										09 19							
Billingshurst	d		08 26										09 26							
Christs Hospital	d		08 32										09 32							
Horsham ■	a		08 37										09 37							
	d	08 00	08 37					09 00					09 37						10 00	
Crawley	d	08 13	08 46					09 13					09 46						10 13	
Three Bridges ■	a	08 16	08 50					09 16					09 50						10 16	
Gatwick Airport ■ ✈	a	08 22	08 55			09 21		09 22					09 55			10 22			10 22	
	d	08 23	08 56			09 23		09 23					09 56			10 23			10 23	
Horley	a	08 26	08 58					09 26					09 58						10 26	
Redhill ■	a	08 36	09 05					09 36					10 05						10 36	
East Croydon	a	08 56	09 19			09 38		09 56					10 19			10 39			10 56	
London Bridge ■ ⊖	a	09 12						10 12											11 12	
Clapham Junction ■	a		09 32			09 48							10 32			10 48				
London Victoria ■ ⊖	a		09 39			09 55							10 39			10 55				

Table 188

Sundays until 9 September

Southampton, Portsmouth and Sussex Coast - Brighton, Gatwick Airport and London

Network Diagram - see first Page of Table 186

		SN ◇1	SN 1	SN ◇1	SN ◇1 H	SN 1	SN 1	SN ◇1	SN ◇1	SN 1	SN 1	SN ◇1	SN 1	SN ◇1	SN ◇1 H	SN 1	SN 1
Eastleigh	d	08 48															
Southampton Airport Parkway	d	08n36															
Southampton Central	d	08n27										09 29					
Swanwick	d											09 46					
Fareham	d	09 02										09 53					
Portchester	d																
Cosham	d	09 11										10 02					
Portsmouth Harbour	d					09 05			09 43							10 05	
Portsmouth & Southsea	d					09 09			09 47							10 09	
Fratton	d					09 13			09 51							10 13	
Hilsea	d																
Bedhampton	d					09 20										10 20	
Havant	d	09 17				09 27			10 00			10 11				10 27	
Warblington	d					09 29										10 29	
Emsworth	d	09 21				09 32			10 04			10 15				10 32	
Southbourne	d					09 35			10 07							10 35	
Nutbourne	d					09 38										10 38	
Bosham	d					09 41										10 41	
Fishbourne (Sussex)	d					09 44										10 44	
Chichester 4	a	09 29				09 47			10 14			10 23				10 47	
	d	09 30				09 48			10 14			10 23				10 48	
Bognor Regis 4	d		09 34		09 52								10 34		10 52		
Barnham	a	09 37	09 40		09 58	09 55			10 22			10 31	10 40		10 58	10 55	
	d	09 38	09 41	09 40	09 59	10 02	10 09		10 22			10 32	10 41	10 40	10 59	11 02	11 09
Bognor Regis	a			09 46			10 15							10 46			11 15
Ford 4	d	09 42	09 45		10 03	10 06						10 36	10 45		11 03	11 06	
Littlehampton 4	a		09 50										10 50				
	d							10 14									
Angmering 3	d	09 48				10 12		10 22				10 42				11 12	
Goring-by-Sea	d	09 52				10 16		10 26				10 46				11 16	
Durrington-on-Sea	d	09 55				10 19		10 29				10 49				11 19	
West Worthing	d	09 57				10 21		10 31				10 51				11 21	
Worthing 4	a	09 59				10 23		10 33	10 37			10 53				11 23	
	d	10 00				10 24			10 41			10 54				11 24	
East Worthing	d	10 02				10 26						10 56				11 26	
Lancing	d	10 05				10 29						10 59				11 29	
Shoreham-by-Sea	d	10 09				10 33			10 47			11 03				11 33	
Southwick	d	10 12				10 36						11 06				11 36	
Fishersgate	d	10 14				10 38						11 08				11 38	
Portslade	d	10 16				10 40						11 10				11 40	
Aldrington	d	10 19				10 43						11 13				11 43	
Hove 2	a	10 21				10 45			10 53			11 15				11 45	
	d	10 21				10 45			10 54		11 01	11 15				11 45	
Brighton 10	a	10 25				10 49					11 05	11 19				11 49	
Preston Park	d																
Burgess Hill	a								11 04								
Haywards Heath 3	a								11 09								
Arundel	d				10 08										11 08		
Amberley	d				10 13										11 13		
Pulborough	d				10 19										11 19		
Billingshurst	d				10 26										11 26		
Christs Hospital	d				10 32										11 32		
Horsham 4	a				10 37										11 37		
	d				10 37					11 00					11 37		
Crawley	d				10 46					11 13					11 46		
Three Bridges 4	a				10 50					11 16					11 50		
Gatwick Airport 10	a				10 55				11 22	11 22					11 55		
	d				10 56				11 23	11 23					11 56		
Horley	a				10 58					11 26					11 58		
Redhill 5	a				11 05					11 36					12 05		
East Croydon	a				11 19				11 38	11 56					12 19		
London Bridge 4	a									12 12							
Clapham Junction 10	a				11 32				11 48						12 32		
London Victoria 15	a				11 39				11 55						12 39		

n Stops at these stations before Eastleigh

Table 188

Sundays until 9 September

Southampton, Portsmouth and Sussex Coast - Brighton, Gatwick Airport and London

Network Diagram - see first Page of Table 186

		SN ◇1	SN ◇1	SN 1	SN 1	SN ◇1	SN 1	SN ◇1	SN ◇1 H	SN 1	SN 1	SN ◇1	SN 1	SN 1	SN ◇1
Eastleigh	d														
Southampton Airport Parkway	d														
Southampton Central	d					10 29									11 28
Swanwick	d					10 46									11 46
Fareham	d					10 53									11 53
Portchester	d														
Cosham	d					11 02									12 02
Portsmouth Harbour	d		10 43							11 05					
Portsmouth & Southsea	d		10 47							11 09					
Fratton	d		10 51							11 13					
Hilsea	d														
Bedhampton	d									11 20					
Havant	d		11 00			11 11				11 27					12 11
Warblington	d									11 29					
Emsworth	d		11 04			11 15				11 32					12 15
Southbourne	d		11 07							11 35					
Nutbourne	d									11 38					
Bosham	d									11 41					
Fishbourne (Sussex)	d									11 44					
Chichester 4	a		11 14			11 23				11 47					12 23
	d		11 14			11 23				11 48					12 23
Bognor Regis 4	d						11 34		11 52						
Barnham	a		11 22			11 31	11 40		11 58	11 55					12 31
	d		11 22			11 32	11 41	11 40	11 59	12 02	12 09				12 32
Bognor Regis	a							11 46			12 15				
Ford 4	d					11 36	11 45		12 03	12 06					12 36
Littlehampton 4	a						11 50								
	d	11 14										12 14			
Angmering 3	d	11 22				11 42				12 12		12 22			12 42
Goring-by-Sea	d	11 26				11 46				12 16		12 26			12 46
Durrington-on-Sea	d	11 29				11 49				12 19		12 29			12 49
West Worthing	d	11 31				11 51				12 21		12 31			12 51
Worthing 4	a	11 33	11 37			11 53				12 23		12 33			12 53
	d		11 41			11 54				12 24		12 41			12 54
East Worthing	d					11 56				12 26					12 56
Lancing	d					11 59				12 29					12 59
Shoreham-by-Sea	d		11 47			12 03				12 33		12 47			13 03
Southwick	d					12 06				12 36					13 06
Fishersgate	d					12 08				12 38					13 08
Portslade	d					12 10				12 40					13 10
Aldrington	d					12 13				12 43					13 13
Hove 2	a		11 53			12 15				12 45		12 53			13 15
	d		11 54		12 01	12 15				12 45		12 54		13 01	13 15
Brighton 10	a				12 05	12 19				12 49				13 05	13 19
Preston Park	d														
Burgess Hill	a		12 04									13 04			
Haywards Heath 3	a		12 09									13 09			
Arundel	d								12 08						
Amberley	d								12 13						
Pulborough	d								12 19						
Billingshurst	d								12 26						
Christs Hospital	d								12 32						
Horsham 4	a								12 37						
	d			12 00					12 37				13 00		
Crawley	d			12 13					12 46				13 13		
Three Bridges 4	a			12 16					12 50				13 16		
Gatwick Airport 10	a		12 22	12 22					12 55			13 22	13 22		
	d		12 23	12 23					12 56			13 23	13 23		
Horley	a			12 26					12 58				13 26		
Redhill 5	a			12 36					13 05				13 36		
East Croydon	a		12 38	12 56					13 19			13 38	13 56		
London Bridge 4	a			13 12									14 12		
Clapham Junction 10	a		12 48						13 32			13 48			
London Victoria 15	a		12 55						13 39			13 55			

Table 188

Sundays until 9 September

Southampton, Portsmouth and Sussex Coast - Brighton, Gatwick Airport and London

Network Diagram - see first Page of Table 186

		SN ■	SN ◇■ ✕	SN ◇■ ✕	SN ■	SN ■	SN ◇■	SN ◇■	SN ■	SN ■	SN ◇■	SN ■	SN ◇■	SN ◇■ ✕
Eastleigh	d													
Southampton Airport Parkway	d													
Southampton Central	d										12 29			
Swanwick	d										12 46			
Fareham	d										12 53			
Portchester	d													
Cosham	d										13 02			
Portsmouth Harbour	d				12 05			12 43						
Portsmouth & Southsea	d				12 09			12 47						
Fratton	d				12 13			12 51						
Hilsea	d													
Bedhampton	d				12 20									
Havant	d				12 27			13 00			13 11			
Warblington	d				12 29									
Emsworth	d				12 32			13 04			13 15			
Southbourne	d				12 35			13 07						
Nutbourne	d				12 38									
Bosham	d				12 41									
Fishbourne (Sussex)	d				12 44									
Chichester ■	a				12 47			13 14			13 23			
	d				12 48			13 14			13 23			
Bognor Regis ■	d	12 34		12 52								13 34		13 52
Barnham	a	12 40		12 58	12 55			13 22			13 31	13 40		13 58
	d	12 41	12 40	12 59	13 02	13 09		13 22			13 32	13 41	13 40	13 59
Bognor Regis	a		12 46			13 15							13 46	
Ford ■	d	12 45		13 03	13 06						13 36	13 45		14 03
Littlehampton ■	a	12 50										13 50		
	d						13 14							
Angmering ■	d				13 12		13 22				13 42			
Goring-by-Sea	d				13 16		13 26				13 46			
Durrington-on-Sea	d				13 19		13 29				13 49			
West Worthing	d				13 21		13 31				13 51			
Worthing ■	a				13 23		13 33	13 37			13 53			
	d				13 24		13 41				13 54			
East Worthing	d				13 26						13 56			
Lancing	d				13 29						13 59			
Shoreham-by-Sea	d				13 33		13 47				14 03			
Southwick	d				13 36						14 06			
Fishersgate	d				13 38						14 08			
Portslade	d				13 40						14 10			
Aldrington	d				13 43						14 13			
Hove ■	a				13 45		13 53				14 15			
	d				13 45		13 54			14 01	14 15			
Brighton ■	a				13 49					14 05	14 19			
Preston Park	d													
Burgess Hill	a						14 04							
Haywards Heath ■	a						14 09							
Arundel	d			13 08										14 08
Amberley	d			13 13										14 13
Pulborough	d			13 19										14 19
Billingshurst	d			13 26										14 26
Christs Hospital	d			13 32										14 32
Horsham ■	a			13 37										14 37
	d			13 37					14 00					14 37
Crawley	d			13 46					14 13					14 46
Three Bridges ■	a			13 50					14 16					14 50
Gatwick Airport ■ ✈	a			13 55			14 22		14 22					14 55
	d			13 56			14 23		14 23					14 56
Horley	a			13 58					14 26					14 58
Redhill ■	a			14 05					14 36					15 05
East Croydon	a			14 19			14 38		14 56					15 19
London Bridge ■ ⊖	a								15 12					
Clapham Junction ■	a			14 32			14 48							15 32
London Victoria ■ ⊖	a			14 39			14 55							15 39

Table 188

Sundays until 9 September

Southampton, Portsmouth and Sussex Coast - Brighton, Gatwick Airport and London

Network Diagram - see first Page of Table 186

		SN ■	SN ■	SN ◇■	SN ◇■	GW ◇	SN ■	SN ■	SN ◇■	SN ■	SN ◇■	SN ◇■ ✕	SN ■	SN ■	SN ◇■	SN ◇■
Eastleigh	d															
Southampton Airport Parkway	d															
Southampton Central	d					13 07			13 29							
Swanwick	d								13 46							
Fareham	d					13 34			13 53							
Portchester	d															
Cosham	d					13 42			14 02							
Portsmouth Harbour	d	13 05			13 43								14 05			14 43
Portsmouth & Southsea	d	13 09			13 47								14 09			14 47
Fratton	d	13 13			13 51								14 13			14 51
Hilsea	d															
Bedhampton	d	13 20											14 20			
Havant	d	13 27			14 00	14 04			14 11				14 27			15 00
Warblington	d	13 29											14 29			
Emsworth	d	13 32			14 04				14 15				14 32			15 04
Southbourne	d	13 35			14 07								14 35			15 07
Nutbourne	d	13 38											14 38			
Bosham	d	13 41											14 41			
Fishbourne (Sussex)	d	13 44											14 44			
Chichester ■	a	13 47			14 14	14 19			14 23				14 47			15 14
	d	13 48			14 14	14 20			14 23				14 48			15 14
Bognor Regis ■	d									14 34		14 52				
Barnham	a	13 55			14 22	14 27			14 31	14 40		14 58	14 55			15 22
	d	14 02	14 09		14 22	14 28			14 32	14 41	14 41	14 59	15 02	15 09		15 22
Bognor Regis	a		14 15								14 47			15 15		
Ford ■	d	14 06							14 36	14 45		15 03	15 06			
Littlehampton ■	a									14 50						
	d			14 14											15 14	
Angmering ■	d	14 12		14 22					14 42				15 12		15 22	
Goring-by-Sea	d	14 16		14 26					14 46				15 16		15 26	
Durrington-on-Sea	d	14 19		14 29					14 49				15 19		15 29	
West Worthing	d	14 21		14 31					14 51				15 21		15 31	
Worthing ■	a	14 23		14 33	14 37	14 45			14 53				15 23		15 33	15 37
	d	14 24		14 41		14 45			14 54				15 24		15 41	
East Worthing	d	14 26							14 56				15 26			
Lancing	d	14 29							14 59				15 29			
Shoreham-by-Sea	d	14 33		14 47		14 52			15 03				15 33		15 47	
Southwick	d	14 36							15 06				15 36			
Fishersgate	d	14 38							15 08				15 38			
Portslade	d	14 40							15 10				15 40			
Aldrington	d	14 43							15 13				15 43			
Hove ■	a	14 45		14 53		15 00			15 15				15 45		15 53	
	d	14 45		14 54		15 00		15 04	15 15				15 45		15 54	
Brighton ■	a	14 49				15 06		15 08	15 19				15 49			
Preston Park	d															
Burgess Hill	a			15 04											16 04	
Haywards Heath ■	a			15 09											16 09	
Arundel	d											15 08				
Amberley	d											15 13				
Pulborough	d											15 19				
Billingshurst	d											15 26				
Christs Hospital	d											15 32				
Horsham ■	a											15 37				
	d						15 00					15 37				
Crawley	d						15 13					15 46				
Three Bridges ■	a						15 16					15 50				
Gatwick Airport ■ ✈	a			15 22			15 22					15 55			16 22	
	d			15 23			15 23					15 56			16 23	
Horley	a						15 26					15 58				
Redhill ■	a						15 36					16 05				
East Croydon	a			15 39			15 56					16 19			16 38	
London Bridge ■ ⊖	a						16 12									
Clapham Junction ■	a			15 48								16 32			16 48	
London Victoria ■ ⊖	a			15 55								16 39			16 55	

Table 188

Sundays
until 9 September

Southampton, Portsmouth and Sussex Coast - Brighton, Gatwick Airport and London

Network Diagram - see first Page of Table 186

		SN 1	SN 1	SN ◇1	SN 1	SN ◇1	SN ◇1	SN 1	SN 1	SN ◇1	SN ◇1	GW ◇	SN 1	SN 1	SN ◇1
Eastleigh	d														
Southampton Airport Parkway	d														
Southampton Central	d			14 29								15 22			15 29
Swanwick	d			14 46											15 46
Fareham	d			14 53								15 51			15 58
Portchester	d														
Cosham	d			15 02								16 01			16 07
Portsmouth Harbour	d							15 05			15 43				
Portsmouth & Southsea	d							15 09			15 47				
Fratton	d							15 13			15 51				
Hilsea	d														
Bedhampton	d							15 20							
Havant	d			15 11				15 27			16 00	16 12			16 16
Warblington	d							15 29							
Emsworth	d			15 15				15 32			16 04				16 20
Southbourne	d							15 35			16 07				
Nutbourne	d							15 38							
Bosham	d							15 41							
Fishbourne (Sussex)	d							15 44							
Chichester 4	a			15 23				15 47			16 14	16 22			16 28
	d			15 23				15 48			16 14	16 23			16 28
Bognor Regis 4	d				15 34		15 52								
Barnham	a			15 31	15 40		15 58	15 55			16 22	16 30			16 36
	d			15 32	15 41	15 40	15 59	16 02	16 09		16 22	16 31			16 38
Bognor Regis	a					15 46			16 15						
Ford 4	d			15 36	15 45		16 03	16 06							16 42
Littlehampton 4	a				15 50										
	d									16 14					
Angmering 3	d			15 42				16 12		16 22					16 48
Goring-by-Sea	d			15 46				16 16		16 26					16 52
Durrington-on-Sea	d			15 49				16 19		16 29					16 55
West Worthing	d			15 51				16 21		16 31					16 57
Worthing 4	a			15 53				16 23		16 33	16 37	16 45			16 59
	d			15 54				16 24			16 41	16 46			17 00
East Worthing	d			15 56				16 26							17 02
Lancing	d			15 59				16 29							17 05
Shoreham-by-Sea	d			16 03				16 33			16 47	16 52			17 09
Southwick	d			16 06				16 36							17 12
Fishersgate	d			16 08				16 38							17 14
Portslade	d			16 10				16 40							17 16
Aldrington	d			16 13				16 43							17 19
Hove 2	a			16 15				16 45			16 53	16 58			17 21
	d		16 01	16 15				16 45			16 54	17 00		17 03	17 22
Brighton 10	a		16 05	16 19				16 49				17 06		17 07	17 26
Preston Park	d										17 04				
Burgess Hill	a										17 09				
Haywards Heath 3	a														
Arundel	d						16 08								
Amberley	d						16 13								
Pulborough	d						16 19								
Billingshurst	d						16 26								
Christs Hospital	d						16 32								
Horsham 4	a						16 37								
	d	16 00					16 37						17 00		
Crawley	d	16 13					16 46						17 13		
Three Bridges 4	a	16 16					16 50						17 16		
Gatwick Airport 10	a	16 22					16 55				17 22		17 22		
	d	16 23					16 56				17 23		17 23		
Horley	a	16 26					16 58						17 26		
Redhill 5	a	16 36					17 05						17 36		
East Croydon	a	16 56					17 19				17 38		17 56		
London Bridge 4	a	17 12											18 12		
Clapham Junction 10	a						17 32				17 48				
London Victoria 15	a						17 39				17 55				

Table 188

Sundays
until 9 September

Southampton, Portsmouth and Sussex Coast - Brighton, Gatwick Airport and London

Network Diagram - see first Page of Table 186

		SN 1	SN ◇1	SN ◇1	SN 1	SN 1	SN ◇1	SN ◇1	SN 1	SN 1	SN ◇1	SN 1
Eastleigh	d											
Southampton Airport Parkway	d											
Southampton Central	d										16 29	
Swanwick	d										16 46	
Fareham	d										16 53	
Portchester	d											
Cosham	d										17 02	
Portsmouth Harbour	d				16 05			16 43				
Portsmouth & Southsea	d				16 09			16 47				
Fratton	d				16 13			16 51				
Hilsea	d											
Bedhampton	d				16 20							
Havant	d				16 27			17 00			17 11	
Warblington	d				16 29							
Emsworth	d				16 32			17 04			17 15	
Southbourne	d				16 35			17 07				
Nutbourne	d				16 38							
Bosham	d				16 41							
Fishbourne (Sussex)	d				16 44							
Chichester 4	a				16 47			17 14			17 23	
	d				16 48			17 14			17 23	
Bognor Regis 4	d	16 34		16 52								17 34
Barnham	a	16 40		16 58	16 55			17 22			17 31	17 40
	d	16 41	16 41	16 59	17 02	17 09		17 22			17 32	17 41
Bognor Regis	a		16 47			17 15						
Ford 4	d	16 45		17 03	17 06						17 36	17 45
Littlehampton 4	a	16 50										17 50
	d						17 14					
Angmering 3	d				17 12		17 22				17 42	
Goring-by-Sea	d				17 16		17 26				17 46	
Durrington-on-Sea	d				17 19		17 29				17 49	
West Worthing	d				17 21		17 31				17 51	
Worthing 4	a				17 23		17 33	17 37			17 53	
	d				17 24			17 41			17 54	
East Worthing	d				17 26						17 56	
Lancing	d				17 29						17 59	
Shoreham-by-Sea	d				17 33			17 47			18 03	
Southwick	d				17 36						18 06	
Fishersgate	d				17 38						18 08	
Portslade	d				17 40						18 10	
Aldrington	d				17 43						18 13	
Hove 2	a				17 45			17 53			18 15	
	d				17 45			17 54		18 01	18 15	
Brighton 10	a				17 49					18 05	18 19	
Preston Park	d							18 04				
Burgess Hill	a							18 09				
Haywards Heath 3	a											
Arundel	d			17 08								
Amberley	d			17 13								
Pulborough	d			17 19								
Billingshurst	d			17 26								
Christs Hospital	d			17 32								
Horsham 4	a			17 37								
	d			17 37					18 00			
Crawley	d			17 46					18 13			
Three Bridges 4	a			17 50					18 16			
Gatwick Airport 10	a			17 55				18 22	18 22			
	d			17 56				18 23	18 23			
Horley	a			17 58					18 26			
Redhill 5	a			18 05					18 36			
East Croydon	a			18 19				18 38	18 56			
London Bridge 4	a								19 12			
Clapham Junction 10	a			18 32				18 48				
London Victoria 15	a			18 39				18 55				

Southampton, Portsmouth and Sussex Coast - Brighton, Gatwick Airport and London

Sundays until 9 September

Network Diagram - see first Page of Table 186

		SN ◇1	SN ◇1	SN 1	SN 1	SN ◇1	SN ◇1	SN 1	SN 1	SN ◇1	SN 1	SN ◇1	SN ◇1	SN 1	SN 1	SN ◇1	SN ◇1	SN 1
Eastleigh	d																	
Southampton Airport Parkway	d																	
Southampton Central	d									17 29								
Swanwick	d									17 46								
Fareham	d									17 53								
Portchester	d																	
Cosham	d									18 02								
Portsmouth Harbour	d			17 05			17 43							18 05			18 43	
Portsmouth & Southsea	d			17 09			17 47							18 09			18 47	
Fratton	d			17 13			17 51							18 13			18 51	
Hilsea	d																	
Bedhampton	d			17 20										18 20				
Havant	d			17 27			18 00			18 11				18 27			19 00	
Warblington	d			17 29										18 29				
Emsworth	d			17 32			18 04			18 15				18 32			19 04	
Southbourne	d			17 35			18 07							18 35			19 07	
Nutbourne	d			17 38										18 38				
Bosham	d			17 41										18 41				
Fishbourne (Sussex)	d			17 44										18 44				
Chichester 4	a			17 47			18 14			18 23				18 47			19 14	
	d			17 48			18 14			18 23				18 48			19 14	
Bognor Regis 4	d		17 52								18 34		18 52					
Barnham	a		17 58	17 55			18 22			18 31	18 40		18 58	18 55			19 22	
	d	17 40	17 59	18 02	18 09		18 22			18 32	18 41	18 41	18 59	19 02	19 09		19 22	
Bognor Regis	a	17 46			18 15							18 47			19 15			
Ford 4	d		18 03	18 06						18 36	18 45		19 03	19 06				
Littlehampton 4	a										18 50							
	d					18 14										19 14		
Angmering 3	d			18 12		18 22				18 42				19 12		19 22		
Goring-by-Sea	d			18 16		18 26				18 46				19 16		19 26		
Durrington-on-Sea	d			18 19		18 29				18 49				19 19		19 29		
West Worthing	d			18 21		18 31				18 51				19 21		19 31		
Worthing 4	a			18 23		18 33	18 37			18 53				19 23		19 33	19 37	
	d			18 24		18 41				18 54				19 24		19 41		
East Worthing	d			18 26						18 56				19 26				
Lancing	d			18 29						18 59				19 29				
Shoreham-by-Sea	d			18 33		18 47				19 03				19 33		19 47		
Southwick	d			18 36						19 06				19 36				
Fishersgate	d			18 38						19 08				19 38				
Portslade	d			18 40						19 10				19 40				
Aldrington	d			18 43						19 13				19 43				
Hove 2	a			18 45		18 53				19 15				19 45		19 53		
	d			18 45		18 54			19 01	19 15				19 45		19 54		
Brighton 10	a			18 49					19 05	19 19				19 49				
Preston Park	d																	
Burgess Hill	a					19 04										20 04		
Haywards Heath 3	a					19 09										20 09		
Arundel	d		18 08										19 08					
Amberley	d		18 13										19 13					
Pulborough	d		18 19										19 19					
Billingshurst	d		18 26										19 26					
Christs Hospital	d		18 32										19 32					
Horsham 4	a		18 37										19 37					
	d		18 37					19 00					19 37					20 00
Crawley	d		18 46					19 13					19 46					20 13
Three Bridges 4	a		18 50					19 16					19 50					20 16
Gatwick Airport 10	a		18 55			19 22		19 22					19 55			20 22		20 22
	d		18 56			19 23		19 23					19 56			20 23		20 23
Horley	a		18 58					19 26					19 58					20 26
Redhill 5	a		19 05					19 36					20 05					20 36
East Croydon	a		19 19			19 38		19 56					20 19			20 38		20 56
London Bridge 4	a							20 12										21 12
Clapham Junction 10	a		19 32			19 48							20 32			20 48		
London Victoria 15	a		19 39			19 55							20 39			20 55		

Southampton, Portsmouth and Sussex Coast - Brighton, Gatwick Airport and London

Sundays until 9 September

Network Diagram - see first Page of Table 186

		SN 1	SN ◇1	SN 1	SN ◇1	SN ◇1	SN 1	SN 1	SN ◇1	SN ◇1	SN 1	SN 1	GW ◇	SN ◇1
Eastleigh	d													19 46
Southampton Airport Parkway	d													19n38
Southampton Central	d		18 29										19 26	19n30
Swanwick	d		18 46											
Fareham	d		18 53										19 49	20 03
Portchester	d													
Cosham	d		19 02										19 58	20 12
Portsmouth Harbour	d						19 05			19 43				
Portsmouth & Southsea	d						19 09			19 47				
Fratton	d						19 13			19 51				
Hilsea	d													
Bedhampton	d						19 20							
Havant	d		19 11				19 27			20 00			20 10	20 18
Warblington	d						19 29							
Emsworth	d		19 15				19 32			20 04				20 22
Southbourne	d						19 35			20 07				
Nutbourne	d						19 38							
Bosham	d						19 41							
Fishbourne (Sussex)	d						19 44							
Chichester 4	a		19 23				19 47			20 14			20 20	20 30
	d		19 23				19 48			20 14			20 21	20 31
Bognor Regis 4	d			19 34		19 52								
Barnham	a		19 31	19 40		19 58	19 55			20 22			20 28	20 38
	d		19 32	19 41	19 40	19 59	20 02	20 09		20 22			20 29	20 39
Bognor Regis	a				19 46			20 15						
Ford 4	d		19 36	19 45		20 03	20 06							20 43
Littlehampton 4	a			19 50										
	d								20 14					
Angmering 3	d		19 42				20 12		20 22					20 49
Goring-by-Sea	d		19 46				20 16		20 26					20 53
Durrington-on-Sea	d		19 49				20 19		20 29					20 56
West Worthing	d		19 51				20 21		20 31					20 58
Worthing 4	a		19 53				20 23		20 33	20 37			20 50	21 00
	d		19 54				20 24		20 41				20 50	21 01
East Worthing	d		19 56				20 26							21 03
Lancing	d		19 59				20 29							21 06
Shoreham-by-Sea	d		20 03				20 33		20 47				20 57	21 10
Southwick	d		20 06				20 36							21 13
Fishersgate	d		20 08				20 38							21 15
Portslade	d		20 10				20 40							21 17
Aldrington	d		20 13				20 43							21 20
Hove 2	a		20 15				20 45		20 53				21 03	21 22
	d	20 01	20 15				20 45		20 54			21 01	21 04	21 22
Brighton 10	a	20 05	20 19				20 49					21 05	21 09	21 26
Preston Park	d													
Burgess Hill	a								21 04					
Haywards Heath 3	a								21 09					
Arundel	d					20 08								
Amberley	d					20 13								
Pulborough	d					20 19								
Billingshurst	d					20 26								
Christs Hospital	d					20 32								
Horsham 4	a					20 37								
	d					20 37					21 00			
Crawley	d					20 46					21 13			
Three Bridges 4	a					20 50					21 16			
Gatwick Airport 10	a					20 55			21 22		21 22			
	d					20 56			21 23		21 23			
Horley	a					20 58					21 26			
Redhill 5	a					21 05					21 36			
East Croydon	a					21 19			21 38		21 56			
London Bridge 4	a										22 12			
Clapham Junction 10	a					21 32			21 48					
London Victoria 15	a					21 39			21 55					

n Stops at these stations before Eastleigh

Table 188

Sundays until 9 September

Southampton, Portsmouth and Sussex Coast - Brighton, Gatwick Airport and London

Network Diagram - see first Page of Table 186

Station		SN ◇■	SN ■	SN ■	SN ◇■	SN ■	SN ■	SN ■	SN ◇■	SN ■	SN ■	SN ◇■	SN ◇■	SN ■	SN ■	SN
Eastleigh	d								20 46							
Southampton Airport Parkway	d								20n38							
Southampton Central	d								20n29							
Swanwick	d															
Fareham	d								21 02							
Portchester	d															
Cosham	d								21 11							
Portsmouth Harbour	d			20 05				20 43						21 05		
Portsmouth & Southsea	d			20 09				20 47						21 09		
Fratton	d			20 13				20 51						21 13		
Hilsea	d															
Bedhampton	d			20 20										21 20		
Havant	d			20 27				21 00	21 17					21 27		
Warblington	d			20 29										21 29		
Emsworth	d			20 32				21 04	21 21					21 32		
Southbourne	d			20 35				21 07						21 35		
Nutbourne	d			20 38										21 38		
Bosham	d			20 41										21 41		
Fishbourne (Sussex)	d			20 44										21 44		
Chichester ■	a			20 47				21 14	21 29					21 47		
	d			20 48				21 14	21 30					21 48		
Bognor Regis ■	d		20 34		20 52						21 34		21 52			22 12
Barnham	a		20 41	20 55	20 58			21 22	21 37		21 40		21 58	21 55		22 18
	d	20 40	20 42	20 56	20 59	21 10		21 22	21 38		21 41	21 40	21 59	22 02	22 09	
Bognor Regis	a	20 46				21 16						21 46			22 15	
Ford ■	d		20 46	21 00	21 03			21 27	21 42		21 45		22 03	22 06		
Littlehampton ■	a		20 51	21 05				21 31			21 50					
	d			21 14				21 42								
Angmering ■	d			21 22				21 52	21 48					22 12		
Goring-by-Sea	d			21 26				21 56	21 52					22 16		
Durrington-on-Sea	d			21 29				21 59	21 55					22 19		
West Worthing	d			21 31				22 01	21 57					22 21		
Worthing ■	a			21 33				22 03	21 59					22 23		
	d			21 34				22 04	22 00					22 24		
East Worthing	d			21 36				22 06	22 02					22 26		
Lancing	d			21 39				22 09	22 05					22 29		
Shoreham-by-Sea	d			21 43				22 13	22 09					22 33		
Southwick	d			21 46				22 16	22 12					22 36		
Fishersgate	d			21 48				22 18	22 14					22 38		
Portslade	d			21 50				22 20	22 16					22 40		
Aldrington	d			21 53				22 23	22 19	←				22 43		
Hove ■	a			21 55				22 25	22 21	22 25				22 45		
	d			21 55				22 25	22 21	22 25				22 45		
Brighton ■	a			21 59				→	22 25	22 29				22 49		
Preston Park	d															
Burgess Hill	a															
Haywards Heath ■	a															
Arundel	d				21 08								22 08			
Amberley	d				21 13								22 13			
Pulborough	d				21 19								22 19			
Billingshurst	d				21 26								22 26			
Christs Hospital	d				21 32								22 32			
Horsham ■	a				21 37								22 37			
	d				21 37		22 00						22 37			
Crawley	d				21 46		22 13						22 46			
Three Bridges ■	a				21 50		22 16						22 50			
Gatwick Airport ■	a				21 55		22 22						22 55			
	d				21 56		22 23						22 56			
Horley	a				21 58		22 26						22 58			
Redhill ■	a				22 05		22 36						23 05			
East Croydon	a				22 19		22 55						23 20			
London Bridge ■	a															
Clapham Junction ■	a				22 32		23 07						23 31			
London Victoria ■	a				22 39		23 14						23 38			

n Stops at these stations before Eastleigh

Table 188

Sundays until 9 September

Southampton, Portsmouth and Sussex Coast - Brighton, Gatwick Airport and London

Network Diagram - see first Page of Table 186

Station		SN ■	SN ■	SN ◇■	SN ■	SN ◇■	SN	SN ■	SN ■	SN ■	SN ■	SN ◇■	SN ◇■	SN ■
Eastleigh	d													
Southampton Airport Parkway	d													
Southampton Central	d			21 30					22 15					22 52
Swanwick	d			21 47					22 32					23 11
Fareham	d			21 54					22 39					23 17
Portchester	d													
Cosham	d			22 03					22 48					23 26
Portsmouth Harbour	d		21 43					22 14			22 43			
Portsmouth & Southsea	d		21 47					22 18			22 47			
Fratton	d		21 51					22 22			22 51			
Hilsea	d													
Bedhampton	d							22 32						
Havant	d		22 00	22 11				22 35	22 54		23 00			23 32
Warblington	d							22 37						
Emsworth	d		22 04	22 15				22 40	22 58		23 04			23 36
Southbourne	d		22 07					22 43			23 07			
Nutbourne	d							22 46						
Bosham	d							22 49						
Fishbourne (Sussex)	d							22 52						
Chichester ■	a		22 14	22 23				22 55	23 06		23 14			23 44
	d		22 14	22 23				22 56	23 07		23 14			23 45
Bognor Regis ■	d													
Barnham	a		22 22	22 31				23 03	23 14		23 23			23 52
	d		22 23	22 32		22 37	22 52	23 04	23 15	23 15	23 24	23 37	23 42	23 53
Bognor Regis	a					22 43	22 59			23 21			23 48	
Ford ■	d		22 27	22 36				23 08	23 20		23 28	23 42		
Littlehampton ■	a		22 32					23 13	23 27		23 33	23 46		00 01
	d		22 42											
Angmering ■	d		22 50	22 42										
Goring-by-Sea	d		22 54	22 46										
Durrington-on-Sea	d		22 57	22 49										
West Worthing	d		22 59	22 51										
Worthing ■	a		23 01	22 53										
	d		23 02	22 54										
East Worthing	d		23 04	22 56										
Lancing	d		23 07	22 59										
Shoreham-by-Sea	d		23 11	23 03										
Southwick	d		23 14	23 06										
Fishersgate	d		23 16	23 08										
Portslade	d		23 18	23 10										
Aldrington	d		23 21	23 13	←									
Hove ■	a		23 24	23 15	23 24									
	d		23 26	23 15	23 26									
Brighton ■	a		→	23 19	23 30									
Preston Park	d													
Burgess Hill	a													
Haywards Heath ■	a													
Arundel	d													
Amberley	d													
Pulborough	d													
Billingshurst	d													
Christs Hospital	d													
Horsham ■	a													
	d	23 03												
Crawley	d	23 16												
Three Bridges ■	a	23 19												
Gatwick Airport ■	a	23 24												
	d	23 25												
Horley	a	23 28												
Redhill ■	a	23 34												
East Croydon	a	23 55												
London Bridge ■	a													
Clapham Junction ■	a	00 11												
London Victoria ■	a	00 19												

Table 188

Sundays from 16 September

Southampton, Portsmouth and Sussex Coast - Brighton, Gatwick Airport and London

Network Diagram - see first Page of Table 186

		SN	SN ■	SN ◇	SN		SN ◇■						SN ■	SN ■	SN ■	SN	SN ■	SN ◇■	SN ◇■	SN ■		SN	SN	SN ■	SN ■
Eastleigh	d																								
Southampton Airport Parkway	d																								
Southampton Central	d																								
Swanwick	d																								
Fareham	d																								
Portchester	d																								
Cosham	d																								
Portsmouth Harbour	d	22p44			23p15																				
Portsmouth & Southsea	d	22p48			23p19																				
Fratton	d	22p52			23p23																				
Hilsea	d	22p56			23p27																				
Bedhampton	d	23p01			23p33																				
Havant	d	23p05			23p36																				
Warblington	d				23p38																				
Emsworth	d				23p41																				
Southbourne	d				23p44																				
Nutbourne	d				23p47																				
Bosham	d				23p50																				
Fishbourne (Sussex)	d				23p53																				
Chichester ■	a	23p16			23p57																				
	d	23p18		23p52	23p57																				
Bognor Regis ■	d																	06 58						07 34	
Barnham	a	23p26		23p59	00 05													07 04						07 40	
	d	23p26		00 01	00 06		00 09							06 06		06 45		07 05		07 28				07 41	
Bognor Regis	a						00 15									06 51				07 34					
Ford ■	d	23p31		00 05	00 10													07 09						07 45	
Littlehampton ■	a	23p35		00 10	00 15									06 13										07 50	
	d	23p40												06 20					07 14				07 40		
Angmering ■	d	23p48																	07 22				07 48		
Goring-by-Sea	d	23p52																	07 26				07 52		
Durrington-on-Sea	d	23p54																	07 29				07 55		
West Worthing	d	23p56																	07 31				07 57		
Worthing ■	a	23p59												06 33					07 33				07 59		
	d	23p59												06 33					07 35				08 00		
East Worthing	d	00 02																					08 02		
Lancing	d	00 05												06 37					07 39				08 05		
Shoreham-by-Sea	d	00 09												06 41					07 43				08 09		
Southwick	d	00 12												06 44					07 46				08 12		
Fishersgate	d	00 14																					08 14		
Portslade	d	00 16												06 48					07 49				08 16		
Aldrington	d	00 18																					08 19		
Hove ■	a	00 20												06 51					07 53				08 21		
	d	00 21												06 51					07 54			07 56	08 21		
Brighton ■	a	00 25												06 55								08 00	08 25		
Preston Park	d																								
Burgess Hill	a																		08 04						
Haywards Heath ■	a																		08 09						
Arundel	d																	07 14							
Amberley	d																	07 19							
Pulborough	d																	07 25							
Billingshurst	d																	07 31							
Christs Hospital	d																	07 38							
Horsham ■	a																	07 42							
	d		23p02										06 04		06 34		07 03	07 42							08 03
Crawley	d		23p14										06 17		06 47		07 16	07 51							08 16
Three Bridges ■	a		23p18										06 20		06 51		07 19	07 54							08 19
Gatwick Airport ■	a		23p22										06 25		06 57		07 24	07 59	08 22						08 24
	d		23p23												06 58		07 25	08 00	08 23						08 25
Horley	a		23p26												07 00		07 28	08 02							08 28
Redhill ■	a		23p36												07 07		07 34	08 09							08 34
East Croydon	a		23p55												07 26		07 56	08 26	08 39						08 56
London Bridge ■	a																08 12								09 12
Clapham Junction ■	a		00 11												07 41			08 37	08 54						
London Victoria ■	a		00 18												07 48			08 46	09 01						

Table 188

Sundays from 16 September

Southampton, Portsmouth and Sussex Coast - Brighton, Gatwick Airport and London

Network Diagram - see first Page of Table 186

		SN ◇■ H	SN ■	SN ■	SN ◇■	SN ◇■		SN ■	SN ◇■	SN ■	SN ◇■	SN ■	SN ◇■ H	SN ■	SN ■		SN ◇■	SN ◇■	SN ■	GW			SN ◇■		SN ■
Eastleigh	d																						08 48		
Southampton Airport Parkway	d																						08n36		
Southampton Central	d								07 29											08 31			08n27		
Swanwick	d								07 46																
Fareham	d								07 53											08 52			09 02		
Portchester	d																								
Cosham	d								08 02											09 00			09 11		
Portsmouth Harbour	d		07 14			07 43								08 14				08 43							
Portsmouth & Southsea	d		07 18			07 47								08 18				08 47							
Fratton	d		07 22			07 51								08 22				08 51							
Hilsea	d																								
Bedhampton	d		07 30											08 30											
Havant	d		07 33			08 00			08 11					08 33				09 00		09 11			09 17		
Warblington	d		07 35											08 35											
Emsworth	d		07 38			08 04			08 15					08 38				09 04					09 21		
Southbourne	d		07 41			08 07								08 41				09 07							
Nutbourne	d		07 43											08 43											
Bosham	d		07 47											08 47											
Fishbourne (Sussex)	d		07 50											08 50											
Chichester ■	a		07 53			08 14			08 23					08 53				09 14		09 22			09 29		
	d		07 53			08 14			08 23					08 53				09 14		09 22			09 30		
Bognor Regis ■	d	07 58								08 36			08 58												09 36
Barnham	a	08 04	08 01			08 22			08 31	08 42			09 04	09 01				09 22		09 30			09 37		09 42
	d	08 05	08 08			08 22		08 26	08 38	08 43	08 43		09 05	09 08				09 22	09 26	09 30			09 38		09 43
Bognor Regis	a							08 32			08 49								09 32						
Ford ■	d	08 09	08 12						08 42	08 47			09 09	09 12									09 42		09 47
Littlehampton ■	a									08 52															09 52
	d				08 14												09 14								
Angmering ■	d		08 18		08 22				08 48					09 18			09 22						09 48		
Goring-by-Sea	d		08 22		08 26				08 52					09 22			09 26						09 52		
Durrington-on-Sea	d		08 25		08 29				08 55					09 25			09 29						09 55		
West Worthing	d		08 27		08 31				08 57					09 27			09 31						09 57		
Worthing ■	a		08 29		08 33	08 37			08 59					09 29			09 33	09 37		09 45			09 59		
	d		08 30		08 41				09 00					09 30			09 41			09 45			10 00		
East Worthing	d		08 32						09 02					09 32									10 02		
Lancing	d		08 35						09 05					09 35									10 05		
Shoreham-by-Sea	d		08 39		08 47				09 09					09 39			09 47			09 52			10 09		
Southwick	d		08 42						09 12					09 42									10 12		
Fishersgate	d		08 44						09 14					09 44									10 14		
Portslade	d		08 46						09 16					09 46									10 16		
Aldrington	d		08 49	←					09 19					09 49	←								10 19		
Hove ■	a		08 51	08 51	08 54				09 21					09 51	09 51		09 54			09 59			10 21		
	d		08 56	08 56	08 54				09 22					09 56	09 56		09 54			09 59			10 21		
Brighton ■	a		→	09 00					09 26					→	10 00					10 05			10 25		
Preston Park	d																								
Burgess Hill	a				09 04												10 04								
Haywards Heath ■	a				09 10												10 10								
Arundel	d	08 14											09 14												
Amberley	d	08 19											09 19												
Pulborough	d	08 25											09 25												
Billingshurst	d	08 31											09 31												
Christs Hospital	d	08 38											09 38												
Horsham ■	a	08 42											09 42												
	d	08 42										09 03	09 42												
Crawley	d	08 51										09 16	09 51												
Three Bridges ■	a	08 54										09 19	09 54												
Gatwick Airport ■	a	08 59			09 21							09 24	09 59				10 22								
	d	09 00			09 23							09 25	10 00				10 23								
Horley	a	09 02										09 28	10 02												
Redhill ■	a	09 09										09 34	10 09												
East Croydon	a	09 26			09 39							09 56	10 26				10 39								
London Bridge ■	a											10 12													
Clapham Junction ■	a	09 37			09 54								10 37				10 54								
London Victoria ■	a	09 46			10 01								10 46				11 01								

n Stops at these stations before Eastleigh

Table 188

Sundays from 16 September

Southampton, Portsmouth and Sussex Coast - Brighton, Gatwick Airport and London

Network Diagram - see first Page of Table 186

		SN ◇1	SN 1	SN ◇1 🚌	SN 1	SN 1	SN 1	SN ◇1	SN ◇1	SN ◇1	SW ◇1	SN 1	SN ◇1	SN 1	SN ◇1 🚌	SN 1	SN 1	SN 1	SN ◇1	SN ◇1
Eastleigh	d										09 22									
Southampton Airport Parkway	d										09 27									
Southampton Central ⛴	d									09 29	09a34									
Swanwick	d									09 46										
Fareham	d									09 53										
Portchester	d																			
Cosham	d									10 02										
Portsmouth Harbour ⛴	d				09 14				09 43							10 14				10 43
Portsmouth & Southsea	d				09 18				09 47							10 18				10 47
Fratton	d				09 22				09 51							10 22				10 51
Hilsea	d																			
Bedhampton	d				09 30											10 30				
Havant	d				09 33				10 00	10 11						10 33				11 00
Warblington	d				09 35											10 35				
Emsworth	d				09 38				10 04	10 15						10 38				11 04
Southbourne	d				09 41				10 07							10 41				11 07
Nutbourne	d				09 43											10 43				
Bosham	d				09 47											10 47				
Fishbourne (Sussex)	d				09 50											10 50				
Chichester 4	a				09 53				10 14	10 23						10 53				11 14
	d				09 53				10 14	10 23						10 53				11 14
Bognor Regis 4	d			09 58								10 34			10 58					
Barnham	a			10 04	10 01				10 22	10 31		10 40			11 04	11 01				11 22
	d	09 44		10 05	10 08		10 15		10 22	10 38		10 41	10 43		11 05	11 08		11 15		11 22
Bognor Regis	a	09 50					10 21						10 49					11 21		
Ford 4	d			10 09	10 12					10 42		10 45			11 09	11 12				
Littlehampton 4	a											10 50								
	d							10 14											11 14	
Angmering 3	d				10 18			10 22		10 48						11 18			11 22	
Goring-by-Sea	d				10 22			10 26		10 52						11 22			11 26	
Durrington-on-Sea	d				10 25			10 29		10 55						11 25			11 29	
West Worthing	d				10 27			10 31		10 57						11 27			11 31	
Worthing 4	a				10 29			10 33	10 37	10 59						11 29			11 33	11 37
	d				10 30				10 41	11 00						11 30				11 41
East Worthing	d				10 32					11 02						11 32				
Lancing	d				10 35					11 05						11 35				
Shoreham-by-Sea	d				10 39				10 47	11 09						11 39				11 47
Southwick	d				10 42					11 12						11 42				
Fishersgate	d				10 44					11 14						11 44				
Portslade	d				10 46					11 16						11 46				
Aldrington	d				10 49	←				11 19						11 49	←			
Hove 2	a				10 51	10 51			10 54	11 21						11 51	11 51			11 54
	d				10 56	10 56			10 54	11 22						11 56	11 56			11 54
Brighton 10	a				→	11 00				11 26						→	12 00			
Preston Park	d																			
Burgess Hill	a								11 04											12 04
Haywards Heath 3	a								11 10											12 10
Arundel	d			10 14											11 14					
Amberley	d			10 19											11 19					
Pulborough	d			10 25											11 25					
Billingshurst	d			10 31											11 31					
Christs Hospital	d			10 38											11 38					
Horsham 4	a			10 42											11 42					
	d		10 03	10 42										11 03	11 42					
Crawley	d		10 16	10 51										11 16	11 51					
Three Bridges 4	a		10 19	10 54										11 19	11 54					
Gatwick Airport 10 ✈	a		10 24	10 59					11 21					11 24	11 59					12 22
	d		10 25	11 00					11 23					11 25	12 00					12 23
Horley	a		10 28	11 02										11 28	12 02					
Redhill 5	a		10 34	11 09										11 34	12 09					
East Croydon	a		10 56	11 26					11 39					11 56	12 26					12 39
London Bridge 4 ⊖	a		11 12											12 12						
Clapham Junction 10	a			11 37					11 54						12 37					12 54
London Victoria 15 ⊖	a			11 46					20 01						12 46					13 01

Table 188

Sundays from 16 September

Southampton, Portsmouth and Sussex Coast - Brighton, Gatwick Airport and London

Network Diagram - see first Page of Table 186

		SN ◇1	SN 1	SN ◇1 🚌	SN 1	SN ◇1 🚌	SN 1	SN 1	SN 1	SN ◇1	SN ◇1	SN ◇1
Eastleigh	d											
Southampton Airport Parkway	d											
Southampton Central ⛴	d	10 29										11 28
Swanwick	d	10 46										11 46
Fareham	d	10 53										11 53
Portchester	d											
Cosham	d	11 02										12 02
Portsmouth Harbour ⛴	d						11 14				11 43	
Portsmouth & Southsea	d						11 18				11 47	
Fratton	d						11 22				11 51	
Hilsea	d											
Bedhampton	d						11 30					
Havant	d	11 11					11 33				12 00	12 11
Warblington	d						11 35					
Emsworth	d	11 15					11 38				12 04	12 15
Southbourne	d						11 41				12 07	
Nutbourne	d						11 43					
Bosham	d						11 47					
Fishbourne (Sussex)	d						11 50					
Chichester 4	a	11 23					11 53				12 14	12 23
	d	11 23					11 53				12 14	12 23
Bognor Regis 4	d		11 34			11 58						
Barnham	a	11 31	11 40			12 04	12 01				12 22	12 31
	d	11 38	11 41	11 43		12 05	12 08		12 15		12 22	12 38
Bognor Regis	a			11 49					12 21			
Ford 4	d	11 42	11 45			12 09	12 12					12 42
Littlehampton 4	a		11 50									
	d									12 14		
Angmering 3	d	11 48					12 18			12 22		12 48
Goring-by-Sea	d	11 52					12 22			12 26		12 52
Durrington-on-Sea	d	11 55					12 25			12 29		12 55
West Worthing	d	11 57					12 27			12 31		12 57
Worthing 4	a	11 59					12 29			12 33	12 37	12 59
	d	12 00					12 30				12 41	13 00
East Worthing	d	12 02					12 32					13 02
Lancing	d	12 05					12 35					13 05
Shoreham-by-Sea	d	12 09					12 39				12 47	13 09
Southwick	d	12 12					12 42					13 12
Fishersgate	d	12 14					12 44					13 14
Portslade	d	12 16					12 46					13 16
Aldrington	d	12 19					12 49	←				13 19
Hove 2	a	12 21					12 51	12 51			12 54	13 21
	d	12 22					12 56	12 56			12 54	13 22
Brighton 10	a	12 26					→	13 00				13 26
Preston Park	d											
Burgess Hill	a										13 04	
Haywards Heath 3	a										13 10	
Arundel	d					12 14						
Amberley	d					12 19						
Pulborough	d					12 25						
Billingshurst	d					12 31						
Christs Hospital	d					12 38						
Horsham 4	a					12 42						
	d				12 03	12 42						
Crawley	d				12 16	12 51						
Three Bridges 4	a				12 19	12 54						
Gatwick Airport 10 ✈	a				12 24	12 59					13 22	
	d				12 25	13 00					13 23	
Horley	a				12 28	13 02						
Redhill 5	a				12 34	13 09						
East Croydon	a				12 56	13 26					13 39	
London Bridge 4 ⊖	a				13 12							
Clapham Junction 10	a					13 37					13 54	
London Victoria 15 ⊖	a					13 46					14 01	

Table 188

Sundays from 16 September

Southampton, Portsmouth and Sussex Coast - Brighton, Gatwick Airport and London

Network Diagram - see first Page of Table 186

Station		SN ■	SN ◇■ H	SN ■	SN ◇■ H	SN ■	SN ■	SN ■	SN ◇■	SN ◇■	SN ◇■	SN ■	SN ◇■ H	SN ■	SN ◇■ H	SN ■	SN ■	SN ■
Eastleigh	d																	
Southampton Airport Parkway	d																	
Southampton Central	d										12 29							
Swanwick	d										12 46							
Fareham	d										12 53							
Portchester	d																	
Cosham	d										13 02							
Portsmouth Harbour	d					12 14				12 43						13 14		
Portsmouth & Southsea	d					12 18				12 47						13 18		
Fratton	d					12 22				12 51						13 22		
Hilsea	d																	
Bedhampton	d					12 30										13 30		
Havant	d					12 33				13 00	13 11					13 33		
Warblington	d					12 35										13 35		
Emsworth	d					12 38				13 04	13 15					13 38		
Southbourne	d					12 41				13 07						13 41		
Nutbourne	d					12 43										13 43		
Bosham	d					12 47										13 47		
Fishbourne (Sussex)	d					12 50										13 50		
Chichester	a					12 53				13 14	13 23					13 53		
	d					12 53				13 14	13 23					13 53		
Bognor Regis	d	12 34			12 58							13 34			13 58			
Barnham	a	12 40			13 04	13 01				13 22	13 31	13 40			14 04	14 01		
	d	12 41	12 43		13 05	13 08		13 15		13 22	13 38	13 41	13 43		14 05	14 08		14 15
Bognor Regis	a		12 49					13 21					13 49					14 21
Ford	d	12 45			13 09	13 12					13 42	13 45			14 09	14 12		
Littlehampton	a	12 50										13 50						
	d								13 14									
Angmering	d					13 18			13 22		13 48					14 18		
Goring-by-Sea	d					13 22			13 26		13 52					14 22		
Durrington-on-Sea	d					13 25			13 29		13 55					14 25		
West Worthing	d					13 27			13 31		13 57					14 27		
Worthing	a					13 29			13 33	13 37	13 59					14 29		
	d					13 30			13 41		14 00					14 30		
East Worthing	d					13 32					14 02					14 32		
Lancing	d					13 35					14 05					14 35		
Shoreham-by-Sea	d					13 39			13 47		14 09					14 39		
Southwick	d					13 42					14 12					14 42		
Fishersgate	d					13 44					14 14					14 44		
Portslade	d					13 46					14 16					14 46		
Aldrington	d					13 49	←				14 19					14 49	←	
Hove	a					13 51	13 51		13 54		14 21					14 51	14 51	
	d					13 56	13 56		13 54		14 22					14 56	14 56	
Brighton	a					→	14 00				14 26					→	15 00	
Preston Park	d																	
Burgess Hill	a								14 04									
Haywards Heath	a								14 10									
Arundel	d				13 14										14 14			
Amberley	d				13 19										14 19			
Pulborough	d				13 25										14 25			
Billingshurst	d				13 31										14 31			
Christs Hospital	d				13 38										14 38			
Horsham	a				13 42										14 42			
	d			13 03	13 42									14 03	14 42			
Crawley	d			13 16	13 51									14 16	14 51			
Three Bridges	a			13 19	13 54									14 19	14 54			
Gatwick Airport	a			13 24	13 59				14 22					14 24	14 59			
	d			13 25	14 00				14 23					14 25	15 00			
Horley	a			13 28	14 02									14 28	15 02			
Redhill	a			13 34	14 09									14 34	15 09			
East Croydon	a			13 56	14 26				14 39					14 56	15 26			
London Bridge	a			14 12										15 12				
Clapham Junction	a				14 37				14 54						15 37			
London Victoria	a				14 46				15 01						15 46			

Table 188

Sundays from 16 September

Southampton, Portsmouth and Sussex Coast - Brighton, Gatwick Airport and London

Network Diagram - see first Page of Table 186

Station		SN ◇■	SN ◇■	GW ◇	SN ◇■	SN ■	SN ◇■ H	SN ■	SN ◇■ H	SN ■	SN ■	SN ■	SN ◇■	SN ◇■	SN ◇■
Eastleigh	d														
Southampton Airport Parkway	d														
Southampton Central	d			13 07	13 29										14 29
Swanwick	d				13 46										14 46
Fareham	d			13 34	13 53										14 53
Portchester	d														
Cosham	d			13 42	14 02										15 02
Portsmouth Harbour	d		13 43							14 14				14 43	
Portsmouth & Southsea	d		13 47							14 18				14 47	
Fratton	d		13 51							14 22				14 51	
Hilsea	d														
Bedhampton	d									14 30					
Havant	d		14 00	14 04	14 11					14 33				15 00	15 11
Warblington	d									14 35					
Emsworth	d		14 04		14 15					14 38				15 04	15 15
Southbourne	d		14 07							14 41				15 07	
Nutbourne	d									14 43					
Bosham	d									14 47					
Fishbourne (Sussex)	d									14 50					
Chichester	a		14 14	14 19	14 23					14 53				15 14	15 23
	d		14 14	14 20	14 23					14 53				15 14	15 23
Bognor Regis	d					14 34			14 58						
Barnham	a		14 22	14 27	14 31	14 40			15 04	15 01				15 22	15 31
	d		14 22	14 28	14 38	14 41	14 43		15 05	15 08		15 15		15 22	15 38
Bognor Regis	a						14 49					15 21			
Ford	d				14 42	14 45			15 09	15 12					15 42
Littlehampton	a					14 50									
	d	14 14											15 14		
Angmering	d	14 22			14 48					15 18			15 22		15 48
Goring-by-Sea	d	14 26			14 52					15 22			15 26		15 52
Durrington-on-Sea	d	14 29			14 55					15 25			15 29		15 55
West Worthing	d	14 31			14 57					15 27			15 31		15 57
Worthing	a	14 33	14 37	14 45	14 59					15 29			15 33	15 37	15 59
	d	14 41		14 45	15 00					15 30			15 41		16 00
East Worthing	d				15 02					15 32					16 02
Lancing	d				15 05					15 35					16 05
Shoreham-by-Sea	d	14 47		14 52	15 09					15 39			15 47		16 09
Southwick	d				15 12					15 42					16 12
Fishersgate	d				15 14					15 44					16 14
Portslade	d				15 16					15 46					16 16
Aldrington	d				15 19					15 49	←				16 19
Hove	a	14 54		15 00	15 21					15 51	15 51		15 54		16 21
	d	14 54		15 00	15 22					15 56	15 56		15 54		16 22
Brighton	a			15 06	15 26					→	16 00				16 26
Preston Park	d														
Burgess Hill	a	15 04											16 04		
Haywards Heath	a	15 10											16 10		
Arundel	d								15 14						
Amberley	d								15 19						
Pulborough	d								15 25						
Billingshurst	d								15 31						
Christs Hospital	d								15 38						
Horsham	a								15 42						
	d							15 03	15 42						
Crawley	d							15 16	15 51						
Three Bridges	a							15 19	15 54						
Gatwick Airport	a	15 22						15 24	15 59				16 22		
	d	15 23						15 25	16 00				16 23		
Horley	a							15 28	16 02						
Redhill	a							15 34	16 09						
East Croydon	a	15 39						15 56	16 26				16 98		
London Bridge	a							16 12							
Clapham Junction	a	15 54							16 37				16 54		
London Victoria	a	16 01							16 46				17 01		

Table 188

Sundays from 16 September

Southampton, Portsmouth and Sussex Coast - Brighton, Gatwick Airport and London

Network Diagram - see first Page of Table 186

Station		SN 1	SN ◇1 H	SN 1	SN ◇1 H	SN 1	SN 1	SN 1	SN ◇1	SN ◇1	GW ◇	SN ◇1	SN 1	SN ◇1 H	SN 1
Eastleigh	d														
Southampton Airport Parkway	d														
Southampton Central ⛴	d										15 22	15 29			
Swanwick	d											15 46			
Fareham	d										15 51	15 58			
Portchester	d														
Cosham	d										16 01	16 07			
Portsmouth Harbour ⛴	d					15 14				15 43					
Portsmouth & Southsea	d					15 18				15 47					
Fratton	d					15 22				15 51					
Hilsea	d														
Bedhampton	d					15 30									
Havant	d					15 33				16 00	16 12	16 16			
Warblington	d					15 35									
Emsworth	d					15 38				16 04		16 20			
Southbourne	d					15 41				16 07					
Nutbourne	d					15 43									
Bosham	d					15 47									
Fishbourne (Sussex)	d					15 50									
Chichester 4	a					15 53				16 14	16 22	16 28			
	d					15 53				16 14	16 23	16 28			
Bognor Regis 4	d	15 34			15 58								16 34		
Barnham	a	15 40			16 04	16 01				16 22	16 30	16 36	16 40		
	d	15 41	15 43		16 05	16 08		16 15		16 22	16 31	16 38	16 41	16 44	
Bognor Regis	a		15 49					16 21						16 50	
Ford 4	d	15 45			16 09	16 12						16 42	16 45		
Littlehampton 4	a	15 50											16 50		
	d								16 14						
Angmering 3	d					16 18			16 22			16 48			
Goring-by-Sea	d					16 22			16 26			16 52			
Durrington-on-Sea	d					16 25			16 29			16 55			
West Worthing	d					16 27			16 31			16 57			
Worthing 4	a					16 29			16 33	16 37	16 45	16 59			
	d					16 30				16 41	16 46	17 00			
East Worthing	d					16 32						17 02			
Lancing	d					16 35						17 05			
Shoreham-by-Sea	d					16 39				16 47	16 52	17 09			
Southwick	d					16 42						17 12			
Fishersgate	d					16 44						17 14			
Portslade	d					16 46						17 16			
Aldrington	d					16 49	←					17 19			
Hove 2	a					16 51	16 51			16 54	16 58	17 21			
	d					16 56	16 56			16 54	17 00	17 22			
Brighton 10	a					→	17 00				17 06	17 26			
Preston Park	d														
Burgess Hill	a									17 04					
Haywards Heath 3	a									17 10					
Arundel	d				16 14										
Amberley	d				16 19										
Pulborough	d				16 25										
Billingshurst	d				16 31										
Christs Hospital	d				16 38										
Horsham 4	a				16 42										
	d			16 03	16 42										17 03
Crawley	d			16 16	16 51										17 16
Three Bridges 4	a			16 19	16 54										17 19
Gatwick Airport 10 ✈	a			16 24	16 59					17 22					17 24
	d			16 25	17 00					17 23					17 25
Horley	a			16 28	17 02										17 28
Redhill 5	a			16 34	17 09										17 34
East Croydon ⇌	a			16 56	17 26					17 39					17 56
London Bridge 4 ⊖	a			17 12											18 12
Clapham Junction 10	a				17 37					17 54					
London Victoria 15 ⊖	a				17 46					18 01					

Table 188

Sundays from 16 September

Southampton, Portsmouth and Sussex Coast - Brighton, Gatwick Airport and London

Network Diagram - see first Page of Table 186

Station		SN ◇1 H	SN 1	SN 1	SN 1	SN ◇1	SN ◇1	SN ◇1	SN 1	SN ◇1 H	SN 1	SN ◇1	SN 1	SN 1	SN 1	SN ◇1	SN ◇1
Eastleigh	d																
Southampton Airport Parkway	d																
Southampton Central ⛴	d							16 29									
Swanwick	d							16 46									
Fareham	d							16 53									
Portchester	d																
Cosham	d							17 02									
Portsmouth Harbour ⛴	d		16 14				16 43						17 14				17 43
Portsmouth & Southsea	d		16 18				16 47						17 18				17 47
Fratton	d		16 22				16 51						17 22				17 51
Hilsea	d																
Bedhampton	d		16 30										17 30				
Havant	d		16 33				17 00	17 11					17 33				18 00
Warblington	d		16 35										17 35				
Emsworth	d		16 38				17 04	17 15					17 38				18 04
Southbourne	d		16 41				17 07						17 41				18 07
Nutbourne	d		16 43										17 43				
Bosham	d		16 47										17 47				
Fishbourne (Sussex)	d		16 50										17 50				
Chichester 4	a		16 53				17 14	17 23					17 53				18 14
	d		16 53				17 14	17 23					17 53				18 14
Bognor Regis 4	d	16 58							17 34			17 58					
Barnham	a	17 04	17 01				17 22	17 31	17 40			18 04	18 01				18 22
	d	17 05	17 08		17 15		17 22	17 38	17 41	17 43		18 05	18 08		18 15		18 22
Bognor Regis	a				17 21					17 49					18 21		
Ford 4	d	17 09	17 12					17 42	17 45			18 09	18 12				
Littlehampton 4	a								17 50								
	d					17 14										18 14	
Angmering 3	d		17 18			17 22		17 48					18 18			18 22	
Goring-by-Sea	d		17 22			17 26		17 52					18 22			18 26	
Durrington-on-Sea	d		17 25			17 29		17 55					18 25			18 29	
West Worthing	d		17 27			17 31		17 57					18 27			18 31	
Worthing 4	a		17 29			17 33	17 37	17 59					18 29			18 33	18 37
	d		17 30				17 41	18 00					18 30				18 41
East Worthing	d		17 32					18 02					18 32				
Lancing	d		17 35					18 05					18 35				
Shoreham-by-Sea	d		17 39				17 47	18 09					18 39				18 47
Southwick	d		17 42					18 12					18 42				
Fishersgate	d		17 44					18 14					18 44				
Portslade	d		17 46					18 16					18 46				
Aldrington	d		17 49	←				18 19					18 49	←			
Hove 2	a		17 51	17 51			17 54	18 21					18 51	18 51			18 54
	d		17 56	17 56			17 54	18 22					18 56	18 56			18 54
Brighton 10	a		→	18 00				18 26					→	19 00			
Preston Park	d																
Burgess Hill	a						18 04										19 04
Haywards Heath 3	a						18 10										19 10
Arundel	d	17 14										18 14					
Amberley	d	17 19										18 19					
Pulborough	d	17 25										18 25					
Billingshurst	d	17 31										18 31					
Christs Hospital	d	17 38										18 38					
Horsham 4	a	17 42										18 42					
	d	17 42									18 03	18 42					
Crawley	d	17 51									18 16	18 51					
Three Bridges 4	a	17 54									18 19	18 54					
Gatwick Airport 10 ✈	a	17 59					18 22				18 24	18 59					19 22
	d	18 00					18 23				18 25	19 00					19 23
Horley	a	18 02									18 28	19 02					
Redhill 5	a	18 09									18 34	19 09					
East Croydon ⇌	a	18 26					18 39				18 56	19 26					19 39
London Bridge 4 ⊖	a										19 12						
Clapham Junction 10	a	18 37					18 54					19 37					19 54
London Victoria 15 ⊖	a	18 46					19 01					19 46					20 01

Table 188

Sundays from 16 September

Southampton, Portsmouth and Sussex Coast - Brighton, Gatwick Airport and London

Network Diagram - see first Page of Table 186

		SN ◇1	SN 1	SN ◇1 ⊼	SN 1	SN ◇1	SN 1	SN 1	SN 1	SN ◇1	SN ◇1	SN ◇1	SN 1
Eastleigh	d												
Southampton Airport Parkway	d												
Southampton Central ⛴	d	17 29										18 29	
Swanwick	d	17 46										18 46	
Fareham	d	17 53										18 53	
Portchester	d												
Cosham	d	18 02										19 02	
Portsmouth Harbour ⛴	d						18 14				18 43		
Portsmouth & Southsea	d						18 18				18 47		
Fratton	d						18 22				18 51		
Hilsea	d												
Bedhampton	d						18 30						
Havant	d	18 11					18 33				19 00	19 11	
Warblington	d						18 35						
Emsworth	d	18 15					18 38				19 04	19 15	
Southbourne	d						18 41				19 07		
Nutbourne	d						18 43						
Bosham	d						18 47						
Fishbourne (Sussex)	d						18 50						
Chichester 4	a	18 23					18 53				19 14	19 23	
	d	18 23					18 53				19 14	19 23	
Bognor Regis 4	d		18 34			18 58							19 34
Barnham	a	18 31	18 40			19 04	19 01				19 22	19 31	19 40
	d	18 38	18 41	18 43		19 05	19 08		19 15		19 22	19 38	19 41
Bognor Regis	a			18 49					19 21				
Ford 4	d	18 42	18 45			19 09	19 12					19 42	19 45
Littlehampton 4	a		18 50										19 50
	d									19 14			
Angmering 3	d	18 48					19 18			19 22		19 48	
Goring-by-Sea	d	18 52					19 22			19 26		19 52	
Durrington-on-Sea	d	18 55					19 25			19 29		19 55	
West Worthing	d	18 57					19 27			19 31		19 57	
Worthing 4	a	18 59					19 29			19 33	19 37	19 59	
	d	19 00					19 30			19 41		20 00	
East Worthing	d	19 02					19 32					20 02	
Lancing	d	19 05					19 35					20 05	
Shoreham-by-Sea	d	19 09					19 39			19 47		20 09	
Southwick	d	19 12					19 42					20 12	
Fishersgate	d	19 14					19 44					20 14	
Portslade	d	19 16					19 46					20 16	
Aldrington	d	19 19					19 49	←				20 19	
Hove 2	a	19 21					19 51	19 51		19 54		20 21	
	d	19 22					19 56	19 56		19 54		20 22	
Brighton 10	a	19 26					→	20 00				20 26	
Preston Park	d												
Burgess Hill	a									20 04			
Haywards Heath 3	a									20 10			
Arundel	d					19 14							
Amberley	d					19 19							
Pulborough	d					19 25							
Billingshurst	d					19 31							
Christs Hospital	d					19 38							
Horsham 4	a					19 42							
	d				19 03	19 42							
Crawley	d				19 16	19 51							
Three Bridges 4	a				19 19	19 54							
Gatwick Airport 10 ✈	a				19 24	19 59				20 22			
	d				19 25	20 00				20 23			
Horley	a				19 28	20 02							
Redhill 5	a				19 34	20 09							
East Croydon	a				19 56	20 26				20 39			
London Bridge 4 ⊖	a				20 12								
Clapham Junction 10	a					20 37				20 54			
London Victoria 15 ⊖	a					20 46				21 01			

Table 188

Sundays from 16 September

Southampton, Portsmouth and Sussex Coast - Brighton, Gatwick Airport and London

Network Diagram - see first Page of Table 186

		SN ◇1 ⊼	SN 1	SN ◇1	SN 1	SN 1	SN 1	SN ◇1	SN ◇1	GW ◇	SN ◇1	SN 1	SN ◇1 ⊼	SN 1
Eastleigh	d										19 46			
Southampton Airport Parkway	d										19n38			
Southampton Central ⛴	d									19 26	19n30			
Swanwick	d													
Fareham	d									19 49	20 03			
Portchester	d													
Cosham	d									19 58	20 12			
Portsmouth Harbour ⛴	d				19 14				19 43					20 14
Portsmouth & Southsea	d				19 18				19 47					20 18
Fratton	d				19 22				19 51					20 22
Hilsea	d													
Bedhampton	d				19 30									20 30
Havant	d				19 33				20 00	20 10	20 18			20 33
Warblington	d				19 35									20 35
Emsworth	d				19 38				20 04		20 22			20 38
Southbourne	d				19 41				20 07					20 41
Nutbourne	d				19 43									20 43
Bosham	d				19 47									20 47
Fishbourne (Sussex)	d				19 50									20 50
Chichester 4	a				19 53				20 14	20 20	20 30			20 53
	d				19 53				20 14	20 21	20 31			20 53
Bognor Regis 4	d			19 58								20 34		
Barnham	a			20 04	20 01				20 22	20 28	20 38	20 41		21 01
	d	19 43		20 05	20 08		20 15		20 22	20 29	20 39	20 42	20 43	21 02
Bognor Regis	a	19 49					20 21						20 49	
Ford 4	d			20 09	20 12						20 43	20 46		21 06
Littlehampton 4	a											20 51		21 11
	d							20 14						21 15
Angmering 3	d				20 18			20 22			20 49			21 23
Goring-by-Sea	d				20 22			20 26			20 53			21 27
Durrington-on-Sea	d				20 25			20 29			20 56			21 30
West Worthing	d				20 27			20 31			20 58			21 32
Worthing 4	a				20 29			20 33	20 37	20 50	21 00			21 34
	d				20 30			20 41		20 50	21 01			21 35
East Worthing	d				20 32						21 03			21 37
Lancing	d				20 35						21 06			21 40
Shoreham-by-Sea	d				20 39			20 47		20 57	21 10			21 44
Southwick	d				20 42						21 13			21 47
Fishersgate	d				20 44						21 15			21 49
Portslade	d				20 46						21 17			21 51
Aldrington	d				20 49	←					21 20			21 54
Hove 2	a				20 51	20 51		20 54		21 03	21 22			21 56
	d				20 56	20 56		20 54		21 04	21 22			21 56
Brighton 10	a				→	21 00				21 09	21 26			22 00
Preston Park	d													
Burgess Hill	a							21 04						
Haywards Heath 3	a							21 10						
Arundel	d			20 14										
Amberley	d			20 19										
Pulborough	d			20 25										
Billingshurst	d			20 31										
Christs Hospital	d			20 38										
Horsham 4	a			20 42										
	d		20 03	20 42										
Crawley	d		20 16	20 51										
Three Bridges 4	a		20 19	20 54										
Gatwick Airport 10 ✈	a		20 24	20 59				21 22						
	d		20 25	21 00				21 23						
Horley	a		20 28	21 02										
Redhill 5	a		20 34	21 09										
East Croydon	a		20 56	21 26				21 39						
London Bridge 4 ⊖	a		21 12											
Clapham Junction 10	a			21 37				21 54						
London Victoria 15 ⊖	a			21 46				22 01						

n Stops at these stations before Eastleigh

Table 188

Sundays from 16 September

Southampton, Portsmouth and Sussex Coast - Brighton, Gatwick Airport and London

Network Diagram - see first Page of Table 186

		SN ■	SN ◇■	SN ■	SN ■	SN ■	SN ◇■	SN ■	SN ■	SN ◇■	SN ◇■	SN ■	SN ■	SN	SN ■	SN ■	SN ◇■	SN ■
Eastleigh	d						20 46											
Southampton Airport Parkway	d						20n38											
Southampton Central	d						20n29										21 30	
Swanwick	d																21 47	
Fareham	d						21 02										21 54	
Portchester	d																	
Cosham	d						21 11										22 03	
Portsmouth Harbour	d					20 43						21 14				21 43		
Portsmouth & Southsea	d					20 47						21 18				21 47		
Fratton	d					20 51						21 22				21 51		
Hilsea	d																	
Bedhampton	d											21 30						
Havant	d					21 00	21 17					21 33				22 00	22 11	
Warblington	d											21 35						
Emsworth	d					21 04	21 21					21 38				22 04	22 15	
Southbourne	d					21 07						21 41				22 07		
Nutbourne	d											21 43						
Bosham	d											21 47						
Fishbourne (Sussex)	d											21 50						
Chichester ■	a					21 14	21 29					21 53				22 14	22 23	
	d					21 14	21 30					21 53				22 14	22 23	
Bognor Regis ■	d		20 58						21 34		21 58			22 12				
Barnham	a		21 04			21 22	21 37		21 40		22 04	22 01		22 18		22 22	22 31	
	d		21 05	21 15		21 22	21 38		21 41	21 43	22 05	22 08	22 15			22 23	22 32	
Bognor Regis	a			21 21						21 49			22 21					
Ford ■	d		21 09			21 27	21 42		21 45		22 09	22 12				22 27	22 36	
Littlehampton ■	a					21 31			21 50							22 32		
	d					21 42										22 42		
Angmering ■	d					21 52	21 48					22 18				22 50	22 42	
Goring-by-Sea	d					21 56	21 52					22 22				22 54	22 46	
Durrington-on-Sea	d					21 59	21 55					22 25				22 57	22 49	
West Worthing	d					22 01	21 57					22 27				22 59	22 51	
Worthing ■	a					22 03	21 59					22 29				23 01	22 53	
	d					22 04	22 00					22 30				23 02	22 54	
East Worthing	d					22 06	22 02					22 32				23 04	22 56	
Lancing	d					22 09	22 05					22 35				23 07	22 59	
Shoreham-by-Sea	d					22 13	22 09					22 39				23 11	23 03	
Southwick	d					22 16	22 12					22 42				23 14	23 06	
Fishersgate	d					22 18	22 14					22 44				23 16	23 08	
Portslade	d					22 20	22 16					22 46				23 18	23 10	
Aldrington	d					22 23	22 19	←				22 49				23 21	23 13	←
Hove ■	a					22 25	22 21	22 25				22 51				23 24	23 15	23 24
	d					22 25	22 21	22 25				22 51				23 26	23 15	23 26
Brighton ■	a					→	22 25	22 29				22 56				→	23 19	23 30
Preston Park	d																	
Burgess Hill	a																	
Haywards Heath ■	a																	
Arundel	d		21 14								22 14							
Amberley	d		21 19								22 19							
Pulborough	d		21 25								22 25							
Billingshurst	d		21 31								22 31							
Christs Hospital	d		21 38								22 38							
Horsham ■	a		21 42								22 42							
	d	21 03	21 42		22 03						22 42				23 03			
Crawley	d	21 16	21 51		22 16						22 51				23 16			
Three Bridges ■	a	21 19	21 54		22 19						22 54				23 19			
Gatwick Airport ■	a	21 24	21 59		22 24						22 59				23 24			
	d	21 25	22 00		22 25						23 00				23 25			
Horley	a	21 28	22 02		22 28						23 02				23 28			
Redhill ■	a	21 34	22 09		22 34						23 09				23 34			
East Croydon	a	21 56	22 26		22 55						23 26				23 55			
London Bridge ■	a	22 12																
Clapham Junction ■	a		22 37		23 07						23 38				00 11			
London Victoria ■	a		22 46		23 14						23 46				00 19			

n Stops at these stations before Eastleigh

Table 188

Sundays from 16 September

Southampton, Portsmouth and Sussex Coast - Brighton, Gatwick Airport and London

Network Diagram - see first Page of Table 186

		SN ◇■	SN	SN ■	SN ■	SN ■	SN ■	SN ◇■	SN ◇■	SN ■
Eastleigh	d									
Southampton Airport Parkway	d									
Southampton Central	d				22 15					22 52
Swanwick	d				22 32					23 11
Fareham	d				22 39					23 17
Portchester	d									
Cosham	d				22 48					23 26
Portsmouth Harbour	d			22 14			22 43			
Portsmouth & Southsea	d			22 18			22 47			
Fratton	d			22 22			22 51			
Hilsea	d									
Bedhampton	d			22 32						
Havant	d			22 35	22 54		23 00			23 32
Warblington	d			22 37						
Emsworth	d			22 40	22 58		23 04			23 36
Southbourne	d			22 43			23 07			
Nutbourne	d			22 46						
Bosham	d			22 49						
Fishbourne (Sussex)	d			22 52						
Chichester ■	a			22 55	23 06		23 14			23 44
	d			22 56	23 07		23 14			23 45
Bognor Regis ■	d									
Barnham	a			23 03	23 14		23 23			23 52
	d	22 43	22 57	23 04	23 15	23 15	23 24	23 37	23 43	23 53
Bognor Regis	a	22 49	23 04			23 21			23 49	
Ford ■	d			23 08	23 20		23 28	23 42		
Littlehampton ■	a			23 13	23 27		23 33	23 46		00 01
	d									
Angmering ■	d									
Goring-by-Sea	d									
Durrington-on-Sea	d									
West Worthing	d									
Worthing ■	a									
	d									
East Worthing	d									
Lancing	d									
Shoreham-by-Sea	d									
Southwick	d									
Fishersgate	d									
Portslade	d									
Aldrington	d									
Hove ■	a									
	d									
Brighton ■	a									
Preston Park	d									
Burgess Hill	a									
Haywards Heath ■	a									
Arundel	d									
Amberley	d									
Pulborough	d									
Billingshurst	d									
Christs Hospital	d									
Horsham ■	a									
	d									
Crawley	d									
Three Bridges ■	a									
Gatwick Airport ■	a									
	d									
Horley	a									
Redhill ■	a									
East Croydon	a									
London Bridge ■	a									
Clapham Junction ■	a									
London Victoria ■	a									

London, Haywards Heath and Brighton - Lewes, Seaford, Eastbourne, Hastings and Ashford

Network Diagram - see first Page of Table 184

Miles	Miles			SN MO ◇■ A	SN MX ◇■	SN MX	SN MO ◇■ A	SN MO ◇■ B	SN MX ◇■	SN ◇■ C	SN	SN ◇■		SN ■	SN	SN ■	SN ■	SN	SN	SN	SN	SN		SN ■	SN ■
—	—	London Victoria ■ ⊖	d	22p47	22p47			22p47	00 05																
—	—	Clapham Junction ■	d	22p53	22p53			22p53	00 11																
—	—	London Bridge ■ ⊖	d																						
—	—	East Croydon	d	23p03	23p03			23p07	00 27																
—	—	Gatwick Airport ■ ✈	d	23p19	23p19			23p29	00 44																
—	0	Haywards Heath ■	d	23p30	23p34			23p41	01 06	01 35												06 07			
—	3	Wivelsfield ■	d	23p34	23p38			23p45														06 11			
—	6¾	Plumpton	d	23p40	23p44			23p51																	
—	9½	Cooksbridge	d																						
0	—	Brighton ■	d			23p34										05 12		05 45			06 00				
0¾	—	London Road (Brighton)	d			23p37												05 48			06 03				
1¾	—	Moulsecoomb	d			23p39												05 50			06 05				
3½	—	Falmer	d			23p43	←											05 54			06 09				
8	12¼	Lewes ■	a	23p48	23p51	23p49	23p48	23p58	01 20	01s49						05 23		06 00			06 15	06 22			
—	—		d	23p59	23p53	23p56	23p59	23p59	01 20							05 23		06 05				06 27			
—	15¾	Southease	d	→																					
—	18½	Newhaven Town ⛴	d			00 04												06 13				06 35			
—	18¾	Newhaven Harbour	d			00 06												06 15				06 37			
—	20¼	Bishopstone	d			00 09												06 18				06 40			
—	21¼	Seaford	a			00 12												06 21				06 43			
11	—	Glynde	d																						
15½	—	Berwick	d		00 02																				
19¾	—	Polegate	d		00 07		00 11	00 11	01s32	02s02						05 35									
21¾	—	Hampden Park ■	d		00 11		00 15	00 15	01s36								05 32								
23¾	—	Eastbourne ■	a		00 16		00 20	00 20	01 41	02 10						05 42	05 37							06 08	
—	—		d		00 22						04 50	05 08		05 15	05 32		05 42			05 53				06 13	
25¾	—	Hampden Park ■	d									05a12			05a36		05a46								06 14
28¾	—	Pevensey & Westham	d		00 29									05 22											06 18
29½	—	Pevensey Bay	d																						06 23
31½	—	Normans Bay	d																						
33¼	—	Cooden Beach	d		00 35																				
34¾	—	Collington	d		00 38																				06 29
35½	—	Bexhill ■	d		00 41						05 05			05 31						06 07					06 32
39¼	—	St Leonards Warrior Sq ■	d		00 47						05 12			05 37						06 14					06 34
40	0	Hastings ■	a		00 50						05 15			05 41						06 18					06 41
—	—		d								05 21								05 47	06 19					06 44
—	1	Ore	d								05 23								05 49						
—	3½	Three Oaks	d																05 55						
—	5	Doleham	d																05 58						
—	9¾	Winchelsea	d																06 04						
—	11¾	Rye	a								05 44								06 08	06 36					
—	—		d								05 44								06 08	06 38					
—	18	Appledore (Kent)	d								05 53								06 17	06 47					
—	21	Ham Street	d								05 58								06 22	06 52					
—	26½	Ashford International	a								06 06								06 30	07 00					

A from 21 May until 10 September
B from 17 September
C from 30 July until 7 September, not from 13 August until 29 August

London, Haywards Heath and Brighton - Lewes, Seaford, Eastbourne, Hastings and Ashford

Network Diagram - see first Page of Table 184

		SN ■	SN	SN ■	SN ■	SN ◇■	SN	SN		SN ■	SN ■	SN ■	SN ◇■	SN	SN	SN	SN	SN ◇■		SN ◇■	SN ◇■	SN ■	SN ■	SN	SN ■
London Victoria ■ ⊖	d												05 32												
Clapham Junction ■	d												05 38												
London Bridge ■ ⊖	d																								
East Croydon	d												05 49												
Gatwick Airport ■ ✈	d												06 20												
Haywards Heath ■	d												06 34									07 10			
Wivelsfield ■	d												06 38									07 14			
Plumpton	d																					07 20			
Cooksbridge	d																					07 24			
Brighton ■	d							06 18			06 26			06 39	06 52	07 00	07 10						07 17	07 25	
London Road (Brighton)	d										06 29			06 42	06 55	07 03	07 13						07 20		
Moulsecoomb	d										06 31			06 44	06 57	07 05	07 15						07 22		
Falmer	d										06 35			06 48	07 01	07 09	07 19						07 26		
Lewes ■	a							06 29			06 41		06 50	06 54	07 08	07 17	07 26					07 29	07 32	07 38	
	d							06 30			06 42		06 51	06 55	07 10							07 31	07 34		
Southease	d																								
Newhaven Town ⛴	d													07 03	07 18								07 42		
Newhaven Harbour	d													07 05	07 23								07 44		
Bishopstone	d													07 08	07 26								07 47		
Seaford	a													07 11	07 29								07 50		
Glynde	d										06 47		06 56									07 36			
Berwick	d										06 53		07 02									07 42			
Polegate	d							06 43			06 58		07 07									07 47			
Hampden Park ■	d		06 24			06 42					07 02		07 11					07 15			07 46	07 51			
Eastbourne ■	a		06 29			06 47		06 50			07 07		07 16					07 20			07 51	07 56			
	d	06 24		06 33	06 47	06 57		06 54		07 02		07 14	07 21							07 38	07 57				08 04
Hampden Park ■	d	06a28			06a51	07a01				07 06		07a18	07 25							07 42	08a01				08a08
Pevensey & Westham	d			06 40						07 11			07 30							07 47					
Pevensey Bay	d																			07 49					
Normans Bay	d			06 45																07 53					
Cooden Beach	d									07 17			07 36							07 56					
Collington	d									07 20			07 39							07 59					
Bexhill ■	d			06 51				07 09		07 22			07 41							08 02					
St Leonards Warrior Sq ■	d			06 57				07 16		07 29			07 48							08 08					
Hastings ■	a			07 00				07 19		07 32			07 51							08 11					
	d							07 20					07 52							08 12					
Ore	d												07a55							08a15					
Three Oaks	d							07 28																	
Doleham	d																								
Winchelsea	d							07 36																	
Rye	a							07 39																	
	d						07 11	07 41																	
Appledore (Kent)	d						07 20	07 50																	
Ham Street	d						07 25	07 55																	
Ashford International	a						07 33	08 03																	

London, Haywards Heath and Brighton - Lewes, Seaford, Eastbourne, Hastings and Ashford

Network Diagram - see first Page of Table 184

		SN	SN	SN ◇1	SN ◇1	SN	SN 1	SN 1	SN	SN	SN ◇1	SN 1	SN	SN ◇1	SN	SN	SN ◇1	SN 1	SN ◇1	SN	SN	SN ◇1
London Victoria	d				06 47									07 47					08 17			
Clapham Junction	d				06 53									07 53					08 23			
London Bridge	d																					
East Croydon	d				07 04									08 03					08 34			
Gatwick Airport	d				07 20									08 20					08 50			
Haywards Heath	d				07 33									08 31					09 10			
Wivelsfield	d				07 37									08 35					09 14			
Plumpton	d				07 43									08 41								
Cooksbridge	d				07 48									08 45								
Brighton	d		07 32			07 40	07 52	08 03	08 10	08 22			08 32		08 38	08 45		08 52		09 10	09 22	
London Road (Brighton)	d					07 43	07 55	08 06	08 13	08 25					08 41	08 48		08 55		09 13	09 25	
Moulsecoomb	d					07 45	07 57	08 08	08 15	08 27					08 43	08 50		08 57		09 15	09 27	
Falmer	d					07 49	08 01	08 12	08 19	08 31					08 47	08 54		09 01		09 19	09 31	
Lewes	a		07 43		07 52	07 56	08 08	08 18	08 26	08 37			08 43	08 50	08 53	09 00		09 07	09 25	09 25	09 37	
	d		07 44		07 53	07 58	08 09	08 19	08 30				08 44	08 51		09 02		09 09	09 25	09 30		
Southease	d																			09 36		
Newhaven Town	d					08 06			08 38							09 10				09 40		
Newhaven Harbour	d					08 08			08 40							09 12				09 42		
Bishopstone	d					08 11			08 43							09 15				09 45		
Seaford	a					08 14			08 46							09 18				09 48		
Glynde	d						08 14	08 24										09 14				
Berwick	d						08 20	08 30										09 20				
Polegate	d		07 57		08 05		08 25	08 35					08 57	09 03				09 25	09 38			
Hampden Park	d			08 06	08 09		08 29	08 39				08 52		09 07			09 17	09 29	09 42			
Eastbourne	a		08 04	08 11	08 14		08 34	08 44				08 57	09 04	09 12			09 22	09 34	09 47			
	d		08 09		08 21		08 40				08 56	09 04	09 09	09 19				09 40				09 55
Hampden Park	d				08 25		08 44				09a00	09a08		09 23				09 44				09a59
Pevensey & Westham	d		08 17		08 30		08 49							09 28				09 49				
Pevensey Bay	d				08 32																	
Normans Bay	d				08 36		08 53											09 53				
Cooden Beach	d				08 39		08 57							09 34				09 57				
Collington	d				08 42		09 00							09 37				10 00				
Bexhill	d		08 25		08 45		09 02						09 24	09 39				10 02				
St Leonards Warrior Sq	d		08 32		08 51		09 09						09 32	09 46				10 09				
Hastings	a		08 35		08 55		09 12						09 35	09 49				10 12				
	d		08 36		08 56		09 13						09 36	09 50				10 13				
Ore	d				08a59		09a16							09a53				10a16				
Three Oaks	d		08 44																			
Doleham	d																					
Winchelsea	d												09 50									
Rye	a		08 54										09 54									
	d	08 13	08 56										09 56									
Appledore (Kent)	d	08 22	09 05										10 05									
Ham Street	d	08 27	09 10										10 10									
Ashford International	a	08 35	09 18										10 18									

London, Haywards Heath and Brighton - Lewes, Seaford, Eastbourne, Hastings and Ashford

Network Diagram - see first Page of Table 184

		SN 1	SN	SN ◇1 A	SN	SN ◇1	SN 1	SN ◇1 A	SN	SN	SN ◇1	SN 1	SN	SN ◇1 A	SN	SN ◇1	SN 1	SN ◇1 A	SN	SN	SN ◇1	SN 1	SN
London Victoria	d			08 47				09 17						09 47				10 17					
Clapham Junction	d			08 53				09 23						09 53				10 23					
London Bridge	d																						
East Croydon	d			09 04				09 33						10 03				10 33					
Gatwick Airport	d			09 20				09 50						10 20				10 50					
Haywards Heath	d			09 35				10 07						10 35				11 07					
Wivelsfield	d							10 11										11 11					
Plumpton	d			09 44										10 44									
Cooksbridge	d			09 49																			
Brighton	d		09 32		09 40		09 52		10 10	10 22			10 32		10 40		10 52		11 10	11 22			11 32
London Road (Brighton)	d				09 43		09 55		10 13	10 25					10 43		10 55		11 13	11 25			
Moulsecoomb	d				09 45		09 57		10 15	10 27					10 45		10 57		11 15	11 27			
Falmer	d				09 49		10 01		10 19	10 31					10 49		11 01		11 19	11 31			
Lewes	a		09 43	09 53	09 55		10 07	10 22	10 25	10 37			10 43	10 52	10 55		11 07	11 22	11 25	11 37			11 43
	d		09 44	09 54	09 58		10 09	10 23	10 28				10 44	10 53	10 58		11 09	11 23	11 28				11 44
Southease	d								10 34										11 34				
Newhaven Town	d				10 06				10 38						11 06				11 38				
Newhaven Harbour	d				10 08				10 40						11 08				11 40				
Bishopstone	d				10 11				10 43						11 11				11 43				
Seaford	a				10 14				10 46						11 14				11 46				
Glynde	d						10 14										11 14						
Berwick	d						10 20										11 20						
Polegate	d		09 57	10 06			10 25	10 35					10 57	11 05			11 25	11 35					11 57
Hampden Park	d	09 52				10 20	10 29	10 39				10 52				11 20	11 29	11 39				11 52	
Eastbourne	a	09 58	10 04	10 14		10 25	10 34	10 44				10 57	11 04	11 13		11 25	11 34	11 44				11 57	12 04
	d	10 04	10 09	10 20			10 40				10 58	11 04	11 09	11 19			11 40				11 58	12 04	12 09
Hampden Park	d	10a08		10 24			10 44				11a02	11a08		11 23			11 44				12a02	12a08	
Pevensey & Westham	d			10 29			10 49							11 28			11 49						
Pevensey Bay	d																						
Normans Bay	d						10 53										11 53						
Cooden Beach	d			10 35			10 57							11 34			11 57						
Collington	d			10 38			11 00							11 37			12 00						
Bexhill	d		10 24	10 40			11 02						11 24	11 39			12 02						12 24
St Leonards Warrior Sq	d		10 31	10 47			11 09						11 31	11 46			12 09						12 31
Hastings	a		10 35	10 50			11 12						11 35	11 49			12 12						12 35
	d		10 36	10 51			11 13						11 36	11 50			12 13						12 36
Ore	d			10a54			11a16							11a53			12a16						
Three Oaks	d		10 44																				12 44
Doleham	d																						
Winchelsea	d												11 50										
Rye	a		10 54										11 54										12 54
	d		10 56										11 56										12 56
Appledore (Kent)	d		11 05										12 05										13 05
Ham Street	d		11 10										12 10										13 10
Ashford International	a		11 18										12 18										13 18

A ⌶ to Lewes

London, Haywards Heath and Brighton - Lewes, Seaford, Eastbourne, Hastings and Ashford

Network Diagram - see first Page of Table 184

		SN	SN	SN	SN	SN	SN	SN	SN	SN	SN	SN	SN	SN	SN	SN	SN	SN	SN	SN	SN	SN	SN
		◇1 A ⊼		◇1	1	◇1			◇1	1		◇1		◇1	1	◇1			◇1	1		◇1	
London Victoria 15 ⊖	d	10 47				11 17						11 47				12 17						12 47	
Clapham Junction 10	d	10 53				11 23						11 53				12 23						12 53	
London Bridge 4 ⊖	d																						
East Croydon	d	11 03				11 33						12 03				12 33						13 03	
Gatwick Airport 10 ✈	d	11 20				11 50						12 20				12 50						13 20	
Haywards Heath 3	d	11 35				12 07						12 35				13 07						13 35	
Wivelsfield 4	d					12 11										13 11							
Plumpton	d	11 44										12 44										13 44	
Cooksbridge	d																						
Brighton 10	d		11 40		11 52		12 10	12 22			12 32		12 40		12 52		13 10	13 22			13 32		13 40
London Road (Brighton)	d		11 43		11 55		12 13	12 25					12 43		12 55		13 13	13 25					13 43
Moulsecoomb	d		11 45		11 57		12 15	12 27					12 45		12 57		13 15	13 27					13 45
Falmer	d		11 49		12 01		12 19	12 31					12 49		13 01		13 19	13 31					13 49
Lewes 4	a	11 52	11 55		12 07	12 22	12 25	12 37			12 43	12 52	12 55		13 07	13 22	13 25	13 37			13 43	13 52	13 55
	d	11 53	11 58		12 09	12 23	12 28				12 44	12 53	12 58		13 09	13 23	13 28				13 44	13 53	13 58
Southease	d						12 34										13 34						
Newhaven Town ⛴	d		12 06				12 38						13 06				13 38						14 06
Newhaven Harbour	d		12 08				12 40						13 08				13 40						14 08
Bishopstone	d		12 11				12 43						13 11				13 43						14 11
Seaford	a		12 14				12 46						13 14				13 46						14 14
Glynde	d				12 14										13 14								
Berwick	d				12 20										13 20								
Polegate	d	12 05			12 25	12 35					12 57	13 05			13 25	13 35					13 57	14 05	
Hampden Park 4	d			12 20	12 29	12 39				12 52				13 20	13 29	13 39				13 52			
Eastbourne 4	a	12 13		12 25	12 34	12 44				12 57	13 04	13 13		13 25	13 34	13 44				13 57	14 04	14 13	
	d	12 19			12 40				12 58	13 04	13 09	13 19			13 40				13 58	14 04	14 09	14 19	
Hampden Park 4	d	12 23			12 44				13a02	13a08		13 23			13 44				14a02	14a08		14 23	
Pevensey & Westham	d	12 28			12 49							13 28			13 49							14 28	
Pevensey Bay	d																						
Normans Bay	d				12 53										13 53								
Cooden Beach	d	12 34			12 57							13 34			13 57							14 34	
Collington	d	12 37			13 00							13 37			14 00							14 37	
Bexhill 4	d	12 39			13 02						13 24	13 39			14 02						14 24	14 39	
St Leonards Warrior Sq 4	d	12 46			13 09						13 31	13 46			14 09						14 31	14 46	
Hastings 4	a	12 49			13 12						13 35	13 49			14 12						14 35	14 49	
	d	12 50			13 13						13 36	13 50			14 13						14 36	14 50	
Ore	d	12a53			13a16							13a53			14a16							14a53	
Three Oaks	d																				14 44		
Doleham	d																						
Winchelsea	d										13 50												
Rye	a										13 54										14 54		
	d										13 56										14 56		
Appledore (Kent)	d										14 05										15 05		
Ham Street	d										14 10										15 10		
Ashford International	a										14 18										15 18		

A ⊼ to Lewes

London, Haywards Heath and Brighton - Lewes, Seaford, Eastbourne, Hastings and Ashford

Network Diagram - see first Page of Table 184

		SN	SN	SN	SN	SN	SN	SN	SN	SN	SN	SN	SN	SN	SN	SN	SN	SN	SN	SN	SN	SN
		◇1	1	◇1			◇1	1		◇1		◇1	1	◇1			◇1	1		◇1		◇1
London Victoria 15 ⊖	d			13 17						13 47				14 17						14 47		
Clapham Junction 10	d			13 23						13 53				14 23						14 53		
London Bridge 4 ⊖	d																					
East Croydon	d			13 33						14 03				14 33						15 03		
Gatwick Airport 10 ✈	d			13 50						14 20				14 50						15 20		
Haywards Heath 3	d			14 07						14 35				15 07						15 35		
Wivelsfield 4	d			14 11										15 11						15 39		
Plumpton	d									14 44										15 45		
Cooksbridge	d																					
Brighton 10	d		13 52		14 10	14 22			14 32		14 40		14 52		15 10	15 22			15 32		15 40	
London Road (Brighton)	d		13 55		14 13	14 25					14 43		14 55		15 13	15 25					15 43	
Moulsecoomb	d		13 57		14 15	14 27					14 45		14 57		15 15	15 27					15 45	
Falmer	d		14 01		14 19	14 31					14 49		15 01		15 19	15 31					15 49	
Lewes 4	a		14 07	14 22	14 25	14 37			14 43	14 52	14 55		15 07	15 22	15 25	15 37			15 43	15 52	15 55	
	d		14 09	14 23	14 28				14 44	14 53	14 58		15 09	15 23	15 28				15 44	15 53	15 58	
Southease	d				14 34										15 34						16 04	
Newhaven Town ⛴	d				14 38						15 06				15 38						16 08	
Newhaven Harbour	d				14 40						15 08				15 40						16 10	
Bishopstone	d				14 43						15 11				15 43						16 13	
Seaford	a				14 46						15 14				15 46						16 16	
Glynde	d		14 14										15 14									
Berwick	d		14 20										15 20									
Polegate	d		14 25	14 35					14 57	15 05			15 25	15 35					15 57	16 05		
Hampden Park 4	d	14 20	14 29	14 39				14 52				15 20	15 29	15 39				15 52				16 20
Eastbourne 4	a	14 25	14 34	14 44				14 57	15 04	15 13		15 25	15 34	15 44				15 57	16 04	16 13		16 25
	d		14 40				14 58	15 04	15 09	15 19			15 40				15 58	16 04	16 09	16 19		
Hampden Park 4	d		14 44				15a02	15a08		15 23			15 44				16a02	16a08		16 23		
Pevensey & Westham	d		14 49							15 28			15 49							16 28		
Pevensey Bay	d									15 30												
Normans Bay	d		14 53							15 34			15 53									
Cooden Beach	d		14 57							15 37			15 57							16 34		
Collington	d		15 00							15 40			16 00							16 37		
Bexhill 4	d		15 02						15 24	15 43			16 02						16 24	16 39		
St Leonards Warrior Sq 4	d		15 09						15 31	15 49			16 09						16 31	16 46		
Hastings 4	a		15 12						15 35	15 52			16 12						16 35	16 49		
	d		15 13						15 36	15 54			16 13						16 36	16 50		
Ore	d		15a16							15a57			16a16							16a53		
Three Oaks	d																		16 44			
Doleham	d																					
Winchelsea	d								15 50													
Rye	a								15 54										16 54			
	d								15 56										16 56			
Appledore (Kent)	d								16 05										17 05			
Ham Street	d								16 10										17 10			
Ashford International	a								16 18										17 18			

London, Haywards Heath and Brighton - Lewes, Seaford, Eastbourne, Hastings and Ashford

Network Diagram - see first Page of Table 184

Station		SN	SN 1	SN ◇1	SN	SN	SN	SN ◇1	SN 1	SN	SN ◇1	SN	SN ◇1	SN 1	SN	SN ◇1 A	SN	SN ◇1	SN 1	SN	SN	SN	SN ◇1 A
London Victoria ⊖	d			15 17							15 47					16 17							16 47
Clapham Junction	d			15 23							15 53					16 23							16 53
London Bridge ⊖	d																						
East Croydon	d			15 33							16 03					16 33							17 03
Gatwick Airport ✈	d			15 50							16 20					16 49							17 20
Haywards Heath	d			16 07							16 35					17 06							17 36
Wivelsfield	d			16 11							16 39					17 10							17 41
Plumpton	d										16 45												17 47
Cooksbridge	d										16 49												17 52
Brighton	d		15 52		16 10	16 22				16 32		16 40		16 52	17 02		17 10			17 20		17 32	
London Road (Brighton)	d		15 55		16 13	16 25						16 43		16 55	17 05		17 13			17 23			
Moulsecoomb	d		15 57		16 15	16 27						16 45		16 57	17 07		17 15			17 25			
Falmer	d		16 01		16 19	16 31						16 49		17 01	17 11		17 19			17 29			
Lewes	a		16 07	16 22	16 25	16 37				16 43	16 54	16 55		17 07	17 17	17 21	17 25			17 35		17 43	17 56
	d		16 09	16 23	16 28					16 44	16 54	16 58		17 09		17 22	17 28			17 36		17 44	17 57
Southease	d				16 34												17 34						
Newhaven Town ⛴	d				16 38							17 06					17 38						
Newhaven Harbour	d				16 40							17 08					17 40						
Bishopstone	d				16 43							17 11					17 43						
Seaford	a				16 46							17 14					17 46						
Glynde	d		16 14											17 14									
Berwick	d		16 20								17 03			17 20		17 31				17 45			
Polegate	d		16 25	16 35						16 57	17 08			17 25		17 36				17 50		17 57	18 09
Hampden Park	d		16 29	16 39					16 52				17 20	17 29		17 40			17 52	17 55			18 13
Eastbourne	a		16 34	16 44					16 57	17 04	17 16		17 25	17 34		17 48			17 57	18 00		18 04	18 18
	d		16 40				16 45	16 58	17 04	17 09	17 21			17 40				17 57	18 01			18 09	18 25
Hampden Park	d		16 44				16a49	17a02	17a08		17 25			17 44				18a01	18a05				18 29
Pevensey & Westham	d		16 49								17 30			17 49									18 34
Pevensey Bay	d										17 32			17 51									
Normans Bay	d		16 53								17 36			17 55									
Cooden Beach	d		16 57								17 39			17 58									18 40
Collington	d		17 00								17 42			18 01									18 43
Bexhill	d		17 02							17 25	17 45			18 04								18 24	18 45
St Leonards Warrior Sq	d		17 09							17 31	17 53			18 10								18 31	18 56
Hastings	a		17 12							17 35	17 57			18 13								18 34	19 00
	d	17 09	17 13							17 36	17 58			18 14								18 36	
Ore	d	17 12	17a16								18a01			18a17									
Three Oaks	d	17 18																				18 44	
Doleham	d	17 21																					
Winchelsea	d	17 27								17 50													
Rye	a	17 30								17 54												18 54	
	d	17 31								17 56											18 31	18 56	
Appledore (Kent)	d	17 40								18 05											18 40	19 05	
Ham Street	d	17 45								18 10											18 45	19 10	
Ashford International	a	17 53								18 18											18 53	19 18	

A [trolley symbol] to Lewes

London, Haywards Heath and Brighton - Lewes, Seaford, Eastbourne, Hastings and Ashford

Network Diagram - see first Page of Table 184

Station		SN	SN ◇1	SN 1	SN 1	SN	SN ◇1	SN 1	SN ◇1 A	SN	SN	SN	SN	SN ◇1	SN 1	SN ◇1 A		SN 1	SN	SN	SN 1	SN
London Victoria ⊖	d								17 35							18 06						
Clapham Junction	d								17 42							18 12						
London Bridge ⊖	d				17 23													18 23				
East Croydon	d				17 36				17 52							18 22		18 37				
Gatwick Airport ✈	d								18 07							18 38						
Haywards Heath	d				18 05				18 18							18 50		19 06				
Wivelsfield	d				18 10				18 23							18 54		19 11				
Plumpton	d								18 29							19 00		19 17				
Cooksbridge	d								18 33							19 05		19 22				
Brighton	d	17 40		17 52		18 08				18 17		18 32	18 38		18 51				19 08	19 22		19 32
London Road (Brighton)	d	17 43		17 55		18 11				18 20			18 41		18 54				19 11	19 25		
Moulsecoomb	d	17 45		17 57		18 13				18 22			18 43		18 56				19 13	19 27		
Falmer	d	17 49		18 01		18 17				18 26			18 47		19 00				19 17	19 31		
Lewes	a	17 55		18 07	18 21	18 23			18 38	18 32		18 44	18 53		19 06	19 09		19 27	19 23	19 37		19 43
	d	18 01		18 08	18 21	18 24			18 38	18 42		18 45	18 54		19 07	19 13	19 16	19 27	19 31	19 40		19 44
Southease	d	18 07											19 00						19 37			
Newhaven Town ⛴	d	18 11				18 33				18 50			19 04			19 21			19 41	19 49		
Newhaven Harbour	d	18 13											19 09						19 44	19a52		
Bishopstone	d	18 16				18 37				18 54			19 12			19 29			19 47			
Seaford	a	18 19				18 40				18 58			19 15			19 34			19 50			
Glynde	d			18 13	18 27												19 21	19 33				
Berwick	d			18 19	18 32												19 27	19 39				
Polegate	d			18 24	18 38				18 51			18 58			19 19		19 32	19 45				19 57
Hampden Park	d		18 20	18 28	18 42			18 52	18 55					19 20			19 36	19 50			19 52	
Eastbourne	a		18 25	18 34	18 49			18 57	19 01			19 05		19 25	19 28		19 41	19 56			19 57	20 04
	d			18 43			18 58	19 04	19 19			19 09					19 51				20 03	20 09
Hampden Park	d			18 47			19a02	19a08	19 23								19 55				20a07	
Pevensey & Westham	d			18 52					19 28			19 17					20 00					
Pevensey Bay	d																					
Normans Bay	d			18 56																		
Cooden Beach	d			19 00					19 34								20 06					
Collington	d			19 03					19 37								20 09					
Bexhill	d			19 05					19 39			19 25					20 11					20 24
St Leonards Warrior Sq	d			19 11					19 45			19 32					20 18					20 31
Hastings	a			19 14					19 48			19 35					20 21					20 34
	d			19 15					19 49			19 36					20 22					20 36
Ore	d			19a18					19a55								20a27					
Three Oaks	d																					20 44
Doleham	d																					
Winchelsea	d											19 50										
Rye	a											19 54										20 54
	d										19 31	19 56										20 56
Appledore (Kent)	d										19 40	20 05										21 05
Ham Street	d										19 45	20 10										21 10
Ashford International	a										19 53	20 18										21 18

A [trolley symbol] to Lewes

Table 189

Mondays to Fridays

London, Haywards Heath and Brighton - Lewes, Seaford, Eastbourne, Hastings and Ashford

Network Diagram - see first Page of Table 184

		SN ◇■ A ✠	SN	SN ◇■	SN ■	SN ◇■ A ✠	SN	SN ■	SN	SN ◇■ A ✠	SN	SN ◇■	SN ◇■	SN	SN	SN ■	SN ◇■	SN ◇■	SN	SN ◇■	SN	SN	SN ■
London Victoria ⊖	d	18 47				19 17				19 47			20 17					20 47		21 17			
Clapham Junction	d	18 53				19 23				19 53			20 23					20 53		21 23			
London Bridge ⊖	d																						
East Croydon	d	19 04				19 33				20 03			20 33					21 04		21 33			
Gatwick Airport ✈	d	19 21				19 49				20 19			20 49					21 19		21 49			
Haywards Heath	d	19 35				20 07				20 36			21 07					21 37		22 08			
Wivelsfield	d	19 39				20 11				20 40			21 11					21 41		22 12			
Plumpton	d	19 45								20 46								21 47					
Cooksbridge	d	19 50								20 50													
Brighton	d		19 40		19 52		20 10		20 30		20 40			21 04	21 30				21 40		22 04	22 28	
London Road (Brighton)	d		19 43		19 55		20 13				20 43			21 07					21 43		22 07		
Moulsecoomb	d		19 45		19 57		20 15				20 45			21 09					21 45		22 09		
Falmer	d		19 49		20 01		20 19				20 49			21 13					21 49		22 13		
Lewes	a	19 54	19 55		20 07	20 22	20 25		20 43	20 55	20 55		21 22	21 19	21 43			21 54	21 55	22 23	22 19	22 39	
	d	19 55	19 58		20 09	20 23	20 28		20 44	20 55	21 00		21 23	21 28	21 44			21 55	21 58	22 23	22 28	22 39	
Southease	d		20 04																22 04				
Newhaven Town ⛴	d		20 08				20 36				21 08			21 36					22 08		22 36		
Newhaven Harbour	d		20 10				20 38				21 10			21 38					22 10		22 38		
Bishopstone	d		20 13				20 41				21 13			21 41					22 13		22 41		
Seaford	a		20 16				20 44				21 16			21 44					22 16		22 44		
Glynde	d				20 14	20 28							21 28							22 29			
Berwick	d				20 20	20 34							21 34							22 34			
Polegate	d	20 07			20 25	20 39			20 57	21 08			21 39		21 57			22 07		22 39		22 52	
Hampden Park	d			20 20	20 29	20 43		20 51				21 20	21 43				21 55			22 43			22 55
Eastbourne	a	20 15		20 25	20 34	20 48		20 56	21 04	21 15		21 25	21 48		22 04		22 00	22 15		22 48		23 03	23 00
	d	20 19						21 04	21 09	21 21					22 09	22 04	22 15	22 21					23 05
Hampden Park	d	20 23						21a08		21 25						22a08	22a19	22 25					23a09
Pevensey & Westham	d	20 28								21 30								22 30					
Pevensey Bay	d																						
Normans Bay	d																						
Cooden Beach	d	20 34								21 36								22 36					
Collington	d	20 37								21 39								22 39					
Bexhill	d	20 40							21 24	21 41					22 23			22 41					
St Leonards Warrior Sq	d	20 46							21 31	21 48					22 31			22 48					
Hastings	a	20 49							21 34	21 53					22 34			22 51					
	d	20 50							21 35	21 54													
Ore	d	20a55							21 37	21a57													
Three Oaks	d								21 43														
Doleham	d								21 46														
Winchelsea	d								21 52														
Rye	a								21 56														
	d								21 56														
Appledore (Kent)	d								22 05														
Ham Street	d								22 10														
Ashford International	a								22 18														

A ✠ to Lewes

Table 189

Mondays to Fridays

London, Haywards Heath and Brighton - Lewes, Seaford, Eastbourne, Hastings and Ashford

Network Diagram - see first Page of Table 184

		SN ◇■	SN	SN ■	SN ■	SN	SN ◇■	SN
London Victoria ⊖	d	21 47					22 47	
Clapham Junction	d	21 53					22 53	
London Bridge ⊖	d							
East Croydon	d	22 03					23 03	
Gatwick Airport ✈	d	22 19					23 19	
Haywards Heath	d	22 34					23 34	
Wivelsfield	d	22 38					23 38	
Plumpton	d	22 44					23 44	
Cooksbridge	d	22 48						
Brighton	d		22 34	23 06		23 28		23 34
London Road (Brighton)	d		22 37	23 09				23 37
Moulsecoomb	d		22 39	23 11				23 39
Falmer	d		22 43	23 15				23 43
Lewes	a	22 53	22 49	23 21		23 39	23 51	23 49
	d	22 53	22 57	23 22		23 39	23 53	23 56
Southease	d		23 03					
Newhaven Town ⛴	d		23 07					00 04
Newhaven Harbour	d		23 09					00 06
Bishopstone	d		23 12					00 09
Seaford	a		23 15					00 12
Glynde	d			23 27				
Berwick	d			23 33			00 02	
Polegate	d	23 06		23 38		23 52	00 07	
Hampden Park	d	23 10		23 42	23 47		00 11	
Eastbourne	a	23 15		23 47	23 52	23 59	00 16	
	d	23 20			23 56		00 22	
Hampden Park	d	23 24			00a01			
Pevensey & Westham	d	23 29					00 29	
Pevensey Bay	d							
Normans Bay	d							
Cooden Beach	d	23 35					00 35	
Collington	d	23 38					00 38	
Bexhill	d	23 40					00 41	
St Leonards Warrior Sq	d	23 47					00 47	
Hastings	a	23 50					00 50	
	d							
Ore	d							
Three Oaks	d							
Doleham	d							
Winchelsea	d							
Rye	a							
	d							
Appledore (Kent)	d							
Ham Street	d							
Ashford International	a							

Table 189

Saturdays

London, Haywards Heath and Brighton - Lewes, Seaford, Eastbourne, Hastings and Ashford

Network Diagram - see first Page of Table 184

		SN ◇1	SN	SN ◇1	SN ◇1 A	SN 1	SN	SN ◇1	SN 1	SN	SN	SN	SN ◇1	SN	SN ◇1	SN ◇1	SN ◇1	SN ◇1	SN 1	SN	SN 1	SN	SN ◇1
London Victoria 15 ⊖	d	22p47		00 05																			
Clapham Junction 10	d	22p53		00 11																			
London Bridge 4 ⊖	d																						
East Croydon	d	23p03		00 24																			
Gatwick Airport 10 ✈	d	23p19		00 42																	06 11		
Haywards Heath 3	d	23p34		01 06	01 35																06 26		
Wivelsfield 4	d	23p38																			06 30		
Plumpton	d	23p44																					
Cooksbridge	d																						
Brighton 10	d		23p34						05 10		05 52			06 10						06 32		06 40	
London Road (Brighton)	d		23p37								05 55			06 13								06 43	
Moulsecoomb	d		23p39								05 57			06 15								06 45	
Falmer	d		23p43								06 01			06 19								06 49	
Lewes 4	a	23p51	23p49	01 20	01s49				05 21		06 07			06 25						06 43	06 41	06 55	
	d	23p53	23p56	01 20					05 21		06 08			06 28						06 45	06 53	06 58	
Southease	d																						
Newhaven Town ⛴	d		00 04								06 16			06 36								07 06	
Newhaven Harbour	d		00 06								06 18			06 38								07 08	
Bishopstone	d		00 09											06 41								07 11	
Seaford	a		00 12								06 23			06 44								07 14	
Glynde	d																						
Berwick	d	00 02																			07 02		
Polegate	d	00 07		01s32	02s02				05 33											06 58	07 07		
Hampden Park 4	d	00 11		01s36															06 52		07 11		07 20
Eastbourne 4	a	00 16		01 41	02 10				05 41										06 57	07 05	07 17		07 25
	d	00 22				05 03		05 38		05 48		05 53	06 04		06 18	06 24	06 45	06 58	07 04	07 09	07 21		
Hampden Park 4	d					05a07				05a52					06 22	06a28		07a02	07a08		07 25		
Pevensey & Westham	d	00 29													06 27						07 30		
Pevensey Bay	d																						
Normans Bay	d														06 31								
Cooden Beach	d	00 35													06 35						07 36		
Collington	d	00 38													06 38						07 39		
Bexhill 4	d	00 41						05 52				06 07	06 18		06 40		07 00			07 24	07 42		
St Leonards Warrior Sq 4	d	00 47						06 00				06 14	06 24		06 49		07 06			07 31	07 48		
Hastings 4	a	00 50						06 04				06 17	06 28		06 53		07 10			07 35	07 51		
	d						05 20	06 05				06 18	06 28		06 54		07 11			07 36	07 52		
Ore	d						05 23	06a08					06a32		06a57		07a14				07a55		
Three Oaks	d						05 29					06 26											
Doleham	d						05 32																
Winchelsea	d						05 38													07 50			
Rye	a						05 41					06 36								07 54			
	d						05 42					06 38								07 56			
Appledore (Kent)	d						05 51					06 47								08 05			
Ham Street	d						05 56					06 52								08 10			
Ashford International	a						06 04					07 00								08 18			

A 28 July, 4 August, 11 August, 1 September, 8 September

Table 189

Saturdays

London, Haywards Heath and Brighton - Lewes, Seaford, Eastbourne, Hastings and Ashford

Network Diagram - see first Page of Table 184

		SN 1	SN	SN	SN ◇1	SN 1	SN	SN 1	SN	SN ◇1	SN 1	SN	SN	SN ◇1	SN 1	SN	SN ◇1	SN	SN ◇1	SN 1	SN ◇1	SN	SN
London Victoria 15 ⊖	d																07 47				08 17		
Clapham Junction 10	d																07 53				08 23		
London Bridge 4 ⊖	d																						
East Croydon	d																08 03				08 33		
Gatwick Airport 10 ✈	d																08 20				08 50		
Haywards Heath 3	d							07 33									08 35				09 07		
Wivelsfield 4	d							07 37													09 11		
Plumpton	d																						
Cooksbridge	d																						
Brighton 10	d	06 52	07 10	07 22			07 32		07 40		07 52	08 10	08 22			08 32		08 40		08 52		09 10	09 22
London Road (Brighton)	d	06 55	07 13	07 25					07 43		07 55	08 13	08 25					08 43		08 55		09 13	09 25
Moulsecoomb	d	06 57	07 15	07 27					07 45		07 57	08 15	08 27					08 45		08 57		09 15	09 27
Falmer	d	07 01	07 19	07 31					07 49		08 01	08 19	08 31					08 49		09 01		09 19	09 31
Lewes 4	a	07 07	07 25	07 37			07 43	07 48	07 55		08 07	08 25	08 37			08 43	08 49	08 55		09 07	09 22	09 25	09 37
	d	07 09	07 28				07 44	07 53	07 58		08 09	08 28				08 44	08 53	08 58		09 09	09 23	09 28	
Southease	d																					09 34	
Newhaven Town ⛴	d		07 36						08 06			08 36						09 06				09 38	
Newhaven Harbour	d		07 38						08 08			08 38						09 08				09 40	
Bishopstone	d		07 41						08 11			08 41						09 11				09 43	
Seaford	a		07 44						08 14			08 44						09 14				09 46	
Glynde	d	07 14									08 14									09 14			
Berwick	d	07 20									08 20									09 20			
Polegate	d	07 25					07 57	08 05			08 25					08 57	09 05			09 25	09 35		
Hampden Park 4	d	07 29				07 52				08 20	08 29				08 52				09 20	09 29	09 39		
Eastbourne 4	a	07 34				07 57	08 05	08 13		08 25	08 34				08 57	09 04	09 13		09 25	09 34	09 44		
	d	07 40			07 58	08 04	08 09	08 18			08 40			08 58	09 04	09 09	09 19			09 40			
Hampden Park 4	d	07 44			08a02	08a08		08 22			08 44			09a02	09a08		09 23			09 44			
Pevensey & Westham	d	07 49						08 28			08 49						09 28			09 49			
Pevensey Bay	d																						
Normans Bay	d	07 53									08 53									09 53			
Cooden Beach	d	07 57						08 34			08 57						09 34			09 57			
Collington	d	08 00						08 37			09 00						09 37			10 00			
Bexhill 4	d	08 02					08 24	08 39			09 02					09 24	09 39			10 02			
St Leonards Warrior Sq 4	d	08 09					08 31	08 46			09 09					09 31	09 46			10 09			
Hastings 4	a	08 12					08 35	08 50			09 12					09 35	09 49			10 12			
	d	08 13					08 36	08 51			09 13					09 36	09 50			10 13			
Ore	d	08a16						08a54			09a16						09a53			10a16			
Three Oaks	d						08 44																
Doleham	d																						
Winchelsea	d															09 50							
Rye	a						08 54									09 54							
	d						08 56									09 56							
Appledore (Kent)	d						09 05									10 05							
Ham Street	d						09 10									10 10							
Ashford International	a						09 18									10 18							

Table 189

London, Haywards Heath and Brighton - Lewes, Seaford, Eastbourne, Hastings and Ashford

Network Diagram - see first Page of Table 184

		SN ◇1		SN 1	SN	SN ◇1	SN	SN ◇1	SN 1	SN ◇1	SN	SN		SN ◇1	SN 1	SN	SN ◇1	SN	SN ◇1	SN 1	SN ◇1	SN		SN	SN ◇1
London Victoria 15 ⊖	d					08 47				09 17							09 47				10 17				
Clapham Junction 10	d					08 53				09 23							09 53				10 23				
London Bridge 4 ⊖	d																								
East Croydon	d					09 03				09 33							10 03				10 33				
Gatwick Airport 10 ✈	d					09 20				09 50							10 20				10 50				
Haywards Heath 3	d					09 35				10 07							10 35				11 07				
Wivelsfield 4	d									10 11											11 11				
Plumpton	d					09 44											10 44								
Cooksbridge	d																								
Brighton 10	d				09 32		09 40		09 52		10 10	10 22				10 32		10 40		10 52		11 10		11 22	
London Road (Brighton)	d						09 43		09 55		10 13	10 25						10 43		10 55		11 13		11 25	
Moulsecoomb	d						09 45		09 57		10 15	10 27						10 45		10 57		11 15		11 27	
Falmer	d						09 49		10 01		10 19	10 31						10 49		11 01		11 19		11 31	
Lewes 4	a				09 43	09 52	09 55		10 07	10 22	10 25	10 37				10 43	10 52	10 55		11 07	11 22	11 25		11 37	
	d				09 44	09 53	09 58		10 09	10 23	10 28					10 44	10 53	10 58		11 09	11 23	11 28			
Southease	d										10 34											11 34			
Newhaven Town	d						10 06				10 38							11 06				11 38			
Newhaven Harbour	d						10 08				10 40							11 08				11 40			
Bishopstone	d						10 11				10 43							11 11				11 43			
Seaford	a						10 14				10 46							11 14				11 46			
Glynde	d								10 14											11 14					
Berwick	d								10 20											11 20					
Polegate	d				09 57	10 05			10 25	10 35						10 57	11 05			11 25	11 35				
Hampden Park 4	d			09 52				10 20	10 29	10 39					10 52				11 20	11 29	11 39				
Eastbourne 4	a			09 57	10 04	10 13		10 25	10 34	10 44					10 57	11 04	11 13		11 25	11 34	11 44				
	d	09 58		10 04	10 09	10 19			10 40					10 58	11 04	11 09	11 19			11 40					11 58
Hampden Park 4	d	10a02		10a08		10 23			10 44					11a02	11a08		11 23			11 44					12a02
Pevensey & Westham	d					10 28			10 49								11 28			11 49					
Pevensey Bay	d																								
Normans Bay	d								10 53											11 53					
Cooden Beach	d					10 34			10 57								11 34			11 57					
Collington	d					10 37			11 00								11 37			12 00					
Bexhill 4	d				10 24	10 39			11 02							11 24	11 39			12 02					
St Leonards Warrior Sq 4	d				10 31	10 46			11 09							11 31	11 46			12 09					
Hastings 4	a				10 35	10 49			11 12							11 35	11 49			12 12					
	d				10 36	10 50			11 13							11 36	11 50			12 13					
Ore	d					10a53			11a16								11a53			12a16					
Three Oaks	d				10 44																				
Doleham	d																								
Winchelsea	d															11 50									
Rye	a				10 54											11 54									
	d				10 56											11 56									
Appledore (Kent)	d				11 05											12 05									
Ham Street	d				11 10											12 10									
Ashford International	a				11 18											12 18									

Table 189

London, Haywards Heath and Brighton - Lewes, Seaford, Eastbourne, Hastings and Ashford

Network Diagram - see first Page of Table 184

		SN 1	SN	SN ◇1	SN	SN ◇1	SN 1	SN ◇1		SN	SN	SN ◇1	SN 1	SN	SN ◇1	SN	SN ◇1	SN 1		SN ◇1	SN	SN	SN ◇1	SN 1	SN
London Victoria 15 ⊖	d			10 47				11 17							11 47					12 17					
Clapham Junction 10	d			10 53				11 23							11 53					12 23					
London Bridge 4 ⊖	d																								
East Croydon	d			11 03				11 33							12 03					12 33					
Gatwick Airport 10 ✈	d			11 20				11 50							12 20					12 50					
Haywards Heath 3	d			11 35				12 07							12 35					13 07					
Wivelsfield 4	d							12 11												13 11					
Plumpton	d			11 44											12 44										
Cooksbridge	d																								
Brighton 10	d		11 32		11 40		11 52			12 10	12 22			12 32		12 40		12 52			13 10	13 22			13 32
London Road (Brighton)	d				11 43		11 55			12 13	12 25					12 43		12 55			13 13	13 25			
Moulsecoomb	d				11 45		11 57			12 15	12 27					12 45		12 57			13 15	13 27			
Falmer	d				11 49		12 01			12 19	12 31					12 49		13 01			13 19	13 31			
Lewes 4	a		11 43	11 52	11 55		12 07	12 22		12 25	12 37			12 43	12 52	12 55		13 07		13 22	13 25	13 37			13 43
	d		11 44	11 53	11 58		12 09	12 23		12 28				12 44	12 53	12 58		13 09		13 23	13 28				13 44
Southease	d									12 34											13 34				
Newhaven Town	d				12 06					12 38						13 06					13 38				
Newhaven Harbour	d				12 08					12 40						13 08					13 40				
Bishopstone	d				12 11					12 43						13 11					13 43				
Seaford	a				12 14					12 46						13 14					13 46				
Glynde	d						12 14											13 14							
Berwick	d						12 20											13 20							
Polegate	d		11 57	12 05			12 25	12 35						12 57	13 05			13 25		13 35					13 57
Hampden Park 4	d	11 52				12 20	12 29	12 39					12 52				13 20	13 29		13 39				13 52	
Eastbourne 4	a	11 57	12 04	12 13		12 25	12 34	12 44					12 57	13 04	13 13		13 25	13 34		13 44				13 57	14 04
	d	12 04	12 09	12 19			12 40					12 58	13 04	13 09	13 19			13 40					13 58	14 04	14 09
Hampden Park 4	d	12a08		12 23			12 44					13a02	13a08		13 23			13 44					14a02	14a08	
Pevensey & Westham	d			12 28			12 49								13 28			13 49							
Pevensey Bay	d																								
Normans Bay	d						12 53											13 53							
Cooden Beach	d			12 34			12 57								13 34			13 57							
Collington	d			12 37			13 00								13 37			14 00							
Bexhill 4	d		12 24	12 39			13 02							13 24	13 39			14 02							14 24
St Leonards Warrior Sq 4	d		12 31	12 46			13 09							13 31	13 46			14 09							14 31
Hastings 4	a		12 35	12 49			13 12							13 35	13 49			14 12							14 35
	d		12 36	12 50			13 13							13 36	13 50			14 13							14 36
Ore	d			12a53			13a16								13a53			14a16							
Three Oaks	d		12 44																						14 44
Doleham	d																								
Winchelsea	d													13 50											
Rye	a		12 54											13 54											14 54
	d		12 56											13 56											14 56
Appledore (Kent)	d		13 05											14 05											15 05
Ham Street	d		13 10											14 10											15 10
Ashford International	a		13 18											14 18											15 18

Table 189

London, Haywards Heath and Brighton - Lewes, Seaford, Eastbourne, Hastings and Ashford

Saturdays

Network Diagram - see first Page of Table 184

		SN ◇1	SN	SN ◇1		SN 1	SN ◇1	SN	SN	SN ◇1	SN 1	SN	SN ◇1	SN		SN ◇1	SN 1	SN ◇1	SN	SN	SN ◇1	SN 1	SN	SN ◇1
London Victoria 15 ⊖	d	12 47					13 17						13 47					14 17						14 47
Clapham Junction 10	d	12 53					13 23						13 53					14 23						14 53
London Bridge 4 ⊖	d																							
East Croydon	d	13 03					13 33						14 03					14 33						15 03
Gatwick Airport 10 ✈	d	13 20					13 50						14 20					14 50						15 20
Haywards Heath 3	d	13 35					14 07						14 35					15 07						15 35
Wivelsfield 4	d						14 11											15 11						
Plumpton	d	13 44											14 44											15 44
Cooksbridge	d																							
Brighton 10	d		13 40			13 52		14 10	14 22			14 32		14 40			14 52		15 10	15 22			15 32	
London Road (Brighton)	d		13 43			13 55		14 13	14 25					14 43			14 55		15 13	15 25				
Moulsecoomb	d		13 45			13 57		14 15	14 27					14 45			14 57		15 15	15 27				
Falmer	d		13 49			14 01		14 19	14 31					14 49			15 01		15 19	15 31				
Lewes 4	a	13 52	13 55			14 07	14 22	14 25	14 37			14 43	14 52	14 55			15 07	15 22	15 25	15 37			15 43	15 52
	d	13 53	13 58			14 09	14 23	14 28				14 44	14 53	14 58			15 09	15 23	15 28				15 44	15 53
Southease	d							14 34											15 34					
Newhaven Town ⛴	d		14 06					14 38						15 06					15 38					
Newhaven Harbour	d		14 08					14 40						15 08					15 40					
Bishopstone	d		14 11					14 43						15 11					15 43					
Seaford	a		14 14					14 46						15 14					15 46					
Glynde	d					14 14											15 14							
Berwick	d					14 20											15 20							
Polegate	d	14 05				14 25	14 35					14 57	15 05				15 25	15 35					15 57	16 05
Hampden Park 4	d			14 20		14 29	14 39				14 52					15 20	15 29	15 39				15 52		
Eastbourne 4	a	14 13		14 25		14 34	14 44				14 57	15 04	15 13			15 25	15 34	15 44				15 57	16 04	16 13
	d	14 19				14 40				14 58	15 04	15 09	15 19				15 40				15 58	16 04	16 09	16 19
Hampden Park 4	d	14 23				14 44				15a02	15a08		15 23				15 44				16a02	16a08		16 23
Pevensey & Westham	d	14 28				14 49							15 28				15 49							16 28
Pevensey Bay	d																							
Normans Bay	d					14 53											15 53							
Cooden Beach	d	14 34				14 57							15 34				15 57							16 34
Collington	d	14 37				15 00							15 37				16 00							16 37
Bexhill 4	d	14 39				15 02						15 24	15 39				16 02						16 24	16 39
St Leonards Warrior Sq 4	d	14 46				15 09						15 31	15 46				16 09						16 31	16 46
Hastings 4	a	14 49				15 12						15 35	15 49				16 12						16 35	16 49
	d	14 50				15 13						15 36	15 50				16 13						16 36	16 50
Ore	d	14a53				15a16							15a53				16a16							16a53
Three Oaks	d																						16 44	
Doleham	d																							
Winchelsea	d											15 50												
Rye	a											15 54											16 54	
	d											15 56											16 56	
Appledore (Kent)	d											16 05											17 05	
Ham Street	d											16 10											17 10	
Ashford International	a											16 18											17 18	

Table 189

London, Haywards Heath and Brighton - Lewes, Seaford, Eastbourne, Hastings and Ashford

Saturdays

Network Diagram - see first Page of Table 184

		SN	SN ◇1	SN 1	SN ◇1	SN	SN	SN ◇1	SN 1	SN		SN ◇1	SN	SN ◇1	SN 1	SN ◇1	SN	SN	SN ◇1	SN 1		SN	SN ◇1	SN	SN ◇1
London Victoria 15 ⊖	d				15 17							15 47				16 17							16 47		
Clapham Junction 10	d				15 23							15 53				16 23							16 53		
London Bridge 4 ⊖	d																								
East Croydon	d				15 33							16 03				16 33							17 03		
Gatwick Airport 10 ✈	d				15 50							16 20				16 50							17 20		
Haywards Heath 3	d				16 07							16 35				17 07							17 35		
Wivelsfield 4	d				16 11											17 11									
Plumpton	d											16 44											17 44		
Cooksbridge	d																								
Brighton 10	d	15 40		15 52		16 10	16 22			16 32			16 40		16 52		17 10	17 22				17 32		17 40	
London Road (Brighton)	d	15 43		15 55		16 13	16 25						16 43		16 55		17 13	17 25						17 43	
Moulsecoomb	d	15 45		15 57		16 15	16 27						16 45		16 57		17 15	17 27						17 45	
Falmer	d	15 49		16 01		16 19	16 31						16 49		17 01		17 19	17 31						17 49	
Lewes 4	a	15 55		16 07	16 22	16 25	16 37			16 43		16 52	16 55		17 07	17 22	17 25	17 37				17 43	17 52	17 55	
	d	15 58		16 09	16 23	16 28				16 44		16 53	16 58		17 09	17 23	17 28					17 44	17 53	17 58	
Southease	d					16 34											17 34								
Newhaven Town ⛴	d	16 06				16 38							17 06				17 38							18 06	
Newhaven Harbour	d	16 08				16 40							17 08				17 40							18 08	
Bishopstone	d	16 11				16 43							17 11				17 43							18 11	
Seaford	a	16 14				16 46							17 14				17 46							18 14	
Glynde	d			16 14											17 14										
Berwick	d			16 20											17 20										
Polegate	d			16 25	16 35					16 57		17 05			17 25	17 35						17 57	18 05		
Hampden Park 4	d		16 20	16 29	16 39				16 52					17 20	17 29	17 39				17 52					18 20
Eastbourne 4	a		16 25	16 34	16 44				16 57	17 04		17 13		17 25	17 34	17 44				17 57		18 04	18 13		18 25
	d			16 40				16 58	17 04	17 09		17 19			17 40				17 58	18 04		18 09	18 19		
Hampden Park 4	d			16 44				17a02	17a08			17 23			17 44				18a02	18a08			18 23		
Pevensey & Westham	d			16 49								17 28			17 49								18 28		
Pevensey Bay	d																								
Normans Bay	d			16 53											17 53										
Cooden Beach	d			16 57								17 34			17 57								18 34		
Collington	d			17 00								17 37			18 00								18 37		
Bexhill 4	d			17 02						17 24		17 39			18 02							18 24	18 39		
St Leonards Warrior Sq 4	d			17 09						17 31		17 46			18 09							18 31	18 46		
Hastings 4	a			17 12						17 35		17 49			18 12							18 35	18 49		
	d			17 13						17 36		17 50			18 13							18 36	18 50		
Ore	d			17a16								17a53			18a16								18a53		
Three Oaks	d																					18 44			
Doleham	d																								
Winchelsea	d									17 50															
Rye	a									17 54												18 54			
	d									17 56												18 56			
Appledore (Kent)	d									18 05												19 05			
Ham Street	d									18 10												19 10			
Ashford International	a									18 18												19 18			

London, Haywards Heath and Brighton - Lewes, Seaford, Eastbourne, Hastings and Ashford

Network Diagram - see first Page of Table 184

Station		SN 1	SN A	SN ◇1	SN	SN	SN ◇1	SN 1	SN	SN ◇1	SN	SN ◇1
London Victoria 15 ⊖	d		17 21							17 47		
Clapham Junction 10	d									17 53		
London Bridge 4 ⊖	d											
East Croydon	d									18 03		
Gatwick Airport 10 ✈	d									18 20		
Haywards Heath 3	d			18 07						18 35		
Wivelsfield 4	d			18 11								
Plumpton	d											
Cooksbridge	d									18 44		
Brighton 10	d	17 52			18 10	18 22			18 32		18 40	
London Road (Brighton)	d	17 55			18 13	18 25					18 43	
Moulsecoomb	d	17 57			18 15	18 27					18 45	
Falmer	d	18 01			18 19	18 31					18 49	
Lewes 4	a	18 07		18 22	18 25	18 37			18 43	18 52	18 55	
	d	18 09		18 23	18 28				18 44	18 53	18 58	
Southease	d				18 34							
Newhaven Town ⛴	d				18 38						19 06	
Newhaven Harbour	d				18 40						19 08	
Bishopstone	d				18 43						19 11	
Seaford	a				18 46						19 14	
Glynde	d	18 14										
Berwick	d	18 20										
Polegate	d	18 25		18 38					18 57	19 05		
Hampden Park 4	d	18 29		18 42				18 52				19 20
Eastbourne 4	a	18 34	18 43	18 47				18 57	19 04	19 13		19 25
	d	18 40					18 58	19 04	19 09	19 19		
Hampden Park 4	d	18 44					19a02	19a08		19 23		
Pevensey & Westham	d	18 49								19 28		
Pevensey Bay	d											
Normans Bay	d	18 53										
Cooden Beach	d	18 57								19 34		
Collington	d	19 00								19 37		
Bexhill 4	d	19 02							19 24	19 39		
St Leonards Warrior Sq 4	d	19 09							19 31	19 46		
Hastings 4	a	19 12							19 35	19 49		
	d	19 13							19 36	19 50		
Ore	d	19a16								19a53		
Three Oaks	d											
Doleham	d											
Winchelsea	d								19 50			
Rye	a								19 54			
	d								19 56			
Appledore (Kent)	d								20 05			
Ham Street	d								20 10			
Ashford International	a								20 18			

Station		SN 1	SN ◇1	SN	SN	SN 1	SN	SN ◇1	SN	SN ◇1	SN 1	SN ◇1 B
London Victoria 15 ⊖	d		18 17					18 47				19 17
Clapham Junction 10	d		18 23					18 53				19 23
London Bridge 4 ⊖	d											
East Croydon	d		18 33					19 03				19 33
Gatwick Airport 10 ✈	d		18 50					19 20				19 50
Haywards Heath 3	d		19 07					19 35				20 07
Wivelsfield 4	d		19 11									20 11
Plumpton	d											
Cooksbridge	d							19 44				
Brighton 10	d	18 52		19 10	19 22		19 32		19 40		19 52	
London Road (Brighton)	d	18 55		19 13	19 25				19 43		19 55	
Moulsecoomb	d	18 57		19 15	19 27				19 45		19 57	
Falmer	d	19 01		19 19	19 31				19 49		20 01	
Lewes 4	a	19 07	19 22	19 25	19 37		19 43	19 52	19 55		20 08	20 22
	d	19 09	19 23	19 28			19 44	19 53	19 58		20 09	20 23
Southease	d			19 34								
Newhaven Town ⛴	d			19 38					20 06			
Newhaven Harbour	d			19 40					20 08			
Bishopstone	d			19 43					20 11			
Seaford	a			19 46					20 14			
Glynde	d	19 14									20 14	20 28
Berwick	d	19 20									20 20	20 34
Polegate	d	19 25	19 35				19 57	20 05			20 25	20 39
Hampden Park 4	d	19 29	19 39			19 52				20 20	20 29	20 43
Eastbourne 4	a	19 34	19 44			19 57	20 04	20 13		20 25	20 34	20 48
	d	19 40				20 04	20 09	20 19				20 54
Hampden Park 4	d	19 44				20a08		20 23				
Pevensey & Westham	d	19 49						20 28				21 01
Pevensey Bay	d											
Normans Bay	d	19 53										
Cooden Beach	d	19 57						20 34				21 07
Collington	d	20 00						20 37				
Bexhill 4	d	20 02					20 24	20 39				21 12
St Leonards Warrior Sq 4	d	20 09					20 31	20 46				21 18
Hastings 4	a	20 12					20 35	20 49				21 21
	d	20 13					20 36	20 50				
Ore	d	20a16						20a53				
Three Oaks	d											
Doleham	d						20 44					
Winchelsea	d											
Rye	a						20 54					
	d						20 56					
Appledore (Kent)	d						21 05					
Ham Street	d						21 10					
Ashford International	a						21 18					

A from 9 June until 1 September

B ◇ to Haywards Heath

London, Haywards Heath and Brighton - Lewes, Seaford, Eastbourne, Hastings and Ashford

Network Diagram - see first Page of Table 184

Station		SN	SN 1	SN	SN ◇1	SN	SN ◇1	SN ◇1	SN	SN 1	SN
London Victoria 15 ⊖	d				19 47			20 17			
Clapham Junction 10	d				19 53			20 23			
London Bridge 4 ⊖	d										
East Croydon	d				20 03			20 33			
Gatwick Airport 10 ✈	d				20 20			20 50			
Haywards Heath 3	d				20 35			21 07			
Wivelsfield 4	d				20 39			21 11			
Plumpton	d				20 45						
Cooksbridge	d										
Brighton 10	d	20 10		20 32		20 40			21 04		21 32
London Road (Brighton)	d	20 13				20 43			21 07		
Moulsecoomb	d	20 15				20 45			21 09		
Falmer	d	20 19				20 49			21 13		
Lewes 4	a	20 25		20 43	20 52	20 55		21 22	21 19		21 43
	d	20 28		20 44	20 53	20 58		21 23	21 28		21 44
Southease	d										
Newhaven Town ⛴	d	20 36				21 06			21 36		
Newhaven Harbour	d	20 38				21 08			21 38		
Bishopstone	d	20 41				21 11			21 41		
Seaford	a	20 44				21 14			21 44		
Glynde	d							21 28			
Berwick	d							21 34			
Polegate	d			20 57	21 05			21 39			21 57
Hampden Park 4	d		20 52				21 20	21 43		21 51	
Eastbourne 4	a		20 57	21 04	21 13		21 25	21 48		21 56	22 04
	d		21 04	21 09	21 19					22 04	22 09
Hampden Park 4	d		21a08		21 23					22a08	
Pevensey & Westham	d				21 28						
Pevensey Bay	d										
Normans Bay	d										
Cooden Beach	d				21 34						
Collington	d				21 37						
Bexhill 4	d			21 23	21 39						22 23
St Leonards Warrior Sq 4	d			21 30	21 46						22 30
Hastings 4	a			21 33	21 49						22 33
	d			21 35	21 50						
Ore	d			21 37	21a53						
Three Oaks	d			21 43							
Doleham	d			21 46							
Winchelsea	d			21 52							
Rye	a			21 56							
	d			21 56							
Appledore (Kent)	d			22 05							
Ham Street	d			22 10							
Ashford International	a			22 18							

Station		SN ◇1	SN ◇1	SN	SN ◇1	SN	SN 1	SN	SN ◇1	SN	SN 1	SN 1
London Victoria 15 ⊖	d		20 47		21 17				21 47			
Clapham Junction 10	d		20 53		21 23				21 53			
London Bridge 4 ⊖	d											
East Croydon	d		21 03		21 33				22 03			
Gatwick Airport 10 ✈	d		21 20		21 49				22 20			
Haywards Heath 3	d		21 34		22 08				22 34			
Wivelsfield 4	d		21 38		22 12				22 38			
Plumpton	d		21 44						22 44			
Cooksbridge	d											
Brighton 10	d			21 40		22 04		22 28		22 34	23 06	
London Road (Brighton)	d			21 43		22 07				22 37	23 09	
Moulsecoomb	d			21 45		22 09				22 39	23 11	
Falmer	d			21 49		22 13				22 43	23 15	
Lewes 4	a		21 51	21 55	22 23	22 19		22 39	22 51	22 49	23 21	
	d		21 53	21 58	22 23	22 28		22 39	22 53	22 56	23 22	
Southease	d											
Newhaven Town ⛴	d			22 06		22 36				23 04		
Newhaven Harbour	d			22 08		22 38				23 06		
Bishopstone	d			22 11		22 41				23 09		
Seaford	a			22 14		22 44				23 12		
Glynde	d				22 29						23 27	
Berwick	d				22 34						23 33	
Polegate	d		22 05		22 39			22 52	23 05		23 38	
Hampden Park 4	d	22 07			22 43		22 55		23 09		23 42	23 47
Eastbourne 4	a	22 12	22 15		22 48		23 00	23 03	23 14		23 47	23 52
	d		22 21				23 05	23 10	23 20			23 56
Hampden Park 4	d		22 25				23a09		23 24			00a01
Pevensey & Westham	d		22 30						23 29			
Pevensey Bay	d											
Normans Bay	d											
Cooden Beach	d		22 36						23 35			
Collington	d		22 39						23 38			
Bexhill 4	d		22 41					23 24	23 40			
St Leonards Warrior Sq 4	d		22 48					23 31	23 47			
Hastings 4	a		22 51					23 34	23 50			
	d											
Ore	d											
Three Oaks	d											
Doleham	d											
Winchelsea	d											
Rye	a											
	d											
Appledore (Kent)	d											
Ham Street	d											
Ashford International	a											

Table 189

Saturdays

London, Haywards Heath and Brighton - Lewes, Seaford, Eastbourne, Hastings and Ashford

Network Diagram - see first Page of Table 184

		SN	SN ◇■	SN
London Victoria ⊖	d		22 47	
Clapham Junction	d		22 53	
London Bridge ⊖	d			
East Croydon	d		23 03	
Gatwick Airport ✈	d		23 20	
Haywards Heath	d		23 34	
Wivelsfield	d		23 38	
Plumpton	d		23 44	
Cooksbridge	d			
Brighton	d	23 28		23 34
London Road (Brighton)	d			23 37
Moulsecoomb	d			23 39
Falmer	d			23 43
Lewes	a	23 39	23 51	23 49
	d	23 39	23 53	23 56
Southease	d			
Newhaven Town ⛴	d			00 04
Newhaven Harbour	d			00 06
Bishopstone	d			00 09
Seaford	a			00 12
Glynde	d			
Berwick	d		00 02	
Polegate	d	23 52	00 07	
Hampden Park	d		00 11	
Eastbourne	a	23 59	00 16	
	d		00 22	
Hampden Park	d			
Pevensey & Westham	d		00 29	
Pevensey Bay	d			
Normans Bay	d			
Cooden Beach	d		00 35	
Collington	d		00 38	
Bexhill	d		00 41	
St Leonards Warrior Sq	d		00 47	
Hastings	a		00 50	
	d			
Ore	d			
Three Oaks	d			
Doleham	d			
Winchelsea	d			
Rye	a			
	d			
Appledore (Kent)	d			
Ham Street	d			
Ashford International	a			

Table 189

Sundays
until 9 September

London, Haywards Heath and Brighton - Lewes, Seaford, Eastbourne, Hastings and Ashford

Network Diagram - see first Page of Table 184

		SN ◇■	SN	SN ◇■	SN ◇■ A	SN ◇■	SN	SN ◇■	SN	SN ■
London Victoria ⊖	d	22p47		00 05						
Clapham Junction	d	22p53		00 11						
London Bridge ⊖	d									
East Croydon	d	23p03		00 24						
Gatwick Airport ✈	d	23p20		00 43						
Haywards Heath	d	23p34		01 06	01 35					
Wivelsfield	d	23p38								
Plumpton	d	23p44								
Cooksbridge	d									
Brighton	d		23p34							07 09
London Road (Brighton)	d		23p37							07 12
Moulsecoomb	d		23p39							07 14
Falmer	d		23p43							07 18
Lewes	a	23p51	23p49	01 20	01s49					07 24
	d	23p53	23p56	01 20						07 25
Southease	d									
Newhaven Town ⛴	d		00 04							
Newhaven Harbour	d		00 06							
Bishopstone	d		00 09							
Seaford	a		00 12							
Glynde	d									07 30
Berwick	d	00 02								07 36
Polegate	d	00 07		01s32	02s02					07 41
Hampden Park	d	00 11		01s36						07 45
Eastbourne	a	00 16		01 41	02 10					07 50
	d	00 22				06 58		07 26	07 30	
Hampden Park	d					07a02		07 30	07a34	
Pevensey & Westham	d	00 29						07 35		
Pevensey Bay	d									
Normans Bay	d									
Cooden Beach	d	00 35						07 41		
Collington	d	00 38						07 44		
Bexhill	d	00 41						07 47		
St Leonards Warrior Sq	d	00 47						07 53		
Hastings	a	00 50						07 56		
	d						07 22	07 57		
Ore	d						07 24	08a00		
Three Oaks	d						07 30			
Doleham	d						07 33			
Winchelsea	d						07 39			
Rye	a						07 43			
	d						07 43			
Appledore (Kent)	d						07 52			
Ham Street	d						07 57			
Ashford International	a						08 06			

		SN	SN	SN ■	SN	SN	SN	SN ◇■	SN	SN ■	SN	SN	SN	SN ◇■
London Victoria ⊖	d													
Clapham Junction	d													
London Bridge ⊖	d													
East Croydon	d													
Gatwick Airport ✈	d													
Haywards Heath	d													
Wivelsfield	d													
Plumpton	d													
Cooksbridge	d													
Brighton	d	07 15		07 43	07 49	08 09			08 20	08 43	08 49	09 09		
London Road (Brighton)	d	07 18		07 46	07 52	08 12				08 46	08 52	09 12		
Moulsecoomb	d	07 20		07 48	07 54	08 14				08 48	08 54	09 14		
Falmer	d	07 24		07 52	07 58	08 18				08 52	08 58	09 18		
Lewes	a	07 31		07 58	08 04	08 24			08 31	08 58	09 04	09 24		
	d	07 32		07 59	08 05	08 25			08 32	08 59	09 05	09 25		
Southease	d				08 11						09 11			
Newhaven Town ⛴	d	07 40			08 15	08 33					09 15	09 33		
Newhaven Harbour	d	07 42			08 17	08 35					09 17	09 35		
Bishopstone	d	07 45			08 20	08 38					09 20	09 38		
Seaford	a	07 48			08 23	08 41					09 23	09 41		
Glynde	d								08 37					
Berwick	d								08 43					
Polegate	d			08 11					08 49	09 11				
Hampden Park	d							08 43	08 53					09 43
Eastbourne	a			08 19				08 49	08 58	09 19				09 49
	d		07 58	08 26			08 34		09 02	09 26			09 34	
Hampden Park	d			08 30			08a38			09 30			09a38	
Pevensey & Westham	d			08 35						09 35				
Pevensey Bay	d													
Normans Bay	d													
Cooden Beach	d			08 41						09 41				
Collington	d			08 44						09 44				
Bexhill	d		08 11	08 46					09 16	09 46				
St Leonards Warrior Sq	d		08 18	08 53					09 23	09 53				
Hastings	a		08 22	08 56					09 26	09 56				
	d		08 22	08 57					09 27	09 57				
Ore	d			09a00						10a00				
Three Oaks	d													
Doleham	d													
Winchelsea	d													
Rye	a		08 39						09 44					
	d		08 41						09 46					
Appledore (Kent)	d		08 50						09 55					
Ham Street	d		08 55						10 00					
Ashford International	a		09 03						10 08					

A 29 July, 5 August, 12 August, 2 September, 9 September

Table 189

Sundays until 9 September

London, Haywards Heath and Brighton - Lewes, Seaford, Eastbourne, Hastings and Ashford

Network Diagram - see first Page of Table 184

		SN	SN ◇■ A ⌶	SN	SN	SN		SN ◇■	SN	SN ◇■ A ⌶	SN	SN	SN	SN ◇■	SN	SN ◇■ A ⌶		SN	SN	SN	SN ◇■	SN	SN ◇■ A ⌶	SN	SN
London Victoria ■ ⊖	d		08 47							09 47						10 47							11 47		
Clapham Junction ■	d		08 53							09 53						10 53							11 53		
London Bridge ■ ⊖	d																								
East Croydon	d		09 03							10 03						11 03							12 03		
Gatwick Airport ■ ✈	d		09 19							10 19						11 19							12 19		
Haywards Heath ■	d		09 30							10 30						11 30							12 30		
Wivelsfield ■	d		09 34							10 34						11 34							12 34		
Plumpton	d		09 40							10 40						11 40							12 40		
Cooksbridge	d																								
Brighton ■	d	09 20		09 29	10 09				10 20		10 29	11 09			11 20			11 29	12 09			12 20		12 29	13 09
London Road (Brighton)	d			09 32	10 12						10 32	11 12						11 32	12 12					12 32	13 12
Moulsecoomb	d			09 34	10 14						10 34	11 14						11 34	12 14					12 34	13 14
Falmer	d			09 38	10 18						10 38	11 18						11 38	12 18					12 38	13 18
Lewes ■	a	09 31	09 48	09 44	10 24				10 31	10 48	10 44	11 24			11 31	11 48		11 44	12 24			12 31	12 48	12 44	13 24
	d	09 32	09 48	09 52	10 25				10 32	10 48	10 52	11 25			11 32	11 48		11 52	12 25			12 32	12 48	12 52	13 25
Southease	d			09 58							10 58							11 58						12 58	
Newhaven Town ⛴	d			10 02	10 33						11 02	11 33						12 02	12 33					13 02	13 33
Newhaven Harbour	d			10 04	10 35						11 04	11 35						12 04	12 35					13 04	13 35
Bishopstone	d			10 07	10 38						11 07	11 38						12 07	12 38					13 07	13 38
Seaford	a			10 10	10 41						11 10	11 41						12 10	12 41					13 10	13 41
Glynde	d	09 37							10 37						11 37							12 37			
Berwick	d	09 43							10 43						11 43							12 43			
Polegate	d	09 49	10 01						10 49	11 01					11 49	12 01						12 49	13 01		
Hampden Park ■	d	09 53						10 43	10 53					11 43	11 53						12 43	12 53			
Eastbourne ■	a	09 58	10 08					10 49	10 58	11 08				11 49	11 58	12 08					12 49	12 58	13 08		
	d	10 02	10 15			10 34			11 02	11 15			11 34		12 02	12 15				12 34		13 02	13 15		
Hampden Park ■	d		10 19			10a38				11 19			11a38			12 19				12a38			13 19		
Pevensey & Westham	d		10 24							11 24						12 24							13 24		
Pevensey Bay	d																								
Normans Bay	d																								
Cooden Beach	d		10 30							11 30						12 30							13 30		
Collington	d		10 33							11 33						12 33							13 33		
Bexhill ■	d	10 16	10 35						11 16	11 35					12 16	12 35						13 16	13 35		
St Leonards Warrior Sq ■	d	10 23	10 42						11 23	11 42					12 23	12 42						13 23	13 42		
Hastings ■	a	10 26	10 45						11 26	11 45					12 26	12 45						13 26	13 45		
	d	10 27	10 46						11 27	11 46					12 27	12 46						13 27	13 46		
Ore	d		10a49							11a49						12a49							13a49		
Three Oaks	d																								
Doleham	d																								
Winchelsea	d																								
Rye	a	10 44							11 44						12 44							13 44			
	d	10 46							11 46						12 46							13 46			
Appledore (Kent)	d	10 55							11 55						12 55							13 55			
Ham Street	d	11 00							12 00						13 00							14 00			
Ashford International	a	11 08							12 08						13 08							14 08			

A ⌶ to Lewes

Table 189

Sundays until 9 September

London, Haywards Heath and Brighton - Lewes, Seaford, Eastbourne, Hastings and Ashford

Network Diagram - see first Page of Table 184

		SN		SN ◇■	SN	SN ◇■ A ⌶	SN	SN	SN	SN ◇■	SN	SN ◇■ A ⌶		SN	SN	SN	SN ◇■	SN	SN ◇■ A ⌶	SN	SN	SN		SN ◇■	SN
London Victoria ■ ⊖	d					12 47						13 47							14 47						
Clapham Junction ■	d					12 53						13 53							14 53						
London Bridge ■ ⊖	d																								
East Croydon	d					13 03						14 03							15 03						
Gatwick Airport ■ ✈	d					13 19						14 19							15 19						
Haywards Heath ■	d					13 30						14 30							15 30						
Wivelsfield ■	d					13 34						14 34							15 34						
Plumpton	d																								
Cooksbridge	d																								
Brighton ■	d				13 20		13 29	14 09			14 20			14 29	15 09			15 20		15 29	16 09				16 20
London Road (Brighton)	d						13 32	14 12						14 32	15 12					15 32	16 12				
Moulsecoomb	d						13 34	14 14						14 34	15 14					15 34	16 14				
Falmer	d						13 38	14 18						14 38	15 18					15 38	16 18				
Lewes ■	a				13 31	13 48	13 44	14 24			14 31	14 48		14 44	15 24			15 31	15 48	15 44	16 24				16 31
	d				13 32	13 48	13 52	14 25			14 32	14 48		14 52	15 25			15 32	15 48	15 52	16 25				16 32
Southease	d						13 58							14 58						15 58					
Newhaven Town ⛴	d						14 02	14 33						15 02	15 33					16 02	16 33				
Newhaven Harbour	d						14 04	14 35						15 04	15 35					16 04	16 35				
Bishopstone	d						14 07	14 38						15 07	15 38					16 07	16 38				
Seaford	a						14 10	14 41						15 10	15 41					16 10	16 41				
Glynde	d				13 37						14 37							15 37							16 37
Berwick	d				13 43						14 43							15 43							16 43
Polegate	d				13 49	14 01					14 49	15 01						15 49	16 01						16 49
Hampden Park ■	d			13 43	13 53					14 43	14 53						15 43	15 53						16 43	16 53
Eastbourne ■	a			13 49	13 58	14 08				14 49	14 58	15 08					15 49	15 58	16 08					16 49	16 58
	d	13 34			14 02	14 15			14 34		15 02	15 15				15 34		16 02	16 15			16 34			17 02
Hampden Park ■	d	13a38				14 19			14a38			15 19				15a38			16 19			16a38			
Pevensey & Westham	d					14 24						15 24							16 24						
Pevensey Bay	d																								
Normans Bay	d																								
Cooden Beach	d					14 30						15 30							16 30						
Collington	d					14 33						15 33							16 33						
Bexhill ■	d				14 16	14 35					15 16	15 35						16 16	16 35						17 16
St Leonards Warrior Sq ■	d				14 23	14 42					15 23	15 42						16 23	16 42						17 23
Hastings ■	a				14 26	14 45					15 26	15 45						16 26	16 45						17 26
	d				14 27	14 46					15 27	15 46						16 27	16 46						17 27
Ore	d					14a49						15a49							16a49						
Three Oaks	d																								
Doleham	d																								
Winchelsea	d																								
Rye	a				14 44						15 44							16 44							17 44
	d				14 46						15 46							16 46							17 46
Appledore (Kent)	d				14 55						15 55							16 55							17 55
Ham Street	d				15 00						16 00							17 00							18 00
Ashford International	a				15 08						16 08							17 08							18 08

A ⌶ to Lewes

Table 189

Sundays until 9 September

London, Haywards Heath and Brighton - Lewes, Seaford, Eastbourne, Hastings and Ashford

Network Diagram - see first Page of Table 184

		SN	SN	SN	SN	SN	SN	SN	SN	SN	SN	SN	SN	SN	SN	SN	SN	SN	SN	SN	SN	SN	SN
		◇1				◇1		◇1				◇1		◇1				◇1		◇1			
		A ⊼						A ⊼						A ⊼						A ⊼			
London Victoria 15 ⊖	d	15 47						16 47						17 47						18 47			
Clapham Junction 10	d	15 53						16 53						17 53						18 53			
London Bridge 4 ⊖	d																						
East Croydon	d	16 03						17 03						18 03						19 03			
Gatwick Airport 10 ✈	d	16 19						17 19						18 19						19 19			
Haywards Heath 3	d	16 30						17 30						18 30						19 30			
Wivelsfield 4	d	16 34						17 34						18 34						19 34			
Plumpton	d	16 40						17 40						18 40						19 40			
Cooksbridge	d																						
Brighton 10	d		16 29	17 09			17 20		17 29	18 09			18 20		18 29	19 09			19 20		19 29	20 09	
London Road (Brighton)	d		16 32	17 12					17 32	18 12					18 32	19 12					19 32	20 12	
Moulsecoomb	d		16 34	17 14					17 34	18 14					18 34	19 14					19 34	20 14	
Falmer	d		16 38	17 18					17 38	18 18					18 38	19 18					19 38	20 18	
Lewes 4	a	16 48	16 44	17 24			17 31	17 48	17 44	18 24			18 31	18 48	18 44	19 24			19 31	19 48	19 44	20 24	
	d	16 48	16 52	17 25			17 32	17 48	17 52	18 25			18 32	18 48	18 52	19 25			19 32	19 48	19 52	20 25	
Southease	d		16 58						17 58						18 58						19 58		
Newhaven Town ⛴	d		17 02	17 33					18 02	18 33					19 02	19 33					20 02	20 33	
Newhaven Harbour	d		17 04	17 35					18 04	18 35					19 04	19 35					20 04	20 35	
Bishopstone	d		17 07	17 38					18 07	18 38					19 07	19 38					20 07	20 38	
Seaford	a		17 10	17 41					18 10	18 41					19 10	19 41					20 10	20 41	
Glynde	d						17 37						18 37						19 37				
Berwick	d						17 43						18 43						19 43				
Polegate	d	17 01					17 49	18 01					18 49	19 01					19 49	20 01			
Hampden Park 4	d					17 43	17 53					18 43	18 53					19 43	19 53				
Eastbourne 4	a	17 08				17 49	17 58	18 08				18 49	18 58	19 08				19 49	19 58	20 08			
	d	17 15			17 34		18 02	18 15			18 34		19 02	19 15			19 34		20 02	20 15			20 34
Hampden Park 4	d	17 19			17a38			18 19			18a38			19 19			19a38			20 19			20a38
Pevensey & Westham	d	17 24						18 24						19 24						20 24			
Pevensey Bay	d																						
Normans Bay	d																						
Cooden Beach	d	17 30						18 30						19 30						20 30			
Collington	d	17 33						18 33						19 33						20 33			
Bexhill 4	d	17 35					18 16	18 35					19 16	19 35					20 16	20 35			
St Leonards Warrior Sq 4	d	17 42					18 23	18 42					19 23	19 42					20 23	20 42			
Hastings 4	a	17 45					18 26	18 45					19 26	19 45					20 26	20 45			
	d	17 46					18 27	18 46					19 27	19 46					20 27	20 46			
Ore	d	17a49						18a49						19a49						20a49			
Three Oaks	d																						
Doleham	d																						
Winchelsea	d																						
Rye	a						18 44						19 44						20 44				
	d						18 46						19 46						20 46				
Appledore (Kent)	d						18 55						19 55						20 55				
Ham Street	d						19 00						20 00						21 00				
Ashford International	a						19 08						20 08						21 08				

A ⊼ to Lewes

Table 189

Sundays until 9 September

London, Haywards Heath and Brighton - Lewes, Seaford, Eastbourne, Hastings and Ashford

Network Diagram - see first Page of Table 184

		SN	SN	SN	SN	SN	SN	SN	SN	SN	SN	SN	SN	SN	SN	SN	SN	SN	SN	SN	SN	SN
		◇1		◇1				1		◇1				1		◇1			1		◇1	
				A ⊼																		
London Victoria 15 ⊖	d			19 47						20 47						21 47					22 47	
Clapham Junction 10	d			19 53						20 53						21 53					22 53	
London Bridge 4 ⊖	d																					
East Croydon	d			20 03						21 03						22 03					23 03	
Gatwick Airport 10 ✈	d			20 19						21 19						22 19					23 19	
Haywards Heath 3	d			20 30						21 30						22 30					23 30	
Wivelsfield 4	d			20 34						21 34						22 34					23 34	
Plumpton	d			20 40						21 40						22 40					23 40	
Cooksbridge	d																					
Brighton 10	d		20 20		20 29	21 09			21 20		21 29	22 09			22 20		22 39	23 09		23 20		23 39
London Road (Brighton)	d				20 32	21 12					21 32	22 12					22 42	23 12				23 42
Moulsecoomb	d				20 34	21 14					21 34	22 14					22 44	23 14				23 44
Falmer	d				20 38	21 18					21 38	22 18					22 48	23 18				23 48
Lewes 4	a		20 31	20 48	20 44	21 24			21 31	21 48	21 44	22 24			22 31	22 48	22 54	23 24		23 31	23 48	23 54
	d		20 32	20 48	20 52	21 25			21 32	21 48	21 52	22 25			22 32	22 59	23 03			23 32	23 59	
Southease	d																					
Newhaven Town ⛴	d				21 00	21 33					22 00	22 33					23 11					
Newhaven Harbour	d				21 04	21 35					22 02	22 35					23 13					
Bishopstone	d				21 07	21 38					22 05	22 38					23 16					
Seaford	a				21 10	21 41					22 08	22 41					23 19					
Glynde	d		20 37						21 37						22 37					23 37		
Berwick	d		20 43						21 43						22 43					23 43		
Polegate	d		20 49	21 01					21 49	22 01					22 49	23 11				23 49	00 11	
Hampden Park 4	d	20 43	20 53					21 43	21 53					22 43	22 53				23 47	23 53	00 15	
Eastbourne 4	a	20 49	20 58	21 08				21 49	21 58	22 08				22 49	22 58	23 19			23 52	23 58	00 20	
	d		21 02	21 15			21 34		22 02	22 15			22 34			23 26						
Hampden Park 4	d			21 19			21a38			22 19			22a38			23 30						
Pevensey & Westham	d			21 24						22 24						23 35						
Pevensey Bay	d																					
Normans Bay	d																					
Cooden Beach	d			21 30						22 30						23 41						
Collington	d			21 33						22 33						23 44						
Bexhill 4	d		21 16	21 35					22 16	22 35						23 46						
St Leonards Warrior Sq 4	d		21 23	21 42					22 23	22 42						23 53						
Hastings 4	a		21 26	21 45					22 26	22 45						23 56						
	d		21 27	21 46																		
Ore	d			21a49																		
Three Oaks	d																					
Doleham	d																					
Winchelsea	d																					
Rye	a		21 44																			
	d		21 46																			
Appledore (Kent)	d		21 55																			
Ham Street	d		22 00																			
Ashford International	a		22 08																			

A ⊼ to Lewes

Table 189

Sundays from 16 September

London, Haywards Heath and Brighton - Lewes, Seaford, Eastbourne, Hastings and Ashford

Network Diagram - see first Page of Table 184

		SN	SN	SN	SN	SN	SN	SN	SN	SN	SN	SN	SN	SN	SN	SN	SN	SN	SN	SN	SN	SN	SN
		◇1		◇1	◇1		◇1		1			1				◇1		1				◇1	
London Victoria 15 ⊖	d	22p47		00 05																			
Clapham Junction 10	d	22p53		00 11																			
London Bridge 4 ⊖	d																						
East Croydon	d	23p03		00 24																			
Gatwick Airport 10 ✈	d	23p20		00 43																			
Haywards Heath 3	d	23p34		01 06																			
Wivelsfield 4	d	23p38																					
Plumpton	d	23p44																					
Cooksbridge	d																						
Brighton 10	d		23p34						07 09	07 15		07 43	07 49	08 09			08 20	08 43	08 49	09 09			09 20
London Road (Brighton)	d		23p37						07 12	07 18		07 46	07 52	08 12				08 46	08 52	09 12			
Moulsecoomb	d		23p39						07 14	07 20		07 48	07 54	08 14				08 48	08 54	09 14			
Falmer	d		23p43						07 18	07 24		07 52	07 58	08 18				08 52	08 58	09 18			
Lewes 4	a	23p51	23p49	01 20					07 24	07 31		07 58	08 04	08 24			08 31	08 58	09 04	09 24			09 31
	d	23p53	23p56	01 20					07 25	07 32		07 59	08 05	08 25			08 32	08 59	09 05	09 25			09 32
Southease	d												08 11						09 11				
Newhaven Town ⛴	d		00 04							07 40			08 15	08 33					09 15	09 33			
Newhaven Harbour	d		00 06							07 42			08 17	08 35					09 17	09 35			
Bishopstone	d		00 09							07 45			08 20	08 38					09 20	09 38			
Seaford	a		00 12							07 48			08 23	08 41					09 23	09 41			
Glynde	d								07 30								08 37						09 37
Berwick	d	00 02							07 36								08 43						09 43
Polegate	d	00 07		01s32					07 41			08 11					08 49	09 11					09 49
Hampden Park 4	d	00 11		01s36					07 45							08 43	08 53					09 43	09 53
Eastbourne 4	a	00 16		01 41					07 50			08 19				08 49	08 58	09 19				09 49	09 58
	d	00 22			06 55		07 26	07 30			07 58	08 26			08 34		09 02	09 26			09 34		10 02
Hampden Park 4	d				06a59		07 30	07a34				08 30			08a38			09 30			09a38		
Pevensey & Westham	d	00 29					07 35					08 35						09 35					
Pevensey Bay	d																						
Normans Bay	d																						
Cooden Beach	d	00 35					07 41					08 41						09 41					
Collington	d	00 38					07 44					08 44						09 44					
Bexhill 4	d	00 41					07 47				08 11	08 46					09 16	09 46					10 16
St Leonards Warrior Sq 4	d	00 47					07 53				08 18	08 53					09 23	09 53					10 23
Hastings 4	a	00 50					07 56				08 22	08 56					09 26	09 56					10 26
	d					07 22	07 57				08 22	08 57					09 27	09 57					10 27
Ore	d					07 24	08a00					09a00						10a00					
Three Oaks	d					07 30																	
Doleham	d					07 33																	
Winchelsea	d					07 39																	
Rye	a					07 43					08 39						09 44						10 44
	d					07 43					08 41						09 46						10 46
Appledore (Kent)	d					07 52					08 50						09 55						10 55
Ham Street	d					07 57					08 55						10 00						11 00
Ashford International	a					08 06					09 03						10 08						11 08

Table 189

Sundays from 16 September

London, Haywards Heath and Brighton - Lewes, Seaford, Eastbourne, Hastings and Ashford

Network Diagram - see first Page of Table 184

		SN	SN	SN	SN	SN	SN	SN	SN	SN	SN	SN	SN	SN	SN	SN	SN	SN	SN	SN	SN	SN	SN
		◇1 A ✠				◇1		◇1 A ✠				◇1		◇1 A ✠				◇1		◇1 A ✠			
London Victoria 15 ⊖	d	08 47						09 47						10 47						11 47			
Clapham Junction 10	d	08 53						09 53						10 53						11 53			
London Bridge 4 ⊖	d																						
East Croydon	d	09 07						10 07						11 07						12 07			
Gatwick Airport 10 ✈	d	09 29						10 29						11 29						12 29			
Haywards Heath 3	d	09 41						10 41						11 41						12 41			
Wivelsfield 4	d	09 45						10 45						11 45						12 45			
Plumpton	d	09 51						10 51						11 51						12 51			
Cooksbridge	d																						
Brighton 10	d		09 39	10 09			10 20		10 39	11 09			11 20		11 39	12 09			12 20		12 39	13 09	
London Road (Brighton)	d		09 42	10 12					10 42	11 12					11 42	12 12					12 42	13 12	
Moulsecoomb	d		09 44	10 14					10 44	11 14					11 44	12 14					12 44	13 14	
Falmer	d		09 48	10 18					10 48	11 18					11 48	12 18					12 48	13 18	
Lewes 4	a	09 58	09 54	10 24			10 31	10 58	10 54	11 24			11 31	11 58	11 54	12 24			12 31	12 58	12 54	13 24	
	d	09 59	10 03	10 25			10 32	10 59	11 03	11 25			11 32	11 59	12 03	12 25			12 32	12 59	13 03	13 25	
Southease	d		10 09						11 09						12 09						13 09		
Newhaven Town ⛴	d		10 13	10 33					11 13	11 33					12 13	12 33					13 13	13 33	
Newhaven Harbour	d		10 15	10 35					11 15	11 35					12 15	12 35					13 15	13 35	
Bishopstone	d		10 18	10 38					11 18	11 38					12 18	12 38					13 18	13 38	
Seaford	a		10 21	10 41					11 21	11 41					12 21	12 41					13 21	13 41	
Glynde	d						10 37						11 37						12 37				
Berwick	d						10 43						11 43						12 43				
Polegate	d	10 11					10 49	11 11					11 49	12 11					12 49	13 11			
Hampden Park 4	d					10 43	10 53					11 43	11 53					12 43	12 53				
Eastbourne 4	a	10 19				10 49	10 58	11 19				11 49	11 58	12 19				12 49	12 58	13 19			
	d	10 26			10 34		11 02	11 26			11 34		12 02	12 26			12 34		13 02	13 26			13 34
Hampden Park 4	d	10 30			10a38			11 30			11a38			12 30			12a38			13 30			13a38
Pevensey & Westham	d	10 35						11 35						12 35						13 35			
Pevensey Bay	d																						
Normans Bay	d																						
Cooden Beach	d	10 41						11 41						12 41						13 41			
Collington	d	10 44						11 44						12 44						13 44			
Bexhill 4	d	10 46					11 16	11 46					12 16	12 46					13 16	13 46			
St Leonards Warrior Sq 4	d	10 53					11 23	11 53					12 23	12 53					13 23	13 53			
Hastings 4	a	10 56					11 26	11 56					12 26	12 56					13 26	13 56			
	d	10 57					11 27	11 57					12 27	12 57					13 27	13 57			
Ore	d	11a00						12a00						13a00						14a00			
Three Oaks	d																						
Doleham	d																						
Winchelsea	d																						
Rye	a						11 44						12 44						13 44				
	d						11 46						12 46						13 46				
Appledore (Kent)	d						11 55						12 55						13 55				
Ham Street	d						12 00						13 00						14 00				
Ashford International	a						12 08						13 08						14 08				

A ✠ to Lewes

Table 189

Sundays from 16 September

London, Haywards Heath and Brighton - Lewes, Seaford, Eastbourne, Hastings and Ashford

Network Diagram - see first Page of Table 184

Station		SN ◇■		SN	SN ◇■ A ✠	SN	SN	SN	SN ◇■	SN	SN ◇■ A ✠	SN		SN	SN	SN ◇■	SN	SN ◇■ A ✠	SN	SN	SN	SN ◇■		SN	SN ◇■ A ✠
London Victoria ■ ⊖	d				12 47						13 47							14 47							15 47
Clapham Junction ■	d				12 53						13 53							14 53							15 53
London Bridge ■ ⊖	d																								
East Croydon	d				13 07						14 07							15 07							16 07
Gatwick Airport ■ ✈	d				13 29						14 29							15 29							16 29
Haywards Heath ■	d				13 41						14 41							15 41							16 41
Wivelsfield ■	d				13 45						14 45							15 45							16 45
Plumpton	d																								16 51
Cooksbridge	d																								
Brighton ■	d			13 20		13 39	14 09			14 20		14 39		15 09			15 20		15 39	16 09				16 20	
London Road (Brighton)	d					13 42	14 12					14 42		15 12					15 42	16 12					
Moulsecoomb	d					13 44	14 14					14 44		15 14					15 44	16 14					
Falmer	d					13 48	14 18					14 48		15 18					15 48	16 18					
Lewes ■	a			13 31	13 56	13 54	14 24			14 31	14 56	14 54		15 24			15 31	15 56	15 54	16 24				16 31	16 58
	d			13 32	13 59	14 03	14 25			14 32	14 59	15 03		15 25			15 32	15 59	16 03	16 25				16 32	16 59
Southease	d					14 09						15 09							16 09						
Newhaven Town ⛴	d					14 13	14 33					15 13		15 33					16 13	16 33					
Newhaven Harbour	d					14 15	14 35					15 15		15 35					16 15	16 35					
Bishopstone	d					14 18	14 38					15 18		15 38					16 18	16 38					
Seaford	a					14 21	14 41					15 21		15 41					16 21	16 41					
Glynde	d			13 37						14 37							15 37							16 37	
Berwick	d			13 43						14 43							15 43							16 43	
Polegate	d			13 49	14 11					14 49	15 11						15 49	16 11						16 49	17 11
Hampden Park ■	d	13 43		13 53					14 43	14 53						15 43	15 53					16 43		16 53	
Eastbourne ■	a	13 49		13 58	14 19				14 49	14 58	15 19					15 49	15 58	16 19				16 49		16 58	17 19
	d			14 02	14 26			14 34		15 02	15 26				15 34		16 02	16 26			16 34			17 02	17 26
Hampden Park ■	d				14 30			14a38			15 30				15a38			16 30			16a38				17 30
Pevensey & Westham	d				14 35						15 35							16 35							17 35
Pevensey Bay	d																								
Normans Bay	d																								
Cooden Beach	d				14 41						15 41							16 41							17 41
Collington	d				14 44						15 44							16 44							17 44
Bexhill ■	d			14 16	14 46					15 16	15 46						16 16	16 46						17 16	17 46
St Leonards Warrior Sq ■	d			14 23	14 53					15 23	15 53						16 23	16 53						17 23	17 53
Hastings ■	a			14 26	14 56					15 26	15 56						16 26	16 56						17 26	17 56
	d			14 27	14 57					15 27	15 57						16 27	16 57						17 27	17 57
Ore	d				15a00						16a00							17a00							18a00
Three Oaks	d																								
Doleham	d																								
Winchelsea	d																								
Rye	a			14 44						15 44							16 44							17 44	
	d			14 46						15 46							16 46							17 46	
Appledore (Kent)	d			14 55						15 55							16 55							17 55	
Ham Street	d			15 00						16 00							17 00							18 00	
Ashford International	a			15 08						16 08							17 08							18 08	

A ✠ to Lewes

Table 189

Sundays from 16 September

London, Haywards Heath and Brighton - Lewes, Seaford, Eastbourne, Hastings and Ashford

Network Diagram - see first Page of Table 184

Station		SN	SN	SN	SN ◇■	SN	SN ◇■ A ✠	SN		SN	SN	SN ◇■	SN	SN ◇■ A ✠	SN	SN	SN	SN ◇■		SN	SN ◇■ A ✠	SN	SN	SN	SN ◇■
London Victoria ■ ⊖	d						16 47							17 47							18 47				
Clapham Junction ■	d						16 53							17 53							18 53				
London Bridge ■ ⊖	d																								
East Croydon	d						17 07							18 07							19 07				
Gatwick Airport ■ ✈	d						17 29							18 29							19 29				
Haywards Heath ■	d						17 41							18 41							19 41				
Wivelsfield ■	d						17 45							18 45							19 45				
Plumpton	d						17 51							18 51							19 51				
Cooksbridge	d																								
Brighton ■	d	16 39	17 09			17 20		17 39		18 09			18 20		18 39	19 09				19 20		19 39	20 09		
London Road (Brighton)	d	16 42	17 12					17 42		18 12					18 42	19 12						19 42	20 12		
Moulsecoomb	d	16 44	17 14					17 44		18 14					18 44	19 14						19 44	20 14		
Falmer	d	16 48	17 18					17 48		18 18					18 48	19 18						19 48	20 18		
Lewes ■	a	16 54	17 24			17 31	17 58	17 54		18 24			18 31	18 58	18 54	19 24				19 31	19 58	19 54	20 24		
	d	17 03	17 25			17 32	17 59	18 03		18 25			18 32	18 59	19 03	19 25				19 32	19 59	20 03	20 25		
Southease	d	17 09						18 09							19 09							20 09			
Newhaven Town ⛴	d	17 13	17 33					18 13		18 33					19 13	19 33						20 13	20 33		
Newhaven Harbour	d	17 15	17 35					18 15		18 35					19 15	19 35						20 15	20 35		
Bishopstone	d	17 18	17 38					18 18		18 38					19 18	19 38						20 18	20 38		
Seaford	a	17 21	17 41					18 21		18 41					19 21	19 41						20 21	20 41		
Glynde	d					17 37							18 37							19 37					
Berwick	d					17 43							18 43							19 43					
Polegate	d					17 49	18 11						18 49	19 11						19 49	20 11				
Hampden Park ■	d				17 43	17 53						18 43	18 53					19 43		19 53					20 43
Eastbourne ■	a				17 49	17 58	18 19					18 49	18 58	19 19				19 49		19 58	20 19				20 49
	d			17 34		18 02	18 26				18 34		19 02	19 26			19 34			20 02	20 26			20 34	
Hampden Park ■	d			17a38			18 30				18a38			19 30			19a38				20 30			20a38	
Pevensey & Westham	d						18 35							19 35							20 35				
Pevensey Bay	d																								
Normans Bay	d																								
Cooden Beach	d						18 41							19 41							20 41				
Collington	d						18 44							19 44							20 44				
Bexhill ■	d					18 16	18 46						19 16	19 46						20 16	20 46				
St Leonards Warrior Sq ■	d					18 23	18 53						19 23	19 53						20 23	20 53				
Hastings ■	a					18 26	18 56						19 26	19 56						20 26	20 56				
	d					18 27	18 57						19 27	19 57						20 27	20 57				
Ore	d						19a00							20a00							21a00				
Three Oaks	d																								
Doleham	d																								
Winchelsea	d																								
Rye	a					18 44							19 44							20 44					
	d					18 46							19 46							20 46					
Appledore (Kent)	d					18 55							19 55							20 55					
Ham Street	d					19 00							20 00							21 00					
Ashford International	a					19 08							20 08							21 08					

A ✠ to Lewes

Table 189

Sundays from 16 September

London, Haywards Heath and Brighton - Lewes, Seaford, Eastbourne, Hastings and Ashford

Network Diagram - see first Page of Table 184

		SN	SN ◇1 A 🚌	SN	SN	SN	SN 1	SN	SN ◇1	SN	SN	SN	SN 1	SN	SN ◇1	SN	SN	SN 1	SN	SN	SN ◇1
London Victoria	d		19 47						20 47						21 47						22 47
Clapham Junction	d		19 53						20 53						21 53						22 53
London Bridge	d																				
East Croydon	d		20 07						21 07						22 07						23 07
Gatwick Airport	d		20 29						21 29						22 29						23 29
Haywards Heath	d		20 41						21 41						22 41						23 41
Wivelsfield	d		20 45						21 45						22 45						23 45
Plumpton	d		20 51						21 51						22 51						23 51
Cooksbridge	d																				
Brighton	d	20 20		20 39	21 09			21 20		21 39	22 09			22 20		22 39	23 09		23 20	23 39	
London Road (Brighton)	d			20 42	21 12					21 42	22 12					22 42	23 12			23 42	
Moulsecoomb	d			20 44	21 14					21 44	22 14					22 44	23 14			23 44	
Falmer	d			20 48	21 18					21 48	22 18					22 48	23 18			23 48	
Lewes	a	20 31	20 58	20 54	21 24			21 31	21 58	21 54	22 24			22 31	22 58	22 54	23 24		23 31	23 54	23 58
	d	20 32	20 59	21 03	21 25			21 32	21 59	22 03	22 25			22 32	22 59	23 03			23 32		23 59
Southease	d			21 09																	
Newhaven Town	d			21 13	21 33					22 11	22 33					23 11					
Newhaven Harbour	d			21 15	21 35					22 13	22 35					23 13					
Bishopstone	d			21 18	21 38					22 16	22 38					23 16					
Seaford	a			21 21	21 41					22 19	22 41					23 19					
Glynde	d	20 37						21 37						22 37					23 37		
Berwick	d	20 43						21 43						22 43					23 43		
Polegate	d	20 49	21 11					21 49	22 11					22 49	23 11				23 49		00 11
Hampden Park	d	20 53					21 43	21 53					22 43	22 53				23 47	23 53		00 15
Eastbourne	a	20 58	21 19				21 49	21 58	22 19				22 49	22 58	23 19			23 52	23 58		00 20
	d	21 02	21 26			21 34		22 02	22 26			22 34			23 26						
Hampden Park	d		21 30			21a38			22 30			22a38			23 30						
Pevensey & Westham	d		21 35						22 35						23 35						
Pevensey Bay	d																				
Normans Bay	d																				
Cooden Beach	d		21 41						22 41						23 41						
Collington	d		21 44						22 44						23 44						
Bexhill	d	21 16	21 46					22 16	22 46						23 46						
St Leonards Warrior Sq	d	21 23	21 53					22 23	22 53						23 53						
Hastings	a	21 26	21 56					22 26	22 56						23 56						
	d	21 27	21 57																		
Ore	d		22a00																		
Three Oaks	d																				
Doleham	d																				
Winchelsea	d																				
Rye	a	21 44																			
	d	21 46																			
Appledore (Kent)	d	21 55																			
Ham Street	d	22 00																			
Ashford International	a	22 08																			

A 🚌 to Lewes

Table 189

Mondays to Fridays

Ashford, Hastings, Eastbourne, Seaford and Lewes - Brighton, Haywards Heath and London

Network Diagram - see first Page of Table 184

Miles	Miles			SN MX 1	SN MX ◇1	SN MO ◇1 A	SN MX ◇1	SN ◇1	SN	SN	SN 1	SN 1	SN	SN 1	SN	SN	SN 1	SN	SN 1	SN ◇1 B 🚌	SN ◇1 B 🚌	SN 1	SN 1
—	0	**Ashford International**	d																				
—	5½	Ham Street	d																				
—	8½	Appledore (Kent)	d																				
—	15¼	Rye	a																				
—	—		d																				
—	17¼	Winchelsea	d																				
—	21½	Doleham	d																				
—	22¾	Three Oaks	d																				
—	25½	Ore	d																				
0	26½	**Hastings**	a																				
—	—		d	23p22							05 07	05 42						05 58		06 15			
0¾	—	**St Leonards Warrior Sq**	d	23p24							05 09	05 45						06 01		06 18			
4½	—	**Bexhill**	d	23p31							05 16	05 52						06 12		06 26			
5¼	—	Collington	d	23p33							05 18	05 54								06 28			
6¾	—	Cooden Beach	d	23p36							05 21	05 57								06 31			
8½	—	Normans Bay	d																				
10½	—	Pevensey Bay	d																				
11¼	—	Pevensey & Westham	d	23p42							05 27	06 03								06 37			
14¼	—	Hampden Park	d	23p47	00 11	00 15					05 32	06 08						06 24		06 42			07 02
16¼	—	**Eastbourne**	a	23p52	00 16	00 20	01 41				05 37	06 13						06 29		06 47			07 07
—	—		d	23p56				05 08		05 32	05 42			06 14			06 24	06 37	06 47	06 57		07 02	
18¼	—	Hampden Park	d	00 01				05 12		05 36	05 46			06a18			06 28		06 51	07 01		07a06	
20¼	—	Polegate	d	00 05				05 16		05 41	05 50						06 33	06 44	06 55	07 05			
24¼	—	Berwick	d								05 55						06 39		07 00				
29	—	Glynde	d														06 45		07 06				
—	0	**Seaford**	d						05 09				05 45			06 30					06 56		
—	1	Bishopstone	d						05 11				05 47			06 32					06 58		
—	2½	Newhaven Harbour	d						05 14				05 50			06 35					07 01		
—	2¾	Newhaven Town	d						05 16				05 52			06 37					07 03		
—	5½	Southease	d																		07 07		
32	9	**Lewes**	a	00 17				05 28	05 25	05 53	06 04		06 01			06 46	06 50	06 57	07 11	07 18	07 14		
—	—		d	00 18				05 29	05 32	05 54	06 05		06 09		06 26	06 47	06 51	06 59	07 12	07 22			
36½	—	Falmer	d	00 25					05 39	06 01			06 16		06 33	06 54		07 06	07 19				
38¼	—	Moulsecoomb	d	00 28					05 42	06 05			06 19		06 36	06 57		07 10	07 22				
39¼	—	London Road (Brighton)	d	00 30					05 44	06 07			06 21		06 38	06 59		07 12	07 24				
40	—	**Brighton**	a	00 34					05 48	06 11			06 25		06 42	07 03		07 16	07 28				
—	11¼	Cooksbridge	d														06 56			07 27			
—	14½	Plumpton	d					05 37			06 13						07 01			07 32			
—	18¼	Wivelsfield	a														07 07			07 39			
—	21¼	**Haywards Heath**	a					05 46			06 23						07 12			07 44			
—	—	**Gatwick Airport**	a					05 58			06 41						07 29						
—	—	East Croydon	a					06 14			06 58						07 45			08 13			
—	—	**London Bridge**	a								07 14						08 01						
—	—	Clapham Junction	a					06 25												08 23			
—	—	**London Victoria**	a					06 32												08 32			

A from 21 May

B 🚌 from Lewes

Table 189

Mondays to Fridays

Ashford, Hastings, Eastbourne, Seaford and Lewes - Brighton, Haywards Heath and London

Network Diagram - see first Page of Table 184

		SN	SN	SN ■	SN ◇■	SN	SN	SN ◇■ A ⊼	SN ◇■	SN	SN	SN	SN	SN ◇■ A ⊼	SN ■	SN ■	SN ◇■	SN ◇■ A ⊼	SN ◇■ A ⊼	SN ■	SN ■	SN	SN
Ashford International	d										06 13	06 38											
Ham Street	d										06 22	06 47											
Appledore (Kent)	d										06 27	06 52											
Rye	a										06 36	07 01											
	d										06 36												
Winchelsea	d										06 40												
Doleham	d										06 46												
Three Oaks	d										06 50												
Ore	d										06 55												
Hastings ■	a										06 58												
	d							06 49			07 12			07 20				07 38					
St Leonards Warrior Sq ■	d							06 52			07 15			07 23				07 40					
Bexhill ■	d							06 59			07 22			07 31				07 47					
Collington	d							07 01						07 33				07 49					
Cooden Beach	d							07 04						07 36				07 52					
Normans Bay	d																	07 55					
Pevensey Bay	d																	07 59					
Pevensey & Westham	d							07 10						07 42				08 01					
Hampden Park ■	d				07 11			07 15						07 46	07 51		08 09	08 06		08 29	08 39		
Eastbourne ■	a				07 16			07 20			07 37			07 51	07 56		08 14	08 11		08 34	08 44		
	d			07 14	07 21			07 32	07 38		07 47			07 57		08 04	08 21	08 18		08 40			
Hampden Park ■	d			07 19	07a25				07a42					08 01		08 08	08a25			08a44			
Polegate	d			07 23				07 39			07 54			08 05		08 12		08 25					
Berwick	d			07 29				07 44						08 11		08 18		08 30					
Glynde	d			07 35										08 16		08 23		08 36					
Seaford	d		07 16				07 33						07 59						08 21				
Bishopstone	d		07 18				07 35						08 01						08 23				
Newhaven Harbour	d		07 21				07 38						08 04						08 26				
Newhaven Town	d		07 23				07 40			07 49			08 06						08 28				
Southease	d		07 27				07 44						08 10						08 32				
Lewes ■	a		07 33	07 41			07 50	07 53		07 57	08 07		08 17	08 22		08 29		08 42	08 39				
	d	07 23	07 34	07 42		07 45	07 51	07 55		07 58	08 07		08 19	08 23		08 30		08 48				08 46	08 58
Falmer	d	07 30	07 41			07 52	07 58			08 05			08 26			08 37						08 53	09 05
Moulsecoomb	d	07 33	07 44			07 55	08 01			08 08			08 29			08 40						08 56	09 08
London Road (Brighton)	d	07 35	07 46			07 57	08 03			08 10			08 32			08 42						08 58	09 10
Brighton ■	a	07 39	07 50			08 01	08 07			08 14	08 20		08 35			08 46						09 02	09 14
Cooksbridge	d			07 48				08 00						08 28									
Plumpton	d			07 53				08 05						08 33									
Wivelsfield ■	a							08 11						08 39				09 00					
Haywards Heath ■	a			08 03				08 16						08 44				09 05					
Gatwick Airport ■	a													08 56				09 22					
East Croydon	a			08 31				08 46						09 14				09 38					
London Bridge ■	a			08 52																			
Clapham Junction ■	a							09 00						09 23				09 48					
London Victoria ■	a							09 09						09 32				09 58					

A ⊼ from Lewes

Table 189

Mondays to Fridays

Ashford, Hastings, Eastbourne, Seaford and Lewes - Brighton, Haywards Heath and London

Network Diagram - see first Page of Table 184

		SN A	SN B	SN	SN	SN ◇■ C ⊼	SN ■	SN ◇■	SN	SN ◇■ C ⊼	SN ■	SN ◇■	SN	SN	SN	SN ◇■	SN ■	SN	SN ◇■	SN	SN ◇■	SN ■
Ashford International	d	07 17	07 17	07 39										08 32				08 52				
Ham Street	d	07 26	07 26	07 48										08 41				09 01				
Appledore (Kent)	d	07 31	07 31	07 53										08 46				09 06				
Rye	a	07 40	07 40	08 02										08 55				09 15				
	d	07 45	07 45											08 55				09 16				
Winchelsea	d	07 48	07 48															09 19				
Doleham	d	07 55	07 55															09 26				
Three Oaks	d	07 58	07 58											09 06				09 29				
Ore	d	08 04	08 04				08 22			08 47							09 20	09 35			09 50	
Hastings ■	a	08 07	08 07				08 25			08 50				09 13			09 23	09 38			09 53	
	d	08 09	08 10				08 26			08 52				09 14			09 24				09 55	
St Leonards Warrior Sq ■	d	08 12	08 13				08 28			08 54				09 17			09 26				09 57	
Bexhill ■	d	08 22	08 22				08 35			09 01				09 24			09 35				10 04	
Collington	d						08 37			09 03							09 37				10 06	
Cooden Beach	d						08 40			09 06							09 40				10 09	
Normans Bay	d						08 43										09 43					
Pevensey Bay	d																					
Pevensey & Westham	d						08 48			09 13							09 48				10 15	
Hampden Park ■	d						08 52	09 07		09 17	09 29	09 42					09 52				10 20	10 29
Eastbourne ■	a	08 37	08 37				08 57	09 12		09 22	09 34	09 47		09 39			09 58				10 25	10 34
	d	08 45	08 45			08 56	09 04	09 19		09 28	09 40			09 47		09 55	10 04		10 20		10 31	10 40
Hampden Park ■	d					09 00	09 08	09a23			09a44					09 59	10 08		10a24			10a44
Polegate	d	08 52	08 52			09 04	09 12			09 35				09 54		10 03	10 12				10 37	
Berwick	d						09 18									10 09	10 18					
Glynde	d						09 23										10 23					
Seaford	d				08 57				09 25						09 58					10 25		
Bishopstone	d				08 59				09 27						10 00					10 27		
Newhaven Harbour	d				09 02				09 30						10 03					10 30		
Newhaven Town	d				09 04				09 32						10 05					10 32		
Southease	d								09 36											10 36		
Lewes ■	a	09 07	09 07		09 13	09 16	09 29		09 44	09 47				10 07	10 14	10 18	10 29			10 44	10 49	
	d	09 07	09 07		09 14	09 18	09 29		09 44	09 48			09 58	10 07	10 14	10 19	10 29			10 44	10 50	
Falmer	d				09 21		09 36		09 51				10 05		10 21		10 36			10 51		
Moulsecoomb	d				09 24		09 39		09 54				10 08		10 24		10 39			10 54		
London Road (Brighton)	d				09 27		09 42		09 57				10 10		10 27		10 42			10 57		
Brighton ■	a	09 20	09 20		09 30		09 45		10 00				10 14	10 20	10 30		10 45			11 00		
Cooksbridge	d					09 23				09 53						10 24						
Plumpton	d					09 28				09 58						10 29						
Wivelsfield ■	a					09 34										10 35						
Haywards Heath ■	a					09 38				10 07						10 40					11 05	
Gatwick Airport ■	a					09 56				10 25						10 55					11 24	
East Croydon	a					10 11				10 41						11 11					11 40	
London Bridge ■	a																					
Clapham Junction ■	a					10 21				10 51						11 21					11 50	
London Victoria ■	a					10 28				10 58						11 28					11 57	

A from 21 May

B until 18 May

C ⊼ from Lewes

Ashford, Hastings, Eastbourne, Seaford and Lewes - Brighton, Haywards Heath and London

Network Diagram - see first Page of Table 184

Station		SN ◇■	SN	SN	SN	SN ◇■	SN ■	SN ◇■	SN	SN ◇■	SN ■	SN ◇■	SN	SN	SN	SN ◇■	SN ■	SN ◇■	SN	SN ◇■	SN ■	SN ◇■	SN
Ashford International	d			09 32										10 32									
Ham Street	d			09 41										10 41									
Appledore (Kent)	d			09 46										10 46									
Rye	a			09 55										10 55									
	d			09 55										10 55									
Winchelsea	d			09 59																			
Doleham	d																						
Three Oaks	d													11 06									
Ore	d						10 22			10 50							11 22			11 50			
Hastings	a			10 13			10 25			10 53				11 13			11 25			11 53			
	d			10 14			10 26			10 55				11 14			11 26			11 55			
St Leonards Warrior Sq	d			10 17			10 28			10 57				11 17			11 28			11 57			
Bexhill	d			10 24			10 35			11 04				11 24			11 35			12 04			
Collington	d						10 37			11 06							11 37			12 06			
Cooden Beach	d						10 40			11 09							11 40			12 09			
Normans Bay	d						10 43										11 43						
Pevensey Bay	d																						
Pevensey & Westham	d						10 48			11 15							11 48			12 15			
Hampden Park	d	10 39					10 52			11 20	11 29	11 39					11 52			12 20	12 29	12 39	
Eastbourne	a	10 44		10 39			10 57			11 25	11 34	11 44		11 39			11 57			12 25	12 34	12 44	
	d			10 47		10 58	11 04	11 19		11 31	11 40			11 47		11 58	12 04	12 19		12 31	12 40		
Hampden Park	d					11 02	11 08	11a23			11a44					12 02	12 08	12a23			12a44		
Polegate	d			10 54		11 06	11 12			11 37				11 54		12 06	12 12			12 37			
Berwick	d						11 18										12 18						
Glynde	d						11 23										12 23						
Seaford	d				10 58				11 25						11 58				12 25				
Bishopstone	d				11 00				11 27						12 00				12 27				
Newhaven Harbour	d				11 03				11 30						12 03				12 30				
Newhaven Town	d				11 05				11 32						12 05				12 32				
Southease	d								11 36										12 36				
Lewes	a			11 07	11 14	11 19	11 29		11 44	11 49				12 07	12 14	12 19	12 29		12 44	12 49			
	d		10 58	11 07	11 14	11 20	11 29		11 44	11 50			11 58	12 07	12 14	12 20	12 29		12 44	12 50			12 58
Falmer	d		11 05		11 21		11 36		11 51				12 05		12 21		12 36		12 51				13 05
Moulsecoomb	d		11 08		11 24		11 39		11 54				12 08		12 24		12 39		12 54				13 08
London Road (Brighton)	d		11 10		11 27		11 42		11 57				12 10		12 27		12 42		12 57				13 10
Brighton	a		11 14	11 20	11 30		11 45		12 00				12 14	12 20	12 30		12 45		13 00				13 14
Cooksbridge	d																						
Plumpton	d					11 28										12 28							
Wivelsfield	a					11 35										12 35							
Haywards Heath	a					11 40				12 05						12 40				13 05			
Gatwick Airport	a					11 55				12 24						12 55				13 24			
East Croydon	a					12 11				12 40						13 11				13 40			
London Bridge	a																						
Clapham Junction	a					12 21				12 50						13 21				13 50			
London Victoria	a					12 28				12 57						13 28				13 57			

Ashford, Hastings, Eastbourne, Seaford and Lewes - Brighton, Haywards Heath and London

Network Diagram - see first Page of Table 184

Station		SN	SN	SN ◇■	SN ■	SN ◇■	SN	SN ◇■	SN ■	SN ◇■	SN	SN	SN	SN ◇■	SN ■	SN ◇■	SN	SN ◇■ A ✕	SN ■	SN ◇■	SN	SN	SN
Ashford International	d	11 32										12 32										13 32	
Ham Street	d	11 41										12 41										13 41	
Appledore (Kent)	d	11 46										12 46										13 46	
Rye	a	11 55										12 55										13 55	
	d	11 55										12 55										13 55	
Winchelsea	d	11 59																				13 59	
Doleham	d																						
Three Oaks	d											13 06											
Ore	d				12 22			12 50							13 22			13 50					
Hastings	a	12 13			12 25			12 53				13 13			13 25			13 53				14 13	
	d	12 14			12 26			12 55				13 14			13 26			13 55				14 14	
St Leonards Warrior Sq	d	12 17			12 28			12 57				13 17			13 28			13 57				14 17	
Bexhill	d	12 24			12 35			13 04				13 24			13 35			14 04				14 24	
Collington	d				12 37			13 06							13 37			14 06					
Cooden Beach	d				12 40			13 09							13 40			14 09					
Normans Bay	d				12 43										13 43								
Pevensey Bay	d																						
Pevensey & Westham	d				12 48			13 15							13 48			14 15					
Hampden Park	d				12 52			13 20	13 29	13 39					13 52			14 20	14 29	14 39			
Eastbourne	a	12 39			12 57			13 25	13 34	13 44		13 39			13 57			14 25	14 34	14 44		14 39	
	d	12 47		12 58	13 04	13 19		13 31	13 40			13 47		13 58	14 04	14 19		14 31	14 40			14 47	
Hampden Park	d			13 02	13 08	13a23			13a44					14 02	14 08	14a23			14a44				
Polegate	d	12 54		13 06	13 12			13 37				13 54		14 06	14 12			14 37				14 54	
Berwick	d				13 18										14 18								
Glynde	d				13 23										14 23								
Seaford	d		12 58				13 25						13 58				14 25						14 58
Bishopstone	d		13 00				13 27						14 00				14 27						15 00
Newhaven Harbour	d		13 03				13 30						14 03				14 30						15 03
Newhaven Town	d		13 05				13 32						14 05				14 32						15 05
Southease	d						13 36										14 36						
Lewes	a	13 07	13 14	13 19	13 29		13 44	13 49				14 07	14 14	14 19	14 29		14 44	14 49				15 07	15 14
	d	13 07	13 14	13 20	13 29		13 44	13 50			13 58	14 07	14 14	14 20	14 29		14 44	14 50			14 58	15 07	15 14
Falmer	d		13 21		13 36		13 51				14 05		14 21		14 36		14 51				15 05		15 21
Moulsecoomb	d		13 24		13 39		13 54				14 08		14 24		14 39		14 54				15 08		15 24
London Road (Brighton)	d		13 27		13 42		13 57				14 10		14 27		14 42		14 57				15 10		15 27
Brighton	a	13 20	13 30		13 45		14 00				14 14	14 20	14 30		14 45		15 00				15 14	15 20	15 30
Cooksbridge	d																						
Plumpton	d			13 28										14 28									
Wivelsfield	a			13 35										14 35									
Haywards Heath	a			13 40				14 05						14 40				15 05					
Gatwick Airport	a			13 55				14 24						14 55				15 24					
East Croydon	a			14 11				14 40						15 11				15 40					
London Bridge	a																						
Clapham Junction	a			14 21				14 50						15 21				15 50					
London Victoria	a			14 28				14 57						15 28				15 57					

A ✕ from Lewes

Table 189

Mondays to Fridays

Ashford, Hastings, Eastbourne, Seaford and Lewes - Brighton, Haywards Heath and London

Network Diagram - see first Page of Table 184

		SN ◇1 A		SN 1	SN ◇1	SN	SN ◇1 A	SN 1	SN ◇1	SN	SN	SN		SN ◇1 A	SN 1	SN ◇1	SN	SN ◇1 A	SN 1	SN ◇1	SN	SN		SN	SN ◇1 A
Ashford International	d										14 32											15 32			
Ham Street	d										14 41											15 41			
Appledore (Kent)	d										14 46											15 46			
Rye	a										14 55											15 55			
	d										14 55											15 55			
Winchelsea	d																					15 59			
Doleham	d																								
Three Oaks	d										15 06														
Ore	d			14 22			14 50								15 20			15 48							
Hastings 4	a			14 25			14 53				15 13				15 23			15 51				16 13			
	d			14 26			14 55				15 14				15 24			15 52				16 14			
St Leonards Warrior Sq 4	d			14 28			14 57				15 17				15 26			15 54				16 17			
Bexhill 4	d			14 35			15 04				15 24				15 33			16 01				16 24			
Collington	d			14 37			15 06								15 35			16 03							
Cooden Beach	d			14 40			15 09								15 38			16 06							
Normans Bay	d			14 43											15 41			16 09							
Pevensey Bay	d														15 45			16 13							
Pevensey & Westham	d			14 48			15 15								15 47			16 15							
Hampden Park 4	d			14 52			15 20	15 29	15 39						15 52			16 20	16 29	16 39					
Eastbourne 4	a			14 57			15 25	15 34	15 44		15 39				15 57			16 25	16 34	16 44		16 39			
	d	14 58		15 04	15 19		15 31	15 40			15 47			15 58	16 04	16 19		16 31	16 40			16 45			16 58
Hampden Park 4	d	15 02		15 08	15a23			15a44						16 02	16 08	16a23			16a44			16 49			17 02
Polegate	d	15 06		15 12			15 37				15 54			16 06	16 12			16 37				16 54			17 06
Berwick	d			15 18											16 18										
Glynde	d			15 23											16 23										
Seaford	d					15 25						15 58					16 25							16 58	
Bishopstone	d					15 27						16 00					16 27							17 00	
Newhaven Harbour	d					15 30						16 03					16 30							17 03	
Newhaven Town	d					15 32						16 05					16 32							17 05	
Southease	d					15 36											16 36								
Lewes 4	a	15 18		15 29		15 44	15 49				16 07	16 14		16 18	16 29		16 44	16 49				17 07		17 14	17 18
	d	15 19		15 29		15 44	15 50			15 58	16 07	16 14		16 20	16 29		16 44	16 50			16 58	17 07		17 14	17 19
Falmer	d			15 36		15 51				16 05		16 21			16 36		16 51				17 05			17 21	
Moulsecoomb	d			15 39		15 54				16 08		16 24			16 39		16 54				17 08			17 24	
London Road (Brighton)	d			15 42		15 57				16 10		16 27			16 42		16 57				17 10			17 27	
Brighton 10	a			15 45		16 00				16 14	16 20	16 30			16 45		17 00				17 14	17 20		17 30	
Cooksbridge	d	15 24												16 25											17 24
Plumpton	d	15 29												16 30											17 29
Wivelsfield 4	a	15 35												16 38											17 35
Haywards Heath 3	a	15 40					16 05							16 42				17 06							17 39
Gatwick Airport 10 ✈	a	15 55					16 25							16 57				17 25							17 54
East Croydon	a	16 11					16 40							17 13				17 41							18 11
London Bridge 4 ⊖	a																								
Clapham Junction 10	a	16 21					16 50							17 22				17 50							18 21
London Victoria 15 ⊖	a	16 28					16 58							17 29				17 58							18 29

A 🛒 from Lewes

Table 189

Mondays to Fridays

Ashford, Hastings, Eastbourne, Seaford and Lewes - Brighton, Haywards Heath and London

Network Diagram - see first Page of Table 184

		SN 1	SN ◇1	SN	SN ◇1 A	SN 1	SN	SN		SN ◇1	SN	SN ◇1 A	SN 1	SN	SN ◇1	SN	SN ◇1	SN 1		SN	SN	SN	SN 1	SN	SN ◇1
Ashford International	d							16 32													17 32	17 58			
Ham Street	d							16 41													17 41	18 07			
Appledore (Kent)	d							16 46													17 46	18 12			
Rye	a							16 55													17 55	18 21			
	d							16 55													17 55				
Winchelsea	d																				17 59				
Doleham	d																								
Three Oaks	d							17 06																	
Ore	d	16 22			16 50								17 22				17 50								
Hastings 4	a	16 25			16 53			17 13					17 25				17 53				18 13				
	d	16 26			16 55			17 14					17 26				17 55				18 14				
St Leonards Warrior Sq 4	d	16 28			16 57			17 17					17 28				17 57				18 17				
Bexhill 4	d	16 35			17 04			17 24					17 35				18 04				18 24				
Collington	d	16 37			17 06								17 37				18 06								
Cooden Beach	d	16 40			17 09								17 40				18 09								
Normans Bay	d	16 43											17 43												
Pevensey Bay	d																								
Pevensey & Westham	d	16 48			17 15								17 48				18 15								
Hampden Park 4	d	16 52			17 20	17 29				17 40			17 52	17 55	18 13		18 20	18 28					18 42		
Eastbourne 4	a	16 57			17 25	17 34		17 39		17 48			17 57	18 00	18 18		18 25	18 34			18 39		18 49		
	d	17 04	17 21		17 31	17 40		17 45				17 57	18 01		18 25		18 31	18 43			18 47				18 58
Hampden Park 4	d	17 08	17a25			17a44						18 01	18 05		18a29			18a47							19 02
Polegate	d	17 12			17 37			17 52				18 05	18 11				18 37				18 54				19 06
Berwick	d	17 18											18 17												
Glynde	d	17 23											18 22												
Seaford	d			17 25							17 58					18 26				18 44				19 02	
Bishopstone	d			17 27							18 00					18 28				18 46				19 04	
Newhaven Harbour	d			17 30							18 03					18 31									
Newhaven Town	d			17 32							18 05					18 33				18 50				19 08	
Southease	d			17 36												18 37									
Lewes 4	a	17 29		17 44	17 49			18 04			18 14	18 17	18 28			18 44	18 49			18 59	19 07			19 17	19 20
	d	17 29		17 44	17 50		17 55	18 07			18 14	18 18	18 28			18 44	18 50			18 59	19 07			19 18	19 21
Falmer	d	17 36		17 51			18 02				18 21		18 35			18 51				19 06				19 25	
Moulsecoomb	d	17 39		17 54			18 05				18 24		18 38			18 54				19 09				19 28	
London Road (Brighton)	d	17 42		17 57			18 07				18 27		18 41			18 57				19 12				19 30	
Brighton 10	a	17 45		18 00			18 11	18 20			18 30		18 44			19 00				19 15	19 21			19 34	
Cooksbridge	d											18 23													19 26
Plumpton	d											18 28					18 58								19 31
Wivelsfield 4	a											18 34					19 06								
Haywards Heath 3	a				18 07							18 38					19 10								19 40
Gatwick Airport 10 ✈	a				18 26							18 56					19 25								19 55
East Croydon	a				18 42							19 12					19 43								20 11
London Bridge 4 ⊖	a																								
Clapham Junction 10	a				18 52							19 21					19 52								20 20
London Victoria 15 ⊖	a				18 59							19 29					19 59								20 28

A 🛒 from Lewes

Ashford, Hastings, Eastbourne, Seaford and Lewes - Brighton, Haywards Heath and London

Network Diagram - see first Page of Table 184

		SN 1	SN ◇1	SN	SN ◇1	SN ◇1	SN	SN	SN	SN 1	SN	SN 1	SN ◇1	SN ◇1	SN	SN 1	SN	SN ◇1	SN	SN 1	SN	SN ◇1
Ashford International	d							18 32	18 58								19 32				19 58	
Ham Street	d							18 41	19 07								19 41				20 07	
Appledore (Kent)	d							18 46	19 12								19 46				20 12	
Rye	a							18 55	19 21								19 55				20 21	
	d							18 55									19 55				20 22	
Winchelsea	d																19 59					
Doleham	d																					
Three Oaks	d							19 06														
Ore	d	18 22			18 50									19 50						20 22		
Hastings 4	a	18 25			18 53			19 13						19 54			20 13			20 25		
	d	18 26			18 55			19 14				19 27		19 55			20 14			20 26	20 39	
St Leonards Warrior Sq 4	d	18 28			18 57			19 17				19 30		19 57			20 17			20 28		
Bexhill 4	d	18 35			19 04			19 24				19 37		20 04			20 24			20 35		
Collington	d	18 37			19 06							19 39		20 06						20 37		
Cooden Beach	d	18 40			19 09							19 42		20 09						20 40		
Normans Bay	d	18 43																				
Pevensey Bay	d																					
Pevensey & Westham	d	18 48			19 15							19 48		20 15						20 46		
Hampden Park 4	d	18 52	18 55		19 20	19 36				19 50		19 52		20 20		20 29		20 43		20 51		
Eastbourne 4	a	18 57	19 01		19 25	19 41		19 44		19 56		19 57		20 25		20 34	20 39	20 48		20 56		
	d	19 04	19 19		19 31	19 51		19 48				20 03	20 19	20 31			20 45			21 04		21 21
Hampden Park 4	d	19 08	19a23			19a55						20 07	20a23							21 08		21a25
Polegate	d	19 12			19 37			19 55				20 11		20 37			20 52			21 12		
Berwick	d	19 18										20 17								21 18		
Glynde	d	19 23										20 22								21 23		
Seaford	d			19 19			19 37				19 58				20 28				20 58			
Bishopstone	d			19 21			19 39				20 00				20 30				21 00			
Newhaven Harbour	d			19 24			19 42				20 03				20 33				21 03			
Newhaven Town	d			19 26			19 44				20 05				20 35				21 05			
Southease	d						19 48								20 39							
Lewes 4	a	19 29		19 35	19 49		19 55	20 07			20 14	20 28		20 49	20 46		21 07		21 14	21 29		
	d	19 29		19 38	19 50		19 57	20 08			20 14	20 28		20 50	20 53		21 07		21 14	21 29		
Falmer	d	19 36		19 45			20 04				20 21	20 35			21 00				21 21	21 36		
Moulsecoomb	d	19 39		19 48			20 07				20 24	20 38			21 03				21 24	21 39		
London Road (Brighton)	d	19 42		19 50			20 09				20 27	20 41			21 05				21 27	21 42		
Brighton 10	a	19 45		19 55			20 13	20 20			20 33	20 44			21 09		21 20		21 33	21 45		
Cooksbridge	d																					
Plumpton	d													20 58								
Wivelsfield 4	a				20 05									21 05								
Haywards Heath 3	a				20 10									21 09								
Gatwick Airport 10 ✈	a				20 25									21 25								
East Croydon	a				20 41									21 41								
London Bridge 4 ⊖	a																					
Clapham Junction 10	a				20 50									21 51								
London Victoria 15 ⊖	a				20 59									21 58								

Ashford, Hastings, Eastbourne, Seaford and Lewes - Brighton, Haywards Heath and London

Network Diagram - see first Page of Table 184

		SN ◇1 A ✠	SN	SN	SN ◇1	SN	SN 1	SN ◇1	SN	SN ◇1	SN	SN ◇1	SN	SN 1	SN	SN ◇1	SN	SN 1	SN 1
Ashford International	d			20 32							21 32				22 32				
Ham Street	d			20 41							21 41				22 41				
Appledore (Kent)	d			20 46							21 46				22 46				
Rye	a			20 55							21 55				22 55				
	d			20 55							21 57				22 55				
Winchelsea	d										22 00				22 58				
Doleham	d														23 05				
Three Oaks	d			21 06											23 08				
Ore	d	20 50						21 22						22 22	23 14				
Hastings 4	a	20 53		21 13				21 25			22 14			22 25	23 17				
	d	20 55		21 14				21 30			22 15			22 26					23 22
St Leonards Warrior Sq 4	d	20 57		21 17				21 32			22 18			22 29					23 24
Bexhill 4	d	21 04		21 24				21 39			22 25			22 38					23 31
Collington	d	21 06						21 41						22 40					23 33
Cooden Beach	d	21 09						21 44						22 43					23 36
Normans Bay	d													22 46					
Pevensey Bay	d																		
Pevensey & Westham	d	21 15						21 50						22 51					23 42
Hampden Park 4	d	21 20			21 43			21 55				22 43		22 55		23 10		23 42	23 47
Eastbourne 4	a	21 25		21 39	21 48			22 00			22 40	22 48		23 00		23 15		23 47	23 52
	d	21 31		21 45			22 04	22 15		22 21	22 45			23 05		23 20			23 56
Hampden Park 4	d						22 08	22 19		22a25				23 09		23a24			00 01
Polegate	d	21 37		21 52			22 12	22 23			22 52			23 13					00 05
Berwick	d						22 18	22 29						23 18					
Glynde	d						22 23							23 24					
Seaford	d		21 28			21 58			22 20				22 58				23 25		
Bishopstone	d		21 30			22 00			22 22				23 00				23 27		
Newhaven Harbour	d		21 33			22 03			22 25				23 03				23 30		
Newhaven Town	d		21 35			22 05			22 27				23 05				23 32		
Southease	d																		
Lewes 4	a	21 49	21 44	22 07		22 14	22 29	22 38	22 35		23 07		23 14	23 29			23 40		00 17
	d	21 50	21 53	22 07		22 14	22 29	22 40	22 42		23 07		23 14	23 30			23 40		00 18
Falmer	d		22 00			22 21	22 36		22 49				23 21	23 37			23 47		00 25
Moulsecoomb	d		22 03			22 24	22 39		22 52				23 24	23 40			23 50		00 28
London Road (Brighton)	d		22 05			22 27	22 42		22 54				23 27	23 42			23 53		00 30
Brighton 10	a		22 09	22 20		22 31	22 45		22 58		23 20		23 31	23 46			23 56		00 34
Cooksbridge	d																		
Plumpton	d							22 48											
Wivelsfield 4	a	22 02						22 54											
Haywards Heath 3	a	22 06						22 58											
Gatwick Airport 10 ✈	a	22 25						23 12											
East Croydon	a	22 41						23 30											
London Bridge 4 ⊖	a																		
Clapham Junction 10	a	22 50						23 42											
London Victoria 15 ⊖	a	22 57						23 52											

A ✠ from Lewes

Table 189

Saturdays

Ashford, Hastings, Eastbourne, Seaford and Lewes - Brighton, Haywards Heath and London

Network Diagram - see first Page of Table 184

		SN ■	SN ◇■	SN ◇■	SN ■	SN	SN	SN ◇■	SN	SN ◇■	SN	SN	SN ◇■	SN ■	SN ■	SN	SN ◇■	SN ■	SN	SN	SN	SN ◇■	SN ■
Ashford International	d																			06 13			
Ham Street	d																			06 22			
Appledore (Kent)	d																			06 27			
Rye	a																			06 36			
	d																			06 51			
Winchelsea	d																			06 54			
Doleham	d																			07 01			
Three Oaks	d																			07 04			
Ore	d													06 22			06 50			07 10			07 22
Hastings ■	a													06 25			06 53			07 13			07 25
	d	23p22												06 26			06 55			07 14			07 26
St Leonards Warrior Sq ■	d	23p24												06 28			06 57			07 17			07 28
Bexhill ■	d	23p31												06 35			07 04			07 24			07 35
Collington	d	23p33												06 37			07 06						07 37
Cooden Beach	d	23p36												06 40			07 09						07 40
Normans Bay	d													06 43									07 43
Pevensey Bay	d																						
Pevensey & Westham	d	23p42												06 48			07 15						07 48
Hampden Park ■	d	23p47	00 11											06 52	07 11		07 20	07 29					07 52
Eastbourne ■	a	23p52	00 16	01 41										06 57	07 17		07 25	07 34		07 39			07 57
	d	23p56			05 03		05 48	06 18		06 24	06 38		06 58	07 04	07 21		07 31	07 40		07 47		07 58	08 04
Hampden Park ■	d	00 01			05 07		05 52	06a22		06 28			07 02	07 08	07a25			07a44				08 02	08 08
Polegate	d	00 05			05 11		05 57			06 32	06 45		07 06	07 12			07 37			07 54		08 06	08 12
Berwick	d									06 38				07 18									08 18
Glynde	d									06 43				07 23									08 23
Seaford	d					05 05			06 28			06 58				07 28					07 58		
Bishopstone	d					05 07			06 30			07 00				07 30					08 00		
Newhaven Harbour	d					05 10			06 33			07 03				07 33					08 03		
Newhaven Town ⛴	d					05 12			06 35			07 05				07 35					08 05		
Southease	d																						
Lewes ■	a	00 17			05 24	05 21	06 10		06 44	06 49	06 57	07 14	07 18	07 29		07 44	07 49			08 07	08 14	08 18	08 29
	d	00 18			05 26	05 28	06 10		06 44	06 50	06 58	07 14	07 20	07 29		07 44	07 50		07 58	08 07	08 14	08 20	08 29
Falmer	d	00 25				05 35	06 18		06 51		07 05	07 21		07 36		07 51			08 05		08 21		08 36
Moulsecoomb	d	00 28				05 38	06 21		06 54		07 09	07 24		07 39		07 54			08 08		08 24		08 39
London Road (Brighton)	d	00 30				05 40	06 24		06 57		07 11	07 27		07 42		07 57			08 10		08 27		08 42
Brighton ■	a	00 34				05 44	06 27		07 00		07 15	07 30		07 45		08 00			08 14	08 20	08 30		08 45
Cooksbridge	d																						
Plumpton	d												07 28									08 28	
Wivelsfield ■	a												07 35									08 35	
Haywards Heath ■	a				05 41					07 05			07 40				08 05					08 40	
Gatwick Airport ■ ✈	a				06 03					07 25			07 55				08 24					08 55	
East Croydon	a									07 41			08 11				08 40					09 11	
London Bridge ■ ⊖	a																						
Clapham Junction ■	a									07 51			08 21				08 50					09 21	
London Victoria ■ ⊖	a									07 58			08 28				08 57					09 28	

Table 189

Saturdays

Ashford, Hastings, Eastbourne, Seaford and Lewes - Brighton, Haywards Heath and London

Network Diagram - see first Page of Table 184

		SN ■	SN A	SN	SN ◇■	SN ■	SN	SN	SN	SN ◇■	SN ■	SN ◇■	SN	SN ◇■	SN ■	SN ◇■	SN	SN	SN	SN ◇■	SN ■	SN ◇■	SN
Ashford International	d							07 32										08 32					
Ham Street	d							07 41										08 41					
Appledore (Kent)	d							07 46										08 46					
Rye	a							07 55										08 55					
	d							07 55										08 55					
Winchelsea	d							07 59															
Doleham	d																						
Three Oaks	d																	09 06					
Ore	d				07 50						08 22			08 50							09 22		
Hastings ■	a				07 53			08 13			08 25			08 53				09 13			09 25		
	d				07 55			08 14			08 26			08 55				09 14			09 26		
St Leonards Warrior Sq ■	d				07 57			08 17			08 28			08 57				09 17			09 28		
Bexhill ■	d				08 04			08 24			08 35			09 04				09 24			09 35		
Collington	d				08 06						08 37			09 06							09 37		
Cooden Beach	d				08 09						08 40			09 09							09 40		
Normans Bay	d										08 43										09 43		
Pevensey Bay	d																						
Pevensey & Westham	d				08 15						08 48			09 15							09 48		
Hampden Park ■	d				08 20	08 29					08 52			09 20	09 29	09 39					09 52		
Eastbourne ■	a				08 25	08 34		08 39			08 57			09 25	09 34	09 44		09 39			09 57		
	d	08 18	08 22		08 31	08 40		08 47		08 58	09 04	09 19		09 31	09 40			09 47		09 58	10 04	10 19	
Hampden Park ■	d	08a22				08a44				09 02	09 08	09a23			09a44					10 02	10 08	10a23	
Polegate	d				08 37			08 54		09 06	09 12			09 37				09 54		10 06	10 12		
Berwick	d										09 18										10 18		
Glynde	d										09 23										10 23		
Seaford	d			08 25					08 58				09 25						09 58				10 25
Bishopstone	d			08 27					09 00				09 27						10 00				10 27
Newhaven Harbour	d			08 30					09 03				09 30						10 03				10 30
Newhaven Town ⛴	d			08 32					09 05				09 32						10 05				10 32
Southease	d			08 36									09 36										10 36
Lewes ■	a			08 44	08 49			09 07	09 14	09 18	09 29		09 44	09 49				10 07	10 14	10 18	10 29		10 44
	d			08 44	08 50		08 58	09 07	09 14	09 20	09 29		09 44	09 50			09 58	10 07	10 14	10 20	10 29		10 44
Falmer	d			08 51			09 05		09 21		09 36		09 51				10 05		10 21		10 36		10 51
Moulsecoomb	d			08 54			09 08		09 24		09 39		09 54				10 08		10 24		10 39		10 54
London Road (Brighton)	d			08 57			09 10		09 27		09 42		09 57				10 10		10 27		10 42		10 57
Brighton ■	a		08 51	09 00			09 14	09 20	09 30		09 45		10 00				10 14	10 20	10 30		10 45		11 00
Cooksbridge	d																						
Plumpton	d									09 28										10 28			
Wivelsfield ■	a									09 35										10 35			
Haywards Heath ■	a				09 05					09 40				10 05						10 40			
Gatwick Airport ■ ✈	a				09 24					09 55				10 24						10 55			
East Croydon	a				09 40					10 11				10 40						11 11			
London Bridge ■ ⊖	a																						
Clapham Junction ■	a				09 50					10 21				10 50						11 21			
London Victoria ■ ⊖	a		09 54		09 57					10 28				10 57						11 28			

A from 9 June until 1 September

Ashford, Hastings, Eastbourne, Seaford and Lewes - Brighton, Haywards Heath and London

Network Diagram - see first Page of Table 184

		SN ◇1	SN 1	SN ◇1	SN	SN	SN	SN ◇1	SN 1	SN ◇1	SN	SN ◇1	SN 1	SN ◇1	SN	SN	SN	SN ◇1	SN 1	SN ◇1	SN	SN ◇1
Ashford International	d					09 32										10 32						
Ham Street	d					09 41										10 41						
Appledore (Kent)	d					09 46										10 46						
Rye	a					09 55										10 55						
	d					09 55										10 55						
Winchelsea	d					09 59																
Doleham	d																					
Three Oaks	d															11 06						
Ore	d	09 50							10 22			10 50							11 22			11 50
Hastings 4	a	09 53				10 13			10 25			10 53				11 13			11 25			11 53
	d	09 55				10 14			10 26			10 55				11 14			11 26			11 55
St Leonards Warrior Sq 4	d	09 57				10 17			10 28			10 57				11 17			11 28			11 57
Bexhill 4	d	10 04				10 24			10 35			11 04				11 24			11 35			12 04
Collington	d	10 06							10 37			11 06							11 37			12 06
Cooden Beach	d	10 09							10 40			11 09							11 40			12 09
Normans Bay	d								10 43										11 43			
Pevensey Bay	d																					
Pevensey & Westham	d	10 15							10 48			11 15							11 48			12 15
Hampden Park 4	d	10 20	10 29	10 39					10 52			11 20	11 29	11 39					11 52			12 20
Eastbourne 4	a	10 25	10 34	10 44		10 39			10 57			11 25	11 34	11 44		11 39			11 57			12 25
	d	10 31	10 40			10 47		10 58	11 04	11 19		11 31	11 40			11 47		11 58	12 04	12 19		12 31
Hampden Park 4	d		10a44					11 02	11 08	11a23			11a44					12 02	12 08	12a23		
Polegate	d	10 37				10 54		11 06	11 12			11 37				11 54		12 06	12 12			12 37
Berwick	d								11 18										12 18			
Glynde	d								11 23										12 23			
Seaford	d						10 58				11 25						11 58				12 25	
Bishopstone	d						11 00				11 27						12 00				12 27	
Newhaven Harbour	d						11 03				11 30						12 03				12 30	
Newhaven Town	d						11 05				11 32						12 05				12 32	
Southease	d										11 36										12 36	
Lewes 4	a	10 49				11 07	11 14	11 18	11 29		11 44	11 49				12 07	12 14	12 18	12 29		12 44	12 49
	d	10 50			10 58	11 07	11 14	11 20	11 29		11 44	11 50			11 58	12 07	12 14	12 20	12 29		12 44	12 50
Falmer	d				11 05		11 21		11 36		11 51				12 05		12 21		12 36		12 51	
Moulsecoomb	d				11 08		11 24		11 39		11 54				12 08		12 24		12 39		12 54	
London Road (Brighton)	d				11 10		11 27		11 42		11 57				12 10		12 27		12 42		12 57	
Brighton 10	a				11 14	11 20	11 30		11 45		12 00				12 14	12 20	12 30		12 45		13 00	
Cooksbridge	d																					
Plumpton	d							11 28										12 28				
Wivelsfield 4	a							11 35										12 35				
Haywards Heath 3	a	11 05						11 40				12 05						12 40				13 05
Gatwick Airport 10	a	11 24						11 55				12 24						12 55				13 24
East Croydon	a	11 40						12 11				12 40						13 11				13 40
London Bridge 4	a																					
Clapham Junction 10	a	11 50						12 21				12 50						13 21				13 50
London Victoria 15	a	11 57						12 28				12 57						13 28				13 57

		SN 1	SN ◇1	SN	SN	SN	SN ◇1	SN 1	SN ◇1	SN	SN ◇1	SN 1	SN ◇1	SN	SN	SN	SN ◇1	SN 1	SN ◇1	SN	SN ◇1	SN 1	SN ◇1
Ashford International	d				11 32										12 32								
Ham Street	d				11 41										12 41								
Appledore (Kent)	d				11 46										12 46								
Rye	a				11 55										12 55								
	d				11 55										12 55								
Winchelsea	d				11 59																		
Doleham	d																						
Three Oaks	d														13 06								
Ore	d							12 22			12 50							13 22			13 50		
Hastings 4	a				12 13			12 25			12 53				13 13			13 25			13 53		
	d				12 14			12 26			12 55				13 14			13 26			13 55		
St Leonards Warrior Sq 4	d				12 17			12 28			12 57				13 17			13 28			13 57		
Bexhill 4	d				12 24			12 35			13 04				13 24			13 35			14 04		
Collington	d							12 37			13 06							13 37			14 06		
Cooden Beach	d							12 40			13 09							13 40			14 09		
Normans Bay	d							12 43										13 43					
Pevensey Bay	d																						
Pevensey & Westham	d							12 48			13 15							13 48			14 15		
Hampden Park 4	d	12 29	12 39					12 52			13 20	13 29	13 39					13 52			14 20	14 29	14 39
Eastbourne 4	a	12 34	12 44		12 39			12 57			13 25	13 34	13 44		13 39			13 57			14 25	14 34	14 44
	d	12 40			12 47		12 58	13 04	13 19		13 31	13 40			13 47		13 58	14 04	14 19		14 31	14 40	
Hampden Park 4	d	12a44					13 02	13 08	13a23			13a44					14 02	14 08	14a23			14a44	
Polegate	d				12 54		13 06	13 12			13 37				13 54		14 06	14 12			14 37		
Berwick	d							13 18										14 18					
Glynde	d							13 23										14 23					
Seaford	d					12 58				13 25						13 58				14 25			
Bishopstone	d					13 00				13 27						14 00				14 27			
Newhaven Harbour	d					13 03				13 30						14 03				14 30			
Newhaven Town	d					13 05				13 32						14 05				14 32			
Southease	d									13 36										14 36			
Lewes 4	a				13 07	13 14	13 19	13 29		13 44	13 49				14 07	14 14	14 19	14 29		14 44	14 49		
	d			12 58	13 07	13 14	13 20	13 29		13 44	13 50			13 58	14 07	14 14	14 20	14 29		14 44	14 50		
Falmer	d			13 05		13 21		13 36		13 51				14 05		14 21		14 36		14 51			
Moulsecoomb	d			13 08		13 24		13 39		13 54				14 08		14 24		14 39		14 54			
London Road (Brighton)	d			13 10		13 27		13 42		13 57				14 10		14 27		14 42		14 57			
Brighton 10	a			13 14	13 20	13 30		13 45		14 00				14 14	14 20	14 30		14 45		15 00			
Cooksbridge	d																						
Plumpton	d						13 28										14 28						
Wivelsfield 4	a						13 35										14 35						
Haywards Heath 3	a						13 40				14 05						14 40				15 05		
Gatwick Airport 10	a						13 55				14 24						14 55				15 24		
East Croydon	a						14 11				14 40						15 11				15 40		
London Bridge 4	a																						
Clapham Junction 10	a						14 21				14 50						15 21				15 50		
London Victoria 15	a						14 28				14 57						15 28				15 57		

Ashford, Hastings, Eastbourne, Seaford and Lewes - Brighton, Haywards Heath and London

Network Diagram - see first Page of Table 184

		SN	SN	SN	SN ◇1	SN 1	SN ◇1	SN	SN ◇1	SN 1	SN ◇1	SN	SN	SN	SN ◇1	SN 1	SN ◇1	SN	SN ◇1	SN 1	SN ◇1	SN
Ashford International	d		13 32										14 32									
Ham Street	d		13 41										14 41									
Appledore (Kent)	d		13 46										14 46									
Rye	a		13 55										14 55									
	d		13 55										14 55									
Winchelsea	d		13 59																			
Doleham	d																					
Three Oaks	d												15 06									
Ore	d					14 22			14 50							15 22			15 50			
Hastings 4	a		14 13			14 25			14 53				15 13			15 25			15 53			
	d		14 14			14 26			14 55				15 14			15 26			15 55			
St Leonards Warrior Sq 4	d		14 17			14 28			14 57				15 17			15 28			15 57			
Bexhill 4	d		14 24			14 35			15 04				15 24			15 35			16 04			
Collington	d					14 37			15 06							15 37			16 06			
Cooden Beach	d					14 40			15 09							15 40			16 09			
Normans Bay	d					14 43										15 43						
Pevensey Bay	d																					
Pevensey & Westham	d					14 48			15 15							15 48			16 15			
Hampden Park 4	d					14 52			15 20	15 29	15 39					15 52			16 20	16 29	16 39	
Eastbourne 4	a		14 39			14 57			15 25	15 34	15 44		15 39			15 57			16 25	16 34	16 44	
	d		14 47		14 58	15 04	15 19		15 31	15 40			15 47		15 58	16 04	16 19		16 31	16 40		
Hampden Park 4	d				15 02	15 08	15a23			15a44					16 02	16 08	16a23			16a44		
Polegate	d		14 54		15 06	15 12			15 37				15 54		16 06	16 12			16 37			
Berwick	d					15 18										16 18						
Glynde	d					15 23										16 23						
Seaford	d			14 58				15 25						15 58				16 25				
Bishopstone	d			15 00				15 27						16 00				16 27				
Newhaven Harbour	d			15 03				15 30						16 03				16 30				
Newhaven Town	d			15 05				15 32						16 05				16 32				
Southease	d							15 36										16 36				
Lewes 4	a		15 07	15 14	15 19	15 29		15 44	15 49				16 07	16 14	16 18	16 29		16 44	16 49			
	d	14 58	15 07	15 14	15 20	15 29		15 44	15 50			15 58	16 07	16 14	16 20	16 29		16 44	16 50			16 58
Falmer	d	15 05		15 21		15 36		15 51				16 05		16 21		16 36		16 51				17 05
Moulsecoomb	d	15 08		15 24		15 39		15 54				16 08		16 24		16 39		16 54				17 08
London Road (Brighton)	d	15 10		15 27		15 42		15 57				16 10		16 27		16 42		16 57				17 10
Brighton 10	a	15 14	15 20	15 30		15 45		16 00				16 14	16 20	16 30		16 45		17 00				17 14
Cooksbridge	d																					
Plumpton	d				15 28										16 28							
Wivelsfield 4	a				15 35										16 35							
Haywards Heath 3	a				15 40				16 05						16 40				17 05			
Gatwick Airport 10	a				15 55				16 24						16 55				17 24			
East Croydon	a				16 11				16 40						17 11				17 40			
London Bridge 4	a																					
Clapham Junction 10	a				16 21				16 50						17 21				17 50			
London Victoria 15	a				16 28				16 57						17 28				17 57			

		SN	SN	SN ◇1	SN 1	SN ◇1	SN	SN ◇1	SN 1	SN ◇1	SN	SN	SN	SN ◇1	SN 1	SN ◇1	SN	SN ◇1	SN 1	SN ◇1	SN	SN	SN
Ashford International	d	15 32										16 32										17 32	
Ham Street	d	15 41										16 41										17 41	
Appledore (Kent)	d	15 46										16 46										17 46	
Rye	a	15 55										16 55										17 55	
	d	15 55										16 55										17 55	
Winchelsea	d	15 59																				17 59	
Doleham	d																						
Three Oaks	d											17 06											
Ore	d				16 22			16 50							17 22			17 50					
Hastings 4	a	16 13			16 25			16 53				17 13			17 25			17 53				18 13	
	d	16 14			16 26			16 55				17 14			17 26			17 55				18 14	
St Leonards Warrior Sq 4	d	16 17			16 28			16 57				17 17			17 28			17 57				18 17	
Bexhill 4	d	16 24			16 35			17 04				17 24			17 35			18 04				18 24	
Collington	d				16 37			17 06							17 37			18 06					
Cooden Beach	d				16 40			17 09							17 40			18 09					
Normans Bay	d				16 43										17 43								
Pevensey Bay	d																						
Pevensey & Westham	d				16 48			17 15							17 48			18 15					
Hampden Park 4	d				16 52			17 20	17 29	17 39					17 52			18 20	18 29	18 42			
Eastbourne 4	a	16 39			16 57			17 25	17 34	17 44		17 39			17 57			18 25	18 34	18 47		18 39	
	d	16 47		16 58	17 04	17 19		17 31	17 40			17 47		17 58	18 04	18 19		18 31	18 40			18 47	
Hampden Park 4	d			17 02	17 08	17a23			17a44					18 02	18 08	18a23			18a44				
Polegate	d	16 54		17 06	17 12			17 37				17 54		18 06	18 12			18 37				18 54	
Berwick	d				17 18										18 18								
Glynde	d				17 23										18 23								
Seaford	d		16 58				17 25						17 58				18 25						18 58
Bishopstone	d		17 00				17 27						18 00				18 27						19 00
Newhaven Harbour	d		17 03				17 30						18 03				18 30						19 03
Newhaven Town	d		17 05				17 32						18 05				18 32						19 05
Southease	d						17 36										18 36						
Lewes 4	a	17 07	17 14	17 18	17 29		17 44	17 49				18 07	18 14	18 18	18 29		18 44	18 49				19 07	19 14
	d	17 07	17 14	17 20	17 29		17 44	17 50			17 58	18 07	18 14	18 20	18 29		18 44	18 50			18 58	19 07	19 14
Falmer	d		17 21		17 36		17 51				18 05		18 21		18 36		18 51				19 05		19 21
Moulsecoomb	d		17 24		17 39		17 54				18 08		18 24		18 39		18 54				19 08		19 24
London Road (Brighton)	d		17 27		17 42		17 57				18 10		18 27		18 42		18 57				19 10		19 27
Brighton 10	a	17 20	17 30		17 45		18 00				18 14	18 20	18 30		18 45		19 00				19 14	19 20	19 30
Cooksbridge	d																						
Plumpton	d			17 28										18 28									
Wivelsfield 4	a			17 35										18 35									
Haywards Heath 3	a			17 40				18 05						18 40				19 05					
Gatwick Airport 10	a			17 55				18 24						18 55				19 25					
East Croydon	a			18 11				18 40						19 11				19 41					
London Bridge 4	a																						
Clapham Junction 10	a			18 21				18 50						19 21				19 51					
London Victoria 15	a			18 28				18 57						19 28				19 58					

Table 189

Ashford, Hastings, Eastbourne, Seaford and Lewes - Brighton, Haywards Heath and London

Network Diagram - see first Page of Table 184

Station		SN ◇1	SN 1	SN ◇1	SN	SN ◇1	SN 1	SN ◇1	SN	SN	SN	SN 1	SN ◇1	SN ◇1	SN	SN 1	SN	SN 1	SN	SN 1	SN ◇1	SN ◇1 A	SN
Ashford International	d									18 32							19 32						
Ham Street	d									18 41							19 41						
Appledore (Kent)	d									18 46							19 46						
Rye	a									18 55							19 55						
	d									18 55							19 55						
Winchelsea	d																19 59						
Doleham	d																						
Three Oaks	d									19 06													
Ore	d		18 22			18 50						19 22		19 50						20 22		20 50	
Hastings	a		18 25			18 53				19 13		19 25		19 53			20 13			20 25		20 53	
	d		18 26			18 55				19 14		19 26		19 55			20 14			20 26		20 55	
St Leonards Warrior Sq	d		18 28			18 57				19 17		19 28		19 57			20 17			20 28		20 57	
Bexhill	d		18 35			19 04				19 24		19 35		20 04			20 24			20 35		21 04	
Collington	d		18 37			19 06						19 37		20 06						20 37		21 06	
Cooden Beach	d		18 40			19 09						19 40		20 09						20 40		21 09	
Normans Bay	d		18 43									19 43								20 43			
Pevensey Bay	d																						
Pevensey & Westham	d		18 48			19 15						19 48		20 15						20 48		21 15	
Hampden Park	d		18 52			19 20	19 29	19 39				19 52		20 20		20 29		20 43		20 52		21 20	
Eastbourne	a		18 57			19 25	19 34	19 44		19 39		19 57		20 25		20 34	20 39	20 48		20 57		21 25	
	d	18 58	19 04	19 19		19 31	19 40			19 47		20 04	20 19	20 31			20 45			21 04	21 19	21 31	
Hampden Park	d	19 02	19 08	19a23			19a44					20 08	20a23							21 08	21a23		
Polegate	d	19 06	19 12			19 37				19 54		20 12		20 37			20 52			21 12		21 37	
Berwick	d		19 18									20 18								21 18			
Glynde	d		19 23									20 23								21 23			
Seaford	d				19 25						19 58				20 28				20 58				21 28
Bishopstone	d				19 27						20 00				20 30				21 00				21 30
Newhaven Harbour	d				19 30						20 03				20 33				21 03				21 33
Newhaven Town	d				19 32						20 05				20 35				21 05				21 35
Southease	d				19 36																		
Lewes	a	19 18	19 29		19 44	19 49				20 07	20 14	20 29		20 49	20 44		21 07		21 14	21 29		21 49	21 44
	d	19 20	19 29		19 44	19 50			19 58	20 07	20 14	20 29		20 50	20 53		21 07		21 14	21 29		21 50	21 53
Falmer	d		19 36		19 51				20 05		20 21	20 36			21 00				21 21	21 36			22 00
Moulsecoomb	d		19 39		19 54				20 08		20 24	20 39			21 03				21 24	21 39			22 03
London Road (Brighton)	d		19 42		19 57				20 10		20 27	20 42			21 05				21 27	21 42			22 05
Brighton	a		19 45		20 00				20 14	20 20	20 30	20 45			21 09		21 20		21 30	21 45			22 10
Cooksbridge	d																						
Plumpton	d	19 28																					
Wivelsfield	a	19 35				20 02								21 04								22 02	
Haywards Heath	a	19 40				20 07								21 09								22 06	
Gatwick Airport	a	19 55				20 25								21 26								22 24	
East Croydon	a	20 11				20 41								21 41								22 40	
London Bridge	a																						
Clapham Junction	a	20 21				20 51								21 51								22 49	
London Victoria	a	20 28				20 58								21 58								22 57	

A 🚌 from Lewes

Table 189

Ashford, Hastings, Eastbourne, Seaford and Lewes - Brighton, Haywards Heath and London

Network Diagram - see first Page of Table 184

Station		SN	SN ◇1	SN	SN 1	SN ◇1	SN	SN ◇1	SN	SN ◇1	SN	SN 1	SN	SN ◇1	SN	SN 1	SN 1
Ashford International	d	20 32							21 32				22 32				
Ham Street	d	20 41							21 41				22 41				
Appledore (Kent)	d	20 46							21 46				22 46				
Rye	a	20 55							21 55				22 55				
	d	20 55							21 57				22 55				
Winchelsea	d								22 00				22 59				
Doleham	d												23 05				
Three Oaks	d	21 06											23 09				
Ore	d				21 22							22 22	23 14				
Hastings	a	21 13			21 25				22 14			22 25	23 17				
	d	21 14			21 26	21 42			22 15			22 26					23 22
St Leonards Warrior Sq	d	21 17			21 28	21 44			22 18			22 29					23 24
Bexhill	d	21 24			21 35	21 51			22 25			22 38					23 31
Collington	d				21 37	21 53						22 40					23 33
Cooden Beach	d				21 40	21 56						22 43					23 36
Normans Bay	d											22 46					
Pevensey Bay	d																
Pevensey & Westham	d				21 46	22 02						22 51					23 42
Hampden Park	d		21 43		21 51	22 07				22 43		22 55		23 09		23 42	23 47
Eastbourne	a	21 39	21 48		21 56	22 12			22 40	22 48		23 00		23 14		23 47	23 52
	d	21 45			22 04	22 18		22 21	22 45			23 05		23 20			23 56
Hampden Park	d				22 08			22a25				23 09		23a24			00 01
Polegate	d	21 52			22 12	22 25			22 52			23 13					00 05
Berwick	d				22 18							23 18					
Glynde	d				22 23							23 24					
Seaford	d			21 58			22 20				22 58				23 25		
Bishopstone	d			22 00			22 22				23 00				23 27		
Newhaven Harbour	d			22 03			22 25				23 03				23 30		
Newhaven Town	d			22 05			22 27				23 05				23 32		
Southease	d																
Lewes	a	22 07		22 14	22 29	22 38	22 35		23 07		23 14	23 29			23 40		00 17
	d	22 07		22 14	22 29	22 40	22 42		23 07		23 14	23 30			23 40		00 18
Falmer	d			22 21	22 36		22 49				23 21	23 37			23 47		00 25
Moulsecoomb	d			22 24	22 39		22 52				23 24	23 40			23 50		00 28
London Road (Brighton)	d			22 27	22 42		22 54				23 27	23 42			23 53		00 30
Brighton	a	22 20		22 31	22 45		22 58		23 20		23 31	23 46			23 56		00 34
Cooksbridge	d																
Plumpton	d					22 48											
Wivelsfield	a					22 54											
Haywards Heath	a					22 58											
Gatwick Airport	a					23 12											
East Croydon	a					23 29											
London Bridge	a																
Clapham Junction	a					23 41											
London Victoria	a					23 52											

Table 189

Sundays until 9 September

Ashford, Hastings, Eastbourne, Seaford and Lewes - Brighton, Haywards Heath and London

Network Diagram - see first Page of Table 184

		SN ■	SN ◇■	SN ◇■	SN ◇■ A 🍴	SN	SN ◇■	SN	SN ■	SN ◇■ A 🍴	SN	SN ■	SN	SN	SN ◇■ A 🍴	SN	SN	SN ■	SN	SN	SN ◇■ A 🍴	SN	SN
Ashford International	d																			08 15			
Ham Street	d																			08 24			
Appledore (Kent)	d																			08 29			
Rye	a																			08 38			
	d																			08 40			
Winchelsea	d																			08 43			
Doleham	d																			08 50			
Three Oaks	d																			08 53			
Ore	d														08 14					08 59	09 14		
Hastings ■	a														08 17					09 02	09 17		
	d	23p22													08 18					09 03	09 18		
St Leonards Warrior Sq ■	d	23p24													08 21					09 06	09 21		
Bexhill ■	d	23p31													08 28					09 13	09 28		
Collington	d	23p33													08 30						09 30		
Cooden Beach	d	23p36													08 33						09 33		
Normans Bay	d																						
Pevensey Bay	d																						
Pevensey & Westham	d	23p42													08 39						09 39		
Hampden Park ■	d	23p47	00 11						07 45						08 43	08 53					09 43	09 53	
Eastbourne ■	a	23p52	00 16	01 41					07 50						08 49	08 58				09 29	09 49	09 58	
	d	23p56			06 58		07 26	07 30		07 55		08 26		08 34	08 59			09 26		09 34	09 59		
Hampden Park ■	d	00 01			07 02		07a30	07 34				08a30		08 38				09a30		09 38			
Polegate	d	00 05			07 06			07 38		08 02				08 42	09 06					09 42	10 06		
Berwick	d							07 44						08 48						09 48			
Glynde	d							07 49						08 53						09 53			
Seaford	d										07 57		08 27				08 57		09 27				09 57
Bishopstone	d										07 59		08 29				08 59		09 29				09 59
Newhaven Harbour	d										08 02		08 32				09 02		09 32				10 02
Newhaven Town	d										08 04		08 34				09 04		09 34				10 04
Southease	d										08 08						09 08						10 08
Lewes ■	a	00 17			07 18			07 55		08 18	08 15		08 43	08 59	09 18		09 15		09 43	09 59	10 18		10 15
	d	00 18			07 22	07 22		07 56		08 22	08 22		08 44	09 00	09 22		09 22		09 44	10 00	10 22		10 22
Falmer	d	00 25				07 29		08 03			08 29		08 51				09 29		09 51				10 29
Moulsecoomb	d	00 28				07 32		08 07			08 32		08 54				09 32		09 54				10 32
London Road (Brighton)	d	00 30				07 34		08 09			08 34		08 56				09 34		09 56				10 34
Brighton ■	a	00 34				07 38		08 13			08 38		09 00	09 12			09 38		10 00	10 12			10 38
Cooksbridge	d																						
Plumpton	d									08 30					09 30						10 30		
Wivelsfield ■	a				07 36					08 36					09 36						10 36		
Haywards Heath ■	a				07 40					08 40					09 40						10 40		
Gatwick Airport ■ ✈	a				07 52					08 52					09 52						10 52		
East Croydon	a				08 09					09 09					10 09						11 09		
London Bridge ■ ⊖	a																						
Clapham Junction ■	a				08 18					09 18					10 18						11 18		
London Victoria ■ ⊖	a				08 25					09 25					10 25						11 25		

A 🍴 from Lewes

Table 189

Sundays until 9 September

Ashford, Hastings, Eastbourne, Seaford and Lewes - Brighton, Haywards Heath and London

Network Diagram - see first Page of Table 184

		SN ◇■	SN	SN	SN ◇■ A 🍴	SN	SN	SN ◇■	SN	SN	SN ◇■ A 🍴	SN	SN	SN ◇■	SN	SN	SN ◇■ A 🍴	SN	SN	SN ◇■	SN	SN	SN ◇■ A 🍴
Ashford International	d			09 21						10 21						11 21						12 21	
Ham Street	d			09 30						10 30						11 30						12 30	
Appledore (Kent)	d			09 35						10 35						11 35						12 35	
Rye	a			09 44						10 44						11 44						12 44	
	d			09 45						10 45						11 45						12 45	
Winchelsea	d																						
Doleham	d																						
Three Oaks	d																						
Ore	d				10 14						11 14						12 14						13 14
Hastings ■	a			10 02	10 17					11 02	11 17					12 02	12 17					13 02	13 17
	d			10 03	10 18					11 03	11 18					12 03	12 18					13 03	13 18
St Leonards Warrior Sq ■	d			10 06	10 21					11 06	11 21					12 06	12 21					13 06	13 21
Bexhill ■	d			10 13	10 28					11 13	11 28					12 13	12 28					13 13	13 28
Collington	d				10 30						11 30						12 30						13 30
Cooden Beach	d				10 33						11 33						12 33						13 33
Normans Bay	d																						
Pevensey Bay	d																						
Pevensey & Westham	d				10 39						11 39						12 39						13 39
Hampden Park ■	d				10 43	10 53					11 43	11 53					12 43	12 53					13 43
Eastbourne ■	a			10 29	10 49	10 58				11 29	11 49	11 58				12 29	12 49	12 58				13 29	13 49
	d	10 15		10 34	10 59			11 15		11 34	11 59			12 15		12 34	12 59			13 15		13 34	13 59
Hampden Park ■	d	10a19		10 38				11a19		11 38				12a19		12 38				13a19		13 38	
Polegate	d			10 42	11 06					11 42	12 06					12 42	13 06					13 42	14 06
Berwick	d			10 48						11 48						12 48						13 48	
Glynde	d			10 53						11 53						12 53						13 53	
Seaford	d		10 27				10 57		11 27				11 57		12 27				12 57		13 27		
Bishopstone	d		10 29				10 59		11 29				11 59		12 29				12 59		13 29		
Newhaven Harbour	d		10 32				11 02		11 32				12 02		12 32				13 02		13 32		
Newhaven Town	d		10 34				11 04		11 34				12 04		12 34				13 04		13 34		
Southease	d						11 08						12 08						13 08				
Lewes ■	a		10 43	10 59	11 18		11 15		11 43	11 59	12 18		12 15		12 43	12 59	13 18		13 15		13 43	13 59	14 18
	d		10 44	11 00	11 22		11 22		11 44	12 00	12 22		12 22		12 44	13 00	13 22		13 22		13 44	14 00	14 22
Falmer	d		10 51				11 29		11 51				12 29		12 51				13 29		13 51		
Moulsecoomb	d		10 54				11 32		11 54				12 32		12 54				13 32		13 54		
London Road (Brighton)	d		10 56				11 34		11 56				12 34		12 56				13 34		13 56		
Brighton ■	a		11 00	11 12			11 38		12 00	12 12			12 38		13 00	13 12			13 38		14 00	14 12	
Cooksbridge	d																						
Plumpton	d				11 30						12 30												
Wivelsfield ■	a				11 36						12 36						13 36						14 36
Haywards Heath ■	a				11 40						12 40						13 40						14 40
Gatwick Airport ■ ✈	a				11 52						12 52						13 52						14 52
East Croydon	a				12 09						13 09						14 09						15 09
London Bridge ■ ⊖	a																						
Clapham Junction ■	a				12 18						13 18						14 18						15 18
London Victoria ■ ⊖	a				12 25						13 25						14 25						15 25

A 🍴 from Lewes

Table 189

Sundays until 9 September

Ashford, Hastings, Eastbourne, Seaford and Lewes - Brighton, Haywards Heath and London

Network Diagram - see first Page of Table 184

		SN		SN	SN	SN	SN	SN	SN	SN	SN	SN		SN	SN	SN	SN	SN	SN	SN	SN	SN		SN	SN
					◇1			◇1			◇1				◇1			◇1			◇1				◇1
								A							A						A				
Ashford International	d						13 21							14 21						15 21					
Ham Street	d						13 30							14 30						15 30					
Appledore (Kent)	d						13 35							14 35						15 35					
Rye	a						13 44							14 44						15 44					
	d						13 45							14 45						15 45					
Winchelsea	d																								
Doleham	d																								
Three Oaks	d																								
Ore	d							14 14							15 14						16 14				
Hastings 4	a						14 02	14 17						15 02	15 17					16 02	16 17				
	d						14 03	14 18						15 03	15 18					16 03	16 18				
St Leonards Warrior Sq 4	d						14 06	14 21						15 06	15 21					16 06	16 21				
Bexhill 4	d						14 13	14 28						15 13	15 28					16 13	16 28				
Collington	d							14 30							15 30						16 30				
Cooden Beach	d							14 33							15 33						16 33				
Normans Bay	d																								
Pevensey Bay	d																								
Pevensey & Westham	d							14 39							15 39						16 39				
Hampden Park 4	d	13 53						14 43	14 53						15 43	15 53					16 43	16 53			
Eastbourne 4	a	13 58					14 29	14 49	14 58					15 29	15 49	15 58				16 29	16 49	16 58			
	d				14 15		14 34	14 59			15 15			15 34	15 59			16 15		16 34	16 59				17 15
Hampden Park 4	d				14a19		14 38				15a19			15 38				16a19		16 38					17a19
Polegate	d						14 42	15 06						15 42	16 06					16 42	17 06				
Berwick	d						14 48							15 48						16 48					
Glynde	d						14 53							15 53						16 53					
Seaford	d			13 57		14 27				14 57		15 27					15 57		16 27					16 57	
Bishopstone	d			13 59		14 29				14 59		15 29					15 59		16 29					16 59	
Newhaven Harbour	d			14 02		14 32				15 02		15 32					16 02		16 32					17 02	
Newhaven Town	d			14 04		14 34				15 04		15 34					16 04		16 34					17 04	
Southease	d			14 08						15 08							16 08							17 08	
Lewes 4	a			14 15		14 43	14 59	15 18		15 15		15 43		15 59	16 18		16 15		16 43	16 59	17 18			17 15	
	d			14 22		14 44	15 00	15 22		15 22		15 44		16 00	16 22		16 22		16 44	17 00	17 22			17 22	
Falmer	d			14 29		14 51				15 29		15 51					16 29		16 51					17 29	
Moulsecoomb	d			14 32		14 54				15 32		15 54					16 32		16 54					17 32	
London Road (Brighton)	d			14 34		14 56				15 34		15 56					16 34		16 56					17 34	
Brighton 10	a			14 38		15 00	15 12			15 38		16 00		16 12			16 38		17 00	17 12				17 38	
Cooksbridge	d																								
Plumpton	d														16 30						17 30				
Wivelsfield 4	a							15 36							16 36						17 36				
Haywards Heath 3	a							15 40							16 40						17 40				
Gatwick Airport 10	a							15 52							16 52						17 52				
East Croydon	a							16 09							17 09						18 09				
London Bridge 4	a																								
Clapham Junction 10	a							16 18							17 18						18 18				
London Victoria 15	a							16 25							17 25						18 25				

A ⊼ from Lewes

Table 189

Sundays until 9 September

Ashford, Hastings, Eastbourne, Seaford and Lewes - Brighton, Haywards Heath and London

Network Diagram - see first Page of Table 184

		SN	SN	SN	SN	SN	SN	SN		SN	SN	SN	SN	SN	SN	SN	SN	SN		SN	SN	SN	SN	SN	SN
				◇1			◇1				◇1			◇1			◇1				◇1			◇1	
				A																					
Ashford International	d		16 21							17 21						18 21							19 21		
Ham Street	d		16 30							17 30						18 30							19 30		
Appledore (Kent)	d		16 35							17 35						18 35							19 35		
Rye	a		16 44							17 44						18 44							19 44		
	d		16 45							17 45						18 45							19 45		
Winchelsea	d																								
Doleham	d																								
Three Oaks	d																								
Ore	d			17 14							18 14						19 14							20 14	
Hastings 4	a		17 02	17 17						18 02	18 17					19 02	19 17						20 02	20 17	
	d		17 03	17 18						18 03	18 18					19 03	19 18						20 03	20 18	
St Leonards Warrior Sq 4	d		17 06	17 21						18 06	18 21					19 06	19 21						20 06	20 21	
Bexhill 4	d		17 13	17 28						18 13	18 28					19 13	19 28						20 13	20 28	
Collington	d			17 30							18 30						19 30							20 30	
Cooden Beach	d			17 33							18 33						19 33							20 33	
Normans Bay	d																								
Pevensey Bay	d																								
Pevensey & Westham	d			17 39							18 39						19 39							20 39	
Hampden Park 4	d			17 43	17 53						18 43	18 53					19 43	19 53						20 43	20 53
Eastbourne 4	a		17 29	17 49	17 58					18 29	18 49	18 58				19 29	19 49	19 58					20 29	20 49	20 58
	d		17 34	17 59			18 15			18 34	18 59			19 15		19 34	19 59				20 15		20 34	20 59	
Hampden Park 4	d		17 38				18a19			18 38				19a19		19 38					20a19		20 38		
Polegate	d		17 42	18 06						18 42	19 06					19 42	20 06						20 42	21 06	
Berwick	d		17 48							18 48						19 48							20 48		
Glynde	d		17 53							18 53						19 53							20 53		
Seaford	d	17 27				17 57		18 27					18 57		19 27					19 57		20 27			
Bishopstone	d	17 29				17 59		18 29					18 59		19 29					19 59		20 29			
Newhaven Harbour	d	17 32				18 02		18 32					19 02		19 32					20 02		20 32			
Newhaven Town	d	17 34				18 04		18 34					19 04		19 34					20 04		20 34			
Southease	d					18 08							19 08							20 08					
Lewes 4	a	17 43	17 59	18 18		18 15		18 43		18 59	19 18		19 15		19 43	19 59	20 18			20 15		20 43	20 59	21 18	
	d	17 44	18 00	18 22		18 22		18 44		19 00	19 22		19 22		19 44	20 00	20 22			20 22		20 44	21 00	21 22	
Falmer	d	17 51				18 29		18 51					19 29		19 51					20 29		20 51			
Moulsecoomb	d	17 54				18 32		18 54					19 32		19 54					20 32		20 54			
London Road (Brighton)	d	17 56				18 34		18 56					19 34		19 56					20 34		20 56			
Brighton 10	a	18 00	18 12			18 38		19 00		19 12			19 38		20 00	20 12				20 38		21 00	21 12		
Cooksbridge	d																								
Plumpton	d			18 30							19 30						20 30							21 30	
Wivelsfield 4	a			18 36							19 36						20 36							21 36	
Haywards Heath 3	a			18 40							19 40						20 40							21 40	
Gatwick Airport 10	a			18 52							19 52						20 52							21 52	
East Croydon	a			19 09							20 09						21 09							22 09	
London Bridge 4	a																								
Clapham Junction 10	a			19 18							20 18						21 18							22 18	
London Victoria 15	a			19 25							20 25						21 25							22 25	

A ⊼ from Lewes

Table 189

Sundays until 9 September

Ashford, Hastings, Eastbourne, Seaford and Lewes - Brighton, Haywards Heath and London

Network Diagram - see first Page of Table 184

Station		SN	SN ◇1	SN	SN	SN	SN 1	SN	SN ◇1	SN	SN	SN	SN 1	SN	SN	SN ◇1	SN 1	SN
Ashford International	d				20 21						21 21			22 32				
Ham Street	d				20 30						21 30			22 41				
Appledore (Kent)	d				20 35						21 35			22 46				
Rye	a				20 44						21 44			22 55				
	d				20 45						21 45			22 55				
Winchelsea	d													22 58				
Doleham	d													23 05				
Three Oaks	d													23 08				
Ore	d						21 14						22 14	23 14				
Hastings 4	a				21 02		21 17				22 02		22 17	23 17				
	d				21 03		21 18				22 03		22 18				23 22	
St Leonards Warrior Sq 4	d				21 06		21 21				22 06		22 21				23 24	
Bexhill 4	d				21 13		21 28				22 13		22 28				23 31	
Collington	d						21 30						22 30				23 33	
Cooden Beach	d						21 33						22 33				23 36	
Normans Bay	d																	
Pevensey Bay	d																	
Pevensey & Westham	d						21 39						22 39				23 42	
Hampden Park 4	d						21 43	21 53					22 43		22 53		23 47	23 53
Eastbourne 4	a				21 29		21 49	21 58			22 29		22 49		22 58		23 52	23 58
	d		21 15		21 34		21 59		22 15		22 34		22 59			23 26		
Hampden Park 4	d		21a19		21 38				22a19		22 38					23a30		
Polegate	d				21 42		22 06				22 42		23 06					
Berwick	d				21 48						22 48							
Glynde	d				21 53						22 53							
Seaford	d	20 57		21 27		21 53				22 27		22 53						
Bishopstone	d	20 59		21 29		21 55				22 29		22 55						
Newhaven Harbour	d	21 02		21 32		21 58				22 32		22 58						
Newhaven Town	d	21 04		21 34		22 00				22 34		23 00						
Southease	d																	
Lewes 4	a	21 13		21 43	21 59	22 09	22 18			22 43	22 59	23 09	23 18					
	d	21 22		21 44	22 00	22 10	22 19			22 44	23 00	23 10	23 19					
Falmer	d	21 29		21 51		22 17	22 26			22 51		23 17	23 26					
Moulsecoomb	d	21 32		21 54		22 20	22 29			22 54		23 20	23 29					
London Road (Brighton)	d	21 34		21 56		22 22	22 31			22 56		23 22	23 31					
Brighton 10	a	21 38		22 00	22 12	22 26	22 35			23 00	23 12	23 26	23 35					
Cooksbridge	d																	
Plumpton	d																	
Wivelsfield 4	a																	
Haywards Heath 3	a																	
Gatwick Airport 10	a																	
East Croydon	a																	
London Bridge 4	a																	
Clapham Junction 10	a																	
London Victoria 15	a																	

Table 189

Sundays from 16 September

Ashford, Hastings, Eastbourne, Seaford and Lewes - Brighton, Haywards Heath and London

Network Diagram - see first Page of Table 184

Station		SN 1	SN ◇1	SN ◇1	SN ◇1 A ⌶	SN	SN ◇1	SN	SN 1	SN ◇1 A ⌶	SN	SN 1	SN	SN	SN ◇1 A ⌶	SN	SN	SN 1	SN	SN	SN ◇1 A ⌶	SN	SN
Ashford International	d																			08 15			
Ham Street	d																			08 24			
Appledore (Kent)	d																			08 29			
Rye	a																			08 38			
	d																			08 40			
Winchelsea	d																			08 43			
Doleham	d																			08 50			
Three Oaks	d																			08 53			
Ore	d														08 14					08 59	09 14		
Hastings 4	a														08 17					09 02	09 17		
	d	23p22													08 18					09 03	09 18		
St Leonards Warrior Sq 4	d	23p24													08 21					09 06	09 21		
Bexhill 4	d	23p31													08 28					09 13	09 28		
Collington	d	23p33													08 30						09 30		
Cooden Beach	d	23p36													08 33						09 33		
Normans Bay	d																						
Pevensey Bay	d																						
Pevensey & Westham	d	23p42													08 39						09 39		
Hampden Park 4	d	23p47	00 11						07 45						08 43	08 53					09 43	09 53	
Eastbourne 4	a	23p52	00 16	01 41					07 50						08 49	08 58				09 29	09 49	09 58	
	d	23p56			06 55		07 26	07 30		07 55		08 26		08 34	08 55			09 26		09 34	09 55		
Hampden Park 4	d	00 01			06 59		07a30	07 34				08a30		08 38				09a30		09 38			
Polegate	d	00 05			07 04			07 38		08 02				08 42	09 02					09 42	10 02		
Berwick	d							07 44						08 48						09 48			
Glynde	d							07 49						08 53						09 53			
Seaford	d										07 53		08 27				08 53		09 27				09 53
Bishopstone	d										07 55		08 29				08 55		09 29				09 55
Newhaven Harbour	d										07 58		08 32				08 58		09 32				09 58
Newhaven Town	d										08 00		08 34				09 00		09 34				10 00
Southease	d										08 04						09 04						10 04
Lewes 4	a	00 17			07 16			07 55		08 14	08 11		08 43	08 59	09 14		09 11		09 43	09 59	10 14		10 11
	d	00 18			07 20	07 22		07 56		08 16	08 18		08 44	09 00	09 16		09 18		09 44	10 00	10 16		10 18
Falmer	d	00 25				07 29		08 03			08 25		08 51				09 25		09 51				10 25
Moulsecoomb	d	00 28				07 32		08 07			08 28		08 54				09 28		09 54				10 28
London Road (Brighton)	d	00 30				07 34		08 09			08 30		08 56				09 30		09 56				10 30
Brighton 10	a	00 34				07 38		08 13			08 34		09 00	09 12			09 34		10 00	10 12			10 34
Cooksbridge	d																						
Plumpton	d									08 24					09 24						10 24		
Wivelsfield 4	a				07 32					08 31					09 31						10 31		
Haywards Heath 3	a				07 36					08 36					09 35						10 35		
Gatwick Airport 10	a				07 51					08 51					09 51						10 51		
East Croydon	a				08 08					09 09					10 09						11 09		
London Bridge 4	a																						
Clapham Junction 10	a				08 23					09 24					10 24						11 24		
London Victoria 15	a				08 30					09 31					10 31						11 31		

A ⌶ from Lewes

Table 189

Sundays from 16 September

Ashford, Hastings, Eastbourne, Seaford and Lewes - Brighton, Haywards Heath and London

Network Diagram - see first Page of Table 184

		SN ◇1	SN	SN	SN ◇1 A ⌶	SN		SN	SN ◇1	SN	SN	SN ◇1 A ⌶	SN	SN	SN ◇1	SN		SN	SN ◇1 A ⌶	SN	SN	SN ◇1	SN	SN	SN ◇1 A ⌶
Ashford International ⇌	d			09 21							10 21							11 21						12 21	
Ham Street	d			09 30							10 30							11 30						12 30	
Appledore (Kent)	d			09 35							10 35							11 35						12 35	
Rye	a			09 44							10 44							11 44						12 44	
	d			09 45							10 45							11 45						12 45	
Winchelsea	d																								
Doleham	d																								
Three Oaks	d																								
Ore	d				10 14							11 14							12 14						13 14
Hastings ■	a			10 02	10 17						11 02	11 17						12 02	12 17					13 02	13 17
	d			10 03	10 18						11 03	11 18						12 03	12 18					13 03	13 18
St Leonards Warrior Sq ■	d			10 06	10 21						11 06	11 21						12 06	12 21					13 06	13 21
Bexhill ■	d			10 13	10 28						11 13	11 28						12 13	12 28					13 13	13 28
Collington	d				10 30							11 30							12 30						13 30
Cooden Beach	d				10 33							11 33							12 33						13 33
Normans Bay	d																								
Pevensey Bay	d																								
Pevensey & Westham	d				10 39							11 39							12 39						13 39
Hampden Park ■	d				10 43	10 53						11 43	11 53						12 43	12 53					13 43
Eastbourne ■	a			10 29	10 49	10 58					11 29	11 49	11 58					12 29	12 49	12 58				13 29	13 49
	d	10 26		10 34	10 55				11 26		11 34	11 55			12 26			12 34	12 55			13 26		13 34	13 55
Hampden Park ■	d	10a30		10 38					11a30		11 38				12a30			12 38				13a30		13 38	
Polegate	d			10 42	11 02						11 42	12 02						12 42	13 02					13 42	14 02
Berwick	d			10 48							11 48							12 48						13 48	
Glynde	d			10 53							11 53							12 53						13 53	
Seaford	d		10 27					10 53		11 27				11 53		12 27					12 53		13 27		
Bishopstone	d		10 29					10 55		11 29				11 55		12 29					12 55		13 29		
Newhaven Harbour	d		10 32					10 58		11 32				11 58		12 32					12 58		13 32		
Newhaven Town ⛴	d		10 34					11 00		11 34				12 00		12 34					13 00		13 34		
Southease	d							11 04						12 04							13 04				
Lewes ■	a		10 43	10 59	11 14			11 11		11 43	11 59	12 14		12 11		12 43		12 59	13 14		13 11		13 43	13 59	14 14
	d		10 44	11 00	11 16			11 18		11 44	12 00	12 16		12 18		12 44		13 00	13 16		13 18		13 44	14 00	14 16
Falmer	d		10 51					11 25		11 51				12 25		12 51					13 25		13 51		
Moulsecoomb	d		10 54					11 28		11 54				12 28		12 54					13 28		13 54		
London Road (Brighton)	d		10 56					11 30		11 56				12 30		12 56					13 30		13 56		
Brighton ■	a		11 00	11 12				11 34		12 00	12 12			12 34		13 00		13 12			13 34		14 00	14 12	
Cooksbridge	d																								
Plumpton	d				11 24							12 24													
Wivelsfield ■	a				11 31							12 31							13 31						14 31
Haywards Heath ■	a				11 35							12 35							13 35						14 35
Gatwick Airport ■ ✈	a				11 51							12 52							13 52						14 52
East Croydon ⇌	a				12 09							13 09							14 09						15 09
London Bridge ■ ⊖	a																								
Clapham Junction ■	a				12 24							13 24							14 24						15 24
London Victoria ■ ⊖	a				12 31							13 31							14 31						15 31

A ⌶ from Lewes

Table 189

Sundays from 16 September

Ashford, Hastings, Eastbourne, Seaford and Lewes - Brighton, Haywards Heath and London

Network Diagram - see first Page of Table 184

		SN		SN	SN ◇1	SN	SN	SN ◇1 A ⌶	SN	SN	SN ◇1	SN		SN	SN ◇1 A ⌶	SN	SN	SN ◇1	SN	SN	SN ◇1 A ⌶	SN		SN	SN ◇1
Ashford International ⇌	d						13 21							14 21						15 21					
Ham Street	d						13 30							14 30						15 30					
Appledore (Kent)	d						13 35							14 35						15 35					
Rye	a						13 44							14 44						15 44					
	d						13 45							14 45						15 45					
Winchelsea	d																								
Doleham	d																								
Three Oaks	d																								
Ore	d							14 14							15 14						16 14				
Hastings ■	a						14 02	14 17						15 02	15 17					16 02	16 17				
	d						14 03	14 18						15 03	15 18					16 03	16 18				
St Leonards Warrior Sq ■	d						14 06	14 21						15 06	15 21					16 06	16 21				
Bexhill ■	d						14 13	14 28						15 13	15 28					16 13	16 28				
Collington	d							14 30							15 30						16 30				
Cooden Beach	d							14 33							15 33						16 33				
Normans Bay	d																								
Pevensey Bay	d																								
Pevensey & Westham	d							14 39							15 39						16 39				
Hampden Park ■	d	13 53						14 43	14 53						15 43	15 53					16 43	16 53			
Eastbourne ■	a	13 58					14 29	14 49	14 58					15 29	15 49	15 58				16 29	16 49	16 58			
	d				14 26		14 34	14 55			15 26			15 34	15 55			16 26		16 34	16 55				17 26
Hampden Park ■	d				14a30		14 38				15a30			15 38				16a30		16 38					17a30
Polegate	d						14 42	15 02						15 42	16 02					16 42	17 02				
Berwick	d						14 48							15 48						16 48					
Glynde	d						14 53							15 53						16 53					
Seaford	d			13 53		14 27				14 53		15 27					15 53		16 27					16 53	
Bishopstone	d			13 55		14 29				14 55		15 29					15 55		16 29					16 55	
Newhaven Harbour	d			13 58		14 32				14 58		15 32					15 58		16 32					16 58	
Newhaven Town ⛴	d			14 00		14 34				15 00		15 34					16 00		16 34					17 00	
Southease	d			14 04						15 04							16 04							17 04	
Lewes ■	a			14 11		14 43	14 59	15 14		15 11		15 43		15 59	16 14		16 11		16 43	16 59	17 14			17 11	
	d			14 18		14 44	15 00	15 16		15 18		15 44		16 00	16 16		16 18		16 44	17 00	17 16			17 18	
Falmer	d			14 25		14 51				15 25		15 51					16 25		16 51					17 25	
Moulsecoomb	d			14 28		14 54				15 28		15 54					16 28		16 54					17 28	
London Road (Brighton)	d			14 30		14 56				15 30		15 56					16 30		16 56					17 30	
Brighton ■	a			14 34		15 00	15 12			15 34		16 00		16 12			16 34		17 00	17 12				17 34	
Cooksbridge	d																								
Plumpton	d														16 24						17 24				
Wivelsfield ■	a							15 31							16 31						17 31				
Haywards Heath ■	a							15 35							16 35						17 35				
Gatwick Airport ■ ✈	a							15 52							16 52						17 52				
East Croydon ⇌	a							16 09							17 09						18 09				
London Bridge ■ ⊖	a																								
Clapham Junction ■	a							16 24							17 24						18 24				
London Victoria ■ ⊖	a							16 31							17 31						18 31				

A ⌶ from Lewes

Table 189

Sundays
from 16 September

Ashford, Hastings, Eastbourne, Seaford and Lewes - Brighton, Haywards Heath and London

Network Diagram - see first Page of Table 184

		SN	SN	SN	SN	SN	SN	SN	SN	SN	SN	SN	SN	SN	SN	SN	SN	SN	SN	SN	SN	SN	SN
				◇1 A 🚌			◇1			◇1			◇1			◇1			◇1			◇1	
Ashford International	d		16 21						17 21						18 21						19 21		
Ham Street	d		16 30						17 30						18 30						19 30		
Appledore (Kent)	d		16 35						17 35						18 35						19 35		
Rye	a		16 44						17 44						18 44						19 44		
	d		16 45						17 45						18 45						19 45		
Winchelsea	d																						
Doleham	d																						
Three Oaks	d																						
Ore	d			17 14						18 14						19 14						20 14	
Hastings 4	a		17 02	17 17					18 02	18 17					19 02	19 17					20 02	20 17	
	d		17 03	17 18					18 03	18 18					19 03	19 18					20 03	20 18	
St Leonards Warrior Sq 4	d		17 06	17 21					18 06	18 21					19 06	19 21					20 06	20 21	
Bexhill 4	d		17 13	17 28					18 13	18 28					19 13	19 28					20 13	20 28	
Collington	d			17 30						18 30						19 30						20 30	
Cooden Beach	d			17 33						18 33						19 33						20 33	
Normans Bay	d																						
Pevensey Bay	d																						
Pevensey & Westham	d			17 39						18 39						19 39						20 39	
Hampden Park 4	d			17 43	17 53					18 43	18 53					19 43	19 53					20 43	20 53
Eastbourne 4	a		17 29	17 49	17 58				18 29	18 49	18 58				19 29	19 49	19 58				20 29	20 49	20 58
	d		17 34	17 55			18 26		18 34	18 55			19 26		19 34	19 55			20 26		20 34	20 55	
Hampden Park 4	d		17 38				18a30		18 38				19a30		19 38				20a30		20 38		
Polegate	d		17 42	18 02					18 42	19 02					19 42	20 02					20 42	21 02	
Berwick	d		17 48						18 48						19 48						20 48		
Glynde	d		17 53						18 53						19 53						20 53		
Seaford	d	17 27				17 53		18 27				18 53		19 27				19 53		20 27			
Bishopstone	d	17 29				17 55		18 29				18 55		19 29				19 55		20 29			
Newhaven Harbour	d	17 32				17 58		18 32				18 58		19 32				19 58		20 32			
Newhaven Town	d	17 34				18 00		18 34				19 00		19 34				20 00		20 34			
Southease	d					18 04						19 04						20 04					
Lewes 4	a	17 43	17 59	18 14		18 12		18 43	18 59	19 14		19 11		19 43	19 59	20 14		20 11		20 43	20 59	21 14	
	d	17 44	18 00	18 16		18 18		18 44	19 00	19 16		19 18		19 44	20 00	20 16		20 18		20 44	21 00	21 16	
Falmer	d	17 51				18 25		18 51				19 25		19 51				20 25		20 51			
Moulsecoomb	d	17 54				18 28		18 54				19 28		19 54				20 28		20 54			
London Road (Brighton)	d	17 56				18 30		18 56				19 30		19 56				20 30		20 56			
Brighton 10	a	18 00	18 12			18 34		19 00	19 12			19 34		20 00	20 12			20 34		21 00	21 12		
Cooksbridge	d																						
Plumpton	d			18 24						19 24						20 24						21 24	
Wivelsfield 4	a			18 31						19 31						20 31						21 31	
Haywards Heath 3	a			18 35						19 35						20 35						21 35	
Gatwick Airport 10 ✈	a			18 52						19 52						20 52						21 52	
East Croydon	a			19 09						20 09						21 09						22 09	
London Bridge 4 ⊖	a																						
Clapham Junction 10	a			19 24						20 24						21 24						22 24	
London Victoria 15 ⊖	a			19 31						20 31						21 31						22 31	

A 🚌 from Lewes

Table 189

Sundays
from 16 September

Ashford, Hastings, Eastbourne, Seaford and Lewes - Brighton, Haywards Heath and London

Network Diagram - see first Page of Table 184

		SN	SN	SN	SN	SN	SN	SN	SN	SN	SN	SN	SN	SN	SN	SN	SN	SN
			◇1				1		◇1				1			◇1	1	
Ashford International	d				20 21						21 21			22 32				
Ham Street	d				20 30						21 30			22 41				
Appledore (Kent)	d				20 35						21 35			22 46				
Rye	a				20 44						21 44			22 55				
	d				20 45						21 45			22 55				
Winchelsea	d													22 58				
Doleham	d													23 05				
Three Oaks	d													23 08				
Ore	d						21 14						22 14	23 14				
Hastings 4	a				21 02		21 17				22 02		22 17	23 17				
	d				21 03		21 18				22 03		22 18				23 22	
St Leonards Warrior Sq 4	d				21 06		21 21				22 06		22 21				23 24	
Bexhill 4	d				21 13		21 28				22 13		22 28				23 31	
Collington	d						21 30						22 30				23 33	
Cooden Beach	d						21 33						22 33				23 36	
Normans Bay	d																	
Pevensey Bay	d																	
Pevensey & Westham	d						21 39						22 39				23 42	
Hampden Park 4	d						21 43	21 53					22 43		22 53		23 47	23 53
Eastbourne 4	a				21 29		21 49	21 58			22 29		22 49		22 58		23 52	23 58
	d		21 26		21 34		21 59		22 26		22 34		22 59			23 26		
Hampden Park 4	d		21a30		21 38				22a30		22 38					23a30		
Polegate	d				21 42		22 06				22 42		23 06					
Berwick	d				21 48						22 48							
Glynde	d				21 53						22 53							
Seaford	d	20 53		21 27		21 53				22 27		22 53						
Bishopstone	d	20 55		21 29		21 55				22 29		22 55						
Newhaven Harbour	d	20 58		21 32		21 58				22 32		22 58						
Newhaven Town	d	21 00		21 34		22 00				22 34		23 00						
Southease	d	21 04																
Lewes 4	a	21 11		21 43	21 59	22 09	22 18			22 43	22 59	23 09	23 18					
	d	21 18		21 44	22 00	22 10	22 19			22 44	23 00	23 10	23 19					
Falmer	d	21 25		21 51		22 17	22 26			22 51		23 17	23 26					
Moulsecoomb	d	21 28		21 54		22 20	22 29			22 54		23 20	23 29					
London Road (Brighton)	d	21 30		21 56		22 22	22 31			22 56		23 22	23 31					
Brighton 10	a	21 34		22 00	22 12	22 26	22 35			23 00	23 12	23 26	23 35					
Cooksbridge	d																	
Plumpton	d																	
Wivelsfield 4	a																	
Haywards Heath 3	a																	
Gatwick Airport 10 ✈	a																	
East Croydon	a																	
London Bridge 4 ⊖	a																	
Clapham Junction 10	a																	
London Victoria 15 ⊖	a																	

until 26 July, 13 Aug to 28 Aug and from 10 Sep

Route Diagram for Table 194

HIGH SPEED SERVICES

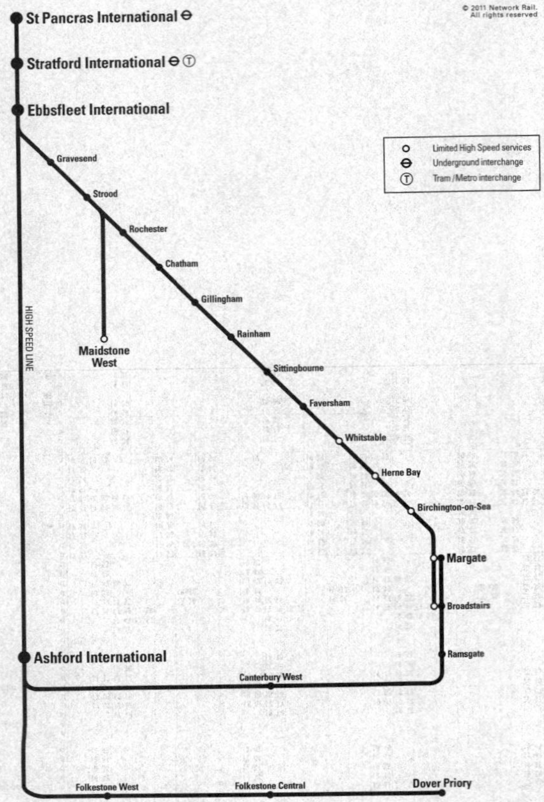

St Pancras International - Kent High Speed Domestic Services

Miles	Miles	Miles			SE A	SE A	SE A	SE MX 1	SE MO B	SE MX	SE MX	SE	SE 1	SE	SE	SE	SE	SE	SE	SE	SE
—	—	—	**St Pancras International** 15 ⊖	d	22p55	23p12	23p25		23p42	23p55	00 12	06 25		06 40	06 55	07 10	07 25	07 40	07 52	08 10	08 25
6	6	6	**Stratford International** ⊖	d	23p02	23p19	23p32		23p49	00 02	00 19	06 32		06 47	07 02	07 17	07 32	07 47	08 02	08 17	08 32
22¼	22¼	22¼	**Ebbsfleet International**	a	23p12	23p30	23p42		23p59	00 12	00 30	06 42		06 58	07 12	07 28	07 42	07 59	08 12	08 29	08 42
—	—	—		d	23p13	23p31	23p43		00 01	00 13	00 31	06 42		06 59	07 13	07 29	07 43	08 00	08 13	08 30	08 43
24¼	—	—	Gravesend 4	d	23p18		23p48			00 18		06 46			07 21		07 48		08 18		08 48
32	—	—	Strood 4	d	23p28		23p58			00 28		06 57			07 31		07 58		08 28		08 58
—	—	—	Maidstone West	d								07a12									
33	—	—	Rochester 4	d	23p33		00 03			00 33					07 36		08 03		08 33		09 03
33½	—	—	Chatham 4	d	23p35		00 05			00 35					07 38		08 05		08 35		09 05
35¼	—	—	Gillingham (Kent) 4	d	23p40		00 10			00 40					07 43		08 10		08 40		09 10
38¼	—	—	Rainham (Kent)	d	23p45		00 15			00 45					07 48		08 15		08 45		09 15
44	—	—	Sittingbourne 4	d	23p53		00 23			00 53					07 57		08 23		08 53		09 23
51¾	—	—	**Faversham** 2	a	00 03		00 33			01 03					08 05		08 33		09 03		09 33
58¾	—	—	Whitstable	d																	
62½	—	—	Herne Bay	d																	
70½	—	—	Birchington-on-Sea	d																	
73½	—	—	Margate 4	d																	
76¾	—	—	**Broadstairs**	a																	
—	56	56	**Ashford International**	a		23p50			00 20		00 50			07 18		07 48		08 20		08 50	
—	—	—		d		23p52		00 03					06 33	07 22		07 50		08 22		08 52	
—	69¼	—	Folkestone West	d		00 05										08 03				09 05	
—	70	—	Folkestone Central	d		00 08										08 06				09 08	
—	77¼	—	**Dover Priory** 4	a		00 20										08 18				09 20	
—	—	—	Deal	a																	
—	—	—	Sandwich	a																	
—	—	70¼	**Canterbury West** 4	a				00 24					06 54	07 38				08 38			
—	—	—		d				00 25					06 55	07 39				08 39			
—	—	87¾	Ramsgate 4	d				00a47					07a17	08 01				08 59			
—	—	87¾	Broadstairs	d										08 06				09 05			
—	—	91	**Margate** 4	a										08 11				09 10			

		SE	SE	SE	SE	SE	SE	SE	SE	SE	SE	SE	SE	SE	SE	SE	SE
St Pancras International 15 ⊖	d	08 40	08 55	09 10	09 25	09 42	09 55	10 10	10 28	10 40	10 52	11 12	11 25	11 42	11 55	12 12	12 22
Stratford International ⊖	d	08 47	09 05	09 17	09 32	09 49	10 02	10 17	10 35	10 47	10 59	11 19	11 32	11 49	12 02	12 19	12 32
Ebbsfleet International	a	08 59	09 15	09 28	09 42	10 00	10 12	10 28	10 45	10 58	11 09	11 30	11 42	12 00	12 12	12 30	12 42
	d	09 00	09 17	09 29	09 43	10 01	10 13	10 29	10 46	10 59	11 13	11 31	11 43	12 01	12 13	12 31	12 43
Gravesend 4	d		09 22		09 48		10 18		10 51		11 18		11 48		12 18		12 48
Strood 4	d		09 32		09 58		10 28		11 01		11 28		11 58		12 28		12 58
Maidstone West	d																
Rochester 4	d		09 37		10 03		10 33		11 06		11 33		12 03		12 33		13 03
Chatham 4	d		09 39		10 05		10 35		11 08		11 35		12 05		12 35		13 05
Gillingham (Kent) 4	d		09 44		10 10		10 40		11 13		11 40		12 10		12 40		13 10
Rainham (Kent)	d		09 49		10 15		10 45		11 18		11 45		12 15		12 45		13 15
Sittingbourne 4	d		09 56		10 23		10 53		11 25		11 53		12 23		12 53		13 23
Faversham 2	a		10 04		10 33		11 03		11 33		12 03		12 33		13 03		13 33
Whitstable	d																
Herne Bay	d																
Birchington-on-Sea	d																
Margate 4	d																
Broadstairs	a																
Ashford International	a	09 20		09 48		10 20		10 48		11 18		11 50		12 20		12 50	
	d	09 22		09 52		10 22		10 52		11 22		11 52		12 22		12 52	
Folkestone West	d			10 05				11 05				12 05				13 05	
Folkestone Central	d			10 08				11 08				12 08				13 08	
Dover Priory 4	a			10 20				11 20				12 20				13 20	
Deal	a																
Sandwich	a																
Canterbury West 4	a	09 38				10 38				11 38				12 38			
	d	09 39				10 39				11 39				12 39			
Ramsgate 4	d	09 59				10 59				11 59				12 59			
Broadstairs	d	10 05				11 05				12 05				13 05			
Margate 4	a	10 10				11 10				12 10				13 10			

A not 14 May

B from 21 May until 23 July

Table 194

Mondays to Fridays

until 26 July, 13 Aug to 28 Aug and from 10 Sep

St Pancras International - Kent High Speed Domestic Services

	SE	SE	SE	SE	SE	SE	SE	SE	SE	SE	SE	SE	SE	SE	SE	SE	SE	SE
St Pancras International d	12 42	12 52	13 12	13 25	13 42	13 55	14 12	14 25	14 42	14 55	15 12	15 25	15 42	15 55	16 10	16 25	16 42	16 55
Stratford International d	12 49	12 58	13 19	13 32	13 49	14 02	14 19	14 32	14 49	15 02	15 19	15 32	15 49	16 02	16 17	16 32	16 49	17 02
Ebbsfleet International a	13 00	13 08	13 30	13 42	14 00	14 12	14 30	14 42	15 00	15 12	15 30	15 42	16 00	16 12	16 28	16 42	17 00	17 12
d	13 01	13 13	13 31	13 43	14 01	14 13	14 31	14 43	15 01	15 13	15 31	15 43	16 01	16 13	16 29	16 43	17 01	17 13
Gravesend d		13 18		13 48		14 18		14 48		15 18		15 48		16 18		16 48		17 18
Strood d		13 28		13 58		14 28		14 58		15 28		15 58		16 28		16 58		17 28
Maidstone West d																		
Rochester d		13 33		14 03		14 33		15 03		15 33		16 03		16 33		17 03		17 34
Chatham d		13 35		14 05		14 35		15 05		15 35		16 05		16 35		17 05		17 37
Gillingham (Kent) d		13 40		14 10		14 40		15 10		15 40		16 10		16 40		17 10		17 43
Rainham (Kent) d		13 45		14 15		14 45		15 15		15 45		16 15		16 45		17 15		17 48
Sittingbourne d		13 53		14 23		14 53		15 23		15 53		16 23		16 53		17 23		17 57
Faversham a		14 03		14 33		15 03		15 33		16 03		16 33		17 03		17 33		18 05
Whitstable d																		
Herne Bay d																		
Birchington-on-Sea d																		
Margate d																		
Broadstairs a																		
Ashford International a	13 20		13 50		14 20		14 50		15 20		15 50		16 20		16 48		17 20	
d	13 22		13 52		14 22		14 52		15 22		15 52		16 22		16 52		17 23	
Folkestone West d			14 05				15 05				16 05				17 05			
Folkestone Central d			14 08				15 08				16 08				17 08			
Dover Priory a			14 20				15 20				16 20				17 20			
Deal a																		
Sandwich a																		
Canterbury West a	13 38				14 38				15 38				16 38				17 39	
d	13 39				14 39				15 39				16 39				17 40	
Ramsgate d	13 59				14 59				15 59				16 59				17 59	
Broadstairs d	14 05				15 05				16 05				17 05				18 05	
Margate a	14 10				15 10				16 10				17 10				18 10	

	SE		SE	SE	SE	SE		SE	SE	SE	SE		SE	SE	SE	SE		SE	SE
St Pancras International d	17 10		17 14	17 18	17 25	17 40		17 44	17 48	17 55	18 10		18 14	18 18	18 25	18 40		18 48	18 55
Stratford International d	17 17		17 21	17 25	17 32	17 47		17 51	17 55	18 02	18 17		18 21	18 25	18 32	18 47		18 55	19 02
Ebbsfleet International a				17 35	17 42				18 05	18 12				18 35	18 42			19 05	19 12
d					17 43					18 13					18 43				19 13
Gravesend d			17 36					18 06					18 38						19 20
Strood d			17 46					18 18					18 49						19 30
Maidstone West d			18a02					18a32					19a05						
Rochester d					18 02					18 31					19 03				19 35
Chatham d					18 05					18 34					19 06				19 38
Gillingham (Kent) d					18 10					18 39					19 11				19 43
Rainham (Kent) d					18 15					18 44					19 16				19 48
Sittingbourne d					18 23					18 52					19 24				19 55
Faversham a					18 31					19 00					19 32				20 04
Whitstable d					18 40					19 09					19 42				
Herne Bay d					18 46					19 15					19 48				
Birchington-on-Sea d					18 55					19 24					19 57				
Margate d					19 02					19 30					20 04				
Broadstairs a					19 08					19 36					20 09				
Ashford International a	17 46					18 16					18 46					19 16			
d	17 50	17 53				18 23	18 20				18 50	18 53				19 23	19 20		
Folkestone West d	18 03						18 33				19 05						19 33		
Folkestone Central d	18 06						18 36				19 08						19 36		
Dover Priory a	18 18						18 47				19 20						19 47		
Deal a							19 06										20 06		
Sandwich a							19 13										20 13		
Canterbury West a		18 09				18 39						19 09				19 39			
d		18 10				18 40						19 10				19 40			
Ramsgate d		18 29				18 59						19 31				19 59			
Broadstairs d		18 35				19 05						19 36				20 05			
Margate a		18 40				19 10						19 41				20 10			

	SE		SE	SE	SE	SE	SE	SE	SE	SE	SE	SE	SE	SE	SE	SE	SE	SE	SE	SE
St Pancras International d	19 10		19 25	19 42	19 55	20 12	20 25	20 42	20 55	21 12	21 25	21 42	21 55	22 12	22 25	22 42	22 55	23 12	23 25	23 55
Stratford International d	19 17		19 32	19 49	20 02	20 19	20 32	20 49	21 02	21 19	21 32	21 49	22 02	22 19	22 32	22 49	23 02	23 19	23 32	00 02
Ebbsfleet International a	19 28		19 42	20 00	20 12	20 30	20 42	21 00	21 12	21 30	21 42	22 00	22 12	22 30	22 42	23 00	23 12	23 30	23 42	00 12
d	19 29		19 45	20 01	20 13	20 31	20 43	21 01	21 13	21 31	21 43	22 01	22 13	22 31	22 43	23 01	23 13	23 31	23 43	00 13
Gravesend d			19 51		20 18		20 48		21 18		21 48		22 18		22 48		23 18		23 48	00 18
Strood d			20 01		20 28		20 58		21 28		21 58		22 28		22 58		23 28		23 58	00 28
Maidstone West d																				
Rochester d			20 08		20 33		21 03		21 33		22 03		22 33		23 03		23 33		00 03	00 33
Chatham d			20 10		20 35		21 05		21 35		22 05		22 35		23 05		23 35		00 05	00 35
Gillingham (Kent) d			20 15		20 40		21 10		21 40		22 10		22 40		23 10		23 40		00 10	00 40
Rainham (Kent) d			20 20		20 45		21 15		21 45		22 15		22 45		23 15		23 45		00 15	00 45
Sittingbourne d			20 27		20 53		21 23		21 53		22 23		22 53		23 23		23 53		00 23	00 53
Faversham a			20 36		21 03		21 33		22 03		22 33		23 03		23 33		00 03		00 33	01 03
Whitstable d																				
Herne Bay d																				
Birchington-on-Sea d																				
Margate d																				
Broadstairs a																				
Ashford International a	19 48			20 20		20 50		21 20		21 50		22 20		22 50		23 20		23 50		
d	19 52	19 55		20 22		20 52		21 22		21 52		22 22		22 52		23 22		23 52		
Folkestone West d	20 05					21 05				22 05				23 05				00 05		
Folkestone Central d	20 08					21 08				22 08				23 08				00 08		
Dover Priory a	20 20					21 20				22 20				23 20				00 20		
Deal a																				
Sandwich a																				
Canterbury West a		20 11		20 38				21 38				22 38				23 38				
d		20 12		20 39				21 39				22 39				23 39				
Ramsgate d		20 32		21 00				21 59				22 59				23a59				
Broadstairs d		20 38		21 05				22 05				23 05								
Margate a		20 43		21 11				22 10				23 10								

Table 194

Mondays to Fridays

27 July to 10 August

St Pancras International - Kent High Speed Domestic Services

	SE	SE	SE	SE	SE	SE	SE	SE	SE	SE	SE	SE	SE	SE	SE	SE	SE	SE	SE	SE	SE	SE
	A	A	A	B	B	B	A	B	B	C	B	B	A	B	B	B	B	B	B	B	B	B
St Pancras International d	22p55	23p12	23p25	23p41	23p47	23p51	23p55	23p56	00§02		00§06	00§11	00§12	00§17	00§21	00§27	00§32	00§36	00§41	00§47	00§51	00§57
Stratford International d	23p02	23p19	23p32	23p50	23p57	00§01	00§02	00§05	00§12		00§16	00§20	00§19	00§27	00§30	00§36	00§42	00§46	00§50	00§57	01§00	01§06
Ebbsfleet International a	23p12	23p30	23p42	00§01	00§07	00§10	00§12	00§16	00§22		00§26	00§31	00§30	00§37	00§41	00§47	00§52	00§56	01§01	01§07	01§11	01§18
d	23p13	23p31	23p43				00§13						00§31						01§03			01§20
Gravesend d	23p18		23p48				00§18															
Strood d	23p28		23p58				00§28															
Maidstone West d																						
Rochester d	23p33		00§03				00§33															
Chatham d	23p35		00§05				00§35															
Gillingham (Kent) d	23p40		00§10				00§40															
Rainham (Kent) d	23p45		00§15				00§45															
Sittingbourne d	23p53		00§23				00§53															
Faversham a	00§03		00§33				01§03															
Whitstable d																						
Herne Bay d																						
Birchington-on-Sea d																						
Margate d																						
Broadstairs a																						
Ashford International a		23p50											00§50						01§29			01§38
d		23p52								00§03												
Folkestone West d		00§05																				
Folkestone Central d		00§08																				
Dover Priory a		00§20																				
Deal a																						
Sandwich a																						
Canterbury West a										00§24												
d										00§25												
Ramsgate d										00a47												
Broadstairs d																						
Margate a																						

	SE	SE	SE	SE	SE	SE	SE	SE	SE	SE	SE	SE	SE	SE	SE	SE	SE	SE	SE	SE	SE
	B	B	B	B	B	B	B	B	B	B	B	B	B	B	B	B	B	B			
St Pancras International d	01§02	01§06	01§11	01§17	01§21	01§27	01§32	01§38	01§44	01§55	02§02	02§32	03§02	03§32	04§02	04§32	05§02	05§32	06 04	06 32	
Stratford International d	01§12	01§16	01§20	01§26	01§30	01§36	01§42	01§48	01§54	02§04	02a08	02a38	03a08	03a38	04a08	04a38	05a08	05§42	06 14	06 42	
Ebbsfleet International a	01§22	01§26	01§33	01§36	01§41	01§47	01§52	01§58	02§04	02§14								05§52	06 24	06 52	
d		01§29	01§35	01§38		01§49		02§00	02§05	02§16								05§56			
Gravesend d				01§43						02§21											
Strood d				01§53						02§31											
Maidstone West d																					
Rochester d				01§57					02§20	02§35											
Chatham d				02§00					02§23	02§38											
Gillingham (Kent) d				02§04					02§27	02§42											
Rainham (Kent) d				02§09					02§32	02§47											
Sittingbourne d				02§17					02§40	02§55											
Faversham a				02§25					02§48	03§03											
Whitstable d																					
Herne Bay d																					
Birchington-on-Sea d																					
Margate d																					
Broadstairs a																					
Ashford International a		01§49	01§54			02§07		02§18										06§16			
d																					06 33
Folkestone West d																					
Folkestone Central d																					
Dover Priory a																					
Deal a																					
Sandwich a																					
Canterbury West a																					06 54
d																					06 55
Ramsgate d																					07a17
Broadstairs d																					
Margate a																					

A 27 Jly

B not 27 Jly

C not 30 Jly, 6 August

Table 194

Mondays to Fridays
27 July to 10 August

St Pancras International - Kent High Speed Domestic Services

		SE	SE	SE	SE	SE	SE	SE	SE	SE	SE	SE	SE	SE	SE	SE	SE	SE	SE	SE	SE	SE	SE	SE
			1 A														1							
St Pancras International 15 ⊖	d	06 52		07 04	07 11	07 18	07 25	07 32	07 39	07 46	07 52	08 04	08 11	08 18	08 25	08 32		08 39	08 46	08 52	09 04	09 11	09 18	09 25
Stratford International ⊖	d	07 03		07 14	07 21	07 28	07 35	07 42	07 49	07 56	08 03	08 14	08 21	08 28	08 35	08 42		08 49	08 56	09 03	09 14	09 21	09 28	09 35
Ebbsfleet International	a	07 13		07 24	07 31	07 38	07 46	07 52	07 59	08 07	08 13	08 24	08 31	08 39	08 46	08 52		09 00	09 07	09 13	09 24	09 31	09 38	09 46
	d			07 30		07 43			08 02			08 30		08 44				09 02			09 30		09 43	
Gravesend 4	d					07 48								08 48									09 48	
Strood 4	d					07 58								08 58									09 58	
Maidstone West	d																							
Rochester 4	d					08 03								09 03									10 03	
Chatham 4	d					08 05								09 05									10 05	
Gillingham (Kent) 4	d					08 10								09 10									10 10	
Rainham (Kent)	d					08 15								09 15									10 15	
Sittingbourne 4	d					08 23								09 23									10 23	
Faversham 2	a					08 33								09 33									10 33	
Whitstable	d																							
Herne Bay	d																							
Birchington-on-Sea	d																							
Margate 4	d																							
Broadstairs	a																							
Ashford International	a			07 51					08 20			08 51						09 20			09 48			
	d		07 03														09 03							
Folkestone West	d																							
Folkestone Central	d																							
Dover Priory 4	a																							
Deal	a																							
Sandwich	a																							
Canterbury West 4	a		07 24														09 21							
	d		07 25														09 22							
Ramsgate 4	d		07a48														09a48							
Broadstairs	d																							
Margate 4	a																							

		SE	SE	SE	SE	SE	SE	SE	SE	SE	SE	SE	SE	SE	SE	SE	SE	SE	SE	SE	SE	SE	SE	SE	SE
			1												1						1				
St Pancras International 15 ⊖	d	09 32		09 39	09 46	09 52	10 04	10 11	10 18	10 25	10 32	10 39	10 46	10 52		11 04	11 11	11 18	11 25	11 32		11 39	11 46	11 52	12 04
Stratford International ⊖	d	09 42		09 49	09 56	10 03	10 14	10 21	10 28	10 35	10 42	10 49	10 56	11 03		11 14	11 21	11 28	11 35	11 42		11 49	11 56	12 03	12 14
Ebbsfleet International	a	09 52		10 00	10 07	10 13	10 24	10 31	10 39	10 46	10 52	10 59	11 07	11 13		11 24	11 31	11 38	11 46	11 52		11 59	12 07	12 13	12 24
	d			10 02			10 30		10 44			11 02				11 30		11 43				12 02			12 30
Gravesend 4	d								10 51									11 48							
Strood 4	d								11 01									11 58							
Maidstone West	d																								
Rochester 4	d								11 06									12 03							
Chatham 4	d								11 08									12 05							
Gillingham (Kent) 4	d								11 13									12 10							
Rainham (Kent)	d								11 18									12 15							
Sittingbourne 4	d								11 25									12 23							
Faversham 2	a								11 33									12 33							
Whitstable	d																								
Herne Bay	d																								
Birchington-on-Sea	d																								
Margate 4	d																								
Broadstairs	a																								
Ashford International	a			10 20			10 51					11 20				11 51						12 20			12 51
	d		10 03												11 03						12 03				
Folkestone West	d																								
Folkestone Central	d																								
Dover Priory 4	a																								
Deal	a																								
Sandwich	a																								
Canterbury West 4	a		10 21												11 21						12 21				
	d		10 22												11 22						12 22				
Ramsgate 4	d		10a44												11a44						12a44				
Broadstairs	d																								
Margate 4	a																								

A not 27 July

Table 194

Mondays to Fridays
27 July to 10 August

St Pancras International - Kent High Speed Domestic Services

		SE	SE	SE	SE	SE	SE	SE	SE	SE	SE	SE	SE	SE	SE	SE	SE	SE	SE	SE	SE	SE	SE	SE	SE
					1										1										
St Pancras International 15 ⊖	d	12 11	12 18	12 25		12 32	12 39	12 46	12 52	13 04	13 11	13 18	13 25	13 32		13 39	13 46	13 52	14 04	14 11	14 18	14 25	14 32	14 39	14 46
Stratford International ⊖	d	12 21	12 28	12 35		12 42	12 49	12 56	13 03	13 14	13 21	13 28	13 35	13 42		13 49	13 56	14 03	14 14	14 21	14 28	14 35	14 42	14 49	14 56
Ebbsfleet International	a	12 31	12 39	12 46		12 52	12 59	13 07	13 13	13 24	13 31	13 38	13 46	13 52		13 59	14 07	14 13	14 24	14 31	14 38	14 46	14 52	14 59	15 07
	d		12 44				13 02			13 30		13 43				14 02			14 30		14 43			15 02	
Gravesend 4	d		12 48									13 48									14 48				
Strood 4	d		12 58									13 58									14 58				
Maidstone West	d																								
Rochester 4	d		13 03									14 03									15 03				
Chatham 4	d		13 05									14 05									15 05				
Gillingham (Kent) 4	d		13 10									14 10									15 10				
Rainham (Kent)	d		13 15									14 15									15 15				
Sittingbourne 4	d		13 23									14 23									15 23				
Faversham 2	a		13 33									14 33									15 33				
Whitstable	d																								
Herne Bay	d																								
Birchington-on-Sea	d																								
Margate 4	d																								
Broadstairs	a																								
Ashford International	a						13 20			13 51						14 20			14 51					15 20	
	d				13 03										14 03										
Folkestone West	d																								
Folkestone Central	d																								
Dover Priory 4	a																								
Deal	a																								
Sandwich	a																								
Canterbury West 4	a				13 21										14 21										
	d				13 22										14 22										
Ramsgate 4	d				13a44										14a44										
Broadstairs	d																								
Margate 4	a																								

		SE	SE	SE	SE	SE	SE	SE	SE	SE	SE	SE	SE	SE	SE	SE	SE	SE	SE	SE	SE	SE	SE	SE	SE
			1						1									1						A	B
St Pancras International 15 ⊖	d	14 52		15 04	15 11	15 18	15 25	15 32		15 39	15 46	15 52	16 04	16 11	16 18	16 25	16 32		16 39	16 46	16 52	17 04	17 11	17 18	17 18
Stratford International ⊖	d	15 03		15 14	15 21	15 28	15 35	15 42		15 49	15 56	16 03	16 14	16 21	16 28	16 35	16 42		16 49	16 56	17 03	17 14	17 21	17 28	17 28
Ebbsfleet International	a	15 13		15 24	15 31	15 38	15 46	15 52		15 59	16 07	16 13	16 24	16 31	16 39	16 46	16 52		16 59	17 07	17 13	17 24	17 31	17 38	17 38
	d			15 30		15 43				16 02			16 30		16 44				17 02			17 30		17 43	17 43
Gravesend 4	d					15 48									16 48									17 48	17 48
Strood 4	d					15 58									16 58									17 58	17 58
Maidstone West	d																								
Rochester 4	d					16 03									17 03									18 03	18 05
Chatham 4	d					16 05									17 05									18 05	18 07
Gillingham (Kent) 4	d					16 10									17 10									18 10	18 12
Rainham (Kent)	d					16 15									17 15									18 15	18 17
Sittingbourne 4	d					16 23									17 23									18 23	18 24
Faversham 2	a					16 33									17 33									18 33	18 33
Whitstable	d																								
Herne Bay	d																								
Birchington-on-Sea	d																								
Margate 4	d																								
Broadstairs	a																								
Ashford International	a			15 51						16 20			16 48						17 20			17 52			
	d		15 03						16 03									17 03							
Folkestone West	d																								
Folkestone Central	d																								
Dover Priory 4	a																								
Deal	a																								
Sandwich	a																								
Canterbury West 4	a		15 21						16 21									17 21							
	d		15 22						16 22									17 22							
Ramsgate 4	d		15a44						16a44									17a44							
Broadstairs	d																								
Margate 4	a																								

A 27 July

B not 27 July

Table 194

Mondays to Fridays

27 July to 10 August

St Pancras International - Kent High Speed Domestic Services

		SE	SE	SE [1]	SE	SE	SE	SE	SE	SE	SE	SE	SE [1]	SE	SE	SE		SE	SE	SE A	SE B	SE	SE	SE [1]	SE
St Pancras International	d	17 25	17 32		17 39	17 46	17 52	18 04	18 11	18 18	18 25	18 32		18 39	18 46	18 52		19 04	19 11	19 18	19 18	19 25	19 32		19 39
Stratford International	d	17 35	17 42		17 49	17 56	18 03	18 14	18 21	18 28	18 35	18 42		18 49	18 56	19 03		19 14	19 21	19 28	19 28	19 35	19 42		19 49
Ebbsfleet International	a	17 46	17 52		17 59	18 07	18 13	18 24	18 31	18 38	18 46	18 52		18 59	19 07	19 13		19 24	19 31	19 38	19 38	19 46	19 52		19 59
	d				18 02			18 30		18 40				19 02				19 30		19 45	19 45				20 02
Gravesend	d									18 45										19 51	19 51				
Strood	d									18 55										20 02	20 01				
Maidstone West	d																								
Rochester	d									19 03										20 06	20 08				
Chatham	d									19 06										20 09	20 10				
Gillingham (Kent)	d									19 11										20 13	20 15				
Rainham (Kent)	d									19 16										20 18	20 20				
Sittingbourne	d									19 24										20 26	20 27				
Faversham	a									19 33										20 34	20 36				
Whitstable	d																								
Herne Bay	d																								
Birchington-on-Sea	d																								
Margate	d																								
Broadstairs	a																								
Ashford International	a				18 20			18 48						19 20				19 51							20 20
	d			18 03									19 03											20 03	
Folkestone West	d																								
Folkestone Central	d																								
Dover Priory	a																								
Deal	a																								
Sandwich	a																								
Canterbury West	a			18 21									19 21											20 21	
	d			18 22									19 22											20 22	
Ramsgate	d			18a44									19a47											20a47	
Broadstairs	d																								
Margate	a																								

		SE	SE		SE	SE	SE	SE	SE	SE [1]	SE	SE	SE		SE	SE	SE	SE	SE	SE	SE	SE	SE	SE
St Pancras International	d	19 46	19 52		20 04	20 11	20 18	20 25	20 32		20 39	20 46	20 52		21 04	21 11	21 18	21 25	21 32	21 39	21 46	21 52	22 04	22 11
Stratford International	d	19 56	20 03		20 14	20 21	20 28	20 35	20 42		20 49	20 56	21 03		21 14	21 21	21 28	21 35	21 42	21 49	21 56	22 03	22 14	22 21
Ebbsfleet International	a	20 07	20 13		20 24	20 31	20 38	20 46	20 52		20 59	21 07	21 13		21 24	21 31	21 38	21 46	21 52	21 59	22 07	22 13	22 24	22 31
	d				20 30		20 43				21 02				21 30		21 43			22 02				
Gravesend	d						20 48										21 48							
Strood	d						20 58										21 58							
Maidstone West	d																							
Rochester	d						21 03										22 03							
Chatham	d						21 05										22 05							
Gillingham (Kent)	d						21 10										22 10							
Rainham (Kent)	d						21 15										22 15							
Sittingbourne	d						21 23										22 23							
Faversham	a						21 33										22 33							
Whitstable	d																							
Herne Bay	d																							
Birchington-on-Sea	d																							
Margate	d																							
Broadstairs	a																							
Ashford International	a				20 51						21 20				21 51					22 20				
	d									21 03														
Folkestone West	d																							
Folkestone Central	d																							
Dover Priory	a																							
Deal	a																							
Sandwich	a																							
Canterbury West	a									21 21														
	d									21 22														
Ramsgate	d									21a47														
Broadstairs	d																							
Margate	a																							

A not 27 July

B 27 July

Table 194

Mondays to Fridays

27 July to 10 August

St Pancras International - Kent High Speed Domestic Services

		SE	SE	SE	SE	SE	SE	SE	SE	SE	SE		SE	SE	SE A	SE B	SE	SE	SE	SE
St Pancras International	d	22 18	22 25	22 32	22 39	22 46	22 52	23 04	23 11	23 16	23 21		23 26	23 32	23 36	23 36	23 41	23 47	23 51	23 56
Stratford International	d	22 28	22 35	22 42	22 47	22 56	23 02	23 14	23 21	23 24	23 30		23 35	23 42	23 46	23 46	23 50	23 57	00 01	00 05
Ebbsfleet International	a	22 38	22 46	22 52	22 57	23 07	23 12	23 24	23 31	23 34	23 41		23 45	23 52	23 56	23 57	00 01	00 07	00 10	00 16
	d																			
Gravesend	d																			
Strood	d																			
Maidstone West	d																			
Rochester	d																			
Chatham	d																			
Gillingham (Kent)	d																			
Rainham (Kent)	d																			
Sittingbourne	d																			
Faversham	a																			
Whitstable	d																			
Herne Bay	d																			
Birchington-on-Sea	d																			
Margate	d																			
Broadstairs	a																			
Ashford International	a																			
	d																			
Folkestone West	d																			
Folkestone Central	d																			
Dover Priory	a																			
Deal	a																			
Sandwich	a																			
Canterbury West	a																			
	d																			
Ramsgate	d																			
Broadstairs	d																			
Margate	a																			

Mondays to Fridays

29 August to 7 September

		SE C	SE D	SE C	SE E	SE F	SE C	SE D	SE [1] G	SE E	SE C		SE F	SE G	SE E	SE	SE	SE		SE	SE [1]			SE	SE
St Pancras International	d	22p55	22p55	23p12	23p12	23p12	23p25	23p25		23p42	23p55		23p55	00 12	00 15	00 48	01 48	02 35		06 24				06 40	06 44
Stratford International	d	23p02	23p03	23p19	23p20	23p20	23p32	23p33		23p50	00 02		00 03	00 20	00a21	00a54	01a54	02a41		06 32				06 47	06 58
Ebbsfleet International	a	23p12	23p13	23p30	23p31	23p31	23p42	23p43		00 01	00 12		00 13	00 31						06 42				06 58	
	d	23p13	23p14	23p31	23p32	23p32	23p43	23p44		00 02	00 13		00 14	00 32						06 42				06 59	
Gravesend	d	23p18	23p18				23p48	23p48			00 18		00 18							06 46					
Strood	d	23p28	23p28				23p58	23p58			00 28		00 28							06 57					07 25
Maidstone West	d																			07a12					07a45
Rochester	d	23p33	23p33				00 03	00 03			00 33		00 33												
Chatham	d	23p35	23p35				00 05	00 05			00 35		00 35												
Gillingham (Kent)	d	23p40	23p40				00 10	00 10			00 40		00 40												
Rainham (Kent)	d	23p45	23p45				00 15	00 15			00 45		00 45												
Sittingbourne	d	23p53	23p53				00 23	00 23			00 53		00 53												
Faversham	a	00 03	00 03				00 33	00 33			01 03		01 03												
Whitstable	d																								
Herne Bay	d																								
Birchington-on-Sea	d																								
Margate	d																								
Broadstairs	a																								
Ashford International	a			23p50	23p50	23p51				00 21				00 51										07 18	
	d			23p52	23p52	23p53			00 03												06 33			07 22	
Folkestone West	d			00 05	00 05	00 06																			
Folkestone Central	d			00 08	00 08	00 08																			
Dover Priory	a			00 20	00 20	00 20																			
Deal	a																								
Sandwich	a																								
Canterbury West	a								00 24												06 54			07 38	
	d								00 25												06 55			07 39	
Ramsgate	d								00a47												07a17			08 01	
Broadstairs	d																							08 06	
Margate	a																							08 11	

A not 27 July

B 27 July

C 29 August

D not 29 August

E 3 September

F not 29 August, 3 September

G not 3 September

Table 194

Mondays to Fridays

29 August to 7 September

St Pancras International - Kent High Speed Domestic Services

Station		SE	SE	SE	SE	SE	SE	SE	SE	SE	SE	SE	SE	SE	SE	SE	SE	SE	SE	SE
St Pancras International	d	06 55	07 09	07 25	07 28	07 40	07 45	07 51	07 58	08 10	08 16	08 21	08 34	08 40	08 47	08 54	09 06	09 15	09 25	09 42
Stratford International	d	07 02	07 17	07 33	07 38	07 48	07 53	08 02	08 13	08 18	08 24	08 29	08 42	08 48	08 55	09 05	09 13	09 25	09 33	09 49
Ebbsfleet International	a	07 12	07 28	07 43	07 48	07 59	08 04	08 12	08 23	08 29	08 35	08 39		08 59	09 05	09 15	09 24	09 35	09 43	10 00
	d	07 13	07 32	07 44		08 00		08 13		08 30		08 43		09 00		09 17	09 28		09 43	10 01
Gravesend	d	07 21		07 48				08 18				08 48				09 22			09 48	
Strood	d	07 31		07 58				08 28				08 58				09 32			09 58	
Maidstone West	d																			
Rochester	d	07 36		08 03				08 33				09 03				09 37			10 03	
Chatham	d	07 38		08 05				08 35				09 05				09 39			10 05	
Gillingham (Kent)	d	07 43		08 10				08 40				09 10				09 44			10 10	
Rainham (Kent)	d	07 48		08 15				08 45				09 15				09 49			10 15	
Sittingbourne	d	07 57		08 23				08 53				09 23				09 56			10 23	
Faversham	a	08 05		08 33				09 03				09 33				10 04			10 33	
Whitstable	d																			
Herne Bay	d																			
Birchington-on-Sea	d																			
Margate	d																			
Broadstairs	a																			
Ashford International	a		07 54			08 20				08 50			09 10	09 20			09 48			10 20
	d		07 55			08 22				08 52				09 22			09 52			10 22
Folkestone West	d		08 08							09 05							10 05			
Folkestone Central	d		08 11							09 08							10 08			
Dover Priory	a		08 21							09 20							10 20			
Deal	a																			
Sandwich	a																			
Canterbury West	a					08 38								09 38						10 38
	d					08 39								09 39						10 39
Ramsgate	d					08 59								09 59						10 59
Broadstairs	d					09 05								10 05						11 05
Margate	a					09 10								10 10						11 10

Station		SE	SE	SE	SE	SE	SE	SE	SE	SE	SE	SE	SE	SE	SE	SE	SE	SE	SE	SE
St Pancras International	d	09 47	09 54	10 10	10 14	10 28	10 40	10 47	10 51	11 11	11 18	11 24	11 41	11 48	11 55	12 11	12 18	12 21	12 41	12 45
Stratford International	d	09 55	10 02	10 17	10 25	10 36	10 47	10 55	10 58	11 19	11 26	11 31	11 49	11 56	12 03	12 19	12 26	12 32	12 49	12 52
Ebbsfleet International	a	10 05	10 12	10 28	10 35	10 46	10 58	11 05	11 08	11 30	11 36	11 41	12 00	12 06	12 13	12 30	12 36	12 42	13 00	13 02
	d		10 13	10 29		10 47	10 59		11 13	11 31		11 44	12 01		12 14	12 31		12 43	13 01	
Gravesend	d		10 18			10 51			11 18			11 48			12 18			12 48		
Strood	d		10 28			11 01			11 28			11 58			12 28			12 58		
Maidstone West	d																			
Rochester	d		10 33			11 06			11 33			12 03			12 33			13 03		
Chatham	d		10 35			11 08			11 35			12 05			12 35			13 05		
Gillingham (Kent)	d		10 40			11 13			11 40			12 10			12 40			13 10		
Rainham (Kent)	d		10 45			11 18			11 45			12 15			12 45			13 15		
Sittingbourne	d		10 53			11 25			11 53			12 23			12 53			13 22		
Faversham	a		11 03			11 33			12 03			12 33			13 03			13 30		
Whitstable	d																			
Herne Bay	d																			
Birchington-on-Sea	d																			
Margate	d																			
Broadstairs	a																			
Ashford International	a			10 48			11 18			11 50			12 20			12 50			13 20	
	d			10 52			11 22			11 52			12 22			12 52			13 22	
Folkestone West	d			11 05						12 05						13 05				
Folkestone Central	d			11 08						12 08						13 08				
Dover Priory	a			11 20						12 20						13 20				
Deal	a																			
Sandwich	a																			
Canterbury West	a						11 38						12 38						13 38	
	d						11 39						12 39						13 39	
Ramsgate	d						11 59						12 59						13 59	
Broadstairs	d						12 05						13 05						14 05	
Margate	a						12 10						13 10						14 10	

Station		SE	SE	SE	SE	SE	SE	SE	SE	SE	SE	SE	SE	SE	SE	SE	SE	SE	SE	SE
St Pancras International	d	12 51	13 11	13 18	13 25	13 41	13 48	13 54	14 12	14 18	14 25	14 41	14 48	14 54	15 11	15 18	15 24	15 41	15 48	15 54
Stratford International	d	12 58	13 19	13 26	13 33	13 49	13 56	14 02	14 19	14 26	14 33	14 49	14 56	15 02	15 19	15 26	15 32	15 49	15 56	16 02
Ebbsfleet International	a	13 08	13 30	13 36	13 43	14 00	14 06	14 12	14 30	14 36	14 43	15 00	15 06	15 12	15 30	15 36	15 42	16 00	16 06	16 12
	d	13 13	13 31		13 44	14 01		14 14	14 31		14 44	15 01		15 14	15 31		15 44	16 01		16 14
Gravesend	d	13 18			13 48			14 18			14 48			15 18			15 48			16 18
Strood	d	13 28			13 58			14 28			14 58			15 28			15 58			16 28
Maidstone West	d																			
Rochester	d	13 33			14 03			14 33			15 03			15 33			16 03			16 33
Chatham	d	13 35			14 05			14 35			15 05			15 35			16 05			16 35
Gillingham (Kent)	d	13 40			14 10			14 40			15 10			15 40			16 10			16 40
Rainham (Kent)	d	13 45			14 15			14 45			15 15			15 45			16 15			16 45
Sittingbourne	d	13 53			14 23			14 53			15 23			15 53			16 23			16 53
Faversham	a	14 03			14 33			15 03			15 33			16 03			16 33			17 03
Whitstable	d																			
Herne Bay	d																			
Birchington-on-Sea	d																			
Margate	d																			
Broadstairs	a																			
Ashford International	a		13 50			14 20			14 50			15 20			15 50			16 20		
	d		13 52			14 22			14 52			15 22			15 52			16 22		
Folkestone West	d		14 05						15 05						16 05					
Folkestone Central	d		14 08						15 08						16 08					
Dover Priory	a		14 20						15 20						16 20					
Deal	a																			
Sandwich	a																			
Canterbury West	a					14 38						15 38						16 38		
	d					14 39						15 39						16 39		
Ramsgate	d					14 59						15 59						16 59		
Broadstairs	d					15 05						16 05						17 05		
Margate	a					15 10						16 10						17 10		

Table 194

Mondays to Fridays

29 August to 7 September

St Pancras International - Kent High Speed Domestic Services

Station		SE	SE	SE	SE	SE	SE	SE		SE	SE	SE	SE	SE		SE	SE	SE	SE		SE
St Pancras International	d	16 09	16 15	16 26	16 41	16 47	16 55	17 10		17 14	17 17		17 25	17 40		17 44	17 47	17 54	18 10		18 14
Stratford International	d	16 17	16 23	16 33	16 49	16 55	17 03	17 18		17 22	17 25		17 32	17 48		17 52	17 55	18 02	18 18		18 22
Ebbsfleet International	a	16 28	16 33	16 43	17 00	17 05	17 13				17 35		17 42				18 05	18 12			
	d	16 29		16 44	17 01		17 14						17 43					18 13			
Gravesend	d			16 48			17 18			17 36						18 06					18 38
Strood	d			16 58			17 28			17 46						18 18					18 49
Maidstone West	d									18a02						18a32					19a05
Rochester	d			17 03			17 34						17 59					18 31			
Chatham	d			17 05			17 37						18 02					18 34			
Gillingham (Kent)	d			17 10			17 43						18 07					18 39			
Rainham (Kent)	d			17 15			17 48						18 12					18 44			
Sittingbourne	d			17 23			17 57						18 19					18 52			
Faversham	a			17 33			18 05						18 27					19 00			
Whitstable	d												18 37					19 09			
Herne Bay	d												18 43					19 15			
Birchington-on-Sea	d												18 52					19 24			
Margate	d											18 53	18 58					19 30			
Broadstairs	a											18 58	19 04					19 36			
Ashford International	a	16 48			17 20			17 46						18 16					18 46		
	d	16 52			17 23			17 50	17 53					18 23	18 20				18 50	18 53	
Folkestone West	d	17 05						18 03							18 33				19 05		
Folkestone Central	d	17 08						18 06							18 36				19 08		
Dover Priory	a	17 20						18 18							18 47				19 20		
Deal	a														19 06						
Sandwich	a														19 13						
Canterbury West	a				17 39				18 09			19 24		18 39						19 09	
	d				17 40				18 10					18 40						19 10	
Ramsgate	d				17 59				18 29					18 59						19 31	
Broadstairs	d				18 05				18 35					19 05						19 36	
Margate	a				18 10				18 40					19 10						19 41	

Station		SE	SE	SE		SE	SE	SE		SE	SE	SE	SE	SE	SE	SE	SE	SE	SE
St Pancras International	d	18 17	18 24	18 40		18 47	18 55	19 09		19 24	19 41	19 54	20 11	20 25	20 41	20 55	21 11	21 25	21 41
Stratford International	d	18 25	18 32	18 48		18 55	19 02	19 17		19 32	19 49	20 02	20 19	20 33	20 49	21 03	21 19	21 33	21 49
Ebbsfleet International	a	18 35	18 42			19 05	19 12	19 28		19 42	20 00	20 12	20 30	20 43	21 00	21 13	21 30	21 43	22 00
	d		18 43				19 13	19 29		19 45	20 01	20 14	20 31	20 44	21 01	21 14	21 31	21 44	22 01
Gravesend	d						19 20			19 51		20 18		20 48		21 18		21 48	
Strood	d						19 30			20 01		20 28		20 58		21 28		21 58	
Maidstone West	d																		
Rochester	d		19 03				19 35			20 08		20 33		21 03		21 33		22 03	
Chatham	d		19 06				19 38			20 10		20 35		21 05		21 35		22 05	
Gillingham (Kent)	d		19 11				19 43			20 15		20 40		21 10		21 40		22 10	
Rainham (Kent)	d		19 16				19 48			20 20		20 45		21 15		21 45		22 15	
Sittingbourne	d		19 24				19 55			20 27		20 53		21 23		21 53		22 23	
Faversham	a		19 32				20 04			20 36		21 03		21 33		22 03		22 33	
Whitstable	d		19 42																
Herne Bay	d		19 48																
Birchington-on-Sea	d		19 57																
Margate	d		20 04																
Broadstairs	a		20 09																
Ashford International	a			19 16				19 48			20 20		20 50		21 20		21 50		22 20
	d			19 23	19 20			19 52	19 55		20 22		20 52		21 22		21 52		22 22
Folkestone West	d				19 33			20 05					21 05				22 05		
Folkestone Central	d				19 36			20 08					21 08				22 08		
Dover Priory	a				19 47			20 20					21 20				22 20		
Deal	a				20 06														
Sandwich	a				20 13														
Canterbury West	a			19 39					20 11		20 38				21 38				22 38
	d			19 40					20 12		20 39				21 39				22 39
Ramsgate	d			19 59					20 32		21 00				21 59				22 59
Broadstairs	d			20 05					20 38		21 05				22 05				23 05
Margate	a			20 10					20 43		21 11				22 10				23 10

Station		SE	SE	SE	SE	SE	SE	SE	SE	SE	SE	SE
St Pancras International	d	21 47	21 55	22 11	22 25	22 42	22 48	22 55	23 12	23 25	23 48	23 55
Stratford International	d	21 55	22 03	22 19	22 33	22 50	22 56	23 03	23 20	23 33	23a54	00 03
Ebbsfleet International	a	22 05	22 13	22 30	22 43	23 01	23 06	23 13	23 31	23 43		00 13
	d		22 14	22 31	22 44	23 02		23 14	23 32	23 44		00 14
Gravesend	d		22 18		22 48			23 18		23 48		00 18
Strood	d		22 28		22 58			23 28		23 58		00 28
Maidstone West	d											
Rochester	d		22 33		23 03			23 33		00 03		00 33
Chatham	d		22 35		23 05			23 35		00 05		00 35
Gillingham (Kent)	d		22 40		23 10			23 40		00 10		00 40
Rainham (Kent)	d		22 45		23 15			23 45		00 15		00 45
Sittingbourne	d		22 53		23 23			23 53		00 23		00 53
Faversham	a		23 03		23 33			00 03		00 33		01 03
Whitstable	d											
Herne Bay	d											
Birchington-on-Sea	d											
Margate	d											
Broadstairs	a											
Ashford International	a			22 50		23 21			23 51			
	d			22 52		23 23			23 53			
Folkestone West	d			23 05					00 06			
Folkestone Central	d			23 08					00 08			
Dover Priory	a			23 20					00 20			
Deal	a											
Sandwich	a											
Canterbury West	a					23 38						
	d					23 39						
Ramsgate	d					23a59						
Broadstairs	d											
Margate	a											

Table 194

Saturdays

until 21 July, 18 Aug and from 15 Sep

St Pancras International - Kent High Speed Domestic Services

		SE	SE	SE	SE	SE ■1	SE	SE ■1	SE	SE A	SE B	SE	SE ■1	SE	SE	SE	SE	SE	SE
St Pancras International	d	22p55	23p12	23p25	23p55		00 12		06 40	06 52	06 55	07 12		07 42	07 52	08 12	08 40	08 50	09 10
Stratford International	d	23p02	23p19	23p32	00 02		00 19		06 47	06 59	07 02	07 19		07 49	07 58	08 19	08 47	09 04	09 17
Ebbsfleet International	a	23p12	23p30	23p42	00 12		00 30		06 58	07 09	07 12	07 30		08 00	08 08	08 30	08 58	09 14	09 28
	d	23p13	23p31	23p43	00 13		00 31		06 59	07 13	07 13	07 31		08 01	08 13	08 31	08 59	09 15	09 29
Gravesend	d	23p18		23p48	00 18					07 17	07 18				08 18			09 20	
Strood	d	23p28		23p58	00 28					07 27	07 28				08 28			09 30	
Maidstone West	d																		
Rochester	d	23p33		00 03	00 33					07 32	07 33				08 33			09 34	
Chatham	d	23p35		00 05	00 35					07 34	07 35				08 35			09 37	
Gillingham (Kent)	d	23p40		00 10	00 40					07 39	07 40				08 40			09 41	
Rainham (Kent)	d	23p45		00 15	00 45					07 44	07 45				08 45			09 46	
Sittingbourne	d	23p53		00 23	00 53					07 51	07 53				08 53			09 54	
Faversham	a	00 03		00 33	01 03					08 03	08 03				09 03			10 03	
Whitstable	d																		
Herne Bay	d																		
Birchington-on-Sea	d																		
Margate	d																		
Broadstairs	a																		
Ashford International	a		23p50				00 50		07 18			07 51		08 20		08 50	09 18		09 48
	d		23p52			00 03		07 03	07 22			07 52	08 03	08 22		08 52	09 22		09 52
Folkestone West	d		00 05									08 05				09 05			10 05
Folkestone Central	d		00 08									08 08				09 08			10 08
Dover Priory	a		00 20									08 20				09 20			10 20
Deal	a																		
Sandwich	a																		
Canterbury West	a					00 24		07 21	07 38				08 21	08 38			09 38		
	d					00 25		07 22	07 39				08 22	08 39			09 39		
Ramsgate	d					00a47		07a44	07 59				08a44	08 59			09 59		
Broadstairs	d								08 05					09 05			10 05		
Margate	a								08 10					09 10			10 10		

		SE	SE	SE	SE	SE	SE	SE	SE	SE	SE	SE	SE	SE	SE	SE	SE	SE
St Pancras International	d	09 25	09 42	09 55	10 12	10 28	10 42	10 52	11 12	11 28	11 42	11 55	12 12	12 28	12 42	12 55	13 12	13 25
Stratford International	d	09 32	09 49	10 02	10 19	10 35	10 49	10 58	11 19	11 35	11 49	12 02	12 19	12 35	12 49	13 06	13 19	13 32
Ebbsfleet International	a	09 42	10 00	10 12	10 30	10 45	11 00	11 08	11 30	11 45	12 00	12 12	12 30	12 45	13 00	13 16	13 30	13 42
	d	09 43	10 01	10 13	10 31	10 46	11 01	11 13	11 31	11 46	12 01	12 13	12 31	12 46	13 01	13 17	13 31	13 43
Gravesend	d	09 48		10 18		10 51		11 18		11 51		12 18		12 51		13 22		13 48
Strood	d	09 58		10 28		11 01		11 28		12 01		12 28		13 01		13 32		13 58
Maidstone West	d																	
Rochester	d	10 03		10 33		11 06		11 33		12 06		12 33		13 06		13 37		14 03
Chatham	d	10 05		10 35		11 08		11 35		12 08		12 35		13 08		13 39		14 05
Gillingham (Kent)	d	10 10		10 40		11 13		11 40		12 13		12 40		13 13		13 44		14 10
Rainham (Kent)	d	10 15		10 45		11 18		11 45		12 18		12 45		13 18		13 49		14 15
Sittingbourne	d	10 23		10 53		11 25		11 53		12 25		12 53		13 25		13 56		14 23
Faversham	a	10 33		11 03		11 34		12 03		12 34		13 03		13 34		14 04		14 33
Whitstable	d																	
Herne Bay	d																	
Birchington-on-Sea	d																	
Margate	d																	
Broadstairs	a																	
Ashford International	a		10 20		10 50		11 20		11 50		12 20		12 50		13 20		13 50	
	d		10 22		10 52		11 22		11 52		12 22		12 52		13 22		13 52	
Folkestone West	d				11 05				12 05				13 05				14 05	
Folkestone Central	d				11 08				12 08				13 08				14 08	
Dover Priory	a				11 20				12 20				13 20				14 20	
Deal	a																	
Sandwich	a																	
Canterbury West	a		10 38				11 38				12 38				13 38			
	d		10 39				11 39				12 39				13 39			
Ramsgate	d		10 59				11 59				12 59				13 59			
Broadstairs	d		11 05				12 05				13 05				14 05			
Margate	a		11 10				12 10				13 10				14 10			

A 19 May

B not 19 May

Table 194

Saturdays

until 21 July, 18 Aug and from 15 Sep

St Pancras International - Kent High Speed Domestic Services

		SE	SE	SE	SE	SE	SE	SE	SE	SE	SE	SE	SE	SE	SE	SE	SE	SE	SE
St Pancras International	d	13 42	13 55	14 12	14 25	14 42	14 55	15 12	15 25	15 42	15 55	16 10	16 28	16 42	16 55	17 12	17 25	17 42	17 55
Stratford International	d	13 49	14 02	14 19	14 32	14 49	15 02	15 19	15 32	15 49	16 02	16 17	16 35	16 49	17 02	17 19	17 32	17 49	18 02
Ebbsfleet International	a	14 00	14 12	14 30	14 42	15 00	15 12	15 30	15 42	16 00	16 12	16 28	16 45	17 00	17 12	17 30	17 42	18 00	18 12
	d	14 01	14 13	14 31	14 43	15 01	15 13	15 31	15 43	16 01	16 13	16 29	16 46	17 01	17 13	17 31	17 43	18 01	18 13
Gravesend	d		14 18		14 48		15 18		15 48		16 18		16 51		17 18		17 48		18 18
Strood	d		14 28		14 58		15 28		15 58		16 28		17 01		17 28		17 58		18 28
Maidstone West	d																		
Rochester	d		14 33		15 03		15 33		16 03		16 33		17 06		17 33		18 03		18 33
Chatham	d		14 35		15 05		15 35		16 05		16 35		17 08		17 35		18 05		18 35
Gillingham (Kent)	d		14 40		15 10		15 40		16 10		16 40		17 13		17 40		18 10		18 40
Rainham (Kent)	d		14 45		15 15		15 45		16 15		16 45		17 18		17 45		18 15		18 45
Sittingbourne	d		14 53		15 23		15 53		16 23		16 53		17 25		17 53		18 23		18 53
Faversham	a		15 03		15 33		16 03		16 33		17 03		17 34		18 03		18 33		19 03
Whitstable	d																		
Herne Bay	d																		
Birchington-on-Sea	d																		
Margate	d																		
Broadstairs	a																		
Ashford International	a	14 20		14 50		15 20		15 50		16 20		16 48		17 20		17 50		18 20	
	d	14 22		14 52		15 22		15 52		16 22		16 52		17 22		17 52		18 22	
Folkestone West	d			15 05				16 05				17 05				18 05			
Folkestone Central	d			15 08				16 08				17 08				18 08			
Dover Priory	a			15 20				16 20				17 20				18 20			
Deal	a																		
Sandwich	a																		
Canterbury West	a	14 38				15 38				16 38				17 38				18 38	
	d	14 39				15 39				16 39				17 39				18 39	
Ramsgate	d	14 59				15 59				16 59				17 59				18 59	
Broadstairs	d	15 05				16 05				17 05				18 05				19 05	
Margate	a	15 10				16 10				17 10				18 10				19 10	

		SE	SE	SE	SE	SE	SE	SE	SE	SE	SE	SE	SE	SE	SE	SE	SE	SE	SE
St Pancras International	d	18 12	18 25	18 42	18 55	19 12	19 25	19 42	19 55	20 12	20 25	20 42	20 55	21 12	21 25	21 42	21 55	22 12	22 25
Stratford International	d	18 19	18 32	18 49	19 02	19 19	19 32	19 49	20 02	20 19	20 32	20 49	21 02	21 19	21 32	21 49	22 02	22 19	22 32
Ebbsfleet International	a	18 30	18 42	19 00	19 12	19 30	19 42	20 00	20 12	20 30	20 42	21 00	21 12	21 30	21 42	22 00	22 12	22 30	22 42
	d	18 31	18 43	19 01	19 13	19 31	19 43	20 01	20 13	20 31	20 43	21 01	21 13	21 31	21 43	22 01	22 13	22 31	22 43
Gravesend	d		18 48		19 18		19 48		20 18		20 48		21 18		21 48		22 18		22 48
Strood	d		18 58		19 28		19 58		20 28		20 58		21 28		21 58		22 28		22 58
Maidstone West	d																		
Rochester	d		19 03		19 33		20 03		20 33		21 03		21 33		22 03		22 33		23 03
Chatham	d		19 05		19 35		20 05		20 35		21 05		21 35		22 05		22 35		23 05
Gillingham (Kent)	d		19 10		19 40		20 10		20 40		21 10		21 40		22 10		22 40		23 10
Rainham (Kent)	d		19 15		19 45		20 15		20 45		21 15		21 45		22 15		22 45		23 15
Sittingbourne	d		19 23		19 53		20 23		20 53		21 23		21 53		22 23		22 53		23 23
Faversham	a		19 33		20 03		20 33		21 03		21 33		22 03		22 31		23 01		23 31
Whitstable	d																		
Herne Bay	d																		
Birchington-on-Sea	d																		
Margate	d																		
Broadstairs	a																		
Ashford International	a	18 50		19 20		19 50		20 20		20 50		21 20		21 50		22 20		22 50	
	d	18 52		19 22		19 52		20 22		20 52		21 22		21 52		22 22		22 52	
Folkestone West	d	19 05				20 05				21 05				22 05				23 05	
Folkestone Central	d	19 08				20 08				21 08				22 08				23 08	
Dover Priory	a	19 20				20 20				21 20				22 20				23 20	
Deal	a																		
Sandwich	a																		
Canterbury West	a			19 38				20 38				21 38				22 38			
	d			19 39				20 39				21 39				22 39			
Ramsgate	d			19 59				20 59				21 59				22 59			
Broadstairs	d			20 05				21 05				22 05				23 05			
Margate	a			20 10				21 10				22 10				23 10			

		SE	SE	SE	SE	SE
St Pancras International	d	22 42	22 55	23 12	23 25	23 55
Stratford International	d	22 49	23 02	23 19	23 32	00 02
Ebbsfleet International	a	23 00	23 12	23 30	23 42	00 12
	d	23 01	23 13	23 31	23 43	00 13
Gravesend	d		23 18		23 48	00 18
Strood	d		23 28		23 58	00 28
Maidstone West	d					
Rochester	d		23 33		00 03	00 33
Chatham	d		23 35		00 05	00 35
Gillingham (Kent)	d		23 40		00 10	00 40
Rainham (Kent)	d		23 45		00 15	00 45
Sittingbourne	d		23 53		00 23	00 53
Faversham	a		00 01		00 31	01 01
Whitstable	d					
Herne Bay	d					
Birchington-on-Sea	d					
Margate	d					
Broadstairs	a					
Ashford International	a	23 20		23 50		
	d	23 22		23 52		
Folkestone West	d			00 05		
Folkestone Central	d			00 08		
Dover Priory	a			00 20		
Deal	a					
Sandwich	a					
Canterbury West	a	23 38				
	d	23 39				
Ramsgate	d	23a59				
Broadstairs	d					
Margate	a					

Table 194

Saturdays
28 July to 11 August

St Pancras International - Kent
High Speed Domestic Services

		SE	SE	SE	SE	SE	SE [1]	SE	SE	SE	SE	SE	SE	SE	SE	SE	SE	SE	SE	SE	SE	SE	SE
St Pancras International [15] ⊖	d	23p41	23p47	23p51	23p56	00 02		00 06	00 11	00 17	00 21	00 27	00 32	00 36	00 41	00 47	00 51	00 57	01 02	01 06	01 11	01 17	01 21
Stratford International ⊖	d	23p50	23p57	00 01	00 05	00 12		00 16	00 20	00 27	00 30	00 36	00 42	00 46	00 50	00 57	01 00	01 06	01 12	01 16	01 20	01 26	01 30
Ebbsfleet International	a	00 01	00 07	00 10	00 16	00 22		00 26	00 31	00 37	00 41	00 47	00 52	00 56	01 01	01 07	01 11	01 18	01 22	01 26	01 33	01 36	01 41
	d														01 03			01 20		01 29	01 35	01 38	
Gravesend [4]	d																					01 43	
Strood [4]	d																					01 53	
Maidstone West	d																						
Rochester [4]	d																					01 57	
Chatham [4]	d																					02 00	
Gillingham (Kent) [4]	d																					02 04	
Rainham (Kent)	d																					02 09	
Sittingbourne [4]	d																					02 17	
Faversham [2]	a																					02 25	
Whitstable	d																						
Herne Bay	d																						
Birchington-on-Sea	d																						
Margate [4]	d																						
Broadstairs	a																						
Ashford International	a														01 29			01 38		01 49	01 54		
	d						00 03																
Folkestone West	d																						
Folkestone Central	d																						
Dover Priory [4]	a																						
Deal	a																						
Sandwich	a																						
Canterbury West [4]	a						00 24																
	d						00 25																
Ramsgate [4]	d						00a47																
Broadstairs	d																						
Margate [4]	a																						

		SE	SE	SE	SE	SE	SE	SE	SE	SE	SE	SE	SE	SE	SE	SE	SE [1]	SE	SE [1]	SE [1]	SE	SE
St Pancras International [15] ⊖	d	01 27	01 32	01 38	01 44	01 55	02 02	02 32	03 02	03 32	04 02	04 32	05 02	05 32	06 04	06 32		06 52			07 04	07 11
Stratford International ⊖	d	01 36	01 42	01 48	01 54	02 04	02a08	02a38	03a08	03a38	04a08	04a38	05a08	05 42	06 14	06 42		07 03			07 14	07 21
Ebbsfleet International	a	01 47	01 52	01 58	02 04	02 14								05 52	06 24	06 52		07 13			07 24	07 31
	d	01 49		02 00	02 05	02 16								05 56							07 30	
Gravesend [4]	d					02 21																
Strood [4]	d					02 31																
Maidstone West	d																					
Rochester [4]	d				02 20	02 35																
Chatham [4]	d				02 23	02 38																
Gillingham (Kent) [4]	d				02 27	02 42																
Rainham (Kent)	d				02 32	02 47																
Sittingbourne [4]	d				02 40	02 55																
Faversham [2]	a				02 48	03 03																
Whitstable	d																					
Herne Bay	d																					
Birchington-on-Sea	d																					
Margate [4]	d																					
Broadstairs	a																					
Ashford International	a	02 07		02 18										06 14							07 51	
	d																06 33		07 03	07 33		
Folkestone West	d																					
Folkestone Central	d																					
Dover Priory [4]	a																					
Deal	a																					
Sandwich	a																					
Canterbury West [4]	a																06 54		07 21	07 54		
	d																06 55		07 22	07 55		
Ramsgate [4]	d																07a15		07a44	08a15		
Broadstairs	d																					
Margate [4]	a																					

Table 194

Saturdays
28 July to 11 August

St Pancras International - Kent
High Speed Domestic Services

		SE	SE	SE	SE [1]	SE	SE	SE	SE	SE	SE	SE	SE	SE [1]	SE	SE	SE	SE	SE	SE	SE	SE	SE [1]
St Pancras International [15] ⊖	d	07 18	07 25	07 32		07 39	07 46	07 52	08 04	08 11	08 18	08 25	08 32		08 39	08 46	08 52	09 04	09 11	09 18	09 25	09 32	
Stratford International ⊖	d	07 28	07 35	07 42		07 49	07 56	08 03	08 14	08 21	08 28	08 35	08 42		08 49	08 56	09 03	09 14	09 21	09 28	09 35	09 42	
Ebbsfleet International	a	07 38	07 46	07 52		07 59	08 07	08 13	08 24	08 31	08 39	08 46	08 52		09 00	09 07	09 13	09 24	09 31	09 38	09 46	09 52	
	d	07 43				08 02			08 30		08 44				09 02			09 30		09 43			
Gravesend [4]	d	07 48									08 48									09 48			
Strood [4]	d	07 58									08 58									09 58			
Maidstone West	d																						
Rochester [4]	d	08 03									09 03									10 03			
Chatham [4]	d	08 05									09 05									10 05			
Gillingham (Kent) [4]	d	08 10									09 10									10 10			
Rainham (Kent)	d	08 15									09 15									10 15			
Sittingbourne [4]	d	08 23									09 23									10 23			
Faversham [2]	a	08 33									09 33									10 33			
Whitstable	d																						
Herne Bay	d																						
Birchington-on-Sea	d																						
Margate [4]	d																						
Broadstairs	a																						
Ashford International	a					08 20			08 51						09 20			09 48					
	d				08 03									09 03									10 03
Folkestone West	d																						
Folkestone Central	d																						
Dover Priory [4]	a																						
Deal	a																						
Sandwich	a																						
Canterbury West [4]	a				08 21									09 21									10 21
	d				08 22									09 22									10 22
Ramsgate [4]	d				08a44									09a48									10a44
Broadstairs	d																						
Margate [4]	a																						

		SE	SE	SE	SE	SE	SE	SE	SE	SE [1]	SE	SE	SE	SE	SE	SE	SE	SE	SE [1]	SE	SE	SE	SE
St Pancras International [15] ⊖	d	09 39	09 46	09 52	10 04	10 11	10 18	10 25	10 32		10 39	10 46	10 52	11 04	11 11	11 18	11 25	11 32		11 39	11 46	11 52	12 04
Stratford International ⊖	d	09 49	09 56	10 03	10 14	10 21	10 28	10 35	10 42		10 49	10 56	11 03	11 14	11 21	11 28	11 35	11 42		11 49	11 56	12 03	12 14
Ebbsfleet International	a	10 00	10 07	10 13	10 24	10 31	10 39	10 46	10 52		10 59	11 07	11 13	11 24	11 31	11 38	11 46	11 52		11 59	12 07	12 13	12 24
	d	10 02			10 30		10 44				11 02			11 30		11 43				12 02			12 30
Gravesend [4]	d						10 48									11 48							
Strood [4]	d						10 58									11 58							
Maidstone West	d																						
Rochester [4]	d						11 03									12 03							
Chatham [4]	d						11 05									12 05							
Gillingham (Kent) [4]	d						11 10									12 10							
Rainham (Kent)	d						11 15									12 15							
Sittingbourne [4]	d						11 23									12 23							
Faversham [2]	a						11 33									12 33							
Whitstable	d																						
Herne Bay	d																						
Birchington-on-Sea	d																						
Margate [4]	d																						
Broadstairs	a																						
Ashford International	a	10 20			10 51						11 20			11 51						12 20			12 51
	d									11 03									12 03				
Folkestone West	d																						
Folkestone Central	d																						
Dover Priory [4]	a																						
Deal	a																						
Sandwich	a																						
Canterbury West [4]	a									11 21									12 21				
	d									11 22									12 22				
Ramsgate [4]	d									11a44									12a44				
Broadstairs	d																						
Margate [4]	a																						

Table 194

Saturdays
28 July to 11 August

St Pancras International - Kent High Speed Domestic Services

		SE	SE		SE	SE	SE ■	SE	SE	SE	SE	SE	SE	SE		SE	SE ■	SE	SE	SE	SE	SE	SE	SE	SE
St Pancras International ⊖	d	12 11	12 18		12 25	12 32		12 39	12 46	12 52	13 04	13 11	13 18	13 25		13 32		13 39	13 46	13 52	14 04	14 11	14 18	14 25	14 32
Stratford International ⊖	d	12 21	12 28		12 35	12 42		12 49	12 56	13 03	13 14	13 21	13 28	13 35		13 42		13 49	13 56	14 03	14 14	14 21	14 28	14 35	14 42
Ebbsfleet International	a	12 31	12 39		12 46	12 52		12 59	13 07	13 13	13 24	13 31	13 38	13 46		13 52		13 59	14 07	14 13	14 24	14 31	14 38	14 46	14 52
	d		12 44					13 02			13 30		13 43					14 02			14 30		14 43		
Gravesend	d		12 48										13 48										14 48		
Strood	d		12 58										13 58										14 58		
Maidstone West	d																								
Rochester	d		13 03										14 03										15 03		
Chatham	d		13 05										14 05										15 05		
Gillingham (Kent)	d		13 10										14 10										15 10		
Rainham (Kent)	d		13 15										14 15										15 15		
Sittingbourne	d		13 23										14 23										15 23		
Faversham	a		13 33										14 33										15 33		
Whitstable	d																								
Herne Bay	d																								
Birchington-on-Sea	d																								
Margate	d																								
Broadstairs	a																								
Ashford International	a							13 20			13 51							14 20			14 51				
	d						13 03										14 03								
Folkestone West	d																								
Folkestone Central	d																								
Dover Priory	a																								
Deal	a																								
Sandwich	a																								
Canterbury West	a						13 21										14 21								
	d						13 22										14 22								
Ramsgate	d						13a44										14a44								
Broadstairs	d																								
Margate	a																								

			SE ■	SE	SE	SE	SE	SE	SE	SE	SE	SE ■		SE	SE	SE	SE	SE	SE	SE	SE	SE ■	SE		SE
St Pancras International ⊖	d			14 39	14 46	14 52	15 04	15 11	15 18	15 25	15 32			15 39	15 46	15 52	16 04	16 11	16 18	16 25	16 32		16 39		16 46
Stratford International ⊖	d			14 49	14 56	15 03	15 14	15 21	15 28	15 35	15 42			15 49	15 56	16 03	16 14	16 21	16 28	16 35	16 42		16 49		16 56
Ebbsfleet International	a			14 59	15 07	15 13	15 24	15 31	15 38	15 46	15 52			15 59	16 07	16 13	16 24	16 31	16 39	16 46	16 52		16 59		17 07
	d			15 02			15 30		15 43					16 02			16 27		16 44				17 02		
Gravesend	d								15 48										16 48						
Strood	d								15 58										16 58						
Maidstone West	d																								
Rochester	d								16 03										17 03						
Chatham	d								16 05										17 05						
Gillingham (Kent)	d								16 10										17 10						
Rainham (Kent)	d								16 15										17 15						
Sittingbourne	d								16 23										17 23						
Faversham	a								16 33										17 33						
Whitstable	d																								
Herne Bay	d																								
Birchington-on-Sea	d																								
Margate	d																								
Broadstairs	a																								
Ashford International	a			15 20			15 51							16 20			16 46						17 20		
	d		15 03									16 03										17 03			
Folkestone West	d																								
Folkestone Central	d																								
Dover Priory	a																								
Deal	a																								
Sandwich	a																								
Canterbury West	a		15 21									16 21										17 21			
	d		15 22									16 22										17 22			
Ramsgate	d		15a44									16a44										17a44			
Broadstairs	d																								
Margate	a																								

Table 194

Saturdays
28 July to 11 August

St Pancras International - Kent High Speed Domestic Services

		SE	SE	SE	SE	SE	SE	SE ■	SE	SE		SE	SE	SE	SE	SE	SE	SE ■	SE	SE	SE		SE ■	SE	SE
St Pancras International ⊖	d	16 52	17 04	17 11	17 18	17 25	17 32		17 39	17 46		17 52	18 04	18 11	18 18	18 25	18 32		18 39	18 46	18 52			19 04	19 11
Stratford International ⊖	d	17 03	17 14	17 21	17 28	17 35	17 42		17 49	17 56		18 03	18 14	18 21	18 28	18 35	18 42		18 49	18 56	19 03			19 14	19 21
Ebbsfleet International	a	17 13	17 24	17 31	17 38	17 46	17 52		17 59	18 07		18 13	18 24	18 31	18 38	18 46	18 52		18 59	19 07	19 13			19 24	19 31
	d		17 30		17 43				18 02				18 30		18 43				19 02					19 30	
Gravesend	d				17 48										18 48										
Strood	d				17 58										18 58										
Maidstone West	d																								
Rochester	d				18 03										19 03										
Chatham	d				18 05										19 05										
Gillingham (Kent)	d				18 10										19 10										
Rainham (Kent)	d				18 15										19 15										
Sittingbourne	d				18 23										19 23										
Faversham	a				18 33										19 33										
Whitstable	d																								
Herne Bay	d																								
Birchington-on-Sea	d																								
Margate	d																								
Broadstairs	a																								
Ashford International	a		17 51						18 20				18 51						19 20					19 51	
	d							18 03										19 03					19 33		
Folkestone West	d																								
Folkestone Central	d																								
Dover Priory	a																								
Deal	a																								
Sandwich	a																								
Canterbury West	a							18 21										19 24					19 54		
	d							18 22										19 25					19 55		
Ramsgate	d							18a44										19a47					20a15		
Broadstairs	d																								
Margate	a																								

		SE	SE	SE	SE ■	SE	SE	SE		SE ■	SE	SE	SE	SE	SE	SE ■	SE	SE	SE		SE ■	SE	SE	SE	SE
St Pancras International ⊖	d	19 18	19 25	19 32		19 39	19 46	19 52			20 04	20 11	20 18	20 25	20 32		20 39	20 46	20 52			21 04	21 11	21 18	21 25
Stratford International ⊖	d	19 28	19 35	19 42		19 49	19 56	20 03			20 14	20 21	20 28	20 35	20 42		20 49	20 56	21 03			21 14	21 21	21 28	21 35
Ebbsfleet International	a	19 38	19 46	19 52		19 59	20 07	20 13			20 24	20 31	20 38	20 46	20 52		20 59	21 07	21 13			21 24	21 31	21 38	21 46
	d	19 43				20 02					20 30		20 43				21 02					21 30		21 43	
Gravesend	d	19 48											20 48											21 48	
Strood	d	19 58											20 58											21 58	
Maidstone West	d																								
Rochester	d	20 03											21 03											22 03	
Chatham	d	20 05											21 05											22 05	
Gillingham (Kent)	d	20 10											21 10											22 10	
Rainham (Kent)	d	20 15											21 15											22 15	
Sittingbourne	d	20 23											21 23											22 23	
Faversham	a	20 33											21 33											22 33	
Whitstable	d																								
Herne Bay	d																								
Birchington-on-Sea	d																								
Margate	d																								
Broadstairs	a																								
Ashford International	a					20 20					20 51						21 20					21 51			
	d				20 03					20 33						21 03					21 34				
Folkestone West	d																								
Folkestone Central	d																								
Dover Priory	a																								
Deal	a																								
Sandwich	a																								
Canterbury West	a				20 24					20 54						21 24					21 55				
	d				20 25					20 55						21 25					21 56				
Ramsgate	d				20a47					21a15						21a47					22a16				
Broadstairs	d																								
Margate	a																								

Table 194

Saturdays

28 July to 11 August

St Pancras International - Kent High Speed Domestic Services

		SE	SE	SE	SE	SE	SE	SE	SE	SE	SE [1]	SE	SE	SE	SE	SE	SE	SE	SE	SE	SE [1]	SE	SE
St Pancras International ⊖	d	21 32	21 39	21 46	21 52	22 04	22 11	22 18	22 25	22 32		22 39	22 46	22 52	23 04	23 11	23 16	23 21	23 26	23 32		23 36	23 41
Stratford International ⊖	d	21 42	21 49	21 56	22 03	22 14	22 21	22 28	22 35	22 42		22 47	22 56	23 02	23 14	23 21	23 26	23 30	23 35	23 42		23 46	23 50
Ebbsfleet International	a	21 52	21 59	22 07	22 13	22 24	22 31	22 40	22 46	22 52		22 57	23 07	23 12	23 24	23 31	23 37	23 41	23 45	23 52		23 56	00 01
	d		22 02																				
Gravesend	d																						
Strood	d																						
Maidstone West	d																						
Rochester	d																						
Chatham	d																						
Gillingham (Kent)	d																						
Rainham (Kent)	d																						
Sittingbourne	d																						
Faversham	a																						
Whitstable	d																						
Herne Bay	d																						
Birchington-on-Sea	d																						
Margate	d																						
Broadstairs	a																						
Ashford International	a		22 20																				
	d										22 34										23 34		
Folkestone West	d																						
Folkestone Central	d																						
Dover Priory	a																						
Deal	a																						
Sandwich	a																						
Canterbury West	a										22 55										23 55		
	d										22 56										23 56		
Ramsgate	d										23a16										00a16		
Broadstairs	d																						
Margate	a																						

		SE	SE	SE
St Pancras International ⊖	d	23 47	23 51	23 56
Stratford International ⊖	d	23 57	00 01	00 05
Ebbsfleet International	a	00 07	00 10	00 16
	d			
Gravesend	d			
Strood	d			
Maidstone West	d			
Rochester	d			
Chatham	d			
Gillingham (Kent)	d			
Rainham (Kent)	d			
Sittingbourne	d			
Faversham	a			
Whitstable	d			
Herne Bay	d			
Birchington-on-Sea	d			
Margate	d			
Broadstairs	a			
Ashford International	a			
	d			
Folkestone West	d			
Folkestone Central	d			
Dover Priory	a			
Deal	a			
Sandwich	a			
Canterbury West	a			
	d			
Ramsgate	d			
Broadstairs	d			
Margate	a			

Table 194

Saturdays

25 August to 8 September

St Pancras International - Kent High Speed Domestic Services

		SE	SE	SE	SE	SE	SE	SE	SE	SE [1]	SE	SE	SE	SE	SE	SE	SE [1]	SE	SE	SE	SE
		A	B	A	B	A	B	A	B		A	B	B	B	B	B		B	A	B	B
St Pancras International ⊖	d	22p55	22p55	23p12	23p12	23p25	23p25	23p55	23p55		00 12	00 12	00 48	01 48	02 35	06 10		06 39	06 40	06 45	06 54
Stratford International ⊖	d	23p02	23p03	23p19	23p20	23p32	23p33	00 02	00 03		00 19	00 20	00a54	01a54	02a41	06 16		06 47	06 47	06 53	07 02
Ebbsfleet International	a	23p12	23p13	23p30	23p31	23p42	23p43	00 12	00 13		00 30	00 31				06 27		06 58	06 58	07 04	07 12
	d	23p13	23p14	23p31	23p32	23p43	23p44	00 13	00 14		00 31	00 32				06 28		06 59	06 59		07 13
Gravesend	d	23p18	23p18			23p48	23p48	00 18	00 18												07 18
Strood	d	23p28	23p28			23p58	23p58	00 28	00 28												07 28
Maidstone West	d																				
Rochester	d	23p33	23p33			00 03	00 03	00 33	00 33												07 33
Chatham	d	23p35	23p35			00 05	00 05	00 35	00 35												07 35
Gillingham (Kent)	d	23p40	23p40			00 10	00 10	00 40	00 40												07 40
Rainham (Kent)	d	23p45	23p45			00 15	00 15	00 45	00 45												07 45
Sittingbourne	d	23p53	23p53			00 23	00 23	00 53	00 53												07 53
Faversham	a	00 03	00 03			00 33	00 33	01 03	01 03												08 03
Whitstable	d																				
Herne Bay	d																				
Birchington-on-Sea	d																				
Margate	d																				
Broadstairs	a																				
Ashford International	a			23p50	23p51						00 50	00 51				06 50		07 18	07 18		
	d			23p52	23p53					00 03						06 52	07 03	07 22	07 22		
Folkestone West	d			00 05	00 06											07 05					
Folkestone Central	d			00 08	00 08											07 08					
Dover Priory	a			00 20	00 20											07 20					
Deal	a																				
Sandwich	a																				
Canterbury West	a									00 24							07 21	07 38	07 38		
	d									00 25							07 22	07 39	07 39		
Ramsgate	d									00a47							07a44	07 59	07 59		
Broadstairs	d																	08 05	08 05		
Margate	a																	08 10	08 10		

		SE	SE	SE	SE	SE	SE [1]	SE	SE	SE	SE	SE	SE	SE	SE	SE	SE	SE	SE	SE	SE
		A	B	A	B	B			B		B	A	B	B	A	B	B	A	B	B	A
St Pancras International ⊖	d	06 55	07 10	07 12	07 14	07 24		07 42	07 47	07 52	08 11	08 12	08 18	08 21	08 40	08 41	08 47	08 50	08 51	09 09	09 10
Stratford International ⊖	d	07 02	07 17	07 19	07 25	07 32		07 49	07 55	07 58	08 19	08 19	08 26	08 32	08 47	08 49	08 55	09 04	08 58	09 17	09 17
Ebbsfleet International	a	07 12	07 28	07 30	07 35	07 42		08 00	08 06	08 08	08 30	08 30	08 36	08 42	08 58	09 00	09 06	09 14	09 08	09 28	09 28
	d	07 13	07 30	07 31		07 46		08 01		08 13	08 31	08 31		08 43	08 59	09 01		09 15	09 13	09 29	09 29
Gravesend	d	07 18				07 51				08 18				08 48				09 20	09 18		
Strood	d	07 28				08 01				08 28				08 58				09 30	09 28		
Maidstone West	d																				
Rochester	d	07 33				08 06				08 33				09 03				09 34	09 33		
Chatham	d	07 35				08 08				08 35				09 05				09 37	09 35		
Gillingham (Kent)	d	07 40				08 13				08 40				09 10				09 41	09 40		
Rainham (Kent)	d	07 45				08 18				08 45				09 15				09 46	09 45		
Sittingbourne	d	07 53				08 25				08 53				09 23				09 54	09 53		
Faversham	a	08 03				08 33				09 03				09 33				10 03	10 03		
Whitstable	d																				
Herne Bay	d																				
Birchington-on-Sea	d																				
Margate	d																				
Broadstairs	a																				
Ashford International	a		07 50	07 51				08 20			08 50	08 50			09 18	09 20				09 48	09 48
	d		07 51	07 52			08 03	08 22			08 52	08 52			09 22	09 22				09 52	09 52
Folkestone West	d		08 04	08 05							09 05	09 05								10 05	10 05
Folkestone Central	d		08 07	08 08							09 08	09 08								10 08	10 08
Dover Priory	a		08 18	08 20							09 20	09 20								10 20	10 20
Deal	a																				
Sandwich	a																				
Canterbury West	a						08 21	08 38							09 38	09 38					
	d						08 22	08 39							09 39	09 39					
Ramsgate	d						08a44	08 59							09 59	09 59					
Broadstairs	d							09 05							10 05	10 05					
Margate	a							09 10							10 10	10 10					

A not from 1 September until 8 September B not 25 August

St Pancras International - Kent
High Speed Domestic Services

Saturdays
25 August to 8 September

Station		SE A	SE B	SE A	SE A	SE B	SE A	SE A	SE B	SE A	SE B	SE A	SE B	SE A	SE A	SE B	SE A	SE A	SE B	SE A	SE B
St Pancras International	d	09 14	09 25	09 25	09 36	09 42	09 47	09 54	09 55	10 11	10 12	10 18	10 28	10 28	10 41	10 42	10 47	10 51	10 52	11 11	11 12
Stratford International	d	09 24	09 32	09 33	09 44	09 49	09 54	10 02	10 02	10 19	10 19	10 26	10 35	10 36	10 49	10 49	10 55	10 58	10 58	11 19	11 19
Ebbsfleet International	a	09 35	09 42	09 43	09 55	10 00	10 04	10 12	10 12	10 30	10 30	10 36	10 45	10 46	11 00	11 00	11 05	11 08	11 08	11 30	11 30
	d		09 43	09 44	09 56	10 01		10 13	10 13	10 31	10 31		10 46	10 47	11 01	11 01		11 13	11 13	11 31	11 31
Gravesend	d		09 48	09 48				10 18	10 18				10 51	10 51				11 18	11 18		
Strood	d		09 58	09 58				10 28	10 28				11 01	11 01				11 28	11 28		
Maidstone West	d																				
Rochester	d		10 03	10 03				10 33	10 33				11 06	11 06				11 33	11 33		
Chatham	d		10 05	10 05				10 35	10 35				11 08	11 08				11 35	11 35		
Gillingham (Kent)	d		10 10	10 10				10 40	10 40				11 13	11 13				11 40	11 40		
Rainham (Kent)	d		10 15	10 15				10 45	10 45				11 18	11 18				11 45	11 45		
Sittingbourne	d		10 23	10 23				10 53	10 53				11 25	11 25				11 53	11 53		
Faversham	a		10 33	10 33				11 03	11 03				11 34	11 34				12 03	12 03		
Whitstable	d																				
Herne Bay	d																				
Birchington-on-Sea	d																				
Margate	d																				
Broadstairs	a																				
Ashford International	a				10 15	10 20				10 50	10 50				11 20	11 20				11 50	11 50
	d				10 22	10 22				10 52	10 52				11 22	11 22				11 52	11 52
Folkestone West	d									11 05	11 05									12 05	12 05
Folkestone Central	d									11 08	11 08									12 08	12 08
Dover Priory	a									11 20	11 20									12 20	12 20
Deal	a																				
Sandwich	a																				
Canterbury West	a				10 38	10 38									11 38	11 38					
	d				10 39	10 39									11 39	11 39					
Ramsgate	d				10 59	10 59									11 59	11 59					
Broadstairs	d				11 05	11 05									12 05	12 05					
Margate	a				11 10	11 10									12 10	12 10					

Station		SE A	SE	SE A	SE B	SE A	SE B	SE A	SE A	SE B	SE A	SE B	SE A	SE A	SE B	SE A	SE	SE A	SE B	SE A	SE B
St Pancras International	d	11 18	11 28	11 41	11 42	11 48	11 55	11 55	12 11	12 12	12 18	12 28	12 28	12 41	12 42	12 47	12 55	13 11	13 12	13 18	13 25
Stratford International	d	11 26	11 35	11 49	11 49	11 56	12 02	12 03	12 19	12 19	12 25	12 35	12 36	12 49	12 49	12 54	13 06	13 19	13 19	13 26	13 32
Ebbsfleet International	a	11 36	11 45	12 00	12 00	12 06	12 12	12 13	12 30	12 30	12 35	12 45	12 46	13 00	13 00	13 04	13 16	13 30	13 30	13 36	13 42
	d		11 46	12 01	12 01		12 13	12 14	12 31	12 31		12 46	12 47	13 01	13 01		13 17	13 31	13 31		13 43
Gravesend	d		11 51				12 18	12 18				12 51	12 51				13 22				13 48
Strood	d		12 01				12 28	12 28				13 01	13 01				13 32				13 58
Maidstone West	d																				
Rochester	d		12 06				12 33	12 33				13 06	13 06				13 37				14 03
Chatham	d		12 08				12 35	12 35				13 08	13 08				13 39				14 05
Gillingham (Kent)	d		12 13				12 40	12 40				13 13	13 13				13 44				14 10
Rainham (Kent)	d		12 18				12 45	12 45				13 18	13 18				13 49				14 15
Sittingbourne	d		12 25				12 53	12 53				13 25	13 25				13 56				14 23
Faversham	a		12 34				13 03	13 03				13 34	13 34				14 04				14 33
Whitstable	d																				
Herne Bay	d																				
Birchington-on-Sea	d																				
Margate	d																				
Broadstairs	a																				
Ashford International	a			12 20	12 20				12 50	12 50				13 20	13 20			13 50	13 50		
	d			12 22	12 22				12 52	12 52				13 22	13 22			13 52	13 52		
Folkestone West	d								13 05	13 05								14 05	14 05		
Folkestone Central	d								13 08	13 08								14 08	14 08		
Dover Priory	a								13 20	13 20								14 20	14 20		
Deal	a																				
Sandwich	a																				
Canterbury West	a			12 38	12 38									13 38	13 38						
	d			12 39	12 39									13 39	13 39						
Ramsgate	d			12 59	12 59									13 59	13 59						
Broadstairs	d			13 05	13 05									14 05	14 05						
Margate	a			13 10	13 10									14 10	14 10						

A not 25 August

B not from 1 September until 8 September

St Pancras International - Kent
High Speed Domestic Services

Saturdays
25 August to 8 September

Station		SE A	SE A	SE B	SE A	SE B	SE A	SE A	SE B	SE A	SE B	SE A	SE A	SE B	SE A	SE B	SE A	SE A	SE B	SE A	SE B
St Pancras International	d	13 25	13 41	13 42	13 48	13 55	13 55	14 11	14 12	14 18	14 25	14 25	14 41	14 42	14 47	14 55	14 55	15 11	15 12	15 18	15 25
Stratford International	d	13 33	13 49	13 49	13 56	14 02	14 03	14 19	14 19	14 26	14 32	14 33	14 49	14 49	14 54	15 02	15 03	15 19	15 19	15 26	15 32
Ebbsfleet International	a	13 43	14 00	14 00	14 06	14 12	14 13	14 30	14 30	14 36	14 42	14 43	15 00	15 00	15 04	15 12	15 13	15 30	15 30	15 36	15 42
	d	13 44	14 01	14 01		14 13	14 14	14 31	14 31		14 43	14 44	15 01	15 01		15 13	15 14	15 31	15 31		15 43
Gravesend	d	13 48				14 18	14 18				14 48	14 48				15 18	15 18				15 48
Strood	d	13 58				14 28	14 28				14 58	14 58				15 28	15 28				15 58
Maidstone West	d																				
Rochester	d	14 03				14 33	14 33				15 03	15 03				15 33	15 33				16 03
Chatham	d	14 05				14 35	14 35				15 05	15 05				15 35	15 35				16 05
Gillingham (Kent)	d	14 10				14 40	14 40				15 10	15 10				15 40	15 40				16 10
Rainham (Kent)	d	14 15				14 45	14 45				15 15	15 15				15 45	15 45				16 15
Sittingbourne	d	14 23				14 53	14 53				15 23	15 23				15 53	15 53				16 23
Faversham	a	14 33				15 03	15 03				15 33	15 33				16 03	16 03				16 33
Whitstable	d																				
Herne Bay	d																				
Birchington-on-Sea	d																				
Margate	d																				
Broadstairs	a																				
Ashford International	a		14 20	14 20				14 50	14 50				15 20	15 20				15 50	15 50		
	d		14 22	14 22				14 52	14 52				15 22	15 22				15 52	15 52		
Folkestone West	d							15 05	15 05									16 05	16 05		
Folkestone Central	d							15 08	15 08									16 08	16 08		
Dover Priory	a							15 20	15 20									16 20	16 20		
Deal	a																				
Sandwich	a																				
Canterbury West	a		14 38	14 38									15 38	15 38							
	d		14 39	14 39									15 39	15 39							
Ramsgate	d		14 59	14 59									15 59	15 59							
Broadstairs	d		15 05	15 05									16 05	16 05							
Margate	a		15 10	15 10									16 10	16 10							

Station		SE A	SE A	SE B	SE A	SE B	SE A	SE A	SE B	SE A	SE A	SE B	SE A	SE B	SE A	SE B	SE A	SE A	SE B	SE A
St Pancras International	d	15 25	15 41	15 42	15 48	15 55	15 55	16 09	16 10	16 15	16 25	16 28	16 41	16 42	16 48	16 55	16 55	17 11	17 12	17 18
Stratford International	d	15 33	15 49	15 49	15 56	16 02	16 03	16 17	16 17	16 22	16 33	16 35	16 49	16 49	16 56	17 02	17 03	17 19	17 19	17 26
Ebbsfleet International	a	15 43	16 00	16 00	16 06	16 12	16 13	16 28	16 28	16 32	16 43	16 45	17 00	17 00	17 06	17 12	17 13	17 30	17 30	17 36
	d	15 44	16 01	16 01		16 13	16 14	16 29	16 29		16 44	16 46	17 01	17 01		17 13	17 14	17 31	17 31	
Gravesend	d	15 48				16 18	16 18				16 48	16 51				17 18	17 18			
Strood	d	15 58				16 28	16 28				16 58	17 01				17 28	17 28			
Maidstone West	d																			
Rochester	d	16 03				16 33	16 33				17 03	17 06				17 33	17 33			
Chatham	d	16 05				16 35	16 35				17 05	17 08				17 35	17 35			
Gillingham (Kent)	d	16 10				16 40	16 40				17 10	17 13				17 40	17 40			
Rainham (Kent)	d	16 15				16 45	16 45				17 15	17 18				17 45	17 45			
Sittingbourne	d	16 23				16 53	16 53				17 23	17 25				17 53	17 53			
Faversham	a	16 33				17 03	17 03				17 33	17 34				18 03	18 03			
Whitstable	d																			
Herne Bay	d																			
Birchington-on-Sea	d																			
Margate	d																			
Broadstairs	a																			
Ashford International	a		16 20	16 20				16 48	16 48				17 20	17 20				17 50	17 50	
	d		16 22	16 22				16 52	16 52				17 22	17 22				17 52	17 52	
Folkestone West	d							17 05	17 05									18 05	18 05	
Folkestone Central	d							17 08	17 08									18 08	18 08	
Dover Priory	a							17 20	17 20									18 20	18 20	
Deal	a																			
Sandwich	a																			
Canterbury West	a		16 38	16 38									17 38	17 38						
	d		16 39	16 39									17 39	17 39						
Ramsgate	d		16 59	16 59									17 59	17 59						
Broadstairs	d		17 05	17 05									18 05	18 05						
Margate	a		17 10	17 10									18 10	18 10						

A not 25 August

B not from 1 September until 8 September

Table 194

Saturdays
25 August to 8 September

St Pancras International - Kent High Speed Domestic Services

		SE A	SE B	SE B	SE A	SE B	SE A	SE B	SE B	SE A	SE B
St Pancras International ⊖	d	17 25	17 25	17 41	17 42	17 48	17 55	17 55	18 11	18 12	18 18
Stratford International ⊖	d	17 32	17 33	17 49	17 49	17 56	18 02	18 03	18 19	18 19	18 26
Ebbsfleet International	a	17 42	17 43	18 00	18 00	18 06	18 12	18 13	18 30	18 30	18 36
	d	17 43	17 44	18 01	18 01		18 13	18 14	18 31	18 31	
Gravesend	d	17 48	17 48				18 18	18 18			
Strood	d	17 58	17 58				18 28	18 28			
Maidstone West	d										
Rochester	d	18 03	18 03				18 33	18 33			
Chatham	d	18 05	18 05				18 35	18 35			
Gillingham (Kent)	d	18 10	18 10				18 40	18 40			
Rainham (Kent)	d	18 15	18 15				18 45	18 45			
Sittingbourne	d	18 23	18 23				18 53	18 53			
Faversham	a	18 33	18 33				19 03	19 03			
Whitstable	d										
Herne Bay	d										
Birchington-on-Sea	d										
Margate	d										
Broadstairs	a										
Ashford International	a			18 20	18 20				18 50	18 50	
	d			18 22	18 22				18 52	18 52	
Folkestone West	d								19 05	19 05	
Folkestone Central	d								19 08	19 08	
Dover Priory	a								19 20	19 20	
Deal	a										
Sandwich	a										
Canterbury West	a			18 38	18 38						
	d			18 39	18 39						
Ramsgate	d			18 59	18 59						
Broadstairs	d			19 05	19 05						
Margate	a			19 10	19 10						

		SE A	SE B	SE B	SE A	SE A	SE B	SE B	SE A	SE B	SE A
St Pancras International ⊖	d	18 25	18 25	18 41	18 42	18 55	18 55	19 11	19 12	19 18	19 25
Stratford International ⊖	d	18 32	18 33	18 49	18 49	19 02	19 03	19 19	19 19	19 26	19 32
Ebbsfleet International	a	18 42	18 43	19 00	19 00	19 12	19 13	19 30	19 30	19 36	19 42
	d	18 43	18 44	19 01	19 01	19 13	19 14	19 31	19 31		19 43
Gravesend	d	18 48	18 48			19 18	19 18				19 48
Strood	d	18 58	18 58			19 28	19 28				19 58
Maidstone West	d										
Rochester	d	19 03	19 03			19 33	19 33				20 03
Chatham	d	19 05	19 05			19 35	19 35				20 05
Gillingham (Kent)	d	19 10	19 10			19 40	19 40				20 10
Rainham (Kent)	d	19 15	19 15			19 45	19 45				20 15
Sittingbourne	d	19 23	19 23			19 53	19 53				20 23
Faversham	a	19 33	19 33			20 03	20 03				20 33
Whitstable	d										
Herne Bay	d										
Birchington-on-Sea	d										
Margate	d										
Broadstairs	a										
Ashford International	a			19 20	19 20			19 50	19 50		
	d			19 22	19 22			19 52	19 52		
Folkestone West	d							20 05	20 05		
Folkestone Central	d							20 08	20 08		
Dover Priory	a							20 20	20 20		
Deal	a										
Sandwich	a										
Canterbury West	a			19 38	19 38						
	d			19 39	19 39						
Ramsgate	d			19 59	19 59						
Broadstairs	d			20 05	20 05						
Margate	a			20 10	20 10						

		SE B	SE B	SE A	SE A	SE B	SE B	SE A	SE B	SE A	SE B
St Pancras International ⊖	d	19 25	19 41	19 42	19 55	19 55	20 11	20 12	20 18	20 25	20 25
Stratford International ⊖	d	19 33	19 49	19 49	20 02	20 03	20 19	20 19	20 26	20 32	20 33
Ebbsfleet International	a	19 43	20 00	20 00	20 12	20 13	20 30	20 30	20 36	20 42	20 43
	d	19 44	20 01	20 01	20 13	20 14	20 31	20 31		20 43	20 44
Gravesend	d	19 48			20 18	20 18				20 48	20 48
Strood	d	19 58			20 28	20 28				20 58	20 58
Maidstone West	d										
Rochester	d	20 03			20 33	20 33				21 03	21 03
Chatham	d	20 05			20 35	20 35				21 05	21 05
Gillingham (Kent)	d	20 10			20 40	20 40				21 10	21 10
Rainham (Kent)	d	20 15			20 45	20 45				21 15	21 15
Sittingbourne	d	20 23			20 53	20 53				21 23	21 23
Faversham	a	20 33			21 03	21 03				21 33	21 33
Whitstable	d										
Herne Bay	d										
Birchington-on-Sea	d										
Margate	d										
Broadstairs	a										
Ashford International	a		20 20	20 20			20 50	20 50			
	d		20 22	20 22			20 52	20 52			
Folkestone West	d						21 05	21 05			
Folkestone Central	d						21 08	21 08			
Dover Priory	a						21 20	21 20			
Deal	a										
Sandwich	a										
Canterbury West	a		20 38	20 38							
	d		20 39	20 39							
Ramsgate	d		20 59	20 59							
Broadstairs	d		21 05	21 05							
Margate	a		21 10	21 10							

		SE B	SE A	SE A	SE B	SE B	SE A	SE B	SE A	SE B
St Pancras International ⊖	d	20 41	20 42	20 55	20 55	21 11	21 12	21 18	21 25	21 25
Stratford International ⊖	d	20 49	20 49	21 02	21 03	21 19	21 19	21 26	21 32	21 33
Ebbsfleet International	a	21 00	21 00	21 12	21 13	21 30	21 30	21 36	21 42	21 43
	d	21 01	21 01	21 13	21 14	21 31	21 31		21 43	21 44
Gravesend	d			21 18	21 18				21 48	21 48
Strood	d			21 28	21 28				21 58	21 58
Maidstone West	d									
Rochester	d			21 33	21 33				22 03	22 03
Chatham	d			21 35	21 35				22 05	22 05
Gillingham (Kent)	d			21 40	21 40				22 10	22 10
Rainham (Kent)	d			21 45	21 45				22 15	22 15
Sittingbourne	d			21 53	21 53				22 23	22 23
Faversham	a			22 03	22 03				22 31	22 31
Whitstable	d									
Herne Bay	d									
Birchington-on-Sea	d									
Margate	d									
Broadstairs	a									
Ashford International	a	21 20	21 20			21 50	21 50			
	d	21 22	21 22			21 52	21 52			
Folkestone West	d					22 05	22 05			
Folkestone Central	d					22 08	22 08			
Dover Priory	a					22 20	22 20			
Deal	a									
Sandwich	a									
Canterbury West	a	21 38	21 38							
	d	21 39	21 39							
Ramsgate	d	21 59	21 59							
Broadstairs	d	22 05	22 05							
Margate	a	22 10	22 10							

A not from 1 September until 8 September
B not 25 August

Table 194

Saturdays
25 August to 8 September

St Pancras International - Kent High Speed Domestic Services

		SE A	SE B	SE B	SE A	SE A	SE B	SE A	SE B	SE A	SE B
St Pancras International ⊖	d	21 41	21 42	21 55	21 55	22 11	22 12	22 17	22 25	22 25	22 42
Stratford International ⊖	d	21 49	21 49	22 02	22 03	22 19	22 19	22 25	22 32	22 33	22 49
Ebbsfleet International	a	22 00	22 00	22 12	22 13	22 30	22 30	22 35	22 42	22 43	23 00
	d	22 01	22 01	22 13	22 14	22 31	22 31		22 43	22 44	23 01
Gravesend	d			22 18	22 18				22 48	22 48	
Strood	d			22 28	22 28				22 58	22 58	
Maidstone West	d										
Rochester	d			22 33	22 33				23 03	23 03	
Chatham	d			22 35	22 35				23 05	23 05	
Gillingham (Kent)	d			22 40	22 40				23 10	23 10	
Rainham (Kent)	d			22 45	22 45				23 15	23 15	
Sittingbourne	d			22 53	22 53				23 23	23 23	
Faversham	a			23 01	23 01				23 31	23 31	
Whitstable	d										
Herne Bay	d										
Birchington-on-Sea	d										
Margate	d										
Broadstairs	a										
Ashford International	a	22 20	22 20			22 50	22 50				23 20
	d	22 22	22 22			22 52	22 52				23 22
Folkestone West	d					23 05	23 05				
Folkestone Central	d					23 08	23 08				
Dover Priory	a					23 20	23 20				
Deal	a										
Sandwich	a										
Canterbury West	a	22 38	22 38								23 38
	d	22 39	22 39								23 39
Ramsgate	d	22 59	22 59								23a59
Broadstairs	d	23 05	23 05								
Margate	a	23 10	23 10								

		SE A	SE B	SE A	SE B	SE A	SE A	SE B	SE A	SE A	SE B
St Pancras International ⊖	d	22 42	22 55	22 55	23 12	23 12	23 18	23 25	23 25	23 55	23 55
Stratford International ⊖	d	22 50	23 02	23 03	23 19	23 20	23 26	23 32	23 33	00 03	00 02
Ebbsfleet International	a	23 01	23 12	23 13	23 30	23 31	23 36	23 42	23 43	00 12	00 12
	d	23 02	23 13	23 14	23 31	23 32		23 43	23 44	00 13	00 13
Gravesend	d		23 18	23 18				23 48	23 48	00 18	00 18
Strood	d		23 28	23 28				23 58	23 58	00 28	00 28
Maidstone West	d										
Rochester	d		23 33	23 33				00 03	00 03	00 32	00 33
Chatham	d		23 35	23 35				00 05	00 05	00 35	00 35
Gillingham (Kent)	d		23 40	23 40				00 10	00 10	00 39	00 40
Rainham (Kent)	d		23 45	23 45				00 15	00 15	00 44	00 45
Sittingbourne	d		23 53	23 53				00 23	00 23	00 52	00 53
Faversham	a		00 01	00 01				00 31	00 31	01 00	01 01
Whitstable	d										
Herne Bay	d										
Birchington-on-Sea	d										
Margate	d										
Broadstairs	a										
Ashford International	a	23 20			23 50	23 50					
	d	23 22			23 52	23 52					
Folkestone West	d				00 05	00 05					
Folkestone Central	d				00 08	00 08					
Dover Priory	a				00 20	00 20					
Deal	a										
Sandwich	a										
Canterbury West	a	23 38									
	d	23 39									
Ramsgate	d	23a59									
Broadstairs	d										
Margate	a										

Sundays
until 22 July, 19 Aug and from 16 Sep

		SE	SE	SE	SE	SE	SE ■	SE	SE	SE
St Pancras International ⊖	d	22p55	23p12	23p25	23p55	00 12		08 42	09 10	09 25
Stratford International ⊖	d	23p02	23p19	23p32	00 02	00 19		08 49	09 17	09 32
Ebbsfleet International	a	23p12	23p30	23p42	00 12	00 30		09 00	09 28	09 42
	d	23p13	23p31	23p43	00 13	00 31		09 01	09 29	09 43
Gravesend	d	23p18		23p48	00 18					09 48
Strood	d	23p28		23p58	00 28					09 58
Maidstone West	d									
Rochester	d	23p33		00 03	00 33					10 03
Chatham	d	23p35		00 05	00 35					10 05
Gillingham (Kent)	d	23p40		00 10	00 40					10 10
Rainham (Kent)	d	23p45		00 15	00 45					10 15
Sittingbourne	d	23p53		00 23	00 53					10 23
Faversham	a	00 01		00 31	01 01					10 33
Whitstable	d									
Herne Bay	d									
Birchington-on-Sea	d									
Margate	d									
Broadstairs	a									
Ashford International	a		23p50			00 50		09 20	09 48	
	d		23p52				09 03	09 22	09 52	
Folkestone West	d		00 05						10 05	
Folkestone Central	d		00 08						10 08	
Dover Priory	a		00 20						10 20	
Deal	a									
Sandwich	a									
Canterbury West	a						09 21	09 38		
	d						09 22	09 39		
Ramsgate	d						09a44	09 59		
Broadstairs	d							10 05		
Margate	a							10 10		

		SE	SE	SE	SE	SE	SE	SE	SE
St Pancras International ⊖	d	09 42	10 10	10 28	10 42	11 12	11 25	11 42	12 12
Stratford International ⊖	d	09 49	10 17	10 35	10 49	11 19	11 32	11 49	12 19
Ebbsfleet International	a	10 00	10 28	10 45	11 00	11 30	11 42	12 00	12 30
	d	10 01	10 29	10 46	11 01	11 31	11 43	12 01	12 31
Gravesend	d			10 51			11 48		
Strood	d			11 01			11 58		
Maidstone West	d								
Rochester	d			11 06			12 03		
Chatham	d			11 08			12 05		
Gillingham (Kent)	d			11 13			12 10		
Rainham (Kent)	d			11 18			12 15		
Sittingbourne	d			11 25			12 23		
Faversham	a			11 34			12 33		
Whitstable	d								
Herne Bay	d								
Birchington-on-Sea	d								
Margate	d								
Broadstairs	a								
Ashford International	a	10 20	10 48		11 20	11 50		12 20	12 50
	d	10 22	10 52		11 22	11 52		12 22	12 52
Folkestone West	d		11 05			12 05			13 05
Folkestone Central	d		11 08			12 08			13 08
Dover Priory	a		11 20			12 20			13 20
Deal	a								
Sandwich	a								
Canterbury West	a	10 38			11 38			12 38	
	d	10 39			11 39			12 39	
Ramsgate	d	10 59			11 59			12 59	
Broadstairs	d	11 05			12 05			13 05	
Margate	a	11 10			12 10			13 10	

A not 25 August
B not from 1 September until 8 September

Table 194

Sundays

until 22 July, 19 Aug and from 16 Sep

St Pancras International - Kent High Speed Domestic Services

		SE	SE	SE	SE	SE	SE	SE	SE	SE	SE	SE	SE	SE	SE	SE	SE	SE
St Pancras International	d	12 28	12 42	12 52	13 12	13 25	13 42	13 55	14 12	14 25	14 42	14 55	15 12	15 25	15 42	15 55	16 10	16 25
Stratford International	d	12 35	12 49	12 58	13 19	13 32	13 49	14 02	14 19	14 32	14 49	15 02	15 19	15 32	15 49	16 02	16 17	16 32
Ebbsfleet International	a	12 45	13 00	13 08	13 30	13 42	14 00	14 12	14 30	14 42	15 00	15 12	15 30	15 42	16 00	16 12	16 28	16 42
	d	12 46	13 01	13 13	13 31	13 43	14 01	14 13	14 31	14 43	15 01	15 13	15 31	15 43	16 01	16 13	16 29	16 43
Gravesend	d	12 51		13 18		13 48		14 18		14 48		15 18		15 48		16 18		16 48
Strood	d	13 01		13 28		13 58		14 28		14 58		15 28		15 58		16 28		16 58
Maidstone West	d																	
Rochester	d	13 06		13 33		14 03		14 33		15 03		15 33		16 03		16 33		17 03
Chatham	d	13 08		13 35		14 05		14 35		15 05		15 35		16 05		16 35		17 05
Gillingham (Kent)	d	13 13		13 40		14 10		14 40		15 10		15 40		16 10		16 40		17 10
Rainham (Kent)	d	13 18		13 45		14 15		14 45		15 15		15 45		16 15		16 45		17 15
Sittingbourne	d	13 25		13 53		14 23		14 53		15 23		15 53		16 23		16 53		17 23
Faversham	a	13 34		14 03		14 33		15 03		15 33		16 03		16 33		17 03		17 33
Whitstable	d																	
Herne Bay	d																	
Birchington-on-Sea	d																	
Margate	d																	
Broadstairs	a																	
Ashford International	a		13 20		13 50		14 20		14 50		15 20		15 50		16 20		16 48	
	d		13 22		13 52		14 22		14 52		15 22		15 52		16 22		16 52	
Folkestone West	d				14 05				15 05				16 05				17 05	
Folkestone Central	d				14 08				15 08				16 08				17 08	
Dover Priory	a				14 20				15 20				16 20				17 20	
Deal	a																	
Sandwich	a																	
Canterbury West	a		13 38				14 38				15 38				16 38			
	d		13 39				14 39				15 39				16 39			
Ramsgate	d		13 59				14 59				15 59				16 59			
Broadstairs	d		14 05				15 05				16 05				17 05			
Margate	a		14 10				15 10				16 10				17 10			

		SE	SE	SE	SE	SE	SE	SE	SE	SE	SE	SE	SE	SE	SE	SE	SE	SE	SE
St Pancras International	d	16 42	16 55	17 12	17 25	17 42	17 58	18 12	18 25	18 42	18 55	19 12	19 25	19 42	19 55	20 12	20 25	20 42	20 55
Stratford International	d	16 49	17 02	17 19	17 32	17 49	18 08	18 19	18 32	18 49	19 02	19 19	19 32	19 49	20 02	20 19	20 32	20 49	21 02
Ebbsfleet International	a	17 00	17 12	17 30	17 42	18 00	18 18	18 30	18 42	19 00	19 12	19 30	19 42	20 00	20 12	20 30	20 42	21 00	21 12
	d	17 01	17 13	17 31	17 43	18 01	18 19	18 31	18 43	19 01	19 13	19 31	19 43	20 01	20 13	20 31	20 43	21 01	21 13
Gravesend	d		17 18		17 48		18 24		18 48		19 18		19 48		20 18		20 48		21 18
Strood	d		17 28		17 58		18 34		18 58		19 28		19 58		20 28		20 58		21 28
Maidstone West	d																		
Rochester	d		17 33		18 03		18 39		19 03		19 33		20 03		20 33		21 03		21 33
Chatham	d		17 35		18 05		18 41		19 05		19 35		20 05		20 35		21 05		21 35
Gillingham (Kent)	d		17 40		18 10		18 46		19 10		19 40		20 10		20 40		21 10		21 40
Rainham (Kent)	d		17 45		18 15		18 51		19 15		19 45		20 15		20 45		21 15		21 45
Sittingbourne	d		17 53		18 23		18 58		19 23		19 53		20 23		20 53		21 23		21 53
Faversham	a		18 03		18 33		19 07		19 33		20 03		20 33		21 03		21 33		22 03
Whitstable	d																		
Herne Bay	d																		
Birchington-on-Sea	d																		
Margate	d																		
Broadstairs	a																		
Ashford International	a	17 20		17 50		18 20		18 50		19 20		19 50		20 20		20 50		21 20	
	d	17 22		17 52		18 22		18 52		19 22		19 52		20 22		20 52		21 22	
Folkestone West	d			18 05				19 05				20 05				21 05			
Folkestone Central	d			18 08				19 08				20 08				21 08			
Dover Priory	a			18 20				19 20				20 20				21 20			
Deal	a																		
Sandwich	a																		
Canterbury West	a	17 38				18 38				19 38				20 38				21 38	
	d	17 39				18 39				19 39				20 39				21 39	
Ramsgate	d	17 59				18 59				19 59				20 59				21 59	
Broadstairs	d	18 05				19 05				20 05				21 05				22 05	
Margate	a	18 10				19 10				20 10				21 10				22 10	

		SE	SE	SE	SE	SE	SE	SE	SE	SE	SE	SE
St Pancras International	d	21 12	21 25	21 42	21 55	22 12	22 25	22 42	22 55	23 12	23 25	23 42
Stratford International	d	21 19	21 32	21 49	22 02	22 19	22 32	22 49	23 02	23 19	23 32	23 49
Ebbsfleet International	a	21 30	21 42	22 00	22 12	22 30	22 42	23 00	23 12	23 30	23 42	23 59
	d	21 31	21 43	22 01	22 13	22 31	22 43	23 01	23 13	23 31	23 43	00 01
Gravesend	d		21 48		22 18		22 48		23 18		23 48	
Strood	d		21 58		22 28		22 58		23 28		23 58	
Maidstone West	d											
Rochester	d		22 03		22 33		23 03		23 33		00 03	
Chatham	d		22 05		22 35		23 05		23 35		00 05	
Gillingham (Kent)	d		22 10		22 40		23 10		23 40		00 10	
Rainham (Kent)	d		22 15		22 45		23 15		23 45		00 15	
Sittingbourne	d		22 23		22 53		23 23		23 53		00 23	
Faversham	a		22 33		23 03		23 31		00 03		00 33	
Whitstable	d											
Herne Bay	d											
Birchington-on-Sea	d											
Margate	d											
Broadstairs	a											
Ashford International	a	21 50		22 20		22 50		23 20		23 50		00 20
	d	21 52		22 22		22 52		23 22		23 52		
Folkestone West	d	22 05				23 05				00 05		
Folkestone Central	d	22 08				23 08				00 08		
Dover Priory	a	22 20				23 20				00 20		
Deal	a											
Sandwich	a											
Canterbury West	a			22 38				23 38				
	d			22 39				23 39				
Ramsgate	d			22 59				23a59				
Broadstairs	d			23 05								
Margate	a			23 10								

Table 194

Sundays

29 July to 12 August

St Pancras International - Kent High Speed Domestic Services

		SE	SE	SE	SE	SE	SE	SE	SE	SE	SE	SE	SE	SE	SE	SE	SE	SE	SE	SE	SE	SE	SE
St Pancras International	d	23p41	23p47	23p51	23p56	00 01	00 06	00 11	00 16	00 21	00 27	00 31	00 36	00 41	00 46	00 51	00 57	01 01	01 06	01 11	01 17	01 21	01 27
Stratford International	d	23p50	23p57	00 01	00 05	00 11	00 16	00 20	00 26	00 30	00 36	00 41	00 46	00 50	00 56	01 00	01 06	01 11	01 16	01 20	01 26	01 30	01 36
Ebbsfleet International	a	00 01	00 07	00 10	00 16	00 21	00 26	00 31	00 36	00 41	00 47	00 51	00 56	01 01	01 06	01 11	01 18	01 21	01 26	01 33	01 36	01 41	01 47
	d													01 03			01 20		01 29	01 35	01 38		01 49
Gravesend	d																				01 43		
Strood	d																				01 54		
Maidstone West	d																						
Rochester	d																				01 58		
Chatham	d																				02 01		
Gillingham (Kent)	d																				02 05		
Rainham (Kent)	d																				02 10		
Sittingbourne	d																				02 18		
Faversham	a																				02 26		
Whitstable	d																						
Herne Bay	d																						
Birchington-on-Sea	d																						
Margate	d																						
Broadstairs	a																						
Ashford International	a													01 29			01 38		01 49	01 54			02 07
	d																						
Folkestone West	d																						
Folkestone Central	d																						
Dover Priory	a																						
Deal	a																						
Sandwich	a																						
Canterbury West	a																						
	d																						
Ramsgate	d																						
Broadstairs	d																						
Margate	a																						

		SE	SE	SE	SE	SE	SE	SE	SE	SE	SE	SE	SE	SE	SE	SE	SE	SE	SE	SE	SE	SE [1]
St Pancras International	d	01 32	01 38	01 44	01 55	02 02	02 32	03 02	03 32	04 02	04 32	05 02	05 32	06 04	06 32	06 52	07 04	07 11	07 18	07 25	07 32	
Stratford International	d	01 42	01 48	01 54	02 04	02a08	02a38	03a08	03a38	04a08	04a38	05a08	05 42	06 14	06 42	07 03	07 14	07 21	07 28	07 35	07 42	
Ebbsfleet International	a	01 52	01 58	02 04	02 14								05 52	06 24	06 52	07 13	07 24	07 31	07 38	07 46	07 52	
	d		02 00	02 05	02 16								05 56				07 30		07 43			
Gravesend	d				02 21														07 48			
Strood	d				02 31														07 58			
Maidstone West	d																					
Rochester	d			02 20	02 35														08 03			
Chatham	d			02 23	02 38														08 05			
Gillingham (Kent)	d			02 27	02 42														08 10			
Rainham (Kent)	d			02 32	02 47														08 15			
Sittingbourne	d			02 40	02 55														08 23			
Faversham	a			02 48	03 03														08 33			
Whitstable	d																					
Herne Bay	d																					
Birchington-on-Sea	d																					
Margate	d																					
Broadstairs	a																					
Ashford International	a		02 18										06 14				07 51					
	d																					08 03
Folkestone West	d																					
Folkestone Central	d																					
Dover Priory	a																					
Deal	a																					
Sandwich	a																					
Canterbury West	a																					08 24
	d																					08 25
Ramsgate	d																					08a47
Broadstairs	d																					
Margate	a																					

Table 194

Sundays 29 July to 12 August

St Pancras International - Kent High Speed Domestic Services

		SE	SE	SE	SE ■	SE	SE	SE	SE	SE	SE ■	SE	SE	SE	SE ■	SE	SE	SE	SE	SE	SE ■	SE	SE	SE
St Pancras International ■ ⊖	d	07 39	07 46	07 52		08 04	08 11	08 18	08 25	08 32		08 39	08 46	08 52		09 04	09 11	09 18	09 25	09 32		09 39	09 46	09 52
Stratford International ⊖	d	07 49	07 56	08 03		08 14	08 21	08 28	08 35	08 42		08 49	08 56	09 03		09 14	09 21	09 28	09 35	09 42		09 49	09 56	10 03
Ebbsfleet International	a	07 59	08 07	08 13		08 24	08 31	08 39	08 46	08 52		09 00	09 07	09 13		09 24	09 31	09 38	09 46	09 52		10 00	10 07	10 13
	d	08 02				08 30		08 44				09 02				09 30		09 43				10 02		
Gravesend ■	d							08 48										09 48						
Strood ■	d							08 58										09 58						
Maidstone West	d																							
Rochester ■	d							09 03										10 03						
Chatham ■	d							09 05										10 05						
Gillingham (Kent) ■	d							09 10										10 10						
Rainham (Kent)	d							09 15										10 15						
Sittingbourne ■	d							09 23										10 23						
Faversham ■	a							09 33										10 33						
Whitstable	d																							
Herne Bay	d																							
Birchington-on-Sea	d																							
Margate ■	d																							
Broadstairs	a																							
Ashford International	a	08 20				08 51						09 20				09 48						10 20		
	d				08 33						09 03				09 33						10 03			
Folkestone West	d																							
Folkestone Central	d																							
Dover Priory ■	a																							
Deal	a																							
Sandwich	a																							
Canterbury West ■	a				08 54						09 21				09 54						10 21			
	d				08 55						09 22				09 55						10 22			
Ramsgate ■	d				09a13						09a44				10a13						10a44			
Broadstairs	d																							
Margate ■	a																							

		SE ■	SE	SE	SE	SE	SE	SE ■	SE	SE	SE	SE ■	SE	SE	SE	SE	SE	SE ■	SE	SE	SE	SE ■	SE	SE	SE
St Pancras International ■ ⊖	d		10 04	10 11	10 18	10 25	10 32		10 39	10 46	10 52		11 04	11 11	11 18	11 25	11 32		11 39	11 46	11 52		12 04	12 11	12 18
Stratford International ⊖	d		10 14	10 21	10 28	10 35	10 42		10 49	10 56	11 03		11 14	11 21	11 28	11 35	11 42		11 49	11 56	12 03		12 14	12 21	12 28
Ebbsfleet International	a		10 24	10 31	10 39	10 46	10 52		10 59	11 07	11 13		11 24	11 31	11 38	11 46	11 52		11 59	12 07	12 13		12 24	12 31	12 39
	d		10 30		10 44				11 02				11 30		11 43				12 02				12 30		12 44
Gravesend ■	d				10 48										11 48										12 48
Strood ■	d				10 58										11 58										12 58
Maidstone West	d																								
Rochester ■	d				11 03										12 03										13 03
Chatham ■	d				11 05										12 05										13 05
Gillingham (Kent) ■	d				11 10										12 10										13 10
Rainham (Kent)	d				11 15										12 15										13 15
Sittingbourne ■	d				11 23										12 23										13 23
Faversham ■	a				11 33										12 33										13 33
Whitstable	d																								
Herne Bay	d																								
Birchington-on-Sea	d																								
Margate ■	d																								
Broadstairs	a																								
Ashford International	a		10 51						11 20				11 51						12 20				12 51		
	d	10 33						11 03				11 33						12 03				12 33			
Folkestone West	d																								
Folkestone Central	d																								
Dover Priory ■	a																								
Deal	a																								
Sandwich	a																								
Canterbury West ■	a	10 54						11 21				11 54						12 21				12 54			
	d	10 55						11 22				11 55						12 22				12 55			
Ramsgate ■	d	11a13						11a44				12a13						12a44				13a13			
Broadstairs	d																								
Margate ■	a																								

Table 194

Sundays 29 July to 12 August

St Pancras International - Kent High Speed Domestic Services

		SE	SE	SE ■	SE	SE	SE	SE ■	SE	SE	SE	SE	SE	SE ■	SE	SE	SE	SE ■	SE	SE	SE	SE	SE
St Pancras International ■ ⊖	d	12 25	12 32		12 39	12 46	12 52		13 04	13 11	13 18	13 25	13 32		13 39	13 46	13 52		14 04	14 11	14 18	14 25	14 32
Stratford International ⊖	d	12 35	12 42		12 49	12 56	13 03		13 14	13 21	13 28	13 35	13 42		13 49	13 56	14 03		14 14	14 21	14 28	14 35	14 42
Ebbsfleet International	a	12 46	12 52		12 59	13 07	13 13		13 24	13 31	13 38	13 46	13 52		13 59	14 07	14 13		14 24	14 31	14 38	14 46	14 52
	d				13 02				13 30		13 43				14 02				14 30		14 43		
Gravesend ■	d										13 48										14 48		
Strood ■	d										13 58										14 58		
Maidstone West	d																						
Rochester ■	d										14 03										15 03		
Chatham ■	d										14 05										15 05		
Gillingham (Kent) ■	d										14 10										15 10		
Rainham (Kent)	d										14 15										15 15		
Sittingbourne ■	d										14 23										15 23		
Faversham ■	a										14 33										15 33		
Whitstable	d																						
Herne Bay	d																						
Birchington-on-Sea	d																						
Margate ■	d																						
Broadstairs	a																						
Ashford International	a				13 20				13 51						14 20				14 51				
	d			13 03				13 33						14 03				14 33					
Folkestone West	d																						
Folkestone Central	d																						
Dover Priory ■	a																						
Deal	a																						
Sandwich	a																						
Canterbury West ■	a			13 21				13 54						14 21				14 54					
	d			13 22				13 55						14 22				14 55					
Ramsgate ■	d			13a44				14a13						14a44				15a13					
Broadstairs	d																						
Margate ■	a																						

		SE ■	SE	SE	SE	SE ■	SE	SE	SE	SE	SE	SE ■	SE	SE	SE	SE ■	SE	SE	SE	SE	SE	SE ■	SE	SE
St Pancras International ■ ⊖	d		14 39	14 46	14 52		15 04	15 11	15 18	15 25	15 32		15 39	15 46	15 52		16 04	16 11	16 18	16 25	16 32		16 39	16 46
Stratford International ⊖	d		14 49	14 56	15 03		15 14	15 21	15 28	15 35	15 42		15 49	15 56	16 03		16 14	16 21	16 28	16 35	16 42		16 49	16 56
Ebbsfleet International	a		14 59	15 07	15 13		15 24	15 31	15 38	15 46	15 52		15 59	16 07	16 13		16 24	16 31	16 39	16 46	16 52		16 59	17 07
	d		15 02				15 30		15 43				16 02				16 29		16 44				17 02	
Gravesend ■	d								15 48										16 48					
Strood ■	d								15 58										16 58					
Maidstone West	d																							
Rochester ■	d								16 03										17 03					
Chatham ■	d								16 05										17 05					
Gillingham (Kent) ■	d								16 10										17 10					
Rainham (Kent)	d								16 15										17 15					
Sittingbourne ■	d								16 23										17 23					
Faversham ■	a								16 33										17 33					
Whitstable	d																							
Herne Bay	d																							
Birchington-on-Sea	d																							
Margate ■	d																							
Broadstairs	a																							
Ashford International	a		15 20				15 51						16 20				16 48						17 20	
	d	15 03				15 33						16 03				16 33						17 03		
Folkestone West	d																							
Folkestone Central	d																							
Dover Priory ■	a																							
Deal	a																							
Sandwich	a																							
Canterbury West ■	a	15 21				15 54						16 21				16 54						17 21		
	d	15 22				15 55						16 22				16 55						17 22		
Ramsgate ■	d	15a44				16a13						16a44				17a13						17a44		
Broadstairs	d																							
Margate ■	a																							

		SE	SE ■	SE	SE	SE	SE	SE	SE ■	SE	SE	SE	SE ■	SE	SE	SE	SE	SE	SE ■	SE	SE	SE	SE ■	SE
St Pancras International ■ ⊖	d	16 52		17 04	17 11	17 18	17 25	17 32		17 39	17 46	17 52		18 04	18 11	18 18	18 25	18 32		18 39	18 46	18 52		19 04
Stratford International ⊖	d	17 03		17 14	17 21	17 28	17 35	17 42		17 49	17 56	18 03		18 14	18 21	18 28	18 35	18 42		18 49	18 56	19 03		19 14
Ebbsfleet International	a	17 13		17 24	17 31	17 38	17 46	17 52		17 59	18 07	18 13		18 24	18 31	18 38	18 46	18 52		18 59	19 07	19 13		19 24
	d			17 30		17 43				18 02				18 30		18 43				19 02				19 30
Gravesend ■	d					17 48										18 48								
Strood ■	d					17 58										18 58								
Maidstone West	d																							
Rochester ■	d					18 03										19 03								
Chatham ■	d					18 05										19 05								
Gillingham (Kent) ■	d					18 10										19 10								
Rainham (Kent)	d					18 15										19 15								
Sittingbourne ■	d					18 23										19 23								
Faversham ■	a					18 33										19 33								
Whitstable	d																							
Herne Bay	d																							
Birchington-on-Sea	d																							
Margate ■	d																							
Broadstairs	a																							
Ashford International	a			17 51						18 20				18 51						19 20				19 51
	d		17 33						18 03				18 33						19 03				19 33	
Folkestone West	d																							
Folkestone Central	d																							
Dover Priory ■	a																							
Deal	a																							
Sandwich	a																							
Canterbury West ■	a		17 54						18 21				18 54						19 21				19 54	
	d		17 55						18 22				18 55						19 22				19 55	
Ramsgate ■	d		18a13						18a44				19a13						19a44				20a13	
Broadstairs	d																							
Margate ■	a																							

St Pancras International - Kent
High Speed Domestic Services

Sundays
29 July to 12 August

		SE	SE	SE	SE	SE 1	SE	SE	SE	SE 1	SE	SE	SE	SE	SE	SE 1	SE	SE	SE	SE 1	SE	SE	SE	SE	SE
St Pancras International	d	19 11	19 18	19 25	19 32		19 39	19 46	19 52		20 04	20 11	20 18	20 25	20 32		20 39	20 46	20 52		21 04	21 11	21 18	21 25	21 32
Stratford International	d	19 21	19 28	19 35	19 42		19 49	19 56	20 03		20 14	20 21	20 28	20 35	20 42		20 49	20 56	21 03		21 14	21 21	21 28	21 35	21 42
Ebbsfleet International	a	19 31	19 38	19 46	19 52		19 59	20 07	20 13		20 24	20 31	20 38	20 46	20 52		20 59	21 07	21 13		21 24	21 31	21 38	21 46	21 52
	d		19 43				20 02				20 30		20 43				21 02				21 30		21 43		
Gravesend	d		19 48										20 48										21 48		
Strood	d		19 58										20 58										21 58		
Maidstone West	d																								
Rochester	d		20 03										21 03										22 03		
Chatham	d		20 05										21 05										22 05		
Gillingham (Kent)	d		20 10										21 10										22 10		
Rainham (Kent)	d		20 15										21 15										22 15		
Sittingbourne	d		20 23										21 23										22 23		
Faversham	a		20 33										21 33										22 33		
Whitstable	d																								
Herne Bay	d																								
Birchington-on-Sea	d																								
Margate	d																								
Broadstairs	a																								
Ashford International	a						20 20				20 51						21 20				21 51				
	d					20 03				20 33						21 03				21 33					
Folkestone West	d																								
Folkestone Central	d																								
Dover Priory	a																								
Deal	a																								
Sandwich	a																								
Canterbury West	a					20 21				20 54						21 21				21 54					
	d					20 22				20 55						21 22				21 55					
Ramsgate	d					20a44				21a13						21a44				22a13					
Broadstairs	d																								
Margate	a																								

		SE	SE 1	SE	SE	SE	SE	SE	SE	SE	SE	SE	SE	SE	SE	SE	SE	SE	SE	SE	SE	SE	SE	SE	SE
St Pancras International	d	21 32		21 39	21 46	21 52	22 04	22 11	22 18	22 25	22 32	22 39	22 46	22 52	23 04	23 11	23 16	23 21	23 26	23 32	23 36	23 41	23 47	23 51	23 56
Stratford International	d	21 42		21 49	21 56	22 03	22 14	22 21	22 28	22 35	22 42	22 47	22 56	23 02	23 14	23 21	23 26	23 30	23 35	23 42	23 46	23 50	23 57	00 01	00 05
Ebbsfleet International	a	21 52		21 59	22 07	22 13	22 24	22 31	22 40	22 46	22 52	22 57	23 07	23 12	23 24	23 31	23 37	23 41	23 45	23 52	23 56	00 01	00 07	00 10	00 16
	d			22 02																					
Gravesend	d																								
Strood	d																								
Maidstone West	d																								
Rochester	d																								
Chatham	d																								
Gillingham (Kent)	d																								
Rainham (Kent)	d																								
Sittingbourne	d																								
Faversham	a																								
Whitstable	d																								
Herne Bay	d																								
Birchington-on-Sea	d																								
Margate	d																								
Broadstairs	a																								
Ashford International	a			22 20																					
	d		22 03																						
Folkestone West	d																								
Folkestone Central	d																								
Dover Priory	a																								
Deal	a																								
Sandwich	a																								
Canterbury West	a		22 21																						
	d		22 22																						
Ramsgate	d		22a44																						
Broadstairs	d																								
Margate	a																								

St Pancras International - Kent
High Speed Domestic Services

Sundays
26 August to 9 September

		SE A	SE B	SE A	SE B	SE A	SE B	SE B	SE A	SE A	SE B	SE B	SE B	SE B	SE B	SE B	SE B	SE 1	SE B	SE A	SE B
St Pancras International	d	22p55	22p55	23p12	23p12	23p25	23p25	23p55	23p55	00 12	00 12	00 15	00 48	01 48	02 48	07 47	08 18		08 41	08 42	08 47
Stratford International	d	23p02	23p03	23p19	23p20	23p32	23p33	00 03	00 02	00 19	00 20	00a21	00a54	01a54	02a54	07 56	08 26		08 49	08 49	08 55
Ebbsfleet International	a	23p12	23p13	23p30	23p31	23p42	23p43	00 12	00 12	00 30	00 31					08 06	08 36		09 00	09 00	09 05
	d	23p13	23p14	23p31	23p32	23p43	23p44	00 13	00 13	00 31	00 32								09 01	09 01	
Gravesend	d	23p18	23p18			23p48	23p48	00 18	00 18												
Strood	d	23p28	23p28			23p58	23p58	00 28	00 28												
Maidstone West	d																				
Rochester	d	23p33	23p33			00 03	00 03	00 32	00 33												
Chatham	d	23p35	23p35			00 05	00 05	00 35	00 35												
Gillingham (Kent)	d	23p40	23p40			00 10	00 10	00 39	00 40												
Rainham (Kent)	d	23p45	23p45			00 15	00 15	00 44	00 45												
Sittingbourne	d	23p53	23p53			00 23	00 23	00 52	00 53												
Faversham	a	00 01	00 01			00 31	00 31	01 00	01 01												
Whitstable	d																				
Herne Bay	d																				
Birchington-on-Sea	d																				
Margate	d																				
Broadstairs	a																				
Ashford International	a			23p50	23p50					00 50	00 51								09 20	09 20	
	d			23p52	23p52													09 03	09 22	09 22	
Folkestone West	d			00 05	00 05																
Folkestone Central	d			00 08	00 08																
Dover Priory	a			00 20	00 20																
Deal	a																				
Sandwich	a																				
Canterbury West	a																	09 21	09 38	09 38	
	d																	09 22	09 39	09 39	
Ramsgate	d																	09a44	09 59	09 59	
Broadstairs	d																		10 05	10 05	
Margate	a																		10 10	10 10	

		SE B	SE A	SE B	SE A	SE B	SE B	SE A	SE B	SE B	SE A	SE B	SE B	SE A	SE B	SE B	SE A	SE B	SE B	SE B	SE A
St Pancras International	d	09 09	09 10	09 17	09 25	09 26	09 36	09 42	09 47	09 55	10 10	10 11	10 14	10 28	10 28	10 41	10 42	10 47	10 52	11 11	11 12
Stratford International	d	09 17	09 17	09 24	09 32	09 33	09 44	09 49	09 55	10 03	10 17	10 19	10 24	10 35	10 36	10 49	10 49	10 55	11 04	11 19	11 19
Ebbsfleet International	a	09 28	09 28	09 34	09 42	09 43	09 55	10 00	10 05	10 13	10 28	10 30	10 35	10 45	10 46	11 00	11 00	11 05	11 13	11 30	11 30
	d	09 29	09 29		09 43	09 44	09 56	10 01			10 29	10 31		10 46	10 47	11 01	11 01			11 31	11 31
Gravesend	d				09 48	09 48								10 51	10 51						
Strood	d				09 58	09 58								11 01	11 01						
Maidstone West	d																				
Rochester	d				10 03	10 03								11 06	11 06						
Chatham	d				10 05	10 05								11 08	11 08						
Gillingham (Kent)	d				10 10	10 10								11 13	11 13						
Rainham (Kent)	d				10 15	10 15								11 18	11 18						
Sittingbourne	d				10 23	10 23								11 25	11 25						
Faversham	a				10 33	10 33								11 34	11 34						
Whitstable	d																				
Herne Bay	d																				
Birchington-on-Sea	d																				
Margate	d																				
Broadstairs	a																				
Ashford International	a	09 48	09 48				10 15	10 20			10 48	10 50				11 20	11 20			11 50	11 50
	d	09 52	09 52				10 22	10 22			10 52	10 52				11 22	11 22			11 52	11 52
Folkestone West	d	10 05	10 05								11 05	11 05								12 05	12 05
Folkestone Central	d	10 08	10 08								11 08	11 08								12 08	12 08
Dover Priory	a	10 20	10 20								11 20	11 20								12 20	12 20
Deal	a																				
Sandwich	a																				
Canterbury West	a						10 38	10 38								11 38	11 38				
	d						10 39	10 39								11 39	11 39				
Ramsgate	d						10 59	10 59								11 59	11 59				
Broadstairs	d						11 05	11 05								12 05	12 05				
Margate	a						11 10	11 10								12 10	12 10				

A not from 2 September until 9 September

B not 26 August

26 August to 9 September

St Pancras International - Kent High Speed Domestic Services

		SE A	SE A	SE B	SE A	SE B	SE A	SE A	SE A	SE B	SE A
St Pancras International	d	11 18	11 25	11 25	11 41	11 42	11 47	11 51	12 11	12 12	12 16
Stratford International	d	11 26	11 32	11 32	11 49	11 49	11 54	11 58	12 19	12 19	12 24
Ebbsfleet International	a	11 36	11 42	11 42	12 00	12 00	12 04	12 08	12 30	12 30	12 34
	d		11 44	11 43	12 01	12 01			12 31	12 31	
Gravesend	d		11 48	11 48							
Strood	d		11 58	11 58							
Maidstone West	d										
Rochester	d		12 03	12 03							
Chatham	d		12 05	12 05							
Gillingham (Kent)	d		12 10	12 10							
Rainham (Kent)	d		12 15	12 15							
Sittingbourne	d		12 23	12 23							
Faversham	a		12 33	12 33							
Whitstable	d										
Herne Bay	d										
Birchington-on-Sea	d										
Margate	d										
Broadstairs	a										
Ashford International	a				12 20	12 20			12 50	12 50	
	d				12 22	12 22			12 52	12 52	
Folkestone West	d								13 05	13 05	
Folkestone Central	d								13 08	13 08	
Dover Priory	a								13 20	13 20	
Deal	a										
Sandwich	a										
Canterbury West	a				12 38	12 38					
	d				12 39	12 39					
Ramsgate	d				12 59	12 59					
Broadstairs	d				13 05	13 05					
Margate	a				13 10	13 10					

		SE A	SE B	SE A	SE B	SE A	SE A	SE B	SE A	SE B	SE A
St Pancras International	d	12 27	12 28	12 41	12 42	12 47	12 51	12 52	13 11	13 12	13 18
Stratford International	d	12 36	12 35	12 49	12 49	12 54	12 58	12 58	13 19	13 19	13 26
Ebbsfleet International	a	12 46	12 45	13 00	13 00	13 04	13 08	13 08	13 30	13 30	13 36
	d	12 47	12 46	13 01	13 01		13 13	13 13	13 31	13 31	
Gravesend	d	12 51	12 51				13 18	13 18			
Strood	d	13 01	13 01				13 28	13 28			
Maidstone West	d										
Rochester	d	13 06	13 06				13 33	13 33			
Chatham	d	13 08	13 08				13 35	13 35			
Gillingham (Kent)	d	13 13	13 13				13 40	13 40			
Rainham (Kent)	d	13 18	13 18				13 45	13 45			
Sittingbourne	d	13 25	13 25				13 53	13 53			
Faversham	a	13 34	13 34				14 03	14 03			
Whitstable	d										
Herne Bay	d										
Birchington-on-Sea	d										
Margate	d										
Broadstairs	a										
Ashford International	a			13 20	13 20				13 50	13 50	
	d			13 22	13 22				13 52	13 52	
Folkestone West	d								14 05	14 05	
Folkestone Central	d								14 08	14 08	
Dover Priory	a								14 20	14 20	
Deal	a										
Sandwich	a										
Canterbury West	a			13 38	13 38						
	d			13 39	13 39						
Ramsgate	d			13 59	13 59						
Broadstairs	d			14 05	14 05						
Margate	a			14 10	14 10						

		SE B	SE A	SE A	SE B	SE A	SE B	SE A	SE A	SE B	SE A
St Pancras International	d	13 25	13 25	13 41	13 42	13 48	13 55	13 55	14 11	14 12	14 18
Stratford International	d	13 32	13 33	13 49	13 49	13 56	14 02	14 03	14 19	14 19	14 26
Ebbsfleet International	a	13 42	13 43	14 00	14 00	14 06	14 12	14 13	14 30	14 30	14 36
	d	13 43	13 44	14 01	14 01		14 13	14 14	14 31	14 31	
Gravesend	d	13 48	13 48				14 18	14 18			
Strood	d	13 58	13 58				14 28	14 28			
Maidstone West	d										
Rochester	d	14 03	14 03				14 33	14 33			
Chatham	d	14 05	14 05				14 35	14 35			
Gillingham (Kent)	d	14 10	14 10				14 40	14 40			
Rainham (Kent)	d	14 15	14 15				14 45	14 45			
Sittingbourne	d	14 23	14 23				14 53	14 53			
Faversham	a	14 33	14 33				15 03	15 03			
Whitstable	d										
Herne Bay	d										
Birchington-on-Sea	d										
Margate	d										
Broadstairs	a										
Ashford International	a			14 20	14 20				14 50	14 50	
	d			14 22	14 22				14 52	14 52	
Folkestone West	d								15 05	15 05	
Folkestone Central	d								15 08	15 08	
Dover Priory	a								15 20	15 20	
Deal	a										
Sandwich	a										
Canterbury West	a			14 38	14 38						
	d			14 39	14 39						
Ramsgate	d			14 59	14 59						
Broadstairs	d			15 05	15 05						
Margate	a			15 10	15 10						

		SE B	SE A	SE A	SE B	SE A	SE B	SE A	SE A	SE B	SE A
St Pancras International	d	14 25	14 25	14 41	14 42	14 48	14 55	14 55	15 11	15 12	15 18
Stratford International	d	14 32	14 33	14 49	14 49	14 56	15 02	15 03	15 19	15 19	15 26
Ebbsfleet International	a	14 42	14 43	15 00	15 00	15 06	15 12	15 13	15 30	15 30	15 36
	d	14 43	14 44	15 01	15 01		15 13	15 14	15 31	15 31	
Gravesend	d	14 48	14 48				15 18	15 18			
Strood	d	14 58	14 58				15 28	15 28			
Maidstone West	d										
Rochester	d	15 03	15 03				15 33	15 33			
Chatham	d	15 05	15 05				15 35	15 35			
Gillingham (Kent)	d	15 10	15 10				15 40	15 40			
Rainham (Kent)	d	15 15	15 15				15 45	15 45			
Sittingbourne	d	15 23	15 23				15 53	15 53			
Faversham	a	15 33	15 33				16 03	16 03			
Whitstable	d										
Herne Bay	d										
Birchington-on-Sea	d										
Margate	d										
Broadstairs	a										
Ashford International	a			15 20	15 20				15 50	15 50	
	d			15 22	15 22				15 52	15 52	
Folkestone West	d								16 05	16 05	
Folkestone Central	d								16 08	16 08	
Dover Priory	a								16 20	16 20	
Deal	a										
Sandwich	a										
Canterbury West	a			15 38	15 38						
	d			15 39	15 39						
Ramsgate	d			15 59	15 59						
Broadstairs	d			16 05	16 05						
Margate	a			16 10	16 10						

A not 26 August

B not from 2 September until 9 September

26 August to 9 September

St Pancras International - Kent High Speed Domestic Services

		SE A	SE B	SE B	SE A	SE B	SE A	SE B	SE B	SE A	SE B
St Pancras International	d	15 25	15 25	15 41	15 42	15 48	15 55	15 55	16 09	16 10	16 12
Stratford International	d	15 32	15 33	15 49	15 49	15 56	16 02	16 03	16 17	16 17	16 22
Ebbsfleet International	a	15 42	15 43	16 00	16 00	16 06	16 12	16 13	16 28	16 28	16 32
	d	15 43	15 44	16 01	16 01		16 13	16 14	16 29	16 29	
Gravesend	d	15 48	15 48				16 18	16 18			
Strood	d	15 58	15 58				16 28	16 28			
Maidstone West	d										
Rochester	d	16 03	16 03				16 33	16 33			
Chatham	d	16 05	16 05				16 35	16 35			
Gillingham (Kent)	d	16 10	16 10				16 40	16 40			
Rainham (Kent)	d	16 15	16 15				16 45	16 45			
Sittingbourne	d	16 23	16 23				16 53	16 53			
Faversham	a	16 33	16 33				17 03	17 03			
Whitstable	d										
Herne Bay	d										
Birchington-on-Sea	d										
Margate	d										
Broadstairs	a										
Ashford International	a			16 20	16 20				16 48	16 48	
	d			16 22	16 22				16 52	16 52	
Folkestone West	d								17 05	17 05	
Folkestone Central	d								17 08	17 08	
Dover Priory	a								17 20	17 20	
Deal	a										
Sandwich	a										
Canterbury West	a			16 38	16 38						
	d			16 39	16 39						
Ramsgate	d			16 59	16 59						
Broadstairs	d			17 05	17 05						
Margate	a			17 10	17 10						

		SE A	SE B	SE B	SE A	SE B	SE A	SE B	SE B	SE A	SE B
St Pancras International	d	16 25	16 25	16 41	16 42	16 48	16 55	16 55	17 11	17 12	17 18
Stratford International	d	16 32	16 33	16 49	16 49	16 56	17 02	17 03	17 19	17 19	17 26
Ebbsfleet International	a	16 42	16 43	17 00	17 00	17 06	17 12	17 13	17 30	17 30	17 36
	d	16 43	16 44	17 01	17 01		17 13	17 14	17 31	17 31	
Gravesend	d	16 48	16 48				17 18	17 18			
Strood	d	16 58	16 58				17 28	17 28			
Maidstone West	d										
Rochester	d	17 03	17 03				17 33	17 33			
Chatham	d	17 05	17 05				17 35	17 35			
Gillingham (Kent)	d	17 10	17 10				17 40	17 40			
Rainham (Kent)	d	17 15	17 15				17 45	17 45			
Sittingbourne	d	17 23	17 23				17 53	17 53			
Faversham	a	17 33	17 33				18 03	18 03			
Whitstable	d										
Herne Bay	d										
Birchington-on-Sea	d										
Margate	d										
Broadstairs	a										
Ashford International	a			17 20	17 20				17 50	17 50	
	d			17 22	17 22				17 52	17 52	
Folkestone West	d								18 05	18 05	
Folkestone Central	d								18 08	18 08	
Dover Priory	a								18 20	18 20	
Deal	a										
Sandwich	a										
Canterbury West	a			17 38	17 38						
	d			17 39	17 39						
Ramsgate	d			17 59	17 59						
Broadstairs	d			18 05	18 05						
Margate	a			18 10	18 10						

		SE A	SE B	SE B	SE A	SE B	SE B	SE A	SE B	SE A	SE B
St Pancras International	d	17 25	17 25	17 41	17 42	17 45	17 48	17 58	18 11	18 12	18 18
Stratford International	d	17 32	17 33	17 49	17 49	17 52	17 55	18 08	18 19	18 19	18 26
Ebbsfleet International	a	17 42	17 43	18 00	18 00	18 04	18 05	18 18	18 30	18 30	18 36
	d	17 43	17 44	18 01	18 01		18 14	18 19	18 31	18 31	
Gravesend	d	17 48	17 48				18 19	18 24			
Strood	d	17 58	17 58				18 29	18 34			
Maidstone West	d										
Rochester	d	18 03	18 03				18 34	18 39			
Chatham	d	18 05	18 05				18 36	18 41			
Gillingham (Kent)	d	18 10	18 10				18 41	18 46			
Rainham (Kent)	d	18 15	18 15				18 46	18 51			
Sittingbourne	d	18 23	18 23				18 54	18 58			
Faversham	a	18 33	18 33				19 04	19 07			
Whitstable	d										
Herne Bay	d										
Birchington-on-Sea	d										
Margate	d										
Broadstairs	a										
Ashford International	a			18 20	18 20				18 50	18 50	
	d			18 22	18 22				18 52	18 52	
Folkestone West	d								19 05	19 05	
Folkestone Central	d								19 08	19 08	
Dover Priory	a								19 20	19 20	
Deal	a										
Sandwich	a										
Canterbury West	a			18 38	18 38						
	d			18 39	18 39						
Ramsgate	d			18 59	18 59						
Broadstairs	d			19 05	19 05						
Margate	a			19 10	19 10						

		SE A	SE B	SE B	SE A	SE A	SE B	SE B	SE A	SE B
St Pancras International	d	18 25	18 27	18 41	18 42	18 55	18 55	19 11	19 12	19 18
Stratford International	d	18 32	18 35	18 49	18 49	19 02	19 03	19 19	19 19	19 26
Ebbsfleet International	a	18 42	18 45	19 00	19 00	19 12	19 13	19 30	19 30	19 36
	d	18 43	18 46	19 01	19 01	19 13	19 14	19 31	19 31	
Gravesend	d	18 48	18 51			19 18	19 18			
Strood	d	18 58	19 01			19 28	19 28			
Maidstone West	d									
Rochester	d	19 03	19 06			19 33	19 33			
Chatham	d	19 05	19 08			19 35	19 35			
Gillingham (Kent)	d	19 10	19 13			19 40	19 40			
Rainham (Kent)	d	19 15	19 18			19 45	19 45			
Sittingbourne	d	19 23	19 25			19 53	19 53			
Faversham	a	19 33	19 34			20 03	20 03			
Whitstable	d									
Herne Bay	d									
Birchington-on-Sea	d									
Margate	d									
Broadstairs	a									
Ashford International	a			19 20	19 20			19 50	19 50	
	d			19 22	19 22			19 52	19 52	
Folkestone West	d							20 05	20 05	
Folkestone Central	d							20 08	20 08	
Dover Priory	a							20 20	20 20	
Deal	a									
Sandwich	a									
Canterbury West	a			19 38	19 38					
	d			19 39	19 39					
Ramsgate	d			19 59	19 59					
Broadstairs	d			20 05	20 05					
Margate	a			20 10	20 10					

A not from 2 September until 9 September

B not 26 August

Sundays

26 August to 9 September

St Pancras International - Kent High Speed Domestic Services

		SE A	SE B	SE B	SE A	SE A	SE B	SE B	SE A	SE B	SE B	SE A	SE B	SE A	SE A	SE B	SE B	SE A	SE B	SE A	SE B
St Pancras International ⊖	d	19 25	19 25	19 41	19 42	19 55	19 55	20 11	20 12	20 18	20 25	20 25	20 41	20 42	20 55	20 55	21 11	21 12	21 18	21 25	21 25
Stratford International ⊖	d	19 32	19 33	19 49	19 49	20 02	20 02	20 19	20 19	20 26	20 32	20 32	20 49	20 49	21 02	21 03	21 19	21 19	21 26	21 32	21 33
Ebbsfleet International	a	19 42	19 43	20 00	20 00	20 12	20 12	20 30	20 30	20 36	20 42	20 42	21 00	21 00	21 12	21 13	21 30	21 30	21 36	21 42	21 43
	d	19 43	19 44	20 01	20 01	20 13	20 14	20 31	20 31		20 44	20 43	21 01	21 01	21 13	21 14	21 31	21 31		21 43	21 44
Gravesend	d	19 48	19 48			20 18	20 18				20 48	20 48			21 18	21 18				21 48	21 48
Strood	d	19 58	19 58			20 28	20 28				20 58	20 58			21 28	21 28				21 58	21 58
Maidstone West	d																				
Rochester	d	20 03	20 03			20 33	20 33				21 03	21 03			21 33	21 33				22 03	22 03
Chatham	d	20 05	20 05			20 35	20 35				21 05	21 05			21 35	21 35				22 05	22 05
Gillingham (Kent)	d	20 10	20 10			20 40	20 40				21 10	21 10			21 40	21 40				22 10	22 10
Rainham (Kent)	d	20 15	20 15			20 45	20 45				21 15	21 15			21 45	21 45				22 15	22 15
Sittingbourne	d	20 23	20 23			20 53	20 53				21 23	21 23			21 53	21 53				22 23	22 23
Faversham	a	20 33	20 33			21 03	21 03				21 33	21 33			22 03	22 03				22 33	22 33
Whitstable	d																				
Herne Bay	d																				
Birchington-on-Sea	d																				
Margate	d																				
Broadstairs	a																				
Ashford International	a			20 20	20 20			20 50	20 50				21 20	21 20			21 50	21 50			
	d			20 22	20 22			20 52	20 52				21 22	21 22			21 52	21 52			
Folkestone West	d							21 05	21 05								22 05	22 05			
Folkestone Central	d							21 08	21 08								22 08	22 08			
Dover Priory	a							21 20	21 20								22 20	22 20			
Deal	a																				
Sandwich	a																				
Canterbury West	a			20 38	20 38								21 38	21 38							
	d			20 39	20 39								21 39	21 39							
Ramsgate	d			20 59	20 59								21 59	21 59							
Broadstairs	d			21 05	21 05								22 05	22 05							
Margate	a			21 10	21 10								22 10	22 10							

		SE B	SE A	SE A	SE B	SE B	SE A	SE B	SE A	SE B	SE A	SE B	SE A	SE B	SE A	SE B	SE B	SE A	SE B	SE A	SE B
St Pancras International ⊖	d	21 41	21 42	21 55	21 55	22 11	22 12	22 18	22 25	22 25	22 42	22 42	22 55	22 55	23 12	23 12	23 18	23 25	23 25	23 42	23 42
Stratford International ⊖	d	21 49	21 49	22 02	22 03	22 19	22 19	22 26	22 32	22 33	22 49	22 50	23 02	23 03	23 19	23 20	23 26	23 32	23 33	23 49	23 50
Ebbsfleet International	a	22 00	22 00	22 12	22 13	22 30	22 30	22 36	22 42	22 43	23 00	23 01	23 12	23 13	23 30	23 31	23 36	23 42	23 43	23 59	00 01
	d	22 01	22 01	22 13	22 14	22 31	22 31		22 43	22 44	23 01	23 02	23 13	23 14	23 31	23 32		23 43	23 44	00 01	00 02
Gravesend	d			22 18	22 18				22 48	22 48			23 18	23 18				23 48	23 48		
Strood	d			22 28	22 28				22 58	22 58			23 28	23 28				23 58	23 58		
Maidstone West	d																				
Rochester	d			22 33	22 33				23 03	23 03			23 33	23 33				00 03	00 03		
Chatham	d			22 35	22 35				23 05	23 05			23 35	23 35				00 05	00 05		
Gillingham (Kent)	d			22 40	22 40				23 10	23 10			23 40	23 40				00 10	00 10		
Rainham (Kent)	d			22 45	22 45				23 15	23 15			23 45	23 45				00 15	00 15		
Sittingbourne	d			22 53	22 53				23 23	23 23			23 53	23 53				00 23	00 23		
Faversham	a			23 03	23 03				23 31	23 31			00 03	00 03				00 33	00 33		
Whitstable	d																				
Herne Bay	d																				
Birchington-on-Sea	d																				
Margate	d																				
Broadstairs	a																				
Ashford International	a	22 20	22 20			22 50	22 50				23 20	23 20			23 50	23 50				00 20	00 21
	d	22 22	22 22			22 52	22 52				23 22	23 22			23 52	23 52					
Folkestone West	d					23 05	23 05								00 05	00 05					
Folkestone Central	d					23 08	23 08								00 08	00 08					
Dover Priory	a					23 20	23 20								00 20	00 20					
Deal	a																				
Sandwich	a																				
Canterbury West	a	22 38	22 38								23 38	23 38									
	d	22 39	22 39								23 39	23 39									
Ramsgate	d	22 59	22 59								23a59	23a59									
Broadstairs	d	23 05	23 05																		
Margate	a	23 10	23 10																		

A not from 2 September until 9 September

B not 26 August

Mondays to Fridays

until 26 July, 13 Aug to 28 Aug and from 10 Sep

Kent - St Pancras International High Speed Domestic Services

Miles	Miles	Miles			SE	SE	SE	SE	SE	SE	SE	SE	SE	SE	SE	SE	SE	SE	SE	SE	SE	SE	SE	SE
—	—	0	Margate	d							05 47										06 48			
—	—	3¼	Broadstairs	d							05 54										06 54			
—	—	5½	Ramsgate	d			05 00				06 00						06 26				07 00			
—	—	20¾	Canterbury West	a			05 23				06 19						06 45				07 19			
—	—	—		d			05 25				06 20						06 50				07 20			
—	—	—	Sandwich	d								05 50				06 18						06 50		
—	—	—	Deal	d								05 56				06 24						06 56		
—	0	—	Dover Priory	d					05 44			06 12				06 42						07 12		
—	7¼	—	Folkestone Central	d					05 56			06 23				06 53						07 23		
—	8	—	Folkestone West	d					05 58			06 26				06 56						07 26		
—	21¼	—	Ashford International	a			05 41		06 11		06 36	06 39				07 09	07 06				07 36	07 39		
—	—	—																						
—	—	—		d	05 13		05 43		06 13		06 43					07 13					07 43			
0	—	—	Broadstairs	d										06 00					06 30					07 00
3¼	—	—	Margate	d										06 05					06 35					07 05
6¼	—	—	Birchington-on-Sea	d										06 10					06 40					07 10
14¼	—	—	Herne Bay	d										06 19					06 49					07 19
18¼	—	—	Whitstable	d										06 25					06 55					07 25
25	—	—	Faversham	a										06 33					07 03					07 33
—	—	—		d		04 56		05 28		05 58				06 34					07 04					07 34
32¾	—	—	Sittingbourne	d		05 07		05 37		06 07				06 42					07 13					07 42
38½	—	—	Rainham (Kent)	d		05 15		05 45		06 15				06 50					07 21					07 50
41½	—	—	Gillingham (Kent)	d		05 20		05 50		06 20				06 55					07 26					07 55
43¼	—	—	Chatham	d		05 24		05 54		06 24				07 00					07 30					08 00
43¾	—	—	Rochester	d		05 27		05 57		06 27				07 03					07 33					08 03
—	—	—	Maidstone West	d											06 56					07 26				
44¾	—	—	Strood	d		05 32		06 02		06 32					07 12					07 42				
52	—	—	Gravesend	d		05 43		06 13		06 43					07 22					07 52				
54	54½	68¾	Ebbsfleet International	a	05 32	05 47	06 02	06 17	06 32	06 47				07 17					07 47					08 17
—	—	—		d	05 33	05 48	06 03	06 18	06 33	06 48			07 06	07 18				07 34	07 48				08 04	08 18
70¾	71¼	85	Stratford International ⊖	a	05 44	05 59	06 14	06 29	06 44	06 59	07 11		07 18	07 29	07 36	07 41		07 45	07 59	08 06	08 11		08 15	08 29
76¾	77¼	91	St Pancras International ⊖	a	05 51	06 06	06 21	06 36	06 51	07 06	07 18		07 25	07 36	07 43	07 48		07 52	08 06	08 13	08 19		08 22	08 36

		SE	SE	SE	SE	SE	SE	SE	SE	SE	SE	SE	SE	SE	SE	SE	SE	SE
Margate	d						07 49				08 53				09 53			
Broadstairs	d						07 55				08 59				09 59			
Ramsgate	d		07 30				08 01				09 05				10 05			
Canterbury West	a		07 49				08 24				09 24				10 24			
	d		07 50				08 25				09 25				10 25			
Sandwich	d																	
Deal	d																	
Dover Priory	d			07 42					08 44				09 44				10 44	
Folkestone Central	d			07 53					08 56				09 56				10 56	
Folkestone West	d			07 56					08 58				09 58				10 58	
Ashford International	a		08 06	08 09			08 41		09 11		09 41		10 11		10 41		11 11	
	d		08 13				08 43		09 13		09 43		10 13		10 43		11 13	
Broadstairs	d																	
Margate	d																	
Birchington-on-Sea	d																	
Herne Bay	d																	
Whitstable	d																	
Faversham	a																	
	d					07 58		08 28		08 58		09 28		09 58		10 28		10 58
Sittingbourne	d					08 06		08 37		09 07		09 37		10 07		10 37		11 07
Rainham (Kent)	d					08 14		08 45		09 15		09 45		10 15		10 45		11 15
Gillingham (Kent)	d					08 19		08 50		09 20		09 50		10 20		10 50		11 20
Chatham	d					08 24		08 54		09 24		09 54		10 24		10 54		11 24
Rochester	d					08 26		08 57		09 27		09 57		10 27		10 57		11 27
Maidstone West	d	07 56																
Strood	d	08 12				08 32		09 02		09 32		10 02		10 32		11 02		11 32
Gravesend	d	08 22				08 43		09 13		09 43		10 13		10 43		11 13		11 43
Ebbsfleet International	a					08 47	09 02	09 17	09 32	09 47	10 02	10 16	10 32	10 47	11 02	11 17	11 32	11 47
	d				08 34	08 48	09 03	09 18	09 33	09 48	10 03	10 17	10 33	10 48	11 03	11 18	11 33	11 48
Stratford International ⊖	a	08 36	08 41		08 45	08 59	09 14	09 29	09 44	09 59	10 14	10 28	10 44	10 59	11 14	11 29	11 44	11 59
St Pancras International ⊖	a	08 43	08 48		08 52	09 07	09 21	09 36	09 51	10 06	10 21	10 35	10 51	11 06	11 21	11 36	11 51	12 06

Table 194

Mondays to Fridays

until 26 July, 13 Aug to 28 Aug and from 10 Sep

Kent - St Pancras International High Speed Domestic Services

		SE	SE	SE	SE	SE	SE	SE	SE A	SE B	SE	SE	SE	SE	SE	SE	SE	SE	SE
Margate	d	10 53				11 53					12 53				13 53				14 53
Broadstairs	d	10 59				11 59					12 59				13 59				14 59
Ramsgate	d	11 05				12 05					13 05				14 05				15 05
Canterbury West	a	11 24				12 24					13 24				14 24				15 24
	d	11 25				12 25					13 25				14 25				15 25
Sandwich	d																		
Deal	d																		
Dover Priory	d			11 44				12 44					13 44				14 44		
Folkestone Central	d			11 56				12 56					13 56				14 56		
Folkestone West	d			11 58				12 58					13 58				14 58		
Ashford International	a	11 41		12 11		12 41		13 11			13 41		14 11		14 41		15 11		15 41
	d	11 43		12 13		12 43		13 13			13 43		14 13		14 43		15 13		15 43
Broadstairs	d																		
Margate	d																		
Birchington-on-Sea	d																		
Herne Bay	d																		
Whitstable	d																		
Faversham	a																		
	d		11 28		11 58		12 28		12 58	12 58		13 28		13 58		14 28		14 58	
Sittingbourne	d		11 37		12 07		12 37		13 07	13 07		13 37		14 07		14 37		15 07	
Rainham (Kent)	d		11 45		12 15		12 45		13 15	13 15		13 45		14 15		14 45		15 15	
Gillingham (Kent)	d		11 50		12 20		12 50		13 20	13 20		13 50		14 20		14 50		15 20	
Chatham	d		11 54		12 24		12 54		13 24	13 24		13 54		14 24		14 54		15 24	
Rochester	d		11 57		12 27		12 57		13 27	13 27		13 57		14 27		14 57		15 27	
Maidstone West	d																		
Strood	d		12 02		12 32		13 02		13 32	13 32		14 02		14 32		15 02		15 32	
Gravesend	d		12 13		12 43		13 13		13 43	13 43		14 13		14 43		15 13		15 43	
Ebbsfleet International	a	12 02	12 17	12 32	12 47	13 02	13 17	13 32	13 47	13 47	14 02	14 17	14 32	14 47	15 02	15 17	15 32	15 47	16 02
	d	12 03	12 18	12 33	12 48	13 03	13 18	13 33	13 51	13 51	14 03	14 18	14 33	14 48	15 03	15 18	15 33	15 51	16 03
Stratford International ⊖	a	12 14	12 29	12 44	12 59	13 14	13 29	13 44	14 01	14 02	14 14	14 29	14 44	14 59	15 14	15 29	15 44	16 02	16 14
St Pancras International ⊖	a	12 21	12 36	12 51	13 06	13 21	13 36	13 51	14 10	14 09	14 21	14 36	14 51	15 06	15 21	15 36	15 51	16 09	16 21

		SE	SE	SE	SE	SE	SE	SE	SE	SE	SE	SE	SE	SE	SE	SE	SE
Margate	d				15 53				16 53				17 53				18 53
Broadstairs	d				15 59				16 59				17 59				18 59
Ramsgate	d				16 05				17 05				18 05				19 05
Canterbury West	a				16 24				17 24				18 24				19 24
	d				16 25				17 25				18 25				19 25
Sandwich	d																
Deal	d																
Dover Priory	d		15 44				16 44				17 44				18 44		
Folkestone Central	d		15 56				16 56				17 56				18 56		
Folkestone West	d		15 58				16 58				17 58				18 58		
Ashford International	a		16 11		16 41		17 11		17 41		18 11		18 41		19 11		19 41
	d		16 13		16 43		17 13		17 43		18 13		18 43		19 13		19 43
Broadstairs	d																
Margate	d																
Birchington-on-Sea	d																
Herne Bay	d																
Whitstable	d																
Faversham	a																
	d	15 28		15 58		16 28		16 58		17 28		17 58		18 28			
Sittingbourne	d	15 37		16 07		16 37		17 07		17 37		18 07		18 37			
Rainham (Kent)	d	15 45		16 15		16 45		17 15		17 45		18 15		18 45			
Gillingham (Kent)	d	15 50		16 20		16 50		17 20		17 50		18 20		18 50			
Chatham	d	15 54		16 24		16 54		17 24		17 54		18 24		18 54			
Rochester	d	15 57		16 27		16 57		17 27		17 57		18 27		18 57			
Maidstone West	d															19 13	
Strood	d	16 02		16 32		17 02		17 32		18 02		18 32		19 02		19 32	
Gravesend	d	16 13		16 43		17 13		17 43		18 13		18 43		19 13		19 43	
Ebbsfleet International	a	16 17	16 32	16 47	17 02	17 17	17 32	17 47	18 02	18 17	18 32	18 47	19 02	19 17	19 32	19 47	20 02
	d	16 18	16 33	16 51	17 03	17 18	17 33	17 48	18 03	18 18	18 33	18 51	19 03	19 18	19 35	19 50	20 03
Stratford International ⊖	a	16 29	16 44	17 02	17 14	17 28	17 44	17 59	18 14	18 29	18 44	19 02	19 14	19 29	19 46	20 01	20 14
St Pancras International ⊖	a	16 36	16 51	17 09	17 21	17 36	17 51	18 06	18 21	18 36	18 51	19 09	19 21	19 36	19 53	20 08	20 21

A until 18 May

B from 21 May

Table 194

Mondays to Fridays

until 26 July, 13 Aug to 28 Aug and from 10 Sep

Kent - St Pancras International High Speed Domestic Services

		SE	SE	SE	SE	SE	SE	SE	SE	SE	SE	SE	SE	SE 1	SE
Margate	d				19 53				20 53				21 53		
Broadstairs	d				19 59				20 59				21 59		
Ramsgate	d				20 05				21 05				22 05	22 24	
Canterbury West	a				20 24				21 24				22 24	22 46	
	d				20 25				21 25				22 25	22 47	
Sandwich	d														
Deal	d														
Dover Priory	d		19 44				20 44				21 44				22 44
Folkestone Central	d		19 56				20 56				21 56				22 56
Folkestone West	d		19 58				20 58				21 58				22 58
Ashford International	a		20 12		20 43		21 11		21 41		22 11		22 41	23 08	23 11
	d		20 13		20 45		21 13		21 43		22 13		22 43		23 13
Broadstairs	d														
Margate	d														
Birchington-on-Sea	d														
Herne Bay	d														
Whitstable	d														
Faversham	a														
	d	19 28		19 58		20 28		20 58		21 28		21 58			
Sittingbourne	d	19 37		20 07		20 37		21 07		21 37		22 07			
Rainham (Kent)	d	19 45		20 15		20 45		21 15		21 45		22 15			
Gillingham (Kent)	d	19 50		20 20		20 50		21 20		21 50		22 20			
Chatham	d	19 54		20 24		20 54		21 24		21 54		22 24			
Rochester	d	19 57		20 27		20 57		21 27		21 57		22 27			
Maidstone West	d														
Strood	d	20 02		20 32		21 02		21 32		22 02		22 32			
Gravesend	d	20 13		20 43		21 13		21 43		22 13		22 43			
Ebbsfleet International	a	20 17	20 33	20 47	21 04	21 17	21 32	21 47	22 02	22 17	22 32	22 47	23 02		23 32
	d	20 18	20 33	20 51	21 05	21 18	21 33	21 48	22 03	22 18	22 33	22 48	23 03		23 33
Stratford International ⊖	a	20 29	20 45	21 02	21 16	21 29	21 44	21 59	22 14	22 29	22 44	22 59	23 14		23 44
St Pancras International ⊖	a	20 36	20 53	21 09	21 23	21 36	21 51	22 06	22 21	22 36	22 51	23 06	23 21		23 52

Mondays to Fridays

27 July to 10 August

		SE A	SE A	SE A	SE MO	SE MX B	SE A	SE A	SE A	SE A	SE A	SE A	SE A	SE A	SE A	SE A	SE A	SE A	SE A	SE A	SE A	SE A	SE A
Margate	d																						
Broadstairs	d																						
Ramsgate	d																						
Canterbury West	a																						
	d																						
Sandwich	d																						
Deal	d																						
Dover Priory	d																						
Folkestone Central	d																						
Folkestone West	d																						
Ashford International	a																						
	d																						
Broadstairs	d																						
Margate	d																						
Birchington-on-Sea	d																						
Herne Bay	d																						
Whitstable	d																						
Faversham	a																						
	d																						
Sittingbourne	d																						
Rainham (Kent)	d																						
Gillingham (Kent)	d																						
Chatham	d																						
Rochester	d																						
Maidstone West	d																						
Strood	d																						
Gravesend	d																						
Ebbsfleet International	a																						
	d	23p40	23p46	23p51	23p55	23p55	00 01	00 06	00 11	00 16	00 21	00 25	00 31	00 36	00 41	00 46	00 51	00 56	01 02	01 08	01 15	01 24	01 32
Stratford International ⊖	a	23p51	23p56	00 01	00 06	00 05	00 11	00 16	00 21	00 26	00 31	00 35	00 41	00 46	00 51	00 56	01 01	01 06	01 12	01 18	01 25	01 34	01 42
St Pancras International ⊖	a	00 01	00 06	00 11	00 15	00 16	00 21	00 26	00 31	00 36	00 41	00 46	00 51	00 56	01 01	01 07	01 11	01 16	01 22	01 28	01 35	01 45	01 52

A not 27 July

B from 31 July until 10 August

Table 194

Kent - St Pancras International High Speed Domestic Services

Mondays to Fridays

27 July to 10 August

		SE	SE	SE A	SE B	SE	SE	SE	SE B	SE A	SE	SE	SE	SE	SE	SE	SE	SE	SE	SE	SE	SE	SE
Margate	d								05 44														
Broadstairs	d								05 49														
Ramsgate	d		05 00	04 55					05 55	05 55													
Canterbury West	a		05 23						06 14	06 14													
	d		05 25						06 15	06 15													
Sandwich	d																						
Deal	d																						
Dover Priory	d																						
Folkestone Central	d																						
Folkestone West	d																						
Ashford International	a		05 41						06 32	06 32													
	d	05 13	05 43			06 13			06 33	06 33		06 43			07 13					07 43			08 13
Broadstairs	d			05 00	05 00								05 58				06 30						
Margate	d			05 05	05 05								06 03				06 35						
Birchington-on-Sea	d												06 08				06 40						
Herne Bay	d			05 17	05 17								06 17				06 49						
Whitstable	d												06 23				06 55						
Faversham	a			05 28	05 28								06 31				07 03						
	d			05 29	05 29			05 58					06 32				07 04						
Sittingbourne	d			05 37	05 37			06 07					06 40				07 13						
Rainham (Kent)	d			05 45	05 45			06 15					06 48				07 21						
Gillingham (Kent)	d			05 50	05 50			06 20					06 54				07 26						
Chatham	d			05 55	05 55			06 24					06 58				07 30						
Rochester	d			05 57	05 57			06 27					07 01				07 33						
Maidstone West	d																						
Strood	d			06 02	06 02			06 32															
Gravesend	d			06 13	06 13			06 43					07 14										
Ebbsfleet International	a	05 32	06 02	06 16	06 16	06 32		06 47	06 52	06 52		07 02	07 17		07 32		07 47			08 02			08 32
	d	05 33	06 04	06 23	06 23	06 34	06 41	06 48	06 54	06 54	07 02	07 09	07 18	07 25	07 34	07 40	07 48	07 55	08 01	08 09	08 16	08 23	08 34
Stratford International	a	05 44	06 14	06 33	06 33	06 45	06 51	06 59	07 04	07 04	07 12	07 19	07 29	07 35	07 45	07 51	07 59	08 05	08 12	08 19	08 26	08 33	08 45
St Pancras International	a	05 50	06 23	06 43	06 43	06 55	07 02	07 07	07 15	07 15	07 22	07 29	07 37	07 43	07 55	08 01	08 09	08 15	08 22	08 29	08 36	08 43	08 55

		SE	SE	SE	SE	SE	SE	SE	SE	SE	SE	SE	SE	SE	SE	SE	SE	SE	SE	SE	SE	SE	SE
Margate	d																						
Broadstairs	d																						
Ramsgate	d																						
Canterbury West	a																						
	d																						
Sandwich	d																						
Deal	d																						
Dover Priory	d																						
Folkestone Central	d																						
Folkestone West	d																						
Ashford International	a																						
	d					08 47			09 13					09 47			10 13					10 47	
Broadstairs	d																						
Margate	d																						
Birchington-on-Sea	d																						
Herne Bay	d																						
Whitstable	d																						
Faversham	a																						
	d		07 58								08 58								09 58				
Sittingbourne	d		08 06								09 07								10 07				
Rainham (Kent)	d		08 14								09 15								10 15				
Gillingham (Kent)	d		08 19								09 20								10 20				
Chatham	d		08 24								09 24								10 24				
Rochester	d		08 26								09 27								10 27				
Maidstone West	d																						
Strood	d		08 32								09 32								10 32				
Gravesend	d		08 43								09 43								10 43				
Ebbsfleet International	a		08 46			09 06			09 32		09 46			10 06			10 32		10 46			11 06	
	d	08 40	08 48	08 55	09 01	09 09	09 16	09 23	09 34	09 40	09 48	09 55	10 01	10 09	10 16	10 23	10 34	10 40	10 48	10 55	11 01	11 09	11 16
Stratford International	a	08 51	08 58	09 05	09 12	09 19	09 26	09 33	09 45	09 51	09 58	10 05	10 12	10 19	10 26	10 33	10 45	10 51	10 58	11 05	11 12	11 19	11 26
St Pancras International	a	09 01	09 08	09 15	09 22	09 29	09 36	09 43	09 55	10 01	10 08	10 15	10 22	10 29	10 36	10 43	10 55	11 01	11 08	11 15	11 22	11 29	11 36

A 27 July

B not 27 July

Table 194

Kent - St Pancras International High Speed Domestic Services

Mondays to Fridays

27 July to 10 August

		SE	SE	SE	SE	SE	SE	SE	SE	SE	SE	SE	SE	SE	SE	SE	SE	SE	SE	SE	SE	SE	SE
Margate	d																						
Broadstairs	d																						
Ramsgate	d																						
Canterbury West	a																						
	d																						
Sandwich	d																						
Deal	d																						
Dover Priory	d																						
Folkestone Central	d																						
Folkestone West	d																						
Ashford International	a																						
	d		11 13					11 47			12 13					12 47			13 13				
Broadstairs	d																						
Margate	d																						
Birchington-on-Sea	d																						
Herne Bay	d																						
Whitstable	d																						
Faversham	a																						
	d				10 58								11 58								12 58		
Sittingbourne	d				11 07								12 07								13 07		
Rainham (Kent)	d				11 15								12 15								13 15		
Gillingham (Kent)	d				11 20								12 20								13 20		
Chatham	d				11 24								12 24								13 24		
Rochester	d				11 27								12 27								13 27		
Maidstone West	d																						
Strood	d				11 32								12 32								13 32		
Gravesend	d				11 43								12 43								13 43		
Ebbsfleet International	a		11 32		11 46			12 06			12 32		12 46			13 06			13 32		13 46		
	d	11 23	11 34	11 40	11 48	11 55	12 01	12 09	12 16	12 23	12 34	12 40	12 48	12 55	13 01	13 09	13 16	13 23	13 34	13 40	13 48	13 55	14 01
Stratford International	a	11 33	11 45	11 51	11 58	12 05	12 12	12 19	12 26	12 33	12 45	12 51	12 58	13 05	13 12	13 19	13 26	13 33	13 45	13 51	13 58	14 05	14 12
St Pancras International	a	11 43	11 55	12 01	12 08	12 15	12 22	12 29	12 36	12 43	12 55	13 01	13 08	13 15	13 22	13 29	13 36	13 43	13 55	14 01	14 08	14 15	14 22

		SE	SE	SE	SE	SE	SE	SE	SE	SE	SE	SE	SE	SE	SE	SE	SE	SE	SE	SE	SE	SE	SE
Margate	d																						
Broadstairs	d																						
Ramsgate	d																						
Canterbury West	a																						
	d																						
Sandwich	d																						
Deal	d																						
Dover Priory	d																						
Folkestone Central	d																						
Folkestone West	d																						
Ashford International	a																						
	d	13 47			14 13					14 47			15 13					15 47			16 13		
Broadstairs	d																						
Margate	d																						
Birchington-on-Sea	d																						
Herne Bay	d																						
Whitstable	d																						
Faversham	a																						
	d						13 58								14 58								15 58
Sittingbourne	d						14 07								15 07								16 07
Rainham (Kent)	d						14 15								15 15								16 15
Gillingham (Kent)	d						14 20								15 20								16 20
Chatham	d						14 24								15 24								16 24
Rochester	d						14 27								15 27								16 27
Maidstone West	d																						
Strood	d						14 32								15 32								16 32
Gravesend	d						14 43								15 43								16 43
Ebbsfleet International	a	14 06			14 32		14 46			15 06			15 32		15 46			16 06			16 32		16 46
	d	14 09	14 16	14 23	14 34	14 40	14 48	14 55	15 01	15 09	15 16	15 23	15 34	15 40	15 48	15 55	16 01	16 09	16 16	16 23	16 34	16 40	16 48
Stratford International	a	14 19	14 26	14 33	14 45	14 51	14 58	15 05	15 12	15 19	15 26	15 33	15 45	15 51	15 58	16 05	16 12	16 19	16 26	16 33	16 45	16 51	16 58
St Pancras International	a	14 29	14 36	14 43	14 55	15 01	15 08	15 15	15 22	15 29	15 36	15 43	15 55	16 01	16 08	16 15	16 22	16 29	16 36	16 43	16 55	17 01	17 08

Table 194

Mondays to Fridays
27 July to 10 August

Kent - St Pancras International High Speed Domestic Services

Station		SE	SE	SE	SE	SE	SE	SE	SE	SE	SE	SE	SE	SE	SE	SE	SE	SE	SE	SE	SE	SE
Margate	d																					
Broadstairs	d																					
Ramsgate	d																					
Canterbury West	a																					
	d																					
Sandwich	d																					
Deal	d																					
Dover Priory	d																					
Folkestone Central	d																					
Folkestone West	d																					
Ashford International	a																					
	d			16 47			17 13					17 47			18 13					18 43		
Broadstairs	d																					
Margate	d																					
Birchington-on-Sea	d																					
Herne Bay	d																					
Whitstable	d																					
Faversham	a																					
	d								16 58								17 58					
Sittingbourne	d								17 07								18 07					
Rainham (Kent)	d								17 15								18 15					
Gillingham (Kent)	d								17 20								18 20					
Chatham	d								17 24								18 24					
Rochester	d								17 27								18 27					
Maidstone West	d																					
Strood	d								17 32								18 32					
Gravesend	d								17 43								18 43					
Ebbsfleet International	a			17 06			17 32		17 46			18 06			18 32		18 46			19 03		
	d	16 55	17 01	17 09	17 16	17 23	17 34	17 40	17 48	17 55	18 01	18 09	18 16	18 23	18 34	18 40	18 48	18 55	19 01	19 09	19 16	19 23
Stratford International ⊖	a	17 05	17 12	17 19	17 26	17 33	17 45	17 51	17 58	18 05	18 12	18 19	18 26	18 33	18 45	18 51	18 58	19 05	19 12	19 19	19 26	19 33
St Pancras International ⊖	a	17 15	17 22	17 29	17 36	17 43	17 55	18 01	18 08	18 15	18 22	18 29	18 36	18 43	18 55	19 01	19 08	19 15	19 22	19 29	19 36	19 43

Station		SE	SE	SE	SE	SE	SE	SE	SE	SE	SE	SE	SE	SE	SE	SE	SE	SE	SE	SE	SE	SE	SE
Margate	d																						
Broadstairs	d																						
Ramsgate	d																						
Canterbury West	a																						
	d																						
Sandwich	d																						
Deal	d																						
Dover Priory	d																						
Folkestone Central	d																						
Folkestone West	d																						
Ashford International	a																						
	d	19 13					19 47			20 13					20 47			21 13					21 47
Broadstairs	d																						
Margate	d																						
Birchington-on-Sea	d																						
Herne Bay	d																						
Whitstable	d																						
Faversham	a																						
	d			18 58								19 58								20 58			
Sittingbourne	d			19 07								20 07								21 07			
Rainham (Kent)	d			19 15								20 15								21 15			
Gillingham (Kent)	d			19 20								20 20								21 20			
Chatham	d			19 24								20 24								21 24			
Rochester	d			19 27								20 27								21 27			
Maidstone West	d																						
Strood	d			19 32								20 32								21 32			
Gravesend	d			19 43								20 43								21 43			
Ebbsfleet International	a	19 32		19 46			20 06			20 32		20 46			21 06			21 32		21 46			22 06
	d	19 34	19 40	19 48	19 55	20 01	20 09	20 16	20 23	20 34	20 40	20 48	20 55	21 01	21 09	21 16	21 23	21 34	21 40	21 48	21 55	22 01	22 09
Stratford International ⊖	a	19 45	19 51	19 58	20 05	20 12	20 19	20 26	20 33	20 45	20 51	20 58	21 05	21 12	21 19	21 26	21 33	21 45	21 51	21 58	22 05	22 12	22 19
St Pancras International ⊖	a	19 55	20 01	20 08	20 15	20 22	20 29	20 36	20 43	20 55	21 01	21 08	21 15	21 22	21 29	21 36	21 43	21 55	22 01	22 08	22 15	22 22	22 29

Table 194

Mondays to Fridays
27 July to 10 August

Kent - St Pancras International High Speed Domestic Services

Station		SE	SE	SE	SE	SE	SE	SE	SE	SE	SE [1]	SE A	SE B	SE	SE	SE	SE	SE	SE	SE	SE B	SE A	SE
Margate	d																						
Broadstairs	d																						
Ramsgate	d										22 24												
Canterbury West	a										22 46												
	d										22 47												
Sandwich	d																						
Deal	d																						
Dover Priory	d																						
Folkestone Central	d																						
Folkestone West	d																						
Ashford International	a										23 08												
	d			22 13						22 43							23 11						
Broadstairs	d																						
Margate	d																						
Birchington-on-Sea	d																						
Herne Bay	d																						
Whitstable	d																						
Faversham	a																						
	d					21 58																	
Sittingbourne	d					22 07																	
Rainham (Kent)	d					22 15																	
Gillingham (Kent)	d					22 20																	
Chatham	d					22 24																	
Rochester	d					22 27																	
Maidstone West	d																						
Strood	d					22 32																	
Gravesend	d					22 43																	
Ebbsfleet International	a			22 32		22 46				23 02							23 30						
	d	22 16	22 23	22 32	22 40	22 47	22 51	22 56	23 01	23 06		23 11	23 13	23 16	23 21	23 26	23 31	23 35	23 40	23 46	23 51	23 52	23 55
Stratford International ⊖	a	22 26	22 33	22 45	22 51	22 58	23 01	23 06	23 11	23 16		23 21	23 23	23 26	23 31	23 36	23 42	23 46	23 51	23 56	00 01	00 02	00 05
St Pancras International ⊖	a	22 36	22 43	22 55	23 01	23 07	23 11	23 15	23 21	23 26		23 31	23 31	23 36	23 41	23 46	23 51	23 56	00 01	00 06	00 11	00 11	00 16

Mondays to Fridays
29 August to 7 September

Station		SE C	SE	SE	SE	SE	SE	SE	SE	SE	SE	SE	SE	SE	SE	SE	SE	SE	SE	SE	SE	SE
Margate	d								05 47										06 48			
Broadstairs	d								05 54										06 54			
Ramsgate	d				05 00				06 00						06 26				07 00			
Canterbury West	a				05 23				06 19						06 45				07 19			
	d				05 25				06 20						06 50				07 20			
Sandwich	d									05 50				06 18						06 50		
Deal	d									05 56				06 24						06 56		
Dover Priory	d						05 44			06 12				06 42						07 12		
Folkestone Central	d						05 56			06 23				06 53						07 23		
Folkestone West	d						05 58			06 26				06 56						07 26		
Ashford International	a				05 41		06 11		06 36	06 39				07 09	07 06				07 36	07 39		
	d		05 13		05 43		06 13		06 43					07 13					07 43			
Broadstairs	d											06 00					06 30					07 00
Margate	d											06 05					06 35					07 05
Birchington-on-Sea	d											06 10					06 40					07 10
Herne Bay	d											06 19					06 49					07 19
Whitstable	d											06 25					06 55					07 25
Faversham	a											06 33					07 03					07 33
	d			04 56		05 28		05 58				06 34					07 04					07 34
Sittingbourne	d			05 07		05 37		06 07				06 42					07 13					07 42
Rainham (Kent)	d			05 15		05 45		06 15				06 50					07 21					07 50
Gillingham (Kent)	d			05 20		05 50		06 20				06 55					07 26					07 55
Chatham	d			05 24		05 54		06 24				07 00					07 30					08 00
Rochester	d			05 27		05 57		06 27				07 03					07 33					08 03
Maidstone West	d												06 56					07 26				
Strood	d			05 32		06 02		06 32					07 12					07 42				
Gravesend	d			05 43		06 13		06 43					07 22					07 52				
Ebbsfleet International	a		05 32	05 47	06 02	06 17	06 32	06 47				07 17					07 47					08 17
	d	23p45	05 33	05 48	06 03	06 18	06 33	06 48			07 06	07 18				07 34	07 48				08 04	08 18
Stratford International ⊖	a	23p56	05 44	05 59	06 14	06 29	06 44	06 59	07 11		07 17	07 29	07 36	07 41		07 45	07 59	08 06	08 11		08 15	08 29
St Pancras International ⊖	a	00 04	05 52	06 07	06 21	06 37	06 51	07 06	07 19		07 25	07 37	07 44	07 49		07 53	08 07	08 14	08 19		08 23	08 37

A 27 July

B not 27 July

C 3 September

Table 194

Mondays to Fridays

29 August to 7 September

Kent - St Pancras International High Speed Domestic Services

		SE	SE	SE	SE	SE	SE	SE	SE	SE	SE	SE	SE	SE	SE	SE	SE	SE	SE	SE
Margate	d						07 49						08 53						09 53	
Broadstairs	d						07 55						08 59						09 59	
Ramsgate	d		07 30				08 01						09 05						10 05	
Canterbury West	a		07 49				08 24						09 24						10 24	
	d		07 50				08 25						09 25						10 25	
Sandwich	d																			
Deal	d																			
Dover Priory	d			07 42						08 44						09 44				
Folkestone Central	d			07 53						08 56						09 56				
Folkestone West	d			07 56						08 58						09 58				
Ashford International	a		08 06	08 09			08 41			09 11			09 41			10 11			10 41	
	d		08 13				08 43			09 13			09 43			10 13			10 43	
Broadstairs	d																			
Margate	d																			
Birchington-on-Sea	d																			
Herne Bay	d																			
Whitstable	d																			
Faversham	a																			
	d					07 58			08 28			08 58			09 28			09 58		
Sittingbourne	d					08 06			08 37			09 07			09 37			10 07		
Rainham (Kent)	d					08 14			08 45			09 15			09 45			10 15		
Gillingham (Kent)	d					08 19			08 50			09 20			09 50			10 20		
Chatham	d					08 24			08 54			09 24			09 54			10 24		
Rochester	d					08 26			08 57			09 27			09 57			10 27		
Maidstone West	d	07 56																		
Strood	d	08 12				08 32			09 02			09 32			10 02			10 32		
Gravesend	d	08 22				08 43			09 13			09 43			10 13			10 43		
Ebbsfleet International	a					08 47	09 02		09 17	09 32		09 47	10 02		10 16	10 32		10 47	11 02	
	d				08 34	08 48	09 03	09 15	09 18	09 33	09 45	09 48	10 03	10 14	10 17	10 33	10 45	10 48	11 03	11 18
Stratford International ⊖	a	08 36	08 41		08 45	08 59	09 14	09 26	09 29	09 44	09 56	09 59	10 14	10 24	10 28	10 44	10 56	10 59	11 14	11 29
St Pancras International ⊖	a	08 44	08 49		08 53	09 06	09 22	09 34	09 41	09 52	10 04	10 07	10 22	10 31	10 39	10 54	11 04	11 07	11 22	11 37

		SE	SE	SE	SE	SE	SE	SE	SE	SE	SE	SE	SE	SE	SE	SE	SE	SE	SE	SE
Margate	d					10 53						11 53						12 53		
Broadstairs	d					10 59						11 59						12 59		
Ramsgate	d					11 05						12 05						13 05		
Canterbury West	a					11 24						12 24						13 24		
	d					11 25						12 25						13 25		
Sandwich	d																			
Deal	d																			
Dover Priory	d		10 44						11 44						12 44					
Folkestone Central	d		10 56						11 56						12 56					
Folkestone West	d		10 58						11 58						12 58					
Ashford International	a		11 11			11 41			12 11			12 41			13 11			13 41		
	d		11 13			11 43			12 13			12 43			13 13			13 43		
Broadstairs	d																			
Margate	d																			
Birchington-on-Sea	d																			
Herne Bay	d																			
Whitstable	d																			
Faversham	a																			
	d	10 28			10 58			11 28			11 58			12 28			12 58			13 28
Sittingbourne	d	10 37			11 07			11 37			12 07			12 37			13 07			13 37
Rainham (Kent)	d	10 45			11 15			11 45			12 15			12 45			13 15			13 45
Gillingham (Kent)	d	10 50			11 20			11 50			12 20			12 50			13 20			13 50
Chatham	d	10 54			11 24			11 54			12 24			12 54			13 24			13 54
Rochester	d	10 57			11 27			11 57			12 27			12 57			13 27			13 57
Maidstone West	d																			
Strood	d	11 02			11 32			12 02			12 32			13 02			13 32			14 02
Gravesend	d	11 13			11 43			12 13			12 43			13 13			13 43			14 13
Ebbsfleet International	a	11 17	11 32		11 47	12 02		12 17	12 32		12 47	13 02		13 17	13 32		13 47	14 02		14 17
	d	11 21	11 33	11 45	11 48	12 03	12 18	12 21	12 33	12 48	12 51	13 03	13 11	13 18	13 33	13 45	13 51	14 03	14 15	14 18
Stratford International ⊖	a	11 32	11 44	11 56	11 59	12 14	12 29	12 32	12 44	12 59	13 02	13 14	13 22	13 29	13 44	13 55	14 02	14 14	14 25	14 29
St Pancras International ⊖	a	11 40	11 52	12 04	12 07	12 24	12 37	12 40	12 51	13 07	13 10	13 22	13 33	13 36	13 52	14 06	14 10	14 22	14 32	14 37

Table 194

Mondays to Fridays

29 August to 7 September

Kent - St Pancras International High Speed Domestic Services

		SE	SE	SE	SE	SE	SE	SE	SE	SE	SE	SE	SE	SE	SE	SE	SE	SE	SE	SE
Margate	d				13 53						14 53							15 53		
Broadstairs	d				13 59						14 59							15 59		
Ramsgate	d				14 05						15 05							16 05		
Canterbury West	a				14 24						15 24							16 24		
	d				14 25						15 25							16 25		
Sandwich	d																			
Deal	d																			
Dover Priory	d	13 44						14 44						15 44						
Folkestone Central	d	13 56						14 56						15 56						
Folkestone West	d	13 58						14 58						15 58						
Ashford International	a	14 11			14 41			15 11			15 41			16 11				16 41		
	d	14 13			14 43			15 13			15 43			16 13				16 43		
Broadstairs	d																			
Margate	d																			
Birchington-on-Sea	d																			
Herne Bay	d																			
Whitstable	d																			
Faversham	a																			
	d			13 58			14 28			14 58			15 28			15 58			16 28	
Sittingbourne	d			14 07			14 37			15 07			15 37			16 07			16 37	
Rainham (Kent)	d			14 15			14 45			15 15			15 45			16 15			16 45	
Gillingham (Kent)	d			14 20			14 50			15 20			15 50			16 20			16 50	
Chatham	d			14 24			14 54			15 24			15 54			16 24			16 54	
Rochester	d			14 27			14 57			15 27			15 57			16 27			16 57	
Maidstone West	d																			
Strood	d			14 32			15 02			15 32			16 02			16 32			17 02	
Gravesend	d			14 43			15 13			15 43			16 13			16 43			17 13	
Ebbsfleet International	a	14 32		14 47	15 02		15 17	15 32		15 47	16 02		16 17	16 32		16 47		17 02	17 17	
	d	14 33	14 45	14 48	15 03	15 18	15 21	15 33	15 48	15 54	16 03	16 15	16 18	16 33	16 38	16 51	16 45	17 03	17 18	17 14
Stratford International ⊖	a	14 44	14 56	14 59	15 14	15 28	15 32	15 44	15 59	16 05	16 14	16 26	16 29	16 44	16 48	17 02	16 55	17 14	17 28	17 24
St Pancras International ⊖	a	14 52	15 04	15 07	15 22	15 37	15 40	15 52	16 08	16 15	16 22	16 33	16 36	16 52	16 56	17 09	17 13	17 22	17 38	17 43

		SE	SE	SE	SE	SE	SE	SE	SE	SE	SE	SE	SE	SE	SE	SE	SE
Margate	d				16 53					17 53				18 53			
Broadstairs	d				16 59					17 59				18 59			
Ramsgate	d				17 05					18 05				19 05			
Canterbury West	a				17 24					18 24				19 24			
	d				17 25					18 25				19 25			
Sandwich	d																
Deal	d																
Dover Priory	d	16 44						17 44				18 44				19 44	
Folkestone Central	d	16 56						17 56				18 56				19 56	
Folkestone West	d	16 58						17 58				18 58				19 58	
Ashford International	a	17 11			17 41			18 11		18 41		19 11		19 41		20 12	
	d	17 13			17 43			18 13		18 43		19 13		19 43		20 13	
Broadstairs	d																
Margate	d																
Birchington-on-Sea	d																
Herne Bay	d																
Whitstable	d																
Faversham	a																
	d		16 58			17 28			17 58		18 28				19 28		19 58
Sittingbourne	d		17 07			17 37			18 07		18 37				19 37		20 07
Rainham (Kent)	d		17 15			17 45			18 15		18 45				19 45		20 15
Gillingham (Kent)	d		17 20			17 50			18 20		18 50				19 50		20 20
Chatham	d		17 24			17 54			18 24		18 54				19 54		20 24
Rochester	d		17 27			17 57			18 27		18 57				19 57		20 27
Maidstone West	d												19 13				
Strood	d		17 32			18 02			18 32		19 02		19 32		20 02		20 32
Gravesend	d		17 43			18 13			18 43		19 13		19 43		20 13		20 43
Ebbsfleet International	a	17 32	17 47		18 02	18 17		18 32	18 47	19 02	19 17	19 32	19 47	20 02	20 17	20 33	20 47
	d	17 33	17 48	17 58	18 03	18 18	18 22	18 33	18 51	19 03	19 18	19 35	19 50	20 03	20 18	20 33	20 51
Stratford International ⊖	a	17 44	17 58	18 09	18 14	18 29	18 32	18 44	19 02	19 14	19 28	19 46	20 01	20 14	20 28	20 45	21 02
St Pancras International ⊖	a	17 52	18 08	18 19	18 22	18 37	18 42	18 52	19 10	19 22	19 39	19 53	20 14	20 22	20 38	20 53	21 10

Table 194

Mondays to Fridays

29 August to 7 September

Kent - St Pancras International High Speed Domestic Services

		SE	SE	SE	SE	SE	SE	SE	SE	SE	SE	SE [1]	SE	SE
Margate [4]	d	19 53				20 53					21 53			
Broadstairs	d	19 59				20 59					21 59			
Ramsgate [4]	d	20 05				21 05					22 05	22 24		
Canterbury West	a	20 24				21 24					22 24	22 46		
	d	20 25				21 25					22 25	22 47		
Sandwich	d													
Deal	d													22 44
Dover Priory	d			20 44					21 44					22 56
Folkestone Central	d			20 56					21 56					22 58
Folkestone West	d			20 58					21 58					23 11
Ashford International	a	20 41		21 11		21 41			22 11		22 41	23 08		23 13
	d	20 43		21 13		21 43			22 13		22 43			
Broadstairs	d													
Margate [4]	d													
Birchington-on-Sea	d													
Herne Bay	d													
Whitstable	d													
Faversham [2]	a													
	d		20 28		20 58			21 28		21 58				
Sittingbourne [4]	d		20 37		21 07			21 37		22 07				
Rainham (Kent)	d		20 45		21 15			21 45		22 15				
Gillingham (Kent) [4]	d		20 50		21 20			21 50		22 20				
Chatham [4]	d		20 54		21 24			21 54		22 24				
Rochester [4]	d		20 57		21 27			21 57		22 27				
Maidstone West	d													
Strood [4]	d		21 02		21 32			22 02		22 32				
Gravesend	d		21 13		21 43			22 13		22 43				
Ebbsfleet International	a	21 02	21 17	21 32	21 47	22 02		22 17	22 32	22 47	23 02			23 32
	d	21 03	21 18	21 33	21 48	22 03	22 14	22 18	22 33	22 48	23 03		23 15	23 33
Stratford International ⊖	a	21 14	21 29	21 44	21 59	22 14	22 24	22 28	22 44	22 59	23 14		23 26	23 44
St Pancras International [4] ⊖	a	21 22	21 36	21 52	22 07	22 22	22 32	22 35	22 52	23 07	23 22		23 34	23 52

Saturdays

until 21 July, 18 Aug and from 15 Sep

		SE	SE	SE	SE	SE	SE	SE	SE	SE	SE	SE	SE	SE	SE	SE	SE	SE	SE	SE
Margate [4]	d				05 53				06 53				07 53				08 53			
Broadstairs	d				05 59				06 59				07 59				08 59			
Ramsgate [4]	d	05 05			06 05				07 05				08 05				09 05			
Canterbury West	a	05 24			06 24				07 24				08 24				09 24			
	d	05 25			06 25				07 25				08 25				09 25			
Sandwich	d																			
Deal	d																			
Dover Priory	d			05 44			06 44				07 44				08 44				09 44	
Folkestone Central	d			05 56			06 56				07 56				08 56				09 56	
Folkestone West	d			05 58			06 58				07 58				08 58				09 58	
Ashford International	a	05 41		06 11	06 41		07 11		07 41		08 11		08 41		09 11		09 41		10 11	
	d	05 43		06 13	06 43		07 13		07 43		08 13		08 43		09 13		09 43		10 13	
Broadstairs	d																			
Margate [4]	d																			
Birchington-on-Sea	d																			
Herne Bay	d																			
Whitstable	d																			
Faversham [2]	a																			
	d		05 28			06 28		06 58		07 28		07 58		08 28		08 58		09 28		09 58
Sittingbourne [4]	d		05 37			06 37		07 07		07 37		08 07		08 37		09 07		09 37		10 07
Rainham (Kent)	d		05 45			06 45		07 15		07 45		08 15		08 45		09 15		09 45		10 15
Gillingham (Kent) [4]	d		05 50			06 50		07 20		07 50		08 20		08 50		09 20		09 50		10 20
Chatham [4]	d		05 54			06 54		07 24		07 54		08 24		08 54		09 24		09 54		10 24
Rochester [4]	d		05 57			06 57		07 27		07 57		08 27		08 57		09 27		09 57		10 27
Maidstone West	d																			
Strood [4]	d		06 02			07 02		07 32		08 02		08 32		09 02		09 32		10 02		10 32
Gravesend	d		06 13			07 13		07 43		08 13		08 43		09 13		09 43		10 13		10 43
Ebbsfleet International	a	06 02	06 17	06 32	07 02	07 17	07 32	07 47	08 02	08 17	08 32	08 47	09 02	09 17	09 32	09 47	10 02	10 17	10 32	10 47
	d	06 03	06 18	06 33	07 03	07 18	07 33	07 48	08 03	08 18	08 33	08 48	09 03	09 18	09 33	09 48	10 03	10 18	10 33	10 48
Stratford International ⊖	a	06 14	06 29	06 44	07 14	07 29	07 44	07 59	08 14	08 29	08 44	08 59	09 14	09 29	09 44	09 59	10 14	10 29	10 44	10 59
St Pancras International [4] ⊖	a	06 21	06 36	06 51	07 21	07 36	07 51	08 06	08 21	08 36	08 51	09 06	09 21	09 36	09 51	10 06	10 21	10 36	10 51	11 06

Table 194

Saturdays

until 21 July, 18 Aug and from 15 Sep

Kent - St Pancras International High Speed Domestic Services

		SE	SE	SE	SE	SE	SE	SE	SE	SE	SE	SE	SE	SE	SE	SE	SE	SE	SE
Margate [4]	d	09 53				10 53				11 53				12 53				13 53	
Broadstairs	d	09 59				10 59				11 59				12 59				13 59	
Ramsgate [4]	d	10 05				11 05				12 05				13 05				14 05	
Canterbury West	a	10 24				11 24				12 24				13 24				14 24	
	d	10 25				11 25				12 25				13 25				14 25	
Sandwich	d																		
Deal	d																		
Dover Priory	d			10 44				11 44				12 44				13 44			
Folkestone Central	d			10 56				11 56				12 56				13 56			
Folkestone West	d			10 58				11 58				12 58				13 58			
Ashford International	a	10 41		11 11		11 41		12 11		12 41		13 11		13 41		14 11		14 41	
	d	10 43		11 13		11 43		12 13		12 43		13 13		13 43		14 13		14 43	
Broadstairs	d																		
Margate [4]	d																		
Birchington-on-Sea	d																		
Herne Bay	d																		
Whitstable	d																		
Faversham [2]	a																		
	d		10 28		10 58		11 28		11 58		12 28		12 58		13 28		13 58		14 28
Sittingbourne [4]	d		10 37		11 07		11 37		12 07		12 37		13 07		13 37		14 07		14 37
Rainham (Kent)	d		10 45		11 15		11 45		12 15		12 45		13 15		13 45		14 15		14 45
Gillingham (Kent) [4]	d		10 50		11 20		11 50		12 20		12 50		13 20		13 50		14 20		14 50
Chatham [4]	d		10 54		11 24		11 54		12 24		12 54		13 24		13 54		14 24		14 54
Rochester [4]	d		10 57		11 27		11 57		12 27		12 57		13 27		13 57		14 27		14 57
Maidstone West	d																		
Strood [4]	d		11 02		11 32		12 02		12 32		13 02		13 32		14 02		14 32		15 02
Gravesend	d		11 13		11 43		12 13		12 43		13 13		13 43		14 13		14 43		15 13
Ebbsfleet International	a	11 02	11 17	11 32	11 47	12 02	12 17	12 32	12 47	13 02	13 17	13 32	13 47	14 02	14 17	14 32	14 47	15 02	15 17
	d	11 03	11 18	11 33	11 48	12 03	12 18	12 33	12 48	13 03	13 18	13 33	13 48	14 03	14 18	14 33	14 51	15 03	15 18
Stratford International ⊖	a	11 14	11 29	11 44	11 59	12 14	12 29	12 44	12 59	13 14	13 29	13 44	13 59	14 14	14 29	14 44	15 02	15 14	15 29
St Pancras International [4] ⊖	a	11 21	11 36	11 51	12 06	12 21	12 36	12 51	13 06	13 21	13 36	13 51	14 06	14 21	14 36	14 51	15 09	15 21	15 36

		SE	SE	SE	SE	SE	SE	SE	SE	SE	SE	SE	SE	SE	SE	SE	SE	SE
Margate [4]	d			14 53				15 53				16 53				17 53		
Broadstairs	d			14 59				15 59				16 59				17 59		
Ramsgate [4]	d			15 05				16 05				17 05				18 05		
Canterbury West	a			15 24				16 24				17 24				18 24		
	d			15 25				16 25				17 25				18 25		
Sandwich	d																	
Deal	d																	
Dover Priory	d	14 44				15 44				16 44				17 44				18 44
Folkestone Central	d	14 56				15 56				16 56				17 56				18 56
Folkestone West	d	14 58				15 58				16 58				17 58				18 58
Ashford International	a	15 11		15 41		16 11		16 41		17 11		17 41		18 11		18 41		19 11
	d	15 13		15 46		16 13		16 43		17 13		17 43		18 13		18 43		19 13
Broadstairs	d																	
Margate [4]	d																	
Birchington-on-Sea	d																	
Herne Bay	d																	
Whitstable	d																	
Faversham [2]	a																	
	d		14 58		15 28		15 58		16 28		16 58		17 28		17 58		18 28	
Sittingbourne [4]	d		15 07		15 37		16 07		16 37		17 07		17 37		18 07		18 37	
Rainham (Kent)	d		15 15		15 45		16 15		16 45		17 15		17 45		18 15		18 45	
Gillingham (Kent) [4]	d		15 20		15 50		16 20		16 50		17 20		17 50		18 20		18 50	
Chatham [4]	d		15 24		15 54		16 24		16 54		17 24		17 54		18 24		18 54	
Rochester [4]	d		15 27		15 57		16 27		16 57		17 27		17 57		18 27		18 57	
Maidstone West	d																	
Strood [4]	d		15 32		16 02		16 32		17 02		17 32		18 02		18 32		19 02	
Gravesend	d		15 43		16 13		16 43		17 13		17 43		18 13		18 43		19 12	
Ebbsfleet International	a	15 32	15 47	16 05	16 17	16 32	16 47	17 02	17 17	17 32	17 47	18 02	18 17	18 32	18 47	19 02	19 16	19 32
	d	15 33	15 51	16 06	16 18	16 33	16 51	17 03	17 18	17 33	17 48	18 03	18 18	18 33	18 51	19 03	19 17	19 35
Stratford International ⊖	a	15 44	16 02	16 17	16 29	16 44	17 02	17 14	17 29	17 44	17 59	18 14	18 29	18 44	19 02	19 14	19 27	19 46
St Pancras International [4] ⊖	a	15 51	16 09	16 24	16 36	16 51	17 09	17 21	17 36	17 51	18 09	18 21	18 36	18 51	19 09	19 21	19 38	19 53

Kent - St Pancras International High Speed Domestic Services

Saturdays
until 21 July, 18 Aug and from 15 Sep

		SE	SE	SE	SE	SE	SE	SE	SE	SE	SE	SE	SE	SE	SE	SE ■1	SE
Margate ■	d		18 53				19 53				20 53				21 53		
Broadstairs	d		18 59				19 59				20 59				21 59		
Ramsgate ■	d		19 05				20 05				21 05				22 05	22 24	
Canterbury West	a		19 24				20 24				21 24				22 24	22 46	
	d		19 25				20 25				21 25				22 25	22 47	
Sandwich	d																
Deal	d																
Dover Priory	d				19 44				20 44				21 44				22 44
Folkestone Central	d				19 56				20 56				21 56				22 56
Folkestone West	d				19 58				20 58				21 58				22 58
Ashford International	a		19 41		20 11		20 41		21 11		21 41		22 11		22 41	23 08	23 11
	d		19 43		20 13		20 43		21 13		21 43		22 13		22 43		23 13
Broadstairs	d																
Margate ■	d																
Birchington-on-Sea	d																
Herne Bay	d																
Whitstable	d																
Faversham ■	a																
	d	18 58		19 28		19 58		20 28		20 58		21 28		21 58			
Sittingbourne ■	d	19 07		19 37		20 07		20 37		21 07		21 37		22 07			
Rainham (Kent)	d	19 15		19 45		20 15		20 45		21 15		21 45		22 15			
Gillingham (Kent) ■	d	19 20		19 50		20 20		20 50		21 20		21 50		22 20			
Chatham ■	d	19 24		19 54		20 24		20 54		21 24		21 54		22 24			
Rochester ■	d	19 27		19 57		20 27		20 57		21 27		21 57		22 27			
Maidstone West	d																
Strood ■	d	19 32		20 02		20 32		21 02		21 32		22 02		22 32			
Gravesend	d	19 43		20 13		20 43		21 13		21 43		22 13		22 43			
Ebbsfleet International	a	19 47	20 02	20 17	20 32	20 47	21 02	21 17	21 32	21 47	22 02	22 17	22 32	22 47	23 02		23 32
	d	19 48	20 03	20 18	20 33	20 51	21 03	21 18	21 33	21 48	22 03	22 18	22 33	22 48	23 03		23 33
Stratford International ⊖	a	19 59	20 14	20 29	20 44	21 02	21 14	21 29	21 44	21 59	22 14	22 29	22 44	22 59	23 14		23 44
St Pancras International ■ ⊖	a	20 06	20 21	20 36	20 51	21 09	21 21	21 36	21 51	22 06	22 21	22 36	22 51	23 06	23 21		23 51

Saturdays
28 July to 11 August

		SE	SE	SE A	SE B	SE	SE	SE	SE	SE	SE	SE	SE	SE	SE	SE	SE	SE	SE	SE	SE	SE	SE
Margate ■	d																						
Broadstairs	d																						
Ramsgate ■	d																						
Canterbury West	a																						
	d																						
Sandwich	d																						
Deal	d																						
Dover Priory	d																						
Folkestone Central	d																						
Folkestone West	d																						
Ashford International	a																						
	d																						
Broadstairs	d																						
Margate ■	d																						
Birchington-on-Sea	d																						
Herne Bay	d																						
Whitstable	d																						
Faversham ■	a																						
	d																						
Sittingbourne ■	d																						
Rainham (Kent)	d																						
Gillingham (Kent) ■	d																						
Chatham ■	d																						
Rochester ■	d																						
Maidstone West	d																						
Strood ■	d																						
Gravesend	d																						
Ebbsfleet International	a																						
	d	23p40	23p46	23p51	23p52	23p55	00 01	00 06	00 11	00 16	00 21	00 25	00 31	00 36	00 41	00 46	00 51	00 56	01 02	01 08	01 15	01 24	01 32
Stratford International ⊖	a	23p51	23p56	00 01	00 02	00 05	00 11	00 16	00 21	00 26	00 31	00 35	00 41	00 46	00 51	00 56	01 01	01 06	01 12	01 18	01 25	01 34	01 42
St Pancras International ■ ⊖	a	00 01	00 06	00 11	00 11	00 16	00 21	00 26	00 31	00 36	00 41	00 46	00 51	00 56	01 01	01 07	01 11	01 16	01 22	01 28	01 35	01 45	01 52

A not 28 July

B not from 4 August until 11 August

Kent - St Pancras International High Speed Domestic Services

Saturdays
28 July to 11 August

		SE	SE	SE	SE	SE	SE	SE	SE	SE	SE	SE	SE	SE	SE	SE	SE	SE	SE	SE	SE	SE	SE
Margate ■	d								05 44														
Broadstairs	d								05 49														
Ramsgate ■	d		05 00						05 55														
Canterbury West	a		05 23						06 14														
	d		05 25						06 15														
Sandwich	d																						
Deal	d																						
Dover Priory	d																						
Folkestone Central	d																						
Folkestone West	d																						
Ashford International	a		05 41						06 31														
	d	05 13	05 43		06 13				06 33		06 47			07 13					07 47			08 13	
Broadstairs	d			05 00								05 54				06 24							
Margate ■	d			05 05								05 59				06 29							
Birchington-on-Sea	d											06 04				06 34							
Herne Bay	d			05 16								06 13				06 43							
Whitstable	d											06 19				06 49							
Faversham ■	a			05 28								06 27				06 57							
	d			05 28			05 58	05 58				06 28				06 58							
Sittingbourne ■	d			05 37			06 07	06 06				06 37				07 07							
Rainham (Kent)	d			05 45			06 15	06 14				06 45				07 15							
Gillingham (Kent) ■	d			05 50			06 20	06 19				06 50				07 20							
Chatham ■	d			05 54			06 24	06 24				06 54				07 24							
Rochester ■	d			05 57			06 27	06 26				06 57				07 27							
Maidstone West	d																						
Strood ■	d			06 02			06 32	06 32				07 02				07 32							
Gravesend	d			06 13			06 43	06 43				07 13				07 43							
Ebbsfleet International	a	05 32	06 02	06 16	06 32		06 47	06 47	06 52		07 06	07 16		07 32		07 46			08 06			08 32	
	d	05 33	06 04	06 23	06 34	06 41	06 48	06 48	06 54	07 01	07 09	07 18	07 23	07 34	07 40	07 48	07 55	08 01	08 09	08 16	08 23	08 34	08 40
Stratford International ⊖	a	05 44	06 14	06 33	06 45	06 51	06 58	06 59	07 04	07 12	07 19	07 28	07 33	07 45	07 51	07 58	08 05	08 12	08 19	08 26	08 33	08 45	08 51
St Pancras International ■ ⊖	a	05 50	06 23	06 43	06 55	07 02	07 07	07 07	07 15	07 22	07 29	07 36	07 43	07 55	08 01	08 08	08 15	08 22	08 29	08 36	08 43	08 55	09 01

		SE	SE	SE	SE	SE	SE	SE	SE	SE	SE	SE	SE	SE	SE	SE	SE	SE	SE	SE	SE	SE	SE
Margate ■	d																						
Broadstairs	d																						
Ramsgate ■	d																						
Canterbury West	a																						
	d																						
Sandwich	d																						
Deal	d																						
Dover Priory	d																						
Folkestone Central	d																						
Folkestone West	d																						
Ashford International	a																						
	d				08 47			09 13					09 47			10 13					10 47		
Broadstairs	d																						
Margate ■	d																						
Birchington-on-Sea	d																						
Herne Bay	d																						
Whitstable	d																						
Faversham ■	a																						
	d	07 58								08 58								09 58					
Sittingbourne ■	d	08 07								09 07								10 07					
Rainham (Kent)	d	08 15								09 15								10 15					
Gillingham (Kent) ■	d	08 20								09 20								10 20					
Chatham ■	d	08 24								09 24								10 24					
Rochester ■	d	08 27								09 27								10 27					
Maidstone West	d																						
Strood ■	d	08 32								09 32								10 32					
Gravesend	d	08 43								09 43								10 43					
Ebbsfleet International	a	08 46			09 06			09 32		09 46			10 06			10 32		10 46			11 06		
	d	08 48	08 55	09 01	09 09	09 16	09 23	09 34	09 40	09 48	09 55	10 01	10 09	10 16	10 23	10 34	10 40	10 48	10 55	11 01	11 09	11 16	11 23
Stratford International ⊖	a	08 58	09 05	09 12	09 19	09 26	09 33	09 45	09 51	09 58	10 05	10 12	10 19	10 26	10 33	10 45	10 51	10 58	11 05	11 12	11 19	11 26	11 33
St Pancras International ■ ⊖	a	09 08	09 15	09 22	09 29	09 36	09 43	09 55	10 01	10 08	10 15	10 22	10 29	10 36	10 43	10 55	11 01	11 08	11 15	11 22	11 29	11 36	11 43

Table 194

Saturdays
28 July to 11 August

Kent - St Pancras International High Speed Domestic Services

		SE	SE	SE	SE		SE	SE	SE	SE	SE	SE	SE	SE	SE	SE		SE	SE	SE	SE	SE	SE	SE	SE
Margate 4	d																								
Broadstairs	d																								
Ramsgate 4	d																								
Canterbury West	a																								
	d																								
Sandwich	d																								
Deal	d																								
Dover Priory	d																								
Folkestone Central	d																								
Folkestone West	d																								
Ashford International	a																								
	d	11 13						11 47			12 13					12 47				13 13					13 47
Broadstairs	d																								
Margate 4	d																								
Birchington-on-Sea	d																								
Herne Bay	d																								
Whitstable	d																								
Faversham 2	a																								
	d			10 58									11 58									12 58			
Sittingbourne 4	d			11 07									12 07									13 07			
Rainham (Kent)	d			11 15									12 15									13 15			
Gillingham (Kent) 4	d			11 20									12 20									13 20			
Chatham 4	d			11 24									12 24									13 24			
Rochester 4	d			11 27									12 27									13 27			
Maidstone West	d																								
Strood 4	d			11 32									12 32									13 32			
Gravesend	d			11 43									12 43									13 43			
Ebbsfleet International	a	11 32		11 46				12 06			12 32		12 46			13 06				13 32		13 46			14 06
	d	11 34	11 40	11 48	11 55		12 01	12 09	12 16	12 23	12 34	12 40	12 48	12 55	13 01	13 09		13 16	13 23	13 34	13 40	13 48	13 55	14 01	14 09
Stratford International ⊖	a	11 45	11 51	11 58	12 05		12 12	12 19	12 26	12 33	12 45	12 51	12 58	13 05	13 12	13 19		13 26	13 33	13 45	13 51	13 58	14 05	14 12	14 19
St Pancras International 4 ⊖	a	11 55	12 01	12 08	12 15		12 22	12 29	12 36	12 43	12 55	13 01	13 08	13 15	13 22	13 29		13 36	13 43	13 55	14 01	14 08	14 15	14 22	14 29

		SE	SE		SE	SE	SE	SE	SE	SE	SE	SE	SE	SE		SE	SE	SE	SE	SE	SE	SE	SE	SE	SE
Margate 4	d																								
Broadstairs	d																								
Ramsgate 4	d																								
Canterbury West	a																								
	d																								
Sandwich	d																								
Deal	d																								
Dover Priory	d																								
Folkestone Central	d																								
Folkestone West	d																								
Ashford International	a																								
	d				14 13					14 47			15 13						15 47			16 13			
Broadstairs	d																								
Margate 4	d																								
Birchington-on-Sea	d																								
Herne Bay	d																								
Whitstable	d																								
Faversham 2	a																								
	d						13 58									14 58									
Sittingbourne 4	d						14 07									15 07									
Rainham (Kent)	d						14 15									15 15									
Gillingham (Kent) 4	d						14 20									15 20									
Chatham 4	d						14 24									15 24									
Rochester 4	d						14 27									15 27									
Maidstone West	d																								
Strood 4	d						14 32									15 32									
Gravesend	d						14 43									15 43									
Ebbsfleet International	a				14 32		14 46			15 06			15 32			15 46			16 06			16 32			
	d	14 16	14 23		14 34	14 40	14 48	14 55	15 01	15 09	15 16	15 23	15 34	15 40		15 48	15 55	16 01	16 09	16 16	16 23	16 34	16 40	16 55	17 01
Stratford International ⊖	a	14 26	14 33		14 45	14 51	14 58	15 05	15 12	15 19	15 26	15 33	15 45	15 51		15 58	16 05	16 12	16 19	16 26	16 33	16 45	16 51	17 05	17 12
St Pancras International 4 ⊖	a	14 36	14 43		14 55	15 01	15 08	15 15	15 22	15 29	15 36	15 43	15 55	16 01		16 08	16 16	16 22	16 29	16 36	16 43	16 55	17 01	17 15	17 22

Table 194

Saturdays
28 July to 11 August

Kent - St Pancras International High Speed Domestic Services

			SE	SE	SE	SE	SE	SE	SE	SE	SE	SE		SE	SE	SE	SE	SE	SE	SE	SE	SE	SE		SE
Margate 4	d																								
Broadstairs	d																								
Ramsgate 4	d																								
Canterbury West	a																								
	d																								
Sandwich	d																								
Deal	d																								
Dover Priory	d																								
Folkestone Central	d																								
Folkestone West	d																								
Ashford International	a																								
	d		16 47			17 13					17 47				18 13					18 47			19 13		
Broadstairs	d																								
Margate 4	d																								
Birchington-on-Sea	d																								
Herne Bay	d																								
Whitstable	d																								
Faversham 2	a																								
	d							16 58									17 58								
Sittingbourne 4	d							17 07									18 07								
Rainham (Kent)	d							17 15									18 15								
Gillingham (Kent) 4	d							17 20									18 20								
Chatham 4	d							17 24									18 24								
Rochester 4	d							17 27									18 27								
Maidstone West	d																								
Strood 4	d							17 32									18 32								
Gravesend	d							17 43									18 43								
Ebbsfleet International	a		17 06			17 32		17 46			18 06				18 32		18 46			19 06			19 32		
	d		17 09	17 16	17 23	17 34	17 40	17 48	17 55	18 01	18 09	18 16		18 23	18 34	18 40	18 48	18 55	19 01	19 09	19 16	19 23	19 34		19 40
Stratford International ⊖	a		17 19	17 26	17 33	17 45	17 51	17 58	18 05	18 12	18 19	18 26		18 33	18 45	18 51	18 58	19 05	19 12	19 19	19 26	19 33	19 45		19 51
St Pancras International 4 ⊖	a		17 29	17 36	17 43	17 55	18 01	18 08	18 15	18 22	18 29	18 36		18 43	18 55	19 01	19 08	19 15	19 22	19 29	19 36	19 43	19 55		20 01

		SE	SE	SE	SE	SE	SE	SE	SE	SE		SE	SE	SE	SE 1	SE	SE	SE	SE	SE	SE		SE	SE	SE 1
Margate 4	d																								
Broadstairs	d																								
Ramsgate 4	d														20 16										21 16
Canterbury West	a														20 34										21 34
	d														20 36										21 36
Sandwich	d																								
Deal	d																								
Dover Priory	d																								
Folkestone Central	d																								
Folkestone West	d																								
Ashford International	a														20 58										21 58
	d				19 47			20 13						20 47				21 13						21 47	
Broadstairs	d																								
Margate 4	d																								
Birchington-on-Sea	d																								
Herne Bay	d																								
Whitstable	d																								
Faversham 2	a																								
	d	18 58								19 58										20 58					
Sittingbourne 4	d	19 07								20 07										21 07					
Rainham (Kent)	d	19 15								20 15										21 15					
Gillingham (Kent) 4	d	19 20								20 20										21 20					
Chatham 4	d	19 24								20 24										21 24					
Rochester 4	d	19 27								20 27										21 27					
Maidstone West	d																								
Strood 4	d	19 32								20 32										21 32					
Gravesend	d	19 43								20 43										21 43					
Ebbsfleet International	a	19 46			20 06			20 32		20 46				21 06				21 32		21 46				22 06	
	d	19 48	19 55	20 01	20 09	20 16	20 23	20 34	20 40	20 48		20 55	21 01	21 09		21 16	21 23	21 34	21 40	21 48	21 55		22 01	22 09	
Stratford International ⊖	a	19 58	20 05	20 12	20 19	20 26	20 33	20 45	20 51	20 58		21 05	21 12	21 19		21 26	21 33	21 45	21 51	21 58	22 05		22 12	22 19	
St Pancras International 4 ⊖	a	20 08	20 15	20 22	20 29	20 36	20 43	20 55	21 01	21 08		21 15	21 22	21 29		21 36	21 43	21 55	22 01	22 08	22 15		22 22	22 29	

Table 194

Kent - St Pancras International
High Speed Domestic Services

Saturdays
28 July to 11 August

		SE	SE	SE	SE	SE	SE	SE	SE	SE	SE 1	SE	SE	SE	SE	SE	SE	SE	SE	SE	SE
Margate	d																				
Broadstairs	d																				
Ramsgate	d										22 24										
Canterbury West	a										22 46										
	d										22 47										
Sandwich	d																				
Deal	d																				
Dover Priory	d																				
Folkestone Central	d																				
Folkestone West	d																				
Ashford International	a										23 08										
	d			22 13						22 43						23 11					
Broadstairs	d																				
Margate	d																				
Birchington-on-Sea	d																				
Herne Bay	d																				
Whitstable	d																				
Faversham	a																				
	d					21 58															
Sittingbourne	d					22 07															
Rainham (Kent)	d					22 15															
Gillingham (Kent)	d					22 20															
Chatham	d					22 24															
Rochester	d					22 27															
Maidstone West	d																				
Strood	d					22 32															
Gravesend	d					22 43															
Ebbsfleet International	a			22 32		22 46				23 02						23 30					
	d	22 16	22 23	22 34	22 40	22 47	22 51	22 56	23 01	23 06		23 11	23 16	23 21	23 26	23 31	23 36	23 40	23 46	23 51	23 55
Stratford International	a	22 26	22 33	22 45	22 51	22 58	23 01	23 06	23 11	23 16		23 21	23 26	23 31	23 36	23 42	23 46	23 51	23 56	00 01	00 06
St Pancras International	a	22 36	22 43	22 55	23 01	23 07	23 11	23 15	23 21	23 26		23 31	23 36	23 41	23 46	23 51	23 56	00 01	00 06	00 11	00 16

Saturdays
25 August to 8 September

		SE A	SE B	SE A	SE B	SE A	SE B	SE A	SE A	SE B	SE A	SE A	SE B	SE A	SE B	SE A	SE A	SE B	SE A	SE B	SE A	SE B
Margate	d									05 53	05 53									06 53	06 53	
Broadstairs	d									05 59	05 59									06 59	06 59	
Ramsgate	d		05 05	05 05						06 05	06 05									07 05	07 05	
Canterbury West	a		05 24	05 24						06 24	06 24									07 24	07 24	
	d		05 25	05 25						06 25	06 25									07 25	07 25	
Sandwich	d																					
Deal	d																					
Dover Priory	d						05 44	05 44							06 44	06 44						
Folkestone Central	d						05 56	05 56							06 56	06 56						
Folkestone West	d						05 58	05 58							06 58	06 58						
Ashford International	a		05 41	05 41			06 11	06 11		06 41	06 41				07 11	07 11				07 41	07 41	
	d	05 13	05 43	05 43			06 13	06 13		06 43	06 43				07 13	07 13				07 43	07 43	
Broadstairs	d																					
Margate	d																					
Birchington-on-Sea	d																					
Herne Bay	d																					
Whitstable	d																					
Faversham	a																					
	d				05 28	05 28			05 58				06 28	06 28				06 58	06 58			07 28
Sittingbourne	d				05 37	05 37			06 07				06 37	06 37				07 07	07 07			07 37
Rainham (Kent)	d				05 45	05 45			06 15				06 45	06 45				07 15	07 15			07 45
Gillingham (Kent)	d				05 50	05 50			06 20				06 50	06 50				07 20	07 20			07 50
Chatham	d				05 54	05 54			06 24				06 54	06 54				07 24	07 24			07 54
Rochester	d				05 57	05 57			06 27				06 57	06 57				07 27	07 27			07 57
Maidstone West	d																					
Strood	d				06 02	06 02			06 32				07 02	07 02				07 32	07 32			08 02
Gravesend	d				06 13	06 13			06 43				07 13	07 13				07 43	07 43			08 13
Ebbsfleet International	a	05 32	06 02	06 02	06 17	06 17	06 32	06 32	06 47	07 02	07 02		07 17	07 17	07 32	07 32		07 47	07 47	08 02	08 02	08 17
	d	05 33	06 03	06 03	06 18	06 18	06 33	06 33	06 48	07 03	07 03	07 15	07 18	07 18	07 33	07 33	07 45	07 48	07 48	08 03	08 03	08 18
Stratford International	a	05 44	06 14	06 14	06 29	06 29	06 44	06 44	06 59	07 14	07 14	07 26	07 29	07 29	07 44	07 44	07 56	07 59	07 59	08 14	08 14	08 29
St Pancras International	a	05 51	06 21	06 22	06 36	06 37	06 51	06 52	07 06	07 21	07 22	07 34	07 36	07 37	07 51	07 52	08 04	08 06	08 07	08 21	08 23	08 36

A not 25 August

B not from 1 September until 8 September

Table 194

Kent - St Pancras International
High Speed Domestic Services

Saturdays
25 August to 8 September

		SE A	SE A	SE	SE	SE A	SE B	SE A	SE A	SE	SE B	SE A	SE A	SE B	SE A	SE B	SE A	SE A	SE A	SE B	SE B
Margate	d						07 53	07 53								08 53	08 53				
Broadstairs	d						07 59	07 59								08 59	08 59				
Ramsgate	d						08 05	08 05								09 05	09 05				
Canterbury West	a						08 24	08 24								09 24	09 24				
	d						08 25	08 25								09 25	09 25				
Sandwich	d																				
Deal	d																				
Dover Priory	d			07 44							08 44	08 44									09 44
Folkestone Central	d			07 56							08 56	08 56									09 56
Folkestone West	d			07 58							08 58	08 58									09 58
Ashford International	a			08 11			08 41	08 41			09 11	09 11				09 41	09 41				10 11
	d			08 13			08 43	08 43			09 13	09 13				09 43	09 43				10 13
Broadstairs	d																				
Margate	d																				
Birchington-on-Sea	d																				
Herne Bay	d																				
Whitstable	d																				
Faversham	a																				
	d		07 28		07 58					08 28				08 58	08 58				09 28	09 28	
Sittingbourne	d		07 37		08 07					08 37				09 07	09 07				09 37	09 37	
Rainham (Kent)	d		07 45		08 15					08 45				09 15	09 15				09 45	09 45	
Gillingham (Kent)	d		07 50		08 20					08 50				09 20	09 20				09 50	09 50	
Chatham	d		07 54		08 24					08 54				09 24	09 24				09 54	09 54	
Rochester	d		07 57		08 27					08 57				09 27	09 27				09 57	09 57	
Maidstone West	d																				
Strood	d		08 02		08 32					09 02				09 32	09 32				10 02	10 02	
Gravesend	d		08 13		08 43					09 13				09 43	09 43				10 12	10 13	
Ebbsfleet International	a		08 17	08 32	08 47		09 02	09 02		09 17	09 32	09 32		09 47	09 47	10 02	10 02		10 16	10 17	10 32
	d	08 18	08 21	08 33	08 48	08 51	09 03	09 03	09 15	09 18	09 33	09 33	09 45	09 48	09 48	10 03	10 03	10 10	10 17	10 18	10 33
Stratford International	a	08 29	08 32	08 44	08 59	09 02	09 14	09 14	09 26	09 29	09 44	09 44	09 56	09 59	09 59	10 14	10 14	10 20	10 27	10 29	10 44
St Pancras International	a	08 37	08 40	08 51	09 06	09 09	09 21	09 22	09 34	09 36	09 51	09 52	10 04	10 06	10 07	10 21	10 22	10 29	10 35	10 36	10 51

		SE A	SE A	SE B	SE A	SE B	SE A	SE B	SE A	SE A	SE B	SE A	SE A	SE B	SE A	SE B	SE A	SE B	SE A	SE A	SE B
Margate	d					09 53	09 53									10 53	10 53				
Broadstairs	d					09 59	09 59									10 59	10 59				
Ramsgate	d					10 05	10 05									11 05	11 05				
Canterbury West	a					10 24	10 24									11 24	11 24				
	d					10 25	10 25									11 25	11 25				
Sandwich	d																				
Deal	d																				
Dover Priory	d	09 44									10 44	10 44									11 44
Folkestone Central	d	09 56									10 56	10 56									11 56
Folkestone West	d	09 58									10 58	10 58									11 58
Ashford International	a	10 11				10 41	10 41				11 11	11 11				11 41	11 41				12 11
	d	10 13				10 43	10 43				11 13	11 13				11 43	11 43				12 13
Broadstairs	d																				
Margate	d																				
Birchington-on-Sea	d																				
Herne Bay	d																				
Whitstable	d																				
Faversham	a																				
	d			09 58	09 58			10 28		10 28				10 58	10 58			11 28		11 28	
Sittingbourne	d			10 07	10 07			10 37		10 37				11 07	11 07			11 37		11 37	
Rainham (Kent)	d			10 15	10 15			10 45		10 45				11 15	11 15			11 45		11 45	
Gillingham (Kent)	d			10 20	10 20			10 50		10 50				11 20	11 20			11 50		11 50	
Chatham	d			10 24	10 24			10 54		10 54				11 24	11 24			11 54		11 54	
Rochester	d			10 27	10 27			10 57		10 57				11 27	11 27			11 57		11 57	
Maidstone West	d																				
Strood	d			10 32	10 32			11 02		11 02				11 32	11 32			12 02		12 02	
Gravesend	d			10 43	10 43			11 13		11 13				11 43	11 43			12 13		12 13	
Ebbsfleet International	a	10 32		10 47	10 47	11 02	11 02	11 17		11 17	11 32	11 32		11 47	11 47	12 02	12 02	12 17		12 17	12 32
	d	10 33	10 45	10 48	10 48	11 03	11 03	11 18	11 18	11 21	11 33	11 33	11 45	11 48	11 48	12 03	12 03	12 18	12 18	12 21	12 33
Stratford International	a	10 44	10 56	10 59	10 59	11 14	11 14	11 29	11 29	11 32	11 44	11 44	11 56	11 59	11 59	12 14	12 14	12 29	12 29	12 32	12 44
St Pancras International	a	10 52	11 04	11 06	11 07	11 21	11 22	11 36	11 37	11 40	11 51	11 52	12 04	12 06	12 07	12 21	12 22	12 36	12 37	12 40	12 51

A not 25 August

B not from 1 September until 8 September

Table 194

Saturdays

25 August to 8 September

Kent - St Pancras International High Speed Domestic Services

		SE A	SE B	SE A	SE A	SE B	SE A	SE B	SE A	SE A	SE B	SE A	SE A	SE B	SE A	SE B	SE A	SE A	SE B	SE A	SE B
Margate	d					11 53	11 53									12 53	12 53				
Broadstairs	d					11 59	11 59									12 59	12 59				
Ramsgate	d					12 05	12 05									13 05	13 05				
Canterbury West	a					12 24	12 24									13 24	13 24				
	d					12 25	12 25									13 25	13 25				
Sandwich	d																				
Deal	d																				
Dover Priory	d	11 44									12 44	12 44									13 44
Folkestone Central	d	11 56									12 56	12 56									13 56
Folkestone West	d	11 58									12 58	12 58									13 58
Ashford International	a	12 11				12 41	12 41				13 11	13 11				13 41	13 41				14 11
	d	12 13				12 43	12 43				13 13	13 13				13 43	13 43				14 13
Broadstairs	d																				
Margate	d																				
Birchington-on-Sea	d																				
Herne Bay	d																				
Whitstable	d																				
Faversham	a																				
	d		11 58	11 58				12 28		12 28				12 58	12 58				13 28	13 28	
Sittingbourne	d		12 07	12 07				12 37		12 37				13 07	13 07				13 37	13 37	
Rainham (Kent)	d		12 15	12 15				12 45		12 45				13 15	13 15				13 45	13 45	
Gillingham (Kent)	d		12 20	12 20				12 50		12 50				13 20	13 20				13 50	13 50	
Chatham	d		12 24	12 24				12 54		12 54				13 24	13 24				13 54	13 54	
Rochester	d		12 27	12 27				12 57		12 57				13 27	13 27				13 57	13 57	
Maidstone West	d																				
Strood	d		12 32	12 32				13 02		13 02				13 32	13 32				14 02	14 02	
Gravesend	d		12 43	12 43				13 13		13 13				13 43	13 43				14 13	14 13	
Ebbsfleet International	a	12 32	12 47	12 47		13 02	13 02	13 17		13 17	13 32	13 32		13 47	13 47	14 02	14 02		14 17	14 17	14 32
	d	12 33	12 48	12 48	12 51	13 03	13 03	13 18	13 18	13 21	13 33	13 33	13 45	13 48	13 48	14 03	14 03	14 15	14 18	14 18	14 33
Stratford International ⊖	a	12 45	12 59	12 59	13 02	13 14	13 14	13 29	13 29	13 32	13 44	13 44	13 56	13 59	13 59	14 14	14 14	14 26	14 29	14 29	14 44
St Pancras International ⊖	a	12 55	13 06	13 07	13 10	13 21	13 22	13 36	13 37	13 40	13 51	13 52	14 04	14 06	14 07	14 21	14 22	14 34	14 36	14 42	14 51

		SE A	SE A	SE B	SE A	SE B	SE A	SE B	SE A	SE A	SE B	SE A	SE A	SE	SE A	SE B	SE A	SE B	SE A	SE B	SE A
Margate	d					13 53	13 53								14 53	14 53					
Broadstairs	d					13 59	13 59								14 59	14 59					
Ramsgate	d					14 05	14 05								15 05	15 05					
Canterbury West	a					14 24	14 24								15 24	15 24					
	d					14 25	14 25								15 25	15 25					
Sandwich	d																				
Deal	d																				
Dover Priory	d	13 44									14 44	14 44								15 44	15 44
Folkestone Central	d	13 56									14 56	14 56								15 56	15 56
Folkestone West	d	13 58									14 58	14 58								15 58	15 58
Ashford International	a	14 11				14 41	14 41				15 11	15 11			15 41	15 41				16 11	16 11
	d	14 13				14 43	14 43				15 13	15 13			15 43	15 46				16 13	16 13
Broadstairs	d																				
Margate	d																				
Birchington-on-Sea	d																				
Herne Bay	d																				
Whitstable	d																				
Faversham	a																				
	d			13 58	13 58			14 28		14 28				14 58				15 28	15 28		
Sittingbourne	d			14 07	14 07			14 37		14 37				15 07				15 37	15 37		
Rainham (Kent)	d			14 15	14 15			14 45		14 45				15 15				15 45	15 45		
Gillingham (Kent)	d			14 20	14 20			14 50		14 50				15 20				15 50	15 50		
Chatham	d			14 24	14 24			14 54		14 54				15 24				15 54	15 54		
Rochester	d			14 27	14 27			14 57		14 57				15 27				15 57	15 57		
Maidstone West	d																				
Strood	d			14 32	14 32			15 02		15 02				15 32				16 02	16 02		
Gravesend	d			14 43	14 43			15 13		15 13				15 43				16 13	16 13		
Ebbsfleet International	a	14 32		14 47	14 47	15 02	15 02	15 17		15 17	15 32	15 32		15 47	16 02	16 05		16 17	16 17	16 32	16 32
	d	14 33	14 44	14 51	14 51	15 03	15 03	15 18	15 18	15 21	15 33	15 33	15 45	15 51	16 03	16 06	16 15	16 18	16 18	16 33	16 33
Stratford International ⊖	a	14 44	14 55	15 02	15 02	15 14	15 14	15 29	15 29	15 32	15 44	15 44	15 55	16 02	16 14	16 17	16 26	16 29	16 29	16 44	16 44
St Pancras International ⊖	a	14 52	15 03	15 09	15 10	15 21	15 22	15 36	15 37	15 40	15 51	15 52	16 06	16 09	16 22	16 24	16 34	16 36	16 37	16 51	16 52

A not 25 August

B not from 1 September until 8 September

Table 194

Saturdays

25 August to 8 September

Kent - St Pancras International High Speed Domestic Services

		SE A	SE B	SE B	SE A	SE A	SE B	SE A	SE B	SE A	SE A	SE B	SE A	SE B	SE A	SE A	SE B	SE A	SE B	SE A
Margate	d			15 53	15 53									16 53	16 53					
Broadstairs	d			15 59	15 59									16 59	16 59					
Ramsgate	d			16 05	16 05									17 05	17 05					
Canterbury West	a			16 24	16 24									17 24	17 24					
	d			16 25	16 25									17 25	17 25					
Sandwich	d																			
Deal	d																			
Dover Priory	d								16 44	16 44									17 44	17 44
Folkestone Central	d								16 56	16 56									17 56	17 56
Folkestone West	d								16 58	16 58									17 58	17 58
Ashford International	a			16 41	16 41				17 11	17 11				17 41	17 41				18 11	18 11
	d			16 43	16 43				17 13	17 13				17 43	17 43				18 13	18 13
Broadstairs	d																			
Margate	d																			
Birchington-on-Sea	d																			
Herne Bay	d																			
Whitstable	d																			
Faversham	a																			
	d		15 58			16 28	16 28					16 58	16 58				17 28	17 28		
Sittingbourne	d		16 07			16 37	16 37					17 07	17 07				17 37	17 37		
Rainham (Kent)	d		16 15			16 45	16 45					17 15	17 15				17 45	17 45		
Gillingham (Kent)	d		16 20			16 50	16 50					17 20	17 20				17 50	17 50		
Chatham	d		16 24			16 54	16 54					17 24	17 24				17 54	17 54		
Rochester	d		16 27			16 57	16 57					17 27	17 27				17 57	17 57		
Maidstone West	d																			
Strood	d		16 32			17 02	17 02					17 32	17 32				18 02	18 02		
Gravesend	d		16 43			17 12	17 13					17 43	17 43				18 13	18 13		
Ebbsfleet International	a		16 47	17 02	17 02	17 16	17 17		17 32	17 32		17 47	17 47	18 02	18 02		18 17	18 17	18 32	18 32
	d	16 44	16 51	17 03	17 03	17 17	17 18	17 13	17 33	17 33	17 45	17 48	17 48	18 03	18 03	18 12	18 18	18 18	18 33	18 33
Stratford International ⊖	a	16 55	17 02	17 14	17 14	17 27	17 29	17 24	17 44	17 44	17 55	17 59	17 58	18 14	18 14	18 22	18 29	18 29	18 44	18 44
St Pancras International ⊖	a	17 06	17 09	17 21	17 22	17 34	17 36	17 37	17 51	17 52	18 03	18 09	18 09	18 21	18 22	18 33	18 36	18 37	18 51	18 52

		SE A	SE B	SE A	SE B	SE A	SE	SE A	SE B	SE A	SE B	SE A	SE B	SE A	SE A	SE B	SE B	SE A	SE A	SE B	SE A
Margate	d				17 53	17 53							18 53	18 53							
Broadstairs	d				17 59	17 59							18 59	18 59							
Ramsgate	d				18 05	18 05							19 05	19 05							
Canterbury West	a				18 24	18 24							19 24	19 24							
	d				18 25	18 25							19 25	19 25							
Sandwich	d																				
Deal	d																				
Dover Priory	d							18 44	18 44								19 44	19 44			
Folkestone Central	d							18 56	18 56								19 56	19 56			
Folkestone West	d							18 58	18 58								19 58	19 58			
Ashford International	a				18 41	18 41		19 11	19 11				19 41	19 41			20 11	20 11			
	d				18 43	18 43		19 13	19 13				19 43	19 43			20 13	20 13			
Broadstairs	d																				
Margate	d																				
Birchington-on-Sea	d																				
Herne Bay	d																				
Whitstable	d																				
Faversham	a																				
	d		17 58	17 58			18 28				18 58	18 58			19 28	19 28			19 58	19 58	
Sittingbourne	d		18 07	18 07			18 37				19 07	19 07			19 37	19 37			20 07	20 07	
Rainham (Kent)	d		18 15	18 15			18 45				19 15	19 15			19 45	19 45			20 15	20 15	
Gillingham (Kent)	d		18 20	18 20			18 50				19 20	19 20			19 50	19 50			20 20	20 20	
Chatham	d		18 24	18 24			18 54				19 24	19 24			19 54	19 54			20 24	20 24	
Rochester	d		18 27	18 27			18 57				19 27	19 27			19 57	19 57			20 27	20 27	
Maidstone West	d																				
Strood	d		18 32	18 32			19 02				19 32	19 32			20 02	20 02			20 32	20 32	
Gravesend	d		18 43	18 43			19 12				19 43	19 43			20 12	20 13			20 43	20 43	
Ebbsfleet International	a		18 47	18 47	19 02	19 02	19 16	19 32	19 32		19 47	19 47	20 02	20 02	20 16	20 17	20 32	20 32	20 47	20 47	
	d	18 45	18 51	18 51	19 03	19 03	19 17	19 33	19 35	19 45	19 48	19 48	20 03	20 03	20 17	20 18	20 33	20 33	20 51	20 51	20 45
Stratford International ⊖	a	18 56	19 02	19 02	19 14	19 14	19 27	19 44	19 46	19 56	19 59	19 59	20 14	20 14	20 27	20 29	20 44	20 44		21 02	20 56
St Pancras International ⊖	a	19 06	19 09	19 10	19 21	19 22	19 38	19 52	19 53	20 03	20 06	20 07	20 21	20 22	20 35	20 36	20 51	20 52	21 06	21 09	21 09

A not 25 August

B not from 1 September until 8 September

Table 194

Kent - St Pancras International High Speed Domestic Services

Saturdays
25 August to 8 September

		SE A	SE B	SE A	SE B	SE A	SE B	SE B	SE A	SE B	SE A	SE B	SE A	SE B	SE A	SE B	SE B	SE A	SE B	SE A	SE B
Margate	d	19 53	19 53								20 53	20 53								21 53	21 53
Broadstairs	d	19 59	19 59								20 59	20 59								21 59	21 59
Ramsgate	d	20 05	20 05								21 05	21 05								22 05	22 05
Canterbury West	a	20 24	20 24								21 24	21 24								22 24	22 24
	d	20 25	20 25								21 25	21 25								22 25	22 25
Sandwich	d																				
Deal	d																				
Dover Priory	d					20 44	20 44								21 44	21 44					
Folkestone Central	d					20 56	20 56								21 56	21 56					
Folkestone West	d					20 58	20 58								21 58	21 58					
Ashford International	a	20 41	20 41			21 11	21 11				21 41	21 41			22 11	22 11				22 41	22 41
	d	20 43	20 47			21 13	21 13				21 43	21 43			22 13	22 13				22 43	22 43
Broadstairs	d																				
Margate	d																				
Birchington-on-Sea	d																				
Herne Bay	d																				
Whitstable	d																				
Faversham	a																				
	d			20 28	20 28				20 58	20 58			21 28	21 28				21 58	21 58		
Sittingbourne	d			20 37	20 37				21 07	21 07			21 37	21 37				22 07	22 07		
Rainham (Kent)	d			20 45	20 45				21 15	21 15			21 45	21 45				22 15	22 15		
Gillingham (Kent)	d			20 50	20 50				21 20	21 20			21 50	21 50				22 20	22 20		
Chatham	d			20 54	20 54				21 24	21 24			21 54	21 54				22 24	22 24		
Rochester	d			20 57	20 57				21 27	21 27			21 57	21 57				22 27	22 27		
Maidstone West	d																				
Strood	d			21 02	21 02				21 32	21 32			22 02	22 02				22 32	22 32		
Gravesend	d			21 13	21 13				21 43	21 43			22 13	22 13				22 43	22 43		
Ebbsfleet International	a	21 02	21 06	21 17	21 17	21 32	21 32		21 47	21 47	22 02	22 02	22 17	22 17	22 32	22 32		22 47	22 47	23 02	23 02
	d	21 03	21 07	21 18	21 21	21 33	21 33	21 45	21 48	21 48	22 03	22 03	22 18	22 18	22 33	22 33	22 45	22 48	22 48	23 03	23 03
Stratford International	a	21 14	21 18	21 29	21 31	21 44	21 44	21 56	21 59	21 59	22 14	22 14	22 29	22 29	22 44	22 44	22 56	22 59	22 59	23 14	23 14
St Pancras International	a	21 21	21 26	21 36	21 42	21 51	21 52	22 03	22 06	22 07	22 21	22 22	22 36	22 37	22 51	22 52	23 03	23 06	23 07	23 21	23 22

		SE 1	SE A	SE B	SE B
Margate	d				
Broadstairs	d				
Ramsgate	d	22 24			
Canterbury West	a	22 46			
	d	22 47			
Sandwich	d				
Deal	d				
Dover Priory	d		22 44	22 44	
Folkestone Central	d		22 56	22 56	
Folkestone West	d		22 58	22 58	
Ashford International	a	23 08	23 11	23 11	
	d		23 13	23 13	
Broadstairs	d				
Margate	d				
Birchington-on-Sea	d				
Herne Bay	d				
Whitstable	d				
Faversham	a				
	d				
Sittingbourne	d				
Rainham (Kent)	d				
Gillingham (Kent)	d				
Chatham	d				
Rochester	d				
Maidstone West	d				
Strood	d				
Gravesend	d				
Ebbsfleet International	a		23 32	23 32	
	d		23 33	23 33	23 45
Stratford International	a		23 44	23 44	23 56
St Pancras International	a		23 51	23 52	00 04

A not from 1 September until 8 September
B not 25 August

Table 194

Kent - St Pancras International High Speed Domestic Services

Sundays
until 22 July, 19 Aug and from 16 Sep

		SE	SE	SE	SE	SE	SE	SE	SE	SE	SE	SE	SE	SE	SE	SE	SE	SE	SE
Margate	d				07 53			08 53			09 53			10 53				11 53	
Broadstairs	d				07 59			08 59			09 59			10 59				11 59	
Ramsgate	d				08 05			09 05			10 05			11 05				12 05	
Canterbury West	a				08 24			09 24			10 24			11 24				12 24	
	d				08 25			09 25			10 25			11 25				12 25	
Sandwich	d																		
Deal	d																		
Dover Priory	d		07 44			08 44			09 44			10 44				11 44			
Folkestone Central	d		07 56			08 56			09 56			10 56				11 56			
Folkestone West	d		07 58			08 58			09 58			10 58				11 58			
Ashford International	a		08 11		08 41	09 11		09 41	10 11		10 41	11 11		11 41		12 11		12 41	
	d	07 43	08 13		08 43	09 13		09 43	10 13		10 43	11 13		11 43		12 13		12 43	
Broadstairs	d																		
Margate	d																		
Birchington-on-Sea	d																		
Herne Bay	d																		
Whitstable	d																		
Faversham	a																		
	d			07 58			08 58			09 58			10 58		11 28		11 58		12 28
Sittingbourne	d			08 07			09 07			10 07			11 07		11 37		12 07		12 37
Rainham (Kent)	d			08 15			09 15			10 15			11 15		11 45		12 15		12 45
Gillingham (Kent)	d			08 20			09 20			10 20			11 20		11 50		12 20		12 50
Chatham	d			08 24			09 24			10 24			11 24		11 54		12 24		12 54
Rochester	d			08 27			09 27			10 27			11 27		11 57		12 27		12 57
Maidstone West	d																		
Strood	d			08 32			09 32			10 32			11 32		12 02		12 32		13 02
Gravesend	d			08 43			09 43			10 43			11 43		12 13		12 43		13 13
Ebbsfleet International	a	08 02	08 32	08 47	09 02	09 32	09 47	10 02	10 32	10 47	11 02	11 32	11 47	12 02	12 17	12 32	12 47	13 02	13 17
	d	08 03	08 33	08 48	09 03	09 33	09 48	10 03	10 33	10 48	11 03	11 33	11 48	12 03	12 18	12 33	12 48	13 03	13 18
Stratford International	a	08 14	08 44	08 59	09 14	09 44	09 59	10 14	10 44	10 59	11 14	11 44	11 59	12 14	12 29	12 44	12 59	13 14	13 29
St Pancras International	a	08 21	08 51	09 06	09 21	09 51	10 06	10 21	10 51	11 06	11 21	11 51	12 06	12 21	12 36	12 51	13 06	13 21	13 36

		SE	SE	SE	SE	SE	SE	SE	SE	SE	SE	SE	SE	SE	SE	SE	SE	SE	SE
Margate	d			12 53				13 53				14 53			15 53				16 53
Broadstairs	d			12 59				13 59				14 59			15 59				16 59
Ramsgate	d			13 05				14 05				15 05			16 05				17 05
Canterbury West	a			13 24				14 24				15 24			16 24				17 24
	d			13 25				14 25				15 25			16 25				17 25
Sandwich	d																		
Deal	d																		
Dover Priory	d	12 44				13 44				14 44				15 44			16 44		
Folkestone Central	d	12 56				13 56				14 56				15 56			16 56		
Folkestone West	d	12 58				13 58				14 58				15 58			16 58		
Ashford International	a	13 11		13 41		14 11		14 41		15 11		15 41		16 11	16 41		17 11		17 41
	d	13 13		13 43		14 13		14 43		15 13		15 43		16 13	16 43		17 13		17 43
Broadstairs	d																		
Margate	d																		
Birchington-on-Sea	d																		
Herne Bay	d																		
Whitstable	d																		
Faversham	a																		
	d		12 58		13 28		13 58		14 28		14 58		15 28			16 28		16 58	
Sittingbourne	d		13 07		13 37		14 07		14 37		15 07		15 37			16 37		17 07	
Rainham (Kent)	d		13 15		13 45		14 15		14 45		15 15		15 45			16 45		17 15	
Gillingham (Kent)	d		13 20		13 50		14 20		14 50		15 20		15 50			16 50		17 20	
Chatham	d		13 24		13 54		14 24		14 54		15 24		15 54			16 54		17 24	
Rochester	d		13 27		13 57		14 27		14 57		15 27		15 57			16 57		17 27	
Maidstone West	d																		
Strood	d		13 32		14 02		14 32		15 02		15 32		16 02			17 02		17 32	
Gravesend	d		13 43		14 13		14 43		15 13		15 43		16 13			17 13		17 43	
Ebbsfleet International	a	13 32	13 47	14 02	14 17	14 32	14 47	15 02	15 17	15 32	15 47	16 02	16 17	16 32	17 02	17 17	17 32	17 47	18 02
	d	13 33	13 51	14 03	14 18	14 33	14 48	15 03	15 18	15 33	15 51	16 03	16 18	16 33	17 03	17 18	17 33	17 48	18 03
Stratford International	a	13 44	14 02	14 14	14 29	14 44	14 59	15 14	15 29	15 44	16 02	16 14	16 29	16 44	17 14	17 29	17 44	17 59	18 14
St Pancras International	a	13 51	14 09	14 21	14 36	14 51	15 06	15 21	15 36	15 51	16 09	16 21	16 36	16 51	17 21	17 36	17 51	18 09	18 21

Table 194

Sundays

until 22 July, 19 Aug and from 16 Sep

Kent - St Pancras International High Speed Domestic Services

		SE	SE	SE	SE	SE	SE	SE	SE	SE	SE	SE	SE	SE	SE	SE	SE	SE
Margate	d				17 53				18 53				19 53				20 53	
Broadstairs	d				17 59				18 59				19 59				20 59	
Ramsgate	d				18 05				19 05				20 05				21 05	
Canterbury West	a				18 24				19 24				20 24				21 24	
	d				18 25				19 25				20 25				21 25	
Sandwich	d																	
Deal	d																	
Dover Priory	d		17 44				18 44				19 44				20 44			
Folkestone Central	d		17 56				18 56				19 56				20 56			
Folkestone West	d		17 58				18 58				19 58				20 58			
Ashford International	a		18 11		18 41		19 11		19 41		20 11		20 41		21 11		21 41	
	d		18 13		18 43		19 13		19 43		20 13		20 43		21 13		21 43	
Broadstairs	d																	
Margate	d																	
Birchington-on-Sea	d																	
Herne Bay	d																	
Whitstable	d																	
Faversham	a																	
	d	17 28		17 58		18 28		18 58		19 28		19 58		20 28		20 58		21 28
Sittingbourne	d	17 37		18 07		18 37		19 07		19 37		20 07		20 37		21 07		21 37
Rainham (Kent)	d	17 45		18 15		18 45		19 15		19 45		20 15		20 45		21 15		21 45
Gillingham (Kent)	d	17 50		18 20		18 50		19 20		19 50		20 20		20 50		21 20		21 50
Chatham	d	17 54		18 24		18 54		19 24		19 54		20 24		20 54		21 24		21 54
Rochester	d	17 57		18 27		18 57		19 27		19 57		20 27		20 57		21 27		21 57
Maidstone West	d																	
Strood	d	18 02		18 32		19 02		19 32		20 02		20 32		21 02		21 32		22 02
Gravesend	d	18 13		18 43		19 13		19 43		20 13		20 43		21 13		21 43		22 13
Ebbsfleet International	a	18 17	18 32	18 47	19 02	19 17	19 32	19 47	20 02	20 17	20 32	20 47	21 02	21 17	21 32	21 47	22 02	22 17
	d	18 18	18 33	18 48	19 03	19 18	19 33	19 48	20 03	20 18	20 33	20 51	21 03	21 18	21 33	21 48	22 03	22 18
Stratford International ⊖	a	18 29	18 44	18 59	19 14	19 29	19 44	19 59	20 14	20 29	20 44	21 02	21 14	21 29	21 44	21 59	22 14	22 29
St Pancras International ⊖	a	18 36	18 51	19 06	19 21	19 36	19 51	20 06	20 21	20 36	20 51	21 09	21 21	21 36	21 51	22 06	22 21	22 36

		SE	SE 1	SE	SE
Margate	d				21 53
Broadstairs	d				21 59
Ramsgate	d		21 40		22 05
Canterbury West	a		22 02		22 24
	d		22 04		22 25
Sandwich	d				
Deal	d				
Dover Priory	d	21 44			
Folkestone Central	d	21 56			
Folkestone West	d	21 58			
Ashford International	a	22 11	22 25		22 41
	d	22 13			22 43
Broadstairs	d				
Margate	d				
Birchington-on-Sea	d				
Herne Bay	d				
Whitstable	d				
Faversham	a				
	d			21 58	
Sittingbourne	d			22 07	
Rainham (Kent)	d			22 15	
Gillingham (Kent)	d			22 20	
Chatham	d			22 24	
Rochester	d			22 27	
Maidstone West	d				
Strood	d			22 32	
Gravesend	d			22 43	
Ebbsfleet International	a	22 32		22 47	23 02
	d	22 33		22 48	23 03
Stratford International ⊖	a	22 44		22 59	23 14
St Pancras International ⊖	a	22 51		23 06	23 21

Table 194

Sundays

29 July to 12 August

Kent - St Pancras International High Speed Domestic Services

		SE	SE	SE	SE	SE	SE	SE	SE	SE	SE	SE	SE	SE	SE	SE	SE	SE	SE	SE	SE	SE	SE
Margate	d																						
Broadstairs	d																						
Ramsgate	d																						
Canterbury West	a																						
	d																						
Sandwich	d																						
Deal	d																						
Dover Priory	d																						
Folkestone Central	d																						
Folkestone West	d																						
Ashford International	a																						
	d																						05 13
Broadstairs	d																						
Margate	d																						
Birchington-on-Sea	d																						
Herne Bay	d																						
Whitstable	d																						
Faversham	a																						
	d																						
Sittingbourne	d																						
Rainham (Kent)	d																						
Gillingham (Kent)	d																						
Chatham	d																						
Rochester	d																						
Maidstone West	d																						
Strood	d																						
Gravesend	d																						
Ebbsfleet International	a																						05 32
	d	23p40	23p46	23p51	23p55	00 01	00 06	00 11	00 16	00 21	00 25	00 31	00 36	00 41	00 46	00 51	00 56	01 02	01 08	01 15	01 24	01 32	05 33
Stratford International ⊖	a	23p51	23p56	00 01	00 06	00 11	00 16	00 21	00 26	00 31	00 35	00 41	00 46	00 51	00 56	01 01	01 06	01 12	01 18	01 25	01 34	01 42	05 44
St Pancras International ⊖	a	00 01	00 06	00 11	00 16	00 21	00 26	00 31	00 36	00 41	00 45	00 51	00 56	01 01	01 07	01 11	01 17	01 22	01 28	01 35	01 45	01 52	05 50

		SE	SE	SE	SE	SE	SE	SE	SE	SE	SE	SE	SE	SE	SE	SE	SE	SE	SE	SE	SE	SE	SE
Margate	d																						
Broadstairs	d																						
Ramsgate	d	05 00					05 55																
Canterbury West	a	05 23					06 14																
	d	05 25					06 15																
Sandwich	d																						
Deal	d																						
Dover Priory	d																						
Folkestone Central	d																						
Folkestone West	d																						
Ashford International	a	05 41					06 31																
	d	05 43		06 13			06 33		06 47			07 13					07 47			08 13			
Broadstairs	d		05 00							05 54				06 24									
Margate	d		05 05							05 59				06 29									
Birchington-on-Sea	d									06 04				06 34									
Herne Bay	d		05 16							06 13				06 43									
Whitstable	d									06 19				06 49									
Faversham	a		05 28							06 27				06 57									
	d		05 28			05 58				06 28				06 58								07 58	
Sittingbourne	d		05 37			06 07				06 37				07 07								08 07	
Rainham (Kent)	d		05 45			06 15				06 45				07 15								08 15	
Gillingham (Kent)	d		05 50			06 20				06 50				07 20								08 20	
Chatham	d		05 54			06 24				06 54				07 24								08 24	
Rochester	d		05 57			06 27				06 57				07 27								08 27	
Maidstone West	d																						
Strood	d		06 02			06 32				07 02				07 32								08 32	
Gravesend	d		06 13			06 43				07 13				07 43								08 43	
Ebbsfleet International	a	06 02	06 16	06 32		06 47	06 52		07 06	07 16		07 32		07 46			08 06			08 32		08 46	
	d	06 04	06 23	06 34	06 41	06 48	06 54	07 01	07 09	07 18	07 23	07 34	07 40	07 48	07 55	08 01	08 09	08 16	08 23	08 34	08 40	08 48	08 55
Stratford International ⊖	a	06 14	06 33	06 45	06 51	06 58	07 04	07 12	07 19	07 28	07 33	07 45	07 51	07 58	08 05	08 12	08 19	08 26	08 33	08 45	08 51	08 58	09 05
St Pancras International ⊖	a	06 23	06 43	06 55	07 02	07 06	07 15	07 22	07 29	07 36	07 43	07 55	08 01	08 08	08 15	08 22	08 29	08 36	08 43	08 55	09 01	09 08	09 15

Table 194

Kent - St Pancras International High Speed Domestic Services

Sundays

29 July to 12 August

		SE	SE	SE	SE	SE	SE	SE	SE	SE	SE	SE	SE	SE	SE	SE	SE	SE	SE	SE	SE	SE	SE
Margate	d																						
Broadstairs	d																						
Ramsgate	d																						
Canterbury West	a																						
	d																						
Sandwich	d																						
Deal	d																						
Dover Priory	d																						
Folkestone Central	d																						
Folkestone West	d																						
Ashford International	a																						
	d		08 47			09 13					09 47			10 13					10 47			11 13	
Broadstairs	d																						
Margate	d																						
Birchington-on-Sea	d																						
Herne Bay	d																						
Whitstable	d																						
Faversham	a																						
	d							08 58								09 58							
Sittingbourne	d							09 07								10 07							
Rainham (Kent)	d							09 15								10 15							
Gillingham (Kent)	d							09 20								10 20							
Chatham	d							09 24								10 24							
Rochester	d							09 27								10 27							
Maidstone West	d																						
Strood	d							09 32								10 32							
Gravesend	d							09 43								10 43							
Ebbsfleet International	a		09 06			09 32		09 46			10 06			10 32		10 46			11 06			11 32	
	d	09 01	09 09	09 16	09 23	09 34	09 40	09 48	09 55	10 01	10 09	10 16	10 23	10 34	10 40	10 48	10 55	11 01	11 09	11 16	11 23	11 34	11 40
Stratford International ⊖	a	09 12	09 19	09 26	09 33	09 45	09 51	09 58	10 05	10 12	10 19	10 26	10 33	10 45	10 51	10 58	11 05	11 12	11 19	11 26	11 33	11 45	11 51
St Pancras International ⊖	a	09 22	09 29	09 36	09 43	09 55	10 01	10 08	10 15	10 22	10 29	10 36	10 43	10 55	11 01	11 08	11 15	11 22	11 29	11 36	11 43	11 55	12 01

		SE	SE	SE	SE	SE	SE	SE	SE	SE	SE	SE	SE	SE	SE	SE	SE	SE	SE	SE	SE	SE	SE
Margate	d																						
Broadstairs	d																						
Ramsgate	d																						
Canterbury West	a																						
	d																						
Sandwich	d																						
Deal	d																						
Dover Priory	d																						
Folkestone Central	d																						
Folkestone West	d																						
Ashford International	a																						
	d				11 47			12 13					12 47			13 13					13 47		
Broadstairs	d																						
Margate	d																						
Birchington-on-Sea	d																						
Herne Bay	d																						
Whitstable	d																						
Faversham	a																						
	d	10 58								11 58								12 58					
Sittingbourne	d	11 07								12 07								13 07					
Rainham (Kent)	d	11 15								12 15								13 15					
Gillingham (Kent)	d	11 20								12 20								13 20					
Chatham	d	11 24								12 24								13 24					
Rochester	d	11 27								12 27								13 27					
Maidstone West	d																						
Strood	d	11 32								12 32								13 32					
Gravesend	d	11 43								12 43								13 43					
Ebbsfleet International	a	11 46			12 06			12 32		12 46			13 06			13 32		13 46			14 06		
	d	11 48	11 55	12 01	12 09	12 16	12 23	12 34	12 40	12 48	12 55	13 01	13 09	13 16	13 23	13 34	13 40	13 48	13 55	14 01	14 09	14 16	14 23
Stratford International ⊖	a	11 58	12 05	12 12	12 19	12 26	12 33	12 45	12 51	12 58	13 05	13 12	13 19	13 26	13 33	13 45	13 51	13 58	14 05	14 12	14 19	14 26	14 33
St Pancras International ⊖	a	12 08	12 15	12 22	12 29	12 36	12 43	12 55	13 01	13 08	13 15	13 22	13 29	13 36	13 43	13 55	14 01	14 08	14 15	14 22	14 29	14 36	14 43

Table 194

Kent - St Pancras International High Speed Domestic Services

Sundays

29 July to 12 August

		SE	SE	SE	SE	SE	SE	SE	SE	SE	SE	SE	SE	SE	SE	SE	SE	SE	SE	SE	SE	SE	SE
Margate	d																						
Broadstairs	d																						
Ramsgate	d																						
Canterbury West	a																						
	d																						
Sandwich	d																						
Deal	d																						
Dover Priory	d																						
Folkestone Central	d																						
Folkestone West	d																						
Ashford International	a																						
	d	14 13					14 47			15 13					15 47			16 13				16 47	
Broadstairs	d																						
Margate	d																						
Birchington-on-Sea	d																						
Herne Bay	d																						
Whitstable	d																						
Faversham	a																						
	d			13 58								14 58											
Sittingbourne	d			14 07								15 07											
Rainham (Kent)	d			14 15								15 15											
Gillingham (Kent)	d			14 20								15 20											
Chatham	d			14 24								15 24											
Rochester	d			14 27								15 27											
Maidstone West	d																						
Strood	d			14 32								15 32											
Gravesend	d			14 43								15 43											
Ebbsfleet International	a	14 32		14 46			15 06			15 32		15 46			16 06			16 32				17 06	
	d	14 34	14 40	14 48	14 55	15 01	15 09	15 16	15 23	15 34	15 40	15 48	15 55	16 01	16 09	16 16	16 23	16 34	16 40	16 55	17 01	17 09	17 16
Stratford International ⊖	a	14 45	14 51	14 58	15 05	15 12	15 19	15 26	15 33	15 45	15 51	15 58	16 05	16 12	16 19	16 26	16 33	16 45	16 51	17 05	17 12	17 19	17 26
St Pancras International ⊖	a	14 55	15 01	15 08	15 15	15 22	15 29	15 36	15 43	15 55	16 01	16 08	16 16	16 22	16 29	16 36	16 43	16 55	17 01	17 15	17 22	17 29	17 36

		SE	SE	SE	SE	SE	SE	SE	SE	SE	SE	SE	SE	SE	SE	SE	SE	SE	SE	SE	SE	SE
Margate	d																					
Broadstairs	d																					
Ramsgate	d																					
Canterbury West	a																					
	d																					
Sandwich	d																					
Deal	d																					
Dover Priory	d																					
Folkestone Central	d																					
Folkestone West	d																					
Ashford International	a																					
	d		17 13					17 47			18 13					18 47			19 13			
Broadstairs	d																					
Margate	d																					
Birchington-on-Sea	d																					
Herne Bay	d																					
Whitstable	d																					
Faversham	a																					
	d				16 58								17 58								18 58	
Sittingbourne	d				17 07								18 07								19 07	
Rainham (Kent)	d				17 15								18 15								19 15	
Gillingham (Kent)	d				17 20								18 20								19 20	
Chatham	d				17 24								18 24								19 24	
Rochester	d				17 27								18 27								19 27	
Maidstone West	d																					
Strood	d				17 32								18 32								19 32	
Gravesend	d				17 43								18 43								19 43	
Ebbsfleet International	a		17 32		17 46			18 06			18 32		18 46			19 06			19 32		19 46	
	d	17 23	17 34	17 40	17 48	17 55	18 01	18 09	18 16	18 23	18 34	18 40	18 48	18 55	19 01	19 09	19 16	19 23	19 34	19 40	19 48	19 55
Stratford International ⊖	a	17 33	17 45	17 51	17 58	18 05	18 12	18 19	18 26	18 33	18 45	18 51	18 58	19 05	19 12	19 19	19 26	19 33	19 45	19 51	19 58	20 05
St Pancras International ⊖	a	17 43	17 55	18 01	18 08	18 15	18 22	18 29	18 36	18 43	18 55	19 01	19 08	19 15	19 22	19 29	19 36	19 43	19 55	20 01	20 08	20 15

29 July to 12 August

Kent - St Pancras International
High Speed Domestic Services

Station		SE	SE	SE	SE	SE	SE	SE	SE	SE	SE	SE	SE	SE	SE	SE	SE	SE	SE	SE	SE	SE	SE
Margate	d																						
Broadstairs	d																						
Ramsgate	d																						
Canterbury West	a																						
	d																						
Sandwich	d																						
Deal	d																						
Dover Priory	d																						
Folkestone Central	d																						
Folkestone West	d																						
Ashford International	a																						
	d		19 47			20 13					20 47			21 13					21 47			22 13	
Broadstairs	d																						
Margate	d																						
Birchington-on-Sea	d																						
Herne Bay	d																						
Whitstable	d																						
Faversham	a																						
	d							19 58								20 58							
Sittingbourne	d							20 07								21 07							
Rainham (Kent)	d							20 15								21 15							
Gillingham (Kent)	d							20 20								21 20							
Chatham	d							20 24								21 24							
Rochester	d							20 27								21 27							
Maidstone West	d																						
Strood	d							20 32								21 32							
Gravesend	d							20 43								21 43							
Ebbsfleet International	a		20 06			20 32		20 46			21 06			21 32		21 46			22 06			22 32	
	d	20 01	20 09	20 16	20 23	20 34	20 40	20 48	20 55	21 01	21 09	21 16	21 23	21 34	21 40	21 48	21 55	22 01	22 09	22 16	22 23	22 34	22 40
Stratford International	a	20 12	20 19	20 26	20 33	20 45	20 51	20 58	21 05	21 12	21 19	21 26	21 33	21 45	21 51	21 58	22 05	22 12	22 19	22 26	22 33	22 45	22 51
St Pancras International	a	20 22	20 29	20 36	20 43	20 55	21 01	21 08	21 15	21 22	21 29	21 36	21 43	21 55	22 01	22 08	22 15	22 22	22 29	22 36	22 43	22 55	23 01

Station		SE	SE	SE	SE	SE	SE 1	SE	SE	SE	SE	SE	SE	SE	SE	SE	SE
Margate	d																
Broadstairs	d																
Ramsgate	d						22 24										
Canterbury West	a						22 46										
	d						22 47										
Sandwich	d																
Deal	d																
Dover Priory	d																
Folkestone Central	d																
Folkestone West	d																
Ashford International	a						23 08										
	d					22 43						23 11					
Broadstairs	d																
Margate	d																
Birchington-on-Sea	d																
Herne Bay	d																
Whitstable	d																
Faversham	a																
	d	21 58															
Sittingbourne	d	22 07															
Rainham (Kent)	d	22 15															
Gillingham (Kent)	d	22 20															
Chatham	d	22 24															
Rochester	d	22 27															
Maidstone West	d																
Strood	d	22 32															
Gravesend	d	22 43															
Ebbsfleet International	a	22 46				23 02						23 30					
	d	22 47	22 51	22 56	23 01	23 06		23 11	23 16	23 21	23 26	23 31	23 36	23 40	23 46	23 51	23 55
Stratford International	a	22 58	23 01	23 06	23 11	23 16		23 21	23 26	23 31	23 36	23 42	23 46	23 51	23 56	00 01	00 06
St Pancras International	a	23 07	23 11	23 15	23 21	23 26		23 31	23 36	23 41	23 46	23 51	23 56	00 01	00 06	00 11	00 15

26 August to 9 September

Kent - St Pancras International
High Speed Domestic Services

Station		SE A	SE A	SE A	SE B	SE A	SE A	SE B	SE A	SE A	SE B	SE A	SE B	SE A	SE A	SE A	SE B	SE A	SE A	SE B	SE A	SE B	SE A
Margate	d												07 53	07 53								08 53	08 53
Broadstairs	d												07 59	07 59								08 59	08 59
Ramsgate	d												08 05	08 05								09 05	09 05
Canterbury West	a												08 24	08 24								09 24	09 24
	d												08 25	08 25								09 25	09 25
Sandwich	d																						
Deal	d																						
Dover Priory	d							07 44	07 44								08 44	08 44					
Folkestone Central	d							07 56	07 56								08 56	08 56					
Folkestone West	d							07 58	07 58								08 58	08 58					
Ashford International	a							08 11	08 11				08 41	08 41			09 11	09 11				09 41	09 41
	d				07 43			08 13	08 13				08 43	08 43			09 13	09 13				09 43	09 43
Broadstairs	d																						
Margate	d																						
Birchington-on-Sea	d																						
Herne Bay	d																						
Whitstable	d																						
Faversham	a																						
	d			06 58			07 28				07 58	07 58				08 28				08 58	08 58		
Sittingbourne	d			07 07			07 37				08 07	08 07				08 37				09 07	09 07		
Rainham (Kent)	d			07 15			07 45				08 15	08 15				08 45				09 15	09 15		
Gillingham (Kent)	d			07 20			07 50				08 20	08 20				08 50				09 20	09 20		
Chatham	d			07 24			07 54				08 24	08 24				08 54				09 24	09 24		
Rochester	d			07 27			07 57				08 27	08 27				08 57				09 27	09 27		
Maidstone West	d																						
Strood	d			07 32			08 02				08 32	08 32				09 02				09 32	09 32		
Gravesend	d			07 43			08 13				08 43	08 43				09 13				09 43	09 43		
Ebbsfleet International	a			07 47	08 02		08 17	08 32	08 32		08 47	08 47	09 02	09 02		09 17	09 32	09 32		09 47	09 47	10 02	10 02
	d	23p45	07 15	07 48	08 03	08 15	08 18	08 33	08 33	08 45	08 48	08 48	09 03	09 03	09 14	09 18	09 33	09 33	09 45	09 48	09 48	10 03	10 03
Stratford International	a	23p56	07 26	07 59	08 14	08 25	08 28	08 44	08 44	08 56	08 59	08 59	09 14	09 14	09 25	09 29	09 44	09 44	09 56	09 59	09 59	10 14	10 14
St Pancras International	a	00 04	07 34	08 07	08 21	08 32	08 35	08 51	08 52	09 04	09 06	09 07	09 21	09 22	09 33	09 42	09 51	09 52	10 04	10 06	10 07	10 21	10 22

Station		SE A	SE A	SE B	SE A	SE A	SE B	SE A	SE B	SE A	SE A	SE B	SE A	SE A	SE B	SE A	SE B	SE A	SE B	SE A
Margate	d								09 53	09 53							10 53	10 53		
Broadstairs	d								09 59	09 59							10 59	10 59		
Ramsgate	d								10 05	10 05							11 05	11 05		
Canterbury West	a								10 24	10 24							11 24	11 24		
	d								10 25	10 25							11 25	11 25		
Sandwich	d																			
Deal	d																			
Dover Priory	d			09 44	09 44							10 44	10 44							
Folkestone Central	d			09 56	09 56							10 56	10 56							
Folkestone West	d			09 58	09 58							10 58	10 58							
Ashford International	a			10 11	10 11				10 41	10 41		11 11	11 11				11 41	11 41		
	d			10 13	10 13				10 43	10 43		11 13	11 13				11 43	11 43		
Broadstairs	d																			
Margate	d																			
Birchington-on-Sea	d																			
Herne Bay	d																			
Whitstable	d																			
Faversham	a																			
	d		09 28				09 58	09 58							10 58	10 58			11 28	
Sittingbourne	d		09 37				10 07	10 07							11 07	11 07			11 37	
Rainham (Kent)	d		09 45				10 15	10 15							11 15	11 15			11 45	
Gillingham (Kent)	d		09 50				10 20	10 20							11 20	11 20			11 50	
Chatham	d		09 54				10 24	10 24							11 24	11 24			11 54	
Rochester	d		09 57				10 27	10 27							11 27	11 27			11 57	
Maidstone West	d																			
Strood	d		10 02				10 32	10 32							11 32	11 32			12 02	
Gravesend	d		10 13				10 43	10 43							11 43	11 43			12 13	
Ebbsfleet International	a		10 17	10 32	10 32		10 47	10 47	11 02	11 02		11 32	11 32		11 47	11 47	12 02	12 02	12 17	
	d	10 16	10 25	10 33	10 33	10 45	10 48	10 48	11 03	11 03	11 18	11 33	11 33	11 45	11 48	11 48	12 03	12 03	12 18	12 18
Stratford International	a	10 26	10 38	10 44	10 44	10 56	10 59	10 59	11 14	11 14	11 29	11 44	11 44	11 56	11 59	11 59	12 14	12 14	12 29	12 29
St Pancras International	a	10 34	10 44	10 51	10 52	11 04	11 06	11 07	11 21	11 22	11 37	11 51	11 52	12 04	12 06	12 07	12 21	12 22	12 36	12 37

A not 26 August

B not from 2 September until 9 September

Table 194

Sundays

26 August to 9 September

Kent - St Pancras International
High Speed Domestic Services

		SE A	SE B	SE A	SE A	SE B	SE A	SE B	SE A	SE B	SE A	SE A	SE B	SE A	SE A	SE	SE B	SE A	SE A	SE B	SE A
Margate	d							11 53	11 53								12 53	12 53			
Broadstairs	d							11 59	11 59								12 59	12 59			
Ramsgate	d							12 05	12 05								13 05	13 05			
Canterbury West	a							12 24	12 24								13 24	13 24			
	d							12 25	12 25								13 25	13 25			
Sandwich	d																				
Deal	d																				
Dover Priory	d		11 44	11 44									12 44	12 44							
Folkestone Central	d		11 56	11 56									12 56	12 56							
Folkestone West	d		11 58	11 58									12 58	12 58							
Ashford International	a		12 11	12 11				12 41	12 41				13 11	13 11			13 41	13 41			
	d		12 13	12 13				12 43	12 43				13 13	13 13			13 43	13 43			
Broadstairs	d																				
Margate	d																				
Birchington-on-Sea	d																				
Herne Bay	d																				
Whitstable	d																				
Faversham	a																				
	d	11 28				11 58	11 58			12 28		12 28				12 58				13 28	13 28
Sittingbourne	d	11 37				12 07	12 07			12 37		12 37				13 07				13 37	13 37
Rainham (Kent)	d	11 45				12 15	12 15			12 45		12 45				13 15				13 45	13 45
Gillingham (Kent)	d	11 50				12 20	12 20			12 50		12 50				13 20				13 50	13 50
Chatham	d	11 54				12 24	12 24			12 54		12 54				13 24				13 54	13 54
Rochester	d	11 57				12 27	12 27			12 57		12 57				13 27				13 57	13 57
Maidstone West	d																				
Strood	d	12 02				12 32	12 32			13 02		13 02				13 32				14 02	14 02
Gravesend	d	12 13				12 43	12 43			13 13		13 13				13 43				14 13	14 13
Ebbsfleet International	a	12 17	12 32	12 32		12 47	12 47	13 02	13 02	13 17		13 17	13 32	13 32		13 47	14 02	14 02		14 17	14 17
	d	12 21	12 33	12 33	12 45	12 48	12 48	13 03	13 03	13 18	13 10	13 21	13 33	13 33	13 45	13 51	14 03	14 03	14 15	14 18	14 18
Stratford International	a	12 32	12 44	12 45	12 56	12 59	12 59	13 14	13 14	13 29	13 21	13 32	13 44	13 44	13 56	14 02	14 14	14 14	14 26	14 29	14 29
St Pancras International	a	12 40	12 51	12 55	13 04	13 06	13 07	13 21	13 22	13 36	13 36	13 40	13 51	13 52	14 06	14 09	14 21	14 22	14 34	14 36	14 44

		SE B	SE A	SE B	SE A	SE A	SE B	SE A	SE B	SE A	SE A	SE B	SE A	SE A	SE B	SE A	SE B	SE A	SE A	SE B	SE A
Margate	d						13 53	13 53									14 53	14 53			
Broadstairs	d						13 59	13 59									14 59	14 59			
Ramsgate	d						14 05	14 05									15 05	15 05			
Canterbury West	a						14 24	14 24									15 24	15 24			
	d						14 25	14 25									15 25	15 25			
Sandwich	d																				
Deal	d																				
Dover Priory	d	13 44	13 44									14 44	14 44								
Folkestone Central	d	13 56	13 56									14 56	14 56								
Folkestone West	d	13 58	13 58									14 58	14 58								
Ashford International	a	14 11	14 11				14 41	14 41				15 11	15 11				15 41	15 41			
	d	14 13	14 13				14 43	14 43				15 13	15 13				15 43	15 43			
Broadstairs	d																				
Margate	d																				
Birchington-on-Sea	d																				
Herne Bay	d																				
Whitstable	d																				
Faversham	a																				
	d			13 58		13 58			14 28		14 28				14 58	14 58				15 28	15 28
Sittingbourne	d			14 07		14 07			14 37		14 37				15 07	15 07				15 37	15 37
Rainham (Kent)	d			14 15		14 15			14 45		14 45				15 15	15 15				15 45	15 45
Gillingham (Kent)	d			14 20		14 20			14 50		14 50				15 20	15 20				15 50	15 50
Chatham	d			14 24		14 24			14 54		14 54				15 24	15 24				15 54	15 54
Rochester	d			14 27		14 27			14 57		14 57				15 27	15 27				15 57	15 57
Maidstone West	d																				
Strood	d			14 32		14 32			15 02		15 02				15 32	15 32				16 02	16 02
Gravesend	d			14 43		14 43			15 13		15 13				15 43	15 43				16 13	16 13
Ebbsfleet International	a	14 32	14 32	14 47		14 47	15 02	15 02	15 17		15 17	15 32	15 32		15 47	15 47	16 02	16 02		16 17	16 17
	d	14 33	14 33	14 48	14 49	14 52	15 03	15 03	15 18	15 18	15 21	15 33	15 33	15 45	15 51	15 51	16 03	16 03	16 15	16 18	16 18
Stratford International	a	14 44	14 44	14 59	15 00	15 03	15 14	15 14	15 29	15 29	15 32	15 44	15 44	15 55	16 02	16 02	16 14	16 14	16 26	16 29	16 29
St Pancras International	a	14 51	14 52	15 06	15 08	15 11	15 21	15 22	15 36	15 37	15 40	15 51	15 52	16 06	16 09	16 12	16 21	16 22	16 34	16 36	16 44

A not 26 August

B not from 2 September until 9 September

Table 194

Sundays

26 August to 9 September

Kent - St Pancras International
High Speed Domestic Services

		SE A	SE B	SE B	SE A	SE B	SE B	SE A	SE A	SE B	SE A	SE B	SE B	SE A	SE B	SE B	SE B	SE A	SE A	SE B	SE B
Margate	d				15 53	15 53								16 53	16 53						
Broadstairs	d				15 59	15 59								16 59	16 59						
Ramsgate	d				16 05	16 05								17 05	17 05						
Canterbury West	a				16 24	16 24								17 24	17 24						
	d				16 25	16 25								17 25	17 25						
Sandwich	d																				
Deal	d																				
Dover Priory	d	15 44	15 44						16 44	16 44									17 44	17 44	
Folkestone Central	d	15 56	15 56						16 56	16 56									17 56	17 56	
Folkestone West	d	15 58	15 58						16 58	16 58									17 58	17 58	
Ashford International	a	16 11	16 11		16 41	16 41			17 11	17 11				17 41	17 41				18 11	18 11	
	d	16 13	16 13		16 43	16 43			17 13	17 13				17 43	17 43				18 13	18 13	
Broadstairs	d																				
Margate	d																				
Birchington-on-Sea	d																				
Herne Bay	d																				
Whitstable	d																				
Faversham	a																				
	d							16 28			16 58		16 58				17 28	17 28			
Sittingbourne	d							16 37			17 07		17 07				17 37	17 37			
Rainham (Kent)	d							16 45			17 15		17 15				17 45	17 45			
Gillingham (Kent)	d							16 50			17 20		17 20				17 50	17 50			
Chatham	d							16 54			17 24		17 24				17 54	17 54			
Rochester	d							16 57			17 27		17 27				17 57	17 57			
Maidstone West	d																				
Strood	d							17 02			17 32		17 32				18 02	18 02			
Gravesend	d							17 13			17 43		17 43				18 12	18 13			
Ebbsfleet International	a	16 32	16 32		17 02	17 02		17 17	17 32	17 32	17 47		17 47	18 02	18 02		18 16	18 17	18 32	18 32	
	d	16 33	16 33	16 48	17 03	17 03	17 14	17 18	17 33	17 33	17 48	17 48	17 55	18 03	18 03	18 14	18 17	18 18	18 33	18 33	18 42
Stratford International	a	16 44	16 44	16 59	17 14	17 14	17 24	17 29	17 44	17 44	17 59	17 59	18 06	18 14	18 14	18 24	18 27	18 29	18 44	18 44	18 53
St Pancras International	a	16 51	16 52	17 06	17 21	17 22	17 31	17 36	17 51	17 52	18 09	18 09	18 13	18 21	18 22	18 31	18 41	18 36	18 51	18 52	19 06

		SE A	SE B	SE A	SE B	SE A	SE B	SE A	SE B	SE A	SE B	SE B	SE A	SE B	SE A	SE B	SE A	SE B	SE B	SE
Margate	d			17 53	17 53								18 53	18 53						
Broadstairs	d			17 59	17 59								18 59	18 59						
Ramsgate	d			18 05	18 05								19 05	19 05						
Canterbury West	a			18 24	18 24								19 24	19 24						
	d			18 25	18 25								19 25	19 25						
Sandwich	d																			
Deal	d																			
Dover Priory	d							18 44	18 44								19 44	19 44		
Folkestone Central	d							18 56	18 56								19 56	19 56		
Folkestone West	d							18 58	18 58								19 58	19 58		
Ashford International	a			18 41	18 41			19 11	19 11				19 41	19 41			20 11	20 11		
	d			18 43	18 43			19 13	19 14				19 43	19 43			20 13	20 13		
Broadstairs	d																			
Margate	d																			
Birchington-on-Sea	d																			
Herne Bay	d																			
Whitstable	d																			
Faversham	a																			
	d	17 58	17 58			18 28	18 28			18 58		18 58			19 28	19 28				19 58
Sittingbourne	d	18 07	18 07			18 37	18 37			19 07		19 07			19 37	19 37				20 07
Rainham (Kent)	d	18 15	18 15			18 45	18 45			19 15		19 15			19 45	19 45				20 15
Gillingham (Kent)	d	18 20	18 20			18 50	18 50			19 20		19 20			19 50	19 50				20 20
Chatham	d	18 24	18 24			18 54	18 54			19 24		19 24			19 54	19 54				20 24
Rochester	d	18 27	18 27			18 57	18 57			19 27		19 27			19 57	19 57				20 27
Maidstone West	d																			
Strood	d	18 32	18 32			19 02	19 02			19 32		19 32			20 02	20 02				20 32
Gravesend	d	18 43	18 43			19 13	19 13			19 43		19 43			20 13	20 13				20 43
Ebbsfleet International	a	18 47	18 47	19 02	19 02	19 17	19 17	19 32	19 34	19 47		19 47	20 02	20 02	20 17	20 17	20 32	20 32		20 47
	d	18 48	18 51	19 03	19 03	19 18	19 18	19 33	19 35	19 48	19 48	19 52	20 03	20 03	20 18	20 18	20 33	20 33	20 45	20 51
Stratford International	a	18 59	19 02	19 14	19 14	19 29	19 29	19 44	19 45	19 59	19 59	20 03	20 14	20 14	20 29	20 29	20 44	20 44	20 55	21 02
St Pancras International	a	19 06	19 10	19 21	19 22	19 36	19 37	19 51	19 52	20 06	20 08	20 14	20 21	20 22	20 36	20 37	20 51	20 52	21 06	21 09

A not from 2 September until 9 September

B not 26 August

Table 194

Sundays

26 August to 9 September

Kent - St Pancras International High Speed Domestic Services

		SE	SE	SE	SE	SE	SE	SE	SE	SE	SE	SE	SE	SE	SE	SE	SE	SE	SE	SE	SE
		A	B	A	B	A	B	A	B	B	A	B	A	B	A	B	1	B	A	B	A
Margate 4	d	19 53	19 53								20 53	20 53									21 53
Broadstairs	d	19 59	19 59								20 59	20 59									21 59
Ramsgate 4	d	20 05	20 05								21 05	21 05					21 40				22 05
Canterbury West	a	20 24	20 24								21 24	21 24					22 02				22 24
	d	20 25	20 25								21 25	21 25					22 04				22 25
Sandwich	d																				
Deal	d																				
Dover Priory	d					20 44	20 44								21 44	21 44					
Folkestone Central	d					20 56	20 56								21 56	21 56					
Folkestone West	d					20 58	20 58								21 58	21 58					
Ashford International	a	20 41	20 41			21 11	21 11				21 41	21 41			22 11	22 11	22 25				22 41
	d	20 43	20 47			21 13	21 13				21 43	21 43			22 13	22 13					22 43
Broadstairs	d																				
Margate 4	d																				
Birchington-on-Sea	d																				
Herne Bay	d																				
Whitstable	d																				
Faversham 2	a																				
	d			20 28	20 28			20 58		20 58			21 28	21 28					21 58	21 58	
Sittingbourne 4	d			20 37	20 37			21 07		21 07			21 37	21 37					22 07	22 07	
Rainham (Kent)	d			20 45	20 45			21 15		21 15			21 45	21 45					22 15	22 15	
Gillingham (Kent) 4	d			20 50	20 50			21 20		21 20			21 50	21 50					22 20	22 20	
Chatham 4	d			20 54	20 54			21 24		21 24			21 54	21 54					22 24	22 24	
Rochester 4	d			20 57	20 57			21 27		21 27			21 57	21 57					22 27	22 27	
Maidstone West	d																				
Strood 4	d			21 02	21 02			21 32		21 32			22 02	22 02					22 32	22 32	
Gravesend	d			21 13	21 13			21 43		21 43			22 13	22 13					22 43	22 43	
Ebbsfleet International	a	21 02	21 06	21 17	21 17	21 32	21 32	21 47		21 47	22 02	22 02	22 17	22 17	22 32	22 32			22 47	22 47	23 02
	d	21 03	21 07	21 18	21 20	21 33	21 33	21 48	21 48	21 51	22 03	22 03	22 18	22 18	22 33	22 33		22 45	22 48	22 48	23 03
Stratford International ⊖	a	21 14	21 18	21 29	21 30	21 44	21 44	21 59	21 59	22 02	22 14	22 14	22 29	22 29	22 44	22 44		22 56	22 59	22 59	23 14
St Pancras International 4 ⊖	a	21 21	21 26	21 36	21 44	21 51	21 52	22 06	22 07	22 10	22 21	22 22	22 36	22 37	22 51	22 52		23 04	23 06	23 07	23 21

		SE	SE
		B	B
Margate 4	d	21 53	
Broadstairs	d	21 59	
Ramsgate 4	d	22 05	
Canterbury West	a	22 24	
	d	22 25	
Sandwich	d		
Deal	d		
Dover Priory	d		
Folkestone Central	d		
Folkestone West	d		
Ashford International	a	22 41	
	d	22 43	
Broadstairs	d		
Margate 4	d		
Birchington-on-Sea	d		
Herne Bay	d		
Whitstable	d		
Faversham 2	a		
	d		
Sittingbourne 4	d		
Rainham (Kent)	d		
Gillingham (Kent) 4	d		
Chatham 4	d		
Rochester 4	d		
Maidstone West	d		
Strood 4	d		
Gravesend	d		
Ebbsfleet International	a	23 02	
	d	23 03	23 45
Stratford International ⊖	a	23 14	23 56
St Pancras International 4 ⊖	a	23 22	00 04

A not from 2 September until 9 September

B not 26 August

Network Diagram for Tables 195, 196

also 199 ⊙

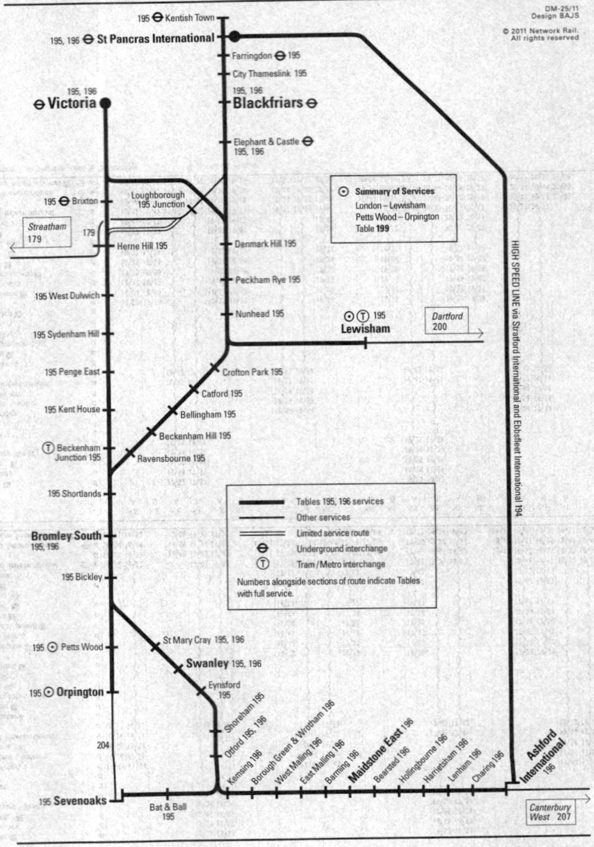

Table 195

Mondays to Fridays

until 27 July, 13 Aug to 28 Aug and from 10 Sep

London Victoria/Kentish Town - Catford, Beckenham Junction, Bromley South, Orpington, Otford and Sevenoaks

Network Diagram - see first Page of Table 195

Miles	Miles	Miles			SE MO A	SE MX B	SE MX C	SE MO ■ A	SE MX ■	SE MO A	SE MX B	SE MX	SE MX ■ C	SE ■ B	SE	SE ■	SE	FC	SE	FC	SE ■	SE	SE ■
0	—	0	**London Victoria** ⊖	d			23p43	23p45	23p52			23p55	00 07	00 07	00 35	05 22			05 40		05 52		06 07
3¼	—	—	Brixton ⊖	d								00 02							05 47				
—	—	—	Kentish Town ⊖	d																05 50			
—	—	—	St Pancras International ⊖	d														05 36		05 54			
—	—	—	Farringdon ⊖	d														05 42		06 00			
—	—	—	City Thameslink	d													05 26	05 44		06 03			
—	0	—	**London Blackfriars** ⊖	d	23p08	23p12				23p38	23p42						05 28	05 47		06 06			
—	1¼	—	Elephant & Castle ⊖	d	23p12	23p16				23p42	23p46						05 32	05 50		06 09			
—	—	—	Loughborough Jn	d																06 13			
4	—	—	Herne Hill	d								00 04			00 43			05a57	05 49	06a17			
5	—	—	West Dulwich	d								00 06							05 51				
5¾	—	—	Sydenham Hill	d								00 08							05 53				
7¼	—	—	Penge East	d								00 11			00 48				05 56				
7¾	—	—	Kent House	d								00 13							05 58				
8¾	—	—	**Beckenham Junction**	d								00 15			00 50				06 00				
—	3¾	4¼	Denmark Hill	d	23p18	23p22	23p52			23p48	23p52						05 39						
—	4½	5	Peckham Rye	d	23p21	23p25	23p55			23p51	23p55						05 41						
—	5¼	5¾	Nunhead	d	23p23	23p27	23p57			23p53	23p57						05 44						
—	—	7½	Lewisham	a																			
—	6½	—	Crofton Park	d	23p26	23p30	23p59			23p56	23p59						05 47						
—	7½	—	Catford	d	23p29	23p33	00 03			23p59	00 03						05 49						
—	8¼	—	Bellingham	d	23p31	23p35	00 05			00 01	00 05						05 52						
—	9	—	Beckenham Hill	d	23p33	23p37	00 07			00 03	00 07						05 54						
—	9½	—	Ravensbourne	d	23p35	23p39	00 09			00 05	00 09						05 56						
10	10½	—	Shortlands	d	23p37	23p41	00 11			00 07	00 11	00 18					05 58		06 03				
11	11½	—	**Bromley South**	d	23p40	23p44	00 14	00 02	00 09	00 10	00 14	00 21	00 25	00 25	00 55	05 39	06 01		06 06		06 09	06 16	06 23
12	12½	—	Bickley	d	23p43	23p47	00 17			00 13	00 17	00 24					06 03		06 09			06 18	
13¾	—	—	Petts Wood	d			00 21					00 29							06 14				
15	—	—	**Orpington**	d			00a25					00a32							06a18				
—	14½	—	St Mary Cray	d	23p47	23p51		00 08	00 15	00 17	00 21		00 31	00 32	01 01	05 45	06 08					06 23	06 30
—	17½	—	**Swanley**	d	23p52	23p56		00a12	00a19	00 22	00 26		00 36	00 36	01a05	05a49	06 12				06a19	06 28	06 34
—	20¼	—	Eynsford	d	23p56	23p59				00 26	00 30		00 40				06 17					06 32	
—	22¾	—	Shoreham (Kent)	d	23p59	00 04				00 30	00 34		00 44				06 20					06 36	
—	24	—	Otford	d	00 03	00 07				00 33	00 37		00a47	00a44			06 23					06 39	06a42
—	25¾	—	Bat & Ball	d	00 06	00 10				00 36	00 40						06 26					06 42	
—	27	—	**Sevenoaks**	a	00 09	00 13				00 39	00 43						06 29					06 45	

		SE	SE ■	FC	FC	SE	SE ■	SE ■	SE	FC	SE	SE ■	SE ■	FC ■	FC	FC ■	SE	SE ■	SE	SE ■	FC D	FC E	FC ■
London Victoria ⊖	d	06 10	06 22			06 30	06 37	06 45			06 50	06 58	07 07				07 10	07 22	07 25	07 36			
Brixton ⊖	d	06 17				06 37					06 57						07 17		07 32				
Kentish Town ⊖	d			05 54	06 08					06 30					06 48						07 08	07 08	
St Pancras International ⊖	d			05 58	06 12					06 34				06 44	06 52	07 04					07 12	07 12	07 16
Farringdon ⊖	d			06 04	06 18					06 40				06 50	06 58	07 10					07 18	07 18	07 22
City Thameslink	d			06 07	06 21				06 39	06 43				06 53	07 01	07 13					07 21	07 21	07 25
London Blackfriars ⊖	d			06 10	06 24				06 42	06 46				06 58	07 04	07 16					07 24	07 24	07 28
Elephant & Castle ⊖	d			06 16	06 27				06 46	06 49				07 02	07 07	07 19					07 28	07 28	07 33
Loughborough Jn	d				06 31					06 53					07 11	07 23							07 37
Herne Hill	d	06 19			06a35	06 39				06a57	06 59				07a15	07a27	07 19		07 34				07a40
West Dulwich	d	06 21				06 41					07 02						07 21		07 36				
Sydenham Hill	d	06 23				06 43					07 04						07 23		07 38				
Penge East	d	06 26				06 46					07 07						07 26		07 41				
Kent House	d	06 28				06 48					07 09						07 28		07 43				
Beckenham Junction	d	06 30				06 50					07 11						07 30		07 45				
Denmark Hill	d			06 22					06 52					07 09							07 34	07 34	
Peckham Rye	d			06 25					06 55					07 12							07 36	07 36	
Nunhead	d			06 27					06 57					07 14							07 39	07 39	
Lewisham	a																						
Crofton Park	d			06 30					07 00					07 17							07 42	07 42	
Catford	d			06 33					07 03					07 20							07 44	07 44	
Bellingham	d			06 35					07 05					07 22							07 47	07 47	
Beckenham Hill	d			06 37					07 07					07 24							07 49	07 49	
Ravensbourne	d			06 39					07 09					07 26							07 51	07 51	
Shortlands	d	06 33		06 41		06 54			07 11		07 14			07 28			07 33		07 48		07 54	07 54	
Bromley South	d	06 37	06 39	06 44		06 57	06 58	07 02	07 14		07 17	07 19	07 23	07 31			07 38	07 40	07 51	07 53	07 57	07 57	
Bickley	d	06 39		06 47		07 00			07 17		07 20			07 34			07 40		07 54		08 00	08 00	
Petts Wood	d	06 44				07 04					07 24						07 49		07 59				
Orpington	d	06a49				07a08					07a28						07a53		08a02				
St Mary Cray	d		06 45	06 51			07 04	07 08	07 21			07 25	07 30	07 38						08 00	08 04	08 04	
Swanley	d		06a49	06 56			07 08	07a12	07 26			07a29	07 34	07 44				07a48		08 04	08 10	08 10	
Eynsford	d			07 00					07 30					07 48							08 15	08 15	
Shoreham (Kent)	d			07 04					07 34					07 52							08 18	08 18	
Otford	d			07 07			07a16		07 37				07a42	07 55						08a12	08 21	08 22	
Bat & Ball	d			07 10					07 40					07 58							08 24	08 25	
Sevenoaks	a			07 14					07 43					08 01							08 27	08 28	

A from 21 May until 23 July
B from 22 May until 27 July
C until 18 May
D until 18 May
E from 21 May until 27 July

Table 195

Mondays to Fridays

until 27 July, 13 Aug to 28 Aug and from 10 Sep

London Victoria/Kentish Town - Catford, Beckenham Junction, Bromley South, Orpington, Otford and Sevenoaks

Network Diagram - see first Page of Table 195

		FC	FC	SE	SE	SE ■	SE	SE ■	SE ■ A	SE ■ B	FC	FC	FC	SE	SE	FC	SE ■	SE	SE ■	FC ■	FC ■	SE	SE
London Victoria ⊖	d			07 40	07 43	07 52	07 55	07 58	08 07	08 07				08 09	08 10		08 22	08 25	08 37			08 39	08 40
Brixton ⊖	d			07 47			08 02								08 17			08 32					08 47
Kentish Town ⊖	d	07 24										07 44									08 20		
St Pancras International ⊖	d	07 28	07 32								07 38	07 48	07 52			08 12				08 16	08 24		
Farringdon ⊖	d	07 34	07 38								07 44	07 54	07 58			08 18				08 22	08 30		
City Thameslink	d	07 37	07 41								07 47	07 57	08 01			08 21				08 25	08 33		
London Blackfriars ⊖	d	07 40	07 44								07 50	08 00	08 04			08 24				08 28	08 36		
Elephant & Castle ⊖	d	07 44	07 47								07 54	08 04	08 07			08 27				08 32			
Loughborough Jn	d		07 51										08 11			08 31							
Herne Hill	d		07a55	07 49			08 04						08a15		08 19	08a36		08 34			08a45		08 48
West Dulwich	d			07 51			08 06								08 21			08 36					08 51
Sydenham Hill	d			07 53			08 08								08 23			08 38					08 53
Penge East	d			07 56			08 11								08 26			08 41					08 56
Kent House	d			07 58			08 13								08 28			08 43					08 58
Beckenham Junction	d			08 00			08 15								08 30			08 45					09 00
Denmark Hill	d	07 50			07 53						08 00	08 10		08 18						08 38		08 48	
Peckham Rye	d	07 53			07 56						08 03	08 13		08 21						08 41		08 51	
Nunhead	d	07 56			07 59						08 06	08 15		08 23						08 43		08 53	
Lewisham	a				08 07									08 30								09 01	
Crofton Park	d										08 09	08 18								08 46			
Catford	d	08 00									08 12	08 21								08 49			
Bellingham	d	08 02									08 15	08 23								08 51			
Beckenham Hill	d										08 17	08 25								08 53			
Ravensbourne	d										08 19	08 27								08 55			
Shortlands	d			08 03							08 22	08 30			08 33			08 48		08 57			09 03
Bromley South	d	08a10		08 06		08a09	08 22	08 28	08 23	08 24	08 25	08 33			08 36		08a39	08 51	08 53	09 00			09 07
Bickley	d			08 09			08 24				08 28	08 35			08 39			08 54		09 03			09 09
Petts Wood	d			08 14			08 29				08 32				08 44			08 59					09 14
Orpington	d			08a19			08a32				08a35				08a47			09a02					09a17
St Mary Cray	d							08 34	08 30	08 31		08 40							09 00	09 07			
Swanley	d							08a39	08 34	08 35		08 44							09 04	09 12			
Eynsford	d											08 49								09 16			
Shoreham (Kent)	d											08 52								09 20			
Otford	d								08a42	08a43		08 55							09a12	09 23			
Bat & Ball	d											08 58								09 26			
Sevenoaks	a											09 01								09 29			

		FC	FC ■	FC	FC	FC	SE ■	SE	SE ■	SE ■	SE	SE	FC	FC	SE ■	SE	SE ■	SE	SE	FC	FC	FC
London Victoria ⊖	d						08 52	08 55	08 58	09 07	09 09	09 10			09 22	09 25	09 37	09 39	09 40			
Brixton ⊖	d							09 02				09 17				09 32			09 47			
Kentish Town ⊖	d			08 36		08 52								09 12						09 26		09 44
St Pancras International ⊖	d	08 28	08 32	08 40	08 44	08 56							09 00	09 16						09 30	09 34	09 48
Farringdon ⊖	d	08 34	08 38	08 46	08 50	09 02							09 06	09 22						09 36	09 40	09 53
City Thameslink	d	08 37	08 41	08 49	08 53	09 05							09 09	09 25						09 39	09 43	09 57
London Blackfriars ⊖	d	08 40	08 44	08 52	08 56	09 08							09 12	09 28						09 42	09 46	10 00
Elephant & Castle ⊖	d	08 44	08 47	08 56	09 00	09 12							09 16	09 31						09 46	09 49	10 03
Loughborough Jn	d		08 51		09 04	09 16								09 35							09 53	10 07
Herne Hill	d		08a57		09a08	09a21		09 04				09 19		09a39		09 34			09 49		09a57	10a11
West Dulwich	d							09 06				09 21				09 36			09 51			
Sydenham Hill	d							09 08				09 23				09 38			09 53			
Penge East	d							09 11				09 26				09 41			09 56			
Kent House	d							09 13				09 28				09 43			09 58			
Beckenham Junction	d							09 15				09 30				09 45			10 00			
Denmark Hill	d	08 52		09 02							09 18		09 22					09 48		09 52		
Peckham Rye	d	08 55									09 21		09 25					09 51		09 55		
Nunhead	d	08 57									09 23		09 27					09 53		09 57		
Lewisham	a										09 31							10 01				
Crofton Park	d	09 00											09 30							10 00		
Catford	d	09 03		09 09									09 33							10 03		
Bellingham	d	09 05											09 35							10 05		
Beckenham Hill	d	09 07											09 37							10 07		
Ravensbourne	d	09 09											09 39							10 09		
Shortlands	d	09 11						09 18				09 33	09 41			09 48			10 03	10 11		
Bromley South	d	09 14		09 18			09a08	09 21	09 19	09 23		09 36	09 44		09a38	09 52	09 53		10 07	10 14		
Bickley	d	09 17		09 20				09 24				09 39	09 47			09 54			10 09	10 17		
Petts Wood	d							09 29				09 44				09 59			10 14			
Orpington	d							09a33				09a47				10a02			10a17			
St Mary Cray	d	09 21		09 25					09 25				09 51				10 00			10 21		
Swanley	d	09 26		09 36					09a29	09 33			09 56				10 04			10 26		
Eynsford	d	09 30		09 40									10 00							10 30		
Shoreham (Kent)	d	09 34		09 44									10 04							10 34		
Otford	d	09 37		09 47						09a41			10 07				10a12			10 37		
Bat & Ball	d	09 40		09 50									10 10							10 40		
Sevenoaks	a	09 45		09 53									10 13							10 43		

A from 21 May until 27 July
B until 18 May

until 27 July, 13 Aug to 28 Aug and from 10 Sep

London Victoria/Kentish Town - Catford, Beckenham Junction, Bromley South, Orpington, Otford and Sevenoaks

Network Diagram - see first Page of Table 195

		SE 1 H	SE	SE 1	SE 1	SE	SE		FC	FC	FC	SE 1 H	SE	SE 1	SE	SE	FC		FC	FC	SE 1 H	SE	SE 1	SE 1	SE
London Victoria 15 ⊖	d	09 52	09 55	09 58	10 07	10 09	10 10					10 22	10 25	10 37	10 39	10 40					10 52	10 55	10 58	11 07	11 09
Brixton ⊖	d		10 02				10 17						10 32			10 47						11 02			
Kentish Town ⊖	d								09 54	10 00	10 14						10 26		10 30	10 44					
St Pancras International 15 ⊖	d								10 00	10 04	10 18						10 30		10 34	10 48					
Farringdon ⊖	d								10 05	10 09	10 24						10 35		10 39	10 54					
City Thameslink 3	d								10 09	10 13	10 27						10 39		10 43	10 57					
London Blackfriars 3 ⊖	d								10 12	10 16	10 30						10 42		10 46	11 00					
Elephant & Castle ⊖	d								10 16	10 19	10 33						10 46		10 49	11 03					
Loughborough Jn	d									10 23	10 37								10 53	11 07					
Herne Hill 4	d		10 04				10 19			10a27	10a41		10 34			10 49			10a57	11a11		11 04			
West Dulwich	d		10 06				10 21						10 36			10 51						11 06			
Sydenham Hill	d		10 08				10 23						10 38			10 53						11 08			
Penge East	d		10 11				10 26						10 41			10 56						11 11			
Kent House 4	d		10 13				10 28						10 43			10 58						11 13			
Beckenham Junction 4 ⇌	d		10 15				10 30						10 45			11 00						11 15			
Denmark Hill 4	d					10 18			10 22						10 48		10 52								11 18
Peckham Rye 4	d					10 21			10 25						10 51		10 55								11 21
Nunhead 4	d					10 23			10 27						10 53		10 57								11 23
Lewisham 4 ⇌	a					10 31									11 01										11 31
Crofton Park	d								10 30								11 00								
Catford	d								10 33								11 03								
Bellingham	d								10 35								11 05								
Beckenham Hill	d								10 37								11 07								
Ravensbourne	d								10 39								11 09								
Shortlands 4	d		10 18				10 33		10 41				10 48			11 03	11 11					11 18			
Bromley South 4	d	10a08	10 21	10 19	10 23		10 36		10 44			10a38	10 51	10 53		11 06	11 14				11a08	11 21	11 19	11 23	
Bickley 4	d		10 24				10 39		10 47				10 54			11 09	11 17					11 24			
Petts Wood 4	d		10 29				10 44						10 59			11 14						11 29			
Orpington 4	d		10a32				10a47						11a02			11a17						11a32			
St Mary Cray	d			10 25					10 51					11 00			11 21						11 25		
Swanley 4	d			10a29	10 33				10 56					11 04			11 26						11a29	11 33	
Eynsford	d								11 00								11 30								
Shoreham (Kent)	d								11 04								11 34								
Otford 4	d				10a41				11 07					11a12			11 37							11a41	
Bat & Ball	d								11 10								11 40								
Sevenoaks 4	a								11 13								11 43								

		SE	FC		FC	FC	SE 1 H	SE	SE 1	SE	SE	FC	FC		FC	SE 1 H	SE	SE 1	SE 1	SE	SE	FC	FC		FC
London Victoria 15 ⊖	d	11 10					11 22	11 25	11 37	11 39	11 40					11 52	11 55	11 58	12 07	12 09	12 10				
Brixton ⊖	d	11 17						11 32			11 47						12 02				12 17				
Kentish Town ⊖	d		10 56		11 00	11 14						11 26	11 30		11 44							11 56	12 00		12 14
St Pancras International 15 ⊖	d		11 00		11 04	11 18						11 30	11 34		11 48							12 00	12 04		12 18
Farringdon ⊖	d		11 05		11 09	11 24						11 35	11 39		11 53							12 05	12 09		12 23
City Thameslink 3	d		11 09		11 13	11 27						11 39	11 43		11 57							12 09	12 13		12 27
London Blackfriars 3 ⊖	d		11 12		11 16	11 30						11 42	11 46		12 00							12 12	12 16		12 30
Elephant & Castle ⊖	d		11 16		11 19	11 33						11 46	11 49		12 03							12 16	12 19		12 33
Loughborough Jn	d				11 23	11 37							11 53		12 07								12 23		12 37
Herne Hill 4	d	11 19			11a27	11a41		11 34			11 49		11a57		12a11		12 04				12 19		12a27		12a41
West Dulwich	d	11 21						11 36			11 51						12 06				12 21				
Sydenham Hill	d	11 23						11 38			11 53						12 08				12 23				
Penge East	d	11 26						11 41			11 56						12 11				12 26				
Kent House 4	d	11 28						11 43			11 58						12 13				12 28				
Beckenham Junction 4 ⇌	d	11 30						11 45			12 00						12 15				12 30				
Denmark Hill 4	d		11 22							11 48		11 52								12 18		12 22			
Peckham Rye 4	d		11 25							11 51		11 55								12 21		12 25			
Nunhead 4	d		11 27							11 53		11 57								12 23		12 27			
Lewisham 4 ⇌	a									12 01										12 31					
Crofton Park	d		11 30									12 00										12 30			
Catford	d		11 33									12 03										12 33			
Bellingham	d		11 35									12 05										12 35			
Beckenham Hill	d		11 37									12 07										12 37			
Ravensbourne	d		11 39									12 09										12 39			
Shortlands 4	d	11 33	11 41					11 48			12 03	12 11					12 18				12 33	12 41			
Bromley South 4	d	11 36	11 44				11a38	11 51	11 53		12 06	12 14				12a08	12 21	12 19	12 23		12 36	12 44			
Bickley 4	d	11 39	11 47					11 54			12 09	12 17					12 24				12 39	12 47			
Petts Wood 4	d	11 44						11 59			12 14						12 29				12 44				
Orpington 4	d	11a47						12a02			12a17						12a32				12a47				
St Mary Cray	d		11 51						12 00			12 21						12 25				12 51			
Swanley 4	d		11 56						12 04			12 26						12a29	12 33			12 56			
Eynsford	d		12 00									12 30										13 00			
Shoreham (Kent)	d		12 04									12 34										13 04			
Otford 4	d		12 07						12a12			12 37							12a41			13 07			
Bat & Ball	d		12 10									12 40										13 10			
Sevenoaks 4	a		12 13									12 43										13 13			

until 27 July, 13 Aug to 28 Aug and from 10 Sep

London Victoria/Kentish Town - Catford, Beckenham Junction, Bromley South, Orpington, Otford and Sevenoaks

Network Diagram - see first Page of Table 195

		SE 1 H	SE	SE 1	SE	SE	FC	FC	FC		SE 1 H	SE	SE 1	SE 1	SE	SE	FC	FC	FC		SE 1 H	SE	SE 1	SE	SE
London Victoria 15 ⊖	d	12 22	12 25	12 37	12 39	12 40					12 52	12 55	12 58	13 07	13 09	13 10					13 22	13 25	13 37	13 39	13 40
Brixton ⊖	d		12 32			12 47						13 02				13 17						13 32			13 47
Kentish Town ⊖	d						12 26	12 30	12 44								12 56	13 00	13 14						
St Pancras International 15 ⊖	d						12 30	12 34	12 48								13 00	13 04	13 18						
Farringdon ⊖	d						12 35	12 39	12 53								13 05	13 09	13 23						
City Thameslink 3	d						12 39	12 43	12 57								13 09	13 13	13 27						
London Blackfriars 3 ⊖	d						12 42	12 46	13 00								13 12	13 16	13 30						
Elephant & Castle ⊖	d						12 46	12 49	13 03								13 16	13 19	13 33						
Loughborough Jn	d							12 53	13 07									13 23	13 37						
Herne Hill 4	d		12 34			12 49		12a57	13a11			13 04				13 19		13a27	13a41			13 34			13 49
West Dulwich	d		12 36			12 51						13 06				13 21						13 36			13 51
Sydenham Hill	d		12 38			12 53						13 08				13 23						13 38			13 53
Penge East	d		12 41			12 56						13 11				13 26						13 41			13 56
Kent House 4	d		12 43			12 58						13 13				13 28						13 43			13 58
Beckenham Junction 4 ⇌	d		12 45			13 00						13 15				13 30						13 45			14 00
Denmark Hill 4	d				12 48		12 52								13 18		13 22							13 48	
Peckham Rye 4	d				12 51		12 55								13 21		13 25							13 51	
Nunhead 4	d				12 53		12 57								13 23		13 27							13 53	
Lewisham 4 ⇌	a				13 01										13 31									14 01	
Crofton Park	d						13 00										13 30								
Catford	d						13 03										13 33								
Bellingham	d						13 05										13 35								
Beckenham Hill	d						13 07										13 37								
Ravensbourne	d						13 09										13 39								
Shortlands 4	d		12 48			13 03	13 11					13 18				13 33	13 41					13 48			14 03
Bromley South 4	d	12a38	12 51	12 53		13 06	13 14				13a08	13 21	13 19	13 23		13 36	13 44				13a38	13 51	13 53		14 06
Bickley 4	d		12 54			13 09	13 17					13 24				13 39	13 47					13 54			14 09
Petts Wood 4	d		12 59			13 14						13 29				13 44						13 59			14 14
Orpington 4	d		13a02			13a17						13a32				13a47						14a02			14a17
St Mary Cray	d			13 00			13 21						13 25				13 51						14 00		
Swanley 4	d			13 04			13 26						13a29	13 33			13 56						14 04		
Eynsford	d						13 30										14 00								
Shoreham (Kent)	d						13 34										14 04								
Otford 4	d			13a12			13 37							13a41			14 07						14a12		
Bat & Ball	d						13 40										14 10								
Sevenoaks 4	a						13 43										14 13								

		FC	FC	FC	SE 1 H		SE	SE 1 A	SE 1 B	SE 1	SE	SE	FC	FC	FC		SE 1 H	SE	SE 1	SE	SE	FC	FC	FC	SE 1 H
London Victoria 15 ⊖	d				13 52		13 55	13 57	13 58	14 07	14 09	14 10					14 22	14 25	14 37	14 39	14 40				14 52
Brixton ⊖	d						14 02					14 17						14 32			14 47				
Kentish Town ⊖	d	13 26	13 30	13 44									13 56	14 00	14 14							14 26	14 30	14 44	
St Pancras International 15 ⊖	d	13 30	13 34	13 48									14 00	14 04	14 18							14 30	14 34	14 48	
Farringdon ⊖	d	13 35	13 39	13 53									14 05	14 09	14 23							14 35	14 39	14 53	
City Thameslink 3	d	13 39	13 43	13 57									14 09	14 13	14 27							14 39	14 43	14 57	
London Blackfriars 3 ⊖	d	13 42	13 46	14 00									14 12	14 16	14 30							14 42	14 46	15 00	
Elephant & Castle ⊖	d	13 46	13 49	14 03									14 16	14 19	14 33							14 46	14 49	15 03	
Loughborough Jn	d		13 53	14 07										14 23	14 37								14 53	15 07	
Herne Hill 4	d		13a57	14a11			14 04					14 19		14a27	14a41			14 34			14 49		14a57	15a11	
West Dulwich	d						14 06					14 21						14 36			14 51				
Sydenham Hill	d						14 08					14 23						14 38			14 53				
Penge East	d						14 11					14 26						14 41			14 56				
Kent House 4	d						14 13					14 28						14 43			14 58				
Beckenham Junction 4 ⇌	d						14 15					14 30						14 45			15 00				
Denmark Hill 4	d	13 52									14 18		14 22							14 48		14 52			
Peckham Rye 4	d	13 55									14 21		14 25							14 51		14 55			
Nunhead 4	d	13 57									14 23		14 27							14 53		14 57			
Lewisham 4 ⇌	a										14 31									15 01					
Crofton Park	d	14 00											14 30									15 00			
Catford	d	14 03											14 33									15 03			
Bellingham	d	14 05											14 35									15 05			
Beckenham Hill	d	14 07											14 37									15 07			
Ravensbourne	d	14 09											14 39									15 09			
Shortlands 4	d	14 11					14 18					14 33	14 41					14 48			15 03	15 11			
Bromley South 4	d	14 14			14a08		14 21	14 18	14 19	14 23		14 36	14 44				14a38	14 51	14 53		15 06	15 14			15a08
Bickley 4	d	14 17					14 24					14 39	14 47					14 54			15 09	15 17			
Petts Wood 4	d						14 29					14 44						14 59			15 14				
Orpington 4	d						14a32					14a47						15a02			15a17				
St Mary Cray	d	14 21						14 24	14 25				14 51						15 00			15 21			
Swanley 4	d	14 26						14a28	14a29	14 33			14 56						15 04			15 26			
Eynsford	d	14 30											15 00									15 30			
Shoreham (Kent)	d	14 34											15 04									15 34			
Otford 4	d	14 37								14a41			15 07						15a12			15 37			
Bat & Ball	d	14 40											15 10									15 40			
Sevenoaks 4	a	14 43											15 13									15 43			

A until 18 May

B from 21 May until 27 July

Table 195

Mondays to Fridays

until 27 July, 13 Aug to 28 Aug and from 10 Sep

London Victoria/Kentish Town - Catford, Beckenham Junction, Bromley South, Orpington, Otford and Sevenoaks

Network Diagram - see first Page of Table 195

		SE	SE 1	SE 1	SE	SE	FC	FC	FC	SE 1 ✠		SE	SE 1	SE	SE	FC	FC	FC	SE 1 ✠	SE		SE	SE 1	SE 1
London Victoria 15 ⊖	d	14 55	14 58	15 07	15 09	15 10				15 22		15 25	15 37	15 39	15 40				15 52			15 55	15 58	16 07
Brixton ⊖	d	15 02				15 17						15 32			15 47							16 02		
Kentish Town ⊖	d						14 56	15 00	15 14							15 26	15 30	15 44						
St Pancras International 15 ⊖	d						15 00	15 04	15 18							15 30	15 34	15 48						
Farringdon ⊖	d						15 05	15 09	15 23							15 35	15 39	15 53						
City Thameslink 3	d						15 09	15 13	15 27							15 39	15 43	15 57						
London Blackfriars 3 ⊖	d						15 12	15 16	15 30							15 42	15 46	16 00						
Elephant & Castle ⊖	d						15 16	15 19	15 33							15 46	15 49	16 03						
Loughborough Jn	d							15 23	15 37								15 53	16 07						
Herne Hill 4	d	15 04				15 19		15a27	15a41			15 34			15 49		15a57	16a11				16 04		
West Dulwich	d	15 06				15 21						15 36			15 51							16 06		
Sydenham Hill	d	15 08				15 23						15 38			15 53							16 08		
Penge East	d	15 11				15 26						15 41			15 56							16 11		
Kent House 4	d	15 13				15 28						15 43			15 58							16 13		
Beckenham Junction 4 🚋	d	15 15				15 30						15 45			16 00					16 12		16 15		
Denmark Hill 4	d				15 18		15 22							15 48		15 52								
Peckham Rye 4	d				15 21		15 25							15 51		15 55								
Nunhead 4	d				15 23		15 27							15 53		15 57								
Lewisham 4 🚋	a				15 31									16 01										
Crofton Park	d						15 30									16 00								
Catford	d						15 33									16 03								
Bellingham	d						15 35									16 05								
Beckenham Hill	d						15 37									16 07								
Ravensbourne	d						15 39									16 09								
Shortlands 4	d	15 18				15 33	15 41					15 48			16 03	16 11						16 18		
Bromley South 4	d	15 21	15 19	15 23		15 36	15 44			15a38		15 51	15 53		16 06	16 14			16a08			16 21	16 19	16 23
Bickley 4	d	15 24				15 39	15 47					15 54			16 09	16 17						16 24		
Petts Wood 4	d	15 29				15 44						15 59			16 14							16 29		
Orpington 4	d	15a32				15a47						16a02			16a17							16a32		
St Mary Cray	d		15 25				15 51						16 00			16 21							16 25	
Swanley 4	d		15a29	15 33			15 56						16 04			16 26							16a29	16 33
Eynsford	d						16 00									16 30								
Shoreham (Kent)	d						16 04									16 34								
Otford 4	d			15a41			16 07						16a12			16 37								16a41
Bat & Ball	d						16 10									16 40								
Sevenoaks 4	a						16 13									16 43								

		SE	SE	FC	FC		SE 1 ✠		SE	SE 1	SE 1	FC	FC	SE	SE	FC	FC		FC 1	FC	SE 1 ✠	SE 1	SE	SE	SE
London Victoria 15 ⊖	d	16 09	16 10				16 22		16 25	16 28	16 37			16 39	16 40						16 57	16 58	16 59	17 04	17 04
Brixton ⊖	d		16 17						16 32						16 47								17 06		
Kentish Town ⊖	d			15 56	16 00							16 10	16 14			16 24	16 30			16 46					
St Pancras International 15 ⊖	d			16 00	16 04							16 14	16 18			16 28	16 34		16 40	16 52					
Farringdon ⊖	d			16 05	16 09							16 19	16 23			16 33	16 39		16 45	16 57					
City Thameslink 3	d			16 09	16 13							16 23	16 27			16 37	16 43		16 49	17 01					
London Blackfriars 3 ⊖	d			16 12	16 16							16 26	16 30			16 42	16 46		16 52	17 04					
Elephant & Castle ⊖	d			16 16	16 19							16 30	16 33			16 46	16 49		16 56	17 08					
Loughborough Jn	d				16 23								16 37				16 53		17 00	17 12					
Herne Hill 4	d		16 19		16a27				16 34				16a41		16 49		16a57		17 06	17a15			17 11		
West Dulwich	d		16 21						16 36						16 51				17 08				17 13		
Sydenham Hill	d		16 23						16 38						16 53				17 10				17 15		
Penge East	d		16 26						16 41						16 56				17 13				17 18		
Kent House 4	d		16 28						16 43						16 58				17 15				17 20		
Beckenham Junction 4 🚋	d		16 30						16 45						17 00				17a20				17 23		
Denmark Hill 4	d	16 18		16 22								16 39		16 48		16 52								17 13	
Peckham Rye 4	d	16 21		16 25								16 42		16 51		16 55								17 16	
Nunhead 4	d	16 23		16 27								16 44		16 53		16 57								17 18	
Lewisham 4 🚋	a	16 31												16 58										17 23	
Crofton Park	d			16 30								16 47				17 00									
Catford	d			16 33								16 50				17 03									
Bellingham	d			16 35								16 52				17 05									
Beckenham Hill	d			16 37								16 54				17 07									
Ravensbourne	d			16 39								16 56				17 09									
Shortlands 4	d		16 33	16 41					16 48			16 58			17 03	17 11							17 26		
Bromley South 4	d		16 36	16 44			16a38		16 51	16 49	16 53	17 01			17 06	17 14					17a13	17 19	17 29		17 24
Bickley 4	d		16 39	16 47					16 54			17 04			17 09	17 17							17 31		
Petts Wood 4	d		16 44						16 59			17 08			17 14								17 36		
Orpington 4	d		16a49						17a04			17a13			17a19								17a41		
St Mary Cray	d			16 51						16 55	17 00					17 21									17 30
Swanley 4	d			16 56						16a59	17 04					17 30									17a34
Eynsford	d			17 00												17 34									
Shoreham (Kent)	d			17 04												17 38									
Otford 4	d			17 07							17a12					17 41						17a35			
Bat & Ball	d			17 10												17 44									
Sevenoaks 4	a			17 14												17 49									

A from 21 May until 27 July

Table 195

Mondays to Fridays

until 27 July, 13 Aug to 28 Aug and from 10 Sep

London Victoria/Kentish Town - Catford, Beckenham Junction, Bromley South, Orpington, Otford and Sevenoaks

Network Diagram - see first Page of Table 195

		SE 1	SE		FC	FC	FC 1	FC	SE 1 ✠	SE 1	SE	SE	SE 1		FC	FC	FC 1	SE	FC	SE 1	SE	SE 1 ✠	SE		SE 1
London Victoria 15 ⊖	d	17 12	17 15						17 27	17 28	17 30	17 34	17 42					17 45		17 54	17 56	17 57	18 00		18 03
Brixton ⊖	d		17 22								17 37							17 52					18 07		
Kentish Town ⊖	d					16 58		17 14							17 18	17 28									
St Pancras International 15 ⊖	d				16 58	17 02	17 14	17 18							17 22	17 32	17 36		17 44						
Farringdon ⊖	d				17 03	17 07	17 19	17 23							17 27	17 37	17 41		17 49						
City Thameslink 3	d				17 07	17 11	17 23	17 27							17 31	17 41	17 45		17 53						
London Blackfriars 3 ⊖	d				17 10	17 14	17 25	17 30							17 36	17 44	17 48		17 56						
Elephant & Castle ⊖	d				17 14	17 18	17 29	17 34							17 40	17 48	17 52		18 00						
Loughborough Jn	d					17 22		17 38								17 52									
Herne Hill 4	d		17 24			17a25	17 36	17a42			17 39					17a55		17 54	18 07				18 10		
West Dulwich	d		17 27								17 42							17 57	18 09				18 12		
Sydenham Hill	d		17 29								17 44							17 59	18 11				18 14		
Penge East	d		17 32								17 47							18 02	18 14				18 17		
Kent House 4	d		17 34								17 49							18 04	18a18				18 20		
Beckenham Junction 4 🚋	d		17 37								17 51							18 06					18 22		
Denmark Hill 4	d				17 20							17 43			17 47						18 06				
Peckham Rye 4	d				17 23							17 46			17 50						18 09				
Nunhead 4	d				17 26							17 49			17 52						18 11				
Lewisham 4 🚋	a											17 55									18 17				
Crofton Park	d				17 29										17 55										
Catford	d				17 32										17 58										
Bellingham	d				17 35										18 01										
Beckenham Hill	d				17 37										18 03										
Ravensbourne	d				17 39										18 05										
Shortlands 4	d		17 40		17 43						17 55				18 07			18 10					18 25		
Bromley South 4	d	17 31	17 43		17 46		17 48		17a43	17 50	17 58		17 59		18 10		18 11	18 15		18 19		18a14	18 28		18 24
Bickley 4	d		17 45				17 50				18 00				18 12			18 18					18 31		
Petts Wood 4	d		17 50								18 05							18 26					18 36		
Orpington 4	d		17a55								18a10							18a32					18a41		
St Mary Cray	d	17 38					17 55			17 57			18 06		18 22		18 18			18 25					
Swanley 4	d	17 42			17 55		17a59			18 01			18 11		18 26		18 22			18a29					
Eynsford	d				18 00										18 31										
Shoreham (Kent)	d				18 03										18 34										
Otford 4	d	17a50			18 06					18a09			18a19		18 38		18a30								18a42
Bat & Ball	d				18 14										18 41										
Sevenoaks 4	a				18 23										18 50										

		FC 1	FC	FC	FC	SE	SE	SE 1	SE 1		SE 1 ✠	SE	SE	SE 1	FC	FC	SE	FC 1	FC			FC	SE 1 ✠	SE 1 B	SE 1 A
London Victoria 15 ⊖	d					18 15	18 18	18 18	18 24		18 27	18 30	18 39	18 42			18 45						18 57	18 58	18 58
Brixton ⊖	d					18 22						18 37					18 52								
Kentish Town ⊖	d			17 48											18 08	18 20			18 34						
St Pancras International 15 ⊖	d	17 56	17 48	17 52	18 04										18 12	18 24		18 30	18 38			18 48			
Farringdon ⊖	d	18 01	17 53	17 57	18 09										18 17	18 29		18 35	18 43			18 53			
City Thameslink 3	d	18 05	17 57	18 01	18 13										18 21	18 33		18 39	18 47			18 57			
London Blackfriars 3 ⊖	d	18 10	18 00	18 04	18 16										18 24	18 36		18 42	18 50			19 00			
Elephant & Castle ⊖	d	18 14	18 05	18 08	18 20										18 28	18 40		18 46	18 54			19 04			
Loughborough Jn	d			18 12	18 24											18 44			18 58			19 08			
Herne Hill 4	d	18 21		18a16	18a27	18 24						18 39				18a47	18 54		19a01			19a11			
West Dulwich	d					18 27						18 42					18 56								
Sydenham Hill	d					18 29						18 44					18 58								
Penge East	d					18 32						18 47					19 01								
Kent House 4	d					18 34						18 49					19 03								
Beckenham Junction 4 🚋	d					18 36						18 51					19 06								
Denmark Hill 4	d		18 15				18 28						18 48		18 34			18 52							
Peckham Rye 4	d		18 18				18 32						18 51		18 38			18 55							
Nunhead 4	d		18 20				18 34						18 54		18 40			18 57							
Lewisham 4 🚋	a						18 42						19 02												
Crofton Park	d		18 23												18 43			19 00							
Catford	d		18 26												18 46			19 03							
Bellingham	d		18 29												18 49			19 05							
Beckenham Hill	d		18 31												18 51			19 07							
Ravensbourne	d		18 33												18 53			19 09							
Shortlands 4	d		18 35			18 39						18 55			18 57		19 09	19 13							
Bromley South 4	d	18 31	18 38			18 42		18 39	18 46		18a43	18 58		18 59	19 00		19 12	19 16					19a13	19 19	19 21
Bickley 4	d		18 40			18 45						19 00			19 03		19 15	19 19							
Petts Wood 4	d					18 54						19 07					19 20								
Orpington 4	d					18a59						19a12					19a25								
St Mary Cray	d	18 38	18 45					18 45	18 52					19 06	19 10			19 23						19 25	19 27
Swanley 4	d	18a42	18 53					18 50	18a56					19 11	19 15			19 29						19a29	19a31
Eynsford	d		18 57												19 19			19 33							
Shoreham (Kent)	d		19 01												19 23			19 37							
Otford 4	d		19 04					18a58						19a19	19 26			19 40							
Bat & Ball	d		19 07												19 29			19 43							
Sevenoaks 4	a		19 12												19 37			19 50							

A from 21 May until 27 July

B until 18 May

until 27 July, 13 Aug to 28 Aug and from 10 Sep

London Victoria/Kentish Town - Catford, Beckenham Junction, Bromley South, Orpington, Otford and Sevenoaks

Network Diagram - see first Page of Table 195

		SE	SE ■	SE	SE	FC	FC	FC	SE ■ H	SE	SE	SE ■	SE	SE	SE	FC	FC	SE ■	SE	SE	SE ■	SE	FC
London Victoria ⊖	d	19 00	19 07	19 09	19 10				19 22	19 25	19 28	19 37	19 39	19 40				19 52	19 55	19 58	20 07	20 10	
Brixton ⊖	d	19 07			19 17					19 32				19 47					20 02			20 17	
Kentish Town ⊖	d					18 54									19 26								19 56
St Pancras International ⊖	d					19 00	19 04	19 18							19 30	19 34	19 48						20 00
Farringdon ⊖	d					19 05	19 09	19 23							19 36	19 39	19 53						20 05
City Thameslink	d					19 09	19 13	19 27							19 39	19 43	19 57						20 09
London Blackfriars ⊖	d					19 12	19 16	19 30							19 42	19 46	20 00						20 12
Elephant & Castle ⊖	d					19 16	19 19	19 33							19 46	19 49	20 03						20 16
Loughborough Jn	d						19 23	19 37								19 53	20 07						
Herne Hill	d	19 09			19 19		19a27	19a41		19 34				19 49		19a57	20a11		20 04			20 19	
West Dulwich	d	19 12			19 21					19 36				19 51					20 06			20 21	
Sydenham Hill	d	19 14			19 23					19 38				19 53					20 08			20 23	
Penge East	d	19 17			19 26					19 41				19 56					20 11			20 26	
Kent House	d	19 19			19 28					19 43				19 58					20 13			20 28	
Beckenham Junction	d	19 21			19 30					19 45				20 00					20 15			20 30	
Denmark Hill	d			19 18		19 22							19 48		19 52								20 22
Peckham Rye	d			19 21		19 25							19 51		19 55								20 25
Nunhead	d			19 23		19 27							19 53		19 57								20 27
Lewisham	a			19 31									20 01										
Crofton Park	d					19 30									20 00								20 30
Catford	d					19 33									20 03								20 33
Bellingham	d					19 35									20 05								20 35
Beckenham Hill	d					19 37									20 07								20 37
Ravensbourne	d					19 39									20 09								20 39
Shortlands	d	19 25			19 33	19 41				19 48				20 03	20 11				20 18			20 33	20 41
Bromley South	d	19 28	19 27		19 36	19 44			19a38	19 51	19 49	19 53		20 06	20 14			20a08	20 21	20 19	20 23	20 36	20 44
Bickley	d	19 30			19 39	19 47				19 54				20 09	20 17				20 24			20 39	20 47
Petts Wood	d	19 35			19 44					19 59				20 14					20 29			20 44	
Orpington	d	19a38			19a48					20a02				20a18					20a32			20a47	
St Mary Cray	d					19 51					19 55	20 00			20 21					20 25			20 51
Swanley	d		19 36			19 56					19a59	20 04			20 26					20a29	20 33		20 56
Eynsford	d					20 00									20 30								21 00
Shoreham (Kent)	d					20 04									20 34								21 04
Otford	d		19a44			20 07						20a12			20 37						20a41		21 07
Bat & Ball	d					20 10									20 40								21 10
Sevenoaks	a					20 13									20 43								21 13

		FC	FC	SE ■	SE	SE ■	FC	FC	FC A	SE ■	SE	SE ■	SE ■	FC	FC	SE ■	SE	SE B	SE ■	SE A	FC	SE
London Victoria ⊖	d			20 22	20 25	20 37				20 52	20 55	20 58	21 07			21 22	21 25	21 43	21 52			21 55
Brixton ⊖	d				20 32						21 02						21 32					22 02
Kentish Town ⊖	d						20 26	20 30						20 56	21 01						21 31	
St Pancras International ⊖	d	20 04	20 18				20 30	20 34	20 48					21 00	21 06						21 36	
Farringdon ⊖	d	20 09	20 23				20 35	20 39	20 53					21 05	21 10						21 40	
City Thameslink	d	20 13	20 27				20 39	20 43	20 57					21 09	21 13						21 43	
London Blackfriars ⊖	d	20 16	20 30				20 42	20 46	21 00					21 12	21 16					21 42	21 46	
Elephant & Castle ⊖	d	20 19	20 33				20 46	20 49	21 03					21 16	21 19					21 46	21 49	
Loughborough Jn	d	20 23	20 37					20 53	21 07						21 23						21 53	
Herne Hill	d	20a27	20a41		20 34			20a57	21a11		21 04				21a27		21 34				21a57	22 04
West Dulwich	d				20 36						21 06						21 36					22 06
Sydenham Hill	d				20 38						21 08						21 38					22 08
Penge East	d				20 41						21 11						21 41					22 11
Kent House	d				20 43						21 13						21 43					22 13
Beckenham Junction	d				20 45						21 15						21 45					22 15
Denmark Hill	d						20 52							21 22				21 52		21 52		
Peckham Rye	d						20 55							21 25				21 55		21 55		
Nunhead	d						20 57							21 27				21 57		21 57		
Lewisham	a																					
Crofton Park	d						21 00							21 30				22 00		22 00		
Catford	d						21 03							21 33				22 03		22 03		
Bellingham	d						21 05							21 35				22 05		22 05		
Beckenham Hill	d						21 07							21 37				22 07		22 07		
Ravensbourne	d						21 09							21 39				22 09		22 09		
Shortlands	d				20 48		21 11				21 18			21 41			21 48	22 11		22 11		22 18
Bromley South	d			20a38	20 51	20 53	21 14			21a09	21 21	21 19	21 23	21 44		21a38	21 51	22 14	22 09	22 14		22 21
Bickley	d				20 54		21 17				21 24			21 47			21 54	22 17		22 17		22 24
Petts Wood	d				20 59						21 29						21 59					22 29
Orpington	d				21a02						21a32						22a02					22a32
St Mary Cray	d					21 00	21 21					21 25	21 30	21 51				22 21	22 15	22 21		
Swanley	d					21 04	21 26					21a29	21 34	21 56				22 26	22a19	22 26		
Eynsford	d						21 30							22 00				22 30		22 30		
Shoreham (Kent)	d						21 34							22 04				22 34		22 34		
Otford	d					21a12	21 37						21a42	22 07				22 37		22 37		
Bat & Ball	d						21 40							22 10				22 40		22 40		
Sevenoaks	a						21 43							22 13				22 43		22 43		

A from 21 May until 27 July

B until 18 May

until 27 July, 13 Aug to 28 Aug and from 10 Sep

London Victoria/Kentish Town - Catford, Beckenham Junction, Bromley South, Orpington, Otford and Sevenoaks

Network Diagram - see first Page of Table 195

		SE ■	SE A	FC	SE B	SE ■	SE	SE B	SE ■	SE A	FC A	SE	SE ■	SE A	FC A	SE B	SE ■	SE	SE B	SE ■	SE A	FC A	SE
London Victoria ⊖	d	22 07			22 13	22 22	22 25	22 43	22 52			22 55	23 07			23 13	23 22	23 25	23 43	23 52			23 55
Brixton ⊖	d						22 32					23 02						23 32					00 02
Kentish Town ⊖	d			22 01							22 31				23 01							23 30	
St Pancras International ⊖	d			22 06							22 36				23 06							23 36	
Farringdon ⊖	d			22 10							22 40				23 10							23 40	
City Thameslink	d			22 13							22 43												
London Blackfriars ⊖	d		22 12	22 16						22 42	22 46			23 12	23 16						23 42	23 46	
Elephant & Castle ⊖	d		22 16	22 19						22 46	22 49			23 16	23 19						23 46	23 49	
Loughborough Jn	d			22 23							22 53				23s23								
Herne Hill	d			22a27			22 34				22a57	23 04			23a27			23 34				23a57	00 04
West Dulwich	d						22 36					23 06						23 36					00 06
Sydenham Hill	d						22 38					23 08						23 38					00 08
Penge East	d						22 41					23 11						23 41					00 11
Kent House	d						22 43					23 13						23 43					00 13
Beckenham Junction	d						22 45					23 15						23 45					00 15
Denmark Hill	d		22 22		22 22			22 52		22 52				23 22		23 22			23 52		23 52		
Peckham Rye	d		22 25		22 25			22 55		22 55				23 25		23 25			23 55		23 55		
Nunhead	d		22 27		22 27			22 57		22 57				23 27		23 27			23 57		23 57		
Lewisham	a																						
Crofton Park	d		22 30		22 30			23 00		23 00				23 30		23 30			23 59		23 59		
Catford	d		22 33		22 33			23 03		23 03				23 33		23 33			00 03		00 03		
Bellingham	d		22 35		22 35			23 05		23 05				23 35		23 35			00 05		00 05		
Beckenham Hill	d		22 37		22 37			23 07		23 07				23 37		23 37			00 07		00 07		
Ravensbourne	d		22 39		22 39			23 09		23 09				23 39		23 39			00 09		00 09		
Shortlands	d		22 41		22 41		22 48	23 11		23 11		23 18		23 41		23 41		23 48	00 11		00 11		00 18
Bromley South	d	22 23	22 44		22 44	22a38	22 51	23 14	23 09	23 14		23 21	23 23	23 44		23 44	23a38	23 51	00 14	00 09	00 14		00 21
Bickley	d		22 47		22 47		22 54	23 17		23 17		23 24		23 47		23 47		23 54	00 17		00 17		00 24
Petts Wood	d						22 59	23 21				23 29				23 54		23 59	00 21				00 29
Orpington	d						23a02	23a25				23a32				23a57		00a02	00a25				00a32
St Mary Cray	d	22 30	22 51		22 51				23 15	23 21			23 30	23 51						00 15	00 21		
Swanley	d	22 34	22 56		22 56				23a19	23 26			23 34	23 56						00a19	00 26		
Eynsford	d		23 00		23 00					23 30				23 59							00 30		
Shoreham (Kent)	d		23 04		23 04					23 34				00 04							00 34		
Otford	d	22a42	23 07		23 07					23 37			23a42	00 07							00 37		
Bat & Ball	d		23 10		23 10					23 40				00 10							00 40		
Sevenoaks	a		23 13		23 13					23 43				00 13							00 43		

Mondays to Fridays

30 July to 10 August

		SE	SE ■	SE	SE	SE ■ C	SE	SE	SE	SE ■	SE ■	SE	FC	SE	FC	SE ■	SE	SE	SE ■	SE	SE	SE ■	FC
London Victoria ⊖	d		23p52		23p55	00 07	00 35	00 45	00 56	01 00	05 22			05 40		05 52	05 57		06 07	06 10	06 14	06 22	
Brixton ⊖	d				00 02			00 52						05 47						06 17			
Kentish Town ⊖	d														05 50								05 54
St Pancras International ⊖	d												05 36		05 54								05 58
Farringdon ⊖	d												05 42		06 00								06 04
City Thameslink	d											05 26	05 44		06 03								06 07
London Blackfriars ⊖	d	23p12		23p42								05 28	05 47		06 06								06 10
Elephant & Castle ⊖	d	23p16		23p46								05 32	05 50		06 09								06 16
Loughborough Jn	d														06 13								
Herne Hill	d				00 04		00 43	00 56					05a57	05 49	06a17					06 19			
West Dulwich	d				00 06			00 58						05 51						06 21			
Sydenham Hill	d				00 08			01 00						05 53						06 23			
Penge East	d				00 11		00 48	01 03						05 56						06 26			
Kent House	d				00 13			01 05						05 58						06 28			
Beckenham Junction	d				00 15		00 50	01 08						06 00						06 30			
Denmark Hill	d	23p22		23p52					01 06			05 39					06 07				06 24		06 22
Peckham Rye	d	23p25		23p55					01 08			05 41									06 29		06 25
Nunhead	d	23p27		23p57					01 11			05 44									06 31		06 27
Lewisham	a																06 15				06 41		
Crofton Park	d	23p30		23p59					01 14			05 47											06 30
Catford	d	23p33		00 03					01 16			05 49											06 33
Bellingham	d	23p35		00 05					01 19			05 52											06 35
Beckenham Hill	d	23p37		00 07					01 21			05 54											06 37
Ravensbourne	d	23p39		00 09					01 23			05 56											06 39
Shortlands	d	23p41		00 11	00 18			01 11	01 25			05 58		06 03						06 33			06 41
Bromley South	d	23p44	00 09	00 14	00 21	00 25	00 55	01 14	01 28	01 16	05 39	06 01		06 06		06 09		06 16	06 23	06 37		06 39	06 44
Bickley	d	23p47		00 17	00 24			01 16	01 30			06 03		06 09				06 18		06 39			06 47
Petts Wood	d				00 29			01 21	01 35					06 14						06 44			
Orpington	d				00a32			01a27	01a42					06a18						06a49			
St Mary Cray	d	23p51	00 15	00 21		00 32	01 01			01 23	05 45	06 08						06 23	06 30			06 45	06 51
Swanley	d	23p56	00a19	00 26		00 36	01a05			01 27	05a49	06 12				06a19		06 28	06 34			06a49	06 56
Eynsford	d	23p59		00 30						01 32		06 17						06 32					07 00
Shoreham (Kent)	d	00 04		00 34						01 35		06 20						06 36					07 04
Otford	d	00 07		00 37		00a44				01a38		06 23						06 39	06a42				07 07
Bat & Ball	d	00 10		00 40								06 26						06 42					07 10
Sevenoaks	a	00 13		00 43								06 29						06 45					07 14

A from 21 May until 27 July

B until 18 May

C not 30 July, 6 August

London Victoria/Kentish Town - Catford, Beckenham Junction, Bromley South, Orpington, Otford and Sevenoaks

Network Diagram - see first Page of Table 195

		FC	SE	SE ■	SE ■	SE	FC	SE	SE ■	SE ■	FC ■	FC	FC ■	SE	SE ■	SE	SE ■	FC	FC ■	FC	FC	SE	SE
London Victoria ■	⊖ d		06 30	06 37	06 45			06 50	06 58	07 07				07 10	07 22	07 25	07 36					07 40	07 43
Brixton	⊖ d		06 37					06 57						07 17		07 32						07 47	
Kentish Town	⊖ d	06 08					06 30					06 48						07 08		07 24			
St Pancras International ■	⊖ d	06 12					06 34				06 44	06 52	07 04					07 12	07 16	07 28	07 32		
Farringdon	⊖ d	06 18					06 40				06 50	06 58	07 10					07 18	07 22	07 34	07 38		
City Thameslink ■	d	06 21				06 39	06 43				06 53	07 01	07 13					07 21	07 25	07 37	07 41		
London Blackfriars ■	⊖ d	06 24				06 42	06 46				06 58	07 04	07 16					07 24	07 28	07 40	07 44		
Elephant & Castle	⊖ d	06 27				06 46	06 49				07 02	07 07	07 19					07 28	07 33	07 44	07 47		
Loughborough Jn	d	06 31					06 53					07 11	07 23						07 37		07 51		
Herne Hill ■	d	06a35	06 39				06a57	06 59				07a15	07a27	07 19		07 34			07a40		07a55	07 49	
West Dulwich	d		06 41					07 02						07 21		07 36						07 51	
Sydenham Hill	d		06 43					07 04						07 23		07 38						07 53	
Penge East	d		06 46					07 07						07 26		07 41						07 56	
Kent House ■	d		06 48					07 09						07 28		07 43						07 58	
Beckenham Junction ■	⇌ d		06 50					07 11						07 30		07 45						08 00	
Denmark Hill ■	d					06 52					07 09							07 34		07 50			07 53
Peckham Rye ■	d					06 55					07 12							07 36		07 53			07 56
Nunhead ■	d					06 57					07 14							07 39		07 56			07 59
Lewisham ■	⇌ a																						08 06
Crofton Park	d					07 00					07 17							07 42					
Catford	d					07 03					07 20							07 44		08 00			
Bellingham	d					07 05					07 22							07 47		08 02			
Beckenham Hill	d					07 07					07 24							07 49					
Ravensbourne	d					07 09					07 26							07 51					
Shortlands ■	d		06 54			07 11		07 14			07 28			07 33		07 48		07 54				08 03	
Bromley South ■	d		06 57	06 58	07 02	07 14		07 17	07 19	07 23	07 31			07 38	07 40	07 51	07 53	07 57		08a10		08 06	
Bickley ■	d		07 00			07 17		07 20			07 34			07 40		07 54		08 00				08 09	
Petts Wood ■	d		07 04					07 24						07 49		07 59						08 14	
Orpington ■	d		07a07					07a28						07a53		08a02						08a19	
St Mary Cray	d			07 04	07 08	07 21			07 25	07 30	07 38						08 00	08 04					
Swanley ■	d			07 08	07a12	07 26			07a29	07 34	07 44				07a48		08 04	08 10					
Eynsford	d					07 30					07 48							08 15					
Shoreham (Kent)	d					07 34					07 52							08 18					
Otford ■	d			07a16		07 37				07a42	07 55						08a12	08 22					
Bat & Ball	d					07 40					07 58							08 25					
Sevenoaks ■	a					07 43					08 01							08 28					

		SE ■	SE	SE ■	SE ■	FC	FC	FC	SE	SE	FC	SE ■	SE	SE ■	FC ■	FC ■	SE	SE	FC	FC ■	FC	FC
London Victoria ■	⊖ d	07 52	07 55	07 58	08 07				08 09	08 10		08 22	08 25	08 37			08 39	08 40				
Brixton	⊖ d		08 02							08 17			08 32					08 47				
Kentish Town	⊖ d						07 44									08 20					08 36	
St Pancras International ■	⊖ d					07 38	07 48	07 52			08 12				08 16	08 24			08 28	08 32	08 40	08 44
Farringdon	⊖ d					07 44	07 54	07 58			08 18				08 22	08 30			08 34	08 38	08 46	08 50
City Thameslink ■	d					07 47	07 57	08 01			08 21				08 25	08 33			08 37	08 41	08 49	08 53
London Blackfriars ■	⊖ d					07 50	08 00	08 04			08 24				08 28	08 36			08 40	08 44	08 52	08 56
Elephant & Castle	⊖ d					07 54	08 04	08 07			08 27				08 32				08 44	08 47	08 56	09 00
Loughborough Jn	d							08 11			08 31									08 51		09 04
Herne Hill ■	d		08 04					08a15		08 19	08a36		08 34			08a45		08 48		08a57		09a08
West Dulwich	d		08 06							08 21			08 36					08 51				
Sydenham Hill	d		08 08							08 23			08 38					08 53				
Penge East	d		08 11							08 26			08 41					08 56				
Kent House ■	d		08 13							08 28			08 43					08 58				
Beckenham Junction ■	⇌ d		08 15							08 30			08 45					09 00				
Denmark Hill ■	d					08 00	08 10		08 18						08 38		08 48		08 52		09 02	
Peckham Rye ■	d					08 03	08 13		08 21						08 41		08 51		08 55			
Nunhead ■	d					08 06	08 15		08 24						08 43		08 53		08 57			
Lewisham ■	⇌ a								08 30								09 01					
Crofton Park	d					08 09	08 18								08 46				09 00			
Catford	d					08 12	08 21								08 49				09 03		09 09	
Bellingham	d					08 15	08 23								08 51				09 05			
Beckenham Hill	d					08 17	08 25								08 53				09 07			
Ravensbourne	d					08 19	08 27								08 55				09 09			
Shortlands ■	d					08 22	08 30			08 33			08 48		08 57			09 03	09 11			
Bromley South ■	d	08a09	08 22	08 28	08 23	08 25	08 33			08 36		08a39	08 51	08 53	09 00			09 07	09 14		09 18	
Bickley ■	d		08 24			08 28	08 35			08 39			08 54		09 03			09 09	09 17		09 20	
Petts Wood ■	d		08 29			08 32				08 44			08 59					09 14				
Orpington ■	d		08a32			08a36				08a47			09a02					09a17				
St Mary Cray	d			08 34	08 30		08 40							09 00	09 07				09 21		09 25	
Swanley ■	d			08a39	08 34		08 44							09 04	09 12				09 26		09 36	
Eynsford	d						08 49								09 16				09 30		09 40	
Shoreham (Kent)	d						08 52								09 20				09 34		09 44	
Otford ■	d				08a42		08 55							09a12	09 23				09 37		09 47	
Bat & Ball	d						08 58								09 26				09 40		09 50	
Sevenoaks ■	a						09 01								09 29				09 45		09 53	

London Victoria/Kentish Town - Catford, Beckenham Junction, Bromley South, Orpington, Otford and Sevenoaks

Network Diagram - see first Page of Table 195

		FC	SE ■	SE	SE ■	SE ■	SE	SE	FC	FC	SE ■	SE	SE ■	SE	SE	FC	FC	FC	SE ■ ⚲	SE	SE ■	SE ■	SE
London Victoria ■	⊖ d		08 52	08 55	08 58	09 07	09 09	09 10			09 22	09 25	09 37	09 39	09 40				09 52	09 55	09 58	10 07	10 09
Brixton	⊖ d			09 02				09 17				09 32			09 47					10 02			
Kentish Town	⊖ d	08 52								09 12						09 26		09 44					
St Pancras International ■	⊖ d	08 56							09 00	09 16						09 30	09 34	09 48					
Farringdon	⊖ d	09 02							09 06	09 22						09 36	09 40	09 53					
City Thameslink ■	d	09 05							09 09	09 25						09 39	09 43	09 57					
London Blackfriars ■	⊖ d	09 08							09 12	09 28						09 42	09 46	10 00					
Elephant & Castle	⊖ d	09 12							09 16	09 31						09 46	09 49	10 03					
Loughborough Jn	d	09 16								09 35							09 53	10 07					
Herne Hill ■	d	09a21		09 04				09 19		09a39		09 34			09 49		09a57	10a11		10 04			
West Dulwich	d			09 06				09 21				09 36			09 51					10 06			
Sydenham Hill	d			09 08				09 23				09 38			09 53					10 08			
Penge East	d			09 11				09 26				09 41			09 56					10 11			
Kent House ■	d			09 13				09 28				09 43			09 58					10 13			
Beckenham Junction ■	⇌ d			09 15				09 30				09 45			10 00					10 15			
Denmark Hill ■	d						09 18		09 22					09 48		09 52							10 18
Peckham Rye ■	d						09 21		09 25					09 51		09 55							10 21
Nunhead ■	d						09 24		09 27					09 53		09 57							10 23
Lewisham ■	⇌ a						09 31							10 01									10 31
Crofton Park	d								09 30							10 00							
Catford	d								09 33							10 03							
Bellingham	d								09 35							10 05							
Beckenham Hill	d								09 37							10 07							
Ravensbourne	d								09 39							10 09							
Shortlands ■	d			09 18				09 33	09 41			09 48			10 03	10 11				10 18			
Bromley South ■	d		09a08	09 21	09 19	09 23		09 36	09 44		09a38	09 52	09 53		10 07	10 14			10a08	10 21	10 19	10 23	
Bickley ■	d			09 24				09 39	09 47			09 54			10 09	10 17				10 24			
Petts Wood ■	d			09 29				09 44				09 59			10 14					10 29			
Orpington ■	d			09a33				09a47				10a02			10a17					10a32			
St Mary Cray	d				09 25				09 51				10 00			10 21					10 25		
Swanley ■	d				09a29	09 33			09 56				10 04			10 26					10a29	10 33	
Eynsford	d								10 00							10 30							
Shoreham (Kent)	d								10 04							10 34							
Otford ■	d					09a41			10 07				10a12			10 37						10a41	
Bat & Ball	d								10 10							10 40							
Sevenoaks ■	a								10 13							10 43							

		SE	FC	FC	FC	SE ■ ⚲	SE	SE ■	SE	SE	FC	FC	FC	SE ■ ⚲	SE	SE ■	SE ■	SE	SE	FC	FC	FC
London Victoria ■	⊖ d	10 10				10 22	10 25	10 37	10 39	10 40				10 52	10 55	10 58	11 07	11 09	11 10			
Brixton	⊖ d	10 17					10 32			10 47					11 02				11 17			
Kentish Town	⊖ d		09 54	10 00	10 14						10 26	10 30	10 44							10 56	11 00	11 14
St Pancras International ■	⊖ d		10 00	10 04	10 18						10 30	10 34	10 48							11 00	11 04	11 18
Farringdon	⊖ d		10 05	10 09	10 24						10 35	10 39	10 54							11 05	11 09	11 24
City Thameslink ■	d		10 09	10 13	10 27						10 39	10 43	10 57							11 09	11 13	11 27
London Blackfriars ■	⊖ d		10 12	10 16	10 30						10 42	10 46	11 00							11 12	11 16	11 30
Elephant & Castle	⊖ d		10 16	10 19	10 33						10 46	10 49	11 03							11 16	11 19	11 33
Loughborough Jn	d			10 23	10 37							10 53	11 07								11 23	11 37
Herne Hill ■	d	10 19		10a27	10a41		10 34			10 49		10a57	11a11		11 04				11 19		11a27	11a41
West Dulwich	d	10 21					10 36			10 51					11 06				11 21			
Sydenham Hill	d	10 23					10 38			10 53					11 08				11 23			
Penge East	d	10 26					10 41			10 56					11 11				11 26			
Kent House ■	d	10 28					10 43			10 58					11 13				11 28			
Beckenham Junction ■	⇌ d	10 30					10 45			11 00					11 15				11 30			
Denmark Hill ■	d		10 22						10 48		10 52							11 18		11 22		
Peckham Rye ■	d		10 25						10 51		10 55							11 21		11 25		
Nunhead ■	d		10 27						10 53		10 57							11 23		11 27		
Lewisham ■	⇌ a								11 01									11 31				
Crofton Park	d		10 30								11 00									11 30		
Catford	d		10 33								11 03									11 33		
Bellingham	d		10 35								11 05									11 35		
Beckenham Hill	d		10 37								11 07									11 37		
Ravensbourne	d		10 39								11 09									11 39		
Shortlands ■	d	10 33	10 41				10 48			11 03	11 11				11 18				11 33	11 41		
Bromley South ■	d	10 36	10 44			10a38	10 51	10 53		11 06	11 14			11a08	11 21	11 19	11 23		11 36	11 44		
Bickley ■	d	10 39	10 47				10 54			11 09	11 17				11 24				11 39	11 47		
Petts Wood ■	d	10 44					10 59			11 14					11 29				11 44			
Orpington ■	d	10a47					11a02			11a17					11a32				11a47			
St Mary Cray	d		10 51					11 00			11 21					11 25				11 51		
Swanley ■	d		10 56					11 04			11 26					11a29	11 33			11 56		
Eynsford	d		11 00								11 30									12 00		
Shoreham (Kent)	d		11 04								11 34									12 04		
Otford ■	d		11 07					11a12			11 37						11a41			12 07		
Bat & Ball	d		11 10								11 40									12 10		
Sevenoaks ■	a		11 13								11 43									12 13		

Table 195

Mondays to Fridays
30 July to 10 August

London Victoria/Kentish Town - Catford, Beckenham Junction, Bromley South, Orpington, Otford and Sevenoaks

Network Diagram - see first Page of Table 195

Station		SE 1	SE	SE 1	SE	SE	FC	FC	FC	SE 1	SE	SE 1	SE 1	SE	SE	FC	FC	FC	SE 1	SE	SE 1	SE	SE
London Victoria 15	⊖ d	11 22	11 25	11 37	11 39	11 40				11 52	11 55	11 58	12 07	12 09	12 10				12 22	12 25	12 37	12 39	12 40
Brixton	⊖ d		11 32			11 47					12 02				12 17					12 32			12 47
Kentish Town	⊖ d						11 26	11 30	11 44							11 56	12 00	12 14					
St Pancras International 15	⊖ d						11 30	11 34	11 48							12 00	12 04	12 18					
Farringdon	⊖ d						11 35	11 39	11 53							12 05	12 09	12 23					
City Thameslink 3	d						11 39	11 43	11 57							12 09	12 13	12 27					
London Blackfriars 3	⊖ d						11 42	11 46	12 00							12 12	12 16	12 30					
Elephant & Castle	⊖ d						11 46	11 49	12 03							12 16	12 19	12 33					
Loughborough Jn	d							11 53	12 07								12 23	12 37					
Herne Hill 4	d		11 34			11 49		11a57	12a11		12 04				12 19		12a27	12a41		12 34			12 49
West Dulwich	d		11 36			11 51					12 06				12 21					12 36			12 51
Sydenham Hill	d		11 38			11 53					12 08				12 23					12 38			12 53
Penge East	d		11 41			11 56					12 11				12 26					12 41			12 56
Kent House 4	d		11 43			11 58					12 13				12 28					12 43			12 58
Beckenham Junction 4	⇌ d		11 45			12 00					12 15				12 30					12 45			13 00
Denmark Hill 4	d				11 48		11 52							12 18		12 22						12 48	
Peckham Rye 4	d				11 51		11 55							12 21		12 25						12 51	
Nunhead 4	d				11 53		11 57							12 23		12 27						12 53	
Lewisham 4	⇌ a				12 01									12 31								13 01	
Crofton Park	d						12 00									12 30							
Catford	d						12 03									12 33							
Bellingham	d						12 05									12 35							
Beckenham Hill	d						12 07									12 37							
Ravensbourne	d						12 09									12 39							
Shortlands 4	d		11 48			12 03	12 11				12 18				12 33	12 41				12 48			13 03
Bromley South 4	d	11a38	11 51	11 53		12 06	12 14			12a08	12 21	12 19	12 23		12 36	12 44			12a38	12 51	12 53		13 06
Bickley 4	d		11 54			12 09	12 17				12 24				12 39	12 47				12 54			13 09
Petts Wood 4	d		11 59			12 14					12 29				12 44					12 59			13 14
Orpington 4	d		12a02			12a17					12a32				12a47					13a02			13a17
St Mary Cray	d			12 00			12 21					12 25				12 51					13 00		
Swanley 4	d			12 04			12 26					12a29	12 33			12 56					13 04		
Eynsford	d						12 30									13 00							
Shoreham (Kent)	d						12 34									13 04							
Otford 4	d			12a12			12 37						12a41			13 07					13a12		
Bat & Ball	d						12 40									13 10							
Sevenoaks 4	a						12 43									13 13							

Station		FC	FC	FC	SE 1	SE	SE 1	SE 1	SE	SE	FC	FC	FC	SE 1	SE	SE 1	SE	SE	FC	FC	FC	SE 1	SE
London Victoria 15	⊖ d				12 52	12 55	12 58	13 07	13 09	13 10				13 22	13 25	13 37	13 39	13 40				13 52	13 55
Brixton	⊖ d					13 02				13 17					13 32			13 47					14 02
Kentish Town	⊖ d	12 26	12 30	12 44							12 56	13 00	13 14						13 26	13 30	13 44		
St Pancras International 15	⊖ d	12 30	12 34	12 48							13 00	13 04	13 18						13 30	13 34	13 48		
Farringdon	⊖ d	12 35	12 39	12 53							13 05	13 09	13 23						13 35	13 39	13 53		
City Thameslink 3	d	12 39	12 43	12 57							13 09	13 13	13 27						13 39	13 43	13 57		
London Blackfriars 3	⊖ d	12 42	12 46	13 00							13 12	13 16	13 30						13 42	13 46	14 00		
Elephant & Castle	⊖ d	12 46	12 49	13 03							13 16	13 19	13 33						13 46	13 49	14 03		
Loughborough Jn	d		12 53	13 07								13 23	13 37							13 53	14 07		
Herne Hill 4	d		12a57	13a11		13 04				13 19		13a27	13a41		13 34			13 49		13a57	14a11		14 04
West Dulwich	d					13 06				13 21					13 36			13 51					14 06
Sydenham Hill	d					13 08				13 23					13 38			13 53					14 08
Penge East	d					13 11				13 26					13 41			13 56					14 11
Kent House 4	d					13 13				13 28					13 43			13 58					14 13
Beckenham Junction 4	⇌ d					13 15				13 30					13 45			14 00					14 15
Denmark Hill 4	d	12 52							13 18		13 22						13 48		13 52				
Peckham Rye 4	d	12 55							13 22		13 25						13 51		13 55				
Nunhead 4	d	12 57							13 24		13 27						13 53		13 57				
Lewisham 4	⇌ a								13 31								14 01						
Crofton Park	d	13 00									13 30								14 00				
Catford	d	13 03									13 33								14 03				
Bellingham	d	13 05									13 35								14 05				
Beckenham Hill	d	13 07									13 37								14 07				
Ravensbourne	d	13 09									13 39								14 09				
Shortlands 4	d	13 11				13 18				13 33	13 41				13 48			14 03	14 11				14 18
Bromley South 4	d	13 14			13a08	13 21	13 19	13 23		13 36	13 44			13a38	13 51	13 53		14 06	14 14			14a08	14 21
Bickley 4	d	13 17				13 24				13 39	13 47				13 54			14 09	14 17				14 24
Petts Wood 4	d					13 29				13 44					13 59			14 14					14 29
Orpington 4	d					13a32				13a47					14a02			14a17					14a32
St Mary Cray	d	13 21					13 25				13 51					14 00			14 21				
Swanley 4	d	13 26					13a29	13 33			13 56					14 04			14 26				
Eynsford	d	13 30									14 00								14 30				
Shoreham (Kent)	d	13 34									14 04								14 34				
Otford 4	d	13 37						13a41			14 07					14a12			14 37				
Bat & Ball	d	13 40									14 10								14 40				
Sevenoaks 4	a	13 43									14 13								14 43				

Table 195

Mondays to Fridays
30 July to 10 August

London Victoria/Kentish Town - Catford, Beckenham Junction, Bromley South, Orpington, Otford and Sevenoaks

Network Diagram - see first Page of Table 195

Station		SE 1	SE 1	SE	SE	FC	FC	FC	SE 1	SE	SE 1	SE	SE	FC	FC	FC	SE 1	SE	SE 1	SE 1	SE	SE
London Victoria 15	⊖ d	13 58	14 07	14 09	14 10				14 22	14 25	14 37	14 39	14 40				14 52	14 55	14 58	15 07	15 09	15 10
Brixton	⊖ d				14 17					14 32			14 47					15 02				15 17
Kentish Town	⊖ d					13 56	14 00	14 14						14 26	14 30	14 44						
St Pancras International 15	⊖ d					14 00	14 04	14 18						14 30	14 34	14 48						
Farringdon	⊖ d					14 05	14 09	14 23						14 35	14 39	14 53						
City Thameslink 3	d					14 09	14 13	14 27						14 39	14 43	14 57						
London Blackfriars 3	⊖ d					14 12	14 16	14 30						14 42	14 46	15 00						
Elephant & Castle	⊖ d					14 16	14 19	14 33						14 46	14 49	15 03						
Loughborough Jn	d						14 23	14 37							14 53	15 07						
Herne Hill 4	d				14 19		14a27	14a41		14 34			14 49		14a57	15a11		15 04				15 19
West Dulwich	d				14 21					14 36			14 51					15 06				15 21
Sydenham Hill	d				14 23					14 38			14 53					15 08				15 23
Penge East	d				14 26					14 41			14 56					15 11				15 26
Kent House 4	d				14 28					14 43			14 58					15 13				15 28
Beckenham Junction 4	⇌ d				14 30					14 45			15 00					15 15				15 30
Denmark Hill 4	d			14 18		14 22						14 48		14 52							15 18	
Peckham Rye 4	d			14 21		14 25						14 51		14 55							15 21	
Nunhead 4	d			14 23		14 27						14 53		14 57							15 23	
Lewisham 4	⇌ a			14 31								15 01									15 31	
Crofton Park	d					14 30								15 00								
Catford	d					14 33								15 03								
Bellingham	d					14 35								15 05								
Beckenham Hill	d					14 37								15 07								
Ravensbourne	d					14 39								15 09								
Shortlands 4	d				14 33	14 41				14 48			15 03	15 11				15 18				15 33
Bromley South 4	d	14 19	14 23		14 36	14 44			14a38	14 51	14 53		15 06	15 14			15a08	15 21	15 19	15 23		15 36
Bickley 4	d				14 39	14 47				14 54			15 09	15 17				15 24				15 39
Petts Wood 4	d				14 44					14 59			15 14					15 29				15 44
Orpington 4	d				14a47					15a02			15a17					15a32				15a47
St Mary Cray	d	14 25				14 51					15 00			15 21					15 25			
Swanley 4	d	14a29	14 33			14 56					15 04			15 26					15a29	15 33		
Eynsford	d					15 00								15 30								
Shoreham (Kent)	d					15 04								15 34								
Otford 4	d		14a41			15 07					15a12			15 37						15a41		
Bat & Ball	d					15 10								15 40								
Sevenoaks 4	a					15 13								15 43								

Station		FC	FC	FC	SE 1	SE	SE 1	SE	SE	FC	FC	FC	SE 1	SE	SE	SE 1	SE 1	SE	SE	FC	FC	SE 1	SE
London Victoria 15	⊖ d				15 22	15 25	15 37	15 39	15 40				15 52		15 55	15 58	16 07	16 09	16 10			16 22	16 25
Brixton	⊖ d					15 32			15 47						16 02				16 17				16 32
Kentish Town	⊖ d	14 56	15 00	15 14						15 26	15 30	15 44								15 56	16 00		
St Pancras International 15	⊖ d	15 00	15 04	15 18						15 30	15 34	15 48								16 00	16 04		
Farringdon	⊖ d	15 05	15 09	15 23						15 35	15 39	15 53								16 05	16 09		
City Thameslink 3	d	15 09	15 13	15 27						15 39	15 43	15 57								16 09	16 13		
London Blackfriars 3	⊖ d	15 12	15 16	15 30						15 42	15 46	16 00								16 12	16 16		
Elephant & Castle	⊖ d	15 16	15 19	15 33						15 46	15 49	16 03								16 16	16 19		
Loughborough Jn	d		15 23	15 37							15 53	16 07									16 23		
Herne Hill 4	d		15a27	15a41		15 34			15 49		15a57	16a11			16 04				16 19		16a27		16 34
West Dulwich	d					15 36			15 51						16 06				16 21				16 36
Sydenham Hill	d					15 38			15 53						16 08				16 23				16 38
Penge East	d					15 41			15 56						16 11				16 26				16 41
Kent House 4	d					15 43			15 58						16 13				16 28				16 43
Beckenham Junction 4	⇌ d					15 45			16 00					16 12	16 15				16 30				16 45
Denmark Hill 4	d	15 22						15 48		15 52								16 18		16 22			
Peckham Rye 4	d	15 25						15 51		15 55								16 21		16 25			
Nunhead 4	d	15 27						15 53		15 57								16 23		16 27			
Lewisham 4	⇌ a							16 01										16 31					
Crofton Park	d	15 30								16 00										16 30			
Catford	d	15 33								16 03										16 33			
Bellingham	d	15 35								16 05										16 35			
Beckenham Hill	d	15 37								16 07										16 37			
Ravensbourne	d	15 39								16 09										16 39			
Shortlands 4	d	15 41				15 48			16 03	16 11					16 18				16 33	16 41			16 48
Bromley South 4	d	15 44			15a38	15 51	15 53		16 06	16 14			16a08		16 21	16 19	16 23		16 36	16 44		16a38	16 51
Bickley 4	d	15 47				15 54			16 09	16 17					16 24				16 39	16 47			16 54
Petts Wood 4	d					15 59			16 14						16 29				16 44				16 59
Orpington 4	d					16a02			16a17						16a32				16a49				17a04
St Mary Cray	d	15 51					16 00			16 21						16 25				16 51			
Swanley 4	d	15 56					16 04			16 26						16a29	16 33			16 56			
Eynsford	d	16 00								16 30										17 00			
Shoreham (Kent)	d	16 04								16 34										17 04			
Otford 4	d	16 07					16a12			16 37							16a41			17 07			
Bat & Ball	d	16 10								16 40										17 10			
Sevenoaks 4	a	16 13								16 43										17 14			

London Victoria/Kentish Town - Catford, Beckenham Junction, Bromley South, Orpington, Otford and Sevenoaks

Network Diagram - see first Page of Table 195

	SE 1	SE 1	FC	FC	SE	SE	FC	FC	FC 1	FC	SE 1 ⌶	SE 1	SE	SE	SE	SE 1	SE	FC	FC	FC 1	FC
London Victoria ⊖ d	16 28	16 37			16 39	16 40					16 57	16 58	16 59	17 04	17 04	17 12	17 15				
Brixton ⊖ d						16 47							17 06				17 22				
Kentish Town ⊖ d			16 10	16 14			16 24	16 30		16 46									16 58		17 14
St Pancras International ⊖ d			16 14	16 18			16 28	16 34	16 40	16 52								16 58	17 02	17 14	17 18
Farringdon ⊖ d			16 19	16 23			16 33	16 39	16 45	16 57								17 03	17 07	17 19	17 23
City Thameslink d			16 23	16 27			16 37	16 43	16 49	17 01								17 07	17 11	17 23	17 27
London Blackfriars ⊖ d			16 26	16 30			16 42	16 46	16 52	17 04								17 10	17 14	17 25	17 30
Elephant & Castle ⊖ d			16 30	16 33			16 46	16 49	16 56	17 08								17 14	17 18	17 29	17 34
Loughborough Jn d				16 37				16 53	17 00	17 12									17 22		17 38
Herne Hill d				16a41		16 49		16a57	17 06	17a15			17 11				17 24		17a25	17 36	17a42
West Dulwich d						16 51			17 08				17 13				17 27				
Sydenham Hill d						16 53			17 10				17 15				17 29				
Penge East d						16 56			17 13				17 18				17 32				
Kent House d						16 58			17 15				17 20				17 34				
Beckenham Junction d						17 00			17a20				17 23				17 37				
Denmark Hill d			16 39		16 48		16 52							17 13				17 20			
Peckham Rye d			16 42		16 51		16 55							17 16				17 23			
Nunhead d			16 44		16 53		16 57							17 18				17 26			
Lewisham a					16 58									17 23							
Crofton Park d			16 47				17 00											17 29			
Catford d			16 50				17 03											17 32			
Bellingham d			16 52				17 05											17 35			
Beckenham Hill d			16 54				17 07											17 37			
Ravensbourne d			16 56				17 09											17 39			
Shortlands d			16 58			17 03	17 11						17 26				17 40	17 43			
Bromley South d	16 49	16 53	17 01			17 06	17 14				17a13	17 19	17 29		17 24	17 31	17 43	17 46		17 48	
Bickley d			17 04			17 09	17 17						17 31				17 45			17 50	
Petts Wood d			17 08			17 14							17 36				17 50				
Orpington d			17a13			17a19							17a41				17a55				
St Mary Cray d	16 55	17 00					17 21								17 30	17 38				17 55	
Swanley d	16a59	17 04					17 30								17a34	17 42		17 55		17a59	
Eynsford d							17 34											18 00			
Shoreham (Kent) d							17 38											18 03			
Otford d		17a12					17 41					17a35				17a50		18 06			
Bat & Ball d							17 44											18 14			
Sevenoaks a							17 49											18 23			

	SE 1 ⌶	SE 1	SE	SE	SE 1	FC	FC	FC 1	SE	FC	SE 1	SE	SE 1 ⌶	SE	SE 1	FC 1	FC	FC	FC	SE	SE	SE 1
London Victoria ⊖ d	17 27	17 28	17 30	17 34	17 42				17 45		17 54	17 56	17 57	18 00	18 03					18 15	18 18	18 18
Brixton ⊖ d			17 37						17 52					18 07						18 22		
Kentish Town ⊖ d						17 18	17 28											17 48				
St Pancras International ⊖ d						17 22	17 32	17 36		17 44						17 56	17 48	17 52	18 04			
Farringdon ⊖ d						17 27	17 37	17 41		17 49						18 01	17 53	17 57	18 09			
City Thameslink d						17 31	17 41	17 45		17 53						18 05	17 57	18 01	18 13			
London Blackfriars ⊖ d						17 36	17 44	17 48		17 56						18 10	18 00	18 04	18 16			
Elephant & Castle ⊖ d						17 40	17 48	17 52		18 00						18 14	18 05	18 08	18 20			
Loughborough Jn d							17 52											18 12	18 24			
Herne Hill d			17 39				17a55		17 54	18 07				18 10		18 21		18a16	18a27	18 24		
West Dulwich d			17 42						17 57	18 09				18 12						18 27		
Sydenham Hill d			17 44						17 59	18 11				18 14						18 29		
Penge East d			17 47						18 02	18 14				18 17						18 32		
Kent House d			17 49						18 04	18a19				18 19						18 34		
Beckenham Junction d			17 51						18 06					18 22						18 36		
Denmark Hill d				17 43		17 47						18 06					18 15				18 28	
Peckham Rye d				17 46		17 50						18 09					18 18				18 32	
Nunhead d				17 49		17 52						18 11					18 20				18 34	
Lewisham a				17 55								18 17									18 42	
Crofton Park d						17 55											18 23					
Catford d						17 58											18 26					
Bellingham d						18 01											18 29					
Beckenham Hill d						18 03											18 31					
Ravensbourne d						18 05											18 33					
Shortlands d			17 55			18 07			18 10					18 25			18 35			18 39		
Bromley South d	17a43	17 50	17 58		17 59	18 10		18 11	18 15		18 19		18a14	18 28	18 24	18 31	18 38			18 42		18 39
Bickley d			18 00			18 12			18 18					18 31			18 40			18 45		
Petts Wood d			18 05						18 26					18 36						18 54		
Orpington d			18a10						18a31					18a41						18a59		
St Mary Cray d		17 57			18 06	18 22		18 18			18 25					18 38	18 45					18 45
Swanley d		18 01			18 11	18 26		18 22			18a29					18a42	18 53					18 50
Eynsford d						18 31											18 57					
Shoreham (Kent) d						18 34											19 01					
Otford d		18a09			18a19	18 38		18a30							18a42		19 04					18a58
Bat & Ball d						18 41											19 07					
Sevenoaks a						18 50											19 12					

London Victoria/Kentish Town - Catford, Beckenham Junction, Bromley South, Orpington, Otford and Sevenoaks

Network Diagram - see first Page of Table 195

	SE 1	SE 1 ⌶	SE	SE	SE 1	FC	FC	SE	FC 1	FC	FC	SE 1 ⌶	SE 1	SE	SE 1	SE	SE	FC	FC	FC	SE 1 ⌶	SE
London Victoria ⊖ d	18 24	18 27	18 30	18 39	18 42			18 45				18 57	18 58	19 00	19 07	19 09	19 10				19 22	19 25
Brixton ⊖ d			18 37					18 52						19 07			19 17					19 32
Kentish Town ⊖ d						18 08	18 20			18 34								18 54				
St Pancras International ⊖ d						18 12	18 24		18 30	18 38	18 48							19 00	19 04	19 18		
Farringdon ⊖ d						18 17	18 29		18 35	18 43	18 53							19 05	19 09	19 23		
City Thameslink d						18 21	18 33		18 39	18 47	18 57							19 09	19 13	19 27		
London Blackfriars ⊖ d						18 24	18 36		18 42	18 50	19 00							19 12	19 16	19 30		
Elephant & Castle ⊖ d						18 28	18 40		18 46	18 54	19 04							19 16	19 19	19 33		
Loughborough Jn d							18 44			18 58	19 08								19 23	19 37		
Herne Hill d			18 39				18a47	18 54		19a01	19a11			19 09			19 19		19a27	19a41		19 34
West Dulwich d			18 42					18 56						19 12			19 21					19 36
Sydenham Hill d			18 44					18 58						19 14			19 23					19 38
Penge East d			18 47					19 01						19 17			19 26					19 41
Kent House d			18 49					19 03						19 19			19 28					19 43
Beckenham Junction d			18 51					19 06						19 21			19 30					19 45
Denmark Hill d				18 48		18 34			18 52							19 18		19 22				
Peckham Rye d				18 51		18 38			18 55							19 21		19 25				
Nunhead d				18 54		18 40			18 57							19 23		19 27				
Lewisham a				19 02												19 31						
Crofton Park d						18 43			19 00									19 30				
Catford d						18 46			19 03									19 33				
Bellingham d						18 49			19 05									19 35				
Beckenham Hill d						18 51			19 07									19 37				
Ravensbourne d						18 53			19 09									19 39				
Shortlands d			18 55			18 57		19 09	19 13					19 25			19 33	19 41				19 48
Bromley South d	18 46	18a43	18 58		18 59	19 00		19 12	19 16			19a13	19 21	19 28	19 27		19 36	19 44			19a38	19 51
Bickley d			19 00			19 03		19 15	19 19					19 30			19 39	19 47				19 54
Petts Wood d			19 07					19 20						19 35			19 44					19 59
Orpington d			19a12					19a25						19a38			19a48					20a02
St Mary Cray d	18 52				19 06	19 10			19 23				19 27					19 51				
Swanley d	18a56				19 11	19 15			19 29				19a31		19 36			19 56				
Eynsford d						19 19			19 33									20 00				
Shoreham (Kent) d						19 23			19 37									20 04				
Otford d					19a19	19 26			19 40						19a44			20 07				
Bat & Ball d						19 29			19 43									20 10				
Sevenoaks a						19 37			19 50									20 13				

	SE	SE 1	SE	SE	SE	FC	FC	SE 1	SE	SE	SE 1	SE	FC	FC	FC	SE 1	SE	SE 1	FC	FC	FC
London Victoria ⊖ d	19 28	19 37	19 39	19 40				19 52	19 55	19 58	20 07	20 10				20 22	20 25	20 37			
Brixton ⊖ d				19 47					20 02			20 17					20 32				
Kentish Town ⊖ d					19 26								19 56						20 26	20 30	
St Pancras International ⊖ d					19 30	19 34	19 48						20 00	20 04	20 18				20 30	20 34	20 48
Farringdon ⊖ d					19 36	19 39	19 53						20 05	20 09	20 23				20 35	20 39	20 53
City Thameslink d					19 39	19 43	19 57						20 09	20 13	20 27				20 39	20 43	20 57
London Blackfriars ⊖ d					19 42	19 46	20 00						20 12	20 16	20 30				20 42	20 46	21 00
Elephant & Castle ⊖ d					19 46	19 49	20 03						20 16	20 19	20 33				20 46	20 49	21 03
Loughborough Jn d						19 53	20 07							20 23	20 37					20 53	21 07
Herne Hill d				19 49		19a57	20a11		20 04			20 19		20a27	20a41		20 34			20a57	21a11
West Dulwich d				19 51					20 06			20 21					20 36				
Sydenham Hill d				19 53					20 08			20 23					20 38				
Penge East d				19 56					20 11			20 26					20 41				
Kent House d				19 58					20 13			20 28					20 43				
Beckenham Junction d				20 00					20 15			20 30					20 45				
Denmark Hill d			19 48		19 52								20 22						20 52		
Peckham Rye d			19 51		19 55								20 25						20 55		
Nunhead d			19 53		19 57								20 27						20 57		
Lewisham a			20 01																		
Crofton Park d					20 00								20 30						21 00		
Catford d					20 03								20 33						21 03		
Bellingham d					20 05								20 35						21 05		
Beckenham Hill d					20 07								20 37						21 07		
Ravensbourne d					20 09								20 39						21 09		
Shortlands d				20 03	20 11				20 18			20 33	20 41				20 48		21 11		
Bromley South d	19 49	19 53		20 06	20 14			20a08	20 21	20 19	20 23	20 36	20 44			20a38	20 51	20 53	21 14		
Bickley d				20 09	20 17				20 24			20 39	20 47				20 54		21 17		
Petts Wood d				20 14					20 29			20 44					20 59				
Orpington d				20a18					20a32			20a47					21a02				
St Mary Cray d	19 55	20 00			20 21					20 25			20 51					21 00	21 21		
Swanley d	19a59	20 04			20 26					20a29	20 33		20 56					21 04	21 26		
Eynsford d					20 30								21 00						21 30		
Shoreham (Kent) d					20 34								21 04						21 34		
Otford d		20a12			20 37						20a41		21 07					21a12	21 37		
Bat & Ball d					20 40								21 10						21 40		
Sevenoaks a					20 43								21 13						21 43		

Table 195

Mondays to Fridays

30 July to 10 August

London Victoria/Kentish Town - Catford, Beckenham Junction, Bromley South, Orpington, Otford and Sevenoaks

Network Diagram - see first Page of Table 195

		SE ■	SE	SE ■	SE ■	FC	FC	SE ■	SE	SE ■	SE	FC
London Victoria	d	20 52	20 55	20 58	21 07			21 22	21 25	21 52		
Brixton	d		21 02						21 32			
Kentish Town	d					20 56	21 01					21 31
St Pancras International	d					21 00	21 06					21 36
Farringdon	d					21 05	21 10					21 40
City Thameslink	d					21 09	21 13					21 43
London Blackfriars	d					21 12	21 16				21 42	21 46
Elephant & Castle	d					21 16	21 19				21 46	21 49
Loughborough Jn	d						21 23					21 53
Herne Hill	d		21 04				21a27		21 34			21a57
West Dulwich	d		21 06						21 36			
Sydenham Hill	d		21 08						21 38			
Penge East	d		21 11						21 41			
Kent House	d		21 13						21 43			
Beckenham Junction	d		21 15						21 45			
Denmark Hill	d					21 22					21 52	
Peckham Rye	d					21 25					21 55	
Nunhead	d					21 27					21 57	
Lewisham	a											
Crofton Park	d					21 30					22 00	
Catford	d					21 33					22 03	
Bellingham	d					21 35					22 05	
Beckenham Hill	d					21 37					22 07	
Ravensbourne	d					21 39					22 09	
Shortlands	d		21 18			21 41			21 48		22 11	
Bromley South	d	21a09	21 21	21 19	21 23	21 44		21a38	21 51	22 09	22 14	
Bickley	d		21 24			21 47			21 54		22 17	
Petts Wood	d		21 29						21 59			
Orpington	d		21a32						22a02			
St Mary Cray	d			21 25	21 30	21 51				22 15	22 21	
Swanley	d			21a29	21 34	21 56				22a19	22 26	
Eynsford	d					22 00					22 30	
Shoreham (Kent)	d					22 04					22 34	
Otford	d				21a42	22 07					22 37	
Bat & Ball	d					22 10					22 40	
Sevenoaks	a					22 13					22 43	

		SE	SE ■	SE	FC	SE ■	SE	SE ■	SE	FC	SE	SE ■
London Victoria	d	21 55	22 07			22 22	22 25	22 52			22 55	23 07
Brixton	d	22 02					22 32				23 02	
Kentish Town	d				22 01					22 31		
St Pancras International	d				22 06					22 36		
Farringdon	d				22 10					22 40		
City Thameslink	d				22 13					22 43		
London Blackfriars	d			22 12	22 16				22 42	22 46		
Elephant & Castle	d			22 16	22 19				22 46	22 49		
Loughborough Jn	d				22 23					22 53		
Herne Hill	d	22 04			22a27		22 34			22a57	23 04	
West Dulwich	d	22 06					22 36				23 06	
Sydenham Hill	d	22 08					22 38				23 08	
Penge East	d	22 11					22 41				23 11	
Kent House	d	22 13					22 43				23 13	
Beckenham Junction	d	22 15					22 45				23 15	
Denmark Hill	d			22 22					22 52			
Peckham Rye	d			22 25					22 55			
Nunhead	d			22 27					22 57			
Lewisham	a											
Crofton Park	d			22 30					23 00			
Catford	d			22 33					23 03			
Bellingham	d			22 35					23 05			
Beckenham Hill	d			22 37					23 07			
Ravensbourne	d			22 39					23 09			
Shortlands	d	22 18		22 41			22 48		23 11		23 18	
Bromley South	d	22 21	22 23	22 44		22a38	22 51	23 09	23 14		23 21	23 23
Bickley	d	22 24		22 47			22 54		23 17		23 24	
Petts Wood	d	22 29					22 59				23 29	
Orpington	d	22a32					23a02				23a32	
St Mary Cray	d		22 30	22 51				23 15	23 21			23 30
Swanley	d		22 34	22 56				23a19	23 26			23 34
Eynsford	d			23 00					23 30			
Shoreham (Kent)	d			23 04					23 34			
Otford	d		22a42	23 07					23 37			23a42
Bat & Ball	d			23 10					23 40			
Sevenoaks	a			23 13					23 43			

		SE	FC	SE ■	SE	SE ■	SE	FC	SE A	SE FO
London Victoria	d			23 22	23 25	23 52			23 55	23 55
Brixton	d				23 32				00 02	00 02
Kentish Town	d		23 01					23 30		
St Pancras International	d		23 06					23 36		
Farringdon	d		23 10					23 40		
City Thameslink	d									
London Blackfriars	d	23 12	23 16				23 42	23 46		
Elephant & Castle	d	23 16	23 19				23 46	23 49		
Loughborough Jn	d		23s23							
Herne Hill	d		23a27		23 34			23a57	00 04	00 04
West Dulwich	d				23 36				00 06	00 06
Sydenham Hill	d				23 38				00 08	00 08
Penge East	d				23 41				00 11	00 11
Kent House	d				23 43				00 13	00 13
Beckenham Junction	d				23 45				00 15	00 15
Denmark Hill	d	23 22					23 52			
Peckham Rye	d	23 25					23 55			
Nunhead	d	23 27					23 57			
Lewisham	a									
Crofton Park	d	23 30					23 59			
Catford	d	23 33					00 03			
Bellingham	d	23 35					00 05			
Beckenham Hill	d	23 37					00 07			
Ravensbourne	d	23 39					00 09			
Shortlands	d	23 41			23 48		00 11		00 18	00 19
Bromley South	d	23 44		23a38	23 51	00 09	00 14		00 21	00 21
Bickley	d	23 47			23 54		00 17		00 24	00 24
Petts Wood	d				23 59				00 29	00 29
Orpington	d				00a02				00a32	00a32
St Mary Cray	d	23 51				00 15	00 21			
Swanley	d	23 56				00a19	00 26			
Eynsford	d	23 59					00 30			
Shoreham (Kent)	d	00 04					00 34			
Otford	d	00 07					00 37			
Bat & Ball	d	00 10					00 40			
Sevenoaks	a	00 13					00 43			

A not 3 August, 10 August

Table 195

Mondays to Fridays

29 August to 7 September

London Victoria/Kentish Town - Catford, Beckenham Junction, Bromley South, Orpington, Otford and Sevenoaks

Network Diagram - see first Page of Table 195

		SE A	SE B	SE ■ A	SE ■ B	SE A	SE B	SE B	SE ■ B	SE	SE	SE ■
London Victoria	d			23p45	23p52			23p55	00 07	00 35	00 45	00 51
Brixton	d							00 02			00s52	
Kentish Town	d											
St Pancras International	d											
Farringdon	d											
City Thameslink	d											
London Blackfriars	d	23p08	23p12			23p38	23p42					
Elephant & Castle	d	23p12	23p16			23p42	23p46					
Loughborough Jn	d											
Herne Hill	d							00 04		00 43	00s54	
West Dulwich	d							00 06			00s57	
Sydenham Hill	d							00 08			01s00	
Penge East	d							00 11		00 48	01s03	
Kent House	d							00 13			01s06	
Beckenham Junction	d							00 15		00 50	01s08	
Denmark Hill	d	23p18	23p22			23p48	23p52					
Peckham Rye	d	23p21	23p25			23p51	23p55					
Nunhead	d	23p23	23p27			23p53	23p57					
Lewisham	a											
Crofton Park	d	23p26	23p30			23p56	23p59					
Catford	d	23p29	23p33			23p59	00 03					
Bellingham	d	23p31	23p35			00 01	00 05					
Beckenham Hill	d	23p33	23p37			00 03	00 07					
Ravensbourne	d	23p35	23p39			00 05	00 09					
Shortlands	d	23p37	23p41			00 07	00 11	00 18			01s12	
Bromley South	d	23p40	23p44	00 02	00 09	00 10	00 14	00 21	00 25	00 55	01s15	01s10
Bickley	d	23p43	23p47			00 13	00 17	00 24			01s18	
Petts Wood	d							00 29			01s25	
Orpington	d							00a32			01a29	
St Mary Cray	d	23p47	23p51	00 08	00 15	00 17	00 21		00 32	01 01		01s17
Swanley	d	23p52	23p56	00a12	00a19	00 22	00 26		00 36	01a05		01s21
Eynsford	d	23p56	23p59			00 26	00 30					01s26
Shoreham (Kent)	d	23p59	00 04			00 30	00 34					01s30
Otford	d	00 03	00 07			00 33	00 37		00a44			01s33
Bat & Ball	d	00 06	00 10			00 36	00 40					
Sevenoaks	a	00 09	00 13			00 39	00 43					

		SE	SE ■	SE	FC	SE	FC	SE ■	SE	SE ■	SE	SE ■
London Victoria	d	00 56	05 22			05 40		05 52		06 07	06 10	06 22
Brixton	d					05 47					06 17	
Kentish Town	d						05 50					
St Pancras International	d				05 36		05 54					
Farringdon	d				05 42		06 00					
City Thameslink	d			05 26	05 44		06 03					
London Blackfriars	d			05 28	05 47		06 06					
Elephant & Castle	d			05 32	05 50		06 09					
Loughborough Jn	d						06 13					
Herne Hill	d				05a57	05 49	06a17				06 19	
West Dulwich	d					05 51					06 21	
Sydenham Hill	d					05 53					06 23	
Penge East	d					05 56					06 26	
Kent House	d					05 58					06 28	
Beckenham Junction	d					06 00					06 30	
Denmark Hill	d	01s05		05 39								
Peckham Rye	d	01s08		05 41								
Nunhead	d	01s10		05 44								
Lewisham	a											
Crofton Park	d	01s13		05 47								
Catford	d	01s16		05 49								
Bellingham	d	01s18		05 52								
Beckenham Hill	d	01s20		05 54								
Ravensbourne	d	01s22		05 56								
Shortlands	d			05 58		06 03					06 33	
Bromley South	d	01s25	05 39	06 01		06 06		06 09	06 16	06 23	06 37	06 39
Bickley	d			06 03		06 09			06 18		06 39	
Petts Wood	d					06 14					06 44	
Orpington	d	01a33				06a18					06a49	
St Mary Cray	d		05 45	06 08					06 23	06 30		06 45
Swanley	d		05a49	06 12				06a19	06 28	06 34		06a49
Eynsford	d			06 17					06 32			
Shoreham (Kent)	d			06 20					06 36			
Otford	d			06 23					06 39	06a42		
Bat & Ball	d			06 26					06 42			
Sevenoaks	a			06 29					06 45			

		FC	FC	SE	SE ■	SE ■	SE	FC	SE	SE ■	SE ■	FC ■
London Victoria	d			06 30	06 37	06 45			06 50	06 58	07 07	
Brixton	d			06 37					06 57			
Kentish Town	d	05 54	06 08					06 30				
St Pancras International	d	05 58	06 12					06 34				06 44
Farringdon	d	06 04	06 18					06 40				06 50
City Thameslink	d	06 07	06 21				06 39	06 43				06 53
London Blackfriars	d	06 10	06 24				06 42	06 46				06 58
Elephant & Castle	d	06 16	06 27				06 46	06 49				07 02
Loughborough Jn	d		06 31					06 53				
Herne Hill	d		06a35	06 39				06a57	06 59			
West Dulwich	d			06 41					07 02			
Sydenham Hill	d			06 43					07 04			
Penge East	d			06 46					07 07			
Kent House	d			06 48					07 09			
Beckenham Junction	d			06 50					07 11			
Denmark Hill	d	06 22					06 52					07 09
Peckham Rye	d	06 25					06 55					07 12
Nunhead	d	06 27					06 57					07 14
Lewisham	a											
Crofton Park	d	06 30					07 00					07 17
Catford	d	06 33					07 03					07 20
Bellingham	d	06 35					07 05					07 22
Beckenham Hill	d	06 37					07 07					07 24
Ravensbourne	d	06 39					07 09					07 26
Shortlands	d	06 41		06 54			07 11		07 14			07 28
Bromley South	d	06 44		06 57	06 58	07 02	07 14		07 17	07 19	07 23	07 31
Bickley	d	06 47		07 00			07 17		07 20			07 34
Petts Wood	d			07 04					07 24			
Orpington	d			07a08					07a28			
St Mary Cray	d	06 51			07 04	07 08	07 21			07 25	07 30	07 38
Swanley	d	06 56			07 08	07a12	07 26			07a29	07 34	07 44
Eynsford	d	07 00					07 30					07 48
Shoreham (Kent)	d	07 04					07 34					07 52
Otford	d	07 07			07a16		07 37				07a42	07 55
Bat & Ball	d	07 10					07 40					07 58
Sevenoaks	a	07 14					07 43					08 01

		FC	FC ■	SE	SE ■	SE	SE ■	FC	FC ■	FC	FC	SE
London Victoria	d			07 10	07 22	07 25	07 36					07 40
Brixton	d			07 17		07 32						07 47
Kentish Town	d	06 48						07 08		07 24		
St Pancras International	d	06 52	07 04					07 12	07 16	07 28	07 32	
Farringdon	d	06 58	07 10					07 18	07 22	07 34	07 38	
City Thameslink	d	07 01	07 13					07 21	07 25	07 37	07 41	
London Blackfriars	d	07 04	07 16					07 24	07 28	07 40	07 44	
Elephant & Castle	d	07 07	07 19					07 28	07 33	07 44	07 47	
Loughborough Jn	d	07 11	07 23						07 37		07 51	
Herne Hill	d	07a15	07a27	07 19		07 34			07a40		07a55	07 49
West Dulwich	d			07 21		07 36						07 51
Sydenham Hill	d			07 23		07 38						07 53
Penge East	d			07 26		07 41						07 56
Kent House	d			07 28		07 43						07 58
Beckenham Junction	d			07 30		07 45						08 00
Denmark Hill	d							07 34		07 50		
Peckham Rye	d							07 36		07 53		
Nunhead	d							07 39		07 56		
Lewisham	a											
Crofton Park	d							07 42				
Catford	d							07 44		08 00		
Bellingham	d							07 47		08 02		
Beckenham Hill	d							07 49				
Ravensbourne	d							07 51				
Shortlands	d			07 33		07 48		07 54				08 03
Bromley South	d			07 38	07 40	07 51	07 53	07 57		08a10		08 06
Bickley	d			07 40		07 54		08 00				08 09
Petts Wood	d			07 49		07 59						08 14
Orpington	d			07a53		08a02						08a19
St Mary Cray	d						08 00	08 04				
Swanley	d				07a48		08 04	08 10				
Eynsford	d							08 15				
Shoreham (Kent)	d							08 18				
Otford	d						08a12	08 22				
Bat & Ball	d							08 25				
Sevenoaks	a							08 28				

A 3 September

B not 3 September

Table 195

Mondays to Fridays
29 August to 7 September

London Victoria/Kentish Town - Catford, Beckenham Junction, Bromley South, Orpington, Otford and Sevenoaks

Network Diagram - see first Page of Table 195

		SE		SE 1	SE	SE 1	SE 1	FC	FC	FC	SE	SE		FC	SE 1	SE	SE 1	FC 1	FC 1	SE	SE	FC		FC 1	FC
London Victoria	d	07 43		07 52	07 55	07 58	08 07				08 09	08 10			08 22	08 25	08 37			08 39	08 40				
Brixton	d				08 02							08 17				08 32					08 47				
Kentish Town	d								07 44										08 20						08 36
St Pancras International	d							07 38	07 48	07 52				08 12				08 16	08 24			08 28		08 32	08 40
Farringdon	d							07 44	07 54	07 58				08 18				08 22	08 30			08 34		08 38	08 46
City Thameslink	d							07 47	07 57	08 01				08 21				08 25	08 33			08 37		08 41	08 49
London Blackfriars	d							07 50	08 00	08 04				08 24				08 28	08 36			08 40		08 44	08 52
Elephant & Castle	d							07 54	08 04	08 07				08 27				08 32				08 44		08 47	08 56
Loughborough Jn	d									08 11				08 31										08 51	
Herne Hill	d				08 04					08a15		08 19		08a36		08 34			08a45		08 48			08a57	
West Dulwich	d				08 06							08 21				08 36					08 51				
Sydenham Hill	d				08 08							08 23				08 38					08 53				
Penge East	d				08 11							08 26				08 41					08 56				
Kent House	d				08 13							08 28				08 43					08 58				
Beckenham Junction	d				08 15							08 30				08 45					09 00				
Denmark Hill	d	07 53						08 00	08 10		08 18							08 38		08 48		08 52			09 02
Peckham Rye	d	07 56						08 03	08 13		08 21							08 41		08 51		08 55			
Nunhead	d	07 59						08 06	08 15		08 23							08 43		08 53		08 57			
Lewisham	a	08 07									08 30									09 01					
Crofton Park	d							08 09	08 18									08 46				09 00			
Catford	d							08 12	08 21									08 49				09 03			09 09
Bellingham	d							08 15	08 23									08 51				09 05			
Beckenham Hill	d							08 17	08 25									08 53				09 07			
Ravensbourne	d							08 19	08 27									08 55				09 09			
Shortlands	d							08 22	08 30			08 33				08 48		08 57			09 03	09 11			
Bromley South	d			08a09	08 22	08 28	08 23	08 25	08 33			08 36			08a39	08 51	08 53	09 00			09 07	09 14			09 18
Bickley	d				08 24			08 28	08 35			08 39				08 54		09 03			09 09	09 17			09 20
Petts Wood	d				08 29			08 32				08 44				08 59					09 14				
Orpington	d				08a32			08a36				08a47				09a02					09a17				
St Mary Cray	d					08 34	08 30		08 40								09 00	09 07				09 21			09 25
Swanley	d					08a39	08 34		08 44								09 04	09 12				09 26			09 36
Eynsford	d								08 49									09 16				09 30			09 40
Shoreham (Kent)	d								08 52									09 20				09 34			09 44
Otford	d						08a42		08 55								09a12	09 23				09 37			09 47
Bat & Ball	d								08 58									09 26				09 40			09 50
Sevenoaks	a								09 01									09 29				09 45			09 53

		FC	FC	SE 1	SE	SE 1	SE 1	SE		SE	FC	FC	SE 1	SE	SE 1	SE	SE	FC		FC	FC	SE 1	SE	SE 1	SE 1
London Victoria	d			08 52	08 55	08 58	09 07	09 09		09 10			09 22	09 25	09 37	09 39	09 40					09 52	09 55	09 58	10 07
Brixton	d				09 02					09 17				09 32			09 47						10 02		
Kentish Town	d		08 52									09 12						09 26			09 44				
St Pancras International	d	08 44	08 56								09 00	09 16						09 30		09 34	09 48				
Farringdon	d	08 50	09 02								09 06	09 22						09 36		09 40	09 53				
City Thameslink	d	08 53	09 05								09 09	09 25						09 39		09 43	09 57				
London Blackfriars	d	08 56	09 08								09 12	09 28						09 42		09 46	10 00				
Elephant & Castle	d	09 00	09 12								09 16	09 31						09 46		09 49	10 03				
Loughborough Jn	d	09 04	09 16									09 35								09 53	10 07				
Herne Hill	d	09a08	09a21		09 04					09 19		09a39		09 34			09 49			09a57	10a11		10 04		
West Dulwich	d				09 06					09 21				09 36			09 51						10 06		
Sydenham Hill	d				09 08					09 23				09 38			09 53						10 08		
Penge East	d				09 11					09 26				09 41			09 56						10 11		
Kent House	d				09 13					09 28				09 43			09 58						10 13		
Beckenham Junction	d				09 15					09 30				09 45			10 00						10 15		
Denmark Hill	d							09 18			09 22					09 48		09 52							
Peckham Rye	d							09 21			09 25					09 51		09 55							
Nunhead	d							09 23			09 27					09 53		09 57							
Lewisham	a							09 31								10 01									
Crofton Park	d										09 30							10 00							
Catford	d										09 33							10 03							
Bellingham	d										09 35							10 05							
Beckenham Hill	d										09 37							10 07							
Ravensbourne	d										09 39							10 09							
Shortlands	d				09 18					09 33	09 41			09 48			10 03	10 11					10 18		
Bromley South	d			09a08	09 21	09 19	09 23			09 36	09 44		09a38	09 52	09 53		10 07	10 14				10a08	10 21	10 19	10 23
Bickley	d				09 24					09 39	09 47			09 54			10 09	10 17					10 24		
Petts Wood	d				09 29					09 44				09 59			10 14						10 29		
Orpington	d				09a33					09a47				10a02			10a17						10a32		
St Mary Cray	d					09 25					09 51				10 00			10 21						10 25	
Swanley	d					09a29	09 33				09 56				10 04			10 26						10a29	10 33
Eynsford	d										10 00							10 30							
Shoreham (Kent)	d										10 04							10 34							
Otford	d						09a41				10 07				10a12			10 37							10a41
Bat & Ball	d										10 10							10 40							
Sevenoaks	a										10 13							10 43							

Table 195

Mondays to Fridays
29 August to 7 September

London Victoria/Kentish Town - Catford, Beckenham Junction, Bromley South, Orpington, Otford and Sevenoaks

Network Diagram - see first Page of Table 195

		SE	SE	FC		FC	FC	SE 1	SE	SE 1	SE	SE	FC	FC		FC	SE 1	SE	SE 1	SE 1	SE	SE	FC	FC	
London Victoria	d	10 09	10 10					10 22	10 25	10 37	10 39	10 40					10 52	10 55	10 58	11 07	11 09	11 10			
Brixton	d		10 17						10 32			10 47						11 02				11 17			
Kentish Town	d			09 54		10 00	10 14						10 26	10 30		10 44							10 56	11 00	
St Pancras International	d			10 00		10 04	10 18						10 30	10 34		10 48							11 00	11 04	
Farringdon	d			10 05		10 09	10 24						10 35	10 39		10 54							11 05	11 09	
City Thameslink	d			10 09		10 13	10 27						10 39	10 43		10 57							11 09	11 13	
London Blackfriars	d			10 12		10 16	10 30						10 42	10 46		11 00							11 12	11 16	
Elephant & Castle	d			10 16		10 19	10 33						10 46	10 49		11 03							11 16	11 19	
Loughborough Jn	d					10 23	10 37							10 53		11 07								11 23	
Herne Hill	d		10 19			10a27	10a41		10 34			10 49		10a57		11a11		11 04				11 19		11a27	
West Dulwich	d		10 21						10 36			10 51						11 06				11 21			
Sydenham Hill	d		10 23						10 38			10 53						11 08				11 23			
Penge East	d		10 26						10 41			10 56						11 11				11 26			
Kent House	d		10 28						10 43			10 58						11 13				11 28			
Beckenham Junction	d		10 30						10 45			11 00						11 15				11 30			
Denmark Hill	d	10 18		10 22							10 48		10 52								11 18		11 22		
Peckham Rye	d	10 21		10 25							10 51		10 55								11 21		11 25		
Nunhead	d	10 23		10 27							10 53		10 57								11 23		11 27		
Lewisham	a	10 31									11 01										11 31				
Crofton Park	d			10 30									11 00										11 30		
Catford	d			10 33									11 03										11 33		
Bellingham	d			10 35									11 05										11 35		
Beckenham Hill	d			10 37									11 07										11 37		
Ravensbourne	d			10 39									11 09										11 39		
Shortlands	d		10 33	10 41					10 48			11 03	11 11					11 18				11 33	11 41		
Bromley South	d		10 36	10 44				10a38	10 51	10 53		11 06	11 14				11a08	11 21	11 19	11 23		11 36	11 44		
Bickley	d		10 39	10 47					10 54			11 09	11 17					11 24				11 39	11 47		
Petts Wood	d		10 44						10 59			11 14						11 29				11 44			
Orpington	d		10a47						11a02			11a17						11a32				11a47			
St Mary Cray	d			10 51						11 00			11 21						11 25				11 51		
Swanley	d			10 56						11 04			11 26						11a29	11 33			11 56		
Eynsford	d			11 00									11 30										12 00		
Shoreham (Kent)	d			11 04									11 34										12 04		
Otford	d			11 07						11a12			11 37							11a41			12 07		
Bat & Ball	d			11 10									11 40										12 10		
Sevenoaks	a			11 13									11 43										12 13		

		FC	SE 1	SE	SE 1	SE	SE	FC	FC	FC		SE 1	SE	SE 1	SE 1	SE	SE	FC	FC	FC	and at the same minutes past each hour until	FC		SE 1
London Victoria	d		11 22	11 25	11 37	11 39	11 40					11 52	11 55	11 58	12 07	12 09	12 10							15 22
Brixton	d			11 32			11 47						12 02				12 17							
Kentish Town	d	11 14						11 26	11 30	11 44								11 56	12 00	12 14		15 14		
St Pancras International	d	11 18						11 30	11 34	11 48								12 00	12 04	12 18		15 18		
Farringdon	d	11 24						11 35	11 39	11 53								12 05	12 09	12 23		15 23		
City Thameslink	d	11 27						11 39	11 43	11 57								12 09	12 13	12 27		15 27		
London Blackfriars	d	11 30						11 42	11 46	12 00								12 12	12 16	12 30		15 30		
Elephant & Castle	d	11 33						11 46	11 49	12 03								12 16	12 19	12 33		15 33		
Loughborough Jn	d	11 37							11 53	12 07									12 23	12 37		15 37		
Herne Hill	d	11a41		11 34			11 49		11a57	12a11			12 04				12 19		12a27	12a41		15a41		
West Dulwich	d			11 36			11 51						12 06				12 21							
Sydenham Hill	d			11 38			11 53						12 08				12 23							
Penge East	d			11 41			11 56						12 11				12 26							
Kent House	d			11 43			11 58						12 13				12 28							
Beckenham Junction	d			11 45			12 00						12 15				12 30							
Denmark Hill	d					11 48		11 52								12 18		12 22						
Peckham Rye	d					11 51		11 55								12 21		12 25						
Nunhead	d					11 53		11 57								12 23		12 27						
Lewisham	a					12 01										12 31								
Crofton Park	d							12 00										12 30						
Catford	d							12 03										12 33						
Bellingham	d							12 05										12 35						
Beckenham Hill	d							12 07										12 37						
Ravensbourne	d							12 09										12 39						
Shortlands	d			11 48			12 03	12 11					12 18				12 33	12 41						
Bromley South	d		11a38	11 51	11 53		12 06	12 14				12a08	12 21	12 19	12 23		12 36	12 44						15a38
Bickley	d			11 54			12 09	12 17					12 24				12 39	12 47						
Petts Wood	d			11 59			12 14						12 29				12 44							
Orpington	d			12a02			12a17						12a32				12a47							
St Mary Cray	d				12 00			12 21						12 25				12 51						
Swanley	d				12 04			12 26						12a29	12 33			12 56						
Eynsford	d							12 30										13 00						
Shoreham (Kent)	d							12 34										13 04						
Otford	d				12a12			12 37							12a41			13 07						
Bat & Ball	d							12 40										13 10						
Sevenoaks	a							12 43										13 13						

London Victoria/Kentish Town - Catford, Beckenham Junction, Bromley South, Orpington, Otford and Sevenoaks

Network Diagram - see first Page of Table 195

Station		SE	SE 1	SE	SE	FC	FC	FC	SE 1		SE	SE	SE 1	SE 1	SE	SE	FC	FC	SE 1		SE	SE 1	SE 1	FC	FC
London Victoria 15 ⊖	d	15 25	15 37	15 39	15 40				15 52			15 55	15 58	16 07	16 09	16 10			16 22		16 25	16 28	16 37		
Brixton ⊖	d	15 32			15 47							16 02				16 17					16 32				
Kentish Town ⊖	d					15 26	15 30	15 44									15 56	16 00						16 10	16 14
St Pancras International 15 ⊖	d					15 30	15 34	15 48									16 00	16 04						16 14	16 18
Farringdon ⊖	d					15 35	15 39	15 53									16 05	16 09						16 19	16 23
City Thameslink 3	d					15 39	15 43	15 57									16 09	16 13						16 23	16 27
London Blackfriars 3 ⊖	d					15 42	15 46	16 00									16 12	16 16						16 26	16 30
Elephant & Castle ⊖	d					15 46	15 49	16 03									16 16	16 19						16 30	16 33
Loughborough Jn	d						15 53	16 07										16 23							16 37
Herne Hill 4	d	15 34			15 49		15a57	16a11				16 04				16 19		16a27			16 34				16a41
West Dulwich	d	15 36			15 51							16 06				16 21					16 36				
Sydenham Hill	d	15 38			15 53							16 08				16 23					16 38				
Penge East	d	15 41			15 56							16 11				16 26					16 41				
Kent House 4	d	15 43			15 58							16 13				16 28					16 43				
Beckenham Junction 4	d	15 45			16 00						16 12	16 15				16 30					16 45				
Denmark Hill 4	d			15 48		15 52									16 18		16 22							16 39	
Peckham Rye 4	d			15 51		15 55									16 21		16 25							16 42	
Nunhead 4	d			15 53		15 57									16 23		16 27							16 44	
Lewisham 4	a			16 01											16 31										
Crofton Park	d					16 00											16 30							16 47	
Catford	d					16 03											16 33							16 50	
Bellingham	d					16 05											16 35							16 52	
Beckenham Hill	d					16 07											16 37							16 54	
Ravensbourne	d					16 09											16 39							16 56	
Shortlands 4	d	15 48			16 03	16 11						16 18				16 33	16 41				16 48			16 58	
Bromley South 4	d	15 51	15 53		16 06	16 14			16a08			16 21	16 19	16 23		16 36	16 44		16a38		16 51	16 49	16 53	17 01	
Bickley 4	d	15 54			16 09	16 17						16 24				16 39	16 47				16 54			17 04	
Petts Wood 4	d	15 59			16 14							16 29				16 44					16 59			17 08	
Orpington 4	d	16a02			16a17							16a32				16a49					17a04			17a13	
St Mary Cray	d		16 00			16 21							16 25				16 51					16 55	17 00		
Swanley 4	d		16 04			16 26							16a29	16 33			16 56					16a59	17 04		
Eynsford	d					16 30											17 00								
Shoreham (Kent)	d					16 34											17 04								
Otford 4	d		16a12			16 37								16a41			17 07						17a12		
Bat & Ball	d					16 40											17 10								
Sevenoaks 4	a					16 43											17 14								

Station		SE	SE	FC	FC		FC 1	FC	SE 1	SE 1	SE	SE	SE	SE 1	SE		FC	FC	FC 1	FC	SE 1	SE 1	SE	SE	SE 1
London Victoria 15 ⊖	d	16 39	16 40						16 57	16 58	16 59	17 04	17 04	17 12	17 15						17 27	17 28	17 30	17 34	17 42
Brixton ⊖	d		16 47								17 06				17 22								17 37		
Kentish Town ⊖	d			16 24	16 30			16 46										16 58		17 14					
St Pancras International 15 ⊖	d			16 28	16 34		16 40	16 52									16 58	17 02	17 14	17 18					
Farringdon ⊖	d			16 33	16 39		16 45	16 57									17 03	17 07	17 19	17 23					
City Thameslink 3	d			16 37	16 43		16 49	17 01									17 07	17 11	17 23	17 27					
London Blackfriars 3 ⊖	d			16 42	16 46		16 52	17 04									17 10	17 14	17 25	17 30					
Elephant & Castle ⊖	d			16 46	16 49		16 56	17 08									17 14	17 18	17 29	17 34					
Loughborough Jn	d				16 53		17 00	17 12										17 22		17 38					
Herne Hill 4	d		16 49		16a57		17 06	17a15			17 11				17 24			17a25	17 36	17a42			17 39		
West Dulwich	d		16 51				17 08				17 13				17 27								17 42		
Sydenham Hill	d		16 53				17 10				17 15				17 29								17 44		
Penge East	d		16 56				17 13				17 18				17 32								17 47		
Kent House 4	d		16 58				17 15				17 20				17 34								17 49		
Beckenham Junction 4	d		17 00				17a20				17 23				17 37								17 51		
Denmark Hill 4	d	16 48		16 52								17 13					17 20							17 43	
Peckham Rye 4	d	16 51		16 55								17 16					17 23							17 46	
Nunhead 4	d	16 53		16 57								17 18					17 26							17 49	
Lewisham 4	a	16 58										17 23												17 55	
Crofton Park	d			17 00													17 29								
Catford	d			17 03													17 32								
Bellingham	d			17 05													17 35								
Beckenham Hill	d			17 07													17 37								
Ravensbourne	d			17 09													17 39								
Shortlands 4	d		17 03	17 11							17 26				17 40		17 43						17 55		
Bromley South 4	d		17 06	17 14					17a13	17 19	17 29		17 24	17 31	17 43		17 46		17 48		17a43	17 50	17 58		17 59
Bickley 4	d		17 09	17 17							17 31				17 45				17 50				18 00		
Petts Wood 4	d		17 14								17 36				17 50								18 05		
Orpington 4	d		17a19								17a41				17a55								18a10		
St Mary Cray	d			17 21									17 30	17 38					17 55			17 57			18 06
Swanley 4	d			17 30									17a34	17 42			17 55		17a59			18 01			18 11
Eynsford	d			17 34													18 00								
Shoreham (Kent)	d			17 38													18 03								
Otford 4	d			17 41						17a35				17a50			18 06					18a09			18a19
Bat & Ball	d			17 44													18 14								
Sevenoaks 4	a			17 49													18 23								

London Victoria/Kentish Town - Catford, Beckenham Junction, Bromley South, Orpington, Otford and Sevenoaks

Network Diagram - see first Page of Table 195

Station		FC	FC	FC 1	SE	FC	SE 1	SE	SE 1	SE		SE 1	FC 1	FC	FC	FC	SE	SE	SE 1	SE 1		SE 1	SE	SE
London Victoria 15 ⊖	d				17 45		17 54	17 56	17 57	18 00		18 03					18 15	18 18	18 18	18 24		18 27	18 30	18 39
Brixton ⊖	d				17 52					18 07							18 22						18 37	
Kentish Town ⊖	d	17 18	17 28												17 48									
St Pancras International 15 ⊖	d	17 22	17 32	17 36		17 44							17 56	17 48	17 52	18 04								
Farringdon ⊖	d	17 27	17 37	17 41		17 49							18 01	17 53	17 57	18 09								
City Thameslink 3	d	17 31	17 41	17 45		17 53							18 05	17 57	18 01	18 13								
London Blackfriars 3 ⊖	d	17 36	17 44	17 48		17 56							18 10	18 00	18 04	18 16								
Elephant & Castle ⊖	d	17 40	17 48	17 52		18 00							18 14	18 05	18 08	18 20								
Loughborough Jn	d		17 52												18 12	18 24								
Herne Hill 4	d		17a55		17 54	18 07				18 10			18 21		18a16	18a27	18 24						18 39	
West Dulwich	d				17 57	18 09				18 12							18 27						18 42	
Sydenham Hill	d				17 59	18 11				18 14							18 29						18 44	
Penge East	d				18 02	18 14				18 17							18 32						18 47	
Kent House 4	d				18 04	18a19				18 20							18 34						18 49	
Beckenham Junction 4	d				18 06					18 22							18 36						18 51	
Denmark Hill 4	d	17 47						18 06						18 15				18 28						18 48
Peckham Rye 4	d	17 50						18 09						18 18				18 32						18 51
Nunhead 4	d	17 52						18 11						18 20				18 34						18 54
Lewisham 4	a							18 17										18 42						19 02
Crofton Park	d	17 55												18 23										
Catford	d	17 58												18 26										
Bellingham	d	18 01												18 29										
Beckenham Hill	d	18 03												18 31										
Ravensbourne	d	18 05												18 33										
Shortlands 4	d	18 07			18 10					18 25				18 35			18 39						18 55	
Bromley South 4	d	18 10		18 11	18 15		18 19		18a14	18 28		18 24	18 31	18 38			18 42		18 39	18 46		18a43	18 58	
Bickley 4	d	18 12			18 18					18 31				18 40			18 45						19 00	
Petts Wood 4	d				18 26					18 36							18 54						19 07	
Orpington 4	d				18a32					18a41							18a59						19a12	
St Mary Cray	d	18 22		18 18			18 25						18 38	18 45					18 45	18 52				
Swanley 4	d	18 26		18 22			18a29						18a42	18 53					18 50	18a56				
Eynsford	d	18 31												18 57										
Shoreham (Kent)	d	18 34												19 01										
Otford 4	d	18 38		18a30								18a42		19 04					18a58					
Bat & Ball	d	18 41												19 07										
Sevenoaks 4	a	18 50												19 12										

Station		SE 1	FC	FC	SE	FC 1	FC		FC	SE 1	SE 1	SE	SE 1	SE	SE	FC	FC		FC	SE 1	SE	SE	SE 1	SE	SE
London Victoria 15 ⊖	d	18 42			18 45					18 57	18 58	19 00	19 07	19 09	19 10					19 22	19 25	19 28	19 37	19 39	19 40
Brixton ⊖	d				18 52							19 07			19 17						19 32				19 47
Kentish Town ⊖	d		18 08	18 20			18 34									18 54									
St Pancras International 15 ⊖	d		18 12	18 24		18 30	18 38		18 48							19 00	19 04		19 18						
Farringdon ⊖	d		18 17	18 29		18 35	18 43		18 53							19 05	19 09		19 23						
City Thameslink 3	d		18 21	18 33		18 39	18 47		18 57							19 09	19 13		19 27						
London Blackfriars 3 ⊖	d		18 24	18 36		18 42	18 50		19 00							19 12	19 16		19 30						
Elephant & Castle ⊖	d		18 28	18 40		18 46	18 54		19 04							19 16	19 19		19 33						
Loughborough Jn	d			18 44			18 58		19 08								19 23		19 37						
Herne Hill 4	d			18a47	18 54		19a01		19a11			19 09			19 19		19a27		19a41		19 34				19 49
West Dulwich	d				18 56							19 12			19 21						19 36				19 51
Sydenham Hill	d				18 58							19 14			19 23						19 38				19 53
Penge East	d				19 01							19 17			19 26						19 41				19 56
Kent House 4	d				19 03							19 19			19 28						19 43				19 58
Beckenham Junction 4	d				19 06							19 21			19 30						19 45				20 00
Denmark Hill 4	d		18 34			18 52								19 18		19 22								19 48	
Peckham Rye 4	d		18 38			18 55								19 21		19 25								19 51	
Nunhead 4	d		18 40			18 57								19 23		19 27								19 53	
Lewisham 4	a													19 31										20 01	
Crofton Park	d		18 43			19 00										19 30									
Catford	d		18 46			19 03										19 33									
Bellingham	d		18 49			19 05										19 35									
Beckenham Hill	d		18 51			19 07										19 37									
Ravensbourne	d		18 53			19 09										19 39									
Shortlands 4	d		18 57		19 09	19 13						19 25			19 33	19 41					19 48				20 03
Bromley South 4	d	18 59	19 00		19 12	19 16				19a13	19 21	19 28	19 27		19 36	19 44				19a38	19 51	19 49	19 53		20 06
Bickley 4	d		19 03		19 15	19 19						19 30			19 39	19 47					19 54				20 09
Petts Wood 4	d				19 20							19 35			19 44						19 59				20 14
Orpington 4	d				19a25							19a38			19a48						20a02				20a18
St Mary Cray	d	19 06	19 10			19 23					19 27					19 51						19 55	20 00		
Swanley 4	d	19 11	19 15			19 29					19a31		19 36			19 56						19a59	20 04		
Eynsford	d		19 19			19 33										20 00									
Shoreham (Kent)	d		19 23			19 37										20 04									
Otford 4	d	19a19	19 26			19 40							19a44			20 07							20a12		
Bat & Ball	d		19 29			19 43										20 10									
Sevenoaks 4	a		19 37			19 50										20 13									

London Victoria/Kentish Town - Catford, Beckenham Junction, Bromley South, Orpington, Otford and Sevenoaks

Mondays to Fridays
29 August to 7 September

Network Diagram - see first Page of Table 195

		SE	FC		FC	SE ■	SE	SE	SE ■	SE	FC	FC	FC		SE ■	SE	SE ■	FC	FC	FC	SE ■	SE	SE ■		SE ■
London Victoria	d					19 52	19 55	19 58	20 07	20 10					20 22	20 25	20 37				20 52	20 55	20 58		21 07
Brixton	d						20 02			20 17						20 32						21 02			
Kentish Town	d	19 26									19 56							20 26	20 30						
St Pancras International	d	19 30	19 34		19 48						20 00	20 04	20 18					20 30	20 34	20 48					
Farringdon	d	19 36	19 39		19 53						20 05	20 09	20 23					20 35	20 39	20 53					
City Thameslink	d	19 39	19 43		19 57						20 09	20 13	20 27					20 39	20 43	20 57					
London Blackfriars	d	19 42	19 46		20 00						20 12	20 16	20 30					20 42	20 46	21 00					
Elephant & Castle	d	19 46	19 49		20 03						20 16	20 19	20 33					20 46	20 49	21 03					
Loughborough Jn	d		19 53		20 07							20 23	20 37						20 53	21 07					
Herne Hill	d		19a57		20a11		20 04			20 19		20a27	20a41			20 34			20a57	21a11		21 04			
West Dulwich	d						20 06			20 21						20 36						21 06			
Sydenham Hill	d						20 08			20 23						20 38						21 08			
Penge East	d						20 11			20 26						20 41						21 11			
Kent House	d						20 13			20 28						20 43						21 13			
Beckenham Junction	d						20 15			20 30						20 45						21 15			
Denmark Hill	d	19 52									20 22							20 52							
Peckham Rye	d	19 55									20 25							20 55							
Nunhead	d	19 57									20 27							20 57							
Lewisham	a																								
Crofton Park	d	20 00									20 30							21 00							
Catford	d	20 03									20 33							21 03							
Bellingham	d	20 05									20 35							21 05							
Beckenham Hill	d	20 07									20 37							21 07							
Ravensbourne	d	20 09									20 39							21 09							
Shortlands	d	20 11					20 18			20 33	20 41					20 48		21 11				21 18			
Bromley South	d	20 14				20a08	20 21	20 19	20 23	20 36	20 44				20a38	20 51	20 53	21 14			21a09	21 21	21 19		21 23
Bickley	d	20 17					20 24			20 39	20 47					20 54		21 17				21 24			
Petts Wood	d						20 29			20 44						20 59						21 29			
Orpington	d						20a32			20a47						21a02						21a32			
St Mary Cray	d	20 21						20 25			20 51						21 00	21 21					21 25		21 30
Swanley	d	20 26						20a29	20 33		20 56						21 04	21 26					21a29		21 34
Eynsford	d	20 30									21 00							21 30							
Shoreham (Kent)	d	20 34									21 04							21 34							
Otford	d	20 37							20a41		21 07						21a12	21 37							21a42
Bat & Ball	d	20 40									21 10							21 40							
Sevenoaks	a	20 43									21 13							21 43							

		FC	FC	SE ■	SE	SE ■	SE	FC	SE		SE ■	SE	FC	SE ■	SE	SE ■	SE	FC	SE		SE ■	SE	FC	SE ■	SE
London Victoria	d			21 22	21 25	21 52			21 55		22 07			22 22	22 25	22 52			22 55		23 07			23 22	23 25
Brixton	d				21 32				22 02						22 32				23 02						23 32
Kentish Town	d	20 56	21 01					21 31					22 01					22 31					23 01		
St Pancras International	d	21 00	21 06					21 36					22 06					22 36					23 06		
Farringdon	d	21 05	21 10					21 40					22 10					22 40					23 10		
City Thameslink	d	21 09	21 13					21 43					22 13					22 43							
London Blackfriars	d	21 12	21 16				21 42	21 46				22 12	22 16				22 42	22 46				23 12	23 16		
Elephant & Castle	d	21 16	21 19				21 46	21 49				22 16	22 19				22 46	22 49				23 16	23 19		
Loughborough Jn	d		21 23					21 53					22 23					22 53					23s23		
Herne Hill	d		21a27		21 34			21a57	22 04				22a27		22 34			22a57	23 04				23a27		23 34
West Dulwich	d				21 36				22 06						22 36				23 06						23 36
Sydenham Hill	d				21 38				22 08						22 38				23 08						23 38
Penge East	d				21 41				22 11						22 41				23 11						23 41
Kent House	d				21 43				22 13						22 43				23 13						23 43
Beckenham Junction	d				21 45				22 15						22 45				23 15						23 45
Denmark Hill	d	21 22					21 52					22 22					22 52					23 22			
Peckham Rye	d	21 25					21 55					22 25					22 55					23 25			
Nunhead	d	21 27					21 57					22 27					22 57					23 27			
Lewisham	a																								
Crofton Park	d	21 30					22 00					22 30					23 00					23 30			
Catford	d	21 33					22 03					22 33					23 03					23 33			
Bellingham	d	21 35					22 05					22 35					23 05					23 35			
Beckenham Hill	d	21 37					22 07					22 37					23 07					23 37			
Ravensbourne	d	21 39					22 09					22 39					23 09					23 39			
Shortlands	d	21 41			21 48		22 11		22 18			22 41			22 48		23 11		23 18			23 41			23 48
Bromley South	d	21 44		21a38	21 51	22 09	22 14		22 21		22 23	22 44		22a38	22 51	23 09	23 14		23 21		23 23	23 44		23a38	23 51
Bickley	d	21 47			21 54		22 17		22 24			22 47			22 54		23 17		23 24			23 47			23 54
Petts Wood	d				21 59				22 29						22 59				23 29						23 59
Orpington	d				22a02				22a32						23a02				23a32						00a02
St Mary Cray	d	21 51				22 15	22 21				22 30	22 51				23 15	23 21				23 30	23 51			
Swanley	d	21 56				22a19	22 26				22 34	22 56				23a19	23 26				23 34	23 56			
Eynsford	d	22 00					22 30					23 00					23 30					23 59			
Shoreham (Kent)	d	22 04					22 34					23 04					23 34					00 04			
Otford	d	22 07					22 37				22a42	23 07					23 37				23a42	00 07			
Bat & Ball	d	22 10					22 40					23 10					23 40					00 10			
Sevenoaks	a	22 13					22 43					23 13					23 43					00 13			

London Victoria/Kentish Town - Catford, Beckenham Junction, Bromley South, Orpington, Otford and Sevenoaks

Mondays to Fridays
29 August to 7 September

Network Diagram - see first Page of Table 195

		SE ■	SE	FC	SE
London Victoria	d	23 52			23 55
Brixton	d				00 02
Kentish Town	d			23 30	
St Pancras International	d			23 36	
Farringdon	d			23 40	
City Thameslink	d				
London Blackfriars	d		23 42	23 46	
Elephant & Castle	d		23 46	23 49	
Loughborough Jn	d				
Herne Hill	d			23a57	00 04
West Dulwich	d				00 06
Sydenham Hill	d				00 08
Penge East	d				00 11
Kent House	d				00 13
Beckenham Junction	d				00 15
Denmark Hill	d		23 52		
Peckham Rye	d		23 55		
Nunhead	d		23 57		
Lewisham	a				
Crofton Park	d		23 59		
Catford	d		00 03		
Bellingham	d		00 05		
Beckenham Hill	d		00 07		
Ravensbourne	d		00 09		
Shortlands	d		00 11		00 18
Bromley South	d	00 09	00 14		00 21
Bickley	d		00 17		00 24
Petts Wood	d				00 29
Orpington	d				00a32
St Mary Cray	d	00 15	00 21		
Swanley	d	00a19	00 26		
Eynsford	d		00 30		
Shoreham (Kent)	d		00 34		
Otford	d		00 37		
Bat & Ball	d		00 40		
Sevenoaks	a		00 43		

Saturdays
until 21 July, 18 Aug and from 15 Sep

		SE	SE	SE ■	SE	SE	SE ■	SE ■	SE	SE ■		FC	SE	SE ■	SE	SE ■	SE	FC	FC	SE		SE	FC	SE	FC
		A	B		A		B	A							B		A					A		B	
London Victoria	d		23p43	23p52		23p55	00 07	00 07	00 35	05 22			05 55	06 07	06 13	06 22				06 25				06 43	
Brixton	d					00 02							06 02							06 32					
Kentish Town	d											05 44							06 14				06 28		06 44
St Pancras International	d											05 48							06 18				06 34		06 48
Farringdon	d											05 53							06 23				06 39		06 53
City Thameslink	d																								
London Blackfriars	d	23p12			23p42							06 00					06 12	06 16	06 30			06 42	06 46		07 00
Elephant & Castle	d	23p16			23p46							06 03					06 16	06 19	06 33			06 46	06 49		07 03
Loughborough Jn	d																						06 53		07 07
Herne Hill	d					00 04			00 43			06a11	06 04					06a27	06a41	06 34			06a57		07a11
West Dulwich	d					00 06							06 06							06 36					
Sydenham Hill	d					00 08							06 08							06 38					
Penge East	d					00 11			00 48				06 11							06 41					
Kent House	d					00 13							06 13							06 43					
Beckenham Junction	d					00 15			00 50				06 15							06 45					
Denmark Hill	d	23p22	23p52		23p52										06 22		06 22					06 52		06 52	
Peckham Rye	d	23p25	23p55		23p55										06 25		06 25					06 55		06 55	
Nunhead	d	23p27	23p57		23p57										06 27		06 27					06 57		06 57	
Lewisham	a																								
Crofton Park	d	23p30	23p59		23p59										06 30		06 30					07 00		07 00	
Catford	d	23p33	00 03		00 03										06 33		06 33					07 03		07 03	
Bellingham	d	23p35	00 05		00 05										06 35		06 35					07 05		07 05	
Beckenham Hill	d	23p37	00 07		00 07										06 37		06 37					07 07		07 07	
Ravensbourne	d	23p39	00 09		00 09										06 39		06 39					07 09		07 09	
Shortlands	d	23p41	00 11		00 11	00 18							06 18		06 41		06 41			06 48		07 11		07 11	
Bromley South	d	23p44	00 14	00 09	00 14	00 21	00 25	00 25	00 55	05 39			06 21	06 23	06 44	06 39	06 44			06 51		07 14		07 14	
Bickley	d	23p47	00 17		00 17	00 24							06 24		06 47		06 47			06 54		07 17		07 17	
Petts Wood	d		00 21			00 29							06 29							06 59					
Orpington	d		00a25			00a32							06a32							07a02					
St Mary Cray	d	23p51		00 15	00 21		00 31	00 32	01 01	05 45				06 30	06 51	06 45	06 51					07 21		07 21	
Swanley	d	23p56		00a19	00 26		00 36	00 36	01a05	05a49				06 34	06 56	06a49	06 56					07 26		07 26	
Eynsford	d	23p59			00 30		00 40								07 00		07 00					07 30		07 30	
Shoreham (Kent)	d	00 04			00 34		00 44								07 04		07 04					07 34		07 34	
Otford	d	00 07			00 37		00a47	00a44						06a42	07 07		07 07					07 37		07 37	
Bat & Ball	d	00 10			00 40										07 10		07 10					07 40		07 40	
Sevenoaks	a	00 13			00 43										07 13		07 13					07 43		07 43	

A not 19 May

B 19 May

London Victoria/Kentish Town - Catford, Beckenham Junction, Bromley South, Orpington, Otford and Sevenoaks

Network Diagram - see first Page of Table 195

		SE	SE 1	SE 1	SE	SE A	FC	SE B	FC	SE 1	SE	SE 1	SE	SE	SE A	FC	SE B	FC	SE 1	SE	SE 1	SE 1	SE
London Victoria 15 ⊖	d	06 55	06 58	07 07	07 10			07 13		07 22	07 25	07 37	07 39	07 40			07 43		07 52	07 55	07 58	08 07	08 09
Brixton ⊖	d	07 02			07 17						07 32			07 47						08 02			
Kentish Town ⊖	d						06 58		07 14							07 28		07 44					
St Pancras International 15 ⊖	d						07 04		07 18							07 34		07 48					
Farringdon ⊖	d						07 09		07 23							07 39		07 53					
City Thameslink 3	d																						
London Blackfriars 3 ⊖	d					07 12	07 16		07 30						07 42	07 46		08 00					
Elephant & Castle ⊖	d					07 16	07 19		07 33						07 46	07 49		08 03					
Loughborough Jn	d						07 23		07 37							07 53		08 07					
Herne Hill 4	d	07 04			07 19		07a27		07a41		07 34			07 49		07a57		08a11		08 04			
West Dulwich	d	07 06			07 21						07 36			07 51						08 06			
Sydenham Hill	d	07 08			07 23						07 38			07 53						08 08			
Penge East	d	07 11			07 26						07 41			07 56						08 11			
Kent House 4	d	07 13			07 28						07 43			07 58						08 13			
Beckenham Junction 4	d	07 15			07 30						07 45			08 00						08 15			
Denmark Hill 4	d					07 22		07 22					07 48		07 52		07 52						08 18
Peckham Rye 4	d					07 25		07 25					07 51		07 55		07 55						08 21
Nunhead 4	d					07 27		07 27					07 53		07 57		07 57						08 23
Lewisham 4	a												08 02										08 31
Crofton Park	d					07 30		07 30							08 00		08 00						
Catford	d					07 33		07 33							08 03		08 03						
Bellingham	d					07 35		07 35							08 05		08 05						
Beckenham Hill	d					07 37		07 37							08 07		08 07						
Ravensbourne	d					07 39		07 39							08 09		08 09						
Shortlands 4	d	07 18			07 33	07 41		07 41			07 48			08 03	08 11		08 11			08 18			
Bromley South 4	d	07 21	07 19	07 23	07 36	07 44		07 44		07a38	07 51	07 53		08 06	08 14		08 14		08a08	08 21	08 19	08 23	
Bickley 4	d	07 24			07 39	07 47		07 47			07 54			08 09	08 17		08 17			08 24			
Petts Wood 4	d	07 29			07 44						07 59			08 14						08 29			
Orpington 4	d	07a32			07a47						08a02			08a17						08a32			
St Mary Cray	d		07 25	07 30		07 51		07 51				08 00			08 21		08 21				08 25		
Swanley 4	d		07a29	07 34		07 56		07 56				08 04			08 26		08 26				08a29	08 33	
Eynsford	d					08 00		08 00							08 30		08 30						
Shoreham (Kent)	d					08 04		08 04							08 34		08 34						
Otford 4	d			07a42		08 07		08 07				08a12			08 37		08 37					08a41	
Bat & Ball	d					08 10		08 10							08 40		08 40						
Sevenoaks 4	a					08 13		08 13							08 43		08 43						

		SE	SE A	FC	SE B	FC	SE 1	SE	SE 1	SE	SE	SE A	FC	SE B	FC	SE 1	SE	SE 1	SE 1	SE	SE	SE A
London Victoria 15 ⊖	d	08 10			08 13		08 22	08 25	08 37	08 39	08 40			08 43		08 52	08 55	08 58	09 07	09 09	09 10	
Brixton ⊖	d	08 17						08 32			08 47						09 02				09 17	
Kentish Town ⊖	d			07 58		08 14							08 28		08 44							
St Pancras International 15 ⊖	d			08 04		08 18							08 34		08 48							
Farringdon ⊖	d			08 09		08 23							08 39		08 53							
City Thameslink 3	d																					
London Blackfriars 3 ⊖	d		08 12	08 16		08 30						08 42	08 46		09 00							09 12
Elephant & Castle ⊖	d		08 16	08 19		08 33						08 46	08 49		09 03							09 16
Loughborough Jn	d			08 23		08 37							08 53		09 07							
Herne Hill 4	d	08 19		08a27		08a41		08 34			08 49		08a57		09a11		09 04				09 19	
West Dulwich	d	08 21						08 36			08 51						09 06				09 21	
Sydenham Hill	d	08 23						08 38			08 53						09 08				09 23	
Penge East	d	08 26						08 41			08 56						09 11				09 26	
Kent House 4	d	08 28						08 43			08 58						09 13				09 28	
Beckenham Junction 4	d	08 30						08 45			09 00						09 15				09 30	
Denmark Hill 4	d		08 22		08 22					08 48		08 52		08 52						09 18		09 22
Peckham Rye 4	d		08 25		08 25					08 51		08 55		08 55						09 21		09 25
Nunhead 4	d		08 27		08 27					08 53		08 57		08 57						09 23		09 27
Lewisham 4	a									09 01										09 31		
Crofton Park	d		08 30		08 30							09 00		09 00								09 30
Catford	d		08 33		08 33							09 03		09 03								09 33
Bellingham	d		08 35		08 35							09 05		09 05								09 35
Beckenham Hill	d		08 37		08 37							09 07		09 07								09 37
Ravensbourne	d		08 39		08 39							09 09		09 09								09 39
Shortlands 4	d	08 33	08 41		08 41			08 48			09 03	09 11		09 11			09 18				09 33	09 41
Bromley South 4	d	08 36	08 44		08 44		08a38	08 51	08 53		09 06	09 14		09 14		09a08	09 21	09 19	09 23		09 36	09 44
Bickley 4	d	08 39	08 47		08 47			08 54			09 09	09 17		09 17			09 24				09 39	09 47
Petts Wood 4	d	08 44						08 59			09 14						09 29				09 44	
Orpington 4	d	08a47						09a02			09a17						09a32				09a47	
St Mary Cray	d		08 51		08 51				09 00			09 21		09 21				09 25				09 51
Swanley 4	d		08 56		08 56				09 04			09 26		09 26				09a29	09 33			09 56
Eynsford	d		09 00		09 00							09 30		09 30								10 00
Shoreham (Kent)	d		09 04		09 04							09 34		09 34								10 04
Otford 4	d		09 07		09 07				09a12			09 37		09 37					09a41			10 07
Bat & Ball	d		09 10		09 10							09 40		09 40								10 10
Sevenoaks 4	a		09 13		09 13							09 43		09 43								10 13

A not 19 May

B 19 May

Table 195

Saturdays

until 21 July, 18 Aug and from 15 Sep

London Victoria/Kentish Town - Catford, Beckenham Junction, Bromley South, Orpington, Otford and Sevenoaks

Network Diagram - see first Page of Table 195

		FC	SE A	FC	SE 1	SE	SE 1	SE	SE	SE B	FC	SE A	FC	and at the same minutes past each hour until	FC	SE 1	SE	SE 1	SE 1	SE	SE	SE B
London Victoria 15 ⊖	d		09 13		09 22	09 25	09 37	09 39	09 40			09 43				18 52	18 55	18 58	19 07	19 09	19 10	
Brixton ⊖	d					09 32			09 47								19 02				19 17	
Kentish Town ⊖	d	08 58		09 14							09 28		09 44		18 44							
St Pancras International 15 ⊖	d	09 04		09 18							09 34		09 48		18 48							
Farringdon ⊖	d	09 09		09 23							09 39		09 53		18 53							
City Thameslink 3	d	09 13		09 27							09 43		09 57		18 57							
London Blackfriars 3 ⊖	d	09 16		09 30						09 42	09 46		10 00		19 00							19 12
Elephant & Castle ⊖	d	09 19		09 33						09 46	09 49		10 03		19 03							19 16
Loughborough Jn	d	09 23		09 37							09 53		10 07		19 07							
Herne Hill 4	d	09a27		09a41		09 34			09 49		09a57		10a11		19a11		19 04				19 19	
West Dulwich	d					09 36			09 51								19 06				19 21	
Sydenham Hill	d					09 38			09 53								19 08				19 23	
Penge East	d					09 41			09 56								19 11				19 26	
Kent House 4	d					09 43			09 58								19 13				19 28	
Beckenham Junction 4	d					09 45			10 00								19 15				19 30	
Denmark Hill 4	d		09 22					09 48		09 52		09 52								19 18		19 22
Peckham Rye 4	d		09 25					09 51		09 55		09 55								19 21		19 25
Nunhead 4	d		09 27					09 53		09 57		09 57								19 23		19 27
Lewisham 4	a							10 01												19 31		
Crofton Park	d		09 30							10 00		10 00										19 30
Catford	d		09 33							10 03		10 03										19 33
Bellingham	d		09 35							10 05		10 05										19 35
Beckenham Hill	d		09 37							10 07		10 07										19 37
Ravensbourne	d		09 39							10 09		10 09										19 39
Shortlands 4	d		09 41			09 48			10 03	10 11		10 11					19 18				19 33	19 41
Bromley South 4	d		09 44		09a38	09 51	09 53		10 06	10 14		10 14				19a08	19 21	19 19	19 23		19 36	19 44
Bickley 4	d		09 47			09 54			10 09	10 17		10 17					19 24				19 39	19 47
Petts Wood 4	d					09 59			10 14								19 29				19 44	
Orpington 4	d					10a02			10a17								19a32				19a48	
St Mary Cray	d		09 51				10 00			10 21		10 21						19 25				19 51
Swanley 4	d		09 56				10 04			10 26		10 26						19a29	19 33			19 56
Eynsford	d		10 00							10 30		10 30										20 00
Shoreham (Kent)	d		10 04							10 34		10 34										20 04
Otford 4	d		10 07				10a12			10 37		10 37							19a41			20 07
Bat & Ball	d		10 10							10 40		10 40										20 10
Sevenoaks 4	a		10 13							10 43		10 43										20 13

		FC	SE A	FC	SE 1	SE	SE 1	SE	SE	SE B	FC	SE A	FC	SE 1	SE	SE 1	SE 1	SE	SE B	FC	SE A	FC
London Victoria 15 ⊖	d		19 13		19 22	19 25	19 37	19 39	19 40			19 43		19 52	19 55	19 58	20 07	20 10			20 13	
Brixton ⊖	d					19 32			19 47						20 02			20 17				
Kentish Town ⊖	d	18 58		19 14							19 28		19 44							19 58		20 14
St Pancras International 15 ⊖	d	19 04		19 18							19 34		19 48							20 04		20 18
Farringdon ⊖	d	19 09		19 23							19 39		19 53							20 09		20 23
City Thameslink 3	d	19 13		19 27							19 43		19 57							20 13		20 27
London Blackfriars 3 ⊖	d	19 16		19 30						19 42	19 46		20 00						20 12	20 16		20 30
Elephant & Castle ⊖	d	19 19		19 33						19 46	19 49		20 03						20 16	20 19		20 33
Loughborough Jn	d	19 23		19 37							19 53		20 07							20 23		20 37
Herne Hill 4	d	19a27		19a41		19 34			19 49		19a57		20a11		20 04			20 19		20a27		20a41
West Dulwich	d					19 36			19 51						20 06			20 21				
Sydenham Hill	d					19 38			19 53						20 08			20 23				
Penge East	d					19 41			19 56						20 11			20 26				
Kent House 4	d					19 43			19 58						20 13			20 28				
Beckenham Junction 4	d					19 45			20 00						20 15			20 30				
Denmark Hill 4	d		19 22					19 48		19 52		19 52							20 22		20 22	
Peckham Rye 4	d		19 25					19 51		19 55		19 55							20 25		20 25	
Nunhead 4	d		19 27					19 53		19 57		19 57							20 27		20 27	
Lewisham 4	a							20 01														
Crofton Park	d		19 30							20 00		20 00							20 30		20 30	
Catford	d		19 33							20 03		20 03							20 33		20 33	
Bellingham	d		19 35							20 05		20 05							20 35		20 35	
Beckenham Hill	d		19 37							20 07		20 07							20 37		20 37	
Ravensbourne	d		19 39							20 09		20 09							20 39		20 39	
Shortlands 4	d		19 41			19 48			20 03	20 11		20 11			20 18			20 33	20 41		20 41	
Bromley South 4	d		19 44		19a38	19 51	19 53		20 06	20 14		20 14		20a08	20 21	20 19	20 23	20 36	20 44		20 44	
Bickley 4	d		19 47			19 54			20 09	20 17		20 17			20 24			20 39	20 47		20 47	
Petts Wood 4	d					19 59			20 14						20 29			20 44				
Orpington 4	d					20a02			20a18						20a32			20a47				
St Mary Cray	d		19 51				20 00			20 21		20 21				20 25	20 30		20 51		20 51	
Swanley 4	d		19 56				20 04			20 26		20 26				20a29	20 34		20 56		20 56	
Eynsford	d		20 00							20 30		20 30							21 00		21 00	
Shoreham (Kent)	d		20 04							20 34		20 34							21 04		21 04	
Otford 4	d		20 07				20a12			20 37		20 37					20a42		21 07		21 07	
Bat & Ball	d		20 10							20 40		20 40							21 10		21 10	
Sevenoaks 4	a		20 13							20 43		20 43							21 13		21 13	

A 19 May

B not 19 May

Table 195

Saturdays
until 21 July, 18 Aug and from 15 Sep

London Victoria/Kentish Town - Catford, Beckenham Junction, Bromley South, Orpington, Otford and Sevenoaks

Network Diagram - see first Page of Table 195

	SE ■	SE	SE	SE ■	SE	FC	FC	SE	SE ■	SE	FC	SE	SE ■	SE	SE	SE ■	SE	FC	SE	SE ■	SE	FC
			A		B					B		A			A		B				B	
London Victoria ⊖ d	20 22	20 25	20 43	20 52				20 55	21 07			21 13	21 22	21 25	21 43	21 52			21 55	22 07		
Brixton ⊖ d		20 32						21 02						21 32					22 02			
Kentish Town ⊖ d						20 31	20 44				21 01							21 31				22 01
St Pancras International ⊖ d						20 36	20 48				21 06							21 36				22 06
Farringdon ⊖ d						20 40	20 53				21 10							21 40				22 10
City Thameslink d						20 43	20 57															
London Blackfriars ⊖ d					20 42	20 46	21 00			21 12	21 16						21 42	21 46			22 12	22 16
Elephant & Castle ⊖ d					20 46	20 49	21 03			21 16	21 19						21 46	21 49			22 16	22 19
Loughborough Jn d						20 53	21 07				21 23							21 53				22 23
Herne Hill d		20 34				20a57	21a11	21 04			21a27			21 34				21a57	22 04			22a27
West Dulwich d		20 36						21 06						21 36					22 06			
Sydenham Hill d		20 38						21 08						21 38					22 08			
Penge East d		20 41						21 11						21 41					22 11			
Kent House d		20 43						21 13						21 43					22 13			
Beckenham Junction d		20 45						21 15						21 45					22 15			
Denmark Hill d			20 52		20 52					21 22		21 22			21 52		21 52				22 22	
Peckham Rye d			20 55		20 55					21 25		21 25			21 55		21 55				22 25	
Nunhead d			20 57		20 57					21 27		21 27			21 57		21 57				22 27	
Lewisham a																						
Crofton Park d			21 00		21 00					21 30		21 30			22 00		22 00				22 30	
Catford d			21 03		21 03					21 33		21 33			22 03		22 03				22 33	
Bellingham d			21 05		21 05					21 35		21 35			22 05		22 05				22 35	
Beckenham Hill d			21 07		21 07					21 37		21 37			22 07		22 07				22 37	
Ravensbourne d			21 09		21 09					21 39		21 39			22 09		22 09				22 39	
Shortlands d		20 48	21 11		21 11			21 18		21 41		21 41		21 48	22 11		22 11		22 18		22 41	
Bromley South d	20a38	20 51	21 14	21 09	21 14			21 21	21 23	21 44		21 44	21a38	21 51	22 14	22 09	22 14		22 21	22 23	22 44	
Bickley d		20 54	21 17		21 17			21 24		21 47		21 47		21 54	22 17		22 17		22 24		22 47	
Petts Wood d		20 59						21 29						21 59					22 29			
Orpington d		21a02						21a32						22a02					22a32			
St Mary Cray d			21 21	21 15	21 21				21 30	21 51		21 51			22 21	22 15	22 21			22 30	22 51	
Swanley d			21 26	21a19	21 26				21 34	21 56		21 56			22 26	22a19	22 26			22 34	22 56	
Eynsford d			21 30		21 30					22 00		22 00			22 30		22 30				23 00	
Shoreham (Kent) d			21 34		21 34					22 04		22 04			22 34		22 34				23 04	
Otford d			21 37		21 37				21a42	22 07		22 07			22 37		22 37			22a42	23 07	
Bat & Ball d			21 40		21 40					22 10		22 10			22 40		22 40				23 10	
Sevenoaks a			21 43		21 43					22 13		22 13			22 43		22 43				23 13	

	SE	SE ■	SE	SE	SE ■	SE	FC	SE	SE ■	SE	FC	SE	SE ■	SE	SE	SE ■	SE	FC	SE
	A			A		B				B		A			A		B		
London Victoria ⊖ d	22 13	22 22	22 25	22 43	22 52			22 55	23 07			23 13	23 22	23 25	23 43	23 52			23 55
Brixton ⊖ d			22 32					23 02						23 32					00 02
Kentish Town ⊖ d							22 31				23 01							23 30	
St Pancras International ⊖ d							22 36				23 06							23 36	
Farringdon ⊖ d							22 40				23 10							23 40	
City Thameslink d																			
London Blackfriars ⊖ d						22 42	22 46			23 12	23 16						23 42	23 46	
Elephant & Castle ⊖ d						22 46	22 49			23 16	23 19						23 46	23 49	
Loughborough Jn d							22 53				23 23								
Herne Hill d			22 34				22a57	23 04			23a27			23 34				23a57	00 04
West Dulwich d			22 36					23 06						23 36					00 06
Sydenham Hill d			22 38					23 08						23 38					00 08
Penge East d			22 41					23 11						23 41					00 11
Kent House d			22 43					23 13						23 43					00 13
Beckenham Junction d			22 45					23 15						23 45					00 15
Denmark Hill d	22 22			22 52		22 52				23 22		23 22			23 52		23 52		
Peckham Rye d	22 25			22 55		22 55				23 25		23 25			23 55		23 55		
Nunhead d	22 27			22 57		22 57				23 27		23 27			23 57		23 57		
Lewisham a																			
Crofton Park d	22 30			23 00		23 00				23 30		23 30			23 58		23 59		
Catford d	22 33			23 03		23 03				23 33		23 33			00 03		00 03		
Bellingham d	22 35			23 05		23 05				23 35		23 35			00 05		00 05		
Beckenham Hill d	22 37			23 07		23 07				23 37		23 37			00 07		00 07		
Ravensbourne d	22 39			23 09		23 09				23 39		23 39			00 09		00 09		
Shortlands d	22 41		22 48	23 11		23 11		23 18		23 41		23 41		23 48	00 11		00 11		00 18
Bromley South d	22 44	22a38	22 51	23 14	23 09	23 14		23 21	23 23	23 44		23 44	23a38	23 51	00 14	00 09	00 14		00 21
Bickley d	22 47		22 54	23 17		23 17		23 24		23 47		23 47		23 54	00 17		00 17		00 24
Petts Wood d			22 59	23 22				23 29				23 52		23 59	00 22				00 29
Orpington d			23a02	23a25				23a32				23a55		00a02	00a25				00a32
St Mary Cray d	22 51				23 15	23 21			23 30	23 51						00 15	00 21		
Swanley d	22 56				23a19	23 26			23 34	23 56						00a19	00 26		
Eynsford d	23 00					23 30				23 59							00 30		
Shoreham (Kent) d	23 04					23 34				00 04							00 34		
Otford d	23 07					23 37			23a42	00 07							00 37		
Bat & Ball d	23 10					23 40				00 10							00 40		
Sevenoaks a	23 13					23 43				00 13							00 43		

A 19 May

B not 19 May

Table 195

Saturdays
28 July to 11 August

London Victoria/Kentish Town - Catford, Beckenham Junction, Bromley South, Orpington, Otford and Sevenoaks

Network Diagram - see first Page of Table 195

	SE	SE ■	SE	SE	SE	SE ■	SE	SE	SE	SE ■	SE ■	FC	SE	SE ■	SE ■	SE	FC	FC	SE	SE	FC	FC
				A	B																	
London Victoria ⊖ d		23p52		23p55	23p55	00 07	00 35	00 45	00 56	01 00	05 22		05 55	06 07	06 22				06 25			
Brixton ⊖ d				00 02	00 02			00 52					06 02						06 32			
Kentish Town ⊖ d												05 44						06 14			06 28	06 44
St Pancras International ⊖ d												05 48						06 18			06 34	06 48
Farringdon ⊖ d												05 53						06 23			06 39	06 53
City Thameslink d																						
London Blackfriars ⊖ d	23p12		23p42									06 00				06 12	06 16	06 30		06 42	06 46	07 00
Elephant & Castle ⊖ d	23p16		23p46									06 03				06 16	06 19	06 33		06 46	06 49	07 03
Loughborough Jn d																					06 53	07 07
Herne Hill d				00 04	00 04		00 43	00 56				06a11	06 04				06a27	06a41	06 34		06a57	07a11
West Dulwich d				00 06	00 06			00 58					06 06						06 36			
Sydenham Hill d				00 08	00 08			01 00					06 08						06 38			
Penge East d				00 11	00 11		00 48	01 03					06 11						06 41			
Kent House d				00 13	00 13			01 05					06 13						06 43			
Beckenham Junction d				00 15	00 15		00 50	01 08					06 15						06 45			
Denmark Hill d	23p22		23p52						01 06							06 22				06 52		
Peckham Rye d	23p25		23p55						01 08							06 25				06 55		
Nunhead d	23p27		23p57						01 11							06 27				06 57		
Lewisham a																						
Crofton Park d	23p30		23p59						01 14							06 30				07 00		
Catford d	23p33		00 03						01 16							06 33				07 03		
Bellingham d	23p35		00 05						01 19							06 35				07 05		
Beckenham Hill d	23p37		00 07						01 21							06 37				07 07		
Ravensbourne d	23p39		00 09						01 23							06 39				07 09		
Shortlands d	23p41		00 11	00 18	00 19			01 11	01 25				06 18			06 41			06 48	07 11		
Bromley South d	23p44	00 09	00 14	00 21	00 21	00 25	00 55	01 14	01 28	01 16	05 39		06 21	06 23	06 39	06 44			06 51	07 14		
Bickley d	23p47		00 17	00 24	00 24			01 16	01 30				06 24			06 47			06 54	07 17		
Petts Wood d				00 29	00 29			01 21	01 35				06 29						06 59			
Orpington d				00a32	00a32			01a27	01a42				06a32						07a02			
St Mary Cray d	23p51	00 15	00 21			00 32	01 01			01 23	05 45			06 30	06 45	06 51				07 21		
Swanley d	23p56	00a19	00 26			00 36	01a05			01 27	05a49			06 34	06a49	06 56				07 26		
Eynsford d	23p59		00 30							01 32						07 00				07 30		
Shoreham (Kent) d	00 04		00 34							01 35						07 04				07 34		
Otford d	00 07		00 37			00a44				01a38				06a42		07 07				07 37		
Bat & Ball d	00 10		00 40													07 10				07 40		
Sevenoaks a	00 13		00 43													07 13				07 43		

	SE	SE ■	SE ■	SE	SE	FC	FC	SE ■	SE	SE ■	SE	SE	SE	FC	FC	SE ■	SE	SE ■	SE ■	SE	SE	SE
London Victoria ⊖ d	06 55	06 58	07 07	07 10				07 22	07 25	07 37	07 39	07 40				07 52	07 55	07 58	08 07	08 09	08 10	
Brixton ⊖ d	07 02			07 17					07 32			07 47					08 02				08 17	
Kentish Town ⊖ d						06 58	07 14							07 28	07 44							
St Pancras International ⊖ d						07 04	07 18							07 34	07 48							
Farringdon ⊖ d						07 09	07 23							07 39	07 53							
City Thameslink d																						
London Blackfriars ⊖ d					07 12	07 16	07 30						07 42	07 46	08 00							08 12
Elephant & Castle ⊖ d					07 16	07 19	07 33						07 46	07 49	08 03							08 16
Loughborough Jn d						07 23	07 37							07 53	08 07							
Herne Hill d	07 04			07 19		07a27	07a41		07 34			07 49		07a57	08a11		08 04				08 19	
West Dulwich d	07 06			07 21					07 36			07 51					08 06				08 21	
Sydenham Hill d	07 08			07 23					07 38			07 53					08 08				08 23	
Penge East d	07 11			07 26					07 41			07 56					08 11				08 26	
Kent House d	07 13			07 28					07 43			07 58					08 13				08 28	
Beckenham Junction d	07 15			07 30					07 45			08 00					08 15				08 30	
Denmark Hill d					07 22						07 48		07 52							08 18		08 22
Peckham Rye d					07 25						07 51		07 55							08 21		08 25
Nunhead d					07 27						07 53		07 57							08 23		08 27
Lewisham a											08 00									08 31		
Crofton Park d					07 30								08 00									08 30
Catford d					07 33								08 03									08 33
Bellingham d					07 35								08 05									08 35
Beckenham Hill d					07 37								08 07									08 37
Ravensbourne d					07 39								08 09									08 39
Shortlands d	07 18			07 33	07 41				07 48			08 03	08 11				08 18				08 33	08 41
Bromley South d	07 21	07 19	07 23	07 36	07 44			07a38	07 51	07 53		08 06	08 14			08a08	08 21	08 19	08 23		08 36	08 44
Bickley d	07 24			07 39	07 47				07 54			08 09	08 17				08 24				08 39	08 47
Petts Wood d	07 29			07 44					07 59			08 14					08 29				08 44	
Orpington d	07a32			07a47					08a02			08a17					08a32				08a47	
St Mary Cray d		07 25	07 30		07 51					08 00			08 21					08 25				08 51
Swanley d		07a29	07 34		07 56					08 04			08 26					08a29	08 33			08 56
Eynsford d					08 00								08 30									09 00
Shoreham (Kent) d					08 04								08 34									09 04
Otford d			07a42		08 07					08a12			08 37						08a41			09 07
Bat & Ball d					08 10								08 40									09 10
Sevenoaks a					08 13								08 43									09 13

A not from 4 August until 11 August

B not 28 July

London Victoria/Kentish Town - Catford, Beckenham Junction, Bromley South, Orpington, Otford and Sevenoaks

Network Diagram - see first Page of Table 195

		FC		FC	SE ■	SE	SE ■	SE	SE	SE	FC	FC		SE ■	SE	SE ■	SE ■	SE	SE	SE	FC	FC		SE ■	SE
London Victoria ⊖	d				08 22	08 25	08 37	08 39	08 40					08 52	08 55	08 58	09 07	09 09	09 10					09 22	09 25
Brixton ⊖	d					08 32			08 47						09 02				09 17						09 32
Kentish Town ⊖	d	07 58		08 14							08 28	08 44									08 58	09 14			
St Pancras International ⊖	d	08 04		08 18							08 34	08 48									09 04	09 18			
Farringdon ⊖	d	08 09		08 23							08 39	08 53									09 09	09 23			
City Thameslink	d																				09 13	09 27			
London Blackfriars ⊖	d	08 16		08 30						08 42	08 46	09 00							09 12	09 16	09 30				
Elephant & Castle ⊖	d	08 19		08 33						08 46	08 49	09 03							09 16	09 19	09 33				
Loughborough Jn	d	08 23		08 37							08 53	09 07									09 23	09 37			
Herne Hill	d	08a27		08a41		08 34			08 49		08a57	09a11			09 04				09 19		09a27	09a41			09 34
West Dulwich	d					08 36			08 51						09 06				09 21						09 36
Sydenham Hill	d					08 38			08 53						09 08				09 23						09 38
Penge East	d					08 41			08 56						09 11				09 26						09 41
Kent House	d					08 43			08 58						09 13				09 28						09 43
Beckenham Junction	d					08 45			09 00						09 15				09 30						09 45
Denmark Hill	d							08 48		08 52								09 18		09 22					
Peckham Rye	d							08 51		08 55								09 21		09 25					
Nunhead	d							08 53		08 57								09 23		09 27					
Lewisham	a							09 01										09 31							
Crofton Park	d									09 00										09 30					
Catford	d									09 03										09 33					
Bellingham	d									09 05										09 35					
Beckenham Hill	d									09 07										09 37					
Ravensbourne	d									09 09										09 39					
Shortlands	d					08 48			09 03	09 11					09 18				09 33	09 41					09 48
Bromley South	d				08a38	08 51	08 53		09 06	09 14				09a08	09 21	09 19	09 23		09 36	09 44				09a38	09 51
Bickley	d					08 54			09 09	09 17					09 24				09 39	09 47					09 54
Petts Wood	d					08 59			09 14						09 29				09 44						09 59
Orpington	d					09a02			09a17						09a32				09a47						10a02
St Mary Cray	d						09 00			09 21						09 25				09 51					
Swanley	d						09 04			09 26						09a29	09 33			09 56					
Eynsford	d									09 30										10 00					
Shoreham (Kent)	d									09 34										10 04					
Otford	d						09a12			09 37							09a41			10 07					
Bat & Ball	d									09 40										10 10					
Sevenoaks	a									09 43										10 13					

		SE ■	SE	SE	SE	FC	FC	SE ■ ✕		SE	SE ■	SE ■	SE	SE	SE	FC	FC	SE ■ ✕		SE	SE ■	SE		SE
London Victoria ⊖	d	09 37	09 39	09 40				09 52		09 55	09 58	10 07	10 09	10 10				10 22		10 25	10 37	10 39	and at the same minutes past each hour until	18 39
Brixton ⊖	d			09 47						10 02				10 17						10 32				
Kentish Town ⊖	d					09 28	09 44									09 58	10 14							
St Pancras International ⊖	d					09 34	09 48									10 04	10 18							
Farringdon ⊖	d					09 39	09 53									10 09	10 23							
City Thameslink	d					09 43	09 57									10 13	10 27							
London Blackfriars ⊖	d				09 42	09 46	10 00								10 12	10 16	10 30							
Elephant & Castle ⊖	d				09 46	09 49	10 03								10 16	10 19	10 33							
Loughborough Jn	d					09 53	10 07									10 23	10 37							
Herne Hill	d			09 49		09a57	10a11			10 04				10 19		10a27	10a41			10 34				
West Dulwich	d			09 51						10 06				10 21						10 36				
Sydenham Hill	d			09 53						10 08				10 23						10 38				
Penge East	d			09 56						10 11				10 26						10 41				
Kent House	d			09 58						10 13				10 28						10 43				
Beckenham Junction	d			10 00						10 15				10 30						10 45				
Denmark Hill	d		09 48		09 52								10 18		10 22							10 48		18 48
Peckham Rye	d		09 51		09 55								10 21		10 25							10 51		18 51
Nunhead	d		09 53		09 57								10 23		10 27							10 53		18 53
Lewisham	a		10 00										10 31									11 01		19 01
Crofton Park	d				10 00										10 30									
Catford	d				10 03										10 33									
Bellingham	d				10 05										10 35									
Beckenham Hill	d				10 07										10 37									
Ravensbourne	d				10 09										10 39									
Shortlands	d			10 03	10 11					10 18				10 33	10 41					10 48				
Bromley South	d	09 53		10 06	10 14			10a08		10 21	10 19	10 23		10 36	10 44			10a38		10 51	10 53			
Bickley	d			10 09	10 17					10 24				10 39	10 47					10 54				
Petts Wood	d			10 14						10 29				10 44						10 59				
Orpington	d			10a17						10a32				10a47						11a02				
St Mary Cray	d	10 00			10 21						10 25				10 51						11 00			
Swanley	d	10 04			10 26						10a29	10 33			10 56						11 04			
Eynsford	d				10 30										11 00									
Shoreham (Kent)	d				10 34										11 04									
Otford	d	10a12			10 37							10a41			11 07						11a12			
Bat & Ball	d				10 40										11 10									
Sevenoaks	a				10 43										11 13									

London Victoria/Kentish Town - Catford, Beckenham Junction, Bromley South, Orpington, Otford and Sevenoaks

Network Diagram - see first Page of Table 195

		SE	SE	FC		FC	SE ■	SE	SE ■	SE ■	SE	SE	SE	FC		FC	SE ■	SE	SE ■	SE	SE	SE	FC	FC	
London Victoria ⊖	d	18 40					18 52	18 55	18 58	19 07	19 09	19 10					19 22	19 25	19 37	19 39	19 40				
Brixton ⊖	d	18 47						19 02				19 17						19 32			19 47				
Kentish Town ⊖	d			18 28		18 44								18 58		19 14							19 28	19 44	
St Pancras International ⊖	d			18 34		18 48								19 04		19 18							19 34	19 48	
Farringdon ⊖	d			18 39		18 53								19 09		19 23							19 39	19 53	
City Thameslink	d			18 43		18 57								19 13		19 27							19 43	19 57	
London Blackfriars ⊖	d		18 42	18 46		19 00							19 12	19 16		19 30						19 42	19 46	20 00	
Elephant & Castle ⊖	d		18 46	18 49		19 03							19 16	19 19		19 33						19 46	19 49	20 03	
Loughborough Jn	d			18 53		19 07								19 23		19 37							19 53	20 07	
Herne Hill	d	18 49		18a57		19a11		19 04				19 19		19a27		19a41		19 34			19 49		19a57	20a11	
West Dulwich	d	18 51						19 06				19 21						19 36			19 51				
Sydenham Hill	d	18 53						19 08				19 23						19 38			19 53				
Penge East	d	18 56						19 11				19 26						19 41			19 56				
Kent House	d	18 58						19 13				19 28						19 43			19 58				
Beckenham Junction	d	19 00						19 15				19 30						19 45			20 00				
Denmark Hill	d		18 52								19 18		19 22							19 48		19 52			
Peckham Rye	d		18 55								19 21		19 25							19 51		19 55			
Nunhead	d		18 57								19 23		19 27							19 53		19 57			
Lewisham	a										19 31									20 01					
Crofton Park	d		19 00										19 30									20 00			
Catford	d		19 03										19 33									20 03			
Bellingham	d		19 05										19 35									20 05			
Beckenham Hill	d		19 07										19 37									20 07			
Ravensbourne	d		19 09										19 39									20 09			
Shortlands	d	19 03	19 11					19 18				19 33	19 41					19 48			20 03	20 11			
Bromley South	d	19 06	19 14				19a08	19 21	19 19	19 23		19 36	19 44				19a38	19 51	19 53		20 06	20 14			
Bickley	d	19 09	19 17					19 24				19 39	19 47					19 54			20 09	20 17			
Petts Wood	d	19 14						19 29				19 44						19 59			20 14				
Orpington	d	19a17						19a32				19a48						20a02			20a18				
St Mary Cray	d		19 21						19 25				19 51						20 00			20 21			
Swanley	d		19 26						19a29	19 33			19 56						20 04			20 26			
Eynsford	d		19 30										20 00									20 30			
Shoreham (Kent)	d		19 34										20 04									20 34			
Otford	d		19 37							19a41			20 07						20a12			20 37			
Bat & Ball	d		19 40										20 10									20 40			
Sevenoaks	a		19 43										20 13									20 43			

		SE ■	SE	SE ■	SE ■	SE	SE	FC	FC	SE ■		SE	SE ■	SE	FC	FC	SE	SE ■	SE	FC		SE ■	SE	SE ■	SE
London Victoria ⊖	d	19 52	19 55	19 58	20 07	20 10				20 22		20 25	20 52				20 55	21 07				21 22	21 25	21 52	
Brixton ⊖	d		20 02			20 17						20 32					21 02						21 32		
Kentish Town ⊖	d							19 58	20 14						20 31	20 44				21 01					
St Pancras International ⊖	d							20 04	20 18						20 36	20 48				21 06					
Farringdon ⊖	d							20 09	20 23						20 40	20 53				21 10					
City Thameslink	d							20 13	20 27						20 43	20 57									
London Blackfriars ⊖	d						20 12	20 16	20 30					20 42	20 46	21 00			21 12	21 16					21 42
Elephant & Castle ⊖	d						20 16	20 19	20 33					20 46	20 49	21 03			21 16	21 19					21 46
Loughborough Jn	d							20 23	20 37						20 53	21 07				21 23					
Herne Hill	d		20 04			20 19		20a27	20a41			20 34			20a57	21a11	21 04			21a27			21 34		
West Dulwich	d		20 06			20 21						20 36					21 06						21 36		
Sydenham Hill	d		20 08			20 23						20 38					21 08						21 38		
Penge East	d		20 11			20 26						20 41					21 11						21 41		
Kent House	d		20 13			20 28						20 43					21 13						21 43		
Beckenham Junction	d		20 15			20 30						20 45					21 15						21 45		
Denmark Hill	d						20 22							20 52					21 22						21 52
Peckham Rye	d						20 25							20 55					21 25						21 55
Nunhead	d						20 27							20 57					21 27						21 57
Lewisham	a																								
Crofton Park	d						20 30							21 00					21 30						22 00
Catford	d						20 33							21 03					21 33						22 03
Bellingham	d						20 35							21 05					21 35						22 05
Beckenham Hill	d						20 37							21 07					21 37						22 07
Ravensbourne	d						20 39							21 09					21 39						22 09
Shortlands	d		20 18			20 33	20 41					20 48		21 11			21 18		21 41				21 48		22 11
Bromley South	d	20a08	20 21	20 19	20 23	20 36	20 44			20a38		20 51	21 09	21 14			21 21	21 23	21 44			21a38	21 51	22 09	22 14
Bickley	d		20 24			20 39	20 47					20 54		21 17			21 24		21 47				21 54		22 17
Petts Wood	d		20 29			20 44						20 59					21 29						21 59		
Orpington	d		20a32			20a47						21a02					21a32						22a02		
St Mary Cray	d			20 25	20 30		20 51						21 15	21 21				21 30	21 51					22 15	22 21
Swanley	d			20a29	20 34		20 56						21a19	21 26				21 34	21 56					22a19	22 26
Eynsford	d						21 00							21 30					22 00						22 30
Shoreham (Kent)	d						21 04							21 34					22 04						22 34
Otford	d				20a42		21 07							21 37				21a42	22 07						22 37
Bat & Ball	d						21 10							21 40					22 10						22 40
Sevenoaks	a						21 13							21 43					22 13						22 43

Table 195

London Victoria/Kentish Town - Catford, Beckenham Junction, Bromley South, Orpington, Otford and Sevenoaks

Saturdays
28 July to 11 August

Network Diagram - see first Page of Table 195

		FC	SE	SE [1]	SE	FC	SE [1]	SE	SE [1]	SE	FC	SE	SE [1]	SE	FC	SE [1]	SE	SE [1]	SE	FC	SE
London Victoria [15] ⊖	d		21 55	22 07			22 22	22 25	22 52			22 55	23 07			23 22	23 25	23 52			23 55
Brixton ⊖	d		22 02					22 32				23 02					23 32				00 02
Kentish Town ⊖	d	21 31				22 01					22 31				23 01					23 30	
St Pancras International [15] ⊖	d	21 36				22 06					22 36				23 06					23 36	
Farringdon ⊖	d	21 40				22 10					22 40				23 10					23 40	
City Thameslink [3]	d																				
London Blackfriars [3] ⊖	d	21 46			22 12	22 16				22 42	22 46			23 12	23 16				23 42	23 46	
Elephant & Castle ⊖	d	21 49			22 16	22 19				22 46	22 49			23 16	23 19				23 46	23 49	
Loughborough Jn	d	21 53				22 23					22 53				23 23						
Herne Hill [4]	d	21a57	22 04			22a27		22 34			22a57	23 04			23a27		23 34			23a57	00 04
West Dulwich	d		22 06					22 36				23 06					23 36				00 06
Sydenham Hill	d		22 08					22 38				23 08					23 38				00 08
Penge East	d		22 11					22 41				23 11					23 41				00 11
Kent House [4]	d		22 13					22 43				23 13					23 43				00 13
Beckenham Junction [4]	d		22 15					22 45				23 15					23 45				00 15
Denmark Hill [4]	d				22 22					22 52				23 22					23 52		
Peckham Rye [4]	d				22 25					22 55				23 25					23 55		
Nunhead [4]	d				22 27					22 57				23 27					23 57		
Lewisham [4]	a																				
Crofton Park	d				22 30					23 00				23 30					23 59		
Catford	d				22 33					23 03				23 33					00 03		
Bellingham	d				22 35					23 05				23 35					00 05		
Beckenham Hill	d				22 37					23 07				23 37					00 07		
Ravensbourne	d				22 39					23 09				23 39					00 09		
Shortlands [4]	d		22 18		22 41			22 48		23 11		23 18		23 41			23 48		00 11		00 18
Bromley South [4]	d		22 21	22 23	22 44		22a38	22 51	23 09	23 14		23 21	23 23	23 44		23a38	23 51	00 09	00 14		00 21
Bickley [4]	d		22 24		22 47			22 54		23 17		23 24		23 47			23 54		00 17		00 24
Petts Wood [4]	d		22 29					22 59				23 29					23 59				00 29
Orpington [4]	d		22a32					23a02				23a32					00a02				00a32
St Mary Cray	d			22 30	22 51				23 15	23 21			23 30	23 51				00 15	00 21		
Swanley [4]	d			22 34	22 56				23a19	23 26			23 34	23 56				00a19	00 26		
Eynsford	d				23 00					23 30				23 59					00 30		
Shoreham (Kent)	d				23 04					23 34				00 04					00 34		
Otford [4]	d			22a42	23 07					23 37			23a42	00 07					00 37		
Bat & Ball	d				23 10					23 40				00 10					00 40		
Sevenoaks [4]	a				23 13					23 43				00 13					00 43		

Saturdays
25 August to 8 September

		SE	SE [1]	SE	SE	SE [1]	SE	SE A	SE [1] A	SE A	SE [1]	FC	SE	SE [1]	SE [1]	SE	FC	FC	SE	SE	FC	FC	SE
London Victoria [15] ⊖	d		23p52		23p55	00 07	00 35	00 45	00 51	00 56	05 22		05 55	06 07	06 22				06 25				06 55
Brixton ⊖	d				00 02			00s52					06 02						06 32				07 02
Kentish Town ⊖	d											05 44						06 14			06 28	06 44	
St Pancras International [15] ⊖	d											05 48						06 18			06 34	06 48	
Farringdon ⊖	d											05 53						06 23			06 39	06 53	
City Thameslink [3]	d																						
London Blackfriars [3] ⊖	d	23p12		23p42								06 00				06 12	06 16	06 30		06 42	06 46	07 00	
Elephant & Castle ⊖	d	23p16		23p46								06 03				06 16	06 19	06 33		06 46	06 49	07 03	
Loughborough Jn	d																				06 53	07 07	
Herne Hill [4]	d				00 04		00 43	00s54				06a11	06 04				06a27	06a41	06 34		06a57	07a11	07 04
West Dulwich	d				00 06			00s57					06 06						06 36				07 06
Sydenham Hill	d				00 08			01s00					06 08						06 38				07 08
Penge East	d				00 11		00 48	01s03					06 11						06 41				07 11
Kent House [4]	d				00 13			01s06					06 13						06 43				07 13
Beckenham Junction [4]	d				00 15		00 50	01s08					06 15						06 45				07 15
Denmark Hill [4]	d	23p22		23p52						01s05						06 22				06 52			
Peckham Rye [4]	d	23p25		23p55						01s08						06 25				06 55			
Nunhead [4]	d	23p27		23p57						01s10						06 27				06 57			
Lewisham [4]	a																						
Crofton Park	d	23p30		23p59						01s13						06 30				07 00			
Catford	d	23p33		00 03						01s16						06 33				07 03			
Bellingham	d	23p35		00 05						01s18						06 35				07 05			
Beckenham Hill	d	23p37		00 07						01s20						06 37				07 07			
Ravensbourne	d	23p39		00 09						01s22						06 39				07 09			
Shortlands [4]	d	23p41		00 11	00 18			01s12					06 18			06 41			06 48	07 11			07 18
Bromley South [4]	d	23p44	00 09	00 14	00 21	00 25	00 55	01s15	01s10	01s25	05 39		06 21	06 23	06 39	06 44			06 51	07 14			07 21
Bickley [4]	d	23p47		00 17	00 24			01s18					06 24			06 47			06 54	07 17			07 24
Petts Wood [4]	d				00 29			01s25					06 29						06 59				07 29
Orpington [4]	d				00a32			01a29		01a33			06a32						07a02				07a32
St Mary Cray	d	23p51	00 15	00 21		00 32	01 01		01s17		05 45			06 30	06 45	06 51				07 21			
Swanley [4]	d	23p56	00a19	00 26		00 36	01a05		01s21		05a49			06 34	06a49	06 56				07 26			
Eynsford	d	23p59		00 30					01s26							07 00				07 30			
Shoreham (Kent)	d	00 04		00 34					01s30							07 04				07 34			
Otford [4]	d	00 07		00 37		00a44			01s33					06a42		07 07				07 37			
Bat & Ball	d	00 10		00 40												07 10				07 40			
Sevenoaks [4]	a	00 13		00 43												07 13				07 43			

A not 25 August

Table 195

London Victoria/Kentish Town - Catford, Beckenham Junction, Bromley South, Orpington, Otford and Sevenoaks

Saturdays
25 August to 8 September

Network Diagram - see first Page of Table 195

		SE [1]	SE [1]	SE	SE	FC	FC	SE [1]	SE	SE [1]	SE	SE	SE	FC	FC	SE [1]	SE	SE [1]	SE [1]	SE	SE	SE	FC
London Victoria [15] ⊖	d	06 58	07 07	07 10				07 22	07 25	07 37	07 39	07 40				07 52	07 55	07 58	08 07	08 09	08 10		
Brixton ⊖	d			07 17					07 32			07 47					08 02				08 17		
Kentish Town ⊖	d					06 58	07 14							07 28	07 44								07 58
St Pancras International [15] ⊖	d					07 04	07 18							07 34	07 48								08 04
Farringdon ⊖	d					07 09	07 23							07 39	07 53								08 09
City Thameslink [3]	d																						
London Blackfriars [3] ⊖	d				07 12	07 16	07 30						07 42	07 46	08 00							08 12	08 16
Elephant & Castle ⊖	d				07 16	07 19	07 33						07 46	07 49	08 03							08 16	08 19
Loughborough Jn	d					07 23	07 37							07 53	08 07								08 23
Herne Hill [4]	d			07 19		07a27	07a41		07 34			07 49		07a57	08a11		08 04				08 19		08a27
West Dulwich	d			07 21					07 36			07 51					08 06				08 21		
Sydenham Hill	d			07 23					07 38			07 53					08 08				08 23		
Penge East	d			07 26					07 41			07 56					08 11				08 26		
Kent House [4]	d			07 28					07 43			07 58					08 13				08 28		
Beckenham Junction [4]	d			07 30					07 45			08 00					08 15				08 30		
Denmark Hill [4]	d				07 22						07 48		07 52							08 18		08 22	
Peckham Rye [4]	d				07 25						07 51		07 55							08 21		08 25	
Nunhead [4]	d				07 27						07 53		07 57							08 23		08 27	
Lewisham [4]	a										08 02									08 31			
Crofton Park	d				07 30								08 00									08 30	
Catford	d				07 33								08 03									08 33	
Bellingham	d				07 35								08 05									08 35	
Beckenham Hill	d				07 37								08 07									08 37	
Ravensbourne	d				07 39								08 09									08 39	
Shortlands [4]	d			07 33	07 41				07 48			08 03	08 11				08 18				08 33	08 41	
Bromley South [4]	d	07 19	07 23	07 36	07 44			07a38	07 51	07 53		08 06	08 14			08a08	08 21	08 19	08 23		08 36	08 44	
Bickley [4]	d			07 39	07 47				07 54			08 09	08 17				08 24				08 39	08 47	
Petts Wood [4]	d			07 44					07 59			08 14					08 29				08 44		
Orpington [4]	d			07a47					08a02			08a17					08a32				08a47		
St Mary Cray	d	07 25	07 30		07 51					08 00			08 21					08 25				08 51	
Swanley [4]	d	07a29	07 34		07 56					08 04			08 26					08a29	08 33			08 56	
Eynsford	d				08 00								08 30									09 00	
Shoreham (Kent)	d				08 04								08 34									09 04	
Otford [4]	d		07a42		08 07					08a12			08 37						08a41			09 07	
Bat & Ball	d				08 10								08 40									09 10	
Sevenoaks [4]	a				08 13								08 43									09 13	

		FC	SE [1]	SE	SE [1]	SE	SE	SE	FC	FC	SE [1]	SE	SE [1]	SE [1]	SE	SE	SE	FC	FC	SE [1]	SE	SE [1]
London Victoria [15] ⊖	d		08 22	08 25	08 37	08 39	08 40				08 52	08 55	08 58	09 07	09 09	09 10				09 22	09 25	09 37
Brixton ⊖	d			08 32			08 47					09 02				09 17					09 32	
Kentish Town ⊖	d	08 14							08 28	08 44								08 58	09 14			
St Pancras International [15] ⊖	d	08 18							08 34	08 48								09 04	09 18			
Farringdon ⊖	d	08 23							08 39	08 53								09 09	09 23			
City Thameslink [3]	d																	09 13	09 27			
London Blackfriars [3] ⊖	d	08 30						08 42	08 46	09 00							09 12	09 16	09 30			
Elephant & Castle ⊖	d	08 33						08 46	08 49	09 03							09 16	09 19	09 33			
Loughborough Jn	d	08 37							08 53	09 07								09 23	09 37			
Herne Hill [4]	d	08a41		08 34			08 49		08a57	09a11		09 04				09 19		09a27	09a41		09 34	
West Dulwich	d			08 36			08 51					09 06				09 21					09 36	
Sydenham Hill	d			08 38			08 53					09 08				09 23					09 38	
Penge East	d			08 41			08 56					09 11				09 26					09 41	
Kent House [4]	d			08 43			08 58					09 13				09 28					09 43	
Beckenham Junction [4]	d			08 45			09 00					09 15				09 30					09 45	
Denmark Hill [4]	d					08 48		08 52							09 18		09 22					
Peckham Rye [4]	d					08 51		08 55							09 21		09 25					
Nunhead [4]	d					08 53		08 57							09 23		09 27					
Lewisham [4]	a					09 01									09 31							
Crofton Park	d							09 00									09 30					
Catford	d							09 03									09 33					
Bellingham	d							09 05									09 35					
Beckenham Hill	d							09 07									09 37					
Ravensbourne	d							09 09									09 39					
Shortlands [4]	d			08 48			09 03	09 11				09 18				09 33	09 41				09 48	
Bromley South [4]	d		08a38	08 51	08 53		09 06	09 14			09a08	09 21	09 19	09 23		09 36	09 44			09a38	09 51	09 53
Bickley [4]	d			08 54			09 09	09 17				09 24				09 39	09 47				09 54	
Petts Wood [4]	d			08 59			09 14					09 29				09 44					09 59	
Orpington [4]	d			09a02			09a17					09a32				09a47					10a02	
St Mary Cray	d				09 00			09 21					09 25				09 51					10 00
Swanley [4]	d				09 04			09 26					09a29	09 33			09 56					10 04
Eynsford	d							09 30									10 00					
Shoreham (Kent)	d							09 34									10 04					
Otford [4]	d				09a12			09 37						09a41			10 07					10a12
Bat & Ball	d							09 40									10 10					
Sevenoaks [4]	a							09 43									10 13					

London Victoria/Kentish Town - Catford, Beckenham Junction, Bromley South, Orpington, Otford and Sevenoaks

Network Diagram - see first Page of Table 195

		SE	SE	SE	FC	FC	and at the same minutes past each hour until	FC	SE 1	SE	SE 1	SE 1	SE	SE	SE	FC	FC	SE 1	SE	SE 1	SE	SE
London Victoria 15 ⊖	d	09 39	09 40						18 52	18 55	18 58	19 07	19 09	19 10				19 22	19 25	19 37	19 39	19 40
Brixton ⊖	d		09 47							19 02				19 17					19 32			19 47
Kentish Town ⊖	d				09 28	09 44		18 44								18 58	19 14					
St Pancras International 15 ⊖	d				09 34	09 48		18 48								19 04	19 18					
Farringdon ⊖	d				09 39	09 53		18 53								19 09	19 23					
City Thameslink 3	d				09 43	09 57		18 57								19 13	19 27					
London Blackfriars 3 ⊖	d			09 42	09 46	10 00		19 00							19 12	19 16	19 30					
Elephant & Castle ⊖	d			09 46	09 49	10 03		19 03							19 16	19 19	19 33					
Loughborough Jn	d				09 53	10 07		19 07								19 23	19 37					
Herne Hill 4	d		09 49		09a57	10a11		19a11		19 04				19 19		19a27	19a41		19 34			19 49
West Dulwich	d		09 51							19 06				19 21					19 36			19 51
Sydenham Hill	d		09 53							19 08				19 23					19 38			19 53
Penge East	d		09 56							19 11				19 26					19 41			19 56
Kent House 4	d		09 58							19 13				19 28					19 43			19 58
Beckenham Junction 4	d		10 00							19 15				19 30					19 45			20 00
Denmark Hill 4	d	09 48		09 52									19 18		19 22						19 48	
Peckham Rye 4	d	09 51		09 55									19 21		19 25						19 51	
Nunhead 4	d	09 53		09 57									19 23		19 27						19 53	
Lewisham 4	a	10 01											19 31								20 01	
Crofton Park	d			10 00											19 30							
Catford	d			10 03											19 33							
Bellingham	d			10 05											19 35							
Beckenham Hill	d			10 07											19 37							
Ravensbourne	d			10 09											19 39							
Shortlands 4	d		10 03	10 11						19 18				19 33	19 41				19 48			20 03
Bromley South 4	d		10 06	10 14					19a08	19 21	19 19	19 23		19 36	19 44			19a38	19 51	19 53		20 06
Bickley 4	d		10 09	10 17						19 24				19 39	19 47				19 54			20 09
Petts Wood 4	d		10 14							19 29				19 44					19 59			20 14
Orpington 4	d		10a17							19a32				19a48					20a02			20a18
St Mary Cray	d			10 21							19 25				19 51					20 00		
Swanley 4	d			10 26							19a29	19 33			19 56					20 04		
Eynsford	d			10 30											20 00							
Shoreham (Kent)	d			10 34											20 04							
Otford 4	d			10 37								19a41			20 07					20a12		
Bat & Ball	d			10 40											20 10							
Sevenoaks 4	a			10 43											20 13							

		SE	FC	FC	SE 1	SE	SE 1	SE 1	SE	SE	FC	FC	SE 1	SE	SE 1	SE	FC	FC	SE	SE 1	SE	FC	SE 1
London Victoria 15 ⊖	d				19 52	19 55	19 58	20 07	20 10				20 22	20 25	20 52				20 55	21 07			21 22
Brixton ⊖	d					20 02			20 17					20 32					21 02				
Kentish Town ⊖	d		19 28	19 44							19 58	20 14					20 31	20 44				21 01	
St Pancras International 15 ⊖	d		19 34	19 48							20 04	20 18					20 36	20 48				21 06	
Farringdon ⊖	d		19 39	19 53							20 09	20 23					20 40	20 53				21 10	
City Thameslink 3	d		19 43	19 57							20 13	20 27					20 43	20 57					
London Blackfriars 3 ⊖	d	19 42	19 46	20 00						20 12	20 16	20 30				20 42	20 46	21 00			21 12	21 16	
Elephant & Castle ⊖	d	19 46	19 49	20 03						20 16	20 19	20 33				20 46	20 49	21 03			21 16	21 19	
Loughborough Jn	d		19 53	20 07							20 23	20 37					20 53	21 07				21 23	
Herne Hill 4	d		19a57	20a11		20 04			20 19		20a27	20a41		20 34			20a57	21a11	21 04			21a27	
West Dulwich	d					20 06			20 21					20 36					21 06				
Sydenham Hill	d					20 08			20 23					20 38					21 08				
Penge East	d					20 11			20 26					20 41					21 11				
Kent House 4	d					20 13			20 28					20 43					21 13				
Beckenham Junction 4	d					20 15			20 30					20 45					21 15				
Denmark Hill 4	d	19 52								20 22						20 52					21 22		
Peckham Rye 4	d	19 55								20 25						20 55					21 25		
Nunhead 4	d	19 57								20 27						20 57					21 27		
Lewisham 4	a																						
Crofton Park	d	20 00								20 30						21 00					21 30		
Catford	d	20 03								20 33						21 03					21 33		
Bellingham	d	20 05								20 35						21 05					21 35		
Beckenham Hill	d	20 07								20 37						21 07					21 37		
Ravensbourne	d	20 09								20 39						21 09					21 39		
Shortlands 4	d	20 11				20 18			20 33	20 41				20 48		21 11			21 18		21 41		
Bromley South 4	d	20 14			20a08	20 21	20 19	20 23	20 36	20 44			20a38	20 51	21 09	21 14			21 21	21 23	21 44		21a38
Bickley 4	d	20 17				20 24			20 39	20 47				20 54		21 17			21 24		21 47		
Petts Wood 4	d					20 29			20 44					20 59					21 29				
Orpington 4	d					20a32			20a47					21a02					21a32				
St Mary Cray	d	20 21					20 25	20 30		20 51					21 15	21 21				21 30	21 51		
Swanley 4	d	20 26					20a29	20 34		20 56					21a19	21 26				21 34	21 56		
Eynsford	d	20 30								21 00						21 30					22 00		
Shoreham (Kent)	d	20 34								21 04						21 34					22 04		
Otford 4	d	20 37						20a42		21 07						21 37				21a42	22 07		
Bat & Ball	d	20 40								21 10						21 40					22 10		
Sevenoaks 4	a	20 43								21 13						21 43					22 13		

London Victoria/Kentish Town - Catford, Beckenham Junction, Bromley South, Orpington, Otford and Sevenoaks

Network Diagram - see first Page of Table 195

		SE	SE 1	SE	FC	SE	SE 1	SE	FC	SE 1	SE	SE 1	SE	FC	SE	SE 1	SE	FC	SE 1	SE	SE 1	SE
London Victoria 15 ⊖	d	21 25	21 52			21 55	22 07			22 22	22 25	22 52			22 55	23 07			23 22	23 25	23 52	
Brixton ⊖	d	21 32				22 02					22 32				23 02					23 32		
Kentish Town ⊖	d				21 31				22 01					22 31				23 01				
St Pancras International 15 ⊖	d				21 36				22 06					22 36				23 06				
Farringdon ⊖	d				21 40				22 10					22 40				23 10				
City Thameslink 3	d																					
London Blackfriars 3 ⊖	d			21 42	21 46			22 12	22 16				22 42	22 46			23 12	23 16				23 42
Elephant & Castle ⊖	d			21 46	21 49			22 16	22 19				22 46	22 49			23 16	23 19				23 46
Loughborough Jn	d				21 53				22 23					22 53				23 23				
Herne Hill 4	d	21 34			21a57	22 04			22a27		22 34			22a57	23 04			23a27		23 34		
West Dulwich	d	21 36				22 06					22 36				23 06					23 36		
Sydenham Hill	d	21 38				22 08					22 38				23 08					23 38		
Penge East	d	21 41				22 11					22 41				23 11					23 41		
Kent House 4	d	21 43				22 13					22 43				23 13					23 43		
Beckenham Junction 4	d	21 45				22 15					22 45				23 15					23 45		
Denmark Hill 4	d			21 52				22 22					22 52				23 22					23 52
Peckham Rye 4	d			21 55				22 25					22 55				23 25					23 55
Nunhead 4	d			21 57				22 27					22 57				23 27					23 57
Lewisham 4	a																					
Crofton Park	d			22 00				22 30					23 00				23 30					23 59
Catford	d			22 03				22 33					23 03				23 33					00 03
Bellingham	d			22 05				22 35					23 05				23 35					00 05
Beckenham Hill	d			22 07				22 37					23 07				23 37					00 07
Ravensbourne	d			22 09				22 39					23 09				23 39					00 09
Shortlands 4	d	21 48		22 11		22 18		22 41			22 48		23 11		23 18		23 41			23 48		00 11
Bromley South 4	d	21 51	22 09	22 14		22 21	22 23	22 44		22a38	22 51	23 09	23 14		23 21	23 23	23 44		23a38	23 51	00 09	00 14
Bickley 4	d	21 54		22 17		22 24		22 47			22 54		23 17		23 24		23 47			23 54		00 17
Petts Wood 4	d	21 59				22 29					22 59				23 29					23 59		
Orpington 4	d	22a02				22a32					23a02				23a32					00a02		
St Mary Cray	d		22 15	22 21			22 30	22 51				23 15	23 21			23 30	23 51				00 15	00 21
Swanley 4	d		22a19	22 26			22 34	22 56				23a19	23 26			23 34	23 56				00a19	00 26
Eynsford	d			22 30				23 00					23 30				23 59					00 30
Shoreham (Kent)	d			22 34				23 04					23 34				00 04					00 34
Otford 4	d			22 37			22a42	23 07					23 37			23a42	00 07					00 37
Bat & Ball	d			22 40				23 10					23 40				00 10					00 40
Sevenoaks 4	a			22 43				23 13					23 43				00 13					00 43

		FC	SE
London Victoria 15 ⊖	d		23 55
Brixton ⊖	d		00 02
Kentish Town ⊖	d	23 30	
St Pancras International 15 ⊖	d	23 36	
Farringdon ⊖	d	23 40	
City Thameslink 3	d		
London Blackfriars 3 ⊖	d	23 46	
Elephant & Castle ⊖	d	23 49	
Loughborough Jn	d		
Herne Hill 4	d	23a57	00 04
West Dulwich	d		00 06
Sydenham Hill	d		00 08
Penge East	d		00 11
Kent House 4	d		00 13
Beckenham Junction 4	d		00 15
Denmark Hill 4	d		
Peckham Rye 4	d		
Nunhead 4	d		
Lewisham 4	a		
Crofton Park	d		
Catford	d		
Bellingham	d		
Beckenham Hill	d		
Ravensbourne	d		
Shortlands 4	d		00 18
Bromley South 4	d		00 21
Bickley 4	d		00 24
Petts Wood 4	d		00 29
Orpington 4	d		00a32
St Mary Cray	d		
Swanley 4	d		
Eynsford	d		
Shoreham (Kent)	d		
Otford 4	d		
Bat & Ball	d		
Sevenoaks 4	a		

Table 195

Sundays

until 22 July, 19 Aug and from 16 Sep

London Victoria/Kentish Town - Catford, Beckenham Junction, Bromley South, Orpington, Otford and Sevenoaks

Network Diagram - see first Page of Table 195

	SE A	SE B	SE ■	SE A	SE	SE ■	SE	SE ■	SE ■	SE	SE	SE ■	SE	SE	SE ■	SE ■	SE	SE	FC	SE ■	SE	FC
London Victoria ⊖ d		23p43	23p52		23p55	00 07	00 35	07 24	07 45		07 51	08 05		08 21	08 24	08 45		08 51		09 05		
Brixton ⊖ d					00 02						07 58			08 28				08 58				
Kentish Town ⊖ d																						09 00
St Pancras International ⊖ d																						09 05
Farringdon ⊖ d																						09 10
City Thameslink d																						
London Blackfriars ⊖ d	23p12			23p42						07 38			08 08				08 38		08 56		09 08	09 15
Elephant & Castle ⊖ d	23p16			23p46						07 42			08 12				08 42		09 00		09 12	09 18
Loughborough Jn d																			09 04			09 22
Herne Hill d					00 04		00 43				08 00			08 30				09 00	09a07			09a26
West Dulwich d					00 06						08 02			08 32				09 02				
Sydenham Hill d					00 08						08 04			08 34				09 04				
Penge East d					00 11		00 48				08 07			08 37				09 07				
Kent House d					00 13						08 09			08 39				09 09				
Beckenham Junction d					00 15		00 50				08 11			08 41				09 11				
Denmark Hill d	23p22	23p52		23p52						07 48			08 18				08 48				09 18	
Peckham Rye d	23p25	23p55		23p55						07 51			08 21				08 51				09 21	
Nunhead d	23p27	23p57		23p57						07 53			08 23				08 53				09 23	
Lewisham a																						
Crofton Park d	23p30	23p58		23p59						07 56			08 26				08 56				09 26	
Catford d	23p33	00 03		00 03						07 59			08 29				08 59				09 29	
Bellingham d	23p35	00 05		00 05						08 01			08 31				09 01				09 31	
Beckenham Hill d	23p37	00 07		00 07						08 03			08 33				09 03				09 33	
Ravensbourne d	23p39	00 09		00 09						08 05			08 35				09 05				09 35	
Shortlands d	23p41	00 11		00 11	00 18					08 07	08 14		08 37	08 44			09 07	09 14			09 37	
Bromley South d	23p44	00 14	00 09	00 14	00 21	00 25	00 55	07 44	08 01	08 10	08 18	08a21	08 40	08 48	08 44	09 01	09 10	09 18		09a21	09 40	
Bickley d	23p47	00 17		00 17	00 24					08 13	08 20		08 43	08 50			09 13	09 20			09 43	
Petts Wood d		00 22			00 29						08 25			08 55				09 25				
Orpington d		00a25			00a32						08a28			08a58				09a28				
St Mary Cray d	23p51		00 15	00 21		00 32	01 01	07 50	08 08	08 17			08 47		08 50	09 08	09 17				09 47	
Swanley d	23p56		00a19	00 26		00 36	01a05	07a54	08 12	08 22			08 52		08a54	09 12	09 22				09 52	
Eynsford d	23p59			00 30						08 26			08 56				09 26				09 56	
Shoreham (Kent) d	00 04			00 34						08 30			09 00				09 30				10 00	
Otford d	00 07			00 37		00a44			08a20	08 33			09 03			09a20	09 33				10 03	
Bat & Ball d	00 10			00 40						08 36			09 06				09 36				10 06	
Sevenoaks a	00 13			00 43						08 39			09 09				09 39				10 09	

	SE	SE ■	FC	SE ■	SE	FC		FC	SE	SE ■	SE	FC	SE	SE ■	SE ■	SE	SE	SE ■	SE	SE	SE ■
London Victoria ⊖ d	09 21	09 24		09 45					20 51	21 05			21 21	21 24	21 45		21 51	22 05		22 21	22 24
Brixton ⊖ d	09 28								20 58				21 28				21 58			22 28	
Kentish Town ⊖ d						09 30		20 30				21 00									
St Pancras International ⊖ d						09 35		20 35				21 05									
Farringdon ⊖ d						09 40		20 40				21 10									
City Thameslink d																					
London Blackfriars ⊖ d			09 26		09 38	09 45		20 45			21 08	21 15				21 38			22 08		
Elephant & Castle ⊖ d			09 30		09 42	09 48		20 48			21 12	21 18				21 42			22 12		
Loughborough Jn d			09 34			09 52		20 52				21 22									
Herne Hill d	09 30		09a37			09a56		20a56	21 00			21a26	21 30				22 00			22 30	
West Dulwich d	09 32								21 02				21 32				22 02			22 32	
Sydenham Hill d	09 34								21 04				21 34				22 04			22 34	
Penge East d	09 37								21 07				21 37				22 07			22 37	
Kent House d	09 39								21 09				21 39				22 09			22 39	
Beckenham Junction d	09 41						and at the same minutes past each hour until		21 11				21 41				22 11			22 41	
Denmark Hill d					09 48						21 18					21 48			22 18		
Peckham Rye d					09 51						21 21					21 51			22 21		
Nunhead d					09 53						21 23					21 53			22 23		
Lewisham a																					
Crofton Park d					09 56						21 26					21 56			22 26		
Catford d					09 59						21 29					21 59			22 29		
Bellingham d					10 01						21 31					22 01			22 31		
Beckenham Hill d					10 03						21 33					22 03			22 33		
Ravensbourne d					10 05						21 35					22 05			22 35		
Shortlands d	09 44				10 07				21 14		21 37		21 44			22 07	22 14		22 37	22 44	
Bromley South d	09 48	09 44		10 01	10 10				21 18	21a21	21 40		21 48	21 44	22 01	22 10	22 18	22a21	22 40	22 48	22 44
Bickley d	09 50				10 13				21 20		21 43		21 50			22 13	22 20		22 43	22 50	
Petts Wood d	09 55								21 25				21 55				22 25			22 55	
Orpington d	09a58								21a28				21a58				22a28			22a58	
St Mary Cray d		09 50		10 08	10 17						21 47			21 50	22 08	22 17			22 47		22 50
Swanley d		09a54		10 12	10 22						21 52			21a54	22 12	22 22			22 52		22a54
Eynsford d					10 26						21 56					22 26			22 56		
Shoreham (Kent) d					10 30						22 00					22 30			23 00		
Otford d				10a20	10 33						22 03				22a20	22 33			23 03		
Bat & Ball d					10 36						22 06					22 36			23 06		
Sevenoaks a					10 39						22 09					22 39			23 09		

A not 20 May

B 20 May

Table 195

Sundays

until 22 July, 19 Aug and from 16 Sep

London Victoria/Kentish Town - Catford, Beckenham Junction, Bromley South, Orpington, Otford and Sevenoaks

Network Diagram - see first Page of Table 195

	SE ■	SE	SE	SE ■	SE	SE	SE ■	SE
London Victoria ⊖ d	22 45		22 51	23 05		23 21	23 45	
Brixton ⊖ d			22 58			23 28		
Kentish Town ⊖ d								
St Pancras International ⊖ d								
Farringdon ⊖ d								
City Thameslink d								
London Blackfriars ⊖ d		22 38			23 08			23 38
Elephant & Castle ⊖ d		22 42			23 12			23 42
Loughborough Jn d								
Herne Hill d			23 00			23 30		
West Dulwich d			23 02			23 32		
Sydenham Hill d			23 04			23 34		
Penge East d			23 07			23 37		
Kent House d			23 09			23 39		
Beckenham Junction d			23 11			23 41		
Denmark Hill d		22 48			23 18			23 48
Peckham Rye d		22 51			23 21			23 51
Nunhead d		22 53			23 23			23 53
Lewisham a								
Crofton Park d		22 56			23 26			23 56
Catford d		22 59			23 29			23 59
Bellingham d		23 01			23 31			00 01
Beckenham Hill d		23 03			23 33			00 03
Ravensbourne d		23 05			23 35			00 05
Shortlands d		23 07	23 14		23 37	23 44		00 07
Bromley South d	23 01	23 10	23 18	23a21	23 40	23 48	00 02	00 10
Bickley d		23 13	23 20		23 43	23 50		00 13
Petts Wood d			23 25			23 55		
Orpington d			23a29			23a59		
St Mary Cray d	23 08	23 17			23 47		00 08	00 17
Swanley d	23 12	23 22			23 52		00a12	00 22
Eynsford d		23 26			23 56			00 26
Shoreham (Kent) d		23 30			23 59			00 30
Otford d	23a20	23 33			00 03			00 33
Bat & Ball d		23 36			00 06			00 36
Sevenoaks a		23 39			00 09			00 39

Sundays

29 July to 12 August

	SE	SE ■	SE	SE	SE ■	SE	SE	SE	SE ■	SE	SE	SE	SE ■	SE	SE	SE ■	SE	SE	SE ■	SE	SE	SE ■
London Victoria ⊖ d		23p52		23p55	00 07	00 35	00 45	00 56	01 00			06 55	07 17		07 25	07 37	07 39		07 52	07 55	08 09	08 17
Brixton ⊖ d				00 02			00 52					07 02			07 32					08 02		
Kentish Town ⊖ d																						
St Pancras International ⊖ d																						
Farringdon ⊖ d																						
City Thameslink d																						
London Blackfriars ⊖ d	23p12		23p42							06 12	06 42			07 12				07 42				
Elephant & Castle ⊖ d	23p16		23p46							06 16	06 46			07 16				07 46				
Loughborough Jn d																						
Herne Hill d				00 04		00 43	00 56					07 04			07 34					08 04		
West Dulwich d				00 06			00 58					07 06			07 36					08 06		
Sydenham Hill d				00 08			01 00					07 08			07 38					08 08		
Penge East d				00 11		00 48	01 03					07 11			07 41					08 11		
Kent House d				00 13			01 05					07 13			07 43					08 13		
Beckenham Junction d				00 15		00 50	01 08					07 15			07 45					08 15		
Denmark Hill d	23p22		23p52					01 06		06 22	06 52			07 22			07 48	07 52			08 18	
Peckham Rye d	23p25		23p55					01 08		06 25	06 55			07 25			07 51	07 55			08 21	
Nunhead d	23p27		23p57					01 11		06 27	06 57			07 27			07 53	07 57			08 23	
Lewisham a																	08 00				08 31	
Crofton Park d	23p30		23p59					01 14		06 30	07 00			07 30				08 00				
Catford d	23p33		00 03					01 16		06 33	07 03			07 33				08 03				
Bellingham d	23p35		00 05					01 19		06 35	07 05			07 35				08 05				
Beckenham Hill d	23p37		00 07					01 21		06 37	07 07			07 37				08 07				
Ravensbourne d	23p39		00 09					01 23		06 39	07 09			07 39				08 09				
Shortlands d	23p41		00 11	00 18			01 11	01 25		06 41	07 11	07 18		07 41	07 48			08 11		08 18		
Bromley South d	23p44	00 09	00 14	00 21	00 25	00 55	01 14	01 28	01 16	06 44	07 14	07 21	07 34	07 44	07 51	07 53		08 14	08a08	08 21		08 34
Bickley d	23p47		00 17	00 24			01 16	01 30		06 47	07 17	07 24		07 47	07 54			08 17		08 24		
Petts Wood d				00 29			01 21	01 35				07 29			07 59					08 29		
Orpington d				00a32			01a27	01a42				07a32			08a02					08a32		
St Mary Cray d	23p51	00 15	00 21		00 32	01 01			01 23	06 51	07 21		07 40	07 51		08 00		08 21				08 40
Swanley d	23p56	00a19	00 26		00 36	01a05			01 27	06 56	07 26		07a44	07 56		08 04		08 26				08a44
Eynsford d	23p59		00 30						01 32	07 00	07 30			08 00				08 30				
Shoreham (Kent) d	00 04		00 34						01 35	07 04	07 34			08 04				08 34				
Otford d	00 07		00 37		00a44				01a38	07 07	07 37			08 07		08a12		08 37				
Bat & Ball d	00 10		00 40							07 10	07 40			08 10				08 40				
Sevenoaks a	00 13		00 43							07 13	07 43			08 13				08 43				

Table 195

Sundays
29 July to 12 August

London Victoria/Kentish Town - Catford, Beckenham Junction, Bromley South, Orpington, Otford and Sevenoaks

Network Diagram - see first Page of Table 195

		SE	SE	SE 1	SE	SE		SE 1	SE	FC	SE	SE 1	SE	FC	SE	FC		SE 1	SE	SE	FC	SE 1 ⌶	SE	FC	SE
London Victoria 15 ⊖	d		08 25	08 37	08 39			08 52	08 55		09 09	09 17			09 25			09 37	09 39			09 52	09 55		10 09
Brixton ⊖	d		08 32						09 02						09 32								10 02		
Kentish Town ⊖	d													09 00							09 30				
St Pancras International 15 ⊖	d													09 05							09 35				
Farringdon ⊖	d													09 10							09 40				
City Thameslink 3	d																								
London Blackfriars 3 ⊖	d	08 12				08 42				08 56			09 12	09 15		09 26				09 42	09 45			09 56	
Elephant & Castle ⊖	d	08 16				08 46				09 00			09 16	09 18		09 30				09 46	09 48			10 00	
Loughborough Jn	d									09 04				09 22		09 34					09 52			10 04	
Herne Hill 4	d		08 34						09 04	09a07				09a26	09 34	09a37					09a56		10 04	10a07	
West Dulwich	d		08 36						09 06						09 36								10 06		
Sydenham Hill	d		08 38						09 08						09 38								10 08		
Penge East	d		08 41						09 11						09 41								10 11		
Kent House 4	d		08 43						09 13						09 43								10 13		
Beckenham Junction 4 ⇌	d		08 45						09 15						09 45								10 15		
Denmark Hill 4	d	08 22			08 48	08 52					09 18		09 22						09 47	09 52					10 18
Peckham Rye 4	d	08 25			08 51	08 55					09 21		09 25						09 51	09 55					10 21
Nunhead 4	d	08 27			08 53	08 57					09 23		09 27						09 52	09 57					10 23
Lewisham 4 ⇌	a				09 01						09 31								10 01						10 31
Crofton Park	d	08 30				09 00							09 30							10 00					
Catford	d	08 33				09 03							09 33							10 03					
Bellingham	d	08 35				09 05							09 35							10 05					
Beckenham Hill	d	08 37				09 07							09 37							10 07					
Ravensbourne	d	08 39				09 09							09 39							10 09					
Shortlands 4	d	08 41	08 48			09 11			09 18				09 41		09 48					10 11			10 18		
Bromley South 4	d	08 44	08 51	08 53		09 14		09a08	09 21			09 34	09 44		09 51			09 53		10 14		10a08	10 21		
Bickley 4	d	08 47	08 54			09 17			09 24				09 47		09 54					10 17			10 24		
Petts Wood 4	d		08 59						09 29						09 59								10 29		
Orpington 4	d		09a02						09a32						10a02								10a32		
St Mary Cray	d	08 51		09 00		09 21						09 40	09 51					10 00		10 21					
Swanley 4	d	08 56		09 04		09 26						09a44	09 56					10 04		10 26					
Eynsford	d	09 00				09 30							10 00							10 30					
Shoreham (Kent)	d	09 04				09 34							10 04							10 34					
Otford 4	d	09 07		09a12		09 37							10 07					10a12		10 37					
Bat & Ball	d	09 10				09 40							10 10							10 40					
Sevenoaks 4	a	09 13				09 43							10 13							10 43					

		SE 1		SE	FC	SE	FC	SE 1	SE		SE		SE	FC	SE 1	SE	FC	SE 1	SE 1	SE	FC		SE	FC
London Victoria 15 ⊖	d	10 17				10 25		10 37	10 39		19 39				19 52	19 55		20 07	20 17				20 25	
Brixton ⊖	d					10 32										20 02							20 32	
Kentish Town ⊖	d				10 00									19 30							20 00			
St Pancras International 15 ⊖	d				10 05									19 35							20 05			
Farringdon ⊖	d				10 10									19 40							20 10			
City Thameslink 3	d																							
London Blackfriars 3 ⊖	d			10 12	10 15		10 26						19 42	19 45			19 56			20 12	20 15			20 26
Elephant & Castle ⊖	d			10 16	10 18		10 30						19 46	19 48			20 00			20 16	20 18			20 30
Loughborough Jn	d				10 22		10 34							19 52			20 04				20 22			20 34
Herne Hill 4	d				10a26	10 34	10a37							19a56		20 04	20a07				20a26		20 34	20a37
West Dulwich	d					10 36										20 06							20 36	
Sydenham Hill	d					10 38										20 08							20 38	
Penge East	d					10 41										20 11							20 41	
Kent House 4	d					10 43				and at						20 13							20 43	
Beckenham Junction 4 ⇌	d					10 45				the same						20 15							20 45	
Denmark Hill 4	d			10 22					10 48	minutes	19 48		19 52							20 22				
Peckham Rye 4	d			10 25					10 51	past	19 51		19 55							20 25				
Nunhead 4	d			10 27					10 53	each	19 53		19 57							20 27				
Lewisham 4 ⇌	a								11 01	hour until	20 01													
Crofton Park	d			10 30									20 00							20 30				
Catford	d			10 33									20 03							20 33				
Bellingham	d			10 35									20 05							20 35				
Beckenham Hill	d			10 37									20 07							20 37				
Ravensbourne	d			10 39									20 09							20 39				
Shortlands 4	d			10 41		10 48							20 11			20 18				20 41			20 48	
Bromley South 4	d	10 34		10 44		10 51		10 53					20 14		20a08	20 21		20 23	20 34	20 44			20 51	
Bickley 4	d			10 47		10 54							20 17			20 24				20 47			20 54	
Petts Wood 4	d					10 59										20 29							20 59	
Orpington 4	d					11a02										20a32							21a02	
St Mary Cray	d	10 40		10 51				11 00					20 21					20 30	20 40	20 51				
Swanley 4	d	10a44		10 56				11 04					20 26					20 34	20a44	20 56				
Eynsford	d			11 00									20 30							21 00				
Shoreham (Kent)	d			11 04									20 34							21 04				
Otford 4	d			11 07				11a12					20 37					20a42		21 07				
Bat & Ball	d			11 10									20 40							21 10				
Sevenoaks 4	a			11 13									20 43							21 13				

Table 195

Sundays
29 July to 12 August

London Victoria/Kentish Town - Catford, Beckenham Junction, Bromley South, Orpington, Otford and Sevenoaks

Network Diagram - see first Page of Table 195

		SE 1	SE	FC	SE	SE 1	SE	FC		SE 1	SE	SE 1	SE	SE	SE 1	SE	SE 1	SE		SE 1	SE	SE	SE 1	SE	SE 1
London Victoria 15 ⊖	d	20 52			20 55	21 07				21 22	21 25	21 52		21 55	22 07		22 22	22 25		22 52		22 55	23 07		23 22
Brixton ⊖	d				21 02						21 32			22 02				22 32				23 02			
Kentish Town ⊖	d			20 30				21 00																	
St Pancras International 15 ⊖	d			20 35				21 05																	
Farringdon ⊖	d			20 40				21 10																	
City Thameslink 3	d																								
London Blackfriars 3 ⊖	d		20 42	20 45			21 12	21 15					21 42			22 12					22 42			23 12	
Elephant & Castle ⊖	d		20 46	20 48			21 16	21 18					21 46			22 16					22 46			23 16	
Loughborough Jn	d			20 52				21 22																	
Herne Hill 4	d			20a56	21 04			21a26			21 34			22 04				22 34				23 04			
West Dulwich	d				21 06						21 36			22 06				22 36				23 06			
Sydenham Hill	d				21 08						21 38			22 08				22 38				23 08			
Penge East	d				21 11						21 41			22 11				22 41				23 11			
Kent House 4	d				21 13						21 43			22 13				22 43				23 13			
Beckenham Junction 4 ⇌	d				21 15						21 45			22 15				22 45				23 15			
Denmark Hill 4	d		20 52				21 22						21 52			22 22					22 52			23 22	
Peckham Rye 4	d		20 55				21 25						21 55			22 25					22 55			23 25	
Nunhead 4	d		20 57				21 27						21 57			22 27					22 57			23 27	
Lewisham 4 ⇌	a																								
Crofton Park	d		21 00				21 30						22 00			22 30					23 00			23 30	
Catford	d		21 03				21 33						22 03			22 33					23 03			23 33	
Bellingham	d		21 05				21 35						22 05			22 35					23 05			23 35	
Beckenham Hill	d		21 07				21 37						22 07			22 37					23 07			23 37	
Ravensbourne	d		21 09				21 39						22 09			22 39					23 09			23 39	
Shortlands 4	d		21 11		21 18		21 41				21 48		22 11	22 18		22 41		22 48			23 11	23 18		23 41	
Bromley South 4	d	21 09	21 14		21 21	21 23	21 44			21a38	21 51	22 09	22 14	22 21	22 23	22 44	22a38	22 51		23 09	23 14	23 21	23 23	23 44	23a38
Bickley 4	d		21 17		21 24		21 47				21 54		22 17	22 24		22 47		22 54			23 17	23 24		23 47	
Petts Wood 4	d				21 29						21 59			22 29				22 59				23 29			
Orpington 4	d				21a32						22a02			22a32				23a02				23a32			
St Mary Cray	d	21 15	21 21			21 30	21 51					22 15	22 21		22 30	22 51				23 15	23 21		23 30	23 51	
Swanley 4	d	21a19	21 26			21 34	21 56					22a19	22 26		22 34	22 56				23a19	23 26		23 34	23 56	
Eynsford	d		21 30				22 00						22 30			23 00					23 30			23 59	
Shoreham (Kent)	d		21 34				22 04						22 34			23 04					23 34			00 04	
Otford 4	d		21 37			21a42	22 07						22 37		22a42	23 07					23 37		23a42	00 07	
Bat & Ball	d		21 40				22 10						22 40			23 10					23 40			00 10	
Sevenoaks 4	a		21 43				22 13						22 43			23 13					23 43			00 13	

		SE	SE 1	SE		SE
London Victoria 15 ⊖	d	23 25	23 52			23 55
Brixton ⊖	d	23 32				00 02
Kentish Town ⊖	d					
St Pancras International 15 ⊖	d					
Farringdon ⊖	d					
City Thameslink 3	d					
London Blackfriars 3 ⊖	d			23 42		
Elephant & Castle ⊖	d			23 46		
Loughborough Jn	d					
Herne Hill 4	d	23 34				00 04
West Dulwich	d	23 36				00 06
Sydenham Hill	d	23 38				00 08
Penge East	d	23 41				00 11
Kent House 4	d	23 43				00 13
Beckenham Junction 4 ⇌	d	23 45				00 15
Denmark Hill 4	d			23 52		
Peckham Rye 4	d			23 55		
Nunhead 4	d			23 57		
Lewisham 4 ⇌	a					
Crofton Park	d			23 59		
Catford	d			00 03		
Bellingham	d			00 05		
Beckenham Hill	d			00 07		
Ravensbourne	d			00 09		
Shortlands 4	d	23 48		00 11		00 18
Bromley South 4	d	23 51	00 09	00 14		00 21
Bickley 4	d	23 54		00 17		00 24
Petts Wood 4	d	23 59				00 29
Orpington 4	d	00a02				00a33
St Mary Cray	d		00 15	00 21		
Swanley 4	d		00a19	00 26		
Eynsford	d			00 30		
Shoreham (Kent)	d			00 34		
Otford 4	d			00 37		
Bat & Ball	d			00 40		
Sevenoaks 4	a			00 43		

Table 195

Sundays
26 August to 9 September

London Victoria/Kentish Town - Catford, Beckenham Junction, Bromley South, Orpington, Otford and Sevenoaks

Network Diagram - see first Page of Table 195

		SE	SE	SE	SE	SE	SE	SE	SE	SE	SE	SE	SE	SE	SE	SE	SE	SE	SE	SE	SE	FC	SE
			1			1		A	1 A	A	1	1			1			1	1				1
London Victoria	d		23p52		23p55	00 07	00 35	00 45	00 51	00 56	07 24	07 45		07 51	08 05		08 21	08 24	08 45		08 51		09 05
Brixton	d				00 02			00s52						07 58			08 28				08 58		
Kentish Town	d																						
St Pancras International	d																						
Farringdon	d																						
City Thameslink	d																						
London Blackfriars	d	23p12		23p42									07 38			08 08				08 38		08 56	
Elephant & Castle	d	23p16		23p46									07 42			08 12				08 42		09 00	
Loughborough Jn	d																					09 04	
Herne Hill	d				00 04		00 43	00s54						08 00			08 30				09 00	09a07	
West Dulwich	d				00 06			00s57						08 02			08 32				09 02		
Sydenham Hill	d				00 08			01s00						08 04			08 34				09 04		
Penge East	d				00 11		00 48	01s03						08 07			08 37				09 07		
Kent House	d				00 13			01s06						08 09			08 39				09 09		
Beckenham Junction	d				00 15		00 50	01s08						08 11			08 41				09 11		
Denmark Hill	d	23p22		23p52						01s05			07 48			08 18				08 48			
Peckham Rye	d	23p25		23p55						01s08			07 51			08 21				08 51			
Nunhead	d	23p27		23p57						01s10			07 53			08 23				08 53			
Lewisham	a																						
Crofton Park	d	23p30		23p59						01s13			07 56			08 26				08 56			
Catford	d	23p33		00 03						01s16			07 59			08 29				08 59			
Bellingham	d	23p35		00 05						01s18			08 01			08 31				09 01			
Beckenham Hill	d	23p37		00 07						01s20			08 03			08 33				09 03			
Ravensbourne	d	23p39		00 09						01s22			08 05			08 35				09 05			
Shortlands	d	23p41		00 11	00 18			01s12					08 07	08 14		08 37	08 44			09 07	09 14		
Bromley South	d	23p44	00 09	00 14	00 21	00 25	00 55	01s15	01s10	01s25	07 44	08 01	08 10	08 18	08a21	08 40	08 48	08 44	09 01	09 10	09 18		09a21
Bickley	d	23p47		00 17	00 24			01s18					08 13	08 20		08 43	08 50			09 13	09 20		
Petts Wood	d				00 29			01s25						08 25			08 55				09 25		
Orpington	d				00a32			01a29		01a33				08a28			08a58				09a28		
St Mary Cray	d	23p51	00 15	00 21		00 32	01 01		01s17		07 50	08 08	08 17			08 47		08 50	09 08	09 17			
Swanley	d	23p56	00a19	00 26		00 36	01a05		01s21		07a54	08 12	08 22			08 52		08a54	09 12	09 22			
Eynsford	d	23p59		00 30					01s26				08 26			08 56				09 26			
Shoreham (Kent)	d	00 04		00 34					01s30				08 30			09 00				09 30			
Otford	d	00 07		00 37		00a44			01s33			08a20	08 33			09 03			09a20	09 33			
Bat & Ball	d	00 10		00 40									08 36			09 06				09 36			
Sevenoaks	a	00 13		00 43									08 39			09 09				09 39			

		SE	FC	SE	SE	FC	SE	SE	FC		FC	SE	SE	SE	FC	SE	SE	SE	SE	SE	SE	SE
					1		1						1				1	1			1	
London Victoria	d			09 21	09 24		09 45					20 51	21 05			21 21	21 24	21 45		21 51	22 05	
Brixton	d			09 28								20 58				21 28				21 58		
Kentish Town	d		09 00						09 30		20 30				21 00							
St Pancras International	d		09 05						09 35		20 35				21 05							
Farringdon	d		09 10						09 40		20 40				21 10							
City Thameslink	d																					
London Blackfriars	d	09 08	09 15			09 26		09 38	09 45		20 45			21 08	21 15				21 38			22 08
Elephant & Castle	d	09 12	09 18			09 30		09 42	09 48		20 48			21 12	21 18				21 42			22 12
Loughborough Jn	d		09 22			09 34			09 52		20 52				21 22							
Herne Hill	d		09a26	09 30		09a37			09a56		20a56	21 00			21a26	21 30				22 00		
West Dulwich	d			09 32								21 02				21 32				22 02		
Sydenham Hill	d			09 34								21 04				21 34				22 04		
Penge East	d			09 37								21 07				21 37				22 07		
Kent House	d			09 39								21 09				21 39				22 09		
Beckenham Junction	d			09 41						and at the same minutes past each hour until		21 11				21 41				22 11		
Denmark Hill	d	09 18						09 48						21 18					21 48			22 18
Peckham Rye	d	09 21						09 51						21 21					21 51			22 21
Nunhead	d	09 23						09 53						21 23					21 53			22 23
Lewisham	a																					
Crofton Park	d	09 26						09 56						21 26					21 56			22 26
Catford	d	09 29						09 59						21 29					21 59			22 29
Bellingham	d	09 31						10 01						21 31					22 01			22 31
Beckenham Hill	d	09 33						10 03						21 33					22 03			22 33
Ravensbourne	d	09 35						10 05						21 35					22 05			22 35
Shortlands	d	09 37		09 44				10 07				21 14		21 37		21 44			22 07	22 14		22 37
Bromley South	d	09 40		09 48	09 44		10 01	10 10				21 18	21a21	21 40		21 48	21 44	22 01	22 10	22 18	22a21	22 40
Bickley	d	09 43		09 50				10 13				21 20		21 43		21 50			22 13	22 20		22 43
Petts Wood	d			09 55								21 25				21 55				22 25		
Orpington	d			09a58								21a28				21a58				22a28		
St Mary Cray	d	09 47			09 50		10 08	10 17						21 47			21 50	22 08	22 17			22 47
Swanley	d	09 52			09a54		10 12	10 22						21 52			21a54	22 12	22 22			22 52
Eynsford	d	09 56						10 26						21 56					22 26			22 56
Shoreham (Kent)	d	10 00						10 30						22 00					22 30			23 00
Otford	d	10 03					10a20	10 33						22 03				22a20	22 33			23 03
Bat & Ball	d	10 06						10 36						22 06					22 36			23 06
Sevenoaks	a	10 09						10 39						22 09					22 39			23 09

A not 26 August

Table 195

Sundays
26 August to 9 September

London Victoria/Kentish Town - Catford, Beckenham Junction, Bromley South, Orpington, Otford and Sevenoaks

Network Diagram - see first Page of Table 195

		SE	SE	SE	SE	SE	SE	SE	SE	SE	SE
			1	1			1			1	
London Victoria	d	22 21	22 24	22 45		22 51	23 05		23 21	23 45	
Brixton	d	22 28				22 58			23 28		
Kentish Town	d										
St Pancras International	d										
Farringdon	d										
City Thameslink	d										
London Blackfriars	d				22 38			23 08			23 38
Elephant & Castle	d				22 42			23 12			23 42
Loughborough Jn	d										
Herne Hill	d	22 30				23 00			23 30		
West Dulwich	d	22 32				23 02			23 32		
Sydenham Hill	d	22 34				23 04			23 34		
Penge East	d	22 37				23 07			23 37		
Kent House	d	22 39				23 09			23 39		
Beckenham Junction	d	22 41				23 11			23 41		
Denmark Hill	d				22 48			23 18			23 48
Peckham Rye	d				22 51			23 21			23 51
Nunhead	d				22 53			23 23			23 53
Lewisham	a										
Crofton Park	d				22 56			23 26			23 56
Catford	d				22 59			23 29			23 59
Bellingham	d				23 01			23 31			00 01
Beckenham Hill	d				23 03			23 33			00 03
Ravensbourne	d				23 05			23 35			00 05
Shortlands	d	22 44			23 07	23 14		23 37	23 44		00 07
Bromley South	d	22 48	22 44	23 01	23 10	23 18	23a21	23 40	23 48	00 02	00 10
Bickley	d	22 50			23 13	23 20		23 43	23 50		00 13
Petts Wood	d	22 55				23 25			23 55		
Orpington	d	22a58				23a29			23a59		
St Mary Cray	d		22 50	23 08	23 17			23 47		00 08	00 17
Swanley	d		22a54	23 12	23 22			23 52		00a12	00 22
Eynsford	d				23 26			23 56			00 26
Shoreham (Kent)	d				23 30			23 59			00 30
Otford	d			23a20	23 33			00 03			00 33
Bat & Ball	d				23 36			00 06			00 36
Sevenoaks	a				23 39			00 09			00 39

Sevenoaks, Otford, Orpington, Bromley South, Beckenham Junction and Catford - Kentish Town/London Victoria

Network Diagram - see first Page of Table 195

Miles	Miles	Miles			SE	SE	SE	SE	SE	SE	SE	SE	FC	SE	SE	FC	SE	SE	SE	SE	SE	FC	SE
						MX		MX															
					■	■	■	■										■	■		■		
					A		A																
—	0	—	Sevenoaks	d													05 40						
—	1¼	—	Bat & Ball	d													05 43						
—	3	—	Otford	d													05 46				06 15		
—	4½	—	Shoreham (Kent)	d													05 49						
—	6½	—	Eynsford	d													05 53						
—	9½	—	Swanley	d	23p32			00 10		04 33							05 58		06 02		06 25		
—	12¼	—	St Mary Cray	d	23p36			00 14		04 37							06 02		06 06				
0	—	—	Orpington	d					04 34		04 55	05 10		05 34	05 40					06 10			
1¼	—	—	Petts Wood	d					04 37		04 58	05 13		05 37	05 43					06 13			
3	14½	—	Bickley	d					04 41	04 41	05 02	05 17		05 41	05 47		06 06			06 17			
4	15½	—	Bromley South	d	23p43	23p50	00 13	00 20	04 44	04 50	05 05	05 20		05 44	05 50		06 10	06 12	06 15	06 20	06 33		
5	16½	—	Shortlands	d					04 47	04 53	05 08	05 23		05 47	05 53		06 13			06 23			
—	17¼	—	Ravensbourne	d					04 49					05 49			06 15						
—	18	—	Beckenham Hill	d					04 51					05 51			06 17						
—	18¾	—	Bellingham	d					04 53					05 53			06 19						
—	19½	—	Catford	d					04 56					05 56			06 22						
—	20½	—	Crofton Park	d					04 58					05 58			06 25						
—	—	0	Lewisham	d																			
—	21¾	1¾	Nunhead	d					05 01					06 01			06 27						
—	22½	2½	Peckham Rye	d					05 04					06 04			06 30						
—	23¼	3¼	Denmark Hill	d					05 07					06 07			06 33						
6¼	—	—	Beckenham Junction	d						04 56	05 11	05 26			05 56					06 26			06 40
7¼	—	—	Kent House	d						04 58	05 13	05 28			05 58					06 28			06 42
7¾	—	—	Penge East	d						05 00	05 15	05 30			06 00					06 30			06 44
9¼	—	—	Sydenham Hill	d						05 03	05 18	05 33			06 03					06 33			06 47
10	—	—	West Dulwich	d						05 05	05 20	05 35			06 05					06 35			06 49
11	—	—	Herne Hill	d						05 08	05 23	05 38	05 54		06 08	06 16				06 38	06 43	06 46	06 52
—	—	—	Loughborough Jn	d												06 19						06 49	
—	25¾	—	Elephant & Castle	d					05 13		05 29		06 00	06 13		06 24	06 40					06 54	
—	27	—	London Blackfriars	d					05 17		05 33		06 04	06 17		06 30	06 48					06 58	
—	—	—	City Thameslink	a					05 19		05 35		06 06	06 19		06 32	06 50					07 00	
—	—	—	Farringdon	a							05 38		06 10			06 36	06 54					07 04	
—	—	—	St Pancras International	a							05 42		06 14			06 40	06 58					07 08	
—	—	—	Kentish Town	a							05 47		06 18			06 44	07 02						
11	—	—	Brixton	d						05 10		05 40			06 10					06 40			06 54
15	—	7½	London Victoria	a	00 02	00 07	00 29	00 38		05 17		05 47			06 18			06 28	06 31	06 47	06 51		07 03

		SE	FC	SE	SE	SE	SE	SE	SE	SE	SE	SE	FC	SE	SE	SE	SE	SE	SE	SE	FC	FC	SE
					■	■		■	■	■						■	■		■		■		
Sevenoaks	d			06 13											06 42								
Bat & Ball	d			06 16											06 48								
Otford	d			06 19				06 38	06 46						06 51		07 01		07 14				
Shoreham (Kent)	d			06 22											06 54								
Eynsford	d			06 26											06 58								
Swanley	d			06 31	06 35			06 48	06 54	06 57					07 03		07 10		07 22	07 23			
St Mary Cray	d			06 35	06 39					07 01					07 07					07 27			
Orpington	d						06 40							06 58				07 08					
Petts Wood	d						06 43							07 01				07 11					
Bickley	d			06 39			06 47							07 05	07 11			07 16					
Bromley South	d			06 42	06 46	06 50	06 50	06 57	07 02	07 08				07 08	07 14	07 16	07 20	07 20	07 31	07 34			07 34
Shortlands	d			06 45			06 53							07 11	07 17			07 23					07 36
Ravensbourne	d			06 47											07 19								
Beckenham Hill	d			06 49											07 21								
Bellingham	d			06 51											07 23								
Catford	d			06 54											07 26								
Crofton Park	d			06 57											07 29								
Lewisham	d	06 41										07 15											
Nunhead	d			06 59								07 20			07 31								
Peckham Rye	d	06 47		07 02								07 23			07 34								
Denmark Hill	d	06 50		07 05								07 29			07 37								
Beckenham Junction	d						06 56				07 08			07 14				07 26					07 39
Kent House	d						06 58				07 11			07 17				07 28					07 42
Penge East	d						07 00				07 14			07 19				07 30					07 44
Sydenham Hill	d						07 03				07 17			07 22				07 33					07 47
West Dulwich	d						07 05				07 19			07 24				07 35					07 49
Herne Hill	d		06 57				07 08				07 22		07 24	07 31				07 38			07 41	07 47	07 52
Loughborough Jn	d		07 00										07 27	07 34								07 50	
Elephant & Castle	d		07 06	07 12				07 16					07 32	07 38	07 44						07 48	07 54	
London Blackfriars	d		07 12	07 18				07 24					07 36	07 42	07 48						07 54	07 58	
City Thameslink	a		07 14	07 20				07 26					07 38	07 44	07 50						07 56	08 00	
Farringdon	a		07 18	07 24				07 30					07 42	07 48	07 54						08 00	08 03	
St Pancras International	a		07 22	07 28				07 34					07 46	07 52	07 58						08 04	08 08	
Kentish Town	a			07 32											08 02							08 14	
Brixton	d						07 10				07 24							07 40					07 54
London Victoria	a	07 04			07 07	07 09	07 19		07 22	07 30	07 33	07 42				07 38	07 43	07 49	07 53	07 55			08 03

A MO from 21 May until 23 July

Sevenoaks, Otford, Orpington, Bromley South, Beckenham Junction and Catford - Kentish Town/London Victoria

Network Diagram - see first Page of Table 195

		SE	SE	SE	SE	SE	SE	FC	SE	SE	SE	SE	SE	SE	FC	SE	SE	SE	SE	SE	SE	FC	SE
					■	■	■			■	■	■						■	■	■	■		
					A	B																	
Sevenoaks	d			07 11													07 36						
Bat & Ball	d			07 14													07 39						
Otford	d			07 18	07 23	07 23					07 38						07 43			07 56			
Shoreham (Kent)	d			07 21													07 46						
Eynsford	d			07 24													07 49						
Swanley	d			07 30	07 32	07 32				07 40	07 47						07 54	07 55	08 02	08 05			
St Mary Cray	d			07 34						07 45							07 59	08 00	08 06				
Orpington	d	07 28							07 38					07 47									
Petts Wood	d	07 31							07 41					07 50									
Bickley	d	07 35		07 39					07 46					07 55			08 03						
Bromley South	d	07 38		07 42	07 40	07 40	07 49		07 50	07 53	07 57			07 58		08 04	08 08	08 06	08 12	08 13	08 16		
Shortlands	d	07 41		07 44					07 53					08 00		08 06	08 10						
Ravensbourne	d			07 47													08 13						
Beckenham Hill	d			07 49													08 15						
Bellingham	d			07 51										08 05			08 17						
Catford	d			07 53										08 08			08 20						
Crofton Park	d			07 56										08 10									
Lewisham	d		07 46										08 05										
Nunhead	d		07 51	07 58									08 11	08 14									
Peckham Rye	d		07 54	08 01									08 13	08 16									
Denmark Hill	d		07 59	08 04									08 17	08 19			08 26		08 30				
Beckenham Junction	d	07 44							07 56			07 59				08 10							08 22
Kent House	d	07 47							07 58			08 02				08 12							08 24
Penge East	d	07 49							08 00			08 04				08 14							08 26
Sydenham Hill	d	07 52							08 03			08 07				08 17							08 29
West Dulwich	d	07 54							08 05			08 09				08 19							08 31
Herne Hill	d	07 57						08 01	08 08			08 13			08 20	08 23						08 32	08 34
Loughborough Jn	d	08 00						08 04				08 16			08 23							08 36	
Elephant & Castle	d	08 05		08 13	07 59	08 00		08 09				08 21		08 25	08 28		08 35	08 31				08 40	
London Blackfriars	d	08 09		08 17	08 04	08 04		08 13				08 25		08 29	08 33		08 42	08 37				08 46	
City Thameslink	a	08 11		08 19	08 06	08 06		08 15				08 27		08 31	08 35		08 44	08 39				08 48	
Farringdon	a	08 15		08 23	08 10	08 10		08 19				08 30		08 35	08 39		08 48	08 43				08 52	
St Pancras International	a	08 19		08 27	08 14	08 14		08 23				08 35		08 39	08 43		08 52	08 47				08 56	
Kentish Town	a			08 32				08 29							08 48		08 57					09 00	
Brixton	d								08 10							08 25							08 36
London Victoria	a		08 11				08 09		08 20	08 17	08 23		08 29			08 35			08 42	08 36	08 39		08 45

		SE	SE	SE	FC	SE	SE	SE	FC	SE	SE	SE	SE	FC	FC	SE	SE	SE	SE	SE	SE	SE
			■		■		■	■		■	■			■			■		■			■
										A	B											
Sevenoaks	d					07 53													08 24			
Bat & Ball	d					07 56													08 27			
Otford	d					08 00	08 09												08 31			08 46
Shoreham (Kent)	d					08 03													08 34			
Eynsford	d					08 06													08 37			
Swanley	d					08 11		08 22											08 42			08 54
St Mary Cray	d					08 16		08 27											08 46			08 58
Orpington	d			08 10								08 26						08 40			08 47	
Petts Wood	d			08 13								08 29						08 43			08 50	
Bickley	d			08 17		08 20						08 33						08 47	08 51		08 55	
Bromley South	d		08 18	08 22		08 26	08 25	08 33				08 36				08 44	08 50	08 50	08 54		08 58	09 05
Shortlands	d		08 20	08 24		08 29						08 39				08 46		08 53	08 56		09 00	
Ravensbourne	d		08 23													08 49					09 03	
Beckenham Hill	d		08 25													08 51					09 05	
Bellingham	d		08 27			08 33										08 53			09 01		09 07	
Catford	d		08 30			08 36										08 56			09 04		09 09	
Crofton Park	d					08 39										08 58					09 12	
Lewisham	d	08 25											08 46							09 06		
Nunhead	d	08 30				08 41							08 52			09 01				09 11	09 14	
Peckham Rye	d	08 33	08 36			08 44							08 55			09 04			09 09	09 14	09 17	
Denmark Hill	d	08 36	08 39			08 47							09 02			09 07			09 12	09 17	09 19	
Beckenham Junction	d			08 28								08 42						08 56				
Kent House	d			08 30						08 42	08 42	08 45						08 58				
Penge East	d									08 44	08 44	08 47						09 00				
Sydenham Hill	d									08 47	08 47	08 50						09 03				
West Dulwich	d			08 35						08 49	08 49	08 52						09 05				
Herne Hill	d			08 38	08 41				08 47	08 52	08 52	08 54		08 57	09 02			09 08				
Loughborough Jn	d								08 50	08 57	08 55				09 05							
Elephant & Castle	d		08 45		08 50	08 54			08 58	09 02	09 02			09 06	09 10	09 14			09 20		09 26	
London Blackfriars	d		08 50		08 54	08 58			09 02	09 06	09 06			09 10	09 14	09 18			09 26		09 30	
City Thameslink	a		08 52		08 56	09 00			09 04	09 08	09 08			09 12	09 16	09 20			09 27		09 32	
Farringdon	a		08 56		09 00	09 04			09 08	09 12	09 12			09 16	09 20	09 24			09 32		09 36	
St Pancras International	a		09 00		09 04	09 08			09 12	09 16	09 16			09 20	09 24	09 28			09 36		09 40	
Kentish Town	a					09 13			09 16							09 34					09 45	
Brixton	d			08 40								08 57						09 10				
London Victoria	a	08 49		08 50			08 53	08 53				09 06	09 11				09 09	09 19		09 29		09 23

A from 21 May until 27 July

B until 18 May

Table 195

Mondays to Fridays
until 27 July, 13 Aug to 28 Aug and from 10 Sep

Sevenoaks, Otford, Orpington, Bromley South, Beckenham Junction and Catford - Kentish Town/London Victoria

Network Diagram - see first Page of Table 195

Station		FC	SE	SE	SE ■	SE ■ ⊼	FC	SE	SE ■	SE	FC	SE A	SE B	FC	SE	SE ■ ⊼	SE	SE ■	SE	FC	SE	FC	SE
Sevenoaks	d			08 43											09 13								09 42
Bat & Ball	d			08 46											09 16								09 46
Otford	d			08 49					09 17						09 21			09 46					09 50
Shoreham (Kent)	d			08 52											09 24								09 53
Eynsford	d			08 56											09 28								09 56
Swanley	d			09 01	09 05				09 26						09 33			09 54					10 01
St Mary Cray	d			09 05	09 09										09 37			09 58					10 05
Orpington	d		08 55					09 10				09 25	09 25				09 40				09 55		
Petts Wood	d		08 58					09 13				09 28	09 28				09 43				09 58		
Bickley	d		09 02	09 09				09 17				09 32	09 32		09 42		09 47				10 02		10 10
Bromley South	d		09 05	09 12	09 15	09 20		09 20	09 34			09 35	09 35		09 45	09 50	09 50	10 05			10 05		10 15
Shortlands	d		09 08	09 15				09 23				09 38	09 38		09 48		09 53				10 08		10 18
Ravensbourne	d			09 17											09 50								10 20
Beckenham Hill	d			09 19											09 52								10 22
Bellingham	d			09 21											09 54								10 24
Catford	d			09 24											09 57								10 27
Crofton Park	d			09 26											09 59								10 29
Lewisham	d									09 38									10 08				
Nunhead	d			09 29						09 43					10 02				10 13				10 32
Peckham Rye	d			09 31						09 45					10 04				10 15				10 34
Denmark Hill	d			09 34						09 49					10 07				10 19				10 37
Beckenham Junction	d		09 11					09 26				09 41	09 41				09 56				10 11		
Kent House	d		09 13					09 28				09 43	09 43				09 58				10 13		
Penge East	d		09 15					09 30				09 45	09 45				10 00				10 15		
Sydenham Hill	d		09 18					09 33				09 48	09 48				10 03				10 18		
West Dulwich	d		09 20					09 35				09 50	09 50				10 05				10 20		
Herne Hill	d	09 20	09 23				09 36	09 38			09 46	09 53	09 53	10 01			10 08			10 16	10 23	10 31	
Loughborough Jn	d	09 23					09 40				09 50			10 04						10 19		10 34	
Elephant & Castle	d	09 30		09 42			09 45				09 55			10 09	10 14					10 24		10 39	10 44
London Blackfriars	d	09 34		09 46			09 50				10 00			10 14	10 18					10 30		10 44	10 48
City Thameslink	a	09 36		09 48			09 52				10 02			10 16	10 20					10 32		10 46	10 50
Farringdon	a	09 40		09 52			09 56				10 06			10 19	10 24					10 35		10 49	10 54
St Pancras International	a	09 44		09 56			10 00				10 10			10 23	10 28					10 40		10 53	10 58
Kentish Town	a	09 48		10 00			10 05				10 14			10 27	10 33					10 44		10 57	11 03
Brixton	d		09 25					09 40				09 55	09 55				10 10				10 25		
London Victoria	a		09 34		09 38	09 43		09 49	09 51	10 00		10 02	10 03			10 07	10 17	10 21	10 28		10 32		

Station		SE ■	SE ■ ⊼	SE	SE	FC	SE	SE ■	SE	SE ■ ⊼	FC	SE	SE	FC	SE	SE ■	SE	SE ■	SE ■ ⊼	FC		FC
Sevenoaks	d						10 02								10 32							
Bat & Ball	d						10 05								10 35							
Otford	d						10 08	10 17							10 38	10 46						
Shoreham (Kent)	d						10 11								10 41							
Eynsford	d						10 15								10 45							
Swanley	d	10 05					10 20	10 26							10 50	10 54		11 05				
St Mary Cray	d	10 09					10 24								10 54	10 58		11 09				
Orpington	d			10 10					10 25			10 40					10 55					
Petts Wood	d			10 13					10 28			10 43					10 58					
Bickley	d			10 17			10 28		10 32			10 47			10 58		11 02					
Bromley South	d	10 15	10 20	10 20			10 31	10 35	10 35	10 50		10 50			11 01	11 05	11 05	11 15	11 20			
Shortlands	d			10 23			10 34		10 38			10 53			11 04		11 08					
Ravensbourne	d						10 36								11 06							
Beckenham Hill	d						10 38								11 08							
Bellingham	d						10 40								11 10						and at the same minutes past each hour until	
Catford	d						10 43								11 13							
Crofton Park	d						10 45								11 15							
Lewisham	d				10 38								11 08									
Nunhead	d				10 43		10 48						11 13		11 18							
Peckham Rye	d				10 45		10 50						11 15		11 20							
Denmark Hill	d				10 49		10 54						11 19		11 24							
Beckenham Junction	d			10 26					10 41			10 56					11 11					
Kent House	d			10 28					10 43			10 58					11 13					
Penge East	d			10 30					10 45			11 00					11 15					
Sydenham Hill	d			10 33					10 48			11 03					11 18					
West Dulwich	d			10 35					10 50			11 05					11 20					
Herne Hill	d			10 38		10 46			10 53		11 01	11 08		11 16			11 23			11 31		15 31
Loughborough Jn	d					10 49					11 04			11 19						11 34		15 34
Elephant & Castle	d					10 54	11 00				11 09			11 24	11 30					11 39		15 39
London Blackfriars	d					11 00	11 04				11 14			11 30	11 34					11 44		15 44
City Thameslink	a					11 02	11 06				11 16			11 32	11 36					11 46		15 46
Farringdon	a					11 06	11 10				11 19			11 36	11 40					11 49		15 49
St Pancras International	a					11 10	11 14				11 23			11 40	11 44					11 53		15 53
Kentish Town	a					11 14	11 19				11 27			11 44	11 49					11 57		15 57
Brixton	d			10 40					10 55			11 10					11 25					
London Victoria	a	10 41	10 37	10 47	10 58			10 51	11 02	11 07		11 17	11 28			11 21	11 32	11 37	11 37			

A until 18 May

B from 21 May until 27 July

Table 195

Mondays to Fridays
until 27 July, 13 Aug to 28 Aug and from 10 Sep

Sevenoaks, Otford, Orpington, Bromley South, Beckenham Junction and Catford - Kentish Town/London Victoria

Network Diagram - see first Page of Table 195

Station		SE	SE	FC	SE	SE ■	SE	SE ■ A	SE ■ B ⊼	FC	SE	SE	FC	SE ■	SE ■	SE	SE	SE ■ ⊼	FC	SE	SE	FC
Sevenoaks	d				15 02									15 32								
Bat & Ball	d				15 05									15 35								
Otford	d				15 08	15 17								15 38	15 46							
Shoreham (Kent)	d				15 11									15 41								
Eynsford	d				15 15									15 45								
Swanley	d				15 20	15 26								15 50	15 54		16 05					
St Mary Cray	d				15 24									15 54	15 58		16 09					
Orpington	d	15 10					15 25				15 40					15 55				16 10		
Petts Wood	d	15 13					15 28				15 43					15 58				16 13		
Bickley	d	15 17			15 28		15 32				15 47			15 58		16 02				16 17		
Bromley South	d	15 20			15 31	15 35	15 35	15 50	15 50		15 50			16 01	16 05	16 05	16 15	16 20		16 20		
Shortlands	d	15 23			15 34		15 38				15 53			16 04		16 08				16 23		
Ravensbourne	d				15 36									16 06								
Beckenham Hill	d				15 38									16 08								
Bellingham	d				15 40									16 10								
Catford	d				15 43									16 13								
Crofton Park	d				15 45									16 15								
Lewisham	d		15 38									16 08									16 38	
Nunhead	d		15 43		15 48							16 13		16 18							16 43	
Peckham Rye	d		15 45		15 50							16 15		16 20							16 45	
Denmark Hill	d		15 49		15 54							16 19		16 24							16 49	
Beckenham Junction	d	15 26					15 41				15 56					16 11				16 26		
Kent House	d	15 28					15 43				15 58					16 13				16 28		
Penge East	d	15 30					15 45				16 00					16 15				16 30		
Sydenham Hill	d	15 33					15 48				16 03					16 18				16 33		
West Dulwich	d	15 35					15 50				16 05					16 20				16 35		
Herne Hill	d	15 38		15 46			15 53			16 01	16 08		16 16			16 23			16 31	16 38		16 50
Loughborough Jn	d			15 49						16 04			16 19						16 34			16 53
Elephant & Castle	d			15 54	16 00					16 09			16 24	16 30					16 39			17 00
London Blackfriars	d			16 00	16 04					16 14			16 30	16 38					16 44			17 04
City Thameslink	a			16 02	16 06					16 16			16 32	16 40					16 46			17 06
Farringdon	a			16 06	16 10					16 19			16 35	16 43					16 49			17 09
St Pancras International	a			16 10	16 14					16 23			16 39	16 47					16 53			17 13
Kentish Town	a			16 14	16 19					16 28			16 44						16 58			17 18
Brixton	d	15 40					15 55				16 10					16 25				16 40		
London Victoria	a	15 47	15 58			15 51	16 02	16 07	16 07		16 17	16 28			16 21	16 32	16 37	16 38		16 47	17 01	

Station		SE ■	SE ■	SE	FC ■	SE	SE ■ ⊼	SE	SE	FC	SE	SE ■	SE	SE ■	SE ■ ⊼	FC	SE	SE ■	SE	FC	SE ■	SE ■	SE
Sevenoaks	d	16 02				16 22					16 32										17 02		
Bat & Ball	d	16 05				16 25					16 35										17 05		
Otford	d	16 08	16 17			16 28					16 38	16 46									17 08	17 17	
Shoreham (Kent)	d	16 11									16 41										17 11		
Eynsford	d	16 15									16 45										17 15		
Swanley	d	16 20	16 26			16 37					16 50	16 54		17 05							17 20	17 26	
St Mary Cray	d	16 24				16 41					16 54	16 58		17 09							17 24		
Orpington	d			16 25				16 40					16 55				17 10						17 24
Petts Wood	d			16 28				16 43					16 58				17 13						17 28
Bickley	d	16 28		16 32				16 47			16 58		17 02				17 17				17 28		17 32
Bromley South	d	16 31	16 35	16 35		16 47	16 50	16 50			17 01	17 05	17 05	17 15	17 20		17 20				17 31	17 35	17 35
Shortlands	d	16 34		16 38				16 53			17 04		17 08				17 23				17 34		17 38
Ravensbourne	d	16 36									17 06										17 36		
Beckenham Hill	d	16 38									17 08										17 38		
Bellingham	d	16 40				16 52					17 10										17 40		
Catford	d	16 43				16 55					17 13										17 43		
Crofton Park	d	16 45									17 15										17 45		
Lewisham	d								17 08										17 38				
Nunhead	d	16 48				16 59			17 13		17 18								17 43		17 48		
Peckham Rye	d	16 50				17 02			17 15		17 20								17 45		17 50		
Denmark Hill	d	16 54				17 05			17 19		17 24								17 49		17 54		
Beckenham Junction	d			16 41				16 56					17 11				17 26	17 30					17 41
Kent House	d			16 43				16 58					17 13				17 28	17 33					17 43
Penge East	d			16 45				17 00					17 15				17 30	17 35					17 45
Sydenham Hill	d			16 48				17 03					17 18				17 33	17 38					17 48
West Dulwich	d			16 50				17 05					17 20				17 35	17 40					17 50
Herne Hill	d			16 53	17 01			17 11		17 21			17 23			17 31	17 38	17 44		17 48			17 53
Loughborough Jn	d									17 24						17 34		17 47		17 51			
Elephant & Castle	d	17 04			17 08	17 12				17 28	17 34					17 39		17 52		17 56	18 00		
London Blackfriars	d	17 08			17 12	17 16				17 32	17 40					17 46		17 56		18 00	18 06		
City Thameslink	a	17 10			17 14	17 18				17 34	17 42					17 48		17 58		18 02	18 08		
Farringdon	a	17 13			17 17	17 23				17 37	17 45					17 51		18 01		18 05	18 11		
St Pancras International	a	17 17			17 21	17 27				17 41	17 49					17 55		18 05		18 09	18 15		
Kentish Town	a					17 32				17 46						18 00				18 14			
Brixton	d			16 55				17 13					17 25				17 40						17 55
London Victoria	a		16 51	17 04			17 07	17 20	17 28			17 23	17 33	17 38	17 37		17 48		17 59			17 53	18 03

A from 21 May until 27 July

B until 18 May

Table 195

Mondays to Fridays

until 27 July, 13 Aug to 28 Aug and from 10 Sep

Sevenoaks, Otford, Orpington, Bromley South, Beckenham Junction and Catford - Kentish Town/London Victoria

Network Diagram - see first Page of Table 195

		SE ■	SE ■	SE ■ H	FC	SE	SE	FC	SE ■	SE ■	SE	SE ■	SE ■ H	FC	SE	SE	FC ■	FC	SE ■	SE ■	SE	SE
Sevenoaks	d								17 32										18 02			18 18
Bat & Ball	d								17 35										18 05			18 21
Otford	d								17 38	17 46									18 08	18 17		18 24
Shoreham (Kent)	d								17 41										18 11			18 27
Eynsford	d								17 45										18 15			18 31
Swanley	d		17 35						17 50	17 54		18 05							18 20	18 26		18 36
St Mary Cray	d		17 39						17 54	17 58		18 09							18 24			18 40
Orpington	d	17 34				17 40					17 55				18 09						18 25	
Petts Wood	d	17 37				17 43					17 58				18 12						18 28	
Bickley	d	17 42				17 47			17 58		18 02				18 17				18 28		18 32	
Bromley South	d	17 45	17 46	17 50		17 50			18 01	18 05	18 05	18 15	18 20		18 20				18 31	18 35	18 35	18 46
Shortlands	d					17 53			18 04		18 08				18 23				18 34		18 38	
Ravensbourne	d								18 06										18 36			
Beckenham Hill	d								18 08										18 38			
Bellingham	d								18 10										18 40			
Catford	d								18 13										18 43			
Crofton Park	d								18 15										18 45			
Lewisham	d						18 08									18 38						
Nunhead	d						18 13		18 18							18 43			18 48			
Peckham Rye	d						18 15		18 20							18 45			18 50			
Denmark Hill	d						18 19		18 23							18 49			18 54			18 59
Beckenham Junction	d	17 49				17 56					18 11				18 26						18 41	
Kent House	d					17 58					18 13				18 28						18 43	
Penge East	d					18 00					18 15				18 30						18 45	
Sydenham Hill	d					18 03					18 18				18 33						18 48	
West Dulwich	d					18 05					18 20				18 35						18 50	
Herne Hill	d				18 06	18 09		18 20			18 24			18 32	18 38		18 41	18 48			18 53	
Loughborough Jn	d				18 09			18 23						18 35				18 51				
Elephant & Castle	d	18 05			18 14			18 28	18 32					18 40			18 48	18 56	19 00			
London Blackfriars	d	18 10			18 18			18 32	18 36					18 44			18 52	19 00	19 06			
City Thameslink	a	18 12			18 20			18 34	18 38					18 46			18 54	19 02	19 08			
Farringdon	a	18 15			18 23			18 37	18 41					18 49			18 57	19 05	19 11			
St Pancras International	a	18 19			18 27			18 41	18 45					18 53			19 01	19 09	19 15			
Kentish Town	a				18 32			18 46										19 14				
Brixton	d					18 11					18 26				18 40						18 55	
London Victoria	a		18 08	18 07		18 18	18 29			18 21	18 33	18 37	18 37		18 48	18 58				18 53	19 03	19 13

		SE ■ H	FC	SE	SE	FC	SE	SE ■	SE	SE	SE	SE ■	SE ■	FC	SE	FC	SE	SE ■	SE	SE ■	FC	SE	FC
Sevenoaks	d						18 32			18 45							19 02						
Bat & Ball	d						18 35			18 48							19 05						
Otford	d						18 38	18 46		18 51							19 08	19 17					
Shoreham (Kent)	d						18 41			18 54							19 11						
Eynsford	d						18 45			18 58							19 15						
Swanley	d						18 50	18 54		19 03	19 05						19 20	19 26					
St Mary Cray	d						18 54	18 58			19 09						19 24						
Orpington	d			18 40					18 55						19 10				19 25			19 40	
Petts Wood	d			18 43					18 58						19 13				19 28			19 43	
Bickley	d			18 47			18 58		19 02						19 17		19 28		19 32			19 47	
Bromley South	d	18 50		18 50			19 01	19 05	19 05	19 11	19 15	19 17	19 20		19 20		19 31	19 35	19 35	19 50		19 50	
Shortlands	d			18 53			19 04		19 08						19 23		19 34		19 38			19 53	
Ravensbourne	d						19 06										19 36						
Beckenham Hill	d						19 08										19 38						
Bellingham	d						19 10										19 40						
Catford	d						19 13										19 43						
Crofton Park	d						19 15										19 45						
Lewisham	d				19 08																		
Nunhead	d				19 13		19 18										19 48						
Peckham Rye	d				19 15		19 20										19 50						
Denmark Hill	d				19 19		19 24			19 28							19 54						
Beckenham Junction	d			18 56					19 11						19 26				19 41			19 56	
Kent House	d			18 58					19 13						19 28				19 43			19 58	
Penge East	d			19 00					19 15						19 30				19 45			20 00	
Sydenham Hill	d			19 03					19 18						19 33				19 48			20 03	
West Dulwich	d			19 05					19 20						19 35				19 50			20 05	
Herne Hill	d		19 02	19 08		19 17			19 23					19 31	19 38	19 47			19 53		20 05	20 08	20 16
Loughborough Jn	d		19 05			19 20								19 34		19 50					20 08		20 19
Elephant & Castle	d		19 10			19 25	19 30							19 39		19 55	20 00				20 13		20 24
London Blackfriars	d		19 18			19 30	19 34							19 46		20 00	20 04				20 18		20 30
City Thameslink	a		19 20			19 32	19 36							19 48		20 02	20 06				20 20		20 32
Farringdon	a		19 23			19 36	19 40							19 51		20 06	20 10				20 23		20 36
St Pancras International	a		19 27			19 40	19 44							19 55		20 10	20 14				20 27		20 40
Kentish Town	a		19 32			19 44	19 49							19 59		20 14	20 19				20 31		20 44
Brixton	d			19 10					19 25						19 40				19 55			20 10	
London Victoria	a	19 07		19 17	19 28			19 21	19 32	19 43	19 37	19 35	19 37		19 47			19 51	20 02	20 07		20 17	

Table 195

Mondays to Fridays

until 27 July, 13 Aug to 28 Aug and from 10 Sep

Sevenoaks, Otford, Orpington, Bromley South, Beckenham Junction and Catford - Kentish Town/London Victoria

Network Diagram - see first Page of Table 195

		SE	SE ■	SE	SE	SE ■	SE ■	FC	SE	FC	SE	SE ■	SE ■	FC	SE	SE A	FC	SE B	SE ■	FC	SE	SE A	SE B
Sevenoaks	d	19 32			19 45						20 02					20 32		20 32				21 02	21 02
Bat & Ball	d	19 35			19 48						20 05					20 35		20 35				21 05	21 05
Otford	d	19 38	19 46		19 51						20 08	20 16				20 38		20 38				21 08	21 08
Shoreham (Kent)	d	19 41			19 54						20 11					20 41		20 41				21 11	21 11
Eynsford	d	19 45			19 58						20 15					20 45		20 45				21 15	21 15
Swanley	d	19 50	19 54		20 03	20 05					20 20	20 24				20 50		20 50	21 10			21 20	21 20
St Mary Cray	d	19 54	19 58			20 09					20 24	20 28				20 54		20 54	21 14			21 24	21 24
Orpington	d			19 55					20 10						20 40						21 10		
Petts Wood	d			19 58					20 13						20 43						21 13		
Bickley	d	19 58		20 02					20 17		20 28				20 47	20 58		20 58			21 17	21 28	21 28
Bromley South	d	20 01	20 05	20 05	20a11	20 15	20 20		20 20		20 31	20 35	20 50		20 50	21 01		21 01	21 20		21 20	21 31	21 31
Shortlands	d	20 04		20 08					20 23		20 34				20 53	21 04		21 04			21 23	21 34	21 34
Ravensbourne	d	20 06									20 36					21 06		21 06				21 36	21 36
Beckenham Hill	d	20 08									20 38					21 08		21 08				21 38	21 38
Bellingham	d	20 10									20 40					21 10		21 10				21 40	21 40
Catford	d	20 13									20 43					21 13		21 13				21 43	21 43
Crofton Park	d	20 15									20 45					21 15		21 15				21 45	21 45
Lewisham	d																						
Nunhead	d	20 18									20 48					21 18		21 18				21 48	21 48
Peckham Rye	d	20 20									20 50					21 20		21 20				21 50	21 50
Denmark Hill	d	20 24									20 54					21 23		21 24				21 53	21 54
Beckenham Junction	d			20 11					20 26						20 56						21 26		
Kent House	d			20 13					20 28						20 58						21 28		
Penge East	d			20 15					20 30						21 00						21 30		
Sydenham Hill	d			20 18					20 33						21 03						21 33		
West Dulwich	d			20 20					20 35						21 05						21 35		
Herne Hill	d			20 23				20 35	20 38	20 46				21 05	21 08		21 16			21 35	21 38		
Loughborough Jn	d							20 38		20 49				21 08			21 19			21 38			
Elephant & Castle	d	20 30						20 43		20 54	21 00			21 13			21 24	21 30		21 43			22 00
London Blackfriars	d	20 34						20 48		21 00	21 04			21 18			21 30	21a34		21 48			22a04
City Thameslink	a	20 36						20 50		21 02	21 06			21 20			21 32			21 50			
Farringdon	a	20 40						20 53		21 06	21 10			21 23			21 36			21 53			
St Pancras International	a	20 44						20 57		21 10	21 14			21 27			21 40			21 57			
Kentish Town	a	20 49						21 01		21 14	21 19			21 31			21 44			22 01			
Brixton	d			20 25					20 40						21 10						21 40		
London Victoria	a		20 21	20 32		20 37	20 38		20 47			20 51	21 07		21 17	21 33			21 37		21 47	22 03	

		SE ■	SE ■	FC	SE	SE A	SE B	SE ■	FC B	SE	SE A	SE B	SE ■	SE ■	FC B	SE	SE A	SE B	SE ■	FC B	SE	SE ■
Sevenoaks	d					21 32	21 32				22 02	22 02					22 32	22 32				
Bat & Ball	d					21 35	21 35				22 05	22 05					22 35	22 35				
Otford	d	21 16				21 38	21 38				22 08	22 08	22 16				22 38	22 38				23 16
Shoreham (Kent)	d					21 41	21 41				22 11	22 11					22 41	22 41				
Eynsford	d					21 45	21 45				22 15	22 15					22 45	22 45				
Swanley	d	21 24				21 50	21 50	22 10			22 20	22 20	22 24				22 50	22 50	23 10			23 24
St Mary Cray	d	21 28				21 54	21 54	22 14			22 24	22 24	22 28				22 54	22 54	23 14			23 28
Orpington	d				21 40					22 10						22 40					23 10	
Petts Wood	d				21 43					22 13						22 43					23 13	
Bickley	d				21 47	21 58	21 58			22 17	22 28	22 28				22 47	22 58	22 58			23 17	
Bromley South	d	21 35	21 50		21 50	22 01	22 01	22 20		22 20	22 31	22 31	22 35	22 50		22 50	23 01	23 01	23 20		23 20	23 35
Shortlands	d				21 53	22 04	22 04			22 23	22 34	22 34				22 53	23 04	23 04			23 23	
Ravensbourne	d					22 06	22 06				22 36	22 36					23 06	23 06				
Beckenham Hill	d					22 08	22 08				22 38	22 38					23 08	23 08				
Bellingham	d					22 10	22 10				22 40	22 40					23 10	23 10				
Catford	d					22 13	22 13				22 43	22 43					23 13	23 13				
Crofton Park	d					22 15	22 15				22 45	22 45					23 15	23 15				
Lewisham	d																					
Nunhead	d					22 18	22 18				22 48	22 48					23 18	23 18				
Peckham Rye	d					22 20	22 20				22 50	22 50					23 20	23 20				
Denmark Hill	d					22 23	22 24				22 53	22 54					23 23	23 24				
Beckenham Junction	d				21 56					22 26						22 56					23 26	
Kent House	d				21 58					22 28						22 58					23 28	
Penge East	d				22 00					22 30						23 00					23 30	
Sydenham Hill	d				22 03					22 33						23 03					23 33	
West Dulwich	d				22 05					22 35						23 05					23 35	
Herne Hill	d			21 57	22 08				22 27	22 38					22 57	23 08				23 27	23 38	
Loughborough Jn	d			22 00					22 30						23 00							
Elephant & Castle	d			22 04			22 30		22 34			23 00			23 04			23 30		23 34		
London Blackfriars	d			22 08			22a34		22 38			23a04			23 08			23a34		23 38		
City Thameslink	a			22 10					22 40													
Farringdon	a			22 13					22 43						23 13					23 43		
St Pancras International	a			22 17					22 47						23 17					23 47		
Kentish Town	a			22 21					22 51						23 21					23 51		
Brixton	d				22 10					22 40						23 10					23 40	
London Victoria	a	21 51	22 07		22 17	22 33		22 37		22 47	23 03		22 51	23 07		23 17	23 33		23 37		23 47	23 51

A until 18 May

B from 21 May until 27 July

Table 195

Mondays to Fridays

until 27 July, 13 Aug to 28 Aug and from 10 Sep

Sevenoaks, Otford, Orpington, Bromley South, Beckenham Junction and Catford - Kentish Town/London Victoria

Network Diagram - see first Page of Table 195

		SE 1
Sevenoaks	d	
Bat & Ball	d	
Otford	d	
Shoreham (Kent)	d	
Eynsford	d	
Swanley	d	
St Mary Cray	d	
Orpington	d	
Petts Wood	d	
Bickley	d	
Bromley South	d	23 50
Shortlands	d	
Ravensbourne	d	
Beckenham Hill	d	
Bellingham	d	
Catford	d	
Crofton Park	d	
Lewisham	d	
Nunhead	d	
Peckham Rye	d	
Denmark Hill	d	
Beckenham Junction	d	
Kent House	d	
Penge East	d	
Sydenham Hill	d	
West Dulwich	d	
Herne Hill	d	
Loughborough Jn	d	
Elephant & Castle ⊖	d	
London Blackfriars ⊖	d	
City Thameslink	a	
Farringdon ⊖	a	
St Pancras International ⊖	a	
Kentish Town ⊖	a	
Brixton ⊖	d	
London Victoria ⊖	a	00 07

Mondays to Fridays

30 July to 10 August

		SE 1 A	SE MO 1	SE 1 A	SE MO 1	SE	SE	SE	SE	FC		SE	SE	FC	SE	SE 1	SE 1	SE	SE 1	FC		SE	SE	FC	SE
Sevenoaks	d														05 40										06 13
Bat & Ball	d														05 43										06 16
Otford	d														05 46				06 15						06 19
Shoreham (Kent)	d														05 49										06 22
Eynsford	d														05 53										06 26
Swanley	d		23p48	00 10			04 33								05 58		06 02		06 25						06 31
St Mary Cray	d		23p52	00 14			04 37								06 02		06 06								06 35
Orpington	d					04 34		04 55	05 10			05 34	05 40					06 10							
Petts Wood	d					04 37		04 58	05 13			05 37	05 43					06 13							
Bickley	d					04 41	04 41	05 02	05 17			05 41	05 47		06 06			06 17							06 39
Bromley South	d	23p50	23p58	00 20	00 23	04 44	04 50	05 05	05 20			05 44	05 50		06 10	06 12	06 15	06 20	06 33						06 42
Shortlands	d					04 47	04 53	05 08	05 23			05 47	05 53		06 13			06 23							06 45
Ravensbourne	d					04 49						05 49			06 15										06 47
Beckenham Hill	d					04 51						05 51			06 17										06 49
Bellingham	d					04 53						05 53			06 19										06 51
Catford	d					04 56						05 56			06 22										06 54
Crofton Park	d					04 58						05 58			06 25										06 57
Lewisham	d																						06 41		
Nunhead	d					05 01						06 01			06 27										06 59
Peckham Rye	d					05 04						06 04			06 30								06 47		07 02
Denmark Hill	d					05 07						06 07			06 33								06 50		07 05
Beckenham Junction	d						04 56	05 11	05 26				05 56					06 26				06 40			
Kent House	d						04 58	05 13	05 28				05 58					06 28				06 42			
Penge East	d						05 00	05 15	05 30				06 00					06 30				06 44			
Sydenham Hill	d						05 03	05 18	05 33				06 03					06 33				06 47			
West Dulwich	d						05 05	05 20	05 35				06 05					06 35				06 49			
Herne Hill	d						05 08	05 23	05 38	05 54			06 08	06 16				06 38	06 43	06 46		06 52		06 57	
Loughborough Jn	d													06 19						06 49				07 00	
Elephant & Castle ⊖	d					05 13		05 29		06 00		06 13		06 24	06 40					06 54				07 06	07 12
London Blackfriars ⊖	d					05 17		05 33		06 04		06 17		06 30	06 48					06 58				07 12	07 18
City Thameslink	a					05 19		05 35		06 06		06 19		06 32	06 50					07 00				07 14	07 20
Farringdon ⊖	a							05 38		06 10				06 36	06 54					07 04				07 18	07 24
St Pancras International ⊖	a							05 42		06 14				06 40	06 58					07 08				07 22	07 28
Kentish Town ⊖	a							05 47		06 18				06 44	07 02										07 32
Brixton ⊖	d						05 10		05 40				06 10					06 40				06 54			
London Victoria ⊖	a	00 07	00 14	00 38	00 39		05 17		05 47				06 18			06 28	06 31	06 47	06 51			07 03	07 04		

A not 30 July, 6 August

Table 195

Mondays to Fridays

30 July to 10 August

Sevenoaks, Otford, Orpington, Bromley South, Beckenham Junction and Catford - Kentish Town/London Victoria

Network Diagram - see first Page of Table 195

		SE 1	SE 1	SE	SE 1	SE 1		SE 1	SE	SE	FC	SE	SE	SE 1	SE 1	SE		SE 1	SE	FC 1	FC	SE	SE	SE	SE
Sevenoaks	d												06 42												07 11
Bat & Ball	d												06 48												07 14
Otford	d				06 38	06 46							06 51		07 01			07 14							07 18
Shoreham (Kent)	d												06 54												07 21
Eynsford	d												06 58												07 24
Swanley	d	06 35			06 48	06 54		06 57					07 03		07 10			07 22	07 23						07 30
St Mary Cray	d	06 39						07 01					07 07						07 27						07 34
Orpington	d			06 40								06 58				07 08							07 28		
Petts Wood	d			06 43								07 01				07 11							07 31		
Bickley	d			06 47								07 05	07 11			07 16							07 35		07 39
Bromley South	d	06 46	06 50	06 50	06 57	07 02		07 08				07 08	07 14	07 16	07 20	07 20		07 31	07 34			07 34	07 38		07 42
Shortlands	d			06 53								07 11	07 17			07 23						07 36	07 41		07 44
Ravensbourne	d												07 19												07 47
Beckenham Hill	d												07 21												07 49
Bellingham	d												07 23												07 51
Catford	d												07 26												07 53
Crofton Park	d												07 29												07 56
Lewisham	d									07 15														07 46	
Nunhead	d									07 20			07 31											07 51	07 58
Peckham Rye	d									07 23			07 34											07 54	08 01
Denmark Hill	d									07 29			07 37											07 59	08 04
Beckenham Junction	d			06 56					07 08			07 14				07 26						07 39	07 44		
Kent House	d			06 58					07 11			07 17				07 28						07 42	07 47		
Penge East	d			07 00					07 14			07 19				07 30						07 44	07 49		
Sydenham Hill	d			07 03					07 17			07 22				07 33						07 47	07 52		
West Dulwich	d			07 05					07 19			07 24				07 35						07 49	07 54		
Herne Hill	d			07 08					07 22		07 24	07 31				07 38				07 41	07 47	07 52	07 57		
Loughborough Jn	d										07 27	07 34									07 50		08 00		
Elephant & Castle ⊖	d				07 16						07 32	07 38	07 44							07 48	07 54		08 05		08 13
London Blackfriars ⊖	d				07 24						07 36	07 42	07 48							07 54	07 58		08 09		08 17
City Thameslink	a				07 26						07 38	07 44	07 50							07 56	08 00		08 11		08 19
Farringdon ⊖	a				07 30						07 42	07 48	07 54							08 00	08 03		08 15		08 23
St Pancras International ⊖	a				07 34						07 46	07 52	07 58							08 04	08 08		08 19		08 27
Kentish Town ⊖	a												08 02								08 14				08 32
Brixton ⊖	d			07 10					07 24							07 40						07 54			
London Victoria ⊖	a	07 07	07 09	07 19		07 22		07 30	07 33	07 42				07 38	07 43	07 49		07 53	07 55			08 03		08 11	

		SE 1		SE 1	FC	SE	SE 1	SE 1	SE 1	SE	SE	FC		SE	SE	SE 1	SE 1	SE 1	SE 1	FC	SE	SE		SE 1	SE
Sevenoaks	d														07 36										
Bat & Ball	d														07 39										
Otford	d	07 23						07 38							07 43			07 56							
Shoreham (Kent)	d														07 46										
Eynsford	d														07 49										
Swanley	d	07 32					07 40	07 47							07 54	07 55	08 02	08 05							
St Mary Cray	d						07 45								07 59	08 00	08 06								
Orpington	d					07 38					07 47														08 10
Petts Wood	d					07 41					07 50														08 13
Bickley	d					07 46					07 55				08 03										08 17
Bromley South	d	07 40		07 49		07 50	07 53	07 57			07 58			08 04	08 08	08 06	08 12	08 13	08 16					08 18	08 22
Shortlands	d					07 53					08 00			08 06	08 10									08 20	08 24
Ravensbourne	d														08 13									08 23	
Beckenham Hill	d														08 15									08 25	
Bellingham	d										08 05				08 17									08 27	
Catford	d										08 08				08 20									08 30	
Crofton Park	d										08 10														
Lewisham	d									08 05												08 25			
Nunhead	d									08 11	08 14											08 30			
Peckham Rye	d									08 13	08 16											08 33		08 36	
Denmark Hill	d									08 17	08 19				08 26		08 30					08 36		08 39	
Beckenham Junction	d					07 56			07 59					08 10							08 22				08 28
Kent House	d					07 58			08 02					08 12							08 24				08 30
Penge East	d					08 00			08 04					08 14							08 26				
Sydenham Hill	d					08 03			08 07					08 17							08 29				
West Dulwich	d					08 05			08 09					08 19							08 31				08 35
Herne Hill	d				08 01	08 08			08 13			08 20		08 23						08 32	08 34				08 38
Loughborough Jn	d				08 04				08 16			08 23								08 36					
Elephant & Castle ⊖	d	08 00			08 09				08 21		08 25	08 28			08 35	08 31				08 40				08 45	
London Blackfriars ⊖	d	08 04			08 13				08 25		08 29	08 33			08 42	08 37				08 46				08 50	
City Thameslink	a	08 06			08 15				08 27		08 31	08 35			08 44	08 39				08 48				08 52	
Farringdon ⊖	a	08 10			08 19				08 30		08 35	08 39			08 48	08 43				08 52				08 56	
St Pancras International ⊖	a	08 14			08 23				08 35		08 39	08 43			08 52	08 47				08 56				09 00	
Kentish Town ⊖	a				08 29							08 48			08 57					09 00					
Brixton ⊖	d					08 10								08 25							08 36				08 40
London Victoria ⊖	a			08 09		08 20	08 17	08 23		08 29				08 35			08 42	08 36	08 39		08 45	08 49			08 50

30 July to 10 August

Sevenoaks, Otford, Orpington, Bromley South, Beckenham Junction and Catford - Kentish Town/London Victoria

Network Diagram - see first Page of Table 195

		FC ■	SE	SE ■	SE ■	FC	SE ■	SE	SE	FC ■	FC	SE	SE ■	SE	SE ■	SE	SE	SE ■	FC	SE	SE	SE ■	SE ■ ⊼
Sevenoaks ■	d		07 53												08 24						08 43		
Bat & Ball	d		07 56												08 27						08 46		
Otford ■	d		08 00	08 09											08 31			08 46			08 49		
Shoreham (Kent)	d		08 03												08 34						08 52		
Eynsford	d		08 06												08 37						08 56		
Swanley ■	d		08 11		08 22										08 42			08 54			09 01	09 05	
St Mary Cray	d		08 16		08 27										08 46			08 58			09 05	09 09	
Orpington ■	d							08 26						08 40			08 47			08 55			
Petts Wood ■	d							08 29						08 43			08 50			08 58			
Bickley ■	d		08 20					08 33						08 47	08 51		08 55			09 02	09 09		
Bromley South ■	d		08 26	08 25	08 33			08 36				08 44	08 50	08 50	08 54		08 58	09 05		09 05	09 12	09 15	09 20
Shortlands ■	d		08 29					08 39				08 46		08 53	08 56		09 00			09 08	09 15		
Ravensbourne	d											08 49					09 03				09 17		
Beckenham Hill	d											08 51					09 05				09 19		
Bellingham	d		08 33									08 53			09 01		09 07				09 21		
Catford	d		08 36									08 56			09 04		09 09				09 24		
Crofton Park	d		08 39									08 58					09 12				09 26		
Lewisham ■	d								08 46							09 06							
Nunhead ■	d		08 41						08 52			09 01				09 11	09 14				09 29		
Peckham Rye ■	d		08 44						08 55			09 04			09 09	09 14	09 17				09 31		
Denmark Hill ■	d		08 47						09 02			09 07			09 12	09 17	09 19				09 34		
Beckenham Junction ■	d							08 42						08 56						09 11			
Kent House ■	d						08 42	08 45						08 58						09 13			
Penge East	d						08 44	08 47						09 00						09 15			
Sydenham Hill	d						08 47	08 50						09 03						09 18			
West Dulwich	d						08 49	08 52						09 05						09 20			
Herne Hill ■	d	08 41				08 47	08 52	08 54		08 57	09 02			09 08					09 20	09 23			
Loughborough Jn	d					08 50	08 57				09 05								09 23				
Elephant & Castle	d	08 50	08 54			08 58	09 02			09 06	09 10	09 14			09 20		09 26		09 30		09 42		
London Blackfriars ■	d	08 54	08 58			09 02	09 06			09 10	09 14	09 18			09 26		09 30		09 34		09 46		
City Thameslink ■	a	08 56	09 00			09 04	09 08			09 12	09 16	09 20			09 27		09 32		09 36		09 48		
Farringdon	a	09 00	09 04			09 08	09 12			09 16	09 20	09 24			09 32		09 36		09 40		09 52		
St Pancras International ■	a	09 04	09 08			09 12	09 16			09 20	09 24	09 28			09 36		09 40		09 44		09 56		
Kentish Town	a		09 13			09 16						09 34					09 45		09 48		10 00		
Brixton	d							08 57						09 10						09 25			
London Victoria ■	a			08 53	08 53			09 06	09 14				09 09	09 19		09 29		09 23		09 34		09 38	09 43

		FC	SE	SE ■	SE	FC	SE	FC	SE	SE ■ ⊼	SE	SE ■	SE	FC	SE	FC	SE	SE ■	SE ■ ⊼	SE	SE	FC
Sevenoaks ■	d								09 13								09 42					
Bat & Ball	d								09 16								09 46					
Otford ■	d			09 17					09 21			09 46					09 50					
Shoreham (Kent)	d								09 24								09 53					
Eynsford	d								09 28								09 56					
Swanley ■	d			09 26					09 33			09 54					10 01	10 05				
St Mary Cray	d								09 37			09 58					10 05	10 09				
Orpington ■	d		09 10				09 25				09 40				09 55					10 10		
Petts Wood ■	d		09 13				09 28				09 43				09 58					10 13		
Bickley ■	d		09 17				09 32		09 42		09 47				10 02		10 10			10 17		
Bromley South ■	d		09 20	09 34			09 35		09 45	09 50	09 50	10 05			10 05		10 15	10 15	10 20	10 20		
Shortlands ■	d		09 23				09 38		09 48		09 53				10 08		10 18			10 23		
Ravensbourne	d								09 50								10 20					
Beckenham Hill	d								09 52								10 22					
Bellingham	d								09 54								10 24					
Catford	d								09 57								10 27					
Crofton Park	d								09 59								10 29					
Lewisham ■	d				09 38								10 08								10 38	
Nunhead ■	d				09 43				10 02				10 13				10 32				10 43	
Peckham Rye ■	d				09 45				10 04				10 15				10 34				10 45	
Denmark Hill ■	d				09 49				10 07				10 19				10 37				10 49	
Beckenham Junction ■	d		09 26				09 41				09 56				10 11					10 26		
Kent House ■	d		09 28				09 43				09 58				10 13					10 28		
Penge East	d		09 30				09 45				10 00				10 15					10 30		
Sydenham Hill	d		09 33				09 48				10 03				10 18					10 33		
West Dulwich	d		09 35				09 50				10 05				10 20					10 35		
Herne Hill ■	d	09 36	09 38			09 46	09 53	10 01			10 08			10 16	10 23	10 31				10 38		10 46
Loughborough Jn	d	09 40				09 50		10 04						10 19		10 34						10 49
Elephant & Castle	d	09 45				09 55		10 09	10 14					10 24		10 39	10 44					10 54
London Blackfriars ■	d	09 50				10 00		10 14	10 18					10 30		10 44	10 48					11 00
City Thameslink ■	a	09 52				10 02		10 16	10 20					10 32		10 46	10 50					11 02
Farringdon	a	09 56				10 06		10 19	10 24					10 35		10 49	10 54					11 06
St Pancras International ■	a	10 00				10 10		10 23	10 28					10 40		10 53	10 58					11 10
Kentish Town	a	10 05				10 14		10 27	10 33					10 44		10 57	11 03					11 14
Brixton	d		09 40				09 55				10 10				10 25					10 40		
London Victoria ■	a		09 49	09 51	10 00		10 02			10 07	10 17	10 21	10 31		10 32			10 41	10 37	10 47	11 03	

30 July to 10 August

Sevenoaks, Otford, Orpington, Bromley South, Beckenham Junction and Catford - Kentish Town/London Victoria

Network Diagram - see first Page of Table 195

		SE	SE ■	SE	SE ■ ⊼	FC	SE	SE	FC	SE	SE ■	SE	SE ■	SE ■ ⊼	FC	SE	SE	FC	SE	SE ■	SE	SE ■ ⊼	FC
Sevenoaks ■	d	10 02								10 32									11 02				
Bat & Ball	d	10 05								10 35									11 05				
Otford ■	d	10 08	10 17							10 38	10 46								11 08	11 17			
Shoreham (Kent)	d	10 11								10 41									11 11				
Eynsford	d	10 15								10 45									11 15				
Swanley ■	d	10 20	10 26							10 50	10 54		11 05						11 20	11 26			
St Mary Cray	d	10 24								10 54	10 58		11 09						11 24				
Orpington ■	d			10 25			10 40					10 55				11 10					11 25		
Petts Wood ■	d			10 28			10 43					10 58				11 13					11 28		
Bickley ■	d	10 28		10 32			10 47			10 58		11 02				11 17			11 28		11 32		
Bromley South ■	d	10 31	10 35	10 35	10 50		10 50			11 01	11 05	11 05	11 15	11 20		11 20			11 31	11 35	11 35	11 50	
Shortlands ■	d	10 34		10 38			10 53			11 04		11 08				11 23			11 34		11 38		
Ravensbourne	d	10 36								11 06									11 36				
Beckenham Hill	d	10 38								11 08									11 38				
Bellingham	d	10 40								11 10									11 40				
Catford	d	10 43								11 13									11 43				
Crofton Park	d	10 45								11 15									11 45				
Lewisham ■	d							11 08									11 38						
Nunhead ■	d	10 48						11 13		11 18							11 43		11 48				
Peckham Rye ■	d	10 50						11 15		11 20							11 45		11 50				
Denmark Hill ■	d	10 54						11 19		11 24							11 49		11 54				
Beckenham Junction ■	d			10 41			10 56					11 11				11 26					11 41		
Kent House ■	d			10 43			10 58					11 13				11 28					11 43		
Penge East	d			10 45			11 00					11 15				11 30					11 45		
Sydenham Hill	d			10 48			11 03					11 18				11 33					11 48		
West Dulwich	d			10 50			11 05					11 20				11 35					11 50		
Herne Hill ■	d			10 53		11 01	11 08		11 16			11 23			11 31	11 38		11 46			11 53		12 01
Loughborough Jn	d					11 04			11 19						11 34			11 49					12 04
Elephant & Castle	d	11 00				11 09			11 24	11 30					11 39			11 54	12 00				12 09
London Blackfriars ■	d	11 04				11 14			11 30	11 34					11 44			12 00	12 04				12 14
City Thameslink ■	a	11 06				11 16			11 32	11 36					11 46			12 02	12 06				12 16
Farringdon	a	11 10				11 19			11 36	11 40					11 49			12 06	12 10				12 19
St Pancras International ■	a	11 14				11 23			11 40	11 44					11 53			12 10	12 14				12 23
Kentish Town	a	11 19				11 27			11 44	11 49					11 57			12 14	12 19				12 27
Brixton	d			10 55			11 10					11 25				11 40					11 55		
London Victoria ■	a		10 51	11 02	11 07		11 17	11 31			11 21	11 32	11 37	11 37		11 47	12 03			11 51	12 02	12 07	

		SE	SE	FC	SE	SE ■	SE	SE ■	SE ■ ⊼	FC	SE	SE	FC	SE	SE ■	SE	SE ■ ⊼	FC	SE	SE	FC	SE	SE ■
Sevenoaks ■	d				11 32									12 02								12 32	
Bat & Ball	d				11 35									12 05								12 35	
Otford ■	d				11 38	11 46								12 08	12 17							12 38	12 46
Shoreham (Kent)	d				11 41									12 11								12 41	
Eynsford	d				11 45									12 15								12 45	
Swanley ■	d				11 50	11 54		12 05						12 20	12 26							12 50	12 54
St Mary Cray	d				11 54	11 58		12 09						12 24								12 54	12 58
Orpington ■	d	11 40					11 55				12 10					12 25			12 40				
Petts Wood ■	d	11 43					11 58				12 13					12 28			12 43				
Bickley ■	d	11 47			11 58		12 02				12 17			12 28		12 32			12 47			12 58	
Bromley South ■	d	11 50			12 01	12 05	12 05	12 15	12 20		12 20			12 31	12 35	12 35	12 50		12 50			13 01	13 05
Shortlands ■	d	11 53			12 04		12 08				12 23			12 34		12 38			12 53			13 04	
Ravensbourne	d				12 06									12 36								13 06	
Beckenham Hill	d				12 08									12 38								13 08	
Bellingham	d				12 10									12 40								13 10	
Catford	d				12 13									12 43								13 13	
Crofton Park	d				12 15									12 45								13 15	
Lewisham ■	d		12 08									12 38								13 08			
Nunhead ■	d		12 13		12 18							12 43		12 48						13 13		13 18	
Peckham Rye ■	d		12 15		12 20							12 45		12 50						13 15		13 20	
Denmark Hill ■	d		12 19		12 24							12 49		12 54						13 19		13 24	
Beckenham Junction ■	d	11 56					12 11				12 26					12 41			12 56				
Kent House ■	d	11 58					12 13				12 28					12 43			12 58				
Penge East	d	12 00					12 15				12 30					12 45			13 00				
Sydenham Hill	d	12 03					12 18				12 33					12 48			13 03				
West Dulwich	d	12 05					12 20				12 35					12 50			13 05				
Herne Hill ■	d	12 08		12 16			12 23			12 31	12 38		12 46			12 53		13 01	13 08		13 16		
Loughborough Jn	d			12 19						12 34			12 49					13 04			13 19		
Elephant & Castle	d			12 24	12 30					12 39			12 54	13 00				13 09			13 24	13 30	
London Blackfriars ■	d			12 30	12 34					12 44			13 00	13 04				13 14			13 30	13 34	
City Thameslink ■	a			12 32	12 36					12 46			13 02	13 06				13 16			13 32	13 36	
Farringdon	a			12 36	12 40					12 49			13 06	13 09				13 19			13 36	13 40	
St Pancras International ■	a			12 40	12 44					12 53			13 10	13 14				13 23			13 40	13 44	
Kentish Town	a			12 44	12 49					12 57			13 14	13 19				13 27			13 44	13 49	
Brixton	d	12 10					12 25				12 40					12 55			13 10				
London Victoria ■	a	12 17	12 31			12 21	12 32	12 37	12 37		12 47	13 01			12 51	13 02	13 07		13 17	13 31			13 21

Sevenoaks, Otford, Orpington, Bromley South, Beckenham Junction and Catford - Kentish Town/London Victoria

Network Diagram - see first Page of Table 195

	SE	SE ■	SE ■ ✠	FC	SE	SE	FC	SE	SE ■	SE	SE ■ ✠	FC	SE	SE	FC	SE	SE ■	SE	SE ■	SE ■ ✠	FC
Sevenoaks ■ d								13 02								13 32					
Bat & Ball d								13 05								13 35					
Otford ■ d								13 08	13 17							13 38	13 46				
Shoreham (Kent) d								13 11								13 41					
Eynsford d								13 15								13 45					
Swanley ■ d		13 05						13 20	13 26							13 50	13 54		14 05		
St Mary Cray d		13 09						13 24								13 54	13 58		14 09		
Orpington ■ d	12 55				13 10					13 25			13 40					13 55			
Petts Wood ■ d	12 58				13 13					13 28			13 43					13 58			
Bickley ■ d	13 02				13 17			13 28		13 32			13 47			13 58		14 02			
Bromley South ■ d	13 05	13 15	13 20		13 20			13 31	13 35	13 35	13 50		13 50			14 01	14 05	14 05	14 15	14 20	
Shortlands ■ d	13 08				13 23			13 34		13 38			13 53			14 04		14 08			
Ravensbourne d								13 36								14 06					
Beckenham Hill d								13 38								14 08					
Bellingham d								13 40								14 10					
Catford d								13 43								14 13					
Crofton Park d								13 45								14 15					
Lewisham ■ d						13 38								14 08							
Nunhead ■ d						13 43		13 48						14 13		14 18					
Peckham Rye ■ d						13 45		13 50						14 15		14 20					
Denmark Hill ■ d						13 49		13 54						14 19		14 24					
Beckenham Junction ■ d	13 11				13 26					13 41			13 56					14 11			
Kent House ■ d	13 13				13 28					13 43			13 58					14 13			
Penge East d	13 15				13 30					13 45			14 00					14 15			
Sydenham Hill d	13 18				13 33					13 48			14 03					14 18			
West Dulwich d	13 20				13 35					13 50			14 05					14 20			
Herne Hill ■ d	13 23			13 31	13 38		13 46			13 53		14 01	14 08		14 16			14 23			14 31
Loughborough Jn d				13 34			13 49					14 04			14 19						14 34
Elephant & Castle ⊖ d				13 39			13 54	14 00				14 09			14 24	14 30					14 39
London Blackfriars ■ ⊖ d				13 44			14 00	14 04				14 14			14 30	14 34					14 44
City Thameslink ■ a				13 46			14 02	14 06				14 16			14 32	14 36					14 46
Farringdon ⊖ a				13 49			14 06	14 10				14 19			14 36	14 40					14 49
St Pancras International ■ ⊖ a				13 53			14 10	14 14				14 23			14 40	14 44					14 53
Kentish Town ⊖ a				13 57			14 14	14 19				14 27			14 44	14 49					14 57
Brixton ⊖ d	13 25				13 40					13 55			14 10					14 25			
London Victoria ■ ⊖ a	13 32	13 37	13 37		13 47	14 01			13 51	14 02	14 07		14 17	14 31			14 21	14 32	14 37	14 37	

	SE	SE	FC	SE	SE ■	SE	SE ■ ✠	FC	SE	SE	FC	SE	SE ■	SE	SE ■	SE ■ ✠	FC	SE	SE	FC	SE	SE ■
Sevenoaks ■ d				14 02								14 32									15 02	
Bat & Ball d				14 05								14 35									15 05	
Otford ■ d				14 08	14 17							14 38	14 46								15 08	15 17
Shoreham (Kent) d				14 11								14 41									15 11	
Eynsford d				14 15								14 45									15 15	
Swanley ■ d				14 20	14 26							14 50	14 54		15 05						15 20	15 26
St Mary Cray d				14 24								14 54	14 58		15 09						15 24	
Orpington ■ d	14 10					14 25			14 40					14 55				15 10				
Petts Wood ■ d	14 13					14 28			14 43					14 58				15 13				
Bickley ■ d	14 17			14 28		14 32			14 47			14 58		15 02				15 17			15 28	
Bromley South ■ d	14 20			14 31	14 35	14 35	14 50		14 50			15 01	15 05	15 05	15 15	15 20		15 20			15 31	15 35
Shortlands ■ d	14 23			14 34		14 38			14 53			15 04		15 08				15 23			15 34	
Ravensbourne d				14 36								15 06									15 36	
Beckenham Hill d				14 38								15 08									15 38	
Bellingham d				14 40								15 10									15 40	
Catford d				14 43								15 13									15 43	
Crofton Park d				14 45								15 15									15 45	
Lewisham ■ d		14 38								15 08									15 38			
Nunhead ■ d		14 43		14 48						15 13		15 18							15 43		15 48	
Peckham Rye ■ d		14 45		14 50						15 15		15 20							15 45		15 50	
Denmark Hill ■ d		14 49		14 54						15 19		15 24							15 49		15 54	
Beckenham Junction ■ d	14 26					14 41			14 56					15 11				15 26				
Kent House ■ d	14 28					14 43			14 58					15 13				15 28				
Penge East d	14 30					14 45			15 00					15 15				15 30				
Sydenham Hill d	14 33					14 48			15 03					15 18				15 33				
West Dulwich d	14 35					14 50			15 05					15 20				15 35				
Herne Hill ■ d	14 38		14 46			14 53		15 01	15 08		15 16			15 23			15 31	15 38		15 46		
Loughborough Jn d			14 49					15 04			15 19						15 34			15 49		
Elephant & Castle ⊖ d			14 54	15 00				15 09			15 24	15 30					15 39			15 54	16 00	
London Blackfriars ■ ⊖ d			15 00	15 04				15 14			15 30	15 34					15 44			16 00	16 04	
City Thameslink ■ a			15 02	15 06				15 16			15 32	15 36					15 46			16 02	16 06	
Farringdon ⊖ a			15 06	15 10				15 19			15 36	15 40					15 49			16 06	16 10	
St Pancras International ■ ⊖ a			15 10	15 14				15 23			15 40	15 44					15 53			16 10	16 14	
Kentish Town ⊖ a			15 14	15 19				15 27			15 44	15 49					15 57			16 14	16 19	
Brixton ⊖ d	14 40					14 55			15 10					15 25				15 40				
London Victoria ■ ⊖ a	14 47	15 01			14 51	15 02	15 07		15 17	15 31			15 21	15 32	15 37	15 37		15 47	16 01			15 51

Table 195

Mondays to Fridays
30 July to 10 August

Sevenoaks, Otford, Orpington, Bromley South, Beckenham Junction and Catford - Kentish Town/London Victoria

Network Diagram - see first Page of Table 195

	SE	SE ■ ✠	FC	SE	SE	FC	SE ■	SE ■	SE	SE	SE ■ ✠	SE	FC	SE	SE	FC	SE ■	SE ■	SE	FC ■	SE
Sevenoaks ■ d							15 32										16 02				16 22
Bat & Ball d							15 35										16 05				16 25
Otford ■ d							15 38	15 46									16 08	16 17			16 28
Shoreham (Kent) d							15 41										16 11				
Eynsford d							15 45										16 15				
Swanley ■ d							15 50	15 54		16 05							16 20	16 26			16 37
St Mary Cray d							15 54	15 58		16 09							16 24				16 41
Orpington ■ d	15 25			15 40					15 55					16 10					16 25		
Petts Wood ■ d	15 28			15 43					15 58					16 13					16 28		
Bickley ■ d	15 32			15 47			15 58		16 02					16 17			16 28		16 32		
Bromley South ■ d	15 35	15 50		15 50			16 01	16 05	16 05	16 15	16 20			16 20			16 31	16 35	16 35		16 47
Shortlands ■ d	15 38			15 53			16 04		16 08					16 23			16 34		16 38		
Ravensbourne d							16 06										16 36				
Beckenham Hill d							16 08										16 38				
Bellingham d							16 10										16 40				16 52
Catford d							16 13										16 43				16 55
Crofton Park d							16 15										16 45				
Lewisham ■ d					16 08							16 16			16 38						
Nunhead ■ d					16 13		16 18								16 43		16 48				16 59
Peckham Rye ■ d					16 15		16 20								16 45		16 50				17 02
Denmark Hill ■ d					16 19		16 24					16 28			16 49		16 54				17 05
Beckenham Junction ■ d	15 41			15 56					16 11					16 26					16 41		
Kent House ■ d	15 43			15 58					16 13					16 28					16 43		
Penge East d	15 45			16 00					16 15					16 30					16 45		
Sydenham Hill d	15 48			16 03					16 18					16 33					16 48		
West Dulwich d	15 50			16 05					16 20					16 35					16 50		
Herne Hill ■ d	15 53		16 01	16 08		16 16			16 23				16 31	16 38		16 50			16 53	17 01	
Loughborough Jn d			16 04			16 19							16 34			16 53					
Elephant & Castle ⊖ d			16 09			16 24	16 30						16 39			17 00	17 04			17 08	17 12
London Blackfriars ■ ⊖ d			16 14			16 30	16 38						16 44			17 04	17 08			17 12	17 16
City Thameslink ■ a			16 16			16 32	16 40						16 46			17 06	17 10			17 14	17 18
Farringdon ⊖ a			16 19			16 35	16 43						16 49			17 09	17 13			17 17	17 23
St Pancras International ■ ⊖ a			16 23			16 39	16 47						16 53			17 13	17 17			17 21	17 27
Kentish Town ⊖ a			16 28			16 44							16 58			17 18					17 32
Brixton ⊖ d	15 55			16 10					16 25					16 40					16 55		
London Victoria ■ ⊖ a	16 02	16 07		16 17	16 31			16 21	16 32	16 37	16 38	16 44		16 47	17 04			16 51	17 04		

	SE ■ ✠	SE	SE	FC	SE	SE ■	SE	SE ■	SE ■ ✠	FC	SE	SE ■	SE	FC	SE ■	SE ■	SE	SE ■	SE ■	SE ■ ✠	FC	SE
Sevenoaks ■ d					16 32										17 02							
Bat & Ball d					16 35										17 05							
Otford ■ d					16 38	16 46									17 08	17 17						
Shoreham (Kent) d					16 41										17 11							
Eynsford d					16 45										17 15							
Swanley ■ d					16 50	16 54		17 05							17 20	17 26			17 35			
St Mary Cray d					16 54	16 58		17 09							17 24				17 39			
Orpington ■ d		16 40					16 55				17 10						17 24	17 34				17 40
Petts Wood ■ d		16 43					16 58				17 13						17 28	17 37				17 43
Bickley ■ d		16 47			16 58		17 02				17 17				17 28		17 32	17 42				17 47
Bromley South ■ d	16 50	16 50			17 01	17 05	17 05	17 15	17 20		17 20				17 31	17 35	17 35	17 45	17 46	17 50		17 50
Shortlands ■ d		16 53			17 04		17 08				17 23				17 34		17 38					17 53
Ravensbourne d					17 06										17 36							
Beckenham Hill d					17 08										17 38							
Bellingham d					17 10										17 40							
Catford d					17 13										17 43							
Crofton Park d					17 15										17 45							
Lewisham ■ d			17 08										17 38									
Nunhead ■ d			17 13		17 18								17 43		17 48							
Peckham Rye ■ d			17 15		17 20								17 45		17 50							
Denmark Hill ■ d			17 19		17 24								17 49		17 54							
Beckenham Junction ■ d		16 56					17 11				17 26	17 30					17 41	17 49				17 56
Kent House ■ d		16 58					17 13				17 28	17 33					17 43					17 58
Penge East d		17 00					17 15				17 30	17 35					17 45					18 00
Sydenham Hill d		17 03					17 18				17 33	17 38					17 48					18 03
West Dulwich d		17 05					17 20				17 35	17 40					17 50					18 05
Herne Hill ■ d		17 11		17 21			17 23			17 31	17 38	17 44		17 48			17 53				18 06	18 09
Loughborough Jn d				17 24						17 34		17 47		17 51							18 09	
Elephant & Castle ⊖ d				17 28	17 34					17 39		17 52		17 56	18 00			18 05			18 14	
London Blackfriars ■ ⊖ d				17 32	17 40					17 46		17 56		18 00	18 06			18 10			18 18	
City Thameslink ■ a				17 34	17 42					17 48		17 58		18 02	18 08			18 12			18 20	
Farringdon ⊖ a				17 37	17 45					17 51		18 01		18 05	18 11			18 15			18 23	
St Pancras International ■ ⊖ a				17 41	17 49					17 55		18 05		18 09	18 15			18 19			18 27	
Kentish Town ⊖ a				17 46						18 00				18 14							18 32	
Brixton ⊖ d		17 13					17 25				17 40						17 55					18 11
London Victoria ■ ⊖ a	17 07	17 20	17 31			17 23	17 33	17 38	17 37		17 48		18 02			17 53	18 03		18 08	18 07		18 18

Table 195

Mondays to Fridays
30 July to 10 August

Sevenoaks, Otford, Orpington, Bromley South, Beckenham Junction and Catford - Kentish Town/London Victoria

Network Diagram - see first Page of Table 195

		SE	FC	SE ■	SE ■	SE	SE ■	SE ■ ⌶	FC	SE	SE	FC ■	FC	SE ■	SE ■	SE	SE	SE ■ ⌶	FC	SE	SE	FC	SE
Sevenoaks ■	d			17 32										18 02			18 18						18 32
Bat & Ball	d			17 35										18 05			18 21						18 35
Otford ■	d			17 38	17 46									18 08	18 17		18 24						18 38
Shoreham (Kent)	d			17 41										18 11			18 27						18 41
Eynsford	d			17 45										18 15			18 31						18 45
Swanley ■	d			17 50	17 54		18 05							18 20	18 26		18 36						18 50
St Mary Cray	d			17 54	17 58		18 09							18 24			18 40						18 54
Orpington ■	d					17 55				18 09						18 25				18 40			
Petts Wood ■	d					17 58				18 12						18 28				18 43			
Bickley ■	d			17 58		18 02				18 17				18 28		18 32				18 47			18 58
Bromley South ■	d			18 01	18 05	18 05	18 15	18 20		18 20				18 31	18 35	18 35	18 46	18 50		18 50			19 01
Shortlands ■	d			18 04		18 08				18 23				18 34		18 38				18 53			19 04
Ravensbourne	d			18 06										18 36									19 06
Beckenham Hill	d			18 08										18 38									19 08
Bellingham	d			18 10										18 40									19 10
Catford	d			18 13										18 43									19 13
Crofton Park	d			18 15										18 45									19 15
Lewisham ■ ⇌	d	18 08									18 38										19 08		
Nunhead ■	d	18 13		18 18							18 43			18 48							19 13		19 18
Peckham Rye ■	d	18 15		18 20							18 45			18 50							19 15		19 20
Denmark Hill ■	d	18 19		18 23							18 49			18 54			18 59				19 19		19 24
Beckenham Junction ■ ⇌	d					18 11				18 26						18 41				18 56			
Kent House ■	d					18 13				18 28						18 43				18 58			
Penge East	d					18 15				18 30						18 45				19 00			
Sydenham Hill	d					18 18				18 33						18 48				19 03			
West Dulwich	d					18 20				18 35						18 50				19 05			
Herne Hill ■	d		18 20			18 24			18 32	18 38		18 41	18 48			18 53			19 02	19 08		19 17	
Loughborough Jn	d		18 23						18 35				18 51						19 05			19 20	
Elephant & Castle ⊖	d		18 28	18 32					18 40			18 48	18 56	19 00					19 10			19 25	19 30
London Blackfriars ■ ⊖	d		18 32	18 36					18 44			18 52	19 00	19 06					19 18			19 30	19 34
City Thameslink ■	a		18 34	18 38					18 46			18 54	19 02	19 08					19 20			19 32	19 36
Farringdon ⊖	a		18 37	18 41					18 49			18 57	19 05	19 11					19 23			19 36	19 40
St Pancras International ■ ⊖	a		18 41	18 45					18 53			19 01	19 09	19 15					19 27			19 40	19 44
Kentish Town ⊖	a		18 46										19 14						19 32			19 44	19 49
Brixton ⊖	d					18 26				18 40						18 55				19 10			
London Victoria ■ ⊖	a	18 32			18 21	18 33	18 37	18 37		18 48	19 01				18 53	19 03	19 13	19 07		19 17	19 31		

		SE ■	SE	SE	SE	SE ■	SE ■	FC	SE	FC	SE	SE ■	SE	SE	SE ■	FC	SE	SE	FC	SE	SE ■	SE
Sevenoaks ■	d			18 45							19 02		19 22							19 32		
Bat & Ball	d			18 48							19 05		19 25							19 35		
Otford ■	d	18 46		18 51							19 08	19 17	19 29							19 38	19 46	
Shoreham (Kent)	d			18 54							19 11		19 32							19 41		
Eynsford	d			18 58							19 15		19 35							19 45		
Swanley ■	d	18 54		19 03	19 05						19 20	19 26	19a43							19 50	19 54	
St Mary Cray	d	18 58			19 09						19 24									19 54	19 58	
Orpington ■	d		18 55						19 10					19 25			19 40					19 55
Petts Wood ■	d		18 58						19 13					19 28			19 43					19 58
Bickley ■	d		19 02						19 17		19 28			19 32			19 47			19 58		20 02
Bromley South ■	d	19 05	19 05	19 11	19 15	19 17	19 20		19 20		19 31	19 35		19 35	19 50		19 50			20 01	20 05	20 05
Shortlands ■	d		19 08						19 23		19 34			19 38			19 53			20 04		20 08
Ravensbourne	d										19 36									20 06		
Beckenham Hill	d										19 38									20 08		
Bellingham	d										19 40									20 10		
Catford	d										19 43									20 13		
Crofton Park	d										19 45									20 15		
Lewisham ■ ⇌	d																	20 10				
Nunhead ■	d										19 48									20 18		
Peckham Rye ■	d										19 50									20 20		
Denmark Hill ■	d			19 28							19 54							20 18		20 24		
Beckenham Junction ■ ⇌	d		19 11						19 26					19 41			19 56					20 11
Kent House ■	d		19 13						19 28					19 43			19 58					20 13
Penge East	d		19 15						19 30					19 45			20 00					20 15
Sydenham Hill	d		19 18						19 33					19 48			20 03					20 18
West Dulwich	d		19 20						19 35					19 50			20 05					20 20
Herne Hill ■	d		19 23					19 31	19 38	19 47				19 53		20 05	20 08		20 16			20 23
Loughborough Jn	d							19 34		19 50						20 08			20 19			
Elephant & Castle ⊖	d							19 39		19 55	20 00					20 13			20 24	20 30		
London Blackfriars ■ ⊖	d							19 46		20 00	20 04					20 18			20 30	20 34		
City Thameslink ■	a							19 48		20 02	20 06					20 20			20 32	20 36		
Farringdon ⊖	a							19 51		20 06	20 10					20 23			20 36	20 40		
St Pancras International ■ ⊖	a							19 55		20 10	20 14					20 27			20 40	20 44		
Kentish Town ⊖	a							19 59		20 14	20 19					20 31			20 44	20 49		
Brixton ⊖	d		19 25						19 40					19 55			20 10					20 25
London Victoria ■ ⊖	a	19 21	19 32	19 43	19 37	19 35	19 37		19 47			19 51		20 02	20 07		20 17	20 31			20 21	20 32

Table 195

Mondays to Fridays
30 July to 10 August

Sevenoaks, Otford, Orpington, Bromley South, Beckenham Junction and Catford - Kentish Town/London Victoria

Network Diagram - see first Page of Table 195

		SE	SE	SE ■	FC	SE	FC	SE	SE ■	SE ■	FC	SE	SE	FC	SE	SE ■	FC	SE	SE	SE ■	SE ■	SE	FC
Sevenoaks ■	d	19 45						20 02							20 32				21 02				
Bat & Ball	d	19 48						20 05							20 35				21 05				
Otford ■	d	19 51						20 08	20 16						20 38				21 08	21 16			
Shoreham (Kent)	d	19 54						20 11							20 41				21 11				
Eynsford	d	19 58						20 15							20 45				21 15				
Swanley ■	d	20 03	20 05					20 20	20 24						20 50	21 10			21 20	21 24			
St Mary Cray	d		20 09					20 24	20 28						20 54	21 14			21 24	21 28			
Orpington ■	d					20 10						20 40						21 10					
Petts Wood ■	d					20 13						20 43						21 13					
Bickley ■	d					20 17		20 28				20 47			20 58			21 17	21 28				
Bromley South ■	d	20a11	20 15	20 20		20 20		20 31	20 35	20 50		20 50			21 01	21 20		21 20	21 31	21 35	21 50		
Shortlands ■	d					20 23		20 34				20 53			21 04			21 23	21 34				
Ravensbourne	d							20 36							21 06				21 36				
Beckenham Hill	d							20 38							21 08				21 38				
Bellingham	d							20 40							21 10				21 40				
Catford	d							20 43							21 13				21 43				
Crofton Park	d							20 45							21 15				21 45				
Lewisham ■ ⇌	d												21 11									21 46	
Nunhead ■	d							20 48							21 18				21 48				
Peckham Rye ■	d							20 50							21 20				21 50				
Denmark Hill ■	d							20 54					21 18		21 24				21 54			21 59	
Beckenham Junction ■ ⇌	d					20 26						20 56						21 26					
Kent House ■	d					20 28						20 58						21 28					
Penge East	d					20 30						21 00						21 30					
Sydenham Hill	d					20 33						21 03						21 33					
West Dulwich	d					20 35						21 05						21 35					
Herne Hill ■	d				20 35	20 38	20 46				21 05	21 08		21 16			21 35	21 38					21 57
Loughborough Jn	d				20 38		20 49				21 08			21 19			21 38						22 00
Elephant & Castle ⊖	d				20 43		20 54	21 00			21 13			21 24	21 30		21 43		22 00				22 04
London Blackfriars ■ ⊖	d				20 48		21 00	21 04			21 18			21 30	21a37		21 48		22a04				22 08
City Thameslink ■	a				20 50		21 02	21 06			21 20			21 32			21 50						22 10
Farringdon ⊖	a				20 53		21 06	21 10			21 23			21 36			21 53						22 13
St Pancras International ■ ⊖	a				20 57		21 10	21 14			21 27			21 40			21 57						22 17
Kentish Town ⊖	a				21 01		21 14	21 19			21 31			21 44			22 01						22 21
Brixton ⊖	d					20 40						21 10						21 40					
London Victoria ■ ⊖	a		20 37	20 38		20 47			20 51	21 07		21 17	21 31			21 37		21 47		21 51	22 07	22 14	

		SE	SE	SE	SE ■	FC	SE	SE	SE ■	SE ■	SE A	FC	SE	SE	SE ■	FC	SE	SE ■	SE ■
Sevenoaks ■	d			21 32				22 02						22 32					
Bat & Ball	d			21 35				22 05						22 35					
Otford ■	d			21 38				22 08	22 16					22 38				23 16	
Shoreham (Kent)	d			21 41				22 11						22 41					
Eynsford	d			21 45				22 15						22 45					
Swanley ■	d			21 50	22 10			22 20	22 24					22 50	23 10			23 24	
St Mary Cray	d			21 54	22 14			22 24	22 28					22 54	23 14			23 28	
Orpington ■	d	21 40					22 10						22 40				23 10		
Petts Wood ■	d	21 43					22 13						22 43				23 13		
Bickley ■	d	21 47		21 58			22 17	22 28					22 47	22 58			23 17		
Bromley South ■	d	21 50		22 01	22 20		22 20	22 31	22 35	22 50			22 50	23 01	23 20		23 20	23 35	23 50
Shortlands ■	d	21 53		22 04			22 23	22 34					22 53	23 04			23 23		
Ravensbourne	d			22 06				22 36						23 06					
Beckenham Hill	d			22 08				22 38						23 08					
Bellingham	d			22 10				22 40						23 10					
Catford	d			22 13				22 43						23 13					
Crofton Park	d			22 15				22 45						23 15					
Lewisham ■ ⇌	d		22 10								22 46								
Nunhead ■	d			22 18				22 48						23 18					
Peckham Rye ■	d			22 20				22 50						23 20					
Denmark Hill ■	d		22 17	22 24				22 54			22 59			23 24					
Beckenham Junction ■ ⇌	d	21 56					22 26						22 56				23 26		
Kent House ■	d	21 58					22 28						22 58				23 28		
Penge East	d	22 00					22 30						23 00				23 30		
Sydenham Hill	d	22 03					22 33						23 03				23 33		
West Dulwich	d	22 05					22 35						23 05				23 35		
Herne Hill ■	d	22 08				22 27	22 38					22 57	23 08			23 27	23 38		
Loughborough Jn	d					22 30						23 00							
Elephant & Castle ⊖	d			22 30		22 34		23 00				23 04		23 30		23 34			
London Blackfriars ■ ⊖	d			22a34		22 38		23a04				23 08		23a34		23 38			
City Thameslink ■	a					22 40													
Farringdon ⊖	a					22 43						23 13				23 43			
St Pancras International ■ ⊖	a					22 47						23 17				23 47			
Kentish Town ⊖	a					22 51						23 21				23 51			
Brixton ⊖	d	22 10					22 40						23 10				23 40		
London Victoria ■ ⊖	a	22 17	22 31		22 37		22 47		22 51	23 07	23 14		23 17		23 37		23 47	23 51	00 07

A not 3 August, 10 August

Table 195

Sevenoaks, Otford, Orpington, Bromley South, Beckenham Junction and Catford - Kentish Town/London Victoria

Mondays to Fridays
29 August to 7 September

Network Diagram - see first Page of Table 195

		SE 1 A	SE 1 B	SE 1 A	SE 1 B	SE	SE	SE	SE	FC	SE	SE	FC	SE	SE 1	SE 1	SE	SE 1	FC	SE	SE	FC	SE
Sevenoaks	d													05 40									06 13
Bat & Ball	d													05 43									06 16
Otford	d													05 46				06 15					06 19
Shoreham (Kent)	d													05 49									06 22
Eynsford	d													05 53									06 26
Swanley	d	23p32			00 10		04 33							05 58		06 02		06 25					06 31
St Mary Cray	d	23p36			00 14		04 37							06 02		06 06							06 35
Orpington	d					04 34		04 55	05 10		05 34	05 40					06 10						
Petts Wood	d					04 37		04 58	05 13		05 37	05 43					06 13						
Bickley	d					04 41	04 41	05 02	05 17		05 41	05 47		06 06			06 17						06 39
Bromley South	d	23p43	23p50	00 13	00 20	04 44	04 50	05 05	05 20		05 44	05 50		06 10	06 12	06 15	06 20	06 33					06 42
Shortlands	d					04 47	04 53	05 08	05 23		05 47	05 53		06 13			06 23						06 45
Ravensbourne	d					04 49					05 49			06 15									06 47
Beckenham Hill	d					04 51					05 51			06 17									06 49
Bellingham	d					04 53					05 53			06 19									06 51
Catford	d					04 56					05 56			06 22									06 54
Crofton Park	d					04 58					05 58			06 25									06 57
Lewisham	d																				06 41		
Nunhead	d					05 01					06 01			06 27									06 59
Peckham Rye	d					05 04					06 04			06 30							06 47		07 02
Denmark Hill	d					05 07					06 07			06 33							06 50		07 05
Beckenham Junction	d						04 56	05 11	05 26			05 56					06 26			06 40			
Kent House	d						04 58	05 13	05 28			05 58					06 28			06 42			
Penge East	d						05 00	05 15	05 30			06 00					06 30			06 44			
Sydenham Hill	d						05 03	05 18	05 33			06 03					06 33			06 47			
West Dulwich	d						05 05	05 20	05 35			06 05					06 35			06 49			
Herne Hill	d						05 08	05 23	05 38	05 54		06 08	06 16				06 38	06 43	06 46	06 52		06 57	
Loughborough Jn	d												06 19						06 49			07 00	
Elephant & Castle	d					05 13		05 29		06 00	06 13		06 24	06 40					06 54			07 06	07 12
London Blackfriars	d					05 17		05 33		06 04	06 17		06 30	06 48					06 58			07 12	07 18
City Thameslink	a					05 19		05 35		06 06	06 19		06 32	06 50					07 00			07 14	07 20
Farringdon	a							05 38		06 10			06 36	06 54					07 04			07 18	07 24
St Pancras International	a							05 42		06 14			06 40	06 58					07 08			07 22	07 28
Kentish Town	a							05 47		06 18			06 44	07 02									07 32
Brixton	d						05 10		05 40			06 10					06 40			06 54			
London Victoria	a	00 02	00 07	00 29	00 38		05 17		05 47			06 18			06 28	06 31	06 47	06 51		07 03	07 04		

		SE 1	SE 1	SE	SE 1	SE 1	SE 1	SE	SE	FC	SE	SE	SE 1	SE 1	SE	SE 1	SE	FC 1	FC	SE	SE	SE	SE
Sevenoaks	d											06 42											07 11
Bat & Ball	d											06 48											07 14
Otford	d				06 38	06 46						06 51		07 01		07 14							07 18
Shoreham (Kent)	d											06 54											07 21
Eynsford	d											06 58											07 24
Swanley	d	06 35			06 48	06 54	06 57					07 03		07 10		07 22	07 23						07 30
St Mary Cray	d	06 39					07 01					07 07					07 27						07 34
Orpington	d			06 40							06 58				07 08						07 28		
Petts Wood	d			06 43							07 01				07 11						07 31		
Bickley	d			06 47							07 05	07 11			07 16						07 35		07 39
Bromley South	d	06 46	06 50	06 50	06 57	07 02	07 08				07 08	07 14	07 16	07 20	07 20	07 31	07 34			07 34	07 38		07 42
Shortlands	d			06 53							07 11	07 17			07 23					07 36	07 41		07 44
Ravensbourne	d											07 19											07 47
Beckenham Hill	d											07 21											07 49
Bellingham	d											07 23											07 51
Catford	d											07 26											07 53
Crofton Park	d											07 29											07 56
Lewisham	d								07 15													07 46	
Nunhead	d								07 20			07 31										07 51	07 58
Peckham Rye	d								07 23			07 34										07 54	08 01
Denmark Hill	d								07 29			07 37										07 59	08 04
Beckenham Junction	d			06 56				07 08			07 14				07 26					07 39	07 44		
Kent House	d			06 58				07 11			07 17				07 28					07 42	07 47		
Penge East	d			07 00				07 14			07 19				07 30					07 44	07 49		
Sydenham Hill	d			07 03				07 17			07 22				07 33					07 47	07 52		
West Dulwich	d			07 05				07 19			07 24				07 35					07 49	07 54		
Herne Hill	d			07 08				07 22		07 24	07 31				07 38			07 41	07 47	07 52	07 57		
Loughborough Jn	d									07 27	07 34								07 50		08 00		
Elephant & Castle	d				07 16					07 32	07 38	07 44						07 48	07 54		08 05		08 13
London Blackfriars	d				07 24					07 36	07 42	07 48						07 54	07 58		08 09		08 17
City Thameslink	a				07 26					07 38	07 44	07 50						07 56	08 00		08 11		08 19
Farringdon	a				07 30					07 42	07 48	07 54						08 00	08 03		08 15		08 23
St Pancras International	a				07 34					07 46	07 52	07 58						08 04	08 08		08 19		08 27
Kentish Town	a											08 02							08 14				08 32
Brixton	d			07 10				07 24							07 40					07 54			
London Victoria	a	07 07	07 09	07 19		07 22	07 30	07 33	07 42				07 38	07 43	07 49	07 53	07 55			08 03		08 11	

A 3 September

B not 3 September

Table 195

Sevenoaks, Otford, Orpington, Bromley South, Beckenham Junction and Catford - Kentish Town/London Victoria

Mondays to Fridays
29 August to 7 September

Network Diagram - see first Page of Table 195

		SE 1	SE 1	FC	SE	SE 1	SE 1	SE 1	SE	SE	FC	SE	SE	SE 1	SE 1	SE 1	SE 1	FC	SE	SE	SE 1	SE
Sevenoaks	d												07 36									
Bat & Ball	d												07 39									
Otford	d	07 23					07 38						07 43			07 56						
Shoreham (Kent)	d												07 46									
Eynsford	d												07 49									
Swanley	d	07 32				07 40	07 47						07 54	07 55	08 02	08 05						
St Mary Cray	d					07 45							07 59	08 00	08 06							
Orpington	d				07 38					07 47												08 10
Petts Wood	d				07 41					07 50												08 13
Bickley	d				07 46					07 55			08 03									08 17
Bromley South	d	07 40	07 49		07 50	07 53	07 57			07 58		08 04	08 08	08 06	08 12	08 13	08 16				08 18	08 22
Shortlands	d				07 53					08 00		08 06	08 10								08 20	08 24
Ravensbourne	d												08 13								08 23	
Beckenham Hill	d												08 15								08 25	
Bellingham	d									08 05			08 17								08 27	
Catford	d									08 08			08 20								08 30	
Crofton Park	d									08 10												
Lewisham	d								08 05											08 25		
Nunhead	d								08 11	08 14										08 30		
Peckham Rye	d								08 13	08 16										08 33	08 36	
Denmark Hill	d								08 17	08 19			08 26		08 30					08 36	08 39	
Beckenham Junction	d				07 56			07 59				08 10							08 22			08 28
Kent House	d				07 58			08 02				08 12							08 24			08 30
Penge East	d				08 00			08 04				08 14							08 26			
Sydenham Hill	d				08 03			08 07				08 17							08 29			
West Dulwich	d				08 05			08 09				08 19							08 31			08 35
Herne Hill	d			08 01	08 08			08 13			08 20	08 23						08 32	08 34			08 38
Loughborough Jn	d			08 04				08 16			08 23							08 36				
Elephant & Castle	d	07 59		08 09				08 21		08 25	08 28		08 35	08 31				08 40			08 45	
London Blackfriars	d	08 04		08 13				08 25		08 29	08 33		08 42	08 37				08 46			08 50	
City Thameslink	a	08 06		08 15				08 27		08 31	08 35		08 44	08 39				08 48			08 52	
Farringdon	a	08 10		08 19				08 30		08 35	08 39		08 48	08 43				08 52			08 56	
St Pancras International	a	08 14		08 23				08 35		08 39	08 43		08 52	08 47				08 56			09 00	
Kentish Town	a			08 29							08 48		08 57					09 00				
Brixton	d				08 10							08 25							08 36			08 40
London Victoria	a		08 09		08 20	08 17	08 23		08 29			08 35			08 42	08 36	08 39		08 45	08 49		08 50

		FC 1	SE	SE 1	SE 1	FC	SE 1	SE	SE	FC 1	FC	SE	SE 1	SE	SE 1	SE	SE	SE 1	FC	SE	SE	SE 1	SE 1
Sevenoaks	d		07 53												08 24						08 43		
Bat & Ball	d		07 56												08 27						08 46		
Otford	d		08 00	08 09											08 31			08 46			08 49		
Shoreham (Kent)	d		08 03												08 34						08 52		
Eynsford	d		08 06												08 37						08 56		
Swanley	d		08 11		08 22										08 42			08 54			09 01	09 05	
St Mary Cray	d		08 16		08 27										08 46			08 58			09 05	09 09	
Orpington	d							08 26						08 40			08 47			08 55			
Petts Wood	d							08 29						08 43			08 50			08 58			
Bickley	d		08 20					08 33						08 47	08 51		08 55			09 02	09 09		
Bromley South	d		08 26	08 25	08 33			08 36				08 44	08 50	08 50	08 54		08 58	09 05		09 05	09 12	09 15	09 20
Shortlands	d		08 29					08 39				08 46		08 53	08 56		09 00			09 08	09 15		
Ravensbourne	d											08 49					09 03				09 17		
Beckenham Hill	d											08 51					09 05				09 19		
Bellingham	d		08 33									08 53			09 01		09 07				09 21		
Catford	d		08 36									08 56			09 04		09 09				09 24		
Crofton Park	d		08 39									08 58					09 12				09 26		
Lewisham	d								08 46							09 06							
Nunhead	d		08 41						08 52			09 01				09 11	09 14				09 29		
Peckham Rye	d		08 44						08 55			09 04			09 09	09 14	09 17				09 31		
Denmark Hill	d		08 47						09 02			09 07			09 12	09 17	09 19				09 34		
Beckenham Junction	d							08 42						08 56						09 11			
Kent House	d						08 42	08 45						08 58						09 13			
Penge East	d						08 44	08 47						09 00						09 15			
Sydenham Hill	d						08 47	08 50						09 03						09 18			
West Dulwich	d						08 49	08 52						09 05						09 20			
Herne Hill	d	08 41				08 47	08 52	08 54		08 57	09 02			09 08					09 20	09 23			
Loughborough Jn	d					08 50	08 57				09 05								09 23				
Elephant & Castle	d	08 50	08 54			08 58	09 02			09 06	09 10	09 14			09 20		09 26		09 30		09 42		
London Blackfriars	d	08 54	08 58			09 02	09 06			09 10	09 14	09 18			09 26		09 30		09 34		09 46		
City Thameslink	a	08 56	09 00			09 04	09 08			09 12	09 16	09 20			09 27		09 32		09 36		09 48		
Farringdon	a	09 00	09 04			09 08	09 12			09 16	09 20	09 24			09 32		09 36		09 40		09 52		
St Pancras International	a	09 04	09 08			09 12	09 16			09 20	09 24	09 28			09 36		09 40		09 44		09 56		
Kentish Town	a		09 13			09 16						09 34					09 45		09 48		10 00		
Brixton	d							08 57						09 10						09 25			
London Victoria	a			08 53	08 53			09 06	09 11				09 09	09 19		09 29		09 23		09 34		09 38	09 43

Sevenoaks, Otford, Orpington, Bromley South, Beckenham Junction and Catford - Kentish Town/London Victoria

Network Diagram - see first Page of Table 195

Station		FC	SE	SE 1	SE	FC	SE	FC	SE	SE 1 ⊼	SE	SE 1	SE	FC	SE	FC	SE	SE 1	SE 1 ⊼	SE	SE	FC
Sevenoaks	d								09 13								09 42					
Bat & Ball	d								09 16								09 46					
Otford	d			09 17					09 21			09 46					09 50					
Shoreham (Kent)	d								09 24								09 53					
Eynsford	d								09 28								09 56					
Swanley	d			09 26					09 33			09 54					10 01	10 05				
St Mary Cray	d								09 37			09 58					10 05	10 09				
Orpington	d		09 10				09 25				09 40				09 55					10 10		
Petts Wood	d		09 13				09 28				09 43				09 58					10 13		
Bickley	d		09 17				09 32		09 42		09 47				10 02		10 10			10 17		
Bromley South	d		09 20	09 34			09 35		09 45	09 50	09 50	10 05			10 05		10 15	10 15	10 20	10 20		
Shortlands	d		09 23				09 38		09 48		09 53				10 08		10 18			10 23		
Ravensbourne	d								09 50								10 20					
Beckenham Hill	d								09 52								10 22					
Bellingham	d								09 54								10 24					
Catford	d								09 57								10 27					
Crofton Park	d								09 59								10 29					
Lewisham	d				09 38								10 08								10 38	
Nunhead	d				09 43				10 02				10 13				10 32				10 43	
Peckham Rye	d				09 45				10 04				10 15				10 34				10 45	
Denmark Hill	d				09 49				10 07				10 19				10 37				10 49	
Beckenham Junction	d		09 26				09 41				09 56				10 11					10 26		
Kent House	d		09 28				09 43				09 58				10 13					10 28		
Penge East	d		09 30				09 45				10 00				10 15					10 30		
Sydenham Hill	d		09 33				09 48				10 03				10 18					10 33		
West Dulwich	d		09 35				09 50				10 05				10 20					10 35		
Herne Hill	d	09 36	09 38			09 46	09 53	10 01			10 08			10 16	10 23	10 31				10 38		10 46
Loughborough Jn	d	09 40				09 50		10 04						10 19		10 34						10 49
Elephant & Castle	d	09 45				09 55		10 09	10 14					10 24		10 39	10 44					10 54
London Blackfriars	d	09 50				10 00		10 14	10 18					10 30		10 44	10 48					11 00
City Thameslink	a	09 52				10 02		10 16	10 20					10 32		10 46	10 50					11 02
Farringdon	a	09 56				10 06		10 19	10 24					10 35		10 49	10 54					11 06
St Pancras International	a	10 00				10 10		10 23	10 28					10 40		10 53	10 58					11 10
Kentish Town	a	10 05				10 14		10 27	10 33					10 44		10 57	11 03					11 14
Brixton	d		09 40				09 55				10 10				10 25					10 40		
London Victoria	a		09 49	09 51	10 00		10 03			10 07	10 17	10 21	10 28		10 32			10 41	10 37	10 47	10 58	

Station		SE	SE 1	SE	SE 1 ⊼	FC	SE	SE	FC	SE	SE 1	SE	SE 1	SE 1 ⊼	FC		FC	SE	SE	FC	SE	SE 1
Sevenoaks	d	10 02								10 32						and at the same minutes past each hour until					15 02	
Bat & Ball	d	10 05								10 35											15 05	
Otford	d	10 08	10 17							10 38	10 46										15 08	15 17
Shoreham (Kent)	d	10 11								10 41											15 11	
Eynsford	d	10 15								10 45											15 15	
Swanley	d	10 20	10 26							10 50	10 54		11 05								15 20	15 26
St Mary Cray	d	10 24								10 54	10 58		11 09								15 24	
Orpington	d			10 25			10 40					10 55						15 10				
Petts Wood	d			10 28			10 43					10 58						15 13				
Bickley	d	10 28		10 32			10 47			10 58		11 02						15 17			15 28	
Bromley South	d	10 31	10 35	10 35	10 50		10 50			11 01	11 05	11 05	11 15	11 20				15 20			15 31	15 35
Shortlands	d	10 34		10 38			10 53			11 04		11 08						15 23			15 34	
Ravensbourne	d	10 36								11 06											15 36	
Beckenham Hill	d	10 38								11 08											15 38	
Bellingham	d	10 40								11 10											15 40	
Catford	d	10 43								11 13											15 43	
Crofton Park	d	10 45								11 15											15 45	
Lewisham	d							11 08											15 38			
Nunhead	d	10 48						11 13		11 18									15 43		15 48	
Peckham Rye	d	10 50						11 15		11 20									15 45		15 50	
Denmark Hill	d	10 54						11 19		11 24									15 49		15 54	
Beckenham Junction	d			10 41			10 56					11 11						15 26				
Kent House	d			10 43			10 58					11 13						15 28				
Penge East	d			10 45			11 00					11 15						15 30				
Sydenham Hill	d			10 48			11 03					11 18						15 33				
West Dulwich	d			10 50			11 05					11 20						15 35				
Herne Hill	d			10 53		11 01	11 08		11 16			11 23			11 31		15 31	15 38		15 46		
Loughborough Jn	d					11 04			11 19						11 34		15 34			15 49		
Elephant & Castle	d	11 00				11 09			11 24	11 30					11 39		15 39			15 54	16 00	
London Blackfriars	d	11 04				11 14			11 30	11 34					11 44		15 44			16 00	16 04	
City Thameslink	a	11 06				11 16			11 32	11 36					11 46		15 46			16 02	16 06	
Farringdon	a	11 10				11 19			11 36	11 40					11 49		15 49			16 06	16 10	
St Pancras International	a	11 14				11 23			11 40	11 44					11 53		15 53			16 10	16 14	
Kentish Town	a	11 19				11 27			11 44	11 49					11 57		15 57			16 14	16 19	
Brixton	d			10 55			11 10					11 25						15 40				
London Victoria	a		10 51	11 02	11 07		11 17	11 28			11 21	11 32	11 37	11 37				15 47	15 58			15 51

Table 195

Mondays to Fridays
29 August to 7 September

Sevenoaks, Otford, Orpington, Bromley South, Beckenham Junction and Catford - Kentish Town/London Victoria

Network Diagram - see first Page of Table 195

Station		SE	SE 1 ⊼	FC	SE	SE	FC	SE 1	SE 1	SE	SE	SE 1 ⊼	FC	SE	SE	FC	SE 1	SE 1	SE	FC 1	SE	SE 1 ⊼	SE
Sevenoaks	d							15 32									16 02				16 22		
Bat & Ball	d							15 35									16 05				16 25		
Otford	d							15 38	15 46								16 08	16 17			16 28		
Shoreham (Kent)	d							15 41									16 11						
Eynsford	d							15 45									16 15						
Swanley	d							15 50	15 54		16 05						16 20	16 26			16 37		
St Mary Cray	d							15 54	15 58		16 09						16 24				16 41		
Orpington	d	15 25			15 40					15 55				16 10					16 25				16 40
Petts Wood	d	15 28			15 43					15 58				16 13					16 28				16 43
Bickley	d	15 32			15 47			15 58		16 02				16 17			16 28		16 32				16 47
Bromley South	d	15 35	15 50		15 50			16 01	16 05	16 05	16 15	16 20		16 20			16 31	16 35	16 35		16 47	16 50	16 50
Shortlands	d	15 38			15 53			16 04		16 08				16 23			16 34		16 38				16 53
Ravensbourne	d							16 06									16 36						
Beckenham Hill	d							16 08									16 38						
Bellingham	d							16 10									16 40				16 52		
Catford	d							16 13									16 43				16 55		
Crofton Park	d							16 15									16 45						
Lewisham	d					16 08									16 38								
Nunhead	d					16 13		16 18							16 43		16 48				16 59		
Peckham Rye	d					16 15		16 20							16 45		16 50				17 02		
Denmark Hill	d					16 19		16 24							16 49		16 54				17 05		
Beckenham Junction	d	15 41			15 56					16 11				16 26					16 41				16 56
Kent House	d	15 43			15 58					16 13				16 28					16 43				16 58
Penge East	d	15 45			16 00					16 15				16 30					16 45				17 00
Sydenham Hill	d	15 48			16 03					16 18				16 33					16 48				17 03
West Dulwich	d	15 50			16 05					16 20				16 35					16 50				17 05
Herne Hill	d	15 53		16 01	16 08		16 16			16 23			16 31	16 38		16 50			16 53	17 01			17 11
Loughborough Jn	d			16 04			16 19						16 34			16 53							
Elephant & Castle	d			16 09			16 24	16 30					16 39			17 00	17 04			17 08	17 12		
London Blackfriars	d			16 14			16 30	16 38					16 44			17 04	17 08			17 12	17 16		
City Thameslink	a			16 16			16 32	16 40					16 46			17 06	17 10			17 14	17 18		
Farringdon	a			16 19			16 35	16 43					16 49			17 09	17 13			17 17	17 23		
St Pancras International	a			16 23			16 39	16 47					16 53			17 13	17 17			17 21	17 27		
Kentish Town	a			16 28			16 44						16 58			17 18					17 32		
Brixton	d	15 55			16 10					16 25				16 40					16 55				17 13
London Victoria	a	16 02	16 07		16 17	16 28			16 21	16 32	16 37	16 38		16 47	17 01			16 51	17 04			17 07	17 20

Station		SE	FC	SE	SE 1	SE	SE 1	SE 1 ⊼	FC	SE	SE 1	SE	FC	SE 1	SE 1	SE	SE 1	SE 1	SE 1 ⊼	FC	SE	SE
Sevenoaks	d			16 32										17 02								
Bat & Ball	d			16 35										17 05								
Otford	d			16 38	16 46									17 08	17 17							
Shoreham (Kent)	d			16 41										17 11								
Eynsford	d			16 45										17 15								
Swanley	d			16 50	16 54		17 05							17 20	17 26			17 35				
St Mary Cray	d			16 54	16 58		17 09							17 24				17 39				
Orpington	d					16 55				17 10						17 24	17 34				17 40	
Petts Wood	d					16 58				17 13						17 28	17 37				17 43	
Bickley	d			16 58		17 02				17 17				17 28		17 32	17 42				17 47	
Bromley South	d			17 01	17 05	17 05	17 15	17 20		17 20				17 31	17 35	17 35	17 45	17 46	17 50		17 50	
Shortlands	d			17 04		17 08				17 23				17 34		17 38					17 53	
Ravensbourne	d			17 06										17 36								
Beckenham Hill	d			17 08										17 38								
Bellingham	d			17 10										17 40								
Catford	d			17 13										17 43								
Crofton Park	d			17 15										17 45								
Lewisham	d	17 08										17 38										18 08
Nunhead	d	17 13		17 18								17 43		17 48								18 13
Peckham Rye	d	17 15		17 20								17 45		17 50								18 15
Denmark Hill	d	17 19		17 24								17 49		17 54								18 19
Beckenham Junction	d					17 11				17 26	17 30					17 41	17 49				17 56	
Kent House	d					17 13				17 28	17 33					17 43					17 58	
Penge East	d					17 15				17 30	17 35					17 45					18 00	
Sydenham Hill	d					17 18				17 33	17 38					17 48					18 03	
West Dulwich	d					17 20				17 35	17 40					17 50					18 05	
Herne Hill	d		17 21			17 23			17 31	17 38	17 44		17 48			17 53				18 06	18 09	
Loughborough Jn	d		17 24						17 34		17 47		17 51							18 09		
Elephant & Castle	d		17 28	17 34					17 39		17 52		17 56	18 00			18 05			18 14		
London Blackfriars	d		17 32	17 40					17 46		17 56		18 00	18 06			18 10			18 18		
City Thameslink	a		17 34	17 42					17 48		17 58		18 02	18 08			18 12			18 20		
Farringdon	a		17 37	17 45					17 51		18 01		18 05	18 11			18 15			18 23		
St Pancras International	a		17 41	17 49					17 55		18 05		18 09	18 15			18 19			18 27		
Kentish Town	a		17 46						18 00				18 14							18 32		
Brixton	d					17 25				17 40						17 55					18 11	
London Victoria	a	17 28			17 23	17 33	17 38	17 37		17 48		17 59			17 53	18 03		18 08	18 07		18 18	18 29

Table 195

Mondays to Fridays
29 August to 7 September

Sevenoaks, Otford, Orpington, Bromley South, Beckenham Junction and Catford - Kentish Town/London Victoria

Network Diagram - see first Page of Table 195

		FC	SE ■	SE ■	SE	SE ■	SE ■	FC	SE	SE	FC ■	FC	SE ■	SE ■	SE	SE	SE ■	FC	SE	SE	FC	SE	SE ■
Sevenoaks	d		17 32										18 02			18 18						18 32	
Bat & Ball	d		17 35										18 05			18 21						18 35	
Otford	d		17 38	17 46									18 08	18 17		18 24						18 38	18 46
Shoreham (Kent)	d		17 41										18 11			18 27						18 41	
Eynsford	d		17 45										18 15			18 31						18 45	
Swanley	d		17 50	17 54		18 05							18 20	18 26		18 36						18 50	18 54
St Mary Cray	d		17 54	17 58		18 09							18 24			18 40						18 54	18 58
Orpington	d				17 55				18 09						18 25				18 40				
Petts Wood	d				17 58				18 12						18 28				18 43				
Bickley	d		17 58		18 02				18 17				18 28		18 32				18 47			18 58	
Bromley South	d		18 01	18 05	18 05	18 15	18 20		18 20				18 31	18 35	18 35	18 46	18 50		18 50			19 01	19 05
Shortlands	d		18 04		18 08				18 23				18 34		18 38				18 53			19 04	
Ravensbourne	d		18 06										18 36									19 06	
Beckenham Hill	d		18 08										18 38									19 08	
Bellingham	d		18 10										18 40									19 10	
Catford	d		18 13										18 43									19 13	
Crofton Park	d		18 15										18 45									19 15	
Lewisham	d									18 38										19 08			
Nunhead	d		18 18							18 43			18 48							19 13		19 18	
Peckham Rye	d		18 20							18 45			18 50							19 15		19 20	
Denmark Hill	d		18 23							18 49			18 54			18 59				19 19		19 24	
Beckenham Junction	d				18 11				18 26						18 41				18 56				
Kent House	d				18 13				18 28						18 43				18 58				
Penge East	d				18 15				18 30						18 45				19 00				
Sydenham Hill	d				18 18				18 33						18 48				19 03				
West Dulwich	d				18 20				18 35						18 50				19 05				
Herne Hill	d	18 20			18 24			18 32	18 38		18 41	18 48			18 53			19 02	19 08		19 17		
Loughborough Jn	d	18 23						18 35				18 51						19 05			19 20		
Elephant & Castle	d	18 28	18 32					18 40			18 48	18 56	19 00					19 10			19 25	19 30	
London Blackfriars	d	18 32	18 36					18 44			18 52	19 00	19 06					19 18			19 30	19 34	
City Thameslink	a	18 34	18 38					18 46			18 54	19 02	19 08					19 20			19 32	19 36	
Farringdon	a	18 37	18 41					18 49			18 57	19 05	19 11					19 23			19 36	19 40	
St Pancras International	a	18 41	18 45					18 53			19 01	19 09	19 15					19 27			19 40	19 44	
Kentish Town	a	18 46										19 14						19 32			19 44	19 49	
Brixton	d				18 26				18 40						18 55				19 10				
London Victoria	a			18 21	18 33	18 37	18 37		18 48	18 58				18 53	19 03	19 13	19 07		19 17	19 28			19 21

		SE	SE	SE	SE ■	SE ■	FC	SE	FC	SE	SE ■	SE	SE ■	FC	SE	FC	SE	SE ■	SE	SE	SE ■	SE ■
Sevenoaks	d		18 45							19 02							19 32			19 45		
Bat & Ball	d		18 48							19 05							19 35			19 48		
Otford	d		18 51							19 08	19 17						19 38	19 46		19 51		
Shoreham (Kent)	d		18 54							19 11							19 41			19 54		
Eynsford	d		18 58							19 15							19 45			19 58		
Swanley	d		19 03	19 05						19 20	19 26						19 50	19 54		20 03	20 05	
St Mary Cray	d			19 09						19 24							19 54	19 58			20 09	
Orpington	d	18 55						19 10				19 25			19 40				19 55			
Petts Wood	d	18 58						19 13				19 28			19 43				19 58			
Bickley	d	19 02						19 17		19 28		19 32			19 47		19 58		20 02			
Bromley South	d	19 05	19 11	19 15	19 17	19 20		19 20		19 31	19 35	19 35	19 50		19 50		20 01	20 05	20 05	20a11	20 15	20 20
Shortlands	d	19 08						19 23		19 34		19 38			19 53		20 04		20 08			
Ravensbourne	d									19 36							20 06					
Beckenham Hill	d									19 38							20 08					
Bellingham	d									19 40							20 10					
Catford	d									19 43							20 13					
Crofton Park	d									19 45							20 15					
Lewisham	d																					
Nunhead	d									19 48							20 18					
Peckham Rye	d									19 50							20 20					
Denmark Hill	d		19 28							19 54							20 24					
Beckenham Junction	d	19 11						19 26				19 41			19 56				20 11			
Kent House	d	19 13						19 28				19 43			19 58				20 13			
Penge East	d	19 15						19 30				19 45			20 00				20 15			
Sydenham Hill	d	19 18						19 33				19 48			20 03				20 18			
West Dulwich	d	19 20						19 35				19 50			20 05				20 20			
Herne Hill	d	19 23					19 31	19 38	19 47			19 53		20 05	20 08	20 16			20 23			
Loughborough Jn	d						19 34		19 50					20 08		20 19						
Elephant & Castle	d						19 39		19 55	20 00				20 13		20 24	20 30					
London Blackfriars	d						19 46		20 00	20 04				20 18		20 30	20 34					
City Thameslink	a						19 48		20 02	20 06				20 20		20 32	20 36					
Farringdon	a						19 51		20 06	20 10				20 23		20 36	20 40					
St Pancras International	a						19 55		20 10	20 14				20 27		20 40	20 44					
Kentish Town	a						19 59		20 14	20 19				20 31		20 44	20 49					
Brixton	d	19 25						19 40				19 55			20 10				20 25			
London Victoria	a	19 32	19 43	19 37	19 35	19 37		19 47			19 51	20 02	20 07		20 17			20 21	20 32		20 37	20 38

Table 195

Mondays to Fridays
29 August to 7 September

Sevenoaks, Otford, Orpington, Bromley South, Beckenham Junction and Catford - Kentish Town/London Victoria

Network Diagram - see first Page of Table 195

		FC	SE	FC	SE	SE ■	SE ■	FC	SE	FC	SE	SE ■	FC	SE	SE	SE ■	SE ■	FC	SE	SE	SE ■	FC	SE
Sevenoaks	d				20 02						20 32				21 02					21 32			
Bat & Ball	d				20 05						20 35				21 05					21 35			
Otford	d				20 08	20 16					20 38				21 08	21 16				21 38			
Shoreham (Kent)	d				20 11						20 41				21 11					21 41			
Eynsford	d				20 15						20 45				21 15					21 45			
Swanley	d				20 20	20 24					20 50	21 10			21 20	21 24				21 50	22 10		
St Mary Cray	d				20 24	20 28					20 54	21 14			21 24	21 28				21 54	22 14		
Orpington	d		20 10						20 40					21 10					21 40				22 10
Petts Wood	d		20 13						20 43					21 13					21 43				22 13
Bickley	d		20 17		20 28				20 47		20 58			21 17	21 28				21 47	21 58			22 17
Bromley South	d		20 20		20 31	20 35	20 50		20 50		21 01	21 20		21 20	21 31	21 35	21 50		21 50	22 01	22 20		22 20
Shortlands	d		20 23		20 34				20 53		21 04			21 23	21 34				21 53	22 04			22 23
Ravensbourne	d				20 36						21 06				21 36					22 06			
Beckenham Hill	d				20 38						21 08				21 38					22 08			
Bellingham	d				20 40						21 10				21 40					22 10			
Catford	d				20 43						21 13				21 43					22 13			
Crofton Park	d				20 45						21 15				21 45					22 15			
Lewisham	d																						
Nunhead	d				20 48						21 18				21 48					22 18			
Peckham Rye	d				20 50						21 20				21 50					22 20			
Denmark Hill	d				20 54						21 24				21 54					22 24			
Beckenham Junction	d		20 26						20 56					21 26					21 56				22 26
Kent House	d		20 28						20 58					21 28					21 58				22 28
Penge East	d		20 30						21 00					21 30					22 00				22 30
Sydenham Hill	d		20 33						21 03					21 33					22 03				22 33
West Dulwich	d		20 35						21 05					21 35					22 05				22 35
Herne Hill	d	20 35	20 38	20 46				21 05	21 08	21 16			21 35	21 38				21 57	22 08			22 27	22 38
Loughborough Jn	d	20 38		20 49				21 08		21 19			21 38					22 00				22 30	
Elephant & Castle	d	20 43		20 54	21 00			21 13		21 24	21 30		21 43		22 00			22 04		22 30		22 34	
London Blackfriars	d	20 48		21 00	21 04			21 18		21 30	21a34		21 48		22a04			22 08		22a34		22 38	
City Thameslink	a	20 50		21 02	21 06			21 20		21 32			21 50					22 10				22 40	
Farringdon	a	20 53		21 06	21 10			21 23		21 36			21 53					22 13				22 43	
St Pancras International	a	20 57		21 10	21 14			21 27		21 40			21 57					22 17				22 47	
Kentish Town	a	21 01		21 14	21 19			21 31		21 44			22 01					22 21				22 51	
Brixton	d		20 40						21 10					21 40					22 10				22 40
London Victoria	a		20 47			20 51	21 07		21 17			21 37		21 47		21 51	22 07		22 17		22 37		22 47

		SE	SE ■	SE ■	FC	SE	SE	SE ■	FC	SE	SE ■	SE ■
Sevenoaks	d	22 02					22 32					
Bat & Ball	d	22 05					22 35					
Otford	d	22 08	22 16				22 38				23 16	
Shoreham (Kent)	d	22 11					22 41					
Eynsford	d	22 15					22 45					
Swanley	d	22 20	22 24				22 50	23 10			23 24	
St Mary Cray	d	22 24	22 28				22 54	23 14			23 28	
Orpington	d					22 40				23 10		
Petts Wood	d					22 43				23 13		
Bickley	d	22 28				22 47	22 58			23 17		
Bromley South	d	22 31	22 35	22 50		22 50	23 01	23 20		23 20	23 35	23 50
Shortlands	d	22 34				22 53	23 04			23 23		
Ravensbourne	d	22 36					23 06					
Beckenham Hill	d	22 38					23 08					
Bellingham	d	22 40					23 10					
Catford	d	22 43					23 13					
Crofton Park	d	22 45					23 15					
Lewisham	d											
Nunhead	d	22 48					23 18					
Peckham Rye	d	22 50					23 20					
Denmark Hill	d	22 54					23 24					
Beckenham Junction	d					22 56				23 26		
Kent House	d					22 58				23 28		
Penge East	d					23 00				23 30		
Sydenham Hill	d					23 03				23 33		
West Dulwich	d					23 05				23 35		
Herne Hill	d				22 57	23 08			23 27	23 38		
Loughborough Jn	d				23 00							
Elephant & Castle	d	23 00			23 04		23 30		23 34			
London Blackfriars	d	23a04			23 08		23a34		23 38			
City Thameslink	a											
Farringdon	a				23 13				23 43			
St Pancras International	a				23 17				23 47			
Kentish Town	a				23 21				23 51			
Brixton	d					23 10				23 40		
London Victoria	a		22 51	23 07		23 17		23 37		23 47	23 51	00 07

Saturdays

until 21 July, 18 Aug and from 15 Sep

Sevenoaks, Otford, Orpington, Bromley South, Beckenham Junction and Catford - Kentish Town/London Victoria

Network Diagram - see first Page of Table 195

	SE [1]	SE [1]	SE A	FC	SE B	SE [1]	FC	SE	SE A	SE B	SE [1]	SE	SE [1]	FC	SE	SE A	SE B	SE A	FC	SE B	SE [1]	SE
Sevenoaks d					05 32				05 55	06 02						06 25				06 32		
Bat & Ball d					05 35				05 58	06 05						06 28				06 35		
Otford d					05 38				06 01	06 08	06 16					06 31				06 38	06 46	
Shoreham (Kent) d					05 41				06 04	06 11						06 34				06 41		
Eynsford d					05 45				06 08	06 15						06 38				06 45		
Swanley d		00 10			05 50	06 05			06 13	06 20	06 24					06 43				06 50	06 54	
St Mary Cray d		00 14			05 54	06 09			06 17	06 24	06 28					06 47				06 54	06 58	
Orpington d			05 44					06 10				06 25			06 40							06 55
Petts Wood d			05 47					06 13				06 28			06 43							06 58
Bickley d			05 51		05 58			06 17	06 21	06 28		06 32			06 47	06 51				06 58		07 02
Bromley South d	23p50	00 20	05 54		06 01	06 16		06 20	06 24	06 31	06 35	06 35	06 50		06 50	06 54				07 01	07 05	07 05
Shortlands d			05 57		06 04			06 23	06 27	06 34		06 38			06 53	06 57				07 04		07 08
Ravensbourne d			05 59		06 06				06 29	06 36						06 59				07 06		
Beckenham Hill d			06 01		06 08				06 31	06 38						07 01				07 08		
Bellingham d			06 03		06 10				06 33	06 40						07 03				07 10		
Catford d			06 06		06 13				06 36	06 43						07 06				07 13		
Crofton Park d			06 08		06 15				06 38	06 45						07 08				07 15		
Lewisham d																	07 08	07 08				
Nunhead d			06 11		06 18				06 41	06 48						07 11	07 13	07 15		07 18		
Peckham Rye d			06 13		06 20				06 43	06 50						07 13	07 15	07 17		07 20		
Denmark Hill d			06 17		06 24				06 47	06 54						07 17	07 19	07 21		07 24		
Beckenham Junction d								06 26				06 41			06 56							07 11
Kent House d								06 28				06 43			06 58							07 13
Penge East d								06 30				06 45			07 00							07 15
Sydenham Hill d								06 33				06 48			07 03							07 18
West Dulwich d								06 35				06 50			07 05							07 20
Herne Hill d				06 01			06 31	06 38				06 53		07 01	07 08				07 16			07 23
Loughborough Jn d							06 34							07 04					07 19			
Elephant & Castle d				06 09	06 30		06 39			07 00				07 09					07 24	07 30		
London Blackfriars d				06 14	06a34		06 44			07a04				07 14					07 30	07a34		
City Thameslink a																						
Farringdon a				06 19			06 49							07 19					07 35			
St Pancras International a				06 23			06 53							07 23					07 40			
Kentish Town a				06 27			06 57							07 27					07 44			
Brixton d								06 40				06 55			07 10							07 25
London Victoria a	00 07	00 38	06 26			06 37		06 47	06 56		06 51	07 02	07 07		07 17	07 26	07 28	07 30			07 21	07 32

	SE [1]	SE [1]	FC	SE	SE A	SE B	SE A	FC	SE B	SE [1]	SE	SE [1]	FC	SE	SE A	SE B	SE A	FC	SE B	SE [1]	SE	SE [1]
Sevenoaks d					06 55				07 02						07 25				07 32			
Bat & Ball d					06 58				07 05						07 28				07 35			
Otford d					07 01				07 08	07 17					07 31				07 38	07 46		
Shoreham (Kent) d					07 04				07 11						07 34				07 41			
Eynsford d					07 08				07 15						07 38				07 45			
Swanley d	07 05				07 13				07 20	07 26					07 43				07 50	07 54		08 05
St Mary Cray d	07 09				07 17				07 24						07 47				07 54	07 58		08 09
Orpington d				07 10							07 25			07 40							07 55	
Petts Wood d				07 13							07 28			07 43							07 58	
Bickley d				07 17	07 21				07 28		07 32			07 47	07 51				07 58		08 02	
Bromley South d	07 15	07 20		07 20	07 24				07 31	07 35	07 35	07 50		07 50	07 54				08 01	08 05	08 05	08 15
Shortlands d				07 23	07 27				07 34		07 38			07 53	07 57				08 04		08 08	
Ravensbourne d					07 29				07 36						07 59				08 06			
Beckenham Hill d					07 31				07 38						08 01				08 08			
Bellingham d					07 33				07 40						08 03				08 10			
Catford d					07 36				07 43						08 06				08 13			
Crofton Park d					07 38				07 45						08 08				08 15			
Lewisham d						07 38	07 38									08 08	08 08					
Nunhead d					07 41	07 43	07 45		07 48						08 11	08 13	08 15		08 18			
Peckham Rye d					07 43	07 45	07 47		07 50						08 13	08 15	08 17		08 20			
Denmark Hill d					07 47	07 49	07 51		07 54						08 17	08 19	08 21		08 24			
Beckenham Junction d				07 26							07 41			07 56							08 11	
Kent House d				07 28							07 43			07 58							08 13	
Penge East d				07 30							07 45			08 00							08 15	
Sydenham Hill d				07 33							07 48			08 03							08 18	
West Dulwich d				07 35							07 50			08 05							08 20	
Herne Hill d			07 31	07 38				07 46			07 53		08 01	08 08				08 16			08 23	
Loughborough Jn d			07 34					07 49					08 04					08 19				
Elephant & Castle d			07 39					07 54	08 00				08 09					08 24	08 30			
London Blackfriars d			07 44					08 00	08a04				08 14					08 30	08a34			
City Thameslink a																						
Farringdon a			07 49					08 05					08 19					08 35				
St Pancras International a			07 53					08 10					08 23					08 40				
Kentish Town a			07 57					08 14					08 27					08 44				
Brixton d				07 40							07 55			08 10							08 25	
London Victoria a	07 37	07 37		07 47	07 56	07 58	08 00			07 51	08 02	08 07		08 17	08 26	08 28	08 30			08 21	08 32	08 37

A 19 May

B not 19 May

Saturdays

until 21 July, 18 Aug and from 15 Sep

Sevenoaks, Otford, Orpington, Bromley South, Beckenham Junction and Catford - Kentish Town/London Victoria

Network Diagram - see first Page of Table 195

	SE [1]	FC	SE	SE A	SE B	SE A	FC	SE B	SE [1]	SE	SE [1]	FC	SE	SE A	SE B	SE A	FC	SE B	SE [1]	SE	SE [1]
Sevenoaks d				07 55				08 02						08 25				08 32			
Bat & Ball d				07 58				08 05						08 28				08 35			
Otford d				08 01				08 08	08 17					08 31				08 38	08 46		
Shoreham (Kent) d				08 04				08 11						08 34				08 41			
Eynsford d				08 08				08 15						08 38				08 45			
Swanley d				08 13				08 20	08 26					08 43				08 50	08 54		09 05
St Mary Cray d				08 17				08 24						08 47				08 54	08 58		09 09
Orpington d			08 10							08 25			08 40							08 55	
Petts Wood d			08 13							08 28			08 43							08 58	
Bickley d			08 17	08 21				08 28		08 32			08 47	08 51				08 58		09 02	
Bromley South d	08 20		08 20	08 24				08 31	08 35	08 35	08 50		08 50	08 54				09 01	09 05	09 05	09 15
Shortlands d			08 23	08 27				08 34		08 38			08 53	08 57				09 04		09 08	
Ravensbourne d				08 29				08 36						08 59				09 06			
Beckenham Hill d				08 31				08 38						09 01				09 08			
Bellingham d				08 33				08 40						09 03				09 10			
Catford d				08 36				08 43						09 06				09 13			
Crofton Park d				08 38				08 45						09 08				09 15			
Lewisham d					08 38	08 38									09 08	09 08					
Nunhead d				08 41	08 43	08 45		08 48						09 11	09 13	09 15		09 18			
Peckham Rye d				08 43	08 45	08 47		08 50						09 13	09 15	09 17		09 20			
Denmark Hill d				08 47	08 49	08 51		08 54						09 17	09 19	09 21		09 24			
Beckenham Junction d			08 26							08 41			08 56							09 11	
Kent House d			08 28							08 43			08 58							09 13	
Penge East d			08 30							08 45			09 00							09 15	
Sydenham Hill d			08 33							08 48			09 03							09 18	
West Dulwich d			08 35							08 50			09 05							09 20	
Herne Hill d		08 31	08 38				08 46			08 53		09 01	09 08				09 16			09 23	
Loughborough Jn d		08 34					08 49					09 04					09 19				
Elephant & Castle d		08 39					08 54	09 00				09 09					09 24	09 30			
London Blackfriars d		08 44					09 00	09a04				09 14					09 30	09a34			
City Thameslink a							09 02					09 16					09 32				
Farringdon a		08 49					09 06					09 19					09 36				
St Pancras International a		08 53					09 10					09 23					09 40				
Kentish Town a		08 57					09 14					09 27					09 44				
Brixton d			08 40							08 55			09 10							09 25	
London Victoria a	08 37		08 47	08 56	08 58	09 00			08 51	09 02	09 07		09 17	09 26	09 28	09 30			09 21	09 32	09 37

	SE [1] ⌶	FC		FC	SE	SE A	FC	SE B	SE [1]	SE	SE [1]	FC	SE	SE A	FC	SE B	SE [1]	SE	SE [1]	SE [1]	FC
Sevenoaks d						18 55		19 02						19 25		19 32					
Bat & Ball d						18 58		19 05						19 28		19 35					
Otford d						19 01		19 08	19 17					19 31		19 38	19 46				
Shoreham (Kent) d						19 04		19 11						19 34		19 41					
Eynsford d						19 08		19 15						19 38		19 45					
Swanley d						19 13		19 20	19 26					19 43		19 50	19 54		20 05		
St Mary Cray d						19 17		19 24						19 47		19 54	19 58		20 09		
Orpington d					19 10					19 25			19 40					19 55			
Petts Wood d					19 13					19 28			19 43					19 58			
Bickley d					19 17	19 21		19 28		19 32			19 47	19 51		19 58		20 02			
Bromley South d	09 20				19 20	19 24		19 31	19 35	19 35	19 50		19 50	19 54		20 01	20 05	20 05	20 15	20 20	
Shortlands d					19 23	19 27		19 34		19 38			19 53	19 57		20 04		20 08			
Ravensbourne d			and at the same minutes past each hour until			19 29		19 36						19 59		20 06					
Beckenham Hill d						19 31		19 38						20 01		20 08					
Bellingham d						19 33		19 40						20 03		20 10					
Catford d						19 36		19 43						20 06		20 13					
Crofton Park d						19 38		19 45						20 08		20 15					
Lewisham d																					
Nunhead d						19 41		19 48						20 11		20 18					
Peckham Rye d						19 43		19 50						20 13		20 20					
Denmark Hill d						19 47		19 54						20 17		20 24					
Beckenham Junction d					19 26					19 41			19 56					20 11			
Kent House d					19 28					19 43			19 58					20 13			
Penge East d					19 30					19 45			20 00					20 15			
Sydenham Hill d					19 33					19 48			20 03					20 18			
West Dulwich d					19 35					19 50			20 05					20 20			
Herne Hill d		09 31		19 31	19 38		19 46			19 53		20 01	20 08		20 16			20 23			20 31
Loughborough Jn d		09 34		19 34			19 49					20 04			20 19						20 34
Elephant & Castle d		09 39		19 39			19 54	20 00				20 09			20 24	20 30					20 39
London Blackfriars d		09 44		19 44			20 00	20a04				20 14			20 30	20a34					20 44
City Thameslink a		09 46		19 46			20 02					20 16			20 32						20 46
Farringdon a		09 49		19 49			20 06					20 19			20 36						20 49
St Pancras International a		09 53		19 53			20 10					20 23			20 40						20 53
Kentish Town a		09 57		19 57			20 14					20 27			20 44						20 57
Brixton d					19 40					19 55			20 10					20 25			
London Victoria a	09 37				19 47	19 56			19 51	20 02	20 07		20 17	20 26			20 21	20 32	20 37	20 37	

A 19 May

B not 19 May

Saturdays

until 21 July, 18 Aug and from 15 Sep

Sevenoaks, Otford, Orpington, Bromley South, Beckenham Junction and Catford - Kentish Town/London Victoria

Network Diagram - see first Page of Table 195

Station		SE	SE A	FC	SE B	SE ■	FC	SE	SE A	FC	SE B	SE ■	SE ■	FC	SE	SE A	SE B	SE ■	FC	SE	SE A	SE B
Sevenoaks	d		19 55		20 02				20 25		20 32					20 55	21 02				21 25	21 32
Bat & Ball	d		19 58		20 05				20 28		20 35					20 58	21 05				21 28	21 35
Otford	d		20 01		20 08				20 31		20 38	20 46				21 01	21 08				21 31	21 38
Shoreham (Kent)	d		20 04		20 11				20 34		20 41					21 04	21 11				21 34	21 41
Eynsford	d		20 08		20 15				20 38		20 45					21 08	21 15				21 38	21 45
Swanley	d		20 13		20 20				20 43		20 50	20 54	21 10			21 13	21 20				21 43	21 50
St Mary Cray	d		20 17		20 24				20 47		20 54	20 58	21 14			21 17	21 24				21 47	21 54
Orpington	d	20 10						20 40							21 10					21 40		
Petts Wood	d	20 13						20 43							21 13					21 43		
Bickley	d	20 17	20 21		20 28			20 47	20 51		20 58				21 17	21 21	21 28			21 47	21 51	21 58
Bromley South	d	20 20	20 24		20 31	20 50		20 50	20 54		21 01	21 05	21 20		21 20	21 24	21 31	21 50		21 50	21 54	22 01
Shortlands	d	20 23	20 27		20 34			20 53	20 57		21 04				21 23	21 27	21 34			21 53	21 57	22 04
Ravensbourne	d		20 29		20 36				20 59		21 06					21 29	21 36				21 59	22 06
Beckenham Hill	d		20 31		20 38				21 01		21 08					21 31	21 38				22 01	22 08
Bellingham	d		20 33		20 40				21 03		21 10					21 33	21 40				22 03	22 10
Catford	d		20 36		20 43				21 06		21 13					21 36	21 43				22 06	22 13
Crofton Park	d		20 38		20 45				21 08		21 15					21 38	21 45				22 08	22 15
Lewisham	d																					
Nunhead	d		20 41		20 48				21 11		21 18					21 41	21 48				22 11	22 18
Peckham Rye	d		20 43		20 50				21 13		21 20					21 43	21 50				22 13	22 20
Denmark Hill	d		20 47		20 54				21 17		21 24					21 47	21 54				22 17	22 24
Beckenham Junction	d	20 26						20 56							21 26					21 56		
Kent House	d	20 28						20 58							21 28					21 58		
Penge East	d	20 30						21 00							21 30					22 00		
Sydenham Hill	d	20 33						21 03							21 33					22 03		
West Dulwich	d	20 35						21 05							21 35					22 05		
Herne Hill	d	20 38		20 46			21 01	21 08		21 16				21 31	21 38				21 57	22 08		
Loughborough Jn	d			20 49			21 04			21 19				21 34					22 00			
Elephant & Castle	d			20 54	21 00		21 09			21 24	21 30			21 39			22 00		22 04			22 30
London Blackfriars	d			21 00	21a04		21 14			21 30	21a34			21 44			22a04		22 08			22a34
City Thameslink	a																					
Farringdon	a			21 05			21 18			21 35				21 48					22 13			
St Pancras International	a			21 10			21 23			21 40				21 53					22 17			
Kentish Town	a			21 14			21 27			21 44				21 57					22 21			
Brixton	d	20 40						21 10							21 40					22 10		
London Victoria	a	20 47	20 56			21 07		21 17	21 26			21 21	21 37		21 47	21 56		22 07		22 17	22 26	

Station		SE ■	SE ■	FC	SE	SE A	SE B	SE ■	FC	SE	SE A	SE B	SE ■	FC	SE	SE ■	SE ■
Sevenoaks	d					21 55	22 02				22 25	22 32					
Bat & Ball	d					21 58	22 05				22 28	22 35					
Otford	d	21 46				22 01	22 08				22 31	22 38				23 16	
Shoreham (Kent)	d					22 04	22 11				22 34	22 41					
Eynsford	d					22 08	22 15				22 38	22 45					
Swanley	d	21 54	22 10			22 13	22 20				22 43	22 50	23 10			23 24	
St Mary Cray	d	21 58	22 14			22 17	22 24				22 47	22 54	23 14			23 28	
Orpington	d				22 10					22 40					23 10		
Petts Wood	d				22 13					22 43					23 13		
Bickley	d				22 17	22 21	22 28			22 47	22 51	22 58			23 17		
Bromley South	d	22 05	22 20		22 20	22 24	22 31	22 50		22 50	22 54	23 01	23 20		23 20	23 35	23 50
Shortlands	d				22 23	22 27	22 34			22 53	22 57	23 04			23 23		
Ravensbourne	d					22 29	22 36				22 59	23 06					
Beckenham Hill	d					22 31	22 38				23 01	23 08					
Bellingham	d					22 33	22 40				23 03	23 10					
Catford	d					22 36	22 43				23 06	23 13					
Crofton Park	d					22 38	22 45				23 08	23 15					
Lewisham	d																
Nunhead	d					22 41	22 48				23 11	23 18					
Peckham Rye	d					22 43	22 50				23 13	23 20					
Denmark Hill	d					22 47	22 54				23 17	23 24					
Beckenham Junction	d				22 26					22 56					23 26		
Kent House	d				22 28					22 58					23 28		
Penge East	d				22 30					23 00					23 30		
Sydenham Hill	d				22 33					23 03					23 33		
West Dulwich	d				22 35					23 05					23 35		
Herne Hill	d			22 27	22 38				22 57	23 08				23 27	23 38		
Loughborough Jn	d			22 30					23 00								
Elephant & Castle	d			22 34			23 00		23 04			23 30		23 34			
London Blackfriars	d			22 38			23a04		23 08			23a34		23 38			
City Thameslink	a																
Farringdon	a			22 42					23 13					23 43			
St Pancras International	a			22 47					23 17					23 47			
Kentish Town	a			22 51					23 21					23 51			
Brixton	d				22 40					23 10					23 40		
London Victoria	a	22 21	22 37		22 47	22 56		23 07		23 17	23 26		23 37		23 47	23 51	00 07

A 19 May

B not 19 May

Saturdays

28 July to 11 August

Sevenoaks, Otford, Orpington, Bromley South, Beckenham Junction and Catford - Kentish Town/London Victoria

Network Diagram - see first Page of Table 195

Station		SE ■	SE ■	FC	SE	SE ■	FC	SE	SE	SE ■	SE	SE ■	FC	SE	SE	FC	SE	SE ■	SE	SE ■	SE ■	FC	SE
Sevenoaks	d				05 32				06 02								06 32						
Bat & Ball	d				05 35				06 05								06 35						
Otford	d				05 38				06 08	06 16							06 38	06 46					
Shoreham (Kent)	d				05 41				06 11								06 41						
Eynsford	d				05 45				06 15								06 45						
Swanley	d		00 10		05 50	06 05			06 20	06 24							06 50	06 54		07 05			
St Mary Cray	d		00 14		05 54	06 09			06 24	06 28							06 54	06 58		07 09			
Orpington	d							06 10			06 25			06 40					06 55				07 10
Petts Wood	d							06 13			06 28			06 43					06 58				07 13
Bickley	d				05 58			06 17	06 28		06 32			06 47			06 58		07 02				07 17
Bromley South	d	23p50	00 20		06 01	06 16		06 20	06 31	06 35	06 35	06 50		06 50			07 01	07 05	07 05	07 15	07 20		07 20
Shortlands	d				06 04			06 23	06 34		06 38			06 53			07 04		07 08				07 23
Ravensbourne	d				06 06				06 36								07 06						
Beckenham Hill	d				06 08				06 38								07 08						
Bellingham	d				06 10				06 40								07 10						
Catford	d				06 13				06 43								07 13						
Crofton Park	d				06 15				06 45								07 15						
Lewisham	d														07 08								
Nunhead	d				06 18				06 48						07 15		07 18						
Peckham Rye	d				06 20				06 50						07 17		07 20						
Denmark Hill	d				06 24				06 54						07 21		07 24						
Beckenham Junction	d							06 26			06 41			06 56					07 11				07 26
Kent House	d							06 28			06 43			06 58					07 13				07 28
Penge East	d							06 30			06 45			07 00					07 15				07 30
Sydenham Hill	d							06 33			06 48			07 03					07 18				07 33
West Dulwich	d							06 35			06 50			07 05					07 20				07 35
Herne Hill	d			06 01			06 31	06 38			06 53		07 01	07 08		07 16			07 23			07 31	07 38
Loughborough Jn	d						06 34						07 04			07 19						07 34	
Elephant & Castle	d			06 09	06 30		06 39		07 00				07 09			07 24	07 30					07 39	
London Blackfriars	d			06 14	06a34		06 44		07a04				07 14			07 30	07a34					07 44	
City Thameslink	a																						
Farringdon	a			06 19			06 49						07 19			07 35						07 49	
St Pancras International	a			06 23			06 53						07 23			07 40						07 53	
Kentish Town	a			06 27			06 57						07 27			07 44						07 57	
Brixton	d							06 40			06 55			07 10					07 25				07 40
London Victoria	a	00 07	00 38			06 37		06 47		06 51	07 02	07 07		07 17	07 33			07 21	07 32	07 37	07 37		07 47

Station		SE	FC	SE	SE ■	SE	SE ■	FC	SE	SE	FC	SE	SE ■	SE	SE ■	SE ■	FC	SE	SE	FC	SE	SE ■	SE
Sevenoaks	d			07 02								07 32									08 02		
Bat & Ball	d			07 05								07 35									08 05		
Otford	d			07 08	07 17							07 38	07 46								08 08	08 17	
Shoreham (Kent)	d			07 11								07 41									08 11		
Eynsford	d			07 15								07 45									08 15		
Swanley	d			07 20	07 26							07 50	07 54		08 05						08 20	08 26	
St Mary Cray	d			07 24								07 54	07 58		08 09						08 24		
Orpington	d					07 25			07 40					07 55				08 10					08 25
Petts Wood	d					07 28			07 43					07 58				08 13					08 28
Bickley	d			07 28		07 32			07 47			07 58		08 02				08 17			08 28		08 32
Bromley South	d			07 31	07 35	07 35	07 50		07 50			08 01	08 05	08 05	08 15	08 20		08 20			08 31	08 35	08 35
Shortlands	d			07 34		07 38			07 53			08 04		08 08				08 23			08 34		08 38
Ravensbourne	d			07 36								08 06									08 36		
Beckenham Hill	d			07 38								08 08									08 38		
Bellingham	d			07 40								08 10									08 40		
Catford	d			07 43								08 13									08 43		
Crofton Park	d			07 45								08 15									08 45		
Lewisham	d	07 38								08 08									08 38				
Nunhead	d	07 45		07 48						08 15		08 18							08 45		08 48		
Peckham Rye	d	07 47		07 50						08 17		08 20							08 47		08 50		
Denmark Hill	d	07 51		07 54						08 21		08 24							08 51		08 54		
Beckenham Junction	d					07 41			07 56					08 11				08 26					08 41
Kent House	d					07 43			07 58					08 13				08 28					08 43
Penge East	d					07 45			08 00					08 15				08 30					08 45
Sydenham Hill	d					07 48			08 03					08 18				08 33					08 48
West Dulwich	d					07 50			08 05					08 20				08 35					08 50
Herne Hill	d		07 46			07 53		08 01	08 08		08 16			08 23			08 31	08 38		08 46			08 53
Loughborough Jn	d		07 49					08 04			08 19						08 34			08 49			
Elephant & Castle	d		07 54	08 00				08 09			08 24	08 30					08 39			08 54	09 00		
London Blackfriars	d		08 00	08a04				08 14			08 30	08a34					08 44			09 00	09a04		
City Thameslink	a																			09 02			
Farringdon	a		08 05					08 19			08 35						08 49			09 06			
St Pancras International	a		08 10					08 23			08 40						08 53			09 10			
Kentish Town	a		08 14					08 27			08 44						08 57			09 14			
Brixton	d					07 55			08 10					08 25				08 40					08 55
London Victoria	a	08 03			07 51	08 02	08 07		08 17	08 33			08 21	08 32	08 37	08 37		08 47	09 03			08 51	09 02

Saturdays
28 July to 11 August

Sevenoaks, Otford, Orpington, Bromley South, Beckenham Junction and Catford - Kentish Town/London Victoria

Network Diagram - see first Page of Table 195

		SE ■		FC	SE	SE	FC	SE	SE ■	SE	SE ■	SE ■		FC		FC	SE	FC	SE	SE ■	SE		SE ■	FC
Sevenoaks ■	d							08 32											19 02					
Bat & Ball	d							08 35											19 05					
Otford ■	d							08 38	08 46										19 08	19 17				
Shoreham (Kent)	d							08 41											19 11					
Eynsford	d							08 45											19 15					
Swanley ■	d							08 50	08 54		09 05								19 20	19 26				
St Mary Cray	d							08 54	08 58		09 09								19 24					
Orpington ■	d				08 40					08 55							19 10				19 25			
Petts Wood ■	d				08 43					08 58							19 13				19 28			
Bickley ■	d				08 47			08 58		09 02							19 17		19 28		19 32			
Bromley South ■	d	08 50			08 50			09 01	09 05	09 05	09 15	09 20					19 20		19 31	19 35	19 35		19 50	
Shortlands ■	d				08 53			09 04		09 08							19 23		19 34		19 38			
Ravensbourne	d							09 06							and at the same minutes past each hour until				19 36					
Beckenham Hill	d							09 08											19 38					
Bellingham	d							09 10											19 40					
Catford	d							09 13											19 43					
Crofton Park	d							09 15											19 45					
Lewisham ■	d					09 08																		
Nunhead ■	d					09 15		09 18											19 48					
Peckham Rye ■	d					09 17		09 20											19 50					
Denmark Hill ■	d					09 21		09 24											19 54					
Beckenham Junction ■	d				08 56					09 11							19 26				19 41			
Kent House ■	d				08 58					09 13							19 28				19 43			
Penge East	d				09 00					09 15							19 30				19 45			
Sydenham Hill	d				09 03					09 18							19 33				19 48			
West Dulwich	d				09 05					09 20							19 35				19 50			
Herne Hill ■	d			09 01	09 08		09 16			09 23				09 31		19 31	19 38	19 46			19 53			20 01
Loughborough Jn	d			09 04			09 19							09 34		19 34		19 49						20 04
Elephant & Castle	d			09 09			09 24	09 30						09 39		19 39		19 54	20 00					20 09
London Blackfriars ■	d			09 14			09 30	09a34						09 44		19 44		20 00	20a04					20 14
City Thameslink ■	a			09 16			09 32							09 46		19 46		20 02						20 16
Farringdon	a			09 19			09 36							09 49		19 49		20 06						20 19
St Pancras International ■	a			09 23			09 40							09 53		19 53		20 10						20 23
Kentish Town	a			09 27			09 44							09 57		19 57		20 14						20 27
Brixton	d				09 10					09 25							19 40				19 55			
London Victoria ■	a	09 07			09 17	09 33			09 21	09 32	09 37	09 37					19 47			19 51	20 02		20 07	

		SE	FC	SE	SE ■	SE	SE ■	SE ■		FC	SE	FC	SE	SE ■	FC	SE	FC	SE		SE ■	SE ■	FC	SE	SE	SE ■
Sevenoaks ■	d			19 32									20 02					20 32						21 02	
Bat & Ball	d			19 35									20 05					20 35						21 05	
Otford ■	d			19 38	19 46								20 08					20 38		20 46				21 08	
Shoreham (Kent)	d			19 41									20 11					20 41						21 11	
Eynsford	d			19 45									20 15					20 45						21 15	
Swanley ■	d			19 50	19 54		20 05						20 20					20 50		20 54	21 10			21 20	
St Mary Cray	d			19 54	19 58		20 09						20 24					20 54		20 58	21 14			21 24	
Orpington ■	d	19 40				19 55					20 10					20 40							21 10		
Petts Wood ■	d	19 43				19 58					20 13					20 43							21 13		
Bickley ■	d	19 47		19 58		20 02					20 17		20 28			20 47		20 58					21 17	21 28	
Bromley South ■	d	19 50		20 01	20 05	20 05	20 15	20 20			20 20		20 31	20 50		20 50		21 01		21 05	21 20		21 20	21 31	21 50
Shortlands ■	d	19 53		20 04		20 08					20 23		20 34			20 53		21 04					21 23	21 34	
Ravensbourne	d			20 06									20 36					21 06						21 36	
Beckenham Hill	d			20 08									20 38					21 08						21 38	
Bellingham	d			20 10									20 40					21 10						21 40	
Catford	d			20 13									20 43					21 13						21 43	
Crofton Park	d			20 15									20 45					21 15						21 45	
Lewisham ■	d																								
Nunhead ■	d			20 18									20 48					21 18						21 48	
Peckham Rye ■	d			20 20									20 50					21 20						21 50	
Denmark Hill ■	d			20 24									20 54					21 24						21 54	
Beckenham Junction ■	d	19 56				20 11					20 26					20 56							21 26		
Kent House ■	d	19 58				20 13					20 28					20 58							21 28		
Penge East	d	20 00				20 15					20 30					21 00							21 30		
Sydenham Hill	d	20 03				20 18					20 33					21 03							21 33		
West Dulwich	d	20 05				20 20					20 35					21 05							21 35		
Herne Hill ■	d	20 08	20 16			20 23				20 31	20 38	20 46			21 01	21 08	21 16					21 31	21 38		
Loughborough Jn	d		20 19							20 34		20 49			21 04		21 19					21 34			
Elephant & Castle	d		20 24	20 30						20 39		20 54	21 00		21 09		21 24	21 30				21 39		22 00	
London Blackfriars ■	d		20 30	20a34						20 44		21 00	21a04		21 14		21 30	21a34				21 44		22a04	
City Thameslink ■	a		20 32							20 46															
Farringdon	a		20 36							20 49		21 05			21 18		21 35					21 48			
St Pancras International ■	a		20 40							20 53		21 10			21 23		21 40					21 53			
Kentish Town	a		20 44							20 57		21 14			21 27		21 44					21 57			
Brixton	d	20 10				20 25					20 40					21 10							21 40		
London Victoria ■	a	20 17			20 21	20 32	20 37	20 37			20 47			21 07		21 17				21 21	21 37		21 47		22 07

Table 195

Saturdays
28 July to 11 August

Sevenoaks, Otford, Orpington, Bromley South, Beckenham Junction and Catford - Kentish Town/London Victoria

Network Diagram - see first Page of Table 195

		FC	SE	SE		SE ■	SE ■	FC	SE	SE	SE ■	FC	SE	SE		SE ■	FC	SE	SE ■	SE ■
Sevenoaks ■	d			21 32						22 02				22 32						
Bat & Ball	d			21 35						22 05				22 35						
Otford ■	d			21 38		21 46				22 08				22 38					23 16	
Shoreham (Kent)	d			21 41						22 11				22 41						
Eynsford	d			21 45						22 15				22 45						
Swanley ■	d			21 50		21 54	22 10			22 20				22 50		23 10			23 24	
St Mary Cray	d			21 54		21 58	22 14			22 24				22 54		23 14			23 28	
Orpington ■	d		21 40						22 10				22 40					23 10		
Petts Wood ■	d		21 43						22 13				22 43					23 13		
Bickley ■	d		21 47	21 58					22 17	22 28			22 47	22 58				23 17		
Bromley South ■	d		21 50	22 01		22 05	22 20		22 20	22 31	22 50		22 50	23 01		23 20		23 20	23 35	23 50
Shortlands ■	d		21 53	22 04					22 23	22 34			22 53	23 04				23 23		
Ravensbourne	d			22 06						22 36				23 06						
Beckenham Hill	d			22 08						22 38				23 08						
Bellingham	d			22 10						22 40				23 10						
Catford	d			22 13						22 43				23 13						
Crofton Park	d			22 15						22 45				23 15						
Lewisham ■	d																			
Nunhead ■	d			22 18						22 48				23 18						
Peckham Rye ■	d			22 20						22 50				23 20						
Denmark Hill ■	d			22 24						22 54				23 24						
Beckenham Junction ■	d		21 56						22 26				22 56					23 26		
Kent House ■	d		21 58						22 28				22 58					23 28		
Penge East	d		22 00						22 30				23 00					23 30		
Sydenham Hill	d		22 03						22 33				23 03					23 33		
West Dulwich	d		22 05						22 35				23 05					23 35		
Herne Hill ■	d	21 57	22 08					22 27	22 38			22 57	23 08				23 27	23 38		
Loughborough Jn	d	22 00						22 30				23 00								
Elephant & Castle	d	22 04		22 30				22 34		23 00		23 04		23 30			23 34			
London Blackfriars ■	d	22 08		22a34				22 38		23a04		23 08		23a34			23 38			
City Thameslink ■	a																			
Farringdon	a	22 13						22 42				23 13					23 43			
St Pancras International ■	a	22 17						22 47				23 17					23 47			
Kentish Town	a	22 21						22 51				23 21					23 51			
Brixton	d		22 10						22 40				23 10					23 40		
London Victoria ■	a		22 17			22 21	22 37		22 47		23 07		23 17			23 37		23 47	23 51	00 07

Saturdays
25 August to 8 September

		SE ■	SE ■	FC	SE	SE ■	FC	SE	SE	SE ■		SE	SE ■	FC	SE	SE	FC	SE	SE ■	SE		SE ■	SE ■	FC	SE
Sevenoaks ■	d				05 32				06 02									06 32							
Bat & Ball	d				05 35				06 05									06 35							
Otford ■	d				05 38				06 08	06 16								06 38	06 46						
Shoreham (Kent)	d				05 41				06 11									06 41							
Eynsford	d				05 45				06 15									06 45							
Swanley ■	d		00 10		05 50	06 05			06 20	06 24								06 50	06 54			07 05			
St Mary Cray	d		00 14		05 54	06 09			06 24	06 28								06 54	06 58			07 09			
Orpington ■	d							06 10				06 25			06 40					06 55					07 10
Petts Wood ■	d							06 13				06 28			06 43					06 58					07 13
Bickley ■	d				05 58			06 17	06 28			06 32			06 47			06 58		07 02					07 17
Bromley South ■	d	23p50	00 20		06 01	06 16		06 20	06 31	06 35		06 35	06 50		06 50			07 01	07 05	07 05		07 15	07 20		07 20
Shortlands ■	d				06 04			06 23	06 34			06 38			06 53			07 04		07 08					07 23
Ravensbourne	d				06 06				06 36									07 06							
Beckenham Hill	d				06 08				06 38									07 08							
Bellingham	d				06 10				06 40									07 10							
Catford	d				06 13				06 43									07 13							
Crofton Park	d				06 15				06 45									07 15							
Lewisham ■	d															07 08									
Nunhead ■	d				06 18				06 48							07 13		07 18							
Peckham Rye ■	d				06 20				06 50							07 15		07 20							
Denmark Hill ■	d				06 24				06 54							07 19		07 24							
Beckenham Junction ■	d							06 26				06 41			06 56					07 11					07 26
Kent House ■	d							06 28				06 43			06 58					07 13					07 28
Penge East	d							06 30				06 45			07 00					07 15					07 30
Sydenham Hill	d							06 33				06 48			07 03					07 18					07 33
West Dulwich	d							06 35				06 50			07 05					07 20					07 35
Herne Hill ■	d			06 01			06 31	06 38				06 53		07 01	07 08		07 16			07 23				07 31	07 38
Loughborough Jn	d						06 34							07 04			07 19							07 34	
Elephant & Castle	d			06 09	06 30		06 39		07 00					07 09			07 24	07 30						07 39	
London Blackfriars ■	d			06 14	06a34		06 44		07a04					07 14			07 30	07a34						07 44	
City Thameslink ■	a																								
Farringdon	a			06 19			06 49							07 19			07 35							07 49	
St Pancras International ■	a			06 23			06 53							07 23			07 40							07 53	
Kentish Town	a			06 27			06 57							07 27			07 44							07 57	
Brixton	d							06 40				06 55			07 10					07 25					07 40
London Victoria ■	a	00 07	00 38			06 37		06 47		06 51		07 02	07 07		07 17	07 28			07 21	07 32		07 37	07 37		07 47

Sevenoaks, Otford, Orpington, Bromley South, Beckenham Junction and Catford - Kentish Town/London Victoria

Network Diagram - see first Page of Table 195

		SE	FC	SE	SE ■	SE		SE ■	FC	SE	SE	FC	SE	SE ■	SE	SE ■		SE ■	FC	SE	SE	FC	SE	SE ■	SE
Sevenoaks ■	d			07 02									07 32										08 02		
Bat & Ball	d			07 05									07 35										08 05		
Otford ■	d			07 08	07 17								07 38	07 46									08 08	08 17	
Shoreham (Kent)	d			07 11									07 41										08 11		
Eynsford	d			07 15									07 45										08 15		
Swanley ■	d			07 20	07 26								07 50	07 54		08 05							08 20	08 26	
St Mary Cray	d			07 24									07 54	07 58		08 09							08 24		
Orpington ■	d					07 25				07 40					07 55					08 10					08 25
Petts Wood ■	d					07 28				07 43					07 58					08 13					08 28
Bickley ■	d			07 28		07 32				07 47			07 58		08 02					08 17			08 28		08 32
Bromley South ■	d			07 31	07 35	07 35		07 50		07 50			08 01	08 05	08 05	08 15		08 20		08 20			08 31	08 35	08 35
Shortlands ■	d			07 34		07 38				07 53			08 04		08 08					08 23			08 34		08 38
Ravensbourne	d			07 36									08 06										08 36		
Beckenham Hill	d			07 38									08 08										08 38		
Bellingham	d			07 40									08 10										08 40		
Catford	d			07 43									08 13										08 43		
Crofton Park	d			07 45									08 15										08 45		
Lewisham ■	d	07 38									08 08										08 38				
Nunhead ■	d	07 43		07 48							08 13		08 18								08 43		08 48		
Peckham Rye ■	d	07 45		07 50							08 15		08 20								08 45		08 50		
Denmark Hill ■	d	07 49		07 54							08 19		08 24								08 49		08 54		
Beckenham Junction ■	d					07 41				07 56					08 11					08 26					08 41
Kent House ■	d					07 43				07 58					08 13					08 28					08 43
Penge East	d					07 45				08 00					08 15					08 30					08 45
Sydenham Hill	d					07 48				08 03					08 18					08 33					08 48
West Dulwich	d					07 50				08 05					08 20					08 35					08 50
Herne Hill ■	d		07 46			07 53			08 01	08 08		08 16			08 23				08 31	08 38		08 46			08 53
Loughborough Jn	d		07 49						08 04			08 19							08 34			08 49			
Elephant & Castle	⊖ d		07 54	08 00					08 09			08 24	08 30						08 39			08 54	09 00		
London Blackfriars ■	⊖ d		08 00	08a04					08 14			08 30	08a34						08 44			09 00	09a04		
City Thameslink ■	a																					09 02			
Farringdon	⊖ a		08 05						08 19			08 35							08 49			09 06			
St Pancras International ■	⊖ a		08 10						08 23			08 40							08 53			09 10			
Kentish Town	⊖ a		08 14						08 27			08 44							08 57			09 14			
Brixton	⊖ d					07 55				08 10					08 25					08 40					08 55
London Victoria ■	⊖ a	07 58			07 51	08 02		08 07		08 17	08 28			08 21	08 32	08 37		08 37		08 47	08 58			08 51	09 02

		SE ■		FC	SE	SE	FC	SE	SE ■	SE	SE ■	SE ■		FC	and at the same minutes past each hour until	FC	SE	FC	SE	SE ■	SE		SE ■	FC
Sevenoaks ■	d							08 32											19 02					
Bat & Ball	d							08 35											19 05					
Otford ■	d							08 38	08 46										19 08	19 17				
Shoreham (Kent)	d							08 41											19 11					
Eynsford	d							08 45											19 15					
Swanley ■	d							08 50	08 54		09 05								19 20	19 26				
St Mary Cray	d							08 54	08 58		09 09								19 24					
Orpington ■	d				08 40					08 55							19 10				19 25			
Petts Wood ■	d				08 43					08 58							19 13				19 28			
Bickley ■	d				08 47			08 58		09 02							19 17		19 28		19 32			
Bromley South ■	d	08 50			08 50			09 01	09 05	09 05	09 15	09 20					19 20		19 31	19 35	19 35		19 50	
Shortlands ■	d				08 53			09 04		09 08							19 23		19 34		19 38			
Ravensbourne	d							09 06											19 36					
Beckenham Hill	d							09 08											19 38					
Bellingham	d							09 10											19 40					
Catford	d							09 13											19 43					
Crofton Park	d							09 15											19 45					
Lewisham ■	d					09 08																		
Nunhead ■	d					09 13		09 18											19 48					
Peckham Rye ■	d					09 15		09 20											19 50					
Denmark Hill ■	d					09 19		09 24											19 54					
Beckenham Junction ■	d				08 56					09 11							19 26				19 41			
Kent House ■	d				08 58					09 13							19 28				19 43			
Penge East	d				09 00					09 15							19 30				19 45			
Sydenham Hill	d				09 03					09 18							19 33				19 48			
West Dulwich	d				09 05					09 20							19 35				19 50			
Herne Hill ■	d			09 01	09 08		09 16			09 23				09 31		19 31	19 38	19 46			19 53			20 01
Loughborough Jn	d			09 04			09 19							09 34		19 34		19 49						20 04
Elephant & Castle	⊖ d			09 09			09 24	09 30						09 39		19 39		19 54	20 00					20 09
London Blackfriars ■	⊖ d			09 14			09 30	09a34						09 44		19 44		20 00	20a04					20 14
City Thameslink ■	a			09 16			09 32							09 46		19 46		20 02						20 16
Farringdon	⊖ a			09 19			09 36							09 49		19 49		20 06						20 19
St Pancras International ■	⊖ a			09 23			09 40							09 53		19 53		20 10						20 23
Kentish Town	⊖ a			09 27			09 44							09 57		19 57		20 14						20 27
Brixton	⊖ d				09 10					09 25							19 40				19 55			
London Victoria ■	⊖ a	09 07			09 17	09 28			09 21	09 32	09 37	09 37					19 47			19 51	20 02		20 07	

Table 195

Saturdays
25 August to 8 September

Sevenoaks, Otford, Orpington, Bromley South, Beckenham Junction and Catford - Kentish Town/London Victoria

Network Diagram - see first Page of Table 195

		SE	FC	SE	SE ■	SE	SE ■	SE ■		FC	SE	FC	SE	SE ■	FC	SE	FC	SE		SE ■	SE ■	FC	SE	SE	SE ■
Sevenoaks ■	d			19 32									20 02					20 32						21 02	
Bat & Ball	d			19 35									20 05					20 35						21 05	
Otford ■	d			19 38	19 46								20 08					20 38		20 46				21 08	
Shoreham (Kent)	d			19 41									20 11					20 41						21 11	
Eynsford	d			19 45									20 15					20 45						21 15	
Swanley ■	d			19 50	19 54		20 05						20 20					20 50		20 54	21 10			21 20	
St Mary Cray	d			19 54	19 58		20 09						20 24					20 54		20 58	21 14			21 24	
Orpington ■	d	19 40				19 55					20 10					20 40							21 10		
Petts Wood ■	d	19 43				19 58					20 13					20 43							21 13		
Bickley ■	d	19 47		19 58		20 02					20 17		20 28			20 47		20 58					21 17	21 28	
Bromley South ■	d	19 50		20 01	20 05	20 05	20 15	20 20			20 20		20 31	20 50		20 50		21 01		21 05	21 20		21 20	21 31	21 50
Shortlands ■	d	19 53		20 04		20 08					20 23		20 34			20 53		21 04					21 23	21 34	
Ravensbourne	d			20 06									20 36					21 06						21 36	
Beckenham Hill	d			20 08									20 38					21 08						21 38	
Bellingham	d			20 10									20 40					21 10						21 40	
Catford	d			20 13									20 43					21 13						21 43	
Crofton Park	d			20 15									20 45					21 15						21 45	
Lewisham ■	d																								
Nunhead ■	d			20 18									20 48					21 18						21 48	
Peckham Rye ■	d			20 20									20 50					21 20						21 50	
Denmark Hill ■	d			20 24									20 54					21 24						21 54	
Beckenham Junction ■	d	19 56				20 11					20 26					20 56							21 26		
Kent House ■	d	19 58				20 13					20 28					20 58							21 28		
Penge East	d	20 00				20 15					20 30					21 00							21 30		
Sydenham Hill	d	20 03				20 18					20 33					21 03							21 33		
West Dulwich	d	20 05				20 20					20 35					21 05							21 35		
Herne Hill ■	d	20 08	20 16			20 23				20 31	20 38	20 46			21 01	21 08	21 16					21 31	21 38		
Loughborough Jn	d		20 19							20 34		20 49			21 04		21 19					21 34			
Elephant & Castle	⊖ d		20 24	20 30						20 39		20 54	21 00		21 09		21 24	21 30				21 39		22 00	
London Blackfriars ■	⊖ d		20 30	20a34						20 44		21 00	21a04		21 14		21 30	21a34				21 44		22a04	
City Thameslink ■	a		20 32							20 46															
Farringdon	⊖ a		20 36							20 49		21 05			21 18		21 35					21 48			
St Pancras International ■	⊖ a		20 40							20 53		21 10			21 23		21 40					21 53			
Kentish Town	⊖ a		20 44							20 57		21 14			21 27		21 44					21 57			
Brixton	⊖ d	20 10				20 25					20 40					21 10							21 40		
London Victoria ■	⊖ a	20 17			20 21	20 32	20 37	20 37			20 47			21 07		21 17				21 21	21 37		21 47		22 07

		FC	SE	SE		SE ■	SE ■	FC	SE	SE	SE ■	FC	SE	SE		SE ■	FC	SE	SE ■	SE ■
Sevenoaks ■	d			21 32						22 02				22 32						
Bat & Ball	d			21 35						22 05				22 35						
Otford ■	d			21 38		21 46				22 08				22 38					23 16	
Shoreham (Kent)	d			21 41						22 11				22 41						
Eynsford	d			21 45						22 15				22 45						
Swanley ■	d			21 50		21 54	22 10			22 20				22 50		23 10			23 24	
St Mary Cray	d			21 54		21 58	22 14			22 24				22 54		23 14			23 28	
Orpington ■	d		21 40						22 10				22 40					23 10		
Petts Wood ■	d		21 43						22 13				22 43					23 13		
Bickley ■	d		21 47	21 58					22 17	22 28			22 47	22 58				23 17		
Bromley South ■	d		21 50	22 01		22 05	22 20		22 20	22 31	22 50		22 50	23 01		23 20		23 20	23 35	23 50
Shortlands ■	d		21 53	22 04					22 23	22 34			22 53	23 04				23 23		
Ravensbourne	d			22 06						22 36				23 06						
Beckenham Hill	d			22 08						22 38				23 08						
Bellingham	d			22 10						22 40				23 10						
Catford	d			22 13						22 43				23 13						
Crofton Park	d			22 15						22 45				23 15						
Lewisham ■	d																			
Nunhead ■	d			22 18						22 48				23 18						
Peckham Rye ■	d			22 20						22 50				23 20						
Denmark Hill ■	d			22 24						22 54				23 24						
Beckenham Junction ■	d		21 56						22 26				22 56					23 26		
Kent House ■	d		21 58						22 28				22 58					23 28		
Penge East	d		22 00						22 30				23 00					23 30		
Sydenham Hill	d		22 03						22 33				23 03					23 33		
West Dulwich	d		22 05						22 35				23 05					23 35		
Herne Hill ■	d	21 57	22 08					22 27	22 38			22 57	23 08				23 27	23 38		
Loughborough Jn	d	22 00						22 30				23 00								
Elephant & Castle	⊖ d	22 04		22 30				22 34		23 00		23 04		23 30			23 34			
London Blackfriars ■	⊖ d	22 08		22a34				22 38		23a04		23 08		23a34			23 38			
City Thameslink ■	a																			
Farringdon	⊖ a	22 13						22 42				23 13					23 43			
St Pancras International ■	⊖ a	22 17						22 47				23 17					23 47			
Kentish Town	⊖ a	22 21						22 51				23 21					23 51			
Brixton	⊖ d		22 10						22 40				23 10					23 40		
London Victoria ■	⊖ a		22 17			22 21	22 37		22 47		23 07		23 17			23 37		23 47	23 51	00 07

Table 195

Sundays

until 22 July, 19 Aug and from 16 Sep

Sevenoaks, Otford, Orpington, Bromley South, Beckenham Junction and Catford - Kentish Town/London Victoria

Network Diagram - see first Page of Table 195

		SE 1	SE	SE	SE	SE 1	SE	SE	SE 1	SE 1	SE	SE	SE 1	SE	SE	SE 1	SE 1	SE	SE	SE 1	SE	SE	SE 1
Sevenoaks 4	d							07 21				07 51			08 21				08 51			09 21	
Bat & Ball	d							07 24				07 54			08 24				08 54			09 24	
Otford 4	d							07 27	07 43			07 57			08 27	08 43			08 57			09 27	09 43
Shoreham (Kent)	d							07 30				08 00			08 30				09 00			09 30	
Eynsford	d							07 34				08 04			08 34				09 04			09 34	
Swanley 4	d					07 32		07 39	07 51			08 09	08 32		08 39	08 51			09 09	09 32		09 39	09 51
St Mary Cray	d					07 36		07 43	07 55			08 13	08 36		08 43	08 55			09 13	09 36		09 43	09 55
Orpington 4	d		06 40	07 02	07 06		07 36				08 06			08 36				09 06			09 36		
Petts Wood 4	d		06 43	07 05	07 09		07 39				08 09			08 39				09 09			09 39		
Bickley 4	d		06 47	07 17	07 13		07 43	07 47			08 13	08 17		08 43	08 47			09 13	09 17		09 43	09 47	
Bromley South 4	d	23p50	06 50	07 20	07 16	07 43	07 46	07 50	08 02	08 13	08 16	08 20	08 43	08 46	08 50	09 02	09 13	09 16	09 20	09 43	09 46	09 50	10 02
Shortlands 4	d		06 53	07 23	07 19		07 49	07 53			08 19	08 23		08 49	08 53			09 19	09 23		09 49	09 53	
Ravensbourne	d		06 55	07 25				07 55				08 25			08 55				09 25			09 55	
Beckenham Hill	d		06 57	07 27				07 57				08 27			08 57				09 27			09 57	
Bellingham	d		06 59	07 29				07 59				08 29			08 59				09 29			09 59	
Catford	d		07 02	07 32				08 02				08 32			09 02				09 32			10 02	
Crofton Park	d		07 04	07 34				08 04				08 34			09 04				09 34			10 04	
Lewisham 4	d																						
Nunhead 4	d		07 07	07 37				08 07				08 37			09 07				09 37			10 07	
Peckham Rye 4	d		07 09	07 39				08 09				08 39			09 09				09 39			10 09	
Denmark Hill 4	d		07 13	07 43				08 13				08 43			09 13				09 43			10 13	
Beckenham Junction 4	d				07 22		07 52				08 22			08 52				09 22			09 52		
Kent House 4	d				07 24		07 54				08 24			08 54				09 24			09 54		
Penge East	d				07 26		07 56				08 26			08 56				09 26			09 56		
Sydenham Hill	d				07 29		07 59				08 29			08 59				09 29			09 59		
West Dulwich	d				07 31		08 01				08 31			09 01				09 31			10 01		
Herne Hill 4	d				07 34		08 04				08 34			09 04				09 34			10 04		
Loughborough Jn	d																						
Elephant & Castle ⊖	d		07 19	07 49				08 19				08 49			09 19				09 49			10 19	
London Blackfriars 3 ⊖	d		07a23	07a53				08a23				08a53			09a23				09a53			10a23	
City Thameslink 3	a																						
Farringdon ⊖	a																						
St Pancras International 15 ⊖	a																						
Kentish Town ⊖	a																						
Brixton ⊖	d				07 36		08 06				08 36			09 06				09 36			10 06		
London Victoria 15 ⊖	a	00 07			07 43	08 03	08 13		08 18	08 29	08 43		09 02	09 13		09 18	09 29	09 43		10 02	10 13		10 18

		SE 1	FC	FC	SE	SE	SE 1	FC	FC	and at the same minutes past each hour until	FC	SE	SE	SE 1	SE 1	FC	FC	SE	SE	SE 1	FC A	FC B
Sevenoaks 4	d					09 51							18 21						18 51			
Bat & Ball	d					09 54							18 24						18 54			
Otford 4	d					09 57							18 27	18 43					18 57			
Shoreham (Kent)	d					10 00							18 30						19 00			
Eynsford	d					10 04							18 34						19 04			
Swanley 4	d					10 09	10 32						18 39	18 51					19 09	19 32		
St Mary Cray	d					10 13	10 36						18 43	18 55					19 13	19 36		
Orpington 4	d				10 06							18 36						19 06				
Petts Wood 4	d				10 09							18 39						19 09				
Bickley 4	d				10 13	10 17						18 43	18 47					19 13	19 17			
Bromley South 4	d	10 13			10 16	10 20	10 43					18 46	18 50	19 02	19 13			19 16	19 20	19 43		
Shortlands 4	d				10 19	10 23						18 49	18 53					19 19	19 23			
Ravensbourne	d					10 25							18 55						19 25			
Beckenham Hill	d					10 27							18 57						19 27			
Bellingham	d					10 29							18 59						19 29			
Catford	d					10 32							19 02						19 32			
Crofton Park	d					10 34							19 04						19 34			
Lewisham 4	d																					
Nunhead 4	d					10 37							19 07						19 37			
Peckham Rye 4	d					10 39							19 09						19 39			
Denmark Hill 4	d					10 43							19 13						19 43			
Beckenham Junction 4	d				10 22							18 52						19 22				
Kent House 4	d				10 24							18 54						19 24				
Penge East	d				10 26							18 56						19 26				
Sydenham Hill	d				10 29							18 59						19 29				
West Dulwich	d				10 31							19 01						19 31				
Herne Hill 4	d		10 14	10 27	10 34			10 44	10 57		18 57	19 04				19 14	19 27	19 34			19 44	19 44
Loughborough Jn	d		10 17	10 30				10 47	11 00		19 00					19 17	19 30				19 47	19 47
Elephant & Castle ⊖	d		10 22	10 34		10 49		10 52	11 04		19 04		19 19			19 22	19 34		19 49		19 52	19 52
London Blackfriars 3 ⊖	d		10 26	10a37		10a53		10 56	11a07		19a07		19a23			19 26	19a37		19a53		19 56	20 03
City Thameslink 3	a																					
Farringdon ⊖	a		10 30					11 00								19 30					20 00	20 07
St Pancras International 15 ⊖	a		10 35					11 05								19 35					20 05	20 13
Kentish Town ⊖	a		10 40					11 10								19 40					20 10	20 17
Brixton ⊖	d				10 36							19 06						19 36				
London Victoria 15 ⊖	a	10 29			10 43		11 02					19 13		19 18	19 29			19 43		20 02		

A from 1 July until 22 July

B until 24 June

Table 195

Sundays

until 22 July, 19 Aug and from 16 Sep

Sevenoaks, Otford, Orpington, Bromley South, Beckenham Junction and Catford - Kentish Town/London Victoria

Network Diagram - see first Page of Table 195

		FC	SE	SE	SE 1	SE 1	FC A	FC B	FC	SE	SE	SE 1	FC A	FC B	FC	SE	SE	SE 1	SE 1	FC A	FC B	FC
Sevenoaks 4	d			19 21							19 51						20 21					
Bat & Ball	d			19 24							19 54						20 24					
Otford 4	d			19 27	19 43						19 57						20 27	20 43				
Shoreham (Kent)	d			19 30							20 00						20 30					
Eynsford	d			19 34							20 04						20 34					
Swanley 4	d			19 39	19 51						20 09	20 32					20 39	20 51				
St Mary Cray	d			19 43	19 55						20 13	20 36					20 43	20 55				
Orpington 4	d		19 36							20 06						20 36						
Petts Wood 4	d		19 39							20 09						20 39						
Bickley 4	d		19 43	19 47						20 13	20 17					20 43	20 47					
Bromley South 4	d		19 46	19 50	20 02	20 13				20 16	20 20	20 43				20 46	20 50	21 02	21 13			
Shortlands 4	d		19 49	19 53						20 19	20 23					20 49	20 53					
Ravensbourne	d			19 55							20 25						20 55					
Beckenham Hill	d			19 57							20 27						20 57					
Bellingham	d			19 59							20 29						20 59					
Catford	d			20 02							20 32						21 02					
Crofton Park	d			20 04							20 34						21 04					
Lewisham 4	d																					
Nunhead 4	d			20 07							20 37						21 07					
Peckham Rye 4	d			20 09							20 39						21 09					
Denmark Hill 4	d			20 13							20 43						21 13					
Beckenham Junction 4	d		19 52							20 22						20 52						
Kent House 4	d		19 54							20 24						20 54						
Penge East	d		19 56							20 26						20 56						
Sydenham Hill	d		19 59							20 29						20 59						
West Dulwich	d		20 01							20 31						21 01						
Herne Hill 4	d	19 57	20 04				20 14	20 14	20 27	20 34			20 44	20 44	20 57	21 04				21 14	21 14	21 27
Loughborough Jn	d	20 00					20 17	20 17	20 30				20 47	20 47	21 00					21 17	21 17	21 30
Elephant & Castle ⊖	d	20 04		20 19			20 22	20 22	20 34		20 49		20 52	20 52	21 04		21 19			21 22	21 22	21 34
London Blackfriars 3 ⊖	d	20a07		20a23			20 26	20 33	20a37		20a53		20 56	21 03	21a07		21a23			21 26	21 33	21a37
City Thameslink 3	a																					
Farringdon ⊖	a						20 30	20 37					21 00	21 07						21 30	21 37	
St Pancras International 15 ⊖	a						20 35	20 43					21 05	21 13						21 35	21 43	
Kentish Town ⊖	a						20 40	20 47					21 10	21 17						21 40	21 47	
Brixton ⊖	d		20 06							20 36						21 06						
London Victoria 15 ⊖	a		20 13		20 18	20 29				20 43		21 02				21 13		21 18	21 29			

		SE	SE	SE 1	FC A	FC B	FC	SE	SE	SE 1	SE 1	FC	SE	SE	SE 1	SE	SE	SE 1	SE 1	SE 1
Sevenoaks 4	d		20 51						21 21					21 51			22 21			
Bat & Ball	d		20 54						21 24					21 54			22 24			
Otford 4	d		20 57						21 27	21 43				21 57			22 27	22 43		
Shoreham (Kent)	d		21 00						21 30					22 00			22 30			
Eynsford	d		21 04						21 34					22 04			22 34			
Swanley 4	d		21 09	21 32					21 39	21 51				22 09	22 32		22 39	22 51		23 32
St Mary Cray	d		21 13	21 36					21 43	21 55				22 13	22 36		22 43	22 55		23 36
Orpington 4	d	21 06						21 36					22 06			22 36				
Petts Wood 4	d	21 09						21 39					22 09			22 39				
Bickley 4	d	21 13	21 17					21 43	21 47				22 13	22 17		22 43	22 47			
Bromley South 4	d	21 16	21 20	21 43				21 46	21 50	22 02	22 13		22 16	22 20	22 43	22 46	22 50	23 02	23 13	23 43
Shortlands 4	d	21 19	21 23					21 49	21 53				22 19	22 23		22 49	22 53			
Ravensbourne	d		21 25						21 55					22 25			22 55			
Beckenham Hill	d		21 27						21 57					22 27			22 57			
Bellingham	d		21 29						21 59					22 29			22 59			
Catford	d		21 32						22 02					22 32			23 02			
Crofton Park	d		21 34						22 04					22 34			23 04			
Lewisham 4	d																			
Nunhead 4	d		21 37						22 07					22 37			23 07			
Peckham Rye 4	d		21 39						22 09					22 39			23 09			
Denmark Hill 4	d		21 43						22 13					22 43			23 13			
Beckenham Junction 4	d	21 22						21 52					22 22			22 52				
Kent House 4	d	21 24						21 54					22 24			22 54				
Penge East	d	21 26						21 56					22 26			22 56				
Sydenham Hill	d	21 29						21 59					22 29			22 59				
West Dulwich	d	21 31						22 01					22 31			23 01				
Herne Hill 4	d	21 34			21 44	21 44	21 57	22 04				22 27	22 34			23 04				
Loughborough Jn	d				21 47	21 47	22 00					22 30								
Elephant & Castle ⊖	d		21 49		21 52	21 52	22 04		22 19			22 34		22 49			23 19			
London Blackfriars 3 ⊖	d		21a53		21 56	22 03	22a07		22a23			22a37		22a53			23a23			
City Thameslink 3	a																			
Farringdon ⊖	a				22 00	22 07														
St Pancras International 15 ⊖	a				22 05	22 13														
Kentish Town ⊖	a				22 10	22 17														
Brixton ⊖	d	21 36						22 06					22 36			23 06				
London Victoria 15 ⊖	a	21 43		22 02				22 13		22 18	22 29		22 43		23 02	23 13		23 18	23 29	00 02

A from 1 July until 22 July

B until 24 June

Sundays

29 July to 12 August

Sevenoaks, Otford, Orpington, Bromley South, Beckenham Junction and Catford - Kentish Town/London Victoria

Network Diagram - see first Page of Table 195

		SE 1	SE 1	SE	SE 1	SE	SE	SE 1	SE 1	SE	SE	SE	SE 1	SE 1	SE	SE	SE	SE 1	SE	SE	SE	SE 1	SE 1
Sevenoaks	d			05 32			06 02					06 32					07 02				07 32		
Bat & Ball	d			05 35			06 05					06 35					07 05				07 35		
Otford	d			05 38			06 08	06 16				06 38	06 46				07 08				07 38	07 46	
Shoreham (Kent)	d			05 41			06 11					06 41					07 11				07 41		
Eynsford	d			05 45			06 15					06 45					07 15				07 45		
Swanley	d			05 50	06 05		06 20	06 24				06 50	06 54	07 10			07 20				07 50	07 54	08 10
St Mary Cray	d			05 54	06 09		06 24	06 28				06 54	06 58	07 14			07 24				07 54	07 58	08 14
Orpington	d					06 10				06 40					07 10				07 40				
Petts Wood	d					06 13				06 43					07 13				07 43				
Bickley	d			05 58		06 17	06 28			06 47		06 58			07 17		07 28		07 47		07 58		
Bromley South	d	23p50	00 23	06 01	06 16	06 20	06 31	06 35	06 50	06 50		07 01	07 05	07 20	07 20		07 31	07 50	07 50		08 01	08 05	08 20
Shortlands	d			06 04		06 23	06 34			06 53		07 04			07 23		07 34		07 53		08 04		
Ravensbourne	d			06 06			06 36					07 06					07 36				08 06		
Beckenham Hill	d			06 08			06 38					07 08					07 38				08 08		
Bellingham	d			06 10			06 40					07 10					07 40				08 10		
Catford	d			06 13			06 43					07 13					07 43				08 13		
Crofton Park	d			06 15			06 45					07 15					07 45				08 15		
Lewisham	d										07 08					07 38				08 08			
Nunhead	d			06 18			06 48				07 15	07 18				07 45	07 48			08 15	08 18		
Peckham Rye	d			06 20			06 50				07 17	07 20				07 47	07 50			08 17	08 20		
Denmark Hill	d			06 24			06 54				07 21	07 24				07 51	07 54			08 21	08 24		
Beckenham Junction	d					06 26				06 56					07 26				07 56				
Kent House	d					06 28				06 58					07 28				07 58				
Penge East	d					06 30				07 00					07 30				08 00				
Sydenham Hill	d					06 33				07 03					07 33				08 03				
West Dulwich	d					06 35				07 05					07 35				08 05				
Herne Hill	d					06 38				07 08					07 38				08 08				
Loughborough Jn	d																						
Elephant & Castle	d			06 30			07 00					07 30					08 00				08 30		
London Blackfriars	d			06a34			07a04					07a34					08a04				08a34		
City Thameslink	a																						
Farringdon	a																						
St Pancras International	a																						
Kentish Town	a																						
Brixton	d					06 40				07 10					07 40				08 10				
London Victoria	a	00 07	00 39		06 37	06 47		06 51	07 07	07 17	07 33		07 21	07 37	07 47	08 03		08 07	08 17	08 33		08 21	08 37

		SE	SE	SE	SE 1	SE	SE	SE	SE 1	SE 1	SE	SE	SE	SE 1	SE	SE	FC	SE	SE 1	SE 1	FC	SE	SE
Sevenoaks	d			08 02				08 32					09 02					09 32					
Bat & Ball	d			08 05				08 35					09 05					09 35					
Otford	d			08 08				08 38	08 46				09 08					09 38	09 46				
Shoreham (Kent)	d			08 11				08 41					09 11					09 41					
Eynsford	d			08 15				08 45					09 15					09 45					
Swanley	d			08 20				08 50	08 54	09 10			09 20					09 50	09 54	10 10			
St Mary Cray	d			08 24				08 54	08 58	09 14			09 24					09 54	09 58	10 14			
Orpington	d	08 10				08 40					09 10				09 40							10 10	
Petts Wood	d	08 13				08 43					09 13				09 43							10 13	
Bickley	d	08 17		08 28		08 47		08 58			09 17		09 28		09 47			09 58				10 17	
Bromley South	d	08 20		08 31	08 50	08 50		09 01	09 05	09 20	09 20		09 31	09 50	09 50			10 01	10 05	10 20		10 20	
Shortlands	d	08 23		08 34		08 53		09 04			09 23		09 34		09 53			10 04				10 23	
Ravensbourne	d			08 36				09 06					09 36					10 06					
Beckenham Hill	d			08 38				09 08					09 38					10 08					
Bellingham	d			08 40				09 10					09 40					10 10					
Catford	d			08 43				09 13					09 43					10 13					
Crofton Park	d			08 45				09 15					09 45					10 15					
Lewisham	d		08 38				09 08					09 38				10 08							10 38
Nunhead	d		08 45	08 48			09 15	09 18				09 45	09 48			10 15		10 18					10 45
Peckham Rye	d		08 47	08 50			09 17	09 20				09 47	09 50			10 17		10 20					10 47
Denmark Hill	d		08 51	08 54			09 21	09 24				09 51	09 54			10 21		10 24					10 51
Beckenham Junction	d	08 26				08 56					09 26				09 56							10 26	
Kent House	d	08 28				08 58					09 28				09 58							10 28	
Penge East	d	08 30				09 00					09 30				10 00							10 30	
Sydenham Hill	d	08 33				09 03					09 33				10 03							10 33	
West Dulwich	d	08 35				09 05					09 35				10 05							10 35	
Herne Hill	d	08 38				09 08					09 38				10 08		10 14				10 27	10 38	
Loughborough Jn	d																10 17				10 30		
Elephant & Castle	d			09 00				09 30					10 00				10 22	10 30			10 34		
London Blackfriars	d			09a04				09a34					10a04				10 26	10a34			10a37		
City Thameslink	a																						
Farringdon	a																10 30						
St Pancras International	a																10 35						
Kentish Town	a																10 40						
Brixton	d	08 40				09 10					09 40				10 10							10 40	
London Victoria	a	08 47	09 03		09 07	09 17	09 33		09 21	09 37	09 47	10 03		10 07	10 17	10 33			10 21	10 37		10 47	11 03

Sundays

29 July to 12 August

Sevenoaks, Otford, Orpington, Bromley South, Beckenham Junction and Catford - Kentish Town/London Victoria

Network Diagram - see first Page of Table 195

		FC	SE	SE 1	FC	and at the same minutes past each hour until	FC	SE	SE	FC	SE	SE 1	SE 1	FC	SE	FC	SE	SE 1	FC	SE	FC
Sevenoaks	d		10 02								18 32						19 02				
Bat & Ball	d		10 05								18 35						19 05				
Otford	d		10 08								18 38	18 46					19 08				
Shoreham (Kent)	d		10 11								18 41						19 11				
Eynsford	d		10 15								18 45						19 15				
Swanley	d		10 20								18 50	18 54	19 10				19 20				
St Mary Cray	d		10 24								18 54	18 58	19 14				19 24				
Orpington	d							18 40							19 10					19 40	
Petts Wood	d							18 43							19 13					19 43	
Bickley	d		10 28					18 47			18 58				19 17		19 28			19 47	
Bromley South	d		10 31	10 50				18 50			19 01	19 05	19 20		19 20		19 31	19 50		19 50	
Shortlands	d		10 34					18 53			19 04				19 23		19 34			19 53	
Ravensbourne	d		10 36								19 06						19 36				
Beckenham Hill	d		10 38								19 08						19 38				
Bellingham	d		10 40								19 10						19 40				
Catford	d		10 43								19 13						19 43				
Crofton Park	d		10 45								19 15						19 45				
Lewisham	d								19 08												
Nunhead	d		10 48						19 15		19 18						19 48				
Peckham Rye	d		10 50						19 17		19 20						19 50				
Denmark Hill	d		10 54						19 21		19 24						19 54				
Beckenham Junction	d							18 56							19 26					19 56	
Kent House	d							18 58							19 28					19 58	
Penge East	d							19 00							19 30					20 00	
Sydenham Hill	d							19 03							19 33					20 03	
West Dulwich	d							19 05							19 35					20 05	
Herne Hill	d	10 44			10 57		18 57	19 08		19 14				19 27	19 38	19 44			19 57	20 08	20 14
Loughborough Jn	d	10 47			11 00		19 00			19 17				19 30		19 47			20 00		20 17
Elephant & Castle	d	10 52	11 00		11 04		19 04			19 22	19 30			19 34		19 52	20 00		20 04		20 22
London Blackfriars	d	10 56	11a04		11a07		19a07			19 26	19a34			19a37		19 56	20a04		20a07		20 26
City Thameslink	a																				
Farringdon	a	11 00								19 30						20 00					20 30
St Pancras International	a	11 05								19 35						20 05					20 35
Kentish Town	a	11 10								19 40						20 10					20 40
Brixton	d							19 10							19 40					20 10	
London Victoria	a			11 07				19 17	19 33			19 21	19 37		19 47			20 07		20 17	

		SE	SE 1	SE 1	FC	SE	SE	FC	SE	SE 1	FC	SE	FC	SE	SE 1	SE 1	FC	SE	FC	SE	SE 1	FC	SE
Sevenoaks	d	19 32							20 02					20 32						21 02			
Bat & Ball	d	19 35							20 05					20 35						21 05			
Otford	d	19 38	19 46						20 08					20 38	20 46					21 08			
Shoreham (Kent)	d	19 41							20 11					20 41						21 11			
Eynsford	d	19 45							20 15					20 45						21 15			
Swanley	d	19 50	19 54	20 10					20 20					20 50	20 54	21 10				21 20			
St Mary Cray	d	19 54	19 58	20 14					20 24					20 54	20 58	21 14				21 24			
Orpington	d					20 10						20 40						21 10					21 40
Petts Wood	d					20 13						20 43						21 13					21 43
Bickley	d	19 58				20 17			20 28			20 47		20 58				21 17		21 28			21 47
Bromley South	d	20 01	20 05	20 20		20 20			20 31	20 50		20 50		21 01	21 05	21 20		21 20		21 31	21 50		21 50
Shortlands	d	20 04				20 23			20 34			20 53		21 04				21 23		21 34			21 53
Ravensbourne	d	20 06							20 36					21 06						21 36			
Beckenham Hill	d	20 08							20 38					21 08						21 38			
Bellingham	d	20 10							20 40					21 10						21 40			
Catford	d	20 13							20 43					21 13						21 43			
Crofton Park	d	20 15							20 45					21 15						21 45			
Lewisham	d						20 32																
Nunhead	d	20 18							20 48					21 18						21 48			
Peckham Rye	d	20 20							20 50					21 20						21 50			
Denmark Hill	d	20 24					20 40		20 54					21 24						21 54			
Beckenham Junction	d					20 26						20 56						21 26					21 56
Kent House	d					20 28						20 58						21 28					21 58
Penge East	d					20 30						21 00						21 30					22 00
Sydenham Hill	d					20 33						21 03						21 33					22 03
West Dulwich	d					20 35						21 05						21 35					22 05
Herne Hill	d				20 27	20 38		20 44			20 57	21 08	21 14				21 27	21 38	21 44			21 57	22 08
Loughborough Jn	d				20 30			20 47			21 00		21 17				21 30		21 47			22 00	
Elephant & Castle	d	20 30			20 34			20 52	21 00		21 04		21 22	21 30			21 34		21 52	22 00		22 04	
London Blackfriars	d	20a34			20a37			20 56	21a04		21a07		21 26	21a34			21a37		21 56	22a04		22a07	
City Thameslink	a																						
Farringdon	a							21 00					21 30						22 00				
St Pancras International	a							21 05					21 35						22 05				
Kentish Town	a							21 10					21 40						22 10				
Brixton	d					20 40						21 10						21 40					22 10
London Victoria	a		20 21	20 37		20 47	20 53			21 07		21 17			21 21	21 37		21 47			22 07		22 17

Sundays
29 July to 12 August

Sevenoaks, Otford, Orpington, Bromley South, Beckenham Junction and Catford - Kentish Town/London Victoria

Network Diagram - see first Page of Table 195

		SE	SE 1	SE 1		FC	SE	SE	SE 1	SE	SE	SE 1	SE	SE 1		SE 1
Sevenoaks 4	d	21 32						22 02			22 32					
Bat & Ball	d	21 35						22 05			22 35					
Otford 4	d	21 38	21 46					22 08			22 38			23 16		
Shoreham (Kent)	d	21 41						22 11			22 41					
Eynsford	d	21 45						22 15			22 45					
Swanley 4	d	21 50	21 54	22 10				22 20			22 50	23 10		23 24		23 48
St Mary Cray	d	21 54	21 58	22 14				22 24			22 54	23 14		23 28		23 52
Orpington 4	d						22 10			22 40			23 10			
Petts Wood 4	d						22 13			22 43			23 13			
Bickley 4	d	21 58					22 17	22 28		22 47	22 58		23 17			
Bromley South 4	d	22 01	22 05	22 20			22 20	22 31	22 50	22 50	23 01	23 20	23 20	23 35		23 58
Shortlands 4	d	22 04					22 23	22 34		22 53	23 04		23 23			
Ravensbourne	d	22 06						22 36			23 06					
Beckenham Hill	d	22 08						22 38			23 08					
Bellingham	d	22 10						22 40			23 10					
Catford	d	22 13						22 43			23 13					
Crofton Park	d	22 15						22 45			23 15					
Lewisham 4	d															
Nunhead 4	d	22 18						22 48			23 18					
Peckham Rye 4	d	22 20						22 50			23 20					
Denmark Hill 4	d	22 24						22 54			23 24					
Beckenham Junction 4	d						22 26			22 56			23 26			
Kent House 4	d						22 28			22 58			23 28			
Penge East	d						22 30			23 00			23 30			
Sydenham Hill	d						22 33			23 03			23 33			
West Dulwich	d						22 35			23 05			23 35			
Herne Hill 4	d					22 27	22 38			23 08			23 38			
Loughborough Jn	d					22 30										
Elephant & Castle	d	22 30				22 34		23 00			23 30					
London Blackfriars 3	d	22a34				22a37		23a04			23a34					
City Thameslink 3	a															
Farringdon	a															
St Pancras International 15	a															
Kentish Town	a															
Brixton	d						22 40			23 10			23 40			
London Victoria 15	a		22 21	22 37			22 47		23 07	23 17		23 37	23 47	23 51		00 14

Sundays
26 August to 9 September

		SE 1	SE	SE	SE	SE 1	SE	SE	SE 1	SE 1		SE	SE	SE 1	SE	SE	SE 1	SE 1 ✕	SE	SE		SE 1	SE	SE	SE 1
Sevenoaks 4	d							07 21					07 51			08 21				08 51				09 21	
Bat & Ball	d							07 24					07 54			08 24				08 54				09 24	
Otford 4	d							07 27	07 43				07 57			08 27	08 43			08 57				09 27	09 43
Shoreham (Kent)	d							07 30					08 00			08 30				09 00				09 30	
Eynsford	d							07 34					08 04			08 34				09 04				09 34	
Swanley 4	d					07 32		07 39	07 51				08 09	08 32		08 39	08 51			09 09		09 32		09 39	09 51
St Mary Cray	d					07 36		07 43	07 55				08 13	08 36		08 43	08 55			09 13		09 36		09 43	09 55
Orpington 4	d		06 40	07 02	07 06		07 36					08 06			08 36				09 06				09 36		
Petts Wood 4	d		06 43	07 05	07 09		07 39					08 09			08 39				09 09				09 39		
Bickley 4	d		06 47	07 17	07 13		07 43	07 47				08 13	08 17		08 43	08 47			09 13	09 17			09 43	09 47	
Bromley South 4	d	23p50	06 50	07 20	07 16	07 43	07 46	07 50	08 02	08 13		08 16	08 20	08 43	08 46	08 50	09 02	09 13	09 16	09 20		09 43	09 46	09 50	10 02
Shortlands 4	d		06 53	07 23	07 19		07 49	07 53				08 19	08 23		08 49	08 53			09 19	09 23			09 49	09 53	
Ravensbourne	d		06 55	07 25				07 55					08 25			08 55				09 25				09 55	
Beckenham Hill	d		06 57	07 27				07 57					08 27			08 57				09 27				09 57	
Bellingham	d		06 59	07 29				07 59					08 29			08 59				09 29				09 59	
Catford	d		07 02	07 32				08 02					08 32			09 02				09 32				10 02	
Crofton Park	d		07 04	07 34				08 04					08 34			09 04				09 34				10 04	
Lewisham 4	d																								
Nunhead 4	d		07 07	07 37				08 07					08 37			09 07				09 37				10 07	
Peckham Rye 4	d		07 09	07 39				08 09					08 39			09 09				09 39				10 09	
Denmark Hill 4	d		07 13	07 43				08 13					08 43			09 13				09 43				10 13	
Beckenham Junction 4	d				07 22		07 52					08 22			08 52				09 22				09 52		
Kent House 4	d				07 24		07 54					08 24			08 54				09 24				09 54		
Penge East	d				07 26		07 56					08 26			08 56				09 26				09 56		
Sydenham Hill	d				07 29		07 59					08 29			08 59				09 29				09 59		
West Dulwich	d				07 31		08 01					08 31			09 01				09 31				10 01		
Herne Hill 4	d				07 34		08 04					08 34			09 04				09 34				10 04		
Loughborough Jn	d																								
Elephant & Castle	d		07 19	07 49				08 19					08 49			09 19				09 49				10 19	
London Blackfriars 3	d		07a23	07a53				08a23					08a53			09a23				09a53				10a23	
City Thameslink 3	a																								
Farringdon	a																								
St Pancras International 15	a																								
Kentish Town	a																								
Brixton	d				07 36		08 06					08 36			09 06				09 36				10 06		
London Victoria 15	a	00 07			07 43	08 03	08 13		08 18	08 29		08 43		09 02	09 13		09 18	09 29	09 43			10 02	10 13		10 18

Sundays
26 August to 9 September

Sevenoaks, Otford, Orpington, Bromley South, Beckenham Junction and Catford - Kentish Town/London Victoria

Network Diagram - see first Page of Table 195

		SE 1 ✕	FC	FC	SE	SE		SE 1	FC	FC		FC	SE	SE	SE 1		SE 1	FC	SE	SE	SE 1	SE	SE	SE 1
Sevenoaks 4	d					09 51								21 21						21 51			22 21	
Bat & Ball	d					09 54								21 24						21 54			22 24	
Otford 4	d					09 57								21 27	21 43					21 57			22 27	22 43
Shoreham (Kent)	d					10 00								21 30						22 00			22 30	
Eynsford	d					10 04								21 34						22 04			22 34	
Swanley 4	d					10 09		10 32						21 39	21 51					22 09	22 32		22 39	22 51
St Mary Cray	d					10 13		10 36						21 43	21 55					22 13	22 36		22 43	22 55
Orpington 4	d				10 06								21 36						22 06			22 36		
Petts Wood 4	d				10 09								21 39						22 09			22 39		
Bickley 4	d				10 13	10 17							21 43	21 47					22 13	22 17		22 43	22 47	
Bromley South 4	d	10 13			10 16	10 20		10 43			and at		21 46	21 50	22 02		22 13		22 16	22 20	22 43	22 46	22 50	23 02
Shortlands 4	d				10 19	10 23					the same		21 49	21 53					22 19	22 23		22 49	22 53	
Ravensbourne	d					10 25					minutes			21 55						22 25			22 55	
Beckenham Hill	d					10 27					past			21 57						22 27			22 57	
Bellingham	d					10 29					each			21 59						22 29			22 59	
Catford	d					10 32					hour until			22 02						22 32			23 02	
Crofton Park	d					10 34								22 04						22 34			23 04	
Lewisham 4	d																							
Nunhead 4	d					10 37								22 07						22 37			23 07	
Peckham Rye 4	d					10 39								22 09						22 39			23 09	
Denmark Hill 4	d					10 43								22 13						22 43			23 13	
Beckenham Junction 4	d				10 22								21 52						22 22			22 52		
Kent House 4	d				10 24								21 54						22 24			22 54		
Penge East	d				10 26								21 56						22 26			22 56		
Sydenham Hill	d				10 29								21 59						22 29			22 59		
West Dulwich	d				10 31								22 01						22 31			23 01		
Herne Hill 4	d		10 14	10 27	10 34				10 44	10 57		21 57	22 04					22 27	22 34			23 04		
Loughborough Jn	d		10 17	10 30					10 47	11 00		22 00						22 30						
Elephant & Castle	d		10 22	10 34		10 49			10 52	11 04		22 04		22 19				22 34		22 49			23 19	
London Blackfriars 3	d		10 26	10a37		10a53			10 56	11a07		22a07		22a23				22a37		22a53			23a23	
City Thameslink 3	a																							
Farringdon	a		10 30						11 00															
St Pancras International 15	a		10 35						11 05															
Kentish Town	a		10 40						11 10															
Brixton	d				10 36								22 06						22 36			23 06		
London Victoria 15	a	10 29			10 43			11 02					22 13		22 18		22 29		22 43		23 02	23 13		23 18

		SE 1		SE 1
Sevenoaks 4	d			
Bat & Ball	d			
Otford 4	d			
Shoreham (Kent)	d			
Eynsford	d			
Swanley 4	d			23 32
St Mary Cray	d			23 36
Orpington 4	d			
Petts Wood 4	d			
Bickley 4	d			
Bromley South 4	d	23 13		23 43
Shortlands 4	d			
Ravensbourne	d			
Beckenham Hill	d			
Bellingham	d			
Catford	d			
Crofton Park	d			
Lewisham 4	d			
Nunhead 4	d			
Peckham Rye 4	d			
Denmark Hill 4	d			
Beckenham Junction 4	d			
Kent House 4	d			
Penge East	d			
Sydenham Hill	d			
West Dulwich	d			
Herne Hill 4	d			
Loughborough Jn	d			
Elephant & Castle	d			
London Blackfriars 3	d			
City Thameslink 3	a			
Farringdon	a			
St Pancras International 15	a			
Kentish Town	a			
Brixton	d			
London Victoria 15	a	23 29		00 02

London - Maidstone East and Ashford International

Mondays to Fridays

until 27 July, 13 Aug to 28 Aug and from 10 Sep

Network Diagram - see first Page of Table 195

Miles	Miles	Miles	Station		SE MO A	SE MX	SE MX B	SE MX C	SE	SE	SE	SE	SE	SE D	SE E	SE	SE	SE	SE	SE	SE	SE	SE
0	—	—	London Victoria ⊖	d	22p45	23p07	00 07	00 07		06 07	06 37	07 07	07 36	08 07	08 07	08 37	09 07	09 37	10 07	10 37	11 07	11 37	12 07
—	0	—	London Blackfriars ⊖195	d																			
—	1¼	—	Elephant & Castle ⊖195	d																			
11	11½	—	Bromley South 195	d	23p01	23p23	00 25	00 25		06 23	06 58	07 23	07 53	08 23	08 24	08 53	09 23	09 53	10 23	10 53	11 23	11 53	12 23
14¾	—	—	St Mary Cray 195	d	23p08	23p30	00 31	00 32		06 30	07 04	07 30	08 00	08 30	08 31	09 00		10 00		11 00		12 00	
17½	—	—	Swanley 195	d	23p12	23p34	00 36	00 36		06 34	07 08	07 34	08 04	08 34	08 35	09 04	09 33	10 04	10 33	11 04	11 33	12 04	12 33
24	—	—	Otford 195	d	23p20	23p42	00 47	00 44		06 42	07 16	07 42	08 12	08 42	08 43	09 12	09 41	10 12	10 41	11 12	11 41	12 12	12 41
27	—	—	Kemsing	d		23p47	00 52	00 49		06 47	07 21	07 47	08 17	08 47	08 48	09 17		10 17		11 17		12 17	
29½	—	—	Borough Green & Wrotham	d	23p28	23p52	00 56	00 54		06 52	07 26	07 52	08 22	08 52	08 53	09 22	09 48	10 22	10 48	11 22	11 48	12 22	12 48
34¾	—	—	West Malling	d	23p34	23p58	01 03	01 00		06 58	07 32	07 58	08 28	08 58	08 59	09 28	09 55	10 28	10 55	11 28	11 55	12 28	12 55
35¾	—	—	East Malling	d	23p37	00 01	01 06	01 03		07 01	07 35	08 01	08 31	09 01	09 02	09 31		10 31		11 31		12 31	
37½	—	—	Barming	d	23p41	00 05	01 09	01 07		07 05	07 39	08 05	08 35	09 05	09 06	09 35		10 35		11 35		12 35	
40	—	—	Maidstone East	a	23p45	00 09	01 13	01 11		07 09	07 43	08 09	08 39	09 10	09 10	09 39	10 02	10 39	11 02	11 39	12 02	12 39	13 02
—	—	—		d	23p46	00 10	01 14	01 12	06 34	07 10	07 44	08 10	08 40	09 10	09 11	09 40	10 03	10 40	11 03	11 40	12 03	12 40	13 03
42¾	—	—	Bearsted	d	23p51	00 15	01 19	01 17	06 39	07 15	07 49	08 15	08 45	09 15	09 16	09 45	10 08	10 45	11 08	11 45	12 08	12 45	13 08
45	—	—	Hollingbourne	d	23p54	00 18	01 22	01 20	06 42	07 18	07 52	08 18	08 48	09 18	09 19	09 48		10 48		11 48		12 48	
47½	—	—	Harrietsham	d	23p58	00 22	01 26	01 24	06 46	07 22	07 56	08 22	08 52	09 22	09 23	09 52		10 52		11 52		12 52	
49¼	—	—	Lenham	d	00 01	00 25	01 29	01 27	06 49	07 25	07 59	08 25	08 55	09 25	09 26	09 55		10 55		11 55		12 55	
53¼	—	—	Charing	d	00 06	00 30	01 34	01 32	06 54	07 30	08 04	08 30	09 00	09 30	09 31	10 00		11 00		12 00		13 00	
59¼	—	56	Ashford International	a	00 15	00 39	01 43	01 41	07 02	07 39	08 13	08 39	09 09	09 40	09 40	10 09	10 27	11 09	11 27	12 09	12 27	13 09	13 27
—	—	—		d																			

Station		SE	SE	SE	SE	SE	SE	SE	SE	SE	SE	SE	SE	SE	FC	SE	SE	SE	SE	SE	SE
London Victoria ⊖	d	12 37	13 07	13 37	14 07	14 37	15 07	15 37	16 07	16 37	16 58	17 12	17 28	17 42		18 03	18 18	18 42	19 07	19 37	20 07
London Blackfriars ⊖195	d														17 48						
Elephant & Castle ⊖195	d														17 52						
Bromley South 195	d	12 53	13 23	13 53	14 23	14 53	15 23	15 53	16 23	16 53	17 19	17 31	17 50	17 59	18 11	18 24	18 39	18 59	19 27	19 53	20 23
St Mary Cray 195	d	13 00		14 00		15 00		16 00		17 00		17 38	17 57	18 06	18 18		18 45	19 06		20 00	
Swanley 195	d	13 04	13 33	14 04	14 33	15 04	15 33	16 04	16 33	17 04		17 42	18 01	18 11	18 22		18 50	19 11	19 36	20 04	20 33
Otford 195	d	13 12	13 41	14 12	14 41	15 12	15 41	16 12	16 41	17 12	17 35	17 51	18 10	18 19	18 31	18 43	18 58	19 19	19 44	20 12	20 41
Kemsing	d	13 17		14 17		15 17		16 17		17 17		17 56		18 24	18 36		19 03	19 24		20 17	
Borough Green & Wrotham	d	13 22	13 48	14 22	14 48	15 22	15 48	16 22	16 48	17 22	17 43	18 00	18 17	18 29	18 41	18 51	19 08	19 29	19 51	20 22	20 48
West Malling	d	13 28	13 55	14 28	14 55	15 28	15 55	16 28	16 55	17 28	17 49	18 07	18 24	18 35	18 47	18 57	19 14	19 35	19 57	20 28	20 55
East Malling	d	13 31		14 31		15 31		16 31		17 31		18 10		18 38	18 50		19 17	19 38		20 31	
Barming	d	13 35		14 35		15 35		16 35		17 35		18 13		18 42	18 54		19 21	19 42		20 35	
Maidstone East	a	13 39	14 02	14 39	15 02	15 39	16 02	16 39	17 02	17 39	17 56	18 17	18 33	18 46	18 58	19 04	19 25	19 46	20 04	20 39	21 02
	d	13 40	14 03	14 40	15 03	15 40	16 03	16 40	17 03	17 40	17 57	18 18		18 47	18 59	19 06	19 26	19 47	20 05	20 40	21 03
Bearsted	d	13 45	14 08	14 45	15 08	15 45	16 08	16 45	17 08	17 45	18 02	18 23		18 52	19 04	19 11	19 31	19 52	20 10	20 45	21 08
Hollingbourne	d	13 48		14 48		15 48	16 11	16 48	17 11	17 48	18 06	18 27		18 55	19 08	19 15	19 34	19 55	20 13	20 48	21 11
Harrietsham	d	13 52		14 52		15 52	16 15	16 52	17 15	17 52	18 09	18 30		18 59	19 11	19 18	19 38	19 59	20 17	20 52	21 15
Lenham	d	13 55		14 55		15 55	16 18	16 55	17 18	17 55	18 13	18 34		19 02	19 15	19 22	19 41	20 02	20 20	20 55	21 18
Charing	d	14 00		15 00		16 00	16 23	17 00	17 23	18 00	18 18	18 39		19 07	19 20	19 27	19 46	20 07	20 25	21 00	21 23
Ashford International	a	14 09	14 27	15 09	15 30	16 09	16 32	17 09	17 34	18 11	18 28	18 50		19 18	19 32	19 40	19 58	20 18	20 34	21 09	21 32
	d																				

Station		SE	SE	SE	SE
London Victoria ⊖	d	20 37	21 07	22 07	23 07
London Blackfriars ⊖195	d				
Elephant & Castle ⊖195	d				
Bromley South 195	d	20 53	21 23	22 23	23 23
St Mary Cray 195	d	21 00	21 30	22 30	23 30
Swanley 195	d	21 04	21 34	22 34	23 34
Otford 195	d	21 12	21 42	22 42	23 42
Kemsing	d	21 17	21 47	22 47	23 47
Borough Green & Wrotham	d	21 22	21 52	22 52	23 52
West Malling	d	21 28	21 58	22 58	23 58
East Malling	d	21 31	22 01	23 01	00 01
Barming	d	21 35	22 05	23 05	00 05
Maidstone East	a	21 39	22 09	23 09	00 09
	d	21 40	22 10	23 10	00 10
Bearsted	d	21 45	22 15	23 15	00 15
Hollingbourne	d	21 48	22 18	23 18	00 18
Harrietsham	d	21 52	22 22	23 22	00 22
Lenham	d	21 55	22 25	23 25	00 25
Charing	d	22 00	22 30	23 30	00 30
Ashford International	a	22 09	22 39	23 39	00 39
	d				

A from 21 May until 23 July
B until 18 May
C from 22 May until 27 July
D from 21 May until 27 July
E until 18 May

London - Maidstone East and Ashford International

Mondays to Fridays

30 July to 10 August

Network Diagram - see first Page of Table 195

Station		SE A	SE MO	SE A	SE	SE	SE	SE	SE	SE	SE	SE	SE	SE	SE	SE	SE	SE	SE	SE	SE	SE	SE
London Victoria ⊖	d	23p07	23p07	00 07	01 00		06 07	06 37	07 07	07 36	08 07	08 37	09 07	09 37	10 07	10 37	11 07	11 37	12 07	12 37	13 07	13 37	14 07
London Blackfriars ⊖195	d																						
Elephant & Castle ⊖195	d																						
Bromley South 195	d	23p23	23p23	00 25	01 16		06 23	06 58	07 23	07 53	08 23	08 53	09 23	09 53	10 23	10 53	11 23	11 53	12 23	12 53	13 23	13 53	14 23
St Mary Cray 195	d	23p30	23p30	00 32	01 23		06 30	07 04	07 30	08 00	08 30	09 00		10 00		11 00		12 00		13 00		14 00	
Swanley 195	d	23p34	23p34	00 36	01 27		06 34	07 08	07 34	08 04	08 34	09 04	09 33	10 04	10 33	11 04	11 33	12 04	12 33	13 04	13 33	14 04	14 33
Otford 195	d	23p42	23p42	00 44	01 38		06 42	07 16	07 42	08 12	08 42	09 12	09 41	10 12	10 41	11 12	11 41	12 12	12 41	13 12	13 41	14 12	14 41
Kemsing	d	23p47	23p47	00 49	01 43		06 47	07 21	07 47	08 17	08 47	09 17		10 17		11 17		12 17		13 17		14 17	
Borough Green & Wrotham	d	23p52	23p52	00 54	01 48		06 52	07 26	07 52	08 22	08 52	09 22	09 48	10 22	10 48	11 22	11 48	12 22	12 48	13 22	13 48	14 22	14 48
West Malling	d	23p58	23p59	01 00	01 54		06 58	07 32	07 58	08 28	08 58	09 28	09 55	10 28	10 55	11 28	11 55	12 28	12 55	13 28	13 55	14 28	14 55
East Malling	d	00 01	00 01	01 03	01 57		07 01	07 35	08 01	08 31	09 01	09 31		10 31		11 31		12 31		13 31		14 31	
Barming	d	00 05	00 05	01 07	02 01		07 05	07 39	08 05	08 35	09 05	09 35		10 35		11 35		12 35		13 35		14 35	
Maidstone East	a	00 09	00 10	01 11	02 05		07 09	07 43	08 09	08 39	09 10	09 39	10 02	10 39	11 02	11 39	12 02	12 39	13 02	13 39	14 02	14 39	15 02
	d	00 10	00 10	01 12	02 06	06 34	07 10	07 44	08 10	08 40	09 10	09 40	10 03	10 40	11 03	11 40	12 03	12 40	13 03	13 40	14 03	14 40	15 03
Bearsted	d	00 15	00 15	01 17	02 11	06 39	07 15	07 49	08 15	08 45	09 15	09 45	10 08	10 45	11 08	11 45	12 08	12 45	13 08	13 45	14 08	14 45	15 08
Hollingbourne	d	00 18	00 18	01 20	02 14	06 42	07 18	07 52	08 18	08 48	09 18	09 48		10 48		11 48		12 48		13 48		14 48	
Harrietsham	d	00 22	00 22	01 24	02 18	06 46	07 22	07 56	08 22	08 52	09 22	09 52		10 52		11 52		12 52		13 52		14 52	
Lenham	d	00 25	00 25	01 27	02 21	06 49	07 25	07 59	08 25	08 55	09 25	09 55		10 55		11 55		12 55		13 55		14 55	
Charing	d	00 30	00 30	01 32	02 26	06 54	07 30	08 04	08 30	09 00	09 30	10 00		11 00		12 00		13 00		14 00		15 00	
Ashford International	a	00 39	00 40	01 41	02 38	07 02	07 39	08 16	08 39	09 09	09 40	10 09	10 28	11 09	11 28	12 09	12 28	13 09	13 28	14 09	14 28	15 09	15 30
	d																						

Station		SE	SE	SE	SE	SE	SE	SE	SE	SE	FC	SE	SE	SE	SE	SE	SE	SE	SE	SE	SE
London Victoria ⊖	d	14 37	15 07	15 37	16 07	16 37	16 58	17 12	17 28	17 42		18 03	18 18	18 42	19 07	19 37	20 07	20 37	21 07	22 07	23 07
London Blackfriars ⊖195	d										17 48										
Elephant & Castle ⊖195	d										17 52										
Bromley South 195	d	14 53	15 23	15 53	16 23	16 53	17 19	17 31	17 50	17 59	18 11	18 24	18 39	18 59	19 27	19 53	20 23	20 53	21 23	22 23	23 23
St Mary Cray 195	d	15 00		16 00		17 00		17 38	17 57	18 06	18 18		18 45	19 06		20 00		21 00	21 30	22 30	23 30
Swanley 195	d	15 04	15 33	16 04	16 33	17 04		17 42	18 01	18 11	18 22		18 50	19 11	19 36	20 04	20 33	21 04	21 34	22 34	23 34
Otford 195	d	15 12	15 41	16 12	16 41	17 12	17 35	17 51	18 10	18 19	18 31	18 43	18 58	19 19	19 44	20 12	20 41	21 12	21 42	22 42	23 42
Kemsing	d	15 17		16 17		17 17		17 56		18 24	18 36		19 03	19 24		20 17		21 17	21 47	22 47	23 47
Borough Green & Wrotham	d	15 22	15 48	16 22	16 48	17 22	17 43	18 00	18 17	18 29	18 41	18 51	19 08	19 29	19 51	20 22	20 48	21 22	21 52	22 52	23 52
West Malling	d	15 28	15 55	16 28	16 55	17 28	17 49	18 07	18 24	18 35	18 47	18 57	19 14	19 35	19 57	20 28	20 55	21 28	21 58	22 58	23 58
East Malling	d	15 31		16 31		17 31		18 10		18 38	18 50		19 17	19 38		20 31		21 31	22 01	23 01	00 01
Barming	d	15 35		16 35		17 35		18 13		18 42	18 54		19 21	19 42		20 35		21 35	22 05	23 05	00 05
Maidstone East	a	15 39	16 02	16 39	17 02	17 39	17 56	18 17	18 33	18 46	18 58	19 04	19 25	19 46	20 04	20 39	21 02	21 39	22 09	23 09	00 09
	d	15 40	16 03	16 40	17 03	17 40	17 57	18 18		18 47	18 59	19 06	19 26	19 47	20 05	20 40	21 03	21 40	22 10	23 10	00 10
Bearsted	d	15 45	16 08	16 45	17 08	17 45	18 02	18 23		18 52	19 04	19 11	19 31	19 52	20 10	20 45	21 08	21 45	22 15	23 15	00 15
Hollingbourne	d	15 48	16 11	16 48	17 11	17 48	18 06	18 27		18 55	19 08	19 15	19 34	19 55	20 13	20 48	21 11	21 48	22 18	23 18	00 18
Harrietsham	d	15 52	16 15	16 52	17 15	17 52	18 09	18 30		18 59	19 11	19 18	19 38	19 59	20 17	20 52	21 15	21 52	22 22	23 22	00 22
Lenham	d	15 55	16 18	16 55	17 18	17 55	18 13	18 34		19 02	19 15	19 22	19 41	20 02	20 20	20 55	21 18	21 55	22 25	23 25	00 25
Charing	d	16 00	16 23	17 00	17 23	18 00	18 18	18 39		19 07	19 20	19 27	19 46	20 07	20 25	21 00	21 23	22 00	22 30	23 30	00 30
Ashford International	a	16 09	16 36	17 09	17 34	18 11	18 30	18 50		19 18	19 32	19 40	19 58	20 18	20 36	21 09	21 36	22 09	22 39	23 39	00 39
	d																				

Mondays to Fridays

29 August to 7 September

Station		SE B	SE C	SE C	SE	SE	SE	SE	SE	SE	SE	SE	SE	SE	SE	SE	SE	SE	SE	SE	SE	SE	SE
London Victoria ⊖	d	22p45	23p07	00 07	00 51		06 07	06 37	07 07	07 36	08 07	08 37	09 07	09 37	10 07	10 37	11 07	11 37	12 07	12 37	13 07	13 37	14 07
London Blackfriars ⊖195	d																						
Elephant & Castle ⊖195	d																						
Bromley South 195	d	23p01	23p23	00 25	01s10		06 23	06 58	07 23	07 53	08 23	08 53	09 23	09 53	10 23	10 53	11 23	11 53	12 23	12 53	13 23	13 53	14 23
St Mary Cray 195	d	23p08	23p30	00 32	01s17		06 30	07 04	07 30	08 00	08 30	09 00		10 00		11 00		12 00		13 00		14 00	
Swanley 195	d	23p12	23p34	00 36	01s21		06 34	07 08	07 34	08 04	08 34	09 04	09 33	10 04	10 33	11 04	11 33	12 04	12 33	13 04	13 33	14 04	14 33
Otford 195	d	23p20	23p42	00 44	01s33		06 42	07 16	07 42	08 12	08 42	09 12	09 41	10 12	10 41	11 12	11 41	12 12	12 41	13 12	13 41	14 12	14 41
Kemsing	d		23p47	00 49	01s37		06 47	07 21	07 47	08 17	08 47	09 17		10 17		11 17		12 17		13 17		14 17	
Borough Green & Wrotham	d	23p28	23p52	00 54	01s42		06 52	07 26	07 52	08 22	08 52	09 22	09 48	10 22	10 48	11 22	11 48	12 22	12 48	13 22	13 48	14 22	14 48
West Malling	d	23p34	23p58	01 00	01s48		06 58	07 32	07 58	08 28	08 58	09 28	09 55	10 28	10 55	11 28	11 55	12 28	12 55	13 28	13 55	14 28	14 55
East Malling	d	23p37	00 01	01 03	01s51		07 01	07 35	08 01	08 31	09 01	09 31		10 31		11 31		12 31		13 31		14 31	
Barming	d	23p41	00 05	01 07	01s55		07 05	07 39	08 05	08 35	09 05	09 35		10 35		11 35		12 35		13 35		14 35	
Maidstone East	a	23p45	00 09	01 11	01s59		07 09	07 43	08 09	08 39	09 10	09 39	10 02	10 39	11 02	11 39	12 02	12 39	13 02	13 39	14 02	14 39	15 02
	d	23p46	00 10	01 12		06 34	07 10	07 44	08 10	08 40	09 10	09 40	10 03	10 40	11 03	11 40	12 03	12 40	13 03	13 40	14 03	14 40	15 03
Bearsted	d	23p51	00 15	01 17	02s04	06 39	07 15	07 49	08 15	08 45	09 15	09 45	10 08	10 45	11 08	11 45	12 08	12 45	13 08	13 45	14 08	14 45	15 08
Hollingbourne	d	23p54	00 18	01 20	02s08	06 42	07 18	07 52	08 18	08 48	09 18	09 48		10 48		11 48		12 48		13 48		14 48	
Harrietsham	d	23p58	00 22	01 24	02s11	06 46	07 22	07 56	08 22	08 52	09 22	09 52		10 52		11 52		12 52		13 52		14 52	
Lenham	d	00 01	00 25	01 27	02s15	06 49	07 25	07 59	08 25	08 55	09 25	09 55		10 55		11 55		12 55		13 55		14 55	
Charing	d	00 06	00 30	01 32	02s20	06 54	07 30	08 04	08 30	09 00	09 30	10 00		11 00		12 00		13 00		14 00		15 00	
Ashford International	a	00 15	00 39	01 41	02 27	07 02	07 39	08 13	08 39	09 09	09 40	10 09	10 27	11 09	11 27	12 09	12 27	13 09	13 27	14 09	14 27	15 09	15 30
	d																						

A not 30 July, 6 August
B 3 September
C not 3 September

Table 196

London - Maidstone East and Ashford International

Mondays to Fridays
29 August to 7 September

Network Diagram - see first Page of Table 195

Station			SE	SE	SE	SE	SE	SE	SE	SE	SE	FC	SE	SE	SE	SE	SE	SE	SE	SE	SE	SE
London Victoria	⊖	d	14 37	15 07	15 37	16 07	16 37	16 58	17 12	17 28	17 42		18 03	18 18	18 42	19 07	19 37	20 07	20 37	21 07	22 07	23 07
London Blackfriars	⊖195	d										17 48										
Elephant & Castle	⊖195	d										17 52										
Bromley South	195	d	14 53	15 23	15 53	16 23	16 53	17 19	17 31	17 50	17 59	18 11	18 24	18 39	18 59	19 27	19 53	20 23	20 53	21 23	22 23	23 23
St Mary Cray	195	d	15 00		16 00		17 00		17 38	17 57	18 06	18 18		18 45	19 06		20 00		21 00	21 30	22 30	23 30
Swanley	195	d	15 04	15 33	16 04	16 33	17 04		17 42	18 01	18 11	18 22		18 50	19 11	19 36	20 04	20 33	21 04	21 34	22 34	23 34
Otford	195	d	15 12	15 41	16 12	16 41	17 12	17 35	17 51	18 10	18 19	18 31	18 43	18 58	19 19	19 44	20 12	20 41	21 12	21 42	22 42	23 42
Kemsing		d	15 17		16 17		17 17		17 56		18 24	18 36		19 03	19 24		20 17		21 17	21 47	22 47	23 47
Borough Green & Wrotham		d	15 22	15 48	16 22	16 48	17 22	17 43	18 00	18 17	18 29	18 41	18 51	19 08	19 29	19 51	20 22	20 48	21 22	21 52	22 52	23 52
West Malling		d	15 28	15 55	16 28	16 55	17 28	17 49	18 07	18 24	18 35	18 47	18 57	19 14	19 35	19 57	20 28	20 55	21 28	21 58	22 58	23 58
East Malling		d	15 31		16 31		17 31		18 10		18 38	18 50		19 17	19 38		20 31		21 31	22 01	23 01	00 01
Barming		d	15 35		16 35		17 35		18 13		18 42	18 54		19 21	19 42		20 35		21 35	22 05	23 05	00 05
Maidstone East		a	15 39	16 02	16 39	17 02	17 39	17 56	18 17	18 33	18 46	18 58	19 04	19 25	19 46	20 04	20 39	21 02	21 39	22 09	23 09	00 09
		d	15 40	16 03	16 40	17 03	17 40	17 57	18 18		18 47	18 59	19 06	19 26	19 47	20 05	20 40	21 03	21 40	22 10	23 10	00 10
Bearsted		d	15 45	16 08	16 45	17 08	17 45	18 02	18 23		18 52	19 04	19 11	19 31	19 52	20 10	20 45	21 08	21 45	22 15	23 15	00 15
Hollingbourne		d	15 48	16 11	16 48	17 11	17 48	18 06	18 27		18 55	19 08	19 15	19 34	19 55	20 13	20 48	21 11	21 48	22 18	23 18	00 18
Harrietsham		d	15 52	16 15	16 52	17 15	17 52	18 09	18 30		18 59	19 11	19 18	19 38	19 59	20 17	20 52	21 15	21 52	22 22	23 22	00 22
Lenham		d	15 55	16 18	16 55	17 18	17 55	18 13	18 34		19 02	19 15	19 22	19 41	20 02	20 20	20 55	21 18	21 55	22 25	23 25	00 25
Charing		d	16 00	16 23	17 00	17 23	18 00	18 18	18 39		19 07	19 20	19 27	19 46	20 07	20 25	21 00	21 23	22 00	22 30	23 30	00 30
Ashford International		a	16 09	16 32	17 09	17 34	18 11	18 28	18 50		19 18	19 32	19 40	19 58	20 18	20 34	21 09	21 32	22 09	22 39	23 39	00 39
		d																				

Saturdays
until 21 July, 18 Aug and from 15 Sep

Station			SE	SE A	SE B	SE	SE	SE	SE	SE	SE	SE	SE	SE	SE	SE	SE	SE	SE	SE	SE	SE	SE	SE
London Victoria	⊖	d	23p07	00 07	00 07		06 07	07 07	07 37	08 07	08 37	09 07	09 37	10 07	10 37	11 07	11 37	12 07	12 37	13 07	13 37	14 07	14 37	15 07
London Blackfriars	⊖195	d																						
Elephant & Castle	⊖195	d																						
Bromley South	195	d	23p23	00 25	00 25		06 23	07 23	07 53	08 23	08 53	09 23	09 53	10 23	10 53	11 23	11 53	12 23	12 53	13 23	13 53	14 23	14 53	15 23
St Mary Cray	195	d	23p30	00 31	00 32		06 30	07 30	08 00		09 00		10 00		11 00		12 00		13 00		14 00		15 00	
Swanley	195	d	23p34	00 36	00 36		06 34	07 34	08 04	08 33	09 04	09 33	10 04	10 33	11 04	11 33	12 04	12 33	13 04	13 33	14 04	14 33	15 04	15 33
Otford	195	d	23p42	00 47	00 44		06 42	07 42	08 12	08 41	09 12	09 41	10 12	10 41	11 12	11 41	12 12	12 41	13 12	13 41	14 12	14 41	15 12	15 41
Kemsing		d	23p47	00 52	00 49		06 47	07 47	08 17		09 17		10 17		11 17		12 17		13 17		14 17		15 17	
Borough Green & Wrotham		d	23p52	00 56	00 54		06 52	07 52	08 22	08 48	09 22	09 48	10 22	10 48	11 22	11 48	12 22	12 48	13 22	13 48	14 22	14 48	15 22	15 48
West Malling		d	23p58	01 03	01 00		06 58	07 58	08 28	08 55	09 28	09 55	10 28	10 55	11 28	11 55	12 28	12 55	13 28	13 55	14 28	14 55	15 28	15 55
East Malling		d	00 01	01 06	01 03		07 01	08 01	08 31		09 31		10 31		11 31		12 31		13 31		14 31		15 31	
Barming		d	00 05	01 09	01 07		07 05	08 05	08 35		09 35		10 35		11 35		12 35		13 35		14 35		15 35	
Maidstone East		a	00 09	01 13	01 11		07 09	08 09	08 39	09 02	09 39	10 02	10 39	11 02	11 39	12 02	12 39	13 02	13 39	14 02	14 39	15 02	15 39	16 02
		d	00 10	01 14	01 12	06 10	07 10	08 10	08 40	09 03	09 40	10 03	10 40	11 03	11 40	12 03	12 40	13 03	13 40	14 03	14 40	15 03	15 40	16 03
Bearsted		d	00 15	01 19	01 17	06 15	07 15	08 15	08 45	09 08	09 45	10 08	10 45	11 08	11 45	12 08	12 45	13 08	13 45	14 08	14 45	15 08	15 45	16 08
Hollingbourne		d	00 18	01 22	01 20	06 18	07 18	08 18	08 48		09 48		10 48		11 48		12 48		13 48		14 48		15 48	
Harrietsham		d	00 22	01 26	01 24	06 22	07 22	08 22	08 52		09 52		10 52		11 52		12 52		13 52		14 52		15 52	
Lenham		d	00 25	01 29	01 27	06 25	07 25	08 25	08 55		09 55		10 55		11 55		12 55		13 55		14 55		15 55	
Charing		d	00 30	01 34	01 32	06 30	07 30	08 30	09 00		10 00		11 00		12 00		13 00		14 00		15 00		16 00	
Ashford International		a	00 39	01 43	01 41	06 39	07 39	08 39	09 09	09 27	10 09	10 27	11 09	11 27	12 09	12 27	13 09	13 27	14 09	14 27	15 09	15 27	16 09	16 27
		d																						

Station			SE	SE	SE	SE	SE	SE	SE	SE	SE	SE	SE	SE	SE
London Victoria	⊖	d	15 37	16 07	16 37	17 07	17 37	18 07	18 37	19 07	19 37	20 07	21 07	22 07	23 07
London Blackfriars	⊖195	d													
Elephant & Castle	⊖195	d													
Bromley South	195	d	15 53	16 23	16 53	17 23	17 53	18 23	18 53	19 23	19 53	20 23	21 23	22 23	23 23
St Mary Cray	195	d	16 00		17 00		18 00		19 00		20 00	20 30	21 30	22 30	23 30
Swanley	195	d	16 04	16 33	17 04	17 33	18 04	18 33	19 04	19 33	20 04	20 34	21 34	22 34	23 34
Otford	195	d	16 12	16 41	17 12	17 41	18 12	18 41	19 12	19 41	20 12	20 42	21 42	22 42	23 42
Kemsing		d	16 17		17 17		18 17		19 17		20 17	20 47	21 47	22 47	23 47
Borough Green & Wrotham		d	16 22	16 48	17 22	17 48	18 22	18 48	19 22	19 48	20 22	20 52	21 52	22 52	23 52
West Malling		d	16 28	16 55	17 28	17 55	18 28	18 55	19 28	19 55	20 28	20 58	21 58	22 58	23 58
East Malling		d	16 31		17 31		18 31		19 31		20 31	21 01	22 01	23 01	00 01
Barming		d	16 35		17 35		18 35		19 35		20 35	21 05	22 05	23 05	00 05
Maidstone East		a	16 39	17 02	17 39	18 02	18 39	19 02	19 39	20 02	20 39	21 09	22 09	23 09	00 09
		d	16 40	17 03	17 40	18 03	18 40	19 03	19 40	20 03	20 40	21 10	22 10	23 10	00 10
Bearsted		d	16 45	17 08	17 45	18 08	18 45	19 08	19 45	20 08	20 45	21 15	22 15	23 15	00 15
Hollingbourne		d	16 48		17 48		18 48		19 48		20 48	21 18	22 18	23 18	00 18
Harrietsham		d	16 52		17 52		18 52		19 52		20 52	21 22	22 22	23 22	00 22
Lenham		d	16 55		17 55		18 55		19 55		20 55	21 25	22 25	23 25	00 25
Charing		d	17 00		18 00		19 00		20 00		21 00	21 30	22 30	23 30	00 30
Ashford International		a	17 09	17 27	18 09	18 27	19 09	19 27	20 09	20 27	21 09	21 39	22 39	23 39	00 39
		d													

A 19 May
B not 19 May

Table 196

London - Maidstone East and Ashford International

Saturdays
28 July to 11 August

Network Diagram - see first Page of Table 195

Station			SE	SE	SE	SE	SE	SE	SE	SE	SE	SE	SE	SE	SE	SE	SE	SE	SE	SE	SE	SE	SE	SE
London Victoria	⊖	d	23p07	00 07	01 00		06 07	07 07	07 37	08 07	08 37	09 07	09 37	10 07	10 37	11 07	11 37	12 07	12 37	13 07	13 37	14 07	14 37	15 07
London Blackfriars	⊖195	d																						
Elephant & Castle	⊖195	d																						
Bromley South	195	d	23p23	00 25	01 16		06 23	07 23	07 53	08 23	08 53	09 23	09 53	10 23	10 53	11 23	11 53	12 23	12 53	13 23	13 53	14 23	14 53	15 23
St Mary Cray	195	d	23p30	00 32	01 23		06 30	07 30	08 00		09 00		10 00		11 00		12 00		13 00		14 00		15 00	
Swanley	195	d	23p34	00 36	01 27		06 34	07 34	08 04	08 33	09 04	09 33	10 04	10 33	11 04	11 33	12 04	12 33	13 04	13 33	14 04	14 33	15 04	15 33
Otford	195	d	23p42	00 44	01 38		06 42	07 42	08 12	08 41	09 12	09 41	10 12	10 41	11 12	11 41	12 12	12 41	13 12	13 41	14 12	14 41	15 12	15 41
Kemsing		d	23p47	00 49	01 43		06 47	07 47	08 17		09 17		10 17		11 17		12 17		13 17		14 17		15 17	
Borough Green & Wrotham		d	23p52	00 54	01 48		06 52	07 52	08 22	08 48	09 22	09 48	10 22	10 48	11 22	11 48	12 22	12 48	13 22	13 48	14 22	14 48	15 22	15 48
West Malling		d	23p58	01 00	01 54		06 58	07 58	08 28	08 55	09 28	09 55	10 28	10 55	11 28	11 55	12 28	12 55	13 28	13 55	14 28	14 55	15 28	15 55
East Malling		d	00 01	01 03	01 57		07 01	08 01	08 31		09 31		10 31		11 31		12 31		13 31		14 31		15 31	
Barming		d	00 05	01 07	02 01		07 05	08 05	08 35		09 35		10 35		11 35		12 35		13 35		14 35		15 35	
Maidstone East		a	00 09	01 11	02 05		07 09	08 09	08 39	09 02	09 39	10 02	10 39	11 02	11 39	12 02	12 39	13 02	13 39	14 02	14 39	15 02	15 39	16 02
		d	00 10	01 12	02 06	06 10	07 10	08 10	08 40	09 03	09 40	10 03	10 40	11 03	11 40	12 03	12 40	13 03	13 40	14 03	14 40	15 03	15 40	16 03
Bearsted		d	00 15	01 17	02 11	06 15	07 15	08 15	08 45	09 08	09 45	10 08	10 45	11 08	11 45	12 08	12 45	13 08	13 45	14 08	14 45	15 08	15 45	16 08
Hollingbourne		d	00 18	01 20	02 14	06 18	07 18	08 18	08 48		09 48		10 48		11 48		12 48		13 48		14 48		15 48	
Harrietsham		d	00 22	01 24	02 18	06 22	07 22	08 22	08 52		09 52		10 52		11 52		12 52		13 52		14 52		15 52	
Lenham		d	00 25	01 27	02 21	06 25	07 25	08 25	08 55		09 55		10 55		11 55		12 55		13 55		14 55		15 55	
Charing		d	00 30	01 32	02 26	06 30	07 30	08 30	09 00		10 00		11 00		12 00		13 00		14 00		15 00		16 00	
Ashford International		a	00 39	01 41	02 38	06 39	07 39	08 39	09 09	09 27	10 09	10 28	11 09	11 28	12 09	12 28	13 09	13 28	14 09	14 28	15 09	15 28	16 09	16 28
		d																						

Station			SE	SE	SE	SE	SE	SE	SE	SE	SE	SE	SE	SE	SE
London Victoria	⊖	d	15 37	16 07	16 37	17 07	17 37	18 07	18 37	19 07	19 37	20 07	21 07	22 07	23 07
London Blackfriars	⊖195	d													
Elephant & Castle	⊖195	d													
Bromley South	195	d	15 53	16 23	16 53	17 23	17 53	18 23	18 53	19 23	19 53	20 23	21 23	22 23	23 23
St Mary Cray	195	d	16 00		17 00		18 00		19 00		20 00	20 30	21 30	22 30	23 30
Swanley	195	d	16 04	16 33	17 04	17 33	18 04	18 33	19 04	19 33	20 04	20 34	21 34	22 34	23 34
Otford	195	d	16 12	16 41	17 12	17 41	18 12	18 41	19 12	19 41	20 12	20 42	21 42	22 42	23 42
Kemsing		d	16 17		17 17		18 17		19 17		20 17	20 47	21 47	22 47	23 47
Borough Green & Wrotham		d	16 22	16 48	17 22	17 48	18 22	18 48	19 22	19 48	20 22	20 52	21 52	22 52	23 52
West Malling		d	16 28	16 55	17 28	17 55	18 28	18 55	19 28	19 55	20 28	20 58	21 58	22 58	23 58
East Malling		d	16 31		17 31		18 31		19 31		20 31	21 01	22 01	23 01	00 01
Barming		d	16 35		17 35		18 35		19 35		20 35	21 05	22 05	23 05	00 05
Maidstone East		a	16 39	17 02	17 39	18 02	18 39	19 02	19 39	20 02	20 39	21 09	22 09	23 09	00 09
		d	16 40	17 03	17 40	18 03	18 40	19 03	19 40	20 03	20 40	21 10	22 10	23 10	00 10
Bearsted		d	16 45	17 08	17 45	18 08	18 45	19 08	19 45	20 08	20 45	21 15	22 15	23 15	00 15
Hollingbourne		d	16 48		17 48		18 48		19 48		20 48	21 18	22 18	23 18	00 18
Harrietsham		d	16 52		17 52		18 52		19 52		20 52	21 22	22 22	23 22	00 22
Lenham		d	16 55		17 55		18 55		19 55		20 55	21 25	22 25	23 25	00 25
Charing		d	17 00		18 00		19 00		20 00		21 00	21 30	22 30	23 30	00 30
Ashford International		a	17 09	17 28	18 09	18 27	19 09	19 28	20 09	20 28	21 09	21 39	22 39	23 39	00 39
		d													

Saturdays
25 August to 8 September

Station			SE	SE	SE A	SE	SE	SE	SE	SE	SE	SE	SE	SE	SE	SE	SE	SE	SE	SE	SE	SE	SE	SE
London Victoria	⊖	d	23p07	00 07	00 51		06 07	07 07	07 37	08 07	08 37	09 07	09 37	10 07	10 37	11 07	11 37	12 07	12 37	13 07	13 37	14 07	14 37	15 07
London Blackfriars	⊖195	d																						
Elephant & Castle	⊖195	d																						
Bromley South	195	d	23p23	00 25	01s10		06 23	07 23	07 53	08 23	08 53	09 23	09 53	10 23	10 53	11 23	11 53	12 23	12 53	13 23	13 53	14 23	14 53	15 23
St Mary Cray	195	d	23p30	00 32	01s17		06 30	07 30	08 00		09 00		10 00		11 00		12 00		13 00		14 00		15 00	
Swanley	195	d	23p34	00 36	01s21		06 34	07 34	08 04	08 33	09 04	09 33	10 04	10 33	11 04	11 33	12 04	12 33	13 04	13 33	14 04	14 33	15 04	15 33
Otford	195	d	23p42	00 44	01s33		06 42	07 42	08 12	08 41	09 12	09 41	10 12	10 41	11 12	11 41	12 12	12 41	13 12	13 41	14 12	14 41	15 12	15 41
Kemsing		d	23p47	00 49	01s37		06 47	07 47	08 17		09 17		10 17		11 17		12 17		13 17		14 17		15 17	
Borough Green & Wrotham		d	23p52	00 54	01s42		06 52	07 52	08 22	08 48	09 22	09 48	10 22	10 48	11 22	11 48	12 22	12 48	13 22	13 48	14 22	14 48	15 22	15 48
West Malling		d	23p58	01 00	01s48		06 58	07 58	08 28	08 55	09 28	09 55	10 28	10 55	11 28	11 55	12 28	12 55	13 28	13 55	14 28	14 55	15 28	15 55
East Malling		d	00 01	01 03	01s51		07 01	08 01	08 31		09 31		10 31		11 31		12 31		13 31		14 31		15 31	
Barming		d	00 05	01 07	01s55		07 05	08 05	08 35		09 35		10 35		11 35		12 35		13 35		14 35		15 35	
Maidstone East		a	00 09	01 11	01s59		07 09	08 09	08 39	09 02	09 39	10 02	10 39	11 02	11 39	12 02	12 39	13 02	13 39	14 02	14 39	15 02	15 39	16 02
		d	00 10	01 12		06 10	07 10	08 10	08 40	09 03	09 40	10 03	10 40	11 03	11 40	12 03	12 40	13 03	13 40	14 03	14 40	15 03	15 40	16 03
Bearsted		d	00 15	01 17	02s04	06 15	07 15	08 15	08 45	09 08	09 45	10 08	10 45	11 08	11 45	12 08	12 45	13 08	13 45	14 08	14 45	15 08	15 45	16 08
Hollingbourne		d	00 18	01 20	02s08	06 18	07 18	08 18	08 48		09 48		10 48		11 48		12 48		13 48		14 48		15 48	
Harrietsham		d	00 22	01 24	02s11	06 22	07 22	08 22	08 52		09 52		10 52		11 52		12 52		13 52		14 52		15 52	
Lenham		d	00 25	01 27	02s15	06 25	07 25	08 25	08 55		09 55		10 55		11 55		12 55		13 55		14 55		15 55	
Charing		d	00 30	01 32	02s20	06 30	07 30	08 30	09 00		10 00		11 00		12 00		13 00		14 00		15 00		16 00	
Ashford International		a	00 39	01 41	02 27	06 39	07 39	08 39	09 09	09 27	10 09	10 27	11 09	11 27	12 09	12 27	13 09	13 27	14 09	14 27	15 09	15 27	16 09	16 27
		d																						

A not 25 August

London - Maidstone East and Ashford International

Saturdays
25 August to 8 September

Network Diagram - see first Page of Table 195

		SE	SE	SE	SE	SE	SE	SE	SE	SE	SE	SE	SE	SE
London Victoria	⊖ d	15 37	16 07	16 37	17 07	17 37	18 07	18 37	19 07	19 37	20 07	21 07	22 07	23 07
London Blackfriars	⊖195 d													
Elephant & Castle	⊖195 d													
Bromley South	195 d	15 53	16 23	16 53	17 23	17 53	18 23	18 53	19 23	19 53	20 23	21 23	22 23	23 23
St Mary Cray	195 d	16 00		17 00		18 00		19 00		20 00	20 30	21 30	22 30	23 30
Swanley	195 d	16 04	16 33	17 04	17 33	18 04	18 33	19 04	19 33	20 04	20 34	21 34	22 34	23 34
Otford	195 d	16 12	16 41	17 12	17 41	18 12	18 41	19 12	19 41	20 12	20 42	21 42	22 42	23 42
Kemsing	d	16 17		17 17		18 17		19 17		20 17	20 47	21 47	22 47	23 47
Borough Green & Wrotham	d	16 22	16 48	17 22	17 48	18 22	18 48	19 22	19 48	20 22	20 52	21 52	22 52	23 52
West Malling	d	16 28	16 55	17 28	17 55	18 28	18 55	19 28	19 55	20 28	20 58	21 58	22 58	23 58
East Malling	d	16 31		17 31		18 31		19 31		20 31	21 01	22 01	23 01	00 01
Barming	d	16 35		17 35		18 35		19 35		20 35	21 05	22 05	23 05	00 05
Maidstone East	a	16 39	17 02	17 39	18 02	18 39	19 02	19 39	20 02	20 39	21 09	22 09	23 09	00 09
	d	16 40	17 03	17 40	18 03	18 40	19 03	19 40	20 03	20 40	21 10	22 10	23 10	00 10
Bearsted	d	16 45	17 08	17 45	18 08	18 45	19 08	19 45	20 08	20 45	21 15	22 15	23 15	00 15
Hollingbourne	d	16 48		17 48		18 48		19 48		20 48	21 18	22 18	23 18	00 18
Harrietsham	d	16 52		17 52		18 52		19 52		20 52	21 22	22 22	23 22	00 22
Lenham	d	16 55		17 55		18 55		19 55		20 55	21 25	22 25	23 25	00 25
Charing	d	17 00		18 00		19 00		20 00		21 00	21 30	22 30	23 30	00 30
Ashford International	a	17 09	17 27	18 09	18 27	19 09	19 27	20 09	20 27	21 09	21 39	22 39	23 39	00 39
	d													

Sundays
until 22 July, 19 Aug and from 16 Sep

		SE	SE	SE	SE	SE	SE	SE	SE	SE	SE	SE	SE	SE	SE	SE	SE	SE	SE
London Victoria	⊖ d	23p07	00 07	07 45	08 45	09 45	10 45	11 45	12 45	13 45	14 45	15 45	16 45	17 45	18 45	19 45	20 45	21 45	22 45
London Blackfriars	⊖195 d																		
Elephant & Castle	⊖195 d																		
Bromley South	195 d	23p23	00 25	08 01	09 01	10 01	11 01	12 01	13 01	14 01	15 01	16 01	17 01	18 01	19 01	20 01	21 01	22 01	23 01
St Mary Cray	195 d	23p30	00 32	08 08	09 08	10 08	11 08	12 08	13 08	14 08	15 08	16 08	17 08	18 08	19 08	20 08	21 08	22 08	23 08
Swanley	195 d	23p34	00 36	08 12	09 12	10 12	11 12	12 12	13 12	14 12	15 12	16 12	17 12	18 12	19 12	20 12	21 12	22 12	23 12
Otford	195 d	23p42	00 44	08 20	09 20	10 20	11 20	12 20	13 20	14 20	15 20	16 20	17 20	18 20	19 20	20 20	21 20	22 20	23 20
Kemsing	d	23p47	00 49																
Borough Green & Wrotham	d	23p52	00 54	08 28	09 28	10 28	11 28	12 28	13 28	14 28	15 28	16 28	17 28	18 28	19 28	20 28	21 28	22 28	23 28
West Malling	d	23p58	01 00	08 34	09 34	10 34	11 34	12 34	13 34	14 34	15 34	16 34	17 34	18 34	19 34	20 34	21 34	22 34	23 34
East Malling	d	00 01	01 03	08 37	09 37	10 37	11 37	12 37	13 37	14 37	15 37	16 37	17 37	18 37	19 37	20 37	21 37	22 37	23 37
Barming	d	00 05	01 07	08 41	09 41	10 41	11 41	12 41	13 41	14 41	15 41	16 41	17 41	18 41	19 41	20 41	21 41	22 41	23 41
Maidstone East	a	00 09	01 11	08 45	09 45	10 45	11 45	12 45	13 45	14 45	15 45	16 45	17 45	18 45	19 45	20 45	21 45	22 45	23 45
	d	00 10	01 12	08 46	09 46	10 46	11 46	12 46	13 46	14 46	15 46	16 46	17 46	18 46	19 46	20 46	21 46	22 46	23 46
Bearsted	d	00 15	01 17	08 51	09 51	10 51	11 51	12 51	13 51	14 51	15 51	16 51	17 51	18 51	19 51	20 51	21 51	22 51	23 51
Hollingbourne	d	00 18	01 20	08 54	09 54	10 54	11 54	12 54	13 54	14 54	15 54	16 54	17 54	18 54	19 54	20 54	21 54	22 54	23 54
Harrietsham	d	00 22	01 24	08 58	09 58	10 58	11 58	12 58	13 58	14 58	15 58	16 58	17 58	18 58	19 58	20 58	21 58	22 58	23 58
Lenham	d	00 25	01 27	09 01	10 01	11 01	12 01	13 01	14 01	15 01	16 01	17 01	18 01	19 01	20 01	21 01	22 01	23 01	00 01
Charing	d	00 30	01 32	09 06	10 06	11 06	12 06	13 06	14 06	15 06	16 06	17 06	18 06	19 06	20 06	21 06	22 06	23 06	00 06
Ashford International	a	00 39	01 41	09 15	10 15	11 15	12 15	13 15	14 15	15 15	16 15	17 15	18 15	19 15	20 15	21 15	22 15	23 15	00 15
	d																		

Sundays
29 July to 12 August

		SE	SE	SE	SE	SE	SE	SE	SE	SE	SE	SE	SE	SE	SE	SE	SE	SE	SE	SE	SE
London Victoria	⊖ d	23p07	00 07	01 00	07 37	08 37	09 37	10 37	11 37	12 37	13 37	14 37	15 37	16 37	17 37	18 37	19 37	20 07	21 07	22 07	23 07
London Blackfriars	⊖195 d																				
Elephant & Castle	⊖195 d																				
Bromley South	195 d	23p23	00 25	01 16	07 53	08 53	09 53	10 53	11 53	12 53	13 53	14 53	15 53	16 53	17 53	18 53	19 53	20 23	21 23	22 23	23 23
St Mary Cray	195 d	23p30	00 32	01 23	08 00	09 00	10 00	11 00	12 00	13 00	14 00	15 00	16 00	17 00	18 00	19 00	20 00	20 30	21 30	22 30	23 30
Swanley	195 d	23p34	00 36	01 27	08 04	09 04	10 04	11 04	12 04	13 04	14 04	15 04	16 04	17 04	18 04	19 04	20 04	20 34	21 34	22 34	23 34
Otford	195 d	23p42	00 44	01 38	08 12	09 12	10 12	11 12	12 12	13 12	14 12	15 12	16 12	17 12	18 12	19 12	20 12	20 42	21 42	22 42	23 42
Kemsing	d	23p47	00 49	01 43	08 17	09 17	10 17	11 17	12 17	13 17	14 17	15 17	16 17	17 17	18 17	19 17	20 17	20 47	21 47	22 47	23 47
Borough Green & Wrotham	d	23p52	00 54	01 48	08 22	09 22	10 22	11 22	12 22	13 22	14 22	15 22	16 22	17 22	18 22	19 22	20 22	20 52	21 52	22 52	23 52
West Malling	d	23p58	01 00	01 54	08 28	09 28	10 28	11 28	12 28	13 28	14 28	15 28	16 28	17 28	18 28	19 28	20 28	20 58	21 58	22 58	23 59
East Malling	d	00 01	01 03	01 57	08 31	09 31	10 31	11 31	12 31	13 31	14 31	15 31	16 31	17 31	18 31	19 31	20 31	21 01	22 01	23 01	00 01
Barming	d	00 05	01 07	02 01	08 35	09 35	10 35	11 35	12 35	13 35	14 35	15 35	16 35	17 35	18 35	19 35	20 35	21 05	22 05	23 05	00 05
Maidstone East	a	00 09	01 11	02 05	08 40	09 40	10 40	11 40	12 40	13 40	14 40	15 40	16 40	17 40	18 40	19 40	20 40	21 10	22 10	23 10	00 10
	d	00 10	01 12	02 06	08 40	09 40	10 40	11 40	12 40	13 40	14 40	15 40	16 40	17 40	18 40	19 40	20 40	21 10	22 10	23 10	00 10
Bearsted	d	00 15	01 17	02 11	08 45	09 45	10 45	11 45	12 45	13 45	14 45	15 45	16 45	17 45	18 45	19 45	20 45	21 15	22 15	23 15	00 15
Hollingbourne	d	00 18	01 20	02 14	08 48	09 48	10 48	11 48	12 48	13 48	14 48	15 48	16 48	17 48	18 48	19 48	20 48	21 18	22 18	23 18	00 18
Harrietsham	d	00 22	01 24	02 18	08 52	09 52	10 52	11 52	12 52	13 52	14 52	15 52	16 52	17 52	18 52	19 52	20 52	21 22	22 22	23 22	00 22
Lenham	d	00 25	01 27	02 21	08 55	09 55	10 55	11 55	12 55	13 55	14 55	15 55	16 55	17 55	18 55	19 55	20 55	21 25	22 25	23 25	00 25
Charing	d	00 30	01 32	02 26	09 00	10 00	11 00	12 00	13 00	14 00	15 00	16 00	17 00	18 00	19 00	20 00	21 00	21 30	22 30	23 30	00 30
Ashford International	a	00 39	01 41	02 38	09 10	10 10	11 10	12 10	13 10	14 10	15 10	16 10	17 10	18 10	19 10	20 10	21 10	21 40	22 40	23 40	00 40
	d																				

London - Maidstone East and Ashford International

Sundays
26 August to 9 September

Network Diagram - see first Page of Table 195

		SE	SE	SE A	SE	SE	SE	SE	SE	SE	SE	SE	SE	SE	SE	SE	SE	SE	SE	SE
London Victoria	⊖ d	23p07	00 07	00 51	07 45	08 45	09 45	10 45	11 45	12 45	13 45	14 45	15 45	16 45	17 45	18 45	19 45	20 45	21 45	22 45
London Blackfriars	⊖195 d																			
Elephant & Castle	⊖195 d																			
Bromley South	195 d	23p23	00 25	01s10	08 01	09 01	10 01	11 01	12 01	13 01	14 01	15 01	16 01	17 01	18 01	19 01	20 01	21 01	22 01	23 01
St Mary Cray	195 d	23p30	00 32	01s17	08 08	09 08	10 08	11 08	12 08	13 08	14 08	15 08	16 08	17 08	18 08	19 08	20 08	21 08	22 08	23 08
Swanley	195 d	23p34	00 36	01s21	08 12	09 12	10 12	11 12	12 12	13 12	14 12	15 12	16 12	17 12	18 12	19 12	20 12	21 12	22 12	23 12
Otford	195 d	23p42	00 44	01s33	08 20	09 20	10 20	11 20	12 20	13 20	14 20	15 20	16 20	17 20	18 20	19 20	20 20	21 20	22 20	23 20
Kemsing	d	23p47	00 49	01s37																
Borough Green & Wrotham	d	23p52	00 54	01s42	08 28	09 28	10 28	11 28	12 28	13 28	14 28	15 28	16 28	17 28	18 28	19 28	20 28	21 28	22 28	23 28
West Malling	d	23p58	01 00	01s48	08 34	09 34	10 34	11 34	12 34	13 34	14 34	15 34	16 34	17 34	18 34	19 34	20 34	21 34	22 34	23 34
East Malling	d	00 01	01 03	01s51	08 37	09 37	10 37	11 37	12 37	13 37	14 37	15 37	16 37	17 37	18 37	19 37	20 37	21 37	22 37	23 37
Barming	d	00 05	01 07	01s55	08 41	09 41	10 41	11 41	12 41	13 41	14 41	15 41	16 41	17 41	18 41	19 41	20 41	21 41	22 41	23 41
Maidstone East	a	00 09	01 11	01s59	08 45	09 45	10 45	11 45	12 45	13 45	14 45	15 45	16 45	17 45	18 45	19 45	20 45	21 45	22 45	23 45
	d	00 10	01 12		08 46	09 46	10 46	11 46	12 46	13 46	14 46	15 46	16 46	17 46	18 46	19 46	20 46	21 46	22 46	23 46
Bearsted	d	00 15	01 17	02s04	08 51	09 51	10 51	11 51	12 51	13 51	14 51	15 51	16 51	17 51	18 51	19 51	20 51	21 51	22 51	23 51
Hollingbourne	d	00 18	01 20	02s08	08 54	09 54	10 54	11 54	12 54	13 54	14 54	15 54	16 54	17 54	18 54	19 54	20 54	21 54	22 54	23 54
Harrietsham	d	00 22	01 24	02s11	08 58	09 58	10 58	11 58	12 58	13 58	14 58	15 58	16 58	17 58	18 58	19 58	20 58	21 58	22 58	23 58
Lenham	d	00 25	01 27	02s15	09 01	10 01	11 01	12 01	13 01	14 01	15 01	16 01	17 01	18 01	19 01	20 01	21 01	22 01	23 01	00 01
Charing	d	00 30	01 32	02s20	09 06	10 06	11 06	12 06	13 06	14 06	15 06	16 06	17 06	18 06	19 06	20 06	21 06	22 06	23 06	00 06
Ashford International	a	00 39	01 41	02 27	09 15	10 15	11 15	12 15	13 15	14 15	15 15	16 15	17 15	18 15	19 15	20 15	21 15	22 15	23 15	00 15
	d																			

A not 26 August

Table 196

Mondays to Fridays

until 27 July, 13 Aug to 28 Aug and from 10 Sep

Ashford International and Maidstone East to London

Network Diagram - see first Page of Table 195

Miles	Miles	Miles				SE	SE	SE	SE	SE	SE A	SE B	SE	SE	SE	SE	SE	SE	SE	SE	SE	SE	SE	SE
14¼	—	0	**Ashford International**		a																			
—	—	—			d	05 20	05 44	05 50	06 03	06 16	06 25	06 25	06 40	06 58	07 15	07 47	08 26	08 47	09 30	09 47	10 30	10 47	11 30	11 47
20¼	—	—	Charing		d	05 28	05 53	05 58	06 11	06 24	06 33	06 33	06 48	07 06	07 23	07 55	08 34	08 55		09 55		10 55		11 55
24¼	—	—	Lenham		d	05 33	05 58	06 03	06 16	06 29	06 38	06 38	06 53	07 11	07 28	08 00	08 39	09 00		10 00		11 00		12 00
26	—	—	Harrietsham		d	05 36	06 01	06 06	06 19	06 32	06 41	06 41	06 56	07 14	07 31	08 03	08 42	09 03		10 03		11 03		12 03
28½	—	—	Hollingbourne		d	05 40	06 04	06 10	06 23	06 36	06 45	06 45	07 00	07 18	07 35	08 07	08 46	09 07		10 07		11 07		12 07
30¾	—	—	Bearsted		d	05 43	06 09	06 13	06 26	06 39	06 48	06 48	07 03	07 21	07 38	08 11	08 49	09 11	09 48	10 11	10 48	11 11	11 48	12 11
33½	—	—	**Maidstone East** 4		a	05 48	06 14	06 20	06 31	06 44	06 53	06 53	07 08	07 26	07 43	08 17	08 54	09 17	09 53	10 17	10 53	11 17	11 53	12 17
—	—	—			d	05 49	06 15	06 20	06 32	06 45	06 54	06 54	07 09	07 27	07 44	08 18	08 55	09 18	09 55	10 18	10 55	11 18	11 55	12 18
36	—	—	Barming		d	05 54		06 25	06 37	06 50	06 59	06 59	07 14	07 32	07 49	08 23		09 23		10 23		11 23		12 23
37¾	—	—	East Malling		d	05 57		06 29	06 41	06 54	07 03	07 03	07 18	07 36		08 26		09 26		10 26		11 26		12 26
38¾	—	—	West Malling		d	06 00	06 22	06 31	06 44	06 57	07 06	07 06	07 21	07 39	07 54	08 29	09 02	09 29	10 02	10 29	11 02	11 29	12 02	12 29
44	—	—	Borough Green & Wrotham		d	06 07	06 30	06 38	06 51	07 04	07 13	07 13	07 28	07 46	08 01	08 36	09 09	09 36	10 09	10 36	11 09	11 36	12 09	12 36
46½	—	—	Kemsing		d				06 55	07 08	07 17	07 17	07 32	07 50		08 40		09 40		10 40		11 40		12 40
49½	—	—	Otford 4	195	a	06 15	06 38	06 46	07 00	07 13	07 22	07 22	07 37	07 55	08 09	08 46	09 17	09 46	10 17	10 46	11 17	11 46	12 17	12 46
56	—	—	Swanley 4	195	a	06 24	06 47	06 54	07 09	07 22	07 31	07 31	07 46	08 04		08 54	09 25	09 54	10 25	10 54	11 25	11 54	12 25	12 54
58¾	—	—	St Mary Cray	195	a											08 58		09 58		10 58		11 58		12 58
62½	0	—	Bromley South 4	195	a	06 33	06 56	07 02	07 19	07 30	07 40	07 40	07 57	08 13	08 25	09 04	09 34	10 04	10 34	11 04	11 34	12 04	12 34	13 04
—	10¼	—	Elephant & Castle	⊖195	a		07 15				07 58	07 59												
—	11½	—	**London Blackfriars** 3	⊖195	a		07 22				08 03	08 04												
73½	—	—	**London Victoria** 15	⊖	a	06 51		07 22	07 43	07 53			08 23	08 36	08 53	09 23	09 51	10 21	10 51	11 21	11 51	12 21	12 51	13 21

			SE	SE	SE	SE	SE	SE	SE	SE	SE	SE	SE	SE	SE	SE	SE	SE	SE	SE	SE
Ashford International		a																			
		d	12 30	12 47	13 30	13 47	14 30	14 47	15 24	15 47	16 26	16 47	17 26	17 49		18 26	18 49	19 19	20 17	21 17	22 17
Charing		d		12 55		13 55		14 55	15 32	15 55	16 34	16 55	17 34	17 57		18 34	18 57	19 27	20 25	21 25	22 25
Lenham		d		13 00		14 00		15 00	15 37	16 00	16 39	17 00	17 39	18 02		18 39	19 02	19 32	20 30	21 30	22 30
Harrietsham		d		13 03		14 03		15 03	15 40	16 03	16 42	17 03	17 42	18 05		18 42	19 05	19 35	20 33	21 33	22 33
Hollingbourne		d		13 07		14 07		15 07	15 44	16 07	16 46	17 07	17 46	18 09		18 46	19 09	19 39	20 37	21 37	22 37
Bearsted		d	12 48	13 11	13 48	14 11	14 48	15 11	15 48	16 11	16 49	17 11	17 49	18 12		18 49	19 12	19 42	20 41	21 41	22 41
Maidstone East 4		a	12 53	13 17	13 53	14 17	14 53	15 17	15 53	16 17	16 54	17 17	17 54	18 17		18 54	19 17	19 47	20 47	21 47	22 47
		d	12 55	13 18	13 55	14 18	14 55	15 18	15 55	16 18	16 55	17 18	17 55	18 18	18 40	18 55	19 18	19 48	20 48	21 48	22 48
Barming		d		13 23		14 23		15 23		16 23		17 23		18 23			19 23	19 53	20 53	21 53	22 53
East Malling		d		13 26		14 26		15 26		16 26		17 26		18 26			19 26	19 56	20 56	21 56	22 56
West Malling		d	13 02	13 29	14 02	14 29	15 02	15 29	16 02	16 29	17 02	17 29	18 02	18 29	18 47	19 02	19 29	19 59	20 59	21 59	22 59
Borough Green & Wrotham		d	13 09	13 36	14 09	14 36	15 09	15 36	16 09	16 36	17 09	17 36	18 09	18 36	18 54	19 09	19 36	20 06	21 06	22 06	23 06
Kemsing		d		13 40		14 40		15 40		16 40		17 40		18 40			19 40	20 10	21 10	22 10	23 10
Otford 4	195	a	13 17	13 46	14 17	14 46	15 17	15 46	16 17	16 46	17 17	17 46	18 17	18 46		19 17	19 46	20 16	21 16	22 16	23 16
Swanley 4	195	a	13 25	13 54	14 25	14 54	15 25	15 54	16 25	16 54	17 25	17 54	18 25	18 54		19 25	19 54	20 24	21 24	22 24	23 24
St Mary Cray	195	a		13 58		14 58		15 58		16 58		17 58		18 58			19 58	20 28	21 28	22 28	23 28
Bromley South 4	195	a	13 34	14 04	14 34	15 04	15 34	16 04	16 34	17 04	17 34	18 05	18 34	19 04	19 16	19 34	20 04	20 34	21 34	22 34	23 34
Elephant & Castle	⊖195	a																			
London Blackfriars 3	⊖195	a																			
London Victoria 15	⊖	a	13 51	14 21	14 51	15 21	15 51	16 21	16 51	17 23	17 53	18 21	18 53	19 21	19 35	19 51	20 21	20 51	21 51	22 51	23 51

Mondays to Fridays

30 July to 10 August

			SE	SE	SE	SE	SE	SE	SE	SE	SE	SE	SE	SE	SE	SE	SE	SE	SE	SE	SE	SE	SE	SE
Ashford International		a																						
		d	05 20	05 44	05 50	06 03	06 16	06 25	06 40	06 58	07 15	07 47	08 26	08 47	09 30	09 47	10 30	10 47	11 30	11 47	12 30	12 47	13 30	13 47
Charing		d	05 28	05 53	05 58	06 11	06 24	06 33	06 48	07 06	07 23	07 55	08 34	08 55		09 55		10 55		11 55		12 55		13 55
Lenham		d	05 33	05 58	06 03	06 16	06 29	06 38	06 53	07 11	07 28	08 00	08 39	09 00		10 00		11 00		12 00		13 00		14 00
Harrietsham		d	05 36	06 01	06 06	06 19	06 32	06 41	06 56	07 14	07 31	08 03	08 42	09 03		10 03		11 03		12 03		13 03		14 03
Hollingbourne		d	05 40	06 04	06 10	06 23	06 36	06 45	07 00	07 18	07 35	08 07	08 46	09 07		10 07		11 07		12 07		13 07		14 07
Bearsted		d	05 43	06 09	06 13	06 26	06 39	06 48	07 03	07 21	07 38	08 11	08 49	09 11	09 48	10 11	10 48	11 11	11 48	12 11	12 48	13 11	13 48	14 11
Maidstone East 4		a	05 48	06 14	06 20	06 31	06 44	06 53	07 08	07 26	07 43	08 17	08 54	09 17	09 53	10 17	10 53	11 17	11 53	12 17	12 53	13 17	13 53	14 17
		d	05 49	06 15	06 20	06 32	06 45	06 54	07 09	07 27	07 44	08 18	08 55	09 18	09 55	10 18	10 55	11 18	11 55	12 18	12 55	13 18	13 55	14 18
Barming		d	05 54		06 25	06 37	06 50	06 59	07 14	07 32	07 49	08 23		09 23		10 23		11 23		12 23		13 23		14 23
East Malling		d	05 57		06 29	06 41	06 54	07 03	07 18	07 36		08 26		09 26		10 26		11 26		12 26		13 26		14 26
West Malling		d	06 00	06 22	06 31	06 44	06 57	07 06	07 21	07 39	07 54	08 29	09 02	09 29	10 02	10 29	11 02	11 29	12 02	12 29	13 02	13 29	14 02	14 29
Borough Green & Wrotham		d	06 07	06 30	06 38	06 51	07 04	07 13	07 28	07 46	08 01	08 36	09 09	09 36	10 09	10 36	11 09	11 36	12 09	12 36	13 09	13 36	14 09	14 36
Kemsing		d				06 55	07 08	07 17	07 32	07 50		08 40		09 40		10 40		11 40		12 40		13 40		14 40
Otford 4	195	a	06 15	06 38	06 46	07 00	07 13	07 22	07 37	07 55	08 09	08 46	09 17	09 46	10 17	10 46	11 17	11 46	12 17	12 46	13 17	13 46	14 17	14 46
Swanley 4	195	a	06 24	06 47	06 54	07 09	07 22	07 31	07 46	08 04		08 54	09 25	09 54	10 25	10 54	11 25	11 54	12 25	12 54	13 25	13 54	14 25	14 54
St Mary Cray	195	a										08 58		09 58		10 58		11 58		12 58		13 58		14 58
Bromley South 4	195	a	06 33	06 56	07 02	07 19	07 30	07 40	07 57	08 13	08 25	09 04	09 34	10 04	10 34	11 04	11 34	12 04	12 34	13 04	13 34	14 04	14 34	15 04
Elephant & Castle	⊖195	a		07 15				07 59																
London Blackfriars 3	⊖195	a		07 22				08 04																
London Victoria 15	⊖	a	06 51		07 22	07 43	07 53		08 23	08 36	08 53	09 23	09 51	10 21	10 51	11 21	11 51	12 21	12 51	13 21	13 51	14 21	14 51	15 21

A from 21 May until 27 July

B until 18 May

Table 196

Mondays to Fridays

30 July to 10 August

Ashford International and Maidstone East to London

Network Diagram - see first Page of Table 195

			SE	SE	SE	SE	SE	SE	SE	SE	SE	SE	SE	SE	SE	SE	SE
Ashford International		a															
		d	14 30	14 47	15 24	15 47	16 24	16 47	17 24	17 49		18 26	18 49	19 19	20 17	21 17	22 17
Charing		d		14 55	15 32	15 55	16 34	16 55	17 34	17 57		18 34	18 57	19 27	20 25	21 25	22 25
Lenham		d		15 00	15 37	16 00	16 39	17 00	17 39	18 02		18 39	19 02	19 32	20 30	21 30	22 30
Harrietsham		d		15 03	15 40	16 03	16 42	17 03	17 42	18 05		18 42	19 05	19 35	20 33	21 33	22 33
Hollingbourne		d		15 07	15 44	16 07	16 46	17 07	17 46	18 09		18 46	19 09	19 39	20 37	21 37	22 37
Bearsted		d	14 48	15 11	15 48	16 11	16 49	17 11	17 49	18 12		18 49	19 12	19 42	20 41	21 41	22 41
Maidstone East 4		a	14 53	15 17	15 53	16 17	16 54	17 17	17 54	18 17		18 54	19 17	19 47	20 47	21 47	22 47
		d	14 55	15 18	15 55	16 18	16 55	17 18	17 55	18 18	18 40	18 55	19 18	19 48	20 48	21 48	22 48
Barming		d		15 23		16 23		17 23		18 23			19 23	19 53	20 53	21 53	22 53
East Malling		d		15 26		16 26		17 26		18 26			19 26	19 56	20 56	21 56	22 56
West Malling		d	15 02	15 29	16 02	16 29	17 02	17 29	18 02	18 29	18 47	19 02	19 29	19 59	20 59	21 59	22 59
Borough Green & Wrotham		d	15 09	15 36	16 09	16 36	17 09	17 36	18 09	18 36	18 54	19 09	19 36	20 06	21 06	22 06	23 06
Kemsing		d		15 40		16 40		17 40		18 40			19 40	20 10	21 10	22 10	23 10
Otford 4	195	a	15 17	15 46	16 17	16 46	17 17	17 46	18 17	18 46		19 17	19 46	20 16	21 16	22 16	23 16
Swanley 4	195	a	15 25	15 54	16 25	16 54	17 25	17 54	18 25	18 54		19 25	19 54	20 24	21 24	22 24	23 24
St Mary Cray	195	a		15 58		16 58		17 58		18 58			19 58	20 28	21 28	22 28	23 28
Bromley South 4	195	a	15 34	16 04	16 34	17 04	17 34	18 05	18 34	19 04	19 16	19 34	20 04	20 34	21 34	22 34	23 34
Elephant & Castle	⊖195	a															
London Blackfriars 3	⊖195	a															
London Victoria 15	⊖	a	15 51	16 21	16 51	17 23	17 53	18 21	18 53	19 21	19 35	19 51	20 21	20 51	21 51	22 51	23 51

Mondays to Fridays

29 August to 7 September

			SE	SE	SE	SE	SE	SE	SE	SE	SE	SE	SE	SE	SE	SE	SE	SE	SE	SE	SE	SE	SE	SE
Ashford International		a																						
		d	05 20	05 44	05 50	06 03	06 16	06 25	06 40	06 58	07 15	07 47	08 26	08 47	09 30	09 47	10 30	10 47	11 30	11 47	12 30	12 47	13 30	13 47
Charing		d	05 28	05 53	05 58	06 11	06 24	06 33	06 48	07 06	07 23	07 55	08 34	08 55		09 55		10 55		11 55		12 55		13 55
Lenham		d	05 33	05 58	06 03	06 16	06 29	06 38	06 53	07 11	07 28	08 00	08 39	09 00		10 00		11 00		12 00		13 00		14 00
Harrietsham		d	05 36	06 01	06 06	06 19	06 32	06 41	06 56	07 14	07 31	08 03	08 42	09 03		10 03		11 03		12 03		13 03		14 03
Hollingbourne		d	05 40	06 04	06 10	06 23	06 36	06 45	07 00	07 18	07 35	08 07	08 46	09 07		10 07		11 07		12 07		13 07		14 07
Bearsted		d	05 43	06 09	06 13	06 26	06 39	06 48	07 03	07 21	07 38	08 11	08 49	09 11	09 48	10 11	10 48	11 11	11 48	12 11	12 48	13 11	13 48	14 11
Maidstone East 4		a	05 48	06 14	06 20	06 31	06 44	06 53	07 08	07 26	07 43	08 17	08 54	09 17	09 53	10 17	10 53	11 17	11 53	12 17	12 53	13 17	13 53	14 17
		d	05 49	06 15	06 20	06 32	06 45	06 54	07 09	07 27	07 44	08 18	08 55	09 18	09 55	10 18	10 55	11 18	11 55	12 18	12 55	13 18	13 55	14 18
Barming		d	05 54		06 25	06 37	06 50	06 59	07 14	07 32	07 49	08 23		09 23		10 23		11 23		12 23		13 23		14 23
East Malling		d	05 57		06 29	06 41	06 54	07 03	07 18	07 36		08 26		09 26		10 26		11 26		12 26		13 26		14 26
West Malling		d	06 00	06 22	06 31	06 44	06 57	07 06	07 21	07 39	07 54	08 29	09 02	09 29	10 02	10 29	11 02	11 29	12 02	12 29	13 02	13 29	14 02	14 29
Borough Green & Wrotham		d	06 07	06 30	06 38	06 51	07 04	07 13	07 28	07 46	08 01	08 36	09 09	09 36	10 09	10 36	11 09	11 36	12 09	12 36	13 09	13 36	14 09	14 36
Kemsing		d				06 55	07 08	07 17	07 32	07 50		08 40		09 40		10 40		11 40		12 40		13 40		14 40
Otford 4	195	a	06 15	06 38	06 46	07 00	07 13	07 22	07 37	07 55	08 09	08 46	09 17	09 46	10 17	10 46	11 17	11 46	12 17	12 46	13 17	13 46	14 17	14 46
Swanley 4	195	a	06 24	06 47	06 54	07 09	07 22	07 31	07 46	08 04		08 54	09 25	09 54	10 25	10 54	11 25	11 54	12 25	12 54	13 25	13 54	14 25	14 54
St Mary Cray	195	a										08 58		09 58		10 58		11 58		12 58		13 58		14 58
Bromley South 4	195	a	06 33	06 56	07 02	07 19	07 30	07 40	07 57	08 13	08 25	09 04	09 34	10 04	10 34	11 04	11 34	12 04	12 34	13 04	13 34	14 04	14 34	15 04
Elephant & Castle	⊖195	a		07 15				07 58																
London Blackfriars 3	⊖195	a		07 22				08 03																
London Victoria 15	⊖	a	06 51		07 22	07 43	07 53		08 23	08 36	08 53	09 23	09 51	10 21	10 51	11 21	11 51	12 21	12 51	13 21	13 51	14 21	14 51	15 21

			SE	SE	SE	SE	SE	SE	SE	SE	SE	SE	SE	SE	SE	SE	SE
Ashford International		a															
		d	14 30	14 47	15 24	15 47	16 26	16 47	17 26	17 49		18 26	18 49	19 19	20 17	21 17	22 17
Charing		d		14 55	15 32	15 55	16 34	16 55	17 34	17 57		18 34	18 57	19 27	20 25	21 25	22 25
Lenham		d		15 00	15 37	16 00	16 39	17 00	17 39	18 02		18 39	19 02	19 32	20 30	21 30	22 30
Harrietsham		d		15 03	15 40	16 03	16 42	17 03	17 42	18 05		18 42	19 05	19 35	20 33	21 33	22 33
Hollingbourne		d		15 07	15 44	16 07	16 46	17 07	17 46	18 09		18 46	19 09	19 39	20 37	21 37	22 37
Bearsted		d	14 48	15 11	15 48	16 11	16 49	17 11	17 49	18 12		18 49	19 12	19 42	20 41	21 41	22 41
Maidstone East 4		a	14 53	15 17	15 53	16 17	16 54	17 17	17 54	18 17		18 54	19 17	19 47	20 47	21 47	22 47
		d	14 55	15 18	15 55	16 18	16 55	17 18	17 55	18 18	18 40	18 55	19 18	19 48	20 48	21 48	22 48
Barming		d		15 23		16 23		17 23		18 23			19 23	19 53	20 53	21 53	22 53
East Malling		d		15 26		16 26		17 26		18 26			19 26	19 56	20 56	21 56	22 56
West Malling		d	15 02	15 29	16 02	16 29	17 02	17 29	18 02	18 29	18 47	19 02	19 29	19 59	20 59	21 59	22 59
Borough Green & Wrotham		d	15 09	15 36	16 09	16 36	17 09	17 36	18 09	18 36	18 54	19 09	19 36	20 06	21 06	22 06	23 06
Kemsing		d		15 40		16 40		17 40		18 40			19 40	20 10	21 10	22 10	23 10
Otford 4	195	a	15 17	15 46	16 17	16 46	17 17	17 46	18 17	18 46		19 17	19 46	20 16	21 16	22 16	23 16
Swanley 4	195	a	15 25	15 54	16 25	16 54	17 25	17 54	18 25	18 54		19 25	19 54	20 24	21 24	22 24	23 24
St Mary Cray	195	a		15 58		16 58		17 58		18 58			19 58	20 28	21 28	22 28	23 28
Bromley South 4	195	a	15 34	16 04	16 34	17 04	17 34	18 05	18 34	19 04	19 16	19 34	20 04	20 34	21 34	22 34	23 34
Elephant & Castle	⊖195	a															
London Blackfriars 3	⊖195	a															
London Victoria 15	⊖	a	15 51	16 21	16 51	17 23	17 53	18 21	18 53	19 21	19 35	19 51	20 21	20 51	21 51	22 51	23 51

Table 196

Ashford International and Maidstone East to London

Saturdays
until 21 July, 18 Aug and from 15 Sep

Network Diagram - see first Page of Table 195

			SE 1	SE 1	SE 1	SE 1	SE 1	SE 1	SE 1	SE 1	SE 1	SE 1	SE 1	SE 1	SE 1	SE 1	SE 1	SE 1	SE 1	SE 1	SE 1	SE 1	SE 1	SE 1
Ashford International	≡	a																						
		d	05 20	05 47	06 30	06 47	07 30	07 47	08 30	08 47	09 30	09 47	10 30	10 47	11 30	11 47	12 30	12 47	13 30	13 47	14 30	14 47	15 30	15 47
Charing		d	05 28	05 55		06 55		07 55		08 55		09 55		10 55		11 55		12 55		13 55		14 55		15 55
Lenham		d	05 33	06 00		07 00		08 00		09 00		10 00		11 00		12 00		13 00		14 00		15 00		16 00
Harrietsham		d	05 36	06 03		07 03		08 03		09 03		10 03		11 03		12 03		13 03		14 03		15 03		16 03
Hollingbourne		d	05 40	06 07		07 07		08 07		09 07		10 07		11 07		12 07		13 07		14 07		15 07		16 07
Bearsted		d	05 43	06 11	06 48	07 11	07 48	08 11	08 48	09 11	09 48	10 11	10 48	11 11	11 48	12 11	12 48	13 11	13 48	14 11	14 48	15 11	15 48	16 11
Maidstone East 4		a	05 48	06 17	06 53	07 17	07 53	08 17	08 53	09 17	09 53	10 17	10 53	11 17	11 53	12 17	12 53	13 17	13 53	14 17	14 53	15 17	15 53	16 17
		d	05 49	06 18	06 55	07 18	07 55	08 18	08 55	09 18	09 55	10 18	10 55	11 18	11 55	12 18	12 55	13 18	13 55	14 18	14 55	15 18	15 55	16 18
Barming		d	05 54	06 23		07 23		08 23		09 23		10 23		11 23		12 23		13 23		14 23		15 23		16 23
East Malling		d	05 58	06 26		07 26		08 26		09 26		10 26		11 26		12 26		13 26		14 26		15 26		16 26
West Malling		d	06 01	06 29	07 02	07 29	08 02	08 29	09 02	09 29	10 02	10 29	11 02	11 29	12 02	12 29	13 02	13 29	14 02	14 29	15 02	15 29	16 02	16 29
Borough Green & Wrotham		d	06 08	06 36	07 09	07 36	08 09	08 36	09 09	09 36	10 09	10 36	11 09	11 36	12 09	12 36	13 09	13 36	14 09	14 36	15 09	15 36	16 09	16 36
Kemsing		d		06 40		07 40		08 40		09 40		10 40		11 40		12 40		13 40		14 40		15 40		16 40
Otford 4	195	a	06 16	06 46	07 17	07 46	08 17	08 46	09 17	09 46	10 17	10 46	11 17	11 46	12 17	12 46	13 17	13 46	14 17	14 46	15 17	15 46	16 17	16 46
Swanley 4	195	a	06 24	06 54	07 25	07 54	08 25	08 54	09 25	09 54	10 25	10 54	11 25	11 54	12 25	12 54	13 25	13 54	14 25	14 54	15 25	15 54	16 25	16 54
St Mary Cray	195	a	06 28	06 58		07 58		08 58		09 58		10 58		11 58		12 58		13 58		14 58		15 58		16 58
Bromley South 4	195	a	06 34	07 04	07 34	08 04	08 34	09 04	09 34	10 04	10 34	11 04	11 34	12 04	12 34	13 04	13 34	14 04	14 34	15 04	15 34	16 04	16 34	17 04
Elephant & Castle	⊖195	a																						
London Blackfriars 3	⊖195	a																						
London Victoria 15	⊖	a	06 51	07 21	07 51	08 21	08 51	09 21	09 51	10 21	10 51	11 21	11 51	12 21	12 51	13 21	13 51	14 21	14 51	15 21	15 51	16 21	16 51	17 21

			SE 1	SE 1	SE 1	SE 1	SE 1	SE 1	SE 1	SE 1	SE 1
Ashford International	≡	a									
		d	16 30	16 47	17 30	17 47	18 30	18 47	19 47	20 47	22 17
Charing		d		16 55		17 55		18 55	19 55	20 55	22 25
Lenham		d		17 00		18 00		19 00	20 00	21 00	22 30
Harrietsham		d		17 03		18 03		19 03	20 03	21 03	22 33
Hollingbourne		d		17 07		18 07		19 07	20 07	21 07	22 37
Bearsted		d	16 48	17 11	17 48	18 11	18 48	19 11	20 11	21 11	22 41
Maidstone East 4		a	16 53	17 17	17 53	18 17	18 53	19 17	20 17	21 17	22 47
		d	16 55	17 18	17 55	18 18	18 55	19 18	20 18	21 18	22 48
Barming		d		17 23		18 23		19 23	20 23	21 23	22 53
East Malling		d		17 26		18 26		19 26	20 26	21 26	22 56
West Malling		d	17 02	17 29	18 02	18 29	19 02	19 29	20 29	21 29	22 59
Borough Green & Wrotham		d	17 09	17 36	18 09	18 36	19 09	19 36	20 36	21 36	23 06
Kemsing		d		17 40		18 40		19 40	20 40	21 40	23 10
Otford 4	195	a	17 17	17 46	18 17	18 46	19 17	19 46	20 46	21 46	23 16
Swanley 4	195	a	17 25	17 54	18 25	18 54	19 25	19 54	20 54	21 54	23 24
St Mary Cray	195	a		17 58		18 58		19 58	20 58	21 58	23 28
Bromley South 4	195	a	17 34	18 04	18 34	19 04	19 34	20 04	21 04	22 04	23 34
Elephant & Castle	⊖195	a									
London Blackfriars 3	⊖195	a									
London Victoria 15	⊖	a	17 51	18 21	18 51	19 21	19 51	20 21	21 21	22 21	23 51

Saturdays
28 July to 11 August

			SE 1	SE 1	SE 1	SE 1	SE 1	SE 1	SE 1	SE 1	SE 1	SE 1	SE 1	SE 1	SE 1	SE 1	SE 1	SE 1	SE 1	SE 1	SE 1	SE 1	SE 1	SE 1
Ashford International	≡	a																						
		d	05 20	05 47	06 30	06 47	07 30	07 47	08 30	08 47	09 30	09 47	10 30	10 47	11 30	11 47	12 30	12 47	13 30	13 47	14 30	14 47	15 30	15 47
Charing		d	05 28	05 55		06 55		07 55		08 55		09 55		10 55		11 55		12 55		13 55		14 55		15 55
Lenham		d	05 33	06 00		07 00		08 00		09 00		10 00		11 00		12 00		13 00		14 00		15 00		16 00
Harrietsham		d	05 36	06 03		07 03		08 03		09 03		10 03		11 03		12 03		13 03		14 03		15 03		16 03
Hollingbourne		d	05 40	06 07		07 07		08 07		09 07		10 07		11 07		12 07		13 07		14 07		15 07		16 07
Bearsted		d	05 43	06 11	06 48	07 11	07 48	08 11	08 48	09 11	09 48	10 11	10 48	11 11	11 48	12 11	12 48	13 11	13 48	14 11	14 48	15 11	15 48	16 11
Maidstone East 4		a	05 48	06 17	06 53	07 17	07 53	08 17	08 53	09 17	09 53	10 17	10 53	11 17	11 53	12 17	12 53	13 17	13 53	14 17	14 53	15 17	15 53	16 17
		d	05 49	06 18	06 55	07 18	07 55	08 18	08 55	09 18	09 55	10 18	10 55	11 18	11 55	12 18	12 55	13 18	13 55	14 18	14 55	15 18	15 55	16 18
Barming		d	05 54	06 23		07 23		08 23		09 23		10 23		11 23		12 23		13 23		14 23		15 23		16 23
East Malling		d	05 58	06 26		07 26		08 26		09 26		10 26		11 26		12 26		13 26		14 26		15 26		16 26
West Malling		d	06 01	06 29	07 02	07 29	08 02	08 29	09 02	09 29	10 02	10 29	11 02	11 29	12 02	12 29	13 02	13 29	14 02	14 29	15 02	15 29	16 02	16 29
Borough Green & Wrotham		d	06 08	06 36	07 09	07 36	08 09	08 36	09 09	09 36	10 09	10 36	11 09	11 36	12 09	12 36	13 09	13 36	14 09	14 36	15 09	15 36	16 09	16 36
Kemsing		d		06 40		07 40		08 40		09 40		10 40		11 40		12 40		13 40		14 40		15 40		16 40
Otford 4	195	a	06 16	06 46	07 17	07 46	08 17	08 46	09 17	09 46	10 17	10 46	11 17	11 46	12 17	12 46	13 17	13 46	14 17	14 46	15 17	15 46	16 17	16 46
Swanley 4	195	a	06 24	06 54	07 25	07 54	08 25	08 54	09 25	09 54	10 25	10 54	11 25	11 54	12 25	12 54	13 25	13 54	14 25	14 54	15 25	15 54	16 25	16 54
St Mary Cray	195	a	06 28	06 58		07 58		08 58		09 58		10 58		11 58		12 58		13 58		14 58		15 58		16 58
Bromley South 4	195	a	06 34	07 04	07 34	08 04	08 34	09 04	09 34	10 04	10 34	11 04	11 34	12 04	12 34	13 04	13 34	14 04	14 34	15 04	15 34	16 04	16 34	17 04
Elephant & Castle	⊖195	a																						
London Blackfriars 3	⊖195	a																						
London Victoria 15	⊖	a	06 51	07 21	07 51	08 21	08 51	09 21	09 51	10 21	10 51	11 21	11 51	12 21	12 51	13 21	13 51	14 21	14 51	15 21	15 51	16 21	16 51	17 21

Table 196

Ashford International and Maidstone East to London

Saturdays
28 July to 11 August

Network Diagram - see first Page of Table 195

			SE 1	SE 1	SE 1	SE 1	SE 1	SE 1	SE 1	SE 1	SE 1
Ashford International	≡	a									
		d	16 30	16 47	17 30	17 47	18 30	18 47	19 47	20 47	22 17
Charing		d		16 55		17 55		18 55	19 55	20 55	22 25
Lenham		d		17 00		18 00		19 00	20 00	21 00	22 30
Harrietsham		d		17 03		18 03		19 03	20 03	21 03	22 33
Hollingbourne		d		17 07		18 07		19 07	20 07	21 07	22 37
Bearsted		d	16 48	17 11	17 48	18 11	18 48	19 11	20 11	21 11	22 41
Maidstone East 4		a	16 53	17 17	17 53	18 17	18 53	19 17	20 17	21 17	22 47
		d	16 55	17 18	17 55	18 18	18 55	19 18	20 18	21 18	22 48
Barming		d		17 23		18 23		19 23	20 23	21 23	22 53
East Malling		d		17 26		18 26		19 26	20 26	21 26	22 56
West Malling		d	17 02	17 29	18 02	18 29	19 02	19 29	20 29	21 29	22 59
Borough Green & Wrotham		d	17 09	17 36	18 09	18 36	19 09	19 36	20 36	21 36	23 06
Kemsing		d		17 40		18 40		19 40	20 40	21 40	23 10
Otford 4	195	a	17 17	17 46	18 17	18 46	19 17	19 46	20 46	21 46	23 16
Swanley 4	195	a	17 25	17 54	18 25	18 54	19 25	19 54	20 54	21 54	23 24
St Mary Cray	195	a		17 58		18 58		19 58	20 58	21 58	23 28
Bromley South 4	195	a	17 34	18 04	18 34	19 04	19 34	20 04	21 04	22 04	23 34
Elephant & Castle	⊖195	a									
London Blackfriars 3	⊖195	a									
London Victoria 15	⊖	a	17 51	18 21	18 51	19 21	19 51	20 21	21 21	22 21	23 51

Saturdays
25 August to 8 September

			SE 1	SE 1	SE 1	SE 1	SE 1	SE 1	SE 1	SE 1	SE 1	SE 1	SE 1	SE 1	SE 1	SE 1	SE 1	SE 1	SE 1	SE 1	SE 1	SE 1	SE 1	SE 1
Ashford International	≡	a																						
		d	05 20	05 47	06 30	06 47	07 30	07 47	08 30	08 47	09 30	09 47	10 30	10 47	11 30	11 47	12 30	12 47	13 30	13 47	14 30	14 47	15 30	15 47
Charing		d	05 28	05 55		06 55		07 55		08 55		09 55		10 55		11 55		12 55		13 55		14 55		15 55
Lenham		d	05 33	06 00		07 00		08 00		09 00		10 00		11 00		12 00		13 00		14 00		15 00		16 00
Harrietsham		d	05 36	06 03		07 03		08 03		09 03		10 03		11 03		12 03		13 03		14 03		15 03		16 03
Hollingbourne		d	05 40	06 07		07 07		08 07		09 07		10 07		11 07		12 07		13 07		14 07		15 07		16 07
Bearsted		d	05 43	06 11	06 48	07 11	07 48	08 11	08 48	09 11	09 48	10 11	10 48	11 11	11 48	12 11	12 48	13 11	13 48	14 11	14 48	15 11	15 48	16 11
Maidstone East 4		a	05 48	06 17	06 53	07 17	07 53	08 17	08 53	09 17	09 53	10 17	10 53	11 17	11 53	12 17	12 53	13 17	13 53	14 17	14 53	15 17	15 53	16 17
		d	05 49	06 18	06 55	07 18	07 55	08 18	08 55	09 18	09 55	10 18	10 55	11 18	11 55	12 18	12 55	13 18	13 55	14 18	14 55	15 18	15 55	16 18
Barming		d	05 54	06 23		07 23		08 23		09 23		10 23		11 23		12 23		13 23		14 23		15 23		16 23
East Malling		d	05 58	06 26		07 26		08 26		09 26		10 26		11 26		12 26		13 26		14 26		15 26		16 26
West Malling		d	06 01	06 29	07 02	07 29	08 02	08 29	09 02	09 29	10 02	10 29	11 02	11 29	12 02	12 29	13 02	13 29	14 02	14 29	15 02	15 29	16 02	16 29
Borough Green & Wrotham		d	06 08	06 36	07 09	07 36	08 09	08 36	09 09	09 36	10 09	10 36	11 09	11 36	12 09	12 36	13 09	13 36	14 09	14 36	15 09	15 36	16 09	16 36
Kemsing		d		06 40		07 40		08 40		09 40		10 40		11 40		12 40		13 40		14 40		15 40		16 40
Otford 4	195	a	06 16	06 46	07 17	07 46	08 17	08 46	09 17	09 46	10 17	10 46	11 17	11 46	12 17	12 46	13 17	13 46	14 17	14 46	15 17	15 46	16 17	16 46
Swanley 4	195	a	06 24	06 54	07 25	07 54	08 25	08 54	09 25	09 54	10 25	10 54	11 25	11 54	12 25	12 54	13 25	13 54	14 25	14 54	15 25	15 54	16 25	16 54
St Mary Cray	195	a	06 28	06 58		07 58		08 58		09 58		10 58		11 58		12 58		13 58		14 58		15 58		16 58
Bromley South 4	195	a	06 34	07 04	07 34	08 04	08 34	09 04	09 34	10 04	10 34	11 04	11 34	12 04	12 34	13 04	13 34	14 04	14 34	15 04	15 34	16 04	16 34	17 04
Elephant & Castle	⊖195	a																						
London Blackfriars 3	⊖195	a																						
London Victoria 15	⊖	a	06 51	07 21	07 51	08 21	08 51	09 21	09 51	10 21	10 51	11 21	11 51	12 21	12 51	13 21	13 51	14 21	14 51	15 21	15 51	16 21	16 51	17 21

			SE 1	SE 1	SE 1	SE 1	SE 1	SE 1	SE 1	SE 1	SE 1
Ashford International	≡	a									
		d	16 30	16 47	17 30	17 47	18 30	18 47	19 47	20 47	22 17
Charing		d		16 55		17 55		18 55	19 55	20 55	22 25
Lenham		d		17 00		18 00		19 00	20 00	21 00	22 30
Harrietsham		d		17 03		18 03		19 03	20 03	21 03	22 33
Hollingbourne		d		17 07		18 07		19 07	20 07	21 07	22 37
Bearsted		d	16 48	17 11	17 48	18 11	18 48	19 11	20 11	21 11	22 41
Maidstone East 4		a	16 53	17 17	17 53	18 17	18 53	19 17	20 17	21 17	22 47
		d	16 55	17 18	17 55	18 18	18 55	19 18	20 18	21 18	22 48
Barming		d		17 23		18 23		19 23	20 23	21 23	22 53
East Malling		d		17 26		18 26		19 26	20 26	21 26	22 56
West Malling		d	17 02	17 29	18 02	18 29	19 02	19 29	20 29	21 29	22 59
Borough Green & Wrotham		d	17 09	17 36	18 09	18 36	19 09	19 36	20 36	21 36	23 06
Kemsing		d		17 40		18 40		19 40	20 40	21 40	23 10
Otford 4	195	a	17 17	17 46	18 17	18 46	19 17	19 46	20 46	21 46	23 16
Swanley 4	195	a	17 25	17 54	18 25	18 54	19 25	19 54	20 54	21 54	23 24
St Mary Cray	195	a		17 58		18 58		19 58	20 58	21 58	23 28
Bromley South 4	195	a	17 34	18 04	18 34	19 04	19 34	20 04	21 04	22 04	23 34
Elephant & Castle	⊖195	a									
London Blackfriars 3	⊖195	a									
London Victoria 15	⊖	a	17 51	18 21	18 51	19 21	19 51	20 21	21 21	22 21	23 51

Table 196

Ashford International and Maidstone East to London

Sundays

until 22 July, 19 Aug and from 16 Sep

Network Diagram - see first Page of Table 195

		SE [1]	SE [1]	SE [1]	SE [1]	SE [1]	SE [1]	SE [1]	SE [1]	SE [1]	SE [1]	SE [1]	SE [1]	SE [1]	SE [1]	SE [1]	SE [1]
Ashford International	a																
	d	06 47	07 47	08 47	09 47	10 47	11 47	12 47	13 47	14 47	15 47	16 47	17 47	18 47	19 47	20 47	21 47
Charing	d	06 55	07 55	08 55	09 55	10 55	11 55	12 55	13 55	14 55	15 55	16 55	17 55	18 55	19 55	20 55	21 55
Lenham	d	07 00	08 00	09 00	10 00	11 00	12 00	13 00	14 00	15 00	16 00	17 00	18 00	19 00	20 00	21 00	22 00
Harrietsham	d	07 03	08 03	09 03	10 03	11 03	12 03	13 03	14 03	15 03	16 03	17 03	18 03	19 03	20 03	21 03	22 03
Hollingbourne	d	07 07	08 07	09 07	10 07	11 07	12 07	13 07	14 07	15 07	16 07	17 07	18 07	19 07	20 07	21 07	22 07
Bearsted	d	07 11	08 11	09 11	10 11	11 11	12 11	13 11	14 11	15 11	16 11	17 11	18 11	19 11	20 11	21 11	22 11
Maidstone East [4]	a	07 16	08 16	09 16	10 16	11 16	12 16	13 16	14 16	15 16	16 16	17 16	18 16	19 16	20 16	21 16	22 16
	d	07 16	08 16	09 16	10 16	11 16	12 16	13 16	14 16	15 16	16 16	17 16	18 16	19 16	20 16	21 16	22 16
Barming	d	07 21	08 21	09 21	10 21	11 21	12 21	13 21	14 21	15 21	16 21	17 21	18 21	19 21	20 21	21 21	22 21
East Malling	d	07 25	08 25	09 25	10 25	11 25	12 25	13 25	14 25	15 25	16 25	17 25	18 25	19 25	20 25	21 25	22 25
West Malling	d	07 28	08 28	09 28	10 28	11 28	12 28	13 28	14 28	15 28	16 28	17 28	18 28	19 28	20 28	21 28	22 28
Borough Green & Wrotham	d	07 35	08 35	09 35	10 35	11 35	12 35	13 35	14 35	15 35	16 35	17 35	18 35	19 35	20 35	21 35	22 35
Kemsing	d																
Otford [4] 195	a	07 43	08 43	09 43	10 43	11 43	12 43	13 43	14 43	15 43	16 43	17 43	18 43	19 43	20 43	21 43	22 43
Swanley [4] 195	a	07 51	08 51	09 51	10 51	11 51	12 51	13 51	14 51	15 51	16 51	17 51	18 51	19 51	20 51	21 51	22 51
St Mary Cray 195	a	07 55	08 55	09 55	10 55	11 55	12 55	13 55	14 55	15 55	16 55	17 55	18 55	19 55	20 55	21 55	22 55
Bromley South [4] 195	a	08 02	09 02	10 02	11 02	12 02	13 02	14 02	15 02	16 02	17 02	18 02	19 02	20 02	21 02	22 02	23 02
Elephant & Castle ⊖195	a																
London Blackfriars [3] ⊖195	a																
London Victoria [15] ⊖	a	08 18	09 18	10 18	11 18	12 18	13 18	14 18	15 18	16 18	17 18	18 18	19 18	20 18	21 18	22 18	23 18

Sundays

29 July to 12 August

		SE [1]	SE [1]	SE [1]	SE [1]	SE [1]	SE [1]	SE [1]	SE [1]	SE [1]	SE [1]	SE [1]	SE [1]	SE [1]	SE [1]	SE [1]	SE [1]	SE [1]	SE [1]
Ashford International	a																		
	d	05 20	05 47	06 47	07 47	08 47	09 47	10 47	11 47	12 47	13 47	14 47	15 47	16 47	17 47	18 47	19 47	20 47	22 17
Charing	d	05 28	05 55	06 55	07 55	08 55	09 55	10 55	11 55	12 55	13 55	14 55	15 55	16 55	17 55	18 55	19 55	20 55	22 25
Lenham	d	05 33	06 00	07 00	08 00	09 00	10 00	11 00	12 00	13 00	14 00	15 00	16 00	17 00	18 00	19 00	20 00	21 00	22 30
Harrietsham	d	05 36	06 03	07 03	08 03	09 03	10 03	11 03	12 03	13 03	14 03	15 03	16 03	17 03	18 03	19 03	20 03	21 03	22 33
Hollingbourne	d	05 40	06 07	07 07	08 07	09 07	10 07	11 07	12 07	13 07	14 07	15 07	16 07	17 07	18 07	19 07	20 07	21 07	22 37
Bearsted	d	05 43	06 11	07 11	08 11	09 11	10 11	11 11	12 11	13 11	14 11	15 11	16 11	17 11	18 11	19 11	20 11	21 11	22 41
Maidstone East [4]	a	05 49	06 17	07 17	08 17	09 17	10 17	11 17	12 17	13 17	14 17	15 17	16 17	17 17	18 17	19 17	20 17	21 17	22 47
	d	05 49	06 18	07 18	08 18	09 18	10 18	11 18	12 18	13 18	14 18	15 18	16 18	17 18	18 18	19 18	20 18	21 18	22 48
Barming	d	05 54	06 23	07 23	08 23	09 23	10 23	11 23	12 23	13 23	14 23	15 23	16 23	17 23	18 23	19 23	20 23	21 23	22 53
East Malling	d	05 58	06 26	07 26	08 26	09 26	10 26	11 26	12 26	13 26	14 26	15 26	16 26	17 26	18 26	19 26	20 26	21 26	22 56
West Malling	d	06 01	06 29	07 29	08 29	09 29	10 29	11 29	12 29	13 29	14 29	15 29	16 29	17 29	18 29	19 29	20 29	21 29	22 59
Borough Green & Wrotham	d	06 08	06 36	07 36	08 36	09 36	10 36	11 36	12 36	13 36	14 36	15 36	16 36	17 36	18 36	19 36	20 36	21 36	23 06
Kemsing	d		06 40	07 40	08 40	09 40	10 40	11 40	12 40	13 40	14 40	15 40	16 40	17 40	18 40	19 40	20 40	21 40	23 10
Otford [4] 195	a	06 16	06 46	07 46	08 46	09 46	10 46	11 46	12 46	13 46	14 46	15 46	16 46	17 46	18 46	19 46	20 46	21 46	23 16
Swanley [4] 195	a	06 24	06 54	07 54	08 54	09 54	10 54	11 54	12 54	13 54	14 54	15 54	16 54	17 54	18 54	19 54	20 54	21 54	23 24
St Mary Cray 195	a	06 28	06 58	07 58	08 58	09 58	10 58	11 58	12 58	13 58	14 58	15 58	16 58	17 58	18 58	19 58	20 58	21 58	23 28
Bromley South [4] 195	a	06 34	07 04	08 04	09 04	10 04	11 04	12 04	13 04	14 04	15 04	16 04	17 04	18 04	19 04	20 04	21 04	22 04	23 34
Elephant & Castle ⊖195	a																		
London Blackfriars [3] ⊖195	a																		
London Victoria [15] ⊖	a	06 51	07 21	08 21	09 21	10 21	11 21	12 21	13 21	14 21	15 21	16 21	17 21	18 21	19 21	20 21	21 21	22 21	23 51

Sundays

26 August to 9 September

		SE [1]	SE [1]	SE [1]	SE [1]	SE [1]	SE [1]	SE [1]	SE [1]	SE [1]	SE [1]	SE [1]	SE [1]	SE [1]	SE [1]	SE [1]	SE [1]
Ashford International	a																
	d	06 47	07 47	08 47	09 47	10 47	11 47	12 47	13 47	14 47	15 47	16 47	17 47	18 47	19 47	20 47	21 47
Charing	d	06 55	07 55	08 55	09 55	10 55	11 55	12 55	13 55	14 55	15 55	16 55	17 55	18 55	19 55	20 55	21 55
Lenham	d	07 00	08 00	09 00	10 00	11 00	12 00	13 00	14 00	15 00	16 00	17 00	18 00	19 00	20 00	21 00	22 00
Harrietsham	d	07 03	08 03	09 03	10 03	11 03	12 03	13 03	14 03	15 03	16 03	17 03	18 03	19 03	20 03	21 03	22 03
Hollingbourne	d	07 07	08 07	09 07	10 07	11 07	12 07	13 07	14 07	15 07	16 07	17 07	18 07	19 07	20 07	21 07	22 07
Bearsted	d	07 11	08 11	09 11	10 11	11 11	12 11	13 11	14 11	15 11	16 11	17 11	18 11	19 11	20 11	21 11	22 11
Maidstone East [4]	a	07 16	08 16	09 16	10 16	11 16	12 16	13 16	14 16	15 16	16 16	17 16	18 16	19 16	20 16	21 16	22 16
	d	07 16	08 16	09 16	10 16	11 16	12 16	13 16	14 16	15 16	16 16	17 16	18 16	19 16	20 16	21 16	22 16
Barming	d	07 21	08 21	09 21	10 21	11 21	12 21	13 21	14 21	15 21	16 21	17 21	18 21	19 21	20 21	21 21	22 21
East Malling	d	07 25	08 25	09 25	10 25	11 25	12 25	13 25	14 25	15 25	16 25	17 25	18 25	19 25	20 25	21 25	22 25
West Malling	d	07 28	08 28	09 28	10 28	11 28	12 28	13 28	14 28	15 28	16 28	17 28	18 28	19 28	20 28	21 28	22 28
Borough Green & Wrotham	d	07 35	08 35	09 35	10 35	11 35	12 35	13 35	14 35	15 35	16 35	17 35	18 35	19 35	20 35	21 35	22 35
Kemsing	d																
Otford [4] 195	a	07 43	08 43	09 43	10 43	11 43	12 43	13 43	14 43	15 43	16 43	17 43	18 43	19 43	20 43	21 43	22 43
Swanley [4] 195	a	07 51	08 51	09 51	10 51	11 51	12 51	13 51	14 51	15 51	16 51	17 51	18 51	19 51	20 51	21 51	22 51
St Mary Cray 195	a	07 55	08 55	09 55	10 55	11 55	12 55	13 55	14 55	15 55	16 55	17 55	18 55	19 55	20 55	21 55	22 55
Bromley South [4] 195	a	08 02	09 02	10 02	11 02	12 02	13 02	14 02	15 02	16 02	17 02	18 02	19 02	20 02	21 02	22 02	23 02
Elephant & Castle ⊖195	a																
London Blackfriars [3] ⊖195	a																
London Victoria [15] ⊖	a	08 18	09 18	10 18	11 18	12 18	13 18	14 18	15 18	16 18	17 18	18 18	19 18	20 18	21 18	22 18	23 18

Table 199

Mondays to Fridays

until 27 July, 13 Aug to 28 Aug and from 10 Sep

London - Lewisham, Hither Green, Petts Wood and Orpington (Summary of Services)

		SE MX	SE MX	SE MO [1] A	SE MX [1]	SE MO A	SE MX B	SE MO A	SE MX	SE MX	SE MO A	SE MX	SE MX	SE MX	SE MX	SE	SE	SE	SE	SE	SE	SE	SE
London Charing Cross [4] ⊖	d		23p36	23p38	23p45	23p46		23p50	23p52		23p56	00 02	00 06	00 10	00 15	00 18	00 48	04 50	04 56	05 02	05 20		05 26
London Waterloo (East) [4] ⊖	d		23p39	23p41	23p48	23p49		23p53	23p55		23p59	00 05	00 09	00 13	00 18	00 21	00 51	04 53	04 59	05 05	05 23		05 29
London Cannon Street [4] ⊖	d																						
London Blackfriars [3] ⊖	d																						
London Bridge [4] ⊖	d		23p44	23p46	23p53	23p54		23p58	23p59		00 04	00 10	00 14	00 18	00 23	00 26	00 56	04a57	05 04	05 10	05a27		05 34
London Victoria [15] ⊖	d	23p25					23p43			23p55													
New Cross [4] ⊖	d							00 04	00 05			00 15		00 23		00 31	01 01		05 09	05 15		05 31	05 39
St Johns	d								00 07													05 33	
Lewisham [4]	a		23p51			00 02		00 07	00 10		00 11	00 19	00 21	00 27		00 35	01 05		05 13	05 19		05 35	05 43
Hither Green [4]	a		23p56			00 07					00 16		00 26	00 31			01 09		05 17				05 47
Petts Wood [4]	a	23p59	00 08			00 20	00 21			00 29			00 38				01 22						
Orpington [4]	a	00 02	00 12	00 01	00 08	00 23	00 25			00 32			00 42		00 46		01 25						

		SE [1]	SE	SE	SE	SE	SE	SE	SE	SE	SE	SE	SE	SE	SE [1]	SE	SE	SE	SE	SE [1]	SE	SE	SE
London Charing Cross [4] ⊖	d	05 30	05 32	05 36	05 39		05 47		05 52	05 56	06 02	06 06		06 09	06 15		06 17		06 26	06 30		06 32	06 36
London Waterloo (East) [4] ⊖	d	05 33	05 35	05 39	05 42		05 50		05 55	05 59	06 05	06 09		06 12	06 18		06 20		06 29	06 33		06 35	06 39
London Cannon Street [4] ⊖	d							05 52					06 12					06 27					
London Blackfriars [3] ⊖	d																						
London Bridge [4] ⊖	d	05 39	05 42	05 44	05 47		05 55	05a55	05a59	06 04	06 10	06 14	06a15	06 17	06 24		06 26	06a30	06 34	06 38		06 40	06 44
London Victoria [15] ⊖	d					05 40										06 10					06 30		
New Cross [4] ⊖	d		05 48		05 52		06 01			06 09	06 15						06 32		06 40			06 46	
St Johns	d						06 03										06 34						
Lewisham [4]	a		05 51	05 52	05 56		06 05			06 13	06 19	06 22		06 26			06 37		06 43			06 49	06 53
Hither Green [4]	a			05 56						06 17		06 27							06 48				06 58
Petts Wood [4]	a			06 08		06 14						06 39				06 44					07 04		07 10
Orpington [4]	a	05 54		06 11		06 18						06 42			06 40	06 49				06 53	07 08		07 13

		SE	SE [1]	SE	SE	SE	SE	SE	SE [1]	SE	SE C	SE D	SE	SE	SE	SE	SE [1]	SE	SE [1]	SE	SE	SE
London Charing Cross [4] ⊖	d	06 39	06 45		06 47	06 52		06 56	07 00		07 02	07 02	07 06				07 10	07 12	07 15	07 17		
London Waterloo (East) [4] ⊖	d	06 42	06 48		06 50	06 55		06 59	07 03		07 05	07 05	07 09				07 13	07 15	07 18	07 20		
London Cannon Street [4] ⊖	d			06 50			07 00								07 10	07 13					07 20	
London Blackfriars [3] ⊖	d																					
London Bridge [4] ⊖	d	06 47	06 53	06 54	06 55	06a59	07 04	07 05	07 08		07 10	07 10	07 14		07 14	07a16	07a18	07 21	07 23	07a24	07 24	
London Victoria [15] ⊖	d									06 50				07 09								07 10
New Cross [4] ⊖	d			06 59	07 02		07 09								07 20							
St Johns	d			07 01	07 04		07 11								07 22							
Lewisham [4]	a	06 56		07 04	07 07		07 14				07 18	07 18		07 24	07 26			07 29				
Hither Green [4]	a			07 08				07 18				08 11	07 23		07 31						07 34	
Petts Wood [4]	a			07 21						07 24			07 36									07 49
Orpington [4]	a		07 09	07 25					07 25	07 28			07 40						07 38		07 48	07 53

		SE	SE D	SE	SE	SE	SE [1]	SE	SE	SE	SE	SE	SE	SE [1]	SE	SE	SE [1]	SE	SE	SE	SE	SE	SE [1]
London Charing Cross [4] ⊖	d				07 26		07 29				07 36		07 39	07 40		07 44					07 48		07 52
London Waterloo (East) [4] ⊖	d				07 29		07 32				07 39		07 42	07 43		07 47					07 51		07 55
London Cannon Street [4] ⊖	d	07 24	07 24	07 27		07 30			07 32	07 36		07 41			07 44		07 47		07 51			07 54	
London Blackfriars [3] ⊖	d																						
London Bridge [4] ⊖	d	07 28	07 28	07 31	07 34	07 34	07 38		07 37	07 40	07 44	07 45	07 47	07a48	07 48	07a51	07 51		07 55		07 56	07 58	08a00
London Victoria [15] ⊖	d							07 25	09a11									07 40		07 43			
New Cross [4] ⊖	d	07 33	07 33	08a38		07 39						07 50			09a03				08 00			08 04	
St Johns	d	07 35	07 35			07 41																08 06	
Lewisham [4]	a	07 38	07 38			07 44				07 48		07 54	07 56						08 04	08 07		08 10	
Hither Green [4]	a		08 31		07 45						07 53	07 58							08 10				
Petts Wood [4]	a							07 59			08 06							08 14	08 23				
Orpington [4]	a						07 53	08 02			08 09						08 08	08 19	08 26		08 15		

		SE	SE	SE	SE [1]	SE	SE	SE	SE	SE	SE	SE	SE	SE [1]	SE	SE	SE	SE [1]	SE	SE
London Charing Cross [4] ⊖	d			07 59	08 00			08 03	08 05		08 11			08 13		08 15		08 17	08 20	
London Waterloo (East) [4] ⊖	d			08 02	08 03			08 06	08 08		08 14			08 16		08 18		08 20	08 23	
London Cannon Street [4] ⊖	d	07 56	08 00				08 05			08 10					08 16		08 19			08 25
London Blackfriars [3] ⊖	d																			
London Bridge [4] ⊖	d	08a00	08 04	08a06	08 09		08a08	08 11	08 13	08 14	08 19			08a20	08 20	08a22	08 23	08 25	08 29	08a28
London Victoria [15] ⊖	d					07 55						08 09	08 10							
New Cross [4] ⊖	d		08 09							08 20					09a38		08 29			
St Johns	d		08 11							08 22							08 31			
Lewisham [4]	a		08 14					08 18		08 25	08 28	08 30					08 33			
Hither Green [4]	a								08 23	08 29							08 38		08 41	
Petts Wood [4]	a					08 29			08 36				08 44				08 51			
Orpington [4]	a				08 25	08 32			08 39				08 47				08 54	08 41		

A from 21 May until 23 July
B until 18 May
C until 18 May
D from 21 May until 27 July

Table 199

Mondays to Fridays

until 27 July, 13 Aug to 28 Aug and from 10 Sep

London - Lewisham, Hither Green, Petts Wood and Orpington (Summary of Services)

		SE	SE	SE	SE	SE	SE	SE	SE	SE	SE	SE	SE	SE	SE	SE	SE	SE	SE	SE	SE	SE	SE
				1			1				1							A	B		1		
London Charing Cross 4	⊖ d	08 23		08 27	08 31		08 33			08 37		08 41				08 44		08 49	08 49		08 53		08 55
London Waterloo (East) 4	⊖ d	08 26		08 30	08 34		08 36			08 40		08 44				08 47		08 52	08 52		08 56		08 58
London Cannon Street 4	⊖ d		08 30			08 36			08 39		08 42				08 47		08 51			08 54		08 56	
London Blackfriars 3	⊖ d																						
London Bridge 4	⊖ d	08 31	08 34	08 35	08 39	08a39	08 41		08 43	08 45	08 46	08 49			08 51	08a52	08 55	08 57	08 57	08 58	09 01	09a00	09 03
London Victoria 15	⊖ d							08 25					08 39	08 40									
New Cross 4	⊖ d	08 38	08 41						08 49						10a08		09 00			09 04			
St Johns	d	08 40	08 43						08 51								09 02			09 06			
Lewisham 4	a	08 43	08 45		08 48				08 54			08 56	09 01				09 05			09 09			
Hither Green 4	a								08 59	08 55							09 10						09 14
Petts Wood 4	a							08 59		09 08				09 14			09 23						
Orpington 4	a			08 53			08 57	09 02		09 11	09 07			09 17			09 26	09 22	09 24		09 20		

		SE	SE	SE	SE	SE	SE	SE	SE	SE	SE	SE	SE	SE	SE	SE	SE	SE	SE	SE	SE	SE	SE
				1				B						1	1								1
London Charing Cross 4	⊖ d			09 00		09 02			09 06		09 11			09 13			09 17				09 26		09 30
London Waterloo (East) 4	⊖ d			09 03		09 05			09 09		09 14			09 16			09 20				09 29		09 33
London Cannon Street 4	⊖ d	09 00	09 03				09 07	09 07		09 09			09 15		09 18			09 20	09 24	09 27		09 30	
London Blackfriars 3	⊖ d																						
London Bridge 4	⊖ d	09 04	09a06	09 08		09 10	09a10	09 11	09 14	09 14	09 19		09 19	09a20	09 22		09a24	09 25	09 28	09a30	09 34	09 34	09 39
London Victoria 15	⊖ d				08 55							09 09				09 10							
New Cross 4	⊖ d	09 09						10a33		09 19			10a38					09 29	09 33			09 39	
St Johns	d	09 11								09 21								09 31	09 35			09 41	
Lewisham 4	a	09 14				09 18				09 24	09 28	09 31						09 34	09 38			09 44	
Hither Green 4	a								09 23	09 28								09 38			09 43		
Petts Wood 4	a				09 29				09 36							09 44		09 51					
Orpington 4	a			09 26	09 33				09 39						09 40	09 47		09 55					09 55

		SE	SE	SE	SE	SE	SE	SE	SE	SE	SE	SE	SE	SE	SE	SE	SE	SE	SE	SE	SE	SE
									1		1								1			
London Charing Cross 4	⊖ d		09 32		09 36		09 39		09 40		09 45		09 47				09 56		10 00		10 02	
London Waterloo (East) 4	⊖ d		09 35		09 39		09 42		09 43		09 48		09 50				09 59		10 03		10 05	
London Cannon Street 4	⊖ d			09 37		09 40				09 47				09 50	09 54	09 57		10 00				10 07
London Blackfriars 3	⊖ d																					
London Bridge 4	⊖ d		09 40	09a40	09 44	09 44	09 47		09a48	09 51	09 53		09a54	09 54	09 58	10a00	10 04	10 04	10 09		10 10	10a10
London Victoria 15	⊖ d	09 25						09 39				09 40								09 55		
New Cross 4	⊖ d					09 49				11a08				09 59	10 03			10 09				
St Johns	d					09 51								10 01	10 05			10 11				
Lewisham 4	a		09 49			09 54	09 56	10 01						10 04	10 08			10 14			10 19	
Hither Green 4	a				09 53	09 58								10 08			10 13					
Petts Wood 4	a	09 59			10 06							10 14		10 21						10 29		
Orpington 4	a	10 02			10 09						10 08	10 17		10 24					10 25	10 32		

		SE	SE	SE	SE	SE	SE	SE	SE	SE	SE	SE	SE	SE	SE	SE	SE	SE	SE	SE	SE	SE	SE
						1 H		1								1							
London Charing Cross 4	⊖ d	10 06		10 09		10 10		10 15		10 17				10 26		10 30		10 32		10 36		10 39	
London Waterloo (East) 4	⊖ d	10 09		10 12		10 13		10 18		10 20				10 29		10 33		10 35		10 39		10 42	
London Cannon Street 4	⊖ d		10 10				10 17				10 20	10 24	10 27		10 30				10 37		10 40		
London Blackfriars 3	⊖ d																						
London Bridge 4	⊖ d	10 14	10 14	10 17		10a18	10 21	10 23		10a24	10 24	10 28	10a30	10 34	10 34	10 39		10 40	10a40	10 44	10 44	10 47	
London Victoria 15	⊖ d				10 09				10 10								10 25						10 39
New Cross 4	⊖ d		10 19				11a38				10 29	10 33			10 39						10 49		
St Johns	d		10 21								10 31	10 35			10 41						10 51		
Lewisham 4	a		10 24	10 26	10 31						10 34	10 38			10 44			10 49			10 54	10 56	11 01
Hither Green 4	a	10 23	10 28								10 38			10 43						10 53	10 58		
Petts Wood 4	a	10 36							10 44		10 51						10 59			11 06			
Orpington 4	a	10 39						10 38	10 47		10 54					10 55	11 02			11 09			

		SE	SE	SE	SE	SE	SE	SE	SE	SE	SE	SE	SE	SE	SE	SE	SE	SE	SE	SE	SE	SE
		1 H		1								1				B					1 H	
London Charing Cross 4	⊖ d	10 40		10 45		10 47				10 56		11 00		11 02			11 06		11 09		11 10	
London Waterloo (East) 4	⊖ d	10 43		10 48		10 50				10 59		11 03		11 05			11 09		11 12		11 13	
London Cannon Street 4	⊖ d		10 47				10 50	10 54	10 57		11 00				11 07	11 07		11 10				11 17
London Blackfriars 3	⊖ d																					
London Bridge 4	⊖ d	10a48	10 51	10 53		10a54	10 54	10 58	11a00	11 04	11 04	11 09		11 10	11a10	11 11	11 14	11 14	11 17		11a18	11 21
London Victoria 15	⊖ d				10 40								10 55							11 09		
New Cross 4	⊖ d		12a08				10 59	11 03			11 09					12a33		11 19				12a38
St Johns	d						11 01	11 05			11 11							11 21				
Lewisham 4	a						11 04	11 08			11 14			11 19				11 24	11 26	11 31		
Hither Green 4	a						11 08			11 13							11 23	11 28				
Petts Wood 4	a				11 14		11 21						11 29				11 36					
Orpington 4	a			11 08	11 17		11 24					11 25	11 32				11 39					

A until 18 May

B from 21 May until 27 July

Table 199

Mondays to Fridays

until 27 July, 13 Aug to 28 Aug and from 10 Sep

London - Lewisham, Hither Green, Petts Wood and Orpington (Summary of Services)

		SE	SE	SE	SE	SE	SE	SE	SE	SE	SE	SE	SE	SE	SE	SE	SE	SE	SE	SE	SE	SE	SE
		1								1								1 H		1			
London Charing Cross 4	⊖ d	11 15		11 17				11 26		11 30		11 32		11 36		11 39		11 40		11 45		11 47	
London Waterloo (East) 4	⊖ d	11 18		11 20				11 29		11 33		11 35		11 39		11 42		11 43		11 48		11 50	
London Cannon Street 4	⊖ d				11 20	11 24	11 27		11 30				11 37		11 40				11 47				11 50
London Blackfriars 3	⊖ d																						
London Bridge 4	⊖ d	11 23		11a24	11 24	11 28	11a30	11 34	11 34	11 39		11 40	11 41	11 44	11 44	11 47		11a48	11 51	11 53		11a54	11 54
London Victoria 15	⊖ d		11 10								11 25						11 39				11 40		
New Cross 4	⊖ d				11 29	11 33			11 39				13a03		11 49				13a08				11 59
St Johns	d				11 31	11 35			11 41						11 51								12 01
Lewisham 4	a				11 33	11 38			11 44			11 49			11 54	11 56	12 01						12 03
Hither Green 4	a				11 38			11 43						11 53	11 58								12 08
Petts Wood 4	a		11 44		11 51						11 59			12 06							12 14		12 21
Orpington 4	a	11 38	11 47		11 54					11 55	12 02			12 09						12 08	12 17		12 24

		SE	SE	SE	SE	SE	SE	SE	SE	SE	SE	SE	SE	SE	SE	SE	SE	SE	SE	SE	SE	SE	SE
						1								1 H		1							
London Charing Cross 4	⊖ d			11 56		12 00		12 02		12 06		12 09		12 10		12 15		12 17				12 26	
London Waterloo (East) 4	⊖ d			11 59		12 03		12 05		12 09		12 12		12 13		12 18		12 20				12 29	
London Cannon Street 4	⊖ d	11 54	11 57		12 00				12 07		12 10				12 17				12 20	12 24	12 27		12 30
London Blackfriars 3	⊖ d																						
London Bridge 4	⊖ d	11 58	12a00	12 04	12 04	12 09		12 10	12 11	12 14	12 14	12 17		12a18	12 21	12 23		12a24	12 24	12 28	12a30	12 34	12 34
London Victoria 15	⊖ d						11 55						12 09				12 10						
New Cross 4	⊖ d	12 03			12 09				13a33		12 19				13a38				12 29	12 33			12 39
St Johns	d	12 05			12 11						12 21								12 31	12 35			12 41
Lewisham 4	a	12 08			12 14			12 19			12 24	12 26	12 31						12 34	12 38			12 44
Hither Green 4	a			12 13						12 23	12 28								12 38			12 43	
Petts Wood 4	a						12 29			12 36							12 44		12 51				
Orpington 4	a					12 25	12 32			12 39						12 38	12 47		12 54				

		SE	SE	SE	SE	SE	SE	SE	SE	SE	SE	SE	SE	SE	SE	SE	SE	SE	SE	SE	SE	SE
		1								1 H		1								1		
London Charing Cross 4	⊖ d	12 30		12 32		12 36		12 39		12 40		12 45		12 47				12 56		13 00		13 02
London Waterloo (East) 4	⊖ d	12 33		12 35		12 39		12 42		12 43		12 48		12 50				12 59		13 03		13 05
London Cannon Street 4	⊖ d				12 37		12 40				12 47				12 50	12 54	12 57		13 00			
London Blackfriars 3	⊖ d																					
London Bridge 4	⊖ d	12 39		12 40	12 41	12 44	12 44	12 47		12a48	12 51	12 53		12a54	12 54	12 58	13a00	13 04	13 04	13 09		13 10
London Victoria 15	⊖ d		12 25						12 39				12 40								12 55	
New Cross 4	⊖ d				14a03		12 49				14a08				12 59	13 03			13 09			
St Johns	d						12 51								13 01	13 05			13 11			
Lewisham 4	a			12 49			12 54	12 56	13 01						13 03	13 08			13 14			13 19
Hither Green 4	a					12 53	12 58								13 08			13 13				
Petts Wood 4	a		12 59			13 06							13 14		13 21						13 29	
Orpington 4	a	12 55	13 02			13 09						13 08	13 17		13 24					13 25	13 32	

		SE	SE	SE	SE	SE	SE	SE	SE	SE	SE	SE	SE	SE	SE	SE	SE	SE	SE	SE	SE	SE	SE
							1 H		1								1						
London Charing Cross 4	⊖ d		13 06		13 09		13 10		13 15		13 17				13 26		13 30		13 32		13 36		13 39
London Waterloo (East) 4	⊖ d		13 09		13 12		13 13		13 18		13 20				13 29		13 33		13 35		13 39		13 42
London Cannon Street 4	⊖ d	13 07		13 10				13 17				13 20	13 24	13 27		13 30				13 37		13 40	
London Blackfriars 3	⊖ d																						
London Bridge 4	⊖ d	13 11	13 14	13 14	13 17		13a18	13 21	13 23		13a24	13 24	13 28	13a30	13 34	13 34	13 39		13 40	13 41	13 44	13 44	13 47
London Victoria 15	⊖ d					13 09				13 10								13 25					
New Cross 4	⊖ d	14a33		13 19				14a38				13 29	13 33			13 39				15a03		13 49	
St Johns	d			13 21								13 31	13 35			13 41						13 51	
Lewisham 4	a			13 24	13 26	13 31						13 34	13 38			13 44			13 49			13 54	13 56
Hither Green 4	a		13 23	13 28								13 38			13 43						13 53	13 58	
Petts Wood 4	a		13 36							13 44		13 51						13 59			14 06		
Orpington 4	a		13 39						13 38	13 47		13 54					13 55	14 02			14 09		

		SE	SE	SE	SE	SE	SE	SE	SE	SE	SE	SE	SE	SE	SE	SE	SE	SE	SE	SE	SE	SE
			1 H		1								1								1 H	
London Charing Cross 4	⊖ d		13 40		13 45		13 47				13 56		14 00		14 02		14 06		14 09		14 10	
London Waterloo (East) 4	⊖ d		13 43		13 48		13 50				13 59		14 03		14 05		14 09		14 12		14 13	
London Cannon Street 4	⊖ d			13 47				13 50	13 54	13 57		14 00				14 07		14 10				14 17
London Blackfriars 3	⊖ d																					
London Bridge 4	⊖ d		13a48	13 51	13 53		13a54	13 54	13 58	14a00	14 04	14 04	14 09		14 10	14 11	14 14	14 14	14 17		14a18	14 21
London Victoria 15	⊖ d	13 39				13 40								13 55						14 09		
New Cross 4	⊖ d			15a08				13 59	14 03			14 09				15a33		14 19				15a38
St Johns	d							14 01	14 05			14 11						14 21				
Lewisham 4	a	14 01						14 04	14 08			14 14			14 19			14 24	14 26	14 31		
Hither Green 4	a							14 08			14 13						14 23	14 28				
Petts Wood 4	a					14 14		14 21						14 29			14 36					
Orpington 4	a				14 08	14 17		14 24					14 25	14 32			14 39					

Table 199

London - Lewisham, Hither Green, Petts Wood and Orpington (Summary of Services)

Mondays to Fridays

until 27 July, 13 Aug to 28 Aug and from 10 Sep

Station	SE	SE	SE	SE	SE	SE	SE	SE	SE	SE	SE	SE	SE	SE	SE	SE	SE	SE	SE	SE	SE	SE
	1								1				A					1 ⊥		1		
London Charing Cross 4 ⊖ d	14 15		14 17				14 26		14 30		14 32			14 36		14 39		14 40		14 45		14 47
London Waterloo (East) 4 ⊖ d	14 18		14 20				14 29		14 33		14 35			14 39		14 42		14 43		14 48		14 50
London Cannon Street 4 ⊖ d				14 20	14 24	14 27		14 30				14 37	14 37		14 40				14 47			
London Blackfriars 3 ⊖ d																						
London Bridge 4 ⊖ d	14 23		14a24	14 24	14 28	14a30	14 34	14 34	14 39		14 40	14a40	14 41	14 44	14 44	14 47		14a48	14 51	14 53		14a54
London Victoria 15 ⊖ d		14 10								14 25							14 39				14 40	
New Cross 4 ⊖ d				14 29	14 33			14 39					16a03		14 49				16a08			
St Johns d				14 31	14 35			14 41							14 51							
Lewisham 4 ⇌ a				14 34	14 38			14 44			14 49				14 54	14 56	15 01					
Hither Green 4 a				14 38			14 43							14 53	14 58							
Petts Wood 4 a		14 44		14 51						14 59				15 06							15 14	
Orpington 4 a	14 38	14 47		14 54					14 55	15 02				15 09						15 08	15 17	

Station	SE	SE	SE	SE	SE	SE	SE	SE	SE	SE	SE	SE	SE	SE	SE	SE	SE	SE	SE	SE	SE	SE
						1								1 ⊥		1						
London Charing Cross 4 ⊖ d				14 56		15 00		15 02		15 06		15 09		15 10		15 15		15 17				15 26
London Waterloo (East) 4 ⊖ d				14 59		15 03		15 05		15 09		15 12		15 13		15 18		15 20				15 29
London Cannon Street 4 ⊖ d	14 50	14 54	14 57		15 00				15 07		15 10				15 17				15 20	15 24	15 27	
London Blackfriars 3 ⊖ d																						
London Bridge 4 ⊖ d	14 54	14 58	15a00	15 04	15 04	15 09		15 10	15 11	15 14	15 14	15 17		15a18	15 21	15 23		15a24	15 24	15 28	15a30	15 34
London Victoria 15 ⊖ d							14 55						15 09				15 10					
New Cross 4 ⊖ d	14 59	15 03			15 09				16a33		15 19				16a38				15 29	15 33		
St Johns d	15 01	15 05			15 11						15 21								15 31	15 35		
Lewisham 4 ⇌ a	15 04	15 08			15 14			15 19			15 24	15 26	15 31						15 34	15 38		
Hither Green 4 a	15 08			15 13						15 23	15 28								15 38			15 43
Petts Wood 4 a	15 21						15 29			15 36							15 44		15 51			
Orpington 4 a	15 24					15 25	15 32			15 39						15 38	15 47		15 54			

Station	SE	SE	SE	SE	SE	SE	SE	SE	SE	SE	SE	SE	SE	SE	SE	SE	SE	SE	SE	SE	SE
		1								1 ⊥		1								1	
London Charing Cross 4 ⊖ d		15 30		15 32		15 36		15 39		15 40		15 45		15 47				15 56		16 00	
London Waterloo (East) 4 ⊖ d		15 33		15 35		15 39		15 42		15 43		15 48		15 50				15 59		16 03	
London Cannon Street 4 ⊖ d	15 30				15 37		15 40				15 47				15 50	15 54	15 57		16 00		
London Blackfriars 3 ⊖ d																					
London Bridge 4 ⊖ d	15 34	15 39		15 40	15 41	15 44	15 44	15 47		15a48	15 51	15 53		15a54	15 54	15 58	16a00	16 04	16 04	16 09	
London Victoria 15 ⊖ d			15 25						15 39				15 40								15 55
New Cross 4 ⊖ d	15 39				17a03		15 49				17a11				15 59	16 03			16 10		
St Johns d	15 41						15 51								16 01	16 05			16 12		
Lewisham 4 ⇌ a	15 44			15 49			15 54	15 56	16 01						16 03	16 08			16 14		
Hither Green 4 a						15 53	15 58								16 08			16 13			
Petts Wood 4 a			15 59			16 06							16 14		16 21						16 29
Orpington 4 a		15 55	16 02			16 09						16 08	16 17		16 24					16 25	16 32

Station	SE	SE	SE	SE	SE	SE	SE	SE	SE	SE	SE	SE	SE	SE	SE	SE	SE	SE	SE	SE	SE
								1 ⊥		1							1				
London Charing Cross 4 ⊖ d	16 02		16 06		16 09			16 10		16 15		16 20			16 26		16 28		16 30		16 32
London Waterloo (East) 4 ⊖ d	16 05		16 09		16 12			16 13		16 18		16 23			16 29		16 31		16 33		16 35
London Cannon Street 4 ⊖ d		16 07		16 10					16 17		16 20		16 24	16 27		16 30				16 35	
London Blackfriars 3 ⊖ d																					
London Bridge 4 ⊖ d	16 10	16 11	16 14	16 14	16 17			16a18	16 21	16a22	16 24	16a28	16 28	16a30	16 34	16 34	16 36		16 38	16a38	16 40
London Victoria 15 ⊖ d						16 09	16 10											16 25			
New Cross 4 ⊖ d		17a33		16 20					17a39		16 30		16 34			16 40					
St Johns d				16 22							16 32		16 36			16 42					
Lewisham 4 ⇌ a	16 19			16 24	16 26	16 31					16 34		16 38			16 44			16 47		
Hither Green 4 a			16 23	16 29							16 39				16 43						16 49
Petts Wood 4 a			16 36				16 44				16 51							16 59			17 03
Orpington 4 a			16 39				16 49				16 57						16 52	17 04			17 06

Station	SE	SE	SE	SE	SE	SE	SE	SE	SE	SE	SE	SE	SE	SE	SE	SE	SE	SE	SE	SE	SE
		1 ⊥		B	A				1	1									1		
London Charing Cross 4 ⊖ d		16 37	16 39						16 41		16 42	16 45		16 49		16 51		16 55	16 57		
London Waterloo (East) 4 ⊖ d		16 40	16 42						16 44		16 45	16 48		16 52		16 54		16 58	16a59		
London Cannon Street 4 ⊖ d	16 39			16 42	16 42			16 44		16 46			16 51		16 54		16 56			16 58	
London Blackfriars 3 ⊖ d																					
London Bridge 4 ⊖ d	16 43	16a44	16a46	16 46	16 46			16a47	16a48	16a49	16 51	16 53	16 55	16 57	16a57	16 59	17 00	17a02		17 02	
London Victoria 15 ⊖ d						16 39	16 40														16 59
New Cross 4 ⊖ d	16 49			16 52	16 52							18a02	17 01							17 08	
St Johns d	16 51												17 03							17 10	
Lewisham 4 ⇌ a	16 53			16 55	16 55	16 58					17 00		17 05			17 07				17 12	
Hither Green 4 a	16 58				17 57						17 05			17 07						17 17	
Petts Wood 4 a							17 14				17 18						17 24				17 36
Orpington 4 a							17 19				17 24						17 27				17 41

A from 21 May until 27 July

B until 18 May

Table 199

London - Lewisham, Hither Green, Petts Wood and Orpington (Summary of Services)

Mondays to Fridays

until 27 July, 13 Aug to 28 Aug and from 10 Sep

Station	SE	SE	SE	SE	SE	SE	SE	SE	SE	SE	SE	SE	SE	SE	SE	SE	SE	SE	SE	SE	SE	SE
	1		1					1						1 ⊥				1		1		1
London Charing Cross 4 ⊖ d		16 59	17 01			17 03			17 06		17 10		17 12	17 14			17 17	17 19			17 21	17 23
London Waterloo (East) 4 ⊖ d		17 02	17 04			17 06			17 09		17 13		17 15	17a17			17 20	17a21			17 24	17 26
London Cannon Street 4 ⊖ d	17 02			17 04	17 06			17 08		17 12		17 16			17 19				17 21	17 24		
London Blackfriars 3 ⊖ d																						
London Bridge 4 ⊖ d	17a05	17a06	17a08	17 08	17a09	17 11		17a11	17 14	17 16	17 19	17a19	17 21		17 23		17a24		17 25	17a27	17a28	17a30
London Victoria 15 ⊖ d							17 04									17 15						
New Cross 4 ⊖ d				17 14						17 22									17 31			
St Johns d										17 24									17 33			
Lewisham 4 ⇌ a				17 17		17 20	17 23			17 26			17 30						17 35			
Hither Green 4 a						17 25			18 21		17 28								17 40			
Petts Wood 4 a						17 39									17 43	17 50						
Orpington 4 a						17 45									17 47	17 55						

Station	SE	SE	SE	SE	SE	SE	SE	SE	SE	SE	SE	SE	SE	SE	SE	SE	SE	SE	SE	SE	SE	SE
			1							1						1 ⊥		1		A	B	1
London Charing Cross 4 ⊖ d				17 26	17 29		17 30		17 32		17 34				17 39	17 41			17 43			17 45
London Waterloo (East) 4 ⊖ d				17 29	17 32		17a32		17 35		17 37				17 42	17a43			17 46			17 48
London Cannon Street 4 ⊖ d	17 26	17 28	17 30					17 34		17 37			17 39	17 41			17 43	17 45		17 47	17 47	
London Blackfriars 3 ⊖ d																						
London Bridge 4 ⊖ d	17 30	17a31	17a33	17 35	17a36			17 39	17 41	17a40	17 43		17a42	17 45	17a46		17 47	17a48	17a50	17 51	17 51	17a52
London Victoria 15 ⊖ d						17 30						17 34										
New Cross 4 ⊖ d	17 36							17 45									17 53			17 58	17 58	
St Johns d								17 47									17 55					
Lewisham 4 ⇌ a	17 39			17 43				17 49			17 52	17 55					17 58			18 01	18 01	
Hither Green 4 a				17 48					17 51								18 03				18 57	
Petts Wood 4 a				18 01		18 05								18 08								
Orpington 4 a				18 07		18 10								18 11								

Station	SE	SE	SE	SE	SE	SE	SE	SE	SE	SE	SE	SE	SE	SE	SE	SE	SE	SE	SE	SE	SE
				1							1					1		1		1	
London Charing Cross 4 ⊖ d		17 47			17 50	17 52		17 54	17 56		17 59				18 01	18 03			18 05	18 07	
London Waterloo (East) 4 ⊖ d		17 50			17 53	17a54		17 57	17 59		18a01				18 04	18a05			18 08	18 10	
London Cannon Street 4 ⊖ d	17 50			17 52			17 56					18 00	18 02				18 04	18 08			18 10
London Blackfriars 3 ⊖ d																					
London Bridge 4 ⊖ d	17a53	17 55		17a55	17a57		18 00	18 02	18 04			18a03	18 06		18a08		18 08	18a11	18a12	18a14	18 14
London Victoria 15 ⊖ d			17 45							17 56				18 00							
New Cross 4 ⊖ d							18 06										18 14				18 20
St Johns d							18 08										18 16				
Lewisham 4 ⇌ a		18 04					18 10		18 13	18 17							18 19				18 23
Hither Green 4 a		18 09						18 12									18 24				
Petts Wood 4 a		18 23	18 26										18 28	18 35							
Orpington 4 a		18 29	18 32										18 32	18 41							

Station	SE	SE	SE	SE	SE	SE	SE	SE	SE	SE	SE	SE	SE	SE	SE	SE	SE	SE	SE	SE	SE	SE
			1						1 ⊥						1			1			1	
London Charing Cross 4 ⊖ d		18 09		18 12	18 14			18 18	18 21					18 23			18 27		18 30		18 32	18 34
London Waterloo (East) 4 ⊖ d		18 12		18 15	18 17			18 21	18a23					18 26			18 30		18 33		18 35	18 37
London Cannon Street 4 ⊖ d	18 12		18 14			18 18	18 21			18 23		18 25			18 28	18 30		18 32		18 34		
London Blackfriars 3 ⊖ d																						
London Bridge 4 ⊖ d	18a15	18 17	18a17	18 21	18 23	18 23	18a24	18 26		18 27		18 29		18a31	18a31	18a33	18a34	18a35	18 38	18 38	18a39	18a41
London Victoria 15 ⊖ d											18 15		18 18									
New Cross 4 ⊖ d				19a38		18 28						18 35								18 44		
St Johns d						18 30						18 37								18 46		
Lewisham 4 ⇌ a		18 26				18 33		18 35				18 40	18 42							18 48		
Hither Green 4 a		18 31			18 35							18 45							18 48			
Petts Wood 4 a		18 43								18 49	18 53								19 02			
Orpington 4 a		18 49								18 53	18 59								19 06			

Station	SE	SE	SE	SE	SE	SE	SE	SE	SE	SE	SE	SE	SE	SE	SE	SE	SE	SE	SE	SE	SE
				1	1 ⊥				1										1		1
London Charing Cross 4 ⊖ d		18 37	18 39		18 41				18 45				18 48		18 52		18 56		19 00		
London Waterloo (East) 4 ⊖ d		18 40	18 42		18 44				18 48				18 51		18 55		18 59		19 03		
London Cannon Street 4 ⊖ d	18 40			18 44				18 46		18 48		18 50		18 54		18 57		19 00			19 04
London Blackfriars 3 ⊖ d																					
London Bridge 4 ⊖ d	18 44	18 46	18 48	18a47	18 50			18a49	18a52	18 52		18 54	18 57	18 58	18a59	19a00	19 04	19 04	19 09		19a07
London Victoria 15 ⊖ d						18 30	18 39				18 45									19 00	
New Cross 4 ⊖ d	18 50		18 55									19 00		19 05				19 09			
St Johns d	18 52											19 02		19 07				19 11			
Lewisham 4 ⇌ a	18 54		18 59				19 02					19 04	19 06	19 10				19 14			
Hither Green 4 a		18 55										19 09					19 14				
Petts Wood 4 a						19 06				19 13	19 19									19 35	
Orpington 4 a					19 06	19 12				19 19	19 25								19 27	19 38	

A until 18 May

B from 21 May until 27 July

Table 199

London - Lewisham, Hither Green, Petts Wood and Orpington (Summary of Services)

Mondays to Fridays

until 27 July, 13 Aug to 28 Aug and from 10 Sep

		SE	SE	SE	SE	SE	SE	SE ■ (trolley)	SE	SE ■	SE	SE	SE	SE	SE	SE	SE	SE ■	SE	SE	SE	SE	SE
London Charing Cross 4 ⊖	d	19 02		19 06		19 09		19 10		19 15		19 17				19 26		19 30		19 32		19 36	
London Waterloo (East) 4 ⊖	d	19 05		19 09		19 12		19 13		19 18		19 20				19 29		19 33		19 35		19 39	
London Cannon Street 4 ⊖	d		19 07		19 10				19 17				19 20	19 24	19 27		19 30				19 37		19 40
London Blackfriars 3 ⊖	d																						
London Bridge 4 ⊖	d	19 10	19a10	19 14	19 14	19 17		19a18	19a20	19 23		19a24	19 24	19 28	19a30	19 34	19 34	19 39		19 40	19a40	19 44	19 44
London Victoria 15 ⊖	d						19 09				19 10								19 25				
New Cross 4 ⊖	d				19 19								19 29	19 33			19 39						19 49
St Johns	d				19 21								19 31	19 35			19 41						19 51
Lewisham 4	a	19 19			19 24	19 26	19 31						19 33	19 38			19 44			19 49			19 55
Hither Green 4	a			19 23	19 28								19 38			19 43						19 53	19 59
Petts Wood 4	a			19 38							19 44		19 51						19 59			20 06	
Orpington 4	a			19 43						19 38	19 48		19 54					19 55	20 02			20 09	

		SE	SE	SE ■ (trolley)	SE	SE ■	SE	SE	SE	SE	SE	SE	SE	SE ■	SE	SE	SE	SE	SE	SE ■ (trolley)	SE	SE ■	SE
London Charing Cross 4 ⊖	d	19 39		19 40		19 45		19 47				19 56		20 00		20 02	20 06		20 09	20 10		20 15	
London Waterloo (East) 4 ⊖	d	19 42		19 43		19 48		19 50				19 59		20 03		20 05	20 09		20 12	20 13		20 18	
London Cannon Street 4 ⊖	d				19 47				19 50	19 54	19 57		20 00					20 10			20 17		
London Blackfriars 3 ⊖	d																						
London Bridge 4 ⊖	d	19 47		19a48	19a50	19 53		19a54	19 54	19 58	20a00	20 04	20 04	20 09		20 10	20 14	20 14	20 17	20a18	20a20	20 23	
London Victoria 15 ⊖	d		19 39				19 40								19 55								20 10
New Cross 4 ⊖	d								19 59	20 03			20 09					20 19					
St Johns	d								20 01	20 05			20 11					20 21					
Lewisham 4	a	19 56	20 01						20 04	20 08			20 14			20 19		20 25	20 26				
Hither Green 4	a								20 08			20 13					20 23	20 29					
Petts Wood 4	a						20 14		20 21						20 29		20 36						20 44
Orpington 4	a					20 08	20 18		20 24					20 25	20 32		20 39					20 38	20 47

		SE	SE	SE	SE	SE ■	SE	SE	SE	SE	SE ■	SE	SE ■	SE	SE	SE	SE ■	SE	SE	SE	SE	SE ■
London Charing Cross 4 ⊖	d		20 17	20 22		20 30		20 32	20 36	20 39	20 40		20 45	20 47	20 52		21 00		21 02	21 06	21 09	21 10
London Waterloo (East) 4 ⊖	d		20 20	20 25		20 33		20 35	20 39	20 42	20 43		20 48	20 50	20 55		21 03		21 05	21 09	21 12	21 13
London Cannon Street 4 ⊖	d	20 20			20 27							20 47				20 57						
London Blackfriars 3 ⊖	d																					
London Bridge 4 ⊖	d	20 24	20 25	20 30	20a30	20 39		20 40	20 44	20 47	20a48	20a50	20 53	20 55	21 00	21a00	21 09		21 10	21 14	21 17	21 19
London Victoria 15 ⊖	d						20 25											20 55				
New Cross 4 ⊖	d	20 29	20 32	20 35				20 45						21 00	21 05				21 15			
St Johns	d	20 31	20 34											21 02								
Lewisham 4	a	20 34	20 36	20 38				20 49		20 56				21 05	21 09				21 19	21 21	21 26	
Hither Green 4	a	20 38		20 44					20 53						21 13					21 26		
Petts Wood 4	a	20 51					20 59		21 06									21 29		21 38		
Orpington 4	a	20 54				20 55	21 02		21 09				21 08				21 25	21 32		21 42		21 34

		SE	SE	SE	SE ■	SE	SE	SE	SE	SE ■	SE ■	SE	SE	SE	SE ■	SE	SE	SE	SE	SE ■	SE	SE	SE
London Charing Cross 4 ⊖	d	21 17	21 22	21 26	21 30		21 32	21 36	21 39	21 40	21 45	21 47	21 52	21 56	22 00		22 02	22 06	22 09	22 10	22 17	22 22	22 26
London Waterloo (East) 4 ⊖	d	21 20	21 25	21 29	21 33		21 35	21 39	21 42	21 43	21 48	21 50	21 55	21 59	22 03		22 05	22 09	22 12	22 13	22 20	22 25	22 29
London Cannon Street 4 ⊖	d																						
London Blackfriars 3 ⊖	d																						
London Bridge 4 ⊖	d	21 25	21 30	21a33	21 39		21 40	21 44	21 47	21a48	21 53	21 55	22 00	22a03	22 09		22 10	22 14	22 17	22 19	22 25	22 30	22a33
London Victoria 15 ⊖	d					21 25										21 55							
New Cross 4 ⊖	d	21 30	21 35				21 45					22 00	22 05				22 15				22 30	22 35	
St Johns	d	21 32										22 02									22 32		
Lewisham 4	a	21 35	21 39				21 49	21 51	21 56			22 05	22 09				22 19	22 21	22 26		22 35	22 39	
Hither Green 4	a		21 43					21 56					22 13					22 26				22 43	
Petts Wood 4	a					21 59		22 08								22 29		22 38					
Orpington 4	a				21 55	22 02		22 12			22 08				22 25	22 32		22 42		22 34			

		SE ■	SE	SE	SE	SE	SE ■	SE ■	SE	SE	SE	SE ■	SE A	SE	SE	SE	SE	SE ■	SE	SE	SE	SE ■
London Charing Cross 4 ⊖	d	22 30		22 32	22 36	22 39	22 40	22 45	22 47	22 52	22 56	23 00			23 02	23 06	23 09	23 10	23 17	23 22	23 26	23 30
London Waterloo (East) 4 ⊖	d	22 33		22 35	22 39	22 42	22 43	22 48	22 50	22 55	22 59	23 03			23 05	23 09	23 12	23 13	23 20	23 25	23 29	23 33
London Cannon Street 4 ⊖	d																					
London Blackfriars 3 ⊖	d																					
London Bridge 4 ⊖	d	22 39		22 40	22 44	22 47	22a48	22 53	22 55	23 00	23a03	23 09			23 10	23 14	23 17	23 19	23 25	23 30	23a33	23 39
London Victoria 15 ⊖	d		22 25										22 43	22 55								
New Cross 4 ⊖	d			22 45					23 00	23 05					23 15				23 30	23 35		
St Johns	d								23 02										23 32			
Lewisham 4	a			22 49	22 51	22 56			23 05	23 09					23 19	23 21	23 26		23 35	23 39		
Hither Green 4	a				22 56					23 13						23 26				23 43		
Petts Wood 4	a		22 59		23 08								23 21	23 29		23 38						
Orpington 4	a	22 54	23 02		23 12			23 08				23 24	23 25	23 32		23 42		23 34				23 54

A until 18 May

Table 199

London - Lewisham, Hither Green, Petts Wood and Orpington (Summary of Services)

Mondays to Fridays

until 27 July, 13 Aug to 28 Aug and from 10 Sep

		SE A	SE	SE	SE	SE	SE ■	SE ■	SE A	SE	SE	SE
London Charing Cross 4 ⊖	d			23 32	23 36	23 39	23 40	23 45		23 52		23 56
London Waterloo (East) 4 ⊖	d			23 35	23 39	23 42	23 43	23 48		23 55		23 59
London Cannon Street 4 ⊖	d											
London Blackfriars 3 ⊖	d											
London Bridge 4 ⊖	d			23 40	23 44	23 47	23a48	23 53		23 59		00a03
London Victoria 15 ⊖	d	23 13	23 25						23 43		23 55	
New Cross 4 ⊖	d			23 45						00 05		
St Johns	d									00 07		
Lewisham 4	a			23 49	23 51	23 56				00 10		
Hither Green 4	a				23 56							
Petts Wood 4	a	23 51	23 59		00 08				00 21		00 29	
Orpington 4	a	23 57	00 02		00 12			00 08	00 25		00 32	

Mondays to Fridays

30 July to 10 August

		SE	SE	SE MO ■	SE ■	SE	SE B	SE MO	SE	SE	SE B	SE MO	SE MO	SE	SE	SE	SE	SE ■	SE	SE	SE	SE	SE
London Charing Cross 4 ⊖	d		23p36	23p40	23p45	23p52			00 02	00 06	00 10	00 10	00 10	00 15	00 18		00 32	00 37		00 44		00 48	
London Waterloo (East) 4 ⊖	d		23p39	23p43	23p48	23p55			00 05	00 09	00 13	00 13	00 13	00 18	00 21		00 35	00 40		00 47		00 51	
London Cannon Street 4 ⊖	d															00 30			00 42				
London Blackfriars 3 ⊖	d																						
London Bridge 4 ⊖	d		23p44	23p49	23p53	23p59			00 10	00 14	00 18	00 18	00 18	00 23	00 26	00 34	00a39	00 45	00 47	00 52		00 56	
London Victoria 15 ⊖	d	23p25					23p55	23p55													00 45		00 56
New Cross 4 ⊖	d					00 05			00 15		00 23	00 23			00 31	00 39				00 57		01 01	
St Johns	d					00 07										00 41							
Lewisham 4	a		23p51			00 10			00 19	00 21	00 27	00 27			00 35	00 44			00 55	01 01		01 05	
Hither Green 4	a		23p56							00 26	00 31	00 33								01 05		01 09	
Petts Wood 4	a	23p59	00 08				00 29	00 29		00 38			00 38								01 21	01 22	01 35
Orpington 4	a	00 02	00 15	00 04	00 08		00 32	00 33		00 45			00 41	00 46				01 00			01 27	01 25	01 42

		SE	SE	SE	SE	SE	SE	SE	SE ■	SE	SE	SE	SE	SE	SE	SE	SE	SE	SE	SE	SE	SE	SE ■
London Charing Cross 4 ⊖	d		04 50	04 56	05 02	05 20		05 26	05 30	05 32	05 36	05 39		05 47		05 52	05 56		06 02	06 06		06 09	06 15
London Waterloo (East) 4 ⊖	d		04 53	04 59	05 05	05 23		05 29	05 33	05 35	05 39	05 42		05 50		05 55	05 59		06 05	06 09		06 12	06 18
London Cannon Street 4 ⊖	d	00 56													05 52						06 12		
London Blackfriars 3 ⊖	d																						
London Bridge 4 ⊖	d	00a59	04a57	05 04	05 10	05a27		05 34	05 39	05 42	05 44	05 47		05 55	05a55	05a59	06 04		06 10	06 14	06a15	06 17	06 24
London Victoria 15 ⊖	d												05 40					05 57					
New Cross 4 ⊖	d			05 09	05 15		05 31	05 39		05 48		05 52		06 01			06 09		06 15				
St Johns	d						05 33							06 03									
Lewisham 4	a			05 13	05 19		05 35	05 43		05 51	05 52	05 56		06 05			06 13	06 15	06 19	06 22		06 26	
Hither Green 4	a			05 17				05 47			05 56						06 17			06 27			
Petts Wood 4	a										06 08		06 14							06 39			
Orpington 4	a								05 54		06 11		06 18							06 42			06 40

		SE	SE	SE	SE	SE	SE ■	SE	SE	SE	SE	SE ■	SE	SE	SE	SE	SE	SE ■	SE	SE	SE	SE
London Charing Cross 4 ⊖	d		06 17			06 26	06 30		06 32	06 36	06 39	06 45		06 47	06 52		06 56	07 00		07 02	07 06	
London Waterloo (East) 4 ⊖	d		06 20			06 29	06 33		06 35	06 39	06 42	06 48		06 50	06 55		06 59	07 03		07 05	07 09	
London Cannon Street 4 ⊖	d				06 27								06 50			07 00						
London Blackfriars 3 ⊖	d																					
London Bridge 4 ⊖	d		06 26		06a30	06 34	06 38		06 40	06 44	06 47	06 53	06 54	06 55	06a59	07 04	07 05	07 08		07 10	07 14	
London Victoria 15 ⊖	d	06 10		06 14				06 30											06 50			07 09
New Cross 4 ⊖	d		06 32			06 40			06 46				06 59	07 02		07 09						
St Johns	d		06 34										07 01	07 04		07 11						
Lewisham 4	a		06 37	06 41		06 43			06 49	06 53	06 55		07 04	07 07		07 14				07 18		07 24
Hither Green 4	a					06 48				06 58			07 08				07 18			08 11	07 23	
Petts Wood 4	a	06 44						07 04		07 10			07 21						07 24		07 36	
Orpington 4	a	06 49					06 53	07 07		07 13		07 09	07 28					07 25	07 28		07 40	

		SE	SE	SE ■	SE	SE ■	SE	SE	SE	SE	SE	SE	SE	SE ■	SE	SE	SE	SE	SE	SE	SE ■	SE	SE
London Charing Cross 4 ⊖	d			07 10	07 12	07 15	07 17					07 26		07 29				07 36		07 39	07 40		07 44
London Waterloo (East) 4 ⊖	d			07 13	07 15	07 18	07 20					07 29		07 32				07 39		07 42	07 43		07 47
London Cannon Street 4 ⊖	d	07 10	07 13					07 20		07 24	07 27		07 30			07 32	07 36		07 41			07 44	
London Blackfriars 3 ⊖	d																						
London Bridge 4 ⊖	d	07 14	07a16	07a18	07 21	07 23	07a24	07 24		07 28	07 31	07 34	07 34	07 38		07 37	07 40	07 44	07 45	07 47	07a48	07 48	07a51
London Victoria 15 ⊖	d								07 10						07 25	09a14							
New Cross 4 ⊖	d	07 20								07 33	08a38		07 39						07 50			09a03	
St Johns	d	07 22								07 35			07 41										
Lewisham 4	a	07 26			07 29					07 38			07 44				07 47		07 54	07 56			
Hither Green 4	a	07 31						07 34		08 31		07 45						07 53	07 58				
Petts Wood 4	a								07 49						07 59			08 06					
Orpington 4	a					07 38		07 48	07 53					07 53	08 02			08 09					

A until 18 May

B not 30 July, 6 August

London - Lewisham, Hither Green, Petts Wood and Orpington (Summary of Services)

	SE 1	SE	SE	SE	SE	SE	SE 1	SE	SE	SE	SE 1	SE	SE	SE	SE	SE	SE	SE	SE	SE 1
London Charing Cross 4 ⊖ d					07 48		07 52			07 59	08 00			08 03	08 05		08 11			08 13
London Waterloo (East) 4 ⊖ d					07 51		07 55			08 02	08 03			08 06	08 08		08 14			08 16
London Cannon Street 4 ⊖ d	07 47		07 51			07 54		07 56	08 00				08 05			08 10				
London Blackfriars 3 ⊖ d																				
London Bridge 4 ⊖ d	07 51		07 55		07 56	07 58	08a00	08a00	08 04	08a06	08 09		08a08	08 11	08 13	08 14	08 19			08a20
London Victoria 15 ⊖ d		07 40		07 43								07 55						08 09	08 10	
New Cross 4 ⊖ d			08 00			08 04			08 09							08 20				
St Johns d						08 06			08 11							08 22				
Lewisham 4 a			08 04	08 06		08 10			08 14					08 18		08 25	08 28	08 30		
Hither Green 4 a			08 10												08 23	08 29				
Petts Wood 4 a		08 14	08 23									08 29			08 36				08 44	
Orpington 4 a	08 08	08 19	08 29		08 15						08 25	08 32			08 39				08 47	

	SE	SE	SE	SE 1	SE	SE	SE	SE	SE 1	SE	SE	SE 1	SE	SE	SE	SE 1	SE	SE	SE	SE	SE	SE
London Charing Cross 4 ⊖ d		08 15		08 17	08 20		08 23		08 27	08 31		08 33			08 37		08 41				08 44	
London Waterloo (East) 4 ⊖ d		08 18		08 20	08 23		08 26		08 30	08 34		08 36			08 40		08 44				08 47	
London Cannon Street 4 ⊖ d	08 16		08 19			08 25		08 30			08 36			08 39		08 42				08 44		08 51
London Blackfriars 3 ⊖ d																						
London Bridge 4 ⊖ d	08 20	08a22	08 23	08 25	08 29	08a28	08 31	08 34	08 35	08 39	08a39	08 41		08 43	08 45	08 46	08 49			08 49	08a52	08 55
London Victoria 15 ⊖ d													08 25					08 39	08 40			
New Cross 4 ⊖ d	09a38		08 29				08 38	08 41						08 49						10a08		09 00
St Johns d			08 31				08 40	08 43						08 51								09 02
Lewisham 4 a			08 33				08 43	08 45		08 50				08 54			08 57	09 01				09 05
Hither Green 4 a			08 38		08 41									08 59	08 55							09 10
Petts Wood 4 a			08 51										08 59		09 08				09 14			09 23
Orpington 4 a			08 57	08 41					08 53			08 57	09 02		09 11	09 07			09 17			09 29

	SE	SE	SE 1	SE	SE	SE	SE	SE 1	SE	SE	SE	SE	SE	SE	SE	SE	SE 1	SE 1	SE	SE	SE	SE
London Charing Cross 4 ⊖ d	08 49		08 53		08 55			09 00		09 02		09 06		09 11			09 13			09 17		
London Waterloo (East) 4 ⊖ d	08 52		08 56		08 58			09 03		09 05		09 09		09 14			09 16			09 20		
London Cannon Street 4 ⊖ d		08 54		08 56		09 00	09 03				09 07		09 09			09 15		09 18			09 20	09 24
London Blackfriars 3 ⊖ d																						
London Bridge 4 ⊖ d	08 57	08 58	09 01	09a00	09 03	09 04	09a06	09 08		09 10	09 11	09 14	09 14	09 19		09 19	09a20	09 22		09a24	09 25	09 28
London Victoria 15 ⊖ d									08 55						09 09				09 10			
New Cross 4 ⊖ d		09 04				09 09					10a33		09 19			10a38					09 29	09 33
St Johns d		09 06				09 11															09 31	09 35
Lewisham 4 a		09 09				09 14				09 18			09 23	09 28	09 31						09 34	09 38
Hither Green 4 a					09 14							09 23	09 28								09 38	
Petts Wood 4 a									09 29			09 36							09 44		09 51	
Orpington 4 a	09 24		09 20					09 26	09 33			09 39						09 40	09 47		09 58	

	SE	SE	SE	SE 1	SE	SE	SE	SE	SE	SE	SE	SE 1	SE	SE 1	SE	SE	SE	SE	SE	SE	SE
London Charing Cross 4 ⊖ d		09 26		09 30		09 32		09 36		09 39		09 40		09 45		09 47				09 56	
London Waterloo (East) 4 ⊖ d		09 29		09 33		09 35		09 39		09 42		09 43		09 48		09 50				09 59	
London Cannon Street 4 ⊖ d	09 28		09 30				09 37		09 40				09 47				09 50	09 54	09 57		10 00
London Blackfriars 3 ⊖ d																					
London Bridge 4 ⊖ d	09a31	09 34		09 39		09 40	09a40	09 44	09 44	09 47		09a48	09 51	09 53		09a54	09 54	09 58	10a00	10 04	10 04
London Victoria 15 ⊖ d					09 25						09 39				09 40						
New Cross 4 ⊖ d			09 39						09 49				11a08				09 59	10 03			10 09
St Johns d			09 41						09 51								10 01	10 05			10 11
Lewisham 4 a			09 44			09 49			09 54	09 56	10 01						10 04	10 08			10 14
Hither Green 4 a		09 44						09 53	09 58								10 08			10 13	
Petts Wood 4 a					09 59			10 06							10 14		10 21				
Orpington 4 a				09 55	10 02			10 09						10 08	10 17		10 27				

	SE 1	SE	SE	SE	SE	SE	SE	SE	SE 1 H	SE	SE 1	SE	SE	SE	SE	SE	SE	SE	SE 1	SE	SE	SE
London Charing Cross 4 ⊖ d	10 00		10 02		10 06		10 09		10 10		10 15		10 17				10 26		10 30		10 32	
London Waterloo (East) 4 ⊖ d	10 03		10 05		10 09		10 12		10 13		10 18		10 20				10 29		10 33		10 35	
London Cannon Street 4 ⊖ d				10 07		10 10				10 17				10 20	10 24	10 27		10 30				10 37
London Blackfriars 3 ⊖ d																						
London Bridge 4 ⊖ d	10 09		10 10	10a10	10 14	10 14	10 17		10a18	10 21	10 23		10a24	10 24	10 28	10a30	10 34	10 34	10 39		10 40	10a40
London Victoria 15 ⊖ d		09 55						10 09				10 10								10 25		
New Cross 4 ⊖ d						10 19				11a38				10 29	10 33			10 39				
St Johns d						10 21								10 31	10 35			10 41				
Lewisham 4 a			10 18			10 24	10 26	10 31						10 34	10 38			10 44			10 48	
Hither Green 4 a					10 23	10 28								10 38			10 43					
Petts Wood 4 a		10 29			10 36							10 44		10 51						10 59		
Orpington 4 a	10 25	10 32			10 39						10 38	10 47		10 57					10 55	11 02		

London - Lewisham, Hither Green, Petts Wood and Orpington (Summary of Services)

	SE	SE	SE	SE	SE 1 H	SE	SE 1	SE	SE	SE	SE	SE	SE	SE	SE 1	SE	SE	SE	SE	SE	SE
London Charing Cross 4 ⊖ d	10 36		10 39		10 40		10 45		10 47				10 56		11 00		11 02		11 06		11 09
London Waterloo (East) 4 ⊖ d	10 39		10 42		10 43		10 48		10 50				10 59		11 03		11 05		11 09		11 12
London Cannon Street 4 ⊖ d		10 40				10 47				10 50	10 54	10 57		11 00				11 07		11 10	
London Blackfriars 3 ⊖ d																					
London Bridge 4 ⊖ d	10 44	10 44	10 47		10a48	10 51	10 53		10a54	10 54	10 58	11a00	11 04	11 04	11 09		11 10	11 11	11 14	11 14	11 17
London Victoria 15 ⊖ d				10 39				10 40								10 55					
New Cross 4 ⊖ d		10 49				12a08				10 59	11 03			11 09				12a33		11 19	
St Johns d		10 51								11 01	11 05			11 11						11 21	
Lewisham 4 a		10 54	10 56	11 01						11 04	11 08			11 14			11 18			11 24	11 26
Hither Green 4 a	10 53	10 58								11 08			11 13						11 23	11 28	
Petts Wood 4 a	11 06							11 14		11 21						11 29			11 36		
Orpington 4 a	11 09						11 08	11 17		11 27					11 25	11 32			11 39		

	SE	SE 1 H	SE	SE 1	SE	SE	SE	SE	SE	SE	SE	SE 1	SE	SE	SE	SE	SE	SE	SE	SE 1 H	SE	SE 1
London Charing Cross 4 ⊖ d		11 10		11 15		11 17				11 26		11 30		11 32		11 36		11 39		11 40		11 45
London Waterloo (East) 4 ⊖ d		11 14		11 18		11 20				11 29		11 33		11 35		11 39		11 42		11 44		11 48
London Cannon Street 4 ⊖ d			11 17				11 20	11 24	11 27		11 30				11 37		11 40				11 47	
London Blackfriars 3 ⊖ d																						
London Bridge 4 ⊖ d		11a19	11 21	11 23		11a24	11 24	11 28	11a30	11 34	11 34	11 39		11 40	11a40	11 44	11 44	11 47		11a49	11 51	11 53
London Victoria 15 ⊖ d	11 09				11 10								11 25						11 39			
New Cross 4 ⊖ d			12a38				11 29	11 33			11 39						11 49				13a08	
St Johns d							11 31	11 35			11 41						11 51					
Lewisham 4 a	11 31						11 34	11 38			11 44			11 48			11 54	11 56	12 01			
Hither Green 4 a							11 39			11 43						11 53	11 58					
Petts Wood 4 a					11 44		11 51						11 59			12 06						
Orpington 4 a				11 38	11 47		11 57					11 55	12 02			12 09						12 08

	SE	SE	SE	SE	SE	SE	SE	SE 1	SE	SE	SE	SE	SE	SE	SE	SE 1 H	SE	SE 1	SE	SE	SE	SE
London Charing Cross 4 ⊖ d		11 47				11 56		12 00		12 02		12 06		12 09		12 10		12 15		12 17		
London Waterloo (East) 4 ⊖ d		11 50				11 59		12 03		12 05		12 09		12 12		12 13		12 18		12 20		
London Cannon Street 4 ⊖ d			11 50	11 54	11 57		12 00				12 07		12 10				12 17				12 20	12 24
London Blackfriars 3 ⊖ d																						
London Bridge 4 ⊖ d		11a54	11 54	11 58	12a00	12 04	12 04	12 09		12 10	12a10	12 14	12 14	12 17		12a18	12 21	12 23		12a24	12 24	12 28
London Victoria 15 ⊖ d	11 40								11 55						12 09				12 10			
New Cross 4 ⊖ d			11 59	12 03			12 09						12 19				13a38				12 29	12 33
St Johns d			12 01	12 05			12 11						12 21								12 31	12 35
Lewisham 4 a			12 04	12 08			12 14			12 18			12 24	12 26	12 31						12 34	12 38
Hither Green 4 a			12 08			12 13						12 23	12 28								12 38	
Petts Wood 4 a	12 14		12 21						12 29			12 36							12 44		12 51	
Orpington 4 a	12 17		12 27					12 25	12 32			12 39						12 38	12 47		12 57	

	SE	SE	SE	SE 1	SE	SE	SE	SE	SE	SE	SE	SE 1 H	SE	SE 1	SE	SE	SE	SE	SE	SE	SE
London Charing Cross 4 ⊖ d		12 26		12 30		12 32		12 36		12 39		12 40		12 45		12 47				12 56	
London Waterloo (East) 4 ⊖ d		12 29		12 33		12 35		12 39		12 42		12 43		12 48		12 50				12 59	
London Cannon Street 4 ⊖ d	12 27		12 30				12 37		12 40				12 47				12 50	12 54	12 57		13 00
London Blackfriars 3 ⊖ d																					
London Bridge 4 ⊖ d	12a30	12 34	12 34	12 39		12 40	12a40	12 44	12 44	12 47		12a48	12 51	12 53		12a54	12 54	12 58	13a00	13 04	13 04
London Victoria 15 ⊖ d					12 25						12 39				12 40						
New Cross 4 ⊖ d			12 39						12 49				14a08				12 59	13 03			13 09
St Johns d			12 41						12 51								13 01	13 05			13 11
Lewisham 4 a			12 44			12 48			12 54	12 56	13 01						13 03	13 08			13 14
Hither Green 4 a		12 43						12 53	12 58								13 08			13 13	
Petts Wood 4 a					12 59			13 06							13 14		13 21				
Orpington 4 a				12 55	13 02			13 09						13 08	13 17		13 27				

	SE 1	SE	SE	SE	SE	SE	SE	SE	SE 1 H	SE	SE 1	SE	SE	SE	SE	SE	SE	SE	SE 1	SE	SE	SE
London Charing Cross 4 ⊖ d	13 00		13 02		13 06		13 09		13 10		13 15		13 17				13 26		13 30		13 32	
London Waterloo (East) 4 ⊖ d	13 03		13 05		13 09		13 12		13 13		13 18		13 20				13 29		13 33		13 35	
London Cannon Street 4 ⊖ d				13 07		13 10				13 17				13 20	13 24	13 27		13 30				13 37
London Blackfriars 3 ⊖ d																						
London Bridge 4 ⊖ d	13 09		13 10	13a10	13 14	13 14	13 17		13a18	13 21	13 23		13a24	13 24	13 28	13a30	13 34	13 34	13 39		13 40	13a40
London Victoria 15 ⊖ d		12 55						13 09				13 10								13 25		
New Cross 4 ⊖ d						13 19				14a38				13 29	13 33			13 39				
St Johns d						13 21								13 31	13 35			13 41				
Lewisham 4 a			13 18			13 24	13 26	13 31						13 34	13 38			13 44			13 48	
Hither Green 4 a					13 23	13 28								13 38			13 43					
Petts Wood 4 a		13 29			13 36							13 44		13 51						13 59		
Orpington 4 a	13 25	13 32			13 39						13 38	13 47		13 57					13 55	14 02		

Table 199

Mondays to Fridays

30 July to 10 August

London - Lewisham, Hither Green, Petts Wood and Orpington (Summary of Services)

Station	SE	SE	SE		SE	SE ■ ✕	SE	SE ■	SE	SE	SE	SE	SE		SE	SE	SE ■	SE	SE	SE	SE	SE	SE	
London Charing Cross ■ ⊖ d	13 36		13 39			13 40		13 45		13 47					13 56		14 00		14 02		14 06		14 09	
London Waterloo (East) ■ ⊖ d	13 39		13 42			13 43		13 48		13 50					13 59		14 03		14 05		14 09		14 12	
London Cannon Street ■ ⊖ d		13 40					13 47				13 50	13 54	13 57			14 00								
London Blackfriars ■ ⊖ d																				14 07		14 10		
London Bridge ■ ⊖ d	13 44	13 44	13 47			13a48	13 51	13 53		13a54	13 54	13 58	14a00		14 04	14 04	14 09		14 10	14a10	14 14	14 14	14 17	
London Victoria ■ ⊖ d					13 39				13 40									13 55						
New Cross ■ ⊖ d		13 49					15a08				13 59	14 03				14 09						14 19		
St Johns d		13 51									14 01	14 05				14 11						14 21		
Lewisham ■ a		13 54	13 56		14 01						14 04	14 08				14 14			14 18			14 24	14 26	
Hither Green ■ a	13 53	13 58									14 08				14 13						14 23	14 28		
Petts Wood ■ a	14 06								14 14		14 21							14 29			14 36			
Orpington ■ a	14 09							14 08	14 17		14 27						14 25	14 32			14 39			

Station	SE	SE ■ ✕	SE	SE ■	SE	SE	SE	SE	SE		SE	SE	SE ■	SE	SE	SE	SE	SE	SE		SE	SE ■ ✕	SE	SE ■
London Charing Cross ■ ⊖ d		14 10		14 15		14 17					14 26		14 30		14 32		14 36		14 39			14 40		14 45
London Waterloo (East) ■ ⊖ d		14 13		14 18		14 20					14 29		14 33		14 35		14 39		14 42			14 43		14 48
London Cannon Street ■ ⊖ d			14 17				14 20	14 24	14 27			14 30				14 37		14 40					14 47	
London Blackfriars ■ ⊖ d																								
London Bridge ■ ⊖ d		14a18	14 21	14 23		14a24	14 24	14 28	14a30		14 34	14 34	14 39		14 40	14 41	14 44	14 44	14 47			14a48	14 51	14 53
London Victoria ■ ⊖ d	14 09				14 10									14 25							14 39			
New Cross ■ ⊖ d			15a38				14 29	14 33				14 39				16a03		14 49					16a08	
St Johns d							14 31	14 35				14 41						14 51						
Lewisham ■ a	14 31						14 34	14 38				14 44			14 48			14 54	14 56		15 01			
Hither Green ■ a							14 38				14 43						14 53	14 58						
Petts Wood ■ a					14 44		14 51							14 59			15 06							
Orpington ■ a				14 38	14 47		14 57						14 55	15 02			15 09							15 08

Station	SE	SE	SE	SE	SE		SE	SE	SE ■	SE	SE	SE	SE	SE	SE		SE	SE ■ ✕	SE	SE ■	SE	SE	SE	SE
London Charing Cross ■ ⊖ d		14 47					14 56		15 00		15 02		15 06		15 09			15 10		15 15		15 17		
London Waterloo (East) ■ ⊖ d		14 50					14 59		15 03		15 05		15 09		15 12			15 13		15 18		15 20		
London Cannon Street ■ ⊖ d			14 50	14 54	14 57			15 00				15 07		15 10					15 17				15 20	15 24
London Blackfriars ■ ⊖ d																								
London Bridge ■ ⊖ d		14a54	14 54	14 58	15a00		15 04	15 04	15 09		15 10	15a10	15 14	15 14	15 17			15a18	15 21	15 23		15a24	15 24	15 28
London Victoria ■ ⊖ d	14 40									14 55							15 09				15 10			
New Cross ■ ⊖ d			14 59	15 03				15 09						15 19					16a38				15 29	15 33
St Johns d			15 01	15 05				15 11						15 21									15 31	15 35
Lewisham ■ a			15 04	15 08				15 14			15 18			15 24	15 26		15 31						15 34	15 38
Hither Green ■ a			15 08				15 13						15 23	15 28									15 38	
Petts Wood ■ a	15 14		15 21							15 29			15 36								15 44		15 51	
Orpington ■ a	15 17		15 27						15 25	15 32			15 39							15 38	15 47		15 57	

Station	SE		SE	SE	SE ■	SE	SE	SE	SE	SE	SE		SE	SE ■ ✕	SE	SE ■	SE	SE	SE	SE	SE		SE	SE
London Charing Cross ■ ⊖ d			15 26		15 30		15 32		15 36		15 39			15 40		15 45		15 47					15 56	
London Waterloo (East) ■ ⊖ d			15 29		15 33		15 35		15 39		15 42			15 43		15 48		15 50					15 59	
London Cannon Street ■ ⊖ d	15 27			15 30				15 37		15 40					15 47				15 50	15 54	15 57			16 00
London Blackfriars ■ ⊖ d																								
London Bridge ■ ⊖ d	15a30		15 34	15 34	15 39		15 40	15a40	15 44	15 44	15 47			15a48	15 51	15 53		15a54	15 54	15 58	16a00		16 04	16 04
London Victoria ■ ⊖ d						15 25							15 39				15 40							
New Cross ■ ⊖ d				15 39						15 49					17a11				15 59	16 03				16 10
St Johns d				15 41						15 51									16 01	16 05				16 12
Lewisham ■ a				15 44			15 48			15 54	15 56		16 01						16 04	16 08				16 14
Hither Green ■ a			15 43						15 53	15 58									16 08				16 13	
Petts Wood ■ a						15 59			16 06								16 14		16 21					
Orpington ■ a					15 55	16 02			16 09							16 08	16 17		16 27					

Station	SE ■	SE	SE	SE	SE	SE	SE		SE	SE	SE ■ ✕	SE	SE ■	SE	SE	SE	SE		SE	SE	SE ■	SE	SE	SE
London Charing Cross ■ ⊖ d	16 00		16 02		16 06		16 09				16 10		16 15		16 20				16 26		16 28		16 30	
London Waterloo (East) ■ ⊖ d	16 03		16 05		16 09		16 12				16 13		16 18		16 23				16 29		16 31		16 33	
London Cannon Street ■ ⊖ d				16 07		16 10						16 17		16 20		16 24	16 27			16 30				16 34
London Blackfriars ■ ⊖ d																								
London Bridge ■ ⊖ d	16 09		16 10	16a10	16 14	16 14	16 17				16a18	16 21	16a22	16 24	16a28	16 28	16a30		16 34	16 34	16 36		16 38	16a37
London Victoria ■ ⊖ d		15 55							16 09	16 10												16 25		
New Cross ■ ⊖ d						16 20						17a39		16 30		16 34				16 40				
St Johns d						16 22								16 32		16 36				16 42				
Lewisham ■ a			16 19			16 24	16 26		16 31					16 34		16 38				16 44			16 47	
Hither Green ■ a					16 23	16 29								16 39					16 43					
Petts Wood ■ a		16 29			16 36					16 44				16 51								16 59		
Orpington ■ a	16 25	16 32			16 39					16 49				16 57							16 52	17 04		

Table 199

Mondays to Fridays

30 July to 10 August

London - Lewisham, Hither Green, Petts Wood and Orpington (Summary of Services)

Station	SE		SE		SE ■ ✕	SE	SE	SE	SE	SE	SE ■	SE ■	SE		SE	SE	SE	SE	SE	SE	SE	SE ■	SE	
London Charing Cross ■ ⊖ d	16 32				16 37	16 39					16 41		16 42		16 45		16 49		16 51		16 55	16 57		
London Waterloo (East) ■ ⊖ d	16 35				16 40	16 42					16 44		16 45		16 48		16 52		16 54		16 58	16a59		
London Cannon Street ■ ⊖ d			16 39				16 42			16 44		16 46				16 51		16 54		16 56			16 58	
London Blackfriars ■ ⊖ d																								
London Bridge ■ ⊖ d	16 40		16 43		16a44	16a46	16 46			16a47	16a48	16a49	16 51		16 53	16 55	16 57	16a57	16 59	17 00	17a02		17 02	
London Victoria ■ ⊖ d								16 39	16 40															
New Cross ■ ⊖ d			16 49				16 52								18a02	17 01							17 08	
St Johns d			16 51													17 03							17 10	
Lewisham ■ a			16 53				16 55	16 58					17 00			17 05			17 07				17 12	
Hither Green ■ a	16 49		16 58				17 57						17 05				17 07						17 17	
Petts Wood ■ a	17 03								17 14				17 18							17 24				
Orpington ■ a	17 06								17 19				17 24							17 27				

Station	SE	SE ■	SE	SE ■	SE	SE	SE	SE	SE ■		SE	SE	SE	SE	SE	SE ■ ✕	SE	SE	SE		SE ■	SE	SE ■	SE
London Charing Cross ■ ⊖ d			16 59	17 01			17 03				17 06		17 10		17 12	17 14			17 17		17 19			17 21
London Waterloo (East) ■ ⊖ d			17 02	17 04			17 06				17 09		17 13		17 15	17a17			17 20		17a21			17 24
London Cannon Street ■ ⊖ d		17 02			17 04	17 06			17 08			17 12		17 16			17 19					17 21	17 24	
London Blackfriars ■ ⊖ d																								
London Bridge ■ ⊖ d		17a05	17a06	17a08	17 08	17a09	17 11		17a11		17 14	17 16	17 19	17a19	17 21		17 23		17a24			17 25	17a27	17a28
London Victoria ■ ⊖ d	16 59							17 04										17 15						
New Cross ■ ⊖ d					17 14							17 22										17 31		
St Johns d												17 24										17 33		
Lewisham ■ a					17 17		17 20	17 23				17 26			17 30							17 35		
Hither Green ■ a							17 25				18 21		17 28									17 40		
Petts Wood ■ a	17 36						17 39										17 43	17 50						
Orpington ■ a	17 41						17 45										17 47	17 55						

Station	SE ■	SE	SE	SE ■	SE		SE	SE	SE	SE	SE	SE ■	SE	SE	SE		SE	SE	SE ■ ✕	SE	SE ■	SE	SE	SE ■
London Charing Cross ■ ⊖ d	17 23				17 26		17 29		17 30		17 32		17 34					17 39	17 41			17 43		17 45
London Waterloo (East) ■ ⊖ d	17 26				17 29		17 32		17a32		17 35		17 37					17 42	17a43			17 46		17 48
London Cannon Street ■ ⊖ d		17 26	17 28	17 30						17 34		17 37			17 39		17 41			17 43	17 45		17 47	
London Blackfriars ■ ⊖ d																								
London Bridge ■ ⊖ d	17a30	17 30	17a31	17a33	17 35		17a36			17 39	17 41	17a40	17 43		17a42		17 45	17a46		17 47	17a48	17a50	17 51	17a52
London Victoria ■ ⊖ d								17 30						17 34										
New Cross ■ ⊖ d		17 36								17 45										17 53			17 58	
St Johns d										17 47										17 55				
Lewisham ■ a		17 39			17 43					17 49			17 52	17 55						17 58			18 01	
Hither Green ■ a					17 48						17 51									18 03			18 57	
Petts Wood ■ a					18 01			18 05									18 08							
Orpington ■ a					18 07			18 10									18 11							

Station	SE		SE	SE	SE ■	SE	SE	SE	SE	SE	SE		SE ■	SE	SE	SE	SE	SE ■	SE	SE ■	SE		SE ■	SE
London Charing Cross ■ ⊖ d			17 47			17 50	17 52		17 54	17 56			17 59				18 01	18 03			18 05		18 07	
London Waterloo (East) ■ ⊖ d			17 50			17 53	17a54		17 57	17 59			18a01				18 04	18a05			18 08		18 10	
London Cannon Street ■ ⊖ d	17 50				17 52			17 56						18 00	18 02				18 04	18 08				18 10
London Blackfriars ■ ⊖ d																								
London Bridge ■ ⊖ d	17a53		17 55		17a55	17a57		18 00	18 02	18 04				18a03	18 06		18a08		18 08	18a11	18a12		18a14	18 14
London Victoria ■ ⊖ d				17 45							17 56					18 00								
New Cross ■ ⊖ d								18 06											18 14					18 20
St Johns d								18 08											18 16					
Lewisham ■ a			18 04					18 10		18 13	18 17								18 19					18 23
Hither Green ■ a			18 09						18 12										18 24					
Petts Wood ■ a			18 23	18 26											18 28	18 35								
Orpington ■ a			18 29	18 31											18 32	18 41								

Station	SE	SE	SE ■	SE	SE	SE	SE		SE	SE ■ ✕	SE	SE	SE	SE	SE	SE ■	SE		SE	SE ■	SE	SE	SE ■	SE
London Charing Cross ■ ⊖ d		18 09		18 12	18 14				18 18	18 21					18 23				18 27		18 30		18 32	18 34
London Waterloo (East) ■ ⊖ d		18 12		18 15	18 17				18 21	18a23					18 26				18 30		18 33		18 35	18 37
London Cannon Street ■ ⊖ d	18 12		18 14			18 18	18 21				18 23		18 25			18 28	18 30			18 32		18 34		
London Blackfriars ■ ⊖ d																								
London Bridge ■ ⊖ d	18a15	18 17	18a17	18 21	18 23	18 23	18a24		18 26		18 27		18 29		18a31	18a31	18a33		18a34	18a35	18 38	18 38	18a39	18a41
London Victoria ■ ⊖ d												18 15		18 18										
New Cross ■ ⊖ d				19a38		18 28							18 35									18 44		
St Johns d						18 30							18 37									18 46		
Lewisham ■ a		18 26				18 33			18 35				18 40	18 42								18 48		
Hither Green ■ a		18 31			18 35								18 45								18 48			
Petts Wood ■ a		18 43									18 49	18 53									19 02			
Orpington ■ a		18 49									18 53	18 59									19 06			

Table 199

Mondays to Fridays

30 July to 10 August

London - Lewisham, Hither Green, Petts Wood and Orpington (Summary of Services)

		SE	SE	SE		SE 1	SE 1 ⌶	SE	SE	SE	SE 1	SE	SE	SE		SE	SE	SE	SE	SE	SE	SE 1	SE	SE 1	
London Charing Cross 4	⊖ d		18 37	18 39			18 41				18 45					18 48		18 52		18 56		19 00			
London Waterloo (East) 4	⊖ d		18 40	18 42			18 44				18 48					18 51		18 55		18 59		19 03			
London Cannon Street 4	⊖ d	18 40				18 44				18 46		18 48		18 50			18 54		18 57		19 00			19 04	
London Blackfriars 3	⊖ d																								
London Bridge 4	⊖ d	18 44	18 46	18 48		18a47	18 50			18a49	18a52	18 52		18 54		18 57	18 58	18a59	19a00	19 04	19 04	19 09		19a07	
London Victoria 15	⊖ d							18 30	18 39				18 45										19 00		
New Cross 4	⊖ d	18 50		18 55										19 00			19 05				19 09				
St Johns	d	18 52												19 02			19 07				19 11				
Lewisham 4	a	18 54		18 59					19 02					19 04		19 06	19 10				19 14				
Hither Green 4	a		18 55											19 09						19 14					
Petts Wood 4	a							19 06				19 13	19 19										19 35		
Orpington 4	a						19 06	19 12				19 19	19 25									19 27	19 38		

		SE	SE	SE	SE	SE	SE	SE 1 ⌶	SE	SE 1		SE	SE	SE	SE	SE	SE	SE	SE 1	SE		SE	SE	SE	SE
London Charing Cross 4	⊖ d	19 02		19 06		19 09		19 10		19 15			19 17				19 26		19 30			19 32		19 36	
London Waterloo (East) 4	⊖ d	19 05		19 09		19 12		19 13		19 18			19 20				19 29		19 33			19 35		19 39	
London Cannon Street 4	⊖ d		19 07		19 10				19 17					19 20	19 24	19 27		19 30					19 37		19 40
London Blackfriars 3	⊖ d																								
London Bridge 4	⊖ d	19 10	19a10	19 14	19 14	19 17		19a18	19a20	19 23			19a24	19 24	19 28	19a30	19 34	19 34	19 39			19 40	19a40	19 44	19 44
London Victoria 15	⊖ d						19 09					19 10								19 25					
New Cross 4	⊖ d				19 19									19 29	19 33			19 39							19 49
St Johns	d				19 21									19 31	19 35			19 41							19 51
Lewisham 4	a	19 18			19 24	19 26	19 31							19 33	19 38			19 44				19 48			19 55
Hither Green 4	a			19 23	19 28									19 38			19 43							19 53	19 59
Petts Wood 4	a			19 38								19 44		19 51						19 59				20 06	
Orpington 4	a			19 43						19 38		19 48		19 57					19 55	20 02				20 09	

		SE	SE	SE 1 ⌶	SE	SE 1		SE	SE	SE	SE	SE	SE	SE	SE 1	SE		SE	SE	SE	SE	SE 1 ⌶	SE	SE 1	SE
London Charing Cross 4	⊖ d	19 39		19 40		19 45			19 47				19 56		20 00			20 02	20 06		20 09	20 10		20 15	
London Waterloo (East) 4	⊖ d	19 42		19 43		19 48			19 50				19 59		20 03			20 05	20 09		20 12	20 13		20 18	
London Cannon Street 4	⊖ d				19 47					19 50	19 54	19 57		20 00						20 10			20 17		
London Blackfriars 3	⊖ d																								
London Bridge 4	⊖ d	19 47		19a48	19a50	19 53			19a54	19 54	19 58	20a00	20 04	20 04	20 09			20 10	20 14	20 14	20 17	20a18	20a20	20 23	
London Victoria 15	⊖ d		19 39					19 40								19 55									20 10
New Cross 4	⊖ d									19 59	20 03			20 09						20 19					
St Johns	d									20 01	20 05			20 11						20 21					
Lewisham 4	a	19 57	20 01							20 04	20 08			20 14				20 18		20 25	20 27				
Hither Green 4	a									20 08			20 13						20 23	20 29					
Petts Wood 4	a							20 14		20 21						20 29			20 36						20 44
Orpington 4	a					20 08		20 18		20 27					20 25	20 32			20 39					20 38	20 47

		SE		SE	SE	SE	SE 1	SE	SE	SE	SE	SE 1		SE	SE 1	SE	SE	SE	SE 1	SE	SE	SE		SE	SE 1
London Charing Cross 4	⊖ d			20 17	20 22		20 30		20 32	20 36	20 39	20 40			20 45	20 47	20 52		21 00		21 02	21 06		21 09	21 10
London Waterloo (East) 4	⊖ d			20 20	20 25		20 33		20 35	20 39	20 42	20 43			20 48	20 50	20 55		21 03		21 05	21 09		21 12	21 13
London Cannon Street 4	⊖ d	20 20				20 27								20 47				20 57							
London Blackfriars 3	⊖ d																								
London Bridge 4	⊖ d	20 24		20 25	20 30	20a30	20 39		20 40	20 44	20 47	20a48		20a50	20 53	20 55	21 00	21a00	21 09		21 10	21 14		21 17	21 19
London Victoria 15	⊖ d							20 25												20 55					
New Cross 4	⊖ d	20 29		20 32	20 35				20 45							21 00	21 05				21 15				
St Johns	d	20 31		20 34												21 02									
Lewisham 4	a	20 34		20 36	20 38				20 49		20 56					21 05	21 09				21 19	21 21		21 26	
Hither Green 4	a	20 38			20 44					20 53							21 13					21 26			
Petts Wood 4	a	20 51						20 59		21 06										21 29		21 38			
Orpington 4	a	20 57					20 55	21 02		21 09					21 08				21 25	21 32		21 42			21 34

		SE	SE	SE	SE	SE 1	SE	SE		SE	SE	SE 1	SE	SE 1	SE	SE	SE	SE 1		SE	SE	SE	SE	SE 1	SE
London Charing Cross 4	⊖ d		21 17	21 22	21 26	21 30		21 32		21 36	21 39	21 40		21 45	21 47	21 52	21 56	22 00			22 02	22 06	22 09	22 10	
London Waterloo (East) 4	⊖ d		21 20	21 25	21 29	21 33		21 35		21 39	21 42	21 43		21 48	21 50	21 55	21 59	22 03			22 05	22 09	22 12	22 13	
London Cannon Street 4	⊖ d	21 16											21 46												22 16
London Blackfriars 3	⊖ d																								
London Bridge 4	⊖ d	21a19	21 25	21 30	21a33	21 39		21 40		21 44	21 47	21a48	21a49	21 53	21 55	22 00	22a03	22 09			22 10	22 14	22 17	22 19	22a19
London Victoria 15	⊖ d						21 25													21 55					
New Cross 4	⊖ d		21 30	21 35				21 45							22 00	22 05					22 15				
St Johns	d		21 32												22 02										
Lewisham 4	a		21 35	21 39				21 49		21 51	21 56				22 05	22 09					22 19	22 21	22 26		
Hither Green 4	a			21 43						21 56						22 13						22 26			
Petts Wood 4	a						21 59			22 08										22 29		22 38			
Orpington 4	a					21 55	22 02			22 15				22 08				22 25		22 32		22 45		22 34	

Table 199

Mondays to Fridays

30 July to 10 August

London - Lewisham, Hither Green, Petts Wood and Orpington (Summary of Services)

		SE	SE	SE		SE 1	SE	SE	SE	SE	SE 1	SE	SE 1	SE		SE	SE	SE 1	SE	SE	SE	SE	SE 1	SE	
London Charing Cross 4	⊖ d	22 17	22 22	22 26		22 30		22 32	22 36	22 39	22 40		22 45	22 47		22 52	22 56	23 00		23 02	23 06	23 09	23 10	23 17	
London Waterloo (East) 4	⊖ d	22 20	22 25	22 29		22 33		22 35	22 39	22 42	22 43		22 48	22 50		22 55	22 59	23 03		23 05	23 09	23 12	23 13	23 20	
London Cannon Street 4	⊖ d											22 46													
London Blackfriars 3	⊖ d																								
London Bridge 4	⊖ d	22 25	22 30	22a33		22 39		22 40	22 44	22 47	22a48	22a49	22 53	22 55		23 00	23a03	23 09		23 10	23 14	23 17	23 19	23 25	
London Victoria 15	⊖ d						22 25												22 55						
New Cross 4	⊖ d	22 30	22 35					22 45						23 00		23 05				23 15				23 30	
St Johns	d	22 32												23 02										23 32	
Lewisham 4	a	22 35	22 39					22 49	22 51	22 56				23 05		23 09				23 19	23 21	23 26		23 35	
Hither Green 4	a		22 43						22 56							23 13					23 26				
Petts Wood 4	a						22 59		23 08										23 29		23 38				
Orpington 4	a					22 54	23 02		23 15				23 08					23 24	23 32		23 45		23 34		

		SE	SE	SE 1	SE	SE	SE	SE	SE 1	SE 1		SE	SE	SE
London Charing Cross 4	⊖ d	23 22	23 26	23 30		23 32	23 36	23 39	23 40	23 45		23 52		23 56
London Waterloo (East) 4	⊖ d	23 25	23 29	23 33		23 35	23 39	23 42	23 43	23 48		23 55		23 59
London Cannon Street 4	⊖ d													
London Blackfriars 3	⊖ d													
London Bridge 4	⊖ d	23 30	23a33	23 39		23 40	23 44	23 47	23a48	23 53		23 59		00a03
London Victoria 15	⊖ d				23 25								23 55	
New Cross 4	⊖ d	23 35				23 45						00 05		
St Johns	d											00 07		
Lewisham 4	a	23 39				23 49	23 51	23 56				00 10		
Hither Green 4	a	23 43					23 56							
Petts Wood 4	a				23 59		00 08						00 29	
Orpington 4	a			23 54	00 02		00 15			00 08			00 32	

Mondays to Fridays

29 August to 7 September

		SE	SE	SE 1	SE 1	SE	SE	SE	SE	SE		SE	SE	SE	SE	SE	SE	SE	SE 1	SE		SE	SE	SE	SE
		A	A	B	A	B	B	A	A	B		A	A	A	A										
London Charing Cross 4	⊖ d		23p36	23p38	23p45	23p46	23p50	23p52		23p56		00 02	00 06	00 10	00 15	00 18		00 32	00 37			00 44	00 48		
London Waterloo (East) 4	⊖ d		23p39	23p41	23p48	23p49	23p53	23p55		23p59		00 05	00 09	00 13	00 18	00 21		00 35	00 40			00 47	00 51		
London Cannon Street 4	⊖ d																00 28			00 41					
London Blackfriars 3	⊖ d																								
London Bridge 4	⊖ d		23p44	23p46	23p53	23p54	23p58	23p59		00 04		00 10	00 14	00 18	00 23	00 26	00 32	00a39	00 45	00 45		00 52	00 56		
London Victoria 15	⊖ d	23p25							23p55															00 45	00 56
New Cross 4	⊖ d						00 04	00 05				00 15		00 23		00 31	00 38					00 57	01 01		
St Johns	d							00 07									00 40								
Lewisham 4	a		23p51			00 02	00 07	00 10		00 11		00 19	00 21	00 27		00 35	00 43			00 52		01 01	01 05		
Hither Green 4	a		23p56			00 07				00 16			00 26	00 31								01s05	01 09		
Petts Wood 4	a	23p59	00 08			00 20			00 29				00 38										01 22	01s25	
Orpington 4	a	00 02	00 12	00 01	00 08	00 23			00 32				00 42		00 46				01 00				01 25	01 29	01 33

		SE	SE	SE	SE	SE		SE	SE	SE 1	SE	SE	SE	SE	SE	SE		SE	SE	SE	SE	SE	SE	SE 1	SE
London Charing Cross 4	⊖ d		04 50	04 56	05 02	05 20			05 26	05 30	05 32	05 36	05 39		05 47			05 52	05 56	06 02	06 06		06 09	06 15	
London Waterloo (East) 4	⊖ d		04 53	04 59	05 05	05 23			05 29	05 33	05 35	05 39	05 42		05 50			05 55	05 59	06 05	06 09		06 12	06 18	
London Cannon Street 4	⊖ d	00 56														05 52						06 12			
London Blackfriars 3	⊖ d																								
London Bridge 4	⊖ d	00a59	04a57	05 04	05 10	05a27			05 34	05 39	05 42	05 44	05 47		05 55	05a55		05a59	06 04	06 10	06 14	06a15	06 17	06 24	
London Victoria 15	⊖ d													05 40											06 10
New Cross 4	⊖ d			05 09	05 15			05 31	05 39		05 48		05 52		06 01				06 09	06 15					
St Johns	d							05 33							06 03										
Lewisham 4	a			05 13	05 19			05 35	05 43		05 51	05 52	05 56		06 05				06 13	06 19	06 22		06 26		
Hither Green 4	a			05 17					05 47			05 56							06 17		06 27				
Petts Wood 4	a											06 08		06 14							06 39				06 44
Orpington 4	a									05 54		06 11		06 18							06 42			06 40	06 49

		SE		SE	SE	SE 1	SE	SE	SE	SE	SE 1	SE		SE	SE	SE	SE	SE 1	SE	SE	SE	SE		SE	SE
London Charing Cross 4	⊖ d	06 17			06 26	06 30		06 32	06 36	06 39	06 45			06 47	06 52		06 56	07 00		07 02	07 06				
London Waterloo (East) 4	⊖ d	06 20			06 29	06 33		06 35	06 39	06 42	06 48			06 50	06 55		06 59	07 03		07 05	07 09				
London Cannon Street 4	⊖ d			06 27								06 50				07 00								07 10	07 13
London Blackfriars 3	⊖ d																								
London Bridge 4	⊖ d	06 26		06a30	06 34	06 38		06 40	06 44	06 47	06 53	06 54		06 55	06a59	07 04	07 05	07 08		07 10	07 14			07 14	07a16
London Victoria 15	⊖ d						06 30												06 50			07 09			
New Cross 4	⊖ d	06 32			06 40			06 46				06 59		07 02		07 09								07 20	
St Johns	d	06 34										07 01		07 04		07 11								07 22	
Lewisham 4	a	06 37			06 43			06 49	06 53	06 56		07 04		07 07		07 14				07 18		07 24		07 26	
Hither Green 4	a				06 48				06 58			07 08					07 18			08 11	07 23			07 31	
Petts Wood 4	a						07 04		07 10			07 21							07 24		07 36				
Orpington 4	a					06 53	07 08		07 13		07 09	07 25						07 25	07 28		07 40				

A not 3 September

B 3 September

Table 199

Mondays to Fridays
29 August to 7 September

London - Lewisham, Hither Green, Petts Wood and Orpington (Summary of Services)

		SE [1]	SE	SE [1]	SE	SE	SE	SE		SE	SE	SE	SE [1]	SE	SE	SE	SE	SE		SE	SE	SE [1]	SE	SE	SE [1]
London Charing Cross 4 ⊖	d	07 10	07 12	07 15	07 17						07 26		07 29					07 36			07 39	07 40		07 44	
London Waterloo (East) 4 ⊖	d	07 13	07 15	07 18	07 20						07 29		07 32					07 39			07 42	07 43		07 47	
London Cannon Street 4 ⊖	d					07 20		07 24		07 27		07 30			07 32	07 32	07 36			07 41			07 44		07 47
London Blackfriars 3 ⊖	d																								
London Bridge 4 ⊖	d	07a18	07 21	07 23	07a24	07 24		07 28		07 31	07 34	07 34	07 38		07a36	07 37	07 40	07 44		07 45	07 47	07a48	07 48	07a51	07 51
London Victoria 15 ⊖	d						07 10							07 25		09a11									
New Cross 4 ⊖	d							07 33		08a38		07 39								07 50			09a03		
St Johns	d							07 35				07 41													
Lewisham 4	a		07 29					07 38				07 44					07 48			07 54	07 56				
Hither Green 4	a					07 34		08 31			07 45							07 53		07 58					
Petts Wood 4	a						07 49							07 59				08 06							
Orpington 4	a			07 38		07 48	07 53						07 53	08 02				08 09							08 08

		SE	SE	SE		SE	SE	SE [1]	SE	SE	SE	SE [1]	SE			SE	SE	SE	SE	SE	SE	SE	SE [1]	SE	
London Charing Cross 4 ⊖	d					07 48		07 52			07 59	08 00					08 03	08 05		08 11			08 13		
London Waterloo (East) 4 ⊖	d					07 51		07 55			08 02	08 03					08 06	08 08		08 14			08 16		
London Cannon Street 4 ⊖	d		07 51				07 54		07 56	08 00						08 05			08 10					08 16	
London Blackfriars 3 ⊖	d																								
London Bridge 4 ⊖	d		07 55			07 56	07 58	08a00	08a00	08 04	08a06	08 09				08a08	08 11	08 13	08 14	08 19			08a20	08 20	
London Victoria 15 ⊖	d	07 40		07 43									07 55								08 09	08 10			
New Cross 4 ⊖	d		08 00				08 04			08 09									08 20					09a38	
St Johns	d						08 06			08 11									08 22						
Lewisham 4	a		08 04	08 07			08 10			08 14							08 18		08 25	08 28	08 30				
Hither Green 4	a		08 10															08 23	08 29						
Petts Wood 4	a	08 14	08 23										08 29					08 36				08 44			
Orpington 4	a	08 19	08 26			08 15						08 25	08 32					08 39				08 47			

		SE	SE	SE [1]	SE	SE	SE	SE	SE [1]	SE		SE	SE [1]	SE	SE	SE	SE [1]	SE	SE	SE		SE	SE	SE	SE
London Charing Cross 4 ⊖	d	08 15		08 17	08 20		08 23		08 27	08 31			08 33			08 37		08 41					08 44		08 49
London Waterloo (East) 4 ⊖	d	08 18		08 20	08 23		08 26		08 30	08 34			08 36			08 40		08 44					08 47		08 52
London Cannon Street 4 ⊖	d		08 19			08 25		08 30				08 36			08 39		08 42					08 47		08 51	
London Blackfriars 3 ⊖	d																								
London Bridge 4 ⊖	d	08a22	08 23	08 25	08 29	08a28	08 31	08 34	08 35	08 39		08a39	08 41		08 43	08 45	08 46	08 49				08 51	08a52	08 55	08 57
London Victoria 15 ⊖	d													08 25					08 39	08 40					
New Cross 4 ⊖	d		08 29				08 38	08 41							08 49							10a08		09 00	
St Johns	d		08 31				08 40	08 43							08 51									09 02	
Lewisham 4	a		08 33				08 43	08 45		08 48					08 54			08 56	09 01					09 05	
Hither Green 4	a		08 38		08 41										08 59	08 55								09 10	
Petts Wood 4	a		08 51											08 59		09 08				09 14				09 23	
Orpington 4	a		08 54	08 41					08 53				08 57	09 02		09 11	09 07			09 17				09 26	09 24

		SE	SE [1]	SE	SE	SE		SE	SE [1]	SE	SE	SE	SE	SE	SE	SE		SE	SE	SE [1]	SE [1]	SE	SE	SE	SE
London Charing Cross 4 ⊖	d		08 53		08 55				09 00		09 02			09 06		09 11				09 13			09 17		
London Waterloo (East) 4 ⊖	d		08 56		08 58				09 03		09 05			09 09		09 14				09 16			09 20		
London Cannon Street 4 ⊖	d	08 54		08 56		09 00		09 03				09 07	09 07		09 09				09 15		09 18			09 20	09 24
London Blackfriars 3 ⊖	d																								
London Bridge 4 ⊖	d	08 58	09 01	09a00	09 03	09 04		09a06	09 08		09 10	09a10	09 11	09 14	09 14	09 19			09 19	09a20	09 22		09a24	09 25	09 28
London Victoria 15 ⊖	d									08 55								09 09				09 10			
New Cross 4 ⊖	d	09 04				09 09							10a33		09 19				10a38					09 29	09 33
St Johns	d	09 06				09 11									09 21									09 31	09 35
Lewisham 4	a	09 09				09 14					09 18				09 24	09 28		09 31						09 34	09 38
Hither Green 4	a				09 14									09 23	09 28									09 38	
Petts Wood 4	a									09 29				09 36								09 44		09 51	
Orpington 4	a		09 20						09 26	09 33				09 39							09 40	09 47		09 55	

		SE		SE	SE	SE [1]	SE	SE	SE	SE	SE	SE		SE	SE [1]	SE	SE [1]	SE	SE	SE	SE	SE		SE	SE
London Charing Cross 4 ⊖	d			09 26		09 30		09 32		09 36		09 39			09 40		09 45		09 47					09 56	
London Waterloo (East) 4 ⊖	d			09 29		09 33		09 35		09 39		09 42			09 43		09 48		09 50					09 59	
London Cannon Street 4 ⊖	d	09 27			09 30				09 37		09 40					09 47				09 50	09 54	09 57			10 00
London Blackfriars 3 ⊖	d																								
London Bridge 4 ⊖	d	09a30		09 34	09 34	09 39		09 40	09a40	09 44	09 44	09 47			09a48	09 51	09 53		09a54	09 54	09 58	10a00		10 04	10 04
London Victoria 15 ⊖	d						09 25							09 39				09 40							
New Cross 4 ⊖	d				09 39						09 49					11a08				09 59	10 03				10 09
St Johns	d				09 41						09 51									10 01	10 05				10 11
Lewisham 4	a				09 44			09 49			09 54	09 56		10 01						10 04	10 08				10 14
Hither Green 4	a			09 43						09 53	09 58									10 08				10 13	
Petts Wood 4	a						09 59			10 06								10 14		10 21					
Orpington 4	a					09 55	10 02			10 09							10 08	10 17		10 24					

Table 199

Mondays to Fridays
29 August to 7 September

London - Lewisham, Hither Green, Petts Wood and Orpington (Summary of Services)

		SE [1]	SE	SE	SE	SE	SE	SE		SE	SE [1] ✕	SE	SE [1]	SE	SE	SE	SE	SE		SE	SE	SE [1]	SE	SE	SE
London Charing Cross 4 ⊖	d	10 00		10 02		10 06		10 09			10 10		10 15		10 17					10 26		10 30		10 32	
London Waterloo (East) 4 ⊖	d	10 03		10 05		10 09		10 12			10 13		10 18		10 20					10 29		10 33		10 35	
London Cannon Street 4 ⊖	d				10 07		10 10					10 17				10 20	10 24	10 27			10 30				10 37
London Blackfriars 3 ⊖	d																								
London Bridge 4 ⊖	d	10 09		10 10	10a10	10 14	10 14	10 17			10a18	10 21	10 23		10a24	10 24	10 28	10a30		10 34	10 34	10 39		10 40	10a40
London Victoria 15 ⊖	d		09 55							10 09				10 10									10 25		
New Cross 4 ⊖	d						10 19					11a38				10 29	10 33				10 39				
St Johns	d						10 21									10 31	10 35				10 41				
Lewisham 4	a			10 19			10 24	10 26		10 31						10 34	10 38				10 44			10 49	
Hither Green 4	a					10 23	10 28									10 38				10 43					
Petts Wood 4	a		10 29			10 36								10 44		10 51							10 59		
Orpington 4	a	10 25	10 32			10 39							10 38	10 47		10 54						10 55	11 02		

		SE	SE	SE		SE	SE [1] ✕	SE	SE [1]	SE	SE	SE	SE	SE		SE	SE	SE [1]	SE	SE	SE	SE	SE	SE	
London Charing Cross 4 ⊖	d	10 36		10 39			10 40		10 45		10 47					10 56		11 00		11 02			11 06		
London Waterloo (East) 4 ⊖	d	10 39		10 42			10 43		10 48		10 50					10 59		11 03		11 05			11 09		
London Cannon Street 4 ⊖	d		10 40					10 47				10 50	10 54	10 57			11 00				11 07	11 07		11 10	
London Blackfriars 3 ⊖	d																								
London Bridge 4 ⊖	d	10 44	10 44	10 47			10a48	10 51	10 53		10a54	10 54	10 58	11a00		11 04	11 04	11 09		11 10	11a10	11 11	11 14	11 14	
London Victoria 15 ⊖	d					10 39				10 40									10 55						
New Cross 4 ⊖	d		10 49					12a08				10 59	11 03				11 09					12a33		11 19	
St Johns	d		10 51									11 01	11 05				11 11							11 21	
Lewisham 4	a		10 54	10 56		11 01						11 04	11 08				11 14			11 19				11 24	
Hither Green 4	a	10 53	10 58									11 08				11 13							11 23	11 28	
Petts Wood 4	a	11 06								11 14		11 21							11 29				11 36		
Orpington 4	a	11 09							11 08	11 17		11 24						11 25	11 32				11 39		

		SE	SE	SE [1] ✕	SE	SE [1]	SE	SE	SE	SE		SE	SE	SE	SE [1]	SE	SE	SE	SE	SE		SE	SE	SE [1] ✕	SE
London Charing Cross 4 ⊖	d	11 09		11 10		11 15		11 17					11 26		11 30		11 32		11 36			11 39		11 40	
London Waterloo (East) 4 ⊖	d	11 12		11 13		11 18		11 20					11 29		11 33		11 35		11 39			11 42		11 43	
London Cannon Street 4 ⊖	d				11 17				11 20	11 24		11 27		11 30				11 37		11 40					11 47
London Blackfriars 3 ⊖	d																								
London Bridge 4 ⊖	d	11 17		11a18	11 21	11 23		11a24	11 24	11 28		11a30	11 34	11 34	11 39		11 40	11 41	11 44	11 44		11 47		11a48	11 51
London Victoria 15 ⊖	d		11 09				11 10									11 25							11 39		
New Cross 4 ⊖	d				12a38				11 29	11 33				11 39				13a03		11 49					13a08
St Johns	d								11 31	11 35				11 41						11 51					
Lewisham 4	a	11 26	11 31						11 33	11 38				11 44			11 49			11 54		11 56	12 01		
Hither Green 4	a								11 38				11 43						11 53	11 58					
Petts Wood 4	a						11 44		11 51							11 59			12 06						
Orpington 4	a					11 38	11 47		11 54						11 55	12 02			12 09						

		SE [1]	SE	SE	SE	SE		SE	SE	SE	SE [1]	SE	SE	SE	SE	SE		SE	SE	SE [1] ✕	SE	SE [1]	SE	SE	SE
London Charing Cross 4 ⊖	d	11 45		11 47					11 56		12 00		12 02		12 06			12 09		12 10		12 15		12 17	
London Waterloo (East) 4 ⊖	d	11 48		11 50					11 59		12 03		12 05		12 09			12 12		12 13		12 18		12 20	
London Cannon Street 4 ⊖	d				11 50	11 54		11 57		12 00				12 07		12 10					12 17				12 20
London Blackfriars 3 ⊖	d																								
London Bridge 4 ⊖	d	11 53		11a54	11 54	11 58		12a00	12 04	12 04	12 09		12 10	12 11	12 14	12 14		12 17		12a18	12 21	12 23		12a24	12 24
London Victoria 15 ⊖	d		11 40									11 55							12 09				12 10		
New Cross 4 ⊖	d				11 59	12 03				12 09				13a33		12 19					13a38				12 29
St Johns	d				12 01	12 05				12 11						12 21									12 31
Lewisham 4	a				12 03	12 08				12 14			12 19			12 24		12 26	12 31						12 34
Hither Green 4	a				12 08				12 13						12 23	12 28									12 38
Petts Wood 4	a		12 14		12 21							12 29			12 36								12 44		12 51
Orpington 4	a	12 08	12 17		12 24						12 25	12 32			12 39							12 38	12 47		12 54

		SE		SE	SE	SE	SE [1]	SE	SE	SE	SE	SE		SE	SE	SE [1] ✕	SE	SE [1]	SE	SE	SE	SE		SE	SE
London Charing Cross 4 ⊖	d				12 26		12 30		12 32		12 36			12 39		12 40		12 45		12 47					12 56
London Waterloo (East) 4 ⊖	d				12 29		12 33		12 35		12 39			12 42		12 43		12 48		12 50					12 59
London Cannon Street 4 ⊖	d	12 24		12 27		12 30				12 37		12 40					12 47				12 50	12 54		12 57	
London Blackfriars 3 ⊖	d																								
London Bridge 4 ⊖	d	12 28		12a30	12 34	12 34	12 39		12 40	12 41	12 44	12 44		12 47		12a48	12 51	12 53		12a54	12 54	12 58		13a00	13 04
London Victoria 15 ⊖	d							12 25							12 39				12 40						
New Cross 4 ⊖	d	12 33				12 39				14a03		12 49					14a08				12 59	13 03			
St Johns	d	12 35				12 41						12 51									13 01	13 05			
Lewisham 4	a	12 38				12 44			12 49			12 54		12 56	13 01						13 03	13 08			
Hither Green 4	a				12 43						12 53	12 58									13 08				13 13
Petts Wood 4	a							12 59			13 06								13 14		13 21				
Orpington 4	a						12 55	13 02			13 09							13 08	13 17		13 24				

London - Lewisham, Hither Green, Petts Wood and Orpington (Summary of Services)

	SE	SE 1	SE	SE	SE	SE	SE		SE	SE	SE 1 ⚒	SE	SE 1	SE	SE	SE	SE		SE	SE	SE	SE 1	SE	SE
London Charing Cross 4 ⊖ d		13 00		13 02		13 06			13 09		13 10		13 15		13 17					13 26		13 30		13 32
London Waterloo (East) 4 ⊖ d		13 03		13 05		13 09			13 12		13 13		13 18		13 20					13 29		13 33		13 35
London Cannon Street 4 ⊖ d	13 00				13 07		13 10					13 17				13 20	13 24		13 27		13 30			
London Blackfriars 3 ⊖ d																								
London Bridge 4 ⊖ d	13 04	13 09		13 10	13 11	13 14	13 14		13 17		13a18	13 21	13 23		13a24	13 24	13 28		13a30	13 34	13 34	13 39		13 40
London Victoria 15 ⊖ d			12 55							13 09				13 10									13 25	
New Cross 4 ⊖ d	13 09				14a33		13 19					14a38				13 29	13 33				13 39			
St Johns d	13 11						13 21									13 31	13 35				13 41			
Lewisham 4 a	13 14			13 19			13 24		13 26	13 31						13 34	13 38				13 44			13 49
Hither Green 4 a						13 23	13 28									13 38				13 43				
Petts Wood 4 a			13 29			13 36								13 44		13 51							13 59	
Orpington 4 a		13 25	13 32			13 39							13 38	13 47		13 54						13 55	14 02	

	SE	SE	SE		SE	SE	SE 1 ⚒	SE	SE 1	SE	SE	SE	SE		SE	SE	SE	SE 1	SE	SE	SE	SE	SE	
London Charing Cross 4 ⊖ d		13 36			13 39		13 40		13 45		13 47					13 56		14 00		14 02		14 06		
London Waterloo (East) 4 ⊖ d		13 39			13 42		13 43		13 48		13 50					13 59		14 03		14 05		14 09		
London Cannon Street 4 ⊖ d	13 37		13 40					13 47				13 50	13 54		13 57		14 00				14 07		14 10	
London Blackfriars 3 ⊖ d																								
London Bridge 4 ⊖ d	13 41	13 44	13 44		13 47		13a48	13 51	13 53		13a54	13 54	13 58		14a00	14 04	14 04	14 09		14 10	14 11	14 14	14 14	
London Victoria 15 ⊖ d						13 39				13 40									13 55					
New Cross 4 ⊖ d	15a03		13 49					15a08				13 59	14 03				14 09				15a33		14 19	
St Johns d			13 51									14 01	14 05				14 11						14 21	
Lewisham 4 a			13 54		13 56	14 01						14 04	14 08				14 14			14 19			14 24	
Hither Green 4 a		13 53	13 58									14 08				14 13						14 23	14 28	
Petts Wood 4 a		14 06								14 14		14 21							14 29			14 36		
Orpington 4 a		14 09							14 08	14 17		14 24						14 25	14 32			14 39		

	SE	SE	SE 1 ⚒	SE	SE 1	SE	SE	SE	SE		SE	SE	SE	SE 1	SE	SE	SE	SE	SE		SE	SE	SE	SE 1 ⚒
London Charing Cross 4 ⊖ d	14 09		14 10		14 15		14 17					14 26		14 30		14 32			14 36			14 39		14 40
London Waterloo (East) 4 ⊖ d	14 12		14 13		14 18		14 20					14 29		14 33		14 35			14 39			14 42		14 43
London Cannon Street 4 ⊖ d				14 17				14 20	14 24		14 27		14 30				14 37	14 37			14 40			
London Blackfriars 3 ⊖ d																								
London Bridge 4 ⊖ d	14 17		14a18	14 21	14 23		14a24	14 24	14 28		14a30	14 34	14 34	14 39		14 40	14a40	14 41	14 44		14 44	14 47		14a48
London Victoria 15 ⊖ d		14 09				14 10									14 25								14 39	
New Cross 4 ⊖ d				15a38				14 29	14 33				14 39					16a03			14 49			
St Johns d								14 31	14 35				14 41								14 51			
Lewisham 4 a	14 26	14 31						14 34	14 38				14 44			14 49					14 54	14 56	15 01	
Hither Green 4 a								14 38				14 43							14 53		14 58			
Petts Wood 4 a						14 44		14 51							14 59				15 06					
Orpington 4 a					14 38	14 47		14 54						14 55	15 02				15 09					

	SE	SE 1	SE	SE	SE		SE	SE	SE	SE	SE 1	SE	SE	SE	SE		SE	SE	SE	SE 1 ⚒	SE	SE 1	SE	SE
London Charing Cross 4 ⊖ d		14 45		14 47					14 56		15 00		15 02		15 06			15 09		15 10		15 15		15 17
London Waterloo (East) 4 ⊖ d		14 48		14 50					14 59		15 03		15 05		15 09			15 12		15 13		15 18		15 20
London Cannon Street 4 ⊖ d	14 47				14 50		14 54	14 57		15 00				15 07			15 10				15 17			
London Blackfriars 3 ⊖ d																								
London Bridge 4 ⊖ d	14 51	14 53		14a54	14 54		14 58	15a00	15 04	15 04	15 09		15 10	15 11	15 14		15 14	15 17		15a18	15 21	15 23		15a24
London Victoria 15 ⊖ d			14 40									14 55							15 09				15 10	
New Cross 4 ⊖ d	16a08				14 59		15 03			15 09				16a33			15 19				16a38			
St Johns d					15 01		15 05			15 11							15 21							
Lewisham 4 a					15 04		15 08			15 14			15 19				15 24	15 26	15 31					
Hither Green 4 a					15 08				15 13						15 23		15 28							
Petts Wood 4 a			15 14		15 21							15 29			15 36								15 44	
Orpington 4 a		15 08	15 17		15 24						15 25	15 32			15 39							15 38	15 47	

	SE		SE	SE	SE	SE	SE 1	SE	SE	SE	SE		SE	SE	SE	SE 1 ⚒	SE	SE 1	SE	SE	SE		SE	SE
London Charing Cross 4 ⊖ d					15 26		15 30		15 32		15 36			15 39		15 40		15 45		15 47				
London Waterloo (East) 4 ⊖ d					15 29		15 33		15 35		15 39			15 42		15 43		15 48		15 50				
London Cannon Street 4 ⊖ d	15 20		15 24	15 27		15 30				15 37			15 40				15 47				15 50		15 54	15 57
London Blackfriars 3 ⊖ d																								
London Bridge 4 ⊖ d	15 24		15 28	15a30	15 34	15 34	15 39		15 40	15 41	15 44		15 44	15 47		15a48	15 51	15 53		15a54	15 54		15 58	16a00
London Victoria 15 ⊖ d								15 25							15 39				15 40					
New Cross 4 ⊖ d	15 29		15 33			15 39				17a03			15 49				17a11				15 59		16 03	
St Johns d	15 31		15 35			15 41							15 51								16 01		16 05	
Lewisham 4 a	15 34		15 38			15 44			15 49				15 54	15 56	16 01						16 03		16 08	
Hither Green 4 a	15 38				15 43						15 53		15 58								16 08			
Petts Wood 4 a	15 51							15 59			16 06								16 14		16 21			
Orpington 4 a	15 54						15 55	16 02			16 09							16 08	16 17		16 24			

Table 199

Mondays to Fridays

29 August to 7 September

London - Lewisham, Hither Green, Petts Wood and Orpington (Summary of Services)

	SE	SE	SE 1	SE	SE	SE	SE		SE	SE	SE	SE	SE 1 ⚒	SE	SE 1	SE	SE		SE	SE	SE	SE	SE 1	SE
London Charing Cross 4 ⊖ d	15 56		16 00		16 02		16 06			16 09			16 10		16 15		16 20				16 26		16 28	
London Waterloo (East) 4 ⊖ d	15 59		16 03		16 05		16 09			16 12			16 13		16 18		16 23				16 29		16 31	
London Cannon Street 4 ⊖ d		16 00				16 07			16 10					16 17		16 20			16 24	16 27		16 30		
London Blackfriars 3 ⊖ d																								
London Bridge 4 ⊖ d	16 04	16 04	16 09		16 10	16 11	16 14		16 14	16 17			16a18	16 21	16a22	16 24	16a28		16 28	16a30	16 34	16 34	16 36	
London Victoria 15 ⊖ d				15 55							16 09	16 10												16 25
New Cross 4 ⊖ d		16 10				17a33			16 20					17a39		16 30			16 34			16 40		
St Johns d		16 12							16 22							16 32			16 36			16 42		
Lewisham 4 a		16 14			16 19				16 24	16 26	16 31					16 34			16 38			16 44		
Hither Green 4 a	16 13						16 23		16 29							16 39					16 43			
Petts Wood 4 a				16 29			16 36					16 44				16 51								16 59
Orpington 4 a			16 25	16 32			16 39					16 49				16 57							16 52	17 04

	SE	SE	SE			SE	SE 1 ⚒	SE	SE	SE	SE	SE	SE 1		SE 1	SE	SE	SE	SE	SE	SE	SE	SE	
London Charing Cross 4 ⊖ d	16 30		16 32				16 37	16 39					16 41			16 42	16 45		16 49		16 51		16 55	
London Waterloo (East) 4 ⊖ d	16 33		16 35				16 40	16 42					16 44			16 45	16 48		16 52		16 54		16 58	
London Cannon Street 4 ⊖ d		16 35				16 39			16 42			16 44			16 46			16 51		16 54		16 56		
London Blackfriars 3 ⊖ d																								
London Bridge 4 ⊖ d	16 38	16a38	16 40			16 43	16a44	16a46	16 46			16a47	16a48		16a49	16 51	16 53	16 55	16 57	16a57	16 59	17 00	17a02	
London Victoria 15 ⊖ d										16 39	16 40													
New Cross 4 ⊖ d						16 49			16 52								18a02	17 01						
St Johns d						16 51												17 03						
Lewisham 4 a	16 47					16 53			16 55	16 58						17 00		17 05			17 07			
Hither Green 4 a			16 49			16 58			17 57							17 05			17 07					
Petts Wood 4 a			17 03								17 14					17 18						17 24		
Orpington 4 a			17 06								17 19					17 24						17 27		

	SE 1	SE	SE	SE 1	SE	SE 1	SE	SE	SE		SE	SE 1	SE	SE	SE	SE	SE	SE 1 ⚒	SE		SE	SE	SE 1	SE
London Charing Cross 4 ⊖ d	16 57				16 59	17 01			17 03				17 06		17 10		17 12	17 14				17 17	17 19	
London Waterloo (East) 4 ⊖ d	16a59				17 02	17 04			17 06				17 09		17 13		17 15	17a17				17 20	17a21	
London Cannon Street 4 ⊖ d		16 58		17 02			17 04	17 06				17 08		17 12		17 16			17 19					17 21
London Blackfriars 3 ⊖ d																								
London Bridge 4 ⊖ d		17 02		17a05	17a06	17a08	17 08	17a09	17 11			17a11	17 14	17 16	17 19	17a19	17 21		17 23			17a24		17 25
London Victoria 15 ⊖ d			16 59								17 04										17 15			
New Cross 4 ⊖ d		17 08					17 14							17 22										17 31
St Johns d		17 10												17 24										17 33
Lewisham 4 a		17 12					17 17		17 20		17 23			17 26			17 30							17 35
Hither Green 4 a		17 17							17 25				18 21		17 28									17 40
Petts Wood 4 a			17 36						17 39										17 43		17 50			
Orpington 4 a			17 41						17 45										17 47		17 55			

	SE 1	SE	SE 1	SE	SE		SE 1	SE	SE	SE	SE	SE	SE	SE 1	SE		SE	SE	SE	SE	SE 1 ⚒	SE	SE 1	SE
London Charing Cross 4 ⊖ d		17 21	17 23					17 26	17 29		17 30		17 32		17 34					17 39	17 41			17 43
London Waterloo (East) 4 ⊖ d		17 24	17 26					17 29	17 32		17a32		17 35		17 37					17 42	17a43			17 46
London Cannon Street 4 ⊖ d	17 24			17 26	17 28		17 30					17 34		17 37				17 39	17 41			17 43	17 45	
London Blackfriars 3 ⊖ d																								
London Bridge 4 ⊖ d	17a27	17a28	17a30	17 30	17a31		17a33	17 35	17a36			17 39	17 41	17a40	17 43			17a42	17 45	17a46		17 47	17a48	17a50
London Victoria 15 ⊖ d										17 30							17 34							
New Cross 4 ⊖ d				17 36								17 45										17 53		
St Johns d												17 47										17 55		
Lewisham 4 a				17 39				17 43				17 49			17 52		17 55					17 58		
Hither Green 4 a								17 48					17 51									18 03		
Petts Wood 4 a								18 01		18 05									18 08					
Orpington 4 a								18 07		18 10									18 11					

	SE		SE 1	SE	SE	SE	SE 1	SE	SE	SE	SE		SE	SE	SE 1	SE	SE	SE	SE	SE 1	SE		SE 1	SE
London Charing Cross 4 ⊖ d			17 45		17 47			17 50	17 52		17 54		17 56		17 59				18 01	18 03				18 05
London Waterloo (East) 4 ⊖ d			17 48		17 50			17 53	17a54		17 57		17 59		18a01				18 04	18a05				18 08
London Cannon Street 4 ⊖ d	17 47			17 50			17 52			17 56						18 00	18 02				18 04		18 08	
London Blackfriars 3 ⊖ d																								
London Bridge 4 ⊖ d	17 51		17a52	17a53	17 55		17a55	17a57		18 00	18 02		18 04			18a03	18 06		18a08		18 08		18a11	18a12
London Victoria 15 ⊖ d						17 45								17 56				18 00						
New Cross 4 ⊖ d	17 58									18 06											18 14			
St Johns d										18 08											18 16			
Lewisham 4 a	18 01				18 04					18 10			18 13	18 17							18 19			
Hither Green 4 a	18 57				18 09						18 12										18 24			
Petts Wood 4 a					18 23	18 26											18 28	18 35						
Orpington 4 a					18 29	18 32											18 32	18 41						

Table 199

London - Lewisham, Hither Green, Petts Wood and Orpington (Summary of Services)

Mondays to Fridays

29 August to 7 September

	SE	SE	SE	SE	SE	SE	SE	SE	SE	SE	SE	SE	SE	SE	SE	SE	SE	SE	SE	SE	SE	SE
	1				1						1 ⊼						1			1		
London Charing Cross 4 ⊖ d	18 07			18 09		18 12	18 14			18 18	18 21					18 23			18 27		18 30	
London Waterloo (East) 4 ⊖ d	18 10			18 12		18 15	18 17			18 21	18a23					18 26			18 30		18 33	
London Cannon Street 4 ⊖ d		18 10	18 12		18 14			18 18	18 21			18 23		18 25			18 28	18 30		18 32		18 34
London Blackfriars 3 ⊖ d																						
London Bridge 4 ⊖ d	18a14	18 14	18a15	18 17	18a17	18 21	18 23	18 23	18a24	18 26		18 27		18 29		18a31	18a31	18a33	18a34	18a35	18 38	18 38
London Victoria 15 ⊖ d													18 15		18 18							
New Cross 4 ⊖ d		18 20				19a38		18 28						18 35								18 44
St Johns d								18 30						18 37								18 46
Lewisham 4 a		18 23		18 26				18 33		18 35				18 40	18 42							18 48
Hither Green 4 a				18 31			18 35							18 45							18 48	
Petts Wood 4 a				18 43								18 49	18 53								19 02	
Orpington 4 a				18 49								18 53	18 59								19 06	

	SE	SE	SE	SE	SE	SE	SE	SE	SE	SE	SE	SE	SE	SE	SE	SE	SE	SE	SE	SE	SE
	1					1	1 ⊼				1										1
London Charing Cross 4 ⊖ d	18 32	18 34		18 37	18 39		18 41				18 45				18 48		18 52		18 56		19 00
London Waterloo (East) 4 ⊖ d	18 35	18 37		18 40	18 42		18 44				18 48				18 51		18 55		18 59		19 03
London Cannon Street 4 ⊖ d			18 40			18 44				18 46		18 48		18 50		18 54		18 57		19 00	
London Blackfriars 3 ⊖ d																					
London Bridge 4 ⊖ d	18a39	18a41	18 44	18 46	18 48	18a47	18 50			18a49	18a52	18 52		18 54	18 57	18 58	18a59	19a00	19 04	19 04	19 09
London Victoria 15 ⊖ d								18 30	18 39				18 45								
New Cross 4 ⊖ d			18 50		18 55									19 00		19 05				19 09	
St Johns d			18 52											19 02		19 07				19 11	
Lewisham 4 a			18 54		18 59				19 02					19 04	19 06	19 10				19 14	
Hither Green 4 a				18 55										19 09					19 14		
Petts Wood 4 a								19 06				19 13	19 19								
Orpington 4 a							19 06	19 12				19 19	19 25								19 27

	SE	SE	SE	SE	SE	SE	SE	SE	SE	SE	SE	SE	SE	SE	SE	SE	SE	SE	SE	SE	SE	SE
		1							1 ⊼		1								1			
London Charing Cross 4 ⊖ d			19 02		19 06		19 09		19 10		19 15		19 17				19 26		19 30		19 32	
London Waterloo (East) 4 ⊖ d			19 05		19 09		19 12		19 13		19 18		19 20				19 29		19 33		19 35	
London Cannon Street 4 ⊖ d		19 04		19 07		19 10				19 17				19 20	19 24	19 27		19 30				19 37
London Blackfriars 3 ⊖ d																						
London Bridge 4 ⊖ d		19a07	19 10	19a10	19 14	19 14	19 17		19a18	19a20	19 23		19a24	19 24	19 28	19a30	19 34	19 34	19 39		19 40	19a40
London Victoria 15 ⊖ d	19 00							19 09				19 10								19 25		
New Cross 4 ⊖ d						19 19								19 29	19 33			19 39				
St Johns d						19 21								19 31	19 35			19 41				
Lewisham 4 a			19 19			19 24	19 26	19 31						19 33	19 38			19 44			19 49	
Hither Green 4 a					19 23	19 28								19 38			19 43					
Petts Wood 4 a	19 35				19 38							19 44		19 51						19 59		
Orpington 4 a	19 38				19 43						19 38	19 48		19 54					19 55	20 02		

	SE	SE	SE	SE	SE	SE	SE	SE	SE	SE	SE	SE	SE	SE	SE	SE	SE	SE	SE	SE	SE	SE
					1 ⊼		1								1						1 ⊼	
London Charing Cross 4 ⊖ d	19 36		19 39		19 40		19 45		19 47				19 56		20 00		20 02	20 06		20 09	20 10	
London Waterloo (East) 4 ⊖ d	19 39		19 42		19 43		19 48		19 50				19 59		20 03		20 05	20 09		20 12	20 13	
London Cannon Street 4 ⊖ d		19 40				19 47				19 50	19 54	19 57		20 00					20 10			20 17
London Blackfriars 3 ⊖ d																						
London Bridge 4 ⊖ d	19 44	19 44	19 47		19a48	19a50	19 53		19a54	19 54	19 58	20a00	20 04	20 04	20 09		20 10	20 14	20 14	20 17	20a18	20a20
London Victoria 15 ⊖ d				19 39				19 40								19 55						
New Cross 4 ⊖ d		19 49								19 59	20 03			20 09					20 19			
St Johns d		19 51								20 01	20 05			20 11					20 21			
Lewisham 4 a		19 55	19 56	20 01						20 04	20 08			20 14			20 19		20 25	20 26		
Hither Green 4 a	19 53	19 59								20 08			20 13					20 23	20 29			
Petts Wood 4 a	20 06							20 14		20 21						20 29		20 36				
Orpington 4 a	20 09						20 08	20 18		20 24					20 25	20 32		20 39				

	SE	SE	SE	SE	SE	SE	SE	SE	SE	SE	SE	SE	SE	SE	SE	SE	SE	SE	SE	SE	SE
	1						1					1		1				1			
London Charing Cross 4 ⊖ d	20 15			20 17	20 22		20 30		20 32	20 36	20 39	20 40		20 45	20 47	20 52		21 00		21 02	21 06
London Waterloo (East) 4 ⊖ d	20 18			20 20	20 25		20 33		20 35	20 39	20 42	20 43		20 48	20 50	20 55		21 03		21 05	21 09
London Cannon Street 4 ⊖ d			20 20			20 27							20 47				20 57				
London Blackfriars 3 ⊖ d																					
London Bridge 4 ⊖ d	20 23		20 24	20 25	20 30	20a30	20 39		20 40	20 44	20 47	20a48	20a50	20 53	20 55	21 00	21a00	21 09		21 10	21 14
London Victoria 15 ⊖ d		20 10						20 25											20 55		
New Cross 4 ⊖ d			20 29	20 32	20 35				20 45						21 00	21 05				21 15	
St Johns d			20 31	20 34											21 02						
Lewisham 4 a			20 34	20 36	20 38				20 49		20 56				21 05	21 09				21 19	21 21
Hither Green 4 a			20 38		20 44					20 53						21 13					21 26
Petts Wood 4 a		20 44	20 51					20 59		21 06									21 29		21 38
Orpington 4 a	20 38	20 47	20 54				20 55	21 02		21 09				21 08				21 25	21 32		21 42

Table 199

London - Lewisham, Hither Green, Petts Wood and Orpington (Summary of Services)

Mondays to Fridays

29 August to 7 September

	SE	SE	SE	SE	SE	SE	SE	SE	SE	SE	SE	SE	SE	SE	SE	SE	SE	SE	SE	SE	SE	SE
		1				1					1	1				1					1	
London Charing Cross 4 ⊖ d	21 09	21 10	21 17	21 22	21 26	21 30		21 32	21 36	21 39	21 40	21 45	21 47	21 52	21 56	22 00		22 02	22 06	22 09	22 10	22 17
London Waterloo (East) 4 ⊖ d	21 12	21 13	21 20	21 25	21 29	21 33		21 35	21 39	21 42	21 43	21 48	21 50	21 55	21 59	22 03		22 05	22 09	22 12	22 13	22 20
London Cannon Street 4 ⊖ d																						
London Blackfriars 3 ⊖ d																						
London Bridge 4 ⊖ d	21 17	21 19	21 25	21 30	21a33	21 39		21 40	21 44	21 47	21a48	21 53	21 55	22 00	22a03	22 09		22 10	22 14	22 17	22 19	22 25
London Victoria 15 ⊖ d							21 25										21 55					
New Cross 4 ⊖ d			21 30	21 35				21 45					22 00	22 05				22 15				22 30
St Johns d			21 32										22 02									22 32
Lewisham 4 a	21 26		21 35	21 39				21 49	21 51	21 56			22 05	22 09				22 19	22 21	22 26		22 35
Hither Green 4 a				21 43					21 56					22 13					22 26			
Petts Wood 4 a							21 59		22 08								22 29		22 38			
Orpington 4 a		21 34				21 55	22 02		22 12			22 08				22 25	22 32		22 42		22 34	

	SE	SE	SE	SE	SE	SE	SE	SE	SE	SE	SE	SE	SE	SE	SE	SE	SE	SE	SE	SE	SE
			1					1	1				1					1			
London Charing Cross 4 ⊖ d	22 22	22 26	22 30		22 32	22 36	22 39	22 40	22 45	22 47	22 52	22 56	23 00		23 02	23 06	23 09	23 10	23 17	23 22	23 26
London Waterloo (East) 4 ⊖ d	22 25	22 29	22 33		22 35	22 39	22 42	22 43	22 48	22 50	22 55	22 59	23 03		23 05	23 09	23 12	23 13	23 20	23 25	23 29
London Cannon Street 4 ⊖ d																					
London Blackfriars 3 ⊖ d																					
London Bridge 4 ⊖ d	22 30	22a33	22 39		22 40	22 44	22 47	22a48	22 53	22 55	23 00	23a03	23 09		23 10	23 14	23 17	23 19	23 25	23 30	23a33
London Victoria 15 ⊖ d				22 25										22 55							
New Cross 4 ⊖ d	22 35				22 45					23 00	23 05				23 15				23 30	23 35	
St Johns d										23 02									23 32		
Lewisham 4 a	22 39				22 49	22 51	22 56			23 05	23 09				23 19	23 21	23 26		23 35	23 39	
Hither Green 4 a	22 43					22 56					23 13					23 26				23 43	
Petts Wood 4 a				22 59		23 08								23 29		23 38					
Orpington 4 a			22 54	23 02		23 12			23 08				23 24	23 32		23 42		23 34			

	SE	SE	SE	SE	SE	SE	SE	SE	SE	SE
	1					1	1			
London Charing Cross 4 ⊖ d	23 30		23 32	23 36	23 39	23 40	23 45	23 52		23 56
London Waterloo (East) 4 ⊖ d	23 33		23 35	23 39	23 42	23 43	23 48	23 55		23 59
London Cannon Street 4 ⊖ d										
London Blackfriars 3 ⊖ d										
London Bridge 4 ⊖ d	23 39		23 40	23 44	23 47	23a48	23 53	23 59		00a03
London Victoria 15 ⊖ d		23 25							23 55	
New Cross 4 ⊖ d			23 45					00 05		
St Johns d								00 07		
Lewisham 4 a			23 49	23 51	23 56			00 10		
Hither Green 4 a				23 56						
Petts Wood 4 a		23 59		00 08					00 29	
Orpington 4 a	23 54	00 02		00 12			00 08		00 32	

Saturdays

until 21 July, 18 Aug and from 15 Sep

	SE	SE	SE	SE	SE	SE	SE	SE	SE	SE	SE	SE	SE	SE	SE	SE	SE	SE	SE	SE	SE	SE
			1	A																		1
London Charing Cross 4 ⊖ d		23p36	23p45		23p52		00 02	00 06	00 10	00 15	00 18	00 48	04 52	05 22	05 26	05 32	05 36	05 39	05 47	05 52	05 56	06 00
London Waterloo (East) 4 ⊖ d		23p39	23p48		23p55		00 05	00 09	00 13	00 18	00 21	00 51	04 55	05 25	05 29	05 35	05 39	05 42	05 50	05 55	05 59	06 03
London Cannon Street 4 ⊖ d																						
London Blackfriars 3 ⊖ d																						
London Bridge 4 ⊖ d		23p44	23p53		23p59		00 10	00 14	00 18	00 23	00 26	00 56	05 00	05 30	05a33	05 40	05 44	05 47	05 55	06 00	06a03	06 08
London Victoria 15 ⊖ d	23p25			23p43		23p55																
New Cross 4 ⊖ d					00 05		00 15		00 23		00 31	01 01	05 05	05 35		05 45			06 00	06 05		
St Johns d					00 07														06 02			
Lewisham 4 a		23p51			00 10		00 19	00 21	00 27		00 35	01 05	05 09	05 39		05 49	05 52	05 56	06 05	06 09		
Hither Green 4 a		23p56						00 26	00 31			01 09	05 13	05 43			05 57			06 13		
Petts Wood 4 a	23p59	00 08		00 21		00 29		00 38				01 22					06 09					
Orpington 4 a	00 02	00 12	00 08	00 25		00 32		00 42		00 46		01 25					06 12					06 23

	SE	SE	SE	SE	SE	SE	SE	SE	SE	SE	SE	SE	SE	SE	SE	SE	SE	SE	SE	SE	SE	SE
															1							
London Charing Cross 4 ⊖ d		06 02	06 06	06 09	06 17	06 22		06 26	06 32	06 36	06 39	06 47	06 52	06 56	07 00		07 02	07 06	07 09		07 17	07 22
London Waterloo (East) 4 ⊖ d		06 05	06 09	06 12	06 20	06 25		06 29	06 35	06 39	06 42	06 50	06 55	06 59	07 03		07 05	07 09	07 12		07 20	07 25
London Cannon Street 4 ⊖ d																						
London Blackfriars 3 ⊖ d																						
London Bridge 4 ⊖ d		06 10	06 14	06 17	06 25	06 30		06a33	06 40	06 44	06 47	06 55	07 00	07a03	07 08		07 10	07 14	07 17		07 25	07 30
London Victoria 15 ⊖ d	05 55						06 25									06 55				07 10		
New Cross 4 ⊖ d		06 15			06 30	06 35			06 45			07 00	07 05				07 15				07 30	07 35
St Johns d					06 32							07 02									07 32	
Lewisham 4 a		06 19	06 22	06 26	06 35	06 39			06 49	06 52	06 56	07 05	07 08				07 19	07 22	07 26		07 35	07 39
Hither Green 4 a			06 27			06 43				06 57			07 14					07 27				07 44
Petts Wood 4 a	06 29		06 39				06 59			07 09						07 29		07 39		07 44		
Orpington 4 a	06 32		06 42				07 02			07 12					07 23	07 32		07 42		07 47		

A 19 May

London - Lewisham, Hither Green, Petts Wood and Orpington (Summary of Services)

	SE	SE ■	SE	SE	SE	SE	SE	SE ■	SE	SE	SE	SE	SE	SE ■	SE	SE	SE	SE	SE	SE	SE
London Charing Cross ⊖ d	07 26	07 30		07 32	07 36	07 39		07 45		07 47	07 52	07 56		08 00		08 02		08 06		08 09	
London Waterloo (East) ⊖ d	07 29	07 33		07 35	07 39	07 42		07 48		07 50	07 55	07 59		08 03		08 05		08 09		08 12	
London Cannon Street ⊖ d													08 00				08 07		08 10		
London Blackfriars ⊖ d																					
London Bridge ⊖ d	07a33	07 38		07 40	07 44	07 47		07 53		07a54	08 00	08a03	08 04	08 08		08 10	08 11	08 14	08 14	08 17	
London Victoria ⊖ d			07 25				07 39		07 40						07 55						08 09
New Cross ⊖ d				07 45							08 05		08 09			08 15	09a33		08 19		
St Johns d													08 11						08 21		
Lewisham a				07 49	07 52	07 56	08 02				08 08		08 13			08 19			08 24	08 26	08 31
Hither Green a					07 57						08 14							08 23	08 28		
Petts Wood a			07 59		08 09				08 14						08 29			08 36			
Orpington a		07 54	08 02		08 12			08 08	08 17					08 23	08 32			08 39			

	SE	SE ■	SE	SE	SE	SE	SE	SE	SE	SE ■	SE	SE	SE	SE	SE	SE	SE	SE ■	SE	SE ■	SE	SE
London Charing Cross ⊖ d		08 15		08 17				08 26		08 30		08 32		08 36		08 39		08 40		08 45		08 47
London Waterloo (East) ⊖ d		08 18		08 20				08 29		08 33		08 35		08 39		08 42		08 43		08 48		08 50
London Cannon Street ⊖ d	08 17				08 20	08 24	08 27		08 30				08 37		08 40				08 47			
London Blackfriars ⊖ d																						
London Bridge ⊖ d	08 21	08 23		08a24	08 24	08 28	08a30	08 34	08 34	08 39		08 40	08 41	08 44	08 44	08 47		08a48	08 51	08 53		08a54
London Victoria ⊖ d			08 10								08 25						08 39				08 40	
New Cross ⊖ d	09a38				08 29	08 33			08 39				10a03		08 49				10a08			
St Johns d					08 31	08 35			08 41						08 51							
Lewisham a					08 34	08 38			08 44			08 49			08 54	08 56	09 01					
Hither Green a					08 38			08 43						08 53	08 58							
Petts Wood a			08 44		08 51						08 59			09 06							09 14	
Orpington a		08 38	08 47		08 54					08 55	09 02			09 09						09 08	09 17	

	SE	SE	SE	SE	SE	SE ■	SE	SE	SE	SE	SE	SE	SE	SE ■		SE ■ ⌶	SE	SE ■	SE	SE
London Charing Cross ⊖ d				08 56		09 00		09 02		09 06		09 09		09 10	and at the same minutes past each hour until	17 10		17 15		17 17
London Waterloo (East) ⊖ d				08 59		09 03		09 05		09 09		09 12		09 13		17 13		17 18		17 20
London Cannon Street ⊖ d	08 50	08 54	08 57		09 00				09 07		09 10						17 17			
London Blackfriars ⊖ d																				
London Bridge ⊖ d	08 54	08 58	09a00	09 04	09 04	09 09		09 10	09 11	09 14	09 14	09 17		09a18		17a18	17 21	17 23		17a24
London Victoria ⊖ d							08 55						09 09						17 10	
New Cross ⊖ d	08 59	09 03			09 09				10a33		09 19						18a38			
St Johns d	09 01	09 05			09 11						09 21									
Lewisham a	09 04	09 08			09 14			09 19			09 24	09 26	09 31							
Hither Green a	09 08			09 13						09 23	09 28									
Petts Wood a	09 21						09 29			09 36									17 44	
Orpington a	09 24					09 25	09 32			09 39								17 38	17 47	

	SE	SE	SE	SE	SE	SE ■	SE	SE	SE	SE	SE	SE	SE	SE ■ ⌶	SE	SE ■	SE	SE	SE	SE	SE	SE
London Charing Cross ⊖ d				17 26		17 30		17 32		17 36		17 39		17 40		17 45		17 47				17 56
London Waterloo (East) ⊖ d				17 29		17 33		17 35		17 39		17 42		17 43		17 48		17 50				17 59
London Cannon Street ⊖ d	17 20	17 24	17 27		17 30				17 37		17 40				17 47				17 50	17 54	17 57	
London Blackfriars ⊖ d																						
London Bridge ⊖ d	17 24	17 28	17a30	17 34	17 34	17 39		17 40	17 41	17 44	17 44	17 47		17a48	17 51	17 53		17a54	17 54	17 58	18a00	18 04
London Victoria ⊖ d							17 25						17 39				17 40					
New Cross ⊖ d	17 29	17 33			17 39				19a03		17 49				19a08				17 59	18 03		
St Johns d	17 31	17 35			17 41						17 51								18 01	18 05		
Lewisham a	17 34	17 38			17 44			17 49			17 54	17 56	18 01						18 04	18 08		
Hither Green a	17 38			17 43						17 53	17 58								18 08			18 13
Petts Wood a	17 51						17 59			18 06							18 14		18 21			
Orpington a	17 54					17 55	18 02			18 09						18 08	18 17		18 24			

	SE	SE ■	SE	SE	SE	SE	SE	SE	SE	SE ■ ⌶	SE	SE ■	SE	SE	SE	SE	SE	SE	SE	SE ■	SE	SE
London Charing Cross ⊖ d		18 00		18 02		18 06		18 09		18 10		18 15		18 17				18 26		18 30		18 32
London Waterloo (East) ⊖ d		18 03		18 05		18 09		18 12		18 13		18 18		18 20				18 29		18 33		18 35
London Cannon Street ⊖ d	18 00				18 07		18 10				18 17				18 20	18 24	18 27		18 30			
London Blackfriars ⊖ d																						
London Bridge ⊖ d	18 04	18 09		18 10	18a10	18 14	18 14	18 17		18a18	18a20	18 23		18a24	18 24	18 28	18a30	18 34	18 34	18 39		18 40
London Victoria ⊖ d			17 55						18 09				18 10								18 25	
New Cross ⊖ d	18 09						18 19								18 29	18 33			18 39			
St Johns d	18 11						18 21								18 31	18 35			18 41			
Lewisham a	18 14			18 19			18 24	18 26	18 31						18 34	18 38			18 44			18 49
Hither Green a						18 23	18 28								18 38			18 43				
Petts Wood a			18 29			18 36							18 44		18 51						18 59	
Orpington a		18 25	18 32			18 39						18 38	18 47		18 54					18 55	19 02	

Table 199

Saturdays

until 21 July, 18 Aug and from 15 Sep

London - Lewisham, Hither Green, Petts Wood and Orpington (Summary of Services)

	SE	SE	SE	SE	SE	SE ■ ⌶	SE	SE ■	SE	SE	SE	SE	SE	SE	SE	SE ■	SE	SE	SE	SE	SE
London Charing Cross ⊖ d		18 36		18 39		18 40		18 45		18 47				18 56		19 00		19 02		19 06	
London Waterloo (East) ⊖ d		18 39		18 42		18 43		18 48		18 50				18 59		19 03		19 05		19 09	
London Cannon Street ⊖ d	18 37		18 40				18 47				18 50	18 54	18 57		19 00				19 07		19 10
London Blackfriars ⊖ d																					
London Bridge ⊖ d	18a40	18 44	18 44	18 47		18a48	18a50	18 53		18a54	18 54	18 58	19a00	19 04	19 04	19 09		19 10	19a10	19 14	19 14
London Victoria ⊖ d					18 39				18 40								18 55				
New Cross ⊖ d			18 49								18 59	19 03			19 09						19 19
St Johns d			18 51								19 01	19 05			19 11						19 21
Lewisham a			18 54	18 56	19 01						19 04	19 08			19 14			19 19			19 24
Hither Green a		18 53	18 58								19 08			19 13						19 23	19 28
Petts Wood a		19 06							19 14		19 21						19 29			19 36	
Orpington a		19 09						19 08	19 17		19 24					19 25	19 32			19 39	

	SE	SE	SE ■ ⌶	SE ■	SE	SE	SE	SE	SE	SE	SE ■	SE	SE	SE	SE	SE	SE	SE ■ ⌶	SE	SE	SE ■	SE
London Charing Cross ⊖ d	19 09		19 10	19 15			19 17			19 26	19 30		19 32	19 36	19 39			19 40	19 47	19 52	19 55	
London Waterloo (East) ⊖ d	19 12		19 13	19 18			19 20			19 29	19 33		19 35	19 39	19 42			19 43	19 50	19 55	19 58	
London Cannon Street ⊖ d						19 20		19 24	19 27													
London Blackfriars ⊖ d																						
London Bridge ⊖ d	19 17		19a18	19 23		19 24	19 25	19 28	19a30	19 34	19 39		19 40	19 44	19 47			19a48	19 55	20 00	20 03	
London Victoria ⊖ d		19 09			19 10							19 25				19 39	19 40					19 55
New Cross ⊖ d						19 29		19 33					19 45						20 00	20 05		
St Johns d						19 31		19 35											20 02			
Lewisham a	19 26	19 31				19 34	19 37	19 38					19 49	19 51	19 56	20 01			20 05	20 09		
Hither Green a						19 38				19 43				19 56						20 13		
Petts Wood a					19 44	19 51						19 59		20 08			20 14					20 29
Orpington a				19 38	19 48	19 54					19 55	20 02		20 12			20 18				20 18	20 32

	SE	SE	SE	SE	SE ■ ⌶	SE	SE	SE	SE ■	SE	SE	SE	SE	SE	SE ■	SE	SE	SE ■	SE	SE	SE
London Charing Cross ⊖ d	19 56	20 02	20 06	20 09	20 10		20 17	20 22	20 25		20 26	20 32	20 36	20 39	20 40	20 47	20 52	20 55		20 56	21 02
London Waterloo (East) ⊖ d	19 59	20 05	20 09	20 12	20 13		20 20	20 25	20 28		20 29	20 35	20 39	20 42	20 43	20 50	20 55	20 58		20 59	21 05
London Cannon Street ⊖ d																					
London Blackfriars ⊖ d																					
London Bridge ⊖ d	20a04	20 10	20 14	20 17	20 19		20 25	20 30	20 33		20a34	20 40	20 44	20 47	20 49	20 55	21 00	21 03		21a04	21 10
London Victoria ⊖ d						20 10				20 25									20 55		
New Cross ⊖ d		20 15					20 30	20 35				20 45				21 00	21 05				21 15
St Johns d							20 32									21 02					
Lewisham a		20 19	20 21	20 26			20 35	20 39				20 49	20 51	20 56		21 05	21 09				21 19
Hither Green a			20 26					20 43					20 56				21 13				
Petts Wood a			20 38			20 44				20 59			21 08						21 29		
Orpington a			20 42		20 34	20 47			20 48	21 02			21 12		21 04			21 18	21 32		

	SE	SE	SE ■	SE	SE	SE ■	SE	SE	SE	SE	SE	SE ■	SE	SE	SE ■	SE	SE	SE	SE	SE	SE ■	SE
London Charing Cross ⊖ d	21 06	21 09	21 10	21 17	21 22	21 25		21 26	21 32	21 36	21 39	21 40	21 47	21 52	21 55		21 56	22 02	22 06	22 09	22 10	22 17
London Waterloo (East) ⊖ d	21 09	21 12	21 13	21 20	21 25	21 28		21 29	21 35	21 39	21 42	21 43	21 50	21 55	21 58		21 59	22 05	22 09	22 12	22 13	22 20
London Cannon Street ⊖ d																						
London Blackfriars ⊖ d																						
London Bridge ⊖ d	21 14	21 17	21 19	21 25	21 30	21 33		21a34	21 40	21 44	21 47	21 49	21 55	22 00	22 03		22a04	22 10	22 14	22 17	22 19	22 25
London Victoria ⊖ d							21 25									21 55						
New Cross ⊖ d				21 30	21 35				21 45				22 00	22 05				22 15				22 30
St Johns d				21 32									22 02									22 32
Lewisham a	21 21	21 26		21 35	21 39				21 49	21 51	21 56		22 05	22 09				22 19	22 21	22 26		22 35
Hither Green a	21 26				21 43					21 56				22 13					22 26			
Petts Wood a	21 38						21 59			22 08						22 29			22 38			
Orpington a	21 42		21 34			21 48	22 02			22 12		22 04			22 18	22 32			22 42		22 34	

	SE	SE ■	SE	SE	SE	SE	SE	SE ■	SE	SE	SE ■	SE A	SE	SE	SE	SE	SE	SE ■	SE	SE	SE ■	SE A
London Charing Cross ⊖ d	22 22	22 25		22 26	22 32	22 36	22 39	22 40	22 47	22 52	22 55			22 56	23 02	23 06	23 09	23 10	23 17	23 22	23 25	
London Waterloo (East) ⊖ d	22 25	22 28		22 29	22 35	22 39	22 42	22 43	22 50	22 55	22 58			22 59	23 05	23 09	23 12	23 13	23 20	23 25	23 28	
London Cannon Street ⊖ d																						
London Blackfriars ⊖ d																						
London Bridge ⊖ d	22 30	22 33		22a34	22 40	22 44	22 47	22 49	22 55	23 00	23 03			23a04	23 10	23 14	23 17	23 19	23 25	23 30	23 33	
London Victoria ⊖ d			22 25									22 43	22 55									23 13
New Cross ⊖ d	22 35				22 45				23 00	23 05					23 15				23 30	23 35		
St Johns d									23 02										23 32			
Lewisham a	22 39				22 49	22 51	22 56		23 05	23 09					23 19	23 21	23 26		23 35	23 39		
Hither Green a	22 43					22 56				23 13						23 26				23 43		
Petts Wood a			22 59			23 08						23 22	23 29			23 38						23 52
Orpington a		22 48	23 02			23 12		23 04			23 18	23 25	23 32			23 42		23 34			23 48	23 55

A 19 May

London - Lewisham, Hither Green, Petts Wood and Orpington (Summary of Services)

Saturdays until 21 July, 18 Aug and from 15 Sep

	SE		SE	SE	SE	SE	SE 1	SE 1	SE A	SE	SE		SE
London Charing Cross ⊖ d			23 26	23 32	23 36	23 39	23 40	23 45		23 52			23 56
London Waterloo (East) ⊖ d			23 29	23 35	23 39	23 42	23 43	23 48		23 55			23 59
London Cannon Street ⊖ d													
London Blackfriars ⊖ d													
London Bridge ⊖ d			23a34	23 40	23 44	23 47	23 49	23 53		23 59			00a04
London Victoria ⊖ d	23 25								23 43		23 55		
New Cross ⊖ d				23 45						00 05			
St Johns d										00 07			
Lewisham a				23 49	23 51	23 55				00 10			
Hither Green a					23 56								
Petts Wood a	23 59				00 08				00 22		00 29		
Orpington a	00 02				00 12		00 04	00 08	00 25		00 32		

Saturdays 28 July to 11 August

	SE	SE B	SE C	SE 1	SE	SE	SE	SE	SE		SE	SE	SE	SE	SE 1	SE	SE	SE	SE		SE	SE	SE	SE
London Charing Cross ⊖ d		23p36	23p36	23p45	23p52		00 02	00 06	00 10		00 15	00 18		00 32	00 37		00 44		00 48				04 52	05 22
London Waterloo (East) ⊖ d		23p39	23p39	23p48	23p55		00 05	00 09	00 13		00 18	00 21		00 35	00 40		00 47		00 51				04 55	05 25
London Cannon Street ⊖ d													00 30			00 42						00 56		
London Blackfriars ⊖ d																								
London Bridge ⊖ d		23p44	23p44	23p53	23p59		00 10	00 14	00 18		00 23	00 26	00 34	00a39	00 45	00 47	00 52		00 56			00a59	05 00	05 30
London Victoria ⊖ d	23p25					23p55												00 45			00 56			
New Cross ⊖ d					00 05		00 15		00 23			00 31	00 39				00 57		01 01				05 05	05 35
St Johns d					00 07								00 41											
Lewisham a		23p51	23p51		00 10		00 19	00 21	00 27			00 35	00 44			00 55	01 01		01 05				05 09	05 39
Hither Green a		23p56	23p56					00 26	00 31								01 05		01 09				05 13	05 43
Petts Wood a	23p59	00 08	00 08			00 29		00 38										01 21	01 24		01 35			
Orpington a	00 02	00 12	00 15	00 08		00 32		00 45			00 46				01 00			01 27	01 27		01 42			

	SE	SE	SE	SE	SE		SE	SE	SE 1	SE	SE	SE	SE	SE	SE		SE	SE	SE	SE	SE	SE	SE	SE
London Charing Cross ⊖ d	05 26	05 32	05 36	05 39	05 47		05 52	05 56	06 00		06 02	06 06	06 09	06 17	06 22			06 26	06 32	06 36	06 39	06 47	06 52	06 56
London Waterloo (East) ⊖ d	05 29	05 35	05 39	05 42	05 50		05 55	05 59	06 03		06 05	06 09	06 12	06 20	06 25			06 29	06 35	06 39	06 42	06 50	06 55	06 59
London Cannon Street ⊖ d																								
London Blackfriars ⊖ d																								
London Bridge ⊖ d	05a33	05 40	05 44	05 47	05 55		06 00	06a03	06 08		06 10	06 14	06 17	06 25	06 30			06a33	06 40	06 44	06 47	06 55	07 00	07a03
London Victoria ⊖ d										05 55							06 25							
New Cross ⊖ d		05 45			06 00		06 05				06 15			06 30	06 35				06 45			07 00	07 05	
St Johns d					06 02									06 32								07 02		
Lewisham a		05 49	05 52	05 56	06 05		06 09				06 19	06 22	06 26	06 35	06 39				06 49	06 52	06 56	07 05	07 08	
Hither Green a			05 57				06 13					06 27			06 43					06 57			07 14	
Petts Wood a			06 09							06 29		06 39					06 59			07 09				
Orpington a			06 12						06 23	06 32		06 42					07 02			07 12				

	SE 1		SE	SE	SE	SE	SE	SE	SE	SE	SE 1		SE	SE	SE	SE	SE	SE 1	SE	SE	SE		SE	SE
London Charing Cross ⊖ d	07 00			07 02	07 06	07 09		07 17	07 22	07 26	07 30			07 32	07 36	07 39		07 45		07 47	07 52		07 56	
London Waterloo (East) ⊖ d	07 03			07 05	07 09	07 12		07 20	07 25	07 29	07 33			07 35	07 39	07 42		07 48		07 50	07 55		07 59	
London Cannon Street ⊖ d																								08 00
London Blackfriars ⊖ d																								
London Bridge ⊖ d	07 08			07 10	07 14	07 17		07 25	07 30	07a33	07 38			07 40	07 44	07 47		07 53		07a54	08 00		08a03	08 04
London Victoria ⊖ d			06 55				07 10						07 25				07 39		07 40					
New Cross ⊖ d				07 15				07 30	07 35					07 45							08 05			08 09
St Johns d								07 32																08 11
Lewisham a				07 19	07 22	07 26		07 35	07 39					07 49	07 52	07 55	08 00				08 08			08 13
Hither Green a					07 27				07 44						07 57						08 14			
Petts Wood a			07 29		07 39		07 44						07 59		08 09				08 14					
Orpington a	07 25		07 32		07 42		07 47				07 54		08 02		08 12			08 08	08 17					

	SE 1	SE	SE	SE	SE	SE	SE		SE	SE	SE 1	SE	SE	SE	SE	SE	SE		SE	SE 1	SE	SE	SE	SE
London Charing Cross ⊖ d	08 00		08 02		08 06		08 09				08 15		08 17				08 26			08 30		08 32		08 36
London Waterloo (East) ⊖ d	08 03		08 05		08 09		08 12				08 18		08 20				08 29			08 33		08 35		08 39
London Cannon Street ⊖ d				08 07		08 10				08 17				08 20	08 24	08 27			08 30				08 37	
London Blackfriars ⊖ d																								
London Bridge ⊖ d	08 08		08 10	08 11	08 14	08 14	08 17			08 21	08 23		08a24	08 24	08 28	08a30	08 34		08 34	08 39		08 40	08 41	08 44
London Victoria ⊖ d		07 55							08 09			08 10									08 25			
New Cross ⊖ d			08 15	09a33		08 19				09a38				08 29	08 33				08 39				10a03	
St Johns d						08 21								08 31	08 35				08 41					
Lewisham a			08 19			08 24	08 26		08 31					08 34	08 38				08 44			08 49		
Hither Green a					08 23	08 28								08 38			08 43							08 53
Petts Wood a		08 29			08 36							08 44		08 51							08 59			09 06
Orpington a	08 23	08 32			08 39						08 38	08 47		08 57						08 55	09 02			09 09

A 19 May

B not from 4 August until 11 August

C not 28 July

London - Lewisham, Hither Green, Petts Wood and Orpington (Summary of Services)

Saturdays 28 July to 11 August

	SE	SE	SE		SE 1	SE	SE 1	SE	SE	SE	SE	SE	SE		SE	SE 1	SE	SE	SE	SE	SE	SE	SE
London Charing Cross ⊖ d		08 39			08 40		08 45		08 47				08 56			09 00		09 02		09 06		09 09	
London Waterloo (East) ⊖ d		08 42			08 43		08 48		08 50				08 59			09 03		09 05		09 09		09 12	
London Cannon Street ⊖ d	08 40					08 47				08 50	08 54	08 57			09 00				09 07		09 10		
London Blackfriars ⊖ d																							
London Bridge ⊖ d	08 44	08 47			08a48	08 51	08 53		08a54	08 54	08 58	09a00	09 04		09 04	09 09		09 10	09 11	09 14	09 14	09 17	
London Victoria ⊖ d			08 39					08 40									08 55						09 09
New Cross ⊖ d	08 49					10a08				08 59	09 03				09 09				10a33		09 19		
St Johns d	08 51									09 01	09 05				09 11						09 21		
Lewisham a	08 54	08 56	09 01							09 04	09 08				09 14			09 19			09 24	09 26	09 31
Hither Green a	08 58									09 08			09 13							09 23	09 28		
Petts Wood a								09 14		09 21							09 29			09 36			
Orpington a							09 08	09 17		09 27						09 25	09 32			09 39			

	SE 1	SE	SE 1	SE	SE	SE	SE	SE	SE		SE	SE 1	SE	SE	SE	SE	SE	SE	SE	SE 1		SE	SE 1	SE
London Charing Cross ⊖ d	09 10		09 15		09 17				09 26			09 30		09 32		09 36		09 39		09 40			09 45	
London Waterloo (East) ⊖ d	09 13		09 18		09 20				09 29			09 33		09 35		09 39		09 42		09 43			09 48	
London Cannon Street ⊖ d		09 17				09 20	09 24	09 27			09 30				09 37		09 40					09 47		
London Blackfriars ⊖ d																								
London Bridge ⊖ d	09a18	09 21	09 23		09a24	09 24	09 28	09a30	09 34		09 34	09 39		09 40	09 41	09 44	09 44	09 47		09a48		09 51	09 53	
London Victoria ⊖ d				09 10									09 25						09 39					09 40
New Cross ⊖ d		10a38				09 29	09 33				09 39				11a03		09 49					11a08		
St Johns d						09 31	09 35				09 41						09 51							
Lewisham a						09 34	09 38				09 44			09 49			09 54	09 56	10 00					
Hither Green a						09 38			09 43							09 53	09 58							
Petts Wood a				09 44		09 51							09 59			10 06								10 14
Orpington a			09 38	09 47		09 57						09 55	10 02			10 09							10 08	10 17

	SE	SE	SE	SE	SE	SE		SE 1	SE	SE	SE	SE	SE	SE	SE	SE 1		SE	SE 1	SE	SE	SE	SE	SE
London Charing Cross ⊖ d	09 47				09 56			10 00		10 02		10 06		10 09		10 10			10 15		10 17			
London Waterloo (East) ⊖ d	09 50				09 59			10 03		10 05		10 09		10 12		10 13			10 18		10 20			
London Cannon Street ⊖ d		09 50	09 54	09 57		10 00					10 07		10 10					10 17				10 20	10 24	10 27
London Blackfriars ⊖ d																								
London Bridge ⊖ d	09a54	09 54	09 58	10a00	10 04	10 04		10 09		10 10	10 11	10 14	10 14	10 17		10a18		10 21	10 23		10a24	10 24	10 28	10a30
London Victoria ⊖ d									09 55						10 09					10 10				
New Cross ⊖ d		09 59	10 03			10 09					11a33		10 19					11a38				10 29	10 33	
St Johns d		10 01	10 05			10 11							10 21									10 31	10 35	
Lewisham a		10 04	10 08			10 14				10 19			10 24	10 26	10 31							10 34	10 38	
Hither Green a		10 08			10 13							10 23	10 28									10 38		
Petts Wood a		10 21							10 29			10 36								10 44		10 51		
Orpington a		10 27						10 25	10 32			10 39							10 38	10 47		10 57		

	SE	SE		SE 1	SE	SE	SE	SE	SE	SE	SE		SE		SE 1	SE	SE 1	SE	SE	SE	SE	SE	SE
London Charing Cross ⊖ d	10 26			10 30		10 32		10 36		10 39		and at the same minutes past each hour until			17 40		17 45		17 47				17 56
London Waterloo (East) ⊖ d	10 29			10 33		10 35		10 39		10 42					17 43		17 48		17 50				17 59
London Cannon Street ⊖ d		10 30					10 37		10 40							17 47				17 50	17 54	17 57	
London Blackfriars ⊖ d																							
London Bridge ⊖ d	10 34	10 34		10 39		10 40	10 41	10 44	10 44	10 47					17a48	17 51	17 53		17a54	17 54	17 58	18a00	18 04
London Victoria ⊖ d					10 25						10 39		17 39					17 40					
New Cross ⊖ d		10 39					12a03		10 49							19a08				17 59	18 03		
St Johns d		10 41							10 51											18 01	18 05		
Lewisham a		10 44				10 49			10 54	10 56	11 01		18 01							18 04	18 08		
Hither Green a	10 43							10 53	10 58											18 08			18 13
Petts Wood a					10 59			11 06										18 14		18 21			
Orpington a				10 55	11 02			11 09									18 08	18 17		18 27			

	SE	SE 1	SE	SE	SE	SE	SE	SE	SE		SE 1	SE	SE 1	SE	SE	SE	SE	SE	SE		SE	SE 1	SE
London Charing Cross ⊖ d		18 00		18 02		18 06		18 09			18 10		18 15		18 17				18 26			18 30	
London Waterloo (East) ⊖ d		18 03		18 05		18 09		18 12			18 13		18 18		18 20				18 29			18 33	
London Cannon Street ⊖ d	18 00				18 07		18 10					18 17				18 20	18 24	18 27			18 30		
London Blackfriars ⊖ d																							
London Bridge ⊖ d	18 04	18 09		18 10	18a10	18 14	18 14	18 17			18a18	18a20	18 23		18a24	18 24	18 28	18a30	18 34		18 34	18 39	
London Victoria ⊖ d			17 55						18 09					18 10									18 25
New Cross ⊖ d	18 09						18 19									18 29	18 33				18 39		
St Johns d	18 11						18 21									18 31	18 35				18 41		
Lewisham a	18 14			18 19			18 24	18 26	18 31							18 34	18 38				18 44		
Hither Green a						18 23	18 28									18 38			18 43				
Petts Wood a			18 29			18 36								18 44		18 51							18 59
Orpington a		18 25	18 32			18 39							18 38	18 47		18 57						18 55	19 02

Table 199

Saturdays
28 July to 11 August

London - Lewisham, Hither Green, Petts Wood and Orpington (Summary of Services)

	SE	SE	SE	SE	SE	SE	SE 1 ⊼	SE	SE 1	SE	SE	SE	SE	SE	SE	SE	SE 1	SE	SE	SE	SE	SE
London Charing Cross 4 ⊖ d	18 32		18 36		18 39		18 40		18 45		18 47				18 56		19 00		19 02		19 06	
London Waterloo (East) 4 ⊖ d	18 35		18 39		18 42		18 43		18 48		18 50				18 59		19 03		19 05		19 09	
London Cannon Street 4 ⊖ d		18 37		18 40				18 47				18 50	18 54	18 57		19 00				19 07		19 10
London Blackfriars 3 ⊖ d																						
London Bridge 4 ⊖ d	18 40	18a40	18 44	18 44	18 47		18a48	18a50	18 53		18a54	18 54	18 58	19a00	19 04	19 04	19 09		19 10	19a10	19 14	19 14
London Victoria 15 ⊖ d						18 39				18 40								18 55				
New Cross 4 ⊖ d				18 49								18 59	19 03			19 09						19 19
St Johns d				18 51								19 01	19 05			19 11						19 21
Lewisham 4 a	18 49			18 54	18 56	19 01						19 04	19 08			19 14			19 19			19 24
Hither Green 4 a			18 53	18 58								19 08			19 13						19 23	19 28
Petts Wood 4 a			19 06							19 14		19 21						19 29			19 36	
Orpington 4 a			19 09						19 08	19 17		19 27					19 25	19 32			19 39	

	SE	SE	SE 1 ⊼	SE 1	SE	SE	SE	SE	SE	SE	SE 1	SE	SE	SE	SE	SE	SE	SE 1 ⊼	SE	SE	SE
London Charing Cross 4 ⊖ d	19 09		19 10	19 15			19 17			19 26	19 30		19 32	19 36	19 39			19 40		19 47	19 52
London Waterloo (East) 4 ⊖ d	19 12		19 13	19 18			19 20			19 29	19 33		19 35	19 39	19 42			19 43		19 50	19 55
London Cannon Street 4 ⊖ d						19 20		19 24	19 27										19 46		
London Blackfriars 3 ⊖ d																					
London Bridge 4 ⊖ d	19 17		19a18	19 23		19 24	19 25	19 28	19a30	19 34	19 39		19 40	19 44	19 47			19a48	19a49	19 55	20 00
London Victoria 15 ⊖ d		19 09			19 10							19 25				19 39	19 40				
New Cross 4 ⊖ d						19 29		19 33					19 45							20 00	20 05
St Johns d						19 31		19 35												20 02	
Lewisham 4 a	19 26	19 31				19 34	19 37	19 38					19 49	19 51	19 56	20 01				20 05	20 09
Hither Green 4 a						19 38				19 43				19 56							20 13
Petts Wood 4 a					19 44	19 51						19 59		20 08			20 14				
Orpington 4 a				19 38	19 48	19 57					19 55	20 02		20 12			20 18				

	SE 1	SE	SE	SE	SE	SE	SE 1 ⊼	SE	SE	SE	SE	SE 1	SE	SE	SE	SE	SE	SE 1	SE	SE	SE	SE 1
London Charing Cross 4 ⊖ d	19 55		19 56	20 02	20 06	20 09	20 10			20 17	20 22	20 25		20 26	20 32	20 36	20 39	20 40		20 47	20 52	20 55
London Waterloo (East) 4 ⊖ d	19 58		19 59	20 05	20 09	20 12	20 13			20 20	20 25	20 28		20 29	20 35	20 39	20 42	20 43		20 50	20 55	20 58
London Cannon Street 4 ⊖ d									20 16										20 46			
London Blackfriars 3 ⊖ d																						
London Bridge 4 ⊖ d	20 03		20a04	20 10	20 14	20 17	20 19		20a19	20 25	20 30	20 33		20a34	20 40	20 44	20 47	20 49	20a49	20 55	21 00	21 03
London Victoria 15 ⊖ d		19 55						20 10					20 25									
New Cross 4 ⊖ d				20 15						20 30	20 35				20 45					21 00	21 05	
St Johns d										20 32										21 02		
Lewisham 4 a				20 19	20 21	20 26				20 35	20 39				20 49	20 51	20 56			21 05	21 09	
Hither Green 4 a					20 26						20 43					20 56					21 13	
Petts Wood 4 a		20 29			20 38			20 44					20 59			21 08						
Orpington 4 a	20 18	20 32			20 42		20 34	20 47				20 48	21 02			21 12		21 04				21 18

	SE	SE	SE	SE	SE	SE 1	SE	SE	SE 1	SE	SE	SE	SE	SE	SE 1	SE	SE	SE 1	SE	SE	SE	SE
London Charing Cross 4 ⊖ d		20 56	21 02	21 06	21 09	21 10	21 17	21 22	21 25		21 26	21 32	21 36	21 39	21 40	21 47	21 52	21 55		21 56	22 02	22 06
London Waterloo (East) 4 ⊖ d		20 59	21 05	21 09	21 12	21 13	21 20	21 25	21 28		21 29	21 35	21 39	21 42	21 43	21 50	21 55	21 58		21 59	22 05	22 09
London Cannon Street 4 ⊖ d																						
London Blackfriars 3 ⊖ d																						
London Bridge 4 ⊖ d		21a04	21 10	21 14	21 17	21 19	21 25	21 30	21 33		21a34	21 40	21 44	21 47	21 49	21 55	22 00	22 03		22a04	22 10	22 14
London Victoria 15 ⊖ d	20 55									21 25									21 55			
New Cross 4 ⊖ d			21 15				21 30	21 35				21 45				22 00	22 05				22 15	
St Johns d							21 32									22 02						
Lewisham 4 a			21 19	21 21	21 26		21 35	21 39				21 49	21 51	21 56		22 05	22 09				22 19	22 21
Hither Green 4 a				21 26				21 43					21 56				22 13					22 26
Petts Wood 4 a	21 29			21 38						21 59			22 08						22 29			22 38
Orpington 4 a	21 32			21 42		21 34			21 48	22 02			22 15		22 04			22 18	22 32			22 45

	SE	SE 1	SE	SE	SE 1	SE	SE	SE	SE	SE	SE 1	SE	SE	SE 1	SE	SE	SE	SE	SE	SE 1	SE
London Charing Cross 4 ⊖ d	22 09	22 10	22 17	22 22	22 25		22 26	22 32	22 36	22 39	22 40	22 47	22 52	22 55		22 56	23 02	23 06	23 09	23 10	23 17
London Waterloo (East) 4 ⊖ d	22 12	22 13	22 20	22 25	22 28		22 29	22 35	22 39	22 42	22 43	22 50	22 55	22 58		22 59	23 05	23 09	23 12	23 13	23 20
London Cannon Street 4 ⊖ d																					
London Blackfriars 3 ⊖ d																					
London Bridge 4 ⊖ d	22 17	22 19	22 25	22 30	22 33		22a34	22 40	22 44	22 47	22 49	22 55	23 00	23 03		23a04	23 10	23 14	23 17	23 19	23 25
London Victoria 15 ⊖ d						22 25									22 55						
New Cross 4 ⊖ d			22 30	22 35				22 45				23 00	23 05				23 15				23 30
St Johns d			22 32									23 02									23 32
Lewisham 4 a	22 26		22 35	22 39				22 49	22 51	22 56		23 05	23 09				23 19	23 21	23 26		23 35
Hither Green 4 a				22 43					22 56				23 13					23 26			
Petts Wood 4 a						22 59			23 08						23 29			23 38			
Orpington 4 a		22 34			22 48	23 02			23 15		23 04			23 18	23 32			23 45		23 34	

Table 199

Saturdays
28 July to 11 August

London - Lewisham, Hither Green, Petts Wood and Orpington (Summary of Services)

	SE	SE 1	SE	SE	SE	SE	SE	SE 1	SE 1	SE	SE	SE
London Charing Cross 4 ⊖ d	23 22	23 25		23 26	23 32	23 36	23 39	23 40	23 45	23 52		23 56
London Waterloo (East) 4 ⊖ d	23 25	23 28		23 29	23 35	23 39	23 42	23 43	23 48	23 55		23 59
London Cannon Street 4 ⊖ d												
London Blackfriars 3 ⊖ d												
London Bridge 4 ⊖ d	23 30	23 33		23a34	23 40	23 44	23 47	23 49	23 53	23 59		00a04
London Victoria 15 ⊖ d			23 25								23 55	
New Cross 4 ⊖ d	23 35				23 45					00 05		
St Johns d										00 07		
Lewisham 4 a	23 39				23 49	23 51	23 56			00 10		
Hither Green 4 a	23 43					23 56						
Petts Wood 4 a			23 59			00 08					00 29	
Orpington 4 a		23 48	00 02			00 15		00 04	00 08		00 32	

Saturdays
25 August to 8 September

	SE	SE	SE 1	SE	SE	SE	SE	SE	SE	SE	SE	SE	SE 1	SE	SE	SE	SE	SE	SE	SE	SE	SE
											A	A	A	A	A		A	A	A			
London Charing Cross 4 ⊖ d		23p36	23p45	23p52		00 02	00 06	00 10	00 15	00 18		00 32	00 37		00 44	00 48				04 52	05 22	05 26
London Waterloo (East) 4 ⊖ d		23p39	23p48	23p55		00 05	00 09	00 13	00 18	00 21		00 35	00 40		00 47	00 51				04 55	05 25	05 29
London Cannon Street 4 ⊖ d											00 28	≀	≀	00 41	≀				00 56			
London Blackfriars 3 ⊖ d											≀	≀	≀	≀	≀				≀			
London Bridge 4 ⊖ d		23p44	23p53	23p59		00 10	00 14	00 18	00 23	00 26	00 32	00a39	00 45	00 45	00 52	00 56			00a59	05 00	05 30	05a33
London Victoria 15 ⊖ d	23p25				23p55						≀		≀	≀			00 45	00 56				
New Cross 4 ⊖ d				00 05		00 15		00 23		00 31	00 38		≀	≀	00 57	01 01	≀	≀		05 05	05 35	
St Johns d				00 07							00 40		≀	≀	≀		≀	≀				
Lewisham 4 a		23p51		00 10		00 19	00 21	00 27		00 35	00 43		≀	00s52	01 01	01 05	≀	≀		05 09	05 39	
Hither Green 4 a		23p56					00 26	00 31					≀		01s05	01 09	≀	≀		05 13	05 43	
Petts Wood 4 a	23p59	00 08			00 29		00 38						≀			01 22	01s25	≀				
Orpington 4 a	00 02	00 12	00 08		00 32		00 42		00 46				01 00			01 25	01 29	01 33				

	SE	SE	SE	SE	SE	SE	SE 1	SE	SE	SE	SE	SE	SE	SE	SE	SE	SE	SE	SE	SE	SE	SE 1
London Charing Cross 4 ⊖ d	05 32	05 36	05 39	05 47	05 52	05 56	06 00		06 02	06 06	06 09	06 17	06 22		06 26	06 32	06 36	06 39	06 47	06 52	06 56	07 00
London Waterloo (East) 4 ⊖ d	05 35	05 39	05 42	05 50	05 55	05 59	06 03		06 05	06 09	06 12	06 20	06 25		06 29	06 35	06 39	06 42	06 50	06 55	06 59	07 03
London Cannon Street 4 ⊖ d																						
London Blackfriars 3 ⊖ d																						
London Bridge 4 ⊖ d	05 40	05 44	05 47	05 55	06 00	06a03	06 08		06 10	06 14	06 17	06 25	06 30		06a33	06 40	06 44	06 47	06 55	07 00	07a03	07 08
London Victoria 15 ⊖ d								05 55						06 25								
New Cross 4 ⊖ d	05 45			06 00	06 05				06 15			06 30	06 35			06 45			07 00	07 05		
St Johns d				06 02								06 32							07 02			
Lewisham 4 a	05 49	05 52	05 56	06 05	06 09				06 19	06 22	06 26	06 35	06 39			06 49	06 52	06 56	07 05	07 08		
Hither Green 4 a		05 57			06 13					06 27			06 43				06 57			07 14		
Petts Wood 4 a		06 09						06 29		06 39				06 59			07 09					
Orpington 4 a		06 12					06 23	06 32		06 42				07 02			07 12					07 23

	SE	SE	SE	SE	SE	SE	SE	SE	SE 1	SE	SE	SE	SE	SE	SE 1	SE	SE	SE	SE	SE	SE 1
London Charing Cross 4 ⊖ d		07 02	07 06	07 09		07 17	07 22	07 26	07 30		07 32	07 36	07 39		07 45		07 47	07 52	07 56		08 00
London Waterloo (East) 4 ⊖ d		07 05	07 09	07 12		07 20	07 25	07 29	07 33		07 35	07 39	07 42		07 48		07 50	07 55	07 59		08 03
London Cannon Street 4 ⊖ d																				08 00	
London Blackfriars 3 ⊖ d																					
London Bridge 4 ⊖ d		07 10	07 14	07 17		07 25	07 30	07a33	07 38		07 40	07 44	07 47		07 53		07a54	08 00	08a03	08 04	08 08
London Victoria 15 ⊖ d	06 55				07 10					07 25				07 39		07 40					
New Cross 4 ⊖ d		07 15				07 30	07 35				07 45							08 05		08 09	
St Johns d						07 32														08 11	
Lewisham 4 a		07 19	07 22	07 26		07 35	07 39				07 49	07 52	07 56	08 02				08 08		08 13	
Hither Green 4 a			07 27				07 44					07 57						08 14			
Petts Wood 4 a	07 29		07 39		07 44					07 59		08 09				08 14					
Orpington 4 a	07 32		07 42		07 47				07 54	08 02		08 12			08 08	08 17					08 23

	SE	SE	SE	SE	SE	SE	SE	SE	SE 1	SE	SE	SE	SE	SE	SE	SE	SE 1	SE	SE	SE	SE	SE
London Charing Cross 4 ⊖ d		08 02		08 06		08 09			08 15		08 17				08 26		08 30		08 32		08 36	
London Waterloo (East) 4 ⊖ d		08 05		08 09		08 12			08 18		08 20				08 29		08 33		08 35		08 39	
London Cannon Street 4 ⊖ d			08 07		08 10			08 17				08 20	08 24	08 27		08 30				08 37		08 40
London Blackfriars 3 ⊖ d																						
London Bridge 4 ⊖ d		08 10	08 11	08 14	08 14	08 17		08 21	08 23		08a24	08 24	08 28	08a30	08 34	08 34	08 39		08 40	08 41	08 44	08 44
London Victoria 15 ⊖ d	07 55						08 09			08 10								08 25				
New Cross 4 ⊖ d		08 15	09a33		08 19			09a38				08 29	08 33			08 39				10a03		08 49
St Johns d					08 21							08 31	08 35			08 41						08 51
Lewisham 4 a		08 19			08 24	08 26	08 31					08 34	08 38			08 44			08 49			08 54
Hither Green 4 a				08 23	08 28							08 38			08 43						08 53	08 58
Petts Wood 4 a	08 29			08 36						08 44		08 51						08 59			09 06	
Orpington 4 a	08 32			08 39					08 38	08 47		08 54					08 55	09 02			09 09	

A not 25 August

Table 199

London - Lewisham, Hither Green, Petts Wood and Orpington (Summary of Services)

Saturdays
25 August to 8 September

Station		SE	SE	SE ■	SE	SE ■	SE	SE	SE	SE	SE	SE	SE	SE ■	SE	SE	SE	SE	SE	SE	SE
London Charing Cross ■ ⊖	d	08 39		08 40		08 45		08 47				08 56		09 00		09 02		09 06		09 09	
London Waterloo (East) ■ ⊖	d	08 42		08 43		08 48		08 50				08 59		09 03		09 05		09 09		09 12	
London Cannon Street ■ ⊖	d				08 47				08 50	08 54	08 57		09 00				09 07		09 10		
London Blackfriars ■ ⊖	d																				
London Bridge ■ ⊖	d	08 47		08a48	08 51	08 53		08a54	08 54	08 58	09a00	09 04	09 04	09 09		09 10	09 11	09 14	09 14	09 17	
London Victoria ■ ⊖	d		08 39				08 40								08 55						09 09
New Cross ■ ⊖	d				10a08				08 59	09 03			09 09				10a33		09 19		
St Johns	d								09 01	09 05			09 11						09 21		
Lewisham ■	a	08 56	09 01						09 04	09 08			09 14			09 19			09 24	09 26	09 31
Hither Green ■	a								09 08			09 13						09 23	09 28		
Petts Wood ■	a						09 14		09 21						09 29			09 36			
Orpington ■	a					09 08	09 17		09 24					09 25	09 32			09 39			

Station		SE ■		SE ■ ⌶	SE	SE ■	SE	SE	SE	SE	SE	SE	SE	SE ■	SE	SE	SE	SE	SE	SE	SE	SE ■ ⌶
London Charing Cross ■ ⊖	d	09 10	and at the same minutes past each hour until	17 10		17 15		17 17				17 26		17 30		17 32		17 36		17 39		17 40
London Waterloo (East) ■ ⊖	d	09 13		17 13		17 18		17 20				17 29		17 33		17 35		17 39		17 42		17 43
London Cannon Street ■ ⊖	d				17 17				17 20	17 24	17 27		17 30				17 37		17 40			
London Blackfriars ■ ⊖	d																					
London Bridge ■ ⊖	d	09a18		17a18	17 21	17 23		17a24	17 24	17 28	17a30	17 34	17 34	17 39		17 40	17 41	17 44	17 44	17 47		17a48
London Victoria ■ ⊖	d						17 10								17 25						17 39	
New Cross ■ ⊖	d				18a38				17 29	17 33			17 39				19a03		17 49			
St Johns	d								17 31	17 35			17 41						17 51			
Lewisham ■	a								17 34	17 38			17 44			17 49			17 54	17 56	18 01	
Hither Green ■	a								17 38			17 43						17 53	17 58			
Petts Wood ■	a						17 44		17 51						17 59			18 06				
Orpington ■	a					17 38	17 47		17 54					17 55	18 02			18 09				

Station		SE	SE ■	SE	SE	SE	SE	SE	SE	SE	SE ■	SE	SE	SE	SE	SE	SE	SE	SE ■ ⌶	SE	SE ■	SE
London Charing Cross ■ ⊖	d		17 45		17 47				17 56		18 00		18 02		18 06		18 09		18 10		18 15	
London Waterloo (East) ■ ⊖	d		17 48		17 50				17 59		18 03		18 05		18 09		18 12		18 13		18 18	
London Cannon Street ■ ⊖	d	17 47				17 50	17 54	17 57		18 00				18 07		18 10				18 17		
London Blackfriars ■ ⊖	d																					
London Bridge ■ ⊖	d	17 51	17 53		17a54	17 54	17 58	18a00	18 04	18 04	18 09		18 10	18a10	18 14	18 14	18 17		18a18	18a20	18 23	
London Victoria ■ ⊖	d			17 40								17 55						18 09				18 10
New Cross ■ ⊖	d	19a08				17 59	18 03			18 09						18 19						
St Johns	d					18 01	18 05			18 11						18 21						
Lewisham ■	a					18 04	18 08			18 14			18 19			18 24	18 26	18 31				
Hither Green ■	a					18 08			18 13						18 23	18 28						
Petts Wood ■	a			18 14		18 21						18 29			18 36							18 44
Orpington ■	a		18 08	18 17		18 24					18 25	18 32			18 39						18 38	18 47

Station		SE	SE	SE	SE	SE	SE	SE ■	SE	SE	SE	SE	SE	SE	SE	SE ■ ⌶	SE	SE ■	SE	SE	SE	SE	SE
London Charing Cross ■ ⊖	d	18 17				18 26		18 30		18 32		18 36		18 39		18 40		18 45		18 47			
London Waterloo (East) ■ ⊖	d	18 20				18 29		18 33		18 35		18 39		18 42		18 43		18 48		18 50			
London Cannon Street ■ ⊖	d		18 20	18 24	18 27		18 30				18 37		18 40				18 47				18 50	18 54	18 57
London Blackfriars ■ ⊖	d																						
London Bridge ■ ⊖	d	18a24	18 24	18 28	18a30	18 34	18 34	18 39		18 40	18a40	18 44	18 44	18 47		18a48	18a50	18 53		18a54	18 54	18 58	19a00
London Victoria ■ ⊖	d								18 25						18 39				18 40				
New Cross ■ ⊖	d		18 29	18 33			18 39						18 49								18 59	19 03	
St Johns	d		18 31	18 35			18 41						18 51								19 01	19 05	
Lewisham ■	a		18 34	18 38			18 44			18 49			18 54	18 56	19 01						19 04	19 08	
Hither Green ■	a		18 38			18 43						18 53	18 58								19 08		
Petts Wood ■	a		18 51						18 59			19 06							19 14		19 21		
Orpington ■	a		18 54					18 55	19 02			19 09						19 08	19 17		19 24		

Station		SE	SE	SE ■	SE	SE	SE	SE	SE	SE	SE	SE ■ ⌶	SE ■	SE	SE	SE	SE	SE	SE	SE ■	SE	SE
London Charing Cross ■ ⊖	d	18 56		19 00		19 02		19 06		19 09		19 10	19 15			19 17			19 26	19 30		19 32
London Waterloo (East) ■ ⊖	d	18 59		19 03		19 05		19 09		19 12		19 13	19 18			19 20			19 29	19 33		19 35
London Cannon Street ■ ⊖	d		19 00				19 07		19 10						19 20		19 24	19 27				
London Blackfriars ■ ⊖	d																					
London Bridge ■ ⊖	d	19 04	19 04	19 09		19 10	19a10	19 14	19 14	19 17		19a18	19 23		19 24	19 25	19 28	19a30	19 34	19 39		19 40
London Victoria ■ ⊖	d				18 55						19 09			19 10							19 25	
New Cross ■ ⊖	d		19 09						19 19						19 29		19 33					19 45
St Johns	d		19 11						19 21						19 31		19 35					
Lewisham ■	a		19 14			19 19			19 24	19 26	19 31				19 34	19 37	19 38					19 49
Hither Green ■	a	19 13						19 23	19 28						19 38				19 43			
Petts Wood ■	a				19 29			19 36						19 44	19 51						19 59	
Orpington ■	a			19 25	19 32			19 39					19 38	19 48	19 54					19 55	20 02	

Table 199

London - Lewisham, Hither Green, Petts Wood and Orpington (Summary of Services)

Saturdays
25 August to 8 September

Station		SE	SE	SE	SE	SE ■ ⌶	SE	SE	SE ■	SE	SE	SE	SE	SE	SE ■ ⌶	SE	SE	SE	SE ■	SE	SE	SE	SE
London Charing Cross ■ ⊖	d	19 36	19 39			19 40	19 47	19 52	19 55		19 56	20 02	20 06	20 09	20 10		20 17	20 22	20 25		20 26	20 32	20 36
London Waterloo (East) ■ ⊖	d	19 39	19 42			19 43	19 50	19 55	19 58		19 59	20 05	20 09	20 12	20 13		20 20	20 25	20 28		20 29	20 35	20 39
London Cannon Street ■ ⊖	d																						
London Blackfriars ■ ⊖	d																						
London Bridge ■ ⊖	d	19 44	19 47			19a48	19 55	20 00	20 03		20a04	20 10	20 14	20 17	20 19		20 25	20 30	20 33		20a34	20 40	20 44
London Victoria ■ ⊖	d			19 39	19 40					19 55						20 10				20 25			
New Cross ■ ⊖	d						20 00	20 05				20 15					20 30	20 35				20 45	
St Johns	d						20 02										20 32						
Lewisham ■	a	19 51	19 56	20 01			20 05	20 09				20 19	20 21	20 26			20 35	20 39				20 49	20 51
Hither Green ■	a	19 56						20 13					20 26					20 43					20 56
Petts Wood ■	a	20 08			20 14					20 29			20 38			20 44				20 59			21 08
Orpington ■	a	20 12			20 18				20 18	20 32			20 42		20 34	20 47			20 48	21 02			21 12

Station		SE	SE ■	SE	SE	SE ■	SE	SE	SE	SE	SE	SE ■	SE	SE	SE ■	SE	SE	SE	SE	SE	SE ■	SE	SE
London Charing Cross ■ ⊖	d	20 39	20 40	20 47	20 52	20 55		20 56	21 02	21 06	21 09	21 10	21 17	21 22	21 25		21 26	21 32	21 36	21 39	21 40	21 47	21 52
London Waterloo (East) ■ ⊖	d	20 42	20 43	20 50	20 55	20 58		20 59	21 05	21 09	21 12	21 13	21 20	21 25	21 28		21 29	21 35	21 39	21 42	21 43	21 50	21 55
London Cannon Street ■ ⊖	d																						
London Blackfriars ■ ⊖	d																						
London Bridge ■ ⊖	d	20 47	20 49	20 55	21 00	21 03		21a04	21 10	21 14	21 17	21 19	21 25	21 30	21 33		21a34	21 40	21 44	21 47	21 49	21 55	22 00
London Victoria ■ ⊖	d						20 55									21 25							
New Cross ■ ⊖	d			21 00	21 05				21 15				21 30	21 35				21 45				22 00	22 05
St Johns	d			21 02									21 32									22 02	
Lewisham ■	a	20 56		21 05	21 09				21 19	21 21	21 26		21 35	21 39				21 49	21 51	21 56		22 05	22 09
Hither Green ■	a				21 13					21 26				21 43					21 56				22 13
Petts Wood ■	a						21 29			21 38						21 59			22 08				
Orpington ■	a		21 04			21 18	21 32			21 42		21 34			21 48	22 02			22 12		22 04		

Station		SE ■	SE	SE	SE	SE	SE	SE ■	SE	SE	SE ■	SE	SE	SE	SE	SE	SE ■	SE	SE	SE ■	SE	SE
London Charing Cross ■ ⊖	d	21 55		21 56	22 02	22 06	22 09	22 10	22 17	22 22	22 25		22 26	22 32	22 36	22 39	22 40	22 47	22 52	22 55		22 56
London Waterloo (East) ■ ⊖	d	21 58		21 59	22 05	22 09	22 12	22 13	22 20	22 25	22 28		22 29	22 35	22 39	22 42	22 43	22 50	22 55	22 58		22 59
London Cannon Street ■ ⊖	d																					
London Blackfriars ■ ⊖	d																					
London Bridge ■ ⊖	d	22 03		22a04	22 10	22 14	22 17	22 19	22 25	22 30	22 33		22a34	22 40	22 44	22 47	22 49	22 55	23 00	23 03		23a04
London Victoria ■ ⊖	d		21 55									22 25									22 55	
New Cross ■ ⊖	d				22 15				22 30	22 35				22 45				23 00	23 05			
St Johns	d								22 32									23 02				
Lewisham ■	a				22 19	22 21	22 26		22 35	22 39				22 49	22 51	22 56		23 05	23 09			
Hither Green ■	a					22 26				22 43					22 56				23 13			
Petts Wood ■	a		22 29			22 38						22 59			23 08						23 29	
Orpington ■	a	22 18	22 32			22 42		22 34			22 48	23 02			23 12		23 04			23 18	23 32	

Station		SE	SE	SE	SE ■	SE	SE	SE ■	SE	SE	SE	SE	SE	SE ■	SE ■	SE	SE	SE
London Charing Cross ■ ⊖	d	23 02	23 06	23 09	23 10	23 17	23 22	23 25		23 26	23 32	23 36	23 39	23 40	23 45	23 52		23 56
London Waterloo (East) ■ ⊖	d	23 05	23 09	23 12	23 13	23 20	23 25	23 28		23 29	23 35	23 39	23 42	23 43	23 48	23 55		23 59
London Cannon Street ■ ⊖	d																	
London Blackfriars ■ ⊖	d																	
London Bridge ■ ⊖	d	23 10	23 14	23 17	23 19	23 25	23 30	23 33		23a34	23 40	23 44	23 47	23 49	23 53	23 59		00a04
London Victoria ■ ⊖	d								23 25								23 55	
New Cross ■ ⊖	d	23 15				23 30	23 35				23 45					00 05		
St Johns	d					23 32										00 07		
Lewisham ■	a	23 19	23 21	23 26		23 35	23 39				23 49	23 51	23 55			00 10		
Hither Green ■	a		23 26				23 43					23 56						
Petts Wood ■	a		23 38						23 59			00 08					00 29	
Orpington ■	a		23 42		23 34			23 48	00 02			00 12		00 04	00 08		00 32	

Sundays
until 22 July, 19 Aug and from 16 Sep

Station		SE	SE	SE ■	SE ■	SE A	SE	SE	SE	SE	SE	SE	SE	SE	SE	SE	SE	SE	SE	SE	SE	SE	SE ■
London Charing Cross ■ ⊖	d		23p36	23p40	23p45		23p52		00 02	00 06	00 10	00 15	00 18	00 48	07 30	07 35	07 46	07 50		07 56	08 00	08 05	08 08
London Waterloo (East) ■ ⊖	d		23p39	23p43	23p48		23p55		00 05	00 09	00 13	00 18	00 21	00 51	07 33	07 38	07 49	07 53		07 59	08 03	08 08	08 11
London Cannon Street ■ ⊖	d																						
London Blackfriars ■ ⊖	d																						
London Bridge ■ ⊖	d		23p44	23p49	23p53		23p59		00 10	00 14	00 18	00 23	00 26	00 56	07a37	07 43	07 54	07 58		08 04	08a07	08 13	08 16
London Victoria ■ ⊖	d	23p25				23p43		23p55											07 51				
New Cross ■ ⊖	d						00 05		00 15		00 23		00 31	01 01		07 49		08 04				08 19	
St Johns	d						00 07									07 51						08 21	
Lewisham ■	a		23p51				00 10		00 19	00 21	00 27		00 35	01 05		07 53	08 02	08 07		08 11		08 23	
Hither Green ■	a		23p56							00 26	00 31			01 09			08 07			08 16			
Petts Wood ■	a	23p59	00 08			00 22		00 29		00 38				01 22			08 20		08 25				
Orpington ■	a	00 02	00 12	00 04	00 08	00 25		00 32		00 42		00 46		01 25			08 23		08 28				08 31

A 20 May

Table 199

Sundays

until 22 July, 19 Aug and from 16 Sep

London - Lewisham, Hither Green, Petts Wood and Orpington (Summary of Services)

		SE	SE	SE	SE ■	SE		SE	SE	SE	SE ■	SE	SE	SE	SE	SE		SE	SE	SE ■	SE	SE	SE	SE ■	SE
London Charing Cross ■ ⊖	d	08 10	08 16	08 20	08 23			08 26	08 30	08 35	08 38	08 40	08 46	08 50		08 56		09 00	09 05	09 08	09 10	09 16	09 20	09 23	
London Waterloo (East) ■ ⊖	d	08 13	08 19	08 23	08 26			08 29	08 33	08 38	08 41	08 43	08 49	08 53		08 59		09 03	09 08	09 11	09 13	09 19	09 23	09 26	
London Cannon Street ■ ⊖	d																								
London Blackfriars ■ ⊖	d																								
London Bridge ■ ⊖	d	08 18	08 24	08 28	08 31			08 34	08a37	08 43	08 46	08 48	08 54	08 58		09 04		09a07	09 13	09 16	09 18	09 24	09 28	09 31	
London Victoria ■ ⊖	d					08 21									08 51										09 21
New Cross ■ ⊖	d			08 34						08 49				09 04					09 19				09 34		
St Johns	d									08 51									09 21						
Lewisham ■ ⇌	a	08 27	08 32	08 37				08 41		08 53		08 57	09 02	09 07		09 11			09 23		09 27	09 32	09 37		
Hither Green ■	a		08 37					08 46					09 07			09 16						09 37			
Petts Wood ■	a		08 50			08 55							09 20		09 25							09 50			09 55
Orpington ■	a		08 53		08 46	08 58					09 01		09 23		09 28					09 31		09 53		09 46	09 58

		SE		SE	SE	SE ■	SE	SE	SE	SE ■		SE ■		SE	SE	SE	SE	SE ■ ✠	SE	SE	SE	SE ■		SE
London Charing Cross ■ ⊖	d	09 26		09 30	09 35	09 38	09 40	09 46	09 50	09 53	and at the same minutes past each hour until	19 53			19 56	20 00	20 05	20 08	20 10	20 16	20 20	20 23		
London Waterloo (East) ■ ⊖	d	09 29		09 33	09 38	09 41	09 43	09 49	09 53	09 56		19 56			19 59	20 03	20 08	20 11	20 13	20 19	20 23	20 26		
London Cannon Street ■ ⊖	d																							
London Blackfriars ■ ⊖	d																							
London Bridge ■ ⊖	d	09 34		09a37	09 43	09 46	09 48	09 54	09 58	10 01		20 01			20 04	20a07	20 13	20 16	20 18	20 24	20 28	20 31		
London Victoria ■ ⊖	d													19 51										20 21
New Cross ■ ⊖	d				09 49				10 04								20 19				20 34			
St Johns	d				09 51												20 21							
Lewisham ■ ⇌	a	09 41			09 53		09 57	10 02	10 07						20 11		20 23		20 27	20 32	20 37			
Hither Green ■	a	09 46						10 07							20 16					20 37				
Petts Wood ■	a							10 20						20 25						20 50				20 55
Orpington ■	a					10 01		10 23		10 16		20 16		20 28				20 31		20 53		20 46		20 58

		SE	SE	SE	SE ■	SE	SE	SE	SE		SE	SE	SE	SE ■	SE	SE	SE	SE ■	SE		SE	SE	SE	SE ■	SE
London Charing Cross ■ ⊖	d	20 26	20 30	20 35	20 38	20 40	20 46	20 50			20 56	21 00	21 05	21 08	21 10	21 16	21 20	21 23			21 26	21 30	21 35	21 38	21 40
London Waterloo (East) ■ ⊖	d	20 29	20 33	20 38	20 41	20 43	20 49	20 53			20 59	21 03	21 08	21 11	21 13	21 19	21 23	21 26			21 29	21 33	21 38	21 41	21 43
London Cannon Street ■ ⊖	d																								
London Blackfriars ■ ⊖	d																								
London Bridge ■ ⊖	d	20 34	20a37	20 43	20 46	20 48	20 54	20 58			21 04	21a07	21 13	21 16	21 18	21 24	21 28	21 31			21 34	21a37	21 43	21 46	21 48
London Victoria ■ ⊖	d								20 51										21 21						
New Cross ■ ⊖	d			20 49				21 04					21 19				21 34						21 49		
St Johns	d			20 51									21 21										21 51		
Lewisham ■ ⇌	a	20 41		20 53		20 57	21 02	21 07			21 11		21 23		21 27	21 32	21 37				21 41		21 53		21 57
Hither Green ■	a	20 46					21 07				21 16					21 37					21 46				
Petts Wood ■	a						21 20		21 25							21 50			21 55					22 01	
Orpington ■	a				21 01		21 23		21 28					21 31		21 53		21 46	21 58						

		SE	SE	SE	SE		SE	SE	SE ■	SE	SE	SE	SE ■	SE	SE		SE	SE	SE ■	SE	SE	SE	SE	SE	SE
London Charing Cross ■ ⊖	d	21 46	21 50		21 56		22 00	22 05	22 08	22 10	22 16	22 20	22 23		22 26		22 30	22 35	22 38	22 40	22 46	22 50		22 56	23 00
London Waterloo (East) ■ ⊖	d	21 49	21 53		21 59		22 03	22 08	22 11	22 13	22 19	22 23	22 26		22 29		22 33	22 38	22 41	22 43	22 49	22 53		22 59	23 03
London Cannon Street ■ ⊖	d																								
London Blackfriars ■ ⊖	d																								
London Bridge ■ ⊖	d	21 54	21 58		22 04		22a07	22 13	22 16	22 18	22 24	22 28	22 31		22 34		22a37	22 43	22 46	22 48	22 54	22 58		23 04	23a07
London Victoria ■ ⊖	d			21 51										22 21									22 51		
New Cross ■ ⊖	d		22 04					22 19				22 34						22 49				23 04			
St Johns	d							22 21										22 51							
Lewisham ■ ⇌	a	22 02	22 07		22 11			22 23		22 27	22 32	22 37			22 41			22 53		22 57	23 02	23 07		23 11	
Hither Green ■	a	22 07			22 16						22 37				22 46						23 07			23 16	
Petts Wood ■	a	22 20		22 25							22 50			22 55							23 20		23 25		
Orpington ■	a	22 23		22 28					22 31		22 53		22 46	22 58					23 01		23 23		23 29		

			SE	SE ■	SE	SE	SE	SE ■	SE	SE	SE		SE	SE ■	SE	SE	SE
London Charing Cross ■ ⊖	d		23 05	23 08	23 10	23 16	23 20	23 23		23 26	23 30		23 35	23 38	23 46	23 50	23 56
London Waterloo (East) ■ ⊖	d		23 08	23 11	23 13	23 19	23 23	23 26		23 29	23 33		23 38	23 41	23 49	23 53	23 59
London Cannon Street ■ ⊖	d																
London Blackfriars ■ ⊖	d																
London Bridge ■ ⊖	d		23 13	23 16	23 18	23 24	23 28	23 31		23 34	23a37		23 43	23 46	23 54	23 58	00 04
London Victoria ■ ⊖	d								23 21								
New Cross ■ ⊖	d		23 19				23 34						23 49			00 04	
St Johns	d		23 21										23 51				
Lewisham ■ ⇌	a		23 23		23 26	23 32	23 37			23 41			23 53		00 02	00 07	00 11
Hither Green ■	a					23 37				23 46					00 07		00 16
Petts Wood ■	a					23 50			23 55						00 20		
Orpington ■	a			23 31		23 53		23 46	23 59					00 01	00 23		

Table 199

Sundays

29 July to 12 August

London - Lewisham, Hither Green, Petts Wood and Orpington (Summary of Services)

		SE	SE	SE ■	SE ■	SE	SE	SE	SE	SE		SE	SE	SE	SE	SE ■	SE	SE	SE	SE		SE	SE	SE	SE
London Charing Cross ■ ⊖	d		23p36	23p40	23p45	23p52		00 02	00 06	00 10		00 15	00 18		00 32	00 37		00 44		00 48				06 26	06 32
London Waterloo (East) ■ ⊖	d		23p39	23p43	23p48	23p55		00 05	00 09	00 13		00 18	00 21		00 35	00 40		00 47		00 51				06 29	06 35
London Cannon Street ■ ⊖	d													00 30			00 42						00 56		
London Blackfriars ■ ⊖	d																								
London Bridge ■ ⊖	d		23p44	23p49	23p53	23p59		00 10	00 14	00 18		00 23	00 26	00 34	00a39	00 45	00 47	00 52		00 56			00a59	06a33	06 40
London Victoria ■ ⊖	d	23p25					23p55												00 45			00 56			
New Cross ■ ⊖	d					00 05		00 15		00 23			00 31	00 39				00 57		01 01					06 45
St Johns	d					00 07								00 41											
Lewisham ■ ⇌	a		23p51			00 10		00 19	00 21	00 27			00 35	00 44			00 55	01 01		01 05					06 49
Hither Green ■	a		23p56						00 26	00 33								01 05		01 09					
Petts Wood ■	a	23p59	00 08				00 29		00 38										01 21	01 22		01 35			
Orpington ■	a	00 02	00 15	00 04	00 08		00 32		00 45			00 46				01 00			01 27	01 25		01 42			

		SE	SE	SE	SE ■	SE		SE	SE	SE	SE	SE	SE ■	SE	SE	SE		SE	SE	SE ■	SE	SE	SE	SE ■	SE
London Charing Cross ■ ⊖	d	06 39	06 52	06 56	07 00			07 02	07 06	07 09	07 22	07 26	07 29		07 31	07 36		07 39		07 45	07 52	07 56		07 59	
London Waterloo (East) ■ ⊖	d	06 42	06 55	06 59	07 03			07 05	07 09	07 12	07 25	07 29	07 32		07 34	07 39		07 42		07 48	07 55	07 59		08 02	
London Cannon Street ■ ⊖	d																						08 00		
London Blackfriars ■ ⊖	d																								
London Bridge ■ ⊖	d	06 47	07 00	07a03	07 08			07 10	07 14	07 17	07 30	07a33	07 38		07 40	07 44		07 47		07 53	08 00	08a03	08 04	08 08	
London Victoria ■ ⊖	d					06 55								07 25					07 39						07 55
New Cross ■ ⊖	d		07 05					07 15			07 35				07 45						08 05		08 09		
St Johns	d																						08 11		
Lewisham ■ ⇌	a	06 56	07 09					07 19	07 22	07 26	07 39				07 49	07 52		07 56	08 00		08 08		08 13		
Hither Green ■	a		07 14						07 27		07 44					07 57					08 14				
Petts Wood ■	a					07 29			07 39					07 59		08 09									08 29
Orpington ■	a				07 25	07 32			07 45				07 54	08 02		08 12				08 08				08 23	08 32

		SE		SE	SE	SE	SE	SE	SE	SE ■	SE	SE		SE	SE	SE	SE	SE	SE	SE	SE	SE		SE ■	SE
London Charing Cross ■ ⊖	d	08 01			08 06		08 09			08 15					08 26		08 31		08 36		08 39			08 40	
London Waterloo (East) ■ ⊖	d	08 04			08 09		08 12			08 18					08 29		08 34		08 39		08 42			08 43	
London Cannon Street ■ ⊖	d			08 07		08 10			08 17		08 24			08 27		08 30		08 37		08 40					08 47
London Blackfriars ■ ⊖	d																								
London Bridge ■ ⊖	d	08 10		08a10	08 14	08 14	08 17		08 21	08 23	08 28			08a30	08 34	08 34	08 40	08a40	08 44	08 44	08 47			08a48	08 51
London Victoria ■ ⊖	d							08 09				08 25										08 39			
New Cross ■ ⊖	d	08 15				08 19			09a38		08 33					08 39				08 49					10a08
St Johns	d					08 21					08 35					08 41				08 51					
Lewisham ■ ⇌	a	08 19				08 24	08 26	08 31			08 38					08 44	08 49			08 54	08 56	09 01			
Hither Green ■	a				08 23	08 28									08 43				08 53	08 58					
Petts Wood ■	a				08 36							08 59							09 06						
Orpington ■	a				08 39					08 38		09 02							09 09						

		SE ■	SE	SE	SE	SE	SE	SE		SE	SE	SE	SE	SE	SE ■		SE ■ ✠		SE	SE ■	SE	SE	SE	SE
London Charing Cross ■ ⊖	d	08 45				08 56		09 01			09 06		09 09		09 10	and at the same minutes past each hour until	18 10			18 15				18 26
London Waterloo (East) ■ ⊖	d	08 48				08 59		09 04			09 09		09 12		09 13		18 13			18 18				18 29
London Cannon Street ■ ⊖	d		08 54		08 57		09 00			09 07		09 10							18 17		18 24		18 27	
London Blackfriars ■ ⊖	d																							
London Bridge ■ ⊖	d	08 53	08 58		09a00	09 04	09 04	09 10		09a10	09 14	09 14	09 17		09a18		18a18		18a20	18 23	18 28		18a30	18 34
London Victoria ■ ⊖	d			08 55										09 09								18 25		
New Cross ■ ⊖	d		09 03				09 09					09 19									18 33			
St Johns	d		09 05				09 11					09 21									18 35			
Lewisham ■ ⇌	a		09 08				09 14	09 19				09 24	09 26	09 31							18 38			
Hither Green ■	a					09 13					09 23	09 28												18 43
Petts Wood ■	a			09 29							09 36											18 59		
Orpington ■	a	09 08		09 32							09 39									18 38		19 02		

		SE	SE	SE		SE	SE	SE	SE	SE ■ ✠	SE	SE ■	SE	SE		SE	SE	SE	SE	SE	SE	SE	SE	SE	
London Charing Cross ■ ⊖	d		18 31			18 36		18 39		18 40		18 45					18 56		19 01		19 06		19 09		
London Waterloo (East) ■ ⊖	d		18 34			18 39		18 42		18 43		18 48					18 59		19 04		19 09		19 12		
London Cannon Street ■ ⊖	d	18 30		18 37			18 40				18 47		18 54			18 57		19 00		19 07		19 10			
London Blackfriars ■ ⊖	d																								
London Bridge ■ ⊖	d	18 34	18 40	18a40		18 44	18 44	18 47		18a48	18a50	18 53	18 58			19a00	19 04	19 04	19 10	19a10	19 14	19 14	19 17		
London Victoria ■ ⊖	d								18 39					18 55										19 09	
New Cross ■ ⊖	d	18 39					18 49						19 03					19 09				19 19			
St Johns	d	18 41					18 51						19 05					19 11				19 21			
Lewisham ■ ⇌	a	18 44	18 49				18 54	18 56	19 01				19 08					19 14	19 19			19 24	19 26	19 31	
Hither Green ■	a					18 53	18 58										19 13				19 23	19 28			
Petts Wood ■	a					19 06								19 29							19 36				
Orpington ■	a					19 09						19 08		19 32							19 39				

London - Lewisham, Hither Green, Petts Wood and Orpington (Summary of Services)

Sundays
29 July to 12 August

		SE ■1 ⌶	SE ■1	SE	SE	SE	SE	SE	SE	SE		SE	SE	SE ■1 ⌶	SE	SE	SE	SE ■1	SE	SE		SE	SE	SE	SE ■1 ⌶
London Charing Cross ■4 ⊖	d	19 10	19 15	19 17				19 26	19 31	19 36		19 39		19 40		19 47	19 52	19 55		19 56		20 01	20 06	20 09	20 10
London Waterloo (East) ■4 ⊖	d	19 13	19 18	19 20				19 29	19 34	19 39		19 42		19 43		19 50	19 55	19 58		19 59		20 04	20 09	20 12	20 13
London Cannon Street ■4 ⊖	d				19 24		19 27																		
London Blackfriars ■3 ⊖	d														19 46										
London Bridge ■4 ⊖	d	19a18	19 23	19 25	19 28		19a30	19 34	19 40	19 44		19 47		19a48	19a49	19 55	20 00	20 03		20a04		20 10	20 14	20 17	20 19
London Victoria ■15 ⊖	d					19 25							19 39						19 55						
New Cross ■4 ⊖	d			19 30	19 33				19 45							20 00	20 05					20 15			
St Johns	d			19 32	19 35											20 02									
Lewisham ■4	a			19 35	19 38				19 49	19 51		19 56	20 01			20 05	20 09					20 19	20 21	20 26	
Hither Green ■4	a							19 43		19 56							20 13						20 26		
Petts Wood ■4	a					19 59				20 08									20 29				20 38		
Orpington ■4	a		19 38			20 02				20 12								20 18	20 32				20 45		20 34

		SE	SE	SE	SE	SE		SE	SE	SE	SE ■1	SE	SE	SE	SE ■1	SE		SE	SE	SE	SE	SE ■1	SE	SE	SE
London Charing Cross ■4 ⊖	d		20 17	20 22		20 26		20 31	20 36	20 39	20 40		20 47	20 52	20 55			20 56	21 01	21 06	21 09	21 10	21 17	21 22	
London Waterloo (East) ■4 ⊖	d		20 20	20 25		20 29		20 34	20 39	20 42	20 43		20 50	20 55	20 58			20 59	21 04	21 09	21 12	21 13	21 20	21 25	
London Cannon Street ■4 ⊖	d	20 16										20 46													
London Blackfriars ■3 ⊖	d																								
London Bridge ■4 ⊖	d	20a19	20 25	20 30		20a34		20 40	20 44	20 47	20 49	20a49	20 55	21 00	21 03			21a04	21 10	21 14	21 17	21 19	21 25	21 30	
London Victoria ■15 ⊖	d				20 25											20 55									21 25
New Cross ■4 ⊖	d		20 30	20 35				20 45					21 00	21 05					21 15				21 30	21 35	
St Johns	d		20 32										21 02										21 32		
Lewisham ■4	a		20 35	20 39				20 49	20 51	20 56			21 05	21 09					21 19	21 21	21 26		21 35	21 39	
Hither Green ■4	a			20 43					20 56					21 13						21 26				21 43	
Petts Wood ■4	a				20 59				21 08							21 29				21 38					21 59
Orpington ■4	a				21 02				21 12		21 04				21 18	21 32				21 45		21 34			22 02

		SE		SE	SE	SE	SE ■1	SE	SE	SE ■1	SE	SE		SE	SE	SE	SE ■1	SE	SE	SE	SE	SE		SE	SE
London Charing Cross ■4 ⊖	d	21 26		21 31	21 36	21 39	21 40	21 47	21 52	21 55		21 56		22 01	22 06	22 09	22 10	22 17	22 22		22 26	22 31		22 36	22 39
London Waterloo (East) ■4 ⊖	d	21 29		21 34	21 39	21 42	21 43	21 50	21 55	21 58		21 59		22 04	22 09	22 12	22 13	22 20	22 25		22 29	22 34		22 39	22 42
London Cannon Street ■4 ⊖	d																								
London Blackfriars ■3 ⊖	d																								
London Bridge ■4 ⊖	d	21a34		21 40	21 44	21 47	21 49	21 55	22 00	22 03		22a04		22 10	22 14	22 17	22 19	22 25	22 30		22a34	22 40		22 44	22 47
London Victoria ■15 ⊖	d										21 55									22 25					
New Cross ■4 ⊖	d			21 45				22 00	22 05					22 15				22 30	22 35			22 45			
St Johns	d							22 02										22 32							
Lewisham ■4	a			21 49	21 51	21 56		22 05	22 09					22 19	22 21	22 26		22 35	22 39			22 49		22 51	22 56
Hither Green ■4	a				21 56				22 13						22 26				22 43					22 56	
Petts Wood ■4	a				22 08						22 29				22 38					22 59				23 08	
Orpington ■4	a				22 12		22 04			22 18	22 32				22 45		22 34			23 02				23 15	

		SE ■1	SE	SE	SE ■1	SE	SE	SE		SE	SE	SE ■1	SE	SE	SE	SE	SE	SE		SE	SE ■1	SE ■1	SE	SE	SE
London Charing Cross ■4 ⊖	d	22 40	22 47	22 52	22 55		22 56	23 01		23 06	23 09	23 10	23 17	23 22		23 26	23 31	23 36		23 39	23 40	23 45	23 52		23 56
London Waterloo (East) ■4 ⊖	d	22 43	22 50	22 55	22 58		22 59	23 04		23 09	23 12	23 13	23 20	23 25		23 29	23 34	23 39		23 42	23 43	23 48	23 55		23 59
London Cannon Street ■4 ⊖	d																								
London Blackfriars ■3 ⊖	d																								
London Bridge ■4 ⊖	d	22 49	22 55	23 00	23 03		23a04	23 10		23 14	23 17	23 19	23 25	23 30		23a34	23 40	23 44		23 47	23 49	23 53	23 59		00a04
London Victoria ■15 ⊖	d					22 55									23 25									23 55	
New Cross ■4 ⊖	d		23 00	23 05				23 15					23 30	23 35			23 45						00 05		
St Johns	d		23 02										23 32										00 07		
Lewisham ■4	a		23 05	23 09				23 19		23 21	23 26		23 35	23 39			23 49	23 51		23 56			00 10		
Hither Green ■4	a			23 13						23 26				23 43				23 56							
Petts Wood ■4	a					23 29				23 38					23 59			00 08						00 29	
Orpington ■4	a	23 04			23 18	23 32				23 45		23 34			00 02			00 15			00 04	00 08		00 33	

Sundays
26 August to 9 September

		SE	SE	SE ■1	SE ■1	SE	SE	SE	SE	SE		SE	SE	SE A	SE A	SE ■1 A	SE A	SE A	SE	SE A		SE A	SE A	SE	SE
London Charing Cross ■4 ⊖	d		23p36	23p40	23p45	23p52		00 02	00 06	00 10		00 15	00 18		00 32	00 37		00 44	00 48					07 30	07 35
London Waterloo (East) ■4 ⊖	d		23p39	23p43	23p48	23p55		00 05	00 09	00 13		00 18	00 21		00 35	00 40		00 47	00 51					07 33	07 38
London Cannon Street ■4 ⊖	d													00 28			00 41						00 56		
London Blackfriars ■3 ⊖	d																								
London Bridge ■4 ⊖	d		23p44	23p49	23p53	23p59		00 10	00 14	00 18		00 23	00 26	00 32	00a39	00 45	00 45	00 52	00 56				00a59	07a37	07 43
London Victoria ■15 ⊖	d	23p25					23p55													00 45		00 56			
New Cross ■4 ⊖	d					00 05		00 15		00 23			00 31	00 38				00 57	01 01						07 49
St Johns	d					00 07								00 40											07 51
Lewisham ■4	a		23p51			00 10		00 19	00 21	00 27			00 35	00 43			00 52	01 01	01 05						07 53
Hither Green ■4	a		23p56						00 26	00 31								01s05	01 09						
Petts Wood ■4	a	23p59	00 08				00 29		00 38										01 22	01s25					
Orpington ■4	a	00 02	00 12	00 04	00 08		00 32		00 42			00 46				01 00			01 25	01 29		01 33			

A not 26 August

London - Lewisham, Hither Green, Petts Wood and Orpington (Summary of Services)

Sundays
26 August to 9 September

		SE	SE	SE	SE	SE		SE	SE ■1	SE	SE	SE	SE ■1	SE	SE	SE		SE	SE ■1	SE	SE	SE	SE	SE	SE
London Charing Cross ■4 ⊖	d	07 46	07 50		07 56	08 00		08 05	08 08	08 10	08 16	08 20	08 23		08 26	08 30		08 35	08 38	08 40	08 46	08 50		08 56	09 00
London Waterloo (East) ■4 ⊖	d	07 49	07 53		07 59	08 03		08 08	08 11	08 13	08 19	08 23	08 26		08 29	08 33		08 38	08 41	08 43	08 49	08 53		08 59	09 03
London Cannon Street ■4 ⊖	d																								
London Blackfriars ■3 ⊖	d																								
London Bridge ■4 ⊖	d	07 54	07 58		08 04	08a07		08 13	08 16	08 18	08 24	08 28	08 31		08 34	08a37		08 43	08 46	08 48	08 54	08 58		09 04	09a07
London Victoria ■15 ⊖	d			07 51										08 21									08 51		
New Cross ■4 ⊖	d		08 04					08 19				08 34						08 49				09 04			
St Johns	d							08 21										08 51							
Lewisham ■4	a	08 02	08 07		08 11			08 23		08 27	08 32	08 37			08 41			08 53		08 57	09 02	09 07		09 11	
Hither Green ■4	a	08 07			08 16						08 37				08 46						09 07			09 16	
Petts Wood ■4	a	08 20		08 25							08 50			08 55							09 20		09 25		
Orpington ■4	a	08 23		08 28					08 31		08 53		08 46	08 58					09 01		09 23		09 28		

		SE		SE ■1	SE	SE	SE	SE ■1	SE	SE	SE	SE		SE ■1	SE	SE	SE	SE ■1		SE ■1	SE		SE	SE
London Charing Cross ■4 ⊖	d	09 05		09 08	09 10	09 16	09 20	09 23		09 26	09 30	09 35		09 38	09 40	09 46	09 50	09 53	and at the same minutes past each hour until	19 53			19 56	20 00
London Waterloo (East) ■4 ⊖	d	09 08		09 11	09 13	09 19	09 23	09 26		09 29	09 33	09 38		09 41	09 43	09 49	09 53	09 56		19 56			19 59	20 03
London Cannon Street ■4 ⊖	d																							
London Blackfriars ■3 ⊖	d																							
London Bridge ■4 ⊖	d	09 13		09 16	09 18	09 24	09 28	09 31		09 34	09a37	09 43		09 46	09 48	09 54	09 58	10 01		20 01			20 04	20a07
London Victoria ■15 ⊖	d								09 21												19 51			
New Cross ■4 ⊖	d	09 19					09 34					09 49					10 04							
St Johns	d	09 21										09 51												
Lewisham ■4	a	09 23			09 27	09 32	09 37			09 41		09 53			09 57	10 02	10 07						20 11	
Hither Green ■4	a					09 37				09 46						10 07							20 16	
Petts Wood ■4	a					09 50			09 55							10 20					20 25			
Orpington ■4	a			09 31		09 53		09 46	09 58					10 01		10 23		10 16		20 16	20 28			

		SE	SE ■1 ⌶	SE	SE	SE	SE ■1	SE		SE	SE	SE	SE ■1	SE	SE	SE	SE	SE		SE	SE	SE ■1	SE	SE	SE
London Charing Cross ■4 ⊖	d	20 05	20 08	20 10	20 16	20 20	20 23			20 26	20 30	20 35	20 38	20 40	20 46	20 50		20 56		21 00	21 05	21 08	21 10	21 16	21 20
London Waterloo (East) ■4 ⊖	d	20 08	20 11	20 13	20 19	20 23	20 26			20 29	20 33	20 38	20 41	20 43	20 49	20 53		20 59		21 03	21 08	21 11	21 13	21 19	21 23
London Cannon Street ■4 ⊖	d																								
London Blackfriars ■3 ⊖	d																								
London Bridge ■4 ⊖	d	20 13	20 16	20 18	20 24	20 28	20 31			20 34	20a37	20 43	20 46	20 48	20 54	20 58		21 04		21a07	21 13	21 16	21 18	21 24	21 28
London Victoria ■15 ⊖	d							20 21									20 51								
New Cross ■4 ⊖	d	20 19				20 34						20 49				21 04					21 19				21 34
St Johns	d	20 21										20 51									21 21				
Lewisham ■4	a	20 23		20 27	20 32	20 37				20 41		20 53		20 57	21 02	21 07		21 11			21 23		21 27	21 32	21 37
Hither Green ■4	a				20 37					20 46					21 07			21 16						21 37	
Petts Wood ■4	a				20 50			20 55							21 20		21 25							21 50	
Orpington ■4	a		20 31		20 53		20 46	20 58					21 01		21 23		21 28					21 31		21 53	

		SE ■1	SE	SE		SE	SE	SE ■1	SE	SE	SE	SE	SE	SE		SE	SE ■1	SE	SE	SE	SE ■1	SE	SE	SE	
London Charing Cross ■4 ⊖	d	21 23		21 26		21 30	21 35	21 38	21 40	21 46	21 50		21 56	22 00		22 05	22 08	22 10	22 16	22 20	22 23		22 26	22 30	
London Waterloo (East) ■4 ⊖	d	21 26		21 29		21 33	21 38	21 41	21 43	21 49	21 53		21 59	22 03		22 08	22 11	22 13	22 19	22 23	22 26		22 29	22 33	
London Cannon Street ■4 ⊖	d																								
London Blackfriars ■3 ⊖	d																								
London Bridge ■4 ⊖	d	21 31		21 34		21a37	21 43	21 46	21 48	21 54	21 58		22 04	22a07		22 13	22 16	22 18	22 24	22 28	22 31		22 34	22a37	
London Victoria ■15 ⊖	d		21 21									21 51										22 21			
New Cross ■4 ⊖	d						21 49				22 04					22 19				22 34					
St Johns	d						21 51									22 21									
Lewisham ■4	a			21 41			21 53		21 57	22 02	22 07		22 11			22 23		22 27	22 32	22 37			22 41		
Hither Green ■4	a			21 46						22 07			22 16						22 37				22 46		
Petts Wood ■4	a		21 55							22 20		22 25							22 50			22 55			
Orpington ■4	a	21 46	21 58					22 01		22 23		22 28					22 31		22 53		22 46	22 58			

		SE	SE ■1	SE	SE	SE	SE	SE	SE	SE		SE ■1	SE	SE	SE	SE ■1	SE	SE	SE	SE		SE ■1	SE	SE	SE
London Charing Cross ■4 ⊖	d	22 35	22 38	22 40	22 46	22 50		22 56	23 00	23 05		23 08	23 10	23 16	23 20	23 23		23 26	23 30	23 35		23 38	23 46	23 50	23 56
London Waterloo (East) ■4 ⊖	d	22 38	22 41	22 43	22 49	22 53		22 59	23 03	23 08		23 11	23 13	23 19	23 23	23 26		23 29	23 33	23 38		23 41	23 49	23 53	23 59
London Cannon Street ■4 ⊖	d																								
London Blackfriars ■3 ⊖	d																								
London Bridge ■4 ⊖	d	22 43	22 46	22 48	22 54	22 58		23 04	23a07	23 13		23 16	23 18	23 24	23 28	23 31		23 34	23a37	23 43		23 46	23 54	23 58	00 04
London Victoria ■15 ⊖	d						22 51										23 21								
New Cross ■4 ⊖	d	22 49				23 04				23 19					23 34					23 49				00 04	
St Johns	d	22 51								23 21										23 51					
Lewisham ■4	a	22 53		22 57	23 02	23 07		23 11		23 23			23 26	23 32	23 37			23 41		23 53			00 02	00 07	00 11
Hither Green ■4	a				23 07			23 16						23 37				23 46					00 07		00 16
Petts Wood ■4	a				23 20		23 25							23 50			23 55						00 20		
Orpington ■4	a		23 01		23 23		23 29					23 31		23 53		23 46	23 59					00 01	00 23		

Table 199

Mondays to Fridays

until 27 July, 13 Aug to 28 Aug and from 10 Sep

Orpington, Petts Wood, Hither Green and Lewisham - London (Summary of Services)

		SE MX	SE MX ■	SE	SE	SE	SE	SE	SE	SE		SE	SE	SE	SE	SE	SE	SE	SE	SE ■		SE	SE	SE	SE
Orpington	d	23p21	23p37	04 34	04 55		05 10	05 14				05 15	05 34			05 40				05 54					
Petts Wood	d	23p24		04 37	04 58		05 13					05 18	05 37			05 43									
Hither Green	d	23p37				05 08			05 23			05 30			05 38										06 08
Lewisham ⇌	d	23p43				05 13			05 28			05 36		05 39	05 43		05 50		05 56				06 09		06 13
St Johns	d													05 41									06 11		
New Cross ⊖	d					05 16			05 31			05 39		05 43	05 46		05 53						06 13		06 16
London Victoria ⊖	a						05 47									06 18									
London Bridge ⊖	d	23p52	23p55			05 22		05 37	05 37	05 42		05 46		05 49	05 53		05 59	06 02	06 06	06 10		06 13	06 19	06 20	06 22
London Blackfriars ⊖	a			05 17	05 32								06 17											06 24	
London Cannon Street ⊖	a								05 41									06 06							
London Waterloo (East) ⊖	d	23p57	23p59			05 27		05 42		05 47		05 50		05 53	05 57		06 04		06 10	06 15		06 18	06 24		06 27
London Charing Cross ⊖	a	00 01	00 03			05 30		05 47		05 50		05 55		05 56	06 01		06 07		06 13	06 18		06 21	06 27		06 30

		SE	SE ■	SE	SE	SE		SE	SE	SE ■	SE	SE	SE	SE	SE ■	SE		SE	SE ■	SE	SE	SE	SE A	SE	SE B
Orpington	d	06 01	06 09	06 10						06 20				06 22	06 24	06 40									
Petts Wood	d	06 04		06 13										06 25		06 43									
Hither Green	d	06 16							06 22					06 38									06 46		06 51
Lewisham ⇌	d	06 22			06 20			06 25	06 27		06 35	06 39	06 41	06 43							06 48	06 50	06 52	06 55	06 57
St Johns	d								06 29			06 41									06 50		06 54		06 59
New Cross ⊖	d	06 25							06 31		06 38	06 43									06 52		06 56		07 01
London Victoria ⊖	a			06 47									07 04			07 19									
London Bridge ⊖	d	06 32	06 25		06 29	06 28		06 34	06 37	06 38	06 44	06 49		06 52	06 40			06 43	06 55	06 57	07 00	07 01	07 03	07 04	07 08
London Blackfriars ⊖	a																			07 03	07 05		07 09		07 14
London Cannon Street ⊖	a					06 32				06 42	06 48														
London Waterloo (East) ⊖	d	06 36	06 30		06 33			06 40	06 42			06 54		06 57	06 45			06 49	07 00			07 06		07 10	
London Charing Cross ⊖	a	06 39	06 33		06 36			06 43	06 45			06 57		07 02	06 49			06 52	07 05			07 11		07 15	

		SE		SE	SE	SE	SE ■	SE	SE ■	SE	SE	SE		SE	SE	SE ■	SE	SE	SE	SE	SE	SE		SE ■	SE
Orpington	d				06 43	06 52	06 54	06 58														07 03		07 04	07 08
Petts Wood	d				06 46	06 55		07 01														07 06			07 11
Hither Green	d	06 56			06 58	07 08												07 11	07 16			07 19			
Lewisham ⇌	d			07 01	07 04						07 08			07 11	07 15			07 17		07 20	07 22	07 25			
St Johns	d																	07 19			07 24				
New Cross ⊖	d			07 04							07 11						07 20	07 21		07 23	07 26				
London Victoria ⊖	a														07 42										07 49
London Bridge ⊖	d	07 07		07 10		07 19	07 10		07 15	07 15	07 18	07 18		07 21		07 21	08 38	07 27	07 27	07 29	07 34			07 23	
London Blackfriars ⊖	a							07 42								07 27		07 33		07 35	07 39			07 29	
London Cannon Street ⊖	a			07 16		07 25				07 21	07 23														
London Waterloo (East) ⊖	d	07 12			07 17		07 15		07 20			07 23		07 26			08 43		07 32			07 37			
London Charing Cross ⊖	a	07 17			07 22		07 20		07 25			07 28		07 31			08 48		07 37			07 42			

		SE	SE ■	SE	SE	SE ■	SE ■	SE		SE	SE	SE	SE	SE	SE ■	SE ■	SE	SE		SE	SE ■	SE	SE ■	SE	SE
Orpington	d	07 11	07 14														07 22	07 28							07 33
Petts Wood	d	07 15															07 25	07 31							07 36
Hither Green	d	07 28											07 32	07 36			07 39								07 49
Lewisham ⇌	d							07 30		07 35			07 38				07 44			07 46					
St Johns	d												07 40												
New Cross ⊖	d									07 38			07 42												
London Victoria ⊖	a																			08 11					
London Bridge ⊖	d	07 38	07 30	07 34	07 36	07 37		07 42		07 44	07 45	07 46	07 48	07 48	07 51	07 52	07 54				07 54	07 58		07 58	08 00
London Blackfriars ⊖	a																	08 08			07 59	08 04			08 06
London Cannon Street ⊖	a	07 44			07 42					07 50		07 52	07 54			07 57									
London Waterloo (East) ⊖	d		07 35	07 39		07 42	07 45	07 47			07 51			07 53	07 56		07 59						08 01	08 03	
London Charing Cross ⊖	a		07 40	07 44		07 47	07 50	07 52			07 56			07 58	08 01		08 04						08 06	08 08	

		SE	SE	SE		SE ■ ✕	SE	SE	SE	SE	SE	SE	SE	SE ■		SE	SE	SE	SE ■	SE	SE ■	SE	SE	SE ■	
Orpington	d	07 38														07 41	07 47						07 52		
Petts Wood	d	07 41														07 44	07 50						07 55		
Hither Green	d											07 52				07 58				08 02					
Lewisham ⇌	d			07 48			07 50	07 55				07 57				08 03		08 05							
St Johns	d			07 50								08 00													
New Cross ⊖	d		07 50	07 53				07 58				08 02													
London Victoria ⊖	a	08 20																08 29							
London Bridge ⊖	d		09 08	08 02			08 02	08 04	08 06		08 06	08 09		08 10					08 11	08 14	08 14	08 18	08 20		
London Blackfriars ⊖	a																08 29		08 17		08 20	08 24	08 26		
London Cannon Street ⊖	a		09 14	08 08				08 10	08 12			08 15													
London Waterloo (East) ⊖	d					08 05	08 07			08 09	08 11		08 13	08 15		08 17				08 19				08 21	
London Charing Cross ⊖	a					08 08	08 12			08 14	08 16		08 18	08 20		08 22				08 24				08 26	

A from 21 May until 27 July

B until 18 May

Table 199

Mondays to Fridays

until 27 July, 13 Aug to 28 Aug and from 10 Sep

Orpington, Petts Wood, Hither Green and Lewisham - London (Summary of Services)

		SE	SE	SE	SE	SE	SE ■ ✕	SE	SE	SE		SE	SE	SE ■	SE	SE	SE	SE	SE	SE ■		SE	SE ■	SE ■	SE
Orpington	d		07 57														08 01	08 10							
Petts Wood	d		08 00														08 04	08 13							
Hither Green	d															08 12	08 17					08 22			
Lewisham ⇌	d				08 08	08 11		08 15								08 17	08 23		08 25						
St Johns	d				08 12											08 21									
New Cross ⊖	d			08 04	08 14			08 18							08 20	08 23									
London Victoria ⊖	a																	08 50	08 49						
London Bridge ⊖	d	08 18		09 18	08 22	08 22	08 24	08 26		08 26		08 28		08 30	09 30	08 30				08 32		08 34	08 34		08 38
London Blackfriars ⊖	a																						08 41		
London Cannon Street ⊖	a				08 28		08 30	08 32				08 35			09 36	08 36				08 38					
London Waterloo (East) ⊖	d	08 23	08 25	09 23		08 27			08 29	08 31			08 33	08 35			08 37					08 39		08 41	08 43
London Charing Cross ⊖	a	08 28	08 30	09 28		08 32			08 34	08 36			08 39	08 40			08 42					08 44		08 46	08 48

		SE	SE	SE	SE ■	SE		SE	SE	SE	SE	SE ■	SE	SE	SE	SE		SE	SE ■	SE	SE ■	SE ■	SE	SE	SE
Orpington	d		08 13												08 21	08 26									
Petts Wood	d		08 16												08 24	08 29									
Hither Green	d													08 32	08 37					08 42					
Lewisham ⇌	d			08 28		08 31		08 35						08 37				08 46							08 48
St Johns	d			08 30										08 40											08 50
New Cross ⊖	d			08 32				08 38					08 38	08 42										08 49	08 52
London Victoria ⊖	a															09 06		09 11							
London Bridge ⊖	d	08 39	08 40	08 42		08 42		08 44	08 46		08 46	08 50	09 51	08 50					08 51	08 54	08 56		08 58	10 01	08 58
London Blackfriars ⊖	a																								
London Cannon Street ⊖	a	08 44	08 46	08 48				08 50	08 52				09 57	08 55					08 57		09 02			10 04	09 04
London Waterloo (East) ⊖	d				08 45	08 47				08 49	08 51	08 55			08 53					08 59		09 01	09 03		
London Charing Cross ⊖	a				08 50	08 52				08 54	08 56	09 00			08 58					09 04		09 04	09 08		

		SE		SE	SE	SE	SE ■	SE	SE	SE	SE	SE ■		SE ■	SE ■	SE	SE A	SE	SE	SE	SE	SE		SE	SE
Orpington	d	08 32		08 40														08 43	08 47	08 52	08 55				
Petts Wood	d	08 35		08 43														08 46	08 50	08 55	08 58				
Hither Green	d							08 50		08 55								08 59		09 08				09 14	
Lewisham ⇌	d				08 52			08 55			08 59							09 04				09 06			09 15
St Johns	d							08 57			09 01							09 07							09 17
New Cross ⊖	d							08 59			09 03						09 04	09 09							09 19
London Victoria ⊖	a			09 19																	09 34	09 29			
London Bridge ⊖	d	09 00			09 01	09 02	09 04	09 06		09 06	09 10	09 12		09 12	09 15	09 18	10 21	09 18		09 21				09 24	09 26
London Blackfriars ⊖	a																		09 30						
London Cannon Street ⊖	a	09 06				09 08	09 10	09 12			09 18	09 18					10 24	09 23							09 32
London Waterloo (East) ⊖	d				09 06				09 08	09 11				09 17	09 20	09 23				09 26				09 29	
London Charing Cross ⊖	a				09 12				09 13	09 16				09 22	09 25	09 28				09 31				09 34	

		SE	SE	SE	SE ■ A	SE ■ B	SE ■	SE		SE	SE	SE	SE	SE	SE	SE ■	SE A	SE B		SE	SE	SE ■ ✕	SE	SE	SE
Orpington	d			09 03	09 04	09 04	09 09	09 10							09 21	09 24	09 25	09 25							
Petts Wood	d			09 06				09 13							09 24		09 28	09 28							
Hither Green	d			09 19										09 28	09 37									09 42	
Lewisham ⇌	d	09 20		09 24						09 26	09 29			09 34						09 38					09 45
St Johns	d			09 26							09 31			09 36											09 47
New Cross ⊖	d		09 19	09 28							09 33		09 33	09 38											09 49
London Victoria ⊖	a							09 49									10 02	10 03		10 00					
London Bridge ⊖	d	09 30	10 31	09 34	09 23	09 23	09 27			09 35	09 39	09 38	10 51	09 45	09 49	09 41					09 42	09 44	09 51	09 52	09 55
London Blackfriars ⊖	a																								
London Cannon Street ⊖	a		10 36	09 40	09 28	09 29					09 45		10 54	09 51							09 48		09 57		10 00
London Waterloo (East) ⊖	d	09 35					09 32			09 40		09 43			09 54	09 46						09 49		09 57	
London Charing Cross ⊖	a	09 40					09 37			09 45		09 48			09 59	09 51						09 54		10 00	

		SE	SE	SE		SE ■ B	SE ■ A	SE	SE	SE	SE	SE	SE	SE		SE	SE ■	SE	SE	SE ■ ✕	SE B	SE	SE	SE	
Orpington	d			09 33		09 38	09 39	09 40								09 51	09 54	09 55							
Petts Wood	d			09 36				09 43								09 54		09 58							
Hither Green	d			09 49										09 58		10 07						10 12			
Lewisham ⇌	d	09 50		09 54					09 56	09 59				10 04					10 08				10 14	10 20	
St Johns	d			09 56						10 01				10 06									10 16		
New Cross ⊖	d		09 49	09 58						10 03			10 03	10 08									10 18		
London Victoria ⊖	a							10 17										10 32	10 28						
London Bridge ⊖	d	09 58	11 01	10 04		09 54	09 55		10 05	10 09	10 08	10 11	11 21	10 14		10 19	10 11			10 13	10 21	10 22	10 24	10 28	
London Blackfriars ⊖	a																								
London Cannon Street ⊖	a		11 06	10 08						10 13		10 15	11 24	10 19							10 24		10 28		
London Waterloo (East) ⊖	d	10 03				09 59	10 00		10 10		10 13					10 24	10 15			10 18		10 27		10 33	
London Charing Cross ⊖	a	10 06				10 02	10 03		10 13		10 16					10 27	10 19			10 22		10 30		10 36	

A until 18 May

B from 21 May until 27 July

until 27 July, 13 Aug to 28 Aug and from 10 Sep

Orpington, Petts Wood, Hither Green and Lewisham - London (Summary of Services)

	SE	SE	SE ■	SE	SE	SE	SE	SE	SE		SE	SE	SE ■	SE	SE	SE ■ ✕	SE	SE	SE		SE	SE	SE ■	SE
Orpington 4 d		10 03	10 09	10 10								10 21	10 24	10 25								10 33	10 39	10 40
Petts Wood 4 d		10 06		10 13								10 24		10 28								10 36		10 43
Hither Green 4 d		10 19									10 28	10 37					10 42					10 49		
Lewisham 4 d		10 24			10 26	10 29					10 34				10 38			10 44	10 50			10 54		
St Johns d		10 26				10 31					10 36							10 46				10 56		
New Cross 4 ⊖ d	10 19	10 28				10 33			10 33		10 38							10 48			10 49	10 58		
London Victoria 15 ⊖ a				10 47										11 02	10 58									11 17
London Bridge 4 ⊖ d	11 31	10 34	10 25		10 35	10 39	10 38	10 41	11 51		10 45	10 49	10 41			10 43	10 52	10 54	10 58		12 01	11 04	10 55	
London Blackfriars 3 ⊖ a																								
London Cannon Street 4 ⊖ a	11 36	10 38				10 43		10 45	11 54		10 50							10 58			12 04	11 08		
London Waterloo (East) 4 ⊖ d			10 30		10 40		10 43					10 54	10 45			10 49	10 57		11 03				11 00	
London Charing Cross 4 ⊖ a			10 33		10 43		10 46					10 57	10 49			10 52	11 00		11 06				11 03	

	SE	SE	SE	SE	SE		SE	SE	SE ■	SE	SE	SE ■ ✕	SE	SE	SE		SE	SE	SE ■	SE	SE	SE	SE	SE
Orpington 4 d								10 51	10 54	10 55								11 03	11 09	11 10				
Petts Wood 4 d								10 54		10 58								11 06		11 13				
Hither Green 4 d							10 58	11 07					11 12					11 19						
Lewisham 4 d	10 56	10 59					11 04				11 08			11 14	11 20			11 24			11 26	11 29		
St Johns d		11 01					11 06							11 16				11 26				11 31		
New Cross 4 ⊖ d		11 03			11 03		11 08							11 18			11 19	11 28				11 33		
London Victoria 15 ⊖ a										11 32	11 28									11 47				
London Bridge 4 ⊖ d	11 05	11 09	11 08	11 11	12 21		11 15	11 19	11 11			11 13	11 22	11 24	11 28		12 31	11 34	11 25		11 35	11 39	11 38	11 41
London Blackfriars 3 ⊖ a																								
London Cannon Street 4 ⊖ a		11 13		11 15	12 24		11 19							11 28			12 36	11 38				11 43		11 45
London Waterloo (East) 4 ⊖ d	11 10		11 13					11 24	11 15			11 19	11 27		11 33				11 30		11 40		11 43	
London Charing Cross 4 ⊖ a	11 13		11 16					11 27	11 19			11 22	11 30		11 36				11 33		11 43		11 46	

	SE		SE	SE	SE ■	SE	SE	SE ■ ✕	SE	SE	SE		SE		SE	SE	SE ■	SE	SE	SE		SE	SE
Orpington 4 d				11 21	11 24	11 25								and at the same minutes past each hour until		14 33	14 39	14 40					
Petts Wood 4 d				11 24		11 28										14 36		14 43					
Hither Green 4 d			11 28	11 37					11 42							14 49							
Lewisham 4 d			11 34				11 38			11 44	11 50					14 54			14 56	14 59			
St Johns d			11 36							11 46						14 56				15 01			
New Cross 4 ⊖ d	11 33		11 38							11 48			11 49		14 49	14 58				15 03			
London Victoria 15 ⊖ a						12 02	11 58											15 17					
London Bridge 4 ⊖ d	12 51		11 45	11 49	11 41			11 43	11 52	11 54	11 58		13 01		16 01	15 04	14 55		15 05	15 09		15 08	15 11
London Blackfriars 3 ⊖ a																							
London Cannon Street 4 ⊖ a	12 54		11 49							11 58			13 06		16 06	15 08				15 13			15 15
London Waterloo (East) 4 ⊖ d				11 54	11 45			11 49	11 57		12 03						15 00		15 10			15 13	
London Charing Cross 4 ⊖ a				11 57	11 49			11 52	12 00		12 06						15 03		15 13			15 16	

	SE	SE	SE	SE ■	SE	SE	SE ■ ✕		SE	SE	SE	SE	SE	SE ■	SE	SE	SE		SE	SE	SE A	SE	SE	SE ■
Orpington 4 d			14 51	14 54	14 55								15 03	15 09	15 10								15 21	15 24
Petts Wood 4 d			14 54		14 58								15 06		15 13								15 24	
Hither Green 4 d		14 58	15 07						15 12				15 19									15 28	15 37	
Lewisham 4 d		15 04				15 08				15 14	15 20		15 24			15 26	15 29					15 34		
St Johns d		15 06								15 16			15 26				15 31					15 36		
New Cross 4 ⊖ d	15 03	15 08								15 18		15 19	15 28				15 33				15 33	15 38		
London Victoria 15 ⊖ a					15 32	15 28									15 47									
London Bridge 4 ⊖ d	16 21	15 15	15 19	15 11			15 13		15 22	15 24	15 28	16 31	15 34	15 25		15 35	15 39		15 38	15 41	16 51	15 45	15 50	15 41
London Blackfriars 3 ⊖ a																								
London Cannon Street 4 ⊖ a	16 24	15 19								15 28		16 36	15 38				15 43			15 45	16 54	15 49		
London Waterloo (East) 4 ⊖ d			15 24	15 15			15 19		15 27		15 33			15 30		15 40			15 43				15 55	15 46
London Charing Cross 4 ⊖ a			15 27	15 19			15 22		15 30		15 36			15 33		15 43			15 46				15 58	15 49

	SE	SE	SE ■ ✕		SE	SE	SE	SE	SE	SE ■	SE	SE	SE		SE	SE	SE A	SE	SE	SE ■	SE	SE	SE ■ ✕	
Orpington 4 d	15 25								15 33	15 39	15 40								15 51	15 54	15 55			
Petts Wood 4 d	15 28								15 36		15 43								15 54		15 58			
Hither Green 4 d					15 42				15 49									15 58	16 07					
Lewisham 4 d		15 38				15 44	15 50		15 54			15 56	15 59					16 04				16 08		
St Johns d						15 46			15 56				16 01					16 06						
New Cross 4 ⊖ d						15 48		15 49	15 58				16 03				16 03	16 08						
London Victoria 15 ⊖ a	16 02	15 58									16 17										16 32	16 28		
London Bridge 4 ⊖ d			15 43		15 53	15 54	15 58	17 01	16 04	15 55		16 05	16 09		16 09	16 12	17 22	16 15	16 19	16 12			16 14	
London Blackfriars 3 ⊖ a																								
London Cannon Street 4 ⊖ a						15 58		17 05	16 08				16 13			16 16	17 26	16 19						
London Waterloo (East) 4 ⊖ d			15 49		15 58		16 03			16 00		16 10			16 14				16 25	16 17			16 20	
London Charing Cross 4 ⊖ a			15 52		16 01		16 06			16 03		16 13			16 18				16 28	16 20			16 24	

A from 21 May until 27 July

Table 199

Mondays to Fridays

until 27 July, 13 Aug to 28 Aug and from 10 Sep

Orpington, Petts Wood, Hither Green and Lewisham - London (Summary of Services)

	SE	SE	SE	SE	SE	SE ■	SE	SE	SE		SE	SE	SE	SE	SE	SE	SE ■	SE	SE		SE ■ ✕	SE A	SE	SE
Orpington 4 d					16 03	16 08	16 10									16 21	16 25	16 25						
Petts Wood 4 d					16 06		16 13									16 24		16 28						
Hither Green 4 d	16 12				16 19										16 28	16 37							16 42	
Lewisham 4 d		16 14	16 20		16 24				16 26			16 29			16 34				16 38					16 44
St Johns d		16 16			16 26							16 31			16 36									16 46
New Cross 4 ⊖ d		16 18		16 20	16 28							16 33		16 34	16 38									16 48
London Victoria 15 ⊖ a							16 47											17 04	17 01					
London Bridge 4 ⊖ d	16 22	16 24	16 29	17 31	16 34	16 25		16 32	16 35		16 38	16 39	16 42	17 52	16 45	16 49	16 42				16 46	16 51	16 52	16 54
London Blackfriars 3 ⊖ a																								
London Cannon Street 4 ⊖ a		16 28		17 36	16 38							16 43	16 46	17 56	16 49							16 54		16 58
London Waterloo (East) 4 ⊖ d	16 28		16 34			16 30		16 38	16 40		16 43					16 55	16 49				16 53		16 57	
London Charing Cross 4 ⊖ a	16 31		16 37			16 33		16 42	16 44		16 46					16 58	16 52				16 56		17 00	

	SE	SE ■	SE	SE	SE		SE	SE	SE	SE	SE	SE	SE	SE	SE ■		SE	SE	SE	SE ■ ✕	SE	SE A	SE	SE
Orpington 4 d	16 33	16 39	16 40											16 51	16 54		16 55							
Petts Wood 4 d	16 36		16 43											16 54			16 58							
Hither Green 4 d	16 50						16 50	16 56					17 00	17 09							17 07			
Lewisham 4 d				16 50					16 56	16 59			17 05					17 08						17 14
St Johns d							16 54			17 01			17 09											17 16
New Cross 4 ⊖ d					16 49		16 56			17 03		17 08	17 11										17 14	17 18
London Victoria 15 ⊖ a			17 20														17 33	17 28						
London Bridge 4 ⊖ d	17 02	16 56		16 59	18 03		17 04	17 06	17 07	17 09	17 09	18 21	17 19		17 12				17 13	17 18	17 22	17 22	18 31	17 25
London Blackfriars 3 ⊖ a																								
London Cannon Street 4 ⊖ a					18 07		17 09		17 11	17 15		18 24	17 24						17 17			17 26	18 35	17 29
London Waterloo (East) 4 ⊖ d	17 07	17 01		17 04				17 11			17 14			17 25	17 16					17 23	17 29			
London Charing Cross 4 ⊖ a	17 10	17 04		17 07				17 15			17 18			17 29	17 20					17 26	17 33			

	SE		SE	SE ■	SE	SE	SE	SE	SE	SE	SE		SE	SE	SE ■	SE	SE ■	SE	SE ■ ✕	SE	SE		SE	SE B
Orpington 4 d			17 03	17 09	17 10	17 13								17 20	17 24	17 24	17 34							
Petts Wood 4 d			17 06		17 13									17 24		17 28	17 37							
Hither Green 4 d			17 19										17 28	17 38										
Lewisham 4 d	17 20		17 24				17 27		17 30				17 35					17 38			17 44		17 50	17 53
St Johns d			17 26										17 37								17 46			
New Cross 4 ⊖ d			17 28						17 33		17 36		17 39								17 48			
London Victoria 15 ⊖ a					17 48											18 03		17 59						
London Bridge 4 ⊖ d	17 30		17 34	17 28			17 36	17 38	17 39	17 42	18 51		17 45	17 49	17 42				17 45	17 52	17 55		18 00	19 01
London Blackfriars 3 ⊖ a																	18 09							
London Cannon Street 4 ⊖ a			17 38	17 32					17 44	17 46	18 54		17 49							17 56	17 59		18 04	19 06
London Waterloo (East) 4 ⊖ d	17 35					17 37	17 41	17 43						17 54	17 47				17 50					
London Charing Cross 4 ⊖ a	17 38					17 40	17 44	17 46						17 57	17 50				17 53					

	SE	SE	SE	SE	SE	SE ■	SE		SE	SE	SE	SE	SE	SE	SE	SE	SE ■		SE	SE	SE ■ ✕	SE	SE	SE ■
Orpington 4 d					17 37	17 39	17 40									17 50	17 54		17 55				18 03	18 09
Petts Wood 4 d					17 40		17 43									17 54			17 58				18 06	
Hither Green 4 d			17 41	17 42	17 53					17 58					18 03	18 07						18 12	18 19	
Lewisham 4 d	17 56	17 59	18 29							18 05	18 08		18 14	18 20	18 59								18 24	
St Johns d					17 57					18 07			18 16										18 26	
New Cross 4 ⊖ d		18 02	18 32		17 59					18 09		18 14	18 18		19 03								18 28	
London Victoria 15 ⊖ a							18 18				18 29								18 33					
London Bridge 4 ⊖ d	18 04	18 09	18 38	17 54	18 06	17 58			18 07	18 16		19 28	18 24	18 28	19 09	18 19	18 10			18 13	18 16	18 23	18 34	18 25
London Blackfriars 3 ⊖ a																								
London Cannon Street 4 ⊖ a		18 13	18 42		18 11					18 20		19 33	18 29		19 13					18 17			18 38	
London Waterloo (East) 4 ⊖ d	18 09			17 59		18 03			18 13					18 33		18 24	18 15				18 21	18 28		18 30
London Charing Cross 4 ⊖ a	18 12			18 03		18 06			18 16					18 37		18 27	18 18				18 25	18 31		18 35

	SE	SE	SE		SE	SE	SE	SE	SE	SE	SE	SE A	SE		SE ■	SE	SE ■ ✕	SE	SE	SE ■	SE A	SE	SE	
Orpington 4 d	18 09												18 21		18 24	18 25						18 33	18 40	
Petts Wood 4 d	18 12												18 24			18 28						18 36	18 43	
Hither Green 4 d			18 21					18 28				18 35	18 37						18 42			18 49		
Lewisham 4 d					18 26			18 35	18 38	18 45	18 50	19 29										18 54		
St Johns d								18 37		18 47												18 56		
New Cross 4 ⊖ d							18 35	18 39		18 49		19 32										18 58		
London Victoria 15 ⊖ a	18 48								18 58							19 03							19 17	
London Bridge 4 ⊖ d		18 31	18 33		18 36	18 38	19 59	18 46		18 55	18 58	19 38	18 49		18 41		18 43	18 43	18 53	18 55	19 01	19 05		
London Blackfriars 3 ⊖ a																								
London Cannon Street 4 ⊖ a		18 35					20 03	18 51		18 59		19 43						18 47			19 06	19 10		
London Waterloo (East) 4 ⊖ d			18 38		18 42	18 45					19 03		18 54		18 46		18 49		18 58	19 00				
London Charing Cross 4 ⊖ a			18 41		18 45	18 48					19 06		18 57		18 49		18 52		19 01	19 04				

A until 18 May

B from 21 May until 27 July

Table 199

Mondays to Fridays

until 27 July, 13 Aug to 28 Aug and from 10 Sep

Orpington, Petts Wood, Hither Green and Lewisham - London (Summary of Services)

		SE	SE	SE	SE	SE	SE ■	SE	SE	SE		SE ■ H	SE	SE	SE	SE	SE ■	SE	SE	SE A		SE	SE	SE	SE
Orpington ■	d					18 50	18 54	18 55								19 03	19 08	19 10							
Petts Wood ■	d					18 54		18 58								19 06		19 13							
Hither Green ■	d				18 59	19 07							19 12			19 19								19 28	
Lewisham ■	d	18 56			19 05				19 08					19 14	19 20	19 24			19 26	19 29				19 34	19 38
St Johns	d				19 07									19 16		19 26								19 36	19 40
New Cross ■	d			19 00	19 09									19 18		19 28				19 32				19 38	19 42
London Victoria ■	a							19 32	19 28									19 47							
London Bridge ■	d	19 05	19 08	20 28	19 15	19 19	19 10			19 12		19 13	19 22	19 24	19 28	19 34	19 25		19 35	19 38		19 38	19 41	19 45	19 49
London Blackfriars ■	a																								
London Cannon Street ■	a			20 31	19 20					19 16				19 28		19 38				19 43			19 45	19 49	
London Waterloo (East) ■	d	19 10	19 13			19 24	19 15					19 18	19 27		19 33		19 30		19 40			19 43			19 54
London Charing Cross ■	a	19 13	19 16			19 27	19 18					19 21	19 30		19 36		19 33		19 43			19 46			19 57

		SE	SE ■	SE	SE ■ H	SE ■		SE	SE	SE	SE	SE	SE	SE	SE ■	SE		SE ■	SE ■	SE	SE	SE	SE	SE	SE
Orpington ■	d	19 21	19 24	19 25		19 39		19 40						19 51	19 54	19 55			20 09	20 10					20 21
Petts Wood ■	d	19 24		19 28				19 43						19 54		19 58				20 13					20 24
Hither Green ■	d	19 37							19 42					20 07							20 12				20 38
Lewisham ■	d	19 43							19 48	19 52	19 56		20 08	20 13							20 18	20 22	20 26	20 38	20 43
St Johns	d												20 10											20 40	
New Cross ■	d								19 51	19 56			20 12								20 21	20 26		20 42	
London Victoria ■	a			20 02				20 17								20 32				20 47					
London Bridge ■	d	19 52	19 41		19 43	19 55			19 58	20 04	20 06	20 11	20 19	20 22	20 11			20 13	20 25		20 28	20 34	20 36	20 49	20 52
London Blackfriars ■	a																								
London Cannon Street ■	a											20 15													
London Waterloo (East) ■	d	19 57	19 46		19 49	20 00			20 03	20 09	20 11		20 24	20 27	20 16			20 19	20 30		20 33	20 39	20 41	20 54	20 57
London Charing Cross ■	a	20 00	19 49		19 52	20 03			20 06	20 12	20 14		20 27	20 30	20 19			20 22	20 33		20 36	20 42	20 44	20 57	21 00

		SE ■		SE	SE	SE ■	SE	SE	SE	SE	SE	SE ■		SE	SE ■	SE ■	SE	SE	SE	SE	SE	SE		SE ■	SE
Orpington ■	d	20 24		20 40							20 51	20 53				21 09	21 10					21 21		21 23	21 40
Petts Wood ■	d			20 43							20 54						21 13					21 24			21 43
Hither Green ■	d						20 42				21 07							21 12				21 37			
Lewisham ■	d						20 48	20 53	20 56	21 08	21 13							21 18	21 23	21 26	21 38	21 43			
St Johns	d									21 10											21 40				
New Cross ■	d						20 51	20 56		21 12								21 21	21 26		21 42				
London Victoria ■	a			21 17													21 47								22 17
London Bridge ■	d	20 40			20 41	20 43	20 58	21 04	21 06	21 19	21 22	21 09		21 11	21 14	21 25		21 28	21 34	21 36	21 49	21 52		21 39	
London Blackfriars ■	a																								
London Cannon Street ■	a				20 45																				
London Waterloo (East) ■	d	20 45				20 48	21 03	21 09	21 11	21 24	21 27	21 14		21 16	21 19	21 30		21 33	21 39	21 41	21 54	21 57		21 44	
London Charing Cross ■	a	20 48				20 51	21 06	21 12	21 14	21 27	21 30	21 18		21 19	21 22	21 33		21 36	21 42	21 44	21 57	22 00		21 48	

		SE	SE ■	SE	SE	SE	SE	SE		SE ■	SE	SE ■	SE ■	SE	SE	SE	SE	SE		SE	SE ■	SE	SE	SE ■	SE
Orpington ■	d							21 51		21 53			22 09	22 10						22 21	22 23	22 40			
Petts Wood ■	d							21 54						22 13						22 24		22 43			
Hither Green ■	d			21 42				22 07							22 12					22 37					22 42
Lewisham ■	d			21 48	21 53	21 56	22 08	22 13							22 18	22 23	22 26	22 38		22 43					22 48
St Johns	d						22 10											22 40							
New Cross ■	d			21 51	21 56		22 12								22 21	22 26		22 42							22 51
London Victoria ■	a													22 47								23 17			
London Bridge ■	d	21 41	21 44	21 58	22 02	22 05	22 19	22 22		22 09	22 11	22 14	22 25		22 28	22 32	22 35	22 49		22 52	22 39		22 41	22 44	22 58
London Blackfriars ■	a																								
London Cannon Street ■	a																								
London Waterloo (East) ■	d	21 46	21 49	22 03	22 07	22 10	22 24	22 27		22 14	22 16	22 19	22 30		22 33	22 37	22 40	22 54		22 57	22 44		22 46	22 49	23 03
London Charing Cross ■	a	21 49	21 52	22 06	22 10	22 13	22 27	22 30		22 18	22 19	22 22	22 33		22 36	22 40	22 43	22 57		23 00	22 48		22 49	22 52	23 06

		SE	SE	SE		SE	SE ■	SE	SE ■	SE ■	SE	SE	SE	SE		SE	SE	SE	SE ■
Orpington ■	d					22 51	22 53			23 09	23 10							23 21	23 37
Petts Wood ■	d					22 54					23 13							23 24	
Hither Green ■	d					23 07						23 12						23 37	
Lewisham ■	d	22 53	22 56	23 08		23 13						23 18	23 23	23 26			23 38	23 43	
St Johns	d			23 10													23 40		
New Cross ■	d	22 56		23 12								23 21	23 26				23 42		
London Victoria ■	a										23 47								
London Bridge ■	d	23 02	23 05	23 19		23 22	23 09	23 11	23 14	23 25		23 28	23 32	23 35		23 41	23 49	23 52	23 55
London Blackfriars ■	a																		
London Cannon Street ■	a																		
London Waterloo (East) ■	d	23 07	23 10	23 24		23 27	23 14	23 16	23 19	23 30		23 33	23 37	23 40		23 46	23 54	23 57	23 59
London Charing Cross ■	a	23 10	23 13	23 27		23 30	23 18	23 19	23 22	23 33		23 36	23 40	23 43		23 49	23 57	00 01	00 03

A from 21 May until 27 July

Table 199

Mondays to Fridays

30 July to 10 August

Orpington, Petts Wood, Hither Green and Lewisham - London (Summary of Services)

		SE	SE ■	SE	SE	SE	SE	SE	SE	SE		SE	SE	SE	SE	SE	SE	SE	SE	SE		SE ■	SE	SE	SE
Orpington ■	d	23p21	23p37	04 34	04 55		05 10	05 14				05 15	05 20	05 34			05 40					05 54			
Petts Wood ■	d	23p24		04 37	04 58		05 13					05 18	05 23	05 37			05 43								
Hither Green ■	d	23p37				05 08			05 23			05 30	05 35			05 38									
Lewisham ■	d	23p43				05 13			05 28			05 36			05 39	05 43		05 50		05 56				06 09	
St Johns	d														05 41									06 11	
New Cross ■	d					05 16			05 31			05 39	05 40		05 43	05 46		05 53						06 13	
London Victoria ■	a						05 47										06 18								
London Bridge ■	d	23p52	23p55			05 22		05 37	05 37	05 42		05 46	05 46		05 49	05 53		05 59	06 02	06 06		06 10	06 13	06 19	06 20
London Blackfriars ■	a			05 17	05 32									06 17											
London Cannon Street ■	a								05 44										06 06						06 24
London Waterloo (East) ■	d	23p57	23p59			05 27		05 42		05 47		05 50	05 50		05 53	05 57		06 04		06 10		06 15	06 18	06 24	
London Charing Cross ■	a	00 04	00 03			05 33		05 47		05 51		05 55	05 53		05 59	06 04		06 10		06 16		06 18	06 24	06 30	

		SE	SE	SE ■	SE	SE		SE	SE	SE	SE ■	SE	SE	SE	SE	SE ■		SE	SE	SE ■	SE	SE	SE	SE	SE
Orpington ■	d		06 01	06 09	06 10						06 20				06 22	06 24		06 40							
Petts Wood ■	d		06 04		06 13										06 25			06 43							
Hither Green ■	d	06 08	06 16							06 22					06 38									06 46	
Lewisham ■	d	06 13	06 22			06 20			06 25	06 27		06 35	06 39	06 41	06 43							06 48	06 50	06 52	06 55
St Johns	d									06 29			06 41									06 50		06 54	
New Cross ■	d	06 16	06 25							06 31		06 38	06 43									06 52		06 56	
London Victoria ■	a				06 47									07 04				07 19							
London Bridge ■	d	06 22	06 32	06 25		06 29		06 28	06 34	06 37	06 38	06 44	06 49		06 52	06 40			06 43	06 55	06 57	07 00	07 01	07 03	07 04
London Blackfriars ■	a																								
London Cannon Street ■	a							06 32			06 42	06 51									07 05	07 06		07 09	
London Waterloo (East) ■	d	06 27	06 36	06 30		06 33			06 40	06 42			06 54		06 57	06 45			06 49	07 00			07 06		07 10
London Charing Cross ■	a	06 33	06 39	06 33		06 39			06 46	06 48			07 00		07 02	06 49			06 55	07 05			07 11		07 15

		SE		SE	SE	SE	SE ■	SE	SE ■	SE	SE	SE		SE	SE	SE ■	SE	SE	SE	SE	SE	SE		SE ■	SE
Orpington ■	d				06 43	06 52	06 54	06 58														07 03		07 04	07 08
Petts Wood ■	d				06 46	06 55		07 01														07 06			07 11
Hither Green ■	d	06 56			06 58	07 08												07 11	07 16			07 18			
Lewisham ■	d			07 01	07 04						07 08			07 11	07 15			07 17		07 20	07 22	07 25			
St Johns	d																	07 19			07 24				
New Cross ■	d			07 04							07 11						07 20	07 21		07 23	07 26				
London Victoria ■	a														07 42										07 49
London Bridge ■	d	07 07		07 10		07 19	07 10		07 15	07 15	07 18	07 18		07 21		07 21	08 38	07 27	07 27	07 29	07 34			07 23	
London Blackfriars ■	a							07 42																	
London Cannon Street ■	a			07 18		07 25				07 21	07 23					07 27		07 33		07 35	07 39			07 29	
London Waterloo (East) ■	d	07 12			07 17		07 15		07 20			07 23		07 26			08 43		07 32			07 37			
London Charing Cross ■	a	07 17			07 22		07 20		07 25			07 28		07 31			08 48		07 37			07 42			

		SE	SE ■	SE	SE	SE ■	SE ■	SE		SE	SE	SE	SE	SE	SE ■	SE ■	SE	SE		SE	SE ■	SE	SE ■	SE	SE
Orpington ■	d	07 11	07 14														07 22	07 28							07 33
Petts Wood ■	d	07 15															07 25	07 31							07 36
Hither Green ■	d	07 28											07 32	07 36			07 39								07 49
Lewisham ■	d							07 30		07 35			07 38				07 44			07 46					
St Johns	d												07 40												
New Cross ■	d									07 38			07 42												
London Victoria ■	a																			08 11					
London Bridge ■	d	07 38	07 30	07 34	07 36	07 37		07 42		07 44	07 45	07 46	07 48	07 48	07 51	07 52	07 54				07 54	07 58		07 58	08 00
London Blackfriars ■	a																	08 08							
London Cannon Street ■	a	07 44			07 43					07 50		07 52	07 54			07 57					07 59	08 05			08 06
London Waterloo (East) ■	d		07 35	07 39		07 42	07 45	07 47			07 51			07 53	07 56		07 59						08 01	08 03	
London Charing Cross ■	a		07 40	07 44		07 47	07 50	07 52			07 56			07 58	08 01		08 04						08 06	08 08	

		SE	SE	SE		SE ■ H	SE	SE	SE	SE	SE	SE	SE	SE ■		SE	SE	SE	SE ■	SE	SE ■	SE	SE	SE ■
Orpington ■	d	07 38														07 41	07 47						07 52	
Petts Wood ■	d	07 41														07 44	07 50						07 55	
Hither Green ■	d											07 52				07 58				08 02				
Lewisham ■	d			07 48			07 50	07 55				07 57				08 03		08 05						
St Johns	d			07 50								08 00												
New Cross ■	d		07 50	07 53				07 58				08 02												
London Victoria ■	a	08 20																08 29						
London Bridge ■	d		09 08	08 02			08 02	08 04	08 06		08 06	08 09		08 10					08 11	08 14	08 14	08 18	08 20	
London Blackfriars ■	a																08 29							
London Cannon Street ■	a		09 14	08 08				08 10	08 12			08 15							08 17		08 20	08 25	08 26	
London Waterloo (East) ■	d					08 05	08 07			08 09	08 11		08 13	08 15		08 17				08 19				08 21
London Charing Cross ■	a					08 08	08 12			08 14	08 16		08 18	08 20		08 22				08 24				08 26

Table 199

Mondays to Fridays
30 July to 10 August

Orpington, Petts Wood, Hither Green and Lewisham - London (Summary of Services)

		SE	SE	SE	SE	SE	SE ■	SE	SE	SE		SE	SE	SE ■	SE	SE	SE	SE	SE	SE ■		SE	SE ■	SE	SE ■
Orpington	d		07 57														08 01	08 10							
Petts Wood	d		08 00														08 04	08 13							
Hither Green	d															08 12	08 17					08 22			
Lewisham	d				08 08	08 11		08 15								08 17	08 23		08 25						
St Johns	d				08 12											08 21									
New Cross	⊖ d			08 04	08 14			08 18							08 20	08 23									
London Victoria	⊖ a																	08 50	08 49						
London Bridge	⊖ d	08 18		09 18	08 22	08 22	08 24	08 26		08 26		08 28		08 30	09 30	08 30				08 32		08 34	08 34	08 38	
London Blackfriars	⊖ a																								
London Cannon Street	⊖ a				08 28		08 30	08 32				08 35			09 36	08 36				08 38			08 41	08 45	
London Waterloo (East)	⊖ d	08 23	08 25	09 23		08 27			08 29	08 31			08 33	08 35			08 37					08 39			08 41
London Charing Cross	⊖ a	08 28	08 30	09 28		08 32			08 34	08 36			08 39	08 40			08 42					08 44			08 46

		SE	SE	SE	SE ■	SE		SE	SE	SE	SE	SE ■	SE	SE	SE	SE		SE	SE ■	SE	SE ■	SE ■	SE	SE	SE
Orpington	d		08 13												08 21	08 26									
Petts Wood	d		08 16												08 24	08 29									
Hither Green	d													08 32	08 37					08 42					
Lewisham	d			08 28		08 31		08 35						08 37				08 46							08 48
St Johns	d			08 30										08 40											08 50
New Cross	⊖ d			08 32				08 38					08 38	08 42										08 49	08 52
London Victoria	⊖ a															09 06		09 14							
London Bridge	⊖ d	08 38	08 40	08 42		08 42		08 44	08 46		08 46	08 50	09 51	08 50					08 51	08 54	08 56		08 58	10 01	08 58
London Blackfriars	⊖ a																								
London Cannon Street	⊖ a		08 46	08 48				08 50	08 52				09 57	08 55					08 57		09 02			10 07	09 04
London Waterloo (East)	⊖ d	08 43			08 45	08 47				08 49	08 51	08 55			08 53					08 59		09 01	09 03		
London Charing Cross	⊖ a	08 48			08 50	08 52				08 54	08 56	09 00			08 58					09 04		09 04	09 09		

		SE		SE	SE	SE	SE ■	SE	SE	SE	SE	SE ■		SE ■	SE ■	SE	SE	SE	SE	SE	SE	SE		SE	SE
Orpington	d	08 32		08 40														08 43	08 47	08 52	08 55				
Petts Wood	d	08 35		08 43														08 46	08 50	08 55	08 58				
Hither Green	d							08 50		08 55								08 59		09 08				09 14	
Lewisham	d				08 52			08 55			08 59							09 04				09 06			09 15
St Johns	d							08 57			09 01							09 07							09 17
New Cross	⊖ d							08 59			09 03						09 04	09 09							09 19
London Victoria	⊖ a			09 19																	09 34	09 29			
London Bridge	⊖ d	09 00			09 01	09 02	09 04	09 06		09 06	09 10	09 12		09 12	09 15	09 18	10 21	09 18		09 21				09 24	09 26
London Blackfriars	⊖ a																		09 30						
London Cannon Street	⊖ a	09 06				09 09	09 10	09 12			09 18	09 18					10 27	09 23							09 32
London Waterloo (East)	⊖ d				09 06				09 08	09 11				09 17	09 20	09 23				09 26				09 29	
London Charing Cross	⊖ a				09 12				09 13	09 16				09 22	09 25	09 28				09 31				09 34	

		SE	SE	SE	SE ■	SE ■	SE	SE		SE	SE	SE	SE	SE ■	SE	SE	SE	SE ■ 🍴		SE	SE	SE	SE	SE	SE
Orpington	d			09 03	09 04	09 09	09 10						09 21	09 24	09 25										09 33
Petts Wood	d			09 06			09 13						09 24		09 28										09 36
Hither Green	d			09 19								09 28	09 37								09 42				09 49
Lewisham	d	09 20		09 24				09 26		09 29		09 34				09 38						09 45	09 50		09 54
St Johns	d			09 26						09 31		09 36										09 47			09 56
New Cross	⊖ d		09 19	09 28						09 33		09 38										09 49		09 49	09 58
London Victoria	⊖ a						09 49								10 02	10 00									
London Bridge	⊖ d	09 30	10 31	09 34	09 23	09 27		09 35		09 39	09 38	09 45	09 49	09 41			09 42	09 44		09 51	09 52	09 55	09 58	11 01	10 04
London Blackfriars	⊖ a																								
London Cannon Street	⊖ a		10 39	09 40	09 29					09 45		09 51					09 48			09 57		10 03		11 07	10 11
London Waterloo (East)	⊖ d	09 35				09 32		09 40			09 43		09 54	09 46				09 49			09 57		10 03		
London Charing Cross	⊖ a	09 40				09 37		09 45			09 48		09 59	09 51				09 54			10 00		10 09		

		SE ■	SE	SE		SE	SE	SE	SE	SE	SE ■	SE	SE	SE ■ 🍴		SE	SE	SE	SE	SE	SE	SE ■	SE	SE
Orpington	d	09 39	09 40							09 51	09 54	09 55									10 03	10 09	10 10	
Petts Wood	d		09 43							09 54		09 58									10 06		10 13	
Hither Green	d								09 58	10 07							10 12				10 19			
Lewisham	d			09 56		09 59			10 04				10 08					10 14	10 20		10 24			10 26
St Johns	d					10 01			10 06									10 16			10 26			
New Cross	⊖ d					10 03			10 08									10 18		10 19	10 28			
London Victoria	⊖ a		10 17									10 32	10 31										10 47	
London Bridge	⊖ d	09 55		10 05		10 09	10 08	10 11	10 14	10 19	10 11			10 13		10 21	10 22	10 24	10 28	11 31	10 34	10 25		10 35
London Blackfriars	⊖ a																							
London Cannon Street	⊖ a					10 16		10 18	10 22							10 27		10 30		11 39	10 41			
London Waterloo (East)	⊖ d	10 00		10 10			10 13			10 24	10 15			10 18			10 27		10 33			10 30		10 40
London Charing Cross	⊖ a	10 03		10 16			10 16			10 27	10 19			10 22			10 30		10 39			10 33		10 46

Table 199

Mondays to Fridays
30 July to 10 August

Orpington, Petts Wood, Hither Green and Lewisham - London (Summary of Services)

		SE	SE	SE	SE	SE	SE ■	SE	SE	SE ■ 🍴		SE	SE	SE	SE	SE	SE	SE ■	SE	SE		SE	SE	SE	SE
Orpington	d					10 21	10 24	10 25									10 33	10 39	10 40						
Petts Wood	d					10 24		10 28									10 36		10 43						
Hither Green	d				10 28	10 37							10 42				10 49								10 58
Lewisham	d	10 29			10 34				10 38					10 44	10 50		10 54			10 56		10 59			11 04
St Johns	d	10 31			10 36									10 46			10 56					11 01			11 06
New Cross	⊖ d	10 33			10 38									10 48		10 49	10 58					11 03			11 08
London Victoria	⊖ a							11 02	11 03										11 17						
London Bridge	⊖ d	10 39	10 38	10 41	10 45	10 49	10 41			10 43		10 51	10 52	10 54	10 58	12 01	11 04	10 55		11 05		11 09	11 08	11 11	11 15
London Blackfriars	⊖ a																								
London Cannon Street	⊖ a	10 46		10 48	10 55							10 57		11 01		12 07	11 11					11 16		11 18	11 22
London Waterloo (East)	⊖ d		10 43			10 54	10 45			10 49			10 57		11 03			11 00		11 10			11 13		
London Charing Cross	⊖ a		10 46			10 57	10 49			10 52			11 00		11 09			11 03		11 16			11 16		

		SE	SE ■	SE	SE	SE ■ 🍴		SE	SE	SE	SE	SE	SE	SE ■	SE	SE		SE	SE	SE	SE	SE	SE ■	SE	SE
Orpington	d	10 51	10 54	10 55									11 03	11 09	11 10							11 21	11 24	11 25	
Petts Wood	d	10 54		10 58									11 06		11 13							11 24		11 28	
Hither Green	d	11 07							11 12				11 19								11 28	11 37			
Lewisham	d				11 08					11 14	11 20		11 24			11 26		11 29			11 34				11 38
St Johns	d									11 16			11 26					11 31			11 36				
New Cross	⊖ d									11 18		11 19	11 28					11 33			11 38				
London Victoria	⊖ a			11 32	11 31										11 47									12 02	12 03
London Bridge	⊖ d	11 19	11 11			11 13		11 21	11 22	11 24	11 28	12 31	11 34	11 25		11 35		11 39	11 38	11 41	11 45	11 49	11 41		
London Blackfriars	⊖ a																								
London Cannon Street	⊖ a							11 27		11 31		12 39	11 41					11 46		11 48	11 52				
London Waterloo (East)	⊖ d	11 26	11 15			11 19			11 28		11 34			11 31		11 40			11 43			11 54	11 45		
London Charing Cross	⊖ a	11 29	11 19			11 22			11 32		11 41			11 34		11 46			11 46			11 57	11 49		

		SE ■ 🍴		SE	SE	SE	SE	SE	SE	SE ■	SE	SE		SE	SE	SE	SE	SE	SE ■	SE	SE	SE ■ 🍴		SE	SE
Orpington	d								11 33	11 39	11 40							11 51	11 54	11 55					
Petts Wood	d								11 36		11 43							11 54		11 58					
Hither Green	d				11 42				11 49								11 58	12 07							12 12
Lewisham	d					11 44	11 50		11 54			11 56		11 59			12 04				12 08				
St Johns	d					11 46			11 56					12 01			12 06								
New Cross	⊖ d					11 48		11 49	11 58					12 03			12 08								
London Victoria	⊖ a										12 17									12 32	12 31				
London Bridge	⊖ d	11 43		11 51	11 52	11 54	11 58	13 01	12 04	11 55		12 05		12 09	12 08	12 11	12 15	12 19	12 11			12 13		12 21	12 22
London Blackfriars	⊖ a																								
London Cannon Street	⊖ a			11 57		12 01		13 07	12 11					12 16		12 18	12 22							12 27	
London Waterloo (East)	⊖ d	11 49			11 57		12 03			12 00		12 10			12 13			12 24	12 15			12 19			12 27
London Charing Cross	⊖ a	11 52			12 00		12 09			12 03		12 16			12 16			12 27	12 19			12 22			12 30

		SE	SE	SE	SE	SE ■	SE	SE		SE	SE	SE	SE	SE	SE ■	SE	SE	SE ■ 🍴		SE	SE	SE	SE	SE	SE
Orpington	d				12 03	12 09	12 10							12 21	12 24	12 25									12 33
Petts Wood	d				12 06		12 13							12 24		12 28									12 36
Hither Green	d				12 19								12 28	12 37							12 42				12 49
Lewisham	d	12 14	12 20		12 24			12 26		12 29			12 34				12 38					12 44	12 50		12 54
St Johns	d	12 16			12 26					12 31			12 36									12 46			12 56
New Cross	⊖ d	12 18		12 19	12 28					12 33			12 38									12 48		12 49	12 58
London Victoria	⊖ a						12 47									13 02	13 01								
London Bridge	⊖ d	12 24	12 28	13 31	12 34	12 25		12 35		12 39	12 38	12 41	12 45	12 49	12 41			12 43		12 51	12 52	12 54	12 58	14 01	13 04
London Blackfriars	⊖ a																								
London Cannon Street	⊖ a	12 31		13 39	12 41					12 46		12 48	12 52							12 57		13 01		14 07	13 11
London Waterloo (East)	⊖ d		12 33			12 30		12 40			12 44			12 54	12 45			12 49			12 57		13 03		
London Charing Cross	⊖ a		12 39			12 33		12 46			12 49			12 57	12 49			12 52			13 00		13 09		

		SE ■	SE	SE		SE	SE	SE	SE	SE	SE ■	SE	SE	SE ■ 🍴		SE	SE	SE	SE	SE	SE	SE ■	SE	SE
Orpington	d	12 39	12 40							12 51	12 54	12 55									13 03	13 09	13 10	
Petts Wood	d		12 43							12 54		12 58									13 06		13 13	
Hither Green	d								12 58	13 07							13 12				13 19			
Lewisham	d			12 56		12 59			13 04				13 08					13 14	13 20		13 24			13 26
St Johns	d					13 01			13 06									13 16			13 26			
New Cross	⊖ d					13 03			13 08									13 18		13 19	13 28			
London Victoria	⊖ a		13 17									13 32	13 31										13 47	
London Bridge	⊖ d	12 55		13 05		13 09	13 08	13 11	13 15	13 19	13 11			13 13		13 21	13 22	13 24	13 28	14 31	13 34	13 25		13 35
London Blackfriars	⊖ a																							
London Cannon Street	⊖ a					13 16		13 18	13 22							13 27		13 31		14 39	13 41			
London Waterloo (East)	⊖ d	13 00		13 10			13 13			13 24	13 15			13 19			13 27		13 33			13 30		13 40
London Charing Cross	⊖ a	13 03		13 16			13 16			13 27	13 19			13 22			13 30		13 39			13 33		13 46

Table 199

Mondays to Fridays
30 July to 10 August

Orpington, Petts Wood, Hither Green and Lewisham - London (Summary of Services)

	SE	SE	SE	SE	SE	SE	SE ■	SE	SE		SE ■ ⊥	SE	SE	SE	SE	SE	SE	SE ■	SE		SE	SE	SE	SE
Orpington ■ d						13 21	13 24	13 25									13 33	13 39	13 40					
Petts Wood ■ d						13 24		13 28									13 36		13 43					
Hither Green ■ d					13 28	13 37							13 42				13 49							
Lewisham ■ ⇌ d	13 29				13 34				13 38					13 44	13 50		13 54				13 56	13 59		
St Johns d	13 31				13 36									13 46			13 56					14 01		
New Cross ■ ⊖ d	13 33			13 33	13 38									13 48		13 49	13 58					14 03		
London Victoria ■ ⊖ a								14 02	14 01										14 17					
London Bridge ■ ⊖ d	13 39	13 38	13 41	14 51	13 45	13 49	13 41				13 43	13 51	13 52	13 54	13 58	15 01	14 04	13 55			14 05	14 09	14 08	14 11
London Blackfriars ■ ⊖ a																								
London Cannon Street ■ ⊖ a	13 46		13 48	14 57	13 52							13 57		14 01		15 07	14 11					14 16		14 18
London Waterloo (East) ■ ⊖ d		13 43				13 54	13 45				13 49		13 57		14 03			14 00			14 10		14 13	
London Charing Cross ■ ⊖ a		13 46				13 57	13 49				13 52		14 00		14 09			14 03			14 16		14 16	

	SE	SE	SE	SE ■	SE		SE	SE ■ ⊥	SE	SE	SE	SE	SE	SE	SE ■		SE	SE	SE	SE	SE	SE	SE	SE
Orpington ■ d			13 51	13 54	13 55									14 03	14 09		14 10							14 21
Petts Wood ■ d			13 54		13 58									14 06			14 13							14 24
Hither Green ■ d		13 58	14 07							14 12				14 19									14 28	14 37
Lewisham ■ ⇌ d		14 04					14 08				14 14	14 20		14 24				14 26	14 29				14 34	
St Johns d		14 06									14 16			14 26					14 31				14 36	
New Cross ■ ⊖ d	14 03	14 08									14 18		14 19	14 28					14 33			14 33	14 38	
London Victoria ■ ⊖ a					14 32		14 31										14 47							
London Bridge ■ ⊖ d	15 21	14 15	14 19	14 11				14 13	14 21	14 22	14 24	14 28	15 31	14 34	14 25			14 35	14 39	14 38	14 41	15 51	14 45	14 49
London Blackfriars ■ ⊖ a																								
London Cannon Street ■ ⊖ a	15 27	14 22							14 27		14 31		15 39	14 41					14 46		14 48	15 57	14 52	
London Waterloo (East) ■ ⊖ d			14 24	14 15				14 19		14 27		14 33			14 30			14 40		14 43				14 54
London Charing Cross ■ ⊖ a			14 27	14 19				14 22		14 30		14 39			14 33			14 46		14 46				14 57

	SE ■		SE	SE	SE ■ ⊥	SE	SE	SE	SE	SE	SE		SE ■	SE	SE	SE	SE	SE	SE	SE	SE		SE ■	SE
Orpington ■ d	14 24		14 25								14 33		14 39	14 40							14 51		14 54	14 55
Petts Wood ■ d			14 28								14 36			14 43							14 54			14 58
Hither Green ■ d							14 42				14 49									14 58	15 07			
Lewisham ■ ⇌ d				14 38				14 44	14 50		14 54				14 56	14 59				15 04				
St Johns d								14 46			14 56					15 01				15 06				
New Cross ■ ⊖ d								14 48		14 49	14 58					15 03			15 03	15 08				
London Victoria ■ ⊖ a			15 02	15 01										15 17										15 32
London Bridge ■ ⊖ d	14 41				14 43	14 51	14 52	14 54	14 58	16 01	15 04		14 55		15 05	15 09	15 08	15 11	16 21	15 15	15 19		15 11	
London Blackfriars ■ ⊖ a																								
London Cannon Street ■ ⊖ a						14 57		15 01		16 09	15 11					15 16		15 18	16 27	15 22				
London Waterloo (East) ■ ⊖ d	14 45				14 49		14 57		15 03				15 00		15 10		15 13				15 24		15 15	
London Charing Cross ■ ⊖ a	14 49				14 52		15 00		15 09				15 03		15 16		15 16				15 27		15 19	

	SE	SE ■ ⊥	SE	SE	SE	SE	SE		SE	SE ■	SE	SE	SE	SE	SE	SE	SE		SE	SE ■	SE	SE	SE ■ ⊥	SE
Orpington ■ d									15 03	15 09	15 10								15 21	15 24	15 25			
Petts Wood ■ d									15 06		15 13								15 24		15 28			
Hither Green ■ d				15 12					15 19								15 28		15 37					
Lewisham ■ ⇌ d	15 08				15 14	15 20			15 24			15 26	15 29				15 34					15 38		
St Johns d					15 16				15 26				15 31				15 36							
New Cross ■ ⊖ d					15 18		15 19		15 28				15 33			15 33	15 38							
London Victoria ■ ⊖ a	15 31										15 47										16 02	16 01		
London Bridge ■ ⊖ d		15 13	15 21	15 22	15 24	15 28	16 31		15 34	15 25		15 35	15 39	15 38	15 41	16 51	15 45		15 50	15 41			15 43	15 51
London Blackfriars ■ ⊖ a																								
London Cannon Street ■ ⊖ a			15 27		15 31		16 39		15 41				15 46		15 48	16 57	15 52							15 57
London Waterloo (East) ■ ⊖ d		15 19		15 27		15 33				15 30		15 40		15 43					15 55	15 46			15 49	
London Charing Cross ■ ⊖ a		15 22		15 30		15 39				15 33		15 46		15 46					15 58	15 49			15 52	

	SE	SE	SE		SE	SE	SE ■	SE	SE	SE	SE	SE	SE		SE	SE ■	SE	SE	SE ■ ⊥	SE	SE	SE	SE	
Orpington ■ d						15 33	15 39	15 40							15 51	15 54	15 55							
Petts Wood ■ d						15 36		15 43							15 54		15 58							
Hither Green ■ d	15 42					15 49							15 58		16 07						16 12			
Lewisham ■ ⇌ d		15 44	15 50			15 54			15 56	15 59			16 04					16 08				16 14	16 16	
St Johns d		15 46				15 56				16 01			16 06									16 16		
New Cross ■ ⊖ d		15 48			15 49	15 58				16 03			16 08									16 18		
London Victoria ■ ⊖ a								16 17									16 32	16 31					16 44	
London Bridge ■ ⊖ d	15 53	15 54	15 58		17 01	16 04	15 55		16 05	16 09	16 09	16 12	16 15		16 19	16 12			16 14	16 21	16 22	16 24		
London Blackfriars ■ ⊖ a																								
London Cannon Street ■ ⊖ a		16 01			17 08	16 11				16 16		16 19	16 22							16 27		16 31		
London Waterloo (East) ■ ⊖ d	15 58		16 03				16 00		16 10		16 14				16 25	16 17			16 20		16 28			
London Charing Cross ■ ⊖ a	16 01		16 09				16 03		16 16		16 18				16 28	16 20			16 24		16 31			

Table 199

Mondays to Fridays
30 July to 10 August

Orpington, Petts Wood, Hither Green and Lewisham - London (Summary of Services)

	SE	SE	SE	SE ■	SE	SE	SE	SE	SE		SE	SE	SE	SE	SE ■	SE	SE	SE ■ ⊥	SE		SE	SE	SE ■	SE
Orpington ■ d			16 03	16 08	16 10									16 21	16 25	16 25						16 33	16 39	16 40
Petts Wood ■ d			16 06		16 13									16 24		16 28						16 36		16 43
Hither Green ■ d			16 19										16 28	16 37					16 42			16 50		
Lewisham ■ ⇌ d	16 20		16 24				16 26		16 29				16 34				16 38				16 44			
St Johns d			16 26						16 31				16 36								16 46			
New Cross ■ ⊖ d		16 20	16 28						16 33			16 34	16 38								16 48			
London Victoria ■ ⊖ a					16 47											17 04	17 04							17 20
London Bridge ■ ⊖ d	16 29	17 31	16 34	16 25		16 32	16 35	16 38	16 39		16 42	17 52	16 45	16 49	16 42			16 46	16 52		16 54	17 02	16 56	
London Blackfriars ■ ⊖ a																								
London Cannon Street ■ ⊖ a		17 39	16 41						16 46		16 49	17 59	16 52								17 01			
London Waterloo (East) ■ ⊖ d	16 34			16 30		16 38	16 40	16 43						16 55	16 49			16 53	16 57			17 07	17 01	
London Charing Cross ■ ⊖ a	16 40			16 33		16 42	16 47	16 46						16 58	16 52			16 56	17 00			17 10	17 04	

	SE	SE	SE	SE	SE		SE	SE	SE	SE	SE	SE ■	SE	SE	SE		SE ■ ⊥	SE	SE	SE	SE	SE	SE	SE ■
Orpington ■ d											16 51	16 54	16 55										17 03	17 09
Petts Wood ■ d											16 54		16 58										17 06	
Hither Green ■ d			16 50	16 56						17 00	17 09							17 07					17 19	
Lewisham ■ ⇌ d	16 50				16 56		16 59			17 05				17 08							17 14	17 20	17 24	
St Johns d			16 54				17 01			17 09											17 16		17 26	
New Cross ■ ⊖ d		16 49	16 56				17 03		17 08	17 11										17 14	17 18		17 28	
London Victoria ■ ⊖ a													17 33	17 31										
London Bridge ■ ⊖ d	16 59	18 03	17 04	17 06	17 07		17 09	17 09	18 21	17 19		17 12			17 13		17 18	17 22	17 22	18 31	17 25	17 30	17 34	17 28
London Blackfriars ■ ⊖ a																								
London Cannon Street ■ ⊖ a		18 10	17 09		17 14		17 18		18 27	17 27					17 20				17 29	18 38	17 32		17 41	17 32
London Waterloo (East) ■ ⊖ d	17 04			17 11				17 14			17 25	17 16					17 23	17 29				17 35		
London Charing Cross ■ ⊖ a	17 10			17 15				17 18			17 29	17 20					17 26	17 33				17 41		

	SE		SE	SE	SE	SE	SE	SE	SE	SE	SE ■		SE	SE ■	SE	SE ■ ⊥	SE	SE	SE	SE	SE		SE	SE
Orpington ■ d	17 10		17 13							17 20	17 24		17 24	17 34										
Petts Wood ■ d	17 13									17 24			17 28	17 37										
Hither Green ■ d									17 28	17 38														17 41
Lewisham ■ ⇌ d				17 27		17 29			17 35						17 38			17 44	17 50	17 53	17 56		17 59	18 29
St Johns d									17 37									17 46						
New Cross ■ ⊖ d						17 33		17 36	17 39									17 48					18 02	18 32
London Victoria ■ ⊖ a	17 48												18 03		18 02									
London Bridge ■ ⊖ d				17 36	17 38	17 39	17 42	18 51	17 45	17 49	17 42					17 45	17 52	17 55	18 00	19 01	18 04		18 09	18 38
London Blackfriars ■ ⊖ a														18 09										
London Cannon Street ■ ⊖ a						17 47	17 49	18 57	17 52								17 59	18 02	18 07	19 09			18 16	18 45
London Waterloo (East) ■ ⊖ d			17 37	17 41	17 43					17 54	17 47					17 50					18 09			
London Charing Cross ■ ⊖ a			17 40	17 47	17 46					17 57	17 50					17 53					18 15			

	SE	SE	SE ■	SE	SE	SE	SE		SE	SE	SE	SE	SE	SE ■	SE	SE	SE ■ ⊥		SE	SE	SE ■	SE	SE	SE
Orpington ■ d		17 37	17 39	17 40									17 50	17 54	17 55					18 03	18 09	18 09		
Petts Wood ■ d		17 40		17 43									17 54		17 58					18 06		18 12		
Hither Green ■ d	17 42	17 53				17 58						18 03	18 07						18 12	18 19				18 21
Lewisham ■ ⇌ d						18 05	18 08			18 14	18 20	18 59								18 24				
St Johns d		17 57				18 07				18 16										18 26				
New Cross ■ ⊖ d		17 59				18 09			18 14	18 18		19 03								18 28				
London Victoria ■ ⊖ a				18 18			18 32								18 33							18 48		
London Bridge ■ ⊖ d	17 54	18 06	17 58		18 07	18 16			19 28	18 24	18 28	19 09	18 19	18 10		18 13	18 16		18 23	18 34	18 25		18 31	18 33
London Blackfriars ■ ⊖ a																								
London Cannon Street ■ ⊖ a		18 11				18 23			19 36	18 32		19 16				18 20				18 41			18 38	
London Waterloo (East) ■ ⊖ d	17 59		18 03		18 13						18 33		18 24	18 15			18 21		18 28		18 30			18 38
London Charing Cross ■ ⊖ a	18 03		18 06		18 16						18 40		18 27	18 18			18 25		18 31		18 35			18 44

	SE	SE	SE		SE	SE	SE	SE	SE	SE	SE	SE ■	SE		SE ■ ⊥	SE	SE	SE	SE ■	SE	SE	SE	SE	
Orpington ■ d											18 21	18 24	18 25							18 33	18 40			
Petts Wood ■ d											18 24		18 28							18 36	18 43			
Hither Green ■ d						18 28				18 35	18 37							18 42		18 49				
Lewisham ■ ⇌ d	18 26	18 29				18 35	18 38	18 45	18 50	19 29										18 54		18 56		
St Johns d						18 37		18 47												18 56				
New Cross ■ ⊖ d		18 32			18 35	18 39		18 49		19 32										18 58				
London Victoria ■ ⊖ a							19 01						19 03								19 17			
London Bridge ■ ⊖ d	18 36	18 38	18 38		19 59	18 46		18 55	18 58	19 38	18 49	18 41			18 43	18 43	18 51	18 53	18 55	19 05		19 05	19 08	
London Blackfriars ■ ⊖ a																								
London Cannon Street ■ ⊖ a		18 45			20 06	18 54		19 02		19 46						18 50	18 57			19 12				
London Waterloo (East) ■ ⊖ d	18 42		18 45						19 03		18 54	18 46			18 49			18 58	19 00			19 10	19 13	
London Charing Cross ■ ⊖ a	18 48		18 48						19 09		18 57	18 49			18 52			19 01	19 04			19 16	19 16	

Table 199

Orpington, Petts Wood, Hither Green and Lewisham - London (Summary of Services)

Mondays to Fridays
30 July to 10 August

		SE	SE	SE	SE	SE ■	SE	SE	SE	SE ■ ✕		SE	SE	SE	SE	SE	SE	SE ■	SE	SE		SE	SE	SE	SE
Orpington	d				18 50	18 54	18 55										19 03	19 08	19 10						
Petts Wood	d				18 54		18 58										19 06		19 13						
Hither Green	d			18 59	19 07									19 12			19 19								19 28
Lewisham	d		18 59	19 05				19 08							19 14	19 20	19 24			19 26		19 29			19 34
St Johns	d			19 07											19 16		19 26								19 36
New Cross	d	19 00	19 03	19 09											19 18		19 28					19 32			19 38
London Victoria	a						19 32	19 31											19 47						
London Bridge	d	20 28	19 09	19 15	19 19	19 10			19 12	19 13		19 21	19 21	19 22	19 24	19 28	19 34	19 25		19 35		19 38	19 38	19 41	19 45
London Blackfriars	a																								
London Cannon Street	a	20 34	19 16	19 22					19 19			19 25	19 28		19 31		19 41					19 46		19 48	19 52
London Waterloo (East)	d				19 24	19 15				19 18				19 27		19 33		19 30		19 40			19 43		
London Charing Cross	a				19 27	19 18				19 21				19 30		19 39		19 33		19 46			19 46		

		SE	SE	SE ■	SE	SE ■ ✕		SE ■	SE	SE	SE	SE	SE	SE	SE	SE		SE	SE ■	SE	SE ■	SE ■	SE	SE	SE
Orpington	d		19 21	19 24	19 25			19 39	19 40									19 51	19 54	19 55		20 09	20 10		
Petts Wood	d		19 24		19 28				19 43									19 54		19 58			20 13		
Hither Green	d		19 37							19 42								20 07						20 12	
Lewisham	d	19 38	19 43							19 48		19 52	19 57		20 08	20 10		20 13						20 18	
St Johns	d	19 40													20 10										
New Cross	d	19 42								19 51		19 56			20 12									20 21	
London Victoria	a				20 02				20 17							20 31				20 32			20 47		
London Bridge	d	19 49	19 52	19 41		19 43		19 55		19 58	19 59	20 04	20 06	20 11	20 19			20 22	20 11		20 13	20 25		20 28	20 32
London Blackfriars	a																								
London Cannon Street	a										20 03			20 18											20 39
London Waterloo (East)	d	19 54	19 57	19 46		19 49		20 00		20 03		20 09	20 11		20 24			20 27	20 16		20 19	20 30		20 33	
London Charing Cross	a	20 00	20 03	19 49		19 52		20 03		20 09		20 15	20 17		20 30			20 33	20 19		20 22	20 33		20 39	

		SE		SE	SE	SE	SE ■	SE	SE	SE ■	SE	SE		SE	SE	SE	SE	SE ■	SE	SE	SE ■	SE ■		SE	SE
Orpington	d					20 21	20 24	20 40									20 51	20 53				21 09		21 10	
Petts Wood	d					20 24		20 43									20 54							21 13	
Hither Green	d					20 38					20 42						21 07								21 12
Lewisham	d	20 22		20 26	20 38	20 43					20 48			20 53	20 57	21 08	21 13			21 11					21 18
St Johns	d				20 40											21 10									
New Cross	d	20 26			20 42						20 51			20 56		21 12									21 21
London Victoria	a							21 17												21 31				21 47	
London Bridge	d	20 34		20 36	20 49	20 52	20 40		20 41	20 43	20 58	20 58		21 04	21 06	21 19	21 22	21 09	21 11		21 14	21 25			21 28
London Blackfriars	a																								
London Cannon Street	a								20 48			21 04													
London Waterloo (East)	d	20 39		20 41	20 54	20 57	20 45			20 48	21 03			21 09	21 11	21 24	21 27	21 14	21 16		21 19	21 30			21 33
London Charing Cross	a	20 45		20 47	21 00	21 03	20 48			20 51	21 09			21 15	21 17	21 30	21 33	21 18	21 22		21 22	21 33			21 39

		SE	SE	SE	SE	SE	SE ■	SE		SE	SE ■	SE	SE	SE	SE	SE	SE	SE		SE	SE ■	SE	SE ■	SE ■	SE
Orpington	d					21 21	21 23	21 40												21 51	21 53			22 09	22 10
Petts Wood	d					21 24		21 43												21 54					22 13
Hither Green	d					21 37							21 42							22 07					
Lewisham	d		21 23	21 27	21 38	21 43						21 46	21 48		21 53	21 57	22 08	22 10		22 13					
St Johns	d				21 40												22 10								
New Cross	d		21 26		21 42								21 51		21 56		22 12								
London Victoria	a							22 17				22 14						22 31							22 47
London Bridge	d	21 28	21 34	21 36	21 49	21 52	21 39			21 41	21 44		21 58	21 58	22 02	22 05	22 19			22 22	22 09	22 11	22 14	22 25	
London Blackfriars	a																								
London Cannon Street	a	21 34												22 04											
London Waterloo (East)	d		21 39	21 41	21 54	21 57	21 44			21 46	21 49		22 03		22 07	22 10	22 24			22 27	22 14	22 16	22 19	22 30	
London Charing Cross	a		21 45	21 47	22 00	22 03	21 48			21 52	21 52		22 09		22 13	22 16	22 30			22 33	22 18	22 22	22 22	22 33	

		SE	SE	SE		SE	SE	SE	SE ■	SE	SE	SE ■	SE A	SE		SE	SE	SE	SE	SE ■	SE	SE ■	SE ■	SE
Orpington	d							22 21	22 23	22 40									22 51	22 53			23 09	23 10
Petts Wood	d							22 24		22 43									22 54					23 13
Hither Green	d	22 12						22 37						22 42					23 07					
Lewisham	d	22 18		22 23		22 26	22 38	22 43					22 46	22 48		22 53	22 56	23 08	23 13					
St Johns	d						22 40											23 10						
New Cross	d	22 21		22 26			22 42							22 51		22 56		23 12						
London Victoria	a									23 17			23 14											23 47
London Bridge	d	22 28	22 28	22 32		22 35	22 49	22 52	22 39		22 41	22 44		22 58		23 02	23 05	23 19	23 22	23 09	23 11	23 14	23 25	
London Blackfriars	a																							
London Cannon Street	a		22 34																					
London Waterloo (East)	d	22 33		22 37		22 40	22 54	22 57	22 44		22 46	22 49		23 03		23 07	23 10	23 24	23 27	23 14	23 16	23 19	23 30	
London Charing Cross	a	22 39		22 43		22 46	23 00	23 03	22 48		22 52	22 52		23 09		23 13	23 16	23 30	23 33	23 18	23 22	23 22	23 33	

A not 3 August, 10 August

Table 199

Orpington, Petts Wood, Hither Green and Lewisham - London (Summary of Services)

Mondays to Fridays
30 July to 10 August

		SE	SE	SE	SE	SE	SE	SE ■
Orpington	d						23 21	23 37
Petts Wood	d						23 24	
Hither Green	d	23 12					23 37	
Lewisham	d	23 18	23 23	23 26		23 38	23 43	
St Johns	d					23 40		
New Cross	d	23 21	23 26			23 42		
London Victoria	a							
London Bridge	d	23 28	23 32	23 35	23 41	23 49	23 52	23 55
London Blackfriars	a							
London Cannon Street	a							
London Waterloo (East)	d	23 33	23 38	23 40	23 46	23 54	23 57	23 59
London Charing Cross	a	23 39	23 46	23 46	23 52	23 59	00 04	00 03

Mondays to Fridays
29 August to 7 September

		SE A	SE ■ A	SE	SE	SE	SE	SE	SE	SE		SE	SE	SE	SE	SE	SE	SE	SE	SE ■		SE	SE	SE	SE
Orpington	d	23p21	23p37	04 34	04 55		05 10	05 14				05 15	05 34			05 40				05 54					
Petts Wood	d	23p24		04 37	04 58		05 13					05 18	05 37			05 43									
Hither Green	d	23p37				05 08			05 23			05 30			05 38										06 08
Lewisham	d	23p43				05 13			05 28			05 36		05 39	05 43		05 50		05 56				06 09		06 13
St Johns	d													05 41									06 11		
New Cross	d					05 16			05 31			05 39		05 43	05 46		05 53						06 13		06 16
London Victoria	a						05 47									06 18									
London Bridge	d	23p52	23p55			05 22		05 37	05 37	05 42		05 46		05 49	05 53		05 59	06 02	06 06	06 10		06 13	06 19	06 20	06 22
London Blackfriars	a			05 17	05 32								06 17												
London Cannon Street	a								05 41									06 06						06 24	
London Waterloo (East)	d	23p57	23p59			05 27		05 42		05 47		05 50		05 53	05 57		06 04		06 10	06 15		06 18	06 24		06 27
London Charing Cross	a	00 01	00 03			05 30		05 47		05 50		05 55		05 56	06 01		06 07		06 13	06 18		06 21	06 27		06 30

		SE	SE ■	SE	SE	SE		SE	SE	SE ■	SE	SE	SE	SE	SE ■	SE		SE	SE ■	SE	SE	SE	SE	SE	SE
Orpington	d	06 01	06 09	06 10						06 20				06 22	06 24	06 40									
Petts Wood	d	06 04		06 13										06 25		06 43									
Hither Green	d	06 16							06 22					06 38									06 46		06 56
Lewisham	d	06 22			06 20			06 25	06 27		06 35	06 39	06 41	06 43							06 48	06 50	06 52	06 55	
St Johns	d								06 29			06 41									06 50		06 54		
New Cross	d	06 25							06 31		06 38	06 43									06 52		06 56		
London Victoria	a			06 47									07 04			07 19									
London Bridge	d	06 32	06 25		06 29	06 28		06 34	06 37	06 38	06 44	06 49		06 52	06 40			06 43	06 55	06 57	07 00	07 01	07 03	07 04	07 07
London Blackfriars	a																								
London Cannon Street	a					06 32				06 42	06 48									07 03	07 05		07 09		
London Waterloo (East)	d	06 36	06 30		06 33			06 40	06 42			06 54		06 57	06 45			06 49	07 00			07 06		07 10	07 12
London Charing Cross	a	06 39	06 33		06 36			06 43	06 45			06 57		07 02	06 49			06 52	07 05			07 11		07 15	07 17

		SE		SE	SE	SE ■	SE	SE ■	SE	SE	SE	SE		SE	SE ■	SE	SE	SE	SE	SE	SE	SE ■		SE	SE
Orpington	d			06 43	06 52	06 54	06 58														07 03	07 04		07 08	07 11
Petts Wood	d			06 46	06 55		07 01														07 06			07 11	07 15
Hither Green	d			06 58	07 08												07 11	07 16			07 19				07 28
Lewisham	d	07 01		07 04						07 08		07 11		07 15			07 17		07 20	07 22	07 25				
St Johns	d																07 19			07 24					
New Cross	d	07 04								07 11						07 20	07 21		07 23	07 26					
London Victoria	a													07 42										07 49	
London Bridge	d	07 10			07 19	07 10		07 15	07 15	07 18	07 18	07 21			07 21	08 38	07 27	07 27	07 29	07 34		07 23			07 38
London Blackfriars	a						07 42																		
London Cannon Street	a	07 16			07 25				07 21	07 23					07 27		07 33		07 35	07 39		07 29			07 44
London Waterloo (East)	d			07 17		07 15		07 20			07 23	07 26				08 43		07 32			07 37				
London Charing Cross	a			07 22		07 20		07 25			07 28	07 31				08 48		07 37			07 42				

		SE ■	SE	SE	SE ■	SE ■	SE	SE		SE	SE	SE	SE	SE ■	SE ■	SE	SE	SE		SE ■	SE	SE ■	SE	SE	SE
Orpington	d	07 14														07 22	07 28							07 33	07 38
Petts Wood	d															07 25	07 31							07 36	07 41
Hither Green	d											07 32	07 36			07 39								07 49	
Lewisham	d						07 30	07 35				07 38				07 44		07 46							
St Johns	d											07 40													
New Cross	d							07 38				07 42													
London Victoria	a																	08 11							08 20
London Bridge	d	07 30	07 34	07 36	07 37		07 42	07 44		07 45	07 46	07 48	07 48	07 51	07 52	07 54				07 54	07 58		07 58	08 00	
London Blackfriars	a																08 08								
London Cannon Street	a			07 42				07 50			07 52	07 54			07 57					07 59	08 03			08 06	
London Waterloo (East)	d	07 35	07 39		07 42	07 45	07 47			07 51			07 53	07 56		07 59						08 01	08 03		
London Charing Cross	a	07 40	07 44		07 47	07 50	07 52			07 56			07 58	08 01		08 04						08 06	08 08		

A not 3 September

Orpington, Petts Wood, Hither Green and Lewisham - London (Summary of Services)

		SE	SE	SE [1] 🍴		SE	SE	SE	SE	SE	SE	SE	SE [1]	SE		SE	SE	SE [1]	SE	SE [1]	SE	SE	SE [1]	SE	
Orpington [4]	d													07 41		07 47						07 52			
Petts Wood [4]	d													07 44		07 50						07 55			
Hither Green [4]	d											07 52			07 58					08 02					
Lewisham [4] ⇌	d		07 48			07 50	07 55				07 57			08 03			08 05								
St Johns	d		07 50								08 00														
New Cross [4] ⊖	d	07 50	07 53				07 58				08 02														
London Victoria [15] ⊖	a																08 29								
London Bridge [4] ⊖	d	09 08	08 02			08 02	08 04	08 06		08 06	08 09		08 10			08 29		08 11	08 14	08 14	08 18	08 20		08 18	
London Blackfriars [3] ⊖	a																								
London Cannon Street [4] ⊖	a	09 14	08 08				08 10	08 12			08 15							08 17		08 20	08 23	08 26			
London Waterloo (East) [4] ⊖	d			08 05		08 07			08 09	08 11		08 13	08 15	08 17					08 19				08 21	08 23	
London Charing Cross [4] ⊖	a			08 08		08 12			08 14	08 16		08 17	08 20	08 22					08 24				08 26	08 28	

		SE	SE	SE	SE	SE [1] 🍴	SE	SE	SE	SE		SE	SE [1]	SE	SE	SE	SE	SE	SE [1]	SE		SE [1]	SE	SE	SE
Orpington [4]	d	07 57														08 01	08 10							08 13	
Petts Wood [4]	d	08 00														08 04	08 13							08 16	
Hither Green [4]	d														08 12	08 17				08 22					08 28
Lewisham [4] ⇌	d			08 08	08 11		08 15								08 17	08 23		08 25							08 30
St Johns	d			08 12											08 21										08 32
New Cross [4] ⊖	d		08 04	08 14			08 18							08 20	08 23										
London Victoria [15] ⊖	a																08 50	08 49							
London Bridge [4] ⊖	d		09 18	08 22	08 22	08 24	08 26		08 26	08 28			08 30	09 30	08 30				08 32	08 34		08 34	08 39	08 40	08 42
London Blackfriars [3] ⊖	a																								
London Cannon Street [4] ⊖	a			08 28		08 30	08 32			08 35				09 36	08 36				08 38			08 41	08 44	08 46	08 48
London Waterloo (East) [4] ⊖	d	08 25	09 23		08 27			08 29	08 31			08 33	08 35			08 37				08 39					
London Charing Cross [4] ⊖	a	08 30	09 28		08 32			08 34	08 36			08 39	08 40			08 42				08 44					

		SE [1]	SE [1]	SE	SE	SE		SE	SE	SE [1]	SE	SE	SE	SE	SE	SE [1]		SE	SE [1]	SE [1]	SE	SE	SE	SE	SE
Orpington [4]	d												08 21	08 26										08 32	08 40
Petts Wood [4]	d												08 24	08 29										08 35	08 43
Hither Green [4]	d											08 32	08 37					08 42							
Lewisham [4] ⇌	d			08 31	08 35							08 37			08 46								08 48		
St Johns	d											08 40											08 50		
New Cross [4] ⊖	d				08 38						08 38	08 42										08 49	08 52		
London Victoria [15] ⊖	a													09 06	09 11										09 19
London Bridge [4] ⊖	d			08 42	08 44	08 46			08 46	08 50	09 51	08 50				08 51		08 54	08 56		08 58	10 01	08 58	09 00	
London Blackfriars [3] ⊖	a																								
London Cannon Street [4] ⊖	a				08 50	08 52					09 57	08 55				08 57			09 02			10 04	09 04	09 06	
London Waterloo (East) [4] ⊖	d	08 41	08 45	08 47				08 49	08 51	08 55			08 53					08 59		09 01	09 03				
London Charing Cross [4] ⊖	a	08 46	08 50	08 52				08 54	08 56	09 00			08 58					09 04		09 04	09 08				

		SE		SE	SE [1]	SE	SE	SE	SE	SE [1]	SE [1]	SE [1]		SE	SE	SE	SE	SE	SE	SE	SE	SE		SE	SE
Orpington [4]	d															08 43	08 47	08 52	08 55						
Petts Wood [4]	d															08 46	08 50	08 55	08 58						
Hither Green [4]	d					08 50		08 55								08 59		09 08			09 14				
Lewisham [4] ⇌	d	08 52				08 55			08 59							09 04				09 06		09 15		09 20	
St Johns	d					08 57			09 01							09 07						09 17			
New Cross [4] ⊖	d					08 59			09 03						09 04	09 09						09 19			09 19
London Victoria [15] ⊖	a																09 30		09 34	09 29					
London Bridge [4] ⊖	d	09 01		09 02	09 04	09 06		09 06	09 10	09 12	09 12	09 15		09 18	10 21	09 18		09 21			09 24	09 26		09 30	10 31
London Blackfriars [3] ⊖	a																								
London Cannon Street [4] ⊖	a			09 07	09 10	09 12			09 18	09 18					10 24	09 23						09 32			10 36
London Waterloo (East) [4] ⊖	d	09 06					09 08	09 11			09 17	09 20		09 23				09 26			09 29			09 35	
London Charing Cross [4] ⊖	a	09 12					09 13	09 16			09 22	09 25		09 28				09 31			09 34			09 40	

		SE	SE [1]	SE [1]	SE	SE	SE	SE		SE	SE	SE	SE [1]	SE	SE	SE	SE [1] 🍴	SE		SE	SE	SE	SE	SE	SE [1]
Orpington [4]	d	09 03	09 04	09 09	09 10							09 21	09 24	09 25										09 33	09 39
Petts Wood [4]	d	09 06			09 13							09 24		09 28										09 36	
Hither Green [4]	d	09 19									09 28	09 37								09 42				09 49	
Lewisham [4] ⇌	d	09 24				09 26	09 29				09 34				09 38						09 45	09 50		09 54	
St Johns	d	09 26					09 31				09 36										09 47			09 56	
New Cross [4] ⊖	d	09 28					09 33			09 33	09 38										09 49		09 49	09 58	
London Victoria [15] ⊖	a				09 49									10 03	10 00										
London Bridge [4] ⊖	d	09 34	09 23	09 27		09 35	09 39	09 38		10 51	09 45	09 49	09 41			09 42	09 44	09 51		09 52	09 55	09 58	11 01	10 04	09 55
London Blackfriars [3] ⊖	a																								
London Cannon Street [4] ⊖	a	09 40	09 29				09 45			10 54	09 51					09 48		09 57			10 00		11 06	10 08	
London Waterloo (East) [4] ⊖	d			09 32		09 40		09 43				09 54	09 46				09 49			09 57		10 03			10 00
London Charing Cross [4] ⊖	a			09 37		09 45		09 48				09 59	09 51				09 54			10 00		10 06			10 03

		SE	SE	SE		SE	SE	SE	SE	SE	SE [1]	SE	SE	SE [1] 🍴		SE	SE	SE	SE	SE	SE [1]	SE	SE	SE	
Orpington [4]	d	09 40								09 51	09 54	09 55								10 03	10 09	10 10			
Petts Wood [4]	d	09 43								09 54		09 58								10 06		10 13			
Hither Green [4]	d								09 58	10 07						10 12				10 19					
Lewisham [4] ⇌	d		09 56	09 59					10 04				10 08				10 14	10 20		10 24			10 26	10 29	
St Johns	d			10 01					10 06								10 16			10 26				10 31	
New Cross [4] ⊖	d			10 03				10 03	10 08								10 18		10 19	10 28				10 33	
London Victoria [15] ⊖	a	10 17										10 32	10 28									10 47			
London Bridge [4] ⊖	d		10 05	10 09		10 08	10 11	11 21	10 14	10 19	10 11			10 13		10 22	10 24	10 28	11 31	10 34	10 25		10 35	10 39	
London Blackfriars [3] ⊖	a																								
London Cannon Street [4] ⊖	a			10 13			10 15	11 24	10 19								10 28		11 36	10 38				10 43	
London Waterloo (East) [4] ⊖	d		10 10			10 13				10 24	10 15			10 18		10 27		10 33			10 30		10 40		
London Charing Cross [4] ⊖	a		10 13			10 16				10 27	10 19			10 22		10 30		10 36			10 33		10 43		

		SE	SE	SE	SE	SE	SE [1]	SE	SE	SE [1] 🍴		SE	SE	SE	SE	SE	SE [1]	SE	SE	SE		SE	SE	SE	SE
Orpington [4]	d					10 21	10 24	10 25								10 33	10 39	10 40							
Petts Wood [4]	d					10 24		10 28								10 36		10 43							
Hither Green [4]	d				10 28	10 37						10 42				10 49									10 58
Lewisham [4] ⇌	d				10 34				10 38				10 44	10 50		10 54			10 56	10 59					11 04
St Johns	d				10 36								10 46			10 56				11 01					11 06
New Cross [4] ⊖	d			10 33	10 38								10 48		10 49	10 58				11 03				11 03	11 08
London Victoria [15] ⊖	a							11 02	10 58									11 17							
London Bridge [4] ⊖	d	10 38	10 41	11 51	10 45	10 49	10 41			10 43		10 52	10 54	10 58	12 01	11 04	10 55		11 05	11 09		11 08	11 11	12 21	11 15
London Blackfriars [3] ⊖	a																								
London Cannon Street [4] ⊖	a		10 45	11 54	10 50								10 58		12 04	11 08				11 13			11 15	12 24	11 19
London Waterloo (East) [4] ⊖	d	10 43				10 54	10 45			10 49		10 57		11 03			11 00		11 10			11 13			
London Charing Cross [4] ⊖	a	10 46				10 57	10 49			10 52		11 00		11 06			11 03		11 13			11 16			

		SE	SE [1]	SE	SE	SE [1] 🍴		SE	SE	SE	SE	SE	SE [1]	SE	SE	SE		SE	SE	SE	SE	SE	SE [1]	SE	SE
Orpington [4]	d	10 51	10 54	10 55								11 03	11 09	11 10								11 21	11 24	11 25	
Petts Wood [4]	d	10 54		10 58								11 06		11 13								11 24		11 28	
Hither Green [4]	d	11 07						11 12				11 19									11 28	11 37			
Lewisham [4] ⇌	d				11 08				11 14	11 20		11 24			11 26	11 29					11 34				11 38
St Johns	d								11 16			11 26				11 31					11 36				
New Cross [4] ⊖	d								11 18		11 19	11 28				11 33				11 33	11 38				
London Victoria [15] ⊖	a			11 32	11 28									11 47										12 02	11 58
London Bridge [4] ⊖	d	11 19	11 11			11 13		11 22	11 24	11 28	12 31	11 34	11 25		11 35	11 39		11 38	11 41	12 51	11 45	11 49	11 41		
London Blackfriars [3] ⊖	a																								
London Cannon Street [4] ⊖	a								11 28		12 36	11 38				11 43			11 45	12 54	11 49				
London Waterloo (East) [4] ⊖	d	11 24	11 15			11 19		11 27		11 33			11 30		11 40			11 43				11 54	11 45		
London Charing Cross [4] ⊖	a	11 27	11 19			11 22		11 30		11 36			11 33		11 43			11 46				11 57	11 49		

		SE [1] 🍴		SE	SE	SE	SE		SE	SE	SE [1]		SE	SE	SE	SE	SE	SE	SE	SE	SE [1]		SE	SE
Orpington [4]	d							and at the same minutes past each hour until		14 33	14 39		14 40							14 51	14 54		14 55	
Petts Wood [4]	d									14 36			14 43							14 54			14 58	
Hither Green [4]	d			11 42						14 49									14 58	15 07				
Lewisham [4] ⇌	d				11 44	11 50				14 54				14 56	14 59				15 04					15 08
St Johns	d				11 46					14 56					15 01				15 06					
New Cross [4] ⊖	d				11 48		11 49		14 49	14 58					15 03			15 03	15 08					
London Victoria [15] ⊖	a												15 17										15 32	15 28
London Bridge [4] ⊖	d	11 43		11 52	11 54	11 58	13 01		16 01	15 04	14 55			15 05	15 09	15 08	15 11	16 21	15 15	15 19	15 11			
London Blackfriars [3] ⊖	a																							
London Cannon Street [4] ⊖	a				11 58		13 06		16 06	15 08					15 13		15 15	16 24	15 19					
London Waterloo (East) [4] ⊖	d	11 49		11 57		12 03					15 00			15 10		15 13				15 24	15 15			
London Charing Cross [4] ⊖	a	11 52		12 00		12 06					15 03			15 13		15 16				15 27	15 19			

		SE [1] 🍴	SE	SE	SE	SE	SE	SE [1]		SE	SE	SE	SE	SE	SE	SE	SE	SE [1]		SE	SE	SE [1] 🍴	SE	SE	SE
Orpington [4]	d						15 03	15 09		15 10							15 21	15 24		15 25					
Petts Wood [4]	d						15 06			15 13							15 24			15 28					
Hither Green [4]	d		15 12				15 19									15 28	15 37						15 42		
Lewisham [4] ⇌	d			15 14	15 20		15 24				15 26	15 29				15 34					15 38			15 44	15 50
St Johns	d			15 16			15 26					15 31				15 36								15 46	
New Cross [4] ⊖	d			15 18		15 19	15 28					15 33			15 33	15 38								15 48	
London Victoria [15] ⊖	a									15 47										16 02	15 58				
London Bridge [4] ⊖	d	15 13	15 22	15 24	15 28	16 31	15 34	15 25			15 35	15 39	15 38	15 41	16 51	15 45	15 50	15 41				15 43	15 53	15 54	15 58
London Blackfriars [3] ⊖	a																								
London Cannon Street [4] ⊖	a			15 28		16 36	15 38					15 43		15 45	16 54	15 49								15 58	
London Waterloo (East) [4] ⊖	d	15 19	15 27		15 33			15 30			15 40		15 43				15 55	15 46				15 49	15 58		16 03
London Charing Cross [4] ⊖	a	15 22	15 30		15 36			15 33			15 43		15 46				15 58	15 49				15 52	16 01		16 06

Table 199

Mondays to Fridays
29 August to 7 September

Orpington, Petts Wood, Hither Green and Lewisham - London (Summary of Services)

		SE	SE	SE ■	SE	SE	SE	SE	SE	SE	SE	SE	SE ■	SE	SE	SE ■ H	SE	SE	SE	SE	SE	SE ■
Orpington	d		15 33	15 39	15 40							15 51	15 54	15 55							16 03	16 08
Petts Wood	d		15 36		15 43							15 54		15 58							16 06	
Hither Green	d		15 49								15 58	16 07					16 12				16 19	
Lewisham	d		15 54			15 56	15 59				16 04				16 08			16 14	16 20		16 24	
St Johns	d		15 56				16 01				16 06							16 16			16 26	
New Cross	d	15 49	15 58				16 03			16 03	16 08							16 18		16 20	16 28	
London Victoria	a				16 17									16 32	16 28							
London Bridge	d	17 01	16 04	15 55		16 05	16 09	16 09	16 12	17 22	16 15	16 19	16 12			16 14	16 22	16 24	16 29	17 31	16 34	16 25
London Blackfriars	a																					
London Cannon Street	a	17 05	16 08				16 13		16 16	17 26	16 19							16 28		17 36	16 38	
London Waterloo (East)	d			16 00		16 10		16 14				16 25	16 17			16 20	16 28		16 34			16 30
London Charing Cross	a			16 03		16 13		16 18				16 28	16 20			16 24	16 31		16 37			16 33

		SE	SE	SE	SE	SE	SE	SE	SE	SE	SE ■	SE	SE	SE ■ H	SE	SE	SE	SE ■	SE	SE	SE	SE	SE
Orpington	d	16 10								16 21	16 25	16 25					16 33	16 39	16 40				
Petts Wood	d	16 13								16 24		16 28					16 36		16 43				
Hither Green	d								16 28	16 37					16 42		16 50					16 50	16 56
Lewisham	d			16 26		16 29			16 34				16 38			16 44				16 50			
St Johns	d					16 31			16 36							16 46						16 54	
New Cross	d					16 33		16 34	16 38							16 48					16 49	16 56	
London Victoria	a	16 47										17 04	17 01						17 20				
London Bridge	d		16 32	16 35	16 38	16 39	16 42	17 52	16 45	16 49	16 42			16 46	16 52	16 54	17 02	16 56		16 59	18 03	17 04	17 06
London Blackfriars	a																						
London Cannon Street	a					16 43	16 46	17 56	16 49							16 58					18 07	17 09	
London Waterloo (East)	d		16 38	16 40	16 43					16 55	16 49			16 53	16 57		17 07	17 01		17 04			17 11
London Charing Cross	a		16 42	16 44	16 46					16 58	16 52			16 56	17 00		17 10	17 04		17 07			17 15

		SE	SE	SE	SE	SE	SE	SE ■	SE	SE	SE	SE ■ H	SE	SE	SE	SE	SE	SE ■	SE	SE	SE	SE	SE
Orpington	d						16 51	16 54	16 55								17 03	17 09	17 10	17 13			
Petts Wood	d						16 54		16 58								17 06		17 13				
Hither Green	d					17 00	17 09						17 07				17 19						
Lewisham	d	16 56	16 59			17 05				17 08					17 14	17 20	17 24				17 27		17 30
St Johns	d		17 01			17 09									17 16		17 26						
New Cross	d		17 03		17 08	17 11								17 14	17 18		17 28						17 33
London Victoria	a								17 33	17 28									17 48				
London Bridge	d	17 07	17 09	17 09	18 21	17 19		17 12			17 13	17 18	17 22	18 31	17 25	17 30	17 34	17 28			17 36	17 38	17 39
London Blackfriars	a																						
London Cannon Street	a	17 11	17 15		18 24	17 24					17 17			18 35	17 29		17 38	17 32					17 44
London Waterloo (East)	d			17 14			17 25	17 16				17 23	17 29			17 35				17 37	17 41	17 43	
London Charing Cross	a			17 18			17 29	17 20				17 26	17 33			17 38				17 40	17 44	17 46	

		SE	SE	SE	SE	SE ■	SE	SE ■	SE	SE ■ H	SE	SE	SE	SE	SE	SE	SE	SE	SE ■	SE	SE	SE
Orpington	d				17 20	17 24	17 24	17 34										17 37	17 39	17 40		
Petts Wood	d				17 24		17 28	17 37										17 40		17 43		
Hither Green	d			17 28	17 38											17 41	17 42	17 53				17 58
Lewisham	d			17 35					17 38		17 44	17 50	17 53	17 56	17 59	18 29						18 05
St Johns	d			17 37							17 46							17 57				18 07
New Cross	d		17 36	17 39							17 48				18 02	18 32		17 59				18 09
London Victoria	a						18 03		17 59											18 18		
London Bridge	d	17 42	18 51	17 45	17 49	17 42				17 45	17 55	18 00	19 01	18 04	18 09	18 38	17 54	18 06	17 58		18 07	18 16
London Blackfriars	a							18 09														
London Cannon Street	a	17 46	18 54	17 49							17 59	18 04	19 06		18 13	18 42		18 11				18 20
London Waterloo (East)	d				17 54	17 47				17 50				18 09			17 59		18 03		18 13	
London Charing Cross	a				17 57	17 50				17 53				18 12			18 03		18 06		18 16	

		SE	SE	SE	SE	SE	SE	SE ■	SE	SE	SE ■ H	SE	SE	SE ■	SE	SE	SE	SE	SE	SE	SE	SE	SE
Orpington	d						17 50	17 54	17 55				18 03	18 09	18 09								
Petts Wood	d						17 54		17 58				18 06		18 12								
Hither Green	d					18 03	18 07					18 12	18 19			18 21				18 28			
Lewisham	d	18 08		18 14	18 20	18 59							18 24				18 26			18 35	18 38	18 45	18 50
St Johns	d			18 16									18 26							18 37		18 47	
New Cross	d		18 14	18 18		19 03							18 28						18 35	18 39		18 49	
London Victoria	a	18 29							18 33						18 48						18 58		
London Bridge	d		19 28	18 24	18 28	19 09	18 19	18 10		18 13	18 16	18 23	18 34	18 25		18 33	18 36	18 38	19 59	18 46		18 55	18 58
London Blackfriars	a																						
London Cannon Street	a		19 33	18 29		19 13				18 17			18 38						20 03	18 51		18 59	
London Waterloo (East)	d				18 33		18 24	18 15			18 21	18 28		18 30		18 38	18 42	18 45					19 03
London Charing Cross	a				18 37		18 27	18 18			18 25	18 31		18 35		18 41	18 45	18 48					19 06

Table 199

Mondays to Fridays
29 August to 7 September

Orpington, Petts Wood, Hither Green and Lewisham - London (Summary of Services)

		SE	SE	SE ■	SE	SE ■ H	SE	SE	SE ■	SE	SE	SE	SE	SE	SE	SE	SE ■	SE	SE	SE	SE ■ H	SE
Orpington	d		18 21	18 24	18 25					18 33	18 40					18 50	18 54	18 55				
Petts Wood	d		18 24		18 28					18 36	18 43					18 54		18 58				
Hither Green	d	18 35	18 37					18 42		18 49					18 59	19 07						19 12
Lewisham	d	19 29								18 54		18 56			19 05				19 08			
St Johns	d									18 56					19 07							
New Cross	d	19 32								18 58				19 00	19 09							
London Victoria	a				19 03						19 17							19 32	19 28			
London Bridge	d	19 38	18 49	18 41		18 43	18 43	18 53	18 55	19 05		19 05	19 08	20 28	19 15	19 19	19 10			19 12	19 13	19 22
London Blackfriars	a																					
London Cannon Street	a	19 43					18 47			19 10				20 31	19 20					19 16		
London Waterloo (East)	d		18 54	18 46		18 49		18 58	19 00			19 10	19 13			19 24	19 15				19 18	19 27
London Charing Cross	a		18 57	18 49		18 52		19 01	19 04			19 13	19 16			19 27	19 18				19 21	19 30

		SE	SE	SE	SE ■	SE	SE	SE	SE	SE	SE	SE	SE	SE ■	SE	SE ■ H	SE ■	SE	SE	SE	SE	SE	SE
Orpington	d			19 03	19 08	19 10							19 21	19 24	19 25		19 39	19 40					
Petts Wood	d			19 06		19 13							19 24		19 28			19 43					
Hither Green	d			19 19							19 28		19 37						19 42				
Lewisham	d	19 14	19 20	19 24			19 26	19 29			19 34	19 38	19 43						19 48	19 52	19 56		20 08
St Johns	d	19 16		19 26							19 36	19 40											20 10
New Cross	d	19 18		19 28				19 32			19 38	19 42							19 51	19 56			20 12
London Victoria	a					19 47									20 02			20 17					
London Bridge	d	19 24	19 28	19 34	19 25		19 35	19 38	19 38	19 41	19 45	19 49	19 52	19 41		19 43	19 55		19 58	20 04	20 06	20 11	20 19
London Blackfriars	a																						
London Cannon Street	a	19 28		19 38				19 43		19 45	19 49											20 15	
London Waterloo (East)	d		19 33		19 30		19 40		19 43			19 54	19 57	19 46		19 49	20 00		20 03	20 09	20 11		20 24
London Charing Cross	a		19 36		19 33		19 43		19 46			19 57	20 00	19 49		19 52	20 03		20 06	20 12	20 14		20 27

		SE	SE ■	SE	SE ■	SE ■	SE	SE	SE	SE	SE	SE	SE ■	SE	SE	SE ■	SE	SE	SE	SE	SE	SE ■	SE
Orpington	d	19 51	19 54	19 55		20 09	20 10					20 21	20 24	20 40							20 51	20 53	
Petts Wood	d	19 54		19 58			20 13					20 24		20 43							20 54		
Hither Green	d	20 07						20 12				20 38					20 42				21 07		
Lewisham	d	20 13						20 18	20 22	20 26	20 38	20 43					20 48	20 53	20 56	21 08	21 13		
St Johns	d										20 40									21 10			
New Cross	d							20 21	20 26		20 42						20 51	20 56		21 12			
London Victoria	a			20 32			20 47							21 17									
London Bridge	d	20 22	20 11		20 13	20 25		20 28	20 34	20 36	20 49	20 52	20 40		20 41	20 43	20 58	21 04	21 06	21 19	21 22	21 09	21 11
London Blackfriars	a																						
London Cannon Street	a														20 45								
London Waterloo (East)	d	20 27	20 16		20 19	20 30		20 33	20 39	20 41	20 54	20 57	20 45			20 48	21 03	21 09	21 11	21 24	21 27	21 14	21 16
London Charing Cross	a	20 30	20 19		20 22	20 33		20 36	20 42	20 44	20 57	21 00	20 48			20 51	21 06	21 12	21 14	21 27	21 30	21 18	21 19

		SE ■	SE ■	SE	SE	SE	SE	SE	SE	SE ■	SE	SE	SE ■	SE	SE	SE	SE	SE	SE ■	SE	SE ■	SE ■
Orpington	d		21 09	21 10					21 21	21 23	21 40							21 51	21 53			22 09
Petts Wood	d			21 13					21 24		21 43							21 54				
Hither Green	d				21 12				21 37					21 42				22 07				
Lewisham	d				21 18	21 23	21 26	21 38	21 43					21 48	21 53	21 56	22 08	22 13				
St Johns	d							21 40									22 10					
New Cross	d				21 21	21 26		21 42						21 51	21 56		22 12					
London Victoria	a			21 47							22 17											
London Bridge	d	21 14	21 25		21 28	21 34	21 36	21 49	21 52	21 39		21 41	21 44	21 58	22 02	22 05	22 19	22 22	22 09	22 11	22 14	22 25
London Blackfriars	a																					
London Cannon Street	a																					
London Waterloo (East)	d	21 19	21 30		21 33	21 39	21 41	21 54	21 57	21 44		21 46	21 49	22 03	22 07	22 10	22 24	22 27	22 14	22 16	22 19	22 30
London Charing Cross	a	21 22	21 33		21 36	21 42	21 44	21 57	22 00	21 48		21 49	21 52	22 06	22 10	22 13	22 27	22 30	22 18	22 19	22 22	22 33

		SE	SE	SE	SE	SE	SE	SE ■	SE	SE	SE ■	SE	SE	SE	SE	SE	SE ■	SE	SE ■	SE ■	SE	SE	SE
Orpington	d	22 10					22 21	22 23	22 40							22 51	22 53			23 09	23 10		
Petts Wood	d	22 13					22 24		22 43							22 54					23 13		
Hither Green	d		22 12				22 37					22 42				23 07						23 12	
Lewisham	d		22 18	22 23	22 26	22 38	22 43					22 48	22 53	22 56	23 08	23 13						23 18	23 23
St Johns	d					22 40									23 10								
New Cross	d		22 21	22 26		22 42						22 51	22 56		23 12							23 21	23 26
London Victoria	a	22 47							23 17												23 47		
London Bridge	d		22 28	22 32	22 35	22 49	22 52	22 39		22 41	22 44	22 58	23 02	23 05	23 19	23 22	23 09	23 11	23 14	23 25		23 28	23 32
London Blackfriars	a																						
London Cannon Street	a																						
London Waterloo (East)	d		22 33	22 37	22 40	22 54	22 57	22 44		22 46	22 49	23 03	23 07	23 10	23 24	23 27	23 14	23 16	23 19	23 30		23 33	23 37
London Charing Cross	a		22 36	22 40	22 43	22 57	23 00	22 48		22 49	22 52	23 06	23 10	23 13	23 27	23 30	23 18	23 19	23 22	23 33		23 36	23 40

29 August to 7 September

Orpington, Petts Wood, Hither Green and Lewisham - London (Summary of Services)

	SE	SE	SE	SE	SE 1
Orpington 4 d				23 21	23 37
Petts Wood 4 d				23 24	
Hither Green 4 d				23 37	
Lewisham 4 ⇌ d	23 26		23 38	23 43	
St Johns d			23 40		
New Cross 4 ⊖ d			23 42		
London Victoria 15 ⊖ a					
London Bridge 4 ⊖ d	23 35	23 41	23 49	23 52	23 55
London Blackfriars 3 ⊖ a					
London Cannon Street 4 ⊖ a					
London Waterloo (East) 4 ⊖ d	23 40	23 46	23 54	23 57	23 59
London Charing Cross 4 ⊖ a	23 43	23 49	23 57	00 01	00 03

Saturdays

until 21 July, 18 Aug and from 15 Sep

	SE	SE 1	SE A	SE	SE	SE	SE	SE	SE	SE	SE	SE	SE	SE	SE	SE	SE	SE 1	SE	SE	SE	SE
Orpington 4 d	23p21	23p37	05 44								05 51	06 10					06 21	06 24	06 25	06 40		
Petts Wood 4 d	23p24		05 47								05 54	06 13					06 24		06 28	06 43		
Hither Green 4 d	23p37					05 42					06 07		06 12				06 37					06 42
Lewisham 4 ⇌ d	23p43				05 39	05 48	05 50	05 56	06 02		06 13		06 18	06 20	06 26	06 32	06 43					06 48
St Johns d					05 41				06 04							06 34						
New Cross 4 ⊖ d					05 43	05 51			06 06				06 21			06 36						06 51
London Victoria 15 ⊖ a			06 26									06 47							07 02	07 17		
London Bridge 4 ⊖ d	23p52	23p55		05 45	05 49	05 57	05 59	06 05	06 12	06 15	06 21		06 27	06 29	06 35	06 42	06 51	06 39			06 45	06 57
London Blackfriars 3 ⊖ a																						
London Cannon Street 4 ⊖ a																						
London Waterloo (East) 4 ⊖ d	23p57	23p59		05 50	05 53	06 02	06 04	06 10	06 17	06 20	06 26		06 32	06 34	06 40	06 47	06 56	06 44			06 50	07 02
London Charing Cross 4 ⊖ a	00 01	00 03		05 53	05 56	06 05	06 07	06 13	06 20	06 25	06 29		06 35	06 37	06 43	06 50	06 59	06 47			06 55	07 05

	SE	SE	SE	SE B	SE A	SE	SE 1	SE	SE	SE 1	SE	SE	SE	SE	SE	SE 1	SE	SE	SE	SE B	SE A	SE
Orpington 4 d						06 51	06 54	06 55		07 09	07 10				07 21	07 24	07 25					
Petts Wood 4 d						06 54		06 58			07 13				07 24		07 28					
Hither Green 4 d						07 07						07 12			07 37							07 42
Lewisham 4 ⇌ d	06 50	06 56	07 02	07 08	07 08	07 13						07 18	07 20	07 26					07 32	07 38	07 38	
St Johns d			07 04																07 34			
New Cross 4 ⊖ d			07 06									07 21							07 36			
London Victoria 15 ⊖ a				07 28	07 30			07 32			07 47						08 02			07 58	08 00	
London Bridge 4 ⊖ d	06 59	07 05	07 12			07 21	07 09		07 15	07 24		07 27	07 29	07 35	07 49	07 39		07 41	07 42			07 52
London Blackfriars 3 ⊖ a																						
London Cannon Street 4 ⊖ a																		07 45				
London Waterloo (East) 4 ⊖ d	07 04	07 10	07 17			07 26	07 14		07 20	07 29		07 32	07 34	07 40	07 54	07 44			07 47			07 57
London Charing Cross 4 ⊖ a	07 07	07 13	07 20			07 29	07 17		07 25	07 33		07 35	07 40	07 43	07 57	07 48			07 50			08 00

	SE		SE	SE 1	SE	SE	SE	SE	SE	SE	SE	SE	SE 1	SE	SE B	SE A	SE 1	SE	SE	SE	SE	SE
Orpington 4 d			07 33	07 39	07 40							07 51	07 54	07 55								
Petts Wood 4 d			07 36		07 43							07 54		07 58								
Hither Green 4 d			07 49								07 58	08 07							08 12			
Lewisham 4 ⇌ d	07 50		07 54				07 56	07 59	07 59		08 04				08 08	08 08				08 14	08 20	
St Johns d			07 56						08 01		08 06									08 16		
New Cross 4 ⊖ d			07 58						08 03		08 08									08 18		08 19
London Victoria 15 ⊖ a					08 17									08 32	08 28	08 30						
London Bridge 4 ⊖ d	07 58		08 04	07 55		08 01	08 05	08 08	08 09	08 11	08 15	08 19	08 11				08 14	08 21	08 22	08 24	08 28	09 31
London Blackfriars 3 ⊖ a																						
London Cannon Street 4 ⊖ a			08 08			08 04			08 13	08 15	08 19							08 24		08 28		09 34
London Waterloo (East) 4 ⊖ d	08 03			08 00			08 10	08 13				08 24	08 15				08 19		08 27		08 33	
London Charing Cross 4 ⊖ a	08 06			08 03			08 13	08 16				08 27	08 19				08 22		08 30		08 36	

	SE	SE 1	SE	SE	SE	SE	SE	SE	SE	SE	SE	SE 1	SE	SE B	SE A	SE 1	SE	SE	SE	SE	SE	SE
Orpington 4 d	08 03	08 09	08 10								08 21	08 24	08 25									08 33
Petts Wood 4 d	08 06		08 13								08 24		08 28									08 36
Hither Green 4 d	08 19									08 28	08 37							08 42				08 49
Lewisham 4 ⇌ d	08 24				08 26	08 29				08 34				08 38	08 38				08 44	08 50		08 54
St Johns d	08 26					08 31				08 36									08 46			08 56
New Cross 4 ⊖ d	08 28					08 33			08 33	08 38									08 48		08 49	08 58
London Victoria 15 ⊖ a			08 47										09 02	08 58	09 00							
London Bridge 4 ⊖ d	08 34	08 25		08 31	08 35	08 39	08 38	08 41	09 51	08 45	08 49	08 41				08 44	08 51	08 52	08 54	08 58	10 01	09 04
London Blackfriars 3 ⊖ a																						
London Cannon Street 4 ⊖ a	08 38			08 34		08 43		08 45	09 54	08 49							08 54		08 58		10 04	09 08
London Waterloo (East) 4 ⊖ d		08 30			08 40		08 43				08 54	08 45				08 49		08 57		09 03		
London Charing Cross 4 ⊖ a		08 33			08 43		08 46				08 57	08 49				08 52		09 00		09 06		

A 19 May

B not 19 May

until 21 July, 18 Aug and from 15 Sep

Orpington, Petts Wood, Hither Green and Lewisham - London (Summary of Services)

	SE 1	SE	SE	SE	SE	SE	SE	SE	SE	SE	SE 1	SE	SE A	SE B	SE 1	SE	SE	SE	SE	SE	SE
Orpington 4 d	08 39	08 40								08 51	08 54	08 55									09 03
Petts Wood 4 d		08 43								08 54		08 58									09 06
Hither Green 4 d									08 58	09 07							09 12				09 19
Lewisham 4 ⇌ d				08 56	08 59				09 04				09 08	09 08				09 14	09 20		09 24
St Johns d					09 01				09 06									09 16			09 26
New Cross 4 ⊖ d					09 03			09 03	09 08									09 18		09 19	09 28
London Victoria 15 ⊖ a		09 17										09 32	09 28	09 30							
London Bridge 4 ⊖ d	08 55		09 01	09 05	09 09	09 08	09 11	10 21	09 15	09 19	09 11				09 14	09 21	09 22	09 24	09 28	10 31	09 34
London Blackfriars 3 ⊖ a																					
London Cannon Street 4 ⊖ a			09 04		09 13		09 15	10 24	09 19							09 24		09 28		10 34	09 38
London Waterloo (East) 4 ⊖ d	09 00			09 10		09 13				09 24	09 15				09 19		09 27		09 33		
London Charing Cross 4 ⊖ a	09 03			09 13		09 16				09 27	09 19				09 22		09 30		09 36		

	SE 1	SE	SE	SE	SE	SE	SE	SE	SE	SE 1	SE	SE A	SE B	SE 1 ⊼	SE	SE	SE	SE	SE	SE 1	SE	SE
Orpington 4 d	09 09	09 10							09 21	09 24	09 25								09 33	09 39	09 40	
Petts Wood 4 d		09 13							09 24		09 28								09 36		09 43	
Hither Green 4 d								09 28	09 37						09 42				09 49			
Lewisham 4 ⇌ d			09 26	09 29				09 34				09 38	09 38			09 44	09 50		09 54			09 56
St Johns d				09 31				09 36								09 46			09 56			
New Cross 4 ⊖ d				09 33			09 33	09 38								09 48		09 49	09 58			
London Victoria 15 ⊖ a		09 47									10 02	09 58	10 00								10 17	
London Bridge 4 ⊖ d	09 25		09 35	09 39	09 38	09 41	10 51	09 45	09 49	09 41				09 44	09 52	09 54	09 58	11 01	10 04	09 55		10 05
London Blackfriars 3 ⊖ a																						
London Cannon Street 4 ⊖ a				09 43		09 45	10 54	09 49								09 58		11 04	10 08			
London Waterloo (East) 4 ⊖ d	09 30		09 40		09 43				09 54	09 45				09 49	09 57		10 03			10 00		10 10
London Charing Cross 4 ⊖ a	09 33		09 43		09 46				09 57	09 49				09 52	10 00		10 06			10 03		10 13

	SE	SE	SE	SE	SE	SE	SE 1	SE	SE A	SE B	SE 1 ⊼		SE 1 ⊼		SE	SE	SE	SE	SE	SE 1	SE	SE
Orpington 4 d						09 51	09 54	09 55				and at the same minutes past each hour until							17 03	17 09	17 10	
Petts Wood 4 d						09 54		09 58											17 06		17 13	
Hither Green 4 d					09 58	10 07									17 12				17 19			
Lewisham 4 ⇌ d	09 59				10 04				10 08	10 08						17 14	17 20		17 24			17 26
St Johns d	10 01				10 06											17 16			17 26			
New Cross 4 ⊖ d	10 03			10 03	10 08											17 18		17 19	17 28			
London Victoria 15 ⊖ a								10 32	10 28	10 30											17 47	
London Bridge 4 ⊖ d	10 09	10 08	10 11	11 21	10 15	10 19	10 11				10 14		17 14		17 22	17 24	17 28	18 31	17 34	17 25		17 35
London Blackfriars 3 ⊖ a																						
London Cannon Street 4 ⊖ a	10 13		10 15	11 24	10 19											17 28		18 34	17 38			
London Waterloo (East) 4 ⊖ d		10 13				10 24	10 15				10 19		17 19		17 27		17 33			17 30		17 40
London Charing Cross 4 ⊖ a		10 16				10 27	10 19				10 22		17 22		17 30		17 36			17 33		17 43

	SE	SE	SE	SE	SE	SE	SE 1	SE	SE A	SE B	SE 1 ⊼	SE	SE	SE	SE	SE	SE 1	SE	SE	SE	SE
Orpington 4 d						17 21	17 24	17 25								17 33	17 39	17 40			
Petts Wood 4 d						17 24		17 28								17 36		17 43			
Hither Green 4 d					17 28	17 37						17 42				17 49					
Lewisham 4 ⇌ d	17 29				17 34				17 38	17 38			17 44	17 50		17 54			17 56	17 59	
St Johns d	17 31				17 36								17 46			17 56				18 01	
New Cross 4 ⊖ d	17 33			17 33	17 38								17 48		17 49	17 58				18 03	
London Victoria 15 ⊖ a								18 02	17 58	18 00								18 17			
London Bridge 4 ⊖ d	17 39	17 38	17 41	18 51	17 45	17 49	17 41				17 44	17 52	17 54	17 58	19 01	18 04	17 55		18 05	18 09	18 08
London Blackfriars 3 ⊖ a																					
London Cannon Street 4 ⊖ a	17 43		17 45	18 54	17 49								17 58		19 04	18 08				18 13	
London Waterloo (East) 4 ⊖ d		17 43				17 54	17 45				17 49	17 57		18 03			18 00		18 10		18 13
London Charing Cross 4 ⊖ a		17 46				17 57	17 49				17 52	18 00		18 06			18 03		18 13		18 16

	SE	SE	SE	SE 1	SE	SE A	SE B	SE 1 ⊼	SE	SE	SE	SE	SE	SE 1	SE	SE	SE	SE	SE	SE	SE	SE 1
Orpington 4 d			17 51	17 54	17 55								18 03	18 09	18 10						18 21	18 24
Petts Wood 4 d			17 54		17 58								18 06		18 13						18 24	
Hither Green 4 d		17 58	18 07						18 12				18 19							18 28	18 37	
Lewisham 4 ⇌ d		18 04				18 08	18 08			18 14	18 20		18 24			18 26	18 29			18 34		
St Johns d		18 06								18 16			18 26				18 31			18 36		
New Cross 4 ⊖ d		18 08								18 18		18 19	18 28				18 33			18 38		
London Victoria 15 ⊖ a					18 32	18 28	18 30								18 47							
London Bridge 4 ⊖ d	18 11	18 15	18 19	18 11				18 14	18 22	18 24	18 28	19a30	18 34	18 25		18 35	18 39	18 38	18 41	18 45	18 49	18 41
London Blackfriars 3 ⊖ a																						
London Cannon Street 4 ⊖ a	18 15	18 19								18 28			18 38				18 43		18 45	18 49		
London Waterloo (East) 4 ⊖ d			18 24	18 15				18 19	18 27		18 33			18 30		18 40		18 43			18 54	18 45
London Charing Cross 4 ⊖ a			18 27	18 19				18 22	18 30		18 36			18 33		18 43		18 46			18 57	18 49

A not 19 May

B 19 May

Table 199

Saturdays

until 21 July, 18 Aug and from 15 Sep

Orpington, Petts Wood, Hither Green and Lewisham - London (Summary of Services)

	SE	SE A	SE B	SE ■ ⊼	SE	SE	SE	SE	SE	SE ■	SE	SE	SE	SE	SE	SE	SE A	SE B	SE	SE ■	SE
Orpington d	18 25								18 33	18 39	18 40								18 51	18 54	18 55
Petts Wood d	18 28								18 36		18 43								18 54		18 58
Hither Green d					18 42				18 49							18 58			19 07		
Lewisham d		18 38	18 38			18 44	18 50		18 54			18 56	18 59			19 04	19 08	19 08	19 12		
St Johns d						18 46			18 56				19 01			19 06					
New Cross ⊖ d						18 48		18 49	18 58				19 03			19 08					
London Victoria ⊖ a	19 02	18 58	19 00								19 17						19 28	19 30			19 32
London Bridge ⊖ d				18 44	18 52	18 54	18 58	20a00	19 04	18 55		19 05	19 09	19 08	19 11	19 15			19 21	19 11	
London Blackfriars ⊖ a																					
London Cannon Street ⊖ a						18 58			19 08				19 13		19 15	19 19					
London Waterloo (East) ⊖ d				18 49	18 57		19 03			19 00		19 10		19 13					19 26	19 15	
London Charing Cross ⊖ a				18 52	19 00		19 06			19 03		19 13		19 16					19 29	19 19	

	SE ■ ⊼	SE ■	SE	SE	SE	SE	SE	SE	SE	SE	SE	SE	SE ■ ⊼	SE ■	SE	SE	SE	SE	SE	SE	SE	SE
Orpington d		19 09	19 10								19 21	19 25	19 28	19 39	19 40						19 51	19 55
Petts Wood d			19 13								19 24	19 28			19 43						19 54	19 58
Hither Green d					19 12						19 37					19 42					20 07	
Lewisham d				19 14	19 18		19 20	19 26		19 38	19 43					19 48	19 53	19 56		20 08	20 13	
St Johns d				19 16						19 40										20 10		
New Cross ⊖ d				19 18		19 19	19 23			19 42						19 51	19 56			20 12		
London Victoria ⊖ a			19 47									20 02			20 17							20 32
London Bridge ⊖ d	19 14	19 25		19a24	19 28	20a30	19 34	19 37	19 41	19 49	19 52		19 44	19 55		19 58	20 04	20 06	20 11	20 19	20 22	
London Blackfriars ⊖ a																						
London Cannon Street ⊖ a																						
London Waterloo (East) ⊖ d	19 19	19 30			19 32		19 39	19 42	19 46	19 54	19 57		19 48	20 00		20 04	20 09	20 11	20 16	20 24	20 27	
London Charing Cross ⊖ a	19 22	19 33			19 35		19 42	19 45	19 49	19 58	20 00		19 51	20 03		20 07	20 12	20 14	20 19	20 28	20 30	

	SE ■	SE ■	SE	SE	SE	SE	SE	SE	SE	SE ■	SE ■	SE	SE	SE	SE	SE	SE	SE	SE ■	SE ■	SE	SE
Orpington d	19 58	20 09	20 10						20 21	20 28	20 39	20 40						20 51	20 58	21 09	21 10	
Petts Wood d			20 13						20 24			20 43						20 54			21 13	
Hither Green d				20 12					20 37				20 42					21 07				21 12
Lewisham d				20 18	20 23	20 26		20 38	20 43				20 48	20 53	20 56		21 08	21 13				21 18
St Johns d								20 40									21 10					
New Cross ⊖ d				20 21	20 26			20 42					20 51	20 56			21 12					21 21
London Victoria ⊖ a			20 47									21 17									21 47	
London Bridge ⊖ d	20 14	20 25		20 28	20 34	20 36	20 41	20 49	20 52	20 44	20 55		20 58	21 04	21 06	21 11	21 19	21 22	21 14	21 25		21 28
London Blackfriars ⊖ a																						
London Cannon Street ⊖ a																						
London Waterloo (East) ⊖ d	20 18	20 30		20 34	20 39	20 41	20 46	20 54	20 57	20 48	21 00		21 04	21 09	21 11	21 16	21 24	21 27	21 18	21 30		21 34
London Charing Cross ⊖ a	20 21	20 33		20 37	20 42	20 44	20 49	20 58	21 00	20 51	21 03		21 07	21 12	21 14	21 19	21 28	21 30	21 21	21 33		21 37

	SE	SE	SE	SE	SE	SE ■	SE ■	SE	SE	SE	SE	SE	SE	SE	SE ■	SE ■	SE	SE	SE	SE	SE
Orpington d					21 21	21 28	21 39	21 40						21 51	21 58	22 09	22 10				
Petts Wood d					21 24			21 43						21 54			22 13				
Hither Green d					21 37				21 42					22 07				22 12			
Lewisham d	21 23	21 26		21 38	21 43				21 48	21 53	21 56		22 08	22 13				22 18	22 23	22 26	
St Johns d				21 40									22 10								
New Cross ⊖ d	21 26			21 42					21 51	21 56			22 12					22 21	22 26		
London Victoria ⊖ a								22 17									22 47				
London Bridge ⊖ d	21 34	21 36	21 41	21 49	21 52	21 44	21 55		21 58	22 02	22 05	22 11	22 19	22 22	22 14	22 25		22 28	22 32	22 35	22 41
London Blackfriars ⊖ a																					
London Cannon Street ⊖ a																					
London Waterloo (East) ⊖ d	21 39	21 41	21 46	21 54	21 57	21 48	22 00		22 04	22 07	22 10	22 16	22 24	22 27	22 18	22 30		22 34	22 37	22 40	22 46
London Charing Cross ⊖ a	21 42	21 44	21 49	21 58	22 00	21 51	22 03		22 07	22 10	22 13	22 19	22 28	22 30	22 21	22 33		22 37	22 40	22 43	22 49

	SE	SE	SE ■	SE ■	SE	SE	SE	SE	SE	SE	SE	SE ■	SE ■	SE	SE	SE	SE	SE	SE	SE	SE ■
Orpington d		22 21	22 28	22 39	22 40						22 51	22 58	23 09	23 10						23 21	23 37
Petts Wood d		22 24			22 43						22 54			23 13						23 24	
Hither Green d		22 37				22 42					23 07				23 12					23 37	
Lewisham d	22 38	22 43				22 48	22 53	22 56		23 08	23 13				23 18	23 23	23 26		23 38	23 43	
St Johns d	22 40									23 10									23 40		
New Cross ⊖ d	22 42					22 51	22 56			23 12					23 21	23 26			23 42		
London Victoria ⊖ a					23 17									23 47							
London Bridge ⊖ d	22 49	22 52	22 44	22 55		22 58	23 02	23 05	23 11	23 19	23 22	23 14	23 25		23 28	23 32	23 35	23 41	23 49	23 52	23 55
London Blackfriars ⊖ a																					
London Cannon Street ⊖ a																					
London Waterloo (East) ⊖ d	22 54	22 57	22 48	23 00		23 04	23 07	23 10	23 16	23 24	23 27	23 18	23 30		23 34	23 37	23 40	23 46	23 54	23 57	23 59
London Charing Cross ⊖ a	22 58	23 00	22 51	23 03		23 07	23 10	23 13	23 20	23 27	23 30	23 21	23 33		23 37	23 40	23 43	23 49	23 57	00 01	00 03

A not 19 May

B 19 May

Table 199

Saturdays

28 July to 11 August

Orpington, Petts Wood, Hither Green and Lewisham - London (Summary of Services)

	SE A	SE B	SE ■	SE	SE	SE	SE	SE	SE	SE	SE	SE	SE	SE	SE	SE	SE	SE ■	SE	SE	SE	SE
Orpington d	23p21	23p21	23p37								05 51	06 10					06 21	06 24	06 25	06 40		
Petts Wood d	23p24	23p24									05 54	06 13					06 24		06 28	06 43		
Hither Green d	23p37	23p37				05 42					06 07		06 12				06 37					06 42
Lewisham d	23p43	23p43			05 39	05 48	05 50	05 56	06 02		06 13		06 18	06 20	06 26	06 32	06 43					06 48
St Johns d					05 41				06 04							06 34						
New Cross ⊖ d					05 43	05 51			06 06				06 21			06 36						06 51
London Victoria ⊖ a												06 47							07 02	07 17		
London Bridge ⊖ d	23p52	23p52	23p55	05 45	05 49	05 57	05 59	06 05	06 12	06 15	06 21		06 27	06 29	06 35	06 42	06 51	06 39			06 45	06 57
London Blackfriars ⊖ a																						
London Cannon Street ⊖ a																						
London Waterloo (East) ⊖ d	23p57	23p57	23p59	05 50	05 53	06 02	06 04	06 10	06 17	06 20	06 26		06 32	06 34	06 40	06 47	06 56	06 44			06 50	07 02
London Charing Cross ⊖ a	00 01	00 04	00 03	05 56	05 59	06 08	06 10	06 16	06 23	06 28	06 32		06 38	06 40	06 46	06 53	07 02	06 47			06 58	07 08

	SE	SE	SE	SE	SE	SE ■	SE	SE	SE ■	SE	SE	SE	SE	SE	SE ■	SE	SE	SE	SE	SE	SE	SE
Orpington d					06 51	06 54	06 55		07 09	07 10				07 21	07 24	07 25						07 33
Petts Wood d					06 54		06 58			07 13				07 24		07 28						07 36
Hither Green d					07 07						07 12			07 37						07 42		07 49
Lewisham d	06 50	06 56	07 02	07 08	07 13						07 18	07 20	07 26					07 32	07 38		07 50	07 54
St Johns d			07 04															07 34				07 56
New Cross ⊖ d			07 06								07 21							07 36				07 58
London Victoria ⊖ a				07 33			07 32			07 47						08 02			08 03			
London Bridge ⊖ d	06 59	07 05	07 12		07 21	07 09		07 15	07 24		07 27	07 29	07 35	07 49	07 39		07 41	07 42		07 52	07 58	08 04
London Blackfriars ⊖ a																						
London Cannon Street ⊖ a																	07 48					08 11
London Waterloo (East) ⊖ d	07 04	07 10	07 17		07 26	07 14		07 20	07 29		07 32	07 34	07 40	07 54	07 44			07 47		07 57	08 03	
London Charing Cross ⊖ a	07 10	07 16	07 23		07 32	07 17		07 28	07 33		07 38	07 43	07 46	07 57	07 48			07 53		08 00	08 09	

	SE ■	SE	SE	SE	SE	SE	SE	SE	SE	SE ■	SE	SE	SE ■	SE	SE	SE	SE	SE	SE	SE ■	SE
Orpington d	07 39	07 40							07 51	07 54	07 55								08 03	08 09	08 10
Petts Wood d		07 43							07 54		07 58								08 06		08 13
Hither Green d								07 58	08 07						08 12				08 19		
Lewisham d				07 56	07 59	07 59		08 04				08 08				08 14	08 20		08 24		
St Johns d						08 01		08 06								08 16			08 26		
New Cross ⊖ d						08 03		08 08								08 18		08 19	08 28		
London Victoria ⊖ a		08 17									08 32	08 33									08 47
London Bridge ⊖ d	07 55		08 01	08 05	08 08	08 09	08 11	08 15	08 19	08 11			08 14	08 21	08 22	08 24	08 28	09 31	08 34	08 25	
London Blackfriars ⊖ a																					
London Cannon Street ⊖ a			08 07			08 16	08 18	08 22						08 27		08 31		09 37	08 41		
London Waterloo (East) ⊖ d	08 00			08 10	08 13				08 24	08 15			08 19		08 27		08 33			08 30	
London Charing Cross ⊖ a	08 03			08 16	08 19				08 27	08 19			08 22		08 30		08 39			08 33	

	SE	SE	SE	SE	SE	SE	SE	SE	SE ■	SE	SE	SE ■	SE	SE	SE	SE	SE	SE	SE ■	SE	SE	SE
Orpington d								08 21	08 24	08 25								08 33	08 39	08 40		
Petts Wood d								08 24		08 28								08 36		08 43		
Hither Green d							08 28	08 37						08 42				08 49				
Lewisham d		08 26	08 29				08 34				08 38				08 44	08 50		08 54				08 56
St Johns d			08 31				08 36								08 46			08 56				
New Cross ⊖ d			08 33			08 33	08 38								08 48		08 49	08 58				
London Victoria ⊖ a										09 02	09 03									09 17		
London Bridge ⊖ d	08 31	08 35	08 39	08 38	08 41	09 51	08 45	08 49	08 41			08 44	08 51	08 52	08 54	08 58	10 01	09 04	08 55		09 01	09 05
London Blackfriars ⊖ a																						
London Cannon Street ⊖ a	08 37		08 46		08 48	09 57	08 52						08 57		09 01		10 07	09 11			09 07	
London Waterloo (East) ⊖ d		08 40		08 43				08 54	08 45			08 49		08 57		09 03			09 00			09 10
London Charing Cross ⊖ a		08 46		08 46				08 57	08 49			08 52		09 00		09 09			09 03			09 16

	SE	SE	SE	SE	SE	SE	SE ■	SE	SE	SE ■	SE	SE	SE	SE	SE	SE	SE ■	SE	SE	SE	SE
Orpington d						08 51	08 54	08 55								09 03	09 09	09 10			
Petts Wood d						08 54		08 58								09 06		09 13			
Hither Green d					08 58	09 07						09 12				09 19					
Lewisham d	08 59				09 04				09 08				09 14	09 20		09 24			09 26	09 29	
St Johns d	09 01				09 06								09 16			09 26				09 31	
New Cross ⊖ d	09 03			09 03	09 08								09 18		09 19	09 28				09 33	
London Victoria ⊖ a								09 32	09 33									09 47			
London Bridge ⊖ d	09 09	09 08	09 11	10 21	09 15	09 19	09 11			09 14	09 21	09 22	09 24	09 28	10 31	09 34	09 25		09 35	09 39	09 38
London Blackfriars ⊖ a																					
London Cannon Street ⊖ a	09 16		09 18	10 27	09 22						09 27		09 31		10 37	09 41				09 46	
London Waterloo (East) ⊖ d		09 13				09 24	09 15			09 19		09 27		09 33			09 30		09 40		09 43
London Charing Cross ⊖ a		09 16				09 27	09 19			09 22		09 30		09 39			09 33		09 43		09 46

A not from 4 August until 11 August

B not 28 July

Orpington, Petts Wood, Hither Green and Lewisham - London (Summary of Services)

	SE	SE	SE	SE	SE ■	SE	SE	SE ■ ⌶	SE		SE	SE	SE	SE	SE ■	SE	SE	SE	SE		SE	SE	SE	SE
Orpington ■ d				09 21	09 24	09 25								09 33	09 39	09 40								09 51
Petts Wood ■ d				09 24		09 28								09 36		09 43								09 54
Hither Green ■ d			09 28	09 37					09 42					09 49									09 58	10 07
Lewisham ■ d			09 34				09 38				09 44	09 50		09 54			09 56	09 59					10 04	
St Johns d			09 36								09 46			09 56				10 01					10 06	
New Cross ■ d		09 33	09 38								09 48		09 49	09 58				10 03				10 03	10 08	
London Victoria ■ a						10 02	10 03									10 17								
London Bridge ■ d	09 41	10 51	09 45	09 49	09 41			09 44	09 52		09 54	09 58	11 01	10 04	09 55		10 05	10 09	10 08		10 11	11 21	10 15	10 19
London Blackfriars ■ a																								
London Cannon Street ■ a	09 48	10 57	09 52								10 01		11 07	10 11				10 16			10 18	11 27	10 22	
London Waterloo (East) ■ d				09 54	09 45			09 49	09 57			10 03			10 00		10 10		10 13					10 24
London Charing Cross ■ a				09 57	09 49			09 52	10 00			10 09			10 03		10 16		10 16					10 27

	SE ■	SE	SE	SE ■ ⌶	SE		SE	SE	SE	SE	SE	SE ■	SE	SE	SE		SE	SE	SE	SE	SE	SE ■	SE	SE
Orpington ■ d	09 54	09 55									10 03	10 09	10 10								10 21	10 24	10 25	
Petts Wood ■ d		09 58									10 06		10 13								10 24		10 28	
Hither Green ■ d							10 12				10 19									10 28	10 37			
Lewisham ■ d			10 08					10 14	10 20		10 24			10 26	10 29					10 34				10 38
St Johns d								10 16			10 26				10 31					10 36				
New Cross ■ d								10 18		10 19	10 28				10 33				10 33	10 38				
London Victoria ■ a		10 32	10 33										10 47										11 02	11 03
London Bridge ■ d	10 11			10 14	10 21		10 22	10 24	10 28	11 31	10 34	10 25		10 35	10 39		10 38	10 41	11 51	10 45	10 49	10 41		
London Blackfriars ■ a																								
London Cannon Street ■ a					10 27			10 31		11 37	10 41				10 46			10 48	11 57	10 52				
London Waterloo (East) ■ d	10 15			10 19			10 27		10 33			10 30		10 40			10 43				10 54	10 45		
London Charing Cross ■ a	10 19			10 22			10 30		10 39			10 33		10 46			10 46				10 57	10 49		

	SE ■ ⌶		SE	SE	SE	SE	SE	SE	SE ■	SE	SE		SE	SE	SE	SE	SE	SE	SE ■	SE	SE		SE ■ ⌶	SE
Orpington ■ d								10 33	10 39	10 40								10 51	10 54	10 55				
Petts Wood ■ d								10 36		10 43								10 54		10 58				
Hither Green ■ d				10 42				10 49									10 58	11 07						
Lewisham ■ d					10 44	10 50		10 54			10 56		10 59				11 04				11 08			
St Johns d					10 46			10 56					11 01				11 06							
New Cross ■ d					10 48		10 49	10 58					11 03			11 03	11 08							
London Victoria ■ a										11 17										11 32	11 33			
London Bridge ■ d	10 44		10 51	10 52	10 54	10 58	12 01	11 04	10 55		11 05		11 09	11 08	11 11	12 21	11 15	11 19	11 11				11 14	11 21
London Blackfriars ■ a																								
London Cannon Street ■ a			10 57		11 01		12 07	11 11					11 16		11 18	12 27	11 22							11 27
London Waterloo (East) ■ d	10 49			10 57		11 03			11 00		11 10			11 13				11 24	11 15				11 19	
London Charing Cross ■ a	10 52			11 00		11 09			11 03		11 16			11 16				11 27	11 19				11 22	

	SE	SE	SE	SE	SE	SE ■	SE		SE	SE	SE	SE	SE	SE	SE	SE ■	SE		SE	SE ■ ⌶	SE	SE	SE	SE
Orpington ■ d					11 03	11 09	11 10								11 21	11 24	11 25							
Petts Wood ■ d					11 06		11 13								11 24		11 28							
Hither Green ■ d	11 12				11 19									11 28	11 37							11 42		
Lewisham ■ d		11 14	11 20		11 24				11 26	11 29				11 34					11 38				11 44	11 50
St Johns d		11 16			11 26					11 31				11 36									11 46	
New Cross ■ d		11 18		11 19	11 28					11 33			11 33	11 38									11 48	
London Victoria ■ a							11 47										12 02		12 03					
London Bridge ■ d	11 22	11 24	11 28	12 31	11 34	11 25			11 35	11 39	11 38	11 41	12 51	11 45	11 49	11 41				11 44	11 51	11 52	11 54	11 58
London Blackfriars ■ a																								
London Cannon Street ■ a		11 31		12 37	11 41					11 46		11 48	12 57	11 52							11 57		12 01	
London Waterloo (East) ■ d	11 27		11 33			11 30			11 40		11 43				11 54	11 45				11 49		11 57		12 03
London Charing Cross ■ a	11 30		11 39			11 33			11 46		11 46				11 57	11 49				11 52		12 00		12 09

	SE	SE	SE ■		SE	SE	SE	SE	SE	SE	SE	SE	SE ■		SE	SE	SE ■ ⌶	SE	SE	SE	SE	SE	SE	
Orpington ■ d		11 33	11 39		11 40							11 51	11 54		11 55								12 03	
Petts Wood ■ d		11 36			11 43							11 54			11 58								12 06	
Hither Green ■ d		11 49									11 58	12 07							12 12				12 19	
Lewisham ■ d		11 54				11 56	11 59				12 04					12 08				12 14	12 20		12 24	
St Johns d		11 56					12 01				12 06									12 16			12 26	
New Cross ■ d	11 49	11 58					12 03			12 03	12 08									12 18		12 19	12 28	
London Victoria ■ a					12 17										12 32	12 33								
London Bridge ■ d	13 01	12 04	11 55			12 05	12 09	12 08	12 11	13 21	12 15	12 19	12 11				12 14	12 21	12 22	12 24	12 28	13 31	12 34	
London Blackfriars ■ a																								
London Cannon Street ■ a	13 07	12 11					12 16		12 18	13 27	12 22							12 27		12 31		13 37	12 41	
London Waterloo (East) ■ d			12 00			12 10		12 13				12 24	12 15				12 19		12 27		12 33			
London Charing Cross ■ a			12 03			12 16		12 16				12 27	12 19				12 22		12 30		12 39			

Orpington, Petts Wood, Hither Green and Lewisham - London (Summary of Services)

	SE ■	SE	SE	SE	SE	SE	SE	SE	SE		SE ■	SE	SE	SE ■ ⌶	SE	SE	SE	SE	SE		SE	SE ■	SE	SE
Orpington ■ d	12 09	12 10							12 21		12 24	12 25									12 33	12 39	12 40	
Petts Wood ■ d		12 13							12 24			12 28									12 36		12 43	
Hither Green ■ d								12 28	12 37							12 42					12 49			
Lewisham ■ d			12 26	12 29				12 34					12 38				12 44	12 50			12 54			12 56
St Johns d				12 31				12 36									12 46				12 56			
New Cross ■ d				12 33			12 33	12 38									12 48		12 49		12 58			
London Victoria ■ a		12 47										13 02	13 03										13 17	
London Bridge ■ d	12 25		12 35	12 39	12 38	12 41	13 51	12 45	12 49		12 41			12 44	12 51	12 52	12 54	12 58	14 01		13 04	12 55		13 05
London Blackfriars ■ a																								
London Cannon Street ■ a				12 46		12 48	13 57	12 52							12 57		13 01		14 07		13 11			
London Waterloo (East) ■ d	12 30		12 40		12 43				12 54		12 45			12 49		12 57		13 03				13 00		13 10
London Charing Cross ■ a	12 33		12 46		12 46				12 57		12 49			12 52		13 00		13 09				13 03		13 16

	SE	SE	SE	SE	SE		SE	SE ■	SE	SE	SE ■ ⌶	SE	SE	SE	SE	SE		SE	SE ■	SE	SE	SE	SE	SE
Orpington ■ d							12 51	12 54	12 55									13 03	13 09	13 10				
Petts Wood ■ d							12 54		12 58									13 06		13 13				
Hither Green ■ d					12 58		13 07						13 12					13 19						
Lewisham ■ d	12 59				13 04					13 08				13 14	13 20			13 24			13 26	13 29		
St Johns d	13 01				13 06									13 16				13 26				13 31		
New Cross ■ d	13 03			13 03	13 08									13 18		13 19		13 28				13 33		
London Victoria ■ a									13 32	13 33										13 47				
London Bridge ■ d	13 09	13 08	13 11	14 21	13 15		13 19	13 11			13 14	13 21	13 22	13 24	13 27	14 31		13 34	13 25		13 35	13 39	13 38	13 41
London Blackfriars ■ a																								
London Cannon Street ■ a	13 16		13 18	14 27	13 22							13 27		13 31		14 37		13 41				13 46		13 48
London Waterloo (East) ■ d		13 13					13 24	13 15			13 19		13 27		13 32				13 30		13 40		13 43	
London Charing Cross ■ a		13 16					13 27	13 19			13 22		13 30		13 39				13 33		13 46		13 46	

	SE	SE		SE	SE ■	SE	SE	SE ■ ⌶	SE	SE	SE	SE		SE	SE	SE ■	SE	SE	SE	SE	SE	SE		SE
Orpington ■ d				13 21	13 24	13 25									13 33	13 39	13 40							
Petts Wood ■ d				13 24		13 28									13 36		13 43							
Hither Green ■ d		13 28		13 37						13 42					13 49									13 58
Lewisham ■ d		13 34					13 38				13 44	13 50			13 54			13 56	13 59					14 04
St Johns d		13 36									13 46				13 56				14 01					14 06
New Cross ■ d	13 33	13 38									13 48			13 49	13 58				14 03			14 03		14 08
London Victoria ■ a						14 02	14 03										14 17							
London Bridge ■ d	14 51	13 45		13 49	13 41			13 44	13 51	13 52	13 54	13 58		15 01	14 04	13 55		14 05	14 09	14 08	14 11	15 21		14 15
London Blackfriars ■ a																								
London Cannon Street ■ a	14 57	13 52							13 57		14 01			15 07	14 11				14 16		14 18	15 27		14 22
London Waterloo (East) ■ d				13 54	13 45			13 49		13 57		14 03				14 00		14 10		14 13				
London Charing Cross ■ a				13 57	13 49			13 52		14 00		14 09				14 03		14 16		14 16				

	SE	SE ■	SE	SE	SE ■ ⌶	SE	SE	SE		SE		SE	SE	SE	SE ■	SE	SE		SE	SE	SE	SE	SE
Orpington ■ d	13 51	13 54	13 55								and at the same minutes past each hour until			17 03	17 09	17 10							
Petts Wood ■ d	13 54		13 58											17 06		17 13							
Hither Green ■ d	14 07						14 12							17 19									17 28
Lewisham ■ d				14 08				14 14		14 20		17 20		17 24			17 26		17 29				17 34
St Johns d								14 16						17 26					17 31				17 36
New Cross ■ d								14 18					17 19	17 28					17 33			17 33	17 38
London Victoria ■ a			14 32	14 33												17 47							
London Bridge ■ d	14 19	14 11			14 14	14 21	14 22	14 24		14 28		17 28	18 31	17 34	17 25		17 35		17 39	17 38	17 41	18 51	17 45
London Blackfriars ■ a																							
London Cannon Street ■ a						14 27		14 31					18 37	17 41					17 46		17 48	18 57	17 52
London Waterloo (East) ■ d	14 24	14 15			14 19		14 27			14 33		17 33			17 30		17 40			17 43			
London Charing Cross ■ a	14 27	14 19			14 22		14 30			14 39		17 39			17 33		17 46			17 46			

	SE	SE ■	SE	SE		SE ■ ⌶	SE	SE	SE	SE	SE	SE	SE ■	SE		SE	SE	SE	SE	SE	SE	SE ■	SE	SE
Orpington ■ d	17 21	17 24	17 25									17 33	17 39	17 40							17 51	17 54	17 55	
Petts Wood ■ d	17 24		17 28									17 36		17 43							17 54		17 58	
Hither Green ■ d	17 37							17 42				17 49								17 58	18 07			
Lewisham ■ d				17 38					17 44	17 50		17 54				17 56	17 59			18 04				18 08
St Johns d									17 46			17 56					18 01			18 06				
New Cross ■ d									17 48		17 49	17 58					18 03			18 08				
London Victoria ■ a			18 02	18 03										18 17									18 32	18 33
London Bridge ■ d	17 49	17 41				17 44	17 51	17 52	17 54	17 58	19 01	18 04	17 55			18 05	18 09	18 08	18 11	18 15	18 19	18 11		
London Blackfriars ■ a																								
London Cannon Street ■ a							17 57		18 01		19 07	18 11					18 16		18 18	18 22				
London Waterloo (East) ■ d	17 54	17 45				17 49		17 57		18 03			18 00			18 10		18 13			18 24	18 15		
London Charing Cross ■ a	17 57	17 49				17 52		18 00		18 09			18 03			18 16		18 16			18 27	18 19		

Table 199

Saturdays
28 July to 11 August

Orpington, Petts Wood, Hither Green and Lewisham - London (Summary of Services)

		SE ■	SE	SE	SE	SE	SE	SE	SE ■	SE	SE	SE	SE	SE	SE	SE	SE ■	SE	SE	SE ■	SE	SE
Orpington	d							18 03	18 09	18 10						18 21	18 24	18 25				
Petts Wood	d							18 06		18 13						18 24		18 28				
Hither Green	d			18 12				18 19							18 28	18 37						18 42
Lewisham	d				18 14	18 20		18 24			18 26	18 29			18 34				18 38			
St Johns	d				18 16			18 26				18 31			18 36							
New Cross	d				18 18		18 19	18 28				18 33			18 38							
London Victoria	a									18 47								19 02	19 03			
London Bridge	d	18 14	18 21	18 22	18 24	18 28	19 31	18 34	18 25		18 35	18 39	18 38	18 41	18 45	18 49	18 41			18 44	18 51	18 52
London Blackfriars	a																					
London Cannon Street	a		18 27		18 31		19 37	18 41				18 46		18 48	18 52						18 57	
London Waterloo (East)	d	18 19		18 27		18 33			18 30		18 40		18 43			18 54	18 45			18 49		18 57
London Charing Cross	a	18 22		18 30		18 39			18 33		18 46		18 46			18 57	18 49			18 52		19 00

		SE	SE	SE	SE	SE ■	SE	SE	SE	SE	SE	SE	SE	SE	SE ■	SE	SE ■	SE	SE ■	SE	SE	SE	SE
Orpington	d				18 33	18 39	18 40							18 51	18 54	18 55			19 09	19 10			
Petts Wood	d				18 36		18 43							18 54		18 58				19 13			
Hither Green	d				18 49							18 58		19 07								19 13	
Lewisham	d	18 44	18 50		18 54			18 56	18 59			19 04	19 08	19 12							19 14	19 18	
St Johns	d	18 46			18 56				19 01			19 06									19 16		
New Cross	d	18 48		18 49	18 58				19 03			19 08									19 18		19 19
London Victoria	a						19 17						19 33			19 32				19 47			
London Bridge	d	18 54	18 58	20 01	19 04	18 55		19 05	19 09	19 08	19 11	19 15		19 21	19 11		19 14	19 19	19 25		19a27	19 28	20 31
London Blackfriars	a																						
London Cannon Street	a	19 01		20 07	19 11				19 16		19 18	19 22						19 25					20 37
London Waterloo (East)	d		19 03			19 00		19 10		19 13				19 26	19 15		19 19		19 30			19 32	
London Charing Cross	a		19 09			19 03		19 16		19 16				19 32	19 19		19 22		19 33			19 38	

		SE	SE	SE	SE	SE	SE	SE ■	SE ■	SE	SE	SE	SE	SE	SE	SE	SE	SE ■	SE ■	SE	SE	SE
Orpington	d					19 21	19 25	19 28	19 39	19 40						19 51	19 55	19 58	20 09	20 10		
Petts Wood	d					19 24	19 28			19 43						19 54	19 58			20 13		
Hither Green	d					19 37					19 43					20 07					20 13	
Lewisham	d	19 21	19 26		19 38	19 43					19 48	19 53	19 57		20 08	20 13					20 18	20 23
St Johns	d				19 40										20 10							
New Cross	d	19 24			19 42						19 51	19 56			20 12						20 21	20 26
London Victoria	a						20 02			20 17							20 32			20 47		
London Bridge	d	19 34	19 37	19 41	19 49	19 52		19 44	19 55		19 58	20 04	20 07	20 11	20 19	20 22		20 14	20 25		20 28	20 34
London Blackfriars	a																					
London Cannon Street	a																					
London Waterloo (East)	d	19 39	19 42	19 46	19 54	19 57		19 48	20 00		20 04	20 09	20 12	20 16	20 24	20 27		20 18	20 30		20 34	20 39
London Charing Cross	a	19 45	19 48	19 52	20 01	20 03		19 51	20 03		20 10	20 15	20 18	20 22	20 31	20 33		20 21	20 33		20 40	20 45

		SE	SE	SE	SE	SE ■	SE ■	SE	SE	SE	SE	SE	SE	SE	SE ■	SE ■	SE	SE	SE	SE	SE	SE	SE
Orpington	d				20 21	20 28	20 39	20 40						20 51	20 58	21 09	21 10						21 21
Petts Wood	d				20 24			20 43						20 54			21 13						21 24
Hither Green	d				20 37				20 43					21 07				21 13					21 37
Lewisham	d	20 27		20 38	20 43				20 48	20 53	20 57		21 08	21 13				21 18	21 23	21 26		21 38	21 43
St Johns	d			20 40									21 10									21 40	
New Cross	d			20 42					20 51	20 56			21 12					21 21	21 26			21 42	
London Victoria	a							21 17									21 47						
London Bridge	d	20 37	20 41	20 49	20 52	20 44	20 55		20 58	21 04	21 07	21 11	21 19	21 22	21 14	21 25		21 28	21 34	21 36	21 41	21 49	21 52
London Blackfriars	a																						
London Cannon Street	a																						
London Waterloo (East)	d	20 42	20 46	20 54	20 57	20 48	21 00		21 04	21 09	21 12	21 16	21 24	21 27	21 18	21 30		21 34	21 39	21 41	21 46	21 54	21 57
London Charing Cross	a	20 48	20 52	21 01	21 03	20 51	21 03		21 10	21 15	21 18	21 22	21 31	21 33	21 21	21 33		21 40	21 45	21 47	21 52	22 01	22 03

		SE ■	SE ■	SE	SE	SE	SE	SE	SE	SE	SE ■	SE ■	SE	SE	SE	SE	SE	SE	SE	SE ■	SE ■	SE	SE
Orpington	d	21 28	21 39	21 40						21 51	21 58	22 09	22 10						22 21	22 28	22 39	22 40	
Petts Wood	d			21 43						21 54			22 13						22 24			22 43	
Hither Green	d				21 43					22 07				22 13					22 37				22 43
Lewisham	d				21 48	21 53	21 56		22 08	22 13				22 18	22 23	22 26		22 38	22 43				22 48
St Johns	d								22 10									22 40					
New Cross	d				21 51	21 56			22 12					22 21	22 26			22 42					22 51
London Victoria	a			22 17									22 47									23 17	
London Bridge	d	21 44	21 55		21 58	22 02	22 05	22 11	22 19	22 22	22 14	22 25		22 28	22 32	22 35	22 41	22 49	22 52	22 44	22 55		22 58
London Blackfriars	a																						
London Cannon Street	a																						
London Waterloo (East)	d	21 48	22 00		22 04	22 07	22 10	22 16	22 24	22 27	22 18	22 30		22 34	22 37	22 40	22 46	22 54	22 57	22 48	23 00		23 04
London Charing Cross	a	21 51	22 03		22 10	22 13	22 16	22 22	22 31	22 33	22 21	22 33		22 40	22 43	22 46	22 52	23 01	23 03	22 51	23 03		23 10

Table 199

Saturdays
28 July to 11 August

Orpington, Petts Wood, Hither Green and Lewisham - London (Summary of Services)

		SE	SE	SE	SE	SE	SE ■	SE ■	SE	SE	SE	SE	SE	SE	SE	SE ■
Orpington	d					22 51	22 58	23 09	23 10						23 21	23 37
Petts Wood	d					22 54			23 13						23 24	
Hither Green	d					23 07				23 13					23 37	
Lewisham	d	22 53	22 56		23 08	23 13				23 18	23 23	23 26		23 38	23 43	
St Johns	d				23 10									23 40		
New Cross	d	22 56			23 12					23 21	23 26			23 42		
London Victoria	a								23 47							
London Bridge	d	23 02	23 05	23 11	23 19	23 22	23 14	23 25		23 28	23 32	23 35	23 41	23 49	23 52	23 55
London Blackfriars	a															
London Cannon Street	a															
London Waterloo (East)	d	23 07	23 10	23 16	23 24	23 27	23 18	23 30		23 34	23 37	23 40	23 46	23 54	23 57	23 59
London Charing Cross	a	23 13	23 16	23 23	23 30	23 33	23 21	23 33		23 40	23 43	23 46	23 52	23 59	00 04	00 03

Saturdays
25 August to 8 September

		SE	SE ■	SE	SE	SE	SE	SE	SE	SE	SE	SE	SE	SE	SE	SE	SE	SE ■	SE	SE	SE	SE	SE
Orpington	d	23p21	23p37								05 51	06 10					06 21	06 24	06 25	06 40			
Petts Wood	d	23p24									05 54	06 13					06 24		06 28	06 43			
Hither Green	d	23p37				05 42					06 07		06 12				06 37					06 42	
Lewisham	d	23p43			05 39	05 48	05 50	05 56	06 02		06 13		06 18	06 20	06 26	06 32	06 43					06 48	06 50
St Johns	d				05 41				06 04							06 34							
New Cross	d				05 43	05 51			06 06				06 21			06 36						06 51	
London Victoria	a											06 47							07 02	07 17			
London Bridge	d	23p52	23p55	05 45	05 49	05 57	05 59	06 05	06 12	06 15	06 21		06 27	06 29	06 35	06 42	06 51	06 39			06 45	06 57	06 59
London Blackfriars	a																						
London Cannon Street	a																						
London Waterloo (East)	d	23p57	23p59	05 50	05 53	06 02	06 04	06 10	06 17	06 20	06 26		06 32	06 34	06 40	06 47	06 56	06 44			06 50	07 02	07 04
London Charing Cross	a	00 01	00 03	05 53	05 56	06 05	06 07	06 13	06 20	06 25	06 29		06 35	06 37	06 43	06 50	06 59	06 47			06 55	07 05	07 07

		SE	SE	SE	SE	SE ■	SE	SE	SE ■	SE	SE	SE	SE	SE	SE ■	SE	SE	SE	SE	SE	SE	SE	SE ■
Orpington	d				06 51	06 54	06 55		07 09	07 10				07 21	07 24	07 25						07 33	07 39
Petts Wood	d				06 54		06 58			07 13				07 24		07 28						07 36	
Hither Green	d				07 07						07 12			07 37						07 42		07 49	
Lewisham	d	06 56	07 02	07 08	07 13						07 18	07 20	07 26					07 32	07 38		07 50	07 54	
St Johns	d		07 04															07 34				07 56	
New Cross	d		07 06								07 21							07 36				07 58	
London Victoria	a			07 28			07 32			07 47						08 02			07 58				
London Bridge	d	07 05	07 12		07 21	07 09		07 15	07 24		07 27	07 29	07 35	07 49	07 39		07 41	07 42		07 52	07 58	08 04	07 55
London Blackfriars	a																						
London Cannon Street	a																07 45					08 08	
London Waterloo (East)	d	07 10	07 17		07 26	07 14		07 20	07 29		07 32	07 34	07 40	07 54	07 44			07 47		07 57	08 03		08 00
London Charing Cross	a	07 13	07 20		07 29	07 17		07 25	07 33		07 35	07 40	07 43	07 57	07 48			07 50		08 00	08 06		08 03

		SE	SE	SE	SE	SE	SE	SE	SE	SE ■	SE	SE	SE ■	SE	SE	SE	SE	SE	SE	SE ■	SE	SE
Orpington	d	07 40							07 51	07 54	07 55								08 03	08 09	08 10	
Petts Wood	d	07 43							07 54		07 58								08 06		08 13	
Hither Green	d							07 58	08 07						08 12				08 19			
Lewisham	d			07 56	07 59	07 59		08 04				08 08				08 14	08 20		08 24			
St Johns	d					08 01		08 06								08 16			08 26			
New Cross	d					08 03		08 08								08 18		08 19	08 28			
London Victoria	a	08 17									08 32	08 28									08 47	
London Bridge	d		08 01	08 05	08 08	08 09	08 11	08 15	08 19	08 11			08 14	08 21	08 22	08 24	08 28	09 31	08 34	08 25		08 31
London Blackfriars	a																					
London Cannon Street	a		08 04			08 13	08 15	08 19						08 24		08 28		09 34	08 38			08 34
London Waterloo (East)	d			08 10	08 13				08 24	08 15			08 19		08 27		08 33			08 30		
London Charing Cross	a			08 13	08 16				08 27	08 19			08 22		08 30		08 36			08 33		

		SE	SE	SE	SE	SE	SE	SE	SE ■	SE	SE	SE ■	SE	SE	SE	SE	SE	SE	SE ■	SE	SE	SE	SE
Orpington	d							08 21	08 24	08 25								08 33	08 39	08 40			
Petts Wood	d							08 24		08 28								08 36		08 43			
Hither Green	d						08 28	08 37						08 42				08 49					
Lewisham	d	08 26	08 29				08 34				08 38				08 44	08 50		08 54				08 56	08 59
St Johns	d		08 31				08 36								08 46			08 56					09 01
New Cross	d		08 33			08 33	08 38								08 48		08 49	08 58					09 03
London Victoria	a									09 02	08 58									09 17			
London Bridge	d	08 35	08 39	08 38	08 41	09 51	08 45	08 49	08 41			08 44	08 51	08 52	08 54	08 58	10 01	09 04	08 55		09 01	09 05	09 09
London Blackfriars	a																						
London Cannon Street	a		08 43		08 45	09 54	08 49						08 54		08 58		10 04	09 08			09 04		09 13
London Waterloo (East)	d	08 40		08 43				08 54	08 45			08 49		08 57		09 03			09 00			09 10	
London Charing Cross	a	08 43		08 46				08 57	08 49			08 52		09 00		09 06			09 03			09 13	

Orpington, Petts Wood, Hither Green and Lewisham - London (Summary of Services)

		SE	SE	SE	SE	SE	SE ■	SE	SE	SE ■	SE	SE	SE	SE	SE	SE	SE ■	SE	SE	SE	SE	SE
Orpington	d					08 51	08 54	08 55								09 03	09 09	09 10				
Petts Wood	d					08 54		08 58								09 06		09 13				
Hither Green	d				08 58	09 07						09 12				09 19						
Lewisham	d				09 04				09 08				09 14	09 20		09 24			09 26	09 29		
St Johns	d				09 06								09 16			09 26				09 31		
New Cross	d			09 03	09 08								09 18		09 19	09 28				09 33		
London Victoria	a							09 32	09 28									09 47				
London Bridge	d	09 08	09 11	10 21	09 15	09 19	09 11			09 14	09 21	09 22	09 24	09 28	10 31	09 34	09 25		09 35	09 39	09 38	09 41
London Blackfriars	a														10 34	09 38				09 43		09 45
London Cannon Street	a		09 15	10 24	09 19						09 24		09 28									
London Waterloo (East)	d	09 13				09 24	09 15			09 19		09 27		09 33			09 30		09 40		09 43	
London Charing Cross	a	09 16				09 27	09 19			09 22		09 30		09 36			09 33		09 43		09 46	

		SE	SE	SE	SE ■	SE	SE	SE ■	SE	SE	SE	SE	SE	SE ■	SE	SE	SE	SE	SE	SE	SE	SE	SE ■
Orpington	d			09 21	09 24	09 25							09 33	09 39	09 40							09 51	09 54
Petts Wood	d			09 24		09 28							09 36		09 43							09 54	
Hither Green	d		09 28	09 37					09 42				09 49								09 58	10 07	
Lewisham	d		09 34				09 38			09 44	09 50		09 54			09 56	09 59				10 04		
St Johns	d		09 36							09 46			09 56				10 01				10 06		
New Cross	d	09 33	09 38							09 48		09 49	09 58				10 03			10 03	10 08		
London Victoria	a					10 02	09 58								10 17								
London Bridge	d	10 51	09 45	09 49	09 41			09 44	09 52	09 54	09 58	11 01	10 04	09 55		10 05	10 09	10 08	10 11	11 21	10 15	10 19	10 11
London Blackfriars	a																10 13		10 15	11 24	10 19		
London Cannon Street	a	10 54	09 49							09 58		11 04	10 08										
London Waterloo (East)	d			09 54	09 45			09 49	09 57		10 03			10 00		10 10		10 13				10 24	10 15
London Charing Cross	a			09 57	09 49			09 52	10 00		10 06			10 03		10 13		10 16				10 27	10 19

		SE	SE	SE ■		SE ■	SE	SE	SE	SE	SE	SE ■	SE	SE	SE	SE	SE	SE	SE	SE	SE ■	SE
Orpington	d	09 55			and at the same minutes past each hour until						17 03	17 09	17 10							17 21	17 24	17 25
Petts Wood	d	09 58									17 06		17 13							17 24		17 28
Hither Green	d						17 12				17 19								17 28	17 37		
Lewisham	d		10 08					17 14	17 20		17 24			17 26	17 29				17 34			
St Johns	d							17 16			17 26				17 31				17 36			
New Cross	d							17 18		17 19	17 28				17 33			17 33	17 38			
London Victoria	a	10 32	10 28										17 47									18 02
London Bridge	d			10 14		17 14	17 22	17 24	17 28	18 31	17 34	17 25		17 35	17 39	17 38	17 41	18 51	17 45	17 49	17 41	
London Blackfriars	a																17 45	18 54	17 49			
London Cannon Street	a							17 28		18 34	17 38				17 43							
London Waterloo (East)	d			10 19		17 19	17 27		17 33			17 30		17 40		17 43				17 54	17 45	
London Charing Cross	a			10 22		17 22	17 30		17 36			17 33		17 43		17 46				17 57	17 49	

		SE	SE ■	SE	SE	SE	SE	SE	SE ■	SE	SE	SE	SE	SE	SE	SE	SE ■	SE	SE	SE ■	SE	SE
Orpington	d							17 33	17 39	17 40						17 51	17 54	17 55				
Petts Wood	d							17 36		17 43						17 54		17 58				
Hither Green	d			17 42				17 49							17 58	18 07					18 12	
Lewisham	d	17 38			17 44	17 50		17 54			17 56	17 59			18 04				18 08			18 14
St Johns	d				17 46			17 56				18 01			18 06							18 16
New Cross	d				17 48		17 49	17 58				18 03			18 08							18 18
London Victoria	a	17 58								18 17								18 32	18 28			
London Bridge	d		17 44	17 52	17 54	17 58	19 01	18 04	17 55		18 05	18 09	18 08	18 11	18 15	18 19	18 11			18 14	18 22	18 24
London Blackfriars	a													18 15	18 19							18 28
London Cannon Street	a				17 58		19 04	18 08				18 13										
London Waterloo (East)	d		17 49	17 57		18 03			18 00		18 10		18 13			18 24	18 15			18 19	18 27	
London Charing Cross	a		17 52	18 00		18 06			18 03		18 13		18 16			18 27	18 19			18 22	18 30	

		SE	SE	SE	SE ■	SE	SE	SE	SE	SE	SE	SE	SE ■	SE	SE	SE ■	SE	SE	SE	SE	SE	SE ■	SE
Orpington	d			18 03	18 09	18 10						18 21	18 24	18 25							18 33	18 39	18 40
Petts Wood	d			18 06		18 13						18 24		18 28							18 36		18 43
Hither Green	d			18 19							18 28	18 37					18 42				18 49		
Lewisham	d	18 20		18 24			18 26	18 29			18 34				18 38			18 44	18 50		18 54		
St Johns	d			18 26				18 31			18 36							18 46			18 56		
New Cross	d		18 19	18 28				18 33			18 38							18 48		18 49	18 58		
London Victoria	a					18 47								19 02	18 58								19 17
London Bridge	d	18 28	19a30	18 34	18 25		18 35	18 39	18 38	18 41	18 45	18 49	18 41			18 44	18 52	18 54	18 58	20a00	19 04	18 55	
London Blackfriars	a																						
London Cannon Street	a			18 38				18 43		18 45	18 49							18 58			19 08		
London Waterloo (East)	d	18 33			18 30		18 40		18 43			18 54	18 45			18 49	18 57		19 03			19 00	
London Charing Cross	a	18 36			18 33		18 43		18 46			18 57	18 49			18 52	19 00		19 06			19 03	

Table 199

Saturdays
25 August to 8 September

Orpington, Petts Wood, Hither Green and Lewisham - London (Summary of Services)

		SE	SE	SE	SE	SE	SE	SE	SE ■	SE	SE ■	SE ■	SE	SE	SE	SE	SE	SE	SE	SE	SE	SE	SE ■
Orpington	d							18 51	18 54	18 55		19 09	19 10								19 21	19 25	19 28
Petts Wood	d							18 54		18 58			19 13								19 24	19 28	
Hither Green	d					18 58		19 07							19 12						19 37		
Lewisham	d	18 56	18 59			19 04	19 08	19 12						19 14	19 18		19 20	19 26		19 38	19 43		
St Johns	d		19 01			19 06								19 16						19 40			
New Cross	d		19 03			19 08								19 18		19 19	19 23			19 42			
London Victoria	a						19 28			19 32			19 47									20 02	
London Bridge	d	19 05	19 09	19 08	19 11	19 15		19 21	19 11		19 14	19 25		19a24	19 28	20a30	19 34	19 37	19 41	19 49	19 52		19 44
London Blackfriars	a																						
London Cannon Street	a		19 13		19 15	19 19																	
London Waterloo (East)	d	19 10		19 13				19 26	19 15		19 19	19 30			19 32		19 39	19 42	19 46	19 54	19 57		19 48
London Charing Cross	a	19 13		19 16				19 29	19 19		19 22	19 33			19 35		19 42	19 45	19 49	19 58	20 00		19 51

		SE ■	SE	SE	SE	SE	SE	SE	SE	SE	SE ■	SE ■	SE	SE	SE	SE	SE	SE	SE	SE ■	SE ■	SE
Orpington	d	19 39	19 40						19 51	19 55	19 58	20 09	20 10						20 21	20 28	20 39	20 40
Petts Wood	d		19 43						19 54	19 58			20 13						20 24			20 43
Hither Green	d			19 42					20 07					20 12					20 37			
Lewisham	d			19 48	19 53	19 56		20 08	20 13					20 18	20 23	20 26		20 38	20 43			
St Johns	d							20 10										20 40				
New Cross	d			19 51	19 56			20 12						20 21	20 26			20 42				
London Victoria	a		20 17							20 32			20 47									21 17
London Bridge	d	19 55		19 58	20 04	20 06	20 11	20 19	20 22		20 14	20 25		20 28	20 34	20 36	20 41	20 49	20 52	20 44	20 55	
London Blackfriars	a																					
London Cannon Street	a																					
London Waterloo (East)	d	20 00		20 04	20 09	20 11	20 16	20 24	20 27		20 18	20 30		20 34	20 39	20 41	20 46	20 54	20 57	20 48	21 00	
London Charing Cross	a	20 03		20 07	20 12	20 14	20 19	20 28	20 30		20 21	20 33		20 37	20 42	20 44	20 49	20 58	21 00	20 51	21 03	

		SE	SE	SE	SE	SE	SE	SE ■	SE ■	SE	SE	SE	SE	SE	SE	SE	SE ■	SE ■	SE	SE	SE	SE	SE
Orpington	d						20 51	20 58	21 09	21 10						21 21	21 28	21 39	21 40				
Petts Wood	d						20 54			21 13						21 24			21 43				
Hither Green	d	20 42					21 07				21 12					21 37				21 42			
Lewisham	d	20 48	20 53	20 56		21 08	21 13				21 18	21 23	21 26		21 38	21 43				21 48	21 53	21 56	
St Johns	d					21 10									21 40								
New Cross	d	20 51	20 56			21 12					21 21	21 26			21 42					21 51	21 56		
London Victoria	a									21 47									22 17				
London Bridge	d	20 58	21 04	21 06	21 11	21 19	21 22	21 14	21 25		21 28	21 34	21 36	21 41	21 49	21 52	21 44	21 55		21 58	22 02	22 05	22 11
London Blackfriars	a																						
London Cannon Street	a																						
London Waterloo (East)	d	21 04	21 09	21 11	21 16	21 24	21 27	21 18	21 30		21 34	21 39	21 41	21 46	21 54	21 57	21 48	22 00		22 04	22 07	22 10	22 16
London Charing Cross	a	21 07	21 12	21 14	21 19	21 28	21 30	21 21	21 33		21 37	21 42	21 44	21 49	21 58	22 00	21 51	22 03		22 07	22 10	22 13	22 19

		SE	SE	SE ■	SE ■	SE	SE	SE	SE	SE	SE	SE	SE ■	SE ■	SE	SE	SE	SE	SE	SE	SE	SE ■
Orpington	d		21 51	21 58	22 09	22 10						22 21	22 28	22 39	22 40						22 51	22 58
Petts Wood	d		21 54			22 13						22 24			22 43						22 54	
Hither Green	d		22 07				22 12					22 37				22 42					23 07	
Lewisham	d	22 08	22 13				22 18	22 23	22 26		22 38	22 43				22 48	22 53	22 56		23 08	23 13	
St Johns	d	22 10									22 40									23 10		
New Cross	d	22 12					22 21	22 26			22 42					22 51	22 56			23 12		
London Victoria	a					22 47									23 17							
London Bridge	d	22 19	22 22	22 14	22 25		22 28	22 32	22 35	22 41	22 49	22 52	22 44	22 55		22 58	23 02	23 05	23 11	23 19	23 22	23 14
London Blackfriars	a																					
London Cannon Street	a																					
London Waterloo (East)	d	22 24	22 27	22 18	22 30		22 34	22 37	22 40	22 46	22 54	22 57	22 48	23 00		23 04	23 07	23 10	23 16	23 24	23 27	23 18
London Charing Cross	a	22 28	22 30	22 21	22 33		22 37	22 40	22 43	22 49	22 58	23 00	22 51	23 03		23 07	23 10	23 13	23 20	23 27	23 30	23 21

		SE ■	SE	SE	SE	SE	SE	SE	SE	SE ■
Orpington	d	23 09	23 10						23 21	23 37
Petts Wood	d		23 13						23 24	
Hither Green	d			23 12					23 37	
Lewisham	d			23 18	23 23	23 26		23 38	23 43	
St Johns	d							23 40		
New Cross	d			23 21	23 26			23 42		
London Victoria	a		23 47							
London Bridge	d	23 25		23 28	23 32	23 35	23 41	23 49	23 52	23 55
London Blackfriars	a									
London Cannon Street	a									
London Waterloo (East)	d	23 30		23 34	23 37	23 40	23 46	23 54	23 57	23 59
London Charing Cross	a	23 33		23 37	23 40	23 43	23 49	23 57	00 01	00 03

Table 199

Sundays

until 22 July, 19 Aug and from 16 Sep

Orpington, Petts Wood, Hither Green and Lewisham - London (Summary of Services)

		SE	SE ■	SE	SE	SE	SE	SE	SE	SE		SE ■	SE	SE	SE	SE	SE	SE	SE	SE ■		SE ■	SE	SE	SE
Orpington	d	23p21	23p37	06 40	07 02	07 06				07 10		07 28	07 36						07 40	07 43		07 58	08 06		
Petts Wood	d	23p24		06 43	07 05	07 09				07 13			07 39						07 43				08 09		
Hither Green	d	23p37							07 12	07 26						07 42			07 56						
Lewisham	d	23p43					07 08		07 18	07 31				07 38		07 48	07 52	07 56	08 01					08 08	
St Johns	d																07 54								
New Cross	d						07 11							07 41			07 56							08 11	
London Victoria	a					07 43							08 13										08 43		
London Bridge	d	23p52	23p55				07 20	07 23	07 26	07 40		07 43		07 50	07 53	07 56	08 04	08 07	08 10	07 59		08 13		08 20	08 23
London Blackfriars	a			07 23	07 53																				
London Cannon Street	a																								
London Waterloo (East)	d	23p57	23p59				07 25	07 28	07 31	07 45		07 48		07 55	07 58	08 01	08 08	08 11	08 15	08 04		08 18		08 25	08 28
London Charing Cross	a	00 01	00 03				07 28	07 31	07 34	07 48		07 52		07 58	08 01	08 04	08 11	08 14	08 18	08 07		08 22		08 28	08 31

		SE	SE	SE	SE	SE ■		SE	SE	SE	SE	SE	SE	SE	SE ■	SE ■		SE	SE	SE	SE	SE	SE	SE	
Orpington	d				08 10	08 28		08 36						08 40	08 43	08 58		09 06						09 10	
Petts Wood	d				08 13			08 39						08 43				09 09						09 13	
Hither Green	d	08 12			08 26						08 42			08 56							09 12			09 26	
Lewisham	d	08 18	08 22	08 26	08 31				08 38		08 48	08 52	08 56	09 01					09 08		09 18	09 22	09 26	09 31	
St Johns	d		08 24									08 54										09 24			
New Cross	d		08 26						08 41			08 56							09 11			09 26			
London Victoria	a							09 13										09 43							
London Bridge	d	08 26	08 34	08 37	08 40	08 43			08 50	08 53	08 56	09 04	09 07	09 10	08 59	09 13			09 20	09 23	09 26	09 34	09 37	09 40	
London Blackfriars	a																								
London Cannon Street	a																								
London Waterloo (East)	d	08 31	08 38	08 41	08 45	08 48			08 55	08 58	09 01	09 08	09 11	09 15	09 04	09 18			09 25	09 28	09 31	09 38	09 41	09 45	
London Charing Cross	a	08 34	08 41	08 44	08 49	08 52			08 58	09 01	09 04	09 11	09 14	09 18	09 07	09 22			09 28	09 31	09 34	09 41	09 44	09 49	

		SE ■		SE ■		SE ■ ⚒	SE	SE	SE	SE	SE	SE	SE	SE ■		SE ■	SE	SE	SE	SE	SE	SE	SE	SE ■
Orpington	d	09 13	and at the same minutes past each hour until	19 13		19 28	19 36						19 40	19 43		19 58	20 06						20 10	20 28
Petts Wood	d						19 39						19 43				20 09						20 13	
Hither Green	d									19 42			19 56							20 12			20 26	
Lewisham	d							19 38		19 48	19 52	19 56	20 01					20 08		20 18	20 22	20 26	20 31	
St Johns	d										19 54										20 24			
New Cross	d							19 41			19 56							20 11			20 26			
London Victoria	a						20 13										20 43							
London Bridge	d	09 29		19 29		19 43		19 50	19 53	19 56	20 04	20 07	20 10	19 59		20 13		20 20	20 23	20 26	20 34	20 37	20 40	20 43
London Blackfriars	a																							
London Cannon Street	a																							
London Waterloo (East)	d	09 34		19 34		19 48		19 55	19 58	20 01	20 08	20 11	20 15	20 04		20 18		20 25	20 28	20 31	20 38	20 41	20 45	20 48
London Charing Cross	a	09 37		19 37		19 52		19 58	20 01	20 04	20 11	20 14	20 18	20 07		20 22		20 28	20 31	20 34	20 41	20 44	20 49	20 52

			SE	SE	SE	SE	SE	SE	SE	SE ■	SE ■		SE	SE	SE	SE	SE	SE	SE	SE ■	SE		SE	SE	SE
Orpington	d		20 36						20 40	20 43	20 58		21 06						21 10	21 28	21 36				
Petts Wood	d		20 39						20 43				21 09						21 13		21 39				
Hither Green	d					20 42			20 56							21 12			21 26						21 42
Lewisham	d			20 38		20 48	20 52	20 56	21 01					21 08		21 18	21 22	21 26	21 31				21 38		21 48
St Johns	d						20 54										21 24								
New Cross	d			20 41			20 56							21 11			21 26						21 41		
London Victoria	a		21 13										21 43								22 13				
London Bridge	d			20 50	20 53	20 56	21 04	21 07	21 10	20 59	21 13			21 20	21 23	21 26	21 34	21 37	21 40	21 43			21 50	21 53	21 56
London Blackfriars	a																								
London Cannon Street	a																								
London Waterloo (East)	d			20 55	20 58	21 01	21 08	21 11	21 15	21 04	21 18			21 25	21 28	21 31	21 38	21 41	21 45	21 48			21 55	21 58	22 01
London Charing Cross	a			20 58	21 01	21 04	21 11	21 14	21 18	21 07	21 22			21 28	21 31	21 34	21 41	21 44	21 49	21 52			21 58	22 01	22 04

		SE	SE	SE	SE ■	SE ■	SE		SE	SE	SE	SE	SE	SE	SE ■	SE	SE		SE	SE	SE	SE	SE	SE ■	SE ■
Orpington	d			21 40	21 43	21 58	22 06							22 10	22 28	22 36							22 40	22 43	22 58
Petts Wood	d			21 43			22 09							22 13		22 39							22 43		
Hither Green	d			21 56							22 12			22 26						22 42			22 56		
Lewisham	d	21 52	21 56	22 01					22 08		22 18	22 22	22 26	22 31			22 38			22 48	22 52	22 56	23 01		
St Johns	d	21 54										22 24									22 54				
New Cross	d	21 56							22 11			22 26					22 41				22 56				
London Victoria	a						22 43									23 13									
London Bridge	d	22 04	22 07	22 10	21 59	22 13			22 20	22 23	22 26	22 34	22 37	22 40	22 43		22 50		22 53	22 56	23 04	23 07	23 10	22 59	23 13
London Blackfriars	a																								
London Cannon Street	a																								
London Waterloo (East)	d	22 08	22 11	22 15	22 04	22 18			22 25	22 28	22 31	22 38	22 41	22 45	22 48		22 55		22 58	23 01	23 08	23 11	23 15	23 04	23 18
London Charing Cross	a	22 11	22 14	22 18	22 07	22 22			22 28	22 31	22 34	22 41	22 44	22 49	22 52		22 58		23 01	23 04	23 11	23 14	23 18	23 07	23 22

		SE	SE		SE	SE	SE	SE
Orpington	d							23 10
Petts Wood	d							23 13
Hither Green	d				23 12			23 26
Lewisham	d	23 08			23 18	23 22	23 26	23 31
St Johns	d					23 24		
New Cross	d	23 11				23 26		
London Victoria	a							
London Bridge	d	23 20	23 23		23 26	23 34	23 37	23 40
London Blackfriars	a							
London Cannon Street	a							
London Waterloo (East)	d	23 25	23 28		23 31	23 38	23 41	23 45
London Charing Cross	a	23 28	23 31		23 34	23 41	23 44	23 49

Table 199

Sundays

29 July to 12 August

Orpington, Petts Wood, Hither Green and Lewisham - London (Summary of Services)

		SE	SE ■	SE	SE	SE	SE	SE	SE	SE ■		SE	SE	SE	SE	SE	SE	SE	SE	SE		SE ■	SE	SE ■	SE
Orpington	d	23p21	23p37		05 51	06 10			06 21	06 24			06 40							06 51		06 54		07 09	07 10
Petts Wood	d	23p24			05 54	06 13			06 24				06 43							06 54					07 13
Hither Green	d	23p37			06 07				06 37						06 42					07 07					
Lewisham	d	23p43			06 13		06 20	06 26				06 31			06 48	06 50	06 56	07 01	07 08	07 13					
St Johns	d											06 33						07 03							
New Cross	d											06 35			06 51			07 05							
London Victoria	a					06 47							07 17						07 33						07 47
London Bridge	d	23p52	23p55	06 15	06 21		06 29	06 35	06 48	06 39		06 42		06 45	06 57	06 59	07 05	07 12		07 21		07 09	07 18	07 24	
London Blackfriars	a																								
London Cannon Street	a																	07 18							
London Waterloo (East)	d	23p57	23p59	06 20	06 26		06 34	06 40	06 53	06 44		06 47		06 50	07 02	07 04	07 10			07 26		07 14	07 22	07 29	
London Charing Cross	a	00 04	00 03	06 26	06 32		06 40	06 46	06 56	06 47		06 53		06 56	07 08	07 10	07 16			07 32		07 17	07 28	07 33	

		SE	SE	SE	SE	SE ■		SE	SE	SE	SE	SE ■	SE	SE	SE	SE		SE	SE	SE	SE	SE	SE ■	SE	SE
Orpington	d				07 21	07 24						07 39	07 40											07 51	
Petts Wood	d				07 24								07 43											07 54	
Hither Green	d	07 12			07 37						07 42										07 58			08 07	
Lewisham	d	07 18	07 20	07 26					07 32	07 38				07 50		07 56		07 59	07 59		08 04	08 08			
St Johns	d								07 34										08 01		08 06				
New Cross	d	07 21							07 36										08 03		08 08				
London Victoria	a									08 03			08 17									08 33			
London Bridge	d	07 27	07 29	07 35	07 49	07 39		07 41	07 42		07 52	07 55		07 58	08 01	08 05		08 08	08 09	08 11	08 15		08 14	08 19	08 21
London Blackfriars	a																								
London Cannon Street	a							07 48							08 07				08 16	08 18	08 22				08 27
London Waterloo (East)	d	07 32	07 34	07 40	07 54	07 44			07 47		07 57	08 00		08 03		08 10		08 13					08 19	08 24	
London Charing Cross	a	07 38	07 43	07 46	07 57	07 48			07 53		08 00	08 03		08 09		08 16		08 19					08 22	08 27	

		SE		SE	SE ■	SE	SE	SE	SE	SE	SE	SE		SE	SE	SE ■	SE	SE	SE	SE	SE ■	SE		SE	SE
Orpington	d				08 09	08 10											08 21				08 39	08 40			
Petts Wood	d					08 13											08 24					08 43			
Hither Green	d	08 12												08 28			08 37		08 42						
Lewisham	d			08 14			08 20		08 26		08 29			08 34	08 38					08 44				08 50	
St Johns	d			08 16							08 31			08 36						08 46					
New Cross	d			08 18						08 19	08 33			08 38						08 48					
London Victoria	a					08 47									09 03							09 17			
London Bridge	d	08 22		08 24	08 25		08 28	08 31	08 35	09 31	08 39	08 41		08 45		08 44	08 49	08 51	08 52	08 54	08 55			08 58	09 01
London Blackfriars	a																								
London Cannon Street	a			08 31				08 37		09 37	08 46	08 48		08 52				08 57		09 01					09 07
London Waterloo (East)	d	08 27			08 30		08 33		08 40							08 49	08 54		08 57		09 00			09 03	
London Charing Cross	a	08 30			08 33		08 39		08 46							08 52	08 57		09 00		09 03			09 09	

		SE	SE	SE	SE	SE	SE	SE ■		SE	SE	SE	SE	SE ■	SE	SE	SE	SE		SE	SE	SE	SE	SE ■ ⚒	SE
Orpington	d									08 51				09 09	09 10										09 21
Petts Wood	d									08 54					09 13										09 24
Hither Green	d					08 58				09 07		09 12										09 28			09 37
Lewisham	d	08 56		08 59		09 04	09 08						09 14			09 20	09 26			09 29		09 34	09 38		
St Johns	d			09 01		09 06							09 16							09 31		09 36			
New Cross	d		08 49	09 03		09 08							09 18					09 19		09 33		09 38			
London Victoria	a						09 33								09 47								10 03		
London Bridge	d	09 05	10 01	09 09	09 11	09 15		09 14		09 19	09 21	09 22	09 24	09 25		09 28	09 35	10 31		09 39	09 41	09 45		09 44	09 49
London Blackfriars	a																								
London Cannon Street	a		10 07	09 16	09 18	09 22					09 27		09 31					10 37		09 46	09 48	09 52			
London Waterloo (East)	d	09 10						09 19		09 24		09 27		09 30		09 33	09 40							09 49	09 54
London Charing Cross	a	09 16						09 22		09 27		09 30		09 33		09 39	09 46							09 52	09 57

		SE	SE	SE		SE ■	SE	SE		SE	SE	SE	SE		SE	SE	SE	SE ■ ⚒	SE	SE	SE	SE	SE ■
Orpington	d					09 39	09 40		and at the same minutes past each hour until										12 51				13 09
Petts Wood	d						09 43												12 54				
Hither Green	d		09 42													12 58			13 07		13 12		
Lewisham	d			09 44				09 50		12 50	12 56		12 59			13 04	13 08					13 14	
St Johns	d			09 46									13 01			13 06						13 16	
New Cross	d			09 48								12 49	13 03			13 08						13 18	
London Victoria	a						10 17										13 33						
London Bridge	d	09 51	09 52	09 54		09 55		09 58		12 58	13 05	14 01	13 09		13 11	13 15		13 14	13 19	13 21	13 22	13 24	13 25
London Blackfriars	a																						
London Cannon Street	a	09 57		10 01								14 07	13 16		13 18	13 22				13 27		13 31	
London Waterloo (East)	d		09 57			10 00		10 03		13 03	13 10							13 19	13 24		13 27		13 30
London Charing Cross	a		10 00			10 03		10 09		13 09	13 16							13 22	13 27		13 30		13 33

Sundays
29 July to 12 August

Orpington, Petts Wood, Hither Green and Lewisham - London (Summary of Services)

		SE	SE	SE	SE	SE	SE	SE	SE	SE 1 ⌶	SE	SE	SE	SE	SE 1	SE	SE	SE	SE	SE	SE	SE	SE
Orpington 4	d	13 10									13 21				13 39	13 40							
Petts Wood 4	d	13 13									13 24					13 43							
Hither Green 4	d							13 28			13 37		13 42									13 58	
Lewisham 4	d		13 20	13 26		13 29		13 34	13 38					13 44			13 50	13 56		13 59		14 04	14 08
St Johns	d					13 31		13 36						13 46						14 01		14 06	
New Cross 4	d				13 19	13 33		13 38						13 48					13 49	14 03		14 08	
London Victoria 15	a	13 47							14 03							14 17							14 33
London Bridge 4	d		13 27	13 35	14 31	13 39	13 41	13 45		13 44	13 49	13 51	13 52	13 54	13 55		13 58	14 05	15 01	14 09	14 11	14 15	
London Blackfriars 3	a																						
London Cannon Street 4	a				14 37	13 46	13 48	13 52				13 57		14 01					15 07	14 16	14 18	14 22	
London Waterloo (East) 4	d		13 33	13 40						13 49	13 54		13 57		14 00		14 03	14 10					
London Charing Cross 4	a		13 39	13 46						13 52	13 57		14 00		14 03		14 09	14 16					

		SE 1 ⌶	SE	SE	SE	SE	SE 1	SE	SE		SE	SE	SE	SE	SE	SE	SE	SE 1 ⌶	SE	SE	SE	SE
Orpington 4	d		13 51				14 09	14 10		and at the same minutes past each hour until									18 21			
Petts Wood 4	d		13 54					14 13											18 24			
Hither Green 4	d		14 07		14 12											18 28			18 37		18 42	
Lewisham 4	d					14 14			14 20		18 20	18 26		18 29		18 34	18 38					18 44
St Johns	d					14 16								18 31		18 36						18 46
New Cross 4	d					14 18							18 19	18 33		18 38						18 48
London Victoria 15	a							14 47									19 03					
London Bridge 4	d	14 14	14 19	14 21	14 22	14 24	14 25		14 28		18 28	18 35	19 31	18 39	18 41	18 45		18 44	18 49	18 51	18 52	18 54
London Blackfriars 3	a																					
London Cannon Street 4	a			14 27		14 31							19 37	18 46	18 48	18 52				18 57		19 01
London Waterloo (East) 4	d	14 19	14 24		14 27		14 30		14 33		18 33	18 40						18 49	18 54		18 57	
London Charing Cross 4	a	14 22	14 27		14 30		14 33		14 39		18 39	18 46						18 52	18 57		19 00	

		SE 1	SE	SE	SE	SE	SE	SE	SE	SE	SE	SE 1 ⌶	SE	SE	SE 1	SE	SE	SE	SE	SE	SE	SE
Orpington 4	d	18 39	18 40											18 51	19 09	19 10						
Petts Wood 4	d		18 43											18 54		19 13						
Hither Green 4	d									18 58				19 07			19 13					
Lewisham 4	d			18 50	18 56		18 59	19 01		19 04	19 08			19 12			19 18		19 21	19 26		19 38
St Johns	d						19 01	19 03		19 06												19 40
New Cross 4	d					18 49	19 03	19 05		19 08								19 19	19 24			19 42
London Victoria 15	a		19 17								19 33					19 47						
London Bridge 4	d	18 55		18 58	19 05	20 01	19 09	19 11	19 11	19 15		19 14	19 19	19 21	19 25		19 28	20 31	19 34	19 37	19 41	19 49
London Blackfriars 3	a																					
London Cannon Street 4	a					20 07	19 16		19 18	19 22			19 25					20 37				
London Waterloo (East) 4	d	19 00		19 03	19 10			19 16				19 18		19 26	19 30		19 32		19 39	19 42	19 46	19 54
London Charing Cross 4	a	19 03		19 09	19 16			19 22				19 22		19 32	19 33		19 38		19 45	19 48	19 52	20 01

		SE	SE 1 ⌶	SE	SE	SE	SE	SE	SE	SE	SE 1	SE 1	SE	SE	SE	SE	SE	SE	SE	SE	SE 1	SE	SE
Orpington 4	d	19 21	19 28	19 40						19 51	19 58	20 09	20 10							20 21	20 28	20 40	
Petts Wood 4	d	19 24		19 43						19 54			20 13							20 24		20 43	
Hither Green 4	d	19 37			19 43					20 07				20 13						20 37			20 43
Lewisham 4	d	19 43			19 48	19 53	19 57		20 08	20 13				20 18	20 23	20 27	20 32		20 38	20 43			20 48
St Johns	d								20 10										20 40				
New Cross 4	d				19 51	19 56			20 12					20 21	20 26				20 42				20 51
London Victoria 15	a			20 17									20 47				20 53					21 17	
London Bridge 4	d	19 52	19 44		19 58	20 04	20 07	20 11	20 19	20 22	20 14	20 25		20 28	20 34	20 37		20 41	20 49	20 52	20 44		20 58
London Blackfriars 3	a																						
London Cannon Street 4	a																						
London Waterloo (East) 4	d	19 57	19 48		20 04	20 09	20 12	20 16	20 24	20 27	20 18	20 30		20 34	20 39	20 42		20 46	20 54	20 57	20 48		21 04
London Charing Cross 4	a	20 03	19 51		20 10	20 15	20 18	20 22	20 31	20 33	20 21	20 33		20 40	20 45	20 48		20 52	21 01	21 03	20 51		21 10

		SE	SE	SE	SE	SE	SE 1	SE 1	SE	SE	SE	SE	SE	SE	SE	SE 1	SE	SE	SE	SE	SE	SE
Orpington 4	d					20 51	20 58	21 09	21 10						21 21	21 28	21 40					
Petts Wood 4	d					20 54			21 13						21 24		21 43					
Hither Green 4	d					21 07				21 13					21 37			21 43				
Lewisham 4	d	20 53	20 57		21 08	21 13				21 18	21 23	21 26		21 38	21 43			21 48	21 53	21 56		22 08
St Johns	d				21 10									21 40								22 10
New Cross 4	d	20 56			21 12					21 21	21 26			21 42				21 51	21 56			22 12
London Victoria 15	a								21 47								22 17					
London Bridge 4	d	21 04	21 07	21 11	21 19	21 22	21 14	21 25		21 28	21 34	21 36	21 41	21 49	21 52	21 44		21 58	22 02	22 05	22 11	22 19
London Blackfriars 3	a																					
London Cannon Street 4	a																					
London Waterloo (East) 4	d	21 09	21 12	21 16	21 24	21 27	21 18	21 30		21 34	21 39	21 41	21 46	21 54	21 57	21 48		22 04	22 07	22 10	22 16	22 24
London Charing Cross 4	a	21 15	21 18	21 22	21 31	21 33	21 21	21 33		21 40	21 45	21 47	21 52	22 01	22 03	21 51		22 10	22 13	22 16	22 22	22 31

Sundays
29 July to 12 August

Orpington, Petts Wood, Hither Green and Lewisham - London (Summary of Services)

		SE	SE 1	SE 1	SE	SE	SE	SE	SE	SE	SE	SE 1	SE	SE	SE	SE	SE	SE	SE	SE 1	SE 1	SE	SE
Orpington 4	d	21 51	21 58	22 09	22 10						22 21	22 28	22 40						22 51	22 58	23 09	23 10	
Petts Wood 4	d	21 54			22 13						22 24		22 43						22 54			23 13	
Hither Green 4	d	22 07				22 13					22 37			22 43					23 07				23 13
Lewisham 4	d	22 13				22 18	22 23	22 26		22 38	22 43			22 48	22 53	22 56		23 08	23 13				23 18
St Johns	d									22 40								23 10					
New Cross 4	d					22 21	22 26			22 42				22 51	22 56			23 12					23 21
London Victoria 15	a				22 47								23 17									23 47	
London Bridge 4	d	22 22	22 14	22 25		22 28	22 32	22 35	22 41	22 49	22 52	22 44		22 58	23 02	23 05	23 11	23 19	23 22	23 14	23 25		23 28
London Blackfriars 3	a																						
London Cannon Street 4	a																						
London Waterloo (East) 4	d	22 27	22 18	22 30		22 34	22 37	22 40	22 46	22 54	22 57	22 48		23 04	23 07	23 10	23 16	23 24	23 27	23 18	23 30		23 34
London Charing Cross 4	a	22 33	22 21	22 33		22 40	22 43	22 46	22 52	23 01	23 03	22 51		23 10	23 13	23 16	23 23	23 30	23 33	23 21	23 33		23 40

		SE	SE	SE	SE	SE	SE 1
Orpington 4	d					23 21	23 37
Petts Wood 4	d					23 24	
Hither Green 4	d					23 37	
Lewisham 4	d	23 23	23 26		23 38	23 43	
St Johns	d				23 40		
New Cross 4	d	23 26			23 42		
London Victoria 15	a						
London Bridge 4	d	23 32	23 35	23 41	23 48	23 52	23 55
London Blackfriars 3	a						
London Cannon Street 4	a						
London Waterloo (East) 4	d	23 37	23 40	23 46	23 52	23 57	23 59
London Charing Cross 4	a	23 43	23 46	23 52	23 58	00 04	00 03

Sundays
26 August to 9 September

		SE	SE 1	SE	SE	SE	SE	SE	SE	SE	SE 1	SE	SE	SE	SE	SE	SE	SE	SE 1	SE 1	SE	SE	SE
Orpington 4	d	23p21	23p37	06 40	07 02	07 06				07 10	07 28	07 36						07 40	07 43	07 58	08 06		
Petts Wood 4	d	23p24		06 43	07 05	07 09				07 13		07 39						07 43			08 09		
Hither Green 4	d	23p37							07 12	07 26					07 42			07 56					
Lewisham 4	d	23p43					07 08		07 18	07 31			07 38		07 48	07 52	07 56	08 01				08 08	
St Johns	d															07 54							
New Cross 4	d						07 11						07 41			07 56						08 11	
London Victoria 15	a					07 43						08 13									08 43		
London Bridge 4	d	23p52	23p55				07 20	07 23	07 26	07 40	07 43		07 50	07 53	07 56	08 04	08 07	08 10	07 59	08 13		08 20	08 23
London Blackfriars 3	a			07 23	07 53																		
London Cannon Street 4	a																						
London Waterloo (East) 4	d	23p57	23p59				07 25	07 28	07 31	07 45	07 48		07 55	07 58	08 01	08 08	08 11	08 15	08 04	08 18		08 25	08 28
London Charing Cross 4	a	00 01	00 03				07 28	07 31	07 34	07 48	07 52		07 58	08 01	08 04	08 11	08 14	08 18	08 07	08 22		08 28	08 31

		SE	SE	SE	SE	SE 1	SE	SE	SE	SE	SE	SE	SE	SE 1	SE 1	SE	SE	SE	SE	SE	SE	SE
Orpington 4	d				08 10	08 28	08 36						08 40	08 43	08 58	09 06						09 10
Petts Wood 4	d				08 13		08 39						08 43			09 09						09 13
Hither Green 4	d	08 12			08 26					08 42			08 56						09 12			09 26
Lewisham 4	d	08 18	08 22	08 26	08 31			08 38		08 48	08 52	08 56	09 01				09 08		09 18	09 22	09 26	09 31
St Johns	d		08 24								08 54									09 24		
New Cross 4	d		08 26					08 41			08 56						09 11			09 26		
London Victoria 15	a						09 13									09 43						
London Bridge 4	d	08 26	08 34	08 37	08 40	08 43		08 50	08 53	08 56	09 04	09 07	09 10	08 59	09 13		09 20	09 23	09 26	09 34	09 37	09 40
London Blackfriars 3	a																					
London Cannon Street 4	a																					
London Waterloo (East) 4	d	08 31	08 38	08 41	08 45	08 48		08 55	08 58	09 01	09 08	09 11	09 15	09 04	09 18		09 25	09 28	09 31	09 38	09 41	09 45
London Charing Cross 4	a	08 34	08 41	08 44	08 49	08 52		08 58	09 01	09 04	09 11	09 14	09 18	09 07	09 22		09 28	09 31	09 34	09 41	09 44	09 49

		SE 1		SE 1	SE 1 ⌶	SE	SE	SE	SE	SE	SE	SE	SE 1	SE 1	SE	SE	SE	SE	SE	SE	SE	SE 1
Orpington 4	d	09 13	and at the same minutes past each hour until	19 13	19 28	19 36						19 40	19 43	19 58	20 06						20 10	20 28
Petts Wood 4	d					19 39						19 43			20 09						20 13	
Hither Green 4	d								19 42			19 56						20 12			20 26	
Lewisham 4	d						19 38		19 48	19 52	19 56	20 01				20 08		20 18	20 22	20 26	20 31	
St Johns	d									19 54									20 24			
New Cross 4	d						19 41			19 56						20 11			20 26			
London Victoria 15	a					20 13									20 43							
London Bridge 4	d	09 29		19 29	19 43		19 50	19 53	19 56	20 04	20 07	20 10	19 59	20 13		20 20	20 23	20 26	20 34	20 37	20 40	20 43
London Blackfriars 3	a																					
London Cannon Street 4	a																					
London Waterloo (East) 4	d	09 34		19 34	19 48		19 55	19 58	20 01	20 08	20 11	20 15	20 04	20 18		20 25	20 28	20 31	20 38	20 41	20 45	20 48
London Charing Cross 4	a	09 37		19 37	19 52		19 58	20 01	20 04	20 11	20 14	20 18	20 07	20 22		20 28	20 31	20 34	20 41	20 44	20 49	20 52

Sundays

26 August to 9 September

Orpington, Petts Wood, Hither Green and Lewisham - London (Summary of Services)

				SE	SE	SE	SE	SE	SE	SE	SE [1]	SE [1]		SE	SE	SE	SE	SE	SE	SE	SE [1]	SE		SE	SE	SE
Orpington [4]		d		20 36						20 40	20 43	20 58		21 06						21 10	21 28	21 36				
Petts Wood [4]		d		20 39						20 43				21 09						21 13		21 39				
Hither Green [4]		d					20 42			20 56							21 12			21 26						21 42
Lewisham [4]	⇌	d			20 38		20 48	20 52	20 56	21 01					21 08		21 18	21 22	21 26	21 31				21 38		21 48
St Johns		d						20 54										21 24								
New Cross [4]	⊖	d			20 41			20 56							21 11			21 26						21 41		
London Victoria [15]	⊖	a		21 13										21 43								22 13				
London Bridge [4]	⊖	d			20 50	20 53	20 56	21 04	21 07	21 10	20 59	21 13			21 20	21 23	21 26	21 34	21 37	21 40	21 43			21 50	21 53	21 56
London Blackfriars [3]	⊖	a																								
London Cannon Street [4]	⊖	a																								
London Waterloo (East) [4]	⊖	d			20 55	20 58	21 01	21 08	21 11	21 15	21 04	21 18			21 25	21 28	21 31	21 38	21 41	21 45	21 48			21 55	21 58	22 01
London Charing Cross [4]	⊖	a			20 58	21 01	21 04	21 11	21 14	21 18	21 07	21 22			21 28	21 31	21 34	21 41	21 44	21 49	21 52			21 58	22 01	22 04

			SE	SE	SE	SE [1]	SE [1]	SE		SE	SE	SE	SE	SE	SE	SE [1]	SE	SE		SE	SE	SE	SE	SE	SE [1]	SE [1]
Orpington [4]		d			21 40	21 43	21 58	22 06							22 10	22 28	22 36							22 40	22 43	22 58
Petts Wood [4]		d			21 43			22 09							22 13		22 39							22 43		
Hither Green [4]		d			21 56							22 12			22 26						22 42			22 56		
Lewisham [4]	⇌	d	21 52	21 56	22 01					22 08		22 18	22 22	22 26	22 31			22 38			22 48	22 52	22 56	23 01		
St Johns		d	21 54										22 24									22 54				
New Cross [4]	⊖	d	21 56							22 11			22 26					22 41				22 56				
London Victoria [15]	⊖	a						22 43									23 13									
London Bridge [4]	⊖	d	22 04	22 07	22 10	21 59	22 13			22 20	22 23	22 26	22 34	22 37	22 40	22 43		22 50		22 53	22 56	23 04	23 07	23 10	22 59	23 13
London Blackfriars [3]	⊖	a																								
London Cannon Street [4]	⊖	a																								
London Waterloo (East) [4]	⊖	d	22 08	22 11	22 15	22 04	22 18			22 25	22 28	22 31	22 38	22 41	22 45	22 48		22 55		22 58	23 01	23 08	23 11	23 15	23 04	23 18
London Charing Cross [4]	⊖	a	22 11	22 14	22 18	22 07	22 22			22 28	22 31	22 34	22 41	22 44	22 49	22 52		22 58		23 01	23 04	23 11	23 14	23 18	23 07	23 22

			SE	SE		SE	SE	SE	SE
Orpington [4]		d							23 10
Petts Wood [4]		d							23 13
Hither Green [4]		d				23 12			23 26
Lewisham [4]	⇌	d	23 08			23 18	23 22	23 26	23 31
St Johns		d					23 24		
New Cross [4]	⊖	d	23 11				23 26		
London Victoria [15]	⊖	a							
London Bridge [4]	⊖	d	23 20	23 23		23 26	23 34	23 37	23 40
London Blackfriars [3]	⊖	a							
London Cannon Street [4]	⊖	a							
London Waterloo (East) [4]	⊖	d	23 25	23 28		23 31	23 38	23 41	23 45
London Charing Cross [4]	⊖	a	23 28	23 31		23 34	23 41	23 44	23 49

Network Diagram for Tables 200, 203, 204 — also 199 ⊙

DM-26/11
Design BAJS

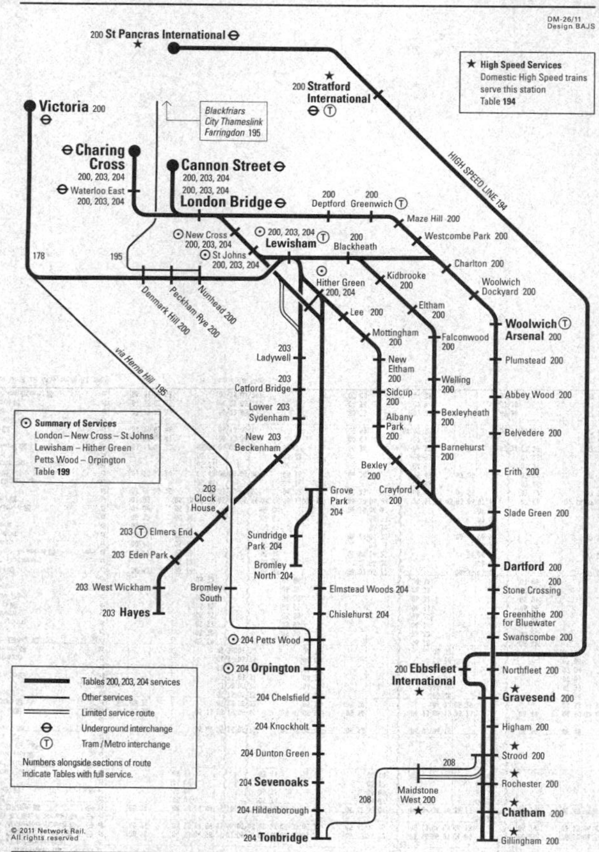

Table 200

Mondays to Fridays

until 27 July, 13 Aug to 28 Aug and from 10 Sep

London - Dartford and Gillingham

Network Diagram - see first Page of Table 200

Miles	Miles	Miles	Miles	Miles			SE MX	SE MO A	SE B	SE MX	SE MO A	SE MO A	SE MX	SE MO A	SE MX	SE MO A	SE MX	SE MX	SE MX	SE MO A	SE MO A	SE MX	SE MX	SE MX
—	—	—	—	0	St Pancras Int'l	d			23p25									23p55						
—	—	—	—	6	Stratford International	d			23p32									00 02						
—	—	—	—	22¼	Ebbsfleet International	d			23p43									00 13						
0	—	0	0	—	London Charing Cross	d	22p39	22p40		23p09	23p10	23p20	23p22	23p26	23p26	23p30	23p32		23p39	23p50	23p56	23p56	00 02	00 10
0¾	—	0¾	0¾	—	London Waterloo (East)	d	22p42	22p43		23p12	23p13	23p23	23p25	23p29	23p29	23p33	23p35		23p42	23p53	23p59	23p59	00 05	00 13
—	0	—	—	—	London Cannon Street	d																		
1¾	1¾	1¾	1¾	—	London Bridge	d	22p47	22p48		23p17	23p18	23p28	23p30	23p34	23p34	23p38	23p40		23p47	23p58	00 04	00 04	00 10	00 18
—	3¾	—	—	—	Deptford	d									23p40	23p44						00 10		
—	4¾	—	—	—	Greenwich	d									23p42	23p46						00 12		
—	5¼	—	—	—	Maze Hill	d									23p45	23p49						00 15		
—	5¾	—	—	—	Westcombe Park	d									23p47	23p51						00 17		
—	—	—	—	0	London Victoria	d																		
—	—	—	—	4¼	Denmark Hill	d																		
—	—	—	—	5	Peckham Rye	d																		
—	—	—	—	5¾	Nunhead	d																		
—	—	4¾	4¾	—	New Cross	d						23p34	23p35				23p45			00 04			00 15	00 23
—	—	5½	5½	—	St Johns	d																		
6	—	6	6	7½	Lewisham	d	22p56	22p57		23p26	23p27	23p38	23p39	23p42			23p49		23p56	00 08	00 12		00 19	00 27
7	—	7	—	8½	Blackheath	d	22p59	23p00		23p29	23p30	23p40					23p52		23p59	00 10			00 22	
—	—	8	—	9½	Kidbrooke	d						23p43					23p55			00 13			00 25	
—	—	9	—	10½	Eltham	d						23p47					23p58			00 17			00 28	
—	—	10¾	—	11¾	Falconwood	d						23p49					00 01			00 19			00 31	
—	—	11¾	—	12¾	Welling	d						23p52					00 03			00 22			00 33	
—	—	12¾	—	14¼	Bexleyheath	d						23p54					00 06			00 24			00 36	
—	—	14	—	15½	Barnehurst	d						23p57					00 08			00 27			00 38	
—	—	—	7¼	—	Hither Green	d							23p44	23p46							00 16			00 32
—	—	—	8	—	Lee	d							23p46	23p48							00 18			00 34
—	—	—	9½	—	Mottingham	d							23p49	23p51							00 21			00 37
—	—	—	10½	—	New Eltham	d							23p51	23p53							00 23			00 39
—	—	—	12	—	Sidcup	d							23p55	23p57							00 27			00 43
—	—	—	13	—	Albany Park	d							23p57	23p59							00 29			00 45
—	—	—	14	—	Bexley	d							23p59	00 01							00 31			00 47
—	—	—	15½	—	Crayford	d							00 03	00 04							00 34			00 51
9	6½	—	—	—	Charlton	d	23p03	23p04		23p33	23p34				23p50	23p54			00 03			00 20		
10	7½	—	—	—	Woolwich Dockyard	d									23p53	23p57						00 23		
10¾	8¼	—	—	—	Woolwich Arsenal	d	23p09	23p10		23p39	23p40				23p56	23p59			00 09			00 26		
11¼	8¾	—	—	—	Plumstead	d									23p58	00 02						00 28		
12¾	10¼	—	—	—	Abbey Wood	d	23p13	23p14		23p43	23p44				00 01	00 05			00 13			00 31		
14¼	11¾	—	—	—	Belvedere	d									00 03	00 07						00 33		
15½	13	—	—	—	Erith	d									00 06	00 10						00 36		
16¾	14¼	—	—	—	Slade Green	d									00 09	00 14						00 39		
18¾	16¼	17	17¼	18½	Dartford	a	23p24	23p24		23p54	23p54	00 04	00 08	00 09	00 14	00 19	00 16		00 24	00 33	00 39	00 44	00 46	00 56
—	—	—	—	—		d	23p25	23p25		23p55	23p55								00 25					
20¾	—	—	19¼	—	Stone Crossing	d	23p29	23p29		23p58	23p59								00 29					
21½	—	—	20	—	Greenhithe for Bluewater	d	23p31	23p31		23p59	00 01								00 31					
22¾	—	—	21¼	—	Swanscombe	d	23p34	23p34		00 04	00 04								00 34					
23½	—	—	22	—	Northfleet	d	23p36	23p36		00 06	00 06								00 36					
25½	—	—	24	24¾	Gravesend	d	23p40	23p40	23p48	00 10	00 10							00 18	00 40					
30	—	—	28½	29¼	Higham	d	23p46	23p46		00 16	00 16								00 46					
32¾	—	—	31¼	32	Strood	d	23p52	23p52	23p58	00 22	00 22							00 28	00 52					
—	—	—	—	—	Maidstone West	d																		
33¾	—	—	32¼	33	Rochester	d	23p56	23p56	00 03	00 26	00 26							00 33	00 56					
34½	—	—	32¾	33½	Chatham	d	23p58	23p58	00 05	00 28	00 28							00 35	00 58					
36	—	—	34½	35¼	Gillingham (Kent)	a	00 03	00 03	00 09	00 33	00 33							00 39	01 03					

A from 21 May until 23 July

B not 14 May

Table 200

Mondays to Fridays

until 27 July, 13 Aug to 28 Aug and from 10 Sep

London - Dartford and Gillingham

Network Diagram - see first Page of Table 200

		SE	SE	SE	SE	SE A	SE B	SE	SE	SE	SE	SE	SE C	SE	SE	SE	SE	SE C	SE	SE	SE	SE
St Pancras Int'l	d												06 25					06 55				
Stratford International	d												06 32					07 02				
Ebbsfleet International	d												06 42					07 13				
London Charing Cross	d	00 18		04 50	04 56	05 02	05 02	05 20	05 26	05 32	05 39	05 52		05 56	06 02	06 09			06 26	06 32	06 39	06 52
London Waterloo (East)	d	00 21		04 53	04 59	05 05	05 05	05 23	05 29	05 35	05 42	05 55		05 59	06 05	06 12			06 29	06 35	06 42	06 55
London Cannon Street	d																06 27					
London Bridge	d	00 26		04 58	05 04	05 10	05 10	05 28	05 34	05 42	05 47	06 01		06 04	06 10	06 17	06 31		06 34	06 40	06 47	07 00
Deptford	d			05 04				05 34				06 07					06 37					07 07
Greenwich	d			05 06				05 36				06 09					06 39					07 09
Maze Hill	d			05 09				05 39				06 12					06 42					07 12
Westcombe Park	d			05 11				05 41				06 14					06 44					07 14
London Victoria	d																					
Denmark Hill	d																					
Peckham Rye	d																					
Nunhead	d																					
New Cross	d	00 31			05 09	05 15	05 15		05 39	05 48	05 52			06 09	06 15				06 40	06 46		
St Johns	d																					
Lewisham	d	00 35			05 13	05 19	05 19		05 43	05 52	05 56			06 13	06 19	06 26			06 44	06 50	06 56	
Blackheath	d	00 38				05 22	05 22			05 54	05 59				06 22	06 29				06 53	06 59	
Kidbrooke	d					05 25	05 25			05 57					06 25					06 56		
Eltham	d					05 28	05 28			06 00					06 28					06 59		
Falconwood	d					05 31	05 31			06 03					06 31					07 01		
Welling	d					05 33	05 33			06 05					06 33					07 04		
Bexleyheath	d					05 36	05 36			06 08					06 36					07 06		
Barnehurst	d					05 38	05 38			06 10					06 38					07 11		
Hither Green	d				05 18				05 48					06 18					06 48			
Lee	d				05 20				05 50					06 20					06 50			
Mottingham	d				05 23				05 53					06 23					06 53			
New Eltham	d				05 25				05 55					06 25					06 55			
Sidcup	d				05 29				05 59					06 29					06 59			
Albany Park	d				05 31				06 01					06 31					07 01			
Bexley	d				05 33				06 03					06 33					07 03			
Crayford	d				05 36				06 06					06 36					07 06			
Charlton	d	00 42		05 14				05 44			06 03	06 17				06 33	06 47				07 03	07 17
Woolwich Dockyard	d			05 17				05 47				06 20					06 50					07 20
Woolwich Arsenal	d	00 47		05 20				05 50			06 09	06 23				06 39	06 53				07 09	07 23
Plumstead	d	00 49		05 22				05 52				06 25					06 55					07 25
Abbey Wood	d	00 53		05 25				05 55			06 13	06 28				06 43	06 58				07 13	07 28
Belvedere	d	00 55		05 27				05 57				06 30					07 00					07 30
Erith	d	00 58		05 30				06 00				06 33					07 03					07 33
Slade Green	d	01 00		05 34				06 04			06 19	06 37					07 07					07 37
Dartford	a	01 05		05 38	05 41	05 47	05 45	06 08	06 11	06 17	06 24	06 44		06 41	06 45	06 54	07 12		07 11	07 18	07 23	07 46
	d	01 06	05 25		05 42	05 55	05 55		06 12		06 25			06 42		06 55			07 12		07 25	
Stone Crossing	d				05 46				06 16					06 46					07 16			
Greenhithe for Bluewater	d	01 10	05 30		05 48	06 00	06 00		06 18		06 30			06 48		07 00			07 18		07 30	
Swanscombe	d				05 51				06 21					06 51					07 21			
Northfleet	d				05 53				06 23					06 53					07 23			
Gravesend	d	01 17	05 37		05a57	06 07	06 07		06a27		06 38		06 46	06 59		07a06		07 21	07 27		07 37	
Higham	d	01 23	05 43			06 13	06 13				06 44			07 05							07 43	
Strood	d	01 29	05 48			06 18	06 18				06 49		06 57	07 17				07 31	07a37		07 48	
Maidstone West	d												07a12									
Rochester	d	01 33	05 52			06 22	06 22				06 53			07 21				07 36			07 52	
Chatham	d	01 35	05 55			06 25	06 25				06 56			07 24				07 38			07 55	
Gillingham (Kent)	a	01 41	05 59			06 29	06 29				07 00			07 28				07 42			07 59	

A not until 18 May, from 21 May

B until 18 May

C not 27 July

Table 200

London - Dartford and Gillingham

Mondays to Fridays

until 27 July, 13 Aug to 28 Aug and from 10 Sep

Network Diagram - see first Page of Table 200

	SE A	SE B	SE	SE C	SE D	SE	SE	SE	SE	SE	SE D	SE C	SE D	SE	SE B	SE	SE	SE	SE	SE	SE	SE
St Pancras Int'l ⊖ d	07 18	07 25													07 52							
Stratford International ⊖ d	07 28	07 32													08 02							
Ebbsfleet International d	07 43	07 43													08 13							
London Charing Cross ⊖ d			06 56	07 02	07 02					07 12						07 26				07 39		
London Waterloo (East) ⊖ d			06 59	07 05	07 05					07 15						07 29				07 42		
London Cannon Street ⊖ d							07 10	07 10	07 13		07 24	07 24	07 24	07 27			07 32	07 36	07 41			07 44
London Bridge ⊖ d			07 05	07 10	07 10		07 14	07 14	07 17	07 21	07 28	07 28	07 28	07 31		07 34	07 37	07 40	07 45	07 47		07 48
Deptford d									07 23								07 43					07 54
Greenwich d									07 25					07 38			07 45					07 59
Maze Hill d									07 28								07 48					08 02
Westcombe Park d									07 30								07 50					08 04
London Victoria ⊖ d						07 09															07 43	
Denmark Hill d																					07 53	
Peckham Rye d																					07 56	
Nunhead d																					07 59	
New Cross ⊖ d							07 20	07 20			07 33	07 33	07 33						07 50			
St Johns d							07 22	07 22			07 35	07 35	07 35									
Lewisham d				07 18	07 18	07 27	07 27	07 27		07 30	07 38	07 38	07 38					07 49	07 54	07 56	08 08	
Blackheath d				07 21	07 21	07 29				07 32	07 41	07 41	07 41					07 52		07 59	08 10	
Kidbrooke d				07 24	07 24						07 44	07 44	07 44					07 55				
Eltham d				07 27	07 27						07 47	07 47	07 47					07 58				
Falconwood d				07 29	07 29						07 50	07 50	07 50					08 01				
Welling d				07 32	07 32						07 52	07 52	07 52					08 03				
Bexleyheath d				07 34	07 34						07 55	07 55	07 55					08 06				
Barnehurst d				07 37	07 37	07 40					07 58	07 59	07 58					08 08				
Hither Green d			07 18		08a11		07 31	07 31					08a31			07 45			07 59			
Lee d			07 20				07 33	07 33								07 47			08 01			
Mottingham d			07 23				07 36	07 36								07 50			08 04			
New Eltham d			07 26				07 39	07 39								07 53			08 07			
Sidcup d			07 29				07 42	07 42								07 56			08 13			
Albany Park d			07 31				07 44	07 44								07 58			08 15			
Bexley d			07 34				07 47	07 47								08 01			08 17			
Crayford d			07 37	07a46			07 50	07 50			08a08	08a08				08 05			08 21			
Charlton d								08a19	07 33	07 37				07 44			07 53		08a50	08 04		08 07
Woolwich Dockyard d									07 36								07 56					08 10
Woolwich Arsenal d									07 39	07 43				07 49			07 59			08 09		08 13
Plumstead d									07 41								08 01					08 15
Abbey Wood d									07 44	07 48				07 53			08 04			08 13		08 18
Belvedere d									07 46								08 06					08 20
Erith d									07 49								08 09					08 23
Slade Green d							07a57		07 52					07a59			08a12			08 20		08a26
Dartford a			07 42			07 48			07 57	07 59						08 11		08 15		08 25	08 27	
Dartford d			07 43							08 00						08 12				08 25		
Stone Crossing d			07 47													08 16						
Greenhithe for Bluewater d			07 49							08 05						08 18				08 30		
Swanscombe d			07 52													08 21						
Northfleet d			07 54													08 23						
Gravesend d	07 48	07 48	07a58							08 12					08 18	08a27				08 37		
Higham d										08 18										08 43		
Strood d	07 58	07 58								08 23					08 28					08 48		
Maidstone West d																						
Rochester d	08 03	08 03								08 27					08 33					08 52		
Chatham d	08 05	08 05								08 30					08 35					08 55		
Gillingham (Kent) a	08 09	08 09								08 35					08 39					08 59		

A 27 July
B not 27 July
C until 18 May
D not until 18 May, from 21 May

Table 200

London - Dartford and Gillingham

Mondays to Fridays

until 27 July, 13 Aug to 28 Aug and from 10 Sep

Network Diagram - see first Page of Table 200

	SE	SE	SE A	SE B	SE	SE	SE	SE	SE	SE	SE	SE B	SE	SE	SE	SE	SE	SE	SE	SE	SE
St Pancras Int'l ⊖ d			08 18	08 25								08 55									
Stratford International ⊖ d			08 28	08 32								09 05									
Ebbsfleet International d			08 44	08 43								09 17									
London Charing Cross ⊖ d					07 59		08 03		08 11				08 20		08 23	08 31			08 41		
London Waterloo (East) ⊖ d					08 02		08 06		08 14				08 23		08 26	08 34			08 44		
London Cannon Street ⊖ d	07 54	07 56				08 05		08 10			08 16			08 25			08 36	08 39			08 47
London Bridge ⊖ d	07 58	08 01			08 07	08 09	08 11	08 14	08 19		08 20		08 29	08 29	08 31	08 39	08 40	08 43	08 49		08 51
Deptford d		08 07				08 15					08 27			08 35			08 46				08 57
Greenwich d		08 09				08 19					08 29			08 39			08 49				08 59
Maze Hill d		08 12				08 22					08 32			08 42			08 52				09 02
Westcombe Park d		08 14				08 24					08 34			08 44			08 54				09 04
London Victoria ⊖ d										08 09										08 39	
Denmark Hill d										08 18										08 48	
Peckham Rye d										08 21										08 51	
Nunhead d										08 23										08 53	
New Cross ⊖ d	08 04							08 20							08 38			08 49			
St Johns d	08 06							08 22							08 40			08 51			
Lewisham d	08 11						08 19	08 25	08 28	08 32					08 43	08 49		08 54	08 56	09 02	
Blackheath d	08 13						08 22		08 31	08 34					08 46	08 52			08 59	09 04	
Kidbrooke d	08 16						08 25			08 37					08 49	08 55				09 07	
Eltham d	08 20						08 28			08 41					08 52	08 58				09 11	
Falconwood d	08 22						08 31			08 43					08 55	09 01				09 13	
Welling d	08 25						08 33			08 46					08 57	09 03				09 16	
Bexleyheath d	08 27						08 36			08 48					09 00	09 06				09 18	
Barnehurst d	08 30						08 38			08 51					09 04	09 08				09 21	
Hither Green d								08 29					08 44					08 59			
Lee d								08 31					08 46					09 01			
Mottingham d								08 34					08 49					09 04			
New Eltham d					08 21			08 37					08 51					09 06			
Sidcup d					08 25			08 40					08 55					09 10			
Albany Park d					08 27			08 42					08 57					09 12			
Bexley d					08 29			08 45					08 59					09 14			
Crayford d					08 33			08 48					09 03					09 18			
Charlton d		08 17				08 27		09a13	08 35		08 37			08 47			08 57	09a45	09 03		09 07
Woolwich Dockyard d		08 20				08 30					08 40			08 50			09 00				09 10
Woolwich Arsenal d		08 23				08 33			08 40		08 43			08 53			09 03		09 09		09 13
Plumstead d		08 25				08 35					08 45			08 55			09 05				09 15
Abbey Wood d		08 28				08 38			08 45		08 48			08 58			09 08		09 13		09 18
Belvedere d		08 30				08 40					08 50			09 00			09 10				09 20
Erith d		08 33				08 43					08 53			09 03			09 13				09 23
Slade Green d	08a35	08 37				08a46					08a56			09 07	09a09		09a16				09a27
Dartford a		08 42			08 38		08 45		08 54	08 58			09 08	09 12		09 15			09 24	09 28	
Dartford d					08 39				08 55				09 09						09 25		
Stone Crossing d					08 43								09 13								
Greenhithe for Bluewater d					08 45				09 00				09 15						09 30		
Swanscombe d					08 48								09 18								
Northfleet d					08 50								09 20								
Gravesend d			08 48	08 48	08a55				09 07			09 22	09a25						09 37		
Higham d									09 13										09 43		
Strood d			08 58	08 58					09 18			09 32							09 48		
Maidstone West d																					
Rochester d			09 03	09 03					09 22			09 37							09 52		
Chatham d			09 05	09 05					09 25			09 39							09 55		
Gillingham (Kent) a			09 09	09 09					09 29			09 43							09 59		

A 27 July
B not 27 July

Table 200

Mondays to Fridays

until 27 July, 13 Aug to 28 Aug and from 10 Sep

London - Dartford and Gillingham

Network Diagram - see first Page of Table 200

		SE	SE	SE A	SE B	SE	SE	SE	SE		SE	SE	SE	SE	SE	SE B	SE	SE	SE		SE	SE	SE	SE	SE
St Pancras Int'l	d			09 18	09 25											09 55									
Stratford International	d			09 28	09 32											10 02									
Ebbsfleet International	d			09 43	09 43											10 13									
London Charing Cross	d					08 55	09 02				09 11						09 26	09 32				09 39			
London Waterloo (East)	d					08 58	09 05				09 14						09 29	09 35				09 42			
London Cannon Street	d	08 54	08 56					09 07	09 09				09 15	09 24	09 27				09 37		09 40			09 47	09 54
London Bridge	d	08 58	09 01			09 03	09 10	09 11	09 14		09 19		09 19	09 28	09 31		09 34	09 40	09 41		09 44	09 47		09 51	09 58
Deptford	d		09 07					09 17					09 25		09 37				09 47					09 57	
Greenwich	d		09 09					09 19					09 29		09 39				09 49					09 59	
Maze Hill	d		09 12					09 22					09 32		09 42				09 52					10 02	
Westcombe Park	d		09 14					09 24					09 34		09 44				09 54					10 04	
London Victoria	d											09 09											09 39		
Denmark Hill	d											09 18											09 48		
Peckham Rye	d											09 21											09 51		
Nunhead	d											09 23											09 53		
New Cross	d	09 04							09 19					09 33							09 49				10 03
St Johns	d	09 06							09 21					09 35							09 51				10 05
Lewisham	d	09 09					09 19		09 24		09 29	09 32		09 38				09 49			09 54	09 56	10 02		10 08
Blackheath	d	09 12					09 22				09 31	09 34		09 41				09 52				09 59	10 04		10 11
Kidbrooke	d	09 15					09 25					09 37		09 44				09 55					10 07		10 14
Eltham	d	09 18					09 28					09 41		09 47				09 58					10 11		10 17
Falconwood	d	09 21					09 31					09 43		09 50				10 01					10 13		10 20
Welling	d	09 23					09 33					09 46		09 52				10 03					10 16		10 22
Bexleyheath	d	09 26					09 36					09 48		09 55				10 06					10 18		10 25
Barnehurst	d	09 32					09 38					09 51		10 02				10 08					10 21		10 32
Hither Green	d					09 15			09 29								09 44				09 59				
Lee	d					09 17			09 31								09 46				10 01				
Mottingham	d					09 20			09 34								09 49				10 04				
New Eltham	d					09 22			09 36								09 51				10 06				
Sidcup	d					09 26			09 40								09 55				10 10				
Albany Park	d					09 28			09 42								09 57				10 12				
Bexley	d					09 30			09 44								09 59				10 14				
Crayford	d					09 33			09 48								10 03				10 18				
Charlton	d		09 17					09 27	10a15		09 37		09 40		09 47				09 57		10a45	10 03		10 07	
Woolwich Dockyard	d		09 20					09 30					09 43		09 50				10 00					10 10	
Woolwich Arsenal	d		09 23					09 33			09 42		09 46		09 53				10 03			10 09		10 13	
Plumstead	d		09 25					09 35					09 48		09 55				10 05					10 15	
Abbey Wood	d		09 28					09 38			09 46		09 51		09 58				10 08			10 13		10 18	
Belvedere	d		09 30					09 40					09 53		10 00				10 10					10 20	
Erith	d		09 33					09 43					09 56		10 03				10 13					10 23	
Slade Green	d	09a42	09 37					09a45					09a59	10a12	10 07				10a16					10a25	10a42
Dartford	a		09 42			09 38	09 45				09 54	09 58			10 12		10 08	10 15				10 24	10 28		
	d					09 39					09 55						10 09					10 25			
Stone Crossing	d					09 43											10 13								
Greenhithe for Bluewater	d					09 45					10 00						10 15					10 30			
Swanscombe	d					09 48											10 18								
Northfleet	d					09 50											10 20								
Gravesend	d			09 48	09 48	09a55					10 07					10 18	10a25					10 37			
Higham	d										10 13											10 43			
Strood	d			09 58	09 58						10 18					10 28						10 48			
Maidstone West	d																								
Rochester	d			10 03	10 03						10 22					10 33						10 52			
Chatham	d			10 05	10 05						10 25					10 35						10 55			
Gillingham (Kent)	a			10 09	10 09						10 29					10 39						10 59			

A 27 July

B not 27 July

Table 200

Mondays to Fridays

until 27 July, 13 Aug to 28 Aug and from 10 Sep

London - Dartford and Gillingham

Network Diagram - see first Page of Table 200

		SE	SE A	SE B	SE		SE	SE	SE	SE C	SE D	SE	SE	SE	SE		SE B	SE	SE	SE	SE	SE	SE	SE	SE
St Pancras Int'l	d		10 18	10 28													10 52								
Stratford International	d		10 28	10 35													10 59								
Ebbsfleet International	d		10 44	10 46													11 13								
London Charing Cross	d				09 56		10 02			10 09	10 09							10 26	10 32			10 39			
London Waterloo (East)	d				09 59		10 05			10 12	10 12							10 29	10 35			10 42			
London Cannon Street	d	09 57						10 07	10 10				10 17	10 24	10 27					10 37	10 40			10 47	10 54
London Bridge	d	10 01			10 04		10 10	10 11	10 14	10 17	10 17		10 21	10 28	10 31			10 34	10 40	10 41	10 44	10 47		10 51	10 58
Deptford	d	10 07						10 17					10 27		10 37					10 47				10 57	
Greenwich	d	10 09						10 19					10 29		10 39					10 49				10 59	
Maze Hill	d	10 12						10 22					10 32		10 42					10 52				11 02	
Westcombe Park	d	10 14						10 24					10 34		10 44					10 54				11 04	
London Victoria	d											10 09											10 39		
Denmark Hill	d											10 18											10 48		
Peckham Rye	d											10 21											10 51		
Nunhead	d											10 23											10 53		
New Cross	d								10 19					10 33							10 49				11 03
St Johns	d								10 21					10 35							10 51				11 05
Lewisham	d						10 19		10 24	10 26	10 26	10 32		10 38					10 49		10 54	10 56	11 02		11 08
Blackheath	d						10 22			10 29	10 29	10 34		10 41					10 52			10 59	11 04		11 11
Kidbrooke	d						10 25					10 37		10 44					10 55				11 07		11 14
Eltham	d						10 28					10 41		10 47					10 58				11 11		11 17
Falconwood	d						10 31					10 43		10 50					11 01				11 13		11 20
Welling	d						10 33					10 46		10 52					11 03				11 16		11 22
Bexleyheath	d						10 36					10 48		10 55					11 06				11 18		11 25
Barnehurst	d						10 38					10 51		11 02					11 08				11 21		11 32
Hither Green	d				10 14				10 29									10 44			10 59				
Lee	d				10 16				10 31									10 46			11 01				
Mottingham	d				10 19				10 34									10 49			11 04				
New Eltham	d				10 21				10 36									10 51			11 06				
Sidcup	d				10 25				10 40									10 55			11 10				
Albany Park	d				10 27				10 42									10 57			11 12				
Bexley	d				10 29				10 44									10 59			11 14				
Crayford	d				10 33				10 48									11 03			11 18				
Charlton	d	10 17						10 27	11a15	10 33	10 33		10 37		10 47					10 57	11a45	11 03		11 07	
Woolwich Dockyard	d	10 20						10 30					10 40		10 50					11 00				11 10	
Woolwich Arsenal	d	10 23						10 33		10 39	10 39		10 43		10 53					11 03		11 09		11 13	
Plumstead	d	10 25						10 35					10 45		10 55					11 05				11 15	
Abbey Wood	d	10 28						10 38		10 43	10 43		10 48		10 58					11 08		11 13		11 18	
Belvedere	d	10 30						10 40					10 50		11 00					11 10				11 20	
Erith	d	10 33						10 43					10 53		11 03					11 13				11 23	
Slade Green	d	10 37						10a46					10a55	11a12	11 07					11a16				11a25	11a42
Dartford	a	10 42			10 38		10 45			10 54	10 54	10 58			11 12			11 08	11 15			11 24	11 28		
	d				10 39					10 55	10 55							11 09				11 25			
Stone Crossing	d				10 43													11 13							
Greenhithe for Bluewater	d				10 45					11 00	11 00							11 15				11 30			
Swanscombe	d				10 48													11 18							
Northfleet	d				10 50													11 20							
Gravesend	d		10 51	10 51	10a55					11 07	11 07						11 18	11a25				11 37			
Higham	d									11 13	11 13											11 43			
Strood	d		11 01	11 01						11 18	11 18						11 28					11 48			
Maidstone West	d																								
Rochester	d		11 06	11 06						11 22	11 23						11 33					11 52			
Chatham	d		11 08	11 08						11 25	11 25						11 35					11 55			
Gillingham (Kent)	a		11 12	11 12						11 29	11 29						11 39					11 59			

A 27 July

B not 27 July

C not until 18 May, from 21 May

D until 18 May

Table 200

Mondays to Fridays

until 27 July, 13 Aug to 28 Aug and from 10 Sep

London - Dartford and Gillingham

Network Diagram - see first Page of Table 200

			SE	SE A	SE B	SE	SE	SE	SE	SE	SE		SE	SE	SE	SE B	SE	SE	SE	SE	SE		SE	SE	SE
St Pancras Int'l ⊖	d			11 18	11 25											11 55									
Stratford International ⊖	d			11 28	11 32											12 02									
Ebbsfleet International	d			11 43	11 43											12 13									
London Charing Cross ⊖	d					10 56	11 02			11 09							11 26	11 32			11 39				
London Waterloo (East) ⊖	d					10 59	11 05			11 12							11 29	11 35			11 42				
London Cannon Street ⊖	d		10 57					11 07	11 10				11 17	11 24	11 27				11 37	11 40				11 47	11 54
London Bridge ⊖	d		11 01			11 04	11 10	11 11	11 14	11 17			11 21	11 28	11 31		11 34	11 40	11 41	11 44	11 47			11 51	11 58
Deptford	d		11 07					11 17					11 27		11 37				11 47					11 57	
Greenwich	d		11 09					11 19					11 29		11 39				11 49					11 59	
Maze Hill	d		11 12					11 22					11 32		11 42				11 52					12 02	
Westcombe Park	d		11 14					11 24					11 34		11 44				11 54					12 04	
London Victoria ⊖	d										11 09												11 39		
Denmark Hill	d										11 18												11 48		
Peckham Rye	d										11 21												11 51		
Nunhead	d										11 23												11 53		
New Cross ⊖	d								11 19					11 33						11 49					12 03
St Johns	d								11 21					11 35						11 51					12 05
Lewisham	d						11 19		11 24	11 26	11 32			11 38				11 49		11 54	11 56		12 02		12 08
Blackheath	d						11 22			11 29	11 34			11 41				11 52			11 59		12 04		12 11
Kidbrooke	d						11 25				11 37			11 44				11 55					12 07		12 14
Eltham	d						11 28				11 41			11 47				11 58					12 11		12 17
Falconwood	d						11 31				11 43			11 50				12 01					12 13		12 20
Welling	d						11 33				11 46			11 52				12 03					12 16		12 22
Bexleyheath	d						11 36				11 48			11 55				12 06					12 18		12 25
Barnehurst	d						11 38				11 51			12 02				12 08					12 21		12 32
Hither Green	d					11 14			11 29								11 44			11 59					
Lee	d					11 16			11 31								11 46			12 01					
Mottingham	d					11 19			11 34								11 49			12 04					
New Eltham	d					11 21			11 36								11 51			12 06					
Sidcup	d					11 25			11 40								11 55			12 10					
Albany Park	d					11 27			11 42								11 57			12 12					
Bexley	d					11 29			11 44								11 59			12 14					
Crayford	d					11 33			11 48								12 03			12 18					
Charlton	d		11 17					11 27	12a15	11 33			11 37		11 47				11 57	12a45	12 03			12 07	
Woolwich Dockyard	d		11 20					11 30					11 40		11 50				12 00					12 10	
Woolwich Arsenal	d		11 23					11 33		11 39			11 43		11 53				12 03		12 09			12 13	
Plumstead	d		11 25					11 35					11 45		11 55				12 05					12 15	
Abbey Wood	d		11 28					11 38		11 43			11 48		11 58				12 08		12 13			12 18	
Belvedere	d		11 30					11 40					11 50		12 00				12 10					12 20	
Erith	d		11 33					11 43					11 53		12 03				12 13					12 23	
Slade Green	d		11 37					11a45					11a55	12a12	12 07				12a16					12a25	12a42
Dartford	a		11 42			11 38	11 45			11 54	11 58				12 12		12 08	12 15			12 24		12 28		
	d					11 39				11 55							12 09				12 25				
Stone Crossing	d					11 43											12 13								
Greenhithe for Bluewater	d					11 45				12 00							12 15				12 30				
Swanscombe	d					11 48											12 18								
Northfleet	d					11 50											12 20								
Gravesend	d			11 48	11 48	11a55				12 07						12 18	12a25				12 37				
Higham	d									12 13											12 43				
Strood	d			11 58	11 58					12 18						12 28					12 48				
Maidstone West	d																								
Rochester	d			12 03	12 03					12 22						12 33					12 52				
Chatham	d			12 05	12 05					12 25						12 35					12 55				
Gillingham (Kent)	a			12 09	12 09					12 29						12 39					12 59				

A 27 July

B not 27 July

Table 200

Mondays to Fridays

until 27 July, 13 Aug to 28 Aug and from 10 Sep

London - Dartford and Gillingham

Network Diagram - see first Page of Table 200

		SE	SE A	SE B	SE	SE	SE		SE	SE	SE	SE	SE	SE	SE B	SE	SE		SE	SE	SE	SE	SE	SE	SE
St Pancras Int'l ⊖	d		12 18	12 22											12 52										
Stratford International ⊖	d		12 28	12 32											12 58										
Ebbsfleet International	d		12 44	12 43											13 13										
London Charing Cross ⊖	d				11 56	12 02				12 09						12 26	12 32				12 39				
London Waterloo (East) ⊖	d				11 59	12 05				12 12						12 29	12 35				12 42				
London Cannon Street ⊖	d	11 57					12 07		12 10			12 17	12 24	12 27					12 37	12 40			12 47	12 54	12 57
London Bridge ⊖	d	12 01			12 04	12 10	12 11		12 14	12 17		12 21	12 28	12 31		12 34	12 40		12 41	12 44	12 47		12 51	12 58	13 01
Deptford	d	12 07					12 17					12 27		12 37					12 47				12 57		13 07
Greenwich	d	12 09					12 19					12 29		12 39					12 49				12 59		13 09
Maze Hill	d	12 12					12 22					12 32		12 42					12 52				13 02		13 12
Westcombe Park	d	12 14					12 24					12 34		12 44					12 54				13 04		13 14
London Victoria ⊖	d										12 09											12 39			
Denmark Hill	d										12 18											12 48			
Peckham Rye	d										12 21											12 51			
Nunhead	d										12 23											12 53			
New Cross ⊖	d								12 19				12 33							12 49				13 03	
St Johns	d								12 21				12 35							12 51				13 05	
Lewisham	d					12 19			12 24	12 26	12 32		12 38				12 49			12 54	12 56	13 02		13 08	
Blackheath	d					12 22				12 29	12 34		12 41				12 52				12 59	13 04		13 11	
Kidbrooke	d					12 25					12 37		12 44				12 55					13 07		13 14	
Eltham	d					12 28					12 41		12 47				12 58					13 11		13 17	
Falconwood	d					12 31					12 43		12 50				13 01					13 13		13 20	
Welling	d					12 33					12 46		12 52				13 03					13 16		13 22	
Bexleyheath	d					12 36					12 48		12 55				13 06					13 18		13 25	
Barnehurst	d					12 38					12 51		13 02				13 08					13 21		13 32	
Hither Green	d				12 14				12 29							12 44				12 59					
Lee	d				12 16				12 31							12 46				13 01					
Mottingham	d				12 19				12 34							12 49				13 04					
New Eltham	d				12 21				12 36							12 51				13 06					
Sidcup	d				12 25				12 40							12 55				13 10					
Albany Park	d				12 27				12 42							12 57				13 12					
Bexley	d				12 29				12 44							12 59				13 14					
Crayford	d				12 33				12 48							13 03				13 18					
Charlton	d	12 17					12 27		13a15	12 33		12 37		12 47					12 57	13a45	13 03		13 07		13 17
Woolwich Dockyard	d	12 20					12 30					12 40		12 50					13 00				13 10		13 20
Woolwich Arsenal	d	12 23					12 33			12 39		12 43		12 53					13 03		13 09		13 13		13 23
Plumstead	d	12 25					12 35					12 45		12 55					13 05				13 15		13 25
Abbey Wood	d	12 28					12 38			12 43		12 48		12 58					13 08		13 13		13 18		13 28
Belvedere	d	12 30					12 40					12 50		13 00					13 10				13 20		13 30
Erith	d	12 33					12 43					12 53		13 03					13 13				13 23		13 33
Slade Green	d	12 37					12a46					12a55	13a12	13 07					13a16				13a25	13a42	13 37
Dartford	a	12 42			12 38	12 45				12 54	12 58			13 12		13 08	13 15				13 24	13 28			13 42
	d				12 39					12 55						13 09					13 25				
Stone Crossing	d				12 43											13 13									
Greenhithe for Bluewater	d				12 45					13 00						13 15					13 30				
Swanscombe	d				12 48											13 18									
Northfleet	d				12 50											13 20									
Gravesend	d		12 48	12 48	12a55					13 07					13 18	13a25					13 37				
Higham	d									13 13											13 43				
Strood	d		12 58	12 58						13 18					13 28						13 48				
Maidstone West	d																								
Rochester	d		13 03	13 03						13 22					13 33						13 52				
Chatham	d		13 05	13 05						13 25					13 35						13 55				
Gillingham (Kent)	a		13 09	13 09						13 29					13 39						13 59				

A 27 July

B not 27 July

Table 200

Mondays to Fridays

until 27 July, 13 Aug to 28 Aug and from 10 Sep

London - Dartford and Gillingham

Network Diagram - see first Page of Table 200

Station		SE A	SE B	SE	SE	SE	SE	SE	SE	SE	SE	SE	SE B	SE	SE	SE	SE	SE	SE	SE	SE	SE
St Pancras Int'l	d	13 18	13 25										13 55									
Stratford International	d	13 28	13 32										14 02									
Ebbsfleet International	d	13 43	13 43										14 13									
London Charing Cross	d			12 56	13 02			13 09						13 26	13 32			13 39				
London Waterloo (East)	d			12 59	13 05			13 12						13 29	13 35			13 42				
London Cannon Street	d					13 07	13 10			13 17	13 24	13 27				13 37	13 40			13 47	13 54	13 57
London Bridge	d			13 04	13 10	13 11	13 14	13 17		13 21	13 28	13 31		13 34	13 40	13 41	13 44	13 47		13 51	13 58	14 01
Deptford	d					13 17				13 27		13 37				13 47				13 57		14 07
Greenwich	d					13 19				13 29		13 39				13 49				13 59		14 09
Maze Hill	d					13 22				13 32		13 42				13 52				14 02		14 12
Westcombe Park	d					13 24				13 34		13 44				13 54				14 04		14 14
London Victoria	d								13 09										13 39			
Denmark Hill	d								13 18										13 48			
Peckham Rye	d								13 21										13 51			
Nunhead	d								13 23										13 53			
New Cross	d						13 19				13 33						13 49				14 03	
St Johns	d						13 21				13 35						13 51				14 05	
Lewisham	d				13 19		13 24	13 26	13 32		13 38				13 49		13 54	13 56	14 02		14 08	
Blackheath	d				13 22			13 29	13 34		13 41				13 52			13 59	14 04		14 11	
Kidbrooke	d				13 25				13 37		13 44				13 55				14 07		14 14	
Eltham	d				13 28				13 41		13 47				13 58				14 11		14 17	
Falconwood	d				13 31				13 43		13 50				14 01				14 13		14 20	
Welling	d				13 33				13 46		13 52				14 03				14 16		14 22	
Bexleyheath	d				13 36				13 48		13 55				14 06				14 18		14 25	
Barnehurst	d				13 38				13 51		14 02				14 08				14 21		14 32	
Hither Green	d			13 14			13 29							13 44			13 59					
Lee	d			13 16			13 31							13 46			14 01					
Mottingham	d			13 19			13 34							13 49			14 04					
New Eltham	d			13 21			13 36							13 51			14 06					
Sidcup	d			13 25			13 40							13 55			14 10					
Albany Park	d			13 27			13 42							13 57			14 12					
Bexley	d			13 29			13 44							13 59			14 14					
Crayford	d			13 33			13 48							14 03			14 18					
Charlton	d					13 27	14a15	13 33		13 37		13 47				13 57	14a45	14 03		14 07		14 17
Woolwich Dockyard	d					13 30				13 40		13 50				14 00				14 10		14 20
Woolwich Arsenal	d					13 33		13 39		13 43		13 53				14 03		14 09		14 13		14 23
Plumstead	d					13 35				13 45		13 55				14 05				14 15		14 25
Abbey Wood	d					13 38		13 43		13 48		13 58				14 08		14 13		14 18		14 28
Belvedere	d					13 40				13 50		14 00				14 10				14 20		14 30
Erith	d					13 43				13 53		14 03				14 13				14 23		14 33
Slade Green	d					13a46				13a55	14a12	14 07				14a16				14a25	14a42	14 37
Dartford	a			13 38	13 45			13 54	13 58			14 12		14 08	14 15			14 24	14 28			14 42
	d			13 39				13 55						14 09				14 25				
Stone Crossing	d			13 43										14 13								
Greenhithe for Bluewater	d			13 45				14 00						14 15				14 30				
Swanscombe	d			13 48										14 18								
Northfleet	d			13 50										14 20								
Gravesend	d	13 48	13 48	13a55				14 07					14 18	14a25				14 37				
Higham	d							14 13										14 43				
Strood	d	13 58	13 58					14 18					14 28					14 48				
Maidstone West	d																					
Rochester	d	14 03	14 03					14 22					14 33					14 52				
Chatham	d	14 05	14 05					14 25					14 35					14 55				
Gillingham (Kent)	a	14 09	14 09					14 29					14 39					14 59				

A 27 July

B not 27 July

Table 200

Mondays to Fridays

until 27 July, 13 Aug to 28 Aug and from 10 Sep

London - Dartford and Gillingham

Network Diagram - see first Page of Table 200

Station		SE A	SE B	SE	SE	SE	SE	SE	SE	SE	SE	SE	SE B	SE	SE	SE	SE	SE	SE	SE	SE	SE	SE A
St Pancras Int'l	d	14 18	14 25										14 55										15 18
Stratford International	d	14 28	14 32										15 02										15 28
Ebbsfleet International	d	14 43	14 43										15 13										15 43
London Charing Cross	d			13 56	14 02			14 09						14 26	14 32			14 39					
London Waterloo (East)	d			13 59	14 05			14 12						14 29	14 35			14 42					
London Cannon Street	d					14 07	14 10			14 17	14 24	14 27				14 37	14 40			14 47	14 54	14 57	
London Bridge	d			14 04	14 10	14 11	14 14	14 17		14 21	14 28	14 31		14 34	14 40	14 41	14 44	14 47		14 51	14 58	15 01	
Deptford	d					14 17				14 27		14 37				14 47				14 57		15 07	
Greenwich	d					14 19				14 29		14 39				14 49				14 59		15 09	
Maze Hill	d					14 22				14 32		14 42				14 52				15 02		15 12	
Westcombe Park	d					14 24				14 34		14 44				14 54				15 04		15 14	
London Victoria	d								14 09										14 39				
Denmark Hill	d								14 18										14 48				
Peckham Rye	d								14 21										14 51				
Nunhead	d								14 23										14 53				
New Cross	d						14 19				14 33						14 49				15 03		
St Johns	d						14 21				14 35						14 51				15 05		
Lewisham	d				14 19		14 24	14 26	14 32		14 38				14 49		14 54	14 56	15 02		15 08		
Blackheath	d				14 22			14 29	14 34		14 41				14 52			14 59	15 04		15 11		
Kidbrooke	d				14 25				14 37		14 44				14 55				15 07		15 14		
Eltham	d				14 28				14 41		14 47				14 58				15 11		15 17		
Falconwood	d				14 31				14 43		14 50				15 01				15 13		15 20		
Welling	d				14 33				14 46		14 52				15 03				15 16		15 22		
Bexleyheath	d				14 36				14 48		14 55				15 06				15 18		15 25		
Barnehurst	d				14 38				14 51		15 02				15 08				15 21		15 32		
Hither Green	d			14 14			14 29							14 44			14 59						
Lee	d			14 16			14 31							14 46			15 01						
Mottingham	d			14 19			14 34							14 49			15 04						
New Eltham	d			14 21			14 36							14 51			15 06						
Sidcup	d			14 25			14 40							14 55			15 10						
Albany Park	d			14 27			14 42							14 57			15 12						
Bexley	d			14 29			14 44							14 59			15 14						
Crayford	d			14 33			14 48							15 03			15 18						
Charlton	d					14 27	15a15	14 33		14 37		14 47				14 57	15a45	15 03		15 07		15 17	
Woolwich Dockyard	d					14 30				14 40		14 50				15 00				15 10		15 20	
Woolwich Arsenal	d					14 33		14 39		14 43		14 53				15 03		15 09		15 13		15 23	
Plumstead	d					14 35				14 45		14 55				15 05				15 15		15 25	
Abbey Wood	d					14 38		14 43		14 48		14 58				15 08		15 13		15 18		15 28	
Belvedere	d					14 40				14 50		15 00				15 10				15 20		15 30	
Erith	d					14 43				14 53		15 03				15 13				15 23		15 33	
Slade Green	d					14a46				14a55	15a12	15 07				15a15				15a25	15a42	15 37	
Dartford	a			14 38	14 45			14 54	14 58			15 12		15 08	15 15			15 24	15 28			15 42	
	d			14 39				14 55						15 09				15 25					
Stone Crossing	d			14 43										15 13									
Greenhithe for Bluewater	d			14 45				15 00						15 15				15 30					
Swanscombe	d			14 48										15 18									
Northfleet	d			14 50										15 20									
Gravesend	d	14 48	14 48	14a55				15 07					15 18	15a25				15 37					15 48
Higham	d							15 13										15 43					
Strood	d	14 58	14 58					15 18					15 28					15 48					15 58
Maidstone West	d																						
Rochester	d	15 03	15 03					15 22					15 33					15 52					16 03
Chatham	d	15 05	15 05					15 25					15 35					15 55					16 05
Gillingham (Kent)	a	15 09	15 09					15 29					15 39					15 59					16 09

A 27 July

B not 27 July

London - Dartford and Gillingham

Mondays to Fridays

until 27 July, 13 Aug to 28 Aug and from 10 Sep

Network Diagram - see first Page of Table 200

Station		SE A	SE	SE	SE		SE	SE	SE	SE	SE B	SE C	SE	SE A	SE		SE	SE	SE	SE	SE	SE	SE B	SE C	SE
St Pancras Int'l	d	15 25												15 55											
Stratford International	d	15 32												16 02											
Ebbsfleet International	d	15 43												16 13											
London Charing Cross	d		14 56	15 02				15 09							15 26		15 32			15 39					
London Waterloo (East)	d		14 59	15 05				15 12							15 29		15 35			15 42					
London Cannon Street	d				15 07		15 10			15 17	15 24	15 24	15 27					15 37	15 40			15 47	15 54	15 54	15 57
London Bridge	d		15 04	15 10	15 11		15 14	15 17		15 21	15 28	15 28	15 31		15 34		15 40	15 41	15 44	15 47		15 51	15 58	15 58	16 01
Deptford	d				15 17					15 27			15 37					15 47				15 57			16 07
Greenwich	d				15 19					15 29			15 39					15 49				15 59			16 09
Maze Hill	d				15 22					15 32			15 42					15 52				16 02			16 12
Westcombe Park	d				15 24					15 34			15 44					15 54				16 04			16 14
London Victoria	d								15 09												15 39				
Denmark Hill	d								15 18												15 48				
Peckham Rye	d								15 21												15 51				
Nunhead	d								15 23												15 53				
New Cross	d						15 19				15 33	15 33							15 49				16 03	16 03	
St Johns	d						15 21				15 35	15 35							15 51				16 05	16 05	
Lewisham	d			15 19			15 24	15 26	15 32		15 38	15 38					15 49		15 54	15 56	16 02		16 08	16 08	
Blackheath	d			15 22				15 29	15 34		15 41	15 41					15 52			15 59	16 04		16 11	16 11	
Kidbrooke	d			15 25					15 37		15 44	15 44					15 55				16 07		16 14	16 14	
Eltham	d			15 28					15 41		15 47	15 47					15 58				16 11		16 17	16 17	
Falconwood	d			15 31					15 43		15 50	15 50					16 01				16 13		16 20	16 20	
Welling	d			15 33					15 46		15 52	15 52					16 03				16 16		16 22	16 22	
Bexleyheath	d			15 36					15 48		15 55	15 55					16 06				16 18		16 25	16 25	
Barnehurst	d			15 38					15 51		15a58	16 02					16 08				16 21		16 33	16 32	
Hither Green	d		15 14				15 29								15 44				15 59						
Lee	d		15 16				15 31								15 46				16 01						
Mottingham	d		15 19				15 34								15 49				16 04						
New Eltham	d		15 21				15 36								15 51				16 06						
Sidcup	d		15 25				15 40								15 55				16 10						
Albany Park	d		15 27				15 42								15 57				16 12						
Bexley	d		15 29				15 44								15 59				16 14						
Crayford	d		15 33				15 48								16 03				16 18						
Charlton	d				15 27		16a15	15 33		15 37			15 47					15 57	16a45	16 03		16 07			16 17
Woolwich Dockyard	d				15 30					15 40			15 50					16 00				16 10			16 20
Woolwich Arsenal	d				15 33			15 39		15 43			15 53					16 03		16 09		16 13			16 23
Plumstead	d				15 35					15 45			15 55					16 05				16 15			16 25
Abbey Wood	d				15 38			15 43		15 48			15 58					16 08		16 13		16 18			16 28
Belvedere	d				15 40					15 50			16 00					16 10				16 20			16 30
Erith	d				15 43					15 53			16 03					16 13				16 23			16 33
Slade Green	d				15a46					15a55		16a12	16 07					16a16				16a25		16a42	16 37
Dartford	a		15 38	15 45				15 54	15 58				16 12		16 08		16 15			16 24	16 28		16 42		16 45
	d		15 39					15 55							16 09					16 25					
Stone Crossing	d		15 43												16 13										
Greenhithe for Bluewater	d		15 45					16 00							16 15					16 30					
Swanscombe	d		15 48												16 18										
Northfleet	d		15 50												16 20										
Gravesend	d	15 48	15a55					16 07						16 18	16a25					16 37					
Higham	d							16 13												16 43					
Strood	d	15 58						16 18						16 28						16 48					
Maidstone West	d																								
Rochester	d	16 03						16 22						16 33						16 52					
Chatham	d	16 05						16 25						16 35						16 55					
Gillingham (Kent)	a	16 09						16 29						16 39						16 59					

A not 27 July
B until 18 May
C not until 18 May, from 21 May

London - Dartford and Gillingham

Mondays to Fridays

until 27 July, 13 Aug to 28 Aug and from 10 Sep

Network Diagram - see first Page of Table 200

Station			SE A	SE B	SE	SE	SE	SE	SE	SE	SE		SE	SE	SE B	SE	SE	SE	SE	SE C	SE D		SE B	SE	SE
St Pancras Int'l	d		16 18	16 25											16 55								17 14		
Stratford International	d		16 28	16 32											17 02								17 21		
Ebbsfleet International	d		16 44	16 43											17 13										
London Charing Cross	d				15 56	16 02			16 09							16 26	16 30								
London Waterloo (East)	d				15 59	16 05			16 12							16 29	16 33								
London Cannon Street	d						16 07	16 10			16 17		16 24	16 27				16 35	16 39	16 42	16 42			16 44	
London Bridge	d				16 04	16 10	16 11	16 14	16 17		16 21		16 28	16 31		16 34	16 38	16 39	16 43	16 46	16 46			16 48	
Deptford	d						16 17				16 27			16 37				16 45							
Greenwich	d						16 20				16 30			16 40				16 48						16 56	
Maze Hill	d						16 23				16 33			16 43				16 51							
Westcombe Park	d						16 25				16 35			16 45				16 53							
London Victoria	d									16 09															16 39
Denmark Hill	d									16 18															16 48
Peckham Rye	d									16 21															16 51
Nunhead	d									16 23															16 53
New Cross	d							16 20					16 34						16 49	16 52	16 52				
St Johns	d							16 22					16 36						16 51						
Lewisham	d					16 19		16 25	16 27	16 32			16 39				16 49		16 54	16 56	16 56				17 02
Blackheath	d					16 22			16 29	16 34			16 42				16 53			16 59	16 59				17 04
Kidbrooke	d					16 25				16 37			16 45				16 56			17 02	17 02				17 07
Eltham	d					16 29				16 41			16 48				16 59			17 06	17 06				17 11
Falconwood	d					16 31				16 43			16 51				17 02			17 08	17 08				17 13
Welling	d					16 34				16 46			16 53				17 04			17 11	17 11				17 16
Bexleyheath	d					16 36				16 48			16 56				17 07			17 13	17 13				17 18
Barnehurst	d					16 39				16 51			17 02				17 11			17 17	17 17				17 21
Hither Green	d				16 14			16 29								16 44			16 58		17a57				
Lee	d				16 16			16 31								16 46			17 00						
Mottingham	d				16 19			16 34								16 49			17 03						
New Eltham	d				16 21			16 37								16 51			17 06						
Sidcup	d				16 25			16 40								16 55			17 09						
Albany Park	d				16 27			16 42								16 57			17 11						
Bexley	d				16 29			16 45								16 59			17 14						
Crayford	d				16 33			16 48								17 03			17 17	17a32					
Charlton	d						16 27	17a15	16 34		16 37			16 47				16 56	17a45					17 02	
Woolwich Dockyard	d						16 30				16 40			16 50				16 59							
Woolwich Arsenal	d						16 33		16 39		16 43			16 53				17 02						17 07	
Plumstead	d						16 35				16 45			16 55				17 04							
Abbey Wood	d						16 39		16 43		16 48			16 59				17 07						17 11	
Belvedere	d						16 41				16 51			17 01				17 10							
Erith	d						16 44				16 53			17 04				17 12							
Slade Green	d						16a46				16a56		17a14	17 07				17 15							
Dartford	a				16 38	16 48			16 54	17 00				17 14		17 08	17 23	17 22						17 26	17 31
	d				16 39				16 55							17 09								17 28	
Stone Crossing	d				16 43											17 13									
Greenhithe for Bluewater	d				16 45				17 00							17 15								17 33	
Swanscombe	d				16 48											17 18									
Northfleet	d				16 50											17 20									
Gravesend	d		16 48	16 48	16a55				17 07						17 18	17a27							17 36	17 40	
Higham	d								17 13															17 46	
Strood	d		16 58	16 58					17 18						17 28								17 46	17 52	
Maidstone West	d																						18a02		
Rochester	d		17 03	17 03					17 22						17 34									17 57	
Chatham	d		17 05	17 05					17 25						17 37									18 00	
Gillingham (Kent)	a		17 09	17 09					17 31						17 41									18 07	

A 27 July
B not 27 July
C until 18 May
D not until 18 May, from 21 May

Table 200

Mondays to Fridays

London - Dartford and Gillingham

until 27 July, 13 Aug to 28 Aug and from 10 Sep

Network Diagram - see first Page of Table 200

		SE	SE	SE	SE	SE	SE A	SE	SE	SE	SE	SE	SE	SE	SE	SE B	SE	SE	SE	SE	SE	SE	SE
St Pancras Int'l ⊖	d						17 18									17 44							
Stratford International ⊖	d						17 28									17 51							
Ebbsfleet International	d						17 43																
London Charing Cross ⊖	d	16 45	16 49		16 51			16 55				17 06	17 10		17 12		17 17				17 29	17 30	17 32
London Waterloo (East) ⊖	d	16 48	16 52		16 54			16 58				17 09	17 13		17 15		17 20				17 32	17 33	17 35
London Cannon Street ⊖	d			16 54		16 58			17 04	17 06				17 16				17 21	17 26	17 28			
London Bridge ⊖	d	16 53	16 57	16 58	16 59	17 02		17 04	17 08	17 10		17 14	17 19	17 20	17 21		17 26	17 25	17 30	17 32	17 37		17 41
Deptford	d	16 59		17 04								17 20		17 26							17 43		
Greenwich	d	17 02		17 07						17 18		17 23		17 29						17 40	17 46		
Maze Hill	d	17 05		17 10								17 26		17 32							17 49		
Westcombe Park	d	17 07		17 12								17 28		17 34							17 51		
London Victoria ⊖	d										17 04												
Denmark Hill	d										17 13												
Peckham Rye	d										17 16												
Nunhead	d										17 18												
New Cross ⊖	d					17 08			17 14									17 31	17 36				
St Johns	d					17 10												17 33					
Lewisham	d				17 08	17 13			17 18		17 25				17 30			17 36	17 40				
Blackheath	d				17 10				17 22		17 28				17 34				17 43			17 49	
Kidbrooke	d				17 13				17 25		17 31				17 37				17 46			17 52	
Eltham	d				17 17				17 29		17 34				17 40				17 50			17 56	
Falconwood	d				17 19				17 31		17 37				17 43				17 52			17 58	
Welling	d				17 22				17 34		17 39				17 45				17 55			18 01	
Bexleyheath	d				17 24				17 36		17 42				17 48				17 58			18 04	
Barnehurst	d				17 27				17 41		17 45				17 51				18 02			18 07	
Hither Green	d		17 07			17 18							17 29					17 41					17 51
Lee	d		17 09			17 20							17 31					17 43					17 53
Mottingham	d		17 12			17 23							17 34					17 46					17 56
New Eltham	d		17 15			17 26		17 20					17 36				17 42	17 48					17 59
Sidcup	d		17a20			17 30		17 26					17a41				17 47	17 52					18a04
Albany Park	d					17 32		17 28									17 49	17 54					
Bexley	d					17 35		17 30									17 52	17 57					
Crayford	d					17 39		17 34									17 55	18a00					
Charlton	d	17 10		17 15		18a05				17 24		17 30		17 37						17 46	17 53		
Woolwich Dockyard	d	17 13		17 18								17 33		17 40							17 56		
Woolwich Arsenal	d	17 16		17 21						17 29		17 36		17 43						17 51	17 59		
Plumstead	d	17 18		17 23								17 38		17 45							18 01		
Abbey Wood	d	17 21		17 26						17 33		17 42		17 48						17 55	18 05		
Belvedere	d	17 24		17 29								17 44		17 51							18 07		
Erith	d	17 26		17 31								17 47		17 53							18 10		
Slade Green	d	17a29		17 34					17a52			17a49		17 56					18a12		18a14		
Dartford	a			17 43	17 38			17 39		17 44	17 54			18 06	18 00		18 00			18 06		18 16	
	d							17 40		17 47							18 02			18 08			
Stone Crossing	d							17 44												18 12			
Greenhithe for Bluewater	d							17 46		17 52							18 07			18 14			
Swanscombe	d							17 49												18 17			
Northfleet	d							17 51												18 19			
Gravesend	d						17 48	17a57		18 00						18 06	18 19			18a27			
Higham	d									18 06							18 25						
Strood	d						17 58			18 14						18 18	18a33						
Maidstone West	d															18a32							
Rochester	d						18 03			18 20													
Chatham	d						18 05			18 23													
Gillingham (Kent)	a						18 09			18 30													

A 27 July

B not 27 July

Table 200

Mondays to Fridays

London - Dartford and Gillingham

until 27 July, 13 Aug to 28 Aug and from 10 Sep

Network Diagram - see first Page of Table 200

		SE	SE	SE	SE	SE	SE A	SE B	SE C	SE	SE	SE	SE	SE	SE	SE	SE	SE D	SE	SE	SE	SE
St Pancras Int'l ⊖	d								18 14									18 18				
Stratford International ⊖	d								18 21									18 28				
Ebbsfleet International	d																	18 40				
London Charing Cross ⊖	d		17 34	17 39							17 50	17 52	17 54	17 56					18 01			18 12
London Waterloo (East) ⊖	d		17 37	17 42							17 53	17 55	17 57	17 59					18 04			18 15
London Cannon Street ⊖	d	17 39				17 43	17 47	17 47		17 50					18 00		18 04			18 10	18 12	
London Bridge ⊖	d	17 43	17 43	17 48		17 47	17 51	17 51		17 54	17 58		18 02	18 04	18 04		18 08		18 10	18 14	18 16	18 21
Deptford	d	17 49									18 04				18 10							18 27
Greenwich	d	17 52								18 02	18 07				18 13						18 24	18 29
Maze Hill	d	17 55									18 10				18 16							18 32
Westcombe Park	d	17 57									18 12				18 18							18 34
London Victoria ⊖	d				17 34											17 56						
Denmark Hill	d				17 43											18 06						
Peckham Rye	d				17 46											18 09						
Nunhead	d				17 49											18 11						
New Cross ⊖	d					17 53	17 58	17 58									18 14			18 20		
St Johns	d					17 55											18 16					
Lewisham	d		17 53		17 56	17 59	18 02	18 02						18 14		18 18	18 20			18 24		
Blackheath	d		17 56		18 00		18 05	18 05				18 09		18 17		18 23				18 27		
Kidbrooke	d		17 59		18 03		18 08	18 08				18 12		18 20		18 26				18 30		
Eltham	d		18 02		18 06		18 12	18 12				18 16		18 23		18 30				18 34		
Falconwood	d		18 05		18 09		18 14	18 14				18 18		18 26		18 32				18 36		
Welling	d		18 07		18 11		18 17	18 17				18 21		18 28		18 35				18 39		
Bexleyheath	d		18 10		18 14		18 20	18 20				18 24		18 31		18 38				18 42		
Barnehurst	d		18 12		18 16		18 23	18 23				18 27		18a36		18 41				18a47		
Hither Green	d					18 03		18a57					18 13				18 25					
Lee	d					18 05							18 15				18 27					
Mottingham	d					18 08							18 18				18 30					
New Eltham	d			18 04		18 11							18 21				18 32		18 26			
Sidcup	d			18 08		18 15							18 25				18 36		18 30			
Albany Park	d			18 10		18 17											18 38		18 32			
Bexley	d			18 13		18 20											18 40		18 35			
Crayford	d			18 16		18a23	18a36						18a32				18 44		18 38			
Charlton	d	18 00								18 08	18 15				18 21		19a10				18 30	18 37
Woolwich Dockyard	d	18 03									18 18				18 24							18 40
Woolwich Arsenal	d	18 06								18 13	18 21				18 27						18 35	18 43
Plumstead	d	18 08									18 23				18 29							18 45
Abbey Wood	d	18 11								18 17	18 26				18 32						18 40	18 48
Belvedere	d	18 14									18 29				18 35							18 50
Erith	d	18 16									18 31				18 37							18 53
Slade Green	d	18 19	18a22								18a36				18 41							18a55
Dartford	a	18 27		18 21	18 25					18 29		18 36			18 48	18 53			18 44		18 52	
	d			18 22						18 31									18 45		18 54	
Stone Crossing	d																		18 49			
Greenhithe for Bluewater	d			18 27						18 36									18 51		18 59	
Swanscombe	d																		18 54			
Northfleet	d																		18 56			
Gravesend	d			18 34					18 38	18a45								18 45	19 02		19a09	
Higham	d			18 40															19 08			
Strood	d			18 45					18 49									18 55	19 14			
Maidstone West	d								19a05													
Rochester	d			18 51														19 03	19 19			
Chatham	d			18 54														19 06	19 22			
Gillingham (Kent)	a			19 02														19 10	19 29			

A until 18 May

B not until 18 May, from 21 May

C not 27 July

D 27 July

Table 200

Mondays to Fridays

London - Dartford and Gillingham

until 27 July, 13 Aug to 28 Aug and from 10 Sep

Network Diagram - see first Page of Table 200

	SE	SE	SE	SE	SE A	SE	SE	SE	SE	SE	SE	SE	SE	SE	SE	SE	SE	SE	SE B	SE A	SE	SE
St Pancras Int'l ⊖ d					18 55														19 18	19 25		
Stratford International ⊖ d					19 02														19 28	19 32		
Ebbsfleet International d					19 13														19 45	19 45		
London Charing Cross ⊖ d	18 14		18 18			18 23				18 34	18 37	18 39				18 48					18 56	19 02
London Waterloo (East) ⊖ d	18 17		18 21			18 26				18 37	18 40	18 42				18 51					18 59	19 05
London Cannon Street ⊖ d		18 21		18 25			18 30		18 34					18 46	18 50		18 54	18 57				
London Bridge ⊖ d	18 23	18 25	18 26	18 29		18 32	18 34		18 38	18 42	18 46	18 48		18 50	18 54	18 57	18 58	19 01			19 04	19 10
Deptford d		18 31								18 48				18 56				19 07				
Greenwich d		18 34					18 42			18 51				18 59				19 10				
Maze Hill d		18 37								18 54				19 02				19 13				
Westcombe Park d		18 39								18 56				19 04				19 15				
London Victoria ⊖ d								18 18					18 39									
Denmark Hill d								18 28					18 48									
Peckham Rye d								18 32					18 51									
Nunhead d								18 34					18 54									
New Cross ⊖ d				18 35					18 44			18 55			19 00		19 05					
St Johns d				18 37					18 46						19 02		19 07					
Lewisham d			18 36	18 41				18 43	18 49			18 59	19 03		19 05	19 07	19 11					19 19
Blackheath d			18 39					18 46	18 52			19 02	19 06			19 10	19 14					19 22
Kidbrooke d			18 42					18 49	18 55			19 05	19 09				19 17					19 25
Eltham d			18 46					18 53	18 59			19 09	19 13				19 21					19 29
Falconwood d			18 48					18 55	19 01			19 11	19 16				19 23					19 31
Welling d			18 51					18 58	19 04			19 14	19 18				19 26					19 34
Bexleyheath d			18 54					19 01	19 07			19 16	19 21				19 29					19 36
Barnehurst d			18 57					19 04	19a12			19a21	19 25				19a34					19 39
Hither Green d	18 35			18 46							18 56				19 09						19 14	
Lee d	18 37			18 48							18 58				19 11						19 16	
Mottingham d	18 40			18 51							19 01				19 14						19 19	
New Eltham d	18 43			18 54		18 48					19 04				19 17						19 22	
Sidcup d	18 47			18 58		18 51					19 08				19 20						19 25	
Albany Park d	18 49			19 00		18 53					19 10				19 22						19 27	
Bexley d	18 51			19 03		18 56					19 13				19 25						19 30	
Crayford d	18a54			19 10		18 59					19 16				19 29						19 33	
Charlton d		18 41		19a40			18 48			18 59				19 06	20a10	19 15		19 18				
Woolwich Dockyard d		18 44								19 02				19 09				19 21				
Woolwich Arsenal d		18 47					18 53			19 05				19 12		19 20		19 24				
Plumstead d		18 49								19 07				19 14				19 26				
Abbey Wood d		18 53					18 57			19 10				19 17		19 24		19 29				
Belvedere d		18 55								19 13				19 19				19 32				
Erith d		18 58								19 15				19 22				19 34				
Slade Green d		19 01								19 18				19a26				19 37				
Dartford a		19 09	19 06			19 04	19 09	19 13		19 28	19 21		19 34			19 34		19 44			19 38	19 48
d						19 05	19 10				19 22					19 35					19 39	
Stone Crossing d						19 09	19 14				19 26										19 43	
Greenhithe for Bluewater d						19 11	19 16				19 29					19 40					19 46	
Swanscombe d						19 14	19 19				19 32										19 49	
Northfleet d						19 16	19 21				19 34										19 51	
Gravesend d					19 20	19a24	19 26				19 38					19 47			19 51	19 51	19a57	
Higham d							19 32				19 44					19 53						
Strood d					19 30		19 38				19a53					19 58			20 01	20 01		
Maidstone West d																						
Rochester d					19 35		19 45									20 03			20 08	20 08		
Chatham d					19 38		19 48									20 05			20 10	20 10		
Gillingham (Kent) a					19 42		19 55									20 13			20 14	20 14		

A not 27 July

B 27 July

Table 200

Mondays to Fridays

London - Dartford and Gillingham

until 27 July, 13 Aug to 28 Aug and from 10 Sep

Network Diagram - see first Page of Table 200

	SE	SE	SE	SE	SE	SE	SE	SE A	SE	SE	SE	SE	SE	SE	SE	SE	SE	SE B	SE A	SE	SE	SE
St Pancras Int'l ⊖ d								19 55										20 18	20 25			
Stratford International ⊖ d								20 02										20 28	20 32			
Ebbsfleet International d								20 13										20 43	20 43			
London Charing Cross ⊖ d			19 09						19 26	19 32			19 39							19 56	20 02	
London Waterloo (East) ⊖ d			19 12						19 29	19 35			19 42							19 59	20 05	
London Cannon Street ⊖ d	19 07	19 10			19 17	19 24	19 27				19 37	19 40			19 47	19 54	19 57					20 10
London Bridge ⊖ d	19 11	19 14	19 17		19 21	19 28	19 31		19 34	19 40	19 41	19 44	19 47		19 51	19 58	20 01			20 04	20 10	20 14
Deptford d	19 17				19 27		19 37				19 47				19 57		20 07					
Greenwich d	19 19				19 29		19 39				19 49				19 59		20 09					
Maze Hill d	19 22				19 32		19 42				19 52				20 02		20 12					
Westcombe Park d	19 24				19 34		19 44				19 54				20 04		20 14					
London Victoria ⊖ d				19 09										19 39								
Denmark Hill d				19 18										19 48								
Peckham Rye d				19 21										19 51								
Nunhead d				19 23										19 53								
New Cross ⊖ d		19 19				19 33						19 49				20 03						20 19
St Johns d		19 21				19 35						19 51				20 05						20 21
Lewisham d		19 24	19 26	19 32		19 38				19 49		19 55	19 56	20 02		20 08					20 19	20 25
Blackheath d			19 29	19 34		19 41				19 52			19 59	20 04		20 11					20 22	
Kidbrooke d				19 37		19 44				19 55				20 07		20 14					20 25	
Eltham d				19 41		19 47				19 58				20 11		20 17					20 28	
Falconwood d				19 43		19 50				20 01				20 13		20 20					20 31	
Welling d				19 46		19 52				20 03				20 16		20 22					20 33	
Bexleyheath d				19 48		19 55				20 06				20 18		20 25					20 36	
Barnehurst d				19 51		19a58				20 08				20 21		20a28					20 38	
Hither Green d		19 29							19 44			20 00								20 14		20 30
Lee d		19 31							19 46			20 02								20 16		20 32
Mottingham d		19 34							19 49			20 05								20 19		20 35
New Eltham d		19 36							19 51			20 07								20 21		20 37
Sidcup d		19 40							19 55			20 11								20 25		20 41
Albany Park d		19 42							19 57			20 13								20 27		20 43
Bexley d		19 44							19 59			20 15								20 29		20 45
Crayford d		19 48							20 03			20 18								20 33		20 48
Charlton d	19 27		19 33		19 37		19 47				19 57		20 03		20 07		20 17					
Woolwich Dockyard d	19 30				19 40		19 50				20 00				20 10		20 20					
Woolwich Arsenal d	19 33		19 39		19 43		19 53				20 03		20 09		20 13		20 23					
Plumstead d	19 35				19 45		19 55				20 05				20 15		20 25					
Abbey Wood d	19 38		19 43		19 48		19 58				20 08		20 13		20 18		20 28					
Belvedere d	19 40				19 50		20 00				20 10				20 20		20 30					
Erith d	19 43				19 53		20 03				20 13				20 23		20 33					
Slade Green d	19a45				19a55		20 07				20a15				20a25		20 37					
Dartford a		19 53	19 55	19 58			20 13		20 08	20 15		20 23	20 25	20 28			20 43			20 38	20 45	20 53
d			19 55						20 09				20 25							20 39		
Stone Crossing d									20 13											20 43		
Greenhithe for Bluewater d			20 00						20 15				20 30							20 45		
Swanscombe d									20 18											20 48		
Northfleet d									20 20											20 50		
Gravesend d			20 07					20 18	20a25				20 37					20 48	20 48	20a55		
Higham d			20 13										20 43									
Strood d			20 18					20 28					20 48					20 58	20 58			
Maidstone West d																						
Rochester d			20 22					20 33					20 52					21 03	21 03			
Chatham d			20 25					20 35					20 55					21 05	21 05			
Gillingham (Kent) a			20 29					20 39					20 59					21 09	21 09			

A not 27 July

B 27 July

Table 200

Mondays to Fridays

until 27 July, 13 Aug to 28 Aug and from 10 Sep

London - Dartford and Gillingham

Network Diagram - see first Page of Table 200

		SE	SE	SE A	SE	SE	SE	SE	SE	SE B		SE A	SE	SE	SE	SE	SE	SE A	SE	SE		SE	SE	SE
St Pancras Int'l	d			20 55						21 18		21 25						21 55						
Stratford International	d			21 02						21 28		21 32						22 02						
Ebbsfleet International	d			21 13						21 43		21 43						22 13						
London Charing Cross	d	20 09			20 22		20 32	20 39					20 52		21 02	21 09			21 22	21 26		21 32	21 39	
London Waterloo (East)	d	20 12			20 25		20 35	20 42					20 55		21 05	21 12			21 25	21 29		21 35	21 42	
London Cannon Street	d		20 17			20 27			20 47					20 57										
London Bridge	d	20 17	20 21		20 30	20 31	20 40	20 47	20 51				21 00	21 01	21 10	21 17	21 20		21 30	21 34		21 40	21 47	21 50
Deptford	d		20 27			20 37			20 57					21 07			21 26			21 40				21 56
Greenwich	d		20 29			20 39			20 59					21 09			21 28			21 42				21 58
Maze Hill	d		20 32			20 42			21 02					21 12			21 31			21 45				22 01
Westcombe Park	d		20 34			20 44			21 04					21 14			21 33			21 47				22 03
London Victoria	d																							
Denmark Hill	d																							
Peckham Rye	d																							
Nunhead	d																							
New Cross	d				20 35		20 45						21 05		21 15				21 35			21 45		
St Johns	d																							
Lewisham	d	20 26			20 39		20 49	20 56					21 09		21 19	21 26			21 39			21 49	21 56	
Blackheath	d	20 29					20 52	20 59							21 22	21 29						21 52	21 59	
Kidbrooke	d						20 55								21 25							21 55		
Eltham	d						20 58								21 28							21 58		
Falconwood	d						21 01								21 31							22 01		
Welling	d						21 03								21 33							22 03		
Bexleyheath	d						21 06								21 36							22 06		
Barnehurst	d						21 08								21 38							22 08		
Hither Green	d				20 44								21 14						21 44					
Lee	d				20 46								21 16						21 46					
Mottingham	d				20 49								21 19						21 49					
New Eltham	d				20 51								21 21						21 51					
Sidcup	d				20 55								21 25						21 55					
Albany Park	d				20 57								21 27						21 57					
Bexley	d				20 59								21 29						21 59					
Crayford	d				21 03								21 33						22 03					
Charlton	d	20 33	20 37			20 47		21 03	21 07					21 17		21 33	21 36			21 50			22 03	22 06
Woolwich Dockyard	d		20 40			20 50			21 10					21 20			21 39			21 53				22 09
Woolwich Arsenal	d	20 39	20 43			20 53		21 09	21 13					21 23		21 39	21 42			21 56			22 09	22 12
Plumstead	d		20 45			20 55			21 15					21 25			21 44			21 58				22 14
Abbey Wood	d	20 43	20 48			20 58		21 13	21 18					21 28		21 43	21 47			22 01			22 13	22 17
Belvedere	d		20 50			21 00			21 20					21 30			21 50			22 03				22 20
Erith	d		20 53			21 03			21 23					21 33			21 52			22 06				22 22
Slade Green	d		20 57			21 07			21 27					21 37			21 56			22 09				22 26
Dartford	a	20 54	21 02		21 08	21 12	21 15	21 24	21 32				21 38	21 42	21 45	21 54	22 00		22 08	22 14		22 16	22 24	22 30
	d	20 55			21 09			21 25					21 39			21 55			22 09				22 25	
Stone Crossing	d				21 13								21 43						22 13					
Greenhithe for Bluewater	d	21 00			21 15			21 30					21 45			22 00			22 15				22 30	
Swanscombe	d				21 18								21 48						22 18					
Northfleet	d				21 20								21 50						22 20					
Gravesend	d	21 07		21 18	21a25			21 37		21 48		21 48	21a55			22 07		22 18	22a25				22 37	
Higham	d	21 13						21 43								22 13							22 43	
Strood	d	21 18		21 28				21 48		21 58		21 58				22 18		22 28					22 48	
Maidstone West	d																							
Rochester	d	21 22		21 33				21 52		22 03		22 03				22 22		22 33					22 52	
Chatham	d	21 25		21 35				21 55		22 05		22 05				22 25		22 35					22 55	
Gillingham (Kent)	a	21 29		21 39				21 59		22 09		22 09				22 29		22 39					22 59	

A not 27 July

B 27 July

Table 200

Mondays to Fridays

until 27 July, 13 Aug to 28 Aug and from 10 Sep

London - Dartford and Gillingham

Network Diagram - see first Page of Table 200

		SE A	SE	SE	SE	SE	SE		SE A	SE	SE	SE	SE	SE	SE	SE	SE		SE A	SE	SE	SE	SE	SE A	SE
St Pancras Int'l	d	22 25							22 55										23 25					23 55	
Stratford International	d	22 32							23 02										23 32					00 02	
Ebbsfleet International	d	22 43							23 13										23 43					00 13	
London Charing Cross	d		21 52	21 56	22 02	22 09				22 22	22 26	22 32	22 39		22 52	22 56	23 02			23 09	23 22	23 26	23 32		23 39
London Waterloo (East)	d		21 55	21 59	22 05	22 12				22 25	22 29	22 35	22 42		22 55	22 59	23 05			23 12	23 25	23 29	23 35		23 42
London Cannon Street	d																								
London Bridge	d		22 00	22 04	22 10	22 17	22 20			22 30	22 34	22 40	22 47	22 50	23 00	23 04	23 10			23 17	23 30	23 34	23 40		23 47
Deptford	d			22 10			22 26				22 40			22 56		23 10						23 40			
Greenwich	d			22 12			22 28				22 42			22 58		23 12						23 42			
Maze Hill	d			22 15			22 31				22 45			23 01		23 15						23 45			
Westcombe Park	d			22 17			22 33				22 47			23 03		23 17						23 47			
London Victoria	d																								
Denmark Hill	d																								
Peckham Rye	d																								
Nunhead	d																								
New Cross	d		22 05		22 15					22 35		22 45			23 05		23 15				23 35		23 45		
St Johns	d																								
Lewisham	d		22 09		22 19	22 26				22 39		22 49	22 56		23 09		23 19			23 26	23 39		23 49		23 56
Blackheath	d				22 22	22 29						22 52	22 59				23 22			23 29			23 52		23 59
Kidbrooke	d				22 25							22 55					23 25						23 55		
Eltham	d				22 28							22 58					23 28						23 58		
Falconwood	d				22 31							23 01					23 31						00 01		
Welling	d				22 33							23 03					23 33						00 03		
Bexleyheath	d				22 36							23 06					23 36						00 06		
Barnehurst	d				22 38							23 08					23 38						00 08		
Hither Green	d		22 14							22 44					23 14						23 44				
Lee	d		22 16							22 46					23 16						23 46				
Mottingham	d		22 19							22 49					23 19						23 49				
New Eltham	d		22 21							22 51					23 21						23 51				
Sidcup	d		22 25							22 55					23 25						23 55				
Albany Park	d		22 27							22 57					23 27						23 57				
Bexley	d		22 29							22 59					23 29						23 59				
Crayford	d		22 33							23 03					23 33						00 03				
Charlton	d			22 20		22 33	22 36				22 50		23 03	23 06		23 20				23 33		23 50			00 03
Woolwich Dockyard	d			22 23			22 39				22 53			23 09		23 23						23 53			
Woolwich Arsenal	d			22 26		22 39	22 42				22 56		23 09	23 12		23 26				23 39		23 56			00 09
Plumstead	d			22 28			22 44				22 58			23 14		23 28						23 58			
Abbey Wood	d			22 31		22 43	22 47				23 01		23 13	23 17		23 31				23 43		00 01			00 13
Belvedere	d			22 33			22 50				23 03			23 20		23 33						00 03			
Erith	d			22 36			22 52				23 06			23 22		23 36						00 06			
Slade Green	d			22 39			22 56				23 09			23 26		23 39						00 09			
Dartford	a		22 38	22 44	22 46	22 54	23 00			23 08	23 14	23 16	23 24	23 30	23 38	23 44	23 46			23 54	00 08	00 14	00 16		00 24
	d		22 39			22 55				23 09			23 25							23 55					00 25
Stone Crossing	d		22 43							23 13			23 29							23 58					00 29
Greenhithe for Bluewater	d		22 45			23 00				23 15			23 31							23 59					00 31
Swanscombe	d		22 48							23 18			23 34							00 04					00 34
Northfleet	d		22 50							23 20			23 36							00 06					00 36
Gravesend	d	22 48	22a55			23 07			23 18	23a25			23 40						23 48	00 10				00 18	00 40
Higham	d					23 13							23 46							00 16					00 46
Strood	d	22 58				23 18			23 28				23 52						23 58	00 22				00 28	00 52
Maidstone West	d																								
Rochester	d	23 03				23 22			23 33				23 56						00 03	00 26				00 33	00 56
Chatham	d	23 05				23 25			23 35				23 58						00 05	00 28				00 35	00 58
Gillingham (Kent)	a	23 09				23 29			23 39				00 03						00 09	00 33				00 39	01 03

A not 27 July

Table 200

Mondays to Fridays

until 27 July, 13 Aug to 28 Aug and from 10 Sep

London - Dartford and Gillingham

Network Diagram - see first Page of Table 200

		SE
St Pancras Int'l	d	
Stratford International	d	
Ebbsfleet International	d	
London Charing Cross	d	23 56
London Waterloo (East)	d	23 59
London Cannon Street	d	
London Bridge	d	00 04
Deptford	d	00 10
Greenwich	d	00 12
Maze Hill	d	00 15
Westcombe Park	d	00 17
London Victoria	d	
Denmark Hill	d	
Peckham Rye	d	
Nunhead	d	
New Cross	d	
St Johns	d	
Lewisham	d	
Blackheath	d	
Kidbrooke	d	
Eltham	d	
Falconwood	d	
Welling	d	
Bexleyheath	d	
Barnehurst	d	
Hither Green	d	
Lee	d	
Mottingham	d	
New Eltham	d	
Sidcup	d	
Albany Park	d	
Bexley	d	
Crayford	d	
Charlton	d	00 20
Woolwich Dockyard	d	00 23
Woolwich Arsenal	d	00 26
Plumstead	d	00 28
Abbey Wood	d	00 31
Belvedere	d	00 33
Erith	d	00 36
Slade Green	d	00 39
Dartford	a	00 44
Stone Crossing	d	
Greenhithe for Bluewater	d	
Swanscombe	d	
Northfleet	d	
Gravesend	d	
Higham	d	
Strood	d	
Maidstone West	d	
Rochester	d	
Chatham	d	
Gillingham (Kent)	a	

Table 200

Mondays to Fridays

30 July to 10 August

London - Dartford and Gillingham

Network Diagram - see first Page of Table 200

		SE A	SE MO	SE A	SE MO	SE	SE A	SE MO	SE MO	SE A		SE	SE A	SE MO	SE	SE A	SE MO	SE	SE	SE		SE	SE	SE	SE
St Pancras Int'l	d																							01 17	01 55
Stratford International	d																							01 26	02 04
Ebbsfleet International	d																							01 38	02 16
London Charing Cross	d	22p39	22p39	23p09	23p09	23p22	23p26	23p26	23p31	23p32		23p39	23p56	23p56	00 02	00 10	00 10	00 18	00 32			00 44			
London Waterloo (East)	d	22p42	22p42	23p12	23p12	23p25	23p29	23p29	23p34	23p35		23p42	23p59	23p59	00 05	00 13	00 13	00 21	00 35			00 47			
London Cannon Street	d																			00 42			00 56		
London Bridge	d	22p47	22p47	23p17	23p17	23p30	23p34	23p35	23p40	23p40		23p47	00 04	00 05	00 10	00 18	00 18	00 26	00 40	00 47		00 52	01 00		
Deptford	d						23p40	23p41					00 10	00 11					00 46				01 06		
Greenwich	d						23p42	23p43					00 12	00 13					00 49				01 09		
Maze Hill	d						23p45	23p47					00 15	00 17					00 53				01 13		
Westcombe Park	d						23p47	23p49					00 17	00 19					00 55				01 15		
London Victoria	d																								
Denmark Hill	d																								
Peckham Rye	d																								
Nunhead	d																								
New Cross	d					23p35			23p45	23p45					00 15	00 23	00 23	00 31				00 57			
St Johns	d																								
Lewisham	d	22p57	22p56	23p27	23p26	23p39			23p50	23p50		23p56			00 19	00 27	00 28	00 35		00 56		01 01			
Blackheath	d	23p00	23p00	23p30	23p30				23p55	23p55		00 01			00 22			00 38		01 00					
Kidbrooke	d								23p58	23p58					00 25					01 03					
Eltham	d								00 01	00 01					00 28					01 06					
Falconwood	d								00 04	00 04					00 31					01 09					
Welling	d								00 06	00 06					00 33					01 11					
Bexleyheath	d								00 09	00 09					00 36					01 14					
Barnehurst	d								00 12	00 12					00 38					01 17					
Hither Green	d					23p44										00 32	00 34					01 06			
Lee	d					23p46										00 34	00 36					01 08			
Mottingham	d					23p49										00 37	00 39					01 11			
New Eltham	d					23p51										00 39	00 41					01 13			
Sidcup	d					23p55										00 43	00 45					01 17			
Albany Park	d					23p57										00 45	00 47					01 19			
Bexley	d					23p59										00 47	00 49					01 21			
Crayford	d					00 03										00 51	00 53					01 25			
Charlton	d	23p05	23p06	23p35	23p36		23p50	23p52				00 06	00 20	00 22				00 43	00 58				01 18		
Woolwich Dockyard	d																								
Woolwich Arsenal	d	23p10	23p10	23p39	23p40		23p56	23p57				00 11	00 26	00 27				00 48	01 04				01 24		
Plumstead	d						23p58	23p59					00 28	00 29				00 50	01 06				01 26		
Abbey Wood	d	23p14	23p15	23p43	23p45		00 01	00 02				00 15	00 31	00 32				00 53	01 09				01 29		
Belvedere	d						00 03	00 04					00 33	00 34				00 55	01 12				01 32		
Erith	d						00 06	00 07					00 36	00 37				00 58	01 14				01 34		
Slade Green	d						00 09	00 09					00 39	00 39				01 00	01 17				01 37		
Dartford	a	23p24	23p24	23p54	23p54	00 11	00 17	00 17	00 22	00 22		00 24	00 47	00 47	00 49	00 59	00 58	01 05	01 25	01 25		01 33	01 45		
	d	23p25	23p25	23p55	23p55							00 25						01 06		01 27					
Stone Crossing	d	23p29	23p29	23p58	23p58							00 29													
Greenhithe for Bluewater	d	23p31	23p31	23p59	23p59							00 31						01 10		01 31					
Swanscombe	d	23p34	23p34	00 04	00 04							00 34													
Northfleet	d	23p36	23p36	00 06	00 06							00 36													
Gravesend	d	23p40	23p40	00 10	00 10							00 40						01 17		01 39				01 43	02 21
Higham	d	23p46	23p46	00 16	00 16							00 46						01 23		01 45					
Strood	d	23p52	23p52	00 22	00 22							00 52						01 29		01 50				01 53	02 31
Maidstone West	d																								
Rochester	d	23p56	23p56	00 26	00 26							00 56						01 33		01 54				01 57	02 35
Chatham	d	23p58	23p58	00 28	00 28							00 58						01 35		01 57				02 00	02 38
Gillingham (Kent)	a	00 06	00 06	00 36	00 36							01 06						01 44		02 04				02 04	02 42

A not 30 July, 6 August

Table 200

London - Dartford and Gillingham

Mondays to Fridays

30 July to 10 August

Network Diagram - see first Page of Table 200

Station		SE	SE	SE	SE	SE		SE	SE	SE	SE	SE	SE	SE	SE	SE		SE	SE	SE	SE	SE	SE	SE	SE
St Pancras Int'l	d																							07 18	
Stratford International	d																							07 28	
Ebbsfleet International	d																							07 43	
London Charing Cross	d		04 50	04 56	05 02	05 20		05 26	05 32	05 39	05 52	05 56		06 02	06 09				06 26	06 32	06 39		06 52		06 56
London Waterloo (East)	d		04 53	04 59	05 05	05 23		05 29	05 35	05 42	05 55	05 59		06 05	06 12				06 29	06 35	06 42		06 55		06 59
London Cannon Street	d																	06 27				06 47			
London Bridge	d		04 58	05 04	05 10	05 28		05 34	05 42	05 47	06 01	06 04		06 10	06 17			06 31	06 34	06 40	06 47		07 00		07 05
Deptford	d		05 04			05 34					06 07							06 37					07 06		
Greenwich	d		05 07			05 37					06 10							06 40				07 01	07 09		
Maze Hill	d		05 10			05 40					06 13														
Westcombe Park	d		05 12			05 42					06 15							06 45					07 14		
London Victoria	d												05 57			06 14									
Denmark Hill	d												06 07			06 24									
Peckham Rye	d															06 29									
Nunhead	d															06 31									
New Cross	d			05 09	05 15			05 39	05 48	05 52		06 09		06 15					06 40	06 46					
St Johns	d																								
Lewisham	d			05 13	05 19			05 43	05 52	05 56		06 13	06 15	06 19	06 26	06 43			06 44	06 50	06 56				
Blackheath	d				05 22				05 54	05 59			06 19	06 22	06 29	06 48				06 54	06 59				
Kidbrooke	d				05 25				05 57					06 25						06 57					
Eltham	d				05 28				06 00					06 28						07 00					
Falconwood	d				05 31				06 03					06 31						07 02					
Welling	d				05 33				06 05					06 33						07 05					
Bexleyheath	d				05 36				06 08					06 36						07 07					
Barnehurst	d				05 38				06 10					06 38						07 11					
Hither Green	d			05 18				05 48				06 18							06 48						07 18
Lee	d			05 20				05 50				06 20							06 50						07 20
Mottingham	d			05 23				05 53				06 23							06 53						07 23
New Eltham	d			05 25				05 55				06 25							06 55						07 26
Sidcup	d			05 29				05 59				06 29							06 59						07 29
Albany Park	d			05 31				06 01				06 31							07 01						07 31
Bexley	d			05 33				06 03				06 33							07 03						07 34
Crayford	d			05 36				06 06				06 36							07 06						07 37
Charlton	d		05 14			05 44				06 03	06 17		06 25		06 33			06 48			07 05	07 09	07 17		
Woolwich Dockyard	d																								
Woolwich Arsenal	d		05 20			05 50				06 09	06 23		06a30		06 39			06 53			07 10	07a13	07 24		
Plumstead	d		05 22			05 52					06 25							06 55					07 26		
Abbey Wood	d		05 25			05 55				06 13	06 28				06 43			06 58			07 15		07 29		
Belvedere	d		05 27			05 57					06 30							07 00					07 31		
Erith	d		05 30			06 00					06 33							07 03					07 34		
Slade Green	d		05 34			06 04				06 19	06 37							07 07					07 37		
Dartford	a		05 41	05 41	05 47	06 11		06 11	06 20	06 24	06 47	06 41		06 48	06 54	07 12		07 15	07 11	07 21	07 23		07 49		07 42
	d	05 25		05 42	05 55			06 12		06 25		06 42			06 55				07 12		07 25				07 43
Stone Crossing	d			05 46				06 16				06 46							07 16						07 47
Greenhithe for Bluewater	d	05 30		05 48	06 00			06 18		06 30		06 48			07 00				07 18		07 30				07 49
Swanscombe	d			05 51				06 21				06 51							07 21						07 52
Northfleet	d			05 53				06 23				06 53							07 23						07 54
Gravesend	d	05 37		06a00	06 07			06a30		06 38		06 59			07a09				07 27		07 37			07 48	07a58
Higham	d	05 43			06 13					06 44		07 05									07 43				
Strood	d	05 48			06 18					06 49		07 17							07a40		07 48			07 58	
Maidstone West	d																								
Rochester	d	05 52			06 22					06 53		07 21									07 52			08 03	
Chatham	d	05 55			06 25					06 56		07 24									07 55			08 05	
Gillingham (Kent)	a	05 59			06 32					07 03		07 31									08 02			08 09	

Table 200

London - Dartford and Gillingham

Mondays to Fridays

30 July to 10 August

Network Diagram - see first Page of Table 200

Station		SE		SE	SE	SE	SE	SE	SE	SE	SE	SE		SE	SE	SE	SE	SE	SE	SE	SE	SE		SE	SE
St Pancras Int'l	d																					08 18			
Stratford International	d																					08 28			
Ebbsfleet International	d																					08 44			
London Charing Cross	d	07 02					07 12			07 26						07 39		07 47						07 59	
London Waterloo (East)	d	07 05					07 15			07 29						07 42								08 02	
London Cannon Street	d				07 10	07 13		07 24	07 27		07 32	07 36		07 39	07 41		07 44			07 54	07 56				08 05
London Bridge	d	07 10			07 14	07 17	07 21	07 28	07 31	07 34	07 37	07 40			07 45	07 47	07 48			07 58	08 01			08 07	08 09
Deptford	d					07 23											07 54								
Greenwich	d					07 26			07 39		07 46						07 59				08 10				08 17
Maze Hill	d																								
Westcombe Park	d					07 31											08 04								
London Victoria	d			07 09															07 43						
Denmark Hill	d																		07 53						
Peckham Rye	d																		07 56						
Nunhead	d																		07 59						
New Cross	d				07 20			07 33							07 50					08 04					
St Johns	d				07 22			07 35												08 06					
Lewisham	d	07 18		07 25	07 27		07 30	07 38				07 48			07 54	07 57			08 07	08 11					
Blackheath	d	07 22		07 29			07 33	07 42				07 52		07 56		08 00		08 06	08 10	08 15					
Kidbrooke	d	07 25						07 45				07 55								08 18					
Eltham	d	07 28						07 48				07 58								08 21					
Falconwood	d	07 31						07 51				08 01								08 24					
Welling	d	07 33						07 53				08 03								08 26					
Bexleyheath	d	07 36						07 56				08 06								08 29					
Barnehurst	d	07 38		07 40				07 59				08 08								08 32					
Hither Green	d	08a11			07 31			08a31		07 45					07 59										
Lee	d				07 33					07 47					08 01										
Mottingham	d				07 36					07 50					08 04										
New Eltham	d				07 39					07 53					08 07									08 21	
Sidcup	d				07 42					07 56					08 13									08 25	
Albany Park	d				07 44					07 58					08 15									08 27	
Bexley	d				07 47					08 01					08 17									08 29	
Crayford	d				07 50					08 05					08 21			08a29						08 33	
Charlton	d				08a18	07 34	07 39		07 45		07 53				08a50	08 05	08 08				08 17				08 24
Woolwich Dockyard	d																								
Woolwich Arsenal	d					07 39	07 45		07 50		07 59					08 10	08 15				08 23				08 30
Plumstead	d					07 41					08 01						08 17				08 25				08 32
Abbey Wood	d					07 44	07 49		07 55		08 04					08 14	08 20				08 28				08 35
Belvedere	d					07 46					08 06						08 22				08 30				08 38
Erith	d					07 49					08 09						08 25				08 33				08 40
Slade Green	d					07 52			08a00		08a15			08a19		08 20	08a28			08a41	08 37				08a44
Dartford	a			07 51		08 00	07 59			08 11		08 18				08 25			08 30		08 45			08 38	
	d						08 00			08 12						08 25								08 39	
Stone Crossing	d									08 16														08 43	
Greenhithe for Bluewater	d						08 05			08 18						08 30								08 45	
Swanscombe	d									08 21														08 48	
Northfleet	d									08 23														08 50	
Gravesend	d						08 12			08a27						08 37						08 48		08a55	
Higham	d						08 18									08 43									
Strood	d						08 23									08 48						08 58			
Maidstone West	d																								
Rochester	d						08 27									08 52						09 03			
Chatham	d						08 30									08 55						09 05			
Gillingham (Kent)	a						08 38									09 02						09 09			

Table 200

London - Dartford and Gillingham

Mondays to Fridays

30 July to 10 August

Network Diagram - see first Page of Table 200

		SE	SE	SE	SE	SE	SE	SE	SE	SE	SE	SE	SE	SE	SE	SE	SE	SE	SE	SE	SE	SE	SE
St Pancras Int'l	d																						09 18
Stratford International	d																						09 28
Ebbsfleet International	d																						09 43
London Charing Cross	d	08 03		08 11			08 19	08 20		08 23	08 29		08 31			08 41				08 47			
London Waterloo (East)	d	08 06		08 14				08 23		08 26			08 34			08 44							
London Cannon Street	d		08 10			08 16			08 25			08 34		08 36	08 39			08 44	08 47		08 54	08 56	
London Bridge	d	08 11	08 14	08 19		08 20		08 29	08 29	08 31			08 39	08 40	08 43	08 49		08 49			08 58	09 01	
Deptford	d					08 28			08 35									08 57					
Greenwich	d					08 31			08 41			08 47		08 51				09 00	09 04			09 10	
Maze Hill	d																						
Westcombe Park	d					08 36												09 05					
London Victoria	d				08 09												08 39						
Denmark Hill	d				08 18												08 48						
Peckham Rye	d				08 21												08 51						
Nunhead	d				08 24												08 53						
New Cross	d		08 20							08 38					08 49						09 04		
St Johns	d		08 22							08 40					08 51						09 06		
Lewisham	d	08 19	08 25	08 28	08 31					08 43			08 50		08 54	08 57	09 02				09 09		
Blackheath	d	08 23		08 31	08 35		08 41			08 47	08 52		08 56			09 00	09 05			09 10	09 15		
Kidbrooke	d				08 38					08 50							09 08				09 18		
Eltham	d	08 28			08 41					08 53			09 02				09 11				09 21		
Falconwood	d	08 31			08 43					08 56			09 04				09 14				09 24		
Welling	d	08 33			08 46					08 58			09 07				09 16				09 26		
Bexleyheath	d	08 36			08 48					09 01			09 09				09 19				09 29		
Barnehurst	d	08 38			08 51		08a56			09 04	09a10		09 14				09 21				09 33		
Hither Green	d		08 29					08 44							08 59								
Lee	d		08 31					08 46							09 01								
Mottingham	d		08 34					08 49							09 04								
New Eltham	d		08 37					08 51							09 06								
Sidcup	d		08 40					08 55							09 10								
Albany Park	d		08 42					08 57							09 12								
Bexley	d		08 45					08 59							09 14								
Crayford	d		08 48					09 03							09 18								
Charlton	d		09a13	08 36		08 39			08 48			08 53		08 57	09a42	09 05		09 08	09 12	09 21		09 17	
Woolwich Dockyard	d																						
Woolwich Arsenal	d			08 41		08 44			08 54			08 59		09 03		09 10		09 13	09 17	09 27		09 23	
Plumstead	d					08 46			08 56					09 05				09 15	09a22	09a32		09 25	
Abbey Wood	d			08 46		08 49			08 59					09 08		09 15		09 19				09 28	
Belvedere	d					08 52			09 01					09 10				09 21				09 30	
Erith	d					08 54			09 04					09 13				09 24				09 33	
Slade Green	d					08a57			09 07	09a15				09a16				09a26			09a45	09 37	
Dartford	a	08 48		08 55	09 01			09 08	09 15			09 17	09 24			09 24	09 31					09 46	
	d			08 56				09 09								09 25							
Stone Crossing	d							09 13															
Greenhithe for Bluewater	d			09 01				09 15								09 30							
Swanscombe	d							09 18															
Northfleet	d							09 20															
Gravesend	d			09 08				09a25								09 37							09 48
Higham	d			09 14												09 43							
Strood	d			09 19												09 48							09 58
Maidstone West	d																						
Rochester	d			09 23												09 52							10 03
Chatham	d			09 26												09 55							10 05
Gillingham (Kent)	a			09 33												10 02							10 09

Table 200

London - Dartford and Gillingham

Mondays to Fridays

30 July to 10 August

Network Diagram - see first Page of Table 200

		SE	SE	SE	SE	SE	SE	SE	SE	SE	SE	SE	SE	SE	SE	SE	SE	SE	SE	SE	SE	SE
St Pancras Int'l	d																					10 18
Stratford International	d																					10 28
Ebbsfleet International	d																					10 44
London Charing Cross	d	08 55	09 02	09 07			09 11					09 22	09 26	09 32			09 39					
London Waterloo (East)	d	08 58	09 05				09 14						09 29	09 35			09 42					
London Cannon Street	d				09 07	09 09			09 15	09 24	09 28				09 37	09 40			09 47	09 54	09 57	
London Bridge	d	09 03	09 10		09 11	09 14	09 19		09 19	09 28	09 32		09 34	09 40	09 41	09 44	09 47		09 51	09 58	10 01	
Deptford	d								09 25										09 57			
Greenwich	d				09 20				09 32		09 41				09 50				10 00		10 10	
Maze Hill	d																					
Westcombe Park	d								09 37										10 05			
London Victoria	d							09 09										09 39				
Denmark Hill	d							09 18										09 48				
Peckham Rye	d							09 21										09 51				
Nunhead	d							09 24										09 53				
New Cross	d					09 19				09 33						09 49				10 03		
St Johns	d									09 35						09 51				10 05		
Lewisham	d		09 19			09 24	09 29	09 32		09 38				09 49		09 54	09 57	10 02		10 08		
Blackheath	d		09 24	09 29			09 32	09 35		09 42		09 48		09 53			10 01	10 06		10 12		
Kidbrooke	d							09 38		09 45								10 09		10 15		
Eltham	d		09 29					09 41		09 49				09 58				10 12		10 19		
Falconwood	d		09 32					09 44		09 51				10 01				10 14		10 21		
Welling	d		09 34					09 46		09 54				10 03				10 17		10 24		
Bexleyheath	d		09 37					09 49		09 56				10 06				10 19		10 26		
Barnehurst	d		09 39	09a45				09 51		10 02				10 08				10 22		10 32		
Hither Green	d	09 15				09 29							09 44			09 59						
Lee	d	09 17				09 31							09 46			10 01						
Mottingham	d	09 20				09 34							09 49			10 04						
New Eltham	d	09 22				09 36							09 52			10 06						
Sidcup	d	09 26				09 40							09 55			10 10						
Albany Park	d	09 28				09 42							09 57			10 12						
Bexley	d	09 30				09 44							10 00			10 14						
Crayford	d	09 33				09 48							10 03			10 18						
Charlton	d				09 27	10a12	09 36		09 41		09 48				09 56	10a42	10 05		10 09		10 17	
Woolwich Dockyard	d																					
Woolwich Arsenal	d				09 33		09 42		09 47		09 53	09 57			10 03		10 10		10 15		10 23	
Plumstead	d				09 35				09 49		09 55	10a02			10 05				10 17		10 25	
Abbey Wood	d				09 38		09 46		09 52		09 58				10 08		10 15		10 20		10 28	
Belvedere	d				09 40				09 55		10 00				10 10				10 22		10 31	
Erith	d				09 43				09 57		10 03				10 13				10 25		10 33	
Slade Green	d				09a46				10a00	10a15	10 07				10a16				10a27	10a45	10 37	
Dartford	a	09 38	09 50				09 54	10 01			10 15		10 08	10 18			10 24	10 31			10 45	
	d	09 39					09 55						10 09				10 25					
Stone Crossing	d	09 43											10 13									
Greenhithe for Bluewater	d	09 45					10 00						10 15				10 30					
Swanscombe	d	09 48											10 18									
Northfleet	d	09 50											10 20									
Gravesend	d	09a55					10 07						10a25				10 37					10 51
Higham	d						10 13										10 43					
Strood	d						10 18										10 48					11 01
Maidstone West	d																					
Rochester	d						10 22										10 52					11 06
Chatham	d						10 25										10 55					11 08
Gillingham (Kent)	a						10 32										11 02					11 12

Table 200

London - Dartford and Gillingham

Mondays to Fridays

30 July to 10 August

Network Diagram - see first Page of Table 200

Station		SE	SE	SE	SE	SE	SE	SE	SE	SE	SE	SE	SE	SE	SE	SE	SE	SE	SE	SE	SE	SE	SE
St Pancras Int'l ⊖	d																			11 18			
Stratford International ⊖	d																			11 28			
Ebbsfleet International	d																			11 43			
London Charing Cross ⊖	d	09 56	10 02			10 09					10 26	10 32			10 39						10 56	11 02	
London Waterloo (East) ⊖	d	09 59	10 05			10 12					10 29	10 35			10 42						10 59	11 05	
London Cannon Street ⊖	d			10 07	10 10			10 17	10 24	10 27			10 37	10 40			10 47	10 54	10 57				11 07
London Bridge ⊖	d	10 04	10 10	10 11	10 14	10 17		10 21	10 28	10 31	10 34	10 40	10 41	10 44	10 47		10 51	10 58	11 01		11 04	11 10	11 11
Deptford	d							10 27									10 57						
Greenwich	d			10 20				10 30		10 40			10 51				11 00		11 10				11 20
Maze Hill	d																						
Westcombe Park	d							10 35									11 05						
London Victoria ⊖	d						10 09									10 39							
Denmark Hill	d						10 18									10 48							
Peckham Rye	d						10 21									10 51							
Nunhead	d						10 23									10 53							
New Cross ⊖	d				10 19				10 33					10 49				11 03					
St Johns	d				10 21				10 35					10 51				11 05					
Lewisham	d		10 19		10 24	10 27	10 32		10 38			10 49		10 54	10 57	11 02		11 08				11 19	
Blackheath	d		10 23			10 31	10 36		10 42			10 53			11 01	11 06		11 12				11 23	
Kidbrooke	d						10 39		10 45							11 09		11 15					
Eltham	d		10 28				10 42		10 49			10 58				11 12		11 19				11 28	
Falconwood	d		10 31				10 44		10 51			11 01				11 14		11 21				11 31	
Welling	d		10 33				10 47		10 54			11 03				11 17		11 24				11 33	
Bexleyheath	d		10 36				10 49		10 56			11 06				11 19		11 26				11 36	
Barnehurst	d		10 38				10 52		11 02			11 08				11 22		11 32				11 38	
Hither Green	d	10 14			10 29						10 44			10 59							11 14		
Lee	d	10 16			10 31						10 46			11 01							11 16		
Mottingham	d	10 19			10 34						10 49			11 04							11 19		
New Eltham	d	10 21			10 36						10 51			11 06							11 21		
Sidcup	d	10 25			10 40						10 55			11 10							11 25		
Albany Park	d	10 27			10 42						10 57			11 12							11 27		
Bexley	d	10 29			10 44						10 59			11 14							11 29		
Crayford	d	10 33			10 48						11 03			11 18							11 33		
Charlton	d			10 26	11a12	10 35		10 39		10 47			10 57	11a42	11 05		11 09		11 17				11 26
Woolwich Dockyard	d																						
Woolwich Arsenal	d			10 33		10 40		10 44		10 53			11 03		11 10		11 14		11 23				11 33
Plumstead	d			10 35				10 46		10 55			11 05				11 16		11 25				11 35
Abbey Wood	d			10 38		10 45		10 49		10 58			11 08		11 15		11 19		11 28				11 38
Belvedere	d			10 40				10 52		11 01			11 10				11 22		11 31				11 40
Erith	d			10 43				10 54		11 03			11 13				11 24		11 33				11 43
Slade Green	d			10a46				10a57	11a15	11 07			11a16				11a27	11a45	11 37				11a46
Dartford	a	10 38	10 48			10 54	11 01			11 15	11 08	11 18			11 24	11 28			11 45		11 38	11 48	
	d	10 39				10 55					11 09				11 25						11 39		
Stone Crossing	d	10 43									11 13										11 43		
Greenhithe for Bluewater	d	10 45				11 00					11 15				11 30						11 45		
Swanscombe	d	10 48									11 18										11 48		
Northfleet	d	10 50									11 20										11 50		
Gravesend	d	10a55				11 07					11a25				11 37					11 48	11a55		
Higham	d					11 13									11 43								
Strood	d					11 18									11 48					11 58			
Maidstone West	d																						
Rochester	d					11 23									11 52					12 03			
Chatham	d					11 25									11 55					12 05			
Gillingham (Kent)	a					11 32									12 02					12 09			

Table 200

London - Dartford and Gillingham

Mondays to Fridays

30 July to 10 August

Network Diagram - see first Page of Table 200

Station		SE	SE	SE	SE	SE	SE	SE	SE	SE	SE	SE	SE	SE	SE	SE	SE	SE	SE	SE	SE	SE	SE
St Pancras Int'l ⊖	d																12 18						
Stratford International ⊖	d																12 28						
Ebbsfleet International	d																12 44						
London Charing Cross ⊖	d		11 09					11 26	11 32			11 39						11 56	12 02			12 09	
London Waterloo (East) ⊖	d		11 12					11 29	11 35			11 42						11 59	12 05			12 12	
London Cannon Street ⊖	d	11 10			11 17	11 24	11 27			11 37	11 40			11 47	11 54	11 57				12 07	12 10		
London Bridge ⊖	d	11 14	11 17		11 21	11 28	11 31	11 34	11 40	11 41	11 44	11 47		11 51	11 58	12 01		12 04	12 10	12 11	12 14	12 17	
Deptford	d				11 27									11 57									
Greenwich	d				11 30		11 40			11 50				12 00		12 09				12 19			
Maze Hill	d															12 13				12 23			
Westcombe Park	d				11 35									12 05									
London Victoria ⊖	d			11 09									11 39										12 09
Denmark Hill	d			11 18									11 48										12 18
Peckham Rye	d			11 21									11 51										12 21
Nunhead	d			11 23									11 53										12 23
New Cross ⊖	d	11 19				11 33					11 49				12 03						12 19		
St Johns	d	11 21				11 35					11 51				12 05						12 21		
Lewisham	d	11 24	11 27	11 32		11 38			11 49		11 54	11 57	12 02		12 08				12 19		12 24	12 27	12 32
Blackheath	d		11 31	11 36		11 42			11 53			12 01	12 06		12 12				12 23			12 30	12 36
Kidbrooke	d			11 39		11 45							12 09		12 15								12 39
Eltham	d			11 42		11 49			11 58				12 12		12 19				12 28				12 42
Falconwood	d			11 44		11 51			12 01				12 14		12 21				12 31				12 44
Welling	d			11 47		11 54			12 03				12 17		12 24				12 33				12 47
Bexleyheath	d			11 49		11 56			12 06				12 19		12 26				12 36				12 49
Barnehurst	d			11 52		12 02			12 08				12 22		12 32				12 38				12 52
Hither Green	d	11 29						11 44			11 59							12 14			12 29		
Lee	d	11 31						11 46			12 01							12 16			12 31		
Mottingham	d	11 34						11 49			12 04							12 19			12 34		
New Eltham	d	11 36						11 51			12 06							12 21			12 36		
Sidcup	d	11 40						11 55			12 10							12 25			12 40		
Albany Park	d	11 42						11 57			12 12							12 27			12 42		
Bexley	d	11 44						11 59			12 14							12 29			12 44		
Crayford	d	11 48						12 03			12 18							12 33			12 48		
Charlton	d	12a12	11 35		11 39		11 47			11 56	12a42	12 05		12 09		12 17				12 27	13a12	12 35	
Woolwich Dockyard	d																						
Woolwich Arsenal	d		11 40		11 44		11 53			12 03		12 10		12 14		12 23				12 32		12 40	
Plumstead	d				11 46		11 55			12 05				12 16		12 26				12 35			
Abbey Wood	d		11 45		11 49		11 58			12 08		12 15		12 19		12 29				12 38		12 44	
Belvedere	d				11 52		12 01			12 10				12 22		12 31				12 40			
Erith	d				11 54		12 03			12 13				12 24		12 34				12 43			
Slade Green	d				11a57	12a15	12 07			12a16				12a27	12a45	12 37				12a46			
Dartford	a		11 54	12 01			12 15	12 08	12 18			12 24	12 31			12 45		12 38	12 48			12 54	13 01
	d		11 55					12 09				12 25						12 39				12 55	
Stone Crossing	d							12 13										12 43					
Greenhithe for Bluewater	d		12 00					12 15				12 30						12 45				13 00	
Swanscombe	d							12 18										12 48					
Northfleet	d							12 20										12 50					
Gravesend	d		12 07					12a25				12 37					12 48	12a55				13 07	
Higham	d		12 13									12 43										13 13	
Strood	d		12 18									12 48					12 58					13 18	
Maidstone West	d																						
Rochester	d		12 22									12 52					13 03					13 22	
Chatham	d		12 25									12 55					13 05					13 25	
Gillingham (Kent)	a		12 32									13 02					13 09					13 32	

Table 200

Mondays to Fridays

London - Dartford and Gillingham

30 July to 10 August

Network Diagram - see first Page of Table 200

		SE		SE	SE	SE	SE	SE	SE	SE	SE	SE		SE	SE	SE	SE	SE	SE	SE	SE	SE		SE	SE
St Pancras Int'l 15 ⊖	d															13 18									
Stratford International ⊖ ⛴	d															13 28									
Ebbsfleet International	d															13 43									
London Charing Cross 4 ⊖	d					12 26	12 32			12 39							12 56	13 02			13 09				
London Waterloo (East) 4 ⊖	d					12 29	12 35			12 42							12 59	13 05			13 12				
London Cannon Street 4 ⊖	d	12 17		12 24	12 27			12 37	12 40			12 47		12 54	12 57				13 07	13 10				13 17	13 24
London Bridge 4 ⊖	d	12 21		12 28	12 31	12 34	12 40	12 41	12 44	12 47		12 51		12 58	13 01		13 04	13 10	13 11	13 14	13 17			13 21	13 28
Deptford	d	12 27										12 57												13 27	
Greenwich 4 ⛴	d	12 30			12 39			12 49				13 00			13 09				13 19					13 30	
Maze Hill	d	12 34			12 43			12 53				13 04			13 13				13 23					13 34	
Westcombe Park	d	12 36										13 06												13 36	
London Victoria 15 ⊖	d										12 39											13 09			
Denmark Hill 4	d										12 48											13 18			
Peckham Rye 4	d										12 51											13 22			
Nunhead 4	d										12 53											13 24			
New Cross 4 ⊖	d			12 33					12 49					13 03						13 19					13 33
St Johns	d			12 35					12 51					13 05						13 21					13 35
Lewisham 4 ⛴	d			12 38			12 49		12 54	12 57	13 02			13 08				13 19		13 24	13 27	13 32			13 38
Blackheath 4	d			12 42			12 53			13 00	13 06			13 12				13 23			13 30	13 36			13 42
Kidbrooke	d			12 45							13 09			13 15								13 39			13 45
Eltham	d			12 49			12 58				13 12			13 19				13 28				13 42			13 49
Falconwood	d			12 51			13 01				13 14			13 21				13 31				13 44			13 51
Welling	d			12 54			13 03				13 17			13 24				13 33				13 47			13 54
Bexleyheath	d			12 56			13 06				13 19			13 26				13 36				13 49			13 56
Barnehurst 4	d			13 02			13 08				13 22			13 32				13 38				13 52			14 02
Hither Green 4	d					12 44			12 59								13 14			13 29					
Lee	d					12 46			13 01								13 16			13 31					
Mottingham	d					12 49			13 04								13 19			13 34					
New Eltham	d					12 51			13 06								13 21			13 36					
Sidcup 4	d					12 55			13 10								13 25			13 40					
Albany Park	d					12 57			13 12								13 27			13 42					
Bexley	d					12 59			13 14								13 29			13 44					
Crayford	d					13 03			13 18								13 33			13 48					
Charlton 4	d	12 39			12 47			12 57	13a42	13 05		13 09			13 17				13 27	14a12	13 35			13 39	
Woolwich Dockyard	d																								
Woolwich Arsenal 4 ⛴	d	12 44			12 53			13 02		13 10		13 14			13 23				13 32		13 40			13 44	
Plumstead	d	12 46			12 56			13 05				13 16			13 26				13 35					13 46	
Abbey Wood	d	12 49			12 59			13 08		13 14		13 19			13 29				13 38		13 44			13 49	
Belvedere	d	12 52			13 01			13 10				13 22			13 31				13 40					13 52	
Erith	d	12 54			13 04			13 13				13 24			13 34				13 43					13 54	
Slade Green 4	d	12a57		13a15	13 07			13a16				13a27		13a45	13 37				13a46					13a57	14a15
Dartford 4	a				13 15	13 08	13 18			13 24	13 31				13 45		13 38	13 48			13 54	14 01			
	d					13 09				13 25							13 39				13 55				
Stone Crossing	d					13 13											13 43								
Greenhithe for Bluewater	d					13 15				13 30							13 45				14 00				
Swanscombe	d					13 18											13 48								
Northfleet	d					13 20											13 50								
Gravesend 4	d					13a25				13 37						13 48	13a55				14 07				
Higham	d									13 43											14 13				
Strood 4	d									13 48						13 58					14 18				
Maidstone West	d																								
Rochester 4	d									13 52						14 03					14 22				
Chatham 4	d									13 55						14 05					14 25				
Gillingham (Kent) 4	a									14 02						14 09					14 32				

Table 200

Mondays to Fridays

London - Dartford and Gillingham

30 July to 10 August

Network Diagram - see first Page of Table 200

		SE	SE	SE	SE	SE	SE	SE		SE	SE	SE	SE	SE	SE	SE	SE	SE		SE	SE	SE	SE	SE	SE
St Pancras Int'l 15 ⊖	d												14 18												
Stratford International ⊖ ⛴	d												14 28												
Ebbsfleet International	d												14 43												
London Charing Cross 4 ⊖	d		13 26	13 32			13 39							13 56	14 02			14 09						14 26	14 32
London Waterloo (East) 4 ⊖	d		13 29	13 35			13 42							13 59	14 05			14 12						14 29	14 35
London Cannon Street 4 ⊖	d	13 27			13 37	13 40				13 47	13 54	13 57				14 07	14 10				14 17	14 24	14 27		
London Bridge 4 ⊖	d	13 31	13 34	13 40	13 41	13 44	13 47			13 51	13 58	14 01		14 04	14 10	14 11	14 14	14 17			14 21	14 28	14 31	14 34	14 40
Deptford	d									13 57											14 27				
Greenwich 4 ⛴	d	13 39			13 49					14 00		14 09				14 19					14 30		14 39		
Maze Hill	d	13 43			13 53					14 04		14 13				14 23					14 34		14 43		
Westcombe Park	d									14 06											14 36				
London Victoria 15 ⊖	d							13 39												14 09					
Denmark Hill 4	d							13 48												14 18					
Peckham Rye 4	d							13 51												14 21					
Nunhead 4	d							13 53												14 23					
New Cross 4 ⊖	d					13 49					14 03						14 19					14 33			
St Johns	d					13 51					14 05						14 21					14 35			
Lewisham 4 ⛴	d			13 49		13 54	13 57	14 02			14 08				14 19		14 24	14 27		14 32		14 38			14 49
Blackheath 4	d			13 53			14 00	14 06			14 12				14 23			14 30		14 36		14 42			14 53
Kidbrooke	d							14 09			14 15									14 39		14 45			
Eltham	d			13 58				14 12			14 19				14 28					14 42		14 49			14 58
Falconwood	d			14 01				14 14			14 21				14 31					14 44		14 51			15 01
Welling	d			14 03				14 17			14 24				14 33					14 47		14 54			15 03
Bexleyheath	d			14 06				14 19			14 26				14 36					14 49		14 56			15 06
Barnehurst 4	d			14 08				14 22			14 32				14 38					14 52		15 02			15 08
Hither Green 4	d		13 44			13 59								14 14			14 29							14 44	
Lee	d		13 46			14 01								14 16			14 31							14 46	
Mottingham	d		13 49			14 04								14 19			14 34							14 49	
New Eltham	d		13 51			14 06								14 21			14 36							14 51	
Sidcup 4	d		13 55			14 10								14 25			14 40							14 55	
Albany Park	d		13 57			14 12								14 27			14 42							14 57	
Bexley	d		13 59			14 14								14 29			14 44							14 59	
Crayford	d		14 03			14 18								14 33			14 48							15 03	
Charlton 4	d	13 47			13 57	14a42	14 05			14 09		14 17				14 27	15a12	14 35			14 39		14 47		
Woolwich Dockyard	d																								
Woolwich Arsenal 4 ⛴	d	13 53			14 02		14 10			14 14		14 23				14 32		14 40			14 44		14 53		
Plumstead	d	13 56			14 05					14 16		14 26				14 35					14 46		14 56		
Abbey Wood	d	13 59			14 08		14 14			14 19		14 29				14 38		14 44			14 49		14 59		
Belvedere	d	14 01			14 10					14 22		14 31				14 40					14 52		15 01		
Erith	d	14 04			14 13					14 24		14 34				14 43					14 54		15 04		
Slade Green 4	d	14 07			14a16					14a27	14a45	14 37				14a46					14a57	15a15	15 07		
Dartford 4	a	14 15	14 08	14 18			14 24	14 31				14 45		14 38	14 48			14 54		15 01			15 15	15 08	15 18
	d		14 09				14 25							14 39				14 55						15 09	
Stone Crossing	d		14 13											14 43										15 13	
Greenhithe for Bluewater	d		14 15				14 30							14 45				15 00						15 15	
Swanscombe	d		14 18											14 48										15 18	
Northfleet	d		14 20											14 50										15 20	
Gravesend 4	d		14a25				14 37						14 48	14a55				15 07						15a25	
Higham	d						14 43											15 13							
Strood 4	d						14 48						14 58					15 18							
Maidstone West	d																								
Rochester 4	d						14 52						15 03					15 22							
Chatham 4	d						14 55						15 05					15 25							
Gillingham (Kent) 4	a						15 02						15 09					15 32							

Table 200

Mondays to Fridays

30 July to 10 August

London - Dartford and Gillingham

Network Diagram - see first Page of Table 200

		SE	SE	SE		SE	SE	SE	SE	SE	SE	SE	SE	SE		SE	SE	SE	SE	SE	SE	SE	SE	SE
St Pancras Int'l	d									15 18														
Stratford International	d									15 28														
Ebbsfleet International	d									15 43														
London Charing Cross	d			14 39							14 56	15 02				15 09					15 26	15 32		
London Waterloo (East)	d			14 42							14 59	15 05				15 12					15 29	15 35		
London Cannon Street	d	14 37	14 40				14 47	14 54	14 57				15 07	15 10				15 17	15 24	15 27			15 37	15 40
London Bridge	d	14 41	14 44	14 47			14 51	14 58	15 01		15 04	15 10	15 11	15 14		15 17		15 21	15 28	15 31	15 34	15 40	15 41	15 44
Deptford	d						14 57											15 27						
Greenwich	d	14 49					15 00		15 09				15 19					15 30		15 39			15 49	
Maze Hill	d	14 52					15 04		15 12				15 22					15 34		15 42			15 52	
Westcombe Park	d						15 06											15 36						
London Victoria	d					14 39											15 09							
Denmark Hill	d					14 48											15 18							
Peckham Rye	d					14 51											15 21							
Nunhead	d					14 53											15 23							
New Cross	d		14 49					15 03						15 19					15 33					15 49
St Johns	d		14 51					15 05						15 21					15 35					15 51
Lewisham	d		14 54	14 57		15 02		15 08				15 19		15 24		15 27	15 32		15 38			15 49		15 54
Blackheath	d			15 00		15 05		15 12				15 23				15 30	15 35		15 42			15 53		
Kidbrooke	d					15 08		15 15									15 38		15 45					
Eltham	d					15 11		15 19				15 28					15 41		15 49			15 58		
Falconwood	d					15 14		15 21				15 31					15 44		15 51			16 01		
Welling	d					15 16		15 24				15 33					15 46		15 54			16 03		
Bexleyheath	d					15 19		15 26				15 36					15 49		15 56			16 06		
Barnehurst	d					15 21		15 32				15 38					15 51		16 02			16 08		
Hither Green	d		14 59								15 14			15 29							15 44			15 59
Lee	d		15 01								15 16			15 31							15 46			16 01
Mottingham	d		15 04								15 19			15 34							15 49			16 04
New Eltham	d		15 06								15 21			15 36							15 51			16 06
Sidcup	d		15 10								15 25			15 40							15 55			16 10
Albany Park	d		15 12								15 27			15 42							15 57			16 12
Bexley	d		15 14								15 29			15 44							15 59			16 14
Crayford	d		15 18								15 33			15 48							16 03			16 18
Charlton	d	14 57	15a42	15 05			15 08		15 17				15 27	16a12		15 35		15 38		15 47			15 57	16a42
Woolwich Dockyard	d																							
Woolwich Arsenal	d	15 03		15 10			15 14		15 23				15 33			15 40		15 44		15 53			16 03	
Plumstead	d	15 05					15 16		15 25				15 35					15 46		15 55			16 05	
Abbey Wood	d	15 08		15 14			15 19		15 28				15 38			15 44		15 49		15 58			16 08	
Belvedere	d	15 10					15 22		15 30				15 40					15 52		16 00			16 10	
Erith	d	15 13					15 24		15 33				15 43					15 54		16 03			16 13	
Slade Green	d	15a16					15a27	15a45	15 37				15a46					15a57	16a15	16 07			16a16	
Dartford	a			15 24		15 31			15 45		15 38	15 48				15 54	16 01			16 15	16 08	16 18		
	d			15 25							15 39					15 55					16 09			
Stone Crossing	d										15 43										16 13			
Greenhithe for Bluewater	d			15 30							15 45					16 00					16 15			
Swanscombe	d										15 48										16 18			
Northfleet	d										15 50										16 20			
Gravesend	d			15 37						15 48	15a55					16 07					16a25			
Higham	d			15 43												16 13								
Strood	d			15 48						15 58						16 18								
Maidstone West	d																							
Rochester	d			15 52						16 03						16 22								
Chatham	d			15 55						16 05						16 25								
Gillingham (Kent)	a			16 02						16 09						16 32								

Table 200

Mondays to Fridays

30 July to 10 August

London - Dartford and Gillingham

Network Diagram - see first Page of Table 200

		SE	SE	SE	SE	SE	SE	SE	SE	SE		SE	SE	SE	SE	SE	SE	SE	SE	SE		SE	SE	SE	SE
St Pancras Int'l	d						16 18																		
Stratford International	d						16 28																		
Ebbsfleet International	d						16 44																		
London Charing Cross	d	15 39						15 56	16 02				16 09					16 26		16 30					
London Waterloo (East)	d	15 42						15 59	16 05				16 12					16 29		16 33					
London Cannon Street	d			15 47	15 54	15 57				16 07		16 10			16 17	16 24	16 27		16 34			16 39	16 42	16 44	
London Bridge	d	15 47		15 51	15 58	16 01		16 04	16 10	16 11		16 14	16 17		16 21	16 28	16 31	16 34	16 39	16 38		16 43	16 46	16 48	
Deptford	d			15 57											16 27										
Greenwich	d			16 00		16 09				16 19					16 30		16 39		16 48					16 57	
Maze Hill	d			16 04		16 12				16 22					16 34		16 42		16 51						
Westcombe Park	d			16 06											16 36										
London Victoria	d		15 39											16 09											16 39
Denmark Hill	d		15 48											16 18											16 48
Peckham Rye	d		15 51											16 21											16 51
Nunhead	d		15 53											16 23											16 53
New Cross	d				16 03							16 20				16 34						16 49	16 52		
St Johns	d				16 05							16 22				16 36						16 51			
Lewisham	d	15 57	16 02		16 08				16 19			16 25	16 27	16 32		16 39				16 49		16 54	16 56		17 01
Blackheath	d	16 00	16 05		16 12				16 23				16 30	16 35		16 43				16 53			17 00		17 05
Kidbrooke	d		16 08		16 15									16 38		16 46							17 03		17 08
Eltham	d		16 11		16 19				16 29					16 41		16 49				16 59			17 06		17 11
Falconwood	d		16 14		16 21				16 31					16 44		16 52				17 02			17 09		17 14
Welling	d		16 16		16 24				16 34					16 46		16 54				17 04			17 11		17 16
Bexleyheath	d		16 19		16 26				16 36					16 49		16 57				17 07			17 14		17 19
Barnehurst	d		16 21		16 33				16 39					16 51		17 02				17 11			17 17		17 22
Hither Green	d							16 14				16 29						16 44				16 58	17a57		
Lee	d							16 16				16 31						16 46				17 00			
Mottingham	d							16 19				16 34						16 49				17 03			
New Eltham	d							16 22				16 37						16 51				17 06			
Sidcup	d							16 25				16 40						16 55				17 09			
Albany Park	d							16 27				16 42						16 57				17 11			
Bexley	d							16 29				16 45						16 59				17 14			
Crayford	d							16 33				16 48						17 03				17 17			
Charlton	d	16 05		16 08		16 17				16 27		17a12	16 35		16 38		16 47		16 56			17a43		17 03	
Woolwich Dockyard	d																								
Woolwich Arsenal	d	16 10		16 14		16 23				16 33			16 40		16 45		16 53		17 02					17 09	
Plumstead	d			16 16		16 25				16 35					16 47		16 55		17 04						
Abbey Wood	d	16 14		16 19		16 28				16 39			16 44		16 50		16 59		17 07					17 14	
Belvedere	d			16 22		16 30				16 41					16 52		17 01		17 10						
Erith	d			16 24		16 33				16 44					16 55		17 04		17 12						
Slade Green	d			16a27		16 37				16a46					16a57	17a15	17 07		17 15						
Dartford	a	16 24	16 31		16 44	16 48		16 38	16 48				16 54	17 00			17 14	17 08	17 22	17 23				17 26	17 31
	d	16 25						16 39					16 55					17 09						17 28	
Stone Crossing	d							16 43										17 13							
Greenhithe for Bluewater	d	16 30						16 45					17 00					17 15						17 33	
Swanscombe	d							16 48										17 18							
Northfleet	d							16 50										17 20							
Gravesend	d	16 37					16 48	16a55					17 07					17a27						17 40	
Higham	d	16 43											17 13											17 46	
Strood	d	16 48					16 58						17 18											17 52	
Maidstone West	d																								
Rochester	d	16 52					17 03						17 22											17 57	
Chatham	d	16 55					17 05						17 25											18 00	
Gillingham (Kent)	a	17 02					17 09						17 32											18 08	

Table 200

Mondays to Fridays

30 July to 10 August

London - Dartford and Gillingham

Network Diagram - see first Page of Table 200

		SE	SE	SE	SE	SE		SE	SE	SE	SE	SE	SE	SE	SE	SE		SE	SE	SE	SE	SE	SE	SE	SE
St Pancras Int'l	d							17 18																	
Stratford International	d							17 28																	
Ebbsfleet International	d							17 43																	
London Charing Cross	d	16 45	16 49		16 51				16 55				17 06	17 10		17 12		17 17				17 29	17 30	17 32	
London Waterloo (East)	d	16 48	16 52		16 54				16 58				17 09	17 13		17 15		17 20				17 32	17 33	17 35	
London Cannon Street	d			16 54		16 58				17 04	17 06				17 16				17 21	17 26	17 28				17 39
London Bridge	d	16 53	16 57	16 58	16 59	17 02			17 04	17 08	17 10		17 14	17 19	17 20	17 21		17 26	17 25	17 30	17 32	17 37		17 41	17 43
Deptford	d	16 59		17 04											17 26							17 43			17 49
Greenwich	d	17 02		17 08							17 19		17 23		17 30						17 40	17 47			17 53
Maze Hill	d	17 05		17 11									17 26		17 33							17 50			17 56
Westcombe Park	d	17 07											17 28									17 52			
London Victoria	d											17 04													
Denmark Hill	d											17 13													
Peckham Rye	d											17 16													
Nunhead	d											17 18													
New Cross	d					17 08				17 14									17 31	17 36					
St Johns	d					17 10													17 33						
Lewisham	d				17 08	17 13				17 18		17 25				17 30			17 36	17 40					
Blackheath	d				17 11					17 22		17 29				17 34				17 44			17 50		
Kidbrooke	d									17 25		17 32				17 37				17 47					
Eltham	d				17 17					17 29		17 35				17 40				17 50			17 56		
Falconwood	d				17 19					17 31		17 37				17 43				17 53			17 58		
Welling	d				17 22					17 34		17 40				17 45				17 55			18 01		
Bexleyheath	d				17 24					17 36		17 42				17 48				17 58			18 04		
Barnehurst	d				17 27					17 41		17 45				17 51				18 02			18 07		
Hither Green	d		17 07			17 18								17 29					17 41					17 51	
Lee	d		17 09			17 20								17 31					17 43					17 53	
Mottingham	d		17 12			17 23								17 34					17 46					17 56	
New Eltham	d		17 15			17 26			17 20					17 36				17 42	17 48					17 59	
Sidcup	d		17a20			17 30			17 26					17a41				17 47	17 52					18a04	
Albany Park	d					17 32			17 28									17 49	17 54						
Bexley	d					17 35			17 30									17 52	17 57						
Crayford	d					17 39			17 34									17 55	18a00						
Charlton	d	17 10		17 15		18a05					17 25		17 31		17 37						17 46	17 55			18 00
Woolwich Dockyard	d																								
Woolwich Arsenal	d	17 16		17 21							17 31		17 36		17 43						17 51	18 00			18 06
Plumstead	d	17 18		17 23									17 38		17 45							18a04			18 08
Abbey Wood	d	17 21		17 26							17 36		17 42		17 48						17 55				18 12
Belvedere	d	17 24		17 29									17 44		17 51										18 14
Erith	d	17 26		17 31									17 47		17 53										18 17
Slade Green	d	17a29		17 34						17a52			17a49		17 56					18a12					18 20
Dartford	a			17 43	17 38				17 39		17 45	17 54			18 06	18 00		18 00			18 06		18 16		18 27
	d								17 40		17 47							18 02			18 08				
Stone Crossing	d								17 44												18 12				
Greenhithe for Bluewater	d								17 46		17 52							18 07			18 14				
Swanscombe	d								17 49												18 17				
Northfleet	d								17 51												18 19				
Gravesend	d							17 48	17a57		18 00							18 19			18a28				
Higham	d										18 06							18 25							
Strood	d							17 58			18 14							18a33							
Maidstone West	d																								
Rochester	d							18 05			18 20														
Chatham	d							18 07			18 23														
Gillingham (Kent)	a							18 11			18 31														

Table 200

Mondays to Fridays

30 July to 10 August

London - Dartford and Gillingham

Network Diagram - see first Page of Table 200

		SE		SE	SE	SE	SE	SE	SE	SE	SE	SE		SE	SE	SE	SE	SE	SE	SE	SE	SE		SE	SE
St Pancras Int'l	d							18 18																	
Stratford International	d							18 28																	
Ebbsfleet International	d							18 40																	
London Charing Cross	d	17 34		17 39						17 50	17 52	17 54			17 56			18 01			18 12	18 14			18 18
London Waterloo (East)	d	17 37		17 42						17 53	17 55	17 57			17 59			18 04			18 15	18 17			18 21
London Cannon Street	d					17 43	17 47		17 50					18 00			18 04		18 10	18 12				18 21	
London Bridge	d	17 43		17 48		17 47	17 51		17 54	17 58		18 02		18 04	18 04		18 08	18 10	18 14	18 16	18 21	18 23		18 25	18 26
Deptford	d													18 10							18 27				
Greenwich	d								18 02	18 07				18 14						18 24	18 30			18 34	
Maze Hill	d									18 10				18 17							18 33			18 37	
Westcombe Park	d									18 12														18 39	
London Victoria	d				17 34											17 56									
Denmark Hill	d				17 43											18 06									
Peckham Rye	d				17 46											18 09									
Nunhead	d				17 49											18 11									
New Cross	d					17 53	17 58										18 14		18 20						
St Johns	d					17 55											18 16								
Lewisham	d	17 53			17 56	17 59	18 02								18 14	18 18	18 20		18 24						18 35
Blackheath	d	17 57			18 00		18 06				18 10				18 18	18 23			18 28						18 39
Kidbrooke	d	18 00					18 09								18 21	18 26			18 31						18 42
Eltham	d	18 03			18 06		18 12				18 16				18 24	18 30			18 34						18 46
Falconwood	d	18 06			18 09		18 15				18 18				18 27	18 32			18 37						18 48
Welling	d	18 08			18 11		18 17				18 21				18 29	18 35			18 39						18 51
Bexleyheath	d	18 11			18 14		18 20				18 24				18 32	18 38			18 42						18 54
Barnehurst	d	18 13			18 16		18 23				18 27				18 36	18 41			18a47						18 57
Hither Green	d					18 03	18a57					18 13					18 25					18 35			
Lee	d					18 05						18 15					18 27					18 37			
Mottingham	d					18 08						18 18					18 30					18 40			
New Eltham	d			18 04		18 11						18 21					18 32	18 26				18 43			
Sidcup	d			18 08		18 15						18 25					18 36	18 30				18 47			
Albany Park	d			18 10		18 17											18 38	18 32				18 49			
Bexley	d			18 13		18 20											18 40	18 35				18 51			
Crayford	d			18 16		18a23						18a32					18 44	18 38				18a54			
Charlton	d								18 07	18 15				18 21			19a08			18 30	18 38			18 42	
Woolwich Dockyard	d																								
Woolwich Arsenal	d								18 13	18 20				18 27						18 35	18 44			18 48	
Plumstead	d									18a24				18 29							18 46			18 50	
Abbey Wood	d								18 18					18 33						18 40	18 49			18 54	
Belvedere	d													18 35										18 56	
Erith	d													18 38										18 59	
Slade Green	d	18a22												18 41	18a45						18a55			19 02	
Dartford	a			18 21	18 25				18 29		18 36			18 48		18 53		18 44		18 52				19 09	19 06
	d			18 22					18 31									18 45		18 54					
Stone Crossing	d																	18 49							
Greenhithe for Bluewater	d			18 27					18 36									18 51		18 59					
Swanscombe	d																	18 54							
Northfleet	d																	18 56							
Gravesend	d			18 34				18 45	18a52									19 02		19a10					
Higham	d			18 40														19 08							
Strood	d			18 45				18 55										19 14							
Maidstone West	d																								
Rochester	d			18 51				19 03										19 19							
Chatham	d			18 54				19 06										19 22							
Gillingham (Kent)	a			19 02				19 10										19 29							

Table 200

Mondays to Fridays

30 July to 10 August

London - Dartford and Gillingham

Network Diagram - see first Page of Table 200

		SE	SE	SE	SE	SE	SE	SE		SE	SE	SE	SE	SE	SE	SE	SE	SE		SE	SE	SE	SE	SE	SE
St Pancras Int'l	d																	19 18							
Stratford International	d																	19 28							
Ebbsfleet International	d																	19 45							
London Charing Cross	d			18 23				18 34		18 37	18 39				18 48					18 56	19 02			19 09	
London Waterloo (East)	d			18 26				18 37		18 40	18 42				18 51					18 59	19 05			19 12	
London Cannon Street	d	18 25	18 25		18 30		18 34						18 46	18 50		18 54	18 57					19 07	19 10		
London Bridge	d	18 29	18 29	18 32	18 34		18 38	18 42		18 46	18 48		18 50	18 54	18 57	18 58	19 01			19 04	19 10	19 11	19 14	19 17	
Deptford	d												18 56				19 07								
Greenwich	d				18 42			18 51					18 59				19 11					19 19			
Maze Hill	d							18 54					19 02				19 14					19 22			
Westcombe Park	d												19 04												
London Victoria	d					18 18						18 39													19 09
Denmark Hill	d					18 28						18 48													19 18
Peckham Rye	d					18 32						18 51													19 21
Nunhead	d					18 34						18 54													19 23
New Cross	d	18 35	18 35				18 44				18 55			19 00		19 05							19 19		
St Johns	d	18 37	18 37				18 46							19 02		19 07							19 21		
Lewisham	d	18 41	18 41			18 43	18 49				18 59	19 03		19 05	19 07	19 11					19 19		19 24	19 27	19 32
Blackheath	d					18 47	18 53				19 03	19 07			19 10	19 15					19 23			19 30	19 35
Kidbrooke	d					18 50	18 56					19 10				19 18									19 38
Eltham	d					18 53	18 59				19 09	19 13				19 21					19 29				19 41
Falconwood	d					18 56	19 02				19 12	19 16				19 24					19 31				19 44
Welling	d					18 58	19 04				19 14	19 18				19 26					19 34				19 46
Bexleyheath	d					19 01	19 07				19 17	19 21				19 29					19 36				19 49
Barnehurst	d					19 04	19a12				19a21	19 25				19 35					19 39				19 51
Hither Green	d	18 46	18 46							18 56				19 09						19 14			19 29		
Lee	d	18 48	18 48							18 58				19 11						19 16			19 31		
Mottingham	d	18 51	18 51							19 01				19 14						19 19			19 34		
New Eltham	d	18 53	18 54	18 48						19 04				19 17						19 22			19 36		
Sidcup	d	18 57	18 58	18 51						19 08				19 20						19 25			19 40		
Albany Park	d	18 59	19 00	18 53						19 10				19 22						19 27			19 42		
Bexley	d	19 01	19 03	18 56						19 13				19 25						19 30			19 44		
Crayford	d	19a05	19 10	18 59						19 16				19 29						19 33			19 48		
Charlton	d		19a40		18 48			18 58					19 07	20a08	19 15		19 18					19 27		19 35	
Woolwich Dockyard	d																								
Woolwich Arsenal	d				18 53			19 04					19 13		19 20		19 24					19 33		19 40	
Plumstead	d							19 06					19a17				19 26					19 35			
Abbey Wood	d				18 57			19 10							19 24		19 29					19 38		19 44	
Belvedere	d							19 12									19 32					19 40			
Erith	d							19 15									19 34					19 43			
Slade Green	d							19 18								19a54	19 37					19a48			
Dartford	a			19 04	19 09	19 14		19 28		19 21		19 34			19 34		19 44			19 38	19 48		19 56	19 55	20 01
	d			19 05	19 10					19 22					19 35					19 39				19 55	
Stone Crossing	d			19 09	19 14					19 26										19 43					
Greenhithe for Bluewater	d			19 11	19 16					19 29					19 40					19 46				20 00	
Swanscombe	d			19 14	19 19					19 32										19 49					
Northfleet	d			19 16	19 21					19 34										19 51					
Gravesend	d			19a24	19 26					19 38					19 47			19 51		19a57				20 07	
Higham	d				19 32					19 44					19 53									20 13	
Strood	d				19 38					19a53					19 58			20 02						20 18	
Maidstone West	d																								
Rochester	d				19 45										20 03			20 06						20 22	
Chatham	d				19 48										20 05			20 09						20 25	
Gillingham (Kent)	a				19 56										20 13			20 13						20 32	

Table 200

Mondays to Fridays

30 July to 10 August

London - Dartford and Gillingham

Network Diagram - see first Page of Table 200

		SE	SE	SE		SE	SE	SE	SE	SE	SE	SE	SE	SE		SE	SE	SE	SE	SE	SE	SE	SE	SE
St Pancras Int'l	d															20 18								
Stratford International	d															20 28								
Ebbsfleet International	d															20 43								
London Charing Cross	d					19 26	19 32			19 39							19 56	20 02		20 09		20 22		20 32
London Waterloo (East)	d					19 29	19 35			19 42							19 59	20 05		20 12		20 25		20 35
London Cannon Street	d	19 17	19 24	19 27				19 37	19 40			19 47	19 54	19 57					20 10		20 17		20 27	
London Bridge	d	19 21	19 28	19 31		19 34	19 40	19 41	19 44	19 47		19 51	19 58	20 01			20 04	20 10	20 14	20 17	20 21	20 30	20 31	20 40
Deptford	d	19 27										19 57									20 27			
Greenwich	d	19 30		19 39				19 49				20 00		20 09							20 30		20 39	
Maze Hill	d	19 33		19 42				19 52				20 03		20 12							20 33		20 42	
Westcombe Park	d	19 35										20 05									20 35			
London Victoria	d										19 39													
Denmark Hill	d										19 48													
Peckham Rye	d										19 51													
Nunhead	d										19 53													
New Cross	d		19 33						19 49				20 03						20 19			20 35		20 45
St Johns	d		19 35						19 51				20 05						20 21					
Lewisham	d		19 38				19 49		19 55	19 57	20 02		20 08					20 19	20 25	20 27		20 39		20 49
Blackheath	d		19 42				19 53			20 00	20 05		20 12					20 22		20 30				20 53
Kidbrooke	d		19 45								20 08		20 15					20 25						20 56
Eltham	d		19 49				19 58				20 11		20 19					20 28						20 59
Falconwood	d		19 51				20 01				20 14		20 21					20 31						21 01
Welling	d		19 54				20 03				20 16		20 24					20 33						21 04
Bexleyheath	d		19 56				20 06				20 19		20 26					20 36						21 06
Barnehurst	d		20a03				20 08				20 21		20a33					20 38						21 09
Hither Green	d					19 44			20 00								20 14		20 30			20 44		
Lee	d					19 46			20 02								20 16		20 32			20 46		
Mottingham	d					19 49			20 05								20 19		20 35			20 49		
New Eltham	d					19 51			20 07								20 21		20 37			20 51		
Sidcup	d					19 55			20 11								20 25		20 41			20 55		
Albany Park	d					19 57			20 13								20 27		20 43			20 57		
Bexley	d					19 59			20 15								20 29		20 45			20 59		
Crayford	d					20 03			20 18								20 33		20 48			21 03		
Charlton	d	19 39		19 47				19 57		20 05		20 09		20 17						20 35	20 39		20 47	
Woolwich Dockyard	d																							
Woolwich Arsenal	d	19 45		19 53				20 03		20 10		20 15		20 23						20 40	20 45		20 53	
Plumstead	d	19 47		19 55				20 05				20 17		20 25							20 47		20 55	
Abbey Wood	d	19 50		19 58				20 08		20 14		20 20		20 28						20 44	20 50		20 58	
Belvedere	d	19 52		20 00				20 10				20 22		20 30							20 52		21 00	
Erith	d	19 55		20 03				20 13				20 25		20 33							20 55		21 03	
Slade Green	d	20a00		20 07				20a18				20a30		20 37							20 57		21 07	
Dartford	a			20 16		20 08	20 18		20 27	20 25	20 32			20 46			20 38	20 48	20 56	20 54	21 05	21 08	21 15	21 18
	d					20 09				20 25							20 39			20 55		21 09		
Stone Crossing	d					20 13											20 43					21 13		
Greenhithe for Bluewater	d					20 15				20 30							20 45			21 00		21 15		
Swanscombe	d					20 18											20 48					21 18		
Northfleet	d					20 20											20 50					21 20		
Gravesend	d					20a25				20 37						20 48	20a55			21 07		21a28		
Higham	d									20 43										21 13				
Strood	d									20 48						20 58				21 18				
Maidstone West	d																							
Rochester	d									20 52						21 03				21 22				
Chatham	d									20 55						21 05				21 25				
Gillingham (Kent)	a									21 02						21 09				21 32				

Table 200

London - Dartford and Gillingham

Mondays to Fridays

30 July to 10 August

Network Diagram - see first Page of Table 200

		SE	SE	SE	SE	SE	SE	SE	SE	SE	SE	SE	SE	SE	SE	SE	SE	SE	SE	SE	SE	SE	SE
St Pancras Int'l ⊖	d			21 18																			
Stratford International ⊖	d			21 28																			
Ebbsfleet International	d			21 43																			
London Charing Cross ⊖	d	20 39			20 52		21 02	21 09		21 22	21 26	21 32	21 39		21 52	21 56	22 02	22 09		22 22	22 26	22 32	22 39
London Waterloo (East) ⊖	d	20 42			20 55		21 05	21 12		21 25	21 29	21 35	21 42		21 55	21 59	22 05	22 12		22 25	22 29	22 35	22 42
London Cannon Street ⊖	d		20 47			20 57			21 16					21 46					22 16				
London Bridge ⊖	d	20 47	20 51		21 00	21 01	21 10	21 17	21 20	21 30	21 34	21 40	21 47	21 50	22 00	22 04	22 10	22 17	22 20	22 30	22 34	22 40	22 47
Deptford	d		20 57						21 26					21 56					22 26				
Greenwich	d		21 00			21 09			21 30		21 42			22 00		22 12			22 30		22 42		
Maze Hill	d		21 03			21 12			21 33		21 45			22 03		22 15			22 33		22 45		
Westcombe Park	d		21 05						21 35					22 05					22 35				
London Victoria ⊖	d																						
Denmark Hill	d																						
Peckham Rye	d																						
Nunhead	d																						
New Cross ⊖	d				21 05		21 15			21 35		21 45			22 05		22 15			22 35		22 45	
St Johns	d																						
Lewisham	d	20 57			21 09		21 19	21 27		21 39		21 49	21 57		22 09		22 19	22 27		22 39		22 49	22 57
Blackheath	d	21 00					21 23	21 30				21 53	22 00				22 23	22 30				22 53	23 00
Kidbrooke	d						21 26					21 56					22 26					22 56	
Eltham	d						21 29					21 59					22 29					22 59	
Falconwood	d						21 31					22 02					22 32					23 02	
Welling	d						21 34					22 04					22 34					23 04	
Bexleyheath	d						21 36					22 07					22 37					23 07	
Barnehurst	d						21 39					22 09					22 39					23 09	
Hither Green	d				21 14					21 44					22 14					22 44			
Lee	d				21 16					21 46					22 16					22 46			
Mottingham	d				21 19					21 49					22 19					22 49			
New Eltham	d				21 21					21 51					22 21					22 51			
Sidcup	d				21 25					21 55					22 25					22 55			
Albany Park	d				21 27					21 57					22 27					22 57			
Bexley	d				21 29					21 59					22 29					22 59			
Crayford	d				21 33					22 03					22 33					23 03			
Charlton	d	21 05	21 09			21 17		21 35	21 39		21 50		22 05	22 09		22 20		22 35	22 39		22 50		23 05
Woolwich Dockyard	d																						
Woolwich Arsenal	d	21 10	21 15			21 23		21 40	21 43		21 56		22 10	22 13		22 26		22 40	22 43		22 56		23 10
Plumstead	d		21 17			21 25			21 45		21 58			22 15		22 28			22 45		22 58		
Abbey Wood	d	21 14	21 20			21 28		21 44	21 48		22 01		22 14	22 18		22 31		22 44	22 48		23 01		23 14
Belvedere	d		21 22			21 30			21 51		22 03			22 21		22 33			22 51		23 03		
Erith	d		21 25			21 33			21 53		22 06			22 23		22 36			22 53		23 06		
Slade Green	d		21 27			21 37			21 56		22 09			22 26		22 39			22 56		23 09		
Dartford	a	21 24	21 35		21 38	21 45	21 48	21 54	22 03	22 08	22 17	22 19	22 24	22 33	22 38	22 47	22 49	22 54	23 03	23 08	23 18	23 20	23 24
	d	21 25			21 39			21 55		22 09			22 25		22 39			22 55		23 09			23 25
Stone Crossing	d				21 43					22 13					22 43					23 13			23 29
Greenhithe for Bluewater	d	21 30			21 45			22 00		22 15			22 30		22 45			23 00		23 15			23 31
Swanscombe	d				21 48					22 18					22 48					23 18			23 34
Northfleet	d				21 50					22 20					22 50					23 20			23 36
Gravesend	d	21 37		21 48	21a58			22 07		22a28			22 37		22a58			23 07		23a28			23 40
Higham	d	21 43						22 13					22 43					23 13					23 46
Strood	d	21 48		21 58				22 18					22 48					23 18					23 52
Maidstone West	d																						
Rochester	d	21 52		22 03				22 22					22 52					23 22					23 56
Chatham	d	21 55		22 05				22 25					22 55					23 25					23 58
Gillingham (Kent)	a	22 02		22 09				22 32					23 02					23 32					00 06

Table 200

London - Dartford and Gillingham

Mondays to Fridays

30 July to 10 August

Network Diagram - see first Page of Table 200

		SE	SE	SE	SE	SE	SE	SE	SE	SE	SE
St Pancras Int'l ⊖	d										
Stratford International ⊖	d										
Ebbsfleet International	d										
London Charing Cross ⊖	d		22 52	22 56	23 02	23 09	23 22	23 26	23 32	23 39	23 56
London Waterloo (East) ⊖	d		22 55	22 59	23 05	23 12	23 25	23 29	23 35	23 42	23 59
London Cannon Street ⊖	d	22 46									
London Bridge ⊖	d	22 50	23 00	23 04	23 10	23 17	23 30	23 34	23 40	23 47	00 04
Deptford	d	22 56		23 10				23 40			00 10
Greenwich	d	23 00		23 12				23 42			00 12
Maze Hill	d	23 03		23 15				23 45			00 15
Westcombe Park	d	23 05		23 17				23 47			00 17
London Victoria ⊖	d										
Denmark Hill	d										
Peckham Rye	d										
Nunhead	d										
New Cross ⊖	d		23 05		23 15		23 35		23 45		
St Johns	d										
Lewisham	d		23 09		23 19	23 27	23 39		23 50	23 56	
Blackheath	d				23 23	23 30			23 55	00 01	
Kidbrooke	d				23 26				23 58		
Eltham	d				23 29				00 01		
Falconwood	d				23 32				00 04		
Welling	d				23 34				00 06		
Bexleyheath	d				23 37				00 09		
Barnehurst	d				23 39				00 12		
Hither Green	d		23 14				23 44				
Lee	d		23 16				23 46				
Mottingham	d		23 19				23 49				
New Eltham	d		23 21				23 51				
Sidcup	d		23 25				23 55				
Albany Park	d		23 27				23 57				
Bexley	d		23 29				23 59				
Crayford	d		23 33				00 03				
Charlton	d	23 09		23 20		23 35		23 50		00 06	00 20
Woolwich Dockyard	d										
Woolwich Arsenal	d	23 13		23 26		23 39		23 56		00 11	00 26
Plumstead	d	23 15		23 28				23 58			00 28
Abbey Wood	d	23 18		23 31		23 43		00 01		00 15	00 31
Belvedere	d	23 21		23 33				00 03			00 33
Erith	d	23 23		23 36				00 06			00 36
Slade Green	d	23 26		23 39				00 09			00 39
Dartford	a	23 33	23 41	23 47	23 49	23 54	00 11	00 17	00 22	00 24	00 47
	d					23 55				00 25	
Stone Crossing	d					23 58				00 29	
Greenhithe for Bluewater	d					23 59				00 31	
Swanscombe	d					00 04				00 34	
Northfleet	d					00 06				00 36	
Gravesend	d					00 10				00 40	
Higham	d					00 16				00 46	
Strood	d					00 22				00 52	
Maidstone West	d										
Rochester	d					00 26				00 56	
Chatham	d					00 28				00 58	
Gillingham (Kent)	a					00 36				01 06	

Table 200

Mondays to Fridays

29 August to 7 September

London - Dartford and Gillingham

Network Diagram - see first Page of Table 200

		SE A	SE B	SE C	SE D	SE A	SE B	SE B	SE A	SE B	SE A	SE B	SE A	SE C	SE E	SE A	SE B	SE B	SE A	SE A	SE A	SE	SE B
St Pancras Int'l ⊖	d			23p25	23p25									23p55	23p55								
Stratford International ⊖	d			23p32	23p33									00 02	00 03								
Ebbsfleet International	d			23p43	23p44									00 13	00 14								
London Charing Cross ⊖	d	22p39	22p40			23p09	23p10	23p20	23p22	23p26	23p26	23p30	23p32			23p39	23p50	23p56	23p56	00 02	00 10	00 18	00 32
London Waterloo (East) ⊖	d	22p42	22p43			23p12	23p13	23p23	23p25	23p29	23p29	23p33	23p35			23p42	23p53	23p59	23p59	00 05	00 13	00 21	00 35
London Cannon Street ⊖	d																						
London Bridge ⊖	d	22p47	22p48			23p17	23p18	23p28	23p30	23p34	23p34	23p38	23p40			23p47	23p58	00 04	00 04	00 10	00 18	00 26	00 40
Deptford	d										23p40	23p44							00 10				00 46
Greenwich	d										23p42	23p46							00 12				00 49
Maze Hill	d										23p45	23p49							00 15				00 53
Westcombe Park	d										23p47	23p51							00 17				00 55
London Victoria ⊖	d																						
Denmark Hill	d																						
Peckham Rye	d																						
Nunhead	d																						
New Cross ⊖	d							23p34	23p35				23p45				00 04			00 15	00 23	00 31	
St Johns	d																						
Lewisham	d	22p56	22p57			23p26	23p27	23p38	23p39	23p42			23p49			23p56	00 08	00 12		00 19	00 27	00 35	
Blackheath	d	22p59	23p00			23p29	23p30	23p40					23p52			23p59	00 10			00 22		00 38	
Kidbrooke	d							23p43					23p55				00 13			00 25			
Eltham	d							23p47					23p58				00 17			00 28			
Falconwood	d							23p49					00 01				00 19			00 31			
Welling	d							23p52					00 03				00 22			00 33			
Bexleyheath	d							23p54					00 06				00 24			00 36			
Barnehurst	d							23p57					00 08				00 27			00 38			
Hither Green	d								23p44	23p46								00 16			00 32		
Lee	d								23p46	23p48								00 18			00 34		
Mottingham	d								23p49	23p51								00 21			00 37		
New Eltham	d								23p51	23p53								00 23			00 39		
Sidcup	d								23p55	23p57								00 27			00 43		
Albany Park	d								23p57	23p59								00 29			00 45		
Bexley	d								23p59	00 01								00 31			00 47		
Crayford	d								00 03	00 04								00 34			00 51		
Charlton	d	23p03	23p04			23p33	23p34				23p50	23p54				00 03			00 20			00 42	00 59
Woolwich Dockyard	d										23p53	23p57							00 23				
Woolwich Arsenal	d	23p09	23p10			23p39	23p40				23p56	23p59				00 09			00 26			00 47	01 04
Plumstead	d										23p58	00 02							00 28			00 49	01s06
Abbey Wood	d	23p13	23p14			23p43	23p44				00 01	00 05				00 13			00 31			00 53	01s09
Belvedere	d										00 03	00 07							00 33			00 55	01s12
Erith	d										00 06	00 10							00 36			00 58	01s15
Slade Green	d										00 09	00 14							00 39			01 00	01s18
Dartford	a	23p24	23p24			23p54	23p54	00 04	00 08	00 09	00 14	00 19	00 16			00 24	00 33	00 39	00 44	00 46	00 56	01 05	01 23
	d	23p25	23p25			23p55	23p55									00 25						01 06	
Stone Crossing	d	23p29	23p29			23p58	23p59									00 29						01 10	
Greenhithe for Bluewater	d	23p31	23p31			23p59	00 01									00 31							
Swanscombe	d	23p34	23p34			00 04	00 04									00 34							
Northfleet	d	23p36	23p36			00 06	00 06									00 36							
Gravesend	d	23p40	23p40	23p48	23p48	00 10	00 10							00 18	00 18	00 40						01 17	
Higham	d	23p46	23p46			00 16	00 16									00 46						01 23	
Strood	d	23p52	23p52	23p58	23p58	00 22	00 22							00 28	00 28	00 52						01 29	
Maidstone West	d																						
Rochester	d	23p56	23p56	00 03	00 03	00 26	00 26							00 33	00 33	00 56						01 33	
Chatham	d	23p58	23p58	00 05	00 05	00 28	00 28							00 35	00 35	00 58						01 35	
Gillingham (Kent)	a	00 03	00 03	00 09	00 09	00 33	00 33							00 39	00 39	01 03						01 41	

A not 3 September
B 3 September
C 29 August
D not 29 August
E not 29 August, 3 September

Table 200

Mondays to Fridays

29 August to 7 September

London - Dartford and Gillingham

Network Diagram - see first Page of Table 200

		SE A	SE	SE	SE	SE	SE	SE	SE	SE	SE	SE	SE	SE	SE	SE	SE	SE	SE	SE	SE	SE	SE
St Pancras Int'l ⊖	d														06 24					06 55			
Stratford International ⊖	d														06 32					07 02			
Ebbsfleet International	d														06 42					07 13			
London Charing Cross ⊖	d	00 32		00 44			04 50	04 56	05 02	05 20	05 26	05 32	05 39	05 52		05 56	06 02	06 09			06 26	06 32	06 39
London Waterloo (East) ⊖	d	00 35		00 47			04 53	04 59	05 05	05 23	05 29	05 35	05 42	05 55		05 59	06 05	06 12			06 29	06 35	06 42
London Cannon Street ⊖	d		00 41		00 56														06 27				
London Bridge ⊖	d	00 40	00 45	00 52	01 00		04 58	05 04	05 10	05 28	05 34	05 42	05 47	06 01		06 04	06 10	06 17	06 31		06 34	06 40	06 47
Deptford	d	00 46			01s06		05 04			05 34				06 07					06 37				
Greenwich	d	00 49			01s08		05 06			05 36				06 09					06 39				
Maze Hill	d	00 52			01s12		05 09			05 39				06 12					06 42				
Westcombe Park	d	00 55			01s15		05 11			05 41				06 14					06 44				
London Victoria ⊖	d																						
Denmark Hill	d																						
Peckham Rye	d																						
Nunhead	d																						
New Cross ⊖	d			00 57				05 09	05 15		05 39	05 48	05 52			06 09	06 15				06 40	06 46	
St Johns	d																						
Lewisham	d		00 53	01 01				05 13	05 19		05 43	05 52	05 56			06 13	06 19	06 26			06 44	06 50	06 56
Blackheath	d		00 57						05 22			05 54	05 59				06 22	06 29				06 53	06 59
Kidbrooke	d		01s00						05 25			05 57					06 25					06 56	
Eltham	d		01s03						05 28			06 00					06 28					06 59	
Falconwood	d		01s06						05 31			06 03					06 31					07 01	
Welling	d		01s09						05 33			06 05					06 33					07 04	
Bexleyheath	d		01s11						05 36			06 08					06 36					07 06	
Barnehurst	d		01s14						05 38			06 10					06 38					07 11	
Hither Green	d			01s05				05 18			05 48					06 18					06 48		
Lee	d			01s08				05 20			05 50					06 20					06 50		
Mottingham	d			01s11				05 23			05 53					06 23					06 53		
New Eltham	d			01s13				05 25			05 55					06 25					06 55		
Sidcup	d			01s16				05 29			05 59					06 29					06 59		
Albany Park	d			01s19				05 31			06 01					06 31					07 01		
Bexley	d			01s21				05 33			06 03					06 33					07 03		
Crayford	d			01s24				05 36			06 06					06 36					07 06		
Charlton	d	00 57			01s17		05 14			05 44			06 03	06 17				06 33	06 47				07 03
Woolwich Dockyard	d						05 17			05 47				06 20					06 50				
Woolwich Arsenal	d	01 04			01s23		05 20			05 50			06 09	06 23				06 39	06 53				07 09
Plumstead	d	01s06			01s26		05 22			05 52				06 25					06 55				
Abbey Wood	d	01s09			01s29		05 25			05 55			06 13	06 28				06 43	06 58				07 13
Belvedere	d	01s12			01s32		05 27			05 57				06 30					07 00				
Erith	d	01s15			01s35		05 30			06 00				06 33					07 03				
Slade Green	d	01s18			01s38		05 34			06 04			06 19	06 37					07 07				
Dartford	a	01 23	01s21	01 30	01 44		05 38	05 41	05 47	06 08	06 11	06 17	06 24	06 44		06 41	06 45	06 54	07 12		07 11	07 18	07 23
	d					05 25		05 42	05 55		06 12		06 25			06 42		06 55			07 12		07 25
Stone Crossing	d							05 46			06 16					06 46					07 16		
Greenhithe for Bluewater	d					05 30		05 48	06 00		06 18		06 30			06 48		07 00			07 18		07 30
Swanscombe	d							05 51			06 21					06 51					07 21		
Northfleet	d							05 53			06 23					06 53					07 23		
Gravesend	d		01s31			05 37		05a57	06 07		06a27		06 38		06 46	06 59		07a06		07 21	07 27		07 37
Higham	d		01s37			05 43			06 13				06 44			07 05							07 43
Strood	d		01s42			05 48			06 18				06 49		06 57	07 17				07 31	07a37		07 48
Maidstone West	d														07a12								
Rochester	d		01s46			05 52			06 22				06 53			07 21				07 36			07 52
Chatham	d		01s48			05 55			06 25				06 56			07 24				07 38			07 55
Gillingham (Kent)	a		01 52			05 59			06 29				07 00			07 28				07 42			07 59

A not 3 September

Table 200

London - Dartford and Gillingham

Mondays to Fridays

29 August to 7 September

Network Diagram - see first Page of Table 200

		SE		SE	SE	SE	SE	SE	SE	SE	SE	SE		SE	SE	SE	SE	SE	SE	SE	SE	SE		SE	SE
St Pancras Int'l ⊖	d			07 25											07 51										
Stratford International ⊖	d			07 33											08 02										
Ebbsfleet International	d			07 44											08 13										
London Charing Cross ⊖	d	06 52			06 56	07 02					07 12					07 26				07 39					
London Waterloo (East) ⊖	d	06 55			06 59	07 05					07 15					07 29				07 42					
London Cannon Street ⊖	d							07 10	07 10	07 13		07 24		07 27			07 32	07 36	07 41			07 44		07 54	07 56
London Bridge ⊖	d	07 00			07 05	07 10		07 14	07 14	07 17	07 21	07 28		07 31		07 34	07 37	07 40	07 45	07 47		07 48		07 58	08 01
Deptford	d	07 07								07 23							07 43					07 54			08 07
Greenwich	d	07 09								07 25				07 38			07 45					07 59			08 09
Maze Hill	d	07 12								07 28							07 48					08 02			08 12
Westcombe Park	d	07 14								07 30							07 50					08 04			08 14
London Victoria ⊖	d						07 09														07 43				
Denmark Hill	d																				07 53				
Peckham Rye	d																				07 56				
Nunhead	d																				07 59				
New Cross ⊖	d							07 20	07 20			07 33							07 50					08 04	
St Johns	d							07 22	07 22			07 35												08 06	
Lewisham	d					07 18	07 27	07 27	07 27		07 30	07 38						07 49	07 54	07 56	08 08			08 11	
Blackheath	d					07 21	07 29				07 32	07 41						07 52		07 59	08 10			08 13	
Kidbrooke	d					07 24						07 44						07 55						08 16	
Eltham	d					07 27						07 47						07 58						08 20	
Falconwood	d					07 29						07 50						08 01						08 22	
Welling	d					07 32						07 52						08 03						08 25	
Bexleyheath	d					07 34						07 55						08 06						08 27	
Barnehurst	d					07 37	07 40					07 58						08 08						08 30	
Hither Green	d				07 18	08a11		07 31	07 31			08a31				07 45			07 59						
Lee	d				07 20			07 33	07 33							07 47			08 01						
Mottingham	d				07 23			07 36	07 36							07 50			08 04						
New Eltham	d				07 26			07 39	07 39							07 53			08 07						
Sidcup	d				07 29			07 42	07 42							07 56			08 13						
Albany Park	d				07 31			07 44	07 44							07 58			08 15						
Bexley	d				07 34			07 47	07 47							08 01			08 17						
Crayford	d				07 37			07 50	07 50							08 05			08 21						
Charlton	d	07 17							08a19	07 33	07 37			07 44			07 53		08a50	08 04		08 07			08 17
Woolwich Dockyard	d	07 20								07 36							07 56					08 10			08 20
Woolwich Arsenal	d	07 23								07 39	07 43			07 49			07 59			08 09		08 13			08 23
Plumstead	d	07 25								07 41							08 01					08 15			08 25
Abbey Wood	d	07 28								07 44	07 48			07 53			08 04			08 13		08 18			08 28
Belvedere	d	07 30								07 46							08 06					08 20			08 30
Erith	d	07 33								07 49							08 09					08 23			08 33
Slade Green	d	07 37						07a57		07 52				07a59			08a12			08 20		08a26		08a35	08 37
Dartford	a	07 46			07 42		07 48			07 57	07 59					08 11		08 15		08 25	08 27				08 42
	d				07 43						08 00					08 12				08 25					
Stone Crossing	d				07 47											08 16									
Greenhithe for Bluewater	d				07 49						08 05					08 18				08 30					
Swanscombe	d				07 52											08 21									
Northfleet	d				07 54											08 23									
Gravesend	d			07 48	07a58						08 12				08 18	08a27				08 37					
Higham	d										08 18									08 43					
Strood	d			07 58							08 23				08 28					08 48					
Maidstone West	d																								
Rochester	d			08 03							08 27				08 33					08 52					
Chatham	d			08 05							08 30				08 35					08 55					
Gillingham (Kent)	a			08 09							08 35				08 39					08 59					

Table 200

London - Dartford and Gillingham

Mondays to Fridays

29 August to 7 September

Network Diagram - see first Page of Table 200

		SE	SE	SE	SE	SE	SE	SE		SE	SE	SE	SE	SE	SE	SE	SE	SE		SE	SE	SE	SE	SE	SE
St Pancras Int'l ⊖	d	08 21									08 54													09 25	
Stratford International ⊖	d	08 29									09 05													09 33	
Ebbsfleet International	d	08 43									09 17													09 43	
London Charing Cross ⊖	d		07 59		08 03		08 11					08 20		08 23	08 31			08 41							08 55
London Waterloo (East) ⊖	d		08 02		08 06		08 14					08 23		08 26	08 34			08 44							08 58
London Cannon Street ⊖	d			08 05		08 10				08 16			08 25			08 36	08 39				08 47	08 54	08 56		
London Bridge ⊖	d		08 07	08 09	08 11	08 14	08 19			08 20		08 29	08 29	08 31	08 39	08 40	08 43	08 49			08 51	08 58	09 01		09 03
Deptford	d			08 15						08 27			08 35			08 46					08 57		09 07		
Greenwich	d			08 19						08 29			08 39			08 49					08 59		09 09		
Maze Hill	d			08 22						08 32			08 42			08 52					09 02		09 12		
Westcombe Park	d			08 24						08 34			08 44			08 54					09 04		09 14		
London Victoria ⊖	d							08 09												08 39					
Denmark Hill	d							08 18												08 48					
Peckham Rye	d							08 21												08 51					
Nunhead	d							08 23												08 53					
New Cross ⊖	d					08 20								08 38			08 49					09 04			
St Johns	d					08 22								08 40			08 51					09 06			
Lewisham	d				08 19	08 25	08 28	08 32						08 43	08 49		08 54	08 56		09 02		09 09			
Blackheath	d				08 22		08 31	08 34						08 46	08 52			08 59		09 04		09 12			
Kidbrooke	d				08 25			08 37						08 49	08 55					09 07		09 15			
Eltham	d				08 28			08 41						08 52	08 58					09 11		09 18			
Falconwood	d				08 31			08 43						08 55	09 01					09 13		09 21			
Welling	d				08 33			08 46						08 57	09 03					09 16		09 23			
Bexleyheath	d				08 36			08 48						09 00	09 06					09 18		09 26			
Barnehurst	d				08 38			08 51						09 04	09 08					09 21		09 32			
Hither Green	d					08 29						08 44					08 59								09 15
Lee	d					08 31						08 46					09 01								09 17
Mottingham	d					08 34						08 49					09 04								09 20
New Eltham	d		08 21			08 37						08 51					09 06								09 22
Sidcup	d		08 25			08 40						08 55					09 10								09 26
Albany Park	d		08 27			08 42						08 57					09 12								09 28
Bexley	d		08 29			08 45						08 59					09 14								09 30
Crayford	d		08 33			08 48						09 03					09 18								09 33
Charlton	d			08 27		09a13	08 35			08 37			08 47			08 57	09a45	09 03			09 07		09 17		
Woolwich Dockyard	d			08 30						08 40			08 50			09 00					09 10		09 20		
Woolwich Arsenal	d			08 33			08 40			08 43			08 53			09 03		09 09			09 13		09 23		
Plumstead	d			08 35						08 45			08 55			09 05					09 15		09 25		
Abbey Wood	d			08 38			08 45			08 48			08 58			09 08		09 13			09 18		09 28		
Belvedere	d			08 40						08 50			09 00			09 10					09 20		09 30		
Erith	d			08 43						08 53			09 03			09 13					09 23		09 33		
Slade Green	d			08a46						08a56			09 07	09a09		09a16					09a27	09a42	09 37		
Dartford	a		08 38		08 45		08 54	08 58				09 08	09 12		09 15			09 24		09 28			09 42		09 38
	d		08 39				08 55					09 09						09 25							09 39
Stone Crossing	d		08 43									09 13													09 43
Greenhithe for Bluewater	d		08 45				09 00					09 15						09 30							09 45
Swanscombe	d		08 48									09 18													09 48
Northfleet	d		08 50									09 20													09 50
Gravesend	d	08 48	08a55				09 07				09 22	09a25						09 37						09 48	09a55
Higham	d						09 13											09 43							
Strood	d	08 58					09 18				09 32							09 48						09 58	
Maidstone West	d																								
Rochester	d	09 03					09 22				09 37							09 52						10 03	
Chatham	d	09 05					09 25				09 39							09 55						10 05	
Gillingham (Kent)	a	09 09					09 29				09 43							09 59						10 09	

Table 200

Mondays to Fridays

29 August to 7 September

London - Dartford and Gillingham

Network Diagram - see first Page of Table 200

	SE	SE	SE	SE	SE	SE	SE	SE	SE	SE	SE	SE	SE	SE	SE	SE	SE	SE	SE	SE	SE
St Pancras Int'l d									09 54										10 28		
Stratford International d									10 02										10 36		
Ebbsfleet International d									10 13										10 47		
London Charing Cross d	09 02			09 11						09 26	09 32			09 39						09 56	10 02
London Waterloo (East) d	09 05			09 14						09 29	09 35			09 42						09 59	10 05
London Cannon Street d		09 07	09 09			09 15	09 24	09 27				09 37	09 40			09 47	09 54	09 57			
London Bridge d	09 10	09 11	09 14	09 19		09 19	09 28	09 31		09 34	09 40	09 41	09 44	09 47		09 51	09 58	10 01		10 04	10 10
Deptford d		09 17				09 25		09 37				09 47				09 57		10 07			
Greenwich d		09 19				09 29		09 39				09 49				09 59		10 09			
Maze Hill d		09 22				09 32		09 42				09 52				10 02		10 12			
Westcombe Park d		09 24				09 34		09 44				09 54				10 04		10 14			
London Victoria d					09 09										09 39						
Denmark Hill d					09 18										09 48						
Peckham Rye d					09 21										09 51						
Nunhead d					09 23										09 53						
New Cross d			09 19				09 33						09 49				10 03				
St Johns d			09 21				09 35						09 51				10 05				
Lewisham d	09 19		09 24	09 29	09 32		09 38				09 49		09 54	09 56	10 02		10 08				10 19
Blackheath d	09 22			09 31	09 34		09 41				09 52			09 59	10 04		10 11				10 22
Kidbrooke d	09 25				09 37		09 44				09 55				10 07		10 14				10 25
Eltham d	09 28				09 41		09 47				09 58				10 11		10 17				10 28
Falconwood d	09 31				09 43		09 50				10 01				10 13		10 20				10 31
Welling d	09 33				09 46		09 52				10 03				10 16		10 22				10 33
Bexleyheath d	09 36				09 48		09 55				10 06				10 18		10 25				10 36
Barnehurst d	09 38				09 51		10 02				10 08				10 21		10 32				10 38
Hither Green d			09 29							09 44			09 59							10 14	
Lee d			09 31							09 46			10 01							10 16	
Mottingham d			09 34							09 49			10 04							10 19	
New Eltham d			09 36							09 51			10 06							10 21	
Sidcup d			09 40							09 55			10 10							10 25	
Albany Park d			09 42							09 57			10 12							10 27	
Bexley d			09 44							09 59			10 14							10 29	
Crayford d			09 48							10 03			10 18							10 33	
Charlton d		09 27	10a15	09 37		09 40		09 47				09 57	10a45	10 03		10 07		10 17			
Woolwich Dockyard d		09 30				09 43		09 50				10 00				10 10		10 20			
Woolwich Arsenal d		09 33		09 42		09 46		09 53				10 03		10 09		10 13		10 23			
Plumstead d		09 35				09 48		09 55				10 05				10 15		10 25			
Abbey Wood d		09 38		09 46		09 51		09 58				10 08		10 13		10 18		10 28			
Belvedere d		09 40				09 53		10 00				10 10				10 20		10 30			
Erith d		09 43				09 56		10 03				10 13				10 23		10 33			
Slade Green d		09a46				09a59	10a12	10 07				10a16				10a25	10a42	10 37			
Dartford a	09 45			09 54	09 58			10 12		10 08	10 15			10 24	10 28			10 42		10 38	10 45
Dartford d				09 55						10 09				10 25						10 39	
Stone Crossing d										10 13										10 43	
Greenhithe for Bluewater d				10 00						10 15				10 30						10 45	
Swanscombe d										10 18										10 48	
Northfleet d										10 20										10 50	
Gravesend d				10 07					10 18	10a25				10 37					10 51	10a55	
Higham d				10 13										10 43							
Strood d				10 18					10 28					10 48					11 01		
Maidstone West d																					
Rochester d				10 22					10 33					10 52					11 06		
Chatham d				10 25					10 35					10 55					11 08		
Gillingham (Kent) a				10 29					10 39					10 59					11 12		

Table 200

Mondays to Fridays

29 August to 7 September

London - Dartford and Gillingham

Network Diagram - see first Page of Table 200

	SE	SE	SE	SE	SE	SE	SE	SE	SE	SE	SE	SE	SE	SE	SE	SE	SE	SE	SE	SE	SE	SE
St Pancras Int'l d								10 51										11 24				
Stratford International d								10 58										11 31				
Ebbsfleet International d								11 13										11 44				
London Charing Cross d			10 09						10 26	10 32			10 39						10 56	11 02		
London Waterloo (East) d			10 12						10 29	10 35			10 42						10 59	11 05		
London Cannon Street d	10 07	10 10			10 17	10 24	10 27				10 37	10 40			10 47	10 54	10 57				11 07	11 10
London Bridge d	10 11	10 14	10 17		10 21	10 28	10 31		10 34	10 40	10 41	10 44	10 47		10 51	10 58	11 01		11 04	11 10	11 11	11 14
Deptford d	10 17				10 27		10 37				10 47				10 57		11 07				11 17	
Greenwich d	10 19				10 29		10 39				10 49				10 59		11 09				11 19	
Maze Hill d	10 22				10 32		10 42				10 52				11 02		11 12				11 22	
Westcombe Park d	10 24				10 34		10 44				10 54				11 04		11 14				11 24	
London Victoria d				10 09										10 39								
Denmark Hill d				10 18										10 48								
Peckham Rye d				10 21										10 51								
Nunhead d				10 23										10 53								
New Cross d		10 19				10 33						10 49				11 03						11 19
St Johns d		10 21				10 35						10 51				11 05						11 21
Lewisham d		10 24	10 26	10 32		10 38				10 49		10 54	10 56	11 02		11 08				11 19		11 24
Blackheath d			10 29	10 34		10 41				10 52			10 59	11 04		11 11				11 22		
Kidbrooke d				10 37		10 44				10 55				11 07		11 14				11 25		
Eltham d				10 41		10 47				10 58				11 11		11 17				11 28		
Falconwood d				10 43		10 50				11 01				11 13		11 20				11 31		
Welling d				10 46		10 52				11 03				11 16		11 22				11 33		
Bexleyheath d				10 48		10 55				11 06				11 18		11 25				11 36		
Barnehurst d				10 51		11 02				11 08				11 21		11 32				11 38		
Hither Green d		10 29							10 44			10 59							11 14			11 29
Lee d		10 31							10 46			11 01							11 16			11 31
Mottingham d		10 34							10 49			11 04							11 19			11 34
New Eltham d		10 36							10 51			11 06							11 21			11 36
Sidcup d		10 40							10 55			11 10							11 25			11 40
Albany Park d		10 42							10 57			11 12							11 27			11 42
Bexley d		10 44							10 59			11 14							11 29			11 44
Crayford d		10 48							11 03			11 18							11 33			11 48
Charlton d	10 27	11a15	10 33		10 37		10 47				10 57	11a45	11 03		11 07		11 17				11 27	12a15
Woolwich Dockyard d	10 30				10 40		10 50				11 00				11 10		11 20				11 30	
Woolwich Arsenal d	10 33		10 39		10 43		10 53				11 03		11 09		11 13		11 23				11 33	
Plumstead d	10 35				10 45		10 55				11 05				11 15		11 25				11 35	
Abbey Wood d	10 38		10 43		10 48		10 58				11 08		11 13		11 18		11 28				11 38	
Belvedere d	10 40				10 50		11 00				11 10				11 20		11 30				11 40	
Erith d	10 43				10 53		11 03				11 13				11 23		11 33				11 43	
Slade Green d	10a46				10a55	11a12	11 07				11a16				11a25	11a42	11 37				11a46	
Dartford a			10 54	10 58			11 12		11 08	11 15			11 24	11 28			11 42		11 38	11 45		
Dartford d			10 55						11 09				11 25						11 39			
Stone Crossing d									11 13										11 43			
Greenhithe for Bluewater d			11 00						11 15				11 30						11 45			
Swanscombe d									11 18										11 48			
Northfleet d									11 20										11 50			
Gravesend d			11 07					11 18	11a25				11 37					11 48	11a55			
Higham d			11 13										11 43									
Strood d			11 18					11 28					11 48					11 58				
Maidstone West d																						
Rochester d			11 22					11 33					11 52					12 03				
Chatham d			11 25					11 35					11 55					12 05				
Gillingham (Kent) a			11 29					11 39					11 59					12 09				

Table 200

London - Dartford and Gillingham

Mondays to Fridays

29 August to 7 September

Network Diagram - see first Page of Table 200

		SE	SE	SE	SE	SE		SE	SE	SE	SE	SE	SE	SE	SE	SE		SE	SE	SE	SE	SE	SE	SE	SE
St Pancras Int'l ⊖	d							11 55											12 21						
Stratford International ⊖ ⛴	d							12 03											12 32						
Ebbsfleet International	d							12 14											12 43						
London Charing Cross ⊖	d	11 09							11 26	11 32			11 39							11 56	12 02			12 09	
London Waterloo (East) ⊖	d	11 12							11 29	11 35			11 42							11 59	12 05			12 12	
London Cannon Street ⊖	d			11 17	11 24	11 27					11 37	11 40			11 47	11 54		11 57				12 07	12 10		
London Bridge ⊖	d	11 17		11 21	11 28	11 31			11 34	11 40	11 41	11 44	11 47		11 51	11 58		12 01		12 04	12 10	12 11	12 14	12 17	
Deptford	d			11 27		11 37					11 47				11 57			12 07				12 17			
Greenwich ⛴	d			11 29		11 39					11 49				11 59			12 09				12 19			
Maze Hill	d			11 32		11 42					11 52				12 02			12 12				12 22			
Westcombe Park	d			11 34		11 44					11 54				12 04			12 14				12 24			
London Victoria ⊖	d		11 09											11 39											12 09
Denmark Hill	d		11 18											11 48											12 18
Peckham Rye	d		11 21											11 51											12 21
Nunhead	d		11 23											11 53											12 23
New Cross ⊖	d				11 33							11 49				12 03							12 19		
St Johns	d				11 35							11 51				12 05							12 21		
Lewisham ⛴	d	11 26	11 32		11 38					11 49		11 54	11 56	12 02		12 08					12 19		12 24	12 26	12 32
Blackheath	d	11 29	11 34		11 41					11 52			11 59	12 04		12 11					12 22			12 29	12 34
Kidbrooke	d		11 37		11 44					11 55				12 07		12 14					12 25				12 37
Eltham	d		11 41		11 47					11 58				12 11		12 17					12 28				12 41
Falconwood	d		11 43		11 50					12 01				12 13		12 20					12 31				12 43
Welling	d		11 46		11 52					12 03				12 16		12 22					12 33				12 46
Bexleyheath	d		11 48		11 55					12 06				12 18		12 25					12 36				12 48
Barnehurst	d		11 51		12 02					12 08				12 21		12 32					12 38				12 51
Hither Green	d								11 44			11 59								12 14			12 29		
Lee	d								11 46			12 01								12 16			12 31		
Mottingham	d								11 49			12 04								12 19			12 34		
New Eltham	d								11 51			12 06								12 21			12 36		
Sidcup	d								11 55			12 10								12 25			12 40		
Albany Park	d								11 57			12 12								12 27			12 42		
Bexley	d								11 59			12 14								12 29			12 44		
Crayford	d								12 03			12 18								12 33			12 48		
Charlton	d	11 33		11 37		11 47					11 57	12a45	12 03		12 07			12 17				12 27	13a15	12 33	
Woolwich Dockyard	d			11 40		11 50					12 00				12 10			12 20				12 30			
Woolwich Arsenal ⛴	d	11 39		11 43		11 53					12 03		12 09		12 13			12 23				12 33		12 39	
Plumstead	d			11 45		11 55					12 05				12 15			12 25				12 35			
Abbey Wood	d	11 43		11 48		11 58					12 08		12 13		12 18			12 28				12 38		12 43	
Belvedere	d			11 50		12 00					12 10				12 20			12 30				12 40			
Erith	d			11 53		12 03					12 13				12 23			12 33				12 43			
Slade Green	d			11a55	12a12	12 07					12a16				12a25	12a42		12 37				12a46			
Dartford	a	11 54	11 58			12 12			12 08	12 15			12 24	12 28				12 42		12 38	12 45			12 54	12 58
	d	11 55							12 09				12 25							12 39				12 55	
Stone Crossing	d								12 13											12 43					
Greenhithe for Bluewater	d	12 00							12 15				12 30							12 45				13 00	
Swanscombe	d								12 18											12 48					
Northfleet	d								12 20											12 50					
Gravesend	d	12 07						12 18	12a25				12 37						12 48	12a55				13 07	
Higham	d	12 13											12 43											13 13	
Strood	d	12 18						12 28					12 48						12 58					13 18	
Maidstone West	d																								
Rochester	d	12 22						12 33					12 52						13 03					13 22	
Chatham	d	12 25						12 35					12 55						13 05					13 25	
Gillingham (Kent)	a	12 29						12 39					12 59						13 09					13 29	

Table 200

London - Dartford and Gillingham

Mondays to Fridays

29 August to 7 September

Network Diagram - see first Page of Table 200

		SE		SE	SE	SE	SE	SE	SE	SE	SE	SE		SE	SE	SE	SE	SE	SE	SE	SE	SE		SE	SE
St Pancras Int'l ⊖	d					12 51											13 25								
Stratford International ⊖ ⛴	d					12 58											13 33								
Ebbsfleet International	d					13 13											13 44								
London Charing Cross ⊖	d						12 26	12 32			12 39							12 56	13 02			13 09			
London Waterloo (East) ⊖	d						12 29	12 35			12 42							12 59	13 05			13 12			
London Cannon Street ⊖	d	12 17		12 24	12 27				12 37	12 40				12 47	12 54	12 57				13 07	13 10				13 17
London Bridge ⊖	d	12 21		12 28	12 31		12 34	12 40	12 41	12 44	12 47			12 51	12 58	13 01		13 04	13 10	13 11	13 14	13 17			13 21
Deptford	d	12 27			12 37				12 47					12 57		13 07				13 17					13 27
Greenwich ⛴	d	12 29			12 39				12 49					12 59		13 09				13 19					13 29
Maze Hill	d	12 32			12 42				12 52					13 02		13 12				13 22					13 32
Westcombe Park	d	12 34			12 44				12 54					13 04		13 14				13 24					13 34
London Victoria ⊖	d											12 39												13 09	
Denmark Hill	d											12 48												13 18	
Peckham Rye	d											12 51												13 21	
Nunhead	d											12 53												13 23	
New Cross ⊖	d			12 33						12 49					13 03						13 19				
St Johns	d			12 35						12 51					13 05						13 21				
Lewisham ⛴	d			12 38				12 49		12 54	12 56	13 02			13 08				13 19		13 24	13 26		13 32	
Blackheath	d			12 41				12 52			12 59	13 04			13 11				13 22			13 29		13 34	
Kidbrooke	d			12 44				12 55				13 07			13 14				13 25					13 37	
Eltham	d			12 47				12 58				13 11			13 17				13 28					13 41	
Falconwood	d			12 50				13 01				13 13			13 20				13 31					13 43	
Welling	d			12 52				13 03				13 16			13 22				13 33					13 46	
Bexleyheath	d			12 55				13 06				13 18			13 25				13 36					13 48	
Barnehurst	d			13 02				13 08				13 21			13 32				13 38					13 51	
Hither Green	d						12 44			12 59								13 14			13 29				
Lee	d						12 46			13 01								13 16			13 31				
Mottingham	d						12 49			13 04								13 19			13 34				
New Eltham	d						12 51			13 06								13 21			13 36				
Sidcup	d						12 55			13 10								13 25			13 40				
Albany Park	d						12 57			13 12								13 27			13 42				
Bexley	d						12 59			13 14								13 29			13 44				
Crayford	d						13 03			13 18								13 33			13 48				
Charlton	d	12 37			12 47				12 57	13a45	13 03			13 07		13 17				13 27	14a15	13 33			13 37
Woolwich Dockyard	d	12 40			12 50				13 00					13 10		13 20				13 30					13 40
Woolwich Arsenal ⛴	d	12 43			12 53				13 03		13 09			13 13		13 23				13 33		13 39			13 43
Plumstead	d	12 45			12 55				13 05					13 15		13 25				13 35					13 45
Abbey Wood	d	12 48			12 58				13 08		13 13			13 18		13 28				13 38		13 43			13 48
Belvedere	d	12 50			13 00				13 10					13 20		13 30				13 40					13 50
Erith	d	12 53			13 03				13 13					13 23		13 33				13 43					13 53
Slade Green	d	12a55		13a12	13 07				13a16					13a25	13a42	13 37				13a46					13a55
Dartford	a				13 12		13 08	13 15			13 24	13 28				13 42		13 38	13 45			13 54		13 58	
	d						13 09				13 25							13 39				13 55			
Stone Crossing	d						13 13											13 43							
Greenhithe for Bluewater	d						13 15				13 30							13 45				14 00			
Swanscombe	d						13 18											13 48							
Northfleet	d						13 20											13 50							
Gravesend	d					13 18	13a25				13 37						13 48	13a55				14 07			
Higham	d										13 43											14 13			
Strood	d					13 28					13 48						13 58					14 18			
Maidstone West	d																								
Rochester	d					13 33					13 52						14 03					14 22			
Chatham	d					13 35					13 55						14 05					14 25			
Gillingham (Kent)	a					13 39					13 59						14 09					14 29			

Table 200

Mondays to Fridays

29 August to 7 September

London - Dartford and Gillingham

Network Diagram - see first Page of Table 200

		SE	SE	SE	SE	SE	SE	SE		SE	SE	SE	SE	SE	SE	SE	SE	SE		SE	SE	SE	SE	SE	SE
St Pancras Int'l	d			13 54											14 25										
Stratford International	d			14 02											14 33										
Ebbsfleet International	d			14 14											14 44										
London Charing Cross	d				13 26	13 32				13 39						13 56	14 02				14 09				
London Waterloo (East)	d				13 29	13 35				13 42						13 59	14 05				14 12				
London Cannon Street	d	13 24	13 27				13 37	13 40				13 47	13 54	13 57				14 07		14 10			14 17	14 24	14 27
London Bridge	d	13 28	13 31		13 34	13 40	13 41	13 44		13 47		13 51	13 58	14 01		14 04	14 10	14 11		14 14	14 17		14 21	14 28	14 31
Deptford	d		13 37				13 47					13 57		14 07				14 17					14 27		14 37
Greenwich	d		13 39				13 49					13 59		14 09				14 19					14 29		14 39
Maze Hill	d		13 42				13 52					14 02		14 12				14 22					14 32		14 42
Westcombe Park	d		13 44				13 54					14 04		14 14				14 24					14 34		14 44
London Victoria	d										13 39											14 09			
Denmark Hill	d										13 48											14 18			
Peckham Rye	d										13 51											14 21			
Nunhead	d										13 53											14 23			
New Cross	d	13 33						13 49					14 03							14 19				14 33	
St Johns	d	13 35						13 51					14 05							14 21				14 35	
Lewisham	d	13 38				13 49		13 54		13 56	14 02		14 08				14 19			14 24	14 26	14 32		14 38	
Blackheath	d	13 41				13 52				13 59	14 04		14 11				14 22				14 29	14 34		14 41	
Kidbrooke	d	13 44				13 55					14 07		14 14				14 25					14 37		14 44	
Eltham	d	13 47				13 58					14 11		14 17				14 28					14 41		14 47	
Falconwood	d	13 50				14 01					14 13		14 20				14 31					14 43		14 50	
Welling	d	13 52				14 03					14 16		14 22				14 33					14 46		14 52	
Bexleyheath	d	13 55				14 06					14 18		14 25				14 36					14 48		14 55	
Barnehurst	d	14 02				14 08					14 21		14 32				14 38					14 51		15 02	
Hither Green	d				13 44			13 59								14 14				14 29					
Lee	d				13 46			14 01								14 16				14 31					
Mottingham	d				13 49			14 04								14 19				14 34					
New Eltham	d				13 51			14 06								14 21				14 36					
Sidcup	d				13 55			14 10								14 25				14 40					
Albany Park	d				13 57			14 12								14 27				14 42					
Bexley	d				13 59			14 14								14 29				14 44					
Crayford	d				14 03			14 18								14 33				14 48					
Charlton	d		13 47				13 57	14a45		14 03		14 07		14 17				14 27		15a15	14 33		14 37		14 47
Woolwich Dockyard	d		13 50				14 00					14 10		14 20				14 30					14 40		14 50
Woolwich Arsenal	d		13 53				14 03			14 09		14 13		14 23				14 33			14 39		14 43		14 53
Plumstead	d		13 55				14 05					14 15		14 25				14 35					14 45		14 55
Abbey Wood	d		13 58				14 08			14 13		14 18		14 28				14 38			14 43		14 48		14 58
Belvedere	d		14 00				14 10					14 20		14 30				14 40					14 50		15 00
Erith	d		14 03				14 13					14 23		14 33				14 43					14 53		15 03
Slade Green	d	14a12	14 07				14a16					14a25	14a42	14 37				14a46					14a55	15a12	15 07
Dartford	a		14 12		14 08	14 15				14 24	14 28			14 42		14 38	14 45				14 54	14 58			15 12
	d				14 09					14 25						14 39					14 55				
Stone Crossing	d				14 13											14 43									
Greenhithe for Bluewater	d				14 15					14 30						14 45					15 00				
Swanscombe	d				14 18											14 48									
Northfleet	d				14 20											14 50									
Gravesend	d			14 18	14a25					14 37					14 48	14a55					15 07				
Higham	d									14 43											15 13				
Strood	d			14 28						14 48					14 58						15 18				
Maidstone West	d																								
Rochester	d			14 33						14 52					15 03						15 22				
Chatham	d			14 35						14 55					15 05						15 25				
Gillingham (Kent)	a			14 39						14 59					15 09						15 29				

Table 200

Mondays to Fridays

29 August to 7 September

London - Dartford and Gillingham

Network Diagram - see first Page of Table 200

		SE	SE	SE		SE	SE	SE	SE	SE	SE	SE	SE	SE		SE	SE	SE	SE	SE	SE	SE	SE	SE	
St Pancras Int'l	d	14 54											15 24											15 54	
Stratford International	d	15 02											15 32											16 02	
Ebbsfleet International	d	15 14											15 44											16 14	
London Charing Cross	d		14 26	14 32				14 39						14 56		15 02			15 09						
London Waterloo (East)	d		14 29	14 35				14 42						14 59		15 05			15 12						
London Cannon Street	d					14 37	14 40			14 47	14 54	14 57					15 07	15 10			15 17	15 24	15 27		
London Bridge	d		14 34	14 40		14 41	14 44	14 47		14 51	14 58	15 01		15 04		15 10	15 11	15 14	15 17		15 21	15 28	15 31		
Deptford	d					14 47				14 57		15 07					15 17				15 27		15 37		
Greenwich	d					14 49				14 59		15 09					15 19				15 29		15 39		
Maze Hill	d					14 52				15 02		15 12					15 22				15 32		15 42		
Westcombe Park	d					14 54				15 04		15 14					15 24				15 34		15 44		
London Victoria	d								14 39											15 09					
Denmark Hill	d								14 48											15 18					
Peckham Rye	d								14 51											15 21					
Nunhead	d								14 53											15 23					
New Cross	d						14 49				15 03							15 19				15 33			
St Johns	d						14 51				15 05							15 21				15 35			
Lewisham	d			14 49			14 54	14 56	15 02		15 08					15 19		15 24	15 26	15 32		15 38			
Blackheath	d			14 52				14 59	15 04		15 11					15 22			15 29	15 34		15 41			
Kidbrooke	d			14 55					15 07		15 14					15 25				15 37		15 44			
Eltham	d			14 58					15 11		15 17					15 28				15 41		15 47			
Falconwood	d			15 01					15 13		15 20					15 31				15 43		15 50			
Welling	d			15 03					15 16		15 22					15 33				15 46		15 52			
Bexleyheath	d			15 06					15 18		15 25					15 36				15 48		15 55			
Barnehurst	d			15 08					15 21		15 32					15 38				15 51		16 02			
Hither Green	d		14 44				14 59							15 14				15 29							
Lee	d		14 46				15 01							15 16				15 31							
Mottingham	d		14 49				15 04							15 19				15 34							
New Eltham	d		14 51				15 06							15 21				15 36							
Sidcup	d		14 55				15 10							15 25				15 40							
Albany Park	d		14 57				15 12							15 27				15 42							
Bexley	d		14 59				15 14							15 29				15 44							
Crayford	d		15 03				15 18							15 33				15 48							
Charlton	d					14 57	15a45	15 03		15 07		15 17					15 27	16a15	15 33		15 37		15 47		
Woolwich Dockyard	d					15 00				15 10		15 20					15 30				15 40		15 50		
Woolwich Arsenal	d					15 03		15 09		15 13		15 23					15 33		15 39		15 43		15 53		
Plumstead	d					15 05				15 15		15 25					15 35				15 45		15 55		
Abbey Wood	d					15 08		15 13		15 18		15 28					15 38		15 43		15 48		15 58		
Belvedere	d					15 10				15 20		15 30					15 40				15 50		16 00		
Erith	d					15 13				15 23		15 33					15 43				15 53		16 03		
Slade Green	d					15a16				15a25	15a42	15 37					15a46				15a55	16a12	16 07		
Dartford	a		15 08	15 15				15 24	15 28			15 42		15 38		15 45			15 54	15 58			16 12		
	d		15 09					15 25						15 39					15 55						
Stone Crossing	d		15 13											15 43											
Greenhithe for Bluewater	d		15 15					15 30						15 45					16 00						
Swanscombe	d		15 18											15 48											
Northfleet	d		15 20											15 50											
Gravesend	d	15 18	15a25					15 37					15 48	15a55					16 07					16 18	
Higham	d							15 43											16 13						
Strood	d	15 28						15 48					15 58						16 18					16 28	
Maidstone West	d																								
Rochester	d	15 33						15 52					16 03						16 22					16 33	
Chatham	d	15 35						15 55					16 05						16 25					16 35	
Gillingham (Kent)	a	15 39						15 59					16 09						16 29					16 39	

Table 200

London - Dartford and Gillingham

Mondays to Fridays

29 August to 7 September

Network Diagram - see first Page of Table 200

		SE	SE	SE	SE	SE	SE	SE	SE	SE		SE	SE	SE	SE	SE	SE	SE	SE	SE		SE	SE	SE	SE
St Pancras Int'l	d											16 26											16 55		
Stratford International	d											16 33											17 03		
Ebbsfleet International	d											16 44											17 14		
London Charing Cross	d	15 26	15 32			15 39							15 56	16 02			16 09							16 26	16 30
London Waterloo (East)	d	15 29	15 35			15 42							15 59	16 05			16 12							16 29	16 33
London Cannon Street	d			15 37	15 40			15 47	15 54	15 57					16 07	16 10			16 17	16 24		16 27			
London Bridge	d	15 34	15 40	15 41	15 44	15 47		15 51	15 58	16 01			16 04	16 10	16 11	16 14	16 17		16 21	16 28		16 31		16 34	16 38
Deptford	d			15 47				15 57		16 07					16 17				16 27			16 37			
Greenwich	d			15 49				15 59		16 09					16 20				16 30			16 40			
Maze Hill	d			15 52				16 02		16 12					16 23				16 33			16 43			
Westcombe Park	d			15 54				16 04		16 14					16 25				16 35			16 45			
London Victoria	d						15 39											16 09							
Denmark Hill	d						15 48											16 18							
Peckham Rye	d						15 51											16 21							
Nunhead	d						15 53											16 23							
New Cross	d				15 49				16 03							16 20				16 34					
St Johns	d				15 51				16 05							16 22				16 36					
Lewisham	d		15 49		15 54	15 56	16 02		16 08					16 19		16 25	16 27	16 32		16 39					16 49
Blackheath	d		15 52			15 59	16 04		16 11					16 22			16 29	16 34		16 42					16 53
Kidbrooke	d		15 55				16 07		16 14					16 25				16 37		16 45					16 56
Eltham	d		15 58				16 11		16 17					16 29				16 41		16 48					16 59
Falconwood	d		16 01				16 13		16 20					16 31				16 43		16 51					17 02
Welling	d		16 03				16 16		16 22					16 34				16 46		16 53					17 04
Bexleyheath	d		16 06				16 18		16 25					16 36				16 48		16 56					17 07
Barnehurst	d		16 08				16 21		16 32					16 39				16 51		17 02					17 11
Hither Green	d	15 44			15 59								16 14			16 29								16 44	
Lee	d	15 46			16 01								16 16			16 31								16 46	
Mottingham	d	15 49			16 04								16 19			16 34								16 49	
New Eltham	d	15 51			16 06								16 21			16 37								16 51	
Sidcup	d	15 55			16 10								16 25			16 40								16 55	
Albany Park	d	15 57			16 12								16 27			16 42								16 57	
Bexley	d	15 59			16 14								16 29			16 45								16 59	
Crayford	d	16 03			16 18								16 33			16 48								17 03	
Charlton	d			15 57	16a45	16 03		16 07		16 17					16 27	17a15	16 34		16 37			16 47			
Woolwich Dockyard	d			16 00				16 10		16 20					16 30				16 40			16 50			
Woolwich Arsenal	d			16 03		16 09		16 13		16 23					16 33		16 39		16 43			16 53			
Plumstead	d			16 05				16 15		16 25					16 35				16 45			16 55			
Abbey Wood	d			16 08		16 13		16 18		16 28					16 39		16 43		16 48			16 59			
Belvedere	d			16 10				16 20		16 30					16 41				16 51			17 01			
Erith	d			16 13				16 23		16 33					16 44				16 53			17 04			
Slade Green	d			16a16				16a25	16a42	16 37					16a46				16a56	17a14		17 07			
Dartford	a	16 08	16 15			16 24	16 28			16 45			16 38	16 48			16 54	17 00				17 14		17 08	17 23
	d	16 09				16 25							16 39				16 55							17 09	
Stone Crossing	d	16 13											16 43											17 13	
Greenhithe for Bluewater	d	16 15				16 30							16 45				17 00							17 15	
Swanscombe	d	16 18											16 48											17 18	
Northfleet	d	16 20											16 50											17 20	
Gravesend	d	16a25				16 37						16 48	16a55				17 07						17 18	17a27	
Higham	d					16 43											17 13								
Strood	d					16 48						16 58					17 18						17 28		
Maidstone West	d																								
Rochester	d					16 52						17 03					17 22						17 34		
Chatham	d					16 55						17 05					17 25						17 37		
Gillingham (Kent)	a					16 59						17 09					17 31						17 41		

Table 200

London - Dartford and Gillingham

Mondays to Fridays

29 August to 7 September

Network Diagram - see first Page of Table 200

		SE	SE	SE	SE	SE		SE	SE	SE	SE	SE	SE	SE	SE	SE		SE	SE	SE	SE	SE	SE	SE	SE
St Pancras Int'l	d				17 14																		17 44		
Stratford International	d				17 22																		17 52		
Ebbsfleet International	d																								
London Charing Cross	d								16 45	16 49		16 51		16 55					17 06	17 10		17 12		17 17	
London Waterloo (East)	d								16 48	16 52		16 54		16 58					17 09	17 13		17 15		17 20	
London Cannon Street	d	16 35	16 39	16 42		16 44					16 54		16 58		17 04	17 06					17 16				17 21
London Bridge	d	16 39	16 43	16 46		16 48			16 53	16 57	16 58	16 59	17 02	17 04	17 08	17 10			17 14	17 19	17 20	17 21		17 26	17 25
Deptford	d	16 45							16 59		17 04								17 20		17 26				
Greenwich	d	16 48				16 56			17 02		17 07					17 18			17 23		17 29				
Maze Hill	d	16 51							17 05		17 10								17 26		17 32				
Westcombe Park	d	16 53							17 07		17 12								17 28		17 34				
London Victoria	d							16 39										17 04							
Denmark Hill	d							16 48										17 13							
Peckham Rye	d							16 51										17 16							
Nunhead	d							16 53										17 18							
New Cross	d		16 49	16 52									17 08		17 14										17 31
St Johns	d		16 51										17 10												17 33
Lewisham	d		16 54	16 56				17 02				17 08	17 13		17 18			17 25				17 30			17 36
Blackheath	d			16 59				17 04				17 10			17 22			17 28				17 34			
Kidbrooke	d			17 02				17 07				17 13			17 25			17 31				17 37			
Eltham	d			17 06				17 11				17 17			17 29			17 34				17 40			
Falconwood	d			17 08				17 13				17 19			17 31			17 37				17 43			
Welling	d			17 11				17 16				17 22			17 34			17 39				17 45			
Bexleyheath	d			17 13				17 18				17 24			17 36			17 42				17 48			
Barnehurst	d			17 17				17 21				17 27			17 41			17 45				17 51			
Hither Green	d		16 58	17a57						17 07			17 18							17 29					17 41
Lee	d		17 00							17 09			17 20							17 31					17 43
Mottingham	d		17 03							17 12			17 23							17 34					17 46
New Eltham	d		17 06							17 15			17 26	17 20						17 36				17 42	17 48
Sidcup	d		17 09							17a20			17 30	17 26						17a41				17 47	17 52
Albany Park	d		17 11										17 32	17 28										17 49	17 54
Bexley	d		17 14										17 35	17 30										17 52	17 57
Crayford	d		17 17										17 39	17 34										17 55	18a00
Charlton	d	16 56	17a45			17 02			17 10		17 15		18a05			17 24			17 30		17 37				
Woolwich Dockyard	d	16 59							17 13		17 18								17 33		17 40				
Woolwich Arsenal	d	17 02				17 07			17 16		17 21					17 29			17 36		17 43				
Plumstead	d	17 04							17 18		17 23								17 38		17 45				
Abbey Wood	d	17 07				17 11			17 21		17 26					17 33			17 42		17 48				
Belvedere	d	17 10							17 24		17 29								17 44		17 51				
Erith	d	17 12							17 26		17 31								17 47		17 53				
Slade Green	d	17 15							17a29		17 34				17a52				17a49		17 56				
Dartford	a	17 22				17 26		17 31			17 43	17 38		17 39		17 44		17 54			18 06	18 00		18 00	
	d					17 28								17 40		17 47								18 02	
Stone Crossing	d													17 44											
Greenhithe for Bluewater	d					17 33								17 46		17 52								18 07	
Swanscombe	d													17 49											
Northfleet	d													17 51											
Gravesend	d				17 36	17 40								17a57		18 00							18 06	18 19	
Higham	d					17 46										18 06								18 25	
Strood	d				17 46	17 52										18 14							18 18	18a33	
Maidstone West	d				18a02																		18a32		
Rochester	d					17 57										18 20									
Chatham	d					18 00										18 23									
Gillingham (Kent)	a					18 07										18 30									

Table 200

Mondays to Fridays

29 August to 7 September

London - Dartford and Gillingham

Network Diagram - see first Page of Table 200

Station		SE		SE	SE	SE	SE	SE	SE	SE	SE	SE	
St Pancras Int'l	d												
Stratford International	d												
Ebbsfleet International	d												
London Charing Cross	d				17 29	17 30	17 32		17 34	17 39			
London Waterloo (East)	d				17 32	17 33	17 35		17 37	17 42			
London Cannon Street	d	17 26		17 28				17 39				17 43	
London Bridge	d	17 30		17 32	17 37		17 41	17 43	17 43	17 48		17 47	
Deptford	d				17 43			17 49					
Greenwich	d			17 40	17 46			17 52					
Maze Hill	d				17 49			17 55					
Westcombe Park	d				17 51			17 57					
London Victoria	d										17 34		
Denmark Hill	d										17 43		
Peckham Rye	d										17 46		
Nunhead	d										17 49		
New Cross	d	17 36										17 53	
St Johns	d											17 55	
Lewisham	d	17 40							17 53		17 56	17 59	
Blackheath	d	17 43				17 49			17 56		18 00		
Kidbrooke	d	17 46				17 52			17 59		18 03		
Eltham	d	17 50				17 56			18 02		18 06		
Falconwood	d	17 52				17 58			18 05		18 09		
Welling	d	17 55				18 01			18 07		18 11		
Bexleyheath	d	17 58				18 04			18 10		18 14		
Barnehurst	d	18 02				18 07			18 12		18 16		
Hither Green	d						17 51					18 03	
Lee	d						17 53					18 05	
Mottingham	d						17 56					18 08	
New Eltham	d						17 59			18 04		18 11	
Sidcup	d						18a04			18 08		18 15	
Albany Park	d									18 10		18 17	
Bexley	d									18 13		18 20	
Crayford	d									18 16		18a23	
Charlton	d			17 46	17 53			18 00					
Woolwich Dockyard	d				17 56			18 03					
Woolwich Arsenal	d			17 51	17 59			18 06					
Plumstead	d				18 01			18 08					
Abbey Wood	d			17 55	18 05			18 11					
Belvedere	d				18 07			18 14					
Erith	d				18 10			18 16					
Slade Green	d	18a12			18a14			18 19	18a22				
Dartford	a			18 06		18 16		18 27		18 21	18 25		
	d			18 08						18 22			
Stone Crossing	d			18 12									
Greenhithe for Bluewater	d			18 14						18 27			
Swanscombe	d			18 17									
Northfleet	d			18 19									
Gravesend	d			18a27						18 34			
Higham	d									18 40			
Strood	d									18 45			
Maidstone West	d												
Rochester	d									18 51			
Chatham	d									18 54			
Gillingham (Kent)	a									19 02			

Station		SE	SE	SE	SE	SE	SE	SE	SE	SE		SE	SE
St Pancras Int'l	d		18 14										
Stratford International	d		18 22										
Ebbsfleet International	d												
London Charing Cross	d				17 50	17 52	17 54	17 56					18 01
London Waterloo (East)	d				17 53	17 55	17 57	17 59					18 04
London Cannon Street	d	17 47		17 50					18 00			18 04	
London Bridge	d	17 51		17 54	17 58		18 02	18 04	18 04			18 08	18 10
Deptford	d				18 04				18 10				
Greenwich	d			18 02	18 07				18 13				
Maze Hill	d				18 10				18 16				
Westcombe Park	d				18 12				18 18				
London Victoria	d									17 56			
Denmark Hill	d									18 06			
Peckham Rye	d									18 09			
Nunhead	d									18 11			
New Cross	d	17 58										18 14	
St Johns	d											18 16	
Lewisham	d	18 02						18 14		18 18		18 20	
Blackheath	d	18 05				18 09		18 17		18 23			
Kidbrooke	d	18 08				18 12		18 20		18 26			
Eltham	d	18 12				18 16		18 23		18 30			
Falconwood	d	18 14				18 18		18 26		18 32			
Welling	d	18 17				18 21		18 28		18 35			
Bexleyheath	d	18 20				18 24		18 31		18 38			
Barnehurst	d	18 23				18 27		18a36		18 41			
Hither Green	d	18a57					18 13					18 25	
Lee	d						18 15					18 27	
Mottingham	d						18 18					18 30	
New Eltham	d						18 21					18 32	18 26
Sidcup	d						18 25					18 36	18 30
Albany Park	d											18 38	18 32
Bexley	d											18 40	18 35
Crayford	d						18a32					18 44	18 38
Charlton	d			18 08	18 15				18 21			19a10	
Woolwich Dockyard	d				18 18				18 24				
Woolwich Arsenal	d			18 13	18 21				18 27				
Plumstead	d				18 23				18 29				
Abbey Wood	d			18 17	18 26				18 32				
Belvedere	d				18 29				18 35				
Erith	d				18 31				18 37				
Slade Green	d				18a36				18 41				
Dartford	a			18 29		18 36			18 48	18 53			18 44
	d			18 31									18 45
Stone Crossing	d												18 49
Greenhithe for Bluewater	d			18 36									18 51
Swanscombe	d												18 54
Northfleet	d												18 56
Gravesend	d		18 38	18a45									19 02
Higham	d												19 08
Strood	d		18 49										19 14
Maidstone West	d		19a05										
Rochester	d												19 19
Chatham	d												19 22
Gillingham (Kent)	a												19 29

Table 200

Mondays to Fridays

29 August to 7 September

London - Dartford and Gillingham

Network Diagram - see first Page of Table 200

Station		SE	SE	SE	SE	SE	SE	SE		SE	SE	SE	SE
St Pancras Int'l	d									18 55			
Stratford International	d									19 02			
Ebbsfleet International	d									19 13			
London Charing Cross	d			18 12	18 14		18 18				18 23		
London Waterloo (East)	d			18 15	18 17		18 21				18 26		
London Cannon Street	d	18 10	18 12			18 21		18 25				18 30	
London Bridge	d	18 14	18 16	18 21	18 23	18 25	18 26	18 29			18 32	18 34	
Deptford	d			18 27		18 31							
Greenwich	d		18 24	18 29		18 34						18 42	
Maze Hill	d			18 32		18 37							
Westcombe Park	d			18 34		18 39							
London Victoria	d												18 18
Denmark Hill	d												18 28
Peckham Rye	d												18 32
Nunhead	d												18 34
New Cross	d	18 20						18 35					
St Johns	d							18 37					
Lewisham	d	18 24					18 36	18 41					18 43
Blackheath	d	18 27					18 39						18 46
Kidbrooke	d	18 30					18 42						18 49
Eltham	d	18 34					18 46						18 53
Falconwood	d	18 36					18 48						18 55
Welling	d	18 39					18 51						18 58
Bexleyheath	d	18 42					18 54						19 01
Barnehurst	d	18a47					18 57						19 04
Hither Green	d				18 35			18 46					
Lee	d				18 37			18 48					
Mottingham	d				18 40			18 51					
New Eltham	d				18 43			18 54			18 48		
Sidcup	d				18 47			18 58			18 51		
Albany Park	d				18 49			19 00			18 53		
Bexley	d				18 51			19 03			18 56		
Crayford	d				18a54			19 10			18 59		
Charlton	d		18 30	18 37		18 41		19a40				18 48	
Woolwich Dockyard	d			18 40		18 44							
Woolwich Arsenal	d		18 35	18 43		18 47						18 53	
Plumstead	d			18 45		18 49							
Abbey Wood	d		18 40	18 48		18 53						18 57	
Belvedere	d			18 50		18 55							
Erith	d			18 53		18 58							
Slade Green	d			18a55		19 01							
Dartford	a		18 52			19 09	19 06				19 04	19 09	19 13
	d		18 54								19 05	19 10	
Stone Crossing	d										19 09	19 14	
Greenhithe for Bluewater	d		18 59								19 11	19 16	
Swanscombe	d										19 14	19 19	
Northfleet	d										19 16	19 21	
Gravesend	d		19a09							19 20	19a24	19 26	
Higham	d											19 32	
Strood	d									19 30		19 38	
Maidstone West	d												
Rochester	d									19 35		19 45	
Chatham	d									19 38		19 48	
Gillingham (Kent)	a									19 42		19 55	

Station		SE	SE	SE	SE	SE		SE	SE	SE	SE	SE	SE
St Pancras Int'l	d												19 24
Stratford International	d												19 32
Ebbsfleet International	d												19 45
London Charing Cross	d		18 34	18 37	18 39					18 48			
London Waterloo (East)	d		18 37	18 40	18 42					18 51			
London Cannon Street	d	18 34						18 46	18 50		18 54	18 57	
London Bridge	d	18 38	18 42	18 46	18 48			18 50	18 54	18 57	18 58	19 01	
Deptford	d		18 48					18 56				19 07	
Greenwich	d		18 51					18 59				19 10	
Maze Hill	d		18 54					19 02				19 13	
Westcombe Park	d		18 56					19 04				19 15	
London Victoria	d					18 39							
Denmark Hill	d					18 48							
Peckham Rye	d					18 51							
Nunhead	d					18 54							
New Cross	d	18 44			18 55				19 00		19 05		
St Johns	d	18 46							19 02		19 07		
Lewisham	d	18 49			18 59	19 03			19 05	19 07	19 11		
Blackheath	d	18 52			19 02	19 06				19 10	19 14		
Kidbrooke	d	18 55			19 05	19 09					19 17		
Eltham	d	18 59			19 09	19 13					19 21		
Falconwood	d	19 01			19 11	19 16					19 23		
Welling	d	19 04			19 14	19 18					19 26		
Bexleyheath	d	19 07			19 16	19 21					19 29		
Barnehurst	d	19a12			19a21	19 25					19a34		
Hither Green	d			18 56					19 09				
Lee	d			18 58					19 11				
Mottingham	d			19 01					19 14				
New Eltham	d			19 04					19 17				
Sidcup	d			19 08					19 20				
Albany Park	d			19 10					19 22				
Bexley	d			19 13					19 25				
Crayford	d			19 16					19 29				
Charlton	d		18 59					19 06	20a10	19 15		19 18	
Woolwich Dockyard	d		19 02					19 09				19 21	
Woolwich Arsenal	d		19 05					19 12		19 20		19 24	
Plumstead	d		19 07					19 14				19 26	
Abbey Wood	d		19 10					19 17		19 24		19 29	
Belvedere	d		19 13					19 19				19 32	
Erith	d		19 15					19 22				19 34	
Slade Green	d		19 18					19a26				19 37	
Dartford	a		19 28	19 21		19 34				19 34		19 44	
	d			19 22						19 35			
Stone Crossing	d			19 26									
Greenhithe for Bluewater	d			19 29						19 40			
Swanscombe	d			19 32									
Northfleet	d			19 34									
Gravesend	d			19 38						19 47			19 51
Higham	d			19 44						19 53			
Strood	d			19a53						19 58			20 01
Maidstone West	d												
Rochester	d									20 03			20 08
Chatham	d									20 05			20 10
Gillingham (Kent)	a									20 13			20 14

Table 200

London - Dartford and Gillingham

Mondays to Fridays

29 August to 7 September

Network Diagram - see first Page of Table 200

Station		SE	SE	SE		SE	SE	SE	SE	SE	SE	SE	SE	SE		SE	SE	SE	SE	SE	SE	SE	SE	SE	
St Pancras Int'l ⊖	d											19 54											20 25		
Stratford International ⊖	d											20 02											20 33		
Ebbsfleet International	d											20 14											20 44		
London Charing Cross ⊖	d	18 56	19 02				19 09						19 26	19 32				19 39						19 56	
London Waterloo (East) ⊖	d	18 59	19 05				19 12						19 29	19 35				19 42						19 59	
London Cannon Street ⊖	d			19 07		19 10			19 17	19 24	19 27					19 37	19 40			19 47	19 54	19 57			
London Bridge ⊖	d	19 04	19 10	19 11		19 14	19 17		19 21	19 28	19 31		19 34	19 40		19 41	19 44	19 47		19 51	19 58	20 01		20 04	
Deptford	d			19 17					19 27		19 37					19 47				19 57		20 07			
Greenwich	d			19 19					19 29		19 39					19 49				19 59		20 09			
Maze Hill	d			19 22					19 32		19 42					19 52				20 02		20 12			
Westcombe Park	d			19 24					19 34		19 44					19 54				20 04		20 14			
London Victoria ⊖	d							19 09											19 39						
Denmark Hill	d							19 18											19 48						
Peckham Rye	d							19 21											19 51						
Nunhead	d							19 23											19 53						
New Cross ⊖	d					19 19				19 33							19 49				20 03				
St Johns	d					19 21				19 35							19 51				20 05				
Lewisham	d		19 19			19 24	19 26	19 32		19 38				19 49			19 55	19 56	20 02		20 08				
Blackheath	d		19 22				19 29	19 34		19 41				19 52				19 59	20 04		20 11				
Kidbrooke	d		19 25					19 37		19 44				19 55					20 07		20 14				
Eltham	d		19 29					19 41		19 47				19 58					20 11		20 17				
Falconwood	d		19 31					19 43		19 50				20 01					20 13		20 20				
Welling	d		19 34					19 46		19 52				20 03					20 16		20 22				
Bexleyheath	d		19 36					19 48		19 55				20 06					20 18		20 25				
Barnehurst	d		19 39					19 51		19a58				20 08					20 21		20a28				
Hither Green	d	19 14				19 29							19 44				20 00							20 14	
Lee	d	19 16				19 31							19 46				20 02							20 16	
Mottingham	d	19 19				19 34							19 49				20 05							20 19	
New Eltham	d	19 22				19 36							19 51				20 07							20 21	
Sidcup	d	19 25				19 40							19 55				20 11							20 25	
Albany Park	d	19 27				19 42							19 57				20 13							20 27	
Bexley	d	19 30				19 44							19 59				20 15							20 29	
Crayford	d	19 33				19 48							20 03				20 18							20 33	
Charlton	d			19 27			19 33		19 37		19 47					19 57		20 03		20 07		20 17			
Woolwich Dockyard	d			19 30					19 40		19 50					20 00				20 10		20 20			
Woolwich Arsenal	d			19 33			19 39		19 43		19 53					20 03		20 09		20 13		20 23			
Plumstead	d			19 35					19 45		19 55					20 05				20 15		20 25			
Abbey Wood	d			19 38			19 43		19 48		19 58					20 08		20 13		20 18		20 28			
Belvedere	d			19 40					19 50		20 00					20 10				20 20		20 30			
Erith	d			19 43					19 53		20 03					20 13				20 23		20 33			
Slade Green	d			19a45					19a55		20 07					20a15				20a25		20 37			
Dartford	a	19 38	19 48			19 53	19 55	19 58			20 13		20 08	20 15			20 23	20 25	20 28			20 43		20 38	
	d	19 39					19 55						20 09					20 25						20 39	
Stone Crossing	d	19 43											20 13											20 43	
Greenhithe for Bluewater	d	19 46					20 00						20 15					20 30						20 45	
Swanscombe	d	19 49											20 18											20 48	
Northfleet	d	19 51											20 20											20 50	
Gravesend	d	19a57					20 07					20 18	20a25					20 37					20 48	20a55	
Higham	d						20 13											20 43							
Strood	d						20 18					20 28						20 48					20 58		
Maidstone West	d																								
Rochester	d						20 22					20 33						20 52					21 03		
Chatham	d						20 25					20 35						20 55					21 05		
Gillingham (Kent)	a						20 29					20 39						20 59					21 09		

Table 200

London - Dartford and Gillingham

Mondays to Fridays

29 August to 7 September

Network Diagram - see first Page of Table 200

Station		SE	SE	SE	SE	SE	SE	SE	SE	SE		SE	SE	SE	SE	SE	SE	SE	SE	SE		SE	SE	SE	SE
St Pancras Int'l ⊖	d					20 55							21 25						21 55						
Stratford International ⊖	d					21 03							21 33						22 03						
Ebbsfleet International	d					21 14							21 44						22 14						
London Charing Cross ⊖	d	20 02		20 09			20 22		20 32	20 39				20 52		21 02	21 09			21 22		21 26	21 32	21 39	
London Waterloo (East) ⊖	d	20 05		20 12			20 25		20 35	20 42				20 55		21 05	21 12			21 25		21 29	21 35	21 42	
London Cannon Street ⊖	d		20 10		20 17			20 27				20 47			20 57										
London Bridge ⊖	d	20 10	20 14	20 17	20 21		20 30	20 31	20 40	20 47		20 51		21 00	21 01	21 10	21 17	21 20		21 30		21 34	21 40	21 47	21 50
Deptford	d				20 27			20 37				20 57			21 07			21 26				21 40			21 56
Greenwich	d				20 29			20 39				20 59			21 09			21 28				21 42			21 58
Maze Hill	d				20 32			20 42				21 02			21 12			21 31				21 45			22 01
Westcombe Park	d				20 34			20 44				21 04			21 14			21 33				21 47			22 03
London Victoria ⊖	d																								
Denmark Hill	d																								
Peckham Rye	d																								
Nunhead	d																								
New Cross ⊖	d		20 19				20 35		20 45					21 05		21 15				21 35			21 45		
St Johns	d		20 21																						
Lewisham	d	20 19	20 25	20 26			20 39		20 49	20 56				21 09		21 19	21 26			21 39			21 49	21 56	
Blackheath	d	20 22		20 29					20 52	20 59						21 22	21 29						21 52	21 59	
Kidbrooke	d	20 25							20 55							21 25							21 55		
Eltham	d	20 28							20 58							21 28							21 58		
Falconwood	d	20 31							21 01							21 31							22 01		
Welling	d	20 33							21 03							21 33							22 03		
Bexleyheath	d	20 36							21 06							21 36							22 06		
Barnehurst	d	20 38							21 08							21 38							22 08		
Hither Green	d		20 30				20 44							21 14						21 44					
Lee	d		20 32				20 46							21 16						21 46					
Mottingham	d		20 35				20 49							21 19						21 49					
New Eltham	d		20 37				20 51							21 21						21 51					
Sidcup	d		20 41				20 55							21 25						21 55					
Albany Park	d		20 43				20 57							21 27						21 57					
Bexley	d		20 45				20 59							21 29						21 59					
Crayford	d		20 48				21 03							21 33						22 03					
Charlton	d			20 33	20 37			20 47		21 03		21 07			21 17		21 33	21 36				21 50		22 03	22 06
Woolwich Dockyard	d				20 40			20 50				21 10			21 20			21 39				21 53			22 09
Woolwich Arsenal	d			20 39	20 43			20 53		21 09		21 13			21 23		21 39	21 42				21 56		22 09	22 12
Plumstead	d				20 45			20 55				21 15			21 25			21 44				21 58			22 14
Abbey Wood	d			20 43	20 48			20 58		21 13		21 18			21 28		21 43	21 47				22 01		22 13	22 17
Belvedere	d				20 50			21 00				21 20			21 30			21 50				22 03			22 20
Erith	d				20 53			21 03				21 23			21 33			21 52				22 06			22 22
Slade Green	d				20 57			21 07				21 27			21 37			21 56				22 09			22 26
Dartford	a	20 45	20 53	20 54	21 02		21 08	21 12	21 15	21 24		21 32		21 38	21 42	21 45	21 54	22 00		22 08		22 14	22 16	22 24	22 30
	d			20 55			21 09			21 25				21 39			21 55			22 09				22 25	
Stone Crossing	d						21 13							21 43						22 13					
Greenhithe for Bluewater	d			21 00			21 15			21 30				21 45			22 00			22 15				22 30	
Swanscombe	d						21 18							21 48						22 18					
Northfleet	d						21 20							21 50						22 20					
Gravesend	d			21 07		21 18	21a25			21 37			21 48	21a55			22 07		22 18	22a25				22 37	
Higham	d			21 13						21 43							22 13							22 43	
Strood	d			21 18		21 28				21 48			21 58				22 18		22 28					22 48	
Maidstone West	d																								
Rochester	d			21 22		21 33				21 52			22 03				22 22		22 33					22 52	
Chatham	d			21 25		21 35				21 55			22 05				22 25		22 35					22 55	
Gillingham (Kent)	a			21 29		21 39				21 59			22 09				22 29		22 39					22 59	

Table 200

Mondays to Fridays

29 August to 7 September

London - Dartford and Gillingham

Network Diagram - see first Page of Table 200

		SE	SE	SE	SE	SE		SE	SE	SE	SE	SE	SE
St Pancras Int'l ⊖	d	22 25							22 55				
Stratford International ⊖	d	22 33							23 03				
Ebbsfleet International	d	22 44							23 14				
London Charing Cross ⊖	d		21 52	21 56	22 02	22 09				22 22	22 26	22 32	22 39
London Waterloo (East) ⊖	d		21 55	21 59	22 05	22 12				22 25	22 29	22 35	22 42
London Cannon Street ⊖	d												
London Bridge ⊖	d		22 00	22 04	22 10	22 17		22 20		22 30	22 34	22 40	22 47
Deptford	d			22 10				22 26			22 40		
Greenwich	d			22 12				22 28			22 42		
Maze Hill	d			22 15				22 31			22 45		
Westcombe Park	d			22 17				22 33			22 47		
London Victoria ⊖	d												
Denmark Hill	d												
Peckham Rye	d												
Nunhead	d												
New Cross ⊖	d		22 05		22 15					22 35		22 45	
St Johns	d												
Lewisham	d		22 09		22 19	22 26				22 39		22 49	22 56
Blackheath	d				22 22	22 29						22 52	22 59
Kidbrooke	d				22 25							22 55	
Eltham	d				22 28							22 58	
Falconwood	d				22 31							23 01	
Welling	d				22 33							23 03	
Bexleyheath	d				22 36							23 06	
Barnehurst	d				22 38							23 08	
Hither Green	d		22 14							22 44			
Lee	d		22 16							22 46			
Mottingham	d		22 19							22 49			
New Eltham	d		22 21							22 51			
Sidcup	d		22 25							22 55			
Albany Park	d		22 27							22 57			
Bexley	d		22 29							22 59			
Crayford	d		22 33							23 03			
Charlton	d			22 20		22 33		22 36			22 50		23 03
Woolwich Dockyard	d			22 23				22 39			22 53		
Woolwich Arsenal	d			22 26		22 39		22 42			22 56		23 09
Plumstead	d			22 28				22 44			22 58		
Abbey Wood	d			22 31		22 43		22 47			23 01		23 13
Belvedere	d			22 33				22 50			23 03		
Erith	d			22 36				22 52			23 06		
Slade Green	d			22 39				22 56			23 09		
Dartford	a		22 38	22 44	22 46	22 54		23 00		23 08	23 14	23 16	23 24
	d		22 39			22 55				23 09			23 25
Stone Crossing	d		22 43							23 13			23 29
Greenhithe for Bluewater	d		22 45			23 00				23 15			23 31
Swanscombe	d		22 48							23 18			23 34
Northfleet	d		22 50							23 20			23 36
Gravesend	d	22 48	22a55			23 07			23 18	23a25			23 40
Higham	d					23 13							23 46
Strood	d	22 58				23 18			23 28				23 52
Maidstone West	d												
Rochester	d	23 03				23 22			23 33				23 56
Chatham	d	23 05				23 25			23 35				23 58
Gillingham (Kent)	a	23 09				23 29			23 39				00 03

		SE	SE	SE		SE	SE	SE	SE	SE	SE	SE	SE
St Pancras Int'l ⊖	d						23 25					23 55	
Stratford International ⊖	d						23 33					00 03	
Ebbsfleet International	d						23 44					00 14	
London Charing Cross ⊖	d		22 52	22 56		23 02		23 09	23 22	23 26	23 32		23 39
London Waterloo (East) ⊖	d		22 55	22 59		23 05		23 12	23 25	23 29	23 35		23 42
London Cannon Street ⊖	d												
London Bridge ⊖	d	22 50	23 00	23 04		23 10		23 17	23 30	23 34	23 40		23 47
Deptford	d	22 56		23 10						23 40			
Greenwich	d	22 58		23 12						23 42			
Maze Hill	d	23 01		23 15						23 45			
Westcombe Park	d	23 03		23 17						23 47			
London Victoria ⊖	d												
Denmark Hill	d												
Peckham Rye	d												
Nunhead	d												
New Cross ⊖	d		23 05			23 15			23 35		23 45		
St Johns	d												
Lewisham	d		23 09			23 19		23 26	23 39		23 49		23 56
Blackheath	d					23 22		23 29			23 52		23 59
Kidbrooke	d					23 25					23 55		
Eltham	d					23 28					23 58		
Falconwood	d					23 31					00 01		
Welling	d					23 33					00 03		
Bexleyheath	d					23 36					00 06		
Barnehurst	d					23 38					00 08		
Hither Green	d		23 14						23 44				
Lee	d		23 16						23 46				
Mottingham	d		23 19						23 49				
New Eltham	d		23 21						23 51				
Sidcup	d		23 25						23 55				
Albany Park	d		23 27						23 57				
Bexley	d		23 29						23 59				
Crayford	d		23 33						00 03				
Charlton	d	23 06		23 20				23 33		23 50			00 03
Woolwich Dockyard	d	23 09		23 23						23 53			
Woolwich Arsenal	d	23 12		23 26				23 39		23 56			00 09
Plumstead	d	23 14		23 28						23 58			
Abbey Wood	d	23 17		23 31				23 43		00 01			00 13
Belvedere	d	23 20		23 33						00 03			
Erith	d	23 22		23 36						00 06			
Slade Green	d	23 26		23 39						00 09			
Dartford	a	23 30	23 38	23 44		23 46		23 54	00 08	00 14	00 16		00 24
	d							23 55					00 25
Stone Crossing	d							23 58					00 29
Greenhithe for Bluewater	d							23 59					00 31
Swanscombe	d							00 04					00 34
Northfleet	d							00 06					00 36
Gravesend	d						23 48	00 10				00 18	00 40
Higham	d							00 16					00 46
Strood	d						23 58	00 22				00 28	00 52
Maidstone West	d												
Rochester	d						00 03	00 26				00 33	00 56
Chatham	d						00 05	00 28				00 35	00 58
Gillingham (Kent)	a						00 09	00 33				00 39	01 03

Table 200

Mondays to Fridays

29 August to 7 September

London - Dartford and Gillingham

Network Diagram - see first Page of Table 200

		SE
St Pancras Int'l ⊖	d	
Stratford International ⊖	d	
Ebbsfleet International	d	
London Charing Cross ⊖	d	23 56
London Waterloo (East) ⊖	d	23 59
London Cannon Street ⊖	d	
London Bridge ⊖	d	00 04
Deptford	d	00 10
Greenwich	d	00 12
Maze Hill	d	00 15
Westcombe Park	d	00 17
London Victoria ⊖	d	
Denmark Hill	d	
Peckham Rye	d	
Nunhead	d	
New Cross ⊖	d	
St Johns	d	
Lewisham	d	
Blackheath	d	
Kidbrooke	d	
Eltham	d	
Falconwood	d	
Welling	d	
Bexleyheath	d	
Barnehurst	d	
Hither Green	d	
Lee	d	
Mottingham	d	
New Eltham	d	
Sidcup	d	
Albany Park	d	
Bexley	d	
Crayford	d	
Charlton	d	00 20
Woolwich Dockyard	d	00 23
Woolwich Arsenal	d	00 26
Plumstead	d	00 28
Abbey Wood	d	00 31
Belvedere	d	00 33
Erith	d	00 36
Slade Green	d	00 39
Dartford	a	00 44
	d	
Stone Crossing	d	
Greenhithe for Bluewater	d	
Swanscombe	d	
Northfleet	d	
Gravesend	d	
Higham	d	
Strood	d	
Maidstone West	d	
Rochester	d	
Chatham	d	
Gillingham (Kent)	a	

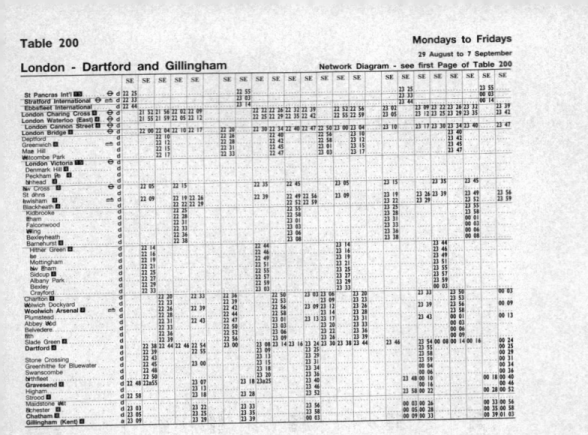

Table 200

London - Dartford and Gillingham

Saturdays

until 21 July, 18 Aug and from 15 Sep

Network Diagram - see first Page of Table 200

Station		SE	SE	SE	SE	SE	SE	SE	SE	SE		SE	SE
St Pancras Int'l	d		23p25					23p55					
Stratford International	d		23p32					00 02					
Ebbsfleet International	d		23p43					00 13					
London Charing Cross	d	22p39		23p09	23p22	23p26	23p32		23p39	23p56		00 02	00 10
London Waterloo (East)	d	22p42		23p12	23p25	23p29	23p35		23p42	23p59		00 05	00 13
London Cannon Street	d												
London Bridge	d	22p47		23p17	23p30	23p34	23p40		23p47	00 04		00 10	00 18
Deptford	d					23p40				00 10			
Greenwich	d					23p42				00 12			
Maze Hill	d					23p45				00 15			
Westcombe Park	d					23p47				00 17			
London Victoria	d												
Denmark Hill	d												
Peckham Rye	d												
Nunhead	d												
New Cross	d				23p35		23p45					00 15	00 23
St Johns	d												
Lewisham	d	22p56		23p26	23p39		23p49		23p56			00 19	00 27
Blackheath	d	22p59		23p29			23p52		23p59			00 22	
Kidbrooke	d						23p55					00 25	
Eltham	d						23p58					00 28	
Falconwood	d						00 01					00 31	
Welling	d						00 03					00 33	
Bexleyheath	d						00 06					00 36	
Barnehurst	d						00 08					00 38	
Hither Green	d				23p44								00 32
Lee	d				23p46								00 34
Mottingham	d				23p49								00 37
New Eltham	d				23p51								00 39
Sidcup	d				23p55								00 43
Albany Park	d				23p57								00 45
Bexley	d				23p59								00 47
Crayford	d				00 03								00 51
Charlton	d	23p03		23p33		23p50			00 03	00 20			
Woolwich Dockyard	d					23p53				00 23			
Woolwich Arsenal	d	23p09		23p39		23p56			00 09	00 26			
Plumstead	d					23p58				00 28			
Abbey Wood	d	23p13		23p43		00 01			00 13	00 31			
Belvedere	d					00 03				00 33			
Erith	d					00 06				00 36			
Slade Green	d					00 09				00 39			
Dartford	a	23p24		23p54	00 08	00 14	00 16		00 24	00 44		00 46	00 56
	d	23p25		23p55					00 25				
Stone Crossing	d	23p29		23p58					00 29				
Greenhithe for Bluewater	d	23p31		23p59					00 31				
Swanscombe	d	23p34		00 04					00 34				
Northfleet	d	23p36		00 06					00 36				
Gravesend	d	23p40	23p48	00 10				00 18	00 40				
Higham	d	23p46		00 16					00 46				
Strood	d	23p52	23p58	00 22				00 28	00 52				
Maidstone West	d												
Rochester	d	23p56	00 03	00 26				00 33	00 56				
Chatham	d	23p58	00 05	00 28				00 35	00 58				
Gillingham (Kent)	a	00 03	00 09	00 33				00 39	01 03				

Station		SE	SE	SE	SE	SE	SE	SE		SE	SE	SE	SE
St Pancras Int'l	d												
Stratford International	d												
Ebbsfleet International	d												
London Charing Cross	d	00 18	04 52		05 22	05 26	05 32	05 39		05 52	05 56	06 02	06 09
London Waterloo (East)	d	00 21	04 55		05 25	05 29	05 35	05 42		05 55	05 59	06 05	06 12
London Cannon Street	d												
London Bridge	d	00 26	05 00		05 30	05 34	05 40	05 47		06 00	06 04	06 10	06 17
Deptford	d					05 40					06 10		
Greenwich	d					05 42					06 12		
Maze Hill	d					05 45					06 15		
Westcombe Park	d					05 47					06 17		
London Victoria	d												
Denmark Hill	d												
Peckham Rye	d												
Nunhead	d												
New Cross	d	00 31	05 05		05 35		05 45			06 05		06 15	
St Johns	d												
Lewisham	d	00 35	05 09		05 39		05 49	05 56		06 09		06 19	06 26
Blackheath	d	00 38					05 52	05 59				06 22	06 29
Kidbrooke	d						05 55					06 25	
Eltham	d						05 58					06 28	
Falconwood	d						06 01					06 31	
Welling	d						06 03					06 33	
Bexleyheath	d						06 06					06 36	
Barnehurst	d						06 08					06 38	
Hither Green	d		05 14		05 44					06 14			
Lee	d		05 16		05 46					06 16			
Mottingham	d		05 19		05 49					06 19			
New Eltham	d		05 21		05 51					06 21			
Sidcup	d		05 25		05 55					06 25			
Albany Park	d		05 27		05 57					06 27			
Bexley	d		05 29		05 59					06 29			
Crayford	d		05 33		06 03					06 33			
Charlton	d	00 42				05 50		06 03			06 20		06 33
Woolwich Dockyard	d					05 53					06 23		
Woolwich Arsenal	d	00 47				05 56		06 09			06 26		06 39
Plumstead	d	00 49				05 58					06 28		
Abbey Wood	d	00 53				06 01		06 13			06 31		06 43
Belvedere	d	00 55				06 03					06 33		
Erith	d	00 58				06 06					06 36		
Slade Green	d	01 00				06 09					06 39		
Dartford	a	01 05	05 38		06 08	06 14	06 16	06 24		06 38	06 44	06 46	06 54
	d	01 06	05 39	05 55	06 09			06 25		06 39			06 55
Stone Crossing	d		05 43		06 13					06 43			
Greenhithe for Bluewater	d	01 10	05 45	06 00	06 15			06 30		06 45			07 00
Swanscombe	d		05 48		06 18					06 48			
Northfleet	d		05 50		06 20					06 50			
Gravesend	d	01 17	05a55	06 07	06a25			06 37		06a55			07 07
Higham	d	01 23		06 13				06 43					07 13
Strood	d	01 29		06 18				06 48					07 18
Maidstone West	d												
Rochester	d	01 33		06 22				06 52					07 22
Chatham	d	01 35		06 25				06 55					07 25
Gillingham (Kent)	a	01 41		06 29				06 59					07 29

Table 200

London - Dartford and Gillingham

Saturdays

until 21 July, 18 Aug and from 15 Sep

Network Diagram - see first Page of Table 200

Station		SE A	SE B	SE	SE	SE		SE	SE	SE	SE	SE	SE
St Pancras Int'l	d	06 52	06 55										07 52
Stratford International	d	06 59	07 02										07 58
Ebbsfleet International	d	07 13	07 13										08 13
London Charing Cross	d			06 22	06 26	06 32		06 39	06 52	06 56	07 02	07 09	
London Waterloo (East)	d			06 25	06 29	06 35		06 42	06 55	06 59	07 05	07 12	
London Cannon Street	d												
London Bridge	d			06 30	06 34	06 40		06 47	07 00	07 04	07 10	07 17	
Deptford	d				06 40					07 10			
Greenwich	d				06 42					07 12			
Maze Hill	d				06 45					07 15			
Westcombe Park	d				06 47					07 17			
London Victoria	d												
Denmark Hill	d												
Peckham Rye	d												
Nunhead	d												
New Cross	d			06 35		06 45			07 05		07 15		
St Johns	d												
Lewisham	d			06 39		06 49		06 56	07 09		07 19	07 26	
Blackheath	d					06 52		06 59			07 22	07 29	
Kidbrooke	d					06 55					07 25		
Eltham	d					06 58					07 28		
Falconwood	d					07 01					07 31		
Welling	d					07 03					07 33		
Bexleyheath	d					07 06					07 36		
Barnehurst	d					07 08					07 38		
Hither Green	d			06 44					07 14				
Lee	d			06 46					07 16				
Mottingham	d			06 49					07 19				
New Eltham	d			06 51					07 21				
Sidcup	d			06 55					07 25				
Albany Park	d			06 57					07 27				
Bexley	d			06 59					07 29				
Crayford	d			07 03					07 33				
Charlton	d				06 50			07 03		07 20		07 33	
Woolwich Dockyard	d				06 53					07 23			
Woolwich Arsenal	d				06 56			07 09		07 26		07 39	
Plumstead	d				06 58					07 28			
Abbey Wood	d				07 01			07 13		07 31		07 43	
Belvedere	d				07 03					07 33			
Erith	d				07 06					07 36			
Slade Green	d				07 09					07 39			
Dartford	a			07 08	07 14	07 16		07 24	07 38	07 44	07 46	07 54	
	d			07 09				07 25	07 39			07 55	
Stone Crossing	d			07 13					07 43				
Greenhithe for Bluewater	d			07 15				07 30	07 45			08 00	
Swanscombe	d			07 18					07 48				
Northfleet	d			07 20					07 50				
Gravesend	d	07 17	07 18	07a25				07 37	07a55			08 07	08 18
Higham	d							07 43				08 13	
Strood	d	07 27	07 28					07 48				08 18	08 28
Maidstone West	d												
Rochester	d	07 32	07 33					07 52				08 22	08 33
Chatham	d	07 34	07 35					07 55				08 25	08 35
Gillingham (Kent)	a	07 38	07 39					07 59				08 29	08 39

Station		SE	SE	SE		SE	SE	SE	SE	SE	SE	SE	SE
St Pancras Int'l	d												
Stratford International	d												
Ebbsfleet International	d												
London Charing Cross	d	07 22	07 26	07 32		07 39		07 52	07 56	08 02			08 09
London Waterloo (East)	d	07 25	07 29	07 35		07 42		07 55	07 59	08 05			08 12
London Cannon Street	d										08 07	08 10	
London Bridge	d	07 30	07 34	07 40		07 47		08 00	08 04	08 10	08 11	08 14	08 17
Deptford	d		07 40						08 10		08 17		
Greenwich	d		07 42						08 12		08 19		
Maze Hill	d		07 45						08 15		08 22		
Westcombe Park	d		07 47						08 17		08 24		
London Victoria	d						07 39						
Denmark Hill	d						07 48						
Peckham Rye	d						07 51						
Nunhead	d						07 53						
New Cross	d	07 35		07 45				08 05		08 15		08 19	
St Johns	d											08 21	
Lewisham	d	07 39		07 49		07 56	08 02	08 09		08 19		08 24	08 26
Blackheath	d			07 52		07 59	08 04			08 22			08 29
Kidbrooke	d			07 55			08 07			08 25			
Eltham	d			07 58			08 11			08 28			
Falconwood	d			08 01			08 13			08 31			
Welling	d			08 03			08 16			08 33			
Bexleyheath	d			08 06			08 18			08 36			
Barnehurst	d			08 08			08 21			08 38			
Hither Green	d	07 44						08 14				08 29	
Lee	d	07 46						08 16				08 31	
Mottingham	d	07 49						08 19				08 34	
New Eltham	d	07 51						08 21				08 36	
Sidcup	d	07 55						08 25				08 40	
Albany Park	d	07 57						08 27				08 42	
Bexley	d	07 59						08 29				08 44	
Crayford	d	08 03						08 33				08 48	
Charlton	d		07 50			08 03			08 20		08 27	09a15	08 33
Woolwich Dockyard	d		07 53						08 23		08 30		
Woolwich Arsenal	d		07 56			08 09			08 26		08 33		08 39
Plumstead	d		07 58						08 28		08 35		
Abbey Wood	d		08 01			08 13			08 31		08 38		08 43
Belvedere	d		08 03						08 33		08 40		
Erith	d		08 06						08 36		08 43		
Slade Green	d		08 09						08 39		08a46		
Dartford	a	08 08	08 14	08 16		08 24	08 29	08 38	08 44	08 46			08 54
	d	08 09				08 25		08 39					08 55
Stone Crossing	d	08 13						08 43					
Greenhithe for Bluewater	d	08 15				08 30		08 45					09 00
Swanscombe	d	08 18						08 48					
Northfleet	d	08 20						08 50					
Gravesend	d	08a25				08 37		08a55					09 07
Higham	d					08 43							09 13
Strood	d					08 48							09 18
Maidstone West	d												
Rochester	d					08 52							09 22
Chatham	d					08 55							09 25
Gillingham (Kent)	a					08 59							09 29

A 19 May

B not 19 May

Table 200

Saturdays

until 21 July, 18 Aug and from 15 Sep

London - Dartford and Gillingham

Network Diagram - see first Page of Table 200

		SE		SE	SE	SE	SE	SE	SE	SE	SE	SE		SE	SE	SE	SE	SE	SE	SE	SE	SE		SE	SE
St Pancras Int'l	d						08 50											09 25							
Stratford International	d						09 04											09 32							
Ebbsfleet International	d						09 15											09 43							
London Charing Cross	d							08 26	08 32			08 39							08 56	09 02				09 09	
London Waterloo (East)	d							08 29	08 35			08 42							08 59	09 05				09 12	
London Cannon Street	d			08 17	08 24	08 27				08 37	08 40				08 47	08 54	08 57				09 07	09 10			
London Bridge	d			08 21	08 28	08 31		08 34	08 40	08 41	08 44	08 47			08 51	08 58	09 01		09 04	09 10	09 11	09 14		09 17	
Deptford	d			08 27		08 37				08 47					08 57		09 07				09 17				
Greenwich	d			08 29		08 39				08 49					08 59		09 09				09 19				
Maze Hill	d			08 32		08 42				08 52					09 02		09 12				09 22				
Westcombe Park	d			08 34		08 44				08 54					09 04		09 14				09 24				
London Victoria	d	08 09												08 39											09 09
Denmark Hill	d	08 18												08 48											09 18
Peckham Rye	d	08 21												08 51											09 21
Nunhead	d	08 23												08 53											09 23
New Cross	d				08 33						08 49					09 03						09 19			
St Johns	d				08 35						08 51					09 05						09 21			
Lewisham	d	08 32			08 38				08 49		08 54	08 56		09 02		09 08				09 19		09 24		09 26	09 32
Blackheath	d	08 34			08 41				08 52			08 59		09 04		09 11				09 22				09 29	09 34
Kidbrooke	d	08 37			08 44				08 55					09 07		09 14				09 25					09 37
Eltham	d	08 41			08 47				08 58					09 11		09 17				09 28					09 41
Falconwood	d	08 43			08 50				09 01					09 13		09 20				09 31					09 43
Welling	d	08 46			08 52				09 03					09 16		09 22				09 33					09 46
Bexleyheath	d	08 48			08 55				09 06					09 18		09 25				09 36					09 48
Barnehurst	d	08 51			09 02				09 08					09 21		09 32				09 38					09 51
Hither Green	d							08 44			08 59								09 14			09 29			
Lee	d							08 46			09 01								09 16			09 31			
Mottingham	d							08 49			09 04								09 19			09 34			
New Eltham	d							08 51			09 06								09 21			09 36			
Sidcup	d							08 55			09 10								09 25			09 40			
Albany Park	d							08 57			09 12								09 27			09 42			
Bexley	d							08 59			09 14								09 29			09 44			
Crayford	d							09 03			09 18								09 33			09 48			
Charlton	d			08 37		08 47				08 57	09a45	09 03			09 07		09 17				09 27	10a15		09 33	
Woolwich Dockyard	d			08 40		08 50				09 00					09 10		09 20				09 30				
Woolwich Arsenal	d			08 43		08 53				09 03		09 09			09 13		09 23				09 33			09 39	
Plumstead	d			08 45		08 55				09 05					09 15		09 25				09 35				
Abbey Wood	d			08 48		08 58				09 08		09 13			09 18		09 28				09 38			09 43	
Belvedere	d			08 50		09 00				09 10					09 20		09 30				09 40				
Erith	d			08 53		09 03				09 13					09 23		09 33				09 43				
Slade Green	d			08a55	09a12	09 07				09a16					09a25	09a42	09 37				09a46				
Dartford	a	08 58				09 12		09 08	09 15			09 24		09 28			09 42		09 38	09 45				09 54	09 58
	d							09 09				09 25							09 39					09 55	
Stone Crossing	d							09 13											09 43						
Greenhithe for Bluewater	d							09 15				09 30							09 45					10 00	
Swanscombe	d							09 18											09 48						
Northfleet	d							09 20											09 50						
Gravesend	d						09 20	09a25				09 37						09 48	09a55					10 07	
Higham	d											09 43												10 13	
Strood	d						09 30					09 48						09 58						10 18	
Maidstone West	d																								
Rochester	d						09 34					09 52						10 03						10 22	
Chatham	d						09 37					09 55						10 05						10 25	
Gillingham (Kent)	a						09 41					09 59						10 09						10 29	

Table 200

Saturdays

until 21 July, 18 Aug and from 15 Sep

London - Dartford and Gillingham

Network Diagram - see first Page of Table 200

		SE	SE	SE	SE	SE	SE	SE		SE	SE	SE	SE	SE	SE	SE	SE	SE		SE	SE	SE	SE	SE	SE
St Pancras Int'l	d				09 55											10 28									
Stratford International	d				10 02											10 35									
Ebbsfleet International	d				10 13											10 46									
London Charing Cross	d					09 26	09 32				09 39						09 56	10 02				10 09			
London Waterloo (East)	d					09 29	09 35				09 42						09 59	10 05				10 12			
London Cannon Street	d	09 17	09 24	09 27				09 37		09 40			09 47	09 54	09 57					10 07	10 10			10 17	10 24
London Bridge	d	09 21	09 28	09 31		09 34	09 40	09 41		09 44	09 47		09 51	09 58	10 01		10 04	10 10		10 11	10 14	10 17		10 21	10 28
Deptford	d	09 27		09 37				09 47					09 57		10 07					10 17				10 27	
Greenwich	d	09 29		09 39				09 49					09 59		10 09					10 19				10 29	
Maze Hill	d	09 32		09 42				09 52					10 02		10 12					10 22				10 32	
Westcombe Park	d	09 34		09 44				09 54					10 04		10 14					10 24				10 34	
London Victoria	d											09 39											10 09		
Denmark Hill	d											09 48											10 18		
Peckham Rye	d											09 51											10 21		
Nunhead	d											09 53											10 23		
New Cross	d		09 33							09 49				10 03							10 19				10 33
St Johns	d		09 35							09 51				10 05							10 21				10 35
Lewisham	d		09 38				09 49			09 54	09 56	10 02		10 08				10 19			10 24	10 26	10 32		10 38
Blackheath	d		09 41				09 52				09 59	10 04		10 11				10 22				10 29	10 34		10 41
Kidbrooke	d		09 44				09 55					10 07		10 14				10 25					10 37		10 44
Eltham	d		09 47				09 58					10 11		10 17				10 28					10 41		10 47
Falconwood	d		09 50				10 01					10 13		10 20				10 31					10 43		10 50
Welling	d		09 52				10 03					10 16		10 22				10 33					10 46		10 52
Bexleyheath	d		09 55				10 06					10 18		10 25				10 36					10 48		10 55
Barnehurst	d		10 02				10 08					10 21		10 32				10 38					10 51		11 02
Hither Green	d					09 44				09 59							10 14				10 29				
Lee	d					09 46				10 01							10 16				10 31				
Mottingham	d					09 49				10 04							10 19				10 34				
New Eltham	d					09 51				10 06							10 21				10 36				
Sidcup	d					09 55				10 10							10 25				10 40				
Albany Park	d					09 57				10 12							10 27				10 42				
Bexley	d					09 59				10 14							10 29				10 44				
Crayford	d					10 03				10 18							10 33				10 48				
Charlton	d	09 37		09 47				09 57		10a45	10 03		10 07		10 17					10 27	11a15	10 33		10 37	
Woolwich Dockyard	d	09 40		09 50				10 00					10 10		10 20					10 30				10 40	
Woolwich Arsenal	d	09 43		09 53				10 03			10 09		10 13		10 23					10 33		10 39		10 43	
Plumstead	d	09 45		09 55				10 05					10 15		10 25					10 35				10 45	
Abbey Wood	d	09 48		09 58				10 08			10 13		10 18		10 28					10 38		10 43		10 48	
Belvedere	d	09 50		10 00				10 10					10 20		10 30					10 40				10 50	
Erith	d	09 53		10 03				10 13					10 23		10 33					10 43				10 53	
Slade Green	d	09a55	10a12	10 07				10a16					10a25	10a42	10 37					10a46				10a55	11a12
Dartford	a			10 12		10 08	10 15				10 24	10 28			10 42		10 38	10 45				10 54	10 58		
	d					10 09					10 25						10 39					10 55			
Stone Crossing	d					10 13											10 43								
Greenhithe for Bluewater	d					10 15					10 30						10 45					11 00			
Swanscombe	d					10 18											10 48								
Northfleet	d					10 20											10 50								
Gravesend	d				10 18	10a25					10 37					10 51	10a55					11 07			
Higham	d										10 43											11 13			
Strood	d				10 28						10 48					11 01						11 18			
Maidstone West	d																								
Rochester	d				10 33						10 52					11 06						11 22			
Chatham	d				10 35						10 55					11 08						11 25			
Gillingham (Kent)	a				10 39						10 59					11 12						11 29			

Table 200

London - Dartford and Gillingham

Saturdays

until 21 July, 18 Aug and from 15 Sep

Network Diagram - see first Page of Table 200

		SE	SE	SE		SE	SE	SE	SE	SE	SE	SE	SE	SE		SE	SE	SE	SE	SE	SE	SE	SE	SE	
St Pancras Int'l	d		10 52											11 28											
Stratford International	d		10 58											11 35											
Ebbsfleet International	d		11 13											11 46											
London Charing Cross	d			10 26		10 32			10 39							10 56	11 02			11 09					
London Waterloo (East)	d			10 29		10 35			10 42							10 59	11 05			11 12					
London Cannon Street	d	10 27					10 37	10 40			10 47	10 54	10 57					11 07	11 10			11 17	11 24	11 27	
London Bridge	d	10 31		10 34		10 40	10 41	10 44	10 47		10 51	10 58	11 01			11 04	11 10	11 11	11 14	11 17		11 21	11 28	11 31	
Deptford	d	10 37					10 47				10 57		11 07					11 17				11 27		11 37	
Greenwich	d	10 39					10 49				10 59		11 09					11 19				11 29		11 39	
Maze Hill	d	10 42					10 52				11 02		11 12					11 22				11 32		11 42	
Westcombe Park	d	10 44					10 54				11 04		11 14					11 24				11 34		11 44	
London Victoria	d									10 39											11 09				
Denmark Hill	d									10 48											11 18				
Peckham Rye	d									10 51											11 21				
Nunhead	d									10 53											11 23				
New Cross	d							10 49				11 03							11 19				11 33		
St Johns	d							10 51				11 05							11 21				11 35		
Lewisham	d					10 49		10 54	10 56	11 02		11 08					11 19		11 24	11 26	11 32		11 38		
Blackheath	d					10 52			10 59	11 04		11 11					11 22			11 29	11 34		11 41		
Kidbrooke	d					10 55				11 07		11 14					11 25				11 37		11 44		
Eltham	d					10 58				11 11		11 17					11 28				11 41		11 47		
Falconwood	d					11 01				11 13		11 20					11 31				11 43		11 50		
Welling	d					11 03				11 16		11 22					11 33				11 46		11 52		
Bexleyheath	d					11 06				11 18		11 25					11 36				11 48		11 55		
Barnehurst	d					11 08				11 21		11 32					11 38				11 51		12 02		
Hither Green	d			10 44				10 59								11 14			11 29						
Lee	d			10 46				11 01								11 16			11 31						
Mottingham	d			10 49				11 04								11 19			11 34						
New Eltham	d			10 51				11 06								11 21			11 36						
Sidcup	d			10 55				11 10								11 25			11 40						
Albany Park	d			10 57				11 12								11 27			11 42						
Bexley	d			10 59				11 14								11 29			11 44						
Crayford	d			11 03				11 18								11 33			11 48						
Charlton	d	10 47					10 57	11a45	11 03		11 07		11 17					11 27	12a15	11 33		11 37		11 47	
Woolwich Dockyard	d	10 50					11 00				11 10		11 20					11 30				11 40		11 50	
Woolwich Arsenal	d	10 53					11 03		11 09		11 13		11 23					11 33		11 39		11 43		11 53	
Plumstead	d	10 55					11 05				11 15		11 25					11 35				11 45		11 55	
Abbey Wood	d	10 58					11 08		11 13		11 18		11 28					11 38		11 43		11 48		11 58	
Belvedere	d	11 00					11 10				11 20		11 30					11 40				11 50		12 00	
Erith	d	11 03					11 13				11 23		11 33					11 43				11 53		12 03	
Slade Green	d	11 07					11a16				11a25	11a42	11 37					11a46				11a55	12a12	12 07	
Dartford	a	11 12		11 08		11 15			11 24	11 28			11 42			11 38	11 45			11 54	11 58			12 12	
	d			11 09					11 25							11 39				11 55					
Stone Crossing	d			11 13												11 43									
Greenhithe for Bluewater	d			11 15					11 30							11 45				12 00					
Swanscombe	d			11 18												11 48									
Northfleet	d			11 20												11 50									
Gravesend	d		11 18	11a25					11 37					11 51		11a55				12 07					
Higham	d								11 43											12 13					
Strood	d		11 28						11 48					12 01						12 18					
Maidstone West	d																								
Rochester	d		11 33						11 52					12 06						12 22					
Chatham	d		11 35						11 55					12 08						12 25					
Gillingham (Kent)	a		11 39						11 59					12 12						12 29					

Table 200

London - Dartford and Gillingham

Saturdays

until 21 July, 18 Aug and from 15 Sep

Network Diagram - see first Page of Table 200

		SE	SE	SE	SE	SE	SE	SE	SE	SE		SE	SE	SE	SE	SE	SE	SE	SE	SE		SE	SE	SE	SE
St Pancras Int'l	d	11 55											12 28											12 55	
Stratford International	d	12 02											12 35											13 06	
Ebbsfleet International	d	12 13											12 46											13 17	
London Charing Cross	d		11 26	11 32			11 39							11 56	12 02			12 09							12 26
London Waterloo (East)	d		11 29	11 35			11 42							11 59	12 05			12 12							12 29
London Cannon Street	d				11 37	11 40			11 47	11 54		11 57				12 07	12 10			12 17		12 24	12 27		
London Bridge	d		11 34	11 40	11 41	11 44	11 47		11 51	11 58		12 01		12 04	12 10	12 11	12 14	12 17		12 21		12 28	12 31		12 34
Deptford	d				11 47				11 57			12 07				12 17				12 27			12 37		
Greenwich	d				11 49				11 59			12 09				12 19				12 29			12 39		
Maze Hill	d				11 52				12 02			12 12				12 22				12 32			12 42		
Westcombe Park	d				11 54				12 04			12 14				12 24				12 34			12 44		
London Victoria	d							11 39											12 09						
Denmark Hill	d							11 48											12 18						
Peckham Rye	d							11 51											12 21						
Nunhead	d							11 53											12 23						
New Cross	d					11 49				12 03							12 19					12 33			
St Johns	d					11 51				12 05							12 21					12 35			
Lewisham	d			11 49		11 54	11 56	12 02		12 08					12 19		12 24	12 26	12 32			12 38			
Blackheath	d			11 52			11 59	12 04		12 11					12 22			12 29	12 34			12 41			
Kidbrooke	d			11 55				12 07		12 14					12 25				12 37			12 44			
Eltham	d			11 58				12 11		12 17					12 28				12 41			12 47			
Falconwood	d			12 01				12 13		12 20					12 31				12 43			12 50			
Welling	d			12 03				12 16		12 22					12 33				12 46			12 52			
Bexleyheath	d			12 06				12 18		12 25					12 36				12 48			12 55			
Barnehurst	d			12 08				12 21		12 32					12 38				12 51			13 02			
Hither Green	d		11 44			11 59								12 14			12 29								12 44
Lee	d		11 46			12 01								12 16			12 31								12 46
Mottingham	d		11 49			12 04								12 19			12 34								12 49
New Eltham	d		11 51			12 06								12 21			12 36								12 51
Sidcup	d		11 55			12 10								12 25			12 40								12 55
Albany Park	d		11 57			12 12								12 27			12 42								12 57
Bexley	d		11 59			12 14								12 29			12 44								12 59
Crayford	d		12 03			12 18								12 33			12 48								13 03
Charlton	d				11 57	12a45	12 03		12 07			12 17				12 27	13a15	12 33		12 37			12 47		
Woolwich Dockyard	d				12 00				12 10			12 20				12 30				12 40			12 50		
Woolwich Arsenal	d				12 03		12 09		12 13			12 23				12 33		12 39		12 43			12 53		
Plumstead	d				12 05				12 15			12 25				12 35				12 45			12 55		
Abbey Wood	d				12 08		12 13		12 18			12 28				12 38		12 43		12 48			12 58		
Belvedere	d				12 10				12 20			12 30				12 40				12 50			13 00		
Erith	d				12 13				12 23			12 33				12 43				12 53			13 03		
Slade Green	d				12a16				12a25	12a42		12 37				12a46				12a55		13a12	13 07		
Dartford	a		12 08	12 15			12 24	12 28				12 42		12 38	12 45			12 54	12 58				13 12		13 08
	d		12 09				12 25							12 39				12 55							13 09
Stone Crossing	d		12 13											12 43											13 13
Greenhithe for Bluewater	d		12 15				12 30							12 45				13 00							13 15
Swanscombe	d		12 18											12 48											13 18
Northfleet	d		12 20											12 50											13 20
Gravesend	d	12 18	12a25				12 37						12 51	12a55				13 07						13 22	13a25
Higham	d						12 43											13 13							
Strood	d	12 28					12 48						13 01					13 18						13 32	
Maidstone West	d																								
Rochester	d	12 33					12 52						13 06					13 22						13 37	
Chatham	d	12 35					12 55						13 08					13 25						13 39	
Gillingham (Kent)	a	12 39					12 59						13 12					13 29						13 43	

Table 200

London - Dartford and Gillingham

Saturdays

until 21 July, 18 Aug and from 15 Sep

Network Diagram - see first Page of Table 200

		SE	SE	SE	SE	SE		SE	SE	SE	SE	SE	SE	SE	SE	SE		SE	SE	SE	SE	SE	SE	SE	SE
St Pancras Int'l	d										13 25											13 55			
Stratford International	d										13 32											14 02			
Ebbsfleet International	d										13 43											14 13			
London Charing Cross	d	12 32			12 39							12 56	13 02			13 09							13 26	13 32	
London Waterloo (East)	d	12 35			12 42							12 59	13 05			13 12							13 29	13 35	
London Cannon Street	d		12 37	12 40				12 47	12 54	12 57				13 07	13 10				13 17	13 24	13 27				13 37
London Bridge	d	12 40	12 41	12 44	12 47			12 51	12 58	13 01		13 04	13 10	13 11	13 14	13 17			13 21	13 28	13 31		13 34	13 40	13 41
Deptford	d		12 47					12 57		13 07				13 17					13 27		13 37				13 47
Greenwich	d		12 49					12 59		13 09				13 19					13 29		13 39				13 49
Maze Hill	d		12 52					13 02		13 12				13 22					13 32		13 42				13 52
Westcombe Park	d		12 54					13 04		13 14				13 24					13 34		13 44				13 54
London Victoria	d					12 39												13 09							
Denmark Hill	d					12 48												13 18							
Peckham Rye	d					12 51												13 21							
Nunhead	d					12 53												13 23							
New Cross	d			12 49					13 03						13 19					13 33					
St Johns	d			12 51					13 05						13 21					13 35					
Lewisham	d	12 49		12 54	12 56	13 02			13 08				13 19		13 24	13 26		13 32		13 38				13 49	
Blackheath	d	12 52			12 59	13 04			13 11				13 22			13 29		13 34		13 41				13 52	
Kidbrooke	d	12 55				13 07			13 14				13 25					13 37		13 44				13 55	
Eltham	d	12 58				13 11			13 17				13 28					13 41		13 47				13 58	
Falconwood	d	13 01				13 13			13 20				13 31					13 43		13 50				14 01	
Welling	d	13 03				13 16			13 22				13 33					13 46		13 52				14 03	
Bexleyheath	d	13 06				13 18			13 25				13 36					13 48		13 55				14 06	
Barnehurst	d	13 08				13 21			13 32				13 38					13 51		14 02				14 08	
Hither Green	d			12 59								13 14			13 29								13 44		
Lee	d			13 01								13 16			13 31								13 46		
Mottingham	d			13 04								13 19			13 34								13 49		
New Eltham	d			13 06								13 21			13 36								13 51		
Sidcup	d			13 10								13 25			13 40								13 55		
Albany Park	d			13 12								13 27			13 42								13 57		
Bexley	d			13 14								13 29			13 44								13 59		
Crayford	d			13 18								13 33			13 48								14 03		
Charlton	d		12 57	13a45	13 03			13 07		13 17				13 27	14a15	13 33			13 37		13 47				13 57
Woolwich Dockyard	d		13 00					13 10		13 20				13 30					13 40		13 50				14 00
Woolwich Arsenal	d		13 03		13 09			13 13		13 23				13 33		13 39			13 43		13 53				14 03
Plumstead	d		13 05					13 15		13 25				13 35					13 45		13 55				14 05
Abbey Wood	d		13 08		13 13			13 18		13 28				13 38		13 43			13 48		13 58				14 08
Belvedere	d		13 10					13 20		13 30				13 40					13 50		14 00				14 10
Erith	d		13 13					13 23		13 33				13 43					13 53		14 03				14 13
Slade Green	d		13a16					13a25	13a42	13 37				13a46					13a55	14a12	14 07				14a16
Dartford	a	13 15			13 24	13 28				13 42		13 38	13 45			13 54		13 58			14 12		14 08	14 15	
	d				13 25							13 39				13 55							14 09		
Stone Crossing	d											13 43											14 13		
Greenhithe for Bluewater	d				13 30							13 45				14 00							14 15		
Swanscombe	d											13 48											14 18		
Northfleet	d											13 50											14 20		
Gravesend	d				13 37						13 48	13a55				14 07						14 18	14a25		
Higham	d				13 43											14 13									
Strood	d				13 48						13 58					14 18						14 28			
Maidstone West	d																								
Rochester	d				13 52						14 03					14 22						14 33			
Chatham	d				13 55						14 05					14 25						14 35			
Gillingham (Kent)	a				13 59						14 09					14 29						14 39			

Table 200

London - Dartford and Gillingham

Saturdays

until 21 July, 18 Aug and from 15 Sep

Network Diagram - see first Page of Table 200

		SE		SE	SE	SE	SE	SE	SE	SE	SE	SE		SE	SE	SE	SE	SE	SE	SE	SE	SE		SE	SE
St Pancras Int'l	d								14 25											14 55					
Stratford International	d								14 32											15 02					
Ebbsfleet International	d								14 43											15 13					
London Charing Cross	d			13 39						13 56	14 02				14 09						14 26	14 32			
London Waterloo (East)	d			13 42						13 59	14 05				14 12						14 29	14 35			
London Cannon Street	d	13 40				13 47	13 54	13 57				14 07		14 10			14 17	14 24	14 27					14 37	14 40
London Bridge	d	13 44		13 47		13 51	13 58	14 01		14 04	14 10	14 11		14 14	14 17		14 21	14 28	14 31		14 34	14 40		14 41	14 44
Deptford	d					13 57		14 07				14 17					14 27		14 37					14 47	
Greenwich	d					13 59		14 09				14 19					14 29		14 39					14 49	
Maze Hill	d					14 02		14 12				14 22					14 32		14 42					14 52	
Westcombe Park	d					14 04		14 14				14 24					14 34		14 44					14 54	
London Victoria	d				13 39											14 09									
Denmark Hill	d				13 48											14 18									
Peckham Rye	d				13 51											14 21									
Nunhead	d				13 53											14 23									
New Cross	d	13 49					14 03							14 19				14 33							14 49
St Johns	d	13 51					14 05							14 21				14 35							14 51
Lewisham	d	13 54		13 56	14 02		14 08				14 19			14 24	14 26	14 32		14 38				14 49			14 54
Blackheath	d			13 59	14 04		14 11				14 22				14 29	14 34		14 41				14 52			
Kidbrooke	d				14 07		14 14				14 25					14 37		14 44				14 55			
Eltham	d				14 11		14 17				14 28					14 41		14 47				14 58			
Falconwood	d				14 13		14 20				14 31					14 43		14 50				15 01			
Welling	d				14 16		14 22				14 33					14 46		14 52				15 03			
Bexleyheath	d				14 18		14 25				14 36					14 48		14 55				15 06			
Barnehurst	d				14 21		14 32				14 38					14 51		15 02				15 08			
Hither Green	d	13 59								14 14				14 29							14 44				14 59
Lee	d	14 01								14 16				14 31							14 46				15 01
Mottingham	d	14 04								14 19				14 34							14 49				15 04
New Eltham	d	14 06								14 21				14 36							14 51				15 06
Sidcup	d	14 10								14 25				14 40							14 55				15 10
Albany Park	d	14 12								14 27				14 42							14 57				15 12
Bexley	d	14 14								14 29				14 44							14 59				15 14
Crayford	d	14 18								14 33				14 48							15 03				15 18
Charlton	d	14a45		14 03		14 07		14 17				14 27		15a15	14 33		14 37		14 47					14 57	15a45
Woolwich Dockyard	d					14 10		14 20				14 30					14 40		14 50					15 00	
Woolwich Arsenal	d			14 09		14 13		14 23				14 33			14 39		14 43		14 53					15 03	
Plumstead	d					14 15		14 25				14 35					14 45		14 55					15 05	
Abbey Wood	d			14 13		14 18		14 28				14 38			14 43		14 48		14 58					15 08	
Belvedere	d					14 20		14 30				14 40					14 50		15 00					15 10	
Erith	d					14 23		14 33				14 43					14 53		15 03					15 13	
Slade Green	d					14a25	14a42	14 37				14a46					14a55	15a12	15 07					15a16	
Dartford	a			14 24	14 28			14 42		14 38	14 45				14 54	14 58			15 12		15 08	15 15			
	d			14 25						14 39					14 55						15 09				
Stone Crossing	d									14 43											15 13				
Greenhithe for Bluewater	d			14 30						14 45					15 00						15 15				
Swanscombe	d									14 48											15 18				
Northfleet	d									14 50											15 20				
Gravesend	d			14 37					14 48	14a55					15 07					15 18	15a25				
Higham	d			14 43											15 13										
Strood	d			14 48					14 58						15 18					15 28					
Maidstone West	d																								
Rochester	d			14 52					15 03						15 22					15 33					
Chatham	d			14 55					15 05						15 25					15 35					
Gillingham (Kent)	a			14 59					15 09						15 29					15 39					

London - Dartford and Gillingham

Saturdays

until 21 July, 18 Aug and from 15 Sep

Network Diagram - see first Page of Table 200

		SE	SE	SE	SE	SE	SE	SE		SE	SE	SE	SE	SE	SE	SE	SE	SE		SE	SE	SE	SE	SE	SE
St Pancras Int'l	d						15 25											15 55							
Stratford International	d						15 32											16 02							
Ebbsfleet International	d						15 43											16 13							
London Charing Cross	d	14 39						14 56		15 02			15 09							15 26	15 32			15 39	
London Waterloo (East)	d	14 42						14 59		15 05			15 12							15 29	15 35			15 42	
London Cannon Street	d			14 47	14 54	14 57					15 07	15 10			15 17	15 24	15 27					15 37	15 40		
London Bridge	d	14 47		14 51	14 58	15 01		15 04		15 10	15 11	15 14	15 17		15 21	15 28	15 31			15 34	15 40	15 41	15 44	15 47	
Deptford	d			14 57		15 07					15 17				15 27		15 37					15 47			
Greenwich	d			14 59		15 09					15 19				15 29		15 39					15 49			
Maze Hill	d			15 02		15 12					15 22				15 32		15 42					15 52			
Westcombe Park	d			15 04		15 14					15 24				15 34		15 44					15 54			
London Victoria	d		14 39											15 09											15 39
Denmark Hill	d		14 48											15 18											15 48
Peckham Rye	d		14 51											15 21											15 51
Nunhead	d		14 53											15 23											15 53
New Cross	d				15 03							15 19				15 33							15 49		
St Johns	d				15 05							15 21				15 35							15 51		
Lewisham	d	14 56	15 02		15 08					15 19		15 24	15 26	15 32		15 38					15 49		15 54	15 56	16 02
Blackheath	d	14 59	15 04		15 11					15 22			15 29	15 34		15 41					15 52			15 59	16 04
Kidbrooke	d		15 07		15 14					15 25				15 37		15 44					15 55				16 07
Eltham	d		15 11		15 17					15 28				15 41		15 47					15 58				16 11
Falconwood	d		15 13		15 20					15 31				15 43		15 50					16 01				16 13
Welling	d		15 16		15 22					15 33				15 46		15 52					16 03				16 16
Bexleyheath	d		15 18		15 25					15 36				15 48		15 55					16 06				16 18
Barnehurst	d		15 21		15 32					15 38				15 51		16 02					16 08				16 21
Hither Green	d							15 14				15 29								15 44			15 59		
Lee	d							15 16				15 31								15 46			16 01		
Mottingham	d							15 19				15 34								15 49			16 04		
New Eltham	d							15 21				15 36								15 51			16 06		
Sidcup	d							15 25				15 40								15 55			16 10		
Albany Park	d							15 27				15 42								15 57			16 12		
Bexley	d							15 29				15 44								15 59			16 14		
Crayford	d							15 33				15 48								16 03			16 18		
Charlton	d	15 03		15 07		15 17					15 27	16a15	15 33		15 37		15 47					15 57	16a45	16 03	
Woolwich Dockyard	d			15 10		15 20					15 30				15 40		15 50					16 00			
Woolwich Arsenal	d	15 09		15 13		15 23					15 33		15 39		15 43		15 53					16 03		16 09	
Plumstead	d			15 15		15 25					15 35				15 45		15 55					16 05			
Abbey Wood	d	15 13		15 18		15 28					15 38		15 43		15 48		15 58					16 08		16 13	
Belvedere	d			15 20		15 30					15 40				15 50		16 00					16 10			
Erith	d			15 23		15 33					15 43				15 53		16 03					16 13			
Slade Green	d			15a25	15a42	15 37					15a46				15a55	16a12	16 07					16a16			
Dartford	a	15 24	15 28			15 42		15 38		15 45			15 54	15 58			16 12			16 08	16 15			16 24	16 28
	d	15 25						15 39					15 55							16 09				16 25	
Stone Crossing	d							15 43												16 13					
Greenhithe for Bluewater	d	15 30						15 45					16 00							16 15				16 30	
Swanscombe	d							15 48												16 18					
Northfleet	d							15 50												16 20					
Gravesend	d	15 37					15 48	15a55					16 07					16 18		16a25				16 37	
Higham	d	15 43											16 13											16 43	
Strood	d	15 48					15 58						16 18					16 28						16 48	
Maidstone West	d																								
Rochester	d	15 52					16 03						16 22					16 33						16 52	
Chatham	d	15 55					16 05						16 25					16 35						16 55	
Gillingham (Kent)	a	15 59					16 09						16 29					16 39						16 59	

London - Dartford and Gillingham

Saturdays

until 21 July, 18 Aug and from 15 Sep

Network Diagram - see first Page of Table 200

		SE	SE	SE		SE	SE	SE	SE	SE	SE	SE	SE	SE		SE	SE	SE	SE	SE	SE	SE	SE	SE
St Pancras Int'l	d					16 28											16 55							
Stratford International	d					16 35											17 02							
Ebbsfleet International	d					16 46											17 13							
London Charing Cross	d						15 56	16 02			16 09							16 26	16 32			16 39		
London Waterloo (East)	d						15 59	16 05			16 12							16 29	16 35			16 42		
London Cannon Street	d	15 47	15 54	15 57					16 07	16 10			16 17	16 24		16 27				16 37	16 40			16 47
London Bridge	d	15 51	15 58	16 01			16 04	16 10	16 11	16 14	16 17		16 21	16 28		16 31		16 34	16 40	16 41	16 44	16 47		16 51
Deptford	d	15 57		16 07					16 17				16 27			16 37				16 47				16 57
Greenwich	d	15 59		16 09					16 19				16 29			16 39				16 49				16 59
Maze Hill	d	16 02		16 12					16 22				16 32			16 42				16 52				17 02
Westcombe Park	d	16 04		16 14					16 24				16 34			16 44				16 54				17 04
London Victoria	d											16 09											16 39	
Denmark Hill	d											16 18											16 48	
Peckham Rye	d											16 21											16 51	
Nunhead	d											16 23											16 53	
New Cross	d		16 03							16 19				16 33							16 49			
St Johns	d		16 05							16 21				16 35							16 51			
Lewisham	d		16 08					16 19		16 24	16 26	16 32		16 38					16 49		16 54	16 56	17 02	
Blackheath	d		16 11					16 22			16 29	16 34		16 41					16 52			16 59	17 04	
Kidbrooke	d		16 14					16 25				16 37		16 44					16 55				17 07	
Eltham	d		16 17					16 28				16 41		16 47					16 58				17 11	
Falconwood	d		16 20					16 31				16 43		16 50					17 01				17 13	
Welling	d		16 22					16 33				16 46		16 52					17 03				17 16	
Bexleyheath	d		16 25					16 36				16 48		16 55					17 06				17 18	
Barnehurst	d		16 32					16 38				16 51		17 02					17 08				17 21	
Hither Green	d						16 14			16 29								16 44			16 59			
Lee	d						16 16			16 31								16 46			17 01			
Mottingham	d						16 19			16 34								16 49			17 04			
New Eltham	d						16 21			16 36								16 51			17 06			
Sidcup	d						16 25			16 40								16 55			17 10			
Albany Park	d						16 27			16 42								16 57			17 12			
Bexley	d						16 29			16 44								16 59			17 14			
Crayford	d						16 33			16 48								17 03			17 18			
Charlton	d	16 07		16 17					16 27	17a15	16 33		16 37			16 47				16 57	17a45	17 03		17 07
Woolwich Dockyard	d	16 10		16 20					16 30				16 40			16 50				17 00				17 10
Woolwich Arsenal	d	16 13		16 23					16 33		16 39		16 43			16 53				17 03		17 09		17 13
Plumstead	d	16 15		16 25					16 35				16 45			16 55				17 05				17 15
Abbey Wood	d	16 18		16 28					16 38		16 43		16 48			16 58				17 08		17 13		17 18
Belvedere	d	16 20		16 30					16 40				16 50			17 00				17 10				17 20
Erith	d	16 23		16 33					16 43				16 53			17 03				17 13				17 23
Slade Green	d	16a25	16a42	16 37					16a46				16a55	17a12		17 07				17a16				17a25
Dartford	a			16 42			16 38	16 45			16 54	16 58				17 12		17 08	17 15			17 24	17 28	
	d						16 39				16 55							17 09				17 25		
Stone Crossing	d						16 43											17 13						
Greenhithe for Bluewater	d						16 45				17 00							17 15				17 30		
Swanscombe	d						16 48											17 18						
Northfleet	d						16 50											17 20						
Gravesend	d					16 51	16a55				17 07						17 18	17a25				17 37		
Higham	d										17 13											17 43		
Strood	d					17 01					17 18						17 28					17 48		
Maidstone West	d																							
Rochester	d					17 06					17 22						17 33					17 52		
Chatham	d					17 08					17 25						17 35					17 55		
Gillingham (Kent)	a					17 12					17 29						17 39					17 59		

Table 200

London - Dartford and Gillingham

Saturdays

until 21 July, 18 Aug and from 15 Sep

Network Diagram - see first Page of Table 200

		SE	SE	SE	SE	SE	SE	SE	SE	SE	SE	SE	SE	SE	SE	SE	SE	SE	SE	SE	SE	SE	SE
St Pancras Int'l ⊖	d			17 25										17 55									
Stratford International ⊖	d			17 32										18 02									
Ebbsfleet International	d			17 43										18 13									
London Charing Cross ⊖	d				16 56	17 02			17 09						17 26	17 32			17 39				
London Waterloo (East) ⊖	d				16 59	17 05			17 12						17 29	17 35			17 42				
London Cannon Street ⊖	d	16 54	16 57				17 07	17 10			17 17	17 24	17 27				17 37	17 40			17 47	17 54	17 57
London Bridge ⊖	d	16 58	17 01		17 04	17 10	17 11	17 14	17 17		17 21	17 28	17 31		17 34	17 40	17 41	17 44	17 47		17 51	17 58	18 01
Deptford	d		17 07				17 17				17 27		17 37				17 47				17 57		18 07
Greenwich	d		17 09				17 19				17 29		17 39				17 49				17 59		18 09
Maze Hill	d		17 12				17 22				17 32		17 42				17 52				18 02		18 12
Westcombe Park	d		17 14				17 24				17 34		17 44				17 54				18 04		18 14
London Victoria ⊖	d									17 09										17 39			
Denmark Hill	d									17 18										17 48			
Peckham Rye	d									17 21										17 51			
Nunhead	d									17 23										17 53			
New Cross ⊖	d	17 03						17 19				17 33						17 49				18 03	
St Johns	d	17 05						17 21				17 35						17 51				18 05	
Lewisham	d	17 08				17 19		17 24	17 26	17 32		17 38				17 49		17 54	17 56	18 02		18 08	
Blackheath	d	17 11				17 22			17 29	17 34		17 41				17 52			17 59	18 04		18 11	
Kidbrooke	d	17 14				17 25				17 37		17 44				17 55				18 07		18 14	
Eltham	d	17 17				17 28				17 41		17 47				17 58				18 11		18 17	
Falconwood	d	17 20				17 31				17 43		17 50				18 01				18 13		18 20	
Welling	d	17 22				17 33				17 46		17 52				18 03				18 16		18 22	
Bexleyheath	d	17 25				17 36				17 48		17 55				18 06				18 18		18 25	
Barnehurst	d	17 32				17 38				17 51		18 02				18 08				18 21		18a28	
Hither Green	d				17 14			17 29							17 44			17 59					
Lee	d				17 16			17 31							17 46			18 01					
Mottingham	d				17 19			17 34							17 49			18 04					
New Eltham	d				17 21			17 36							17 51			18 06					
Sidcup	d				17 25			17 40							17 55			18 10					
Albany Park	d				17 27			17 42							17 57			18 12					
Bexley	d				17 29			17 44							17 59			18 14					
Crayford	d				17 33			17 48							18 03			18 18					
Charlton	d		17 17				17 27	18a15	17 33		17 37		17 47				17 57	18a45	18 03		18 07		18 17
Woolwich Dockyard	d		17 20				17 30				17 40		17 50				18 00				18 10		18 20
Woolwich Arsenal	d		17 23				17 33		17 39		17 43		17 53				18 03		18 09		18 13		18 23
Plumstead	d		17 25				17 35				17 45		17 55				18 05				18 15		18 25
Abbey Wood	d		17 28				17 38		17 43		17 48		17 58				18 08		18 13		18 18		18 28
Belvedere	d		17 30				17 40				17 50		18 00				18 10				18 20		18 30
Erith	d		17 33				17 43				17 53		18 03				18 13				18 23		18 33
Slade Green	d	17a42	17 37				17a46				17a55	18a12	18 07				18a16				18a25		18 37
Dartford	a		17 42		17 38	17 45			17 54	17 58			18 12		18 08	18 15			18 24	18 28			18 42
	d				17 39				17 55						18 09				18 25				
Stone Crossing	d				17 43										18 13								
Greenhithe for Bluewater	d				17 45				18 00						18 15				18 30				
Swanscombe	d				17 48										18 18								
Northfleet	d				17 50										18 20								
Gravesend	d			17 48	17a55				18 07					18 18	18a25				18 37				
Higham	d								18 13										18 43				
Strood	d			17 58					18 18					18 28					18 48				
Maidstone West	d																						
Rochester	d			18 03					18 22					18 33					18 52				
Chatham	d			18 05					18 25					18 35					18 55				
Gillingham (Kent)	a			18 09					18 29					18 39					18 59				

Table 200

London - Dartford and Gillingham

Saturdays

until 21 July, 18 Aug and from 15 Sep

Network Diagram - see first Page of Table 200

		SE	SE	SE	SE	SE	SE	SE	SE	SE	SE	SE	SE	SE	SE	SE	SE	SE	SE	SE	SE	SE	SE
St Pancras Int'l ⊖	d	18 25										18 55										19 25	
Stratford International ⊖	d	18 32										19 02										19 32	
Ebbsfleet International	d	18 43										19 13										19 43	
London Charing Cross ⊖	d		17 56	18 02			18 09						18 26	18 32			18 39						18 56
London Waterloo (East) ⊖	d		17 59	18 05			18 12						18 29	18 35			18 42						18 59
London Cannon Street ⊖	d				18 07	18 10			18 17	18 24	18 27				18 37	18 40			18 47	18 54	18 57		
London Bridge ⊖	d		18 04	18 10	18 11	18 14	18 17		18 21	18 28	18 31		18 34	18 40	18 41	18 44	18 47		18 51	18 58	19 01		19 04
Deptford	d				18 17				18 27		18 37				18 47				18 57		19 07		
Greenwich	d				18 19				18 29		18 39				18 49				18 59		19 09		
Maze Hill	d				18 22				18 32		18 42				18 52				19 02		19 12		
Westcombe Park	d				18 24				18 34		18 44				18 54				19 04		19 14		
London Victoria ⊖	d							18 09										18 39					
Denmark Hill	d							18 18										18 48					
Peckham Rye	d							18 21										18 51					
Nunhead	d							18 23										18 53					
New Cross ⊖	d					18 19				18 33						18 49				19 03			
St Johns	d					18 21				18 35						18 51				19 05			
Lewisham	d			18 19		18 24	18 26	18 32		18 38				18 49		18 54	18 56	19 02		19 08			
Blackheath	d			18 22			18 29	18 34		18 41				18 52			18 59	19 04		19 11			
Kidbrooke	d			18 25				18 37		18 44				18 55				19 07		19 14			
Eltham	d			18 28				18 41		18 47				18 58				19 11		19 17			
Falconwood	d			18 31				18 43		18 50				19 01				19 13		19 20			
Welling	d			18 33				18 46		18 52				19 03				19 16		19 22			
Bexleyheath	d			18 36				18 48		18 55				19 06				19 18		19 25			
Barnehurst	d			18 38				18 51		18a58				19 08				19 21		19a28			
Hither Green	d		18 14			18 29							18 44			18 59							19 14
Lee	d		18 16			18 31							18 46			19 01							19 16
Mottingham	d		18 19			18 34							18 49			19 04							19 19
New Eltham	d		18 21			18 36							18 51			19 06							19 21
Sidcup	d		18 25			18 40							18 55			19 10							19 25
Albany Park	d		18 27			18 42							18 57			19 12							19 27
Bexley	d		18 29			18 44							18 59			19 14							19 29
Crayford	d		18 33			18 48							19 03			19 18							19 33
Charlton	d				18 27	19a15	18 33		18 37		18 47				18 57	19a45	19 03		19 07		19 17		
Woolwich Dockyard	d				18 30				18 40		18 50				19 00				19 10		19 20		
Woolwich Arsenal	d				18 33		18 39		18 43		18 53				19 03		19 09		19 13		19 23		
Plumstead	d				18 35				18 45		18 55				19 05				19 15		19 25		
Abbey Wood	d				18 38		18 43		18 48		18 58				19 08		19 13		19 18		19 28		
Belvedere	d				18 40				18 50		19 00				19 10				19 20		19 30		
Erith	d				18 43				18 53		19 03				19 13				19 23		19 33		
Slade Green	d				18a45				18a56		19 07				19a15				19a26		19 37		
Dartford	a		18 38	18 45			18 54	18 58			19 12		19 08	19 15			19 24	19 28			19 42		19 38
	d		18 39				18 55						19 09				19 25						19 39
Stone Crossing	d		18 43										19 13										19 43
Greenhithe for Bluewater	d		18 45				19 00						19 15				19 30						19 45
Swanscombe	d		18 48										19 18										19 48
Northfleet	d		18 50										19 20										19 50
Gravesend	d	18 48	18a55				19 07					19 18	19a25				19 37					19 48	19a55
Higham	d						19 13										19 43						
Strood	d	18 58					19 18					19 28					19 48					19 58	
Maidstone West	d																						
Rochester	d	19 03					19 22					19 33					19 52					20 03	
Chatham	d	19 05					19 25					19 35					19 55					20 05	
Gillingham (Kent)	a	19 09					19 29					19 39					19 59					20 09	

London - Dartford and Gillingham

Saturdays

until 21 July, 18 Aug and from 15 Sep

Network Diagram - see first Page of Table 200

		SE		SE	SE	SE	SE	SE	SE	SE	SE	SE		SE	SE	SE	SE	SE	SE	SE	SE	SE		SE	SE
St Pancras Int'l ⊖	d									19 55							20 25							20 55	
Stratford International ⊖	d									20 02							20 32							21 02	
Ebbsfleet International	d									20 13							20 43							21 13	
London Charing Cross ⊖	d	19 02				19 09					19 26	19 32		19 39				19 52	19 56	20 02	20 09				20 22
London Waterloo (East) ⊖	d	19 05				19 12					19 29	19 35		19 42				19 55	19 59	20 05	20 12				20 25
London Cannon Street ⊖	d			19 07	19 10			19 24	19 27																
London Bridge ⊖	d	19 10		19 11	19 14	19 17		19 28	19 31		19 34	19 40		19 47		19 50		20 00	20 05	20 10	20 17	20 20			20 30
Deptford	d			19 17					19 37							19 56			20 11			20 26			
Greenwich	d			19 19					19 39							19 58			20 13			20 28			
Maze Hill	d			19 22					19 42							20 01			20 16			20 31			
Westcombe Park	d			19 24					19 44							20 03			20 18			20 33			
London Victoria ⊖	d						19 09								19 39										
Denmark Hill	d						19 18								19 48										
Peckham Rye	d						19 21								19 51										
Nunhead	d						19 23								19 53										
New Cross ⊖	d				19 19			19 33				19 45						20 05		20 15					20 35
St Johns	d				19 21			19 35																	
Lewisham	d	19 19			19 24	19 26	19 32	19 38				19 49		19 56	20 02			20 09		20 19	20 26				20 39
Blackheath	d	19 22				19 29	19 34	19 41				19 52		19 59	20 04					20 22	20 29				
Kidbrooke	d	19 25					19 37	19 44				19 55			20 07					20 25					
Eltham	d	19 28					19 41	19 47				19 58			20 11					20 28					
Falconwood	d	19 31					19 43	19 50				20 01			20 13					20 31					
Welling	d	19 33					19 46	19 52				20 03			20 16					20 33					
Bexleyheath	d	19 36					19 48	19 55				20 06			20 18					20 36					
Barnehurst	d	19 38					19 51	19a58				20 08			20 21					20 38					
Hither Green	d				19 29						19 44							20 14							20 44
Lee	d				19 31						19 46							20 16							20 46
Mottingham	d				19 34						19 49							20 19							20 49
New Eltham	d				19 36						19 51							20 21							20 51
Sidcup	d				19 40						19 55							20 25							20 55
Albany Park	d				19 42						19 57							20 27							20 57
Bexley	d				19 44						19 59							20 29							20 59
Crayford	d				19 48						20 03							20 33							21 03
Charlton	d			19 27	20a15	19 33			19 47					20 03		20 06			20 20		20 33	20 36			
Woolwich Dockyard	d			19 30					19 50							20 09			20 23			20 39			
Woolwich Arsenal	d			19 33		19 39			19 53					20 09		20 12			20 26		20 39	20 42			
Plumstead	d			19 35					19 55							20 14			20 28			20 44			
Abbey Wood	d			19 38		19 43			19 58					20 13		20 17			20 31		20 43	20 47			
Belvedere	d			19 40					20 00							20 20			20 34			20 50			
Erith	d			19 43					20 03							20 22			20 36			20 52			
Slade Green	d			19 46					20 07							20 26			20 39			20 56			
Dartford	a	19 45		19 52		19 54	19 58		20 12		20 08	20 15		20 24	20 28	20 31		20 38	20 44	20 46	20 54	21 01			21 08
	d					19 55					20 09			20 25				20 39			20 55				21 09
Stone Crossing	d										20 13							20 43							21 13
Greenhithe for Bluewater	d					20 00					20 15			20 30				20 45			21 00				21 15
Swanscombe	d										20 18							20 48							21 18
Northfleet	d										20 20							20 50							21 20
Gravesend	d					20 07				20 18	20a25			20 37			20 48	20a55			21 07			21 18	21a25
Higham	d					20 13								20 43							21 13				
Strood	d					20 18				20 28				20 48			20 58				21 18			21 28	
Maidstone West	d																								
Rochester	d					20 22				20 33				20 52			21 03				21 22			21 33	
Chatham	d					20 25				20 35				20 55			21 05				21 25			21 35	
Gillingham (Kent)	a					20 29				20 39				20 59			21 09				21 29			21 39	

London - Dartford and Gillingham

Saturdays

until 21 July, 18 Aug and from 15 Sep

Network Diagram - see first Page of Table 200

		SE	SE	SE	SE	SE	SE	SE		SE	SE	SE	SE	SE	SE	SE	SE	SE		SE	SE	SE	SE	SE	SE
St Pancras Int'l ⊖	d					21 25						21 55									22 25				
Stratford International ⊖	d					21 32						22 02									22 32				
Ebbsfleet International	d					21 43						22 13									22 43				
London Charing Cross ⊖	d	20 26	20 32	20 39			20 52	20 56		21 02	21 09		21 22	21 26	21 32	21 39	21 52	21 56		22 02		22 09	22 22	22 26	22 32
London Waterloo (East) ⊖	d	20 29	20 35	20 42			20 55	20 59		21 05	21 12		21 25	21 29	21 35	21 42	21 55	21 59		22 05		22 12	22 25	22 29	22 35
London Cannon Street ⊖	d																								
London Bridge ⊖	d	20 35	20 40	20 47	20 50		21 00	21 05		21 10	21 17		21 30	21 35	21 40	21 47	22 00	22 05		22 10		22 17	22 30	22 35	22 40
Deptford	d	20 41			20 56			21 11						21 41				22 11						22 41	
Greenwich	d	20 43			20 58			21 13						21 43				22 13						22 43	
Maze Hill	d	20 46			21 01			21 16						21 46				22 16						22 46	
Westcombe Park	d	20 48			21 03			21 18						21 48				22 18						22 48	
London Victoria ⊖	d																								
Denmark Hill	d																								
Peckham Rye	d																								
Nunhead	d																								
New Cross ⊖	d		20 45				21 05			21 15			21 35		21 45		22 05			22 15			22 35		22 45
St Johns	d																								
Lewisham	d		20 49	20 56			21 09			21 19	21 26		21 39		21 49	21 56	22 09			22 19		22 26	22 39		22 49
Blackheath	d		20 52	20 59						21 22	21 29				21 52	21 59				22 22		22 29			22 52
Kidbrooke	d		20 55							21 25					21 55					22 25					22 55
Eltham	d		20 58							21 28					21 58					22 28					22 58
Falconwood	d		21 01							21 31					22 01					22 31					23 01
Welling	d		21 03							21 33					22 03					22 33					23 03
Bexleyheath	d		21 06							21 36					22 06					22 36					23 06
Barnehurst	d		21 08							21 38					22 08					22 38					23 08
Hither Green	d						21 14						21 44				22 14						22 44		
Lee	d						21 16						21 46				22 16						22 46		
Mottingham	d						21 19						21 49				22 19						22 49		
New Eltham	d						21 21						21 51				22 21						22 51		
Sidcup	d						21 25						21 55				22 25						22 55		
Albany Park	d						21 27						21 57				22 27						22 57		
Bexley	d						21 29						21 59				22 29						22 59		
Crayford	d						21 33						22 03				22 33						23 03		
Charlton	d	20 50		21 03	21 06			21 20			21 33			21 50		22 03		22 20				22 33		22 50	
Woolwich Dockyard	d	20 53			21 09			21 23						21 53				22 23						22 53	
Woolwich Arsenal	d	20 56		21 09	21 12			21 26			21 39			21 56		22 09		22 26				22 39		22 56	
Plumstead	d	20 58			21 14			21 28						21 58				22 28						22 58	
Abbey Wood	d	21 01		21 13	21 17			21 31			21 43			22 01		22 13		22 31				22 43		23 01	
Belvedere	d	21 04			21 20			21 34						22 04				22 34						23 04	
Erith	d	21 06			21 22			21 36						22 06				22 36						23 06	
Slade Green	d	21 09			21 26			21 39						22 09				22 39						23 09	
Dartford	a	21 14	21 16	21 24	21 31		21 38	21 44		21 46	21 54		22 08	22 14	22 16	22 24	22 38	22 44		22 46		22 54	23 08	23 14	23 16
	d			21 25			21 39				21 55		22 09			22 25						22 55			
Stone Crossing	d						21 43						22 13			22 29						22 59			
Greenhithe for Bluewater	d			21 30			21 45				22 00		22 15			22 31						23 01			
Swanscombe	d						21 48						22 18			22 34						23 04			
Northfleet	d						21 50						22 20			22 36						23 06			
Gravesend	d			21 37		21 48	21a55				22 07	22 18	22a25			22 40					22 48	23 10			
Higham	d			21 43							22 13					22 46						23 16			
Strood	d			21 48		21 58					22 18	22 28				22 52					22 58	23 22			
Maidstone West	d																								
Rochester	d			21 52		22 03					22 22	22 33				22 56					23 03	23 26			
Chatham	d			21 55		22 05					22 25	22 35				22 58					23 05	23 28			
Gillingham (Kent)	a			21 59		22 09					22 29	22 39				23 03					23 09	23 33			

Table 200

until 21 July, 18 Aug and from 15 Sep

London - Dartford and Gillingham

Network Diagram - see first Page of Table 200

		SE	SE	SE	SE	SE	SE	SE	SE	SE	SE	SE	SE	SE
St Pancras Int'l	d	22 55					23 25					23 55		
Stratford International	d	23 02					23 32					00 02		
Ebbsfleet International	d	23 13					23 43					00 13		
London Charing Cross	d		22 39	22 52	22 56	23 02		23 09	23 22	23 26	23 32		23 39	23 56
London Waterloo (East)	d		22 42	22 55	22 59	23 05		23 12	23 25	23 29	23 35		23 42	23 59
London Cannon Street	d													
London Bridge	d		22 47	23 00	23 05	23 10		23 17	23 30	23 35	23 40		23 47	00 05
Deptford	d				23 11					23 41				00 11
Greenwich	d				23 13					23 43				00 13
Maze Hill	d				23 16					23 46				00 16
Westcombe Park	d				23 18					23 48				00 18
London Victoria	d													
Denmark Hill	d													
Peckham Rye	d													
Nunhead	d													
New Cross	d			23 05		23 15			23 35		23 45			
St Johns	d													
Lewisham	d		22 56	23 09		23 19		23 26	23 39		23 49		23 56	
Blackheath	d		22 59			23 22		23 29			23 52		23 58	
Kidbrooke	d					23 25					23 55			
Eltham	d					23 28					23 58			
Falconwood	d					23 31					00 01			
Welling	d					23 33					00 03			
Bexleyheath	d					23 36					00 06			
Barnehurst	d					23 38					00 08			
Hither Green	d			23 14					23 44					
Lee	d			23 16					23 46					
Mottingham	d			23 19					23 49					
New Eltham	d			23 21					23 51					
Sidcup	d			23 25					23 55					
Albany Park	d			23 27					23 57					
Bexley	d			23 29					23 59					
Crayford	d			23 33					00 03					
Charlton	d		23 03		23 20			23 33		23 50			00 03	00 20
Woolwich Dockyard	d				23 23					23 53				00 23
Woolwich Arsenal	d		23 09		23 26			23 39		23 56			00 09	00 26
Plumstead	d				23 28					23 58				00 28
Abbey Wood	d		23 13		23 31			23 43		00 01			00 13	00 31
Belvedere	d				23 34					00 04				00 34
Erith	d				23 36					00 06				00 36
Slade Green	d				23 39					00 09				00 39
Dartford	a		23 24	23 38	23 44	23 46		23 54	00 08	00 14	00 16		00 24	00 44
	d		23 25					23 55					00 25	
Stone Crossing	d		23 29					23 58					00 29	
Greenhithe for Bluewater	d		23 31					23 59					00 31	
Swanscombe	d		23 34					00 04					00 34	
Northfleet	d		23 36					00 06					00 36	
Gravesend	d	23 18	23 40				23 48	00 10				00 18	00 40	
Higham	d		23 46					00 16					00 46	
Strood	d	23 28	23 52				23 58	00 22				00 28	00 52	
Maidstone West	d													
Rochester	d	23 33	23 56				00 03	00 26				00 33	00 56	
Chatham	d	23 35	23 58				00 05	00 28				00 35	00 58	
Gillingham (Kent)	a	23 39	00 03				00 09	00 33				00 39	01 03	

Table 200

28 July to 11 August

London - Dartford and Gillingham

Network Diagram - see first Page of Table 200

		SE A	SE B	SE A	SE B	SE A	SE B	SE A	SE B	SE A	SE B	SE A	SE B	SE A	SE B	SE	SE	SE	SE	SE	SE	SE	SE
St Pancras Int'l	d																						01 17
Stratford International	d																						01 26
Ebbsfleet International	d																						01 38
London Charing Cross	d	22p39	22p39	23p09	23p09	23p22	23p22	23p26	23p26	23p32	23p32	23p39	23p39	23p56	23p56	00 02	00 10	00 18	00 32		00 44		
London Waterloo (East)	d	22p42	22p42	23p12	23p12	23p25	23p25	23p29	23p29	23p35	23p35	23p42	23p42	23p59	23p59	00 05	00 13	00 21	00 35		00 47		
London Cannon Street	d																			00 42		00 56	
London Bridge	d	22p47	22p47	23p17	23p17	23p30	23p30	23p34	23p34	23p40	23p40	23p47	23p47	00 04	00 04	00 10	00 18	00 26	00 40	00 47	00 52	01 00	
Deptford	d							23p40	23p40					00 10	00 10				00 46			01 06	
Greenwich	d							23p42	23p42					00 12	00 12				00 49			01 09	
Maze Hill	d							23p45	23p45					00 15	00 15				00 53			01 13	
Westcombe Park	d							23p47	23p47					00 17	00 17				00 55			01 15	
London Victoria	d																						
Denmark Hill	d																						
Peckham Rye	d																						
Nunhead	d																						
New Cross	d					23p35	23p35			23p45	23p45					00 15	00 23	00 31			00 57		
St Johns	d																						
Lewisham	d	22p56	22p57	23p26	23p27	23p39	23p39			23p49	23p50	23p56	23p56			00 19	00 27	00 35		00 56	01 01		
Blackheath	d	22p59	23p00	23p29	23p30					23p52	23p55	23p59	00 01			00 22		00 38		01 00			
Kidbrooke	d									23p55	23p58					00 25				01 03			
Eltham	d									23p58	00 01					00 28				01 06			
Falconwood	d									00 01	00 04					00 31				01 09			
Welling	d									00 03	00 06					00 33				01 11			
Bexleyheath	d									00 06	00 09					00 36				01 14			
Barnehurst	d									00 08	00 12					00 38				01 17			
Hither Green	d					23p44	23p44										00 32				01 06		
Lee	d					23p46	23p46										00 34				01 08		
Mottingham	d					23p49	23p49										00 37				01 11		
New Eltham	d					23p51	23p51										00 39				01 13		
Sidcup	d					23p55	23p55										00 43				01 17		
Albany Park	d					23p57	23p57										00 45				01 19		
Bexley	d					23p59	23p59										00 47				01 21		
Crayford	d					00 03	00 03										00 51				01 25		
Charlton	d	23p03	23p05	23p33	23p35			23p50	23p50			00 03	00 06	00 20	00 20			00 42	00 58			01 18	
Woolwich Dockyard	d							23p53						00 23									
Woolwich Arsenal	d	23p09	23p10	23p39	23p39			23p56	23p56			00 09	00 11	00 26	00 26			00 47	01 04			01 24	
Plumstead	d							23p58	23p58					00 28	00 28			00 49	01 06			01 26	
Abbey Wood	d	23p13	23p14	23p43	23p43			00 01	00 01			00 13	00 15	00 31	00 31			00 53	01 09			01 29	
Belvedere	d							00 03	00 03					00 33	00 33			00 55	01 12			01 32	
Erith	d							00 06	00 06					00 36	00 36			00 58	01 14			01 34	
Slade Green	d							00 09	00 09					00 39	00 39			01 00	01 17			01 37	
Dartford	a	23p24	23p24	23p54	23p54	00 08	00 11	00 14	00 17	00 16	00 22	00 24	00 24	00 44	00 47	00 49	00 59	01 05	01 25	01 25	01 33	01 45	
	d	23p25	23p25	23p55	23p55							00 25	00 25					01 06		01 27			
Stone Crossing	d	23p29	23p29	23p58	23p58							00 29	00 29										
Greenhithe for Bluewater	d	23p31	23p31	23p59	23p59							00 31	00 31					01 10		01 31			
Swanscombe	d	23p34	23p34	00 04	00 04							00 34	00 34										
Northfleet	d	23p36	23p36	00 06	00 06							00 36	00 36										
Gravesend	d	23p40	23p40	00 10	00 10							00 40	00 40					01 17		01 39			01 43
Higham	d	23p46	23p46	00 16	00 16							00 46	00 46					01 23		01 45			
Strood	d	23p52	23p52	00 22	00 22							00 52	00 52					01 29		01 50			01 53
Maidstone West	d																						
Rochester	d	23p56	23p56	00 26	00 26							00 56	00 56					01 33		01 54			01 57
Chatham	d	23p58	23p58	00 28	00 28							00 58	00 58					01 35		01 57			02 00
Gillingham (Kent)	a	00 03	00 06	00 33	00 36							01 03	01 06					01 44		02 04			02 04

A not from 4 August until 11 August

B not 28 July

Table 200

London - Dartford and Gillingham

Saturdays

28 July to 11 August

Network Diagram - see first Page of Table 200

	SE	SE	SE	SE	SE		SE	SE	SE	SE	SE	SE
St Pancras Int'l d	01 55											
Stratford International d	02 04											
Ebbsfleet International d	02 16											
London Charing Cross d		04 52		05 22	05 26		05 32	05 39	05 52	05 56	06 02	06 09
London Waterloo (East) d		04 55		05 25	05 29		05 35	05 42	05 55	05 59	06 05	06 12
London Cannon Street d												
London Bridge d		05 00		05 30	05 34		05 40	05 47	06 00	06 04	06 10	06 17
Deptford d					05 40					06 10		
Greenwich d					05 43					06 13		
Maze Hill d					05 46					06 16		
Westcombe Park d					05 48					06 18		
London Victoria d												
Denmark Hill d												
Peckham Rye d												
Nunhead d												
New Cross d		05 05		05 35			05 45		06 05		06 15	
St Johns d												
Lewisham d		05 09		05 39			05 50	05 57	06 09		06 20	06 27
Blackheath d							05 54	06 00			06 24	06 30
Kidbrooke d							05 57				06 27	
Eltham d							06 00				06 30	
Falconwood d							06 02				06 32	
Welling d							06 05				06 35	
Bexleyheath d							06 07				06 37	
Barnehurst d							06 10				06 40	
Hither Green d		05 14		05 44					06 14			
Lee d		05 16		05 46					06 16			
Mottingham d		05 19		05 49					06 19			
New Eltham d		05 21		05 51					06 21			
Sidcup d		05 25		05 55					06 25			
Albany Park d		05 27		05 57					06 27			
Bexley d		05 29		05 59					06 29			
Crayford d		05 33		06 03					06 33			
Charlton d					05 51			06 05		06 21		06 35
Woolwich Dockyard d												
Woolwich Arsenal d					05 56			06 11		06 26		06 41
Plumstead d					05 58					06 28		
Abbey Wood d					06 01			06 15		06 31		06 45
Belvedere d					06 03					06 33		
Erith d					06 06					06 36		
Slade Green d					06 09					06 39		
Dartford a		05 38		06 08	06 17		06 19	06 24	06 38	06 47	06 49	06 54
Dartford d		05 39	05 55	06 09				06 25	06 39			06 55
Stone Crossing d		05 43		06 13					06 43			
Greenhithe for Bluewater d		05 45	06 00	06 15				06 30	06 45			07 00
Swanscombe d		05 48		06 18					06 48			
Northfleet d		05 50		06 20					06 50			
Gravesend d	02 21	05a58	06 07	06a28				06 37	06a58			07 07
Higham d			06 13					06 43				07 13
Strood d	02 31		06 18					06 48				07 18
Maidstone West d												
Rochester d	02 35		06 22					06 52				07 22
Chatham d	02 38		06 25					06 55				07 25
Gillingham (Kent) a	02 42		06 29					07 02				07 32

	SE	SE	SE		SE	SE	SE	SE	SE	SE	SE	SE
St Pancras Int'l d						07 18						
Stratford International d						07 28						
Ebbsfleet International d						07 43						
London Charing Cross d	06 22	06 26	06 32		06 39		06 52	06 56	07 02	07 09	07 22	07 26
London Waterloo (East) d	06 25	06 29	06 35		06 42		06 55	06 59	07 05	07 12	07 25	07 29
London Cannon Street d												
London Bridge d	06 30	06 34	06 40		06 47		07 00	07 04	07 10	07 17	07 30	07 34
Deptford d		06 40						07 10				07 40
Greenwich d		06 43						07 13				07 43
Maze Hill d												
Westcombe Park d		06 48						07 18				07 48
London Victoria d												
Denmark Hill d												
Peckham Rye d												
Nunhead d												
New Cross d	06 35		06 45				07 05		07 15		07 35	
St Johns d												
Lewisham d	06 39		06 50		06 57		07 09		07 20	07 27	07 39	
Blackheath d			06 54		07 00				07 24	07 31		
Kidbrooke d			06 57						07 27			
Eltham d			07 00						07 30			
Falconwood d			07 02						07 32			
Welling d			07 05						07 35			
Bexleyheath d			07 07						07 37			
Barnehurst d			07 10						07 40			
Hither Green d	06 44						07 14				07 44	
Lee d	06 46						07 16				07 46	
Mottingham d	06 49						07 19				07 49	
New Eltham d	06 51						07 21				07 51	
Sidcup d	06 55						07 25				07 55	
Albany Park d	06 57						07 27				07 57	
Bexley d	06 59						07 30				08 00	
Crayford d	07 03						07 33				08 03	
Charlton d		06 51			07 05			07 21		07 35		07 51
Woolwich Dockyard d												
Woolwich Arsenal d		06 56			07 11			07 26		07 41		07 56
Plumstead d		06 58						07 28				07 58
Abbey Wood d		07 01			07 15			07 31		07 45		08 01
Belvedere d		07 03						07 33				08 03
Erith d		07 06						07 36				08 06
Slade Green d		07 09						07 39				08 09
Dartford a	07 08	07 17	07 20		07 24		07 38	07 47	07 49	07 54	08 08	08 17
Dartford d	07 09				07 25		07 39			07 55	08 09	
Stone Crossing d	07 13						07 43				08 13	
Greenhithe for Bluewater d	07 15				07 30		07 45			08 00	08 15	
Swanscombe d	07 18						07 48				08 18	
Northfleet d	07 20						07 50				08 20	
Gravesend d	07a28				07 37	07 48	07a58			08 07	08a28	
Higham d					07 43					08 13		
Strood d					07 48	07 58				08 18		
Maidstone West d												
Rochester d					07 52	08 03				08 22		
Chatham d					07 55	08 05				08 25		
Gillingham (Kent) a					08 02	08 09				08 32		

Table 200

London - Dartford and Gillingham

Saturdays

28 July to 11 August

Network Diagram - see first Page of Table 200

	SE		SE	SE	SE	SE	SE	SE	SE	SE	SE	
St Pancras Int'l d						08 18						
Stratford International d						08 28						
Ebbsfleet International d						08 44						
London Charing Cross d	07 32		07 39				07 52	07 56	08 02			
London Waterloo (East) d	07 35		07 42				07 55	07 59	08 05			
London Cannon Street d					07 55					08 07	08 10	
London Bridge d	07 40		07 47				08 00	08 04	08 10	08 11	08 14	
Deptford d								08 10				
Greenwich d					08 06			08 13		08 20		
Maze Hill d												
Westcombe Park d								08 18				
London Victoria d				07 39								
Denmark Hill d				07 48								
Peckham Rye d				07 51								
Nunhead d				07 53								
New Cross d	07 45						08 05		08 15		08 19	
St Johns d											08 21	
Lewisham d	07 50		07 57	08 01			08 09		08 19		08 24	
Blackheath d	07 54		08 01	08 04					08 23			
Kidbrooke d	07 57			08 07								
Eltham d	08 00			08 11					08 29			
Falconwood d	08 02			08 13					08 31			
Welling d	08 05			08 16					08 34			
Bexleyheath d	08 07			08 18					08 36			
Barnehurst d	08 10			08 21					08 39			
Hither Green d							08 14				08 29	
Lee d							08 16				08 31	
Mottingham d							08 19				08 34	
New Eltham d							08 21				08 36	
Sidcup d							08 25				08 40	
Albany Park d							08 27				08 42	
Bexley d							08 30				08 44	
Crayford d							08 34				08 48	
Charlton d			08 05		08 13			08 21		08 26	09a12	
Woolwich Dockyard d												
Woolwich Arsenal d			08 11		08a17			08 26		08 33		
Plumstead d								08 28		08 35		
Abbey Wood d			08 15					08 31		08 38		
Belvedere d								08 33		08 40		
Erith d								08 36		08 43		
Slade Green d								08 39		08a46		
Dartford a	08 19		08 24	08 32			08 39	08 47	08 49			
Dartford d			08 25				08 40					
Stone Crossing d							08 44					
Greenhithe for Bluewater d			08 30				08 46					
Swanscombe d							08 49					
Northfleet d							08 51					
Gravesend d			08 37			08 48	08a59					
Higham d			08 43									
Strood d			08 48			08 58						
Maidstone West d												
Rochester d			08 52			09 03						
Chatham d			08 55			09 05						
Gillingham (Kent) a			09 02			09 09						

	SE	SE	SE	SE	SE	SE	SE	SE	SE		SE	SE
St Pancras Int'l d												
Stratford International d												
Ebbsfleet International d												
London Charing Cross d	08 09					08 26	08 32				08 39	
London Waterloo (East) d	08 12					08 29	08 35				08 42	
London Cannon Street d			08 17	08 24	08 27			08 37	08 40			
London Bridge d	08 17		08 21	08 28	08 31	08 34	08 40	08 41	08 44		08 47	
Deptford d			08 27									
Greenwich d			08 30		08 40			08 50				
Maze Hill d												
Westcombe Park d			08 35									
London Victoria d		08 09										08 39
Denmark Hill d		08 18										08 48
Peckham Rye d		08 21										08 51
Nunhead d		08 23										08 53
New Cross d				08 33					08 49			
St Johns d				08 35					08 51			
Lewisham d	08 27	08 32		08 38			08 49		08 54		08 57	09 02
Blackheath d	08 31	08 36		08 42			08 53				09 01	09 06
Kidbrooke d		08 39		08 45								09 09
Eltham d		08 42		08 49			08 59					09 12
Falconwood d		08 44		08 51			09 01					09 14
Welling d		08 47		08 54			09 04					09 17
Bexleyheath d		08 49		08 56			09 06					09 19
Barnehurst d		08 52		09 02			09 09					09 22
Hither Green d						08 44			08 59			
Lee d						08 46			09 01			
Mottingham d						08 49			09 04			
New Eltham d						08 51			09 06			
Sidcup d						08 55			09 10			
Albany Park d						08 57			09 12			
Bexley d						08 59			09 14			
Crayford d						09 03			09 18			
Charlton d	08 35		08 39		08 47			08 56	09a42		09 05	
Woolwich Dockyard d												
Woolwich Arsenal d	08 41		08 45		08 53			09 03			09 11	
Plumstead d			08 47		08 55			09 05				
Abbey Wood d	08 45		08 50		08 58			09 08			09 15	
Belvedere d			08 52		09 01			09 10				
Erith d			08 55		09 03			09 13				
Slade Green d			08a57	09a12	09 07			09a16				
Dartford a	08 54	09 01			09 15	09 08	09 18				09 24	09 31
Dartford d	08 55					09 09					09 25	
Stone Crossing d						09 13						
Greenhithe for Bluewater d	09 00					09 15					09 30	
Swanscombe d						09 18						
Northfleet d						09 20						
Gravesend d	09 07					09a25					09 37	
Higham d	09 13										09 43	
Strood d	09 18										09 48	
Maidstone West d												
Rochester d	09 22										09 52	
Chatham d	09 25										09 55	
Gillingham (Kent) a	09 32										10 02	

Table 200

Saturdays

28 July to 11 August

London - Dartford and Gillingham

Network Diagram - see first Page of Table 200

Station		SE	SE	SE	SE	SE	SE	SE	SE	SE	SE	SE	SE	SE	SE	SE	SE	SE	SE	SE	SE	SE	SE
St Pancras Int'l 15 ⊖	d				09 18																		
Stratford International ⊖ ⛴	d				09 28																		
Ebbsfleet International	d				09 43																		
London Charing Cross 4 ⊖	d					08 56	09 02			09 09					09 26	09 32			09 39				
London Waterloo (East) 4 ⊖	d					08 59	09 05			09 12					09 29	09 35			09 42				
London Cannon Street 4 ⊖	d	08 47	08 54	08 57				09 07	09 10			09 17	09 24	09 27			09 37	09 40			09 47	09 54	09 57
London Bridge 4 ⊖	d	08 51	08 58	09 01		09 04	09 10	09 11	09 14	09 17		09 21	09 28	09 31	09 34	09 40	09 41	09 44	09 47		09 51	09 58	10 01
Deptford	d	08 57										09 27									09 57		
Greenwich 4 ⛴	d	09 00		09 10				09 20				09 30		09 40			09 50				10 00		10 10
Maze Hill	d																						
Westcombe Park	d	09 05										09 35									10 05		
London Victoria 15 ⊖	d										09 09									09 39			
Denmark Hill 4	d										09 18									09 48			
Peckham Rye 4	d										09 21									09 51			
Nunhead 4	d										09 23									09 53			
New Cross 4 ⊖	d		09 03						09 19				09 33					09 49				10 03	
St Johns	d		09 05						09 21				09 35					09 51				10 05	
Lewisham 4 ⛴	d		09 08				09 19		09 24	09 27	09 32		09 38			09 49		09 54	09 57	10 02		10 08	
Blackheath 4	d		09 12				09 23			09 31	09 36		09 42			09 53			10 01	10 06		10 12	
Kidbrooke	d		09 15								09 39		09 45							10 09		10 15	
Eltham	d		09 19				09 29				09 42		09 49			09 59				10 12		10 19	
Falconwood	d		09 21				09 31				09 44		09 51			10 01				10 14		10 21	
Welling	d		09 24				09 34				09 47		09 54			10 04				10 17		10 24	
Bexleyheath	d		09 26				09 36				09 49		09 56			10 06				10 20		10 26	
Barnehurst 4	d		09 32				09 39				09 52		10 02			10 09				10 22		10 32	
Hither Green 4	d					09 14			09 29						09 44			09 59					
Lee	d					09 16			09 31						09 46			10 01					
Mottingham	d					09 19			09 34						09 49			10 04					
New Eltham	d					09 21			09 36						09 51			10 06					
Sidcup 4	d					09 25			09 40						09 55			10 10					
Albany Park	d					09 27			09 42						09 57			10 12					
Bexley	d					09 29			09 44						09 59			10 14					
Crayford	d					09 33			09 48						10 03			10 18					
Charlton 4	d	09 09		09 17				09 26	10a12	09 35		09 39		09 47			09 56	10a42	10 05		10 09		10 17
Woolwich Dockyard	d																						
Woolwich Arsenal 4 ⛴	d	09 15		09 23				09 33		09 41		09 45		09 53			10 03		10 11		10 15		10 23
Plumstead	d	09 17		09 25				09 35				09 47		09 55			10 05				10 17		10 25
Abbey Wood	d	09 20		09 28				09 38		09 45		09 50		09 58			10 08		10 15		10 20		10 28
Belvedere	d	09 22		09 31				09 40				09 52		10 01			10 10				10 22		10 31
Erith	d	09 25		09 33				09 43				09 55		10 03			10 13				10 25		10 33
Slade Green 4	d	09a27	09a42	09 37				09a46				09a57	10a12	10 07			10a16				10a27	10a42	10 37
Dartford 4	a			09 45		09 38	09 48			09 54	10 01			10 15	10 08	10 18			10 24	10 32			10 45
	d					09 39				09 55					10 09				10 25				
Stone Crossing	d					09 43									10 13								
Greenhithe for Bluewater	d					09 45				10 00					10 15				10 30				
Swanscombe	d					09 48									10 18								
Northfleet	d					09 50									10 20								
Gravesend 4	d				09 48	09a55				10 07					10a25				10 37				
Higham	d									10 13									10 43				
Strood 4	d				09 58					10 18									10 48				
Maidstone West	d																						
Rochester 4	d				10 03					10 22									10 52				
Chatham 4	d				10 05					10 25									10 55				
Gillingham (Kent) 4	a				10 09					10 32									11 02				

Table 200

Saturdays

28 July to 11 August

London - Dartford and Gillingham

Network Diagram - see first Page of Table 200

Station		SE	SE	SE	SE	SE	SE	SE	SE	SE	SE	SE	SE	SE	SE	SE	SE	SE	SE	SE	SE	SE
St Pancras Int'l 15 ⊖	d	10 18																			11 18	
Stratford International ⊖ ⛴	d	10 28																			11 28	
Ebbsfleet International	d	10 44																			11 43	
London Charing Cross 4 ⊖	d		09 56	10 02			10 09					10 26	10 32			10 39						10 56
London Waterloo (East) 4 ⊖	d		09 59	10 05			10 12					10 29	10 35			10 42						10 59
London Cannon Street 4 ⊖	d				10 07	10 10			10 17	10 24	10 27			10 37	10 40			10 47	10 54	10 57		
London Bridge 4 ⊖	d		10 04	10 10	10 11	10 14	10 17		10 21	10 28	10 31	10 34	10 40	10 41	10 44	10 47		10 51	10 58	11 01		11 04
Deptford	d								10 27									10 57				
Greenwich 4 ⛴	d				10 20				10 30		10 40			10 50				11 00		11 10		
Maze Hill	d																					
Westcombe Park	d								10 35									11 05				
London Victoria 15 ⊖	d							10 09									10 39					
Denmark Hill 4	d							10 18									10 48					
Peckham Rye 4	d							10 21									10 51					
Nunhead 4	d							10 23									10 53					
New Cross 4 ⊖	d					10 19				10 33					10 49				11 03			
St Johns	d					10 21				10 35					10 51				11 05			
Lewisham 4 ⛴	d			10 19		10 24	10 27	10 32		10 38			10 49		10 54	10 57	11 02		11 08			
Blackheath 4	d			10 23			10 31	10 36		10 42			10 53			11 01	11 06		11 12			
Kidbrooke	d							10 39		10 45							11 09		11 15			
Eltham	d			10 29				10 42		10 49			10 59				11 12		11 19			
Falconwood	d			10 31				10 44		10 51			11 01				11 14		11 21			
Welling	d			10 34				10 47		10 54			11 04				11 17		11 24			
Bexleyheath	d			10 36				10 49		10 56			11 06				11 19		11 26			
Barnehurst 4	d			10 39				10 52		11 02			11 09				11 22		11 32			
Hither Green 4	d		10 14			10 29						10 44			10 59							11 14
Lee	d		10 16			10 31						10 46			11 01							11 16
Mottingham	d		10 19			10 34						10 49			11 04							11 19
New Eltham	d		10 21			10 36						10 51			11 06							11 21
Sidcup 4	d		10 25			10 40						10 55			11 10							11 25
Albany Park	d		10 27			10 42						10 57			11 12							11 27
Bexley	d		10 29			10 44						10 59			11 14							11 29
Crayford	d		10 33			10 48						11 03			11 18							11 33
Charlton 4	d				10 26	11a12	10 35		10 39		10 47			10 56	11a42	11 05		11 09		11 17		
Woolwich Dockyard	d																					
Woolwich Arsenal 4 ⛴	d				10 33		10 41		10 45		10 53			11 03		11 11		11 15		11 23		
Plumstead	d				10 35				10 47		10 55			11 05				11 17		11 25		
Abbey Wood	d				10 38		10 45		10 50		10 58			11 08		11 15		11 20		11 28		
Belvedere	d				10 40				10 52		11 01			11 10				11 22		11 31		
Erith	d				10 43				10 55		11 03			11 13				11 25		11 33		
Slade Green 4	d				10a46				10a57	11a12	11 07			11a16				11a27	11a42	11 37		
Dartford 4	a		10 38	10 48			10 54	11 01			11 15	11 08	11 18			11 24	11 31			11 45		11 38
	d		10 39				10 55					11 09				11 25						11 39
Stone Crossing	d		10 43									11 13										11 43
Greenhithe for Bluewater	d		10 45				11 00					11 15				11 30						11 45
Swanscombe	d		10 48									11 18										11 48
Northfleet	d		10 50									11 20										11 50
Gravesend 4	d	10 48	10a55				11 07					11a25				11 37					11 48	11a55
Higham	d						11 13									11 43						
Strood 4	d	10 58					11 18									11 48					11 58	
Maidstone West	d																					
Rochester 4	d	11 03					11 22									11 52					12 03	
Chatham 4	d	11 05					11 25									11 55					12 05	
Gillingham (Kent) 4	a	11 09					11 32									12 02					12 09	

Table 200

London - Dartford and Gillingham

Saturdays

28 July to 11 August

Network Diagram - see first Page of Table 200

		SE	SE	SE	SE	SE	SE	SE	SE	SE		SE	SE	SE	SE	SE	SE	SE	SE	SE		SE	SE	SE	SE
St Pancras Int'l	d																			12 18					
Stratford International	d																			12 28					
Ebbsfleet International	d																			12 44					
London Charing Cross	d	11 02			11 09					11 26		11 32			11 39							11 56	12 02		
London Waterloo (East)	d	11 05			11 12					11 29		11 35			11 42							11 59	12 05		
London Cannon Street	d		11 07	11 10			11 17	11 24	11 27				11 37	11 40			11 47	11 54	11 57					12 07	12 10
London Bridge	d	11 10	11 11	11 14	11 17		11 21	11 28	11 31	11 34		11 40	11 41	11 44	11 47		11 51	11 58	12 01			12 04	12 10	12 11	12 14
Deptford	d						11 27										11 57								
Greenwich	d		11 20				11 30		11 40				11 50				12 00		12 09					12 19	
Maze Hill	d																		12 13					12 23	
Westcombe Park	d						11 35										12 05								
London Victoria	d					11 09										11 39									
Denmark Hill	d					11 18										11 48									
Peckham Rye	d					11 21										11 51									
Nunhead	d					11 23										11 53									
New Cross	d			11 19				11 33						11 49				12 03							12 19
St Johns	d			11 21				11 35						11 51				12 05							12 21
Lewisham	d	11 19		11 24	11 27	11 32		11 38				11 49		11 54	11 57	12 02		12 08					12 19		12 24
Blackheath	d	11 23			11 31	11 36		11 42				11 53			12 01	12 06		12 12					12 23		
Kidbrooke	d					11 39		11 45								12 09		12 15							
Eltham	d	11 29				11 42		11 49				11 59				12 12		12 19					12 29		
Falconwood	d	11 31				11 44		11 51				12 01				12 14		12 21					12 31		
Welling	d	11 34				11 47		11 54				12 04				12 17		12 24					12 34		
Bexleyheath	d	11 36				11 49		11 56				12 06				12 19		12 26					12 36		
Barnehurst	d	11 39				11 52		12 02				12 09				12 22		12 32					12 39		
Hither Green	d			11 29						11 44				11 59								12 14			12 29
Lee	d			11 31						11 46				12 01								12 16			12 31
Mottingham	d			11 34						11 49				12 04								12 19			12 34
New Eltham	d			11 36						11 51				12 06								12 21			12 36
Sidcup	d			11 40						11 55				12 10								12 25			12 40
Albany Park	d			11 42						11 57				12 12								12 27			12 42
Bexley	d			11 44						11 59				12 14								12 29			12 44
Crayford	d			11 48						12 03				12 18								12 33			12 48
Charlton	d		11 26	12a12	11 35		11 39		11 47				11 56	12a42	12 05		12 09		12 17					12 27	13a12
Woolwich Dockyard	d																								
Woolwich Arsenal	d		11 33		11 41		11 45		11 53				12 03		12 11		12 15		12 23					12 32	
Plumstead	d		11 35				11 47		11 55				12 05				12 17		12 26					12 35	
Abbey Wood	d		11 38		11 45		11 50		11 58				12 08		12 15		12 20		12 29					12 38	
Belvedere	d		11 40				11 52		12 01				12 10				12 22		12 31					12 40	
Erith	d		11 43				11 55		12 03				12 13				12 25		12 34					12 43	
Slade Green	d		11a46				11a57	12a12	12 07				12a16				12a27	12a42	12 37					12a46	
Dartford	a	11 48			11 54	12 01			12 15	12 08		12 15			12 24	12 31			12 45			12 38	12 48		
	d				11 55					12 09					12 25							12 39			
Stone Crossing	d									12 13												12 43			
Greenhithe for Bluewater	d				12 00					12 15					12 30							12 45			
Swanscombe	d									12 18												12 48			
Northfleet	d									12 20												12 50			
Gravesend	d				12 07					12a25					12 37					12 48		12a55			
Higham	d				12 13										12 43										
Strood	d				12 18										12 48					12 58					
Maidstone West	d																								
Rochester	d				12 22										12 52					13 03					
Chatham	d				12 25										12 55					13 05					
Gillingham (Kent)	a				12 32										13 02					13 09					

Table 200

London - Dartford and Gillingham

Saturdays

28 July to 11 August

Network Diagram - see first Page of Table 200

		SE	SE	SE	SE	SE		SE	SE	SE	SE	SE	SE	SE	SE	SE		SE	SE	SE	SE	SE	SE	SE	SE
St Pancras Int'l	d																	13 18							
Stratford International	d																	13 28							
Ebbsfleet International	d																	13 43							
London Charing Cross	d	12 09						12 26	12 32			12 39							12 56	13 02			13 09		
London Waterloo (East)	d	12 12						12 29	12 35			12 42							12 59	13 05			13 12		
London Cannon Street	d			12 17	12 24	12 27				12 37	12 40			12 47	12 54	12 57					13 07	13 10			13 17
London Bridge	d	12 17		12 21	12 28	12 31		12 34	12 40	12 41	12 44	12 47		12 51	12 58	13 01			13 04	13 10	13 11	13 14	13 17		13 21
Deptford	d			12 27										12 57											13 27
Greenwich	d			12 30		12 39				12 49				13 00		13 09					13 19				13 30
Maze Hill	d			12 34		12 43				12 53				13 04		13 13					13 23				13 34
Westcombe Park	d			12 36										13 06											13 36
London Victoria	d		12 09										12 39											13 09	
Denmark Hill	d		12 18										12 48											13 18	
Peckham Rye	d		12 21										12 51											13 21	
Nunhead	d		12 23										12 53											13 23	
New Cross	d				12 33						12 49				13 03							13 19			
St Johns	d				12 35						12 51				13 05							13 21			
Lewisham	d	12 27	12 32		12 38				12 49		12 54	12 57	13 02		13 08					13 19		13 24	13 27	13 32	
Blackheath	d	12 31	12 36		12 42				12 53			13 01	13 06		13 12					13 23			13 31	13 36	
Kidbrooke	d		12 39		12 45								13 09		13 15									13 39	
Eltham	d		12 42		12 49				12 59				13 12		13 19					13 29				13 42	
Falconwood	d		12 44		12 51				13 01				13 14		13 21					13 31				13 44	
Welling	d		12 47		12 54				13 04				13 17		13 24					13 34				13 47	
Bexleyheath	d		12 49		12 56				13 06				13 19		13 26					13 36				13 49	
Barnehurst	d		12 52		13 02				13 09				13 22		13 32					13 39				13 52	
Hither Green	d							12 44			12 59								13 14			13 29			
Lee	d							12 46			13 01								13 16			13 31			
Mottingham	d							12 49			13 04								13 19			13 34			
New Eltham	d							12 51			13 06								13 21			13 36			
Sidcup	d							12 55			13 10								13 25			13 40			
Albany Park	d							12 57			13 12								13 27			13 42			
Bexley	d							12 59			13 14								13 29			13 44			
Crayford	d							13 03			13 18								13 33			13 48			
Charlton	d	12 35		12 39		12 47				12 57	13a42	13 05		13 09		13 17					13 27	14a12	13 35		13 39
Woolwich Dockyard	d																								
Woolwich Arsenal	d	12 41		12 44		12 53				13 02		13 11		13 14		13 23					13 32		13 41		13 44
Plumstead	d			12 46		12 56				13 05				13 16		13 26					13 35				13 46
Abbey Wood	d	12 45		12 49		12 59				13 08		13 15		13 19		13 29					13 38		13 45		13 49
Belvedere	d			12 52		13 01				13 10				13 22		13 31					13 40				13 52
Erith	d			12 54		13 04				13 13				13 24		13 34					13 43				13 54
Slade Green	d			12a57	13a12	13 07				13a16				13a27	13a42	13 37					13a46				13a57
Dartford	a	12 54	13 01			13 15		13 08	13 18			13 24	13 31			13 45			13 38	13 48			13 54	14 01	
	d	12 55						13 09				13 25							13 39				13 55		
Stone Crossing	d							13 13											13 43						
Greenhithe for Bluewater	d	13 00						13 15				13 30							13 45				14 00		
Swanscombe	d							13 18											13 48						
Northfleet	d							13 20											13 50						
Gravesend	d	13 07						13a25				13 37						13 48	13a55				14 07		
Higham	d	13 13										13 43											14 13		
Strood	d	13 18										13 48						13 58					14 18		
Maidstone West	d																								
Rochester	d	13 22										13 52						14 03					14 22		
Chatham	d	13 25										13 55						14 05					14 25		
Gillingham (Kent)	a	13 32										14 02						14 09					14 32		

Table 200

London - Dartford and Gillingham

Saturdays

28 July to 11 August

Network Diagram - see first Page of Table 200

		SE		SE	SE	SE	SE	SE	SE	SE	SE	SE		SE	SE	SE	SE	SE	SE	SE	SE	SE		SE	SE
St Pancras Int'l	d														14 18										
Stratford International	d														14 28										
Ebbsfleet International	d														14 43										
London Charing Cross	d				13 26	13 32			13 39							13 56	14 02			14 09					
London Waterloo (East)	d				13 29	13 35			13 42							13 59	14 05			14 12					
London Cannon Street	d	13 24		13 27			13 37	13 40			13 47	13 54		13 57				14 07	14 10			14 17		14 24	14 27
London Bridge	d	13 28		13 31	13 34	13 40	13 41	13 44	13 47		13 51	13 58		14 01		14 04	14 10	14 11	14 14	14 17		14 21		14 28	14 31
Deptford	d										13 57											14 27			
Greenwich	d			13 39			13 49				14 00			14 09				14 19				14 30			14 39
Maze Hill	d			13 43			13 53				14 04			14 13				14 23				14 34			14 43
Westcombe Park	d										14 06											14 36			
London Victoria	d									13 39											14 09				
Denmark Hill	d									13 48											14 18				
Peckham Rye	d									13 51											14 21				
Nunhead	d									13 53											14 23				
New Cross	d	13 33						13 49				14 03							14 19					14 33	
St Johns	d	13 35						13 51				14 05							14 21					14 35	
Lewisham	d	13 38				13 49		13 54	13 57	14 02		14 08					14 19		14 24	14 27	14 32			14 38	
Blackheath	d	13 42				13 53			14 01	14 06		14 12					14 23			14 31	14 36			14 42	
Kidbrooke	d	13 45								14 09		14 15									14 39			14 45	
Eltham	d	13 49				13 59				14 12		14 19					14 29				14 42			14 49	
Falconwood	d	13 51				14 01				14 14		14 21					14 31				14 44			14 51	
Welling	d	13 54				14 04				14 17		14 24					14 34				14 47			14 54	
Bexleyheath	d	13 56				14 06				14 19		14 26					14 36				14 49			14 56	
Barnehurst	d	14 02				14 09				14 22		14 32					14 39				14 52			15 02	
Hither Green	d				13 44			13 59								14 14			14 29						
Lee	d				13 46			14 01								14 16			14 31						
Mottingham	d				13 49			14 04								14 19			14 34						
New Eltham	d				13 51			14 06								14 21			14 36						
Sidcup	d				13 55			14 10								14 25			14 40						
Albany Park	d				13 57			14 12								14 27			14 42						
Bexley	d				13 59			14 14								14 29			14 44						
Crayford	d				14 03			14 18								14 33			14 48						
Charlton	d			13 47			13 57	14a42	14 05		14 09			14 17				14 27	15a12	14 35		14 39			14 47
Woolwich Dockyard	d																								
Woolwich Arsenal	d			13 53			14 02		14 11		14 14			14 23				14 32		14 41		14 44			14 53
Plumstead	d			13 56			14 05				14 16			14 26				14 35				14 46			14 56
Abbey Wood	d			13 59			14 08		14 15		14 19			14 29				14 38		14 45		14 49			14 59
Belvedere	d			14 01			14 10				14 22			14 31				14 40				14 52			15 01
Erith	d			14 04			14 13				14 24			14 34				14 43				14 54			15 04
Slade Green	d	14a12		14 07			14a16				14a27	14a42		14 37				14a46				14a57		15a12	15 07
Dartford	a			14 15	14 08	14 18			14 24	14 31				14 45		14 38	14 48			14 54	15 01				15 15
	d				14 09				14 25							14 39				14 55					
Stone Crossing	d				14 13											14 43									
Greenhithe for Bluewater	d				14 15				14 30							14 45				15 00					
Swanscombe	d				14 18											14 48									
Northfleet	d				14 20											14 50									
Gravesend	d				14a25				14 37						14 48	14a55				15 07					
Higham	d								14 43											15 13					
Strood	d								14 48						14 58					15 18					
Maidstone West	d																								
Rochester	d								14 52						15 03					15 22					
Chatham	d								14 55						15 05					15 25					
Gillingham (Kent)	a								15 02						15 09					15 32					

Table 200

London - Dartford and Gillingham

Saturdays

28 July to 11 August

Network Diagram - see first Page of Table 200

		SE	SE	SE	SE	SE	SE	SE		SE	SE	SE	SE	SE	SE	SE	SE	SE		SE	SE	SE	SE	SE	SE
St Pancras Int'l	d											15 18													
Stratford International	d											15 28													
Ebbsfleet International	d											15 43													
London Charing Cross	d	14 26	14 32			14 39							14 56	15 02			15 09						15 26	15 32	
London Waterloo (East)	d	14 29	14 35			14 42							14 59	15 05			15 12						15 29	15 35	
London Cannon Street	d			14 37	14 40			14 47		14 54	14 57				15 07	15 10				15 17	15 24	15 27			15 37
London Bridge	d	14 34	14 40	14 41	14 44	14 47		14 51		14 58	15 01		15 04	15 10	15 11	15 14	15 17			15 21	15 28	15 31	15 34	15 40	15 41
Deptford	d							14 57												15 27					
Greenwich	d			14 49				15 00			15 09				15 19					15 30		15 39			15 49
Maze Hill	d			14 53				15 04			15 13				15 23					15 34		15 43			15 53
Westcombe Park	d							15 06												15 36					
London Victoria	d						14 39											15 09							
Denmark Hill	d						14 48											15 18							
Peckham Rye	d						14 51											15 21							
Nunhead	d						14 53											15 23							
New Cross	d				14 49					15 03						15 19					15 33				
St Johns	d				14 51					15 05						15 21					15 35				
Lewisham	d		14 49		14 54	14 57	15 02			15 08				15 19		15 24	15 27	15 32			15 38			15 49	
Blackheath	d		14 53			15 01	15 06			15 12				15 23			15 31	15 36			15 42			15 53	
Kidbrooke	d						15 09			15 15								15 39			15 45				
Eltham	d		14 59				15 12			15 19				15 29				15 42			15 49			15 59	
Falconwood	d		15 01				15 14			15 21				15 31				15 44			15 51			16 01	
Welling	d		15 04				15 17			15 24				15 34				15 47			15 54			16 04	
Bexleyheath	d		15 06				15 19			15 26				15 36				15 49			15 56			16 06	
Barnehurst	d		15 09				15 22			15 32				15 39				15 52			16 02			16 09	
Hither Green	d	14 44			14 59								15 14			15 29							15 44		
Lee	d	14 46			15 01								15 16			15 31							15 46		
Mottingham	d	14 49			15 04								15 19			15 34							15 49		
New Eltham	d	14 51			15 06								15 21			15 36							15 51		
Sidcup	d	14 55			15 10								15 25			15 40							15 55		
Albany Park	d	14 57			15 12								15 27			15 42							15 57		
Bexley	d	14 59			15 14								15 29			15 44							15 59		
Crayford	d	15 03			15 18								15 33			15 48							16 03		
Charlton	d			14 57	15a42	15 05		15 09			15 17				15 27	16a12	15 35			15 39		15 47			15 57
Woolwich Dockyard	d																								
Woolwich Arsenal	d			15 02		15 11		15 14			15 23				15 32		15 41			15 44		15 53			16 02
Plumstead	d			15 05				15 16			15 26				15 35					15 46		15 56			16 05
Abbey Wood	d			15 08		15 15		15 19			15 29				15 38		15 45			15 49		15 59			16 08
Belvedere	d			15 10				15 22			15 31				15 40					15 52		16 01			16 10
Erith	d			15 13				15 24			15 34				15 43					15 54		16 04			16 13
Slade Green	d			15a16				15a27		15a42	15 37				15a46					15a57	16a12	16 07			16a16
Dartford	a	15 08	15 18			15 24	15 31				15 45		15 38	15 48			15 54	16 01				16 15	16 08	16 18	
	d	15 09				15 25							15 39				15 55						16 09		
Stone Crossing	d	15 13											15 43										16 13		
Greenhithe for Bluewater	d	15 15				15 30							15 45				16 00						16 15		
Swanscombe	d	15 18											15 48										16 18		
Northfleet	d	15 20											15 50										16 20		
Gravesend	d	15a25				15 37						15 48	15a55				16 07						16a25		
Higham	d					15 43											16 13								
Strood	d					15 48						15 58					16 18								
Maidstone West	d																								
Rochester	d					15 52						16 03					16 22								
Chatham	d					15 55						16 05					16 25								
Gillingham (Kent)	a					16 02						16 09					16 32								

Table 200

Saturdays

28 July to 11 August

London - Dartford and Gillingham

Network Diagram - see first Page of Table 200

		SE	SE	SE		SE	SE	SE	SE	SE	SE	SE	SE	SE		SE	SE	SE	SE	SE	SE	SE	SE	SE
St Pancras Int'l	d								16 18															
Stratford International	d								16 28															
Ebbsfleet International	d								16 44															
London Charing Cross	d		15 39							15 56	16 02			16 09						16 26	16 32			16 39
London Waterloo (East)	d		15 42							15 59	16 05			16 12						16 29	16 35			16 42
London Cannon Street	d	15 40				15 47	15 54	15 57				16 07	16 10				16 17	16 24	16 27			16 37	16 40	
London Bridge	d	15 44	15 47			15 51	15 58	16 01		16 04	16 10	16 11	16 14	16 17			16 21	16 28	16 31	16 34	16 40	16 41	16 44	16 47
Deptford	d					15 57											16 27							
Greenwich	d					16 00		16 09				16 19					16 30		16 39			16 49		
Maze Hill	d					16 04		16 13				16 23					16 34		16 43			16 53		
Westcombe Park	d					16 06											16 36							
London Victoria	d			15 39												16 09								
Denmark Hill	d			15 48												16 18								
Peckham Rye	d			15 51												16 21								
Nunhead	d			15 53												16 23								
New Cross	d	15 49					16 03						16 19					16 33					16 49	
St Johns	d	15 51					16 05						16 21					16 35					16 51	
Lewisham	d	15 54	15 57	16 02			16 08				16 19		16 24	16 27		16 32		16 38			16 49		16 54	16 57
Blackheath	d		16 01	16 06			16 12				16 23			16 31		16 36		16 42			16 53			17 01
Kidbrooke	d			16 09			16 15									16 39		16 45						
Eltham	d			16 12			16 19				16 29					16 42		16 49			16 59			
Falconwood	d			16 14			16 21				16 31					16 44		16 51			17 01			
Welling	d			16 17			16 24				16 34					16 47		16 54			17 04			
Bexleyheath	d			16 19			16 26				16 36					16 49		16 56			17 06			
Barnehurst	d			16 22			16 32				16 39					16 52		17 02			17 09			
Hither Green	d	15 59								16 14			16 29							16 44			16 59	
Lee	d	16 01								16 16			16 31							16 46			17 01	
Mottingham	d	16 04								16 19			16 34							16 49			17 04	
New Eltham	d	16 06								16 21			16 36							16 51			17 06	
Sidcup	d	16 10								16 25			16 40							16 55			17 10	
Albany Park	d	16 12								16 27			16 42							16 57			17 12	
Bexley	d	16 14								16 29			16 44							16 59			17 14	
Crayford	d	16 18								16 33			16 48							17 03			17 18	
Charlton	d	16a42	16 05			16 09		16 17				16 27	17a12	16 35			16 39		16 47			16 57	17a42	17 05
Woolwich Dockyard	d																							
Woolwich Arsenal	d		16 11			16 14		16 23				16 32		16 41			16 44		16 53			17 02		17 11
Plumstead	d					16 16		16 26				16 35					16 46		16 56			17 05		
Abbey Wood	d		16 15			16 19		16 29				16 38		16 45			16 49		16 59			17 08		17 15
Belvedere	d					16 22		16 31				16 40					16 52		17 01			17 10		
Erith	d					16 24		16 34				16 43					16 54		17 04			17 13		
Slade Green	d					16a27	16a42	16 37				16a46					16a57	17a12	17 07			17a16		
Dartford	a		16 24	16 31				16 45		16 38	16 48			16 54		17 01			17 15	17 08	17 18			17 24
	d		16 25							16 39				16 55						17 09				17 25
Stone Crossing	d									16 43										17 13				
Greenhithe for Bluewater	d		16 30							16 45				17 00						17 15				17 30
Swanscombe	d									16 48										17 18				
Northfleet	d									16 50										17 20				
Gravesend	d		16 37						16 48	16a55				17 07						17a25				17 37
Higham	d		16 43											17 13										17 43
Strood	d		16 48						16 58					17 18										17 48
Maidstone West	d																							
Rochester	d		16 52						17 03					17 22										17 52
Chatham	d		16 55						17 05					17 25										17 55
Gillingham (Kent)	a		17 02						17 09					17 32										18 02

Table 200

Saturdays

28 July to 11 August

London - Dartford and Gillingham

Network Diagram - see first Page of Table 200

		SE	SE	SE	SE	SE	SE	SE	SE	SE		SE	SE	SE	SE	SE	SE	SE	SE	SE		SE	SE	SE	SE
St Pancras Int'l	d					17 18																			
Stratford International	d					17 28																			
Ebbsfleet International	d					17 43																			
London Charing Cross	d						16 56	17 02				17 09					17 26	17 32				17 39			
London Waterloo (East)	d						16 59	17 05				17 12					17 29	17 35				17 42			
London Cannon Street	d		16 47	16 54	16 57				17 07	17 10				17 17	17 24	17 27			17 37	17 40				17 47	17 54
London Bridge	d		16 51	16 58	17 01		17 04	17 10	17 11	17 14		17 17		17 21	17 28	17 31	17 34	17 40	17 41	17 44		17 47		17 51	17 58
Deptford	d		16 57											17 27										17 57	
Greenwich	d		17 00		17 09				17 19					17 30		17 39			17 49					18 00	
Maze Hill	d		17 04		17 13				17 23					17 34		17 43			17 53					18 04	
Westcombe Park	d		17 06											17 36										18 06	
London Victoria	d	16 39											17 09										17 39		
Denmark Hill	d	16 48											17 18										17 48		
Peckham Rye	d	16 51											17 21										17 51		
Nunhead	d	16 53											17 23										17 53		
New Cross	d			17 03						17 19					17 33					17 49					18 03
St Johns	d			17 05						17 21					17 35					17 51					18 05
Lewisham	d	17 02		17 08				17 19		17 24		17 27	17 32		17 38			17 49		17 54		17 57	18 02		18 08
Blackheath	d	17 06		17 12				17 23				17 31	17 36		17 42			17 53				18 01	18 06		18 12
Kidbrooke	d	17 09		17 15									17 39		17 45								18 09		18 15
Eltham	d	17 12		17 19				17 29					17 42		17 49			17 59					18 12		18 19
Falconwood	d	17 14		17 21				17 31					17 44		17 51			18 01					18 14		18 21
Welling	d	17 17		17 24				17 34					17 47		17 54			18 04					18 17		18 24
Bexleyheath	d	17 19		17 26				17 36					17 49		17 56			18 06					18 19		18 26
Barnehurst	d	17 22		17 32				17 39					17 52		18 02			18 09					18 22		18a33
Hither Green	d						17 14			17 29							17 44			17 59					
Lee	d						17 16			17 31							17 46			18 01					
Mottingham	d						17 19			17 34							17 49			18 04					
New Eltham	d						17 21			17 36							17 51			18 06					
Sidcup	d						17 25			17 40							17 55			18 10					
Albany Park	d						17 27			17 42							17 57			18 12					
Bexley	d						17 29			17 44							17 59			18 14					
Crayford	d						17 33			17 48							18 03			18 18					
Charlton	d		17 09		17 17				17 27	18a12		17 35		17 39		17 47			17 57	18a42		18 05		18 09	
Woolwich Dockyard	d																								
Woolwich Arsenal	d		17 14		17 23				17 32			17 41		17 44		17 53			18 02			18 11		18 14	
Plumstead	d		17 16		17 26				17 35					17 46		17 56			18 05					18 16	
Abbey Wood	d		17 19		17 29				17 38			17 45		17 49		17 59			18 08			18 15		18 19	
Belvedere	d		17 22		17 31				17 40					17 52		18 01			18 10					18 22	
Erith	d		17 24		17 34				17 43					17 54		18 04			18 13					18 24	
Slade Green	d		17a27	17a42	17 37				17a46					17a57	18a12	18 07			18a16					18a27	
Dartford	a	17 31			17 45		17 38	17 48				17 54	18 01			18 15	18 08	18 18				18 24	18 31		
	d						17 39					17 55					18 09					18 25			
Stone Crossing	d						17 43										18 13								
Greenhithe for Bluewater	d						17 45					18 00					18 15					18 30			
Swanscombe	d						17 48										18 18								
Northfleet	d						17 50										18 20								
Gravesend	d					17 48	17a55					18 07					18a25					18 37			
Higham	d											18 13										18 43			
Strood	d					17 58						18 18										18 48			
Maidstone West	d																								
Rochester	d					18 03						18 22										18 52			
Chatham	d					18 05						18 25										18 55			
Gillingham (Kent)	a					18 09						18 32										19 02			

Saturdays

28 July to 11 August

London - Dartford and Gillingham

Network Diagram - see first Page of Table 200

		SE	SE	SE	SE	SE		SE	SE	SE	SE	SE	SE	SE	SE	SE		SE	SE	SE	SE	SE	SE	SE	SE
St Pancras Int'l ⊖	d		18 18																					19 18	
Stratford International ⊖	d		18 28																					19 28	
Ebbsfleet International	d		18 43																					19 43	
London Charing Cross ⊖	d			17 56	18 02				18 09					18 26	18 32				18 39						18 56
London Waterloo (East) ⊖	d			17 59	18 05				18 12					18 29	18 35				18 42						18 59
London Cannon Street ⊖	d	17 57				18 07		18 10			18 17	18 24	18 27			18 37		18 40			18 47	18 54	18 57		
London Bridge ⊖	d	18 01		18 04	18 10	18 11		18 14	18 17		18 21	18 28	18 31	18 34	18 40	18 41		18 44	18 47		18 51	18 58	19 01		19 04
Deptford	d										18 27										18 57				
Greenwich	d	18 09				18 19					18 30		18 39			18 49					19 00		19 09		
Maze Hill	d	18 13				18 23					18 34		18 43			18 53					19 04		19 13		
Westcombe Park	d										18 36										19 06				
London Victoria ⊖	d									18 09										18 39					
Denmark Hill	d									18 18										18 48					
Peckham Rye	d									18 21										18 51					
Nunhead	d									18 23										18 53					
New Cross ⊖	d							18 19				18 33						18 49				19 03			
St Johns	d							18 21				18 35						18 51				19 05			
Lewisham	d				18 19			18 24	18 27	18 32		18 38			18 49			18 54	18 57	19 02		19 08			
Blackheath	d				18 23				18 31	18 36		18 42			18 53				19 01	19 06		19 12			
Kidbrooke	d									18 39		18 45								19 09		19 15			
Eltham	d				18 29					18 42		18 49			18 59					19 12		19 19			
Falconwood	d				18 31					18 44		18 51			19 01					19 14		19 21			
Welling	d				18 34					18 47		18 54			19 04					19 17		19 24			
Bexleyheath	d				18 36					18 49		18 56			19 06					19 19		19 26			
Barnehurst	d				18 39					18 52		19a03			19 09					19 22		19a33			
Hither Green	d			18 14				18 29						18 44				18 59							19 14
Lee	d			18 16				18 31						18 46				19 01							19 16
Mottingham	d			18 19				18 34						18 49				19 04							19 19
New Eltham	d			18 21				18 36						18 51				19 06							19 21
Sidcup	d			18 25				18 40						18 55				19 10							19 25
Albany Park	d			18 27				18 42						18 57				19 12							19 27
Bexley	d			18 29				18 44						18 59				19 14							19 29
Crayford	d			18 33				18 48						19 03				19 18							19 33
Charlton	d	18 17				18 27		19a12	18 35		18 39		18 47			18 57		19a42	19 05		19 09		19 17		
Woolwich Dockyard	d																								
Woolwich Arsenal	d	18 23				18 32			18 41		18 44		18 53			19 02			19 11		19 14		19 23		
Plumstead	d	18 26				18 35					18 46		18 56			19 05					19 16		19 26		
Abbey Wood	d	18 29				18 38			18 45		18 49		18 59			19 08			19 15		19 19		19 29		
Belvedere	d	18 31				18 40					18 52		19 01			19 10					19 22		19 31		
Erith	d	18 34				18 43					18 54		19 04			19 13					19 24		19 34		
Slade Green	d	18 37				18a48					19a00		19 07			19a18					19a30		19 37		
Dartford	a	18 45		18 38	18 48				18 54	19 01			19 15	19 08	19 18				19 24	19 31			19 45		19 38
	d			18 39					18 55					19 09					19 25						19 39
Stone Crossing	d			18 43										19 13											19 43
Greenhithe for Bluewater	d			18 45					19 00					19 15					19 30						19 45
Swanscombe	d			18 48										19 18											19 48
Northfleet	d			18 50										19 20											19 50
Gravesend	d		18 48	18a55					19 07					19a25					19 37					19 48	19a55
Higham	d								19 13										19 43						
Strood	d		18 58						19 18										19 48					19 58	
Maidstone West	d																								
Rochester	d		19 03						19 22										19 52					20 03	
Chatham	d		19 05						19 25										19 55					20 05	
Gillingham (Kent)	a		19 09						19 32										20 02					20 09	

Table 200

Saturdays

28 July to 11 August

London - Dartford and Gillingham

Network Diagram - see first Page of Table 200

		SE		SE	SE	SE	SE	SE	SE	SE	SE	SE		SE	SE	SE	SE	SE	SE	SE	SE	SE		SE	SE
St Pancras Int'l ⊖	d															20 18									
Stratford International ⊖	d															20 28									
Ebbsfleet International	d															20 43									
London Charing Cross ⊖	d	19 02				19 09				19 26	19 32	19 39					19 52	19 56	20 02	20 09		20 22		20 26	20 32
London Waterloo (East) ⊖	d	19 05				19 12				19 29	19 35	19 42					19 55	19 59	20 05	20 12		20 25		20 29	20 35
London Cannon Street ⊖	d			19 07	19 10			19 24	19 27						19 46						20 16				
London Bridge ⊖	d	19 10		19 11	19 14	19 17		19 28	19 31	19 34	19 40	19 47			19 50		20 00	20 05	20 10	20 17	20 20	20 30		20 35	20 40
Deptford	d			19 17					19 37									20 11						20 41	
Greenwich	d			19 19					19 40						19 58			20 13			20 28			20 43	
Maze Hill	d			19 23					19 44						20 02			20 17			20 32			20 47	
Westcombe Park	d			19 25					19 46									20 19						20 49	
London Victoria ⊖	d						19 09							19 39											
Denmark Hill	d						19 18							19 48											
Peckham Rye	d						19 21							19 51											
Nunhead	d						19 23							19 53											
New Cross ⊖	d				19 19			19 33			19 45						20 05		20 15			20 35			20 45
St Johns	d				19 21			19 35																	
Lewisham	d	19 19			19 24	19 26	19 32	19 38			19 49	19 56		20 02			20 09		20 20	20 26		20 39			20 50
Blackheath	d	19 23				19 30	19 36	19 42			19 53	20 00		20 06					20 24	20 30					20 54
Kidbrooke	d						19 39	19 45						20 09					20 27						20 57
Eltham	d	19 29					19 42	19 49			19 59			20 12					20 30						21 00
Falconwood	d	19 31					19 44	19 51			20 01			20 14					20 32						21 02
Welling	d	19 34					19 47	19 54			20 04			20 17					20 35						21 05
Bexleyheath	d	19 36					19 49	19 56			20 06			20 19					20 37						21 07
Barnehurst	d	19 39					19 52	20a03			20 09			20 22					20 40						21 10
Hither Green	d				19 29					19 44							20 14					20 44			
Lee	d				19 31					19 46							20 16					20 46			
Mottingham	d				19 34					19 49							20 19					20 49			
New Eltham	d				19 36					19 51							20 21					20 51			
Sidcup	d				19 40					19 55							20 25					20 55			
Albany Park	d				19 42					19 57							20 27					20 57			
Bexley	d				19 44					19 59							20 29					20 59			
Crayford	d				19 48					20 03							20 33					21 03			
Charlton	d			19 27	20a12	19 36			19 49			20 06			20 09			20 22		20 36	20 39			20 52	
Woolwich Dockyard	d																								
Woolwich Arsenal	d			19 33		19 40			19 54			20 10			20 14			20 27		20 40	20 44			20 57	
Plumstead	d			19 35					19 56						20 16			20 29			20 46			20 59	
Abbey Wood	d			19 38		19 45			19 59			20 15			20 19			20 32		20 45	20 49			21 02	
Belvedere	d			19 40					20 02						20 22			20 34			20 52			21 04	
Erith	d			19 43					20 04						20 24			20 37			20 54			21 07	
Slade Green	d			19 46					20 07						20 27			20 39			20 57			21 09	
Dartford	a	19 48		19 55		19 54	20 01		20 15	20 08	20 18	20 24		20 31	20 34		20 38	20 47	20 49	20 54	21 04	21 08		21 17	21 19
	d					19 55				20 09		20 25					20 39			20 55		21 09			
Stone Crossing	d									20 13							20 43					21 13			
Greenhithe for Bluewater	d					20 00				20 15		20 30					20 45			21 00		21 15			
Swanscombe	d									20 18							20 48					21 18			
Northfleet	d									20 20							20 50					21 20			
Gravesend	d					20 07				20a25		20 37				20 48	20a58			21 07		21a28			
Higham	d					20 13						20 43								21 13					
Strood	d					20 18						20 48				20 58				21 18					
Maidstone West	d																								
Rochester	d					20 22						20 52				21 03				21 22					
Chatham	d					20 25						20 55				21 05				21 25					
Gillingham (Kent)	a					20 32						21 02				21 09				21 32					

London - Dartford and Gillingham

Saturdays

28 July to 11 August

Network Diagram - see first Page of Table 200

		SE	SE	SE	SE	SE	SE	SE	SE	SE	SE	SE
St Pancras Int'l	d			21 18								
Stratford International	d			21 28								
Ebbsfleet International	d			21 43								
London Charing Cross	d	20 39			20 52	20 56	21 02	21 09	21 22	21 26	21 32	21 39
London Waterloo (East)	d	20 42			20 55	20 59	21 05	21 12	21 25	21 29	21 35	21 42
London Cannon Street	d		20 46									
London Bridge	d	20 47	20 50		21 00	21 05	21 10	21 17	21 30	21 35	21 40	21 47
Deptford	d					21 11				21 41		
Greenwich	d		20 58			21 13				21 43		
Maze Hill	d		21 02			21 17				21 47		
Westcombe Park	d					21 19				21 49		
London Victoria	d											
Denmark Hill	d											
Peckham Rye	d											
Nunhead	d											
New Cross	d				21 05		21 15		21 35		21 45	
St Johns	d											
Lewisham	d	20 56			21 09		21 20	21 26	21 39		21 50	21 56
Blackheath	d	21 00					21 24	21 30			21 54	22 00
Kidbrooke	d						21 27				21 57	
Eltham	d						21 30				22 00	
Falconwood	d						21 32				22 02	
Welling	d						21 35				22 05	
Bexleyheath	d						21 37				22 07	
Barnehurst	d						21 40				22 10	
Hither Green	d				21 14				21 44			
Lee	d				21 16				21 46			
Mottingham	d				21 19				21 49			
New Eltham	d				21 21				21 51			
Sidcup	d				21 25				21 55			
Albany Park	d				21 27				21 57			
Bexley	d				21 29				21 59			
Crayford	d				21 33				22 03			
Charlton	d	21 06	21 09			21 22		21 36		21 52		22 06
Woolwich Dockyard	d											
Woolwich Arsenal	d	21 10	21 14			21 27		21 40		21 57		22 10
Plumstead	d		21 16			21 29				21 59		
Abbey Wood	d	21 15	21 19			21 32		21 45		22 02		22 15
Belvedere	d		21 22			21 34				22 04		
Erith	d		21 24			21 37				22 07		
Slade Green	d		21 27			21 39				22 09		
Dartford	a	21 24	21 34		21 38	21 47	21 49	21 54	22 08	22 17	22 19	22 24
	d	21 25			21 39			21 55	22 09			22 25
Stone Crossing	d				21 43				22 13			22 29
Greenhithe for Bluewater	d	21 30			21 45			22 00	22 15			22 31
Swanscombe	d				21 48				22 18			22 34
Northfleet	d				21 50				22 20			22 36
Gravesend	d	21 37		21 48	21a58			22 07	22a28			22 40
Higham	d	21 43						22 13				22 46
Strood	d	21 48		21 58				22 18				22 52
Maidstone West	d											
Rochester	d	21 52		22 03				22 22				22 56
Chatham	d	21 55		22 05				22 25				22 58
Gillingham (Kent)	a	22 02		22 09				22 32				23 06

		SE	SE	SE	SE	SE	SE	SE	SE	SE	SE	SE
St Pancras Int'l	d											
Stratford International	d											
Ebbsfleet International	d											
London Charing Cross	d	21 52	21 56	22 02	22 09	22 22	22 26	22 32	22 39	22 52	22 56	23 02
London Waterloo (East)	d	21 55	21 59	22 05	22 12	22 25	22 29	22 35	22 42	22 55	22 59	23 05
London Cannon Street	d											
London Bridge	d	22 00	22 05	22 10	22 17	22 30	22 35	22 40	22 47	23 00	23 05	23 10
Deptford	d		22 11				22 41				23 11	
Greenwich	d		22 13				22 43				23 13	
Maze Hill	d		22 17				22 47				23 17	
Westcombe Park	d		22 19				22 49				23 19	
London Victoria	d											
Denmark Hill	d											
Peckham Rye	d											
Nunhead	d											
New Cross	d	22 05		22 15		22 35		22 45		23 05		23 15
St Johns	d											
Lewisham	d	22 09		22 20	22 26	22 39		22 50	22 56	23 09		23 20
Blackheath	d			22 24	22 30			22 54	23 00			23 24
Kidbrooke	d			22 27				22 57				23 27
Eltham	d			22 30				23 00				23 30
Falconwood	d			22 32				23 02				23 32
Welling	d			22 35				23 05				23 35
Bexleyheath	d			22 37				23 07				23 37
Barnehurst	d			22 40				23 10				23 40
Hither Green	d	22 14				22 44				23 14		
Lee	d	22 16				22 46				23 16		
Mottingham	d	22 19				22 49				23 19		
New Eltham	d	22 21				22 51				23 21		
Sidcup	d	22 25				22 55				23 25		
Albany Park	d	22 27				22 57				23 27		
Bexley	d	22 29				22 59				23 29		
Crayford	d	22 33				23 03				23 33		
Charlton	d		22 22		22 36		22 52		23 06		23 22	
Woolwich Dockyard	d											
Woolwich Arsenal	d		22 27		22 40		22 57		23 10		23 27	
Plumstead	d		22 29				22 59				23 29	
Abbey Wood	d		22 32		22 45		23 02		23 15		23 32	
Belvedere	d		22 34				23 04				23 34	
Erith	d		22 37				23 07				23 37	
Slade Green	d		22 39				23 09				23 39	
Dartford	a	22 41	22 47	22 49	22 54	23 11	23 17	23 19	23 24	23 41	23 47	23 49
	d				22 55				23 25			
Stone Crossing	d				22 59				23 29			
Greenhithe for Bluewater	d				23 01				23 31			
Swanscombe	d				23 04				23 34			
Northfleet	d				23 06				23 36			
Gravesend	d				23 10				23 40			
Higham	d				23 16				23 46			
Strood	d				23 22				23 52			
Maidstone West	d											
Rochester	d				23 26				23 56			
Chatham	d				23 28				23 58			
Gillingham (Kent)	a				23 33				00 06			

London - Dartford and Gillingham

Saturdays

28 July to 11 August

Network Diagram - see first Page of Table 200

		SE	SE	SE	SE	SE	SE
St Pancras Int'l	d						
Stratford International	d						
Ebbsfleet International	d						
London Charing Cross	d	23 09	23 22	23 26	23 32	23 39	23 56
London Waterloo (East)	d	23 12	23 25	23 29	23 35	23 42	23 59
London Cannon Street	d						
London Bridge	d	23 17	23 30	23 35	23 40	23 47	00 05
Deptford	d			23 41			00 11
Greenwich	d			23 43			00 13
Maze Hill	d			23 47			00 17
Westcombe Park	d			23 49			00 19
London Victoria	d						
Denmark Hill	d						
Peckham Rye	d						
Nunhead	d						
New Cross	d		23 35		23 45		
St Johns	d						
Lewisham	d	23 26	23 39		23 50	23 56	
Blackheath	d	23 30			23 55	00 01	
Kidbrooke	d				23 58		
Eltham	d				00 01		
Falconwood	d				00 04		
Welling	d				00 06		
Bexleyheath	d				00 09		
Barnehurst	d				00 12		
Hither Green	d		23 44				
Lee	d		23 46				
Mottingham	d		23 49				
New Eltham	d		23 51				
Sidcup	d		23 55				
Albany Park	d		23 57				
Bexley	d		23 59				
Crayford	d		00 03				
Charlton	d	23 36		23 52		00 06	00 22
Woolwich Dockyard	d						
Woolwich Arsenal	d	23 40		23 57		00 11	00 27
Plumstead	d			23 59			00 29
Abbey Wood	d	23 45		00 02		00 15	00 32
Belvedere	d			00 04			00 34
Erith	d			00 07			00 37
Slade Green	d			00 09			00 39
Dartford	a	23 54	00 11	00 17	00 22	00 24	00 47
	d	23 55				00 25	
Stone Crossing	d	23 58				00 29	
Greenhithe for Bluewater	d	23 59				00 31	
Swanscombe	d	00 04				00 34	
Northfleet	d	00 06				00 36	
Gravesend	d	00 10				00 40	
Higham	d	00 16				00 46	
Strood	d	00 22				00 52	
Maidstone West	d						
Rochester	d	00 26				00 56	
Chatham	d	00 28				00 58	
Gillingham (Kent)	a	00 36				01 06	

Table 200

Saturdays

25 August to 8 September

London - Dartford and Gillingham

Network Diagram - see first Page of Table 200

Station		SE	SE A	SE B	SE	SE	SE	SE	SE A	SE B	SE	SE	SE	SE	SE	SE B	SE B	SE B	SE B	SE	SE	SE	SE
St Pancras Int'l	d		23p25	23p25					23p55	23p55													
Stratford International	d		23p32	23p33					00 02	00 03													
Ebbsfleet International	d		23p43	23p44					00 13	00 14													
London Charing Cross	d	22p39			23p09	23p22	23p26	23p32			23p39	23p56	00 02	00 10	00 18	00 32		00 44		04 52		05 22	05 26
London Waterloo (East)	d	22p42			23p12	23p25	23p29	23p35			23p42	23p59	00 05	00 13	00 21	00 35		00 47		04 55		05 25	05 29
London Cannon Street	d																00 41		00 56				
London Bridge	d	22p47			23p17	23p30	23p34	23p40			23p47	00 04	00 10	00 18	00 26	00 40	00 45	00 52	01 00	05 00		05 30	05 34
Deptford	d						23p40					00 10				00 46			01s06				05 40
Greenwich	d						23p42					00 12				00 49			01s08				05 42
Maze Hill	d						23p45					00 15				00 52			01s12				05 45
Westcombe Park	d						23p47					00 17				00 55			01s14				05 47
London Victoria	d																						
Denmark Hill	d																						
Peckham Rye	d																						
Nunhead	d																						
New Cross	d					23p35		23p45					00 15	00 23	00 31			00 57		05 05		05 35	
St Johns	d																						
Lewisham	d	22p56			23p26	23p39		23p49			23p56		00 19	00 27	00 35		00s52	01 01		05 09		05 39	
Blackheath	d	22p59			23p29			23p52			23p59		00 22		00 38		00s55						
Kidbrooke	d							23p55					00 25				00s59						
Eltham	d							23p58					00 28				01s02						
Falconwood	d							00 01					00 31				01s05						
Welling	d							00 03					00 33				01s08						
Bexleyheath	d							00 06					00 36				01s11						
Barnehurst	d							00 08					00 38				01s14						
Hither Green	d					23p44								00 32				01s05		05 14		05 44	
Lee	d					23p46								00 34				01s08		05 16		05 46	
Mottingham	d					23p49								00 37				01s11		05 19		05 49	
New Eltham	d					23p51								00 39				01s13		05 21		05 51	
Sidcup	d					23p55								00 43				01s16		05 25		05 55	
Albany Park	d					23p57								00 45				01s19		05 27		05 57	
Bexley	d					23p59								00 47				01s21		05 29		05 59	
Crayford	d					00 03								00 51				01s24		05 33		06 03	
Charlton	d	23p03			23p33		23p50				00 03	00 20			00 42	00 57			01s17				05 50
Woolwich Dockyard	d						23p53					00 23											05 53
Woolwich Arsenal	d	23p09			23p39		23p56				00 09	00 26			00 47	01 04			01s22				05 56
Plumstead	d						23p58					00 28			00 49	01s06			01s26				05 58
Abbey Wood	d	23p13			23p43		00 01				00 13	00 31			00 53	01s09			01s29				06 01
Belvedere	d						00 03					00 33			00 55	01s12			01s32				06 03
Erith	d						00 06					00 36			00 58	01s15			01s35				06 06
Slade Green	d						00 09					00 39			01 00	01s18			01s38				06 09
Dartford	a	23p24			23p54	00 08	00 14	00 16			00 24	00 44	00 46	00 56	01 05	01 23	01s21	01 30	01 44	05 38		06 08	06 14
	d	23p25			23p55						00 25				01 06					05 39	05 55	06 09	
Stone Crossing	d	23p29			23p58						00 29									05 43		06 13	
Greenhithe for Bluewater	d	23p31			23p59						00 31				01 10					05 45	06 00	06 15	
Swanscombe	d	23p34			00 04						00 34									05 48		06 18	
Northfleet	d	23p36			00 06						00 36									05 50		06 20	
Gravesend	d	23p40	23p48	23p48	00 10				00 18	00 18	00 40				01 17		01s31			05a55	06 07	06a25	
Higham	d	23p46			00 16						00 46				01 23		01s37				06 13		
Strood	d	23p52	23p58	23p58	00 22				00 28	00 28	00 52				01 29		01s42				06 18		
Maidstone West	d																						
Rochester	d	23p56	00 03	00 03	00 26				00 33	00 33	00 56				01 33		01s46				06 22		
Chatham	d	23p58	00 05	00 05	00 28				00 35	00 35	00 58				01 35		01s48				06 25		
Gillingham (Kent)	a	00 03	00 09	00 09	00 33				00 39	00 39	01 03				01 41		01 52				06 29		

A not from 1 September until 8 September

B not 25 August

Table 200

Saturdays

25 August to 8 September

London - Dartford and Gillingham

Network Diagram - see first Page of Table 200

Station		SE	SE	SE	SE	SE	SE	SE A	SE B	SE	SE	SE	SE	SE A	SE	SE	SE	SE	SE	SE	SE	SE	SE
St Pancras Int'l	d							06 54	06 55					07 24					07 52				
Stratford International	d							07 02	07 02					07 32					07 58				
Ebbsfleet International	d							07 13	07 13					07 46					08 13				
London Charing Cross	d	05 32	05 39	05 52	05 56	06 02	06 09			06 22	06 26	06 32	06 39		06 52	06 56	07 02	07 09		07 22	07 26	07 32	07 39
London Waterloo (East)	d	05 35	05 42	05 55	05 59	06 05	06 12			06 25	06 29	06 35	06 42		06 55	06 59	07 05	07 12		07 25	07 29	07 35	07 42
London Cannon Street	d																						
London Bridge	d	05 40	05 47	06 00	06 04	06 10	06 17			06 30	06 34	06 40	06 47		07 00	07 04	07 10	07 17		07 30	07 34	07 40	07 47
Deptford	d				06 10						06 40					07 10					07 40		
Greenwich	d				06 12						06 42					07 12					07 42		
Maze Hill	d				06 15						06 45					07 15					07 45		
Westcombe Park	d				06 17						06 47					07 17					07 47		
London Victoria	d																						
Denmark Hill	d																						
Peckham Rye	d																						
Nunhead	d																						
New Cross	d	05 45		06 05		06 15				06 35		06 45			07 05		07 15			07 35		07 45	
St Johns	d																						
Lewisham	d	05 49	05 56	06 09		06 19	06 26			06 39		06 49	06 56		07 09		07 19	07 26		07 39		07 49	07 56
Blackheath	d	05 52	05 59			06 22	06 29					06 52	06 59				07 22	07 29				07 52	07 59
Kidbrooke	d	05 55				06 25						06 55					07 25					07 55	
Eltham	d	05 58				06 28						06 58					07 28					07 58	
Falconwood	d	06 01				06 31						07 01					07 31					08 01	
Welling	d	06 03				06 33						07 03					07 33					08 03	
Bexleyheath	d	06 06				06 36						07 06					07 36					08 06	
Barnehurst	d	06 08				06 38						07 08					07 38					08 08	
Hither Green	d			06 14						06 44					07 14					07 44			
Lee	d			06 16						06 46					07 16					07 46			
Mottingham	d			06 19						06 49					07 19					07 49			
New Eltham	d			06 21						06 51					07 21					07 51			
Sidcup	d			06 25						06 55					07 25					07 55			
Albany Park	d			06 27						06 57					07 27					07 57			
Bexley	d			06 29						06 59					07 29					07 59			
Crayford	d			06 33						07 03					07 33					08 03			
Charlton	d		06 03		06 20		06 33				06 50		07 03			07 20		07 33			07 50		08 03
Woolwich Dockyard	d				06 23						06 53					07 23					07 53		
Woolwich Arsenal	d		06 09		06 26		06 39				06 56		07 09			07 26		07 39			07 56		08 09
Plumstead	d				06 28						06 58					07 28					07 58		
Abbey Wood	d		06 13		06 31		06 43				07 01		07 13			07 31		07 43			08 01		08 13
Belvedere	d				06 33						07 03					07 33					08 03		
Erith	d				06 36						07 06					07 36					08 06		
Slade Green	d				06 39						07 09					07 39					08 09		
Dartford	a	06 16	06 24	06 38	06 44	06 46	06 54			07 08	07 14	07 16	07 24		07 38	07 44	07 46	07 54		08 08	08 14	08 16	08 24
	d		06 25	06 39			06 55			07 09			07 25		07 39			07 55		08 09			08 25
Stone Crossing	d			06 43						07 13					07 43					08 13			
Greenhithe for Bluewater	d		06 30	06 45			07 00			07 15			07 30		07 45			08 00		08 15			08 30
Swanscombe	d			06 48						07 18					07 48					08 18			
Northfleet	d			06 50						07 20					07 50					08 20			
Gravesend	d		06 37	06a55			07 07	07 18	07 18	07a25			07 37	07 51	07a55			08 07	08 18	08a25			08 37
Higham	d		06 43				07 13						07 43					08 13					08 43
Strood	d		06 48				07 18	07 28	07 28				07 48	08 01				08 18	08 28				08 48
Maidstone West	d																						
Rochester	d		06 52				07 22	07 33	07 33				07 52	08 06				08 22	08 33				08 52
Chatham	d		06 55				07 25	07 35	07 35				07 55	08 08				08 25	08 35				08 55
Gillingham (Kent)	a		06 59				07 29	07 39	07 39				07 59	08 12				08 29	08 39				08 59

A not 25 August

B not from 1 September until 8 September

Table 200

Saturdays

London - Dartford and Gillingham

25 August to 8 September

Network Diagram - see first Page of Table 200

		SE	SE A	SE	SE	SE	SE	SE	SE	SE	SE	SE	SE	SE A	SE B	SE	SE	SE	SE	SE	SE	SE
St Pancras Int'l	d		08 21											08 51	08 50							
Stratford International	d		08 32											08 58	09 04							
Ebbsfleet International	d		08 43											09 13	09 15							
London Charing Cross	d			07 52	07 56	08 02			08 09							08 26	08 32			08 39		
London Waterloo (East)	d			07 55	07 59	08 05			08 12							08 29	08 35			08 42		
London Cannon Street	d						08 07	08 10			08 17	08 24	08 27					08 37	08 40			08 47
London Bridge	d			08 00	08 04	08 10	08 11	08 14	08 17		08 21	08 28	08 31			08 34	08 40	08 41	08 44	08 47		08 51
Deptford	d				08 10		08 17				08 27		08 37					08 47				08 57
Greenwich	d				08 12		08 19				08 29		08 39					08 49				08 59
Maze Hill	d				08 15		08 22				08 32		08 42					08 52				09 02
Westcombe Park	d				08 17		08 24				08 34		08 44					08 54				09 04
London Victoria	d	07 39								08 09											08 39	
Denmark Hill	d	07 48								08 18											08 48	
Peckham Rye	d	07 51								08 21											08 51	
Nunhead	d	07 53								08 23											08 53	
New Cross	d			08 05		08 15		08 19				08 33							08 49			
St Johns	d							08 21				08 35							08 51			
Lewisham	d	08 02		08 09		08 19		08 24	08 26	08 32		08 38					08 49		08 54	08 56	09 02	
Blackheath	d	08 04				08 22			08 29	08 34		08 41					08 52			08 59	09 04	
Kidbrooke	d	08 07				08 25				08 37		08 44					08 55				09 07	
Eltham	d	08 11				08 28				08 41		08 47					08 58				09 11	
Falconwood	d	08 13				08 31				08 43		08 50					09 01				09 13	
Welling	d	08 16				08 33				08 46		08 52					09 03				09 16	
Bexleyheath	d	08 18				08 36				08 48		08 55					09 06				09 18	
Barnehurst	d	08 21				08 38				08 51		09 02					09 08				09 21	
Hither Green	d			08 14				08 29								08 44			08 59			
Lee	d			08 16				08 31								08 46			09 01			
Mottingham	d			08 19				08 34								08 49			09 04			
New Eltham	d			08 21				08 36								08 51			09 06			
Sidcup	d			08 25				08 40								08 55			09 10			
Albany Park	d			08 27				08 42								08 57			09 12			
Bexley	d			08 29				08 44								08 59			09 14			
Crayford	d			08 33				08 48								09 03			09 18			
Charlton	d				08 20		08 27	09a15	08 33		08 37		08 47					08 57	09a45	09 03		09 07
Woolwich Dockyard	d				08 23		08 30				08 40		08 50					09 00				09 10
Woolwich Arsenal	d				08 26		08 33		08 39		08 43		08 53					09 03		09 09		09 13
Plumstead	d				08 28		08 35				08 45		08 55					09 05				09 15
Abbey Wood	d				08 31		08 38		08 43		08 48		08 58					09 08		09 13		09 18
Belvedere	d				08 33		08 40				08 50		09 00					09 10				09 20
Erith	d				08 36		08 43				08 53		09 03					09 13				09 23
Slade Green	d				08 39		08a46				08a55	09a12	09 07					09a16				09a25
Dartford	a	08 29		08 38	08 44	08 46			08 54	08 58			09 12			09 08	09 15			09 24	09 28	
	d			08 39					08 55							09 09				09 25		
Stone Crossing	d			08 43												09 13						
Greenhithe for Bluewater	d			08 45					09 00							09 15				09 30		
Swanscombe	d			08 48												09 18						
Northfleet	d			08 50												09 20						
Gravesend	d		08 48	08a55					09 07					09 18	09 20	09a25				09 37		
Higham	d								09 13											09 43		
Strood	d		08 58						09 18					09 28	09 30					09 48		
Maidstone West	d																					
Rochester	d		09 03						09 22					09 33	09 34					09 52		
Chatham	d		09 05						09 25					09 35	09 37					09 55		
Gillingham (Kent)	a		09 09						09 29					09 39	09 41					09 59		

A not 25 August

B not from 1 September until 8 September

Table 200

Saturdays

London - Dartford and Gillingham

25 August to 8 September

Network Diagram - see first Page of Table 200

		SE	SE	SE A	SE B	SE	SE	SE	SE	SE	SE	SE	SE	SE	SE B	SE A	SE	SE	SE	SE	SE	SE	SE
St Pancras Int'l	d			09 25	09 25										09 54	09 55							
Stratford International	d			09 32	09 33										10 02	10 02							
Ebbsfleet International	d			09 43	09 44										10 13	10 13							
London Charing Cross	d					08 56	09 02			09 09							09 26	09 32			09 39		
London Waterloo (East)	d					08 59	09 05			09 12							09 29	09 35			09 42		
London Cannon Street	d	08 54	08 57					09 07	09 10			09 17	09 24	09 27					09 37	09 40			09 47
London Bridge	d	08 58	09 01			09 04	09 10	09 11	09 14	09 17		09 21	09 28	09 31			09 34	09 40	09 41	09 44	09 47		09 51
Deptford	d		09 07					09 17				09 27		09 37					09 47				09 57
Greenwich	d		09 09					09 19				09 29		09 39					09 49				09 59
Maze Hill	d		09 12					09 22				09 32		09 42					09 52				10 02
Westcombe Park	d		09 14					09 24				09 34		09 44					09 54				10 04
London Victoria	d										09 09											09 39	
Denmark Hill	d										09 18											09 48	
Peckham Rye	d										09 21											09 51	
Nunhead	d										09 23											09 53	
New Cross	d	09 03							09 19				09 33							09 49			
St Johns	d	09 05							09 21				09 35							09 51			
Lewisham	d	09 08					09 19		09 24	09 26	09 32		09 38					09 49		09 54	09 56	10 02	
Blackheath	d	09 11					09 22			09 29	09 34		09 41					09 52			09 59	10 04	
Kidbrooke	d	09 14					09 25				09 37		09 44					09 55				10 07	
Eltham	d	09 17					09 28				09 41		09 47					09 58				10 11	
Falconwood	d	09 20					09 31				09 43		09 50					10 01				10 13	
Welling	d	09 22					09 33				09 46		09 52					10 03				10 16	
Bexleyheath	d	09 25					09 36				09 48		09 55					10 06				10 18	
Barnehurst	d	09 32					09 38				09 51		10 02					10 08				10 21	
Hither Green	d					09 14			09 29								09 44			09 59			
Lee	d					09 16			09 31								09 46			10 01			
Mottingham	d					09 19			09 34								09 49			10 04			
New Eltham	d					09 21			09 36								09 51			10 06			
Sidcup	d					09 25			09 40								09 55			10 10			
Albany Park	d					09 27			09 42								09 57			10 12			
Bexley	d					09 29			09 44								09 59			10 14			
Crayford	d					09 33			09 48								10 03			10 18			
Charlton	d		09 17					09 27	10a15	09 33		09 37		09 47					09 57	10a45	10 03		10 07
Woolwich Dockyard	d		09 20					09 30				09 40		09 50					10 00				10 10
Woolwich Arsenal	d		09 23					09 33		09 39		09 43		09 53					10 03		10 09		10 13
Plumstead	d		09 25					09 35				09 45		09 55					10 05				10 15
Abbey Wood	d		09 28					09 38		09 43		09 48		09 58					10 08		10 13		10 18
Belvedere	d		09 30					09 40				09 50		10 00					10 10				10 20
Erith	d		09 33					09 43				09 53		10 03					10 13				10 23
Slade Green	d	09a42	09 37					09a46				09a55	10a12	10 07					10a16				10a25
Dartford	a		09 42			09 38	09 45			09 54	09 58			10 12			10 08	10 15			10 24	10 28	
	d					09 39				09 55							10 09				10 25		
Stone Crossing	d					09 43											10 13						
Greenhithe for Bluewater	d					09 45				10 00							10 15				10 30		
Swanscombe	d					09 48											10 18						
Northfleet	d					09 50											10 20						
Gravesend	d			09 48	09 48	09a55				10 07					10 18	10 18	10a25				10 37		
Higham	d									10 13											10 43		
Strood	d			09 58	09 58					10 18					10 28	10 28					10 48		
Maidstone West	d																						
Rochester	d			10 03	10 03					10 22					10 33	10 33					10 52		
Chatham	d			10 05	10 05					10 25					10 35	10 35					10 55		
Gillingham (Kent)	a			10 09	10 09					10 29					10 39	10 39					10 59		

A not from 1 September until 8 September

B not 25 August

Table 200

Saturdays

25 August to 8 September

London - Dartford and Gillingham

Network Diagram - see first Page of Table 200

		SE	SE	SE A		SE B	SE	SE	SE	SE	SE	SE	SE	SE		SE	SE B	SE A	SE	SE	SE	SE	SE	SE
St Pancras Int'l	d			10 28		10 28											10 51	10 52						
Stratford International	d			10 35		10 36											10 58	10 58						
Ebbsfleet International	d			10 46		10 47											11 13	11 13						
London Charing Cross	d						09 56	10 02			10 09								10 26	10 32			10 39	
London Waterloo (East)	d						09 59	10 05			10 12								10 29	10 35			10 42	
London Cannon Street	d	09 54	09 57						10 07	10 10			10 17	10 24		10 27					10 37	10 40		
London Bridge	d	09 58	10 01				10 04	10 10	10 11	10 14	10 17		10 21	10 28		10 31			10 34	10 40	10 41	10 44	10 47	
Deptford	d		10 07						10 17				10 27			10 37					10 47			
Greenwich	d		10 09						10 19				10 29			10 39					10 49			
Maze Hill	d		10 12						10 22				10 32			10 42					10 52			
Westcombe Park	d		10 14						10 24				10 34			10 44					10 54			
London Victoria	d											10 09												10 39
Denmark Hill	d											10 18												10 48
Peckham Rye	d											10 21												10 51
Nunhead	d											10 23												10 53
New Cross	d	10 03								10 19				10 33								10 49		
St Johns	d	10 05								10 21				10 35								10 51		
Lewisham	d	10 08						10 19		10 24	10 26	10 32		10 38						10 49		10 54	10 56	11 02
Blackheath	d	10 11						10 22			10 29	10 34		10 41						10 52			10 59	11 04
Kidbrooke	d	10 14						10 25				10 37		10 44						10 55				11 07
Eltham	d	10 17						10 28				10 41		10 47						10 58				11 11
Falconwood	d	10 20						10 31				10 43		10 50						11 01				11 13
Welling	d	10 22						10 33				10 46		10 52						11 03				11 16
Bexleyheath	d	10 25						10 36				10 48		10 55						11 06				11 18
Barnehurst	d	10 32						10 38				10 51		11 02						11 08				11 21
Hither Green	d						10 14			10 29									10 44			10 59		
Lee	d						10 16			10 31									10 46			11 01		
Mottingham	d						10 19			10 34									10 49			11 04		
New Eltham	d						10 21			10 36									10 51			11 06		
Sidcup	d						10 25			10 40									10 55			11 10		
Albany Park	d						10 27			10 42									10 57			11 12		
Bexley	d						10 29			10 44									10 59			11 14		
Crayford	d						10 33			10 48									11 03			11 18		
Charlton	d		10 17						10 27	11a15	10 33		10 37			10 47					10 57	11a45	11 03	
Woolwich Dockyard	d		10 20						10 30				10 40			10 50					11 00			
Woolwich Arsenal	d		10 23						10 33		10 39		10 43			10 53					11 03		11 09	
Plumstead	d		10 25						10 35				10 45			10 55					11 05			
Abbey Wood	d		10 28						10 38		10 43		10 48			10 58					11 08		11 13	
Belvedere	d		10 30						10 40				10 50			11 00					11 10			
Erith	d		10 33						10 43				10 53			11 03					11 13			
Slade Green	d	10a42	10 37						10a46				10a55	11a12		11 07					11a16			
Dartford	a		10 42				10 38	10 45			10 54	10 58				11 12			11 08	11 15			11 24	11 28
	d						10 39				10 55								11 09				11 25	
Stone Crossing	d						10 43												11 13					
Greenhithe for Bluewater	d						10 45				11 00								11 15				11 30	
Swanscombe	d						10 48												11 18					
Northfleet	d						10 50												11 20					
Gravesend	d			10 51		10 51	10a55				11 07						11 18	11 18	11a25				11 37	
Higham	d										11 13												11 43	
Strood	d			11 01		11 01					11 18						11 28	11 28					11 48	
Maidstone West	d																							
Rochester	d			11 06		11 06					11 22						11 33	11 33					11 52	
Chatham	d			11 08		11 08					11 25						11 35	11 35					11 55	
Gillingham (Kent)	a			11 12		11 12					11 29						11 39	11 39					11 59	

A not from 1 September until 8 September

B not 25 August

Table 200

Saturdays

25 August to 8 September

London - Dartford and Gillingham

Network Diagram - see first Page of Table 200

		SE	SE	SE	SE	SE	SE	SE	SE	SE		SE	SE	SE	SE	SE A	SE B	SE	SE	SE		SE	SE	SE	SE
St Pancras Int'l	d				11 28											11 55	11 55								
Stratford International	d				11 35											12 02	12 03								
Ebbsfleet International	d				11 46											12 13	12 14								
London Charing Cross	d					10 56	11 02			11 09								11 26	11 32				11 39		
London Waterloo (East)	d					10 59	11 05			11 12								11 29	11 35				11 42		
London Cannon Street	d	10 47	10 54	10 57				11 07	11 10				11 17	11 24	11 27					11 37		11 40			11 47
London Bridge	d	10 51	10 58	11 01		11 04	11 10	11 11	11 14	11 17			11 21	11 28	11 31			11 34	11 40	11 41		11 44	11 47		11 51
Deptford	d	10 57		11 07				11 17					11 27		11 37					11 47					11 57
Greenwich	d	10 59		11 09				11 19					11 29		11 39					11 49					11 59
Maze Hill	d	11 02		11 12				11 22					11 32		11 42					11 52					12 02
Westcombe Park	d	11 04		11 14				11 24					11 34		11 44					11 54					12 04
London Victoria	d											11 09												11 39	
Denmark Hill	d											11 18												11 48	
Peckham Rye	d											11 21												11 51	
Nunhead	d											11 23												11 53	
New Cross	d		11 03						11 19					11 33								11 49			
St Johns	d		11 05						11 21					11 35								11 51			
Lewisham	d		11 08				11 19		11 24	11 26		11 32		11 38					11 49			11 54	11 56	12 02	
Blackheath	d		11 11				11 22			11 29		11 34		11 41					11 52				11 59	12 04	
Kidbrooke	d		11 14				11 25					11 37		11 44					11 55					12 07	
Eltham	d		11 17				11 28					11 41		11 47					11 58					12 11	
Falconwood	d		11 20				11 31					11 43		11 50					12 01					12 13	
Welling	d		11 22				11 33					11 46		11 52					12 03					12 16	
Bexleyheath	d		11 25				11 36					11 48		11 55					12 06					12 18	
Barnehurst	d		11 32				11 38					11 51		12 02					12 08					12 21	
Hither Green	d					11 14			11 29									11 44				11 59			
Lee	d					11 16			11 31									11 46				12 01			
Mottingham	d					11 19			11 34									11 49				12 04			
New Eltham	d					11 21			11 36									11 51				12 06			
Sidcup	d					11 25			11 40									11 55				12 10			
Albany Park	d					11 27			11 42									11 57				12 12			
Bexley	d					11 29			11 44									11 59				12 14			
Crayford	d					11 33			11 48									12 03				12 18			
Charlton	d	11 07		11 17				11 27	12a15	11 33			11 37		11 47					11 57		12a45	12 03		12 07
Woolwich Dockyard	d	11 10		11 20				11 30					11 40		11 50					12 00					12 10
Woolwich Arsenal	d	11 13		11 23				11 33		11 39			11 43		11 53					12 03			12 09		12 13
Plumstead	d	11 15		11 25				11 35					11 45		11 55					12 05					12 15
Abbey Wood	d	11 18		11 28				11 38		11 43			11 48		11 58					12 08			12 13		12 18
Belvedere	d	11 20		11 30				11 40					11 50		12 00					12 10					12 20
Erith	d	11 23		11 33				11 43					11 53		12 03					12 13					12 23
Slade Green	d	11a25	11a42	11 37				11a46					11a55	12a12	12 07					12a16					12a25
Dartford	a			11 42		11 38	11 45			11 54		11 58			12 12			12 08	12 15				12 24	12 28	
	d					11 39				11 55								12 09					12 25		
Stone Crossing	d					11 43												12 13							
Greenhithe for Bluewater	d					11 45				12 00								12 15					12 30		
Swanscombe	d					11 48												12 18							
Northfleet	d					11 50												12 20							
Gravesend	d				11 51	11a55				12 07						12 18	12 18	12a25					12 37		
Higham	d									12 13													12 43		
Strood	d				12 01					12 18						12 28	12 28						12 48		
Maidstone West	d																								
Rochester	d				12 06					12 22						12 33	12 33						12 52		
Chatham	d				12 08					12 25						12 35	12 35						12 55		
Gillingham (Kent)	a				12 12					12 29						12 39	12 39						12 59		

A not from 1 September until 8 September

B not 25 August

Table 200

London - Dartford and Gillingham

Saturdays

25 August to 8 September

Network Diagram - see first Page of Table 200

		SE	SE	SE A	SE B	SE		SE	SE	SE	SE	SE	SE	SE	SE	SE		SE	SE	SE	SE	SE	SE	SE	SE
St Pancras Int'l	d			12 28	12 28											12 55									
Stratford International	d			12 35	12 36											13 06									
Ebbsfleet International	d			12 46	12 47											13 17									
London Charing Cross	d					11 56		12 02			12 09							12 26	12 32			12 39			
London Waterloo (East)	d					11 59		12 05			12 12							12 29	12 35			12 42			
London Cannon Street	d	11 54	11 57						12 07	12 10			12 17	12 24	12 27					12 37	12 40			12 47	12 54
London Bridge	d	11 58	12 01			12 04		12 10	12 11	12 14	12 17		12 21	12 28	12 31			12 34	12 40	12 41	12 44	12 47		12 51	12 58
Deptford	d		12 07						12 17				12 27		12 37					12 47				12 57	
Greenwich	d		12 09						12 19				12 29		12 39					12 49				12 59	
Maze Hill	d		12 12						12 22				12 32		12 42					12 52				13 02	
Westcombe Park	d		12 14						12 24				12 34		12 44					12 54				13 04	
London Victoria	d											12 09											12 39		
Denmark Hill	d											12 18											12 48		
Peckham Rye	d											12 21											12 51		
Nunhead	d											12 23											12 53		
New Cross	d	12 03								12 19				12 33							12 49				13 03
St Johns	d	12 05								12 21				12 35							12 51				13 05
Lewisham	d	12 08						12 19		12 24	12 26	12 32		12 38					12 49		12 54	12 56	13 02		13 08
Blackheath	d	12 11						12 22			12 29	12 34		12 41					12 52			12 59	13 04		13 11
Kidbrooke	d	12 14						12 25				12 37		12 44					12 55				13 07		13 14
Eltham	d	12 17						12 28				12 41		12 47					12 58				13 11		13 17
Falconwood	d	12 20						12 31				12 43		12 50					13 01				13 13		13 20
Welling	d	12 22						12 33				12 46		12 52					13 03				13 16		13 22
Bexleyheath	d	12 25						12 36				12 48		12 55					13 06				13 18		13 25
Barnehurst	d	12 32						12 38				12 51		13 02					13 08				13 21		13 32
Hither Green	d					12 14				12 29								12 44			12 59				
Lee	d					12 16				12 31								12 46			13 01				
Mottingham	d					12 19				12 34								12 49			13 04				
New Eltham	d					12 21				12 36								12 51			13 06				
Sidcup	d					12 25				12 40								12 55			13 10				
Albany Park	d					12 27				12 42								12 57			13 12				
Bexley	d					12 29				12 44								12 59			13 14				
Crayford	d					12 33				12 48								13 03			13 18				
Charlton	d		12 17						12 27	13a15	12 33		12 37		12 47					12 57	13a45	13 03		13 07	
Woolwich Dockyard	d		12 20						12 30				12 40		12 50					13 00				13 10	
Woolwich Arsenal	d		12 23						12 33		12 39		12 43		12 53					13 03		13 09		13 13	
Plumstead	d		12 25						12 35				12 45		12 55					13 05				13 15	
Abbey Wood	d		12 28						12 38		12 43		12 48		12 58					13 08		13 13		13 18	
Belvedere	d		12 30						12 40				12 50		13 00					13 10				13 20	
Erith	d		12 33						12 43				12 53		13 03					13 13				13 23	
Slade Green	d	12a42	12 37						12a46				12a55	13a12	13 07					13a16				13a25	13a42
Dartford	a		12 42			12 38		12 45			12 54	12 58			13 12			13 08	13 15			13 24	13 28		
	d					12 39					12 55							13 09				13 25			
Stone Crossing	d					12 43												13 13							
Greenhithe for Bluewater	d					12 45					13 00							13 15				13 30			
Swanscombe	d					12 48												13 18							
Northfleet	d					12 50												13 20							
Gravesend	d			12 51	12 51	12a55					13 07					13 22		13a25				13 37			
Higham	d										13 13											13 43			
Strood	d			13 01	13 01						13 18					13 32						13 48			
Maidstone West	d																								
Rochester	d			13 06	13 06						13 22					13 37						13 52			
Chatham	d			13 08	13 08						13 25					13 39						13 55			
Gillingham (Kent)	a			13 12	13 12						13 29					13 43						13 59			

A not from 1 September until 8 September

B not 25 August

Table 200

London - Dartford and Gillingham

Saturdays

25 August to 8 September

Network Diagram - see first Page of Table 200

		SE		SE A	SE B	SE	SE	SE	SE	SE	SE	SE		SE	SE	SE A	SE B	SE	SE	SE	SE	SE		SE	SE
St Pancras Int'l	d			13 25	13 25											13 55	13 55								
Stratford International	d			13 32	13 33											14 02	14 03								
Ebbsfleet International	d			13 43	13 44											14 13	14 14								
London Charing Cross	d					12 56	13 02			13 09								13 26	13 32			13 39			
London Waterloo (East)	d					12 59	13 05			13 12								13 29	13 35			13 42			
London Cannon Street	d	12 57						13 07	13 10			13 17		13 24	13 27					13 37	13 40				13 47
London Bridge	d	13 01				13 04	13 10	13 11	13 14	13 17		13 21		13 28	13 31			13 34	13 40	13 41	13 44	13 47			13 51
Deptford	d	13 07						13 17				13 27			13 37					13 47					13 57
Greenwich	d	13 09						13 19				13 29			13 39					13 49					13 59
Maze Hill	d	13 12						13 22				13 32			13 42					13 52					14 02
Westcombe Park	d	13 14						13 24				13 34			13 44					13 54					14 04
London Victoria	d										13 09													13 39	
Denmark Hill	d										13 18													13 48	
Peckham Rye	d										13 21													13 51	
Nunhead	d										13 23													13 53	
New Cross	d								13 19					13 33							13 49				
St Johns	d								13 21					13 35							13 51				
Lewisham	d						13 19		13 24	13 26	13 32			13 38					13 49		13 54	13 56		14 02	
Blackheath	d						13 22			13 29	13 34			13 41					13 52			13 59		14 04	
Kidbrooke	d						13 25				13 37			13 44					13 55					14 07	
Eltham	d						13 28				13 41			13 47					13 58					14 11	
Falconwood	d						13 31				13 43			13 50					14 01					14 13	
Welling	d						13 33				13 46			13 52					14 03					14 16	
Bexleyheath	d						13 36				13 48			13 55					14 06					14 18	
Barnehurst	d						13 38				13 51			14 02					14 08					14 21	
Hither Green	d					13 14			13 29									13 44			13 59				
Lee	d					13 16			13 31									13 46			14 01				
Mottingham	d					13 19			13 34									13 49			14 04				
New Eltham	d					13 21			13 36									13 51			14 06				
Sidcup	d					13 25			13 40									13 55			14 10				
Albany Park	d					13 27			13 42									13 57			14 12				
Bexley	d					13 29			13 44									13 59			14 14				
Crayford	d					13 33			13 48									14 03			14 18				
Charlton	d	13 17						13 27	14a15	13 33		13 37			13 47					13 57	14a45	14 03			14 07
Woolwich Dockyard	d	13 20						13 30				13 40			13 50					14 00					14 10
Woolwich Arsenal	d	13 23						13 33		13 39		13 43			13 53					14 03		14 09			14 13
Plumstead	d	13 25						13 35				13 45			13 55					14 05					14 15
Abbey Wood	d	13 28						13 38		13 43		13 48			13 58					14 08		14 13			14 18
Belvedere	d	13 30						13 40				13 50			14 00					14 10					14 20
Erith	d	13 33						13 43				13 53			14 03					14 13					14 23
Slade Green	d	13 37						13a46				13a55		14a12	14 07					14a16					14a25
Dartford	a	13 42				13 38	13 45			13 54	13 58				14 12			14 08	14 15			14 24		14 28	
	d					13 39				13 55								14 09				14 25			
Stone Crossing	d					13 43												14 13							
Greenhithe for Bluewater	d					13 45				14 00								14 15				14 30			
Swanscombe	d					13 48												14 18							
Northfleet	d					13 50												14 20							
Gravesend	d			13 48	13 48	13a55				14 07						14 18	14 18	14a25				14 37			
Higham	d									14 13												14 43			
Strood	d			13 58	13 58					14 18						14 28	14 28					14 48			
Maidstone West	d																								
Rochester	d			14 03	14 03					14 22						14 33	14 33					14 52			
Chatham	d			14 05	14 05					14 25						14 35	14 35					14 55			
Gillingham (Kent)	a			14 09	14 09					14 29						14 39	14 39					14 59			

A not from 1 September until 8 September

B not 25 August

Table 200

Saturdays

25 August to 8 September

London - Dartford and Gillingham

Network Diagram - see first Page of Table 200

Station		SE	SE	SE A	SE B	SE	SE	SE	SE	SE	SE	SE	SE	SE	SE A	SE B	SE	SE	SE	SE	SE	SE	SE
St Pancras Int'l ⊖	d			14 25	14 25										14 55	14 55							
Stratford International ⊖	d			14 32	14 33										15 02	15 03							
Ebbsfleet International	d			14 43	14 44										15 13	15 14							
London Charing Cross ⊖	d					13 56	14 02			14 09							14 26	14 32			14 39		
London Waterloo (East) ⊖	d					13 59	14 05			14 12							14 29	14 35			14 42		
London Cannon Street ⊖	d	13 54	13 57					14 07	14 10			14 17	14 24	14 27					14 37	14 40			14 47
London Bridge ⊖	d	13 58	14 01			14 04	14 10	14 11	14 14	14 17		14 21	14 28	14 31			14 34	14 40	14 41	14 44	14 47		14 51
Deptford	d		14 07					14 17				14 27		14 37					14 47				14 57
Greenwich	d		14 09					14 19				14 29		14 39					14 49				14 59
Maze Hill	d		14 12					14 22				14 32		14 42					14 52				15 02
Westcombe Park	d		14 14					14 24				14 34		14 44					14 54				15 04
London Victoria ⊖	d										14 09											14 39	
Denmark Hill	d										14 18											14 48	
Peckham Rye	d										14 21											14 51	
Nunhead	d										14 23											14 53	
New Cross ⊖	d	14 03							14 19				14 33							14 49			
St Johns	d	14 05							14 21				14 35							14 51			
Lewisham	d	14 08					14 19		14 24	14 26	14 32		14 38					14 49		14 54	14 56	15 02	
Blackheath	d	14 11					14 22			14 29	14 34		14 41					14 52			14 59	15 04	
Kidbrooke	d	14 14					14 25				14 37		14 44					14 55				15 07	
Eltham	d	14 17					14 28				14 41		14 47					14 58				15 11	
Falconwood	d	14 20					14 31				14 43		14 50					15 01				15 13	
Welling	d	14 22					14 33				14 46		14 52					15 03				15 16	
Bexleyheath	d	14 25					14 36				14 48		14 55					15 06				15 18	
Barnehurst	d	14 32					14 38				14 51		15 02					15 08				15 21	
Hither Green	d					14 14			14 29								14 44			14 59			
Lee	d					14 16			14 31								14 46			15 01			
Mottingham	d					14 19			14 34								14 49			15 04			
New Eltham	d					14 21			14 36								14 51			15 06			
Sidcup	d					14 25			14 40								14 55			15 10			
Albany Park	d					14 27			14 42								14 57			15 12			
Bexley	d					14 29			14 44								14 59			15 14			
Crayford	d					14 33			14 48								15 03			15 18			
Charlton	d		14 17					14 27	15a15	14 33		14 37		14 47					14 57	15a45	15 03		15 07
Woolwich Dockyard	d		14 20					14 30				14 40		14 50					15 00				15 10
Woolwich Arsenal	d		14 23					14 33		14 39		14 43		14 53					15 03		15 09		15 13
Plumstead	d		14 25					14 35				14 45		14 55					15 05				15 15
Abbey Wood	d		14 28					14 38		14 43		14 48		14 58					15 08		15 13		15 18
Belvedere	d		14 30					14 40				14 50		15 00					15 10				15 20
Erith	d		14 33					14 43				14 53		15 03					15 13				15 23
Slade Green	d	14a42	14 37					14a46				14a55	15a12	15 07					15a16				15a25
Dartford	a		14 42			14 38	14 45			14 54	14 58			15 12			15 08	15 15			15 24	15 28	
	d					14 39				14 55							15 09				15 25		
Stone Crossing	d					14 43											15 13						
Greenhithe for Bluewater	d					14 45				15 00							15 15				15 30		
Swanscombe	d					14 48											15 18						
Northfleet	d					14 50											15 20						
Gravesend	d			14 48	14 48	14a55				15 07					15 18	15 18	15a25				15 37		
Higham	d									15 13											15 43		
Strood	d			14 58	14 58					15 18					15 28	15 28					15 48		
Maidstone West	d																						
Rochester	d			15 03	15 03					15 22					15 33	15 33					15 52		
Chatham	d			15 05	15 05					15 25					15 35	15 35					15 55		
Gillingham (Kent)	a			15 09	15 09					15 29					15 39	15 39					15 59		

A not from 1 September until 8 September

B not 25 August

Table 200

Saturdays

25 August to 8 September

London - Dartford and Gillingham

Network Diagram - see first Page of Table 200

Station		SE	SE	SE A	SE B	SE	SE	SE	SE	SE	SE	SE	SE	SE	SE A	SE B	SE	SE	SE	SE	SE	SE
St Pancras Int'l ⊖	d			15 25	15 25										15 55	15 55						
Stratford International ⊖	d			15 32	15 33										16 02	16 03						
Ebbsfleet International	d			15 43	15 44										16 13	16 14						
London Charing Cross ⊖	d					14 56	15 02			15 09							15 26	15 32			15 39	
London Waterloo (East) ⊖	d					14 59	15 05			15 12							15 29	15 35			15 42	
London Cannon Street ⊖	d	14 54	14 57					15 07	15 10			15 17	15 24	15 27					15 37	15 40		
London Bridge ⊖	d	14 58	15 01			15 04	15 10	15 11	15 14	15 17		15 21	15 28	15 31			15 34	15 40	15 41	15 44	15 47	
Deptford	d		15 07					15 17				15 27		15 37					15 47			
Greenwich	d		15 09					15 19				15 29		15 39					15 49			
Maze Hill	d		15 12					15 22				15 32		15 42					15 52			
Westcombe Park	d		15 14					15 24				15 34		15 44					15 54			
London Victoria ⊖	d										15 09											15 39
Denmark Hill	d										15 18											15 48
Peckham Rye	d										15 21											15 51
Nunhead	d										15 23											15 53
New Cross ⊖	d	15 03							15 19				15 33							15 49		
St Johns	d	15 05							15 21				15 35							15 51		
Lewisham	d	15 08					15 19		15 24	15 26	15 32		15 38					15 49		15 54	15 56	16 02
Blackheath	d	15 11					15 22			15 29	15 34		15 41					15 52			15 59	16 04
Kidbrooke	d	15 14					15 25				15 37		15 44					15 55				16 07
Eltham	d	15 17					15 28				15 41		15 47					15 58				16 11
Falconwood	d	15 20					15 31				15 43		15 50					16 01				16 13
Welling	d	15 22					15 33				15 46		15 52					16 03				16 16
Bexleyheath	d	15 25					15 36				15 48		15 55					16 06				16 18
Barnehurst	d	15 32					15 38				15 51		16 02					16 08				16 21
Hither Green	d					15 14			15 29								15 44			15 59		
Lee	d					15 16			15 31								15 46			16 01		
Mottingham	d					15 19			15 34								15 49			16 04		
New Eltham	d					15 21			15 36								15 51			16 06		
Sidcup	d					15 25			15 40								15 55			16 10		
Albany Park	d					15 27			15 42								15 57			16 12		
Bexley	d					15 29			15 44								15 59			16 14		
Crayford	d					15 33			15 48								16 03			16 18		
Charlton	d		15 17					15 27	16a15	15 33		15 37		15 47					15 57	16a45	16 03	
Woolwich Dockyard	d		15 20					15 30				15 40		15 50					16 00			
Woolwich Arsenal	d		15 23					15 33		15 39		15 43		15 53					16 03		16 09	
Plumstead	d		15 25					15 35				15 45		15 55					16 05			
Abbey Wood	d		15 28					15 38		15 43		15 48		15 58					16 08		16 13	
Belvedere	d		15 30					15 40				15 50		16 00					16 10			
Erith	d		15 33					15 43				15 53		16 03					16 13			
Slade Green	d	15a42	15 37					15a46				15a55	16a12	16 07					16a16			
Dartford	a		15 42			15 38	15 45			15 54	15 58			16 12			16 08	16 15			16 24	16 28
	d					15 39				15 55							16 09				16 25	
Stone Crossing	d					15 43											16 13					
Greenhithe for Bluewater	d					15 45				16 00							16 15				16 30	
Swanscombe	d					15 48											16 18					
Northfleet	d					15 50											16 20					
Gravesend	d			15 48	15 48	15a55				16 07					16 18	16 18	16a25				16 37	
Higham	d									16 13											16 43	
Strood	d			15 58	15 58					16 18					16 28	16 28					16 48	
Maidstone West	d																					
Rochester	d			16 03	16 03					16 22					16 33	16 33					16 52	
Chatham	d			16 05	16 05					16 25					16 35	16 35					16 55	
Gillingham (Kent)	a			16 09	16 09					16 29					16 39	16 39					16 59	

A not from 1 September until 8 September

B not 25 August

Table 200

London - Dartford and Gillingham

Saturdays

25 August to 8 September

Network Diagram - see first Page of Table 200

		SE	SE	SE	SE A	SE B	SE	SE	SE	SE	SE	SE	SE	SE	SE	SE B	SE A	SE	SE	SE	SE	SE	SE
St Pancras Int'l	d				16 25	16 28										16 55	16 55						
Stratford International	d				16 33	16 35										17 02	17 03						
Ebbsfleet International	d				16 44	16 46										17 13	17 14						
London Charing Cross	d						15 56	16 02			16 09							16 26	16 32			16 39	
London Waterloo (East)	d						15 59	16 05			16 12							16 29	16 35			16 42	
London Cannon Street	d	15 47	15 54	15 57					16 07	16 10			16 17	16 24	16 27					16 37	16 40		
London Bridge	d	15 51	15 58	16 01			16 04	16 10	16 11	16 14	16 17		16 21	16 28	16 31			16 34	16 40	16 41	16 44	16 47	
Deptford	d	15 57		16 07					16 17				16 27		16 37					16 47			
Greenwich	d	15 59		16 09					16 19				16 29		16 39					16 49			
Maze Hill	d	16 02		16 12					16 22				16 32		16 42					16 52			
Westcombe Park	d	16 04		16 14					16 24				16 34		16 44					16 54			
London Victoria	d											16 09											16 39
Denmark Hill	d											16 18											16 48
Peckham Rye	d											16 21											16 51
Nunhead	d											16 23											16 53
New Cross	d		16 03							16 19				16 33							16 49		
St Johns	d		16 05							16 21				16 35							16 51		
Lewisham	d		16 08					16 19		16 24	16 26	16 32		16 38					16 49		16 54	16 56	17 02
Blackheath	d		16 11					16 22			16 29	16 34		16 41					16 52			16 59	17 04
Kidbrooke	d		16 14					16 25				16 37		16 44					16 55				17 07
Eltham	d		16 17					16 28				16 41		16 47					16 58				17 11
Falconwood	d		16 20					16 31				16 43		16 50					17 01				17 13
Welling	d		16 22					16 33				16 46		16 52					17 03				17 16
Bexleyheath	d		16 25					16 36				16 48		16 55					17 06				17 18
Barnehurst	d		16 32					16 38				16 51		17 02					17 08				17 21
Hither Green	d						16 14			16 29								16 44			16 59		
Lee	d						16 16			16 31								16 46			17 01		
Mottingham	d						16 19			16 34								16 49			17 04		
New Eltham	d						16 21			16 36								16 51			17 06		
Sidcup	d						16 25			16 40								16 55			17 10		
Albany Park	d						16 27			16 42								16 57			17 12		
Bexley	d						16 29			16 44								16 59			17 14		
Crayford	d						16 33			16 48								17 03			17 18		
Charlton	d	16 07		16 17					16 27	17a15	16 33		16 37		16 47					16 57	17a45	17 03	
Woolwich Dockyard	d	16 10		16 20					16 30				16 40		16 50					17 00			
Woolwich Arsenal	d	16 13		16 23					16 33		16 39		16 43		16 53					17 03		17 09	
Plumstead	d	16 15		16 25					16 35				16 45		16 55					17 05			
Abbey Wood	d	16 18		16 28					16 38		16 43		16 48		16 58					17 08		17 13	
Belvedere	d	16 20		16 30					16 40				16 50		17 00					17 10			
Erith	d	16 23		16 33					16 43				16 53		17 03					17 13			
Slade Green	d	16a25	16a42	16 37					16a46				16a55	17a12	17 07					17a16			
Dartford	a			16 42			16 38	16 45			16 54	16 58			17 12			17 08	17 15			17 24	17 28
	d						16 39				16 55							17 09				17 25	
Stone Crossing	d						16 43											17 13					
Greenhithe for Bluewater	d						16 45				17 00							17 15				17 30	
Swanscombe	d						16 48											17 18					
Northfleet	d						16 50											17 20					
Gravesend	d				16 48	16 51	16a55				17 07					17 18	17 18	17a25				17 37	
Higham	d										17 13											17 43	
Strood	d				16 58	17 01					17 18					17 28	17 28					17 48	
Maidstone West	d																						
Rochester	d				17 03	17 06					17 22					17 33	17 33					17 52	
Chatham	d				17 05	17 08					17 25					17 35	17 35					17 55	
Gillingham (Kent)	a				17 09	17 12					17 29					17 39	17 39					17 59	

A not 25 August

B not from 1 September until 8 September

Table 200

London - Dartford and Gillingham

Saturdays

25 August to 8 September

Network Diagram - see first Page of Table 200

		SE	SE	SE	SE A	SE B	SE	SE	SE	SE	SE	SE	SE	SE	SE	SE A	SE B	SE	SE	SE	SE	SE	SE
St Pancras Int'l	d				17 25	17 25										17 55	17 55						
Stratford International	d				17 32	17 33										18 02	18 03						
Ebbsfleet International	d				17 43	17 44										18 13	18 14						
London Charing Cross	d						16 56	17 02			17 09							17 26	17 32			17 39	
London Waterloo (East)	d						16 59	17 05			17 12							17 29	17 35			17 42	
London Cannon Street	d	16 47	16 54	16 57					17 07	17 10			17 17	17 24	17 27					17 37	17 40		
London Bridge	d	16 51	16 58	17 01			17 04	17 10	17 11	17 14	17 17		17 21	17 28	17 31			17 34	17 40	17 41	17 44	17 47	
Deptford	d	16 57		17 07					17 17				17 27		17 37					17 47			
Greenwich	d	16 59		17 09					17 19				17 29		17 39					17 49			
Maze Hill	d	17 02		17 12					17 22				17 32		17 42					17 52			
Westcombe Park	d	17 04		17 14					17 24				17 34		17 44					17 54			
London Victoria	d											17 09											17 39
Denmark Hill	d											17 18											17 48
Peckham Rye	d											17 21											17 51
Nunhead	d											17 23											17 53
New Cross	d		17 03							17 19				17 33							17 49		
St Johns	d		17 05							17 21				17 35							17 51		
Lewisham	d		17 08					17 19		17 24	17 26	17 32		17 38					17 49		17 54	17 56	18 02
Blackheath	d		17 11					17 22			17 29	17 34		17 41					17 52			17 59	18 04
Kidbrooke	d		17 14					17 25				17 37		17 44					17 55				18 07
Eltham	d		17 17					17 28				17 41		17 47					17 58				18 11
Falconwood	d		17 20					17 31				17 43		17 50					18 01				18 13
Welling	d		17 22					17 33				17 46		17 52					18 03				18 16
Bexleyheath	d		17 25					17 36				17 48		17 55					18 06				18 18
Barnehurst	d		17 32					17 38				17 51		18 02					18 08				18 21
Hither Green	d						17 14			17 29								17 44			17 59		
Lee	d						17 16			17 31								17 46			18 01		
Mottingham	d						17 19			17 34								17 49			18 04		
New Eltham	d						17 21			17 36								17 51			18 06		
Sidcup	d						17 25			17 40								17 55			18 10		
Albany Park	d						17 27			17 42								17 57			18 12		
Bexley	d						17 29			17 44								17 59			18 14		
Crayford	d						17 33			17 48								18 03			18 18		
Charlton	d	17 07		17 17					17 27	18a15	17 33		17 37		17 47					17 57	18a45	18 03	
Woolwich Dockyard	d	17 10		17 20					17 30				17 40		17 50					18 00			
Woolwich Arsenal	d	17 13		17 23					17 33		17 39		17 43		17 53					18 03		18 09	
Plumstead	d	17 15		17 25					17 35				17 45		17 55					18 05			
Abbey Wood	d	17 18		17 28					17 38		17 43		17 48		17 58					18 08		18 13	
Belvedere	d	17 20		17 30					17 40				17 50		18 00					18 10			
Erith	d	17 23		17 33					17 43				17 53		18 03					18 13			
Slade Green	d	17a25	17a42	17 37					17a46				17a55	18a12	18 07					18a16			
Dartford	a			17 42			17 38	17 45			17 54	17 58			18 12			18 08	18 15			18 24	18 28
	d						17 39				17 55							18 09				18 25	
Stone Crossing	d						17 43											18 13					
Greenhithe for Bluewater	d						17 45				18 00							18 15				18 30	
Swanscombe	d						17 48											18 18					
Northfleet	d						17 50											18 20					
Gravesend	d				17 48	17 48	17a55				18 07					18 18	18 18	18a25				18 37	
Higham	d										18 13											18 43	
Strood	d				17 58	17 58					18 18					18 28	18 28					18 48	
Maidstone West	d																						
Rochester	d				18 03	18 03					18 22					18 33	18 33					18 52	
Chatham	d				18 05	18 05					18 25					18 35	18 35					18 55	
Gillingham (Kent)	a				18 09	18 09					18 29					18 39	18 39					18 59	

A not from 1 September until 8 September

B not 25 August

Table 200

Saturdays

25 August to 8 September

London - Dartford and Gillingham

Network Diagram - see first Page of Table 200

Station		SE		SE	SE	SE A	SE B	SE	SE	SE	SE	SE	
St Pancras Int'l	d					18 25	18 25						
Stratford International	d					18 32	18 33						
Ebbsfleet International	d					18 43	18 44						
London Charing Cross	d							17 56	18 02			18 09	
London Waterloo (East)	d							17 59	18 05			18 12	
London Cannon Street	d	17 47		17 54	17 57					18 07	18 10		
London Bridge	d	17 51		17 58	18 01			18 04	18 10	18 11	18 14	18 17	
Deptford	d	17 57			18 07					18 17			
Greenwich	d	17 59			18 09					18 19			
Maze Hill	d	18 02			18 12					18 22			
Westcombe Park	d	18 04			18 14					18 24			
London Victoria	d												
Denmark Hill	d												
Peckham Rye	d												
Nunhead	d												
New Cross	d			18 03							18 19		
St Johns	d			18 05							18 21		
Lewisham	d			18 08					18 19		18 24	18 26	
Blackheath	d			18 11					18 22			18 29	
Kidbrooke	d			18 14					18 25				
Eltham	d			18 17					18 28				
Falconwood	d			18 20					18 31				
Welling	d			18 22					18 33				
Bexleyheath	d			18 25					18 36				
Barnehurst	d			18a28					18 38				
Hither Green	d							18 14			18 29		
Lee	d							18 16			18 31		
Mottingham	d							18 19			18 34		
New Eltham	d							18 21			18 36		
Sidcup	d							18 25			18 40		
Albany Park	d							18 27			18 42		
Bexley	d							18 29			18 44		
Crayford	d							18 33			18 48		
Charlton	d	18 07			18 17					18 27	19a15	18 33	
Woolwich Dockyard	d	18 10			18 20					18 30			
Woolwich Arsenal	d	18 13			18 23					18 33		18 39	
Plumstead	d	18 15			18 25					18 35			
Abbey Wood	d	18 18			18 28					18 38		18 43	
Belvedere	d	18 20			18 30					18 40			
Erith	d	18 23			18 33					18 43			
Slade Green	d	18a25			18 37					18a45			
Dartford	a				18 42			18 38	18 45			18 54	
	d							18 39				18 55	
Stone Crossing	d							18 43					
Greenhithe for Bluewater	d							18 45				19 00	
Swanscombe	d							18 48					
Northfleet	d							18 50					
Gravesend	d					18 48	18 48	18a55				19 07	
Higham	d											19 13	
Strood	d					18 58	18 58					19 18	
Maidstone West	d												
Rochester	d					19 03	19 03					19 22	
Chatham	d					19 05	19 05					19 25	
Gillingham (Kent)	a					19 09	19 09					19 29	

Station		SE	SE	SE	SE	SE A	SE B	SE	SE	SE		SE	SE
St Pancras Int'l	d					18 55	18 55						
Stratford International	d					19 02	19 03						
Ebbsfleet International	d					19 13	19 14						
London Charing Cross	d							18 26	18 32				18 39
London Waterloo (East)	d							18 29	18 35				18 42
London Cannon Street	d		18 17	18 24	18 27					18 37		18 40	
London Bridge	d		18 21	18 28	18 31			18 34	18 40	18 41		18 44	18 47
Deptford	d		18 27		18 37					18 47			
Greenwich	d		18 29		18 39					18 49			
Maze Hill	d		18 32		18 42					18 52			
Westcombe Park	d		18 34		18 44					18 54			
London Victoria	d	18 09											
Denmark Hill	d	18 18											
Peckham Rye	d	18 21											
Nunhead	d	18 23											
New Cross	d			18 33								18 49	
St Johns	d			18 35								18 51	
Lewisham	d	18 32		18 38					18 49			18 54	18 56
Blackheath	d	18 34		18 41					18 52				18 59
Kidbrooke	d	18 37		18 44					18 55				
Eltham	d	18 41		18 47					18 58				
Falconwood	d	18 43		18 50					19 01				
Welling	d	18 46		18 52					19 03				
Bexleyheath	d	18 48		18 55					19 06				
Barnehurst	d	18 51		18a58					19 08				
Hither Green	d							18 44				18 59	
Lee	d							18 46				19 01	
Mottingham	d							18 49				19 04	
New Eltham	d							18 51				19 06	
Sidcup	d							18 55				19 10	
Albany Park	d							18 57				19 12	
Bexley	d							18 59				19 14	
Crayford	d							19 03				19 18	
Charlton	d		18 37		18 47					18 57		19a45	19 03
Woolwich Dockyard	d		18 40		18 50					19 00			
Woolwich Arsenal	d		18 43		18 53					19 03			19 09
Plumstead	d		18 45		18 55					19 05			
Abbey Wood	d		18 48		18 58					19 08			19 13
Belvedere	d		18 50		19 00					19 10			
Erith	d		18 53		19 03					19 13			
Slade Green	d		18a56		19 07					19a15			
Dartford	a	18 58			19 12			19 08	19 15				19 24
	d							19 09					19 25
Stone Crossing	d							19 13					
Greenhithe for Bluewater	d							19 15					19 30
Swanscombe	d							19 18					
Northfleet	d							19 20					
Gravesend	d					19 18	19 18	19a25					19 37
Higham	d												19 43
Strood	d					19 28	19 28						19 48
Maidstone West	d												
Rochester	d					19 33	19 33						19 52
Chatham	d					19 35	19 35						19 55
Gillingham (Kent)	a					19 39	19 39						19 59

A not from 1 September until 8 September

B not 25 August

Table 200

Saturdays

25 August to 8 September

London - Dartford and Gillingham

Network Diagram - see first Page of Table 200

Station		SE	SE	SE	SE	SE A	SE B	SE		SE	SE	SE	SE
St Pancras Int'l	d					19 25	19 25						
Stratford International	d					19 32	19 33						
Ebbsfleet International	d					19 43	19 44						
London Charing Cross	d							18 56		19 02			19 09
London Waterloo (East)	d							18 59		19 05			19 12
London Cannon Street	d		18 47	18 54	18 57						19 07	19 10	
London Bridge	d		18 51	18 58	19 01			19 04		19 10	19 11	19 14	19 17
Deptford	d		18 57		19 07						19 17		
Greenwich	d		18 59		19 09						19 19		
Maze Hill	d		19 02		19 12						19 22		
Westcombe Park	d		19 04		19 14						19 24		
London Victoria	d	18 39											
Denmark Hill	d	18 48											
Peckham Rye	d	18 51											
Nunhead	d	18 53											
New Cross	d			19 03								19 19	
St Johns	d			19 05								19 21	
Lewisham	d	19 02		19 08						19 19		19 24	19 26
Blackheath	d	19 04		19 11						19 22			19 29
Kidbrooke	d	19 07		19 14						19 25			
Eltham	d	19 11		19 17						19 28			
Falconwood	d	19 13		19 20						19 31			
Welling	d	19 16		19 22						19 33			
Bexleyheath	d	19 18		19 25						19 36			
Barnehurst	d	19 21		19a28						19 38			
Hither Green	d							19 14				19 29	
Lee	d							19 16				19 31	
Mottingham	d							19 19				19 34	
New Eltham	d							19 21				19 36	
Sidcup	d							19 25				19 40	
Albany Park	d							19 27				19 42	
Bexley	d							19 29				19 44	
Crayford	d							19 33				19 48	
Charlton	d		19 07		19 17						19 27	20a15	19 33
Woolwich Dockyard	d		19 10		19 20						19 30		
Woolwich Arsenal	d		19 13		19 23						19 33		19 39
Plumstead	d		19 15		19 25						19 35		
Abbey Wood	d		19 18		19 28						19 38		19 43
Belvedere	d		19 20		19 30						19 40		
Erith	d		19 23		19 33						19 43		
Slade Green	d		19a26		19 37						19 46		
Dartford	a	19 28			19 42			19 38		19 45	19 52		19 54
	d							19 39					19 55
Stone Crossing	d							19 43					
Greenhithe for Bluewater	d							19 45					20 00
Swanscombe	d							19 48					
Northfleet	d							19 50					
Gravesend	d					19 48	19 48	19a55					20 07
Higham	d												20 13
Strood	d					19 58	19 58						20 18
Maidstone West	d												
Rochester	d					20 03	20 03						20 22
Chatham	d					20 05	20 05						20 25
Gillingham (Kent)	a					20 09	20 09						20 29

Station		SE	SE	SE	SE A	SE B		SE	SE	SE	SE	SE	SE A
St Pancras Int'l	d				19 55	19 55							20 25
Stratford International	d				20 02	20 03							20 32
Ebbsfleet International	d				20 13	20 14							20 43
London Charing Cross	d							19 26	19 32	19 39			
London Waterloo (East)	d							19 29	19 35	19 42			
London Cannon Street	d		19 24	19 27									
London Bridge	d		19 28	19 31				19 34	19 40	19 47		19 50	
Deptford	d			19 37								19 56	
Greenwich	d			19 39								19 58	
Maze Hill	d			19 42								20 01	
Westcombe Park	d			19 44								20 03	
London Victoria	d	19 09									19 39		
Denmark Hill	d	19 18									19 48		
Peckham Rye	d	19 21									19 51		
Nunhead	d	19 23									19 53		
New Cross	d		19 33						19 45				
St Johns	d		19 35										
Lewisham	d	19 32	19 38						19 49	19 56	20 02		
Blackheath	d	19 34	19 41						19 52	19 59	20 04		
Kidbrooke	d	19 37	19 44						19 55		20 07		
Eltham	d	19 41	19 47						19 58		20 11		
Falconwood	d	19 43	19 50						20 01		20 13		
Welling	d	19 46	19 52						20 03		20 16		
Bexleyheath	d	19 48	19 55						20 06		20 18		
Barnehurst	d	19 51	19a58						20 08		20 21		
Hither Green	d							19 44					
Lee	d							19 46					
Mottingham	d							19 49					
New Eltham	d							19 51					
Sidcup	d							19 55					
Albany Park	d							19 57					
Bexley	d							19 59					
Crayford	d							20 03					
Charlton	d			19 47						20 03		20 06	
Woolwich Dockyard	d			19 50								20 09	
Woolwich Arsenal	d			19 53						20 09		20 12	
Plumstead	d			19 55								20 14	
Abbey Wood	d			19 58						20 13		20 17	
Belvedere	d			20 00								20 20	
Erith	d			20 03								20 22	
Slade Green	d			20 07								20 26	
Dartford	a	19 58		20 12				20 08	20 15	20 24	20 28	20 31	
	d							20 09		20 25			
Stone Crossing	d							20 13					
Greenhithe for Bluewater	d							20 15		20 30			
Swanscombe	d							20 18					
Northfleet	d							20 20					
Gravesend	d				20 18	20 18		20a25		20 37			20 48
Higham	d									20 43			
Strood	d				20 28	20 28				20 48			20 58
Maidstone West	d												
Rochester	d				20 33	20 33				20 52			21 03
Chatham	d				20 35	20 35				20 55			21 05
Gillingham (Kent)	a				20 39	20 39				20 59			21 09

A not from 1 September until 8 September

B not 25 August

Table 200

London - Dartford and Gillingham

Saturdays

25 August to 8 September

Network Diagram - see first Page of Table 200

		SE A	SE	SE		SE	SE	SE	SE B	SE A	SE	SE	SE	SE		SE	SE B	SE A	SE	SE	SE	SE	SE B	SE A
St Pancras Int'l	d	20 25							20 55	20 55							21 25	21 25					21 55	21 55
Stratford International	d	20 33							21 02	21 03							21 32	21 33					22 02	22 03
Ebbsfleet International	d	20 44							21 13	21 14							21 43	21 44					22 13	22 14
London Charing Cross	d		19 52	19 56		20 02	20 09				20 22	20 26	20 32	20 39					20 52	20 56	21 02	21 09		
London Waterloo (East)	d		19 55	19 59		20 05	20 12				20 25	20 29	20 35	20 42					20 55	20 59	21 05	21 12		
London Cannon Street	d																							
London Bridge	d		20 00	20 05		20 10	20 17	20 20			20 30	20 35	20 40	20 47		20 50			21 00	21 05	21 10	21 17		
Deptford	d			20 11				20 26				20 41				20 56				21 11				
Greenwich	d			20 13				20 28				20 43				20 58				21 13				
Maze Hill	d			20 16				20 31				20 46				21 01				21 16				
Westcombe Park	d			20 18				20 33				20 48				21 03				21 18				
London Victoria	d																							
Denmark Hill	d																							
Peckham Rye	d																							
Nunhead	d																							
New Cross	d		20 05			20 15					20 35		20 45						21 05		21 15			
St Johns	d																							
Lewisham	d		20 09			20 19	20 26				20 39		20 49	20 56					21 09		21 19	21 26		
Blackheath	d					20 22	20 29						20 52	20 59							21 22	21 29		
Kidbrooke	d					20 25							20 55								21 25			
Eltham	d					20 28							20 58								21 28			
Falconwood	d					20 31							21 01								21 31			
Welling	d					20 33							21 03								21 33			
Bexleyheath	d					20 36							21 06								21 36			
Barnehurst	d					20 38							21 08								21 38			
Hither Green	d		20 14								20 44								21 14					
Lee	d		20 16								20 46								21 16					
Mottingham	d		20 19								20 49								21 19					
New Eltham	d		20 21								20 51								21 21					
Sidcup	d		20 25								20 55								21 25					
Albany Park	d		20 27								20 57								21 27					
Bexley	d		20 29								20 59								21 29					
Crayford	d		20 33								21 03								21 33					
Charlton	d			20 20			20 33	20 36				20 50		21 03		21 06				21 20		21 33		
Woolwich Dockyard	d			20 23				20 39				20 53				21 09				21 23				
Woolwich Arsenal	d			20 26			20 39	20 42				20 56		21 09		21 12				21 26		21 39		
Plumstead	d			20 28				20 44				20 58				21 14				21 28				
Abbey Wood	d			20 31			20 43	20 47				21 01		21 13		21 17				21 31		21 43		
Belvedere	d			20 34				20 50				21 04				21 20				21 34				
Erith	d			20 36				20 52				21 06				21 22				21 36				
Slade Green	d			20 39				20 56				21 09				21 26				21 39				
Dartford	a		20 38	20 44		20 46	20 54	21 01			21 08	21 14	21 16	21 24		21 31			21 38	21 44	21 46	21 54		
	d		20 39				20 55				21 09			21 25					21 39			21 55		
Stone Crossing	d		20 43								21 13								21 43					
Greenhithe for Bluewater	d		20 45				21 00				21 15			21 30					21 45			22 00		
Swanscombe	d		20 48								21 18								21 48					
Northfleet	d		20 50								21 20								21 50					
Gravesend	d	20 48	20a55				21 07		21 18	21 18	21a25			21 37			21 48	21 48	21a55			22 07	22 18	22 18
Higham	d						21 13							21 43								22 13		
Strood	d	20 58					21 18		21 28	21 28				21 48			21 58	21 58				22 18	22 28	22 28
Maidstone West	d																							
Rochester	d	21 03					21 22		21 33	21 33				21 52			22 03	22 03				22 22	22 33	22 33
Chatham	d	21 05					21 25		21 35	21 35				21 55			22 05	22 05				22 25	22 35	22 35
Gillingham (Kent)	a	21 09					21 29		21 39	21 39				21 59			22 09	22 09				22 29	22 39	22 39

A not 25 August

B not from 1 September until 8 September

Table 200

London - Dartford and Gillingham

Saturdays

25 August to 8 September

Network Diagram - see first Page of Table 200

		SE	SE	SE	SE	SE	SE	SE	SE A	SE B		SE	SE	SE	SE	SE A	SE B	SE	SE	SE		SE	SE A	SE B	SE
St Pancras Int'l	d								22 25	22 25						22 55	22 55						23 25	23 25	
Stratford International	d								22 32	22 33						23 02	23 03						23 32	23 33	
Ebbsfleet International	d								22 43	22 44						23 13	23 14						23 43	23 44	
London Charing Cross	d	21 22	21 26	21 32	21 39	21 52	21 56	22 02				22 09	22 22	22 26	22 32			22 39	22 52	22 56		23 02			23 09
London Waterloo (East)	d	21 25	21 29	21 35	21 42	21 55	21 59	22 05				22 12	22 25	22 29	22 35			22 42	22 55	22 59		23 05			23 12
London Cannon Street	d																								
London Bridge	d	21 30	21 35	21 40	21 47	22 00	22 05	22 10				22 17	22 30	22 35	22 40			22 47	23 00	23 05		23 10			23 17
Deptford	d		21 41				22 11							22 41						23 11					
Greenwich	d		21 43				22 13							22 43						23 13					
Maze Hill	d		21 46				22 16							22 46						23 16					
Westcombe Park	d		21 48				22 18							22 48						23 18					
London Victoria	d																								
Denmark Hill	d																								
Peckham Rye	d																								
Nunhead	d																								
New Cross	d	21 35		21 45		22 05		22 15					22 35		22 45				23 05			23 15			
St Johns	d																								
Lewisham	d	21 39		21 49	21 56	22 09		22 19				22 26	22 39		22 49			22 56	23 09			23 19			23 26
Blackheath	d			21 52	21 59			22 22				22 29			22 52			22 59				23 22			23 29
Kidbrooke	d			21 55				22 25							22 55							23 25			
Eltham	d			21 58				22 28							22 58							23 28			
Falconwood	d			22 01				22 31							23 01							23 31			
Welling	d			22 03				22 33							23 03							23 33			
Bexleyheath	d			22 06				22 36							23 06							23 36			
Barnehurst	d			22 08				22 38							23 08							23 38			
Hither Green	d	21 44				22 14							22 44						23 14						
Lee	d	21 46				22 16							22 46						23 16						
Mottingham	d	21 49				22 19							22 49						23 19						
New Eltham	d	21 51				22 21							22 51						23 21						
Sidcup	d	21 55				22 25							22 55						23 25						
Albany Park	d	21 57				22 27							22 57						23 27						
Bexley	d	21 59				22 29							22 59						23 29						
Crayford	d	22 03				22 33							23 03						23 33						
Charlton	d		21 50		22 03		22 20					22 33		22 50				23 03		23 20					23 33
Woolwich Dockyard	d		21 53				22 23							22 53						23 23					
Woolwich Arsenal	d		21 56		22 09		22 26					22 39		22 56				23 09		23 26					23 39
Plumstead	d		21 58				22 28							22 58						23 28					
Abbey Wood	d		22 01		22 13		22 31					22 43		23 01				23 13		23 31					23 43
Belvedere	d		22 04				22 34							23 04						23 34					
Erith	d		22 06				22 36							23 06						23 36					
Slade Green	d		22 09				22 39							23 09						23 39					
Dartford	a	22 08	22 14	22 16	22 24	22 38	22 44	22 46				22 54	23 08	23 14	23 16			23 24	23 38	23 44		23 46			23 54
	d	22 09			22 25							22 55						23 25							23 55
Stone Crossing	d	22 13			22 29							22 59						23 29							23 58
Greenhithe for Bluewater	d	22 15			22 31							23 01						23 31							23 59
Swanscombe	d	22 18			22 34							23 04						23 34							00 04
Northfleet	d	22 20			22 36							23 06						23 36							00 06
Gravesend	d	22a25			22 40				22 48	22 48		23 10				23 18	23 18	23 40					23 48	23 48	00 10
Higham	d				22 46							23 16						23 46							00 16
Strood	d				22 52				22 58	22 58		23 22				23 28	23 28	23 52					23 58	23 58	00 22
Maidstone West	d																								
Rochester	d				22 56				23 03	23 03		23 26				23 33	23 33	23 56					00 03	00 03	00 26
Chatham	d				22 58				23 05	23 05		23 28				23 35	23 35	23 58					00 05	00 05	00 28
Gillingham (Kent)	a				23 03				23 09	23 09		23 33				23 39	23 39	00 03					00 09	00 09	00 33

A not from 1 September until 8 September

B not 25 August

Table 200

London - Dartford and Gillingham

Saturdays

25 August to 8 September

Network Diagram - see first Page of Table 200

		SE	SE	SE	SE A	SE B	SE	SE
St Pancras Int'l ⊖	d				23 55	23 55		
Stratford International ⊖ ⛴	d				00 03	00 02		
Ebbsfleet International	d				00 13	00 13		
London Charing Cross ⊖	d	23 22	23 26	23 32			23 39	23 56
London Waterloo (East) ⊖	d	23 25	23 29	23 35			23 42	23 59
London Cannon Street ⊖	d							
London Bridge ⊖	d	23 30	23 35	23 40			23 47	00 05
Deptford	d		23 41					00 11
Greenwich ⛴	d		23 43					00 13
Maze Hill	d		23 46					00 16
Westcombe Park	d		23 48					00 18
London Victoria ⊖	d							
Denmark Hill	d							
Peckham Rye	d							
Nunhead	d							
New Cross ⊖	d	23 35		23 45				
St Johns	d							
Lewisham ⛴	d	23 39		23 49			23 56	
Blackheath	d			23 52			23 58	
Kidbrooke	d			23 55				
Eltham	d			23 58				
Falconwood	d			00 01				
Welling	d			00 03				
Bexleyheath	d			00 06				
Barnehurst	d			00 08				
Hither Green	d	23 44						
Lee	d	23 46						
Mottingham	d	23 49						
New Eltham	d	23 51						
Sidcup	d	23 55						
Albany Park	d	23 57						
Bexley	d	23 59						
Crayford	d	00 03						
Charlton	d		23 50				00 03	00 20
Woolwich Dockyard	d		23 53					00 23
Woolwich Arsenal ⛴	d		23 56				00 09	00 26
Plumstead	d		23 58					00 28
Abbey Wood	d		00 01				00 13	00 31
Belvedere	d		00 04					00 34
Erith	d		00 06					00 36
Slade Green	d		00 09					00 39
Dartford	a	00 08	00 14	00 16			00 24	00 44
	d						00 25	
Stone Crossing	d						00 29	
Greenhithe for Bluewater	d						00 31	
Swanscombe	d						00 34	
Northfleet	d						00 36	
Gravesend	d				00 18	00 18	00 40	
Higham	d						00 46	
Strood	d				00 28	00 28	00 52	
Maidstone West	d							
Rochester	d				00 32	00 33	00 56	
Chatham	d				00 35	00 35	00 58	
Gillingham (Kent)	a				00 39	00 39	01 03	

A not 25 August

B not from 1 September until 8 September

Table 200

London - Dartford and Gillingham

Sundays

until 22 July, 19 Aug and from 16 Sep

Network Diagram - see first Page of Table 200

		SE	SE	SE	SE	SE	SE	SE	SE	SE	SE	SE	SE	SE	SE	SE	SE	SE	SE	SE	SE	SE	SE
St Pancras Int'l ⊖	d		23p25					23p55															
Stratford International ⊖ ⛴	d		23p32					00 02															
Ebbsfleet International	d		23p43					00 13															
London Charing Cross ⊖	d	22p39		23p09	23p22	23p26	23p32		23p39	23p56	00 02	00 10	00 18		07 30		07 50	07 56	08 00	08 10	08 20	08 26	08 30
London Waterloo (East) ⊖	d	22p42		23p12	23p25	23p29	23p35		23p42	23p59	00 05	00 13	00 21		07 33		07 53	07 59	08 03	08 13	08 23	08 29	08 33
London Cannon Street ⊖	d																						
London Bridge ⊖	d	22p47		23p17	23p30	23p35	23p40		23p47	00 05	00 10	00 18	00 26		07 38		07 58	08 04	08 08	08 18	08 28	08 34	08 38
Deptford	d					23p41				00 11					07 44				08 14				08 44
Greenwich ⛴	d					23p43				00 13					07 46				08 16				08 46
Maze Hill	d					23p46				00 16					07 49				08 19				08 49
Westcombe Park	d					23p48				00 18					07 51				08 21				08 51
London Victoria ⊖	d																						
Denmark Hill	d																						
Peckham Rye	d																						
Nunhead	d																						
New Cross ⊖	d				23p35		23p45				00 15	00 23	00 31				08 04				08 34		
St Johns	d																						
Lewisham ⛴	d	22p56		23p26	23p39		23p49		23p56		00 19	00 27	00 35				08 08	08 12		08 27	08 38	08 42	
Blackheath	d	22p59		23p29			23p52		23p58		00 22		00 38				08 10			08 30	08 40		
Kidbrooke	d						23p55				00 25						08 13				08 43		
Eltham	d						23p58				00 28						08 17				08 47		
Falconwood	d						00 01				00 31						08 19				08 49		
Welling	d						00 03				00 33						08 22				08 52		
Bexleyheath	d						00 06				00 36						08 24				08 54		
Barnehurst	d						00 08				00 38						08 27				08 57		
Hither Green	d				23p44							00 32						08 16				08 46	
Lee	d				23p46							00 34						08 18				08 48	
Mottingham	d				23p49							00 37						08 21				08 51	
New Eltham	d				23p51							00 39						08 23				08 53	
Sidcup	d				23p55							00 43						08 27				08 57	
Albany Park	d				23p57							00 45						08 29				08 59	
Bexley	d				23p59							00 47						08 31				09 01	
Crayford	d				00 03							00 51						08 34				09 04	
Charlton	d	23p03		23p33		23p50			00 03	00 20			00 42		07 54				08 24	08 34			08 54
Woolwich Dockyard	d					23p53				00 23					07 57				08 27				08 57
Woolwich Arsenal ⛴	d	23p09		23p39		23p56			00 09	00 26			00 47		08 00				08 30	08 40			09 00
Plumstead	d					23p58				00 28			00 49		08 02				08 32				09 02
Abbey Wood	d	23p13		23p43		00 01			00 13	00 31			00 53		08 05				08 35	08 44			09 05
Belvedere	d					00 04				00 34			00 55		08 07				08 37				09 07
Erith	d					00 06				00 36			00 58		08 10				08 40				09 10
Slade Green	d					00 09				00 39			01 00		08 14				08 44				09 14
Dartford	a	23p24		23p54	00 08	00 14	00 16		00 24	00 44	00 46	00 56	01 05		08 19		08 33	08 39	08 49	08 54	09 03	09 09	09 19
	d	23p25		23p55					00 25				01 06	07 55		08 25		08 40		08 55		09 10	
Stone Crossing	d	23p29		23p58					00 29					07 59		08 29		08 44				09 14	
Greenhithe for Bluewater	d	23p31		23p59					00 31				01 10	08 01		08 31		08 46		09 00		09 16	
Swanscombe	d	23p34		00 04					00 34					08 04		08 34		08 49				09 19	
Northfleet	d	23p36		00 06					00 36					08 06		08 36		08 51				09 21	
Gravesend	d	23p40	23p48	00 10				00 18	00 40				01 17	08 10		08 40		08a55		09 07		09a25	
Higham	d	23p46		00 16					00 46				01 23	08 16		08 46				09 13			
Strood	d	23p52	23p58	00 22				00 28	00 52				01 29	08 22		08 52				09 18			
Maidstone West	d																						
Rochester	d	23p56	00 03	00 26				00 33	00 56				01 33	08 26		08 56				09 23			
Chatham	d	23p58	00 05	00 28				00 35	00 58				01 35	08 28		08 58				09 26			
Gillingham (Kent)	a	00 03	00 09	00 33				00 39	01 03				01 41	08 33		09 03				09 30			

Table 200

London - Dartford and Gillingham

Sundays

until 22 July, 19 Aug and from 16 Sep

Network Diagram - see first Page of Table 200

		SE	SE	SE	SE	SE		SE	SE	SE	SE	SE	SE	SE	SE	SE		SE	SE	SE	SE	SE	SE	SE	SE
St Pancras Int'l	d			09 25												10 28									
Stratford International	d			09 32												10 35									
Ebbsfleet International	d			09 43												10 46									
London Charing Cross	d	08 40	08 50		08 56	09 00		09 10		09 20	09 26	09 30	09 40		09 50			09 56	10 00	10 10		10 20	10 26	10 30	10 40
London Waterloo (East)	d	08 43	08 53		08 59	09 03		09 13		09 23	09 29	09 33	09 43		09 53			09 59	10 03	10 13		10 23	10 29	10 33	10 43
London Cannon Street	d																								
London Bridge	d	08 48	08 58		09 04	09 08		09 18	09 23	09 28	09 34	09 38	09 48	09 53	09 58			10 04	10 08	10 18	10 23	10 28	10 34	10 38	10 48
Deptford	d					09 14			09 29			09 44		09 59					10 14		10 29			10 44	
Greenwich	d					09 16			09 31			09 46		10 01					10 16		10 31			10 46	
Maze Hill	d					09 19			09 34			09 49		10 04					10 19		10 34			10 49	
Westcombe Park	d					09 21			09 36			09 51		10 06					10 21		10 36			10 51	
London Victoria	d																								
Denmark Hill	d																								
Peckham Rye	d																								
Nunhead	d																								
New Cross	d		09 04							09 34					10 04							10 34			
St Johns	d																								
Lewisham	d	08 57	09 08		09 12			09 27		09 38	09 42		09 57		10 08			10 12		10 27		10 38	10 42		10 57
Blackheath	d	09 00	09 10					09 30		09 40			10 00		10 10					10 30		10 40			11 00
Kidbrooke	d		09 13							09 43					10 13							10 43			
Eltham	d		09 17							09 47					10 17							10 47			
Falconwood	d		09 19							09 49					10 19							10 49			
Welling	d		09 22							09 52					10 22							10 52			
Bexleyheath	d		09 24							09 54					10 24							10 54			
Barnehurst	d		09 27							09 57					10 27							10 57			
Hither Green	d				09 16						09 46							10 16					10 46		
Lee	d				09 18						09 48							10 18					10 48		
Mottingham	d				09 21						09 51							10 21					10 51		
New Eltham	d				09 23						09 53							10 23					10 53		
Sidcup	d				09 27						09 57							10 27					10 57		
Albany Park	d				09 29						09 59							10 29					10 59		
Bexley	d				09 31						10 01							10 31					11 01		
Crayford	d				09 34						10 04							10 34					11 04		
Charlton	d	09 04				09 24		09 34	09 39			09 54	10 04	10 09					10 24	10 34	10 39			10 54	11 04
Woolwich Dockyard	d					09 27			09 42			09 57		10 12					10 27		10 42			10 57	
Woolwich Arsenal	d	09 10				09 30		09 40	09 45			10 00	10 10	10 15					10 30	10 40	10 45			11 00	11 10
Plumstead	d					09 32			09a47			10 02		10a17					10 32		10a47			11 02	
Abbey Wood	d	09 14				09 35		09 44				10 05	10 14						10 35	10 44				11 05	11 14
Belvedere	d					09 37						10 07							10 37					11 07	
Erith	d					09 40						10 10							10 40					11 10	
Slade Green	d					09 44						10 14							10 44					11 14	
Dartford	a	09 24	09 33		09 39	09 49		09 54		10 03	10 09	10 19	10 24		10 33			10 39	10 49	10 54		11 03	11 09	11 19	11 24
	d	09 25			09 40			09 55			10 10		10 25					10 40		10 55			11 10		11 25
Stone Crossing	d				09 44						10 14							10 44					11 14		
Greenhithe for Bluewater	d	09 30			09 46			10 00			10 16		10 30					10 46		11 00			11 16		11 30
Swanscombe	d				09 49						10 19							10 49					11 19		
Northfleet	d				09 51						10 21							10 51					11 21		
Gravesend	d	09 37		09 48	09a55			10 07			10a25		10 37			10 51		10a55		11 07			11a25		11 37
Higham	d	09 43						10 13					10 43							11 13					11 43
Strood	d	09 48		09 58				10 18					10 48			11 01				11 18					11 48
Maidstone West	d																								
Rochester	d	09 52		10 03				10 23					10 52			11 06				11 23					11 52
Chatham	d	09 55		10 05				10 26					10 55			11 08				11 26					11 55
Gillingham (Kent)	a	10 02		10 09				10 30					11 02			11 12				11 30					12 02

Table 200

London - Dartford and Gillingham

Sundays

until 22 July, 19 Aug and from 16 Sep

Network Diagram - see first Page of Table 200

		SE		SE	SE	SE	SE	SE	SE	SE	SE	SE		SE	SE	SE	SE	SE	SE	SE	SE	SE		SE	SE
St Pancras Int'l	d				11 25												12 28							12 52	
Stratford International	d				11 32												12 35							12 58	
Ebbsfleet International	d				11 43												12 46							13 13	
London Charing Cross	d			10 50		10 56	11 00	11 10		11 20	11 26	11 30		11 40		11 50		11 56	12 00	12 10		12 20			12 26
London Waterloo (East)	d			10 53		10 59	11 03	11 13		11 23	11 29	11 33		11 43		11 53		11 59	12 03	12 13		12 23			12 29
London Cannon Street	d																								
London Bridge	d	10 53		10 58		11 04	11 08	11 18	11 23	11 28	11 34	11 38		11 48	11 53	11 58		12 04	12 08	12 18	12 23	12 28			12 34
Deptford	d	10 59					11 14		11 29			11 44			11 59				12 14		12 29				
Greenwich	d	11 01					11 16		11 31			11 46			12 01				12 16		12 31				
Maze Hill	d	11 04					11 19		11 34			11 49			12 04				12 19		12 34				
Westcombe Park	d	11 06					11 21		11 36			11 51			12 06				12 21		12 36				
London Victoria	d																								
Denmark Hill	d																								
Peckham Rye	d																								
Nunhead	d																								
New Cross	d			11 04						11 34						12 04						12 34			
St Johns	d																								
Lewisham	d			11 08		11 12		11 27		11 38	11 42			11 57		12 08		12 12		12 27		12 38			12 42
Blackheath	d			11 10				11 30		11 40				12 00		12 10				12 30		12 40			
Kidbrooke	d			11 13						11 43						12 13						12 43			
Eltham	d			11 17						11 47						12 17						12 47			
Falconwood	d			11 19						11 49						12 19						12 49			
Welling	d			11 22						11 52						12 22						12 52			
Bexleyheath	d			11 24						11 54						12 24						12 54			
Barnehurst	d			11 27						11 57						12 27						12 57			
Hither Green	d					11 16					11 46							12 16							12 46
Lee	d					11 18					11 48							12 18							12 48
Mottingham	d					11 21					11 51							12 21							12 51
New Eltham	d					11 23					11 53							12 23							12 53
Sidcup	d					11 27					11 57							12 27							12 57
Albany Park	d					11 29					11 59							12 29							12 59
Bexley	d					11 31					12 01							12 31							13 01
Crayford	d					11 34					12 04							12 34							13 04
Charlton	d	11 09					11 24	11 34	11 39			11 54		12 04	12 09				12 24	12 34	12 39				
Woolwich Dockyard	d	11 12					11 27		11 42			11 57			12 12				12 27		12 42				
Woolwich Arsenal	d	11 15					11 30	11 40	11 45			12 00		12 10	12 15				12 30	12 40	12 45				
Plumstead	d	11a17					11 32		11a47			12 02			12a17				12 32		12a47				
Abbey Wood	d						11 35	11 44				12 05		12 14					12 35	12 44					
Belvedere	d						11 37					12 07							12 37						
Erith	d						11 40					12 10							12 40						
Slade Green	d						11 44					12 14							12 44						
Dartford	a			11 33		11 39	11 49	11 54		12 03	12 09	12 19		12 24		12 33		12 39	12 49	12 54		13 03			13 09
	d					11 40		11 55			12 10			12 25				12 40		12 55					13 10
Stone Crossing	d					11 44					12 14							12 44							13 14
Greenhithe for Bluewater	d					11 46		12 00			12 16			12 30				12 46		13 00					13 16
Swanscombe	d					11 49					12 19							12 49							13 19
Northfleet	d					11 51					12 21							12 51							13 21
Gravesend	d				11 48	11a55		12 07			12a25			12 37			12 51	12a55		13 07				13 18	13a25
Higham	d							12 13						12 43						13 13					
Strood	d				11 58			12 18						12 48			13 01			13 18				13 28	
Maidstone West	d																								
Rochester	d				12 03			12 23						12 52			13 06			13 23				13 33	
Chatham	d				12 05			12 26						12 55			13 08			13 26				13 35	
Gillingham (Kent)	a				12 09			12 30						13 02			13 12			13 30				13 39	

Table 200

Sundays

until 22 July, 19 Aug and from 16 Sep

London - Dartford and Gillingham

Network Diagram - see first Page of Table 200

		SE	SE	SE	SE	SE	SE	SE		SE	SE	SE	SE	SE	SE	SE	SE	SE		SE	SE	SE	SE	SE	SE
St Pancras Int'l ⊖	d					13 25							13 55							14 25					
Stratford International ⊖	d					13 32							14 02							14 32					
Ebbsfleet International	d					13 43							14 13							14 43					
London Charing Cross ⊖	d	12 30	12 40		12 50		12 56	13 00		13 10		13 20		13 26	13 30	13 40		13 50			13 56	14 00	14 10		14 20
London Waterloo (East) ⊖	d	12 33	12 43		12 53		12 59	13 03		13 13		13 23		13 29	13 33	13 43		13 53			13 59	14 03	14 13		14 23
London Cannon Street ⊖	d																								
London Bridge ⊖	d	12 38	12 48	12 53	12 58		13 04	13 08		13 18	13 23	13 28		13 34	13 38	13 48	13 53	13 58			14 04	14 08	14 18	14 23	14 28
Deptford	d	12 44		12 59				13 14			13 29				13 44		13 59					14 14		14 29	
Greenwich	d	12 46		13 01				13 16			13 31				13 46		14 01					14 16		14 31	
Maze Hill	d	12 49		13 04				13 19			13 34				13 49		14 04					14 19		14 34	
Westcombe Park	d	12 51		13 06				13 21			13 36				13 51		14 06					14 21		14 36	
London Victoria ⊖	d																								
Denmark Hill	d																								
Peckham Rye	d																								
Nunhead	d																								
New Cross ⊖	d				13 04							13 34						14 04							14 34
St Johns	d																								
Lewisham	d		12 57		13 08		13 12			13 27		13 38		13 42		13 57		14 08			14 12		14 27		14 38
Blackheath	d		13 00		13 10					13 30		13 40				14 00		14 10					14 30		14 40
Kidbrooke	d				13 13							13 43						14 13							14 43
Eltham	d				13 17							13 47						14 17							14 47
Falconwood	d				13 19							13 49						14 19							14 49
Welling	d				13 22							13 52						14 22							14 52
Bexleyheath	d				13 24							13 54						14 24							14 54
Barnehurst	d				13 27							13 57						14 27							14 57
Hither Green	d						13 16							13 46							14 16				
Lee	d						13 18							13 48							14 18				
Mottingham	d						13 21							13 51							14 21				
New Eltham	d						13 23							13 53							14 23				
Sidcup	d						13 27							13 57							14 27				
Albany Park	d						13 29							13 59							14 29				
Bexley	d						13 31							14 01							14 31				
Crayford	d						13 34							14 04							14 34				
Charlton	d	12 54	13 04	13 09				13 24		13 34	13 39				13 54	14 04	14 09					14 24	14 34	14 39	
Woolwich Dockyard	d	12 57		13 12				13 27			13 42				13 57		14 12					14 27		14 42	
Woolwich Arsenal	d	13 00	13 10	13 15				13 30		13 40	13 45				14 00	14 10	14 15					14 30	14 40	14 45	
Plumstead	d	13 02		13a17				13 32			13a47				14 02		14a17					14 32		14a47	
Abbey Wood	d	13 05	13 14					13 35		13 44					14 05	14 14						14 35	14 44		
Belvedere	d	13 07						13 37							14 07							14 37			
Erith	d	13 10						13 40							14 10							14 40			
Slade Green	d	13 14						13 44							14 14							14 44			
Dartford	a	13 19	13 24		13 33		13 39	13 49		13 54		14 03		14 09	14 19	14 24		14 33			14 39	14 49	14 54		15 03
	d		13 25				13 40			13 55				14 10		14 25					14 40		14 55		
Stone Crossing	d						13 44							14 14							14 44				
Greenhithe for Bluewater	d		13 30				13 46			14 00				14 16		14 30					14 46		15 00		
Swanscombe	d						13 49							14 19							14 49				
Northfleet	d						13 51							14 21							14 51				
Gravesend	d		13 37			13 48	13a55			14 07			14 18	14a25		14 37				14 48	14a55		15 07		
Higham	d		13 43							14 13						14 43							15 13		
Strood	d		13 48			13 58				14 18			14 28			14 48				14 58			15 18		
Maidstone West	d																								
Rochester	d		13 52			14 03				14 23			14 33			14 52				15 03			15 23		
Chatham	d		13 55			14 05				14 26			14 35			14 55				15 05			15 26		
Gillingham (Kent)	a		14 02			14 09				14 30			14 39			15 02				15 09			15 30		

Table 200

Sundays

until 22 July, 19 Aug and from 16 Sep

London - Dartford and Gillingham

Network Diagram - see first Page of Table 200

		SE	SE	SE		SE	SE	SE	SE	SE	SE	SE	SE	SE		SE	SE	SE	SE	SE	SE	SE	SE	SE	
St Pancras Int'l ⊖	d	14 55							15 25							15 55						16 25			
Stratford International ⊖	d	15 02							15 32							16 02						16 32			
Ebbsfleet International	d	15 13							15 43							16 13						16 43			
London Charing Cross ⊖	d		14 26	14 30		14 40		14 50		14 56	15 00	15 10		15 20			15 26	15 30	15 40		15 50		15 56	16 00	
London Waterloo (East) ⊖	d		14 29	14 33		14 43		14 53		14 59	15 03	15 13		15 23			15 29	15 33	15 43		15 53		15 59	16 03	
London Cannon Street ⊖	d																								
London Bridge ⊖	d		14 34	14 38		14 48	14 53	14 58		15 04	15 08	15 18	15 23	15 28			15 34	15 38	15 48	15 53	15 58		16 04	16 08	
Deptford	d			14 44			14 59				15 14		15 29					15 44		15 59				16 14	
Greenwich	d			14 46			15 01				15 16		15 31					15 46		16 01				16 16	
Maze Hill	d			14 49			15 04				15 19		15 34					15 49		16 04				16 19	
Westcombe Park	d			14 51			15 06				15 21		15 36					15 51		16 06				16 21	
London Victoria ⊖	d																								
Denmark Hill	d																								
Peckham Rye	d																								
Nunhead	d																								
New Cross ⊖	d							15 04						15 34							16 04				
St Johns	d																								
Lewisham	d		14 42			14 57		15 08		15 12		15 27		15 38			15 42		15 57		16 08		16 12		
Blackheath	d					15 00		15 10				15 30		15 40					16 00		16 10				
Kidbrooke	d							15 13						15 43							16 13				
Eltham	d							15 17						15 47							16 17				
Falconwood	d							15 19						15 49							16 19				
Welling	d							15 22						15 52							16 22				
Bexleyheath	d							15 24						15 54							16 24				
Barnehurst	d							15 27						15 57							16 27				
Hither Green	d		14 46							15 16							15 46						16 16		
Lee	d		14 48							15 18							15 48						16 18		
Mottingham	d		14 51							15 21							15 51						16 21		
New Eltham	d		14 53							15 23							15 53						16 23		
Sidcup	d		14 57							15 27							15 57						16 27		
Albany Park	d		14 59							15 29							15 59						16 29		
Bexley	d		15 01							15 31							16 01						16 31		
Crayford	d		15 04							15 34							16 04						16 34		
Charlton	d			14 54		15 04	15 09				15 24	15 34	15 39					15 54	16 04	16 09				16 24	
Woolwich Dockyard	d			14 57			15 12				15 27		15 42					15 57		16 12				16 27	
Woolwich Arsenal	d			15 00		15 10	15 15				15 30	15 40	15 45					16 00	16 10	16 15				16 30	
Plumstead	d			15 02			15a17				15 32		15a47					16 02		16a17				16 32	
Abbey Wood	d			15 05		15 14					15 35	15 44						16 05	16 14					16 35	
Belvedere	d			15 07							15 37							16 07						16 37	
Erith	d			15 10							15 40							16 10						16 40	
Slade Green	d			15 14							15 44							16 14						16 44	
Dartford	a		15 09	15 19		15 24		15 33		15 39	15 49	15 54		16 03			16 09	16 19	16 24		16 33		16 39	16 49	
	d		15 10			15 25				15 40		15 55					16 10		16 25				16 40		
Stone Crossing	d		15 14							15 44							16 14						16 44		
Greenhithe for Bluewater	d		15 16			15 30				15 46		16 00					16 16		16 30				16 46		
Swanscombe	d		15 19							15 49							16 19						16 49		
Northfleet	d		15 21							15 51							16 21						16 51		
Gravesend	d	15 18	15a25			15 37			15 48	15a55		16 07				16 18	16a25		16 37			16 48	16a55		
Higham	d					15 43						16 13							16 43						
Strood	d	15 28				15 48			15 58			16 18				16 28			16 48			16 58			
Maidstone West	d																								
Rochester	d	15 33				15 52			16 03			16 23				16 33			16 52			17 03			
Chatham	d	15 35				15 55			16 05			16 26				16 35			16 55			17 05			
Gillingham (Kent)	a	15 39				16 02			16 09			16 30				16 39			17 02			17 09			

Table 200

London - Dartford and Gillingham

Sundays

until 22 July, 19 Aug and from 16 Sep

Network Diagram - see first Page of Table 200

		SE	SE	SE	SE	SE	SE	SE	SE	SE		SE	SE	SE	SE	SE	SE	SE	SE	SE		SE	SE	SE	SE
St Pancras Int'l ⊖	d				16 55							17 25						17 58							18 25
Stratford International ⊖	d				17 02							17 32						18 08							18 32
Ebbsfleet International	d				17 13							17 43						18 19							18 43
London Charing Cross ⊖	d	16 10		16 20		16 26	16 30	16 40		16 50			16 56	17 00	17 10		17 20		17 26	17 30		17 40		17 50	
London Waterloo (East) ⊖	d	16 13		16 23		16 29	16 33	16 43		16 53			16 59	17 03	17 13		17 23		17 29	17 33		17 43		17 53	
London Cannon Street ⊖	d																								
London Bridge ⊖	d	16 18	16 23	16 28		16 34	16 38	16 48	16 53	16 58			17 04	17 08	17 18	17 23	17 28		17 34	17 38		17 48	17 53	17 58	
Deptford	d		16 29				16 44		16 59					17 14		17 29				17 44			17 59		
Greenwich	d		16 31				16 46		17 01					17 16		17 31				17 46			18 01		
Maze Hill	d		16 34				16 49		17 04					17 19		17 34				17 49			18 04		
Westcombe Park	d		16 36				16 51		17 06					17 21		17 36				17 51			18 06		
London Victoria ⊖	d																								
Denmark Hill	d																								
Peckham Rye	d																								
Nunhead	d																								
New Cross ⊖	d			16 34						17 04							17 34							18 04	
St Johns	d																								
Lewisham	d	16 27		16 38		16 42		16 57		17 08			17 12		17 27		17 38		17 42			17 57		18 08	
Blackheath	d	16 30		16 40				17 00		17 10					17 30		17 40					18 00		18 10	
Kidbrooke	d			16 43						17 13							17 43							18 13	
Eltham	d			16 47						17 17							17 47							18 17	
Falconwood	d			16 49						17 19							17 49							18 19	
Welling	d			16 52						17 22							17 52							18 22	
Bexleyheath	d			16 54						17 24							17 54							18 24	
Barnehurst	d			16 57						17 27							17 57							18 27	
Hither Green	d					16 46							17 16						17 46						
Lee	d					16 48							17 18						17 48						
Mottingham	d					16 51							17 21						17 51						
New Eltham	d					16 53							17 23						17 53						
Sidcup	d					16 57							17 27						17 57						
Albany Park	d					16 59							17 29						17 59						
Bexley	d					17 01							17 31						18 01						
Crayford	d					17 04							17 34						18 04						
Charlton	d	16 34	16 39				16 54	17 04	17 09					17 24	17 34	17 39				17 54		18 04	18 09		
Woolwich Dockyard	d		16 42				16 57		17 12					17 27		17 42				17 57			18 12		
Woolwich Arsenal	d	16 40	16 45				17 00	17 10	17 15					17 30	17 40	17 45				18 00		18 10	18 15		
Plumstead	d		16a47				17 02		17a17					17 32		17a47				18 02			18a17		
Abbey Wood	d	16 44					17 05	17 14						17 35	17 44					18 05		18 14			
Belvedere	d						17 07							17 37						18 07					
Erith	d						17 10							17 40						18 10					
Slade Green	d						17 14							17 44						18 14					
Dartford	a	16 54		17 03		17 09	17 19	17 24		17 33			17 39	17 49	17 54		18 03		18 09	18 19		18 24		18 33	
	d	16 55				17 10		17 25					17 40		17 55				18 10			18 25			
Stone Crossing	d					17 14							17 44						18 14						
Greenhithe for Bluewater	d	17 00				17 16		17 30					17 46		18 00				18 16			18 30			
Swanscombe	d					17 19							17 49						18 19						
Northfleet	d					17 21							17 51						18 21						
Gravesend	d	17 07			17 18	17a25		17 37				17 48	17a55		18 07			18 24	18a25			18 37			18 48
Higham	d	17 13						17 43							18 13							18 43			
Strood	d	17 18			17 28			17 48				17 58			18 18			18 34				18 48			18 58
Maidstone West	d																								
Rochester	d	17 23			17 33			17 52				18 03			18 23			18 39				18 52			19 03
Chatham	d	17 26			17 35			17 55				18 05			18 26			18 41				18 55			19 05
Gillingham (Kent)	a	17 30			17 39			18 02				18 09			18 30			18 45				19 02			19 09

Table 200

London - Dartford and Gillingham

Sundays

until 22 July, 19 Aug and from 16 Sep

Network Diagram - see first Page of Table 200

		SE	SE	SE	SE	SE		SE	SE	SE	SE	SE	SE	SE	SE	SE		SE	SE	SE	SE	SE	SE	
St Pancras Int'l ⊖	d							18 55								19 25						19 55		
Stratford International ⊖	d							19 02								19 32						20 02		
Ebbsfleet International	d							19 13								19 43						20 13		
London Charing Cross ⊖	d	17 56	18 00	18 10		18 20			18 26	18 30	18 40		18 50	18 56	19 00			19 10	19 20	19 26	19 30		19 40	
London Waterloo (East) ⊖	d	17 59	18 03	18 13		18 23			18 29	18 33	18 43		18 53	18 59	19 03			19 13	19 23	19 29	19 33		19 43	
London Cannon Street ⊖	d																							
London Bridge ⊖	d	18 04	18 08	18 18	18 23	18 28			18 34	18 38	18 48	18 53	18 58	19 04	19 08			19 18	19 28	19 34	19 38		19 48	
Deptford	d		18 14		18 29					18 44		18 59			19 14						19 44			
Greenwich	d		18 16		18 31					18 46		19 01			19 16						19 46			
Maze Hill	d		18 19		18 34					18 49		19 04			19 19						19 49			
Westcombe Park	d		18 21		18 36					18 51		19 06			19 21						19 51			
London Victoria ⊖	d																							
Denmark Hill	d																							
Peckham Rye	d																							
Nunhead	d																							
New Cross ⊖	d					18 34							19 04						19 34					
St Johns	d																							
Lewisham	d	18 12		18 27		18 38			18 42		18 57		19 08	19 12				19 27	19 38	19 42			19 57	
Blackheath	d			18 30		18 40					19 00		19 10					19 30	19 40				20 00	
Kidbrooke	d					18 43							19 13						19 43					
Eltham	d					18 47							19 17						19 47					
Falconwood	d					18 49							19 19						19 49					
Welling	d					18 52							19 22						19 52					
Bexleyheath	d					18 54							19 24						19 54					
Barnehurst	d					18 57							19 27						19 57					
Hither Green	d	18 16							18 46					19 16						19 46				and at the same minutes past each hour until
Lee	d	18 18							18 48					19 18						19 48				
Mottingham	d	18 21							18 51					19 21						19 51				
New Eltham	d	18 23							18 53					19 23						19 53				
Sidcup	d	18 27							18 57					19 27						19 57				
Albany Park	d	18 29							18 59					19 29						19 59				
Bexley	d	18 31							19 01					19 31						20 01				
Crayford	d	18 34							19 04					19 34						20 04				
Charlton	d		18 24	18 34	18 39					18 54	19 04	19 09			19 24			19 34			19 54		20 04	
Woolwich Dockyard	d		18 27		18 42					18 57		19 12			19 27						19 57			
Woolwich Arsenal	d		18 30	18 40	18 45					19 00	19 10	19 15			19 30			19 40			20 00		20 10	
Plumstead	d		18 32		18a47					19 02		19a17			19 32						20 02			
Abbey Wood	d		18 35	18 44						19 05	19 14				19 35			19 44			20 05		20 14	
Belvedere	d		18 37							19 07					19 37						20 07			
Erith	d		18 40							19 10					19 40						20 10			
Slade Green	d		18 44							19 14					19 44						20 14			
Dartford	a	18 39	18 49	18 54		19 03			19 09	19 19	19 24		19 33	19 39	19 49			19 54	20 03	20 09	20 19		20 24	
	d	18 40		18 55					19 10		19 25							19 55					20 25	
Stone Crossing	d	18 44							19 14		19 29							19 59					20 29	
Greenhithe for Bluewater	d	18 46		19 00					19 16		19 31							20 01					20 31	
Swanscombe	d	18 49							19 19		19 34							20 04					20 34	
Northfleet	d	18 51							19 21		19 36							20 06					20 36	
Gravesend	d	18a55		19 07				19 18	19a25		19 40					19 48		20 10				20 18	20 40	
Higham	d			19 13							19 46							20 16					20 46	
Strood	d			19 18				19 28			19 52					19 58		20 22				20 28	20 52	
Maidstone West	d																							
Rochester	d			19 23				19 33			19 56					20 03		20 26				20 33	20 56	
Chatham	d			19 26				19 35			19 58					20 05		20 28				20 35	20 58	
Gillingham (Kent)	a			19 30				19 39			20 03					20 09		20 33				20 39	21 03	

Table 200

Sundays

until 22 July, 19 Aug and from 16 Sep

London - Dartford and Gillingham

Network Diagram - see first Page of Table 200

Station		SE	SE	SE	SE	SE	SE	SE	SE	SE	SE	SE
St Pancras Int'l ⊖	d					23 25						
Stratford International ⊖ ⛴	d					23 32						
Ebbsfleet International	d					23 43						
London Charing Cross ⊖	d	22 40	22 50	22 56	23 00		23 10	23 20	23 26	23 30	23 50	23 56
London Waterloo (East) ⊖	d	22 43	22 53	22 59	23 03		23 13	23 23	23 29	23 33	23 53	23 59
London Cannon Street ⊖	d											
London Bridge ⊖	d	22 48	22 58	23 04	23 08		23 18	23 28	23 34	23 38	23 58	00 04
Deptford	d				23 14					23 44		
Greenwich ⛴	d				23 16					23 46		
Maze Hill	d				23 19					23 49		
Westcombe Park	d				23 21					23 51		
London Victoria ⊖	d											
Denmark Hill	d											
Peckham Rye	d											
Nunhead	d											
New Cross ⊖	d		23 04					23 34			00 04	
St Johns	d											
Lewisham ⛴	d	22 57	23 08	23 12			23 27	23 38	23 42		00 08	00 12
Blackheath	d	23 00	23 10				23 30	23 40			00 10	
Kidbrooke	d		23 13					23 43			00 13	
Eltham	d		23 17					23 47			00 17	
Falconwood	d		23 19					23 49			00 19	
Welling	d		23 22					23 52			00 22	
Bexleyheath	d		23 24					23 54			00 24	
Barnehurst	d		23 27					23 57			00 27	
Hither Green	d			23 16					23 46			00 16
Lee	d			23 18					23 48			00 18
Mottingham	d			23 21					23 51			00 21
New Eltham	d			23 23					23 53			00 23
Sidcup	d			23 27					23 57			00 27
Albany Park	d			23 29					23 59			00 29
Bexley	d			23 31					00 01			00 31
Crayford	d			23 34					00 04			00 34
Charlton	d	23 04			23 24		23 34			23 54		
Woolwich Dockyard	d				23 27					23 57		
Woolwich Arsenal ⛴	d	23 10			23 30		23 40			23 59		
Plumstead	d				23 32					00 02		
Abbey Wood	d	23 14			23 35		23 44			00 05		
Belvedere	d				23 37					00 07		
Erith	d				23 40					00 10		
Slade Green	d				23 44					00 14		
Dartford	a	23 24	23 33	23 39	23 49		23 54	00 04	00 09	00 19	00 33	00 39
	d	23 25					23 55					
Stone Crossing	d	23 29					23 59					
Greenhithe for Bluewater	d	23 31					00 01					
Swanscombe	d	23 34					00 04					
Northfleet	d	23 36					00 06					
Gravesend	d	23 40				23 48	00 10					
Higham	d	23 46					00 16					
Strood	d	23 52				23 58	00 22					
Maidstone West	d											
Rochester	d	23 56				00 03	00 26					
Chatham	d	23 58				00 05	00 28					
Gillingham (Kent)	a	00 03				00 09	00 33					

Table 200

Sundays

29 July to 12 August

London - Dartford and Gillingham

Network Diagram - see first Page of Table 200

Station		SE	SE	SE	SE	SE	SE	SE	SE	SE
St Pancras Int'l ⊖	d									
Stratford International ⊖ ⛴	d									
Ebbsfleet International	d									
London Charing Cross ⊖	d	22p39	23p09	23p22	23p26	23p32	23p39	23p56	00 02	00 10
London Waterloo (East) ⊖	d	22p42	23p12	23p25	23p29	23p35	23p42	23p59	00 05	00 13
London Cannon Street ⊖	d									
London Bridge ⊖	d	22p47	23p17	23p30	23p35	23p40	23p47	00 05	00 10	00 18
Deptford	d				23p41			00 11		
Greenwich ⛴	d				23p43			00 13		
Maze Hill	d				23p47			00 17		
Westcombe Park	d				23p49			00 19		
London Victoria ⊖	d									
Denmark Hill	d									
Peckham Rye	d									
Nunhead	d									
New Cross ⊖	d			23p35		23p45			00 15	00 23
St Johns	d									
Lewisham ⛴	d	22p56	23p26	23p39		23p50	23p56		00 19	00 28
Blackheath	d	23p00	23p30			23p55	00 01		00 22	
Kidbrooke	d					23p58			00 25	
Eltham	d					00 01			00 28	
Falconwood	d					00 04			00 31	
Welling	d					00 06			00 33	
Bexleyheath	d					00 09			00 36	
Barnehurst	d					00 12			00 38	
Hither Green	d			23p44						00 34
Lee	d			23p46						00 36
Mottingham	d			23p49						00 39
New Eltham	d			23p51						00 41
Sidcup	d			23p55						00 45
Albany Park	d			23p57						00 47
Bexley	d			23p59						00 49
Crayford	d			00 03						00 53
Charlton	d	23p06	23p36		23p52		00 06	00 22		
Woolwich Dockyard	d									
Woolwich Arsenal ⛴	d	23p10	23p40		23p57		00 11	00 27		
Plumstead	d				23p59			00 29		
Abbey Wood	d	23p15	23p45		00 02		00 15	00 32		
Belvedere	d				00 04			00 34		
Erith	d				00 07			00 37		
Slade Green	d				00 09			00 39		
Dartford	a	23p24	23p54	00 11	00 17	00 22	00 24	00 47	00 49	01 01
	d	23p25	23p55				00 25			
Stone Crossing	d	23p29	23p58				00 29			
Greenhithe for Bluewater	d	23p31	23p59				00 31			
Swanscombe	d	23p34	00 04				00 34			
Northfleet	d	23p36	00 06				00 36			
Gravesend	d	23p40	00 10				00 40			
Higham	d	23p46	00 16				00 46			
Strood	d	23p52	00 22				00 52			
Maidstone West	d									
Rochester	d	23p56	00 26				00 56			
Chatham	d	23p58	00 28				00 58			
Gillingham (Kent)	a	00 06	00 36				01 06			

Station		SE	SE	SE	SE	SE	SE	SE	SE		SE	SE	SE
St Pancras Int'l ⊖	d						01 17	01 55					
Stratford International ⊖ ⛴	d						01 26	02 04					
Ebbsfleet International	d						01 38	02 16					
London Charing Cross ⊖	d	00 18	00 32		00 44							06 26	06 32
London Waterloo (East) ⊖	d	00 21	00 35		00 47							06 29	06 35
London Cannon Street ⊖	d			00 42		00 56							
London Bridge ⊖	d	00 26	00 40	00 47	00 52	01 00						06 34	06 40
Deptford	d		00 46			01 06						06 40	
Greenwich ⛴	d		00 49			01 09						06 43	
Maze Hill	d		00 53			01 13							
Westcombe Park	d		00 55			01 15						06 48	
London Victoria ⊖	d												
Denmark Hill	d												
Peckham Rye	d												
Nunhead	d												
New Cross ⊖	d	00 31			00 57								06 45
St Johns	d												
Lewisham ⛴	d	00 35		00 56	01 01								06 50
Blackheath	d	00 38		01 00									06 54
Kidbrooke	d			01 03									06 57
Eltham	d			01 06									07 00
Falconwood	d			01 09									07 02
Welling	d			01 11									07 05
Bexleyheath	d			01 14									07 07
Barnehurst	d			01 17						and every 30 minutes until			07 10
Hither Green	d				01 06								
Lee	d				01 08								
Mottingham	d				01 11								
New Eltham	d				01 13								
Sidcup	d				01 17								
Albany Park	d				01 19								
Bexley	d				01 21								
Crayford	d				01 25								
Charlton	d	00 43	00 58			01 18						06 51	
Woolwich Dockyard	d												
Woolwich Arsenal ⛴	d	00 48	01 04			01 24						06 56	
Plumstead	d	00 50	01 06			01 26						06 58	
Abbey Wood	d	00 53	01 09			01 29						07 01	
Belvedere	d	00 55	01 12			01 32						07 03	
Erith	d	00 58	01 14			01 34						07 06	
Slade Green	d	01 00	01 17			01 37						07 09	
Dartford	a	01 05	01 25	01 25	01 33	01 45						07 17	07 20
	d	01 06		01 27					05 39		07 09		
Stone Crossing	d								05 43		07 13		
Greenhithe for Bluewater	d	01 10		01 31					05 45		07 15		
Swanscombe	d								05 48		07 18		
Northfleet	d								05 50		07 20		
Gravesend	d	01 17		01 39			01 43	02 21	05a55		07a25		
Higham	d	01 23		01 45									
Strood	d	01 29		01 50			01 54	02 31					
Maidstone West	d												
Rochester	d	01 33		01 54			01 58	02 35					
Chatham	d	01 35		01 57			02 01	02 38					
Gillingham (Kent)	a	01 44		02 04			02 05	02 42					

London - Dartford and Gillingham

Sundays

29 July to 12 August

Network Diagram - see first Page of Table 200

		SE	SE	SE	SE	SE	SE	SE		SE	SE	SE	SE	SE	SE	SE	SE	SE		SE	SE	SE	SE	SE	SE
St Pancras Int'l ⊖	d		07 18												08 18										
Stratford International ⊖	d		07 28												08 28										
Ebbsfleet International	d		07 43												08 44										
London Charing Cross ⊖	d	06 39		06 52	06 56	07 02	07 09	07 22		07 26	07 31	07 39				07 52	07 56	08 01				08 09			
London Waterloo (East) ⊖	d	06 42		06 55	06 59	07 05	07 12	07 25		07 29	07 34	07 42				07 55	07 59	08 04				08 12			
London Cannon Street ⊖	d													07 55						08 07	08 10			08 17	08 24
London Bridge ⊖	d	06 47		07 00	07 04	07 10	07 17	07 30		07 34	07 40	07 47				08 00	08 04	08 10		08 11	08 14	08 17		08 21	08 28
Deptford	d				07 10					07 40							08 10							08 27	
Greenwich	d				07 13					07 43				08 06			08 13			08 20				08 30	
Maze Hill	d																								
Westcombe Park	d				07 18					07 48							08 18							08 35	
London Victoria ⊖	d												07 39										08 09		
Denmark Hill	d												07 48										08 18		
Peckham Rye	d												07 51										08 21		
Nunhead	d												07 53										08 23		
New Cross ⊖	d			07 05		07 15		07 35			07 45					08 05		08 15			08 19				08 33
St Johns	d																				08 21				08 35
Lewisham	d	06 57		07 09		07 20	07 27	07 39			07 50	07 57	08 01			08 09		08 19			08 24	08 27	08 32		08 39
Blackheath	d	07 00				07 24	07 31				07 54	08 01	08 04					08 23				08 31	08 36		08 43
Kidbrooke	d					07 27					07 57		08 07										08 39		08 46
Eltham	d					07 30					08 00		08 11					08 29					08 42		08 49
Falconwood	d					07 32					08 02		08 13					08 31					08 44		08 52
Welling	d					07 35					08 05		08 16					08 34					08 47		08 54
Bexleyheath	d					07 37					08 07		08 18					08 36					08 49		08 57
Barnehurst	d					07 40					08 10		08 21					08 39					08 52		09 02
Hither Green	d			07 14				07 44								08 14					08 29				
Lee	d			07 16				07 46								08 16					08 31				
Mottingham	d			07 19				07 49								08 19					08 34				
New Eltham	d			07 21				07 51								08 21					08 36				
Sidcup	d			07 25				07 55								08 25					08 40				
Albany Park	d			07 27				07 57								08 27					08 42				
Bexley	d			07 29				07 59								08 29					08 44				
Crayford	d			07 33				08 03								08 33					08 48				
Charlton	d	07 05			07 21		07 35			07 51		08 05		08 13			08 21			08 26	09a12	08 35		08 39	
Woolwich Dockyard	d																								
Woolwich Arsenal	d	07 11			07 26		07 41			07 56		08 11		08a17			08 26			08 33		08 41		08 45	
Plumstead	d				07 28					07 58							08 28			08 35				08 47	
Abbey Wood	d	07 15			07 31		07 45			08 01		08 15					08 31			08 38		08 45		08 50	
Belvedere	d				07 33					08 03							08 33			08 40				08 52	
Erith	d				07 36					08 06							08 36			08 43				08 55	
Slade Green	d				07 39					08 09							08 39			08a46				08a57	09a15
Dartford	a	07 24		07 38	07 47	07 49	07 54	08 08		08 17	08 19	08 24	08 32			08 38	08 47	08 49				08 54	09 01		
	d	07 25		07 39			07 55	08 09				08 25				08 39						08 55			
Stone Crossing	d			07 43				08 13								08 43									
Greenhithe for Bluewater	d	07 30		07 45			08 00	08 15				08 30				08 45						09 00			
Swanscombe	d			07 48				08 18								08 48									
Northfleet	d			07 50				08 20								08 50									
Gravesend	d	07 37	07 48	07a58			08 07	08a28				08 37			08 48	08a58						09 07			
Higham	d	07 43					08 13					08 43										09 13			
Strood	d	07 48	07 58				08 18					08 48			08 58							09 18			
Maidstone West	d																								
Rochester	d	07 52	08 03				08 22					08 52			09 03							09 22			
Chatham	d	07 55	08 05				08 25					08 55			09 05							09 25			
Gillingham (Kent)	a	08 02	08 09				08 32					09 02			09 09							09 32			

London - Dartford and Gillingham

Sundays

29 July to 12 August

Network Diagram - see first Page of Table 200

		SE	SE	SE		SE	SE	SE	SE	SE	SE	SE	SE	SE		SE	SE	SE	SE	SE	SE	SE	SE	SE
St Pancras Int'l ⊖	d												09 18											
Stratford International ⊖	d												09 28											
Ebbsfleet International	d												09 43											
London Charing Cross ⊖	d		08 26	08 31				08 39						08 56		09 01			09 09					09 26
London Waterloo (East) ⊖	d		08 29	08 34				08 42						08 59		09 04			09 12					09 29
London Cannon Street ⊖	d	08 27				08 37	08 40			08 47	08 54	08 57					09 07	09 10			09 17	09 24	09 27	
London Bridge ⊖	d	08 31	08 34	08 40		08 41	08 44	08 47		08 51	08 58	09 01		09 04		09 10	09 11	09 14	09 17		09 21	09 28	09 31	09 34
Deptford	d									08 57											09 27			
Greenwich	d	08 40				08 50				09 00		09 10					09 20				09 30		09 40	
Maze Hill	d																							
Westcombe Park	d									09 05											09 35			
London Victoria ⊖	d								08 39											09 09				
Denmark Hill	d								08 48											09 18				
Peckham Rye	d								08 51											09 21				
Nunhead	d								08 53											09 23				
New Cross ⊖	d						08 49				09 03							09 19				09 33		
St Johns	d						08 51				09 05							09 21				09 35		
Lewisham	d			08 49			08 54	08 57	09 02		09 09					09 19		09 24	09 27	09 32		09 39		
Blackheath	d			08 53				09 01	09 06		09 13					09 23			09 31	09 36		09 43		
Kidbrooke	d								09 09		09 16									09 39		09 46		
Eltham	d			08 59					09 12		09 19					09 29				09 42		09 49		
Falconwood	d			09 01					09 14		09 22					09 31				09 44		09 52		
Welling	d			09 04					09 17		09 24					09 34				09 47		09 54		
Bexleyheath	d			09 06					09 19		09 27					09 36				09 49		09 57		
Barnehurst	d			09 09					09 22		09 32					09 39				09 52		10 02		
Hither Green	d		08 44				08 59							09 14				09 29						09 44
Lee	d		08 46				09 01							09 16				09 31						09 46
Mottingham	d		08 49				09 04							09 19				09 34						09 49
New Eltham	d		08 51				09 06							09 21				09 36						09 51
Sidcup	d		08 55				09 10							09 25				09 40						09 55
Albany Park	d		08 57				09 12							09 27				09 42						09 57
Bexley	d		08 59				09 14							09 29				09 44						09 59
Crayford	d		09 03				09 18							09 33				09 48						10 03
Charlton	d	08 47				08 56	09a42	09 05		09 09		09 17					09 26	10a12	09 35		09 39		09 47	
Woolwich Dockyard	d																							
Woolwich Arsenal	d	08 53				09 03		09 11		09 15		09 23					09 33		09 41		09 45		09 53	
Plumstead	d	08 55				09 05				09 17		09 25					09 35				09 47		09 55	
Abbey Wood	d	08 58				09 08		09 15		09 20		09 28					09 38		09 45		09 50		09 58	
Belvedere	d	09 01				09 10				09 22		09 31					09 40				09 52		10 01	
Erith	d	09 03				09 13				09 25		09 33					09 43				09 55		10 03	
Slade Green	d	09 07				09a16				09a27	09a45	09 37					09a46				09a57	10a15	10 07	
Dartford	a	09 15	09 08	09 18				09 24	09 31			09 45		09 38		09 48			09 54	10 01			10 15	10 08
	d		09 09					09 25						09 39					09 55					10 09
Stone Crossing	d		09 13											09 43										10 13
Greenhithe for Bluewater	d		09 15					09 30						09 45					10 00					10 15
Swanscombe	d		09 18											09 48										10 18
Northfleet	d		09 20											09 50										10 20
Gravesend	d		09a25					09 37					09 48	09a55					10 07					10a25
Higham	d							09 43											10 13					
Strood	d							09 48					09 58						10 18					
Maidstone West	d																							
Rochester	d							09 52					10 03						10 22					
Chatham	d							09 55					10 05						10 25					
Gillingham (Kent)	a							10 02					10 09						10 32					

Table 200

Sundays

29 July to 12 August

London - Dartford and Gillingham

Network Diagram - see first Page of Table 200

Station		SE	SE	SE	SE	SE	SE	SE	SE	SE		SE	SE	SE	SE	SE	SE	SE	SE	SE		SE	SE	SE	SE
St Pancras Int'l	d									10 18															
Stratford International	d									10 28															
Ebbsfleet International	d									10 44															
London Charing Cross	d	09 31			09 39							09 56	10 01			10 09						10 26	10 31		
London Waterloo (East)	d	09 34			09 42							09 59	10 04			10 12						10 29	10 34		
London Cannon Street	d		09 37	09 40			09 47	09 54	09 57					10 07	10 10			10 17	10 24	10 27				10 37	10 40
London Bridge	d	09 40	09 41	09 44	09 47		09 51	09 58	10 01			10 04	10 10	10 11	10 14	10 17		10 21	10 28	10 31		10 34	10 40	10 41	10 44
Deptford	d						09 57											10 27							
Greenwich	d		09 50				10 00		10 10					10 20				10 30		10 40				10 50	
Maze Hill	d																								
Westcombe Park	d						10 05											10 35							
London Victoria	d					09 39											10 09								
Denmark Hill	d					09 47											10 18								
Peckham Rye	d					09 51											10 21								
Nunhead	d					09 52											10 23								
New Cross	d			09 49				10 03							10 19				10 33						10 49
St Johns	d			09 51				10 05							10 21				10 35						10 51
Lewisham	d	09 49		09 54	09 57	10 03		10 09					10 19		10 24	10 27	10 32		10 39				10 49		10 54
Blackheath	d	09 53			10 01	10 07		10 13					10 23			10 31	10 36		10 43				10 53		
Kidbrooke	d					10 10		10 16									10 39		10 46						
Eltham	d	09 59				10 13		10 19					10 29				10 42		10 49				10 59		
Falconwood	d	10 01				10 15		10 22					10 31				10 44		10 52				11 01		
Welling	d	10 04				10 18		10 24					10 34				10 47		10 54				11 04		
Bexleyheath	d	10 06				10 20		10 27					10 36				10 49		10 57				11 06		
Barnehurst	d	10 09				10 23		10 32					10 39				10 52		11 02				11 09		
Hither Green	d			09 59								10 14			10 29							10 44			10 59
Lee	d			10 01								10 16			10 31							10 46			11 01
Mottingham	d			10 04								10 19			10 34							10 49			11 04
New Eltham	d			10 06								10 21			10 36							10 51			11 06
Sidcup	d			10 10								10 25			10 40							10 55			11 10
Albany Park	d			10 12								10 27			10 42							10 57			11 12
Bexley	d			10 14								10 29			10 44							10 59			11 14
Crayford	d			10 18								10 33			10 48							11 03			11 18
Charlton	d		09 56	10a42	10 05		10 09		10 17					10 26	11a12	10 35		10 39		10 47				10 56	11a42
Woolwich Dockyard	d																								
Woolwich Arsenal	d		10 03		10 11		10 15		10 23					10 33		10 41		10 45		10 53				11 03	
Plumstead	d		10 05				10 17		10 25					10 35				10 47		10 55				11 05	
Abbey Wood	d		10 08		10 15		10 20		10 28					10 38		10 45		10 50		10 58				11 08	
Belvedere	d		10 10				10 22		10 31					10 40				10 52		11 01				11 10	
Erith	d		10 13				10 25		10 33					10 43				10 55		11 03				11 13	
Slade Green	d		10a16				10a27	10a45	10 37					10a46				10a57	11a15	11 07				11a16	
Dartford	a	10 18			10 24	10 32			10 45			10 38	10 48			10 54	11 01			11 15		11 08	11 18		
	d				10 25							10 39				10 55						11 09			
Stone Crossing	d											10 43										11 13			
Greenhithe for Bluewater	d				10 30							10 45				11 00						11 15			
Swanscombe	d											10 48										11 18			
Northfleet	d											10 50										11 20			
Gravesend	d				10 37					10 48		10a55				11 07						11a25			
Higham	d				10 43											11 13									
Strood	d				10 48					10 58						11 18									
Maidstone West	d																								
Rochester	d				10 52					11 03						11 22									
Chatham	d				10 55					11 05						11 25									
Gillingham (Kent)	a				11 02					11 09						11 32									

Table 200

Sundays

29 July to 12 August

London - Dartford and Gillingham

Network Diagram - see first Page of Table 200

Station		SE	SE	SE	SE	SE		SE	SE	SE	SE	SE	SE	SE	SE	SE		SE	SE	SE	SE	SE	SE	SE	SE
St Pancras Int'l	d							11 18																	
Stratford International	d							11 28																	
Ebbsfleet International	d							11 43																	
London Charing Cross	d	10 39							10 56	11 01			11 09						11 26	11 31			11 39		
London Waterloo (East)	d	10 42							10 59	11 04			11 12						11 29	11 34			11 42		
London Cannon Street	d			10 47	10 54	10 57					11 07	11 10			11 17	11 24		11 27			11 37	11 40			11 47
London Bridge	d	10 47		10 51	10 58	11 01			11 04	11 10	11 11	11 14	11 17		11 21	11 28		11 31	11 34	11 40	11 41	11 44	11 47		11 51
Deptford	d			10 57											11 27										11 57
Greenwich	d			11 00		11 10					11 20				11 30			11 40			11 50				12 00
Maze Hill	d																								
Westcombe Park	d			11 05											11 35										12 05
London Victoria	d		10 39											11 09										11 39	
Denmark Hill	d		10 48											11 18										11 48	
Peckham Rye	d		10 51											11 21										11 51	
Nunhead	d		10 53											11 23										11 53	
New Cross	d				11 03							11 19				11 33						11 49			
St Johns	d				11 05							11 21				11 35						11 51			
Lewisham	d	10 57	11 02		11 09					11 19		11 24	11 27	11 32		11 39				11 49		11 54	11 57	12 02	
Blackheath	d	11 01	11 06		11 13					11 23			11 31	11 36		11 43				11 53			12 01	12 06	
Kidbrooke	d		11 09		11 16									11 39		11 46								12 09	
Eltham	d		11 12		11 19					11 29				11 42		11 49				11 59				12 12	
Falconwood	d		11 14		11 22					11 31				11 44		11 52				12 01				12 14	
Welling	d		11 17		11 24					11 34				11 47		11 54				12 04				12 17	
Bexleyheath	d		11 19		11 27					11 36				11 49		11 57				12 06				12 19	
Barnehurst	d		11 22		11 32					11 39				11 52		12 02				12 09				12 22	
Hither Green	d								11 14			11 29							11 44			11 59			
Lee	d								11 16			11 31							11 46			12 01			
Mottingham	d								11 19			11 34							11 49			12 04			
New Eltham	d								11 21			11 36							11 51			12 06			
Sidcup	d								11 25			11 40							11 55			12 10			
Albany Park	d								11 27			11 42							11 57			12 12			
Bexley	d								11 29			11 44							11 59			12 14			
Crayford	d								11 33			11 48							12 03			12 18			
Charlton	d	11 05		11 09		11 17					11 26	12a12	11 35		11 39			11 47			11 56	12a42	12 05		12 09
Woolwich Dockyard	d																								
Woolwich Arsenal	d	11 11		11 15		11 23					11 33		11 41		11 45			11 53			12 03		12 11		12 15
Plumstead	d			11 17		11 25					11 35				11 47			11 55			12 05				12 17
Abbey Wood	d	11 15		11 20		11 28					11 38		11 45		11 50			11 58			12 08		12 15		12 20
Belvedere	d			11 22		11 31					11 40				11 52			12 01			12 10				12 22
Erith	d			11 25		11 33					11 43				11 55			12 03			12 13				12 25
Slade Green	d			11a27	11a45	11 37					11a46				11a57	12a15		12 07			12a16				12a27
Dartford	a	11 24	11 31			11 45			11 38	11 48			11 54	12 01				12 15	12 08	12 18			12 24	12 31	
	d	11 25							11 39				11 55						12 09				12 25		
Stone Crossing	d								11 43										12 13						
Greenhithe for Bluewater	d	11 30							11 45				12 00						12 15				12 30		
Swanscombe	d								11 48										12 18						
Northfleet	d								11 50										12 20						
Gravesend	d	11 37						11 48	11a55				12 07						12a25				12 37		
Higham	d	11 43											12 13										12 43		
Strood	d	11 48						11 58					12 18										12 48		
Maidstone West	d																								
Rochester	d	11 52						12 03					12 22										12 52		
Chatham	d	11 55						12 05					12 25										12 55		
Gillingham (Kent)	a	12 02						12 09					12 32										13 02		

London - Dartford and Gillingham

Sundays
29 July to 12 August

Network Diagram - see first Page of Table 200

		SE		SE	SE	SE	SE	SE	SE	SE	SE	SE		SE	SE	SE	SE	SE	SE	SE	SE	SE		SE	SE
St Pancras Int'l ⊖	d				12 18																				
Stratford International ⊖	d				12 28																				
Ebbsfleet International	d				12 44																				
London Charing Cross ⊖	d					11 56	12 01			12 09						12 26	12 31			12 39					
London Waterloo (East) ⊖	d					11 59	12 04			12 12						12 29	12 34			12 42					
London Cannon Street ⊖	d	11 54		11 57				12 07	12 10			12 17		12 24	12 27			12 37	12 40			12 47		12 54	12 57
London Bridge ⊖	d	11 58		12 01		12 04	12 10	12 11	12 14	12 17		12 21		12 28	12 31	12 34	12 40	12 41	12 44	12 47		12 51		12 58	13 01
Deptford	d											12 27										12 57			
Greenwich	d			12 09				12 19				12 30			12 39			12 49				13 00			13 09
Maze Hill	d			12 13				12 23				12 34			12 43			12 53				13 04			13 13
Westcombe Park	d											12 36										13 06			
London Victoria ⊖	d										12 09										12 39				
Denmark Hill	d										12 18										12 48				
Peckham Rye	d										12 21										12 51				
Nunhead	d										12 23										12 53				
New Cross ⊖	d	12 03							12 19					12 33					12 49					13 03	
St Johns	d	12 05							12 21					12 35					12 51					13 05	
Lewisham	d	12 09					12 19		12 24	12 27	12 32			12 39			12 49		12 54	12 57	13 02			13 09	
Blackheath	d	12 13					12 23			12 31	12 36			12 43			12 53			13 01	13 06			13 13	
Kidbrooke	d	12 16									12 39			12 46							13 09			13 16	
Eltham	d	12 19					12 29				12 42			12 49			12 59				13 12			13 19	
Falconwood	d	12 22					12 31				12 44			12 52			13 01				13 14			13 22	
Welling	d	12 24					12 34				12 47			12 54			13 04				13 17			13 24	
Bexleyheath	d	12 27					12 36				12 49			12 57			13 06				13 19			13 27	
Barnehurst	d	12 32					12 39				12 52			13 02			13 09				13 22			13 32	
Hither Green	d					12 14			12 29							12 44			12 59						
Lee	d					12 16			12 31							12 46			13 01						
Mottingham	d					12 19			12 34							12 49			13 04						
New Eltham	d					12 21			12 36							12 51			13 06						
Sidcup	d					12 25			12 40							12 55			13 10						
Albany Park	d					12 27			12 42							12 57			13 12						
Bexley	d					12 29			12 44							12 59			13 14						
Crayford	d					12 33			12 48							13 03			13 18						
Charlton	d			12 17				12 27	13a12	12 35		12 39			12 47			12 57	13a42	13 05		13 09			13 17
Woolwich Dockyard	d																								
Woolwich Arsenal	d			12 23				12 32		12 41		12 44			12 53			13 02		13 11		13 14			13 23
Plumstead	d			12 26				12 35				12 46			12 56			13 05				13 16			13 26
Abbey Wood	d			12 29				12 38		12 45		12 49			12 59			13 08		13 15		13 19			13 29
Belvedere	d			12 31				12 40				12 52			13 01			13 10				13 22			13 31
Erith	d			12 34				12 43				12 54			13 04			13 13				13 24			13 34
Slade Green	d	12a45		12 37				12a46				12a57		13a15	13 07			13a16				13a27		13a45	13 37
Dartford	a			12 45		12 38	12 48			12 54	13 01				13 15	13 08	13 18			13 24	13 31				13 45
	d					12 39				12 55						13 09				13 25					
Stone Crossing	d					12 43										13 13									
Greenhithe for Bluewater	d					12 45				13 00						13 15				13 30					
Swanscombe	d					12 48										13 18									
Northfleet	d					12 50										13 20									
Gravesend	d				12 48	12a55				13 07						13a25				13 37					
Higham	d									13 13										13 43					
Strood	d				12 58					13 18										13 48					
Maidstone West	d																								
Rochester	d				13 03					13 22										13 52					
Chatham	d				13 05					13 25										13 55					
Gillingham (Kent)	a				13 09					13 32										14 02					

Table 200

London - Dartford and Gillingham

Sundays
29 July to 12 August

Network Diagram - see first Page of Table 200

		SE	SE	SE	SE	SE	SE	SE		SE	SE	SE	SE	SE	SE	SE	SE	SE		SE	SE	SE	SE	SE	SE
St Pancras Int'l ⊖	d	13 18																					14 18		
Stratford International ⊖	d	13 28																					14 28		
Ebbsfleet International	d	13 43																					14 43		
London Charing Cross ⊖	d		12 56	13 01			13 09						13 26	13 31			13 39							13 56	14 01
London Waterloo (East) ⊖	d		12 59	13 04			13 12						13 29	13 34			13 42							13 59	14 04
London Cannon Street ⊖	d				13 07	13 10				13 17	13 24	13 27			13 37	13 40				13 47	13 54	13 57			
London Bridge ⊖	d		13 04	13 10	13 11	13 14	13 17			13 21	13 28	13 31	13 34	13 40	13 41	13 44	13 47			13 51	13 58	14 01		14 04	14 10
Deptford	d									13 27										13 57					
Greenwich	d				13 19					13 30		13 39			13 49					14 00		14 09			
Maze Hill	d				13 23					13 34		13 43			13 53					14 04		14 13			
Westcombe Park	d									13 36										14 06					
London Victoria ⊖	d							13 09										13 39							
Denmark Hill	d							13 18										13 48							
Peckham Rye	d							13 21										13 51							
Nunhead	d							13 23										13 53							
New Cross ⊖	d					13 19					13 33					13 49					14 03				
St Johns	d					13 21					13 35					13 51					14 05				
Lewisham	d			13 19		13 24	13 27	13 32			13 39			13 49		13 54	13 57	14 02			14 09				14 19
Blackheath	d			13 23			13 31	13 36			13 43			13 53			14 01	14 06			14 13				14 23
Kidbrooke	d							13 39			13 46							14 09			14 16				
Eltham	d			13 29				13 42			13 49			13 59				14 12			14 19				14 29
Falconwood	d			13 31				13 44			13 52			14 01				14 14			14 22				14 31
Welling	d			13 34				13 47			13 54			14 04				14 17			14 24				14 34
Bexleyheath	d			13 36				13 49			13 57			14 06				14 19			14 27				14 36
Barnehurst	d			13 39				13 52			14 02			14 09				14 22			14 32				14 39
Hither Green	d		13 14			13 29							13 44			13 59								14 14	
Lee	d		13 16			13 31							13 46			14 01								14 16	
Mottingham	d		13 19			13 34							13 49			14 04								14 19	
New Eltham	d		13 21			13 36							13 51			14 06								14 21	
Sidcup	d		13 25			13 40							13 55			14 10								14 25	
Albany Park	d		13 27			13 42							13 57			14 12								14 27	
Bexley	d		13 29			13 44							13 59			14 14								14 29	
Crayford	d		13 33			13 48							14 03			14 18								14 33	
Charlton	d				13 27	14a12	13 35			13 39		13 47			13 57	14a42	14 05			14 09		14 17			
Woolwich Dockyard	d																								
Woolwich Arsenal	d				13 32		13 41			13 44		13 53			14 02		14 11			14 14		14 23			
Plumstead	d				13 35					13 46		13 56			14 05					14 16		14 26			
Abbey Wood	d				13 38		13 45			13 49		13 59			14 08		14 15			14 19		14 29			
Belvedere	d				13 40					13 52		14 01			14 10					14 22		14 31			
Erith	d				13 43					13 54		14 04			14 13					14 24		14 34			
Slade Green	d				13a46					13a57	14a15	14 07			14a16					14a27	14a45	14 37			
Dartford	a		13 38	13 48			13 54	14 01				14 15	14 08	14 18			14 24	14 31				14 45		14 38	14 48
	d		13 39				13 55						14 09				14 25							14 39	
Stone Crossing	d		13 43										14 13											14 43	
Greenhithe for Bluewater	d		13 45				14 00						14 15				14 30							14 45	
Swanscombe	d		13 48										14 18											14 48	
Northfleet	d		13 50										14 20											14 50	
Gravesend	d	13 48	13a55				14 07						14a25				14 37						14 48	14a55	
Higham	d						14 13										14 43								
Strood	d	13 58					14 18										14 48						14 58		
Maidstone West	d																								
Rochester	d	14 03					14 22										14 52						15 03		
Chatham	d	14 05					14 25										14 55						15 05		
Gillingham (Kent)	a	14 09					14 32										15 02						15 09		

Table 200

Sundays

29 July to 12 August

London - Dartford and Gillingham

Network Diagram - see first Page of Table 200

Station		SE	SE	SE	SE	SE	SE	SE	SE	SE	SE	SE	SE	SE	SE	SE	SE	SE	SE	SE	SE	SE
St Pancras Int'l	d																	15 18				
Stratford International	d																	15 28				
Ebbsfleet International	d																	15 43				
London Charing Cross	d			14 09					14 26	14 31			14 39						14 56	15 01		
London Waterloo (East)	d			14 12					14 29	14 34			14 42						14 59	15 04		
London Cannon Street	d	14 07	14 10			14 17	14 24	14 27			14 37	14 40			14 47	14 54	14 57				15 07	15 10
London Bridge	d	14 11	14 14	14 17		14 21	14 28	14 31	14 34	14 40	14 41	14 44	14 47		14 51	14 58	15 01		15 04	15 10	15 11	15 14
Deptford	d					14 27									14 57							
Greenwich	d	14 19				14 30		14 39			14 49				15 00		15 09				15 19	
Maze Hill	d	14 23				14 34		14 43			14 53				15 04		15 13				15 23	
Westcombe Park	d					14 36									15 06							
London Victoria	d				14 09									14 39								
Denmark Hill	d				14 18									14 48								
Peckham Rye	d				14 21									14 51								
Nunhead	d				14 23									14 53								
New Cross	d		14 19				14 33					14 49				15 03						15 19
St Johns	d		14 21				14 35					14 51				15 05						15 21
Lewisham	d		14 24	14 27	14 32		14 39			14 49		14 54	14 57	15 02		15 09				15 19		15 24
Blackheath	d			14 31	14 36		14 43			14 53			15 01	15 06		15 13				15 23		
Kidbrooke	d				14 39		14 46							15 09		15 16						
Eltham	d				14 42		14 49			14 59				15 12		15 19				15 29		
Falconwood	d				14 44		14 52			15 01				15 14		15 22				15 31		
Welling	d				14 47		14 54			15 04				15 17		15 24				15 34		
Bexleyheath	d				14 49		14 57			15 06				15 19		15 27				15 36		
Barnehurst	d				14 52		15 02			15 09				15 22		15 32				15 39		
Hither Green	d		14 29						14 44			14 59							15 14			15 29
Lee	d		14 31						14 46			15 01							15 16			15 31
Mottingham	d		14 34						14 49			15 04							15 19			15 34
New Eltham	d		14 36						14 51			15 06							15 21			15 36
Sidcup	d		14 40						14 55			15 10							15 25			15 40
Albany Park	d		14 42						14 57			15 12							15 27			15 42
Bexley	d		14 44						14 59			15 14							15 29			15 44
Crayford	d		14 48						15 03			15 18							15 33			15 48
Charlton	d	14 27	15a12	14 35		14 39		14 47			14 57	15a42	15 05		15 09		15 17				15 27	16a12
Woolwich Dockyard	d																					
Woolwich Arsenal	d	14 32		14 41		14 44		14 53			15 02		15 11		15 14		15 23				15 32	
Plumstead	d	14 35				14 46		14 56			15 05				15 16		15 26				15 35	
Abbey Wood	d	14 38		14 45		14 49		14 59			15 08		15 15		15 19		15 29				15 38	
Belvedere	d	14 40				14 52		15 01			15 10				15 22		15 31				15 40	
Erith	d	14 43				14 54		15 04			15 13				15 24		15 34				15 43	
Slade Green	d	14a46				14a57	15a15	15 07			15a16				15a27	15a45	15 37				15a46	
Dartford	a			14 54	15 01			15 15	15 08	15 18			15 24	15 31			15 45		15 38	15 48		
	d			14 55					15 09				15 25						15 39			
Stone Crossing	d								15 13										15 43			
Greenhithe for Bluewater	d			15 00					15 15				15 30						15 45			
Swanscombe	d								15 18										15 48			
Northfleet	d								15 20										15 50			
Gravesend	d			15 07					15a25				15 37					15 48	15a55			
Higham	d			15 13									15 43									
Strood	d			15 18									15 48					15 58				
Maidstone West	d																					
Rochester	d			15 22									15 52					16 03				
Chatham	d			15 25									15 55					16 05				
Gillingham (Kent)	a			15 32									16 02					16 09				

Table 200

Sundays

29 July to 12 August

London - Dartford and Gillingham

Network Diagram - see first Page of Table 200

Station		SE	SE	SE	SE	SE	SE	SE	SE	SE	SE	SE	SE	SE	SE	SE	SE	SE	SE	SE	SE	SE	SE
St Pancras Int'l	d															16 18							
Stratford International	d															16 28							
Ebbsfleet International	d															16 44							
London Charing Cross	d	15 09					15 26	15 31			15 39						15 56	16 01			16 09		
London Waterloo (East)	d	15 12					15 29	15 34			15 42						15 59	16 04			16 12		
London Cannon Street	d			15 17	15 24	15 27			15 37	15 40			15 47	15 54	15 57				16 07	16 10			16 17
London Bridge	d	15 17		15 21	15 28	15 31	15 34	15 40	15 41	15 44	15 47		15 51	15 58	16 01		16 04	16 10	16 11	16 14	16 17		16 21
Deptford	d			15 27									15 57										16 27
Greenwich	d			15 30		15 39			15 49				16 00		16 09				16 19				16 30
Maze Hill	d			15 34		15 43			15 53				16 04		16 13				16 23				16 34
Westcombe Park	d			15 36									16 06										16 36
London Victoria	d		15 09									15 39										16 09	
Denmark Hill	d		15 18									15 48										16 18	
Peckham Rye	d		15 21									15 51										16 21	
Nunhead	d		15 23									15 53										16 23	
New Cross	d				15 33					15 49				16 03						16 19			
St Johns	d				15 35					15 51				16 05						16 21			
Lewisham	d	15 27	15 32		15 39			15 49		15 54	15 57	16 02		16 09				16 19		16 24	16 27	16 32	
Blackheath	d	15 31	15 36		15 43			15 53			16 01	16 06		16 13				16 23			16 31	16 36	
Kidbrooke	d		15 39		15 46							16 09		16 16								16 39	
Eltham	d		15 42		15 49			15 59				16 12		16 19				16 29				16 42	
Falconwood	d		15 44		15 52			16 01				16 14		16 22				16 31				16 44	
Welling	d		15 47		15 54			16 04				16 17		16 24				16 34				16 47	
Bexleyheath	d		15 49		15 57			16 06				16 19		16 27				16 36				16 49	
Barnehurst	d		15 52		16 02			16 09				16 22		16 32				16 39				16 52	
Hither Green	d						15 44			15 59							16 14			16 29			
Lee	d						15 46			16 01							16 16			16 31			
Mottingham	d						15 49			16 04							16 19			16 34			
New Eltham	d						15 51			16 06							16 21			16 36			
Sidcup	d						15 55			16 10							16 25			16 40			
Albany Park	d						15 57			16 12							16 27			16 42			
Bexley	d						15 59			16 14							16 29			16 44			
Crayford	d						16 03			16 18							16 33			16 48			
Charlton	d	15 35		15 39		15 47			15 57	16a42	16 05		16 09		16 17				16 27	17a12	16 35		16 39
Woolwich Dockyard	d																						
Woolwich Arsenal	d	15 41		15 44		15 53			16 02		16 11		16 14		16 23				16 32		16 41		16 44
Plumstead	d			15 46		15 56			16 05				16 16		16 26				16 35				16 46
Abbey Wood	d	15 45		15 49		15 59			16 08		16 15		16 19		16 29				16 38		16 45		16 49
Belvedere	d			15 52		16 01			16 10				16 22		16 31				16 40				16 52
Erith	d			15 54		16 04			16 13				16 24		16 34				16 43				16 54
Slade Green	d			15a57	16a15	16 07			16a16				16a27	16a45	16 37				16a46				16a57
Dartford	a	15 54	16 01			16 15	16 08	16 18			16 24	16 31			16 45		16 38	16 48			16 54	17 01	
	d	15 55					16 09				16 25						16 39				16 55		
Stone Crossing	d						16 13										16 43						
Greenhithe for Bluewater	d	16 00					16 15				16 30						16 45				17 00		
Swanscombe	d						16 18										16 48						
Northfleet	d						16 20										16 50						
Gravesend	d	16 07					16a25				16 37					16 48	16a55				17 07		
Higham	d	16 13									16 43										17 13		
Strood	d	16 18									16 48					16 58					17 18		
Maidstone West	d																						
Rochester	d	16 22									16 52					17 03					17 22		
Chatham	d	16 25									16 55					17 05					17 25		
Gillingham (Kent)	a	16 32									17 02					17 09					17 32		

Table 200

Sundays

29 July to 12 August

London - Dartford and Gillingham

Network Diagram - see first Page of Table 200

		SE	SE	SE	SE	SE		SE	SE	SE	SE	SE	SE	SE	SE	SE		SE	SE	SE	SE	SE	SE	SE	SE
St Pancras Int'l 15 ⊖	d													17 18											
Stratford International ⊖	d													17 28											
Ebbsfleet International	d													17 43											
London Charing Cross 4 ⊖	d			16 26	16 31				16 39						16 56	17 01				17 09					17 26
London Waterloo (East) 4 ⊖	d			16 29	16 34				16 42						16 59	17 04				17 12					17 29
London Cannon Street 4 ⊖	d	16 24	16 27			16 37		16 40			16 47	16 54	16 57					17 07	17 10			17 17	17 24	17 27	
London Bridge 4 ⊖	d	16 28	16 31	16 34	16 40	16 41		16 44	16 47		16 51	16 58	17 01		17 04	17 10		17 11	17 14	17 17		17 21	17 28	17 31	17 34
Deptford	d										16 57											17 27			
Greenwich 4	d		16 39			16 49					17 00		17 09					17 19				17 30		17 39	
Maze Hill	d		16 43			16 53					17 04		17 13					17 23				17 34		17 43	
Westcombe Park	d										17 06											17 36			
London Victoria 15 ⊖	d									16 39											17 09				
Denmark Hill 4	d									16 48											17 18				
Peckham Rye 4	d									16 51											17 21				
Nunhead 4	d									16 53											17 23				
New Cross 4 ⊖	d	16 33						16 49				17 03							17 19				17 33		
St Johns	d	16 35						16 51				17 05							17 21				17 35		
Lewisham 4	d	16 39			16 49			16 54	16 57	17 02		17 09				17 19			17 24	17 27	17 32		17 39		
Blackheath 4	d	16 43			16 53				17 01	17 06		17 13				17 23				17 31	17 36		17 43		
Kidbrooke	d	16 46								17 09		17 16									17 39		17 46		
Eltham	d	16 49			16 59					17 12		17 19				17 29					17 42		17 49		
Falconwood	d	16 52			17 01					17 14		17 22				17 31					17 44		17 52		
Welling	d	16 54			17 04					17 17		17 24				17 34					17 47		17 54		
Bexleyheath	d	16 57			17 06					17 19		17 27				17 36					17 49		17 57		
Barnehurst 4	d	17 02			17 09					17 22		17 32				17 39					17 52		18 02		
Hither Green 4	d			16 44				16 59							17 14				17 29						17 44
Lee	d			16 46				17 01							17 16				17 31						17 46
Mottingham	d			16 49				17 04							17 19				17 34						17 49
New Eltham	d			16 51				17 06							17 21				17 36						17 51
Sidcup 4	d			16 55				17 10							17 25				17 40						17 55
Albany Park	d			16 57				17 12							17 27				17 42						17 57
Bexley	d			16 59				17 14							17 29				17 44						17 59
Crayford	d			17 03				17 18							17 33				17 48						18 03
Charlton 4	d		16 47			16 57		17a42	17 05		17 09		17 17					17 27	18a12	17 35		17 39		17 47	
Woolwich Dockyard	d																								
Woolwich Arsenal 4	d		16 53			17 02			17 11		17 14		17 23					17 32		17 41		17 44		17 53	
Plumstead	d		16 56			17 05					17 16		17 26					17 35				17 46		17 56	
Abbey Wood	d		16 59			17 08			17 15		17 19		17 29					17 38		17 45		17 49		17 59	
Belvedere	d		17 01			17 10					17 22		17 31					17 40				17 52		18 01	
Erith	d		17 04			17 13					17 24		17 34					17 43				17 54		18 04	
Slade Green 4	d	17a15	17 07			17a16					17a27	17a45	17 37					17a46				17a57	18a15	18 07	
Dartford 4	a		17 15	17 08	17 18				17 24	17 31			17 45		17 38	17 48				17 54	18 01			18 15	18 08
	d			17 09					17 25						17 39					17 55					18 09
Stone Crossing	d			17 13											17 43										18 13
Greenhithe for Bluewater	d			17 15					17 30						17 45					18 00					18 15
Swanscombe	d			17 18											17 48										18 18
Northfleet	d			17 20											17 50										18 20
Gravesend 4	d			17a25					17 37					17 48	17a55					18 07					18a25
Higham	d								17 43											18 13					
Strood 4	d								17 48					17 58						18 18					
Maidstone West	d																								
Rochester 4	d								17 52					18 03						18 22					
Chatham 4	d								17 55					18 05						18 25					
Gillingham (Kent) 4	a								18 02					18 09						18 32					

Table 200

Sundays

29 July to 12 August

London - Dartford and Gillingham

Network Diagram - see first Page of Table 200

		SE		SE	SE	SE	SE	SE	SE	SE	SE	SE		SE	SE	SE	SE	SE	SE	SE	SE	SE		SE	SE
St Pancras Int'l 15 ⊖	d										18 18														
Stratford International ⊖	d										18 28														
Ebbsfleet International	d										18 43														
London Charing Cross 4 ⊖	d	17 31				17 39						17 56		18 01			18 09					18 26		18 31	
London Waterloo (East) 4 ⊖	d	17 34				17 42						17 59		18 04			18 12					18 29		18 34	
London Cannon Street 4 ⊖	d			17 37	17 40			17 47	17 54	17 57					18 07	18 10			18 17	18 24	18 27				18 37
London Bridge 4 ⊖	d	17 40		17 41	17 44	17 47		17 51	17 58	18 01		18 04		18 10	18 11	18 14	18 17		18 21	18 28	18 31	18 34		18 40	18 41
Deptford	d							17 57											18 27						
Greenwich 4	d			17 49				18 00		18 09					18 19				18 30		18 39				18 49
Maze Hill	d			17 53				18 04		18 13					18 23				18 34		18 43				18 53
Westcombe Park	d							18 06											18 36						
London Victoria 15 ⊖	d						17 39											18 09							
Denmark Hill 4	d						17 48											18 18							
Peckham Rye 4	d						17 51											18 21							
Nunhead 4	d						17 53											18 23							
New Cross 4 ⊖	d				17 49				18 03							18 19				18 33					
St Johns	d				17 51				18 05							18 21				18 35					
Lewisham 4	d	17 49			17 54	17 57	18 02		18 09					18 19		18 24	18 27	18 32		18 39				18 49	
Blackheath 4	d	17 53				18 01	18 06		18 13					18 23			18 31	18 36		18 43				18 53	
Kidbrooke	d						18 09		18 16									18 39		18 46					
Eltham	d	17 59					18 12		18 19					18 29				18 42		18 49				18 59	
Falconwood	d	18 01					18 14		18 22					18 31				18 44		18 52				19 01	
Welling	d	18 04					18 17		18 24					18 34				18 47		18 54				19 04	
Bexleyheath	d	18 06					18 19		18 27					18 36				18 49		18 57				19 06	
Barnehurst 4	d	18 09					18 22		18a32					18 39				18 52		19a02				19 09	
Hither Green 4	d				17 59							18 14				18 29						18 44			
Lee	d				18 01							18 16				18 31						18 46			
Mottingham	d				18 04							18 19				18 34						18 49			
New Eltham	d				18 06							18 21				18 36						18 51			
Sidcup 4	d				18 10							18 25				18 40						18 55			
Albany Park	d				18 12							18 27				18 42						18 57			
Bexley	d				18 14							18 29				18 44						18 59			
Crayford	d				18 18							18 33				18 48						19 03			
Charlton 4	d			17 57	18a42	18 05		18 09		18 17					18 27	19a12	18 35		18 39		18 47				18 57
Woolwich Dockyard	d																								
Woolwich Arsenal 4	d			18 02		18 11		18 14		18 23					18 32		18 41		18 44		18 53				19 02
Plumstead	d			18 05				18 16		18 26					18 35				18 46		18 56				19 05
Abbey Wood	d			18 08		18 15		18 19		18 29					18 38		18 45		18 49		18 59				19 08
Belvedere	d			18 10				18 22		18 31					18 40				18 52		19 01				19 10
Erith	d			18 13				18 24		18 34					18 43				18 54		19 04				19 13
Slade Green 4	d			18a16				18a27		18 37					18a48				19a00		19 07				19a18
Dartford 4	a	18 18				18 24	18 31			18 45		18 38		18 48			18 54	19 01			19 15	19 08		19 18	
	d					18 25						18 39					18 55					19 09			
Stone Crossing	d											18 43										19 13			
Greenhithe for Bluewater	d					18 30						18 45					19 00					19 15			
Swanscombe	d											18 48										19 18			
Northfleet	d											18 50										19 20			
Gravesend 4	d					18 37					18 48	18a55					19 07					19a25			
Higham	d					18 43											19 13								
Strood 4	d					18 48					18 58						19 18								
Maidstone West	d																								
Rochester 4	d					18 52					19 03						19 22								
Chatham 4	d					18 55					19 05						19 25								
Gillingham (Kent) 4	a					19 02					19 09						19 32								

Table 200

Sundays

29 July to 12 August

London - Dartford and Gillingham

Network Diagram - see first Page of Table 200

Station		SE	SE	SE	SE	SE	SE	SE		SE	SE	SE	SE	SE	SE	SE	SE	SE		SE	SE	SE	SE	SE	SE
St Pancras Int'l ⊖	d							19 18																20 18	
Stratford International ⊖	d							19 28																20 28	
Ebbsfleet International	d							19 43																20 43	
London Charing Cross ⊖	d		18 39							18 56	19 01			19 09				19 26		19 31	19 39				19 52
London Waterloo (East) ⊖	d		18 42							18 59	19 04			19 12				19 29		19 34	19 42				19 55
London Cannon Street ⊖	d	18 40			18 47	18 54	18 57					19 07	19 10			19 24	19 27						19 46		
London Bridge ⊖	d	18 44	18 47		18 51	18 58	19 01			19 04	19 10	19 11	19 14	19 17		19 28	19 31	19 34		19 40	19 47		19 50		20 00
Deptford	d				18 57							19 17					19 37								
Greenwich	d				19 00		19 09					19 19					19 40						19 58		
Maze Hill	d				19 04		19 13					19 23					19 44						20 02		
Westcombe Park	d				19 06							19 25					19 46								
London Victoria ⊖	d			18 39											19 09							19 39			
Denmark Hill	d			18 48											19 18							19 48			
Peckham Rye	d			18 51											19 21							19 51			
Nunhead	d			18 53											19 23							19 53			
New Cross ⊖	d	18 49				19 03							19 19			19 33				19 45					20 05
St Johns	d	18 51				19 05							19 21			19 35									
Lewisham	d	18 54	18 57	19 02		19 09					19 19		19 24	19 26	19 32	19 39				19 49	19 56	20 02			20 09
Blackheath	d		19 01	19 06		19 13					19 23			19 30	19 36	19 43				19 53	20 00	20 06			
Kidbrooke	d			19 09		19 16									19 39	19 46						20 09			
Eltham	d			19 12		19 19					19 29				19 42	19 49				19 59		20 12			
Falconwood	d			19 14		19 22					19 31				19 44	19 52				20 01		20 14			
Welling	d			19 17		19 24					19 34				19 47	19 54				20 04		20 17			
Bexleyheath	d			19 19		19 27					19 36				19 49	19 57				20 06		20 19			
Barnehurst	d			19 22		19a32					19 39				19 52	20a02				20 09		20 22			
Hither Green	d	18 59								19 14			19 29					19 44							20 14
Lee	d	19 01								19 16			19 31					19 46							20 16
Mottingham	d	19 04								19 19			19 34					19 49							20 19
New Eltham	d	19 06								19 21			19 36					19 51							20 21
Sidcup	d	19 10								19 25			19 40					19 55							20 25
Albany Park	d	19 12								19 27			19 42					19 57							20 27
Bexley	d	19 14								19 29			19 44					19 59							20 29
Crayford	d	19 18								19 33			19 48					20 03							20 33
Charlton	d	19a42	19 05		19 09		19 17					19 27	20a12	19 36			19 49				20 06		20 09		
Woolwich Dockyard	d																								
Woolwich Arsenal	d		19 11		19 14		19 23					19 33		19 40			19 54				20 10		20 14		
Plumstead	d				19 16		19 26					19 35					19 56						20 16		
Abbey Wood	d		19 15		19 19		19 29					19 38		19 45			19 59				20 15		20 19		
Belvedere	d				19 22		19 31					19 40					20 02						20 22		
Erith	d				19 24		19 34					19 43					20 04						20 24		
Slade Green	d				19a30		19 37					19 46					20 07						20 27		
Dartford	a		19 24	19 31			19 45			19 38	19 48	19 55		19 54	20 01		20 15	20 08		20 18	20 24	20 31	20 37		20 38
	d		19 25							19 39				19 55				20 09			20 25				20 38
Stone Crossing	d									19 43								20 13							20 42
Greenhithe for Bluewater	d		19 30							19 45				20 00				20 15			20 30				20 45
Swanscombe	d									19 48								20 18							20 48
Northfleet	d									19 50								20 20							20 50
Gravesend	d		19 37					19 48		19a55				20 07				20a25			20 37			20 48	20a58
Higham	d		19 43											20 13							20 43				
Strood	d		19 48					19 58						20 18							20 48			20 58	
Maidstone West	d																								
Rochester	d		19 52					20 03						20 22							20 52			21 03	
Chatham	d		19 55					20 05						20 25							20 55			21 05	
Gillingham (Kent)	a		20 02					20 09						20 32							21 02			21 09	

Table 200

Sundays

29 July to 12 August

London - Dartford and Gillingham

Network Diagram - see first Page of Table 200

Station		SE	SE	SE		SE	SE	SE	SE	SE	SE	SE	SE	SE		SE	SE	SE	SE	SE	SE	SE	SE	SE	
St Pancras Int'l ⊖	d											21 18													
Stratford International ⊖	d											21 28													
Ebbsfleet International	d											21 43													
London Charing Cross ⊖	d	19 56	20 01	20 09			20 22	20 26	20 31	20 39			20 52	20 56		21 01	21 09	21 22	21 26	21 31	21 39	21 52	21 56	22 01	
London Waterloo (East) ⊖	d	19 59	20 04	20 12			20 25	20 29	20 34	20 42			20 55	20 59		21 04	21 12	21 25	21 29	21 34	21 42	21 55	21 59	22 04	
London Cannon Street ⊖	d					20 16					20 46														
London Bridge ⊖	d	20 05	20 10	20 17		20 20	20 30	20 35	20 40	20 47	20 50		21 00	21 05		21 10	21 17	21 30	21 35	21 40	21 47	22 00	22 05	22 10	
Deptford	d	20 11						20 41						21 11					21 41				22 11		
Greenwich	d	20 13				20 28		20 43			20 58			21 13					21 43				22 13		
Maze Hill	d	20 17				20 32		20 47			21 02			21 17					21 47				22 17		
Westcombe Park	d	20 19						20 49						21 19					21 49				22 19		
London Victoria ⊖	d																								
Denmark Hill	d																								
Peckham Rye	d																								
Nunhead	d																								
New Cross ⊖	d		20 15				20 35		20 45				21 05			21 15		21 35		21 45		22 05		22 15	
St Johns	d																								
Lewisham	d		20 20	20 26			20 39		20 50	20 56			21 09			21 20	21 26	21 39		21 50	21 56	22 09		22 20	
Blackheath	d		20 24	20 30					20 54	21 00						21 24	21 30			21 54	22 00			22 24	
Kidbrooke	d		20 27						20 57							21 27				21 57				22 27	
Eltham	d		20 30						21 00							21 30				22 00				22 30	
Falconwood	d		20 32						21 02							21 32				22 02				22 32	
Welling	d		20 35						21 05							21 35				22 05				22 35	
Bexleyheath	d		20 37						21 07							21 37				22 07				22 37	
Barnehurst	d		20 40						21 10							21 40				22 10				22 40	
Hither Green	d						20 44						21 14					21 44				22 14			
Lee	d						20 46						21 16					21 46				22 16			
Mottingham	d						20 49						21 19					21 49				22 19			
New Eltham	d						20 51						21 21					21 51				22 21			
Sidcup	d						20 55						21 25					21 55				22 25			
Albany Park	d						20 57						21 27					21 57				22 27			
Bexley	d						20 59						21 29					21 59				22 29			
Crayford	d						21 03						21 33					22 03				22 33			
Charlton	d	20 22		20 36		20 39		20 52		21 06	21 09			21 22			21 36		21 52		22 06		22 22		
Woolwich Dockyard	d																								
Woolwich Arsenal	d	20 27		20 40		20 44		20 57		21 10	21 14			21 27			21 40		21 57		22 10		22 27		
Plumstead	d	20 29				20 46		20 59			21 16			21 29					21 59				22 29		
Abbey Wood	d	20 32		20 45		20 49		21 02		21 15	21 19			21 32			21 45		22 02		22 15		22 32		
Belvedere	d	20 34				20 52		21 04			21 22			21 34					22 04				22 34		
Erith	d	20 37				20 54		21 07			21 24			21 37					22 07				22 37		
Slade Green	d	20 39				20 57		21 09			21 27			21 39					22 09				22 39		
Dartford	a	20 47	20 49	20 54		21 07	21 08	21 17	21 19	21 24	21 37		21 38	21 47		21 49	21 54	22 08	22 17	22 19	22 24	22 41	22 47	22 49	
	d			20 55			21 09			21 25			21 39				21 55	22 09			22 25				
Stone Crossing	d						21 13						21 43					22 13			22 29				
Greenhithe for Bluewater	d			21 00			21 15			21 30			21 45				22 00	22 15			22 31				
Swanscombe	d						21 18						21 48					22 18			22 34				
Northfleet	d						21 20						21 50					22 20			22 36				
Gravesend	d			21 07			21a28			21 37		21 48	21a58				22 07	22a28			22 40				
Higham	d			21 13						21 43							22 13				22 46				
Strood	d			21 18						21 48		21 58					22 18				22 52				
Maidstone West	d																								
Rochester	d			21 22						21 52		22 03					22 22				22 56				
Chatham	d			21 25						21 55		22 05					22 25				22 58				
Gillingham (Kent)	a			21 32						22 02		22 09					22 32				23 06				

London - Dartford and Gillingham

Sundays
29 July to 12 August

Network Diagram - see first Page of Table 200

Station		SE	SE	SE	SE	SE	SE	SE	SE	SE	SE	SE	SE	SE	SE
St Pancras Int'l	d														
Stratford International	d														
Ebbsfleet International	d														
London Charing Cross	d	22 09	22 22	22 26	22 31	22 39	22 52	22 56	23 01	23 09	23 22	23 26	23 31	23 39	23 56
London Waterloo (East)	d	22 12	22 25	22 29	22 34	22 42	22 55	22 59	23 04	23 12	23 25	23 29	23 34	23 42	23 59
London Cannon Street	d														
London Bridge	d	22 17	22 30	22 35	22 40	22 47	23 00	23 05	23 10	23 17	23 30	23 35	23 40	23 47	00 05
Deptford	d			22 41				23 11				23 41			00 11
Greenwich	d			22 43				23 13				23 43			00 13
Maze Hill	d			22 47				23 17				23 47			00 17
Westcombe Park	d			22 49				23 19				23 49			00 19
London Victoria	d														
Denmark Hill	d														
Peckham Rye	d														
Nunhead	d														
New Cross	d		22 35		22 45		23 05		23 15		23 35		23 45		
St Johns	d														
Lewisham	d	22 26	22 39		22 50	22 56	23 09		23 20	23 26	23 39		23 50	23 56	
Blackheath	d	22 30			22 54	23 00			23 24	23 30			23 55	00 01	
Kidbrooke	d				22 57				23 27				23 58		
Eltham	d				23 00				23 30				00 01		
Falconwood	d				23 02				23 32				00 04		
Welling	d				23 05				23 35				00 06		
Bexleyheath	d				23 07				23 37				00 09		
Barnehurst	d				23 10				23 40				00 12		
Hither Green	d		22 44				23 14				23 44				
Lee	d		22 46				23 16				23 46				
Mottingham	d		22 49				23 19				23 49				
New Eltham	d		22 51				23 21				23 51				
Sidcup	d		22 55				23 25				23 55				
Albany Park	d		22 57				23 27				23 57				
Bexley	d		22 59				23 29				23 59				
Crayford	d		23 03				23 33				00 03				
Charlton	d	22 36		22 52		23 06		23 22		23 36		23 52		00 06	00 22
Woolwich Dockyard	d														
Woolwich Arsenal	d	22 40		22 57		23 10		23 27		23 40		23 57		00 11	00 27
Plumstead	d			22 59				23 29				23 59			00 29
Abbey Wood	d	22 45		23 02		23 15		23 32		23 45		00 02		00 15	00 32
Belvedere	d			23 04				23 34				00 04			00 34
Erith	d			23 07				23 37				00 07			00 37
Slade Green	d			23 09				23 39				00 09			00 39
Dartford	a	22 54	23 11	23 17	23 19	23 24	23 41	23 47	23 50	23 54	00 11	00 17	00 22	00 24	00 47
	d	22 55				23 25				23 55				00 25	
Stone Crossing	d	22 59				23 29				23 58				00 29	
Greenhithe for Bluewater	d	23 01				23 31				23 59				00 31	
Swanscombe	d	23 04				23 34				00 04				00 34	
Northfleet	d	23 06				23 36				00 06				00 36	
Gravesend	d	23 10				23 40				00 10				00 40	
Higham	d	23 16				23 46				00 16				00 46	
Strood	d	23 22				23 52				00 22				00 52	
Maidstone West	d														
Rochester	d	23 26				23 56				00 26				00 56	
Chatham	d	23 28				23 58				00 28				00 58	
Gillingham (Kent)	a	23 36				00 06				00 36				01 06	

London - Dartford and Gillingham

Sundays
26 August to 9 September

Network Diagram - see first Page of Table 200

Station		SE	SE A	SE B	SE	SE	SE	SE	SE B	SE A
St Pancras Int'l	d		23p25	23p25					23p55	23p55
Stratford International	d		23p32	23p33					00 03	00 02
Ebbsfleet International	d		23p43	23p44					00 13	00 13
London Charing Cross	d	22p39			23p09	23p22	23p26	23p32		
London Waterloo (East)	d	22p42			23p12	23p25	23p29	23p35		
London Cannon Street	d									
London Bridge	d	22p47			23p17	23p30	23p35	23p40		
Deptford	d						23p41			
Greenwich	d						23p43			
Maze Hill	d						23p46			
Westcombe Park	d						23p48			
London Victoria	d									
Denmark Hill	d									
Peckham Rye	d									
Nunhead	d									
New Cross	d					23p35		23p45		
St Johns	d									
Lewisham	d	22p56			23p26	23p39		23p49		
Blackheath	d	22p59			23p29			23p52		
Kidbrooke	d							23p55		
Eltham	d							23p58		
Falconwood	d							00 01		
Welling	d							00 03		
Bexleyheath	d							00 06		
Barnehurst	d							00 08		
Hither Green	d					23p44				
Lee	d					23p46				
Mottingham	d					23p49				
New Eltham	d					23p51				
Sidcup	d					23p55				
Albany Park	d					23p57				
Bexley	d					23p59				
Crayford	d					00 03				
Charlton	d	23p03			23p33		23p50			
Woolwich Dockyard	d						23p53			
Woolwich Arsenal	d	23p09			23p39		23p56			
Plumstead	d						23p58			
Abbey Wood	d	23p13			23p43		00 01			
Belvedere	d						00 04			
Erith	d						00 06			
Slade Green	d						00 09			
Dartford	a	23p24			23p54	00 08	00 14	00 16		
	d	23p25			23p55					
Stone Crossing	d	23p29			23p58					
Greenhithe for Bluewater	d	23p31			23p59					
Swanscombe	d	23p34			00 04					
Northfleet	d	23p36			00 06					
Gravesend	d	23p40	23p48	23p48	00 10				00 18	00 18
Higham	d	23p46			00 16					
Strood	d	23p52	23p58	23p58	00 22				00 28	00 28
Maidstone West	d									
Rochester	d	23p56	00 03	00 03	00 26				00 32	00 33
Chatham	d	23p58	00 05	00 05	00 28				00 35	00 35
Gillingham (Kent)	a	00 03	00 09	00 09	00 33				00 39	00 39

Station		SE	SE	SE	SE	SE	SE B	SE B	SE B	SE B	SE	SE	SE	SE
St Pancras Int'l	d													
Stratford International	d													
Ebbsfleet International	d													
London Charing Cross	d	23p39	23p56	00 02	00 10	00 18	00 32		00 44			07 30		07 50
London Waterloo (East)	d	23p42	23p59	00 05	00 13	00 21	00 35		00 47			07 33		07 53
London Cannon Street	d							00 41		00 56				
London Bridge	d	23p47	00 05	00 10	00 18	00 26	00 40	00 45	00 52	01 00		07 38		07 58
Deptford	d		00 11				00 46			01s06		07 44		
Greenwich	d		00 13				00 49			01s08		07 46		
Maze Hill	d		00 16				00 53			01s12		07 49		
Westcombe Park	d		00 18				00 55			01s15		07 51		
London Victoria	d													
Denmark Hill	d													
Peckham Rye	d													
Nunhead	d													
New Cross	d			00 15	00 23	00 31			00 57					08 04
St Johns	d													
Lewisham	d	23p56		00 19	00 27	00 35		00 53	01 01					08 08
Blackheath	d	23p58		00 22		00 38		00 57						08 10
Kidbrooke	d			00 25				01s00						08 13
Eltham	d			00 28				01s03						08 17
Falconwood	d			00 31				01s06						08 19
Welling	d			00 33				01s09						08 22
Bexleyheath	d			00 36				01s11						08 24
Barnehurst	d			00 38				01s14						08 27
Hither Green	d				00 32				01s05					
Lee	d				00 34				01s08					
Mottingham	d				00 37				01s11					
New Eltham	d				00 39				01s13					
Sidcup	d				00 43				01s16					
Albany Park	d				00 45				01s19					
Bexley	d				00 47				01s21					
Crayford	d				00 51				01s24					
Charlton	d	00 03	00 20			00 42	00 59			01s17		07 54		
Woolwich Dockyard	d		00 23									07 57		
Woolwich Arsenal	d	00 09	00 26			00 47	01 04			01s23		08 00		
Plumstead	d		00 28			00 49	01s06			01s26		08 02		
Abbey Wood	d	00 13	00 31			00 53	01s09			01s29		08 05		
Belvedere	d		00 34			00 55	01s12			01s32		08 07		
Erith	d		00 36			00 58	01s15			01s35		08 10		
Slade Green	d		00 39			01 00	01s18			01s38		08 14		
Dartford	a	00 24	00 44	00 46	00 56	01 05	01 23	01s21	01 30	01 44		08 19		08 33
	d	00 25				01 06					07 55		08 25	
Stone Crossing	d	00 29									07 59		08 29	
Greenhithe for Bluewater	d	00 31				01 10					08 01		08 31	
Swanscombe	d	00 34									08 04		08 34	
Northfleet	d	00 36									08 06		08 36	
Gravesend	d	00 40				01 17		01s31			08 10		08 40	
Higham	d	00 46				01 23		01s37			08 16		08 46	
Strood	d	00 52				01 29		01s42			08 22		08 52	
Maidstone West	d													
Rochester	d	00 56				01 33		01s46			08 26		08 56	
Chatham	d	00 58				01 35		01s48			08 28		08 58	
Gillingham (Kent)	a	01 03				01 41		01 52			08 33		09 03	

A not from 2 September until 9 September

B not 26 August

Table 200

Sundays

26 August to 9 September

London - Dartford and Gillingham

Network Diagram - see first Page of Table 200

		SE	SE	SE	SE	SE		SE	SE	SE	SE A	SE B	SE	SE	SE	SE		SE	SE	SE	SE	SE	SE	SE A	SE B
St Pancras Int'l	d										09 25	09 26												10 28	10 28
Stratford International	d										09 32	09 33												10 35	10 36
Ebbsfleet International	d										09 43	09 44												10 46	10 47
London Charing Cross	d	07 56	08 00	08 10	08 20	08 26		08 30	08 40	08 50			08 56	09 00	09 10			09 20	09 26	09 30	09 40		09 50		
London Waterloo (East)	d	07 59	08 03	08 13	08 23	08 29		08 33	08 43	08 53			08 59	09 03	09 13			09 23	09 29	09 33	09 43		09 53		
London Cannon Street	d																								
London Bridge	d	08 04	08 08	08 18	08 28	08 34		08 38	08 48	08 58			09 04	09 08	09 18	09 23		09 28	09 34	09 38	09 48	09 53	09 58		
Deptford	d		08 14					08 44						09 14		09 29				09 44		09 59			
Greenwich	d		08 16					08 46						09 16		09 31				09 46		10 01			
Maze Hill	d		08 19					08 49						09 19		09 34				09 49		10 04			
Westcombe Park	d		08 21					08 51						09 21		09 36				09 51		10 06			
London Victoria	d																								
Denmark Hill	d																								
Peckham Rye	d																								
Nunhead	d																								
New Cross	d				08 34					09 04								09 34					10 04		
St Johns	d																								
Lewisham	d	08 12		08 27	08 38	08 42			08 57	09 08			09 12		09 27			09 38	09 42		09 57		10 08		
Blackheath	d			08 30	08 40				09 00	09 10					09 30			09 40			10 00		10 10		
Kidbrooke	d				08 43					09 13								09 43					10 13		
Eltham	d				08 47					09 17								09 47					10 17		
Falconwood	d				08 49					09 19								09 49					10 19		
Welling	d				08 52					09 22								09 52					10 22		
Bexleyheath	d				08 54					09 24								09 54					10 24		
Barnehurst	d				08 57					09 27								09 57					10 27		
Hither Green	d	08 16				08 46							09 16						09 46						
Lee	d	08 18				08 48							09 18						09 48						
Mottingham	d	08 21				08 51							09 21						09 51						
New Eltham	d	08 23				08 53							09 23						09 53						
Sidcup	d	08 27				08 57							09 27						09 57						
Albany Park	d	08 29				08 59							09 29						09 59						
Bexley	d	08 31				09 01							09 31						10 01						
Crayford	d	08 34				09 04							09 34						10 04						
Charlton	d		08 24	08 34				08 54	09 04					09 24	09 34	09 39				09 54	10 04	10 09			
Woolwich Dockyard	d		08 27					08 57						09 27		09 42				09 57		10 12			
Woolwich Arsenal	d		08 30	08 40				09 00	09 10					09 30	09 40	09 45				10 00	10 10	10 15			
Plumstead	d		08 32					09 02						09 32		09a47				10 02		10a17			
Abbey Wood	d		08 35	08 44				09 05	09 14					09 35	09 44					10 05	10 14				
Belvedere	d		08 37					09 07						09 37						10 07					
Erith	d		08 40					09 10						09 40						10 10					
Slade Green	d		08 44					09 14						09 44						10 14					
Dartford	a	08 39	08 49	08 54	09 03	09 09		09 19	09 24	09 33			09 39	09 49	09 54			10 03	10 09	10 19	10 24		10 33		
	d	08 40		08 55		09 10			09 25				09 40		09 55				10 10		10 25				
Stone Crossing	d	08 44				09 14							09 44						10 14						
Greenhithe for Bluewater	d	08 46		09 00		09 16			09 30				09 46		10 00				10 16		10 30				
Swanscombe	d	08 49				09 19							09 49						10 19						
Northfleet	d	08 51				09 21							09 51						10 21						
Gravesend	d	08a55		09 07		09a25			09 37		09 48	09 48	09a55		10 07				10a25		10 37			10 51	10 51
Higham	d			09 13					09 43						10 13						10 43				
Strood	d			09 18					09 48		09 58	09 58			10 18						10 48			11 01	11 01
Maidstone West	d																								
Rochester	d			09 23					09 52		10 03	10 03			10 23						10 52			11 06	11 06
Chatham	d			09 26					09 55		10 05	10 05			10 26						10 55			11 08	11 08
Gillingham (Kent)	a			09 30					10 02		10 09	10 09			10 30						11 02			11 12	11 12

A not from 2 September until 9 September

B not 26 August

Table 200

Sundays

26 August to 9 September

London - Dartford and Gillingham

Network Diagram - see first Page of Table 200

		SE		SE	SE	SE	SE	SE	SE	SE	SE	SE		SE A	SE B	SE	SE	SE	SE	SE	SE	SE		SE	SE
St Pancras Int'l	d													11 25	11 25										
Stratford International	d													11 32	11 32										
Ebbsfleet International	d													11 44	11 43										
London Charing Cross	d	09 56		10 00	10 10		10 20	10 26	10 30	10 40		10 50				10 56	11 00	11 10		11 20	11 26	11 30		11 40	
London Waterloo (East)	d	09 59		10 03	10 13		10 23	10 29	10 33	10 43		10 53				10 59	11 03	11 13		11 23	11 29	11 33		11 43	
London Cannon Street	d																								
London Bridge	d	10 04		10 08	10 18	10 23	10 28	10 34	10 38	10 48	10 53	10 58				11 04	11 08	11 18	11 23	11 28	11 34	11 38		11 48	11 53
Deptford	d			10 14		10 29			10 44		10 59						11 14		11 29			11 44			11 59
Greenwich	d			10 16		10 31			10 46		11 01						11 16		11 31			11 46			12 01
Maze Hill	d			10 19		10 34			10 49		11 04						11 19		11 34			11 49			12 04
Westcombe Park	d			10 21		10 36			10 51		11 06						11 21		11 36			11 51			12 06
London Victoria	d																								
Denmark Hill	d																								
Peckham Rye	d																								
Nunhead	d																								
New Cross	d						10 34					11 04								11 34					
St Johns	d																								
Lewisham	d	10 12			10 27		10 38	10 42		10 57		11 08				11 12		11 27		11 38	11 42			11 57	
Blackheath	d				10 30		10 40			11 00		11 10						11 30		11 40				12 00	
Kidbrooke	d						10 43					11 13								11 43					
Eltham	d						10 47					11 17								11 47					
Falconwood	d						10 49					11 19								11 49					
Welling	d						10 52					11 22								11 52					
Bexleyheath	d						10 54					11 24								11 54					
Barnehurst	d						10 57					11 27								11 57					
Hither Green	d	10 16						10 46								11 16					11 46				
Lee	d	10 18						10 48								11 18					11 48				
Mottingham	d	10 21						10 51								11 21					11 51				
New Eltham	d	10 23						10 53								11 23					11 53				
Sidcup	d	10 27						10 57								11 27					11 57				
Albany Park	d	10 29						10 59								11 29					11 59				
Bexley	d	10 31						11 01								11 31					12 01				
Crayford	d	10 34						11 04								11 34					12 04				
Charlton	d			10 24	10 34	10 39			10 54	11 04	11 09						11 24	11 34	11 39			11 54		12 04	12 09
Woolwich Dockyard	d			10 27		10 42			10 57		11 12						11 27		11 42			11 57			12 12
Woolwich Arsenal	d			10 30	10 40	10 45			11 00	11 10	11 15						11 30	11 40	11 45			12 00		12 10	12 15
Plumstead	d			10 32		10a47			11 02		11a17						11 32		11a47			12 02			12a17
Abbey Wood	d			10 35	10 44				11 05	11 14							11 35	11 44				12 05		12 14	
Belvedere	d			10 37					11 07								11 37					12 07			
Erith	d			10 40					11 10								11 40					12 10			
Slade Green	d			10 44					11 14								11 44					12 14			
Dartford	a	10 39		10 49	10 54		11 03	11 09	11 19	11 24		11 33				11 39	11 49	11 54		12 03	12 09	12 19		12 24	
	d	10 40			10 55			11 10		11 25						11 40		11 55			12 10			12 25	
Stone Crossing	d	10 44						11 14								11 44					12 14				
Greenhithe for Bluewater	d	10 46			11 00			11 16		11 30						11 46		12 00			12 16			12 30	
Swanscombe	d	10 49						11 19								11 49					12 19				
Northfleet	d	10 51						11 21								11 51					12 21				
Gravesend	d	10a55			11 07			11a25		11 37				11 48	11 48	11a55		12 07			12a25			12 37	
Higham	d				11 13					11 43								12 13						12 43	
Strood	d				11 18					11 48				11 58	11 58			12 18						12 48	
Maidstone West	d																								
Rochester	d				11 23					11 52				12 03	12 03			12 23						12 52	
Chatham	d				11 26					11 55				12 05	12 05			12 26						12 55	
Gillingham (Kent)	a				11 30					12 02				12 09	12 09			12 30						13 02	

A not 26 August

B not from 2 September until 9 September

Table 200

London - Dartford and Gillingham

Sundays

26 August to 9 September

Network Diagram - see first Page of Table 200

Station		SE	SE A	SE B	SE	SE	SE	SE		SE	SE A	SE B	SE	SE	SE	SE	SE	SE B		SE A	SE	SE	SE	SE	SE
St Pancras Int'l	d		12 27	12 28							12 51	12 52						13 25		13 25					
Stratford International	d		12 36	12 35							12 58	12 58						13 32		13 33					
Ebbsfleet International	d		12 47	12 46							13 13	13 13						13 43		13 44					
London Charing Cross	d	11 50			11 56	12 00	12 10			12 20			12 26	12 30	12 40		12 50				12 56	13 00	13 10		13 20
London Waterloo (East)	d	11 53			11 59	12 03	12 13			12 23			12 29	12 33	12 43		12 53				12 59	13 03	13 13		13 23
London Cannon Street	d																								
London Bridge	d	11 58			12 04	12 08	12 18	12 23		12 28			12 34	12 38	12 48	12 53	12 58				13 04	13 08	13 18	13 23	13 28
Deptford	d					12 14		12 29						12 44		12 59						13 14		13 29	
Greenwich	d					12 16		12 31						12 46		13 01						13 16		13 31	
Maze Hill	d					12 19		12 34						12 49		13 04						13 19		13 34	
Westcombe Park	d					12 21		12 36						12 51		13 06						13 21		13 36	
London Victoria	d																								
Denmark Hill	d																								
Peckham Rye	d																								
Nunhead	d																								
New Cross	d	12 04								12 34							13 04								13 34
St Johns	d																								
Lewisham	d	12 08			12 12		12 27			12 38			12 42		12 57		13 08				13 12		13 27		13 38
Blackheath	d	12 10					12 30			12 40					13 00		13 10						13 30		13 40
Kidbrooke	d	12 13								12 43							13 13								13 43
Eltham	d	12 17								12 47							13 17								13 47
Falconwood	d	12 19								12 49							13 19								13 49
Welling	d	12 22								12 52							13 22								13 52
Bexleyheath	d	12 24								12 54							13 24								13 54
Barnehurst	d	12 27								12 57							13 27								13 57
Hither Green	d				12 16								12 46								13 16				
Lee	d				12 18								12 48								13 18				
Mottingham	d				12 21								12 51								13 21				
New Eltham	d				12 23								12 53								13 23				
Sidcup	d				12 27								12 57								13 27				
Albany Park	d				12 29								12 59								13 29				
Bexley	d				12 31								13 01								13 31				
Crayford	d				12 34								13 04								13 34				
Charlton	d					12 24	12 34	12 39						12 54	13 04	13 09						13 24	13 34	13 39	
Woolwich Dockyard	d					12 27		12 42						12 57		13 12						13 27		13 42	
Woolwich Arsenal	d					12 30	12 40	12 45						13 00	13 10	13 15						13 30	13 40	13 45	
Plumstead	d					12 32		12a47						13 02		13a17						13 32		13a47	
Abbey Wood	d					12 35	12 44							13 05	13 14							13 35	13 44		
Belvedere	d					12 37								13 07								13 37			
Erith	d					12 40								13 10								13 40			
Slade Green	d					12 44								13 14								13 44			
Dartford	a	12 33			12 39	12 49	12 54			13 03			13 09	13 19	13 24		13 33				13 39	13 49	13 54		14 03
	d				12 40		12 55						13 10		13 25						13 40		13 55		
Stone Crossing	d				12 44								13 14								13 44				
Greenhithe for Bluewater	d				12 46		13 00						13 16		13 30						13 46		14 00		
Swanscombe	d				12 49								13 19								13 49				
Northfleet	d				12 51								13 21								13 51				
Gravesend	d		12 51	12 51	12a55		13 07				13 18	13 18	13a25		13 37			13 48		13 48	13a55		14 07		
Higham	d						13 13								13 43								14 13		
Strood	d		13 01	13 01			13 18				13 28	13 28			13 48			13 58		13 58			14 18		
Maidstone West	d																								
Rochester	d		13 06	13 06			13 23				13 33	13 33			13 52			14 03		14 03			14 23		
Chatham	d		13 08	13 08			13 26				13 35	13 35			13 55			14 05		14 05			14 26		
Gillingham (Kent)	a		13 12	13 12			13 30				13 39	13 39			14 02			14 09		14 09			14 30		

A not 26 August

B not from 2 September until 9 September

Table 200

London - Dartford and Gillingham

Sundays

26 August to 9 September

Network Diagram - see first Page of Table 200

Station		SE A	SE B	SE		SE	SE	SE	SE	SE A	SE B	SE	SE	SE		SE	SE	SE A	SE B	SE	SE	SE	SE	SE	
St Pancras Int'l	d	13 55	13 55							14 25	14 25							14 55	14 55						
Stratford International	d	14 02	14 03							14 32	14 33							15 02	15 03						
Ebbsfleet International	d	14 13	14 14							14 43	14 44							15 13	15 14						
London Charing Cross	d			13 26		13 30	13 40		13 50			13 56	14 00	14 10			14 20			14 26	14 30	14 40		14 50	
London Waterloo (East)	d			13 29		13 33	13 43		13 53			13 59	14 03	14 13			14 23			14 29	14 33	14 43		14 53	
London Cannon Street	d																								
London Bridge	d			13 34		13 38	13 48	13 53	13 58			14 04	14 08	14 18		14 23	14 28			14 34	14 38	14 48	14 53	14 58	
Deptford	d					13 44		13 59					14 14			14 29					14 44		14 59		
Greenwich	d					13 46		14 01					14 16			14 31					14 46		15 01		
Maze Hill	d					13 49		14 04					14 19			14 34					14 49		15 04		
Westcombe Park	d					13 51		14 06					14 21			14 36					14 51		15 06		
London Victoria	d																								
Denmark Hill	d																								
Peckham Rye	d																								
Nunhead	d																								
New Cross	d								14 04								14 34							15 04	
St Johns	d																								
Lewisham	d			13 42			13 57		14 08			14 12		14 27			14 38			14 42		14 57		15 08	
Blackheath	d						14 00		14 10					14 30			14 40					15 00		15 10	
Kidbrooke	d								14 13								14 43							15 13	
Eltham	d								14 17								14 47							15 17	
Falconwood	d								14 19								14 49							15 19	
Welling	d								14 22								14 52							15 22	
Bexleyheath	d								14 24								14 54							15 24	
Barnehurst	d								14 27								14 57							15 27	
Hither Green	d			13 46								14 16								14 46					
Lee	d			13 48								14 18								14 48					
Mottingham	d			13 51								14 21								14 51					
New Eltham	d			13 53								14 23								14 53					
Sidcup	d			13 57								14 27								14 57					
Albany Park	d			13 59								14 29								14 59					
Bexley	d			14 01								14 31								15 01					
Crayford	d			14 04								14 34								15 04					
Charlton	d					13 54	14 04	14 09					14 24	14 34		14 39					14 54	15 04	15 09		
Woolwich Dockyard	d					13 57		14 12					14 27			14 42					14 57		15 12		
Woolwich Arsenal	d					14 00	14 10	14 15					14 30	14 40		14 45					15 00	15 10	15 15		
Plumstead	d					14 02		14a17					14 32			14a47					15 02		15a17		
Abbey Wood	d					14 05	14 14						14 35	14 44							15 05	15 14			
Belvedere	d					14 07							14 37								15 07				
Erith	d					14 10							14 40								15 10				
Slade Green	d					14 14							14 44								15 14				
Dartford	a			14 09		14 19	14 24		14 33			14 39	14 49	14 54			15 03			15 09	15 19	15 24		15 33	
	d			14 10			14 25					14 40		14 55						15 10		15 25			
Stone Crossing	d			14 14								14 44								15 14					
Greenhithe for Bluewater	d			14 16			14 30					14 46		15 00						15 16		15 30			
Swanscombe	d			14 19								14 49								15 19					
Northfleet	d			14 21								14 51								15 21					
Gravesend	d	14 18	14 18	14a25			14 37			14 48	14 48	14a55		15 07				15 18	15 18	15a25		15 37			
Higham	d						14 43							15 13								15 43			
Strood	d	14 28	14 28				14 48			14 58	14 58			15 18				15 28	15 28			15 48			
Maidstone West	d																								
Rochester	d	14 33	14 33				14 52			15 03	15 03			15 23				15 33	15 33			15 52			
Chatham	d	14 35	14 35				14 55			15 05	15 05			15 26				15 35	15 35			15 55			
Gillingham (Kent)	a	14 39	14 39				15 02			15 09	15 09			15 30				15 39	15 39			16 02			

A not from 2 September until 9 September

B not 26 August

Table 200

Sundays

26 August to 9 September

London - Dartford and Gillingham

Network Diagram - see first Page of Table 200

		SE A	SE B	SE	SE	SE	SE	SE	SE A	SE B	SE	SE	SE	SE	SE	SE A	SE B	SE	SE	SE	SE	SE	SE A
St Pancras Int'l	d	15 25	15 25						15 55	15 55						16 25	16 25						16 55
Stratford International	d	15 32	15 33						16 02	16 03						16 32	16 33						17 02
Ebbsfleet International	d	15 43	15 44						16 13	16 14						16 43	16 44						17 13
London Charing Cross	d			14 56	15 00	15 10		15 20			15 26	15 30	15 40		15 50			15 56	16 00	16 10		16 20	
London Waterloo (East)	d			14 59	15 03	15 13		15 23			15 29	15 33	15 43		15 53			15 59	16 03	16 13		16 23	
London Cannon Street	d																						
London Bridge	d			15 04	15 08	15 18	15 23	15 28			15 34	15 38	15 48	15 53	15 58			16 04	16 08	16 18	16 23	16 28	
Deptford	d				15 14		15 29					15 44		15 59					16 14		16 29		
Greenwich	d				15 16		15 31					15 46		16 01					16 16		16 31		
Maze Hill	d				15 19		15 34					15 49		16 04					16 19		16 34		
Westcombe Park	d				15 21		15 36					15 51		16 06					16 21		16 36		
London Victoria	d																						
Denmark Hill	d																						
Peckham Rye	d																						
Nunhead	d																						
New Cross	d							15 34							16 04							16 34	
St Johns	d																						
Lewisham	d			15 12		15 27		15 38			15 42		15 57		16 08			16 12		16 27		16 38	
Blackheath	d					15 30		15 40					16 00		16 10					16 30		16 40	
Kidbrooke	d							15 43							16 13							16 43	
Eltham	d							15 47							16 17							16 47	
Falconwood	d							15 49							16 19							16 49	
Welling	d							15 52							16 22							16 52	
Bexleyheath	d							15 54							16 24							16 54	
Barnehurst	d							15 57							16 27							16 57	
Hither Green	d			15 16							15 46							16 16					
Lee	d			15 18							15 48							16 18					
Mottingham	d			15 21							15 51							16 21					
New Eltham	d			15 23							15 53							16 23					
Sidcup	d			15 27							15 57							16 27					
Albany Park	d			15 29							15 59							16 29					
Bexley	d			15 31							16 01							16 31					
Crayford	d			15 34							16 04							16 34					
Charlton	d				15 24	15 34	15 39					15 54	16 04	16 09					16 24	16 34	16 39		
Woolwich Dockyard	d				15 27		15 42					15 57		16 12					16 27		16 42		
Woolwich Arsenal	d				15 30	15 40	15 45					16 00	16 10	16 15					16 30	16 40	16 45		
Plumstead	d				15 32		15a47					16 02		16a17					16 32		16a47		
Abbey Wood	d				15 35	15 44						16 05	16 14						16 35	16 44			
Belvedere	d				15 37							16 07							16 37				
Erith	d				15 40							16 10							16 40				
Slade Green	d				15 44							16 14							16 44				
Dartford	a			15 39	15 49	15 54		16 03			16 09	16 19	16 24		16 33			16 39	16 49	16 54		17 03	
	d			15 40		15 55					16 10		16 25					16 40		16 55			
Stone Crossing	d			15 44							16 14							16 44					
Greenhithe for Bluewater	d			15 46		16 00					16 16		16 30					16 46		17 00			
Swanscombe	d			15 49							16 19							16 49					
Northfleet	d			15 51							16 21							16 51					
Gravesend	d	15 48	15 48	15a55		16 07			16 18	16 18	16a25		16 37			16 48	16 48	16a55		17 07			17 18
Higham	d					16 13							16 43							17 13			
Strood	d	15 58	15 58			16 18			16 28	16 28			16 48			16 58	16 58			17 18			17 28
Maidstone West	d																						
Rochester	d	16 03	16 03			16 23			16 33	16 33			16 52			17 03	17 03			17 23			17 33
Chatham	d	16 05	16 05			16 26			16 35	16 35			16 55			17 05	17 05			17 26			17 35
Gillingham (Kent)	a	16 09	16 09			16 30			16 39	16 39			17 02			17 09	17 09			17 30			17 39

A not from 2 September until 9 September

B not 26 August

Table 200

Sundays

26 August to 9 September

London - Dartford and Gillingham

Network Diagram - see first Page of Table 200

		SE A	SE	SE	SE	SE	SE	SE B	SE A	SE	SE	SE	SE	SE	SE A	SE B	SE	SE	SE	SE	SE	SE B	SE A
St Pancras Int'l	d	16 55						17 25	17 25						17 48	17 58						18 25	18 27
Stratford International	d	17 03						17 32	17 33						17 55	18 08						18 32	18 35
Ebbsfleet International	d	17 14						17 43	17 44						18 14	18 19						18 43	18 46
London Charing Cross	d		16 26	16 30	16 40		16 50			16 56	17 00	17 10		17 20			17 26	17 30	17 40		17 50		
London Waterloo (East)	d		16 29	16 33	16 43		16 53			16 59	17 03	17 13		17 23			17 29	17 33	17 43		17 53		
London Cannon Street	d																						
London Bridge	d		16 34	16 38	16 48	16 53	16 58			17 04	17 08	17 18	17 23	17 28			17 34	17 38	17 48	17 53	17 58		
Deptford	d			16 44		16 59					17 14		17 29					17 44		17 59			
Greenwich	d			16 46		17 01					17 16		17 31					17 46		18 01			
Maze Hill	d			16 49		17 04					17 19		17 34					17 49		18 04			
Westcombe Park	d			16 51		17 06					17 21		17 36					17 51		18 06			
London Victoria	d																						
Denmark Hill	d																						
Peckham Rye	d																						
Nunhead	d																						
New Cross	d						17 04							17 34							18 04		
St Johns	d																						
Lewisham	d		16 42		16 57		17 08			17 12		17 27		17 38			17 42		17 57		18 08		
Blackheath	d				17 00		17 10					17 30		17 40					18 00		18 10		
Kidbrooke	d						17 13							17 43							18 13		
Eltham	d						17 17							17 47							18 17		
Falconwood	d						17 19							17 49							18 19		
Welling	d						17 22							17 52							18 22		
Bexleyheath	d						17 24							17 54							18 24		
Barnehurst	d						17 27							17 57							18 27		
Hither Green	d		16 46							17 16							17 46						
Lee	d		16 48							17 18							17 48						
Mottingham	d		16 51							17 21							17 51						
New Eltham	d		16 53							17 23							17 53						
Sidcup	d		16 57							17 27							17 57						
Albany Park	d		16 59							17 29							17 59						
Bexley	d		17 01							17 31							18 01						
Crayford	d		17 04							17 34							18 04						
Charlton	d			16 54	17 04	17 09					17 24	17 34	17 39					17 54	18 04	18 09			
Woolwich Dockyard	d			16 57		17 12					17 27		17 42					17 57		18 12			
Woolwich Arsenal	d			17 00	17 10	17 15					17 30	17 40	17 45					18 00	18 10	18 15			
Plumstead	d			17 02		17a17					17 32		17a47					18 02		18a17			
Abbey Wood	d			17 05	17 14						17 35	17 44						18 05	18 14				
Belvedere	d			17 07							17 37							18 07					
Erith	d			17 10							17 40							18 10					
Slade Green	d			17 14							17 44							18 14					
Dartford	a		17 09	17 19	17 24		17 33			17 39	17 49	17 54		18 03			18 09	18 19	18 24		18 33		
	d		17 10		17 25					17 40		17 55					18 10		18 25				
Stone Crossing	d		17 14							17 44							18 14						
Greenhithe for Bluewater	d		17 16		17 30					17 46		18 00					18 16		18 30				
Swanscombe	d		17 19							17 49							18 19						
Northfleet	d		17 21							17 51							18 21						
Gravesend	d	17 18	17a25		17 37			17 48	17 48	17a55		18 07			18 19	18 24	18a25		18 37			18 48	18 51
Higham	d				17 43							18 13							18 43				
Strood	d	17 28			17 48			17 58	17 58			18 18			18 29	18 34			18 48			18 58	19 01
Maidstone West	d																						
Rochester	d	17 33			17 52			18 03	18 03			18 23			18 34	18 39			18 52			19 03	19 06
Chatham	d	17 35			17 55			18 05	18 05			18 26			18 36	18 41			18 55			19 05	19 08
Gillingham (Kent)	a	17 39			18 02			18 09	18 09			18 30			18 40	18 45			19 02			19 09	19 12

A not 26 August

B not from 2 September until 9 September

Table 200

Sundays

26 August to 9 September

London - Dartford and Gillingham

Network Diagram - see first Page of Table 200

		SE		SE	SE	SE	SE	SE A	SE B	SE	SE	SE		SE	SE	SE	SE	SE A	SE B	SE	SE	SE		SE	SE A
St Pancras Int'l ⊖	d							18 55	18 55									19 25	19 25						19 55
Stratford International ⊖	d							19 02	19 03									19 32	19 33						20 02
Ebbsfleet International	d							19 13	19 14									19 43	19 44						20 13
London Charing Cross ⊖	d	17 56		18 00	18 10		18 20			18 26	18 30	18 40			18 50	18 56	19 00			19 10	19 20	19 26		19 30	
London Waterloo (East) ⊖	d	17 59		18 03	18 13		18 23			18 29	18 33	18 43			18 53	18 59	19 03			19 13	19 23	19 29		19 33	
London Cannon Street ⊖	d																								
London Bridge ⊖	d	18 04		18 08	18 18	18 23	18 28			18 34	18 38	18 48		18 53	18 58	19 04	19 08			19 18	19 28	19 34		19 38	
Deptford	d			18 14		18 29					18 44			18 59			19 14							19 44	
Greenwich	d			18 16		18 31					18 46			19 01			19 16							19 46	
Maze Hill	d			18 19		18 34					18 49			19 04			19 19							19 49	
Westcombe Park	d			18 21		18 36					18 51			19 06			19 21							19 51	
London Victoria ⊖	d																								
Denmark Hill	d																								
Peckham Rye	d																								
Nunhead	d																								
New Cross ⊖	d						18 34								19 04						19 34				
St Johns	d																								
Lewisham	d	18 12			18 27		18 38			18 42		18 57			19 08	19 12				19 27	19 38	19 42			
Blackheath	d				18 30		18 40					19 00			19 10					19 30	19 40				
Kidbrooke	d						18 43								19 13						19 43				
Eltham	d						18 47								19 17						19 47				
Falconwood	d						18 49								19 19						19 49				
Welling	d						18 52								19 22						19 52				
Bexleyheath	d						18 54								19 24						19 54				
Barnehurst	d						18 57								19 27						19 57				
Hither Green	d	18 16								18 46						19 16						19 46			
Lee	d	18 18								18 48						19 18						19 48			
Mottingham	d	18 21								18 51						19 21						19 51			
New Eltham	d	18 23								18 53						19 23						19 53			
Sidcup	d	18 27								18 57						19 27						19 57			
Albany Park	d	18 29								18 59						19 29						19 59			
Bexley	d	18 31								19 01						19 31						20 01			
Crayford	d	18 34								19 04						19 34						20 04			
Charlton	d			18 24	18 34	18 39					18 54	19 04		19 09			19 24			19 34				19 54	
Woolwich Dockyard	d			18 27		18 42					18 57			19 12			19 27							19 57	
Woolwich Arsenal	d			18 30	18 40	18 45					19 00	19 10		19 15			19 30			19 40				20 00	
Plumstead	d			18 32		18a47					19 02			19a17			19 32							20 02	
Abbey Wood	d			18 35	18 44						19 05	19 14					19 35			19 44				20 05	
Belvedere	d			18 37							19 07						19 37							20 07	
Erith	d			18 40							19 10						19 40							20 10	
Slade Green	d			18 44							19 14						19 44							20 14	
Dartford	a	18 39		18 49	18 54		19 03			19 09	19 19	19 24			19 33	19 39	19 49			19 54	20 03	20 09		20 19	
	d	18 40			18 55					19 10		19 25								19 55					
Stone Crossing	d	18 44								19 14		19 29								19 59					
Greenhithe for Bluewater	d	18 46			19 00					19 16		19 31								20 01					
Swanscombe	d	18 49								19 19		19 34								20 04					
Northfleet	d	18 51								19 21		19 36								20 06					
Gravesend	d	18a55			19 07			19 18	19 18	19a25		19 40						19 48	19 48	20 10					20 18
Higham	d				19 13							19 46								20 16					
Strood	d				19 18			19 28	19 28			19 52						19 58	19 58	20 22					20 28
Maidstone West	d																								
Rochester	d				19 23			19 33	19 33			19 56						20 03	20 03	20 26					20 33
Chatham	d				19 26			19 35	19 35			19 58						20 05	20 05	20 28					20 35
Gillingham (Kent)	a				19 30			19 39	19 39			20 03						20 09	20 09	20 33					20 39

A not from 2 September until 9 September

B not 26 August

Table 200

Sundays

26 August to 9 September

London - Dartford and Gillingham

Network Diagram - see first Page of Table 200

		SE A	SE	SE	SE	SE	SE A	SE B		SE	SE	SE	SE	SE B	SE A	SE	SE	SE		SE	SE B	SE A	SE	SE	SE
St Pancras Int'l ⊖	d	19 55					20 25	20 25						20 55	20 55						21 25	21 25			
Stratford International ⊖	d	20 02					20 32	20 32						21 02	21 03						21 32	21 33			
Ebbsfleet International	d	20 14					20 44	20 43						21 13	21 14						21 43	21 44			
London Charing Cross ⊖	d		19 40	19 50	19 56	20 00				20 10	20 20	20 26	20 30			20 40	20 50	20 56		21 00			21 10	21 20	21 26
London Waterloo (East) ⊖	d		19 43	19 53	19 59	20 03				20 13	20 23	20 29	20 33			20 43	20 53	20 59		21 03			21 13	21 23	21 29
London Cannon Street ⊖	d																								
London Bridge ⊖	d		19 48	19 58	20 04	20 08				20 18	20 28	20 34	20 38			20 48	20 58	21 04		21 08			21 18	21 28	21 34
Deptford	d					20 14							20 44							21 14					
Greenwich	d					20 16							20 46							21 16					
Maze Hill	d					20 19							20 49							21 19					
Westcombe Park	d					20 21							20 51							21 21					
London Victoria ⊖	d																								
Denmark Hill	d																								
Peckham Rye	d																								
Nunhead	d																								
New Cross ⊖	d			20 04							20 34						21 04							21 34	
St Johns	d																								
Lewisham	d		19 57	20 08	20 12					20 27	20 38	20 42				20 57	21 08	21 12					21 27	21 38	21 42
Blackheath	d		20 00	20 10						20 30	20 40					21 00	21 10						21 30	21 40	
Kidbrooke	d			20 13							20 43						21 13							21 43	
Eltham	d			20 17							20 47						21 17							21 47	
Falconwood	d			20 19							20 49						21 19							21 49	
Welling	d			20 22							20 52						21 22							21 52	
Bexleyheath	d			20 24							20 54						21 24							21 54	
Barnehurst	d			20 27							20 57						21 27							21 57	
Hither Green	d				20 16							20 46						21 16							21 46
Lee	d				20 18							20 48						21 18							21 48
Mottingham	d				20 21							20 51						21 21							21 51
New Eltham	d				20 23							20 53						21 23							21 53
Sidcup	d				20 27							20 57						21 27							21 57
Albany Park	d				20 29							20 59						21 29							21 59
Bexley	d				20 31							21 01						21 31							22 01
Crayford	d				20 34							21 04						21 34							22 04
Charlton	d		20 04			20 24				20 34			20 54			21 04				21 24			21 34		
Woolwich Dockyard	d					20 27							20 57							21 27					
Woolwich Arsenal	d		20 10			20 30				20 40			21 00			21 10				21 30			21 40		
Plumstead	d					20 32							21 02							21 32					
Abbey Wood	d		20 14			20 35				20 44			21 05			21 14				21 35			21 44		
Belvedere	d					20 37							21 07							21 37					
Erith	d					20 40							21 10							21 40					
Slade Green	d					20 44							21 14							21 44					
Dartford	a		20 24	20 33	20 39	20 49				20 54	21 03	21 09	21 19			21 24	21 33	21 39		21 49			21 54	22 03	22 09
	d		20 25							20 55						21 25							21 55		
Stone Crossing	d		20 29							20 59						21 29							21 59		
Greenhithe for Bluewater	d		20 31							21 01						21 31							22 01		
Swanscombe	d		20 34							21 04						21 34							22 04		
Northfleet	d		20 36							21 06						21 36							22 06		
Gravesend	d	20 18	20 40				20 48	20 48		21 10				21 18	21 18	21 40					21 48	21 48	22 10		
Higham	d		20 46							21 16						21 46							22 16		
Strood	d	20 28	20 52				20 58	20 58		21 22				21 28	21 28	21 52					21 58	21 58	22 22		
Maidstone West	d																								
Rochester	d	20 33	20 56				21 03	21 03		21 26				21 33	21 33	21 56					22 03	22 03	22 26		
Chatham	d	20 35	20 58				21 05	21 05		21 28				21 35	21 35	21 58					22 05	22 05	22 28		
Gillingham (Kent)	a	20 39	21 03				21 09	21 09		21 33				21 39	21 39	22 03					22 09	22 09	22 33		

A not 26 August

B not from 2 September until 9 September

Table 200

Sundays

26 August to 9 September

London - Dartford and Gillingham

Network Diagram - see first Page of Table 200

		SE	SE A	SE B		SE	SE	SE	SE	SE A	SE B	SE	SE	SE		SE	SE A	SE B	SE	SE	SE	SE	SE A	SE B
St Pancras Int'l	d		21 55	21 55						22 25	22 25						22 55	22 55					23 25	23 25
Stratford International	d		22 02	22 03						22 32	22 33						23 02	23 03					23 32	23 33
Ebbsfleet International	d		22 13	22 14						22 43	22 44						23 13	23 14					23 43	23 44
London Charing Cross	d	21 30				21 40	21 50	21 56	22 00			22 10	22 20	22 26		22 30			22 40	22 50	22 56	23 00		
London Waterloo (East)	d	21 33				21 43	21 53	21 59	22 03			22 13	22 23	22 29		22 33			22 43	22 53	22 59	23 03		
London Cannon Street	d																							
London Bridge	d	21 38				21 48	21 58	22 04	22 08			22 18	22 28	22 34		22 38			22 48	22 58	23 04	23 08		
Deptford	d	21 44							22 14							22 44						23 14		
Greenwich	d	21 46							22 16							22 46						23 16		
Maze Hill	d	21 49							22 19							22 49						23 19		
Westcombe Park	d	21 51							22 21							22 51						23 21		
London Victoria	d																							
Denmark Hill	d																							
Peckham Rye	d																							
Nunhead	d																							
New Cross	d						22 04						22 34							23 04				
St Johns	d																							
Lewisham	d					21 57	22 08	22 12				22 27	22 38	22 42					22 57	23 08	23 12			
Blackheath	d					22 00	22 10					22 30	22 40						23 00	23 10				
Kidbrooke	d						22 13						22 43							23 13				
Eltham	d						22 17						22 47							23 17				
Falconwood	d						22 19						22 49							23 19				
Welling	d						22 22						22 52							23 22				
Bexleyheath	d						22 24						22 54							23 24				
Barnehurst	d						22 27						22 57							23 27				
Hither Green	d							22 16						22 46							23 16			
Lee	d							22 18						22 48							23 18			
Mottingham	d							22 21						22 51							23 21			
New Eltham	d							22 23						22 53							23 23			
Sidcup	d							22 27						22 57							23 27			
Albany Park	d							22 29						22 59							23 29			
Bexley	d							22 31						23 01							23 31			
Crayford	d							22 34						23 04							23 34			
Charlton	d	21 54				22 04			22 24			22 34				22 54			23 04			23 24		
Woolwich Dockyard	d	21 57							22 27							22 57						23 27		
Woolwich Arsenal	d	22 00				22 10			22 30			22 40				23 00			23 10			23 30		
Plumstead	d	22 02							22 32							23 02						23 32		
Abbey Wood	d	22 05				22 14			22 35			22 44				23 05			23 14			23 35		
Belvedere	d	22 07							22 37							23 07						23 37		
Erith	d	22 10							22 40							23 10						23 40		
Slade Green	d	22 14							22 44							23 14						23 44		
Dartford	a	22 19				22 24	22 33	22 39	22 49			22 54	23 03	23 09		23 19			23 24	23 33	23 39	23 49		
	d					22 25						22 55							23 25					
Stone Crossing	d					22 29						22 59							23 29					
Greenhithe for Bluewater	d					22 31						23 01							23 31					
Swanscombe	d					22 34						23 04							23 34					
Northfleet	d					22 36						23 06							23 36					
Gravesend	d		22 18	22 18		22 40				22 48	22 48	23 10					23 18	23 18	23 40				23 48	23 48
Higham	d					22 46						23 16							23 46					
Strood	d		22 28	22 28		22 52				22 58	22 58	23 22					23 28	23 28	23 52				23 58	23 58
Maidstone West	d																							
Rochester	d		22 33	22 33		22 56				23 03	23 03	23 26					23 33	23 33	23 56				00 03	00 03
Chatham	d		22 35	22 35		22 58				23 05	23 05	23 28					23 35	23 35	23 58				00 05	00 05
Gillingham (Kent)	a		22 39	22 39		23 03				23 09	23 09	23 33					23 39	23 39	00 03				00 09	00 09

A not from 2 September until 9 September

B not 26 August

Table 200

Sundays

26 August to 9 September

London - Dartford and Gillingham

Network Diagram - see first Page of Table 200

		SE	SE	SE	SE	SE	SE
St Pancras Int'l	d						
Stratford International	d						
Ebbsfleet International	d						
London Charing Cross	d	23 10	23 20	23 26	23 30	23 50	23 56
London Waterloo (East)	d	23 13	23 23	23 29	23 33	23 53	23 59
London Cannon Street	d						
London Bridge	d	23 18	23 28	23 34	23 38	23 58	00 04
Deptford	d				23 44		
Greenwich	d				23 46		
Maze Hill	d				23 49		
Westcombe Park	d				23 51		
London Victoria	d						
Denmark Hill	d						
Peckham Rye	d						
Nunhead	d						
New Cross	d		23 34			00 04	
St Johns	d						
Lewisham	d	23 27	23 38	23 42		00 08	00 12
Blackheath	d	23 30	23 40			00 10	
Kidbrooke	d		23 43			00 13	
Eltham	d		23 47			00 17	
Falconwood	d		23 49			00 19	
Welling	d		23 52			00 22	
Bexleyheath	d		23 54			00 24	
Barnehurst	d		23 57			00 27	
Hither Green	d			23 46			00 16
Lee	d			23 48			00 18
Mottingham	d			23 51			00 21
New Eltham	d			23 53			00 23
Sidcup	d			23 57			00 27
Albany Park	d			23 59			00 29
Bexley	d			00 01			00 31
Crayford	d			00 04			00 34
Charlton	d	23 34			23 54		
Woolwich Dockyard	d				23 57		
Woolwich Arsenal	d	23 40			23 59		
Plumstead	d				00 02		
Abbey Wood	d	23 44			00 05		
Belvedere	d				00 07		
Erith	d				00 10		
Slade Green	d				00 14		
Dartford	a	23 54	00 04	00 09	00 19	00 33	00 39
	d	23 55					
Stone Crossing	d	23 59					
Greenhithe for Bluewater	d	00 01					
Swanscombe	d	00 04					
Northfleet	d	00 06					
Gravesend	d	00 10					
Higham	d	00 16					
Strood	d	00 22					
Maidstone West	d						
Rochester	d	00 26					
Chatham	d	00 28					
Gillingham (Kent)	a	00 33					

Mondays to Fridays

Gillingham and Dartford - London

until 27 July, 13 Aug to 28 Aug and from 10 Sep

Network Diagram - see first Page of Table 200

Miles	Miles	Miles	Miles	Miles			SE	SE	SE	SE	SE	SE	SE	SE	SE A	SE	SE	SE	SE	SE	SE	SE	SE	SE
0	—	—	0	0	Gillingham (Kent) [4]	d	04 09			04 34		04 54			05 20			05 24	05 45					
1¾	—	—	1¾	1¾	Chatham [4]	d	04 13			04 38		04 58			05 24			05 28	05 49					
2¼	—	—	2¼	2¼	Rochester [4]	d	04 15			04 40		05 00			05 27			05 30	05 51					
—	—	—	—	—	Maidstone West	d																		
3¼	—	—	3¼	3¼	Strood [4]	d	04 20			04 45		05 05			05 32			05 35						
6	—	—	6	6	Higham	d	04 25			04 50		05 10						05 40						
10½	—	—	10½	10½	Gravesend [4]	d	04 33			04 58		05 18		05 28	05 43			05 48						
12½	—	—	12½	—	Northfleet	d				05 02				05 32										
13¼	—	—	13¼	—	Swanscombe	d				05 04				05 34										
14½	—	—	14½	—	Greenhithe for Bluewater	d	04 38			05 07		05 23		05 37				05 53						
15¼	—	—	15¼	—	Stone Crossing	d				05 09				05 39										
17¼	0	0	17¼	0	Dartford [4]	a	04 43			05 13		05 28		05 43				05 58						
—	—	—	—	—		d	04 44		05 01	05 14	05 22	05 29	05 31	05 44		05 52	05 56	05 59		06 01		06 13	06 16	
19¼	2	—	—	—	Slade Green [4]	d			05 05				05 35							06 05			06 20	
20½	3¼	—	—	—	Erith	d			05 08				05 38							06 08			06 23	
21¾	4½	—	—	—	Belvedere	d			05 10				05 40							06 10			06 25	
23¼	6	—	—	—	Abbey Wood	d			05 13			05 38	05 43					06 08		06 13			06 28	
24¾	7½	—	—	—	Plumstead	d			05 16				05 46							06 16			06 31	
25¼	8	—	—	—	Woolwich Arsenal [4]	d			05 19			05 43	05 49					06 13		06 19			06 34	
26	8¾	—	—	—	Woolwich Dockyard	d			05 22				05 52							06 22			06 37	
27	9¾	—	—	—	Charlton [4]	d			05 25			05 47	05 55					06 17		06 25			06 40	
—	—	—	19	—	Crayford	d	04 48			05 18				05 48			06 01							
—	—	—	20½	—	Bexley	d	04 51			05 21				05 51			06 04							
—	—	—	21½	—	Albany Park	d	04 54			05 24				05 54			06 07							
—	—	—	22½	—	Sidcup [4]	d	04 57			05 27				05 57			06 10							
—	—	—	24	—	New Eltham	d	05 00			05 30				06 00			06 13							
—	—	—	25	—	Mottingham	d	05 02			05 32				06 02			06 16							
—	—	—	26½	—	Lee	d	05 05			05 35				06 05			06 19							
—	—	—	27¼	—	Hither Green [4]	d	05 08	05 23		05 38				06 08			06 22							
—	—	3	—	3	Barnehurst [4]	d					05 29					05 59					06 14	06 20		
—	—	4¼	—	4¼	Bexleyheath	d					05 31					06 01					06 16	06 22		
—	—	5¾	—	5¾	Welling	d					05 34					06 04					06 19	06 25		
—	—	6¾	—	6¾	Falconwood	d					05 37					06 07					06 22	06 28		
—	—	8	—	8	Eltham	d					05 40					06 10					06 25	06 31		
—	—	9	—	9	Kidbrooke	d					05 43					06 13					06 28	06 34		
29	—	10	—	10	Blackheath [4]	d					05 46	05 52				06 16		06 22			06 31	06 37		
30	—	11	28½	11	Lewisham [4]	d	05 13	05 28		05 43	05 50	05 56		06 13		06 20	06 27	06 25			06 35	06 41		06 48
—	—	11½	29	—	St Johns	d											06 29							06 50
—	—	12¼	29¾	—	New Cross [4]	d	05 16	05 31		05 46	05 53			06 16			06 31				06 38			06 52
—	—	—	—	12¾	Nunhead [4]	d																		
—	—	—	—	13½	Peckham Rye [4]	d																06 47		
—	—	—	—	14¼	Denmark Hill [4]	d																06 50		
—	—	—	—	18½	London Victoria [15]	a																07 04		
—	10½	—	—	—	Westcombe Park	d			05 27				05 57							06 27			06 42	
—	11	—	—	—	Maze Hill	d			05 29				05 59							06 29			06 44	
—	12	—	—	—	Greenwich [4]	d			05 32				06 02							06 32			06 47	
—	12½	—	—	—	Deptford	a			05 34				06 04							06 34			06 49	
34¼	15½	15¼	32¾	—	London Bridge [4]	a	05 22	05 36	05 41	05 52	05 58	06 05	06 12	06 22		06 28	06 37	06 34	06 27	06 42	06 43		06 56	06 58
—	16¼	—	—	—	London Cannon Street [4]	a		05 41											06 32		06 48		07 03	07 05
35¼	—	16¼	33¾	—	London Waterloo (East) [4]	a	05 26		05 46	05 57	06 03	06 10	06 17	06 26		06 33	06 41	06 39		06 48				
—	—	—	—	—	London Charing Cross [4]	a	05 30		05 50	06 01	06 07	06 13	06 21	06 30		06 36	06 45	06 43		06 52				
—	—	—	—	12½	Ebbsfleet International	a									05 47									
—	—	—	—	29¼	Stratford International	a									05 59									
—	—	—	—	35¼	St Pancras Int'l [15]	a									06 06									

A not 27 July

Mondays to Fridays

Gillingham and Dartford - London

until 27 July, 13 Aug to 28 Aug and from 10 Sep

Network Diagram - see first Page of Table 200

		SE	SE A	SE B	SE C	SE	SE D	SE	SE	SE	SE	SE	SE	SE	SE	SE	SE A	SE B	SE [1]	SE	SE	SE
Gillingham (Kent) [4]	d		05 50	05 50		05 54						06 07					06 20	06 20	06 34			
Chatham [4]	d		05 54	05 55		05 58						06 11					06 24	06 24	06 38			
Rochester [4]	d		05 57	05 57		06 00						06 13					06 27	06 27	06 41			
Maidstone West	d																					
Strood [4]	d		06 02	06 02		06 05						06 18					06 32	06 32				
Higham	d					06 10						06 23										
Gravesend [4]	d	06 05	06 13	06 13		06 18						06 31				06 34	06 43	06 43				
Northfleet	d	06 09														06 38						
Swanscombe	d	06 11														06 40						
Greenhithe for Bluewater	d	06 14				06 23						06 37				06 43						
Stone Crossing	d	06 16														06 45						
Dartford [4]	a	06 20				06 28						06 41				06 49						
	d	06 21				06 29		06 31		06 31	06 39	06 42				06 50						
Slade Green [4]	d									06 36											06 55	
Erith	d									06 39											06 57	
Belvedere	d									06 41											07 00	
Abbey Wood	d					06 38				06 45		06 51									07 03	
Plumstead	d									06 48											07 06	
Woolwich Arsenal [4]	d					06 43				06 51		06 56									07 09	
Woolwich Dockyard	d									06 53											07 12	
Charlton [4]	d					06 47				06 57											07 15	
Crayford	d				06 25		06 30	06 35							06 50	06 55						
Bexley	d				06 28		06 33	06 38							06 53	06 58						
Albany Park	d				06 31		06 36	06 41							06 56	07 01						
Sidcup [4]	d				06 34		06 39	06 44							06 59	07 04						
New Eltham	d				06 38		06 43	06 47							07 02	07 07						
Mottingham	d				06 40		06 45	06 50							07 05	07 10						
Lee	d				06 43		06 48	06 53							07 08	07 13						
Hither Green [4]	d				06 46		06 51	06 56						07 08	07 11	07 16						
Barnehurst [4]	d	06 28							06 39		06 49		06 53									07 00
Bexleyheath	d	06 31							06 41		06 52		06 56									07 03
Welling	d	06 34							06 44		06 55		06 59									07 06
Falconwood	d	06 37							06 47		06 57		07 01									07 08
Eltham	d	06 40							06 50		07 00		07 04									07 11
Kidbrooke	d	06 43							06 53		07 03		07 07									07 14
Blackheath [4]	d	06 47				06 52			06 57		07 08	07 05	07 11									07 18
Lewisham [4]	d	06 50			06 52	06 55	06 57		07 01		07 11	07 08	07 15		07 17					07 20		07 22
St Johns	d				06 54		06 59								07 19							07 24
New Cross [4]	d				06 56		07 01		07 04			07 11			07 21					07 23		07 26
Nunhead [4]	d												07 20									
Peckham Rye [4]	d												07 23									
Denmark Hill [4]	d												07 29									
London Victoria [15]	a												07 42									
Westcombe Park	d									06 59											07 17	
Maze Hill	d									07 01											07 19	
Greenwich [4]	d									07 05											07 23	
Deptford	a									07 07											07 25	
London Bridge [4]	a	07 00			07 02	07 03	07 07	07 06	07 09	07 14	07 20	07 17		07 18	07 26	07 26			07 20	07 28	07 33	07 33
London Cannon Street [4]	a				07 09		07 14		07 16	07 21		07 23		07 25	07 33				07 27	07 35		07 39
London Waterloo (East) [4]	a	07 05				07 09		07 11			07 25					07 31					07 38	
London Charing Cross [4]	a	07 11				07 15		07 17			07 31					07 37					07 44	
Ebbsfleet International	a		06 17	06 16													06 47	06 47				
Stratford International	a		06 29	06 33													06 59	06 59				
St Pancras Int'l [15]	a		06 36	06 43													07 06	07 07				

A not 27 July
B 27 July
C from 21 May until 27 July
D until 18 May

Table 200

Mondays to Fridays

until 27 July, 13 Aug to 28 Aug and from 10 Sep

Gillingham and Dartford - London

Network Diagram - see first Page of Table 200

Station		SE	SE	SE	SE	SE	SE		SE	SE	SE	SE	SE	SE	SE	SE	SE		SE	SE	SE	SE	SE	SE	SE
															A	■							B		
Gillingham (Kent) ■	d								06 38						06 54	07 04									
Chatham ■	d								06 42						06 58	07 08									
Rochester ■	d								06 44						07 01	07 11									
Maidstone West	d																						06 56		
Strood ■	d								06 49					06 57									07 12		
Higham	d								06 54					07 02											
Gravesend ■	d		06 47						07 02					07 09	07 14							07 17	07 22		
Northfleet	d		06 51																			07 21			
Swanscombe	d		06 53																			07 23			
Greenhithe for Bluewater	d		06 56						07 07					07 16								07 26			
Stone Crossing	d		06 58																			07 28			
Dartford ■	a		07 02						07 12					07 21								07 33			
	d	07 00	07 03			07 05			07 12	07 17			07 20	07 23						07 25		07 34			07 36
Slade Green ■	d					07 09					07 19									07 29					
Erith	d					07 12					07 22									07 32					
Belvedere	d					07 14					07 24									07 34					
Abbey Wood	d		07 12			07 18					07 28			07 34						07 38					
Plumstead	d					07 21					07 31									07 41					
Woolwich Arsenal ■	d		07 17			07 24					07 34			07 39						07 44					
Woolwich Dockyard	d					07 26					07 36									07 46					
Charlton ■	d		07 22			07 30					07 40			07 44						07 50					
Crayford	d						07 10		07 17												07 30	07 38			
Bexley	d						07 13		07 20												07 33	07 41			
Albany Park	d						07 16		07 22												07 36	07 44			
Sidcup ■	d						07 19		07 25												07 39	07 47			
New Eltham	d						07 23		07 28												07 43	07 50			
Mottingham	d						07 25		07 31												07 45				
Lee	d						07 28		07 34												07 48				
Hither Green ■	d			07 28			07 32		07 36								07 49				07 52				
Barnehurst ■	d	07 08			07 13					07 24			07 28						07 33					07 38	07 44
Bexleyheath	d	07 11			07 16					07 26			07 31						07 36					07 41	07 46
Welling	d	07 14			07 19					07 29			07 34						07 39					07 44	07 49
Falconwood	d	07 16			07 21					07 32			07 36						07 41					07 46	07 52
Eltham	d	07 19			07 24					07 35			07 39						07 44					07 49	07 55
Kidbrooke	d	07 22			07 27					07 38			07 42						07 47					07 52	07 58
Blackheath ■	d	07 27			07 31					07 42			07 47						07 51					07 57	08 02
Lewisham ■	d	07 30			07 35		07 38			07 46		07 48	07 50						07 55		07 57				08 05
St Johns	d						07 40					07 50									08 00				
New Cross ■	d				07 38		07 42					07 53							07 58		08 02				
Nunhead ■	d									07 51															08 11
Peckham Rye ■	d									07 54															08 13
Denmark Hill ■	d									07 59															08 17
London Victoria ■	a									08 11															08 29
Westcombe Park	d					07 32					07 42									07 52					
Maze Hill	d					07 34					07 44									07 54					
Greenwich ■	d		07 28			07 37					07 47			07 51						07 57					
Deptford	a					07 39					07 49									07 59					
London Bridge ■	a	07 40	07 35	07 37	07 43	07 45	07 47		07 47		07 57	08 01	08 00	07 57		07 51	07 59		08 03	08 05	08 08	08 05			
London Cannon Street ■	a		07 42	07 44	07 50	07 52	07 54					08 08		08 04		07 57	08 06		08 10	08 12	08 15				
London Waterloo (East) ■	a	07 46							07 52		08 02		08 06									08 10		08 12	
London Charing Cross ■	a	07 52							07 58		08 08		08 12									08 16		08 18	
Ebbsfleet International	a														07 17										
Stratford International	a														07 29								07 36		
St Pancras Int'l ■	a														07 37								07 43		

A 27 July

B not 27 July

Table 200

Mondays to Fridays

until 27 July, 13 Aug to 28 Aug and from 10 Sep

Gillingham and Dartford - London

Network Diagram - see first Page of Table 200

Station		SE	SE		SE	SE	SE	SE	SE	SE	SE	SE	SE		SE	SE	SE	SE	SE	SE	SE	SE	SE		SE
												■									A				
Gillingham (Kent) ■	d										07 12	07 19													
Chatham ■	d										07 16	07 24													
Rochester ■	d										07 18														
Maidstone West	d																				07 26				
Strood ■	d						07 18				07 23										07 42				
Higham	d						07 23				07 28														
Gravesend ■	d						07 31				07 36									07 48	07 52				
Northfleet	d										07 40									07 52					
Swanscombe	d										07 42									07 54					
Greenhithe for Bluewater	d						07 37				07 45									07 57					
Stone Crossing	d										07 47									07 59					
Dartford ■	a						07 42				07 51									08 03					
	d					07 40	07 43		07 45		07 52				07 56				08 02	08 04					08 06
Slade Green ■	d		07 39						07 50								07 59					08 00			08 10
Erith	d		07 42						07 52								08 02								08 13
Belvedere	d		07 44						07 55								08 04								08 15
Abbey Wood	d		07 48				07 52		07 58								08 08			08 14					08 18
Plumstead	d		07 51						08 01								08 11								08 21
Woolwich Arsenal ■	d		07 54				07 57		08 05								08 14			08 19					08 24
Woolwich Dockyard	d		07 56						08 07								08 16								08 27
Charlton ■	d		08 00				08 03		08 11								08 20			08 24					08 30
Crayford	d									07 50	07 56														
Bexley	d									07 53	07 59														
Albany Park	d									07 56	08 02														
Sidcup ■	d	07 51								07 59	08 05					08 11									
New Eltham	d	07 54								08 03	08 09					08 14									
Mottingham	d	07 56								08 05						08 16									
Lee	d	07 59								08 08						08 19									
Hither Green ■	d	08 02								08 12						08 22									
Barnehurst ■	d					07 48		07 53					07 58		08 04				08 09			08 13	08 13		
Bexleyheath	d					07 51		07 56					08 01		08 06				08 11			08 16	08 16		
Welling	d					07 54		07 59					08 04		08 09				08 14			08 19	08 19		
Falconwood	d					07 56		08 01					08 06		08 12				08 17			08 21	08 21		
Eltham	d					07 59		08 04					08 09		08 15				08 20			08 24	08 24		
Kidbrooke	d					08 02		08 07					08 12		08 18				08 23			08 27	08 27		
Blackheath ■	d					08 07		08 11					08 17		08 22				08 27			08 31	08 31		
Lewisham ■	d				08 08	08 11		08 15		08 17					08 25			08 28	08 31			08 35	08 35		
St Johns	d				08 12					08 21								08 30							
New Cross ■	d				08 14			08 18		08 23								08 32				08 38	08 38		
Nunhead ■	d														08 30										
Peckham Rye ■	d														08 33										
Denmark Hill ■	d														08 36										
London Victoria ■	a														08 49										
Westcombe Park	d		08 02						08 13								08 22								08 32
Maze Hill	d		08 04						08 15								08 24								08 34
Greenwich ■	d		08 07				08 11		08 19								08 27			08 31					08 37
Deptford	a		08 09						08 21								08 29								08 39
London Bridge ■	a	08 13	08 16		08 20	08 20	08 17	08 25	08 27	08 29	08 25	08 09				08 33	08 37	08 41	08 40	08 38		08 43	08 43		08 45
London Cannon Street ■	a				08 28		08 24	08 32	08 35	08 36		08 17						08 48		08 44		08 50	08 50		08 52
London Waterloo (East) ■	a	08 18	08 22			08 26					08 30		08 32			08 38	08 42		08 46						
London Charing Cross ■	a	08 24	08 28			08 32					08 36		08 39			08 44	08 48		08 52						
Ebbsfleet International	a																								
Stratford International	a																				08 06				
St Pancras Int'l ■	a																				08 13				

A not 27 July

Gillingham and Dartford - London

Mondays to Fridays

until 27 July, 13 Aug to 28 Aug and from 10 Sep

Network Diagram - see first Page of Table 200

		SE	SE	SE	SE	SE	SE	SE	SE	SE	SE	SE	SE	SE	SE	SE	SE	SE	SE	SE	SE	SE	SE
				1	1							A						A	B				
Gillingham (Kent) 4	d		07 38	07 46	08 03									08 08				08 19	08 19				
Chatham 4	d		07 42	07 50	08 08									08 12				08 24	08 24				
Rochester 4	d		07 44		08 11									08 14				08 26	08 26				
Maidstone West	d											07 56											
Strood 4	d		07 49								07 58	08 12		08 19				08 32	08 32				
Higham	d		07 54								08 03			08 24									
Gravesend 4	d		08 02								08 17	08 22		08 33			08 06	08 43	08 43				
Northfleet	d													08 37			08 10						
Swanscombe	d													08 39			08 12						
Greenhithe for Bluewater	d		08 08								08 23			08 42			08 15						
Stone Crossing	d													08 44			08 17						
Dartford 4	a		08 12								08 27			08 49			08 21						
	d		08 13								08 29			08 49			08 22			08 24			
Slade Green 4	d					08 17		08 17									08 27				08 31	08 31	
Erith	d							08 19													08 33		
Belvedere	d							08 22													08 36		
Abbey Wood	d							08 25									08 34				08 39		
Plumstead	d							08 28													08 42		
Woolwich Arsenal 4	d							08 31									08 40				08 45		
Woolwich Dockyard	d							08 34													08 47		
Charlton 4	d							08 37								08 37	08 45				08 50		
Crayford	d	08 10	08 17							08 28	08 34			08 54		09 07							
Bexley	d	08 13	08 20							08 31	08 37			08 57		09 10							
Albany Park	d	08 16	08 23							08 34	08 40			09 00		09 13							
Sidcup 4	d	08 19	08 26				08 31			08 37	08 43			09 03		09 16							
New Eltham	d	08 23	08 30				08 34			08 41	08 46			09 06		09 19							
Mottingham	d	08 25					08 36			08 43	08 49			09 08		09 21							
Lee	d	08 28					08 39			08 46	08 52			09 11		09 24							
Hither Green 4	d	08 32					08 42			08 50	08 55		08 59	09 14	09 19	09 28							
Barnehurst 4	d					08 24														08 30		08 37	08 37
Bexleyheath	d					08 27														08 33		08 40	08 40
Welling	d					08 30														08 36		08 43	08 43
Falconwood	d					08 32														08 38		08 45	08 45
Eltham	d					08 35														08 41		08 48	08 48
Kidbrooke	d					08 38														08 44		08 51	08 51
Blackheath 4	d					08 42														08 48		08 55	08 55
Lewisham 4	d	08 37				08 46			08 48	08 55			09 04		09 24	09 34				08 52		08 59	08 59
St Johns	d	08 40							08 50	08 57			09 07		09 26	09 36						09 01	09 01
New Cross 4 ⊖	d	08 42							08 52	08 59			09 09		09 28	09 38						09 03	09 03
Nunhead 4	d					08 52																	
Peckham Rye 4	d					08 55																	
Denmark Hill 4	d					09 02																	
London Victoria 15 ⊖	a					09 11																	
Westcombe Park	d							08 39													08 52		
Maze Hill	d							08 41													08 54		
Greenwich 4	d							08 45									08 51				08 58		
Deptford	a							08 47													09 00		
London Bridge 4 ⊖	a	08 49	08 45	08 31	08 49		08 52	08 56	08 57	09 05	09 05		09 17	09 23	09 33	09 44	09 00			09 00	09 07	09 09	09 09
London Cannon Street 4 ⊖	a	08 55		08 38	08 57				09 04	09 12			09 23		09 40	09 51	09 08				09 14	09 18	09 18
London Waterloo (East) 4 ⊖	a		08 50				08 58	09 02			09 10			09 28						09 05			
London Charing Cross 4 ⊖	a		08 56				09 04	09 08			09 16			09 34						09 12			
Ebbsfleet International	a																	08 47	08 46				
Stratford International ⊖	a											08 36						08 59	08 58				
St Pancras Int'l 15 ⊖	a											08 43						09 07	09 08				

A not 27 July

B 27 July

Gillingham and Dartford - London

Mondays to Fridays

until 27 July, 13 Aug to 28 Aug and from 10 Sep

Network Diagram - see first Page of Table 200

		SE	SE	SE	SE	SE	SE	SE	SE	SE	SE	SE	SE	SE	SE	SE	SE	SE	SE	SE	SE	SE	SE
		1											A										
Gillingham (Kent) 4	d	08 24											08 50										
Chatham 4	d	08 28											08 54										
Rochester 4	d	08 31											08 57										
Maidstone West	d																						
Strood 4	d												09 02										
Higham	d																						
Gravesend 4	d							09 02				08 48	09 13								09 32		
Northfleet	d							09 06													09 36		
Swanscombe	d							09 08													09 38		
Greenhithe for Bluewater	d							09 11				08 53									09 41		
Stone Crossing	d							09 13													09 43		
Dartford 4	a							09 17				08 58									09 47		
	d		08 38			08 52		09 18				08 58			09 01	09 08			09 22		09 48		
Slade Green 4	d			08 39			08 47				08 54				09 05		09 15			09 17			
Erith	d			08 41							08 56				09 08		09 18						
Belvedere	d			08 44							08 59				09 10		09 20						
Abbey Wood	d			08 47							09 02	09 07			09 13		09 23						
Plumstead	d			08 50							09 05				09 16		09 26						
Woolwich Arsenal 4	d			08 53							09 08	09 12			09 19		09 29						
Woolwich Dockyard	d			08 56							09 10				09 22		09 32						
Charlton 4	d			08 59						09 07	09 13	09 17			09 25		09 35						09 40
Crayford	d							09 22		09 37											09 52		10 07
Bexley	d							09 25		09 40											09 55		10 10
Albany Park	d							09 28		09 43											09 58		10 13
Sidcup 4	d							09 31		09 46											10 01		10 16
New Eltham	d							09 34		09 49											10 04		10 19
Mottingham	d							09 36		09 51											10 06		10 21
Lee	d							09 39		09 54											10 09		10 24
Hither Green 4	d							09 42	09 49	09 58											10 12	10 19	10 28
Barnehurst 4	d		08 45			08 59	09a04							09 08		09 16			09 29	09a34			
Bexleyheath	d		08 47			09 01								09 10		09 19			09 31				
Welling	d		08 50			09 04								09 13		09 22			09 34				
Falconwood	d		08 53			09 07								09 16		09 24			09 37				
Eltham	d		08 56			09 10								09 19		09 27			09 40				
Kidbrooke	d		08 59			09 13								09 22		09 30			09 43				
Blackheath 4	d		09 02			09 16						09 21		09 25		09 34			09 46				
Lewisham 4	d		09 06		09 15	09 20			09 54	10 04		09 26		09 29		09 38		09 45	09 50			10 24	10 34
St Johns	d				09 17				09 56	10 06				09 31				09 47				10 26	10 36
New Cross 4 ⊖	d				09 19				09 58	10 08				09 33				09 49				10 28	10 38
Nunhead 4	d		09 11													09 43							
Peckham Rye 4	d		09 14													09 45							
Denmark Hill 4	d		09 17													09 49							
London Victoria 15 ⊖	a		09 29													10 00							
Westcombe Park	d			09 01							09 15				09 27		09 37						
Maze Hill	d			09 03							09 17				09 29		09 39						
Greenwich 4	d			09 07							09 21				09 32		09 42						
Deptford	a			09 09							09 23				09 34		09 44						
London Bridge 4 ⊖	a	09 11		09 17	09 25	09 29		09 52	10 04	10 14	09 29	09 34		09 38	09 41		09 50	09 54	09 58		10 22	10 34	10 44
London Cannon Street 4 ⊖	a	09 18			09 32				10 08	10 19	09 36			09 45	09 48		09 57	10 00				10 38	10 50
London Waterloo (East) 4 ⊖	a			09 22		09 34		09 56				09 39							10 02		10 26		
London Charing Cross 4 ⊖	a			09 28		09 40		10 00				09 45							10 06		10 30		
Ebbsfleet International	a												09 17										
Stratford International ⊖	a												09 29										
St Pancras Int'l 15 ⊖	a												09 36										

A not 27 July

Table 200

Gillingham and Dartford - London

Mondays to Fridays

until 27 July, 13 Aug to 28 Aug and from 10 Sep

Network Diagram - see first Page of Table 200

Station		SE	SE	SE A	SE B	SE	SE	SE	SE	SE	SE	SE C	SE C	SE	SE	SE	SE	SE	SE A	SE D	SE	SE
Gillingham (Kent)	d		08 54	09 20	09 20													09 24	09 50			
Chatham	d		08 58	09 24	09 24													09 28	09 54			
Rochester	d		09 00	09 27	09 27													09 30	09 57			
Maidstone West	d																					
Strood	d		09 05	09 32	09 32													09 35	10 02			
Higham	d		09 10															09 40				
Gravesend	d		09 18	09 43	09 43									10 02				09 48	10 13			
Northfleet	d													10 06								
Swanscombe	d													10 08								
Greenhithe for Bluewater	d		09 23											10 11				09 53				
Stone Crossing	d													10 13								
Dartford	a		09 28											10 17				09 58				
	d		09 29				09 31	09 38			09 52			10 18				09 59			10 01	10 08
Slade Green	d	09 25					09 35		09 45			09 47	09 47				09 55				10 05	
Erith	d	09 28					09 38		09 48								09 58				10 08	
Belvedere	d	09 30					09 40		09 50								10 00				10 10	
Abbey Wood	d	09 33	09 38				09 43		09 53								10 03	10 07			10 13	
Plumstead	d	09 36					09 46		09 56								10 06				10 16	
Woolwich Arsenal	d	09 39	09 43				09 49		09 59								10 09	10 12			10 19	
Woolwich Dockyard	d	09 42					09 52		10 02								10 12				10 22	
Charlton	d	09 45	09 47				09 55		10 05							10 07	10 15	10 17			10 25	
Crayford	d													10 22		10 37						
Bexley	d													10 25		10 40						
Albany Park	d													10 28		10 43						
Sidcup	d													10 31		10 46						
New Eltham	d													10 34		10 49						
Mottingham	d													10 36		10 51						
Lee	d													10 39		10 54						
Hither Green	d													10 42	10 49	10 58						
Barnehurst	d					09 38		09 46			09 59	10a04	10 08							10 08		10 16
Bexleyheath	d					09 40		09 49			10 01		10 10							10 10		10 19
Welling	d					09 43		09 52			10 04		10 13							10 13		10 22
Falconwood	d					09 46		09 54			10 07		10 16							10 16		10 24
Eltham	d					09 49		09 57			10 10		10 19							10 19		10 27
Kidbrooke	d					09 52		10 00			10 13		10 22							10 22		10 30
Blackheath	d		09 52			09 55		10 04			10 16		10 25					10 21		10 25		10 34
Lewisham	d		09 56			09 59		10 08		10 14	10 20		10 29		10 54	11 04		10 26		10 29		10 38
St Johns	d					10 01				10 16			10 31		10 56	11 06				10 31		
New Cross	d					10 03				10 18			10 33		10 58	11 08				10 33		
Nunhead	d							10 13														10 43
Peckham Rye	d							10 15														10 45
Denmark Hill	d							10 19														10 49
London Victoria	a							10 28														10 58
Westcombe Park	d	09 47					09 57		10 07								10 17				10 27	
Maze Hill	d	09 49					09 59		10 09								10 19				10 29	
Greenwich	d	09 52					10 02		10 12								10 22				10 32	
Deptford	a	09 54					10 04		10 14								10 24				10 34	
London Bridge	a	10 00	10 05			10 08	10 11		10 20	10 24	10 28		10 38	10 52	11 04	11 14	10 30	10 35		10 38	10 41	
London Cannon Street	a	10 04				10 13	10 15		10 24	10 28			10 43		11 08	11 19	10 36			10 43	10 45	
London Waterloo (East)	a		10 09								10 32			10 56				10 39				
London Charing Cross	a		10 13								10 36			11 00				10 43				
Ebbsfleet International	a			09 47	09 46														10 16			
Stratford International	a			09 59	09 58														10 28			
St Pancras Int'l	a			10 06	10 08														10 35			

A not 27 July
B 27 July
C from 21 May until 27 July
D until 18 May

Table 200

Gillingham and Dartford - London

Mondays to Fridays

until 27 July, 13 Aug to 28 Aug and from 10 Sep

Network Diagram - see first Page of Table 200

Station		SE	SE	SE	SE	SE	SE	SE	SE	SE	SE A	SE B	SE	SE	SE	SE	SE	SE	SE	SE	SE	SE	SE
Gillingham (Kent)	d									09 54	10 20	10 20											
Chatham	d									09 58	10 24	10 24											
Rochester	d									10 00	10 27	10 27											
Maidstone West	d																						
Strood	d									10 05	10 32	10 32											
Higham	d									10 10													
Gravesend	d					10 32				10 18	10 43	10 43								11 02			
Northfleet	d					10 36														11 06			
Swanscombe	d					10 38														11 08			
Greenhithe for Bluewater	d					10 41				10 23										11 11			
Stone Crossing	d					10 43														11 13			
Dartford	a					10 47				10 28										11 17			
	d			10 22		10 48				10 29				10 31	10 38			10 52		11 18			
Slade Green	d	10 15			10 17				10 25					10 35		10 45			10 47				10 55
Erith	d	10 18							10 28					10 38		10 48							10 58
Belvedere	d	10 20							10 30					10 40		10 50							11 00
Abbey Wood	d	10 23							10 33	10 38				10 43		10 53							11 03
Plumstead	d	10 26							10 36					10 46		10 56							11 06
Woolwich Arsenal	d	10 29							10 39	10 43				10 49		10 59							11 09
Woolwich Dockyard	d	10 32							10 42					10 52		11 02							11 12
Charlton	d	10 35						10 37	10 45	10 47				10 55		11 05						11 07	11 15
Crayford	d					10 52		11 07												11 22		11 37	
Bexley	d					10 55		11 10												11 25		11 40	
Albany Park	d					10 58		11 13												11 28		11 43	
Sidcup	d					11 01		11 16												11 31		11 46	
New Eltham	d					11 04		11 19												11 34		11 49	
Mottingham	d					11 06		11 21												11 36		11 51	
Lee	d					11 09		11 24												11 39		11 54	
Hither Green	d					11 12	11 19	11 28												11 42	11 49	11 58	
Barnehurst	d			10 29	10a34								10 38		10 46			10 59	11a04				
Bexleyheath	d			10 31									10 40		10 49			11 01					
Welling	d			10 34									10 43		10 52			11 04					
Falconwood	d			10 37									10 46		10 54			11 07					
Eltham	d			10 40									10 49		10 57			11 10					
Kidbrooke	d			10 43									10 52		11 00			11 13					
Blackheath	d			10 46						10 52			10 55		11 04			11 16					
Lewisham	d		10 44	10 50			11 24	11 34		10 56			10 59		11 08		11 14	11 20			11 54	12 04	
St Johns	d		10 46				11 26	11 36					11 01				11 16				11 56	12 06	
New Cross	d		10 48				11 28	11 38					11 03				11 18				11 58	12 08	
Nunhead	d														11 13								
Peckham Rye	d														11 15								
Denmark Hill	d														11 19								
London Victoria	a														11 28								
Westcombe Park	d	10 37							10 47					10 57		11 07							11 17
Maze Hill	d	10 39							10 49					10 59		11 09							11 19
Greenwich	d	10 42							10 52					11 02		11 12							11 22
Deptford	a	10 44							10 54					11 04		11 14							11 24
London Bridge	a	10 50	10 54	10 58		11 22	11 34	11 44	11 00	11 05			11 08	11 11		11 20	11 24	11 28		11 52	12 04	12 14	11 30
London Cannon Street	a	10 54	10 58				11 38	11 49	11 06				11 13	11 15		11 24	11 28				12 08	12 19	11 36
London Waterloo (East)	a			11 02		11 26				11 09								11 32		11 56			
London Charing Cross	a			11 06		11 30				11 13								11 36		12 00			
Ebbsfleet International	a										10 47	10 46											
Stratford International	a										10 59	10 58											
St Pancras Int'l	a										11 06	11 08											

A not 27 July
B 27 July

Table 200

Gillingham and Dartford - London

Mondays to Fridays

until 27 July, 13 Aug to 28 Aug and from 10 Sep

Network Diagram - see first Page of Table 200

Station		SE	SE A		SE	SE	SE	SE	SE	SE	SE	SE	SE		SE	SE	SE	SE A	SE B	SE	SE	SE	SE		SE
Gillingham (Kent)	d	10 24	10 50														10 54	11 20	11 20						
Chatham	d	10 28	10 54														10 58	11 24	11 24						
Rochester	d	10 30	10 57														11 00	11 27	11 27						
Maidstone West	d																								
Strood	d	10 35	11 02														11 05	11 32	11 32						
Higham	d	10 40															11 10								
Gravesend	d	10 48	11 13									11 32					11 18	11 43	11 43						
Northfleet	d											11 36													
Swanscombe	d											11 38													
Greenhithe for Bluewater	d	10 53										11 41					11 23								
Stone Crossing	d											11 43													
Dartford	a	10 58										11 47					11 28								
	d	10 59				11 01	11 08			11 22		11 48					11 29				11 31	11 38			
Slade Green	d					11 05		11 15			11 17					11 25					11 35		11 45		
Erith	d					11 08		11 18								11 28					11 38		11 48		
Belvedere	d					11 10		11 20								11 30					11 40		11 50		
Abbey Wood	d	11 08				11 13		11 23								11 33	11 38				11 43		11 53		
Plumstead	d					11 16		11 26								11 36					11 46		11 56		
Woolwich Arsenal	d	11 13				11 19		11 29								11 39	11 43				11 49		11 59		
Woolwich Dockyard	d					11 22		11 32								11 42					11 52		12 02		
Charlton	d	11 17				11 25		11 35							11 37	11 45	11 47				11 55		12 05		
Crayford	d											11 52			12 07										
Bexley	d											11 55			12 10										
Albany Park	d											11 58			12 13										
Sidcup	d											12 01			12 16										
New Eltham	d											12 04			12 19										
Mottingham	d											12 06			12 21										
Lee	d											12 09			12 24										
Hither Green	d											12 12	12 19		12 28										
Barnehurst	d				11 08		11 16			11 29	11a34									11 38		11 46			
Bexleyheath	d				11 10		11 19			11 31										11 40		11 49			
Welling	d				11 13		11 22			11 34										11 43		11 52			
Falconwood	d				11 16		11 24			11 37										11 46		11 54			
Eltham	d				11 19		11 27			11 40										11 49		11 57			
Kidbrooke	d				11 22		11 30			11 43										11 52		12 00			
Blackheath	d	11 22			11 25		11 34			11 46							11 52			11 55		12 04			
Lewisham	d	11 26			11 29		11 38		11 44	11 50			12 24		12 34		11 56			11 59		12 08			12 14
St Johns	d				11 31				11 46				12 26		12 36					12 01					12 16
New Cross	d				11 33				11 48				12 28		12 38					12 03					12 18
Nunhead	d						11 43															12 13			
Peckham Rye	d						11 45															12 15			
Denmark Hill	d						11 49															12 19			
London Victoria	a						11 58															12 28			
Westcombe Park	d					11 27		11 37								11 47					11 57		12 07		
Maze Hill	d					11 29		11 39								11 49					11 59		12 09		
Greenwich	d					11 32		11 42								11 52					12 02		12 12		
Deptford	a					11 34		11 44								11 54					12 04		12 14		
London Bridge	a	11 35			11 38	11 41		11 50	11 54	11 58		12 22	12 34		12 44	12 00	12 05			12 08	12 11		12 20		12 24
London Cannon Street	a				11 43	11 45		11 54	11 58				12 38		12 49	12 04				12 13	12 15		12 24		12 28
London Waterloo (East)	a	11 39								12 02		12 26					12 09								
London Charing Cross	a	11 43								12 06		12 30					12 13								
Ebbsfleet International	a		11 17															11 47	11 46						
Stratford International	a		11 29															11 59	11 58						
St Pancras Int'l	a		11 36															12 06	12 08						

A not 27 July

B 27 July

Table 200

Gillingham and Dartford - London

Mondays to Fridays

until 27 July, 13 Aug to 28 Aug and from 10 Sep

Network Diagram - see first Page of Table 200

Station		SE	SE A	SE A	SE	SE	SE	SE	SE		SE B	SE	SE	SE	SE	SE	SE	SE	SE		SE	SE	SE	SE	SE B
Gillingham (Kent)	d								11 24		11 50													11 54	12 20
Chatham	d								11 28		11 54													11 58	12 24
Rochester	d								11 30		11 57													12 00	12 27
Maidstone West	d																								
Strood	d								11 35		12 02													12 05	12 32
Higham	d								11 40															12 10	
Gravesend	d				12 02				11 48		12 13								12 32					12 18	12 43
Northfleet	d				12 06														12 36						
Swanscombe	d				12 08														12 38						
Greenhithe for Bluewater	d				12 11				11 53										12 41					12 23	
Stone Crossing	d				12 13														12 43						
Dartford	a				12 17				11 58										12 47					12 28	
	d	11 52			12 18				11 59				12 01	12 08			12 22		12 48					12 29	
Slade Green	d		11 47	11 47				11 55					12 05		12 15			12 17					12 25		
Erith	d							11 58					12 08		12 18								12 28		
Belvedere	d							12 00					12 10		12 20								12 30		
Abbey Wood	d							12 03	12 08				12 13		12 23								12 33	12 38	
Plumstead	d							12 06					12 16		12 26								12 36		
Woolwich Arsenal	d							12 09	12 13				12 19		12 29								12 39	12 43	
Woolwich Dockyard	d							12 12					12 22		12 32								12 42		
Charlton	d						12 07	12 15	12 17				12 25		12 35							12 37	12 45	12 47	
Crayford	d				12 22		12 37												12 52			13 07			
Bexley	d				12 25		12 40												12 55			13 10			
Albany Park	d				12 28		12 43												12 58			13 13			
Sidcup	d				12 31		12 46												13 01			13 16			
New Eltham	d				12 34		12 49												13 04			13 19			
Mottingham	d				12 36		12 51												13 06			13 21			
Lee	d				12 39		12 54												13 09			13 24			
Hither Green	d				12 42	12 49	12 58												13 12		13 19	13 28			
Barnehurst	d	11 59	12a04	12 08								12 08		12 16			12 29	12 38							
Bexleyheath	d	12 01		12 10								12 10		12 19			12 31	12 40							
Welling	d	12 04		12 13								12 13		12 22			12 34	12 43							
Falconwood	d	12 07		12 16								12 16		12 24			12 37	12 46							
Eltham	d	12 10		12 19								12 19		12 27			12 40	12 49							
Kidbrooke	d	12 13		12 22								12 22		12 30			12 43	12 52							
Blackheath	d	12 16		12 25					12 22			12 25		12 34			12 46	12 55						12 52	
Lewisham	d	12 20		12 29		12 54	13 04		12 26			12 29		12 38		12 44	12 50	12 59			13 24	13 34		12 56	
St Johns	d			12 31		12 56	13 06					12 31				12 46		13 01			13 26	13 36			
New Cross	d			12 33		12 58	13 08					12 33				12 48		13 03			13 28	13 38			
Nunhead	d													12 43											
Peckham Rye	d													12 45											
Denmark Hill	d													12 49											
London Victoria	a													12 58											
Westcombe Park	d							12 17					12 27		12 37								12 47		
Maze Hill	d							12 19					12 29		12 39								12 49		
Greenwich	d							12 22					12 32		12 42								12 52		
Deptford	a							12 24					12 34		12 44								12 54		
London Bridge	a	12 28		12 38	12 52	13 04	13 14	12 30	12 35			12 38	12 41		12 50	12 54	12 58	13 08	13 22		13 34	13 44	13 00	13 05	
London Cannon Street	a			12 43		13 08	13 19	12 36				12 43	12 45		12 54	12 58		13 13			13 38	13 49	13 06		
London Waterloo (East)	a	12 32			12 56				12 39								13 02		13 26					13 09	
London Charing Cross	a	12 36			13 00				12 43								13 06		13 30					13 13	
Ebbsfleet International	a										12 17														12 47
Stratford International	a										12 29														12 59
St Pancras Int'l	a										12 36														13 06

A from 21 May until 27 July

B not 27 July

Table 200

Mondays to Fridays

until 27 July, 13 Aug to 28 Aug and from 10 Sep

Network Diagram - see first Page of Table 200

Gillingham and Dartford - London

		SE A	SE	SE	SE		SE	SE	SE	SE	SE	SE	SE	SE	SE B		SE	SE	SE	SE	SE	SE	SE	SE	SE
Gillingham (Kent)	d	12 20												12 24	12 50										
Chatham	d	12 24												12 28	12 54										
Rochester	d	12 27												12 30	12 57										
Maidstone West	d																								
Strood	d	12 32												12 35	13 02										
Higham	d													12 40											
Gravesend	d	12 43								13 02				12 48	13 13								13 32		
Northfleet	d									13 06													13 36		
Swanscombe	d									13 08													13 38		
Greenhithe for Bluewater	d									13 11				12 53									13 41		
Stone Crossing	d									13 13													13 43		
Dartford	a									13 17				12 58									13 47		
	d		12 31	12 38				12 52		13 18				12 59			13 01	13 08			13 22		13 48		
Slade Green	d		12 35		12 45				12 47				12 55				13 05		13 15			13 17			
Erith	d		12 38		12 48								12 58				13 08		13 18						
Belvedere	d		12 40		12 50								13 00				13 10		13 20						
Abbey Wood	d		12 43		12 53								13 03	13 08			13 13		13 23						
Plumstead	d		12 46		12 56								13 06				13 16		13 26						
Woolwich Arsenal	d		12 49		12 59								13 09	13 13			13 19		13 29						
Woolwich Dockyard	d		12 52		13 02								13 12				13 22		13 32						
Charlton	d		12 55		13 05							13 07	13 15	13 17			13 25		13 35						13 37
Crayford	d									13 22		13 37											13 52		14 07
Bexley	d									13 25		13 40											13 55		14 10
Albany Park	d									13 28		13 43											13 58		14 13
Sidcup	d									13 31		13 46											14 01		14 16
New Eltham	d									13 34		13 49											14 04		14 19
Mottingham	d									13 36		13 51											14 06		14 21
Lee	d									13 39		13 54											14 09		14 24
Hither Green	d									13 42	13 49	13 58											14 12	14 19	14 28
Barnehurst	d			12 46				12 59	13 08									13 16			13 29	13 38			
Bexleyheath	d			12 49				13 01	13 10									13 19			13 31	13 40			
Welling	d			12 52				13 04	13 13									13 22			13 34	13 43			
Falconwood	d			12 54				13 07	13 16									13 24			13 37	13 46			
Eltham	d			12 57				13 10	13 19									13 27			13 40	13 49			
Kidbrooke	d			13 00				13 13	13 22									13 30			13 43	13 52			
Blackheath	d			13 04				13 16	13 25					13 22				13 34			13 46	13 55			
Lewisham	d			13 08			13 14	13 20	13 29		13 54	14 04		13 26				13 38		13 44	13 50	13 59		14 24	14 34
St Johns	d						13 16		13 31		13 56	14 06								13 46		14 01		14 26	14 36
New Cross	d						13 18		13 33		13 58	14 08								13 48		14 03		14 28	14 38
Nunhead	d			13 13														13 43							
Peckham Rye	d			13 15														13 45							
Denmark Hill	d			13 19														13 49							
London Victoria	a			13 28														13 58							
Westcombe Park	d		12 57		13 07								13 17				13 27		13 37						
Maze Hill	d		12 59		13 09								13 19				13 29		13 39						
Greenwich	d		13 02		13 12								13 22				13 32		13 42						
Deptford	a		13 04		13 14								13 24				13 34		13 44						
London Bridge	a		13 11		13 20		13 24	13 28	13 38	13 52	14 04	14 14	13 30	13 35			13 41		13 50	13 54	13 58	14 08	14 22	14 34	14 44
London Cannon Street	a		13 15		13 24		13 28		13 43		14 08	14 19	13 36				13 45		13 54	13 58		14 13		14 38	14 49
London Waterloo (East)	a							13 32		13 56				13 39							14 02		14 26		
London Charing Cross	a							13 36		14 00				13 43							14 06		14 30		
Ebbsfleet International	a	12 46													13 17										
Stratford International	a	12 58													13 29										
St Pancras Int'l	a	13 08													13 36										

A 27 July

B not 27 July

Table 200

Mondays to Fridays

until 27 July, 13 Aug to 28 Aug and from 10 Sep

Network Diagram - see first Page of Table 200

Gillingham and Dartford - London

			SE	SE	SE A	SE B	SE C	SE	SE	SE	SE		SE	SE	SE	SE	SE	SE	SE	SE D	SE		SE	SE	SE
Gillingham (Kent)	d			12 54	13 20	13 20	13 20												13 24	13 50					
Chatham	d			12 58	13 24	13 24	13 24												13 28	13 54					
Rochester	d			13 00	13 27	13 27	13 27												13 30	13 57					
Maidstone West	d																								
Strood	d			13 05	13 32	13 32	13 32												13 35	14 02					
Higham	d			13 10															13 40						
Gravesend	d			13 18	13 43	13 43	13 43								14 02				13 48	14 13					
Northfleet	d														14 06										
Swanscombe	d														14 08										
Greenhithe for Bluewater	d			13 23											14 11				13 53						
Stone Crossing	d														14 13										
Dartford	a			13 28											14 17				13 58						
	d			13 29				13 31	13 38				13 52		14 18				13 59		14 01		14 08		
Slade Green	d		13 25					13 35		13 45				13 47				13 55			14 05			14 15	
Erith	d		13 28					13 38		13 48								13 58			14 08			14 18	
Belvedere	d		13 30					13 40		13 50								14 00			14 10			14 20	
Abbey Wood	d		13 33	13 38				13 43		13 53								14 03	14 08		14 13			14 23	
Plumstead	d		13 36					13 46		13 56								14 06			14 16			14 26	
Woolwich Arsenal	d		13 39	13 43				13 49		13 59								14 09	14 13		14 19			14 29	
Woolwich Dockyard	d		13 42					13 52		14 02								14 12			14 22			14 32	
Charlton	d		13 45	13 47				13 55		14 05							14 07	14 15	14 17		14 25			14 35	
Crayford	d														14 22		14 37								
Bexley	d														14 25		14 40								
Albany Park	d														14 28		14 43								
Sidcup	d														14 31		14 46								
New Eltham	d														14 34		14 49								
Mottingham	d														14 36		14 51								
Lee	d														14 39		14 54								
Hither Green	d														14 42	14 49	14 58								
Barnehurst	d								13 46				13 59	14 08									14 16		
Bexleyheath	d								13 49				14 01	14 10									14 19		
Welling	d								13 52				14 04	14 13									14 22		
Falconwood	d								13 54				14 07	14 16									14 24		
Eltham	d								13 57				14 10	14 19									14 27		
Kidbrooke	d								14 00				14 13	14 22									14 30		
Blackheath	d			13 52					14 04				14 16	14 25					14 22				14 34		
Lewisham	d			13 56					14 08		14 14		14 20	14 29		14 54	15 04		14 26				14 38		14 44
St Johns	d										14 16			14 31		14 56	15 06								14 46
New Cross	d										14 18			14 33		14 58	15 08								14 48
Nunhead	d								14 13														14 43		
Peckham Rye	d								14 15														14 45		
Denmark Hill	d								14 19														14 49		
London Victoria	a								14 28														14 58		
Westcombe Park	d		13 47					13 57		14 07								14 17			14 27			14 37	
Maze Hill	d		13 49					13 59		14 09								14 19			14 29			14 39	
Greenwich	d		13 52					14 02		14 12								14 22			14 32			14 42	
Deptford	a		13 54					14 04		14 14								14 24			14 34			14 44	
London Bridge	a		14 00	14 05				14 11		14 20	14 24		14 28	14 38	14 52	15 04	15 14	14 30	14 35		14 41			14 50	14 54
London Cannon Street	a		14 06					14 15		14 24	14 28			14 43		15 08	15 19	14 36			14 45			14 54	14 58
London Waterloo (East)	a			14 09									14 32		14 56				14 39						
London Charing Cross	a			14 13									14 36		15 00				14 43						
Ebbsfleet International	a				13 46	13 47	13 47													14 17					
Stratford International	a				13 58	14 01	14 02													14 29					
St Pancras Int'l	a				14 08	14 10	14 09													14 36					

A 27 July

B until 18 May

C from 21 May until 26 July

D not 27 July

Table 200

Mondays to Fridays

Gillingham and Dartford - London

until 27 July, 13 Aug to 28 Aug and from 10 Sep

Network Diagram - see first Page of Table 200

		SE	SE	SE	SE	SE	SE	SE	SE A	SE B	SE	SE	SE	SE	SE	SE	SE	SE	SE	SE	SE	SE A	SE
Gillingham (Kent)	d							13 54	14 20	14 20											14 24	14 50	
Chatham	d							13 58	14 24	14 24											14 28	14 54	
Rochester	d							14 00	14 27	14 27											14 30	14 57	
Maidstone West	d																						
Strood	d							14 05	14 32	14 32											14 35	15 02	
Higham	d							14 10													14 40		
Gravesend	d			14 32				14 18	14 43	14 43							15 02				14 48	15 13	
Northfleet	d			14 36													15 06						
Swanscombe	d			14 38													15 08						
Greenhithe for Bluewater	d			14 41				14 23									15 11				14 53		
Stone Crossing	d			14 43													15 13						
Dartford	a			14 47				14 28									15 17				14 58		
	d	14 22		14 48				14 29			14 31	14 38			14 52		15 18				14 59		15 01
Slade Green	d		14 17				14 25				14 35		14 45			14 47				14 55			15 05
Erith	d						14 28				14 38		14 48							14 58			15 08
Belvedere	d						14 30				14 40		14 50							15 00			15 10
Abbey Wood	d						14 33	14 38			14 43		14 53							15 03	15 08		15 13
Plumstead	d						14 36				14 46		14 56							15 06			15 16
Woolwich Arsenal	d						14 39	14 43			14 49		14 59							15 09	15 13		15 19
Woolwich Dockyard	d						14 42				14 52		15 02							15 12			15 22
Charlton	d					14 37	14 45	14 47			14 55		15 05						15 07	15 15	15 17		15 25
Crayford	d			14 52		15 07											15 22		15 37				
Bexley	d			14 55		15 10											15 25		15 40				
Albany Park	d			14 58		15 13											15 28		15 43				
Sidcup	d			15 01		15 16											15 31		15 46				
New Eltham	d			15 04		15 19											15 34		15 49				
Mottingham	d			15 06		15 21											15 36		15 51				
Lee	d			15 09		15 24											15 39		15 54				
Hither Green	d			15 12	15 19	15 28											15 42	15 49	15 58				
Barnehurst	d	14 29	14 38									14 46			14 59	15 08							
Bexleyheath	d	14 31	14 40									14 49			15 01	15 10							
Welling	d	14 34	14 43									14 52			15 04	15 13							
Falconwood	d	14 37	14 46									14 54			15 07	15 16							
Eltham	d	14 40	14 49									14 57			15 10	15 19							
Kidbrooke	d	14 43	14 52									15 00			15 13	15 22							
Blackheath	d	14 46	14 55					14 52				15 04			15 16	15 25					15 22		
Lewisham	d	14 50	14 59		15 24	15 34		14 56				15 08		15 14	15 20	15 29		15 54	16 04		15 26		
St Johns	d		15 01		15 26	15 36								15 16		15 31		15 56	16 06				
New Cross	d		15 03		15 28	15 38								15 18		15 33		15 58	16 08				
Nunhead	d											15 13											
Peckham Rye	d											15 15											
Denmark Hill	d											15 19											
London Victoria	a											15 28											
Westcombe Park	d						14 47				14 57		15 07							15 17			15 27
Maze Hill	d						14 49				14 59		15 09							15 19			15 29
Greenwich	d						14 52				15 02		15 12							15 22			15 32
Deptford	a						14 54				15 04		15 14							15 24			15 34
London Bridge	a	14 58	15 08	15 22	15 34	15 44	15 00	15 05			15 11		15 20	15 24	15 28	15 38	15 52	16 04	16 15	15 30	15 35		15 41
London Cannon Street	a		15 13		15 38	15 49	15 06				15 15		15 24	15 28		15 43		16 08	16 19	15 36			15 45
London Waterloo (East)	a	15 02		15 26				15 09							15 32		15 57				15 39		
London Charing Cross	a	15 06		15 30				15 13							15 36		16 01				15 43		
Ebbsfleet International	a								14 47	14 46												15 17	
Stratford International	a								14 59	14 58												15 29	
St Pancras Int'l	a								15 06	15 08												15 36	

A not 27 July

B 27 July

Table 200

Mondays to Fridays

Gillingham and Dartford - London

until 27 July, 13 Aug to 28 Aug and from 10 Sep

Network Diagram - see first Page of Table 200

		SE	SE	SE	SE	SE A	SE A	SE	SE	SE	SE	SE	SE B	SE C	SE D	SE	SE	SE	SE	SE	SE	SE
Gillingham (Kent)	d											14 54	15 20	15 20								
Chatham	d											14 58	15 24	15 24								
Rochester	d											15 00	15 27	15 27								
Maidstone West	d																					
Strood	d											15 05	15 32	15 32								
Higham	d											15 10										
Gravesend	d							15 32				15 18	15 43	15 43								16 02
Northfleet	d							15 36														16 06
Swanscombe	d							15 38														16 08
Greenhithe for Bluewater	d							15 41				15 23										16 11
Stone Crossing	d							15 43														16 13
Dartford	a							15 47				15 28										16 17
	d	15 08			15 22			15 48				15 29				15 31	15 38			15 52		16 18
Slade Green	d		15 15			15 17	15 17				15 25					15 35		15 45			15 47	
Erith	d		15 18								15 28					15 38		15 48				
Belvedere	d		15 20								15 30					15 40		15 50				
Abbey Wood	d		15 23								15 33	15 38				15 43		15 53				
Plumstead	d		15 26								15 36					15 46		15 56				
Woolwich Arsenal	d		15 29								15 39	15 43				15 49		15 59				
Woolwich Dockyard	d		15 32								15 42					15 52		16 02				
Charlton	d		15 35							15 37	15 45	15 47				15 55		16 05				
Crayford	d							15 52		16 07												16 22
Bexley	d							15 55		16 10												16 25
Albany Park	d							15 58		16 13												16 28
Sidcup	d							16 01		16 16												16 31
New Eltham	d							16 04		16 19												16 34
Mottingham	d							16 06		16 21												16 36
Lee	d							16 09		16 24												16 39
Hither Green	d							16 12	16 19	16 28												16 42
Barnehurst	d	15 16			15 29	15a34	15 38								15 38		15 46			15 59	16 08	
Bexleyheath	d	15 19			15 31		15 40								15 40		15 49			16 01	16 10	
Welling	d	15 22			15 34		15 43								15 43		15 52			16 04	16 13	
Falconwood	d	15 24			15 37		15 46								15 46		15 54			16 07	16 16	
Eltham	d	15 27			15 40		15 49								15 49		15 57			16 10	16 19	
Kidbrooke	d	15 30			15 43		15 52								15 52		16 00			16 13	16 22	
Blackheath	d	15 34			15 46		15 55					15 52			15 55		16 04			16 16	16 25	
Lewisham	d	15 38		15 44	15 50		15 59		16 24	16 34		15 56			15 59		16 08		16 14	16 20	16 29	
St Johns	d			15 46			16 01		16 26	16 36					16 01				16 16		16 31	
New Cross	d			15 48			16 03		16 28	16 38					16 03				16 18		16 33	
Nunhead	d	15 43															16 13					
Peckham Rye	d	15 45															16 15					
Denmark Hill	d	15 49															16 19					
London Victoria	a	15 58															16 28					
Westcombe Park	d		15 37								15 47					15 57		16 07				
Maze Hill	d		15 39								15 49					15 59		16 09				
Greenwich	d		15 42								15 52					16 02		16 12				
Deptford	a		15 44								15 54					16 04		16 14				
London Bridge	a		15 50	15 54	15 58		16 09	16 22	16 34	16 44	16 00	16 05			16 09	16 12		16 20	16 24	16 29	16 39	16 52
London Cannon Street	a		15 54	15 58			16 13		16 38	16 49	16 06				16 13	16 16		16 24	16 28		16 43	
London Waterloo (East)	a				16 02			16 27				16 09								16 33		16 56
London Charing Cross	a				16 06			16 31				16 13								16 37		17 00
Ebbsfleet International	a												15 46	15 47								
Stratford International	a												15 58	16 02								
St Pancras Int'l	a												16 08	16 09								

A from 21 May until 27 July

B 27 July

C not 27 July

D until 18 May

Table 200

Gillingham and Dartford - London

Mondays to Fridays

until 27 July, 13 Aug to 28 Aug and from 10 Sep

Network Diagram - see first Page of Table 200

		SE	SE	SE	SE	SE A	SE	SE	SE		SE	SE	SE	SE	SE	SE	SE	SE	SE		SE	SE	SE	SE	SE B
Gillingham (Kent)	d				15 24	15 50												15 54							16 20
Chatham	d				15 28	15 54												15 58							16 24
Rochester	d				15 30	15 57												16 00							16 27
Maidstone West	d																								
Strood	d				15 35	16 02												16 05							16 32
Higham	d				15 40													16 10							
Gravesend	d				15 48	16 13												16 18						16 32	16 43
Northfleet	d																							16 36	
Swanscombe	d																							16 38	
Greenhithe for Bluewater	d				15 53													16 23						16 41	
Stone Crossing	d																							16 43	
Dartford	a				15 58													16 28						16 48	
	d				15 59		16 01	16 08				16 22		16 42				16 29	16 31		16 38			16 52	
Slade Green	d			15 55			16 05		16 15				16 17				16 25		16 35			16 44			
Erith	d			15 58			16 08		16 18								16 28		16 38			16 46			
Belvedere	d			16 00			16 10		16 20								16 30		16 40			16 49			
Abbey Wood	d			16 03	16 08		16 13		16 23								16 33	16 38	16 43			16 52			
Plumstead	d			16 06			16 16		16 26								16 36		16 46			16 55			
Woolwich Arsenal	d			16 09	16 13		16 19		16 29								16 39	16 43	16 49			16 58			
Woolwich Dockyard	d			16 12			16 22		16 32								16 42		16 52			17 00			
Charlton	d		16 07	16 15	16 17		16 25		16 35							16 37	16 45	16 47	16 55			17 03			
Crayford	d		16 37											16 46		17 07									
Bexley	d		16 40											16 49		17 10									
Albany Park	d		16 43											16 52		17 13									
Sidcup	d	16 38	16 46											16 55		17 16									
New Eltham	d	16 41	16 49											16 58		17 19									
Mottingham	d	16 43	16 51											17 00		17 21									
Lee	d	16 46	16 54											17 03		17 24									
Hither Green	d	16 50	17 00											17 07	17 19	17 28									
Barnehurst	d							16 16				16 29	16 38								16 46			16 59	
Bexleyheath	d							16 19				16 31	16 40								16 49			17 01	
Welling	d							16 22				16 34	16 43								16 52			17 04	
Falconwood	d							16 24				16 37	16 46								16 54			17 07	
Eltham	d							16 27				16 40	16 49								16 57			17 10	
Kidbrooke	d							16 30				16 43	16 52								17 00			17 13	
Blackheath	d				16 22			16 34				16 46	16 55					16 52			17 04			17 16	
Lewisham	d		17 05		16 26			16 38			16 44	16 50	16 59		17 24	17 35		16 56			17 08		17 14	17 20	
St Johns	d	16 54	17 09								16 46		17 01		17 26	17 37							17 16		
New Cross	d	16 56	17 11								16 48		17 03		17 28	17 39							17 18		
Nunhead	d							16 43													17 13				
Peckham Rye	d							16 45													17 15				
Denmark Hill	d							16 49													17 19				
London Victoria	a							17 01													17 28				
Westcombe Park	d			16 17			16 27		16 37								16 47		16 57			17 05			
Maze Hill	d			16 19			16 29		16 39								16 49		16 59			17 07			
Greenwich	d			16 22			16 32		16 42								16 52		17 02			17 11			
Deptford	a			16 24			16 34		16 44								16 54		17 04			17 13			
London Bridge	a	17 04	17 18	16 30	16 35		16 42		16 50		16 54	16 58	17 09	17 21	17 34	17 45	17 01	17 07	17 13			17 21	17 24	17 29	
London Cannon Street	a	17 09	17 24	16 36			16 46		16 54		16 58		17 15		17 38	17 49	17 05	17 11	17 17			17 26	17 29		
London Waterloo (East)	a				16 39							17 03		17 28										17 34	
London Charing Cross	a				16 44							17 07		17 33										17 38	
Ebbsfleet International	a					16 17																			16 46
Stratford International	a					16 29																			16 58
St Pancras Int'l	a					16 36																			17 08

A not 27 July

B 27 July

Table 200

Gillingham and Dartford - London

Mondays to Fridays

until 27 July, 13 Aug to 28 Aug and from 10 Sep

Network Diagram - see first Page of Table 200

		SE A	SE	SE	SE		SE	SE	SE	SE	SE	SE A	SE	SE	SE		SE	SE	SE	SE	SE	SE	SE	SE	SE A
Gillingham (Kent)	d	16 20			16 24							16 50												16 54	17 20
Chatham	d	16 24			16 28							16 54												16 58	17 24
Rochester	d	16 27			16 30							16 57												17 00	17 27
Maidstone West	d																								
Strood	d	16 32			16 35							17 02												17 05	17 32
Higham	d				16 40																			17 10	
Gravesend	d	16 43			16 48						17 02	17 13							17 32					17 18	17 43
Northfleet	d										17 06								17 36						
Swanscombe	d										17 08								17 38						
Greenhithe for Bluewater	d				16 53						17 11								17 41					17 23	
Stone Crossing	d										17 13								17 43						
Dartford	a				16 58						17 17								17 47					17 28	
	d				16 59		17 01	17 08			17 18		17 22						17 48					17 29	
Slade Green	d		16 47	16 55			17 05															17 15	17 25		
Erith	d			16 58			17 08															17 18	17 28		
Belvedere	d			17 00			17 10															17 20	17 30		
Abbey Wood	d			17 03	17 08		17 13															17 23	17 33	17 38	
Plumstead	d			17 06			17 16															17 26	17 36		
Woolwich Arsenal	d			17 09	17 13		17 19															17 29	17 39	17 43	
Woolwich Dockyard	d			17 12			17 22															17 32	17 42		
Charlton	d			17 15	17 17		17 25														17 30	17 35	17 45	17 47	
Crayford	d										17 22						17 37		17 52		18 01				
Bexley	d										17 25						17 40		17 55		18 04				
Albany Park	d										17 28						17 43		17 58		18 07				
Sidcup	d										17 31						17 46		18 01		18 10				
New Eltham	d										17 34						17 49		18 04		18 13				
Mottingham	d										17 36						17 51		18 06		18 15				
Lee	d										17 39						17 54		18 09		18 18				
Hither Green	d									17 41	17 42			17 53			17 58	18 03	18 12	18 19	18 21				
Barnehurst	d		17 08					17 16		18 10			17 29		17 38			18 38							
Bexleyheath	d		17 10					17 19		18 12			17 31		17 40			18 40							
Welling	d		17 13					17 22		18 15			17 34		17 43			18 43							
Falconwood	d		17 16					17 24		18 18			17 37		17 46			18 46							
Eltham	d		17 19					17 27		18 20			17 40		17 49			18 49							
Kidbrooke	d		17 22					17 30		18 23			17 43		17 52			18 52							
Blackheath	d		17 25		17 22			17 34					17 46		17 55			18 55						17 52	
Lewisham	d		17 30		17 27			17 38	17 44	18 29			17 50		17 59		18 05	18 59		18 24				17 56	
St Johns	d								17 46					17 57			18 07			18 26					
New Cross	d		17 33						17 48	18 32				17 59	18 02		18 09	19 03		18 28					
Nunhead	d							17 43																	
Peckham Rye	d							17 45																	
Denmark Hill	d							17 49																	
London Victoria	a							17 59																	
Westcombe Park	d			17 17			17 27															17 37	17 47		
Maze Hill	d			17 19			17 29															17 39	17 49		
Greenwich	d			17 22			17 32															17 42	17 52		
Deptford	a			17 24			17 34															17 44	17 54		
London Bridge	a		17 39	17 31	17 35		17 42		17 55	18 38	17 53		18 00	18 06	18 09		18 16	19 08	18 22	18 34	18 33	17 52	18 03	18 04	
London Cannon Street	a		17 44	17 36			17 46		17 59	18 42			18 04	18 11	18 13		18 20	19 13		18 38		17 56	18 07		
London Waterloo (East)	a				17 40						17 58								18 27		18 37			18 08	
London Charing Cross	a				17 44						18 03								18 31		18 41			18 12	
Ebbsfleet International	a	16 47										17 17													17 47
Stratford International	a	17 02										17 28													17 59
St Pancras Int'l	a	17 09										17 36													18 06

A not 27 July

Table 200

Mondays to Fridays

Gillingham and Dartford - London

until 27 July, 13 Aug to 28 Aug and from 10 Sep

Network Diagram - see first Page of Table 200

Station		SE A	SE	SE	SE	SE	SE	SE	SE	SE	SE	SE	SE	SE	SE	SE B	SE	SE C	SE	SE	SE	SE
Gillingham (Kent)	d	17 20								17 24								17 50				
Chatham	d	17 24								17 28								17 54				
Rochester	d	17 27								17 30								17 57				
Maidstone West	d																					
Strood	d	17 32								17 35								18 02				
Higham	d									17 40												
Gravesend	d	17 43								17 48							18 02	18 13				18 32
Northfleet	d																18 06					18 36
Swanscombe	d																18 08					18 38
Greenhithe for Bluewater	d									17 53							18 11					18 41
Stone Crossing	d																18 13					18 43
Dartford	a									17 58							18 17					18 47
	d			17 31	17 38			17 52		17 59	18 01		18 08				18 18		18 22			18 48
Slade Green	d		17 29	17 35		17 45			17 55		18 05			18 15								
Erith	d			17 38		17 48			17 57		18 08			18 18								
Belvedere	d			17 40		17 50			18 00		18 10			18 20								
Abbey Wood	d			17 43		17 53			18 03	18 08	18 13			18 23								
Plumstead	d			17 46		17 56			18 06		18 16			18 26								
Woolwich Arsenal	d			17 49		17 59			18 09	18 13	18 19			18 29								
Woolwich Dockyard	d			17 52		18 02			18 11		18 22			18 32								
Charlton	d			17 55		18 05			18 14	18 17	18 25			18 35								
Crayford	d																18 22				18 37	18 52
Bexley	d																18 25				18 40	18 55
Albany Park	d																18 28				18 43	18 58
Sidcup	d											18 20					18 31				18 46	19 01
New Eltham	d											18 23					18 34				18 49	19 04
Mottingham	d																18 36				18 51	19 06
Lee	d																18 39				18 54	19 09
Hither Green	d											18 28				18 35	18 42			18 49	18 59	19 12
Barnehurst	d		17 38		17 46			17 59					18 16			19 08			18 29			
Bexleyheath	d		17 40		17 49			18 01					18 19			19 10			18 31			
Welling	d		17 43		17 52			18 04					18 22			19 13			18 34			
Falconwood	d		17 46		17 54			18 07					18 24			19 16			18 37			
Eltham	d		17 49		17 57			18 10					18 27			19 19			18 40			
Kidbrooke	d		17 52		18 00			18 13					18 30			19 22			18 43			
Blackheath	d		17 55		18 04			18 16		18 22			18 34			19 25			18 46			
Lewisham	d		17 59		18 08		18 14	18 20		18 26		18 35	18 38		18 45	19 29			18 50	18 54	19 05	
St Johns	d						18 16					18 37			18 47					18 56	19 07	
New Cross	d		18 02				18 18					18 39			18 49	19 32				18 58	19 09	
Nunhead	d				18 13								18 43									
Peckham Rye	d				18 15								18 45									
Denmark Hill	d				18 19								18 49									
London Victoria	a				18 29								18 58									
Westcombe Park	d			17 57		18 07			18 16		18 27			18 37								
Maze Hill	d			17 59		18 09			18 18		18 29			18 39								
Greenwich	d			18 02		18 12			18 22		18 32			18 42								
Deptford	a			18 04		18 14			18 24		18 34			18 44								
London Bridge	a		18 09	18 13		18 20	18 24	18 28	18 31	18 35	18 43	18 46		18 50	18 55	19 38	18 52		18 58	19 04	19 15	19 22
London Cannon Street	a		18 13	18 17		18 24	18 29		18 35		18 47	18 51		18 54	18 59	19 43				19 10	19 20	
London Waterloo (East)	a							18 32		18 41							18 57		19 02			19 26
London Charing Cross	a							18 37		18 45							19 01		19 06			19 30
Ebbsfleet International	a	17 46																18 17				
Stratford International	a	17 58																18 29				
St Pancras Int'l	a	18 08																18 36				

A 27 July
B until 18 May
C not 27 July

Table 200

Mondays to Fridays

Gillingham and Dartford - London

until 27 July, 13 Aug to 28 Aug and from 10 Sep

Network Diagram - see first Page of Table 200

Station		SE	SE	SE	SE	SE	SE A	SE B	SE	SE	SE	SE	SE	SE	SE C	SE	SE D	SE	SE B	SE	SE	SE	SE
Gillingham (Kent)	d					17 54	18 20	18 20						18 24					18 50			18 54	
Chatham	d					17 58	18 24	18 24						18 28					18 54			18 58	
Rochester	d					18 00	18 27	18 27						18 30					18 57			19 00	
Maidstone West	d																						
Strood	d					18 05	18 32	18 32						18 35					19 02			19 05	
Higham	d					18 10								18 40								19 10	
Gravesend	d					18 18	18 43	18 43						18 48				19 02	19 13			19 18	
Northfleet	d																	19 06					
Swanscombe	d																	19 08					
Greenhithe for Bluewater	d					18 23								18 53				19 11				19 23	
Stone Crossing	d																	19 13					
Dartford	a					18 28								18 58				19 17				19 28	
	d					18 29			18 31	18 38			18 52	18 59		19 01		19 18			19 22	19 29	19 31
Slade Green	d				18 25				18 35			18 51				19 05				19 20			19 35
Erith	d				18 28				18 38			18 53				19 08				19 23			19 38
Belvedere	d				18 30				18 40			18 56				19 10				19 25			19 40
Abbey Wood	d				18 33	18 38			18 43			18 59		19 08		19 13				19 28		19 38	19 43
Plumstead	d				18 36				18 46			19 02				19 16				19 31			19 46
Woolwich Arsenal	d				18 39	18 43			18 49			19 05		19 13		19 19				19 34		19 43	19 49
Woolwich Dockyard	d				18 42				18 52			19 07				19 22				19 37			19 52
Charlton	d			18 37	18 45	18 47			18 55			19 10		19 17		19 25				19 40		19 47	19 55
Crayford	d	18 55		19 07													19 07	19 22					
Bexley	d			19 10													19 10	19 25					
Albany Park	d			19 13													19 13	19 28					
Sidcup	d			19 16													19 16	19 31					
New Eltham	d			19 19													19 19	19 34					
Mottingham	d			19 21													19 21	19 36					
Lee	d			19 24													19 24	19 39					
Hither Green	d		19 19	19 28													19 28	19 42					
Barnehurst	d	19a07								18 46			18 59		19 08						19 30		
Bexleyheath	d									18 49			19 01		19 10						19 32		
Welling	d									18 52			19 04		19 13						19 35		
Falconwood	d									18 54			19 07		19 16						19 38		
Eltham	d									18 57			19 10		19 19						19 41		
Kidbrooke	d									19 00			19 13		19 22						19 44		
Blackheath	d					18 52				19 04			19 16	19 22	19 25						19 48	19 52	
Lewisham	d		19 24	19 34		18 56				19 08	19 14		19 20	19 26	19 29		19 34	19 48			19 52	19 56	
St Johns	d		19 26	19 36							19 16						19 36						
New Cross	d		19 28	19 38							19 18				19 32		19 38	19 51			19 56		
Nunhead	d									19 13													
Peckham Rye	d									19 15													
Denmark Hill	d									19 19													
London Victoria	a									19 28													
Westcombe Park	d				18 47				18 57			19 12				19 27				19 42			19 57
Maze Hill	d				18 49				18 59			19 14				19 29				19 44			19 59
Greenwich	d				18 52				19 02			19 18				19 32				19 47			20 02
Deptford	a				18 54				19 04			19 20				19 34				19 49			20 04
London Bridge	a		19 34	19 44	19 00	19 05			19 11		19 24	19 27	19 28	19 35	19 38	19 41	19 44	19 57		19 59	20 03	20 06	20 11
London Cannon Street	a		19 38	19 49	19 06				19 16		19 28	19 33			19 43	19 45	19 49			20 03			20 15
London Waterloo (East)	a					19 09							19 32	19 39				20 02			20 08	20 11	
London Charing Cross	a					19 13							19 36	19 43				20 06			20 12	20 14	
Ebbsfleet International	a						18 46	18 47											19 17				
Stratford International	a						18 58	19 02											19 29				
St Pancras Int'l	a						19 08	19 09											19 36				

A 27 July
B not 27 July
C from 21 May until 27 July
D until 18 May

Table 200

Mondays to Fridays

until 27 July, 13 Aug to 28 Aug and from 10 Sep

Gillingham and Dartford - London

Network Diagram - see first Page of Table 200

		SE	SE A	SE B	SE	SE	SE	SE	SE	SE	SE B	SE	SE	SE	SE	SE	SE A	SE B	SE	SE	SE	SE
Gillingham (Kent)	d		19 20				19 24				19 50		19 54				20 20	20 20		20 24		
Chatham	d		19 24				19 28				19 54		19 58				20 24	20 24		20 28		
Rochester	d		19 27				19 30				19 57		20 00				20 27	20 27		20 30		
Maidstone West	d			19 13																		
Strood	d		19 32	19 32			19 35				20 02		20 05				20 32	20 32		20 35		
Higham	d						19 40						20 10							20 40		
Gravesend	d	19 32	19 43	19 43			19 48			20 02	20 13		20 18			20 32	20 43	20 43		20 48		
Northfleet	d	19 36								20 06						20 36						
Swanscombe	d	19 38								20 08						20 38						
Greenhithe for Bluewater	d	19 41					19 53			20 11			20 23			20 41				20 53		
Stone Crossing	d	19 43								20 13						20 43						
Dartford	a	19 47					19 58			20 17			20 28			20 47				20 58		
	d	19 48				19 55	19 59	20 01	20 16	20 18		20 25	20 29	20 31	20 46	20 48			20 55	20 59	21 01	21 16
Slade Green	d				19 50			20 05	20 20					20 35	20 50						21 05	21 20
Erith	d				19 53			20 08	20 23					20 38	20 53						21 08	21 23
Belvedere	d				19 55			20 10	20 25					20 40	20 55						21 10	21 25
Abbey Wood	d				19 58		20 08	20 13	20 28				20 38	20 43	20 58					21 08	21 13	21 28
Plumstead	d				20 01			20 16	20 31					20 46	21 01						21 16	21 31
Woolwich Arsenal	d				20 04		20 13	20 19	20 34				20 43	20 49	21 04					21 13	21 19	21 34
Woolwich Dockyard	d				20 07			20 22	20 37					20 52	21 07						21 22	21 37
Charlton	d				20 10		20 17	20 25	20 40				20 47	20 55	21 10					21 17	21 25	21 40
Crayford	d	19 52								20 22						20 52						
Bexley	d	19 55								20 25						20 55						
Albany Park	d	19 58								20 28						20 58						
Sidcup	d	20 01								20 31						21 01						
New Eltham	d	20 04								20 34						21 04						
Mottingham	d	20 06								20 36						21 06						
Lee	d	20 09								20 39						21 09						
Hither Green	d	20 12								20 42						21 12						
Barnehurst	d					20 02						20 32							21 02			
Bexleyheath	d					20 04						20 34							21 04			
Welling	d					20 07						20 37							21 07			
Falconwood	d					20 10						20 40							21 10			
Eltham	d					20 12						20 42							21 12			
Kidbrooke	d					20 15						20 45							21 15			
Blackheath	d					20 19	20 22					20 49	20 52						21 19	21 22		
Lewisham	d	20 18				20 22	20 26			20 48		20 53	20 56			21 18			21 23	21 26		
St Johns	d																					
New Cross	d	20 21				20 26				20 51		20 56				21 21			21 26			
Nunhead	d																					
Peckham Rye	d																					
Denmark Hill	d																					
London Victoria	a																					
Westcombe Park	d				20 12			20 27	20 42					20 57	21 12						21 27	21 42
Maze Hill	d				20 14			20 29	20 44					20 59	21 14						21 29	21 44
Greenwich	d				20 17			20 32	20 47					21 02	21 17						21 32	21 47
Deptford	a				20 19			20 34	20 49					21 04	21 19						21 34	21 49
London Bridge	a	20 27			20 27	20 33	20 36	20 41	20 57	20 57		21 03	21 06	21 11	21 27	21 27			21 33	21 36	21 41	21 57
London Cannon Street	a				20 31			20 45														
London Waterloo (East)	a	20 32				20 38	20 40			21 02		21 08	21 10	21 15		21 32			21 38	21 40	21 45	
London Charing Cross	a	20 36				20 42	20 44			21 06		21 12	21 14	21 19		21 36			21 42	21 44	21 49	
Ebbsfleet International	a		19 46	19 47							20 17						20 46	20 47				
Stratford International	a		19 58	20 01							20 29						20 58	21 02				
St Pancras Int'l	a		20 08	20 08							20 36						21 08	21 09				

A 27 Jly

B not 27 Jly

Table 200

Mondays to Fridays

until 27 July, 13 Aug to 28 Aug and from 10 Sep

Gillingham and Dartford - London

Network Diagram - see first Page of Table 200

		SE	SE A	SE	SE	SE	SE	SE	SE A	SE B	SE	SE	SE	SE	SE A	SE	SE	SE	SE	SE B	SE A	SE	SE
Gillingham (Kent)	d		20 50		20 54				21 20	21 20		21 24			21 50		21 54			22 20	22 20		22 24
Chatham	d		20 54		20 58				21 24	21 24		21 28			21 54		21 58			22 24	22 24		22 28
Rochester	d		20 57		21 00				21 27	21 27		21 30			21 57		22 00			22 27	22 27		22 30
Maidstone West	d																						
Strood	d		21 02		21 05				21 32	21 32		21 35			22 02		22 05			22 32	22 32		22 35
Higham	d				21 10							21 40					22 10						22 40
Gravesend	d	21 02	21 13		21 18			21 32	21 43	21 43		21 48		22 02	22 13		22 18		22 32	22 43	22 43		22 48
Northfleet	d	21 06						21 36						22 06					22 36				
Swanscombe	d	21 08						21 38						22 08					22 38				
Greenhithe for Bluewater	d	21 11			21 23			21 41				21 53		22 11			22 23		22 41				22 53
Stone Crossing	d	21 13						21 43						22 13					22 43				
Dartford	a	21 17			21 28			21 47				21 58		22 17			22 28		22 47				22 58
	d	21 18		21 25	21 29	21 31	21 46	21 48			21 55	21 59	22 01	22 18		22 25	22 29	22 31	22 48			22 55	22 59
Slade Green	d					21 35	21 50						22 05					22 35					
Erith	d					21 38	21 53						22 08					22 38					
Belvedere	d					21 40	21 55						22 10					22 40					
Abbey Wood	d				21 38	21 43	21 58					22 08	22 13				22 38	22 43					23 08
Plumstead	d					21 46	22 01						22 16					22 46					
Woolwich Arsenal	d				21 43	21 49	22 04					22 13	22 19				22 43	22 49					23 13
Woolwich Dockyard	d					21 52	22 07						22 22					22 52					
Charlton	d				21 47	21 55	22 10					22 17	22 25				22 47	22 55					23 17
Crayford	d	21 22						21 52						22 22					22 52				
Bexley	d	21 25						21 55						22 25					22 55				
Albany Park	d	21 28						21 58						22 28					22 58				
Sidcup	d	21 31						22 01						22 31					23 01				
New Eltham	d	21 34						22 04						22 34					23 04				
Mottingham	d	21 36						22 06						22 36					23 06				
Lee	d	21 39						22 09						22 39					23 09				
Hither Green	d	21 42						22 12						22 42					23 12				
Barnehurst	d			21 32							22 02					22 32						23 02	
Bexleyheath	d			21 34							22 04					22 34						23 04	
Welling	d			21 37							22 07					22 37						23 07	
Falconwood	d			21 40							22 10					22 40						23 10	
Eltham	d			21 42							22 12					22 42						23 12	
Kidbrooke	d			21 45							22 15					22 45						23 15	
Blackheath	d			21 49	21 52						22 19	22 22				22 49	22 52					23 19	23 22
Lewisham	d	21 48		21 53	21 56			22 18			22 23	22 26		22 48		22 53	22 56		23 18			23 23	23 26
St Johns	d																						
New Cross	d	21 51		21 56				22 21			22 26			22 51		22 56			23 21			23 26	
Nunhead	d																						
Peckham Rye	d																						
Denmark Hill	d																						
London Victoria	a																						
Westcombe Park	d					21 57	22 12						22 27					22 57					
Maze Hill	d					21 59	22 14						22 29					22 59					
Greenwich	d					22 02	22 17						22 32					23 02					
Deptford	a					22 04	22 19						22 34					23 04					
London Bridge	a	21 57		22 01	22 05	22 11	22 27	22 27			22 31	22 35	22 41	22 57		23 01	23 05	23 11	23 27			23 31	23 35
London Cannon Street	a																						
London Waterloo (East)	a	22 02		22 06	22 09	22 15		22 32			22 36	22 39	22 45	23 02		23 06	23 09	23 15	23 32			23 36	23 39
London Charing Cross	a	22 06		22 10	22 13	22 19		22 36			22 40	22 43	22 49	23 06		23 10	23 13	23 19	23 36			23 40	23 43
Ebbsfleet International	a		21 17						21 47	21 46					22 17					22 46	22 47		
Stratford International	a		21 29						21 59	21 58					22 29					22 58	22 59		
St Pancras Int'l	a		21 36						22 06	22 08					22 36					23 07	23 06		

A not 27 Jly

B 27 Jly

Table 200

Mondays to Fridays

until 27 July, 13 Aug to 28 Aug and from 10 Sep

Gillingham and Dartford - London

Network Diagram - see first Page of Table 200

Station		SE	SE
Gillingham (Kent)	d		22 54
Chatham	d		22 58
Rochester	d		23 00
Maidstone West	d		
Strood	d		23 05
Higham	d		23 10
Gravesend	d		23 18
Northfleet	d		
Swanscombe	d		
Greenhithe for Bluewater	d		23 23
Stone Crossing	d		
Dartford	a		23 28
	d	23 01	
Slade Green	d	23 05	
Erith	d	23 08	
Belvedere	d	23 10	
Abbey Wood	d	23 13	
Plumstead	d	23 16	
Woolwich Arsenal	d	23 19	
Woolwich Dockyard	d	23 22	
Charlton	d	23 25	
Crayford	d		
Bexley	d		
Albany Park	d		
Sidcup	d		
New Eltham	d		
Mottingham	d		
Lee	d		
Hither Green	d		
Barnehurst	d		
Bexleyheath	d		
Welling	d		
Falconwood	d		
Eltham	d		
Kidbrooke	d		
Blackheath	d		
Lewisham	d		
St Johns	d		
New Cross	d		
Nunhead	d		
Peckham Rye	d		
Denmark Hill	d		
London Victoria	a		
Westcombe Park	d	23 27	
Maze Hill	d	23 29	
Greenwich	d	23 32	
Deptford	a	23 34	
London Bridge	a	23 41	
London Cannon Street	a		
London Waterloo (East)	a	23 45	
London Charing Cross	a	23 49	
Ebbsfleet International	a		
Stratford International	a		
St Pancras Int'l	a		

Table 200

Mondays to Fridays

30 July to 10 August

Gillingham and Dartford - London

Network Diagram - see first Page of Table 200

Station		SE	SE	SE	SE	SE	SE	SE	SE	SE	SE	SE	SE	SE	SE	SE	SE	SE	SE	SE	SE	SE	SE
		A	A	A	MO	A																	
Gillingham (Kent)	d							04 09			04 34		04 54					05 24	05 45				
Chatham	d							04 13			04 38		04 58					05 28	05 49				
Rochester	d							04 15			04 40		05 00					05 30	05 51				
Maidstone West	d																						
Strood	d							04 20			04 45		05 05					05 35					
Higham	d							04 25			04 50		05 10					05 40					
Gravesend	d							04 33			04 58		05 18		05 28			05 48					
Northfleet	d										05 02				05 32								
Swanscombe	d										05 04				05 34								
Greenhithe for Bluewater	d							04 38			05 07		05 23		05 37			05 53					
Stone Crossing	d										05 09				05 39								
Dartford	a							04 43			05 13		05 28		05 43			05 58					
	d							04 44		05 01	05 14	05 22	05 28	05 31	05 44	05 52	05 56	05 58		06 01		06 13	
Slade Green	d									05 05				05 36						06 05			
Erith	d									05 08				05 38						06 08			
Belvedere	d									05 10				05 41						06 10			
Abbey Wood	d									05 13			05 37	05 44				06 07		06 13			
Plumstead	d									05 16				05 47						06 16			
Woolwich Arsenal	d									05 20			05 42	05 50				06 12		06 20			
Woolwich Dockyard	d																						
Charlton	d	23p45	23p54	00 07	00 11	00 15	00 26			05 24			05 47	05 54				06 17		06 24			06 31
Crayford	d							04 48			05 18				05 48		06 03						
Bexley	d							04 51			05 21				05 51		06 06						
Albany Park	d							04 54			05 24				05 54		06 08						
Sidcup	d							04 57			05 27				05 57		06 11						
New Eltham	d							05 00			05 30				06 00		06 14						
Mottingham	d							05 02			05 32				06 02		06 17						
Lee	d							05 05			05 35				06 05		06 20						
Hither Green	d							05 08	05 23		05 38				06 08		06 22						
Barnehurst	d											05 29				05 59					06 13	06 20	06a55
Bexleyheath	d											05 31				06 01					06 15	06 22	
Welling	d											05 34				06 04					06 18	06 25	
Falconwood	d											05 37				06 07					06 21	06 28	
Eltham	d											05 40				06 09					06 24	06 30	
Kidbrooke	d											05 43				06 12					06 27		
Blackheath	d											05 46	05 52			06 16		06 22			06 31	06 37	
Lewisham	d							05 13	05 28		05 43	05 50	05 56		06 13	06 20	06 27	06 25			06 35	06 41	
St Johns	d																06 29						
New Cross	d							05 16	05 31		05 46	05 53			06 16		06 31				06 38		
Nunhead	d																						
Peckham Rye	d																					06 47	
Denmark Hill	d																					06 50	
London Victoria	a																					07 04	
Westcombe Park	d									05 26				05 56						06 26			
Maze Hill	d									05 29				05 59						06 29			
Greenwich	d									05 32				06 02						06 32			
Deptford	a									05 34				06 04						06 34			
London Bridge	a							05 22	05 36	05 41	05 52	05 58	06 05	06 12	06 22	06 28	06 37	06 34	06 27	06 42	06 43		
London Cannon Street	a			00 22	00 34		00 41		05 44										06 32		06 51		
London Waterloo (East)	a							05 26		05 46	05 57	06 03	06 10	06 17	06 26	06 33	06 41	06 39		06 48			
London Charing Cross	a	00 08	00 16			00 33		05 33		05 51	06 04	06 10	06 16	06 24	06 33	06 39	06 48	06 46		06 55			
Ebbsfleet International	a																						
Stratford International	a																						
St Pancras Int'l	a																						

A not 30 July, 6 August

30 July to 10 August

Gillingham and Dartford - London

Network Diagram - see first Page of Table 200

		SE	SE	SE	SE	SE		SE	SE	SE	SE	SE	SE	SE	SE	SE		SE	SE	SE [1]	SE	SE	SE	SE	SE
Gillingham (Kent)	d				05 50			05 54					06 07						06 20	06 34					
Chatham	d				05 55			05 58					06 11						06 24	06 38					
Rochester	d				05 57			06 00					06 13						06 27	06 41					
Maidstone West	d																								
Strood	d				06 02			06 05					06 18						06 32						
Higham	d							06 10					06 23												
Gravesend	d			06 05	06 13			06 18					06 31					06 34	06 43						
Northfleet	d			06 09														06 38							
Swanscombe	d			06 11														06 40							
Greenhithe for Bluewater	d			06 14				06 23					06 37					06 43							
Stone Crossing	d			06 16														06 45							
Dartford	a			06 20				06 28					06 41					06 49							
	d	06 16		06 21				06 28	06 31		06 31	06 39	06 42					06 50						07 00	
Slade Green	d	06 20									06 36											06 55			
Erith	d	06 23									06 39											06 57			
Belvedere	d	06 25									06 41											07 00			
Abbey Wood	d	06 28						06 37			06 45		06 51									07 03			
Plumstead	d	06 31									06 48											07 06			
Woolwich Arsenal	d	06 35						06 42			06 51		06 55									07 09			
Woolwich Dockyard	d																								
Charlton	d	06 39						06 47			06 57		07 00									07 14			
Crayford	d					06 25			06 35							06 50		06 55							
Bexley	d					06 28			06 38							06 53		06 58							
Albany Park	d					06 31			06 41							06 56		07 01							
Sidcup	d					06 34			06 44							06 59		07 04							
New Eltham	d					06 38			06 47							07 02		07 07							
Mottingham	d					06 40			06 50							07 05		07 10							
Lee	d					06 43			06 53							07 08		07 13							
Hither Green	d					06 46			06 56						07 08	07 11		07 16							
Barnehurst	d			06 28						06 37		06 48		06 53									06 59	07 07	07 13
Bexleyheath	d			06 31						06 39		06 51		06 56									07 01	07 10	07 15
Welling	d			06 34						06 42		06 54		06 59									07 04	07 13	07 18
Falconwood	d			06 37						06 45		06 56		07 01									07 07	07 16	07 21
Eltham	d			06 40						06 48		06 59		07 04									07 10	07 19	07 24
Kidbrooke	d									06 51		07 02		07 07									07 13	07 22	07 27
Blackheath	d			06 47				06 52		06 57		07 08		07 11									07 18	07 27	07 31
Lewisham	d		06 48	06 50		06 52		06 55		07 01		07 11	07 08	07 15		07 17					07 20		07 22	07 30	07 35
St Johns	d		06 50			06 54										07 19							07 24		
New Cross	d		06 52			06 56				07 04			07 11			07 21					07 23		07 26		07 38
Nunhead	d													07 20											
Peckham Rye	d													07 23											
Denmark Hill	d													07 29											
London Victoria	a													07 42											
Westcombe Park	d	06 41									06 59											07 16			
Maze Hill	d	06 44									07 01											07 19			
Greenwich	d	06 47									07 06											07 23			
Deptford	a	06 49									07 08											07 25			
London Bridge	a	06 56	06 58	07 00		07 02		07 03	07 06	07 09	07 14	07 20	07 17		07 18	07 26		07 26		07 20	07 28	07 33	07 33	07 40	07 43
London Cannon Street	a	07 05	07 06			07 09				07 18	07 21		07 23		07 25	07 33				07 27	07 35		07 39		07 50
London Waterloo (East)	a			07 05				07 09	07 11			07 25						07 31				07 38		07 46	
London Charing Cross	a			07 11				07 15	07 17			07 31						07 37				07 44		07 52	
Ebbsfleet International	a				06 16														06 47						
Stratford International	a				06 33														06 59						
St Pancras Int'l	a				06 43														07 07						

Table 200

Mondays to Fridays

30 July to 10 August

Gillingham and Dartford - London

Network Diagram - see first Page of Table 200

		SE		SE	SE	SE	SE	SE	SE	SE	SE	SE		SE	SE	SE [1]	SE	SE	SE	SE	SE	SE		SE	SE
Gillingham (Kent)	d							06 38							06 54	07 04									
Chatham	d							06 42							06 58	07 08									
Rochester	d							06 44							07 01	07 11									
Maidstone West	d																								
Strood	d							06 49						06 57											
Higham	d							06 54						07 02											
Gravesend	d			06 47				07 02						07 09	07 14						07 17				
Northfleet	d			06 51																	07 21				
Swanscombe	d			06 53																	07 23				
Greenhithe for Bluewater	d			06 56				07 07						07 16							07 26				
Stone Crossing	d			06 58																	07 28				
Dartford	a			07 02				07 12						07 21							07 33				
	d			07 03		07 05		07 12	07 17			07 20		07 23					07 25		07 34			07 36	
Slade Green	d					07 09				07 19									07 29						
Erith	d					07 12				07 21									07 32						
Belvedere	d					07 14				07 24									07 34						
Abbey Wood	d			07 12		07 18				07 27				07 32					07 38						
Plumstead	d					07 21				07 30									07 41						
Woolwich Arsenal	d	07 15		07 17		07 24				07 33				07 38					07 44						
Woolwich Dockyard	d																								
Charlton	d			07 22		07 30				07 39				07 44					07 50						
Crayford	d						07 10	07 17												07 30	07 38				
Bexley	d						07 13	07 20												07 33	07 41				
Albany Park	d						07 16	07 22												07 36	07 44				
Sidcup	d						07 19	07 25												07 39	07 47				07 51
New Eltham	d						07 23	07 28												07 43	07 50				07 54
Mottingham	d						07 25	07 31												07 45					07 56
Lee	d						07 28	07 34												07 48					07 59
Hither Green	d				07 28		07 32	07 36									07 49			07 52					08 02
Barnehurst	d	07a35							07 24			07 27						07 33				07 38		07 44	
Bexleyheath	d								07 26			07 30						07 35				07 41		07 46	
Welling	d								07 29			07 33						07 38				07 44		07 49	
Falconwood	d								07 32			07 36						07 41				07 46		07 52	
Eltham	d								07 34			07 39						07 44				07 49		07 55	
Kidbrooke	d								07 37			07 42						07 47				07 52			
Blackheath	d								07 42			07 47						07 51				07 57		08 02	
Lewisham	d						07 38		07 46		07 48	07 50						07 55		07 57				08 05	
St Johns	d						07 40				07 50									08 00					
New Cross	d						07 42				07 53							07 58		08 02					
Nunhead	d								07 51															08 11	
Peckham Rye	d								07 54															08 13	
Denmark Hill	d								07 59															08 17	
London Victoria	a								08 11															08 29	
Westcombe Park	d									07 41									07 52						
Maze Hill	d					07 33				07 43									07 54						
Greenwich	d			07 28		07 37				07 47				07 51					07 59						
Deptford	a					07 39				07 49															
London Bridge	a			07 35	07 37	07 45	07 47	07 47		07 57	08 01	08 00		07 57		07 51	07 59	08 03	08 05	08 08	08 05				08 13
London Cannon Street	a			07 43	07 44	07 52	07 54				08 08			08 05		07 57	08 06	08 10	08 12	08 15					
London Waterloo (East)	a							07 52		08 02		08 06									08 10	08 12			08 18
London Charing Cross	a							07 58		08 08		08 12									08 16	08 18			08 24
Ebbsfleet International	a														07 17										
Stratford International	a														07 29										
St Pancras Int'l	a														07 37										

Gillingham and Dartford - London

Mondays to Fridays

30 July to 10 August

Network Diagram - see first Page of Table 200

Station		SE	SE	SE	SE	SE	SE	SE		SE	SE [1]	SE	SE	SE	SE	SE	SE	SE		SE	SE	SE	SE	SE	SE [1]
Gillingham (Kent) [4]	d									07 12	07 19													07 38	07 46
Chatham [4]	d									07 16	07 24													07 42	07 50
Rochester [4]	d									07 18														07 44	
Maidstone West	d																								
Strood [4]	d				07 18					07 23														07 49	
Higham	d				07 23					07 28														07 54	
Gravesend [4]	d				07 31					07 36								07 48						08 02	
Northfleet	d									07 40								07 52							
Swanscombe	d									07 42								07 54							
Greenhithe for Bluewater	d				07 37					07 45								07 57						08 08	
Stone Crossing	d									07 47								07 59							
Dartford [4]	a				07 42					07 51								08 03						08 12	
	d			07 40	07 43		07 45			07 52			07 56				08 02	08 04				08 06		08 13	
Slade Green [4]	d	07 39					07 50								07 59					08 01		08 10			
Erith	d	07 41					07 52								08 01							08 13			
Belvedere	d	07 44					07 55								08 04							08 15			
Abbey Wood	d	07 47			07 52		07 58								08 07			08 14				08 18			
Plumstead	d	07 50					08 01								08 10							08 21			
Woolwich Arsenal [4]	d	07 54			07 58		08 05								08 14			08 19				08 25			
Woolwich Dockyard	d																								
Charlton [4]	d	07 59			08 07		08 10								08 19			08 26				08 30			
Crayford	d							07 50		07 56													08 10	08 17	
Bexley	d							07 53		07 59													08 13	08 20	
Albany Park	d							07 56		08 02													08 16	08 23	
Sidcup [4]	d							07 59		08 05				08 11									08 19	08 26	
New Eltham	d							08 03		08 09				08 14									08 23	08 30	
Mottingham	d							08 05						08 16									08 25		
Lee	d							08 08						08 19									08 28		
Hither Green [4]	d							08 12						08 22									08 32		
Barnehurst [4]	d			07 48		07 53						07 58	08 04				08 09			08 13	08 13				
Bexleyheath	d			07 51		07 55						08 01	08 06				08 11			08 16	08 16				
Welling	d			07 54		07 58						08 04	08 09				08 14			08 19	08 19				
Falconwood	d			07 56		08 01						08 06	08 12				08 17			08 21	08 21				
Eltham	d			07 59		08 04						08 09	08 15				08 20			08 24	08 24				
Kidbrooke	d					08 07						08 12					08 23								
Blackheath [4]	d			08 07		08 11						08 17	08 22				08 27			08 31	08 31				
Lewisham [4]	d		08 08	08 11		08 15		08 17					08 25			08 28	08 31			08 35	08 35		08 37		
St Johns	d		08 12					08 21								08 30							08 40		
New Cross [4]	d		08 14			08 18		08 23								08 32				08 38	08 38		08 42		
Nunhead [4]	d												08 30												
Peckham Rye [4]	d												08 33												
Denmark Hill [4]	d												08 36												
London Victoria [15]	a												08 49												
Westcombe Park	d						08 12																		
Maze Hill	d	08 03					08 14								08 23							08 35			
Greenwich [4]	d	08 07					08 19								08 27							08 39			
Deptford	a	08 09					08 21								08 29										
London Bridge [4]	a	08 16	08 20	08 20	08 17	08 25	08 27	08 29		08 25	08 09			08 33	08 37	08 41	08 40	08 38		08 43	08 43	08 45	08 49	08 45	08 31
London Cannon Street [4]	a		08 28		08 25	08 32	08 35	08 36			08 17					08 48		08 45		08 50	08 50	08 52	08 55		08 38
London Waterloo (East) [4]	a	08 22		08 26						08 30		08 32		08 38	08 42		08 46							08 50	
London Charing Cross [4]	a	08 28		08 32						08 36		08 39		08 44	08 48		08 52							08 56	
Ebbsfleet International	a																								
Stratford International	a																								
St Pancras Int'l [15]	a																								

Gillingham and Dartford - London

Mondays to Fridays

30 July to 10 August

Network Diagram - see first Page of Table 200

Station		SE [1]	SE	SE		SE	SE	SE	SE	SE	SE	SE	SE	SE		SE	SE	SE	SE	SE	SE [1]	SE	SE	SE	
Gillingham (Kent) [4]	d	08 03									08 08					08 19					08 24				
Chatham [4]	d	08 08									08 12					08 24					08 28				
Rochester [4]	d	08 11									08 14					08 26					08 31				
Maidstone West	d																								
Strood [4]	d								07 58		08 19					08 32									
Higham	d								08 03		08 24														
Gravesend [4]	d								08 17		08 33			08 06		08 43									
Northfleet	d										08 37			08 10											
Swanscombe	d										08 39			08 12											
Greenhithe for Bluewater	d								08 23		08 42			08 15											
Stone Crossing	d										08 44			08 17											
Dartford [4]	a								08 27		08 49			08 21											
	d								08 29		08 49			08 22			08 24					08 38			
Slade Green [4]	d		08 17			08 17								08 27				08 31	08 31				08 39		
Erith	d					08 19												08 33					08 41		
Belvedere	d					08 22												08 36					08 44		
Abbey Wood	d					08 25								08 34				08 39					08 47		
Plumstead	d					08 28												08 42					08 50		
Woolwich Arsenal [4]	d					08 31								08 39				08 45					08 54		
Woolwich Dockyard	d																								
Charlton [4]	d					08 36							08 39	08 45				08 51					08 59		
Crayford	d							08 28	08 34		08 54		09 07												
Bexley	d							08 31	08 37		08 57		09 10												
Albany Park	d							08 34	08 40		09 00		09 13												
Sidcup [4]	d			08 31				08 37	08 43		09 03		09 16												
New Eltham	d			08 34				08 41	08 46		09 06		09 19												
Mottingham	d			08 36				08 43	08 49		09 08		09 21												
Lee	d			08 39				08 46	08 52		09 11		09 24												
Hither Green [4]	d			08 42				08 50	08 55	08 59	09 14	09 19	09 28												
Barnehurst [4]	d		08 23														08 30		08 37	08 37		08 45			
Bexleyheath	d		08 26														08 33		08 39	08 39		08 47			
Welling	d		08 29														08 36		08 42	08 42		08 50			
Falconwood	d		08 31														08 38		08 45	08 45		08 53			
Eltham	d		08 34														08 41		08 48	08 48		08 55			
Kidbrooke	d		08 37																08 51	08 51		08 58			
Blackheath [4]	d		08 42														08 48		08 55	08 55		09 02			
Lewisham [4]	d		08 46				08 48	08 55		09 04		09 24	09 34				08 52		08 59	08 59		09 06		09 15	
St Johns	d						08 50	08 57		09 07		09 26	09 36						09 01	09 01				09 17	
New Cross [4]	d						08 52	08 59		09 09		09 28	09 38						09 03	09 03				09 19	
Nunhead [4]	d		08 52																			09 11			
Peckham Rye [4]	d		08 55																			09 14			
Denmark Hill [4]	d		09 02																			09 17			
London Victoria [15]	a		09 14																			09 29			
Westcombe Park	d					08 38												08 53							
Maze Hill	d					08 41												08 55					09 03		
Greenwich [4]	d					08 45								08 51				08 59					09 07		
Deptford	a					08 47																	09 09		
London Bridge [4]	a	08 51		08 52		08 56	08 57	09 05	09 05	09 17	09 23	09 33	09 44	09 00			09 00	09 07	09 09	09 09	09 11		09 17	09 25	
London Cannon Street [4]	a	08 57					09 04	09 12		09 23		09 40	09 51	09 09				09 14	09 18	09 18	09 18			09 32	
London Waterloo (East) [4]	a			08 58		09 02			09 10		09 28						09 05						09 22		
London Charing Cross [4]	a			09 04		09 09			09 16		09 34						09 12						09 28		
Ebbsfleet International	a															08 46									
Stratford International	a															08 58									
St Pancras Int'l [15]	a															09 08									

Table 200

Gillingham and Dartford - London

Mondays to Fridays

30 July to 10 August

Network Diagram - see first Page of Table 200

		SE	SE	SE	SE	SE	SE	SE	SE	SE		SE	SE	SE	SE	SE	SE	SE	SE	SE		SE	SE	SE	SE
Gillingham (Kent)	d																					08 54	09 20		
Chatham	d																					08 58	09 24		
Rochester	d																					09 00	09 27		
Maidstone West	d																								
Strood	d																					09 05	09 32		
Higham	d																					09 10			
Gravesend	d			09 02				08 48									09 32					09 18	09 43		
Northfleet	d			09 06													09 36								
Swanscombe	d			09 08													09 38								
Greenhithe for Bluewater	d			09 11				08 53									09 41					09 23			
Stone Crossing	d			09 13													09 43								
Dartford	a			09 17				08 58									09 47					09 28			
	d	08 52		09 18				08 58		09 01		09 08			09 22		09 48					09 28			09 31
Slade Green	d		08 45				08 54			09 05			09 13			09 17				09 23					09 36
Erith	d						08 56			09 08			09 15							09 26					09 38
Belvedere	d						08 59			09 10			09 18							09 28					09 41
Abbey Wood	d						09 02	09 07		09 13			09 21							09 31		09 37			09 44
Plumstead	d						09 05			09 16			09 24							09 34					09 47
Woolwich Arsenal	d						09 08	09 12		09 20			09 27							09 38		09 42			09 50
Woolwich Dockyard	d																								
Charlton	d					09 08	09 13	09 16		09 25			09 32						09 41	09 43		09 46			09 56
Crayford	d			09 22		09 37											09 52		10 07						
Bexley	d			09 25		09 40											09 55		10 10						
Albany Park	d			09 28		09 43											09 58		10 13						
Sidcup	d			09 31		09 46											10 01		10 16						
New Eltham	d			09 34		09 49											10 04		10 19						
Mottingham	d			09 36		09 51											10 06		10 21						
Lee	d			09 39		09 54											10 09		10 24						
Hither Green	d			09 42	09 49	09 58											10 12	10 19	10 28						
Barnehurst	d	08 59	09a07						09 07			09 15			09 29	09a37								09 37	
Bexleyheath	d	09 01							09 09			09 18			09 31									09 39	
Welling	d	09 04							09 12			09 21			09 34									09 42	
Falconwood	d	09 07							09 15			09 23			09 37									09 45	
Eltham	d	09 09							09 18			09 26			09 39									09 48	
Kidbrooke	d								09 21			09 29												09 51	
Blackheath	d	09 16						09 22	09 25			09 34			09 46							09 52		09 55	
Lewisham	d	09 20			09 54	10 04		09 26	09 29			09 38		09 45	09 50			10 24	10 34			09 56		09 59	
St Johns	d				09 56	10 06			09 31					09 47				10 26	10 36					10 01	
New Cross	d				09 58	10 08			09 33					09 49				10 28	10 38					10 03	
Nunhead	d											09 43													
Peckham Rye	d											09 45													
Denmark Hill	d											09 49													
London Victoria	a											10 00													
Westcombe Park	d						09 15													09 45					
Maze Hill	d						09 17			09 30			09 38							09 48					10 00
Greenwich	d						09 21			09 34			09 44							09 52					10 04
Deptford	a						09 23													09 54					
London Bridge	a	09 29		09 52	10 04	10 14	09 29	09 34	09 38	09 41			09 50	09 54	09 58		10 22	10 34	10 44	10 00		10 05		10 08	10 11
London Cannon Street	a				10 11	10 22	09 36		09 45	09 48			09 57	10 03				10 41	10 55	10 07				10 16	10 18
London Waterloo (East)	a	09 34		09 56				09 39							10 02		10 26					10 09			
London Charing Cross	a	09 40		10 00				09 45							10 09		10 30					10 16			
Ebbsfleet International	a																						09 46		
Stratford International	a																						09 58		
St Pancras Int'l	a																						10 08		

Table 200

Gillingham and Dartford - London

Mondays to Fridays

30 July to 10 August

Network Diagram - see first Page of Table 200

		SE	SE	SE	SE	SE		SE	SE	SE	SE	SE	SE	SE	SE	SE		SE	SE	SE	SE	SE	SE	SE	SE
Gillingham (Kent)	d											09 24												09 54	10 20
Chatham	d											09 28												09 58	10 24
Rochester	d											09 30												10 00	10 27
Maidstone West	d																								
Strood	d											09 35												10 05	10 32
Higham	d											09 40												10 10	
Gravesend	d							10 02				09 48								10 32				10 18	10 43
Northfleet	d							10 06												10 36					
Swanscombe	d							10 08												10 38					
Greenhithe for Bluewater	d							10 11				09 53								10 41				10 23	
Stone Crossing	d							10 13												10 43					
Dartford	a							10 17				09 58								10 47				10 28	
	d	09 38			09 52			10 18				09 58	10 01	10 08				10 22		10 48				10 28	
Slade Green	d		09 43			09 47					09 53		10 06		10 13				10 17				10 23		
Erith	d		09 45								09 56		10 08		10 15								10 26		
Belvedere	d		09 48								09 58		10 11		10 18								10 28		
Abbey Wood	d		09 51								10 01	10 07	10 14		10 21								10 31	10 37	
Plumstead	d		09 54								10 04		10 17		10 24								10 34		
Woolwich Arsenal	d		09 57								10 08	10 12	10 20		10 27								10 38	10 42	
Woolwich Dockyard	d																								
Charlton	d		10 02							10 09	10 13	10 16	10 26		10 32							10 39	10 43	10 46	
Crayford	d							10 22		10 37										10 52		11 07			
Bexley	d							10 25		10 40										10 55		11 10			
Albany Park	d							10 28		10 43										10 58		11 13			
Sidcup	d							10 31		10 46										11 01		11 16			
New Eltham	d							10 34		10 49										11 04		11 19			
Mottingham	d							10 36		10 51										11 06		11 21			
Lee	d							10 39		10 54										11 09		11 24			
Hither Green	d							10 42	10 49	10 58										11 12	11 19	11 28			
Barnehurst	d	09 45			09 58	10 07								10 15				10 28	10a37						
Bexleyheath	d	09 47			10 01	10 09								10 17				10 31							
Welling	d	09 50			10 04	10 12								10 20				10 34							
Falconwood	d	09 53			10 06	10 15								10 23				10 36							
Eltham	d	09 55			10 09	10 18								10 25				10 39							
Kidbrooke	d	09 58				10 21								10 28											
Blackheath	d	10 03			10 16	10 25						10 22		10 33				10 46						10 52	
Lewisham	d	10 08		10 14	10 20	10 29			10 54	11 04		10 26		10 38		10 44		10 50			11 24	11 34		10 56	
St Johns	d			10 16		10 31			10 56	11 06						10 46					11 26	11 36			
New Cross	d			10 18		10 33			10 58	11 08						10 48					11 28	11 38			
Nunhead	d	10 13												10 43											
Peckham Rye	d	10 15												10 45											
Denmark Hill	d	10 19												10 49											
London Victoria	a	10 31												11 03											
Westcombe Park	d										10 15												10 45		
Maze Hill	d		10 08								10 18		10 30		10 38								10 48		
Greenwich	d		10 14								10 22		10 34		10 44								10 52		
Deptford	a										10 24												10 54		
London Bridge	a		10 20	10 23	10 28	10 38		10 52	11 04	11 14	10 30	10 35	10 41		10 50	10 54		10 58		11 22	11 34	11 44	11 00	11 05	
London Cannon Street	a		10 27	10 30		10 46			11 11	11 22	10 39		10 48		10 57	11 01					11 41	11 52	11 07		
London Waterloo (East)	a				10 32			10 56				10 39						11 02		11 26				11 09	
London Charing Cross	a				10 39			11 00				10 46						11 09		11 32				11 16	
Ebbsfleet International	a																								10 46
Stratford International	a																								10 58
St Pancras Int'l	a																								11 08

Table 200

Mondays to Fridays

30 July to 10 August

Gillingham and Dartford - London

Network Diagram - see first Page of Table 200

Station		SE		SE	SE	SE	SE	SE	SE	SE	SE	SE	
Gillingham (Kent)	d												
Chatham	d												
Rochester	d												
Maidstone West	d												
Strood	d												
Higham	d												
Gravesend	d									11 02			
Northfleet	d									11 06			
Swanscombe	d									11 08			
Greenhithe for Bluewater	d									11 11			
Stone Crossing	d									11 13			
Dartford	a									11 17			
	d			10 31	10 38			10 52		11 18			
Slade Green	d			10 36		10 43			10 47				
Erith	d			10 38		10 45							
Belvedere	d			10 41		10 48							
Abbey Wood	d			10 44		10 51							
Plumstead	d			10 47		10 54							
Woolwich Arsenal	d			10 50		10 57							
Woolwich Dockyard	d												
Charlton	d			10 56		11 02						11 09	
Crayford	d									11 22		11 37	
Bexley	d									11 25		11 40	
Albany Park	d									11 28		11 43	
Sidcup	d									11 31		11 46	
New Eltham	d									11 34		11 49	
Mottingham	d									11 36		11 51	
Lee	d									11 39		11 54	
Hither Green	d									11 42	11 49	11 58	
Barnehurst	d	10 37			10 45			10 58	11a07				
Bexleyheath	d	10 39			10 47			11 01					
Welling	d	10 42			10 50			11 04					
Falconwood	d	10 45			10 53			11 06					
Eltham	d	10 48			10 55			11 09					
Kidbrooke	d	10 51			10 58								
Blackheath	d	10 55			11 03			11 16					
Lewisham	d	10 59			11 08		11 14	11 20			11 54	12 04	
St Johns	d	11 01					11 16				11 56	12 06	
New Cross	d	11 03					11 18				11 58	12 08	
Nunhead	d				11 13								
Peckham Rye	d				11 15								
Denmark Hill	d				11 19								
London Victoria	a				11 31								
Westcombe Park	d												
Maze Hill	d			11 00		11 08							
Greenwich	d			11 04		11 14							
Deptford	a												
London Bridge	a	11 08		11 11		11 20	11 24	11 28		11 52	12 04	12 14	
London Cannon Street	a	11 16		11 18		11 27	11 31				12 11	12 22	
London Waterloo (East)	a							11 32		11 56			
London Charing Cross	a							11 41		12 00			
Ebbsfleet International	a												
Stratford International	a												
St Pancras Int'l	a												

Station		SE	SE	SE	SE	SE	SE	SE	SE	SE		SE	SE
Gillingham (Kent)	d		10 24										
Chatham	d		10 28										
Rochester	d		10 30										
Maidstone West	d												
Strood	d		10 35										
Higham	d		10 40										
Gravesend	d		10 48									11 32	
Northfleet	d											11 36	
Swanscombe	d											11 38	
Greenhithe for Bluewater	d		10 53									11 41	
Stone Crossing	d											11 43	
Dartford	a		10 58									11 47	
	d		10 58		11 01	11 08			11 22			11 48	
Slade Green	d	10 53			11 06		11 13			11 17			
Erith	d	10 56			11 08		11 15						
Belvedere	d	10 58			11 11		11 18						
Abbey Wood	d	11 01	11 07		11 14		11 21						
Plumstead	d	11 04			11 17		11 24						
Woolwich Arsenal	d	11 08	11 12		11 20		11 27						
Woolwich Dockyard	d												
Charlton	d	11 13	11 16		11 26		11 32						
Crayford	d											11 52	
Bexley	d											11 55	
Albany Park	d											11 58	
Sidcup	d											12 01	
New Eltham	d											12 04	
Mottingham	d											12 06	
Lee	d											12 09	
Hither Green	d											12 12	12 19
Barnehurst	d			11 07		11 15			11 28	11a37			
Bexleyheath	d			11 09		11 17			11 31				
Welling	d			11 12		11 20			11 34				
Falconwood	d			11 15		11 23			11 36				
Eltham	d			11 18		11 25			11 39				
Kidbrooke	d			11 21		11 28							
Blackheath	d		11 22	11 25		11 33			11 46				
Lewisham	d		11 26	11 29		11 38		11 44	11 50				12 24
St Johns	d			11 31				11 46					12 26
New Cross	d			11 33				11 48					12 28
Nunhead	d					11 43							
Peckham Rye	d					11 45							
Denmark Hill	d					11 49							
London Victoria	a					12 03							
Westcombe Park	d	11 15											
Maze Hill	d	11 18			11 30		11 38						
Greenwich	d	11 22			11 34		11 44						
Deptford	a	11 24											
London Bridge	a	11 30	11 35	11 38	11 41		11 50	11 54	11 58			12 22	12 34
London Cannon Street	a	11 39		11 46	11 48		11 57	12 01					12 41
London Waterloo (East)	a		11 39						12 02			12 26	
London Charing Cross	a		11 46						12 09			12 30	
Ebbsfleet International	a												
Stratford International	a												
St Pancras Int'l	a												

Table 200

Mondays to Fridays

30 July to 10 August

Gillingham and Dartford - London

Network Diagram - see first Page of Table 200

Station		SE	SE	SE	SE	SE	SE	SE		SE	SE	SE	SE
Gillingham (Kent)	d			10 54	11 20								
Chatham	d			10 58	11 24								
Rochester	d			11 00	11 27								
Maidstone West	d												
Strood	d			11 05	11 32								
Higham	d			11 10									
Gravesend	d			11 18	11 43								
Northfleet	d												
Swanscombe	d												
Greenhithe for Bluewater	d			11 23									
Stone Crossing	d												
Dartford	a			11 28									
	d			11 28			11 31	11 38				11 52	
Slade Green	d		11 23				11 36			11 43			11 47
Erith	d		11 26				11 38			11 45			
Belvedere	d		11 28				11 41			11 48			
Abbey Wood	d		11 31	11 37			11 44			11 51			
Plumstead	d		11 34				11 47			11 54			
Woolwich Arsenal	d		11 38	11 42			11 50			11 58			
Woolwich Dockyard	d												
Charlton	d	11 39	11 43	11 46			11 56			12 07			
Crayford	d	12 07											
Bexley	d	12 10											
Albany Park	d	12 13											
Sidcup	d	12 16											
New Eltham	d	12 19											
Mottingham	d	12 21											
Lee	d	12 24											
Hither Green	d	12 28											
Barnehurst	d					11 37		11 45				11 58	12 07
Bexleyheath	d					11 39		11 47				12 01	12 09
Welling	d					11 42		11 50				12 04	12 12
Falconwood	d					11 45		11 53				12 06	12 15
Eltham	d					11 48		11 55				12 09	12 18
Kidbrooke	d					11 51		11 58					12 21
Blackheath	d			11 52		11 55		12 03				12 16	12 25
Lewisham	d	12 34		11 56		11 59		12 08			12 14	12 20	12 29
St Johns	d	12 36				12 01					12 16		12 31
New Cross	d	12 38				12 03					12 18		12 33
Nunhead	d							12 13					
Peckham Rye	d							12 15					
Denmark Hill	d							12 19					
London Victoria	a							12 31					
Westcombe Park	d		11 45										
Maze Hill	d		11 48				12 00						
Greenwich	d		11 52				12 04			12 13			
Deptford	a		11 54										
London Bridge	a	12 44	12 00	12 05		12 08	12 11			12 20	12 24	12 28	12 38
London Cannon Street	a	12 52	12 07			12 16	12 18			12 27	12 31		12 46
London Waterloo (East)	a			12 09								12 32	
London Charing Cross	a			12 16								12 39	
Ebbsfleet International	a				11 46								
Stratford International	a				11 58								
St Pancras Int'l	a				12 08								

Station		SE	SE	SE	SE	SE		SE	SE	SE	SE	SE	SE
Gillingham (Kent)	d					11 24							
Chatham	d					11 28							
Rochester	d					11 30							
Maidstone West	d												
Strood	d					11 35							
Higham	d					11 40							
Gravesend	d	12 02				11 48							
Northfleet	d	12 06											
Swanscombe	d	12 08											
Greenhithe for Bluewater	d	12 11				11 53							
Stone Crossing	d	12 13											
Dartford	a	12 17				11 58							
	d	12 18				11 58			12 01	12 08			12 22
Slade Green	d				11 53				12 05		12 13		
Erith	d				11 56				12 08		12 15		
Belvedere	d				11 58				12 10		12 18		
Abbey Wood	d				12 01	12 07			12 13		12 21		
Plumstead	d				12 04				12 16		12 24		
Woolwich Arsenal	d				12 08	12 12			12 19		12 28		
Woolwich Dockyard	d												
Charlton	d			12 09	12 13	12 16			12 26		12 37		
Crayford	d	12 22		12 37									
Bexley	d	12 25		12 40									
Albany Park	d	12 28		12 43									
Sidcup	d	12 31		12 46									
New Eltham	d	12 34		12 49									
Mottingham	d	12 36		12 51									
Lee	d	12 39		12 54									
Hither Green	d	12 42	12 49	12 58									
Barnehurst	d							12 07		12 15			12 28
Bexleyheath	d							12 09		12 17			12 31
Welling	d							12 12		12 20			12 34
Falconwood	d							12 15		12 23			12 36
Eltham	d							12 18		12 25			12 39
Kidbrooke	d							12 21		12 28			
Blackheath	d					12 22		12 25		12 33			12 46
Lewisham	d		12 54	13 04		12 26		12 29		12 38		12 44	12 50
St Johns	d		12 56	13 06				12 31				12 46	
New Cross	d		12 58	13 08				12 33				12 48	
Nunhead	d									12 43			
Peckham Rye	d									12 45			
Denmark Hill	d									12 49			
London Victoria	a									13 01			
Westcombe Park	d				12 15								
Maze Hill	d												
Greenwich	d				12 22				12 33		12 43		
Deptford	a				12 24								
London Bridge	a	12 52	13 04	13 14	12 30	12 35		12 38	12 41		12 50	12 54	12 58
London Cannon Street	a		13 11	13 22	12 39			12 46	12 48		12 57	13 01	
London Waterloo (East)	a	12 56				12 39							13 02
London Charing Cross	a	13 00				12 46							13 09
Ebbsfleet International	a												
Stratford International	a												
St Pancras Int'l	a												

Table 200

Mondays to Fridays

30 July to 10 August

Gillingham and Dartford - London

Network Diagram - see first Page of Table 200

		SE	SE	SE		SE	SE	SE	SE	SE	SE	SE	SE	SE		SE	SE	SE	SE	SE	SE	SE	SE	SE	
Gillingham (Kent)	d							11 54	12 20													12 24			
Chatham	d							11 58	12 24													12 28			
Rochester	d							12 00	12 27													12 30			
Maidstone West	d																								
Strood	d							12 05	12 32													12 35			
Higham	d							12 10														12 40			
Gravesend	d		12 32					12 18	12 43									13 02				12 48			
Northfleet	d		12 36															13 06							
Swanscombe	d		12 38															13 08							
Greenhithe for Bluewater	d		12 41					12 23										13 11				12 53			
Stone Crossing	d		12 43															13 13							
Dartford	a		12 47					12 28										13 17				12 58			
	d		12 48					12 28			12 31	12 38				12 52		13 18				12 58		13 01	
Slade Green	d	12 17					12 23				12 35		12 43				12 47				12 53			13 05	
Erith	d						12 26				12 38		12 45								12 56			13 08	
Belvedere	d						12 28				12 40		12 48								12 58			13 10	
Abbey Wood	d						12 31	12 37			12 43		12 51								13 01	13 07		13 13	
Plumstead	d						12 34				12 46		12 54								13 04			13 16	
Woolwich Arsenal	d						12 38	12 42			12 49		12 58								13 08	13 12		13 19	
Woolwich Dockyard	d																								
Charlton	d					12 39	12 43	12 46			12 56		13 07							13 09	13 13	13 16		13 26	
Crayford	d		12 52			13 07												13 22		13 37					
Bexley	d		12 55			13 10												13 25		13 40					
Albany Park	d		12 58			13 13												13 28		13 43					
Sidcup	d		13 01			13 16												13 31		13 46					
New Eltham	d		13 04			13 19												13 34		13 49					
Mottingham	d		13 06			13 21												13 36		13 51					
Lee	d		13 09			13 24												13 39		13 54					
Hither Green	d		13 12	13 19		13 28												13 42	13 49	13 58					
Barnehurst	d	12a37								12 37		12 45				12 58	13a07						13 07		
Bexleyheath	d									12 39		12 47				13 01							13 09		
Welling	d									12 42		12 50				13 04							13 12		
Falconwood	d									12 45		12 53				13 06							13 15		
Eltham	d									12 48		12 55				13 09							13 18		
Kidbrooke	d									12 51		12 58											13 21		
Blackheath	d							12 52		12 55		13 03				13 16						13 22	13 25		
Lewisham	d			13 24		13 34		12 56		12 59		13 08		13 14		13 20			13 54	14 04		13 26	13 29		
St Johns	d			13 26		13 36				13 01				13 16					13 56	14 06			13 31		
New Cross	d			13 28		13 38				13 03				13 18					13 58	14 08			13 33		
Nunhead	d											13 13													
Peckham Rye	d											13 15													
Denmark Hill	d											13 19													
London Victoria	a											13 31													
Westcombe Park	d						12 45														13 15				
Maze Hill	d																								
Greenwich	d						12 52				13 03		13 13								13 22			13 33	
Deptford	a						12 54														13 24				
London Bridge	a		13 22	13 34		13 44	13 00	13 05		13 08	13 11		13 20	13 24		13 28		13 52	14 04	14 14	13 30	13 35	13 38	13 41	
London Cannon Street	a			13 41		13 52	13 07			13 16	13 18		13 27	13 31					14 11	14 22	13 39		13 46	13 48	
London Waterloo (East)	a		13 26					13 09								13 32		13 56				13 39			
London Charing Cross	a		13 30					13 16								13 39		14 00				13 46			
Ebbsfleet International	a								12 46																
Stratford International	a								12 58																
St Pancras Int'l	a								13 08																

Table 200

Mondays to Fridays

30 July to 10 August

Gillingham and Dartford - London

Network Diagram - see first Page of Table 200

		SE	SE	SE	SE	SE	SE	SE	SE	SE		SE	SE	SE	SE	SE	SE	SE	SE	SE		SE	SE	SE	SE
Gillingham (Kent)	d											12 54	13 20												
Chatham	d											12 58	13 24												
Rochester	d											13 00	13 27												
Maidstone West	d																								
Strood	d											13 05	13 32												
Higham	d											13 10													
Gravesend	d						13 32					13 18	13 43									14 02			
Northfleet	d						13 36															14 06			
Swanscombe	d						13 38															14 08			
Greenhithe for Bluewater	d						13 41					13 23										14 11			
Stone Crossing	d						13 43															14 13			
Dartford	a						13 47					13 28										14 17			
	d	13 08			13 22		13 48					13 28			13 31	13 38			13 52			14 18			
Slade Green	d		13 13			13 17				13 23					13 35		13 43			13 47					13 53
Erith	d		13 15							13 26					13 38		13 45								13 56
Belvedere	d		13 18							13 28					13 40		13 48								13 58
Abbey Wood	d		13 21							13 31		13 37			13 43		13 51								14 01
Plumstead	d		13 24							13 34					13 46		13 54								14 04
Woolwich Arsenal	d		13 28							13 38		13 42			13 49		13 58								14 08
Woolwich Dockyard	d																								
Charlton	d		13 37						13 39	13 43		13 46			13 56		14 07							14 09	14 13
Crayford	d						13 52		14 07													14 22		14 37	
Bexley	d						13 55		14 10													14 25		14 40	
Albany Park	d						13 58		14 13													14 28		14 43	
Sidcup	d						14 01		14 16													14 31		14 46	
New Eltham	d						14 04		14 19													14 34		14 49	
Mottingham	d						14 06		14 21													14 36		14 51	
Lee	d						14 09		14 24													14 39		14 54	
Hither Green	d						14 12	14 19	14 28													14 42	14 49	14 58	
Barnehurst	d	13 15			13 28	13a37								13 37		13 45			13 58	14a07					
Bexleyheath	d	13 17			13 31									13 39		13 47			14 01						
Welling	d	13 20			13 34									13 42		13 50			14 04						
Falconwood	d	13 23			13 36									13 45		13 53			14 06						
Eltham	d	13 25			13 39									13 48		13 55			14 09						
Kidbrooke	d	13 28												13 51		13 58									
Blackheath	d	13 33			13 46							13 52		13 55		14 03			14 16						
Lewisham	d	13 38		13 44	13 50			14 24	14 34			13 56		13 59		14 08		14 14	14 20				14 54	15 04	
St Johns	d			13 46				14 26	14 36					14 01				14 16					14 56	15 06	
New Cross	d			13 48				14 28	14 38					14 03				14 18					14 58	15 08	
Nunhead	d	13 43														14 13									
Peckham Rye	d	13 45														14 15									
Denmark Hill	d	13 49														14 19									
London Victoria	a	14 01														14 31									
Westcombe Park	d									13 45															14 15
Maze Hill	d																								
Greenwich	d		13 43							13 52					14 03		14 13								14 22
Deptford	a									13 54															14 24
London Bridge	a		13 50	13 54	13 58		14 22	14 34	14 44	14 00		14 05		14 08	14 11		14 20	14 24	14 28			14 52	15 04	15 14	14 30
London Cannon Street	a		13 57	14 01				14 41	14 52	14 07				14 16	14 18		14 27	14 31					15 11	15 22	14 39
London Waterloo (East)	a				14 02		14 26					14 09							14 32			14 56			
London Charing Cross	a				14 09		14 30					14 16							14 39			15 00			
Ebbsfleet International	a												13 46												
Stratford International	a												13 58												
St Pancras Int'l	a												14 08												

Table 200

Mondays to Fridays

30 July to 10 August

Gillingham and Dartford - London

Network Diagram - see first Page of Table 200

		SE	SE	SE	SE	SE	SE	SE	SE	SE	SE	SE	SE	SE	SE	SE	SE	SE	SE	SE	SE	SE	SE	SE
Gillingham (Kent)	d	13 24													13 54	14 20								
Chatham	d	13 28													13 58	14 24								
Rochester	d	13 30													14 00	14 27								
Maidstone West	d																							
Strood	d	13 35													14 05	14 32								
Higham	d	13 40													14 10									
Gravesend	d	13 48									14 32				14 18	14 43								
Northfleet	d										14 36													
Swanscombe	d										14 38													
Greenhithe for Bluewater	d	13 53									14 41				14 23									
Stone Crossing	d										14 43													
Dartford	a	13 58									14 47				14 28									
	d	13 58		14 01	14 08				14 22		14 48				14 28			14 31	14 38				14 52	
Slade Green	d			14 05		14 13				14 17				14 23				14 35			14 43			14 47
Erith	d			14 08		14 15								14 26				14 38			14 45			
Belvedere	d			14 10		14 18								14 28				14 40			14 48			
Abbey Wood	d	14 07		14 13		14 21								14 31	14 37			14 43			14 51			
Plumstead	d			14 16		14 24								14 34				14 46		14 51	14 54			
Woolwich Arsenal	d	14 12		14 19		14 28								14 38	14 42			14 49		14 55	14 59			
Woolwich Dockyard	d																							
Charlton	d	14 16		14 26		14 37							14 39	14 43	14 46			14 56		15 01	15 07			
Crayford	d										14 52		15 07											
Bexley	d										14 55		15 10											
Albany Park	d										14 58		15 13											
Sidcup	d										15 01		15 16											
New Eltham	d										15 04		15 19											
Mottingham	d										15 06		15 21											
Lee	d										15 09		15 24											
Hither Green	d										15 12	15 19	15 28											
Barnehurst	d		14 07		14 15				14 28	14a37							14 37		14 45				14 59	15a07
Bexleyheath	d		14 09		14 17				14 31								14 39		14 47				15 01	
Welling	d		14 12		14 20				14 34								14 42		14 50				15 04	
Falconwood	d		14 15		14 23				14 36								14 45		14 53				15 07	
Eltham	d		14 18		14 25				14 39								14 48		14 55				15 09	
Kidbrooke	d		14 21		14 28												14 51		14 58					
Blackheath	d	14 22	14 25		14 33				14 46						14 52		14 55		15 03				15 16	
Lewisham	d	14 26	14 29		14 38			14 44	14 50			15 24	15 34		14 56		14 59		15 08			15 14	15 20	
St Johns	d		14 31					14 46				15 26	15 36				15 01					15 16		
New Cross	d		14 33					14 48				15 28	15 38				15 03					15 18		
Nunhead	d				14 43														15 13					
Peckham Rye	d				14 45														15 15					
Denmark Hill	d				14 49														15 19					
London Victoria	a				15 01														15 31					
Westcombe Park	d													14 45										
Maze Hill	d																							
Greenwich	d			14 33		14 43								14 52				15 03		15 08	15 13			
Deptford	a													14 54										
London Bridge	a	14 35	14 38	14 41		14 50		14 54	14 58		15 22	15 34	15 44	15 00	15 05		15 08	15 11			15 20	15 24	15 28	
London Cannon Street	a		14 46	14 48		14 57		15 01				15 41	15 52	15 07			15 16	15 18		15 25	15 27	15 31		
London Waterloo (East)	a	14 39							15 02		15 26				15 09								15 32	
London Charing Cross	a	14 46							15 09		15 30				15 16								15 39	
Ebbsfleet International	a															14 46								
Stratford International	a															14 58								
St Pancras Int'l	a															15 08								

Table 200

Mondays to Fridays

30 July to 10 August

Gillingham and Dartford - London

Network Diagram - see first Page of Table 200

		SE	SE	SE	SE	SE	SE	SE	SE	SE	SE	SE	SE	SE	SE	SE	SE	SE	SE	SE	SE	SE
Gillingham (Kent)	d					14 24												14 54	15 20			
Chatham	d					14 28												14 58	15 24			
Rochester	d					14 30												15 00	15 27			
Maidstone West	d																					
Strood	d					14 35												15 05	15 32			
Higham	d					14 40												15 10				
Gravesend	d	15 02				14 48								15 32				15 18	15 43			
Northfleet	d	15 06												15 36								
Swanscombe	d	15 08												15 38								
Greenhithe for Bluewater	d	15 11				14 53								15 41				15 23				
Stone Crossing	d	15 13												15 43								
Dartford	a	15 17				14 58								15 47				15 28				
	d	15 18				14 58		15 01	15 08			15 22		15 48				15 28		15 31	15 38	
Slade Green	d				14 53			15 05		15 15			15 17				15 23			15 35		
Erith	d				14 56			15 08		15 18							15 26			15 38		
Belvedere	d				14 58			15 10		15 20							15 28			15 40		
Abbey Wood	d				15 01	15 07		15 13		15 23							15 31	15 37		15 43		
Plumstead	d				15 04			15 16		15 26							15 34			15 46		
Woolwich Arsenal	d				15 08	15 12		15 19		15 29							15 38	15 42		15 49		
Woolwich Dockyard	d																					
Charlton	d			15 08	15 13	15 16		15 26		15 36						15 38	15 43	15 46		15 56		
Crayford	d	15 22		15 37										15 52		16 07						
Bexley	d	15 25		15 40										15 55		16 10						
Albany Park	d	15 28		15 43										15 58		16 13						
Sidcup	d	15 31		15 46										16 01		16 16						
New Eltham	d	15 34		15 49										16 04		16 19						
Mottingham	d	15 36		15 51										16 06		16 21						
Lee	d	15 39		15 54										16 09		16 24						
Hither Green	d	15 42	15 49	15 58										16 12	16 19	16 28						
Barnehurst	d						15 07		15 15			15 29	15 37								15 45	
Bexleyheath	d						15 09		15 18			15 31	15 39								15 48	
Welling	d						15 12		15 21			15 34	15 42								15 51	
Falconwood	d						15 15		15 23			15 37	15 45								15 53	
Eltham	d						15 18		15 26			15 39	15 48								15 56	
Kidbrooke	d						15 21		15 29				15 51								15 59	
Blackheath	d					15 22	15 25		15 34			15 46	15 55					15 52			16 04	
Lewisham	d		15 54	16 04		15 26	15 29		15 38		15 44	15 50	15 59		16 24	16 34		15 56			16 08	
St Johns	d		15 56	16 06			15 31				15 46		16 01		16 26	16 36						
New Cross	d		15 58	16 08			15 33				15 48		16 03		16 28	16 38						
Nunhead	d								15 43												16 13	
Peckham Rye	d								15 45												16 15	
Denmark Hill	d								15 49												16 19	
London Victoria	a								16 01												16 31	
Westcombe Park	d				15 15												15 45					
Maze Hill	d																					
Greenwich	d				15 22			15 33		15 43							15 52			16 03		16 07
Deptford	a				15 24												15 54					
London Bridge	a	15 52	16 04	16 15	15 30	15 35	15 38	15 41		15 50	15 54	15 58	16 09	16 22	16 34	16 44	16 00	16 05		16 12		
London Cannon Street	a		16 11	16 22	15 39		15 46	15 48		15 57	16 01		16 16		16 41	16 52	16 09			16 19		16 25
London Waterloo (East)	a	15 57				15 39						16 02		16 27				16 09				
London Charing Cross	a	16 01				15 46						16 09		16 31				16 16				
Ebbsfleet International	a																		15 46			
Stratford International	a																		15 58			
St Pancras Int'l	a																		16 08			

Table 200

Gillingham and Dartford - London

Network Diagram - see first Page of Table 200

		SE	SE	SE	SE	SE	SE	SE		SE	SE	SE	SE	SE	SE	SE	SE	SE		SE	SE	SE	SE	SE	SE
Gillingham (Kent)	d											15 24													15 54
Chatham	d											15 28													15 58
Rochester	d											15 30													16 00
Maidstone West	d																								
Strood	d											15 35													16 05
Higham	d											15 40													16 10
Gravesend	d						16 02					15 48													16 18
Northfleet	d						16 06																		
Swanscombe	d						16 08																		
Greenhithe for Bluewater	d						16 11					15 53													16 23
Stone Crossing	d						16 13																		
Dartford	a						16 17					15 58													16 28
	d				15 52		16 18					15 58		16 01	16 08			16 22			16 42				16 28
Slade Green	d	15 45				15 47					15 53			16 05		16 15				16 17				16 23	
Erith	d	15 48									15 56			16 08		16 18								16 26	
Belvedere	d	15 50									15 58			16 10		16 20								16 28	
Abbey Wood	d	15 53									16 01	16 07		16 13		16 23								16 31	16 37
Plumstead	d	15 56									16 04			16 16		16 26								16 34	
Woolwich Arsenal	d	15 59									16 08	16 12		16 19		16 29								16 38	16 42
Woolwich Dockyard	d																								
Charlton	d	16 06								16 08	16 13	16 16		16 26		16 36							16 38	16 43	16 46
Crayford	d						16 22			16 37											16 46		17 07		
Bexley	d						16 25			16 40											16 49		17 10		
Albany Park	d						16 28			16 43											16 52		17 13		
Sidcup	d						16 31	16 38		16 46											16 55		17 16		
New Eltham	d						16 34	16 41		16 49											16 58		17 19		
Mottingham	d						16 36	16 43		16 51											17 00		17 21		
Lee	d						16 39	16 46		16 54											17 03		17 24		
Hither Green	d						16 42	16 50		17 00											17 07	17 19	17 28		
Barnehurst	d				15 59	16a07							16 07		16 15			16 29		16a37					
Bexleyheath	d				16 01								16 09		16 18			16 31							
Welling	d				16 04								16 12		16 21			16 34							
Falconwood	d				16 07								16 15		16 23			16 37							
Eltham	d				16 09								16 18		16 26			16 39							
Kidbrooke	d												16 21		16 29										
Blackheath	d		16 10		16 16							16 22	16 25		16 34			16 46							16 52
Lewisham	d		16 16	16 14	16 20					17 05		16 26	16 29		16 38		16 44	16 50				17 24	17 35		16 56
St Johns	d			16 16				16 54		17 09			16 31				16 46					17 26	17 37		
New Cross	d			16 18				16 56		17 11			16 33				16 48					17 28	17 39		
Nunhead	d														16 43										
Peckham Rye	d														16 45										
Denmark Hill	d		16 28												16 49										
London Victoria	a		16 44												17 04										
Westcombe Park	d										16 15													16 45	
Maze Hill	d																								
Greenwich	d	16 13									16 22			16 33		16 43								16 52	
Deptford	a										16 24													16 54	
London Bridge	a	16 20		16 24	16 29		16 52	17 04		17 18	16 30	16 35	16 39	16 42		16 50	16 54	16 58			17 21	17 34	17 45	17 01	17 07
London Cannon Street	a	16 27		16 31				17 09		17 27	16 39		16 46	16 49		16 57	17 01					17 41	17 52	17 08	17 14
London Waterloo (East)	a				16 33		16 56					16 39						17 03			17 28				
London Charing Cross	a				16 40		17 00					16 47						17 10			17 33				
Ebbsfleet International	a																								
Stratford International	a																								
St Pancras Int'l	a																								

Table 200

Gillingham and Dartford - London

Network Diagram - see first Page of Table 200

		SE	SE	SE		SE	SE	SE	SE	SE	SE	SE	SE	SE		SE	SE	SE	SE	SE	SE	SE	SE	SE	
Gillingham (Kent)	d									16 20			16 24												
Chatham	d									16 24			16 28												
Rochester	d									16 27			16 30												
Maidstone West	d																								
Strood	d									16 32			16 35												
Higham	d												16 40												
Gravesend	d								16 32	16 43			16 48								17 02				
Northfleet	d								16 36												17 06				
Swanscombe	d								16 38												17 08				
Greenhithe for Bluewater	d								16 41				16 53								17 11				
Stone Crossing	d								16 43												17 13				
Dartford	a								16 48				16 58								17 17				
	d		16 31				16 38		16 52				16 58			17 01		17 08			17 18	17 22			
Slade Green	d		16 35	16 44							16 47	16 53				17 05									
Erith	d		16 38	16 46								16 56				17 08									
Belvedere	d		16 40	16 49								16 58				17 10									
Abbey Wood	d		16 43	16 52								17 01	17 07			17 13									
Plumstead	d		16 46	16 55								17 04				17 16									
Woolwich Arsenal	d		16 49	16 58								17 08	17 12			17 19									
Woolwich Dockyard	d																								
Charlton	d		16 56	17 05								17 13	17 16			17 26									
Crayford	d																				17 22				
Bexley	d																				17 25				
Albany Park	d																				17 28				
Sidcup	d																				17 31				
New Eltham	d																				17 34				
Mottingham	d																				17 36				
Lee	d																				17 39				
Hither Green	d																			17 41	17 42		17 53		
Barnehurst	d	16 37					16 45		16 59		17a06			17 07				17 15		18 10		17 29		17 37	
Bexleyheath	d	16 39					16 48		17 01					17 09				17 18		18 12		17 31		17 39	
Welling	d	16 42					16 51		17 04					17 12				17 21		18 15		17 34		17 42	
Falconwood	d	16 45					16 53		17 07					17 15				17 23				17 37		17 45	
Eltham	d	16 48					16 56		17 10					17 18				17 26		18 19		17 39		17 48	
Kidbrooke	d	16 51					16 59							17 21				17 29		18 22				17 51	
Blackheath	d	16 55				17 00	17 04		17 16				17 22	17 25			17 29	17 34		18 26		17 46		17 55	
Lewisham	d	16 59					17 08	17 14	17 20				17 27	17 29				17 38	17 44	18 29		17 50		17 59	
St Johns	d	17 01						17 16											17 46				17 57		
New Cross	d	17 03						17 18						17 33					17 48	18 32			17 59	18 02	
Nunhead	d						17 13											17 43							
Peckham Rye	d						17 15											17 45							
Denmark Hill	d						17 19											17 49							
London Victoria	a						17 31											18 02							
Westcombe Park	d											17 15													
Maze Hill	d																								
Greenwich	d		17 04	17 11								17 22				17 33									
Deptford	a											17 24													
London Bridge	a	17 09	17 13	17 21				17 24	17 29			17 31	17 35	17 39		17 42			17 55	18 38	17 53	18 00	18 06	18 09	
London Cannon Street	a	17 18	17 20	17 29				17 32				17 39		17 47		17 49			18 02	18 45		18 07	18 11	18 16	
London Waterloo (East)	a								17 34				17 40								17 58				
London Charing Cross	a					17 25			17 41				17 47				17 53				18 03				
Ebbsfleet International	a									16 46															
Stratford International	a									16 58															
St Pancras Int'l	a									17 08															

Table 200

Mondays to Fridays

30 July to 10 August

Gillingham and Dartford - London

Network Diagram - see first Page of Table 200

		SE	SE	SE	SE	SE	SE	SE	SE	SE	SE	SE	SE	SE	SE	SE	SE	SE	SE	SE	SE	SE	SE
Gillingham (Kent)	d								16 54	17 20								17 24					
Chatham	d								16 58	17 24								17 28					
Rochester	d								17 00	17 27								17 30					
Maidstone West	d																						
Strood	d								17 05	17 32								17 35					
Higham	d								17 10									17 40					
Gravesend	d			17 32					17 18	17 43								17 48					
Northfleet	d			17 36																			
Swanscombe	d			17 38																			
Greenhithe for Bluewater	d			17 41					17 23									17 53					
Stone Crossing	d			17 43																			
Dartford	a			17 47					17 28									17 58					
	d			17 48					17 28			17 31	17 38			17 52		17 58		18 01		18 08	
Slade Green	d						17 15	17 25			17 29	17 35		17 46			17 54			18 05			18 15
Erith	d						17 18	17 27				17 38		17 48			17 56			18 08			18 18
Belvedere	d						17 20	17 30				17 40		17 51			17 59			18 10			18 20
Abbey Wood	d						17 23	17 33	17 37			17 43		17 54			18 02	18 07		18 13			18 23
Plumstead	d						17 26	17 36				17 46		17 57			18 05			18 16			18 26
Woolwich Arsenal	d						17 29	17 39	17 42			17 49		18 00			18 08	18 12		18 19			18 29
Woolwich Dockyard	d																						
Charlton	d					17 31	17 36	17 43	17 46			17 56		18 07			18 13	18 16		18 26			18 36
Crayford	d	17 37		17 52		18 01																	
Bexley	d	17 40		17 55		18 04																	
Albany Park	d	17 43		17 58		18 07																	
Sidcup	d	17 46		18 01		18 10															18 20		
New Eltham	d	17 49		18 04		18 13															18 23		
Mottingham	d	17 51		18 06		18 15																	
Lee	d	17 54		18 09		18 18																	
Hither Green	d	17 58	18 03	18 12	18 19	18 21															18 28		
Barnehurst	d		18 37								17 37		17 45			17 59			18 10			18 15	
Bexleyheath	d		18 39								17 39		17 47			18 01			18 12			18 18	
Welling	d		18 42								17 42		17 50			18 04			18 15			18 21	
Falconwood	d		18 45								17 45		17 53			18 07						18 23	
Eltham	d		18 48								17 48		17 55			18 09			18 19			18 26	
Kidbrooke	d		18 51								17 51		17 58						18 22			18 29	
Blackheath	d		18 55						17 52		17 55		18 03			18 16		18 22	18 26			18 34	
Lewisham	d	18 05	18 59		18 24				17 56		17 59		18 08		18 14	18 20		18 26	18 29		18 35	18 38	
St Johns	d	18 07			18 26										18 16						18 37		
New Cross	d	18 09	19 03		18 28						18 02				18 18				18 32		18 39		
Nunhead	d												18 13									18 43	
Peckham Rye	d												18 15									18 45	
Denmark Hill	d												18 19									18 49	
London Victoria	a												18 32									19 01	
Westcombe Park	d							17 46									18 15						
Maze Hill	d																						
Greenwich	d						17 43	17 54				18 04		18 13			18 22			18 35			18 43
Deptford	a							17 56									18 24						
London Bridge	a	18 16	19 08	18 22	18 34	18 33	17 52	18 03	18 04		18 09	18 13		18 20	18 24	18 28	18 31	18 35	18 38	18 43	18 46		18 50
London Cannon Street	a	18 23	19 16		18 41		17 59	18 10			18 16	18 20		18 27	18 32		18 38		18 45	18 50	18 54		18 57
London Waterloo (East)	a			18 27		18 37			18 08							18 32		18 41					
London Charing Cross	a			18 31		18 44			18 15							18 40		18 48					
Ebbsfleet International	a									17 46													
Stratford International	a									17 58													
St Pancras Int'l	a									18 08													

Table 200

Mondays to Fridays

30 July to 10 August

Gillingham and Dartford - London

Network Diagram - see first Page of Table 200

		SE	SE	SE	SE	SE	SE	SE	SE	SE	SE	SE	SE	SE	SE	SE	SE	SE	SE	SE	SE	SE	SE
Gillingham (Kent)	d											17 54	18 20									18 24	
Chatham	d											17 58	18 24									18 28	
Rochester	d											18 00	18 27									18 30	
Maidstone West	d																						
Strood	d											18 05	18 32									18 35	
Higham	d											18 10										18 40	
Gravesend	d			18 02				18 32				18 18	18 43									18 48	
Northfleet	d			18 06				18 36															
Swanscombe	d			18 08				18 38															
Greenhithe for Bluewater	d			18 11				18 41				18 24										18 53	
Stone Crossing	d			18 13				18 43															
Dartford	a			18 17				18 47				18 28										18 58	
	d			18 18	18 22			18 48				18 29			18 31	18 38					18 52	18 59	
Slade Green	d										18 23				18 35			18 45		18 50			
Erith	d										18 26				18 38					18 52			
Belvedere	d										18 28				18 40					18 55			
Abbey Wood	d										18 31	18 37			18 43					18 58		19 07	
Plumstead	d										18 34				18 46					19 01			
Woolwich Arsenal	d										18 38	18 42			18 49			18 58		19 04		19 12	
Woolwich Dockyard	d																						
Charlton	d									18 38	18 43	18 46			18 56			19 04		19 09		19 16	
Crayford	d			18 22			18 37	18 52		19 07													
Bexley	d			18 25			18 40	18 55		19 10													
Albany Park	d			18 28			18 43	18 58		19 13													
Sidcup	d			18 31			18 46	19 01		19 16													
New Eltham	d			18 34			18 49	19 04		19 19													
Mottingham	d			18 36			18 51	19 06		19 21													
Lee	d			18 39			18 54	19 09		19 24													
Hither Green	d		18 35	18 42		18 49	18 59	19 12	19 19	19 28													
Barnehurst	d		19 07		18 29									18 37		18 45					18 59		19 07
Bexleyheath	d		19 09		18 31									18 39		18 47					19 01		19 09
Welling	d		19 12		18 34									18 42		18 50					19 04		19 12
Falconwood	d		19 15		18 37									18 45		18 53					19 07		19 15
Eltham	d		19 18		18 39									18 48		18 55					19 09		19 18
Kidbrooke	d		19 21											18 51		18 58							19 21
Blackheath	d		19 25		18 46							18 52		18 55		19 03					19 16	19 22	19 25
Lewisham	d	18 45	19 29		18 50	18 54	19 05		19 24	19 34		18 56		18 59		19 08			19 14		19 20	19 26	19 29
St Johns	d	18 47				18 56	19 07		19 26	19 36									19 16				
New Cross	d	18 49	19 32			18 58	19 09		19 28	19 38				19 03					19 18				19 32
Nunhead	d															19 13							
Peckham Rye	d															19 15							
Denmark Hill	d															19 19							
London Victoria	a															19 31							
Westcombe Park	d										18 45									19 11			
Maze Hill	d																						
Greenwich	d										18 52				19 03		19 12	19 12		19 18			
Deptford	a										18 54									19 20			
London Bridge	a	18 55	19 38	18 52	18 58	19 04	19 15	19 22	19 34	19 44	19 00	19 05		19 08	19 11		19 19	19 19	19 24	19 27	19 28	19 35	19 38
London Cannon Street	a	19 02	19 46			19 12	19 22		19 41	19 52	19 09			19 16	19 19		19 25	19 28	19 31	19 36			19 46
London Waterloo (East)	a			18 57	19 02			19 26				19 09									19 32	19 39	
London Charing Cross	a			19 01	19 09			19 30				19 16									19 39	19 46	
Ebbsfleet International	a												18 46										
Stratford International	a												18 58										
St Pancras Int'l	a												19 08										

Table 200

Gillingham and Dartford - London

Mondays to Fridays

30 July to 10 August

Network Diagram - see first Page of Table 200

		SE		SE	SE	SE	SE	SE	SE	SE	SE	SE		SE	SE	SE	SE	SE	SE	SE	SE	SE		SE	SE
Gillingham (Kent)	d								18 54						19 20			19 24						19 54	
Chatham	d								18 58						19 24			19 28						19 58	
Rochester	d								19 00						19 27			19 30						20 00	
Maidstone West	d																								
Strood	d								19 05						19 32			19 35						20 05	
Higham	d								19 10									19 40						20 10	
Gravesend	d					19 02			19 18					19 32	19 43			19 48			20 02			20 18	
Northfleet	d					19 06								19 36							20 06				
Swanscombe	d					19 08								19 38							20 08				
Greenhithe for Bluewater	d					19 11			19 23					19 41				19 53			20 11			20 23	
Stone Crossing	d					19 13								19 43							20 13				
Dartford	a					19 17			19 28					19 47				19 58			20 17			20 28	
	d	19 01			19 15	19 18		19 22	19 28	19 31				19 48			19 55	19 59	20 01	20 16	20 18	20 25		20 28	20 31
Slade Green	d	19 05			19 20		19 20			19 35	19 48					19 57			20 05	20 20					20 35
Erith	d	19 08			19 23		19 23			19 38	19 51								20 08	20 23					20 38
Belvedere	d	19 10			19 25		19 25			19 40	19 53								20 10	20 25					20 40
Abbey Wood	d	19 13			19 28		19 28		19 37	19 43	19 56							20 07	20 13	20 28				20 37	20 43
Plumstead	d	19 16			19 31		19 31			19 46	19 59								20 16	20 31					20 46
Woolwich Arsenal	d	19 19			19 34		19 34		19 42	19 49	20 02					20 08		20 12	20 19	20 34				20 42	20 49
Woolwich Dockyard	d																								
Charlton	d	19 26			19 41		19 41		19 47	19 56	20 09					20 13		20 16	20 26	20 40				20 47	20 56
Crayford	d			19 07		19 22								19 52							20 22				
Bexley	d			19 10		19 25								19 55							20 25				
Albany Park	d			19 13		19 28								19 58							20 28				
Sidcup	d			19 16		19 31								20 01							20 31				
New Eltham	d			19 19		19 34								20 04							20 34				
Mottingham	d			19 21		19 36								20 06							20 36				
Lee	d			19 24		19 39								20 09							20 39				
Hither Green	d			19 28		19 42								20 12							20 42				
Barnehurst	d							19 29									20 01					20 32			
Bexleyheath	d							19 31									20 04					20 34			
Welling	d							19 34									20 07					20 37			
Falconwood	d							19 37									20 09					20 40			
Eltham	d							19 40									20 12					20 42			
Kidbrooke	d							19 43									20 15					20 45			
Blackheath	d							19 48	19 53			20 05					20 19	20 22				20 49		20 53	
Lewisham	d			19 34		19 48		19 52	19 57			20 10		20 18			20 22	20 26			20 48	20 53		20 57	
St Johns	d			19 36																					
New Cross	d			19 38		19 51		19 56						20 21			20 26				20 51	20 56			
Nunhead	d																								
Peckham Rye	d																								
Denmark Hill	d											20 18													
London Victoria	a											20 31													
Westcombe Park	d				19 43		19 43				20 11									20 42					
Maze Hill	d																								
Greenwich	d	19 33			19 51		19 51			20 03	20 18					20 23			20 33	20 49					21 03
Deptford	a				19 53		19 53				20 20									20 51					
London Bridge	a	19 41		19 44	19 59	19 57	19 59	20 03	20 06	20 11	20 27			20 27		20 29	20 33	20 36	20 41	20 57	20 57	21 03		21 06	21 11
London Cannon Street	a	19 48		19 52	20 03		20 06			20 18	20 34					20 39			20 48	21 04					
London Waterloo (East)	a					20 02		20 08	20 11					20 32			20 38	20 40			21 02	21 08		21 10	21 15
London Charing Cross	a					20 09		20 15	20 17					20 39			20 45	20 47			21 09	21 15		21 17	21 22
Ebbsfleet International	a														19 46										
Stratford International	a														19 58										
St Pancras Int'l	a														20 08										

Table 200

Gillingham and Dartford - London

Mondays to Fridays

30 July to 10 August

Network Diagram - see first Page of Table 200

		SE	SE	SE	SE	SE	SE	SE		SE	SE	SE	SE	SE	SE	SE	SE	SE		SE	SE	SE	SE	SE A	SE
Gillingham (Kent)	d				20 20		20 24							20 54						21 20		21 24			
Chatham	d				20 24		20 28							20 58						21 24		21 28			
Rochester	d				20 27		20 30							21 00						21 27		21 30			
Maidstone West	d																								
Strood	d				20 32		20 35							21 05						21 32		21 35			
Higham	d						20 40							21 10								21 40			
Gravesend	d			20 32	20 43		20 48					21 02		21 18				21 32		21 43		21 48			22 02
Northfleet	d			20 36								21 06						21 36							22 06
Swanscombe	d			20 38								21 08						21 38							22 08
Greenhithe for Bluewater	d			20 41			20 53					21 11		21 23				21 41				21 53			22 11
Stone Crossing	d			20 43								21 13						21 43							22 13
Dartford	a			20 47			20 58					21 17		21 28				21 47				21 58			22 17
	d		20 46	20 48		20 55	20 58	21 01		21 16		21 18	21 25	21 28	21 31	21 46		21 48			21 55	21 58	22 01		22 18
Slade Green	d		20 50					21 05		21 20					21 35	21 50							22 05		
Erith	d		20 53					21 08		21 23					21 38	21 53							22 08		
Belvedere	d		20 55					21 10		21 25					21 40	21 55							22 10		
Abbey Wood	d		20 58				21 07	21 13		21 28				21 37	21 43	21 58						22 07	22 13		
Plumstead	d		21 01					21 16		21 31					21 46	22 01							22 16		
Woolwich Arsenal	d		21 04				21 12	21 19		21 34				21 42	21 49	22 04						22 12	22 19		
Woolwich Dockyard	d																								
Charlton	d	21 01	21 10				21 17	21 26		21 41				21 47	21 56	22 11						22 18	22 25		
Crayford	d			20 52								21 22						21 52							22 22
Bexley	d			20 55								21 25						21 55							22 25
Albany Park	d			20 58								21 28						21 58							22 28
Sidcup	d			21 01								21 31						22 01							22 31
New Eltham	d			21 04								21 34						22 04							22 34
Mottingham	d			21 06								21 36						22 06							22 36
Lee	d			21 09								21 39						22 09							22 39
Hither Green	d			21 12								21 42						22 12							22 42
Barnehurst	d					21 02							21 32								22 02				
Bexleyheath	d					21 04							21 34								22 04				
Welling	d					21 07							21 37								22 07				
Falconwood	d					21 10							21 40								22 10				
Eltham	d					21 12							21 42								22 12				
Kidbrooke	d					21 15							21 45								22 15				
Blackheath	d	21 07				21 19	21 23				21 41		21 49	21 53			22 05				22 19	22 23		22 41	
Lewisham	d	21 11		21 18		21 23	21 27				21 46	21 48	21 53	21 57			22 10	22 18			22 23	22 26		22 46	22 48
St Johns	d																								
New Cross	d			21 21		21 26						21 51	21 56					22 21			22 26				22 51
Nunhead	d																								
Peckham Rye	d																								
Denmark Hill	d	21 18									21 59						22 17							22 59	
London Victoria	a	21 31									22 14						22 31							23 14	
Westcombe Park	d		21 12							21 43						22 13							22 27		
Maze Hill	d									21 45					21 59	22 15							22 29		
Greenwich	d		21 19					21 33		21 49					22 04	22 19							22 33		
Deptford	a		21 21							21 51						22 21							22 35		
London Bridge	a		21 27	21 27		21 33	21 36	21 41		21 57		21 57	22 01	22 05	22 11	22 27		22 27			22 31	22 35	22 41		22 57
London Cannon Street	a		21 34							22 04						22 34									
London Waterloo (East)	a			21 32		21 38	21 40	21 45				22 02	22 06	22 09	22 15			22 32			22 36	22 39	22 45		23 02
London Charing Cross	a			21 39		21 45	21 47	21 52				22 09	22 13	22 16	22 22			22 39			22 43	22 46	22 52		23 09
Ebbsfleet International	a				20 46															21 46					
Stratford International	a				20 58															21 58					
St Pancras Int'l	a				21 08															22 08					

A not 3 August, 10 August

Gillingham and Dartford - London

Mondays to Fridays

30 July to 10 August

Network Diagram - see first Page of Table 200

		SE	SE	SE		SE	SE	SE	SE	SE	SE	SE	SE	SE		SE
Gillingham (Kent) 4	d		21 54				22 20			22 24		22 54				
Chatham 4	d		21 58				22 24			22 28		22 58				
Rochester 4	d		22 00				22 27			22 30		23 00				
Maidstone West	d															
Strood 4	d		22 05				22 32			22 35		23 05				
Higham	d		22 10							22 40		23 10				
Gravesend 4	d		22 18			22 32	22 43			22 48		23 18				
Northfleet	d					22 36										
Swanscombe	d					22 38										
Greenhithe for Bluewater	d		22 23			22 41				22 53		23 23				
Stone Crossing	d					22 43										
Dartford 4	a		22 28			22 47				22 58		23 28				
	d	22 25	22 28	22 31		22 48		22 55		22 58	23 01					
Slade Green 4	d			22 35							23 05					
Erith	d			22 38							23 08					
Belvedere	d			22 40							23 10					
Abbey Wood	d		22 37	22 43						23 07	23 13					
Plumstead	d			22 46							23 16					
Woolwich Arsenal 4 ⛴	d		22 42	22 49						23 12	23 19					
Woolwich Dockyard	d															
Charlton 4	d		22 48	22 55					23 07	23 17	23 25		23 32	23 45		23 54
Crayford	d					22 52										
Bexley	d					22 55										
Albany Park	d					22 58										
Sidcup 4	d					23 01										
New Eltham	d					23 04										
Mottingham	d					23 06										
Lee	d					23 09										
Hither Green 4	d					23 12										
Barnehurst 4	d	22 32						23 02								
Bexleyheath	d	22 34						23 04								
Welling	d	22 37						23 07								
Falconwood	d	22 40						23 10								
Eltham	d	22 42						23 12								
Kidbrooke	d	22 45						23 15								
Blackheath 4	d	22 49	22 53					23 19		23 23						
Lewisham 4 ⛴	d	22 53	22 56			23 18		23 23		23 26						
St Johns	d															
New Cross 4 ⊖	d	22 56				23 21		23 26								
Nunhead 4	d															
Peckham Rye 4	d															
Denmark Hill 4	d															
London Victoria 15 ⊖	a															
Westcombe Park	d			22 57							23 27					
Maze Hill	d			22 59							23 29					
Greenwich 4 ⛴	d			23 03							23 33					
Deptford	a			23 05							23 35					
London Bridge 4 ⊖	a	23 01	23 05	23 11		23 27		23 31		23 35	23 41					
London Cannon Street 4 ⊖	a								23 22				23 48			
London Waterloo (East) 4 ⊖	a	23 06	23 09	23 15		23 32		23 36		23 39	23 45					
London Charing Cross 4 ⊖	a	23 13	23 16	23 22		23 39		23 46		23 46	23 52			00 08		00 16
Ebbsfleet International	a						22 46									
Stratford International ⊖ ⛴	a						22 58									
St Pancras Int'l 15 ⊖	a						23 07									

Table 200

Gillingham and Dartford - London

Mondays to Fridays

29 August to 7 September

Network Diagram - see first Page of Table 200

		SE A	SE B	SE A	SE	SE	SE	SE	SE	SE		SE	SE	SE	SE	SE	SE	SE	SE	SE		SE	SE	SE	SE
Gillingham (Kent) 4	d					04 09			04 34			04 54			05 20			05 24	05 45						
Chatham 4	d					04 13			04 38			04 58			05 24			05 28	05 49						
Rochester 4	d					04 15			04 40			05 00			05 27			05 30	05 51						
Maidstone West	d																								
Strood 4	d					04 20			04 45			05 05			05 32			05 35							
Higham	d					04 25			04 50			05 10						05 40							
Gravesend 4	d					04 33			04 58			05 18		05 28	05 43			05 48							
Northfleet	d								05 02					05 32											
Swanscombe	d								05 04					05 34											
Greenhithe for Bluewater	d					04 38			05 07			05 23		05 37				05 53							
Stone Crossing	d								05 09					05 39											
Dartford 4	a					04 43			05 13			05 28		05 43				05 58							
	d					04 44		05 01	05 14	05 22		05 29	05 31	05 44		05 52	05 56	05 59		06 01			06 13	06 16	
Slade Green 4	d							05 05					05 35							06 05				06 20	
Erith	d							05 08					05 38							06 08				06 23	
Belvedere	d							05 10					05 40							06 10				06 25	
Abbey Wood	d							05 13				05 38	05 43					06 08		06 13				06 28	
Plumstead	d							05 16					05 46							06 16				06 31	
Woolwich Arsenal 4 ⛴	d							05 19				05 43	05 49					06 13		06 19				06 34	
Woolwich Dockyard	d							05 22					05 52							06 22				06 37	
Charlton 4	d	00 07	00 11	00 15	00 26			05 25				05 47	05 55					06 17		06 25				06 40	
Crayford	d					04 48			05 18					05 48			06 01								
Bexley	d					04 51			05 21					05 51			06 04								
Albany Park	d					04 54			05 24					05 54			06 07								
Sidcup 4	d					04 57			05 27					05 57			06 10								
New Eltham	d					05 00			05 30					06 00			06 13								
Mottingham	d					05 02			05 32					06 02			06 16								
Lee	d					05 05			05 35					06 05			06 19								
Hither Green 4	d					05 08	05 23		05 38					06 08			06 22								
Barnehurst 4	d									05 29						05 59						06 14	06 20		
Bexleyheath	d									05 31						06 01						06 16	06 22		
Welling	d									05 34						06 04						06 19	06 25		
Falconwood	d									05 37						06 07						06 22	06 28		
Eltham	d									05 40						06 10						06 25	06 31		
Kidbrooke	d									05 43						06 13						06 28	06 34		
Blackheath 4	d									05 46		05 52				06 16		06 22				06 31	06 37		
Lewisham 4 ⛴	d					05 13	05 28		05 43	05 50		05 56		06 13		06 20	06 27	06 25				06 35	06 41		06 48
St Johns	d																06 29								06 50
New Cross 4 ⊖	d					05 16	05 31		05 46	05 53				06 16			06 31					06 38			06 52
Nunhead 4	d																								
Peckham Rye 4	d																						06 47		
Denmark Hill 4	d																						06 50		
London Victoria 15 ⊖	a																						07 04		
Westcombe Park	d							05 27					05 57							06 27				06 42	
Maze Hill	d							05 29					05 59							06 29				06 44	
Greenwich 4 ⛴	d							05 32					06 02							06 32				06 47	
Deptford	a							05 34					06 04							06 34				06 49	
London Bridge 4 ⊖	a					05 22	05 36	05 41	05 52	05 58		06 05	06 12	06 22		06 28	06 37	06 34	06 27	06 42		06 43		06 56	06 58
London Cannon Street 4 ⊖	a	00 19	00 31		00 38		05 41												06 32			06 48		07 03	07 05
London Waterloo (East) 4 ⊖	a					05 26		05 46	05 57	06 03		06 10	06 17	06 26		06 33	06 41	06 39		06 48					
London Charing Cross 4 ⊖	a			00 30		05 30		05 50	06 01	06 07		06 13	06 21	06 30		06 36	06 45	06 43		06 52					
Ebbsfleet International	a														05 47										
Stratford International ⊖ ⛴	a														05 59										
St Pancras Int'l 15 ⊖	a														06 07										

A not 3 September

B 3 September

Table 200

Mondays to Fridays

29 August to 7 September

Gillingham and Dartford - London

Network Diagram - see first Page of Table 200

		SE	SE	SE	SE	SE		SE	SE	SE	SE	SE	SE	SE	SE	SE		SE ■	SE	SE	SE	SE	SE	SE	SE
Gillingham (Kent)	d		05 50		05 54						06 07					06 20		06 34							
Chatham	d		05 54		05 58						06 11					06 24		06 38							
Rochester	d		05 57		06 00						06 13					06 27		06 41							
Maidstone West	d																								
Strood	d		06 02		06 05						06 18					06 32									
Higham	d				06 10						06 23														
Gravesend	d	06 05	06 13		06 18						06 31				06 34	06 43							06 47		
Northfleet	d	06 09													06 38								06 51		
Swanscombe	d	06 11													06 40								06 53		
Greenhithe for Bluewater	d	06 14			06 23						06 37				06 43								06 56		
Stone Crossing	d	06 16													06 45								06 58		
Dartford	a	06 20			06 28						06 41				06 49								07 02		
	d	06 21			06 29	06 31			06 31	06 39	06 42				06 50							07 00	07 03		
Slade Green	d								06 36											06 55					
Erith	d								06 39											06 57					
Belvedere	d								06 41											07 00					
Abbey Wood	d				06 38				06 45		06 51									07 03			07 12		
Plumstead	d								06 48											07 06					
Woolwich Arsenal	d				06 43				06 51		06 56									07 09			07 17		
Woolwich Dockyard	d								06 53											07 12					
Charlton	d				06 47				06 57											07 15			07 22		
Crayford	d			06 25		06 35								06 50	06 55										
Bexley	d			06 28		06 38								06 53	06 58										
Albany Park	d			06 31		06 41								06 56	07 01										
Sidcup	d			06 34		06 44								06 59	07 04										
New Eltham	d			06 38		06 47								07 02	07 07										
Mottingham	d			06 40		06 50								07 05	07 10										
Lee	d			06 43		06 53								07 08	07 13										
Hither Green	d			06 46		06 56							07 08	07 11	07 16									07 28	
Barnehurst	d	06 28						06 39		06 49		06 53									07 00	07 08			07 13
Bexleyheath	d	06 31						06 41		06 52		06 56									07 03	07 11			07 16
Welling	d	06 34						06 44		06 55		06 59									07 06	07 14			07 19
Falconwood	d	06 37						06 47		06 57		07 01									07 08	07 16			07 21
Eltham	d	06 40						06 50		07 00		07 04									07 11	07 19			07 24
Kidbrooke	d	06 43						06 53		07 03		07 07									07 14	07 22			07 27
Blackheath	d	06 47			06 52			06 57		07 08	07 05	07 11									07 18	07 27			07 31
Lewisham	d	06 50		06 52	06 55			07 01		07 11	07 08	07 15		07 17					07 20		07 22	07 30			07 35
St Johns	d			06 54										07 19							07 24				
New Cross	d			06 56				07 04			07 11			07 21					07 23		07 26				07 38
Nunhead	d											07 20													
Peckham Rye	d											07 23													
Denmark Hill	d											07 29													
London Victoria	a											07 42													
Westcombe Park	d								06 59											07 17					
Maze Hill	d								07 01											07 19					
Greenwich	d								07 05											07 23			07 28		
Deptford	a								07 07											07 25					
London Bridge	a	07 00		07 02	07 03	07 06		07 09	07 14	07 20	07 17		07 18	07 26	07 26			07 20	07 28	07 33	07 33	07 40	07 35	07 37	07 43
London Cannon Street	a			07 09				07 16	07 21		07 23		07 25	07 33				07 27	07 35		07 39		07 42	07 44	07 50
London Waterloo (East)	a	07 05			07 09	07 11				07 25					07 31					07 38		07 46			
London Charing Cross	a	07 11			07 15	07 17				07 31					07 37					07 44		07 52			
Ebbsfleet International	a		06 17													06 47									
Stratford International	a		06 29													06 59									
St Pancras Int'l	a		06 37													07 06									

Table 200

Mondays to Fridays

29 August to 7 September

Gillingham and Dartford - London

Network Diagram - see first Page of Table 200

		SE		SE	SE	SE ■	SE	SE	SE	SE	SE	SE		SE	SE	SE	SE	SE	SE	SE	SE	SE		SE	SE
Gillingham (Kent)	d				06 38	07 04																			
Chatham	d				06 42	07 08																			
Rochester	d				06 44	07 11																			
Maidstone West	d																	06 56							
Strood	d				06 49						06 57							07 12							
Higham	d				06 54						07 02														
Gravesend	d				07 02						07 09						07 17	07 22							
Northfleet	d																07 21								
Swanscombe	d																07 23								
Greenhithe for Bluewater	d				07 07						07 16						07 26								
Stone Crossing	d																07 28								
Dartford	a				07 12						07 21						07 33								
	d	07 05			07 12		07 17			07 20	07 23				07 25		07 34			07 36					07 40
Slade Green	d	07 09						07 19							07 29							07 39			
Erith	d	07 12						07 22							07 32							07 42			
Belvedere	d	07 14						07 24							07 34							07 44			
Abbey Wood	d	07 18						07 28			07 34				07 38							07 48			
Plumstead	d	07 21						07 31							07 41							07 51			
Woolwich Arsenal	d	07 24						07 34			07 39				07 44							07 54			
Woolwich Dockyard	d	07 26						07 36							07 46							07 56			
Charlton	d	07 30						07 40			07 44				07 50							08 00			
Crayford	d			07 10	07 17											07 30	07 38								
Bexley	d			07 13	07 20											07 33	07 41								
Albany Park	d			07 16	07 22											07 36	07 44								
Sidcup	d			07 19	07 25											07 39	07 47				07 51				
New Eltham	d			07 23	07 28											07 43	07 50				07 54				
Mottingham	d			07 25	07 31											07 45					07 56				
Lee	d			07 28	07 34											07 48					07 59				
Hither Green	d			07 32	07 36							07 49				07 52					08 02				
Barnehurst	d						07 24			07 28				07 33					07 38	07 44					07 48
Bexleyheath	d						07 26			07 31				07 36					07 41	07 46					07 51
Welling	d						07 29			07 34				07 39					07 44	07 49					07 54
Falconwood	d						07 32			07 36				07 41					07 46	07 52					07 56
Eltham	d						07 35			07 39				07 44					07 49	07 55					07 59
Kidbrooke	d						07 38			07 42				07 47					07 52	07 58					08 02
Blackheath	d						07 42			07 47				07 51					07 57	08 02					08 07
Lewisham	d			07 38			07 46		07 48	07 50				07 55		07 57				08 05				08 08	08 11
St Johns	d			07 40					07 50							08 00								08 12	
New Cross	d			07 42					07 53					07 58		08 02								08 14	
Nunhead	d						07 51													08 11					
Peckham Rye	d						07 54													08 13					
Denmark Hill	d						07 59													08 17					
London Victoria	a						08 11													08 29					
Westcombe Park	d	07 32						07 42							07 52							08 02			
Maze Hill	d	07 34						07 44							07 54							08 04			
Greenwich	d	07 37						07 47			07 51				07 57							08 07			
Deptford	a	07 39						07 49							07 59							08 09			
London Bridge	a	07 45		07 47	07 47	07 51		07 57	08 01	08 00	07 57	07 59		08 03	08 05	08 08	08 05				08 13	08 16		08 20	08 20
London Cannon Street	a	07 52		07 54		07 57			08 08		08 03	08 06		08 10	08 12	08 15								08 28	
London Waterloo (East)	a				07 52			08 02		08 06							08 10		08 12		08 18	08 22			08 26
London Charing Cross	a				07 58			08 08		08 12							08 16		08 17		08 24	08 28			08 32
Ebbsfleet International	a																								
Stratford International	a																	07 36							
St Pancras Int'l	a																	07 44							

Table 200

Gillingham and Dartford - London

Mondays to Fridays

29 August to 7 September

Network Diagram - see first Page of Table 200

Station		SE	SE	SE	SE	SE	SE 1	SE	SE	SE	SE	SE	SE	SE	SE	SE	SE	SE	SE	SE	SE 1	SE 1	SE
Gillingham (Kent)	d					07 12	07 19												07 38	07 46	08 03	
Chatham	d					07 16	07 24												07 42	07 50	08 08	
Rochester	d					07 18													07 44		08 11	
Maidstone West	d														07 26							
Strood	d	07 18				07 23									07 42					07 49			
Higham	d	07 23				07 28														07 54			
Gravesend	d	07 31				07 36								07 48	07 52					08 02			
Northfleet	d					07 40								07 52									
Swanscombe	d					07 42								07 54									
Greenhithe for Bluewater	d	07 37				07 45								07 57						08 08			
Stone Crossing	d					07 47								07 59									
Dartford	a	07 42				07 51								08 03						08 12			
	d	07 43		07 45		07 52			07 56				08 02	08 04				08 06		08 13			
Slade Green	d			07 50							07 59					08 00		08 10					08 17
Erith	d			07 52							08 02							08 13					
Belvedere	d			07 55							08 04							08 15					
Abbey Wood	d	07 52		07 58							08 08			08 14				08 18					
Plumstead	d			08 01							08 11							08 21					
Woolwich Arsenal	d	07 57		08 05							08 14			08 19				08 24					
Woolwich Dockyard	d			08 07							08 16							08 27					
Charlton	d	08 03		08 11							08 20			08 24				08 30					
Crayford	d				07 50	07 56													08 10	08 17			
Bexley	d				07 53	07 59													08 13	08 20			
Albany Park	d				07 56	08 02													08 16	08 23			
Sidcup	d				07 59	08 05				08 11									08 19	08 26			
New Eltham	d				08 03	08 09				08 14									08 23	08 30			
Mottingham	d				08 05					08 16									08 25				
Lee	d				08 08					08 19									08 28				
Hither Green	d				08 12					08 22									08 32				
Barnehurst	d		07 53					07 58	08 04				08 09			08 13	08 13						08 24
Bexleyheath	d		07 56					08 01	08 06				08 11			08 16	08 16						08 27
Welling	d		07 59					08 04	08 09				08 14			08 19	08 19						08 30
Falconwood	d		08 01					08 06	08 12				08 17			08 21	08 21						08 32
Eltham	d		08 04					08 09	08 15				08 20			08 24	08 24						08 35
Kidbrooke	d		08 07					08 12	08 18				08 23			08 27	08 27						08 38
Blackheath	d		08 11					08 17	08 22				08 27			08 31	08 31						08 42
Lewisham	d		08 15		08 17				08 25			08 28	08 31			08 35	08 35		08 37				08 46
St Johns	d				08 21							08 30							08 40				
New Cross	d		08 18		08 23							08 32				08 38	08 38		08 42				
Nunhead	d								08 30														08 52
Peckham Rye	d								08 33														08 55
Denmark Hill	d								08 36														09 02
London Victoria	a								08 49														09 11
Westcombe Park	d			08 13							08 22							08 32					
Maze Hill	d			08 15							08 24							08 34					
Greenwich	d	08 11		08 19							08 27			08 31				08 37					
Deptford	a			08 21							08 29							08 39					
London Bridge	a	08 17	08 25	08 27	08 29	08 25	08 09			08 33	08 37	08 41	08 40	08 38		08 43	08 43	08 45	08 49	08 45	08 31	08 49	
London Cannon Street	a	08 23	08 32	08 35	08 36		08 17					08 48		08 44		08 50	08 50	08 52	08 55		08 38	08 57	
London Waterloo (East)	a					08 30		08 32		08 38	08 42		08 46							08 50			
London Charing Cross	a					08 36		08 39		08 44	08 48		08 52							08 56			
Ebbsfleet International	a																						
Stratford International	a														08 06								
St Pancras Int'l	a														08 14								

Table 200

Gillingham and Dartford - London

Mondays to Fridays

29 August to 7 September

Network Diagram - see first Page of Table 200

Station		SE	SE	SE	SE	SE	SE	SE	SE	SE	SE	SE	SE	SE	SE	SE	SE	SE 1	SE	SE	SE	SE
Gillingham (Kent)	d								08 08				08 19					08 24				
Chatham	d								08 12				08 24					08 28				
Rochester	d								08 14				08 26					08 31				
Maidstone West	d						07 56															
Strood	d					07 58	08 12		08 19				08 32									
Higham	d					08 03			08 24													
Gravesend	d					08 17	08 22		08 33			08 06	08 43									
Northfleet	d								08 37			08 10										
Swanscombe	d								08 39			08 12										
Greenhithe for Bluewater	d					08 23			08 42			08 15										
Stone Crossing	d								08 44			08 17										
Dartford	a					08 27			08 49			08 21										
	d					08 29			08 49			08 22		08 24					08 38			08 52
Slade Green	d		08 17									08 27			08 31	08 31				08 39		
Erith	d		08 19												08 33					08 41		
Belvedere	d		08 22												08 36					08 44		
Abbey Wood	d		08 25									08 34			08 39					08 47		
Plumstead	d		08 28												08 42					08 50		
Woolwich Arsenal	d		08 31									08 40			08 45					08 53		
Woolwich Dockyard	d		08 34												08 47					08 56		
Charlton	d		08 37								08 37	08 45			08 50					08 59		
Crayford	d				08 28	08 34			08 54		09 07											
Bexley	d				08 31	08 37			08 57		09 10											
Albany Park	d				08 34	08 40			09 00		09 13											
Sidcup	d	08 31			08 37	08 43			09 03		09 16											
New Eltham	d	08 34			08 41	08 46			09 06		09 19											
Mottingham	d	08 36			08 43	08 49			09 08		09 21											
Lee	d	08 39			08 46	08 52			09 11		09 24											
Hither Green	d	08 42			08 50	08 55		08 59	09 14	09 19	09 28											
Barnehurst	d													08 30		08 37	08 37		08 45			08 59
Bexleyheath	d													08 33		08 40	08 40		08 47			09 01
Welling	d													08 36		08 43	08 43		08 50			09 04
Falconwood	d													08 38		08 45	08 45		08 53			09 07
Eltham	d													08 41		08 48	08 48		08 56			09 10
Kidbrooke	d													08 44		08 51	08 51		08 59			09 13
Blackheath	d													08 48		08 55	08 55		09 02			09 16
Lewisham	d			08 48	08 55			09 04		09 24	09 34			08 52		08 59	08 59		09 06		09 15	09 20
St Johns	d			08 50	08 57			09 07		09 26	09 36					09 01	09 01				09 17	
New Cross	d			08 52	08 59			09 09		09 28	09 38					09 03	09 03				09 19	
Nunhead	d																		09 11			
Peckham Rye	d																		09 14			
Denmark Hill	d																		09 17			
London Victoria	a																		09 29			
Westcombe Park	d		08 39												08 52					09 01		
Maze Hill	d		08 41												08 54					09 03		
Greenwich	d		08 45									08 51			08 58					09 07		
Deptford	a		08 47												09 00					09 09		
London Bridge	a	08 52	08 56	08 57	09 05	09 05		09 17	09 23	09 33	09 44	09 00		09 00	09 07	09 09	09 09	09 11		09 17	09 25	09 29
London Cannon Street	a			09 04	09 12			09 23		09 40	09 51	09 07			09 14	09 18	09 18	09 18			09 32	
London Waterloo (East)	a	08 58	09 02			09 10			09 28					09 05						09 22		09 34
London Charing Cross	a	09 04	09 08			09 16			09 34					09 12						09 28		09 40
Ebbsfleet International	a												08 47									
Stratford International	a						08 36						08 59									
St Pancras Int'l	a						08 44						09 06									

Table 200

Mondays to Fridays

29 August to 7 September

Gillingham and Dartford - London

Network Diagram - see first Page of Table 200

Station		SE	SE	SE	SE	SE	SE	SE	SE	SE		SE	SE	SE	SE	SE	SE	SE	SE	SE		SE	SE	SE	SE
Gillingham (Kent)	d							08 50														08 54	09 20		
Chatham	d							08 54														08 58	09 24		
Rochester	d							08 57														09 00	09 27		
Maidstone West	d																								
Strood	d							09 02														09 05	09 32		
Higham	d																					09 10			
Gravesend	d		09 02				08 48	09 13									09 32					09 18	09 43		
Northfleet	d		09 06														09 36								
Swanscombe	d		09 08														09 38								
Greenhithe for Bluewater	d		09 11				08 53										09 41					09 23			
Stone Crossing	d		09 13														09 43								
Dartford	a		09 17				08 58										09 47					09 28			
	d		09 18				08 58			09 01		09 08			09 22		09 48					09 29			09 31
Slade Green	d	08 47				08 54				09 05			09 15			09 17				09 25					09 35
Erith	d					08 56				09 08			09 18							09 28					09 38
Belvedere	d					08 59				09 10			09 20							09 30					09 40
Abbey Wood	d					09 02	09 07			09 13			09 23							09 33		09 38			09 43
Plumstead	d					09 05				09 16			09 26							09 36					09 46
Woolwich Arsenal	d					09 08	09 12			09 19			09 29							09 39		09 43			09 49
Woolwich Dockyard	d					09 10				09 22			09 32							09 42					09 52
Charlton	d				09 07	09 13	09 17			09 25			09 35						09 40	09 45		09 47			09 55
Crayford	d		09 22		09 37												09 52		10 07						
Bexley	d		09 25		09 40												09 55		10 10						
Albany Park	d		09 28		09 43												09 58		10 13						
Sidcup	d		09 31		09 46												10 01		10 16						
New Eltham	d		09 34		09 49												10 04		10 19						
Mottingham	d		09 36		09 51												10 06		10 21						
Lee	d		09 39		09 54												10 09		10 24						
Hither Green	d		09 42	09 49	09 58												10 12	10 19	10 28						
Barnehurst	d	09a04							09 08			09 16			09 29	09a34								09 38	
Bexleyheath	d								09 10			09 19			09 31									09 40	
Welling	d								09 13			09 22			09 34									09 43	
Falconwood	d								09 16			09 24			09 37									09 46	
Eltham	d								09 19			09 27			09 40									09 49	
Kidbrooke	d								09 22			09 30			09 43									09 52	
Blackheath	d						09 21		09 25			09 34			09 46							09 52		09 55	
Lewisham	d			09 54	10 04		09 26		09 29			09 38		09 45	09 50			10 24	10 34			09 56		09 59	
St Johns	d			09 56	10 06				09 31					09 47				10 26	10 36					10 01	
New Cross	d			09 58	10 08				09 33					09 49				10 28	10 38					10 03	
Nunhead	d											09 43													
Peckham Rye	d											09 45													
Denmark Hill	d											09 49													
London Victoria	a											10 00													
Westcombe Park	d					09 15				09 27			09 37							09 47					09 57
Maze Hill	d					09 17				09 29			09 39							09 49					09 59
Greenwich	d					09 21				09 32			09 42							09 52					10 02
Deptford	a					09 23				09 34			09 44							09 54					10 04
London Bridge	a		09 52	10 04	10 14	09 29	09 34		09 38	09 41			09 50	09 54	09 58		10 22	10 34	10 44	10 00		10 05		10 08	10 11
London Cannon Street	a			10 08	10 19	09 36			09 45	09 48			09 57	10 00				10 38	10 50	10 04				10 13	10 15
London Waterloo (East)	a		09 56				09 39								10 02		10 26					10 09			
London Charing Cross	a		10 00				09 45								10 06		10 30					10 13			
Ebbsfleet International	a							09 17															09 47		
Stratford International	a							09 29															09 59		
St Pancras Int'l	a							09 41															10 07		

Table 200

Mondays to Fridays

29 August to 7 September

Gillingham and Dartford - London

Network Diagram - see first Page of Table 200

Station		SE	SE	SE	SE	SE		SE	SE	SE	SE	SE	SE	SE	SE	SE		SE	SE	SE	SE	SE	SE	SE	SE
Gillingham (Kent)	d												09 24	09 50											
Chatham	d												09 28	09 54											
Rochester	d												09 30	09 57											
Maidstone West	d																								
Strood	d												09 35	10 02											
Higham	d												09 40												
Gravesend	d								10 02				09 48	10 13								10 32			
Northfleet	d								10 06													10 36			
Swanscombe	d								10 08													10 38			
Greenhithe for Bluewater	d								10 11				09 53									10 41			
Stone Crossing	d								10 13													10 43			
Dartford	a								10 17				09 58									10 47			
	d	09 38			09 52				10 18				09 59		10 01	10 08				10 22		10 48			
Slade Green	d		09 45			09 47		09 47				09 55			10 05			10 15			10 17				10 25
Erith	d		09 48									09 58			10 08			10 18							10 28
Belvedere	d		09 50									10 00			10 10			10 20							10 30
Abbey Wood	d		09 53									10 03	10 07		10 13			10 23							10 33
Plumstead	d		09 56									10 06			10 16			10 26							10 36
Woolwich Arsenal	d		09 59									10 09	10 12		10 19			10 29							10 39
Woolwich Dockyard	d		10 02									10 12			10 22			10 32							10 42
Charlton	d		10 05								10 07	10 15	10 17		10 25			10 35						10 37	10 45
Crayford	d								10 22		10 37											10 52		11 07	
Bexley	d								10 25		10 40											10 55		11 10	
Albany Park	d								10 28		10 43											10 58		11 13	
Sidcup	d								10 31		10 46											11 01		11 16	
New Eltham	d								10 34		10 49											11 04		11 19	
Mottingham	d								10 36		10 51											11 06		11 21	
Lee	d								10 39		10 54											11 09		11 24	
Hither Green	d								10 42	10 49	10 58											11 12	11 19	11 28	
Barnehurst	d	09 46			09 59	10a04		10 08								10 16				10 29	10a34				
Bexleyheath	d	09 49			10 01			10 10								10 19				10 31					
Welling	d	09 52			10 04			10 13								10 22				10 34					
Falconwood	d	09 54			10 07			10 16								10 24				10 37					
Eltham	d	09 57			10 10			10 19								10 27				10 40					
Kidbrooke	d	10 00			10 13			10 22								10 30				10 43					
Blackheath	d	10 04			10 16			10 25					10 21			10 34				10 46					
Lewisham	d	10 08		10 14	10 20			10 29		10 54	11 04		10 26			10 38			10 44	10 50			11 24	11 34	
St Johns	d			10 16				10 31		10 56	11 06								10 46				11 26	11 36	
New Cross	d			10 18				10 33		10 58	11 08								10 48				11 28	11 38	
Nunhead	d	10 13														10 43									
Peckham Rye	d	10 15														10 45									
Denmark Hill	d	10 19														10 49									
London Victoria	a	10 28														10 58									
Westcombe Park	d		10 07									10 17			10 27			10 37							10 47
Maze Hill	d		10 09									10 19			10 29			10 39							10 49
Greenwich	d		10 12									10 22			10 32			10 42							10 52
Deptford	a		10 14									10 24			10 34			10 44							10 54
London Bridge	a		10 20	10 24	10 28			10 38	10 52	11 04	11 14	10 30	10 35		10 41			10 50	10 54	10 58		11 22	11 34	11 44	11 00
London Cannon Street	a		10 24	10 28				10 43		11 08	11 19	10 36			10 45			10 54	10 58				11 38	11 49	11 06
London Waterloo (East)	a				10 32				10 56				10 39							11 02		11 26			
London Charing Cross	a				10 36				11 00				10 43							11 06		11 30			
Ebbsfleet International	a													10 16											
Stratford International	a													10 28											
St Pancras Int'l	a													10 39											

Table 200

Gillingham and Dartford - London

Mondays to Fridays

29 August to 7 September

Network Diagram - see first Page of Table 200

Station		SE		SE	SE	SE	SE	SE	SE	SE	SE	SE		SE	SE	SE	SE	SE	SE	SE	SE	SE		SE	SE
Gillingham (Kent) ■	d	09 54		10 20													10 24	10 50							
Chatham ■	d	09 58		10 24													10 28	10 54							
Rochester ■	d	10 00		10 27													10 30	10 57							
Maidstone West	d																								
Strood ■	d	10 05		10 32													10 35	11 02							
Higham	d	10 10															10 40								
Gravesend ■	d	10 18		10 43								11 02					10 48	11 13							
Northfleet	d											11 06													
Swanscombe	d											11 08													
Greenhithe for Bluewater	d	10 23										11 11					10 53								
Stone Crossing	d											11 13													
Dartford ■	a	10 28										11 17					10 58								
	d	10 29				10 31	10 38			10 52		11 18					10 59			11 01	11 08				11 22
Slade Green ■	d					10 35		10 45			10 47					10 55				11 05		11 15			
Erith	d					10 38		10 48								10 58				11 08		11 18			
Belvedere	d					10 40		10 50								11 00				11 10		11 20			
Abbey Wood	d	10 38				10 43		10 53								11 03	11 08			11 13		11 23			
Plumstead	d					10 46		10 56								11 06				11 16		11 26			
Woolwich Arsenal ■	d	10 43				10 49		10 59								11 09	11 13			11 19		11 29			
Woolwich Dockyard	d					10 52		11 02								11 12				11 22		11 32			
Charlton ■	d	10 47				10 55		11 05							11 07	11 15	11 17			11 25		11 35			
Crayford	d											11 22			11 37										
Bexley	d											11 25			11 40										
Albany Park	d											11 28			11 43										
Sidcup ■	d											11 31			11 46										
New Eltham	d											11 34			11 49										
Mottingham	d											11 36			11 51										
Lee	d											11 39			11 54										
Hither Green ■	d											11 42		11 49	11 58										
Barnehurst ■	d				10 38		10 46			10 59	11a04								11 08		11 16				11 29
Bexleyheath	d				10 40		10 49			11 01									11 10		11 19				11 31
Welling	d				10 43		10 52			11 04									11 13		11 22				11 34
Falconwood	d				10 46		10 54			11 07									11 16		11 24				11 37
Eltham	d				10 49		10 57			11 10									11 19		11 27				11 40
Kidbrooke	d				10 52		11 00			11 13									11 22		11 30				11 43
Blackheath ■	d	10 52			10 55		11 04			11 16							11 22		11 25		11 34				11 46
Lewisham ■	d	10 56			10 59		11 08		11 14	11 20				11 54	12 04		11 26		11 29		11 38			11 44	11 50
St Johns	d				11 01				11 16					11 56	12 06				11 31					11 46	
New Cross ■	⊖ d				11 03				11 18					11 58	12 08				11 33					11 48	
Nunhead ■	d						11 13														11 43				
Peckham Rye ■	d						11 15														11 45				
Denmark Hill ■	d						11 19														11 49				
London Victoria ■	⊖ a						11 28														11 58				
Westcombe Park	d					10 57		11 07								11 17				11 27		11 37			
Maze Hill	d					10 59		11 09								11 19				11 29		11 39			
Greenwich ■	d					11 02		11 12								11 22				11 32		11 42			
Deptford	a					11 04		11 14								11 24				11 34		11 44			
London Bridge ■	⊖ a	11 05			11 08	11 11		11 20	11 24	11 28		11 52		12 04	12 14	11 30	11 35		11 38	11 41		11 50		11 54	11 58
London Cannon Street ■	⊖ a				11 13	11 15		11 24	11 28					12 08	12 19	11 36			11 43	11 45		11 54		11 58	
London Waterloo (East) ■	⊖ a	11 09								11 32		11 56					11 39								12 02
London Charing Cross ■	⊖ a	11 13								11 36		12 00					11 43								12 06
Ebbsfleet International	a			10 47														11 17							
Stratford International	⊖ a			10 59														11 32							
St Pancras Int'l ■	⊖ a			11 07														11 40							

Table 200

Gillingham and Dartford - London

Mondays to Fridays

29 August to 7 September

Network Diagram - see first Page of Table 200

Station		SE	SE	SE	SE	SE	SE	SE		SE	SE	SE	SE	SE	SE	SE	SE	SE		SE	SE	SE	SE	SE	SE
Gillingham (Kent) ■	d						10 54	11 20															11 24	11 50	
Chatham ■	d						10 58	11 24															11 28	11 54	
Rochester ■	d						11 00	11 27															11 30	11 57	
Maidstone West	d																								
Strood ■	d						11 05	11 32															11 35	12 02	
Higham	d						11 10																11 40		
Gravesend ■	d		11 32				11 18	11 43										12 02					11 48	12 13	
Northfleet	d		11 36															12 06							
Swanscombe	d		11 38															12 08							
Greenhithe for Bluewater	d		11 41				11 23											12 11					11 53		
Stone Crossing	d		11 43															12 13							
Dartford ■	a		11 47				11 28											12 17					11 58		
	d		11 48				11 29				11 31	11 38			11 52			12 18					11 59		12 01
Slade Green ■	d	11 17				11 25					11 35		11 45			11 47	11 47					11 55			12 05
Erith	d					11 28					11 38		11 48									11 58			12 08
Belvedere	d					11 30					11 40		11 50									12 00			12 10
Abbey Wood	d					11 33	11 38				11 43		11 53									12 03	12 08		12 13
Plumstead	d					11 36					11 46		11 56									12 06			12 16
Woolwich Arsenal ■	d					11 39	11 43				11 49		11 59									12 09	12 13		12 19
Woolwich Dockyard	d					11 42					11 52		12 02									12 12			12 22
Charlton ■	d				11 37	11 45	11 47				11 55		12 05								12 07	12 15	12 17		12 25
Crayford	d		11 52		12 07													12 22			12 37				
Bexley	d		11 55		12 10													12 25			12 40				
Albany Park	d		11 58		12 13													12 28			12 43				
Sidcup ■	d		12 01		12 16													12 31			12 46				
New Eltham	d		12 04		12 19													12 34			12 49				
Mottingham	d		12 06		12 21													12 36			12 51				
Lee	d		12 09		12 24													12 39			12 54				
Hither Green ■	d		12 12	12 19	12 28													12 42		12 49	12 58				
Barnehurst ■	d	11a34								11 38		11 46			11 59	12a04	12 08								
Bexleyheath	d									11 40		11 49			12 01		12 10								
Welling	d									11 43		11 52			12 04		12 13								
Falconwood	d									11 46		11 54			12 07		12 16								
Eltham	d									11 49		11 57			12 10		12 19								
Kidbrooke	d									11 52		12 00			12 13		12 22								
Blackheath ■	d						11 52			11 55		12 04			12 16		12 25						12 22		
Lewisham ■	d			12 24	12 34		11 56			11 59		12 08		12 14	12 20		12 29			12 54	13 04		12 26		
St Johns	d			12 26	12 36					12 01				12 16			12 31			12 56	13 06				
New Cross ■	⊖ d			12 28	12 38					12 03				12 18			12 33			12 58	13 08				
Nunhead ■	d											12 13													
Peckham Rye ■	d											12 15													
Denmark Hill ■	d											12 19													
London Victoria ■	⊖ a											12 28													
Westcombe Park	d					11 47					11 57		12 07									12 17			12 27
Maze Hill	d					11 49					11 59		12 09									12 19			12 29
Greenwich ■	d					11 52					12 02		12 12									12 22			12 32
Deptford	a					11 54					12 04		12 14									12 24			12 34
London Bridge ■	⊖ a		12 22	12 34	12 44	12 00	12 05			12 08	12 11		12 20	12 24	12 28		12 38	12 52		13 04	13 14	12 30	12 35		12 41
London Cannon Street ■	⊖ a			12 38	12 49	12 04				12 13	12 15		12 24	12 28			12 43			13 08	13 19	12 36			12 45
London Waterloo (East) ■	⊖ a		12 26				12 09								12 32			12 56					12 39		
London Charing Cross ■	⊖ a		12 30				12 13								12 36			13 00					12 43		
Ebbsfleet International	a							11 47																12 17	
Stratford International	⊖ a							11 59																12 32	
St Pancras Int'l ■	⊖ a							12 07																12 40	

Table 200

Mondays to Fridays

29 August to 7 September

Gillingham and Dartford - London

Network Diagram - see first Page of Table 200

		SE	SE	SE		SE	SE	SE	SE	SE	SE	SE	SE	SE		SE	SE	SE	SE	SE	SE	SE	SE	SE	
Gillingham (Kent)	d											11 54	12 20												
Chatham	d											11 58	12 24												
Rochester	d											12 00	12 27												
Maidstone West	d																								
Strood	d											12 05	12 32												
Higham	d											12 10													
Gravesend	d							12 32				12 18	12 43								13 02				
Northfleet	d							12 36													13 06				
Swanscombe	d							12 38													13 08				
Greenhithe for Bluewater	d							12 41				12 23									13 11				
Stone Crossing	d							12 43													13 13				
Dartford	a							12 47				12 28									13 17				
	d	12 08				12 22		12 48				12 29		12 31		12 38			12 52		13 18				
Slade Green	d		12 15				12 17				12 25			12 35			12 45			12 47				12 55	
Erith	d		12 18								12 28			12 38			12 48							12 58	
Belvedere	d		12 20								12 30			12 40			12 50							13 00	
Abbey Wood	d		12 23								12 33	12 38		12 43			12 53							13 03	
Plumstead	d		12 26								12 36			12 46			12 56							13 06	
Woolwich Arsenal	d		12 29								12 39	12 43		12 49			12 59							13 09	
Woolwich Dockyard	d		12 32								12 42			12 52			13 02							13 12	
Charlton	d		12 35							12 37	12 45	12 47		12 55			13 05						13 07	13 15	
Crayford	d							12 52		13 07											13 22		13 37		
Bexley	d							12 55		13 10											13 25		13 40		
Albany Park	d							12 58		13 13											13 28		13 43		
Sidcup	d							13 01		13 16											13 31		13 46		
New Eltham	d							13 04		13 19											13 34		13 49		
Mottingham	d							13 06		13 21											13 36		13 51		
Lee	d							13 09		13 24											13 39		13 54		
Hither Green	d							13 12	13 19	13 28											13 42	13 49	13 58		
Barnehurst	d	12 16				12 29	12 38									12 46			12 59	13 08					
Bexleyheath	d	12 19				12 31	12 40									12 49			13 01	13 10					
Welling	d	12 22				12 34	12 43									12 52			13 04	13 13					
Falconwood	d	12 24				12 37	12 46									12 54			13 07	13 16					
Eltham	d	12 27				12 40	12 49									12 57			13 10	13 19					
Kidbrooke	d	12 30				12 43	12 52									13 00			13 13	13 22					
Blackheath	d	12 34				12 46	12 55					12 52				13 04			13 16	13 25					
Lewisham	d	12 38		12 44		12 50	12 59		13 24	13 34		12 56				13 08		13 14	13 20	13 29		13 54	14 04		
St Johns	d			12 46			13 01		13 26	13 36								13 16		13 31		13 56	14 06		
New Cross	d			12 48			13 03		13 28	13 38								13 18		13 33		13 58	14 08		
Nunhead	d	12 43														13 13									
Peckham Rye	d	12 45														13 15									
Denmark Hill	d	12 49														13 19									
London Victoria	a	12 58														13 28									
Westcombe Park	d		12 37								12 47			12 57			13 07							13 17	
Maze Hill	d		12 39								12 49			12 59			13 09							13 19	
Greenwich	d		12 42								12 52			13 02			13 12							13 22	
Deptford	a		12 44								12 54			13 04			13 14							13 24	
London Bridge	a		12 50	12 54		12 58	13 08	13 22	13 34	13 44	13 00	13 05		13 11			13 20	13 24	13 28	13 38	13 52	14 04	14 14	13 30	
London Cannon Street	a		12 54	12 58			13 13		13 38	13 49	13 06			13 15			13 24	13 28		13 43		14 08	14 19	13 36	
London Waterloo (East)	a					13 02		13 26				13 09							13 32		13 56				
London Charing Cross	a					13 06		13 30				13 13							13 36		14 00				
Ebbsfleet International	a												12 47												
Stratford International	a												13 02												
St Pancras Int'l	a												13 10												

Table 200

Mondays to Fridays

29 August to 7 September

Gillingham and Dartford - London

Network Diagram - see first Page of Table 200

		SE	SE	SE	SE	SE	SE	SE	SE	SE		SE	SE	SE	SE	SE	SE	SE	SE	SE		SE	SE	SE	SE
Gillingham (Kent)	d	12 24	12 50												12 54	13 20									
Chatham	d	12 28	12 54												12 58	13 24									
Rochester	d	12 30	12 57												13 00	13 27									
Maidstone West	d																								
Strood	d	12 35	13 02												13 05	13 32									
Higham	d	12 40													13 10										
Gravesend	d	12 48	13 13							13 32					13 18	13 43								14 02	
Northfleet	d									13 36														14 06	
Swanscombe	d									13 38														14 08	
Greenhithe for Bluewater	d	12 53								13 41					13 23									14 11	
Stone Crossing	d									13 43														14 13	
Dartford	a	12 58								13 47					13 28									14 17	
	d	12 59		13 01	13 08			13 22		13 48					13 29		13 31	13 38				13 52		14 18	
Slade Green	d			13 05		13 15			13 17					13 25			13 35		13 45				13 47		
Erith	d			13 08		13 18								13 28			13 38		13 48						
Belvedere	d			13 10		13 20								13 30			13 40		13 50						
Abbey Wood	d	13 08		13 13		13 23								13 33	13 38		13 43		13 53						
Plumstead	d			13 16		13 26								13 36			13 46		13 56						
Woolwich Arsenal	d	13 13		13 19		13 29								13 39	13 43		13 49		13 59						
Woolwich Dockyard	d			13 22		13 32								13 42			13 52		14 02						
Charlton	d	13 17		13 25		13 35							13 37	13 45	13 47		13 55		14 05						
Crayford	d									13 52			14 07											14 22	
Bexley	d									13 55			14 10											14 25	
Albany Park	d									13 58			14 13											14 28	
Sidcup	d									14 01			14 16											14 31	
New Eltham	d									14 04			14 19											14 34	
Mottingham	d									14 06			14 21											14 36	
Lee	d									14 09			14 24											14 39	
Hither Green	d									14 12		14 19	14 28											14 42	14 49
Barnehurst	d				13 16			13 29	13 38									13 46				13 59	14 08		
Bexleyheath	d				13 19			13 31	13 40									13 49				14 01	14 10		
Welling	d				13 22			13 34	13 43									13 52				14 04	14 13		
Falconwood	d				13 24			13 37	13 46									13 54				14 07	14 16		
Eltham	d				13 27			13 40	13 49									13 57				14 10	14 19		
Kidbrooke	d				13 30			13 43	13 52									14 00				14 13	14 22		
Blackheath	d	13 22			13 34			13 46	13 55						13 52			14 04				14 16	14 25		
Lewisham	d	13 26			13 38		13 44	13 50	13 59			14 24	14 34		13 56			14 08		14 14		14 20	14 29		14 54
St Johns	d						13 46		14 01			14 26	14 36							14 16			14 31		14 56
New Cross	d						13 48		14 03			14 28	14 38							14 18			14 33		14 58
Nunhead	d				13 43													14 13							
Peckham Rye	d				13 45													14 15							
Denmark Hill	d				13 49													14 19							
London Victoria	a				13 58													14 28							
Westcombe Park	d			13 27		13 37								13 47			13 57		14 07						
Maze Hill	d			13 29		13 39								13 49			13 59		14 09						
Greenwich	d			13 32		13 42								13 52			14 02		14 12						
Deptford	a			13 34		13 44								13 54			14 04		14 14						
London Bridge	a	13 35		13 41		13 50	13 54	13 58	14 08	14 22		14 34	14 44	14 00	14 05		14 11		14 20	14 24		14 28	14 38	14 52	15 04
London Cannon Street	a			13 45		13 54	13 58		14 13			14 38	14 49	14 06			14 15		14 24	14 28			14 43		15 08
London Waterloo (East)	a	13 39						14 02		14 26					14 09							14 32		14 56	
London Charing Cross	a	13 43						14 06		14 30					14 13							14 36		15 00	
Ebbsfleet International	a		13 17													13 47									
Stratford International	a		13 29													14 02									
St Pancras Int'l	a		13 36													14 10									

Table 200

Gillingham and Dartford - London

Mondays to Fridays

29 August to 7 September

Network Diagram - see first Page of Table 200

		SE	SE	SE	SE	SE		SE	SE	SE	SE	SE	SE	SE	SE	SE		SE	SE	SE	SE	SE	SE	SE	SE
Gillingham (Kent)	d			13 24	13 50													13 54	14 20						
Chatham	d			13 28	13 54													13 58	14 24						
Rochester	d			13 30	13 57													14 00	14 27						
Maidstone West	d																								
Strood	d			13 35	14 02													14 05	14 32						
Higham	d			13 40														14 10							
Gravesend	d			13 48	14 13								14 32					14 18	14 43						
Northfleet	d												14 36												
Swanscombe	d												14 38												
Greenhithe for Bluewater	d			13 53									14 41					14 23							
Stone Crossing	d												14 43												
Dartford	a			13 58									14 47					14 28							
	d			13 59		14 01		14 08			14 22		14 48					14 29		14 31	14 38			14 52	
Slade Green	d		13 55			14 05			14 15			14 17				14 25				14 35		14 45			14 47
Erith	d		13 58			14 08			14 18							14 28				14 38		14 48			
Belvedere	d		14 00			14 10			14 20							14 30				14 40		14 50			
Abbey Wood	d		14 03	14 08		14 13			14 23							14 33		14 38		14 43		14 53			
Plumstead	d		14 06			14 16			14 26							14 36				14 46		14 56			
Woolwich Arsenal	d		14 09	14 13		14 19			14 29							14 39		14 43		14 49		14 59			
Woolwich Dockyard	d		14 12			14 22			14 32							14 42				14 52		15 02			
Charlton	d	14 07	14 15	14 17		14 25			14 35						14 37	14 45		14 47		14 55		15 05			
Crayford	d	14 37											14 52		15 07										
Bexley	d	14 40											14 55		15 10										
Albany Park	d	14 43											14 58		15 13										
Sidcup	d	14 46											15 01		15 16										
New Eltham	d	14 49											15 04		15 19										
Mottingham	d	14 51											15 06		15 21										
Lee	d	14 54											15 09		15 24										
Hither Green	d	14 58											15 12	15 19	15 28										
Barnehurst	d							14 16			14 29	14 38									14 46			14 59	15 08
Bexleyheath	d							14 19			14 31	14 40									14 49			15 01	15 10
Welling	d							14 22			14 34	14 43									14 52			15 04	15 13
Falconwood	d							14 24			14 37	14 46									14 54			15 07	15 16
Eltham	d							14 27			14 40	14 49									14 57			15 10	15 19
Kidbrooke	d							14 30			14 43	14 52									15 00			15 13	15 22
Blackheath	d			14 22				14 34			14 46	14 55						14 52			15 04			15 16	15 25
Lewisham	d	15 04		14 26				14 38		14 44	14 50	14 59		15 24	15 34			14 56			15 08		15 14	15 20	15 29
St Johns	d	15 06								14 46		15 01		15 26	15 36								15 16		15 31
New Cross	d	15 08								14 48		15 03		15 28	15 38								15 18		15 33
Nunhead	d							14 43													15 13				
Peckham Rye	d							14 45													15 15				
Denmark Hill	d							14 49													15 19				
London Victoria	a							14 58													15 28				
Westcombe Park	d		14 17			14 27			14 37							14 47				14 57		15 07			
Maze Hill	d		14 19			14 29			14 39							14 49				14 59		15 09			
Greenwich	d		14 22			14 32			14 42							14 52				15 02		15 12			
Deptford	a		14 24			14 34			14 44							14 54				15 04		15 14			
London Bridge	a	15 14	14 30	14 35		14 41			14 50	14 54	14 58	15 08	15 22	15 34	15 44	15 00		15 05		15 11		15 20	15 24	15 28	15 38
London Cannon Street	a	15 19	14 36			14 45			14 54	14 58		15 13		15 38	15 49	15 06				15 15		15 24	15 28		15 43
London Waterloo (East)	a			14 39							15 02		15 26					15 09						15 32	
London Charing Cross	a			14 43							15 06		15 30					15 13						15 36	
Ebbsfleet International	a				14 17														14 47						
Stratford International	a				14 29														14 59						
St Pancras Int'l	a				14 37														15 07						

Table 200

Gillingham and Dartford - London

Mondays to Fridays

29 August to 7 September

Network Diagram - see first Page of Table 200

		SE		SE	SE	SE	SE	SE	SE	SE	SE	SE		SE	SE	SE	SE	SE	SE	SE	SE	SE		SE	SE
Gillingham (Kent)	d						14 24	14 50													14 54	15 20			
Chatham	d						14 28	14 54													14 58	15 24			
Rochester	d						14 30	14 57													15 00	15 27			
Maidstone West	d																								
Strood	d						14 35	15 02													15 05	15 32			
Higham	d						14 40														15 10				
Gravesend	d	15 02					14 48	15 13									15 32				15 18	15 43			
Northfleet	d	15 06															15 36								
Swanscombe	d	15 08															15 38								
Greenhithe for Bluewater	d	15 11					14 53										15 41				15 23				
Stone Crossing	d	15 13															15 43								
Dartford	a	15 17					14 58										15 47				15 28				
	d	15 18					14 59		15 01	15 08				15 22			15 48				15 29			15 31	15 38
Slade Green	d					14 55			15 05		15 15				15 17	15 17				15 25				15 35	
Erith	d					14 58			15 08		15 18									15 28				15 38	
Belvedere	d					15 00			15 10		15 20									15 30				15 40	
Abbey Wood	d					15 03	15 08		15 13		15 23									15 33	15 38			15 43	
Plumstead	d					15 06			15 16		15 26									15 36				15 46	
Woolwich Arsenal	d					15 09	15 13		15 19		15 29									15 39	15 43			15 49	
Woolwich Dockyard	d					15 12			15 22		15 32									15 42				15 52	
Charlton	d				15 07	15 15	15 17		15 25		15 35								15 37	15 45	15 47			15 55	
Crayford	d	15 22			15 37												15 52		16 07						
Bexley	d	15 25			15 40												15 55		16 10						
Albany Park	d	15 28			15 43												15 58		16 13						
Sidcup	d	15 31			15 46												16 01		16 16						
New Eltham	d	15 34			15 49												16 04		16 19						
Mottingham	d	15 36			15 51												16 06		16 21						
Lee	d	15 39			15 54												16 09		16 24						
Hither Green	d	15 42		15 49	15 58												16 12	16 19	16 28						
Barnehurst	d									15 16				15 29	15a34	15 38									15 46
Bexleyheath	d									15 19				15 31		15 40									15 49
Welling	d									15 22				15 34		15 43									15 52
Falconwood	d									15 24				15 37		15 46									15 54
Eltham	d									15 27				15 40		15 49									15 57
Kidbrooke	d									15 30				15 43		15 52									16 00
Blackheath	d						15 22			15 34				15 46		15 55					15 52				16 04
Lewisham	d			15 54	16 04		15 26			15 38		15 44		15 50		15 59		16 24	16 34		15 56				16 08
St Johns	d			15 56	16 06							15 46				16 01		16 26	16 36						
New Cross	d			15 58	16 08							15 48				16 03		16 28	16 38						
Nunhead	d									15 43															16 13
Peckham Rye	d									15 45															16 15
Denmark Hill	d									15 49															16 19
London Victoria	a									15 58															16 28
Westcombe Park	d					15 17			15 27		15 37									15 47				15 57	
Maze Hill	d					15 19			15 29		15 39									15 49				15 59	
Greenwich	d					15 22			15 32		15 42									15 52				16 02	
Deptford	a					15 24			15 34		15 44									15 54				16 04	
London Bridge	a	15 52		16 04	16 15	15 30	15 35		15 41		15 50	15 54		15 58		16 09	16 22	16 34	16 44	16 00	16 05			16 12	
London Cannon Street	a			16 08	16 19	15 36			15 45		15 54	15 58				16 13		16 38	16 49	16 06				16 16	
London Waterloo (East)	a	15 57					15 39							16 02			16 27				16 09				
London Charing Cross	a	16 01					15 43							16 06			16 31				16 13				
Ebbsfleet International	a							15 17														15 47			
Stratford International	a							15 32														16 05			
St Pancras Int'l	a							15 40														16 15			

Table 200

Mondays to Fridays

29 August to 7 September

Gillingham and Dartford - London

Network Diagram - see first Page of Table 200

		SE	SE	SE	SE	SE	SE	SE		SE	SE	SE	SE	SE	SE	SE	SE	SE		SE	SE	SE	SE	SE	SE
Gillingham (Kent)	d										15 24	15 50												15 54	
Chatham	d										15 28	15 54												15 58	
Rochester	d										15 30	15 57												16 00	
Maidstone West	d																								
Strood	d										15 35	16 02												16 05	
Higham	d										15 40													16 10	
Gravesend	d					16 02					15 48	16 13												16 18	
Northfleet	d					16 06																			
Swanscombe	d					16 08																			
Greenhithe for Bluewater	d					16 11					15 53													16 23	
Stone Crossing	d					16 13																			
Dartford	a					16 17					15 58													16 28	
	d			15 52		16 18					15 59		16 01	16 08			16 22			16 42				16 29	16 31
Slade Green	d	15 45			15 47					15 55			16 05		16 15			16 17					16 25		16 35
Erith	d	15 48								15 58			16 08		16 18								16 28		16 38
Belvedere	d	15 50								16 00			16 10		16 20								16 30		16 40
Abbey Wood	d	15 53								16 03	16 08		16 13		16 23								16 33	16 38	16 43
Plumstead	d	15 56								16 06			16 16		16 26								16 36		16 46
Woolwich Arsenal	d	15 59								16 09	16 13		16 19		16 29								16 39	16 43	16 49
Woolwich Dockyard	d	16 02								16 12			16 22		16 32								16 42		16 52
Charlton	d	16 05						16 07		16 15	16 17		16 25		16 35							16 37	16 45	16 47	16 55
Crayford	d					16 22		16 37												16 46		17 07			
Bexley	d					16 25		16 40												16 49		17 10			
Albany Park	d					16 28		16 43												16 52		17 13			
Sidcup	d					16 31	16 38	16 46												16 55		17 16			
New Eltham	d					16 34	16 41	16 49												16 58		17 19			
Mottingham	d					16 36	16 43	16 51												17 00		17 21			
Lee	d					16 39	16 46	16 54												17 03		17 24			
Hither Green	d					16 42	16 50	17 00												17 07	17 19	17 28			
Barnehurst	d			15 59	16 08									16 16			16 29	16 38							
Bexleyheath	d			16 01	16 10									16 19			16 31	16 40							
Welling	d			16 04	16 13									16 22			16 34	16 43							
Falconwood	d			16 07	16 16									16 24			16 37	16 46							
Eltham	d			16 10	16 19									16 27			16 40	16 49							
Kidbrooke	d			16 13	16 22									16 30			16 43	16 52							
Blackheath	d			16 16	16 25						16 22			16 34			16 46	16 55						16 52	
Lewisham	d		16 14	16 20	16 29			17 05			16 26			16 38		16 44	16 50	16 59			17 24	17 35		16 56	
St Johns	d		16 16		16 31		16 54	17 09								16 46		17 01			17 26	17 37			
New Cross	d		16 18		16 33		16 56	17 11								16 48		17 03			17 28	17 39			
Nunhead	d													16 43											
Peckham Rye	d													16 45											
Denmark Hill	d													16 49											
London Victoria	a													17 01											
Westcombe Park	d	16 07								16 17			16 27		16 37								16 47		16 57
Maze Hill	d	16 09								16 19			16 29		16 39								16 49		16 59
Greenwich	d	16 12								16 22			16 32		16 42								16 52		17 02
Deptford	a	16 14								16 24			16 34		16 44								16 54		17 04
London Bridge	a	16 20	16 24	16 29	16 39	16 52	17 04	17 18		16 30	16 35		16 42		16 50	16 54	16 58	17 09		17 21	17 34	17 45	17 01	17 07	17 13
London Cannon Street	a	16 24	16 28		16 43		17 09	17 24		16 36			16 46		16 54	16 58		17 15			17 38	17 49	17 05	17 11	17 17
London Waterloo (East)	a			16 33		16 56					16 39						17 03			17 28					
London Charing Cross	a			16 37		17 00					16 44						17 07			17 33					
Ebbsfleet International	a											16 17													
Stratford International	a											16 29													
St Pancras Int'l	a											16 36													

Table 200

Mondays to Fridays

29 August to 7 September

Gillingham and Dartford - London

Network Diagram - see first Page of Table 200

		SE	SE	SE		SE	SE	SE	SE	SE	SE	SE	SE	SE		SE	SE	SE	SE	SE	SE	SE	SE	SE	
Gillingham (Kent)	d						16 20			16 24							16 50								
Chatham	d						16 24			16 28							16 54								
Rochester	d						16 27			16 30							16 57								
Maidstone West	d																								
Strood	d						16 32			16 35							17 02								
Higham	d									16 40															
Gravesend	d					16 32	16 43			16 48						17 02	17 13						17 32		
Northfleet	d					16 36										17 06							17 36		
Swanscombe	d					16 38										17 08							17 38		
Greenhithe for Bluewater	d					16 41				16 53						17 11							17 41		
Stone Crossing	d					16 43										17 13							17 43		
Dartford	a					16 48				16 58						17 17							17 47		
	d	16 38				16 52				16 59	17 01	17 08				17 18		17 22					17 48		
Slade Green	d		16 44					16 47	16 55		17 05														
Erith	d		16 46						16 58		17 08														
Belvedere	d		16 49						17 00		17 10														
Abbey Wood	d		16 52						17 03	17 08	17 13														
Plumstead	d		16 55						17 06		17 16														
Woolwich Arsenal	d		16 58						17 09	17 13	17 19														
Woolwich Dockyard	d		17 00						17 12		17 22														
Charlton	d		17 03						17 15	17 17	17 25														
Crayford	d															17 22					17 37		17 52		
Bexley	d															17 25					17 40		17 55		
Albany Park	d															17 28					17 43		17 58		
Sidcup	d															17 31					17 46		18 01		
New Eltham	d															17 34					17 49		18 04		
Mottingham	d															17 36					17 51		18 06		
Lee	d															17 39					17 54		18 09		
Hither Green	d													17 41		17 42			17 53		17 58	18 03	18 12	18 19	
Barnehurst	d	16 46				16 59		17 08				17 16		18 10				17 29		17 38		18 38			
Bexleyheath	d	16 49				17 01		17 10				17 19		18 12				17 31		17 40		18 40			
Welling	d	16 52				17 04		17 13				17 22		18 15				17 34		17 43		18 43			
Falconwood	d	16 54				17 07		17 16				17 24		18 18				17 37		17 46		18 46			
Eltham	d	16 57				17 10		17 19				17 27		18 20				17 40		17 49		18 49			
Kidbrooke	d	17 00				17 13		17 22				17 30		18 23				17 43		17 52		18 52			
Blackheath	d	17 04				17 16		17 25		17 22		17 34						17 46		17 55		18 55			
Lewisham	d	17 08		17 14		17 20		17 30		17 27		17 38	17 44	18 29				17 50		17 59	18 05	18 59		18 24	
St Johns	d			17 16									17 46						17 57		18 07			18 26	
New Cross	d			17 18				17 33					17 48	18 32					17 59	18 02	18 09	19 03		18 28	
Nunhead	d	17 13										17 43													
Peckham Rye	d	17 15										17 45													
Denmark Hill	d	17 19										17 49													
London Victoria	a	17 28										17 59													
Westcombe Park	d		17 05						17 17		17 27														
Maze Hill	d		17 07						17 19		17 29														
Greenwich	d		17 11						17 22		17 32														
Deptford	a		17 13						17 24		17 34														
London Bridge	a		17 21	17 24		17 29		17 39	17 31	17 35	17 42		17 55	18 38		17 53		18 00	18 06	18 09	18 16	19 08	18 22	18 34	
London Cannon Street	a		17 26	17 29				17 44	17 36		17 46		17 59	18 42				18 04	18 11	18 13	18 20	19 13		18 38	
London Waterloo (East)	a					17 34				17 40						17 58							18 27		
London Charing Cross	a					17 38				17 44						18 03							18 31		
Ebbsfleet International	a						16 47										17 17								
Stratford International	a						17 02										17 28								
St Pancras Int'l	a						17 09										17 38								

Table 200

Gillingham and Dartford - London

Mondays to Fridays

29 August to 7 September

Network Diagram - see first Page of Table 200

		SE	SE	SE	SE	SE	SE	SE	SE	SE		SE	SE	SE	SE	SE	SE	SE	SE	SE		SE	SE	SE	SE
Gillingham (Kent)	d				16 54	17 20									17 24									17 50	
Chatham	d				16 58	17 24									17 28									17 54	
Rochester	d				17 00	17 27									17 30									17 57	
Maidstone West	d																								
Strood	d				17 05	17 32									17 35									18 02	
Higham	d				17 10										17 40										
Gravesend	d				17 18	17 43									17 48								18 02	18 13	
Northfleet	d																						18 06		
Swanscombe	d																						18 08		
Greenhithe for Bluewater	d				17 23										17 53								18 11		
Stone Crossing	d																						18 13		
Dartford	a				17 28										17 58								18 17		
	d				17 29			17 31	17 38				17 52		17 59	18 01		18 08					18 18		18 22
Slade Green	d		17 15	17 25			17 29	17 35		17 45				17 55		18 05			18 15						
Erith	d		17 18	17 28				17 38		17 48				17 57		18 08			18 18						
Belvedere	d		17 20	17 30				17 40		17 50				18 00		18 10			18 20						
Abbey Wood	d		17 23	17 33	17 38			17 43		17 53				18 03	18 08	18 13			18 23						
Plumstead	d		17 26	17 36				17 46		17 56				18 06		18 16			18 26						
Woolwich Arsenal	d		17 29	17 39	17 43			17 49		17 59				18 09	18 13	18 19			18 29						
Woolwich Dockyard	d		17 32	17 42				17 52		18 02				18 11		18 22			18 32						
Charlton	d	17 30	17 35	17 45	17 47			17 55		18 05				18 14	18 17	18 25			18 35						
Crayford	d	18 01																					18 22		
Bexley	d	18 04																					18 25		
Albany Park	d	18 07																					18 28		
Sidcup	d	18 10															18 20						18 31		
New Eltham	d	18 13															18 23						18 34		
Mottingham	d	18 15																					18 36		
Lee	d	18 18																					18 39		
Hither Green	d	18 21															18 28					18 35	18 42		
Barnehurst	d						17 38		17 46				17 59					18 16				19 08			18 29
Bexleyheath	d						17 40		17 49				18 01					18 19				19 10			18 31
Welling	d						17 43		17 52				18 04					18 22				19 13			18 34
Falconwood	d						17 46		17 54				18 07					18 24				19 16			18 37
Eltham	d						17 49		17 57				18 10					18 27				19 19			18 40
Kidbrooke	d						17 52		18 00				18 13					18 30				19 22			18 43
Blackheath	d				17 52		17 55		18 04				18 16		18 22			18 34				19 25			18 46
Lewisham	d				17 56		17 59		18 08			18 14	18 20		18 26		18 35	18 38		18 45		19 29			18 50
St Johns	d											18 16					18 37			18 47					
New Cross ⊖	d						18 02					18 18					18 39			18 49		19 32			
Nunhead	d								18 13									18 43							
Peckham Rye	d								18 15									18 45							
Denmark Hill	d								18 19									18 49							
London Victoria ⊖	a								18 29									18 58							
Westcombe Park	d		17 37	17 47				17 57		18 07				18 16		18 27			18 37						
Maze Hill	d		17 39	17 49				17 59		18 09				18 18		18 29			18 39						
Greenwich	d		17 42	17 52				18 02		18 12				18 22		18 32			18 42						
Deptford	a		17 44	17 54				18 04		18 14				18 24		18 34			18 44						
London Bridge ⊖	a	18 33	17 52	18 03	18 04		18 09	18 13		18 20		18 24	18 28	18 31	18 35	18 43	18 46		18 50	18 55		19 38	18 52		18 58
London Cannon Street ⊖	a		17 56	18 07			18 13	18 17		18 24		18 29		18 35		18 47	18 51		18 54	18 59		19 43			
London Waterloo (East) ⊖	a	18 37			18 08								18 32		18 41								18 57		19 02
London Charing Cross ⊖	a	18 41			18 12								18 37		18 45								19 01		19 06
Ebbsfleet International	a					17 47																		18 17	
Stratford International ⊖	a					17 58																		18 29	
St Pancras Int'l ⊖	a					18 08																		18 37	

Table 200

Gillingham and Dartford - London

Mondays to Fridays

29 August to 7 September

Network Diagram - see first Page of Table 200

		SE	SE	SE	SE	SE		SE	SE	SE	SE	SE	SE	SE	SE	SE		SE	SE	SE	SE	SE	SE	SE	SE
Gillingham (Kent)	d								17 54	18 20						18 24					18 50			18 54	
Chatham	d								17 58	18 24						18 28					18 54			18 58	
Rochester	d								18 00	18 27						18 30					18 57			19 00	
Maidstone West	d																								
Strood	d								18 05	18 32						18 35					19 02			19 05	
Higham	d								18 10							18 40								19 10	
Gravesend	d			18 32					18 18	18 43						18 48				19 02	19 13			19 18	
Northfleet	d			18 36																19 06					
Swanscombe	d			18 38																19 08					
Greenhithe for Bluewater	d			18 41					18 23							18 53				19 11				19 23	
Stone Crossing	d			18 43																19 13					
Dartford	a			18 47					18 28							18 58				19 17				19 28	
	d			18 48					18 29		18 31	18 38			18 52	18 59			19 01	19 18			19 22	19 29	19 31
Slade Green	d							18 25			18 35			18 51					19 05			19 20			19 35
Erith	d							18 28			18 38			18 53					19 08			19 23			19 38
Belvedere	d							18 30			18 40			18 56					19 10			19 25			19 40
Abbey Wood	d							18 33	18 38		18 43			18 59		19 08			19 13			19 28		19 38	19 43
Plumstead	d							18 36			18 46			19 02					19 16			19 31			19 46
Woolwich Arsenal	d							18 39	18 43		18 49			19 05		19 13			19 19			19 34		19 43	19 49
Woolwich Dockyard	d							18 42			18 52			19 07					19 22			19 37			19 52
Charlton	d					18 37		18 45	18 47		18 55			19 10		19 17			19 25			19 40		19 47	19 55
Crayford	d		18 37	18 52		19 07														19 22					
Bexley	d		18 40	18 55		19 10														19 25					
Albany Park	d		18 43	18 58		19 13														19 28					
Sidcup	d		18 46	19 01		19 16														19 31					
New Eltham	d		18 49	19 04		19 19														19 34					
Mottingham	d		18 51	19 06		19 21														19 36					
Lee	d		18 54	19 09		19 24														19 39					
Hither Green	d	18 49	18 59	19 12	19 19	19 28														19 42					
Barnehurst	d											18 46			18 59			19 08					19 30		
Bexleyheath	d											18 49			19 01			19 10					19 32		
Welling	d											18 52			19 04			19 13					19 35		
Falconwood	d											18 54			19 07			19 16					19 38		
Eltham	d											18 57			19 10			19 19					19 41		
Kidbrooke	d											19 00			19 13			19 22					19 44		
Blackheath	d								18 52			19 04			19 16	19 22		19 25					19 48	19 52	
Lewisham	d	18 54	19 05		19 24	19 34			18 56			19 08	19 14		19 20	19 26		19 29		19 48			19 52	19 56	
St Johns	d	18 56	19 07		19 26	19 36							19 16												
New Cross ⊖	d	18 58	19 09		19 28	19 38							19 18					19 32		19 51			19 56		
Nunhead	d											19 13													
Peckham Rye	d											19 15													
Denmark Hill	d											19 19													
London Victoria ⊖	a											19 28													
Westcombe Park	d							18 47			18 57			19 12					19 27			19 42			19 57
Maze Hill	d							18 49			18 59			19 14					19 29			19 44			19 59
Greenwich	d							18 52			19 02			19 18					19 32			19 47			20 02
Deptford	a							18 54			19 04			19 20					19 34			19 49			20 04
London Bridge ⊖	a	19 04	19 15	19 22	19 34	19 44		19 00	19 05		19 11		19 24	19 27	19 28	19 35		19 38	19 41	19 57		19 59	20 03	20 06	20 11
London Cannon Street ⊖	a	19 10	19 20		19 38	19 49		19 06			19 16		19 28	19 33				19 43	19 45			20 03			20 15
London Waterloo (East) ⊖	a			19 26					19 09						19 32	19 39				20 02			20 08	20 11	
London Charing Cross ⊖	a			19 30					19 13						19 36	19 43				20 06			20 12	20 14	
Ebbsfleet International	a									18 47											19 17				
Stratford International ⊖	a									19 02											19 28				
St Pancras Int'l ⊖	a									19 10											19 39				

Table 200

Gillingham and Dartford - London

Mondays to Fridays

29 August to 7 September

Network Diagram - see first Page of Table 200

Station		SE		SE	SE	SE	SE	SE	SE	SE	SE	SE		SE	SE	SE	SE	SE	SE	SE	SE	SE		SE	SE
Gillingham (Kent)	d						19 24				19 50			19 54				20 20		20 24					20 50
Chatham	d						19 28				19 54			19 58				20 24		20 28					20 54
Rochester	d						19 30				19 57			20 00				20 27		20 30					20 57
Maidstone West	d			19 13																					
Strood	d			19 32			19 35				20 02			20 05				20 32		20 35					21 02
Higham	d						19 40							20 10						20 40					
Gravesend	d	19 32		19 43			19 48			20 02	20 13			20 18			20 32	20 43		20 48				21 02	21 13
Northfleet	d	19 36								20 06							20 36							21 06	
Swanscombe	d	19 38								20 08							20 38							21 08	
Greenhithe for Bluewater	d	19 41					19 53			20 11				20 23			20 41			20 53				21 11	
Stone Crossing	d	19 43								20 13							20 43							21 13	
Dartford	a	19 47					19 58			20 17				20 28			20 47			20 58				21 17	
	d	19 48				19 55	19 59	20 01	20 16	20 18		20 25		20 29	20 31	20 46	20 48		20 55	20 59	21 01	21 16		21 18	
Slade Green	d				19 50			20 05	20 20						20 35	20 50					21 05	21 20			
Erith	d				19 53			20 08	20 23						20 38	20 53					21 08	21 23			
Belvedere	d				19 55			20 10	20 25						20 40	20 55					21 10	21 25			
Abbey Wood	d				19 58		20 08	20 13	20 28					20 38	20 43	20 58				21 08	21 13	21 28			
Plumstead	d				20 01			20 16	20 31						20 46	21 01					21 16	21 31			
Woolwich Arsenal	d				20 04		20 13	20 19	20 34					20 43	20 49	21 04				21 13	21 19	21 34			
Woolwich Dockyard	d				20 07			20 22	20 37						20 52	21 07					21 22	21 37			
Charlton	d				20 10		20 17	20 25	20 40					20 47	20 55	21 10				21 17	21 25	21 40			
Crayford	d	19 52								20 22							20 52							21 22	
Bexley	d	19 55								20 25							20 55							21 25	
Albany Park	d	19 58								20 28							20 58							21 28	
Sidcup	d	20 01								20 31							21 01							21 31	
New Eltham	d	20 04								20 34							21 04							21 34	
Mottingham	d	20 06								20 36							21 06							21 36	
Lee	d	20 09								20 39							21 09							21 39	
Hither Green	d	20 12								20 42							21 12							21 42	
Barnehurst	d					20 02						20 32							21 02						
Bexleyheath	d					20 04						20 34							21 04						
Welling	d					20 07						20 37							21 07						
Falconwood	d					20 10						20 40							21 10						
Eltham	d					20 12						20 42							21 12						
Kidbrooke	d					20 15						20 45							21 15						
Blackheath	d					20 19	20 22					20 49		20 52					21 19	21 22					
Lewisham	d	20 18				20 22	20 26			20 48		20 53		20 56			21 18		21 23	21 26				21 48	
St Johns	d																								
New Cross	d	20 21				20 26				20 51		20 56					21 21		21 26					21 51	
Nunhead	d																								
Peckham Rye	d																								
Denmark Hill	d																								
London Victoria	a																								
Westcombe Park	d				20 12			20 27	20 42						20 57	21 12					21 27	21 42			
Maze Hill	d				20 14			20 29	20 44						20 59	21 14					21 29	21 44			
Greenwich	d				20 17			20 32	20 47						21 02	21 17					21 32	21 47			
Deptford	a				20 19			20 34	20 49						21 04	21 19					21 34	21 49			
London Bridge	a	20 27			20 27	20 33	20 36	20 41	20 57	20 57		21 03		21 06	21 11	21 27	21 27		21 33	21 36	21 41	21 57		21 57	
London Cannon Street	a				20 31			20 45																	
London Waterloo (East)	a	20 32				20 38	20 40			21 02		21 08		21 10	21 15		21 32		21 38	21 40	21 45			22 02	
London Charing Cross	a	20 36				20 42	20 44			21 06		21 12		21 14	21 19		21 36		21 42	21 44	21 49			22 06	
Ebbsfleet International	a			19 47							20 17							20 47							21 17
Stratford International	a			20 01							20 28							21 02							21 29
St Pancras Int'l	a			20 14							20 38							21 10							21 36

Table 200

Gillingham and Dartford - London

Mondays to Fridays

29 August to 7 September

Network Diagram - see first Page of Table 200

Station		SE	SE	SE	SE	SE	SE	SE		SE	SE	SE	SE	SE	SE	SE	SE	SE		SE	SE	SE	SE		
Gillingham (Kent)	d		20 54				21 20			21 24			21 50		21 54			22 20			22 24		22 54		
Chatham	d		20 58				21 24			21 28			21 54		21 58			22 24			22 28		22 58		
Rochester	d		21 00				21 27			21 30			21 57		22 00			22 27			22 30		23 00		
Maidstone West	d																								
Strood	d		21 05				21 32			21 35			22 02		22 05			22 32			22 35		23 05		
Higham	d		21 10							21 40					22 10						22 40		23 10		
Gravesend	d		21 18			21 32	21 43			21 48		22 02	22 13		22 18		22 32	22 43			22 48		23 18		
Northfleet	d					21 36						22 06					22 36								
Swanscombe	d					21 38						22 08					22 38								
Greenhithe for Bluewater	d		21 23			21 41				21 53		22 11			22 23		22 41				22 53		23 23		
Stone Crossing	d					21 43						22 13					22 43								
Dartford	a		21 28			21 47				21 58		22 17			22 28		22 47				22 58		23 28		
	d	21 25	21 29	21 31	21 46	21 48		21 55		21 59	22 01	22 18		22 25	22 29	22 31	22 48			22 55	22 59	23 01			
Slade Green	d			21 35	21 50						22 05					22 35						23 05			
Erith	d			21 38	21 53						22 08					22 38						23 08			
Belvedere	d			21 40	21 55						22 10					22 40						23 10			
Abbey Wood	d		21 38	21 43	21 58					22 08	22 13				22 38	22 43					23 08	23 13			
Plumstead	d			21 46	22 01						22 16					22 46						23 16			
Woolwich Arsenal	d		21 43	21 49	22 04					22 13	22 19				22 43	22 49					23 13	23 19			
Woolwich Dockyard	d			21 52	22 07						22 22					22 52						23 22			
Charlton	d		21 47	21 55	22 10					22 17	22 25				22 47	22 55					23 17	23 25			
Crayford	d					21 52						22 22					22 52								
Bexley	d					21 55						22 25					22 55								
Albany Park	d					21 58						22 28					22 58								
Sidcup	d					22 01						22 31					23 01								
New Eltham	d					22 04						22 34					23 04								
Mottingham	d					22 06						22 36					23 06								
Lee	d					22 09						22 39					23 09								
Hither Green	d					22 12						22 42					23 12								
Barnehurst	d	21 32						22 02						22 32						23 02					
Bexleyheath	d	21 34						22 04						22 34						23 04					
Welling	d	21 37						22 07						22 37						23 07					
Falconwood	d	21 40						22 10						22 40						23 10					
Eltham	d	21 42						22 12						22 42						23 12					
Kidbrooke	d	21 45						22 15						22 45						23 15					
Blackheath	d	21 49	21 52					22 19		22 22				22 49	22 52					23 19	23 22				
Lewisham	d	21 53	21 56			22 18		22 23		22 26		22 48		22 53	22 56		23 18			23 23	23 26				
St Johns	d																								
New Cross	d	21 56				22 21		22 26				22 51		22 56			23 21			23 26					
Nunhead	d																								
Peckham Rye	d																								
Denmark Hill	d																								
London Victoria	a																								
Westcombe Park	d			21 57	22 12						22 27					22 57						23 27			
Maze Hill	d			21 59	22 14						22 29					22 59						23 29			
Greenwich	d			22 02	22 17						22 32					23 02						23 32			
Deptford	a			22 04	22 19						22 34					23 04						23 34			
London Bridge	a	22 01	22 05	22 11	22 27	22 27		22 31		22 35	22 41	22 57		23 01	23 05	23 11	23 27			23 31	23 35	23 41			
London Cannon Street	a																								
London Waterloo (East)	a	22 06	22 09	22 15		22 32		22 36		22 39	22 45	23 02		23 06	23 09	23 15	23 32			23 36	23 39	23 45			
London Charing Cross	a	22 10	22 13	22 19		22 36		22 40		22 43	22 49	23 06		23 10	23 13	23 19	23 36			23 40	23 43	23 49			
Ebbsfleet International	a						21 47						22 17					22 47							
Stratford International	a						21 59						22 28					22 59							
St Pancras Int'l	a						22 07						22 35					23 07							

Table 200

Gillingham and Dartford - London

Saturdays

until 21 July, 18 Aug and from 15 Sep

Network Diagram - see first Page of Table 200

		SE	SE	SE	SE	SE	SE	SE	SE	SE		SE	SE	SE	SE	SE	SE A	SE B	SE	SE		SE	SE	SE A	SE B
Gillingham (Kent)	d				04 48				05 18				05 50		05 54							06 24			
Chatham	d				04 52				05 22				05 54		05 58							06 28			
Rochester	d				04 54				05 24				05 57		06 00							06 30			
Maidstone West	d																								
Strood	d				04 59				05 29				06 02		06 05							06 35			
Higham	d				05 04				05 34						06 10							06 40			
Gravesend	d				05 12				05 42			06 02	06 13		06 18				06 32			06 48			
Northfleet	d				05 15				05 45			06 06							06 36						
Swanscombe	d				05 17				05 47			06 08							06 38						
Greenhithe for Bluewater	d				05 21				05 51			06 11			06 23				06 41			06 53			
Stone Crossing	d				05 23				05 53			06 13							06 43						
Dartford	a				05 27				05 57			06 17			06 28				06 47			06 58			
	d	05 05	05 18	05 22	05 29	05 35	05 48	05 52	05 59	06 05		06 18		06 22	06 29	06 35	06 38	06 38	06 48	06 52		06 59	07 01	07 08	07 08
Slade Green	d	05 10				05 40				06 10						06 40							07 05		
Erith	d	05 12				05 42				06 12						06 42							07 08		
Belvedere	d	05 15				05 45				06 15						06 45							07 10		
Abbey Wood	d	05 18			05 38	05 48			06 08	06 18					06 38	06 48						07 08	07 13		
Plumstead	d	05 21				05 51				06 21						06 51							07 16		
Woolwich Arsenal	d	05 24			05 43	05 54			06 13	06 24					06 43	06 54						07 13	07 19		
Woolwich Dockyard	d	05 26				05 56				06 26						06 56							07 22		
Charlton	d	05 29			05 47	05 59			06 17	06 29					06 47	06 59						07 17	07 25		
Crayford	d		05 22				05 52					06 22							06 52						
Bexley	d		05 25				05 55					06 25							06 55						
Albany Park	d		05 28				05 58					06 28							06 58						
Sidcup	d		05 31				06 01					06 31							07 01						
New Eltham	d		05 34				06 04					06 34							07 04						
Mottingham	d		05 36				06 06					06 36							07 06						
Lee	d		05 39				06 09					06 39							07 09						
Hither Green	d		05 42				06 12					06 42							07 12						
Barnehurst	d			05 29				05 59						06 29			06 46	06 46		06 59				07 16	07 16
Bexleyheath	d			05 31				06 01						06 31			06 49	06 49		07 01				07 19	07 19
Welling	d			05 34				06 04						06 34			06 52	06 52		07 04				07 22	07 22
Falconwood	d			05 37				06 07						06 37			06 54	06 54		07 07				07 24	07 24
Eltham	d			05 40				06 10						06 40			06 57	06 57		07 10				07 27	07 27
Kidbrooke	d			05 43				06 13						06 43			07 00	07 00		07 13				07 30	07 30
Blackheath	d			05 46	05 52			06 16	06 22					06 46	06 52		07 04	07 04		07 16		07 22		07 34	07 34
Lewisham	d		05 48	05 50	05 56		06 18	06 20	06 26			06 48		06 50	06 56		07 08	07 08	07 18	07 20		07 26		07 38	07 38
St Johns	d																								
New Cross	d		05 51				06 21					06 51							07 21						
Nunhead	d																07 13	07 15						07 43	07 45
Peckham Rye	d																07 15	07 17						07 45	07 47
Denmark Hill	d																07 19	07 21						07 49	07 51
London Victoria	a																07 28	07 30						07 58	08 00
Westcombe Park	d	05 31				06 01				06 31						07 01							07 27		
Maze Hill	d	05 33				06 03				06 33						07 03							07 29		
Greenwich	d	05 37				06 07				06 37						07 07							07 32		
Deptford	a	05 39				06 09				06 39						07 09							07 34		
London Bridge	a	05 45	05 56	05 59	06 05	06 15	06 26	06 29	06 35	06 45		06 56		06 59	07 05	07 15			07 26	07 29		07 35	07 41		
London Cannon Street	a																						07 45		
London Waterloo (East)	a	05 49	06 01	06 03	06 09	06 19	06 31	06 33	06 39	06 49		07 01		07 03	07 09	07 19			07 31	07 33		07 39			
London Charing Cross	a	05 53	06 05	06 07	06 13	06 25	06 35	06 37	06 43	06 55		07 05		07 07	07 13	07 25			07 35	07 40		07 43			
Ebbsfleet International	a												06 17												
Stratford International	a												06 29												
St Pancras Int'l	a												06 36												

A not 19 May

B 19 May

Table 200

Gillingham and Dartford - London

Saturdays

until 21 July, 18 Aug and from 15 Sep

Network Diagram - see first Page of Table 200

		SE	SE	SE	SE	SE		SE	SE	SE	SE	SE A	SE B	SE	SE	SE		SE	SE	SE	SE	SE	SE	SE	SE
Gillingham (Kent)	d		06 50					06 54								07 20						07 24			
Chatham	d		06 54					06 58								07 24						07 28			
Rochester	d		06 57					07 00								07 27						07 30			
Maidstone West	d																								
Strood	d		07 02					07 05								07 32						07 35			
Higham	d							07 10														07 40			
Gravesend	d	07 02	07 13					07 18							07 32	07 43						07 48			
Northfleet	d	07 06													07 36										
Swanscombe	d	07 08													07 38										
Greenhithe for Bluewater	d	07 11						07 23							07 41							07 53			
Stone Crossing	d	07 13													07 43										
Dartford	a	07 17						07 28							07 47							07 58			
	d	07 18		07 22				07 29		07 31		07 38	07 38		07 48				07 52			07 59		08 01	
Slade Green	d				07 25					07 35				07 45						07 55				08 05	
Erith	d				07 28					07 38				07 48						07 58				08 08	
Belvedere	d				07 30					07 40				07 50						08 00				08 10	
Abbey Wood	d				07 33			07 38		07 43				07 53						08 03		08 08		08 13	
Plumstead	d				07 36					07 46				07 56						08 06				08 16	
Woolwich Arsenal	d				07 39			07 43		07 49				07 59						08 09		08 13		08 19	
Woolwich Dockyard	d				07 42					07 52				08 02						08 12				08 22	
Charlton	d				07 45			07 47		07 55				08 05						08 15		08 17		08 25	
Crayford	d	07 22									07 37				07 52										08 07
Bexley	d	07 25									07 40				07 55										08 10
Albany Park	d	07 28									07 43				07 58										08 13
Sidcup	d	07 31									07 46				08 01										08 16
New Eltham	d	07 34									07 49				08 04										08 19
Mottingham	d	07 36									07 51				08 06										08 21
Lee	d	07 39									07 54				08 09										08 24
Hither Green	d	07 42				07 49					07 58				08 12						08 19				08 28
Barnehurst	d			07 29					07 38			07 46	07 46						07 59				08 08		
Bexleyheath	d			07 31					07 40			07 49	07 49						08 01				08 10		
Welling	d			07 34					07 43			07 52	07 52						08 04				08 13		
Falconwood	d			07 37					07 46			07 54	07 54						08 07				08 16		
Eltham	d			07 40					07 49			07 57	07 57						08 10				08 19		
Kidbrooke	d			07 43					07 52			08 00	08 00						08 13				08 22		
Blackheath	d			07 46				07 52	07 55			08 04	08 04						08 16			08 22	08 25		
Lewisham	d			07 50		07 54		07 56	07 59		08 04	08 08	08 08					08 14	08 20		08 24	08 26	08 29		08 34
St Johns	d					07 56			08 01		08 06							08 16			08 26		08 31		08 36
New Cross	d					07 58			08 03		08 08							08 18			08 28		08 33		08 38
Nunhead	d											08 13	08 15												
Peckham Rye	d											08 15	08 17												
Denmark Hill	d											08 19	08 21												
London Victoria	a											08 28	08 30												
Westcombe Park	d				07 47					07 57				08 07						08 17				08 27	
Maze Hill	d				07 49					07 59				08 09						08 19				08 29	
Greenwich	d				07 52					08 02				08 12						08 22				08 32	
Deptford	a				07 54					08 04				08 14						08 24				08 34	
London Bridge	a	07 52		07 58	08 00	08 04		08 05	08 08	08 11	08 14			08 20	08 22			08 24	08 28	08 30	08 34	08 35	08 38	08 41	08 44
London Cannon Street	a				08 04	08 08			08 13	08 15	08 19			08 24				08 28		08 34	08 38		08 43	08 45	08 49
London Waterloo (East)	a	07 56		08 02				08 09							08 26				08 32			08 39			
London Charing Cross	a	08 00		08 06				08 13							08 30				08 36			08 43			
Ebbsfleet International	a		07 17													07 47									
Stratford International	a		07 29													07 59									
St Pancras Int'l	a		07 36													08 06									

A not 19 May

B 19 May

Table 200

Saturdays

until 21 July, 18 Aug and from 15 Sep

Gillingham and Dartford - London

Network Diagram - see first Page of Table 200

		SE A		SE B	SE	SE	SE	SE	SE	SE	SE	SE		SE	SE	SE	SE	SE	SE	SE	SE A	SE B		SE	SE
Gillingham (Kent)	d						07 50										07 54	08 20							
Chatham	d						07 54										07 58	08 24							
Rochester	d						07 57										08 00	08 27							
Maidstone West	d																								
Strood	d						08 02										08 05	08 32							
Higham	d																08 10								
Gravesend	d					08 02	08 13					08 32					08 18	08 43							
Northfleet	d					08 06						08 36													
Swanscombe	d					08 08						08 38													
Greenhithe for Bluewater	d					08 11						08 41					08 23								
Stone Crossing	d					08 13						08 43													
Dartford	a					08 17						08 47					08 28								
	d	08 08		08 08		08 18			08 22			08 48					08 29			08 31	08 38	08 38			
Slade Green	d				08 15											08 25				08 35				08 45	
Erith	d				08 18											08 28				08 38				08 48	
Belvedere	d				08 20											08 30				08 40				08 50	
Abbey Wood	d				08 23											08 33	08 38			08 43				08 53	
Plumstead	d				08 26											08 36				08 46				08 56	
Woolwich Arsenal	d				08 29											08 39	08 43			08 49				08 59	
Woolwich Dockyard	d				08 32											08 42				08 52				09 02	
Charlton	d				08 35										08 37	08 45	08 47			08 55				09 05	
Crayford	d					08 22					08 37	08 52			09 07										
Bexley	d					08 25					08 40	08 55			09 10										
Albany Park	d					08 28					08 43	08 58			09 13										
Sidcup	d					08 31					08 46	09 01			09 16										
New Eltham	d					08 34					08 49	09 04			09 19										
Mottingham	d					08 36					08 51	09 06			09 21										
Lee	d					08 39					08 54	09 09			09 24										
Hither Green	d					08 42				08 49	08 58	09 12		09 19	09 28										
Barnehurst	d	08 16		08 16					08 29										08 38		08 46	08 46			
Bexleyheath	d	08 19		08 19					08 31										08 40		08 49	08 49			
Welling	d	08 22		08 22					08 34										08 43		08 52	08 52			
Falconwood	d	08 24		08 24					08 37										08 46		08 54	08 54			
Eltham	d	08 27		08 27					08 40										08 49		08 57	08 57			
Kidbrooke	d	08 30		08 30					08 43										08 52		09 00	09 00			
Blackheath	d	08 34		08 34					08 46								08 52		08 55		09 04	09 04			
Lewisham	d	08 38		08 38				08 44	08 50	08 54	09 04			09 24	09 34		08 56		08 59		09 08	09 08			09 14
St Johns	d							08 46		08 56	09 06			09 26	09 36				09 01						09 16
New Cross	d							08 48		08 58	09 08			09 28	09 38				09 03						09 18
Nunhead	d	08 43		08 45																	09 13	09 15			
Peckham Rye	d	08 45		08 47																	09 15	09 17			
Denmark Hill	d	08 49		08 51																	09 19	09 21			
London Victoria	a	08 58		09 00																	09 28	09 30			
Westcombe Park	d				08 37											08 47				08 57				09 07	
Maze Hill	d				08 39											08 49				08 59				09 09	
Greenwich	d				08 42											08 52				09 02				09 12	
Deptford	a				08 44											08 54				09 04				09 14	
London Bridge	a				08 50	08 52		08 54	08 58	09 04	09 14	09 22		09 34	09 44	09 00	09 05		09 08	09 11				09 20	09 24
London Cannon Street	a				08 54			08 58		09 08	09 19			09 38	09 49	09 04			09 13	09 15				09 24	09 28
London Waterloo (East)	a					08 56			09 02			09 26					09 09								
London Charing Cross	a					09 00			09 06			09 30					09 13								
Ebbsfleet International	a						08 17											08 47							
Stratford International	a						08 29											08 59							
St Pancras Int'l	a						08 36											09 06							

A not 19 May

B 19 May

Table 200

Saturdays

until 21 July, 18 Aug and from 15 Sep

Gillingham and Dartford - London

Network Diagram - see first Page of Table 200

		SE	SE	SE	SE	SE	SE	SE		SE	SE	SE A	SE B	SE	SE	SE	SE	SE		SE	SE	SE	SE	SE	SE
Gillingham (Kent)	d							08 24		08 50													08 54	09 20	
Chatham	d							08 28		08 54													08 58	09 24	
Rochester	d							08 30		08 57													09 00	09 27	
Maidstone West	d																								
Strood	d							08 35		09 02													09 05	09 32	
Higham	d							08 40															09 10		
Gravesend	d			09 02				08 48		09 13								09 32					09 18	09 43	
Northfleet	d			09 06														09 36							
Swanscombe	d			09 08														09 38							
Greenhithe for Bluewater	d			09 11				08 53										09 41					09 23		
Stone Crossing	d			09 13														09 43							
Dartford	a			09 17				08 58										09 47					09 28		
	d	08 52		09 18				08 59			09 01	09 08	09 08			09 22		09 48					09 29		09 31
Slade Green	d		08 47				08 55				09 05			09 15			09 17					09 25			09 35
Erith	d						08 58				09 08			09 18								09 28			09 38
Belvedere	d						09 00				09 10			09 20								09 30			09 40
Abbey Wood	d						09 03	09 08			09 13			09 23								09 33	09 38		09 43
Plumstead	d						09 06				09 16			09 26								09 36			09 46
Woolwich Arsenal	d						09 09	09 13			09 19			09 29								09 39	09 43		09 49
Woolwich Dockyard	d						09 12				09 22			09 32								09 42			09 52
Charlton	d					09 07	09 15	09 17			09 25			09 35							09 37	09 45	09 47		09 55
Crayford	d			09 22		09 37												09 52			10 07				
Bexley	d			09 25		09 40												09 55			10 10				
Albany Park	d			09 28		09 43												09 58			10 13				
Sidcup	d			09 31		09 46												10 01			10 16				
New Eltham	d			09 34		09 49												10 04			10 19				
Mottingham	d			09 36		09 51												10 06			10 21				
Lee	d			09 39		09 54												10 09			10 24				
Hither Green	d			09 42	09 49	09 58												10 12		10 19	10 28				
Barnehurst	d	08 59	09 08									09 16	09 16			09 29	09 38								
Bexleyheath	d	09 01	09 10									09 19	09 19			09 31	09 40								
Welling	d	09 04	09 13									09 22	09 22			09 34	09 43								
Falconwood	d	09 07	09 16									09 24	09 24			09 37	09 46								
Eltham	d	09 10	09 19									09 27	09 27			09 40	09 49								
Kidbrooke	d	09 13	09 22									09 30	09 30			09 43	09 52								
Blackheath	d	09 16	09 25					09 22				09 34	09 34			09 46	09 55						09 52		
Lewisham	d	09 20	09 29		09 54	10 04		09 26				09 38	09 38		09 44	09 50	09 59			10 24	10 34		09 56		
St Johns	d		09 31		09 56	10 06									09 46		10 01			10 26	10 36				
New Cross	d		09 33		09 58	10 08									09 48		10 03			10 28	10 38				
Nunhead	d											09 43	09 45												
Peckham Rye	d											09 45	09 47												
Denmark Hill	d											09 49	09 51												
London Victoria	a											09 58	10 00												
Westcombe Park	d						09 17				09 27			09 37								09 47			09 57
Maze Hill	d						09 19				09 29			09 39								09 49			09 59
Greenwich	d						09 22				09 32			09 42								09 52			10 02
Deptford	a						09 24				09 34			09 44								09 54			10 04
London Bridge	a	09 28	09 38	09 52	10 04	10 14	09 30	09 35			09 41			09 50	09 54	09 58	10 08	10 22		10 34	10 44	10 00	10 05		10 11
London Cannon Street	a		09 43		10 08	10 19	09 34				09 45			09 54	09 58		10 13			10 38	10 49	10 04			10 15
London Waterloo (East)	a	09 32		09 56				09 39								10 02		10 26					10 09		
London Charing Cross	a	09 36		10 00				09 43								10 06		10 30					10 13		
Ebbsfleet International	a									09 17														09 47	
Stratford International	a									09 29														09 59	
St Pancras Int'l	a									09 36														10 06	

A not 19 May

B 19 May

Table 200

Gillingham and Dartford - London

Saturdays

until 21 July, 18 Aug and from 15 Sep

Network Diagram - see first Page of Table 200

		SE A	SE B	SE		SE	SE	SE	SE	SE	SE	SE	SE	SE		SE	SE A	SE B	SE	SE	SE	SE	SE	SE
Gillingham (Kent)	d												09 24	09 50										
Chatham	d												09 28	09 54										
Rochester	d												09 30	09 57										
Maidstone West	d																							
Strood	d												09 35	10 02										
Higham	d												09 40											
Gravesend	d								10 02				09 48	10 13									10 32	
Northfleet	d								10 06														10 36	
Swanscombe	d								10 08														10 38	
Greenhithe for Bluewater	d								10 11				09 53										10 41	
Stone Crossing	d								10 13														10 43	
Dartford	a								10 17				09 58										10 47	
	d	09 38	09 38				09 52		10 18				09 59			10 01	10 08	10 08			10 22		10 48	
Slade Green	d			09 45				09 47				09 55				10 05			10 15			10 17		
Erith	d			09 48								09 58				10 08			10 18					
Belvedere	d			09 50								10 00				10 10			10 20					
Abbey Wood	d			09 53								10 03	10 08			10 13			10 23					
Plumstead	d			09 56								10 06				10 16			10 26					
Woolwich Arsenal	d			09 59								10 09	10 13			10 19			10 29					
Woolwich Dockyard	d			10 02								10 12				10 22			10 32					
Charlton	d			10 05							10 07	10 15	10 17			10 25			10 35					
Crayford	d								10 22		10 37												10 52	
Bexley	d								10 25		10 40												10 55	
Albany Park	d								10 28		10 43												10 58	
Sidcup	d								10 31		10 46												11 01	
New Eltham	d								10 34		10 49												11 04	
Mottingham	d								10 36		10 51												11 06	
Lee	d								10 39		10 54												11 09	
Hither Green	d								10 42	10 49	10 58												11 12	11 19
Barnehurst	d	09 46	09 46				09 59	10 08									10 16	10 16			10 29	10 38		
Bexleyheath	d	09 49	09 49				10 01	10 10									10 19	10 19			10 31	10 40		
Welling	d	09 52	09 52				10 04	10 13									10 22	10 22			10 34	10 43		
Falconwood	d	09 54	09 54				10 07	10 16									10 24	10 24			10 37	10 46		
Eltham	d	09 57	09 57				10 10	10 19									10 27	10 27			10 40	10 49		
Kidbrooke	d	10 00	10 00				10 13	10 22									10 30	10 30			10 43	10 52		
Blackheath	d	10 04	10 04				10 16	10 25									10 34	10 34			10 46	10 55		
Lewisham	d	10 08	10 08			10 14	10 20	10 29		10 54	11 04		10 22				10 38	10 38		10 44	10 50	10 59		11 24
St Johns	d					10 16		10 31		10 56	11 06		10 26							10 46		11 01		11 26
New Cross	d					10 18		10 33		10 58	11 08									10 48		11 03		11 28
Nunhead	d	10 13	10 15														10 43	10 45						
Peckham Rye	d	10 15	10 17														10 45	10 47						
Denmark Hill	d	10 19	10 21														10 49	10 51						
London Victoria	a	10 28	10 30														10 58	11 00						
Westcombe Park	d			10 07								10 17				10 27			10 37					
Maze Hill	d			10 09								10 19				10 29			10 39					
Greenwich	d			10 12								10 22				10 32			10 42					
Deptford	a			10 14								10 24				10 34			10 44					
London Bridge	a			10 20		10 24	10 28	10 38	10 52	11 04	11 14	10 30	10 35			10 41			10 50	10 54	10 58	11 08	11 22	11 34
London Cannon Street	a			10 24		10 28		10 43		11 08	11 19	10 34				10 45			10 54	10 58		11 13		11 38
London Waterloo (East)	a						10 32		10 56				10 39								11 02		11 26	
London Charing Cross	a						10 36		11 00				10 43								11 06		11 30	
Ebbsfleet International	a													10 17										
Stratford International	a													10 29										
St Pancras Int'l	a													10 36										

A not 19 May

B 19 May

Table 200

Gillingham and Dartford - London

Saturdays

until 21 July, 18 Aug and from 15 Sep

Network Diagram - see first Page of Table 200

		SE	SE	SE	SE	SE	SE A	SE B	SE	SE		SE	SE	SE	SE	SE	SE	SE	SE	SE		SE A	SE B	SE	SE
Gillingham (Kent)	d			09 54	10 20													10 24	10 50						
Chatham	d			09 58	10 24													10 28	10 54						
Rochester	d			10 00	10 27													10 30	10 57						
Maidstone West	d																								
Strood	d			10 05	10 32													10 35	11 02						
Higham	d			10 10														10 40							
Gravesend	d			10 18	10 43									11 02				10 48	11 13						
Northfleet	d													11 06											
Swanscombe	d													11 08											
Greenhithe for Bluewater	d			10 23										11 11				10 53							
Stone Crossing	d													11 13											
Dartford	a			10 28										11 17				10 58							
	d			10 29		10 31	10 38	10 38				10 52		11 18				10 59		11 01		11 08	11 08		
Slade Green	d		10 25			10 35			10 45				10 47				10 55			11 05				11 15	
Erith	d		10 28			10 38			10 48								10 58			11 08				11 18	
Belvedere	d		10 30			10 40			10 50								11 00			11 10				11 20	
Abbey Wood	d		10 33	10 38		10 43			10 53								11 03	11 08		11 13				11 23	
Plumstead	d		10 36			10 46			10 56								11 06			11 16				11 26	
Woolwich Arsenal	d		10 39	10 43		10 49			10 59								11 09	11 13		11 19				11 29	
Woolwich Dockyard	d		10 42			10 52			11 02								11 12			11 22				11 32	
Charlton	d	10 37	10 45	10 47		10 55			11 05							11 07	11 15	11 17		11 25				11 35	
Crayford	d	11 07												11 22		11 37									
Bexley	d	11 10												11 25		11 40									
Albany Park	d	11 13												11 28		11 43									
Sidcup	d	11 16												11 31		11 46									
New Eltham	d	11 19												11 34		11 49									
Mottingham	d	11 21												11 36		11 51									
Lee	d	11 24												11 39		11 54									
Hither Green	d	11 28												11 42	11 49	11 58									
Barnehurst	d						10 46	10 46				10 59	11 08									11 16	11 16		
Bexleyheath	d						10 49	10 49				11 01	11 10									11 19	11 19		
Welling	d						10 52	10 52				11 04	11 13									11 22	11 22		
Falconwood	d						10 54	10 54				11 07	11 16									11 24	11 24		
Eltham	d						10 57	10 57				11 10	11 19									11 27	11 27		
Kidbrooke	d						11 00	11 00				11 13	11 22									11 30	11 30		
Blackheath	d			10 52			11 04	11 04				11 16	11 25					11 22				11 34	11 34		
Lewisham	d	11 34		10 56			11 08	11 08		11 14		11 20	11 29		11 54	12 04		11 26				11 38	11 38		11 44
St Johns	d	11 36								11 16			11 31		11 56	12 06									11 46
New Cross	d	11 38								11 18			11 33		11 58	12 08									11 48
Nunhead	d						11 13	11 15														11 43	11 45		
Peckham Rye	d						11 15	11 17														11 45	11 47		
Denmark Hill	d						11 19	11 21														11 49	11 51		
London Victoria	a						11 28	11 30														11 58	12 00		
Westcombe Park	d		10 47			10 57			11 07								11 17			11 27				11 37	
Maze Hill	d		10 49			10 59			11 09								11 19			11 29				11 39	
Greenwich	d		10 52			11 02			11 12								11 22			11 32				11 42	
Deptford	a		10 54			11 04			11 14								11 24			11 34				11 44	
London Bridge	a	11 44	11 00	11 05		11 11			11 20	11 24		11 28	11 38	11 52	12 04	12 14	11 30	11 35		11 41				11 50	11 54
London Cannon Street	a	11 49	11 04			11 15			11 24	11 28			11 43		12 08	12 19	11 34			11 45				11 54	11 58
London Waterloo (East)	a			11 09								11 32		11 56				11 39							
London Charing Cross	a			11 13								11 36		12 00				11 43							
Ebbsfleet International	a				10 47														11 17						
Stratford International	a				10 59														11 29						
St Pancras Int'l	a				11 06														11 36						

A not 19 May

B 19 May

Table 200

Saturdays

until 21 July, 18 Aug and from 15 Sep

Gillingham and Dartford - London

Network Diagram - see first Page of Table 200

		SE	SE	SE	SE	SE		SE	SE	SE	SE	SE A	SE B	SE	SE	SE		SE	SE	SE	SE	SE	SE	SE	SE
Gillingham (Kent)	d								10 54	11 20													11 24	11 50	
Chatham	d								10 58	11 24													11 28	11 54	
Rochester	d								11 00	11 27													11 30	11 57	
Maidstone West	d																								
Strood	d								11 05	11 32													11 35	12 02	
Higham	d								11 10														11 40		
Gravesend	d			11 32					11 18	11 43									12 02				11 48	12 13	
Northfleet	d			11 36															12 06						
Swanscombe	d			11 38															12 08						
Greenhithe for Bluewater	d			11 41					11 23										12 11				11 53		
Stone Crossing	d			11 43															12 13						
Dartford	a			11 47					11 28										12 17				11 58		
	d	11 22		11 48					11 29		11 31	11 38	11 38			11 52			12 18				11 59		12 01
Slade Green	d		11 17					11 25			11 35			11 45				11 47				11 55			12 05
Erith	d							11 28			11 38			11 48								11 58			12 08
Belvedere	d							11 30			11 40			11 50								12 00			12 10
Abbey Wood	d							11 33	11 38		11 43			11 53								12 03	12 08		12 13
Plumstead	d							11 36			11 46			11 56								12 06			12 16
Woolwich Arsenal	d							11 39	11 43		11 49			11 59								12 09	12 13		12 19
Woolwich Dockyard	d							11 42			11 52			12 02								12 12			12 22
Charlton	d					11 37		11 45	11 47		11 55			12 05							12 07	12 15	12 17		12 25
Crayford	d			11 52		12 07													12 22		12 37				
Bexley	d			11 55		12 10													12 25		12 40				
Albany Park	d			11 58		12 13													12 28		12 43				
Sidcup	d			12 01		12 16													12 31		12 46				
New Eltham	d			12 04		12 19													12 34		12 49				
Mottingham	d			12 06		12 21													12 36		12 51				
Lee	d			12 09		12 24													12 39		12 54				
Hither Green	d			12 12	12 19	12 28													12 42	12 49	12 58				
Barnehurst	d	11 29	11 38									11 46	11 46			11 59		12 08							
Bexleyheath	d	11 31	11 40									11 49	11 49			12 01		12 10							
Welling	d	11 34	11 43									11 52	11 52			12 04		12 13							
Falconwood	d	11 37	11 46									11 54	11 54			12 07		12 16							
Eltham	d	11 40	11 49									11 57	11 57			12 10		12 19							
Kidbrooke	d	11 43	11 52									12 00	12 00			12 13		12 22							
Blackheath	d	11 46	11 55						11 52			12 04	12 04			12 16		12 25					12 22		
Lewisham	d	11 50	11 59		12 24	12 34			11 56			12 08	12 08		12 14	12 20		12 29		12 54	13 04		12 26		
St Johns	d		12 01		12 26	12 36									12 16			12 31		12 56	13 06				
New Cross	d		12 03		12 28	12 38									12 18			12 33		12 58	13 08				
Nunhead	d											12 13	12 15												
Peckham Rye	d											12 15	12 17												
Denmark Hill	d											12 19	12 21												
London Victoria	a											12 28	12 30												
Westcombe Park	d							11 47			11 57			12 07								12 17			12 27
Maze Hill	d							11 49			11 59			12 09								12 19			12 29
Greenwich	d							11 52			12 02			12 12								12 22			12 32
Deptford	a							11 54			12 04			12 14								12 24			12 34
London Bridge	a	11 58	12 08	12 22	12 34	12 44		12 00	12 05		12 11			12 20	12 24	12 28		12 38	12 52	13 04	13 14	12 30	12 35		12 41
London Cannon Street	a		12 13		12 38	12 49		12 04			12 15			12 24	12 28			12 43		13 08	13 19	12 34			12 45
London Waterloo (East)	a	12 02		12 26					12 09							12 32			12 56				12 39		
London Charing Cross	a	12 06		12 30					12 13							12 36			13 00				12 43		
Ebbsfleet International	a									11 47														12 17	
Stratford International	a									11 59														12 29	
St Pancras Int'l	a									12 06														12 36	

A not 19 May

B 19 May

Table 200

Saturdays

until 21 July, 18 Aug and from 15 Sep

Gillingham and Dartford - London

Network Diagram - see first Page of Table 200

		SE A		SE B	SE	SE	SE	SE	SE	SE	SE	SE		SE	SE	SE	SE A	SE B	SE	SE	SE	SE		SE	SE
Gillingham (Kent)	d													11 54	12 20										
Chatham	d													11 58	12 24										
Rochester	d													12 00	12 27										
Maidstone West	d																								
Strood	d													12 05	12 32										
Higham	d													12 10											
Gravesend	d								12 32					12 18	12 43									13 02	
Northfleet	d								12 36															13 06	
Swanscombe	d								12 38															13 08	
Greenhithe for Bluewater	d								12 41					12 23										13 11	
Stone Crossing	d								12 43															13 13	
Dartford	a								12 47					12 28										13 17	
	d	12 08		12 08			12 22		12 48					12 29		12 31	12 38	12 38			12 52			13 18	
Slade Green	d				12 15			12 17				12 25				12 35			12 45			12 47			
Erith	d				12 18							12 28				12 38			12 48						
Belvedere	d				12 20							12 30				12 40			12 50						
Abbey Wood	d				12 23							12 33		12 38		12 43			12 53						
Plumstead	d				12 26							12 36				12 46			12 56						
Woolwich Arsenal	d				12 29							12 39		12 43		12 49			12 59						
Woolwich Dockyard	d				12 32							12 42				12 52			13 02						
Charlton	d				12 35						12 37	12 45		12 47		12 55			13 05						
Crayford	d								12 52		13 07													13 22	
Bexley	d								12 55		13 10													13 25	
Albany Park	d								12 58		13 13													13 28	
Sidcup	d								13 01		13 16													13 31	
New Eltham	d								13 04		13 19													13 34	
Mottingham	d								13 06		13 21													13 36	
Lee	d								13 09		13 24													13 39	
Hither Green	d								13 12	13 19	13 28													13 42	13 49
Barnehurst	d	12 16		12 16			12 29	12 38									12 46	12 46			12 59	13 08			
Bexleyheath	d	12 19		12 19			12 31	12 40									12 49	12 49			13 01	13 10			
Welling	d	12 22		12 22			12 34	12 43									12 52	12 52			13 04	13 13			
Falconwood	d	12 24		12 24			12 37	12 46									12 54	12 54			13 07	13 16			
Eltham	d	12 27		12 27			12 40	12 49									12 57	12 57			13 10	13 19			
Kidbrooke	d	12 30		12 30			12 43	12 52									13 00	13 00			13 13	13 22			
Blackheath	d	12 34		12 34			12 46	12 55						12 52			13 04	13 04			13 16	13 25			
Lewisham	d	12 38		12 38		12 44	12 50	12 59		13 24	13 34			12 56			13 08	13 08		13 14	13 20	13 29			13 54
St Johns	d					12 46		13 01		13 26	13 36									13 16		13 31			13 56
New Cross	d					12 48		13 03		13 28	13 38									13 18		13 33			13 58
Nunhead	d	12 43		12 45													13 13	13 15							
Peckham Rye	d	12 45		12 47													13 15	13 17							
Denmark Hill	d	12 49		12 51													13 19	13 21							
London Victoria	a	12 58		13 00													13 28	13 30							
Westcombe Park	d				12 37							12 47				12 57			13 07						
Maze Hill	d				12 39							12 49				12 59			13 09						
Greenwich	d				12 42							12 52				13 02			13 12						
Deptford	a				12 44							12 54				13 04			13 14						
London Bridge	a				12 50	12 54	12 58	13 08	13 22	13 34	13 44	13 00		13 05		13 11			13 20	13 24	13 28	13 38		13 52	14 04
London Cannon Street	a				12 54	12 58		13 13		13 38	13 49	13 04				13 15			13 24	13 28		13 43			14 08
London Waterloo (East)	a						13 02		13 26					13 09							13 33			13 56	
London Charing Cross	a						13 06		13 30					13 13							13 36			14 00	
Ebbsfleet International	a														12 47										
Stratford International	a														12 59										
St Pancras Int'l	a														13 06										

A not 19 May

B 19 May

Table 200

Gillingham and Dartford - London

Saturdays

until 21 July, 18 Aug and from 15 Sep

Network Diagram - see first Page of Table 200

		SE	SE	SE	SE	SE	SE A	SE B	SE	SE	SE	SE	SE	SE	SE	SE	SE	SE	SE	SE A	SE B	SE	SE
Gillingham (Kent)	d			12 24	12 50												12 54	13 20					
Chatham	d			12 28	12 54												12 58	13 24					
Rochester	d			12 30	12 57												13 00	13 27					
Maidstone West	d																						
Strood	d			12 35	13 02												13 05	13 32					
Higham	d			12 40													13 10						
Gravesend	d			12 48	13 13								13 32				13 18	13 43					
Northfleet	d												13 36										
Swanscombe	d												13 38										
Greenhithe for Bluewater	d			12 53									13 41				13 23						
Stone Crossing	d												13 43										
Dartford	a			12 58									13 47				13 28						
	d			12 59		13 01	13 08	13 08			13 22		13 48				13 29		13 31	13 38	13 38		
Slade Green	d		12 55			13 05			13 15			13 17				13 25			13 35			13 45	
Erith	d		12 58			13 08			13 18							13 28			13 38			13 48	
Belvedere	d		13 00			13 10			13 20							13 30			13 40			13 50	
Abbey Wood	d		13 03	13 08		13 13			13 23							13 33	13 38		13 43			13 53	
Plumstead	d		13 06			13 16			13 26							13 36			13 46			13 56	
Woolwich Arsenal	d		13 09	13 13		13 19			13 29							13 39	13 43		13 49			13 59	
Woolwich Dockyard	d		13 12			13 22			13 32							13 42			13 52			14 02	
Charlton	d	13 07	13 15	13 17		13 25			13 35						13 37	13 45	13 47		13 55			14 05	
Crayford	d	13 37											13 52		14 07								
Bexley	d	13 40											13 55		14 10								
Albany Park	d	13 43											13 58		14 13								
Sidcup	d	13 46											14 01		14 16								
New Eltham	d	13 49											14 04		14 19								
Mottingham	d	13 51											14 06		14 21								
Lee	d	13 54											14 09		14 24								
Hither Green	d	13 58											14 12	14 19	14 28								
Barnehurst	d						13 16	13 16			13 29	13 38								13 46	13 46		
Bexleyheath	d						13 19	13 19			13 31	13 40								13 49	13 49		
Welling	d						13 22	13 22			13 34	13 43								13 52	13 52		
Falconwood	d						13 24	13 24			13 37	13 46								13 54	13 54		
Eltham	d						13 27	13 27			13 40	13 49								13 57	13 57		
Kidbrooke	d						13 30	13 30			13 43	13 52								14 00	14 00		
Blackheath	d			13 22			13 34	13 34			13 46	13 55					13 52			14 04	14 04		
Lewisham	d	14 04		13 26			13 38	13 38		13 44	13 50	13 59		14 24	14 34		13 56			14 08	14 08		14 14
St Johns	d	14 06								13 46		14 01		14 26	14 36								14 16
New Cross	d	14 08								13 48		14 03		14 28	14 38								14 18
Nunhead	d						13 43	13 45												14 13	14 15		
Peckham Rye	d						13 45	13 47												14 15	14 17		
Denmark Hill	d						13 49	13 51												14 19	14 21		
London Victoria	a						13 58	14 00												14 28	14 30		
Westcombe Park	d		13 17			13 27			13 37							13 47			13 57			14 07	
Maze Hill	d		13 19			13 29			13 39							13 49			13 59			14 09	
Greenwich	d		13 22			13 32			13 42							13 52			14 02			14 12	
Deptford	a		13 24			13 34			13 44							13 54			14 04			14 14	
London Bridge	a	14 14	13 30	13 35		13 41			13 50	13 54	13 58	14 08	14 22	14 34	14 44	14 00	14 05		14 11			14 20	14 24
London Cannon Street	a	14 19	13 34			13 45			13 54	13 58		14 13		14 38	14 49	14 04			14 15			14 24	14 28
London Waterloo (East)	a			13 39							14 02		14 26				14 09						
London Charing Cross	a			13 43							14 06		14 30				14 13						
Ebbsfleet International	a				13 17													13 47					
Stratford International	a				13 29													13 59					
St Pancras Int'l	a				13 36													14 06					

A not 19 May

B 19 May

Table 200

Gillingham and Dartford - London

Saturdays

until 21 July, 18 Aug and from 15 Sep

Network Diagram - see first Page of Table 200

		SE	SE	SE	SE	SE	SE	SE	SE	SE	SE A	SE B	SE	SE	SE	SE	SE	SE	SE	SE	SE	SE
Gillingham (Kent)	d							13 24	13 50												13 54	14 20
Chatham	d							13 28	13 54												13 58	14 24
Rochester	d							13 30	13 57												14 00	14 27
Maidstone West	d																					
Strood	d							13 35	14 02												14 05	14 32
Higham	d							13 40													14 10	
Gravesend	d			14 02				13 48	14 13								14 32				14 18	14 43
Northfleet	d			14 06													14 36					
Swanscombe	d			14 08													14 38					
Greenhithe for Bluewater	d			14 11				13 53									14 41				14 23	
Stone Crossing	d			14 13													14 43					
Dartford	a			14 17				13 58									14 47				14 28	
	d	13 52		14 18				13 59		14 01	14 08	14 08			14 22		14 48				14 29	
Slade Green	d		13 47				13 55			14 05			14 15			14 17				14 25		
Erith	d						13 58			14 08			14 18							14 28		
Belvedere	d						14 00			14 10			14 20							14 30		
Abbey Wood	d						14 03	14 08		14 13			14 23							14 33	14 38	
Plumstead	d						14 06			14 16			14 26							14 36		
Woolwich Arsenal	d						14 09	14 13		14 19			14 29							14 39	14 43	
Woolwich Dockyard	d						14 12			14 22			14 32							14 42		
Charlton	d					14 07	14 15	14 17		14 25			14 35						14 37	14 45	14 47	
Crayford	d			14 22		14 37											14 52		15 07			
Bexley	d			14 25		14 40											14 55		15 10			
Albany Park	d			14 28		14 43											14 58		15 13			
Sidcup	d			14 31		14 46											15 01		15 16			
New Eltham	d			14 34		14 49											15 04		15 19			
Mottingham	d			14 36		14 51											15 06		15 21			
Lee	d			14 39		14 54											15 09		15 24			
Hither Green	d			14 42	14 49	14 58											15 12	15 19	15 28			
Barnehurst	d	13 59	14 08								14 16	14 16			14 29	14 38						
Bexleyheath	d	14 01	14 10								14 19	14 19			14 31	14 40						
Welling	d	14 04	14 13								14 22	14 22			14 34	14 43						
Falconwood	d	14 07	14 16								14 24	14 24			14 37	14 46						
Eltham	d	14 10	14 19								14 27	14 27			14 40	14 49						
Kidbrooke	d	14 13	14 22								14 30	14 30			14 43	14 52						
Blackheath	d	14 16	14 25					14 22			14 34	14 34			14 46	14 55					14 52	
Lewisham	d	14 20	14 29		14 54	15 04		14 26			14 38	14 38		14 44	14 50	14 59		15 24	15 34		14 56	
St Johns	d		14 31		14 56	15 06								14 46		15 01		15 26	15 36			
New Cross	d		14 33		14 58	15 08								14 48		15 03		15 28	15 38			
Nunhead	d										14 43	14 45										
Peckham Rye	d										14 45	14 47										
Denmark Hill	d										14 49	14 51										
London Victoria	a										14 58	15 00										
Westcombe Park	d						14 17			14 27			14 37							14 47		
Maze Hill	d						14 19			14 29			14 39							14 49		
Greenwich	d						14 22			14 32			14 42							14 52		
Deptford	a						14 24			14 34			14 44							14 54		
London Bridge	a	14 28	14 38	14 52	15 04	15 14	14 30	14 35		14 41			14 50	14 54	14 58	15 08	15 22	15 34	15 44	15 00	15 05	
London Cannon Street	a		14 43		15 08	15 19	14 34			14 45			14 54	14 58		15 13		15 38	15 49	15 04		
London Waterloo (East)	a	14 32		14 56				14 39							15 02		15 26				15 09	
London Charing Cross	a	14 36		15 00				14 43							15 06		15 30				15 13	
Ebbsfleet International	a								14 17													14 47
Stratford International	a								14 29													15 02
St Pancras Int'l	a								14 36													15 09

A not 19 May

B 19 May

Table 200

Saturdays

until 21 July, 18 Aug and from 15 Sep

Gillingham and Dartford - London

Network Diagram - see first Page of Table 200

		SE	SE A	SE B	SE	SE	SE	SE	SE	SE		SE	SE	SE	SE	SE	SE A	SE B	SE	SE		SE	SE	SE	SE
Gillingham (Kent)	d													14 24	14 50										
Chatham	d													14 28	14 54										
Rochester	d													14 30	14 57										
Maidstone West	d																								
Strood	d													14 35	15 02										
Higham	d													14 40											
Gravesend	d								15 02					14 48	15 13									15 32	
Northfleet	d								15 06															15 36	
Swanscombe	d								15 08															15 38	
Greenhithe for Bluewater	d								15 11					14 53										15 41	
Stone Crossing	d								15 13															15 43	
Dartford	a								15 17					14 58										15 47	
	d	14 31	14 38	14 38			14 52		15 18					14 59		15 01	15 08	15 08				15 22		15 48	
Slade Green	d	14 35			14 45			14 47					14 55			15 05			15 15				15 17		
Erith	d	14 38			14 48								14 58			15 08			15 18						
Belvedere	d	14 40			14 50								15 00			15 10			15 20						
Abbey Wood	d	14 43			14 53								15 03	15 08		15 13			15 23						
Plumstead	d	14 46			14 56								15 06			15 16			15 26						
Woolwich Arsenal	d	14 49			14 59								15 09	15 13		15 19			15 29						
Woolwich Dockyard	d	14 52			15 02								15 12			15 22			15 32						
Charlton	d	14 55			15 05							15 07	15 15	15 17		15 25			15 35						
Crayford	d								15 22			15 37												15 52	
Bexley	d								15 25			15 40												15 55	
Albany Park	d								15 28			15 43												15 58	
Sidcup	d								15 31			15 46												16 01	
New Eltham	d								15 34			15 49												16 04	
Mottingham	d								15 36			15 51												16 06	
Lee	d								15 39			15 54												16 09	
Hither Green	d								15 42	15 49		15 58												16 12	16 19
Barnehurst	d		14 46	14 46			14 59	15 08									15 16	15 16				15 29	15 38		
Bexleyheath	d		14 49	14 49			15 01	15 10									15 19	15 19				15 31	15 40		
Welling	d		14 52	14 52			15 04	15 13									15 22	15 22				15 34	15 43		
Falconwood	d		14 54	14 54			15 07	15 16									15 24	15 24				15 37	15 46		
Eltham	d		14 57	14 57			15 10	15 19									15 27	15 27				15 40	15 49		
Kidbrooke	d		15 00	15 00			15 13	15 22									15 30	15 30				15 43	15 52		
Blackheath	d		15 04	15 04			15 16	15 25						15 22			15 34	15 34				15 46	15 55		
Lewisham	d		15 08	15 08		15 14	15 20	15 29		15 54		16 04		15 26			15 38	15 38		15 44		15 50	15 59		16 24
St Johns	d					15 16		15 31		15 56		16 06								15 46			16 01		16 26
New Cross	d					15 18		15 33		15 58		16 08								15 48			16 03		16 28
Nunhead	d		15 13	15 15													15 43	15 45							
Peckham Rye	d		15 15	15 17													15 45	15 47							
Denmark Hill	d		15 19	15 21													15 49	15 51							
London Victoria	a		15 28	15 30													15 58	16 00							
Westcombe Park	d	14 57			15 07								15 17			15 27			15 37						
Maze Hill	d	14 59			15 09								15 19			15 29			15 39						
Greenwich	d	15 02			15 12								15 22			15 32			15 42						
Deptford	a	15 04			15 14								15 24			15 34			15 44						
London Bridge	a	15 11			15 20	15 24	15 28	15 38	15 52	16 04		16 14	15 30	15 35		15 41			15 50	15 54		15 58	16 08	16 22	16 34
London Cannon Street	a	15 15			15 24	15 28		15 43		16 08		16 19	15 34			15 45			15 54	15 58			16 13		16 38
London Waterloo (East)	a						15 32		15 56					15 39								16 02		16 26	
London Charing Cross	a						15 36		16 00					15 43								16 06		16 30	
Ebbsfleet International	a														15 17										
Stratford International	a														15 29										
St Pancras Int'l	a														15 36										

A not 19 May

B 19 May

Table 200

Saturdays

until 21 July, 18 Aug and from 15 Sep

Gillingham and Dartford - London

Network Diagram - see first Page of Table 200

		SE	SE	SE	SE	SE		SE A	SE B	SE	SE	SE	SE	SE	SE	SE		SE	SE	SE	SE	SE A	SE B	SE	SE
Gillingham (Kent)	d			14 54	15 20														15 24	15 50					
Chatham	d			14 58	15 24														15 28	15 54					
Rochester	d			15 00	15 27														15 30	15 57					
Maidstone West	d																								
Strood	d			15 05	15 32														15 35	16 02					
Higham	d			15 10															15 40						
Gravesend	d			15 18	15 43									16 02					15 48	16 13					
Northfleet	d													16 06											
Swanscombe	d													16 08											
Greenhithe for Bluewater	d			15 23										16 11					15 53						
Stone Crossing	d													16 13											
Dartford	a			15 28										16 17					15 58						
	d			15 29		15 31		15 38	15 38			15 52		16 18					15 59		16 01	16 08	16 08		
Slade Green	d		15 25			15 35				15 45			15 47					15 55			16 05			16 15	
Erith	d		15 28			15 38				15 48								15 58			16 08			16 18	
Belvedere	d		15 30			15 40				15 50								16 00			16 10			16 20	
Abbey Wood	d		15 33	15 38		15 43				15 53								16 03	16 08		16 13			16 23	
Plumstead	d		15 36			15 46				15 56								16 06			16 16			16 26	
Woolwich Arsenal	d		15 39	15 43		15 49				15 59								16 09	16 13		16 19			16 29	
Woolwich Dockyard	d		15 42			15 52				16 02								16 12			16 22			16 32	
Charlton	d	15 37	15 45	15 47		15 55				16 05						16 07		16 15	16 17		16 25			16 35	
Crayford	d	16 07												16 22		16 37									
Bexley	d	16 10												16 25		16 40									
Albany Park	d	16 13												16 28		16 43									
Sidcup	d	16 16												16 31		16 46									
New Eltham	d	16 19												16 34		16 49									
Mottingham	d	16 21												16 36		16 51									
Lee	d	16 24												16 39		16 54									
Hither Green	d	16 28												16 42	16 49	16 58									
Barnehurst	d							15 46	15 46			15 59	16 08									16 16	16 16		
Bexleyheath	d							15 49	15 49			16 01	16 10									16 19	16 19		
Welling	d							15 52	15 52			16 04	16 13									16 22	16 22		
Falconwood	d							15 54	15 54			16 07	16 16									16 24	16 24		
Eltham	d							15 57	15 57			16 10	16 19									16 27	16 27		
Kidbrooke	d							16 00	16 00			16 13	16 22									16 30	16 30		
Blackheath	d			15 52				16 04	16 04			16 16	16 25						16 22			16 34	16 34		
Lewisham	d	16 34		15 56				16 08	16 08		16 14	16 20	16 29		16 54	17 04			16 26			16 38	16 38		16 44
St Johns	d	16 36									16 16		16 31		16 56	17 06									16 46
New Cross	d	16 38									16 18		16 33		16 58	17 08									16 48
Nunhead	d							16 13	16 15													16 43	16 45		
Peckham Rye	d							16 15	16 17													16 45	16 47		
Denmark Hill	d							16 19	16 21													16 49	16 51		
London Victoria	a							16 28	16 30													16 58	17 00		
Westcombe Park	d		15 47			15 57				16 07								16 17			16 27			16 37	
Maze Hill	d		15 49			15 59				16 09								16 19			16 29			16 39	
Greenwich	d		15 52			16 02				16 12								16 22			16 32			16 42	
Deptford	a		15 54			16 04				16 14								16 24			16 34			16 44	
London Bridge	a	16 44	16 00	16 05		16 11				16 20	16 24	16 28	16 38	16 52	17 04	17 14		16 30	16 35		16 41			16 50	16 54
London Cannon Street	a	16 49	16 04			16 15				16 24	16 28		16 43		17 08	17 19		16 34			16 45			16 54	16 58
London Waterloo (East)	a			16 09								16 32		16 56					16 39						
London Charing Cross	a			16 13								16 36		17 00					16 43						
Ebbsfleet International	a				15 47															16 17					
Stratford International	a				16 02															16 29					
St Pancras Int'l	a				16 09															16 36					

A not 19 May

B 19 May

Gillingham and Dartford - London

Saturdays

until 21 July, 18 Aug and from 15 Sep

Network Diagram - see first Page of Table 200

Station		SE	SE	SE	SE	SE	SE	SE	SE	SE	SE A	SE B	SE	SE	SE	SE	SE	SE	SE	SE	SE	SE
Gillingham (Kent)	d							15 54	16 20												16 24	16 50
Chatham	d							15 58	16 24												16 28	16 54
Rochester	d							16 00	16 27												16 30	16 57
Maidstone West	d																					
Strood	d							16 05	16 32												16 35	17 02
Higham	d							16 10													16 40	
Gravesend	d			16 32				16 18	16 43								17 02				16 48	17 13
Northfleet	d			16 36													17 06					
Swanscombe	d			16 38													17 08					
Greenhithe for Bluewater	d			16 41				16 23									17 11				16 53	
Stone Crossing	d			16 43													17 13					
Dartford	a			16 47				16 28									17 17				16 58	
	d	16 22		16 48				16 29		16 31	16 38	16 38			16 52		17 18				16 59	
Slade Green	d		16 17				16 25			16 35			16 45			16 47				16 55		
Erith	d						16 28			16 38			16 48							16 58		
Belvedere	d						16 30			16 40			16 50							17 00		
Abbey Wood	d						16 33	16 38		16 43			16 53							17 03	17 08	
Plumstead	d						16 36			16 46			16 56							17 06		
Woolwich Arsenal	d						16 39	16 43		16 49			16 59							17 09	17 13	
Woolwich Dockyard	d						16 42			16 52			17 02							17 12		
Charlton	d					16 37	16 45	16 47		16 55			17 05						17 07	17 15	17 17	
Crayford	d			16 52		17 07											17 22		17 37			
Bexley	d			16 55		17 10											17 25		17 40			
Albany Park	d			16 58		17 13											17 28		17 43			
Sidcup	d			17 01		17 16											17 31		17 46			
New Eltham	d			17 04		17 19											17 34		17 49			
Mottingham	d			17 06		17 21											17 36		17 51			
Lee	d			17 09		17 24											17 39		17 54			
Hither Green	d			17 12	17 19	17 28											17 42	17 49	17 58			
Barnehurst	d	16 29	16 38								16 46	16 46			16 59	17 08						
Bexleyheath	d	16 31	16 40								16 49	16 49			17 01	17 10						
Welling	d	16 34	16 43								16 52	16 52			17 04	17 13						
Falconwood	d	16 37	16 46								16 54	16 54			17 07	17 16						
Eltham	d	16 40	16 49								16 57	16 57			17 10	17 19						
Kidbrooke	d	16 43	16 52								17 00	17 00			17 13	17 22						
Blackheath	d	16 46	16 55					16 52			17 04	17 04			17 16	17 25					17 22	
Lewisham	d	16 50	16 59		17 24	17 34		16 56			17 08	17 08		17 14	17 20	17 29		17 54	18 04		17 26	
St Johns	d		17 01		17 26	17 36								17 16		17 31		17 56	18 06			
New Cross	d		17 03		17 28	17 38								17 18		17 33		17 58	18 08			
Nunhead	d										17 13	17 15										
Peckham Rye	d										17 15	17 17										
Denmark Hill	d										17 19	17 21										
London Victoria	a										17 28	17 30										
Westcombe Park	d						16 47			16 57			17 07							17 17		
Maze Hill	d						16 49			16 59			17 09							17 19		
Greenwich	d						16 52			17 02			17 12							17 22		
Deptford	a						16 54			17 04			17 14							17 24		
London Bridge	a	16 58	17 08	17 22	17 34	17 44	17 00	17 05		17 11			17 20	17 24	17 28	17 38	17 52	18 04	18 14	17 30	17 35	
London Cannon Street	a		17 13		17 38	17 49	17 04			17 15			17 24	17 28		17 43		18 08	18 19	17 34		
London Waterloo (East)	a	17 02		17 26				17 09							17 32		17 56				17 39	
London Charing Cross	a	17 06		17 30				17 13							17 36		18 00				17 43	
Ebbsfleet International	a								16 47													17 17
Stratford International	a								17 02													17 29
St Pancras Int'l	a								17 09													17 36

A not 19 May

B 19 May

Gillingham and Dartford - London

Saturdays

until 21 July, 18 Aug and from 15 Sep

Network Diagram - see first Page of Table 200

Station		SE	SE A	SE B	SE	SE	SE	SE	SE	SE	SE	SE	SE	SE	SE	SE A	SE B	SE	SE	SE	SE	SE	SE
Gillingham (Kent)	d												16 54	17 20									
Chatham	d												16 58	17 24									
Rochester	d												17 00	17 27									
Maidstone West	d																						
Strood	d												17 05	17 32									
Higham	d												17 10										
Gravesend	d								17 32				17 18	17 43								18 02	
Northfleet	d								17 36													18 06	
Swanscombe	d								17 38													18 08	
Greenhithe for Bluewater	d								17 41				17 23									18 11	
Stone Crossing	d								17 43													18 13	
Dartford	a								17 47				17 28									18 17	
	d	17 01	17 08	17 08			17 22		17 48				17 29		17 31	17 38	17 38			17 52		18 18	
Slade Green	d	17 05			17 15			17 17				17 25			17 35			17 45			17 47		
Erith	d	17 08			17 18							17 28			17 38			17 48					
Belvedere	d	17 10			17 20							17 30			17 40			17 50					
Abbey Wood	d	17 13			17 23							17 33	17 38		17 43			17 53					
Plumstead	d	17 16			17 26							17 36			17 46			17 56					
Woolwich Arsenal	d	17 19			17 29							17 39	17 43		17 49			17 59					
Woolwich Dockyard	d	17 22			17 32							17 42			17 52			18 02					
Charlton	d	17 25			17 35						17 37	17 45	17 47		17 55			18 05					
Crayford	d								17 52		18 07											18 22	
Bexley	d								17 55		18 10											18 25	
Albany Park	d								17 58		18 13											18 28	
Sidcup	d								18 01		18 16											18 31	
New Eltham	d								18 04		18 19											18 34	
Mottingham	d								18 06		18 21											18 36	
Lee	d								18 09		18 24											18 39	
Hither Green	d								18 12	18 19	18 28											18 42	18 49
Barnehurst	d		17 16	17 16			17 29	17 38								17 46	17 46			17 59	18 08		
Bexleyheath	d		17 19	17 19			17 31	17 40								17 49	17 49			18 01	18 10		
Welling	d		17 22	17 22			17 34	17 43								17 52	17 52			18 04	18 13		
Falconwood	d		17 24	17 24			17 37	17 46								17 54	17 54			18 07	18 16		
Eltham	d		17 27	17 27			17 40	17 49								17 57	17 57			18 10	18 19		
Kidbrooke	d		17 30	17 30			17 43	17 52								18 00	18 00			18 13	18 22		
Blackheath	d		17 34	17 34			17 46	17 55					17 52			18 04	18 04			18 16	18 25		
Lewisham	d		17 38	17 38		17 44	17 50	17 59		18 24	18 34		17 56			18 08	18 08		18 14	18 20	18 29		18 54
St Johns	d					17 46		18 01		18 26	18 36								18 16		18 31		18 56
New Cross	d					17 48		18 03		18 28	18 38								18 18		18 33		18 58
Nunhead	d		17 43	17 45												18 13	18 15						
Peckham Rye	d		17 45	17 47												18 15	18 17						
Denmark Hill	d		17 49	17 51												18 19	18 21						
London Victoria	a		17 58	18 00												18 28	18 30						
Westcombe Park	d	17 27			17 37							17 47			17 57			18 07					
Maze Hill	d	17 29			17 39							17 49			17 59			18 09					
Greenwich	d	17 32			17 42							17 52			18 02			18 12					
Deptford	a	17 34			17 44							17 54			18 04			18 14					
London Bridge	a	17 41			17 50	17 54	17 58	18 08	18 22	18 34	18 44	18 00	18 05		18 11			18 20	18 24	18 28	18 38	18 52	19 04
London Cannon Street	a	17 45			17 54	17 58		18 13		18 38	18 49	18 04			18 15			18 24	18 28		18 43		19 08
London Waterloo (East)	a						18 02		18 26				18 09							18 32		18 56	
London Charing Cross	a						18 06		18 30				18 13							18 36		19 00	
Ebbsfleet International	a													17 47									
Stratford International	a													17 59									
St Pancras Int'l	a													18 09									

A not 19 May

B 19 May

Table 200

Saturdays

until 21 July, 18 Aug and from 15 Sep

Gillingham and Dartford - London

Network Diagram - see first Page of Table 200

		SE	SE	SE	SE	SE	SE A	SE B	SE	SE	SE	SE	SE	SE	SE	SE A	SE B	SE	SE	SE	SE	SE
Gillingham (Kent)	d			17 24	17 50									17 54					18 20			18 24
Chatham	d			17 28	17 54									17 58					18 24			18 28
Rochester	d			17 30	17 57									18 00					18 27			18 30
Maidstone West	d																					
Strood	d			17 35	18 02									18 05					18 32			18 35
Higham	d			17 40										18 10								18 40
Gravesend	d			17 48	18 13									18 18				18 32	18 43			18 48
Northfleet	d																	18 36				
Swanscombe	d																	18 38				
Greenhithe for Bluewater	d			17 53										18 23				18 41				18 53
Stone Crossing	d																	18 43				
Dartford	a			17 58										18 28				18 47				18 58
	d			17 59		18 01	18 08	18 08			18 22			18 29	18 31	18 38	18 38	18 48			18 52	18 59
Slade Green	d		17 55			18 05			18 15			18 17	18 25		18 35					18 55		
Erith	d		17 58			18 08			18 18				18 28		18 38					18 58		
Belvedere	d		18 00			18 10			18 20				18 30		18 40					19 00		
Abbey Wood	d		18 03	18 08		18 13			18 23				18 33	18 38	18 43					19 03		19 08
Plumstead	d		18 06			18 16			18 26				18 36		18 46					19 06		
Woolwich Arsenal	d		18 09	18 13		18 19			18 29				18 39	18 43	18 49					19 09		19 13
Woolwich Dockyard	d		18 12			18 22			18 32				18 42		18 52					19 12		
Charlton	d	18 07	18 15	18 17		18 25			18 35				18 45	18 47	18 55					19 15		19 17
Crayford	d	18 37																18 52				
Bexley	d	18 40																18 55				
Albany Park	d	18 43																18 58				
Sidcup	d	18 46																19 01				
New Eltham	d	18 49																19 04				
Mottingham	d	18 51																19 06				
Lee	d	18 54																19 09				
Hither Green	d	18 58																19 12				
Barnehurst	d						18 16	18 16			18 29	18 38				18 46	18 46				18 59	
Bexleyheath	d						18 19	18 19			18 31	18 40				18 49	18 49				19 01	
Welling	d						18 22	18 22			18 34	18 43				18 52	18 52				19 04	
Falconwood	d						18 24	18 24			18 37	18 46				18 54	18 54				19 07	
Eltham	d						18 27	18 27			18 40	18 49				18 57	18 57				19 10	
Kidbrooke	d						18 30	18 30			18 43	18 52				19 00	19 00				19 13	
Blackheath	d			18 22			18 34	18 34			18 46	18 55		18 52		19 04	19 04				19 16	19 22
Lewisham	d	19 04		18 26			18 38	18 38		18 44	18 50	18 59		18 56		19 08	19 08	19 18			19 20	19 26
St Johns	d	19 06								18 46		19 01										
New Cross	d	19 08								18 48		19 03									19 23	
Nunhead	d						18 43	18 45								19 13	19 15					
Peckham Rye	d						18 45	18 47								19 15	19 17					
Denmark Hill	d						18 49	18 51								19 19	19 21					
London Victoria	a						18 58	19 00								19 28	19 30					
Westcombe Park	d		18 17			18 27			18 37				18 47		18 57					19 17		
Maze Hill	d		18 19			18 29			18 39				18 49		18 59					19 19		
Greenwich	d		18 22			18 32			18 42				18 52		19 02					19 22		
Deptford	a		18 24			18 34			18 44				18 54		19 04					19 24		
London Bridge	a	19 14	18 30	18 35		18 41			18 50	18 54	18 58	19 08	19 00	19 05	19 11			19 27		19 30	19 33	19 36
London Cannon Street	a	19 19	18 34			18 45			18 54	18 58		19 13	19 04		19 15							
London Waterloo (East)	a			18 39							19 02			19 09				19 32			19 39	19 42
London Charing Cross	a			18 43							19 06			19 13				19 35			19 42	19 45
Ebbsfleet International	a				18 17														18 47			
Stratford International	a				18 29														19 02			
St Pancras Int'l	a				18 36														19 09			

A not 19 May

B 19 May

Table 200

Saturdays

until 21 July, 18 Aug and from 15 Sep

Gillingham and Dartford - London

Network Diagram - see first Page of Table 200

		SE	SE	SE	SE	SE	SE	SE	SE	SE	SE	SE	SE	SE	SE	SE	SE	SE	SE	SE	SE	SE	SE
Gillingham (Kent)	d			18 50			18 54			19 20			19 24			19 50		19 54			20 20		20 24
Chatham	d			18 54			18 58			19 24			19 28			19 54		19 58			20 24		20 28
Rochester	d			18 57			19 00			19 27			19 30			19 57		20 00			20 27		20 30
Maidstone West	d																						
Strood	d			19 02			19 05			19 32			19 35			20 02		20 05			20 32		20 35
Higham	d						19 10						19 40					20 10					20 40
Gravesend	d		19 02	19 12			19 18		19 32	19 43			19 48		20 02	20 13		20 18		20 32	20 43		20 48
Northfleet	d		19 06						19 36						20 06					20 36			
Swanscombe	d		19 08						19 38						20 08					20 38			
Greenhithe for Bluewater	d		19 11				19 23		19 41				19 53		20 11			20 23		20 41			20 53
Stone Crossing	d		19 13						19 43						20 13					20 43			
Dartford	a		19 17				19 28		19 47				19 58		20 17			20 28		20 47			20 58
	d	19 01	19 18			19 25	19 29	19 31	19 48			19 55	19 59	20 01	20 18		20 25	20 29	20 31	20 48		20 55	20 59
Slade Green	d	19 05			19 25			19 35			19 55			20 05					20 35				
Erith	d	19 08			19 28			19 38			19 58			20 08					20 38				
Belvedere	d	19 10			19 30			19 40			20 00			20 10					20 40				
Abbey Wood	d	19 13			19 33		19 38	19 43			20 03		20 08	20 13				20 38	20 43				21 08
Plumstead	d	19 16			19 36			19 46			20 06			20 16					20 46				
Woolwich Arsenal	d	19 19			19 39		19 43	19 49			20 09		20 13	20 19				20 43	20 49				21 13
Woolwich Dockyard	d	19 22			19 42			19 52			20 12			20 22					20 52				
Charlton	d	19 25			19 45		19 47	19 55			20 15		20 17	20 25				20 47	20 55				21 17
Crayford	d		19 22						19 52						20 22					20 52			
Bexley	d		19 25						19 55						20 25					20 55			
Albany Park	d		19 28						19 58						20 28					20 58			
Sidcup	d		19 31						20 01						20 31					21 01			
New Eltham	d		19 34						20 04						20 34					21 04			
Mottingham	d		19 36						20 06						20 36					21 06			
Lee	d		19 39						20 09						20 39					21 09			
Hither Green	d		19 42						20 12						20 42					21 12			
Barnehurst	d					19 32						20 02					20 32					21 02	
Bexleyheath	d					19 34						20 04					20 34					21 04	
Welling	d					19 37						20 07					20 37					21 07	
Falconwood	d					19 40						20 10					20 40					21 10	
Eltham	d					19 42						20 12					20 42					21 12	
Kidbrooke	d					19 45						20 15					20 45					21 15	
Blackheath	d					19 49	19 52					20 19	20 22				20 49	20 52				21 19	21 22
Lewisham	d		19 48			19 53	19 56		20 18			20 23	20 26		20 48		20 53	20 56		21 18		21 23	21 26
St Johns	d																						
New Cross	d		19 51			19 56			20 21			20 26			20 51		20 56			21 21		21 26	
Nunhead	d																						
Peckham Rye	d																						
Denmark Hill	d																						
London Victoria	a																						
Westcombe Park	d	19 27			19 47			19 57			20 17			20 27					20 57				
Maze Hill	d	19 29			19 49			19 59			20 19			20 29					20 59				
Greenwich	d	19 32			19 52			20 02			20 22			20 32					21 02				
Deptford	a	19 34			19 54			20 04			20 24			20 34					21 04				
London Bridge	a	19 41	19 57		20 00	20 03	20 06	20 11	20 27		20 30	20 33	20 36	20 41	20 57		21 03	21 06	21 11	21 27		21 33	21 36
London Cannon Street	a																						
London Waterloo (East)	a	19 45	20 04			20 08	20 10	20 15	20 34			20 38	20 40	20 45	21 04		21 08	21 10	21 15	21 34		21 38	21 40
London Charing Cross	a	19 49	20 07			20 12	20 14	20 19	20 37			20 42	20 44	20 49	21 07		21 12	21 14	21 19	21 37		21 42	21 44
Ebbsfleet International	a			19 16						19 47						20 17					20 47		
Stratford International	a			19 27						19 59						20 29					21 02		
St Pancras Int'l	a			19 38						20 06						20 36					21 09		

Table 200

Saturdays

Gillingham and Dartford - London

until 21 July, 18 Aug and from 15 Sep

Network Diagram - see first Page of Table 200

		SE	SE	SE	SE	SE	SE	SE	SE	SE	SE	SE	SE	SE	SE	SE	SE	SE	SE	SE	SE	SE	SE
Gillingham (Kent)	d			20 50		20 54			21 20		21 24			21 50		21 54			22 20		22 24		22 54
Chatham	d			20 54		20 58			21 24		21 28			21 54		21 58			22 24		22 28		22 58
Rochester	d			20 57		21 00			21 27		21 30			21 57		22 00			22 27		22 30		23 00
Maidstone West	d																						
Strood	d			21 02		21 05			21 32		21 35			22 02		22 05			22 32		22 35		23 05
Higham	d					21 10					21 40					22 10					22 40		23 10
Gravesend	d		21 02	21 13		21 18		21 32	21 43		21 48		22 02	22 13		22 18		22 32	22 43		22 48		23 18
Northfleet	d		21 06					21 36					22 06					22 36					
Swanscombe	d		21 08					21 38					22 08					22 38					
Greenhithe for Bluewater	d		21 11			21 23		21 41			21 53		22 11			22 23		22 41			22 53		23 23
Stone Crossing	d		21 13					21 43					22 13					22 43					
Dartford	a		21 17			21 28		21 47			21 58		22 17			22 28		22 47			22 58		23 28
	d	21 01	21 18		21 25	21 29	21 31	21 48		21 55	21 59	22 01	22 18		22 25	22 29	22 31	22 48		22 55	22 59	23 01	
Slade Green	d	21 05					21 35					22 05					22 35					23 05	
Erith	d	21 08					21 38					22 08					22 38					23 08	
Belvedere	d	21 10					21 40					22 10					22 40					23 10	
Abbey Wood	d	21 13				21 38	21 43				22 08	22 13				22 38	22 43				23 08	23 13	
Plumstead	d	21 16					21 46					22 16					22 46					23 16	
Woolwich Arsenal	d	21 19				21 43	21 49				22 13	22 19				22 43	22 49				23 13	23 19	
Woolwich Dockyard	d	21 22					21 52					22 22					22 52					23 22	
Charlton	d	21 25				21 47	21 55				22 17	22 25				22 47	22 55				23 17	23 25	
Crayford	d		21 22					21 52					22 22					22 52					
Bexley	d		21 25					21 55					22 25					22 55					
Albany Park	d		21 28					21 58					22 28					22 58					
Sidcup	d		21 31					22 01					22 31					23 01					
New Eltham	d		21 34					22 04					22 34					23 04					
Mottingham	d		21 36					22 06					22 36					23 06					
Lee	d		21 39					22 09					22 39					23 09					
Hither Green	d		21 42					22 12					22 42					23 12					
Barnehurst	d				21 32					22 02					22 32					23 02			
Bexleyheath	d				21 34					22 04					22 34					23 04			
Welling	d				21 37					22 07					22 37					23 07			
Falconwood	d				21 40					22 10					22 40					23 10			
Eltham	d				21 42					22 12					22 42					23 12			
Kidbrooke	d				21 45					22 15					22 45					23 15			
Blackheath	d				21 49	21 52				22 19	22 22				22 49	22 52				23 19	23 22		
Lewisham	d		21 48		21 53	21 56		22 18		22 23	22 26		22 48		22 53	22 56		23 18		23 23	23 26		
St Johns	d																						
New Cross	d		21 51		21 56			22 21		22 26			22 51		22 56			23 21		23 26			
Nunhead	d																						
Peckham Rye	d																						
Denmark Hill	d																						
London Victoria	a																						
Westcombe Park	d	21 27					21 57					22 27					22 57					23 27	
Maze Hill	d	21 29					21 59					22 29					22 59					23 29	
Greenwich	d	21 32					22 02					22 32					23 02					23 32	
Deptford	a	21 34					22 04					22 34					23 04					23 34	
London Bridge	a	21 41	21 57		22 01	22 05	22 11	22 27		22 31	22 35	22 41	22 57		23 01	23 05	23 11	23 27		23 31	23 35	23 41	
London Cannon Street	a																						
London Waterloo (East)	a	21 45	22 04		22 06	22 09	22 15	22 34		22 36	22 39	22 45	23 04		23 06	23 09	23 15	23 34		23 36	23 39	23 45	
London Charing Cross	a	21 49	22 07		22 10	22 13	22 19	22 37		22 40	22 43	22 49	23 07		23 10	23 13	23 20	23 37		23 40	23 43	23 49	
Ebbsfleet International	a			21 17					21 47					22 17					22 47				
Stratford International	a			21 29					21 59					22 29					22 59				
St Pancras Int'l	a			21 36					22 06					22 36					23 06				

Table 200

Saturdays

Gillingham and Dartford - London

28 July to 11 August

Network Diagram - see first Page of Table 200

		SE A	SE A	SE	SE	SE	SE	SE	SE	SE	SE	SE	SE	SE	SE	SE	SE	SE	SE	SE	SE	SE	SE
Gillingham (Kent)	d									04 48				05 18			05 50		05 54				06 19
Chatham	d									04 52				05 22			05 54		05 58				06 24
Rochester	d									04 54				05 24			05 57		06 00				06 26
Maidstone West	d																						
Strood	d									04 59				05 29			06 02		06 05				06 32
Higham	d									05 04				05 34					06 10				
Gravesend	d									05 12				05 42		06 02	06 13		06 18			06 32	06 43
Northfleet	d									05 15				05 45		06 06						06 36	
Swanscombe	d									05 17				05 47		06 08						06 38	
Greenhithe for Bluewater	d									05 21				05 51		06 11			06 23			06 41	
Stone Crossing	d									05 23				05 53		06 13						06 43	
Dartford	a									05 27				05 57		06 17			06 28			06 47	
	d						05 05	05 18	05 22	05 28	05 35	05 48	05 52	05 58	06 05	06 18		06 22	06 28	06 35	06 38	06 48	
Slade Green	d						05 10				05 40				06 10					06 40			
Erith	d						05 12				05 42				06 12					06 42			
Belvedere	d						05 15				05 45				06 15					06 45			
Abbey Wood	d						05 18			05 37	05 48			06 07	06 18				06 37	06 48			
Plumstead	d						05 21				05 51				06 21					06 51			
Woolwich Arsenal	d						05 24			05 42	05 54			06 12	06 24				06 42	06 54			
Woolwich Dockyard	d																						
Charlton	d	23p45	23p54	00 07	00 15	00 26	05 29			05 47	05 59			06 17	06 29				06 47	06 59			
Crayford	d							05 23				05 53				06 22						06 52	
Bexley	d							05 26				05 56				06 25						06 55	
Albany Park	d							05 29				05 59				06 28						06 58	
Sidcup	d							05 32				06 02				06 31						07 01	
New Eltham	d							05 35				06 05				06 34						07 04	
Mottingham	d							05 37				06 07				06 36						07 06	
Lee	d							05 40				06 10				06 39						07 09	
Hither Green	d							05 42				06 12				06 42						07 12	
Barnehurst	d								05 28				05 58					06 28			06 45		
Bexleyheath	d								05 31				06 01					06 31			06 48		
Welling	d								05 34				06 04					06 34			06 51		
Falconwood	d								05 36				06 06					06 36			06 53		
Eltham	d								05 39				06 09					06 39			06 56		
Kidbrooke	d								05 42				06 12					06 42			06 59		
Blackheath	d								05 46	05 52			06 16	06 22				06 46	06 52		07 04		
Lewisham	d							05 48	05 50	05 56		06 18	06 20	06 26		06 48		06 50	06 56		07 08	07 18	
St Johns	d																						
New Cross	d							05 51				06 21				06 51						07 21	
Nunhead	d																				07 15		
Peckham Rye	d																				07 17		
Denmark Hill	d																				07 21		
London Victoria	a																				07 33		
Westcombe Park	d						05 31				06 01				06 31					07 01			
Maze Hill	d						05 33				06 03				06 33					07 03			
Greenwich	d						05 37				06 07				06 37					07 07			
Deptford	a						05 39				06 09				06 39					07 09			
London Bridge	a						05 45	05 56	05 59	06 05	06 15	06 26	06 29	06 35	06 45	06 56		06 59	07 05	07 15		07 26	
London Cannon Street	a			00 22		00 41																	
London Waterloo (East)	a						05 49	06 01	06 03	06 09	06 19	06 31	06 33	06 39	06 49	07 01		07 03	07 09	07 19		07 31	
London Charing Cross	a	00 08	00 16		00 33		05 56	06 08	06 10	06 16	06 28	06 38	06 40	06 46	06 58	07 08		07 10	07 16	07 28		07 38	
Ebbsfleet International	a																06 16						06 47
Stratford International	a																06 33						06 59
St Pancras Int'l	a																06 43						07 07

A not 28 July

Table 200

Saturdays
28 July to 11 August

Gillingham and Dartford - London

Network Diagram - see first Page of Table 200

Station		SE	SE	SE	SE	SE		SE	SE	SE	SE	SE	SE	SE	SE	SE		SE	SE	SE	SE	SE	SE	SE	SE
Gillingham (Kent)	d	06 20		06 24					06 50				06 54								07 20				
Chatham	d	06 24		06 28					06 54				06 58								07 24				
Rochester	d	06 27		06 30					06 57				07 00								07 27				
Maidstone West	d																								
Strood	d	06 32		06 35					07 02				07 05								07 32				
Higham	d			06 40									07 10												
Gravesend	d	06 43		06 48				07 02	07 13				07 18							07 32	07 43				
Northfleet	d							07 06												07 36					
Swanscombe	d							07 08												07 38					
Greenhithe for Bluewater	d			06 53				07 11					07 23							07 41					
Stone Crossing	d							07 13												07 43					
Dartford	a			06 58				07 17					07 28							07 47					
	d		06 52	06 58	07 01	07 08		07 18		07 22			07 28		07 31			07 38		07 48			07 52		
Slade Green	d				07 05						07 23				07 36				07 43					07 53	
Erith	d				07 08						07 26				07 38				07 45					07 56	
Belvedere	d				07 10						07 28				07 41				07 48					07 58	
Abbey Wood	d			07 07	07 13						07 31		07 37		07 44				07 51					08 01	
Plumstead	d				07 16						07 34				07 47				07 54					08 04	
Woolwich Arsenal	d			07 12	07 19						07 38		07 42		07 50				07 57					08 08	
Woolwich Dockyard	d																								
Charlton	d			07 16	07 24						07 43		07 46		07 56				08 02					08 13	
Crayford	d							07 22								07 38				07 52					
Bexley	d							07 25								07 41				07 55					
Albany Park	d							07 28								07 44				07 58					
Sidcup	d							07 31								07 47				08 01					
New Eltham	d							07 34								07 50				08 04					
Mottingham	d							07 36								07 52				08 06					
Lee	d							07 39								07 55				08 09					
Hither Green	d							07 42				07 49				07 58				08 12					08 19
Barnehurst	d		06 58			07 15				07 28				07 37				07 45					07 58		
Bexleyheath	d		07 01			07 17				07 31				07 39				07 47					08 01		
Welling	d		07 04			07 20				07 34				07 42				07 50					08 04		
Falconwood	d		07 06			07 23				07 36				07 45				07 53					08 06		
Eltham	d		07 09			07 25				07 39				07 48				07 55					08 09		
Kidbrooke	d		07 12			07 28								07 51				07 58							
Blackheath	d		07 16	07 22		07 33				07 46			07 52	07 55				08 03					08 16		
Lewisham	d		07 20	07 26		07 38				07 50		07 54	07 56	07 59		08 04		08 08				08 14	08 20		08 24
St Johns	d											07 56		08 01		08 06						08 16			08 26
New Cross	d											07 58		08 03		08 08						08 18			08 28
Nunhead	d					07 45												08 15							
Peckham Rye	d					07 47												08 17							
Denmark Hill	d					07 51												08 21							
London Victoria	a					08 03												08 33							
Westcombe Park	d				07 26						07 45													08 15	
Maze Hill	d				07 29						07 48				08 00				08 08					08 18	
Greenwich	d				07 33						07 52				08 04				08 14					08 22	
Deptford	a				07 35						07 54													08 24	
London Bridge	a		07 29	07 35	07 41			07 52		07 58	08 00	08 04	08 05	08 08	08 11	08 14			08 20	08 22		08 24	08 28	08 30	08 34
London Cannon Street	a				07 48						08 07	08 11		08 16	08 18	08 22			08 27			08 31		08 37	08 41
London Waterloo (East)	a		07 33	07 39				07 56		08 02			08 09							08 26			08 32		
London Charing Cross	a		07 43	07 46				08 00		08 09			08 16							08 30			08 39		
Ebbsfleet International	a	06 47							07 16												07 46				
Stratford International	a	06 58							07 28												07 58				
St Pancras Int'l	a	07 07							07 36												08 08				

Table 200

Saturdays
28 July to 11 August

Gillingham and Dartford - London

Network Diagram - see first Page of Table 200

Station		SE		SE	SE	SE	SE	SE	SE	SE	SE	SE		SE	SE	SE	SE	SE	SE	SE	SE	SE		SE	SE
Gillingham (Kent)	d	07 24																		07 54	08 20				
Chatham	d	07 28																		07 58	08 24				
Rochester	d	07 30																		08 00	08 27				
Maidstone West	d																								
Strood	d	07 35																		08 05	08 32				
Higham	d	07 40																		08 10					
Gravesend	d	07 48						08 02								08 32				08 18	08 43				
Northfleet	d							08 06								08 36									
Swanscombe	d							08 08								08 38									
Greenhithe for Bluewater	d	07 53						08 11								08 41				08 23					
Stone Crossing	d							08 13								08 43									
Dartford	a	07 58						08 17								08 47				08 28					
	d	07 58			08 01		08 08	08 18		08 22						08 48				08 28				08 31	08 38
Slade Green	d				08 06							08 13							08 23					08 36	
Erith	d				08 08							08 15							08 26					08 38	
Belvedere	d				08 11							08 18							08 28					08 41	
Abbey Wood	d	08 07			08 14							08 21							08 31	08 37				08 44	
Plumstead	d				08 17							08 24							08 34					08 47	
Woolwich Arsenal	d	08 12			08 20						08 19	08 27							08 38	08 42				08 50	
Woolwich Dockyard	d																								
Charlton	d	08 16			08 26							08 32						08 39	08 43	08 46				08 56	
Crayford	d					08 08		08 22							08 38	08 52		09 07							
Bexley	d					08 11		08 25							08 41	08 55		09 10							
Albany Park	d					08 14		08 28							08 44	08 58		09 13							
Sidcup	d					08 17		08 31							08 47	09 01		09 16							
New Eltham	d					08 20		08 34							08 50	09 04		09 19							
Mottingham	d					08 22		08 36							08 52	09 06		09 21							
Lee	d					08 25		08 39							08 55	09 09		09 24							
Hither Green	d					08 28		08 42						08 49	08 58	09 12	09 19	09 28							
Barnehurst	d			08 07			08 15			08 28	08a37											08 37			08 45
Bexleyheath	d			08 09			08 17			08 31												08 39			08 47
Welling	d			08 12			08 20			08 34												08 42			08 50
Falconwood	d			08 15			08 23			08 36												08 45			08 53
Eltham	d			08 18			08 25			08 39												08 48			08 55
Kidbrooke	d			08 21			08 28															08 51			08 58
Blackheath	d	08 22		08 25			08 33			08 46										08 52		08 55			09 03
Lewisham	d	08 26		08 29		08 34	08 38		08 44	08 50				08 54	09 04		09 24	09 34		08 56		08 59			09 08
St Johns	d			08 31		08 36			08 46					08 56	09 06		09 26	09 36				09 01			
New Cross	d			08 33		08 38			08 48					08 58	09 08		09 28	09 38				09 03			
Nunhead	d						08 45																		09 15
Peckham Rye	d						08 47																		09 17
Denmark Hill	d						08 51																		09 21
London Victoria	a						09 03																		09 33
Westcombe Park	d																		08 45						
Maze Hill	d				08 30							08 38							08 48					09 00	
Greenwich	d				08 34							08 44							08 52					09 04	
Deptford	a																		08 54						
London Bridge	a	08 35		08 38	08 41	08 44		08 52	08 54	08 58		08 50		09 04	09 14	09 22	09 34	09 44	09 00	09 05		09 08		09 11	
London Cannon Street	a			08 46	08 48	08 52			09 01			08 57		09 11	09 22		09 41	09 52	09 07			09 16		09 18	
London Waterloo (East)	a	08 39						08 56		09 02						09 26				09 09					
London Charing Cross	a	08 46						09 00		09 09						09 30				09 16					
Ebbsfleet International	a																				08 46				
Stratford International	a																				08 58				
St Pancras Int'l	a																				09 08				

Table 200

Gillingham and Dartford - London

28 July to 11 August

Network Diagram - see first Page of Table 200

		SE	SE	SE	SE	SE	SE	SE		SE	SE	SE	SE	SE	SE	SE	SE	SE		SE	SE	SE	SE	SE	SE
Gillingham (Kent)	d										08 24													08 54	09 20
Chatham	d										08 28													08 58	09 24
Rochester	d										08 30													09 00	09 27
Maidstone West	d																								
Strood	d										08 35													09 05	09 32
Higham	d										08 40													09 10	
Gravesend	d					09 02					08 48									09 32				09 18	09 43
Northfleet	d					09 06														09 36					
Swanscombe	d					09 08														09 38					
Greenhithe for Bluewater	d					09 11					08 53									09 41				09 23	
Stone Crossing	d					09 13														09 43					
Dartford	a					09 17					08 58									09 47				09 28	
	d			08 52		09 18					08 58		09 01	09 08			09 22			09 48				09 28	
Slade Green	d	08 43			08 47					08 53			09 06		09 13			09 17					09 23		
Erith	d	08 45								08 56			09 08		09 15								09 26		
Belvedere	d	08 48								08 58			09 11		09 18								09 28		
Abbey Wood	d	08 51								09 01	09 07		09 14		09 21								09 31	09 37	
Plumstead	d	08 54								09 04			09 17		09 24								09 34		
Woolwich Arsenal	d	08 57								09 08	09 12		09 20		09 27								09 38	09 42	
Woolwich Dockyard	d																								
Charlton	d	09 02						09 09		09 13	09 16		09 26		09 32							09 39	09 43	09 46	
Crayford	d					09 22		09 37												09 52		10 07			
Bexley	d					09 25		09 40												09 55		10 10			
Albany Park	d					09 28		09 43												09 58		10 13			
Sidcup	d					09 31		09 46												10 01		10 16			
New Eltham	d					09 34		09 49												10 04		10 19			
Mottingham	d					09 36		09 51												10 06		10 21			
Lee	d					09 39		09 54												10 09		10 24			
Hither Green	d					09 42	09 49	09 58												10 12	10 19	10 28			
Barnehurst	d			08 58	09 07							09 07		09 15			09 28	09 37							
Bexleyheath	d			09 01	09 09							09 09		09 17			09 31	09 39							
Welling	d			09 04	09 12							09 12		09 20			09 34	09 42							
Falconwood	d			09 06	09 15							09 15		09 23			09 36	09 45							
Eltham	d			09 09	09 18							09 18		09 25			09 39	09 48							
Kidbrooke	d				09 21							09 21		09 28				09 51							
Blackheath	d			09 16	09 25						09 22	09 25		09 33			09 46	09 55						09 52	
Lewisham	d		09 14	09 20	09 29		09 54	10 04			09 26	09 29		09 38		09 44	09 50	09 59			10 24	10 34		09 56	
St Johns	d		09 16		09 31		09 56	10 06				09 31				09 46		10 01			10 26	10 36			
New Cross	d		09 18		09 33		09 58	10 08				09 33				09 48		10 03			10 28	10 38			
Nunhead	d													09 45											
Peckham Rye	d													09 47											
Denmark Hill	d													09 51											
London Victoria	a													10 03											
Westcombe Park	d									09 15													09 45		
Maze Hill	d	09 08								09 18			09 30		09 38								09 48		
Greenwich	d	09 14								09 22			09 34		09 44								09 52		
Deptford	a									09 24													09 54		
London Bridge	a	09 20	09 24	09 28	09 38	09 52	10 04	10 14		09 30	09 35	09 38	09 41		09 50	09 54	09 58	10 08		10 22	10 34	10 44	10 00	10 05	
London Cannon Street	a	09 27	09 31		09 46		10 11	10 22		09 37		09 46	09 48		09 57	10 01		10 16			10 41	10 52	10 07		
London Waterloo (East)	a			09 32		09 56					09 39						10 02			10 26				10 09	
London Charing Cross	a			09 39		10 00					09 43						10 09			10 30				10 16	
Ebbsfleet International	a																								09 46
Stratford International	a																								09 58
St Pancras Int'l	a																								10 08

Table 200

Gillingham and Dartford - London

28 July to 11 August

Network Diagram - see first Page of Table 200

		SE	SE	SE		SE	SE	SE	SE	SE	SE	SE	SE	SE		SE	SE	SE	SE	SE	SE	SE	SE	SE
Gillingham (Kent)	d													09 24										
Chatham	d													09 28										
Rochester	d													09 30										
Maidstone West	d																							
Strood	d													09 35										
Higham	d													09 40										
Gravesend	d									10 02				09 48									10 32	
Northfleet	d									10 06													10 36	
Swanscombe	d									10 08													10 38	
Greenhithe for Bluewater	d									10 11				09 53									10 41	
Stone Crossing	d									10 13													10 43	
Dartford	a									10 17				09 58									10 47	
	d		09 31	09 38				09 52		10 18				09 58			10 01	10 08			10 22		10 48	
Slade Green	d		09 36			09 43			09 47				09 53				10 06		10 13			10 17		
Erith	d		09 38			09 45							09 56				10 08		10 15					
Belvedere	d		09 41			09 48							09 58				10 11		10 18					
Abbey Wood	d		09 44			09 51							10 01	10 07			10 14		10 21					
Plumstead	d		09 47			09 54							10 04				10 17		10 24					
Woolwich Arsenal	d		09 50			09 57							10 08	10 12			10 20		10 27					
Woolwich Dockyard	d																							
Charlton	d		09 56			10 02						10 09	10 13	10 16			10 26		10 32					
Crayford	d									10 22		10 37											10 52	
Bexley	d									10 25		10 40											10 55	
Albany Park	d									10 28		10 43											10 58	
Sidcup	d									10 31		10 46											11 01	
New Eltham	d									10 34		10 49											11 04	
Mottingham	d									10 36		10 51											11 06	
Lee	d									10 39		10 54											11 09	
Hither Green	d									10 42	10 49	10 58											11 12	11 19
Barnehurst	d	09 37		09 45				09 58	10 07							10 07		10 15			10 28	10 37		
Bexleyheath	d	09 39		09 47				10 01	10 09							10 09		10 17			10 31	10 39		
Welling	d	09 42		09 50				10 04	10 12							10 12		10 20			10 34	10 42		
Falconwood	d	09 45		09 53				10 06	10 15							10 15		10 23			10 36	10 45		
Eltham	d	09 48		09 55				10 09	10 18							10 18		10 25			10 39	10 48		
Kidbrooke	d	09 51		09 58					10 21							10 21		10 28				10 51		
Blackheath	d	09 55		10 03				10 16	10 25					10 22		10 25		10 33			10 46	10 55		
Lewisham	d	09 59		10 08			10 14	10 20	10 29		10 54	11 04		10 26		10 29		10 38		10 44	10 50	10 59		11 24
St Johns	d	10 01					10 16		10 31		10 56	11 06				10 31				10 46		11 01		11 26
New Cross	d	10 03					10 18		10 33		10 58	11 08				10 33				10 48		11 03		11 28
Nunhead	d			10 15														10 45						
Peckham Rye	d			10 17														10 47						
Denmark Hill	d			10 21														10 51						
London Victoria	a			10 33														11 03						
Westcombe Park	d												10 15											
Maze Hill	d		10 00			10 08							10 18				10 30		10 38					
Greenwich	d		10 04			10 14							10 22				10 34		10 44					
Deptford	a												10 24											
London Bridge	a	10 08	10 11			10 20	10 24	10 28	10 38	10 52	11 04	11 14	10 30	10 35		10 38	10 41		10 50	10 54	10 58	11 08	11 22	11 34
London Cannon Street	a	10 16	10 18			10 27	10 31		10 46		11 11	11 22	10 37			10 46	10 48		10 57	11 01		11 16		11 41
London Waterloo (East)	a							10 32		10 56				10 39							11 02		11 26	
London Charing Cross	a							10 39		11 00				10 46							11 09		11 30	
Ebbsfleet International	a																							
Stratford International	a																							
St Pancras Int'l	a																							

Table 200

Saturdays

28 July to 11 August

Gillingham and Dartford - London

Network Diagram - see first Page of Table 200

Station		SE	SE	SE	SE	SE	SE	SE	SE	SE		SE	SE	SE	SE	SE	SE	SE	SE	SE		SE	SE	SE	SE
Gillingham (Kent)	d			09 54	10 20													10 24							
Chatham	d			09 58	10 24													10 28							
Rochester	d			10 00	10 27													10 30							
Maidstone West	d																								
Strood	d			10 05	10 32													10 35							
Higham	d			10 10														10 40							
Gravesend	d			10 18	10 43									11 02				10 48							
Northfleet	d													11 06											
Swanscombe	d													11 08											
Greenhithe for Bluewater	d			10 23										11 11				10 53							
Stone Crossing	d													11 13											
Dartford	a			10 28										11 17				10 58							
	d			10 28			10 31	10 38				10 52		11 18				10 58		11 01		11 08			11 22
Slade Green	d		10 23				10 36		10 43				10 47				10 53			11 06			11 13		
Erith	d		10 26				10 38		10 45								10 56			11 08			11 15		
Belvedere	d		10 28				10 41		10 48								10 58			11 11			11 18		
Abbey Wood	d		10 31	10 37			10 44		10 51								11 01	11 07		11 14			11 21		
Plumstead	d		10 34				10 47		10 54								11 04			11 17			11 24		
Woolwich Arsenal	d		10 38	10 42			10 50		10 57								11 08	11 12		11 20			11 27		
Woolwich Dockyard	d																								
Charlton	d	10 39	10 43	10 46			10 56		11 02							11 09	11 13	11 16		11 26			11 32		
Crayford	d	11 07												11 22		11 37									
Bexley	d	11 10												11 25		11 40									
Albany Park	d	11 13												11 28		11 43									
Sidcup	d	11 16												11 31		11 46									
New Eltham	d	11 19												11 34		11 49									
Mottingham	d	11 21												11 36		11 51									
Lee	d	11 24												11 39		11 54									
Hither Green	d	11 28												11 42	11 49	11 58									
Barnehurst	d					10 37		10 45				10 58	11 07						11 07			11 15			11 28
Bexleyheath	d					10 39		10 47				11 01	11 09						11 09			11 17			11 31
Welling	d					10 42		10 50				11 04	11 12						11 12			11 20			11 34
Falconwood	d					10 45		10 53				11 06	11 15						11 15			11 23			11 36
Eltham	d					10 48		10 55				11 09	11 18						11 18			11 25			11 39
Kidbrooke	d					10 51		10 58					11 21						11 21			11 28			
Blackheath	d			10 52		10 55		11 03				11 16	11 25					11 22	11 25			11 33			11 46
Lewisham	d	11 34		10 56		10 59		11 08		11 14		11 20	11 29		11 54	12 04		11 26	11 29			11 38		11 44	11 50
St Johns	d	11 36				11 01				11 16			11 31		11 56	12 06			11 31					11 46	
New Cross	d	11 38				11 03				11 18			11 33		11 58	12 08			11 33					11 48	
Nunhead	d							11 15														11 45			
Peckham Rye	d							11 17														11 47			
Denmark Hill	d							11 21														11 51			
London Victoria	a							11 33														12 03			
Westcombe Park	d		10 45														11 15								
Maze Hill	d		10 48				11 00		11 08								11 18			11 30			11 38		
Greenwich	d		10 52				11 04		11 14								11 22			11 34			11 44		
Deptford	a		10 54														11 24								
London Bridge	a	11 44	11 00	11 05		11 08	11 11		11 20	11 24		11 28	11 38	11 52	12 04	12 14	11 30	11 35	11 38	11 41			11 50	11 54	11 58
London Cannon Street	a	11 52	11 07			11 16	11 18		11 27	11 31			11 46		12 11	12 22	11 37		11 46	11 48			11 57	12 01	
London Waterloo (East)	a			11 09								11 32		11 56				11 39							12 02
London Charing Cross	a			11 16								11 39		12 00				11 46							12 09
Ebbsfleet International	a				10 46																				
Stratford International	a				10 58																				
St Pancras Int'l	a				11 08																				

Table 200

Saturdays

28 July to 11 August

Gillingham and Dartford - London

Network Diagram - see first Page of Table 200

Station		SE	SE	SE	SE	SE		SE	SE	SE	SE	SE	SE	SE	SE	SE		SE	SE	SE	SE	SE	SE	SE	SE
Gillingham (Kent)	d							10 54	11 20													11 24			
Chatham	d							10 58	11 24													11 28			
Rochester	d							11 00	11 27													11 30			
Maidstone West	d																								
Strood	d							11 05	11 32													11 35			
Higham	d							11 10														11 40			
Gravesend	d		11 32					11 18	11 43									12 02				11 48			
Northfleet	d		11 36															12 06							
Swanscombe	d		11 38															12 08							
Greenhithe for Bluewater	d		11 41					11 23										12 11				11 53			
Stone Crossing	d		11 43															12 13							
Dartford	a		11 47					11 28										12 17				11 58			
	d		11 48					11 28			11 31	11 38			11 52			12 18				11 58		12 01	12 08
Slade Green	d	11 17				11 23					11 36		11 43			11 47					11 53			12 05	
Erith	d					11 26					11 38		11 45								11 56			12 08	
Belvedere	d					11 28					11 41		11 48								11 58			12 10	
Abbey Wood	d					11 31		11 37			11 44		11 51								12 01	12 07		12 13	
Plumstead	d					11 34					11 47		11 54								12 04			12 16	
Woolwich Arsenal	d					11 38		11 42			11 50		11 58								12 08	12 12		12 19	
Woolwich Dockyard	d																								
Charlton	d				11 39	11 43		11 46			11 56		12 07							12 09	12 13	12 16		12 26	
Crayford	d		11 52		12 07													12 22		12 37					
Bexley	d		11 55		12 10													12 25		12 40					
Albany Park	d		11 58		12 13													12 28		12 43					
Sidcup	d		12 01		12 16													12 31		12 46					
New Eltham	d		12 04		12 19													12 34		12 49					
Mottingham	d		12 06		12 21													12 36		12 51					
Lee	d		12 09		12 24													12 39		12 54					
Hither Green	d		12 12	12 19	12 28													12 42	12 49	12 58					
Barnehurst	d	11 37								11 37		11 45			11 58	12 07							12 07		12 15
Bexleyheath	d	11 39								11 39		11 47			12 01	12 09							12 09		12 17
Welling	d	11 42								11 42		11 50			12 04	12 12							12 12		12 20
Falconwood	d	11 45								11 45		11 53			12 06	12 15							12 15		12 23
Eltham	d	11 48								11 48		11 55			12 09	12 18							12 18		12 25
Kidbrooke	d	11 51								11 51		11 58				12 21							12 21		12 28
Blackheath	d	11 55						11 52		11 55		12 03			12 16	12 25						12 22	12 25		12 33
Lewisham	d	11 59		12 24	12 34			11 56		11 59		12 08		12 14	12 20	12 29			12 54	13 04		12 26	12 29		12 38
St Johns	d	12 01		12 26	12 36					12 01				12 16		12 31			12 56	13 06			12 31		
New Cross	d	12 03		12 28	12 38					12 03				12 18		12 33			12 58	13 08			12 33		
Nunhead	d											12 15													12 45
Peckham Rye	d											12 17													12 47
Denmark Hill	d											12 21													12 51
London Victoria	a											12 33													13 03
Westcombe Park	d					11 45															12 15				
Maze Hill	d					11 48					12 00														
Greenwich	d					11 52					12 04		12 13								12 22			12 33	
Deptford	a					11 54															12 24				
London Bridge	a	12 08	12 22	12 34	12 44	12 00		12 05		12 08	12 11		12 20	12 24	12 28	12 38		12 52	13 04	13 14	12 30	12 35	12 38	12 41	
London Cannon Street	a	12 16		12 41	12 52	12 07				12 16	12 18		12 27	12 31		12 46			13 11	13 22	12 37		12 46	12 48	
London Waterloo (East)	a		12 26					12 09							12 32			12 56				12 39			
London Charing Cross	a		12 30					12 16							12 39			13 00				12 46			
Ebbsfleet International	a								11 46																
Stratford International	a								11 58																
St Pancras Int'l	a								12 08																

Table 200

Gillingham and Dartford - London

Saturdays

28 July to 11 August

Network Diagram - see first Page of Table 200

		SE		SE	SE	SE	SE	SE	SE	SE	SE	SE		SE	SE	SE	SE	SE	SE	SE	SE	SE		SE	SE
Gillingham (Kent)	d										11 54	12 20													
Chatham	d										11 58	12 24													
Rochester	d										12 00	12 27													
Maidstone West	d																								
Strood	d										12 05	12 32													
Higham	d										12 10														
Gravesend	d						12 32				12 18	12 43									13 02				
Northfleet	d						12 36														13 06				
Swanscombe	d						12 38														13 08				
Greenhithe for Bluewater	d						12 41				12 23										13 11				
Stone Crossing	d						12 43														13 13				
Dartford	a						12 47				12 28										13 17				
	d				12 22		12 48				12 28				12 31	12 38			12 52		13 18				
Slade Green	d	12 13				12 17				12 23					12 35		12 43			12 47					12 53
Erith	d	12 15								12 26					12 38		12 45								12 56
Belvedere	d	12 18								12 28					12 40		12 48								12 58
Abbey Wood	d	12 21								12 31	12 37				12 43		12 51								13 01
Plumstead	d	12 24								12 34					12 46		12 54								13 04
Woolwich Arsenal	d	12 28								12 38	12 42				12 49		12 58								13 08
Woolwich Dockyard	d																								
Charlton	d	12 37							12 39	12 43	12 46				12 56		13 07							13 09	13 13
Crayford	d						12 52		13 07												13 22			13 37	
Bexley	d						12 55		13 10												13 25			13 40	
Albany Park	d						12 58		13 13												13 28			13 43	
Sidcup	d						13 01		13 16												13 31			13 46	
New Eltham	d						13 04		13 19												13 34			13 49	
Mottingham	d						13 06		13 21												13 36			13 51	
Lee	d						13 09		13 24												13 39			13 54	
Hither Green	d						13 12	13 19	13 28												13 42	13 49		13 58	
Barnehurst	d				12 28	12 37								12 37		12 45			12 58	13 07					
Bexleyheath	d				12 31	12 39								12 39		12 47			13 01	13 09					
Welling	d				12 34	12 42								12 42		12 50			13 04	13 12					
Falconwood	d				12 36	12 45								12 45		12 53			13 06	13 15					
Eltham	d				12 39	12 48								12 48		12 55			13 09	13 18					
Kidbrooke	d					12 51								12 51		12 58				13 21					
Blackheath	d				12 46	12 55					12 52			12 55		13 03			13 16	13 25					
Lewisham	d			12 44	12 50	12 59		13 24	13 34		12 56			12 59		13 08		13 14	13 20	13 29		13 54		14 04	
St Johns	d			12 46		13 01		13 26	13 36					13 01				13 16		13 31		13 56		14 06	
New Cross	d			12 48		13 03		13 28	13 38					13 03				13 18		13 33		13 58		14 08	
Nunhead	d															13 15									
Peckham Rye	d															13 17									
Denmark Hill	d															13 21									
London Victoria	a															13 33									
Westcombe Park	d									12 45															13 15
Maze Hill	d																								
Greenwich	d	12 43								12 52					13 03		13 13								13 22
Deptford	a									12 54															13 24
London Bridge	a	12 50		12 54	12 58	13 08	13 22	13 34	13 44	13 00	13 05			13 08	13 11		13 20	13 24	13 27	13 38	13 52	14 04		14 14	13 30
London Cannon Street	a	12 57		13 01		13 16		13 41	13 52	13 07				13 16	13 18		13 27	13 31		13 46		14 11		14 22	13 37
London Waterloo (East)	a				13 02		13 26				13 09								13 32		13 56				
London Charing Cross	a				13 09		13 30				13 16								13 39		14 00				
Ebbsfleet International	a											12 46													
Stratford International	a											12 58													
St Pancras Int'l	a											13 08													

Table 200

Gillingham and Dartford - London

Saturdays

28 July to 11 August

Network Diagram - see first Page of Table 200

		SE	SE	SE	SE	SE	SE	SE		SE	SE	SE	SE	SE	SE	SE	SE	SE		SE	SE	SE	SE	SE	SE
Gillingham (Kent)	d	12 24													12 54	13 20									
Chatham	d	12 28													12 58	13 24									
Rochester	d	12 30													13 00	13 27									
Maidstone West	d																								
Strood	d	12 35													13 05	13 32									
Higham	d	12 40													13 10										
Gravesend	d	12 48									13 32				13 18	13 43									14 02
Northfleet	d										13 36														14 06
Swanscombe	d										13 38														14 08
Greenhithe for Bluewater	d	12 53									13 41				13 23										14 11
Stone Crossing	d										13 43														14 13
Dartford	a	12 58									13 47				13 28										14 17
	d	12 58		13 01	13 08			13 22			13 48				13 28			13 31		13 38			13 52		14 18
Slade Green	d			13 05		13 13				13 17				13 23				13 35			13 43			13 47	
Erith	d			13 08		13 15								13 26				13 38			13 45				
Belvedere	d			13 10		13 18								13 28				13 40			13 48				
Abbey Wood	d	13 07		13 13		13 21								13 31	13 37			13 43			13 51				
Plumstead	d			13 16		13 24								13 34				13 46			13 54				
Woolwich Arsenal	d	13 12		13 19		13 28								13 38	13 42			13 49			13 58				
Woolwich Dockyard	d																								
Charlton	d	13 16		13 26		13 37							13 39	13 43	13 46			13 56			14 07				
Crayford	d										13 52		14 07												14 22
Bexley	d										13 55		14 10												14 25
Albany Park	d										13 58		14 13												14 28
Sidcup	d										14 01		14 16												14 31
New Eltham	d										14 04		14 19												14 34
Mottingham	d										14 06		14 21												14 36
Lee	d										14 09		14 24												14 39
Hither Green	d										14 12	14 19	14 28												14 42
Barnehurst	d		13 07		13 15			13 28		13 37							13 37			13 45			13 58	14 07	
Bexleyheath	d		13 09		13 17			13 31		13 39							13 39			13 47			14 01	14 09	
Welling	d		13 12		13 20			13 34		13 42							13 42			13 50			14 04	14 12	
Falconwood	d		13 15		13 23			13 36		13 45							13 45			13 53			14 06	14 15	
Eltham	d		13 18		13 25			13 39		13 48							13 48			13 55			14 09	14 18	
Kidbrooke	d		13 21		13 28					13 51							13 51			13 58				14 21	
Blackheath	d	13 22	13 25		13 33			13 46		13 55					13 52		13 55			14 03			14 16	14 25	
Lewisham	d	13 26	13 29		13 38		13 44	13 50		13 59		14 24	14 34		13 56		13 59			14 08		14 14	14 20	14 29	
St Johns	d		13 31				13 46			14 01		14 26	14 36				14 01					14 16		14 31	
New Cross	d		13 33				13 48			14 03		14 28	14 38				14 03					14 18		14 33	
Nunhead	d				13 45															14 15					
Peckham Rye	d				13 47															14 17					
Denmark Hill	d				13 51															14 21					
London Victoria	a				14 03															14 33					
Westcombe Park	d													13 45											
Maze Hill	d																								
Greenwich	d			13 33		13 43								13 52				14 03			14 13				
Deptford	a													13 54											
London Bridge	a	13 35	13 38	13 41		13 50	13 54	13 58		14 08	14 22	14 34	14 44	14 00	14 05		14 08	14 11			14 20	14 24	14 28	14 38	14 52
London Cannon Street	a		13 46	13 48		13 57	14 01			14 16		14 41	14 52	14 07			14 16	14 18			14 27	14 31		14 46	
London Waterloo (East)	a	13 39						14 02			14 26				14 09								14 32		14 56
London Charing Cross	a	13 46						14 09			14 30				14 16								14 39		15 00
Ebbsfleet International	a															13 46									
Stratford International	a															13 58									
St Pancras Int'l	a															14 08									

Table 200

Saturdays
28 July to 11 August

Gillingham and Dartford - London

Network Diagram - see first Page of Table 200

Station		SE	SE	SE		SE	SE	SE	SE	SE	SE	SE	SE	SE		SE	SE	SE	SE	SE	SE	SE	SE	SE
Gillingham (Kent) 4	d					13 24													13 54	14 20				
Chatham 4	d					13 28													13 58	14 24				
Rochester 4	d					13 30													14 00	14 27				
Maidstone West	d																							
Strood 4	d					13 35													14 05	14 32				
Higham	d					13 40													14 10					
Gravesend 4	d					13 48								14 32					14 18	14 43				
Northfleet	d													14 36										
Swanscombe	d													14 38										
Greenhithe for Bluewater	d					13 53								14 41					14 23					
Stone Crossing	d													14 43										
Dartford 4	a					13 58								14 47					14 28					
	d					13 58		14 01	14 08			14 22		14 48					14 28			14 31	14 38	
Slade Green 4	d			13 53				14 05		14 13			14 17					14 23				14 35		14 43
Erith	d			13 56				14 08		14 15								14 26				14 38		14 45
Belvedere	d			13 58				14 10		14 18								14 28				14 40		14 48
Abbey Wood	d			14 01		14 07		14 13		14 21								14 31	14 37			14 43		14 51
Plumstead	d			14 04				14 16		14 24								14 34				14 46		14 54
Woolwich Arsenal 4	d			14 08		14 12		14 19		14 28								14 38	14 42			14 49		14 58
Woolwich Dockyard	d																							
Charlton 4	d		14 09	14 13		14 16		14 26		14 37							14 39	14 43	14 46			14 56		15 07
Crayford	d		14 37											14 52			15 07							
Bexley	d		14 40											14 55			15 10							
Albany Park	d		14 43											14 58			15 13							
Sidcup 4	d		14 46											15 01			15 16							
New Eltham	d		14 49											15 04			15 19							
Mottingham	d		14 51											15 06			15 21							
Lee	d		14 54											15 09			15 24							
Hither Green 4	d	14 49	14 58											15 12		15 19	15 28							
Barnehurst 4	d						14 07		14 15			14 28	14 37								14 37		14 45	
Bexleyheath	d						14 09		14 17			14 31	14 39								14 39		14 47	
Welling	d						14 12		14 20			14 34	14 42								14 42		14 50	
Falconwood	d						14 15		14 23			14 36	14 45								14 45		14 53	
Eltham	d						14 18		14 25			14 39	14 48								14 48		14 55	
Kidbrooke	d						14 21		14 28				14 51								14 51		14 58	
Blackheath 4	d					14 22	14 25		14 33			14 46	14 55						14 52		14 55		15 03	
Lewisham 4	d	14 54	15 04			14 26	14 29		14 38		14 44	14 50	14 59			15 24	15 34		14 56		14 59		15 08	
St Johns	d	14 56	15 06				14 31				14 46		15 01			15 26	15 36				15 01			
New Cross 4	d	14 58	15 08				14 33				14 48		15 03			15 28	15 38				15 03			
Nunhead 4	d								14 45														15 15	
Peckham Rye 4	d								14 47														15 17	
Denmark Hill 4	d								14 51														15 21	
London Victoria 15	a								15 03														15 33	
Westcombe Park	d			14 15														14 45						
Maze Hill	d																							
Greenwich 4	d			14 22				14 33		14 43								14 52				15 03		15 13
Deptford	a			14 24														14 54						
London Bridge 4	a	15 04	15 14	14 30		14 35	14 38	14 41		14 50	14 54	14 58	15 08	15 22		15 34	15 44	15 00	15 05		15 08	15 11		15 20
London Cannon Street 4	a	15 11	15 22	14 37			14 46	14 48		14 57	15 01		15 16			15 41	15 52	15 07			15 16	15 18		15 27
London Waterloo (East) 4	a					14 39						15 02		15 26					15 09					
London Charing Cross 4	a					14 46						15 09		15 30					15 16					
Ebbsfleet International	a																			14 46				
Stratford International	a																			14 58				
St Pancras Int'l 15	a																			15 08				

Table 200

Saturdays
28 July to 11 August

Gillingham and Dartford - London

Network Diagram - see first Page of Table 200

Station		SE	SE	SE	SE	SE	SE	SE	SE	SE		SE	SE	SE	SE	SE	SE	SE	SE	SE		SE	SE	SE	SE
Gillingham (Kent) 4	d								14 24														14 54	15 20	
Chatham 4	d								14 28														14 58	15 24	
Rochester 4	d								14 30														15 00	15 27	
Maidstone West	d																								
Strood 4	d								14 35														15 05	15 32	
Higham	d								14 40														15 10		
Gravesend 4	d				15 02				14 48									15 32					15 18	15 43	
Northfleet	d				15 06													15 36							
Swanscombe	d				15 08													15 38							
Greenhithe for Bluewater	d				15 11				14 53									15 41					15 23		
Stone Crossing	d				15 13													15 43							
Dartford 4	a				15 17				14 58									15 47					15 28		
	d		14 52		15 18				14 58			15 01	15 08			15 22		15 48					15 28		
Slade Green 4	d			14 47				14 53				15 05		15 13			15 17					15 23			
Erith	d							14 56				15 08		15 15								15 26			
Belvedere	d							14 58				15 10		15 18								15 28			
Abbey Wood	d							15 01	15 07			15 13		15 21								15 31	15 37		
Plumstead	d							15 04				15 16		15 24								15 34			
Woolwich Arsenal 4	d							15 08	15 12			15 19		15 28								15 38	15 42		
Woolwich Dockyard	d																								
Charlton 4	d						15 09	15 13	15 16			15 26		15 37						15 39		15 43	15 46		
Crayford	d				15 22		15 37											15 52		16 07					
Bexley	d				15 25		15 40											15 55		16 10					
Albany Park	d				15 28		15 43											15 58		16 13					
Sidcup 4	d				15 31		15 46											16 01		16 16					
New Eltham	d				15 34		15 49											16 04		16 19					
Mottingham	d				15 36		15 51											16 06		16 21					
Lee	d				15 39		15 54											16 09		16 24					
Hither Green 4	d				15 42	15 49	15 58											16 12	16 19	16 28					
Barnehurst 4	d		14 58	15 07						15 07			15 15			15 28	15 37								15 37
Bexleyheath	d		15 01	15 09						15 09			15 17			15 31	15 39								15 39
Welling	d		15 04	15 12						15 12			15 20			15 34	15 42								15 42
Falconwood	d		15 06	15 15						15 15			15 23			15 36	15 45								15 45
Eltham	d		15 09	15 18						15 18			15 25			15 39	15 48								15 48
Kidbrooke	d			15 21						15 21			15 28				15 51								15 51
Blackheath 4	d		15 16	15 25					15 22	15 25			15 33			15 46	15 55						15 52		15 55
Lewisham 4	d	15 14	15 20	15 29		15 54	16 04		15 26	15 29			15 38		15 44	15 50	15 59		16 24	16 34			15 56		15 59
St Johns	d	15 16		15 31		15 56	16 06			15 31					15 46		16 01		16 26	16 36					16 01
New Cross 4	d	15 18		15 33		15 58	16 08			15 33					15 48		16 03		16 28	16 38					16 03
Nunhead 4	d												15 45												
Peckham Rye 4	d												15 47												
Denmark Hill 4	d												15 51												
London Victoria 15	a												16 03												
Westcombe Park	d							15 15														15 45			
Maze Hill	d																								
Greenwich 4	d							15 22				15 33		15 43								15 52			
Deptford	a							15 24														15 54			
London Bridge 4	a	15 24	15 28	15 38	15 52	16 04	16 14	15 30	15 35	15 38		15 41		15 50	15 54	15 58	16 08	16 22	16 34	16 44		16 00	16 05		16 08
London Cannon Street 4	a	15 31		15 46		16 11	16 22	15 37		15 46		15 48		15 57	16 01		16 16		16 41	16 52		16 07			16 16
London Waterloo (East) 4	a		15 32		15 56				15 39							16 02		16 26					16 09		
London Charing Cross 4	a		15 39		16 00				15 46							16 09		16 30					16 16		
Ebbsfleet International	a																							15 46	
Stratford International	a																							15 58	
St Pancras Int'l 15	a																							16 08	

Table 200

Gillingham and Dartford - London

Saturdays

28 July to 11 August

Network Diagram - see first Page of Table 200

		SE	SE	SE	SE	SE		SE	SE	SE	SE	SE	SE	SE	SE	SE		SE	SE	SE	SE	SE	SE	SE	SE
Gillingham (Kent)	d												15 24												
Chatham	d												15 28												
Rochester	d												15 30												
Maidstone West	d																								
Strood	d												15 35												
Higham	d												15 40												
Gravesend	d								16 02				15 48									16 32			
Northfleet	d								16 06													16 36			
Swanscombe	d								16 08													16 38			
Greenhithe for Bluewater	d								16 11				15 53									16 41			
Stone Crossing	d								16 13													16 43			
Dartford	a								16 17				15 58									16 47			
	d	15 31	15 38			15 52			16 18				15 58		16 01	16 08				16 22		16 48			
Slade Green	d	15 35		15 43				15 47				15 53			16 05			16 13			16 17				16 23
Erith	d	15 38		15 45								15 56			16 08			16 15							16 26
Belvedere	d	15 40		15 48								15 58			16 10			16 18							16 28
Abbey Wood	d	15 43		15 51								16 01	16 07		16 13			16 21							16 31
Plumstead	d	15 46		15 54								16 04			16 16			16 24							16 34
Woolwich Arsenal	d	15 49		15 58								16 08	16 12		16 19			16 28							16 38
Woolwich Dockyard	d																								
Charlton	d	15 56		16 07							16 09	16 13	16 16		16 26			16 37						16 39	16 43
Crayford	d								16 22		16 37											16 52		17 07	
Bexley	d								16 25		16 40											16 55		17 10	
Albany Park	d								16 28		16 43											16 58		17 13	
Sidcup	d								16 31		16 46											17 01		17 16	
New Eltham	d								16 34		16 49											17 04		17 19	
Mottingham	d								16 36		16 51											17 06		17 21	
Lee	d								16 39		16 54											17 09		17 24	
Hither Green	d								16 42	16 49	16 58											17 12	17 19	17 28	
Barnehurst	d		15 45			15 58		16 07						16 07		16 15				16 28	16 37				
Bexleyheath	d		15 47			16 01		16 09						16 09		16 17				16 31	16 39				
Welling	d		15 50			16 04		16 12						16 12		16 20				16 34	16 42				
Falconwood	d		15 53			16 06		16 15						16 15		16 23				16 36	16 45				
Eltham	d		15 55			16 09		16 18						16 18		16 25				16 39	16 48				
Kidbrooke	d		15 58					16 21						16 21		16 28					16 51				
Blackheath	d		16 03			16 16		16 25					16 22	16 25		16 33				16 46	16 55				
Lewisham	d		16 08		16 14	16 20		16 29		16 54	17 04		16 26	16 29		16 38			16 44	16 50	16 59		17 24	17 34	
St Johns	d				16 16			16 31		16 56	17 06			16 31					16 46		17 01		17 26	17 36	
New Cross	d				16 18			16 33		16 58	17 08			16 33					16 48		17 03		17 28	17 38	
Nunhead	d		16 15													16 45									
Peckham Rye	d		16 17													16 47									
Denmark Hill	d		16 21													16 51									
London Victoria	a		16 33													17 03									
Westcombe Park	d											16 15													16 45
Maze Hill	d																								
Greenwich	d	16 03		16 13								16 22			16 33			16 43							16 52
Deptford	a											16 24													16 54
London Bridge	a	16 11		16 20	16 24	16 28		16 38	16 52	17 04	17 14	16 30	16 35	16 38	16 41			16 50	16 54	16 58	17 08	17 22	17 34	17 44	17 00
London Cannon Street	a	16 18		16 27	16 31			16 46		17 11	17 22	16 37		16 46	16 48			16 57	17 01		17 16		17 41	17 52	17 07
London Waterloo (East)	a					16 32			16 56				16 39							17 02		17 26			
London Charing Cross	a					16 39			17 00				16 46							17 09		17 30			
Ebbsfleet International	a																								
Stratford International	a																								
St Pancras Int'l	a																								

Table 200

Gillingham and Dartford - London

Saturdays

28 July to 11 August

Network Diagram - see first Page of Table 200

		SE		SE	SE	SE	SE	SE	SE	SE	SE	SE		SE	SE	SE	SE	SE	SE	SE	SE	SE		SE	SE
Gillingham (Kent)	d	15 54		16 20													16 24								
Chatham	d	15 58		16 24													16 28								
Rochester	d	16 00		16 27													16 30								
Maidstone West	d																								
Strood	d	16 05		16 32													16 35								
Higham	d	16 10															16 40								
Gravesend	d	16 18		16 43								17 02					16 48								
Northfleet	d											17 06													
Swanscombe	d											17 08													
Greenhithe for Bluewater	d	16 23										17 11					16 53								
Stone Crossing	d											17 13													
Dartford	a	16 28										17 17					16 58								
	d	16 28				16 31	16 38			16 52		17 18					16 58		17 01	17 08				17 22	
Slade Green	d					16 35		16 43			16 47					16 53			17 05		17 13				17 17
Erith	d					16 38		16 45								16 56			17 08		17 15				
Belvedere	d					16 40		16 48								16 58			17 10		17 18				
Abbey Wood	d	16 37				16 43		16 51								17 01	17 07		17 13		17 21				
Plumstead	d					16 46		16 54								17 04			17 16		17 24				
Woolwich Arsenal	d	16 42				16 49		16 58								17 08	17 12		17 19		17 28				
Woolwich Dockyard	d																								
Charlton	d	16 46				16 56		17 07							17 09	17 13	17 16		17 26		17 37				
Crayford	d											17 22			17 37										
Bexley	d											17 25			17 40										
Albany Park	d											17 28			17 43										
Sidcup	d											17 31			17 46										
New Eltham	d											17 34			17 49										
Mottingham	d											17 36			17 51										
Lee	d											17 39			17 54										
Hither Green	d											17 42		17 49	17 58										
Barnehurst	d				16 37		16 45			16 58	17 07							17 07		17 15				17 28	17 37
Bexleyheath	d				16 39		16 47			17 01	17 09							17 09		17 17				17 31	17 39
Welling	d				16 42		16 50			17 04	17 12							17 12		17 20				17 34	17 42
Falconwood	d				16 45		16 53			17 06	17 15							17 15		17 23				17 36	17 45
Eltham	d				16 48		16 55			17 09	17 18							17 18		17 25				17 39	17 48
Kidbrooke	d				16 51		16 58				17 21							17 21		17 28					17 51
Blackheath	d	16 52			16 55		17 03			17 16	17 25						17 22	17 25		17 33				17 46	17 55
Lewisham	d	16 56			16 59		17 08		17 14	17 20	17 29			17 54	18 04		17 26	17 29		17 38		17 44		17 50	17 59
St Johns	d				17 01				17 16		17 31			17 56	18 06			17 31				17 46			18 01
New Cross	d				17 03				17 18		17 33			17 58	18 08			17 33				17 48			18 03
Nunhead	d						17 15													17 45					
Peckham Rye	d						17 17													17 47					
Denmark Hill	d						17 21													17 51					
London Victoria	a						17 33													18 03					
Westcombe Park	d															17 15									
Maze Hill	d																								
Greenwich	d					17 03		17 13								17 22			17 33		17 43				
Deptford	a															17 24									
London Bridge	a	17 05			17 08	17 11		17 20	17 24	17 28	17 38	17 52		18 04	18 14	17 30	17 35	17 38	17 41		17 50	17 54		17 58	18 08
London Cannon Street	a				17 16	17 18		17 27	17 31		17 46			18 11	18 22	17 37		17 46	17 48		17 57	18 01			18 16
London Waterloo (East)	a	17 09								17 32		17 56					17 39							18 02	
London Charing Cross	a	17 16								17 39		18 00					17 46							18 09	
Ebbsfleet International	a			16 46																					
Stratford International	a																								
St Pancras Int'l	a																								

Table 200

Saturdays

28 July to 11 August

Gillingham and Dartford - London

Network Diagram - see first Page of Table 200

		SE	SE	SE	SE	SE	SE	SE	SE	SE	SE	SE	SE	SE	SE	SE	SE	SE	SE	SE	SE	SE	SE
Gillingham (Kent)	d					16 54	17 20												17 24				
Chatham	d					16 58	17 24												17 28				
Rochester	d					17 00	17 27												17 30				
Maidstone West	d																						
Strood	d					17 05	17 32												17 35				
Higham	d					17 10													17 40				
Gravesend	d	17 32				17 18	17 43								18 02				17 48				
Northfleet	d	17 36													18 06								
Swanscombe	d	17 38													18 08								
Greenhithe for Bluewater	d	17 41				17 23									18 11				17 53				
Stone Crossing	d	17 43													18 13								
Dartford	a	17 47				17 28									18 17				17 58				
	d	17 48				17 28			17 31	17 38			17 52		18 18				17 58		18 01	18 08	
Slade Green	d				17 23				17 35		17 43			17 47				17 53			18 05		18 13
Erith	d				17 26				17 38		17 45							17 56			18 08		18 15
Belvedere	d				17 28				17 40		17 48							17 58			18 10		18 18
Abbey Wood	d				17 31	17 37			17 43		17 51							18 01	18 07		18 13		18 21
Plumstead	d				17 34				17 46		17 54							18 04			18 16		18 24
Woolwich Arsenal ⇌	d				17 38	17 42			17 49		17 58							18 08	18 12		18 19		18 28
Woolwich Dockyard	d																						
Charlton	d			17 39	17 43	17 46			17 56		18 07						18 09	18 13	18 16		18 26		18 37
Crayford	d	17 52		18 07											18 22		18 37						
Bexley	d	17 55		18 10											18 25		18 40						
Albany Park	d	17 58		18 13											18 28		18 43						
Sidcup	d	18 01		18 16											18 31		18 46						
New Eltham	d	18 04		18 19											18 34		18 49						
Mottingham	d	18 06		18 21											18 36		18 51						
Lee	d	18 09		18 24											18 39		18 54						
Hither Green	d	18 12	18 19	18 28											18 42	18 49	18 58						
Barnehurst	d							17 37		17 45			17 58	18 07						18 07		18 15	
Bexleyheath	d							17 39		17 47			18 01	18 09						18 09		18 17	
Welling	d							17 42		17 50			18 04	18 12						18 12		18 20	
Falconwood	d							17 45		17 53			18 06	18 15						18 15		18 23	
Eltham	d							17 48		17 55			18 09	18 18						18 18		18 25	
Kidbrooke	d							17 51		17 58				18 21						18 21		18 28	
Blackheath	d					17 52		17 55		18 03			18 16	18 25					18 22	18 25		18 33	
Lewisham ⇌	d		18 24	18 34		17 56		17 59		18 08		18 14	18 20	18 29		18 54	19 04		18 26	18 29		18 38	
St Johns	d		18 26	18 36				18 01				18 16		18 31		18 56	19 06			18 31			
New Cross ⊖	d		18 28	18 38				18 03				18 18		18 33		18 58	19 08			18 33			
Nunhead	d									18 15												18 45	
Peckham Rye	d									18 17												18 47	
Denmark Hill	d									18 21												18 51	
London Victoria ⊖	a									18 33												19 03	
Westcombe Park	d				17 45													18 15					
Maze Hill	d																						
Greenwich ⇌	d				17 52				18 03		18 13							18 22			18 33		18 43
Deptford	a				17 54													18 24					
London Bridge ⊖	a	18 22	18 34	18 44	18 00	18 05		18 08	18 11		18 20	18 24	18 28	18 38	18 52	19 04	19 14	18 30	18 35	18 38	18 41		18 50
London Cannon Street ⊖	a		18 41	18 52	18 07			18 16	18 18		18 27	18 31		18 46		19 11	19 22	18 37		18 46	18 48		18 57
London Waterloo (East) ⊖	a	18 26				18 09							18 32		18 56				18 39				
London Charing Cross ⊖	a	18 30				18 16							18 39		19 00				18 46				
Ebbsfleet International	a						17 46																
Stratford International ⊖ ⇌	a						17 58																
St Pancras Int'l ⊖	a						18 08																

Table 200

Saturdays

28 July to 11 August

Gillingham and Dartford - London

Network Diagram - see first Page of Table 200

		SE	SE	SE	SE	SE	SE	SE	SE	SE	SE	SE	SE	SE	SE	SE	SE	SE	SE	SE	SE	SE
Gillingham (Kent)	d					17 54						18 20			18 24					18 54		
Chatham	d					17 58						18 24			18 28					18 58		
Rochester	d					18 00						18 27			18 30					19 00		
Maidstone West	d																					
Strood	d					18 05						18 32			18 35					19 05		
Higham	d					18 10									18 40					19 10		
Gravesend	d					18 18					18 32	18 43			18 48		19 02			19 18		19 32
Northfleet	d										18 36						19 06					19 36
Swanscombe	d										18 38						19 08					19 38
Greenhithe for Bluewater	d					18 23					18 41				18 53		19 11			19 23		19 41
Stone Crossing	d										18 43						19 13					19 43
Dartford	a					18 28					18 47				18 58		19 17			19 28		19 47
	d		18 22			18 28		18 31	18 38		18 48			18 52	18 58	19 01	19 18		19 25	19 28	19 31	19 48
Slade Green	d			18 17	18 23			18 35					18 53			19 05		19 23			19 35	
Erith	d				18 26			18 38					18 56			19 08		19 26			19 38	
Belvedere	d				18 28			18 40					18 58			19 10		19 28			19 40	
Abbey Wood	d				18 31	18 37		18 43					19 01		19 07	19 13		19 31		19 37	19 43	
Plumstead	d				18 34			18 46					19 04			19 16		19 34			19 46	
Woolwich Arsenal ⇌	d				18 38	18 42		18 49		18 55			19 08		19 12	19 19		19 38		19 42	19 49	
Woolwich Dockyard	d																					
Charlton	d				18 43	18 46		18 56		19 01			19 13		19 16	19 26		19 43		19 47	19 56	
Crayford	d										18 52						19 22					19 52
Bexley	d										18 55						19 25					19 55
Albany Park	d										18 58						19 28					19 58
Sidcup	d										19 01						19 31					20 01
New Eltham	d										19 04						19 34					20 04
Mottingham	d										19 06						19 36					20 06
Lee	d										19 09						19 39					20 09
Hither Green	d										19 13						19 43					20 13
Barnehurst	d		18 28	18 37			18 37		18 45					18 58					19 31			
Bexleyheath	d		18 31	18 39			18 39		18 47					19 01					19 34			
Welling	d		18 34	18 42			18 42		18 50					19 04					19 37			
Falconwood	d		18 36	18 45			18 45		18 53					19 06					19 39			
Eltham	d		18 39	18 48			18 48		18 55					19 09					19 42			
Kidbrooke	d			18 51			18 51		18 58					19 12					19 45			
Blackheath	d		18 46	18 55		18 52	18 55		19 03					19 17	19 22				19 49	19 53		
Lewisham ⇌	d	18 44	18 50	18 59		18 56	18 59		19 08		19 18			19 21	19 26		19 48		19 53	19 57		20 18
St Johns	d	18 46		19 01			19 01															
New Cross ⊖	d	18 48		19 03			19 03							19 24			19 51		19 56			20 21
Nunhead	d								19 15													
Peckham Rye	d								19 17													
Denmark Hill	d								19 21													
London Victoria ⊖	a								19 33													
Westcombe Park	d				18 45								19 15					19 45				
Maze Hill	d																					
Greenwich ⇌	d				18 52			19 03		19 09			19 22			19 33		19 52			20 03	
Deptford	a				18 54								19 24					19 54				
London Bridge ⊖	a	18 54	18 58	19 08	19 00	19 05	19 08	19 11		19 18	19 27		19 30	19 33	19 36	19 41	19 57	20 00	20 03	20 07	20 11	20 27
London Cannon Street ⊖	a	19 01		19 16	19 07		19 16	19 18		19 25			19 37					20 07				
London Waterloo (East) ⊖	a		19 02			19 09					19 32			19 39	19 42	19 45	20 04		20 08	20 11	20 15	20 34
London Charing Cross ⊖	a		19 09			19 16					19 38			19 45	19 48	19 52	20 10		20 15	20 18	20 22	20 40
Ebbsfleet International	a											18 46										
Stratford International ⊖ ⇌	a											18 58										
St Pancras Int'l ⊖	a											19 08										

Table 200

Saturdays

28 July to 11 August

Gillingham and Dartford - London

Network Diagram - see first Page of Table 200

		SE	SE	SE	SE	SE	SE	SE	SE	SE
Gillingham (Kent) 4	d	19 20			19 24				19 54	
Chatham 4	d	19 24			19 28				19 58	
Rochester 4	d	19 27			19 30				20 00	
Maidstone West	d									
Strood 4	d	19 32			19 35				20 05	
Higham	d				19 40				20 10	
Gravesend 4	d	19 43			19 48		20 02		20 18	
Northfleet	d						20 06			
Swanscombe	d						20 08			
Greenhithe for Bluewater	d				19 53		20 11		20 23	
Stone Crossing	d						20 13			
Dartford 4	a				19 58		20 17		20 28	
	d			19 55	19 58	20 01	20 18	20 25	20 28	20 31
Slade Green 4	d		19 53			20 05				20 35
Erith	d		19 56			20 08				20 38
Belvedere	d		19 58			20 10				20 40
Abbey Wood	d		20 01		20 07	20 13			20 37	20 43
Plumstead	d		20 04			20 16				20 46
Woolwich Arsenal 4	d		20 08		20 12	20 19			20 42	20 49
Woolwich Dockyard	d									
Charlton 4	d		20 13		20 17	20 25			20 47	20 55
Crayford	d						20 22			
Bexley	d						20 25			
Albany Park	d						20 28			
Sidcup 4	d						20 31			
New Eltham	d						20 34			
Mottingham	d						20 36			
Lee	d						20 39			
Hither Green 4	d						20 43			
Barnehurst 4	d			20 01				20 31		
Bexleyheath	d			20 04				20 34		
Welling	d			20 07				20 37		
Falconwood	d			20 09				20 39		
Eltham	d			20 12				20 42		
Kidbrooke	d			20 15				20 45		
Blackheath 4	d			20 19	20 23			20 49	20 53	
Lewisham 4	d			20 23	20 27		20 48	20 53	20 57	
St Johns	d									
New Cross 4	d			20 26			20 51	20 56		
Nunhead 4	d									
Peckham Rye 4	d									
Denmark Hill 4	d									
London Victoria 15	a									
Westcombe Park	d		20 15			20 27				20 57
Maze Hill	d					20 29				20 59
Greenwich 4	d		20 22			20 33				21 03
Deptford	a		20 24			20 35				21 05
London Bridge 4	a		20 30	20 33	20 37	20 41	20 57	21 03	21 07	21 11
London Cannon Street 4	a		20 37							
London Waterloo (East) 4	a			20 38	20 41	20 45	21 04	21 08	21 11	21 15
London Charing Cross 4	a			20 45	20 48	20 52	21 10	21 15	21 18	21 22
Ebbsfleet International	a	19 46								
Stratford International	a	19 58								
St Pancras Int'l 15	a	20 08								

			SE	SE	SE	SE	SE	SE	SE	SE	SE		SE	SE	SE	SE
Gillingham (Kent) 4	d			20 20		20 24				20 54				21 20		21 24
Chatham 4	d			20 24		20 28				20 58				21 24		21 28
Rochester 4	d			20 27		20 30				21 00				21 27		21 30
Maidstone West	d															
Strood 4	d			20 32		20 35				21 05				21 32		21 35
Higham	d					20 40				21 10						21 40
Gravesend 4	d		20 32	20 43		20 48		21 02		21 18			21 32	21 43		21 48
Northfleet	d		20 36					21 06					21 36			
Swanscombe	d		20 38					21 08					21 38			
Greenhithe for Bluewater	d		20 41			20 53		21 11		21 23			21 41			21 53
Stone Crossing	d		20 43					21 13					21 43			
Dartford 4	a		20 47			20 58		21 17		21 28			21 47			21 58
	d		20 48		20 55	20 58	21 01	21 18	21 25	21 28	21 31		21 48		21 55	21 58
Slade Green 4	d						21 05				21 35					
Erith	d						21 08				21 38					
Belvedere	d						21 10				21 40					
Abbey Wood	d					21 07	21 13			21 37	21 43					22 07
Plumstead	d						21 16				21 46					
Woolwich Arsenal 4	d					21 12	21 19			21 42	21 49					22 12
Woolwich Dockyard	d															
Charlton 4	d					21 17	21 25			21 47	21 55					22 17
Crayford	d		20 52					21 22					21 52			
Bexley	d		20 55					21 25					21 55			
Albany Park	d		20 58					21 28					21 58			
Sidcup 4	d		21 01					21 31					22 01			
New Eltham	d		21 04					21 34					22 04			
Mottingham	d		21 06					21 36					22 06			
Lee	d		21 09					21 39					22 09			
Hither Green 4	d		21 13					21 43					22 13			
Barnehurst 4	d				21 01				21 31						22 01	
Bexleyheath	d				21 04				21 34						22 04	
Welling	d				21 07				21 37						22 07	
Falconwood	d				21 09				21 39						22 09	
Eltham	d				21 12				21 42						22 12	
Kidbrooke	d				21 15				21 45						22 15	
Blackheath 4	d				21 19	21 22			21 49	21 52					22 19	22 22
Lewisham 4	d		21 18		21 23	21 26		21 48	21 53	21 56			22 18		22 23	22 26
St Johns	d															
New Cross 4	d		21 21		21 26			21 51	21 56				22 21		22 26	
Nunhead 4	d															
Peckham Rye 4	d															
Denmark Hill 4	d															
London Victoria 15	a															
Westcombe Park	d						21 27				21 57					
Maze Hill	d						21 29				21 59					
Greenwich 4	d						21 33				22 03					
Deptford	a						21 35				22 05					
London Bridge 4	a		21 27		21 33	21 36	21 41	21 57	22 01	22 05	22 11		22 27		22 31	22 35
London Cannon Street 4	a															
London Waterloo (East) 4	a		21 34		21 38	21 40	21 45	22 04	22 06	22 09	22 15		22 34		22 36	22 39
London Charing Cross 4	a		21 40		21 45	21 47	21 52	22 10	22 13	22 16	22 22		22 40		22 43	22 46
Ebbsfleet International	a			20 46										21 46		
Stratford International	a			20 58										21 58		
St Pancras Int'l 15	a			21 08										22 08		

Table 200

Saturdays

28 July to 11 August

Gillingham and Dartford - London

Network Diagram - see first Page of Table 200

		SE	SE	SE	SE	SE		SE	SE	SE	SE	SE	SE
Gillingham (Kent) 4	d				21 54				22 20		22 24		22 54
Chatham 4	d				21 58				22 24		22 28		22 58
Rochester 4	d				22 00				22 27		22 30		23 00
Maidstone West	d												
Strood 4	d				22 05				22 32		22 35		23 05
Higham	d				22 10						22 40		23 10
Gravesend 4	d		22 02		22 18			22 32	22 43		22 48		23 18
Northfleet	d		22 06					22 36					
Swanscombe	d		22 08					22 38					
Greenhithe for Bluewater	d		22 11		22 23			22 41			22 53		23 23
Stone Crossing	d		22 13					22 43					
Dartford 4	a		22 17		22 28			22 47			22 58		23 28
	d	22 01	22 18	22 25	22 28	22 31		22 48		22 55	22 58	23 01	
Slade Green 4	d	22 05				22 35						23 05	
Erith	d	22 08				22 38						23 08	
Belvedere	d	22 10				22 40						23 10	
Abbey Wood	d	22 13			22 37	22 43					23 07	23 13	
Plumstead	d	22 16				22 46						23 16	
Woolwich Arsenal 4	d	22 19			22 42	22 49					23 12	23 19	
Woolwich Dockyard	d												
Charlton 4	d	22 25			22 47	22 55					23 17	23 25	
Crayford	d		22 22					22 52					
Bexley	d		22 25					22 55					
Albany Park	d		22 28					22 58					
Sidcup 4	d		22 31					23 01					
New Eltham	d		22 34					23 04					
Mottingham	d		22 36					23 06					
Lee	d		22 39					23 09					
Hither Green 4	d		22 43					23 13					
Barnehurst 4	d			22 31						23 01			
Bexleyheath	d			22 34						23 04			
Welling	d			22 37						23 07			
Falconwood	d			22 39						23 09			
Eltham	d			22 42						23 12			
Kidbrooke	d			22 45						23 15			
Blackheath 4	d			22 49	22 52					23 19	23 22		
Lewisham 4	d		22 48	22 53	22 56			23 18		23 23	23 26		
St Johns	d												
New Cross 4	d		22 51	22 56				23 21		23 26			
Nunhead 4	d												
Peckham Rye 4	d												
Denmark Hill 4	d												
London Victoria 15	a												
Westcombe Park	d	22 27				22 57						23 27	
Maze Hill	d	22 29				22 59						23 29	
Greenwich 4	d	22 33				23 03						23 33	
Deptford	a	22 35				23 05						23 35	
London Bridge 4	a	22 41	22 57	23 01	23 05	23 11		23 27		23 31	23 35	23 41	
London Cannon Street 4	a												
London Waterloo (East) 4	a	22 45	23 04	23 06	23 09	23 15		23 34		23 36	23 39	23 45	
London Charing Cross 4	a	22 52	23 10	23 13	23 16	23 23		23 40		23 43	23 46	23 52	
Ebbsfleet International	a								22 46				
Stratford International	a								22 58				
St Pancras Int'l 15	a								23 07				

Table 200

Saturdays

25 August to 22 September

Gillingham and Dartford - London

Network Diagram - see first Page of Table 200

		SE A	SE A	SE A	SE	SE	SE	SE	SE	SE		SE	SE	SE	SE	SE B	SE A	SE	SE	SE		SE	SE	SE A	SE
Gillingham (Kent)	d							04 48					05 18			05 50	05 50		05 54					06 20	
Chatham	d							04 52					05 22			05 54	05 54		05 58					06 24	
Rochester	d							04 54					05 24			05 57	05 57		06 00					06 27	
Maidstone West	d																								
Strood	d							04 59					05 29			06 02	06 02		06 05					06 32	
Higham	d							05 04					05 34						06 10						
Gravesend	d							05 12					05 42		06 02	06 13	06 13		06 18				06 32	06 43	
Northfleet	d							05 15					05 45		06 06								06 36		
Swanscombe	d							05 17					05 47		06 08								06 38		
Greenhithe for Bluewater	d							05 21					05 51		06 11				06 23				06 41		
Stone Crossing	d							05 23					05 53		06 13								06 43		
Dartford	a							05 27					05 57		06 17				06 28				06 47		
	d				05 05	05 18	05 22	05 29	05 35	05 48		05 52	05 59	06 05	06 18			06 22	06 29	06 35		06 38	06 48		06 52
Slade Green	d				05 10				05 40					06 10						06 40					
Erith	d				05 12				05 42					06 12						06 42					
Belvedere	d				05 15				05 45					06 15						06 45					
Abbey Wood	d				05 18			05 38	05 48				06 08	06 18					06 38	06 48					
Plumstead	d				05 21				05 51					06 21						06 51					
Woolwich Arsenal	d				05 24			05 43	05 54				06 13	06 24					06 43	06 54					
Woolwich Dockyard	d				05 26				05 56					06 26						06 56					
Charlton	d	00 07	00 15	00 26	05 29			05 47	05 59				06 17	06 29					06 47	06 59					
Crayford	d					05 22				05 52					06 22								06 52		
Bexley	d					05 25				05 55					06 25								06 55		
Albany Park	d					05 28				05 58					06 28								06 58		
Sidcup	d					05 31				06 01					06 31								07 01		
New Eltham	d					05 34				06 04					06 34								07 04		
Mottingham	d					05 36				06 06					06 36								07 06		
Lee	d					05 39				06 09					06 39								07 09		
Hither Green	d					05 42				06 12					06 42								07 12		
Barnehurst	d						05 29					05 59						06 29				06 46			06 59
Bexleyheath	d						05 31					06 01						06 31				06 49			07 01
Welling	d						05 34					06 04						06 34				06 52			07 04
Falconwood	d						05 37					06 07						06 37				06 54			07 07
Eltham	d						05 40					06 10						06 40				06 57			07 10
Kidbrooke	d						05 43					06 13						06 43				07 00			07 13
Blackheath	d						05 46	05 52				06 16	06 22					06 46	06 52			07 04			07 16
Lewisham	d					05 48	05 50	05 56		06 18		06 20	06 26		06 48			06 50	06 56			07 08	07 18		07 20
St Johns	d																						07 21		
New Cross	d					05 51				06 21					06 51										
Nunhead	d																					07 13			
Peckham Rye	d																					07 15			
Denmark Hill	d																					07 19			
London Victoria	a																					07 28			
Westcombe Park	d				05 31				06 01					06 31						07 01					
Maze Hill	d				05 33				06 03					06 33						07 03					
Greenwich	d				05 37				06 07					06 37						07 07					
Deptford	a				05 39				06 09					06 39						07 09					
London Bridge	a				05 45	05 56	05 59	06 05	06 15	06 26		06 29	06 35	06 45	06 56			06 59	07 05	07 15			07 26		07 29
London Cannon Street	a	00 19		00 38																					
London Waterloo (East)	a				05 49	06 01	06 03	06 09	06 19	06 31		06 33	06 39	06 49	07 01			07 03	07 09	07 19			07 31		07 33
London Charing Cross	a		00 30		05 53	06 05	06 07	06 13	06 25	06 35		06 37	06 43	06 55	07 05			07 07	07 13	07 25			07 35		07 40
Ebbsfleet International	a															06 17	06 17							06 47	
Stratford International	a															06 29	06 29							06 59	
St Pancras Int'l	a															06 36	06 37							07 06	

A 1 September, 8 September

B not from 1 September until 8 September

Table 200

Saturdays

25 August to 22 September

Gillingham and Dartford - London

Network Diagram - see first Page of Table 200

		SE	SE	SE	SE	SE A		SE B	SE	SE	SE	SE	SE	SE	SE	SE		SE	SE	SE A	SE B	SE	SE	SE	SE
Gillingham (Kent)	d	06 24				06 50		06 50				06 54								07 20	07 20				
Chatham	d	06 28				06 54		06 54				06 58								07 24	07 24				
Rochester	d	06 30				06 57		06 57				07 00								07 27	07 27				
Maidstone West	d																								
Strood	d	06 35				07 02		07 02				07 05								07 32	07 32				
Higham	d	06 40										07 10													
Gravesend	d	06 48			07 02	07 13		07 13				07 18							07 32	07 43	07 43				
Northfleet	d				07 06														07 36						
Swanscombe	d				07 08														07 38						
Greenhithe for Bluewater	d	06 53			07 11							07 23							07 41						
Stone Crossing	d				07 13														07 43						
Dartford	a	06 58			07 17							07 28							07 47						
	d	06 59	07 01	07 08	07 18				07 22			07 29		07 31		07 38			07 48				07 52		
Slade Green	d		07 05							07 25				07 35				07 45						07 55	
Erith	d		07 08							07 28				07 38				07 48						07 58	
Belvedere	d		07 10							07 30				07 40				07 50						08 00	
Abbey Wood	d	07 08	07 13							07 33		07 38		07 43				07 53						08 03	
Plumstead	d		07 16							07 36				07 46				07 56						08 06	
Woolwich Arsenal	d	07 13	07 19							07 39		07 43		07 49				07 59						08 09	
Woolwich Dockyard	d		07 22							07 42				07 52				08 02						08 12	
Charlton	d	07 17	07 25							07 45		07 47		07 55				08 05						08 15	
Crayford	d				07 22										07 37				07 52						
Bexley	d				07 25										07 40				07 55						
Albany Park	d				07 28										07 43				07 58						
Sidcup	d				07 31										07 46				08 01						
New Eltham	d				07 34										07 49				08 04						
Mottingham	d				07 36										07 51				08 06						
Lee	d				07 39										07 54				08 09						
Hither Green	d				07 42						07 49				07 58				08 12						08 19
Barnehurst	d			07 16					07 29				07 38			07 46							07 59		
Bexleyheath	d			07 19					07 31				07 40			07 49							08 01		
Welling	d			07 22					07 34				07 43			07 52							08 04		
Falconwood	d			07 24					07 37				07 46			07 54							08 07		
Eltham	d			07 27					07 40				07 49			07 57							08 10		
Kidbrooke	d			07 30					07 43				07 52			08 00							08 13		
Blackheath	d	07 22		07 34					07 46			07 52	07 55			08 04							08 16		
Lewisham	d	07 26		07 38					07 50		07 54	07 56	07 59		08 04	08 08						08 14	08 20		08 24
St Johns	d										07 56		08 01		08 06							08 16			08 26
New Cross	d										07 58		08 03		08 08							08 18			08 28
Nunhead	d			07 43												08 13									
Peckham Rye	d			07 45												08 15									
Denmark Hill	d			07 49												08 19									
London Victoria	a			07 58												08 28									
Westcombe Park	d		07 27							07 47				07 57				08 07						08 17	
Maze Hill	d		07 29							07 49				07 59				08 09						08 19	
Greenwich	d		07 32							07 52				08 02				08 12						08 22	
Deptford	a		07 34							07 54				08 04				08 14						08 24	
London Bridge	a	07 35	07 41		07 52				07 58	08 00	08 04	08 05	08 08	08 11	08 14			08 20	08 22			08 24	08 28	08 30	08 34
London Cannon Street	a		07 45							08 04	08 08		08 13	08 15	08 19			08 24				08 28		08 34	08 38
London Waterloo (East)	a	07 39			07 56				08 02			08 09							08 26				08 32		
London Charing Cross	a	07 43			08 00				08 06			08 13							08 30				08 36		
Ebbsfleet International	a					07 17		07 17												07 47	07 47				
Stratford International	a					07 29		07 29												07 59	07 59				
St Pancras Int'l	a					07 36		07 37												08 06	08 07				

A not from 1 September until 8 September

B 1 September, 8 September

Table 200

Gillingham and Dartford - London

Saturdays

25 August to 22 September

Network Diagram - see first Page of Table 200

		SE		SE	SE	SE	SE	SE	SE	SE A	SE B	SE		SE	SE	SE	SE	SE	SE	SE	SE	SE		SE	SE
Gillingham (Kent)	d	07 24								07 50	07 50										07 54	08 20			
Chatham	d	07 28								07 54	07 54										07 58	08 24			
Rochester	d	07 30								07 57	07 57										08 00	08 27			
Maidstone West	d																								
Strood	d	07 35								08 02	08 02										08 05	08 32			
Higham	d	07 40																			08 10				
Gravesend	d	07 48							08 02	08 13	08 13						08 32				08 18	08 43			
Northfleet	d								08 06								08 36								
Swanscombe	d								08 08								08 38								
Greenhithe for Bluewater	d	07 53							08 11								08 41				08 23				
Stone Crossing	d								08 13								08 43								
Dartford	a	07 58							08 17								08 47				08 28				
	d	07 59			08 01		08 08		08 18					08 22			08 48				08 29				08 31
Slade Green	d				08 05			08 15												08 25					08 35
Erith	d				08 08			08 18												08 28					08 38
Belvedere	d				08 10			08 20												08 30					08 40
Abbey Wood	d	08 08			08 13			08 23												08 33	08 38				08 43
Plumstead	d				08 16			08 26												08 36					08 46
Woolwich Arsenal	d	08 13			08 19			08 29												08 39	08 43				08 49
Woolwich Dockyard	d				08 22			08 32												08 42					08 52
Charlton	d	08 17			08 25			08 35											08 37	08 45	08 47				08 55
Crayford	d					08 07			08 22							08 37	08 52		09 07						
Bexley	d					08 10			08 25							08 40	08 55		09 10						
Albany Park	d					08 13			08 28							08 43	08 58		09 13						
Sidcup	d					08 16			08 31							08 46	09 01		09 16						
New Eltham	d					08 19			08 34							08 49	09 04		09 19						
Mottingham	d					08 21			08 36							08 51	09 06		09 21						
Lee	d					08 24			08 39							08 54	09 09		09 24						
Hither Green	d					08 28			08 42						08 49	08 58	09 12	09 19	09 28						
Barnehurst	d			08 08			08 16							08 29										08 38	
Bexleyheath	d			08 10			08 19							08 31										08 40	
Welling	d			08 13			08 22							08 34										08 43	
Falconwood	d			08 16			08 24							08 37										08 46	
Eltham	d			08 19			08 27							08 40										08 49	
Kidbrooke	d			08 22			08 30							08 43										08 52	
Blackheath	d	08 22		08 25			08 34							08 46							08 52			08 55	
Lewisham	d	08 26		08 29		08 34	08 38					08 44		08 50	08 54	09 04		09 24	09 34		08 56			08 59	
St Johns	d			08 31		08 36						08 46			08 56	09 06		09 26	09 36					09 01	
New Cross	d			08 33		08 38						08 48			08 58	09 08		09 28	09 38					09 03	
Nunhead	d						08 43																		
Peckham Rye	d						08 45																		
Denmark Hill	d						08 49																		
London Victoria	a						08 58																		
Westcombe Park	d				08 27			08 37												08 47					08 57
Maze Hill	d				08 29			08 39												08 49					08 59
Greenwich	d				08 32			08 42												08 52					09 02
Deptford	a				08 34			08 44												08 54					09 04
London Bridge	a	08 35		08 38	08 41	08 44		08 50	08 52			08 54		08 58	09 04	09 14	09 22	09 34	09 44	09 00	09 05			09 08	09 11
London Cannon Street	a			08 43	08 45	08 49		08 54				08 58			09 08	09 19		09 38	09 49	09 04				09 13	09 15
London Waterloo (East)	a	08 39							08 56					09 02			09 26				09 09				
London Charing Cross	a	08 43							09 00					09 06			09 30				09 13				
Ebbsfleet International	a									08 17	08 17											08 47			
Stratford International	a									08 29	08 32											08 59			
St Pancras Int'l	a									08 36	08 40											09 06			

A not from 1 September until 8 September

B 1 September, 8 September

Table 200

Gillingham and Dartford - London

Saturdays

25 August to 22 September

Network Diagram - see first Page of Table 200

		SE	SE	SE	SE	SE	SE	SE		SE	SE	SE	SE	SE	SE	SE	SE	SE		SE	SE	SE	SE	SE	SE
Gillingham (Kent)	d											08 24	08 50												08 54
Chatham	d											08 28	08 54												08 58
Rochester	d											08 30	08 57												09 00
Maidstone West	d																								
Strood	d											08 35	09 02												09 05
Higham	d											08 40													09 10
Gravesend	d						09 02					08 48	09 13								09 32				09 18
Northfleet	d						09 06														09 36				
Swanscombe	d						09 08														09 38				
Greenhithe for Bluewater	d						09 11					08 53									09 41				09 23
Stone Crossing	d						09 13														09 43				
Dartford	a						09 17					08 58									09 47				09 28
	d	08 38			08 52		09 18					08 59		09 01	09 08			09 22			09 48				09 29
Slade Green	d		08 45			08 47					08 55			09 05		09 15				09 17				09 25	
Erith	d		08 48								08 58			09 08		09 18								09 28	
Belvedere	d		08 50								09 00			09 10		09 20								09 30	
Abbey Wood	d		08 53								09 03	09 08		09 13		09 23								09 33	09 38
Plumstead	d		08 56								09 06			09 16		09 26								09 36	
Woolwich Arsenal	d		08 59								09 09	09 13		09 19		09 29								09 39	09 43
Woolwich Dockyard	d		09 02								09 12			09 22		09 32								09 42	
Charlton	d		09 05							09 07	09 15	09 17		09 25		09 35							09 37	09 45	09 47
Crayford	d						09 22			09 37											09 52		10 07		
Bexley	d						09 25			09 40											09 55		10 10		
Albany Park	d						09 28			09 43											09 58		10 13		
Sidcup	d						09 31			09 46											10 01		10 16		
New Eltham	d						09 34			09 49											10 04		10 19		
Mottingham	d						09 36			09 51											10 06		10 21		
Lee	d						09 39			09 54											10 09		10 24		
Hither Green	d						09 42	09 49		09 58											10 12	10 19	10 28		
Barnehurst	d	08 46			08 59	09 08									09 16			09 29		09 38					
Bexleyheath	d	08 49			09 01	09 10									09 19			09 31		09 40					
Welling	d	08 52			09 04	09 13									09 22			09 34		09 43					
Falconwood	d	08 54			09 07	09 16									09 24			09 37		09 46					
Eltham	d	08 57			09 10	09 19									09 27			09 40		09 49					
Kidbrooke	d	09 00			09 13	09 22									09 30			09 43		09 52					
Blackheath	d	09 04			09 16	09 25						09 22			09 34			09 46		09 55					09 52
Lewisham	d	09 08		09 14	09 20	09 29		09 54		10 04		09 26			09 38		09 44	09 50		09 59		10 24	10 34		09 56
St Johns	d			09 16		09 31		09 56		10 06							09 46			10 01		10 26	10 36		
New Cross	d			09 18		09 33		09 58		10 08							09 48			10 03		10 28	10 38		
Nunhead	d	09 13													09 43										
Peckham Rye	d	09 15													09 45										
Denmark Hill	d	09 19													09 49										
London Victoria	a	09 28													09 58										
Westcombe Park	d		09 07								09 17			09 27		09 37								09 47	
Maze Hill	d		09 09								09 19			09 29		09 39								09 49	
Greenwich	d		09 12								09 22			09 32		09 42								09 52	
Deptford	a		09 14								09 24			09 34		09 44								09 54	
London Bridge	a		09 20	09 24	09 28	09 38	09 52	10 04		10 14	09 30	09 35		09 41		09 50	09 54	09 58		10 08	10 22	10 34	10 44	10 00	10 05
London Cannon Street	a		09 24	09 28		09 43		10 08		10 19	09 34			09 45		09 54	09 58			10 13		10 38	10 49	10 04	
London Waterloo (East)	a				09 32		09 56					09 39						10 02			10 26				10 09
London Charing Cross	a				09 36		10 00					09 43						10 06			10 30				10 13
Ebbsfleet International	a												09 17												
Stratford International	a												09 29												
St Pancras Int'l	a												09 36												

Table 200

Saturdays

25 August to 22 September

Gillingham and Dartford - London

Network Diagram - see first Page of Table 200

Station		SE A	SE B	SE		SE	SE	SE	SE	SE	SE	SE	SE	SE		SE	SE B	SE A	SE	SE	SE	SE	SE	SE
Gillingham (Kent)	d	09 20	09 20													09 24	09 50	09 50						
Chatham	d	09 24	09 24													09 28	09 54	09 54						
Rochester	d	09 27	09 27													09 30	09 57	09 57						
Maidstone West	d																							
Strood	d	09 32	09 32													09 35	10 02	10 02						
Higham	d															09 40								
Gravesend	d	09 43	09 43								10 02					09 48	10 12	10 13						
Northfleet	d										10 06													
Swanscombe	d										10 08													
Greenhithe for Bluewater	d										10 11					09 53								
Stone Crossing	d										10 13													
Dartford	a										10 17					09 58								
	d			09 31		09 38			09 52		10 18					09 59			10 01	10 08			10 22	
Slade Green	d			09 35			09 45			09 47				09 55					10 05		10 15			10 17
Erith	d			09 38			09 48							09 58					10 08		10 18			
Belvedere	d			09 40			09 50							10 00					10 10		10 20			
Abbey Wood	d			09 43			09 53							10 03		10 08			10 13		10 23			
Plumstead	d			09 46			09 56							10 06					10 16		10 26			
Woolwich Arsenal	d			09 49			09 59							10 09		10 13			10 19		10 29			
Woolwich Dockyard	d			09 52			10 02							10 12					10 22		10 32			
Charlton	d			09 55			10 05						10 07	10 15		10 17			10 25		10 35			
Crayford	d										10 22		10 37											
Bexley	d										10 25		10 40											
Albany Park	d										10 28		10 43											
Sidcup	d										10 31		10 46											
New Eltham	d										10 34		10 49											
Mottingham	d										10 36		10 51											
Lee	d										10 39		10 54											
Hither Green	d										10 42	10 49	10 58											
Barnehurst	d					09 46			09 59	10 08										10 16			10 29	10 38
Bexleyheath	d					09 49			10 01	10 10										10 19			10 31	10 40
Welling	d					09 52			10 04	10 13										10 22			10 34	10 43
Falconwood	d					09 54			10 07	10 16										10 24			10 37	10 46
Eltham	d					09 57			10 10	10 19										10 27			10 40	10 49
Kidbrooke	d					10 00			10 13	10 22										10 30			10 43	10 52
Blackheath	d					10 04			10 16	10 25						10 22				10 34			10 46	10 55
Lewisham	d					10 08		10 14	10 20	10 29		10 54	11 04			10 26				10 38		10 44	10 50	10 59
St Johns	d							10 16		10 31		10 56	11 06									10 46		11 01
New Cross	d							10 18		10 33		10 58	11 08									10 48		11 03
Nunhead	d					10 13														10 43				
Peckham Rye	d					10 15														10 45				
Denmark Hill	d					10 19														10 49				
London Victoria	a					10 28														10 58				
Westcombe Park	d			09 57			10 07							10 17					10 27		10 37			
Maze Hill	d			09 59			10 09							10 19					10 29		10 39			
Greenwich	d			10 02			10 12							10 22					10 32		10 42			
Deptford	a			10 04			10 14							10 24					10 34		10 44			
London Bridge	a			10 11			10 20	10 24	10 28	10 38	10 52	11 04	11 14	10 30		10 35			10 41		10 50	10 54	10 58	11 08
London Cannon Street	a			10 15			10 24	10 28		10 43		11 08	11 19	10 34					10 45		10 54	10 58		11 13
London Waterloo (East)	a								10 32		10 56					10 39							11 02	
London Charing Cross	a								10 36		11 00					10 43							11 06	
Ebbsfleet International	a	09 47	09 47														10 16	10 17						
Stratford International	a	09 59	09 59														10 27	10 29						
St Pancras Int'l	a	10 06	10 07														10 35	10 36						

A not from 1 September until 8 September

B 1 September, 8 September

Table 200

Saturdays

25 August to 22 September

Gillingham and Dartford - London

Network Diagram - see first Page of Table 200

Station		SE	SE	SE	SE	SE	SE A	SE B	SE	SE		SE	SE	SE	SE	SE	SE	SE	SE	SE		SE A	SE B	SE	SE
Gillingham (Kent)	d					09 54	10 20	10 20												10 24		10 50	10 50		
Chatham	d					09 58	10 24	10 24												10 28		10 54	10 54		
Rochester	d					10 00	10 27	10 27												10 30		10 57	10 57		
Maidstone West	d																								
Strood	d					10 05	10 32	10 32												10 35		11 02	11 02		
Higham	d					10 10														10 40					
Gravesend	d	10 32				10 18	10 43	10 43								11 02				10 48		11 13	11 13		
Northfleet	d	10 36														11 06									
Swanscombe	d	10 38														11 08									
Greenhithe for Bluewater	d	10 41				10 23										11 11				10 53					
Stone Crossing	d	10 43														11 13									
Dartford	a	10 47				10 28										11 17				10 58					
	d	10 48				10 29			10 31	10 38				10 52		11 18				10 59				11 01	11 08
Slade Green	d				10 25				10 35			10 45			10 47				10 55					11 05	
Erith	d				10 28				10 38			10 48							10 58					11 08	
Belvedere	d				10 30				10 40			10 50							11 00					11 10	
Abbey Wood	d				10 33	10 38			10 43			10 53							11 03	11 08				11 13	
Plumstead	d				10 36				10 46			10 56							11 06					11 16	
Woolwich Arsenal	d				10 39	10 43			10 49			10 59							11 09	11 13				11 19	
Woolwich Dockyard	d				10 42				10 52			11 02							11 12					11 22	
Charlton	d			10 37	10 45	10 47			10 55			11 05						11 07	11 15	11 17				11 25	
Crayford	d	10 52		11 07												11 22		11 37							
Bexley	d	10 55		11 10												11 25		11 40							
Albany Park	d	10 58		11 13												11 28		11 43							
Sidcup	d	11 01		11 16												11 31		11 46							
New Eltham	d	11 04		11 19												11 34		11 49							
Mottingham	d	11 06		11 21												11 36		11 51							
Lee	d	11 09		11 24												11 39		11 54							
Hither Green	d	11 12	11 19	11 28												11 42	11 49	11 58							
Barnehurst	d									10 46				10 59	11 08										11 16
Bexleyheath	d									10 49				11 01	11 10										11 19
Welling	d									10 52				11 04	11 13										11 22
Falconwood	d									10 54				11 07	11 16										11 24
Eltham	d									10 57				11 10	11 19										11 27
Kidbrooke	d									11 00				11 13	11 22										11 30
Blackheath	d					10 52				11 04				11 16	11 25					11 22					11 34
Lewisham	d		11 24	11 34		10 56				11 08			11 14	11 20	11 29		11 54	12 04		11 26					11 38
St Johns	d		11 26	11 36									11 16		11 31		11 56	12 06							
New Cross	d		11 28	11 38									11 18		11 33		11 58	12 08							
Nunhead	d									11 13															11 43
Peckham Rye	d									11 15															11 45
Denmark Hill	d									11 19															11 49
London Victoria	a									11 28															11 58
Westcombe Park	d				10 47				10 57			11 07							11 17					11 27	
Maze Hill	d				10 49				10 59			11 09							11 19					11 29	
Greenwich	d				10 52				11 02			11 12							11 22					11 32	
Deptford	a				10 54				11 04			11 14							11 24					11 34	
London Bridge	a	11 22	11 34	11 44	11 00	11 05			11 11			11 20	11 24	11 28	11 38	11 52	12 04	12 14	11 30	11 35				11 41	
London Cannon Street	a		11 38	11 49	11 04				11 15			11 24	11 28		11 43		12 08	12 19	11 34					11 45	
London Waterloo (East)	a	11 26				11 09								11 32		11 56				11 39					
London Charing Cross	a	11 30				11 13								11 36		12 00				11 43					
Ebbsfleet International	a						10 47	10 47														11 17	11 17		
Stratford International	a						10 59	10 59														11 29	11 32		
St Pancras Int'l	a						11 06	11 07														11 36	11 40		

A not from 1 September until 8 September

B 1 September, 8 September

Gillingham and Dartford - London

Saturdays

25 August to 22 September

Network Diagram - see first Page of Table 200

		SE	SE	SE	SE	SE	SE	SE	SE	SE	SE A	SE B	SE	SE	SE	SE	SE	SE	SE	SE	SE	SE	SE
Gillingham (Kent)	d									10 54	11 20	11 20											11 24
Chatham	d									10 58	11 24	11 24											11 28
Rochester	d									11 00	11 27	11 27											11 30
Maidstone West	d																						
Strood	d									11 05	11 32	11 32											11 35
Higham	d									11 10													11 40
Gravesend	d					11 32				11 18	11 43	11 43							12 02				11 48
Northfleet	d					11 36													12 06				
Swanscombe	d					11 38													12 08				
Greenhithe for Bluewater	d					11 41				11 23									12 11				11 53
Stone Crossing	d					11 43													12 13				
Dartford	a					11 47				11 28									12 17				11 58
	d			11 22		11 48				11 29			11 31	11 38			11 52		12 18				11 59
Slade Green	d	11 15			11 17				11 25				11 35		11 45			11 47				11 55	
Erith	d	11 18							11 28				11 38		11 48							11 58	
Belvedere	d	11 20							11 30				11 40		11 50							12 00	
Abbey Wood	d	11 23							11 33	11 38			11 43		11 53							12 03	12 08
Plumstead	d	11 26							11 36				11 46		11 56							12 06	
Woolwich Arsenal	d	11 29							11 39	11 43			11 49		11 59							12 09	12 13
Woolwich Dockyard	d	11 32							11 42				11 52		12 02							12 12	
Charlton	d	11 35						11 37	11 45	11 47			11 55		12 05						12 07	12 15	12 17
Crayford	d					11 52		12 07											12 22		12 37		
Bexley	d					11 55		12 10											12 25		12 40		
Albany Park	d					11 58		12 13											12 28		12 43		
Sidcup	d					12 01		12 16											12 31		12 46		
New Eltham	d					12 04		12 19											12 34		12 49		
Mottingham	d					12 06		12 21											12 36		12 51		
Lee	d					12 09		12 24											12 39		12 54		
Hither Green	d					12 12	12 19	12 28											12 42	12 49	12 58		
Barnehurst	d			11 29	11 38									11 46			11 59	12 08					
Bexleyheath	d			11 31	11 40									11 49			12 01	12 10					
Welling	d			11 34	11 43									11 52			12 04	12 13					
Falconwood	d			11 37	11 46									11 54			12 07	12 16					
Eltham	d			11 40	11 49									11 57			12 10	12 19					
Kidbrooke	d			11 43	11 52									12 00			12 13	12 22					
Blackheath	d			11 46	11 55					11 52				12 04			12 16	12 25					12 22
Lewisham	d		11 44	11 50	11 59		12 24	12 34		11 56				12 08		12 14	12 20	12 29		12 54	13 04		12 26
St Johns	d		11 46		12 01		12 26	12 36								12 16		12 31		12 56	13 06		
New Cross	d		11 48		12 03		12 28	12 38								12 18		12 33		12 58	13 08		
Nunhead	d													12 13									
Peckham Rye	d													12 15									
Denmark Hill	d													12 19									
London Victoria	a													12 28									
Westcombe Park	d	11 37							11 47				11 57		12 07							12 17	
Maze Hill	d	11 39							11 49				11 59		12 09							12 19	
Greenwich	d	11 42							11 52				12 02		12 12							12 22	
Deptford	a	11 44							11 54				12 04		12 14							12 24	
London Bridge	a	11 50	11 54	11 58	12 08	12 22	12 34	12 44	12 00	12 05			12 11		12 20	12 24	12 28	12 38	12 52	13 04	13 14	12 30	12 35
London Cannon Street	a	11 54	11 58		12 13		12 38	12 49	12 04				12 15		12 24	12 28		12 43		13 08	13 19	12 34	
London Waterloo (East)	a			12 02		12 26				12 09							12 32		12 56				12 39
London Charing Cross	a			12 06		12 30				12 13							12 36		13 00				12 43
Ebbsfleet International	a										11 47	11 47											
Stratford International	a										11 59	11 59											
St Pancras Int'l	a										12 06	12 07											

A not from 1 September until 8 September

B 1 September, 8 September

Gillingham and Dartford - London

Saturdays

25 August to 22 September

Network Diagram - see first Page of Table 200

		SE A	SE B	SE	SE	SE	SE	SE	SE	SE	SE	SE	SE	SE	SE A	SE B	SE	SE	SE	SE	SE	SE
Gillingham (Kent)	d	11 50	11 50											11 54	12 20	12 20						
Chatham	d	11 54	11 54											11 58	12 24	12 24						
Rochester	d	11 57	11 57											12 00	12 27	12 27						
Maidstone West	d																					
Strood	d	12 02	12 02											12 05	12 32	12 32						
Higham	d													12 10								
Gravesend	d	12 13	12 13							12 32				12 18	12 43	12 43						
Northfleet	d									12 36												
Swanscombe	d									12 38												
Greenhithe for Bluewater	d									12 41				12 23								
Stone Crossing	d									12 43												
Dartford	a									12 47				12 28								
	d			12 01	12 08			12 22		12 48				12 29			12 31	12 38			12 52	
Slade Green	d			12 05		12 15			12 17				12 25				12 35		12 45			12 47
Erith	d			12 08		12 18							12 28				12 38		12 48			
Belvedere	d			12 10		12 20							12 30				12 40		12 50			
Abbey Wood	d			12 13		12 23							12 33	12 38			12 43		12 53			
Plumstead	d			12 16		12 26							12 36				12 46		12 56			
Woolwich Arsenal	d			12 19		12 29							12 39	12 43			12 49		12 59			
Woolwich Dockyard	d			12 22		12 32							12 42				12 52		13 02			
Charlton	d			12 25		12 35						12 37	12 45	12 47			12 55		13 05			
Crayford	d									12 52		13 07										
Bexley	d									12 55		13 10										
Albany Park	d									12 58		13 13										
Sidcup	d									13 01		13 16										
New Eltham	d									13 04		13 19										
Mottingham	d									13 06		13 21										
Lee	d									13 09		13 24										
Hither Green	d									13 12	13 19	13 28										
Barnehurst	d				12 16			12 29	12 38									12 46			12 59	13 08
Bexleyheath	d				12 19			12 31	12 40									12 49			13 01	13 10
Welling	d				12 22			12 34	12 43									12 52			13 04	13 13
Falconwood	d				12 24			12 37	12 46									12 54			13 07	13 16
Eltham	d				12 27			12 40	12 49									12 57			13 10	13 19
Kidbrooke	d				12 30			12 43	12 52									13 00			13 13	13 22
Blackheath	d				12 34			12 46	12 55					12 52				13 04			13 16	13 25
Lewisham	d				12 38		12 44	12 50	12 59		13 24	13 34		12 56				13 08		13 14	13 20	13 29
St Johns	d						12 46		13 01		13 26	13 36								13 16		13 31
New Cross	d						12 48		13 03		13 28	13 38								13 18		13 33
Nunhead	d				12 43													13 13				
Peckham Rye	d				12 45													13 15				
Denmark Hill	d				12 49													13 19				
London Victoria	a				12 58													13 28				
Westcombe Park	d			12 27		12 37							12 47				12 57		13 07			
Maze Hill	d			12 29		12 39							12 49				12 59		13 09			
Greenwich	d			12 32		12 42							12 52				13 02		13 12			
Deptford	a			12 34		12 44							12 54				13 04		13 14			
London Bridge	a			12 41		12 50	12 54	12 58	13 08	13 22	13 34	13 44	13 00	13 05			13 11		13 20	13 24	13 28	13 38
London Cannon Street	a			12 45		12 54	12 58		13 13		13 38	13 49	13 04				13 15		13 24	13 28		13 43
London Waterloo (East)	a							13 02		13 26				13 09							13 33	
London Charing Cross	a							13 06		13 30				13 13							13 36	
Ebbsfleet International	a	12 17	12 17												12 47	12 47						
Stratford International	a	12 29	12 32												12 59	12 59						
St Pancras Int'l	a	12 36	12 40												13 06	13 07						

A not from 1 September until 8 September

B 1 September, 8 September

Table 200

Saturdays

25 August to 22 September

Gillingham and Dartford - London

Network Diagram - see first Page of Table 200

		SE	SE	SE	SE	SE	SE A	SE B	SE	SE	SE	SE	SE	SE	SE	SE	SE	SE	SE	SE A	SE B	SE	SE
Gillingham (Kent)	d					12 24	12 50	12 50											12 54	13 20	13 20		
Chatham	d					12 28	12 54	12 54											12 58	13 24	13 24		
Rochester	d					12 30	12 57	12 57											13 00	13 27	13 27		
Maidstone West	d																						
Strood	d					12 35	13 02	13 02											13 05	13 32	13 32		
Higham	d					12 40													13 10				
Gravesend	d	13 02				12 48	13 13	13 13							13 32				13 18	13 43	13 43		
Northfleet	d	13 06													13 36								
Swanscombe	d	13 08													13 38								
Greenhithe for Bluewater	d	13 11				12 53									13 41				13 23				
Stone Crossing	d	13 13													13 43								
Dartford	a	13 17				12 58									13 47				13 28				
	d	13 18				12 59			13 01	13 08			13 22		13 48				13 29			13 31	13 38
Slade Green	d				12 55				13 05		13 15			13 17				13 25				13 35	
Erith	d				12 58				13 08		13 18							13 28				13 38	
Belvedere	d				13 00				13 10		13 20							13 30				13 40	
Abbey Wood	d				13 03	13 08			13 13		13 23							13 33	13 38			13 43	
Plumstead	d				13 06				13 16		13 26							13 36				13 46	
Woolwich Arsenal	d				13 09	13 13			13 19		13 29							13 39	13 43			13 49	
Woolwich Dockyard	d				13 12				13 22		13 32							13 42				13 52	
Charlton	d			13 07	13 15	13 17			13 25		13 35						13 37	13 45	13 47			13 55	
Crayford	d	13 22		13 37											13 52		14 07						
Bexley	d	13 25		13 40											13 55		14 10						
Albany Park	d	13 28		13 43											13 58		14 13						
Sidcup	d	13 31		13 46											14 01		14 16						
New Eltham	d	13 34		13 49											14 04		14 19						
Mottingham	d	13 36		13 51											14 06		14 21						
Lee	d	13 39		13 54											14 09		14 24						
Hither Green	d	13 42	13 49	13 58											14 12	14 19	14 28						
Barnehurst	d									13 16			13 29	13 38									13 46
Bexleyheath	d									13 19			13 31	13 40									13 49
Welling	d									13 22			13 34	13 43									13 52
Falconwood	d									13 24			13 37	13 46									13 54
Eltham	d									13 27			13 40	13 49									13 57
Kidbrooke	d									13 30			13 43	13 52									14 00
Blackheath	d					13 22				13 34			13 46	13 55					13 52				14 04
Lewisham	d		13 54	14 04		13 26				13 38		13 44	13 50	13 59		14 24	14 34		13 56				14 08
St Johns	d		13 56	14 06								13 46		14 01		14 26	14 36						
New Cross	d		13 58	14 08								13 48		14 03		14 28	14 38						
Nunhead	d									13 43													14 13
Peckham Rye	d									13 45													14 15
Denmark Hill	d									13 49													14 19
London Victoria	a									13 58													14 28
Westcombe Park	d				13 17				13 27		13 37							13 47				13 57	
Maze Hill	d				13 19				13 29		13 39							13 49				13 59	
Greenwich	d				13 22				13 32		13 42							13 52				14 02	
Deptford	a				13 24				13 34		13 44							13 54				14 04	
London Bridge	a	13 52	14 04	14 14	13 30	13 35			13 41		13 50	13 54	13 58	14 08	14 22	14 34	14 44	14 00	14 05			14 11	
London Cannon Street	a		14 08	14 19	13 34				13 45		13 54	13 58		14 13		14 38	14 49	14 04				14 15	
London Waterloo (East)	a	13 56				13 39							14 02		14 26				14 09				
London Charing Cross	a	14 00				13 43							14 06		14 30				14 13				
Ebbsfleet International	a						13 17	13 17												13 47	13 47		
Stratford International	a						13 29	13 32												13 59	13 59		
St Pancras Int'l	a						13 36	13 40												14 06	14 07		

A not from 1 September until 8 September **B** 1 September, 8 September

Table 200

Saturdays

25 August to 22 September

Gillingham and Dartford - London

Network Diagram - see first Page of Table 200

		SE	SE	SE	SE	SE	SE	SE	SE	SE	SE A	SE B	SE	SE	SE	SE	SE	SE	SE	SE	SE	SE
Gillingham (Kent)	d									13 24	13 50	13 50										
Chatham	d									13 28	13 54	13 54										
Rochester	d									13 30	13 57	13 57										
Maidstone West	d																					
Strood	d									13 35	14 02	14 02										
Higham	d									13 40												
Gravesend	d					14 02				13 48	14 13	14 13							14 32			
Northfleet	d					14 06													14 36			
Swanscombe	d					14 08													14 38			
Greenhithe for Bluewater	d					14 11				13 53									14 41			
Stone Crossing	d					14 13													14 43			
Dartford	a					14 17				13 58									14 47			
	d			13 52		14 18				13 59			14 01	14 08			14 22		14 48			
Slade Green	d	13 45			13 47				13 55				14 05		14 15			14 17				14 25
Erith	d	13 48							13 58				14 08		14 18							14 28
Belvedere	d	13 50							14 00				14 10		14 20							14 30
Abbey Wood	d	13 53							14 03	14 08			14 13		14 23							14 33
Plumstead	d	13 56							14 06				14 16		14 26							14 36
Woolwich Arsenal	d	13 59							14 09	14 13			14 19		14 29							14 39
Woolwich Dockyard	d	14 02							14 12				14 22		14 32							14 42
Charlton	d	14 05						14 07	14 15	14 17			14 25		14 35						14 37	14 45
Crayford	d					14 22		14 37											14 52		15 07	
Bexley	d					14 25		14 40											14 55		15 10	
Albany Park	d					14 28		14 43											14 58		15 13	
Sidcup	d					14 31		14 46											15 01		15 16	
New Eltham	d					14 34		14 49											15 04		15 19	
Mottingham	d					14 36		14 51											15 06		15 21	
Lee	d					14 39		14 54											15 09		15 24	
Hither Green	d					14 42	14 49	14 58											15 12	15 19	15 28	
Barnehurst	d			13 59	14 08									14 16			14 29	14 38				
Bexleyheath	d			14 01	14 10									14 19			14 31	14 40				
Welling	d			14 04	14 13									14 22			14 34	14 43				
Falconwood	d			14 07	14 16									14 24			14 37	14 46				
Eltham	d			14 10	14 19									14 27			14 40	14 49				
Kidbrooke	d			14 13	14 22									14 30			14 43	14 52				
Blackheath	d			14 16	14 25					14 22				14 34			14 46	14 55				
Lewisham	d		14 14	14 20	14 29		14 54	15 04		14 26				14 38		14 44	14 50	14 59		15 24	15 34	
St Johns	d		14 16		14 31		14 56	15 06								14 46		15 01		15 26	15 36	
New Cross	d		14 18		14 33		14 58	15 08								14 48		15 03		15 28	15 38	
Nunhead	d													14 43								
Peckham Rye	d													14 45								
Denmark Hill	d													14 49								
London Victoria	a													14 58								
Westcombe Park	d	14 07							14 17				14 27		14 37							14 47
Maze Hill	d	14 09							14 19				14 29		14 39							14 49
Greenwich	d	14 12							14 22				14 32		14 42							14 52
Deptford	a	14 14							14 24				14 34		14 44							14 54
London Bridge	a	14 20	14 24	14 28	14 38	14 52	15 04	15 14	14 30	14 35			14 41		14 50	14 54	14 58	15 08	15 22	15 34	15 44	15 00
London Cannon Street	a	14 24	14 28		14 43		15 08	15 19	14 34				14 45		14 54	14 58		15 13		15 38	15 49	15 04
London Waterloo (East)	a			14 32		14 56				14 39							15 02		15 26			
London Charing Cross	a			14 36		15 00				14 43							15 06		15 30			
Ebbsfleet International	a										14 17	14 17										
Stratford International	a										14 29	14 29										
St Pancras Int'l	a										14 36	14 42										

A not from 1 September until 8 September **B** 1 September, 8 September

Table 200

Saturdays

Gillingham and Dartford - London

25 August to 22 September

Network Diagram - see first Page of Table 200

		SE	SE A	SE B	SE	SE	SE	SE	SE	SE	SE	SE	SE	SE	SE	SE A	SE B	SE	SE	SE	SE	SE	SE
Gillingham (Kent)	d	13 54	14 20	14 20											14 24	14 50	14 50						
Chatham	d	13 58	14 24	14 24											14 28	14 54	14 54						
Rochester	d	14 00	14 27	14 27											14 30	14 57	14 57						
Maidstone West	d																						
Strood	d	14 05	14 32	14 32											14 35	15 02	15 02						
Higham	d	14 10													14 40								
Gravesend	d	14 18	14 43	14 43							15 02				14 48	15 13	15 13						
Northfleet	d										15 06												
Swanscombe	d										15 08												
Greenhithe for Bluewater	d	14 23									15 11				14 53								
Stone Crossing	d										15 13												
Dartford	a	14 28									15 17				14 58								
	d	14 29			14 31	14 38			14 52		15 18				14 59			15 01	15 08			15 22	
Slade Green	d				14 35		14 45			14 47				14 55				15 05		15 15			15 17
Erith	d				14 38		14 48							14 58				15 08		15 18			
Belvedere	d				14 40		14 50							15 00				15 10		15 20			
Abbey Wood	d	14 38			14 43		14 53							15 03	15 08			15 13		15 23			
Plumstead	d				14 46		14 56							15 06				15 16		15 26			
Woolwich Arsenal	d	14 43			14 49		14 59							15 09	15 13			15 19		15 29			
Woolwich Dockyard	d				14 52		15 02							15 12				15 22		15 32			
Charlton	d	14 47			14 55		15 05						15 07	15 15	15 17			15 25		15 35			
Crayford	d										15 22		15 37										
Bexley	d										15 25		15 40										
Albany Park	d										15 28		15 43										
Sidcup	d										15 31		15 46										
New Eltham	d										15 34		15 49										
Mottingham	d										15 36		15 51										
Lee	d										15 39		15 54										
Hither Green	d										15 42	15 49	15 58										
Barnehurst	d					14 46			14 59	15 08									15 16			15 29	15 38
Bexleyheath	d					14 49			15 01	15 10									15 19			15 31	15 40
Welling	d					14 52			15 04	15 13									15 22			15 34	15 43
Falconwood	d					14 54			15 07	15 16									15 24			15 37	15 46
Eltham	d					14 57			15 10	15 19									15 27			15 40	15 49
Kidbrooke	d					15 00			15 13	15 22									15 30			15 43	15 52
Blackheath	d	14 52				15 04			15 16	15 25					15 22				15 34			15 46	15 55
Lewisham	d	14 56				15 08		15 14	15 20	15 29		15 54	16 04		15 26				15 38		15 44	15 50	15 59
St Johns	d							15 16		15 31		15 56	16 06								15 46		16 01
New Cross	d							15 18		15 33		15 58	16 08								15 48		16 03
Nunhead	d					15 13													15 43				
Peckham Rye	d					15 15													15 45				
Denmark Hill	d					15 19													15 49				
London Victoria	a					15 28													15 58				
Westcombe Park	d				14 57		15 07							15 17				15 27		15 37			
Maze Hill	d				14 59		15 09							15 19				15 29		15 39			
Greenwich	d				15 02		15 12							15 22				15 32		15 42			
Deptford	a				15 04		15 14							15 24				15 34		15 44			
London Bridge	a	15 05			15 11		15 20	15 24	15 28	15 38	15 52	16 04	16 14	15 30	15 35			15 41		15 50	15 54	15 58	16 08
London Cannon Street	a				15 15		15 24	15 28		15 43		16 08	16 19	15 34				15 45		15 54	15 58		16 13
London Waterloo (East)	a	15 09							15 32		15 56				15 39							16 02	
London Charing Cross	a	15 13							15 36		16 00				15 43							16 06	
Ebbsfleet International	a		14 47	14 47												15 17	15 17						
Stratford International	a		15 02	15 02												15 29	15 32						
St Pancras Int'l	a		15 09	15 10												15 36	15 40						

A not from 1 September until 8 September

B 1 September, 8 September

Table 200

Saturdays

Gillingham and Dartford - London

25 August to 22 September

Network Diagram - see first Page of Table 200

		SE	SE	SE	SE	SE	SE	SE	SE	SE	SE	SE	SE	SE	SE	SE	SE	SE	SE A	SE B	SE	SE	SE
Gillingham (Kent)	d					14 54	15 20											15 24	15 50	15 50			
Chatham	d					14 58	15 24											15 28	15 54	15 54			
Rochester	d					15 00	15 27											15 30	15 57	15 57			
Maidstone West	d																						
Strood	d					15 05	15 32											15 35	16 02	16 02			
Higham	d					15 10												15 40					
Gravesend	d	15 32				15 18	15 43							16 02				15 48	16 13	16 13			
Northfleet	d	15 36												16 06									
Swanscombe	d	15 38												16 08									
Greenhithe for Bluewater	d	15 41				15 23								16 11				15 53					
Stone Crossing	d	15 43												16 13									
Dartford	a	15 47				15 28								16 17				15 58					
	d	15 48				15 29		15 31	15 38			15 52		16 18				15 59			16 01	16 08	
Slade Green	d				15 25			15 35		15 45			15 47				15 55				16 05		16 15
Erith	d				15 28			15 38		15 48							15 58				16 08		16 18
Belvedere	d				15 30			15 40		15 50							16 00				16 10		16 20
Abbey Wood	d				15 33	15 38		15 43		15 53							16 03	16 08			16 13		16 23
Plumstead	d				15 36			15 46		15 56							16 06				16 16		16 26
Woolwich Arsenal	d				15 39	15 43		15 49		15 59							16 09	16 13			16 19		16 29
Woolwich Dockyard	d				15 42			15 52		16 02							16 12				16 22		16 32
Charlton	d			15 37	15 45	15 47		15 55		16 05						16 07	16 15	16 17			16 25		16 35
Crayford	d	15 52		16 07										16 22		16 37							
Bexley	d	15 55		16 10										16 25		16 40							
Albany Park	d	15 58		16 13										16 28		16 43							
Sidcup	d	16 01		16 16										16 31		16 46							
New Eltham	d	16 04		16 19										16 34		16 49							
Mottingham	d	16 06		16 21										16 36		16 51							
Lee	d	16 09		16 24										16 39		16 54							
Hither Green	d	16 12	16 19	16 28										16 42	16 49	16 58							
Barnehurst	d								15 46			15 59	16 08									16 16	
Bexleyheath	d								15 49			16 01	16 10									16 19	
Welling	d								15 52			16 04	16 13									16 22	
Falconwood	d								15 54			16 07	16 16									16 24	
Eltham	d								15 57			16 10	16 19									16 27	
Kidbrooke	d								16 00			16 13	16 22									16 30	
Blackheath	d					15 52			16 04			16 16	16 25					16 22				16 34	
Lewisham	d		16 24	16 34		15 56			16 08		16 14	16 20	16 29		16 54	17 04		16 26				16 38	
St Johns	d		16 26	16 36							16 16		16 31		16 56	17 06							
New Cross	d		16 28	16 38							16 18		16 33		16 58	17 08							
Nunhead	d								16 13													16 43	
Peckham Rye	d								16 15													16 45	
Denmark Hill	d								16 19													16 49	
London Victoria	a								16 28													16 58	
Westcombe Park	d				15 47			15 57		16 07							16 17				16 27		16 37
Maze Hill	d				15 49			15 59		16 09							16 19				16 29		16 39
Greenwich	d				15 52			16 02		16 12							16 22				16 32		16 42
Deptford	a				15 54			16 04		16 14							16 24				16 34		16 44
London Bridge	a	16 22	16 34	16 44	16 00	16 05		16 11		16 20	16 24	16 28	16 38	16 52	17 04	17 14	16 30	16 35			16 41		16 50
London Cannon Street	a		16 38	16 49	16 04			16 15		16 24	16 28		16 43		17 08	17 19	16 34				16 45		16 54
London Waterloo (East)	a	16 26				16 09						16 32		16 56				16 39					
London Charing Cross	a	16 30				16 13						16 36		17 00				16 43					
Ebbsfleet International	a						15 47												16 17	16 17			
Stratford International	a						16 02												16 29	16 29			
St Pancras Int'l	a						16 09												16 36	16 37			

A not from 1 September until 8 September

B 1 September, 8 September

Table 200

Saturdays

25 August to 22 September

Gillingham and Dartford - London

Network Diagram - see first Page of Table 200

		SE		SE	SE	SE	SE	SE	SE	SE	SE A	SE B		SE	SE	SE	SE	SE	SE	SE	SE	SE		SE	SE
Gillingham (Kent)	d									15 54	16 20	16 20													16 24
Chatham	d									15 58	16 24	16 24													16 28
Rochester	d									16 00	16 27	16 27													16 30
Maidstone West	d																								
Strood	d									16 05	16 32	16 32													16 35
Higham	d									16 10															16 40
Gravesend	d					16 32				16 18	16 43	16 43								17 02					16 48
Northfleet	d					16 36														17 06					
Swanscombe	d					16 38														17 08					
Greenhithe for Bluewater	d					16 41				16 23										17 11					16 53
Stone Crossing	d					16 43														17 13					
Dartford	a					16 47				16 28										17 17					16 58
	d			16 22		16 48				16 29				16 31	16 38			16 52		17 18					16 59
Slade Green	d				16 17				16 25					16 35		16 45			16 47					16 55	
Erith	d								16 28					16 38		16 48								16 58	
Belvedere	d								16 30					16 40		16 50								17 00	
Abbey Wood	d								16 33	16 38				16 43		16 53								17 03	17 08
Plumstead	d								16 36					16 46		16 56								17 06	
Woolwich Arsenal	d								16 39	16 43				16 49		16 59								17 09	17 13
Woolwich Dockyard	d								16 42					16 52		17 02								17 12	
Charlton	d							16 37	16 45	16 47				16 55		17 05						17 07		17 15	17 17
Crayford	d					16 52		17 07												17 22		17 37			
Bexley	d					16 55		17 10												17 25		17 40			
Albany Park	d					16 58		17 13												17 28		17 43			
Sidcup	d					17 01		17 16												17 31		17 46			
New Eltham	d					17 04		17 19												17 34		17 49			
Mottingham	d					17 06		17 21												17 36		17 51			
Lee	d					17 09		17 24												17 39		17 54			
Hither Green	d					17 12	17 19	17 28												17 42	17 49	17 58			
Barnehurst	d			16 29	16 38										16 46			16 59	17 08						
Bexleyheath	d			16 31	16 40										16 49			17 01	17 10						
Welling	d			16 34	16 43										16 52			17 04	17 13						
Falconwood	d			16 37	16 46										16 54			17 07	17 16						
Eltham	d			16 40	16 49										16 57			17 10	17 19						
Kidbrooke	d			16 43	16 52										17 00			17 13	17 22						
Blackheath	d			16 46	16 55					16 52					17 04			17 16	17 25						17 22
Lewisham	d	16 44		16 50	16 59		17 24	17 34		16 56					17 08		17 14	17 20	17 29		17 54	18 04			17 26
St Johns	d	16 46			17 01		17 26	17 36									17 16		17 31		17 56	18 06			
New Cross	d	16 48			17 03		17 28	17 38									17 18		17 33		17 58	18 08			
Nunhead	d														17 13										
Peckham Rye	d														17 15										
Denmark Hill	d														17 19										
London Victoria	a														17 28										
Westcombe Park	d								16 47					16 57		17 07								17 17	
Maze Hill	d								16 49					16 59		17 09								17 19	
Greenwich	d								16 52					17 02		17 12								17 22	
Deptford	a								16 54					17 04		17 14								17 24	
London Bridge	a	16 54		16 58	17 08	17 22	17 34	17 44	17 00	17 05				17 11		17 20	17 24	17 28	17 38	17 52	18 04	18 14		17 30	17 35
London Cannon Street	a	16 58			17 13		17 38	17 49	17 04					17 15		17 24	17 28		17 43		18 08	18 19		17 34	
London Waterloo (East)	a			17 02		17 26				17 09								17 32		17 56					17 39
London Charing Cross	a			17 06		17 30				17 13								17 36		18 00					17 43
Ebbsfleet International	a										16 47	16 47													
Stratford International	a										17 02														
St Pancras Int'l	a										17 09														

A not from 1 September until 8 September

B 1 September, 8 September

Table 200

Saturdays

25 August to 22 September

Gillingham and Dartford - London

Network Diagram - see first Page of Table 200

		SE A	SE B	SE	SE	SE	SE	SE		SE	SE	SE	SE	SE	SE	SE A	SE B	SE		SE	SE	SE	SE	SE	SE
Gillingham (Kent)	d	16 50	16 50												16 54	17 20	17 20								
Chatham	d	16 54	16 54												16 58	17 24	17 24								
Rochester	d	16 57	16 57												17 00	17 27	17 27								
Maidstone West	d																								
Strood	d	17 02	17 02												17 05	17 32	17 32								
Higham	d														17 10										
Gravesend	d	17 12	17 13								17 32				17 18	17 43	17 43								18 02
Northfleet	d										17 36														18 06
Swanscombe	d										17 38														18 08
Greenhithe for Bluewater	d										17 41				17 23										18 11
Stone Crossing	d										17 43														18 13
Dartford	a										17 47				17 28										18 17
	d			17 01	17 08			17 22			17 48				17 29			17 31		17 38			17 52		18 18
Slade Green	d			17 05		17 15				17 17				17 25				17 35			17 45			17 47	
Erith	d			17 08		17 18								17 28				17 38			17 48				
Belvedere	d			17 10		17 20								17 30				17 40			17 50				
Abbey Wood	d			17 13		17 23								17 33	17 38			17 43			17 53				
Plumstead	d			17 16		17 26								17 36				17 46			17 56				
Woolwich Arsenal	d			17 19		17 29								17 39	17 43			17 49			17 59				
Woolwich Dockyard	d			17 22		17 32								17 42				17 52			18 02				
Charlton	d			17 25		17 35							17 37	17 45	17 47			17 55			18 05				
Crayford	d										17 52		18 07												18 22
Bexley	d										17 55		18 10												18 25
Albany Park	d										17 58		18 13												18 28
Sidcup	d										18 01		18 16												18 31
New Eltham	d										18 04		18 19												18 34
Mottingham	d										18 06		18 21												18 36
Lee	d										18 09		18 24												18 39
Hither Green	d										18 12	18 19	18 28												18 42
Barnehurst	d				17 16			17 29		17 38										17 46			17 59	18 08	
Bexleyheath	d				17 19			17 31		17 40										17 49			18 01	18 10	
Welling	d				17 22			17 34		17 43										17 52			18 04	18 13	
Falconwood	d				17 24			17 37		17 46										17 54			18 07	18 16	
Eltham	d				17 27			17 40		17 49										17 57			18 10	18 19	
Kidbrooke	d				17 30			17 43		17 52										18 00			18 13	18 22	
Blackheath	d				17 34			17 46		17 55					17 52					18 04			18 16	18 25	
Lewisham	d				17 38		17 44	17 50		17 59		18 24	18 34		17 56					18 08		18 14	18 20	18 29	
St Johns	d						17 46			18 01		18 26	18 36									18 16		18 31	
New Cross	d						17 48			18 03		18 28	18 38									18 18		18 33	
Nunhead	d				17 43															18 13					
Peckham Rye	d				17 45															18 15					
Denmark Hill	d				17 49															18 19					
London Victoria	a				17 58															18 28					
Westcombe Park	d			17 27		17 37								17 47				17 57			18 07				
Maze Hill	d			17 29		17 39								17 49				17 59			18 09				
Greenwich	d			17 32		17 42								17 52				18 02			18 12				
Deptford	a			17 34		17 44								17 54				18 04			18 14				
London Bridge	a			17 41		17 50	17 54	17 58		18 08	18 22	18 34	18 44	18 00	18 05			18 11			18 20	18 24	18 28	18 38	18 52
London Cannon Street	a			17 45		17 54	17 58			18 13		18 38	18 49	18 04				18 15			18 24	18 28		18 43	
London Waterloo (East)	a							18 02			18 26				18 09								18 32		18 56
London Charing Cross	a							18 06			18 30				18 13								18 36		19 00
Ebbsfleet International	a	17 16	17 17													17 47	17 47								
Stratford International	a	17 27	17 29													17 58	17 59								
St Pancras Int'l	a	17 34	17 36													18 09	18 09								

A 1 September, 8 September

B not from 1 September until 8 September

Gillingham and Dartford - London

Saturdays

25 August to 22 September

Network Diagram - see first Page of Table 200

		SE	SE	SE		SE	SE A	SE B	SE	SE	SE	SE	SE	SE		SE	SE	SE	SE	SE	SE A	SE B	SE	SE
Gillingham (Kent)	d					17 24	17 50	17 50									17 54				18 20	18 20		
Chatham	d					17 28	17 54	17 54									17 58				18 24	18 24		
Rochester	d					17 30	17 57	17 57									18 00				18 27	18 27		
Maidstone West	d																							
Strood	d					17 35	18 02	18 02									18 05				18 32	18 32		
Higham	d					17 40											18 10							
Gravesend	d					17 48	18 13	18 13									18 18			18 32	18 43	18 43		
Northfleet	d																			18 36				
Swanscombe	d																			18 38				
Greenhithe for Bluewater	d					17 53											18 23			18 41				
Stone Crossing	d																			18 43				
Dartford	a					17 58											18 28			18 47				
	d					17 59			18 01	18 08			18 22				18 29	18 31	18 38	18 48				18 52
Slade Green	d			17 55					18 05		18 15			18 17		18 25		18 35					18 55	
Erith	d			17 58					18 08		18 18					18 28		18 38					18 58	
Belvedere	d			18 00					18 10		18 20					18 30		18 40					19 00	
Abbey Wood	d			18 03		18 08			18 13		18 23					18 33	18 38	18 43					19 03	
Plumstead	d			18 06					18 16		18 26					18 36		18 46					19 06	
Woolwich Arsenal	d			18 09		18 13			18 19		18 29					18 39	18 43	18 49					19 09	
Woolwich Dockyard	d			18 12					18 22		18 32					18 42		18 52					19 12	
Charlton	d		18 07	18 15		18 17			18 25		18 35					18 45	18 47	18 55					19 15	
Crayford	d		18 37																	18 52				
Bexley	d		18 40																	18 55				
Albany Park	d		18 43																	18 58				
Sidcup	d		18 46																	19 01				
New Eltham	d		18 49																	19 04				
Mottingham	d		18 51																	19 06				
Lee	d		18 54																	19 09				
Hither Green	d	18 49	18 58																	19 12				
Barnehurst	d									18 16			18 29	18 38					18 46					18 59
Bexleyheath	d									18 19			18 31	18 40					18 49					19 01
Welling	d									18 22			18 34	18 43					18 52					19 04
Falconwood	d									18 24			18 37	18 46					18 54					19 07
Eltham	d									18 27			18 40	18 49					18 57					19 10
Kidbrooke	d									18 30			18 43	18 52					19 00					19 13
Blackheath	d					18 22				18 34			18 46	18 55			18 52		19 04					19 16
Lewisham	d	18 54	19 04			18 26				18 38		18 44	18 50	18 59			18 56		19 08	19 18				19 20
St Johns	d	18 56	19 06									18 46		19 01										
New Cross ⊖	d	18 58	19 08									18 48		19 03										19 23
Nunhead	d									18 43									19 13					
Peckham Rye	d									18 45									19 15					
Denmark Hill	d									18 49									19 19					
London Victoria ⊖	a									18 58									19 28					
Westcombe Park	d			18 17					18 27		18 37					18 47		18 57					19 17	
Maze Hill	d			18 19					18 29		18 39					18 49		18 59					19 19	
Greenwich	d			18 22					18 32		18 42					18 52		19 02					19 22	
Deptford	a			18 24					18 34		18 44					18 54		19 04					19 24	
London Bridge ⊖	a	19 04	19 14	18 30		18 35			18 41		18 50	18 54	18 58	19 08		19 00	19 05	19 11		19 27			19 30	19 33
London Cannon Street ⊖	a	19 08	19 19	18 34					18 45		18 54	18 58		19 13		19 04		19 15						
London Waterloo (East) ⊖	a					18 39							19 02				19 09			19 32				19 39
London Charing Cross ⊖	a					18 43							19 06				19 13			19 35				19 42
Ebbsfleet International	a						18 17	18 17													18 47	18 47		
Stratford International ⊖	a						18 29	18 29													19 02	19 02		
St Pancras Int'l ⊖	a						18 36	18 37													19 09	19 10		

A not from 1 September until 8 September

B 1 September, 8 September

Gillingham and Dartford - London

Saturdays

25 August to 22 September

Network Diagram - see first Page of Table 200

		SE	SE	SE	SE	SE	SE	SE	SE	SE		SE A	SE B	SE	SE	SE	SE	SE	SE B	SE A		SE	SE	SE	SE
Gillingham (Kent)	d	18 24			18 50			18 54				19 20	19 20			19 24			19 50	19 50			19 54		
Chatham	d	18 28			18 54			18 58				19 24	19 24			19 28			19 54	19 54			19 58		
Rochester	d	18 30			18 57			19 00				19 27	19 27			19 30			19 57	19 57			20 00		
Maidstone West	d																								
Strood	d	18 35			19 02			19 05				19 32	19 32			19 35			20 02	20 02			20 05		
Higham	d	18 40						19 10								19 40							20 10		
Gravesend	d	18 48		19 02	19 12			19 18		19 32		19 43	19 43			19 48		20 02	20 12	20 13			20 18		20 32
Northfleet	d			19 06						19 36								20 06							20 36
Swanscombe	d			19 08						19 38								20 08							20 38
Greenhithe for Bluewater	d	18 53		19 11				19 23		19 41						19 53		20 11					20 23		20 41
Stone Crossing	d			19 13						19 43								20 13							20 43
Dartford	a	18 58		19 17				19 28		19 47						19 58		20 17					20 28		20 47
	d	18 59	19 01	19 18			19 25	19 29	19 31	19 48					19 55	19 59	20 01	20 18				20 25	20 29	20 31	20 48
Slade Green	d		19 05			19 25			19 35					19 55			20 05							20 35	
Erith	d		19 08			19 28			19 38					19 58			20 08							20 38	
Belvedere	d		19 10			19 30			19 40					20 00			20 10							20 40	
Abbey Wood	d	19 08	19 13			19 33		19 38	19 43					20 03		20 08	20 13						20 38	20 43	
Plumstead	d		19 16			19 36			19 46					20 06			20 16							20 46	
Woolwich Arsenal	d	19 13	19 19			19 39		19 43	19 49					20 09		20 13	20 19						20 43	20 49	
Woolwich Dockyard	d		19 22			19 42			19 52					20 12			20 22							20 52	
Charlton	d	19 17	19 25			19 45		19 47	19 55					20 15		20 17	20 25						20 47	20 55	
Crayford	d			19 22						19 52								20 22							20 52
Bexley	d			19 25						19 55								20 25							20 55
Albany Park	d			19 28						19 58								20 28							20 58
Sidcup	d			19 31						20 01								20 31							21 01
New Eltham	d			19 34						20 04								20 34							21 04
Mottingham	d			19 36						20 06								20 36							21 06
Lee	d			19 39						20 09								20 39							21 09
Hither Green	d			19 42						20 12								20 42							21 12
Barnehurst	d						19 32								20 02							20 32			
Bexleyheath	d						19 34								20 04							20 34			
Welling	d						19 37								20 07							20 37			
Falconwood	d						19 40								20 10							20 40			
Eltham	d						19 42								20 12							20 42			
Kidbrooke	d						19 45								20 15							20 45			
Blackheath	d	19 22					19 49	19 52							20 19	20 22						20 49	20 52		
Lewisham	d	19 26		19 48			19 53	19 56		20 18					20 23	20 26		20 48				20 53	20 56		21 18
St Johns	d																								
New Cross ⊖	d			19 51			19 56			20 21					20 26			20 51				20 56			21 21
Nunhead	d																								
Peckham Rye	d																								
Denmark Hill	d																								
London Victoria ⊖	a																								
Westcombe Park	d		19 27			19 47			19 57					20 17			20 27							20 57	
Maze Hill	d		19 29			19 49			19 59					20 19			20 29							20 59	
Greenwich	d		19 32			19 52			20 02					20 22			20 32							21 02	
Deptford	a		19 34			19 54			20 04					20 24			20 34							21 04	
London Bridge ⊖	a	19 36	19 41	19 57		20 00	20 03	20 06	20 11	20 27				20 30	20 33	20 36	20 41	20 57				21 03	21 06	21 11	21 27
London Cannon Street ⊖	a																								
London Waterloo (East) ⊖	a	19 42	19 45	20 04			20 08	20 10	20 15	20 34					20 38	20 40	20 45	21 04				21 08	21 10	21 15	21 34
London Charing Cross ⊖	a	19 45	19 49	20 07			20 12	20 14	20 19	20 37					20 42	20 44	20 49	21 07				21 12	21 14	21 19	21 37
Ebbsfleet International	a				19 16							19 47	19 47						20 16	20 17					
Stratford International ⊖	a				19 27							19 59	19 59						20 27	20 29					
St Pancras Int'l ⊖	a				19 38							20 06	20 07						20 35	20 36					

A not from 1 September until 8 September

B 1 September, 8 September

Saturdays

25 August to 22 September

Gillingham and Dartford - London

Network Diagram - see first Page of Table 200

		SE A	SE B	SE	SE	SE	SE	SE B	SE A	SE	SE	SE	SE	SE B	SE A	SE	SE	SE	SE	SE B	SE A	SE	SE
Gillingham (Kent)	d	20 20	20 20		20 24			20 50	20 50		20 54			21 20	21 20		21 24			21 50	21 50		21 54
Chatham	d	20 24	20 24		20 28			20 54	20 54		20 58			21 24	21 24		21 28			21 54	21 54		21 58
Rochester	d	20 27	20 27		20 30			20 57	20 57		21 00			21 27	21 27		21 30			21 57	21 57		22 00
Maidstone West	d																						
Strood	d	20 32	20 32		20 35			21 02	21 02		21 05			21 32	21 32		21 35			22 02	22 02		22 05
Higham	d				20 40						21 10						21 40						22 10
Gravesend	d	20 43	20 43		20 48		21 02	21 13	21 13		21 18		21 32	21 43	21 43		21 48		22 02	22 13	22 13		22 18
Northfleet	d						21 06						21 36						22 06				
Swanscombe	d						21 08						21 38						22 08				
Greenhithe for Bluewater	d				20 53		21 11				21 23		21 41				21 53		22 11				22 23
Stone Crossing	d						21 13						21 43						22 13				
Dartford	a				20 58		21 17				21 28		21 47				21 58		22 17				22 28
	d			20 55	20 59	21 01	21 18			21 25	21 29	21 31	21 48			21 55	21 59	22 01	22 18			22 25	22 29
Slade Green	d					21 05						21 35						22 05					
Erith	d					21 08						21 38						22 08					
Belvedere	d					21 10						21 40						22 10					
Abbey Wood	d				21 08	21 13					21 38	21 43					22 08	22 13					22 38
Plumstead	d					21 16						21 46						22 16					
Woolwich Arsenal	d				21 13	21 19					21 43	21 49					22 13	22 19					22 43
Woolwich Dockyard	d					21 22						21 52						22 22					
Charlton	d				21 17	21 25					21 47	21 55					22 17	22 25					22 47
Crayford	d						21 22						21 52						22 22				
Bexley	d						21 25						21 55						22 25				
Albany Park	d						21 28						21 58						22 28				
Sidcup	d						21 31						22 01						22 31				
New Eltham	d						21 34						22 04						22 34				
Mottingham	d						21 36						22 06						22 36				
Lee	d						21 39						22 09						22 39				
Hither Green	d						21 42						22 12						22 42				
Barnehurst	d			21 02						21 32						22 02						22 32	
Bexleyheath	d			21 04						21 34						22 04						22 34	
Welling	d			21 07						21 37						22 07						22 37	
Falconwood	d			21 10						21 40						22 10						22 40	
Eltham	d			21 12						21 42						22 12						22 42	
Kidbrooke	d			21 15						21 45						22 15						22 45	
Blackheath	d			21 19	21 22					21 49	21 52					22 19	22 22					22 49	22 52
Lewisham	d			21 23	21 26		21 48			21 53	21 56		22 18			22 23	22 26		22 48			22 53	22 56
St Johns	d																						
New Cross	d			21 26			21 51			21 56			22 21			22 26			22 51			22 56	
Nunhead	d																						
Peckham Rye	d																						
Denmark Hill	d																						
London Victoria	a																						
Westcombe Park	d					21 27						21 57						22 27					
Maze Hill	d					21 29						21 59						22 29					
Greenwich	d					21 32						22 02						22 32					
Deptford	a					21 34						22 04						22 34					
London Bridge	a			21 33	21 36	21 41	21 57			22 01	22 05	22 11	22 27			22 31	22 35	22 41	22 57			23 01	23 05
London Cannon Street	a																						
London Waterloo (East)	a			21 38	21 40	21 45	22 04			22 06	22 09	22 15	22 34			22 36	22 39	22 45	23 04			23 06	23 09
London Charing Cross	a			21 42	21 44	21 49	22 07			22 10	22 13	22 19	22 37			22 40	22 43	22 49	23 07			23 10	23 13
Ebbsfleet International	a	20 47	20 47					21 17	21 17					21 47	21 47					22 17	22 17		
Stratford International	a		21 02					21 29	21 31					21 59	21 59					22 29	22 29		
St Pancras Int'l	a	21 06	21 09					21 36	21 42					22 06	22 07					22 36	22 37		

A 1 September, 8 September

B not from 1 September until 8 September

Table 200

Saturdays

25 August to 22 September

Gillingham and Dartford - London

Network Diagram - see first Page of Table 200

		SE	SE	SE A	SE B	SE	SE	SE	SE
Gillingham (Kent)	d			22 20	22 20		22 24		22 54
Chatham	d			22 24	22 24		22 28		22 58
Rochester	d			22 27	22 27		22 30		23 00
Maidstone West	d								
Strood	d			22 32	22 32		22 35		23 05
Higham	d						22 40		23 10
Gravesend	d		22 32	22 43	22 43		22 48		23 18
Northfleet	d		22 36						
Swanscombe	d		22 38						
Greenhithe for Bluewater	d		22 41				22 53		23 23
Stone Crossing	d		22 43						
Dartford	a		22 47				22 58		23 28
	d	22 31	22 48			22 55	22 59	23 01	
Slade Green	d	22 35						23 05	
Erith	d	22 38						23 08	
Belvedere	d	22 40						23 10	
Abbey Wood	d	22 43					23 08	23 13	
Plumstead	d	22 46						23 16	
Woolwich Arsenal	d	22 49					23 13	23 19	
Woolwich Dockyard	d	22 52						23 22	
Charlton	d	22 55					23 17	23 25	
Crayford	d		22 52						
Bexley	d		22 55						
Albany Park	d		22 58						
Sidcup	d		23 01						
New Eltham	d		23 04						
Mottingham	d		23 06						
Lee	d		23 09						
Hither Green	d		23 12						
Barnehurst	d					23 02			
Bexleyheath	d					23 04			
Welling	d					23 07			
Falconwood	d					23 10			
Eltham	d					23 12			
Kidbrooke	d					23 15			
Blackheath	d					23 19	23 22		
Lewisham	d		23 18			23 23	23 26		
St Johns	d								
New Cross	d		23 21			23 26			
Nunhead	d								
Peckham Rye	d								
Denmark Hill	d								
London Victoria	a								
Westcombe Park	d	22 57						23 27	
Maze Hill	d	22 59						23 29	
Greenwich	d	23 02						23 32	
Deptford	a	23 04						23 34	
London Bridge	a	23 11	23 27			23 31	23 35	23 41	
London Cannon Street	a								
London Waterloo (East)	a	23 15	23 34			23 36	23 39	23 45	
London Charing Cross	a	23 20	23 37			23 40	23 43	23 49	
Ebbsfleet International	a			22 47	22 47				
Stratford International	a			22 59	22 59				
St Pancras Int'l	a			23 06	23 07				

A not from 1 September until 8 September

B 1 September, 8 September

Table 200

Gillingham and Dartford - London

Sundays

until 22 July, 19 Aug and from 16 Sep

Network Diagram - see first Page of Table 200

Station		SE	SE	SE	SE	SE	SE	SE	SE	SE		SE	SE	SE	SE	SE	SE	SE	SE	SE		SE	SE	SE	SE
Gillingham (Kent)	d							06 45					07 15	07 20				07 45						08 15	08 20
Chatham	d							06 49					07 19	07 24				07 49						08 19	08 24
Rochester	d							06 51					07 21	07 27				07 51						08 21	08 27
Maidstone West	d																								
Strood	d							06 56					07 26	07 32				07 56						08 26	08 32
Higham	d							07 01					07 31					08 01						08 31	
Gravesend	d							07 09					07 39	07 43				08 09						08 39	08 43
Northfleet	d							07 12					07 42					08 12						08 42	
Swanscombe	d							07 14					07 44					08 14						08 44	
Greenhithe for Bluewater	d							07 18					07 48					08 18						08 48	
Stone Crossing	d							07 20					07 50					08 20						08 50	
Dartford	a							07 24					07 54					08 24						08 54	
	d	06 40	06 43	06 48	07 10	07 13	07 18	07 29	07 40	07 43		07 48	07 59		08 10	08 13	08 18	08 29		08 40		08 43	08 48	08 59	
Slade Green	d		06 48			07 18				07 48						08 18						08 48			
Erith	d		06 50			07 20				07 50						08 20						08 50			
Belvedere	d		06 53			07 23				07 53						08 23						08 53			
Abbey Wood	d		06 56			07 26		07 38		07 56			08 08			08 26		08 38				08 56		09 08	
Plumstead	d		06 59			07 29				07 59						08 29			08 47			08 59			
Woolwich Arsenal	d		07 02			07 32		07 43		08 02			08 13			08 32		08 43	08 50			09 02		09 13	
Woolwich Dockyard	d		07 04			07 34				08 04						08 34			08 52			09 04			
Charlton	d		07 07			07 37		07 47		08 07			08 17			08 37		08 47	08 55			09 07		09 17	
Crayford	d			06 52			07 22					07 52					08 22						08 52		
Bexley	d			06 55			07 25					07 55					08 25						08 55		
Albany Park	d			06 58			07 28					07 58					08 28						08 58		
Sidcup	d			07 01			07 31					08 01					08 31						09 01		
New Eltham	d			07 04			07 34					08 04					08 34						09 04		
Mottingham	d			07 06			07 36					08 06					08 36						09 06		
Lee	d			07 09			07 39					08 09					08 39						09 09		
Hither Green	d			07 12			07 42					08 12					08 42						09 12		
Barnehurst	d	06 47			07 17				07 47						08 17					08 47					
Bexleyheath	d	06 49			07 19				07 49						08 19					08 49					
Welling	d	06 52			07 22				07 52						08 22					08 52					
Falconwood	d	06 55			07 25				07 55						08 25					08 55					
Eltham	d	06 58			07 28				07 58						08 28					08 58					
Kidbrooke	d	07 01			07 31				08 01						08 31					09 01					
Blackheath	d	07 04			07 34			07 52	08 04				08 22		08 34			08 52		09 04				09 22	
Lewisham	d	07 08		07 18	07 38		07 48	07 56	08 08			08 18	08 26		08 38		08 48	08 56		09 08			09 18	09 26	
St Johns	d																								
New Cross ⊖	d	07 11			07 41				08 11						08 41					09 11					
Nunhead	d																								
Peckham Rye	d																								
Denmark Hill	d																								
London Victoria ⊖	a																								
Westcombe Park	d		07 09			07 39				08 09						08 39			08 57			09 09			
Maze Hill	d		07 11			07 41				08 11						08 41			08 59			09 11			
Greenwich	d		07 15			07 45				08 15						08 45			09 03			09 15			
Deptford	a		07 17			07 47				08 17						08 47			09 05			09 17			
London Bridge ⊖	a	07 19	07 23	07 26	07 49	07 53	07 56	08 06	08 19	08 23		08 26	08 36		08 49	08 53	08 56	09 06	09 11	09 19		09 23	09 26	09 36	
London Cannon Street ⊖	a																								
London Waterloo (East) ⊖	a	07 25	07 27	07 30	07 55	07 57	08 00	08 11	08 25	08 27		08 30	08 41		08 55	08 57	09 00	09 11		09 25		09 27	09 30	09 41	
London Charing Cross ⊖	a	07 28	07 31	07 34	07 58	08 01	08 04	08 14	08 28	08 31		08 34	08 44		08 58	09 01	09 04	09 14		09 28		09 31	09 34	09 44	
Ebbsfleet International	a													07 47											08 47
Stratford International ⊖	a																								08 59
St Pancras Int'l ⊖	a																								09 06

Table 200

Gillingham and Dartford - London

Sundays

until 22 July, 19 Aug and from 16 Sep

Network Diagram - see first Page of Table 200

Station		SE	SE	SE	SE	SE		SE	SE	SE	SE	SE	SE	SE	SE	SE		SE	SE	SE	SE	SE	SE	SE	SE
Gillingham (Kent)	d					08 54						09 20	09 24						09 54					10 20	10 24
Chatham	d					08 58						09 24	09 28						09 58					10 24	10 28
Rochester	d					09 00						09 27	09 30						10 00					10 27	10 30
Maidstone West	d																								
Strood	d					09 05						09 32	09 35						10 05					10 32	10 35
Higham	d					09 10							09 40						10 10						10 40
Gravesend	d				09 02	09 18					09 32	09 43	09 48					10 02	10 18				10 32	10 43	10 48
Northfleet	d				09 06						09 36							10 06					10 36		
Swanscombe	d				09 08						09 38							10 08					10 38		
Greenhithe for Bluewater	d				09 11	09 23					09 41		09 53					10 11	10 23				10 41		10 53
Stone Crossing	d				09 13						09 43							10 13					10 43		
Dartford	a				09 17	09 28					09 47		09 58					10 17	10 28				10 47		10 58
	d		09 10	09 13	09 18	09 29			09 40	09 43	09 48		09 59		10 10	10 13		10 18	10 29		10 40	10 43	10 48		10 59
Slade Green	d			09 18						09 48						10 18						10 48			
Erith	d			09 20						09 50						10 20						10 50			
Belvedere	d			09 23						09 53						10 23						10 53			
Abbey Wood	d			09 26		09 38				09 56			10 08			10 26			10 38			10 56			11 08
Plumstead	d	09 17		09 29				09 47		09 59				10 17		10 29				10 47		10 59			
Woolwich Arsenal	d	09 20		09 32		09 43		09 50		10 02			10 13	10 20		10 32			10 43	10 50		11 02			11 13
Woolwich Dockyard	d	09 22		09 34				09 52		10 04				10 22		10 34				10 52		11 04			
Charlton	d	09 25		09 37		09 47		09 55		10 07			10 17	10 25		10 37			10 47	10 55		11 07			11 17
Crayford	d				09 22						09 52							10 22					10 52		
Bexley	d				09 25						09 55							10 25					10 55		
Albany Park	d				09 28						09 58							10 28					10 58		
Sidcup	d				09 31						10 01							10 31					11 01		
New Eltham	d				09 34						10 04							10 34					11 04		
Mottingham	d				09 36						10 06							10 36					11 06		
Lee	d				09 39						10 09							10 39					11 09		
Hither Green	d				09 42						10 12							10 42					11 12		
Barnehurst	d		09 17						09 47						10 17						10 47				
Bexleyheath	d		09 19						09 49						10 19						10 49				
Welling	d		09 22						09 52						10 22						10 52				
Falconwood	d		09 25						09 55						10 25						10 55				
Eltham	d		09 28						09 58						10 28						10 58				
Kidbrooke	d		09 31						10 01						10 31						11 01				
Blackheath	d		09 34			09 52			10 04				10 22		10 34				10 52		11 04				11 22
Lewisham	d		09 38		09 48	09 56			10 08		10 18		10 26		10 38			10 48	10 56		11 08		11 18		11 26
St Johns	d																								
New Cross ⊖	d		09 41						10 11						10 41						11 11				
Nunhead	d																								
Peckham Rye	d																								
Denmark Hill	d																								
London Victoria ⊖	a																								
Westcombe Park	d	09 27		09 39				09 57		10 09				10 27		10 39				10 57		11 09			
Maze Hill	d	09 29		09 41				09 59		10 11				10 29		10 41				10 59		11 11			
Greenwich	d	09 33		09 45				10 03		10 15				10 33		10 45				11 03		11 15			
Deptford	a	09 35		09 47				10 05		10 17				10 35		10 47				11 05		11 17			
London Bridge ⊖	a	09 41	09 49	09 53	09 56	10 06		10 11	10 19	10 23	10 26		10 36	10 41	10 49	10 53		10 56	11 06	11 11	11 19	11 23	11 26		11 36
London Cannon Street ⊖	a																								
London Waterloo (East) ⊖	a		09 55	09 57	10 00	10 11			10 25	10 27	10 30		10 41		10 55	10 57		11 00	11 11		11 25	11 27	11 30		11 41
London Charing Cross ⊖	a		09 58	10 01	10 04	10 14			10 28	10 31	10 34		10 44		10 58	11 01		11 04	11 14		11 28	11 31	11 34		11 44
Ebbsfleet International	a											09 47												10 47	
Stratford International ⊖	a											09 59												10 59	
St Pancras Int'l ⊖	a											10 06												11 06	

Table 200

Sundays

until 22 July, 19 Aug and from 16 Sep

Gillingham and Dartford - London

Network Diagram - see first Page of Table 200

		SE	SE	SE	SE	SE	SE	SE	SE	SE	SE	SE	SE	SE	SE	SE	SE	SE	SE	SE	SE	SE
Gillingham (Kent)	d					10 54					11 20	11 24					11 50	11 54				
Chatham	d					10 58					11 24	11 28					11 54	11 58				
Rochester	d					11 00					11 27	11 30					11 57	12 00				
Maidstone West	d																					
Strood	d					11 05					11 32	11 35					12 02	12 05				
Higham	d					11 10						11 40						12 10				
Gravesend	d				11 02	11 18				11 32	11 43	11 48				12 02	12 13	12 18				12 32
Northfleet	d				11 06					11 36						12 06						12 36
Swanscombe	d				11 08					11 38						12 08						12 38
Greenhithe for Bluewater	d				11 11	11 23				11 41		11 53				12 11		12 23				12 41
Stone Crossing	d				11 13					11 43						12 13						12 43
Dartford	a				11 17	11 28				11 47		11 58				12 17		12 28				12 47
	d		11 10	11 13	11 18	11 29		11 40	11 43	11 48		11 59		12 10	12 13	12 18		12 29		12 40	12 43	12 48
Slade Green	d			11 18					11 48						12 18						12 48	
Erith	d			11 20					11 50						12 20						12 50	
Belvedere	d			11 23					11 53						12 23						12 53	
Abbey Wood	d			11 26		11 38			11 56			12 08			12 26			12 38			12 56	
Plumstead	d	11 17		11 29			11 47		11 59				12 17		12 29				12 47		12 59	
Woolwich Arsenal	d	11 20		11 32		11 43	11 50		12 02			12 13	12 20		12 32			12 43	12 50		13 02	
Woolwich Dockyard	d	11 22		11 34			11 52		12 04				12 22		12 34				12 52		13 04	
Charlton	d	11 25		11 37		11 47	11 55		12 07			12 17	12 25		12 37			12 47	12 55		13 07	
Crayford	d				11 22					11 52						12 22						12 52
Bexley	d				11 25					11 55						12 25						12 55
Albany Park	d				11 28					11 58						12 28						12 58
Sidcup	d				11 31					12 01						12 31						13 01
New Eltham	d				11 34					12 04						12 34						13 04
Mottingham	d				11 36					12 06						12 36						13 06
Lee	d				11 39					12 09						12 39						13 09
Hither Green	d				11 42					12 12						12 42						13 12
Barnehurst	d		11 17					11 47						12 17						12 47		
Bexleyheath	d		11 19					11 49						12 19						12 49		
Welling	d		11 22					11 52						12 22						12 52		
Falconwood	d		11 25					11 55						12 25						12 55		
Eltham	d		11 28					11 58						12 28						12 58		
Kidbrooke	d		11 31					12 01						12 31						13 01		
Blackheath	d		11 34			11 52		12 04				12 22		12 34				12 52		13 04		
Lewisham	d		11 38		11 48	11 56		12 08		12 18		12 26		12 38		12 48		12 56		13 08		13 18
St Johns	d																					
New Cross	d		11 41					12 11						12 41						13 11		
Nunhead	d																					
Peckham Rye	d																					
Denmark Hill	d																					
London Victoria	a																					
Westcombe Park	d	11 27		11 39			11 57		12 09				12 27		12 39				12 57		13 09	
Maze Hill	d	11 29		11 41			11 59		12 11				12 29		12 41				12 59		13 11	
Greenwich	d	11 33		11 45			12 03		12 15				12 33		12 45				13 03		13 15	
Deptford	a	11 35		11 47			12 05		12 17				12 35		12 47				13 05		13 17	
London Bridge	a	11 41	11 49	11 53	11 56	12 06	12 11	12 19	12 23	12 26		12 36	12 41	12 49	12 53	12 56		13 06	13 11	13 19	13 23	13 26
London Cannon Street	a																					
London Waterloo (East)	a		11 55	11 57	12 00	12 11		12 25	12 27	12 30		12 41		12 55	12 57	13 00		13 11		13 25	13 27	13 30
London Charing Cross	a		11 58	12 01	12 04	12 14		12 28	12 31	12 34		12 44		12 58	13 01	13 04		13 14		13 28	13 31	13 34
Ebbsfleet International	a										11 47						12 17					
Stratford International	a										11 59						12 29					
St Pancras Int'l	a										12 06						12 36					

Table 200

Sundays

until 22 July, 19 Aug and from 16 Sep

Gillingham and Dartford - London

Network Diagram - see first Page of Table 200

		SE	SE	SE	SE	SE	SE	SE	SE	SE	SE	SE	SE	SE	SE	SE	SE	SE	SE	SE	SE	SE	SE
Gillingham (Kent)	d	12 20	12 24					12 50	12 54					13 20	13 24					13 50	13 54		
Chatham	d	12 24	12 28					12 54	12 58					13 24	13 28					13 54	13 58		
Rochester	d	12 27	12 30					12 57	13 00					13 27	13 30					13 57	14 00		
Maidstone West	d																						
Strood	d	12 32	12 35					13 02	13 05					13 32	13 35					14 02	14 05		
Higham	d		12 40						13 10						13 40						14 10		
Gravesend	d	12 43	12 48				13 02	13 13	13 18				13 32	13 43	13 48				14 02	14 13	14 18		
Northfleet	d						13 06						13 36						14 06				
Swanscombe	d						13 08						13 38						14 08				
Greenhithe for Bluewater	d		12 53				13 11		13 23				13 41		13 53				14 11		14 23		
Stone Crossing	d						13 13						13 43						14 13				
Dartford	a		12 58				13 17		13 28				13 47		13 58				14 17		14 28		
	d		12 59		13 10	13 13	13 18		13 29		13 40	13 43	13 48		13 59		14 10	14 13	14 18		14 29		14 40
Slade Green	d					13 18						13 48						14 18					
Erith	d					13 20						13 50						14 20					
Belvedere	d					13 23						13 53						14 23					
Abbey Wood	d		13 08			13 26			13 38			13 56			14 08			14 26			14 38		
Plumstead	d			13 17		13 29				13 47		13 59				14 17		14 29				14 47	
Woolwich Arsenal	d		13 13	13 20		13 32			13 43	13 50		14 02			14 13	14 20		14 32			14 43	14 50	
Woolwich Dockyard	d			13 22		13 34				13 52		14 04				14 22		14 34				14 52	
Charlton	d		13 17	13 25		13 37			13 47	13 55		14 07			14 17	14 25		14 37			14 47	14 55	
Crayford	d						13 22						13 52						14 22				
Bexley	d						13 25						13 55						14 25				
Albany Park	d						13 28						13 58						14 28				
Sidcup	d						13 31						14 01						14 31				
New Eltham	d						13 34						14 04						14 34				
Mottingham	d						13 36						14 06						14 36				
Lee	d						13 39						14 09						14 39				
Hither Green	d						13 42						14 12						14 42				
Barnehurst	d				13 17						13 47						14 17						14 47
Bexleyheath	d				13 19						13 49						14 19						14 49
Welling	d				13 22						13 52						14 22						14 52
Falconwood	d				13 25						13 55						14 25						14 55
Eltham	d				13 28						13 58						14 28						14 58
Kidbrooke	d				13 31						14 01						14 31						15 01
Blackheath	d		13 22		13 34				13 52		14 04				14 22		14 34				14 52		15 04
Lewisham	d		13 26		13 38		13 48		13 56		14 08		14 18		14 26		14 38		14 48		14 56		15 08
St Johns	d																						
New Cross	d				13 41						14 11						14 41						15 11
Nunhead	d																						
Peckham Rye	d																						
Denmark Hill	d																						
London Victoria	a																						
Westcombe Park	d			13 27		13 39				13 57		14 09				14 27		14 39				14 57	
Maze Hill	d			13 29		13 41				13 59		14 11				14 29		14 41				14 59	
Greenwich	d			13 33		13 45				14 03		14 15				14 33		14 45				15 03	
Deptford	a			13 35		13 47				14 05		14 17				14 35		14 47				15 05	
London Bridge	a		13 36	13 41	13 49	13 53	13 56		14 06	14 11	14 19	14 23	14 26		14 36	14 41	14 49	14 53	14 56		15 06	15 11	15 19
London Cannon Street	a																						
London Waterloo (East)	a		13 41		13 55	13 57	14 00		14 11		14 25	14 27	14 30		14 41		14 55	14 57	15 00		15 11		15 25
London Charing Cross	a		13 44		13 58	14 01	14 04		14 14		14 28	14 31	14 34		14 44		14 58	15 01	15 04		15 14		15 28
Ebbsfleet International	a	12 47						13 17						13 47						14 17			
Stratford International	a	12 59						13 29						14 02						14 29			
St Pancras Int'l	a	13 06						13 36						14 09						14 36			

Table 200

Gillingham and Dartford - London

Sundays

until 22 July, 19 Aug and from 16 Sep

Network Diagram - see first Page of Table 200

		SE	SE	SE	SE	SE	SE	SE	SE	SE	SE	SE	SE	SE	SE	SE	SE	SE	SE	SE	SE	SE
Gillingham (Kent)	d			14 20	14 24					14 50	14 54					15 20	15 24					15 50
Chatham	d			14 24	14 28					14 54	14 58					15 24	15 28					15 54
Rochester	d			14 27	14 30					14 57	15 00					15 27	15 30					15 57
Maidstone West	d																					
Strood	d			14 32	14 35					15 02	15 05					15 32	15 35					16 02
Higham	d				14 40						15 10						15 40					
Gravesend	d		14 32	14 43	14 48				15 02	15 13	15 18				15 32	15 43	15 48				16 02	16 13
Northfleet	d		14 36						15 06						15 36						16 06	
Swanscombe	d		14 38						15 08						15 38						16 08	
Greenhithe for Bluewater	d		14 41		14 53				15 11		15 23				15 41		15 53				16 11	
Stone Crossing	d		14 43						15 13						15 43						16 13	
Dartford	a		14 47		14 58				15 17		15 28				15 47		15 58				16 17	
	d	14 43	14 48		14 59		15 10	15 13	15 18		15 29		15 40	15 43	15 48		15 59		16 10	16 13	16 18	
Slade Green	d	14 48						15 18						15 48						16 18		
Erith	d	14 50						15 20						15 50						16 20		
Belvedere	d	14 53						15 23						15 53						16 23		
Abbey Wood	d	14 56			15 08			15 26			15 38			15 56			16 08			16 26		
Plumstead	d	14 59				15 17		15 29				15 47		15 59				16 17		16 29		
Woolwich Arsenal	d	15 02			15 13	15 20		15 32			15 43	15 50		16 02			16 13	16 20		16 32		
Woolwich Dockyard	d	15 04				15 22		15 34				15 52		16 04				16 22		16 34		
Charlton	d	15 07			15 17	15 25		15 37			15 47	15 55		16 07			16 17	16 25		16 37		
Crayford	d		14 52						15 22						15 52						16 22	
Bexley	d		14 55						15 25						15 55						16 25	
Albany Park	d		14 58						15 28						15 58						16 28	
Sidcup	d		15 01						15 31						16 01						16 31	
New Eltham	d		15 04						15 34						16 04						16 34	
Mottingham	d		15 06						15 36						16 06						16 36	
Lee	d		15 09						15 39						16 09						16 39	
Hither Green	d		15 12						15 42						16 12						16 42	
Barnehurst	d						15 17						15 47						16 17			
Bexleyheath	d						15 19						15 49						16 19			
Welling	d						15 22						15 52						16 22			
Falconwood	d						15 25						15 55						16 25			
Eltham	d						15 28						15 58						16 28			
Kidbrooke	d						15 31						16 01						16 31			
Blackheath	d				15 22		15 34				15 52		16 04				16 22		16 34			
Lewisham	d		15 18		15 26		15 38		15 48		15 56		16 08		16 18		16 26		16 38		16 48	
St Johns	d																					
New Cross	d						15 41						16 11						16 41			
Nunhead	d																					
Peckham Rye	d																					
Denmark Hill	d																					
London Victoria	a																					
Westcombe Park	d	15 09				15 27		15 39				15 57		16 09				16 27		16 39		
Maze Hill	d	15 11				15 29		15 41				15 59		16 11				16 29		16 41		
Greenwich	d	15 15				15 33		15 45				16 03		16 15				16 33		16 45		
Deptford	a	15 17				15 35		15 47				16 05		16 17				16 35		16 47		
London Bridge	a	15 23	15 26		15 36	15 41	15 49	15 53	15 56		16 06	16 11	16 19	16 23	16 26		16 36	16 41	16 49	16 53	16 56	
London Cannon Street	a																					
London Waterloo (East)	a	15 27	15 30		15 41		15 55	15 57	16 00		16 11		16 25	16 27	16 30		16 41		16 55	16 57	17 00	
London Charing Cross	a	15 31	15 34		15 44		15 58	16 01	16 04		16 14		16 28	16 31	16 34		16 44		16 58	17 01	17 04	
Ebbsfleet International	a			14 47						15 17						15 47						16 17
Stratford International	a			14 59						15 29						16 02						16 29
St Pancras Int'l	a			15 06						15 36						16 09						16 36

Table 200

Gillingham and Dartford - London

Sundays

until 22 July, 19 Aug and from 16 Sep

Network Diagram - see first Page of Table 200

		SE	SE	SE	SE	SE	SE	SE	SE	SE	SE	SE	SE	SE	SE	SE	SE	SE	SE	SE	SE	SE	SE
Gillingham (Kent)	d	15 54					16 20	16 24					16 50	16 54					17 20	17 24			
Chatham	d	15 58					16 24	16 28					16 54	16 58					17 24	17 28			
Rochester	d	16 00					16 27	16 30					16 57	17 00					17 27	17 30			
Maidstone West	d																						
Strood	d	16 05					16 32	16 35					17 02	17 05					17 32	17 35			
Higham	d	16 10						16 40						17 10						17 40			
Gravesend	d	16 18				16 32	16 43	16 48				17 02	17 13	17 18				17 32	17 43	17 48			
Northfleet	d					16 36						17 06						17 36					
Swanscombe	d					16 38						17 08						17 38					
Greenhithe for Bluewater	d	16 23				16 41		16 53				17 11		17 23				17 41		17 53			
Stone Crossing	d					16 43						17 13						17 43					
Dartford	a	16 28				16 47		16 58				17 17		17 28				17 47		17 58			
	d	16 29		16 40	16 43	16 48		16 59		17 10	17 13	17 18		17 29		17 40	17 43	17 48		17 59		18 10	18 13
Slade Green	d				16 48						17 18						17 48						18 18
Erith	d				16 50						17 20						17 50						18 20
Belvedere	d				16 53						17 23						17 53						18 23
Abbey Wood	d	16 38			16 56			17 08			17 26			17 38			17 56			18 08			18 26
Plumstead	d		16 47		16 59				17 17		17 29				17 47		17 59				18 17		18 29
Woolwich Arsenal	d	16 43	16 50		17 02			17 13	17 20		17 32			17 43	17 50		18 02			18 13	18 20		18 32
Woolwich Dockyard	d		16 52		17 04				17 22		17 34				17 52		18 04				18 22		18 34
Charlton	d	16 47	16 55		17 07			17 17	17 25		17 37			17 47	17 55		18 07			18 17	18 25		18 37
Crayford	d					16 52						17 22						17 52					
Bexley	d					16 55						17 25						17 55					
Albany Park	d					16 58						17 28						17 58					
Sidcup	d					17 01						17 31						18 01					
New Eltham	d					17 04						17 34						18 04					
Mottingham	d					17 06						17 36						18 06					
Lee	d					17 09						17 39						18 09					
Hither Green	d					17 12						17 42						18 12					
Barnehurst	d			16 47						17 17						17 47						18 17	
Bexleyheath	d			16 49						17 19						17 49						18 19	
Welling	d			16 52						17 22						17 52						18 22	
Falconwood	d			16 55						17 25						17 55						18 25	
Eltham	d			16 58						17 28						17 58						18 28	
Kidbrooke	d			17 01						17 31						18 01						18 31	
Blackheath	d	16 52		17 04				17 22		17 34				17 52		18 04				18 22		18 34	
Lewisham	d	16 56		17 08		17 18		17 26		17 38		17 48		17 56		18 08		18 18		18 26		18 38	
St Johns	d																						
New Cross	d			17 11						17 41						18 11						18 41	
Nunhead	d																						
Peckham Rye	d																						
Denmark Hill	d																						
London Victoria	a																						
Westcombe Park	d		16 57		17 09				17 27		17 39				17 57		18 09				18 27		18 39
Maze Hill	d		16 59		17 11				17 29		17 41				17 59		18 11				18 29		18 41
Greenwich	d		17 03		17 15				17 33		17 45				18 03		18 15				18 33		18 45
Deptford	a		17 05		17 17				17 35		17 47				18 05		18 17				18 35		18 47
London Bridge	a	17 06	17 11	17 19	17 23	17 26		17 36	17 41	17 49	17 53	17 56		18 06	18 11	18 19	18 23	18 26		18 36	18 41	18 49	18 53
London Cannon Street	a																						
London Waterloo (East)	a	17 11		17 25	17 27	17 30		17 41		17 55	17 57	18 00		18 11		18 25	18 27	18 30		18 41		18 55	18 57
London Charing Cross	a	17 14		17 28	17 31	17 34		17 44		17 58	18 01	18 04		18 14		18 28	18 31	18 34		18 44		18 58	19 01
Ebbsfleet International	a						16 47						17 17						17 47				
Stratford International	a												17 29						17 59				
St Pancras Int'l	a												17 36						18 09				

Table 200

Sundays

until 22 July, 19 Aug and from 16 Sep

Gillingham and Dartford - London

Network Diagram - see first Page of Table 200

		SE	SE	SE	SE	SE		SE	SE	SE	SE	SE	SE	SE	SE	SE		SE	SE	SE	SE	SE	SE	SE	SE
Gillingham (Kent)	d		17 50	17 54					18 20	18 24				18 50	18 54					19 20	19 24				19 45
Chatham	d		17 54	17 58					18 24	18 28				18 54	18 58					19 24	19 28				19 49
Rochester	d		17 57	18 00					18 27	18 30				18 57	19 00					19 27	19 30				19 51
Maidstone West	d																								
Strood	d		18 02	18 05					18 32	18 35				19 02	19 05					19 32	19 35				19 56
Higham	d			18 10						18 40					19 10						19 40				20 01
Gravesend	d	18 02	18 13	18 18				18 32	18 43	18 48			19 02	19 13	19 18				19 32	19 43	19 48				20 09
Northfleet	d	18 06						18 36					19 06						19 36						20 12
Swanscombe	d	18 08						18 38					19 08						19 38						20 14
Greenhithe for Bluewater	d	18 11		18 23				18 41		18 53			19 11		19 23				19 41		19 53				20 18
Stone Crossing	d	18 13						18 43					19 13						19 43						20 20
Dartford	a	18 17		18 28				18 47		18 58			19 17		19 28				19 47		19 58				20 24
	d	18 18		18 29	18 40	18 43		18 48		18 59	19 10	19 13	19 18		19 29	19 40		19 43	19 48		19 59	20 10	20 13	20 18	20 29
Slade Green	d					18 48						19 18						19 48					20 18		
Erith	d					18 50						19 20						19 50					20 20		
Belvedere	d					18 53						19 23						19 53					20 23		
Abbey Wood	d			18 38		18 56				19 08		19 26			19 38			19 56			20 08		20 26		20 38
Plumstead	d					18 59						19 29						19 59					20 29		
Woolwich Arsenal	d			18 43		19 02				19 13		19 32			19 43			20 02			20 13		20 32		20 43
Woolwich Dockyard	d					19 04						19 34						20 04					20 34		
Charlton	d			18 47		19 07				19 17		19 37			19 47			20 07			20 17		20 37		20 47
Crayford	d	18 22						18 52					19 22						19 52					20 22	
Bexley	d	18 25						18 55					19 25						19 55					20 25	
Albany Park	d	18 28						18 58					19 28						19 58					20 28	
Sidcup	d	18 31						19 01					19 31						20 01					20 31	
New Eltham	d	18 34						19 04					19 34						20 04					20 34	
Mottingham	d	18 36						19 06					19 36						20 06					20 36	
Lee	d	18 39						19 09					19 39						20 09					20 39	
Hither Green	d	18 42						19 12					19 42						20 12					20 42	
Barnehurst	d				18 47						19 17					19 47						20 17			
Bexleyheath	d				18 49						19 19					19 49						20 19			
Welling	d				18 52						19 22					19 52						20 22			
Falconwood	d				18 55						19 25					19 55						20 25			
Eltham	d				18 58						19 28					19 58						20 28			
Kidbrooke	d				19 01						19 31					20 01						20 31			
Blackheath	d			18 52	19 04					19 22	19 34				19 52	20 04					20 22	20 34			20 52
Lewisham	d	18 48		18 56	19 08			19 18		19 26	19 38		19 48		19 56	20 08			20 18		20 26	20 38		20 48	20 56
St Johns	d																								
New Cross	d				19 11						19 41					20 11						20 41			
Nunhead	d																								
Peckham Rye	d																								
Denmark Hill	d																								
London Victoria	a																								
Westcombe Park	d					19 09						19 39						20 09					20 39		
Maze Hill	d					19 11						19 41						20 11					20 41		
Greenwich	d					19 15						19 45						20 15					20 45		
Deptford	a					19 17						19 47						20 17					20 47		
London Bridge	a	18 56		19 06	19 19	19 23		19 26		19 36	19 49	19 53	19 56		20 06	20 19		20 23	20 26		20 36	20 49	20 53	20 56	21 06
London Cannon Street	a																								
London Waterloo (East)	a	19 00		19 11	19 25	19 27		19 30		19 41	19 55	19 57	20 00		20 11	20 25		20 27	20 30		20 41	20 55	20 57	21 00	21 11
London Charing Cross	a	19 04		19 14	19 28	19 31		19 34		19 44	19 58	20 01	20 04		20 14	20 28		20 31	20 34		20 44	20 58	21 01	21 04	21 14
Ebbsfleet International	a		18 17						18 47					19 17						19 47					
Stratford International	a		18 29						18 59					19 29						19 59					
St Pancras Int'l	a		18 36						19 06					19 36						20 06					

Table 200

Sundays

until 22 July, 19 Aug and from 16 Sep

Gillingham and Dartford - London

Network Diagram - see first Page of Table 200

		SE		SE	SE	SE	SE	SE	SE	SE	SE	SE		SE	SE	SE	SE	SE	SE	SE	SE	SE		SE	SE
Gillingham (Kent)	d	19 50					20 15	20 20				20 45		20 50				21 15	21 20					21 45	21 50
Chatham	d	19 54					20 19	20 24				20 49		20 54				21 19	21 24					21 49	21 54
Rochester	d	19 57					20 21	20 27				20 51		20 57				21 21	21 27					21 51	21 57
Maidstone West	d																								
Strood	d	20 02					20 26	20 32				20 56		21 02				21 26	21 32					21 56	22 02
Higham	d						20 31					21 01						21 31						22 01	
Gravesend	d	20 13					20 39	20 43				21 09		21 13				21 39	21 43					22 09	22 13
Northfleet	d						20 42					21 12						21 42						22 12	
Swanscombe	d						20 44					21 14						21 44						22 14	
Greenhithe for Bluewater	d						20 48					21 18						21 48						22 18	
Stone Crossing	d						20 50					21 20						21 50						22 20	
Dartford	a						20 54					21 24						21 54						22 24	
	d			20 40	20 43	20 48	20 59		21 10	21 13	21 18	21 29			21 40	21 43	21 48	21 59		22 10	22 13	22 18		22 29	
Slade Green	d				20 48					21 18						21 48					22 18				
Erith	d				20 50					21 20						21 50					22 20				
Belvedere	d				20 53					21 23						21 53					22 23				
Abbey Wood	d				20 56		21 08			21 26		21 38				21 56		22 08			22 26			22 38	
Plumstead	d				20 59					21 29						21 59					22 29				
Woolwich Arsenal	d				21 02		21 13			21 32		21 43				22 02		22 13			22 32			22 43	
Woolwich Dockyard	d				21 04					21 34						22 04					22 34				
Charlton	d				21 07		21 17			21 37		21 47				22 07		22 17			22 37			22 47	
Crayford	d					20 52					21 22						21 52					22 22			
Bexley	d					20 55					21 25						21 55					22 25			
Albany Park	d					20 58					21 28						21 58					22 28			
Sidcup	d					21 01					21 31						22 01					22 31			
New Eltham	d					21 04					21 34						22 04					22 34			
Mottingham	d					21 06					21 36						22 06					22 36			
Lee	d					21 09					21 39						22 09					22 39			
Hither Green	d					21 12					21 42						22 12					22 42			
Barnehurst	d			20 47					21 17						21 47					22 17					
Bexleyheath	d			20 49					21 19						21 49					22 19					
Welling	d			20 52					21 22						21 52					22 22					
Falconwood	d			20 55					21 25						21 55					22 25					
Eltham	d			20 58					21 28						21 58					22 28					
Kidbrooke	d			21 01					21 31						22 01					22 31					
Blackheath	d			21 04			21 22		21 34			21 52			22 04			22 22		22 34				22 52	
Lewisham	d			21 08		21 18	21 26		21 38		21 48	21 56			22 08		22 18	22 26		22 38		22 48		22 56	
St Johns	d																								
New Cross	d			21 11					21 41						22 11					22 41					
Nunhead	d																								
Peckham Rye	d																								
Denmark Hill	d																								
London Victoria	a																								
Westcombe Park	d				21 09					21 39						22 09					22 39				
Maze Hill	d				21 11					21 41						22 11					22 41				
Greenwich	d				21 15					21 45						22 15					22 45				
Deptford	a				21 17					21 47						22 17					22 47				
London Bridge	a			21 19	21 23	21 26	21 36		21 49	21 53	21 56	22 06			22 19	22 23	22 26	22 36		22 49	22 53	22 56		23 06	
London Cannon Street	a																								
London Waterloo (East)	a			21 25	21 27	21 30	21 41		21 55	21 57	22 00	22 11			22 25	22 27	22 30	22 41		22 55	22 57	23 00		23 11	
London Charing Cross	a			21 28	21 31	21 34	21 44		21 58	22 01	22 04	22 14			22 28	22 31	22 34	22 44		22 58	23 01	23 04		23 14	
Ebbsfleet International	a	20 17						20 47						21 17					21 47						22 17
Stratford International	a	20 29						21 02						21 29					21 59						22 29
St Pancras Int'l	a	20 36						21 09						21 36					22 06						22 36

Table 200

Gillingham and Dartford - London

Sundays

until 22 July, 19 Aug and from 16 Sep

Network Diagram - see first Page of Table 200

		SE	SE	SE	SE	SE
Gillingham (Kent)	d				22 15	22 20
Chatham	d				22 19	22 24
Rochester	d				22 21	22 27
Maidstone West	d					
Strood	d				22 26	22 32
Higham	d				22 31	
Gravesend	d				22 39	22 43
Northfleet	d				22 42	
Swanscombe	d				22 44	
Greenhithe for Bluewater	d				22 48	
Stone Crossing	d				22 50	
Dartford	a				22 54	
	d	22 40	22 43	22 48	22 59	
Slade Green	d		22 48			
Erith	d		22 50			
Belvedere	d		22 53			
Abbey Wood	d		22 56		23 08	
Plumstead	d		22 59			
Woolwich Arsenal	d		23 02		23 13	
Woolwich Dockyard	d		23 04			
Charlton	d		23 07		23 17	
Crayford	d			22 52		
Bexley	d			22 55		
Albany Park	d			22 58		
Sidcup	d			23 01		
New Eltham	d			23 04		
Mottingham	d			23 06		
Lee	d			23 09		
Hither Green	d			23 12		
Barnehurst	d	22 47				
Bexleyheath	d	22 49				
Welling	d	22 52				
Falconwood	d	22 55				
Eltham	d	22 58				
Kidbrooke	d	23 01				
Blackheath	d	23 04			23 22	
Lewisham	d	23 08		23 18	23 26	
St Johns	d					
New Cross	d	23 11				
Nunhead	d					
Peckham Rye	d					
Denmark Hill	d					
London Victoria	a					
Westcombe Park	d		23 09			
Maze Hill	d		23 11			
Greenwich	d		23 15			
Deptford	a		23 17			
London Bridge	a	23 19	23 23	23 26	23 36	
London Cannon Street	a					
London Waterloo (East)	a	23 25	23 27	23 30	23 41	
London Charing Cross	a	23 28	23 31	23 34	23 44	
Ebbsfleet International	a					22 47
Stratford International	a					22 59
St Pancras Int'l	a					23 06

Table 200

Gillingham and Dartford - London

Sundays

29 July to 12 August

Network Diagram - see first Page of Table 200

		SE	SE	SE	SE	SE	SE	SE	SE	SE		SE	SE	SE	SE	SE	SE	SE	SE	SE		SE	SE	SE	SE
Gillingham (Kent)	d				05 18			05 50		05 54						06 20		06 24					06 50		
Chatham	d				05 22			05 54		05 58						06 24		06 28					06 54		
Rochester	d				05 24			05 57		06 00						06 27		06 30					06 57		
Maidstone West	d																								
Strood	d				05 29			06 02		06 05						06 32		06 35					07 02		
Higham	d				05 34					06 10								06 40							
Gravesend	d				05 42		06 02	06 13		06 18					06 32	06 43		06 48				07 02	07 13		
Northfleet	d				05 45		06 06								06 36							07 06			
Swanscombe	d				05 47		06 08								06 38							07 08			
Greenhithe for Bluewater	d				05 51		06 11			06 23					06 41			06 53				07 11			
Stone Crossing	d				05 53		06 13								06 43							07 13			
Dartford	a				05 57		06 17			06 28					06 47			06 58				07 17			
	d		05 35	05 52	05 58	06 05	06 18		06 22	06 28			06 35	06 38	06 48		06 52	06 58	07 01	07 08		07 18		07 22	
Slade Green	d		05 40			06 10							06 40						07 05						07 23
Erith	d		05 42			06 12							06 42						07 08						07 26
Belvedere	d		05 45			06 15							06 45						07 10						07 28
Abbey Wood	d		05 48		06 07	06 18				06 37			06 48					07 07	07 13						07 31
Plumstead	d		05 51			06 21							06 51						07 16						07 34
Woolwich Arsenal	d		05 54		06 12	06 24				06 42			06 54					07 12	07 19						07 38
Woolwich Dockyard	d																								
Charlton	d	00 26	05 59		06 17	06 29				06 47			06 59					07 16	07 24						07 43
Crayford	d						06 22								06 52							07 22			
Bexley	d						06 25								06 55							07 25			
Albany Park	d						06 28								06 58							07 28			
Sidcup	d						06 31								07 01							07 31			
New Eltham	d						06 34								07 04							07 34			
Mottingham	d						06 36								07 06							07 36			
Lee	d						06 39								07 09							07 39			
Hither Green	d						06 42								07 12							07 42			
Barnehurst	d			05 58					06 28					06 45			06 58			07 15				07 28	
Bexleyheath	d			06 01					06 31					06 48			07 01			07 17				07 31	
Welling	d			06 04					06 34					06 51			07 04			07 20				07 34	
Falconwood	d			06 06					06 36					06 53			07 06			07 23				07 36	
Eltham	d			06 09					06 39					06 56			07 09			07 25				07 39	
Kidbrooke	d			06 12					06 42					06 59			07 12			07 28					
Blackheath	d			06 16	06 22				06 46	06 52				07 04			07 16	07 22		07 33				07 46	
Lewisham	d			06 20	06 26		06 48		06 50	06 56		07 01		07 08	07 18		07 20	07 26		07 38				07 50	
St Johns	d											07 03													
New Cross	d						06 51					07 05			07 21										
Nunhead	d													07 15						07 45					
Peckham Rye	d													07 17						07 47					
Denmark Hill	d													07 21						07 51					
London Victoria	a													07 33						08 03					
Westcombe Park	d		06 01			06 31							07 01						07 26						07 45
Maze Hill	d		06 03			06 33							07 03						07 29						07 48
Greenwich	d		06 07			06 37							07 07						07 33						07 52
Deptford	a		06 09			06 39							07 09						07 35						07 54
London Bridge	a		06 15	06 29	06 35	06 45	06 56		06 59	07 05		07 11	07 15		07 26		07 29	07 35	07 41			07 52		07 58	08 00
London Cannon Street	a	00 41										07 18							07 48						08 07
London Waterloo (East)	a		06 19	06 33	06 39	06 49	07 01		07 03	07 09			07 22		07 31		07 33	07 39				07 56		08 02	
London Charing Cross	a		06 26	06 40	06 46	06 56	07 08		07 10	07 16			07 28		07 38		07 43	07 46				08 00		08 09	
Ebbsfleet International	a							06 16								06 47							07 16		
Stratford International	a							06 33								06 58							07 28		
St Pancras Int'l	a							06 43								07 06							07 36		

Table 200

Sundays

29 July to 12 August

Gillingham and Dartford - London

Network Diagram - see first Page of Table 200

		SE	SE	SE	SE	SE		SE	SE	SE	SE	SE	SE	SE	SE	SE		SE	SE	SE	SE	SE	SE	SE	SE
Gillingham (Kent)	d	06 54								07 20				07 24											
Chatham	d	06 58								07 24				07 28											
Rochester	d	07 00								07 27				07 30											
Maidstone West	d																								
Strood	d	07 05								07 32				07 35											
Higham	d	07 10												07 40											
Gravesend	d	07 18							07 32	07 43				07 48						08 02					
Northfleet	d								07 36											08 06					
Swanscombe	d								07 38											08 08					
Greenhithe for Bluewater	d	07 23							07 41					07 53						08 11					
Stone Crossing	d								07 43											08 13					
Dartford	a	07 28							07 47					07 58						08 17					
	d	07 28		07 31		07 38			07 48			07 52		07 58		08 01			08 08	08 18		08 22			
Slade Green	d			07 36				07 43					07 53			08 06								08 13	
Erith	d			07 38				07 45					07 56			08 08								08 15	
Belvedere	d			07 41				07 48					07 58			08 11								08 18	
Abbey Wood	d	07 37		07 44				07 51					08 01	08 07		08 14								08 21	
Plumstead	d			07 47				07 54					08 04			08 17								08 24	
Woolwich Arsenal	d	07 42		07 50				07 57					08 08	08 12		08 20							08 19	08 27	
Woolwich Dockyard	d																								
Charlton	d	07 46		07 56				08 02					08 13	08 16		08 26								08 32	
Crayford	d				07 38				07 52									08 08		08 22					08 38
Bexley	d				07 41				07 55									08 11		08 25					08 41
Albany Park	d				07 44				07 58									08 14		08 28					08 44
Sidcup	d				07 47				08 01									08 17		08 31					08 47
New Eltham	d				07 50				08 04									08 20		08 34					08 50
Mottingham	d				07 52				08 06									08 22		08 36					08 52
Lee	d				07 55				08 09									08 25		08 39					08 55
Hither Green	d				07 58				08 12									08 28		08 42					08 58
Barnehurst	d		07 37			07 45						07 58			08 07				08 15			08 28	08a37		
Bexleyheath	d		07 39			07 47						08 01			08 09				08 17			08 31			
Welling	d		07 42			07 50						08 04			08 12				08 20			08 34			
Falconwood	d		07 45			07 53						08 06			08 15				08 23			08 36			
Eltham	d		07 48			07 55						08 09			08 18				08 25			08 39			
Kidbrooke	d		07 51			07 58									08 21				08 28						
Blackheath	d	07 52	07 55			08 03						08 16		08 22	08 25				08 33			08 46			
Lewisham	d	07 56	07 59		08 04	08 08					08 14	08 20		08 26	08 29			08 34	08 38		08 44	08 50			09 04
St Johns	d		08 01		08 06						08 16				08 31			08 36			08 46				09 06
New Cross	d		08 03		08 08						08 18				08 33			08 38			08 48				09 08
Nunhead	d					08 15													08 45						
Peckham Rye	d					08 17													08 47						
Denmark Hill	d					08 21													08 51						
London Victoria	a					08 33													09 03						
Westcombe Park	d												08 15												
Maze Hill	d			08 00				08 08					08 18			08 30								08 38	
Greenwich	d			08 04				08 14					08 22			08 34								08 44	
Deptford	a												08 24												
London Bridge	a	08 05	08 08	08 11	08 14			08 20	08 22		08 24	08 28	08 30	08 35	08 38	08 41		08 44		08 52	08 54	08 58		08 50	09 14
London Cannon Street	a		08 16	08 18	08 22			08 27			08 31		08 37		08 46	08 48		08 52			09 01			08 57	09 22
London Waterloo (East)	a	08 09							08 26			08 32		08 39						08 56		09 02			
London Charing Cross	a	08 16							08 30			08 39		08 46						09 00		09 09			
Ebbsfleet International	a									07 46															
Stratford International	a									07 58															
St Pancras Int'l	a									08 08															

Table 200

Sundays

29 July to 12 August

Gillingham and Dartford - London

Network Diagram - see first Page of Table 200

		SE		SE	SE	SE	SE	SE	SE	SE	SE	SE		SE	SE	SE	SE	SE	SE	SE	SE	SE		SE	SE
Gillingham (Kent)	d					07 54	08 20											08 24							
Chatham	d					07 58	08 24											08 28							
Rochester	d					08 00	08 27											08 30							
Maidstone West	d																								
Strood	d					08 05	08 32											08 35							
Higham	d					08 10												08 40							
Gravesend	d	08 32				08 18	08 43									09 02			08 48						
Northfleet	d	08 36														09 06									
Swanscombe	d	08 38														09 08									
Greenhithe for Bluewater	d	08 41				08 23										09 11			08 53						
Stone Crossing	d	08 43														09 13									
Dartford	a	08 47				08 28										09 17			08 58						
	d	08 48				08 28			08 31	08 38				08 52		09 18			08 58		09 01	09 08			
Slade Green	d				08 23				08 36		08 43				08 47			08 53			09 06			09 13	
Erith	d				08 26				08 38		08 45							08 56			09 08			09 15	
Belvedere	d				08 28				08 41		08 48							08 58			09 11			09 18	
Abbey Wood	d				08 31	08 37			08 44		08 51							09 01	09 07		09 14			09 21	
Plumstead	d				08 34				08 47		08 54							09 04			09 17			09 24	
Woolwich Arsenal	d				08 38	08 42			08 50		08 57							09 08	09 12		09 20			09 27	
Woolwich Dockyard	d																								
Charlton	d			08 39	08 43	08 46			08 56		09 02						09 09	09 13	09 16		09 26			09 32	
Crayford	d	08 52		09 07												09 22	09 37								
Bexley	d	08 55		09 10												09 25	09 40								
Albany Park	d	08 58		09 13												09 28	09 43								
Sidcup	d	09 01		09 16												09 31	09 46								
New Eltham	d	09 04		09 19												09 34	09 49								
Mottingham	d	09 06		09 21												09 36	09 51								
Lee	d	09 09		09 24												09 39	09 54								
Hither Green	d	09 12		09 28												09 42	09 58								
Barnehurst	d							08 37		08 45				08 58	09a07					09 07		09 15			
Bexleyheath	d							08 39		08 47				09 01						09 09		09 17			
Welling	d							08 42		08 50				09 04						09 12		09 20			
Falconwood	d							08 45		08 53				09 06						09 15		09 23			
Eltham	d							08 48		08 55				09 09						09 18		09 25			
Kidbrooke	d							08 51		08 58										09 21		09 28			
Blackheath	d					08 52		08 55		09 03				09 16					09 22	09 25		09 33			
Lewisham	d			09 34		08 56		08 59		09 08		09 14		09 20			10 04		09 26	09 29		09 38			09 44
St Johns	d			09 36				09 01				09 16					10 06			09 31					09 46
New Cross	d			09 38				09 03				09 18					10 08			09 33					09 48
Nunhead	d									09 15												09 45			
Peckham Rye	d									09 17												09 47			
Denmark Hill	d									09 21												09 51			
London Victoria	a									09 33												10 03			
Westcombe Park	d				08 45													09 15							
Maze Hill	d				08 48				09 00		09 08							09 18			09 30			09 38	
Greenwich	d				08 52				09 04		09 14							09 22			09 34			09 44	
Deptford	a				08 54													09 24							
London Bridge	a	09 22		09 44	09 00	09 05		09 08	09 11		09 20	09 24		09 28		09 52	10 14	09 30	09 35	09 38	09 41			09 50	09 54
London Cannon Street	a			09 52	09 07			09 16	09 18		09 27	09 31					10 22	09 37		09 46	09 48			09 57	10 01
London Waterloo (East)	a	09 26				09 09								09 32		09 56			09 39						
London Charing Cross	a	09 30				09 16								09 39		10 00			09 46						
Ebbsfleet International	a						08 46																		
Stratford International	a						08 58																		
St Pancras Int'l	a						09 08																		

Table 200

Gillingham and Dartford - London

Sundays

29 July to 12 August

Network Diagram - see first Page of Table 200

Station		SE	SE	SE	SE	SE	SE	SE		SE	SE	SE	SE	SE	SE	SE	SE	SE		SE	SE	SE	SE	SE	SE
Gillingham (Kent)	d						08 54	09 20													09 24				
Chatham	d						08 58	09 24													09 28				
Rochester	d						09 00	09 27													09 30				
Maidstone West	d																								
Strood	d						09 05	09 32													09 35				
Higham	d						09 10														09 40				
Gravesend	d			09 32			09 18	09 43									10 02				09 48				
Northfleet	d			09 36													10 06								
Swanscombe	d			09 38													10 08								
Greenhithe for Bluewater	d			09 41			09 23										10 11				09 53				
Stone Crossing	d			09 43													10 13								
Dartford	a			09 47			09 28										10 17				09 58				
	d	09 22		09 48			09 28				09 31	09 38			09 52		10 18				09 58		10 01	10 08	
Slade Green	d		09 17			09 23					09 36		09 43			09 47				09 53			10 06		10 13
Erith	d					09 26					09 38		09 45							09 56			10 08		10 15
Belvedere	d					09 28					09 41		09 48							09 58			10 11		10 18
Abbey Wood	d					09 31	09 37				09 44		09 51							10 01	10 07		10 14		10 21
Plumstead	d					09 34					09 47		09 54							10 04			10 17		10 24
Woolwich Arsenal	d					09 38	09 42				09 50		09 57							10 08	10 12		10 20		10 27
Woolwich Dockyard	d																								
Charlton	d				09 39	09 43	09 46				09 56		10 02					10 09		10 13	10 16		10 26		10 32
Crayford	d			09 52	10 07												10 22	10 37							
Bexley	d			09 55	10 10												10 25	10 40							
Albany Park	d			09 58	10 13												10 28	10 43							
Sidcup	d			10 01	10 16												10 31	10 46							
New Eltham	d			10 04	10 19												10 34	10 49							
Mottingham	d			10 06	10 21												10 36	10 51							
Lee	d			10 09	10 24												10 39	10 54							
Hither Green	d			10 12	10 28												10 42	10 58							
Barnehurst	d	09 28	09a37							09 37		09 45			09 58	10a07						10 07		10 15	
Bexleyheath	d	09 31								09 39		09 47			10 01							10 09		10 17	
Welling	d	09 34								09 42		09 50			10 04							10 12		10 20	
Falconwood	d	09 36								09 45		09 53			10 06							10 15		10 23	
Eltham	d	09 39								09 48		09 55			10 09							10 18		10 25	
Kidbrooke	d									09 51		09 58										10 21		10 28	
Blackheath	d	09 46					09 52			09 55		10 03			10 16						10 22	10 25		10 33	
Lewisham	d	09 50			10 34		09 56			09 59		10 08		10 14	10 20			11 04			10 26	10 29		10 38	
St Johns	d				10 36					10 01				10 16				11 06				10 31			
New Cross	d				10 38					10 03				10 18				11 08				10 33			
Nunhead	d											10 15												10 45	
Peckham Rye	d											10 17												10 47	
Denmark Hill	d											10 21												10 51	
London Victoria	a											10 33												11 03	
Westcombe Park	d					09 45														10 15					
Maze Hill	d					09 48					10 00		10 08							10 18			10 30		10 38
Greenwich	d					09 52					10 04		10 14							10 22			10 34		10 44
Deptford	a					09 54														10 24					
London Bridge	a	09 58		10 22	10 44	10 00	10 05			10 08	10 11		10 20	10 24	10 28		10 52	11 14		10 30	10 35	10 38	10 41		10 50
London Cannon Street	a				10 52	10 07				10 16	10 18		10 27	10 31				11 22		10 37		10 46	10 48		10 57
London Waterloo (East)	a	10 02		10 26			10 09								10 32		10 56				10 39				
London Charing Cross	a	10 09		10 30			10 16								10 39		11 00				10 46				
Ebbsfleet International	a							09 46																	
Stratford International	a							09 58																	
St Pancras Int'l	a							10 08																	

Table 200

Gillingham and Dartford - London

Sundays

29 July to 12 August

Network Diagram - see first Page of Table 200

Station		SE	SE	SE		SE	SE	SE	SE	SE	SE	SE	SE	SE		SE	SE	SE	SE	SE	SE	SE	SE	SE	
Gillingham (Kent)	d								09 54	10 20												10 24			
Chatham	d								09 58	10 24												10 28			
Rochester	d								10 00	10 27												10 30			
Maidstone West	d																								
Strood	d								10 05	10 32												10 35			
Higham	d								10 10													10 40			
Gravesend	d					10 32			10 18	10 43									11 02			10 48			
Northfleet	d					10 36													11 06						
Swanscombe	d					10 38													11 08						
Greenhithe for Bluewater	d					10 41			10 23										11 11			10 53			
Stone Crossing	d					10 43													11 13						
Dartford	a					10 47			10 28										11 17			10 58			
	d		10 22			10 48			10 28			10 31	10 38				10 52		11 18			10 58		11 01	
Slade Green	d			10 17				10 23				10 36		10 43				10 47			10 53			11 06	
Erith	d							10 26				10 38		10 45							10 56			11 08	
Belvedere	d							10 28				10 41		10 48							10 58			11 11	
Abbey Wood	d							10 31	10 37			10 44		10 51							11 01	11 07		11 14	
Plumstead	d							10 34				10 47		10 54							11 04			11 17	
Woolwich Arsenal	d							10 38	10 42			10 50		10 57							11 08	11 12		11 20	
Woolwich Dockyard	d																								
Charlton	d						10 39	10 43	10 46			10 56		11 02						11 09	11 13	11 16		11 26	
Crayford	d					10 52	11 07												11 22	11 37					
Bexley	d					10 55	11 10												11 25	11 40					
Albany Park	d					10 58	11 13												11 28	11 43					
Sidcup	d					11 01	11 16												11 31	11 46					
New Eltham	d					11 04	11 19												11 34	11 49					
Mottingham	d					11 06	11 21												11 36	11 51					
Lee	d					11 09	11 24												11 39	11 54					
Hither Green	d					11 12	11 28												11 42	11 58					
Barnehurst	d		10 28	10a37							10 37		10 45				10 58	11a07					11 07		
Bexleyheath	d		10 31								10 39		10 47				11 01						11 09		
Welling	d		10 34								10 42		10 50				11 04						11 12		
Falconwood	d		10 36								10 45		10 53				11 06						11 15		
Eltham	d		10 39								10 48		10 55				11 09						11 18		
Kidbrooke	d										10 51		10 58										11 21		
Blackheath	d		10 46						10 52		10 55		11 03				11 16					11 22	11 25		
Lewisham	d	10 44	10 50				11 34		10 56		10 59		11 08			11 14	11 20			12 04		11 26	11 29		
St Johns	d	10 46					11 36				11 01					11 16				12 06			11 31		
New Cross	d	10 48					11 38				11 03					11 18				12 08			11 33		
Nunhead	d												11 15												
Peckham Rye	d												11 17												
Denmark Hill	d												11 21												
London Victoria	a												11 33												
Westcombe Park	d							10 45													11 15				
Maze Hill	d							10 48				11 00		11 08							11 18			11 30	
Greenwich	d							10 52				11 04		11 14							11 22			11 34	
Deptford	a							10 54													11 24				
London Bridge	a	10 54	10 58			11 22	11 44	11 00	11 05		11 08	11 11		11 20		11 24	11 28		11 52	12 14	11 30	11 35	11 38	11 41	
London Cannon Street	a	11 01					11 52	11 07			11 16	11 18		11 27		11 31				12 22	11 37		11 46	11 48	
London Waterloo (East)	a		11 02			11 26			11 09								11 32		11 56			11 39			
London Charing Cross	a		11 09			11 30			11 16								11 39		12 00			11 46			
Ebbsfleet International	a									10 46															
Stratford International	a									10 58															
St Pancras Int'l	a									11 08															

Table 200

Sundays

29 July to 12 August

Gillingham and Dartford - London

Network Diagram - see first Page of Table 200

		SE	SE	SE	SE	SE	SE	SE	SE	SE	SE	SE	SE	SE	SE	SE	SE	SE	SE	SE	SE	SE	SE
Gillingham (Kent)	d									10 54	11 20											11 24	
Chatham	d									10 58	11 24											11 28	
Rochester	d									11 00	11 27											11 30	
Maidstone West	d																						
Strood	d									11 05	11 32											11 35	
Higham	d									11 10												11 40	
Gravesend	d						11 32			11 18	11 43								12 02			11 48	
Northfleet	d						11 36												12 06				
Swanscombe	d						11 38												12 08				
Greenhithe for Bluewater	d						11 41			11 23									12 11			11 53	
Stone Crossing	d						11 43												12 13				
Dartford	a						11 47			11 28									12 17			11 58	
	d	11 08			11 22		11 48			11 28			11 31	11 38			11 52		12 18			11 58	
Slade Green	d		11 13			11 17			11 23				11 36		11 43			11 47			11 53		
Erith	d		11 15						11 26				11 38		11 45						11 56		
Belvedere	d		11 18						11 28				11 41		11 48						11 58		
Abbey Wood	d		11 21						11 31	11 37			11 44		11 51						12 01	12 07	
Plumstead	d		11 24						11 34				11 47		11 54						12 04		
Woolwich Arsenal	d		11 27						11 38	11 42			11 50		11 58						12 08	12 12	
Woolwich Dockyard	d																						
Charlton	d		11 32					11 39	11 43	11 46			11 56		12 07					12 09	12 13	12 16	
Crayford	d						11 52	12 07											12 22	12 37			
Bexley	d						11 55	12 10											12 25	12 40			
Albany Park	d						11 58	12 13											12 28	12 43			
Sidcup	d						12 01	12 16											12 31	12 46			
New Eltham	d						12 04	12 19											12 34	12 49			
Mottingham	d						12 06	12 21											12 36	12 51			
Lee	d						12 09	12 24											12 39	12 54			
Hither Green	d						12 12	12 28											12 42	12 58			
Barnehurst	d	11 15			11 28	11a37						11 37		11 45			11 58	12a07					12 07
Bexleyheath	d	11 17			11 31							11 39		11 47			12 01						12 09
Welling	d	11 20			11 34							11 42		11 50			12 04						12 12
Falconwood	d	11 23			11 36							11 45		11 53			12 06						12 15
Eltham	d	11 25			11 39							11 48		11 55			12 09						12 18
Kidbrooke	d	11 28										11 51		11 58									12 21
Blackheath	d	11 33			11 46					11 52		11 55		12 03			12 16					12 22	12 25
Lewisham	d	11 38		11 44	11 50			12 34		11 56		11 59		12 08		12 14	12 20			13 04		12 26	12 29
St Johns	d			11 46				12 36				12 01				12 16				13 06			12 31
New Cross	d			11 48				12 38				12 03				12 18				13 08			12 33
Nunhead	d	11 45												12 15									
Peckham Rye	d	11 47												12 17									
Denmark Hill	d	11 51												12 21									
London Victoria	a	12 03												12 33									
Westcombe Park	d								11 45												12 15		
Maze Hill	d		11 38						11 48				12 00										
Greenwich	d		11 44						11 52				12 04		12 13						12 22		
Deptford	a								11 54												12 24		
London Bridge	a		11 50	11 54	11 58		12 22	12 44	12 00	12 05		12 08	12 11		12 20	12 24	12 28		12 52	13 14	12 30	12 35	12 38
London Cannon Street	a		11 57	12 01				12 52	12 07			12 16	12 18		12 27	12 31				13 22	12 37		12 46
London Waterloo (East)	a				12 02		12 26			12 09							12 32		12 56			12 39	
London Charing Cross	a				12 09		12 30			12 16							12 39		13 00			12 46	
Ebbsfleet International	a										11 46												
Stratford International	a										11 58												
St Pancras Int'l	a										12 08												

Table 200

Sundays

29 July to 12 August

Gillingham and Dartford - London

Network Diagram - see first Page of Table 200

		SE	SE	SE	SE	SE	SE	SE	SE	SE	SE	SE	SE	SE	SE	SE	SE	SE	SE	SE	SE	SE	SE
Gillingham (Kent)	d										11 54	12 20											12 24
Chatham	d										11 58	12 24											12 28
Rochester	d										12 00	12 27											12 30
Maidstone West	d																						
Strood	d										12 05	12 32											12 35
Higham	d										12 10												12 40
Gravesend	d							12 32			12 18	12 43								13 02			12 48
Northfleet	d							12 36												13 06			
Swanscombe	d							12 38												13 08			
Greenhithe for Bluewater	d							12 41			12 23									13 11			12 53
Stone Crossing	d							12 43												13 13			
Dartford	a							12 47			12 28									13 17			12 58
	d	12 01	12 08			12 22		12 48			12 28			12 31	12 38			12 52		13 18			12 58
Slade Green	d	12 05		12 13			12 17			12 23				12 35		12 43			12 47			12 53	
Erith	d	12 08		12 15						12 26				12 38		12 45						12 56	
Belvedere	d	12 10		12 18						12 28				12 40		12 48						12 58	
Abbey Wood	d	12 13		12 21						12 31	12 37			12 43		12 51						13 01	13 07
Plumstead	d	12 16		12 24						12 34				12 46		12 54						13 04	
Woolwich Arsenal	d	12 19		12 28						12 38	12 42			12 49		12 58						13 08	13 12
Woolwich Dockyard	d																						
Charlton	d	12 26		12 37					12 39	12 43	12 46			12 56		13 07					13 09	13 13	13 16
Crayford	d							12 52	13 07											13 22	13 37		
Bexley	d							12 55	13 10											13 25	13 40		
Albany Park	d							12 58	13 13											13 28	13 43		
Sidcup	d							13 01	13 16											13 31	13 46		
New Eltham	d							13 04	13 19											13 34	13 49		
Mottingham	d							13 06	13 21											13 36	13 51		
Lee	d							13 09	13 24											13 39	13 54		
Hither Green	d							13 12	13 28											13 42	13 58		
Barnehurst	d		12 15			12 28	12a37						12 37		12 45			12 58	13a07				
Bexleyheath	d		12 17			12 31							12 39		12 47			13 01					
Welling	d		12 20			12 34							12 42		12 50			13 04					
Falconwood	d		12 23			12 36							12 45		12 53			13 06					
Eltham	d		12 25			12 39							12 48		12 55			13 09					
Kidbrooke	d		12 28										12 51		12 58								
Blackheath	d		12 33			12 46					12 52		12 55		13 03			13 16					13 22
Lewisham	d		12 38		12 44	12 50			13 34		12 56		12 59		13 08		13 14	13 20			14 04		13 26
St Johns	d				12 46				13 36				13 01				13 16				14 06		
New Cross	d				12 48				13 38				13 03				13 18				14 08		
Nunhead	d		12 45												13 15								
Peckham Rye	d		12 47												13 17								
Denmark Hill	d		12 51												13 21								
London Victoria	a		13 03												13 33								
Westcombe Park	d									12 45												13 15	
Maze Hill	d																						
Greenwich	d	12 33		12 43						12 52				13 03		13 13						13 22	
Deptford	a									12 54												13 24	
London Bridge	a	12 41		12 50	12 54	12 58		13 22	13 44	13 00	13 05		13 08	13 11		13 20	13 24	13 27		13 52	14 14	13 30	13 35
London Cannon Street	a	12 48		12 57	13 01				13 52	13 07			13 16	13 18		13 27	13 31				14 22	13 37	
London Waterloo (East)	a					13 02		13 26			13 09							13 33		13 56			13 39
London Charing Cross	a					13 09		13 30			13 16							13 39		14 00			13 46
Ebbsfleet International	a											12 46											
Stratford International	a											12 58											
St Pancras Int'l	a											13 08											

Table 200

Sundays

29 July to 12 August

Gillingham and Dartford - London

Network Diagram - see first Page of Table 200

Station		SE		SE	SE	SE	SE	SE	SE	SE	SE	SE		SE	SE	SE	SE	SE	SE	SE	SE	SE		SE	SE
Gillingham (Kent)	d													12 54	13 20										
Chatham	d													12 58	13 24										
Rochester	d													13 00	13 27										
Maidstone West	d																								
Strood	d													13 05	13 32										
Higham	d													13 10											
Gravesend	d									13 32				13 18	13 43									14 02	
Northfleet	d									13 36														14 06	
Swanscombe	d									13 38														14 08	
Greenhithe for Bluewater	d									13 41				13 23										14 11	
Stone Crossing	d									13 43														14 13	
Dartford	a									13 47				13 28										14 17	
	d			13 01	13 08			13 22		13 48				13 28			13 31	13 38			13 52			14 18	
Slade Green	d			13 05		13 13			13 17			13 23					13 35		13 43			13 47			
Erith	d			13 08		13 15						13 26					13 38		13 45						
Belvedere	d			13 10		13 18						13 28					13 40		13 48						
Abbey Wood	d			13 13		13 21						13 31		13 37			13 43		13 51						
Plumstead	d			13 16		13 24						13 34					13 46		13 54						
Woolwich Arsenal	d			13 19		13 28						13 38		13 42			13 49		13 58						
Woolwich Dockyard	d																								
Charlton	d			13 26		13 37					13 39	13 43		13 46			13 56		14 07						14 09
Crayford	d									13 52	14 07													14 22	14 37
Bexley	d									13 55	14 10													14 25	14 40
Albany Park	d									13 58	14 13													14 28	14 43
Sidcup	d									14 01	14 16													14 31	14 46
New Eltham	d									14 04	14 19													14 34	14 49
Mottingham	d									14 06	14 21													14 36	14 51
Lee	d									14 09	14 24													14 39	14 54
Hither Green	d									14 12	14 28													14 42	14 58
Barnehurst	d	13 07			13 15			13 28	13a37							13 37		13 45			13 58	14a07			
Bexleyheath	d	13 09			13 17			13 31								13 39		13 47			14 01				
Welling	d	13 12			13 20			13 34								13 42		13 50			14 04				
Falconwood	d	13 15			13 23			13 36								13 45		13 53			14 06				
Eltham	d	13 18			13 25			13 39								13 48		13 55			14 09				
Kidbrooke	d	13 21			13 28											13 51		13 58							
Blackheath	d	13 25			13 33			13 46						13 52		13 55		14 03			14 16				
Lewisham	d	13 29			13 38		13 44	13 50			14 34			13 56		13 59		14 08		14 14	14 20				15 04
St Johns	d	13 31					13 46				14 36					14 01				14 16					15 06
New Cross	d	13 33					13 48				14 38					14 03				14 18					15 08
Nunhead	d				13 45													14 15							
Peckham Rye	d				13 47													14 17							
Denmark Hill	d				13 51													14 21							
London Victoria	a				14 03													14 33							
Westcombe Park	d											13 45													
Maze Hill	d																								
Greenwich	d			13 33		13 43						13 52					14 03		14 13						
Deptford	a											13 54													
London Bridge	a	13 38		13 41		13 50	13 54	13 58		14 22	14 44	14 00		14 05		14 08	14 11		14 20	14 24	14 28			14 52	15 14
London Cannon Street	a	13 46		13 48		13 57	14 01				14 52	14 07				14 16	14 18		14 27	14 31					15 22
London Waterloo (East)	a							14 02		14 26				14 09							14 32			14 56	
London Charing Cross	a							14 09		14 30				14 16							14 39			15 00	
Ebbsfleet International	a														13 46										
Stratford International	a														13 58										
St Pancras Int'l	a														14 08										

Table 200

Sundays

29 July to 12 August

Gillingham and Dartford - London

Network Diagram - see first Page of Table 200

Station		SE	SE	SE	SE	SE	SE	SE		SE	SE	SE	SE	SE	SE	SE	SE	SE		SE	SE	SE	SE	SE	SE
Gillingham (Kent)	d		13 24												13 54	14 20									
Chatham	d		13 28												13 58	14 24									
Rochester	d		13 30												14 00	14 27									
Maidstone West	d																								
Strood	d		13 35												14 05	14 32									
Higham	d		13 40												14 10										
Gravesend	d		13 48									14 32			14 18	14 43									15 02
Northfleet	d											14 36													15 06
Swanscombe	d											14 38													15 08
Greenhithe for Bluewater	d		13 53									14 41			14 23										15 11
Stone Crossing	d											14 43													15 13
Dartford	a		13 58									14 47			14 28										15 17
	d		13 58		14 01	14 08				14 22		14 48			14 28			14 31		14 38			14 52		15 18
Slade Green	d	13 53			14 05		14 13				14 17			14 23				14 35			14 43			14 47	
Erith	d	13 56			14 08		14 15							14 26				14 38			14 45				
Belvedere	d	13 58			14 10		14 18							14 28				14 40			14 48				
Abbey Wood	d	14 01	14 07		14 13		14 21							14 31	14 37			14 43			14 51				
Plumstead	d	14 04			14 16		14 24							14 34				14 46			14 54				
Woolwich Arsenal	d	14 08	14 12		14 19		14 28							14 38	14 42			14 49			14 58				
Woolwich Dockyard	d																								
Charlton	d	14 13	14 16		14 26		14 37						14 39	14 43	14 46			14 56			15 07				
Crayford	d											14 52	15 07												15 22
Bexley	d											14 55	15 10												15 25
Albany Park	d											14 58	15 13												15 28
Sidcup	d											15 01	15 16												15 31
New Eltham	d											15 04	15 19												15 34
Mottingham	d											15 06	15 21												15 36
Lee	d											15 09	15 24												15 39
Hither Green	d											15 12	15 28												15 42
Barnehurst	d			14 07		14 15				14 28	14a37						14 37			14 45			14 58	15a07	
Bexleyheath	d			14 09		14 17				14 31							14 39			14 47			15 01		
Welling	d			14 12		14 20				14 34							14 42			14 50			15 04		
Falconwood	d			14 15		14 23				14 36							14 45			14 53			15 06		
Eltham	d			14 18		14 25				14 39							14 48			14 55			15 09		
Kidbrooke	d			14 21		14 28											14 51			14 58					
Blackheath	d		14 22	14 25		14 33				14 46					14 52		14 55			15 03			15 16		
Lewisham	d		14 26	14 29		14 38		14 44		14 50			15 34		14 56		14 59			15 08		15 14	15 20		
St Johns	d			14 31				14 46					15 36				15 01					15 16			
New Cross	d			14 33				14 48					15 38				15 03					15 18			
Nunhead	d					14 45														15 15					
Peckham Rye	d					14 47														15 17					
Denmark Hill	d					14 51														15 21					
London Victoria	a					15 03														15 33					
Westcombe Park	d	14 15												14 45											
Maze Hill	d																								
Greenwich	d	14 22			14 33		14 43							14 52				15 03			15 13				
Deptford	a	14 24												14 54											
London Bridge	a	14 30	14 35	14 38	14 41		14 50	14 54		14 58		15 22	15 44	15 00	15 05		15 08	15 11			15 20	15 24	15 28		15 52
London Cannon Street	a	14 37		14 46	14 48		14 57	15 01					15 52	15 07			15 16	15 18			15 27	15 31			
London Waterloo (East)	a		14 39							15 02		15 26			15 09								15 32		15 56
London Charing Cross	a		14 46							15 09		15 30			15 16								15 39		16 00
Ebbsfleet International	a															14 46									
Stratford International	a															14 58									
St Pancras Int'l	a															15 08									

Table 200

Gillingham and Dartford - London

Sundays

29 July to 12 August

Network Diagram - see first Page of Table 200

		SE	SE	SE	SE	SE	SE	SE	SE	SE	SE	SE	SE	SE	SE	SE	SE	SE	SE	SE	SE	SE
Gillingham (Kent)	d			14 24											14 54	15 20						
Chatham	d			14 28											14 58	15 24						
Rochester	d			14 30											15 00	15 27						
Maidstone West	d																					
Strood	d			14 35											15 05	15 32						
Higham	d			14 40											15 10							
Gravesend	d			14 48								15 32			15 18	15 43						
Northfleet	d											15 36										
Swanscombe	d											15 38										
Greenhithe for Bluewater	d			14 53								15 41			15 23							
Stone Crossing	d											15 43										
Dartford	a			14 58								15 47			15 28							
	d			14 58		15 01	15 08			15 22		15 48			15 28			15 31	15 38			15 52
Slade Green	d		14 53			15 05		15 13			15 17			15 23				15 35		15 43		
Erith	d		14 56			15 08		15 15						15 26				15 38		15 45		
Belvedere	d		14 58			15 10		15 18						15 28				15 40		15 48		
Abbey Wood	d		15 01	15 07		15 13		15 21						15 31	15 37			15 43		15 51		
Plumstead	d		15 04			15 16		15 24						15 34				15 46		15 54		
Woolwich Arsenal	d		15 08	15 12		15 19		15 28						15 38	15 42			15 49		15 58		
Woolwich Dockyard	d																					
Charlton	d	15 09	15 13	15 16		15 26		15 37					15 39	15 43	15 46			15 56		16 07		
Crayford	d	15 37										15 52	16 07									
Bexley	d	15 40										15 55	16 10									
Albany Park	d	15 43										15 58	16 13									
Sidcup	d	15 46										16 01	16 16									
New Eltham	d	15 49										16 04	16 19									
Mottingham	d	15 51										16 06	16 21									
Lee	d	15 54										16 09	16 24									
Hither Green	d	15 58										16 12	16 28									
Barnehurst	d				15 07		15 15			15 28	15a37						15 37		15 45			15 58
Bexleyheath	d				15 09		15 17			15 31							15 39		15 47			16 01
Welling	d				15 12		15 20			15 34							15 42		15 50			16 04
Falconwood	d				15 15		15 23			15 36							15 45		15 53			16 06
Eltham	d				15 18		15 25			15 39							15 48		15 55			16 09
Kidbrooke	d				15 21		15 28										15 51		15 58			
Blackheath	d			15 22	15 25		15 33			15 46					15 52		15 55		16 03			16 16
Lewisham	d	16 04		15 26	15 29		15 38		15 44	15 50			16 34		15 56		15 59		16 08		16 14	16 20
St Johns	d	16 06			15 31				15 46				16 36				16 01				16 16	
New Cross	d	16 08			15 33				15 48				16 38				16 03				16 18	
Nunhead	d						15 45												16 15			
Peckham Rye	d						15 47												16 17			
Denmark Hill	d						15 51												16 21			
London Victoria	a						16 03												16 33			
Westcombe Park	d		15 15											15 45								
Maze Hill	d																					
Greenwich	d		15 22			15 33		15 43						15 52				16 03		16 13		
Deptford	a		15 24											15 54								
London Bridge	a	16 14	15 30	15 35	15 38	15 41		15 50	15 54	15 58		16 22	16 44	16 00	16 05		16 08	16 11		16 20	16 24	16 28
London Cannon Street	a	16 22	15 37		15 46	15 48		15 57	16 01				16 52	16 07			16 16	16 18		16 27	16 31	
London Waterloo (East)	a			15 39						16 02		16 26			16 09							16 32
London Charing Cross	a			15 46						16 09		16 30			16 16							16 39
Ebbsfleet International	a															15 46						
Stratford International	a															15 58						
St Pancras Int'l	a															16 08						

Table 200

Gillingham and Dartford - London

Sundays

29 July to 12 August

Network Diagram - see first Page of Table 200

		SE	SE	SE	SE	SE	SE	SE	SE	SE	SE	SE	SE	SE	SE	SE	SE	SE	SE	SE	SE	SE	SE
Gillingham (Kent)	d					15 24										15 54	16 20					
Chatham	d					15 28										15 58	16 24					
Rochester	d					15 30										16 00	16 27					
Maidstone West	d																						
Strood	d					15 35										16 05	16 32					
Higham	d					15 40										16 10						
Gravesend	d		16 02			15 48								16 32			16 18	16 43					
Northfleet	d		16 06											16 36									
Swanscombe	d		16 08											16 38									
Greenhithe for Bluewater	d		16 11			15 53								16 41			16 23						
Stone Crossing	d		16 13											16 43									
Dartford	a		16 17			15 58								16 47			16 28						
	d		16 18			15 58		16 01	16 08			16 22		16 48			16 28			16 31	16 38		
Slade Green	d	15 47			15 53			16 05		16 13			16 17			16 23				16 35		16 43	
Erith	d				15 56			16 08		16 15						16 26				16 38		16 45	
Belvedere	d				15 58			16 10		16 18						16 28				16 40		16 48	
Abbey Wood	d				16 01	16 07		16 13		16 21						16 31	16 37			16 43		16 51	
Plumstead	d				16 04			16 16		16 24						16 34				16 46		16 54	
Woolwich Arsenal	d				16 08	16 12		16 19		16 28						16 38	16 42			16 49		16 58	
Woolwich Dockyard	d																						
Charlton	d			16 09	16 13	16 16		16 26		16 37					16 39	16 43	16 46			16 56		17 07	
Crayford	d		16 22	16 37										16 52	17 07								
Bexley	d		16 25	16 40										16 55	17 10								
Albany Park	d		16 28	16 43										16 58	17 13								
Sidcup	d		16 31	16 46										17 01	17 16								
New Eltham	d		16 34	16 49										17 04	17 19								
Mottingham	d		16 36	16 51										17 06	17 21								
Lee	d		16 39	16 54										17 09	17 24								
Hither Green	d		16 42	16 58										17 12	17 28								
Barnehurst	d	16a07					16 07		16 15			16 28	16a37						16 37		16 45		
Bexleyheath	d						16 09		16 17			16 31							16 39		16 47		
Welling	d						16 12		16 20			16 34							16 42		16 50		
Falconwood	d						16 15		16 23			16 36							16 45		16 53		
Eltham	d						16 18		16 25			16 39							16 48		16 55		
Kidbrooke	d						16 21		16 28										16 51		16 58		
Blackheath	d					16 22	16 25		16 33			16 46					16 52		16 55		17 03		
Lewisham	d			17 04		16 26	16 29		16 38		16 44	16 50			17 34		16 56		16 59		17 08		17 14
St Johns	d			17 06			16 31				16 46				17 36				17 01				17 16
New Cross	d			17 08			16 33				16 48				17 38				17 03				17 18
Nunhead	d								16 45												17 15		
Peckham Rye	d								16 47												17 17		
Denmark Hill	d								16 51												17 21		
London Victoria	a								17 03												17 33		
Westcombe Park	d				16 15											16 45							
Maze Hill	d																						
Greenwich	d				16 22			16 33		16 43						16 52				17 03		17 13	
Deptford	a				16 24											16 54							
London Bridge	a		16 52	17 14	16 30	16 35	16 38	16 41		16 50	16 54	16 58		17 22	17 44	17 00	17 05		17 08	17 11		17 20	17 24
London Cannon Street	a			17 22	16 37		16 46	16 48		16 57	17 01				17 52	17 07			17 16	17 18		17 27	17 31
London Waterloo (East)	a		16 56			16 39						17 02		17 26			17 09						
London Charing Cross	a		17 00			16 46						17 09		17 30			17 16						
Ebbsfleet International	a																	16 46					
Stratford International	a																						
St Pancras Int'l	a																						

Table 200

Gillingham and Dartford - London

Sundays

29 July to 12 August

Network Diagram - see first Page of Table 200

		SE	SE	SE	SE	SE		SE	SE	SE	SE	SE	SE	SE	SE	SE		SE	SE	SE	SE	SE	SE	SE	SE
Gillingham (Kent)	d							16 24												16 54	17 20				
Chatham	d							16 28												16 58	17 24				
Rochester	d							16 30												17 00	17 27				
Maidstone West	d																								
Strood	d							16 35												17 05	17 32				
Higham	d							16 40												17 10					
Gravesend	d			17 02				16 48								17 32				17 18	17 43				
Northfleet	d			17 06												17 36									
Swanscombe	d			17 08												17 38									
Greenhithe for Bluewater	d			17 11				16 53								17 41				17 23					
Stone Crossing	d			17 13												17 43									
Dartford	a			17 17				16 58								17 47				17 28					
	d	16 52		17 18				16 58		17 01	17 08			17 22		17 48				17 28			17 31	17 38	
Slade Green	d		16 47			16 53				17 05		17 13			17 17				17 23				17 35		17 43
Erith	d					16 56				17 08		17 15							17 26				17 38		17 45
Belvedere	d					16 58				17 10		17 18							17 28				17 40		17 48
Abbey Wood	d					17 01		17 07		17 13		17 21							17 31	17 37			17 43		17 51
Plumstead	d					17 04				17 16		17 24							17 34				17 46		17 54
Woolwich Arsenal	d					17 08		17 12		17 19		17 28							17 38	17 42			17 49		17 58
Woolwich Dockyard	d																								
Charlton	d				17 09	17 13		17 16		17 26		17 37						17 39	17 43	17 46			17 56		18 07
Crayford	d			17 22	17 37											17 52		18 07							
Bexley	d			17 25	17 40											17 55		18 10							
Albany Park	d			17 28	17 43											17 58		18 13							
Sidcup	d			17 31	17 46											18 01		18 16							
New Eltham	d			17 34	17 49											18 04		18 19							
Mottingham	d			17 36	17 51											18 06		18 21							
Lee	d			17 39	17 54											18 09		18 24							
Hither Green	d			17 42	17 58											18 12		18 28							
Barnehurst	d	16 58	17a07						17 07		17 15			17 28	17a37							17 37		17 45	
Bexleyheath	d	17 01							17 09		17 17			17 31								17 39		17 47	
Welling	d	17 04							17 12		17 20			17 34								17 42		17 50	
Falconwood	d	17 06							17 15		17 23			17 36								17 45		17 53	
Eltham	d	17 09							17 18		17 25			17 39								17 48		17 55	
Kidbrooke	d								17 21		17 28											17 51		17 58	
Blackheath	d	17 16						17 22	17 25		17 33			17 46						17 52		17 55		18 03	
Lewisham	d	17 20			18 04			17 26	17 29		17 38		17 44	17 50				18 34		17 56		17 59		18 08	
St Johns	d				18 06				17 31				17 46					18 36				18 01			
New Cross	d				18 08				17 33				17 48					18 38				18 03			
Nunhead	d										17 45													18 15	
Peckham Rye	d										17 47													18 17	
Denmark Hill	d										17 51													18 21	
London Victoria	a										18 03													18 33	
Westcombe Park	d					17 15													17 45						
Maze Hill	d																								
Greenwich	d					17 22				17 33		17 43							17 52				18 03		18 13
Deptford	a					17 24													17 54						
London Bridge	a	17 28		17 52	18 14	17 30		17 35	17 38	17 41		17 50	17 54	17 58		18 22		18 44	18 00	18 05		18 08	18 11		18 20
London Cannon Street	a				18 22	17 37			17 46	17 48		17 57	18 01					18 52	18 07			18 16	18 18		18 27
London Waterloo (East)	a	17 32		17 56				17 39						18 02		18 26				18 09					
London Charing Cross	a	17 39		18 00				17 46						18 09		18 30				18 16					
Ebbsfleet International	a																				17 46				
Stratford International	a																				17 58				
St Pancras Int'l	a																				18 08				

Table 200

Gillingham and Dartford - London

Sundays

29 July to 12 August

Network Diagram - see first Page of Table 200

		SE		SE	SE	SE	SE	SE	SE	SE	SE	SE		SE	SE	SE	SE	SE	SE	SE	SE	SE		SE	SE
Gillingham (Kent)	d								17 24										17 54						
Chatham	d								17 28										17 58						
Rochester	d								17 30										18 00						
Maidstone West	d																								
Strood	d								17 35										18 05						
Higham	d								17 40										18 10						
Gravesend	d					18 02			17 48										18 18						18 32
Northfleet	d					18 06																			18 36
Swanscombe	d					18 08																			18 38
Greenhithe for Bluewater	d					18 11			17 53										18 23						18 41
Stone Crossing	d					18 13																			18 43
Dartford	a					18 17			17 58										18 28						18 47
	d			17 52		18 18			17 58		18 01	18 08				18 22			18 28		18 31	18 38			18 48
Slade Green	d				17 47			17 53			18 05			18 13			18 17	18 23			18 35				
Erith	d							17 56			18 08			18 15				18 26			18 38				
Belvedere	d							17 58			18 10			18 18				18 28			18 40				
Abbey Wood	d							18 01	18 07		18 13			18 21				18 31	18 37		18 43				
Plumstead	d							18 04			18 16			18 24				18 34			18 46				
Woolwich Arsenal	d							18 08	18 12		18 19			18 28				18 38	18 42		18 49			18 55	
Woolwich Dockyard	d																								
Charlton	d						18 09	18 13	18 16		18 26			18 37				18 43	18 46		18 56			19 01	
Crayford	d					18 22	18 37																		18 52
Bexley	d					18 25	18 40																		18 55
Albany Park	d					18 28	18 43																		18 58
Sidcup	d					18 31	18 46																		19 01
New Eltham	d					18 34	18 49																		19 04
Mottingham	d					18 36	18 51																		19 06
Lee	d					18 39	18 54																		19 09
Hither Green	d					18 42	18 58																		19 13
Barnehurst	d			17 58	18a07					18 07		18 15				18 28	18a37			18 37		18 45			
Bexleyheath	d			18 01						18 09		18 17				18 31				18 39		18 47			
Welling	d			18 04						18 12		18 20				18 34				18 42		18 50			
Falconwood	d			18 06						18 15		18 23				18 36				18 45		18 53			
Eltham	d			18 09						18 18		18 25				18 39				18 48		18 55			
Kidbrooke	d									18 21		18 28								18 51		18 58			
Blackheath	d			18 16					18 22	18 25		18 33				18 46			18 52	18 55		19 03			
Lewisham	d	18 14		18 20			19 04		18 26	18 29		18 38			18 44	18 50			18 56	18 59		19 08			19 18
St Johns	d	18 16					19 06			18 31					18 46					19 01					
New Cross	d	18 18					19 08			18 33					18 48					19 03					
Nunhead	d											18 45										19 15			
Peckham Rye	d											18 47										19 17			
Denmark Hill	d											18 51										19 21			
London Victoria	a											19 03										19 33			
Westcombe Park	d							18 15										18 45							
Maze Hill	d																								
Greenwich	d							18 22			18 33			18 43				18 52			19 03			19 09	
Deptford	a							18 24										18 54							
London Bridge	a	18 24		18 28		18 52	19 14	18 30	18 35	18 38	18 41			18 50	18 54	18 58		19 00	19 05	19 08	19 11			19 18	19 27
London Cannon Street	a	18 31					19 22	18 37		18 46	18 48			18 57	19 01			19 07		19 16	19 18			19 25	
London Waterloo (East)	a			18 32		18 56			18 39							19 02			19 09						19 32
London Charing Cross	a			18 39		19 00			18 46							19 09			19 16						19 38
Ebbsfleet International	a																								
Stratford International	a																								
St Pancras Int'l	a																								

Table 200

Sundays

29 July to 12 August

Gillingham and Dartford - London

Network Diagram - see first Page of Table 200

		SE	SE	SE	SE	SE	SE	SE		SE	SE	SE	SE	SE	SE	SE	SE	SE		SE	SE	SE	SE	SE	SE
Gillingham (Kent) 4	d	18 20			18 24						18 54			19 20			19 24						19 54		
Chatham 4	d	18 24			18 28						18 58			19 24			19 28						19 58		
Rochester 4	d	18 27			18 30						19 00			19 27			19 30						20 00		
Maidstone West	d																								
Strood 4	d	18 32			18 35						19 05			19 32			19 35						20 05		
Higham	d				18 40						19 10						19 40						20 10		
Gravesend 4	d	18 43			18 48		19 02				19 18		19 32	19 43			19 48				20 02		20 18		20 32
Northfleet	d						19 06						19 36								20 06				20 36
Swanscombe	d						19 08						19 38								20 08				20 38
Greenhithe for Bluewater	d				18 53		19 11				19 23		19 41				19 53				20 11		20 23		20 41
Stone Crossing	d						19 13						19 43								20 13				20 43
Dartford 4	a				18 58		19 17				19 28		19 47				19 58				20 17		20 28		20 47
	d			18 52	18 58	19 01	19 18			19 25	19 28	19 31	19 48			19 55	19 58	20 01			20 18	20 25	20 28	20 31	20 48
Slade Green 4	d		18 53			19 05		19 23				19 35			19 53			20 05						20 35	
Erith	d		18 56			19 08		19 26				19 38			19 56			20 08						20 38	
Belvedere	d		18 58			19 10		19 28				19 40			19 58			20 10						20 40	
Abbey Wood	d		19 01		19 07	19 13		19 31			19 37	19 43			20 01		20 07	20 13					20 37	20 43	
Plumstead	d		19 04			19 16		19 34				19 46			20 04			20 16						20 46	
Woolwich Arsenal 4 ⇌	d		19 08		19 12	19 19		19 38			19 42	19 49			20 08		20 12	20 19					20 42	20 49	
Woolwich Dockyard	d																								
Charlton 4	d		19 13		19 16	19 26		19 43			19 47	19 56			20 13		20 17	20 25					20 47	20 55	
Crayford	d						19 22						19 52								20 22				20 52
Bexley	d						19 25						19 55								20 25				20 55
Albany Park	d						19 28						19 58								20 28				20 58
Sidcup 4	d						19 31						20 01								20 31				21 01
New Eltham	d						19 34						20 04								20 34				21 04
Mottingham	d						19 36						20 06								20 36				21 06
Lee	d						19 39						20 09								20 39				21 09
Hither Green 4	d						19 43						20 13								20 43				21 13
Barnehurst 4	d			18 58						19 31						20 01						20 31			
Bexleyheath	d			19 01						19 34						20 04						20 34			
Welling	d			19 04						19 37						20 07						20 37			
Falconwood	d			19 06						19 39						20 09						20 39			
Eltham	d			19 09						19 42						20 12						20 42			
Kidbrooke	d			19 12						19 45						20 15						20 45			
Blackheath 4	d			19 17	19 22					19 49	19 53					20 19	20 23			20 28		20 49	20 53		
Lewisham 4 ⇌	d			19 21	19 26		19 48			19 53	19 57		20 18			20 23	20 27			20 32	20 48	20 53	20 57		21 18
St Johns	d																								
New Cross 4 ⊖	d			19 24			19 51			19 56			20 21			20 26					20 51	20 56			21 21
Nunhead 4	d																								
Peckham Rye 4	d																			20 40					
Denmark Hill 4	d																			20 53					
London Victoria 15 ⊖	a																								
Westcombe Park	d		19 15					19 45							20 15			20 27						20 57	
Maze Hill	d																	20 29						20 59	
Greenwich 4 ⇌	d		19 22			19 33		19 52				20 03			20 22			20 33						21 03	
Deptford	a		19 24					19 54							20 24			20 35						21 05	
London Bridge 4 ⊖	a		19 30	19 33	19 36	19 41	19 57	20 00		20 03	20 07	20 11	20 27		20 30	20 33	20 37	20 41			20 57	21 03	21 07	21 11	21 27
London Cannon Street 4 ⊖	a		19 37					20 07							20 37										
London Waterloo (East) 4 ⊖	a			19 39	19 42	19 45	20 04			20 08	20 11	20 15	20 34			20 38	20 41	20 45			21 04	21 08	21 11	21 15	21 34
London Charing Cross 4 ⊖	a			19 45	19 48	19 52	20 10			20 15	20 18	20 22	20 40			20 45	20 48	20 52			21 10	21 15	21 18	21 22	21 40
Ebbsfleet International	a	18 46												19 46											
Stratford International ⊖ ⇌	a	18 58												19 58											
St Pancras Int'l 15 ⊖	a	19 08												20 08											

Table 200

Sundays

29 July to 12 August

Gillingham and Dartford - London

Network Diagram - see first Page of Table 200

		SE	SE	SE		SE	SE	SE	SE	SE	SE	SE	SE	SE		SE	SE	SE	SE	SE	SE	SE	SE	SE	
Gillingham (Kent) 4	d	20 20		20 24					20 54			21 20		21 24					21 54			22 20		22 24	
Chatham 4	d	20 24		20 28					20 58			21 24		21 28					21 58			22 24		22 28	
Rochester 4	d	20 27		20 30					21 00			21 27		21 30					22 00			22 27		22 30	
Maidstone West	d																								
Strood 4	d	20 32		20 35					21 05			21 32		21 35					22 05			22 32		22 35	
Higham	d			20 40					21 10					21 40					22 10					22 40	
Gravesend 4	d	20 43		20 48			21 02		21 18		21 32	21 43		21 48			22 02		22 18		22 32	22 43		22 48	
Northfleet	d						21 06				21 36						22 06				22 36				
Swanscombe	d						21 08				21 38						22 08				22 38				
Greenhithe for Bluewater	d			20 53			21 11		21 23		21 41			21 53			22 11		22 23		22 41			22 53	
Stone Crossing	d						21 13				21 43						22 13				22 43				
Dartford 4	a			20 58			21 17		21 28		21 47			21 58			22 17		22 28		22 47			22 58	
	d		20 55	20 58		21 01	21 18	21 25	21 28	21 31	21 48		21 55	21 58		22 01	22 18	22 25	22 28	22 31	22 48		22 55	22 58	
Slade Green 4	d					21 05				21 35						22 05				22 35					
Erith	d					21 08				21 38						22 08				22 38					
Belvedere	d					21 10				21 40						22 10				22 40					
Abbey Wood	d			21 07		21 13			21 37	21 43				22 07		22 13			22 37	22 43				23 07	
Plumstead	d					21 16				21 46						22 16				22 46					
Woolwich Arsenal 4 ⇌	d			21 12		21 19			21 42	21 49				22 12		22 19			22 42	22 49				23 12	
Woolwich Dockyard	d																								
Charlton 4	d			21 17		21 25			21 47	21 55				22 17		22 25			22 47	22 55				23 17	
Crayford	d						21 22				21 52						22 22				22 52				
Bexley	d						21 25				21 55						22 25				22 55				
Albany Park	d						21 28				21 58						22 28				22 58				
Sidcup 4	d						21 31				22 01						22 31				23 01				
New Eltham	d						21 34				22 04						22 34				23 04				
Mottingham	d						21 36				22 06						22 36				23 06				
Lee	d						21 39				22 09						22 39				23 09				
Hither Green 4	d						21 43				22 13						22 43				23 13				
Barnehurst 4	d		21 01					21 31					22 01					22 31					23 01		
Bexleyheath	d		21 04					21 34					22 04					22 34					23 04		
Welling	d		21 07					21 37					22 07					22 37					23 07		
Falconwood	d		21 09					21 39					22 09					22 39					23 09		
Eltham	d		21 12					21 42					22 12					22 42					23 12		
Kidbrooke	d		21 15					21 45					22 15					22 45					23 15		
Blackheath 4	d		21 19	21 22				21 49	21 52				22 19	22 22				22 49	22 52				23 19	23 22	
Lewisham 4 ⇌	d		21 23	21 26			21 48	21 53	21 56		22 18		22 23	22 26			22 48	22 53	22 56		23 18		23 23	23 26	
St Johns	d																								
New Cross 4 ⊖	d		21 26				21 51	21 56			22 21		22 26				22 51	22 56			23 21		23 26		
Nunhead 4	d																								
Peckham Rye 4	d																								
Denmark Hill 4	d																								
London Victoria 15 ⊖	a																								
Westcombe Park	d					21 27				21 57						22 27				22 57					
Maze Hill	d					21 29				21 59						22 29				22 59					
Greenwich 4 ⇌	d					21 33				22 03						22 33				23 03					
Deptford	a					21 35				22 05						22 35				23 05					
London Bridge 4 ⊖	a		21 33	21 36		21 41	21 57	22 01	22 05	22 11	22 27		22 31	22 35		22 41	22 57	23 01	23 05	23 11	23 27		23 31	23 35	
London Cannon Street 4 ⊖	a																								
London Waterloo (East) 4 ⊖	a		21 38	21 40		21 45	22 04	22 06	22 09	22 15	22 34		22 36	22 39		22 45	23 04	23 06	23 09	23 15	23 34		23 36	23 39	
London Charing Cross 4 ⊖	a		21 45	21 47		21 52	22 10	22 13	22 16	22 22	22 40		22 43	22 46		22 52	23 10	23 13	23 16	23 23	23 40		23 43	23 46	
Ebbsfleet International	a	20 46										21 46										22 46			
Stratford International ⊖ ⇌	a	20 58										21 58										22 58			
St Pancras Int'l 15 ⊖	a	21 08										22 08										23 07			

Table 200

Sundays
29 July to 12 August

Gillingham and Dartford - London

Network Diagram - see first Page of Table 200

Station		SE	SE
Gillingham (Kent)	d		22 54
Chatham	d		22 58
Rochester	d		23 00
Maidstone West	d		
Strood	d		23 05
Higham	d		23 10
Gravesend	d		23 18
Northfleet	d		
Swanscombe	d		
Greenhithe for Bluewater	d		23 23
Stone Crossing	d		
Dartford	a		23 31
	d	23 01	
Slade Green	d	23 05	
Erith	d	23 08	
Belvedere	d	23 10	
Abbey Wood	d	23 13	
Plumstead	d	23 16	
Woolwich Arsenal	d	23 19	
Woolwich Dockyard	d		
Charlton	d	23 25	
Crayford	d		
Bexley	d		
Albany Park	d		
Sidcup	d		
New Eltham	d		
Mottingham	d		
Lee	d		
Hither Green	d		
Barnehurst	d		
Bexleyheath	d		
Welling	d		
Falconwood	d		
Eltham	d		
Kidbrooke	d		
Blackheath	d		
Lewisham	d		
St Johns	d		
New Cross	d		
Nunhead	d		
Peckham Rye	d		
Denmark Hill	d		
London Victoria	a		
Westcombe Park	d	23 27	
Maze Hill	d	23 29	
Greenwich	d	23 33	
Deptford	a	23 35	
London Bridge	a	23 41	
London Cannon Street	a		
London Waterloo (East)	a	23 45	
London Charing Cross	a	23 52	
Ebbsfleet International	a		
Stratford International	a		
St Pancras Int'l	a		

Table 200

Sundays
26 August to 9 September

Gillingham and Dartford - London

Network Diagram - see first Page of Table 200

Station		SE A	SE	SE	SE	SE	SE	SE	SE	SE	SE	SE	SE	SE B	SE A	SE	SE	SE	SE	SE A	SE	SE	SE
Gillingham (Kent)	d								06 45				07 15	07 20	07 20				07 45	07 50			
Chatham	d								06 49				07 19	07 24	07 24				07 49	07 54			
Rochester	d								06 51				07 21	07 27	07 27				07 51	07 57			
Maidstone West	d																						
Strood	d								06 56				07 26	07 32	07 32				07 56	08 02			
Higham	d								07 01				07 31						08 01				
Gravesend	d								07 09				07 39	07 43	07 43				08 09	08 13			
Northfleet	d								07 12				07 42						08 12				
Swanscombe	d								07 14				07 44						08 14				
Greenhithe for Bluewater	d								07 18				07 48						08 18				
Stone Crossing	d								07 20				07 50						08 20				
Dartford	a								07 24				07 54						08 24				
	d		06 40	06 43	06 48	07 10	07 13	07 18	07 29	07 40	07 43	07 48	07 59			08 10	08 13	08 18	08 29			08 40	08 43
Slade Green	d			06 48			07 18				07 48						08 18						08 48
Erith	d			06 50			07 20				07 50						08 20						08 50
Belvedere	d			06 53			07 23				07 53						08 23						08 53
Abbey Wood	d			06 56			07 26		07 38		07 56		08 08				08 26		08 38				08 56
Plumstead	d			06 59			07 29				07 59						08 29				08 47		08 59
Woolwich Arsenal	d			07 02			07 32		07 43		08 02		08 13				08 32		08 43		08 50		09 02
Woolwich Dockyard	d			07 04			07 34				08 04						08 34				08 52		09 04
Charlton	d	00 26		07 07			07 37		07 47		08 07		08 17				08 37		08 47		08 55		09 07
Crayford	d				06 52			07 22				07 52						08 22					
Bexley	d				06 55			07 25				07 55						08 25					
Albany Park	d				06 58			07 28				07 58						08 28					
Sidcup	d				07 01			07 31				08 01						08 31					
New Eltham	d				07 04			07 34				08 04						08 34					
Mottingham	d				07 06			07 36				08 06						08 36					
Lee	d				07 09			07 39				08 09						08 39					
Hither Green	d				07 12			07 42				08 12						08 42					
Barnehurst	d		06 47			07 17				07 47						08 17						08 47	
Bexleyheath	d		06 49			07 19				07 49						08 19						08 49	
Welling	d		06 52			07 22				07 52						08 22						08 52	
Falconwood	d		06 55			07 25				07 55						08 25						08 55	
Eltham	d		06 58			07 28				07 58						08 28						08 58	
Kidbrooke	d		07 01			07 31				08 01						08 31						09 01	
Blackheath	d		07 04			07 34			07 52	08 04			08 22			08 34			08 52			09 04	
Lewisham	d		07 08		07 18	07 38		07 48	07 56	08 08		08 18	08 26			08 38		08 48	08 56			09 08	
St Johns	d																						
New Cross	d		07 11			07 41				08 11						08 41						09 11	
Nunhead	d																						
Peckham Rye	d																						
Denmark Hill	d																						
London Victoria	a																						
Westcombe Park	d			07 09			07 39				08 09						08 39				08 57		09 09
Maze Hill	d			07 11			07 41				08 11						08 41				08 59		09 11
Greenwich	d			07 15			07 45				08 15						08 45				09 03		09 15
Deptford	a			07 17			07 47				08 17						08 47				09 05		09 17
London Bridge	a		07 19	07 23	07 26	07 49	07 53	07 56	08 06	08 19	08 23	08 26	08 36			08 49	08 53	08 56	09 06		09 11	09 19	09 23
London Cannon Street	a	00 38																					
London Waterloo (East)	a		07 25	07 27	07 30	07 55	07 57	08 00	08 11	08 25	08 27	08 30	08 41			08 55	08 57	09 00	09 11			09 25	09 27
London Charing Cross	a		07 28	07 31	07 34	07 58	08 01	08 04	08 14	08 28	08 31	08 34	08 44			08 58	09 01	09 04	09 14			09 28	09 31
Ebbsfleet International	a													07 47	07 47					08 17			
Stratford International	a														07 59					08 28			
St Pancras Int'l	a														08 07					08 35			

A not 26 August

B not from 2 September until 9 September

Table 200

Sundays

26 August to 9 September

Gillingham and Dartford - London

Network Diagram - see first Page of Table 200

		SE	SE	SE A	SE B	SE	SE	SE	SE	SE B	SE	SE	SE	SE	SE	SE A	SE B	SE	SE	SE	SE	SE	SE B
Gillingham (Kent)	d		08 15	08 20	08 20					08 50	08 54					09 20	09 20	09 24					09 50
Chatham	d		08 19	08 24	08 24					08 54	08 58					09 24	09 24	09 28					09 54
Rochester	d		08 21	08 27	08 27					08 57	09 00					09 27	09 27	09 30					09 57
Maidstone West	d																						
Strood	d		08 26	08 32	08 32					09 02	09 05					09 32	09 32	09 35					10 02
Higham	d		08 31								09 10							09 40					
Gravesend	d		08 39	08 43	08 43				09 02	09 13	09 18				09 32	09 43	09 43	09 48				10 02	10 13
Northfleet	d		08 42						09 06						09 36							10 06	
Swanscombe	d		08 44						09 08						09 38							10 08	
Greenhithe for Bluewater	d		08 48						09 11		09 23				09 41			09 53				10 11	
Stone Crossing	d		08 50						09 13						09 43							10 13	
Dartford	a		08 54						09 17		09 28				09 47			09 58				10 17	
	d	08 48	08 59				09 10	09 13	09 18		09 29		09 40	09 43	09 48			09 59		10 10	10 13	10 18	
Slade Green	d							09 18						09 48							10 18		
Erith	d							09 20						09 50							10 20		
Belvedere	d							09 23						09 53							10 23		
Abbey Wood	d		09 08					09 26			09 38			09 56				10 08			10 26		
Plumstead	d					09 17		09 29				09 47		09 59					10 17		10 29		
Woolwich Arsenal	d		09 13			09 20		09 32			09 43	09 50		10 02				10 13	10 20		10 32		
Woolwich Dockyard	d					09 22		09 34				09 52		10 04					10 22		10 34		
Charlton	d		09 17			09 25		09 37			09 47	09 55		10 07				10 17	10 25		10 37		
Crayford	d	08 52							09 22						09 52							10 22	
Bexley	d	08 55							09 25						09 55							10 25	
Albany Park	d	08 58							09 28						09 58							10 28	
Sidcup	d	09 01							09 31						10 01							10 31	
New Eltham	d	09 04							09 34						10 04							10 34	
Mottingham	d	09 06							09 36						10 06							10 36	
Lee	d	09 09							09 39						10 09							10 39	
Hither Green	d	09 12							09 42						10 12							10 42	
Barnehurst	d						09 17						09 47							10 17			
Bexleyheath	d						09 19						09 49							10 19			
Welling	d						09 22						09 52							10 22			
Falconwood	d						09 25						09 55							10 25			
Eltham	d						09 28						09 58							10 28			
Kidbrooke	d						09 31						10 01							10 31			
Blackheath	d		09 22				09 34				09 52		10 04					10 22		10 34			
Lewisham	d	09 18	09 26				09 38		09 48		09 56		10 08		10 18			10 26		10 38		10 48	
St Johns	d																						
New Cross	d						09 41						10 11							10 41			
Nunhead	d																						
Peckham Rye	d																						
Denmark Hill	d																						
London Victoria	a																						
Westcombe Park	d					09 27		09 39				09 57		10 09					10 27		10 39		
Maze Hill	d					09 29		09 41				09 59		10 11					10 29		10 41		
Greenwich	d					09 33		09 45				10 03		10 15					10 33		10 45		
Deptford	a					09 35		09 47				10 05		10 17					10 35		10 47		
London Bridge	a	09 26	09 36			09 41	09 49	09 53	09 56		10 06	10 11	10 19	10 23	10 26			10 36	10 41	10 49	10 53	10 56	
London Cannon Street	a																						
London Waterloo (East)	a	09 30	09 41				09 55	09 57	10 00		10 11		10 25	10 27	10 30			10 41		10 55	10 57	11 00	
London Charing Cross	a	09 34	09 44				09 58	10 01	10 04		10 14		10 28	10 31	10 34			10 44		10 58	11 01	11 04	
Ebbsfleet International	a			08 47	08 47					09 17						09 47	09 47						10 17
Stratford International	a			08 59	08 59					09 29						09 59	09 59						10 38
St Pancras Int'l	a			09 06	09 07					09 42						10 06	10 07						10 44

A not from 2 September until 9 September

B not 26 August

Table 200

Sundays

26 August to 9 September

Gillingham and Dartford - London

Network Diagram - see first Page of Table 200

		SE	SE	SE	SE	SE	SE A	SE B	SE	SE	SE	SE	SE	SE B	SE	SE	SE	SE	SE	SE A	SE B	SE
Gillingham (Kent)	d	09 54					10 20	10 20	10 24					10 50	10 54					11 20	11 20	11 24
Chatham	d	09 58					10 24	10 24	10 28					10 54	10 58					11 24	11 24	11 28
Rochester	d	10 00					10 27	10 27	10 30					10 57	11 00					11 27	11 27	11 30
Maidstone West	d																					
Strood	d	10 05					10 32	10 32	10 35					11 02	11 05					11 32	11 32	11 35
Higham	d	10 10							10 40						11 10							11 40
Gravesend	d	10 18				10 32	10 43	10 43	10 48				11 02	11 13	11 18				11 32	11 43	11 43	11 48
Northfleet	d					10 36							11 06						11 36			
Swanscombe	d					10 38							11 08						11 38			
Greenhithe for Bluewater	d	10 23				10 41			10 53				11 11		11 23				11 41			11 53
Stone Crossing	d					10 43							11 13						11 43			
Dartford	a	10 28				10 47			10 58				11 17		11 28				11 47			11 58
	d	10 29		10 40	10 43	10 48			10 59		11 10	11 13	11 18		11 29		11 40	11 43	11 48			11 59
Slade Green	d				10 48							11 18						11 48				
Erith	d				10 50							11 20						11 50				
Belvedere	d				10 53							11 23						11 53				
Abbey Wood	d	10 38			10 56				11 08			11 26			11 38			11 56				12 08
Plumstead	d		10 47		10 59					11 17		11 29				11 47		11 59				
Woolwich Arsenal	d	10 43	10 50		11 02				11 13	11 20		11 32			11 43	11 50		12 02				12 13
Woolwich Dockyard	d		10 52		11 04					11 22		11 34				11 52		12 04				
Charlton	d	10 47	10 55		11 07				11 17	11 25		11 37			11 47	11 55		12 07				12 17
Crayford	d					10 52							11 22						11 52			
Bexley	d					10 55							11 25						11 55			
Albany Park	d					10 58							11 28						11 58			
Sidcup	d					11 01							11 31						12 01			
New Eltham	d					11 04							11 34						12 04			
Mottingham	d					11 06							11 36						12 06			
Lee	d					11 09							11 39						12 09			
Hither Green	d					11 12							11 42						12 12			
Barnehurst	d			10 47							11 17						11 47					
Bexleyheath	d			10 49							11 19						11 49					
Welling	d			10 52							11 22						11 52					
Falconwood	d			10 55							11 25						11 55					
Eltham	d			10 58							11 28						11 58					
Kidbrooke	d			11 01							11 31						12 01					
Blackheath	d	10 52		11 04					11 22		11 34				11 52		12 04					12 22
Lewisham	d	10 56		11 08		11 18			11 26		11 38		11 48		11 56		12 08		12 18			12 26
St Johns	d																					
New Cross	d			11 11							11 41						12 11					
Nunhead	d																					
Peckham Rye	d																					
Denmark Hill	d																					
London Victoria	a																					
Westcombe Park	d		10 57		11 09					11 27		11 39				11 57		12 09				
Maze Hill	d		10 59		11 11					11 29		11 41				11 59		12 11				
Greenwich	d		11 03		11 15					11 33		11 45				12 03		12 15				
Deptford	a		11 05		11 17					11 35		11 47				12 05		12 17				
London Bridge	a	11 06	11 11	11 19	11 23	11 26			11 36	11 41	11 49	11 53	11 56		12 06	12 11	12 19	12 23	12 26			12 36
London Cannon Street	a																					
London Waterloo (East)	a	11 11		11 25	11 27	11 30			11 41		11 55	11 57	12 00		12 11		12 25	12 27	12 30			12 41
London Charing Cross	a	11 14		11 28	11 31	11 34			11 44		11 58	12 01	12 04		12 14		12 28	12 31	12 34			12 44
Ebbsfleet International	a						10 47	10 47						11 17						11 47	11 47	
Stratford International	a						10 59	10 59												11 59	11 59	
St Pancras Int'l	a						11 06	11 07												12 06	12 07	

A not from 2 September until 9 September

B not 26 August

Table 200

Gillingham and Dartford - London

Sundays

26 August to 9 September

Network Diagram - see first Page of Table 200

		SE	SE	SE	SE	SE A	SE B	SE	SE	SE	SE	SE	SE A	SE B	SE	SE	SE	SE	SE	SE A	SE B	SE	SE
Gillingham (Kent)	d					11 50	11 50	11 54					12 20	12 20	12 24					12 50	12 50	12 54	
Chatham	d					11 54	11 54	11 58					12 24	12 24	12 28					12 54	12 54	12 58	
Rochester	d					11 57	11 57	12 00					12 27	12 27	12 30					12 57	12 57	13 00	
Maidstone West	d																						
Strood	d					12 02	12 02	12 05					12 32	12 32	12 35					13 02	13 02	13 05	
Higham	d							12 10							12 40							13 10	
Gravesend	d				12 02	12 13	12 13	12 18				12 32	12 43	12 43	12 48				13 02	13 13	13 13	13 18	
Northfleet	d				12 06							12 36							13 06				
Swanscombe	d				12 08							12 38							13 08				
Greenhithe for Bluewater	d				12 11			12 23				12 41			12 53				13 11			13 23	
Stone Crossing	d				12 13							12 43							13 13				
Dartford	a				12 17			12 28				12 47			12 58				13 17			13 28	
	d		12 10	12 13	12 18			12 29		12 40	12 43	12 48			12 59		13 10	13 13	13 18			13 29	
Slade Green	d			12 18							12 48							13 18					
Erith	d			12 20							12 50							13 20					
Belvedere	d			12 23							12 53							13 23					
Abbey Wood	d			12 26				12 38			12 56				13 08			13 26				13 38	
Plumstead	d	12 17		12 29					12 47		12 59					13 17		13 29					13 47
Woolwich Arsenal	d	12 20		12 32				12 43	12 50		13 02				13 13	13 20		13 32				13 43	13 50
Woolwich Dockyard	d	12 22		12 34					12 52		13 04					13 22		13 34					13 52
Charlton	d	12 25		12 37				12 47	12 55		13 07				13 17	13 25		13 37				13 47	13 55
Crayford	d				12 22							12 52							13 22				
Bexley	d				12 25							12 55							13 25				
Albany Park	d				12 28							12 58							13 28				
Sidcup	d				12 31							13 01							13 31				
New Eltham	d				12 34							13 04							13 34				
Mottingham	d				12 36							13 06							13 36				
Lee	d				12 39							13 09							13 39				
Hither Green	d				12 42							13 12							13 42				
Barnehurst	d		12 17							12 47							13 17						
Bexleyheath	d		12 19							12 49							13 19						
Welling	d		12 22							12 52							13 22						
Falconwood	d		12 25							12 55							13 25						
Eltham	d		12 28							12 58							13 28						
Kidbrooke	d		12 31							13 01							13 31						
Blackheath	d		12 34					12 52		13 04					13 22		13 34					13 52	
Lewisham	d		12 38		12 48			12 56		13 08		13 18			13 26		13 38		13 48			13 56	
St Johns	d																						
New Cross	d		12 41							13 11							13 41						
Nunhead	d																						
Peckham Rye	d																						
Denmark Hill	d																						
London Victoria	a																						
Westcombe Park	d	12 27		12 39					12 57		13 09					13 27		13 39					13 57
Maze Hill	d	12 29		12 41					12 59		13 11					13 29		13 41					13 59
Greenwich	d	12 33		12 45					13 03		13 15					13 33		13 45					14 03
Deptford	a	12 35		12 47					13 05		13 17					13 35		13 47					14 05
London Bridge	a	12 41	12 49	12 53	12 56			13 06	13 11	13 19	13 23	13 26			13 36	13 41	13 49	13 53	13 56			14 06	14 11
London Cannon Street	a																						
London Waterloo (East)	a		12 55	12 57	13 00			13 11		13 25	13 27	13 30			13 41		13 55	13 57	14 00			14 11	
London Charing Cross	a		12 58	13 01	13 04			13 14		13 28	13 31	13 34			13 44		13 58	14 01	14 04			14 14	
Ebbsfleet International	a					12 17	12 17						12 47	12 47						13 17	13 17		
Stratford International	a					12 29	12 32						12 59	12 59						13 29	13 32		
St Pancras Int'l	a					12 36	12 40						13 06	13 07						13 36	13 40		

A not from 2 September until 9 September B not 26 August

Table 200

Gillingham and Dartford - London

Sundays

26 August to 9 September

Network Diagram - see first Page of Table 200

		SE	SE	SE	SE	SE	SE	SE	SE	SE	SE A	SE B	SE	SE	SE	SE	SE	SE A	SE B	SE	SE	SE
Gillingham (Kent)	d				13 20	13 24					13 50	13 50	13 54					14 20	14 20	14 24		
Chatham	d				13 24	13 28					13 54	13 54	13 58					14 24	14 24	14 28		
Rochester	d				13 27	13 30					13 57	13 57	14 00					14 27	14 27	14 30		
Maidstone West	d																					
Strood	d				13 32	13 35					14 02	14 02	14 05					14 32	14 32	14 35		
Higham	d					13 40							14 10							14 40		
Gravesend	d			13 32	13 43	13 48				14 02	14 13	14 13	14 18				14 32	14 43	14 43	14 48		
Northfleet	d			13 36						14 06							14 36					
Swanscombe	d			13 38						14 08							14 38					
Greenhithe for Bluewater	d			13 41		13 53				14 11			14 23				14 41			14 53		
Stone Crossing	d			13 43						14 13							14 43					
Dartford	a			13 47		13 58				14 17			14 28				14 47			14 58		
	d	13 40	13 43	13 48		13 59		14 10	14 13	14 18			14 29		14 40	14 43	14 48			14 59		15 10
Slade Green	d		13 48						14 18							14 48						
Erith	d		13 50						14 20							14 50						
Belvedere	d		13 53						14 23							14 53						
Abbey Wood	d		13 56			14 08			14 26				14 38			14 56				15 08		
Plumstead	d		13 59				14 17		14 29					14 47		14 59					15 17	
Woolwich Arsenal	d		14 02			14 13	14 20		14 32				14 43	14 50		15 02				15 13	15 20	
Woolwich Dockyard	d		14 04				14 22		14 34					14 52		15 04					15 22	
Charlton	d		14 07			14 17	14 25		14 37				14 47	14 55		15 07				15 17	15 25	
Crayford	d			13 52						14 22							14 52					
Bexley	d			13 55						14 25							14 55					
Albany Park	d			13 58						14 28							14 58					
Sidcup	d			14 01						14 31							15 01					
New Eltham	d			14 04						14 34							15 04					
Mottingham	d			14 06						14 36							15 06					
Lee	d			14 09						14 39							15 09					
Hither Green	d			14 12						14 42							15 12					
Barnehurst	d	13 47						14 17							14 47							15 17
Bexleyheath	d	13 49						14 19							14 49							15 19
Welling	d	13 52						14 22							14 52							15 22
Falconwood	d	13 55						14 25							14 55							15 25
Eltham	d	13 58						14 28							14 58							15 28
Kidbrooke	d	14 01						14 31							15 01							15 31
Blackheath	d	14 04				14 22		14 34					14 52		15 04					15 22		15 34
Lewisham	d	14 08		14 18		14 26		14 38		14 48			14 56		15 08		15 18			15 26		15 38
St Johns	d																					
New Cross	d	14 11						14 41							15 11							15 41
Nunhead	d																					
Peckham Rye	d																					
Denmark Hill	d																					
London Victoria	a																					
Westcombe Park	d		14 09				14 27		14 39					14 57		15 09					15 27	
Maze Hill	d		14 11				14 29		14 41					14 59		15 11					15 29	
Greenwich	d		14 15				14 33		14 45					15 03		15 15					15 33	
Deptford	a		14 17				14 35		14 47					15 05		15 17					15 35	
London Bridge	a	14 19	14 23	14 26		14 36	14 41	14 49	14 53	14 56			15 06	15 11	15 19	15 23	15 26			15 36	15 41	15 49
London Cannon Street	a																					
London Waterloo (East)	a	14 25	14 27	14 30		14 41		14 55	14 57	15 00			15 11		15 25	15 27	15 30			15 41		15 55
London Charing Cross	a	14 28	14 31	14 34		14 44		14 58	15 01	15 04			15 14		15 28	15 31	15 34			15 44		15 58
Ebbsfleet International	a				13 47						14 17	14 17						14 47	14 47			
Stratford International	a				14 02						14 29	14 29						14 59	15 03			
St Pancras Int'l	a				14 09						14 36	14 44						15 06	15 11			

A not from 2 September until 9 September B not 26 August

Table 200

Sundays

26 August to 9 September

Gillingham and Dartford - London

Network Diagram - see first Page of Table 200

Station		SE	SE	SE A	SE B	SE	SE	SE	SE	SE	SE A	SE B	SE	SE	SE	SE	SE	SE A	SE B	SE	SE	SE	SE
Gillingham (Kent)	d			14 50	14 50	14 54					15 20	15 20	15 24					15 50	15 50	15 54			
Chatham	d			14 54	14 54	14 58					15 24	15 24	15 28					15 54	15 54	15 58			
Rochester	d			14 57	14 57	15 00					15 27	15 27	15 30					15 57	15 57	16 00			
Maidstone West	d																						
Strood	d			15 02	15 02	15 05					15 32	15 32	15 35					16 02	16 02	16 05			
Higham	d					15 10							15 40							16 10			
Gravesend	d		15 02	15 13	15 13	15 18				15 32	15 43	15 43	15 48				16 02	16 13	16 13	16 18			
Northfleet	d		15 06							15 36							16 06						
Swanscombe	d		15 08							15 38							16 08						
Greenhithe for Bluewater	d		15 11			15 23				15 41			15 53				16 11			16 23			
Stone Crossing	d		15 13							15 43							16 13						
Dartford	a		15 17			15 28				15 47			15 58				16 17			16 28			
	d	15 13	15 18			15 29		15 40	15 43	15 48			15 59		16 10	16 13	16 18			16 29		16 40	16 43
Slade Green	d	15 18							15 48							16 18							16 48
Erith	d	15 20							15 50							16 20							16 50
Belvedere	d	15 23							15 53							16 23							16 53
Abbey Wood	d	15 26				15 38			15 56				16 08			16 26				16 38			16 56
Plumstead	d	15 29					15 47		15 59					16 17		16 29					16 47		16 59
Woolwich Arsenal ⇌	d	15 32				15 43	15 50		16 02				16 13	16 20		16 32				16 43	16 50		17 02
Woolwich Dockyard	d	15 34					15 52		16 04					16 22		16 34					16 52		17 04
Charlton	d	15 37				15 47	15 55		16 07				16 17	16 25		16 37				16 47	16 55		17 07
Crayford	d		15 22							15 52							16 22						
Bexley	d		15 25							15 55							16 25						
Albany Park	d		15 28							15 58							16 28						
Sidcup	d		15 31							16 01							16 31						
New Eltham	d		15 34							16 04							16 34						
Mottingham	d		15 36							16 06							16 36						
Lee	d		15 39							16 09							16 39						
Hither Green	d		15 42							16 12							16 42						
Barnehurst	d							15 47							16 17							16 47	
Bexleyheath	d							15 49							16 19							16 49	
Welling	d							15 52							16 22							16 52	
Falconwood	d							15 55							16 25							16 55	
Eltham	d							15 58							16 28							16 58	
Kidbrooke	d							16 01							16 31							17 01	
Blackheath	d					15 52		16 04					16 22		16 34					16 52		17 04	
Lewisham ⇌	d		15 48			15 56		16 08		16 18			16 26		16 38		16 48			16 56		17 08	
St Johns	d																						
New Cross ⊖	d							16 11							16 41							17 11	
Nunhead	d																						
Peckham Rye	d																						
Denmark Hill	d																						
London Victoria ⊖	a																						
Westcombe Park	d	15 39					15 57		16 09					16 27		16 39					16 57		17 09
Maze Hill	d	15 41					15 59		16 11					16 29		16 41					16 59		17 11
Greenwich ⇌	d	15 45					16 03		16 15					16 33		16 45					17 03		17 15
Deptford	a	15 47					16 05		16 17					16 35		16 47					17 05		17 17
London Bridge ⊖	a	15 53	15 56			16 06	16 11	16 19	16 23	16 26			16 36	16 41	16 49	16 53	16 56			17 06	17 11	17 19	17 23
London Cannon Street ⊖	a																						
London Waterloo (East) ⊖	a	15 57	16 00			16 11		16 25	16 27	16 30			16 41		16 55	16 57	17 00			17 11		17 25	17 27
London Charing Cross ⊖	a	16 01	16 04			16 14		16 28	16 31	16 34			16 44		16 58	17 01	17 04			17 14		17 28	17 31
Ebbsfleet International	a			15 17	15 17						15 47	15 47						16 17	16 17				
Stratford International ⊖ ⇌	a			15 29	15 32						16 02	16 02						16 29	16 29				
St Pancras Int'l ⊖	a			15 36	15 40						16 09	16 12						16 36	16 44				

A not from 2 September until 9 September

B not 26 August

Table 200

Sundays

26 August to 9 September

Gillingham and Dartford - London

Network Diagram - see first Page of Table 200

Station		SE	SE	SE	SE	SE	SE	SE	SE A	SE B	SE	SE	SE	SE	SE	SE B	SE A	SE	SE	SE	SE	SE	SE A
Gillingham (Kent)	d		16 20	16 24					16 50	16 50	16 54					17 20	17 20	17 24					17 50
Chatham	d		16 24	16 28					16 54	16 54	16 58					17 24	17 24	17 28					17 54
Rochester	d		16 27	16 30					16 57	16 57	17 00					17 27	17 27	17 30					17 57
Maidstone West	d																						
Strood	d		16 32	16 35					17 02	17 02	17 05					17 32	17 32	17 35					18 02
Higham	d			16 40							17 10							17 40					
Gravesend	d	16 32	16 43	16 48				17 02	17 12	17 13	17 18				17 32	17 43	17 43	17 48				18 02	18 12
Northfleet	d	16 36						17 06							17 36							18 06	
Swanscombe	d	16 38						17 08							17 38							18 08	
Greenhithe for Bluewater	d	16 41		16 53				17 11			17 23				17 41			17 53				18 11	
Stone Crossing	d	16 43						17 13							17 43							18 13	
Dartford	a	16 47		16 58				17 17			17 28				17 47			17 58				18 17	
	d	16 48		16 59		17 10	17 13	17 18			17 29		17 40	17 43	17 48			17 59		18 10	18 13	18 18	
Slade Green	d						17 18							17 48							18 18		
Erith	d						17 20							17 50							18 20		
Belvedere	d						17 23							17 53							18 23		
Abbey Wood	d			17 08			17 26				17 38			17 56				18 08			18 26		
Plumstead	d				17 17		17 29					17 47		17 59					18 17		18 29		
Woolwich Arsenal ⇌	d			17 13	17 20		17 32				17 43	17 50		18 02				18 13	18 20		18 32		
Woolwich Dockyard	d				17 22		17 34					17 52		18 04					18 22		18 34		
Charlton	d			17 17	17 25		17 37				17 47	17 55		18 07				18 17	18 25		18 37		
Crayford	d	16 52						17 22							17 52							18 22	
Bexley	d	16 55						17 25							17 55							18 25	
Albany Park	d	16 58						17 28							17 58							18 28	
Sidcup	d	17 01						17 31							18 01							18 31	
New Eltham	d	17 04						17 34							18 04							18 34	
Mottingham	d	17 06						17 36							18 06							18 36	
Lee	d	17 09						17 39							18 09							18 39	
Hither Green	d	17 12						17 42							18 12							18 42	
Barnehurst	d					17 17							17 47							18 17			
Bexleyheath	d					17 19							17 49							18 19			
Welling	d					17 22							17 52							18 22			
Falconwood	d					17 25							17 55							18 25			
Eltham	d					17 28							17 58							18 28			
Kidbrooke	d					17 31							18 01							18 31			
Blackheath	d			17 22		17 34					17 52		18 04					18 22		18 34			
Lewisham ⇌	d	17 18		17 26		17 38		17 48			17 56		18 08		18 18			18 26		18 38		18 48	
St Johns	d																						
New Cross ⊖	d					17 41							18 11							18 41			
Nunhead	d																						
Peckham Rye	d																						
Denmark Hill	d																						
London Victoria ⊖	a																						
Westcombe Park	d				17 27		17 39					17 57		18 09					18 27		18 39		
Maze Hill	d				17 29		17 41					17 59		18 11					18 29		18 41		
Greenwich ⇌	d				17 33		17 45					18 03		18 15					18 33		18 45		
Deptford	a				17 35		17 47					18 05		18 17					18 35		18 47		
London Bridge ⊖	a	17 26		17 36	17 41	17 49	17 53	17 56			18 06	18 11	18 19	18 23	18 26			18 36	18 41	18 49	18 53	18 56	
London Cannon Street ⊖	a																						
London Waterloo (East) ⊖	a	17 30		17 41		17 55	17 57	18 00			18 11		18 25	18 27	18 30			18 41		18 55	18 57	19 00	
London Charing Cross ⊖	a	17 34		17 44		17 58	18 01	18 04			18 14		18 28	18 31	18 34			18 44		18 58	19 01	19 04	
Ebbsfleet International	a		16 47						17 16	17 17						17 47	17 47						18 16
Stratford International ⊖ ⇌	a									17 29						17 59	18 06						18 27
St Pancras Int'l ⊖	a									17 36						18 09	18 13						18 41

A not 26 August

B not from 2 September until 9 September

Table 200

Gillingham and Dartford - London

Sundays

26 August to 9 September

Network Diagram - see first Page of Table 200

Station		SE A	SE	SE	SE	SE	SE A	SE B	SE	SE	SE	SE	SE A	SE B	SE	SE	SE	SE	SE A	SE B	SE	SE
Gillingham (Kent)	d	17 50	17 54				18 20	18 20	18 24				18 50	18 50	18 54				19 20	19 20	19 24	
Chatham	d	17 54	17 58				18 24	18 24	18 28				18 54	18 54	18 58				19 24	19 24	19 28	
Rochester	d	17 57	18 00				18 27	18 27	18 30				18 57	18 57	19 00				19 27	19 27	19 30	
Maidstone West	d																					
Strood	d	18 02	18 05				18 32	18 32	18 35				19 02	19 02	19 05				19 32	19 32	19 35	
Higham	d		18 10						18 40						19 10						19 40	
Gravesend	d	18 13	18 18			18 32	18 43	18 43	18 48			19 02	19 13	19 13	19 18			19 32	19 43	19 43	19 48	
Northfleet	d					18 36						19 06						19 36				
Swanscombe	d					18 38						19 08						19 38				
Greenhithe for Bluewater	d		18 23			18 41			18 53			19 11			19 23			19 41			19 53	
Stone Crossing	d					18 43						19 13						19 43				
Dartford	a		18 28			18 47			18 58			19 17			19 28			19 47			19 58	
	d		18 29	18 40	18 43	18 48			18 59	19 10	19 13	19 18			19 29	19 40	19 43	19 48			19 59	20 10
Slade Green	d				18 48						19 18						19 48					
Erith	d				18 50						19 20						19 50					
Belvedere	d				18 53						19 23						19 53					
Abbey Wood	d		18 38		18 56				19 08		19 26				19 38		19 56				20 08	
Plumstead	d				18 59						19 29						19 59					
Woolwich Arsenal	d		18 43		19 02				19 13		19 32				19 43		20 02				20 13	
Woolwich Dockyard	d				19 04						19 34						20 04					
Charlton	d		18 47		19 07				19 17		19 37				19 47		20 07				20 17	
Crayford	d					18 52						19 22						19 52				
Bexley	d					18 55						19 25						19 55				
Albany Park	d					18 58						19 28						19 58				
Sidcup	d					19 01						19 31						20 01				
New Eltham	d					19 04						19 34						20 04				
Mottingham	d					19 06						19 36						20 06				
Lee	d					19 09						19 39						20 09				
Hither Green	d					19 12						19 42						20 12				
Barnehurst	d			18 47						19 17						19 47						20 17
Bexleyheath	d			18 49						19 19						19 49						20 19
Welling	d			18 52						19 22						19 52						20 22
Falconwood	d			18 55						19 25						19 55						20 25
Eltham	d			18 58						19 28						19 58						20 28
Kidbrooke	d			19 01						19 31						20 01						20 31
Blackheath	d		18 52	19 04					19 22	19 34					19 52	20 04					20 22	20 34
Lewisham	d		18 56	19 08		19 18			19 26	19 38		19 48			19 56	20 08		20 18			20 26	20 38
St Johns	d																					
New Cross	d			19 11						19 41						20 11						20 41
Nunhead	d																					
Peckham Rye	d																					
Denmark Hill	d																					
London Victoria	a																					
Westcombe Park	d				19 09						19 39						20 09					
Maze Hill	d				19 11						19 41						20 11					
Greenwich	d				19 15						19 45						20 15					
Deptford	a				19 17						19 47						20 17					
London Bridge	a		19 06	19 19	19 23	19 26			19 36	19 49	19 53	19 56			20 06	20 19	20 23	20 26			20 36	20 49
London Cannon Street	a																					
London Waterloo (East)	a		19 11	19 25	19 27	19 30			19 41	19 55	19 57	20 00			20 11	20 25	20 27	20 30			20 41	20 55
London Charing Cross	a		19 14	19 28	19 31	19 34			19 44	19 58	20 01	20 04			20 14	20 28	20 31	20 34			20 44	20 58
Ebbsfleet International	a	18 17					18 47	18 47					19 17	19 17					19 47	19 47		
Stratford International	a	18 29					18 59	19 02					19 29	19 29					19 59	20 03		
St Pancras Int'l	a	18 36					19 06	19 10					19 36	19 37					20 06	20 14		

A not from 2 September until 9 September

B not 26 August

Table 200

Gillingham and Dartford - London

Sundays

26 August to 9 September

Network Diagram - see first Page of Table 200

Station		SE	SE	SE	SE A	SE B	SE	SE	SE	SE	SE	SE	SE	SE	SE	SE A	SE B	SE	SE	SE	SE	SE A	SE B
Gillingham (Kent)	d			19 45	19 50	19 50				20 15	20 20				20 45	20 50	20 50				21 15	21 20	21 20
Chatham	d			19 49	19 54	19 54				20 19	20 24				20 49	20 54	20 54				21 19	21 24	21 24
Rochester	d			19 51	19 57	19 57				20 21	20 27				20 51	20 57	20 57				21 21	21 27	21 27
Maidstone West	d																						
Strood	d			19 56	20 02	20 02				20 26	20 32				20 56	21 02	21 02				21 26	21 32	21 32
Higham	d			20 01						20 31					21 01						21 31		
Gravesend	d			20 09	20 13	20 13				20 39	20 43				21 09	21 13	21 13				21 39	21 43	21 43
Northfleet	d			20 12						20 42					21 12						21 42		
Swanscombe	d			20 14						20 44					21 14						21 44		
Greenhithe for Bluewater	d			20 18						20 48					21 18						21 48		
Stone Crossing	d			20 20						20 50					21 20						21 50		
Dartford	a			20 24						20 54					21 24						21 54		
	d	20 13	20 18	20 29			20 40	20 43	20 48	20 59		21 10	21 13	21 18	21 29			21 40	21 43	21 48	21 59		
Slade Green	d	20 18						20 48					21 18						21 48				
Erith	d	20 20						20 50					21 20						21 50				
Belvedere	d	20 23						20 53					21 23						21 53				
Abbey Wood	d	20 26		20 38				20 56		21 08			21 26		21 38				21 56		22 08		
Plumstead	d	20 29						20 59					21 29						21 59				
Woolwich Arsenal	d	20 32		20 43				21 02		21 13			21 32		21 43				22 02		22 13		
Woolwich Dockyard	d	20 34						21 04					21 34						22 04				
Charlton	d	20 37		20 47				21 07		21 17			21 37		21 47				22 07		22 17		
Crayford	d		20 22						20 52					21 22						21 52			
Bexley	d		20 25						20 55					21 25						21 55			
Albany Park	d		20 28						20 58					21 28						21 58			
Sidcup	d		20 31						21 01					21 31						22 01			
New Eltham	d		20 34						21 04					21 34						22 04			
Mottingham	d		20 36						21 06					21 36						22 06			
Lee	d		20 39						21 09					21 39						22 09			
Hither Green	d		20 42						21 12					21 42						22 12			
Barnehurst	d						20 47					21 17						21 47					
Bexleyheath	d						20 49					21 19						21 49					
Welling	d						20 52					21 22						21 52					
Falconwood	d						20 55					21 25						21 55					
Eltham	d						20 58					21 28						21 58					
Kidbrooke	d						21 01					21 31						22 01					
Blackheath	d			20 52			21 04			21 22		21 34			21 52			22 04			22 22		
Lewisham	d		20 48	20 56			21 08		21 18	21 26		21 38		21 48	21 56			22 08		22 18	22 26		
St Johns	d																						
New Cross	d						21 11					21 41						22 11					
Nunhead	d																						
Peckham Rye	d																						
Denmark Hill	d																						
London Victoria	a																						
Westcombe Park	d	20 39						21 09					21 39						22 09				
Maze Hill	d	20 41						21 11					21 41						22 11				
Greenwich	d	20 45						21 15					21 45						22 15				
Deptford	a	20 47						21 17					21 47						22 17				
London Bridge	a	20 53	20 56	21 06			21 19	21 23	21 26	21 36		21 49	21 53	21 56	22 06			22 19	22 23	22 26	22 36		
London Cannon Street	a																						
London Waterloo (East)	a	20 57	21 00	21 11			21 25	21 27	21 30	21 41		21 55	21 57	22 00	22 11			22 25	22 27	22 30	22 41		
London Charing Cross	a	21 01	21 04	21 14			21 28	21 31	21 34	21 44		21 58	22 01	22 04	22 14			22 28	22 31	22 34	22 44		
Ebbsfleet International	a				20 17	20 17					20 47					21 17	21 17					21 47	21 47
Stratford International	a				20 29	20 29					21 02					21 29	21 30					21 59	22 02
St Pancras Int'l	a				20 36	20 37					21 09					21 36	21 44					22 06	22 10

A not from 2 September until 9 September

B not 26 August

Table 200

Sundays

26 August to 9 September

Gillingham and Dartford - London

Network Diagram - see first Page of Table 200

		SE	SE	SE	SE	SE A	SE B	SE	SE	SE	SE	SE A	SE B
Gillingham (Kent)	d				21 45	21 50	21 50				22 15	22 20	22 20
Chatham	d				21 49	21 54	21 54				22 19	22 24	22 24
Rochester	d				21 51	21 57	21 57				22 21	22 27	22 27
Maidstone West	d												
Strood	d				21 56	22 02	22 02				22 26	22 32	22 32
Higham	d				22 01						22 31		
Gravesend	d				22 09	22 13	22 13				22 39	22 43	22 43
Northfleet	d				22 12						22 42		
Swanscombe	d				22 14						22 44		
Greenhithe for Bluewater	d				22 18						22 48		
Stone Crossing	d				22 20						22 50		
Dartford	a				22 24						22 54		
	d	22 10	22 13	22 18	22 29			22 40	22 43	22 48	22 59		
Slade Green	d		22 18						22 48				
Erith	d		22 20						22 50				
Belvedere	d		22 23						22 53				
Abbey Wood	d		22 26		22 38				22 56		23 08		
Plumstead	d		22 29						22 59				
Woolwich Arsenal	d		22 32		22 43				23 02		23 13		
Woolwich Dockyard	d		22 34						23 04				
Charlton	d		22 37		22 47				23 07		23 17		
Crayford	d			22 22						22 52			
Bexley	d			22 25						22 55			
Albany Park	d			22 28						22 58			
Sidcup	d			22 31						23 01			
New Eltham	d			22 34						23 04			
Mottingham	d			22 36						23 06			
Lee	d			22 39						23 09			
Hither Green	d			22 42						23 12			
Barnehurst	d	22 17						22 47					
Bexleyheath	d	22 19						22 49					
Welling	d	22 22						22 52					
Falconwood	d	22 25						22 55					
Eltham	d	22 28						22 58					
Kidbrooke	d	22 31						23 01					
Blackheath	d	22 34			22 52			23 04			23 22		
Lewisham	d	22 38		22 48	22 56			23 08		23 18	23 26		
St Johns	d												
New Cross	d	22 41						23 11					
Nunhead	d												
Peckham Rye	d												
Denmark Hill	d												
London Victoria	a												
Westcombe Park	d		22 39						23 09				
Maze Hill	d		22 41						23 11				
Greenwich	d		22 45						23 15				
Deptford	a		22 47						23 17				
London Bridge	a	22 49	22 53	22 56	23 06			23 19	23 23	23 26	23 36		
London Cannon Street	a												
London Waterloo (East)	a	22 55	22 57	23 00	23 11			23 25	23 27	23 30	23 41		
London Charing Cross	a	22 58	23 01	23 04	23 14			23 28	23 31	23 34	23 44		
Ebbsfleet International	a					22 17	22 17					22 47	22 47
Stratford International	a					22 29	22 29					22 59	22 59
St Pancras Int'l	a					22 36	22 37					23 06	23 07

A not from 2 September until 9 September

B not 26 August

Table 203

Mondays to Fridays

until 27 July, 13 Aug to 28 Aug and from 10 Sep

London - Hayes (Kent) via Catford Bridge

Network Diagram - see first Page of Table 200

Miles	Miles			SE MO A	SE MX	SE	SE	SE	SE	SE	SE	SE	SE	SE	SE	SE	SE	SE	SE	SE	SE	SE
0	—	London Charing Cross	d	23p35	23p52		05 47	06 17	06 47		07 17		07 44		08 15		08 44			09 17		09 47
0¾	—	London Waterloo (East)	d	23p38	23p55		05 50	06 20	06 50		07 20		07 47		08 18		08 47			09 20		09 50
—	0	London Cannon Street	d							07 00		07 30		08 00		08 30		09 00	09 03		09 30	
1¾	0¾	London Bridge	d	23p43	23p59		05 55	06 26	06 55	07 04	07 25	07 34	07 53	08 04	08 23	08 34	08 53	09 04	09 07	09 25	09 34	09 55
4¾	—	New Cross	d	23p49	00 05	05 31	06 01	06 32	07 02	07 09		07 39		08 09		08 41		09 09			09 39	
5½	—	St Johns	d	23p51	00 07	05 33	06 03	06 34	07 04	07 11		07 41		08 11		08 43		09 11			09 41	
6	—	Lewisham	d	23p54	00 10	05 36	06 06	06 38	07 08	07 16		07 44		08 17		08 46		09 14			09 44	
6¾	—	Ladywell	d	23p57	00 13	05 39	06 09	06 41	07 11	07 19	07 34	07 47	08 04	08 20	08 34	08 49	09 04	09 17	09 22	09 34	09 47	10 04
7½	—	Catford Bridge	d	23p59	00 15	05 41	06 11	06 43	07 13	07 21	07 36	07 49	08 06	08 22	08 36	08 51	09 06	09 19	09 24	09 36	09 49	10 06
9	—	Lower Sydenham	d	00 02	00 18	05 44	06 14	06 46	07 16	07 24	07 39	07 52	08 09	08 25	08 39	08 54	09 09	09 22	09 27	09 39	09 52	10 09
9½	—	New Beckenham	d	00 04	00 20	05 46	06 16	06 48	07 18	07 26	07 41	07 54	08 11	08 27	08 41	08 56	09 11	09 24	09a29	09 41	09 54	10 11
10¼	—	Clock House	d	00 06	00 23	05 48	06 18	06 50	07 20	07 29	07 43	07 57	08 13	08 29	08 43	08 58	09 13	09 27		09 43	09 57	10 13
11	—	Elmers End	d	00 09	00 25	05 51	06 21	06 53	07 23	07 31	07 46	07 59	08 16	08 32	08 46	09 01	09 16	09 29		09 46	09 59	10 16
12½	—	Eden Park	d	00 12	00 29	05 54	06 24	06 56	07 26	07 35	07 49	08 03	08 19	08 35	08 49	09 04	09 19	09 33		09 49	10 03	10 19
13¼	—	West Wickham	d	00 15	00 31	05 57	06 27	06 59	07 29	07 37	07 52	08 05	08 22	08 38	08 52	09 07	09 22	09 35		09 52	10 05	10 22
14½	—	Hayes (Kent)	a	00 18	00 34	06 00	06 30	07 02	07 32	07 40	07 56	08 08	08 25	08 41	08 55	09 10	09 25	09 38		09 55	10 08	10 25

		SE		SE	SE	SE	SE	SE	SE	SE	SE	SE	SE	SE	SE	SE	SE	SE	SE	SE	SE
London Charing Cross	d		and at the same minutes past each hour until		15 17		15 47		16 20		16 39		16 59		17 21		17 43		18 05		18 27	
London Waterloo (East)	d				15 20		15 50		16 23		16 42		17 02		17 24		17 46		18 08		18 30	
London Cannon Street	d	10 00		15 00		15 30		16 00		16 30		16 51		17 12		17 34		17 56		18 18		18 40
London Bridge	d	10 04		15 04	15 25	15 34	15 55	16 04	16 29	16 34	16 47	16 55	17 07	17 16	17 29	17 39	17 52	18 00	18 13	18 23	18 35	18 44
New Cross	d	10 09		15 09		15 39		16 10		16 40		17 01		17 22		17 45		18 06		18 28		18 50
St Johns	d	10 11		15 11		15 41		16 12		16 42		17 03		17 24		17 47		18 08		18 30		18 52
Lewisham	d	10 14		15 14		15 44		16 15		16 45		17 06		17 27		17 50		18 11		18 33		18 55
Ladywell	d	10 17		15 17	15 34	15 47	16 04	16 18	16 38	16 48	16 57	17 09	17 17	17 30	17 40	17 53	18 01	18 14	18 23	18 36	18 45	18 58
Catford Bridge	d	10 19		15 19	15 36	15 49	16 06	16 20	16 40	16 50	16 59	17 11	17 19	17 32	17 42	17 55	18 03	18 16	18 25	18 38	18 47	19 00
Lower Sydenham	d	10 22		15 22	15 39	15 52	16 09	16 23	16 43	16 53	17 02	17 14	17 22	17 35	17 45	17 58	18 06	18 19	18 28	18 41	18 50	19 03
New Beckenham	d	10 24		15 24	15 41	15 54	16 11	16 25	16 45	16 55	17 04	17 16	17 24	17 37	17 47	18 00	18 08	18 21	18 30	18 43	18 52	19 05
Clock House	d	10 27		15 27	15 43	15 57	16 13	16 27	16 48	16 57	17 07	17 18	17 27	17 39	17 49	18 02	18 11	18 23	18 33	18 46	18 55	19 07
Elmers End	d	10 29		15 29	15 46	15 59	16 16	16 30	16 51	17 00	17 10	17 21	17 30	17 42	17 52	18 05	18 14	18 26	18 36	18 49	18 58	19 10
Eden Park	d	10 33		15 33	15 49	16 03	16 19	16 34	16 54	17 04	17 13	17 25	17 33	17 46	17 56	18 09	18 17	18 30	18 39	18 52	19 01	19 14
West Wickham	d	10 35		15 35	15 52	16 05	16 22	16 36	16 57	17 06	17 16	17 27	17 36	17 48	17 58	18 11	18 20	18 32	18 42	18 55	19 04	19 16
Hayes (Kent)	a	10 38		15 38	15 55	16 08	16 25	16 42	17 02	17 12	17 21	17 32	17 42	17 54	18 03	18 16	18 26	18 38	18 47	19 00	19 10	19 22

		SE	SE	SE	SE	SE	SE	SE	SE		SE	SE
London Charing Cross	d	18 52		19 17		19 47		20 17	20 47	and every 30 minutes until	23 17	23 52
London Waterloo (East)	d	18 55		19 20		19 50		20 20	20 50		23 20	23 55
London Cannon Street	d		19 00		19 30		20 00					
London Bridge	d	19 00	19 04	19 25	19 34	19 55	20 04	20 25	20 55		23 25	23 59
New Cross	d		19 09		19 39		20 09	20 32	21 00		23 30	00 05
St Johns	d		19 11		19 41		20 11	20 34	21 02		23 32	00 07
Lewisham	d		19 14		19 44		20 14	20 37	21 05		23 35	00 10
Ladywell	d	19 09	19 17	19 34	19 47	20 04	20 17	20 40	21 08		23 38	00 13
Catford Bridge	d	19 11	19 19	19 36	19 49	20 06	20 19	20 42	21 10		23 40	00 15
Lower Sydenham	d	19 14	19 22	19 39	19 52	20 09	20 22	20 45	21 13		23 43	00 18
New Beckenham	d	19 16	19 24	19 41	19 54	20 11	20 24	20 47	21 15		23 45	00 20
Clock House	d	19 19	19 27	19 43	19 57	20 13	20 27	20 50	21 18		23 48	00 23
Elmers End	d	19 22	19 29	19 46	19 59	20 16	20 29	20 52	21 20		23 50	00 25
Eden Park	d	19 25	19 33	19 49	20 03	20 19	20 33	20 56	21 24		23 54	00 29
West Wickham	d	19 28	19 35	19 52	20 05	20 22	20 35	20 58	21 26		23 56	00 31
Hayes (Kent)	a	19 33	19 39	19 55	20 09	20 25	20 39	21 01	21 29		23 59	00 34

Mondays to Fridays

30 July to 10 August

		SE	SE	SE	SE	SE	SE	SE	SE	SE	SE	SE	SE	SE	SE	SE	SE	SE	SE	SE	SE	SE	SE
London Charing Cross	d	23p17	23p52			05 47	06 17	06 47		07 17		07 44		08 15		08 44			09 17		09 47		10 17
London Waterloo (East)	d	23p20	23p55			05 50	06 20	06 50		07 20		07 47		08 18		08 47			09 20		09 50		10 20
London Cannon Street	d			00 30					07 00		07 30		08 00		08 30		09 00	09 03		09 30		10 00	
London Bridge	d	23p25	23p59	00 34		05 55	06 26	06 55	07 04	07 25	07 34	07 53	08 04	08 23	08 34	08 53	09 04	09 07	09 25		09 55	10 04	10 25
New Cross	d	23p30	00 05	00 39	05 31	06 01	06 32	07 02	07 09		07 39		08 09		08 41		09 09			09 39		10 09	
St Johns	d	23p32	00 07	00 41	05 33	06 03	06 34	07 04	07 11		07 41		08 11		08 43		09 11			09 41		10 11	
Lewisham	d	23p35	00 10	00 44	05 36	06 06	06 38	07 08	07 16		07 44		08 17		08 46		09 14			09 44		10 14	
Ladywell	d	23p38	00 13	00 47	05 39	06 09	06 41	07 11	07 19	07 34	07 47	08 04	08 20	08 34	08 49	09 04	09 17	09 22	09 34	09 47	10 04	10 17	10 34
Catford Bridge	d	23p40	00 15	00 49	05 41	06 11	06 43	07 13	07 21	07 36	07 49	08 06	08 22	08 36	08 51	09 06	09 19	09 24	09 36	09 49	10 06	10 19	10 36
Lower Sydenham	d	23p43	00 18	00 52	05 44	06 14	06 46	07 16	07 24	07 39	07 52	08 09	08 25	08 39	08 54	09 09	09 22	09 27	09 39	09 52	10 09	10 22	10 39
New Beckenham	d	23p45	00 20	00 54	05 46	06 16	06 48	07 18	07 26	07 41	07 54	08 11	08 27	08 41	08 56	09 11	09 24	09a29	09 41	09 54	10 11	10 24	10 41
Clock House	d	23p48	00 23	00 57	05 48	06 18	06 50	07 20	07 29	07 43	07 57	08 13	08 29	08 43	08 58	09 13	09 27		09 43	09 57	10 13	10 27	10 43
Elmers End	d	23p50	00 25	00 59	05 51	06 21	06 53	07 23	07 31	07 46	07 59	08 16	08 32	08 46	09 01	09 16	09 29		09 46	09 59	10 16	10 29	10 46
Eden Park	d	23p54	00 29	01 03	05 54	06 24	06 56	07 26	07 35	07 49	08 03	08 19	08 35	08 49	09 04	09 19	09 33		09 49	10 03	10 19	10 33	10 49
West Wickham	d	23p56	00 31	01 05	05 57	06 27	06 59	07 29	07 37	07 52	08 05	08 22	08 38	08 52	09 07	09 22	09 35		09 52	10 05	10 22	10 35	10 52
Hayes (Kent)	a	00 02	00 37	01 11	06 03	06 33	07 05	07 35	07 43	07 56	08 11	08 25	08 44	08 55	09 13	09 25	09 41		09 55	10 11	10 25	10 41	10 55

A from 21 May until 23 July

London - Hayes (Kent) via Catford Bridge

Mondays to Fridays

30 July to 10 August

Network Diagram - see first Page of Table 200

Station		SE		SE	SE	SE	SE	SE	SE	SE	SE	SE	SE	SE	SE	SE	SE	SE	SE	SE	SE	SE
London Charing Cross	d		and at the same minutes past each hour until		15 47		16 20		16 39		16 59		17 21		17 43		18 05		18 27		18 52	
London Waterloo (East)	d				15 50		16 23		16 42		17 02		17 24		17 46		18 08		18 30		18 55	
London Cannon Street	d	10 30		15 30		16 00		16 30		16 51		17 12		17 34		17 56		18 18		18 40		19 00
London Bridge	d	10 34		15 34	15 55	16 04	16 29	16 34	16 47	16 55	17 07	17 16	17 29	17 39	17 52	18 00	18 13	18 23	18 35	18 44	19 00	19 04
New Cross	d	10 39		15 39		16 10		16 40		17 01		17 22		17 45		18 06		18 28		18 50		19 09
St Johns	d	10 41		15 41		16 12		16 42		17 03		17 24		17 47		18 08		18 30		18 52		19 11
Lewisham	d	10 44		15 44		16 15		16 45		17 06		17 27		17 50		18 11		18 33		18 55		19 14
Ladywell	d	10 47		15 47	16 04	16 18	16 38	16 48	16 57	17 09	17 17	17 30	17 40	17 53	18 01	18 14	18 23	18 36	18 45	18 58	19 09	19 17
Catford Bridge	d	10 49		15 49	16 06	16 20	16 40	16 50	16 59	17 11	17 19	17 32	17 42	17 55	18 03	18 16	18 25	18 38	18 47	19 00	19 11	19 19
Lower Sydenham	d	10 52		15 52	16 09	16 23	16 43	16 53	17 02	17 14	17 22	17 35	17 45	17 58	18 06	18 19	18 28	18 41	18 50	19 03	19 14	19 22
New Beckenham	d	10 54		15 54	16 11	16 25	16 45	16 55	17 04	17 16	17 24	17 37	17 47	18 00	18 08	18 21	18 30	18 43	18 52	19 05	19 16	19 24
Clock House	d	10 57		15 57	16 13	16 27	16 48	16 57	17 07	17 18	17 27	17 39	17 49	18 02	18 11	18 23	18 33	18 46	18 55	19 07	19 19	19 27
Elmers End	d	10 59		15 59	16 16	16 30	16 51	17 00	17 10	17 21	17 30	17 42	17 52	18 05	18 14	18 26	18 36	18 49	18 58	19 10	19 22	19 29
Eden Park	d	11 03		16 03	16 19	16 34	16 54	17 04	17 13	17 25	17 33	17 46	17 56	18 09	18 17	18 30	18 39	18 52	19 01	19 14	19 25	19 33
West Wickham	d	11 05		16 05	16 22	16 36	16 57	17 06	17 16	17 27	17 36	17 48	17 58	18 11	18 20	18 32	18 42	18 55	19 04	19 16	19 28	19 35
Hayes (Kent)	a	11 11		16 11	16 25	16 42	17 02	17 12	17 21	17 32	17 42	17 54	18 03	18 16	18 26	18 38	18 47	19 00	19 10	19 22	19 33	19 42

Station		SE	SE	SE	SE	SE	SE		SE	SE
London Charing Cross	d	19 17		19 47		20 17	20 47	and every 30 minutes until	23 17	23 52
London Waterloo (East)	d	19 20		19 50		20 20	20 50		23 20	23 55
London Cannon Street	d		19 30		20 00					
London Bridge	d	19 25	19 34	19 55	20 04	20 25	20 55		23 25	23 59
New Cross	d		19 39		20 09	20 32	21 00		23 30	00 05
St Johns	d		19 41		20 11	20 34	21 02		23 32	00 07
Lewisham	d		19 44		20 14	20 37	21 05		23 35	00 10
Ladywell	d	19 34	19 47	20 04	20 17	20 40	21 08		23 38	00 13
Catford Bridge	d	19 36	19 49	20 06	20 19	20 42	21 10		23 40	00 15
Lower Sydenham	d	19 39	19 52	20 09	20 22	20 45	21 13		23 43	00 18
New Beckenham	d	19 41	19 54	20 11	20 24	20 47	21 15		23 45	00 20
Clock House	d	19 43	19 57	20 13	20 27	20 50	21 18		23 48	00 23
Elmers End	d	19 46	19 59	20 16	20 29	20 52	21 20		23 50	00 25
Eden Park	d	19 49	20 03	20 19	20 33	20 56	21 24		23 54	00 29
West Wickham	d	19 52	20 05	20 22	20 35	20 58	21 26		23 56	00 31
Hayes (Kent)	a	19 55	20 12	20 25	20 42	21 04	21 32		00 02	00 37

Mondays to Fridays

29 August to 7 September

Station		SE A	SE B	SE	SE	SE	SE	SE	SE	SE	SE	SE	SE	SE	SE	SE	SE	SE	SE	SE	SE
London Charing Cross	d	23p35	23p52			05 47	06 17	06 47		07 17		07 44		08 15		08 44			09 17		09 47
London Waterloo (East)	d	23p38	23p55			05 50	06 20	06 50		07 20		07 47		08 18		08 47			09 20		09 50
London Cannon Street	d	⌇	⌇	00 28					07 00		07 30		08 00		08 30		09 00	09 03		09 30	
London Bridge	d	23p43	23p59	00 32		05 55	06 26	06 55	07 04	07 25	07 34	07 53	08 04	08 23	08 34	08 53	09 04	09 07	09 25	09 34	09 55
New Cross	d	23p49	00 05	00 38	05 31	06 01	06 32	07 02	07 09		07 39		08 09		08 41		09 09			09 39	
St Johns	d	23p51	00 07	00 40	05 33	06 03	06 34	07 04	07 11		07 41		08 11		08 43		09 11			09 41	
Lewisham	d	23p54	00 10	00 43	05 36	06 06	06 38	07 08	07 16		07 44		08 17		08 46		09 14			09 44	
Ladywell	d	23p57	00 13	00s46	05 39	06 09	06 41	07 11	07 19	07 34	07 47	08 04	08 20	08 34	08 49	09 04	09 17	09 22	09 34	09 47	10 04
Catford Bridge	d	23p59	00 15	00s49	05 41	06 11	06 43	07 13	07 21	07 36	07 49	08 06	08 22	08 36	08 51	09 06	09 19	09 24	09 36	09 49	10 06
Lower Sydenham	d	00 02	00 18	00s52	05 44	06 14	06 46	07 16	07 24	07 39	07 52	08 09	08 25	08 39	08 54	09 09	09 22	09 27	09 39	09 52	10 09
New Beckenham	d	00 04	00 20	00s55	05 46	06 16	06 48	07 18	07 26	07 41	07 54	08 11	08 27	08 41	08 56	09 11	09 24	09a29	09 41	09 54	10 11
Clock House	d	00 06	00 23	00s58	05 48	06 18	06 50	07 20	07 29	07 43	07 57	08 13	08 29	08 43	08 58	09 13	09 27		09 43	09 57	10 13
Elmers End	d	00 09	00 25	01s01	05 51	06 21	06 53	07 23	07 31	07 46	07 59	08 16	08 32	08 46	09 01	09 16	09 29		09 46	09 59	10 16
Eden Park	d	00 12	00 29	01s05	05 54	06 24	06 56	07 26	07 35	07 49	08 03	08 19	08 35	08 49	09 04	09 19	09 33		09 49	10 03	10 19
West Wickham	d	00 15	00 31	01s08	05 57	06 27	06 59	07 29	07 37	07 52	08 05	08 22	08 38	08 52	09 07	09 22	09 35		09 52	10 05	10 22
Hayes (Kent)	a	00 18	00 34	01 12	06 00	06 30	07 02	07 32	07 40	07 56	08 08	08 25	08 41	08 55	09 10	09 25	09 38		09 55	10 08	10 25

Station		SE		SE	SE	SE	SE	SE	SE	SE	SE	SE	SE	SE	SE	SE	SE	SE	SE	SE	SE	SE
London Charing Cross	d		and at the same minutes past each hour until		15 17		15 47		16 20		16 39		16 59		17 21		17 43		18 05		18 27	
London Waterloo (East)	d				15 20		15 50		16 23		16 42		17 02		17 24		17 46		18 08		18 30	
London Cannon Street	d	10 00		15 00		15 30		16 00		16 30		16 51		17 12		17 34		17 56		18 18		18 40
London Bridge	d	10 04		15 04	15 25	15 34	15 55	16 04	16 29	16 34	16 47	16 55	17 07	17 16	17 29	17 39	17 52	18 00	18 13	18 23	18 35	18 44
New Cross	d	10 09		15 09		15 39		16 10		16 40		17 01		17 22		17 45		18 06		18 28		18 50
St Johns	d	10 11		15 11		15 41		16 12		16 42		17 03		17 24		17 47		18 08		18 30		18 52
Lewisham	d	10 14		15 14		15 44		16 15		16 45		17 06		17 27		17 50		18 11		18 33		18 55
Ladywell	d	10 17		15 17	15 34	15 47	16 04	16 18	16 38	16 48	16 57	17 09	17 17	17 30	17 40	17 53	18 01	18 14	18 23	18 36	18 45	18 58
Catford Bridge	d	10 19		15 19	15 36	15 49	16 06	16 20	16 40	16 50	16 59	17 11	17 19	17 32	17 42	17 55	18 03	18 16	18 25	18 38	18 47	19 00
Lower Sydenham	d	10 22		15 22	15 39	15 52	16 09	16 23	16 43	16 53	17 02	17 14	17 22	17 35	17 45	17 58	18 06	18 19	18 28	18 41	18 50	19 03
New Beckenham	d	10 24		15 24	15 41	15 54	16 11	16 25	16 45	16 55	17 04	17 16	17 24	17 37	17 47	18 00	18 08	18 21	18 30	18 43	18 52	19 05
Clock House	d	10 27		15 27	15 43	15 57	16 13	16 27	16 48	16 57	17 07	17 18	17 27	17 39	17 49	18 02	18 11	18 23	18 33	18 46	18 55	19 07
Elmers End	d	10 29		15 29	15 46	15 59	16 16	16 30	16 51	17 00	17 10	17 21	17 30	17 42	17 52	18 05	18 14	18 26	18 36	18 49	18 58	19 10
Eden Park	d	10 33		15 33	15 49	16 03	16 19	16 34	16 54	17 04	17 13	17 25	17 33	17 46	17 56	18 09	18 17	18 30	18 39	18 52	19 01	19 14
West Wickham	d	10 35		15 35	15 52	16 05	16 22	16 36	16 57	17 06	17 16	17 27	17 36	17 48	17 58	18 11	18 20	18 32	18 42	18 55	19 04	19 16
Hayes (Kent)	a	10 38		15 38	15 55	16 08	16 25	16 42	17 02	17 12	17 21	17 32	17 42	17 54	18 03	18 16	18 26	18 38	18 47	19 00	19 10	19 22

A 3 September

B not 3 September

London - Hayes (Kent) via Catford Bridge

Mondays to Fridays

29 August to 7 September

Network Diagram - see first Page of Table 200

Station		SE	SE	SE	SE	SE	SE	SE	SE		SE	SE
London Charing Cross	d	18 52		19 17		19 47		20 17	20 47	and every 30 minutes until	23 17	23 52
London Waterloo (East)	d	18 55		19 20		19 50		20 20	20 50		23 20	23 55
London Cannon Street	d		19 00		19 30		20 00					
London Bridge	d	19 00	19 04	19 25	19 34	19 55	20 04	20 25	20 55		23 25	23 59
New Cross	d		19 09		19 39		20 09	20 32	21 00		23 30	00 05
St Johns	d		19 11		19 41		20 11	20 34	21 02		23 32	00 07
Lewisham	d		19 14		19 44		20 14	20 37	21 05		23 35	00 10
Ladywell	d	19 09	19 17	19 34	19 47	20 04	20 17	20 40	21 08		23 38	00 13
Catford Bridge	d	19 11	19 19	19 36	19 49	20 06	20 19	20 42	21 10		23 40	00 15
Lower Sydenham	d	19 14	19 22	19 39	19 52	20 09	20 22	20 45	21 13		23 43	00 18
New Beckenham	d	19 16	19 24	19 41	19 54	20 11	20 24	20 47	21 15		23 45	00 20
Clock House	d	19 19	19 27	19 43	19 57	20 13	20 27	20 50	21 18		23 48	00 23
Elmers End	d	19 22	19 29	19 46	19 59	20 16	20 29	20 52	21 20		23 50	00 25
Eden Park	d	19 25	19 33	19 49	20 03	20 19	20 33	20 56	21 24		23 54	00 29
West Wickham	d	19 28	19 35	19 52	20 05	20 22	20 35	20 58	21 26		23 56	00 31
Hayes (Kent)	a	19 33	19 39	19 55	20 09	20 25	20 39	21 01	21 29		23 59	00 34

Saturdays

until 21 July, 18 Aug and from 15 Sep

Station		SE	SE		SE	SE	SE	SE	SE	SE	SE		SE	SE	SE		SE	SE
London Charing Cross	d	23p52	05 47	and every 30 minutes until	07 17	07 47		08 17		08 47		and at the same minutes past each hour until		19 17	19 47	and every 30 minutes until	23 17	23 52
London Waterloo (East)	d	23p55	05 50		07 20	07 50		08 20		08 50				19 20	19 50		23 20	23 55
London Cannon Street	d						08 00		08 30		09 00		19 00					
London Bridge	d	23p59	05 55		07 25	07 55	08 04	08 25	08 34	08 55	09 04		19 04	19 25	19 55		23 25	23 59
New Cross	d	00 05	06 00		07 30		08 09		08 39		09 09		19 09		20 00		23 30	00 05
St Johns	d	00 07	06 02		07 32		08 11		08 41		09 11		19 11		20 02		23 32	00 07
Lewisham	d	00 10	06 05		07 35		08 14		08 44		09 14		19 14	19 37	20 05		23 35	00 10
Ladywell	d	00 13	06 08		07 38	08 04	08 17	08 34	08 47	09 04	09 17		19 17	19 40	20 08		23 38	00 13
Catford Bridge	d	00 15	06 10		07 40	08 06	08 19	08 36	08 49	09 06	09 19		19 19	19 42	20 10		23 40	00 15
Lower Sydenham	d	00 18	06 13		07 43	08 09	08 22	08 39	08 52	09 09	09 22		19 22	19 45	20 13		23 43	00 18
New Beckenham	d	00 20	06 15		07 45	08 11	08 24	08 41	08 54	09 11	09 24		19 24	19 47	20 15		23 45	00 20
Clock House	d	00 23	06 18		07 48	08 13	08 27	08 43	08 57	09 13	09 27		19 27	19 50	20 18		23 48	00 23
Elmers End	d	00 25	06 20		07 50	08 16	08 29	08 46	08 59	09 16	09 29		19 29	19 52	20 20		23 50	00 25
Eden Park	d	00 29	06 24		07 54	08 19	08 33	08 49	09 03	09 19	09 33		19 33	19 56	20 24		23 54	00 29
West Wickham	d	00 31	06 26		07 56	08 22	08 35	08 52	09 05	09 22	09 35		19 35	19 58	20 26		23 56	00 31
Hayes (Kent)	a	00 34	06 29		07 59	08 25	08 41	08 55	09 08	09 25	09 38		19 38	20 01	20 29		23 59	00 34

Saturdays

28 July to 11 August

Station		SE A	SE B	SE A	SE	SE		SE	SE	SE	SE	SE	SE	SE		SE	SE	SE		SE
London Charing Cross	d	23p17	23p52	23p52		05 47	and every 30 minutes until	07 17	07 47		08 17		08 47		and at the same minutes past each hour until		19 17	19 47	and every 30 minutes until	23 17
London Waterloo (East)	d	23p20	23p55	23p55		05 50		07 20	07 50		08 20		08 50				19 20	19 50		23 20
London Cannon Street	d	⌇	⌇	⌇	00 30					08 00		08 30		09 00		19 00				
London Bridge	d	23p25	23p59	23p59	00 34	05 55		07 25	07 55	08 04	08 25	08 34	08 55	09 04		19 04	19 25	19 55		23 25
New Cross	d	23p30	00 05	00 05	00 39	06 00		07 30		08 09		08 39		09 09		19 09		20 00		23 30
St Johns	d	23p32	00 07	00 07	00 41	06 02		07 32		08 11		08 41		09 11		19 11		20 02		23 32
Lewisham	d	23p35	00 10	00 10	00 44	06 05		07 35		08 14		08 44		09 14		19 14	19 37	20 05		23 35
Ladywell	d	23p38	00 13	00 13	00 47	06 08		07 38	08 04	08 17	08 34	08 47	09 04	09 17		19 17	19 40	20 08		23 38
Catford Bridge	d	23p40	00 15	00 15	00 49	06 10		07 40	08 06	08 19	08 36	08 49	09 06	09 19		19 19	19 42	20 10		23 40
Lower Sydenham	d	23p43	00 18	00 18	00 52	06 13		07 43	08 09	08 22	08 39	08 52	09 09	09 22		19 22	19 45	20 13		23 43
New Beckenham	d	23p45	00 20	00 20	00 54	06 15		07 45	08 11	08 24	08 41	08 54	09 11	09 24		19 24	19 47	20 15		23 45
Clock House	d	23p48	00 23	00 23	00 57	06 18		07 48	08 13	08 27	08 43	08 57	09 13	09 27		19 27	19 50	20 18		23 48
Elmers End	d	23p50	00 25	00 25	00 59	06 20		07 50	08 16	08 29	08 46	08 59	09 16	09 29		19 29	19 52	20 20		23 50
Eden Park	d	23p54	00 29	00 29	01 03	06 24		07 54	08 19	08 33	08 49	09 03	09 19	09 33		19 33	19 56	20 24		23 54
West Wickham	d	23p56	00 31	00 31	01 05	06 26		07 56	08 22	08 35	08 52	09 05	09 22	09 35		19 35	19 58	20 26		23 56
Hayes (Kent)	a	00 02	00 34	00 37	01 11	06 32		08 02	08 25	08 44	08 55	09 11	09 25	09 41		19 41	20 04	20 32		00 02

Station		SE
London Charing Cross	d	23 52
London Waterloo (East)	d	23 55
London Cannon Street	d	
London Bridge	d	23 59
New Cross	d	00 05
St Johns	d	00 07
Lewisham	d	00 10
Ladywell	d	00 13
Catford Bridge	d	00 15
Lower Sydenham	d	00 18
New Beckenham	d	00 20
Clock House	d	00 23
Elmers End	d	00 25
Eden Park	d	00 29
West Wickham	d	00 31
Hayes (Kent)	a	00 37

A not 28 July

B not from 4 August until 11 August

Table 203

London - Hayes (Kent) via Catford Bridge

Saturdays

25 August to 8 September

Network Diagram - see first Page of Table 200

		SE	SE A	SE		SE	SE	SE	SE	SE	SE	SE		SE	SE	SE		SE	SE
London Charing Cross	d	23p52		05 47	and every 30 minutes until	07 17	07 47		08 17		08 47		and at the same minutes past each hour until		19 17	19 47	and every 30 minutes until	23 17	23 52
London Waterloo (East)	d	23p55		05 50		07 20	07 50		08 20		08 50				19 20	19 50		23 20	23 55
London Cannon Street	d		00 28					08 00		08 30		09 00		19 00					
London Bridge	d	23p59	00 32	05 55		07 25	07 55	08 04	08 25	08 34	08 55	09 04		19 04	19 25	19 55		23 25	23 59
New Cross	d	00 05	00 38	06 00		07 30		08 09		08 39		09 09		19 09		20 00		23 30	00 05
St Johns	d	00 07	00 40	06 02		07 32		08 11		08 41		09 11		19 11		20 02		23 32	00 07
Lewisham	d	00 10	00 43	06 05		07 35		08 14		08 44		09 14		19 14	19 37	20 05		23 35	00 10
Ladywell	d	00 13	00s46	06 08		07 38	08 04	08 17	08 34	08 47	09 04	09 17		19 17	19 40	20 08		23 38	00 13
Catford Bridge	d	00 15	00s49	06 10		07 40	08 06	08 19	08 36	08 49	09 06	09 19		19 19	19 42	20 10		23 40	00 15
Lower Sydenham	d	00 18	00s52	06 13		07 43	08 09	08 22	08 39	08 52	09 09	09 22		19 22	19 45	20 13		23 43	00 18
New Beckenham	d	00 20	00s55	06 15		07 45	08 11	08 24	08 41	08 54	09 11	09 24		19 24	19 47	20 15		23 45	00 20
Clock House	d	00 23	00s58	06 18		07 48	08 13	08 27	08 43	08 57	09 13	09 27		19 27	19 50	20 18		23 48	00 23
Elmers End	d	00 25	01s01	06 20		07 50	08 16	08 29	08 46	08 59	09 16	09 29		19 29	19 52	20 20		23 50	00 25
Eden Park	d	00 29	01s05	06 24		07 54	08 19	08 33	08 49	09 03	09 19	09 33		19 33	19 56	20 24		23 54	00 29
West Wickham	d	00 31	01s08	06 26		07 56	08 22	08 35	08 52	09 05	09 22	09 35		19 35	19 58	20 26		23 56	00 31
Hayes (Kent)	a	00 34	01 12	06 29		07 59	08 25	08 41	08 55	09 08	09 25	09 38		19 38	20 01	20 29		23 59	00 34

Sundays

until 22 July, 19 Aug and from 16 Sep

		SE	SE		SE	SE
London Charing Cross	d	23p52	07 35	and every 30 minutes until	23 05	23 35
London Waterloo (East)	d	23p55	07 38		23 08	23 38
London Cannon Street	d					
London Bridge	d	23p59	07 43		23 13	23 43
New Cross	d	00 05	07 49		23 19	23 49
St Johns	d	00 07	07 51		23 21	23 51
Lewisham	d	00 10	07 54		23 24	23 54
Ladywell	d	00 13	07 57		23 27	23 57
Catford Bridge	d	00 15	07 59		23 29	23 59
Lower Sydenham	d	00 18	08 02		23 32	00 02
New Beckenham	d	00 20	08 04		23 34	00 04
Clock House	d	00 23	08 06		23 36	00 06
Elmers End	d	00 25	08 09		23 39	00 09
Eden Park	d	00 29	08 12		23 42	00 12
West Wickham	d	00 31	08 15		23 45	00 15
Hayes (Kent)	a	00 34	08 18		23 48	00 18

Sundays

29 July to 12 August

		SE	SE	SE	SE	SE		SE	SE		SE	SE
London Charing Cross	d	23p17	23p52				and every 30 minutes until		19 17	and every 30 minutes until	23 17	23 52
London Waterloo (East)	d	23p20	23p55						19 20		23 20	23 55
London Cannon Street	d			00 30	08 00	08 30		19 00				
London Bridge	d	23p25	23p59	00 34	08 04	08 34		19 04	19 25		23 25	23 59
New Cross	d	23p30	00 05	00 39	08 09	08 39		19 09	19 30		23 30	00 05
St Johns	d	23p32	00 07	00 41	08 11	08 41		19 11	19 32		23 32	00 07
Lewisham	d	23p35	00 10	00 44	08 14	08 44		19 14	19 35		23 35	00 10
Ladywell	d	23p38	00 13	00 47	08 17	08 47		19 17	19 38		23 38	00 13
Catford Bridge	d	23p40	00 15	00 49	08 19	08 49		19 19	19 40		23 40	00 15
Lower Sydenham	d	23p43	00 18	00 52	08 22	08 52		19 22	19 43		23 43	00 18
New Beckenham	d	23p45	00 20	00 54	08 24	08 54		19 24	19 45		23 45	00 20
Clock House	d	23p48	00 23	00 57	08 27	08 57		19 27	19 48		23 48	00 23
Elmers End	d	23p50	00 25	00 59	08 29	08 59		19 29	19 50		23 50	00 25
Eden Park	d	23p54	00 29	01 03	08 33	09 03		19 33	19 54		23 54	00 29
West Wickham	d	23p56	00 31	01 05	08 35	09 05		19 35	19 56		23 56	00 31
Hayes (Kent)	a	00 02	00 37	01 11	08 44	09 11		19 41	20 02		00 02	00 37

Sundays

26 August to 9 September

		SE	SE B	SE		SE	SE
London Charing Cross	d	23p52		07 35	and every 30 minutes until	23 05	23 35
London Waterloo (East)	d	23p55		07 38		23 08	23 38
London Cannon Street	d		00 28				
London Bridge	d	23p59	00 32	07 43		23 13	23 43
New Cross	d	00 05	00 38	07 49		23 19	23 49
St Johns	d	00 07	00 40	07 51		23 21	23 51
Lewisham	d	00 10	00 43	07 54		23 24	23 54
Ladywell	d	00 13	00s46	07 57		23 27	23 57
Catford Bridge	d	00 15	00s49	07 59		23 29	23 59
Lower Sydenham	d	00 18	00s52	08 02		23 32	00 02
New Beckenham	d	00 20	00s55	08 04		23 34	00 04
Clock House	d	00 23	00s58	08 06		23 36	00 06
Elmers End	d	00 25	01s01	08 09		23 39	00 09
Eden Park	d	00 29	01s05	08 12		23 42	00 12
West Wickham	d	00 31	01s08	08 15		23 45	00 15
Hayes (Kent)	a	00 34	01 12	08 18		23 48	00 18

A not 25 August

B not 26 August

Table 203

Hayes (Kent) - London via Catford Bridge

Mondays to Fridays

until 27 July, 13 Aug to 28 Aug and then from 10 Sep

Network Diagram - see first Page of Table 200

Miles	Miles			SE	SE	SE	SE	SE	SE	SE	SE	SE
0	—	Hayes (Kent)	d	05 15	05 45	06 15	06 23	06 45	06 55	07 13	07 23	07 33
1¼	—	West Wickham	d	05 18	05 48	06 18	06 26	06 48	06 58	07 16	07 26	07 36
2	—	Eden Park	d	05 20	05 50	06 20	06 28	06 50	07 00	07 18	07 28	07 38
3½	—	Elmers End	d	05 24	05 54	06 24	06 32	06 54	07 04	07 22	07 32	07 42
4¼	—	Clock House	d	05 26	05 56	06 26	06 34	06 56	07 06	07 24	07 34	07 44
5	—	New Beckenham	d	05 28	05 58	06 28	06 37	06 59	07 09	07 27	07 37	07 47
5½	—	Lower Sydenham	d	05 30	06 00	06 30	06 39	07 01	07 11	07 29	07 39	07 49
7	—	Catford Bridge	d	05 33	06 03	06 33	06 42	07 04	07 14	07 32	07 42	07 52
7¾	—	Ladywell	d	05 35	06 05	06 35	06 44	07 06	07 16	07 34	07 44	07 54
8½	—	Lewisham	d	05 39	06 09	06 39	06 48		07 20		07 48	
9	—	St Johns	a	05 41	06 11	06 41	06 50				07 50	
9¾	—	New Cross	a	05 43	06 13	06 43	06 52		07 23		07 52	
12¾	0	London Bridge	a	05 48	06 18	06 48	06 58	07 17	07 28	07 44	08 01	
—	0¾	London Cannon Street	a				07 05		07 35		08 08	
13¾	—	London Waterloo (East)	a	05 53	06 24	06 53		07 22		07 50		08 08
14½	—	London Charing Cross	a	05 56	06 27	06 57		07 28		07 56		08 14

		SE	SE	SE	SE	SE	SE	SE	SE	SE	SE	SE
Hayes (Kent)	d	07 43	07 53	08 03	08 13	08 23	08 33	08 50	09 08	09 20	09 38	09 50
West Wickham	d	07 46	07 56	08 06	08 16	08 26	08 36	08 53	09 11	09 23	09 41	09 53
Eden Park	d	07 48	07 58	08 08	08 18	08 28	08 38	08 55	09 13	09 25	09 43	09 55
Elmers End	d	07 52	08 02	08 12	08 22	08 32	08 42	08 59	09 17	09 29	09 47	09 59
Clock House	d	07 54	08 04	08 14	08 24	08 34	08 44	09 01	09 19	09 31	09 49	10 01
New Beckenham	d	07 57	08 07	08 17	08 27	08 37	08 47	09 04	09 21	09 34	09 51	10 03
Lower Sydenham	d	07 59	08 09	08 19	08 29	08 39	08 49	09 06	09 23	09 36	09 53	10 05
Catford Bridge	d	08 02	08 12	08 22	08 32	08 42	08 52	09 09	09 26	09 39	09 56	10 08
Ladywell	d	08 04	08 14	08 24	08 34	08 44	08 54	09 11	09 28	09 41	09 58	10 10
Lewisham	d	08 08		08 28		08 48		09 15		09 45		10 14
St Johns	a	08 12		08 30		08 50		09 17		09 47		10 16
New Cross	a	08 14		08 32		08 52		09 19		09 49		10 18
London Bridge	a	08 20		08 41		08 57		09 25	09 37	09 54	10 07	10 24
London Cannon Street	a	08 28		08 48		09 04		09 32		10 00		10 28
London Waterloo (East)	a		08 28		08 48		09 07		09 42		10 12	
London Charing Cross	a		08 34		08 54		09 13		09 48		10 16	

		SE	SE		SE	SE	SE	SE	SE	SE	SE	SE	SE	SE	SE	SE	SE	SE	SE	SE	SE
Hayes (Kent)	d	10 08	10 20	and at the same minutes past each hour until	15 20	15 38	15 50		16 08	16 20	16 38	16 50	17 08	17 20	17 37	17 47	18 08	18 21	18 38	18 50	19 05
West Wickham	d	10 11	10 23		15 23	15 41	15 53		16 11	16 23	16 41	16 53	17 11	17 23	17 40	17 50	18 11	18 24	18 41	18 53	19 08
Eden Park	d	10 13	10 25		15 25	15 43	15 55		16 13	16 25	16 43	16 55	17 13	17 25	17 42	17 52	18 13	18 26	18 43	18 55	19 10
Elmers End	d	10 17	10 29		15 29	15 47	15 59		16 17	16 29	16 47	16 59	17 17	17 29	17 46	17 56	18 17	18 30	18 47	18 59	19 17
Clock House	d	10 19	10 31		15 31	15 49	16 01		16 19	16 31	16 49	17 01	17 19	17 31	17 48	17 58	18 19	18 32	18 49	19 01	19 19
New Beckenham	d	10 21	10 33		15 33	15 51	16 03	16 15	16 21	16 33	16 51	17 03	17 21	17 33	17 50	18 00	18 21	18 34	18 51	19 03	19 21
Lower Sydenham	d	10 23	10 35		15 35	15 53	16 05	16 17	16 23	16 35	16 53	17 05	17 23	17 35	17 52	18 02	18 23	18 36	18 53	19 05	19 23
Catford Bridge	d	10 26	10 38		15 38	15 56	16 08	16 20	16 26	16 38	16 56	17 08	17 26	17 38	17 55	18 05	18 26	18 39	18 56	19 08	19 26
Ladywell	d	10 28	10 40		15 40	15 58	16 10	16 22	16 28	16 40	16 58	17 10	17 28	17 40	17 57	18 07	18 28	18 41	18 58	19 10	19 28
Lewisham	d		10 44		15 44		16 14			16 44		17 14		17 44		18 14		18 45		19 14	
St Johns	a		10 46		15 46		16 16			16 46		17 16		17 46		18 16		18 47		19 16	
New Cross	a		10 48		15 48		16 18			16 48		17 18		17 48		18 18		18 49		19 18	
London Bridge	a	10 37	10 54		15 54	16 09	16 24	16 32	16 37	16 54	17 08	17 24	17 38	17 55	18 07	18 24	18 38	18 55	19 07	19 24	19 37
London Cannon Street	a		10 58		15 58		16 28			16 58		17 29		17 59		18 29		18 59		19 28	
London Waterloo (East)	a	10 42				16 13		16 37	16 42		17 13		17 42		18 12		18 44		19 12		19 42
London Charing Cross	a	10 46				16 18		16 42	16 46		17 18		17 46		18 16		18 48		19 16		19 46

		SE		SE
Hayes (Kent)	d	19 14	and every 30 minutes until	23 14
West Wickham	d	19 17		23 17
Eden Park	d	19 19		23 19
Elmers End	d	19 23		23 23
Clock House	d	19 25		23 25
New Beckenham	d	19 27		23 27
Lower Sydenham	d	19 29		23 29
Catford Bridge	d	19 32		23 32
Ladywell	d	19 34		23 34
Lewisham	d	19 38		23 38
St Johns	a	19 40		23 40
New Cross	a	19 42		23 42
London Bridge	a	19 49		23 49
London Cannon Street	a			
London Waterloo (East)	a	19 53		23 53
London Charing Cross	a	19 57		23 57

Mondays to Fridays

30 July to 10 August

		SE	SE	SE	SE	SE	SE	SE	SE	SE
Hayes (Kent)	d	05 15	05 45	06 15	06 23	06 45	06 55	07 13	07 23	07 33
West Wickham	d	05 18	05 48	06 18	06 26	06 48	06 58	07 16	07 26	07 36
Eden Park	d	05 20	05 50	06 20	06 28	06 50	07 00	07 18	07 28	07 38
Elmers End	d	05 24	05 54	06 24	06 32	06 54	07 04	07 22	07 32	07 42
Clock House	d	05 26	05 56	06 26	06 34	06 56	07 06	07 24	07 34	07 44
New Beckenham	d	05 28	05 58	06 28	06 37	06 59	07 09	07 27	07 37	07 47
Lower Sydenham	d	05 30	06 00	06 30	06 39	07 01	07 11	07 29	07 39	07 49
Catford Bridge	d	05 33	06 03	06 33	06 42	07 04	07 14	07 32	07 42	07 52
Ladywell	d	05 35	06 05	06 35	06 44	07 06	07 16	07 34	07 44	07 54
Lewisham	d	05 39	06 09	06 39	06 48		07 20		07 48	
St Johns	a	05 41	06 11	06 41	06 50				07 50	
New Cross	a	05 43	06 13	06 43	06 52		07 23		07 52	
London Bridge	a	05 48	06 18	06 48	06 58	07 17	07 28	07 44	08 01	
London Cannon Street	a				07 06		07 35		08 08	
London Waterloo (East)	a	05 53	06 24	06 53		07 22		07 50		08 08
London Charing Cross	a	05 59	06 30	07 00		07 28		07 56		08 14

		SE	SE	SE	SE	SE	SE	SE	SE	SE	SE	SE	SE	SE
Hayes (Kent)	d	07 43	07 53	08 03	08 13	08 23	08 33	08 50	09 08	09 20	09 38	09 50	10 08	10 20
West Wickham	d	07 46	07 56	08 06	08 16	08 26	08 36	08 53	09 11	09 23	09 41	09 53	10 11	10 23
Eden Park	d	07 48	07 58	08 08	08 18	08 28	08 38	08 55	09 13	09 25	09 43	09 55	10 13	10 25
Elmers End	d	07 52	08 02	08 12	08 22	08 32	08 42	08 59	09 17	09 29	09 47	09 59	10 17	10 29
Clock House	d	07 54	08 04	08 14	08 24	08 34	08 44	09 01	09 19	09 31	09 49	10 01	10 19	10 31
New Beckenham	d	07 57	08 07	08 17	08 27	08 37	08 47	09 04	09 21	09 34	09 51	10 03	10 21	10 33
Lower Sydenham	d	07 59	08 09	08 19	08 29	08 39	08 49	09 06	09 23	09 36	09 53	10 05	10 23	10 35
Catford Bridge	d	08 02	08 12	08 22	08 32	08 42	08 52	09 09	09 26	09 39	09 56	10 08	10 26	10 38
Ladywell	d	08 04	08 14	08 24	08 34	08 44	08 54	09 11	09 28	09 41	09 58	10 10	10 28	10 40
Lewisham	d	08 08		08 28		08 48		09 15		09 45		10 14		10 44
St Johns	a	08 12		08 30		08 50		09 17		09 47		10 16		10 46
New Cross	a	08 14		08 32		08 52		09 19		09 49		10 18		10 48
London Bridge	a	08 20		08 41		08 57		09 25	09 37	09 54	10 07	10 23	10 37	10 54
London Cannon Street	a	08 28		08 48		09 04		09 32		10 03		10 30		11 01
London Waterloo (East)	a		08 28		08 48		09 07		09 42		10 12		10 42	
London Charing Cross	a		08 34		08 54		09 13		09 48		10 16		10 46	

		SE	SE	SE	SE	SE	SE	SE	SE	SE	SE	SE	SE	SE	SE
Hayes (Kent)	d	10 38	10 50	11 08	11 20	11 38	11 50	12 08	12 20	12 38	12 50	13 08	13 20	13 38	13 50
West Wickham	d	10 41	10 53	11 11	11 23	11 41	11 53	12 11	12 23	12 41	12 53	13 11	13 23	13 41	13 53
Eden Park	d	10 43	10 55	11 13	11 25	11 43	11 55	12 13	12 25	12 43	12 55	13 13	13 25	13 43	13 55
Elmers End	d	10 47	10 59	11 17	11 29	11 47	11 59	12 17	12 29	12 47	12 59	13 17	13 29	13 47	13 59
Clock House	d	10 49	11 01	11 19	11 31	11 49	12 01	12 19	12 31	12 49	13 01	13 19	13 31	13 49	14 01
New Beckenham	d	10 51	11 03	11 21	11 33	11 51	12 03	12 21	12 33	12 51	13 03	13 21	13 33	13 51	14 03
Lower Sydenham	d	10 53	11 05	11 23	11 35	11 53	12 05	12 23	12 35	12 53	13 05	13 23	13 35	13 53	14 05
Catford Bridge	d	10 56	11 08	11 26	11 38	11 56	12 08	12 26	12 38	12 56	13 08	13 26	13 38	13 56	14 08
Ladywell	d	10 58	11 10	11 28	11 40	11 58	12 10	12 28	12 40	12 58	13 10	13 28	13 40	13 58	14 10
Lewisham	d		11 14		11 44		12 14		12 44		13 14		13 44		14 14
St Johns	a		11 16		11 46		12 16		12 46		13 16		13 46		14 16
New Cross	a		11 18		11 48		12 18		12 48		13 18		13 48		14 18
London Bridge	a	11 07	11 24	11 37	11 54	12 07	12 24	12 37	12 54	13 07	13 24	13 37	13 54	14 07	14 24
London Cannon Street	a		11 31		12 01		12 31		13 01		13 31		14 01		14 31
London Waterloo (East)	a	11 12		11 42		12 12		12 42		13 12		13 42		14 12	
London Charing Cross	a	11 16		11 46		12 16		12 49		13 16		13 46		14 16	

		SE	SE	SE	SE	SE	SE	SE	SE
Hayes (Kent)	d	14 08	14 20	14 38	14 50	15 08	15 20	15 38	15 50
West Wickham	d	14 11	14 23	14 41	14 53	15 11	15 23	15 41	15 53
Eden Park	d	14 13	14 25	14 43	14 55	15 13	15 25	15 43	15 55
Elmers End	d	14 17	14 29	14 47	14 59	15 17	15 29	15 47	15 59
Clock House	d	14 19	14 31	14 49	15 01	15 19	15 31	15 49	16 01
New Beckenham	d	14 21	14 33	14 51	15 03	15 21	15 33	15 51	16 03
Lower Sydenham	d	14 23	14 35	14 53	15 05	15 23	15 35	15 53	16 05
Catford Bridge	d	14 26	14 38	14 56	15 08	15 26	15 38	15 56	16 08
Ladywell	d	14 28	14 40	14 58	15 10	15 28	15 40	15 58	16 10
Lewisham	d		14 44		15 14		15 44		16 14
St Johns	a		14 46		15 16		15 46		16 16
New Cross	a		14 48		15 18		15 48		16 18
London Bridge	a	14 37	14 54	15 07	15 24	15 37	15 54	16 09	16 24
London Cannon Street	a		15 01		15 31		16 01		16 31
London Waterloo (East)	a	14 42		15 12		15 42		16 13	
London Charing Cross	a	14 46		15 16		15 46		16 18	

Hayes (Kent) - London via Catford Bridge

Mondays to Fridays

30 July to 10 August

Network Diagram - see first Page of Table 200

		SE		SE	SE	SE	SE	SE	SE	SE	SE	SE		SE	SE	SE	SE	SE		SE	SE
Hayes (Kent)	d			16 08	16 20	16 38	16 50	17 08	17 20	17 37	17 47	18 08		18 21	18 38	18 50	19 05	19 14		22 44	23 14
West Wickham	d			16 11	16 23	16 41	16 53	17 11	17 23	17 40	17 50	18 11		18 24	18 41	18 53	19 08	19 17		22 47	23 17
Eden Park	d			16 13	16 25	16 43	16 55	17 13	17 25	17 42	17 52	18 13		18 26	18 43	18 55	19 10	19 19		22 49	23 19
Elmers End	d			16 17	16 29	16 47	16 59	17 17	17 29	17 46	17 56	18 17		18 30	18 47	18 59	19 17	19 23		22 53	23 23
Clock House	d			16 19	16 31	16 49	17 01	17 19	17 31	17 48	17 58	18 19		18 32	18 49	19 01	19 19	19 25		22 55	23 25
New Beckenham	d	16 14		16 21	16 33	16 51	17 03	17 21	17 33	17 50	18 00	18 21		18 34	18 51	19 03	19 21	19 27	and every 30 minutes until	22 57	23 27
Lower Sydenham	d	16 16		16 23	16 35	16 53	17 05	17 23	17 35	17 52	18 02	18 23		18 36	18 53	19 05	19 23	19 29		22 59	23 29
Catford Bridge	d	16 19		16 26	16 38	16 56	17 08	17 26	17 38	17 55	18 05	18 26		18 39	18 56	19 08	19 26	19 32		23 02	23 32
Ladywell	d	16 21		16 28	16 40	16 58	17 10	17 28	17 40	17 57	18 07	18 28		18 41	18 58	19 10	19 28	19 34		23 04	23 34
Lewisham	d				16 44		17 14		17 44		18 14			18 45		19 14		19 38		23 08	23 38
St Johns	a				16 46		17 16		17 46		18 16			18 47		19 16		19 40		23 10	23 40
New Cross	a				16 48		17 18		17 48		18 18			18 49		19 18		19 42		23 12	23 42
London Bridge	a	16 32		16 37	16 54	17 08	17 24	17 38	17 55	18 07	18 24	18 38		18 55	19 07	19 24	19 37	19 49		23 19	23 49
London Cannon Street	a				17 01		17 32		18 02		18 32			19 02		19 31					
London Waterloo (East)	a	16 37		16 42		17 13		17 42		18 12		18 44			19 12		19 42	19 53		23 23	23 53
London Charing Cross	a	16 42		16 46		17 18		17 46		18 16		18 48			19 16		19 46	20 00		23 30	23 59

Mondays to Fridays

29 August to 7 September

		SE	SE	SE	SE	SE	SE	SE	SE	SE		SE	SE	SE	SE	SE	SE	SE	SE	SE	SE		SE	SE
Hayes (Kent)	d	05 15	05 45	06 15	06 23	06 45	06 55	07 13	07 23	07 33		07 43	07 53	08 03	08 13	08 23	08 33	08 50	09 08	09 20	09 38		09 50	10 08
West Wickham	d	05 18	05 48	06 18	06 26	06 48	06 58	07 16	07 26	07 36		07 46	07 56	08 06	08 16	08 26	08 36	08 53	09 11	09 23	09 41		09 53	10 11
Eden Park	d	05 20	05 50	06 20	06 28	06 50	07 00	07 18	07 28	07 38		07 48	07 58	08 08	08 18	08 28	08 38	08 55	09 13	09 25	09 43		09 55	10 13
Elmers End	d	05 24	05 54	06 24	06 32	06 54	07 04	07 22	07 32	07 42		07 52	08 02	08 12	08 22	08 32	08 42	08 59	09 17	09 29	09 47		09 59	10 17
Clock House	d	05 26	05 56	06 26	06 34	06 56	07 06	07 24	07 34	07 44		07 54	08 04	08 14	08 24	08 34	08 44	09 01	09 19	09 31	09 49		10 01	10 19
New Beckenham	d	05 28	05 58	06 28	06 37	06 59	07 09	07 27	07 37	07 47		07 57	08 07	08 17	08 27	08 37	08 47	09 04	09 21	09 34	09 51		10 03	10 21
Lower Sydenham	d	05 30	06 00	06 30	06 39	07 01	07 11	07 29	07 39	07 49		07 59	08 09	08 19	08 29	08 39	08 49	09 06	09 23	09 36	09 53		10 05	10 23
Catford Bridge	d	05 33	06 03	06 33	06 42	07 04	07 14	07 32	07 42	07 52		08 02	08 12	08 22	08 32	08 42	08 52	09 09	09 26	09 39	09 56		10 08	10 26
Ladywell	d	05 35	06 05	06 35	06 44	07 06	07 16	07 34	07 44	07 54		08 04	08 14	08 24	08 34	08 44	08 54	09 11	09 28	09 41	09 58		10 10	10 28
Lewisham	d	05 39	06 09	06 39	06 48		07 20		07 48			08 08		08 28		08 48		09 15		09 45			10 14	
St Johns	a	05 41	06 11	06 41	06 50				07 50			08 12		08 30		08 50		09 17		09 47			10 16	
New Cross	a	05 43	06 13	06 43	06 52		07 23		07 52			08 14		08 32		08 52		09 19		09 49			10 18	
London Bridge	a	05 48	06 18	06 48	06 58	07 17	07 28	07 44	08 01			08 20		08 41		08 57		09 25	09 37	09 54	10 07		10 24	10 37
London Cannon Street	a				07 05		07 35		08 08			08 28		08 48		09 04		09 32		10 00			10 28	
London Waterloo (East)	a	05 53	06 24	06 53		07 22		07 50		08 08			08 28		08 48		09 07		09 42		10 12			10 42
London Charing Cross	a	05 56	06 27	06 57		07 28		07 56		08 14			08 34		08 54		09 13		09 48		10 16			10 46

		SE		SE	SE	SE	SE		SE	SE	SE	SE	SE	SE	SE	SE	SE		SE	SE	SE	SE
Hayes (Kent)	d	10 20		15 20	15 38	15 50			16 08	16 20	16 38	16 50	17 08	17 20	17 37	17 47	18 08		18 21	18 38	18 50	19 05
West Wickham	d	10 23		15 23	15 41	15 53			16 11	16 23	16 41	16 53	17 11	17 23	17 40	17 50	18 11		18 24	18 41	18 53	19 08
Eden Park	d	10 25		15 25	15 43	15 55			16 13	16 25	16 43	16 55	17 13	17 25	17 42	17 52	18 13		18 26	18 43	18 55	19 10
Elmers End	d	10 29		15 29	15 47	15 59			16 17	16 29	16 47	16 59	17 17	17 29	17 46	17 56	18 17		18 30	18 47	18 59	19 17
Clock House	d	10 31	and at the same minutes past each hour until	15 31	15 49	16 01			16 19	16 31	16 49	17 01	17 19	17 31	17 48	17 58	18 19		18 32	18 49	19 01	19 19
New Beckenham	d	10 33		15 33	15 51	16 03	16 15		16 21	16 33	16 51	17 03	17 21	17 33	17 50	18 00	18 21		18 34	18 51	19 03	19 21
Lower Sydenham	d	10 35		15 35	15 53	16 05	16 17		16 23	16 35	16 53	17 05	17 23	17 35	17 52	18 02	18 23		18 36	18 53	19 05	19 23
Catford Bridge	d	10 38		15 38	15 56	16 08	16 20		16 26	16 38	16 56	17 08	17 26	17 38	17 55	18 05	18 26		18 39	18 56	19 08	19 26
Ladywell	d	10 40		15 40	15 58	16 10	16 22		16 28	16 40	16 58	17 10	17 28	17 40	17 57	18 07	18 28		18 41	18 58	19 10	19 28
Lewisham	d	10 44		15 44		16 14				16 44		17 14		17 44		18 14			18 45		19 14	
St Johns	a	10 46		15 46		16 16				16 46		17 16		17 46		18 16			18 47		19 16	
New Cross	a	10 48		15 48		16 18				16 48		17 18		17 48		18 18			18 49		19 18	
London Bridge	a	10 54		15 54	16 09	16 24	16 32		16 37	16 54	17 08	17 24	17 38	17 55	18 07	18 24	18 38		18 55	19 07	19 24	19 37
London Cannon Street	a	10 58		15 58		16 28				16 58		17 29		17 59		18 29			18 59		19 28	
London Waterloo (East)	a				16 13		16 37		16 42		17 13		17 42		18 12		18 44			19 12		19 42
London Charing Cross	a				16 18		16 42		16 46		17 18		17 46		18 16		18 48			19 16		19 46

		SE		SE
Hayes (Kent)	d	19 14		23 14
West Wickham	d	19 17		23 17
Eden Park	d	19 19		23 19
Elmers End	d	19 23		23 23
Clock House	d	19 25		23 25
New Beckenham	d	19 27	and every 30 minutes until	23 27
Lower Sydenham	d	19 29		23 29
Catford Bridge	d	19 32		23 32
Ladywell	d	19 34		23 34
Lewisham	d	19 38		23 38
St Johns	a	19 40		23 40
New Cross	a	19 42		23 42
London Bridge	a	19 49		23 49
London Cannon Street	a			
London Waterloo (East)	a	19 53		23 53
London Charing Cross	a	19 57		23 57

Hayes (Kent) - London via Catford Bridge

Saturdays

until 21 July, 18 Aug and from 15 Sep

Network Diagram - see first Page of Table 200

		SE	SE		SE	SE	SE	SE	SE		SE		SE	SE	SE		SE		SE	SE
Hayes (Kent)	d	05 15	05 38		07 08	07 36	07 50	08 08	08 20		08 38		18 38	18 50	19 14		22 14		22 44	23 14
West Wickham	d	05 18	05 41		07 11	07 39	07 53	08 11	08 23		08 41		18 41	18 53	19 17		22 17		22 47	23 17
Eden Park	d	05 20	05 43		07 13	07 41	07 55	08 13	08 25		08 43		18 43	18 55	19 19		22 19		22 49	23 19
Elmers End	d	05 24	05 47		07 17	07 45	07 59	08 17	08 29		08 47		18 47	18 59	19 23		22 23		22 53	23 23
Clock House	d	05 26	05 49		07 19	07 47	08 01	08 19	08 31		08 49	and at the same minutes past each hour until	18 49	19 01	19 25		22 25		22 55	23 25
New Beckenham	d	05 28	05 51	and every 30 minutes until	07 21	07 49	08 03	08 21	08 33		08 51		18 51	19 03	19 27	and every 30 minutes until	22 27		22 57	23 27
Lower Sydenham	d	05 30	05 53		07 23	07 51	08 05	08 23	08 35		08 53		18 53	19 05	19 29		22 29		22 59	23 29
Catford Bridge	d	05 33	05 56		07 26	07 54	08 08	08 26	08 38		08 56		18 56	19 08	19 32		22 32		23 02	23 32
Ladywell	d	05 35	05 58		07 28	07 56	08 10	08 28	08 40		08 58		18 58	19 10	19 34		22 34		23 04	23 34
Lewisham	d	05 39	06 02		07 32	07 59	08 14		08 44					19 14	19 38		22 38		23 08	23 38
St Johns	a	05 41	06 04		07 34		08 16		08 46					19 16	19 40		22 40		23 10	23 40
New Cross	a	05 43	06 06		07 36		08 18		08 48					19 18	19 42		22 42		23 12	23 42
London Bridge	a	05 48	06 12		07 42	08 07	08 24	08 37	08 54		09 07		19 07	19 24	19 49		22 49		23 19	23 49
London Cannon Street	a						08 28		08 58											
London Waterloo (East)	a	05 53	06 16		07 46	08 12		08 42			09 12		19 12		19 53		22 53		23 23	23 53
London Charing Cross	a	05 56	06 20		07 50	08 16		08 46			09 16		19 16		19 58		22 58		23 27	23 57

Saturdays

28 July to 11 August

		SE	SE		SE	SE	SE	SE	SE		SE		SE	SE	SE		SE		SE	SE
Hayes (Kent)	d	05 15	05 38		07 08	07 36	07 50	08 08	08 20		08 38		18 38	18 50	19 14		22 14		22 44	23 14
West Wickham	d	05 18	05 41		07 11	07 39	07 53	08 11	08 23		08 41		18 41	18 53	19 17		22 17		22 47	23 17
Eden Park	d	05 20	05 43		07 13	07 41	07 55	08 13	08 25		08 43		18 43	18 55	19 19		22 19		22 49	23 19
Elmers End	d	05 24	05 47		07 17	07 45	07 59	08 17	08 29		08 47		18 47	18 59	19 23		22 23		22 53	23 23
Clock House	d	05 26	05 49		07 19	07 47	08 01	08 19	08 31		08 49	and at the same minutes past each hour until	18 49	19 01	19 25		22 25		22 55	23 25
New Beckenham	d	05 28	05 51	and every 30 minutes until	07 21	07 49	08 03	08 21	08 33		08 51		18 51	19 03	19 27	and every 30 minutes until	22 27		22 57	23 27
Lower Sydenham	d	05 30	05 53		07 23	07 51	08 05	08 23	08 35		08 53		18 53	19 05	19 29		22 29		22 59	23 29
Catford Bridge	d	05 33	05 56		07 26	07 54	08 08	08 26	08 38		08 56		18 56	19 08	19 32		22 32		23 02	23 32
Ladywell	d	05 35	05 58		07 28	07 56	08 10	08 28	08 40		08 58		18 58	19 10	19 34		22 34		23 04	23 34
Lewisham	d	05 39	06 02		07 32	07 59	08 14		08 44					19 14	19 38		22 38		23 08	23 38
St Johns	a	05 41	06 04		07 34		08 16		08 46					19 16	19 40		22 40		23 10	23 40
New Cross	a	05 43	06 06		07 36		08 18		08 48					19 18	19 42		22 42		23 12	23 42
London Bridge	a	05 48	06 12		07 42	08 07	08 24	08 37	08 54		09 07		19 07	19 27	19 49		22 49		23 19	23 49
London Cannon Street	a						08 31		09 01											
London Waterloo (East)	a	05 53	06 16		07 46	08 12		08 42			09 12		19 12		19 53		22 53		23 23	23 53
London Charing Cross	a	05 59	06 23		07 53	08 19		08 46			09 16		19 16		20 01		23 01		23 30	23 59

Saturdays

25 August to 8 September

		SE	SE		SE	SE	SE	SE	SE		SE		SE	SE	SE		SE		SE	SE
Hayes (Kent)	d	05 15	05 38		07 08	07 36	07 50	08 08	08 20		08 38		18 38	18 50	19 14		22 14		22 44	23 14
West Wickham	d	05 18	05 41		07 11	07 39	07 53	08 11	08 23		08 41		18 41	18 53	19 17		22 17		22 47	23 17
Eden Park	d	05 20	05 43		07 13	07 41	07 55	08 13	08 25		08 43		18 43	18 55	19 19		22 19		22 49	23 19
Elmers End	d	05 24	05 47		07 17	07 45	07 59	08 17	08 29		08 47		18 47	18 59	19 23		22 23		22 53	23 23
Clock House	d	05 26	05 49		07 19	07 47	08 01	08 19	08 31		08 49	and at the same minutes past each hour until	18 49	19 01	19 25		22 25		22 55	23 25
New Beckenham	d	05 28	05 51	and every 30 minutes until	07 21	07 49	08 03	08 21	08 33		08 51		18 51	19 03	19 27	and every 30 minutes until	22 27		22 57	23 27
Lower Sydenham	d	05 30	05 53		07 23	07 51	08 05	08 23	08 35		08 53		18 53	19 05	19 29		22 29		22 59	23 29
Catford Bridge	d	05 33	05 56		07 26	07 54	08 08	08 26	08 38		08 56		18 56	19 08	19 32		22 32		23 02	23 32
Ladywell	d	05 35	05 58		07 28	07 56	08 10	08 28	08 40		08 58		18 58	19 10	19 34		22 34		23 04	23 34
Lewisham	d	05 39	06 02		07 32	07 59	08 14		08 44					19 14	19 38		22 38		23 08	23 38
St Johns	a	05 41	06 04		07 34		08 16		08 46					19 16	19 40		22 40		23 10	23 40
New Cross	a	05 43	06 06		07 36		08 18		08 48					19 18	19 42		22 42		23 12	23 42
London Bridge	a	05 48	06 12		07 42	08 07	08 24	08 37	08 54		09 07		19 07	19 24	19 49		22 49		23 19	23 49
London Cannon Street	a						08 28		08 58											
London Waterloo (East)	a	05 53	06 16		07 46	08 12		08 42			09 12		19 12		19 53		22 53		23 23	23 53
London Charing Cross	a	05 56	06 20		07 50	08 16		08 46			09 16		19 16		19 58		22 58		23 27	23 57

Sundays

until 22 July, 19 Aug and from 16 Sep

		SE		SE
Hayes (Kent)	d	07 28		22 58
West Wickham	d	07 31		23 01
Eden Park	d	07 33		23 03
Elmers End	d	07 37		23 07
Clock House	d	07 39		23 09
New Beckenham	d	07 41	and every 30 minutes until	23 11
Lower Sydenham	d	07 43		23 13
Catford Bridge	d	07 46		23 16
Ladywell	d	07 48		23 18
Lewisham	d	07 52		23 22
St Johns	a	07 54		23 24
New Cross	a	07 56		23 26
London Bridge	a	08 03		23 33
London Cannon Street	a			
London Waterloo (East)	a	08 08		23 38
London Charing Cross	a	08 11		23 41

Table 203

Sundays

29 July to 12 August

Hayes (Kent) - London via Catford Bridge

Network Diagram - see first Page of Table 200

			SE	SE	SE	SE	SE		SE	SE	SE		SE		SE	SE
Hayes (Kent)		d	06 08	06 38	07 08	07 36	07 50	and every 30 minutes until	18 20	18 38	19 14	and every 30 minutes until	22 14		22 44	23 14
Wst Wkham		d	06 11	06 41	07 11	07 39	07 53		18 23	18 41	19 17		22 17		22 47	23 17
Ben Park		d	06 13	06 43	07 13	07 41	07 55		18 25	18 43	19 19		22 19		22 49	23 19
Eners Ed ■	⇌	d	06 17	06 47	07 17	07 45	07 59		18 29	18 47	19 23		22 23		22 53	23 23
Clock House		d	06 19	06 49	07 19	07 47	08 01		18 31	18 49	19 25		22 25		22 55	23 25
Nw Beckenham ■		d	06 21	06 51	07 21	07 49	08 03		18 33	18 51	19 27		22 27		22 57	23 27
bwer Sydenham		d	06 23	06 53	07 23	07 51	08 05		18 35	18 53	19 29		22 29		22 59	23 29
Catford Bridge		d	06 26	06 56	07 26	07 54	08 08		18 38	18 56	19 32		22 32		23 02	23 32
ldywell		d	06 28	06 58	07 28	07 56	08 10		18 40	18 58	19 34		22 34		23 04	23 34
Lewisham ■	⇌	d	06 31	07 01	07 32	07 59	08 14		18 44	19 01	19 38		22 38		23 08	23 38
St dhns		a	06 33	07 03	07 34		08 16		18 46	19 03	19 40		22 40		23 10	23 40
Nw Cross ■	⊖	a	06 35	07 05	07 36		08 18		18 48	19 05	19 42		22 42		23 12	23 42
London Bridge ■	⊖	a	06 42	07 11	07 42	08 07	08 24		18 54	19 11	19 49		22 49		23 19	23 48
London Cannon Street ■	⊖	a		07 18			08 31		19 01							
London Waterloo (East) ■	⊖	a	06 46		07 46	08 12				19 15	19 53		22 53		23 23	23 52
London Charing Cross ■	⊖	a	06 53		07 53	08 19				19 22	20 01		23 01		23 30	23 58

Sundays

26 August to 9 September

			SE		SE
Hayes (Kent)		d	07 28	and every 30 minutes until	22 58
Wst Wkham		d	07 31		23 01
Ben Park		d	07 33		23 03
Eners Ed ■	⇌	d	07 37		23 07
Clock House		d	07 39		23 09
Nw Beckenham ■		d	07 41		23 11
bwer Sydenham		d	07 43		23 13
Catford Bridge		d	07 46		23 16
ldywell		d	07 48		23 18
Lewisham ■	⇌	d	07 52		23 22
St dhns		a	07 54		23 24
Nw Cross ■	⊖	a	07 56		23 26
London Bridge ■	⊖	a	08 03		23 33
London Cannon Street ■	⊖	a			
London Waterloo (East) ■	⊖	a	08 08		23 38
London Charing Cross ■	⊖	a	08 11		23 41

Table 204

Mondays to Fridays

until 27 July, 13 Aug to 28 Aug and from 10 Sep

London Charing Cross/Cannon Street - Grove Park, Orpington, Sevenoaks and Tonbridge, Grove Park - Bromley North

Network Diagram - see first Page of Table 200

Miles	Miles				SE MO ■ A	SE MX ■	SE MX	SE MO ■ A	SE MX ■	SE MX ■	SE MX	SE MO A	SE MX		SE MX	SE MX	SE	SE ■	SE	SE	SE	SE ■	SE ■		SE	SE
0	—	London Charing Cross ■	⊖	d	23p23	23p30	23p36	23p38	23p40	23p45		23p46	00 06		00 15		00 48	05 30	05 36		06 06	06 15	06 30			06 36
0¾	—	London Waterloo (East) ■	⊖	d	23p26	23p33	23p39	23p41	23p43	23p48		23p49	00 09		00 18		00 51	05 33	05 39		06 09	06 18	06 33			06 39
—	—	London Cannon Street ■	⊖	d																						
1¾	—	London Bridge ■	⊖	d	23p31	23p39	23p44	23p46	23p49	23p53		23p54	00 14		00 23		00 56	05 39	05 44		06 14	06 24	06 38			06 44
4¾	—	Nw Cross ■	⊖	d													01 01									
5½	—	St dhns		d																						
6	—	Lewisham ■	⇌	d			23p52					00 03	00 22				01 05		05 52		06 23					06 53
7¼	—	Hither Green ■		d			23p56					00 07	00 26				01 09		05 56		06 27					06 58
9	0	Grove Park ■		d			23p59				00 07	00 11	00 30			00 37	01 13		06 00	06 16	06 30				06 36	07 02
—	1¼	Sundridge Park		d							00 10					00 40				06 19					06 39	
—	1¾	Bromley North		a							00 12					00 42				06 21					06 41	
10¼	—	Enstead Wods		d			00 03					00 14	00 33				01 16		06 03		06 33					07 05
11¼	—	Chislehurst		d			00 05					00 17	00 35				01 19		06 05		06 36					07 07
12¾	—	Petts Wod ■		d			00 08					00 20	00 38				01 22		06 08		06 39					07 10
13¾	—	Orpington ■		a	23p46	23p54	00 12	00 01		00 08		00 23	00 42		00 46		01 25	05 54	06 11		06 42	06 40	06 53			07 13
—	—			d	23p46	23p54		00 02		00 09					00 46			05 55	06 12		06 44	06 40	06 54			07 14
15¼	—	Chelsfield ■		d	23p49	23p57									00 49			05 58	06 15		06 47					07 17
16½	—	Knockholt		d															06 18		06 50					07 20
20½	—	Dunton Green		d											00 56				06 23		06 55					07 25
22	—	Sevenoaks ■		a	23p57	00 05		00 11	00 11	00 18					00 59			06 05	06 26		06 59	06 49	07 03			07 28
—	—			d	23p57	00 05		00 12	00 12	00 19					00 59			06 06				06 50	07 03			
27	—	Hildenborough		d		00 11									01 05			06 12					07 09			
29½	—	Tonbridge ■		a	00 05	00 15		00 20	00 20	00 27					01 10			06 16				06 58	07 13			

			SE ■	SE	SE	SE ■	SE	SE	SE ■		SE ■	SE	SE ■	SE	SE ■	SE	SE ■	SE	SE		SE	SE ■ B	SE ■ C	SE ■	SE	SE ■
London Charing Cross ■	⊖	d	06 45			07 00		07 06	07 10		07 15		07 29			07 36	07 40	07 48				07 52	07 52	08 00	08 05	08 13
London Waterloo (East) ■	⊖	d	06 48			07 03		07 09	07 13		07 18		07 32			07 39	07 43	07 51				07 55	07 55	08 03	08 08	08 16
London Cannon Street ■	⊖	d			06 50							07 20			07 47						07 51					
London Bridge ■	⊖	d	06 53		06 54	07 08		07 14	07 19		07 23	07 24	07 38		07 51	07 44	07 49	07 56			07 55	08 01	08 01	08 09	08 13	08 21
Nw Cross ■	⊖	d			06 59																08 00					
St dhns		d			07 01																					
Lewisham ■	⇌	d			07 04																08 05					
Hither Green ■		d			07 08			07 23				07 35				07 53					08 10				08 23	
Grove Park ■		d		07 06	07 12		07 25	07 27				07 38		07 46		07 57			08 06		08 14				08 27	
Sundridge Park		d		07 09			07 28							07 49					08 09							
Bromley North		a		07 11			07 30							07 51					08 11							
Enstead Wods		d			07 15			07 30				07 41				08 00					08 17				08 30	
Chislehurst		d			07 18			07 33				07 44				08 03					08 20				08 32	
Petts Wod ■		d			07 21			07 36								08 06					08 23				08 36	
Orpington ■		a	07 09		07 25	07 25		07 40			07 38	07 48	07 53		08 08	08 09		08 15			08 26			08 25	08 39	
		d	07 10			07 26		07 42			07 39		07 54		08 09	08 12								08 26	08 45	
Chelsfield ■		d						07 45					07 57			08 15									08 48	
Knockholt		d						07 48					08 00												08 51	
Dunton Green		d						07 53								08 21									08 56	
Sevenoaks ■		a	07 19			07 35		08 00	07 42		07 48		08 06		08 18	08 24	08 11					08 27		08 35	08 59	08 44
		d	07 19			07 35			07 43		07 49		08 07		08 19		08 12					08 28		08 35		08 45
Hildenborough		d				07 41							08 13											08 41		
Tonbridge ■		a	07 27			07 45			07 51		07 58		08 17		08 27		08 20					08 36	08 37	08 47		08 53

			SE ■	SE	SE		SE ■	SE ■	SE ■	SE	SE	SE B	SE C	SE ■	SE		SE	SE ■	SE	SE ■	SE ■	SE	SE	SE ■	SE	
London Charing Cross ■	⊖	d	08 17				08 27	08 33			08 37	08 49	08 49	08 53				09 00	09 06	09 13				09 30		
London Waterloo (East) ■	⊖	d	08 20				08 30	08 36			08 40	08 52	08 52	08 56				09 03	09 09	09 16				09 33		
London Cannon Street ■	⊖	d			08 19				08 42								08 51				09 18		09 20			
London Bridge ■	⊖	d	08 25		08 23		08 35	08 41	08 46		08 45	08 57	08 57	09 01			08 55	09 08	09 14	09 21	09 22		09 25	09 39		
Nw Cross ■	⊖	d			08 29												09 00						09 29			
St dhns		d			08 31												09 02						09 31			
Lewisham ■	⇌	d			08 34												09 06						09 34			
Hither Green ■		d			08 38						08 55						09 10		09 23				09 38			
Grove Park ■		d		08 26	08 42					08 46	08 59				09 06		09 14		09 27			09 35	09 42		09 55	
Sundridge Park		d		08 29						08 49					09 09							09 38			09 58	
Bromley North		a		08 31						08 51					09 11							09 40			10 00	
Enstead Wods		d			08 45						09 02						09 17		09 30				09 45			
Chislehurst		d			08 48						09 05						09 20		09 33				09 48			
Petts Wod ■		d			08 51						09 08						09 23		09 36				09 51			
Orpington ■		a	08 41		08 54		08 53	08 57	09 07		09 11	09 22	09 24	09 20			09 26	09 26	09 39		09 40		09 55	09 55		
		d	08 42				08 54	08 58	09 07		09 12			09 21				09 26	09 42		09 41			09 56		
Chelsfield ■		d									09 15								09 45							
Knockholt		d									09 18								09 48							
Dunton Green		d									09 23								09 53							
Sevenoaks ■		a	08 51				09 03	09 07	09 17		09 26			09 30				09 35	09 57	09 43	09 50			10 05		
		d	08 52				09 03	09 07	09 17					09 31				09 35		09 44	09 50			10 05		
Hildenborough		d					09 09											09 41						10 11		
Tonbridge ■		a	09 00				09 13	09 18	09 25					09 40				09 46		09 52	09 58			10 15		

A from 21 May until 23 uly

B until 18 May

C from 21 May until 27 uly

until 27 July, 13 Aug to 28 Aug and from 10 Sep

London Charing Cross/Cannon Street - Grove Park, Orpington, Sevenoaks and Tonbridge, Grove Park - Bromley North

Network Diagram - see first Page of Table 200

		SE	SE ■	SE ■	SE	SE ■	SE	SE	SE ■ ⊼	SE ■		SE	SE	SE ■	SE	SE	SE ■ ⊼	SE ■	SE	SE ■		SE	SE	SE ■ ⊼	SE ■
London Charing Cross ■ ⊖	d	09 36	09 40	09 45		10 00		10 06	10 10	10 15				10 30		10 36	10 40	10 45		11 00			11 06	11 10	11 15
London Waterloo (East) ■ ⊖	d	09 39	09 43	09 48		10 03		10 09	10 13	10 18				10 33		10 39	10 43	10 48		11 03			11 09	11 13	11 18
London Cannon Street ■ ⊖	d				09 50								10 20						10 50						
London Bridge ■ ⊖	d	09 44	09 49	09 53	09 54	10 09		10 14	10 19	10 23			10 24	10 39		10 44	10 49	10 53	10 54	11 09			11 14	11 19	11 23
New Cross ■ ⊖	d				09 59								10 29						10 59						
St Johns	d				10 01								10 31						11 01						
Lewisham ■	d				10 04								10 34						11 04						
Hither Green ■	d	09 53			10 08			10 23					10 38			10 53			11 08				11 23		
Grove Park ■	d	09 57			10 12		10 15	10 27				10 35	10 42		10 55	10 57			11 12			11 15	11 27		
Sundridge Park	d						10 18					10 38			10 58							11 18			
Bromley North	a						10 20					10 40			11 00							11 20			
Elmstead Woods	d	10 00			10 15			10 30					10 45			11 00			11 15				11 30		
Chislehurst	d	10 03			10 18			10 33					10 48			11 03			11 18				11 33		
Petts Wood ■	d	10 06			10 21			10 36					10 51			11 06			11 21				11 36		
Orpington ■	a	10 09		10 08	10 24	10 25		10 39		10 38			10 54	10 55		11 09		11 08	11 24	11 25			11 39		11 38
	d	10 12		10 09		10 26		10 42		10 39				10 56		11 12		11 09		11 26			11 42		11 39
Chelsfield ■	d	10 15						10 45								11 15							11 45		
Knockholt	d	10 18						10 48								11 18							11 48		
Dunton Green	d	10 23						10 53								11 23							11 53		
Sevenoaks ■	a	10 26	10 11	10 18		10 35		10 56	10 41	10 48				11 05		11 26	11 11	11 18		11 35			11 56	11 41	11 48
	d		10 12	10 19		10 35			10 42	10 49				11 05			11 12	11 19		11 35				11 42	11 49
Hildenborough	d					10 41								11 11						11 41					
Tonbridge ■	a		10 20	10 27		10 45			10 50	10 57				11 15			11 20	11 27		11 45				11 50	11 57

		SE	SE	SE ■	SE	SE		SE ■ ⊼	SE ■	SE	SE ■	SE	SE	SE ■ ⊼	SE ■	SE		SE	SE ■	SE	SE	SE ■ ⊼	SE ■	SE	SE ■
London Charing Cross ■ ⊖	d			11 30		11 36		11 40	11 45		12 00		12 06	12 10	12 15				12 30		12 36	12 40	12 45		13 00
London Waterloo (East) ■ ⊖	d			11 33		11 39		11 43	11 48		12 03		12 09	12 13	12 18				12 33		12 39	12 43	12 48		13 03
London Cannon Street ■ ⊖	d		11 20							11 50								12 20						12 50	
London Bridge ■ ⊖	d		11 24	11 39		11 44		11 49	11 53	11 54	12 09		12 14	12 19	12 23			12 24	12 39		12 44	12 49	12 53	12 54	13 09
New Cross ■ ⊖	d		11 29							11 59								12 29						12 59	
St Johns	d		11 31							12 01								12 31						13 01	
Lewisham ■	d		11 34							12 04								12 34						13 04	
Hither Green ■	d		11 38			11 53				12 08			12 23					12 38			12 53			13 08	
Grove Park ■	d	11 35	11 42		11 55	11 57				12 12		12 15	12 27			12 35		12 42		12 55	12 57			13 12	
Sundridge Park	d	11 38			11 58							12 18				12 38				12 58					
Bromley North	a	11 40			12 00							12 20				12 40				13 00					
Elmstead Woods	d		11 45			12 00				12 15			12 30					12 45			13 00			13 15	
Chislehurst	d		11 48			12 03				12 18			12 33					12 48			13 03			13 18	
Petts Wood ■	d		11 51			12 06				12 21			12 36					12 51			13 06			13 21	
Orpington ■	a		11 54	11 55		12 09			12 08	12 24	12 25		12 39		12 38			12 54	12 55		13 09		13 08	13 24	13 25
	d			11 56		12 12			12 09		12 26		12 42		12 39				12 56		13 12		13 09		13 26
Chelsfield ■	d					12 15							12 45								13 15				
Knockholt	d					12 18							12 48								13 18				
Dunton Green	d					12 23							12 53								13 23				
Sevenoaks ■	a			12 05		12 26		12 11	12 18		12 35		12 56	12 41	12 48				13 05		13 26	13 11	13 18		13 35
	d			12 05				12 12	12 19		12 35			12 42	12 49				13 05			13 12	13 19		13 35
Hildenborough	d			12 11							12 41								13 11						13 41
Tonbridge ■	a			12 15				12 20	12 27		12 45			12 50	12 57				13 15			13 20	13 27		13 45

		SE		SE	SE ■ ⊼	SE ■	SE	SE	SE ■	SE	SE	SE ■ ⊼		SE ■	SE	SE ■	SE	SE	SE ■ ⊼	SE ■	SE	SE		SE ■	SE
London Charing Cross ■ ⊖	d			13 06	13 10	13 15			13 30		13 36	13 40		13 45		14 00		14 06	14 10	14 15				14 30	
London Waterloo (East) ■ ⊖	d			13 09	13 13	13 18			13 33		13 39	13 43		13 48		14 03		14 09	14 13	14 18				14 33	
London Cannon Street ■ ⊖	d							13 20							13 50							14 20			
London Bridge ■ ⊖	d			13 14	13 19	13 23		13 24	13 39		13 44	13 49		13 53	13 54	14 09		14 14	14 19	14 23		14 24		14 39	
New Cross ■ ⊖	d							13 29							13 59							14 29			
St Johns	d							13 31							14 01							14 31			
Lewisham ■	d							13 34							14 04							14 34			
Hither Green ■	d			13 23				13 38			13 53				14 08			14 23				14 38			
Grove Park ■	d	13 15		13 27			13 35	13 42		13 55	13 57				14 12		14 15	14 27			14 35	14 42			14 55
Sundridge Park	d	13 18					13 38			13 58							14 18				14 38				14 58
Bromley North	a	13 20					13 40			14 00							14 20				14 40				15 00
Elmstead Woods	d			13 30				13 45			14 00				14 15			14 30				14 45			
Chislehurst	d			13 33				13 48			14 03				14 18			14 33				14 48			
Petts Wood ■	d			13 36				13 51			14 06				14 21			14 36				14 51			
Orpington ■	a			13 39		13 38		13 54	13 55		14 09			14 08	14 24	14 25		14 39		14 38		14 54		14 55	
	d			13 42		13 39			13 56		14 12			14 09		14 26		14 42		14 39				14 56	
Chelsfield ■	d			13 45							14 15							14 45							
Knockholt	d			13 48							14 18							14 48							
Dunton Green	d			13 53							14 23							14 53							
Sevenoaks ■	a			13 56	13 41	13 48			14 05		14 26	14 11		14 18		14 35		14 56	14 41	14 48				15 05	
	d				13 42	13 49			14 05			14 12		14 19		14 35			14 42	14 49				15 05	
Hildenborough	d								14 11							14 41								15 11	
Tonbridge ■	a				13 50	13 57			14 15			14 20		14 27		14 45			14 50	14 57				15 16	

Table 204

Mondays to Fridays

until 27 July, 13 Aug to 28 Aug and from 10 Sep

London Charing Cross/Cannon Street - Grove Park, Orpington, Sevenoaks and Tonbridge, Grove Park - Bromley North

Network Diagram - see first Page of Table 200

		SE	SE ■ ⊼	SE ■	SE	SE ■	SE	SE		SE ■ ⊼	SE ■	SE	SE	SE ■	SE	SE	SE ■ ⊼	SE ■		SE	SE ■	SE	SE	SE ■ ⊼	SE ■
London Charing Cross ■ ⊖	d	14 36	14 40	14 45		15 00		15 06		15 10	15 15			15 30		15 36	15 40	15 45			16 00		16 06	16 10	16 15
London Waterloo (East) ■ ⊖	d	14 39	14 43	14 48		15 03		15 09		15 13	15 18			15 33		15 39	15 43	15 48			16 03		16 09	16 13	16 18
London Cannon Street ■ ⊖	d				14 50								15 20							15 50					
London Bridge ■ ⊖	d	14 44	14 49	14 53	14 54	15 09		15 14		15 19	15 23		15 24	15 39		15 44	15 49	15 53		15 54	16 09		16 14	16 19	16 23
New Cross ■ ⊖	d				14 59								15 29							15 59					
St Johns	d				15 01								15 31							16 01					
Lewisham ■	d				15 04								15 34							16 04					
Hither Green ■	d	14 53			15 08			15 23					15 38			15 53				16 08			16 23		
Grove Park ■	d	14 57			15 12		15 15	15 27				15 35	15 42		15 55	15 57				16 12		16 15	16 27		
Sundridge Park	d						15 18					15 38			15 58							16 18			
Bromley North	a						15 20					15 40			16 00							16 20			
Elmstead Woods	d	15 00			15 15			15 30					15 45			16 00				16 15			16 30		
Chislehurst	d	15 03			15 18			15 33					15 48			16 03				16 18			16 33		
Petts Wood ■	d	15 06			15 21			15 36					15 51			16 06				16 21			16 36		
Orpington ■	a	15 09		15 08	15 24	15 25		15 39			15 38		15 54	15 55		16 09		16 08		16 24	16 25		16 39		
	d	15 12		15 09		15 26		15 42			15 39			15 56		16 12		16 09			16 26		16 42		
Chelsfield ■	d	15 15						15 45								16 15							16 45		
Knockholt	d	15 18						15 48								16 18							16 48		
Dunton Green	d	15 23						15 53								16 23							16 53		
Sevenoaks ■	a	15 26	15 11	15 18		15 35		15 56		15 41	15 48			16 05		16 26	16 11	16 18			16 35		16 58	16 42	16 46
	d		15 12	15 19		15 35				15 42	15 49			16 05			16 12	16 19			16 35			16 43	16 47
Hildenborough	d					15 41								16 11							16 41				
Tonbridge ■	a		15 20	15 27		15 45				15 50	15 57			16 15			16 20	16 27			16 45			16 51	16 55

		SE ■	SE	SE		SE	SE ■ ⊼	SE ■	SE	SE	SE ■	SE	SE ■	SE ■		SE	SE	SE ■ ⊼	SE	SE ■	SE ■	SE	SE	SE ■ ⊼	
London Charing Cross ■ ⊖	d	16 28				16 32	16 37	16 41		16 42	16 57			17 01			17 03	17 14			17 23		17 26	17 41	
London Waterloo (East) ■ ⊖	d	16 31				16 35	16 40	16 44		16 45	17 00			17 04			17 06	17 18			17 26		17 29	17 44	
London Cannon Street ■ ⊖	d			16 20								16 56	17 02						17 19	17 24					
London Bridge ■ ⊖	d	16 36		16 24		16 40	16 45	16 49		16 51		17 00	17 06	17 09			17 11		17 23	17 28	17 31		17 35		
New Cross ■ ⊖	d			16 30																					
St Johns	d			16 32																					
Lewisham ■	d			16 35						17 01							17 21						17 44		
Hither Green ■	d			16 39		16 50				17 06							17 26						17 49		
Grove Park ■	d		16 35	16 43		16 54			16 57	17 10		17 15				17 17	17 30		17 35			17 40	17 53		
Sundridge Park	d		16 38						17 00							17 20						17 43			
Bromley North	a		16 40						17 02							17 22						17 45			
Elmstead Woods	d			16 46		16 57				17 13		17 18					17 33		17 38				17 56		
Chislehurst	d			16 48		17 00				17 15		17 21					17 35		17 40				17 58		
Petts Wood ■	d			16 51		17 03				17 19		17 24					17 40		17 44				18 02		
Orpington ■	a	16 52		16 57		17 06				17 24		17 27					17 45		17 47				18 07		
	d	16 53				17 07						17 28							17 50						
Chelsfield ■	d					17 10						17 31		17 28					17 53		17 50				
Knockholt	d					17 13						17 34							17 56						
Dunton Green	d					17 18						17 39							18 01						
Sevenoaks ■	a	17 02				17 23	17 09	17 13			17 27	17 44	17 31	17 37				17 45	18 07	17 53	17 59			18 11	
	d	17 03					17 10	17 14			17 27		17 32	17 37				17 46		17 54	17 59			18 11	
Hildenborough	d	17 09												17 43						18 00	18 05				
Tonbridge ■	a	17 13					17 18	17 22			17 35		17 40	17 48				17 54		18 04	18 09			18 19	

		SE	SE ■	SE ■	SE	SE	SE ■	SE	SE ■	SE ■		SE	SE	SE ■ ⊼	SE	SE ■	SE	SE	SE ■	SE ■ ⊼		SE	SE ■	SE ■	SE ■ A
London Charing Cross ■ ⊖	d			17 45		17 47	18 03			18 07			18 09	18 21				18 30	18 32	18 41			18 45		19 00
London Waterloo (East) ■ ⊖	d			17 48		17 50	18 06			18 10			18 12	18 24				18 33	18 35	18 44			18 48		19 03
London Cannon Street ■ ⊖	d	17 41	17 45					18 02	18 08						18 23	18 32						18 48		19 04	
London Bridge ■ ⊖	d	17 45	17 49	17 53		17 55		18 06	18 12	18 15			18 17		18 27	18 36		18 38	18 40	18 50		18 52	18 53	19 09	19 09
New Cross ■ ⊖	d																								
St Johns	d																								
Lewisham ■	d					18 05							18 27												
Hither Green ■	d					18 10							18 31					18 49							
Grove Park ■	d	17 59			18 03	18 14		18 20				18 23	18 35		18 41		18 45	18 53				19 05			
Sundridge Park	d				18 06							18 26					18 48								
Bromley North	a				18 08							18 28					18 50								
Elmstead Woods	d	18 02				18 17		18 23					18 38		18 44			18 56				19 08			
Chislehurst	d	18 05				18 20		18 25					18 40		18 46			18 58				19 10			
Petts Wood ■	d	18 08				18 23		18 29					18 44		18 50			19 03				19 14			
Orpington ■	a	18 11				18 29		18 32					18 49		18 53			19 06		19 06		19 19			19 27
	d	18 12						18 34							18 58			19 12		19 07					19 28
Chelsfield ■	d	18 15		18 12				18 37		18 34					19 01			19 15	18 58						19 31
Knockholt	d	18 18						18 40							19 04			19 18							
Dunton Green	d	18 23						18 45							19 09			19 23							
Sevenoaks ■	a	18 28	18 15	18 21			18 33	18 50	18 37	18 42				18 52	19 14	19 00		19 28	19 06	19 16			19 20	19 32	19 38
	d		18 16	18 21			18 34		18 38	18 43				18 52		19 00			19 06	19 17			19 21	19 33	19 39
Hildenborough	d			18 27					18 44	18 49									19 12					19 40	19 45
Tonbridge ■	a		18 24	18 32			18 42		18 48	18 54				19 00		19 08			19 17	19 25			19 29	19 44	19 50

A until 18 May

Table 204

Mondays to Fridays

until 27 July, 13 Aug to 28 Aug and from 10 Sep

London Charing Cross/Cannon Street - Grove Park, Orpington, Sevenoaks and Tonbridge, Grove Park - Bromley North

Network Diagram - see first Page of Table 200

	SE 1 A	SE	SE	SE 1 H	SE 1	SE	SE	SE 1	SE	SE	SE 1 H	SE 1	SE	SE 1	SE	SE	SE 1 H	SE 1	SE	SE	SE 1	SE
London Charing Cross ⊖ d	19 00		19 06	19 10	19 15			19 30		19 36	19 40	19 45		20 00		20 06	20 10	20 15			20 30	20 36
London Waterloo (East) ⊖ d	19 03		19 09	19 13	19 18			19 33		19 39	19 43	19 48		20 03		20 09	20 13	20 18			20 33	20 39
London Cannon Street ⊖ d							19 20						19 50							20 20		
London Bridge ⊖ d	19 09		19 14	19 19	19 23		19 24	19 39		19 44	19 49	19 53	19 54	20 09		20 14	20 19	20 23		20 24	20 39	20 44
New Cross ⊖ d							19 29						19 59							20 29		
St Johns d							19 31						20 01							20 31		
Lewisham d							19 34						20 04							20 34		
Hither Green d			19 23				19 38			19 53			20 08			20 23				20 38		20 53
Grove Park d		19 08	19 27			19 32	19 42		19 52	19 57			20 12		20 17	20 27			20 37	20 42		20 57
Sundridge Park d		19 11				19 35			19 55						20 20				20 40			
Bromley North a		19 13				19 37			19 57						20 22				20 42			
Elmstead Woods d			19 30				19 45			20 00			20 15			20 30				20 45		21 00
Chislehurst d			19 33				19 48			20 03			20 18			20 33				20 48		21 03
Petts Wood d			19 38				19 51			20 06			20 21			20 36				20 51		21 06
Orpington a	19 27		19 43		19 38		19 54	19 55		20 09		20 08	20 24	20 25		20 39		20 38		20 54	20 55	21 09
Orpington d	19 28		19 44		19 39			19 56		20 12		20 09		20 26		20 42		20 39			20 56	21 12
Chelsfield d	19 31		19 47							20 15						20 45						21 15
Knockholt d			19 50							20 18						20 48						21 18
Dunton Green d			19 55							20 23						20 53						21 23
Sevenoaks a	19 38		19 58	19 41	19 48			20 05		20 26	20 11	20 18		20 35		20 56	20 41	20 48			21 05	21 26
Sevenoaks d	19 39			19 42	19 49			20 05			20 12	20 19		20 35			20 42	20 49			21 05	
Hildenborough d	19 45							20 11						20 41							21 11	
Tonbridge a	19 52			19 53	19 57			20 15			20 20	20 27		20 45			20 50	20 57			21 15	

	SE 1	SE 1	SE 1	SE	SE	SE 1	SE 1	SE	SE	SE 1	SE 1	SE 1	SE	SE	SE 1	SE 1	SE	SE	SE 1	SE 1	SE 1
London Charing Cross ⊖ d	20 40	20 45	21 00		21 06	21 10	21 30		21 36	21 40	21 45	22 00		22 06	22 10	22 30		22 36	22 40	22 45	23 00
London Waterloo (East) ⊖ d	20 43	20 48	21 03		21 09	21 13	21 33		21 39	21 43	21 48	22 03		22 09	22 13	22 33		22 39	22 43	22 48	23 03
London Cannon Street ⊖ d																					
London Bridge ⊖ d	20 49	20 53	21 09		21 14	21 19	21 39		21 44	21 49	21 53	22 09		22 14	22 19	22 39		22 44	22 49	22 53	23 09
New Cross ⊖ d																					
St Johns d																					
Lewisham d					21 22				21 52					22 22				22 52			
Hither Green d					21 26				21 56					22 26				22 56			
Grove Park d				21 07	21 30			21 37	22 00				22 07	22 30			22 37	23 00			
Sundridge Park d				21 10				21 40					22 10				22 40				
Bromley North a				21 12				21 42					22 12				22 42				
Elmstead Woods d					21 33				22 03					22 33				23 03			
Chislehurst d					21 35				22 05					22 35				23 05			
Petts Wood d					21 38				22 08					22 38				23 08			
Orpington a		21 08	21 25		21 42	21 34	21 55		22 12		22 08	22 25		22 42	22 34	22 54		23 12		23 08	23 24
Orpington d		21 09	21 26		21 43	21 35	21 56				22 09	22 26			22 35	22 54				23 09	23 24
Chelsfield d					21 46		21 59					22 29				22 57					23 27
Knockholt d					21 49																
Dunton Green d					21 54																
Sevenoaks a	21 11	21 18	21 35		21 57	21 44	22 06			22 11	22 18	22 36			22 44	23 05			23 11	23 18	23 35
Sevenoaks d	21 12	21 19	21 35			21 44	22 07			22 12	22 19	22 37			22 44	23 05			23 12	23 19	23 35
Hildenborough d			21 41				22 13					22 43				23 11					23 41
Tonbridge a	21 20	21 27	21 45			21 52	22 17			22 20	22 27	22 47			22 52	23 15			23 20	23 27	23 45

	SE	SE	SE 1	SE 1	SE	SE	SE 1	SE 1
London Charing Cross ⊖ d		23 06	23 10	23 30		23 36	23 40	23 45
London Waterloo (East) ⊖ d		23 09	23 13	23 33		23 39	23 43	23 48
London Cannon Street ⊖ d								
London Bridge ⊖ d		23 14	23 19	23 39		23 44	23 49	23 53
New Cross ⊖ d								
St Johns d								
Lewisham d		23 22				23 52		
Hither Green d		23 26				23 56		
Grove Park d	23 07	23 30			23 37	23 59		
Sundridge Park d	23 10				23 40			
Bromley North a	23 12				23 42			
Elmstead Woods d		23 33				00 03		
Chislehurst d		23 35				00 05		
Petts Wood d		23 38				00 08		
Orpington a		23 42	23 34	23 54		00 12		00 08
Orpington d			23 35	23 54				00 09
Chelsfield d				23 57				
Knockholt d								
Dunton Green d								
Sevenoaks a			23 44	00 05			00 11	00 18
Sevenoaks d			23 44	00 05			00 12	00 19
Hildenborough d				00 11				
Tonbridge a			23 52	00 15			00 20	00 27

A from 21 May until 27 July

Table 204

Mondays to Fridays

30 July to 10 August

London Charing Cross/Cannon Street - Grove Park, Orpington, Sevenoaks and Tonbridge, Grove Park - Bromley North

Network Diagram - see first Page of Table 200

	SE 1 A	SE	SE 1 A	SE MO 1	SE 1 A	SE MO 1	SE A	SE	SE MO	SE	SE A	SE 1	SE	SE 1	SE	SE	SE	SE 1	SE 1	SE	SE	SE 1
London Charing Cross ⊖ d	23p30	23p36	23p40	23p40	23p45	23p45		00 06	00 10	00 15		00 37	00 48	05 30	05 36		06 06	06 15	06 30		06 36	06 45
London Waterloo (East) ⊖ d	23p33	23p39	23p43	23p43	23p48	23p48		00 09	00 13	00 18		00 40	00 51	05 33	05 39		06 09	06 18	06 33		06 39	06 48
London Cannon Street ⊖ d																						
London Bridge ⊖ d	23p39	23p44	23p49	23p49	23p53	23p53		00 14	00 18	00 23		00 45	00 56	05 39	05 44		06 14	06 24	06 38		06 44	06 53
New Cross ⊖ d													01 01									
St Johns d																						
Lewisham d		23p52						00 22					01 05		05 52		06 23				06 53	
Hither Green d		23p56						00 26					01 09		05 56		06 27				06 58	
Grove Park d		23p59					00 07	00 30	00 29		00 37		01 13		06 00	06 16	06 30			06 36	07 02	
Sundridge Park d							00 10				00 40					06 19				06 39		
Bromley North a							00 12				00 42					06 21				06 41		
Elmstead Woods d		00 03						00 33	00 32				01 16		06 03		06 33				07 05	
Chislehurst d		00 05						00 35	00 35				01 19		06 05		06 36				07 07	
Petts Wood d		00 08						00 38	00 38				01 22		06 08		06 39				07 10	
Orpington a	23p54	00 15		00 04	00 08	00 08		00 45	00 41	00 46		01 00	01 25	05 54	06 11		06 42	06 40	06 53		07 13	07 09
Orpington d	23p54			00 05	00 09	00 09			00 42	00 46		01 01	01 26	05 55	06 12		06 44	06 40	06 54		07 14	07 10
Chelsfield d	23p57					00 12			00 45	00 49			01 29	05 58	06 15		06 47				07 17	
Knockholt d													01 32		06 18		06 50				07 20	
Dunton Green d										00 56			01 37		06 23		06 55				07 25	
Sevenoaks a	00 05		00 11	00 14	00 18	00 19			00 52	00 59		01 10	01 40	06 05	06 29		07 02	06 49	07 03		07 31	07 19
Sevenoaks d	00 05		00 12	00 14	00 19	00 20			00 53	00 59		01 11	01 40	06 06				06 50	07 03			07 19
Hildenborough d	00 11								00 59	01 05			01 46	06 12					07 09			
Tonbridge a	00 15		00 20	00 22	00 27	00 28			01 04	01 13		01 19	01 50	06 16				06 58	07 13			07 27

	SE 1	SE	SE	SE	SE	SE 1	SE 1	SE	SE 1	SE	SE 1	SE	SE 1	SE	SE 1	SE 1	SE	SE	SE	SE 1	SE 1	SE
London Charing Cross ⊖ d	07 00				07 06	07 10	07 15		07 29			07 36	07 40	07 48	07 52	08 00			08 05	08 13	08 17	
London Waterloo (East) ⊖ d	07 03				07 09	07 13	07 18		07 32			07 39	07 43	07 51	07 55	08 03			08 08	08 16	08 20	
London Cannon Street ⊖ d			06 50					07 20			07 47							07 51				
London Bridge ⊖ d	07 08		06 54		07 14	07 19	07 23	07 24	07 38		07 51	07 44	07 49	07 56	08 01	08 09		07 55	08 13	08 21	08 25	
New Cross ⊖ d			06 59															08 00				
St Johns d			07 01																			
Lewisham d			07 04															08 05				
Hither Green d			07 08		07 23			07 35				07 53						08 10	08 23			
Grove Park d		07 06	07 12	07 25	07 27			07 38		07 46		07 57					08 06	08 14	08 27			08 26
Sundridge Park d		07 09		07 28						07 49							08 09					08 29
Bromley North a		07 11		07 30						07 51							08 11					08 31
Elmstead Woods d			07 15		07 30			07 41				08 00						08 17	08 30			
Chislehurst d			07 18		07 33			07 44				08 03						08 20	08 32			
Petts Wood d			07 21		07 36							08 06						08 23	08 36			
Orpington a	07 25		07 28		07 40		07 38	07 48	07 53		08 08	08 09		08 15		08 25		08 29	08 39		08 41	
Orpington d	07 26				07 42		07 39		07 54		08 09	08 12				08 26			08 45		08 42	
Chelsfield d					07 45				07 57			08 15							08 48			
Knockholt d					07 48				08 00										08 51			
Dunton Green d					07 53							08 21							08 56			
Sevenoaks a	07 35				08 00	07 42	07 48		08 06		08 18	08 24	08 11			08 35			08 59	08 44	08 51	
Sevenoaks d	07 35					07 43	07 49		08 07		08 19		08 12			08 35				08 45	08 52	
Hildenborough d	07 41								08 13							08 41						
Tonbridge a	07 45					07 51	07 58		08 17		08 27		08 20		08 37	08 47				08 53	09 00	

	SE 1	SE	SE 1	SE 1	SE	SE	SE	SE 1	SE 1	SE	SE	SE	SE 1	SE 1	SE 1	SE	SE	SE	SE	SE 1	SE 1
London Charing Cross ⊖ d	08 27		08 33			08 37	08 49	08 53	09 00			09 06	09 13		09 30				09 36	09 40	09 45
London Waterloo (East) ⊖ d	08 30		08 36			08 40	08 52	08 56	09 03			09 09	09 16		09 33				09 39	09 43	09 48
London Cannon Street ⊖ d		08 19		08 42							08 51			09 18			09 20				
London Bridge ⊖ d	08 35	08 23	08 41	08 46		08 45	08 57	09 01	09 08		08 55	09 14	09 21	09 22	09 39		09 25		09 44	09 49	09 53
New Cross ⊖ d		08 29									09 00						09 29				
St Johns d		08 31									09 02						09 31				
Lewisham d		08 34									09 06						09 34				
Hither Green d		08 38				08 55					09 10	09 23					09 38		09 53		
Grove Park d		08 42			08 46	08 59				09 06	09 14	09 27				09 35	09 42	09 55	09 57		
Sundridge Park d					08 49					09 09						09 38		09 58			
Bromley North a					08 51					09 11						09 40		10 00			
Elmstead Woods d		08 45				09 02					09 17	09 30					09 45		10 00		
Chislehurst d		08 48				09 05					09 20	09 33					09 47		10 03		
Petts Wood d		08 51				09 08					09 23	09 36					09 51		10 06		
Orpington a	08 53	08 57	08 57	09 07		09 11	09 24	09 20	09 26		09 29	09 39		09 40	09 55		09 58		10 09		10 08
Orpington d	08 54		08 58	09 07		09 12		09 21	09 26			09 42		09 41	09 56				10 12		10 09
Chelsfield d						09 15						09 45							10 15		
Knockholt d						09 18						09 48							10 18		
Dunton Green d						09 23						09 53							10 23		
Sevenoaks a	09 03		09 07	09 17		09 26		09 30	09 35			09 57	09 43	09 50	10 05				10 26	10 11	10 18
Sevenoaks d	09 03		09 07	09 17				09 31	09 35				09 44	09 50	10 05					10 12	10 19
Hildenborough d	09 09								09 41						10 11						
Tonbridge a	09 13		09 18	09 25				09 40	09 46				09 52	09 58	10 15					10 20	10 27

A not 30 July, 6 August

Table 204

Mondays to Fridays
30 July to 10 August

London Charing Cross/Cannon Street - Grove Park, Orpington, Sevenoaks and Tonbridge, Grove Park - Bromley North

Network Diagram - see first Page of Table 200

		SE 1	SE	SE	SE	SE 1 ⊼	SE 1	SE 1		SE	SE	SE	SE	SE 1 ⊼	SE 1	SE 1	SE	SE		SE	SE 1 ⊼	SE 1	SE 1	SE	SE
London Charing Cross 4 ⊖	d	10 00			10 06	10 10	10 15	10 30					10 36	10 40	10 45	11 00				11 06	11 10	11 15	11 30		
London Waterloo (East) 4 ⊖	d	10 03			10 09	10 13	10 18	10 33					10 39	10 43	10 48	11 03				11 09	11 14	11 18	11 33		
London Cannon Street 4 ⊖	d		09 50								10 20						10 50								11 20
London Bridge 4 ⊖	d	10 09	09 54		10 14	10 19	10 23	10 39			10 24		10 44	10 49	10 53	11 09	10 54			11 14	11 19	11 23	11 39		11 24
New Cross 4 ⊖	d		09 59								10 29						10 59								11 29
St Johns	d		10 01								10 31						11 01								11 31
Lewisham 4	d		10 04								10 34						11 04								11 34
Hither Green 4	d		10 08		10 23						10 38		10 53				11 08			11 23					11 39
Grove Park 4	d		10 12	10 15	10 27					10 35	10 42	10 55	10 57				11 12	11 15		11 27				11 35	11 42
Sundridge Park	d			10 18						10 38		10 58						11 18						11 38	
Bromley North	a			10 20						10 40		11 00						11 20						11 40	
Elmstead Woods	d		10 15		10 30						10 45		11 00				11 15			11 30					11 45
Chislehurst	d		10 18		10 33						10 48		11 03				11 18			11 33					11 48
Petts Wood 4	d		10 21		10 36						10 51		11 06				11 21			11 36					11 51
Orpington 4	a	10 25	10 27		10 39		10 38	10 55			10 57		11 09		11 08	11 25	11 27			11 39		11 38	11 55		11 57
	d	10 26			10 42		10 39	10 56					11 12		11 09	11 26				11 42		11 39	11 56		
Chelsfield 3	d				10 45								11 15							11 45					
Knockholt	d				10 48								11 18							11 48					
Dunton Green	d				10 53								11 23							11 53					
Sevenoaks 4	a	10 35			10 56	10 41	10 48	11 05					11 26	11 11	11 18	11 35				11 56	11 42	11 48	12 05		
	d	10 35				10 42	10 49	11 05						11 12	11 19	11 35					11 42	11 49	12 05		
Hildenborough	d	10 41						11 11								11 41							12 11		
Tonbridge 4	a	10 45				10 50	10 57	11 15						11 20	11 27	11 45					11 50	11 57	12 15		

		SE	SE	SE 1 ⊼		SE 1	SE 1	SE	SE	SE	SE 1 ⊼	SE 1	SE 1	SE		SE	SE	SE	SE 1 ⊼	SE 1	SE 1	SE	SE	SE
London Charing Cross 4 ⊖	d		11 36	11 40		11 45	12 00			12 06	12 10	12 15	12 30					12 36	12 40	12 45	13 00			13 06
London Waterloo (East) 4 ⊖	d		11 39	11 44		11 48	12 03			12 09	12 13	12 18	12 33					12 39	12 43	12 48	13 03			13 09
London Cannon Street 4 ⊖	d							11 50								12 20						12 50		
London Bridge 4 ⊖	d		11 44	11 49		11 53	12 09	11 54		12 14	12 19	12 23	12 39			12 24		12 44	12 49	12 53	13 09	12 54		13 14
New Cross 4 ⊖	d							11 59								12 29						12 59		
St Johns	d							12 01								12 31						13 01		
Lewisham 4	d							12 04								12 34						13 04		
Hither Green 4	d		11 53					12 08		12 23						12 38		12 53				13 08		13 23
Grove Park 4	d	11 55	11 57					12 12	12 15	12 27				12 35		12 42	12 55	12 57				13 12	13 15	13 27
Sundridge Park	d	11 58							12 18					12 38			12 58						13 18	
Bromley North	a	12 00							12 20					12 40			13 00						13 20	
Elmstead Woods	d		12 00					12 15		12 30						12 45		13 00				13 15		13 30
Chislehurst	d		12 03					12 17		12 33						12 48		13 03				13 17		13 33
Petts Wood 4	d		12 06					12 21		12 36						12 51		13 06				13 21		13 36
Orpington 4	a		12 09			12 08	12 25	12 27		12 39		12 38	12 55			12 57		13 09		13 08	13 25	13 27		13 39
	d		12 12			12 09	12 26			12 42		12 39	12 56					13 12		13 09	13 26			13 42
Chelsfield 3	d		12 15							12 45								13 15						13 45
Knockholt	d		12 18							12 48								13 18						13 48
Dunton Green	d		12 23							12 53								13 23						13 53
Sevenoaks 4	a		12 26	12 12		12 18	12 35			12 56	12 41	12 48	13 05					13 26	13 11	13 18	13 35			13 56
	d			12 12		12 19	12 35				12 42	12 49	13 05						13 12	13 19	13 35			
Hildenborough	d						12 41						13 11								13 41			
Tonbridge 4	a			12 20		12 27	12 45				12 50	12 57	13 15						13 20	13 27	13 45			

		SE 1 ⊼	SE 1	SE 1	SE	SE	SE	SE	SE 1 ⊼	SE 1		SE 1	SE	SE	SE	SE 1 ⊼	SE 1	SE 1	SE	SE		SE	SE	SE 1 ⊼	SE 1
London Charing Cross 4 ⊖	d	13 10	13 15	13 30				13 36	13 40	13 45		14 00			14 06	14 10	14 15	14 30					14 36	14 40	14 45
London Waterloo (East) 4 ⊖	d	13 13	13 18	13 33				13 39	13 43	13 48		14 03			14 09	14 13	14 18	14 33					14 39	14 43	14 48
London Cannon Street 4 ⊖	d					13 20							13 50							14 20					
London Bridge 4 ⊖	d	13 19	13 23	13 39		13 24		13 44	13 49	13 53		14 09	13 54		14 14	14 19	14 23	14 39		14 24			14 44	14 49	14 53
New Cross 4 ⊖	d					13 29							13 59							14 29					
St Johns	d					13 31							14 01							14 31					
Lewisham 4	d					13 34							14 04							14 34					
Hither Green 4	d					13 38		13 53					14 08		14 23					14 38			14 53		
Grove Park 4	d				13 35	13 42	13 55	13 57					14 12	14 15	14 27				14 35	14 42		14 55	14 57		
Sundridge Park	d				13 38		13 58							14 18					14 38			14 58			
Bromley North	a				13 40		14 00							14 20					14 40			15 00			
Elmstead Woods	d					13 45		14 00					14 15		14 30					14 45			15 00		
Chislehurst	d					13 48		14 03					14 18		14 33					14 47			15 03		
Petts Wood 4	d					13 51		14 06					14 21		14 36					14 51			15 06		
Orpington 4	a		13 38	13 55		13 57		14 09		14 08		14 25	14 27		14 39		14 38	14 55		14 57			15 09		15 08
	d		13 39	13 56				14 12		14 09		14 26			14 42		14 39	14 56					15 12		15 09
Chelsfield 3	d							14 15							14 45								15 15		
Knockholt	d							14 18							14 48								15 18		
Dunton Green	d							14 23							14 53								15 23		
Sevenoaks 4	a	13 41	13 48	14 05				14 26	14 11	14 18		14 35			14 56	14 41	14 48	15 05					15 26	15 11	15 18
	d	13 42	13 49	14 05					14 12	14 19		14 35				14 42	14 49	15 05						15 12	15 19
Hildenborough	d			14 11								14 41						15 11							
Tonbridge 4	a	13 50	13 57	14 15					14 20	14 27		14 45				14 50	14 57	15 16						15 20	15 27

Table 204

Mondays to Fridays
30 July to 10 August

London Charing Cross/Cannon Street - Grove Park, Orpington, Sevenoaks and Tonbridge, Grove Park - Bromley North

Network Diagram - see first Page of Table 200

		SE 1	SE	SE	SE	SE 1 ⊼		SE 1	SE 1	SE	SE	SE	SE	SE 1 ⊼	SE 1	SE 1		SE	SE	SE	SE 1 ⊼	SE 1	SE 1	SE	SE
London Charing Cross 4 ⊖	d	15 00			15 06	15 10		15 15	15 30				15 36	15 40	15 45	16 00				16 06	16 10	16 15	16 28		
London Waterloo (East) 4 ⊖	d	15 03			15 09	15 13		15 18	15 33				15 39	15 43	15 48	16 03				16 09	16 13	16 18	16 31		
London Cannon Street 4 ⊖	d		14 50								15 20							15 50							16 20
London Bridge 4 ⊖	d	15 09	14 54		15 14	15 19		15 23	15 39		15 24		15 44	15 49	15 53	16 09		15 54		16 14	16 19	16 23	16 36		16 24
New Cross 4 ⊖	d		14 59								15 29							15 59							16 30
St Johns	d		15 01								15 31							16 01							16 32
Lewisham 4	d		15 04								15 34							16 04							16 35
Hither Green 4	d		15 08		15 23						15 38		15 53					16 08		16 23					16 39
Grove Park 4	d		15 12	15 15	15 27					15 35	15 42	15 55	15 57					16 12	16 15	16 27				16 35	16 43
Sundridge Park	d			15 18						15 38		15 58							16 18					16 38	
Bromley North	a			15 20						15 40		16 00							16 20					16 40	
Elmstead Woods	d		15 15		15 30						15 45		16 00					16 15		16 30					16 46
Chislehurst	d		15 17		15 33						15 47		16 03					16 18		16 33					16 48
Petts Wood 4	d		15 21		15 36						15 51		16 06					16 21		16 36					16 51
Orpington 4	a	15 25	15 27		15 39			15 38	15 55		15 57		16 09		16 08	16 25		16 27		16 39			16 52		16 57
	d	15 26			15 42			15 39	15 56				16 12		16 09	16 26				16 42			16 53		
Chelsfield 3	d				15 45								16 15							16 45					
Knockholt	d				15 48								16 18							16 48					
Dunton Green	d				15 53								16 23							16 53					
Sevenoaks 4	a	15 35			15 56	15 41		15 48	16 05				16 26	16 11	16 18	16 35				16 58	16 42	16 46	17 02		
	d	15 35				15 42		15 49	16 05					16 12	16 19	16 35					16 43	16 47	17 03		
Hildenborough	d	15 41							16 11							16 41							17 09		
Tonbridge 4	a	15 45				15 50		15 57	16 15					16 20	16 27	16 45					16 51	16 55	17 13		

		SE		SE 1 ⊼	SE 1	SE	SE	SE 1	SE	SE 1	SE 1	SE		SE	SE 1 ⊼	SE	SE 1	SE 1	SE	SE	SE 1 ⊼	SE		SE 1	SE 1
London Charing Cross 4 ⊖	d	16 32		16 37	16 41		16 42	16 57			17 01			17 03	17 14			17 23		17 26	17 41				17 45
London Waterloo (East) 4 ⊖	d	16 35		16 40	16 44		16 45	17 00			17 04			17 06	17 18			17 26		17 29	17 44				17 48
London Cannon Street 4 ⊖	d								16 56	17 02						17 19	17 24					17 41		17 45	
London Bridge 4 ⊖	d	16 40		16 45	16 49		16 51		17 00	17 06	17 09			17 11		17 23	17 28	17 31		17 35		17 45		17 49	17 53
New Cross 4 ⊖	d																								
St Johns	d																								
Lewisham 4	d						17 01							17 21						17 44					
Hither Green 4	d	16 50					17 06							17 26						17 49					
Grove Park 4	d	16 54				16 57	17 10		17 15			17 17		17 30		17 35			17 40	17 53		17 59			
Sundridge Park	d					17 00						17 20							17 43						
Bromley North	a					17 02						17 22							17 45						
Elmstead Woods	d	16 57					17 13		17 18					17 33		17 38				17 56		18 02			
Chislehurst	d	17 00					17 15		17 21					17 35		17 40				17 58		18 05			
Petts Wood 4	d	17 03					17 19		17 24					17 40		17 44				18 02		18 08			
Orpington 4	a	17 06					17 24		17 27					17 45		17 47				18 07		18 11			
	d	17 07							17 28							17 50						18 12			
Chelsfield 3	d	17 10							17 31		17 28					17 53		17 50				18 15			18 12
Knockholt	d	17 13							17 34							17 56						18 18			
Dunton Green	d	17 18							17 39							18 01						18 23			
Sevenoaks 4	a	17 23		17 09	17 13			17 27	17 44	17 31	17 37				17 45	18 07	17 53	17 59			18 11	18 28		18 15	18 21
	d			17 10	17 14			17 27		17 32	17 37				17 46		17 54	17 59			18 11			18 16	18 21
Hildenborough	d										17 43						18 00	18 05							18 27
Tonbridge 4	a			17 18	17 22			17 35		17 40	17 48				17 54		18 04	18 09			18 19			18 24	18 32

		SE	SE	SE 1	SE	SE 1	SE 1	SE		SE	SE 1 ⊼	SE	SE 1	SE	SE	SE 1	SE 1 ⊼	SE		SE 1	SE 1	SE 1	SE	SE	SE 1 ⊼
London Charing Cross 4 ⊖	d		17 47	18 03			18 07			18 09	18 21				18 30	18 32	18 41			18 45		19 00		19 06	19 10
London Waterloo (East) 4 ⊖	d		17 50	18 06			18 10			18 12	18 24				18 33	18 35	18 44			18 48		19 03		19 09	19 13
London Cannon Street 4 ⊖	d				18 02	18 08						18 23	18 32					18 48			19 04				
London Bridge 4 ⊖	d		17 55		18 06	18 12	18 15			18 17		18 27	18 36		18 38	18 40	18 50	18 52		18 53	19 09	19 09		19 14	19 19
New Cross 4 ⊖	d																								
St Johns	d																								
Lewisham 4	d		18 05							18 27															
Hither Green 4	d		18 10							18 31					18 49									19 23	
Grove Park 4	d	18 03	18 14		18 20			18 23		18 35		18 41		18 45	18 53			19 05					19 08	19 27	
Sundridge Park	d	18 06						18 26						18 48									19 11		
Bromley North	a	18 08						18 28						18 50									19 13		
Elmstead Woods	d		18 17		18 23					18 38		18 44			18 56			19 08						19 30	
Chislehurst	d		18 20		18 25					18 40		18 46			18 58			19 10						19 33	
Petts Wood 4	d		18 23		18 29					18 44		18 50			19 03			19 14						19 38	
Orpington 4	a		18 29		18 32					18 49		18 53			19 06		19 06	19 19				19 27		19 43	
	d				18 34							18 58			19 12		19 07					19 28		19 44	
Chelsfield 3	d				18 37		18 34					19 01			19 15	18 58						19 31		19 47	
Knockholt	d				18 40							19 04			19 18									19 50	
Dunton Green	d				18 45							19 09			19 23									19 55	
Sevenoaks 4	a			18 33	18 50	18 37	18 42				18 52	19 14	19 00		19 28	19 06	19 16			19 20	19 32	19 38		19 58	19 41
	d			18 34		18 38	18 43				18 52		19 00			19 06	19 17			19 21	19 33	19 39			19 42
Hildenborough	d					18 44	18 49									19 12					19 40	19 45			
Tonbridge 4	a			18 42		18 48	18 54				19 00		19 08			19 17	19 25			19 29	19 44	19 52			19 53

Left page

Table 204

Mondays to Fridays
30 July to 10 August

London Charing Cross/Cannon Street - Grove Park, Orpington, Sevenoaks and Tonbridge, Grove Park - Bromley North

Network Diagram - see first Page of Table 200

		SE ■	SE ■	SE	SE	SE	SE	SE ■ (bicycle)	SE ■	SE ■	SE	SE	SE	SE ■ (bicycle)	SE ■	SE ■	SE	SE	SE	SE ■	SE ■	SE ■
London Charing Cross	d	19 15	19 30				19 36	19 40	19 45	20 00			20 06	20 10	20 15	20 30			20 36	20 40	20 45	21 00
London Waterloo (East)	d	19 18	19 33				19 39	19 43	19 48	20 03			20 09	20 13	20 18	20 33			20 39	20 43	20 48	21 03
London Cannon Street	d				19 20						19 50							20 20				
London Bridge	d	19 23	19 39		19 24		19 44	19 49	19 53	20 09	19 54		20 14	20 19	20 23	20 39		20 24	20 44	20 49	20 53	21 09
New Cross	d				19 29						19 59							20 29				
St Johns	d				19 31						20 01							20 31				
Lewisham	d				19 34						20 04							20 34				
Hither Green	d				19 38		19 53				20 08		20 23					20 38	20 53			
Grove Park	d			19 32	19 42	19 52	19 57				20 12	20 17	20 27				20 37	20 42	20 57			
Sundridge Park	d			19 35		19 55						20 20					20 40					
Bromley North	a			19 37		19 57						20 22					20 42					
Elmstead Woods	d				19 45		20 00				20 15		20 30					20 45	21 00			
Chislehurst	d				19 47		20 03				20 18		20 33					20 48	21 03			
Petts Wood	d				19 51		20 06				20 21		20 36					20 51	21 06			
Orpington	a	19 38	19 55		19 57		20 09		20 08	20 25	20 27		20 39		20 38	20 55		20 57	21 09		21 08	21 25
	d	19 39	19 56				20 12		20 09	20 26			20 42		20 39	20 56			21 12		21 09	21 26
Chelsfield	d						20 15						20 45						21 15			
Knockholt	d						20 18						20 48						21 18			
Dunton Green	d						20 23						20 53						21 23			
Sevenoaks	a	19 48	20 05				20 26	20 11	20 18	20 35			20 56	20 41	20 48	21 05			21 26	21 11	21 18	21 35
	d	19 49	20 05					20 12	20 19	20 35				20 42	20 49	21 05				21 12	21 19	21 35
Hildenborough	d		20 11							20 41						21 11						21 41
Tonbridge	a	19 57	20 15					20 20	20 27	20 45				20 50	20 57	21 15				21 20	21 27	21 45

		SE	SE	SE ■	SE ■	SE	SE	SE ■	SE ■	SE ■	SE	SE	SE ■	SE ■	SE	SE	SE ■	SE ■	SE ■	SE	SE	SE ■	SE ■
London Charing Cross	d		21 06	21 10	21 30		21 36	21 40	21 45	22 00		22 06	22 10	22 30		22 36	22 40	22 45	23 00		23 06	23 10	23 30
London Waterloo (East)	d		21 09	21 13	21 33		21 39	21 43	21 48	22 03		22 09	22 13	22 33		22 39	22 43	22 48	23 03		23 09	23 13	23 33
London Cannon Street	d																						
London Bridge	d		21 14	21 19	21 39		21 44	21 49	21 53	22 09		22 14	22 19	22 39		22 44	22 49	22 53	23 09		23 14	23 19	23 39
New Cross	d																						
St Johns	d																						
Lewisham	d		21 22				21 52					22 22				22 52					23 22		
Hither Green	d		21 26				21 56					22 26				22 56					23 26		
Grove Park	d	21 07	21 30			21 37	22 00				22 07	22 30			22 37	23 00				23 07	23 30		
Sundridge Park	d	21 10				21 40					22 10				22 40					23 10			
Bromley North	a	21 12				21 42					22 12				22 42					23 12			
Elmstead Woods	d		21 33				22 03					22 33				23 03					23 33		
Chislehurst	d		21 35				22 05					22 35				23 05					23 35		
Petts Wood	d		21 38				22 08					22 38				23 08					23 38		
Orpington	a		21 42	21 34	21 55		22 15		22 08	22 25		22 45	22 34	22 54		23 15		23 08	23 24		23 45	23 34	23 54
	d		21 43	21 35	21 56				22 09	22 26			22 35	22 54				23 09	23 24			23 35	23 54
Chelsfield	d		21 46		21 59					22 29				22 57					23 27				23 57
Knockholt	d		21 49																				
Dunton Green	d		21 54																				
Sevenoaks	a		22 00	21 44	22 06			22 11	22 18	22 36			22 44	23 05			23 11	23 18	23 35			23 44	00 05
	d			21 44	22 07			22 12	22 19	22 37			22 44	23 05			23 12	23 19	23 35			23 44	00 05
Hildenborough	d				22 13					22 43				23 11					23 41				00 11
Tonbridge	a			21 52	22 17			22 20	22 27	22 47			22 52	23 15			23 20	23 27	23 45			23 52	00 15

		SE	SE	SE ■	SE ■
London Charing Cross	d		23 36	23 40	23 45
London Waterloo (East)	d		23 39	23 43	23 48
London Cannon Street	d				
London Bridge	d		23 44	23 49	23 53
New Cross	d				
St Johns	d				
Lewisham	d		23 52		
Hither Green	d		23 56		
Grove Park	d	23 37	23 59		
Sundridge Park	d	23 40			
Bromley North	a	23 42			
Elmstead Woods	d		00 03		
Chislehurst	d		00 05		
Petts Wood	d		00 08		
Orpington	a		00 15		00 08
	d				00 09
Chelsfield	d				
Knockholt	d				
Dunton Green	d				
Sevenoaks	a			00 11	00 18
	d			00 12	00 19
Hildenborough	d				
Tonbridge	a			00 20	00 27

Right page

Table 204

Mondays to Fridays
29 August to 7 September

London Charing Cross/Cannon Street - Grove Park, Orpington, Sevenoaks and Tonbridge, Grove Park - Bromley North

Network Diagram - see first Page of Table 200

		SE ■ A	SE ■ B	SE B	SE ■ A	SE ■ B	SE ■ B	SE B	SE A	SE B	SE B	SE B	SE ■	SE	SE	SE ■	SE	SE	SE	SE ■	SE ■	SE	SE
London Charing Cross	d	23p23	23p30	23p36	23p38	23p40	23p45		23p46	00 06	00 15		00 37	00 48	00 48	05 30	05 36		06 06	06 15	06 30		06 36
London Waterloo (East)	d	23p26	23p33	23p39	23p41	23p43	23p48		23p49	00 09	00 18		00 40	00 51	00 51	05 33	05 39		06 09	06 18	06 33		06 39
London Cannon Street	d																						
London Bridge	d	23p31	23p39	23p44	23p46	23p49	23p53		23p54	00 14	00 23		00 45	00 56	00 56	05 39	05 44		06 14	06 24	06 38		06 44
New Cross	d													01 01	01 01								
St Johns	d																						
Lewisham	d			23p52					00 03	00 22				01 05	01 05		05 52		06 23				06 53
Hither Green	d			23p56					00 07	00 26				01 09	01 09		05 56		06 27				06 58
Grove Park	d			23p59				00 07	00 11	00 30		00 37		01 13	01 13		06 00	06 16	06 30			06 36	07 02
Sundridge Park	d							00 10				00 40						06 19				06 39	
Bromley North	a							00 12				00 42						06 21				06 41	
Elmstead Woods	d			00 03					00 14	00 33				01 16	01 16		06 03		06 33				07 05
Chislehurst	d			00 05					00 17	00 35				01 18	01 19		06 05		06 36				07 07
Petts Wood	d			00 08					00 20	00 38				01 22	01 22		06 08		06 39				07 10
Orpington	a	23p46	23p54	00 12	00 01		00 08		00 23	00 42	00 46		01 00	01 25	01 25	05 54	06 11		06 42	06 40	06 53		07 13
	d	23p46	23p54		00 02		00 09				00 46		01 01	01 26		05 55	06 12		06 44	06 40	06 54		07 14
Chelsfield	d	23p49	23p57								00 49			01s29		05 58	06 15		06 47				07 17
Knockholt	d													01s32			06 18		06 50				07 20
Dunton Green	d										00 56			01s37			06 23		06 55				07 25
Sevenoaks	a	23p57	00 05		00 11	00 11	00 18				00 59		01s10	01s40		06 05	06 26		06 59	06 49	07 03		07 28
	d	23p57	00 05		00 12	00 12	00 19				00 59					06 06				06 50	07 03		
Hildenborough	d		00 11								01 05			01s46		06 12					07 09		
Tonbridge	a	00 05	00 15		00 20	00 20	00 27				01 10		01s19	01s50		06 16				06 58	07 13		

		SE ■	SE	SE	SE ■	SE	SE	SE ■	SE ■	SE	SE ■	SE	SE ■	SE	SE ■	SE	SE	SE	SE ■	SE ■	SE	SE ■	SE ■
London Charing Cross	d	06 45			07 00		07 06	07 10	07 15		07 29			07 36	07 40	07 48			07 52	08 00	08 05	08 13	08 17
London Waterloo (East)	d	06 48			07 03		07 09	07 13	07 18		07 32			07 39	07 43	07 51			07 55	08 03	08 08	08 16	08 20
London Cannon Street	d			06 50						07 20			07 47					07 51					
London Bridge	d	06 53		06 54	07 08		07 14	07 19	07 23	07 24	07 38		07 51	07 44	07 49	07 56		07 55	08 01	08 09	08 13	08 21	08 25
New Cross	d			06 59														08 00					
St Johns	d			07 01																			
Lewisham	d			07 04														08 05					
Hither Green	d			07 08			07 23			07 35				07 53				08 10			08 23		
Grove Park	d		07 06	07 12		07 25	07 27			07 38		07 46		07 57			08 06	08 14			08 27		
Sundridge Park	d		07 09			07 28						07 49					08 09						
Bromley North	a		07 11			07 30						07 51					08 11						
Elmstead Woods	d			07 15			07 30			07 41				08 00				08 17			08 30		
Chislehurst	d			07 18			07 33			07 44				08 03				08 20			08 32		
Petts Wood	d			07 21			07 36							08 06				08 23			08 36		
Orpington	a	07 09		07 25	07 25		07 40		07 38	07 48	07 53		08 08	08 09		08 15		08 26		08 25	08 39		08 41
	d	07 10			07 26		07 42		07 39		07 54		08 09	08 12						08 26	08 45		08 42
Chelsfield	d						07 45				07 57			08 15							08 48		
Knockholt	d						07 48				08 00										08 51		
Dunton Green	d						07 53							08 21							08 56		
Sevenoaks	a	07 19			07 35		08 00	07 42	07 48		08 06		08 18	08 24	08 11					08 35	08 59	08 44	08 51
	d	07 19			07 35			07 43	07 49		08 07		08 19		08 12					08 35		08 45	08 52
Hildenborough	d				07 41						08 13									08 41			
Tonbridge	a	07 27			07 45			07 51	07 58		08 17		08 27		08 20				08 37	08 47		08 53	09 00

		SE	SE	SE ■	SE ■	SE ■	SE	SE	SE	SE ■	SE	SE	SE ■	SE	SE ■	SE ■	SE	SE	SE ■	SE	SE	SE ■
London Charing Cross	d			08 27	08 33			08 37	08 49	08 53			09 00	09 06	09 13				09 30		09 36	09 40
London Waterloo (East)	d			08 30	08 36			08 40	08 52	08 56			09 03	09 09	09 16				09 33		09 39	09 43
London Cannon Street	d		08 19			08 42						08 51				09 18		09 20				
London Bridge	d		08 23	08 35	08 41	08 46		08 45	08 57	09 01		08 55	09 08	09 14	09 21	09 22		09 25	09 39		09 44	09 49
New Cross	d		08 29									09 00						09 29				
St Johns	d		08 31									09 02						09 31				
Lewisham	d		08 34									09 06						09 34				
Hither Green	d		08 38					08 55				09 10		09 23				09 38			09 53	
Grove Park	d	08 26	08 42				08 46	08 59			09 06	09 14		09 27			09 35	09 42		09 55	09 57	
Sundridge Park	d	08 29					08 49				09 09						09 38			09 58		
Bromley North	a	08 31					08 51				09 11						09 40			10 00		
Elmstead Woods	d		08 45					09 02				09 17		09 30				09 45			10 00	
Chislehurst	d		08 48					09 05				09 20		09 33				09 48			10 03	
Petts Wood	d		08 51					09 08				09 23		09 36				09 51			10 06	
Orpington	a		08 54	08 53	08 57	09 07		09 11	09 24	09 20		09 26	09 26	09 39		09 40		09 55	09 55		10 09	
	d			08 54	08 58	09 07		09 12		09 21			09 26	09 42		09 41			09 56		10 12	
Chelsfield	d							09 15						09 45							10 15	
Knockholt	d							09 18						09 48							10 18	
Dunton Green	d							09 23						09 53							10 23	
Sevenoaks	a			09 03	09 07	09 17		09 26		09 30			09 35	09 57	09 43	09 50			10 05		10 26	10 11
	d			09 03	09 07	09 17				09 31			09 35		09 44	09 50			10 05			10 12
Hildenborough	d			09 09									09 41						10 11			
Tonbridge	a			09 13	09 18	09 25				09 40			09 46		09 52	09 58			10 15			10 20

A 3 September

B not 3 September

Table 204

Mondays to Fridays
29 August to 7 September

London Charing Cross/Cannon Street - Grove Park, Orpington, Sevenoaks and Tonbridge, Grove Park - Bromley North

Network Diagram - see first Page of Table 200

		SE ■	SE	SE ■	SE	SE	SE ■ ⌶	SE ■	SE	SE	SE ■	SE	SE	SE ■ ⌶	SE ■	SE	SE ■	SE	SE	SE ■ ⌶	SE ■	SE	SE
London Charing Cross ■ ⊖	d	09 45		10 00		10 06	10 10	10 15			10 30		10 36	10 40	10 45		11 00		11 06	11 10	11 15		
London Waterloo (East) ■ ⊖	d	09 48		10 03		10 09	10 13	10 18			10 33		10 39	10 43	10 48		11 03		11 09	11 13	11 18		
London Cannon Street ■ ⊖	d		09 50							10 20						10 50							11 20
London Bridge ■ ⊖	d	09 53	09 54	10 09		10 14	10 19	10 23		10 24	10 39		10 44	10 49	10 53	10 54	11 09		11 14	11 19	11 23		11 24
New Cross ■ ⊖	d		09 59							10 29						10 59							11 29
St Johns	d		10 01							10 31						11 01							11 31
Lewisham ■ ⇌	d		10 04							10 34						11 04							11 34
Hither Green ■	d		10 08			10 23				10 38			10 53			11 08			11 23				11 38
Grove Park ■	d		10 12		10 15	10 27			10 35	10 42		10 55	10 57			11 12		11 15	11 27			11 35	11 42
Sundridge Park	d				10 18				10 38			10 58						11 18				11 38	
Bromley North	a				10 20				10 40			11 00						11 20				11 40	
Elmstead Woods	d		10 15			10 30				10 45			11 00			11 15			11 30				11 45
Chislehurst	d		10 18			10 33				10 48			11 03			11 18			11 33				11 48
Petts Wood ■	d		10 21			10 36				10 51			11 06			11 21			11 36				11 51
Orpington ■	a	10 08	10 24	10 25		10 39		10 38		10 54	10 55		11 09		11 08	11 24	11 25		11 39		11 38		11 54
	d	10 09		10 26		10 42		10 39			10 56		11 12		11 09		11 26		11 42		11 39		
Chelsfield ■	d					10 45							11 15						11 45				
Knockholt	d					10 48							11 18						11 48				
Dunton Green	d					10 53							11 23						11 53				
Sevenoaks ■	a	10 18		10 35		10 56	10 41	10 48			11 05		11 26	11 11	11 18		11 35		11 56	11 41	11 48		
	d	10 19		10 35			10 42	10 49			11 05			11 12	11 19		11 35			11 42	11 49		
Hildenborough	d			10 41							11 11						11 41						
Tonbridge ■	a	10 27		10 45			10 50	10 57			11 15			11 20	11 27		11 45			11 50	11 57		

		SE ■	SE	SE	SE ■ ⌶	SE ■	SE	SE ■	SE	SE	SE ■ ⌶	SE ■	SE	SE	SE ■	SE	SE	SE ■ ⌶	SE ■	SE	SE ■	SE
London Charing Cross ■ ⊖	d	11 30		11 36	11 40	11 45		12 00		12 06	12 10	12 15			12 30		12 36	12 40	12 45		13 00	
London Waterloo (East) ■ ⊖	d	11 33		11 39	11 43	11 48		12 03		12 09	12 13	12 18			12 33		12 39	12 43	12 48		13 03	
London Cannon Street ■ ⊖	d						11 50							12 20						12 50		
London Bridge ■ ⊖	d	11 39		11 44	11 49	11 53	11 54	12 09		12 14	12 19	12 23		12 24	12 39		12 44	12 49	12 53	12 54	13 09	
New Cross ■ ⊖	d						11 59							12 29						12 59		
St Johns	d						12 01							12 31						13 01		
Lewisham ■ ⇌	d						12 04							12 34						13 04		
Hither Green ■	d			11 53			12 08			12 23				12 38			12 53			13 08		
Grove Park ■	d		11 55	11 57			12 12		12 15	12 27			12 35	12 42		12 55	12 57			13 12		13 15
Sundridge Park	d		11 58						12 18				12 38			12 58						13 18
Bromley North	a		12 00						12 20				12 40			13 00						13 20
Elmstead Woods	d			12 00			12 15			12 30				12 45			13 00			13 15		
Chislehurst	d			12 03			12 18			12 33				12 48			13 03			13 18		
Petts Wood ■	d			12 06			12 21			12 36				12 51			13 06			13 21		
Orpington ■	a	11 55		12 09		12 08	12 24	12 25		12 39		12 38		12 54	12 55		13 09		13 08	13 24	13 25	
	d	11 56		12 12		12 09		12 26		12 42		12 39			12 56		13 12		13 09		13 26	
Chelsfield ■	d			12 15						12 45							13 15					
Knockholt	d			12 18						12 48							13 18					
Dunton Green	d			12 23						12 53							13 23					
Sevenoaks ■	a	12 05		12 26	12 11	12 18		12 35		12 56	12 41	12 48			13 05		13 26	13 11	13 18		13 35	
	d	12 05			12 12	12 19		12 35			12 42	12 49			13 05			13 12	13 19		13 35	
Hildenborough	d	12 11						12 41							13 11						13 41	
Tonbridge ■	a	12 15			12 20	12 27		12 45			12 50	12 57			13 15			13 20	13 27		13 45	

		SE	SE ■ ⌶	SE ■	SE	SE	SE ■	SE	SE	SE ■ ⌶	SE ■	SE	SE ■	SE	SE	SE ■ ⌶	SE ■	SE	SE	SE ■	SE	SE	SE ■ ⌶
London Charing Cross ■ ⊖	d	13 06	13 10	13 15			13 30		13 36	13 40	13 45		14 00		14 06	14 10	14 15			14 30		14 36	14 40
London Waterloo (East) ■ ⊖	d	13 09	13 13	13 18			13 33		13 39	13 43	13 48		14 03		14 09	14 13	14 18			14 33		14 39	14 43
London Cannon Street ■ ⊖	d					13 20						13 50							14 20				
London Bridge ■ ⊖	d	13 14	13 19	13 23		13 24	13 39		13 44	13 49	13 53	13 54	14 09		14 14	14 19	14 23		14 24	14 39		14 44	14 49
New Cross ■ ⊖	d					13 29						13 59							14 29				
St Johns	d					13 31						14 01							14 31				
Lewisham ■ ⇌	d					13 34						14 04							14 34				
Hither Green ■	d	13 23				13 38			13 53			14 08			14 23				14 38			14 53	
Grove Park ■	d	13 27			13 35	13 42		13 55	13 57			14 12		14 15	14 27			14 35	14 42		14 55	14 57	
Sundridge Park	d				13 38			13 58						14 18				14 38			14 58		
Bromley North	a				13 40			14 00						14 20				14 40			15 00		
Elmstead Woods	d	13 30				13 45			14 00			14 15			14 30				14 45			15 00	
Chislehurst	d	13 33				13 48			14 03			14 18			14 33				14 48			15 03	
Petts Wood ■	d	13 36				13 51			14 06			14 21			14 36				14 51			15 06	
Orpington ■	a	13 39		13 38		13 54	13 55		14 09		14 08	14 24	14 25		14 39		14 38		14 54	14 55		15 09	
	d	13 42		13 39			13 56		14 12		14 09		14 26		14 42		14 39			14 56		15 12	
Chelsfield ■	d	13 45							14 15						14 45							15 15	
Knockholt	d	13 48							14 18						14 48							15 18	
Dunton Green	d	13 53							14 23						14 53							15 23	
Sevenoaks ■	a	13 56	13 41	13 48			14 05		14 26	14 11	14 18		14 35		14 56	14 41	14 48			15 05		15 26	15 11
	d		13 42	13 49			14 05			14 12	14 19		14 35			14 42	14 49			15 05			15 12
Hildenborough	d						14 11						14 41							15 11			
Tonbridge ■	a		13 50	13 57			14 15			14 20	14 27		14 45			14 50	14 57			15 16			15 20

Table 204

Mondays to Fridays
29 August to 7 September

London Charing Cross/Cannon Street - Grove Park, Orpington, Sevenoaks and Tonbridge, Grove Park - Bromley North

Network Diagram - see first Page of Table 200

		SE ■	SE	SE ■	SE	SE	SE ■ ⌶	SE ■	SE	SE	SE ■	SE	SE	SE ■ ⌶	SE ■	SE	SE ■	SE	SE	SE ■ ⌶	SE ■	SE ■	SE
London Charing Cross ■ ⊖	d	14 45		15 00		15 06	15 10	15 15			15 30		15 36	15 40	15 45		16 00		16 06	16 10	16 15	16 28	
London Waterloo (East) ■ ⊖	d	14 48		15 03		15 09	15 13	15 18			15 33		15 39	15 43	15 48		16 03		16 09	16 13	16 18	16 31	
London Cannon Street ■ ⊖	d		14 50							15 20						15 50							
London Bridge ■ ⊖	d	14 53	14 54	15 09		15 14	15 19	15 23		15 24	15 39		15 44	15 49	15 53	15 54	16 09		16 14	16 19	16 23	16 36	
New Cross ■ ⊖	d		14 59							15 29						15 59							
St Johns	d		15 01							15 31						16 01							
Lewisham ■ ⇌	d		15 04							15 34						16 04							
Hither Green ■	d		15 08			15 23				15 38			15 53			16 08			16 23				
Grove Park ■	d		15 12		15 15	15 27			15 35	15 42		15 55	15 57			16 12		16 15	16 27				16 35
Sundridge Park	d				15 18				15 38			15 58						16 18					16 38
Bromley North	a				15 20				15 40			16 00						16 20					16 40
Elmstead Woods	d		15 15			15 30				15 45			16 00			16 15			16 30				
Chislehurst	d		15 18			15 33				15 48			16 03			16 18			16 33				
Petts Wood ■	d		15 21			15 36				15 51			16 06			16 21			16 36				
Orpington ■	a	15 08	15 24	15 25		15 39		15 38		15 54	15 55		16 09		16 08	16 24	16 25		16 39			16 52	
	d	15 09		15 26		15 42		15 39			15 56		16 12		16 09		16 26		16 42			16 53	
Chelsfield ■	d					15 45							16 15						16 45				
Knockholt	d					15 48							16 18						16 48				
Dunton Green	d					15 53							16 23						16 53				
Sevenoaks ■	a	15 18		15 35		15 56	15 41	15 48			16 05		16 26	16 11	16 18		16 35		16 58	16 42	16 46	17 02	
	d	15 19		15 35			15 42	15 49			16 05			16 12	16 19		16 35			16 43	16 47	17 03	
Hildenborough	d			15 41							16 11						16 41					17 09	
Tonbridge ■	a	15 27		15 45			15 50	15 57			16 15			16 20	16 27		16 45			16 51	16 55	17 13	

		SE	SE	SE ■ ⌶	SE ■	SE	SE	SE ■	SE	SE ■	SE ■	SE	SE	SE ■ ⌶	SE	SE ■	SE ■	SE	SE	SE ■ ⌶	SE	SE ■
London Charing Cross ■ ⊖	d		16 32	16 37	16 41		16 42	16 57			17 01		17 03	17 14			17 23		17 26	17 41		
London Waterloo (East) ■ ⊖	d		16 35	16 40	16 44		16 45	17 00			17 04		17 06	17 18			17 26		17 29	17 44		
London Cannon Street ■ ⊖	d	16 20							16 56	17 02					17 19	17 24					17 41	17 45
London Bridge ■ ⊖	d	16 24	16 40	16 45	16 49		16 51		17 00	17 06	17 09		17 11		17 23	17 28	17 31		17 35		17 45	17 49
New Cross ■ ⊖	d	16 30																				
St Johns	d	16 32																				
Lewisham ■ ⇌	d	16 35					17 01						17 21						17 44			
Hither Green ■	d	16 39	16 50				17 06						17 26						17 49			
Grove Park ■	d	16 43	16 54			16 57	17 10		17 15			17 17	17 30		17 35			17 40	17 53		17 59	
Sundridge Park	d					17 00						17 20						17 43				
Bromley North	a					17 02						17 22						17 45				
Elmstead Woods	d	16 46	16 57				17 13		17 18				17 33		17 38				17 56		18 02	
Chislehurst	d	16 48	17 00				17 15		17 21				17 35		17 40				17 58		18 05	
Petts Wood ■	d	16 51	17 03				17 19		17 24				17 40		17 44				18 02		18 08	
Orpington ■	a	16 57	17 06				17 24		17 27				17 45		17 47				18 07		18 11	
	d		17 07						17 28						17 50						18 12	
Chelsfield ■	d		17 10						17 31		17 28				17 53		17 50				18 15	
Knockholt	d		17 13						17 34						17 56						18 18	
Dunton Green	d		17 18						17 39						18 01						18 23	
Sevenoaks ■	a		17 23	17 09	17 13			17 27	17 44	17 31	17 37			17 45	18 07	17 53	17 59			18 11	18 28	18 15
	d			17 10	17 14			17 27		17 32	17 37			17 46		17 54	17 59			18 11		18 16
Hildenborough	d										17 43					18 00	18 05					
Tonbridge ■	a			17 18	17 22			17 35		17 40	17 48			17 54		18 04	18 09			18 19		18 24

		SE ■	SE	SE	SE ■	SE	SE ■	SE ■	SE	SE	SE ■ ⌶	SE	SE ■	SE	SE	SE ■	SE ■ ⌶	SE	SE ■	SE ■	SE ■	SE	SE
London Charing Cross ■ ⊖	d	17 45		17 47	18 03			18 07		18 09	18 21				18 30	18 32	18 41		18 45		19 00		19 06
London Waterloo (East) ■ ⊖	d	17 48		17 50	18 06			18 10		18 12	18 24				18 33	18 35	18 44		18 48		19 03		19 09
London Cannon Street ■ ⊖	d					18 02	18 08					18 23	18 32					18 48		19 04			
London Bridge ■ ⊖	d	17 53		17 55		18 06	18 12	18 15		18 17		18 27	18 36		18 38	18 40	18 50	18 52	18 53	19 09	19 09		19 14
New Cross ■ ⊖	d																						
St Johns	d																						
Lewisham ■ ⇌	d			18 05						18 27													
Hither Green ■	d			18 10						18 31					18 49								19 23
Grove Park ■	d		18 03	18 14		18 20			18 23	18 35		18 41		18 45	18 53			19 05				19 08	19 27
Sundridge Park	d		18 06						18 26					18 48								19 11	
Bromley North	a		18 08						18 28					18 50								19 13	
Elmstead Woods	d			18 17		18 23				18 38		18 44			18 56			19 08					19 30
Chislehurst	d			18 20		18 25				18 40		18 46			18 58			19 10					19 33
Petts Wood ■	d			18 23		18 29				18 44		18 50			19 03			19 14					19 38
Orpington ■	a			18 29		18 32				18 49		18 53			19 06		19 06	19 19			19 27		19 43
	d					18 34						18 58			19 12		19 07				19 28		19 44
Chelsfield ■	d	18 12				18 37		18 34				19 01			19 15	18 58					19 31		19 47
Knockholt	d					18 40						19 04			19 18								19 50
Dunton Green	d					18 45						19 09			19 23								19 55
Sevenoaks ■	a	18 21			18 33	18 50	18 37	18 42			18 52	19 14	19 00		19 28	19 06	19 16		19 20	19 32	19 38		19 58
	d	18 21			18 34		18 38	18 43			18 52		19 00			19 06	19 17		19 21	19 33	19 39		
Hildenborough	d	18 27					18 44	18 49								19 12				19 40	19 45		
Tonbridge ■	a	18 32			18 42		18 48	18 54			19 00		19 08			19 17	19 25		19 29	19 44	19 52		

Table 204

Mondays to Fridays

29 August to 7 September

London Charing Cross/Cannon Street - Grove Park, Orpington, Sevenoaks and Tonbridge, Grove Park - Bromley North

Network Diagram - see first Page of Table 200

	SE 1 ⌶	SE 1	SE	SE	SE 1	SE	SE	SE 1 ⌶	SE 1	SE	SE 1	SE	SE	SE 1 ⌶	SE 1	SE	SE	SE 1	SE	SE 1	SE 1
London Charing Cross ⊖ d	19 10	19 15			19 30		19 36	19 40	19 45		20 00		20 06	20 10	20 15			20 30	20 36	20 40	20 45
London Waterloo (East) ⊖ d	19 13	19 18			19 33		19 39	19 43	19 48		20 03		20 09	20 13	20 18			20 33	20 39	20 43	20 48
London Cannon Street ⊖ d				19 20						19 50							20 20				
London Bridge ⊖ d	19 19	19 23		19 24	19 39		19 44	19 49	19 53	19 54	20 09		20 14	20 19	20 23		20 24	20 39	20 44	20 49	20 53
New Cross ⊖ d				19 29						19 59							20 29				
St Johns d				19 31						20 01							20 31				
Lewisham d				19 34						20 04							20 34				
Hither Green d				19 38			19 53			20 08			20 23				20 38		20 53		
Grove Park d			19 32	19 42		19 52	19 57			20 12		20 17	20 27			20 37	20 42		20 57		
Sundridge Park d			19 35			19 55						20 20				20 40					
Bromley North a			19 37			19 57						20 22				20 42					
Elmstead Woods d				19 45			20 00			20 15			20 30				20 45		21 00		
Chislehurst d				19 48			20 03			20 18			20 33				20 48		21 03		
Petts Wood d				19 51			20 06			20 21			20 36				20 51		21 06		
Orpington a		19 38		19 54	19 55		20 09		20 08	20 24	20 25		20 39		20 38		20 54	20 55	21 09		21 08
Orpington d		19 39			19 56		20 12		20 09		20 26		20 42		20 39			20 56	21 12		21 09
Chelsfield d							20 15						20 45						21 15		
Knockholt d							20 18						20 48						21 18		
Dunton Green d							20 23						20 53						21 23		
Sevenoaks a	19 41	19 48			20 05		20 26	20 11	20 18		20 35		20 56	20 41	20 48			21 05	21 26	21 11	21 18
Sevenoaks d	19 42	19 49			20 05			20 12	20 19		20 35			20 42	20 49			21 05		21 12	21 19
Hildenborough d					20 11						20 41							21 11			
Tonbridge a	19 53	19 57			20 15			20 20	20 27		20 45			20 50	20 57			21 15		21 20	21 27

	SE 1	SE	SE	SE 1	SE 1	SE	SE	SE 1	SE 1	SE 1	SE	SE	SE 1	SE 1	SE	SE	SE 1	SE 1	SE 1	SE	SE	SE 1
London Charing Cross ⊖ d	21 00		21 06	21 10	21 30		21 36	21 40	21 45	22 00		22 06	22 10	22 30		22 36	22 40	22 45	23 00		23 06	23 10
London Waterloo (East) ⊖ d	21 03		21 09	21 13	21 33		21 39	21 43	21 48	22 03		22 09	22 13	22 33		22 39	22 43	22 48	23 03		23 09	23 13
London Cannon Street ⊖ d																						
London Bridge ⊖ d	21 09		21 14	21 19	21 39		21 44	21 49	21 53	22 09		22 14	22 19	22 39		22 44	22 49	22 53	23 09		23 14	23 19
New Cross ⊖ d																						
St Johns d																						
Lewisham d			21 22				21 52					22 22				22 52					23 22	
Hither Green d			21 26				21 56					22 26				22 56					23 26	
Grove Park d		21 07	21 30			21 37	22 00				22 07	22 30			22 37	23 00				23 07	23 30	
Sundridge Park d		21 10				21 40					22 10				22 40					23 10		
Bromley North a		21 12				21 42					22 12				22 42					23 12		
Elmstead Woods d			21 33				22 03					22 33				23 03					23 33	
Chislehurst d			21 35				22 05					22 35				23 05					23 35	
Petts Wood d			21 38				22 08					22 38				23 08					23 38	
Orpington a	21 25		21 42	21 34	21 55		22 12		22 08	22 25		22 42	22 34	22 54		23 12		23 08	23 24		23 42	23 34
Orpington d	21 26		21 43	21 35	21 56				22 09	22 26			22 35	22 54				23 09	23 24			23 35
Chelsfield d			21 46		21 59					22 29				22 57					23 27			
Knockholt d			21 49																			
Dunton Green d			21 54																			
Sevenoaks a	21 35		21 57	21 44	22 06			22 11	22 18	22 36			22 44	23 05			23 11	23 18	23 35			23 44
Sevenoaks d	21 35			21 44	22 07			22 12	22 19	22 37			22 44	23 05			23 12	23 19	23 35			23 44
Hildenborough d	21 41				22 13					22 43				23 11					23 41			
Tonbridge a	21 45			21 52	22 17			22 20	22 27	22 47			22 52	23 15			23 20	23 27	23 45			23 52

	SE 1	SE	SE	SE 1	SE 1
London Charing Cross ⊖ d	23 30		23 36	23 40	23 45
London Waterloo (East) ⊖ d	23 33		23 39	23 43	23 48
London Cannon Street ⊖ d					
London Bridge ⊖ d	23 39		23 44	23 49	23 53
New Cross ⊖ d					
St Johns d					
Lewisham d			23 52		
Hither Green d			23 56		
Grove Park d		23 37	23 59		
Sundridge Park d		23 40			
Bromley North a		23 42			
Elmstead Woods d			00 03		
Chislehurst d			00 05		
Petts Wood d			00 08		
Orpington a	23 54		00 12		00 08
Orpington d	23 54				00 09
Chelsfield d	23 57				
Knockholt d					
Dunton Green d					
Sevenoaks a	00 05			00 11	00 18
Sevenoaks d	00 05			00 12	00 19
Hildenborough d	00 11				
Tonbridge a	00 15			00 20	00 27

Table 204

Saturdays

until 21 July, 18 Aug and from 15 Sep

London Charing Cross/Cannon Street - Grove Park, Orpington, Sevenoaks and Tonbridge, Grove Park - Bromley North

Network Diagram - see first Page of Table 200

	SE 1	SE	SE 1	SE 1	SE	SE	SE	SE	SE	SE	SE 1	SE	SE	SE	SE	SE 1	SE	SE	SE 1	SE	SE	SE
London Charing Cross ⊖ d	23p30	23p36	23p40	23p45		00 06	00 15		00 48	05 36	06 00		06 06		06 36	07 00		07 06	07 30			07 36
London Waterloo (East) ⊖ d	23p33	23p39	23p43	23p48		00 09	00 18		00 51	05 39	06 03		06 09		06 39	07 03		07 09	07 33			07 39
London Cannon Street ⊖ d																						
London Bridge ⊖ d	23p39	23p44	23p49	23p53		00 14	00 23		00 56	05 44	06 08		06 14		06 44	07 08		07 14	07 38			07 44
New Cross ⊖ d									01 01													
St Johns d																						
Lewisham d		23p52				00 22			01 05	05 53			06 23		06 53			07 23				07 53
Hither Green d		23p56				00 26			01 09	05 57			06 27		06 57			07 27				07 57
Grove Park d		23p59			00 07	00 30		00 37	01 13	06 01		06 07	06 31	06 37	07 01		07 07	07 31		07 35	07 55	08 01
Sundridge Park d					00 10			00 40				06 10		06 40			07 10			07 38	07 58	
Bromley North a					00 12			00 42				06 12		06 42			07 12			07 40	08 00	
Elmstead Woods d		00 03				00 33			01 16	06 04			06 34		07 04			07 34				08 04
Chislehurst d		00 05				00 35			01 19	06 06			06 36		07 06			07 36				08 06
Petts Wood d		00 08				00 38			01 22	06 09			06 39		07 09			07 39				08 09
Orpington a	23p54	00 12		00 08		00 42	00 46		01 25	06 12	06 23		06 42		07 12	07 23		07 42	07 54			08 12
Orpington d	23p54			00 09			00 46			06 13	06 24		06 43		07 13	07 24		07 43	07 54			08 13
Chelsfield d	23p57						00 49			06 16			06 46		07 16			07 46				08 16
Knockholt d										06 19			06 49		07 19			07 49				08 19
Dunton Green d							00 56			06 24			06 54		07 24			07 54				08 24
Sevenoaks a	00 05		00 11	00 18			00 59			06 27	06 33		06 57		07 27	07 33		07 57	08 02			08 27
Sevenoaks d	00 05		00 12	00 19			00 59				06 33					07 33			08 03			
Hildenborough d	00 11						01 05				06 39					07 39			08 09			
Tonbridge a	00 15		00 20	00 27			01 10				06 43					07 43			08 14			

	SE 1	SE 1	SE	SE	SE 1	SE	SE	SE 1	SE	SE	SE 1	SE 1	SE	SE 1	SE	SE	SE 1	SE 1	SE	SE	SE 1	SE
London Charing Cross ⊖ d	07 45	08 00		08 06	08 15			08 30		08 36	08 40	08 45		09 00		09 06	09 10	09 15			09 30	
London Waterloo (East) ⊖ d	07 48	08 03		08 09	08 18			08 33		08 39	08 43	08 48		09 03		09 09	09 13	09 18			09 33	
London Cannon Street ⊖ d							08 20						08 50							09 20		
London Bridge ⊖ d	07 53	08 08		08 14	08 23		08 24	08 39		08 44	08 49	08 53	08 54	09 09		09 14	09 19	09 23		09 24	09 39	
New Cross ⊖ d							08 29						08 59							09 29		
St Johns d							08 31						09 01							09 31		
Lewisham d							08 34						09 04							09 34		
Hither Green d				08 23			08 38			08 53			09 08			09 23				09 38		
Grove Park d			08 15	08 27		08 35	08 42		08 55	08 57			09 12		09 15	09 27			09 35	09 42		09 55
Sundridge Park d			08 18			08 38			08 58						09 18				09 38			09 58
Bromley North a			08 20			08 40			09 00						09 20				09 40			10 00
Elmstead Woods d				08 30			08 45			09 00			09 15			09 30				09 45		
Chislehurst d				08 33			08 48			09 03			09 18			09 33				09 48		
Petts Wood d				08 36			08 51			09 06			09 21			09 36				09 51		
Orpington a	08 08	08 23		08 39	08 38		08 54	08 55		09 09		09 08	09 24	09 25		09 39		09 38		09 54	09 55	
Orpington d	08 09	08 24		08 42	08 39			08 56		09 12		09 09		09 26		09 42		09 39			09 56	
Chelsfield d				08 45						09 15						09 45						
Knockholt d				08 48						09 18						09 48						
Dunton Green d				08 53						09 23						09 53						
Sevenoaks a	08 18	08 33		08 56	08 48			09 05		09 26	09 11	09 18		09 35		09 56	09 41	09 48			10 05	
Sevenoaks d	08 19	08 33			08 49			09 05			09 12	09 19		09 35			09 42	09 49			10 05	
Hildenborough d		08 39						09 11						09 41							10 11	
Tonbridge a	08 27	08 43			08 57			09 15			09 20	09 27		09 45			09 50	09 57			10 15	

	SE	SE 1	SE 1	SE	SE 1	SE	SE	SE 1 ⌶	SE 1	SE	SE	SE 1	SE	SE	SE 1 ⌶	SE 1	SE	SE 1	SE	SE	SE 1 ⌶
London Charing Cross ⊖ d	09 36	09 40	09 45		10 00		10 06	10 10	10 15			10 30		10 36	10 40	10 45		11 00		11 06	11 10
London Waterloo (East) ⊖ d	09 39	09 43	09 48		10 03		10 09	10 13	10 18			10 33		10 39	10 43	10 48		11 03		11 09	11 13
London Cannon Street ⊖ d				09 50							10 20						10 50				
London Bridge ⊖ d	09 44	09 49	09 53	09 54	10 09		10 14	10 19	10 23		10 24	10 39		10 44	10 49	10 53	10 54	11 09		11 14	11 19
New Cross ⊖ d				09 59							10 29						10 59				
St Johns d				10 01							10 31						11 01				
Lewisham d				10 04							10 34						11 04				
Hither Green d	09 53			10 08			10 23				10 38			10 53			11 08			11 23	
Grove Park d	09 57			10 12		10 15	10 27			10 35	10 42		10 55	10 57			11 12		11 15	11 27	
Sundridge Park d						10 18				10 38			10 58						11 18		
Bromley North a						10 20				10 40			11 00						11 20		
Elmstead Woods d	10 00			10 15			10 30				10 45			11 00			11 15			11 30	
Chislehurst d	10 03			10 18			10 33				10 48			11 03			11 18			11 33	
Petts Wood d	10 06			10 21			10 36				10 51			11 06			11 21			11 36	
Orpington a	10 09		10 08	10 24	10 25		10 39		10 38		10 54	10 55		11 09		11 08	11 24	11 25		11 39	
Orpington d	10 12		10 09		10 26		10 42		10 39			10 56		11 12		11 09		11 26		11 42	
Chelsfield d	10 15						10 45							11 15						11 45	
Knockholt d	10 18						10 48							11 18						11 48	
Dunton Green d	10 23						10 53							11 23						11 53	
Sevenoaks a	10 26	10 11	10 18		10 35		10 56	10 41	10 48			11 05		11 26	11 11	11 18		11 35		11 56	11 41
Sevenoaks d		10 12	10 19		10 35			10 42	10 49			11 05			11 12	11 19		11 35			11 42
Hildenborough d					10 41							11 11						11 41			
Tonbridge a		10 20	10 27		10 45			10 50	10 57			11 15			11 20	11 27		11 45			11 50

Saturdays

until 21 July, 18 Aug and from 15 Sep

London Charing Cross/Cannon Street - Grove Park, Orpington, Sevenoaks and Tonbridge, Grove Park - Bromley North

Network Diagram - see first Page of Table 200

		SE ■	SE	SE	SE ■	SE	SE	SE ■ ⚲	SE ■	SE	SE ■	SE	SE	SE ■ ⚲	SE ■	SE	SE	SE ■	SE	SE	SE ■ ⚲	SE ■	SE
London Charing Cross ■ ⊖	d	11 15			11 30		11 36	11 40	11 45		12 00		12 06	12 10	12 15			12 30		12 36	12 40	12 45	
London Waterloo (East) ■ ⊖	d	11 18			11 33		11 39	11 43	11 48		12 03		12 09	12 13	12 18			12 33		12 39	12 43	12 48	
London Cannon Street ■ ⊖	d			11 20						11 50							12 20						12 50
London Bridge ■ ⊖	d	11 23		11 24	11 39		11 44	11 49	11 53	11 54	12 09		12 14	12 19	12 23		12 24	12 39		12 44	12 49	12 53	12 54
New Cross ■ ⊖	d			11 29						11 59							12 29						12 59
St Johns	d			11 31						12 01							12 31						13 01
Lewisham ■	d			11 34						12 04							12 34						13 04
Hither Green ■	d			11 38			11 53			12 08			12 23				12 38			12 53			13 08
Grove Park ■	d		11 35	11 42		11 55	11 57			12 12		12 15	12 27			12 35	12 42		12 55	12 57			13 12
Sundridge Park	d		11 38			11 58						12 18				12 38			12 58				
Bromley North	a		11 40			12 00						12 20				12 40			13 00				
Elmstead Woods	d			11 45			12 00			12 15			12 30				12 45			13 00			13 15
Chislehurst	d			11 48			12 03			12 18			12 33				12 48			13 03			13 18
Petts Wood ■	d			11 51			12 06			12 21			12 36				12 51			13 06			13 21
Orpington ■	a	11 38		11 54	11 55		12 09		12 08	12 24	12 25		12 39		12 38		12 54	12 55		13 09		13 08	13 24
	d	11 39			11 56		12 12		12 09		12 26		12 42		12 39			12 56		13 12		13 09	
Chelsfield ■	d						12 15						12 45							13 15			
Knockholt	d						12 18						12 48							13 18			
Dunton Green	d						12 23						12 53							13 23			
Sevenoaks ■	a	11 48			12 05		12 26	12 11	12 18		12 35		12 56	12 41	12 48			13 05		13 26	13 11	13 18	
	d	11 49			12 05			12 12	12 19		12 35			12 42	12 49			13 05			13 12	13 19	
Hildenborough	d				12 11						12 41							13 11					
Tonbridge ■	a	11 57			12 15			12 20	12 27		12 45			12 50	12 57			13 15			13 20	13 27	

		SE ■	SE	SE	SE ■ ⚲	SE ■	SE	SE	SE ■	SE	SE	SE ■ ⚲	SE ■	SE	SE ■	SE	SE	SE ■ ⚲	SE ■	SE	SE	SE ■
London Charing Cross ■ ⊖	d	13 00		13 06	13 10	13 15			13 30		13 36	13 40	13 45		14 00		14 06	14 10	14 15			14 30
London Waterloo (East) ■ ⊖	d	13 03		13 09	13 13	13 18			13 33		13 39	13 43	13 48		14 03		14 09	14 13	14 18			14 33
London Cannon Street ■ ⊖	d							13 20						13 50							14 20	
London Bridge ■ ⊖	d	13 09		13 14	13 19	13 23		13 24	13 39		13 44	13 49	13 53	13 54	14 09		14 14	14 19	14 23		14 24	14 39
New Cross ■ ⊖	d							13 29						13 59							14 29	
St Johns	d							13 31						14 01							14 31	
Lewisham ■	d							13 34						14 04							14 34	
Hither Green ■	d			13 23				13 38			13 53			14 08			14 23				14 38	
Grove Park ■	d		13 15	13 27			13 35	13 42		13 55	13 57			14 12		14 15	14 27			14 35	14 42	
Sundridge Park	d		13 18				13 38			13 58						14 18				14 38		
Bromley North	a		13 20				13 40			14 00						14 20				14 40		
Elmstead Woods	d			13 30				13 45			14 00			14 15			14 30				14 45	
Chislehurst	d			13 33				13 48			14 03			14 18			14 33				14 48	
Petts Wood ■	d			13 36				13 51			14 06			14 21			14 36				14 51	
Orpington ■	a	13 25		13 39		13 38		13 54	13 55		14 09		14 08	14 24	14 25		14 39		14 38		14 54	14 55
	d	13 26		13 42		13 39			13 56		14 12		14 09		14 26		14 42		14 39			14 56
Chelsfield ■	d			13 45							14 15						14 45					
Knockholt	d			13 48							14 18						14 48					
Dunton Green	d			13 53							14 23						14 53					
Sevenoaks ■	a	13 35		13 56	13 41	13 48			14 05		14 26	14 11	14 18		14 35		14 56	14 41	14 48			15 05
	d	13 35			13 42	13 49			14 05			14 12	14 19		14 35			14 42	14 49			15 05
Hildenborough	d	13 41							14 11						14 41							15 11
Tonbridge ■	a	13 45			13 50	13 57			14 15			14 20	14 27		14 45			14 50	14 57			15 15

		SE	SE	SE ■ ⚲	SE ■	SE	SE ■	SE	SE	SE ■ ⚲	SE ■	SE	SE	SE ■	SE	SE	SE ■ ⚲	SE ■	SE	SE ■	SE	SE	SE ■ ⚲
London Charing Cross ■ ⊖	d		14 36	14 40	14 45		15 00		15 06	15 10	15 15			15 30		15 36	15 40	15 45		16 00		16 06	16 10
London Waterloo (East) ■ ⊖	d		14 39	14 43	14 48		15 03		15 09	15 13	15 18			15 33		15 39	15 43	15 48		16 03		16 09	16 13
London Cannon Street ■ ⊖	d					14 50							15 20						15 50				
London Bridge ■ ⊖	d		14 44	14 49	14 53	14 54	15 09		15 14	15 19	15 23		15 24	15 39		15 44	15 49	15 53	15 54	16 09		16 14	16 19
New Cross ■ ⊖	d					14 59							15 29						15 59				
St Johns	d					15 01							15 31						16 01				
Lewisham ■	d					15 04							15 34						16 04				
Hither Green ■	d		14 53			15 08			15 23				15 38			15 53			16 08			16 23	
Grove Park ■	d	14 55	14 57			15 12		15 15	15 27			15 35	15 42		15 55	15 57			16 12		16 15	16 27	
Sundridge Park	d	14 58						15 18				15 38			15 58						16 18		
Bromley North	a	15 00						15 20				15 40			16 00						16 20		
Elmstead Woods	d		15 00			15 15			15 30				15 45			16 00			16 15			16 30	
Chislehurst	d		15 03			15 18			15 33				15 48			16 03			16 18			16 33	
Petts Wood ■	d		15 06			15 21			15 36				15 51			16 06			16 21			16 36	
Orpington ■	a		15 09		15 08	15 24	15 25		15 39		15 38		15 54	15 55		16 09		16 08	16 24	16 25		16 39	
	d		15 12		15 09		15 26		15 42		15 39			15 56		16 12		16 09		16 26		16 42	
Chelsfield ■	d		15 15						15 45							16 15						16 45	
Knockholt	d		15 18						15 48							16 18						16 48	
Dunton Green	d		15 23						15 53							16 23						16 53	
Sevenoaks ■	a		15 26	15 11	15 18		15 35		15 56	15 41	15 48			16 05		16 26	16 11	16 18		16 35		16 56	16 41
	d			15 12	15 19		15 35			15 42	15 49			16 05			16 12	16 19		16 35			16 42
Hildenborough	d						15 41							16 11						16 41			
Tonbridge ■	a			15 20	15 27		15 45			15 50	15 57			16 15			16 20	16 27		16 45			16 50

Table 204

Saturdays

until 21 July, 18 Aug and from 15 Sep

London Charing Cross/Cannon Street - Grove Park, Orpington, Sevenoaks and Tonbridge, Grove Park - Bromley North

Network Diagram - see first Page of Table 200

		SE ■	SE	SE	SE ■	SE	SE	SE ■ ⚲	SE ■	SE	SE ■	SE	SE	SE ■ ⚲	SE ■	SE	SE	SE ■	SE	SE	SE ■ ⚲	SE ■	SE
London Charing Cross ■ ⊖	d	16 15			16 30		16 36	16 40	16 45		17 00		17 06	17 10	17 15			17 30		17 36	17 40	17 45	
London Waterloo (East) ■ ⊖	d	16 18			16 33		16 39	16 43	16 48		17 03		17 09	17 13	17 18			17 33		17 39	17 43	17 48	
London Cannon Street ■ ⊖	d			16 20						16 50							17 20						17 50
London Bridge ■ ⊖	d	16 23		16 24	16 39		16 44	16 49	16 53	16 54	17 09		17 14	17 19	17 23		17 24	17 39		17 44	17 49	17 53	17 54
New Cross ■ ⊖	d			16 29						16 59							17 29						17 59
St Johns	d			16 31						17 01							17 31						18 01
Lewisham ■	d			16 34						17 04							17 34						18 04
Hither Green ■	d			16 38			16 53			17 08			17 23				17 38			17 53			18 08
Grove Park ■	d		16 35	16 42		16 55	16 57			17 12		17 15	17 27			17 35	17 42		17 55	17 57			18 12
Sundridge Park	d		16 38			16 58						17 18				17 38			17 58				
Bromley North	a		16 40			17 00						17 20				17 40			18 00				
Elmstead Woods	d			16 45			17 00			17 15			17 30				17 45			18 00			18 15
Chislehurst	d			16 48			17 03			17 18			17 33				17 48			18 03			18 18
Petts Wood ■	d			16 51			17 06			17 21			17 36				17 51			18 06			18 21
Orpington ■	a	16 38		16 54	16 55		17 09		17 08	17 24	17 25		17 39		17 38		17 54	17 55		18 09		18 08	18 24
	d	16 39			16 56		17 12		17 09		17 26		17 42		17 39			17 56		18 12		18 09	
Chelsfield ■	d						17 15						17 45							18 15			
Knockholt	d						17 18						17 48							18 18			
Dunton Green	d						17 23						17 53							18 23			
Sevenoaks ■	a	16 48			17 05		17 26	17 11	17 18		17 35		17 56	17 41	17 48			18 05		18 26	18 11	18 18	
	d	16 49			17 05			17 12	17 19		17 35			17 42	17 49			18 05			18 12	18 19	
Hildenborough	d				17 11						17 41							18 11					
Tonbridge ■	a	16 57			17 15			17 20	17 27		17 45			17 50	17 57			18 15			18 20	18 27	

		SE ■	SE	SE	SE ■ ⚲	SE ■	SE	SE	SE ■	SE	SE	SE ■ ⚲	SE ■	SE	SE ■	SE	SE	SE ■ ⚲	SE ■	SE	SE	SE ■
London Charing Cross ■ ⊖	d	18 00		18 06	18 10	18 15			18 30		18 36	18 40	18 45		19 00		19 06	19 10	19 15			19 30
London Waterloo (East) ■ ⊖	d	18 03		18 09	18 13	18 18			18 33		18 39	18 43	18 48		19 03		19 09	19 13	19 18			19 33
London Cannon Street ■ ⊖	d							18 20						18 50							19 20	
London Bridge ■ ⊖	d	18 09		18 14	18 19	18 23		18 24	18 39		18 44	18 49	18 53	18 54	19 09		19 14	19 19	19 23		19 24	19 39
New Cross ■ ⊖	d							18 29						18 59							19 29	
St Johns	d							18 31						19 01							19 31	
Lewisham ■	d							18 34						19 04							19 34	
Hither Green ■	d			18 23				18 38			18 53			19 09			19 23				19 38	
Grove Park ■	d		18 15	18 27			18 35	18 42		18 55	18 57			19 12		19 15	19 27			19 35	19 42	
Sundridge Park	d		18 18				18 38			18 58						19 18				19 38		
Bromley North	a		18 20				18 40			19 00						19 20				19 40		
Elmstead Woods	d			18 30				18 45			19 00			19 15			19 30				19 45	
Chislehurst	d			18 33				18 48			19 03			19 18			19 33				19 48	
Petts Wood ■	d			18 36				18 51			19 06			19 21			19 36				19 51	
Orpington ■	a	18 25		18 39		18 38		18 54	18 55		19 09		19 08	19 24	19 25		19 39		19 38		19 54	19 55
	d	18 26		18 42		18 39			18 56		19 12		19 09		19 26		19 42		19 39			19 56
Chelsfield ■	d			18 45							19 15						19 45					
Knockholt	d			18 48							19 18						19 48					
Dunton Green	d			18 53							19 23						19 53					
Sevenoaks ■	a	18 35		18 56	18 41	18 48			19 05		19 26	19 11	19 18		19 35		19 56	19 41	19 49			20 05
	d	18 35			18 42	18 49			19 05			19 12	19 19		19 35			19 42	19 49			20 05
Hildenborough	d	18 41							19 11						19 41							20 11
Tonbridge ■	a	18 45			18 50	18 58			19 15			19 20	19 27		19 45			19 50	19 58			20 15

		SE	SE	SE ■ ⚲	SE ■	SE	SE	SE ■ ⚲	SE ■	SE	SE	SE ■	SE ■	SE	SE	SE ■	SE ■	SE	SE	SE ■	SE ■	SE	SE
London Charing Cross ■ ⊖	d		19 36	19 40	19 55		20 06	20 10	20 25		20 36	20 40	20 55		21 06	21 10	21 25		21 36	21 40	21 55		22 06
London Waterloo (East) ■ ⊖	d		19 39	19 43	19 58		20 09	20 13	20 28		20 39	20 43	20 58		21 09	21 13	21 28		21 39	21 43	21 58		22 09
London Cannon Street ■ ⊖	d																						
London Bridge ■ ⊖	d		19 44	19 49	20 03		20 14	20 19	20 33		20 44	20 49	21 03		21 14	21 19	21 33		21 44	21 49	22 03		22 14
New Cross ■ ⊖	d																						
St Johns	d																						
Lewisham ■	d		19 52				20 22				20 52				21 22				21 52				22 22
Hither Green ■	d		19 56				20 26				20 56				21 26				21 56				22 26
Grove Park ■	d	19 55	20 00			20 15	20 30			20 37	21 00			21 07	21 30			21 37	22 00			22 07	22 30
Sundridge Park	d	19 58				20 18				20 40				21 10				21 40				22 10	
Bromley North	a	20 00				20 20				20 42				21 12				21 42				22 12	
Elmstead Woods	d		20 03				20 33				21 03				21 33				22 03				22 33
Chislehurst	d		20 05				20 35				21 05				21 35				22 05				22 35
Petts Wood ■	d		20 08				20 38				21 08				21 38				22 08				22 38
Orpington ■	a		20 12		20 18		20 42	20 34	20 48		21 12	21 04	21 18		21 42	21 34	21 48		22 12	22 04	22 18		22 42
	d		20 13		20 21		20 43	20 35	20 51		21 13	21 05	21 21		21 43	21 35	21 51			22 05	22 21		
Chelsfield ■	d		20 16				20 46				21 16				21 46								
Knockholt	d		20 19				20 49				21 19				21 49								
Dunton Green	d		20 24				20 54				21 24				21 54								
Sevenoaks ■	a		20 27	20 11	20 30		20 57	20 44	21 00		21 27	21 14	21 30		21 57	21 44	22 00			22 14	22 30		
	d			20 12	20 31			20 44	21 01			21 14	21 31			21 44	22 01			22 14	22 31		
Hildenborough	d								21 07								22 07						
Tonbridge ■	a			20 20	20 39			20 52	21 11			21 22	21 39			21 52	22 11			22 22	22 39		

Table 204

Saturdays

until 21 July, 18 Aug and from 15 Sep

London Charing Cross/Cannon Street - Grove Park, Orpington, Sevenoaks and Tonbridge, Grove Park - Bromley North

Network Diagram - see first Page of Table 200

		SE ■	SE ■	SE	SE	SE ■	SE ■	SE	SE	SE ■	SE ■	SE	SE	SE ■	SE ■
London Charing Cross	d	22 10	22 25		22 36	22 40	22 55		23 06	23 10	23 25		23 36	23 40	23 45
London Waterloo (East)	d	22 13	22 28		22 39	22 43	22 58		23 09	23 13	23 28		23 39	23 43	23 48
London Cannon Street	d														
London Bridge	d	22 19	22 33		22 44	22 49	23 03		23 14	23 19	23 33		23 44	23 49	23 53
New Cross	d														
St Johns	d														
Lewisham	d				22 52				23 22				23 52		
Hither Green	d				22 56				23 26				23 56		
Grove Park	d			22 37	23 00			23 07	23 30			23 37	23 59		
Sundridge Park	d			22 40				23 10				23 40			
Bromley North	a			22 42				23 12				23 42			
Elmstead Woods	d				23 03				23 33				00 03		
Chislehurst	d				23 05				23 35				00 05		
Petts Wood	d				23 08				23 38				00 08		
Orpington	a	22 34	22 48		23 12	23 04	23 18		23 42	23 34	23 48		00 12	00 04	00 08
	d	22 35	22 49			23 05	23 19			23 35	23 49			00 05	00 09
Chelsfield	d		22 52								23 52				
Knockholt	d														
Dunton Green	d														
Sevenoaks	a	22 44	22 59			23 14	23 28			23 44	23 59			00 14	00 18
	d	22 44	23 00			23 14	23 28			23 44	23 59			00 14	00 19
Hildenborough	d		23 06								00 06				
Tonbridge	a	22 52	23 10			23 22	23 36			23 52	00 10			00 22	00 27

Saturdays

28 July to 11 August

		SE ■	SE A	SE B	SE ■	SE ■	SE	SE	SE	SE	SE ■	SE	SE	SE ■	SE	SE	SE	SE	SE ■	SE	SE	SE ■	SE
London Charing Cross	d	23p30	23p36	23p36	23p40	23p45		00 06	00 15		00 37	00 48	05 36	06 00		06 06		06 36	07 00		07 06	07 30	
London Waterloo (East)	d	23p33	23p39	23p39	23p43	23p48		00 09	00 18		00 40	00 51	05 39	06 03		06 09		06 39	07 03		07 09	07 33	
London Cannon Street	d																						
London Bridge	d	23p39	23p44	23p44	23p49	23p53		00 14	00 23		00 45	00 56	05 44	06 08		06 14		06 44	07 08		07 14	07 38	
New Cross	d											01 01											
St Johns	d																						
Lewisham	d		23p52	23p52				00 22				01 05	05 53			06 23		06 53			07 23		
Hither Green	d		23p56	23p56				00 26				01 09	05 57			06 27		06 57			07 27		
Grove Park	d		23p59	23p59			00 07	00 30		00 37		01 13	06 01		06 07	06 31	06 37	07 01		07 07	07 31		07 35
Sundridge Park	d						00 10			00 40					06 10		06 40			07 10			07 38
Bromley North	a						00 12			00 42					06 12		06 42			07 12			07 40
Elmstead Woods	d		00 03	00 03				00 33				01 16	06 04			06 34		07 04			07 34		
Chislehurst	d		00 05	00 05				00 35				01 19	06 06			06 36		07 06			07 36		
Petts Wood	d		00 08	00 08				00 38				01 24	06 09			06 39		07 09			07 39		
Orpington	a	23p54	00 12	00 15		00 08		00 45	00 46		01 00	01 27	06 12	06 23		06 42		07 12	07 25		07 42	07 54	
	d	23p54				00 09			00 46		01 01	01 28	06 13	06 24		06 43		07 13	07 26		07 43	07 54	
Chelsfield	d	23p57							00 49			01 31	06 16			06 46		07 16			07 46		
Knockholt	d											01 34	06 19			06 49		07 19			07 49		
Dunton Green	d								00 56			01 39	06 24			06 54		07 24			07 54		
Sevenoaks	a	00 05			00 11	00 18			00 59		01 10	01 42	06 30	06 33		07 00		07 30	07 35		08 00	08 02	
	d	00 05			00 12	00 19			00 59		01 11	01 42		06 33					07 35			08 03	
Hildenborough	d	00 11							01 05			01 48		06 39					07 41			08 09	
Tonbridge	a	00 15			00 20	00 27			01 13		01 19	01 52		06 43					07 45			08 14	

		SE	SE	SE ■	SE ■	SE	SE	SE ■	SE ■	SE	SE	SE	SE	SE ■	SE ■	SE ■	SE	SE	SE	SE ■	SE ■	SE ■	SE
London Charing Cross	d		07 36	07 45	08 00		08 06	08 15	08 30				08 36	08 40	08 45	09 00			09 06	09 10	09 15	09 30	
London Waterloo (East)	d		07 39	07 48	08 03		08 09	08 18	08 33				08 39	08 43	08 48	09 03			09 09	09 13	09 18	09 33	
London Cannon Street	d										08 20						08 50						
London Bridge	d		07 44	07 53	08 08		08 14	08 23	08 39		08 24		08 44	08 49	08 53	09 09	08 54		09 14	09 19	09 23	09 39	
New Cross	d										08 29						08 59						
St Johns	d										08 31						09 01						
Lewisham	d		07 53								08 34						09 04						
Hither Green	d		07 57				08 23				08 38		08 53				09 08		09 23				
Grove Park	d	07 55	08 01			08 15	08 27			08 35	08 42	08 55	08 57				09 12	09 15	09 27				09 35
Sundridge Park	d	07 58				08 18				08 38		08 58						09 18					09 38
Bromley North	a	08 00				08 20				08 40		09 00						09 20					09 40
Elmstead Woods	d		08 04				08 30				08 45		09 00				09 15		09 30				
Chislehurst	d		08 06				08 33				08 48		09 03				09 18		09 33				
Petts Wood	d		08 09				08 36				08 51		09 06				09 21		09 36				
Orpington	a		08 12	08 08	08 23		08 39	08 38	08 55		08 57		09 09		09 08	09 25	09 27		09 39		09 38	09 55	
	d		08 13	08 09	08 24		08 42	08 39	08 56				09 12		09 09	09 26			09 42		09 39	09 56	
Chelsfield	d		08 16				08 45						09 15						09 45				
Knockholt	d		08 19				08 48						09 18						09 48				
Dunton Green	d		08 24				08 53						09 23						09 53				
Sevenoaks	a		08 30	08 18	08 33		08 56	08 48	09 05				09 26	09 11	09 18	09 35			09 56	09 41	09 48	10 05	
	d			08 19	08 33			08 49	09 05					09 12	09 19	09 35				09 42	09 49	10 05	
Hildenborough	d				08 39				09 11							09 41						10 11	
Tonbridge	a			08 27	08 43			08 57	09 15					09 20	09 27	09 45				09 50	09 57	10 15	

A not from 4 August until 11 August

B not 28 July

Table 204

Saturdays

28 July to 11 August

London Charing Cross/Cannon Street - Grove Park, Orpington, Sevenoaks and Tonbridge, Grove Park - Bromley North

Network Diagram - see first Page of Table 200

		SE	SE	SE	SE ■	SE ■	SE ■	SE	SE	SE	SE ■ ✕	SE ■	SE ■	SE	SE	SE	SE	SE ■ ✕	SE ■	SE ■	SE	SE
London Charing Cross	d			09 36	09 40	09 45	10 00			10 06	10 10	10 15	10 30				10 36	10 40	10 45	11 00		
London Waterloo (East)	d			09 39	09 43	09 48	10 03			10 09	10 13	10 18	10 33				10 39	10 43	10 48	11 03		
London Cannon Street	d	09 20						09 50							10 20						10 50	
London Bridge	d	09 24		09 44	09 49	09 53	10 09	09 54		10 14	10 19	10 23	10 39		10 24		10 44	10 49	10 53	11 09	10 54	
New Cross	d	09 29						09 59							10 29						10 59	
St Johns	d	09 31						10 01							10 31						11 01	
Lewisham	d	09 34						10 04							10 34						11 04	
Hither Green	d	09 38		09 53				10 08		10 23					10 38		10 53				11 08	
Grove Park	d	09 42	09 55	09 57				10 12	10 15	10 27				10 35	10 42	10 55	10 57				11 12	11 15
Sundridge Park	d		09 58						10 18					10 38		10 58						11 18
Bromley North	a		10 00						10 20					10 40		11 00						11 20
Elmstead Woods	d	09 45		10 00				10 15		10 30					10 45		11 00				11 15	
Chislehurst	d	09 48		10 03				10 18		10 33					10 48		11 03				11 18	
Petts Wood	d	09 51		10 06				10 21		10 36					10 51		11 06				11 21	
Orpington	a	09 57		10 09		10 08	10 25	10 27		10 39		10 38	10 55		10 57		11 09		11 08	11 25	11 27	
	d			10 12		10 09	10 26			10 42		10 39	10 56				11 12		11 09	11 26		
Chelsfield	d			10 15						10 45							11 15					
Knockholt	d			10 18						10 48							11 18					
Dunton Green	d			10 23						10 53							11 23					
Sevenoaks	a			10 26	10 11	10 18	10 35			10 56	10 41	10 48	11 05				11 26	11 11	11 18	11 35		
	d				10 12	10 19	10 35				10 42	10 49	11 05					11 12	11 19	11 35		
Hildenborough	d						10 41						11 11							11 41		
Tonbridge	a				10 20	10 27	10 45				10 50	10 57	11 15					11 20	11 27	11 45		

		SE	SE ■ ✕	SE ■	SE ■	SE	SE	SE	SE	SE ■ ✕	SE ■	SE ■	SE	SE	SE	SE ■ ✕	SE ■	SE ■	SE	SE	SE	SE	SE ■ ✕
London Charing Cross	d	11 06	11 10	11 15	11 30				11 36	11 40	11 45	12 00			12 06	12 10	12 15	12 30				12 36	12 40
London Waterloo (East)	d	11 09	11 13	11 18	11 33				11 39	11 43	11 48	12 03			12 09	12 13	12 18	12 33				12 39	12 43
London Cannon Street	d						11 20						11 50							12 20			
London Bridge	d	11 14	11 19	11 23	11 39		11 24		11 44	11 49	11 53	12 09	11 54		12 14	12 19	12 23	12 39		12 24		12 44	12 49
New Cross	d						11 29						11 59							12 29			
St Johns	d						11 31						12 01							12 31			
Lewisham	d						11 34						12 04							12 34			
Hither Green	d	11 23					11 38		11 53				12 08		12 23					12 38		12 53	
Grove Park	d	11 27				11 35	11 42	11 55	11 57				12 12	12 15	12 27				12 35	12 42	12 55	12 57	
Sundridge Park	d					11 38		11 58						12 18					12 38		12 58		
Bromley North	a					11 40		12 00						12 20					12 40		13 00		
Elmstead Woods	d	11 30					11 45		12 00				12 15		12 30					12 45		13 00	
Chislehurst	d	11 33					11 48		12 03				12 18		12 33					12 48		13 03	
Petts Wood	d	11 36					11 51		12 06				12 21		12 36					12 51		13 06	
Orpington	a	11 39		11 38	11 55		11 57		12 09		12 08	12 25	12 27		12 39		12 38	12 55		12 57		13 09	
	d	11 42		11 39	11 56				12 12		12 09	12 26			12 42		12 39	12 56				13 12	
Chelsfield	d	11 45							12 15						12 45							13 15	
Knockholt	d	11 48							12 18						12 48							13 18	
Dunton Green	d	11 53							12 23						12 53							13 23	
Sevenoaks	a	11 56	11 41	11 48	12 05				12 26	12 11	12 18	12 35			12 56	12 41	12 48	13 05				13 26	13 11
	d		11 42	11 49	12 05					12 12	12 19	12 35				12 42	12 49	13 05					13 12
Hildenborough	d				12 11							12 41						13 11					
Tonbridge	a		11 50	11 57	12 15					12 20	12 27	12 45				12 50	12 57	13 15					13 20

		SE ■	SE ■	SE	SE	SE	SE ■ ✕	SE ■	SE ■	SE	SE	SE	SE	SE ■ ✕	SE ■	SE ■	SE	SE	SE	SE ■ ✕	SE ■	SE ■
London Charing Cross	d	12 45	13 00			13 06	13 10	13 15	13 30				13 36	13 40	13 45	14 00			14 06	14 10	14 15	14 30
London Waterloo (East)	d	12 48	13 03			13 09	13 13	13 18	13 33				13 39	13 43	13 48	14 03			14 09	14 13	14 18	14 33
London Cannon Street	d			12 50							13 20						13 50					
London Bridge	d	12 53	13 09	12 54		13 14	13 19	13 23	13 39		13 24		13 44	13 49	13 53	14 09	13 54		14 14	14 19	14 23	14 39
New Cross	d			12 59							13 29						13 59					
St Johns	d			13 01							13 31						14 01					
Lewisham	d			13 04							13 34						14 04					
Hither Green	d			13 08		13 23					13 38		13 53				14 08		14 23			
Grove Park	d			13 12	13 15	13 27				13 35	13 42	13 55	13 57				14 12	14 15	14 27			
Sundridge Park	d				13 18					13 38		13 58						14 18				
Bromley North	a				13 20					13 40		14 00						14 20				
Elmstead Woods	d			13 15		13 30					13 45		14 00				14 15		14 30			
Chislehurst	d			13 18		13 33					13 48		14 03				14 18		14 33			
Petts Wood	d			13 21		13 36					13 51		14 06				14 21		14 36			
Orpington	a	13 08	13 25	13 27		13 39		13 38	13 55		13 57		14 09		14 08	14 25	14 27		14 39		14 38	14 55
	d	13 09	13 26			13 42		13 39	13 56				14 12		14 09	14 26			14 42		14 39	14 56
Chelsfield	d					13 45							14 15						14 45			
Knockholt	d					13 48							14 18						14 48			
Dunton Green	d					13 53							14 23						14 53			
Sevenoaks	a	13 18	13 35			13 56	13 41	13 48	14 05				14 26	14 11	14 18	14 35			14 56	14 41	14 48	15 05
	d	13 19	13 35				13 42	13 49	14 05					14 12	14 19	14 35				14 42	14 49	15 05
Hildenborough	d		13 41						14 11							14 41						15 11
Tonbridge	a	13 27	13 45				13 50	13 57	14 15					14 20	14 27	14 45				14 50	14 57	15 15

Table 204

Saturdays
28 July to 11 August

London Charing Cross/Cannon Street - Grove Park, Orpington, Sevenoaks and Tonbridge, Grove Park - Bromley North

Network Diagram - see first Page of Table 200

		SE	SE	SE	SE	SE 1 ⌶	SE 1	SE 1	SE	SE		SE	SE 1 ⌶	SE 1	SE 1	SE	SE	SE	SE	SE 1 ⌶		SE 1	SE 1	SE	SE
London Charing Cross 4 ⊖	d				14 36	14 40	14 45	15 00				15 06	15 10	15 15	15 30				15 36	15 40		15 45	16 00		
London Waterloo (East) 4 ⊖	d				14 39	14 43	14 48	15 03				15 09	15 13	15 18	15 33				15 39	15 43		15 48	16 03		
London Cannon Street 4 ⊖	d		14 20						14 50								15 20							15 50	
London Bridge 4 ⊖	d		14 24		14 44	14 49	14 53	15 09	14 54			15 14	15 19	15 23	15 39		15 24		15 44	15 49		15 53	16 09	15 54	
New Cross 4 ⊖	d		14 29						14 59								15 29							15 59	
St Johns	d		14 31						15 01								15 31							16 01	
Lewisham 4	d		14 34						15 04								15 34							16 04	
Hither Green 4	d		14 38		14 53				15 08			15 23					15 38		15 53					16 08	
Grove Park 4	d	14 35	14 42	14 55	14 57				15 12	15 15		15 27				15 35	15 42	15 55	15 57					16 12	16 15
Sundridge Park	d	14 38		14 58						15 18						15 38		15 58							16 18
Bromley North	a	14 40		15 00						15 20						15 40		16 00							16 20
Elmstead Woods	d		14 45		15 00				15 15			15 30					15 45		16 00					16 15	
Chislehurst	d		14 48		15 03				15 18			15 33					15 48		16 03					16 18	
Petts Wood 4	d		14 51		15 06				15 21			15 36					15 51		16 06					16 21	
Orpington 4	a		14 57		15 09		15 08	15 25	15 27			15 39		15 38	15 55		15 57		16 09			16 08	16 25	16 27	
	d				15 12		15 09	15 26				15 42		15 39	15 56				16 12			16 09	16 26		
Chelsfield 3	d				15 15							15 45							16 15						
Knockholt	d				15 18							15 48							16 18						
Dunton Green	d				15 23							15 53							16 23						
Sevenoaks 4	a				15 26	15 11	15 18	15 35				15 56	15 41	15 48	16 05				16 26	16 11		16 18	16 35		
	d					15 12	15 19	15 35					15 42	15 49	16 05					16 12		16 19	16 35		
Hildenborough	d							15 41							16 11								16 41		
Tonbridge 4	a					15 20	15 27	15 45					15 50	15 57	16 15					16 20		16 27	16 45		

		SE	SE 1 ⌶	SE 1	SE 1	SE		SE	SE	SE	SE 1 ⌶	SE 1	SE 1	SE	SE	SE		SE 1 ⌶	SE 1	SE 1	SE	SE	SE	SE	SE 1 ⌶
London Charing Cross 4 ⊖	d	16 06	16 10	16 15	16 30					16 36	16 40	16 45	17 00			17 06		17 10	17 15	17 30				17 36	17 40
London Waterloo (East) 4 ⊖	d	16 09	16 13	16 18	16 33					16 39	16 43	16 48	17 03			17 09		17 13	17 18	17 33				17 39	17 43
London Cannon Street 4 ⊖	d							16 20						16 50								17 20			
London Bridge 4 ⊖	d	16 14	16 19	16 23	16 39			16 24		16 44	16 49	16 53	17 09	16 54		17 14		17 19	17 23	17 39		17 24		17 44	17 49
New Cross 4 ⊖	d							16 29						16 59								17 29			
St Johns	d							16 31						17 01								17 31			
Lewisham 4	d							16 34						17 04								17 34			
Hither Green 4	d	16 23						16 38		16 53				17 08		17 23						17 38		17 53	
Grove Park 4	d	16 27				16 35		16 42	16 55	16 57				17 12	17 15	17 27					17 35	17 42	17 55	17 57	
Sundridge Park	d					16 38			16 58						17 18						17 38		17 58		
Bromley North	a					16 40			17 00						17 20						17 40		18 00		
Elmstead Woods	d	16 30						16 45		17 00				17 15		17 30						17 45		18 00	
Chislehurst	d	16 33						16 48		17 03				17 18		17 33						17 48		18 03	
Petts Wood 4	d	16 36						16 51		17 06				17 21		17 36						17 51		18 06	
Orpington 4	a	16 39		16 38	16 55			16 57		17 09		17 08	17 25	17 27		17 39			17 38	17 55		17 57		18 09	
	d	16 42		16 39	16 56					17 12		17 09	17 26			17 42			17 39	17 56				18 12	
Chelsfield 3	d	16 45								17 15						17 45								18 15	
Knockholt	d	16 48								17 18						17 48								18 18	
Dunton Green	d	16 53								17 23						17 53								18 23	
Sevenoaks 4	a	16 56	16 41	16 48	17 05					17 26	17 11	17 18	17 35			17 56		17 41	17 48	18 05				18 26	18 11
	d		16 42	16 49	17 05						17 12	17 19	17 35					17 42	17 49	18 05					18 12
Hildenborough	d				17 11								17 41							18 11					
Tonbridge 4	a		16 50	16 57	17 15						17 20	17 27	17 45					17 50	17 57	18 15					18 20

		SE 1		SE 1	SE	SE	SE	SE 1 ⌶	SE 1	SE 1	SE	SE		SE	SE	SE 1 ⌶	SE 1	SE 1	SE	SE	SE	SE 1 ⌶		SE 1	SE 1
London Charing Cross 4 ⊖	d	17 45		18 00			18 06	18 10	18 15	18 30					18 36	18 40	18 45	19 00			19 06	19 10		19 15	19 30
London Waterloo (East) 4 ⊖	d	17 48		18 03			18 09	18 13	18 18	18 33					18 39	18 43	18 48	19 03			19 09	19 13		19 18	19 33
London Cannon Street 4 ⊖	d				17 50							18 20							18 50						
London Bridge 4 ⊖	d	17 53		18 09	17 54		18 14	18 19	18 23	18 39		18 24			18 44	18 49	18 53	19 09	18 54		19 14	19 19		19 23	19 39
New Cross 4 ⊖	d				17 59							18 29							18 59						
St Johns	d				18 01							18 31							19 01						
Lewisham 4	d				18 04							18 34							19 04						
Hither Green 4	d				18 08		18 23					18 38			18 53				19 08		19 23				
Grove Park 4	d				18 12	18 15	18 27				18 35	18 42		18 55	18 57				19 12	19 15	19 27				
Sundridge Park	d					18 18					18 38			18 58						19 18					
Bromley North	a					18 20					18 40			19 00						19 20					
Elmstead Woods	d				18 15		18 30					18 45			19 00				19 15		19 30				
Chislehurst	d				18 18		18 33					18 48			19 03				19 18		19 33				
Petts Wood 4	d				18 21		18 36					18 51			19 06				19 21		19 36				
Orpington 4	a	18 08		18 25	18 27		18 39		18 38	18 55		18 57			19 09		19 08	19 25	19 27		19 39			19 38	19 55
	d	18 09		18 26			18 42		18 39	18 56					19 12		19 09	19 26			19 42			19 39	19 56
Chelsfield 3	d						18 45								19 15						19 45				
Knockholt	d						18 48								19 18						19 48				
Dunton Green	d						18 53								19 23						19 53				
Sevenoaks 4	a	18 18		18 35			18 56	18 41	18 48	19 05					19 26	19 11	19 18	19 35			19 56	19 41		19 49	20 05
	d	18 19		18 35				18 42	18 49	19 05						19 12	19 19	19 35				19 42		19 49	20 05
Hildenborough	d			18 41						19 11								19 41							20 11
Tonbridge 4	a	18 27		18 45				18 50	18 58	19 15						19 20	19 27	19 45				19 50		19 58	20 15

Table 204

Saturdays
28 July to 11 August

London Charing Cross/Cannon Street - Grove Park, Orpington, Sevenoaks and Tonbridge, Grove Park - Bromley North

Network Diagram - see first Page of Table 200

		SE	SE	SE	SE	SE 1 ⌶	SE 1	SE		SE	SE 1 ⌶	SE 1	SE	SE	SE 1	SE 1	SE	SE		SE 1	SE 1	SE	SE	SE 1	SE 1
London Charing Cross 4 ⊖	d				19 36	19 40	19 55			20 06	20 10	20 25		20 36	20 40	20 55		21 06		21 10	21 25		21 36	21 40	21 55
London Waterloo (East) 4 ⊖	d				19 39	19 43	19 58			20 09	20 13	20 28		20 39	20 43	20 58		21 09		21 13	21 28		21 39	21 43	21 58
London Cannon Street 4 ⊖	d		19 20																						
London Bridge 4 ⊖	d		19 24		19 44	19 49	20 03			20 14	20 19	20 33		20 44	20 49	21 03		21 14		21 19	21 33		21 44	21 49	22 03
New Cross 4 ⊖	d		19 29																						
St Johns	d		19 31																						
Lewisham 4	d		19 34		19 52					20 22				20 52				21 22					21 52		
Hither Green 4	d		19 38		19 56					20 26				20 56				21 26					21 56		
Grove Park 4	d	19 35	19 42	19 55	20 00			20 15		20 30			20 37	21 00			21 07	21 30				21 37	22 00		
Sundridge Park	d	19 38		19 58				20 18					20 40				21 10					21 40			
Bromley North	a	19 40		20 00				20 20					20 42				21 12					21 42			
Elmstead Woods	d		19 45		20 03					20 33				21 03				21 33					22 03		
Chislehurst	d		19 48		20 05					20 35				21 05				21 35					22 05		
Petts Wood 4	d		19 51		20 08					20 38				21 08				21 38					22 08		
Orpington 4	a		19 57		20 12		20 18			20 42	20 34	20 48		21 12	21 04	21 18		21 42		21 34	21 48		22 15	22 04	22 18
	d				20 13		20 21			20 43	20 35	20 51		21 13	21 05	21 21		21 43		21 35	21 51			22 05	22 21
Chelsfield 3	d				20 16					20 46				21 16				21 46							
Knockholt	d				20 19					20 49				21 19				21 49							
Dunton Green	d				20 24					20 54				21 24				21 54							
Sevenoaks 4	a				20 30	20 11	20 30			21 00	20 44	21 00		21 30	21 14	21 30		22 00		21 44	22 00			22 14	22 30
	d					20 12	20 31				20 44	21 01			21 14	21 31				21 44	22 01			22 14	22 31
Hildenborough	d											21 07									22 07				
Tonbridge 4	a					20 20	20 39				20 52	21 11			21 22	21 39				21 52	22 11			22 22	22 39

		SE	SE	SE 1		SE 1	SE	SE	SE 1	SE 1	SE	SE	SE 1	SE 1		SE	SE	SE 1	SE 1
London Charing Cross 4 ⊖	d		22 06	22 10		22 25		22 36	22 40	22 55		23 06	23 10	23 25			23 36	23 40	23 45
London Waterloo (East) 4 ⊖	d		22 09	22 13		22 28		22 39	22 43	22 58		23 09	23 13	23 28			23 39	23 43	23 48
London Cannon Street 4 ⊖	d																		
London Bridge 4 ⊖	d		22 14	22 19		22 33		22 44	22 49	23 03		23 14	23 19	23 33			23 44	23 49	23 53
New Cross 4 ⊖	d																		
St Johns	d																		
Lewisham 4	d		22 22					22 52				23 22					23 52		
Hither Green 4	d		22 26					22 56				23 26					23 56		
Grove Park 4	d	22 07	22 30				22 37	23 00			23 07	23 30				23 37	23 59		
Sundridge Park	d	22 10					22 40				23 10					23 40			
Bromley North	a	22 12					22 42				23 12					23 42			
Elmstead Woods	d		22 33					23 03				23 33					00 03		
Chislehurst	d		22 35					23 05				23 35					00 05		
Petts Wood 4	d		22 38					23 08				23 38					00 08		
Orpington 4	a		22 45	22 34		22 48		23 15	23 04	23 18		23 45	23 34	23 48			00 15	00 04	00 08
	d			22 35		22 49			23 05	23 19			23 35	23 49				00 05	00 09
Chelsfield 3	d					22 52								23 52					
Knockholt	d																		
Dunton Green	d																		
Sevenoaks 4	a			22 44		22 59			23 14	23 28			23 44	23 59				00 14	00 18
	d			22 44		23 00			23 14	23 28			23 44	23 59				00 14	00 19
Hildenborough	d					23 06								00 06					
Tonbridge 4	a			22 52		23 10			23 22	23 36			23 52	00 10				00 22	00 27

Saturdays
25 August to 8 September

		SE 1	SE	SE 1	SE 1	SE	SE	SE	SE	SE 1 A		SE A	SE	SE	SE 1	SE	SE	SE	SE	SE 1		SE	SE	SE 1	SE
London Charing Cross 4 ⊖	d	23p30	23p36	23p40	23p45		00 06	00 15		00 37		00 48	00 48	05 36	06 00		06 06		06 36	07 00			07 06	07 30	
London Waterloo (East) 4 ⊖	d	23p33	23p39	23p43	23p48		00 09	00 18		00 40		00 51	00 51	05 39	06 03		06 09		06 39	07 03			07 09	07 33	
London Cannon Street 4 ⊖	d																								
London Bridge 4 ⊖	d	23p39	23p44	23p49	23p53		00 14	00 23		00 45		00 56	00 56	05 44	06 08		06 14		06 44	07 08			07 14	07 38	
New Cross 4 ⊖	d											01 01	01 01												
St Johns	d																								
Lewisham 4	d		23p52				00 22					01 05	01 05	05 53			06 23		06 53				07 23		
Hither Green 4	d		23p56				00 26					01 09	01 09	05 57			06 27		06 57				07 27		
Grove Park 4	d		23p59			00 07	00 30		00 37			01 13	01 13	06 01		06 07	06 31	06 37	07 01			07 07	07 31		07 35
Sundridge Park	d					00 10			00 40							06 10		06 40				07 10			07 38
Bromley North	a					00 12			00 42							06 12		06 42				07 12			07 40
Elmstead Woods	d		00 03				00 33					01 16	01 16	06 04			06 34		07 04				07 34		
Chislehurst	d		00 05				00 35					01 18	01 19	06 06			06 36		07 06				07 36		
Petts Wood 4	d		00 08				00 38					01 22	01 22	06 09			06 39		07 09				07 39		
Orpington 4	a	23p54	00 12		00 08		00 42	00 46		01 00		01 25	01 25	06 12	06 23		06 42		07 12	07 23			07 42	07 54	
	d	23p54			00 09			00 46		01 01		01 26		06 13	06 24		06 43		07 13	07 24			07 43	07 54	
Chelsfield 3	d	23p57						00 49				01s29		06 16			06 46		07 16				07 46		
Knockholt	d											01s32		06 19			06 49		07 19				07 49		
Dunton Green	d							00 56				01s37		06 24			06 54		07 24				07 54		
Sevenoaks 4	a	00 05		00 11	00 18			00 59		01s10		01s40		06 27	06 33		06 57		07 27	07 33			07 57	08 02	
	d	00 05		00 12	00 19			00 59							06 33					07 33				08 03	
Hildenborough	d	00 11						01 05				01s46			06 39					07 39				08 09	
Tonbridge 4	a	00 15		00 20	00 27			01 10		01s19		01s50			06 43					07 43				08 14	

A not 25 August

London Charing Cross/Cannon Street - Grove Park, Orpington, Sevenoaks and Tonbridge, Grove Park - Bromley North

Network Diagram - see first Page of Table 200

		SE	SE	SE 1	SE 1	SE	SE	SE 1	SE	SE	SE 1	SE	SE	SE 1	SE 1	SE	SE 1	SE	SE	SE 1	SE 1	SE	SE
London Charing Cross 4 ⊖	d		07 36	07 45	08 00		08 06	08 15			08 30		08 36	08 40	08 45		09 00		09 06	09 10	09 15		
London Waterloo (East) 4 ⊖	d		07 39	07 48	08 03		08 09	08 18			08 33		08 39	08 43	08 48		09 03		09 09	09 13	09 18		
London Cannon Street 4 ⊖	d									08 20						08 50							09 20
London Bridge 4 ⊖	d		07 44	07 53	08 08		08 14	08 23		08 24	08 39		08 44	08 49	08 53	08 54	09 09		09 14	09 19	09 23		09 24
New Cross 4 ⊖	d									08 29						08 59							09 29
St Johns	d									08 31						09 01							09 31
Lewisham 4 ⇌	d		07 53							08 34						09 04							09 34
Hither Green 4	d		07 57				08 23			08 38			08 53			09 08			09 23				09 38
Grove Park 4	d	07 55	08 01			08 15	08 27		08 35	08 42		08 55	08 57			09 12		09 15	09 27			09 35	09 42
Sundridge Park	d	07 58				08 18			08 38			08 58						09 18				09 38	
Bromley North	a	08 00				08 20			08 40			09 00						09 20				09 40	
Elmstead Woods	d		08 04				08 30			08 45			09 00			09 15			09 30				09 45
Chislehurst	d		08 06				08 33			08 48			09 03			09 18			09 33				09 48
Petts Wood 4	d		08 09				08 36			08 51			09 06			09 21			09 36				09 51
Orpington 4	a		08 12	08 08	08 23		08 39	08 38		08 54	08 55		09 09		09 08	09 24	09 25		09 39		09 38		09 54
	d		08 13	08 09	08 24		08 42	08 39			08 56		09 12		09 09		09 26		09 42		09 39		
Chelsfield 3	d		08 16				08 45						09 15						09 45				
Knockholt	d		08 19				08 48						09 18						09 48				
Dunton Green	d		08 24				08 53						09 23						09 53				
Sevenoaks 4	a		08 27	08 18	08 33		08 56	08 48			09 05		09 26	09 11	09 18		09 35		09 56	09 41	09 48		
	d			08 19	08 33			08 49			09 05			09 12	09 19		09 35			09 42	09 49		
Hildenborough	d				08 39						09 11						09 41						
Tonbridge 4	a			08 27	08 43			08 57			09 15			09 20	09 27		09 45			09 50	09 57		

		SE 1	SE	SE	SE 1	SE 1	SE	SE 1	SE	SE	SE 1 H	SE 1	SE	SE	SE 1	SE	SE	SE 1 H	SE 1	SE	SE 1	SE
London Charing Cross 4 ⊖	d	09 30		09 36	09 40	09 45		10 00		10 06	10 10	10 15			10 30		10 36	10 40	10 45		11 00	
London Waterloo (East) 4 ⊖	d	09 33		09 39	09 43	09 48		10 03		10 09	10 13	10 18			10 33		10 39	10 43	10 48		11 03	
London Cannon Street 4 ⊖	d						09 50							10 20						10 50		
London Bridge 4 ⊖	d	09 39		09 44	09 49	09 53	09 54	10 09		10 14	10 19	10 23		10 24	10 39		10 44	10 49	10 53	10 54	11 09	
New Cross 4 ⊖	d						09 59							10 29						10 59		
St Johns	d						10 01							10 31						11 01		
Lewisham 4 ⇌	d						10 04							10 34						11 04		
Hither Green 4	d			09 53			10 08			10 23				10 38			10 53			11 08		
Grove Park 4	d		09 55	09 57			10 12		10 15	10 27			10 35	10 42		10 55	10 57			11 12		11 15
Sundridge Park	d		09 58						10 18				10 38			10 58						11 18
Bromley North	a		10 00						10 20				10 40			11 00						11 20
Elmstead Woods	d			10 00			10 15			10 30				10 45			11 00			11 15		
Chislehurst	d			10 03			10 18			10 33				10 48			11 03			11 18		
Petts Wood 4	d			10 06			10 21			10 36				10 51			11 06			11 21		
Orpington 4	a	09 55		10 09		10 08	10 24	10 25		10 39		10 38		10 54	10 55		11 09		11 08	11 24	11 25	
	d	09 56		10 12		10 09		10 26		10 42		10 39			10 56		11 12		11 09		11 26	
Chelsfield 3	d			10 15						10 45							11 15					
Knockholt	d			10 18						10 48							11 18					
Dunton Green	d			10 23						10 53							11 23					
Sevenoaks 4	a	10 05		10 26	10 11	10 18		10 35		10 56	10 41	10 48			11 05		11 26	11 11	11 18		11 35	
	d	10 05			10 12	10 19		10 35			10 42	10 49			11 05			11 12	11 19		11 35	
Hildenborough	d	10 11						10 41							11 11						11 41	
Tonbridge 4	a	10 15			10 20	10 27		10 45			10 50	10 57			11 15			11 20	11 27		11 45	

		SE	SE 1 H	SE 1	SE	SE	SE 1	SE	SE	SE 1 H	SE 1	SE	SE 1	SE	SE	SE 1 H	SE 1	SE	SE	SE 1	SE	SE	SE 1 H
London Charing Cross 4 ⊖	d	11 06	11 10	11 15			11 30		11 36	11 40	11 45		12 00		12 06	12 10	12 15			12 30		12 36	12 40
London Waterloo (East) 4 ⊖	d	11 09	11 13	11 18			11 33		11 39	11 43	11 48		12 03		12 09	12 13	12 18			12 33		12 39	12 43
London Cannon Street 4 ⊖	d					11 20						11 50							12 20				
London Bridge 4 ⊖	d	11 14	11 19	11 23		11 24	11 39		11 44	11 49	11 53	11 54	12 09		12 14	12 19	12 23		12 24	12 39		12 44	12 49
New Cross 4 ⊖	d					11 29						11 59							12 29				
St Johns	d					11 31						12 01							12 31				
Lewisham 4 ⇌	d					11 34						12 04							12 34				
Hither Green 4	d	11 23				11 38			11 53			12 08			12 23				12 38			12 53	
Grove Park 4	d	11 27			11 35	11 42		11 55	11 57			12 12		12 15	12 27			12 35	12 42		12 55	12 57	
Sundridge Park	d				11 38			11 58						12 18				12 38			12 58		
Bromley North	a				11 40			12 00						12 20				12 40			13 00		
Elmstead Woods	d	11 30				11 45			12 00			12 15			12 30				12 45			13 00	
Chislehurst	d	11 33				11 48			12 03			12 18			12 33				12 48			13 03	
Petts Wood 4	d	11 36				11 51			12 06			12 21			12 36				12 51			13 06	
Orpington 4	a	11 39		11 38		11 54	11 55		12 09		12 08	12 24	12 25		12 39		12 38		12 54	12 55		13 09	
	d	11 42		11 39			11 56		12 12		12 09		12 26		12 42		12 39			12 56		13 12	
Chelsfield 3	d	11 45							12 15						12 45							13 15	
Knockholt	d	11 48							12 18						12 48							13 18	
Dunton Green	d	11 53							12 23						12 53							13 23	
Sevenoaks 4	a	11 56	11 41	11 48			12 05		12 26	12 11	12 18		12 35		12 56	12 41	12 48			13 05		13 26	13 11
	d		11 42	11 49			12 05			12 12	12 19		12 35			12 42	12 49			13 05			13 12
Hildenborough	d						12 11						12 41							13 11			
Tonbridge 4	a		11 50	11 57			12 15			12 20	12 27		12 45			12 50	12 57			13 15			13 20

Table 204

Saturdays

25 August to 8 September

London Charing Cross/Cannon Street - Grove Park, Orpington, Sevenoaks and Tonbridge, Grove Park - Bromley North

Network Diagram - see first Page of Table 200

		SE 1	SE	SE 1	SE	SE	SE 1 H	SE 1	SE	SE	SE 1	SE	SE	SE 1 H	SE 1	SE	SE 1	SE	SE	SE 1 H	SE 1	SE
London Charing Cross 4 ⊖	d	12 45		13 00		13 06	13 10	13 15			13 30		13 36	13 40	13 45		14 00		14 06	14 10	14 15	
London Waterloo (East) 4 ⊖	d	12 48		13 03		13 09	13 13	13 18			13 33		13 39	13 43	13 48		14 03		14 09	14 13	14 18	
London Cannon Street 4 ⊖	d		12 50							13 20						13 50						
London Bridge 4 ⊖	d	12 53	12 54	13 09		13 14	13 19	13 23		13 24	13 39		13 44	13 49	13 53	13 54	14 09		14 14	14 19	14 23	
New Cross 4 ⊖	d		12 59							13 29						13 59						
St Johns	d		13 01							13 31						14 01						
Lewisham 4 ⇌	d		13 04							13 34						14 04						
Hither Green 4	d		13 08			13 23				13 38			13 53			14 08			14 23			
Grove Park 4	d		13 12		13 15	13 27			13 35	13 42		13 55	13 57			14 12		14 15	14 27			14 35
Sundridge Park	d				13 18				13 38			13 58						14 18				14 38
Bromley North	a				13 20				13 40			14 00						14 20				14 40
Elmstead Woods	d		13 15			13 30				13 45			14 00			14 15			14 30			
Chislehurst	d		13 18			13 33				13 48			14 03			14 18			14 33			
Petts Wood 4	d		13 21			13 36				13 51			14 06			14 21			14 36			
Orpington 4	a	13 08	13 24	13 25		13 39		13 38		13 54	13 55		14 09		14 08	14 24	14 25		14 39		14 38	
	d	13 09		13 26		13 42		13 39			13 56		14 12		14 09		14 26		14 42		14 39	
Chelsfield 3	d					13 45							14 15						14 45			
Knockholt	d					13 48							14 18						14 48			
Dunton Green	d					13 53							14 23						14 53			
Sevenoaks 4	a	13 18		13 35		13 56	13 41	13 48			14 05		14 26	14 11	14 18		14 35		14 56	14 41	14 48	
	d	13 19		13 35			13 42	13 49			14 05			14 12	14 19		14 35			14 42	14 49	
Hildenborough	d			13 41							14 11						14 41					
Tonbridge 4	a	13 27		13 45			13 50	13 57			14 15			14 20	14 27		14 45			14 50	14 57	

		SE	SE 1	SE	SE	SE 1 H	SE 1	SE	SE 1	SE	SE	SE 1 H	SE 1	SE	SE	SE 1	SE	SE	SE 1 H	SE 1	SE	SE 1	SE
London Charing Cross 4 ⊖	d		14 30		14 36	14 40	14 45		15 00		15 06	15 10	15 15			15 30		15 36	15 40	15 45		16 00	
London Waterloo (East) 4 ⊖	d		14 33		14 39	14 43	14 48		15 03		15 09	15 13	15 18			15 33		15 39	15 43	15 48		16 03	
London Cannon Street 4 ⊖	d	14 20						14 50							15 20						15 50		
London Bridge 4 ⊖	d	14 24	14 39		14 44	14 49	14 53	14 54	15 09		15 14	15 19	15 23		15 24	15 39		15 44	15 49	15 53	15 54	16 09	
New Cross 4 ⊖	d	14 29						14 59							15 29						15 59		
St Johns	d	14 31						15 01							15 31						16 01		
Lewisham 4 ⇌	d	14 34						15 04							15 34						16 04		
Hither Green 4	d	14 38			14 53			15 08			15 23				15 38			15 53			16 08		
Grove Park 4	d	14 42		14 55	14 57			15 12		15 15	15 27			15 35	15 42		15 55	15 57			16 12		16 15
Sundridge Park	d			14 58						15 18				15 38			15 58						16 18
Bromley North	a			15 00						15 20				15 40			16 00						16 20
Elmstead Woods	d	14 45			15 00			15 15			15 30				15 45			16 00			16 15		
Chislehurst	d	14 48			15 03			15 18			15 33				15 48			16 03			16 18		
Petts Wood 4	d	14 51			15 06			15 21			15 36				15 51			16 06			16 21		
Orpington 4	a	14 54	14 55		15 09		15 08	15 24	15 25		15 39		15 38		15 54	15 55		16 09		16 08	16 24	16 25	
	d		14 56		15 12		15 09		15 26		15 42		15 39			15 56		16 12		16 09		16 26	
Chelsfield 3	d				15 15						15 45							16 15					
Knockholt	d				15 18						15 48							16 18					
Dunton Green	d				15 23						15 53							16 23					
Sevenoaks 4	a		15 05		15 26	15 11	15 18		15 35		15 56	15 41	15 48			16 05		16 26	16 11	16 18		16 35	
	d		15 05			15 12	15 19		15 35			15 42	15 49			16 05			16 12	16 19		16 35	
Hildenborough	d		15 11						15 41							16 11						16 41	
Tonbridge 4	a		15 15			15 20	15 27		15 45			15 50	15 57			16 15			16 20	16 27		16 45	

		SE	SE 1 H	SE 1	SE	SE	SE 1	SE	SE	SE 1 H	SE 1	SE	SE 1	SE	SE	SE 1 H	SE 1	SE	SE	SE 1	SE	SE	SE 1 H
London Charing Cross 4 ⊖	d	16 06	16 10	16 15			16 30		16 36	16 40	16 45		17 00		17 06	17 10	17 15			17 30		17 36	17 40
London Waterloo (East) 4 ⊖	d	16 09	16 13	16 18			16 33		16 39	16 43	16 48		17 03		17 09	17 13	17 18			17 33		17 39	17 43
London Cannon Street 4 ⊖	d					16 20						16 50							17 20				
London Bridge 4 ⊖	d	16 14	16 19	16 23		16 24	16 39		16 44	16 49	16 53	16 54	17 09		17 14	17 19	17 23		17 24	17 39		17 44	17 49
New Cross 4 ⊖	d					16 29						16 59							17 29				
St Johns	d					16 31						17 01							17 31				
Lewisham 4 ⇌	d					16 34						17 04							17 34				
Hither Green 4	d	16 23				16 38			16 53			17 08			17 23				17 38			17 53	
Grove Park 4	d	16 27			16 35	16 42		16 55	16 57			17 12		17 15	17 27			17 35	17 42		17 55	17 57	
Sundridge Park	d				16 38			16 58						17 18				17 38			17 58		
Bromley North	a				16 40			17 00						17 20				17 40			18 00		
Elmstead Woods	d	16 30				16 45			17 00			17 15			17 30				17 45			18 00	
Chislehurst	d	16 33				16 48			17 03			17 18			17 33				17 48			18 03	
Petts Wood 4	d	16 36				16 51			17 06			17 21			17 36				17 51			18 06	
Orpington 4	a	16 39		16 38		16 54	16 55		17 09		17 08	17 24	17 25		17 39		17 38		17 54	17 55		18 09	
	d	16 42		16 39			16 56		17 12		17 09		17 26		17 42		17 39			17 56		18 12	
Chelsfield 3	d	16 45							17 15						17 45							18 15	
Knockholt	d	16 48							17 18						17 48							18 18	
Dunton Green	d	16 53							17 23						17 53							18 23	
Sevenoaks 4	a	16 56	16 41	16 48			17 05		17 26	17 11	17 18		17 35		17 56	17 41	17 48			18 05		18 26	18 11
	d		16 42	16 49			17 05			17 12	17 19		17 35			17 42	17 49			18 05			18 12
Hildenborough	d						17 11						17 41							18 11			
Tonbridge 4	a		16 50	16 57			17 15			17 20	17 27		17 45			17 50	17 57			18 15			18 20

Table 204

Saturdays
25 August to 8 September

London Charing Cross/Cannon Street - Grove Park, Orpington, Sevenoaks and Tonbridge, Grove Park - Bromley North

Network Diagram - see first Page of Table 200

		SE 1		SE	SE 1	SE	SE	SE 1 ⊼	SE 1	SE	SE	SE 1	
London Charing Cross 4 ⊖	d	17 45			18 00		18 06	18 10	18 15			18 30	
London Waterloo (East) 4 ⊖	d	17 48			18 03		18 09	18 13	18 18			18 33	
London Cannon Street 4 ⊖	d			17 50							18 20		
London Bridge 4 ⊖	d	17 53		17 54	18 09		18 14	18 19	18 23		18 24	18 39	
New Cross 4 ⊖	d			17 59							18 29		
St Johns	d			18 01							18 31		
Lewisham 4	d			18 04							18 34		
Hither Green 4	d			18 08			18 23				18 38		
Grove Park 4	d			18 12		18 15	18 27			18 35	18 42		
Sundridge Park	d					18 18				18 38			
Bromley North	a					18 20				18 40			
Elmstead Woods	d			18 15			18 30				18 45		
Chislehurst	d			18 18			18 33				18 48		
Petts Wood 4	d			18 21			18 36				18 51		
Orpington 4	a	18 08		18 24	18 25		18 39		18 38		18 54	18 55	
	d	18 09			18 26		18 42		18 39			18 56	
Chelsfield 3	d						18 45						
Knockholt	d						18 48						
Dunton Green	d						18 53						
Sevenoaks 4	a	18 18			18 35		18 56	18 41	18 48			19 05	
	d	18 19			18 35			18 42	18 49			19 05	
Hildenborough	d				18 41							19 11	
Tonbridge 4	a	18 27			18 45			18 50	18 58			19 15	

		SE	SE	SE 1 ⊼	SE 1	SE	SE 1	SE	SE	SE 1 ⊼		SE 1	SE
London Charing Cross 4 ⊖	d		18 36	18 40	18 45		19 00		19 06	19 10		19 15	
London Waterloo (East) 4 ⊖	d		18 39	18 43	18 48		19 03		19 09	19 13		19 18	
London Cannon Street 4 ⊖	d					18 50							
London Bridge 4 ⊖	d		18 44	18 49	18 53	18 54	19 09		19 14	19 19		19 23	
New Cross 4 ⊖	d					18 59							
St Johns	d					19 01							
Lewisham 4	d					19 04							
Hither Green 4	d		18 53			19 09			19 23				
Grove Park 4	d	18 55	18 57			19 12		19 15	19 27				19 35
Sundridge Park	d	18 58						19 18					19 38
Bromley North	a	19 00						19 20					19 40
Elmstead Woods	d		19 00			19 15			19 30				
Chislehurst	d		19 03			19 18			19 33				
Petts Wood 4	d		19 06			19 21			19 36				
Orpington 4	a		19 09		19 08	19 24	19 25		19 39			19 38	
	d		19 12		19 09		19 26		19 42			19 39	
Chelsfield 3	d		19 15						19 45				
Knockholt	d		19 18						19 48				
Dunton Green	d		19 23						19 53				
Sevenoaks 4	a		19 26	19 11	19 18		19 35		19 56	19 41		19 49	
	d			19 12	19 19		19 35			19 42		19 49	
Hildenborough	d						19 41						
Tonbridge 4	a			19 20	19 27		19 45			19 50		19 58	

		SE	SE 1	SE	SE	SE 1 ⊼	SE 1	SE		SE	SE 1 ⊼	SE 1	SE
London Charing Cross 4 ⊖	d		19 30		19 36	19 40	19 55			20 06	20 10	20 25	
London Waterloo (East) 4 ⊖	d		19 33		19 39	19 43	19 58			20 09	20 13	20 28	
London Cannon Street 4 ⊖	d	19 20											
London Bridge 4 ⊖	d	19 24	19 39		19 44	19 49	20 03			20 14	20 19	20 33	
New Cross 4 ⊖	d	19 29											
St Johns	d	19 31											
Lewisham 4	d	19 34			19 52					20 22			
Hither Green 4	d	19 38			19 56					20 26			
Grove Park 4	d	19 42		19 55	20 00			20 15		20 30			20 37
Sundridge Park	d			19 58				20 18					20 40
Bromley North	a			20 00				20 20					20 42
Elmstead Woods	d	19 45			20 03					20 33			
Chislehurst	d	19 48			20 05					20 35			
Petts Wood 4	d	19 51			20 08					20 38			
Orpington 4	a	19 54	19 55		20 12		20 18			20 42	20 34	20 48	
	d		19 56		20 13		20 21			20 43	20 35	20 51	
Chelsfield 3	d				20 16					20 46			
Knockholt	d				20 19					20 49			
Dunton Green	d				20 24					20 54			
Sevenoaks 4	a		20 05		20 27	20 11	20 30			20 57	20 44	21 00	
	d		20 05			20 12	20 31				20 44	21 01	
Hildenborough	d		20 11									21 07	
Tonbridge 4	a		20 15			20 20	20 39				20 52	21 11	

		SE	SE 1	SE 1	SE	SE		SE 1	SE 1	SE	SE	SE 1	SE 1
London Charing Cross 4 ⊖	d	20 36	20 40	20 55		21 06		21 10	21 25		21 36	21 40	21 55
London Waterloo (East) 4 ⊖	d	20 39	20 43	20 58		21 09		21 13	21 28		21 39	21 43	21 58
London Cannon Street 4 ⊖	d												
London Bridge 4 ⊖	d	20 44	20 49	21 03		21 14		21 19	21 33		21 44	21 49	22 03
New Cross 4 ⊖	d												
St Johns	d												
Lewisham 4	d	20 52				21 22					21 52		
Hither Green 4	d	20 56				21 26					21 56		
Grove Park 4	d	21 00			21 07	21 30				21 37	22 00		
Sundridge Park	d				21 10					21 40			
Bromley North	a				21 12					21 42			
Elmstead Woods	d	21 03				21 33					22 03		
Chislehurst	d	21 05				21 35					22 05		
Petts Wood 4	d	21 08				21 38					22 08		
Orpington 4	a	21 12	21 04	21 18		21 42		21 34	21 48		22 12	22 04	22 18
	d	21 13	21 05	21 21		21 43		21 35	21 51			22 05	22 21
Chelsfield 3	d	21 16				21 46							
Knockholt	d	21 19				21 49							
Dunton Green	d	21 24				21 54							
Sevenoaks 4	a	21 27	21 14	21 30		21 57		21 44	22 00			22 14	22 30
	d		21 14	21 31				21 44	22 01			22 14	22 31
Hildenborough	d								22 07				
Tonbridge 4	a		21 22	21 39				21 52	22 11			22 22	22 39

		SE	SE	SE 1		SE 1	SE	SE	SE 1	SE 1
London Charing Cross 4 ⊖	d		22 06	22 10		22 25		22 36	22 40	22 55
London Waterloo (East) 4 ⊖	d		22 09	22 13		22 28		22 39	22 43	22 58
London Cannon Street 4 ⊖	d									
London Bridge 4 ⊖	d		22 14	22 19		22 33		22 44	22 49	23 03
New Cross 4 ⊖	d									
St Johns	d									
Lewisham 4	d		22 22					22 52		
Hither Green 4	d		22 26					22 56		
Grove Park 4	d	22 07	22 30				22 37	23 00		
Sundridge Park	d	22 10					22 40			
Bromley North	a	22 12					22 42			
Elmstead Woods	d		22 33					23 03		
Chislehurst	d		22 35					23 05		
Petts Wood 4	d		22 38					23 08		
Orpington 4	a		22 42	22 34		22 48		23 12	23 04	23 18
	d			22 35		22 49			23 05	23 19
Chelsfield 3	d					22 52				
Knockholt	d									
Dunton Green	d									
Sevenoaks 4	a			22 44		22 59			23 14	23 28
	d			22 44		23 00			23 14	23 28
Hildenborough	d					23 06				
Tonbridge 4	a			22 52		23 10			23 22	23 36

		SE	SE	SE 1	SE 1		SE	SE	SE 1	SE 1
London Charing Cross 4 ⊖	d		23 06	23 10	23 25			23 36	23 40	23 45
London Waterloo (East) 4 ⊖	d		23 09	23 13	23 28			23 39	23 43	23 48
London Cannon Street 4 ⊖	d									
London Bridge 4 ⊖	d		23 14	23 19	23 33			23 44	23 49	23 53
New Cross 4 ⊖	d									
St Johns	d									
Lewisham 4	d		23 22					23 52		
Hither Green 4	d		23 26					23 56		
Grove Park 4	d	23 07	23 30				23 37	23 59		
Sundridge Park	d	23 10					23 40			
Bromley North	a	23 12					23 42			
Elmstead Woods	d		23 33					00 03		
Chislehurst	d		23 35					00 05		
Petts Wood 4	d		23 38					00 08		
Orpington 4	a		23 42	23 34	23 48			00 12	00 04	00 08
	d			23 35	23 49				00 05	00 09
Chelsfield 3	d				23 52					
Knockholt	d									
Dunton Green	d									
Sevenoaks 4	a			23 44	23 59				00 14	00 18
	d			23 44	23 59				00 14	00 19
Hildenborough	d				00 06					
Tonbridge 4	a			23 52	00 10				00 22	00 27

Table 204

Sundays
until 22 July, 19 Aug and from 16 Sep

London Charing Cross/Cannon Street - Grove Park, Orpington, Sevenoaks and Tonbridge, Grove Park - Bromley North

Network Diagram - see first Page of Table 200

		SE 1	SE	SE 1	SE 1	SE	SE	SE	SE	SE		SE
London Charing Cross 4 ⊖	d	23p25	23p36	23p40	23p45		00 06	00 15		00 48		07 46
London Waterloo (East) 4 ⊖	d	23p28	23p39	23p43	23p48		00 09	00 18		00 51		07 49
London Cannon Street 4 ⊖	d											
London Bridge 4 ⊖	d	23p33	23p44	23p49	23p53		00 14	00 23		00 56		07 54
New Cross 4 ⊖	d									01 01		
St Johns	d											
Lewisham 4	d		23p52				00 22			01 05		08 03
Hither Green 4	d		23p56				00 26			01 09		08 07
Grove Park 4	d		23p59			00 07	00 30		00 37	01 13		08 11
Sundridge Park	d					00 10			00 40			
Bromley North	a					00 12			00 42			
Elmstead Woods	d		00 03				00 33			01 16		08 14
Chislehurst	d		00 05				00 35			01 19		08 17
Petts Wood 4	d		00 08				00 38			01 22		08 20
Orpington 4	a	23p48	00 12	00 04	00 08		00 42	00 46		01 25		08 23
	d	23p49		00 05	00 09			00 46				
Chelsfield 3	d	23p52						00 49				
Knockholt	d											
Dunton Green	d							00 56				
Sevenoaks 4	a	23p59		00 14	00 18			00 59				
	d	23p59		00 14	00 19			00 59				
Hildenborough	d	00 06						01 05				
Tonbridge 4	a	00 10		00 22	00 27			01 10				

		SE 1	SE	SE 1	SE 1	SE	SE 1	SE	SE 1		SE 1	SE
London Charing Cross 4 ⊖	d	08 08	08 16	08 23	08 38	08 46	09 08	09 16	09 23		09 38	09 46
London Waterloo (East) 4 ⊖	d	08 11	08 19	08 26	08 41	08 49	09 11	09 19	09 26		09 41	09 49
London Cannon Street 4 ⊖	d											
London Bridge 4 ⊖	d	08 16	08 24	08 31	08 46	08 54	09 16	09 24	09 31		09 46	09 54
New Cross 4 ⊖	d											
St Johns	d											
Lewisham 4	d		08 33			09 03		09 33				10 03
Hither Green 4	d		08 37			09 07		09 37				10 07
Grove Park 4	d		08 41			09 11		09 41				10 11
Sundridge Park	d											
Bromley North	a											
Elmstead Woods	d		08 44			09 14		09 44				10 14
Chislehurst	d		08 47			09 17		09 47				10 17
Petts Wood 4	d		08 50			09 20		09 50				10 20
Orpington 4	a	08 31	08 53	08 46	09 01	09 23	09 31	09 53	09 46		10 01	10 23
	d	08 32	08 54	08 46	09 02		09 32	09 54	09 46		10 02	
Chelsfield 3	d		08 57					09 57				
Knockholt	d		09 00					10 00				
Dunton Green	d		09 05					10 05				
Sevenoaks 4	a	08 41	09 08	08 55	09 11		09 41	10 08	09 55		10 11	
	d	08 42		08 56	09 12		09 42		09 56		10 12	
Hildenborough	d	08 48					09 48					
Tonbridge 4	a	08 52		09 04	09 20		09 52		10 04		10 20	

		SE 1		SE 1	SE 1 ⊼	SE	SE 1		SE 1	SE	SE 1	SE	SE 1
London Charing Cross 4 ⊖	d	09 53		19 53	20 08	20 16	20 23		20 38	20 46	21 08	21 16	21 23
London Waterloo (East) 4 ⊖	d	09 56		19 56	20 11	20 19	20 26		20 41	20 49	21 11	21 19	21 26
London Cannon Street 4 ⊖	d												
London Bridge 4 ⊖	d	10 01		20 01	20 16	20 24	20 31		20 46	20 54	21 16	21 24	21 31
New Cross 4 ⊖	d												
St Johns	d												
Lewisham 4	d		and at			20 33				21 03		21 33	
Hither Green 4	d		the same			20 37				21 07		21 37	
Grove Park 4	d		minutes			20 41				21 11		21 41	
Sundridge Park	d		past										
Bromley North	a		each										
Elmstead Woods	d		hour until			20 44				21 14		21 44	
Chislehurst	d					20 47				21 17		21 47	
Petts Wood 4	d					20 50				21 20		21 50	
Orpington 4	a	10 16		20 16	20 31	20 53	20 46		21 01	21 23	21 31	21 53	21 46
	d	10 16		20 16	20 32	20 54	20 46		21 02		21 32	21 54	21 46
Chelsfield 3	d					20 57						21 57	
Knockholt	d					21 00						22 00	
Dunton Green	d					21 05						22 05	
Sevenoaks 4	a	10 25		20 25	20 41	21 08	20 55		21 11		21 41	22 08	21 55
	d	10 26		20 26	20 42		20 56		21 12		21 42		21 56
Hildenborough	d				20 48						21 48		
Tonbridge 4	a	10 34		20 34	20 52		21 04		21 20		21 52		22 04

		SE 1	SE	SE 1	SE		SE 1	SE 1	SE	SE 1	SE	SE 1
London Charing Cross 4 ⊖	d	21 38	21 46	22 08	22 16		22 23	22 38	22 46	23 08	23 16	23 23
London Waterloo (East) 4 ⊖	d	21 41	21 49	22 11	22 19		22 26	22 41	22 49	23 11	23 19	23 26
London Cannon Street 4 ⊖	d											
London Bridge 4 ⊖	d	21 46	21 54	22 16	22 24		22 31	22 46	22 54	23 16	23 24	23 31
New Cross 4 ⊖	d											
St Johns	d											
Lewisham 4	d		22 03		22 33				23 03		23 33	
Hither Green 4	d		22 07		22 37				23 07		23 37	
Grove Park 4	d		22 11		22 41				23 11		23 41	
Sundridge Park	d											
Bromley North	a											
Elmstead Woods	d		22 14		22 44				23 14		23 44	
Chislehurst	d		22 17		22 47				23 17		23 47	
Petts Wood 4	d		22 20		22 50				23 20		23 50	
Orpington 4	a	22 01	22 23	22 31	22 53		22 46	23 01	23 23	23 31	23 53	23 46
	d	22 02		22 32			22 46	23 02		23 32		23 46
Chelsfield 3	d						22 49					23 49
Knockholt	d											
Dunton Green	d											
Sevenoaks 4	a	22 11		22 41			22 57	23 11		23 41		23 57
	d	22 12		22 42			22 57	23 12		23 42		23 57
Hildenborough	d			22 48						23 48		
Tonbridge 4	a	22 20		22 52			23 05	23 20		23 52		00 05

		SE 1	SE
London Charing Cross 4 ⊖	d	23 38	23 46
London Waterloo (East) 4 ⊖	d	23 41	23 49
London Cannon Street 4 ⊖	d		
London Bridge 4 ⊖	d	23 46	23 54
New Cross 4 ⊖	d		
St Johns	d		
Lewisham 4	d		00 03
Hither Green 4	d		00 07
Grove Park 4	d		00 11
Sundridge Park	d		
Bromley North	a		
Elmstead Woods	d		00 14
Chislehurst	d		00 17
Petts Wood 4	d		00 20
Orpington 4	a	00 01	00 23
	d	00 02	
Chelsfield 3	d		
Knockholt	d		
Dunton Green	d		
Sevenoaks 4	a	00 11	
	d	00 12	
Hildenborough	d		
Tonbridge 4	a	00 20	

Table 204

Sundays

29 July to 12 August

London Charing Cross/Cannon Street - Grove Park, Orpington, Sevenoaks and Tonbridge, Grove Park - Bromley North

Network Diagram - see first Page of Table 200

	SE 1	SE	SE 1	SE 1	SE	SE	SE	SE	SE 1	SE	SE	SE	SE 1	SE	SE 1	SE	SE 1	SE 1	SE	SE 1	SE	SE 1
London Charing Cross ⊖ d	23p25	23p36	23p40	23p45		00 06	00 15		00 37	00 48			07 00	07 06	07 29	07 36	07 45	07 59	08 06	08 15	08 36	08 40
London Waterloo (East) ⊖ d	23p28	23p39	23p43	23p48		00 09	00 18		00 40	00 51			07 03	07 09	07 32	07 39	07 48	08 02	08 09	08 18	08 39	08 43
London Cannon Street ⊖ d																						
London Bridge ⊖ d	23p33	23p44	23p49	23p53		00 14	00 23		00 45	00 56			07 08	07 14	07 38	07 44	07 53	08 08	08 14	08 23	08 44	08 49
New Cross ⊖ d										01 01												
St Johns d																						
Lewisham d		23p52				00 22				01 05				07 23		07 53						
Hither Green d		23p56				00 26				01 09				07 27		07 57			08 23		08 53	
Grove Park d		23p59			00 07	00 30		00 37		01 13				07 31		08 01			08 27		08 57	
Sundridge Park d					00 10			00 40														
Bromley North a					00 12			00 42														
Elmstead Woods d		00 03				00 33				01 16				07 34		08 04			08 30		09 00	
Chislehurst d		00 05				00 35				01 19				07 36		08 06			08 33		09 03	
Petts Wood d		00 08				00 38				01 22				07 39		08 09			08 36		09 06	
Orpington a	23p48	00 15	00 04	00 08		00 45	00 46		01 00	01 25			07 25	07 45	07 54	08 12	08 08	08 23	08 39	08 38	09 09	
d	23p49		00 05	00 09			00 46		01 01	01 26	06 13	07 13	07 26		07 54	08 13	08 09	08 24		08 39	09 12	
Chelsfield d	23p52						00 49			01 29	06 16	07 16				08 16					09 15	
Knockholt d										01 32	06 19	07 19				08 19					09 18	
Dunton Green d							00 56			01 37	06 24	07 24				08 24					09 23	
Sevenoaks a	23p59		00 14	00 18			00 59		01 10	01 40	06 27	07 27	07 35		08 02	08 30	08 18	08 33		08 48	09 26	09 11
d	23p59		00 14	00 19			00 59		01 11	01 40			07 35		08 03		08 19	08 33		08 49		09 12
Hildenborough d	00 06						01 05			01 46			07 41		08 09			08 39				
Tonbridge a	00 10		00 22	00 27			01 13		01 19	01 50			07 45		08 14		08 27	08 43		08 57		09 20

	SE 1	SE	SE 1		SE 1 (trolley)	SE 1	SE	SE 1 (trolley)	SE 1	SE	SE 1 (trolley)	SE 1	SE	SE 1 (trolley)	SE 1	SE	SE 1 (trolley)	SE	SE 1	SE 1	SE
London Charing Cross ⊖ d	08 45	09 06	09 10	and at the same minutes past each hour until	18 10	18 15	18 36	18 40	18 45	19 06	19 10	19 15	19 36	19 40	19 55	20 06	20 10	20 36	20 40	20 55	21 06
London Waterloo (East) ⊖ d	08 48	09 09	09 13		18 13	18 18	18 39	18 43	18 48	19 09	19 13	19 18	19 39	19 43	19 58	20 09	20 13	20 39	20 43	20 58	21 09
London Cannon Street ⊖ d																					
London Bridge ⊖ d	08 53	09 14	09 19		18 19	18 23	18 44	18 49	18 53	19 14	19 19	19 23	19 44	19 49	20 03	20 14	20 19	20 44	20 49	21 03	21 14
New Cross ⊖ d																					
St Johns d																					
Lewisham d													19 52			20 22		20 52			21 22
Hither Green d		09 23					18 53			19 23			19 56			20 26		20 56			21 26
Grove Park d		09 27					18 57			19 27			20 00			20 30		21 00			21 30
Sundridge Park d																					
Bromley North a																					
Elmstead Woods d		09 30					19 00			19 30			20 03			20 33		21 03			21 33
Chislehurst d		09 33					19 03			19 33			20 05			20 35		21 05			21 35
Petts Wood d		09 36					19 06			19 36			20 08			20 38		21 08			21 38
Orpington a	09 08	09 39				18 38	19 09		19 08	19 39		19 38	20 12		20 18	20 45	20 34	21 12	21 04	21 18	21 45
d	09 09					18 39	19 12		19 09			19 39	20 13		20 21		20 35	21 13	21 05	21 21	
Chelsfield d							19 15						20 16					21 16			
Knockholt d							19 18						20 19					21 19			
Dunton Green d							19 23						20 24					21 24			
Sevenoaks a	09 18		09 41		18 41	18 48	19 26	19 11	19 18		19 41	19 49	20 30	20 11	20 30		20 44	21 30	21 14	21 30	
d	09 19		09 42		18 42	18 49		19 12	19 19		19 42	19 49		20 12	20 31		20 44		21 14	21 31	
Hildenborough d																					
Tonbridge a	09 27		09 50		18 50	18 58		19 20	19 27		19 50	19 58		20 20	20 39		20 52		21 22	21 39	

	SE 1	SE	SE 1	SE 1	SE	SE 1	SE	SE 1	SE 1	SE	SE 1	SE	SE 1	SE 1
London Charing Cross ⊖ d	21 10	21 36	21 40	21 55	22 06	22 10	22 36	22 40	22 55	23 06	23 10	23 36	23 40	23 45
London Waterloo (East) ⊖ d	21 13	21 39	21 43	21 58	22 09	22 13	22 39	22 43	22 58	23 09	23 13	23 39	23 43	23 48
London Cannon Street ⊖ d														
London Bridge ⊖ d	21 19	21 44	21 49	22 03	22 14	22 19	22 44	22 49	23 03	23 14	23 19	23 44	23 49	23 53
New Cross ⊖ d														
St Johns d														
Lewisham d		21 52			22 22		22 52			23 22		23 52		
Hither Green d		21 56			22 26		22 56			23 26		23 56		
Grove Park d		22 00			22 30		23 00			23 30		23 59		
Sundridge Park d														
Bromley North a														
Elmstead Woods d		22 03			22 33		23 03			23 33		00 03		
Chislehurst d		22 05			22 35		23 05			23 35		00 05		
Petts Wood d		22 08			22 38		23 08			23 38		00 08		
Orpington a	21 34	22 12	22 04	22 18	22 45	22 34	23 15	23 04	23 18	23 45	23 34	00 15	00 04	00 08
d	21 35	22 13	22 05	22 19		22 35		23 05	23 19		23 35		00 05	00 09
Chelsfield d		22 16		22 22					23 22					00 12
Knockholt d		22 19												
Dunton Green d		22 24												
Sevenoaks a	21 44	22 30	22 14	22 30		22 44		23 14	23 30		23 44		00 14	00 19
d	21 44		22 14	22 31		22 44		23 14	23 31		23 44		00 14	00 20
Hildenborough d														
Tonbridge a	21 52		22 22	22 39		22 52		23 22	23 39		23 52		00 22	00 28

Table 204

Sundays

26 August to 9 September

London Charing Cross/Cannon Street - Grove Park, Orpington, Sevenoaks and Tonbridge, Grove Park - Bromley North

Network Diagram - see first Page of Table 200

	SE 1	SE	SE 1	SE 1	SE	SE	SE	SE	SE 1 A	SE A	SE	SE	SE 1	SE	SE 1	SE 1	SE	SE 1	SE	SE 1	SE 1	SE
London Charing Cross ⊖ d	23p25	23p36	23p40	23p45		00 06	00 15		00 37	00 48	00 48	07 46	08 08	08 16	08 23	08 38	08 46	09 08	09 16	09 23	09 38	09 46
London Waterloo (East) ⊖ d	23p28	23p39	23p43	23p48		00 09	00 18		00 40	00 51	00 51	07 49	08 11	08 19	08 26	08 41	08 49	09 11	09 19	09 26	09 41	09 49
London Cannon Street ⊖ d																						
London Bridge ⊖ d	23p33	23p44	23p49	23p53		00 14	00 23		00 45	00 56	00 56	07 54	08 16	08 24	08 31	08 46	08 54	09 16	09 24	09 31	09 46	09 54
New Cross ⊖ d										01 01	01 01											
St Johns d																						
Lewisham d		23p52				00 22				01 05	01 05	08 03		08 33			09 03		09 33			10 03
Hither Green d		23p56				00 26				01 09	01 09	08 07		08 37			09 07		09 37			10 07
Grove Park d		23p59			00 07	00 30		00 37		01 13	01 13	08 11		08 41			09 11		09 41			10 11
Sundridge Park d					00 10			00 40														
Bromley North a					00 12			00 42														
Elmstead Woods d		00 03				00 33				01 16	01 16	08 14		08 44			09 14		09 44			10 14
Chislehurst d		00 05				00 35				01 18	01 19	08 17		08 47			09 17		09 47			10 17
Petts Wood d		00 08				00 38				01 22	01 22	08 20		08 50			09 20		09 50			10 20
Orpington a	23p48	00 12	00 04	00 08		00 42	00 46		01 00	01 25	01 25	08 23	08 31	08 53	08 46	09 01	09 23	09 31	09 53	09 46	10 01	10 23
d	23p49		00 05	00 09			00 46		01 01	01 26			08 32	08 54	08 46	09 02		09 32	09 54	09 46	10 02	
Chelsfield d	23p52						00 49			01s29				08 57					09 57			
Knockholt d										01s32				09 00					10 00			
Dunton Green d							00 56			01s37				09 05					10 05			
Sevenoaks a	23p59		00 14	00 18			00 59		01s10	01s40			08 41	09 08	08 55	09 11		09 41	10 08	09 55	10 11	
d	23p59		00 14	00 19			00 59						08 42		08 56	09 12		09 42		09 56	10 12	
Hildenborough d	00 06						01 05			01s46			08 48					09 48				
Tonbridge a	00 10		00 22	00 27			01 10		01s20	01s50			08 52		09 04	09 20		09 52		10 04	10 20	

	SE 1		SE 1	SE 1 (trolley)	SE	SE 1	SE 1	SE	SE 1	SE	SE 1	SE 1	SE	SE 1	SE	SE 1	SE 1	SE	SE 1	SE	SE 1
London Charing Cross ⊖ d	09 53	and at the same minutes past each hour until	19 53	20 08	20 16	20 23	20 38	20 46	21 08	21 16	21 23	21 38	21 46	22 08	22 16	22 23	22 38	22 46	23 08	23 16	23 23
London Waterloo (East) ⊖ d	09 56		19 56	20 11	20 19	20 26	20 41	20 49	21 11	21 19	21 26	21 41	21 49	22 11	22 19	22 26	22 41	22 49	23 11	23 19	23 26
London Cannon Street ⊖ d																					
London Bridge ⊖ d	10 01		20 01	20 16	20 24	20 31	20 46	20 54	21 16	21 24	21 31	21 46	21 54	22 16	22 24	22 31	22 46	22 54	23 16	23 24	23 31
New Cross ⊖ d																					
St Johns d																					
Lewisham d					20 33			21 03		21 33			22 03		22 33			23 03		23 33	
Hither Green d					20 37			21 07		21 37			22 07		22 37			23 07		23 37	
Grove Park d					20 41			21 11		21 41			22 11		22 41			23 11		23 41	
Sundridge Park d																					
Bromley North a																					
Elmstead Woods d					20 44			21 14		21 44			22 14		22 44			23 14		23 44	
Chislehurst d					20 47			21 17		21 47			22 17		22 47			23 17		23 47	
Petts Wood d					20 50			21 20		21 50			22 20		22 50			23 20		23 50	
Orpington a	10 16		20 16	20 31	20 53	20 46	21 01	21 23	21 31	21 53	21 46	22 01	22 23	22 31	22 53	22 46	23 01	23 23	23 31	23 53	23 46
d	10 16		20 16	20 32	20 54	20 46	21 02		21 32	21 54	21 46	22 02		22 32		22 46	23 02		23 32		23 46
Chelsfield d					20 57					21 57						22 49					23 49
Knockholt d					21 00					22 00											
Dunton Green d					21 05					22 05											
Sevenoaks a	10 25		20 25	20 41	21 08	20 55	21 11		21 41	22 08	21 55	22 11		22 41		22 57	23 11		23 41		23 57
d	10 26		20 26	20 42		20 56	21 12		21 42		21 56	22 12		22 42		22 57	23 12		23 42		23 57
Hildenborough d				20 48					21 48					22 48					23 48		
Tonbridge a	10 34		20 34	20 52		21 04	21 20		21 52		22 04	22 20		22 52		23 05	23 20		23 52		00 05

	SE 1	SE
London Charing Cross ⊖ d	23 38	23 46
London Waterloo (East) ⊖ d	23 41	23 49
London Cannon Street ⊖ d		
London Bridge ⊖ d	23 46	23 54
New Cross ⊖ d		
St Johns d		
Lewisham d		00 03
Hither Green d		00 07
Grove Park d		00 11
Sundridge Park d		
Bromley North a		
Elmstead Woods d		00 14
Chislehurst d		00 17
Petts Wood d		00 20
Orpington a	00 01	00 23
d	00 02	
Chelsfield d		
Knockholt d		
Dunton Green d		
Sevenoaks a	00 11	
d	00 12	
Hildenborough d		
Tonbridge a	00 20	

A not 26 August

Table 204

Mondays to Fridays

until 27 July, 13 Aug to 28 Aug and from 10 Sep

Bromley North to Grove Park, Tonbridge, Sevenoaks, Orpington and Grove Park - London Cannon Street/Charing Cross

Network Diagram - see first Page of Table 200

Miles	Miles			SE MX	SE MX ■	SE MX	SE	SE	SE ■	SE	SE ■	SE	SE	SE ■	SE ■	SE ■	SE	SE	SE	SE ■	SE ■	SE ■	SE
0	—	Tonbridge	d		23p14		04 52		05 32		05 50			06 00	06 06	06 19				06 32	06 40	06 44	
2½	—	Hildenborough	d		23p18		04 56		05 36					06 04		06 23				06 36			
7½	—	Sevenoaks	a		23p24		05 02		05 42		05 58			06 10	06 14	06 30				06 43	06 48	06 52	
—	—		d		23p25		05 03		05 43		05 59		06 02	06 11	06 15	06 32			06 36	06 44	06 49	06 53	
1½	—	Dunton Green	d										06 05						06 39				
5½	—	Knockholt	d										06 10						06 44				
6¾	—	Chelsfield	d		23p32		05 10		05 50				06 13						06 47				
8¾	—	Orpington	a		23p36		05 13		05 53		06 08		06 16	06 19	06 23				06 50	06 53		07 02	
—	—		d	23p21	23p37		05 14	05 15	05 54	06 01	06 09		06 22	06 20	06 24			06 43	06 52	06 54		07 04	07 03
9¼	—	Petts Wood	d	23p24				05 18		06 04			06 25					06 46	06 55				07 06
10¾	—	Chislehurst	d	23p27				05 21		06 07			06 28					06 49	06 58				07 09
11¾	—	Elmstead Woods	d	23p29				05 23		06 09			06 30					06 51	07 00				07 11
—	0	Bromley North	d			00 23						06 25					06 45						
—	0½	Sundridge Park	d			00 25						06 27					06 47						
13	1¾	Grove Park	d	23p33		00a28		05 27		06 12		06a30	06 34				06a50	06 54	07 04				07 15
14¾	—	Hither Green	d	23p37				05 30		06 16			06 38					06 58	07 08				07 19
16	—	Lewisham	d	23p43				05 36		06 22			06 43					07 04					07 25
16½	—	St Johns	a																				
17¼	—	New Cross	a					05 39		06 25													
20¼	—	London Bridge	a	23p52	23p54		05 37	05 45	06 09	06 31	06 24		06 51	06 38	06 39	06 54			07 18	07 09	07 14	07 22	
—	—	London Cannon Street	a											06 42					07 25			07 29	
21¼	—	London Waterloo (East)	a	23p56	23p59		05 41	05 50	06 14	06 36	06 29		06 56		06 44	06 59		07 16		07 14	07 19		07 36
22	—	London Charing Cross	a	00 01	00 03		05 47	05 55	06 18	06 39	06 33		07 02		06 49	07 05		07 22		07 20	07 25		07 42

		SE	SE	SE ■	SE ■	SE ■	SE	SE	SE	SE ■	SE ■	SE ■	SE	SE	SE	SE ■	SE ■	SE	SE ■	SE	SE	SE	SE ■
Tonbridge	d			06 51	07 02	07 11				07 15	07 23	07 31				07 35	07 42		07 51				07 59
Hildenborough	d			06 55		07 15				07 20		07 35				07 40			07 55				
Sevenoaks	a			07 02	07 10	07 22				07 26	07 31	07 42				07 46	07 50		08 02				08 07
	d		06 56	07 03	07 11	07 23			07 17	07 27	07 32	07 43			07 37	07 47	07 51		08 03			07 57	08 08
Dunton Green	d		06 59						07 20						07 40							08 00	
Knockholt	d		07 04						07 25						07 45							08 05	
Chelsfield	d		07 07			07 32			07 28			07 52			07 48				08 12			08 08	
Orpington	a		07 10	07 13					07 31						07 51							08 12	
	d		07 11	07 14			07 22		07 33				07 41		07 52			07 57		08 01		08 13	
Petts Wood	d		07 15				07 25		07 36				07 44		07 55			08 00		08 04		08 16	
Chislehurst	d		07 18				07 28		07 39				07 47		07 59			08 03		08 07		08 20	
Elmstead Woods	d		07 20				07 31		07 41				07 50		08 01			08 06		08 10		08 22	
Bromley North	d	07 15						07 35						07 55							08 15		
Sundridge Park	d	07 17						07 37						07 57							08 17		
Grove Park	d	07a20	07 24				07 34	07a40	07 45				07 53	08a00	08 05			08 09		08 13	08a20	08 26	
Hither Green	d		07 28				07 39		07 49				07 58							08 17			
Lewisham	d						07 44						08 03							08 23			
St Johns	a																						
New Cross	a																						
London Bridge	a		07 37	07 29	07 36	07 50	07 53		07 59	07 53		08 09			08 18	08 13			08 29			08 39	08 33
London Cannon Street	a		07 44						08 06	07 59					08 26	08 20						08 46	08 41
London Waterloo (East)	a			07 34	07 41	07 55	07 58				08 00	08 14	08 16				08 20	08 24	08 34	08 36			
London Charing Cross	a			07 40	07 47	08 01	08 04				08 06	08 20	08 22				08 26	08 30	08 40	08 42			

		SE ■	SE	SE	SE	SE ■	SE ■	SE ■	SE ■	SE ■	SE	SE	SE	SE ■ A	SE ■ B	SE	SE ■	SE	SE	SE ■	SE ■	SE
Tonbridge	d	08 04				08 11	08 15	08 22	08 35	08 40				08 43	08 44		08 50			09 02	09 10	
Hildenborough	d					08 15	08 20		08 39					08 48	08 48					09 06		
Sevenoaks	a	08 12				08 22	08 26	08 30	08 45	08 48				08 54	08 54		08 58			09 13	09 18	
	d	08 12			08 17	08 23	08 27	08 31	08 45	08 49			08 37	08 55	08 55		08 59		09 06	09 14	09 19	
Dunton Green	d				08 20								08 40						09 09			
Knockholt	d				08 25								08 45						09 14			
Chelsfield	d				08 28	08 32			08 53				08 48						09 17			
Orpington	a				08 31								08 51	09 03	09 03		09 08		09 20	09 24		
	d		08 21		08 32						08 43		08 52	09 04	09 04	09 03	09 09		09 21	09 24		09 33
Petts Wood	d		08 24		08 35						08 46		08 55			09 06			09 24			09 36
Chislehurst	d		08 27		08 39						08 49		08 58			09 09			09 27			09 39
Elmstead Woods	d		08 29		08 41						08 51		09 00			09 11			09 30			09 41
Bromley North	d			08 35								08 55						09 25				
Sundridge Park	d			08 37								08 57						09 27				
Grove Park	d		08 33	08a40	08 45						08 55	09a00	09 04			09 15		09a30	09 33			09 45
Hither Green	d		08 37								08 59		09 08			09 19			09 37			09 49
Lewisham	d										09 04					09 24						09 54
St Johns	a										09 07					09 26						09 56
New Cross	a										09 09					09 28						09 58
London Bridge	a				08 59	08 49	08 55		09 11	09 14	09 17		09 20	09 22	09 22	09 33	09 26		09 49	09 40	09 43	10 04
London Cannon Street	a				09 06		09 02				09 23			09 29	09 28	09 40						10 08
London Waterloo (East)	a	08 40	08 52			08 54		09 00	09 16	09 19			09 25				09 31		09 53	09 45	09 48	
London Charing Cross	a	08 46	08 58			09 00		09 04	09 22	09 25			09 31				09 37		09 59	09 51	09 54	

A from 21 May until 27 July

B until 18 May

Table 204

Mondays to Fridays

until 27 July, 13 Aug to 28 Aug and from 10 Sep

Bromley North to Grove Park, Tonbridge, Sevenoaks, Orpington and Grove Park - London Cannon Street/Charing Cross

Network Diagram - see first Page of Table 200

		SE ■ A	SE ■ B	SE	SE	SE ■	SE ■	SE	SE	SE ■	SE	SE	SE ■	SE ■	SE	SE ■	SE	SE	SE ■	SE ■	SE	SE	SE ■
Tonbridge	d	09 19	09 20			09 32	09 40			09 50			10 02	10 10		10 20			10 32	10 40			10 50
Hildenborough	d					09 36							10 06						10 36				
Sevenoaks	a	09 27	09 28			09 43	09 48			09 58			10 13	10 18		10 28			10 43	10 48			10 58
	d	09 28	09 29		09 36	09 44	09 49			09 59		10 06	10 14	10 19		10 29		10 36	10 44	10 49			10 59
Dunton Green	d				09 39							10 09						10 39					
Knockholt	d				09 44							10 14						10 44					
Chelsfield	d				09 47							10 17						10 47					
Orpington	a	09 37	09 38		09 50	09 53				10 08		10 20	10 23			10 38		10 50	10 53				11 08
	d	09 38	09 39		09 51	09 54			10 03	10 09		10 21	10 24		10 33	10 39		10 51	10 54			11 03	11 09
Petts Wood	d				09 54				10 06			10 24			10 36			10 54				11 06	
Chislehurst	d				09 57				10 09			10 27			10 39			10 57				11 09	
Elmstead Woods	d				09 59				10 11			10 29			10 41			10 59				11 11	
Bromley North	d			09 45				10 05			10 25						10 45				11 05		
Sundridge Park	d			09 47				10 07			10 27						10 47				11 07		
Grove Park	d			09a50	10 03			10a10	10 15		10a30	10 33			10 45		10a50	11 03			11a10	11 15	
Hither Green	d				10 07				10 19			10 37			10 49			11 07				11 19	
Lewisham	d								10 24						10 54							11 24	
St Johns	a								10 26						10 56							11 26	
New Cross	a								10 28						10 58							11 28	
London Bridge	a	09 54	09 55		10 19	10 10	10 13		10 34	10 25		10 49	10 40	10 43	11 04	10 55		11 19	11 10	11 13		11 34	11 25
London Cannon Street	a								10 38						11 08							11 38	
London Waterloo (East)	a	09 58	09 59		10 23	10 15	10 18			10 29		10 53	10 45	10 48		10 59		11 23	11 15	11 18			11 29
London Charing Cross	a	10 02	10 03		10 27	10 19	10 22			10 33		10 57	10 49	10 52		11 03		11 27	11 19	11 22			11 33

		SE	SE	SE ■	SE ■	SE	SE ■	SE	SE	SE ■	SE ■	SE	SE	SE ■	SE	SE	SE ■	SE ■	SE	SE ■	SE	SE	SE ■
Tonbridge	d			11 02	11 10		11 20			11 32	11 40			11 50			12 02	12 10		12 20			12 32
Hildenborough	d			11 06						11 36							12 06						12 36
Sevenoaks	a			11 13	11 18		11 28			11 43	11 48			11 58			12 13	12 18		12 28			12 43
	d		11 06	11 14	11 19		11 29		11 36	11 44	11 49			11 59		12 06	12 14	12 19		12 29		12 36	12 44
Dunton Green	d		11 09						11 39							12 09						12 39	
Knockholt	d		11 14						11 44							12 14						12 44	
Chelsfield	d		11 17						11 47							12 17						12 47	
Orpington	a		11 20	11 23			11 38		11 50	11 53				12 08		12 20	12 23			12 38		12 50	12 53
	d		11 21	11 24		11 33	11 39		11 51	11 54			12 03	12 09		12 21	12 24		12 33	12 39		12 51	12 54
Petts Wood	d		11 24			11 36			11 54				12 06			12 24			12 36			12 54	
Chislehurst	d		11 27			11 39			11 57				12 09			12 27			12 39			12 57	
Elmstead Woods	d		11 29			11 41			11 59				12 11			12 29			12 41			12 59	
Bromley North	d	11 25						11 45				12 05			12 25						12 45		
Sundridge Park	d	11 27						11 47				12 07			12 27						12 47		
Grove Park	d	11a30	11 33			11 45		11a50	12 03			12a10	12 15		12a30	12 33			12 45		12a50	13 03	
Hither Green	d		11 37			11 49			12 07				12 19			12 37			12 49			13 07	
Lewisham	d					11 54							12 24						12 54				
St Johns	a					11 56							12 26						12 56				
New Cross	a					11 58							12 28						12 58				
London Bridge	a		11 49	11 40	11 43	12 04	11 55		12 19	12 10	12 13		12 34	12 25		12 49	12 40	12 43	13 04	12 55		13 19	13 10
London Cannon Street	a					12 08							12 38						13 08				
London Waterloo (East)	a		11 53	11 45	11 48		11 59		12 23	12 15	12 18			12 29		12 53	12 45	12 48		12 59		13 23	13 15
London Charing Cross	a		11 57	11 49	11 52		12 03		12 27	12 19	12 22			12 33		12 57	12 49	12 52		13 03		13 27	13 19

		SE ■	SE	SE	SE ■	SE	SE	SE ■	SE ■	SE	SE ■	SE	SE	SE ■	SE ■	SE	SE	SE ■	SE	SE	SE ■	SE ■
Tonbridge	d	12 40			12 50			13 02	13 10		13 20			13 32	13 40			13 50			14 02	14 10
Hildenborough	d							13 06						13 36							14 06	
Sevenoaks	a	12 48			12 58			13 13	13 18		13 28			13 43	13 48			13 58			14 13	14 18
	d	12 49			12 59		13 06	13 14	13 19		13 29		13 36	13 44	13 49			13 59		14 06	14 14	14 19
Dunton Green	d						13 09						13 39							14 09		
Knockholt	d						13 14						13 44							14 14		
Chelsfield	d						13 17						13 47							14 17		
Orpington	a				13 08		13 20	13 23			13 38		13 50	13 53				14 08		14 20	14 23	
	d			13 03	13 09		13 21	13 24		13 33	13 39		13 51	13 54			14 03	14 09		14 21	14 24	
Petts Wood	d			13 06			13 24			13 36			13 54				14 06			14 24		
Chislehurst	d			13 09			13 27			13 39			13 57				14 09			14 27		
Elmstead Woods	d			13 11			13 29			13 41			13 59				14 11			14 29		
Bromley North	d		13 05			13 25						13 45				14 05			14 25			
Sundridge Park	d		13 07			13 27						13 47				14 07			14 27			
Grove Park	d		13a10	13 15		13a30	13 33			13 45		13a50	14 03			14a10	14 15		14a30	14 33		
Hither Green	d			13 19			13 37			13 49			14 07				14 19			14 37		
Lewisham	d			13 24						13 54							14 24					
St Johns	a			13 26						13 56							14 26					
New Cross	a			13 28						13 58							14 28					
London Bridge	a	13 13		13 34	13 25		13 49	13 40	13 43	14 04	13 55		14 19	14 10	14 13		14 34	14 25		14 49	14 40	14 43
London Cannon Street	a			13 38						14 08							14 38					
London Waterloo (East)	a	13 18			13 29		13 53	13 45	13 48		13 59		14 23	14 15	14 18			14 29		14 53	14 45	14 48
London Charing Cross	a	13 22			13 33		13 57	13 49	13 52		14 03		14 27	14 19	14 22			14 33		14 57	14 49	14 52

A from 21 May until 27 July

B until 18 May

until 27 July, 13 Aug to 28 Aug and from 10 Sep

Bromley North to Grove Park, Tonbridge, Sevenoaks, Orpington and Grove Park - London Cannon Street/Charing Cross

Network Diagram - see first Page of Table 200

		SE	SE 1	SE	SE	SE 1	SE 1 H	SE	SE	SE 1	SE	SE	SE 1	SE 1 H	SE	SE 1	SE	SE	SE 1	SE 1 H	SE	SE	SE 1
Tonbridge	d		14 20			14 32	14 40			14 50			15 02	15 10		15 20			15 32	15 40			15 50
Hildenborough	d					14 36							15 06						15 36				
Sevenoaks	a		14 28			14 43	14 48			14 58			15 13	15 18		15 28			15 43	15 48			15 58
	d		14 29		14 36	14 44	14 49			14 59		15 06	15 14	15 19		15 29		15 36	15 44	15 49			15 59
Dunton Green	d				14 39							15 09						15 39					
Knockholt	d				14 44							15 14						15 44					
Chelsfield	d				14 47							15 17						15 47					
Orpington	a		14 38		14 50	14 53				15 08		15 20	15 23			15 38		15 50	15 53				16 07
	d	14 33	14 39		14 51	14 54			15 03	15 09		15 21	15 24		15 33	15 39		15 51	15 54			16 03	16 08
Petts Wood	d	14 36			14 54				15 06			15 24			15 36			15 54				16 06	
Chislehurst	d	14 39			14 57				15 09			15 27			15 39			15 57				16 09	
Elmstead Woods	d	14 41			14 59				15 11			15 29			15 41			15 59				16 11	
Bromley North	d			14 45				15 05			15 25						15 45				16 05		
Sundridge Park	d			14 47				15 07			15 27						15 47				16 07		
Grove Park	d	14 45		14a50	15 03			15a10	15 15		15a30	15 33			15 45		15a50	16 03			16a10	16 15	
Hither Green	d	14 49			15 07				15 19			15 37			15 49			16 07				16 19	
Lewisham	d	14 54							15 24						15 54							16 24	
St Johns	a	14 56							15 26						15 56							16 26	
New Cross	a	14 58							15 28						15 58							16 28	
London Bridge	a	15 04	14 55		15 19	15 10	15 13		15 34	15 25		15 49	15 40	15 43	16 04	15 55		16 19	16 11	16 14		16 34	16 25
London Cannon Street	a	15 08							15 38						16 08							16 38	
London Waterloo (East)	a		14 59		15 23	15 15	15 18			15 29		15 55	15 45	15 48		15 59		16 24	16 16	16 20			16 29
London Charing Cross	a		15 03		15 27	15 19	15 22			15 33		15 58	15 49	15 52		16 03		16 28	16 20	16 24			16 33

		SE	SE	SE 1	SE 1 H	SE	SE 1	SE	SE	SE 1	SE 1 H	SE	SE	SE 1	SE	SE	SE	SE 1	SE 1 H	SE	SE 1	SE
Tonbridge	d			16 02	16 10		16 20			16 32	16 40			16 50				17 02	17 10		17 20	
Hildenborough	d			16 06						16 36								17 06				
Sevenoaks	a			16 13	16 18		16 28			16 43	16 48			16 58				17 13	17 18		17 28	
	d		16 06	16 14	16 19		16 29		16 36	16 44	16 52			16 59			17 05	17 14	17 19		17 29	
Dunton Green	d		16 09						16 39								17 08					
Knockholt	d		16 14						16 44								17 13					
Chelsfield	d		16 17	16 21					16 47								17 16					
Orpington	a		16 20	16 24			16 38		16 50	16 53				17 08			17 19	17 23			17 38	
	d		16 21	16 25		16 33	16 39		16 51	16 54			17 03	17 09	17 13		17 20	17 24		17 37	17 39	
Petts Wood	d		16 24			16 36			16 54				17 06				17 24			17 40		
Chislehurst	d		16 27			16 39			16 57				17 09				17 27			17 43		
Elmstead Woods	d		16 29			16 41			16 59				17 11				17 29			17 45		
Bromley North	d	16 25						16 45				17 07				17 27						17 50
Sundridge Park	d	16 27						16 47				17 09				17 29						17 52
Grove Park	d	16a30	16 33			16 45		16a50	17 03			17a12	17 15			17a32	17 34			17 49		17a55
Hither Green	d		16 37			16 50			17 09				17 19				17 38			17 53		
Lewisham	d												17 24									
St Johns	a												17 26							17 57		
New Cross	a												17 28							17 59		
London Bridge	a		16 48	16 42	16 46	17 01	16 56			17 11	17 17		17 34	17 27			17 49	17 41	17 44	18 06	17 58	
London Cannon Street	a												17 38	17 32						18 11		
London Waterloo (East)	a		16 54	16 48	16 52	17 06	17 00		17 24	17 16	17 22				17 36		17 53	17 46	17 50		18 02	
London Charing Cross	a		16 58	16 52	16 56	17 10	17 04		17 29	17 20	17 26				17 40		17 57	17 50	17 53		18 06	

		SE	SE 1	SE 1 H	SE	SE 1	SE	SE	SE 1	SE 1 H	SE 1	SE	SE	SE	SE	SE 1	SE 1 H	SE	SE 1	SE	SE	SE 1	SE 1 H
Tonbridge	d		17 32	17 40		17 50			18 02	18 10	18 23					18 32	18 40		18 50			19 02	19 10
Hildenborough	d		17 36						18 06							18 36						19 06	
Sevenoaks	a		17 43	17 48		17 58			18 13	18 18	18 31					18 43	18 48		18 59			19 13	19 18
	d	17 35	17 44	17 49		17 59		18 05	18 14	18 19	18 32				18 35	18 44	18 49		18 59		19 06	19 14	19 19
Dunton Green	d	17 38						18 08							18 38						19 09		
Knockholt	d	17 43						18 13							18 43						19 14		
Chelsfield	d	17 46						18 16							18 46						19 17		
Orpington	a	17 49	17 53			18 08		18 19	18 23						18 49	18 53			19 08		19 20	19 23	
	d	17 50	17 54		18 03	18 09		18 21	18 24				18 33		18 50	18 54		19 03	19 08		19 21	19 24	
Petts Wood	d	17 54			18 06			18 24					18 36		18 54			19 06			19 24		
Chislehurst	d	17 57			18 09			18 27					18 39		18 57			19 09			19 27		
Elmstead Woods	d	17 59			18 11			18 29					18 41		18 59			19 11			19 29		
Bromley North	d						18 13					18 33		18 55						19 18			
Sundridge Park	d						18 15					18 35		18 57						19 20			
Grove Park	d	18 03			18 15		18a18	18 33				18a38	18 45	19a00	19 03			19 15		19a23	19 33		
Hither Green	d	18 07			18 19			18 37					18 49		19 07			19 19			19 37		
Lewisham	d				18 24								18 54					19 24			19 43		
St Johns	a				18 26								18 56					19 26					
New Cross	a				18 28								18 58					19 28					
London Bridge	a	18 18	18 09	18 16	18 34	18 25		18 48	18 40	18 43	18 55		19 04		19 19	19 10	19 13	19 34	19 25		19 52	19 40	19 43
London Cannon Street	a				18 38								19 10					19 38					
London Waterloo (East)	a	18 23	18 14	18 20		18 29		18 53	18 45	18 48	18 59				19 23	19 14	19 17		19 29		19 56	19 45	19 48
London Charing Cross	a	18 27	18 18	18 25		18 35		18 57	18 49	18 52	19 04				19 27	19 18	19 21		19 33		20 00	19 49	19 52

until 27 July, 13 Aug to 28 Aug and from 10 Sep

Bromley North to Grove Park, Tonbridge, Sevenoaks, Orpington and Grove Park - London Cannon Street/Charing Cross

Network Diagram - see first Page of Table 200

		SE 1	SE	SE	SE 1	SE 1	SE 1	SE	SE	SE 1	SE 1	SE	SE	SE	SE 1	SE 1	SE 1	SE	SE	SE 1	SE 1	SE	SE
Tonbridge	d	19 20			19 32	19 40	19 51			20 02	20 10				20 32	20 40	20 50			21 02	21 10		
Hildenborough	d				19 36					20 06					20 36					21 06			
Sevenoaks	a	19 28			19 43	19 48	19 59			20 13	20 18				20 43	20 48	20 58			21 13	21 18		
	d	19 29		19 36	19 44	19 49	20 00		20 06	20 14	20 19			20 35	20 44	20 49	20 59		21 05	21 14	21 19		21 35
Dunton Green	d			19 39					20 09					20 38					21 08				21 38
Knockholt	d			19 44					20 14					20 43					21 13				21 43
Chelsfield	d			19 47					20 17					20 46					21 16				21 46
Orpington	a	19 38		19 50	19 53		20 08		20 20	20 23				20 49	20 52		21 08		21 19	21 22			21 49
	d	19 39		19 51	19 54		20 09		20 21	20 24				20 51	20 53		21 09		21 21	21 23			21 51
Petts Wood	d			19 54					20 24					20 54					21 24				21 54
Chislehurst	d			19 57					20 27					20 57					21 27				21 57
Elmstead Woods	d			19 59					20 29					20 59					21 29				21 59
Bromley North	d		19 42					20 02				20 27	20 53					21 23				21 53	
Sundridge Park	d		19 44					20 04				20 29	20 55					21 25				21 55	
Grove Park	d		19a47	20 03				20a07	20 34			20a32	20a58	21 03				21a28	21 33			21a58	22 03
Hither Green	d			20 07					20 38					21 07					21 37				22 07
Lewisham	d			20 13					20 43					21 13					21 43				22 13
St Johns	a																						
New Cross	a																						
London Bridge	a	19 54		20 22	20 10	20 13	20 24		20 52	20 39	20 42			21 22	21 08	21 13	21 24		21 52	21 38	21 43		22 22
London Cannon Street	a																						
London Waterloo (East)	a	19 59		20 26	20 15	20 18	20 29		20 56	20 44	20 47			21 26	21 13	21 18	21 29		21 56	21 43	21 48		22 26
London Charing Cross	a	20 03		20 30	20 19	20 22	20 33		21 00	20 48	20 51			21 30	21 18	21 22	21 33		22 00	21 48	21 52		22 30

		SE 1	SE 1	SE 1	SE	SE	SE 1	SE 1	SE	SE	SE 1	SE 1	SE 1	SE	SE	SE 1	SE
Tonbridge	d	21 32	21 40	21 50			22 02	22 10			22 31	22 40	22 50			23 14	
Hildenborough	d	21 36					22 06				22 35					23 18	
Sevenoaks	a	21 43	21 48	21 58			22 13	22 18			22 41	22 48	22 58			23 24	
	d	21 44	21 49	21 59		22 05	22 14	22 19			22 42	22 49	22 59			23 25	
Dunton Green	d					22 08											
Knockholt	d					22 13											
Chelsfield	d					22 16					22 49					23 32	
Orpington	a	21 52		22 08		22 19	22 22				22 52		23 08			23 36	
	d	21 53		22 09		22 21	22 23			22 51	22 53		23 09		23 21	23 37	
Petts Wood	d					22 24				22 54					23 24		
Chislehurst	d					22 27				22 57					23 27		
Elmstead Woods	d					22 29				22 59					23 29		
Bromley North	d				22 23				22 53					23 23			23 53
Sundridge Park	d				22 25				22 55					23 25			23 55
Grove Park	d				22a28	22 33			22a58	23 03				23a28	23 33		23a58
Hither Green	d					22 37				23 07					23 37		
Lewisham	d					22 43				23 13					23 43		
St Johns	a																
New Cross	a																
London Bridge	a	22 08	22 13	22 24		22 52	22 38	22 43		23 22	23 08	23 13	23 24		23 52	23 54	
London Cannon Street	a																
London Waterloo (East)	a	22 13	22 18	22 29		22 56	22 43	22 48		23 26	23 13	23 18	23 29		23 56	23 59	
London Charing Cross	a	22 18	22 22	22 33		23 00	22 48	22 52		23 30	23 18	23 22	23 33		00 01	00 03	

Mondays to Fridays

30 July to 10 August

		SE	SE 1	SE A	SE	SE	SE	SE 1	SE	SE 1	SE	SE	SE 1	SE 1	SE 1	SE	SE	SE	SE 1	SE 1	SE 1	SE	SE
Tonbridge	d		23p14		04 52		04 56	05 32		05 50			06 00	06 06	06 19				06 32	06 40	06 44		
Hildenborough	d		23p18		04 56		05 00	05 36					06 04		06 23				06 36				
Sevenoaks	a		23p24		05 02		05 06	05 42		05 58			06 10	06 14	06 30				06 43	06 48	06 52		
	d		23p25		05 03		05 07	05 43		05 59		06 02	06 11	06 15	06 32			06 36	06 44	06 49	06 53		
Dunton Green	d											06 05						06 39					
Knockholt	d											06 10						06 44					
Chelsfield	d		23p32		05 10		05 14	05 50				06 13						06 47					
Orpington	a		23p36		05 13		05 18	05 53		06 08		06 16	06 19	06 23				06 50	06 53		07 02		
	d	23p21	23p37		05 14	05 15	05 20	05 54	06 01	06 09		06 22	06 20	06 24			06 43	06 52	06 54		07 04	07 03	
Petts Wood	d	23p24				05 18	05 23		06 04			06 25					06 46	06 55				07 06	
Chislehurst	d	23p27				05 21	05 26		06 07			06 28					06 49	06 58				07 09	
Elmstead Woods	d	23p29				05 23	05 28		06 09			06 30					06 51	07 00				07 11	
Bromley North	d			00 23							06 25					06 45							07 15
Sundridge Park	d			00 25							06 27					06 47							07 17
Grove Park	d	23p33		00a28		05 27	05 31		06 12		06a30	06 34				06a50	06 54	07 04				07 14	07a20
Hither Green	d	23p37				05 30	05 35		06 16			06 38					06 58	07 08				07 18	
Lewisham	d	23p43				05 36			06 22			06 43					07 04					07 25	
St Johns	a																						
New Cross	a					05 39	05 40		06 25														
London Bridge	a	23p52	23p54		05 37	05 45	05 45	06 09	06 31	06 24		06 51	06 38	06 39	06 54			07 18	07 09	07 14	07 22		
London Cannon Street	a												06 42					07 25			07 29		
London Waterloo (East)	a	23p56	23p59		05 41	05 50	05 50	06 14	06 36	06 29		06 56		06 44	06 59		07 16		07 14	07 19		07 36	
London Charing Cross	a	00 04	00 03		05 47	05 55	05 53	06 18	06 39	06 33		07 02		06 49	07 05		07 22		07 20	07 25		07 42	

A not 30 July, 6 August

Table 204

Mondays to Fridays

30 July to 10 August

Bromley North to Grove Park, Tonbridge, Sevenoaks, Orpington and Grove Park - London Cannon Street/Charing Cross

Network Diagram - see first Page of Table 200

	SE	SE [1]	SE [1]	SE [1]	SE	SE	SE	SE [1]	SE [1]	SE [1]	SE	SE	SE	SE [1]	SE [1]	SE	SE [1]	SE	SE	SE	SE [1]	SE [1]
Tonbridge [4] d		06 51	07 02	07 11				07 15	07 23	07 31				07 35	07 42		07 51				07 59	08 04
Hildenborough d		06 55		07 15				07 20		07 35				07 40			07 55					
Sevenoaks [4] a		07 02	07 10	07 22				07 26	07 31	07 42				07 46	07 50		08 02				08 07	08 12
d	06 56	07 03	07 11	07 23			07 17	07 27	07 32	07 43			07 37	07 47	07 51		08 03			07 57	08 08	08 12
Dunton Green d	06 59						07 20						07 40							08 00		
Knockholt d	07 04						07 25						07 45							08 05		
Chelsfield [3] d	07 07			07 32			07 28			07 52			07 48				08 12			08 08		
Orpington [4] a	07 10	07 13					07 31						07 51							08 12		
d	07 11	07 14			07 22		07 33				07 41		07 52			07 57		08 01		08 13		
Petts Wood [4] d	07 15				07 25		07 36				07 44		07 55			08 00		08 04		08 16		
Chislehurst d	07 18				07 28		07 39				07 47		07 59			08 03		08 07		08 20		
Elmstead Woods d	07 20				07 31		07 41				07 50		08 01			08 06		08 10		08 22		
Bromley North d						07 35						07 55							08 15			
Sundridge Park d						07 37						07 57							08 17			
Grove Park [4] d	07 24				07 34	07a40	07 45				07 53	08a00	08 05			08 09		08 13	08a20	08 26		
Hither Green [4] d	07 28				07 39		07 49				07 58							08 17				
Lewisham [4] d					07 44						08 03							08 23				
St Johns a																						
New Cross [4] a																						
London Bridge [4] a	07 37	07 29	07 36	07 50	07 53		07 59	07 53		08 09			08 18	08 13			08 29			08 39	08 33	
London Cannon Street [4] a	07 44						08 06	07 59					08 26	08 20						08 46	08 41	
London Waterloo (East) [4] a		07 34	07 41	07 55	07 58				08 00	08 14	08 16				08 20	08 24	08 34	08 36				08 40
London Charing Cross [4] a		07 40	07 47	08 01	08 04				08 06	08 20	08 22				08 26	08 30	08 40	08 42				08 46

	SE	SE	SE	SE [1]	SE [1]	SE [1]	SE [1]	SE [1]	SE	SE	SE	SE [1]	SE	SE [1]	SE	SE	SE [1]	SE [1] ⚒	SE	SE [1]	SE
Tonbridge [4] d				08 11	08 15	08 22	08 35	08 40				08 43		08 50			09 02	09 10		09 20	
Hildenborough d				08 15	08 20		08 39					08 48					09 06				
Sevenoaks [4] a				08 22	08 26	08 30	08 45	08 48				08 54		08 58			09 13	09 18		09 28	
d			08 17	08 23	08 27	08 31	08 45	08 49			08 37	08 55		08 59		09 06	09 14	09 19		09 29	
Dunton Green d			08 20								08 40					09 09					
Knockholt d			08 25								08 45					09 14					
Chelsfield [3] d			08 28	08 32			08 53				08 48					09 17					
Orpington [4] a			08 31								08 51	09 03		09 08		09 20	09 24			09 38	
d	08 21		08 32						08 43		08 52	09 04	09 03	09 09		09 21	09 24		09 33	09 39	
Petts Wood [4] d	08 24		08 35						08 46		08 55		09 06			09 24			09 36		
Chislehurst d	08 27		08 39						08 49		08 58		09 09			09 27			09 39		
Elmstead Woods d	08 29		08 41						08 51		09 00		09 11			09 30			09 41		
Bromley North d		08 35								08 55					09 25						09 45
Sundridge Park d		08 37								08 57					09 27						09 47
Grove Park [4] d	08 33	08a40	08 45						08 55	09a00	09 04		09 15		09a30	09 33			09 45		09a50
Hither Green [4] d	08 37								08 59		09 08		09 19			09 37			09 49		
Lewisham [4] d									09 04				09 24						09 54		
St Johns a									09 07				09 26						09 56		
New Cross [4] a									09 09				09 28						09 58		
London Bridge [4] a			08 59	08 49	08 55		09 11	09 14	09 17		09 20	09 22	09 33	09 26		09 49	09 40	09 43	10 04	09 55	
London Cannon Street [4] a			09 06		09 02				09 23			09 29	09 40						10 11		
London Waterloo (East) [4] a	08 52			08 54		09 00	09 16	09 19			09 25			09 31		09 53	09 45	09 48		09 59	
London Charing Cross [4] a	08 58			09 00		09 04	09 22	09 25			09 31			09 37		09 59	09 51	09 54		10 03	

	SE	SE [1]	SE [1] ⚒	SE	SE	SE [1]	SE	SE	SE [1]	SE [1] ⚒	SE	SE [1]	SE	SE	SE [1]	SE [1] ⚒	SE	SE	SE [1]	SE	SE	SE [1]
Tonbridge [4] d		09 32	09 40			09 50			10 02	10 10		10 20			10 32	10 40			10 50			11 02
Hildenborough d		09 36							10 06						10 36							11 06
Sevenoaks [4] a		09 43	09 48			09 58			10 13	10 18		10 28			10 43	10 48			10 58			11 13
d	09 36	09 44	09 49			09 59		10 06	10 14	10 19		10 29		10 36	10 44	10 49			10 59		11 06	11 14
Dunton Green d	09 39							10 09						10 39							11 09	
Knockholt d	09 44							10 14						10 44							11 14	
Chelsfield [3] d	09 47							10 17						10 47							11 17	
Orpington [4] a	09 50	09 53				10 08		10 20	10 23			10 38		10 50	10 53				11 08		11 20	11 23
d	09 51	09 54			10 03	10 09		10 21	10 24		10 33	10 39		10 51	10 54			11 03	11 09		11 21	11 24
Petts Wood [4] d	09 54				10 06			10 24			10 36			10 54				11 06			11 24	
Chislehurst d	09 57				10 09			10 27			10 39			10 57				11 09			11 27	
Elmstead Woods d	09 59				10 11			10 29			10 41			10 59				11 11			11 29	
Bromley North d				10 05			10 25						10 45				11 05			11 25		
Sundridge Park d				10 07			10 27						10 47				11 07			11 27		
Grove Park [4] d	10 03			10a10	10 15		10a30	10 33			10 45		10a50	11 03			11a10	11 15		11a30	11 33	
Hither Green [4] d	10 07				10 19			10 37			10 49			11 07				11 19			11 37	
Lewisham [4] d					10 24						10 54							11 24				
St Johns a					10 26						10 56							11 26				
New Cross [4] a					10 28						10 58							11 28				
London Bridge [4] a	10 19	10 10	10 13		10 34	10 25		10 49	10 40	10 43	11 04	10 55		11 19	11 10	11 13		11 34	11 25		11 49	11 40
London Cannon Street [4] a					10 41						11 11							11 41				
London Waterloo (East) [4] a	10 23	10 15	10 18			10 29		10 53	10 45	10 48		10 59		11 24	11 15	11 18			11 30		11 53	11 45
London Charing Cross [4] a	10 27	10 19	10 22			10 33		10 57	10 49	10 52		11 03		11 29	11 19	11 22			11 34		11 57	11 49

Table 204

Mondays to Fridays

30 July to 10 August

Bromley North to Grove Park, Tonbridge, Sevenoaks, Orpington and Grove Park - London Cannon Street/Charing Cross

Network Diagram - see first Page of Table 200

	SE [1] ⚒	SE	SE [1]	SE	SE	SE [1]	SE [1] ⚒	SE	SE	SE [1]	SE	SE	SE [1]	SE [1] ⚒	SE	SE [1]	SE	SE	SE [1]	SE [1] ⚒	SE
Tonbridge [4] d	11 10		11 20			11 32	11 40			11 50			12 02	12 10		12 20			12 32	12 40	
Hildenborough d						11 36							12 06						12 36		
Sevenoaks [4] a	11 18		11 28			11 43	11 48			11 58			12 13	12 18		12 28			12 43	12 48	
d	11 19		11 29		11 36	11 44	11 49			11 59		12 06	12 14	12 19		12 29		12 36	12 44	12 49	
Dunton Green d					11 39							12 09						12 39			
Knockholt d					11 44							12 14						12 44			
Chelsfield [3] d					11 47							12 17						12 47			
Orpington [4] a			11 38		11 50	11 53				12 08		12 20	12 23			12 38		12 50	12 53		
d		11 33	11 39		11 51	11 54			12 03	12 09		12 21	12 24		12 33	12 39		12 51	12 54		
Petts Wood [4] d		11 36			11 54				12 06			12 24			12 36			12 54			
Chislehurst d		11 39			11 57				12 09			12 27			12 39			12 57			
Elmstead Woods d		11 41			11 59				12 11			12 29			12 41			12 59			
Bromley North d				11 45				12 05			12 25						12 45				13 05
Sundridge Park d				11 47				12 07			12 27						12 47				13 07
Grove Park [4] d		11 45		11a50	12 03			12a10	12 15		12a30	12 33			12 45		12a50	13 03			13a10
Hither Green [4] d		11 49			12 07				12 19			12 37			12 49			13 07			
Lewisham [4] d		11 54							12 24						12 54						
St Johns a		11 56							12 26						12 56						
New Cross [4] a		11 58							12 28						12 58						
London Bridge [4] a	11 43	12 04	11 55		12 19	12 10	12 13		12 34	12 25		12 49	12 40	12 43	13 04	12 55		13 19	13 10	13 13	
London Cannon Street [4] a		12 11							12 41						13 11						
London Waterloo (East) [4] a	11 48		11 59		12 23	12 15	12 18			12 29		12 53	12 45	12 48		12 59		13 23	13 15	13 18	
London Charing Cross [4] a	11 52		12 03		12 27	12 19	12 22			12 33		12 57	12 49	12 52		13 03		13 27	13 19	13 22	

	SE	SE [1]	SE	SE	SE [1]	SE [1] ⚒	SE	SE [1]	SE	SE	SE [1]	SE [1] ⚒	SE	SE	SE [1]	SE	SE	SE [1]	SE [1] ⚒	SE	SE [1]	SE
Tonbridge [4] d		12 50			13 02	13 10		13 20			13 32	13 40			13 50			14 02	14 10		14 20	
Hildenborough d					13 06						13 36							14 06				
Sevenoaks [4] a		12 58			13 13	13 18		13 28			13 43	13 48			13 58			14 13	14 18		14 28	
d		12 59		13 06	13 14	13 19		13 29		13 36	13 44	13 49			13 59		14 06	14 14	14 19		14 29	
Dunton Green d				13 09						13 39							14 09					
Knockholt d				13 14						13 44							14 14					
Chelsfield [3] d				13 17						13 47							14 17					
Orpington [4] a		13 08		13 20	13 23			13 38		13 50	13 53				14 08		14 20	14 23			14 38	
d	13 03	13 09		13 21	13 24		13 33	13 39		13 51	13 54			14 03	14 09		14 21	14 24		14 33	14 39	
Petts Wood [4] d	13 06			13 24			13 36			13 54				14 06			14 24			14 36		
Chislehurst d	13 09			13 27			13 39			13 57				14 09			14 27			14 39		
Elmstead Woods d	13 11			13 29			13 41			13 59				14 11			14 29			14 41		
Bromley North d			13 25						13 45				14 05			14 25						14 45
Sundridge Park d			13 27						13 47				14 07			14 27						14 47
Grove Park [4] d	13 15		13a30	13 33			13 45		13a50	14 03			14a10	14 15		14a30	14 33			14 45		14a50
Hither Green [4] d	13 19			13 37			13 49			14 07				14 19			14 37			14 49		
Lewisham [4] d	13 24						13 54							14 24						14 54		
St Johns a	13 26						13 56							14 26						14 56		
New Cross [4] a	13 28						13 58							14 28						14 58		
London Bridge [4] a	13 34	13 25		13 49	13 40	13 43	14 04	13 55		14 19	14 10	14 13		14 34	14 25		14 49	14 40	14 43	15 04	14 55	
London Cannon Street [4] a	13 41						14 11							14 41						15 11		
London Waterloo (East) [4] a		13 29		13 53	13 45	13 48		13 59		14 23	14 15	14 18			14 29		14 53	14 45	14 48		14 59	
London Charing Cross [4] a		13 33		13 57	13 49	13 52		14 03		14 27	14 19	14 22			14 33		14 57	14 49	14 52		15 03	

	SE	SE [1]	SE [1] ⚒	SE	SE	SE [1]	SE	SE	SE [1]	SE [1] ⚒	SE	SE [1]	SE	SE	SE [1]	SE [1] ⚒	SE	SE	SE [1]	SE	SE	SE [1]
Tonbridge [4] d		14 32	14 40			14 50			15 02	15 10		15 20			15 32	15 40			15 50			16 02
Hildenborough d		14 36							15 06						15 36							16 06
Sevenoaks [4] a		14 43	14 48			14 58			15 13	15 18		15 28			15 43	15 48			15 58			16 13
d	14 36	14 44	14 49			14 59		15 06	15 14	15 19		15 29		15 36	15 44	15 49			15 59		16 06	16 14
Dunton Green d	14 39							15 09						15 39							16 09	
Knockholt d	14 44							15 14						15 44							16 14	
Chelsfield [3] d	14 47							15 17						15 47							16 17	16 21
Orpington [4] a	14 50	14 53				15 08		15 20	15 23			15 38		15 50	15 53				16 07		16 20	16 24
d	14 51	14 54			15 03	15 09		15 21	15 24		15 33	15 39		15 51	15 54			16 03	16 08		16 21	16 25
Petts Wood [4] d	14 54				15 06			15 24			15 36			15 54				16 06			16 24	
Chislehurst d	14 57				15 09			15 27			15 39			15 57				16 09			16 27	
Elmstead Woods d	14 59				15 11			15 29			15 41			15 59				16 11			16 29	
Bromley North d				15 05			15 25						15 45				16 05			16 25		
Sundridge Park d				15 07			15 27						15 47				16 07			16 27		
Grove Park [4] d	15 03			15a10	15 15		15a30	15 33			15 45		15a50	16 03			16a10	16 15		16a30	16 33	
Hither Green [4] d	15 07				15 19			15 37			15 49			16 07				16 19			16 37	
Lewisham [4] d					15 24						15 54							16 24				
St Johns a					15 26						15 56							16 26				
New Cross [4] a					15 28						15 58							16 28				
London Bridge [4] a	15 19	15 10	15 13		15 34	15 25		15 49	15 40	15 43	16 04	15 55		16 19	16 11	16 14		16 34	16 25		16 48	16 42
London Cannon Street [4] a					15 41						16 11							16 41				
London Waterloo (East) [4] a	15 23	15 15	15 18			15 29		15 55	15 45	15 48		15 59		16 24	16 16	16 20			16 29		16 54	16 48
London Charing Cross [4] a	15 27	15 19	15 22			15 33		15 58	15 49	15 52		16 03		16 28	16 20	16 24			16 33		16 58	16 52

Table 204

Mondays to Fridays
30 July to 10 August

Bromley North to Grove Park, Tonbridge, Sevenoaks, Orpington and Grove Park - London Cannon Street/Charing Cross

Network Diagram - see first Page of Table 200

		SE 1 ⌶		SE	SE 1	SE	SE	SE 1	SE 1 ⌶	SE	SE	SE 1		SE	SE	SE	SE 1	SE 1 ⌶	SE	SE 1	SE	SE		SE 1	SE 1 ⌶
Tonbridge 4	d	16 10			16 20			16 32	16 40			16 50					17 02	17 10		17 20				17 32	17 40
Hildenborough	d							16 36									17 06							17 36	
Sevenoaks 4	a	16 18			16 28			16 43	16 48			16 58					17 13	17 18		17 28				17 43	17 48
	d	16 19			16 29		16 36	16 44	16 52			16 59				17 05	17 14	17 19		17 29		17 35		17 44	17 49
Dunton Green	d						16 39									17 08						17 38			
Knockholt	d						16 44									17 13						17 43			
Chelsfield 3	d						16 47									17 16						17 46			
Orpington 4	a				16 38		16 50	16 53				17 08				17 19	17 23			17 38		17 49		17 53	
	d			16 33	16 39		16 51	16 54			17 03	17 09		17 13		17 20	17 24		17 37	17 39		17 50		17 54	
Petts Wood 4	d			16 36			16 54				17 06					17 24			17 40			17 54			
Chislehurst	d			16 39			16 57				17 09					17 27			17 43			17 57			
Elmstead Woods	d			16 41			16 59				17 11					17 29			17 45			17 59			
Bromley North	d					16 45				17 07					17 27						17 50				
Sundridge Park	d					16 47				17 09					17 29						17 52				
Grove Park 4	d			16 45		16a50	17 03			17a12	17 15				17a32	17 34			17 49		17a55	18 03			
Hither Green 4	d			16 50			17 09				17 19					17 38			17 53			18 07			
Lewisham 4	d										17 24								17 57						
St Johns	a										17 26								17 59						
New Cross 4	⊖ a										17 28														
London Bridge 4	⊖ a	16 46		17 01	16 56			17 11	17 17		17 34	17 27				17 49	17 41	17 44	18 06	17 58		18 18		18 09	18 16
London Cannon Street 4	⊖ a										17 41	17 32							18 11						
London Waterloo (East) 4	⊖ a	16 52		17 06	17 00		17 24	17 16	17 22					17 36		17 53	17 46	17 50		18 02		18 23		18 14	18 20
London Charing Cross 4	⊖ a	16 56		17 10	17 04		17 29	17 20	17 26					17 40		17 57	17 50	17 53		18 06		18 27		18 18	18 25

		SE	SE 1	SE	SE	SE 1	SE 1 ⌶	SE 1		SE	SE	SE	SE	SE 1	SE 1 ⌶	SE	SE 1	SE		SE	SE 1	SE 1 ⌶	SE 1	SE	SE
Tonbridge 4	d		17 50			18 02	18 10	18 23						18 32	18 40		18 50				19 02	19 10	19 20		
Hildenborough	d					18 06								18 36							19 06				
Sevenoaks 4	a		17 58			18 13	18 18	18 31						18 43	18 48		18 59				19 13	19 18	19 28		
	d		17 59		18 05	18 14	18 19	18 32					18 35	18 44	18 49		18 59			19 06	19 14	19 19	19 29		19 36
Dunton Green	d				18 08								18 38							19 09					19 39
Knockholt	d				18 13								18 43							19 14					19 44
Chelsfield 3	d				18 16								18 46							19 17					19 47
Orpington 4	a		18 08		18 19	18 23							18 49	18 53			19 08			19 20	19 23		19 38		19 50
	d	18 03	18 09		18 21	18 24					18 33		18 50	18 54		19 03	19 08			19 21	19 24		19 39		19 51
Petts Wood 4	d	18 06			18 24						18 36		18 54			19 06				19 24					19 54
Chislehurst	d	18 09			18 27						18 39		18 57			19 09				19 27					19 57
Elmstead Woods	d	18 11			18 29						18 41		18 59			19 11				19 29					19 59
Bromley North	d			18 13						18 33		18 55						19 18						19 42	
Sundridge Park	d			18 15						18 35		18 57						19 20						19 44	
Grove Park 4	d	18 15		18a18	18 33					18a38	18 45	19a00	19 03			19 15		19a23		19 33				19a47	20 03
Hither Green 4	d	18 19			18 37						18 49		19 07			19 19				19 37					20 07
Lewisham 4	d	18 24									18 54					19 24				19 43					20 13
St Johns	a	18 26									18 56					19 26									
New Cross 4	⊖ a	18 28									18 58					19 28									
London Bridge 4	⊖ a	18 34	18 25		18 48	18 40	18 43	18 55			19 04		19 19	19 10	19 13	19 34	19 25			19 52	19 40	19 43	19 54		20 22
London Cannon Street 4	⊖ a	18 41									19 12					19 41									
London Waterloo (East) 4	⊖ a		18 29		18 53	18 45	18 48	18 59					19 23	19 14	19 17		19 29			19 56	19 45	19 48	19 59		20 26
London Charing Cross 4	⊖ a		18 35		18 57	18 49	18 52	19 04					19 27	19 18	19 21		19 33			20 03	19 49	19 52	20 03		20 33

		SE 1	SE 1	SE 1		SE	SE	SE 1	SE 1	SE	SE	SE	SE 1	SE 1		SE 1	SE	SE	SE 1	SE 1	SE	SE	SE 1	SE 1	
Tonbridge 4	d	19 32	19 40	19 51				20 02	20 10				20 32	20 40		20 50			21 02	21 10			21 32	21 40	
Hildenborough	d	19 36						20 06					20 36						21 06				21 36		
Sevenoaks 4	a	19 43	19 48	19 59				20 13	20 18				20 43	20 48		20 58			21 13	21 18			21 43	21 48	
	d	19 44	19 49	20 00			20 06	20 14	20 19			20 35	20 44	20 49		20 59		21 05	21 14	21 19		21 35	21 44	21 49	
Dunton Green	d						20 09					20 38						21 08				21 38			
Knockholt	d						20 14					20 43						21 13				21 43			
Chelsfield 3	d						20 17					20 46						21 16				21 46			
Orpington 4	a	19 53		20 08			20 20	20 23				20 49	20 52			21 08		21 19	21 22			21 49	21 52		
	d	19 54		20 09			20 21	20 24				20 51	20 53			21 09		21 21	21 23			21 51	21 53		
Petts Wood 4	d						20 24					20 54						21 24				21 54			
Chislehurst	d						20 27					20 57						21 27				21 57			
Elmstead Woods	d						20 29					20 59						21 29				21 59			
Bromley North	d					20 02				20 27	20 53						21 23				21 53				
Sundridge Park	d					20 04				20 29	20 55						21 25				21 55				
Grove Park 4	d					20a07	20 34			20a32	20a58	21 03					21a28	21 33			21a58	22 03			
Hither Green 4	d						20 38					21 07						21 37				22 07			
Lewisham 4	d						20 43					21 13						21 43				22 13			
St Johns	a																								
New Cross 4	⊖ a																								
London Bridge 4	⊖ a	20 10	20 13	20 24			20 52	20 39	20 42			21 22	21 08	21 13		21 24		21 52	21 38	21 43		22 22	22 08	22 13	
London Cannon Street 4	⊖ a																								
London Waterloo (East) 4	⊖ a	20 15	20 18	20 29			20 56	20 44	20 47			21 26	21 13	21 18		21 29		21 56	21 43	21 48		22 26	22 13	22 18	
London Charing Cross 4	⊖ a	20 19	20 22	20 33			21 03	20 48	20 51			21 33	21 18	21 22		21 33		22 03	21 48	21 52		22 33	22 18	22 22	

Table 204

Mondays to Fridays
30 July to 10 August

Bromley North to Grove Park, Tonbridge, Sevenoaks, Orpington and Grove Park - London Cannon Street/Charing Cross

Network Diagram - see first Page of Table 200

		SE 1	SE	SE	SE 1	SE 1	SE	SE	SE 1	SE 1		SE 1	SE	SE	SE 1	SE
Tonbridge 4	d	21 50			22 02	22 10			22 31	22 40		22 50			23 14	
Hildenborough	d				22 06				22 35						23 18	
Sevenoaks 4	a	21 58			22 13	22 18			22 41	22 48		22 58			23 24	
	d	21 59		22 05	22 14	22 19			22 42	22 49		22 59			23 25	
Dunton Green	d			22 08												
Knockholt	d			22 13												
Chelsfield 3	d			22 16					22 49						23 32	
Orpington 4	a	22 08		22 19	22 22				22 52			23 08			23 36	
	d	22 09		22 21	22 23			22 51	22 53			23 09		23 21	23 37	
Petts Wood 4	d			22 24				22 54						23 24		
Chislehurst	d			22 27				22 57						23 27		
Elmstead Woods	d			22 29				22 59						23 29		
Bromley North	d		22 23				22 53						23 23			23 53
Sundridge Park	d		22 25				22 55						23 25			23 55
Grove Park 4	d		22a28	22 33			22a58	23 03					23a28	23 33		23a58
Hither Green 4	d			22 37				23 07						23 37		
Lewisham 4	d			22 43				23 13						23 43		
St Johns	a															
New Cross 4	⊖ a															
London Bridge 4	⊖ a	22 24		22 52	22 38	22 43		23 22	23 08	23 13		23 24		23 52	23 54	
London Cannon Street 4	⊖ a															
London Waterloo (East) 4	⊖ a	22 29		22 56	22 43	22 48		23 26	23 13	23 18		23 29		23 56	23 59	
London Charing Cross 4	⊖ a	22 33		23 03	22 48	22 52		23 33	23 18	23 22		23 33		00 04	00 03	

Mondays to Fridays
29 August to 7 September

		SE A	SE 1 A	SE A	SE	SE	SE 1	SE	SE 1	SE		SE	SE 1	SE 1	SE 1	SE	SE	SE	SE 1	SE 1		SE 1	SE	SE	SE
Tonbridge 4	d		23p14		04 52		05 32		05 50				06 00	06 06	06 19				06 32	06 40		06 44			
Hildenborough	d		23p18		04 56		05 36						06 04		06 23				06 36						
Sevenoaks 4	a		23p24		05 02		05 42		05 58				06 10	06 14	06 30				06 43	06 48		06 52			
	d		23p25		05 03		05 43		05 59			06 02	06 11	06 15	06 32			06 36	06 44	06 49		06 53			06 56
Dunton Green	d											06 05						06 39							06 59
Knockholt	d											06 10						06 44							07 04
Chelsfield 3	d		23p32		05 10		05 50					06 13						06 47							07 07
Orpington 4	a		23p36		05 13		05 53		06 08			06 16	06 19	06 23				06 50	06 53			07 02			07 10
	d	23p21	23p37		05 14	05 15	05 54	06 01	06 09			06 22	06 20	06 24			06 43	06 52	06 54			07 04	07 03		07 11
Petts Wood 4	d	23p24				05 18		06 04				06 25					06 46	06 55					07 06		07 15
Chislehurst	d	23p27				05 21		06 07				06 28					06 49	06 58					07 09		07 18
Elmstead Woods	d	23p29				05 23		06 09				06 30					06 51	07 00					07 11		07 20
Bromley North	d			00 23						06 25						06 45								07 15	
Sundridge Park	d			00 25						06 27						06 47								07 17	
Grove Park 4	d	23p33		00a28		05 27		06 12		06a30		06 34				06a50	06 54	07 04					07 15	07a20	07 24
Hither Green 4	d	23p37				05 30		06 16				06 38					06 58	07 08					07 19		07 28
Lewisham 4	d	23p43				05 36		06 22				06 43					07 04						07 25		
St Johns	a																								
New Cross 4	⊖ a					05 39		06 25																	
London Bridge 4	⊖ a	23p52	23p54		05 37	05 45	06 09	06 31	06 24			06 51	06 38	06 39	06 54			07 18	07 09	07 14		07 22			07 37
London Cannon Street 4	⊖ a												06 42					07 25				07 29			07 44
London Waterloo (East) 4	⊖ a	23p56	23p59		05 41	05 50	06 14	06 36	06 29			06 56		06 44	06 59		07 16		07 14	07 19			07 36		
London Charing Cross 4	⊖ a	00 01	00 03		05 47	05 55	06 18	06 39	06 33			07 02		06 49	07 05		07 22		07 20	07 25			07 42		

		SE 1	SE 1	SE 1	SE	SE		SE	SE 1	SE 1	SE 1	SE	SE	SE	SE 1	SE 1		SE	SE 1	SE	SE	SE	SE 1	SE 1	SE
Tonbridge 4	d	06 51	07 02	07 11					07 15	07 23	07 31				07 35	07 42			07 51				07 59	08 04	
Hildenborough	d	06 55		07 15					07 20		07 35				07 40				07 55						
Sevenoaks 4	a	07 02	07 10	07 22					07 26	07 31	07 42				07 46	07 50			08 02				08 07	08 12	
	d	07 03	07 11	07 23				07 17	07 27	07 32	07 43			07 37	07 47	07 51			08 03			07 57	08 08	08 12	
Dunton Green	d							07 20						07 40								08 00			
Knockholt	d							07 25						07 45								08 05			
Chelsfield 3	d			07 32				07 28			07 52			07 48					08 12			08 08			
Orpington 4	a	07 13						07 31						07 51								08 12			
	d	07 14			07 22			07 33				07 41		07 52				07 57		08 01		08 13			08 21
Petts Wood 4	d				07 25			07 36				07 44		07 55				08 00		08 04		08 16			08 24
Chislehurst	d				07 28			07 39				07 47		07 59				08 03		08 07		08 20			08 27
Elmstead Woods	d				07 31			07 41				07 50		08 01				08 06		08 10		08 22			08 29
Bromley North	d					07 35							07 55								08 15				
Sundridge Park	d					07 37							07 57								08 17				
Grove Park 4	d				07 34	07a40		07 45				07 53	08a00	08 05				08 09		08 13	08a20	08 26			08 33
Hither Green 4	d				07 39			07 49				07 58								08 17					08 37
Lewisham 4	d				07 44							08 03								08 23					
St Johns	a																								
New Cross 4	⊖ a																								
London Bridge 4	⊖ a	07 29	07 36	07 50	07 53			07 59	07 53		08 09			08 18	08 13				08 29			08 39	08 33		
London Cannon Street 4	⊖ a							08 06	07 59					08 26	08 20							08 46	08 41		
London Waterloo (East) 4	⊖ a	07 34	07 41	07 55	07 58					08 00	08 14	08 16				08 20		08 24	08 34	08 36				08 40	08 52
London Charing Cross 4	⊖ a	07 40	07 47	08 01	08 04					08 06	08 20	08 22				08 26		08 30	08 40	08 42				08 46	08 58

A not 3 September

Bromley North to Grove Park, Tonbridge, Sevenoaks, Orpington and Grove Park - London Cannon Street/Charing Cross

Network Diagram - see first Page of Table 200

		SE		SE	SE ■	SE ■	SE ■	SE ■	SE ■	SE	SE	SE		SE ■	SE	SE ■	SE	SE	SE ■	SE ■ ✠	SE	SE ■		SE	SE
Tonbridge ■	d				08 11	08 15	08 22	08 35	08 40					08 43		08 50			09 02	09 10		09 20			
Hildenborough	d				08 15	08 20		08 39						08 48					09 06						
Sevenoaks ■	a				08 22	08 26	08 30	08 45	08 48					08 54		08 58			09 13	09 18		09 28			
	d			08 17	08 23	08 27	08 31	08 45	08 49			08 37		08 55		08 59		09 06	09 14	09 19		09 29			09 36
Dunton Green	d			08 20								08 40						09 09							09 39
Knockholt	d			08 25								08 45						09 14							09 44
Chelsfield ■	d			08 28	08 32			08 53				08 48						09 17							09 47
Orpington ■	a			08 31								08 51		09 03		09 08		09 20	09 24			09 38			09 50
	d			08 32						08 43		08 52		09 04	09 03	09 09		09 21	09 24		09 33	09 39			09 51
Petts Wood ■	d			08 35						08 46		08 55			09 06			09 24			09 36				09 54
Chislehurst	d			08 39						08 49		08 58			09 09			09 27			09 39				09 57
Elmstead Woods	d			08 41						08 51		09 00			09 11			09 30			09 41				09 59
Bromley North	d	08 35									08 55						09 25							09 45	
Sundridge Park	d	08 37									08 57						09 27							09 47	
Grove Park ■	d	08a40		08 45						08 55	09a00	09 04			09 15		09a30	09 33			09 45			09a50	10 03
Hither Green ■	d									08 59		09 08			09 19			09 37			09 49				10 07
Lewisham ■	d									09 04					09 24						09 54				
St Johns	a									09 07					09 26						09 56				
New Cross ■	a									09 09					09 28						09 58				
London Bridge ■	a			08 59	08 49	08 55		09 11	09 14	09 17		09 20		09 22	09 33	09 26		09 49	09 40	09 43	10 04	09 55			10 19
London Cannon Street ■	a			09 06		09 02				09 23				09 29	09 40						10 08				
London Waterloo (East) ■	a				08 54		09 00	09 16	09 19			09 25				09 31		09 53	09 45	09 48		09 59			10 23
London Charing Cross ■	a				09 00		09 04	09 22	09 25			09 31				09 37		09 59	09 51	09 54		10 03			10 27

		SE ■	SE ■ ✠	SE	SE	SE ■	SE	SE		SE ■	SE ■ ✠	SE	SE ■	SE	SE	SE ■	SE ■ ✠	SE		SE	SE ■	SE	SE	SE ■	SE ■ ✠
Tonbridge ■	d	09 32	09 40			09 50				10 02	10 10		10 20			10 32	10 40				10 50			11 02	11 10
Hildenborough	d	09 36								10 06						10 36								11 06	
Sevenoaks ■	a	09 43	09 48			09 58				10 13	10 18		10 28			10 43	10 48				10 58			11 13	11 18
	d	09 44	09 49			09 59		10 06		10 14	10 19		10 29		10 36	10 44	10 49				10 59		11 06	11 14	11 19
Dunton Green	d							10 09							10 39								11 09		
Knockholt	d							10 14							10 44								11 14		
Chelsfield ■	d							10 17							10 47								11 17		
Orpington ■	a	09 53				10 08		10 20		10 23			10 38		10 50	10 53					11 08		11 20	11 23	
	d	09 54			10 03	10 09		10 21		10 24		10 33	10 39		10 51	10 54				11 03	11 09		11 21	11 24	
Petts Wood ■	d				10 06			10 24				10 36			10 54					11 06			11 24		
Chislehurst	d				10 09			10 27				10 39			10 57					11 09			11 27		
Elmstead Woods	d				10 11			10 29				10 41			10 59					11 11			11 29		
Bromley North	d			10 05			10 25							10 45				11 05				11 25			
Sundridge Park	d			10 07			10 27							10 47				11 07				11 27			
Grove Park ■	d			10a10	10 15		10a30	10 33				10 45		10a50	11 03			11a10		11 15		11a30	11 33		
Hither Green ■	d				10 19			10 37				10 49			11 07					11 19			11 37		
Lewisham ■	d				10 24							10 54								11 24					
St Johns	a				10 26							10 56								11 26					
New Cross ■	a				10 28							10 58								11 28					
London Bridge ■	a	10 10	10 13		10 34	10 25		10 49		10 40	10 43	11 04	10 55		11 19	11 10	11 13			11 34	11 25		11 49	11 40	11 43
London Cannon Street ■	a				10 38							11 08								11 38					
London Waterloo (East) ■	a	10 15	10 18			10 29		10 53		10 45	10 48		10 59		11 23	11 15	11 18				11 29		11 53	11 45	11 48
London Charing Cross ■	a	10 19	10 22			10 33		10 57		10 49	10 52		11 03		11 27	11 19	11 22				11 33		11 57	11 49	11 52

		SE	SE ■	SE		SE	SE ■	SE ■ ✠	SE	SE	SE ■	SE	SE	SE ■		SE ■ ✠	SE	SE ■	SE	SE	SE ■	SE ■ ✠	SE	SE
Tonbridge ■	d		11 20				11 32	11 40			11 50			12 02		12 10		12 20			12 32	12 40		
Hildenborough	d						11 36							12 06							12 36			
Sevenoaks ■	a		11 28				11 43	11 48			11 58			12 13		12 18		12 28			12 43	12 48		
	d		11 29			11 36	11 44	11 49			11 59		12 06	12 14		12 19		12 29		12 36	12 44	12 49		
Dunton Green	d					11 39							12 09							12 39				
Knockholt	d					11 44							12 14							12 44				
Chelsfield ■	d					11 47							12 17							12 47				
Orpington ■	a		11 38			11 50	11 53				12 08		12 20	12 23				12 38		12 50	12 53			
	d	11 33	11 39			11 51	11 54			12 03	12 09		12 21	12 24			12 33	12 39		12 51	12 54			13 03
Petts Wood ■	d	11 36				11 54				12 06			12 24				12 36			12 54				13 06
Chislehurst	d	11 39				11 57				12 09			12 27				12 39			12 57				13 09
Elmstead Woods	d	11 41				11 59				12 11			12 29				12 41			12 59				13 11
Bromley North	d			11 45					12 05			12 25							12 45				13 05	
Sundridge Park	d			11 47					12 07			12 27							12 47				13 07	
Grove Park ■	d	11 45		11a50		12 03			12a10	12 15		12a30	12 33				12 45		12a50	13 03			13a10	13 15
Hither Green ■	d	11 49				12 07				12 19			12 37				12 49			13 07				13 19
Lewisham ■	d	11 54								12 24							12 54							13 24
St Johns	a	11 56								12 26							12 56							13 26
New Cross ■	a	11 58								12 28							12 58							13 28
London Bridge ■	a	12 04	11 55			12 19	12 10	12 13		12 34	12 25		12 49	12 40		12 43	13 04	12 55		13 19	13 10	13 13		13 34
London Cannon Street ■	a	12 08								12 38							13 08							13 38
London Waterloo (East) ■	a		11 59			12 23	12 15	12 18			12 29		12 53	12 45		12 48		12 59		13 23	13 15	13 18		
London Charing Cross ■	a		12 03			12 27	12 19	12 22			12 33		12 57	12 49		12 52		13 03		13 27	13 19	13 22		

Table 204

Mondays to Fridays

29 August to 7 September

Bromley North to Grove Park, Tonbridge, Sevenoaks, Orpington and Grove Park - London Cannon Street/Charing Cross

Network Diagram - see first Page of Table 200

		SE ■	SE	SE	SE ■	SE ■ ✠	SE	SE ■	SE	SE		SE ■	SE ■ ✠	SE	SE	SE ■	SE	SE	SE ■	SE ■ ✠		SE	SE ■	SE	SE
Tonbridge ■	d	12 50			13 02	13 10		13 20				13 32	13 40			13 50			14 02	14 10			14 20		
Hildenborough	d				13 06							13 36							14 06						
Sevenoaks ■	a	12 58			13 13	13 18		13 28				13 43	13 48			13 58			14 13	14 18			14 28		
	d	12 59		13 06	13 14	13 19		13 29		13 36		13 44	13 49			13 59		14 06	14 14	14 19			14 29		14 36
Dunton Green	d			13 09						13 39								14 09							14 39
Knockholt	d			13 14						13 44								14 14							14 44
Chelsfield ■	d			13 17						13 47								14 17							14 47
Orpington ■	a	13 08		13 20	13 23			13 38		13 50		13 53				14 08		14 20	14 23				14 38		14 50
	d	13 09		13 21	13 24		13 33	13 39		13 51		13 54			14 03	14 09		14 21	14 24			14 33	14 39		14 51
Petts Wood ■	d			13 24			13 36			13 54					14 06			14 24				14 36			14 54
Chislehurst	d			13 27			13 39			13 57					14 09			14 27				14 39			14 57
Elmstead Woods	d			13 29			13 41			13 59					14 11			14 29				14 41			14 59
Bromley North	d		13 25						13 45					14 05			14 25							14 45	
Sundridge Park	d		13 27						13 47					14 07			14 27							14 47	
Grove Park ■	d		13a30	13 33			13 45		13a50	14 03				14a10	14 15		14a30	14 33				14 45		14a50	15 03
Hither Green ■	d			13 37			13 49			14 07					14 19			14 37				14 49			15 07
Lewisham ■	d						13 54								14 24							14 54			
St Johns	a						13 56								14 26							14 56			
New Cross ■	a						13 58								14 28							14 58			
London Bridge ■	a	13 25		13 49	13 40	13 43	14 04	13 55		14 19		14 10	14 13		14 34	14 25		14 49	14 40	14 43		15 04	14 55		15 19
London Cannon Street ■	a						14 08								14 38							15 08			
London Waterloo (East) ■	a	13 29		13 53	13 45	13 48		13 59		14 23		14 15	14 18			14 29		14 53	14 45	14 48			14 59		15 23
London Charing Cross ■	a	13 33		13 57	13 49	13 52		14 03		14 27		14 19	14 22			14 33		14 57	14 49	14 52			15 03		15 27

		SE ■	SE ■ ✠	SE	SE	SE ■		SE	SE	SE ■	SE ■ ✠	SE	SE ■	SE	SE	SE ■		SE ■ ✠	SE	SE	SE ■	SE	SE	SE ■	SE ■ ✠
Tonbridge ■	d	14 32	14 40			14 50				15 02	15 10		15 20			15 32		15 40			15 50			16 02	16 10
Hildenborough	d	14 36								15 06						15 36								16 06	
Sevenoaks ■	a	14 43	14 48			14 58				15 13	15 18		15 28			15 43		15 48			15 58			16 13	16 18
	d	14 44	14 49			14 59			15 06	15 14	15 19		15 29		15 36	15 44		15 49			15 59		16 06	16 14	16 19
Dunton Green	d								15 09						15 39								16 09		
Knockholt	d								15 14						15 44								16 14		
Chelsfield ■	d								15 17						15 47								16 17	16 21	
Orpington ■	a	14 53				15 08			15 20	15 23			15 38		15 50	15 53					16 07		16 20	16 24	
	d	14 54			15 03	15 09			15 21	15 24		15 33	15 39		15 51	15 54				16 03	16 08		16 21	16 25	
Petts Wood ■	d				15 06				15 24			15 36			15 54					16 06			16 24		
Chislehurst	d				15 09				15 27			15 39			15 57					16 09			16 27		
Elmstead Woods	d				15 11				15 29			15 41			15 59					16 11			16 29		
Bromley North	d			15 05				15 25						15 45					16 05			16 25			
Sundridge Park	d			15 07				15 27						15 47					16 07			16 27			
Grove Park ■	d			15a10	15 15			15a30	15 33			15 45		15a50	16 03				16a10	16 15		16a30	16 33		
Hither Green ■	d				15 19				15 37			15 49			16 07					16 19			16 37		
Lewisham ■	d				15 24							15 54								16 24					
St Johns	a				15 26							15 56								16 26					
New Cross ■	a				15 28							15 58								16 28					
London Bridge ■	a	15 10	15 13		15 34	15 25			15 49	15 40	15 43	16 04	15 55		16 19	16 11		16 14		16 34	16 25		16 48	16 42	16 46
London Cannon Street ■	a				15 38							16 08								16 38					
London Waterloo (East) ■	a	15 15	15 18			15 29			15 55	15 45	15 48		15 59		16 24	16 16		16 20			16 29		16 54	16 48	16 52
London Charing Cross ■	a	15 19	15 22			15 33			15 58	15 49	15 52		16 03		16 28	16 20		16 24			16 33		16 58	16 52	16 56

		SE		SE ■	SE	SE	SE ■	SE ■ ✠	SE	SE	SE ■	SE		SE	SE	SE ■	SE ■ ✠	SE	SE ■	SE	SE	SE ■		SE ■ ✠	SE
Tonbridge ■	d			16 20			16 32	16 40			16 50					17 02	17 10		17 20			17 32		17 40	
Hildenborough	d						16 36									17 06						17 36			
Sevenoaks ■	a			16 28			16 43	16 48			16 58					17 13	17 18		17 28			17 43		17 48	
	d			16 29		16 36	16 44	16 52			16 59				17 05	17 14	17 19		17 29		17 35	17 44		17 49	
Dunton Green	d					16 39									17 08						17 38				
Knockholt	d					16 44									17 13						17 43				
Chelsfield ■	d					16 47									17 16						17 46				
Orpington ■	a			16 38		16 50	16 53				17 08				17 19	17 23			17 38		17 49	17 53			
	d	16 33		16 39		16 51	16 54			17 03	17 09	17 13			17 20	17 24		17 37	17 39		17 50	17 54			18 03
Petts Wood ■	d	16 36				16 54				17 06					17 24			17 40			17 54				18 06
Chislehurst	d	16 39				16 57				17 09					17 27			17 43			17 57				18 09
Elmstead Woods	d	16 41				16 59				17 11					17 29			17 45			17 59				18 11
Bromley North	d				16 45				17 07					17 27						17 50					
Sundridge Park	d				16 47				17 09					17 29						17 52					
Grove Park ■	d	16 45			16a50	17 03			17a12	17 15				17a32	17 34			17 49		17a55	18 03				18 15
Hither Green ■	d	16 50				17 09				17 19					17 38			17 53			18 07				18 19
Lewisham ■	d									17 24															18 24
St Johns	a									17 26								17 57							18 26
New Cross ■	a									17 28								17 59							18 28
London Bridge ■	a	17 01		16 56			17 11	17 17		17 34	17 27				17 49	17 41	17 44	18 06	17 58		18 18	18 09		18 16	18 34
London Cannon Street ■	a									17 38	17 32							18 11							18 38
London Waterloo (East) ■	a	17 06		17 00		17 24	17 16	17 22				17 36			17 53	17 46	17 50		18 02		18 23	18 14		18 20	
London Charing Cross ■	a	17 10		17 04		17 29	17 20	17 26				17 40			17 57	17 50	17 53		18 06		18 27	18 18		18 25	

Table 204

Mondays to Fridays
29 August to 7 September

Bromley North to Grove Park, Tonbridge, Sevenoaks, Orpington and Grove Park - London Cannon Street/Charing Cross

Network Diagram - see first Page of Table 200

Station		SE ■	SE	SE	SE ■	SE ■ H	SE ■	SE	SE	SE	SE	SE ■	SE ■ H	SE	SE ■	SE	SE	SE ■	SE ■ H	SE ■	SE	SE	SE ■
Tonbridge ■	d	17 50			18 02	18 10	18 23					18 32	18 40		18 50			19 02	19 10	19 20			19 32
Hildenborough	d				18 06							18 36						19 06					19 36
Sevenoaks ■	a	17 58			18 13	18 18	18 31					18 43	18 48		18 59			19 13	19 18	19 28			19 43
	d	17 59		18 05	18 14	18 19	18 32				18 35	18 44	18 49		18 59		19 06	19 14	19 19	19 29		19 36	19 44
Dunton Green	d			18 08							18 38						19 09					19 39	
Knockholt	d			18 13							18 43						19 14					19 44	
Chelsfield ■	d			18 16							18 46						19 17					19 47	
Orpington ■	a	18 08		18 19	18 23						18 49	18 53			19 08		19 20	19 23		19 38		19 50	19 53
	d	18 09		18 21	18 24				18 33		18 50	18 54		19 03	19 08		19 21	19 24		19 39		19 51	19 54
Petts Wood ■	d			18 24					18 36		18 54			19 06			19 24					19 54	
Chislehurst	d			18 27					18 39		18 57			19 09			19 27					19 57	
Elmstead Woods	d			18 29					18 41		18 59			19 11			19 29					19 59	
Bromley North	d		18 13					18 33		18 55						19 18					19 42		
Sundridge Park	d		18 15					18 35		18 57						19 20					19 44		
Grove Park ■	d		18a18	18 33				18a38	18 45	19a00	19 03			19 15		19a23	19 33				19a47	20 03	
Hither Green ■	d			18 37					18 49		19 07			19 19			19 37					20 07	
Lewisham ■	d								18 54					19 24			19 43					20 13	
St Johns	a								18 56					19 26									
New Cross ■	a								18 58					19 28									
London Bridge ■	a	18 25		18 48	18 40	18 43	18 55		19 04		19 19	19 10	19 13	19 34	19 25		19 52	19 40	19 43	19 54		20 22	20 10
London Cannon Street ■	a								19 10					19 38									
London Waterloo (East) ■	a	18 29		18 53	18 45	18 48	18 59				19 23	19 14	19 17		19 29		19 56	19 45	19 48	19 59		20 26	20 15
London Charing Cross ■	a	18 35		18 57	18 49	18 52	19 04				19 27	19 18	19 21		19 33		20 00	19 49	19 52	20 03		20 30	20 19

Station		SE ■	SE ■	SE	SE	SE ■	SE ■	SE	SE	SE	SE ■	SE ■	SE ■	SE	SE	SE ■	SE ■	SE	SE	SE ■	SE ■	SE ■
Tonbridge ■	d	19 40	19 51			20 02	20 10				20 32	20 40	20 50			21 02	21 10			21 32	21 40	21 50
Hildenborough	d					20 06					20 36					21 06				21 36		
Sevenoaks ■	a	19 48	19 59			20 13	20 18				20 43	20 48	20 58			21 13	21 18			21 43	21 48	21 58
	d	19 49	20 00		20 06	20 14	20 19			20 35	20 44	20 49	20 59		21 05	21 14	21 19		21 35	21 44	21 49	21 59
Dunton Green	d				20 09					20 38					21 08				21 38			
Knockholt	d				20 14					20 43					21 13				21 43			
Chelsfield ■	d				20 17					20 46					21 16				21 46			
Orpington ■	a		20 08		20 20	20 23				20 49	20 52		21 08		21 19	21 22			21 49	21 52		22 08
	d		20 09		20 21	20 24				20 51	20 53		21 09		21 21	21 23			21 51	21 53		22 09
Petts Wood ■	d				20 24					20 54					21 24				21 54			
Chislehurst	d				20 27					20 57					21 27				21 57			
Elmstead Woods	d				20 29					20 59					21 29				21 59			
Bromley North	d			20 02				20 27	20 53					21 23				21 53				
Sundridge Park	d			20 04				20 29	20 55					21 25				21 55				
Grove Park ■	d			20a07	20 34			20a32	20a58	21 03				21a28	21 33			21a58	22 03			
Hither Green ■	d				20 38					21 07					21 37				22 07			
Lewisham ■	d				20 43					21 13					21 43				22 13			
St Johns	a																					
New Cross ■	a																					
London Bridge ■	a	20 13	20 24		20 52	20 39	20 42			21 22	21 08	21 13	21 24		21 52	21 38	21 43		22 22	22 08	22 13	22 24
London Cannon Street ■	a																					
London Waterloo (East) ■	a	20 18	20 29		20 56	20 44	20 47			21 26	21 13	21 18	21 29		21 56	21 43	21 48		22 26	22 13	22 18	22 29
London Charing Cross ■	a	20 22	20 33		21 00	20 48	20 51			21 30	21 18	21 22	21 33		22 00	21 48	21 52		22 30	22 18	22 22	22 33

Station		SE	SE	SE ■	SE ■	SE	SE	SE ■	SE ■	SE ■	SE	SE	SE ■	SE
Tonbridge ■	d			22 02	22 10			22 31	22 40	22 50			23 14	
Hildenborough	d			22 06				22 35					23 18	
Sevenoaks ■	a			22 13	22 18			22 41	22 48	22 58			23 24	
	d		22 05	22 14	22 19			22 42	22 49	22 59			23 25	
Dunton Green	d		22 08											
Knockholt	d		22 13											
Chelsfield ■	d		22 16					22 49					23 32	
Orpington ■	a		22 19	22 22				22 52		23 08			23 36	
	d		22 21	22 23			22 51	22 53		23 09		23 21	23 37	
Petts Wood ■	d		22 24				22 54					23 24		
Chislehurst	d		22 27				22 57					23 27		
Elmstead Woods	d		22 29				22 59					23 29		
Bromley North	d	22 23				22 53					23 23			23 53
Sundridge Park	d	22 25				22 55					23 25			23 55
Grove Park ■	d	22a28	22 33			22a58	23 03				23a28	23 33		23a58
Hither Green ■	d		22 37				23 07					23 37		
Lewisham ■	d		22 43				23 13					23 43		
St Johns	a													
New Cross ■	a													
London Bridge ■	a		22 52	22 38	22 43		23 22	23 08	23 13	23 24		23 52	23 54	
London Cannon Street ■	a													
London Waterloo (East) ■	a		22 56	22 43	22 48		23 26	23 13	23 18	23 29		23 56	23 59	
London Charing Cross ■	a		23 00	22 48	22 52		23 30	23 18	23 22	23 33		00 01	00 03	

Table 204

Saturdays
until 21 July, 18 Aug and from 15 Sep

Bromley North to Grove Park, Tonbridge, Sevenoaks, Orpington and Grove Park - London Cannon Street/Charing Cross

Network Diagram - see first Page of Table 200

Station		SE	SE ■	SE	SE	SE	SE	SE ■	SE	SE	SE ■	SE ■	SE	SE	SE ■	SE	SE ■	SE	SE	SE ■	SE ■	SE	SE
Tonbridge ■	d		23p14					06 02			06 32	06 50			07 02		07 20			07 32	07 40		
Hildenborough	d		23p18					06 06			06 36				07 06					07 36			
Sevenoaks ■	a		23p24					06 13			06 43	06 58			07 13		07 28			07 43	07 48		
	d		23p25		05 36		06 06	06 14		06 36	06 44	06 59		07 06	07 14		07 29		07 36	07 44	07 49		
Dunton Green	d				05 39		06 09			06 39				07 09					07 39				
Knockholt	d				05 44		06 14			06 44				07 14					07 44				
Chelsfield ■	d		23p32		05 47		06 17			06 47				07 17					07 47				
Orpington ■	a		23p36		05 50		06 20	06 23		06 50	06 53	07 08		07 20	07 23		07 38		07 50	07 53			
	d	23p21	23p37		05 51		06 21	06 24		06 51	06 54	07 09		07 21	07 24	07 33	07 39		07 51	07 54			08 03
Petts Wood ■	d	23p24			05 54		06 24			06 54				07 24		07 36			07 54				08 06
Chislehurst	d	23p27			05 57		06 27			06 57				07 27		07 39			07 57				08 09
Elmstead Woods	d	23p29			05 59		06 29			06 59				07 29		07 41			07 59				08 11
Bromley North	d			00 23		06 23			06 53				07 23					07 45				08 05	
Sundridge Park	d			00 25		06 25			06 55				07 25					07 47				08 07	
Grove Park ■	d	23p33		00a28	06 03	06a28	06 33		06a58	07 03			07a28	07 33		07 45		07a50	08 03			08a10	08 15
Hither Green ■	d	23p37			06 07		06 37			07 07				07 37		07 49			08 07				08 19
Lewisham ■	d	23p43			06 13		06 43			07 13						07 54							08 24
St Johns	a															07 56							08 26
New Cross ■	a															07 58							08 28
London Bridge ■	a	23p52	23p54		06 21		06 51	06 39		07 21	07 09	07 24		07 49	07 39	08 04	07 55		08 19	08 10	08 13		08 34
London Cannon Street ■	a															08 08							08 38
London Waterloo (East) ■	a	23p56	23p59		06 25		06 55	06 43		07 25	07 13	07 29		07 53	07 43		07 59		08 23	08 15	08 19		
London Charing Cross ■	a	00 01	00 03		06 29		06 59	06 47		07 29	07 17	07 33		07 57	07 48		08 03		08 27	08 19	08 22		

Station		SE ■	SE	SE	SE ■	SE ■	SE	SE ■	SE	SE	SE ■	SE ■	SE	SE	SE ■	SE	SE	SE ■	SE ■ H	SE	SE ■	SE	SE
Tonbridge ■	d	07 50			08 02	08 10		08 20			08 32	08 40			08 50			09 02	09 10		09 20		
Hildenborough	d				08 06						08 36							09 06					
Sevenoaks ■	a	07 58			08 13	08 18		08 28			08 43	08 48			08 58			09 13	09 18		09 28		
	d	07 59		08 06	08 14	08 19		08 29		08 36	08 44	08 49			08 59		09 06	09 14	09 19		09 29		09 36
Dunton Green	d			08 09						08 39							09 09						09 39
Knockholt	d			08 14						08 44							09 14						09 44
Chelsfield ■	d			08 17						08 47							09 17						09 47
Orpington ■	a	08 08		08 20	08 23			08 38		08 50	08 53				09 08		09 20	09 23			09 38		09 50
	d	08 09		08 21	08 24		08 33	08 39		08 51	08 54			09 03	09 09		09 21	09 24		09 33	09 39		09 51
Petts Wood ■	d			08 24			08 36			08 54				09 06			09 24			09 36			09 54
Chislehurst	d			08 27			08 39			08 57				09 09			09 27			09 39			09 57
Elmstead Woods	d			08 29			08 41			08 59				09 11			09 29			09 41			09 59
Bromley North	d		08 25						08 45				09 05			09 25						09 45	
Sundridge Park	d		08 27						08 47				09 07			09 27						09 47	
Grove Park ■	d		08a30	08 33			08 45		08a50	09 03			09a10	09 15		09a30	09 33			09 45		09a50	10 03
Hither Green ■	d			08 37			08 49			09 07				09 19			09 37			09 49			10 07
Lewisham ■	d						08 54							09 24						09 54			
St Johns	a						08 56							09 26						09 56			
New Cross ■	a						08 58							09 28						09 58			
London Bridge ■	a	08 25		08 49	08 40	08 43	09 04	08 55		09 19	09 10	09 13		09 34	09 25		09 49	09 40	09 43	10 04	09 55		10 19
London Cannon Street ■	a						09 08							09 38						10 08			
London Waterloo (East) ■	a	08 29		08 53	08 45	08 49		08 59		09 23	09 15	09 19			09 29		09 53	09 45	09 49		09 59		10 23
London Charing Cross ■	a	08 33		08 57	08 49	08 52		09 03		09 27	09 19	09 22			09 33		09 57	09 49	09 52		10 03		10 27

Station		SE ■	SE ■ H	SE	SE	SE ■	SE	SE	SE ■	SE ■ H	SE	SE ■	SE	SE	SE ■	SE ■ H	SE	SE	SE ■	SE	SE	SE ■
Tonbridge ■	d	09 32	09 40			09 50			10 02	10 10		10 20			10 32	10 40			10 50			11 02
Hildenborough	d	09 36							10 06						10 36							11 06
Sevenoaks ■	a	09 43	09 48			09 58			10 13	10 18		10 28			10 43	10 48			10 58			11 13
	d	09 44	09 49			09 59		10 06	10 14	10 19		10 29		10 36	10 44	10 49			10 59		11 06	11 14
Dunton Green	d							10 09						10 39							11 09	
Knockholt	d							10 14						10 44							11 14	
Chelsfield ■	d							10 17						10 47							11 17	
Orpington ■	a	09 53				10 08		10 20	10 23			10 38		10 50	10 53				11 08		11 20	11 23
	d	09 54			10 03	10 09		10 21	10 24		10 33	10 39		10 51	10 54			11 03	11 09		11 21	11 24
Petts Wood ■	d				10 06			10 24			10 36			10 54				11 06			11 24	
Chislehurst	d				10 09			10 27			10 39			10 57				11 09			11 27	
Elmstead Woods	d				10 11			10 29			10 41			10 59				11 11			11 29	
Bromley North	d			10 05			10 25						10 45				11 05			11 25		
Sundridge Park	d			10 07			10 27						10 47				11 07			11 27		
Grove Park ■	d			10a10	10 15		10a30	10 33			10 45		10a50	11 03			11a10	11 15		11a30	11 33	
Hither Green ■	d				10 19			10 37			10 49			11 07				11 19			11 37	
Lewisham ■	d				10 24						10 54							11 24				
St Johns	a				10 26						10 56							11 26				
New Cross ■	a				10 28						10 58							11 28				
London Bridge ■	a	10 10	10 13		10 34	10 25		10 49	10 40	10 43	11 04	10 55		11 19	11 10	11 13		11 34	11 25		11 49	11 40
London Cannon Street ■	a				10 38						11 08							11 38				
London Waterloo (East) ■	a	10 15	10 19			10 29		10 53	10 45	10 49		10 59		11 23	11 15	11 19			11 29		11 53	11 45
London Charing Cross ■	a	10 19	10 22			10 33		10 57	10 49	10 52		11 03		11 27	11 19	11 22			11 33		11 57	11 49

Table 204

Saturdays

until 21 July, 18 Aug and from 15 Sep

Bromley North to Grove Park, Tonbridge, Sevenoaks, Orpington and Grove Park - London Cannon Street/Charing Cross

Network Diagram - see first Page of Table 200

		SE 1 ⚭	SE	SE 1	SE	SE	SE 1	SE 1 ⚭		SE	SE	SE 1	SE	SE	SE 1	SE 1 ⚭	SE	SE 1		SE	SE	SE 1	SE 1 ⚭	SE	SE
Tonbridge 4	d	11 10		11 20			11 32	11 40				11 50			12 02	12 10		12 20				12 32	12 40		
Hildenborough	d						11 36								12 06							12 36			
Sevenoaks 4	a	11 18		11 28			11 43	11 48				11 58			12 13	12 18		12 28				12 43	12 48		
	d	11 19		11 29		11 36	11 44	11 49				11 59		12 06	12 14	12 19		12 29			12 36	12 44	12 49		
Dunton Green	d					11 39								12 09							12 39				
Knockholt	d					11 44								12 14							12 44				
Chelsfield 3	d					11 47								12 17							12 47				
Orpington 4	a			11 38		11 50	11 53					12 08		12 20	12 23			12 38			12 50	12 53			
	d		11 33	11 39		11 51	11 54				12 03	12 09		12 21	12 24		12 33	12 39			12 51	12 54			13 03
Petts Wood 4	d		11 36			11 54					12 06			12 24			12 36				12 54				13 06
Chislehurst	d		11 39			11 57					12 09			12 27			12 39				12 57				13 09
Elmstead Woods	d		11 41			11 59					12 11			12 29			12 41				12 59				13 11
Bromley North	d				11 45					12 05			12 25							12 45				13 05	
Sundridge Park	d				11 47					12 07			12 27							12 47				13 07	
Grove Park 4	d		11 45		11a50	12 03				12a10	12 15		12a30	12 33			12 45			12a50	13 03			13a10	13 15
Hither Green 4	d		11 49			12 07					12 19			12 37			12 49				13 07				13 19
Lewisham 4	d		11 54								12 24						12 54								13 24
St Johns	a		11 56								12 26						12 56								13 26
New Cross 4 ⊖	a		11 58								12 28						12 58								13 28
London Bridge 4 ⊖	a	11 43	12 04	11 55		12 19	12 10	12 13			12 34	12 25		12 49	12 40	12 43	13 04	12 55			13 19	13 10	13 13		13 34
London Cannon Street 4 ⊖	a		12 08								12 38						13 08								13 38
London Waterloo (East) 4 ⊖	a	11 49		11 59		12 23	12 15	12 19				12 29		12 53	12 45	12 49		12 59			13 23	13 15	13 19		
London Charing Cross 4 ⊖	a	11 52		12 03		12 27	12 19	12 22				12 33		12 57	12 49	12 52		13 03			13 27	13 19	13 22		

		SE 1	SE	SE		SE 1	SE 1 ⚭	SE	SE 1	SE	SE	SE 1	SE 1 ⚭	SE		SE	SE 1	SE	SE	SE 1	SE 1 ⚭	SE	SE 1	SE	
Tonbridge 4	d	12 50				13 02	13 10		13 20			13 32	13 40				13 50			14 02	14 10		14 20		
Hildenborough	d					13 06						13 36								14 06					
Sevenoaks 4	a	12 58				13 13	13 18		13 28			13 43	13 48				13 58			14 13	14 18		14 28		
	d	12 59		13 06		13 14	13 19		13 29		13 36	13 44	13 49				13 59		14 06	14 14	14 19		14 29		
Dunton Green	d			13 09							13 39								14 09						
Knockholt	d			13 14							13 44								14 14						
Chelsfield 3	d			13 17							13 47								14 17						
Orpington 4	a	13 08		13 20		13 23			13 38		13 50	13 53					14 08		14 20	14 23			14 38		
	d	13 09		13 21		13 24		13 33	13 39		13 51	13 54				14 03	14 09		14 21	14 24		14 33	14 39		
Petts Wood 4	d			13 24				13 36			13 54					14 06			14 24			14 36			
Chislehurst	d			13 27				13 39			13 57					14 09			14 27			14 39			
Elmstead Woods	d			13 29				13 41			13 59					14 11			14 29			14 41			
Bromley North	d		13 25							13 45				14 05				14 25						14 45	
Sundridge Park	d		13 27							13 47				14 07				14 27						14 47	
Grove Park 4	d		13a30	13 33				13 45		13a50	14 03			14a10		14 15		14a30	14 33			14 45		14a50	
Hither Green 4	d			13 37				13 49			14 07					14 19			14 37			14 49			
Lewisham 4	d							13 54								14 24						14 54			
St Johns	a							13 56								14 26						14 56			
New Cross 4 ⊖	a							13 58								14 28						14 58			
London Bridge 4 ⊖	a	13 25		13 49		13 40	13 43	14 04	13 55		14 19	14 10	14 13			14 34	14 25		14 49	14 40	14 43	15 04	14 55		
London Cannon Street 4 ⊖	a							14 08								14 38						15 08			
London Waterloo (East) 4 ⊖	a	13 29		13 53		13 45	13 49		13 59		14 23	14 15	14 19				14 29		14 53	14 45	14 49		14 59		
London Charing Cross 4 ⊖	a	13 33		13 57		13 49	13 52		14 03		14 27	14 19	14 22				14 33		14 57	14 49	14 52		15 03		

		SE	SE 1	SE 1 ⚭	SE	SE	SE 1	SE	SE	SE 1		SE 1 ⚭	SE	SE 1	SE	SE	SE 1	SE 1 ⚭	SE	SE		SE 1	SE	SE	SE 1
Tonbridge 4	d		14 32	14 40			14 50			15 02		15 10		15 20			15 32	15 40				15 50			16 02
Hildenborough	d		14 36							15 06							15 36								16 06
Sevenoaks 4	a		14 43	14 48			14 58			15 13		15 18		15 28			15 43	15 48				15 58			16 13
	d	14 36	14 44	14 49			14 59		15 06	15 14		15 19		15 29		15 36	15 44	15 49				15 59		16 06	16 14
Dunton Green	d	14 39							15 09							15 39								16 09	
Knockholt	d	14 44							15 14							15 44								16 14	
Chelsfield 3	d	14 47							15 17							15 47								16 17	
Orpington 4	a	14 50	14 53				15 08		15 20	15 23				15 38		15 50	15 53					16 08		16 20	16 23
	d	14 51	14 54			15 03	15 09		15 21	15 24			15 33	15 39		15 51	15 54			16 03		16 09		16 21	16 24
Petts Wood 4	d	14 54				15 06			15 24				15 36			15 54				16 06				16 24	
Chislehurst	d	14 57				15 09			15 27				15 39			15 57				16 09				16 27	
Elmstead Woods	d	14 59				15 11			15 29				15 41			15 59				16 11				16 29	
Bromley North	d				15 05			15 25							15 45				16 05				16 25		
Sundridge Park	d				15 07			15 27							15 47				16 07				16 27		
Grove Park 4	d	15 03			15a10	15 15		15a30	15 33				15 45		15a50	16 03			16a10	16 15			16a30	16 33	
Hither Green 4	d	15 07				15 19			15 37				15 49			16 07				16 19				16 37	
Lewisham 4	d					15 24							15 54							16 24					
St Johns	a					15 26							15 56							16 26					
New Cross 4 ⊖	a					15 28							15 58							16 28					
London Bridge 4 ⊖	a	15 19	15 10	15 13		15 34	15 25		15 49	15 40		15 43	16 04	15 55		16 19	16 10	16 13		16 34		16 25		16 49	16 40
London Cannon Street 4 ⊖	a					15 38							16 08							16 38					
London Waterloo (East) 4 ⊖	a	15 23	15 15	15 19			15 29		15 53	15 45		15 49		15 59		16 23	16 15	16 19				16 29		16 53	16 45
London Charing Cross 4 ⊖	a	15 27	15 19	15 22			15 33		15 57	15 49		15 52		16 03		16 27	16 19	16 22				16 33		16 57	16 49

Table 204

Saturdays

until 21 July, 18 Aug and from 15 Sep

Bromley North to Grove Park, Tonbridge, Sevenoaks, Orpington and Grove Park - London Cannon Street/Charing Cross

Network Diagram - see first Page of Table 200

		SE 1 ⚭	SE	SE 1	SE	SE		SE 1	SE 1 ⚭	SE	SE	SE 1	SE	SE	SE 1	SE 1 ⚭		SE	SE 1	SE	SE	SE 1	SE 1 ⚭	SE	SE
Tonbridge 4	d	16 10		16 20				16 32	16 40			16 50			17 02	17 10			17 20			17 32	17 40		
Hildenborough	d							16 36							17 06							17 36			
Sevenoaks 4	a	16 18		16 28				16 43	16 48			16 58			17 13	17 18			17 28			17 43	17 48		
	d	16 19		16 29		16 36		16 44	16 49			16 59		17 06	17 14	17 19			17 29		17 36	17 44	17 49		
Dunton Green	d					16 39								17 09							17 39				
Knockholt	d					16 44								17 14							17 44				
Chelsfield 3	d					16 47								17 17							17 47				
Orpington 4	a			16 38		16 50		16 53				17 08		17 20	17 23				17 38		17 50	17 53			
	d		16 33	16 39		16 51		16 54			17 03	17 09		17 21	17 24			17 33	17 39		17 51	17 54			18 03
Petts Wood 4	d		16 36			16 54					17 06			17 24				17 36			17 54				18 06
Chislehurst	d		16 39			16 57					17 09			17 27				17 39			17 57				18 09
Elmstead Woods	d		16 41			16 59					17 11			17 29				17 41			17 59				18 11
Bromley North	d				16 45					17 05			17 25							17 45				18 05	
Sundridge Park	d				16 47					17 07			17 27							17 47				18 07	
Grove Park 4	d		16 45		16a50	17 03				17a10	17 15		17a30	17 33				17 45		17a50	18 03			18a10	18 15
Hither Green 4	d		16 49			17 07					17 19			17 37				17 49			18 07				18 19
Lewisham 4	d		16 54								17 24							17 54							18 24
St Johns	a		16 56								17 26							17 56							18 26
New Cross 4 ⊖	a		16 58								17 28							17 58							18 28
London Bridge 4 ⊖	a	16 43	17 04	16 55		17 19		17 10	17 13		17 34	17 25		17 49	17 40	17 43		18 04	17 55		18 19	18 10	18 13		18 34
London Cannon Street 4 ⊖	a		17 08								17 38							18 08							18 38
London Waterloo (East) 4 ⊖	a	16 49		16 59		17 23		17 15	17 19			17 29		17 53	17 45	17 49			17 59		18 23	18 15	18 19		
London Charing Cross 4 ⊖	a	16 52		17 03		17 27		17 19	17 22			17 33		17 57	17 49	17 52			18 03		18 27	18 19	18 22		

		SE 1		SE	SE	SE 1	SE 1 ⚭	SE	SE 1	SE	SE	SE 1		SE 1 ⚭	SE 1	SE	SE	SE	SE 1 ⚭	SE 1	SE	SE		SE 1	SE 1
Tonbridge 4	d	17 50				18 02	18 10		18 20			18 32		18 40	18 50				19 10	19 18				19 40	19 50
Hildenborough	d					18 06						18 36								19 22					
Sevenoaks 4	a	17 58				18 13	18 18		18 28			18 43		18 48	18 58				19 18	19 28				19 48	19 58
	d	17 59			18 06	18 14	18 19		18 29		18 36	18 44		18 49	18 59			19 06	19 19	19 29		19 36		19 49	19 59
Dunton Green	d				18 09						18 39							19 09				19 39			
Knockholt	d				18 14						18 44							19 14				19 44			
Chelsfield 3	d				18 17						18 47							19 17				19 47			
Orpington 4	a	18 08			18 20	18 23			18 38		18 50	18 53			19 08			19 20	19 27	19 38		19 50		19 57	20 08
	d	18 09			18 21	18 24		18 33	18 39		18 51	18 54			19 09			19 21	19 28	19 39		19 51		19 58	20 09
Petts Wood 4	d				18 24			18 36			18 54							19 24				19 54			
Chislehurst	d				18 27			18 39			18 57							19 27				19 57			
Elmstead Woods	d				18 29			18 41			18 59							19 29				19 59			
Bromley North	d			18 25						18 45						19 05	19 25				19 45				
Sundridge Park	d			18 27						18 47						19 07	19 27				19 47				
Grove Park 4	d			18a30	18 33			18 45		18a50	19 03					19a10	19a30	19 33			19a50	20 03			
Hither Green 4	d				18 37			18 49			19 07							19 37				20 07			
Lewisham 4	d							18 54			19 12							19 43				20 13			
St Johns	a							18 56																	
New Cross 4 ⊖	a							18 58																	
London Bridge 4 ⊖	a	18 25			18 49	18 40	18 43	19 04	18 55		19 21	19 10		19 13	19 24			19 52	19 43	19 54		20 22		20 13	20 24
London Cannon Street 4 ⊖	a							19 08																	
London Waterloo (East) 4 ⊖	a	18 29			18 53	18 45	18 49		18 59		19 25	19 15		19 19	19 29			19 56	19 48	19 59		20 26		20 18	20 29
London Charing Cross 4 ⊖	a	18 33			18 57	18 49	18 52		19 03		19 29	19 19		19 22	19 33			20 00	19 51	20 03		20 30		20 21	20 33

		SE	SE	SE	SE 1	SE 1	SE	SE		SE 1	SE 1	SE	SE	SE 1	SE 1	SE	SE	SE 1		SE 1	SE	SE	SE 1	SE 1	SE
Tonbridge 4	d				20 10	20 18				20 40	20 50			21 10	21 18			21 40		21 50			22 10	22 18	
Hildenborough	d					20 22									21 22									22 22	
Sevenoaks 4	a				20 18	20 28				20 48	20 58			21 18	21 28			21 48		21 58			22 18	22 28	
	d			20 06	20 19	20 29		20 36		20 49	20 59		21 06	21 19	21 29		21 36	21 49		21 59		22 06	22 19	22 29	
Dunton Green	d			20 09				20 39					21 09				21 39					22 09			
Knockholt	d			20 14				20 44					21 14				21 44					22 14			
Chelsfield 3	d			20 17				20 47					21 17				21 47					22 17			
Orpington 4	a			20 20	20 27	20 38		20 50		20 57	21 08		21 20	21 27	21 38		21 50	21 57		22 08		22 20	22 27	22 38	
	d			20 21	20 28	20 39		20 51		20 58	21 09		21 21	21 28	21 39		21 51	21 58		22 09		22 21	22 28	22 39	
Petts Wood 4	d			20 24				20 54					21 24				21 54					22 24			
Chislehurst	d			20 27				20 57					21 27				21 57					22 27			
Elmstead Woods	d			20 29				20 59					21 29				21 59					22 29			
Bromley North	d	20 05	20 25				20 53					21 23				21 53					22 23				22 53
Sundridge Park	d	20 07	20 27				20 55					21 25				21 55					22 25				22 55
Grove Park 4	d	20a10	20a30	20 33			20a58	21 03				21a28	21 33			21a58	22 03				22a28	22 33			22a58
Hither Green 4	d			20 37				21 07					21 37				22 07					22 37			
Lewisham 4	d			20 43				21 13					21 43				22 13					22 43			
St Johns	a																								
New Cross 4 ⊖	a																								
London Bridge 4 ⊖	a			20 52	20 43	20 54		21 22		21 13	21 24		21 52	21 43	21 54		22 22	22 13		22 24		22 52	22 43	22 54	
London Cannon Street 4 ⊖	a																								
London Waterloo (East) 4 ⊖	a			20 56	20 48	20 59		21 26		21 18	21 29		21 56	21 48	21 59		22 26	22 18		22 29		22 56	22 48	22 59	
London Charing Cross 4 ⊖	a			21 00	20 51	21 03		21 30		21 21	21 33		22 00	21 51	22 03		22 30	22 21		22 33		23 00	22 51	23 03	

Table 204

Saturdays
until 21 July, 18 Aug and from 15 Sep

Bromley North to Grove Park, Tonbridge, Sevenoaks, Orpington and Grove Park - London Cannon Street/Charing Cross

Network Diagram - see first Page of Table 200

		SE	SE 1	SE 1		SE	SE	SE 1	SE
Tonbridge 4	d		22 40	22 50				23 14	
Hildenborough	d							23 18	
Sevenoaks 4	a		22 48	22 58				23 24	
	d		22 49	22 59				23 25	
Dunton Green	d								
Knockholt	d								
Chelsfield 3	d							23 32	
Orpington 4	a		22 57	23 08				23 36	
	d	22 51	22 58	23 09			23 21	23 37	
Petts Wood 4	d	22 54					23 24		
Chislehurst	d	22 57					23 27		
Elmstead Woods	d	22 59					23 29		
Bromley North	d					23 23			23 53
Sundridge Park	d					23 25			23 55
Grove Park 4	d	23 03				23a28	23 33		23a58
Hither Green 4	d	23 07					23 37		
Lewisham 4	d	23 13					23 43		
St Johns	a								
New Cross 4	⊖ a								
London Bridge 4	⊖ a	23 22	23 13	23 24			23 52	23 54	
London Cannon Street 4	⊖ a								
London Waterloo (East) 4	⊖ a	23 26	23 18	23 29			23 56	23 59	
London Charing Cross 4	⊖ a	23 30	23 21	23 33			00 01	00 03	

Saturdays
28 July to 11 August

		SE A	SE B	SE 1	SE	SE	SE	SE	SE 1	SE		SE	SE 1	SE 1	SE	SE	SE 1	SE	SE 1	SE		SE	SE 1	SE 1	SE
Tonbridge 4	d			23p14					06 02				06 32	06 50			07 02		07 20				07 32	07 40	
Hildenborough	d			23p18					06 06				06 36				07 06						07 36		
Sevenoaks 4	a			23p24					06 13				06 43	06 58			07 13		07 28				07 43	07 48	
	d			23p25		05 36		06 06	06 14			06 36	06 44	06 59		07 06	07 14		07 29			07 36	07 44	07 49	
Dunton Green	d					05 39		06 09				06 39				07 09						07 39			
Knockholt	d					05 44		06 14				06 44				07 14						07 44			
Chelsfield 3	d			23p32		05 47		06 17				06 47				07 17						07 47			
Orpington 4	a			23p36		05 50		06 20	06 23			06 50	06 53	07 08		07 20	07 23		07 38			07 50	07 53		
	d	23p21	23p21	23p37		05 51		06 21	06 24			06 51	06 54	07 09		07 21	07 24	07 33	07 39			07 51	07 54		
Petts Wood 4	d	23p24	23p24			05 54		06 24				06 54				07 24		07 36				07 54			
Chislehurst	d	23p27	23p27			05 57		06 27				06 57				07 27		07 39				07 57			
Elmstead Woods	d	23p29	23p29			05 59		06 29				06 59				07 29		07 41				07 59			
Bromley North	d				00 23		06 23			06 53					07 23					07 45					08 05
Sundridge Park	d				00 25		06 25			06 55					07 25					07 47					08 07
Grove Park 4	d	23p33	23p33		00a28	06 03	06a28	06 33		06a58		07 03			07a28	07 33		07 45		07a50		08 03			08a10
Hither Green 4	d	23p37	23p37			06 07		06 37				07 07				07 37		07 49				08 07			
Lewisham 4	d	23p43	23p43			06 13		06 43				07 13						07 54							
St Johns	a																	07 56							
New Cross 4	⊖ a																	07 58							
London Bridge 4	⊖ a	23p52	23p52	23p54		06 21		06 51	06 39			07 21	07 09	07 24		07 49	07 39	08 04	07 55			08 19	08 10	08 13	
London Cannon Street 4	⊖ a																	08 11							
London Waterloo (East) 4	⊖ a	23p56	23p56	23p59		06 25		06 55	06 43			07 25	07 13	07 29		07 53	07 43		07 59			08 23	08 15	08 19	
London Charing Cross 4	⊖ a	00 01	00 04	00 03		06 32		07 02	06 47			07 32	07 17	07 33		07 57	07 48		08 03			08 27	08 19	08 22	

		SE	SE 1	SE	SE	SE 1		SE 1	SE	SE 1	SE	SE	SE 1	SE 1	SE	SE		SE 1	SE	SE	SE 1	SE 1 H	SE	SE 1	SE
Tonbridge 4	d		07 50			08 02		08 10		08 20			08 32	08 40				08 50			09 02	09 10		09 20	
Hildenborough	d					08 06							08 36								09 06				
Sevenoaks 4	a		07 58			08 13		08 18		08 28			08 43	08 48				08 58			09 13	09 18		09 28	
	d		07 59		08 06	08 14		08 19		08 29		08 36	08 44	08 49				08 59		09 06	09 14	09 19		09 29	
Dunton Green	d				08 09							08 39								09 09					
Knockholt	d				08 14							08 44								09 14					
Chelsfield 3	d				08 17							08 47								09 17					
Orpington 4	a		08 08		08 20	08 23				08 38		08 50	08 53					09 08		09 20	09 23			09 38	
	d	08 03	08 09		08 21	08 24			08 33	08 39		08 51	08 54			09 03		09 09		09 21	09 24		09 33	09 39	
Petts Wood 4	d	08 06			08 24				08 36			08 54				09 06				09 24			09 36		
Chislehurst	d	08 09			08 27				08 39			08 57				09 09				09 27			09 39		
Elmstead Woods	d	08 11			08 29				08 41			08 59				09 11				09 29			09 41		
Bromley North	d			08 25							08 45				09 05				09 25						09 45
Sundridge Park	d			08 27							08 47				09 07				09 27						09 47
Grove Park 4	d	08 15		08a30	08 33				08 45		08a50	09 03			09a10	09 15			09a30	09 33			09 45		09a50
Hither Green 4	d	08 19			08 37				08 49			09 07				09 19				09 37			09 49		
Lewisham 4	d	08 24							08 54							09 24							09 54		
St Johns	a	08 26							08 56							09 26							09 56		
New Cross 4	⊖ a	08 28							08 58							09 28							09 58		
London Bridge 4	⊖ a	08 34	08 25		08 49	08 40		08 43	09 04	08 55		09 19	09 10	09 13		09 34		09 25		09 49	09 40	09 43	10 04	09 55	
London Cannon Street 4	⊖ a	08 41							09 11							09 41							10 11		
London Waterloo (East) 4	⊖ a		08 29		08 53	08 45		08 49		08 59		09 23	09 15	09 19				09 29		09 53	09 45	09 49		09 59	
London Charing Cross 4	⊖ a		08 33		08 57	08 49		08 52		09 03		09 27	09 19	09 22				09 33		09 57	09 49	09 52		10 03	

A not from 4 August until 11 August

B not 28 July

Table 204

Saturdays
28 July to 11 August

Bromley North to Grove Park, Tonbridge, Sevenoaks, Orpington and Grove Park - London Cannon Street/Charing Cross

Network Diagram - see first Page of Table 200

		SE		SE 1	SE 1 H	SE	SE	SE 1	SE	SE	SE 1	SE 1 H		SE	SE 1	SE	SE	SE 1	SE 1 H	SE	SE	SE 1		SE	SE
Tonbridge 4	d			09 32	09 40			09 50			10 02	10 10			10 20			10 32	10 40			10 50			
Hildenborough	d			09 36							10 06							10 36							
Sevenoaks 4	a			09 43	09 48			09 58			10 13	10 18			10 28			10 43	10 48			10 58			
	d	09 36		09 44	09 49			09 59		10 06	10 14	10 19			10 29		10 36	10 44	10 49			10 59			11 06
Dunton Green	d	09 39								10 09							10 39								11 09
Knockholt	d	09 44								10 14							10 44								11 14
Chelsfield 3	d	09 47								10 17							10 47								11 17
Orpington 4	a	09 50		09 53				10 08		10 20	10 23				10 38		10 50	10 53				11 08			11 20
	d	09 51		09 54			10 03	10 09		10 21	10 24			10 33	10 39		10 51	10 54			11 03	11 09			11 21
Petts Wood 4	d	09 54					10 06			10 24				10 36			10 54				11 06				11 24
Chislehurst	d	09 57					10 09			10 27				10 39			10 57				11 09				11 27
Elmstead Woods	d	09 59					10 11			10 29				10 41			10 59				11 11				11 29
Bromley North	d					10 05			10 25							10 45				11 05				11 25	
Sundridge Park	d					10 07			10 27							10 47				11 07				11 27	
Grove Park 4	d	10 03				10a10	10 15		10a30	10 33				10 45		10a50	11 03			11a10	11 15			11a30	11 33
Hither Green 4	d	10 07					10 19			10 37				10 49			11 07				11 19				11 37
Lewisham 4	d						10 24							10 54							11 24				
St Johns	a						10 26							10 56							11 26				
New Cross 4	⊖ a						10 28							10 58							11 28				
London Bridge 4	⊖ a	10 19		10 10	10 13		10 34	10 25		10 49	10 40	10 43		11 04	10 55		11 19	11 10	11 13		11 34	11 25			11 49
London Cannon Street 4	⊖ a						10 41							11 11							11 41				
London Waterloo (East) 4	⊖ a	10 23		10 15	10 19			10 29		10 53	10 45	10 49			10 59		11 23	11 15	11 19			11 29			11 53
London Charing Cross 4	⊖ a	10 27		10 19	10 22			10 33		10 57	10 49	10 52			11 03		11 27	11 19	11 22			11 33			11 57

		SE 1	SE 1 H	SE	SE 1	SE	SE	SE 1		SE 1 H	SE	SE	SE 1	SE	SE	SE 1	SE 1 H	SE		SE 1	SE	SE	SE 1	SE 1 H	SE
Tonbridge 4	d	11 02	11 10		11 20			11 32		11 40			11 50			12 02	12 10			12 20			12 32	12 40	
Hildenborough	d	11 06						11 36								12 06							12 36		
Sevenoaks 4	a	11 13	11 18		11 28			11 43		11 48			11 58			12 13	12 18			12 28			12 43	12 48	
	d	11 14	11 19		11 29		11 36	11 44		11 49			11 59		12 06	12 14	12 19			12 29		12 36	12 44	12 49	
Dunton Green	d						11 39								12 09							12 39			
Knockholt	d						11 44								12 14							12 44			
Chelsfield 3	d						11 47								12 17							12 47			
Orpington 4	a	11 23			11 38		11 50	11 53					12 08		12 20	12 23				12 38		12 50	12 53		
	d	11 24		11 33	11 39		11 51	11 54				12 03	12 09		12 21	12 24		12 33		12 39		12 51	12 54		
Petts Wood 4	d			11 36			11 54					12 06			12 24			12 36				12 54			
Chislehurst	d			11 39			11 57					12 09			12 27			12 39				12 57			
Elmstead Woods	d			11 41			11 59					12 11			12 29			12 41				12 59			
Bromley North	d					11 45					12 05			12 25							12 45				13 05
Sundridge Park	d					11 47					12 07			12 27							12 47				13 07
Grove Park 4	d			11 45		11a50	12 03				12a10	12 15		12a30	12 33			12 45			12a50	13 03			13a10
Hither Green 4	d			11 49			12 07					12 19			12 37			12 49				13 07			
Lewisham 4	d			11 54								12 24						12 54							
St Johns	a			11 56								12 26						12 56							
New Cross 4	⊖ a			11 58								12 28						12 58							
London Bridge 4	⊖ a	11 40	11 43	12 04	11 55		12 19	12 10		12 13		12 34	12 25		12 49	12 40	12 43	13 04		12 55		13 19	13 10	13 13	
London Cannon Street 4	⊖ a			12 11								12 41						13 11							
London Waterloo (East) 4	⊖ a	11 45	11 49		11 59		12 23	12 15		12 19			12 29		12 53	12 45	12 49			12 59		13 23	13 15	13 19	
London Charing Cross 4	⊖ a	11 49	11 52		12 03		12 27	12 19		12 22			12 33		12 57	12 49	12 52			13 03		13 27	13 19	13 22	

		SE	SE 1	SE		SE	SE 1	SE 1 H	SE	SE 1	SE	SE	SE 1	SE 1 H		SE	SE	SE 1	SE	SE	SE 1	SE 1 H	SE	SE 1
Tonbridge 4	d		12 50				13 02	13 10		13 20			13 32	13 40				13 50			14 02	14 10		14 20
Hildenborough	d						13 06						13 36								14 06			
Sevenoaks 4	a		12 58				13 13	13 18		13 28			13 43	13 48				13 58			14 13	14 18		14 28
	d		12 59			13 06	13 14	13 19		13 29		13 36	13 44	13 49				13 59		14 06	14 14	14 19		14 29
Dunton Green	d					13 09						13 39								14 09				
Knockholt	d					13 14						13 44								14 14				
Chelsfield 3	d					13 17						13 47								14 17				
Orpington 4	a		13 08			13 20	13 23			13 38		13 50	13 53					14 08		14 20	14 23			14 38
	d	13 03	13 09			13 21	13 24		13 33	13 39		13 51	13 54				14 03	14 09		14 21	14 24		14 33	14 39
Petts Wood 4	d	13 06				13 24			13 36			13 54					14 06			14 24			14 36	
Chislehurst	d	13 09				13 27			13 39			13 57					14 09			14 27			14 39	
Elmstead Woods	d	13 11				13 29			13 41			13 59					14 11			14 29			14 41	
Bromley North	d			13 25							13 45					14 05			14 25					
Sundridge Park	d			13 27							13 47					14 07			14 27					
Grove Park 4	d	13 15		13a30		13 33			13 45		13a50	14 03				14a10	14 15		14a30	14 33			14 45	
Hither Green 4	d	13 19				13 37			13 49			14 07					14 19			14 37			14 49	
Lewisham 4	d	13 24							13 54								14 24						14 54	
St Johns	a	13 26							13 56								14 26						14 56	
New Cross 4	⊖ a	13 28							13 58								14 28						14 58	
London Bridge 4	⊖ a	13 34	13 25			13 49	13 40	13 43	14 04	13 55		14 19	14 10	14 13			14 34	14 25		14 49	14 40	14 43	15 04	14 55
London Cannon Street 4	⊖ a	13 41							14 11								14 41						15 11	
London Waterloo (East) 4	⊖ a		13 29			13 53	13 45	13 49		13 59		14 23	14 15	14 19				14 29		14 53	14 45	14 49		14 59
London Charing Cross 4	⊖ a		13 33			13 57	13 49	13 52		14 03		14 27	14 19	14 22				14 33		14 57	14 49	14 52		15 03

Table 204

Saturdays
28 July to 11 August

Bromley North to Grove Park, Tonbridge, Sevenoaks, Orpington and Grove Park - London Cannon Street/Charing Cross

Network Diagram - see first Page of Table 200

Station		SE	SE	SE 1	SE 1 ⊼	SE	SE	SE 1	SE	SE	SE 1	SE 1 ⊼	SE	SE 1	SE	SE	SE 1	SE 1 ⊼	SE	SE	SE 1	SE	SE
Tonbridge	d			14 32	14 40			14 50			15 02	15 10		15 20			15 32	15 40			15 50		
Hildenborough	d			14 36							15 06						15 36						
Sevenoaks	a			14 43	14 48			14 58			15 13	15 18		15 28			15 43	15 48			15 58		
	d		14 36	14 44	14 49			14 59		15 06	15 14	15 19		15 29		15 36	15 44	15 49			15 59		16 06
Dunton Green	d		14 39							15 09						15 39							16 09
Knockholt	d		14 44							15 14						15 44							16 14
Chelsfield	d		14 47							15 17						15 47							16 17
Orpington	a		14 50	14 53				15 08		15 20	15 23			15 38		15 50	15 53				16 08		16 20
	d		14 51	14 54			15 03	15 09		15 21	15 24		15 33	15 39		15 51	15 54			16 03	16 09		16 21
Petts Wood	d		14 54				15 06			15 24			15 36			15 54				16 06			16 24
Chislehurst	d		14 57				15 09			15 27			15 39			15 57				16 09			16 27
Elmstead Woods	d		14 59				15 11			15 29			15 41			15 59				16 11			16 29
Bromley North	d	14 45				15 05			15 25						15 45				16 05			16 25	
Sundridge Park	d	14 47				15 07			15 27						15 47				16 07			16 27	
Grove Park	d	14a50	15 03			15a10	15 15		15a30	15 33			15 45		15a50	16 03			16a10	16 15		16a30	16 33
Hither Green	d		15 07				15 19			15 37			15 49			16 07				16 19			16 37
Lewisham	d						15 24						15 54							16 24			
St Johns	a						15 26						15 56							16 26			
New Cross	a						15 28						15 58							16 28			
London Bridge	a		15 19	15 10	15 13		15 34	15 25		15 49	15 40	15 43	16 04	15 55		16 19	16 10	16 13		16 34	16 25		16 49
London Cannon Street	a						15 41						16 11							16 41			
London Waterloo (East)	a		15 23	15 15	15 19			15 29		15 53	15 45	15 49		15 59		16 23	16 15	16 19			16 29		16 53
London Charing Cross	a		15 27	15 19	15 22			15 33		15 57	15 49	15 52		16 03		16 27	16 19	16 22			16 33		16 57

Station		SE 1	SE 1 ⊼	SE	SE 1	SE	SE	SE 1	SE 1 ⊼	SE	SE	SE 1	SE	SE	SE 1	SE 1 ⊼	SE	SE 1	SE	SE	SE 1	SE 1 ⊼	SE
Tonbridge	d	16 02	16 10		16 20			16 32	16 40			16 50			17 02	17 10		17 20			17 32	17 40	
Hildenborough	d	16 06						16 36							17 06						17 36		
Sevenoaks	a	16 13	16 18		16 28			16 43	16 48			16 58			17 13	17 18		17 28			17 43	17 48	
	d	16 14	16 19		16 29		16 36	16 44	16 49			16 59		17 06	17 14	17 19		17 29		17 36	17 44	17 49	
Dunton Green	d						16 39							17 09						17 39			
Knockholt	d						16 44							17 14						17 44			
Chelsfield	d						16 47							17 17						17 47			
Orpington	a	16 23			16 38		16 50	16 53				17 08		17 20	17 23			17 38		17 50	17 53		
	d	16 24		16 33	16 39		16 51	16 54			17 03	17 09		17 21	17 24		17 33	17 39		17 51	17 54		
Petts Wood	d			16 36			16 54				17 06			17 24			17 36			17 54			
Chislehurst	d			16 39			16 57				17 09			17 27			17 39			17 57			
Elmstead Woods	d			16 41			16 59				17 11			17 29			17 41			17 59			
Bromley North	d					16 45				17 05			17 25						17 45				18 05
Sundridge Park	d					16 47				17 07			17 27						17 47				18 07
Grove Park	d			16 45		16a50	17 03			17a10	17 15		17a30	17 33			17 45		17a50	18 03			18a10
Hither Green	d			16 49			17 07				17 19			17 37			17 49			18 07			
Lewisham	d			16 54							17 24						17 54						
St Johns	a			16 56							17 26						17 56						
New Cross	a			16 58							17 28						17 58						
London Bridge	a	16 40	16 43	17 04	16 55		17 19	17 10	17 13		17 34	17 25		17 49	17 40	17 43	18 04	17 55		18 19	18 10	18 13	
London Cannon Street	a			17 11							17 41						18 11						
London Waterloo (East)	a	16 45	16 49		16 59		17 23	17 15	17 19			17 29		17 53	17 45	17 49		17 59		18 23	18 15	18 19	
London Charing Cross	a	16 49	16 52		17 03		17 27	17 19	17 22			17 33		17 57	17 49	17 52		18 03		18 27	18 19	18 22	

Station		SE	SE 1	SE	SE	SE 1	SE 1 ⊼	SE	SE 1	SE	SE	SE 1	SE 1 ⊼	SE 1	SE	SE	SE	SE 1 ⊼	SE 1	SE	SE	SE 1
Tonbridge	d		17 50			18 02	18 10		18 20			18 32	18 40	18 50				19 10	19 18			19 40
Hildenborough	d					18 06						18 36							19 22			
Sevenoaks	a		17 58			18 13	18 18		18 28			18 43	18 48	18 58				19 18	19 28			19 48
	d		17 59		18 06	18 14	18 19		18 29		18 36	18 44	18 49	18 59			19 06	19 19	19 29		19 36	19 49
Dunton Green	d				18 09						18 39						19 09				19 39	
Knockholt	d				18 14						18 44						19 14				19 44	
Chelsfield	d				18 17						18 47						19 17				19 47	
Orpington	a		18 08		18 20	18 23			18 38		18 50	18 53		19 08			19 20	19 27	19 38		19 50	19 57
	d	18 03	18 09		18 21	18 24		18 33	18 39		18 51	18 54		19 09			19 21	19 28	19 39		19 51	19 58
Petts Wood	d	18 06			18 24			18 36			18 54						19 24				19 54	
Chislehurst	d	18 09			18 27			18 39			18 57						19 27				19 57	
Elmstead Woods	d	18 11			18 29			18 41			18 59						19 29				19 59	
Bromley North	d			18 25						18 45					19 05	19 25				19 45		
Sundridge Park	d			18 27						18 47					19 07	19 27				19 47		
Grove Park	d	18 15		18a30	18 33			18 45		18a50	19 03				19a10	19a30	19 33			19a50	20 03	
Hither Green	d	18 19			18 37			18 49			19 07						19 37				20 07	
Lewisham	d	18 24						18 54			19 12						19 43				20 13	
St Johns	a	18 26						18 56														
New Cross	a	18 28						18 58														
London Bridge	a	18 34	18 25		18 49	18 40	18 43	19 04	18 55		19 21	19 10	19 13	19 24			19 52	19 43	19 54		20 22	20 13
London Cannon Street	a	18 41						19 11														
London Waterloo (East)	a		18 29		18 53	18 45	18 49		18 59		19 25	19 15	19 19	19 29			19 56	19 48	19 59		20 26	20 18
London Charing Cross	a		18 33		18 57	18 49	18 52		19 03		19 32	19 19	19 22	19 33			20 03	19 51	20 03		20 33	20 21

Table 204

Saturdays
28 July to 11 August

Bromley North to Grove Park, Tonbridge, Sevenoaks, Orpington and Grove Park - London Cannon Street/Charing Cross

Network Diagram - see first Page of Table 200

Station		SE 1	SE	SE	SE	SE 1	SE 1	SE	SE	SE 1	SE 1	SE	SE	SE 1	SE 1	SE	SE	SE 1	SE 1	SE	SE	SE 1	SE 1
Tonbridge	d	19 50				20 10	20 18			20 40	20 50			21 10	21 18			21 40	21 50			22 10	22 18
Hildenborough	d						20 22								21 22								22 22
Sevenoaks	a	19 58				20 18	20 28			20 48	20 58			21 18	21 28			21 48	21 58			22 18	22 28
	d	19 59			20 06	20 19	20 29		20 36	20 49	20 59		21 06	21 19	21 29		21 36	21 49	21 59		22 06	22 19	22 29
Dunton Green	d				20 09				20 39				21 09				21 39				22 09		
Knockholt	d				20 14				20 44				21 14				21 44				22 14		
Chelsfield	d				20 17				20 47				21 17				21 47				22 17		
Orpington	a	20 08			20 20	20 27	20 38		20 50	20 57	21 08		21 20	21 27	21 38		21 50	21 57	22 08		22 20	22 27	22 38
	d	20 09			20 21	20 28	20 39		20 51	20 58	21 09		21 21	21 28	21 39		21 51	21 58	22 09		22 21	22 28	22 39
Petts Wood	d				20 24				20 54				21 24				21 54				22 24		
Chislehurst	d				20 27				20 57				21 27				21 57				22 27		
Elmstead Woods	d				20 29				20 59				21 29				21 59				22 29		
Bromley North	d		20 05	20 25				20 53				21 23				21 53				22 23			
Sundridge Park	d		20 07	20 27				20 55				21 25				21 55				22 25			
Grove Park	d		20a10	20a30	20 33			20a58	21 03			21a28	21 33			21a58	22 03			22a28	22 33		
Hither Green	d				20 37				21 07				21 37				22 07				22 37		
Lewisham	d				20 43				21 13				21 43				22 13				22 43		
St Johns	a																						
New Cross	a																						
London Bridge	a	20 24			20 52	20 43	20 54		21 22	21 13	21 24		21 52	21 43	21 54		22 22	22 13	22 24		22 52	22 43	22 54
London Cannon Street	a																						
London Waterloo (East)	a	20 29			20 56	20 48	20 59		21 26	21 18	21 29		21 56	21 48	21 59		22 26	22 18	22 29		22 56	22 48	22 59
London Charing Cross	a	20 33			21 03	20 51	21 03		21 33	21 21	21 33		22 03	21 51	22 03		22 33	22 21	22 33		23 03	22 51	23 03

Station		SE	SE	SE 1	SE 1	SE	SE	SE 1	SE
Tonbridge	d			22 40	22 50			23 14	
Hildenborough	d							23 18	
Sevenoaks	a			22 48	22 58			23 24	
	d			22 49	22 59			23 25	
Dunton Green	d								
Knockholt	d								
Chelsfield	d							23 32	
Orpington	a			22 57	23 08			23 36	
	d		22 51	22 58	23 09		23 21	23 37	
Petts Wood	d		22 54				23 24		
Chislehurst	d		22 57				23 27		
Elmstead Woods	d		22 59				23 29		
Bromley North	d	22 53				23 23			23 53
Sundridge Park	d	22 55				23 25			23 55
Grove Park	d	22a58	23 03			23a28	23 33		23a58
Hither Green	d		23 07				23 37		
Lewisham	d		23 13				23 43		
St Johns	a								
New Cross	a								
London Bridge	a		23 22	23 13	23 24		23 52	23 54	
London Cannon Street	a								
London Waterloo (East)	a		23 26	23 18	23 29		23 56	23 59	
London Charing Cross	a		23 33	23 21	23 33		00 04	00 03	

Saturdays
25 August to 8 September

Station		SE	SE 1	SE	SE	SE	SE	SE 1	SE	SE	SE 1	SE 1	SE	SE	SE 1	SE	SE 1	SE	SE	SE 1	SE 1	SE	SE
Tonbridge	d		23p14					06 02			06 32	06 50			07 02		07 20			07 32	07 40		
Hildenborough	d		23p18					06 06			06 36				07 06					07 36			
Sevenoaks	a		23p24					06 13			06 43	06 58			07 13		07 28			07 43	07 48		
	d		23p25		05 36		06 06	06 14		06 36	06 44	06 59		07 06	07 14		07 29		07 36	07 44	07 49		
Dunton Green	d				05 39		06 09			06 39				07 09					07 39				
Knockholt	d				05 44		06 14			06 44				07 14					07 44				
Chelsfield	d		23p32		05 47		06 17			06 47				07 17					07 47				
Orpington	a		23p36		05 50		06 20	06 23		06 50	06 53	07 08		07 20	07 23		07 38		07 50	07 53			
	d	23p21	23p37		05 51		06 21	06 24		06 51	06 54	07 09		07 21	07 24	07 33	07 39		07 51	07 54			08 03
Petts Wood	d	23p24			05 54		06 24			06 54				07 24		07 36			07 54				08 06
Chislehurst	d	23p27			05 57		06 27			06 57				07 27		07 39			07 57				08 09
Elmstead Woods	d	23p29			05 59		06 29			06 59				07 29		07 41			07 59				08 11
Bromley North	d			00 23		06 23			06 53				07 23					07 45				08 05	
Sundridge Park	d			00 25		06 25			06 55				07 25					07 47				08 07	
Grove Park	d	23p33		00a28	06 03	06a28	06 33		06a58	07 03			07a28	07 33		07 45		07a50	08 03			08a10	08 15
Hither Green	d	23p37			06 07		06 37			07 07				07 37		07 49			08 07				08 19
Lewisham	d	23p43			06 13		06 43			07 13						07 54							08 24
St Johns	a															07 56							08 26
New Cross	a															07 58							08 28
London Bridge	a	23p52	23p54		06 21		06 51	06 39		07 21	07 09	07 24		07 49	07 39	08 04	07 55		08 19	08 10	08 13		08 34
London Cannon Street	a															08 08							08 38
London Waterloo (East)	a	23p56	23p59		06 25		06 55	06 43		07 25	07 13	07 29		07 53	07 43		07 59		08 23	08 15	08 19		
London Charing Cross	a	00 01	00 03		06 29		06 59	06 47		07 29	07 17	07 33		07 57	07 48		08 03		08 27	08 19	08 22		

Table 204

Saturdays

25 August to 8 September

Bromley North to Grove Park, Tonbridge, Sevenoaks, Orpington and Grove Park - London Cannon Street/Charing Cross

Network Diagram - see first Page of Table 200

		SE ■	SE	SE	SE ■	SE ■	SE	SE ■	SE	SE	SE ■	SE ■	SE	SE	SE ■	SE	SE	SE ■	SE ■ ✠	SE	SE ■	SE	SE
Tonbridge ■	d	07 50			08 02	08 10		08 20			08 32	08 40			08 50			09 02	09 10		09 20		
Hildenborough	d				08 06						08 36							09 06					
Sevenoaks ■	a	07 58			08 13	08 18		08 28			08 43	08 48			08 58			09 13	09 18		09 28		
	d	07 59		08 06	08 14	08 19		08 29		08 36	08 44	08 49			08 59		09 06	09 14	09 19		09 29		09 36
Dunton Green	d			08 09						08 39							09 09						09 39
Knockholt	d			08 14						08 44							09 14						09 44
Chelsfield ■	d			08 17						08 47							09 17						09 47
Orpington ■	a	08 08		08 20	08 23			08 38		08 50	08 53				09 08		09 20	09 23			09 38		09 50
	d	08 09		08 21	08 24		08 33	08 39		08 51	08 54			09 03	09 09		09 21	09 24		09 33	09 39		09 51
Petts Wood ■	d			08 24			08 36			08 54				09 06			09 24			09 36			09 54
Chislehurst	d			08 27			08 39			08 57				09 09			09 27			09 39			09 57
Elmstead Woods	d			08 29			08 41			08 59				09 11			09 29			09 41			09 59
Bromley North	d		08 25						08 45				09 05			09 25						09 45	
Sundridge Park	d		08 27						08 47				09 07			09 27						09 47	
Grove Park ■	d		08a30	08 33			08 45		08a50	09 03			09a10	09 15		09a30	09 33			09 45		09a50	10 03
Hither Green ■	d			08 37			08 49			09 07				09 19			09 37			09 49			10 07
Lewisham ■ ⇌	d						08 54							09 24						09 54			
St Johns	a						08 56							09 26						09 56			
New Cross ■ ⊖	a						08 58							09 28						09 58			
London Bridge ■ ⊖	a	08 25		08 49	08 40	08 43	09 04	08 55		09 19	09 10	09 13		09 34	09 25		09 49	09 40	09 43	10 04	09 55		10 19
London Cannon Street ■ ⊖	a						09 08							09 38						10 08			
London Waterloo (East) ■ ⊖	a	08 29		08 53	08 45	08 49		08 59		09 23	09 15	09 19			09 29		09 53	09 45	09 49		09 59		10 23
London Charing Cross ■ ⊖	a	08 33		08 57	08 49	08 52		09 03		09 27	09 19	09 22			09 33		09 57	09 49	09 52		10 03		10 27

		SE ■	SE ■ ✠	SE	SE	SE ■	SE	SE	SE ■	SE ■ ✠	SE	SE ■	SE	SE	SE ■	SE ■ ✠	SE	SE	SE ■	SE	SE	SE ■
Tonbridge ■	d	09 32	09 40			09 50			10 02	10 10		10 20			10 32	10 40			10 50			11 02
Hildenborough	d	09 36							10 06						10 36							11 06
Sevenoaks ■	a	09 43	09 48			09 58			10 13	10 18		10 28			10 43	10 48			10 58			11 13
	d	09 44	09 49			09 59		10 06	10 14	10 19		10 29		10 36	10 44	10 49			10 59		11 06	11 14
Dunton Green	d							10 09						10 39							11 09	
Knockholt	d							10 14						10 44							11 14	
Chelsfield ■	d							10 17						10 47							11 17	
Orpington ■	a	09 53				10 08		10 20	10 23			10 38		10 50	10 53				11 08		11 20	11 23
	d	09 54			10 03	10 09		10 21	10 24		10 33	10 39		10 51	10 54			11 03	11 09		11 21	11 24
Petts Wood ■	d				10 06			10 24			10 36			10 54				11 06			11 24	
Chislehurst	d				10 09			10 27			10 39			10 57				11 09			11 27	
Elmstead Woods	d				10 11			10 29			10 41			10 59				11 11			11 29	
Bromley North	d			10 05			10 25						10 45				11 05			11 25		
Sundridge Park	d			10 07			10 27						10 47				11 07			11 27		
Grove Park ■	d			10a10	10 15		10a30	10 33			10 45		10a50	11 03			11a10	11 15		11a30	11 33	
Hither Green ■	d				10 19			10 37			10 49			11 07				11 19			11 37	
Lewisham ■ ⇌	d				10 24						10 54							11 24				
St Johns	a				10 26						10 56							11 26				
New Cross ■ ⊖	a				10 28						10 58							11 28				
London Bridge ■ ⊖	a	10 10	10 13		10 34	10 25		10 49	10 40	10 43	11 04	10 55		11 19	11 10	11 13		11 34	11 25		11 49	11 40
London Cannon Street ■ ⊖	a				10 38						11 08							11 38				
London Waterloo (East) ■ ⊖	a	10 15	10 19			10 29		10 53	10 45	10 49		10 59		11 23	11 15	11 19			11 29		11 53	11 45
London Charing Cross ■ ⊖	a	10 19	10 22			10 33		10 57	10 49	10 52		11 03		11 27	11 19	11 22			11 33		11 57	11 49

		SE ■ ✠	SE	SE ■	SE	SE	SE ■	SE ■ ✠	SE	SE	SE ■	SE	SE	SE ■	SE ■ ✠	SE	SE ■	SE	SE	SE ■	SE ■ ✠	SE	SE
Tonbridge ■	d	11 10		11 20			11 32	11 40			11 50			12 02	12 10		12 20			12 32	12 40		
Hildenborough	d						11 36							12 06						12 36			
Sevenoaks ■	a	11 18		11 28			11 43	11 48			11 58			12 13	12 18		12 28			12 43	12 48		
	d	11 19		11 29		11 36	11 44	11 49			11 59		12 06	12 14	12 19		12 29		12 36	12 44	12 49		
Dunton Green	d					11 39							12 09						12 39				
Knockholt	d					11 44							12 14						12 44				
Chelsfield ■	d					11 47							12 17						12 47				
Orpington ■	a			11 38		11 50	11 53				12 08		12 20	12 23			12 38		12 50	12 53			
	d		11 33	11 39		11 51	11 54			12 03	12 09		12 21	12 24		12 33	12 39		12 51	12 54			13 03
Petts Wood ■	d		11 36			11 54				12 06			12 24			12 36			12 54				13 06
Chislehurst	d		11 39			11 57				12 09			12 27			12 39			12 57				13 09
Elmstead Woods	d		11 41			11 59				12 11			12 29			12 41			12 59				13 11
Bromley North	d				11 45				12 05			12 25						12 45				13 05	
Sundridge Park	d				11 47				12 07			12 27						12 47				13 07	
Grove Park ■	d		11 45		11a50	12 03			12a10	12 15		12a30	12 33			12 45		12a50	13 03			13a10	13 15
Hither Green ■	d		11 49			12 07				12 19			12 37			12 49			13 07				13 19
Lewisham ■ ⇌	d		11 54							12 24						12 54							13 24
St Johns	a		11 56							12 26						12 56							13 26
New Cross ■ ⊖	a		11 58							12 28						12 58							13 28
London Bridge ■ ⊖	a	11 43	12 04	11 55		12 19	12 10	12 13		12 34	12 25		12 49	12 40	12 43	13 04	12 55		13 19	13 10	13 13		13 34
London Cannon Street ■ ⊖	a		12 08							12 38						13 08							13 38
London Waterloo (East) ■ ⊖	a	11 49		11 59		12 23	12 15	12 19			12 29		12 53	12 45	12 49		12 59		13 23	13 15	13 19		
London Charing Cross ■ ⊖	a	11 52		12 03		12 27	12 19	12 22			12 33		12 57	12 49	12 52		13 03		13 27	13 19	13 22		

Table 204

Saturdays

25 August to 8 September

Bromley North to Grove Park, Tonbridge, Sevenoaks, Orpington and Grove Park - London Cannon Street/Charing Cross

Network Diagram - see first Page of Table 200

		SE ■	SE	SE	SE ■	SE ■ ✠	SE	SE ■	SE	SE	SE ■	SE ■ ✠	SE	SE	SE ■	SE	SE	SE ■	SE ■ ✠	SE	SE ■	SE
Tonbridge ■	d	12 50			13 02	13 10		13 20			13 32	13 40			13 50			14 02	14 10		14 20	
Hildenborough	d				13 06						13 36							14 06				
Sevenoaks ■	a	12 58			13 13	13 18		13 28			13 43	13 48			13 58			14 13	14 18		14 28	
	d	12 59		13 06	13 14	13 19		13 29		13 36	13 44	13 49			13 59		14 06	14 14	14 19		14 29	
Dunton Green	d			13 09						13 39							14 09					
Knockholt	d			13 14						13 44							14 14					
Chelsfield ■	d			13 17						13 47							14 17					
Orpington ■	a	13 08		13 20	13 23			13 38		13 50	13 53				14 08		14 20	14 23			14 38	
	d	13 09		13 21	13 24		13 33	13 39		13 51	13 54			14 03	14 09		14 21	14 24		14 33	14 39	
Petts Wood ■	d			13 24			13 36			13 54				14 06			14 24			14 36		
Chislehurst	d			13 27			13 39			13 57				14 09			14 27			14 39		
Elmstead Woods	d			13 29			13 41			13 59				14 11			14 29			14 41		
Bromley North	d		13 25						13 45				14 05			14 25						14 45
Sundridge Park	d		13 27						13 47				14 07			14 27						14 47
Grove Park ■	d		13a30	13 33			13 45		13a50	14 03			14a10	14 15		14a30	14 33			14 45		14a50
Hither Green ■	d			13 37			13 49			14 07				14 19			14 37			14 49		
Lewisham ■ ⇌	d						13 54							14 24						14 54		
St Johns	a						13 56							14 26						14 56		
New Cross ■ ⊖	a						13 58							14 28						14 58		
London Bridge ■ ⊖	a	13 25		13 49	13 40	13 43	14 04	13 55		14 19	14 10	14 13		14 34	14 25		14 49	14 40	14 43	15 04	14 55	
London Cannon Street ■ ⊖	a						14 08							14 38						15 08		
London Waterloo (East) ■ ⊖	a	13 29		13 53	13 45	13 49		13 59		14 23	14 15	14 19			14 29		14 53	14 45	14 49		14 59	
London Charing Cross ■ ⊖	a	13 33		13 57	13 49	13 52		14 03		14 27	14 19	14 22			14 33		14 57	14 49	14 52		15 03	

		SE	SE ■	SE ■ ✠	SE	SE	SE ■	SE	SE	SE ■	SE ■ ✠	SE	SE ■	SE	SE	SE ■	SE ■ ✠	SE	SE	SE ■	SE	SE	SE ■
Tonbridge ■	d		14 32	14 40			14 50			15 02	15 10		15 20			15 32	15 40			15 50			16 02
Hildenborough	d		14 36							15 06						15 36							16 06
Sevenoaks ■	a		14 43	14 48			14 58			15 13	15 18		15 28			15 43	15 48			15 58			16 13
	d	14 36	14 44	14 49			14 59		15 06	15 14	15 19		15 29		15 36	15 44	15 49			15 59		16 06	16 14
Dunton Green	d	14 39							15 09						15 39							16 09	
Knockholt	d	14 44							15 14						15 44							16 14	
Chelsfield ■	d	14 47							15 17						15 47							16 17	
Orpington ■	a	14 50	14 53				15 08		15 20	15 23			15 38		15 50	15 53				16 08		16 20	16 23
	d	14 51	14 54			15 03	15 09		15 21	15 24		15 33	15 39		15 51	15 54			16 03	16 09		16 21	16 24
Petts Wood ■	d	14 54				15 06			15 24			15 36			15 54				16 06			16 24	
Chislehurst	d	14 57				15 09			15 27			15 39			15 57				16 09			16 27	
Elmstead Woods	d	14 59				15 11			15 29			15 41			15 59				16 11			16 29	
Bromley North	d				15 05			15 25						15 45				16 05			16 25		
Sundridge Park	d				15 07			15 27						15 47				16 07			16 27		
Grove Park ■	d	15 03			15a10	15 15		15a30	15 33			15 45		15a50	16 03			16a10	16 15		16a30	16 33	
Hither Green ■	d	15 07				15 19			15 37			15 49			16 07				16 19			16 37	
Lewisham ■ ⇌	d					15 24						15 54							16 24				
St Johns	a					15 26						15 56							16 26				
New Cross ■ ⊖	a					15 28						15 58							16 28				
London Bridge ■ ⊖	a	15 19	15 10	15 13		15 34	15 25		15 49	15 40	15 43	16 04	15 55		16 19	16 10	16 13		16 34	16 25		16 49	16 40
London Cannon Street ■ ⊖	a					15 38						16 08							16 38				
London Waterloo (East) ■ ⊖	a	15 23	15 15	15 19			15 29		15 53	15 45	15 49		15 59		16 23	16 15	16 19			16 29		16 53	16 45
London Charing Cross ■ ⊖	a	15 27	15 19	15 22			15 33		15 57	15 49	15 52		16 03		16 27	16 19	16 22			16 33		16 57	16 49

		SE ■ ✠	SE	SE ■	SE	SE	SE ■	SE ■ ✠	SE	SE	SE ■	SE	SE	SE ■	SE ■ ✠	SE	SE ■	SE	SE	SE ■	SE ■ ✠	SE	SE
Tonbridge ■	d	16 10		16 20			16 32	16 40			16 50			17 02	17 10		17 20			17 32	17 40		
Hildenborough	d						16 36							17 06						17 36			
Sevenoaks ■	a	16 18		16 28			16 43	16 48			16 58			17 13	17 18		17 28			17 43	17 48		
	d	16 19		16 29		16 36	16 44	16 49			16 59		17 06	17 14	17 19		17 29		17 36	17 44	17 49		
Dunton Green	d					16 39							17 09						17 39				
Knockholt	d					16 44							17 14						17 44				
Chelsfield ■	d					16 47							17 17						17 47				
Orpington ■	a			16 38		16 50	16 53				17 08		17 20	17 23			17 38		17 50	17 53			
	d		16 33	16 39		16 51	16 54			17 03	17 09		17 21	17 24		17 33	17 39		17 51	17 54			18 03
Petts Wood ■	d		16 36			16 54				17 06			17 24			17 36			17 54				18 06
Chislehurst	d		16 39			16 57				17 09			17 27			17 39			17 57				18 09
Elmstead Woods	d		16 41			16 59				17 11			17 29			17 41			17 59				18 11
Bromley North	d				16 45				17 05			17 25						17 45				18 05	
Sundridge Park	d				16 47				17 07			17 27						17 47				18 07	
Grove Park ■	d		16 45		16a50	17 03			17a10	17 15		17a30	17 33			17 45		17a50	18 03			18a10	18 15
Hither Green ■	d		16 49			17 07				17 19			17 37			17 49			18 07				18 19
Lewisham ■ ⇌	d		16 54							17 24						17 54							18 24
St Johns	a		16 56							17 26						17 56							18 26
New Cross ■ ⊖	a		16 58							17 28						17 58							18 28
London Bridge ■ ⊖	a	16 43	17 04	16 55		17 19	17 10	17 13		17 34	17 25		17 49	17 40	17 43	18 04	17 55		18 19	18 10	18 13		18 34
London Cannon Street ■ ⊖	a		17 08							17 38						18 08							18 38
London Waterloo (East) ■ ⊖	a	16 49		16 59		17 23	17 15	17 19			17 29		17 53	17 45	17 49		17 59		18 23	18 15	18 19		
London Charing Cross ■ ⊖	a	16 52		17 03		17 27	17 19	17 22			17 33		17 57	17 49	17 52		18 03		18 27	18 19	18 22		

Saturdays

25 August to 8 September

Bromley North to Grove Park, Tonbridge, Sevenoaks, Orpington and Grove Park - London Cannon Street/Charing Cross

Network Diagram - see first Page of Table 200

	SE ■		SE	SE	SE ■	SE ■ ⚒	SE	SE ■	SE	SE	SE ■		SE ■ ⚒	SE ■	SE	SE	SE	SE ■ ⚒	SE ■	SE	SE		SE ■	SE ■
Tonbridge ■ d	17 50				18 02	18 10		18 20			18 32		18 40	18 50				19 10	19 18				19 40	19 50
Hildenborough d					18 06						18 36								19 22					
Sevenoaks ■ a	17 58				18 13	18 18		18 28			18 43		18 48	18 58				19 18	19 28				19 48	19 58
d	17 59			18 06	18 14	18 19		18 29		18 36	18 44		18 49	18 59			19 06	19 19	19 29		19 36		19 49	19 59
Dunton Green d				18 09						18 39							19 09				19 39			
Knockholt d				18 14						18 44							19 14				19 44			
Chelsfield ■ d				18 17						18 47							19 17				19 47			
Orpington ■ a	18 08			18 20	18 23			18 38		18 50	18 53			19 08			19 20	19 27	19 38		19 50		19 57	20 08
d	18 09			18 21	18 24		18 33	18 39		18 51	18 54			19 09			19 21	19 28	19 39		19 51		19 58	20 09
Petts Wood ■ d				18 24			18 36			18 54							19 24				19 54			
Chislehurst d				18 27			18 39			18 57							19 27				19 57			
Elmstead Woods d				18 29			18 41			18 59							19 29				19 59			
Bromley North d			18 25						18 45						19 05	19 25				19 45				
Sundridge Park d			18 27						18 47						19 07	19 27				19 47				
Grove Park ■ d			18a30	18 33			18 45		18a50	19 03					19a10	19a30	19 33			19a50	20 03			
Hither Green ■ d				18 37			18 49			19 07							19 37				20 07			
Lewisham ■ d							18 54			19 12							19 43				20 13			
St Johns a							18 56																	
New Cross ■ a							18 58																	
London Bridge ■ a	18 25			18 49	18 40	18 43	19 04	18 55		19 21	19 10		19 13	19 24			19 52	19 43	19 54		20 22		20 13	20 24
London Cannon Street ■ a							19 08																	
London Waterloo (East) ■ a	18 29			18 53	18 45	18 49		18 59		19 25	19 15		19 19	19 29			19 56	19 48	19 59		20 26		20 18	20 29
London Charing Cross ■ a	18 33			18 57	18 49	18 52		19 03		19 29	19 19		19 22	19 33			20 00	19 51	20 03		20 30		20 21	20 33

	SE	SE	SE	SE ■	SE ■	SE	SE		SE ■	SE ■	SE	SE	SE ■	SE ■	SE	SE	SE ■		SE ■	SE	SE	SE ■	SE ■	SE
Tonbridge ■ d				20 10	20 18				20 40	20 50			21 10	21 18			21 40		21 50			22 10	22 18	
Hildenborough d					20 22									21 22									22 22	
Sevenoaks ■ a				20 18	20 28				20 48	20 58			21 18	21 28			21 48		21 58			22 18	22 28	
d			20 06	20 19	20 29		20 36		20 49	20 59		21 06	21 19	21 29		21 36	21 49		21 59		22 06	22 19	22 29	
Dunton Green d			20 09				20 39					21 09				21 39					22 09			
Knockholt d			20 14				20 44					21 14				21 44					22 14			
Chelsfield ■ d			20 17				20 47					21 17				21 47					22 17			
Orpington ■ a			20 20	20 27	20 38		20 50		20 57	21 08		21 20	21 27	21 38		21 50	21 57		22 08		22 20	22 27	22 38	
d			20 21	20 28	20 39		20 51		20 58	21 09		21 21	21 28	21 39		21 51	21 58		22 09		22 21	22 28	22 39	
Petts Wood ■ d			20 24				20 54					21 24				21 54					22 24			
Chislehurst d			20 27				20 57					21 27				21 57					22 27			
Elmstead Woods d			20 29				20 59					21 29				21 59					22 29			
Bromley North d	20 05	20 25				20 53					21 23				21 53					22 23				22 53
Sundridge Park d	20 07	20 27				20 55					21 25				21 55					22 25				22 55
Grove Park ■ d	20a10	20a30	20 33			20a58	21 03				21a28	21 33			21a58	22 03				22a28	22 33			22a58
Hither Green ■ d			20 37				21 07					21 37				22 07					22 37			
Lewisham ■ d			20 43				21 13					21 43				22 13					22 43			
St Johns a																								
New Cross ■ a																								
London Bridge ■ a			20 52	20 43	20 54		21 22		21 13	21 24		21 52	21 43	21 54		22 22	22 13		22 24		22 52	22 43	22 54	
London Cannon Street ■ a																								
London Waterloo (East) ■ a			20 56	20 48	20 59		21 26		21 18	21 29		21 56	21 48	21 59		22 26	22 18		22 29		22 56	22 48	22 59	
London Charing Cross ■ a			21 00	20 51	21 03		21 30		21 21	21 33		22 00	21 51	22 03		22 30	22 21		22 33		23 00	22 51	23 03	

	SE	SE ■	SE ■		SE	SE	SE ■	SE
Tonbridge ■ d		22 40	22 50				23 14	
Hildenborough d							23 18	
Sevenoaks ■ a		22 48	22 58				23 24	
d		22 49	22 59				23 25	
Dunton Green d								
Knockholt d								
Chelsfield ■ d							23 32	
Orpington ■ a		22 57	23 08				23 36	
d	22 51	22 58	23 09			23 21	23 37	
Petts Wood ■ d	22 54					23 24		
Chislehurst d	22 57					23 27		
Elmstead Woods d	22 59					23 29		
Bromley North d					23 23			23 53
Sundridge Park d					23 25			23 55
Grove Park ■ d	23 03				23a28	23 33		23a58
Hither Green ■ d	23 07					23 37		
Lewisham ■ d	23 13					23 43		
St Johns a								
New Cross ■ a								
London Bridge ■ a	23 22	23 13	23 24			23 52	23 54	
London Cannon Street ■ a								
London Waterloo (East) ■ a	23 26	23 18	23 29			23 56	23 59	
London Charing Cross ■ a	23 30	23 21	23 33			00 01	00 03	

Sundays

until 22 July, 19 Aug and from 16 Sep

Bromley North to Grove Park, Tonbridge, Sevenoaks, Orpington and Grove Park - London Cannon Street/Charing Cross

Network Diagram - see first Page of Table 200

	SE	SE ■	SE	SE	SE ■	SE	SE ■	SE ■	SE	SE ■		SE	SE ■	SE ■	SE	SE ■		SE ■	SE ■ ⚒		SE	SE ■	SE ■
Tonbridge ■ d		23p14			07 10		07 23	07 38		08 10			08 25	08 38		08 55		18 55	19 10			19 25	19 38
Hildenborough d		23p18						07 42						08 42									19 42
Sevenoaks ■ a		23p24			07 18		07 31	07 48		08 18			08 33	08 48		09 03		19 03	19 18			19 33	19 48
d		23p25			07 19		07 32	07 49		08 19		08 25	08 33	08 49		09 03		19 03	19 19		19 25	19 33	19 49
Dunton Green d												08 28									19 28		
Knockholt d												08 33									19 33		
Chelsfield ■ d		23p32					07 39					08 36									19 36		
Orpington ■ a		23p36			07 27		07 42	07 57		08 27		08 39	08 42	08 57		09 12	and at the same minutes past each hour until	19 12	19 27		19 39	19 42	19 57
d	23p21	23p37		07 10	07 28	07 40	07 43	07 58	08 10	08 28		08 40	08 43	08 58	09 10	09 13		19 13	19 28		19 40	19 43	19 58
Petts Wood ■ d	23p24			07 13		07 43			08 13			08 43			09 13						19 43		
Chislehurst d	23p27			07 16		07 46			08 16			08 46			09 16						19 46		
Elmstead Woods d	23p29			07 18		07 48			08 18			08 48			09 18						19 48		
Bromley North d			00 23																				
Sundridge Park d			00 25																				
Grove Park ■ d	23p33		00a28	07 22		07 52			08 22			08 52			09 22						19 52		
Hither Green ■ d	23p37			07 26		07 56			08 26			08 56			09 26						19 56		
Lewisham ■ d	23p43			07 31		08 01			08 31			09 01			09 31						20 01		
St Johns a																							
New Cross ■ a																							
London Bridge ■ a	23p52	23p54		07 39	07 43	08 09	07 58	08 13	08 39	08 43		09 09	08 58	09 13	09 39	09 28		19 28	19 43		20 09	19 58	20 13
London Cannon Street ■ a																							
London Waterloo (East) ■ a	23p56	23p59		07 44	07 48	08 14	08 03	08 18	08 44	08 48		09 14	09 03	09 18	09 44	09 33		19 33	19 48		20 14	20 03	20 18
London Charing Cross ■ a	00 01	00 03		07 48	07 52	08 18	08 07	08 22	08 49	08 52		09 18	09 07	09 22	09 49	09 37		19 37	19 52		20 18	20 07	20 22

	SE		SE
Tonbridge ■ d			
Hildenborough d			
Sevenoaks ■ a			
d			
Dunton Green d			
Knockholt d			
Chelsfield ■ d			
Orpington ■ a		and at the same minutes past each hour until	
d	20 10		23 10
Petts Wood ■ d	20 13		23 13
Chislehurst d	20 16		23 16
Elmstead Woods d	20 18		23 18
Bromley North d			
Sundridge Park d			
Grove Park ■ d	20 22		23 22
Hither Green ■ d	20 26		23 26
Lewisham ■ d	20 31		23 31
St Johns a			
New Cross ■ a			
London Bridge ■ a	20 39		23 39
London Cannon Street ■ a			
London Waterloo (East) ■ a	20 44		23 44
London Charing Cross ■ a	20 49		23 49

Sundays

29 July to 12 August

	SE	SE ■	SE	SE	SE	SE ■	SE	SE ■	SE ■		SE	SE ■	SE ■	SE ■	SE	SE ■	SE ■	SE		SE		SE ■	SE ■ ⚒
Tonbridge ■ d		23p14				06 02		06 32	06 50			07 02	07 20	07 40		07 50	08 10					18 20	18 40
Hildenborough d		23p18				06 06		06 36				07 06											
Sevenoaks ■ a		23p24				06 13		06 43	06 58			07 13	07 28	07 48		07 58	08 18					18 28	18 48
d		23p25		05 36		06 14	06 36	06 44	06 59			07 14	07 29	07 49	07 36	07 59	08 19					18 29	18 49
Dunton Green d				05 39			06 39								07 39								
Knockholt d				05 44			06 44								07 44								
Chelsfield ■ d		23p32		05 47			06 47								07 47								
Orpington ■ a		23p36		05 50		06 23	06 50	06 53	07 08			07 23	07 38		07 50	08 08			and at the same minutes past each hour until			18 38	
d	23p21	23p37		05 51	06 21	06 24	06 51	06 54	07 09		07 21	07 24	07 39		07 51	08 09		08 21		18 21		18 39	
Petts Wood ■ d	23p24			05 54	06 24		06 54				07 24				07 54			08 24		18 24			
Chislehurst d	23p27			05 57	06 27		06 57				07 27				07 57			08 27		18 27			
Elmstead Woods d	23p29			05 59	06 29		06 59				07 29				07 59			08 29		18 29			
Bromley North d			00 23																				
Sundridge Park d			00 25																				
Grove Park ■ d	23p33		00a28	06 03	06 33		07 03				07 33				08 03			08 33		18 33			
Hither Green ■ d	23p37			06 07	06 37		07 07				07 37				08 07			08 37		18 37			
Lewisham ■ d	23p43			06 13			07 13																
St Johns a																							
New Cross ■ a																							
London Bridge ■ a	23p52	23p54		06 21	06 48	06 39	07 21	07 09	07 24		07 49	07 39	07 55	08 13	08 19	08 25	08 43	08 49		18 49		18 55	19 13
London Cannon Street ■ a																							
London Waterloo (East) ■ a	23p56	23p59		06 25	06 52	06 43	07 25	07 13	07 29		07 53	07 43	07 59	08 19	08 23	08 29	08 49	08 53		18 53		18 59	19 18
London Charing Cross ■ a	00 04	00 03		06 32	06 56	06 47	07 32	07 17	07 33		07 57	07 48	08 03	08 22	08 27	08 33	08 52	08 57		18 57		19 03	19 22

Table 204

Sundays
29 July to 12 August

Bromley North to Grove Park, Tonbridge, Sevenoaks, Orpington and Grove Park - London Cannon Street/Charing Cross

Network Diagram - see first Page of Table 200

		SE	SE ■	SE	SE ■	SE	SE ■		SE ■	SE ■	SE	SE ■
Tonbridge 4	d		18 50		19 10		19 40	and at the same minutes past each hour until	22 40	22 50		23 14
Hildenborough	d											23 18
Sevenoaks 4	a		18 58		19 18		19 48		22 48	22 58		23 24
	d	18 36	18 59		19 19	19 36	19 49		22 49	22 59		23 25
Dunton Green	d	18 39				19 39						
Knockholt	d	18 44				19 44						
Chelsfield 3	d	18 47				19 47						23 32
Orpington 4	a	18 50	19 08		19 27	19 50	19 57		22 57	23 08		23 36
	d	18 51	19 09	19 21	19 28	19 51	19 58		22 58	23 09	23 21	23 37
Petts Wood 4	d	18 54		19 24		19 54					23 24	
Chislehurst	d	18 57		19 27		19 57					23 27	
Elmstead Woods	d	18 59		19 29		19 59					23 29	
Bromley North	d											
Sundridge Park	d											
Grove Park 4	d	19 03		19 33		20 03					23 33	
Hither Green 4	d	19 07		19 37		20 07					23 37	
Lewisham 4	d	19 12		19 43		20 13					23 43	
St Johns	a											
New Cross 4 ⊖	a											
London Bridge 4 ⊖	a	19 21	19 24	19 52	19 43	20 22	20 13		23 13	23 24	23 52	23 54
London Cannon Street 4 ⊖	a											
London Waterloo (East) 4 ⊖	a	19 25	19 29	19 56	19 48	20 26	20 18		23 18	23 29	23 56	23 59
London Charing Cross 4 ⊖	a	19 32	19 33	20 03	19 51	20 33	20 21		23 21	23 33	00 04	00 03

Sundays
26 August to 9 September

		SE	SE ■	SE	SE	SE ■	SE	SE ■	SE ■	SE	SE ■	SE	SE ■	SE ■	SE	SE ■		SE ■	SE ■	SE	SE ■	SE ■
Tonbridge 4	d		23p14			07 10		07 23	07 38		08 10		08 25	08 38		08 55	and at the same minutes past each hour until	18 55	19 10		19 25	19 38
Hildenborough	d		23p18						07 42					08 42								19 42
Sevenoaks 4	a		23p24			07 18		07 31	07 48		08 18		08 33	08 48		09 03		19 03	19 18		19 33	19 48
	d		23p25			07 19		07 32	07 49		08 19	08 25	08 33	08 49		09 03		19 03	19 19	19 25	19 33	19 49
Dunton Green	d											08 28								19 28		
Knockholt	d											08 33								19 33		
Chelsfield 3	d		23p32					07 39				08 36								19 36		
Orpington 4	a		23p36			07 27		07 42	07 57		08 27	08 39	08 42	08 57		09 12		19 12	19 27	19 39	19 42	19 57
	d	23p21	23p37		07 10	07 28	07 40	07 43	07 58	08 10	08 28	08 40	08 43	08 58	09 10	09 13		19 13	19 28	19 40	19 43	19 58
Petts Wood 4	d	23p24			07 13		07 43			08 13		08 43			09 13					19 43		
Chislehurst	d	23p27			07 16		07 46			08 16		08 46			09 16					19 46		
Elmstead Woods	d	23p29			07 18		07 48			08 18		08 48			09 18					19 48		
Bromley North	d			00 23																		
Sundridge Park	d			00 25																		
Grove Park 4	d	23p33		00a28	07 22		07 52			08 22		08 52			09 22					19 52		
Hither Green 4	d	23p37			07 26		07 56			08 26		08 56			09 26					19 56		
Lewisham 4	d	23p43			07 31		08 01			08 31		09 01			09 31					20 01		
St Johns	a																					
New Cross 4 ⊖	a																					
London Bridge 4 ⊖	a	23p52	23p54		07 39	07 43	08 09	07 58	08 13	08 39	08 43	09 09	08 58	09 13	09 39	09 28		19 28	19 43	20 09	19 58	20 13
London Cannon Street 4 ⊖	a																					
London Waterloo (East) 4 ⊖	a	23p56	23p59		07 44	07 48	08 14	08 03	08 18	08 44	08 48	09 14	09 03	09 18	09 44	09 33		19 33	19 48	20 14	20 03	20 18
London Charing Cross 4 ⊖	a	00 01	00 03		07 48	07 52	08 18	08 07	08 22	08 49	08 52	09 18	09 07	09 22	09 49	09 37		19 37	19 52	20 18	20 07	20 22

		SE		SE
Tonbridge 4	d		and at the same minutes past each hour until	
Hildenborough	d			
Sevenoaks 4	a			
	d			
Dunton Green	d			
Knockholt	d			
Chelsfield 3	d			
Orpington 4	a			
	d	20 10		23 10
Petts Wood 4	d	20 13		23 13
Chislehurst	d	20 16		23 16
Elmstead Woods	d	20 18		23 18
Bromley North	d			
Sundridge Park	d			
Grove Park 4	d	20 22		23 22
Hither Green 4	d	20 26		23 26
Lewisham 4	d	20 31		23 31
St Johns	a			
New Cross 4 ⊖	a			
London Bridge 4 ⊖	a	20 39		23 39
London Cannon Street 4 ⊖	a			
London Waterloo (East) 4 ⊖	a	20 44		23 44
London Charing Cross 4 ⊖	a	20 49		23 49

Network Diagram for Tables 206, 207, 208

DM-27/11
Design BAJS

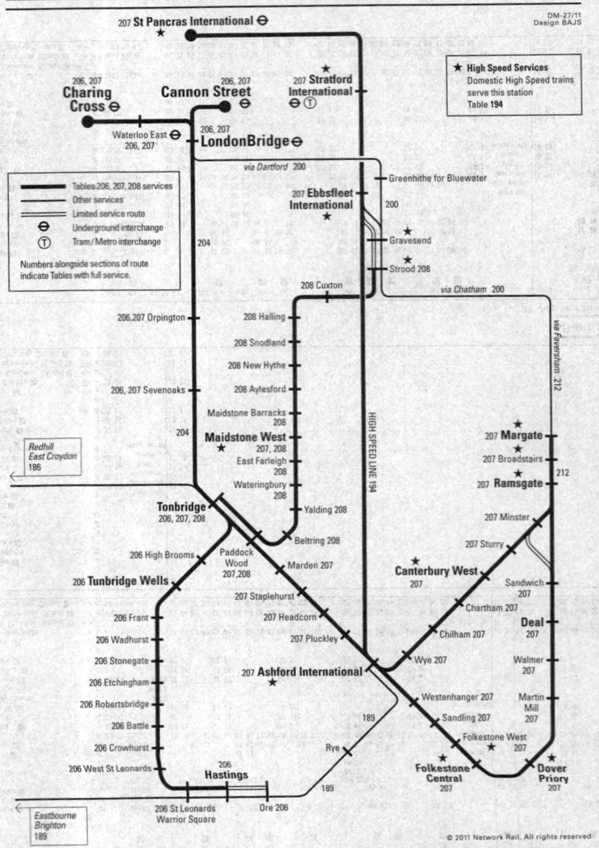

Table 206

Mondays to Fridays

until 27 July, 13 Aug to 28 Aug and from 10 Sep

London and Tonbridge - Tunbridge Wells and Hastings

Network Diagram - see first Page of Table 206

Miles	Station		SE MO 1 A	SE MX 1	SE MO 1 A	SE MX 1	SE MX 1	SE 1	SE 1	SE 1	SE 1	SE 1	SE 1	SE 1	SE 1	SE 1	SE 1	SE 1	SE 1	SE 1	SE 1	SE 1	SE 1
—	London Charing Cross ⊖	d	22p23	22p45	23p23	23p30	23p45						06 15		06 45	07 00	07 15	07 29		08 00	08 17	08 27	
0¼	London Waterloo (East) ⊖	d	22p26	22p48	23p26	23p33	23p48						06 18		06 48	07 03	07 18	07 32		08 03	08 20	08 30	
—	London Cannon Street ⊖	d																	07 47				08 42
1¾	London Bridge ⊖	d	22p31	22p53	23p31	23p39	23p53						06 24		06 53	07 08	07 23	07 38	07 51	08 09	08 25	08 35	08 46
13¾	Orpington	d	22p46	23p09	23p46	23p54	00 09						06 40		07 10	07 26	07 39	07 54	08 09	08 26	08 42	08 54	09 07
22	Sevenoaks	d	22p57	23p19	23p57	00 05	00 19						06 50		07 19	07 35	07 49	08 07	08 19	08 35	08 52	09 03	09 17
29½	Tonbridge	a	23p05	23p27	00 05	00 15	00 27						06 58		07 27	07 45	07 58	08 17	08 27	08 47	09 00	09 13	09 25
—		d	23p06	23p28	00 06	00 16	00 27	05 00	05 30	06 08	06 20	06 35	06 58	07 18	07 31	07 46	07 59	08 17	08 27	08 48	09 00	09 16	09 26
33	High Brooms	d	23p12	23p35	00 12	00 22	00 34	05 06	05 36	06 14	06 26	06 41	07 04	07 24	07 37	07 55	08 05	08 23	08 34	08 54	09 06	09 23	09 35
34½	Tunbridge Wells	a	23p15	23p39	00 15	00 26	00 38	05 10	05 40	06 17	06 30	06 45	07 08	07 28	07 41	08 02	08 08	08 30	08 40	08 58	09 10	09 27	09 39
—		d	23p17	23p40	00 17		00 40			06 18		06 46			07 42		08 13		08 49		09 14		09 42
36¾	Frant	d	23p22	23p45	00 22		00 45			06 23		06 51			07 47		08 18				09 19		
39¼	Wadhurst	d	23p27	23p50	00 27		00 50			06 28		06 57			07 52		08 24		08 57		09 25		09 50
43¼	Stonegate	d	23p33	23p56	00 33		00 56			06 34		07 03			07 58		08 30				09 31		
47½	Etchingham	d	23p38	00 01	00 38		01 00			06 38		07 08			08 02		08 34		09 05		09 36		
49¼	Robertsbridge	d	23p42	00 05	00 42		01 04			06 42		07 13			08 06		08 38		09 09		09 40		
55½	Battle	d	23p50	00 13	00 50		01 12			06 50		07 21			08 15		08 46		09 17		09 48		10 06
57½	Crowhurst	d	23p53	00 16	00 53		01 15			06 54		07 24			08 18		08 49				09 51		
60¾	West St Leonards	d	23p58	00 21	00 58		01 20			06 59		07 31			08 23		08 54				09 57		
—	St Leonards Warrior Sq	d	00 01	00 25	01 01		01 23			07 03		07 34			08 26		08 57		09 28		10 00		10 16
62½	Hastings	a	00 04	00 28	01 04		01 26			07 07		07 38			08 30		09 01		09 32		10 03		10 20
63½	Ore	a								07 12													

Station		SE 1	SE 1	SE 1	SE 1	SE 1	SE 1	SE 1	SE 1	SE 1	SE 1	SE 1	SE 1	SE 1	SE 1	SE 1	SE 1	SE 1	SE 1	SE 1	SE 1	SE 1	SE 1
London Charing Cross ⊖	d	09 00		09 30	09 45	10 00	10 15	10 30	10 45	11 00	11 15	11 30	11 45	12 00	12 15	12 30	12 45	13 00	13 15	13 30	13 45	14 00	14 15
London Waterloo (East) ⊖	d	09 03		09 33	09 48	10 03	10 18	10 33	10 48	11 03	11 18	11 33	11 48	12 03	12 18	12 33	12 48	13 03	13 18	13 33	13 48	14 03	14 18
London Cannon Street ⊖	d		09 18																				
London Bridge ⊖	d	09 08	09 22	09 39	09 53	10 09	10 23	10 39	10 53	11 09	11 23	11 39	11 53	12 09	12 23	12 39	12 53	13 09	13 23	13 39	13 53	14 09	14 23
Orpington	d	09 26	09 41	09 56	10 09	10 26	10 39	10 56	11 09	11 26	11 39	11 56	12 09	12 26	12 39	12 56	13 09	13 26	13 39	13 56	14 09	14 26	14 39
Sevenoaks	d	09 35	09 50	10 05	10 19	10 35	10 49	11 05	11 19	11 35	11 49	12 05	12 19	12 35	12 49	13 05	13 19	13 35	13 49	14 05	14 19	14 35	14 49
Tonbridge	a	09 46	09 58	10 15	10 27	10 45	10 57	11 15	11 27	11 45	11 57	12 15	12 27	12 45	12 57	13 15	13 27	13 45	13 57	14 15	14 27	14 45	14 57
	d	09 46	09 59	10 16	10 28	10 46	11 01	11 16	11 28	11 46	11 58	12 16	12 28	12 46	12 58	13 16	13 28	13 46	13 58	14 16	14 28	14 46	14 58
High Brooms	d	09 53	10 05	10 23	10 35	10 54	11 07	11 23	11 35	11 53	12 05	12 23	12 35	12 53	13 05	13 23	13 35	13 53	14 05	14 23	14 35	14 53	15 05
Tunbridge Wells	a	09 57	10 09	10 27	10 39	10 57	11 11	11 27	11 39	11 57	12 09	12 27	12 39	12 57	13 09	13 27	13 39	13 57	14 09	14 27	14 39	14 57	15 09
	d		10 13		10 40		11 12		11 40		12 10		12 40		13 10		13 40		14 10		14 40		15 10
Frant	d		10 18				11 17				12 15				13 15				14 15				15 15
Wadhurst	d		10 22		10 48		11 22		11 48		12 20		12 48		13 20		13 48		14 20		14 48		15 20
Stonegate	d		10 28				11 28				12 26				13 26				14 26				15 26
Etchingham	d		10 33				11 32				12 31				13 31				14 31				15 31
Robertsbridge	d		10 37				11 36				12 35				13 35				14 35				15 35
Battle	d		10 45		11 04		11 44		12 04		12 43		13 04		13 43		14 04		14 43		15 04		15 43
Crowhurst	d		10 48				11 48				12 46				13 46				14 46				15 46
West St Leonards	d		10 53				11 53				12 51				13 51				14 51				15 51
St Leonards Warrior Sq	d		10 57		11 14		11 56		12 15		12 55		13 15		13 55		14 15		14 55		15 15		15 55
Hastings	a		11 00		11 17		12 00		12 18		12 59		13 18		13 59		14 18		14 59		15 18		15 59
Ore	a																						

Station		SE 1	SE 1	SE 1	SE 1	SE 1	SE 1	SE 1	SE 1	SE 1	SE 1	SE 1	SE 1	SE 1	SE 1	SE 1		SE 1	SE 1	SE 1	SE 1	SE 1
London Charing Cross ⊖	d	14 30	14 45	15 00	15 15	15 30	15 45	16 00	16 15	16 28	16 41		17 01	17 19	17 23			17 45	17 59	18 07		18 32
London Waterloo (East) ⊖	d	14 33	14 48	15 03	15 18	15 33	15 48	16 03	16 18	16 31	16 44		17 04	17 22	17 26			17 48	18 02	18 10		18 35
London Cannon Street ⊖	d											17 02					17 37				18 28	
London Bridge ⊖	d	14 39	14 53	15 09	15 23	15 39	15 53	16 09	16 23	16 36	16 49	17 06	17 09		17 31		17 42	17 53		18 15	18 32	18 40
Orpington	d	14 56	15 09	15 26	15 39	15 56	16 09	16 26		16 53												
Sevenoaks	d	15 05	15 19	15 35	15 49	16 05	16 19	16 35	16 47	17 03	17 14	17 32	17 37		17 59			18 21		18 43		19 06
Tonbridge	a	15 16	15 27	15 45	15 57	16 15	16 27	16 45	16 55	17 13	17 22	17 40	17 48		18 09			18 32		18 54		19 17
	d	15 16	15 28	15 46	15 58	16 16	16 28	16 46	16 55	17 13	17 22	17 41	17 48		18 11			18 32		18 54		19 17
High Brooms	d	15 23	15 35	15 53	16 05	16 23	16 35	16 53	17 01	17 21	17 28	17 47	17 54	18 04	18 17		18 21	18 38	18 42	19 00	19 09	19 23
Tunbridge Wells	a	15 27	15 39	15 57	16 09	16 27	16 39	16 59	17 05	17 26	17 32	17 50	18 00	18 08	18 22		18 24	18 44	18 46	19 06	19 13	19 29
	d		15 40		16 14		16 40		17 05		17 38	17 52		18 08		18 29	18 33		18 49		19 20	
Frant	d				16 19		16 45		17 10			17 57		18 13			18 38		18 54		19 25	
Wadhurst	d		15 48		16 25		16 49		17 15		17 46	18 02		18 18		18 37	18 43		18 59		19 30	
Stonegate	d				16 31		16 55		17 21			18 08		18 24			18 49		19 05		19 36	
Etchingham	d				16 35		17 00		17 25		17 55	18 13		18 28		18 46	18 54		19 10		19 41	
Robertsbridge	d				16 39		17 04		17 29		17 59	18 17		18 32			18 58		19 14		19 45	
Battle	d		16 04		16 47		17 12		17 37		18 07	18 25		18 40		18 56	19 06		19 22		19 53	
Crowhurst	d				16 50		17 15		17 40			18 28		18 43			19 09		19 26		19 56	
West St Leonards	d		16 12		16 55		17 21		17 45			18 34		18 48			19 15		19 34		20 01	
St Leonards Warrior Sq	d		16 15		16 58		17 24		17 48		18 17	18 37		18 51		19 06	19 18		19 37		20 05	
Hastings	a		16 18		17 01		17 28		17 55		18 24	18 43		18 54		19 12	19 23		19 42		20 08	
Ore	a													19 00							20 15	

A from 21 May until 23 July

Table 206

Mondays to Fridays

until 27 July, 13 Aug to 28 Aug and from 10 Sep

London and Tonbridge - Tunbridge Wells and Hastings

Network Diagram - see first Page of Table 206

Station		SE 1	SE 1	SE 1	SE 1	SE 1	SE 1	SE 1	SE 1	SE 1	SE 1	SE 1	SE 1	SE 1	SE 1	SE 1	SE 1	SE 1	SE 1
London Charing Cross ⊖	d	18 45		19 15	19 30	19 45	20 00	20 15	20 30	20 45	21 00	21 30	21 45	22 00	22 30	22 45	23 00	23 30	23 45
London Waterloo (East) ⊖	d	18 48		19 18	19 33	19 48	20 03	20 18	20 33	20 48	21 03	21 33	21 48	22 03	22 33	22 48	23 03	23 33	23 48
London Cannon Street ⊖	d		19 04																
London Bridge ⊖	d	18 53	19 09	19 23	19 39	19 53	20 09	20 23	20 39	20 53	21 09	21 39	21 53	22 09	22 39	22 53	23 09	23 39	23 53
Orpington	d			19 39	19 56	20 09	20 26	20 39	20 56	21 09	21 26	21 56	22 09	22 26	22 54	23 09	23 24	23 54	00 09
Sevenoaks	d	19 21	19 33	19 49	20 05	20 19	20 35	20 49	21 05	21 19	21 35	22 07	22 19	22 37	23 05	23 19	23 35	00 05	00 19
Tonbridge	a	19 29	19 44	19 57	20 15	20 27	20 45	20 57	21 15	21 27	21 45	22 17	22 27	22 47	23 15	23 27	23 45	00 15	00 27
	d	19 30	19 45	19 58	20 16	20 28	20 46	20 58	21 16	21 28	21 46	22 17	22 28	22 47	23 16	23 28	23 46	00 16	00 27
High Brooms	d	19 36	19 53	20 05	20 23	20 35	20 53	21 05	21 23	21 35	21 53	22 24	22 35	22 54	23 22	23 35	23 52	00 22	00 34
Tunbridge Wells	a	19 39	19 56	20 09	20 27	20 39	20 57	21 09	21 27	21 39	21 57	22 27	22 39	22 58	23 26	23 39	23 56	00 26	00 38
	d	19 41	19 57	20 11		20 40		21 10		21 40			22 40			23 40			00 40
Frant	d	19 46	20 02	20 16		20 45		21 15		21 45			22 45			23 45			00 45
Wadhurst	d	19 50	20 07	20 21		20 50		21 20		21 50			22 50			23 50			00 50
Stonegate	d	19 56	20 13	20 27		20 56		21 26		21 56			22 56			23 56			00 56
Etchingham	d	20 01	20 18	20 32		21 01		21 31		22 01			23 01			00 01			01 00
Robertsbridge	d	20 05	20 22	20 36		21 05		21 36		22 05			23 05			00 05			01 04
Battle	d	20 13	20 29	20 44		21 13		21 44		22 13			23 13			00 13			01 12
Crowhurst	d	20 16		20 47		21 16		21 47		22 16			23 16			00 16			01 15
West St Leonards	d	20 21		20 53		21 21		21 52		22 21			23 21			00 21			01 20
St Leonards Warrior Sq	d	20 25	20 39	20 56		21 25		21 56		22 25			23 25			00 25			01 23
Hastings	a	20 30	20 43	21 00		21 29		21 59		22 29			23 29			00 28			01 26
Ore	a																		

Mondays to Fridays

30 July to 10 August

Station		SE 1 A	SE MO 1	SE 1 A	SE 1 A	SE MO 1	SE 1	SE	SE 1	SE 1	SE 1	SE 1	SE 1	SE 1	SE 1	SE 1	SE 1	SE 1	SE 1	SE 1	SE 1	SE 1	SE 1
London Charing Cross ⊖	d	22p45	22p55	23p30	23p45	23p45	00 37	00 48						06 15		06 45	07 00	07 15	07 29		08 00	08 17	08 27
London Waterloo (East) ⊖	d	22p48	22p58	23p33	23p48	23p48	00 40	00 51						06 18		06 48	07 03	07 18	07 32		08 03	08 20	08 30
London Cannon Street ⊖	d																			07 47			
London Bridge ⊖	d	22p53	23p03	23p39	23p53	23p53	00 45	00 56						06 24		06 53	07 08	07 23	07 38	07 51	08 09	08 25	08 35
Orpington	d	23p09	23p19	23p54	00 09	00 09	01 01	01 26						06 40		07 10	07 26	07 39	07 54	08 09	08 26	08 42	08 54
Sevenoaks	d	23p19	23p31	00 05	00 19	00 20	01 11	01 40						06 50		07 19	07 35	07 49	08 07	08 19	08 35	08 52	09 03
Tonbridge	a	23p27	23p39	00 15	00 27	00 28	01 19	01 50						06 58		07 27	07 45	07 58	08 17	08 27	08 47	09 00	09 13
	d	23p28	23p40	00 16	00 27	00 28	01 20	01 51	05 00	05 30	06 08	06 20	06 35	06 58	07 18	07 31	07 46	07 59	08 17	08 27	08 48	09 00	09 16
High Brooms	d	23p35	23p46	00 22	00 34	00 34	01 26	01 57	05 06	05 36	06 14	06 26	06 41	07 04	07 24	07 37	07 55	08 05	08 23	08 34	08 54	09 06	09 23
Tunbridge Wells	a	23p39	23p49	00 26	00 38	00 38	01 30	02 04	05 10	05 40	06 17	06 30	06 45	07 08	07 28	07 41	08 02	08 08	08 30	08 40	08 58	09 10	09 27
	d	23p40	23p51		00 40	00 39	01 31				06 18		06 46			07 42		08 13		08 49		09 14	
Frant	d	23p45	23p56		00 45	00 44					06 23		06 51			07 47		08 18				09 19	
Wadhurst	d	23p50	00 01		00 50	00 49	01 39				06 28		06 57			07 52		08 24		08 57		09 25	
Stonegate	d	23p56	00 07		00 56	00 55					06 34		07 03			07 58		08 30				09 31	
Etchingham	d	00 01	00 12		01 00	00 59					06 38		07 08			08 02		08 34		09 05		09 36	
Robertsbridge	d	00 05	00 16		01 04	01 03					06 42		07 13			08 06		08 38		09 09		09 40	
Battle	d	00 13	00 23		01 12	01 11	01 55				06 50		07 21			08 15		08 46		09 17		09 48	
Crowhurst	d	00 16	00 27		01 15	01 15					06 54		07 24			08 18		08 49				09 51	
West St Leonards	d	00 21	00 32		01 20	01 20					06 59		07 31			08 23		08 54				09 57	
St Leonards Warrior Sq	d	00 25	00 36		01 23	01 23	02 06				07 03		07 34			08 26		08 57		09 28		10 00	
Hastings	a	00 28	00 39		01 26	01 26	02 12				07 07		07 38			08 30		09 01		09 32		10 03	
Ore	a										07 12												

Station		SE 1	SE 1	SE 1	SE 1	SE 1	SE 1	SE 1	SE 1	SE 1	SE 1	SE 1	SE 1	SE 1	SE 1	SE 1	SE 1	SE 1	SE 1	SE 1	SE 1	SE 1	SE 1
London Charing Cross ⊖	d		09 00		09 30	09 45	10 00	10 15	10 30	10 45	11 00	11 15	11 30	11 45	12 00	12 15	12 30	12 45	13 00	13 15	13 30	13 45	14 00
London Waterloo (East) ⊖	d		09 03		09 33	09 48	10 03	10 18	10 33	10 48	11 03	11 18	11 33	11 48	12 03	12 18	12 33	12 48	13 03	13 18	13 33	13 48	14 03
London Cannon Street ⊖	d	08 42		09 18																			
London Bridge ⊖	d	08 46	09 08	09 22	09 39	09 53	10 09	10 23	10 39	10 53	11 09	11 23	11 39	11 53	12 09	12 23	12 39	12 53	13 09	13 23	13 39	13 53	14 09
Orpington	d	09 07	09 26	09 41	09 56	10 09	10 26	10 39	10 56	11 09	11 26	11 39	11 56	12 09	12 26	12 39	12 56	13 09	13 26	13 39	13 56	14 09	14 26
Sevenoaks	d	09 17	09 35	09 50	10 05	10 19	10 35	10 49	11 05	11 19	11 35	11 49	12 05	12 19	12 35	12 49	13 05	13 19	13 35	13 49	14 05	14 19	14 35
Tonbridge	a	09 25	09 46	09 58	10 15	10 27	10 45	10 57	11 15	11 27	11 45	11 57	12 15	12 27	12 45	12 57	13 15	13 27	13 45	13 57	14 15	14 27	14 45
	d	09 26	09 46	09 59	10 16	10 28	10 46	11 01	11 16	11 28	11 46	11 58	12 16	12 28	12 46	12 58	13 16	13 28	13 46	13 58	14 16	14 28	14 46
High Brooms	d	09 35	09 53	10 05	10 23	10 35	10 54	11 07	11 23	11 35	11 53	12 05	12 23	12 35	12 53	13 05	13 23	13 35	13 53	14 05	14 23	14 35	14 53
Tunbridge Wells	a	09 39	09 57	10 09	10 27	10 39	10 57	11 11	11 27	11 39	11 57	12 09	12 27	12 39	12 57	13 09	13 27	13 39	13 57	14 09	14 27	14 39	14 57
	d	09 42		10 13		10 40		11 12		11 40		12 10		12 40		13 10		13 40		14 10		14 40	
Frant	d			10 18				11 17				12 15				13 15				14 15			
Wadhurst	d	09 50		10 22		10 48		11 22		11 48		12 20		12 48		13 20		13 48		14 20		14 48	
Stonegate	d			10 28				11 28				12 26				13 26				14 26			
Etchingham	d			10 33				11 32				12 31				13 31				14 31			
Robertsbridge	d			10 37				11 36				12 35				13 35				14 35			
Battle	d	10 06		10 45		11 04		11 44		12 04		12 43		13 04		13 43		14 04		14 43		15 04	
Crowhurst	d			10 48				11 48				12 46				13 46				14 46			
West St Leonards	d			10 53				11 53				12 51				13 51				14 51			
St Leonards Warrior Sq	d	10 16		10 57		11 14		11 56		12 15		12 55		13 15		13 55		14 15		14 55		15 15	
Hastings	a	10 20		11 00		11 17		12 00		12 18		12 59		13 18		13 59		14 18		14 59		15 18	
Ore	a																						

A not 30 July, 6 August

London and Tonbridge - Tunbridge Wells and Hastings

Network Diagram - see first Page of Table 206

		SE	SE	SE	SE	SE	SE	SE	SE	SE	SE	SE	SE	SE	SE	SE	SE		SE	SE	SE	SE
		1	1	1	1	1	1	1	1	1	1	1	1	1	1	1	1		1	1	1	1
London Charing Cross ⊖	d	14 15	14 30	14 45	15 00	15 15	15 30	15 45	16 00	16 15	16 28	16 41		17 01	17 19	17 23			17 45	17 59	18 07	
London Waterloo (East) ⊖	d	14 18	14 33	14 48	15 03	15 18	15 33	15 48	16 03	16 18	16 31	16 44		17 04	17 22	17 26			17 48	18 02	18 10	
London Cannon Street ⊖	d												17 02				17 37					18 28
London Bridge ⊖	d	14 23	14 39	14 53	15 09	15 23	15 39	15 53	16 09	16 23	16 36	16 49	17 06	17 09		17 31	17 42		17 53		18 15	18 32
Orpington	d	14 39	14 56	15 09	15 26	15 39	15 56	16 09	16 26		16 53											
Sevenoaks	d	14 49	15 05	15 19	15 35	15 49	16 05	16 19	16 35	16 47	17 03	17 14	17 32	17 37		17 59			18 21		18 43	
Tonbridge	a	14 57	15 16	15 27	15 45	15 57	16 15	16 27	16 45	16 55	17 13	17 22	17 40	17 48		18 09			18 32		18 54	
	d	14 58	15 16	15 28	15 46	15 58	16 16	16 28	16 46	16 55	17 13	17 22	17 41	17 48		18 11			18 32		18 54	
High Brooms	d	15 05	15 23	15 35	15 53	16 05	16 23	16 35	16 53	17 01	17 21	17 28	17 47	17 54	18 04	18 17	18 21		18 38	18 42	19 00	19 09
Tunbridge Wells	a	15 09	15 27	15 39	15 57	16 09	16 27	16 39	16 59	17 05	17 26	17 32	17 50	18 00	18 08	18 22	18 24		18 44	18 46	19 06	19 13
	d	15 10		15 40		16 14		16 40		17 05		17 38	17 52		18 08		18 29	18 33		18 49		19 20
Frant	d	15 15				16 19		16 45		17 10			17 57		18 13			18 38		18 54		19 25
Wadhurst	d	15 20		15 48		16 25		16 49		17 15		17 46	18 02		18 18		18 37	18 43		18 59		19 30
Stonegate	d	15 26				16 31		16 55		17 21			18 08		18 24			18 49		19 05		19 36
Etchingham	d	15 31				16 35		17 00		17 25		17 55	18 13		18 28		18 46	18 54		19 10		19 41
Robertsbridge	d	15 35				16 39		17 04		17 29		17 59	18 17		18 32			18 58		19 14		19 45
Battle	d	15 43		16 04		16 47		17 12		17 37		18 07	18 25		18 40		18 56	19 06		19 22		19 53
Crowhurst	d	15 46				16 50		17 15		17 40			18 28		18 43			19 09		19 26		19 56
West St Leonards	d	15 51		16 12		16 55		17 21		17 45			18 34		18 48			19 15		19 34		20 01
St Leonards Warrior Sq	d	15 55		16 15		16 58		17 24		17 48		18 17	18 37		18 51		19 06	19 18		19 37		20 05
Hastings	a	15 59		16 22		17 01		17 28		17 55		18 24	18 43		18 54		19 12	19 23		19 42		20 08
Ore	a														19 00							20 15

		SE	SE	SE	SE	SE	SE	SE	SE	SE	SE	SE	SE	SE	SE	SE	SE	SE	SE	SE
		1	1	1	1	1	1	1	1	1	1	1	1	1	1	1	1	1	1	1
London Charing Cross ⊖	d	18 32	18 45		19 15	19 30	19 45	20 00	20 15	20 30	20 45	21 00	21 30	21 45	22 00	22 30	22 45	23 00	23 30	23 45
London Waterloo (East) ⊖	d	18 35	18 48		19 18	19 33	19 48	20 03	20 18	20 33	20 48	21 03	21 33	21 48	22 03	22 33	22 48	23 03	23 33	23 48
London Cannon Street ⊖	d			19 04																
London Bridge ⊖	d	18 40	18 53	19 09	19 23	19 39	19 53	20 09	20 23	20 39	20 53	21 09	21 39	21 53	22 09	22 39	22 53	23 09	23 39	23 53
Orpington	d				19 39	19 56	20 09	20 26	20 39	20 56	21 09	21 26	21 56	22 09	22 26	22 54	23 09	23 24	23 54	00 09
Sevenoaks	d	19 06	19 21	19 33	19 49	20 05	20 19	20 35	20 49	21 05	21 19	21 35	22 07	22 19	22 37	23 05	23 19	23 35	00 05	00 19
Tonbridge	a	19 17	19 29	19 44	19 57	20 15	20 27	20 45	20 57	21 15	21 27	21 45	22 17	22 27	22 47	23 15	23 27	23 45	00 15	00 27
	d	19 17	19 30	19 45	19 58	20 16	20 28	20 46	20 58	21 16	21 28	21 46	22 17	22 28	22 47	23 16	23 28	23 46	00 16	00 27
High Brooms	d	19 23	19 36	19 53	20 05	20 23	20 35	20 53	21 05	21 23	21 35	21 53	22 24	22 35	22 54	23 22	23 35	23 52	00 22	00 34
Tunbridge Wells	a	19 29	19 39	19 56	20 09	20 27	20 39	20 57	21 09	21 27	21 39	21 57	22 27	22 39	22 58	23 26	23 39	23 56	00 26	00 38
	d		19 41	19 57	20 11		20 40		21 10		21 40			22 40			23 40			00 40
Frant	d		19 46	20 02	20 16		20 45		21 15		21 45			22 45			23 45			00 45
Wadhurst	d		19 50	20 07	20 21		20 50		21 20		21 50			22 50			23 50			00 50
Stonegate	d		19 56	20 13	20 27		20 56		21 26		21 56			22 56			23 56			00 56
Etchingham	d		20 01	20 18	20 32		21 01		21 31		22 01			23 01			00 01			01 00
Robertsbridge	d		20 05	20 22	20 36		21 05		21 36		22 05			23 05			00 05			01 04
Battle	d		20 13	20 29	20 44		21 13		21 44		22 13			23 13			00 13			01 12
Crowhurst	d		20 16		20 47		21 16		21 47		22 16			23 16			00 16			01 15
West St Leonards	d		20 21		20 53		21 21		21 52		22 21			23 21			00 21			01 20
St Leonards Warrior Sq	d		20 25	20 39	20 56		21 25		21 56		22 25			23 25			00 25			01 23
Hastings	a		20 30	20 43	21 00		21 29		21 59		22 29			23 29			00 28			01 26
Ore	a																			

Mondays to Fridays
29 August to 7 September

		SE	SE	SE	SE	SE	SE	SE	SE	SE	SE	SE	SE	SE	SE	SE	SE	SE	SE	SE	SE	SE	SE
		1	1	1	1	1	1		1	1	1	1	1	1	1	1	1	1	1	1	1	1	1
		A	B	A	B	B																	
London Charing Cross ⊖	d	22p23	22p45	23p23	23p30	23p45	00 37	00 48						06 15		06 45	07 00	07 15	07 29		08 00	08 17	08 27
London Waterloo (East) ⊖	d	22p26	22p48	23p26	23p33	23p48	00 40	00 51						06 18		06 48	07 03	07 18	07 32		08 03	08 20	08 30
London Cannon Street ⊖	d																			07 47			
London Bridge ⊖	d	22p31	22p53	23p31	23p39	23p53	00 45	00 56						06 24		06 53	07 08	07 23	07 38	07 51	08 09	08 25	08 35
Orpington	d	22p46	23p09	23p46	23p54	00 09	01 01	01 26						06 40		07 10	07 26	07 39	07 54	08 09	08 26	08 42	08 54
Sevenoaks	d	22p57	23p19	23p57	00 05	00 19	01s10	01s40						06 50		07 19	07 35	07 49	08 07	08 19	08 35	08 52	09 03
Tonbridge	a	23p05	23p27	00 05	00 15	00 27	01s19	01s50						06 58		07 27	07 45	07 58	08 17	08 27	08 47	09 00	09 13
	d	23p06	23p28	00 06	00 16	00 27			05 00	05 30	06 08	06 20	06 35	06 58	07 18	07 31	07 46	07 59	08 17	08 27	08 48	09 00	09 16
High Brooms	d	23p12	23p35	00 12	00 22	00 34	01s26	01s57	05 06	05 36	06 14	06 26	06 41	07 04	07 24	07 37	07 55	08 05	08 23	08 34	08 54	09 06	09 23
Tunbridge Wells	a	23p15	23p39	00 15	00 26	00 38	01s30	02 00	05 10	05 40	06 17	06 30	06 45	07 08	07 28	07 41	08 02	08 08	08 30	08 40	08 58	09 10	09 27
	d	23p17	23p40	00 17		00 40					06 18		06 46			07 42		08 13		08 49		09 14	
Frant	d	23p22	23p45	00 22		00 45					06 23		06 51			07 47		08 18				09 19	
Wadhurst	d	23p27	23p50	00 27		00 50	01s38				06 28		06 57			07 52		08 24		08 57		09 25	
Stonegate	d	23p33	23p56	00 33		00 56					06 34		07 03			07 58		08 30				09 31	
Etchingham	d	23p38	00 01	00 38		01 00					06 38		07 08			08 02		08 34		09 05		09 36	
Robertsbridge	d	23p42	00 05	00 42		01 04					06 42		07 13			08 06		08 38		09 09		09 40	
Battle	d	23p50	00 13	00 50		01 12	01s54				06 50		07 21			08 15		08 46		09 17		09 48	
Crowhurst	d	23p53	00 16	00 53		01 15					06 54		07 24			08 18		08 49				09 51	
West St Leonards	d	23p58	00 21	00 58		01 20					06 59		07 31			08 23		08 54				09 57	
St Leonards Warrior Sq	d	00 01	00 25	01 01		01 23	02s04				07 03		07 34			08 26		08 57		09 28		10 00	
Hastings	a	00 04	00 28	01 04		01 26	02 07				07 07		07 38			08 30		09 01		09 32		10 03	
Ore	a										07 12												

A 3 September

B not 3 September

London and Tonbridge - Tunbridge Wells and Hastings

Network Diagram - see first Page of Table 206

		SE	SE	SE	SE	SE	SE	SE	SE	SE	SE	SE	SE	SE	SE	SE	SE	SE	SE	SE	SE	SE	SE
		1	1	1	1	1	1	1	1	1	1	1	1	1	1	1	1	1	1	1	1	1	1
London Charing Cross ⊖	d		09 00		09 30	09 45	10 00	10 15	10 30	10 45	11 00	11 15	11 30	11 45	12 00	12 15	12 30	12 45	13 00	13 15	13 30	13 45	14 00
London Waterloo (East) ⊖	d		09 03		09 33	09 48	10 03	10 18	10 33	10 48	11 03	11 18	11 33	11 48	12 03	12 18	12 33	12 48	13 03	13 18	13 33	13 48	14 03
London Cannon Street ⊖	d	08 42		09 18																			
London Bridge ⊖	d	08 46	09 08	09 22	09 39	09 53	10 09	10 23	10 39	10 53	11 09	11 23	11 39	11 53	12 09	12 23	12 39	12 53	13 09	13 23	13 39	13 53	14 09
Orpington	d	09 07	09 26	09 41	09 56	10 09	10 26	10 39	10 56	11 09	11 26	11 39	11 56	12 09	12 26	12 39	12 56	13 09	13 26	13 39	13 56	14 09	14 26
Sevenoaks	d	09 17	09 35	09 50	10 05	10 19	10 35	10 49	11 05	11 19	11 35	11 49	12 05	12 19	12 35	12 49	13 05	13 19	13 35	13 49	14 05	14 19	14 35
Tonbridge	a	09 25	09 46	09 58	10 15	10 27	10 45	10 57	11 15	11 27	11 45	11 57	12 15	12 27	12 45	12 57	13 15	13 27	13 45	13 57	14 15	14 27	14 45
	d	09 26	09 46	09 59	10 16	10 28	10 46	11 01	11 16	11 28	11 46	11 58	12 16	12 28	12 46	12 58	13 16	13 28	13 46	13 58	14 16	14 28	14 46
High Brooms	d	09 35	09 53	10 05	10 23	10 35	10 54	11 07	11 23	11 35	11 53	12 05	12 23	12 35	12 53	13 05	13 23	13 35	13 53	14 05	14 23	14 35	14 53
Tunbridge Wells	a	09 39	09 57	10 09	10 27	10 39	10 57	11 11	11 27	11 39	11 57	12 09	12 27	12 39	12 57	13 09	13 27	13 39	13 57	14 09	14 27	14 39	14 57
	d	09 42		10 13		10 40		11 12		11 40		12 10		12 40		13 10		13 40		14 10		14 40	
Frant	d			10 18				11 17				12 15				13 15				14 15			
Wadhurst	d	09 50		10 22		10 48		11 22		11 48		12 20		12 48		13 20		13 48		14 20		14 48	
Stonegate	d			10 28				11 28				12 26				13 26				14 26			
Etchingham	d			10 33				11 32				12 31				13 31				14 31			
Robertsbridge	d			10 37				11 36				12 35				13 35				14 35			
Battle	d	10 06		10 45		11 04		11 44		12 04		12 43		13 04		13 43		14 04		14 43		15 04	
Crowhurst	d			10 48				11 48				12 46				13 46				14 46			
West St Leonards	d			10 53				11 53				12 51				13 51				14 51			
St Leonards Warrior Sq	d	10 16		10 57		11 14		11 56		12 15		12 55		13 15		13 55		14 15		14 55		15 15	
Hastings	a	10 20		11 00		11 17		12 00		12 18		12 59		13 18		13 59		14 18		14 59		15 18	
Ore	a																						

		SE	SE	SE	SE	SE	SE	SE	SE	SE	SE	SE	SE	SE	SE	SE	SE		SE	SE	SE	SE
		1	1	1	1	1	1	1	1	1	1	1	1	1	1	1	1		1	1	1	1
London Charing Cross ⊖	d	14 15	14 30	14 45	15 00	15 15	15 30	15 45	16 00	16 15	16 28	16 41		17 01	17 19	17 23			17 45	17 59	18 07	
London Waterloo (East) ⊖	d	14 18	14 33	14 48	15 03	15 18	15 33	15 48	16 03	16 18	16 31	16 44		17 04	17 22	17 26			17 48	18 02	18 10	
London Cannon Street ⊖	d												17 02				17 37					18 28
London Bridge ⊖	d	14 23	14 39	14 53	15 09	15 23	15 39	15 53	16 09	16 23	16 36	16 49	17 06	17 09		17 31	17 42		17 53		18 15	18 32
Orpington	d	14 39	14 56	15 09	15 26	15 39	15 56	16 09	16 26		16 53											
Sevenoaks	d	14 49	15 05	15 19	15 35	15 49	16 05	16 19	16 35	16 47	17 03	17 14	17 32	17 37		17 59			18 21		18 43	
Tonbridge	a	14 57	15 16	15 27	15 45	15 57	16 15	16 27	16 45	16 55	17 13	17 22	17 40	17 48		18 09			18 32		18 54	
	d	14 58	15 16	15 28	15 46	15 58	16 16	16 28	16 46	16 55	17 13	17 22	17 41	17 48		18 11			18 32		18 54	
High Brooms	d	15 05	15 23	15 35	15 53	16 05	16 23	16 35	16 53	17 01	17 21	17 28	17 47	17 54	18 04	18 17	18 21		18 38	18 42	19 00	19 09
Tunbridge Wells	a	15 09	15 27	15 39	15 57	16 09	16 27	16 39	16 59	17 05	17 26	17 32	17 50	18 00	18 08	18 22	18 24		18 44	18 46	19 06	19 13
	d	15 10		15 40		16 14		16 40		17 05		17 38	17 52		18 08		18 29	18 33		18 49		19 20
Frant	d	15 15				16 19		16 45		17 10			17 57		18 13			18 38		18 54		19 25
Wadhurst	d	15 20		15 48		16 25		16 49		17 15		17 46	18 02		18 18		18 37	18 43		18 59		19 30
Stonegate	d	15 26				16 31		16 55		17 21			18 08		18 24			18 49		19 05		19 36
Etchingham	d	15 31				16 35		17 00		17 25		17 55	18 13		18 28		18 46	18 54		19 10		19 41
Robertsbridge	d	15 35				16 39		17 04		17 29		17 59	18 17		18 32			18 58		19 14		19 45
Battle	d	15 43		16 04		16 47		17 12		17 37		18 07	18 25		18 40		18 56	19 06		19 22		19 53
Crowhurst	d	15 46				16 50		17 15		17 40			18 28		18 43			19 09		19 26		19 56
West St Leonards	d	15 51		16 12		16 55		17 21		17 45			18 34		18 48			19 15		19 34		20 01
St Leonards Warrior Sq	d	15 55		16 15		16 58		17 24		17 48		18 17	18 37		18 51		19 06	19 18		19 37		20 05
Hastings	a	15 59		16 18		17 01		17 28		17 55		18 24	18 43		18 54		19 12	19 23		19 42		20 08
Ore	a														19 00							20 15

		SE	SE	SE	SE	SE	SE	SE	SE	SE	SE	SE	SE	SE	SE	SE	SE	SE	SE	SE
		1	1	1	1	1	1	1	1	1	1	1	1	1	1	1	1	1	1	1
London Charing Cross ⊖	d	18 32	18 45		19 15	19 30	19 45	20 00	20 15	20 30	20 45	21 00	21 30	21 45	22 00	22 30	22 45	23 00	23 30	23 45
London Waterloo (East) ⊖	d	18 35	18 48		19 18	19 33	19 48	20 03	20 18	20 33	20 48	21 03	21 33	21 48	22 03	22 33	22 48	23 03	23 33	23 48
London Cannon Street ⊖	d			19 04																
London Bridge ⊖	d	18 40	18 53	19 09	19 23	19 39	19 53	20 09	20 23	20 39	20 53	21 09	21 39	21 53	22 09	22 39	22 53	23 09	23 39	23 53
Orpington	d				19 39	19 56	20 09	20 26	20 39	20 56	21 09	21 26	21 56	22 09	22 26	22 54	23 09	23 24	23 54	00 09
Sevenoaks	d	19 06	19 21	19 33	19 49	20 05	20 19	20 35	20 49	21 05	21 19	21 35	22 07	22 19	22 37	23 05	23 19	23 35	00 05	00 19
Tonbridge	a	19 17	19 29	19 44	19 57	20 15	20 27	20 45	20 57	21 15	21 27	21 45	22 17	22 27	22 47	23 15	23 27	23 45	00 15	00 27
	d	19 17	19 30	19 45	19 58	20 16	20 28	20 46	20 58	21 16	21 28	21 46	22 17	22 28	22 47	23 16	23 28	23 46	00 16	00 27
High Brooms	d	19 23	19 36	19 53	20 05	20 23	20 35	20 53	21 05	21 23	21 35	21 53	22 24	22 35	22 54	23 22	23 35	23 52	00 22	00 34
Tunbridge Wells	a	19 29	19 39	19 56	20 09	20 27	20 39	20 57	21 09	21 27	21 39	21 57	22 27	22 39	22 58	23 26	23 39	23 56	00 26	00 38
	d		19 41	19 57	20 11		20 40		21 10		21 40			22 40			23 40			00 40
Frant	d		19 46	20 02	20 16		20 45		21 15		21 45			22 45			23 45			00 45
Wadhurst	d		19 50	20 07	20 21		20 50		21 20		21 50			22 50			23 50			00 50
Stonegate	d		19 56	20 13	20 27		20 56		21 26		21 56			22 56			23 56			00 56
Etchingham	d		20 01	20 18	20 32		21 01		21 31		22 01			23 01			00 01			01 00
Robertsbridge	d		20 05	20 22	20 36		21 05		21 36		22 05			23 05			00 05			01 04
Battle	d		20 13	20 29	20 44		21 13		21 44		22 13			23 13			00 13			01 12
Crowhurst	d		20 16		20 47		21 16		21 47		22 16			23 16			00 16			01 15
West St Leonards	d		20 21		20 53		21 21		21 52		22 21			23 21			00 21			01 20
St Leonards Warrior Sq	d		20 25	20 39	20 56		21 25		21 56		22 25			23 25			00 25			01 23
Hastings	a		20 30	20 43	21 00		21 29		21 59		22 29			23 29			00 28			01 26
Ore	a																			

Saturdays

until 21 July, 18 Aug and from 15 Sep

London and Tonbridge - Tunbridge Wells and Hastings

Network Diagram - see first Page of Table 206

		SE	SE	SE	SE	SE	SE	SE	SE	SE	SE	SE	SE	SE	SE	SE	SE	SE	SE	SE	SE	SE	SE
London Charing Cross ⊖	d	22p45	23p30	23p45				07 45	08 15	08 30	08 45	09 00	09 15	09 30	09 45	10 00	10 15	10 30	10 45	11 00	11 15	11 30	11 45
London Waterloo (East) ⊖	d	22p48	23p33	23p48				07 48	08 18	08 33	08 48	09 03	09 18	09 33	09 48	10 03	10 18	10 33	10 48	11 03	11 18	11 33	11 48
London Cannon Street ⊖	d																						
London Bridge ⊖	d	22p53	23p39	23p53				07 53	08 23	08 39	08 53	09 09	09 23	09 39	09 53	10 09	10 23	10 39	10 53	11 09	11 23	11 39	11 53
Orpington	d	23p09	23p54	00 09				08 09	08 39	08 56	09 09	09 26	09 39	09 56	10 09	10 26	10 39	10 56	11 09	11 26	11 39	11 56	12 09
Sevenoaks	d	23p19	00 05	00 19				08 19	08 49	09 05	09 19	09 35	09 49	10 05	10 19	10 35	10 49	11 05	11 19	11 35	11 49	12 05	12 19
Tonbridge	a	23p27	00 15	00 27				08 27	08 57	09 15	09 27	09 45	09 57	10 15	10 27	10 45	10 57	11 15	11 27	11 45	11 57	12 15	12 27
	d	23p28	00 16	00 27	06 58	07 28	07 58	08 28	08 58	09 16	09 28	09 46	09 58	10 16	10 28	10 46	10 58	11 16	11 28	11 46	11 58	12 16	12 28
High Brooms	d	23p35	00 22	00 34	07 05	07 35	08 05	08 35	09 05	09 23	09 35	09 53	10 05	10 23	10 35	10 53	11 05	11 23	11 35	11 53	12 05	12 23	12 35
Tunbridge Wells	a	23p39	00 26	00 38	07 09	07 39	08 09	08 39	09 09	09 27	09 39	09 57	10 09	10 27	10 39	10 57	11 09	11 27	11 39	11 57	12 09	12 27	12 39
	d	23p40		00 40	07 10		08 10	08 40	09 10		09 40		10 10		10 40		11 10		11 40		12 10		12 40
Frant	d	23p45		00 45	07 15		08 15	08 45	09 15				10 15				11 15				12 15		
Wadhurst	d	23p50		00 50	07 20		08 20	08 50	09 20		09 48		10 20		10 48		11 20		11 48		12 20		12 48
Stonegate	d	23p56		00 56	07 26		08 26	08 56	09 26				10 26				11 26				12 26		
Etchingham	d	00 01		01 00	07 31		08 31	09 01	09 31				10 31				11 31				12 31		
Robertsbridge	d	00 05		01 04	07 35		08 35	09 05	09 35				10 35				11 35				12 35		
Battle	d	00 13		01 12	07 43		08 43	09 13	09 43		10 04		10 43		11 04		11 43		12 04		12 43		13 04
Crowhurst	d	00 16		01 15	07 46		08 46	09 16	09 46				10 46				11 46				12 46		
West St Leonards	d	00 21		01 20	07 51		08 51	09 21	09 51				10 51				11 51				12 51		
St Leonards Warrior Sq	d	00 25		01 23	07 55		08 55	09 25	09 55		10 15		10 55		11 15		11 55		12 15		12 55		13 15
Hastings	a	00 28		01 26	07 59		08 59	09 29	09 59		10 18		10 59		11 18		11 59		12 18		12 59		13 18
Ore	a																						

		SE	SE	SE	SE	SE	SE	SE	SE	SE	SE	SE	SE	SE	SE	SE	SE	SE	SE	SE	SE	SE	SE
London Charing Cross ⊖	d	12 00	12 15	12 30	12 45	13 00	13 15	13 30	13 45	14 00	14 15	14 30	14 45	15 00	15 15	15 30	15 45	16 00	16 15	16 30	16 45	17 00	17 15
London Waterloo (East) ⊖	d	12 03	12 18	12 33	12 48	13 03	13 18	13 33	13 48	14 03	14 18	14 33	14 48	15 03	15 18	15 33	15 48	16 03	16 18	16 33	16 48	17 03	17 18
London Cannon Street ⊖	d																						
London Bridge ⊖	d	12 09	12 23	12 39	12 53	13 09	13 23	13 39	13 53	14 09	14 23	14 39	14 53	15 09	15 23	15 39	15 53	16 09	16 23	16 39	16 53	17 09	17 23
Orpington	d	12 26	12 39	12 56	13 09	13 26	13 39	13 56	14 09	14 26	14 39	14 56	15 09	15 26	15 39	15 56	16 09	16 26	16 39	16 56	17 09	17 26	17 39
Sevenoaks	d	12 35	12 49	13 05	13 19	13 35	13 49	14 05	14 19	14 35	14 49	15 05	15 19	15 35	15 49	16 05	16 19	16 35	16 49	17 05	17 19	17 35	17 49
Tonbridge	a	12 45	12 57	13 15	13 27	13 45	13 57	14 15	14 27	14 45	14 57	15 15	15 27	15 45	15 57	16 15	16 27	16 45	16 57	17 15	17 27	17 45	17 57
	d	12 46	12 58	13 16	13 28	13 46	13 58	14 16	14 28	14 46	14 58	15 16	15 28	15 46	15 58	16 16	16 28	16 46	16 58	17 16	17 28	17 46	17 58
High Brooms	d	12 53	13 05	13 23	13 35	13 53	14 05	14 23	14 35	14 53	15 05	15 23	15 35	15 53	16 05	16 23	16 35	16 53	17 05	17 23	17 35	17 53	18 05
Tunbridge Wells	a	12 57	13 09	13 27	13 39	13 57	14 09	14 27	14 39	14 57	15 09	15 27	15 39	15 57	16 09	16 27	16 39	16 57	17 09	17 27	17 39	17 57	18 09
	d		13 10		13 40		14 10		14 40		15 10		15 40		16 10		16 40		17 10		17 40		18 10
Frant	d		13 15				14 15				15 15				16 15				17 15				18 15
Wadhurst	d		13 20		13 48		14 20		14 48		15 20		15 48		16 20		16 48		17 20		17 48		18 20
Stonegate	d		13 26				14 26				15 26				16 26				17 26				18 26
Etchingham	d		13 31				14 31				15 31				16 31				17 31				18 31
Robertsbridge	d		13 35				14 35				15 35				16 35				17 35				18 35
Battle	d		13 43		14 04		14 43		15 04		15 43		16 04		16 43		17 04		17 43		18 04		18 43
Crowhurst	d		13 46				14 46				15 46				16 46				17 46				18 46
West St Leonards	d		13 51				14 51				15 51				16 51				17 51				18 51
St Leonards Warrior Sq	d		13 55		14 15		14 55		15 15		15 55		16 15		16 55		17 15		17 55		18 15		18 55
Hastings	a		13 59		14 18		14 59		15 18		15 59		16 18		16 59		17 18		17 59		18 18		18 59
Ore	a																						

		SE	SE	SE	SE	SE	SE	SE	SE	SE	SE	SE	SE	SE	SE	SE	SE	SE	SE
London Charing Cross ⊖	d	17 30	17 45	18 00	18 15	18 30	18 45	19 00	19 15	19 30	19 55	20 25	20 55	21 25	21 55	22 25	22 55	23 25	23 45
London Waterloo (East) ⊖	d	17 33	17 48	18 03	18 18	18 33	18 48	19 03	19 18	19 33	19 58	20 28	20 58	21 28	21 58	22 28	22 58	23 28	23 48
London Cannon Street ⊖	d																		
London Bridge ⊖	d	17 39	17 53	18 09	18 23	18 39	18 53	19 09	19 23	19 39	20 03	20 33	21 03	21 33	22 03	22 33	23 03	23 33	23 53
Orpington	d	17 56	18 09	18 26	18 39	18 56	19 09	19 26	19 39	19 56	20 21	20 51	21 21	21 51	22 21	22 49	23 19	23 49	00 09
Sevenoaks	d	18 05	18 19	18 35	18 49	19 05	19 19	19 35	19 49	20 05	20 31	21 01	21 31	22 01	22 31	23 00	23 28	23 59	00 19
Tonbridge	a	18 15	18 27	18 45	18 58	19 15	19 27	19 45	19 58	20 15	20 39	21 11	21 39	22 11	22 39	23 10	23 36	00 10	00 27
	d	18 16	18 28	18 46	18 58	19 16	19 28	19 46	19 58	20 16	20 40	21 11	21 40	22 11	22 40	23 11	23 37	00 11	00 27
High Brooms	d	18 23	18 35	18 53	19 05	19 23	19 35	19 53	20 05	20 23	20 46	21 19	21 46	22 19	22 46	23 17	23 43	00 17	00 34
Tunbridge Wells	a	18 27	18 39	18 57	19 09	19 27	19 39	19 57	20 09	20 27	20 50	21 23	21 50	22 23	22 50	23 21	23 47	00 21	00 38
	d		18 40		19 10		19 40		20 10		20 51		21 51		22 51		23 48		00 39
Frant	d				19 15				20 15		20 56		21 56		22 56		23 53		00 44
Wadhurst	d		18 48		19 20		19 48		20 20		21 01		22 01		23 01		23 58		00 49
Stonegate	d				19 26				20 26		21 07		22 07		23 07		00 04		00 55
Etchingham	d				19 31				20 31		21 12		22 12		23 12		00 09		00 59
Robertsbridge	d				19 35				20 35		21 16		22 16		23 16		00 13		01 03
Battle	d		19 04		19 43		20 04		20 43		21 24		22 24		23 24		00 21		01 11
Crowhurst	d				19 46				20 46		21 27		22 27		23 27		00 24		01 15
West St Leonards	d				19 51				20 51		21 32		22 32		23 33		00 29		01 20
St Leonards Warrior Sq	d		19 15		19 55		20 15		20 55		21 36		22 36		23 36		00 33		01 23
Hastings	a		19 18		19 59		20 18		20 59		21 39		22 39		23 39		00 36		01 26
Ore	a																		

Saturdays

28 July to 11 August

London and Tonbridge - Tunbridge Wells and Hastings

Network Diagram - see first Page of Table 206

		SE	SE	SE	SE	SE	SE	SE	SE	SE	SE	SE	SE	SE	SE	SE	SE	SE	SE	SE	SE	SE	SE
London Charing Cross ⊖	d	22p45	23p30	23p45	00 37	00 48				07 45	08 15	08 30	08 45	09 00	09 15	09 30	09 45	10 00	10 15	10 30	10 45	11 00	11 15
London Waterloo (East) ⊖	d	22p48	23p33	23p48	00 40	00 51				07 48	08 18	08 33	08 48	09 03	09 18	09 33	09 48	10 03	10 18	10 33	10 48	11 03	11 18
London Cannon Street ⊖	d																						
London Bridge ⊖	d	22p53	23p39	23p53	00 45	00 56				07 53	08 23	08 39	08 53	09 09	09 23	09 39	09 53	10 09	10 23	10 39	10 53	11 09	11 23
Orpington	d	23p09	23p54	00 09	01 01	01 28				08 09	08 39	08 56	09 09	09 26	09 39	09 56	10 09	10 26	10 39	10 56	11 09	11 26	11 39
Sevenoaks	d	23p19	00 05	00 19	01 11	01 42				08 19	08 49	09 05	09 19	09 35	09 49	10 05	10 19	10 35	10 49	11 05	11 19	11 35	11 49
Tonbridge	a	23p27	00 15	00 27	01 19	01 52				08 27	08 57	09 15	09 27	09 45	09 57	10 15	10 27	10 45	10 57	11 15	11 27	11 45	11 57
	d	23p28	00 16	00 27	01 20	01 53	06 58	07 28	07 58	08 28	08 58	09 16	09 28	09 46	09 58	10 16	10 28	10 46	10 58	11 16	11 28	11 46	11 58
High Brooms	d	23p35	00 22	00 34	01 26	01 59	07 05	07 35	08 05	08 35	09 05	09 23	09 35	09 53	10 05	10 23	10 35	10 53	11 05	11 23	11 35	11 53	12 05
Tunbridge Wells	a	23p39	00 26	00 38	01 30	02 06	07 09	07 39	08 09	08 39	09 09	09 27	09 39	09 57	10 09	10 27	10 39	10 57	11 09	11 27	11 39	11 57	12 09
	d	23p40		00 40	01 31		07 10		08 10	08 40	09 10		09 40		10 10		10 40		11 10		11 40		12 10
Frant	d	23p45		00 45			07 15		08 15	08 45	09 15				10 15				11 15				12 15
Wadhurst	d	23p50		00 50	01 39		07 20		08 20	08 50	09 20		09 48		10 20		10 48		11 20		11 48		12 20
Stonegate	d	23p56		00 56			07 26		08 26	08 56	09 26				10 26				11 26				12 26
Etchingham	d	00 01		01 00			07 31		08 31	09 01	09 31				10 31				11 31				12 31
Robertsbridge	d	00 05		01 04			07 35		08 35	09 05	09 35				10 35				11 35				12 35
Battle	d	00 13		01 12	01 55		07 43		08 43	09 13	09 43		10 04		10 43		11 04		11 43		12 04		12 43
Crowhurst	d	00 16		01 15			07 46		08 46	09 16	09 46				10 46				11 46				12 46
West St Leonards	d	00 21		01 20			07 51		08 51	09 21	09 51				10 51				11 51				12 51
St Leonards Warrior Sq	d	00 25		01 23	02 06		07 55		08 55	09 25	09 55		10 15		10 55		11 15		11 55		12 15		12 55
Hastings	a	00 28		01 26	02 12		07 59		08 59	09 29	09 59		10 18		10 59		11 18		11 59		12 18		12 59
Ore	a																						

		SE	SE	SE	SE	SE	SE	SE	SE	SE	SE	SE	SE	SE	SE	SE	SE	SE	SE	SE	SE	SE	SE
London Charing Cross ⊖	d	11 30	11 45	12 00	12 15	12 30	12 45	13 00	13 15	13 30	13 45	14 00	14 15	14 30	14 45	15 00	15 15	15 30	15 45	16 00	16 15	16 30	16 45
London Waterloo (East) ⊖	d	11 33	11 48	12 03	12 18	12 33	12 48	13 03	13 18	13 33	13 48	14 03	14 18	14 33	14 48	15 03	15 18	15 33	15 48	16 03	16 18	16 33	16 48
London Cannon Street ⊖	d																						
London Bridge ⊖	d	11 39	11 53	12 09	12 23	12 39	12 53	13 09	13 23	13 39	13 53	14 09	14 23	14 39	14 53	15 09	15 23	15 39	15 53	16 09	16 23	16 39	16 53
Orpington	d	11 56	12 09	12 26	12 39	12 56	13 09	13 26	13 39	13 56	14 09	14 26	14 39	14 56	15 09	15 26	15 39	15 56	16 09	16 26	16 39	16 56	17 09
Sevenoaks	d	12 05	12 19	12 35	12 49	13 05	13 19	13 35	13 49	14 05	14 19	14 35	14 49	15 05	15 19	15 35	15 49	16 05	16 19	16 35	16 49	17 05	17 19
Tonbridge	a	12 15	12 27	12 45	12 57	13 15	13 27	13 45	13 57	14 15	14 27	14 45	14 57	15 15	15 27	15 45	15 57	16 15	16 27	16 45	16 57	17 15	17 27
	d	12 16	12 28	12 46	12 58	13 16	13 28	13 46	13 58	14 16	14 28	14 46	14 58	15 16	15 28	15 46	15 58	16 16	16 28	16 46	16 58	17 16	17 28
High Brooms	d	12 23	12 35	12 53	13 05	13 23	13 35	13 53	14 05	14 23	14 35	14 53	15 05	15 23	15 35	15 53	16 05	16 23	16 35	16 53	17 05	17 23	17 35
Tunbridge Wells	a	12 27	12 39	12 57	13 09	13 27	13 39	13 57	14 09	14 27	14 39	14 57	15 09	15 27	15 39	15 57	16 09	16 27	16 39	16 57	17 09	17 27	17 39
	d		12 40		13 10		13 40		14 10		14 40		15 10		15 40		16 10		16 40		17 10		17 40
Frant	d				13 15				14 15				15 15				16 15				17 15		
Wadhurst	d		12 48		13 20		13 48		14 20		14 48		15 20		15 48		16 20		16 48		17 20		17 48
Stonegate	d				13 26				14 26				15 26				16 26				17 26		
Etchingham	d				13 31				14 31				15 31				16 31				17 31		
Robertsbridge	d				13 35				14 35				15 35				16 35				17 35		
Battle	d		13 04		13 43		14 04		14 43		15 04		15 43		16 04		16 43		17 04		17 43		18 04
Crowhurst	d				13 46				14 46				15 46				16 46				17 46		
West St Leonards	d				13 51				14 51				15 51				16 51				17 51		
St Leonards Warrior Sq	d		13 15		13 55		14 15		14 55		15 15		15 55		16 15		16 55		17 15		17 55		18 15
Hastings	a		13 18		13 59		14 18		14 59		15 18		15 59		16 18		16 59		17 18		17 59		18 18
Ore	a																						

		SE	SE	SE	SE	SE	SE	SE	SE	SE	SE	SE	SE	SE	SE	SE	SE	SE	SE	SE	SE
London Charing Cross ⊖	d	17 00	17 15	17 30	17 45	18 00	18 15	18 30	18 45	19 00	19 15	19 30	19 55	20 25	20 55	21 25	21 55	22 25	22 55	23 25	23 45
London Waterloo (East) ⊖	d	17 03	17 18	17 33	17 48	18 03	18 18	18 33	18 48	19 03	19 18	19 33	19 58	20 28	20 58	21 28	21 58	22 28	22 58	23 28	23 48
London Cannon Street ⊖	d																				
London Bridge ⊖	d	17 09	17 23	17 39	17 53	18 09	18 23	18 39	18 53	19 09	19 23	19 39	20 03	20 33	21 03	21 33	22 03	22 33	23 03	23 33	23 53
Orpington	d	17 26	17 39	17 56	18 09	18 26	18 39	18 56	19 09	19 26	19 39	19 56	20 21	20 51	21 21	21 51	22 21	22 49	23 19	23 49	00 09
Sevenoaks	d	17 35	17 49	18 05	18 19	18 35	18 49	19 05	19 19	19 35	19 49	20 05	20 31	21 01	21 31	22 01	22 31	23 00	23 28	23 59	00 19
Tonbridge	a	17 45	17 57	18 15	18 27	18 45	18 58	19 15	19 27	19 45	19 58	20 15	20 39	21 11	21 39	22 11	22 39	23 10	23 36	00 10	00 27
	d	17 46	17 58	18 16	18 28	18 46	18 58	19 16	19 28	19 46	19 58	20 16	20 40	21 11	21 40	22 11	22 40	23 11	23 37	00 11	00 27
High Brooms	d	17 53	18 05	18 23	18 35	18 53	19 05	19 23	19 35	19 53	20 05	20 23	20 46	21 19	21 46	22 19	22 46	23 17	23 43	00 17	00 34
Tunbridge Wells	a	17 57	18 09	18 27	18 39	18 57	19 09	19 27	19 39	19 57	20 09	20 27	20 50	21 23	21 50	22 23	22 50	23 21	23 47	00 21	00 38
	d		18 10		18 40		19 10		19 40		20 10		20 51		21 51		22 51		23 48		00 39
Frant	d		18 15				19 15				20 15		20 56		21 56		22 56		23 53		00 44
Wadhurst	d		18 20		18 48		19 20		19 48		20 20		21 01		22 01		23 01		23 58		00 49
Stonegate	d		18 26				19 26				20 26		21 07		22 07		23 07		00 04		00 55
Etchingham	d		18 31				19 31				20 31		21 12		22 12		23 12		00 09		00 59
Robertsbridge	d		18 35				19 35				20 35		21 16		22 16		23 16		00 13		01 03
Battle	d		18 43		19 04		19 43		20 04		20 43		21 24		22 24		23 24		00 21		01 11
Crowhurst	d		18 46				19 46				20 46		21 27		22 27		23 27		00 24		01 15
West St Leonards	d		18 51				19 51				20 51		21 32		22 32		23 33		00 29		01 20
St Leonards Warrior Sq	d		18 55		19 15		19 55		20 15		20 55		21 36		22 36		23 36		00 33		01 23
Hastings	a		18 59		19 18		19 59		20 18		20 59		21 39		22 39		23 39		00 36		01 26
Ore	a																				

London and Tonbridge - Tunbridge Wells and Hastings

Saturdays
25 August to 8 September

Network Diagram - see first Page of Table 206

	SE	SE	SE	SE A	SE A	SE	SE	SE	SE	SE	SE
London Charing Cross ⊖ d	22p45	23p30	23p45	00 37	00 48				07 45	08 15	08 30
London Waterloo (East) ⊖ d	22p48	23p33	23p48	00 40	00 51				07 48	08 18	08 33
London Cannon Street ⊖ d				⌇	⌇						
London Bridge ⊖ d	22p53	23p39	23p53	00 45	00 56				07 53	08 23	08 39
Orpington d	23p09	23p54	00 09	01 01	01 26				08 09	08 39	08 56
Sevenoaks d	23p19	00 05	00 19	01s10	01s40				08 19	08 49	09 05
Tonbridge a	23p27	00 15	00 27	01s19	01s50				08 27	08 57	09 15
d	23p28	00 16	00 27	⌇	⌇	06 58	07 28	07 58	08 28	08 58	09 16
High Brooms d	23p35	00 22	00 34	01s26	01s57	07 05	07 35	08 05	08 35	09 05	09 23
Tunbridge Wells a	23p39	00 26	00 38	01s30	02 00	07 09	07 39	08 09	08 39	09 09	09 27
d	23p40		00 40	⌇		07 10		08 10	08 40	09 10	
Frant d	23p45		00 45	⌇		07 15		08 15	08 45	09 15	
Wadhurst d	23p50		00 50	01s38		07 20		08 20	08 50	09 20	
Stonegate d	23p56		00 56	⌇		07 26		08 26	08 56	09 26	
Etchingham d	00 01		01 00	⌇		07 31		08 31	09 01	09 31	
Robertsbridge d	00 05		01 04	⌇		07 35		08 35	09 05	09 35	
Battle d	00 13		01 12	01s54		07 43		08 43	09 13	09 43	
Crowhurst d	00 16		01 15	⌇		07 46		08 46	09 16	09 46	
West St Leonards d	00 21		01 20	⌇		07 51		08 51	09 21	09 51	
St Leonards Warrior Sq d	00 25		01 23	02s04		07 55		08 55	09 25	09 55	
Hastings a	00 28		01 26	02 07		07 59		08 59	09 29	09 59	
Ore a											

	SE	SE	SE	SE	SE	SE	SE	SE	SE	SE	SE
London Charing Cross ⊖ d	08 45	09 00	09 15	09 30	09 45	10 00	10 15	10 30	10 45	11 00	11 15
London Waterloo (East) ⊖ d	08 48	09 03	09 18	09 33	09 48	10 03	10 18	10 33	10 48	11 03	11 18
London Cannon Street ⊖ d											
London Bridge ⊖ d	08 53	09 09	09 23	09 39	09 53	10 09	10 23	10 39	10 53	11 09	11 23
Orpington d	09 09	09 26	09 39	09 56	10 09	10 26	10 39	10 56	11 09	11 26	11 39
Sevenoaks d	09 19	09 35	09 49	10 05	10 19	10 35	10 49	11 05	11 19	11 35	11 49
Tonbridge a	09 27	09 45	09 57	10 15	10 27	10 45	10 57	11 15	11 27	11 45	11 57
d	09 28	09 46	09 58	10 16	10 28	10 46	10 58	11 16	11 28	11 46	11 58
High Brooms d	09 35	09 53	10 05	10 23	10 35	10 53	11 05	11 23	11 35	11 53	12 05
Tunbridge Wells a	09 39	09 57	10 09	10 27	10 39	10 57	11 09	11 27	11 39	11 57	12 09
d	09 40		10 10		10 40		11 10		11 40		12 10
Frant d			10 15				11 15				12 15
Wadhurst d	09 48		10 20		10 48		11 20		11 48		12 20
Stonegate d			10 26				11 26				12 26
Etchingham d			10 31				11 31				12 31
Robertsbridge d			10 35				11 35				12 35
Battle d	10 04		10 43		11 04		11 43		12 04		12 43
Crowhurst d			10 46				11 46				12 46
West St Leonards d			10 51				11 51				12 51
St Leonards Warrior Sq d	10 15		10 55		11 15		11 55		12 15		12 55
Hastings a	10 18		10 59		11 18		11 59		12 18		12 59
Ore a											

	SE	SE	SE	SE	SE	SE	SE	SE	SE	SE	SE
London Charing Cross ⊖ d	11 30	11 45	12 00	12 15	12 30	12 45	13 00	13 15	13 30	13 45	14 00
London Waterloo (East) ⊖ d	11 33	11 48	12 03	12 18	12 33	12 48	13 03	13 18	13 33	13 48	14 03
London Cannon Street ⊖ d											
London Bridge ⊖ d	11 39	11 53	12 09	12 23	12 39	12 53	13 09	13 23	13 39	13 53	14 09
Orpington d	11 56	12 09	12 26	12 39	12 56	13 09	13 26	13 39	13 56	14 09	14 26
Sevenoaks d	12 05	12 19	12 35	12 49	13 05	13 19	13 35	13 49	14 05	14 19	14 35
Tonbridge a	12 15	12 27	12 45	12 57	13 15	13 27	13 45	13 57	14 15	14 27	14 45
d	12 16	12 28	12 46	12 58	13 16	13 28	13 46	13 58	14 16	14 28	14 46
High Brooms d	12 23	12 35	12 53	13 05	13 23	13 35	13 53	14 05	14 23	14 35	14 53
Tunbridge Wells a	12 27	12 39	12 57	13 09	13 27	13 39	13 57	14 09	14 27	14 39	14 57
d		12 40		13 10		13 40		14 10		14 40	
Frant d				13 15				14 15			
Wadhurst d		12 48		13 20		13 48		14 20		14 48	
Stonegate d				13 26				14 26			
Etchingham d				13 31				14 31			
Robertsbridge d				13 35				14 35			
Battle d		13 04		13 43		14 04		14 43		15 04	
Crowhurst d				13 46				14 46			
West St Leonards d				13 51				14 51			
St Leonards Warrior Sq d		13 15		13 55		14 15		14 55		15 15	
Hastings a		13 18		13 59		14 18		14 59		15 18	
Ore a											

	SE	SE	SE	SE	SE	SE	SE	SE	SE	SE	SE
London Charing Cross ⊖ d	14 15	14 30	14 45	15 00	15 15	15 30	15 45	16 00	16 15	16 30	16 45
London Waterloo (East) ⊖ d	14 18	14 33	14 48	15 03	15 18	15 33	15 48	16 03	16 18	16 33	16 48
London Cannon Street ⊖ d											
London Bridge ⊖ d	14 23	14 39	14 53	15 09	15 23	15 39	15 53	16 09	16 23	16 39	16 53
Orpington d	14 39	14 56	15 09	15 26	15 39	15 56	16 09	16 26	16 39	16 56	17 09
Sevenoaks d	14 49	15 05	15 19	15 35	15 49	16 05	16 19	16 35	16 49	17 05	17 19
Tonbridge a	14 57	15 15	15 27	15 45	15 57	16 15	16 27	16 45	16 57	17 15	17 27
d	14 58	15 16	15 28	15 46	15 58	16 16	16 28	16 46	16 58	17 16	17 28
High Brooms d	15 05	15 23	15 35	15 53	16 05	16 23	16 35	16 53	17 05	17 23	17 35
Tunbridge Wells a	15 09	15 27	15 39	15 57	16 09	16 27	16 39	16 57	17 09	17 27	17 39
d	15 10		15 40		16 10		16 40		17 10		17 40
Frant d	15 15				16 15				17 15		
Wadhurst d	15 20		15 48		16 20		16 48		17 20		17 48
Stonegate d	15 26				16 26				17 26		
Etchingham d	15 31				16 31				17 31		
Robertsbridge d	15 35				16 35				17 35		
Battle d	15 43		16 04		16 43		17 04		17 43		18 04
Crowhurst d	15 46				16 46				17 46		
West St Leonards d	15 51				16 51				17 51		
St Leonards Warrior Sq d	15 55		16 15		16 55		17 15		17 55		18 15
Hastings a	15 59		16 18		16 59		17 18		17 59		18 18
Ore a											

	SE	SE	SE	SE	SE	SE	SE	SE	SE	SE
London Charing Cross ⊖ d	17 00	17 15	17 30	17 45	18 00	18 15	18 30	18 45	19 00	19 15
London Waterloo (East) ⊖ d	17 03	17 18	17 33	17 48	18 03	18 18	18 33	18 48	19 03	19 18
London Cannon Street ⊖ d										
London Bridge ⊖ d	17 09	17 23	17 39	17 53	18 09	18 23	18 39	18 53	19 09	19 23
Orpington d	17 26	17 39	17 56	18 09	18 26	18 39	18 56	19 09	19 26	19 39
Sevenoaks d	17 35	17 49	18 05	18 19	18 35	18 49	19 05	19 19	19 35	19 49
Tonbridge a	17 45	17 57	18 15	18 27	18 45	18 58	19 15	19 27	19 45	19 58
d	17 46	17 58	18 16	18 28	18 46	18 58	19 16	19 28	19 46	19 58
High Brooms d	17 53	18 05	18 23	18 35	18 53	19 05	19 23	19 35	19 53	20 05
Tunbridge Wells a	17 57	18 09	18 27	18 39	18 57	19 09	19 27	19 39	19 57	20 09
d		18 10		18 40		19 10		19 40		20 10
Frant d		18 15				19 15				20 15
Wadhurst d		18 20		18 48		19 20		19 48		20 20
Stonegate d		18 26				19 26				20 26
Etchingham d		18 31				19 31				20 31
Robertsbridge d		18 35				19 35				20 35
Battle d		18 43		19 04		19 43		20 04		20 43
Crowhurst d		18 46				19 46				20 46
West St Leonards d		18 51				19 51				20 51
St Leonards Warrior Sq d		18 55		19 15		19 55		20 15		20 55
Hastings a		18 59		19 18		19 59		20 18		20 59
Ore a										

	SE	SE	SE	SE	SE	SE	SE	SE	SE	SE
London Charing Cross ⊖ d	19 30	19 55	20 25	20 55	21 25	21 55	22 25	22 55	23 25	23 45
London Waterloo (East) ⊖ d	19 33	19 58	20 28	20 58	21 28	21 58	22 28	22 58	23 28	23 48
London Cannon Street ⊖ d										
London Bridge ⊖ d	19 39	20 03	20 33	21 03	21 33	22 03	22 33	23 03	23 33	23 53
Orpington d	19 56	20 21	20 51	21 21	21 51	22 21	22 49	23 19	23 49	00 09
Sevenoaks d	20 05	20 31	21 01	21 31	22 01	22 31	23 00	23 28	23 59	00 19
Tonbridge a	20 15	20 39	21 11	21 39	22 11	22 39	23 10	23 36	00 10	00 27
d	20 16	20 40	21 11	21 40	22 11	22 40	23 11	23 37	00 11	00 27
High Brooms d	20 23	20 46	21 19	21 46	22 19	22 46	23 17	23 43	00 17	00 34
Tunbridge Wells a	20 27	20 50	21 23	21 50	22 23	22 50	23 21	23 47	00 21	00 38
d		20 51		21 51		22 51		23 48		00 39
Frant d		20 56		21 56		22 56		23 53		00 44
Wadhurst d		21 01		22 01		23 01		23 58		00 49
Stonegate d		21 07		22 07		23 07		00 04		00 55
Etchingham d		21 12		22 12		23 12		00 09		00 59
Robertsbridge d		21 16		22 16		23 16		00 13		01 03
Battle d		21 24		22 24		23 24		00 21		01 11
Crowhurst d		21 27		22 27		23 27		00 24		01 15
West St Leonards d		21 32		22 32		23 33		00 29		01 20
St Leonards Warrior Sq d		21 36		22 36		23 36		00 33		01 23
Hastings a		21 39		22 39		23 39		00 36		01 26
Ore a										

A not 25 August

London and Tonbridge - Tunbridge Wells and Hastings

Sundays
until 22 July, 19 Aug and from 16 Sep

Network Diagram - see first Page of Table 206

	SE	SE	SE	SE	SE	SE	SE	SE	SE	SE	SE
London Charing Cross ⊖ d	22p55	23p25	23p45		08 23		09 23	09 53	10 23	10 53	11 23
London Waterloo (East) ⊖ d	22p58	23p28	23p48		08 26		09 26	09 56	10 26	10 56	11 26
London Cannon Street ⊖ d											
London Bridge ⊖ d	23p03	23p33	23p53		08 31		09 31	10 01	10 31	11 01	11 31
Orpington d	23p19	23p49	00 09		08 46		09 46	10 16	10 46	11 16	11 46
Sevenoaks d	23p28	23p59	00 19		08 56		09 56	10 26	10 56	11 26	11 56
Tonbridge a	23p36	00 10	00 27		09 04		10 04	10 34	11 04	11 34	12 04
d	23p37	00 11	00 27	08 25	09 04	09 34	10 04	10 34	11 04	11 34	12 04
High Brooms d	23p43	00 17	00 34	08 31	09 10	09 40	10 10	10 40	11 10	11 40	12 10
Tunbridge Wells a	23p47	00 21	00 38	08 35	09 14	09 44	10 14	10 44	11 14	11 44	12 14
d	23p48		00 39		09 15	09 45	10 15	10 45	11 15	11 45	12 15
Frant d	23p53		00 44		09 20		10 20		11 20		12 20
Wadhurst d	23p58		00 49		09 25	09 52	10 25	10 52	11 25	11 52	12 25
Stonegate d	00 04		00 55		09 31		10 31		11 31		12 31
Etchingham d	00 09		00 59		09 36		10 36		11 36		12 36
Robertsbridge d	00 13		01 03		09 40		10 40		11 40		12 40
Battle d	00 21		01 11		09 48	10 08	10 48	11 08	11 48	12 08	12 48
Crowhurst d	00 24		01 15		09 51		10 51		11 51		12 51
West St Leonards d	00 29		01 20		09 56		10 56		11 56		12 56
St Leonards Warrior Sq d	00 33		01 23		10 00	10 18	11 00	11 18	12 00	12 18	13 00
Hastings a	00 36		01 26		10 03	10 21	11 03	11 21	12 03	12 21	13 03
Ore a											

	SE	SE	SE	SE	SE	SE	SE	SE	SE	SE	SE
London Charing Cross ⊖ d	11 53	12 23	12 53	13 23	13 53	14 23	14 53	15 23	15 53	16 23	16 53
London Waterloo (East) ⊖ d	11 56	12 26	12 56	13 26	13 56	14 26	14 56	15 26	15 56	16 26	16 56
London Cannon Street ⊖ d											
London Bridge ⊖ d	12 01	12 31	13 01	13 31	14 01	14 31	15 01	15 31	16 01	16 31	17 01
Orpington d	12 16	12 46	13 16	13 46	14 16	14 46	15 16	15 46	16 16	16 46	17 16
Sevenoaks d	12 26	12 56	13 26	13 56	14 26	14 56	15 26	15 56	16 26	16 56	17 26
Tonbridge a	12 34	13 04	13 34	14 04	14 34	15 04	15 34	16 04	16 34	17 04	17 34
d	12 34	13 04	13 34	14 04	14 34	15 04	15 34	16 04	16 34	17 04	17 34
High Brooms d	12 40	13 10	13 40	14 10	14 40	15 10	15 40	16 10	16 40	17 10	17 40
Tunbridge Wells a	12 44	13 14	13 44	14 14	14 44	15 14	15 44	16 14	16 44	17 14	17 44
d	12 45	13 15	13 45	14 15	14 45	15 15	15 45	16 15	16 45	17 15	17 45
Frant d		13 20		14 20		15 20		16 20		17 20	
Wadhurst d	12 52	13 25	13 52	14 25	14 52	15 25	15 52	16 25	16 52	17 25	17 52
Stonegate d		13 31		14 31		15 31		16 31		17 31	
Etchingham d		13 36		14 36		15 36		16 36		17 36	
Robertsbridge d		13 40		14 40		15 40		16 40		17 40	
Battle d	13 08	13 48	14 08	14 48	15 08	15 48	16 08	16 48	17 08	17 48	18 08
Crowhurst d		13 51		14 51		15 51		16 51		17 51	
West St Leonards d		13 56		14 56		15 56		16 56		17 56	
St Leonards Warrior Sq d	13 18	14 00	14 18	15 00	15 18	16 00	16 18	17 00	17 18	18 00	18 18
Hastings a	13 21	14 03	14 21	15 03	15 21	16 03	16 21	17 03	17 21	18 03	18 21
Ore a											

	SE	SE	SE	SE	SE	SE	SE	SE	SE	SE
London Charing Cross ⊖ d	17 23	17 53	18 23	18 53	19 23	19 53	20 23	21 23	22 23	23 23
London Waterloo (East) ⊖ d	17 26	17 56	18 26	18 56	19 26	19 56	20 26	21 26	22 26	23 26
London Cannon Street ⊖ d										
London Bridge ⊖ d	17 31	18 01	18 31	19 01	19 31	20 01	20 31	21 31	22 31	23 31
Orpington d	17 46	18 16	18 46	19 16	19 46	20 16	20 46	21 46	22 46	23 46
Sevenoaks d	17 56	18 26	18 56	19 26	19 56	20 26	20 56	21 56	22 57	23 57
Tonbridge a	18 04	18 34	19 04	19 34	20 04	20 34	21 04	22 04	23 05	00 05
d	18 04	18 34	19 04	19 34	20 04	20 34	21 04	22 04	23 06	00 06
High Brooms d	18 10	18 40	19 10	19 40	20 10	20 40	21 10	22 10	23 12	00 12
Tunbridge Wells a	18 14	18 44	19 14	19 44	20 14	20 44	21 14	22 14	23 15	00 15
d	18 15	18 45	19 15	19 45	20 15		21 15	22 15	23 17	00 17
Frant d	18 20		19 20		20 20		21 20	22 20	23 22	00 22
Wadhurst d	18 25	18 52	19 25	19 52	20 25		21 25	22 25	23 27	00 27
Stonegate d	18 31		19 31		20 31		21 31	22 31	23 33	00 33
Etchingham d	18 36		19 36		20 36		21 36	22 36	23 38	00 38
Robertsbridge d	18 40		19 40		20 40		21 40	22 40	23 42	00 42
Battle d	18 48	19 08	19 48	20 08	20 48		21 48	22 48	23 50	00 50
Crowhurst d	18 51		19 51		20 51		21 51	22 51	23 53	00 53
West St Leonards d	18 56		19 56		20 56		21 56	22 56	23 58	00 58
St Leonards Warrior Sq d	19 00	19 18	20 00	20 18	21 00		22 00	23 00	00 01	01 01
Hastings a	19 03	19 21	20 03	20 21	21 03		22 03	23 03	00 04	01 04
Ore a										

Sundays
29 July to 12 August

	SE	SE	SE	SE	SE	SE	SE	SE	SE	SE	SE
London Charing Cross ⊖ d	22p55	23p25	23p45	00 37	00 48		07 45	08 15	08 45	09 15	09 45
London Waterloo (East) ⊖ d	22p58	23p28	23p48	00 40	00 51		07 48	08 18	08 48	09 18	09 48
London Cannon Street ⊖ d											
London Bridge ⊖ d	23p03	23p33	23p53	00 45	00 56		07 53	08 23	08 53	09 23	09 53
Orpington d	23p19	23p49	00 09	01 01	01 26		08 09	08 39	09 09	09 39	10 09
Sevenoaks d	23p28	23p59	00 19	01 11	01 40		08 19	08 49	09 19	09 49	10 19
Tonbridge a	23p36	00 10	00 27	01 19	01 50		08 27	08 57	09 27	09 57	10 27
d	23p37	00 11	00 27	01 20	01 51	07 58	08 28	08 58	09 28	09 58	10 28
High Brooms d	23p43	00 17	00 34	01 26	01 57	08 05	08 35	09 05	09 35	10 05	10 35
Tunbridge Wells a	23p47	00 21	00 38	01 30	02 04	08 09	08 39	09 09	09 39	10 09	10 39
d	23p48		00 39	01 31		08 10	08 40	09 10	09 40	10 10	10 40
Frant d	23p53		00 44			08 15	08 45	09 15		10 15	
Wadhurst d	23p58		00 49	01 39		08 20	08 50	09 20	09 48	10 20	10 48
Stonegate d	00 04		00 55			08 26	08 56	09 26		10 26	
Etchingham d	00 09		00 59			08 31	09 01	09 31		10 31	
Robertsbridge d	00 13		01 03			08 35	09 05	09 35		10 35	
Battle d	00 21		01 11	01 55		08 43	09 13	09 43	10 04	10 43	11 04
Crowhurst d	00 24		01 15			08 46	09 16	09 46		10 46	
West St Leonards d	00 29		01 20			08 51	09 23	09 51		10 53	
St Leonards Warrior Sq d	00 33		01 23	02 06		08 58	09 27	09 58	10 15	10 57	11 15
Hastings a	00 36		01 26	02 12		09 02	09 30	10 02	10 18	11 01	11 18
Ore a											

	SE	SE	SE	SE	SE	SE	SE	SE	SE	SE	SE
London Charing Cross ⊖ d	10 15	10 45	11 15	11 45	12 15	12 45	13 15	13 45	14 15	14 45	15 15
London Waterloo (East) ⊖ d	10 18	10 48	11 18	11 48	12 18	12 48	13 18	13 48	14 18	14 48	15 18
London Cannon Street ⊖ d											
London Bridge ⊖ d	10 23	10 53	11 23	11 53	12 23	12 53	13 23	13 53	14 23	14 53	15 23
Orpington d	10 39	11 09	11 39	12 09	12 39	13 09	13 39	14 09	14 39	15 09	15 39
Sevenoaks d	10 49	11 19	11 49	12 19	12 49	13 19	13 49	14 19	14 49	15 19	15 49
Tonbridge a	10 57	11 27	11 57	12 27	12 57	13 27	13 57	14 27	14 57	15 27	15 57
d	10 58	11 28	11 58	12 28	12 58	13 28	13 58	14 28	14 58	15 28	15 58
High Brooms d	11 05	11 35	12 05	12 35	13 05	13 35	14 05	14 35	15 05	15 35	16 05
Tunbridge Wells a	11 09	11 39	12 09	12 39	13 09	13 39	14 09	14 39	15 09	15 39	16 09
d	11 10	11 40	12 10	12 40	13 10	13 40	14 10	14 40	15 10	15 40	16 10
Frant d	11 15		12 15		13 15		14 15		15 15		16 15
Wadhurst d	11 20	11 48	12 20	12 48	13 20	13 48	14 20	14 48	15 20	15 48	16 20
Stonegate d	11 26		12 26		13 26		14 26		15 26		16 26
Etchingham d	11 31		12 31		13 31		14 31		15 31		16 31
Robertsbridge d	11 35		12 35		13 35		14 35		15 35		16 35
Battle d	11 43	12 04	12 43	13 04	13 43	14 04	14 43	15 04	15 43	16 04	16 43
Crowhurst d	11 46		12 46		13 46		14 46		15 46		16 46
West St Leonards d	11 53		12 53		13 53		14 53		15 53		16 53
St Leonards Warrior Sq d	11 57	12 15	12 57	13 15	13 57	14 15	14 57	15 15	15 57	16 15	16 57
Hastings a	12 01	12 18	13 01	13 18	14 01	14 18	15 01	15 18	16 01	16 18	17 01
Ore a											

Table 206

Sundays
29 July to 12 August

London and Tonbridge - Tunbridge Wells and Hastings

Network Diagram - see first Page of Table 206

	SE	SE	SE	SE	SE	SE	SE	SE	SE	SE	SE	SE	SE
London Charing Cross ⊖ d	15 45	16 15	16 45	17 15	17 45	18 15	18 45	19 15	19 55	20 55	21 55	22 55	23 45
London Waterloo (East) ⊖ d	15 48	16 18	16 48	17 18	17 48	18 18	18 48	19 18	19 58	20 58	21 58	22 58	23 48
London Cannon Street ⊖ d													
London Bridge ⊖ d	15 53	16 23	16 53	17 23	17 53	18 23	18 53	19 23	20 03	21 03	22 03	23 03	23 53
Orpington d	16 09	16 39	17 09	17 39	18 09	18 39	19 09	19 39	20 21	21 21	22 19	23 19	00 09
Sevenoaks d	16 19	16 49	17 19	17 49	18 19	18 49	19 19	19 49	20 31	21 31	22 31	23 31	00 20
Tonbridge a	16 27	16 57	17 27	17 57	18 27	18 58	19 27	19 58	20 39	21 39	22 39	23 39	00 28
Tonbridge d	16 28	16 58	17 28	17 58	18 28	18 58	19 28	19 58	20 40	21 40	22 40	23 40	00 28
High Brooms d	16 35	17 05	17 35	18 05	18 35	19 05	19 35	20 05	20 46	21 46	22 46	23 46	00 34
Tunbridge Wells a	16 39	17 09	17 39	18 09	18 39	19 09	19 39	20 09	20 50	21 50	22 49	23 49	00 38
Tunbridge Wells d	16 40	17 10	17 40	18 10	18 40	19 10	19 40	20 10	20 51	21 51	22 51	23 51	00 39
Frant d		17 15		18 15		19 15		20 15	20 56	21 56	22 56	23 56	00 44
Wadhurst d	16 48	17 20	17 48	18 20	18 48	19 20	19 48	20 20	21 01	22 01	23 01	00 01	00 49
Stonegate d		17 26		18 26		19 26		20 26	21 07	22 07	23 07	00 07	00 55
Etchingham d		17 31		18 31		19 31		20 31	21 12	22 12	23 11	00 12	00 59
Robertsbridge d		17 35		18 35		19 35		20 35	21 16	22 16	23 15	00 16	01 03
Battle d	17 04	17 43	18 04	18 43	19 04	19 43	20 04	20 43	21 24	22 24	23 23	00 23	01 11
Crowhurst d		17 46		18 46		19 46		20 46	21 27	22 27	23 27	00 27	01 15
West St Leonards d		17 53		18 53		19 53		20 53	21 32	22 32	23 32	00 32	01 20
St Leonards Warrior Sq d	17 15	17 57	18 15	18 57	19 15	19 57	20 15	20 57	21 36	22 36	23 36	00 36	01 23
Hastings a	17 18	18 01	18 18	19 01	19 18	20 01	20 18	21 01	21 39	22 39	23 39	00 39	01 26
Ore a													

Sundays
26 August to 9 September

	SE	SE	SE	SE A	SE A	SE	SE	SE	SE	SE	SE	SE	SE	SE	SE	SE	SE	SE	SE	SE	SE	SE
London Charing Cross ⊖ d	22p55	23p25	23p45	00 37	00 48		08 23		09 23	09 53	10 23	10 53	11 23	11 53	12 23	12 53	13 23	13 53	14 23	14 53	15 23	15 53
London Waterloo (East) ⊖ d	22p58	23p28	23p48	00 40	00 51		08 26		09 26	09 56	10 26	10 56	11 26	11 56	12 26	12 56	13 26	13 56	14 26	14 56	15 26	15 56
London Cannon Street ⊖ d																						
London Bridge ⊖ d	23p03	23p33	23p53	00 45	00 56		08 31		09 31	10 01	10 31	11 01	11 31	12 01	12 31	13 01	13 31	14 01	14 31	15 01	15 31	16 01
Orpington d	23p19	23p49	00 09	01 01	01 26		08 46		09 46	10 16	10 46	11 16	11 46	12 16	12 46	13 16	13 46	14 16	14 46	15 16	15 46	16 16
Sevenoaks d	23p28	23p59	00 19	01s10	01s40		08 56		09 56	10 26	10 56	11 26	11 56	12 26	12 56	13 26	13 56	14 26	14 56	15 26	15 56	16 26
Tonbridge a	23p36	00 10	00 27	01s20	01s50		09 04		10 04	10 34	11 04	11 34	12 04	12 34	13 04	13 34	14 04	14 34	15 04	15 34	16 04	16 34
Tonbridge d	23p37	00 11	00 27			08 25	09 04	09 34	10 04	10 34	11 04	11 34	12 04	12 34	13 04	13 34	14 04	14 34	15 04	15 34	16 04	16 34
High Brooms d	23p43	00 17	00 34	01s27	01s57	08 31	09 10	09 40	10 10	10 40	11 10	11 40	12 10	12 40	13 10	13 40	14 10	14 40	15 10	15 40	16 10	16 40
Tunbridge Wells a	23p47	00 21	00 38	01s31	02 00	08 35	09 14	09 44	10 14	10 44	11 14	11 44	12 14	12 44	13 14	13 44	14 14	14 44	15 14	15 44	16 14	16 44
Tunbridge Wells d	23p48		00 39				09 15	09 45	10 15	10 45	11 15	11 45	12 15	12 45	13 15	13 45	14 15	14 45	15 15	15 45	16 15	16 45
Frant d	23p53		00 44				09 20		10 20		11 20		12 20		13 20		14 20		15 20		16 20	
Wadhurst d	23p58		00 49	01s39			09 25	09 52	10 25	10 52	11 25	11 52	12 25	12 52	13 25	13 52	14 25	14 52	15 25	15 52	16 25	16 52
Stonegate d	00 04		00 55				09 31		10 31		11 31		12 31		13 31		14 31		15 31		16 31	
Etchingham d	00 09		00 59				09 36		10 36		11 36		12 36		13 36		14 36		15 36		16 36	
Robertsbridge d	00 13		01 03				09 40		10 40		11 40		12 40		13 40		14 40		15 40		16 40	
Battle d	00 21		01 11	01s54			09 48	10 08	10 48	11 08	11 48	12 08	12 48	13 08	13 48	14 08	14 48	15 08	15 48	16 08	16 48	17 08
Crowhurst d	00 24		01 15				09 51		10 51		11 51		12 51		13 51		14 51		15 51		16 51	
West St Leonards d	00 29		01 20				09 56		10 56		11 56		12 56		13 56		14 56		15 56		16 56	
St Leonards Warrior Sq d	00 33		01 23	02s04			10 00	10 18	11 00	11 18	12 00	12 18	13 00	13 18	14 00	14 18	15 00	15 18	16 00	16 18	17 00	17 18
Hastings a	00 36		01 26	02 07			10 03	10 21	11 03	11 21	12 03	12 21	13 03	13 21	14 03	14 21	15 03	15 21	16 03	16 21	17 03	17 21
Ore a																						

	SE	SE	SE	SE	SE	SE	SE	SE	SE	SE	SE	SE
London Charing Cross ⊖ d	16 23	16 53	17 23	17 53	18 23	18 53	19 23	19 53	20 23	21 23	22 23	23 23
London Waterloo (East) ⊖ d	16 26	16 56	17 26	17 56	18 26	18 56	19 26	19 56	20 26	21 26	22 26	23 26
London Cannon Street ⊖ d												
London Bridge ⊖ d	16 31	17 01	17 31	18 01	18 31	19 01	19 31	20 01	20 31	21 31	22 31	23 31
Orpington d	16 46	17 16	17 46	18 16	18 46	19 16	19 46	20 16	20 46	21 46	22 46	23 46
Sevenoaks d	16 56	17 26	17 56	18 26	18 56	19 26	19 56	20 26	20 56	21 56	22 57	23 57
Tonbridge a	17 04	17 34	18 04	18 34	19 04	19 34	20 04	20 34	21 04	22 04	23 05	00 05
Tonbridge d	17 04	17 34	18 04	18 34	19 04	19 34	20 04	20 34	21 04	22 04	23 06	00 06
High Brooms d	17 10	17 40	18 10	18 40	19 10	19 40	20 10	20 40	21 10	22 10	23 12	00 12
Tunbridge Wells a	17 14	17 44	18 14	18 44	19 14	19 44	20 14	20 44	21 14	22 14	23 15	00 15
Tunbridge Wells d	17 15	17 45	18 15	18 45	19 15	19 45	20 15		21 15	22 15	23 17	00 17
Frant d	17 20		18 20		19 20		20 20		21 20	22 20	23 22	00 22
Wadhurst d	17 25	17 52	18 25	18 52	19 25	19 52	20 25		21 25	22 25	23 27	00 27
Stonegate d	17 31		18 31		19 31		20 31		21 31	22 31	23 33	00 33
Etchingham d	17 36		18 36		19 36		20 36		21 36	22 36	23 38	00 38
Robertsbridge d	17 40		18 40		19 40		20 40		21 40	22 40	23 42	00 42
Battle d	17 48	18 08	18 48	19 08	19 48	20 08	20 48		21 48	22 48	23 50	00 50
Crowhurst d	17 51		18 51		19 51		20 51		21 51	22 51	23 53	00 53
West St Leonards d	17 56		18 56		19 56		20 56		21 56	22 56	23 58	00 58
St Leonards Warrior Sq d	18 00	18 18	19 00	19 18	20 00	20 18	21 00		22 00	23 00	00 01	01 01
Hastings a	18 03	18 21	19 03	19 21	20 03	20 21	21 03		22 03	23 03	00 04	01 04
Ore a												

A not 26 August

Table 206

Mondays to Fridays
until 27 July, 13 Aug to 28 Aug and from 10 Sep

Hastings and Tunbridge Wells - Tonbridge and London

Network Diagram - see first Page of Table 206

Miles		SE MX	SE	SE	SE	SE	SE	SE	SE	SE	SE	SE A 🚌	SE B 🚌	SE	SE A 🚌	SE	SE	SE	SE	SE	SE	SE
0	Ore d											06 12			06 37						07 40	
1	Hastings d	22p10			05 17		05 37	05 48		06 03		06 20	06 28		06 41		07 01		07 25		07 44	
1¾	St Leonards Warrior Sq d	22p13			05 20		05 40	05 51		06 06		06 23	06 31		06 44		07 04		07 28		07 47	
2¾	West St Leonards d	22p16			05 23		05 43			06 09			06 34		06 47		07 07		07 31		07 50	
6	Crowhurst d	22p22			05 29		05 49			06 15			06 40		06 53		07 13		07 37		07 56	
8	Battle d	22p26			05 33		05 53	06 01		06 19		06 33	06 44		06 57		07 17		07 41		08 00	
14¼	Robertsbridge d	22p33			05 40		06 00			06 27		06 40			07 05		07 25		07 48		08 07	
16	Etchingham d	22p37			05 44		06 04	06 10		06 31		06 44	06 53		07 09		07 29		07 52		08 11	
19¾	Stonegate d	22p42			05 49		06 09			06 36		06 50			07 14		07 34		07 57		08 17	
24¼	Wadhurst d	22p49			05 56		06 16	06 21		06 43		06 57	07 04		07 21		07 41		08 04		08 24	
26¾	Frant d	22p53			06 00		06 20			06 47		07 01			07 25		07 45		08 08		08 28	
29	Tunbridge Wells a	22p58			06 06		06 25	06 29		06 53		07 06	07 11		07 31		07 51		08 13		08 33	
—	Tunbridge Wells d	22p59	05 21	05 50	06 09	06 21	06 34		06 40	06 56	07 00	07 16		07 20	07 36	07 40	07 56	08 00	08 18	08 25	08 40	08 51
30½	High Brooms d	23p02	05 24	05 53	06 12	06 24	06 37		06 44	07 00	07 04	07 20		07 24	07 40	07 44	08 00	08 04	08 22	08 28	08 43	08 54
34	Tonbridge a	23p08	05 30	05 59	06 18	06 30	06 44		06 50		07 10			07 30		07 50		08 10		08 34	08 49	09 00
41½	Sevenoaks a	23p24	05 42	06 10	06 30	06 43	06 52		07 02		07 22			07 42		08 02		08 22		08 45	08 58	09 13
49¾	Orpington a	23p36	05 53	06 19		06 53	07 02		07 13												09 08	09 24
61¾	London Bridge ⊖ a	23p54	06 09	06 38	06 54	07 09	07 22		07 29		07 50			08 09	08 24	08 29		08 49	09 03	09 11	09 26	09 40
—	London Cannon Street ⊖ a			06 42			07 29								08 30				09 10			
62¾	London Waterloo (East) ⊖ a	23p59	06 14		06 59	07 14			07 34	07 44	07 55	08 04		08 14		08 34	08 44	08 54		09 16	09 31	09 45
63½	London Charing Cross ⊖ a	00 03	06 18		07 05	07 20			07 40	07 50	08 01	08 08		08 20		08 40	08 50	09 00		09 22	09 37	09 51

	SE C	SE D	SE	SE	SE	SE	SE	SE	SE	SE	SE	SE	SE	SE	SE	SE	SE	SE	SE	SE	SE	SE
Ore d																						
Hastings d	08 13	08 15		08 47		09 29		09 50		10 31		10 50		11 31		11 50		12 31		12 50		13 31
St Leonards Warrior Sq d	08 16	08 18		08 50		09 32		09 53		10 34		10 53		11 34		11 53		12 34		12 53		13 34
West St Leonards d	08 19	08 21		08 53				09 56				10 56				11 56				12 56		
Crowhurst d	08 25	08 27		08 58				10 02				11 02				12 02				13 02		
Battle d	08 29	08 31		09 02		09 42		10 06		10 44		11 06		11 44		12 06		12 44		13 06		13 44
Robertsbridge d	08 37	08 38		09 09				10 13				11 13				12 13				13 13		
Etchingham d	08 41	08 42		09 13				10 17				11 17				12 17				13 17		
Stonegate d	08 46	08 47		09 18				10 23				11 23				12 23				13 23		
Wadhurst d	08 53	08 54		09 25		09 58		10 30		11 00		11 29		12 00		12 29		13 00		13 29		14 00
Frant d	08 57	08 58		09 29				10 34				11 33				12 33				13 33		
Tunbridge Wells a	09 02	09 03		09 34		10 05		10 39		11 07		11 38		12 07		12 38		13 07		13 38		14 07
Tunbridge Wells d	09 08	09 09	09 21	09 39	09 51	10 09	10 21	10 39	10 51	11 09	11 21	11 39	11 51	12 09	12 21	12 39	12 51	13 09	13 21	13 39	13 51	14 09
High Brooms d	09 11	09 12	09 24	09 42	09 54	10 12	10 24	10 43	10 54	11 12	11 24	11 42	11 54	12 12	12 24	12 42	12 54	13 12	13 24	13 42	13 54	14 12
Tonbridge a	09 17	09 18	09 30	09 48	10 00	10 18	10 30	10 49	11 00	11 18	11 30	11 48	12 00	12 18	12 30	12 48	13 00	13 18	13 30	13 48	14 00	14 18
Sevenoaks a	09 27	09 28	09 43	09 58	10 13	10 28	10 43	10 58	11 13	11 28	11 43	11 58	12 13	12 28	12 43	12 58	13 13	13 28	13 43	13 58	14 13	14 28
Orpington a	09 37	09 38	09 53	10 08	10 23	10 38	10 53	11 08	11 23	11 38	11 53	12 08	12 23	12 38	12 53	13 08	13 23	13 38	13 53	14 08	14 23	14 38
London Bridge ⊖ a	09 54	09 55	10 10	10 25	10 40	10 55	11 10	11 25	11 40	11 55	12 10	12 25	12 40	12 55	13 10	13 25	13 40	13 55	14 10	14 25	14 40	14 55
London Cannon Street ⊖ a																						
London Waterloo (East) ⊖ a	09 58	09 59	10 15	10 29	10 45	10 59	11 15	11 29	11 45	11 59	12 15	12 29	12 45	12 59	13 15	13 29	13 45	13 59	14 15	14 29	14 45	14 59
London Charing Cross ⊖ a	10 02	10 03	10 19	10 33	10 49	11 03	11 19	11 33	11 49	12 03	12 19	12 33	12 49	13 03	13 19	13 33	13 49	14 03	14 19	14 33	14 49	15 03

	SE	SE	SE	SE	SE	SE	SE	SE	SE	SE	SE	SE	SE	SE	SE	SE	SE	SE	SE	SE	SE
Ore d																					
Hastings d		13 50		14 31		14 50		15 31		15 45		16 19		16 50		17 19		17 50		18 19	
St Leonards Warrior Sq d		13 53		14 34		14 53		15 34		15 48		16 21		16 53		17 22		17 53		18 22	
West St Leonards d		13 56				14 56				15 51		16 25		16 56		17 25		17 56		18 25	
Crowhurst d		14 02				15 02				15 57		16 30		17 02		17 31		18 02		18 31	
Battle d		14 06		14 44		15 06		15 44		16 01		16 34		17 06		17 35		18 06		18 35	
Robertsbridge d		14 13				15 13				16 08		16 41		17 13		17 42		18 13		18 42	
Etchingham d		14 17				15 17				16 12		16 45		17 17		17 46		18 17		18 46	
Stonegate d		14 23				15 23				16 17		16 50		17 23		17 52		18 23		18 51	
Wadhurst d		14 29		15 00		15 29		16 00		16 24		16 57		17 29		17 59		18 29		18 58	
Frant d		14 33				15 33				16 28		17 01		17 33		18 03		18 33		19 02	
Tunbridge Wells a		14 38		15 07		15 38		16 07		16 33		17 06		17 38		18 08		18 39		19 07	
Tunbridge Wells d	14 21	14 39	14 51	15 09	15 21	15 39	15 51	16 09	16 21	16 36	16 51	17 06	17 21	17 39	17 49	18 13	18 19	18 39	18 51	19 09	19 21
High Brooms d	14 24	14 42	14 54	15 12	15 24	15 42	15 54	16 12	16 24	16 39	16 55	17 10	17 24	17 42	17 52	18 16	18 22	18 42	18 54	19 12	19 24
Tonbridge a	14 30	14 48	15 00	15 18	15 30	15 48	16 00	16 18	16 30	16 46	17 01	17 16	17 30	17 49	17 59	18 22	18 28	18 50	19 00	19 18	19 30
Sevenoaks a	14 43	14 58	15 13	15 28	15 43	15 58	16 13	16 28	16 43	16 58	17 13	17 28	17 43	17 58	18 13	18 31	18 43	18 59	19 13	19 28	19 43
Orpington a	14 53	15 08	15 23	15 38	15 53	16 07	16 24	16 38	16 53	17 08	17 23	17 38	17 53	18 08	18 23		18 53	19 08	19 23	19 38	19 53
London Bridge ⊖ a	15 10	15 25	15 40	15 55	16 11	16 25	16 42	16 56	17 11	17 27	17 41	17 58	18 09	18 25	18 40	18 55	19 10	19 25	19 40	19 54	20 10
London Cannon Street ⊖ a										17 32											
London Waterloo (East) ⊖ a	15 15	15 29	15 45	15 59	16 16	16 29	16 48	17 00	17 16		17 46	18 02	18 14	18 29	18 45	18 59	19 14	19 29	19 45	19 59	20 15
London Charing Cross ⊖ a	15 19	15 33	15 49	16 03	16 20	16 33	16 52	17 04	17 20		17 50	18 06	18 18	18 35	18 49	19 04	19 18	19 33	19 49	20 03	20 19

A 🚌 from Hastings
B 🚌 from Tunbridge Wells
C from 21 May until 27 July
D until 18 May

Table 206

Hastings and Tunbridge Wells - Tonbridge and London

Mondays to Fridays
until 27 July, 13 Aug to 28 Aug and from 10 Sep

Network Diagram - see first Page of Table 206

Station		SE	SE	SE	SE	SE	SE	SE	SE	SE	SE	SE	SE
Ore	d												
Hastings	d	18 46			19 50			20 50			21 50	22 10	
St Leonards Warrior Sq	d	18 49			19 53			20 53			21 53	22 13	
West St Leonards	d	18 52			19 56			20 56			21 56	22 16	
Crowhurst	d	18 58			20 02			21 02			22 02	22 22	
Battle	d	19 02			20 06			21 06			22 06	22 26	
Robertsbridge	d	19 09			20 14			21 14			22 14	22 33	
Etchingham	d	19 12			20 17			21 17			22 17	22 37	
Stonegate	d	19 18			20 23			21 23			22 23	22 42	
Wadhurst	d	19 24			20 29			21 29			22 29	22 49	
Frant	d	19 28			20 33			21 33			22 33	22 53	
Tunbridge Wells	a	19 33			20 38			21 38			22 38	22 58	
	d	19 38	19 51	20 21	20 39	20 51	21 21	21 39	21 51	22 21	22 39	22 59	23 33
High Brooms	d	19 41	19 54	20 24	20 42	20 54	21 24	21 42	21 54	22 24	22 42	23 02	23 36
Tonbridge	a	19 47	20 00	20 30	20 48	21 00	21 30	21 48	22 00	22 30	22 48	23 08	23 42
Sevenoaks	a	19 59	20 13	20 43	20 58	21 13	21 43	21 58	22 13	22 41	22 58	23 24	
Orpington	a	20 08	20 23	20 52	21 08	21 22	21 52	22 08	22 22	22 52	23 08	23 36	
London Bridge ⊖	a	20 24	20 39	21 08	21 24	21 38	22 08	22 24	22 38	23 08	23 24	23 54	
London Cannon Street ⊖	a												
London Waterloo (East) ⊖	a	20 29	20 44	21 13	21 29	21 43	22 13	22 29	22 43	23 13	23 29	23 59	
London Charing Cross ⊖	a	20 33	20 48	21 18	21 33	21 48	22 18	22 33	22 48	23 18	23 33	00 03	

Mondays to Fridays
30 July to 10 August

Station		SE	SE	SE	SE	SE	SE	SE	SE	SE	SE	SE A ⌶	SE B ⌶	SE	SE	SE	SE	SE	SE	SE	SE	SE	SE
Ore	d											06 12			06 37						07 40		
Hastings	d	22p10			05 17		05 37	05 48		06 03		06 20	06 28		06 41		07 01		07 25		07 44		08 14
St Leonards Warrior Sq	d	22p13			05 20		05 40	05 51		06 06		06 23	06 31		06 44		07 04		07 28		07 47		08 17
West St Leonards	d	22p16			05 23		05 43			06 09			06 34		06 47		07 07		07 31		07 50		08 20
Crowhurst	d	22p22			05 29		05 49			06 15			06 40		06 53		07 13		07 37		07 56		08 26
Battle	d	22p26			05 33		05 53	06 01		06 19		06 33	06 44		06 57		07 17		07 41		08 00		08 30
Robertsbridge	d	22p33			05 40		06 00			06 27		06 40			07 05		07 25		07 48		08 07		08 38
Etchingham	d	22p37			05 44		06 04	06 10		06 31		06 44	06 53		07 09		07 29		07 52		08 11		08 42
Stonegate	d	22p42			05 49		06 09			06 36		06 50			07 14		07 34		07 57		08 17		08 47
Wadhurst	d	22p49			05 56		06 16	06 21		06 43		06 57	07 04		07 21		07 41		08 04		08 24		08 54
Frant	d	22p53			06 00		06 20			06 47		07 01			07 25		07 45		08 08		08 28		08 58
Tunbridge Wells	a	22p58			06 06		06 25	06 29		06 53		07 06	07 11		07 31		07 51		08 13		08 33		09 03
	d	22p59	05 21	05 50	06 09	06 21	06 34		06 40	06 56	07 00	07 16		07 20	07 36	07 40	07 56	08 00	08 18	08 25	08 40	08 51	09 09
High Brooms	d	23p02	05 24	05 53	06 12	06 24	06 37		06 44	07 00	07 04	07 20		07 24	07 40	07 44	08 00	08 04	08 22	08 28	08 43	08 54	09 12
Tonbridge	a	23p08	05 30	05 59	06 18	06 30	06 44		06 50		07 10			07 30		07 50		08 10		08 34	08 49	09 00	09 18
Sevenoaks	a	23p24	05 42	06 10	06 30	06 43	06 52		07 02		07 22			07 42		08 02		08 22		08 45	08 58	09 13	09 28
Orpington	a	23p36	05 53	06 19		06 53	07 02		07 13												09 08	09 24	09 38
London Bridge ⊖	a	23p54	06 09	06 38	06 54	07 09	07 22		07 29		07 50			08 09	08 24	08 29		08 49	09 03	09 11	09 26	09 40	09 55
London Cannon Street ⊖	a			06 42			07 29								08 30				09 10				
London Waterloo (East) ⊖	a	23p59	06 14		06 59	07 14			07 34	07 44	07 55	08 04		08 14		08 34	08 44	08 54		09 16	09 31	09 45	09 59
London Charing Cross ⊖	a	00 03	06 18		07 05	07 20			07 40	07 50	08 01	08 08		08 20		08 40	08 50	09 00		09 22	09 37	09 51	10 03

Station		SE	SE	SE	SE	SE	SE	SE	SE	SE	SE	SE	SE	SE	SE	SE	SE	SE	SE	SE	SE	SE	SE
Ore	d																						
Hastings	d		08 47		09 29		09 50		10 31		10 50		11 31		11 50		12 31		12 50		13 31		13 50
St Leonards Warrior Sq	d		08 50		09 32		09 53		10 34		10 53		11 34		11 53		12 34		12 53		13 34		13 53
West St Leonards	d		08 53				09 56				10 56				11 56				12 56				13 56
Crowhurst	d		08 58				10 02				11 02				12 02				13 02				14 02
Battle	d		09 02		09 42		10 06		10 44		11 06		11 44		12 06		12 44		13 06		13 44		14 06
Robertsbridge	d		09 09				10 13				11 13				12 13				13 13				14 13
Etchingham	d		09 13				10 17				11 17				12 17				13 17				14 17
Stonegate	d		09 18				10 23				11 23				12 23				13 23				14 23
Wadhurst	d		09 25		09 58		10 30		11 00		11 29		12 00		12 29		13 00		13 29		14 00		14 29
Frant	d		09 29				10 34				11 33				12 33				13 33				14 33
Tunbridge Wells	a		09 34		10 05		10 39		11 07		11 38		12 07		12 38		13 07		13 38		14 07		14 38
	d	09 21	09 39	09 51	10 09	10 21	10 39	10 51	11 09	11 21	11 39	11 51	12 09	12 21	12 39	12 51	13 09	13 21	13 39	13 51	14 09	14 21	14 39
High Brooms	d	09 24	09 42	09 54	10 12	10 24	10 43	10 54	11 12	11 24	11 42	11 54	12 12	12 24	12 42	12 54	13 12	13 24	13 42	13 54	14 12	14 24	14 42
Tonbridge	a	09 30	09 48	10 00	10 18	10 30	10 49	11 00	11 18	11 30	11 48	12 00	12 18	12 30	12 48	13 00	13 18	13 30	13 48	14 00	14 18	14 30	14 48
Sevenoaks	a	09 43	09 58	10 13	10 28	10 43	10 58	11 13	11 28	11 43	11 58	12 13	12 28	12 43	12 58	13 13	13 28	13 43	13 58	14 13	14 28	14 43	14 58
Orpington	a	09 53	10 08	10 23	10 38	10 53	11 08	11 23	11 38	11 53	12 08	12 23	12 38	12 53	13 08	13 23	13 38	13 53	14 08	14 23	14 38	14 53	15 08
London Bridge ⊖	a	10 10	10 25	10 40	10 55	11 10	11 25	11 40	11 55	12 10	12 25	12 40	12 55	13 10	13 25	13 40	13 55	14 10	14 25	14 40	14 55	15 10	15 25
London Cannon Street ⊖	a																						
London Waterloo (East) ⊖	a	10 15	10 29	10 45	10 59	11 15	11 30	11 45	11 59	12 15	12 29	12 45	12 59	13 15	13 29	13 45	13 59	14 15	14 29	14 45	14 59	15 15	15 29
London Charing Cross ⊖	a	10 19	10 33	10 49	11 03	11 19	11 34	11 49	12 03	12 19	12 33	12 49	13 03	13 19	13 33	13 49	14 03	14 19	14 33	14 49	15 03	15 19	15 33

A ⌶ from Hastings
B ⌶ from Tunbridge Wells

Table 206

Hastings and Tunbridge Wells - Tonbridge and London

Mondays to Fridays
30 July to 10 August

Network Diagram - see first Page of Table 206

Station		SE	SE	SE	SE	SE	SE	SE	SE	SE	SE	SE	SE	SE	SE	SE	SE	SE	SE	SE	SE	SE
Ore	d																					
Hastings	d		14 31		14 50		15 31		15 45		16 19		16 50		17 19		17 50		18 19		18 46	
St Leonards Warrior Sq	d		14 34		14 53		15 34		15 48		16 21		16 53		17 22		17 53		18 22		18 49	
West St Leonards	d				14 56				15 51		16 25		16 56		17 25		17 56		18 25		18 52	
Crowhurst	d				15 02				15 57		16 30		17 02		17 31		18 02		18 31		18 58	
Battle	d		14 44		15 06		15 44		16 01		16 34		17 06		17 35		18 06		18 35		19 02	
Robertsbridge	d				15 13				16 08		16 41		17 13		17 42		18 13		18 42		19 09	
Etchingham	d				15 17				16 12		16 45		17 17		17 46		18 17		18 46		19 12	
Stonegate	d				15 23				16 17		16 50		17 23		17 52		18 23		18 51		19 18	
Wadhurst	d		15 00		15 29		16 00		16 24		16 57		17 29		17 59		18 29		18 58		19 24	
Frant	d				15 33				16 28		17 01		17 33		18 03		18 33		19 02		19 28	
Tunbridge Wells	a		15 07		15 38		16 07		16 33		17 06		17 38		18 08		18 39		19 07		19 33	
	d	14 51	15 09	15 21	15 39	15 51	16 09	16 21	16 36	16 51	17 06	17 21	17 39	17 49	18 13	18 19	18 39	18 51	19 09	19 21	19 38	19 51
High Brooms	d	14 54	15 12	15 24	15 42	15 54	16 12	16 24	16 39	16 55	17 10	17 24	17 42	17 52	18 16	18 22	18 42	18 54	19 12	19 24	19 41	19 54
Tonbridge	a	15 00	15 18	15 30	15 48	16 00	16 18	16 30	16 46	17 01	17 16	17 30	17 49	17 59	18 22	18 28	18 50	19 00	19 18	19 30	19 47	20 00
Sevenoaks	a	15 13	15 28	15 43	15 58	16 13	16 28	16 43	16 58	17 13	17 28	17 43	17 58	18 13	18 31	18 43	18 59	19 13	19 28	19 43	19 59	20 13
Orpington	a	15 23	15 38	15 53	16 07	16 24	16 38	16 53	17 08	17 23	17 38	17 53	18 08	18 23		18 53	19 08	19 23	19 38	19 53	20 08	20 23
London Bridge ⊖	a	15 40	15 55	16 11	16 25	16 42	16 56	17 11	17 27	17 41	17 58	18 09	18 25	18 40	18 55	19 10	19 25	19 40	19 54	20 10	20 24	20 39
London Cannon Street ⊖	a								17 32													
London Waterloo (East) ⊖	a	15 45	15 59	16 16	16 29	16 48	17 00	17 16		17 46	18 02	18 14	18 29	18 45	18 59	19 14	19 29	19 45	19 59	20 15	20 29	20 44
London Charing Cross ⊖	a	15 49	16 03	16 20	16 33	16 52	17 04	17 20		17 50	18 06	18 18	18 35	18 49	19 04	19 18	19 33	19 49	20 03	20 19	20 33	20 48

Station		SE	SE	SE	SE	SE	SE	SE	SE	SE	SE
Ore	d										
Hastings	d		19 50			20 50			21 50	22 10	
St Leonards Warrior Sq	d		19 53			20 53			21 53	22 13	
West St Leonards	d		19 56			20 56			21 56	22 16	
Crowhurst	d		20 02			21 02			22 02	22 22	
Battle	d		20 06			21 06			22 06	22 26	
Robertsbridge	d		20 14			21 14			22 14	22 33	
Etchingham	d		20 17			21 17			22 17	22 37	
Stonegate	d		20 23			21 23			22 23	22 42	
Wadhurst	d		20 29			21 29			22 29	22 49	
Frant	d		20 33			21 33			22 33	22 53	
Tunbridge Wells	a		20 38			21 38			22 38	22 58	
	d	20 21	20 39	20 51	21 21	21 39	21 51	22 21	22 39	22 59	23 33
High Brooms	d	20 24	20 42	20 54	21 24	21 42	21 54	22 24	22 42	23 02	23 36
Tonbridge	a	20 30	20 48	21 00	21 30	21 48	22 00	22 30	22 48	23 08	23 42
Sevenoaks	a	20 43	20 58	21 13	21 43	21 58	22 13	22 41	22 58	23 24	
Orpington	a	20 52	21 08	21 22	21 52	22 08	22 22	22 52	23 08	23 36	
London Bridge ⊖	a	21 08	21 24	21 38	22 08	22 24	22 38	23 08	23 24	23 54	
London Cannon Street ⊖	a										
London Waterloo (East) ⊖	a	21 13	21 29	21 43	22 13	22 29	22 43	23 13	23 29	23 59	
London Charing Cross ⊖	a	21 18	21 33	21 48	22 18	22 33	22 48	23 18	23 33	00 03	

Mondays to Fridays
29 August to 7 September

Station		SE A	SE	SE	SE	SE	SE	SE	SE	SE	SE	SE B ⌶	SE C ⌶	SE	SE B ⌶	SE	SE	SE	SE	SE	SE	SE	SE
Ore	d											06 12			06 37						07 40		
Hastings	d	22p10			05 17		05 37	05 48		06 03		06 20	06 28		06 41		07 01		07 25		07 44		08 14
St Leonards Warrior Sq	d	22p13			05 20		05 40	05 51		06 06		06 23	06 31		06 44		07 04		07 28		07 47		08 17
West St Leonards	d	22p16			05 23		05 43			06 09			06 34		06 47		07 07		07 31		07 50		08 20
Crowhurst	d	22p22			05 29		05 49			06 15			06 40		06 53		07 13		07 37		07 56		08 26
Battle	d	22p26			05 33		05 53	06 01		06 19		06 33	06 44		06 57		07 17		07 41		08 00		08 30
Robertsbridge	d	22p33			05 40		06 00			06 27		06 40			07 05		07 25		07 48		08 07		08 38
Etchingham	d	22p37			05 44		06 04	06 10		06 31		06 44	06 53		07 09		07 29		07 52		08 11		08 42
Stonegate	d	22p42			05 49		06 09			06 36		06 50			07 14		07 34		07 57		08 17		08 47
Wadhurst	d	22p49			05 56		06 16	06 21		06 43		06 57	07 04		07 21		07 41		08 04		08 24		08 54
Frant	d	22p53			06 00		06 20			06 47		07 01			07 25		07 45		08 08		08 28		08 58
Tunbridge Wells	a	22p58			06 06		06 25	06 29		06 53		07 06	07 11		07 31		07 51		08 13		08 33		09 03
	d	22p59	05 21	05 50	06 09	06 21	06 34		06 40	06 56	07 00	07 16		07 20	07 36	07 40	07 56	08 00	08 18	08 25	08 40	08 51	09 09
High Brooms	d	23p02	05 24	05 53	06 12	06 24	06 37		06 44	07 00	07 04	07 20		07 24	07 40	07 44	08 00	08 04	08 22	08 28	08 43	08 54	09 12
Tonbridge	a	23p08	05 30	05 59	06 18	06 30	06 44		06 50		07 10			07 30		07 50		08 10		08 34	08 49	09 00	09 18
Sevenoaks	a	23p24	05 42	06 10	06 30	06 43	06 52		07 02		07 22			07 42		08 02		08 22		08 45	08 58	09 13	09 28
Orpington	a	23p36	05 53	06 19		06 53	07 02		07 13												09 08	09 24	09 38
London Bridge ⊖	a	23p54	06 09	06 38	06 54	07 09	07 22		07 29		07 50			08 09	08 24	08 29		08 49	09 03	09 11	09 26	09 40	09 55
London Cannon Street ⊖	a			06 42			07 29								08 30				09 10				
London Waterloo (East) ⊖	a	23p59	06 14		06 59	07 14			07 34	07 44	07 55	08 04		08 14		08 34	08 44	08 54		09 16	09 31	09 45	09 59
London Charing Cross ⊖	a	00 03	06 18		07 05	07 20			07 40	07 50	08 01	08 08		08 20		08 40	08 50	09 00		09 22	09 37	09 51	10 03

A not 3 September
B ⌶ from Hastings
C ⌶ from Tunbridge Wells

Table 206

Mondays to Fridays

29 August to 7 September

Hastings and Tunbridge Wells - Tonbridge and London

Network Diagram - see first Page of Table 206

		SE 1	SE 1	SE 1	SE 1	SE 1	SE 1	SE 1	SE 1	SE 1	SE 1	SE 1	SE 1	SE 1	SE 1	SE 1	SE 1	SE 1	SE 1	SE 1	SE 1	SE 1	SE 1
Ore	d																						
Hastings 4	d		08 47		09 29		09 50		10 31		10 50		11 31		11 50		12 31		12 50		13 31		13 50
St Leonards Warrior Sq 4	d		08 50		09 32		09 53		10 34		10 53		11 34		11 53		12 34		12 53		13 34		13 53
West St Leonards	d		08 53				09 56				10 56				11 56				12 56				13 56
Crowhurst	d		08 58				10 02				11 02				12 02				13 02				14 02
Battle	d		09 02		09 42		10 06		10 44		11 06		11 44		12 06		12 44		13 06		13 44		14 06
Robertsbridge	d		09 09				10 13				11 13				12 13				13 13				14 13
Etchingham	d		09 13				10 17				11 17				12 17				13 17				14 17
Stonegate	d		09 18				10 23				11 23				12 23				13 23				14 23
Wadhurst	d		09 25		09 58		10 30		11 00		11 29		12 00		12 29		13 00		13 29		14 00		14 29
Frant	d		09 29				10 34				11 33				12 33				13 33				14 33
Tunbridge Wells 4	a		09 34		10 05		10 39		11 07		11 38		12 07		12 38		13 07		13 38		14 07		14 38
	d	09 21	09 39	09 51	10 09	10 21	10 39	10 51	11 09	11 21	11 39	11 51	12 09	12 21	12 39	12 51	13 09	13 21	13 39	13 51	14 09	14 21	14 39
High Brooms	d	09 24	09 42	09 54	10 12	10 24	10 43	10 54	11 12	11 24	11 42	11 54	12 12	12 24	12 42	12 54	13 12	13 24	13 42	13 54	14 12	14 24	14 42
Tonbridge 4	a	09 30	09 48	10 00	10 18	10 30	10 49	11 00	11 18	11 30	11 48	12 00	12 18	12 30	12 48	13 00	13 18	13 30	13 48	14 00	14 18	14 30	14 48
Sevenoaks 4	a	09 43	09 58	10 13	10 28	10 43	10 58	11 13	11 28	11 43	11 58	12 13	12 28	12 43	12 58	13 13	13 28	13 43	13 58	14 13	14 28	14 43	14 58
Orpington 4	a	09 53	10 08	10 23	10 38	10 53	11 08	11 23	11 38	11 53	12 08	12 23	12 38	12 53	13 08	13 23	13 38	13 53	14 08	14 23	14 38	14 53	15 08
London Bridge 4 ⊖	a	10 10	10 25	10 40	10 55	11 10	11 25	11 40	11 55	12 10	12 25	12 40	12 55	13 10	13 25	13 40	13 55	14 10	14 25	14 40	14 55	15 10	15 25
London Cannon Street 4 ⊖	a																						
London Waterloo (East) 4 ⊖	a	10 15	10 29	10 45	10 59	11 15	11 29	11 45	11 59	12 15	12 29	12 45	12 59	13 15	13 29	13 45	13 59	14 15	14 29	14 45	14 59	15 15	15 29
London Charing Cross 4 ⊖	a	10 19	10 33	10 49	11 03	11 19	11 33	11 49	12 03	12 19	12 33	12 49	13 03	13 19	13 33	13 49	14 03	14 19	14 33	14 49	15 03	15 19	15 33

		SE 1	SE 1	SE 1	SE 1	SE 1	SE 1	SE 1	SE 1	SE 1	SE 1	SE 1	SE 1	SE 1	SE 1	SE 1	SE 1	SE 1	SE 1	SE 1	SE 1	SE 1
Ore	d																					
Hastings 4	d		14 31		14 50		15 31		15 45		16 19		16 50		17 19		17 50		18 19		18 46	
St Leonards Warrior Sq 4	d		14 34		14 53		15 34		15 48		16 21		16 53		17 22		17 53		18 22		18 49	
West St Leonards	d				14 56				15 51		16 25		16 56		17 25		17 56		18 25		18 52	
Crowhurst	d				15 02				15 57		16 30		17 02		17 31		18 02		18 31		18 58	
Battle	d		14 44		15 06		15 44		16 01		16 34		17 06		17 35		18 06		18 35		19 02	
Robertsbridge	d				15 13				16 08		16 41		17 13		17 42		18 13		18 42		19 09	
Etchingham	d				15 17				16 12		16 45		17 17		17 46		18 17		18 46		19 12	
Stonegate	d				15 23				16 17		16 50		17 23		17 52		18 23		18 51		19 18	
Wadhurst	d		15 00		15 29		16 00		16 24		16 57		17 29		17 59		18 29		18 58		19 24	
Frant	d				15 33				16 28		17 01		17 33		18 03		18 33		19 02		19 28	
Tunbridge Wells 4	a		15 07		15 38		16 07		16 33		17 06		17 38		18 08		18 39		19 07		19 33	
	d	14 51	15 09	15 21	15 39	15 51	16 09	16 21	16 36	16 51	17 06	17 21	17 39	17 49	18 13	18 19	18 39	18 51	19 09	19 21	19 38	19 51
High Brooms	d	14 54	15 12	15 24	15 42	15 54	16 12	16 24	16 39	16 55	17 10	17 24	17 42	17 52	18 16	18 22	18 42	18 54	19 12	19 24	19 41	19 54
Tonbridge 4	a	15 00	15 18	15 30	15 48	16 00	16 18	16 30	16 46	17 01	17 16	17 30	17 49	17 59	18 22	18 28	18 50	19 00	19 18	19 30	19 47	20 00
Sevenoaks 4	a	15 13	15 28	15 43	15 58	16 13	16 28	16 43	16 58	17 13	17 28	17 43	17 58	18 13	18 31	18 43	18 59	19 13	19 28	19 43	19 59	20 13
Orpington 4	a	15 23	15 38	15 53	16 07	16 24	16 38	16 53	17 08	17 23	17 38	17 53	18 08	18 23		18 53	19 08	19 23	19 38	19 53	20 08	20 23
London Bridge 4 ⊖	a	15 40	15 55	16 11	16 25	16 42	16 56	17 11	17 27	17 41	17 58	18 09	18 25	18 40	18 55	19 10	19 25	19 40	19 54	20 10	20 24	20 39
London Cannon Street 4 ⊖	a								17 32													
London Waterloo (East) 4 ⊖	a	15 45	15 59	16 16	16 29	16 48	17 00	17 16		17 46	18 02	18 14	18 29	18 45	18 59	19 14	19 29	19 45	19 59	20 15	20 29	20 44
London Charing Cross 4 ⊖	a	15 49	16 03	16 20	16 33	16 52	17 04	17 20		17 50	18 06	18 18	18 35	18 49	19 04	19 18	19 33	19 49	20 03	20 19	20 33	20 48

		SE 1	SE 1	SE 1	SE 1	SE 1	SE 1	SE 1	SE 1	SE 1	SE 1
Ore	d										
Hastings 4	d		19 50			20 50			21 50	22 10	
St Leonards Warrior Sq 4	d		19 53			20 53			21 53	22 13	
West St Leonards	d		19 56			20 56			21 56	22 16	
Crowhurst	d		20 02			21 02			22 02	22 22	
Battle	d		20 06			21 06			22 06	22 26	
Robertsbridge	d		20 14			21 14			22 14	22 33	
Etchingham	d		20 17			21 17			22 17	22 37	
Stonegate	d		20 23			21 23			22 23	22 42	
Wadhurst	d		20 29			21 29			22 29	22 49	
Frant	d		20 33			21 33			22 33	22 53	
Tunbridge Wells 4	a		20 38			21 38			22 38	22 58	
	d	20 21	20 39	20 51	21 21	21 39	21 51	22 21	22 39	22 59	23 33
High Brooms	d	20 24	20 42	20 54	21 24	21 42	21 54	22 24	22 42	23 02	23 36
Tonbridge 4	a	20 30	20 48	21 00	21 30	21 48	22 00	22 30	22 48	23 08	23 42
Sevenoaks 4	a	20 43	20 58	21 13	21 43	21 58	22 13	22 41	22 58	23 24	
Orpington 4	a	20 52	21 08	21 22	21 52	22 08	22 22	22 52	23 08	23 36	
London Bridge 4 ⊖	a	21 08	21 24	21 38	22 08	22 24	22 38	23 08	23 24	23 54	
London Cannon Street 4 ⊖	a										
London Waterloo (East) 4 ⊖	a	21 13	21 29	21 43	22 13	22 29	22 43	23 13	23 29	23 59	
London Charing Cross 4 ⊖	a	21 18	21 33	21 48	22 18	22 33	22 48	23 18	23 33	00 03	

Table 206

Saturdays

until 21 July, 18 Aug and from 15 Sep

Hastings and Tunbridge Wells - Tonbridge and London

Network Diagram - see first Page of Table 206

		SE 1	SE	SE 1	SE 1	SE 1	SE 1	SE 1	SE 1	SE 1	SE 1	SE 1	SE 1	SE 1	SE 1	SE 1	SE 1	SE 1	SE 1	SE 1	SE 1	SE 1	SE 1
Ore	d																						
Hastings 4	d	22p10		05 50	06 20		06 50		07 20		07 50		08 20		08 50		09 31		09 50		10 31		10 50
St Leonards Warrior Sq 4	d	22p13		05 53	06 23		06 53		07 23		07 53		08 23		08 53		09 34		09 53		10 34		10 53
West St Leonards	d	22p16		05 56	06 26		06 56		07 26		07 56		08 26		08 56				09 56				10 56
Crowhurst	d	22p22		06 02	06 32		07 02		07 32		08 02		08 32		09 02				10 02				11 02
Battle	d	22p26		06 06	06 36		07 06		07 36		08 06		08 36		09 06		09 44		10 06		10 44		11 06
Robertsbridge	d	22p33		06 13	06 43		07 13		07 44		08 13		08 44		09 14				10 13				11 13
Etchingham	d	22p37		06 17	06 47		07 17		07 47		08 17		08 47		09 17				10 17				11 17
Stonegate	d	22p42		06 23	06 53		07 23		07 53		08 23		08 53		09 23				10 23				11 23
Wadhurst	d	22p49		06 29	06 59		07 29		07 59		08 29		08 59		09 29		10 00		10 29		11 00		11 29
Frant	d	22p53		06 33	07 03		07 33		08 03		08 33		09 03		09 33				10 33				11 33
Tunbridge Wells 4	a	22p58		06 38	07 08		07 38		08 08		08 38		09 08		09 38		10 07		10 38		11 07		11 38
	d	22p59	05 48	06 39	07 09	07 21	07 39	07 51	08 09	08 21	08 39	08 51	09 09	09 21	09 39	09 51	10 09	10 21	10 39	10 51	11 09	11 21	11 39
High Brooms	d	23p02	05 51	06 42	07 12	07 24	07 42	07 54	08 12	08 24	08 42	08 54	09 12	09 24	09 42	09 54	10 12	10 24	10 42	10 54	11 12	11 24	11 42
Tonbridge 4	a	23p08	05 57	06 48	07 18	07 30	07 48	08 00	08 18	08 30	08 48	09 00	09 18	09 30	09 48	10 00	10 18	10 30	10 48	11 00	11 18	11 30	11 48
Sevenoaks 4	a	23p24		06 58	07 28	07 43	07 58	08 13	08 28	08 43	08 58	09 13	09 28	09 43	09 58	10 13	10 28	10 43	10 58	11 13	11 28	11 43	11 58
Orpington 4	a	23p36		07 08	07 38	07 53	08 08	08 23	08 38	08 53	09 08	09 23	09 38	09 53	10 08	10 23	10 38	10 53	11 08	11 23	11 38	11 53	12 08
London Bridge 4 ⊖	a	23p54		07 24	07 55	08 10	08 25	08 40	08 55	09 10	09 25	09 40	09 55	10 10	10 25	10 40	10 55	11 10	11 25	11 40	11 55	12 10	12 25
London Cannon Street 4 ⊖	a																						
London Waterloo (East) 4 ⊖	a	23p59		07 29	07 59	08 15	08 29	08 45	08 59	09 15	09 29	09 45	09 59	10 15	10 29	10 45	10 59	11 15	11 29	11 45	11 59	12 15	12 29
London Charing Cross 4 ⊖	a	00 03		07 33	08 03	08 19	08 33	08 49	09 03	09 19	09 33	09 49	10 03	10 19	10 33	10 49	11 03	11 19	11 33	11 49	12 03	12 19	12 33

		SE 1	SE 1	SE 1	SE 1	SE 1	SE 1	SE 1	SE 1	SE 1	SE 1	SE 1	SE 1	SE 1	SE 1	SE 1	SE 1	SE 1	SE 1	SE 1	SE 1	SE 1	SE 1
Ore	d																						
Hastings 4	d		11 31		11 50		12 31		12 50		13 31		13 50		14 31		14 50		15 31		15 50		16 31
St Leonards Warrior Sq 4	d		11 34		11 53		12 34		12 53		13 34		13 53		14 34		14 53		15 34		15 53		16 34
West St Leonards	d				11 56				12 56				13 56				14 56				15 56		
Crowhurst	d				12 02				13 02				14 02				15 02				16 02		
Battle	d		11 44		12 06		12 44		13 06		13 44		14 06		14 44		15 06		15 44		16 06		16 44
Robertsbridge	d				12 13				13 13				14 13				15 13				16 13		
Etchingham	d				12 17				13 17				14 17				15 17				16 17		
Stonegate	d				12 23				13 23				14 23				15 23				16 23		
Wadhurst	d		12 00		12 29		13 00		13 29		14 00		14 29		15 00		15 29		16 00		16 29		17 00
Frant	d				12 33				13 33				14 33				15 33				16 33		
Tunbridge Wells 4	a		12 07		12 38		13 07		13 38		14 07		14 38		15 07		15 38		16 07		16 38		17 07
	d	11 51	12 09	12 21	12 39	12 51	13 09	13 21	13 39	13 51	14 09	14 21	14 39	14 51	15 09	15 21	15 39	15 51	16 09	16 21	16 39	16 51	17 09
High Brooms	d	11 54	12 12	12 24	12 42	12 54	13 12	13 24	13 42	13 54	14 12	14 24	14 42	14 54	15 12	15 24	15 42	15 54	16 12	16 24	16 42	16 54	17 12
Tonbridge 4	a	12 00	12 18	12 30	12 48	13 00	13 18	13 30	13 48	14 00	14 18	14 30	14 48	15 00	15 18	15 30	15 48	16 00	16 18	16 30	16 48	17 00	17 18
Sevenoaks 4	a	12 13	12 28	12 43	12 58	13 13	13 28	13 43	13 58	14 13	14 28	14 43	14 58	15 13	15 28	15 43	15 58	16 13	16 28	16 43	16 58	17 13	17 28
Orpington 4	a	12 23	12 38	12 53	13 08	13 23	13 38	13 53	14 08	14 23	14 38	14 53	15 08	15 23	15 38	15 53	16 08	16 23	16 38	16 53	17 08	17 23	17 38
London Bridge 4 ⊖	a	12 40	12 55	13 10	13 25	13 40	13 55	14 10	14 25	14 40	14 55	15 10	15 25	15 40	15 55	16 10	16 25	16 40	16 55	17 10	17 25	17 40	17 55
London Cannon Street 4 ⊖	a																						
London Waterloo (East) 4 ⊖	a	12 45	12 59	13 15	13 29	13 45	13 59	14 15	14 29	14 45	14 59	15 15	15 29	15 45	15 59	16 15	16 29	16 45	16 59	17 15	17 29	17 45	17 59
London Charing Cross 4 ⊖	a	12 49	13 03	13 19	13 33	13 49	14 03	14 19	14 33	14 49	15 03	15 19	15 33	15 49	16 03	16 19	16 33	16 49	17 03	17 19	17 33	17 49	18 03

		SE 1	SE 1	SE 1	SE 1	SE 1	SE 1	SE 1	SE 1	SE 1	SE 1	SE 1	SE 1	SE 1	SE 1	SE 1	SE 1
Ore	d																
Hastings 4	d		16 50		17 20		17 50		18 50		19 50		20 50		21 50	22 10	
St Leonards Warrior Sq 4	d		16 53		17 23		17 53		18 53		19 53		20 53		21 53	22 13	
West St Leonards	d		16 56		17 26		17 56		18 56		19 56		20 56		21 56	22 16	
Crowhurst	d		17 02		17 32		18 02		19 02		20 02		21 02		22 02	22 22	
Battle	d		17 06		17 36		18 06		19 06		20 06		21 06		22 06	22 26	
Robertsbridge	d		17 13		17 44		18 13		19 13		20 13		21 13		22 13	22 33	
Etchingham	d		17 17		17 47		18 17		19 17		20 17		21 17		22 17	22 37	
Stonegate	d		17 23		17 53		18 23		19 23		20 23		21 23		22 23	22 42	
Wadhurst	d		17 29		17 59		18 29		19 29		20 29		21 29		22 29	22 49	
Frant	d		17 33		18 03		18 33		19 33		20 33		21 33		22 33	22 53	
Tunbridge Wells 4	a		17 38		18 08		18 38		19 38		20 38		21 38		22 38	22 58	
	d	17 21	17 39	17 51	18 09	18 21	18 39	19 08	19 39	20 08	20 39	21 05	21 39	22 05	22 39	22 59	23 33
High Brooms	d	17 24	17 42	17 54	18 12	18 24	18 42	19 11	19 42	20 11	20 42	21 08	21 42	22 08	22 42	23 02	23 36
Tonbridge 4	a	17 30	17 48	18 00	18 18	18 30	18 48	19 17	19 48	20 17	20 48	21 14	21 48	22 14	22 48	23 08	23 45
Sevenoaks 4	a	17 43	17 58	18 13	18 28	18 43	18 58	19 28	19 58	20 28	20 58	21 28	21 58	22 28	22 58	23 24	
Orpington 4	a	17 53	18 08	18 23	18 38	18 53	19 08	19 38	20 08	20 38	21 08	21 38	22 08	22 38	23 08	23 36	
London Bridge 4 ⊖	a	18 10	18 25	18 40	18 55	19 10	19 24	19 54	20 24	20 54	21 24	21 54	22 24	22 54	23 24	23 54	
London Cannon Street 4 ⊖	a																
London Waterloo (East) 4 ⊖	a	18 15	18 29	18 45	18 59	19 15	19 29	19 59	20 29	20 59	21 29	21 59	22 29	22 59	23 29	23 59	
London Charing Cross 4 ⊖	a	18 19	18 33	18 49	19 03	19 19	19 33	20 03	20 33	21 03	21 33	22 03	22 33	23 03	23 33	00 03	

Table 206

Saturdays
28 July to 11 August

Hastings and Tunbridge Wells - Tonbridge and London

Network Diagram - see first Page of Table 206

		SE ■	SE	SE ■	SE ■	SE ■	SE ■	SE ■	SE ■	SE ■	SE ■	SE ■	SE ■	SE ■	SE ■	SE ■	SE ■	SE ■	SE ■	SE ■	SE ■	SE ■	SE ■
Ore	d																						
Hastings ■	d	22p10		05 50	06 20		06 50		07 20		07 50		08 20		08 50		09 31		09 50		10 31		10 50
St Leonards Warrior Sq ■	d	22p13		05 53	06 23		06 53		07 23		07 53		08 23		08 53		09 34		09 53		10 34		10 53
West St Leonards	d	22p16		05 56	06 26		06 56		07 26		07 56		08 26		08 56				09 56				10 56
Crowhurst	d	22p22		06 02	06 32		07 02		07 32		08 02		08 32		09 02				10 02				11 02
Battle	d	22p26		06 06	06 36		07 06		07 36		08 06		08 36		09 06		09 44		10 06		10 44		11 06
Robertsbridge	d	22p33		06 13	06 43		07 13		07 44		08 13		08 44		09 14				10 13				11 13
Etchingham	d	22p37		06 17	06 47		07 17		07 47		08 17		08 47		09 17				10 17				11 17
Stonegate	d	22p42		06 23	06 53		07 23		07 53		08 23		08 53		09 23				10 23				11 23
Wadhurst	d	22p49		06 29	06 59		07 29		07 59		08 29		08 59		09 29		10 00		10 29		11 00		11 29
Frant	d	22p53		06 33	07 03		07 33		08 03		08 33		09 03		09 33				10 33				11 33
Tunbridge Wells ■	a	22p58		06 38	07 08		07 38		08 08		08 38		09 08		09 38		10 07		10 38		11 07		11 38
	d	22p59	05 48	06 39	07 09	07 21	07 39	07 51	08 09	08 21	08 39	08 51	09 09	09 21	09 39	09 51	10 09	10 21	10 39	10 51	11 09	11 21	11 39
High Brooms	d	23p02	05 51	06 42	07 12	07 24	07 42	07 54	08 12	08 24	08 42	08 54	09 12	09 24	09 42	09 54	10 12	10 24	10 42	10 54	11 12	11 24	11 42
Tonbridge ■	a	23p08	05 57	06 48	07 18	07 30	07 48	08 00	08 18	08 30	08 48	09 00	09 18	09 30	09 48	10 00	10 18	10 30	10 48	11 00	11 18	11 30	11 48
Sevenoaks ■	a	23p24		06 58	07 28	07 43	07 58	08 13	08 28	08 43	08 58	09 13	09 28	09 43	09 58	10 13	10 28	10 43	10 58	11 13	11 28	11 43	11 58
Orpington ■	a	23p36		07 08	07 38	07 53	08 08	08 23	08 38	08 53	09 08	09 23	09 38	09 53	10 08	10 23	10 38	10 53	11 08	11 23	11 38	11 53	12 08
London Bridge ■ ⊖	a	23p54		07 24	07 55	08 10	08 25	08 40	08 55	09 10	09 25	09 40	09 55	10 10	10 25	10 40	10 55	11 10	11 25	11 40	11 55	12 10	12 25
London Cannon Street ■ ⊖	a																						
London Waterloo (East) ■ ⊖	a	23p59		07 29	07 59	08 15	08 29	08 45	08 59	09 15	09 29	09 45	09 59	10 15	10 29	10 45	10 59	11 15	11 29	11 45	11 59	12 15	12 29
London Charing Cross ■ ⊖	a	00 03		07 33	08 03	08 19	08 33	08 49	09 03	09 19	09 33	09 49	10 03	10 19	10 33	10 49	11 03	11 19	11 33	11 49	12 03	12 19	12 33

		SE ■	SE ■	SE ■	SE ■	SE ■	SE ■	SE ■	SE ■	SE ■	SE ■	SE ■	SE ■	SE ■	SE ■	SE ■	SE ■	SE ■	SE ■	SE ■	SE ■	SE ■	SE ■
Ore	d																						
Hastings ■	d		11 31		11 50		12 31		12 50		13 31		13 50		14 31		14 50		15 31		15 50		16 31
St Leonards Warrior Sq ■	d		11 34		11 53		12 34		12 53		13 34		13 53		14 34		14 53		15 34		15 53		16 34
West St Leonards	d				11 56				12 56				13 56				14 56				15 56		
Crowhurst	d				12 02				13 02				14 02				15 02				16 02		
Battle	d		11 44		12 06		12 44		13 06		13 44		14 06		14 44		15 06		15 44		16 06		16 44
Robertsbridge	d				12 13				13 13				14 13				15 13				16 13		
Etchingham	d				12 17				13 17				14 17				15 17				16 17		
Stonegate	d				12 23				13 23				14 23				15 23				16 23		
Wadhurst	d		12 00		12 29		13 00		13 29		14 00		14 29		15 00		15 29		16 00		16 29		17 00
Frant	d				12 33				13 33				14 33				15 33				16 33		
Tunbridge Wells ■	a		12 07		12 38		13 07		13 38		14 07		14 38		15 07		15 38		16 07		16 38		17 07
	d	11 51	12 09	12 21	12 39	12 51	13 09	13 21	13 39	13 51	14 09	14 21	14 39	14 51	15 09	15 21	15 39	15 51	16 09	16 21	16 39	16 51	17 09
High Brooms	d	11 54	12 12	12 24	12 42	12 54	13 12	13 24	13 42	13 54	14 12	14 24	14 42	14 54	15 12	15 24	15 42	15 54	16 12	16 24	16 42	16 54	17 12
Tonbridge ■	a	12 00	12 18	12 30	12 48	13 00	13 18	13 30	13 48	14 00	14 18	14 30	14 48	15 00	15 18	15 30	15 48	16 00	16 18	16 30	16 48	17 00	17 18
Sevenoaks ■	a	12 13	12 28	12 43	12 58	13 13	13 28	13 43	13 58	14 13	14 28	14 43	14 58	15 13	15 28	15 43	15 58	16 13	16 28	16 43	16 58	17 13	17 28
Orpington ■	a	12 23	12 38	12 53	13 08	13 23	13 38	13 53	14 08	14 23	14 38	14 53	15 08	15 23	15 38	15 53	16 08	16 23	16 38	16 53	17 08	17 23	17 38
London Bridge ■ ⊖	a	12 40	12 55	13 10	13 25	13 40	13 55	14 10	14 25	14 40	14 55	15 10	15 25	15 40	15 55	16 10	16 25	16 40	16 55	17 10	17 25	17 40	17 55
London Cannon Street ■ ⊖	a																						
London Waterloo (East) ■ ⊖	a	12 45	12 59	13 15	13 29	13 45	13 59	14 15	14 29	14 45	14 59	15 15	15 29	15 45	15 59	16 15	16 29	16 45	16 59	17 15	17 29	17 45	17 59
London Charing Cross ■ ⊖	a	12 49	13 03	13 19	13 33	13 49	14 03	14 19	14 33	14 49	15 03	15 19	15 33	15 49	16 03	16 19	16 33	16 49	17 03	17 19	17 33	17 49	18 03

		SE ■	SE ■	SE ■	SE ■	SE ■	SE ■	SE ■	SE ■	SE ■	SE ■	SE ■	SE ■	SE ■	SE ■	SE ■	SE ■	SE ■
Ore	d																	
Hastings ■	d		16 50		17 20		17 50		18 50		19 50		20 50		21 50	22 10		22 45
St Leonards Warrior Sq ■	d		16 53		17 23		17 53		18 53		19 53		20 53		21 53	22 13		22 48
West St Leonards	d		16 56		17 26		17 56		18 56		19 56		20 56		21 56	22 16		22 51
Crowhurst	d		17 02		17 32		18 02		19 02		20 02		21 02		22 02	22 22		22 56
Battle	d		17 06		17 36		18 06		19 06		20 06		21 06		22 06	22 26		23 00
Robertsbridge	d		17 13		17 44		18 13		19 13		20 13		21 13		22 13	22 33		23 08
Etchingham	d		17 17		17 47		18 17		19 17		20 17		21 17		22 17	22 37		23 12
Stonegate	d		17 23		17 53		18 23		19 23		20 23		21 23		22 23	22 42		23 18
Wadhurst	d		17 29		17 59		18 29		19 29		20 29		21 29		22 29	22 49		23 24
Frant	d		17 33		18 03		18 33		19 33		20 33		21 33		22 33	22 53		23 28
Tunbridge Wells ■	a		17 38		18 08		18 38		19 38		20 38		21 38		22 38	22 58		23 34
	d	17 21	17 39	17 51	18 09	18 21	18 39	19 08	19 39	20 08	20 39	21 05	21 39	22 05	22 39	22 59	23 33	23 35
High Brooms	d	17 24	17 42	17 54	18 12	18 24	18 42	19 11	19 42	20 11	20 42	21 08	21 42	22 08	22 42	23 02	23 36	23 38
Tonbridge ■	a	17 30	17 48	18 00	18 18	18 30	18 48	19 17	19 48	20 17	20 48	21 14	21 48	22 14	22 48	23 08	23 45	23 45
Sevenoaks ■	a	17 43	17 58	18 13	18 28	18 43	18 58	19 28	19 58	20 28	20 58	21 28	21 58	22 28	22 58	23 24		
Orpington ■	a	17 53	18 08	18 23	18 38	18 53	19 08	19 38	20 08	20 38	21 08	21 38	22 08	22 38	23 08	23 36		
London Bridge ■ ⊖	a	18 10	18 25	18 40	18 55	19 10	19 24	19 54	20 24	20 54	21 24	21 54	22 24	22 54	23 24	23 54		
London Cannon Street ■ ⊖	a																	
London Waterloo (East) ■ ⊖	a	18 15	18 29	18 45	18 59	19 15	19 29	19 59	20 29	20 59	21 29	21 59	22 29	22 59	23 29	23 59		
London Charing Cross ■ ⊖	a	18 19	18 33	18 49	19 03	19 19	19 33	20 03	20 33	21 03	21 33	22 03	22 33	23 03	23 33	00 03		

Table 206

Saturdays
25 August to 8 September

Hastings and Tunbridge Wells - Tonbridge and London

Network Diagram - see first Page of Table 206

		SE ■	SE	SE ■	SE ■	SE ■	SE ■	SE ■	SE ■	SE ■	SE ■	SE ■	SE ■	SE ■	SE ■	SE ■	SE ■	SE ■	SE ■	SE ■	SE ■	SE ■	SE ■
Ore	d																						
Hastings ■	d	22p10		05 50	06 20		06 50		07 20		07 50		08 20		08 50		09 31		09 50		10 31		10 50
St Leonards Warrior Sq ■	d	22p13		05 53	06 23		06 53		07 23		07 53		08 23		08 53		09 34		09 53		10 34		10 53
West St Leonards	d	22p16		05 56	06 26		06 56		07 26		07 56		08 26		08 56				09 56				10 56
Crowhurst	d	22p22		06 02	06 32		07 02		07 32		08 02		08 32		09 02				10 02				11 02
Battle	d	22p26		06 06	06 36		07 06		07 36		08 06		08 36		09 06		09 44		10 06		10 44		11 06
Robertsbridge	d	22p33		06 13	06 43		07 13		07 44		08 13		08 44		09 14				10 13				11 13
Etchingham	d	22p37		06 17	06 47		07 17		07 47		08 17		08 47		09 17				10 17				11 17
Stonegate	d	22p42		06 23	06 53		07 23		07 53		08 23		08 53		09 23				10 23				11 23
Wadhurst	d	22p49		06 29	06 59		07 29		07 59		08 29		08 59		09 29		10 00		10 29		11 00		11 29
Frant	d	22p53		06 33	07 03		07 33		08 03		08 33		09 03		09 33				10 33				11 33
Tunbridge Wells ■	a	22p58		06 38	07 08		07 38		08 08		08 38		09 08		09 38		10 07		10 38		11 07		11 38
	d	22p59	05 48	06 39	07 09	07 21	07 39	07 51	08 09	08 21	08 39	08 51	09 09	09 21	09 39	09 51	10 09	10 21	10 39	10 51	11 09	11 21	11 39
High Brooms	d	23p02	05 51	06 42	07 12	07 24	07 42	07 54	08 12	08 24	08 42	08 54	09 12	09 24	09 42	09 54	10 12	10 24	10 42	10 54	11 12	11 24	11 42
Tonbridge ■	a	23p08	05 57	06 48	07 18	07 30	07 48	08 00	08 18	08 30	08 48	09 00	09 18	09 30	09 48	10 00	10 18	10 30	10 48	11 00	11 18	11 30	11 48
Sevenoaks ■	a	23p24		06 58	07 28	07 43	07 58	08 13	08 28	08 43	08 58	09 13	09 28	09 43	09 58	10 13	10 28	10 43	10 58	11 13	11 28	11 43	11 58
Orpington ■	a	23p36		07 08	07 38	07 53	08 08	08 23	08 38	08 53	09 08	09 23	09 38	09 53	10 08	10 23	10 38	10 53	11 08	11 23	11 38	11 53	12 08
London Bridge ■ ⊖	a	23p54		07 24	07 55	08 10	08 25	08 40	08 55	09 10	09 25	09 40	09 55	10 10	10 25	10 40	10 55	11 10	11 25	11 40	11 55	12 10	12 25
London Cannon Street ■ ⊖	a																						
London Waterloo (East) ■ ⊖	a	23p59		07 29	07 59	08 15	08 29	08 45	08 59	09 15	09 29	09 45	09 59	10 15	10 29	10 45	10 59	11 15	11 29	11 45	11 59	12 15	12 29
London Charing Cross ■ ⊖	a	00 03		07 33	08 03	08 19	08 33	08 49	09 03	09 19	09 33	09 49	10 03	10 19	10 33	10 49	11 03	11 19	11 33	11 49	12 03	12 19	12 33

		SE ■	SE ■	SE ■	SE ■	SE ■	SE ■	SE ■	SE ■	SE ■	SE ■	SE ■	SE ■	SE ■	SE ■	SE ■	SE ■	SE ■	SE ■	SE ■	SE ■	SE ■	SE ■
Ore	d																						
Hastings ■	d		11 31		11 50		12 31		12 50		13 31		13 50		14 31		14 50		15 31		15 50		16 31
St Leonards Warrior Sq ■	d		11 34		11 53		12 34		12 53		13 34		13 53		14 34		14 53		15 34		15 53		16 34
West St Leonards	d				11 56				12 56				13 56				14 56				15 56		
Crowhurst	d				12 02				13 02				14 02				15 02				16 02		
Battle	d		11 44		12 06		12 44		13 06		13 44		14 06		14 44		15 06		15 44		16 06		16 44
Robertsbridge	d				12 13				13 13				14 13				15 13				16 13		
Etchingham	d				12 17				13 17				14 17				15 17				16 17		
Stonegate	d				12 23				13 23				14 23				15 23				16 23		
Wadhurst	d		12 00		12 29		13 00		13 29		14 00		14 29		15 00		15 29		16 00		16 29		17 00
Frant	d				12 33				13 33				14 33				15 33				16 33		
Tunbridge Wells ■	a		12 07		12 38		13 07		13 38		14 07		14 38		15 07		15 38		16 07		16 38		17 07
	d	11 51	12 09	12 21	12 39	12 51	13 09	13 21	13 39	13 51	14 09	14 21	14 39	14 51	15 09	15 21	15 39	15 51	16 09	16 21	16 39	16 51	17 09
High Brooms	d	11 54	12 12	12 24	12 42	12 54	13 12	13 24	13 42	13 54	14 12	14 24	14 42	14 54	15 12	15 24	15 42	15 54	16 12	16 24	16 42	16 54	17 12
Tonbridge ■	a	12 00	12 18	12 30	12 48	13 00	13 18	13 30	13 48	14 00	14 18	14 30	14 48	15 00	15 18	15 30	15 48	16 00	16 18	16 30	16 48	17 00	17 18
Sevenoaks ■	a	12 13	12 28	12 43	12 58	13 13	13 28	13 43	13 58	14 13	14 28	14 43	14 58	15 13	15 28	15 43	15 58	16 13	16 28	16 43	16 58	17 13	17 28
Orpington ■	a	12 23	12 38	12 53	13 08	13 23	13 38	13 53	14 08	14 23	14 38	14 53	15 08	15 23	15 38	15 53	16 08	16 23	16 38	16 53	17 08	17 23	17 38
London Bridge ■ ⊖	a	12 40	12 55	13 10	13 25	13 40	13 55	14 10	14 25	14 40	14 55	15 10	15 25	15 40	15 55	16 10	16 25	16 40	16 55	17 10	17 25	17 40	17 55
London Cannon Street ■ ⊖	a																						
London Waterloo (East) ■ ⊖	a	12 45	12 59	13 15	13 29	13 45	13 59	14 15	14 29	14 45	14 59	15 15	15 29	15 45	15 59	16 15	16 29	16 45	16 59	17 15	17 29	17 45	17 59
London Charing Cross ■ ⊖	a	12 49	13 03	13 19	13 33	13 49	14 03	14 19	14 33	14 49	15 03	15 19	15 33	15 49	16 03	16 19	16 33	16 49	17 03	17 19	17 33	17 49	18 03

		SE ■	SE ■	SE ■	SE ■	SE ■	SE ■	SE ■	SE ■	SE ■	SE ■	SE ■	SE ■	SE ■	SE ■	SE ■	SE ■
Ore	d																
Hastings ■	d		16 50		17 20		17 50		18 50		19 50		20 50		21 50	22 10	
St Leonards Warrior Sq ■	d		16 53		17 23		17 53		18 53		19 53		20 53		21 53	22 13	
West St Leonards	d		16 56		17 26		17 56		18 56		19 56		20 56		21 56	22 16	
Crowhurst	d		17 02		17 32		18 02		19 02		20 02		21 02		22 02	22 22	
Battle	d		17 06		17 36		18 06		19 06		20 06		21 06		22 06	22 26	
Robertsbridge	d		17 13		17 44		18 13		19 13		20 13		21 13		22 13	22 33	
Etchingham	d		17 17		17 47		18 17		19 17		20 17		21 17		22 17	22 37	
Stonegate	d		17 23		17 53		18 23		19 23		20 23		21 23		22 23	22 42	
Wadhurst	d		17 29		17 59		18 29		19 29		20 29		21 29		22 29	22 49	
Frant	d		17 33		18 03		18 33		19 33		20 33		21 33		22 33	22 53	
Tunbridge Wells ■	a		17 38		18 08		18 38		19 38		20 38		21 38		22 38	22 58	
	d	17 21	17 39	17 51	18 09	18 21	18 39	19 08	19 39	20 08	20 39	21 05	21 39	22 05	22 39	22 59	23 33
High Brooms	d	17 24	17 42	17 54	18 12	18 24	18 42	19 11	19 42	20 11	20 42	21 08	21 42	22 08	22 42	23 02	23 36
Tonbridge ■	a	17 30	17 48	18 00	18 18	18 30	18 48	19 17	19 48	20 17	20 48	21 14	21 48	22 14	22 48	23 08	23 45
Sevenoaks ■	a	17 43	17 58	18 13	18 28	18 43	18 58	19 28	19 58	20 28	20 58	21 28	21 58	22 28	22 58	23 24	
Orpington ■	a	17 53	18 08	18 23	18 38	18 53	19 08	19 38	20 08	20 38	21 08	21 38	22 08	22 38	23 08	23 36	
London Bridge ■ ⊖	a	18 10	18 25	18 40	18 55	19 10	19 24	19 54	20 24	20 54	21 24	21 54	22 24	22 54	23 24	23 54	
London Cannon Street ■ ⊖	a																
London Waterloo (East) ■ ⊖	a	18 15	18 29	18 45	18 59	19 15	19 29	19 59	20 29	20 59	21 29	21 59	22 29	22 59	23 29	23 59	
London Charing Cross ■ ⊖	a	18 19	18 33	18 49	19 03	19 19	19 33	20 03	20 33	21 03	21 33	22 03	22 33	23 03	23 33	00 03	

Table 206

Hastings and Tunbridge Wells - Tonbridge and London

Sundays

until 22 July, 19 Aug and from 16 Sep

Network Diagram - see first Page of Table 206

		SE	SE	SE	SE	SE	SE	SE	SE	SE	SE	SE	SE	SE	SE	SE	SE	SE	SE	SE	SE	SE	SE
Ore	d																						
Hastings	d	22p10	07 27		08 27	09 08	09 27	10 08	10 27	11 08	11 27	12 08	12 27	13 08	13 27	14 08	14 27	15 08	15 27	16 08	16 27	17 08	17 27
St Leonards Warrior Sq	d	22p13	07 29		08 29	09 11	09 29	10 11	10 29	11 11	11 29	12 11	12 29	13 11	13 29	14 11	14 29	15 11	15 29	16 11	16 29	17 11	17 29
West St Leonards	d	22p16	07 33		08 33		09 33		10 33		11 33		12 33		13 33		14 33		15 33		16 33		17 33
Crowhurst	d	22p22	07 38		08 38		09 38		10 38		11 38		12 38		13 38		14 38		15 38		16 38		17 38
Battle	d	22p26	07 43		08 43	09 21	09 43	10 21	10 43	11 21	11 43	12 21	12 43	13 21	13 43	14 21	14 43	15 21	15 43	16 21	16 43	17 21	17 43
Robertsbridge	d	22p33	07 50		08 50		09 50		10 50		11 50		12 50		13 50		14 50		15 50		16 50		17 50
Etchingham	d	22p37	07 53		08 53		09 53		10 53		11 53		12 53		13 53		14 53		15 53		16 53		17 53
Stonegate	d	22p42	07 59		08 59		09 59		10 59		11 59		12 59		13 59		14 59		15 59		16 59		17 59
Wadhurst	d	22p49	08 05		09 05	09 37	10 05	10 37	11 05	11 37	12 05	12 37	13 05	13 37	14 05	14 37	15 05	15 37	16 05	16 37	17 05	17 37	18 05
Frant	d	22p53	08 09		09 09		10 09		11 09		12 09		13 09		14 09		15 09		16 09		17 09		18 09
Tunbridge Wells	a	22p58	08 14		09 14	09 44	10 14	10 44	11 14	11 44	12 14	12 44	13 14	13 44	14 14	14 44	15 14	15 44	16 14	16 44	17 14	17 44	18 14
	d	22p59	08 15	08 45	09 15	09 45	10 15	10 45	11 15	11 45	12 15	12 45	13 15	13 45	14 15	14 45	15 15	15 45	16 15	16 45	17 15	17 45	18 15
High Brooms	d	23p02	08 18	08 48	09 18	09 48	10 18	10 48	11 18	11 48	12 18	12 48	13 18	13 48	14 18	14 48	15 18	15 48	16 18	16 48	17 18	17 48	18 18
Tonbridge	a	23p08	08 24	08 54	09 24	09 54	10 24	10 54	11 24	11 54	12 24	12 54	13 24	13 54	14 24	14 54	15 24	15 54	16 24	16 54	17 24	17 54	18 24
Sevenoaks	a	23p24	08 33	09 03	09 33	10 03	10 33	11 03	11 33	12 03	12 33	13 03	13 33	14 03	14 33	15 03	15 33	16 03	16 33	17 03	17 33	18 03	18 33
Orpington	a	23p36	08 42	09 12	09 42	10 12	10 42	11 12	11 42	12 12	12 42	13 12	13 42	14 12	14 42	15 12	15 42	16 12	16 42	17 12	17 42	18 12	18 42
London Bridge ⊖	a	23p54	08 58	09 28	09 58	10 28	10 58	11 28	11 58	12 28	12 58	13 28	13 58	14 28	14 58	15 28	15 58	16 28	16 58	17 28	17 58	18 28	18 58
London Cannon Street ⊖	a																						
London Waterloo (East) ⊖	a	23p59	09 03	09 33	10 03	10 33	11 03	11 33	12 03	12 33	13 03	13 33	14 03	14 33	15 03	15 33	16 03	16 33	17 03	17 33	18 03	18 33	19 03
London Charing Cross ⊖	a	00 03	09 07	09 37	10 07	10 37	11 07	11 37	12 07	12 37	13 07	13 37	14 07	14 37	15 07	15 37	16 07	16 37	17 07	17 37	18 07	18 37	19 07

		SE	SE	SE	SE	SE	SE	SE
Ore	d							
Hastings	d	18 08	18 27	19 27		20 27	21 27	22 27
St Leonards Warrior Sq	d	18 11	18 29	19 29		20 29	21 29	22 29
West St Leonards	d		18 33	19 33		20 33	21 33	22 33
Crowhurst	d		18 38	19 38		20 38	21 38	22 38
Battle	d	18 21	18 43	19 43		20 43	21 43	22 43
Robertsbridge	d		18 50	19 50		20 50	21 50	22 50
Etchingham	d		18 53	19 53		20 53	21 53	22 53
Stonegate	d		18 59	19 59		20 59	21 59	22 59
Wadhurst	d	18 37	19 05	20 05		21 05	22 05	23 05
Frant	d		19 09	20 09		21 09	22 09	23 09
Tunbridge Wells	a	18 44	19 14	20 14		21 14	22 14	23 14
	d	18 45	19 15	20 15	20 53	21 15	22 15	23 15
High Brooms	d	18 48	19 18	20 18	20 56	21 18	22 18	23 18
Tonbridge	a	18 54	19 24	20 24	21 02	21 24	22 24	23 24
Sevenoaks	a	19 03	19 33	20 33		21 33	22 33	
Orpington	a	19 12	19 42	20 42		21 42	22 42	
London Bridge ⊖	a	19 28	19 58	20 58		21 58	22 58	
London Cannon Street ⊖	a							
London Waterloo (East) ⊖	a	19 33	20 03	21 03		22 03	23 03	
London Charing Cross ⊖	a	19 37	20 07	21 07		22 07	23 07	

Sundays

29 July to 12 August

		SE	SE	SE	SE	SE	SE	SE	SE	SE	SE	SE	SE	SE	SE	SE	SE	SE	SE	SE	SE	SE	SE
Ore	d																						
Hastings	d	22p10		05 50	06 20	06 50	07 20	07 50	08 13	08 50	09 31	09 50	10 31	10 50	11 31	11 50	12 31	12 50	13 31	13 50	14 31	14 50	15 31
St Leonards Warrior Sq	d	22p13		05 53	06 23	06 53	07 23	07 53	08 16	08 53	09 34	09 53	10 34	10 53	11 34	11 53	12 34	12 53	13 34	13 53	14 34	14 53	15 34
West St Leonards	d	22p16		05 56	06 26	06 56	07 26	07 56	08 26	08 56		09 56		10 56		11 56		12 56		13 56		14 56	
Crowhurst	d	22p22		06 02	06 32	07 02	07 32	08 02	08 32	09 02		10 02		11 02		12 02		13 02		14 02		15 02	
Battle	d	22p26		06 06	06 36	07 06	07 36	08 06	08 36	09 06	09 44	10 06	10 44	11 06	11 44	12 06	12 44	13 06	13 44	14 06	14 44	15 06	15 44
Robertsbridge	d	22p33		06 13	06 43	07 13	07 44	08 13	08 44	09 14		10 13		11 13		12 13		13 13		14 13		15 13	
Etchingham	d	22p37		06 17	06 47	07 17	07 47	08 17	08 47	09 17		10 17		11 17		12 17		13 17		14 17		15 17	
Stonegate	d	22p42		06 23	06 53	07 23	07 53	08 23	08 53	09 23		10 23		11 23		12 23		13 23		14 23		15 23	
Wadhurst	d	22p49		06 29	06 59	07 29	07 59	08 29	08 59	09 29	10 00	10 29	11 00	11 29	12 00	12 29	13 00	13 29	14 00	14 29	15 00	15 29	16 00
Frant	d	22p53		06 33	07 03	07 33	08 03	08 33	09 03	09 33		10 33		11 33		12 33		13 33		14 33		15 33	
Tunbridge Wells	a	22p58		06 38	07 08	07 38	08 08	08 38	09 08	09 38	10 07	10 38	11 07	11 38	12 07	12 38	13 07	13 38	14 07	14 38	15 07	15 38	16 07
	d	22p59	05 48	06 39	07 09	07 39	08 09	08 39	09 09	09 39	10 09	10 39	11 09	11 39	12 09	12 39	13 09	13 39	14 09	14 39	15 09	15 39	16 09
High Brooms	d	23p02	05 51	06 42	07 12	07 42	08 12	08 42	09 12	09 42	10 12	10 42	11 12	11 42	12 12	12 42	13 12	13 42	14 12	14 42	15 12	15 42	16 12
Tonbridge	a	23p08	05 57	06 48	07 18	07 48	08 18	08 48	09 18	09 48	10 18	10 48	11 18	11 48	12 18	12 48	13 18	13 48	14 18	14 48	15 18	15 48	16 18
Sevenoaks	a	23p24		06 58	07 28	07 58	08 28	08 58	09 28	09 58	10 28	10 58	11 28	11 58	12 28	12 58	13 28	13 58	14 28	14 58	15 28	15 58	16 28
Orpington	a	23p36		07 08	07 38	08 08	08 38	09 08	09 38	10 08	10 38	11 08	11 38	12 08	12 38	13 08	13 38	14 08	14 38	15 08	15 38	16 08	16 38
London Bridge ⊖	a	23p54		07 24	07 55	08 25	08 55	09 25	09 55	10 25	10 55	11 25	11 55	12 25	12 55	13 25	13 55	14 25	14 55	15 25	15 55	16 25	16 55
London Cannon Street ⊖	a																						
London Waterloo (East) ⊖	a	23p59		07 29	07 59	08 29	08 59	09 29	09 59	10 29	10 59	11 29	11 59	12 29	12 59	13 29	13 59	14 29	14 59	15 29	15 59	16 29	16 59
London Charing Cross ⊖	a	00 03		07 33	08 03	08 33	09 03	09 33	10 03	10 33	11 03	11 33	12 03	12 33	13 03	13 33	14 03	14 33	15 03	15 33	16 03	16 33	17 03

Table 206

Hastings and Tunbridge Wells - Tonbridge and London

Sundays

29 July to 12 August

Network Diagram - see first Page of Table 206

		SE	SE	SE	SE	SE	SE	SE	SE	SE	SE
Ore	d										
Hastings	d	15 50	16 31	16 50	17 31	17 50	18 50	19 50	20 50	21 50	22 10
St Leonards Warrior Sq	d	15 53	16 34	16 53	17 34	17 53	18 53	19 53	20 53	21 53	22 13
West St Leonards	d	15 56		16 56		17 56	18 56	19 56	20 56	21 56	22 16
Crowhurst	d	16 02		17 02		18 02	19 02	20 02	21 02	22 02	22 22
Battle	d	16 06	16 44	17 06	17 44	18 06	19 06	20 06	21 06	22 06	22 26
Robertsbridge	d	16 13		17 13		18 13	19 13	20 13	21 13	22 13	22 33
Etchingham	d	16 17		17 17		18 17	19 17	20 17	21 17	22 17	22 37
Stonegate	d	16 23		17 23		18 23	19 23	20 23	21 23	22 23	22 42
Wadhurst	d	16 29	17 00	17 29	18 00	18 29	19 29	20 29	21 29	22 29	22 49
Frant	d	16 33		17 33		18 33	19 33	20 33	21 33	22 33	22 53
Tunbridge Wells	a	16 38	17 07	17 38	18 07	18 38	19 38	20 38	21 38	22 38	22 58
	d	16 39	17 09	17 39	18 09	18 39	19 39	20 39	21 39	22 39	22 59
High Brooms	d	16 42	17 12	17 42	18 12	18 42	19 42	20 42	21 42	22 42	23 02
Tonbridge	a	16 48	17 18	17 48	18 18	18 48	19 48	20 48	21 48	22 48	23 08
Sevenoaks	a	16 58	17 28	17 58	18 28	18 58	19 58	20 58	21 58	22 58	23 24
Orpington	a	17 08	17 38	18 08	18 38	19 08	20 08	21 08	22 08	23 08	23 36
London Bridge ⊖	a	17 25	17 55	18 25	18 55	19 24	20 24	21 24	22 24	23 24	23 54
London Cannon Street ⊖	a										
London Waterloo (East) ⊖	a	17 29	17 59	18 29	18 59	19 29	20 29	21 29	22 29	23 29	23 59
London Charing Cross ⊖	a	17 33	18 03	18 33	19 03	19 33	20 33	21 33	22 33	23 33	00 03

Sundays

26 August to 9 September

		SE	SE	SE	SE	SE	SE	SE	SE	SE	SE	SE	SE	SE	SE	SE	SE	SE	SE	SE	SE	SE	SE
Ore	d																						
Hastings	d	22p10	07 27		08 27	09 08	09 27	10 08	10 27	11 08	11 27	12 08	12 27	13 08	13 27	14 08	14 27	15 08	15 27	16 08	16 27	17 08	17 27
St Leonards Warrior Sq	d	22p13	07 29		08 29	09 11	09 29	10 11	10 29	11 11	11 29	12 11	12 29	13 11	13 29	14 11	14 29	15 11	15 29	16 11	16 29	17 11	17 29
West St Leonards	d	22p16	07 33		08 33		09 33		10 33		11 33		12 33		13 33		14 33		15 33		16 33		17 33
Crowhurst	d	22p22	07 38		08 38		09 38		10 38		11 38		12 38		13 38		14 38		15 38		16 38		17 38
Battle	d	22p26	07 43		08 43	09 21	09 43	10 21	10 43	11 21	11 43	12 21	12 43	13 21	13 43	14 21	14 43	15 21	15 43	16 21	16 43	17 21	17 43
Robertsbridge	d	22p33	07 50		08 50		09 50		10 50		11 50		12 50		13 50		14 50		15 50		16 50		17 50
Etchingham	d	22p37	07 53		08 53		09 53		10 53		11 53		12 53		13 53		14 53		15 53		16 53		17 53
Stonegate	d	22p42	07 59		08 59		09 59		10 59		11 59		12 59		13 59		14 59		15 59		16 59		17 59
Wadhurst	d	22p49	08 05		09 05	09 37	10 05	10 37	11 05	11 37	12 05	12 37	13 05	13 37	14 05	14 37	15 05	15 37	16 05	16 37	17 05	17 37	18 05
Frant	d	22p53	08 09		09 09		10 09		11 09		12 09		13 09		14 09		15 09		16 09		17 09		18 09
Tunbridge Wells	a	22p58	08 14		09 14	09 44	10 14	10 44	11 14	11 44	12 14	12 44	13 14	13 44	14 14	14 44	15 14	15 44	16 14	16 44	17 14	17 44	18 14
	d	22p59	08 15	08 45	09 15	09 45	10 15	10 45	11 15	11 45	12 15	12 45	13 15	13 45	14 15	14 45	15 15	15 45	16 15	16 45	17 15	17 45	18 15
High Brooms	d	23p02	08 18	08 48	09 18	09 48	10 18	10 48	11 18	11 48	12 18	12 48	13 18	13 48	14 18	14 48	15 18	15 48	16 18	16 48	17 18	17 48	18 18
Tonbridge	a	23p08	08 24	08 54	09 24	09 54	10 24	10 54	11 24	11 54	12 24	12 54	13 24	13 54	14 24	14 54	15 24	15 54	16 24	16 54	17 24	17 54	18 24
Sevenoaks	a	23p24	08 33	09 03	09 33	10 03	10 33	11 03	11 33	12 03	12 33	13 03	13 33	14 03	14 33	15 03	15 33	16 03	16 33	17 03	17 33	18 03	18 33
Orpington	a	23p36	08 42	09 12	09 42	10 12	10 42	11 12	11 42	12 12	12 42	13 12	13 42	14 12	14 42	15 12	15 42	16 12	16 42	17 12	17 42	18 12	18 42
London Bridge ⊖	a	23p54	08 58	09 28	09 58	10 28	10 58	11 28	11 58	12 28	12 58	13 28	13 58	14 28	14 58	15 28	15 58	16 28	16 58	17 28	17 58	18 28	18 58
London Cannon Street ⊖	a																						
London Waterloo (East) ⊖	a	23p59	09 03	09 33	10 03	10 33	11 03	11 33	12 03	12 33	13 03	13 33	14 03	14 33	15 03	15 33	16 03	16 33	17 03	17 33	18 03	18 33	19 03
London Charing Cross ⊖	a	00 03	09 07	09 37	10 07	10 37	11 07	11 37	12 07	12 37	13 07	13 37	14 07	14 37	15 07	15 37	16 07	16 37	17 07	17 37	18 07	18 37	19 07

		SE	SE	SE	SE	SE	SE	SE
Ore	d							
Hastings	d	18 08	18 27	19 27		20 27	21 27	22 27
St Leonards Warrior Sq	d	18 11	18 29	19 29		20 29	21 29	22 29
West St Leonards	d		18 33	19 33		20 33	21 33	22 33
Crowhurst	d		18 38	19 38		20 38	21 38	22 38
Battle	d	18 21	18 43	19 43		20 43	21 43	22 43
Robertsbridge	d		18 50	19 50		20 50	21 50	22 50
Etchingham	d		18 53	19 53		20 53	21 53	22 53
Stonegate	d		18 59	19 59		20 59	21 59	22 59
Wadhurst	d	18 37	19 05	20 05		21 05	22 05	23 05
Frant	d		19 09	20 09		21 09	22 09	23 09
Tunbridge Wells	a	18 44	19 14	20 14		21 14	22 14	23 14
	d	18 45	19 15	20 15	20 53	21 15	22 15	23 15
High Brooms	d	18 48	19 18	20 18	20 56	21 18	22 18	23 18
Tonbridge	a	18 54	19 24	20 24	21 02	21 24	22 24	23 24
Sevenoaks	a	19 03	19 33	20 33		21 33	22 33	
Orpington	a	19 12	19 42	20 42		21 42	22 42	
London Bridge ⊖	a	19 28	19 58	20 58		21 58	22 58	
London Cannon Street ⊖	a							
London Waterloo (East) ⊖	a	19 33	20 03	21 03		22 03	23 03	
London Charing Cross ⊖	a	19 37	20 07	21 07		22 07	23 07	

Table 207

Mondays to Fridays

until 27 July, 13 Aug to 28 Aug and then from 10 Sep

London and Tonbridge - Ashford International, Folkestone, Dover, Canterbury West, Ramsgate and Margate

Network Diagram - see first Page of Table 206

Miles	Miles	Miles	Miles			SE MX ■	SE MO ■ A	SE MX ■	SE B	SE MO ■ A	SE MX ■		SE MO ■ A	SE MO A	SE MX ■	SE MO ■ A	SE MX ■		SE MX	SE ■	SE	SE ■	SE
—	—	—	0	St Pancras Intl. ⊖	d				23p12					23p42					00 12				
—	—	—	6	Stratford International ⊖	d				23p19					23p49					00 19				
—	—	—	22¾	Ebbsfleet International	d				23p31					00 01					00 31				
0	—	—	—	London Charing Cross ⊖	d	21p40	22p08	22p10		22p38	22p40		23p08		23p10	23p38	23p40						
0¾	—	—	—	London Waterloo (East) ⊖	d	21p43	22p11	22p13		22p41	22p43		23p11		23p13	23p41	23p43						
—	—	—	—	London Cannon Street ⊖	d																		
1¾	—	—	—	London Bridge ⊖	d	21p49	22p16	22p19		22p46	22p49		23p16		23p19	23p46	23p49						
13¾	—	—	—	Orpington	d		22p32	22p35		23p02			23p32		23p35	00 02							
22	—	—	—	Sevenoaks	d	22p12	22p42	22p44		23p12	23p12		23p42		23p44	00 12	00 12						
29½	—	—	—	Tonbridge	a	22p20	22p52	22p52		23p20	23p20		23p52		23p52	00 20	00 20						
—	—	—	—		d	22p20	22p52	22p53		23p20	23p20		23p52		23p53	00 20	00 20			04 50			
34¾	—	—	—	Paddock Wood	d	22p28	23p00	23p00		23p28	23p28		23p59		23p59	00 28	00 28			04 58	05 42		06 20
—	—	—	—	Maidstone West 194	a																06 01		06 39
39½	—	—	—	Marden	d	22p33	23p05	23p06		23p33	23p33		00 05		00 06	00 33	00 33			05 03			
41¾	—	—	—	Staplehurst	d	22p37	23p09	23p10		23p37	23p37		00 09		00 10	00 37	00 37			05 07			
45¼	—	—	—	Headcorn	d	22p43	23p15	23p15		23p43	23p43		00 15		00 15	00 43	00 43			05 13			
50½	—	—	—	Pluckley	d	22p49		23p21		23p49	23p49				00 21	00 49	00 49			05 19			
56	0	—	56	Ashford International	a	22p56	23p26	23p29	23p50	23p56	23p56		00 26	00 20	00 29	00 58	00 56		00 50	05 27			
—	—	—	—		d	23p00	23p30	23p32	23p52	00 01	00 01	00 03			00 32		01 00	01 03		05 30		06 02	
—	4¼	—	—	Wye	d							00 09						01 09					
—	9	—	—	Chilham	d							00 15						01 15					
—	11	—	—	Chartham	d							00 19						01 19					
—	14¼	—	—	Canterbury West	d							00 25						01a24					
—	16½	—	—	Sturry	d							00 29											
64¼	—	—	—	Westenhanger	d	23p08	23p38	23p41			00 09				00 41		01 08			05 38		06 10	
65½	—	—	—	Sandling	d	23p11	23p41	23p43		00 11	00 12				00 43		01 11			05 41		06 13	
69¼	—	—	—	Folkestone West	d	23p17	23p47	23p49	00 05	00 17	00 18				00 49		01 17			05 47		06 19	
70	—	—	—	Folkestone Central	d	23p20	23p50	23p52	00 08	00 19	00 21				00 52		01 20			05 50		06 22	
77¼	—	—	—	Dover Priory	a	23p31	00 01	00 05	00 20	00 30	00 32				01 03		01 31			06 01		06 33	
—	—	—	—		d	23p32	00 02	00 06												06 02			
82¼	—	—	—	Martin Mill	d	23p41	00 11	00 15												06 11			
85	—	—	—	Walmer	d	23p45	00 15	00 19												06 15			
86½	—	—	—	Deal	d	23p49	00 19	00 23												06 19			
90¾	—	—	—	Sandwich	d	23p56	00 26	00 30												06 26			
—	25½	4¾	—	Minster	d							00 41											
99	29½	—	—	Ramsgate	a	00 08	00 38	00 42				00 47								06 38			
101¼	31¾	—	—	Broadstairs	a																		
104½	35	—	—	Margate	a																		

		SE ■	SE ■	SE ■	SE	SE C	SE ■	SE C	SE D	SE C	SE ■	SE D	SE	SE ■	SE C	SE ■		SE D	SE	SE C	SE ■		SE D
St Pancras Intl. ⊖	d					06 25		06 40	07 04	07 10		07 39			07 40			08 04		08 10			08 39
Stratford International ⊖	d					06 32		06 47	07 14	07 17		07 49			07 47			08 14		08 17			08 49
Ebbsfleet International	d					06 42		06 59	07 30	07 29		08 02			08 00			08 30		08 30			09 02
London Charing Cross ⊖	d			05 30							06 30					07 10					07 40		
London Waterloo (East) ⊖	d			05 33							06 33					07 13					07 43		
London Cannon Street ⊖	d																						
London Bridge ⊖	d			05 39							06 38					07 19					07 49		
Orpington	d			05 55							06 54												
Sevenoaks	d			06 06							07 03					07 43					08 12		
Tonbridge	a			06 16							07 13					07 51					08 20		
	d			06 20							07 14					07 51					08 20		
Paddock Wood	d			06 28	06 50						07 22		07 40			07 59			08 10		08 28		
Maidstone West 194	a				07 09	07 12							07 59						08 29				
Marden	d			06 33							07 27					08 04					08 33		
Staplehurst	d			06 37							07 31					08 08					08 37		
Headcorn	d			06 43							07 37					08 14					08 43		
Pluckley	d			06 49							07 43					08 20					08 49		
Ashford International	a			06 58				07 18	07 51	07 48	07 51	08 20			08 20	08 27		08 51		08 50	08 57		09 20
	d	06 30	06 33	07 00			07 03	07 22		07 50	07 52			07 58	08 22	08 31	08 34			08 52	09 00	09 03	
Wye	d		06 39				07 09				07 58						08 40					09 09	
Chilham	d		06 45				07 15				08 04						08 46						
Chartham	d		06 49				07 19				08 08						08 50						
Canterbury West	d		06 55				07a24	07 39			08 15				08 39		08a55					09 22	
Sturry	d		06 59					07 44			08 19											09 26	
Westenhanger	d	06 38		07 08										08 08		08 39					09 08		
Sandling	d	06 41		07 11										08 11		08 42					09 11		
Folkestone West	d	06 47		07 17						08 03				08 17		08 47				09 05	09 17		
Folkestone Central	d	06 50		07 20						08 06				08 20		08 50				09 08	09 20		
Dover Priory	a	07 00		07 31						08 18				08 31		09 01				09 20	09 31		
	d	07 07		07 50										08 32							09 32		
Martin Mill	d	07 16		07 59										08 41							09 41		
Walmer	d	07 20		08 04										08 45							09 45		
Deal	d	07 25		08 08										08 49							09 49		
Sandwich	d	07 32		08 16										08 56							09 56		
Minster	d		07 11					07 55			08 31											09 38	
Ramsgate	a	07 44	07 17	08 29				08 00			08 38			09 08	08 59						10 08	09 44	
Broadstairs	a							08 06							09 04								
Margate	a							08 11							09 10								

A from 21 May until 23 July
B not 14 May
C not 27 July
D 27 July

Table 207

Mondays to Fridays

until 27 July, 13 Aug to 28 Aug and then from 10 Sep

London and Tonbridge - Ashford International, Folkestone, Dover, Canterbury West, Ramsgate and Margate

Network Diagram - see first Page of Table 206

		SE A	SE ■		SE	SE B	SE A	SE ■		SE ■	SE B	SE A	SE ■		SE	SE B	SE A	SE ■		SE B	SE A	SE ■ C ⌶	
St Pancras Intl. ⊖	d	08 40				09 04	09 10				09 39	09 42				10 04	10 10			10 39	10 40		
Stratford International ⊖	d	08 47				09 14	09 17				09 49	09 49				10 14	10 17			10 49	10 47		
Ebbsfleet International	d	09 00				09 30	09 29				10 02	10 01				10 30	10 29			11 02	10 59		
London Charing Cross ⊖	d		08 13					08 33		08 53			09 13					09 40				10 10	
London Waterloo (East) ⊖	d		08 16					08 36		08 56			09 16					09 43				10 13	
London Cannon Street ⊖	d																						
London Bridge ⊖	d		08 21					08 41		09 01			09 21					09 49				10 19	
Orpington	d							08 58		09 21													
Sevenoaks	d		08 45					09 07		09 31			09 44					10 12				10 42	
Tonbridge	a		08 53					09 18		09 40			09 52					10 20				10 50	
	d		08 53		09 03			09 20		09 42			09 52		10 03			10 20				10 50	
Paddock Wood	d		09 01		09 10			09 28					10 00		10 10			10 28				10 58	
Maidstone West 194	a				09 29										10 29								
Marden	d		09 06					09 33					10 05					10 33				11 03	
Staplehurst	d		09 10					09 37					10 09					10 37				11 07	
Headcorn	d		09 16					09 43					10 15					10 43				11 13	
Pluckley	d		09 22					09 49					10 21					10 49				11 19	
Ashford International	a	09 20	09 29			09 48	09 48	09 56		10 12	10 20	10 20	10 28			10 51	10 48	10 56		11 20	11 18	11 26	
	d	09 22	09 33	09 36			09 52	10 00	10 03			10 22	10 32	10 34			10 52	11 00	11 03		11 22	11 30	11 33
Wye	d			09 42					10 09					10 40					11 09				11 39
Chilham	d			09 48										10 46									11 45
Chartham	d			09 52										10 50									11 49
Canterbury West	d	09 39		09a57					10 22			10 39		10a55					11 22		11 39		11a54
Sturry	d								10 26										11 26				
Westenhanger	d		09 41					10 08					10 40					11 08				11 38	
Sandling	d		09 44					10 11					10 43					11 11				11 41	
Folkestone West	d		09 49				10 05	10 17					10 48				11 05	11 17				11 47	
Folkestone Central	d		09 52				10 08	10 20					10 51				11 08	11 20				11 50	
Dover Priory	a		10 03				10 20	10 31					11 02				11 20	11 31				12 01	
	d							10 32										11 32					
Martin Mill	d							10 41										11 41					
Walmer	d							10 45										11 45					
Deal	d							10 49										11 49					
Sandwich	d							10 56										11 56					
Minster	d								10 38										11 38				
Ramsgate	a	09 59						11 08	10 44			10 59						12 08	11 44		11 59		
Broadstairs	a	10 04										11 04									12 04		
Margate	a	10 10										11 10									12 10		

		SE D	SE B	SE E	SE A	SE ■ C ⌶		SE B	SE A	SE ■ C ⌶		SE	SE B	SE A	SE ■ C ⌶		SE B	SE A	SE ■ C ⌶		SE	SE B
St Pancras Intl. ⊖	d		11 04		11 12			11 39	11 42				12 04	12 12			12 39	12 42				13 04
Stratford International ⊖	d		11 14		11 19			11 49	11 49				12 14	12 19			12 49	12 49				13 14
Ebbsfleet International	d		11 30		11 31			12 02	12 01				12 30	12 31			13 02	13 01				13 30
London Charing Cross ⊖	d					10 40				11 10					11 40				12 10			
London Waterloo (East) ⊖	d					10 43				11 13					11 43				12 13			
London Cannon Street ⊖	d																					
London Bridge ⊖	d					10 49				11 19					11 49				12 19			
Orpington	d																					
Sevenoaks	d					11 12				11 42					12 12				12 42			
Tonbridge	a					11 20				11 50					12 20				12 50			
	d	11 03		11 04		11 20				11 50		12 03			12 20				12 50		13 03	
Paddock Wood	d	11 10		11 11		11 28				11 58		12 10			12 28				12 58		13 10	
Maidstone West 194	a	11 30		11 30								12 29									13 29	
Marden	d					11 33				12 03					12 33				13 03			
Staplehurst	d					11 37				12 07					12 37				13 07			
Headcorn	d					11 43				12 13					12 43				13 13			
Pluckley	d					11 49				12 19					12 49				13 19			
Ashford International	a		11 51		11 50	11 56		12 20	12 20	12 26			12 51	12 50	12 56		13 20	13 20	13 26			13 51
	d				11 52	12 00	12 03		12 22	12 30	12 33			12 52	13 00	13 03		13 22	13 30	13 33		
Wye	d						12 09				12 39					13 09				13 39		
Chilham	d										12 45									13 45		
Chartham	d										12 49									13 49		
Canterbury West	d						12 22		12 39		12a54					13 22		13 39		13a54		
Sturry	d						12 26									13 26						
Westenhanger	d					12 08				12 38					13 08				13 38			
Sandling	d					12 11				12 41					13 11				13 41			
Folkestone West	d				12 05	12 17				12 47				13 05	13 17				13 47			
Folkestone Central	d				12 08	12 20				12 50				13 08	13 20				13 50			
Dover Priory	a				12 20	12 31				13 01				13 20	13 31				14 01			
	d					12 32									13 32							
Martin Mill	d					12 41									13 41							
Walmer	d					12 45									13 45							
Deal	d					12 49									13 49							
Sandwich	d					12 56									13 56							
Minster	d						12 38									13 38						
Ramsgate	a					13 08	12 44		12 59						14 08	13 44		13 59				
Broadstairs	a								13 04									14 04				
Margate	a								13 10									14 10				

A not 27 July
B 27 July
C ⌶ to Ashford International
D from 21 May until 27 July
E until 18 May

Table 207

Mondays to Fridays

until 27 July, 13 Aug to 28 Aug and then from 10 Sep

London and Tonbridge - Ashford International, Folkestone, Dover, Canterbury West, Ramsgate and Margate

Network Diagram - see first Page of Table 206

	SE A	SE ■ B ⊥		SE C	SE A	SE ■ B ⊥		SE	SE C	SE A	SE ■ B ⊥		SE C	SE A	SE ■ B ⊥		SE	SE C	SE A	SE ■ B ⊥		SE C
St Pancras Intl. ■ ⊖ d	13 12			13 39	13 42				14 04	14 12			14 39	14 42				15 04	15 12			15 39
Stratford International ⊖ d	13 19			13 49	13 49				14 14	14 19			14 49	14 49				15 14	15 19			15 49
Ebbsfleet International d	13 31			14 02	14 01				14 30	14 31			15 02	15 01				15 30	15 31			16 02
London Charing Cross ■ ⊖ d		12 40				13 10					13 40				14 10					14 40		
London Waterloo (East) ■ ⊖ d		12 43				13 13					13 43				14 13					14 43		
London Cannon Street ■ ⊖ d																						
London Bridge ■ ⊖ d		12 49				13 19					13 49				14 19					14 49		
Orpington ■ d																						
Sevenoaks ■ d		13 12				13 42					14 12				14 42					15 12		
Tonbridge ■ a		13 20				13 50					14 20				14 50					15 20		
d		13 20				13 50		14 03			14 20				14 50		15 03			15 20		
Paddock Wood ■ d		13 28				13 58		14 10			14 28				14 58		15 10			15 28		
Maidstone West ■ 194 a								14 29									15 29					
Marden d		13 33				14 03					14 33				15 03					15 33		
Staplehurst d		13 37				14 07					14 37				15 07					15 37		
Headcorn d		13 43				14 13					14 43				15 13					15 43		
Pluckley d		13 49				14 19					14 49				15 19					15 49		
Ashford International a	13 50	13 56		14 20	14 20	14 26			14 51	14 50	14 56		15 20	15 20	15 26			15 51	15 50	15 56		16 20
d	13 52	14 00	14 03		14 22	14 30	14 33			14 52	15 00	15 03		15 22	15 30	15 33			15 52	16 00	16 03	
Wye d			14 09				14 39					15 09				15 39					16 09	
Chilham d							14 45									15 45						
Chartham d							14 49									15 49						
Canterbury West ■ d			14 22		14 39		14a54					15 22		15 39		15a54					16 22	
Sturry d			14 26									15 26									16 26	
Westenhanger d		14 08				14 38					15 08				15 38					16 08		
Sandling d		14 11				14 41					15 11				15 41					16 11		
Folkestone West d	14 05	14 17				14 47				15 05	15 17				15 47				16 05	16 17		
Folkestone Central d	14 08	14 20				14 50				15 08	15 20				15 50				16 08	16 20		
Dover Priory ■ a	14 20	14 31				15 01				15 20	15 31				16 01				16 20	16 31		
d		14 32									15 32				16 02					16 32		
Martin Mill d		14 41									15 41				16 11					16 41		
Walmer d		14 45									15 45				16 15					16 45		
Deal d		14 49									15 49				16 19					16 49		
Sandwich d		14 56									15 56				16 26					16 56		
Minster ■ d			14 38								16 08	15 38								17 08	16 38	
Ramsgate ■ a		15 08	14 44		14 59						16 14	15 44		15 59	16 38					17 14	16 44	
Broadstairs a					15 04									16 04								
Margate ■ a					15 10									16 10								

	SE A	SE ■ B ⊥		SE	SE C	SE A	SE ■ B ⊥		SE C	SE A	SE ■ B ⊥		SE	SE C	SE A		SE ■ B ⊥		SE ■	SE ■	SE
St Pancras Intl. ■ ⊖ d	15 42				16 04	16 10			16 39	16 42				17 04	17 10						
Stratford International ⊖ d	15 49				16 14	16 17			16 49	16 49				17 14	17 17						
Ebbsfleet International d	16 01				16 30	16 29			17 02	17 01				17 30							
London Charing Cross ■ ⊖ d		15 10					15 40				16 10						16 37				
London Waterloo (East) ■ ⊖ d		15 13					15 43				16 13						16 40				
London Cannon Street ■ ⊖ d																			16 46	17 08	
London Bridge ■ ⊖ d		15 19					15 49				16 19						16 45		16 50	17 12	
Orpington ■ d																					
Sevenoaks ■ d		15 42					16 12				16 43						17 10				
Tonbridge ■ a		15 50					16 20				16 51						17 18				
d		15 50		16 03			16 20				16 51						17 18				
Paddock Wood ■ d		15 58		16 10			16 28				16 59		17 02				17 26				17 30
Maidstone West ■ 194 a				16 29									17 21								17 49
Marden d		16 03					16 33				17 04						17 32				
Staplehurst d		16 07					16 37				17 08						17 36				
Headcorn d		16 13					16 43				17 14						17 42				
Pluckley d		16 19					16 49				17 20						17 48				
Ashford International a	16 20	16 26			16 48	16 48	16 56		17 20	17 20	17 27			17 52	17 46		17 56				
d	16 22	16 30	16 35			16 52	17 00	17 03		17 23	17 31	17 35			17 50	17 53	18 00	18 03			
Wye d			16 41					17 09				17 41						18 09			
Chilham d			16 47					17 15				17 47						18 15			
Chartham d			16 51					17 19				17 51						18 19			
Canterbury West ■ d	16 39		16a56					17 25		17 40		17a58				18 10		18 25			
Sturry d								17 29										18 29			
Westenhanger d		16 38					17 08				17 39						18 08				
Sandling d		16 41					17 11				17 42						18 11				
Folkestone West d		16 47				17 05	17 17				17 47				18 03		18 17				
Folkestone Central d		16 50				17 08	17 20				17 50				18 06		18 20				
Dover Priory ■ a		17 01				17 20	17 31				18 01				18 18		18 31				
d		17 02					17 32				18 02						18 32				
Martin Mill d		17 11					17 41				18 11						18 41				
Walmer d		17 15					17 45				18 15						18 45				
Deal d		17 19					17 49				18 19						18 49				
Sandwich d		17 26					17 56				18 26						18 56				
Minster ■ d								17 41										18 41			
Ramsgate ■ a	16 59	17 38					18 08	17 47		17 59	18 40					18 29	19 10	18 49			
Broadstairs a	17 04									18 04						18 34					
Margate ■ a	17 10									18 10						18 40			18 28	18 55	

A not 27 July

B ⊥ to Ashford International

C 27 July

Table 207

Mondays to Fridays

until 27 July, 13 Aug to 28 Aug and then from 10 Sep

London and Tonbridge - Ashford International, Folkestone, Dover, Canterbury West, Ramsgate and Margate

Network Diagram - see first Page of Table 206

	SE ■	SE A	SE A	SE B	SE A		SE	SE ■ C ⊥	SE ■	SE ■	SE A	SE A	SE B	SE A		SE ■	SE ■ C ⊥	SE ■	SE	SE A	SE A	SE B
St Pancras Intl. ■ ⊖ d		17 14	17 25	17 39	17 40						17 44	17 55	18 04	18 10						18 14	18 25	18 39
Stratford International ⊖ d		17 21	17 32	17 49	17 47						17 51	18 02	18 14	18 17						18 21	18 32	18 49
Ebbsfleet International d			17 43	18 02								18 13	18 30								18 43	19 02
London Charing Cross ■ ⊖ d	16 57							17 14									17 41					
London Waterloo (East) ■ ⊖ d	17 00							17 18									17 44					
London Cannon Street ■ ⊖ d									17 24	17 30						17 45		17 52				
London Bridge ■ ⊖ d									17 28	17 34						17 49		17 56				
Orpington ■ d																						
Sevenoaks ■ d	17 27							17 46	17 54							18 16	18 11					
Tonbridge ■ a	17 35							17 54	18 04							18 24	18 19					
d	17 36							17 54	18 05							18 25	18 20					
Paddock Wood ■ d	17 43						17 52	18 02	18 12							18 32	18 28		18 42			
Maidstone West ■ 194 a		18 02					18 11				18 32								19 01	19 05		
Marden d	17 49							18 08	18 18							18 38	18 33					
Staplehurst d	17 53							18 12	18 22							18 42	18 37					
Headcorn d	17 59							18 18	18 28							18 48	18 43					
Pluckley d	18 05								18 34							18 54	18 49					
Ashford International a	18 15			18 20	18 16			18 30	18 42				18 48	18 46		19 01	18 58					19 20
d					18 20	18 23		18 32	18 44					18 50	18 53	19 03	19 04					
Wye d								18 38								19 09						
Chilham d								18 44								19 15						
Chartham d								18 48								19 19						
Canterbury West ■ d						18 40		18 54							19 10	19 25						
Sturry d								18 59								19 29						
Westenhanger d									18 53								19 12					
Sandling d									18 56								19 15					
Folkestone West d					18 33				19 01					19 05			19 20					
Folkestone Central d					18 36				19 04					19 08			19 23					
Dover Priory ■ a					18 47				19 15					19 20			19 34					
d					18 50				19 16								19 35					
Martin Mill d									19 26								19 44					
Walmer d									19 30								19 48					
Deal d					19 07				19 35								19 53					
Sandwich d					19a13				19 41								19 59					
Minster ■ d								19 10								19 41						
Ramsgate ■ a						18 59		19 19	19 56						19 30	19 49	20 14					
Broadstairs a						19 04									19 36							
Margate ■ a			19 01			19 10				19 19		19 29			19 41			19 36			20 03	

	SE ■	SE A		SE ■	SE ■	SE ■ C ⊥	SE B	SE	SE ■	SE ■	SE A		SE ■ C ⊥		SE B	SE	SE A	SE ■ C ⊥		SE B	SE A
St Pancras Intl. ■ ⊖ d		18 40					19 04				19 10				19 39		19 42			20 04	20 12
Stratford International ⊖ d		18 47					19 14				19 17				19 49		19 49			20 14	20 19
Ebbsfleet International d							19 30				19 29				20 02		20 01			20 30	20 31
London Charing Cross ■ ⊖ d	18 03					18 21							18 41					19 10			
London Waterloo (East) ■ ⊖ d	18 06					18 24							18 44					19 13			
London Cannon Street ■ ⊖ d				18 08	18 14				18 32	18 44											
London Bridge ■ ⊖ d				18 12	18 18				18 36	18 48			18 50					19 19			
Orpington ■ d													19 07								
Sevenoaks ■ d	18 34			18 38		18 52			19 00				19 17					19 42			
Tonbridge ■ a	18 42			18 48		19 00			19 08				19 25					19 53			
d	18 43			18 49		19 01			19 09				19 25					19 54			
Paddock Wood ■ d	18 50			18 56		19 09		19 12	19 17				19 33			19 42		20 01			
Maidstone West ■ 194 a								19 31								20 01					
Marden d	18 56			19 02					19 23				19 38					20 07			
Staplehurst d	19 00			19 06		19 17			19 27				19 42					20 11			
Headcorn d	19 06			19 12		19 23			19 33				19 48					20 17			
Pluckley d				19 18					19 39				19 54					20 23			
Ashford International a	19 18	19 16		19 27		19 35	19 51		19 49		19 48		20 02		20 20		20 20	20 31		20 51	20 50
d	19 23	19 20	19 23	19 29		19 37					19 52	19 55	20 06	20 08			20 22	20 37	20 40		20 52
Wye d				19 36										20 14					20 46		
Chilham d				19 42															20 52		
Chartham d				19 45															20 56		
Canterbury West ■ d			19 40	19 52								20 12		20 27			20 39		21a02		
Sturry d				19 56										20 31							
Westenhanger d	19 31					19 45							20 14					20 45			
Sandling d	19 34					19 48							20 17					20 48			
Folkestone West d	19 40	19 33				19 54					20 05		20 23					20 54			21 05
Folkestone Central d	19a44	19 36				19 57					20 08		20 26					20 57			21 08
Dover Priory ■ a		19 47				20 08					20 20		20 37					21 08			21 20
d		19 50				20 09							20 38								
Martin Mill d						20 18							20 47								
Walmer d						20 23							20 51								
Deal d		20 07				20 27							20 55								
Sandwich d		20a13				20 34							21 02								
Minster ■ d				20 08										20 43							
Ramsgate ■ a			19 59	20 18		20 48						20 32	21 16	20 52			20 59				
Broadstairs a			20 04									20 37					21 05				
Margate ■ a			20 10		19 59					20 31		20 43					21 11				

A not 27 July

B 27 July

C ⊥ to Ashford International

until 27 July, 13 Aug to 28 Aug and then from 10 Sep

London and Tonbridge - Ashford International, Folkestone, Dover, Canterbury West, Ramsgate and Margate

Network Diagram - see first Page of Table 206

		SE 1 A ⚲		SE	SE B	SE C	SE 1 A ⚲	SE B	SE C	SE 1		SE	SE B	SE C	SE 1	SE C	SE 1		SE	SE C	SE 1	SE C
St Pancras Intl. [15] ⊖	d				20 39	20 42		21 04	21 12				21 39	21 42		22 12				22 42		23 12
Stratford International ⊖	d				20 49	20 49		21 14	21 19				21 49	21 49		22 19				22 49		23 19
Ebbsfleet International	d				21 02	21 01		21 30	21 31				22 02	22 01		22 31				23 01		23 31
London Charing Cross [4] ⊖	d	19 40					20 10			20 40					21 10		21 40				22 10	
London Waterloo (East) [4] ⊖	d	19 43					20 13			20 43					21 13		21 43				22 13	
London Cannon Street [4] ⊖	d																					
London Bridge [4] ⊖	d	19 49					20 19			20 49					21 19		21 49				22 19	
Orpington [4]	d														21 35						22 35	
Sevenoaks [4]	d	20 12					20 42			21 12					21 44		22 12				22 44	
Tonbridge [4]	a	20 20					20 50			21 20					21 52		22 20				22 52	
	d	20 20		20 33			20 50			21 20		21 33			21 53		22 20		22 33		22 53	
Paddock Wood [4]	d	20 28		20 40			20 58			21 28		21 40			22 00		22 28		22 40		23 00	
Maidstone West [4] 194	a			20 59								21 59							22 59			
Marden	d	20 33					21 03			21 33					22 06		22 33				23 06	
Staplehurst	d	20 37					21 07			21 37					22 10		22 37				23 10	
Headcorn	d	20 43					21 13			21 43					22 15		22 43				23 15	
Pluckley	d	20 49					21 19			21 49					22 21		22 49				23 21	
Ashford International	a	20 56			21 20	21 20	21 26	21 51	21 50	21 56			22 20	22 20	22 29	22 50	22 56			23 20	23 29	23 50
	d	21 00	21 03			21 22	21 30		21 52	22 00	22 03			22 22	22 32	22 52	23 00	23 03		23 22	23 32	23 52
Wye	d		21 09								22 09							23 09				
Chilham	d		21 15								22 15							23 15				
Chartham	d		21 19								22 19							23 19				
Canterbury West [4]	d		21 25			21 39					22 25			22 39				23 25		23 39		
Sturry	d		21 29								22 29							23 29				
Westenhanger	d	21 08					21 38			22 08					22 41		23 08				23 41	
Sandling	d	21 11					21 41			22 11					22 43		23 11				23 43	
Folkestone West	d	21 17					21 47		22 05	22 17					22 49	23 05	23 17				23 49	00 05
Folkestone Central	d	21 20					21 50		22 08	22 20					22 52	23 08	23 20				23 52	00 08
Dover Priory [4]	a	21 31					22 01		22 20	22 31					23 03	23 20	23 31				00 05	00 20
	d	21 32								22 32							23 32				00 06	
Martin Mill	d	21 41								22 41							23 41				00 15	
Walmer	d	21 45								22 45							23 45				00 19	
Deal	d	21 49								22 49							23 49				00 23	
Sandwich	d	21 56								22 56							23 56				00 30	
Minster [4]	d		21 41								22 41							23 41				
Ramsgate [4]	a	22 08	21 47			21 59				23 08	22 47			22 59			00 08	23 47		23 59	00 42	
Broadstairs	a					22 04								23 04								
Margate [4]	a					22 10								23 10								

		SE 1	SE 1 D	SE 1	SE 1	SE 1 D
St Pancras Intl. [15] ⊖	d					
Stratford International ⊖	d					
Ebbsfleet International	d					
London Charing Cross [4] ⊖	d	22 40	22 40	23 10	23 40	23 40
London Waterloo (East) [4] ⊖	d	22 43	22 43	23 13	23 43	23 43
London Cannon Street [4] ⊖	d					
London Bridge [4] ⊖	d	22 49	22 49	23 19	23 49	23 49
Orpington [4]	d			23 35		
Sevenoaks [4]	d	23 12	23 12	23 44	00 12	00 12
Tonbridge [4]	a	23 20	23 20	23 52	00 20	00 20
	d	23 20	23 20	23 53	00 20	00 20
Paddock Wood [4]	d	23 28	23 28	23 59	00 28	00 28
Maidstone West [4] 194	a					
Marden	d	23 33	23 33	00 06	00 33	00 33
Staplehurst	d	23 37	23 37	00 10	00 37	00 37
Headcorn	d	23 43	23 43	00 15	00 43	00 43
Pluckley	d	23 49	23 49	00 21	00 49	00 49
Ashford International	a	23 56	23 56	00 29	00 56	00 56
	d	00 01	00 03	00 32	01 00	01 03
Wye	d		00 09			01 09
Chilham	d		00 15			01 15
Chartham	d		00 19			01 19
Canterbury West [4]	d		00 25			01a24
Sturry	d		00 29			
Westenhanger	d	00 09		00 41	01 08	
Sandling	d	00 12		00 43	01 11	
Folkestone West	d	00 18		00 49	01 17	
Folkestone Central	d	00 21		00 52	01 20	
Dover Priory [4]	a	00 32		01 03	01 31	
	d					
Martin Mill	d					
Walmer	d					
Deal	d					
Sandwich	d					
Minster [4]	d		00 41			
Ramsgate [4]	a		00 47			
Broadstairs	a					
Margate [4]	a					

A ⚲ to Ashford International
B 27 July
C not 27 July
D not 27 July. 1 to Ashford International 1 from Ashford International

30 July to 10 August

London and Tonbridge - Ashford International, Folkestone, Dover, Canterbury West, Ramsgate and Margate

Network Diagram - see first Page of Table 206

		SE 1 A	SE 1 A	SE MO 1		SE 1 A		SE MO 1	SE MO 1	SE 1 A	SE MO 1	SE 1 A		SE	SE	SE MO	SE	SE	SE	SE	SE 1	SE	SE
St Pancras Intl. [15] ⊖	d													00 41	00 57		01 06	01 11	01 27	01 38		05 32	
Stratford International ⊖	d													00 50	01 06		01 16	01 20	01 36	01 48		05 42	
Ebbsfleet International	d													01 03	01 20		01 29	01 35	01 49	02 00		05 56	
London Charing Cross [4] ⊖	d	21p40	22p10	22p10		22p40		22p40	23p10	23p10	23p40	23p40											
London Waterloo (East) [4] ⊖	d	21p43	22p13	22p13		22p43		22p43	23p13	23p13	23p43	23p43											
London Cannon Street [4] ⊖	d																						
London Bridge [4] ⊖	d	21p49	22p19	22p19		22p49		22p49	23p19	23p19	23p49	23p49											
Orpington [4]	d		22p35	22p35				23p05	23p35	23p35	00 05												
Sevenoaks [4]	d	22p12	22p44	22p44		23p12		23p14	23p44	23p44	00 14	00 12											
Tonbridge [4]	a	22p20	22p52	22p52		23p20		23p22	23p52	23p52	00 22	00 20											
	d	22p20	22p53	22p53		23p20		23p23	23p53	23p53	00 23	00 20									04 50		
Paddock Wood [4]	d	22p28	23p00	23p00		23p28		23p30	23p59	23p59	00 30	00 28									04 58		05 42
Maidstone West [4] 194	a																						06 01
Marden	d	22p33	23p06	23p05		23p33		23p35	00 05	00 06	00 35	00 33									05 03		
Staplehurst	d	22p37	23p10	23p09		23p37		23p39	00 09	00 10	00 39	00 37									05 07		
Headcorn	d	22p43	23p15	23p14		23p43		23p44	00 14	00 15	00 44	00 43									05 13		
Pluckley	d	22p49	23p21	23p20		23p49		23p50	00 20	00 21	00 50	00 49									05 19		
Ashford International	a	22p56	23p29	23p28		23p56		23p58	00 28	00 29	00 58	00 56		01 29	01 38		01 49	01 54	02 07	02 18	05 27	06 16	
	d	23p00	23p32	23p31	23p35	00 01	00 03	00 03	00 31	00 32	01 01	01 00	01 03			01 05					05 30		
Wye	d				23p41		00 09	00 09					01 09			01 11							
Chilham	d				23p47		00 15	00 15					01 15			01 17							
Chartham	d				23p51		00 19	00 19					01 19			01 21							
Canterbury West [4]	d				23p57		00 25	00 25					01a24			01a26							
Sturry	d						00 29	00 29															
Westenhanger	d	23p08	23p41	23p40		00 09			00 40	00 41	01 10	01 08									05 38		
Sandling	d	23p11	23p43	23p42		00 12			00 42	00 43	01 12	01 11									05 41		
Folkestone West	d	23p17	23p49	23p47		00 18			00 47	00 49	01 17	01 17									05 47		
Folkestone Central	d	23p20	23p52	23p50		00 21			00 50	00 52	01 20	01 20									05 50		
Dover Priory [4]	a	23p31	00 05	00 01		00 32			01 01	01 03	01 31	01 31									06 01		
	d	23p32	00 06	00 02																	06 02		
Martin Mill	d	23p41	00 15	00 11																	06 11		
Walmer	d	23p45	00 19	00 15																	06 15		
Deal	d	23p49	00 23	00 19																	06 19		
Sandwich	d	23p56	00 30	00 26																	06 26		
Minster [4]	d						00 41	00 41															
Ramsgate [4]	a	00 08	00 42	00 38	00 15		00 47	00 47													06 38		
Broadstairs	a																						
Margate [4]	a																						

		SE 1	SE	SE 1	SE 1	SE 1	SE	SE 1	SE 1	SE	SE	SE	SE 1	SE 1		SE	SE	SE 1		SE 1		SE	SE
St Pancras Intl. [15] ⊖	d									07 04	07 39					08 04						08 39	
Stratford International ⊖	d									07 14	07 49					08 14						08 49	
Ebbsfleet International	d									07 30	08 02					08 30						09 02	
London Charing Cross [4] ⊖	d					05 30			06 30					07 10				07 40		08 13			
London Waterloo (East) [4] ⊖	d					05 33			06 33					07 13				07 43		08 16			
London Cannon Street [4] ⊖	d																						
London Bridge [4] ⊖	d					05 39			06 38					07 19				07 49		08 21			
Orpington [4]	d					05 55			06 54														
Sevenoaks [4]	d					06 06			07 03					07 43				08 12		08 45			
Tonbridge [4]	a					06 16			07 13					07 51				08 20		08 53			
	d					06 20			07 14					07 51				08 20		08 53			09 03
Paddock Wood [4]	d		06 20			06 28	06 50		07 22			07 40		07 59			08 10	08 28		09 01			09 10
Maidstone West [4] 194	a		06 39				07 09					07 59					08 29						09 29
Marden	d					06 33			07 27					08 04				08 33		09 06			
Staplehurst	d					06 37			07 31					08 08				08 37		09 10			
Headcorn	d					06 43			07 37					08 14				08 43		09 16			
Pluckley	d					06 49			07 43					08 20				08 49		09 22			
Ashford International	a					06 58			07 51	07 51	08 20			08 27		08 51		08 57		09 29		09 20	
	d	06 02		06 29	06 33	07 00		07 03	07 52				07 58	08 31	08 34			09 00	09 03	09 33	09 36		
Wye	d				06 39			07 09	07 58						08 40				09 09		09 42		
Chilham	d				06 45			07 15	08 04						08 46						09 48		
Chartham	d				06 49			07 19	08 08						08 50						09 52		
Canterbury West [4]	d				06 55			07 25	08 15						08 56				09 22		09 58		
Sturry	d				06 59			07 29	08 19										09 26				
Westenhanger	d	06 10		06 38		07 08							08 08	08 40				09 08		09 41			
Sandling	d	06 13		06 41		07 11							08 11	08 43				09 11		09 44			
Folkestone West	d	06 19		06 47		07 17							08 17	08 48				09 17		09 49			
Folkestone Central	d	06 22		06 50		07 20							08 20	08 50				09 20		09 52			
Dover Priory [4]	a	06 33		07 00		07 31							08 31	09 02				09 31		10 03			
	d			07 07		07 50							08 32					09 32					
Martin Mill	d			07 16		07 59							08 41					09 41					
Walmer	d			07 20		08 04							08 45					09 45					
Deal	d			07 25		08 08							08 49					09 49					
Sandwich	d			07 32		08 16							08 56					09 56					
Minster [4]	d				07 11			07 41	08 31										09 38				
Ramsgate [4]	a			07 44	07 17	08 29		07 48	08 38				09 08		09 19			10 08	09 44		10 19		
Broadstairs	a																						
Margate [4]	a																						

A not 30 July, 6 August

Table 207

Mondays to Fridays
30 July to 10 August

London and Tonbridge - Ashford International, Folkestone, Dover, Canterbury West, Ramsgate and Margate

Network Diagram - see first Page of Table 206

		SE 1		SE 1	SE	SE 1		SE	SE	SE 1		SE	SE 1 A		SE	SE	SE 1 A		SE	SE 1 A		SE
St Pancras Intl. 15 ⊖	d				09 04			09 39				10 04			10 39				11 04			11 39
Stratford International ⊖	d				09 14			09 49				10 14			10 49				11 14			11 49
Ebbsfleet International	d				09 30			10 02				10 30			11 02				11 30			12 02
London Charing Cross 4 ⊖	d	08 33		08 53		09 13				09 40			10 10				10 40			11 10		
London Waterloo (East) 4 ⊖	d	08 36		08 56		09 16				09 43			10 13				10 43			11 14		
London Cannon Street 4 ⊖	d																					
London Bridge 4 ⊖	d	08 41		09 01		09 21				09 49			10 19				10 49			11 19		
Orpington 4	d	08 58		09 21																		
Sevenoaks 4	d	09 07		09 31		09 44				10 12			10 42				11 12			11 42		
Tonbridge 4	a	09 18		09 40		09 52				10 20			10 50				11 20			11 50		
	d	09 20		09 42		09 52			10 03	10 20			10 50			11 03	11 20			11 50		
Paddock Wood 4	d	09 28				10 00			10 10	10 28			10 58			11 10	11 28			11 58		
Maidstone West 4 194	a								10 29							11 30						
Marden	d	09 33				10 05				10 33			11 03				11 33			12 03		
Staplehurst	d	09 37				10 09				10 37			11 07				11 37			12 07		
Headcorn	d	09 43				10 15				10 43			11 13				11 43			12 13		
Pluckley	d	09 49				10 21				10 49			11 19				11 49			12 19		
Ashford International	a	09 56		10 12	09 48	10 28		10 20		10 56		10 51	11 26		11 20		11 56		11 51	12 26		12 20
	d	10 00	10 03			10 32	10 34			11 00	11 03		11 30	11 33			12 00	12 03		12 30	12 33	
Wye	d		10 09				10 40				11 09			11 39				12 09			12 39	
Chilham	d						10 46							11 45							12 45	
Chartham	d						10 50							11 49							12 49	
Canterbury West 4	d		10 22				10 56				11 22			11 55				12 22			12 55	
Sturry	d		10 26								11 26							12 26				
Westenhanger	d	10 08				10 40				11 08			11 38				12 08			12 38		
Sandling	d	10 11				10 43				11 11			11 41				12 11			12 41		
Folkestone West	d	10 17				10 48				11 17			11 47				12 17			12 47		
Folkestone Central	d	10 20				10 51				11 20			11 50				12 20			12 50		
Dover Priory 4	a	10 31				11 02				11 31			12 01				12 31			13 01		
	d	10 32								11 32							12 32					
Martin Mill	d	10 41								11 41							12 41					
Walmer	d	10 45								11 45							12 45					
Deal	d	10 49								11 49							12 49					
Sandwich	d	10 56								11 56							12 56					
Minster 4	d		10 38								11 38							12 38				
Ramsgate 4	a	11 08	10 44				11 19			12 08	11 44			12 15			13 08	12 44			13 15	
Broadstairs	a																					
Margate 4	a																					

		SE	SE 1 A		SE	SE 1 A		SE	SE	SE 1 A		SE	SE 1 A		SE	SE	SE 1 A		SE	SE 1 A		SE	SE
St Pancras Intl. 15 ⊖	d				12 04			12 39				13 04			13 39				14 04			14 39	
Stratford International ⊖	d				12 14			12 49				13 14			13 49				14 14			14 49	
Ebbsfleet International	d				12 30			13 02				13 30			14 02				14 30			15 02	
London Charing Cross 4 ⊖	d		11 40			12 10				12 40			13 10				13 40			14 10			
London Waterloo (East) 4 ⊖	d		11 44			12 13				12 43			13 13				13 43			14 13			
London Cannon Street 4 ⊖	d																						
London Bridge 4 ⊖	d		11 49			12 19				12 49			13 19				13 49			14 19			
Orpington 4	d																						
Sevenoaks 4	d		12 12			12 42				13 12			13 42				14 12			14 42			
Tonbridge 4	a		12 20			12 50				13 20			13 50				14 20			14 50			
	d	12 03	12 20			12 50			13 03	13 20			13 50			14 03	14 20			14 50			15 03
Paddock Wood 4	d	12 10	12 28			12 58			13 10	13 28			13 58			14 10	14 28			14 58			15 10
Maidstone West 4 194	a	12 29							13 29							14 29							15 29
Marden	d		12 33			13 03				13 33			14 03				14 33			15 03			
Staplehurst	d		12 37			13 07				13 37			14 07				14 37			15 07			
Headcorn	d		12 43			13 13				13 43			14 13				14 43			15 13			
Pluckley	d		12 49			13 19				13 49			14 19				14 49			15 19			
Ashford International	a		12 56		12 51	13 26		13 20		13 56		13 51	14 26		14 20		14 56		14 51	15 27		15 20	
	d		13 00	13 03		13 30	13 33			14 00	14 03		14 30	14 33			15 00	15 03		15 30	15 33		
Wye	d			13 09			13 39				14 09			14 39				15 09			15 40		
Chilham	d						13 45							14 45							15 46		
Chartham	d						13 49							14 49							15 50		
Canterbury West 4	d			13 22			13 55				14 22			14 55				15 22			15 55		
Sturry	d			13 26							14 26							15 26					
Westenhanger	d		13 08			13 38				14 08			14 38				15 08			15 39			
Sandling	d		13 11			13 41				14 11			14 41				15 11			15 42			
Folkestone West	d		13 17			13 47				14 17			14 47				15 17			15 47			
Folkestone Central	d		13 20			13 50				14 20			14 50				15 20			15 50			
Dover Priory 4	a		13 31			14 01				14 31			15 01				15 31			16 01			
	d		13 32							14 32							15 32			16 02			
Martin Mill	d		13 41							14 41							15 41			16 11			
Walmer	d		13 45							14 45							15 45			16 15			
Deal	d		13 49							14 49							15 49			16 19			
Sandwich	d		13 56							14 56							15 56			16 26			
Minster 4	d			13 38							14 38						16 08	15 38					
Ramsgate 4	a		14 08	13 44			14 15			15 08	14 44			15 19			16 14	15 44		16 38	16 19		
Broadstairs	a																						
Margate 4	a																						

A 🚆 to Ashford International

Table 207

Mondays to Fridays
30 July to 10 August

London and Tonbridge - Ashford International, Folkestone, Dover, Canterbury West, Ramsgate and Margate

Network Diagram - see first Page of Table 206

		SE 1 A		SE	SE 1 A		SE	SE	SE 1 A		SE	SE 1 A		SE	SE	SE 1 A		SE 1	SE	SE 1	SE	SE 1	SE
St Pancras Intl. 15 ⊖	d			15 04			15 39				16 04			16 39					17 04				17 39
Stratford International ⊖	d			15 14			15 49				16 14			16 49					17 14				17 49
Ebbsfleet International	d			15 30			16 02				16 30			17 02					17 30				18 02
London Charing Cross 4 ⊖	d	14 40			15 10				15 40			16 10				16 37						16 57	
London Waterloo (East) 4 ⊖	d	14 43			15 13				15 43			16 13				16 40						17 00	
London Cannon Street 4 ⊖	d																	16 46		17 08			
London Bridge 4 ⊖	d	14 49			15 19				15 49			16 19				16 45		16 50		17 12			
Orpington 4	d																						
Sevenoaks 4	d	15 12			15 42				16 12			16 43				17 10						17 27	
Tonbridge 4	a	15 20			15 50				16 20			16 51				17 18						17 35	
	d	15 20			15 50			16 03	16 20			16 51				17 18						17 36	
Paddock Wood 4	d	15 28			15 58			16 10	16 28			16 59			17 02	17 26					17 30	17 43	
Maidstone West 4 194	a							16 29							17 21						17 49		
Marden	d	15 33			16 03				16 33			17 04				17 32						17 49	
Staplehurst	d	15 37			16 07				16 37			17 08				17 36						17 53	
Headcorn	d	15 43			16 13				16 43			17 14				17 42						17 59	
Pluckley	d	15 49			16 19				16 49			17 20				17 48						18 05	
Ashford International	a	15 56		15 51	16 27		16 20		16 56		16 48	17 27		17 20		17 56			17 52			18 15	18 20
	d	16 00	16 03		16 30	16 35			17 00	17 03		17 31	17 35			18 00	18 03						
Wye	d		16 09			16 41				17 09			17 41				18 09						
Chilham	d					16 47				17 15			17 47				18 15						
Chartham	d					16 51				17 19			17 51				18 19						
Canterbury West 4	d		16 22			16 57				17 25			17 57				18 25						
Sturry	d		16 26							17 29							18 29						
Westenhanger	d	16 08			16 39				17 08			17 39				18 08							
Sandling	d	16 11			16 42				17 11			17 42				18 11							
Folkestone West	d	16 17			16 47				17 17			17 47				18 17							
Folkestone Central	d	16 20			16 50				17 20			17 50				18 20							
Dover Priory 4	a	16 31			17 01				17 31			18 01				18 31							
	d	16 32			17 02				17 32			18 02				18 32							
Martin Mill	d	16 41			17 11				17 41			18 11				18 41							
Walmer	d	16 45			17 15				17 45			18 15				18 45							
Deal	d	16 49			17 19				17 49			18 19				18 49							
Sandwich	d	16 56			17 26				17 56			18 26				18 56							
Minster 4	d	17 08	16 38							17 41							18 41						
Ramsgate 4	a	17 14	16 44		17 38	17 19			18 08	17 47		18 40	18 19			19 10	18 49						
Broadstairs	a																						
Margate 4	a																	18 28		18 55			

		SE	SE 1 A	SE 1	SE 1	SE 1	SE 1 A	SE 1	SE	SE	SE	SE 1	SE 1	SE 1	SE 1 A	SE	SE	SE 1	SE 1	SE 1 A		SE
St Pancras Intl. 15 ⊖	d								18 04	18 39						19 04						19 39
Stratford International ⊖	d								18 14	18 49						19 14						19 49
Ebbsfleet International	d								18 30	19 02						19 30						20 02
London Charing Cross 4 ⊖	d		17 14				17 41					18 03			18 21					18 41		
London Waterloo (East) 4 ⊖	d		17 18				17 44					18 06			18 24					18 44		
London Cannon Street 4 ⊖	d			17 24	17 30	17 45		17 52					18 08	18 14				18 32	18 44			
London Bridge 4 ⊖	d			17 28	17 34	17 49		17 56					18 12	18 18				18 36	18 48	18 50		
Orpington 4	d																			19 07		
Sevenoaks 4	d		17 46	17 54		18 16	18 11					18 34	18 38		18 52			19 00		19 17		
Tonbridge 4	a		17 54	18 04		18 24	18 19					18 42	18 48		19 00			19 08		19 25		
	d		17 54	18 05		18 25	18 20					18 43	18 49		19 01			19 09		19 25		
Paddock Wood 4	d	17 52	18 02	18 12		18 32	18 28				18 42	18 50	18 56		19 09		19 12	19 17		19 33		
Maidstone West 4 194	a	18 11									19 01						19 31					
Marden	d		18 08	18 18		18 38	18 33					18 56	19 02					19 23		19 38		
Staplehurst	d		18 12	18 22		18 42	18 37					19 00	19 06		19 17			19 27		19 42		
Headcorn	d		18 18	18 28		18 48	18 43					19 06	19 12		19 23			19 33		19 48		
Pluckley	d			18 34		18 54	18 49						19 18					19 39		19 54		
Ashford International	a		18 30	18 42		19 01	18 58		18 48	19 20		19 18	19 27		19 35	19 51		19 49		20 02		20 20
	d		18 32	18 44		19 03	19 04					19 23	19 29		19 37					20 06	20 08	
Wye	d		18 38			19 09							19 36								20 14	
Chilham	d		18 44			19 15							19 42									
Chartham	d		18 48			19 19							19 45									
Canterbury West 4	d		18 54			19 25							19 52								20 27	
Sturry	d		18 59			19 29							19 56								20 31	
Westenhanger	d			18 53			19 12					19 31			19 45					20 14		
Sandling	d			18 56			19 15					19 34			19 48					20 17		
Folkestone West	d			19 01			19 20					19 40			19 54					20 23		
Folkestone Central	d			19 04			19 23					19a44			19 57					20 26		
Dover Priory 4	a			19 15			19 34								20 08					20 37		
	d			19 16			19 35								20 09					20 38		
Martin Mill	d			19 26			19 44								20 18					20 47		
Walmer	d			19 30			19 48								20 23					20 51		
Deal	d			19 35			19 53								20 27					20 55		
Sandwich	d			19 41			19 59								20 34					21 02		
Minster 4	d		19 10			19 41							20 08								20 43	
Ramsgate 4	a		19 19	19 56		19 49	20 14						20 19		20 48					21 16	20 52	
Broadstairs	a																					
Margate 4	a				19 19			19 36						19 59					20 31			

A 🚆 to Ashford International

Table 207

Mondays to Fridays
30 July to 10 August

London and Tonbridge - Ashford International, Folkestone, Dover, Canterbury West, Ramsgate and Margate

Network Diagram - see first Page of Table 206

Station		SE	SE ■ A ♮		SE ■ A ♮		SE	SE	SE ■ A ♮	SE	SE ■		SE	SE	SE ■	SE	SE ■		SE	SE ■	SE ■		SE ■
St Pancras Intl. ⊖	d						20 04			20 39			21 04			21 39							
Stratford International ⊖	d						20 14			20 49			21 14			21 49							
Ebbsfleet International	d						20 30			21 02			21 30			22 02							
London Charing Cross ⊖	d		19 10		19 40				20 10		20 40				21 10		21 40			22 10	22 40		23 10
London Waterloo (East) ⊖	d		19 13		19 43				20 13		20 43				21 13		21 43			22 13	22 43		23 13
London Cannon Street ⊖	d																						
London Bridge ⊖	d		19 19		19 49				20 19		20 49				21 19		21 49			22 19	22 49		23 19
Orpington	d														21 35					22 35			23 35
Sevenoaks	d		19 42		20 12				20 42		21 12				21 44		22 12			22 44	23 12		23 44
Tonbridge	a		19 53		20 20				20 50		21 20				21 52		22 20			22 52	23 20		23 52
	d		19 54		20 20			20 33	20 50		21 20			21 33	21 53		22 20		22 33	22 53	23 20		23 53
Paddock Wood	d	19 42	20 01		20 28			20 40	20 58		21 28			21 40	22 00		22 28		22 40	23 00	23 28		23 59
Maidstone West 194	a	20 01						20 59						21 59					22 59				
Marden	d		20 07		20 33				21 03		21 33				22 06		22 33			23 06	23 33		00 06
Staplehurst	d		20 11		20 37				21 07		21 37				22 10		22 37			23 10	23 37		00 10
Headcorn	d		20 17		20 43				21 13		21 43				22 15		22 43			23 15	23 43		00 15
Pluckley	d		20 23		20 49				21 19		21 49				22 21		22 49			23 21	23 49		00 21
Ashford International	a		20 31		20 56		20 51		21 26	21 20	21 56		21 51		22 29	22 20	22 56			23 29	23 56		00 29
	d		20 37	20 40	21 00	21 03			21 30		22 00	22 03			22 32		23 00	23 03		23 32	00 01	00 03	00 32
Wye	d			20 46		21 09						22 09						23 09				00 09	
Chilham	d			20 52		21 15						22 15						23 15				00 15	
Chartham	d			20 56		21 19						22 19						23 19				00 19	
Canterbury West	d			21 02		21 25						22 25						23 25				00 25	
Sturry	d					21 29						22 29						23 29				00 29	
Westenhanger	d		20 45		21 08				21 38		22 08				22 41		23 08			23 41	00 09		00 41
Sandling	d		20 48		21 11				21 41		22 11				22 43		23 11			23 43	00 12		00 43
Folkestone West	d		20 54		21 17				21 47		22 17				22 49		23 17			23 49	00 18		00 49
Folkestone Central	d		20 57		21 20				21 50		22 20				22 52		23 20			23 52	00 21		00 52
Dover Priory	a		21 08		21 31				22 01		22 31				23 03		23 31			00 05	00 32		01 03
	d				21 32						22 32						23 32			00 06			
Martin Mill	d				21 41						22 41						23 41			00 15			
Walmer	d				21 45						22 45						23 45			00 19			
Deal	d				21 49						22 49						23 49			00 23			
Sandwich	d				21 56						22 56						23 56			00 30			
Minster	d					21 41						22 41						23 41				00 41	
Ramsgate	a			21 21	22 08	21 47					23 08	22 47					00 08	23 47		00 42		00 47	
Broadstairs	a																						
Margate	a																						

Station		SE ■	
St Pancras Intl. ⊖	d		
Stratford International ⊖	d		
Ebbsfleet International	d		
London Charing Cross ⊖	d	23 40	
London Waterloo (East) ⊖	d	23 43	
London Cannon Street ⊖	d		
London Bridge ⊖	d	23 49	
Orpington	d		
Sevenoaks	d	00 12	
Tonbridge	a	00 20	
	d	00 20	
Paddock Wood	d	00 28	
Maidstone West 194	a		
Marden	d	00 33	
Staplehurst	d	00 37	
Headcorn	d	00 43	
Pluckley	d	00 49	
Ashford International	a	00 56	
	d	01 00	01 03
Wye	d		01 09
Chilham	d		01 15
Chartham	d		01 19
Canterbury West	d		01a24
Sturry	d		
Westenhanger	d	01 08	
Sandling	d	01 11	
Folkestone West	d	01 17	
Folkestone Central	d	01 20	
Dover Priory	a	01 31	
	d		
Martin Mill	d		
Walmer	d		
Deal	d		
Sandwich	d		
Minster	d		
Ramsgate	a		
Broadstairs	a		
Margate	a		

A ♮ to Ashford International

Table 207

Mondays to Fridays
29 August to 7 September

London and Tonbridge - Ashford International, Folkestone, Dover, Canterbury West, Ramsgate and Margate

Network Diagram - see first Page of Table 206

Station		SE ■ A	SE ■ B	SE ■ A	SE C	SE B	SE D	SE ■ B	SE ■ A		SE ■ B	SE B	SE ■ A	SE ■ B	SE ■ A		SE A	SE ■	SE	SE ■	SE	SE ■	SE ■
St Pancras Intl. ⊖	d				23p12	23p12	23p12					23p42					00 12						
Stratford International ⊖	d				23p19	23p20	23p20					23p50					00 20						
Ebbsfleet International	d				23p31	23p32	23p32					00 02					00 32						
London Charing Cross ⊖	d	21p40	22p08	22p10				22p38	22p40		23p08		23p10	23p38	23p40								
London Waterloo (East) ⊖	d	21p43	22p11	22p13				22p41	22p43		23p11		23p13	23p41	23p43								
London Cannon Street ⊖	d																						
London Bridge ⊖	d	21p49	22p16	22p19				22p46	22p49		23p16		23p19	23p46	23p49								
Orpington	d		22p32	22p35				23p02			23p32		23p35	00 02									
Sevenoaks	d	22p12	22p42	22p44				23p12	23p12		23p42		23p44	00 12	00 12								
Tonbridge	a	22p20	22p52	22p52				23p20	23p20		23p52		23p52	00 20	00 20								
	d	22p20	22p52	22p53				23p20	23p20		23p52		23p53	00 20	00 20			04 50					
Paddock Wood	d	22p28	23p00	23p00				23p28	23p28		23p59		23p59	00 28	00 28			04 58	05 42		06 20		
Maidstone West 194	a																		06 01		06 39		
Marden	d	22p33	23p05	23p06				23p33	23p33		00 05		00 06	00 33	00 33			05 03					
Staplehurst	d	22p37	23p09	23p10				23p37	23p37		00 09		00 10	00 37	00 37			05 07					
Headcorn	d	22p43	23p15	23p15				23p43	23p43		00 15		00 15	00 43	00 43			05 13					
Pluckley	d	22p49		23p21				23p49	23p49				00 21	00 49	00 49			05 19					
Ashford International	a	22p56	23p26	23p29	23p50	23p50	23p51	23p56	23p56		00 26	00 21	00 29	00 58	00 56		00 51	05 27					
	d	23p00	23p30	23p32	23p52	23p52	23p53	00 01	00 01	00 03			00 32		01 00	01 03		05 30		06 02		06 30	06 33
Wye	d									00 09						01 09							06 39
Chilham	d									00 15						01 15							06 45
Chartham	d									00 19						01 19							06 49
Canterbury West	d									00 25						01a24							06 55
Sturry	d									00 29													06 59
Westenhanger	d	23p08	23p38	23p41					00 09				00 41		01 08			05 38		06 10		06 38	
Sandling	d	23p11	23p41	23p43				00 11	00 12				00 43		01 11			05 41		06 13		06 41	
Folkestone West	d	23p17	23p47	23p49	00 05	00 05	00 06	00 17	00 18				00 49		01 17			05 47		06 19		06 47	
Folkestone Central	d	23p20	23p50	23p52	00 08	00 08	00 08	00 19	00 21				00 52		01 20			05 50		06 22		06 50	
Dover Priory	a	23p31	00 01	00 05	00 20	00 20	00 20	00 30	00 32				01 03		01 31			06 01		06 33		07 00	
	d	23p32	00 02	00 06														06 02				07 07	
Martin Mill	d	23p41	00 11	00 15														06 11				07 16	
Walmer	d	23p45	00 15	00 19														06 15				07 20	
Deal	d	23p49	00 19	00 23														06 19				07 25	
Sandwich	d	23p56	00 26	00 30														06 26				07 32	
Minster	d									00 41													07 11
Ramsgate	a	00 08	00 38	00 42						00 47								06 38				07 44	07 17
Broadstairs	a																						
Margate	a																						

Station		SE ■	SE	SE	SE ■	SE	SE ■	SE	SE	SE	SE ■	SE	SE ■		SE	SE	SE ■		SE	SE	SE ■		SE
St Pancras Intl. ⊖	d			06 24		06 40		06 44	07 09			07 40				08 10			08 34	08 40			
Stratford International ⊖	d			06 32		06 47		06 58	07 17			07 48				08 18			08 42	08 48			
Ebbsfleet International	d			06 42		06 59			07 32			08 00				08 30				09 00			
London Charing Cross ⊖	d	05 30					06 30						07 10				07 40				08 13		
London Waterloo (East) ⊖	d	05 33					06 33						07 13				07 43				08 16		
London Cannon Street ⊖	d																						
London Bridge ⊖	d	05 39					06 38						07 19				07 49				08 21		
Orpington	d	05 55					06 54																
Sevenoaks	d	06 06					07 03						07 43				08 12				08 45		
Tonbridge	a	06 16					07 13						07 51				08 20				08 53		
	d	06 20					07 14						07 51				08 20				08 53		09 03
Paddock Wood	d	06 28	06 50				07 22			07 40			07 59		08 10		08 28				09 01		09 10
Maidstone West 194	a		07 09	07 12				07 45		07 59					08 29								09 29
Marden	d	06 33					07 27						08 04				08 33				09 06		
Staplehurst	d	06 37					07 31						08 08				08 37				09 10		
Headcorn	d	06 43					07 37						08 14				08 43				09 16		
Pluckley	d	06 49					07 43						08 20				08 49				09 22		
Ashford International	a	06 58				07 18	07 51		07 54			08 20	08 27			08 50	08 57		09 10	09 20	09 29		
	d	07 00			07 03	07 22	07 52		07 55		07 58	08 22	08 31	08 34		08 52	09 00	09 03		09 22	09 33	09 36	
Wye	d				07 09		07 58							08 40				09 09				09 42	
Chilham	d				07 15		08 04							08 46								09 48	
Chartham	d				07 19		08 08							08 50								09 52	
Canterbury West	d				07a24	07 39	08 15					08 39		08a55				09 22		09 39		09a57	
Sturry	d					07 44	08 19											09 26					
Westenhanger	d	07 08									08 08		08 39				09 08				09 41		
Sandling	d	07 11									08 11		08 42				09 11				09 44		
Folkestone West	d	07 17							08 08		08 17		08 47			09 05	09 17				09 49		
Folkestone Central	d	07 20							08 11		08 20		08 50			09 08	09 20				09 52		
Dover Priory	a	07 31							08 21		08 31		09 01			09 20	09 31				10 03		
	d	07 50									08 32						09 32						
Martin Mill	d	07 59									08 41						09 41						
Walmer	d	08 04									08 45						09 45						
Deal	d	08 08									08 49						09 49						
Sandwich	d	08 16									08 56						09 56						
Minster	d					07 55	08 31											09 38					
Ramsgate	a	08 29				08 00	08 38				09 08	08 57					10 08	09 44		09 59			
Broadstairs	a					08 06						09 04								10 04			
Margate	a					08 11						09 10								10 10			

A not 3 September
B 3 September
C 29 August
D not 29 August, 3 September

London and Tonbridge - Ashford International, Folkestone, Dover, Canterbury West, Ramsgate and Margate

Network Diagram - see first Page of Table 206

	SE	SE 1		SE 1	SE	SE 1		SE	SE	SE 1		SE	SE 1 A 🛒		SE	SE	SE 1 A 🛒		SE	SE 1 A 🛒	
St Pancras Intl. d	09 06				09 42				10 10			10 40				11 11			11 41		
Stratford International d	09 13				09 49				10 17			10 47				11 19			11 49		
Ebbsfleet International d	09 28				10 01				10 29			10 59				11 31			12 01		
London Charing Cross d		08 33		08 53		09 13				09 40			10 10				10 40			11 10	
London Waterloo (East) d		08 36		08 56		09 16				09 43			10 13				10 43			11 13	
London Cannon Street d																					
London Bridge d		08 41		09 01		09 21				09 49			10 19				10 49			11 19	
Orpington d		08 58		09 21																	
Sevenoaks d		09 07		09 31		09 44				10 12			10 42				11 12			11 42	
Tonbridge a		09 18		09 40		09 52				10 20			10 50				11 20			11 50	
Tonbridge d		09 20		09 42		09 52		10 03		10 20			10 50		11 03		11 20			11 50	
Paddock Wood d		09 28				10 00		10 10		10 28			10 58		11 10		11 28			11 58	
Maidstone West 194 a								10 29							11 30						
Marden d		09 33				10 05				10 33			11 03				11 33			12 03	
Staplehurst d		09 37				10 09				10 37			11 07				11 37			12 07	
Headcorn d		09 43				10 15				10 43			11 13				11 43			12 13	
Pluckley d		09 49				10 21				10 49			11 19				11 49			12 19	
Ashford International a	09 48	09 56		10 12	10 20	10 28			10 48	10 56		11 18	11 26			11 50	11 56		12 20	12 26	
Ashford International d	09 52	10 00	10 03		10 22	10 32	10 34		10 52	11 00	11 03	11 22	11 30	11 33		11 52	12 00	12 03	12 22	12 30	12 33
Wye d			10 09				10 40				11 09			11 39				12 09			12 39
Chilham d							10 46							11 45							12 45
Chartham d							10 50							11 49							12 49
Canterbury West d			10 22		10 39		10a55				11 22	11 39		11a54				12 22	12 39		12a54
Sturry d			10 26								11 26							12 26			
Westenhanger d		10 08				10 40				11 08			11 38				12 08			12 38	
Sandling d		10 11				10 43				11 11			11 41				12 11			12 41	
Folkestone West d	10 05	10 17				10 48			11 05	11 17			11 47			12 05	12 17			12 47	
Folkestone Central d	10 08	10 20				10 51			11 08	11 20			11 50			12 08	12 20			12 50	
Dover Priory a	10 20	10 31				11 02			11 20	11 31			12 01			12 20	12 31			13 01	
Dover Priory d		10 32								11 32							12 32				
Martin Mill d		10 41								11 41							12 41				
Walmer d		10 45								11 45							12 45				
Deal d		10 49								11 49							12 49				
Sandwich d		10 56								11 56							12 56				
Minster d			10 38								11 38							12 38			
Ramsgate a		11 08	10 44		10 59					12 08	11 44	11 59					13 08	12 44	12 59		
Broadstairs a					11 04							12 04							13 04		
Margate a					11 10							12 10							13 10		

	SE	SE	SE 1 A 🛒		SE	SE 1 A 🛒		SE	SE	SE 1 A 🛒		SE	SE 1 A 🛒		SE	SE	SE 1 A 🛒		SE	SE 1 A 🛒		SE
St Pancras Intl. d		12 11			12 41				13 11			13 41				14 12			14 41			
Stratford International d		12 19			12 49				13 19			13 49				14 19			14 49			
Ebbsfleet International d		12 31			13 01				13 31			14 01				14 31			15 01			
London Charing Cross d			11 40			12 10				12 40			13 10				13 40			14 10		
London Waterloo (East) d			11 43			12 13				12 43			13 13				13 43			14 13		
London Cannon Street d																						
London Bridge d			11 49			12 19				12 49			13 19				13 49			14 19		
Orpington d																						
Sevenoaks d			12 12			12 42				13 12			13 42				14 12			14 42		
Tonbridge a			12 20			12 50				13 20			13 50				14 20			14 50		
Tonbridge d	12 03		12 20			12 50		13 03		13 20			13 50		14 03		14 20			14 50		15 03
Paddock Wood d	12 10		12 28			12 58		13 10		13 28			13 58		14 10		14 28			14 58		15 10
Maidstone West 194 a	12 29							13 29							14 29							15 29
Marden d			12 33			13 03				13 33			14 03				14 33			15 03		
Staplehurst d			12 37			13 07				13 37			14 07				14 37			15 07		
Headcorn d			12 43			13 13				13 43			14 13				14 43			15 13		
Pluckley d			12 49			13 19				13 49			14 19				14 49			15 19		
Ashford International a		12 50	12 56		13 20	13 26			13 50	13 56		14 20	14 26			14 50	14 56		15 20	15 26		
Ashford International d		12 52	13 00	13 03	13 22	13 30	13 33		13 52	14 00	14 03	14 22	14 30	14 33		14 52	15 00	15 03	15 22	15 30	15 33	
Wye d				13 09			13 39				14 09			14 39				15 09			15 39	
Chilham d							13 45							14 45							15 45	
Chartham d							13 49							14 49							15 49	
Canterbury West d				13 22	13 39		13a54				14 22	14 39		14a54				15 22	15 39		15a54	
Sturry d				13 26							14 26							15 26				
Westenhanger d			13 08			13 38				14 08			14 38				15 08			15 38		
Sandling d			13 11			13 41				14 11			14 41				15 11			15 41		
Folkestone West d		13 05	13 17			13 47			14 05	14 17			14 47			15 05	15 17			15 47		
Folkestone Central d		13 08	13 20			13 50			14 08	14 20			14 50			15 08	15 20			15 50		
Dover Priory a		13 20	13 31			14 01			14 20	14 31			15 01			15 20	15 31			16 01		
Dover Priory d			13 32							14 32							15 32			16 02		
Martin Mill d			13 41							14 41							15 41			16 11		
Walmer d			13 45							14 45							15 45			16 15		
Deal d			13 49							14 49							15 49			16 19		
Sandwich d			13 56							14 56							15 56			16 26		
Minster d				13 38							14 38						16 08	15 38				
Ramsgate a			14 08	13 44	13 59					15 08	14 44	14 59					16 14	15 44	15 59	16 38		
Broadstairs a					14 04							15 04							16 04			
Margate a					14 10							15 10							16 10			

A 🛒 to Ashford International

Table 207

Mondays to Fridays
29 August to 7 September

London and Tonbridge - Ashford International, Folkestone, Dover, Canterbury West, Ramsgate and Margate

Network Diagram - see first Page of Table 206

	SE	SE 1 A 🛒		SE	SE 1 A 🛒		SE	SE	SE 1 A 🛒		SE	SE 1 A 🛒		SE	SE		SE 1 A 🛒		SE 1	SE 1	SE	SE 1
St Pancras Intl. d	15 11			15 41				16 09			16 41				17 10							
Stratford International d	15 19			15 49				16 17			16 49				17 18							
Ebbsfleet International d	15 31			16 01				16 29			17 01											
London Charing Cross d		14 40			15 10				15 40			16 10					16 37					16 57
London Waterloo (East) d		14 43			15 13				15 43			16 13					16 40					17 00
London Cannon Street d																			16 46	17 08		
London Bridge d		14 49			15 19				15 49			16 19					16 45		16 50	17 12		
Orpington d																						
Sevenoaks d		15 12			15 42				16 12			16 43					17 10					17 27
Tonbridge a		15 20			15 50				16 20			16 51					17 18					17 35
Tonbridge d		15 20			15 50		16 03		16 20			16 51					17 18					17 36
Paddock Wood d		15 28			15 58		16 10		16 28			16 59		17 02			17 26				17 30	17 43
Maidstone West 194 a							16 29							17 21							17 49	
Marden d		15 33			16 03				16 33			17 04					17 32					17 49
Staplehurst d		15 37			16 07				16 37			17 08					17 36					17 53
Headcorn d		15 43			16 13				16 43			17 14					17 42					17 59
Pluckley d		15 49			16 19				16 49			17 20					17 48					18 05
Ashford International a	15 50	15 56		16 20	16 26			16 48	16 56		17 20	17 27			17 46		17 56					18 15
Ashford International d	15 52	16 00	16 03	16 22	16 30	16 35		16 52	17 00	17 03	17 23	17 31	17 35		17 50	17 53	18 00	18 03				
Wye d			16 09			16 41				17 09			17 41					18 09				
Chilham d						16 47				17 15			17 47					18 15				
Chartham d						16 51				17 19			17 51					18 19				
Canterbury West d			16 22	16 39		16a56				17 25	17 40		17a58			18 10		18 25				
Sturry d			16 26							17 29								18 29				
Westenhanger d		16 08			16 38				17 08			17 39					18 08					
Sandling d		16 11			16 41				17 11			17 42					18 11					
Folkestone West d	16 05	16 17			16 47			17 05	17 17			17 47			18 03		18 17					
Folkestone Central d	16 08	16 20			16 50			17 08	17 20			17 50			18 06		18 20					
Dover Priory a	16 20	16 31			17 01			17 20	17 31			18 01			18 18		18 31					
Dover Priory d		16 32			17 02				17 32			18 02					18 32					
Martin Mill d		16 41			17 11				17 41			18 11					18 41					
Walmer d		16 45			17 15				17 45			18 15					18 45					
Deal d		16 49			17 19				17 49			18 19					18 49					
Sandwich d		16 56			17 26				17 56			18 26					18 56					
Minster d		17 08	16 38							17 41								18 41				
Ramsgate a		17 14	16 44	16 59	17 38				18 08	17 47	17 59	18 40				18 29	19 10	18 49				
Broadstairs a				17 04							18 04					18 34						
Margate a				17 10							18 10					18 40			18 28	18 55		

	SE	SE	SE		SE	SE 1 A 🛒	SE 1	SE 1	SE	SE	SE		SE 1	SE 1 A 🛒	SE 1	SE	SE	SE	SE 1	SE		SE 1
St Pancras Intl. d	17 14	17 25	17 40						17 44	17 54	18 10						18 14	18 24		18 40		
Stratford International d	17 22	17 32	17 48						17 52	18 02	18 18						18 22	18 32		18 48		
Ebbsfleet International d		17 43								18 13								18 43				
London Charing Cross d						17 14								17 41					18 03			
London Waterloo (East) d						17 18								17 44					18 06			
London Cannon Street d							17 24	17 30					17 45		17 52							18 08
London Bridge d							17 28	17 34					17 49		17 56							18 12
Orpington d																						
Sevenoaks d						17 46	17 54						18 16	18 11					18 34			18 38
Tonbridge a						17 54	18 04						18 24	18 19					18 42			18 48
Tonbridge d						17 54	18 05						18 25	18 20					18 43			18 49
Paddock Wood d					17 52	18 02	18 12						18 32	18 28		18 42			18 50			18 56
Maidstone West 194 a	18 02				18 11				18 32							19 01	19 05					
Marden d						18 08	18 18						18 38	18 33					18 56			19 02
Staplehurst d						18 12	18 22						18 42	18 37					19 00			19 06
Headcorn d						18 18	18 28						18 48	18 43					19 06			19 12
Pluckley d							18 34						18 54	18 49								19 18
Ashford International a			18 16			18 30	18 42				18 46		19 01	18 58					19 18	19 16		19 27
Ashford International d			18 20	18 23		18 32	18 44				18 50	18 53	19 03	19 04					19 23	19 20	19 23	19 29
Wye d						18 38							19 09									19 36
Chilham d						18 44							19 15									19 42
Chartham d						18 48							19 19									19 45
Canterbury West d				18 40		18 54						19 10	19 25								19 40	19 52
Sturry d						18 59							19 29									19 56
Westenhanger d							18 53							19 12					19 31			
Sandling d							18 56							19 15					19 34			
Folkestone West d			18 33				19 01				19 05			19 20					19 40	19 33		
Folkestone Central d			18 36				19 04				19 08			19 23					19a44	19 36		
Dover Priory a			18 47				19 15				19 20			19 34						19 47		
Dover Priory d			18 50				19 16							19 35						19 50		
Martin Mill d							19 26							19 44								
Walmer d							19 30							19 48								
Deal d			19 07				19 35							19 53						20 07		
Sandwich d			19a13				19 41							19 59						20a13		
Minster d						19 10							19 41									20 08
Ramsgate a				18 59		19 19	19 56					19 30	19 49	20 14							19 59	20 18
Broadstairs a				19 04								19 36									20 04	
Margate a		18 57		19 10				19 19		19 29		19 41			19 36			20 03			20 10	

A 🛒 to Ashford International

Table 207

Mondays to Fridays

29 August to 7 September

London and Tonbridge - Ashford International, Folkestone, Dover, Canterbury West, Ramsgate and Margate

Network Diagram - see first Page of Table 206

	SE ■	SE ■ A	SE	SE ■	SE ■	SE		SE ■ A		SE	SE	SE ■ A		SE	SE ■ A		SE	SE	SE ■ A	SE
St Pancras Intl. 15 ⊖ d						19 09				19 41				20 11				20 41		21 11
Stratford International ⊖ d						19 17				19 49				20 19				20 49		21 19
Ebbsfleet International d						19 29				20 01				20 31				21 01		21 31
London Charing Cross 4 ⊖ d		18 21						18 41				19 10			19 40				20 10	
London Waterloo (East) 4 ⊖ d		18 24						18 44				19 13			19 43				20 13	
London Cannon Street 4 ⊖ d	18 14			18 32	18 44															
London Bridge 4 ⊖ d	18 18			18 36	18 48			18 50				19 19			19 49				20 19	
Orpington 4 d								19 07												
Sevenoaks 4 d		18 52		19 00				19 17				19 42			20 12				20 42	
Tonbridge 4 a		19 00		19 08				19 25				19 53			20 20				20 50	
d		19 01		19 09				19 25				19 54			20 20		20 33		20 50	
Paddock Wood 4 d		19 09	19 12	19 17				19 33			19 42	20 01			20 28		20 40		20 58	
Maidstone West 4 194 a			19 31								20 01						20 59			
Marden d				19 23				19 38				20 07			20 33				21 03	
Staplehurst d		19 17		19 27				19 42				20 11			20 37				21 07	
Headcorn d		19 23		19 33				19 48				20 17			20 43				21 13	
Pluckley d				19 39				19 54				20 23			20 49				21 19	
Ashford International a		19 35		19 49		19 48		20 02		20 20		20 31		20 50	20 56			21 20	21 26	21 50
d		19 37				19 52	19 55	20 06	20 08	20 22		20 37	20 40	20 52	21 00	21 03		21 22	21 30	21 52
Wye d									20 14				20 46			21 09				
Chilham d													20 52			21 15				
Chartham d													20 56			21 19				
Canterbury West 4 d							20 12		20 27	20 39			21a02			21 25		21 39		
Sturry d									20 31							21 29				
Westenhanger d		19 45						20 14				20 45			21 08				21 38	
Sandling d		19 48						20 17				20 48			21 11				21 41	
Folkestone West d		19 54				20 05		20 23				20 54		21 05	21 17				21 47	22 05
Folkestone Central d		19 57				20 08		20 26				20 57		21 08	21 20				21 50	22 08
Dover Priory 4 a		20 08				20 20		20 37				21 08		21 20	21 31				22 01	22 20
d		20 09						20 38							21 32					
Martin Mill d		20 18						20 47							21 41					
Walmer d		20 23						20 51							21 45					
Deal d		20 27						20 55							21 49					
Sandwich d		20 34						21 02							21 56					
Minster 4 d									20 43							21 41				
Ramsgate 4 a		20 48					20 32	21 16	20 52	20 59					22 08	21 47		21 59		
Broadstairs a							20 37			21 05								22 04		
Margate 4 a	19 59				20 31		20 43			21 11								22 10		

	SE ■		SE	SE	SE ■	SE	SE ■		SE	SE	SE ■	SE	SE ■		SE ■	SE ■	
St Pancras Intl. 15 ⊖ d				21 41		22 11				22 42		23 12					
Stratford International ⊖ d				21 49		22 19				22 50		23 20					
Ebbsfleet International d				22 01		22 31				23 02		23 32					
London Charing Cross 4 ⊖ d	20 40				21 10		21 40				22 10		22 40		23 10	23 40	
London Waterloo (East) 4 ⊖ d	20 43				21 13		21 43				22 13		22 43		23 13	23 43	
London Cannon Street 4 ⊖ d																	
London Bridge 4 ⊖ d	20 49				21 19		21 49				22 19		22 49		23 19	23 49	
Orpington 4 d					21 35						22 35				23 35		
Sevenoaks 4 d	21 12				21 44		22 12				22 44		23 12		23 44	00 12	
Tonbridge 4 a	21 20				21 52		22 20				22 52		23 20		23 52	00 20	
d	21 20		21 33		21 53		22 20		22 33		22 53		23 20		23 53	00 20	
Paddock Wood 4 d	21 28		21 40		22 00		22 28		22 40		23 00		23 28		23 59	00 28	
Maidstone West 4 194 a			21 59						22 59								
Marden d	21 33				22 06		22 33				23 06		23 33		00 06	00 33	
Staplehurst d	21 37				22 10		22 37				23 10		23 37		00 10	00 37	
Headcorn d	21 43				22 15		22 43				23 15		23 43		00 15	00 43	
Pluckley d	21 49				22 21		22 49				23 21		23 49		00 21	00 49	
Ashford International a	21 56			22 20	22 29	22 50	22 56			23 21	23 29	23 51	23 56		00 29	00 56	
d	22 00	22 03		22 22	22 32	22 52	23 00	23 03		23 23	23 32	23 53	00 01	00 03	00 32	01 00	01 03
Wye d		22 09						23 09						00 09			01 09
Chilham d		22 15						23 15						00 15			01 15
Chartham d		22 19						23 19						00 19			01 19
Canterbury West 4 d		22 25		22 39				23 25		23 39				00 25			01a24
Sturry d		22 29						23 29						00 29			
Westenhanger d	22 08				22 41		23 08				23 41		00 09		00 41	01 08	
Sandling d	22 11				22 43		23 11				23 43		00 12		00 43	01 11	
Folkestone West d	22 17				22 49	23 05	23 17				23 49	00 06	00 18		00 49	01 17	
Folkestone Central d	22 20				22 52	23 08	23 20				23 52	00 08	00 21		00 52	01 20	
Dover Priory 4 a	22 31				23 03	23 20	23 31				00 05	00 20	00 32		01 03	01 31	
d	22 32						23 32				00 06						
Martin Mill d	22 41						23 41				00 15						
Walmer d	22 45						23 45				00 19						
Deal d	22 49						23 49				00 23						
Sandwich d	22 56						23 56				00 30						
Minster 4 d		22 41						23 41						00 41			
Ramsgate 4 a	23 08	22 47		22 59			00 08	23 47		23 59	00 42			00 47			
Broadstairs a				23 04													
Margate 4 a				23 10													

A to Ashford International

Table 207

Saturdays

until 21 July, 18 Aug and from 15 Sep

London and Tonbridge - Ashford International, Folkestone, Dover, Canterbury West, Ramsgate and Margate

Network Diagram - see first Page of Table 206

	SE ■	SE ■	SE	SE ■		SE ■	SE ■		SE	SE ■	SE	SE ■	SE ■	SE ■	SE	SE ■	SE	SE ■	SE	SE ■	SE
St Pancras Intl. 15 ⊖ d			23p12						00 12						06 40				07 12		07 42
Stratford International ⊖ d			23p19						00 19						06 47				07 19		07 49
Ebbsfleet International d			23p31						00 31						06 59				07 31		08 01
London Charing Cross 4 ⊖ d	21p40	22p10		22p40		23p10	23p40									06 00					
London Waterloo (East) 4 ⊖ d	21p43	22p13		22p43		23p13	23p43									06 03					
London Cannon Street 4 ⊖ d																					
London Bridge 4 ⊖ d	21p49	22p19		22p49		23p19	23p49									06 08					
Orpington 4 d		22p35				23p35										06 24					
Sevenoaks 4 d	22p12	22p44		23p12		23p44	00 12									06 33					
Tonbridge 4 a	22p20	22p52		23p20		23p52	00 20									06 43					
d	22p20	22p53		23p20		23p53	00 20				06 03			06 20		06 50	07 03				
Paddock Wood 4 d	22p28	23p00		23p28		23p59	00 28				06 10			06 28		06 58	07 10				
Maidstone West 4 194 a											06 29						07 29				
Marden d	22p33	23p06		23p33		00 06	00 33							06 33		07 03					
Staplehurst d	22p37	23p10		23p37		00 10	00 37							06 37		07 07					
Headcorn d	22p43	23p15		23p43		00 15	00 43							06 43		07 13					
Pluckley d	22p49	23p21		23p49		00 21	00 49							06 49		07 19					
Ashford International a	22p56	23p29	23p50	23p56		00 29	00 56		00 50					06 56	07 18	07 26			07 51		08 20
d	23p00	23p32	23p52	00 01	00 03	00 32	01 00	01 03		01 03		06 30	06 33	07 03	07 22	07 30		07 33	07 52	08 03	08 22
Wye d					00 09			01 09		01 09			06 39	07 09				07 39		08 09	
Chilham d					00 15			01 15		01 15			06 45					07 45			
Chartham d					00 19			01 19		01 19			06 49					07 49			
Canterbury West 4 d					00 25			01a24		01a24			06a54	07 22	07 39			07a54		08 22	08 39
Sturry d					00 29									07 26						08 26	
Westenhanger d	23p08	23p41		00 09		00 41	01 08					06 38				07 38					
Sandling d	23p11	23p43		00 12		00 43	01 11					06 41				07 41					
Folkestone West d	23p17	23p49	00 05	00 18		00 49	01 17					06 47				07 47			08 05		
Folkestone Central d	23p20	23p52	00 08	00 21		00 52	01 20					06 50				07 50			08 08		
Dover Priory 4 a	23p31	00 05	00 20	00 32		01 03	01 31					07 01				08 01			08 20		
d	23p32	00 06										07 02				08 02					
Martin Mill d	23p41	00 15										07 11				08 11					
Walmer d	23p45	00 19										07 15				08 15					
Deal d	23p49	00 23										07 19				08 19					
Sandwich d	23p56	00 30										07 26				08 26					
Minster 4 d					00 41									07 38						08 38	
Ramsgate 4 a	00 08	00 42			00 47							07 38		07 44	07 59	08 38				08 44	08 59
Broadstairs a															08 04						09 04
Margate 4 a															08 10						09 10

	SE ■		SE	SE	SE ■	SE	SE ■		SE	SE	SE ■	SE	SE ■		SE	SE	SE ■	SE	SE ■ A		SE	SE
St Pancras Intl. 15 ⊖ d				08 12		08 40				09 10		09 42				10 12		10 42				11 12
Stratford International ⊖ d				08 19		08 47				09 17		09 49				10 19		10 49				11 19
Ebbsfleet International d				08 31		08 59				09 29		10 01				10 31		11 01				11 31
London Charing Cross 4 ⊖ d	07 00				07 30		08 00				08 40		09 10				09 40		10 10			
London Waterloo (East) 4 ⊖ d	07 03				07 33		08 03				08 43		09 13				09 43		10 13			
London Cannon Street 4 ⊖ d																						
London Bridge 4 ⊖ d	07 08				07 38		08 08				08 49		09 19				09 49		10 19			
Orpington 4 d	07 24				07 54		08 24															
Sevenoaks 4 d	07 33				08 03		08 33				09 12		09 42				10 12		10 42			
Tonbridge 4 a	07 43				08 14		08 43				09 20		09 50				10 20		10 50			
d	07 50		08 03		08 20		08 50		09 03		09 20		09 50		10 03		10 20		10 50		11 03	
Paddock Wood 4 d	07 58		08 10		08 28		08 58		09 10		09 28		09 58		10 10		10 28		10 58		11 10	
Maidstone West 4 194 a			08 29						09 29						10 29						11 29	
Marden d	08 03				08 33		09 03				09 33		10 03				10 33		11 03			
Staplehurst d	08 07				08 37		09 07				09 37		10 07				10 37		11 07			
Headcorn d	08 13				08 43		09 13				09 43		10 13				10 43		11 13			
Pluckley d	08 19				08 49		09 19				09 49		10 19				10 49		11 19			
Ashford International a	08 27			08 50	08 56	09 18	09 26			09 48	09 56	10 20	10 26			10 50	10 56	11 20	11 26			11 50
d	08 31	08 34		08 52	09 03	09 22	09 30	09 33		09 52	10 03	10 22	10 30	10 33		10 52	11 03	11 22	11 30	11 33		11 52
Wye d		08 40			09 09			09 39			10 09			10 39			11 09			11 39		
Chilham d		08 46						09 45						10 45						11 45		
Chartham d		08 50						09 49						10 49						11 49		
Canterbury West 4 d		08a55			09 22	09 39		09a54			10 22	10 39		10a54			11 22	11 39		11a54		
Sturry d					09 26						10 26						11 26					
Westenhanger d	08 39						09 38						10 38						11 38			
Sandling d	08 42						09 41						10 41						11 41			
Folkestone West d	08 47			09 05			09 47			10 05			10 47			11 05			11 47			12 05
Folkestone Central d	08 50			09 08			09 50			10 08			10 50			11 08			11 50			12 08
Dover Priory 4 a	09 01			09 20			10 01			10 20			11 01			11 20			12 01			12 20
d	09 02						10 02						11 02						12 02			
Martin Mill d	09 11						10 11						11 11						12 11			
Walmer d	09 15						10 15						11 15						12 15			
Deal d	09 19						10 19						11 19						12 19			
Sandwich d	09 26						10 26						11 26						12 26			
Minster 4 d					09 38						10 38						11 38					
Ramsgate 4 a	09 38				09 48	09 59	10 38				10 44	10 59	11 38				11 44	11 59	12 38			
Broadstairs a						10 04						11 04						12 04				
Margate 4 a						10 10						11 10						12 10				

A to Ashford International

Table 207

London and Tonbridge - Ashford International, Folkestone, Dover, Canterbury West, Ramsgate and Margate

Saturdays

until 21 July, 18 Aug and from 15 Sep

Network Diagram - see first Page of Table 206

		SE 1 A	SE		SE 1 A	SE	SE	SE 1 A	SE		SE 1 A	SE	SE	SE 1 A	SE		SE 1 A	SE	SE	SE 1 A	SE
St Pancras Intl. 15 ⊖	d		11 42				12 12		12 42				13 12		13 42				14 12		14 42
Stratford International ⊖	d		11 49				12 19		12 49				13 19		13 49				14 19		14 49
Ebbsfleet International	d		12 01				12 31		13 01				13 31		14 01				14 31		15 01
London Charing Cross 4 ⊖	d	10 40			11 10			11 40			12 10			12 40			13 10			13 40	
London Waterloo (East) 4 ⊖	d	10 43			11 13			11 43			12 13			12 43			13 13			13 43	
London Cannon Street 4 ⊖	d																				
London Bridge 4 ⊖	d	10 49			11 19			11 49			12 19			12 49			13 19			13 49	
Orpington 4	d																				
Sevenoaks 4	d	11 12			11 42			12 12			12 42			13 12			13 42			14 12	
Tonbridge 4	a	11 20			11 50			12 20			12 50			13 20			13 50			14 20	
	d	11 20			11 50	12 03		12 20			12 50	13 03		13 20			13 50	14 03		14 20	
Paddock Wood 4	d	11 28			11 58	12 10		12 28			12 58	13 10		13 28			13 58	14 10		14 28	
Maidstone West 4 194	a					12 29						13 29						14 29			
Marden	d	11 33			12 03			12 33			13 03			13 33			14 03			14 33	
Staplehurst	d	11 37			12 07			12 37			13 07			13 37			14 07			14 37	
Headcorn	d	11 43			12 13			12 43			13 13			13 43			14 13			14 43	
Pluckley	d	11 49			12 19			12 49			13 19			13 49			14 19			14 49	
Ashford International	a	11 56	12 20		12 26		12 50	12 56	13 20		13 26		13 50	13 56	14 20		14 26		14 50	14 56	15 20
	d	12 03	12 22	12 30	12 33		12 52	13 03	13 22	13 30	13 33		13 52	14 03	14 22	14 30	14 33		14 52	15 03	15 22
Wye	d	12 09			12 39			13 09			13 39			14 09			14 39			15 09	
Chilham	d				12 45						13 45						14 45				
Chartham	d				12 49						13 49						14 49				
Canterbury West 4	d	12 22	12 39		12a54			13 22	13 39		13a54			14 22	14 39		14a54			15 22	15 39
Sturry	d	12 26						13 26						14 26						15 26	
Westenhanger	d			12 38						13 38						14 38					
Sandling	d			12 41						13 41						14 41					
Folkestone West	d			12 47			13 05			13 47			14 05			14 47			15 05		
Folkestone Central	d			12 50			13 08			13 50			14 08			14 50			15 08		
Dover Priory 4	a			13 01			13 20			14 01			14 20			15 01			15 20		
	d			13 02						14 02						15 02					
Martin Mill	d			13 11						14 11						15 11					
Walmer	d			13 15						14 15						15 15					
Deal	d			13 19						14 19						15 19					
Sandwich	d			13 26						14 26						15 26					
Minster 4	d	12 38						13 38						14 38						15 38	
Ramsgate 4	a	12 44	12 59	13 38				13 44	13 59	14 38				14 44	14 59	15 38				15 44	15 59
Broadstairs	a		13 04						14 04						15 04						16 04
Margate 4	a		13 10						14 10						15 10						16 10

			SE 1 A	SE	SE	SE 1 A	SE		SE 1 A	SE	SE	SE 1 A	SE		SE 1 A	SE	SE	SE 1 A	SE		SE 1 A	SE	SE
St Pancras Intl. 15 ⊖	d				15 12		15 42				16 10		16 42				17 12		17 42				18 12
Stratford International ⊖	d				15 19		15 49				16 17		16 49				17 19		17 49				18 19
Ebbsfleet International	d				15 31		16 01				16 29		17 01				17 31		18 01				18 31
London Charing Cross 4 ⊖	d		14 10			14 40			15 10			15 40			16 10			16 40			17 10		
London Waterloo (East) 4 ⊖	d		14 13			14 43			15 13			15 43			16 13			16 43			17 13		
London Cannon Street 4 ⊖	d																						
London Bridge 4 ⊖	d		14 19			14 49			15 19			15 49			16 19			16 49			17 19		
Orpington 4	d																						
Sevenoaks 4	d		14 42			15 12			15 42			16 12			16 42			17 12			17 42		
Tonbridge 4	a		14 50			15 20			15 50			16 20			16 50			17 20			17 50		
	d		14 50	15 03		15 20			15 50	16 03		16 20			16 50	17 03		17 20			17 50	18 03	
Paddock Wood 4	d		14 58	15 10		15 28			15 58	16 10		16 28			16 58	17 10		17 28			17 58	18 10	
Maidstone West 4 194	a			15 29						16 29						17 29						18 29	
Marden	d		15 03			15 33			16 03			16 33			17 03			17 33			18 03		
Staplehurst	d		15 07			15 37			16 07			16 37			17 07			17 37			18 07		
Headcorn	d		15 13			15 43			16 13			16 43			17 13			17 43			18 13		
Pluckley	d		15 19			15 49			16 19			16 49			17 19			17 49			18 19		
Ashford International	a		15 26		15 50	15 56	16 20		16 26		16 48	16 56	17 20		17 26		17 50	17 56	18 20		18 26		18 50
	d	15 30	15 33		15 52	16 03	16 22	16 30	16 33		16 52	17 03	17 22	17 30	17 33		17 52	18 03	18 22	18 30	18 33		18 52
Wye	d		15 39			16 09			16 39			17 09			17 39			18 09			18 39		
Chilham	d		15 45						16 45						17 45						18 45		
Chartham	d		15 49						16 49						17 49						18 49		
Canterbury West 4	d		15a54			16 22	16 39		16a54			17 22	17 39		17a54			18 22	18 39		18a54		
Sturry	d					16 26						17 26						18 26					
Westenhanger	d	15 38						16 38						17 38						18 38			
Sandling	d	15 41						16 41						17 41						18 41			
Folkestone West	d	15 47			16 05			16 47			17 05			17 47			18 05			18 47			19 05
Folkestone Central	d	15 50			16 08			16 50			17 08			17 50			18 08			18 50			19 08
Dover Priory 4	a	16 01			16 20			17 01			17 20			18 01			18 20			19 01			19 20
	d	16 02						17 02						18 02						19 02			
Martin Mill	d	16 11						17 11						18 11						19 11			
Walmer	d	16 15						17 15						18 15						19 15			
Deal	d	16 19						17 19						18 19						19 19			
Sandwich	d	16 26						17 26						18 26						19 26			
Minster 4	d					16 38						17 38						18 38					
Ramsgate 4	a	16 38				16 44	16 59	17 38				17 44	17 59	18 38				18 44	18 59	19 38			
Broadstairs	a						17 04						18 04						19 04				
Margate 4	a						17 10						18 10						19 10				

A to Ashford International

Table 207

London and Tonbridge - Ashford International, Folkestone, Dover, Canterbury West, Ramsgate and Margate

Saturdays

until 21 July, 18 Aug and from 15 Sep

Network Diagram - see first Page of Table 206

		SE 1 A	SE	SE 1 A	SE	SE	SE 1 A	SE	SE 1 A	SE	SE	SE 1 A	SE	SE 1 A	SE	SE	SE 1	SE	SE 1	SE	SE	SE 1	SE
St Pancras Intl. 15 ⊖	d		18 42			19 12		19 42			20 12		20 42			21 12		21 42			22 12		22 42
Stratford International ⊖	d		18 49			19 19		19 49			20 19		20 49			21 19		21 49			22 19		22 49
Ebbsfleet International	d		19 01			19 31		20 01			20 31		21 01			21 31		22 01			22 31		23 01
London Charing Cross 4 ⊖	d	17 40		18 10			18 40		19 10			19 40		20 10			20 40		21 10			21 40	
London Waterloo (East) 4 ⊖	d	17 43		18 13			18 43		19 13			19 43		20 13			20 43		21 13			21 43	
London Cannon Street 4 ⊖	d																						
London Bridge 4 ⊖	d	17 49		18 19			18 49		19 19			19 49		20 19			20 49		21 19			21 49	
Orpington 4	d													20 35			21 05		21 35			22 05	
Sevenoaks 4	d	18 12		18 42			19 12		19 42			20 12		20 44			21 14		21 44			22 14	
Tonbridge 4	a	18 20		18 50			19 20		19 50			20 20		20 52			21 22		21 52			22 22	
	d	18 20		18 50	19 03		19 20		19 50	20 03		20 20		20 53	21 03		21 23		21 53	22 03		22 23	
Paddock Wood 4	d	18 28		18 58	19 10		19 28		19 58	20 10		20 28		21 00	21 10		21 30		22 00	22 10		22 30	
Maidstone West 4 194	a				19 29					20 29					21 29					22 29			
Marden	d	18 33		19 03			19 33		20 03			20 33		21 05			21 35		22 05			22 35	
Staplehurst	d	18 37		19 07			19 37		20 07			20 37		21 09			21 39		22 09			22 39	
Headcorn	d	18 43		19 13			19 43		20 13			20 43		21 14			21 44		22 14			22 44	
Pluckley	d	18 49		19 19			19 49		20 19			20 49		21 20			21 50		22 20			22 50	
Ashford International	a	18 56	19 20	19 26		19 50	19 56	20 20	20 26		20 50	20 56	21 20	21 28		21 50	21 58	22 20	22 28		22 50	22 58	23 20
	d	19 03	19 22	19 30		19 52	20 03	20 22	20 30		20 52	21 03	21 22	21 31		21 52	22 03	22 22	22 31		22 52	23 03	23 22
Wye	d	19 09					20 09					21 09					22 09					23 09	
Chilham	d	19 15					20 15					21 15					22 15					23 15	
Chartham	d	19 19					20 19					21 19					22 19					23 19	
Canterbury West 4	d	19 25	19 39				20 25	20 39				21 25	21 39				22 25	22 39				23 25	23 39
Sturry	d	19 29					20 29					21 29					22 29					23 29	
Westenhanger	d			19 38					20 38					21 40					22 40				
Sandling	d			19 41					20 41					21 42					22 42				
Folkestone West	d			19 47		20 05			20 47		21 05			21 47		22 05			22 47		23 05		
Folkestone Central	d			19 50		20 08			20 50		21 08			21 50		22 08			22 50		23 08		
Dover Priory 4	a			20 01		20 20			21 01		21 20			22 01		22 20			23 01		23 20		
	d			20 02					21 02					22 02					23 02				
Martin Mill	d			20 11					21 11					22 11					23 11				
Walmer	d			20 15					21 15					22 15					23 15				
Deal	d			20 19					21 19					22 19					23 19				
Sandwich	d			20 26					21 26					22 26					23 26				
Minster 4	d	19 41					20 41					21 41					22 41					23 41	
Ramsgate 4	a	19 47	19 59	20 38			20 47	20 59	21 38			21 47	21 59	22 38			22 48	22 59	23 38			23 47	23 59
Broadstairs	a		20 04					21 04					22 04					23 04					
Margate 4	a		20 10					21 10					22 10					23 10					

		SE 1	SE	SE 1	SE 1		SE 1
St Pancras Intl. 15 ⊖	d		23 12				
Stratford International ⊖	d		23 19				
Ebbsfleet International	d		23 31				
London Charing Cross 4 ⊖	d	22 10		22 40	23 10		23 40
London Waterloo (East) 4 ⊖	d	22 13		22 43	23 13		23 43
London Cannon Street 4 ⊖	d						
London Bridge 4 ⊖	d	22 19		22 49	23 19		23 49
Orpington 4	d	22 35		23 05	23 35		00 05
Sevenoaks 4	d	22 44		23 14	23 44		00 14
Tonbridge 4	a	22 52		23 22	23 52		00 22
	d	22 53		23 23	23 53		00 23
Paddock Wood 4	d	23 00		23 30	23 59		00 30
Maidstone West 4 194	a						
Marden	d	23 05		23 35	00 05		00 35
Staplehurst	d	23 09		23 39	00 09		00 39
Headcorn	d	23 14		23 44	00 14		00 44
Pluckley	d	23 20		23 50	00 20		00 50
Ashford International	a	23 28	23 50	23 58	00 28		00 58
	d	23 31	23 52	00 03	00 31	01 01	01 04
Wye	d			00 09			01 10
Chilham	d			00 15			01 16
Chartham	d			00 19			01 20
Canterbury West 4	d			00 25			01a25
Sturry	d			00 29			
Westenhanger	d	23 40			00 40	01 10	
Sandling	d	23 42			00 42	01 12	
Folkestone West	d	23 47	00 05		00 47	01 17	
Folkestone Central	d	23 50	00 08		00 50	01 20	
Dover Priory 4	a	00 01	00 20		01 01	01 31	
	d	00 02					
Martin Mill	d	00 11					
Walmer	d	00 15					
Deal	d	00 19					
Sandwich	d	00 26					
Minster 4	d			00 41			
Ramsgate 4	a	00 38		00 47			
Broadstairs	a						
Margate 4	a						

A to Ashford International

London and Tonbridge - Ashford International, Folkestone, Dover, Canterbury West, Ramsgate and Margate

Network Diagram - see first Page of Table 206

	SE ■	SE ■	SE ■	SE ■ A	SE ■	SE ■	SE ■	SE ■ A	SE		SE	SE ■	SE	SE	SE	SE	SE	SE	SE ■		SE ■	SE ■	SE ■	SE
St Pancras Intl. ⊖ d									00 41		00 57		01 06	01 11	01 27	01 38	05 32							
Stratford International ⊖ d									00 50		01 06		01 16	01 20	01 36	01 48	05 42							
Ebbsfleet International d									01 03		01 20		01 29	01 35	01 49	02 00	05 56							
London Charing Cross ■ ⊖ d	21p40	22p10	22p40	22p40		23p10	23p40	23p40															06 00	
London Waterloo (East) ■ ⊖ d	21p43	22p13	22p43	22p43		23p13	23p43	23p43															06 03	
London Cannon Street ■ ⊖ d																								
London Bridge ■ ⊖ d	21p49	22p19	22p49	22p49		23p19	23p49	23p49															06 08	
Orpington ■ d		22p35				23p35																	06 24	
Sevenoaks ■ d	22p12	22p44	23p12	23p12		23p44	00 12	00 12															06 33	
Tonbridge ■ a	22p20	22p52	23p20	23p20		23p52	00 20	00 20															06 43	
d	22p20	22p53	23p20	23p20		23p53	00 20	00 20										06 03				06 20	06 50	07 03
Paddock Wood ■ d	22p28	23p00	23p28	23p28		23p59	00 28	00 28										06 10				06 28	06 58	07 10
Maidstone West ■ 194 a																		06 29						07 29
Marden d	22p33	23p06	23p33	23p33		00 06	00 33	00 33														06 33	07 03	
Staplehurst d	22p37	23p10	23p37	23p37		00 10	00 37	00 37														06 37	07 07	
Headcorn d	22p43	23p15	23p43	23p43		00 15	00 43	00 43														06 43	07 13	
Pluckley d	22p49	23p21	23p49	23p49		00 21	00 49	00 49														06 49	07 19	
Ashford International a	22p56	23p29	23p56	23p56		00 29	00 56	00 56	01 29		01 38		01 49	01 54	02 07	02 18	06 14					06 56	07 26	
d	23p00	23p32	00 01	00 03	00 03	00 32	01 00	01 03				01 03							06 30		06 33	07 03	07 30	
Wye d				00 09	00 09			01 09				01 09									06 39	07 09		
Chilham d				00 15	00 15			01 15				01 15									06 45			
Chartham d				00 19	00 19			01 19				01 19									06 49			
Canterbury West ■ d				00 25	00 25			01a24				01a24									06 55	07 22		
Sturry d				00 29	00 29																	07 26		
Westenhanger d	23p08	23p41	00 09			00 41	01 08												06 38				07 38	
Sandling d	23p11	23p43	00 12			00 43	01 11												06 41				07 41	
Folkestone West d	23p17	23p49	00 18			00 49	01 17												06 47				07 47	
Folkestone Central d	23p20	23p52	00 21			00 52	01 20												06 50				07 50	
Dover Priory ■ a	23p31	00 05	00 32			01 03	01 31												07 01				08 01	
d	23p32	00 06																	07 02				08 02	
Martin Mill d	23p41	00 15																	07 11				08 11	
Walmer d	23p45	00 19																	07 15				08 15	
Deal d	23p49	00 23																	07 19				08 19	
Sandwich d	23p56	00 30																	07 26				08 26	
Minster ■ d				00 41	00 41																	07 38		
Ramsgate ■ a	00 08	00 42		00 47	00 47														07 38		07 15	07 44	08 38	
Broadstairs a																								
Margate ■ a																								

	SE	SE ■	SE	SE ■	SE ■		SE ■		SE	SE ■	SE	SE	SE ■	SE ■			SE	SE ■	SE	SE	SE ■	SE ■		SE
St Pancras Intl. ⊖ d	07 04		07 39								08 04	08 39							09 04	09 39				
Stratford International ⊖ d	07 14		07 49								08 14	08 49							09 14	09 49				
Ebbsfleet International d	07 30		08 02								08 30	09 02							09 30	10 02				
London Charing Cross ■ ⊖ d							07 00			07 30				08 00				08 40				09 10		
London Waterloo (East) ■ ⊖ d							07 03			07 33				08 03				08 43				09 13		
London Cannon Street ■ ⊖ d																								
London Bridge ■ ⊖ d							07 08			07 38				08 08				08 49				09 19		
Orpington ■ d							07 26			07 54				08 24										
Sevenoaks ■ d							07 35			08 03				08 33				09 12				09 42		
Tonbridge ■ a							07 45			08 14				08 43				09 20				09 50		
d							07 50		08 03	08 20				08 50			09 03	09 20				09 50		10 03
Paddock Wood ■ d							07 58		08 10	08 28				08 58			09 10	09 28				09 58		10 10
Maidstone West ■ 194 a									08 29								09 29							10 29
Marden d							08 03			08 33				09 03				09 33				10 03		
Staplehurst d							08 07			08 37				09 07				09 37				10 07		
Headcorn d							08 13			08 43				09 13				09 43				10 13		
Pluckley d							08 19			08 49				09 19				09 49				10 19		
Ashford International a	07 51		08 20				08 27			08 56	08 51	09 20		09 26				09 56	09 48	10 20		10 26		
d		07 33		08 00	08 03		08 31	08 34		09 00			09 03	09 30	09 33			10 00			10 03	10 30	10 33	
Wye d		07 39			08 09			08 40					09 09		09 39						10 09		10 39	
Chilham d		07 45						08 46							09 45								10 45	
Chartham d		07 49						08 50							09 49								10 49	
Canterbury West ■ d		07 55			08 22			08 56					09 22		09 55						10 22		10 55	
Sturry d					08 26								09 26								10 26			
Westenhanger d							08 39							09 38								10 38		
Sandling d							08 42							09 41								10 41		
Folkestone West d				08 13			08 47			09 13				09 47				10 13				10 47		
Folkestone Central d				08 16			08 50			09 16				09 50				10 16				10 50		
Dover Priory ■ a				08 28			09 01			09 28				10 01				10 28				11 01		
d							09 02							10 02								11 02		
Martin Mill d							09 11							10 11								11 11		
Walmer d							09 15							10 15								11 15		
Deal d							09 19							10 19								11 19		
Sandwich d							09 26							10 26								11 26		
Minster ■ d					08 38								09 38								10 38			
Ramsgate ■ a		08 15			08 44		09 38	09 15					09 48	10 38	10 15						10 44	11 38	11 15	
Broadstairs a																								
Margate ■ a																								

A not 28 July. ■ to Ashford International ■ from Ashford International

London and Tonbridge - Ashford International, Folkestone, Dover, Canterbury West, Ramsgate and Margate

Network Diagram - see first Page of Table 206

	SE ■		SE	SE	SE ■	SE ■ A ♨		SE	SE ■ A ♨	SE	SE		SE ■	SE ■ A ♨		SE	SE ■ A ♨	SE	SE	SE ■	SE ■ A ♨			SE
St Pancras Intl. ⊖ d			10 04	10 39						11 04	11 39							12 04	12 39					
Stratford International ⊖ d			10 14	10 49						11 14	11 49							12 14	12 49					
Ebbsfleet International d			10 30	11 02						11 30	12 02							12 30	13 02					
London Charing Cross ■ ⊖ d	09 40					10 10			10 40					11 10			11 40				12 10			
London Waterloo (East) ■ ⊖ d	09 43					10 13			10 43					11 13			11 43				12 13			
London Cannon Street ■ ⊖ d																								
London Bridge ■ ⊖ d	09 49					10 19			10 49					11 19			11 49				12 19			
Orpington ■ d																								
Sevenoaks ■ d	10 12					10 42			11 12					11 42			12 12				12 42			
Tonbridge ■ a	10 20					10 50			11 20					11 50			12 20				12 50			
d	10 20					10 50		11 03	11 20					11 50		12 03	12 20				12 50			13 03
Paddock Wood ■ d	10 28					10 58		11 10	11 28					11 58		12 10	12 28				12 58			13 10
Maidstone West ■ 194 a								11 29								12 29								13 29
Marden d	10 33					11 03			11 33					12 03			12 33				13 03			
Staplehurst d	10 37					11 07			11 37					12 07			12 37				13 07			
Headcorn d	10 43					11 13			11 43					12 13			12 43				13 13			
Pluckley d	10 49					11 19			11 49					12 19			12 49				13 19			
Ashford International a	10 56		10 51	11 20		11 26			11 56	11 51	12 20			12 26			12 56	12 51	13 20		13 26			
d	11 00				11 03	11 30	11 33		12 00				12 03	12 30	12 33		13 00			13 03	13 30	13 33		
Wye d					11 09		11 39						12 09		12 39					13 09		13 39		
Chilham d							11 45								12 45							13 45		
Chartham d							11 49								12 49							13 49		
Canterbury West ■ d					11 22		11 55						12 22		12 55					13 22		13 55		
Sturry d					11 26								12 26							13 26				
Westenhanger d						11 38								12 38							13 38			
Sandling d						11 41								12 41							13 41			
Folkestone West d	11 13					11 47			12 13					12 47			13 13				13 47			
Folkestone Central d	11 16					11 50			12 16					12 50			13 16				13 50			
Dover Priory ■ a	11 28					12 01			12 28					13 01			13 28				14 01			
d						12 02								13 02							14 02			
Martin Mill d						12 11								13 11							14 11			
Walmer d						12 15								13 15							14 15			
Deal d						12 19								13 19							14 19			
Sandwich d						12 26								13 26							14 26			
Minster ■ d					11 38								12 38							13 38				
Ramsgate ■ a					11 44	12 38	12 15						12 44	13 38	13 15					13 44	14 38	14 15		
Broadstairs a																								
Margate ■ a																								

	SE ■ A ♨	SE	SE	SE ■	SE ■ A ♨		SE	SE ■ A ♨		SE	SE	SE ■	SE ■ A ♨		SE	SE ■ A ♨	SE	SE		SE ■	SE ■ A ♨		SE	SE ■ A ♨
St Pancras Intl. ⊖ d		13 04	13 39							14 04	14 39						15 04	15 39						
Stratford International ⊖ d		13 14	13 49							14 14	14 49						15 14	15 49						
Ebbsfleet International d		13 30	14 02							14 30	15 02						15 30	16 02						
London Charing Cross ■ ⊖ d	12 40				13 10			13 40					14 10			14 40					15 10			15 40
London Waterloo (East) ■ ⊖ d	12 43				13 13			13 43					14 13			14 43					15 13			15 43
London Cannon Street ■ ⊖ d																								
London Bridge ■ ⊖ d	12 49				13 19			13 49					14 19			14 49					15 19			15 49
Orpington ■ d																								
Sevenoaks ■ d	13 12				13 42			14 12					14 42			15 12					15 42			16 12
Tonbridge ■ a	13 20				13 50			14 20					14 50			15 20					15 50			16 20
d	13 20				13 50		14 03	14 20					14 50		15 03	15 20					15 50		16 03	16 20
Paddock Wood ■ d	13 28				13 58		14 10	14 28					14 58		15 10	15 28					15 58		16 10	16 28
Maidstone West ■ 194 a							14 29								15 29								16 29	
Marden d	13 33				14 03			14 33					15 03			15 33					16 03			16 33
Staplehurst d	13 37				14 07			14 37					15 07			15 37					16 07			16 37
Headcorn d	13 43				14 13			14 43					15 13			15 43					16 13			16 43
Pluckley d	13 49				14 19			14 49					15 19			15 49					16 19			16 49
Ashford International a	13 56	13 51	14 20		14 26			14 56		14 51	15 20		15 26			15 56	15 51	16 20			16 26			16 56
d	14 00			14 03	14 30	14 33		15 00				15 03	15 30	15 33		16 00				16 03	16 30	16 33		17 00
Wye d				14 09		14 39						15 09		15 39						16 09		16 39		
Chilham d						14 45								15 45								16 45		
Chartham d						14 49								15 49								16 49		
Canterbury West ■ d				14 22		14 55						15 22		15 55						16 22		16 55		
Sturry d				14 26								15 26								16 26				
Westenhanger d					14 38								15 38								16 38			
Sandling d					14 41								15 41								16 41			
Folkestone West d	14 13				14 47			15 13					15 47			16 13					16 47			17 13
Folkestone Central d	14 16				14 50			15 16					15 50			16 16					16 50			17 16
Dover Priory ■ a	14 28				15 01			15 28					16 01			16 28					17 01			17 28
d					15 02								16 02								17 02			
Martin Mill d					15 11								16 11								17 11			
Walmer d					15 15								16 15								17 15			
Deal d					15 19								16 19								17 19			
Sandwich d					15 26								16 26								17 26			
Minster ■ d				14 38								15 38								16 38				
Ramsgate ■ a				14 44	15 38	15 15						15 44	16 38	16 15						16 44	17 38	17 15		
Broadstairs a																								
Margate ■ a																								

A ♨ to Ashford International

Table 207

Saturdays
28 July to 11 August

London and Tonbridge - Ashford International, Folkestone, Dover, Canterbury West, Ramsgate and Margate

Network Diagram - see first Page of Table 206

		SE	SE	SE ■	SE ■ A ⌶		SE	SE ■ A ⌶	SE	SE	SE ■	SE ■ A ⌶		SE	SE ■ A ⌶	SE	SE	SE ■	SE ■ A ⌶	SE	SE	SE ■	SE ■ A ⌶
St Pancras Intl. ■ ⊖	d	16 04	16 39						17 04	17 39						18 04	18 39				19 04		
Stratford International ⊖	d	16 14	16 49						17 14	17 49						18 14	18 49				19 14		
Ebbsfleet International	d	16 27	17 02						17 30	18 02						18 30	19 02				19 30		
London Charing Cross ■ ⊖	d				16 10			16 40				17 10			17 40				18 10				18 40
London Waterloo (East) ■ ⊖	d				16 13			16 43				17 13			17 43				18 13				18 43
London Cannon Street ■ ⊖	d																						
London Bridge ■ ⊖	d				16 19			16 49				17 19			17 49				18 19				18 49
Orpington ■	d																						
Sevenoaks ■	d				16 42			17 12				17 42			18 12				18 42				19 12
Tonbridge ■	a				16 50			17 20				17 50			18 20				18 50				19 20
	d				16 50		17 03	17 20				17 50		18 03	18 20				18 50	19 03			19 20
Paddock Wood ■	d				16 58		17 10	17 28				17 58		18 10	18 28				18 58	19 10			19 28
Maidstone West ■ 194	a						17 29							18 29						19 29			
Marden	d				17 03			17 33				18 03			18 33				19 03				19 33
Staplehurst	d				17 07			17 37				18 07			18 37				19 07				19 37
Headcorn	d				17 13			17 43				18 13			18 43				19 13				19 43
Pluckley	d				17 19			17 49				18 19			18 49				19 19				19 49
Ashford International	a	16 46	17 20		17 26			17 56	17 51	18 20		18 26			18 56	18 51	19 20		19 26		19 51		19 56
	d			17 03	17 30	17 33		18 00			18 03	18 30	18 33		19 00			19 03	19 30			19 33	20 00
Wye	d			17 09		17 39					18 09		18 39					19 09				19 39	
Chilham	d					17 45							18 45					19 15				19 45	
Chartham	d					17 49							18 49					19 19				19 49	
Canterbury West ■	d			17 22		17 55					18 22		18 55					19 25				19 55	
Sturry	d			17 26							18 26							19 29					
Westenhanger	d				17 38							18 38							19 38				
Sandling	d				17 41							18 41							19 41				
Folkestone West	d				17 47			18 13				18 47			19 13				19 47				20 13
Folkestone Central	d				17 50			18 16				18 50			19 16				19 50				20 16
Dover Priory ■	a				18 01			18 28				19 01			19 28				20 01				20 28
	d				18 02							19 02							20 02				
Martin Mill	d				18 11							19 11							20 11				
Walmer	d				18 15							19 15							20 15				
Deal	d				18 19							19 19							20 19				
Sandwich	d				18 26							19 26							20 26				
Minster ■	d			17 38							18 38							19 41					
Ramsgate ■	a			17 44	18 38	18 15					18 44	19 38	19 15					19 47	20 38			20 15	
Broadstairs	a																						
Margate ■	a																						

		SE	SE ■	SE ■ A ⌶	SE	SE	SE ■	SE ■ A ⌶	SE	SE ■	SE ■ A ⌶	SE	SE	SE ■	SE ■	SE ■	SE	SE	SE ■	SE ■	SE ■	SE ■
St Pancras Intl. ■ ⊖	d	19 39				20 04			20 39				21 04				21 39					
Stratford International ⊖	d	19 49				20 14			20 49				21 14				21 49					
Ebbsfleet International	d	20 02				20 30			21 02				21 30				22 02					
London Charing Cross ■ ⊖	d			19 10				19 40			20 10				20 40	21 10				21 40	22 10	
London Waterloo (East) ■ ⊖	d			19 13				19 43			20 13				20 43	21 13				21 43	22 13	
London Cannon Street ■ ⊖	d																					
London Bridge ■ ⊖	d			19 19				19 49			20 19				20 49	21 19				21 49	22 19	
Orpington ■	d										20 35				21 05	21 35				22 05	22 35	
Sevenoaks ■	d			19 42				20 12			20 44				21 14	21 44				22 14	22 44	
Tonbridge ■	a			19 50				20 20			20 52				21 22	21 52				22 22	22 52	
	d			19 50	20 03			20 20			20 53	21 03			21 23	21 53		22 03		22 23	22 53	
Paddock Wood ■	d			19 58	20 10			20 28			21 00	21 10			21 30	22 00		22 10		22 30	23 00	
Maidstone West ■ 194	a				20 29							21 29						22 29				
Marden	d			20 03				20 33			21 05				21 35	22 05				22 35	23 05	
Staplehurst	d			20 07				20 37			21 09				21 39	22 09				22 39	23 09	
Headcorn	d			20 13				20 43			21 14				21 44	22 14				22 44	23 14	
Pluckley	d			20 19				20 49			21 20				21 50	22 20				22 50	23 20	
Ashford International	a	20 20		20 26		20 51		20 56	21 20		21 28		21 51		21 58	22 28	22 20			22 58	23 28	
	d		20 03	20 30			20 33	21 00		21 03	21 31			21 34	22 01	22 31			22 34	23 01	23 31	23 34
Wye	d		20 09				20 39			21 09				21 40					22 40			23 40
Chilham	d		20 15				20 45			21 15				21 46					22 46			23 46
Chartham	d		20 19				20 49			21 19				21 50					22 50			23 50
Canterbury West ■	d		20 25				20 55			21 25				21 56					22 56			23 56
Sturry	d		20 29							21 29												
Westenhanger	d			20 38							21 40					22 40					23 40	
Sandling	d			20 41							21 42					22 42					23 42	
Folkestone West	d			20 47				21 13			21 47				22 14	22 47				23 14	23 47	
Folkestone Central	d			20 50				21 16			21 50				22 17	22 50				23 17	23 50	
Dover Priory ■	a			21 01				21 28			22 01				22 28	23 01				23 28	00 01	
	d			21 02							22 02					23 02					00 02	
Martin Mill	d			21 11							22 11					23 11					00 11	
Walmer	d			21 15							22 15					23 15					00 15	
Deal	d			21 19							22 19					23 19					00 19	
Sandwich	d			21 26							22 26					23 26					00 26	
Minster ■	d		20 41							21 41												
Ramsgate ■	a		20 47	21 38			21 15			21 47	22 38			22 16		23 38			23 16		00 38	00 16
Broadstairs	a																					
Margate ■	a																					

A ⌶ to Ashford International

Table 207

Saturdays
28 July to 11 August

London and Tonbridge - Ashford International, Folkestone, Dover, Canterbury West, Ramsgate and Margate

Network Diagram - see first Page of Table 206

		SE ■	SE ■	SE ■	
St Pancras Intl. ■ ⊖	d				
Stratford International ⊖	d				
Ebbsfleet International	d				
London Charing Cross ■ ⊖	d	22 40	23 10	23 40	
London Waterloo (East) ■ ⊖	d	22 43	23 13	23 43	
London Cannon Street ■ ⊖	d				
London Bridge ■ ⊖	d	22 49	23 19	23 49	
Orpington ■	d	23 05	23 35	00 05	
Sevenoaks ■	d	23 14	23 44	00 14	
Tonbridge ■	a	23 22	23 52	00 22	
	d	23 23	23 53	00 23	
Paddock Wood ■	d	23 30	23 59	00 30	
Maidstone West ■ 194	a				
Marden	d	23 35	00 05	00 35	
Staplehurst	d	23 39	00 09	00 39	
Headcorn	d	23 44	00 14	00 44	
Pluckley	d	23 50	00 20	00 50	
Ashford International	a	23 57	00 28	00 58	
	d	00 03	00 31	01 01	01 04
Wye	d	00 09			01 10
Chilham	d	00 15			01 16
Chartham	d	00 19			01 20
Canterbury West ■	d	00 25			01a25
Sturry	d	00 29			
Westenhanger	d		00 40	01 10	
Sandling	d		00 42	01 12	
Folkestone West	d		00 47	01 17	
Folkestone Central	d		00 50	01 20	
Dover Priory ■	a		01 01	01 31	
	d				
Martin Mill	d				
Walmer	d				
Deal	d				
Sandwich	d				
Minster ■	d	00 41			
Ramsgate ■	a	00 47			
Broadstairs	a				
Margate ■	a				

Saturdays
25 August to 8 September

		SE ■	SE ■	SE A	SE B	SE ■		SE ■	SE ■		SE A	SE B	SE ■	SE	SE ■	SE ■	SE B	SE ■	SE B	SE A	SE ■	SE	SE ■
St Pancras Intl. ■ ⊖	d			23p12	23p12						00 12	00 12					06 10		06 39	06 40			
Stratford International ⊖	d			23p19	23p20						00 19	00 20					06 16		06 47	06 47			
Ebbsfleet International	d			23p31	23p32						00 31	00 32					06 28		06 59	06 59			
London Charing Cross ■ ⊖	d	21p40	22p10			22p40		23p10	23p40												06 00		
London Waterloo (East) ■ ⊖	d	21p43	22p13			22p43		23p13	23p43												06 03		
London Cannon Street ■ ⊖	d																						
London Bridge ■ ⊖	d	21p49	22p19			22p49		23p19	23p49												06 08		
Orpington ■	d		22p35					23p35													06 24		
Sevenoaks ■	d	22p12	22p44			23p12		23p44	00 12												06 33		
Tonbridge ■	a	22p20	22p52			23p20		23p52	00 20												06 43		
	d	22p20	22p53			23p20		23p53	00 20					06 03				06 20			06 50	07 03	
Paddock Wood ■	d	22p28	23p00			23p28		23p59	00 28					06 10				06 28			06 58	07 10	
Maidstone West ■ 194	a													06 29								07 29	
Marden	d	22p33	23p06			23p33		00 06	00 33									06 33			07 03		
Staplehurst	d	22p37	23p10			23p37		00 10	00 37									06 37			07 07		
Headcorn	d	22p43	23p15			23p43		00 15	00 43									06 43			07 13		
Pluckley	d	22p49	23p21			23p49		00 21	00 49									06 49			07 19		
Ashford International	a	22p56	23p29	23p50	23p51	23p56		00 29	00 56		00 50	00 51					06 50	06 56	07 18	07 18	07 26		
	d	23p00	23p32	23p52	23p53	00 01	00 03	00 32	01 00	01 03			01 03		06 30	06 33	06 52	07 03	07 22	07 22	07 30		07 33
Wye	d						00 09			01 09			01 09			06 39		07 09					07 39
Chilham	d						00 15			01 15			01 15			06 45							07 45
Chartham	d						00 19			01 19			01 19			06 49							07 49
Canterbury West ■	d						00 25			01a24			01a24			06a54		07 22	07 39	07 39			07a54
Sturry	d						00 29											07 26					
Westenhanger	d	23p08	23p41			00 09		00 41	01 08						06 38						07 38		
Sandling	d	23p11	23p43			00 12		00 43	01 11						06 41						07 41		
Folkestone West	d	23p17	23p49	00 05	00 06	00 18		00 49	01 17						06 47		07 05				07 47		
Folkestone Central	d	23p20	23p52	00 08	00 08	00 21		00 52	01 20						06 50		07 08				07 50		
Dover Priory ■	a	23p31	00 05	00 20	00 20	00 32		01 03	01 31						07 01		07 20				08 01		
	d	23p32	00 06												07 02						08 02		
Martin Mill	d	23p41	00 15												07 11						08 11		
Walmer	d	23p45	00 19												07 15						08 15		
Deal	d	23p49	00 23												07 19						08 19		
Sandwich	d	23p56	00 30												07 26						08 26		
Minster ■	d						00 41											07 38					
Ramsgate ■	a	00 08	00 42				00 47								07 38			07 44	07 59	07 59	08 38		
Broadstairs	a																		08 04	08 04			
Margate ■	a																		08 10	08 10			

A not from 1 September until 8 September

B not 25 August

Saturdays
25 August to 8 September

London and Tonbridge - Ashford International, Folkestone, Dover, Canterbury West, Ramsgate and Margate

Network Diagram - see first Page of Table 206

	SE	SE	SE	SE	SE		SE	SE	SE	SE	SE	SE	SE		SE	SE	SE	SE	SE	SE	SE	
	A	B	■1		■1			A	B	■1	B	A	■1			A	B	■1	A	B	■1	
St Pancras Intl. ■15 ⊖ d	07 10	07 12		07 42				08 11	08 12		08 40	08 41				09 09	09 10		09 36	09 42		
Stratford International ⊖ d	07 17	07 19		07 49				08 19	08 19		08 47	08 49				09 17	09 17		09 44	09 49		
Ebbsfleet International d	07 30	07 31		08 01				08 31	08 31		08 59	09 01				09 29	09 29		09 56	10 01		
London Charing Cross ■4 ⊖ d					07 00					07 30			08 00					08 40			09 10	
London Waterloo (East) ■4 ⊖ d					07 03					07 33			08 03					08 43			09 13	
London Cannon Street ■4 ⊖ d																						
London Bridge ■4 ⊖ d					07 08					07 38			08 08					08 49			09 19	
Orpington ■4 d					07 24					07 54			08 24									
Sevenoaks ■4 d					07 33					08 03			08 33					09 12			09 42	
Tonbridge ■4 a					07 43					08 14			08 43					09 20			09 50	
d					07 50		08 03			08 20			08 50		09 03			09 20			09 50	
Paddock Wood ■4 d					07 58		08 10			08 28			08 58		09 10			09 28			09 58	
Maidstone West ■4 194 a							08 29								09 29							
Marden d					08 03					08 33			09 03					09 33			10 03	
Staplehurst d					08 07					08 37			09 07					09 37			10 07	
Headcorn d					08 13					08 43			09 13					09 43			10 13	
Pluckley d					08 19					08 49			09 19					09 49			10 19	
Ashford International a	07 50	07 51		08 20	08 27			08 50	08 50	08 56	09 18	09 20	09 26			09 48	09 48	09 56	10 15	10 20	10 26	
d	07 51	07 52	08 03	08 22	08 31	08 34		08 52	08 52	09 03	09 22	09 22	09 30	09 33		09 52	09 52	10 03	10 22	10 22	10 30	10 33
Wye d			08 09			08 40				09 09				09 39				10 09				10 39
Chilham d						08 46								09 45								10 45
Chartham d						08 50								09 49								10 49
Canterbury West ■4 d			08 22	08 39		08a55				09 22	09 39	09 39		09a54				10 22	10 39	10 39		10a54
Sturry d			08 26							09 26								10 26				
Westenhanger d					08 39								09 38								10 38	
Sandling d					08 42								09 41								10 41	
Folkestone West d	08 04	08 05			08 47			09 05	09 05				09 47			10 05	10 05				10 47	
Folkestone Central d	08 07	08 08			08 50			09 08	09 08				09 50			10 08	10 08				10 50	
Dover Priory ■4 a	08 18	08 20			09 01			09 20	09 20				10 01			10 20	10 20				11 01	
d					09 02								10 02								11 02	
Martin Mill d					09 11								10 11								11 11	
Walmer d					09 15								10 15								11 15	
Deal d					09 19								10 19								11 19	
Sandwich d					09 26								10 26								11 26	
Minster ■4 d			08 38							09 38								10 38				
Ramsgate ■4 a			08 44	08 59	09 38					09 48	09 59	09 59	10 38					10 44	10 59	10 59	11 38	
Broadstairs a				09 04							10 04	10 04							11 04	11 04		
Margate ■4 a				09 10							10 10	10 10							11 10	11 10		

	SE	SE	SE	SE	SE	SE	SE		SE	SE	SE	SE	SE	SE	SE		SE	SE	SE	SE	SE
		A	B	■1	A	B	■1 C 🛒			A	B	■1 C 🛒	A	B	■1 C 🛒			A	B	■1 C 🛒	A
St Pancras Intl. ■15 ⊖ d		10 11	10 12		10 41	10 42				11 11	11 12		11 41	11 42				12 11	12 12		12 41
Stratford International ⊖ d		10 19	10 19		10 49	10 49				11 19	11 19		11 49	11 49				12 19	12 19		12 49
Ebbsfleet International d		10 31	10 31		11 01	11 01				11 31	11 31		12 01	12 01				12 31	12 31		13 01
London Charing Cross ■4 ⊖ d				09 40			10 10					10 40			11 10					11 40	
London Waterloo (East) ■4 ⊖ d				09 43			10 13					10 43			11 13					11 43	
London Cannon Street ■4 ⊖ d																					
London Bridge ■4 ⊖ d				09 49			10 19					10 49			11 19					11 49	
Orpington ■4 d																					
Sevenoaks ■4 d				10 12			10 42					11 12			11 42					12 12	
Tonbridge ■4 a				10 20			10 50					11 20			11 50					12 20	
d	10 03			10 20			10 50		11 03			11 20			11 50		12 03			12 20	
Paddock Wood ■4 d	10 10			10 28			10 58		11 10			11 28			11 58		12 10			12 28	
Maidstone West ■4 194 a	10 29								11 29								12 29				
Marden d				10 33			11 03					11 33			12 03					12 33	
Staplehurst d				10 37			11 07					11 37			12 07					12 37	
Headcorn d				10 43			11 13					11 43			12 13					12 43	
Pluckley d				10 49			11 19					11 49			12 19					12 49	
Ashford International a		10 50	10 50	10 56	11 20	11 20	11 26			11 50	11 50	11 56	12 20	12 20	12 26			12 50	12 50	12 56	13 20
d		10 52	10 52	11 03	11 22	11 22	11 30	11 33		11 52	11 52	12 03	12 22	12 22	12 30	12 33		12 52	12 52	13 03	13 22
Wye d				11 09				11 39				12 09				12 39				13 09	
Chilham d								11 45								12 45					
Chartham d								11 49								12 49					
Canterbury West ■4 d				11 22	11 39	11 39		11a54				12 22	12 39	12 39		12a54				13 22	13 39
Sturry d				11 26								12 26								13 26	
Westenhanger d							11 38								12 38						
Sandling d							11 41								12 41						
Folkestone West d		11 05	11 05				11 47			12 05	12 05				12 47			13 05	13 05		
Folkestone Central d		11 08	11 08				11 50			12 08	12 08				12 50			13 08	13 08		
Dover Priory ■4 a		11 20	11 20				12 01			12 20	12 20				13 01			13 20	13 20		
d							12 02								13 02						
Martin Mill d							12 11								13 11						
Walmer d							12 15								13 15						
Deal d							12 19								13 19						
Sandwich d							12 26								13 26						
Minster ■4 d				11 38								12 38								13 38	
Ramsgate ■4 a				11 44	11 59	11 59	12 38					12 44	12 59	12 59	13 38					13 44	13 59
Broadstairs a					12 04	12 04							13 04	13 04							14 04
Margate ■4 a					12 10	12 10							13 10	13 10							14 10

A not 25 August
B not from 1 September until 8 September
C 🛒 to Ashford International

Saturdays
25 August to 8 September

London and Tonbridge - Ashford International, Folkestone, Dover, Canterbury West, Ramsgate and Margate

Network Diagram - see first Page of Table 206

	SE	SE		SE	SE	SE	SE	SE	SE	SE		SE	SE	SE	SE	SE	SE	SE		SE	SE	SE
	A	■1 B 🛒			C	A	■1 B 🛒	C	A	■1 B 🛒			C	A	■1 B 🛒	C	A	■1 B 🛒			C	A
St Pancras Intl. ■15 ⊖ d	12 42				13 11	13 12		13 41	13 42				14 11	14 12		14 41	14 42				15 11	15 12
Stratford International ⊖ d	12 49				13 19	13 19		13 49	13 49				14 19	14 19		14 49	14 49				15 19	15 19
Ebbsfleet International d	13 01				13 31	13 31		14 01	14 01				14 31	14 31		15 01	15 01				15 31	15 31
London Charing Cross ■4 ⊖ d		12 10					12 40			13 10					13 40			14 10				
London Waterloo (East) ■4 ⊖ d		12 13					12 43			13 13					13 43			14 13				
London Cannon Street ■4 ⊖ d																						
London Bridge ■4 ⊖ d		12 19					12 49			13 19					13 49			14 19				
Orpington ■4 d																						
Sevenoaks ■4 d		12 42					13 12			13 42					14 12			14 42				
Tonbridge ■4 a		12 50					13 20			13 50					14 20			14 50				
d		12 50		13 03			13 20			13 50		14 03			14 20			14 50		15 03		
Paddock Wood ■4 d		12 58		13 10			13 28			13 58		14 10			14 28			14 58		15 10		
Maidstone West ■4 194 a				13 29								14 29								15 29		
Marden d		13 03					13 33			14 03					14 33			15 03				
Staplehurst d		13 07					13 37			14 07					14 37			15 07				
Headcorn d		13 13					13 43			14 13					14 43			15 13				
Pluckley d		13 19					13 49			14 19					14 49			15 19				
Ashford International a	13 20	13 26			13 50	13 50	13 56	14 20	14 20	14 26			14 50	14 50	14 56	15 20	15 20	15 26			15 50	15 50
d	13 22	13 30	13 33		13 52	13 52	14 03	14 22	14 22	14 30	14 33		14 52	14 52	15 03	15 22	15 22	15 30	15 33		15 52	15 52
Wye d			13 39				14 09				14 39				15 09				15 39			
Chilham d			13 45								14 45								15 45			
Chartham d			13 49								14 49								15 49			
Canterbury West ■4 d	13 39		13a54				14 22	14 39	14 39		14a54				15 22	15 39	15 39		15a54			
Sturry d							14 26								15 26							
Westenhanger d		13 38								14 38								15 38				
Sandling d		13 41								14 41								15 41				
Folkestone West d		13 47			14 05	14 05				14 47			15 05	15 05				15 47			16 05	16 05
Folkestone Central d		13 50			14 08	14 08				14 50			15 08	15 08				15 50			16 08	16 08
Dover Priory ■4 a		14 01			14 20	14 20				15 01			15 20	15 20				16 01			16 20	16 20
d		14 02								15 02								16 02				
Martin Mill d		14 11								15 11								16 11				
Walmer d		14 15								15 15								16 15				
Deal d		14 19								15 19								16 19				
Sandwich d		14 26								15 26								16 26				
Minster ■4 d							14 38								15 38							
Ramsgate ■4 a	13 59	14 38					14 44	14 59	14 59	15 38					15 44	15 59	15 59	16 38				
Broadstairs a	14 04							15 04	15 04							16 04	16 04					
Margate ■4 a	14 10							15 10	15 10							16 10	16 10					

	SE	SE	SE	SE		SE	SE	SE	SE	SE	SE	SE		SE	SE	SE	SE	SE	SE	SE		SE
	■1 B 🛒	C	A	■1 B 🛒			C	A	■1 B 🛒	C	A	■1 B 🛒			C	A	■1 B 🛒	C	A	■1 B 🛒		
St Pancras Intl. ■15 ⊖ d		15 41	15 42				16 09	16 10		16 41	16 42				17 11	17 12		17 41	17 42			
Stratford International ⊖ d		15 49	15 49				16 17	16 17		16 49	16 49				17 19	17 19		17 49	17 49			
Ebbsfleet International d		16 01	16 01				16 29	16 29		17 01	17 01				17 31	17 31		18 01	18 01			
London Charing Cross ■4 ⊖ d	14 40			15 10					15 40			16 10					16 40			17 10		
London Waterloo (East) ■4 ⊖ d	14 43			15 13					15 43			16 13					16 43			17 13		
London Cannon Street ■4 ⊖ d																						
London Bridge ■4 ⊖ d	14 49			15 19					15 49			16 19					16 49			17 19		
Orpington ■4 d																						
Sevenoaks ■4 d	15 12			15 42					16 12			16 42					17 12			17 42		
Tonbridge ■4 a	15 20			15 50					16 20			16 50					17 20			17 50		
d	15 20			15 50		16 03			16 20			16 50		17 03			17 20			17 50		18 03
Paddock Wood ■4 d	15 28			15 58		16 10			16 28			16 58		17 10			17 28			17 58		18 10
Maidstone West ■4 194 a						16 29								17 29								18 29
Marden d	15 33			16 03					16 33			17 03					17 33			18 03		
Staplehurst d	15 37			16 07					16 37			17 07					17 37			18 07		
Headcorn d	15 43			16 13					16 43			17 13					17 43			18 13		
Pluckley d	15 49			16 19					16 49			17 19					17 49			18 19		
Ashford International a	15 56	16 20	16 20	16 26			16 48	16 48	16 56	17 20	17 20	17 26			17 50	17 50	17 56	18 20	18 20	18 26		
d	16 03	16 22	16 22	16 30	16 33		16 52	16 52	17 03	17 22	17 22	17 30	17 33		17 52	17 52	18 03	18 22	18 22	18 30	18 33	
Wye d	16 09				16 39				17 09				17 39				18 09				18 39	
Chilham d					16 45								17 45								18 45	
Chartham d					16 49								17 49								18 49	
Canterbury West ■4 d	16 22	16 39	16 39		16a54				17 22	17 39	17 39		17a54				18 22	18 39	18 39		18a54	
Sturry d	16 26								17 26								18 26					
Westenhanger d				16 38								17 38								18 38		
Sandling d				16 41								17 41								18 41		
Folkestone West d				16 47			17 05	17 05				17 47			18 05	18 05				18 47		
Folkestone Central d				16 50			17 08	17 08				17 50			18 08	18 08				18 50		
Dover Priory ■4 a				17 01			17 20	17 20				18 01			18 20	18 20				19 01		
d				17 02								18 02								19 02		
Martin Mill d				17 11								18 11								19 11		
Walmer d				17 15								18 15								19 15		
Deal d				17 19								18 19								19 19		
Sandwich d				17 26								18 26								19 26		
Minster ■4 d	16 38								17 38								18 38					
Ramsgate ■4 a	16 44	16 59	16 59	17 38					17 44	17 59	17 59	18 38					18 44	18 59	18 59	19 38		
Broadstairs a		17 04	17 04							18 04	18 04							19 04	19 04			
Margate ■4 a		17 10	17 10							18 10	18 10							19 10	19 10			

A not from 1 September until 8 September
B 🛒 to Ashford International
C not 25 August

Table 207

Saturdays
25 August to 8 September

London and Tonbridge - Ashford International, Folkestone, Dover, Canterbury West, Ramsgate and Margate

Network Diagram - see first Page of Table 206

		SE A	SE B	SE ■ C	SE A	SE B	SE ■ C	SE	SE A	SE B	SE ■ C	SE A	SE B	SE ■ C	SE	SE A	SE B	SE ■ C	SE A	SE B	SE ■ C	SE
St Pancras Intl. ⊖	d	18 11	18 12		18 41	18 42			19 11	19 12		19 41	19 42			20 11	20 12		20 41	20 42		
Stratford International ⊖	d	18 19	18 19		18 49	18 49			19 19	19 19		19 49	19 49			20 19	20 19		20 49	20 49		
Ebbsfleet International	d	18 31	18 31		19 01	19 01			19 31	19 31		20 01	20 01			20 31	20 31		21 01	21 01		
London Charing Cross ⊖	d			17 40			18 10				18 40			19 10				19 40			20 10	
London Waterloo (East) ⊖	d			17 43			18 13				18 43			19 13				19 43			20 13	
London Cannon Street ⊖	d																					
London Bridge ⊖	d			17 49			18 19				18 49			19 19				19 49			20 19	
Orpington	d																				20 35	
Sevenoaks	d			18 12			18 42				19 12			19 42				20 12			20 44	
Tonbridge	a			18 20			18 50				19 20			19 50				20 20			20 52	
	d			18 20			18 50	19 03			19 20			19 50	20 03			20 20			20 53	21 03
Paddock Wood	d			18 28			18 58	19 10			19 28			19 58	20 10			20 28			21 00	21 10
Maidstone West 194	a							19 29							20 29							21 29
Marden	d			18 33			19 03				19 33			20 03				20 33			21 05	
Staplehurst	d			18 37			19 07				19 37			20 07				20 37			21 09	
Headcorn	d			18 43			19 13				19 43			20 13				20 43			21 14	
Pluckley	d			18 49			19 19				19 49			20 19				20 49			21 20	
Ashford International	a	18 50	18 50	18 56	19 20	19 20	19 26		19 50	19 50	19 56	20 20	20 20	20 26		20 50	20 50	20 56	21 20	21 20	21 28	
	d	18 52	18 52	19 03	19 22	19 22	19 30		19 52	19 52	20 03	20 22	20 22	20 30		20 52	20 52	21 03	21 22	21 22	21 31	
Wye	d			19 09							20 09							21 09				
Chilham	d			19 15							20 15							21 15				
Chartham	d			19 19							20 19							21 19				
Canterbury West	d			19 25	19 39	19 39					20 25	20 39	20 39					21 25	21 39	21 39		
Sturry	d			19 29							20 29							21 29				
Westenhanger	d						19 38							20 38							21 40	
Sandling	d						19 41							20 41							21 42	
Folkestone West	d	19 05	19 05				19 47		20 05	20 05				20 47		21 05	21 05				21 47	
Folkestone Central	d	19 08	19 08				19 50		20 08	20 08				20 50		21 08	21 08				21 50	
Dover Priory	a	19 20	19 20				20 01		20 20	20 20				21 01		21 20	21 20				22 01	
	d						20 02							21 02							22 02	
Martin Mill	d						20 11							21 11							22 11	
Walmer	d						20 15							21 15							22 15	
Deal	d						20 19							21 19							22 19	
Sandwich	d						20 26							21 26							22 26	
Minster	d			19 41							20 41							21 41				
Ramsgate	a			19 47	19 59	19 59	20 38				20 47	20 59	20 59	21 38				21 47	21 59	21 59	22 38	
Broadstairs	a				20 04	20 04						21 04	21 04						22 04	22 04		
Margate	a				20 10	20 10						21 10	21 10						22 10	22 10		

		SE A	SE B	SE ■	SE A	SE B	SE ■	SE	SE A	SE B	SE ■	SE B	SE A	SE ■	SE B	SE A	SE ■	SE ■		SE ■
St Pancras Intl. ⊖	d	21 11	21 12		21 41	21 42			22 11	22 12		22 42	22 42		23 12	23 12				
Stratford International ⊖	d	21 19	21 19		21 49	21 49			22 19	22 19		22 49	22 50		23 19	23 20				
Ebbsfleet International	d	21 31	21 31		22 01	22 01			22 31	22 31		23 01	23 02		23 31	23 32				
London Charing Cross ⊖	d			20 40			21 10				21 40			22 10			22 40	23 10		23 40
London Waterloo (East) ⊖	d			20 43			21 13				21 43			22 13			22 43	23 13		23 43
London Cannon Street ⊖	d																			
London Bridge ⊖	d			20 49			21 19				21 49			22 19			22 49	23 19		23 49
Orpington	d			21 05			21 35				22 05			22 35			23 05	23 35		00 05
Sevenoaks	d			21 14			21 44				22 14			22 44			23 14	23 44		00 14
Tonbridge	a			21 22			21 52				22 22			22 52			23 22	23 52		00 22
	d			21 23			21 53	22 03			22 23			22 53			23 23	23 53		00 23
Paddock Wood	d			21 30			22 00	22 10			22 30			23 00			23 30	23 59		00 30
Maidstone West 194	a							22 29												
Marden	d			21 35			22 05				22 35			23 05			23 35	00 05		00 35
Staplehurst	d			21 39			22 09				22 39			23 09			23 39	00 09		00 39
Headcorn	d			21 44			22 14				22 44			23 14			23 44	00 14		00 44
Pluckley	d			21 50			22 20				22 50			23 20			23 50	00 20		00 50
Ashford International	a	21 50	21 50	21 58	22 20	22 20	22 28		22 50	22 50	22 58	23 20	23 20	23 28	23 50	23 50	23 58	00 28		00 58
	d	21 52	21 52	22 03	22 22	22 22	22 31		22 52	22 52	23 03	23 22	23 22	23 31	23 52	23 52	00 03	00 31	01 01	01 04
Wye	d			22 09							23 09						00 09			01 10
Chilham	d			22 15							23 15						00 15			01 16
Chartham	d			22 19							23 19						00 19			01 20
Canterbury West	d			22 25	22 39	22 39					23 25	23 39	23 39				00 25			01a25
Sturry	d			22 29							23 29						00 29			
Westenhanger	d						22 40							23 40				00 40	01 10	
Sandling	d						22 42							23 42				00 42	01 12	
Folkestone West	d	22 05	22 05				22 47		23 05	23 05				23 47	00 05	00 05		00 47	01 17	
Folkestone Central	d	22 08	22 08				22 50		23 08	23 08				23 50	00 08	00 08		00 50	01 20	
Dover Priory	a	22 20	22 20				23 01		23 20	23 20				00 01	00 20	00 20		01 01	01 31	
	d						23 02							00 02						
Martin Mill	d						23 11							00 11						
Walmer	d						23 15							00 15						
Deal	d						23 19							00 19						
Sandwich	d						23 26							00 26						
Minster	d			22 41							23 41						00 41			
Ramsgate	a			22 48	22 59	22 59	23 38				23 47	23 59	23 59	00 38			00 47			
Broadstairs	a				23 04	23 04														
Margate	a				23 10	23 10														

A not 25 August
B not from 1 September until 8 September
C ⌶ to Ashford International

Table 207

Sundays
until 22 July, 19 Aug and from 16 Sep

London and Tonbridge - Ashford International, Folkestone, Dover, Canterbury West, Ramsgate and Margate

Network Diagram - see first Page of Table 206

		SE ■	SE	SE ■	SE ■		SE ■	SE	SE	SE	SE ■	SE ■	SE ■	SE	SE	SE ■		SE	SE ■	SE	SE	SE ■	
St Pancras Intl. ⊖	d		23p12					00 12							08 42			09 10			09 42		
Stratford International ⊖	d		23p19					00 19							08 49			09 17			09 49		
Ebbsfleet International	d		23p31					00 31							09 01			09 29			10 01		
London Charing Cross ⊖	d	22p10		22p40	23p10		23p40									08 08			08 38			09 08	
London Waterloo (East) ⊖	d	22p13		22p43	23p13		23p43									08 11			08 41			09 11	
London Cannon Street ⊖	d																						
London Bridge ⊖	d	22p19		22p49	23p19		23p49									08 16			08 46			09 16	
Orpington	d	22p35		23p05	23p35		00 05									08 32			09 02			09 32	
Sevenoaks	d	22p44		23p14	23p44		00 14									08 42			09 12			09 42	
Tonbridge	a	22p52		23p22	23p52		00 22									08 52			09 20			09 52	
	d	22p53		23p23	23p53		00 23		06 26				08 20			08 52			09 20			09 52	
Paddock Wood	d	23p00		23p30	23p59		00 30		06 34	07 34			08 28	08 34		09 00			09 28	09 34		10 00	
Maidstone West 194	a								06 53	07 53				08 53						09 53			
Marden	d	23p05		23p35	00 05		00 35						08 33			09 05			09 33			10 05	
Staplehurst	d	23p09		23p39	00 09		00 39						08 37			09 09			09 37			10 09	
Headcorn	d	23p14		23p44	00 14		00 44						08 43			09 15			09 43			10 15	
Pluckley	d	23p20		23p50	00 20		00 50						08 49						09 49				
Ashford International	a	23p28	23p50	23p58	00 28		00 58	00 50					08 56		09 20	09 26		09 48	09 56		10 20	10 26	
	d	23p31	23p52	00 03	00 31	01 01	01 04				08 30	08 33	09 03		09 22	09 30	09 33	09 52	10 03		10 22	10 30	10 33
Wye	d			00 09			01 10					08 39	09 09				09 39		10 09				10 39
Chilham	d			00 15			01 16					08 45					09 45						10 45
Chartham	d			00 19			01 20					08 49					09 49						10 49
Canterbury West	d			00 25			01a25					08a54	09 22		09 39		09a54		10 22		10 39		10a54
Sturry	d			00 29									09 26						10 26				
Westenhanger	d	23p40			00 40	01 10					08 38					09 38						10 38	
Sandling	d	23p42			00 42	01 12					08 41					09 41						10 41	
Folkestone West	d	23p47	00 05		00 47	01 17					08 47					09 47		10 05				10 47	
Folkestone Central	d	23p50	00 08		00 50	01 20					08 50					09 50		10 08				10 50	
Dover Priory	a	00 01	00 20		01 01	01 31					09 01					10 01		10 20				11 01	
	d	00 02									09 02					10 02						11 02	
Martin Mill	d	00 11									09 11					10 11						11 11	
Walmer	d	00 15									09 15					10 15						11 15	
Deal	d	00 19									09 19					10 19						11 19	
Sandwich	d	00 26									09 26					10 26						11 26	
Minster	d			00 41									09 38						10 38				
Ramsgate	a	00 38		00 47							09 38		09 44		09 59	10 38			10 44		10 59	11 38	
Broadstairs	a														10 04						11 04		
Margate	a														10 10						11 10		

		SE	SE ■	SE	SE	SE ■ A		SE	SE ■ A	SE	SE	SE ■ A		SE	SE ■ A	SE	SE	SE ■ A		SE	SE ■ A	SE	SE
St Pancras Intl. ⊖	d	10 10			10 42			11 12			11 42			12 12			12 42			13 12			13 42
Stratford International ⊖	d	10 17			10 49			11 19			11 49			12 19			12 49			13 19			13 49
Ebbsfleet International	d	10 29			11 01			11 31			12 01			12 31			13 01			13 31			14 01
London Charing Cross ⊖	d		09 38			10 08			10 38			11 08			11 38			12 08			12 38		
London Waterloo (East) ⊖	d		09 41			10 11			10 41			11 11			11 41			12 11			12 41		
London Cannon Street ⊖	d																						
London Bridge ⊖	d		09 46			10 16			10 46			11 16			11 46			12 16			12 46		
Orpington	d		10 02			10 32			11 02			11 32			12 02			12 32			13 02		
Sevenoaks	d		10 12			10 42			11 12			11 42			12 12			12 42			13 12		
Tonbridge	a		10 20			10 52			11 20			11 52			12 20			12 52			13 20		
	d		10 20			10 52			11 20			11 52			12 20			12 52			13 20		
Paddock Wood	d		10 28	10 34		11 00			11 28	11 34		12 00			12 28	12 34		13 00			13 28	13 34	
Maidstone West 194	a			10 53						11 53						12 53						13 53	
Marden	d		10 33			11 05			11 33			12 05			12 33			13 05			13 33		
Staplehurst	d		10 37			11 09			11 37			12 09			12 37			13 09			13 37		
Headcorn	d		10 43			11 15			11 43			12 15			12 43			13 15			13 43		
Pluckley	d		10 49						11 49						12 49						13 49		
Ashford International	a	10 48	10 56		11 20	11 26		11 50	11 56		12 20	12 26		12 50	12 56		13 20	13 26		13 50	13 56		14 20
	d	10 52	11 03		11 22	11 30	11 33	11 52	12 03		12 22	12 30	12 33	12 52	13 03		13 22	13 30	13 33	13 52	14 03		14 22
Wye	d		11 09				11 39		12 09				12 39		13 09				13 39		14 09		
Chilham	d						11 45						12 45						13 45				
Chartham	d						11 49						12 49						13 49				
Canterbury West	d		11 22		11 39		11a54		12 22		12 39		12a54		13 22		13 39		13a54		14 22		14 39
Sturry	d		11 26						12 26						13 26						14 26		
Westenhanger	d					11 38						12 38						13 38					
Sandling	d					11 41						12 41						13 41					
Folkestone West	d	11 05				11 47		12 05				12 47		13 05				13 47		14 05			
Folkestone Central	d	11 08				11 50		12 08				12 50		13 08				13 50		14 08			
Dover Priory	a	11 20				12 01		12 20				13 01		13 20				14 01		14 20			
	d					12 02						13 02						14 02					
Martin Mill	d					12 11						13 11						14 11					
Walmer	d					12 15						13 15						14 15					
Deal	d					12 19						13 19						14 19					
Sandwich	d					12 26						13 26						14 26					
Minster	d		11 38						12 38						13 38						14 38		
Ramsgate	a		11 44		11 59	12 38			12 44		12 59	13 38			13 44		13 59	14 38			14 44		14 59
Broadstairs	a				12 04						13 04						14 04						15 04
Margate	a				12 10						13 10						14 10						15 10

A ⌶ to Ashford International

Table 207

Sundays
until 22 July, 19 Aug and from 16 Sep

London and Tonbridge - Ashford International, Folkestone, Dover, Canterbury West, Ramsgate and Margate

Network Diagram - see first Page of Table 206

Station		SE 1 A ⚒		SE	SE 1 A ⚒	SE	SE	SE 1 A ⚒		SE	SE 1 A ⚒	SE	SE	SE 1 A ⚒		SE	SE 1 A ⚒	SE	SE	SE 1 A ⚒		SE
St Pancras Intl. 15 ⊖	d			14 12			14 42			15 12			15 42			16 10			16 42			17 12
Stratford International ⊖	d			14 19			14 49			15 19			15 49			16 17			16 49			17 19
Ebbsfleet International	d			14 31			15 01			15 31			16 01			16 29			17 01			17 31
London Charing Cross 4 ⊖	d	13 08			13 38			14 08			14 38			15 08			15 38			16 08		
London Waterloo (East) 4 ⊖	d	13 11			13 41			14 11			14 41			15 11			15 41			16 11		
London Cannon Street 4 ⊖	d																					
London Bridge 4 ⊖	d	13 16			13 46			14 16			14 46			15 16			15 46			16 16		
Orpington 4	d	13 32			14 02			14 32			15 02			15 32			16 02			16 32		
Sevenoaks 4	d	13 42			14 12			14 42			15 12			15 42			16 12			16 42		
Tonbridge 4	a	13 52			14 20			14 52			15 20			15 52			16 20			16 52		
	d	13 52			14 20			14 52			15 20			15 52			16 20			16 52		
Paddock Wood 4	d	14 00			14 28	14 34		15 00			15 28	15 34		16 00			16 28	16 34		17 00		
Maidstone West 4 194	a					14 53						15 53						16 53				
Marden	d	14 05			14 33			15 05			15 33			16 05			16 33			17 05		
Staplehurst	d	14 09			14 37			15 09			15 37			16 09			16 37			17 09		
Headcorn	d	14 15			14 43			15 15			15 43			16 15			16 43			17 15		
Pluckley	d				14 49						15 49						16 49					
Ashford International	a	14 26		14 50	14 56		15 20	15 26		15 50	15 56		16 20	16 26		16 48	16 56		17 20	17 26		17 50
	d	14 30	14 33	14 52	15 03		15 22	15 30	15 33	15 52	16 03		16 22	16 30	16 33	16 52	17 03		17 22	17 30	17 33	17 52
Wye	d		14 39		15 09				15 39		16 09				16 39		17 09				17 39	
Chilham	d		14 45						15 45						16 45						17 45	
Chartham	d		14 49						15 49						16 49						17 49	
Canterbury West 4	d		14a54		15 22		15 39		15a54		16 22		16 39		16a54		17 22		17 39		17a54	
Sturry	d				15 26						16 26						17 26					
Westenhanger	d	14 38						15 38						16 38						17 38		
Sandling	d	14 41						15 41						16 41						17 41		
Folkestone West	d	14 47		15 05				15 47		16 05				16 47		17 05				17 47		18 05
Folkestone Central	d	14 50		15 08				15 50		16 08				16 50		17 08				17 50		18 08
Dover Priory 4	a	15 01		15 20				16 01		16 20				17 01		17 20				18 01		18 20
	d	15 02						16 02						17 02						18 02		
Martin Mill	d	15 11						16 11						17 11						18 11		
Walmer	d	15 15						16 15						17 15						18 15		
Deal	d	15 19						16 19						17 19						18 19		
Sandwich	d	15 26						16 26						17 26						18 26		
Minster 4	d				15 38						16 38						17 38					
Ramsgate 4	a	15 38			15 44		15 59	16 38			16 44		16 59	17 38			17 44		17 59	18 38		
Broadstairs	a						16 04						17 04						18 04			
Margate 4	a						16 10						17 10						18 10			

Station		SE 1 A ⚒	SE	SE	SE 1 A ⚒	SE	SE 1 A ⚒	SE	SE	SE 1 A ⚒	SE	SE 1 A ⚒	SE	SE	SE 1 A ⚒	SE	SE 1 A ⚒	SE	SE	SE 1 A ⚒	SE	SE 1	SE
St Pancras Intl. 15 ⊖	d			17 42		18 12			18 42		19 12			19 42		20 12			20 42		21 12		
Stratford International ⊖	d			17 49		18 19			18 49		19 19			19 49		20 19			20 49		21 19		
Ebbsfleet International	d			18 01		18 31			19 01		19 31			20 01		20 31			21 01		21 31		
London Charing Cross 4 ⊖	d	16 38			17 08		17 38			18 08		18 38			19 08		19 38			20 08		20 38	
London Waterloo (East) 4 ⊖	d	16 41			17 11		17 41			18 11		18 41			19 11		19 41			20 11		20 41	
London Cannon Street 4 ⊖	d																						
London Bridge 4 ⊖	d	16 46			17 16		17 46			18 16		18 46			19 16		19 46			20 16		20 46	
Orpington 4	d	17 02			17 32		18 02			18 32		19 02			19 32		20 02			20 32		21 02	
Sevenoaks 4	d	17 12			17 42		18 12			18 42		19 12			19 42		20 12			20 42		21 12	
Tonbridge 4	a	17 20			17 52		18 20			18 52		19 20			19 52		20 20			20 52		21 20	
	d	17 20			17 52		18 20			18 52		19 20			19 52		20 20			20 52		21 20	
Paddock Wood 4	d	17 28	17 34		18 00		18 28	18 34		19 00		19 28	19 34		20 00		20 28	20 34		21 00		21 28	21 34
Maidstone West 4 194	a		17 53					18 53					19 53					20 53					21 53
Marden	d	17 33			18 05		18 33			19 05		19 33			20 05		20 33			21 05		21 33	
Staplehurst	d	17 37			18 09		18 37			19 09		19 37			20 09		20 37			21 09		21 37	
Headcorn	d	17 43			18 15		18 43			19 15		19 43			20 15		20 43			21 15		21 43	
Pluckley	d	17 49					18 49					19 49					20 49					21 49	
Ashford International	a	17 56		18 20	18 26	18 50	18 56		19 20	19 26	19 50	19 56		20 20	20 26	20 50	20 56		21 20	21 26	21 50	21 56	
	d	18 03		18 22	18 30	18 52	19 03		19 22	19 30	19 52	20 03		20 22	20 30	20 52	21 03		21 22	21 30	21 52	22 03	
Wye	d	18 09					19 09					20 09					21 09					22 09	
Chilham	d	18 15					19 15					20 15					21 15					22 15	
Chartham	d	18 19					19 19					20 19					21 19					22 19	
Canterbury West 4	d	18 25		18 39			19 25		19 39			20 25		20 39			21 25		21 39			22 25	
Sturry	d	18 29					19 29					20 29					21 29					22 29	
Westenhanger	d				18 38					19 38					20 38					21 38			
Sandling	d				18 41					19 41					20 41					21 41			
Folkestone West	d				18 47	19 05				19 47	20 05				20 47	21 05				21 47	22 05		
Folkestone Central	d				18 50	19 08				19 50	20 08				20 50	21 08				21 50	22 08		
Dover Priory 4	a				19 01	19 20				20 01	20 20				21 01	21 20				22 01	22 20		
	d				19 02					20 02					21 02					22 02			
Martin Mill	d				19 11					20 11					21 11					22 11			
Walmer	d				19 15					20 15					21 15					22 15			
Deal	d				19 19					20 19					21 19					22 19			
Sandwich	d				19 26					20 26					21 26					22 26			
Minster 4	d	18 41					19 41					20 41					21 41					22 41	
Ramsgate 4	a	18 47		18 59	19 38		19 47		19 59	20 38		20 47		20 59	21 38		21 47		21 59	22 38		22 47	
Broadstairs	a			19 04					20 04					21 04					22 04				
Margate 4	a			19 10					20 10					21 10					22 10				

A ⚒ to Ashford International

Table 207

Sundays
until 22 July, 19 Aug and from 16 Sep

London and Tonbridge - Ashford International, Folkestone, Dover, Canterbury West, Ramsgate and Margate

Network Diagram - see first Page of Table 206

Station		SE	SE 1	SE	SE 1	SE	SE 1	SE	SE 1	SE 1	SE 1	SE
St Pancras Intl. 15 ⊖	d	21 42		22 12		22 42		23 12				23 42
Stratford International ⊖	d	21 49		22 19		22 49		23 19				23 49
Ebbsfleet International	d	22 01		22 31		23 01		23 31				00 01
London Charing Cross 4 ⊖	d		21 08		21 38		22 08		22 38	23 08	23 38	
London Waterloo (East) 4 ⊖	d		21 11		21 41		22 11		22 41	23 11	23 41	
London Cannon Street 4 ⊖	d											
London Bridge 4 ⊖	d		21 16		21 46		22 16		22 46	23 16	23 46	
Orpington 4	d		21 32		22 02		22 32		23 02	23 32	00 02	
Sevenoaks 4	d		21 42		22 12		22 42		23 12	23 42	00 12	
Tonbridge 4	a		21 52		22 20		22 52		23 20	23 52	00 20	
	d		21 52		22 20		22 52		23 20	23 52	00 20	
Paddock Wood 4	d		22 00		22 28		23 00		23 28	23 59	00 28	
Maidstone West 4 194	a											
Marden	d		22 05		22 33		23 05		23 33	00 05	00 33	
Staplehurst	d		22 09		22 37		23 09		23 37	00 09	00 37	
Headcorn	d		22 15		22 43		23 15		23 43	00 15	00 43	
Pluckley	d				22 49				23 49		00 49	
Ashford International	a	22 20	22 26	22 50	22 56	23 20	23 26	23 50	23 56	00 26	00 58	00 20
	d	22 22	22 30	22 52	23 03	23 22	23 30	23 52	00 01			
Wye	d				23 09							
Chilham	d				23 15							
Chartham	d				23 19							
Canterbury West 4	d	22 39			23 25	23 39						
Sturry	d				23 29							
Westenhanger	d		22 38				23 38					
Sandling	d		22 41				23 41		00 11			
Folkestone West	d		22 47	23 05			23 47	00 05	00 17			
Folkestone Central	d		22 50	23 08			23 50	00 08	00 19			
Dover Priory 4	a		23 01	23 20			00 01	00 20	00 30			
	d		23 02				00 02					
Martin Mill	d		23 11				00 11					
Walmer	d		23 15				00 15					
Deal	d		23 19				00 19					
Sandwich	d		23 26				00 26					
Minster 4	d				23 41							
Ramsgate 4	a	22 59	23 39		23 47	23 59	00 38					
Broadstairs	a	23 04										
Margate 4	a	23 10										

Sundays
29 July to 12 August

Station		SE 1	SE 1	SE 1	SE 1	SE 1		SE	SE	SE	SE	SE	SE	SE	SE	SE	SE	SE	SE 1	SE 1	SE 1	SE	SE
St Pancras Intl. 15 ⊖	d							00 41	00 57	01 06	01 11	01 27	01 38	05 32		07 04		07 39				08 04	
Stratford International ⊖	d							00 50	01 06	01 16	01 20	01 36	01 48	05 42		07 14		07 49				08 14	
Ebbsfleet International	d							01 03	01 20	01 29	01 35	01 49	02 00	05 56		07 30		08 02				08 30	
London Charing Cross 4 ⊖	d	22p10		22p40	23p10	23p40															07 00		
London Waterloo (East) 4 ⊖	d	22p13		22p43	23p13	23p43															07 03		
London Cannon Street 4 ⊖	d																						
London Bridge 4 ⊖	d	22p19		22p49	23p19	23p49															07 08		
Orpington 4	d	22p35		23p05	23p35	00 05															07 26		
Sevenoaks 4	d	22p44		23p14	23p44	00 14															07 35		
Tonbridge 4	a	22p52		23p22	23p52	00 22															07 45		
	d	22p53		23p23	23p53	00 23									06 03						07 50		
Paddock Wood 4	d	23p00		23p30	23p59	00 30									06 10		07 10				07 58		08 10
Maidstone West 4 194	a														06 24		07 29						08 29
Marden	d	23p05		23p35	00 05	00 35															08 03		
Staplehurst	d	23p09		23p39	00 09	00 39															08 07		
Headcorn	d	23p14		23p44	00 14	00 44															08 13		
Pluckley	d	23p20		23p50	00 20	00 50															08 19		
Ashford International	a	23p28		23p57	00 28	00 58		01 29	01 38	01 49	01 54	02 07	02 18	06 14		07 51		08 20			08 26	08 51	
	d	23p31	23p34	00 03	00 31	01 01	01 04												08 00	08 03	08 30		
Wye	d		23p40	00 09			01 10													08 09			
Chilham	d		23p46	00 15			01 16													08 15			
Chartham	d		23p50	00 19			01 20													08 19			
Canterbury West 4	d		23p56	00 25			01a25													08 25			
Sturry	d			00 29																08 29			
Westenhanger	d	23p40			00 40	01 10															08 38		
Sandling	d	23p42			00 42	01 12															08 41		
Folkestone West	d	23p47			00 47	01 17													08 13		08 47		
Folkestone Central	d	23p50			00 50	01 20													08 16		08 50		
Dover Priory 4	a	00 01			01 01	01 31													08 28		09 01		
	d	00 02																			09 02		
Martin Mill	d	00 11																			09 11		
Walmer	d	00 15																			09 15		
Deal	d	00 19																			09 19		
Sandwich	d	00 26																			09 26		
Minster 4	d			00 41																08 41			
Ramsgate 4	a	00 38	00 16	00 47																08 47	09 38		
Broadstairs	a																						
Margate 4	a																						

Table 207

Sundays
29 July to 12 August

London and Tonbridge - Ashford International, Folkestone, Dover, Canterbury West, Ramsgate and Margate

Network Diagram - see first Page of Table 206

	SE 1	SE 1	SE	SE 1	SE 1	SE	SE	SE 1	SE 1		SE 1		SE	SE	SE	SE 1		SE 1 A		SE	SE	SE
St Pancras Intl. ⊖ d			08 39			09 04							09 39	10 04						10 39	11 04	
Stratford International ⊖ d			08 49			09 14							09 49	10 14						10 49	11 14	
Ebbsfleet International d			09 02			09 30							10 02	10 30						11 02	11 30	
London Charing Cross ⊖ d		07 29			07 59				08 40		09 10					09 40		10 10				
London Waterloo (East) ⊖ d		07 32			08 02				08 43		09 13					09 43		10 13				
London Cannon Street ⊖ d																						
London Bridge ⊖ d		07 38			08 08				08 49		09 19					09 49		10 19				
Orpington d		07 54			08 24																	
Sevenoaks d		08 03			08 33				09 12		09 42					10 12		10 42				
Tonbridge a		08 14			08 43				09 20		09 50					10 20		10 50				
Tonbridge d		08 20			08 50				09 20		09 50					10 20		10 50				
Paddock Wood d		08 28			08 58		09 10		09 28		09 58				10 10	10 28		10 58				11 10
Maidstone West 194 a							09 29								10 29							11 29
Marden d		08 33			09 03				09 33		10 03					10 33		11 03				
Staplehurst d		08 37			09 07				09 37		10 07					10 37		11 07				
Headcorn d		08 43			09 13				09 43		10 13					10 43		11 13				
Pluckley d		08 49			09 19				09 49		10 19					10 49		11 19				
Ashford International a		08 56	09 20		09 26	09 48			09 56		10 26		10 20	10 51		10 56		11 26		11 20	11 51	
Ashford International d	08 33	09 00		09 03	09 30			09 33	10 00	10 03	10 30	10 33				11 00	11 03	11 30	11 33			
Wye d	08 39			09 09				09 39		10 09		10 39					11 09		11 39			
Chilham d	08 45							09 45				10 45							11 45			
Chartham d	08 49							09 49				10 49							11 49			
Canterbury West d	08 55			09 22				09 55		10 22		10 55					11 22		11 55			
Sturry d				09 26						10 26							11 26					
Westenhanger d					09 38						10 38							11 38				
Sandling d					09 41						10 41							11 41				
Folkestone West d		09 16			09 47				10 16		10 47					11 16		11 47				
Folkestone Central d		09 19			09 50				10 19		10 50					11 19		11 50				
Dover Priory a		09 29			10 01				10 29		11 01					11 29		12 01				
Dover Priory d					10 02						11 02							12 02				
Martin Mill d					10 11						11 11							12 11				
Walmer d					10 15						11 15							12 15				
Deal d					10 19						11 19							12 19				
Sandwich d					10 26						11 26							12 26				
Minster d				09 38						10 38							11 38					
Ramsgate a	09 13			09 44	10 38			10 13		10 44	11 38	11 13					11 44	12 38	12 13			
Broadstairs a																						
Margate a																						

	SE 1 A		SE 1 A		SE	SE	SE	SE 1 A		SE 1 A		SE	SE	SE	SE 1 A		SE 1 A		SE	SE	SE
St Pancras Intl. ⊖ d					11 39	12 04						12 39	13 04						13 39	14 04	
Stratford International ⊖ d					11 49	12 14						12 49	13 14						13 49	14 14	
Ebbsfleet International d					12 02	12 30						13 02	13 30						14 02	14 30	
London Charing Cross ⊖ d	10 40		11 10					11 40		12 10					12 40		13 10				
London Waterloo (East) ⊖ d	10 43		11 13					11 43		12 13					12 43		13 13				
London Cannon Street ⊖ d																					
London Bridge ⊖ d	10 49		11 19					11 49		12 19					12 49		13 19				
Orpington d																					
Sevenoaks d	11 12		11 42					12 12		12 42					13 12		13 42				
Tonbridge a	11 20		11 50					12 20		12 50					13 20		13 50				
Tonbridge d	11 20		11 50					12 20		12 50					13 20		13 50				
Paddock Wood d	11 28		11 58				12 10	12 28		12 58				13 10	13 28		13 58				14 10
Maidstone West 194 a							12 29							13 29							14 29
Marden d	11 33		12 03					12 33		13 03					13 33		14 03				
Staplehurst d	11 37		12 07					12 37		13 07					13 37		14 07				
Headcorn d	11 43		12 13					12 43		13 13					13 43		14 13				
Pluckley d	11 49		12 19					12 49		13 19					13 49		14 19				
Ashford International a	11 56		12 26		12 20	12 51		12 56		13 26		13 20	13 51		13 56		14 26		14 20	14 51	
Ashford International d	12 00	12 03	12 30	12 33				13 00	13 03	13 30	13 33				14 00	14 03	14 30	14 33			
Wye d		12 09		12 39					13 09		13 39					14 09		14 39			
Chilham d				12 45							13 45							14 45			
Chartham d				12 49							13 49							14 49			
Canterbury West d		12 22		12 55					13 22		13 55					14 22		14 55			
Sturry d		12 26							13 26							14 26					
Westenhanger d			12 38							13 38							14 38				
Sandling d			12 41							13 41							14 41				
Folkestone West d	12 16		12 47					13 13		13 47					14 16		14 47				
Folkestone Central d	12 19		12 50					13 16		13 50					14 19		14 50				
Dover Priory a	12 29		13 01					13 28		14 01					14 29		15 01				
Dover Priory d			13 02							14 02							15 02				
Martin Mill d			13 11							14 11							15 11				
Walmer d			13 15							14 15							15 15				
Deal d			13 19							14 19							15 19				
Sandwich d			13 26							14 26							15 26				
Minster d		12 38							13 38							14 38					
Ramsgate a		12 44	13 38	13 13					13 44	14 38	14 13					14 44	15 38	15 13			
Broadstairs a																					
Margate a																					

A 🛒 to Ashford International

Table 207

Sundays
29 July to 12 August

London and Tonbridge - Ashford International, Folkestone, Dover, Canterbury West, Ramsgate and Margate

Network Diagram - see first Page of Table 206

	SE 1 A		SE 1 A		SE	SE	SE	SE 1 A		SE 1 A		SE	SE	SE	SE 1 A		SE 1 A		SE	SE	SE
St Pancras Intl. ⊖ d					14 39	15 04						15 39	16 04						16 39	17 04	
Stratford International ⊖ d					14 49	15 14						15 49	16 14						16 49	17 14	
Ebbsfleet International d					15 02	15 30						16 02	16 29						17 02	17 30	
London Charing Cross ⊖ d	13 40		14 10					14 40		15 10					15 40		16 10				
London Waterloo (East) ⊖ d	13 43		14 13					14 43		15 13					15 43		16 13				
London Cannon Street ⊖ d																					
London Bridge ⊖ d	13 49		14 19					14 49		15 19					15 49		16 19				
Orpington d																					
Sevenoaks d	14 12		14 42					15 12		15 42					16 12		16 42				
Tonbridge a	14 20		14 50					15 20		15 50					16 20		16 50				
Tonbridge d	14 20		14 50					15 20		15 50					16 20		16 50				
Paddock Wood d	14 28		14 58				15 10	15 28		15 58				16 10	16 28		16 58				17 10
Maidstone West 194 a							15 29							16 29							17 29
Marden d	14 33		15 03					15 33		16 03					16 33		17 03				
Staplehurst d	14 37		15 07					15 37		16 07					16 37		17 07				
Headcorn d	14 43		15 13					15 43		16 13					16 43		17 13				
Pluckley d	14 49		15 19					15 49		16 19					16 49		17 19				
Ashford International a	14 56		15 26		15 20	15 51		15 56		16 26		16 20	16 48		16 56		17 26		17 20	17 51	
Ashford International d	15 00	15 03	15 30	15 33				16 00	16 03	16 30	16 33				17 00	17 03	17 30	17 33			
Wye d		15 09		15 39					16 09		16 39					17 09		17 39			
Chilham d				15 45							16 45							17 45			
Chartham d				15 49							16 49							17 49			
Canterbury West d		15 22		15 55					16 22		16 55					17 22		17 55			
Sturry d		15 26							16 26							17 26					
Westenhanger d			15 38							16 38							17 38				
Sandling d			15 41							16 41							17 41				
Folkestone West d	15 16		15 47					16 13		16 47					17 13		17 47				
Folkestone Central d	15 19		15 50					16 16		16 50					17 16		17 50				
Dover Priory a	15 29		16 01					16 28		17 01					17 28		18 01				
Dover Priory d			16 02							17 02							18 02				
Martin Mill d			16 11							17 11							18 11				
Walmer d			16 15							17 15							18 15				
Deal d			16 19							17 19							18 19				
Sandwich d			16 26							17 26							18 26				
Minster d		15 38							16 38							17 38					
Ramsgate a		15 44	16 38	16 13					16 44	17 38	17 13					17 44	18 38	18 13			
Broadstairs a																					
Margate a																					

	SE 1 A		SE 1 A		SE	SE	SE	SE 1 A		SE 1 A		SE	SE	SE	SE 1 A		SE 1 A		SE	SE	SE
St Pancras Intl. ⊖ d					17 39	18 04						18 39	19 04						19 39	20 04	
Stratford International ⊖ d					17 49	18 14						18 49	19 14						19 49	20 14	
Ebbsfleet International d					18 02	18 30						19 02	19 30						20 02	20 30	
London Charing Cross ⊖ d	16 40		17 10					17 40		18 10					18 40		19 10				
London Waterloo (East) ⊖ d	16 43		17 13					17 43		18 13					18 43		19 13				
London Cannon Street ⊖ d																					
London Bridge ⊖ d	16 49		17 19					17 49		18 19					18 49		19 19				
Orpington d																					
Sevenoaks d	17 12		17 42					18 12		18 42					19 12		19 42				
Tonbridge a	17 20		17 50					18 20		18 50					19 20		19 50				
Tonbridge d	17 20		17 50					18 20		18 50					19 20		19 50				
Paddock Wood d	17 28		17 58				18 10	18 28		18 58				19 10	19 28		19 58				20 10
Maidstone West 194 a							18 29							19 29							20 29
Marden d	17 33		18 03					18 33		19 03					19 33		20 03				
Staplehurst d	17 37		18 07					18 37		19 07					19 37		20 07				
Headcorn d	17 43		18 13					18 43		19 13					19 43		20 13				
Pluckley d	17 49		18 19					18 49		19 19					19 49		20 19				
Ashford International a	17 56		18 26		18 20	18 51		18 56		19 26		19 20	19 51		19 56		20 26		20 20	20 51	
Ashford International d	18 00	18 03	18 30	18 33				19 00	19 03	19 30	19 33				20 00	20 03	20 30	20 33			
Wye d		18 09		18 39					19 09		19 39					20 09		20 39			
Chilham d				18 45					19 15		19 45					20 15		20 45			
Chartham d				18 49					19 19		19 49					20 19		20 49			
Canterbury West d		18 22		18 55					19 25		19 55					20 25		20 55			
Sturry d		18 26							19 29							20 29					
Westenhanger d			18 38							19 38							20 38				
Sandling d			18 41							19 41							20 41				
Folkestone West d	18 13		18 47					19 13		19 47					20 13		20 47				
Folkestone Central d	18 16		18 50					19 16		19 50					20 16		20 50				
Dover Priory a	18 28		19 01					19 28		20 01					20 28		21 01				
Dover Priory d			19 02							20 02							21 02				
Martin Mill d			19 11							20 11							21 11				
Walmer d			19 15							20 15							21 15				
Deal d			19 19							20 19							21 19				
Sandwich d			19 26							20 26							21 26				
Minster d		18 38							19 41							20 41					
Ramsgate a		18 44	19 38	19 13					19 47	20 38	20 13					20 47	21 38	21 13			
Broadstairs a																					
Margate a																					

A 🛒 to Ashford International

Table 207

Sundays 29 July to 12 August

London and Tonbridge - Ashford International, Folkestone, Dover, Canterbury West, Ramsgate and Margate

Network Diagram - see first Page of Table 206

	SE ■ A ⌶		SE ■ A ⌶		SE	SE	SE	SE ■		SE ■	
St Pancras Intl. ⊖ d					20 39	21 04					
Stratford International ⊖ d					20 49	21 14					
Ebbsfleet International d					21 02	21 30					
London Charing Cross ⊖ d	19 40		20 10					20 40		21 10	
London Waterloo (East) ⊖ d	19 43		20 13					20 43		21 13	
London Cannon Street ⊖ d											
London Bridge ⊖ d	19 49		20 19					20 49		21 19	
Orpington d			20 35					21 05		21 35	
Sevenoaks d	20 12		20 44					21 14		21 44	
Tonbridge a	20 20		20 52					21 22		21 52	
d	20 20		20 53					21 23		21 53	
Paddock Wood d	20 28		21 00				21 10	21 30		22 00	
Maidstone West 194 a							21 29				
Marden d	20 33		21 05					21 35		22 05	
Staplehurst d	20 37		21 09					21 39		22 09	
Headcorn d	20 43		21 14					21 44		22 14	
Pluckley d	20 49		21 20					21 50		22 20	
Ashford International a	20 56		21 28		21 20	21 51		21 57		22 28	
d	21 00	21 03	21 31	21 35				22 01	22 04	22 31	22 35
Wye d		21 09		21 41					22 10		22 41
Chilham d		21 15		21 47					22 16		22 47
Chartham d		21 19		21 51					22 20		22 51
Canterbury West d		21 25		21 57					22 26		22 57
Sturry d		21 29							22 30		
Westenhanger d			21 40							22 40	
Sandling d			21 42							22 42	
Folkestone West d	21 13		21 47					22 14		22 47	
Folkestone Central d	21 16		21 50					22 17		22 50	
Dover Priory a	21 28		22 01					22 28		23 01	
d			22 02							23 03	
Martin Mill d			22 11							23 12	
Walmer d			22 15							23 16	
Deal d			22 19							23 20	
Sandwich d			22 26							23 27	
Minster d		21 41							22 42		
Ramsgate a		21 47	22 38	22 15					22 48	23 39	23 15
Broadstairs a											
Margate a											

	SE	SE	SE ■		SE ■		SE ■	SE ■	SE ■
St Pancras Intl. ⊖ d	21 39								
Stratford International ⊖ d	21 49								
Ebbsfleet International d	22 02								
London Charing Cross ⊖ d			21 40		22 10		22 40	23 10	23 40
London Waterloo (East) ⊖ d			21 43		22 13		22 43	23 13	23 43
London Cannon Street ⊖ d									
London Bridge ⊖ d			21 49		22 19		22 49	23 19	23 49
Orpington d			22 05		22 35		23 05	23 35	00 05
Sevenoaks d			22 14		22 44		23 14	23 44	00 14
Tonbridge a			22 22		22 52		23 22	23 52	00 22
d			22 23		22 53		23 23	23 53	00 23
Paddock Wood d		22 10	22 30		23 00		23 30	23 59	00 30
Maidstone West 194 a		22 29							
Marden d			22 35		23 05		23 35	00 05	00 35
Staplehurst d			22 39		23 09		23 39	00 09	00 39
Headcorn d			22 44		23 14		23 44	00 14	00 44
Pluckley d			22 50		23 20		23 50	00 20	00 50
Ashford International a	22 20		22 57		23 28		23 58	00 28	00 58
d			23 01	23 04	23 31	23 35	00 03	00 31	01 01
Wye d				23 10		23 41	00 09		
Chilham d				23 16		23 47	00 15		
Chartham d				23 20		23 51	00 19		
Canterbury West d				23 26		23 57	00 25		
Sturry d				23 30			00 29		
Westenhanger d					23 40			00 40	01 10
Sandling d					23 42			00 42	01 12
Folkestone West d			23 14		23 47			00 47	01 17
Folkestone Central d			23 17		23 50			00 50	01 20
Dover Priory a			23 28		00 01			01 01	01 31
d					00 02				
Martin Mill d					00 11				
Walmer d					00 15				
Deal d					00 19				
Sandwich d					00 26				
Minster d				23 42			00 41		
Ramsgate a				23 48	00 38	00 15	00 47		
Broadstairs a									
Margate a									

Sundays 26 August to 9 September

	SE ■	SE B	SE C	SE ■	SE ■	SE ■		SE B	SE C	SE	SE	SE ■
St Pancras Intl. ⊖ d		23p12	23p12					00 12	00 12			
Stratford International ⊖ d		23p19	23p20					00 19	00 20			
Ebbsfleet International d		23p31	23p32					00 31	00 32			
London Charing Cross ⊖ d	22p10			22p40	23p10	23p40						
London Waterloo (East) ⊖ d	22p13			22p43	23p13	23p43						
London Cannon Street ⊖ d												
London Bridge ⊖ d	22p19			22p49	23p19	23p49						
Orpington d	22p35			23p05	23p35	00 05						
Sevenoaks d	22p44			23p14	23p44	00 14						
Tonbridge a	22p52			23p22	23p52	00 22						
d	22p53			23p23	23p53	00 23				06 26		
Paddock Wood d	23p00			23p30	23p59	00 30				06 34	07 34	
Maidstone West 194 a										06 53	07 53	
Marden d	23p05			23p35	00 05	00 35						
Staplehurst d	23p09			23p39	00 09	00 39						
Headcorn d	23p14			23p44	00 14	00 44						
Pluckley d	23p20			23p50	00 20	00 50						
Ashford International a	23p28	23p50	23p50	23p58	00 28	00 58		00 50	00 51			
d	23p31	23p52	23p52	00 03	00 31	01 01	01 04					08 30
Wye d				00 09			01 10					
Chilham d				00 15			01 16					
Chartham d				00 19			01 20					
Canterbury West d				00 25			01a25					
Sturry d				00 29								
Westenhanger d	23p40				00 40	01 10						08 38
Sandling d	23p42				00 42	01 12						08 41
Folkestone West d	23p47	00 05	00 05		00 47	01 17						08 47
Folkestone Central d	23p50	00 08	00 08		00 50	01 20						08 50
Dover Priory a	00 01	00 20	00 20		01 01	01 31						09 01
d	00 02											09 02
Martin Mill d	00 11											09 11
Walmer d	00 15											09 15
Deal d	00 19											09 19
Sandwich d	00 26											09 26
Minster d				00 41								
Ramsgate a	00 38			00 47								09 38
Broadstairs a												
Margate a												

	SE ■	SE ■	SE	SE C	SE B	SE ■		SE C	SE B	SE ■
St Pancras Intl. ⊖ d				08 41	08 42			09 09	09 10	
Stratford International ⊖ d				08 49	08 49			09 17	09 17	
Ebbsfleet International d				09 01	09 01			09 29	09 29	
London Charing Cross ⊖ d						08 08				08 38
London Waterloo (East) ⊖ d						08 11				08 41
London Cannon Street ⊖ d										
London Bridge ⊖ d						08 16				08 46
Orpington d						08 32				09 02
Sevenoaks d						08 42				09 12
Tonbridge a						08 52				09 20
d		08 20				08 52				09 20
Paddock Wood d		08 28	08 34			09 00				09 28
Maidstone West 194 a			08 53							
Marden d		08 33				09 05				09 33
Staplehurst d		08 37				09 09				09 37
Headcorn d		08 43				09 15				09 43
Pluckley d		08 49								09 49
Ashford International a		08 56		09 20	09 20	09 26		09 48	09 48	09 56
d	08 33	09 03		09 22	09 22	09 30	09 33	09 52	09 52	10 03
Wye d	08 39	09 09					09 39			10 09
Chilham d	08 45						09 45			
Chartham d	08 49						09 49			
Canterbury West d	08a54	09 22		09 39	09 39		09a54			10 22
Sturry d		09 26								10 26
Westenhanger d						09 38				
Sandling d						09 41				
Folkestone West d						09 47		10 05	10 05	
Folkestone Central d						09 50		10 08	10 08	
Dover Priory a						10 01		10 20	10 20	
d						10 02				
Martin Mill d						10 11				
Walmer d						10 15				
Deal d						10 19				
Sandwich d						10 26				
Minster d		09 38								10 38
Ramsgate a		09 44		09 59	09 59	10 38				10 44
Broadstairs a				10 04	10 04					
Margate a				10 10	10 10					

A ⌶ to Ashford International B not from 2 September until 9 September C not 26 August

Table 207

Sundays 26 August to 9 September

London and Tonbridge - Ashford International, Folkestone, Dover, Canterbury West, Ramsgate and Margate

Network Diagram - see first Page of Table 206

	SE	SE A	SE B	SE ■		SE B	SE A	SE ■	SE	SE A	SE B
St Pancras Intl. ⊖ d		09 36	09 42			10 10	10 11			10 41	10 42
Stratford International ⊖ d		09 44	09 49			10 17	10 19			10 49	10 49
Ebbsfleet International d		09 56	10 01			10 29	10 31			11 01	11 01
London Charing Cross ⊖ d				09 08				09 38			
London Waterloo (East) ⊖ d				09 11				09 41			
London Cannon Street ⊖ d											
London Bridge ⊖ d				09 16				09 46			
Orpington d				09 32				10 02			
Sevenoaks d				09 42				10 12			
Tonbridge a				09 52				10 20			
d				09 52				10 20			
Paddock Wood d	09 34			10 00				10 28	10 34		
Maidstone West 194 a	09 53								10 53		
Marden d				10 05				10 33			
Staplehurst d				10 09				10 37			
Headcorn d				10 15				10 43			
Pluckley d								10 49			
Ashford International a		10 15	10 20	10 26		10 48	10 50	10 56		11 20	11 20
d		10 22	10 22	10 30	10 33	10 52	10 52	11 03		11 22	11 22
Wye d					10 39			11 09			
Chilham d					10 45						
Chartham d					10 49						
Canterbury West d		10 39	10 39		10a54			11 22		11 39	11 39
Sturry d								11 26			
Westenhanger d				10 38							
Sandling d				10 41							
Folkestone West d				10 47		11 05	11 05				
Folkestone Central d				10 50		11 08	11 08				
Dover Priory a				11 01		11 20	11 20				
d				11 02							
Martin Mill d				11 11							
Walmer d				11 15							
Deal d				11 19							
Sandwich d				11 26							
Minster d								11 38			
Ramsgate a		10 59	10 59	11 38				11 44		11 59	11 59
Broadstairs a		11 04	11 04							12 04	12 04
Margate a		11 10	11 10							12 10	12 10

	SE ■ C ⌶		SE A	SE B	SE ■ C ⌶	SE	SE A	SE B	SE ■ C ⌶		SE A
St Pancras Intl. ⊖ d			11 11	11 12			11 41	11 42			12 11
Stratford International ⊖ d			11 19	11 19			11 49	11 49			12 19
Ebbsfleet International d			11 31	11 31			12 01	12 01			12 31
London Charing Cross ⊖ d	10 08				10 38				11 08		
London Waterloo (East) ⊖ d	10 11				10 41				11 11		
London Cannon Street ⊖ d											
London Bridge ⊖ d	10 16				10 46				11 16		
Orpington d	10 32				11 02				11 32		
Sevenoaks d	10 42				11 12				11 42		
Tonbridge a	10 52				11 20				11 52		
d	10 52				11 20				11 52		
Paddock Wood d	11 00				11 28	11 34			12 00		
Maidstone West 194 a						11 53					
Marden d	11 05				11 33				12 05		
Staplehurst d	11 09				11 37				12 09		
Headcorn d	11 15				11 43				12 15		
Pluckley d					11 49						
Ashford International a	11 26		11 50	11 50	11 56		12 20	12 20	12 26		12 50
d	11 30	11 33	11 52	11 52	12 03		12 22	12 22	12 30	12 33	12 52
Wye d		11 39			12 09					12 39	
Chilham d		11 45								12 45	
Chartham d		11 49								12 49	
Canterbury West d		11a54			12 22		12 39	12 39		12a54	
Sturry d					12 26						
Westenhanger d	11 38								12 38		
Sandling d	11 41								12 41		
Folkestone West d	11 47		12 05	12 05					12 47		13 05
Folkestone Central d	11 50		12 08	12 08					12 50		13 08
Dover Priory a	12 01		12 20	12 20					13 01		13 20
d	12 02								13 02		
Martin Mill d	12 11								13 11		
Walmer d	12 15								13 15		
Deal d	12 19								13 19		
Sandwich d	12 26								13 26		
Minster d					12 38						
Ramsgate a	12 38				12 44		12 59	12 59	13 38		
Broadstairs a							13 04	13 04			
Margate a							13 10	13 10			

	SE B	SE ■ C ⌶	SE	SE A	SE B	SE ■ C ⌶		SE A	SE B	SE ■ C ⌶	SE
St Pancras Intl. ⊖ d	12 12			12 41	12 42			13 11	13 12		
Stratford International ⊖ d	12 19			12 49	12 49			13 19	13 19		
Ebbsfleet International d	12 31			13 01	13 01			13 31	13 31		
London Charing Cross ⊖ d		11 38				12 08				12 38	
London Waterloo (East) ⊖ d		11 41				12 11				12 41	
London Cannon Street ⊖ d											
London Bridge ⊖ d		11 46				12 16				12 46	
Orpington d		12 02				12 32				13 02	
Sevenoaks d		12 12				12 42				13 12	
Tonbridge a		12 20				12 52				13 20	
d		12 20				12 52				13 20	
Paddock Wood d		12 28	12 34			13 00				13 28	13 34
Maidstone West 194 a			12 53								13 53
Marden d		12 33				13 05				13 33	
Staplehurst d		12 37				13 09				13 37	
Headcorn d		12 43				13 15				13 43	
Pluckley d		12 49								13 49	
Ashford International a	12 50	12 56		13 20	13 20	13 26		13 50	13 50	13 56	
d	12 52	13 03		13 22	13 22	13 30	13 33	13 52	13 52	14 03	
Wye d		13 09					13 39			14 09	
Chilham d							13 45				
Chartham d							13 49				
Canterbury West d		13 22		13 39	13 39		13a54			14 22	
Sturry d		13 26								14 26	
Westenhanger d						13 38					
Sandling d						13 41					
Folkestone West d	13 05					13 47		14 05	14 05		
Folkestone Central d	13 08					13 50		14 08	14 08		
Dover Priory a	13 20					14 01		14 20	14 20		
d						14 02					
Martin Mill d						14 11					
Walmer d						14 15					
Deal d						14 19					
Sandwich d						14 26					
Minster d		13 38								14 38	
Ramsgate a		13 44		13 59	13 59	14 38				14 44	
Broadstairs a				14 04	14 04						
Margate a				14 10	14 10						

	SE A	SE B	SE ■ C ⌶		SE A	SE B	SE ■ C ⌶	SE	SE A	SE B
St Pancras Intl. ⊖ d	13 41	13 42			14 11	14 12			14 41	14 42
Stratford International ⊖ d	13 49	13 49			14 19	14 19			14 49	14 49
Ebbsfleet International d	14 01	14 01			14 31	14 31			15 01	15 01
London Charing Cross ⊖ d			13 08				13 38			
London Waterloo (East) ⊖ d			13 11				13 41			
London Cannon Street ⊖ d										
London Bridge ⊖ d			13 16				13 46			
Orpington d			13 32				14 02			
Sevenoaks d			13 42				14 12			
Tonbridge a			13 52				14 20			
d			13 52				14 20			
Paddock Wood d			14 00				14 28	14 34		
Maidstone West 194 a								14 53		
Marden d			14 05				14 33			
Staplehurst d			14 09				14 37			
Headcorn d			14 15				14 43			
Pluckley d							14 49			
Ashford International a	14 20	14 20	14 26		14 50	14 50	14 56		15 20	15 20
d	14 22	14 22	14 30	14 33	14 52	14 52	15 03		15 22	15 22
Wye d				14 39			15 09			
Chilham d				14 45						
Chartham d				14 49						
Canterbury West d	14 39	14 39		14a54			15 22		15 39	15 39
Sturry d							15 26			
Westenhanger d			14 38							
Sandling d			14 41							
Folkestone West d			14 47		15 05	15 05				
Folkestone Central d			14 50		15 08	15 08				
Dover Priory a			15 01		15 20	15 20				
d			15 02							
Martin Mill d			15 11							
Walmer d			15 15							
Deal d			15 19							
Sandwich d			15 26							
Minster d							15 38			
Ramsgate a	14 59	14 59	15 38				15 44		15 59	15 59
Broadstairs a	15 04	15 04							16 04	16 04
Margate a	15 10	15 10							16 10	16 10

A not 26 August B not from 2 September until 9 September C ⌶ to Ashford International

London and Tonbridge - Ashford International, Folkestone, Dover, Canterbury West, Ramsgate and Margate

Network Diagram - see first Page of Table 206

			SE [1] A 🛒	SE B	SE C	SE [1] A 🛒	SE	SE B	SE C		SE [1] A 🛒	SE B	SE C	SE [1] A 🛒	SE	SE B	SE C		SE [1] A 🛒	SE B	SE C	SE [1] A 🛒	SE
St Pancras Intl. [15] ⊖	d			15 11	15 12			15 41	15 42			16 09	16 10			16 41	16 42			17 11	17 12		
Stratford International ⊖	d			15 19	15 19			15 49	15 49			16 17	16 17			16 49	16 49			17 19	17 19		
Ebbsfleet International	d			15 31	15 31			16 01	16 01			16 29	16 29			17 01	17 01			17 31	17 31		
London Charing Cross [4] ⊖	d		14 08			14 38					15 08			15 38					16 08			16 38	
London Waterloo (East) [4] ⊖	d		14 11			14 41					15 11			15 41					16 11			16 41	
London Cannon Street [4] ⊖	d																						
London Bridge [4] ⊖	d		14 16			14 46					15 16			15 46					16 16			16 46	
Orpington [4]	d		14 32			15 02					15 32			16 02					16 32			17 02	
Sevenoaks [4]	d		14 42			15 12					15 42			16 12					16 42			17 12	
Tonbridge [4]	a		14 52			15 20					15 52			16 20					16 52			17 20	
	d		14 52			15 20					15 52			16 20					16 52			17 20	
Paddock Wood [4]	d		15 00			15 28	15 34				16 00			16 28	16 34				17 00			17 28	17 34
Maidstone West [4] 194	a						15 53								16 53								17 53
Marden	d		15 05			15 33					16 05			16 33					17 05			17 33	
Staplehurst	d		15 09			15 37					16 09			16 37					17 09			17 37	
Headcorn	d		15 15			15 43					16 15			16 43					17 15			17 43	
Pluckley	d					15 49								16 49								17 49	
Ashford International	a		15 26	15 50	15 50	15 56		16 20	16 20		16 26	16 48	16 48	16 56		17 20	17 20		17 26	17 50	17 50	17 56	
	d	15 30	15 33	15 52	15 52	16 03		16 22	16 22	16 30	16 33	16 52	16 52	17 03		17 22	17 22	17 30	17 33	17 52	17 52	18 03	
Wye	d		15 39			16 09					16 39			17 09					17 39			18 09	
Chilham	d		15 45								16 45								17 45			18 15	
Chartham	d		15 49								16 49								17 49			18 19	
Canterbury West [4]	d		15a54			16 22		16 39	16 39		16a54			17 22		17 39	17 39		17a54			18 25	
Sturry	d					16 26								17 26								18 29	
Westenhanger	d	15 38								16 38								17 38					
Sandling	d	15 41								16 41								17 41					
Folkestone West	d	15 47		16 05	16 05					16 47		17 05	17 05					17 47		18 05	18 05		
Folkestone Central	d	15 50		16 08	16 08					16 50		17 08	17 08					17 50		18 08	18 08		
Dover Priory [4]	a	16 01		16 20	16 20					17 01		17 20	17 20					18 01		18 20	18 20		
	d	16 02								17 02								18 02					
Martin Mill	d	16 11								17 11								18 11					
Walmer	d	16 15								17 15								18 15					
Deal	d	16 19								17 19								18 19					
Sandwich	d	16 26								17 26								18 26					
Minster [4]	d					16 38								17 38								18 41	
Ramsgate [4]	a	16 38				16 44		16 59	16 59	17 38				17 44		17 59	17 59	18 38				18 47	
Broadstairs	a							17 04	17 04							18 04	18 04						
Margate [4]	a							17 10	17 10							18 10	18 10						

		SE B	SE C	SE [1] A 🛒	SE B	SE C	SE [1] A 🛒	SE	SE B	SE C	SE [1] A 🛒	SE B	SE C	SE [1] A 🛒	SE	SE B	SE C	SE [1] A 🛒	SE B	SE C	SE [1] A 🛒	SE	SE B
St Pancras Intl. [15] ⊖	d	17 41	17 42		18 11	18 12			18 41	18 42		19 11	19 12			19 41	19 42		20 11	20 12			20 41
Stratford International ⊖	d	17 49	17 49		18 19	18 19			18 49	18 49		19 19	19 19			19 49	19 49		20 19	20 19			20 49
Ebbsfleet International	d	18 01	18 01		18 31	18 31			19 01	19 01		19 31	19 31			20 01	20 01		20 31	20 31			21 01
London Charing Cross [4] ⊖	d			17 08			17 38				18 08			18 38				19 08			19 38		
London Waterloo (East) [4] ⊖	d			17 11			17 41				18 11			18 41				19 11			19 41		
London Cannon Street [4] ⊖	d																						
London Bridge [4] ⊖	d			17 16			17 46				18 16			18 46				19 16			19 46		
Orpington [4]	d			17 32			18 02				18 32			19 02				19 32			20 02		
Sevenoaks [4]	d			17 42			18 12				18 42			19 12				19 42			20 12		
Tonbridge [4]	a			17 52			18 20				18 52			19 20				19 52			20 20		
	d			17 52			18 20				18 52			19 20				19 52			20 20		
Paddock Wood [4]	d			18 00			18 28	18 34			19 00			19 28	19 34			20 00			20 28	20 34	
Maidstone West [4] 194	a							18 53							19 53							20 53	
Marden	d			18 05			18 33				19 05			19 33				20 05			20 33		
Staplehurst	d			18 09			18 37				19 09			19 37				20 09			20 37		
Headcorn	d			18 15			18 43				19 15			19 43				20 15			20 43		
Pluckley	d						18 49							19 49							20 49		
Ashford International	a	18 20	18 20	18 26	18 50	18 50	18 56		19 20	19 20	19 26	19 50	19 50	19 56		20 20	20 20	20 26	20 50	20 50	20 56		21 20
	d	18 22	18 22	18 30	18 52	18 52	19 03		19 22	19 22	19 30	19 52	19 52	20 03		20 22	20 22	20 30	20 52	20 52	21 03		21 22
Wye	d						19 09							20 09							21 09		
Chilham	d						19 15							20 15							21 15		
Chartham	d						19 19							20 19							21 19		
Canterbury West [4]	d	18 39	18 39				19 25		19 39	19 39				20 25		20 39	20 39				21 25		21 39
Sturry	d						19 29							20 29							21 29		
Westenhanger	d			18 38							19 38							20 38					
Sandling	d			18 41							19 41							20 41					
Folkestone West	d			18 47	19 05	19 05					19 47	20 05	20 05					20 47	21 05	21 05			
Folkestone Central	d			18 50	19 08	19 08					19 50	20 08	20 08					20 50	21 08	21 08			
Dover Priory [4]	a			19 01	19 20	19 20					20 01	20 20	20 20					21 01	21 20	21 20			
	d			19 02							20 02							21 02					
Martin Mill	d			19 11							20 11							21 11					
Walmer	d			19 15							20 15							21 15					
Deal	d			19 19							20 19							21 19					
Sandwich	d			19 26							20 26							21 26					
Minster [4]	d						19 41							20 41							21 41		
Ramsgate [4]	a	18 59	18 59	19 38			19 47		19 59	19 59	20 38			20 47		20 59	20 59	21 38			21 47		21 59
Broadstairs	a	19 04	19 04						20 04	20 04						21 04	21 04						22 04
Margate [4]	a	19 10	19 10						20 10	20 10						21 10	21 10						22 10

A 🛒 to Ashford International

B not 26 August

C not from 2 September until 9 September

London and Tonbridge - Ashford International, Folkestone, Dover, Canterbury West, Ramsgate and Margate

Network Diagram - see first Page of Table 206

		SE A	SE [1] B 🛒	SE C	SE A	SE [1]	SE	SE C	SE A	SE [1]	SE C	SE A	SE [1]	SE A	SE C	SE [1]	SE A	SE C	SE [1]	SE [1]	SE [1]	SE A
St Pancras Intl. [15] ⊖	d	20 42		21 11	21 12			21 41	21 42		22 11	22 12		22 42	22 42		23 12	23 12				23 42
Stratford International ⊖	d	20 49		21 19	21 19			21 49	21 49		22 19	22 19		22 49	22 50		23 19	23 20				23 49
Ebbsfleet International	d	21 01		21 31	21 31			22 01	22 01		22 31	22 31		23 01	23 02		23 31	23 32				00 01
London Charing Cross [4] ⊖	d		20 08			20 38				21 08			21 38			22 08			22 38	23 08	23 38	
London Waterloo (East) [4] ⊖	d		20 11			20 41				21 11			21 41			22 11			22 41	23 11	23 41	
London Cannon Street [4] ⊖	d																					
London Bridge [4] ⊖	d		20 16			20 46				21 16			21 46			22 16			22 46	23 16	23 46	
Orpington [4]	d		20 32			21 02				21 32			22 02			22 32			23 02	23 32	00 02	
Sevenoaks [4]	d		20 42			21 12				21 42			22 12			22 42			23 12	23 42	00 12	
Tonbridge [4]	a		20 52			21 20				21 52			22 20			22 52			23 20	23 52	00 20	
	d		20 52			21 20				21 52			22 20			22 52			23 20	23 52	00 20	
Paddock Wood [4]	d		21 00			21 28	21 34			22 00			22 28			23 00			23 28	23 59	00 28	
Maidstone West [4] 194	a						21 53															
Marden	d		21 05			21 33				22 05			22 33			23 05			23 33	00 05	00 33	
Staplehurst	d		21 09			21 37				22 09			22 37			23 09			23 37	00 09	00 37	
Headcorn	d		21 15			21 43				22 15			22 43			23 15			23 43	00 15	00 43	
Pluckley	d					21 49							22 49						23 49		00 49	
Ashford International	a	21 20	21 26	21 50	21 50	21 56		22 20	22 20	22 26	22 50	22 50	22 56	23 20	23 20	23 26	23 50	23 50	23 56	00 26	00 58	00 20
	d	21 22	21 30	21 52	21 52	22 03		22 22	22 22	22 30	22 52	22 52	23 03	23 22	23 22	23 30	23 52	23 52	00 01			
Wye	d					22 09							23 09									
Chilham	d					22 15							23 15									
Chartham	d					22 19							23 19									
Canterbury West [4]	d	21 39				22 25		22 39	22 39				23 25	23 39	23 39							
Sturry	d					22 29							23 29									
Westenhanger	d		21 38							22 38						23 38						
Sandling	d		21 41							22 41						23 41			00 11			
Folkestone West	d		21 47	22 05	22 05					22 47	23 05	23 05				23 47	00 05	00 05	00 17			
Folkestone Central	d		21 50	22 08	22 08					22 50	23 08	23 08				23 50	00 08	00 08	00 19			
Dover Priory [4]	a		22 01	22 20	22 20					23 01	23 20	23 20				00 01	00 20	00 20	00 30			
	d		22 02							23 02						00 02						
Martin Mill	d		22 11							23 11						00 11						
Walmer	d		22 15							23 15						00 15						
Deal	d		22 19							23 19						00 19						
Sandwich	d		22 26							23 26						00 26						
Minster [4]	d					22 41							23 41									
Ramsgate [4]	a	21 59	22 38			22 47		22 59	22 59	23 39			23 47	23 59	23 59	00 38						
Broadstairs	a	22 04						23 04	23 04													
Margate [4]	a	22 10						23 10	23 10													

		SE C
St Pancras Intl. [15] ⊖	d	23 42
Stratford International ⊖	d	23 50
Ebbsfleet International	d	00 02
London Charing Cross [4] ⊖	d	
London Waterloo (East) [4] ⊖	d	
London Cannon Street [4] ⊖	d	
London Bridge [4] ⊖	d	
Orpington [4]	d	
Sevenoaks [4]	d	
Tonbridge [4]	a	
	d	
Paddock Wood [4]	d	
Maidstone West [4] 194	a	
Marden	d	
Staplehurst	d	
Headcorn	d	
Pluckley	d	
Ashford International	a	00 21
	d	
Wye	d	
Chilham	d	
Chartham	d	
Canterbury West [4]	d	
Sturry	d	
Westenhanger	d	
Sandling	d	
Folkestone West	d	
Folkestone Central	d	
Dover Priory [4]	a	
	d	
Martin Mill	d	
Walmer	d	
Deal	d	
Sandwich	d	
Minster [4]	d	
Ramsgate [4]	a	
Broadstairs	a	
Margate [4]	a	

A not from 2 September until 9 September

B 🛒 to Ashford International

C not 26 August

until 27 July, 13 Aug to 28 Aug and then from 10 Sep

Margate, Ramsgate, Canterbury West, Dover, Folkestone, Ashford International - Tonbridge and London

Network Diagram - see first Page of Table 206

Miles	Miles	Miles	Miles			SE MX ■	SE A	SE B	SE	SE ■	SE ■	SE B	SE A	SE ■	SE	SE ■	SE A	SE B	SE A	SE	SE ■	SE ■	SE A
0	0	—	—	Margate ■	d																		
3¼	3¼	—	—	Broadstairs	d																		
5½	5½	—	—	Ramsgate ■	d	21p22						05 00	05 00			04 50	04 55				05 36		05 55
—	9½	0	—	Minster ■	d							05 06	05 06								05 42		
13¾	—	4¾	—	Sandwich	d	21p34										05 04							
18	—	—	—	Deal	d	21p40										05 10							
19½	—	—	—	Walmer	d	21p43										05 13							
22¼	—	—	—	Martin Mill	d	21p48										05 17							
27¼	—	—	—	Dover Priory ■	a	21p56										05 26							
—	—	—	—		d	21p57				04 37						05 27		05 44				05 45	
34½	—	—	—	Folkestone Central	d	22p09				04 49						05 39		05 56					
35¼	—	—	—	Folkestone West	d	22p11				04 51						05 42		05 58					
39	—	—	—	Sandling	d	22p16				04 56						05 47							
40¼	—	—	—	Westenhanger	d	22p19				04 59						05 49							
—	18½	—	—	Sturry	d							05 18	05 18								05 54		
—	20¾	—	—	Canterbury West ■	d							05 25	05 25	05 36							06 00		06 15
—	24	—	—	Chartham	d									05 41							06 05		
—	26	—	—	Chilham	d									05 44							06 08		
—	30¾	—	—	Wye	d									05 51							06 15		
48½	35	—	0	Ashford International	a	22p28				05 08		05 41	05 41	05 57		05 59		06 11			06 21		06 32
—	—	—	—		d	22p33	05 13	05 13		05 13	05 29	05 43	05 43			06 03		06 13	06 13		06 24		06 33
54	—	—	—	Pluckley	d	22p39				05 19	05 35					06 09					06 30		
59¼	—	—	—	Headcorn	d	22p46				05 26	05 42					06 16					06 37		
62¾	—	—	—	Staplehurst	d	22p51				05 31	05 47					06 21					06 42		
65	—	—	—	Marden	d	22p55				05 35	05 51					06 25					06 46		
—	—	—	—	Maidstone West ■ 194	d				05 18						05 56					06 26			
69¾	—	—	—	Paddock Wood ■	d	23p01			05a37	05 42	05 58				06a15	06 32				06a45	06 53		
75	—	—	—	Tonbridge ■	a	23p10				05 49	06 05					06 39					07 01		
—	—	—	—		d	23p14				05 50	06 06					06 40					07 02		
82¼	—	—	—	Sevenoaks ■	a	23p24				05 58	06 14					06 48					07 10		
90¾	—	—	—	Orpington ■	a	23p36				06 08	06 23												
102¾	—	—	—	London Bridge ■ ⊖	a	23p54				06 24	06 39					07 14					07 36	07 51	
—	—	—	—	London Cannon Street ■ ⊖	a																	07 57	
103¾	—	—	—	London Waterloo (East) ■ ⊖	a	23p59				06 29	06 44					07 19					07 41		
104½	—	—	—	London Charing Cross ■ ⊖	a	00 03				06 33	06 49					07 25					07 47		
—	—	—	33¼	Ebbsfleet International	a		05 32	05 32				06 02	06 02				06 16	06 32	06 32				06 52
—	—	—	50	Stratford International ⊖	a		05 44	05 44				06 14	06 14				06 33	06 44	06 45				07 04
—	—	—	56	St Pancras Intl. ■ ⊖	a		05 50	05 51				06 21	06 23				06 43	06 51	06 55				07 15

		SE ■	SE B	SE B	SE A	SE ■	SE B	SE	SE ■	SE ■	SE B	SE B	SE A	SE ■	SE ■	SE B	SE	SE ■	SE B	SE B	SE A	SE ■	SE ■
Margate ■	d		05 47																06 48				
Broadstairs	d		05 54																06 54				
Ramsgate ■	d	05 26	06 00						06 08			06 26		06 12	06 42				07 00				06 59
Minster ■	d								06 17						06 48								
Sandwich	d	05 40		05 50							06 18			06 26						06 50			
Deal	d	05 46		05 56							06 24			06 32						06 56			
Walmer	d	05 49												06 35									
Martin Mill	d	05 53												06 39									
Dover Priory ■	a	06 02		06 10							06 38			06 48						07 10			
	d	06 04		06 12						06 24	06 42			06 49						07 12			
Folkestone Central	d	06 15		06 23						06 36	06 53			07 00				07 14		07 23			
Folkestone West	d	06 18		06 26						06 38	06 56			07 03				07 17		07 26			
Sandling	d	06 23								06 43				07 08				07 22					
Westenhanger	d	06 26								06 46				07 11				07 25					
Sturry	d								06 29						07 00								
Canterbury West ■	d		06 20						06 34			06 50			07 06				07 20				
Chartham	d								06 39						07 11								
Chilham	d								06 42						07 14								
Wye	d								06 49						07 21								
Ashford International	a	06 35	06 36	06 39					06 55	06 55	07 09	07 06		07 20	07 27			07 34	07 36	07 39			
	d	06 38	06 43		06 43	06 45			06 57	07 03	07 13		07 13	07 22	07 29			07 38	07 43		07 43	07 45	
Pluckley	d	06 44				06 51			07 04	07 09				07 28				07 44				07 51	
Headcorn	d	06 51				06 58			07 11	07 16				07 35	07 40			07 51				07 58	
Staplehurst	d	06 56				07 03			07 16	07 22				07 40	07 45			07 56				08 03	
Marden	d	07 00				07 07			07 20	07 26				07 44	07 49			08 00				08 07	
Maidstone West ■ 194	d						06 56	07 01								07 26	07 41						
Paddock Wood ■	d	07 07				07 14		07a20	07 27	07 33				07 51	07 55		08a00	08 07				08 14	
Tonbridge ■	a	07 14				07 21			07 34	07 41				07 58	08 03			08 14				08 21	
	d	07 15				07 23			07 35	07 42				07 59	08 04			08 15				08 22	
Sevenoaks ■	a	07 26				07 31			07 46	07 50				08 07	08 12			08 26				08 30	
Orpington ■	a																						
London Bridge ■ ⊖	a	07 53							08 13					08 33				08 55					08 49
London Cannon Street ■ ⊖	a	07 59							08 20					08 41				09 02					08 57
London Waterloo (East) ■ ⊖	a					08 00				08 20					08 40							09 00	
London Charing Cross ■ ⊖	a					08 06				08 26					08 46							09 04	
Ebbsfleet International	a				07 02								07 32								08 02		
Stratford International ⊖	a		07 11		07 19		07 36				07 41		07 45			08 06			08 11		08 19		
St Pancras Intl. ■ ⊖	a		07 18		07 29		07 43				07 48		07 55			08 13			08 19		08 29		

A 27 dly

B not 27 dly

until 27 July, 13 Aug to 28 Aug and then from 10 Sep

Margate, Ramsgate, Canterbury West, Dover, Folkestone, Ashford International - Tonbridge and London

Network Diagram - see first Page of Table 206

		SE ■	SE ■	SE ■	SE A	SE A	SE A	SE B	SE	SE ■ C ⌶	SE ■ C ⌶	SE A	SE B	SE ■ C ⌶	SE ■ C ⌶	SE A	SE B	SE	SE ■ C ⌶	SE ■ C ⌶	SE A	SE B
Margate ■	d											07 49									08 53	
Broadstairs	d											07 55									08 59	
Ramsgate ■	d	06 49	07 10	07 19		07 30				07 22		08 01		07 40	08 16				08 05	08 40	09 05	
Minster ■	d		07 16									08 07		07 53					08 16	08 46		
Sandwich	d	07 01								07 34				08 01					08 25			
Deal	d	07 07								07 40				08 07					08 31			
Walmer	d	07 10								07 43				08 10					08 34			
Martin Mill	d	07 15								07 48				08 15					08 38			
Dover Priory ■	a	07 23								07 56				08 23					08 47			
	d	07 24					07 42			07 57				08 24		08 44			08 57			
Folkestone Central	d	07 36					07 53			08 09				08 36		08 56			09 09			
Folkestone West	d	07 38					07 56			08 11				08 38		08 58			09 11			
Sandling	d	07 43								08 16				08 43					09 16			
Westenhanger	d	07 46								08 19				08 46					09 19			
Sturry	d		07 28									08 19								08 58		
Canterbury West ■	d		07 36			07 50					08 00	08 25			08 36					09 07	09 25	
Chartham	d		07 41								08 05				08 41							
Chilham	d		07 44								08 08				08 44							
Wye	d		07 51								08 15				08 51					09 19		
Ashford International	a	07 55	07 58			08 06	08 09			08 28	08 21	08 41		08 55	08 58	09 11			09 28	09 25	09 41	
	d	08 03				08 13		08 13		08 33		08 43	08 47	09 03		09 13	09 13		09 33		09 43	09 47
Pluckley	d	08 09								08 39				09 09					09 39			
Headcorn	d	08 16								08 46				09 16					09 46			
Staplehurst	d	08 21								08 51				09 21					09 51			
Marden	d	08 25								08 55				09 25					09 55			
Maidstone West ■ 194	d				07 56				08 18									09 28				
Paddock Wood ■	d	08 31							08 37	09 01				09 31				09 47	10 01			
Tonbridge ■	a	08 39							08 45	09 09				09 39				09 57	10 09			
	d	08 40								09 10				09 40					10 10			
Sevenoaks ■	a	08 48								09 18				09 48					10 18			
Orpington ■	a																					
London Bridge ■ ⊖	a	09 14		09 11						09 43				10 13					10 43			
London Cannon Street ■ ⊖	a			09 18																		
London Waterloo (East) ■ ⊖	a	09 19								09 48				10 18					10 48			
London Charing Cross ■ ⊖	a	09 25								09 54				10 22					10 52			
Ebbsfleet International	a							08 32				09 02	09 06			09 32	09 32				10 02	10 06
Stratford International ⊖	a				08 36	08 41		08 45				09 14	09 19			09 44	09 45				10 14	10 19
St Pancras Intl. ■ ⊖	a				08 43	08 48		08 55				09 21	09 29			09 51	09 55				10 21	10 29

		SE ■ C ⌶	SE ■ C ⌶	SE A	SE B	SE	SE ■ C ⌶	SE ■ C ⌶	SE A	SE B	SE ■ C ⌶	SE ■ C ⌶	SE A	SE B	SE	SE ■ C ⌶	SE ■ C ⌶	SE A	SE B	SE ■ C ⌶	SE ■ C ⌶	SE A
Margate ■	d								09 53									10 53				
Broadstairs	d								09 59									10 59				
Ramsgate ■	d						09 22	09 40	10 05							10 22	10 40	11 05				
Minster ■	d							09 46									10 46					
Sandwich	d						09 34									10 34						
Deal	d						09 40									10 40						
Walmer	d						09 43									10 43						
Martin Mill	d						09 48									10 48						
Dover Priory ■	a						09 56									10 56						
	d	09 24		09 44			09 57				10 24		10 44			10 57				11 24		11 44
Folkestone Central	d	09 36		09 56			10 09				10 36		10 56			11 09				11 36		11 56
Folkestone West	d	09 38		09 58			10 11				10 38		10 58			11 11				11 38		11 58
Sandling	d	09 43					10 16				10 43					11 16				11 43		
Westenhanger	d	09 46					10 19				10 46					11 19				11 46		
Sturry	d							09 58									10 58					
Canterbury West ■	d		09 36					10 07	10 25			10 36					11 07	11 25			11 36	
Chartham	d		09 41									10 41									11 41	
Chilham	d		09 44									10 44									11 44	
Wye	d		09 51					10 19				10 51					11 19				11 51	
Ashford International	a	09 55	09 58	10 11			10 28	10 25	10 41		10 55	10 58	11 11			11 28	11 25	11 41		11 55	11 58	12 11
	d	10 03		10 13	10 13		10 33		10 43	10 47	11 03		11 13	11 13		11 33		11 43	11 47	12 03		12 13
Pluckley	d	10 09					10 39				11 09					11 39				12 09		
Headcorn	d	10 16					10 46				11 16					11 46				12 16		
Staplehurst	d	10 21					10 51				11 21					11 51				12 21		
Marden	d	10 25					10 55				11 25					11 55				12 25		
Maidstone West ■ 194	d					10 28									11 28							
Paddock Wood ■	d	10 31				10 47	11 01				11 31				11 47	12 01				12 31		
Tonbridge ■	a	10 39				10 55	11 09				11 39				11 55	12 09				12 39		
	d	10 40					11 10				11 40					12 10				12 40		
Sevenoaks ■	a	10 48					11 18				11 48					12 18				12 48		
Orpington ■	a																					
London Bridge ■ ⊖	a	11 13					11 43				12 13					12 43				13 13		
London Cannon Street ■ ⊖	a																					
London Waterloo (East) ■ ⊖	a	11 18					11 48				12 18					12 48				13 18		
London Charing Cross ■ ⊖	a	11 22					11 52				12 22					12 52				13 22		
Ebbsfleet International	a			10 32	10 32				11 02	11 06			11 32	11 32				12 02	12 06			12 32
Stratford International ⊖	a			10 44	10 45				11 14	11 19			11 44	11 45				12 14	12 19			12 44
St Pancras Intl. ■ ⊖	a			10 51	10 55				11 21	11 29			11 51	11 55				12 21	12 29			12 51

A not 27 dly

B 27 dly

C ⌶ from Ashford International

Table 207

Mondays to Fridays

until 27 July, 13 Aug to 28 Aug and then from 10 Sep

Margate, Ramsgate, Canterbury West, Dover, Folkestone, Ashford International - Tonbridge and London

Network Diagram - see first Page of Table 206

Station		SE A	SE	SE 1 B 🍴	SE 1 B 🍴	SE C	SE A	SE 1 B 🍴	SE 1 B 🍴	SE C	SE A	SE D	SE E	SE 1 B 🍴	SE 1 B 🍴	SE C	SE A	SE 1 B 🍴	SE 1 B 🍴	SE C	SE A	SE
Margate	d					11 53										12 53						
Broadstairs	d					11 59										12 59						
Ramsgate	d			11 22	11 40	12 05								12 22	12 40	13 05						
Minster	d				11 46										12 46							
Sandwich	d			11 34										12 34								
Deal	d			11 40										12 40								
Walmer	d			11 43										12 43								
Martin Mill	d			11 48										12 48								
Dover Priory	a			11 56										12 56								
	d			11 57				12 24		12 44				12 57				13 24		13 44		
Folkestone Central	d			12 09				12 36		12 56				13 09				13 36		13 56		
Folkestone West	d			12 11				12 38		12 58				13 11				13 38		13 58		
Sandling	d			12 16				12 43						13 16				13 43				
Westenhanger	d			12 19				12 46						13 19				13 46				
Sturry	d				11 58										12 58							
Canterbury West	d				12 07	12 25			12 36						13 07	13 25			13 36			
Chartham	d								12 41										13 41			
Chilham	d								12 44										13 44			
Wye	d				12 19				12 51						13 19				13 51			
Ashford International	a			12 28	12 25	12 41		12 55	12 58	13 11				13 28	13 25	13 41		13 55	13 58	14 11		
	d	12 13		12 33		12 43	12 47	13 03		13 13	13 13			13 33		13 43	13 47	14 03		14 13	14 13	
Pluckley	d			12 39				13 09						13 39				14 09				
Headcorn	d			12 46				13 16						13 46				14 16				
Staplehurst	d			12 51				13 21						13 51				14 21				
Marden	d			12 55				13 25						13 55				14 25				
Maidstone West 194	d		12 28									13 28	13 28									14 28
Paddock Wood	d		12 47	13 01				13 31				13 47	13 47	14 01				14 31				14 47
Tonbridge	a		12 58	13 09				13 39				13 55	13 56	14 09				14 39				14 55
	d			13 10				13 40						14 10				14 40				
Sevenoaks	a			13 18				13 48						14 18				14 48				
Orpington	a																					
London Bridge ⊖	a			13 43				14 13						14 43				15 13				
London Cannon Street ⊖	a																					
London Waterloo (East) ⊖	a			13 48				14 18						14 48				15 18				
London Charing Cross ⊖	a			13 52				14 22						14 52				15 22				
Ebbsfleet International	a	12 32				13 02	13 06			13 32	13 32					14 02	14 06			14 32	14 32	
Stratford International ⊖	a	12 45				13 14	13 19			13 44	13 45					14 14	14 19			14 44	14 45	
St Pancras Intl. ⊖	a	12 55				13 21	13 29			13 51	13 55					14 21	14 29			14 51	14 55	

Station		SE 1 B 🍴	SE 1 B 🍴	SE C	SE A	SE 1 B 🍴	SE 1 B 🍴	SE C	SE A	SE	SE 1 B 🍴	SE 1 B 🍴	SE C	SE A	SE 1 B 🍴	SE 1 B 🍴	SE C	SE A	SE	SE 1 B 🍴	SE 1 B 🍴	SE C	SE A
Margate	d			13 53									14 53									15 53	
Broadstairs	d			13 59									14 59									15 59	
Ramsgate	d	13 22	13 40	14 05							14 22	14 40	15 05							15 22	15 40	16 05	
Minster	d		13 46									14 46									15 46		
Sandwich	d	13 34									14 34									15 34			
Deal	d	13 40									14 40									15 40			
Walmer	d	13 43									14 43									15 43			
Martin Mill	d	13 48									14 48									15 48			
Dover Priory	a	13 56									14 56									15 56			
	d	13 57				14 24		14 44			14 57				15 24		15 44			15 57			
Folkestone Central	d	14 09				14 36		14 56			15 09				15 36		15 56			16 09			
Folkestone West	d	14 11				14 38		14 58			15 11				15 38		15 58			16 11			
Sandling	d	14 16				14 43					15 16				15 43					16 16			
Westenhanger	d	14 19				14 46					15 19				15 46					16 19			
Sturry	d		13 58									14 58									15 58		
Canterbury West	d		14 07	14 25			14 36					15 04	15 25			15 36					16 04	16 25	
Chartham	d						14 41									15 41							
Chilham	d						14 44									15 44							
Wye	d		14 19				14 51					15 16				15 51					16 16		
Ashford International	a	14 28	14 25	14 41		14 55	14 58	15 11			15 28	15 22	15 41		15 55	15 58	16 11			16 28	16 22	16 41	
	d	14 33		14 43	14 47	15 03		15 13	15 13		15 33		15 43	15 47	16 03		16 13	16 13		16 33		16 43	16 47
Pluckley	d	14 39				15 09					15 39				16 09					16 39			
Headcorn	d	14 46				15 16					15 46				16 16					16 46			
Staplehurst	d	14 51				15 21					15 51				16 21					16 51			
Marden	d	14 55				15 25					15 55				16 25					16 55			
Maidstone West 194	d									15 28									16 33				
Paddock Wood	d	15 01				15 31				15 47	16 01				16 31				16a52	17 01			
Tonbridge	a	15 09				15 39				15 55	16 09				16 39					17 09			
	d	15 10				15 40					16 10				16 40					17 10			
Sevenoaks	a	15 18				15 48					16 18				16 48					17 18			
Orpington	a																						
London Bridge ⊖	a	15 43				16 14					16 46				17 17					17 44			
London Cannon Street ⊖	a																						
London Waterloo (East) ⊖	a	15 48				16 20					16 52				17 22					17 50			
London Charing Cross ⊖	a	15 52				16 24					16 56				17 26					17 53			
Ebbsfleet International	a			15 02	15 06			15 32	15 32				16 02	16 06			16 32	16 32				17 02	17 06
Stratford International ⊖	a			15 14	15 19			15 44	15 45				16 14	16 19			16 44	16 45				17 14	17 19
St Pancras Intl. ⊖	a			15 21	15 29			15 51	15 55				16 21	16 29			16 51	16 55				17 21	17 29

A 27 July
B 🍴 from Ashford International
C not 27 July
D from 21 May until 27 July
E until 18 May

Table 207

Mondays to Fridays

until 27 July, 13 Aug to 28 Aug and then from 10 Sep

Margate, Ramsgate, Canterbury West, Dover, Folkestone, Ashford International - Tonbridge and London

Network Diagram - see first Page of Table 206

Station		SE	SE 1 A 🍴	SE 1 A 🍴	SE B	SE C	SE	SE 1 A 🍴	SE 1 A 🍴	SE B	SE C	SE 1 A 🍴	SE 1 A 🍴	SE B	SE C	SE	SE 1 A 🍴	SE 1 A 🍴	SE B	SE C	SE	SE 1	SE 1
Margate	d									16 53									17 53				
Broadstairs	d									16 59									17 59				
Ramsgate	d		15 50					16 22	16 40	17 05		16 50					17 22	17 40	18 05			17 50	
Minster	d								16 46									17 46					
Sandwich	d		16 02					16 34				17 02					17 34					18 02	
Deal	d		16 08					16 40				17 08					17 40					18 08	
Walmer	d		16 11					16 43				17 11					17 43					18 11	
Martin Mill	d		16 16					16 48				17 16					17 48					18 16	
Dover Priory	a		16 24					16 56				17 24					17 56					18 24	
	d		16 24		16 44			16 57				17 24		17 44			17 57					18 24	
Folkestone Central	d		16 36		16 56			17 09				17 36		17 56			18 09					18 36	
Folkestone West	d		16 38		16 58			17 11				17 38		17 58			18 11					18 38	
Sandling	d		16 43					17 16				17 43					18 16					18 43	
Westenhanger	d		16 46					17 19				17 46					18 19					18 46	
Sturry	d								16 58									17 58					
Canterbury West	d			16 36					17 04	17 25			17 36					18 04	18 25				18 36
Chartham	d			16 41									17 41										18 41
Chilham	d			16 44									17 44										18 44
Wye	d			16 51					17 16				17 51					18 16					18 51
Ashford International	a		16 55	16 58	17 11			17 28	17 22	17 41		17 55	17 58	18 11			18 28	18 23	18 41			18 55	18 58
	d		17 03		17 13	17 13		17 33		17 43	17 47	18 03		18 13	18 13		18 33		18 43	18 43		19 03	
Pluckley	d		17 09					17 39				18 09					18 39					19 09	
Headcorn	d		17 16					17 46				18 16					18 46					19 16	
Staplehurst	d		17 21					17 51				18 21					18 51					19 21	
Marden	d		17 25					17 55				18 25					18 55					19 25	
Maidstone West 194	d	16 58					17 28									18 18					18 48		
Paddock Wood	d	17a17	17 31				17a47	18 01				18 31				18a37	19 01				19a07	19 31	
Tonbridge	a		17 39					18 09				18 39					19 09					19 39	
	d		17 40					18 10				18 40					19 10					19 40	
Sevenoaks	a		17 48					18 18				18 48					19 18					19 48	
Orpington	a																						
London Bridge ⊖	a		18 16					18 43				19 13					19 43					20 13	
London Cannon Street ⊖	a																						
London Waterloo (East) ⊖	a		18 20					18 48				19 17					19 48					20 18	
London Charing Cross ⊖	a		18 25					18 52				19 21					19 52					20 22	
Ebbsfleet International	a				17 32	17 32				18 02	18 06			18 32	18 32				19 02	19 03			
Stratford International ⊖	a				17 44	17 45				18 14	18 19			18 44	18 45				19 14	19 19			
St Pancras Intl. ⊖	a				17 51	17 55				18 21	18 29			18 51	18 55				19 21	19 29			

Station		SE B	SE C	SE B	SE	SE 1	SE 1	SE B	SE C	SE	SE 1	SE 1	SE B	SE C	SE 1	SE 1	SE B	SE C	SE	SE 1	SE 1	SE B
Margate	d							18 53									19 53					
Broadstairs	d							18 59									19 59					
Ramsgate	d					18 22	18 40	19 05							19 22	19 40	20 05					
Minster	d						18 46									19 46						
Sandwich	d					18 34									19 34							
Deal	d					18 40									19 40							
Walmer	d					18 43									19 43							
Martin Mill	d					18 48									19 48							
Dover Priory	a					18 56									19 56							
	d	18 44				18 57					19 24		19 44		19 57					20 24		20 44
Folkestone Central	d	18 56				19 09					19 36		19 56		20 09					20 36		20 56
Folkestone West	d	18 58				19 11					19 38		19 58		20 11					20 38		20 58
Sandling	d					19 16					19 43				20 16					20 43		
Westenhanger	d					19 19					19 46				20 19					20 46		
Sturry	d						18 58									19 58						
Canterbury West	d						19 07	19 25				19 36				20 07	20 25				20 36	
Chartham	d											19 41									20 41	
Chilham	d											19 44									20 44	
Wye	d						19 19					19 51				20 19					20 51	
Ashford International	a	19 11				19 29	19 26	19 41			19 55	19 58	20 12		20 28	20 25	20 43			20 55	20 58	21 11
	d	19 13	19 13			19 33		19 43	19 47		20 03		20 13	20 13	20 33		20 45	20 47		21 03		21 13
Pluckley	d					19 39					20 09				20 39					21 09		
Headcorn	d					19 46					20 16				20 46					21 16		
Staplehurst	d					19 51					20 21				20 51					21 21		
Marden	d					19 55					20 25				20 55					21 25		
Maidstone West 194	d			19 13	19 18					19 58									20 58			
Paddock Wood	d				19a37	20 01				20 17	20 31				21 01				21 17	21 31		
Tonbridge	a					20 09				20 25	20 39				21 09				21 25	21 39		
	d					20 10					20 40				21 10					21 40		
Sevenoaks	a					20 18					20 48				21 18					21 48		
Orpington	a																					
London Bridge ⊖	a					20 42					21 13				21 43					22 13		
London Cannon Street ⊖	a																					
London Waterloo (East) ⊖	a					20 47					21 18				21 48					22 18		
London Charing Cross ⊖	a					20 51					21 22				21 52					22 22		
Ebbsfleet International	a	19 32	19 32	19 47				20 02	20 06				20 33	20 32			21 04	21 06				21 32
Stratford International ⊖	a	19 46	19 45	20 01				20 14	20 19				20 45	20 45			21 16	21 19				21 44
St Pancras Intl. ⊖	a	19 53	19 55	20 08				20 21	20 29				20 53	20 55			21 23	21 29				21 51

A 🍴 from Ashford International
B not 27 July
C 27 July

Table 207

Mondays to Fridays

until 27 July, 13 Aug to 28 Aug and then from 10 Sep

Margate, Ramsgate, Canterbury West, Dover, Folkestone, Ashford International - Tonbridge and London

Network Diagram - see first Page of Table 206

		SE	SE ■1	SE ■1	SE	SE	SE	SE ■1	SE ■1	SE	SE	SE ■1	SE	SE	SE ■1	SE	SE	SE ■1
		A			B	A				B	A		B	A		A	B	
Margate ■4	d				20 53								21 53					
Broadstairs	d				20 59								21 59					
Ramsgate ■4	d		20 22	20 40	21 05							21 22	22 05		22 24			22 45
Minster ■4	d			20 46											22 30			
Sandwich	d		20 34									21 34						22 57
Deal	d		20 40									21 40						23 03
Walmer	d		20 43									21 43						23 06
Martin Mill	d		20 48									21 48						23 11
Dover Priory ■4	a		20 56									21 56						23 19
	d		20 57					21 24		21 44		21 57					22 44	23 24
Folkestone Central	d		21 09					21 36		21 56		22 09					22 56	23 36
Folkestone West	d		21 11					21 38		21 58		22 11					22 58	23 38
Sandling	d		21 16					21 43				22 16						23 43
Westenhanger	d		21 19					21 46				22 19						23 46
Sturry	d			20 58											22 42			
Canterbury West ■4	d			21 07	21 25				21 36				22 25		22 47			
Chartham	d								21 41						22 52			
Chilham	d								21 44						22 55			
Wye	d			21 19					21 51						23 02			
Ashford International	a		21 28	21 25	21 41			21 55	21 58	22 11		22 28	22 41		23 08		23 11	23 55
	d	21 13	21 33		21 43	21 47		22 03		22 13	22 13	22 33	22 43	22 43		23 11	23 13	
Pluckley	d		21 39					22 09				22 39						
Headcorn	d		21 46					22 16				22 46						
Staplehurst	d		21 51					22 21				22 51						
Marden	d		21 55					22 25				22 55						
Maidstone West ■4 194	d						21 58											
Paddock Wood ■4	d		22 01				22 17	22 31				23 01						
Tonbridge ■4	a		22 09				22 25	22 39				23 10						
	d		22 10					22 40				23 14						
Sevenoaks ■4	a		22 18					22 48				23 24						
Orpington ■4	a											23 36						
London Bridge ■4 ⊖	a		22 43					23 13				23 54						
London Cannon Street ■4 ⊖	a																	
London Waterloo (East) ■4 ⊖	a		22 48					23 18				23 59						
London Charing Cross ■4 ⊖	a		22 52					23 22				00 03						
Ebbsfleet International	a	21 32			22 02	22 06				22 32	22 32		23 02	23 02		23 30	23 32	
Stratford International ⊖	a	21 45			22 14	22 19				22 44	22 45		23 14	23 16		23 42	23 44	
St Pancras Intl. ■15 ⊖	a	21 55			22 21	22 29				22 51	22 55		23 21	23 26		23 51	23 52	

Mondays to Fridays

30 July to 10 August

		SE ■1	SE	SE	SE ■1	SE ■1	SE	SE ■1	SE	SE ■1	SE	SE	SE ■1	SE	SE ■1	SE ■1	SE	SE ■1	SE	SE ■1	SE ■1	SE	SE ■1
		C																					
Margate ■4	d													05 44									
Broadstairs	d													05 49									
Ramsgate ■4	d	21p22					05 00			04 50			05 36	05 55		05 26				06 08			06 12
Minster ■4	d						05 06						05 42							06 17			
Sandwich	d	21p34								05 04						05 40							06 26
Deal	d	21p40								05 10						05 46							06 32
Walmer	d	21p43								05 13						05 49							06 35
Martin Mill	d	21p48								05 17						05 53							06 39
Dover Priory ■4	a	21p56								05 26						06 02							06 48
	d	21p57			04 37					05 27					05 45	06 04					06 24		06 49
Folkestone Central	d	22p09			04 49					05 39						06 15					06 36		07 00
Folkestone West	d	22p11			04 51					05 42						06 18					06 38		07 03
Sandling	d	22p16			04 56					05 47						06 23					06 43		07 08
Westenhanger	d	22p19			04 59					05 49						06 26					06 46		07 11
Sturry	d						05 18						05 54							06 29			
Canterbury West ■4	d						05 25	05 36					06 00	06 15						06 34			
Chartham	d							05 41					06 05							06 39			
Chilham	d							05 44					06 08							06 42			
Wye	d							05 51					06 15							06 49			
Ashford International	a	22p28			05 08		05 41	05 57		05 59			06 21	06 32		06 35				06 55	06 55		07 20
	d	22p33	05 13		05 13	05 29	05 43			06 03	06 13		06 24	06 33		06 38	06 43	06 45		06 57	07 03	07 13	07 22
Pluckley	d	22p39			05 19	05 35				06 09			06 30			06 44		06 51		07 04	07 09		07 28
Headcorn	d	22p46			05 26	05 42				06 16			06 37			06 51		06 58		07 11	07 16		07 35
Staplehurst	d	22p51			05 31	05 47				06 21			06 42			06 56		07 03		07 16	07 22		07 40
Marden	d	22p55			05 35	05 51				06 25			06 46			07 00		07 07		07 20	07 26		07 44
Maidstone West ■4 194	d			05 18					05 56			06 26							07 01				
Paddock Wood ■4	d	23p01		05a37	05 42	05 58			06a15	06 32		06a45	06 53			07 07		07 14	07a20	07 27	07 33		07 51
Tonbridge ■4	a	23p10			05 49	06 05				06 39			07 01			07 14		07 21		07 34	07 41		07 58
	d	23p14			05 50	06 06				06 40			07 02			07 15		07 23		07 35	07 42		07 59
Sevenoaks ■4	a	23p24			05 58	06 14				06 48			07 10			07 26		07 31		07 46	07 50		08 07
Orpington ■4	a	23p36			06 08	06 23																	
London Bridge ■4 ⊖	a	23p54			06 24	06 39				07 14			07 36		07 51	07 53				08 13			08 33
London Cannon Street ■4 ⊖	a														07 57	07 59				08 20			08 41
London Waterloo (East) ■4 ⊖	a	23p59			06 29	06 44				07 19			07 41					08 00			08 20		
London Charing Cross ■4 ⊖	a	00 03			06 33	06 49				07 25			07 47					08 06			08 26		
Ebbsfleet International	a		05 32				06 02				06 32			06 52			07 02					07 32	
Stratford International ⊖	a		05 44				06 14				06 45			07 04			07 19					07 45	
St Pancras Intl. ■15 ⊖	a		05 50				06 23				06 55			07 15			07 29					07 55	

A 27 July

B not 27 July

C not 30 July, 6 August

Table 207

Mondays to Fridays

30 July to 10 August

Margate, Ramsgate, Canterbury West, Dover, Folkestone, Ashford International - Tonbridge and London

Network Diagram - see first Page of Table 206

		SE ■1	SE	SE ■1	SE	SE ■1	SE ■1	SE ■1	SE ■1	SE ■1	SE	SE	SE ■1	SE ■1	SE	SE ■1	SE ■1	SE	SE	SE ■1	SE ■1	SE
													A ⌶	A ⌶		A ⌶	A ⌶			A ⌶	A ⌶	
Margate ■4	d																					
Broadstairs	d																					
Ramsgate ■4	d	06 42					06 59	06 49	07 10	07 19			07 22	07 30		07 40	08 13			08 05	08 40	
Minster ■4	d	06 48							07 16					07 36		07 53	08 20			08 16	08 46	
Sandwich	d							07 01					07 34			08 01				08 25		
Deal	d							07 07					07 40			08 07				08 31		
Walmer	d							07 10					07 43			08 10				08 34		
Martin Mill	d							07 15					07 48			08 15				08 38		
Dover Priory ■4	a							07 23					07 56			08 23				08 47		
	d							07 24					07 57			08 24				08 57		
Folkestone Central	d			07 14				07 36					08 09			08 36				09 09		
Folkestone West	d			07 17				07 38					08 11			08 38				09 11		
Sandling	d			07 22				07 43					08 16			08 43				09 16		
Westenhanger	d			07 25				07 46					08 19			08 46				09 19		
Sturry	d	07 00							07 28					07 48			08 31				08 58	
Canterbury West ■4	d	07 06							07 36					08 00			08 36				09 07	
Chartham	d	07 11							07 41					08 05			08 41					
Chilham	d	07 14							07 44					08 08			08 44					
Wye	d	07 21							07 51					08 15			08 51				09 19	
Ashford International	a	07 27		07 34				07 55	07 58				08 28	08 21		08 55	08 58			09 28	09 25	
	d	07 29		07 38	07 43	07 45		08 03			08 13		08 33		08 47	09 03		09 13		09 33		09 47
Pluckley	d			07 44		07 51		08 09					08 39			09 09				09 39		
Headcorn	d	07 40		07 51		07 58		08 16					08 46			09 16				09 46		
Staplehurst	d	07 45		07 56		08 03		08 21					08 51			09 21				09 51		
Marden	d	07 49		08 00		08 07		08 25					08 55			09 25				09 55		
Maidstone West ■4 194	d		07 41									08 18							09 28			
Paddock Wood ■4	d	07 55	08a00	08 07		08 14		08 31				08 37	09 01			09 31			09 47	10 01		
Tonbridge ■4	a	08 03		08 14		08 21		08 39				08 45	09 09			09 39			09 57	10 09		
	d	08 04		08 15		08 22		08 40					09 10			09 40				10 10		
Sevenoaks ■4	a	08 12		08 26		08 30		08 48					09 18			09 48				10 18		
Orpington ■4	a																					
London Bridge ■4 ⊖	a			08 55			08 51	09 14		09 11			09 43			10 13				10 43		
London Cannon Street ■4 ⊖	a			09 02			08 57			09 18												
London Waterloo (East) ■4 ⊖	a	08 40				09 00		09 19					09 48			10 18				10 48		
London Charing Cross ■4 ⊖	a	08 46				09 04		09 25					09 54			10 22				10 52		
Ebbsfleet International	a				08 02						08 32				09 06			09 32				10 06
Stratford International ⊖	a				08 19						08 45				09 19			09 45				10 19
St Pancras Intl. ■15 ⊖	a				08 29						08 55				09 29			09 55				10 29

		SE ■1	SE ■1	SE	SE	SE ■1	SE ■1	SE	SE ■1	SE ■1	SE	SE	SE ■1	SE ■1	SE	SE ■1	SE ■1	SE	SE	SE ■1	SE ■1	SE
		A ⌶	A ⌶			A ⌶	A ⌶		A ⌶	A ⌶			A ⌶	A ⌶		A ⌶	A ⌶			A ⌶	A ⌶	
Margate ■4	d																					
Broadstairs	d																					
Ramsgate ■4	d	09 16				09 22	09 40		10 16				10 22	10 40		11 16				11 22	11 40	
Minster ■4	d						09 46							10 46							11 46	
Sandwich	d					09 34							10 34							11 34		
Deal	d					09 40							10 40							11 40		
Walmer	d					09 43							10 43							11 43		
Martin Mill	d					09 48							10 48							11 48		
Dover Priory ■4	a					09 56							10 56							11 56		
	d		09 24			09 57				10 24			10 57				11 24			11 57		
Folkestone Central	d		09 36			10 09				10 36			11 09				11 36			12 09		
Folkestone West	d		09 38			10 11				10 38			11 11				11 38			12 11		
Sandling	d		09 43			10 16				10 43			11 16				11 43			12 16		
Westenhanger	d		09 46			10 19				10 46			11 19				11 46			12 19		
Sturry	d						09 58							10 58							11 58	
Canterbury West ■4	d	09 36					10 07		10 36					11 07		11 36					12 07	
Chartham	d	09 41							10 41							11 41						
Chilham	d	09 44							10 44							11 44						
Wye	d	09 51					10 19		10 51					11 19		11 51					12 19	
Ashford International	a	09 58	09 55			10 28	10 25		10 58	10 55			11 28	11 25		11 58	11 55			12 28	12 25	
	d	10 03		10 13		10 33		10 47	11 03		11 13		11 33		11 47	12 03		12 13		12 33		12 47
Pluckley	d	10 09				10 39			11 09				11 39			12 09				12 39		
Headcorn	d	10 16				10 46			11 16				11 46			12 16				12 46		
Staplehurst	d	10 21				10 51			11 21				11 51			12 21				12 51		
Marden	d	10 25				10 55			11 25				11 55			12 25				12 55		
Maidstone West ■4 194	d				10 28							11 28							12 28			
Paddock Wood ■4	d	10 31			10 47	11 01			11 31			11 47	12 01			12 31			12 47	13 01		
Tonbridge ■4	a	10 39			10 55	11 09			11 39			11 55	12 09			12 39			12 58	13 09		
	d	10 40				11 10			11 40				12 10			12 40				13 10		
Sevenoaks ■4	a	10 48				11 18			11 48				12 18			12 48				13 18		
Orpington ■4	a																					
London Bridge ■4 ⊖	a	11 13				11 43			12 13				12 43			13 13				13 43		
London Cannon Street ■4 ⊖	a																					
London Waterloo (East) ■4 ⊖	a	11 18				11 48			12 18				12 48			13 18				13 48		
London Charing Cross ■4 ⊖	a	11 22				11 52			12 22				12 52			13 22				13 52		
Ebbsfleet International	a			10 32				11 06			11 32				12 06			12 32				13 06
Stratford International ⊖	a			10 45				11 19			11 45				12 19			12 45				13 19
St Pancras Intl. ■15 ⊖	a			10 55				11 29			11 55				12 29			12 55				13 29

A ⌶ from Ashford International

Table 207

Mondays to Fridays

30 July to 10 August

Margate, Ramsgate, Canterbury West, Dover, Folkestone, Ashford International - Tonbridge and London

Network Diagram - see first Page of Table 206

		SE 1 A ⌶	SE 1 A ⌶	SE	SE	SE 1 A ⌶	SE 1 A ⌶	SE	SE 1 A ⌶	SE 1 A ⌶	SE	SE	SE 1 A ⌶	SE 1 A ⌶	SE	SE 1 A ⌶	SE 1 A ⌶	SE	SE	SE 1 A ⌶	SE 1 A ⌶	SE
Margate [4]	d																					
Broadstairs	d																					
Ramsgate [4]	d	12 16				12 22	12 40		13 16				13 22	13 40		14 16				14 22	14 40	
Minster [4]	d						12 46							13 46							14 46	
Sandwich	d					12 34							13 34							14 34		
Deal	d					12 40							13 40							14 40		
Walmer	d					12 43							13 43							14 43		
Martin Mill	d					12 48							13 48							14 48		
Dover Priory [4]	a					12 56							13 56							14 56		
	d		12 24			12 57				13 24			13 57				14 24			14 57		
Folkestone Central	d		12 36			13 09				13 36			14 09				14 36			15 09		
Folkestone West	d		12 38			13 11				13 38			14 11				14 38			15 11		
Sandling	d		12 43			13 16				13 43			14 16				14 43			15 16		
Westenhanger	d		12 46			13 19				13 46			14 19				14 46			15 19		
Sturry	d						12 58							13 58							14 58	
Canterbury West [4]	d	12 36					13 07		13 36					14 07		14 36					15 04	
Chartham	d	12 41							13 41							14 41						
Chilham	d	12 44							13 44							14 44						
Wye	d	12 51					13 19		13 51					14 19		14 51					15 16	
Ashford International	a	12 58	12 55			13 28	13 25		13 58	13 55			14 28	14 25		14 58	14 55			15 28	15 22	
	d	13 03		13 13		13 33		13 47	14 03		14 13		14 33		14 47	15 03		15 13		15 33		15 47
Pluckley	d	13 09				13 39			14 09				14 39			15 09				15 39		
Headcorn	d	13 16				13 46			14 16				14 46			15 16				15 46		
Staplehurst	d	13 21				13 51			14 21				14 51			15 21				15 51		
Marden	d	13 25				13 55			14 25				14 55			15 25				15 55		
Maidstone West [4] 194	d				13 28							14 28							15 28			
Paddock Wood [4]	d	13 31			13 47	14 01			14 31			14 47	15 01			15 31			15 47	16 01		
Tonbridge [4]	a	13 39			13 55	14 09			14 39			14 55	15 09			15 39			15 55	16 09		
	d	13 40				14 10			14 40				15 10			15 40				16 10		
Sevenoaks [4]	a	13 48				14 18			14 48				15 18			15 48				16 18		
Orpington [4]	a																					
London Bridge [4] ⊖	a	14 13				14 43			15 13				15 43			16 14				16 46		
London Cannon Street [4] ⊖	a																					
London Waterloo (East) [4] ⊖	a	14 18				14 48			15 18				15 48			16 20				16 52		
London Charing Cross [4] ⊖	a	14 22				14 52			15 22				15 52			16 24				16 56		
Ebbsfleet International	a			13 32				14 06			14 32				15 06			15 32				16 06
Stratford International ⊖	a			13 45				14 19			14 45				15 19			15 45				16 19
St Pancras Intl. [15] ⊖	a			13 55				14 29			14 55				15 29			15 55				16 29

		SE 1 A ⌶	SE 1 A ⌶	SE	SE	SE 1 A ⌶	SE 1 A ⌶	SE	SE	SE 1 A ⌶	SE 1 A ⌶	SE	SE	SE 1 A ⌶	SE 1 A ⌶	SE	SE 1 A ⌶	SE 1 A ⌶	SE	SE	SE 1 A ⌶	SE 1 A ⌶	SE
Margate [4]	d																						
Broadstairs	d																						
Ramsgate [4]	d	15 16				15 22	15 40			15 50	16 16			16 22	16 40		16 50	17 16			17 22	17 40	
Minster [4]	d						15 46								16 46							17 46	
Sandwich	d					15 34				16 02				16 34			17 02				17 34		
Deal	d					15 40				16 08				16 40			17 08				17 40		
Walmer	d					15 43				16 11				16 43			17 11				17 43		
Martin Mill	d					15 48				16 16				16 48			17 16				17 48		
Dover Priory [4]	a					15 56				16 24				16 56			17 24				17 56		
	d		15 24			15 57				16 24				16 57			17 24				17 57		
Folkestone Central	d		15 36			16 09				16 36				17 09			17 36				18 09		
Folkestone West	d		15 38			16 11				16 38				17 11			17 38				18 11		
Sandling	d		15 43			16 16				16 43				17 16			17 43				18 16		
Westenhanger	d		15 46			16 19				16 46				17 19			17 46				18 19		
Sturry	d						15 58								16 58							17 58	
Canterbury West [4]	d	15 36					16 04				16 36				17 04			17 36				18 04	
Chartham	d	15 41									16 41							17 41					
Chilham	d	15 44									16 44							17 44					
Wye	d	15 51					16 16				16 51				17 16			17 51				18 16	
Ashford International	a	15 58	15 55			16 28	16 22			16 55	16 58			17 28	17 22		17 55	17 58			18 28	18 22	
	d	16 03		16 13		16 33		16 47		17 03		17 13		17 33		17 47	18 03		18 13		18 33		18 43
Pluckley	d	16 09				16 39				17 09				17 39			18 09				18 39		
Headcorn	d	16 16				16 46				17 16				17 46			18 16				18 46		
Staplehurst	d	16 21				16 51				17 21				17 51			18 21				18 51		
Marden	d	16 25				16 55				17 25				17 55			18 25				18 55		
Maidstone West [4] 194	d				16 33				16 58				17 28							18 18			
Paddock Wood [4]	d	16 31			16a52	17 01			17a17	17 31			17a47	18 01			18 31			18a37	19 01		
Tonbridge [4]	a	16 39				17 09				17 39				18 09			18 39				19 09		
	d	16 40				17 10				17 40				18 10			18 40				19 10		
Sevenoaks [4]	a	16 48				17 18				17 48				18 18			18 48				19 18		
Orpington [4]	a																						
London Bridge [4] ⊖	a	17 17				17 44				18 16				18 43			19 13				19 43		
London Cannon Street [4] ⊖	a																						
London Waterloo (East) [4] ⊖	a	17 22				17 50				18 20				18 48			19 17				19 48		
London Charing Cross [4] ⊖	a	17 26				17 53				18 25				18 52			19 21				19 52		
Ebbsfleet International	a			16 32				17 06				17 32				18 06			18 32				19 03
Stratford International ⊖	a			16 45				17 19				17 45				18 19			18 45				19 19
St Pancras Intl. [15] ⊖	a			16 55				17 29				17 55				18 29			18 55				19 29

A ⌶ from Ashford International

Table 207

Mondays to Fridays

30 July to 10 August

Margate, Ramsgate, Canterbury West, Dover, Folkestone, Ashford International - Tonbridge and London

Network Diagram - see first Page of Table 206

		SE	SE 1	SE 1	SE	SE	SE 1	SE 1	SE	SE	SE 1	SE 1	SE	SE 1	SE 1	SE	SE	SE 1	SE 1	SE	SE 1	SE 1
Margate [4]	d																					
Broadstairs	d																					
Ramsgate [4]	d		17 50	18 16			18 22	18 40			19 14			19 22	19 40			20 14			20 22	20 40
Minster [4]	d							18 46							19 46							20 46
Sandwich	d		18 02				18 34							19 34							20 34	
Deal	d		18 08				18 40							19 40							20 40	
Walmer	d		18 11				18 43							19 43							20 43	
Martin Mill	d		18 16				18 48							19 48							20 48	
Dover Priory [4]	a		18 24				18 56							19 56							20 56	
	d		18 24				18 57					19 24		19 57					20 24		20 57	
Folkestone Central	d		18 36				19 09					19 36		20 09					20 36		21 09	
Folkestone West	d		18 38				19 11					19 38		20 11					20 38		21 11	
Sandling	d		18 43				19 16					19 43		20 16					20 43		21 16	
Westenhanger	d		18 46				19 19					19 46		20 19					20 46		21 19	
Sturry	d							18 58							19 58							20 58
Canterbury West [4]	d			18 36				19 07			19 36				20 07			20 36				21 07
Chartham	d			18 41							19 41							20 41				
Chilham	d			18 44							19 44							20 44				
Wye	d			18 51				19 19			19 51				20 19			20 51				21 19
Ashford International	a		18 55	18 58			19 29	19 26			19 58	19 55		20 28	20 25			20 58	20 55		21 28	21 25
	d		19 03		19 13		19 33		19 47		20 03		20 13	20 33		20 47		21 03		21 13	21 33	
Pluckley	d		19 09				19 39				20 09			20 39				21 09			21 39	
Headcorn	d		19 16				19 46				20 16			20 46				21 16			21 46	
Staplehurst	d		19 21				19 51				20 21			20 51				21 21			21 51	
Marden	d		19 25				19 55				20 25			20 55				21 25			21 55	
Maidstone West [4] 194	d	18 48				19 18				19 58							20 58					
Paddock Wood [4]	d	19a07	19 31			19a37	20 01			20 17	20 31			21 01			21 17	21 31			22 01	
Tonbridge [4]	a		19 39				20 09			20 25	20 39			21 09			21 25	21 39			22 09	
	d		19 40				20 10				20 40			21 10				21 40			22 10	
Sevenoaks [4]	a		19 48				20 18				20 48			21 18				21 48			22 18	
Orpington [4]	a																					
London Bridge [4] ⊖	a		20 13				20 42				21 13			21 43				22 13			22 43	
London Cannon Street [4] ⊖	a																					
London Waterloo (East) [4] ⊖	a		20 18				20 47				21 18			21 48				22 18			22 48	
London Charing Cross [4] ⊖	a		20 22				20 51				21 22			21 52				22 22			22 52	
Ebbsfleet International	a				19 32				20 06				20 32			21 06				21 32		
Stratford International ⊖	a				19 45				20 19				20 45			21 19				21 45		
St Pancras Intl. [15] ⊖	a				19 55				20 29				20 55			21 29				21 55		

		SE	SE	SE 1	SE 1	SE	SE 1	SE	SE 1	SE	SE 1
Margate [4]	d										
Broadstairs	d										
Ramsgate [4]	d			21 16			21 22		22 24		22 45
Minster [4]	d								22 30		
Sandwich	d						21 34				22 57
Deal	d						21 40				23 03
Walmer	d						21 43				23 06
Martin Mill	d						21 48				23 11
Dover Priory [4]	a						21 56				23 19
	d				21 24		21 57				23 24
Folkestone Central	d				21 36		22 09				23 36
Folkestone West	d				21 38		22 11				23 38
Sandling	d				21 43		22 16				23 43
Westenhanger	d				21 46		22 19				23 46
Sturry	d								22 42		
Canterbury West [4]	d			21 36					22 47		
Chartham	d			21 41					22 52		
Chilham	d			21 44					22 55		
Wye	d			21 51					23 02		
Ashford International	a			21 58	21 55		22 28		23 08		23 55
	d	21 47		22 03		22 13	22 33	22 43		23 11	
Pluckley	d			22 09			22 39				
Headcorn	d			22 16			22 46				
Staplehurst	d			22 21			22 51				
Marden	d			22 25			22 55				
Maidstone West [4] 194	d		21 58								
Paddock Wood [4]	d		22 17	22 31			23 01				
Tonbridge [4]	a		22 25	22 39			23 10				
	d			22 40			23 14				
Sevenoaks [4]	a			22 48			23 24				
Orpington [4]	a						23 36				
London Bridge [4] ⊖	a			23 13			23 54				
London Cannon Street [4] ⊖	a										
London Waterloo (East) [4] ⊖	a			23 18			23 59				
London Charing Cross [4] ⊖	a			23 22			00 03				
Ebbsfleet International	a	22 06				22 32		23 02		23 30	
Stratford International ⊖	a	22 19				22 45		23 16		23 42	
St Pancras Intl. [15] ⊖	a	22 29				22 55		23 26		23 51	

Table 207

Mondays to Fridays
29 August to 7 September

Margate, Ramsgate, Canterbury West, Dover, Folkestone, Ashford International - Tonbridge and London

Network Diagram - see first Page of Table 206

Station		SE ■ A	SE	SE	SE ■	SE ■	SE	SE ■	SE	SE ■	SE	SE	SE ■	SE ■	SE ■	SE	SE	SE ■	SE	SE	SE ■	SE ■
Margate	d															05 47						
Broadstairs	d															05 54						
Ramsgate	d	21p22					05 00			04 50			05 36		05 26	06 00					06 08	
Minster	d						05 06						05 42								06 17	
Sandwich	d	21p34								05 04					05 40		05 50					
Deal	d	21p40								05 10					05 46		05 56					
Walmer	d	21p43								05 13					05 49							
Martin Mill	d	21p48								05 17					05 53							
Dover Priory	a	21p56								05 26					06 02		06 10					
	d	21p57			04 37					05 27	05 44			05 45	06 04		06 12					06 24
Folkestone Central	d	22p09			04 49					05 39	05 56				06 15		06 23					06 36
Folkestone West	d	22p11			04 51					05 42	05 58				06 18		06 26					06 38
Sandling	d	22p16			04 56					05 47					06 23							06 43
Westenhanger	d	22p19			04 59					05 49					06 26							06 46
Sturry	d						05 18						05 54								06 29	
Canterbury West	d						05 25	05 36					06 00			06 20					06 34	
Chartham	d							05 41					06 05								06 39	
Chilham	d							05 44					06 08								06 42	
Wye	d							05 51					06 15								06 49	
Ashford International	a	22p28			05 08		05 41	05 57		05 59	06 11		06 21		06 35	06 36	06 39				06 55	06 55
	d	22p33	05 13		05 13	05 29	05 43			06 03	06 13		06 24		06 38	06 43		06 45			06 57	07 03
Pluckley	d	22p39			05 19	05 35				06 09			06 30		06 44			06 51			07 04	07 09
Headcorn	d	22p46			05 26	05 42				06 16			06 37		06 51			06 58			07 11	07 16
Staplehurst	d	22p51			05 31	05 47				06 21			06 42		06 56			07 03			07 16	07 22
Marden	d	22p55			05 35	05 51				06 25			06 46		07 00			07 07			07 20	07 26
Maidstone West 194	d			05 18					05 56			06 26							06 56	07 01		
Paddock Wood	d	23p01		05a37	05 42	05 58			06a15	06 32		06a45	06 53		07 07			07 14		07a20	07 27	07 33
Tonbridge	a	23p10			05 49	06 05				06 39			07 01		07 14			07 21			07 34	07 41
	d	23p14			05 50	06 06				06 40			07 02		07 15			07 23			07 35	07 42
Sevenoaks	a	23p24			05 58	06 14				06 48			07 10		07 26			07 31			07 46	07 50
Orpington	a	23p36			06 08	06 23																
London Bridge	a	23p54			06 24	06 39				07 14			07 36	07 51	07 53						08 13	
London Cannon Street	a													07 57	07 59						08 20	
London Waterloo (East)	a	23p59			06 29	06 44				07 19			07 41					08 00				08 20
London Charing Cross	a	00 03			06 33	06 49				07 25			07 47					08 06				08 26
Ebbsfleet International	a		05 32				06 02				06 32											
Stratford International	a		05 44				06 14				06 44					07 11			07 36			
St Pancras Intl.	a		05 52				06 21				06 51					07 19			07 44			

Station		SE	SE	SE ■	SE ■	SE	SE	SE ■	SE	SE	SE ■	SE ■	SE ■	SE ■	SE ■	SE	SE	SE	SE	SE ■ B ✠	SE ■ B ✠	SE
Margate	d								06 48													07 49
Broadstairs	d								06 54													07 55
Ramsgate	d		06 26	06 12	06 42				07 00			06 59	06 49	07 10	07 19		07 30			07 22		08 01
Minster	d				06 48									07 16								08 07
Sandwich	d	06 18		06 26						06 50			07 01							07 34		
Deal	d	06 24		06 32						06 56			07 07							07 40		
Walmer	d			06 35									07 10							07 43		
Martin Mill	d			06 39									07 15							07 48		
Dover Priory	a	06 38		06 48						07 10			07 23							07 56		
	d	06 42		06 49						07 12			07 24					07 42		07 57		
Folkestone Central	d	06 53		07 00				07 14		07 23			07 36					07 53		08 09		
Folkestone West	d	06 56		07 03				07 17		07 26			07 38					07 56		08 11		
Sandling	d			07 08				07 22					07 43							08 16		
Westenhanger	d			07 11				07 25					07 46							08 19		
Sturry	d				07 00									07 28								08 19
Canterbury West	d		06 50		07 06				07 20					07 36			07 50				08 00	08 25
Chartham	d				07 11									07 41							08 05	
Chilham	d				07 14									07 44							08 08	
Wye	d				07 21									07 51							08 15	
Ashford International	a	07 09	07 06	07 20	07 27			07 34	07 36	07 39			07 55	07 58			08 06	08 09		08 28	08 21	08 41
	d	07 13		07 22	07 29			07 38	07 43		07 45		08 03				08 13			08 33		08 43
Pluckley	d			07 28				07 44			07 51		08 09							08 39		
Headcorn	d			07 35	07 40			07 51			07 58		08 16							08 46		
Staplehurst	d			07 40	07 45			07 56			08 03		08 21							08 51		
Marden	d			07 44	07 49			08 00			08 07		08 25							08 55		
Maidstone West 194	d					07 26	07 41									07 56			08 18			
Paddock Wood	d			07 51	07 55		08a00	08 07			08 14		08 31						08 37	09 01		
Tonbridge	a			07 58	08 03			08 14			08 21		08 39						08 45	09 09		
	d			07 59	08 04			08 15			08 22		08 40							09 10		
Sevenoaks	a			08 07	08 12			08 26			08 30		08 48							09 18		
Orpington	a																					
London Bridge	a			08 33				08 55				08 49	09 14		09 11					09 43		
London Cannon Street	a			08 41				09 02				08 57			09 18							
London Waterloo (East)	a				08 40						09 00		09 19							09 48		
London Charing Cross	a				08 46						09 04		09 25							09 54		
Ebbsfleet International	a																					09 02
Stratford International	a	07 41				08 06			08 11							08 36	08 41					09 14
St Pancras Intl.	a	07 49				08 14			08 19							08 44	08 49					09 22

A not 3 September

B ✠ from Ashford International

Table 207

Mondays to Fridays
29 August to 7 September

Margate, Ramsgate, Canterbury West, Dover, Folkestone, Ashford International - Tonbridge and London

Network Diagram - see first Page of Table 206

Station		SE ■ A ✠	SE ■ A ✠	SE	SE	SE ■ A ✠	SE ■ A ✠	SE	SE ■ A ✠	SE ■ A ✠	SE	SE	SE ■ A ✠	SE ■ A ✠	SE	SE ■ A ✠	SE ■ A ✠	SE	SE	SE ■ A ✠	SE ■ A ✠	SE
Margate	d							08 53							09 53							10 53
Broadstairs	d							08 59							09 59							10 59
Ramsgate	d	07 40	08 16			08 05	08 40	09 05					09 22	09 40	10 05					10 22	10 40	11 05
Minster	d	07 53				08 16	08 46							09 46							10 46	
Sandwich	d	08 01				08 25							09 34							10 34		
Deal	d	08 07				08 31							09 40							10 40		
Walmer	d	08 10				08 34							09 43							10 43		
Martin Mill	d	08 15				08 38							09 48							10 48		
Dover Priory	a	08 23				08 47							09 56							10 56		
	d	08 24		08 44		08 57			09 24		09 44		09 57			10 24		10 44		10 57		
Folkestone Central	d	08 36		08 56		09 09			09 36		09 56		10 09			10 36		10 56		11 09		
Folkestone West	d	08 38		08 58		09 11			09 38		09 58		10 11			10 38		10 58		11 11		
Sandling	d	08 43				09 16			09 43				10 16			10 43				11 16		
Westenhanger	d	08 46				09 19			09 46				10 19			10 46				11 19		
Sturry	d						08 58							09 58							10 58	
Canterbury West	d		08 36				09 07	09 25		09 36				10 07	10 25		10 36				11 07	11 25
Chartham	d		08 41							09 41							10 41					
Chilham	d		08 44							09 44							10 44					
Wye	d		08 51				09 19			09 51				10 19			10 51				11 19	
Ashford International	a	08 55	08 58	09 11		09 28	09 25	09 41	09 55	09 58	10 11		10 28	10 25	10 41	10 55	10 58	11 11		11 28	11 25	11 41
	d	09 03		09 13		09 33		09 43	10 03		10 13		10 33		10 43	11 03		11 13		11 33		11 43
Pluckley	d	09 09				09 39			10 09				10 39			11 09				11 39		
Headcorn	d	09 16				09 46			10 16				10 46			11 16				11 46		
Staplehurst	d	09 21				09 51			10 21				10 51			11 21				11 51		
Marden	d	09 25				09 55			10 25				10 55			11 25				11 55		
Maidstone West 194	d				09 28							10 28							11 28			
Paddock Wood	d	09 31			09 47	10 01			10 31			10 47	11 01			11 31			11 47	12 01		
Tonbridge	a	09 39			09 57	10 09			10 39			10 55	11 09			11 39			11 55	12 09		
	d	09 40				10 10			10 40				11 10			11 40				12 10		
Sevenoaks	a	09 48				10 18			10 48				11 18			11 48				12 18		
Orpington	a																					
London Bridge	a	10 13				10 43			11 13				11 43			12 13				12 43		
London Cannon Street	a																					
London Waterloo (East)	a	10 18				10 48			11 18				11 48			12 18				12 48		
London Charing Cross	a	10 22				10 52			11 22				11 52			12 22				12 52		
Ebbsfleet International	a			09 32				10 02			10 32				11 02			11 32				12 02
Stratford International	a			09 44				10 14			10 44				11 14			11 44				12 14
St Pancras Intl.	a			09 52				10 22			10 54				11 22			11 52				12 24

Station		SE ■ A ✠	SE ■ A ✠	SE	SE	SE ■ A ✠	SE ■ A ✠	SE	SE ■ A ✠	SE ■ A ✠	SE	SE	SE ■ A ✠	SE ■ A ✠	SE	SE ■ A ✠	SE ■ A ✠	SE	SE	SE ■ A ✠	SE ■ A ✠	SE
Margate	d							11 53							12 53							13 53
Broadstairs	d							11 59							12 59							13 59
Ramsgate	d					11 22	11 40	12 05					12 22	12 40	13 05					13 22	13 40	14 05
Minster	d						11 46							12 46							13 46	
Sandwich	d					11 34							12 34							13 34		
Deal	d					11 40							12 40							13 40		
Walmer	d					11 43							12 43							13 43		
Martin Mill	d					11 48							12 48							13 48		
Dover Priory	a					11 56							12 56							13 56		
	d	11 24		11 44		11 57			12 24		12 44		12 57			13 24		13 44		13 57		
Folkestone Central	d	11 36		11 56		12 09			12 36		12 56		13 09			13 36		13 56		14 09		
Folkestone West	d	11 38		11 58		12 11			12 38		12 58		13 11			13 38		13 58		14 11		
Sandling	d	11 43				12 16			12 43				13 16			13 43				14 16		
Westenhanger	d	11 46				12 19			12 46				13 19			13 46				14 19		
Sturry	d						11 58							12 58							13 58	
Canterbury West	d		11 36				12 07	12 25		12 36				13 07	13 25		13 36				14 07	14 25
Chartham	d		11 41							12 41							13 41					
Chilham	d		11 44							12 44							13 44					
Wye	d		11 51				12 19			12 51				13 19			13 51				14 19	
Ashford International	a	11 55	11 58	12 11		12 28	12 25	12 41	12 55	12 58	13 11		13 28	13 25	13 41	13 55	13 58	14 11		14 28	14 25	14 41
	d	12 03		12 13		12 33		12 43	13 03		13 13		13 33		13 43	14 03		14 13		14 33		14 43
Pluckley	d	12 09				12 39			13 09				13 39			14 09				14 39		
Headcorn	d	12 16				12 46			13 16				13 46			14 16				14 46		
Staplehurst	d	12 21				12 51			13 21				13 51			14 21				14 51		
Marden	d	12 25				12 55			13 25				13 55			14 25				14 55		
Maidstone West 194	d				12 28							13 28							14 28			
Paddock Wood	d	12 31			12 47	13 01			13 31			13 47	14 01			14 31			14 47	15 01		
Tonbridge	a	12 39			12 58	13 09			13 39			13 55	14 09			14 39			14 55	15 09		
	d	12 40				13 10			13 40				14 10			14 40				15 10		
Sevenoaks	a	12 48				13 18			13 48				14 18			14 48				15 18		
Orpington	a																					
London Bridge	a	13 13				13 43			14 13				14 43			15 13				15 43		
London Cannon Street	a																					
London Waterloo (East)	a	13 18				13 48			14 18				14 48			15 18				15 48		
London Charing Cross	a	13 22				13 52			14 22				14 52			15 22				15 52		
Ebbsfleet International	a			12 32				13 02			13 32				14 02			14 32				15 02
Stratford International	a			12 44				13 14			13 44				14 14			14 44				15 14
St Pancras Intl.	a			12 51				13 22			13 52				14 22			14 52				15 22

A ✠ from Ashford International

Margate, Ramsgate, Canterbury West, Dover, Folkestone, Ashford International - Tonbridge and London

Network Diagram - see first Page of Table 206

		SE ■ A ⌶	SE ■ A ⌶	SE	SE	SE ■ A ⌶	SE ■ A ⌶	SE	SE ■ A ⌶	SE ■ A ⌶		SE	SE	SE ■ A ⌶	SE ■ A ⌶	SE	SE	SE ■ A ⌶	SE ■ A ⌶	SE		SE	SE ■ A ⌶	SE ■ A ⌶	SE
Margate ■	d							14 53								15 53									16 53
Broadstairs	d							14 59								15 59									16 59
Ramsgate ■	d					14 22	14 40	15 05						15 22	15 40	16 05		15 50					16 22	16 40	17 05
Minster ■	d						14 46								15 46									16 46	
Sandwich	d					14 34								15 34				16 02					16 34		
Deal	d					14 40								15 40				16 08					16 40		
Walmer	d					14 43								15 43				16 11					16 43		
Martin Mill	d					14 48								15 48				16 16					16 48		
Dover Priory ■	a					14 56								15 56				16 24					16 56		
	d	14 24		14 44		14 57			15 24			15 44		15 57				16 24		16 44			16 57		
Folkestone Central	d	14 36		14 56		15 09			15 36			15 56		16 09				16 36		16 56			17 09		
Folkestone West	d	14 38		14 58		15 11			15 38			15 58		16 11				16 38		16 58			17 11		
Sandling	d	14 43				15 16			15 43					16 16				16 43					17 16		
Westenhanger	d	14 46				15 19			15 46					16 19				16 46					17 19		
Sturry	d						14 58								15 58									16 58	
Canterbury West ■	d		14 36				15 04	15 25		15 36					16 04	16 25			16 36					17 04	17 25
Chartham	d		14 41							15 41									16 41						
Chilham	d		14 44							15 44									16 44						
Wye	d		14 51				15 16			15 51					16 16				16 51					17 16	
Ashford International	a	14 55	14 58	15 11		15 28	15 22	15 41	15 55	15 58		16 11		16 28	16 22	16 41		16 55	16 58	17 11			17 28	17 22	17 41
	d	15 03		15 13		15 33		15 43	16 03			16 13		16 33		16 43		17 03		17 13			17 33		17 43
Pluckley	d	15 09				15 39			16 09					16 39				17 09					17 39		
Headcorn	d	15 16				15 46			16 16					16 46				17 16					17 46		
Staplehurst	d	15 21				15 51			16 21					16 51				17 21					17 51		
Marden	d	15 25				15 55			16 25					16 55				17 25					17 55		
Maidstone West ■ 194	d				15 28								16 33				16 58					17 28			
Paddock Wood ■	d	15 31			15 47	16 01			16 31				16a52	17 01			17a17	17 31				17a47	18 01		
Tonbridge ■	a	15 39			15 55	16 09			16 39					17 09				17 39					18 09		
	d	15 40				16 10			16 40					17 10				17 40					18 10		
Sevenoaks ■	a	15 48				16 18			16 48					17 18				17 48					18 18		
Orpington ■	a																								
London Bridge ■ ⊖	a	16 14				16 46			17 17					17 44				18 16					18 43		
London Cannon Street ■ ⊖	a																								
London Waterloo (East) ■ ⊖	a	16 20				16 52			17 22					17 50				18 20					18 48		
London Charing Cross ■ ⊖	a	16 24				16 56			17 26					17 53				18 25					18 52		
Ebbsfleet International	a			15 32				16 02				16 32				17 02				17 32					18 02
Stratford International ⊖	a			15 44				16 14				16 44				17 14				17 44					18 14
St Pancras Intl. ■ ⊖	a			15 52				16 22				16 52				17 22				17 52					18 22

		SE ■ A ⌶	SE ■ A ⌶	SE	SE	SE ■ A ⌶	SE ■ A ⌶		SE	SE	SE ■	SE ■	SE	SE	SE	SE ■	SE ■		SE	SE	SE ■	SE ■	SE	SE ■	SE ■
Margate ■	d								17 53										18 53						
Broadstairs	d								17 59										18 59						
Ramsgate ■	d	16 50				17 22	17 40		18 05		17 50					18 22	18 40		19 05					19 22	19 40
Minster ■	d						17 46										18 46								19 46
Sandwich	d	17 02				17 34					18 02					18 34								19 34	
Deal	d	17 08				17 40					18 08					18 40								19 40	
Walmer	d	17 11				17 43					18 11					18 43								19 43	
Martin Mill	d	17 16				17 48					18 16					18 48								19 48	
Dover Priory ■	a	17 24				17 56					18 24					18 56								19 56	
	d	17 24		17 44		17 57					18 24		18 44			18 57					19 24		19 44	19 57	
Folkestone Central	d	17 36		17 56		18 09					18 36		18 56			19 09					19 36		19 56	20 09	
Folkestone West	d	17 38		17 58		18 11					18 38		18 58			19 11					19 38		19 58	20 11	
Sandling	d	17 43				18 16					18 43					19 16					19 43			20 16	
Westenhanger	d	17 46				18 19					18 46					19 19					19 46			20 19	
Sturry	d						17 58										18 58								19 58
Canterbury West ■	d		17 36				18 04		18 25			18 36					19 07		19 25			19 36			20 07
Chartham	d		17 41									18 41										19 41			
Chilham	d		17 44									18 44										19 44			
Wye	d		17 51				18 16					18 51					19 19					19 51			20 19
Ashford International	a	17 55	17 58	18 11		18 28	18 23		18 41		18 55	18 58	19 11			19 29	19 26		19 41		19 55	19 58	20 12	20 28	20 25
	d	18 03		18 13		18 33			18 43		19 03		19 13			19 33			19 43		20 03		20 13	20 33	
Pluckley	d	18 09				18 39					19 09					19 39					20 09			20 39	
Headcorn	d	18 16				18 46					19 16					19 46					20 16			20 46	
Staplehurst	d	18 21				18 51					19 21					19 51					20 21			20 51	
Marden	d	18 25				18 55					19 25					19 55					20 25			20 55	
Maidstone West ■ 194	d				18 18					18 48				19 13	19 18					19 58					
Paddock Wood ■	d	18 31			18a37	19 01				19a07	19 31				19a37	20 01				20 17	20 31			21 01	
Tonbridge ■	a	18 39				19 09					19 39					20 09				20 25	20 39			21 09	
	d	18 40				19 10					19 40					20 10					20 40			21 10	
Sevenoaks ■	a	18 48				19 18					19 48					20 18					20 48			21 18	
Orpington ■	a																								
London Bridge ■ ⊖	a	19 13				19 43					20 13					20 42					21 13			21 43	
London Cannon Street ■ ⊖	a																								
London Waterloo (East) ■ ⊖	a	19 17				19 48					20 18					20 47					21 18			21 48	
London Charing Cross ■ ⊖	a	19 21				19 52					20 22					20 51					21 22			21 52	
Ebbsfleet International	a			18 32					19 02				19 32	19 47					20 02				20 33		
Stratford International ⊖	a			18 44					19 14				19 46	20 01					20 14				20 45		
St Pancras Intl. ■ ⊖	a			18 52					19 22				19 53	20 14					20 22				20 53		

A ⌶ from Ashford International

Margate, Ramsgate, Canterbury West, Dover, Folkestone, Ashford International - Tonbridge and London

Network Diagram - see first Page of Table 206

		SE	SE		SE ■	SE ■	SE	SE ■	SE ■	SE	SE	SE ■	SE ■		SE	SE ■	SE	SE ■	SE	SE ■
Margate ■	d	19 53								20 53							21 53			
Broadstairs	d	19 59								20 59							21 59			
Ramsgate ■	d	20 05						20 22	20 40	21 05						21 22	22 05	22 24		22 45
Minster ■	d								20 46									22 30		
Sandwich	d							20 34								21 34				22 57
Deal	d							20 40								21 40				23 03
Walmer	d							20 43								21 43				23 06
Martin Mill	d							20 48								21 48				23 11
Dover Priory ■	a							20 56								21 56				23 19
	d				20 24		20 44	20 57				21 24			21 44	21 57			22 44	23 24
Folkestone Central	d				20 36		20 56	21 09				21 36			21 56	22 09			22 56	23 36
Folkestone West	d				20 38		20 58	21 11				21 38			21 58	22 11			22 58	23 38
Sandling	d				20 43			21 16				21 43				22 16				23 43
Westenhanger	d				20 46			21 19				21 46				22 19				23 46
Sturry	d								20 58									22 42		
Canterbury West ■	d	20 25				20 36			21 07	21 25			21 36				22 25	22 47		
Chartham	d					20 41							21 41					22 52		
Chilham	d					20 44							21 44					22 55		
Wye	d					20 51			21 19				21 51					23 02		
Ashford International	a	20 41			20 55	20 58	21 11	21 28	21 25	21 41		21 55	21 58		22 11	22 28	22 41	23 08	23 11	23 55
	d	20 43			21 03		21 13	21 33		21 43		22 03			22 13	22 33	22 43		23 13	
Pluckley	d				21 09			21 39				22 09				22 39				
Headcorn	d				21 16			21 46				22 16				22 46				
Staplehurst	d				21 21			21 51				22 21				22 51				
Marden	d				21 25			21 55				22 25				22 55				
Maidstone West ■ 194	d		20 58								21 58									
Paddock Wood ■	d		21 17		21 31			22 01			22 17	22 31				23 01				
Tonbridge ■	a		21 25		21 39			22 09			22 25	22 39				23 10				
	d				21 40			22 10				22 40				23 14				
Sevenoaks ■	a				21 48			22 18				22 48				23 24				
Orpington ■	a															23 36				
London Bridge ■ ⊖	a				22 13			22 43				23 13				23 54				
London Cannon Street ■ ⊖	a																			
London Waterloo (East) ■ ⊖	a				22 18			22 48				23 18				23 59				
London Charing Cross ■ ⊖	a				22 22			22 52				23 22				00 03				
Ebbsfleet International	a	21 02					21 32			22 02					22 32		23 02		23 32	
Stratford International ⊖	a	21 14					21 44			22 14					22 44		23 14		23 44	
St Pancras Intl. ■ ⊖	a	21 22					21 52			22 22					22 52		23 22		23 52	

Saturdays

until 21 July, 18 Aug and from 15 Sep

		SE ■	SE ■	SE	SE	SE	SE ■	SE ■	SE	SE ■		SE	SE	SE ■	SE	SE ■	SE ■	SE	SE	SE ■ A ⌶		SE	SE ■ A ⌶	SE ■ A ⌶	SE
Margate ■	d								05 53						06 53							07 53			
Broadstairs	d								05 59						06 59							07 59			
Ramsgate ■	d	21p22		05 05			05 32		06 05	05 50				06 40	07 05	06 50				07 40		08 05	07 50		
Minster ■	d						05 38							06 46						07 46					
Sandwich	d	21p34								06 02						07 02							08 02		
Deal	d	21p40								06 08						07 08							08 08		
Walmer	d	21p43								06 11						07 11							08 11		
Martin Mill	d	21p48								06 16						07 16							08 16		
Dover Priory ■	a	21p56								06 24						07 24							08 24		
	d	21p57	04 50		05 44			05 50		06 24		06 44				07 24		07 44					08 24		08 44
Folkestone Central	d	22p09	05 02		05 56			06 02		06 36		06 56				07 36		07 56					08 36		08 56
Folkestone West	d	22p11	05 04		05 58			06 04		06 38		06 58				07 38		07 58					08 38		08 58
Sandling	d	22p16	05 09					06 09		06 43						07 43							08 43		
Westenhanger	d	22p19	05 12					06 12		06 46						07 46							08 46		
Sturry	d						05 50							06 58						07 58					
Canterbury West ■	d			05 25			05 56		06 25					07 04	07 25		07 36			08 07		08 25		08 36	
Chartham	d						06 01							07 09			07 41							08 41	
Chilham	d						06 04							07 12			07 44							08 44	
Wye	d						06 11							07 19			07 51			08 19				08 51	
Ashford International	a	22p28	05 21	05 41	06 11		06 17	06 21	06 41	06 55		07 11		07 26	07 41	07 55	07 58	08 11		08 25		08 41	08 55	08 58	09 11
	d	22p33	05 25	05 43	06 13		06 25		06 43	07 03		07 13		07 33	07 43	08 03		08 13		08 33		08 43	09 03		09 13
Pluckley	d	22p39	05 31				06 31			07 09				07 39		08 09				08 39			09 09		
Headcorn	d	22p46	05 38				06 38			07 16				07 46		08 16				08 46			09 16		
Staplehurst	d	22p51	05 43				06 43			07 21				07 51		08 21				08 51			09 21		
Marden	d	22p55	05 47				06 47			07 25				07 55		08 25				08 55			09 25		
Maidstone West ■ 194	d					06 28							07 28						08 28						
Paddock Wood ■	d	23p01	05 53			06 47	06 53			07 31			07 47	08 01		08 31			08 47	09 01			09 31		
Tonbridge ■	a	23p10	06 01			06 55	07 01			07 39			07 55	08 09		08 39			08 55	09 09			09 39		
	d	23p14	06 02				07 02			07 40				08 10		08 40				09 10			09 40		
Sevenoaks ■	a	23p24	06 13				07 13			07 48				08 18		08 48				09 18			09 48		
Orpington ■	a	23p36	06 23				07 23																		
London Bridge ■ ⊖	a	23p54	06 39				07 39			08 13				08 43		09 13				09 43			10 13		
London Cannon Street ■ ⊖	a																								
London Waterloo (East) ■ ⊖	a	23p59	06 43				07 43			08 19				08 49		09 19				09 49			10 19		
London Charing Cross ■ ⊖	a	00 03	06 47				07 48			08 22				08 52		09 22				09 52			10 22		
Ebbsfleet International	a			06 02	06 32				07 02			07 32			08 02			08 32				09 02			09 32
Stratford International ⊖	a			06 14	06 44				07 14			07 44			08 14			08 44				09 14			09 44
St Pancras Intl. ■ ⊖	a			06 21	06 51				07 21			07 51			08 21			08 51				09 21			09 51

A ⌶ from Ashford International

Table 207

Saturdays

until 21 July, 18 Aug and from 15 Sep

Margate, Ramsgate, Canterbury West, Dover, Folkestone, Ashford International - Tonbridge and London

Network Diagram - see first Page of Table 206

		SE	SE 1 A ⌶	SE	SE 1 A ⌶	SE 1 A ⌶	SE	SE	SE 1 A ⌶	SE	SE 1 A ⌶	SE 1 A ⌶	SE	SE	SE 1 A ⌶	SE	SE 1 A ⌶	SE 1 A ⌶	SE	SE	SE 1 A ⌶	SE
Margate 4	d			08 53						09 53						10 53						11 53
Broadstairs	d			08 59						09 59						10 59						11 59
Ramsgate 4	d		08 40	09 05	08 50				09 40	10 05	09 50				10 40	11 05	10 50				11 40	12 05
Minster 4	d		08 46						09 46						10 46						11 46	
Sandwich	d				09 02						10 02						11 02					
Deal	d				09 08						10 08						11 08					
Walmer	d				09 11						10 11						11 11					
Martin Mill	d				09 16						10 16						11 16					
Dover Priory 4	a				09 24						10 24						11 24					
	d				09 24		09 44				10 24		10 44				11 24		11 44			
Folkestone Central	d				09 36		09 56				10 36		10 56				11 36		11 56			
Folkestone West	d				09 38		09 58				10 38		10 58				11 38		11 58			
Sandling	d				09 43						10 43						11 43					
Westenhanger	d				09 46						10 46						11 46					
Sturry	d		08 58						09 58						10 58						11 58	
Canterbury West 4	d		09 07	09 25		09 36			10 07	10 25		10 36			11 07	11 25		11 36			12 07	12 25
Chartham	d					09 41						10 41						11 41				
Chilham	d					09 44						10 44						11 44				
Wye	d		09 19			09 51			10 19			10 51			11 19			11 51			12 19	
Ashford International	a		09 25	09 41	09 55	09 58	10 11		10 25	10 41	10 55	10 58	11 11		11 25	11 41	11 55	11 58	12 11		12 25	12 41
	d		09 33	09 43	10 03		10 13		10 33	10 43	11 03		11 13		11 33	11 43	12 03		12 13		12 33	12 43
Pluckley	d		09 39		10 09				10 39		11 09				11 39		12 09				12 39	
Headcorn	d		09 46		10 16				10 46		11 16				11 46		12 16				12 46	
Staplehurst	d		09 51		10 21				10 51		11 21				11 51		12 21				12 51	
Marden	d		09 55		10 25				10 55		11 25				11 55		12 25				12 55	
Maidstone West 4 194	d	09 28						10 28						11 28						12 28		
Paddock Wood 4	d	09 47	10 01		10 31			10 47	11 01		11 31			11 47	12 01		12 31			12 47	13 01	
Tonbridge 4	a	09 55	10 09		10 39			10 55	11 09		11 39			11 55	12 09		12 39			12 55	13 09	
	d		10 10		10 40				11 10		11 40				12 10		12 40				13 10	
Sevenoaks 4	a		10 18		10 48				11 18		11 48				12 18		12 48				13 18	
Orpington 4	a																					
London Bridge 4 ⊖	a		10 43		11 13				11 43		12 13				12 43		13 13				13 43	
London Cannon Street 4 ⊖	a																					
London Waterloo (East) 4 ⊖	a		10 49		11 19				11 49		12 19				12 49		13 19				13 49	
London Charing Cross 4 ⊖	a		10 52		11 22				11 52		12 22				12 52		13 22				13 52	
Ebbsfleet International	a			10 02			10 32			11 02			11 32			12 02			12 32			13 02
Stratford International ⊖	a			10 14			10 44			11 14			11 44			12 14			12 44			13 14
St Pancras Intl. 15 ⊖	a			10 21			10 51			11 21			11 51			12 21			12 51			13 21

		SE 1 A ⌶	SE 1 A ⌶	SE	SE	SE 1 A ⌶	SE	SE 1 A ⌶	SE 1 A ⌶	SE	SE	SE 1 A ⌶	SE	SE 1 A ⌶	SE 1 A ⌶	SE	SE	SE 1 A ⌶	SE	SE 1 A ⌶	SE 1 A ⌶	SE
Margate 4	d						12 53						13 53						14 53			
Broadstairs	d						12 59						13 59						14 59			
Ramsgate 4	d	11 50				12 40	13 05	12 50				13 40	14 05	13 50				14 40	15 05	14 50		
Minster 4	d					12 46						13 46						14 46				
Sandwich	d	12 02						13 02						14 02						15 02		
Deal	d	12 08						13 08						14 08						15 08		
Walmer	d	12 11						13 11						14 11						15 11		
Martin Mill	d	12 16						13 16						14 16						15 16		
Dover Priory 4	a	12 24						13 24						14 24						15 24		
	d	12 24		12 44				13 24		13 44				14 24		14 44				15 24		15 44
Folkestone Central	d	12 36		12 56				13 36		13 56				14 36		14 56				15 36		15 56
Folkestone West	d	12 38		12 58				13 38		13 58				14 38		14 58				15 38		15 58
Sandling	d	12 43						13 43						14 43						15 43		
Westenhanger	d	12 46						13 46						14 46						15 46		
Sturry	d					12 58						13 58						14 58				
Canterbury West 4	d		12 36			13 07	13 25		13 36			14 07	14 25		14 36			15 07	15 25		15 36	
Chartham	d		12 41						13 41						14 41						15 41	
Chilham	d		12 44						13 44						14 44						15 44	
Wye	d		12 51			13 19			13 51			14 19			14 51			15 19			15 51	
Ashford International	a	12 55	12 58	13 11		13 25	13 41	13 55	13 58	14 11		14 25	14 41	14 55	14 58	15 11		15 25	15 41	15 55	15 58	16 11
	d	13 03		13 13		13 33	13 43	14 03		14 13		14 33	14 43	15 03		15 13		15 33	15 46	16 03		16 13
Pluckley	d	13 09				13 39		14 09				14 39		15 09				15 39		16 09		
Headcorn	d	13 16				13 46		14 16				14 46		15 16				15 46		16 16		
Staplehurst	d	13 21				13 51		14 21				14 51		15 21				15 51		16 21		
Marden	d	13 25				13 55		14 25				14 55		15 25				15 55		16 25		
Maidstone West 4 194	d				13 28						14 28						15 28					
Paddock Wood 4	d	13 31			13 47	14 01		14 31			14 47	15 01		15 31			15 47	16 01		16 31		
Tonbridge 4	a	13 39			13 55	14 09		14 39			14 55	15 09		15 39			15 55	16 09		16 39		
	d	13 40				14 10		14 40				15 10		15 40				16 10		16 40		
Sevenoaks 4	a	13 48				14 18		14 48				15 18		15 48				16 18		16 48		
Orpington 4	a																					
London Bridge 4 ⊖	a	14 13				14 43		15 13				15 43		16 13				16 43		17 13		
London Cannon Street 4 ⊖	a																					
London Waterloo (East) 4 ⊖	a	14 19				14 49		15 19				15 49		16 19				16 49		17 19		
London Charing Cross 4 ⊖	a	14 22				14 52		15 22				15 52		16 22				16 52		17 22		
Ebbsfleet International	a			13 32			14 02			14 32			15 02			15 32			16 05			16 32
Stratford International ⊖	a			13 44			14 14			14 44			15 14			15 44			16 17			16 44
St Pancras Intl. 15 ⊖	a			13 51			14 21			14 51			15 21			15 51			16 24			16 51

A ⌶ from Ashford International

Table 207

Saturdays

until 21 July, 18 Aug and from 15 Sep

Margate, Ramsgate, Canterbury West, Dover, Folkestone, Ashford International - Tonbridge and London

Network Diagram - see first Page of Table 206

		SE	SE 1 A ⌶	SE	SE 1 A ⌶	SE 1 A ⌶	SE	SE	SE 1 A ⌶	SE	SE 1 A ⌶	SE 1 A ⌶	SE	SE	SE 1 A ⌶	SE	SE 1	SE 1	SE	SE	SE 1	SE
Margate 4	d			15 53						16 53						17 53						18 53
Broadstairs	d			15 59						16 59						17 59						18 59
Ramsgate 4	d		15 40	16 05	15 50				16 40	17 05	16 50				17 40	18 05	17 50				18 40	19 05
Minster 4	d		15 46						16 46						17 46						18 46	
Sandwich	d				16 02						17 02						18 02					
Deal	d				16 08						17 08						18 08					
Walmer	d				16 11						17 11						18 11					
Martin Mill	d				16 16						17 16						18 16					
Dover Priory 4	a				16 24						17 24						18 24					
	d				16 24		16 44				17 24		17 44				18 24		18 44			
Folkestone Central	d				16 36		16 56				17 36		17 56				18 36		18 56			
Folkestone West	d				16 38		16 58				17 38		17 58				18 38		18 58			
Sandling	d				16 43						17 43						18 43					
Westenhanger	d				16 46						17 46						18 46					
Sturry	d		15 58						16 58						17 58						18 58	
Canterbury West 4	d		16 07	16 25		16 36			17 07	17 25		17 36			18 07	18 25		18 36			19 07	19 25
Chartham	d					16 41						17 41						18 41				
Chilham	d					16 44						17 44						18 44				
Wye	d		16 19			16 51			17 19			17 51			18 19			18 51			19 19	
Ashford International	a		16 25	16 41	16 55	16 58	17 11		17 25	17 41	17 55	17 58	18 11		18 25	18 41	18 55	18 58	19 11		19 25	19 41
	d		16 33	16 43	17 03		17 13		17 33	17 43	18 03		18 13		18 33	18 43	19 03		19 13		19 33	19 43
Pluckley	d		16 39		17 09				17 39		18 09				18 39		19 09				19 39	
Headcorn	d		16 46		17 16				17 46		18 16				18 46		19 16				19 46	
Staplehurst	d		16 51		17 21				17 51		18 21				18 51		19 21				19 51	
Marden	d		16 55		17 25				17 55		18 25				18 55		19 25				19 55	
Maidstone West 4 194	d	16 28						17 28						18 28						19 28		
Paddock Wood 4	d	16 47	17 01		17 31			17 47	18 01		18 31			18 47	19 01		19 31			19 47	20 01	
Tonbridge 4	a	16 55	17 09		17 39			17 55	18 09		18 39			18 55	19 09		19 39			19 55	20 09	
	d		17 10		17 40				18 10		18 40				19 10		19 40				20 10	
Sevenoaks 4	a		17 18		17 48				18 18		18 48				19 18		19 48				20 18	
Orpington 4	a														19 27		19 57				20 27	
London Bridge 4 ⊖	a		17 43		18 13				18 43		19 13				19 43		20 13				20 43	
London Cannon Street 4 ⊖	a																					
London Waterloo (East) 4 ⊖	a		17 49		18 19				18 49		19 19				19 48		20 18				20 48	
London Charing Cross 4 ⊖	a		17 52		18 22				18 52		19 22				19 51		20 21				20 51	
Ebbsfleet International	a			17 02			17 32			18 02			18 32			19 02			19 32			20 02
Stratford International ⊖	a			17 14			17 44			18 14			18 44			19 14			19 46			20 14
St Pancras Intl. 15 ⊖	a			17 21			17 51			18 21			18 51			19 21			19 53			20 21

		SE 1	SE 1	SE	SE	SE 1	SE	SE 1	SE	SE	SE 1	SE	SE 1	SE	SE	SE 1	SE	SE 1	SE	SE 1
Margate 4	d						19 53					20 53					21 53			
Broadstairs	d						19 59					20 59					21 59			
Ramsgate 4	d	18 50				19 40	20 05	19 50			20 40	21 05	20 50			21 22	22 05	22 24		22 45
Minster 4	d					19 46					20 46							22 30		
Sandwich	d	19 02						20 02					21 02			21 34				22 57
Deal	d	19 08						20 08					21 08			21 40				23 03
Walmer	d	19 11						20 11					21 11			21 43				23 06
Martin Mill	d	19 16						20 16					21 16			21 48				23 11
Dover Priory 4	a	19 24						20 24					21 24			21 56				23 19
	d	19 24		19 44				20 24	20 44				21 24	21 44		21 57			22 44	23 24
Folkestone Central	d	19 36		19 56				20 36	20 56				21 36	21 56		22 09			22 56	23 36
Folkestone West	d	19 38		19 58				20 38	20 58				21 38	21 58		22 11			22 58	23 38
Sandling	d	19 43						20 43					21 43			22 16				23 43
Westenhanger	d	19 46						20 46					21 46			22 19				23 46
Sturry	d					19 58					20 58							22 42		
Canterbury West 4	d		19 36			20 04	20 25				21 04	21 25					22 25	22 47		
Chartham	d		19 41			20 09					21 09							22 52		
Chilham	d		19 44			20 12					21 12							22 55		
Wye	d		19 51			20 19					21 19							23 02		
Ashford International	a	19 55	19 58	20 11		20 25	20 41	20 55	21 11		21 25	21 41	21 55	22 11		22 28	22 41	23 08	23 11	23 55
	d	20 03		20 13		20 33	20 43	21 03	21 13		21 33	21 43	22 03	22 13		22 33	22 43		23 13	
Pluckley	d	20 09				20 39		21 09			21 39		22 09			22 39				
Headcorn	d	20 16				20 46		21 16			21 46		22 16			22 46				
Staplehurst	d	20 21				20 51		21 21			21 51		22 21			22 51				
Marden	d	20 25				20 55		21 25			21 55		22 25			22 55				
Maidstone West 4 194	d				20 28					21 28					22 28					
Paddock Wood 4	d	20 31			20 47	21 01		21 31		21 47	22 01		22 31		22 47	23 01				
Tonbridge 4	a	20 39			20 55	21 09		21 39		21 55	22 09		22 39		22 55	23 10				
	d	20 40				21 10		21 40			22 10		22 40			23 14				
Sevenoaks 4	a	20 48				21 18		21 48			22 18		22 48			23 24				
Orpington 4	a	20 57				21 27		21 57			22 27		22 57			23 36				
London Bridge 4 ⊖	a	21 13				21 43		22 13			22 43		23 13			23 54				
London Cannon Street 4 ⊖	a																			
London Waterloo (East) 4 ⊖	a	21 18				21 48		22 18			22 48		23 18			23 59				
London Charing Cross 4 ⊖	a	21 21				21 51		22 21			22 51		23 21			00 03				
Ebbsfleet International	a			20 32			21 02		21 32			22 02		22 32			23 02		23 32	
Stratford International ⊖	a			20 44			21 14		21 44			22 14		22 44			23 14		23 44	
St Pancras Intl. 15 ⊖	a			20 51			21 21		21 51			22 21		22 51			23 21		23 51	

A ⌶ from Ashford International

Margate, Ramsgate, Canterbury West, Dover, Folkestone, Ashford International - Tonbridge and London

Network Diagram - see first Page of Table 206

		SE ■	SE	SE ■	SE	SE	SE	SE ■	SE ■	SE	SE	SE ■	SE	SE	SE ■	SE ■	SE	SE ■	SE ■	SE	SE	SE ■ A ✠	SE ■ ✠
Margate ■	d									05 44													
Broadstairs	d									05 49													
Ramsgate ■	d	21p22			05 00			05 32		05 55		05 50			06 40			06 50	07 16			07 40	
Minster ■	d				05 06			05 38							06 46							07 46	
Sandwich	d	21p34										06 02						07 02					
Deal	d	21p40										06 08						07 08					
Walmer	d	21p43										06 11						07 11					
Martin Mill	d	21p48										06 16						07 16					
Dover Priory ■	a	21p56										06 24						07 24					
	d	21p57		04 50					05 50			06 24						07 24					
Folkestone Central	d	22p09		05 02					06 02			06 36						07 36					
Folkestone West	d	22p11		05 04					06 04			06 38						07 38					
Sandling	d	22p16		05 09					06 09			06 43						07 43					
Westenhanger	d	22p19		05 12					06 12			06 46						07 46					
Sturry	d				05 18			05 50							06 58							07 58	
Canterbury West ■	d				05 25			05 56		06 15					07 04				07 36			08 07	
Chartham	d							06 01							07 09				07 41				
Chilham	d							06 04							07 12				07 44				
Wye	d							06 11							07 19				07 51			08 19	
Ashford International	a	22p28		05 21	05 41			06 17	06 21	06 31		06 55			07 25			07 55	07 58			08 25	
	d	22p33	05 13	05 25	05 43	06 13		06 25		06 33	06 47	07 03	07 13		07 33	07 33	07 47	08 03		08 13		08 33	08 33
Pluckley	d	22p39		05 31				06 31				07 09			07 39	07 39		08 09				08 39	08 39
Headcorn	d	22p46		05 38				06 38				07 16			07 46	07 46		08 16				08 46	08 46
Staplehurst	d	22p51		05 43				06 43				07 21			07 51	07 51		08 21				08 51	08 51
Marden	d	22p55		05 47				06 47				07 25			07 55	07 55		08 25				08 55	08 55
Maidstone West ■ 194	d						06 28							07 28							08 28		
Paddock Wood ■	d	23p01		05 53			06 47	06 53				07 31		07 47	08 01	08 01		08 31			08 47	09 01	09 01
Tonbridge ■	a	23p10		06 01			06 55	07 01				07 39		07 55	08 09	08 09		08 39			08 55	09 09	09 09
	d	23p14		06 02				07 02				07 40			08 10	08 10		08 40				09 10	09 10
Sevenoaks ■	a	23p24		06 13				07 13				07 48			08 18	08 18		08 48				09 18	09 18
Orpington ■	a	23p36		06 23				07 23															
London Bridge ■ ⊖	a	23p54		06 39				07 39				08 13			08 43	08 43		09 13				09 43	09 43
London Cannon Street ■ ⊖	a																						
London Waterloo (East) ■ ⊖	a	23p59		06 43				07 43				08 19			08 49	08 49		09 19				09 49	09 49
London Charing Cross ■ ⊖	a	00 03		06 47				07 48				08 22			08 52	08 52		09 22				09 52	09 52
Ebbsfleet International	a		05 32		06 02	06 32				06 52	07 06		07 32				08 06			08 32			
Stratford International ⊖	a		05 44		06 14	06 45				07 04	07 19		07 45				08 19			08 45			
St Pancras Intl. ■ ⊖	a		05 50		06 23	06 55				07 15	07 29		07 55				08 29			08 55			

		SE	SE ■ A ✠	SE ■ A ✠	SE	SE	SE ■ A ✠	SE ■ A ✠	SE	SE ■ A ✠	SE ■ A ✠	SE	SE	SE ■ A ✠	SE ■ A ✠	SE	SE ■ A ✠	SE ■ A ✠	SE	SE	SE ■ A ✠	SE ■ A ✠	SE
Margate ■	d																						
Broadstairs	d																						
Ramsgate ■	d		07 50	08 16			08 40			08 50	09 16			09 40			09 50	10 16			10 40		
Minster ■	d						08 46							09 46							10 46		
Sandwich	d		08 02							09 02							10 02						
Deal	d		08 08							09 08							10 08						
Walmer	d		08 11							09 11							10 11						
Martin Mill	d		08 16							09 16							10 16						
Dover Priory ■	a		08 24							09 24							10 24						
	d		08 24					08 56		09 24					09 56		10 24					10 56	
Folkestone Central	d		08 36					09 09		09 36					10 09		10 36					11 09	
Folkestone West	d		08 38					09 11		09 38					10 11		10 38					11 11	
Sandling	d		08 43							09 43							10 43						
Westenhanger	d		08 46							09 46							10 46						
Sturry	d						08 58							09 58							10 58		
Canterbury West ■	d			08 36			09 07				09 36			10 07				10 36			11 07		
Chartham	d			08 41							09 41							10 41					
Chilham	d			08 44							09 44							10 44					
Wye	d			08 51			09 19				09 51			10 19				10 51			11 19		
Ashford International	a		08 55	08 58			09 25	09 28		09 55	09 58			10 25	10 28		10 55	10 58			11 25	11 28	
	d	08 47	09 03		09 13		09 33		09 47	10 03		10 13		10 33		10 47	11 03		11 13		11 33		11 47
Pluckley	d		09 09				09 39			10 09				10 39			11 09				11 39		
Headcorn	d		09 16				09 46			10 16				10 46			11 16				11 46		
Staplehurst	d		09 21				09 51			10 21				10 51			11 21				11 51		
Marden	d		09 25				09 55			10 25				10 55			11 25				11 55		
Maidstone West ■ 194	d					09 28							10 28							11 28			
Paddock Wood ■	d		09 31			09 47	10 01			10 31			10 47	11 01			11 31			11 47	12 01		
Tonbridge ■	a		09 39			09 55	10 09			10 39			10 55	11 09			11 39			11 55	12 09		
	d		09 40				10 10			10 40				11 10			11 40				12 10		
Sevenoaks ■	a		09 48				10 18			10 48				11 18			11 48				12 18		
Orpington ■	a																						
London Bridge ■ ⊖	a		10 13				10 43			11 13				11 43			12 13				12 43		
London Cannon Street ■ ⊖	a																						
London Waterloo (East) ■ ⊖	a		10 19				10 49			11 19				11 49			12 19				12 49		
London Charing Cross ■ ⊖	a		10 22				10 52			11 22				11 52			12 22				12 52		
Ebbsfleet International	a	09 06			09 32				10 06			10 32				11 06			11 32				12 06
Stratford International ⊖	a	09 19			09 45				10 19			10 45				11 19			11 45				12 19
St Pancras Intl. ■ ⊖	a	09 29			09 55				10 29			10 55				11 29			11 55				12 29

		SE ■ A ✠	SE ■ A ✠	SE	SE	SE ■ A ✠	SE ■ A ✠	SE	SE ■ A ✠	SE ■ A ✠	SE	SE	SE ■ A ✠	SE ■ A ✠	SE	SE ■ A ✠	SE ■ A ✠	SE	SE	SE ■ A ✠	SE ■ A ✠	SE
Margate ■	d																					
Broadstairs	d																					
Ramsgate ■	d	10 50	11 16			11 40			11 50	12 16			12 40			12 50	13 16			13 40		
Minster ■	d					11 46							12 46							13 46		
Sandwich	d	11 02							12 02							13 02						
Deal	d	11 08							12 08							13 08						
Walmer	d	11 11							12 11							13 11						
Martin Mill	d	11 16							12 16							13 16						
Dover Priory ■	a	11 24							12 24							13 24						
	d	11 24					11 56		12 24					12 56		13 24					13 56	
Folkestone Central	d	11 36					12 09		12 36					13 09		13 36					14 09	
Folkestone West	d	11 38					12 11		12 38					13 11		13 38					14 11	
Sandling	d	11 43							12 43							13 43						
Westenhanger	d	11 46							12 46							13 46						
Sturry	d					11 58							12 58							13 58		
Canterbury West ■	d		11 36			12 07				12 36			13 07				13 36			14 07		
Chartham	d		11 41							12 41							13 41					
Chilham	d		11 44							12 44							13 44					
Wye	d		11 51			12 19				12 51			13 19				13 51			14 19		
Ashford International	a	11 55	11 58			12 25	12 28		12 55	12 58			13 25	13 28		13 55	13 58			14 25	14 28	
	d	12 03		12 13		12 33		12 47	13 03		13 13		13 33		13 47	14 03		14 13		14 33		14 47
Pluckley	d	12 09				12 39			13 09				13 39			14 09				14 39		
Headcorn	d	12 16				12 46			13 16				13 46			14 16				14 46		
Staplehurst	d	12 21				12 51			13 21				13 51			14 21				14 51		
Marden	d	12 25				12 55			13 25				13 55			14 25				14 55		
Maidstone West ■ 194	d				12 28							13 28							14 28			
Paddock Wood ■	d	12 31			12 47	13 01			13 31			13 47	14 01			14 31			14 47	15 01		
Tonbridge ■	a	12 39			12 55	13 09			13 39			13 55	14 09			14 39			14 55	15 09		
	d	12 40				13 10			13 40				14 10			14 40				15 10		
Sevenoaks ■	a	12 48				13 18			13 48				14 18			14 48				15 18		
Orpington ■	a																					
London Bridge ■ ⊖	a	13 13				13 43			14 13				14 43			15 13				15 43		
London Cannon Street ■ ⊖	a																					
London Waterloo (East) ■ ⊖	a	13 19				13 49			14 19				14 49			15 19				15 49		
London Charing Cross ■ ⊖	a	13 22				13 52			14 22				14 52			15 22				15 52		
Ebbsfleet International	a			12 32				13 06			13 32				14 06			14 32				15 06
Stratford International ⊖	a			12 45				13 19			13 45				14 19			14 45				15 19
St Pancras Intl. ■ ⊖	a			12 55				13 29			13 55				14 29			14 55				15 29

		SE ■ A ✠	SE ■ A ✠	SE	SE	SE ■ A ✠	SE ■ A ✠	SE	SE ■ A ✠	SE ■ A ✠	SE	SE	SE ■ A ✠	SE ■ A ✠	SE	SE ■ A ✠	SE ■ A ✠	SE	SE	SE ■ A ✠	SE ■ A ✠	SE
Margate ■	d																					
Broadstairs	d																					
Ramsgate ■	d	13 50	14 16			14 40			14 50	15 16			15 40			15 50	16 16			16 40		
Minster ■	d					14 46							15 46							16 46		
Sandwich	d	14 02							15 02							16 02						
Deal	d	14 08							15 08							16 08						
Walmer	d	14 11							15 11							16 11						
Martin Mill	d	14 16							15 16							16 16						
Dover Priory ■	a	14 24							15 24							16 24						
	d	14 24					14 56		15 24					15 56		16 24					16 56	
Folkestone Central	d	14 36					15 09		15 36					16 09		16 36					17 09	
Folkestone West	d	14 38					15 11		15 38					16 11		16 38					17 11	
Sandling	d	14 43							15 43							16 43						
Westenhanger	d	14 46							15 46							16 46						
Sturry	d					14 58							15 58							16 58		
Canterbury West ■	d		14 36			15 07				15 36			16 07				16 36			17 07		
Chartham	d		14 41							15 41							16 41					
Chilham	d		14 44							15 44							16 44					
Wye	d		14 51			15 19				15 51			16 19				16 51			17 19		
Ashford International	a	14 55	14 58			15 25	15 28		15 55	15 58			16 25	16 28		16 55	16 58			17 25	17 28	
	d	15 03		15 13		15 33		15 47	16 03		16 13		16 33		16 47	17 03		17 13		17 33		17 47
Pluckley	d	15 09				15 39			16 09				16 39			17 09				17 39		
Headcorn	d	15 16				15 46			16 16				16 46			17 16				17 46		
Staplehurst	d	15 21				15 51			16 21				16 51			17 21				17 51		
Marden	d	15 25				15 55			16 25				16 55			17 25				17 55		
Maidstone West ■ 194	d				15 28							16 28							17 28			
Paddock Wood ■	d	15 31			15 47	16 01			16 31			16 47	17 01			17 31			17 47	18 01		
Tonbridge ■	a	15 39			15 55	16 09			16 39			16 55	17 09			17 39			17 55	18 09		
	d	15 40				16 10			16 40				17 10			17 40				18 10		
Sevenoaks ■	a	15 48				16 18			16 48				17 18			17 48				18 18		
Orpington ■	a																					
London Bridge ■ ⊖	a	16 13				16 43			17 13				17 43			18 13				18 43		
London Cannon Street ■ ⊖	a																					
London Waterloo (East) ■ ⊖	a	16 19				16 49			17 19				17 49			18 19				18 49		
London Charing Cross ■ ⊖	a	16 22				16 52			17 22				17 52			18 22				18 52		
Ebbsfleet International	a			15 32				16 06			16 32				17 06			17 32				18 06
Stratford International ⊖	a			15 45				16 19			16 45				17 19			17 45				18 19
St Pancras Intl. ■ ⊖	a			15 55				16 29			16 55				17 29			17 55				18 29

A ✠ from Ashford International

Table 207

Saturdays

28 July to 11 August

Margate, Ramsgate, Canterbury West, Dover, Folkestone, Ashford International - Tonbridge and London

Network Diagram - see first Page of Table 206

		SE 1 A ⊼	SE 1 A ⊼	SE	SE	SE 1 A ⊼	SE 1 A ⊼	SE	SE 1	SE 1	SE	SE	SE 1	SE 1	SE	SE 1	SE 1	SE	SE	SE 1	SE 1	SE	SE 1
Margate 4	d																						
Broadstairs	d																						
Ramsgate 4	d	16 50	17 16			17 40			17 50	18 16			18 40			18 50	19 16			19 40			19 50
Minster 4	d					17 46							18 46							19 46			
Sandwich	d	17 02							18 02							19 02							20 02
Deal	d	17 08							18 08							19 08							20 08
Walmer	d	17 11							18 11							19 11							20 11
Martin Mill	d	17 16							18 16							19 16							20 16
Dover Priory 4	a	17 24							18 24							19 24							20 24
	d	17 24					17 56		18 24					18 56		19 24					19 56		20 24
Folkestone Central	d	17 36					18 09		18 36					19 09		19 36					20 09		20 36
Folkestone West	d	17 38					18 11		18 38					19 11		19 38					20 11		20 38
Sandling	d	17 43							18 43							19 43							20 43
Westenhanger	d	17 46							18 46							19 46							20 46
Sturry	d					17 58							18 58							19 58			
Canterbury West 4	d		17 36			18 07				18 36			19 07				19 36			20 07			
Chartham	d		17 41							18 41							19 41						
Chilham	d		17 44							18 44							19 44						
Wye	d		17 51			18 19				18 51			19 19				19 51			20 19			
Ashford International	a	17 55	17 58			18 25	18 28		18 55	18 58			19 25	19 28		19 55	19 58			20 25	20 28		20 55
	d	18 03		18 13		18 33		18 47	19 03		19 13		19 33		19 47	20 03		20 13		20 33		20 47	21 03
Pluckley	d	18 09				18 39			19 09				19 39			20 09				20 39			21 09
Headcorn	d	18 16				18 46			19 16				19 46			20 16				20 46			21 16
Staplehurst	d	18 21				18 51			19 21				19 51			20 21				20 51			21 21
Marden	d	18 25				18 55			19 25				19 55			20 25				20 55			21 25
Maidstone West 4 194	d				18 28							19 28							20 28				
Paddock Wood 4	d	18 31			18 47	19 01			19 31			19 47	20 01			20 31			20 47	21 01			21 31
Tonbridge 4	a	18 39			18 55	19 09			19 39			19 55	20 09			20 39			20 55	21 09			21 39
	d	18 40				19 10			19 40				20 10			20 40				21 10			21 40
Sevenoaks 4	a	18 48				19 18			19 48				20 18			20 48				21 18			21 48
Orpington 4	a					19 27			19 57				20 27			20 57				21 27			21 57
London Bridge 4 ⊖	a	19 13				19 43			20 13				20 43			21 13				21 43			22 13
London Cannon Street 4 ⊖	a																						
London Waterloo (East) 4 ⊖	a	19 19				19 48			20 18				20 48			21 18				21 48			22 18
London Charing Cross 4 ⊖	a	19 22				19 51			20 21				20 51			21 21				21 51			22 21
Ebbsfleet International	a			18 32				19 06			19 32				20 06			20 32				21 06	
Stratford International ⊖	a			18 45				19 19			19 45				20 19			20 45				21 19	
St Pancras Intl. 15 ⊖	a			18 55				19 29			19 55				20 29			20 55				21 29	

		SE 1	SE	SE	SE 1	SE 1	SE	SE 1	SE 1	SE	SE	SE 1	SE	SE 1	SE	SE 1
Margate 4	d															
Broadstairs	d															
Ramsgate 4	d	20 16			20 40			20 50	21 16			21 22		22 24		22 45
Minster 4	d				20 46									22 30		
Sandwich	d							21 02				21 34				22 57
Deal	d							21 08				21 40				23 03
Walmer	d							21 11				21 43				23 06
Martin Mill	d							21 16				21 48				23 11
Dover Priory 4	a							21 24				21 56				23 19
	d					20 56		21 24				21 57				23 24
Folkestone Central	d					21 09		21 36				22 09				23 36
Folkestone West	d					21 11		21 38				22 11				23 38
Sandling	d							21 43				22 16				23 43
Westenhanger	d							21 46				22 19				23 46
Sturry	d				20 58									22 42		
Canterbury West 4	d	20 36			21 07				21 36					22 47		
Chartham	d	20 41							21 41					22 52		
Chilham	d	20 44							21 44					22 55		
Wye	d	20 51			21 19				21 51					23 02		
Ashford International	a	20 58			21 25	21 28		21 55	21 58			22 28		23 08		23 55
	d		21 13		21 33		21 47	22 03		22 13		22 33	22 43		23 11	
Pluckley	d				21 39			22 09				22 39				
Headcorn	d				21 46			22 16				22 46				
Staplehurst	d				21 51			22 21				22 51				
Marden	d				21 55			22 25				22 55				
Maidstone West 4 194	d			21 28							22 28					
Paddock Wood 4	d			21 47	22 01			22 31			22 47	23 01				
Tonbridge 4	a			21 55	22 09			22 39			22 55	23 10				
	d				22 10			22 40								
Sevenoaks 4	a				22 18			22 48								
Orpington 4	a				22 27			22 57								
London Bridge 4 ⊖	a				22 43			23 13								
London Cannon Street 4 ⊖	a															
London Waterloo (East) 4 ⊖	a				22 48			23 18								
London Charing Cross 4 ⊖	a				22 51			23 21								
Ebbsfleet International	a		21 32				22 06			22 32			23 02		23 30	
Stratford International ⊖	a		21 45				22 19			22 45			23 16		23 42	
St Pancras Intl. 15 ⊖	a		21 55				22 29			22 55			23 26		23 51	

A ⊼ from Ashford International

Table 207

Saturdays

25 August to 8 September

Margate, Ramsgate, Canterbury West, Dover, Folkestone, Ashford International - Tonbridge and London

Network Diagram - see first Page of Table 206

		SE 1	SE A	SE 1	SE B	SE A	SE B	SE A	SE	SE 1	SE 1	SE B	SE A	SE 1	SE B	SE A	SE	SE 1	SE B	SE A	SE 1	SE 1	SE
Margate 4	d											05 53	05 53						06 53	06 53			
Broadstairs	d											05 59	05 59						06 59	06 59			
Ramsgate 4	d	21p22			05 05	05 05				05 32		06 05	06 05	05 50				06 40	07 05	07 05	06 50		
Minster 4	d									05 38								06 46					
Sandwich	d	21p34												06 02							07 02		
Deal	d	21p40												06 08							07 08		
Walmer	d	21p43												06 11							07 11		
Martin Mill	d	21p48												06 16							07 16		
Dover Priory 4	a	21p56												06 24							07 24		
	d	21p57		04 50			05 44	05 44			05 50			06 24	06 44	06 44					07 24		07 44
Folkestone Central	d	22p09		05 02			05 56	05 56			06 02			06 36	06 56	06 56					07 36		07 56
Folkestone West	d	22p11		05 04			05 58	05 58			06 04			06 38	06 58	06 58					07 38		07 58
Sandling	d	22p16		05 09							06 09			06 43							07 43		
Westenhanger	d	22p19		05 12							06 12			06 46							07 46		
Sturry	d									05 50								06 58					
Canterbury West 4	d				05 25	05 25				05 56		06 25	06 25					07 04	07 25	07 25		07 36	
Chartham	d									06 01								07 09				07 41	
Chilham	d									06 04								07 12				07 44	
Wye	d									06 11								07 19				07 51	
Ashford International	a	22p28		05 21	05 41	05 41	06 11	06 11		06 17	06 21	06 41	06 41	06 55	07 11	07 11		07 26	07 41	07 41	07 55	07 58	08 11
	d	22p33	05 13	05 25	05 43	05 43	06 13	06 13		06 25		06 43	06 43	07 03	07 13	07 13		07 33	07 43	07 43	08 03		08 13
Pluckley	d	22p39		05 31						06 31				07 09				07 39			08 09		
Headcorn	d	22p46		05 38						06 38				07 16				07 46			08 16		
Staplehurst	d	22p51		05 43						06 43				07 21				07 51			08 21		
Marden	d	22p55		05 47						06 47				07 25				07 55			08 25		
Maidstone West 4 194	d								06 28								07 28						
Paddock Wood 4	d	23p01		05 53					06 47	06 53				07 31			07 47	08 01			08 31		
Tonbridge 4	a	23p10		06 01					06 55	07 01				07 39			07 55	08 09			08 39		
	d	23p14		06 02						07 02				07 40				08 10			08 40		
Sevenoaks 4	a	23p24		06 13						07 13				07 48				08 18			08 48		
Orpington 4	a	23p36		06 23						07 23													
London Bridge 4 ⊖	a	23p54		06 39						07 39				08 13				08 43			09 13		
London Cannon Street 4 ⊖	a																						
London Waterloo (East) 4 ⊖	a	23p59		06 43						07 43				08 19				08 49			09 19		
London Charing Cross 4 ⊖	a	00 03		06 47						07 48				08 22				08 52			09 22		
Ebbsfleet International	a		05 32		06 02	06 02	06 32	06 32				07 02	07 02		07 32	07 32			08 02	08 02			08 32
Stratford International ⊖	a		05 44		06 14	06 14	06 44	06 44				07 14	07 14		07 44	07 44			08 14	08 14			08 44
St Pancras Intl. 15 ⊖	a		05 51		06 21	06 22	06 51	06 52				07 21	07 22		07 51	07 52			08 21	08 23			08 51

		SE	SE 1 C ⊼	SE B	SE A	SE 1 C ⊼	SE 1 C ⊼	SE B	SE A	SE	SE 1 C ⊼	SE B	SE A	SE 1 C ⊼	SE 1 C ⊼	SE B	SE A	SE	SE 1 C ⊼	SE B	SE A	SE 1 C ⊼	SE 1 C ⊼
Margate 4	d			07 53	07 53							08 53	08 53							09 53	09 53		
Broadstairs	d			07 59	07 59							08 59	08 59							09 59	09 59		
Ramsgate 4	d		07 40	08 05	08 05	07 50					08 40	09 05	09 05	08 50					09 40	10 05	10 05	09 50	
Minster 4	d		07 46								08 46								09 46				
Sandwich	d					08 02								09 02								10 02	
Deal	d					08 08								09 08								10 08	
Walmer	d					08 11								09 11								10 11	
Martin Mill	d					08 16								09 16								10 16	
Dover Priory 4	a					08 24								09 24								10 24	
	d					08 24		08 44	08 44					09 24		09 44	09 44					10 24	
Folkestone Central	d					08 36		08 56	08 56					09 36		09 56	09 56					10 36	
Folkestone West	d					08 38		08 58	08 58					09 38		09 58	09 58					10 38	
Sandling	d					08 43								09 43								10 43	
Westenhanger	d					08 46								09 46								10 46	
Sturry	d		07 58								08 58								09 58				
Canterbury West 4	d		08 07	08 25	08 25		08 36				09 07	09 25	09 25		09 36				10 07	10 25	10 25		10 36
Chartham	d						08 41								09 41								10 41
Chilham	d						08 44								09 44								10 44
Wye	d		08 19				08 51				09 19				09 51				10 19				10 51
Ashford International	a		08 25	08 41	08 41	08 55	08 58	09 11	09 11		09 25	09 41	09 41	09 55	09 58	10 11	10 11		10 25	10 41	10 41	10 55	10 58
	d		08 33	08 43	08 43	09 03		09 13	09 13		09 33	09 43	09 43	10 03		10 13	10 13		10 33	10 43	10 43	11 03	
Pluckley	d		08 39			09 09					09 39			10 09					10 39			11 09	
Headcorn	d		08 46			09 16					09 46			10 16					10 46			11 16	
Staplehurst	d		08 51			09 21					09 51			10 21					10 51			11 21	
Marden	d		08 55			09 25					09 55			10 25					10 55			11 25	
Maidstone West 4 194	d	08 28								09 28								10 28					
Paddock Wood 4	d	08 47	09 01			09 31				09 47	10 01			10 31				10 47	11 01			11 31	
Tonbridge 4	a	08 55	09 09			09 39				09 55	10 09			10 39				10 55	11 09			11 39	
	d		09 10			09 40					10 10			10 40					11 10			11 40	
Sevenoaks 4	a		09 18			09 48					10 18			10 48					11 18			11 48	
Orpington 4	a																						
London Bridge 4 ⊖	a		09 43			10 13					10 43			11 13					11 43			12 13	
London Cannon Street 4 ⊖	a																						
London Waterloo (East) 4 ⊖	a		09 49			10 19					10 49			11 19					11 49			12 19	
London Charing Cross 4 ⊖	a		09 52			10 22					10 52			11 22					11 52			12 22	
Ebbsfleet International	a			09 02	09 02			09 32	09 32			10 02	10 02			10 32	10 32			11 02	11 02		
Stratford International ⊖	a			09 14	09 14			09 44	09 44			10 14	10 14			10 44	10 44			11 14	11 14		
St Pancras Intl. 15 ⊖	a			09 21	09 22			09 51	09 52			10 21	10 22			10 51	10 52			11 21	11 22		

A not 25 August

B not from 1 September until 8 September

C ⊼ from Ashford International

Margate, Ramsgate, Canterbury West, Dover, Folkestone, Ashford International - Tonbridge and London

Network Diagram - see first Page of Table 206

		SE	SE	SE	SE	SE	SE	SE	SE	SE	SE	SE	SE	SE	SE	SE	SE	SE	SE	SE	SE	SE
					1			1	1				1			1	1				1	
		A	B		C	A	B	C	C	A	B		C	A	B	C	C	A	B		C	A
					⚒			⚒	⚒				⚒			⚒	⚒				⚒	
Margate	d					10 53	10 53							11 53	11 53							12 53
Broadstairs	d					10 59	10 59							11 59	11 59							12 59
Ramsgate	d				10 40	11 05	11 05	10 50					11 40	12 05	12 05	11 50					12 40	13 05
Minster	d				10 46								11 46								12 46	
Sandwich	d							11 02								12 02						
Deal	d							11 08								12 08						
Walmer	d							11 11								12 11						
Martin Mill	d							11 16								12 16						
Dover Priory	a							11 24								12 24						
	d	10 44	10 44					11 24		11 44	11 44					12 24		12 44	12 44			
Folkestone Central	d	10 56	10 56					11 36		11 56	11 56					12 36		12 56	12 56			
Folkestone West	d	10 58	10 58					11 38		11 58	11 58					12 38		12 58	12 58			
Sandling	d							11 43								12 43						
Westenhanger	d							11 46								12 46						
Sturry	d				10 58								11 58								12 58	
Canterbury West	d				11 07	11 25	11 25		11 36				12 07	12 25	12 25		12 36				13 07	13 25
Chartham	d								11 41								12 41					
Chilham	d								11 44								12 44					
Wye	d				11 19				11 51				12 19				12 51				13 19	
Ashford International	a	11 11	11 11		11 25	11 41	11 41	11 55	11 58	12 11	12 11		12 25	12 41	12 41	12 55	12 58	13 11	13 11		13 25	13 41
	d	11 13	11 13		11 33	11 43	11 43	12 03		12 13	12 13		12 33	12 43	12 43	13 03		13 13	13 13		13 33	13 43
Pluckley	d				11 39			12 09					12 39			13 09					13 39	
Headcorn	d				11 46			12 16					12 46			13 16					13 46	
Staplehurst	d				11 51			12 21					12 51			13 21					13 51	
Marden	d				11 55			12 25					12 55			13 25					13 55	
Maidstone West 194	d			11 28								12 28								13 28		
Paddock Wood	d			11 47	12 01			12 31				12 47	13 01			13 31				13 47	14 01	
Tonbridge	a			11 55	12 09			12 39				12 55	13 09			13 39				13 55	14 09	
	d				12 10			12 40					13 10			13 40					14 10	
Sevenoaks	a				12 18			12 48					13 18			13 48					14 18	
Orpington	a																					
London Bridge	a				12 43			13 13					13 43			14 13					14 43	
London Cannon Street	a																					
London Waterloo (East)	a				12 49			13 19					13 49			14 19					14 49	
London Charing Cross	a				12 52			13 22					13 52			14 22					14 52	
Ebbsfleet International	a	11 32	11 32			12 02	12 02			12 32	12 32			13 02	13 02			13 32	13 32			14 02
Stratford International	a	11 44	11 44			12 14	12 14			12 44	12 45			13 14	13 14			13 44	13 44			14 14
St Pancras Intl.	a	11 51	11 52			12 21	12 22			12 51	12 55			13 21	13 22			13 51	13 52			14 21

		SE	SE	SE	SE	SE	SE	SE	SE	SE	SE	SE	SE	SE	SE	SE	SE	SE	SE	SE	SE	SE	SE
			1	1				1			1	1				1			1	1			
		B	C	C	A	B		C	A	B	C	C	A	B		C	B	A	C	C	A	B	
			⚒	⚒				⚒			⚒	⚒				⚒			⚒	⚒			
Margate	d	12 53							13 53	13 53							14 53	14 53					
Broadstairs	d	12 59							13 59	13 59							14 59	14 59					
Ramsgate	d	13 05	12 50					13 40	14 05	14 05	13 50					14 40	15 05	15 05	14 50				
Minster	d							13 46								14 46							
Sandwich	d		13 02								14 02								15 02				
Deal	d		13 08								14 08								15 08				
Walmer	d		13 11								14 11								15 11				
Martin Mill	d		13 16								14 16								15 16				
Dover Priory	a		13 24								14 24								15 24				
	d		13 24		13 44	13 44					14 24		14 44	14 44					15 24		15 44	15 44	
Folkestone Central	d		13 36		13 56	13 56					14 36		14 56	14 56					15 36		15 56	15 56	
Folkestone West	d		13 38		13 58	13 58					14 38		14 58	14 58					15 38		15 58	15 58	
Sandling	d		13 43								14 43								15 43				
Westenhanger	d		13 46								14 46								15 46				
Sturry	d							13 58								14 58							
Canterbury West	d	13 25		13 36				14 07	14 25	14 25		14 36				15 07	15 25	15 25		15 36			
Chartham	d			13 41								14 41								15 41			
Chilham	d			13 44								14 44								15 44			
Wye	d			13 51				14 19				14 51				15 19				15 51			
Ashford International	a	13 41	13 55	13 58	14 11	14 11		14 25	14 41	14 41	14 55	14 58	15 11	15 11		15 25	15 41	15 41	15 55	15 58	16 11	16 11	
	d	13 43	14 03		14 13	14 13		14 33	14 43	14 43	15 03		15 13	15 13		15 33	15 43	15 46	16 03		16 13	16 13	
Pluckley	d		14 09					14 39			15 09					15 39			16 09				
Headcorn	d		14 16					14 46			15 16					15 46			16 16				
Staplehurst	d		14 21					14 51			15 21					15 51			16 21				
Marden	d		14 25					14 55			15 25					15 55			16 25				
Maidstone West 194	d						14 28								15 28								16 28
Paddock Wood	d		14 31				14 47	15 01			15 31				15 47	16 01			16 31				16 47
Tonbridge	a		14 39				14 55	15 09			15 39				15 55	16 09			16 39				16 55
	d		14 40					15 10			15 40					16 10			16 40				
Sevenoaks	a		14 48					15 18			15 48					16 18			16 48				
Orpington	a																						
London Bridge	a		15 13					15 43			16 13					16 43			17 13				
London Cannon Street	a																						
London Waterloo (East)	a		15 19					15 49			16 19					16 49			17 19				
London Charing Cross	a		15 22					15 52			16 22					16 52			17 22				
Ebbsfleet International	a	14 02			14 32	14 32			15 02	15 02			15 32	15 32			16 02	16 05			16 32	16 32	
Stratford International	a	14 14			14 44	14 44			15 14	15 14			15 44	15 44			16 14	16 17			16 44	16 44	
St Pancras Intl.	a	14 22			14 51	14 52			15 21	15 22			15 51	15 52			16 22	16 24			16 51	16 52	

A not from 1 September until 8 September B not 25 August C ⚒ from Ashford International

Table 207

Saturdays
25 August to 8 September

Margate, Ramsgate, Canterbury West, Dover, Folkestone, Ashford International - Tonbridge and London

Network Diagram - see first Page of Table 206

		SE	SE	SE	SE	SE	SE	SE	SE	SE	SE	SE	SE	SE	SE	SE	SE	SE	SE	SE	SE	SE	SE
		1			1	1				1			1	1				1			1	1	
		A	B	C	A	A	B	C		A	B	C	A	A	B	C		A	B	C			C
		⚒			⚒	⚒				⚒			⚒	⚒				⚒					
Margate	d		15 53	15 53							16 53	16 53							17 53	17 53			
Broadstairs	d		15 59	15 59							16 59	16 59							17 59	17 59			
Ramsgate	d	15 40	16 05	16 05	15 50					16 40	17 05	17 05	16 50					17 40	18 05	18 05	17 50		
Minster	d	15 46								16 46								17 46					
Sandwich	d				16 02								17 02								18 02		
Deal	d				16 08								17 08								18 08		
Walmer	d				16 11								17 11								18 11		
Martin Mill	d				16 16								17 16								18 16		
Dover Priory	a				16 24								17 24								18 24		
	d				16 24		16 44	16 44					17 24		17 44	17 44					18 24		18 44
Folkestone Central	d				16 36		16 56	16 56					17 36		17 56	17 56					18 36		18 56
Folkestone West	d				16 38		16 58	16 58					17 38		17 58	17 58					18 38		18 58
Sandling	d				16 43								17 43								18 43		
Westenhanger	d				16 46								17 46								18 46		
Sturry	d	15 58								16 58								17 58					
Canterbury West	d	16 07	16 25	16 25		16 36				17 07	17 25	17 25		17 36				18 07	18 25	18 25		18 36	
Chartham	d					16 41								17 41								18 41	
Chilham	d					16 44								17 44								18 44	
Wye	d	16 19				16 51				17 19				17 51				18 19				18 51	
Ashford International	a	16 25	16 41	16 41	16 55	16 58	17 11	17 11		17 25	17 41	17 41	17 55	17 58	18 11	18 11		18 25	18 41	18 41	18 55	18 58	19 11
	d	16 33	16 43	16 43	17 03		17 13	17 13		17 33	17 43	17 43	18 03		18 13	18 13		18 33	18 43	18 43	19 03		19 13
Pluckley	d	16 39			17 09					17 39			18 09					18 39			19 09		
Headcorn	d	16 46			17 16					17 46			18 16					18 46			19 16		
Staplehurst	d	16 51			17 21					17 51			18 21					18 51			19 21		
Marden	d	16 55			17 25					17 55			18 25					18 55			19 25		
Maidstone West 194	d								17 28								18 28						
Paddock Wood	d	17 01			17 31				17 47	18 01			18 31				18 47	19 01			19 31		
Tonbridge	a	17 09			17 39				17 55	18 09			18 39				18 55	19 09			19 39		
	d	17 10			17 40					18 10			18 40					19 10			19 40		
Sevenoaks	a	17 18			17 48					18 18			18 48					19 18			19 48		
Orpington	a																	19 27			19 57		
London Bridge	a	17 43			18 13					18 43			19 13					19 43			20 13		
London Cannon Street	a																						
London Waterloo (East)	a	17 49			18 19					18 49			19 19					19 48			20 18		
London Charing Cross	a	17 52			18 22					18 52			19 22					19 51			20 21		
Ebbsfleet International	a		17 02	17 02			17 32	17 32			18 02	18 02			18 32	18 32			19 02	19 02			19 32
Stratford International	a		17 14	17 14			17 44	17 44			18 14	18 14			18 44	18 44			19 14	19 14			19 44
St Pancras Intl.	a		17 21	17 22			17 51	17 52			18 21	18 22			18 51	18 52			19 21	19 22			19 52

		SE	SE	SE	SE	SE	SE	SE	SE	SE	SE	SE	SE	SE	SE	SE	SE	SE	SE	SE	SE	SE
				1			1	1				1			1				1			1
		B			B	C			B	C			B	C		B	C			B	C	
Margate	d				18 53	18 53							19 53	19 53						20 53	20 53	
Broadstairs	d				18 59	18 59							19 59	19 59						20 59	20 59	
Ramsgate	d			18 40	19 05	19 05	18 50					19 40	20 05	20 05	19 50				20 40	21 05	21 05	20 50
Minster	d			18 46								19 46							20 46			
Sandwich	d						19 02								20 02							21 02
Deal	d						19 08								20 08							21 08
Walmer	d						19 11								20 11							21 11
Martin Mill	d						19 16								20 16							21 16
Dover Priory	a						19 24								20 24							21 24
	d	18 44					19 24		19 44	19 44					20 24	20 44	20 44					21 24
Folkestone Central	d	18 56					19 36		19 56	19 56					20 36	20 56	20 56					21 36
Folkestone West	d	18 58					19 38		19 58	19 58					20 38	20 58	20 58					21 38
Sandling	d						19 43								20 43							21 43
Westenhanger	d						19 46								20 46							21 46
Sturry	d			18 58								19 58							20 58			
Canterbury West	d			19 07	19 25	19 25		19 36				20 04	20 25	20 25					21 04	21 25	21 25	
Chartham	d							19 41				20 09							21 09			
Chilham	d							19 44				20 12							21 12			
Wye	d			19 19				19 51				20 19							21 19			
Ashford International	a	19 11		19 25	19 41	19 41	19 55	19 58	20 11	20 11		20 25	20 41	20 41	20 55	21 11	21 11		21 25	21 41	21 41	21 55
	d	19 13		19 33	19 43	19 43	20 03		20 13	20 13		20 33	20 43	20 47	21 03	21 13	21 13		21 33	21 43	21 43	22 03
Pluckley	d			19 39			20 09					20 39			21 09				21 39			22 09
Headcorn	d			19 46			20 16					20 46			21 16				21 46			22 16
Staplehurst	d			19 51			20 21					20 51			21 21				21 51			22 21
Marden	d			19 55			20 25					20 55			21 25				21 55			22 25
Maidstone West 194	d		19 28								20 28							21 28				
Paddock Wood	d		19 47	20 01			20 31				20 47	21 01			21 31			21 47	22 01			22 31
Tonbridge	a		19 55	20 09			20 39				20 55	21 09			21 39			21 55	22 09			22 39
	d			20 10			20 40					21 10			21 40				22 10			22 40
Sevenoaks	a			20 18			20 48					21 18			21 48				22 18			22 48
Orpington	a			20 27			20 57					21 27			21 57				22 27			22 57
London Bridge	a			20 43			21 13					21 43			22 13				22 43			23 13
London Cannon Street	a																					
London Waterloo (East)	a			20 48			21 18					21 48			22 18				22 48			23 18
London Charing Cross	a			20 51			21 21					21 51			22 21				22 51			23 21
Ebbsfleet International	a	19 32			20 02	20 02			20 32	20 32			21 02	21 06		21 32	21 32			22 02	22 02	
Stratford International	a	19 46			20 14	20 14			20 44	20 44			21 14	21 18		21 44	21 44			22 14	22 14	
St Pancras Intl.	a	19 53			20 21	20 22			20 51	20 52			21 21	21 26		21 51	21 52			22 21	22 22	

A ⚒ from Ashford International B not from 1 September until 8 September C not 25 August

Table 207

Saturdays
25 August to 8 September

Margate, Ramsgate, Canterbury West, Dover, Folkestone, Ashford International - Tonbridge and London

Network Diagram - see first Page of Table 206

		SE A	SE B	SE	SE ■	SE A	SE B	SE ■	SE A	SE B	SE ■
Margate ■	d					21 53	21 53				
Broadstairs	d					21 59	21 59				
Ramsgate ■	d				21 22	22 05	22 05	22 24			22 45
Minster ■	d							22 30			
Sandwich	d				21 34						22 57
Deal	d				21 40						23 03
Walmer	d				21 43						23 06
Martin Mill	d				21 48						23 11
Dover Priory ■	a				21 56						23 19
	d	21 44	21 44		21 57				22 44	22 44	23 24
Folkestone Central	d	21 56	21 56		22 09				22 56	22 56	23 36
Folkestone West	d	21 58	21 58		22 11				22 58	22 58	23 38
Sandling	d				22 16						23 43
Westenhanger	d				22 19						23 46
Sturry	d							22 42			
Canterbury West ■	d					22 25	22 25	22 47			
Chartham	d							22 52			
Chilham	d							22 55			
Wye	d							23 02			
Ashford International	a	22 11	22 11		22 28	22 41	22 41	23 08	23 11	23 11	23 55
	d	22 13	22 13		22 33	22 43	22 43		23 13	23 13	
Pluckley	d				22 39						
Headcorn	d				22 46						
Staplehurst	d				22 51						
Marden	d				22 55						
Maidstone West ■ 194	d			22 28							
Paddock Wood ■	d			22 47	23 01						
Tonbridge ■	a			22 55	23 10						
	d				23 14						
Sevenoaks ■	a				23 24						
Orpington ■	a				23 36						
London Bridge ■ ⊖	a				23 54						
London Cannon Street ■ ⊖	a										
London Waterloo (East) ■ ⊖	a				23 59						
London Charing Cross ■ ⊖	a				00 03						
Ebbsfleet International	a	22 32	22 32			23 02	23 02		23 32	23 32	
Stratford International ⊖	a	22 44	22 44			23 14	23 14		23 44	23 44	
St Pancras Intl. ■ ⊖	a	22 51	22 52			23 21	23 22		23 51	23 52	

Sundays
until 22 July, 19 Aug and from 16 Sep

		SE ■	SE ■	SE	SE ■	SE ■	SE	SE	SE ■	SE	SE ■ C	SE	SE	SE ■ C	SE	SE ■ C	SE	SE	SE ■ C	SE ■ C	SE	SE ■ C	SE
Margate ■	d											07 53					08 53						09 53
Broadstairs	d											07 59					08 59						09 59
Ramsgate ■	d	21p22							06 50		07 40	08 05		07 50		08 40	09 05		08 50			09 40	10 05
Minster ■	d										07 46					08 46						09 46	
Sandwich	d	21p34							07 02					08 02					09 02				
Deal	d	21p40							07 08					08 08					09 08				
Walmer	d	21p43							07 11					08 11					09 11				
Martin Mill	d	21p48							07 16					08 16					09 16				
Dover Priory ■	a	21p56							07 24					08 24					09 24				
	d	21p57							07 24	07 44				08 24	08 44				09 24		09 44		
Folkestone Central	d	22p09							07 36	07 56				08 36	08 56				09 36		09 56		
Folkestone West	d	22p11							07 38	07 58				08 38	08 58				09 38		09 58		
Sandling	d	22p16							07 43					08 43					09 43				
Westenhanger	d	22p19							07 46					08 46					09 46				
Sturry	d										07 58					08 58						09 58	
Canterbury West ■	d										08 04	08 25				09 04	09 25			09 36		10 07	10 25
Chartham	d										08 09					09 09				09 41			
Chilham	d										08 12					09 12				09 44			
Wye	d										08 19					09 19				09 51		10 19	
Ashford International	a	22p28							07 55	08 11	08 25	08 41		08 55	09 11	09 25	09 41		09 55	09 58	10 11	10 25	10 41
	d	22p33	06 33		07 03	07 33	07 43		08 03	08 13	08 33	08 43		09 03	09 13	09 33	09 43		10 03		10 13	10 33	10 43
Pluckley	d	22p39	06 39			07 39					08 39					09 39						10 39	
Headcorn	d	22p46	06 46		07 14	07 46			08 14		08 46			09 14		09 46			10 14			10 46	
Staplehurst	d	22p51	06 51		07 19	07 51			08 19		08 51			09 19		09 51			10 19			10 51	
Marden	d	22p55	06 55		07 23	07 55			08 23		08 55			09 23		09 55			10 23			10 55	
Maidstone West ■ 194	d			07 03				08 03					09 03					10 03					
Paddock Wood ■	d	23p01	07 01	07a22	07 29	08 01		08a22	08 29		09 01		09a22	09 29		10 01		10a22	10 29			11 01	
Tonbridge ■	a	23p10	07 09		07 38	08 09			08 38		09 09			09 38		10 09			10 38			11 09	
	d	23p14	07 10		07 38	08 10			08 38		09 10			09 38		10 10			10 38			11 10	
Sevenoaks ■	a	23p24	07 18		07 48	08 18			08 48		09 18			09 48		10 18			10 48			11 18	
Orpington ■	a	23p36	07 27		07 57	08 27			08 57		09 27			09 57		10 27			10 57			11 27	
London Bridge ■ ⊖	a	23p54	07 43		08 13	08 43			09 13		09 43			10 13		10 43			11 13			11 43	
London Cannon Street ■ ⊖	a																						
London Waterloo (East) ■ ⊖	a	23p59	07 48		08 18	08 48			09 18		09 48			10 18		10 48			11 18			11 48	
London Charing Cross ■ ⊖	a	00 03	07 52		08 22	08 52			09 22		09 52			10 22		10 52			11 22			11 52	
Ebbsfleet International	a						08 02			08 32		09 02			09 32		10 02				10 32		11 02
Stratford International ⊖	a						08 14			08 44		09 14			09 44		10 14				10 44		11 14
St Pancras Intl. ■ ⊖	a						08 21			08 51		09 21			09 51		10 21				10 51		11 21

A not from 1 September until 8 September B not 25 August C ⚌ from Ashford International

Table 207

Sundays
until 22 July, 19 Aug and from 16 Sep

Margate, Ramsgate, Canterbury West, Dover, Folkestone, Ashford International - Tonbridge and London

Network Diagram - see first Page of Table 206

		SE	SE ■ A	SE ■ A	SE	SE ■ A	SE	SE	SE ■ A	SE ■ A	SE	SE ■ A	SE	SE	SE ■ A	SE ■ A	SE	SE ■ A	SE	SE	SE ■ A	SE ■ A	SE
Margate ■	d						10 53						11 53						12 53				
Broadstairs	d						10 59						11 59						12 59				
Ramsgate ■	d		09 50			10 40	11 05		10 50			11 40	12 05		11 50			12 40	13 05		12 50		
Minster ■	d					10 46						11 46						12 46					
Sandwich	d		10 02						11 02						12 02						13 02		
Deal	d		10 08						11 08						12 08						13 08		
Walmer	d		10 11						11 11						12 11						13 11		
Martin Mill	d		10 16						11 16						12 16						13 16		
Dover Priory ■	a		10 24						11 24						12 24						13 24		
	d		10 24		10 44				11 24		11 44				12 24		12 44				13 24		13 44
Folkestone Central	d		10 36		10 56				11 36		11 56				12 36		12 56				13 36		13 56
Folkestone West	d		10 38		10 58				11 38		11 58				12 38		12 58				13 38		13 58
Sandling	d		10 43						11 43						12 43						13 43		
Westenhanger	d		10 46						11 46						12 46						13 46		
Sturry	d					10 58						11 58						12 58					
Canterbury West ■	d			10 36		11 07	11 25			11 36		12 07	12 25			12 36		13 07	13 25			13 36	
Chartham	d			10 41						11 41						12 41						13 41	
Chilham	d			10 44						11 44						12 44						13 44	
Wye	d			10 51		11 19				11 51		12 19				12 51		13 19				13 51	
Ashford International	a		10 55	10 58	11 11	11 25	11 41		11 55	11 58	12 11	12 25	12 41		12 55	12 58	13 11	13 25	13 41		13 55	13 58	14 11
	d		11 03		11 13	11 33	11 43		12 03		12 13	12 33	12 43		13 03		13 13	13 33	13 43		14 03		14 13
Pluckley	d					11 39						12 39						13 39					
Headcorn	d		11 14			11 46			12 14			12 46			13 14			13 46			14 14		
Staplehurst	d		11 19			11 51			12 19			12 51			13 19			13 51			14 19		
Marden	d		11 23			11 55			12 23			12 55			13 23			13 55			14 23		
Maidstone West ■ 194	d	11 03						12 03						13 03						14 03			
Paddock Wood ■	d	11a22	11 29			12 01		12a22	12 29			13 01		13a22	13 29			14 01		14a22	14 29		
Tonbridge ■	a		11 38			12 09			12 38			13 09			13 38			14 09			14 38		
	d		11 38			12 10			12 38			13 10			13 38			14 10			14 38		
Sevenoaks ■	a		11 48			12 18			12 48			13 18			13 48			14 18			14 48		
Orpington ■	a		11 57			12 27			12 57			13 27			13 57			14 27			14 57		
London Bridge ■ ⊖	a		12 13			12 43			13 13			13 43			14 13			14 43			15 13		
London Cannon Street ■ ⊖	a																						
London Waterloo (East) ■ ⊖	a		12 18			12 48			13 18			13 48			14 18			14 48			15 18		
London Charing Cross ■ ⊖	a		12 22			12 52			13 22			13 52			14 22			14 52			15 22		
Ebbsfleet International	a				11 32		12 02				12 32		13 02				13 32		14 02				14 32
Stratford International ⊖	a				11 44		12 14				12 44		13 14				13 44		14 14				14 44
St Pancras Intl. ■ ⊖	a				11 51		12 21				12 51		13 21				13 51		14 21				14 51

		SE ■ A	SE	SE	SE ■ A	SE ■ A	SE	SE ■ A	SE	SE	SE ■ A	SE ■ A	SE	SE ■ A	SE	SE	SE ■ A	SE ■ A	SE	SE ■ A	SE	SE
Margate ■	d		13 53						14 53						15 53						16 53	
Broadstairs	d		13 59						14 59						15 59						16 59	
Ramsgate ■	d	13 40	14 05		13 50			14 40	15 05		14 50			15 40	16 05		15 50			16 40	17 05	
Minster ■	d	13 46						14 46						15 46						16 46		
Sandwich	d				14 02						15 02						16 02					
Deal	d				14 08						15 08						16 08					
Walmer	d				14 11						15 11						16 11					
Martin Mill	d				14 16						15 16						16 16					
Dover Priory ■	a				14 24						15 24						16 24					
	d				14 24		14 44				15 24		15 44				16 24		16 44			
Folkestone Central	d				14 36		14 56				15 36		15 56				16 36		16 56			
Folkestone West	d				14 38		14 58				15 38		15 58				16 38		16 58			
Sandling	d				14 43						15 43						16 43					
Westenhanger	d				14 46						15 46						16 46					
Sturry	d	13 58						14 58						15 58						16 58		
Canterbury West ■	d	14 07	14 25			14 36		15 07	15 25			15 36		16 07	16 25			16 36		17 07	17 25	
Chartham	d					14 41						15 41						16 41				
Chilham	d					14 44						15 44						16 44				
Wye	d	14 19				14 51		15 19				15 51		16 19				16 51		17 19		
Ashford International	a	14 25	14 41		14 55	14 58	15 11	15 25	15 41		15 55	15 58	16 11	16 25	16 41		16 55	16 58	17 11	17 25	17 41	
	d	14 33	14 43		15 03		15 13	15 33	15 43		16 03		16 13	16 33	16 43		17 03		17 13	17 33	17 43	
Pluckley	d	14 39						15 39						16 39						17 39		
Headcorn	d	14 46			15 14			15 46			16 14			16 46			17 14			17 46		
Staplehurst	d	14 51			15 19			15 51			16 19			16 51			17 19			17 51		
Marden	d	14 55			15 23			15 55			16 23			16 55			17 23			17 55		
Maidstone West ■ 194	d			15 03						16 03						17 03						18 03
Paddock Wood ■	d	15 01		15a22	15 29			16 01		16a22	16 29			17 01		17a22	17 29			18 01		18a22
Tonbridge ■	a	15 09			15 38			16 09			16 38			17 09			17 38			18 09		
	d	15 10			15 38			16 10			16 38			17 10			17 38			18 10		
Sevenoaks ■	a	15 18			15 48			16 18			16 48			17 18			17 48			18 18		
Orpington ■	a	15 27			15 57			16 27			16 57			17 27			17 57			18 27		
London Bridge ■ ⊖	a	15 43			16 13			16 43			17 13			17 43			18 13			18 43		
London Cannon Street ■ ⊖	a																					
London Waterloo (East) ■ ⊖	a	15 48			16 18			16 48			17 18			17 48			18 18			18 48		
London Charing Cross ■ ⊖	a	15 52			16 22			16 52			17 22			17 52			18 22			18 52		
Ebbsfleet International	a		15 02				15 32		16 02				16 32		17 02				17 32		18 02	
Stratford International ⊖	a		15 14				15 44		16 14				16 44		17 14				17 44		18 14	
St Pancras Intl. ■ ⊖	a		15 21				15 51		16 21				16 51		17 21				17 51		18 21	

A ⚌ from Ashford International

Table 207

Sundays

until 22 July, 19 Aug and from 16 Sep

Margate, Ramsgate, Canterbury West, Dover, Folkestone, Ashford International - Tonbridge and London

Network Diagram - see first Page of Table 206

		SE ■ A	SE ■ A	SE	SE ■ A	SE	SE	SE ■	SE ■	SE	SE ■	SE	SE	SE ■	SE	SE ■	SE	SE	SE ■	SE	SE ■	SE	SE
Margate ■	d					17 53						18 53					19 53					20 53	
Broadstairs	d					17 59						18 59					19 59					20 59	
Ramsgate ■	d	16 50			17 40	18 05		17 50			18 40	19 05		18 50		19 40	20 05		19 50		20 40	21 05	
Minster ■	d				17 46						18 46					19 46					20 46		
Sandwich	d	17 02						18 02						19 02					20 02				
Deal	d	17 08						18 08						19 08					20 08				
Walmer	d	17 11						18 11						19 11					20 11				
Martin Mill	d	17 16						18 16						19 16					20 16				
Dover Priory ■	a	17 24						18 24						19 24					20 24				
	d	17 24		17 44				18 24		18 44				19 24	19 44				20 24	20 44			
Folkestone Central	d	17 36		17 56				18 36		18 56				19 36	19 56				20 36	20 56			
Folkestone West	d	17 38		17 58				18 38		18 58				19 38	19 58				20 38	20 58			
Sandling	d	17 43						18 43						19 43					20 43				
Westenhanger	d	17 46						18 46						19 46					20 46				
Sturry	d				17 58						18 58					19 58					20 58		
Canterbury West ■	d		17 36		18 07	18 25			18 36		19 04	19 25				20 04	20 25				21 04	21 25	
Chartham	d		17 41						18 41		19 09					20 09					21 09		
Chilham	d		17 44						18 44		19 12					20 12					21 12		
Wye	d		17 51		18 19				18 51		19 19					20 19					21 19		
Ashford International	a	17 55	17 58	18 11	18 25	18 41		18 55	18 58	19 11	19 25	19 41		19 55	20 11	20 25	20 41		20 55	21 11	21 25	21 41	
	d	18 03		18 13	18 33	18 43		19 03		19 13	19 33	19 43		20 03	20 13	20 33	20 43		21 03	21 13	21 33	21 43	
Pluckley	d				18 39						19 39					20 39					21 39		
Headcorn	d	18 14			18 46			19 14			19 46			20 14		20 46			21 14		21 46		
Staplehurst	d	18 19			18 51			19 19			19 51			20 19		20 51			21 19		21 51		
Marden	d	18 23			18 55			19 23			19 55			20 23		20 55			21 23		21 55		
Maidstone West ■ 194	d						19 03						20 03					21 03					22 03
Paddock Wood ■	d	18 29			19 01		19a22	19 29			20 01		20a22	20 29		21 01		21a22	21 29		22 01		22 23
Tonbridge ■	a	18 38			19 09			19 38			20 09			20 38		21 09			21 38		22 09		22 32
	d	18 38			19 10			19 38			20 10			20 38		21 10			21 38		22 10		
Sevenoaks ■	a	18 48			19 18			19 48			20 18			20 48		21 18			21 48		22 18		
Orpington ■	a	18 57			19 27			19 57			20 27			20 57		21 27			21 57		22 27		
London Bridge ■	a	19 13			19 43			20 13			20 43			21 13		21 43			22 13		22 43		
London Cannon Street ■	a																						
London Waterloo (East) ■	a	19 18			19 48			20 18			20 48			21 18		21 48			22 18		22 48		
London Charing Cross ■	a	19 22			19 52			20 22			20 52			21 22		21 52			22 22		22 52		
Ebbsfleet International	a			18 32		19 02				19 32		20 02			20 32		21 02			21 32		22 02	
Stratford International	a			18 44		19 14				19 44		20 14			20 44		21 14			21 44		22 14	
St Pancras Intl. ■	a			18 51		19 21				19 51		20 21			20 51		21 21			21 51		22 21	

		SE ■	SE	SE ■	SE	SE ■
Margate ■	d				21 53	
Broadstairs	d				21 59	
Ramsgate ■	d	20 50		21 40	22 05	21 50
Minster ■	d			21 46		
Sandwich	d	21 02				22 02
Deal	d	21 08				22 08
Walmer	d	21 11				22 11
Martin Mill	d	21 16				22 16
Dover Priory ■	a	21 24				22 24
	d	21 24	21 44			22 24
Folkestone Central	d	21 36	21 56			22 36
Folkestone West	d	21 38	21 58			22 38
Sandling	d	21 43				22 43
Westenhanger	d	21 46				22 46
Sturry	d			21 58		
Canterbury West ■	d			22 04	22 25	
Chartham	d			22 09		
Chilham	d			22 12		
Wye	d			22 19		
Ashford International	a	21 55	22 11	22 25	22 41	22 55
	d	22 03	22 13		22 43	
Pluckley	d					
Headcorn	d	22 14				
Staplehurst	d	22 19				
Marden	d	22 23				
Maidstone West ■ 194	d					
Paddock Wood ■	d	22 29				
Tonbridge ■	a	22 38				
	d	22 38				
Sevenoaks ■	a	22 48				
Orpington ■	a	22 57				
London Bridge ■	a	23 13				
London Cannon Street ■	a					
London Waterloo (East) ■	a	23 18				
London Charing Cross ■	a	23 22				
Ebbsfleet International	a		22 32		23 02	
Stratford International	a		22 44		23 14	
St Pancras Intl. ■	a		22 51		23 21	

A ✠ from Ashford International

Table 207

Sundays

29 July to 12 August

Margate, Ramsgate, Canterbury West, Dover, Folkestone, Ashford International - Tonbridge and London

Network Diagram - see first Page of Table 206

		SE	SE ■	SE	SE	SE	SE ■	SE ■	SE	SE	SE ■	SE	SE ■	SE	SE ■	SE	SE ■	SE ■	SE	SE	SE ■ A	SE ■ A	SE
Margate ■	d																				07 29		
Broadstairs	d																				07 34		
Ramsgate ■	d			05 00			05 32		05 55		05 50				06 40		06 50	07 16			07 40		
Minster ■	d			05 06			05 38								06 46						07 46		
Sandwich	d										06 02						07 02						
Deal	d										06 08						07 08						
Walmer	d										06 11						07 11						
Martin Mill	d										06 16						07 16						
Dover Priory ■	a										06 24						07 24						
	d		04 50					05 50			06 24		06 56				07 24					07 56	
Folkestone Central	d		05 02					06 02			06 36		07 09				07 36					08 09	
Folkestone West	d		05 04					06 04			06 38		07 11				07 38					08 11	
Sandling	d		05 09					06 09			06 43						07 43						
Westenhanger	d		05 12					06 12			06 46						07 46						
Sturry	d			05 18			05 50								06 58						07 58		
Canterbury West ■	d			05 25			05 56		06 15						07 04			07 36			08 07		
Chartham	d						06 01								07 09			07 41					
Chilham	d						06 04								07 12			07 44					
Wye	d						06 11								07 19			07 51			08 19		
Ashford International	a		05 21	05 41			06 17	06 21	06 31		06 55		07 28		07 25		07 55	07 58			08 25	08 28	
	d	05 13	05 25	05 43	06 13		06 25		06 33	06 47	07 03	07 13			07 33	07 47	08 03		08 13		08 33		08 47
Pluckley	d		05 31				06 31				07 09				07 39		08 09				08 39		
Headcorn	d		05 38				06 38				07 16				07 46		08 16				08 46		
Staplehurst	d		05 43				06 43				07 21				07 51		08 21				08 51		
Marden	d		05 47				06 47				07 25				07 55		08 25				08 55		
Maidstone West ■ 194	d					06 28								07 28						08 28			
Paddock Wood ■	d		05 53			06a47	06 53				07 31			07a47	08 01		08 31			08a47	09 01		
Tonbridge ■	a		06 01				07 01				07 39				08 09		08 39				09 09		
	d		06 02				07 02				07 40				08 10		08 40				09 10		
Sevenoaks ■	a		06 13				07 13				07 48				08 18		08 48				09 18		
Orpington ■	a		06 23				07 23																
London Bridge ■	a		06 39				07 39				08 13				08 43		09 13				09 43		
London Cannon Street ■	a																						
London Waterloo (East) ■	a		06 43				07 43				08 19				08 49		09 19				09 49		
London Charing Cross ■	a		06 47				07 48				08 22				08 52		09 22				09 52		
Ebbsfleet International	a	05 32		06 02	06 32				06 52	07 06		07 32				08 06			08 32				09 06
Stratford International	a	05 44		06 14	06 45				07 04	07 19		07 45				08 19			08 45				09 19
St Pancras Intl. ■	a	05 50		06 23	06 55				07 15	07 29		07 55				08 29			08 55				09 29

		SE ■ A	SE ■ A	SE	SE	SE ■ A	SE ■ A	SE	SE ■ A	SE ■ A	SE	SE	SE ■ A	SE ■ A	SE	SE ■ A	SE ■ A	SE	SE	SE ■ A	SE ■ A	SE
Margate ■	d																					
Broadstairs	d																					
Ramsgate ■	d	07 50	08 16			08 40			08 50	09 16			09 40			09 50	10 16			10 40		
Minster ■	d					08 46							09 46							10 46		
Sandwich	d	08 02							09 02							10 02						
Deal	d	08 08							09 08							10 08						
Walmer	d	08 11							09 11							10 11						
Martin Mill	d	08 16							09 16							10 16						
Dover Priory ■	a	08 24							09 24							10 24						
	d	08 24					08 56		09 24					09 56		10 24					10 56	
Folkestone Central	d	08 36					09 09		09 36					10 09		10 36					11 09	
Folkestone West	d	08 38					09 11		09 38					10 11		10 38					11 11	
Sandling	d	08 43							09 43							10 43						
Westenhanger	d	08 46							09 46							10 46						
Sturry	d					08 58							09 58							10 58		
Canterbury West ■	d		08 36			09 07				09 36			10 07				10 36			11 07		
Chartham	d		08 41							09 41							10 41					
Chilham	d		08 44							09 44							10 44					
Wye	d		08 51			09 19				09 51			10 19				10 51			11 19		
Ashford International	a	08 55	08 58			09 25	09 28		09 55	09 58			10 25	10 28		10 55	10 58			11 25	11 28	
	d	09 03		09 13		09 33		09 47	10 03		10 13		10 33		10 47	11 03		11 13		11 33		11 47
Pluckley	d	09 09				09 39			10 09				10 39			11 09				11 39		
Headcorn	d	09 16				09 46			10 16				10 46			11 16				11 46		
Staplehurst	d	09 21				09 51			10 21				10 51			11 21				11 51		
Marden	d	09 25				09 55			10 25				10 55			11 25				11 55		
Maidstone West ■ 194	d				09 28							10 28							11 28			
Paddock Wood ■	d	09 31			09a47	10 01			10 31			10a47	11 01			11 31			11a47	12 01		
Tonbridge ■	a	09 39				10 09			10 39				11 09			11 39				12 09		
	d	09 40				10 10			10 40				11 10			11 40				12 10		
Sevenoaks ■	a	09 48				10 18			10 48				11 18			11 48				12 18		
Orpington ■	a																					
London Bridge ■	a	10 13				10 43			11 13				11 43			12 13				12 43		
London Cannon Street ■	a																					
London Waterloo (East) ■	a	10 19				10 49			11 19				11 49			12 19				12 49		
London Charing Cross ■	a	10 22				10 52			11 22				11 52			12 22				12 52		
Ebbsfleet International	a			09 32				10 06			10 32				11 06			11 32				12 06
Stratford International	a			09 45				10 19			10 45				11 19			11 45				12 19
St Pancras Intl. ■	a			09 55				10 29			10 55				11 29			11 55				12 29

A ✠ from Ashford International

Table 207

Sundays

29 July to 12 August

Margate, Ramsgate, Canterbury West, Dover, Folkestone, Ashford International - Tonbridge and London

Network Diagram - see first Page of Table 206

	SE 1 A ⌶	SE 1 A ⌶	SE	SE	SE 1 A ⌶	SE 1 A ⌶	SE	SE 1 A ⌶	SE 1 A ⌶	SE	SE	SE 1 A ⌶	SE 1 A ⌶	SE	SE 1 A ⌶	SE 1 A ⌶	SE	SE	SE 1 A ⌶	SE 1 A ⌶	SE
Margate d																					
Broadstairs d																					
Ramsgate d	10 50	11 16			11 40			11 50	12 16			12 40			12 50	13 16			13 40		
Minster d					11 46							12 46							13 46		
Sandwich d	11 02							12 02							13 02						
Deal d	11 08							12 08							13 08						
Walmer d	11 11							12 11							13 11						
Martin Mill d	11 16							12 16							13 16						
Dover Priory a	11 24							12 24							13 24						
d	11 24					11 56		12 24					12 56		13 24					13 56	
Folkestone Central d	11 36					12 09		12 36					13 09		13 36					14 09	
Folkestone West d	11 38					12 11		12 38					13 11		13 38					14 11	
Sandling d	11 43							12 43							13 43						
Westenhanger d	11 46							12 46							13 46						
Sturry d					11 58							12 58							13 58		
Canterbury West d		11 36			12 07				12 36			13 07				13 36			14 07		
Chartham d		11 41							12 41							13 41					
Chilham d		11 44							12 44							13 44					
Wye d		11 51			12 19				12 51			13 19				13 51			14 19		
Ashford International a	11 55	11 58			12 25	12 28		12 55	12 58			13 25	13 28		13 55	13 58			14 25	14 28	
d	12 03		12 13		12 33		12 47	13 03		13 13		13 33		13 47	14 03		14 13		14 33		14 47
Pluckley d	12 09				12 39			13 09				13 39			14 09				14 39		
Headcorn d	12 16				12 46			13 16				13 46			14 16				14 46		
Staplehurst d	12 21				12 51			13 21				13 51			14 21				14 51		
Marden d	12 25				12 55			13 25				13 55			14 25				14 55		
Maidstone West 194 d				12 28							13 28							14 28			
Paddock Wood d	12 31			12a47	13 01			13 31			13a47	14 01			14 31			14a47	15 01		
Tonbridge a	12 39				13 09			13 39				14 09			14 39				15 09		
d	12 40				13 10			13 40				14 10			14 40				15 10		
Sevenoaks a	12 48				13 18			13 48				14 18			14 48				15 18		
Orpington a																					
London Bridge ⊖ a	13 13				13 43			14 13				14 43			15 13				15 43		
London Cannon Street ⊖ a																					
London Waterloo (East) ⊖ a	13 19				13 49			14 19				14 49			15 19				15 49		
London Charing Cross ⊖ a	13 22				13 52			14 22				14 52			15 22				15 52		
Ebbsfleet International a			12 32				13 06			13 32				14 06			14 32				15 06
Stratford International ⊖ a			12 45				13 19			13 45				14 19			14 45				15 19
St Pancras Intl. ⊖ a			12 55				13 29			13 55				14 29			14 55				15 29

	SE 1 A ⌶	SE 1 A ⌶	SE	SE	SE 1 A ⌶	SE 1 A ⌶	SE	SE 1 A ⌶	SE 1 A ⌶	SE	SE	SE 1 A ⌶	SE 1 A ⌶	SE	SE 1 A ⌶	SE 1 A ⌶	SE	SE	SE 1 A ⌶	SE 1 A ⌶	SE
Margate d																					
Broadstairs d																					
Ramsgate d	13 50	14 16			14 40			14 50	15 16			15 40			15 50	16 16			16 40		
Minster d					14 46							15 46							16 46		
Sandwich d	14 02							15 02							16 02						
Deal d	14 08							15 08							16 08						
Walmer d	14 11							15 11							16 11						
Martin Mill d	14 16							15 16							16 16						
Dover Priory a	14 24							15 24							16 24						
d	14 24					14 56		15 24					15 56		16 24					16 56	
Folkestone Central d	14 36					15 09		15 36					16 09		16 36					17 09	
Folkestone West d	14 38					15 11		15 38					16 11		16 38					17 11	
Sandling d	14 43							15 43							16 43						
Westenhanger d	14 46							15 46							16 46						
Sturry d					14 58							15 58							16 58		
Canterbury West d		14 36			15 07				15 36			16 07				16 36			17 07		
Chartham d		14 41							15 41							16 41					
Chilham d		14 44							15 44							16 44					
Wye d		14 51			15 19				15 51			16 19				16 51			17 19		
Ashford International a	14 55	14 58			15 25	15 28		15 55	15 58			16 25	16 28		16 55	16 58			17 25	17 28	
d	15 03		15 13		15 33		15 47	16 03		16 13		16 33		16 47	17 03		17 13		17 33		17 47
Pluckley d	15 09				15 39			16 09				16 39			17 09				17 39		
Headcorn d	15 16				15 46			16 16				16 46			17 16				17 46		
Staplehurst d	15 21				15 51			16 21				16 51			17 21				17 51		
Marden d	15 25				15 55			16 25				16 55			17 25				17 55		
Maidstone West 194 d				15 28							16 28							17 28			
Paddock Wood d	15 31			15a47	16 01			16 31			16a47	17 01			17 31			17a47	18 01		
Tonbridge a	15 39				16 09			16 39				17 09			17 39				18 09		
d	15 40				16 10			16 40				17 10			17 40				18 10		
Sevenoaks a	15 48				16 18			16 48				17 18			17 48				18 18		
Orpington a																					
London Bridge ⊖ a	16 13				16 43			17 13				17 43			18 13				18 43		
London Cannon Street ⊖ a																					
London Waterloo (East) ⊖ a	16 19				16 49			17 19				17 49			18 19				18 49		
London Charing Cross ⊖ a	16 22				16 52			17 22				17 52			18 22				18 52		
Ebbsfleet International a			15 32				16 06			16 32				17 06			17 32				18 06
Stratford International ⊖ a			15 45				16 19			16 45				17 19			17 45				18 19
St Pancras Intl. ⊖ a			15 55				16 29			16 55				17 29			17 55				18 29

A ⌶ from Ashford International

Table 207

Sundays

29 July to 12 August

Margate, Ramsgate, Canterbury West, Dover, Folkestone, Ashford International - Tonbridge and London

Network Diagram - see first Page of Table 206

	SE 1 A ⌶	SE 1 A ⌶	SE	SE	SE 1 A ⌶	SE 1 A ⌶	SE	SE 1	SE 1	SE	SE	SE 1	SE 1	SE	SE 1	SE 1	SE	SE	SE 1	SE 1	SE
Margate d																					
Broadstairs d																					
Ramsgate d	16 50	17 16			17 40			17 50	18 16			18 40			18 50	19 16			19 40		
Minster d					17 46							18 46							19 46		
Sandwich d	17 02							18 02							19 02						
Deal d	17 08							18 08							19 08						
Walmer d	17 11							18 11							19 11						
Martin Mill d	17 16							18 16							19 16						
Dover Priory a	17 24							18 24							19 24						
d	17 24					17 56		18 24					18 56		19 24					19 56	
Folkestone Central d	17 36					18 09		18 36					19 09		19 36					20 09	
Folkestone West d	17 38					18 11		18 38					19 11		19 38					20 11	
Sandling d	17 43							18 43							19 43						
Westenhanger d	17 46							18 46							19 46						
Sturry d					17 58							18 58							19 58		
Canterbury West d		17 36			18 07				18 36			19 07				19 36			20 04		
Chartham d		17 41							18 41							19 41			20 09		
Chilham d		17 44							18 44							19 44			20 12		
Wye d		17 51			18 19				18 51			19 19				19 51			20 19		
Ashford International a	17 55	17 58			18 25	18 28		18 55	18 58			19 25	19 28		19 55	19 58			20 25	20 28	
d	18 03		18 13		18 33		18 47	19 03		19 13		19 33		19 47	20 03		20 13		20 33		20 47
Pluckley d	18 09				18 39			19 09				19 39			20 09				20 39		
Headcorn d	18 16				18 46			19 16				19 46			20 16				20 46		
Staplehurst d	18 21				18 51			19 21				19 51			20 21				20 51		
Marden d	18 25				18 55			19 25				19 55			20 25				20 55		
Maidstone West 194 d				18 28							19 28							20 28			
Paddock Wood d	18 31			18a47	19 01			19 31			19a47	20 01			20 31			20a47	21 01		
Tonbridge a	18 39				19 09			19 39				20 09			20 39				21 09		
d	18 40				19 10			19 40				20 10			20 40				21 10		
Sevenoaks a	18 48				19 18			19 48				20 18			20 48				21 18		
Orpington a					19 27			19 57				20 27			20 57				21 27		
London Bridge ⊖ a	19 13				19 43			20 13				20 43			21 13				21 43		
London Cannon Street ⊖ a																					
London Waterloo (East) ⊖ a	19 18				19 48			20 18				20 48			21 18				21 48		
London Charing Cross ⊖ a	19 22				19 51			20 21				20 51			21 21				21 51		
Ebbsfleet International a			18 32				19 06			19 32				20 06			20 32				21 06
Stratford International ⊖ a			18 45				19 19			19 45				20 19			20 45				21 19
St Pancras Intl. ⊖ a			18 55				19 29			19 55				20 29			20 55				21 29

	SE 1	SE 1	SE	SE	SE 1	SE 1	SE	SE 1	SE 1	SE	SE	SE 1	SE	SE 1	SE	SE 1
Margate d																
Broadstairs d																
Ramsgate d	19 50	20 16			20 40			20 50	21 16			21 22		22 24		22 45
Minster d					20 46									22 30		
Sandwich d	20 02							21 02				21 34				22 57
Deal d	20 08							21 08				21 40				23 03
Walmer d	20 11							21 11				21 43				23 06
Martin Mill d	20 16							21 16				21 48				23 11
Dover Priory a	20 24							21 24				21 56				23 19
d	20 24					20 56		21 24				21 57				23 24
Folkestone Central d	20 36					21 09		21 36				22 09				23 36
Folkestone West d	20 38					21 11		21 38				22 11				23 38
Sandling d	20 43							21 43				22 16				23 43
Westenhanger d	20 46							21 46				22 19				23 46
Sturry d					20 58									22 42		
Canterbury West d		20 36			21 04				21 36					22 47		
Chartham d					21 09									22 52		
Chilham d					21 12									22 55		
Wye d					21 19									23 02		
Ashford International a	20 55	20 58			21 25	21 28		21 55	21 58			22 28		23 08		23 55
d	21 03		21 13		21 33		21 47	22 03		22 13		22 33	22 43		23 11	
Pluckley d	21 09				21 39			22 09				22 39				
Headcorn d	21 16				21 46			22 16				22 46				
Staplehurst d	21 21				21 51			22 21				22 51				
Marden d	21 25				21 55			22 25				22 55				
Maidstone West 194 d				21 28							22 28					
Paddock Wood d	21 31			21a47	22 01			22 31			22 47	23 01				
Tonbridge a	21 39				22 09			22 39			22 55	23 12				
d	21 40				22 10			22 40								
Sevenoaks a	21 48				22 18			22 48								
Orpington a	21 57				22 27			22 57								
London Bridge ⊖ a	22 13				22 43			23 13								
London Cannon Street ⊖ a																
London Waterloo (East) ⊖ a	22 18				22 48			23 18								
London Charing Cross ⊖ a	22 21				22 51			23 21								
Ebbsfleet International a			21 32				22 06			22 32			23 02		23 30	
Stratford International ⊖ a			21 45				22 19			22 45			23 16		23 42	
St Pancras Intl. ⊖ a			21 55				22 29			22 55			23 26		23 51	

A ⌶ from Ashford International

Table 207

Sundays
26 August to 9 September

Margate, Ramsgate, Canterbury West, Dover, Folkestone, Ashford International - Tonbridge and London

Network Diagram - see first Page of Table 206

Station		SE 1	SE 1	SE	SE 1	SE 1	SE A	SE	SE 1	SE A	SE B	SE 1 C 🛒	SE A	SE B	SE	SE 1 C 🛒	SE A	SE B	SE 1 C 🛒	SE A	SE B	SE
Margate	d												07 53	07 53						08 53	08 53	
Broadstairs	d												07 59	07 59						08 59	08 59	
Ramsgate	d	21p22							06 50			07 40	08 05	08 05		07 50			08 40	09 05	09 05	
Minster	d											07 46							08 46			
Sandwich	d	21p34							07 02							08 02						
Deal	d	21p40							07 08							08 08						
Walmer	d	21p43							07 11							08 11						
Martin Mill	d	21p48							07 16							08 16						
Dover Priory	a	21p56							07 24							08 24						
	d	21p57							07 24	07 44	07 44					08 24	08 44	08 44				
Folkestone Central	d	22p09							07 36	07 56	07 56					08 36	08 56	08 56				
Folkestone West	d	22p11							07 38	07 58	07 58					08 38	08 58	08 58				
Sandling	d	22p16							07 43							08 43						
Westenhanger	d	22p19							07 46							08 46						
Sturry	d											07 58							08 58			
Canterbury West	d											08 04	08 25	08 25					09 04	09 25	09 25	
Chartham	d											08 09							09 09			
Chilham	d											08 12							09 12			
Wye	d											08 19							09 19			
Ashford International	a	22p28							07 55	08 11	08 11	08 25	08 41	08 41		08 55	09 11	09 11	09 25	09 41	09 41	
	d	22p33	06 33		07 03	07 33	07 43		08 03	08 13	08 13	08 33	08 43	08 43		09 03	09 13	09 13	09 33	09 43	09 43	
Pluckley	d	22p39	06 39			07 39						08 39							09 39			
Headcorn	d	22p46	06 46		07 14	07 46			08 14			08 46				09 14			09 46			
Staplehurst	d	22p51	06 51		07 19	07 51			08 19			08 51				09 19			09 51			
Marden	d	22p55	06 55		07 23	07 55			08 23			08 55				09 23			09 55			
Maidstone West 194	d			07 03				08 03							09 03							10 03
Paddock Wood	d	23p01	07 01	07a22	07 29	08 01		08a22	08 29			09 01			09a22	09 29			10 01			10a22
Tonbridge	a	23p10	07 09		07 38	08 09			08 38			09 09				09 38			10 09			
	d	23p14	07 10		07 38	08 10			08 38			09 10				09 38			10 10			
Sevenoaks	a	23p24	07 18		07 48	08 18			08 48			09 18				09 48			10 18			
Orpington	a	23p36	07 27		07 57	08 27			08 57			09 27				09 57			10 27			
London Bridge	a	23p54	07 43		08 13	08 43			09 13			09 43				10 13			10 43			
London Cannon Street	a																					
London Waterloo (East)	a	23p59	07 48		08 18	08 48			09 18			09 48				10 18			10 48			
London Charing Cross	a	00 03	07 52		08 22	08 52			09 22			09 52				10 22			10 52			
Ebbsfleet International	a						08 02			08 32	08 32		09 02	09 02			09 32	09 32		10 02	10 02	
Stratford International	a						08 14			08 44	08 44		09 14	09 14			09 44	09 44		10 14	10 14	
St Pancras Intl.	a						08 21			08 51	08 52		09 21	09 22			09 51	09 52		10 21	10 22	

Station		SE 1 C 🛒	SE 1 C 🛒	SE A	SE B	SE 1 C 🛒	SE A	SE B	SE	SE 1 C 🛒	SE 1 C 🛒	SE A	SE B	SE 1 C 🛒	SE A	SE B	SE	SE 1 C 🛒	SE 1 C 🛒	SE A	SE B	SE 1 C 🛒	SE A
Margate	d						09 53	09 53							10 53	10 53							11 53
Broadstairs	d						09 59	09 59							10 59	10 59							11 59
Ramsgate	d	08 50				09 40	10 05	10 05		09 50				10 40	11 05	11 05		10 50				11 40	12 05
Minster	d					09 46								10 46								11 46	
Sandwich	d	09 02								10 02								11 02					
Deal	d	09 08								10 08								11 08					
Walmer	d	09 11								10 11								11 11					
Martin Mill	d	09 16								10 16								11 16					
Dover Priory	a	09 24								10 24								11 24					
	d	09 24		09 44	09 44					10 24		10 44	10 44					11 24		11 44	11 44		
Folkestone Central	d	09 36		09 56	09 56					10 36		10 56	10 56					11 36		11 56	11 56		
Folkestone West	d	09 38		09 58	09 58					10 38		10 58	10 58					11 38		11 58	11 58		
Sandling	d	09 43								10 43								11 43					
Westenhanger	d	09 46								10 46								11 46					
Sturry	d					09 58								10 58								11 58	
Canterbury West	d		09 36			10 07	10 25	10 25			10 36			11 07	11 25	11 25			11 36			12 07	12 25
Chartham	d		09 41								10 41								11 41				
Chilham	d		09 44								10 44								11 44				
Wye	d		09 51			10 19					10 51			11 19					11 51			12 19	
Ashford International	a	09 55	09 58	10 11	10 11	10 25	10 41	10 41		10 55	10 58	11 11	11 11	11 25	11 41	11 41		11 55	11 58	12 11	12 11	12 25	12 41
	d	10 03		10 13	10 13	10 33	10 43	10 43		11 03		11 13	11 13	11 33	11 43	11 43		12 03		12 13	12 13	12 33	12 43
Pluckley	d					10 39								11 39								12 39	
Headcorn	d	10 14				10 46				11 14				11 46				12 14				12 46	
Staplehurst	d	10 19				10 51				11 19				11 51				12 19				12 51	
Marden	d	10 23				10 55				11 23				11 55				12 23				12 55	
Maidstone West 194	d								11 03								12 03						
Paddock Wood	d	10 29				11 01			11a22	11 29				12 01			12a22	12 29				13 01	
Tonbridge	a	10 38				11 09				11 38				12 09				12 38				13 09	
	d	10 38				11 10				11 38				12 10				12 38				13 10	
Sevenoaks	a	10 48				11 18				11 48				12 18				12 48				13 18	
Orpington	a	10 57				11 27				11 57				12 27				12 57				13 27	
London Bridge	a	11 13				11 43				12 13				12 43				13 13				13 43	
London Cannon Street	a																						
London Waterloo (East)	a	11 18				11 48				12 18				12 48				13 18				13 48	
London Charing Cross	a	11 22				11 52				12 22				12 52				13 22				13 52	
Ebbsfleet International	a			10 32	10 32		11 02	11 02				11 32	11 32		12 02	12 02				12 32	12 32		13 02
Stratford International	a			10 44	10 44		11 14	11 14				11 44	11 44		12 14	12 14				12 44	12 45		13 14
St Pancras Intl.	a			10 51	10 52		11 21	11 22				11 51	11 52		12 21	12 22				12 51	12 55		13 21

A not from 2 September until 9 September
B not 26 August
C 🛒 from Ashford International

Table 207

Sundays
26 August to 9 September

Margate, Ramsgate, Canterbury West, Dover, Folkestone, Ashford International - Tonbridge and London

Network Diagram - see first Page of Table 206

Station		SE A	SE	SE 1 B 🛒	SE 1 B 🛒	SE C	SE A	SE 1 B 🛒	SE C	SE A	SE	SE 1 B 🛒	SE 1 B 🛒	SE C	SE A	SE 1 B 🛒	SE C	SE A	SE	SE 1 B 🛒	SE 1 B 🛒	SE C
Margate	d	11 53							12 53	12 53							13 53	13 53				
Broadstairs	d	11 59							12 59	12 59							13 59	13 59				
Ramsgate	d	12 05		11 50				12 40	13 05	13 05		12 50				13 40	14 05	14 05		13 50		
Minster	d							12 46								13 46						
Sandwich	d			12 02								13 02								14 02		
Deal	d			12 08								13 08								14 08		
Walmer	d			12 11								13 11								14 11		
Martin Mill	d			12 16								13 16								14 16		
Dover Priory	a			12 24								13 24								14 24		
	d			12 24		12 44	12 44					13 24		13 44	13 44					14 24		14 44
Folkestone Central	d			12 36		12 56	12 56					13 36		13 56	13 56					14 36		14 56
Folkestone West	d			12 38		12 58	12 58					13 38		13 58	13 58					14 38		14 58
Sandling	d			12 43								13 43								14 43		
Westenhanger	d			12 46								13 46								14 46		
Sturry	d							12 58								13 58						
Canterbury West	d	12 25			12 36			13 07	13 25	13 25			13 36			14 07	14 25	14 25			14 36	
Chartham	d				12 41								13 41								14 41	
Chilham	d				12 44								13 44								14 44	
Wye	d				12 51			13 19					13 51			14 19					14 51	
Ashford International	a	12 41		12 55	12 58	13 11	13 11	13 25	13 41	13 41		13 55	13 58	14 11	14 11	14 25	14 41	14 41		14 55	14 58	15 11
	d	12 43		13 03		13 13	13 13	13 33	13 43	13 43		14 03		14 13	14 13	14 33	14 43	14 43		15 03		15 13
Pluckley	d							13 39								14 39						
Headcorn	d			13 14				13 46				14 14				14 46				15 14		
Staplehurst	d			13 19				13 51				14 19				14 51				15 19		
Marden	d			13 23				13 55				14 23				14 55				15 23		
Maidstone West 194	d		13 03								14 03								15 03			
Paddock Wood	d		13a22	13 29				14 01			14a22	14 29				15 01			15a22	15 29		
Tonbridge	a			13 38				14 09				14 38				15 09				15 38		
	d			13 38				14 10				14 38				15 10				15 38		
Sevenoaks	a			13 48				14 18				14 48				15 18				15 48		
Orpington	a			13 57				14 27				14 57				15 27				15 57		
London Bridge	a			14 13				14 43				15 13				15 43				16 13		
London Cannon Street	a																					
London Waterloo (East)	a			14 18				14 48				15 18				15 48				16 18		
London Charing Cross	a			14 22				14 52				15 22				15 52				16 22		
Ebbsfleet International	a	13 02				13 32	13 32		14 02	14 02				14 32	14 32		15 02	15 02				15 32
Stratford International	a	13 14				13 44	13 44		14 14	14 14				14 44	14 44		15 14	15 14				15 44
St Pancras Intl.	a	13 22				13 51	13 52		14 21	14 22				14 51	14 52		15 21	15 22				15 51

Station		SE A	SE 1 B 🛒	SE C	SE A	SE	SE 1 B 🛒	SE 1 B 🛒	SE C	SE A	SE 1 B 🛒	SE C	SE A	SE	SE 1 B 🛒	SE 1 B 🛒	SE C	SE A	SE 1 B 🛒	SE C	SE A	SE
Margate	d			14 53	14 53							15 53	15 53							16 53	16 53	
Broadstairs	d			14 59	14 59							15 59	15 59							16 59	16 59	
Ramsgate	d		14 40	15 05	15 05		14 50				15 40	16 05	16 05		15 50				16 40	17 05	17 05	
Minster	d		14 46								15 46								16 46			
Sandwich	d						15 02								16 02							
Deal	d						15 08								16 08							
Walmer	d						15 11								16 11							
Martin Mill	d						15 16								16 16							
Dover Priory	a						15 24								16 24							
	d	14 44					15 24		15 44	15 44					16 24		16 44	16 44				
Folkestone Central	d	14 56					15 36		15 56	15 56					16 36		16 56	16 56				
Folkestone West	d	14 58					15 38		15 58	15 58					16 38		16 58	16 58				
Sandling	d						15 43								16 43							
Westenhanger	d						15 46								16 46							
Sturry	d		14 58								15 58								16 58			
Canterbury West	d		15 07	15 25	15 25			15 36			16 07	16 25	16 25			16 36			17 07	17 25	17 25	
Chartham	d							15 41								16 41						
Chilham	d							15 44								16 44						
Wye	d		15 19					15 51			16 19					16 51			17 19			
Ashford International	a	15 11	15 25	15 41	15 41		15 55	15 58	16 11	16 11	16 25	16 41	16 41		16 55	16 58	17 11	17 11	17 25	17 41	17 41	
	d	15 13	15 33	15 43	15 43		16 03		16 13	16 13	16 33	16 43	16 43		17 03		17 13	17 13	17 33	17 43	17 43	
Pluckley	d		15 39								16 39								17 39			
Headcorn	d		15 46				16 14				16 46				17 14				17 46			
Staplehurst	d		15 51				16 19				16 51				17 19				17 51			
Marden	d		15 55				16 23				16 55				17 23				17 55			
Maidstone West 194	d					16 03								17 03								18 03
Paddock Wood	d		16 01			16a22	16 29				17 01			17a22	17 29				18 01			18a22
Tonbridge	a		16 09				16 38				17 09				17 38				18 09			
	d		16 10				16 38				17 10				17 38				18 10			
Sevenoaks	a		16 18				16 48				17 18				17 48				18 18			
Orpington	a		16 27				16 57				17 27				17 57				18 27			
London Bridge	a		16 43				17 13				17 43				18 13				18 43			
London Cannon Street	a																					
London Waterloo (East)	a		16 48				17 18				17 48				18 18				18 48			
London Charing Cross	a		16 52				17 22				17 52				18 22				18 52			
Ebbsfleet International	a	15 32		16 02	16 02				16 32	16 32		17 02	17 02				17 32	17 32		18 02	18 02	
Stratford International	a	15 44		16 14	16 14				16 44	16 44		17 14	17 14				17 44	17 44		18 14	18 14	
St Pancras Intl.	a	15 52		16 21	16 22				16 51	16 52		17 21	17 22				17 51	17 52		18 21	18 22	

A not 26 August
B 🛒 from Ashford International
C not from 2 September until 9 September

Table 207

Margate, Ramsgate, Canterbury West, Dover, Folkestone, Ashford International - Tonbridge and London

Sundays

26 August to 9 September

Network Diagram - see first Page of Table 206

		SE ■ A ⚒	SE ■ A ⚒	SE B	SE C	SE ■ A ⚒	SE B	SE C	SE	SE ■	SE ■	SE B	SE C	SE ■	SE B	SE C	SE	SE ■	SE B	SE C	SE ■	SE B	SE C
Margate ■	d						17 53	17 53							18 53	18 53						19 53	19 53
Broadstairs	d						17 59	17 59							18 59	18 59						19 59	19 59
Ramsgate ■	d	16 50				17 40	18 05	18 05		17 50				18 40	19 05	19 05		18 50			19 40	20 05	20 05
Minster ■	d					17 46								18 46							19 46		
Sandwich	d	17 02								18 02								19 02					
Deal	d	17 08								18 08								19 08					
Walmer	d	17 11								18 11								19 11					
Martin Mill	d	17 16								18 16								19 16					
Dover Priory ■	a	17 24								18 24								19 24					
	d	17 24		17 44	17 44					18 24		18 44	18 44					19 24	19 44	19 44			
Folkestone Central	d	17 36		17 56	17 56					18 36		18 56	18 56					19 36	19 56	19 56			
Folkestone West	d	17 38		17 58	17 58					18 38		18 58	18 58					19 38	19 58	19 58			
Sandling	d	17 43								18 43								19 43					
Westenhanger	d	17 46								18 46								19 46					
Sturry	d					17 58								18 58							19 58		
Canterbury West ■	d		17 36			18 07	18 25	18 25			18 36			19 04	19 25	19 25					20 04	20 25	20 25
Chartham	d		17 41								18 41			19 09							20 09		
Chilham	d		17 44								18 44			19 12							20 12		
Wye	d		17 51			18 19					18 51			19 19							20 19		
Ashford International	a	17 55	17 58	18 11	18 11	18 25	18 41	18 41		18 55	18 58	19 11	19 11	19 25	19 41	19 41		19 55	20 11	20 11	20 25	20 41	20 41
	d		18 03	18 13	18 13	18 33	18 43	18 43			19 03	19 13	19 14	19 33	19 43	19 43		20 03	20 13	20 13	20 33	20 43	20 47
Pluckley	d					18 39								19 39							20 39		
Headcorn	d		18 14			18 46					19 14			19 46				20 14			20 46		
Staplehurst	d		18 19			18 51					19 19			19 51				20 19			20 51		
Marden	d		18 23			18 55					19 23			19 55				20 23			20 55		
Maidstone West ■ 194	d								19 03								20 03						
Paddock Wood ■	d		18 29			19 01			19a22		19 29			20 01			20a22	20 29			21 01		
Tonbridge ■	a		18 38			19 09					19 38			20 09				20 38			21 09		
	d		18 38			19 10					19 38			20 10				20 38			21 10		
Sevenoaks ■	a		18 48			19 18					19 48			20 18				20 48			21 18		
Orpington ■	a		18 57			19 27					19 57			20 27				20 57			21 27		
London Bridge ■ ⊖	a		19 13			19 43					20 13			20 43				21 13			21 43		
London Cannon Street ■ ⊖	a																						
London Waterloo (East) ■ ⊖	a		19 18			19 48					20 18			20 48				21 18			21 48		
London Charing Cross ■ ⊖	a		19 22			19 52					20 22			20 52				21 22			21 52		
Ebbsfleet International	a			18 32	18 32		19 02	19 02				19 32	19 34		20 02	20 02			20 32	20 32		21 02	21 06
Stratford International ⊖	a			18 44	18 44		19 14	19 14				19 44	19 45		20 14	20 14			20 44	20 44		21 14	21 18
St Pancras Intl. ■ ⊖	a			18 51	18 52		19 21	19 22				19 51	19 52		20 21	20 22			20 51	20 52		21 21	21 26

		SE	SE ■	SE B	SE C	SE ■	SE B	SE C	SE	SE ■	SE B	SE C	SE ■	SE B	SE C	SE ■
Margate ■	d						20 53	20 53						21 53	21 53	
Broadstairs	d						20 59	20 59						21 59	21 59	
Ramsgate ■	d		19 50			20 40	21 05	21 05		20 50			21 40	22 05	22 05	21 50
Minster ■	d					20 46							21 46			
Sandwich	d		20 02							21 02						22 02
Deal	d		20 08							21 08						22 08
Walmer	d		20 11							21 11						22 11
Martin Mill	d		20 16							21 16						22 16
Dover Priory ■	a		20 24							21 24						22 24
	d		20 24	20 44	20 44					21 24	21 44	21 44				22 24
Folkestone Central	d		20 36	20 56	20 56					21 36	21 56	21 56				22 36
Folkestone West	d		20 38	20 58	20 58					21 38	21 58	21 58				22 38
Sandling	d		20 43							21 43						22 43
Westenhanger	d		20 46							21 46						22 46
Sturry	d					20 58							21 58			
Canterbury West ■	d					21 04	21 25	21 25					22 04	22 25	22 25	
Chartham	d					21 09							22 09			
Chilham	d					21 12							22 12			
Wye	d					21 19							22 19			
Ashford International	a		20 55	21 11	21 11	21 25	21 41	21 41		21 55	22 11	22 11	22 25	22 41	22 41	22 55
	d		21 03	21 13	21 13	21 33	21 43	21 43		22 03	22 13	22 13		22 43	22 43	
Pluckley	d					21 39										
Headcorn	d		21 14			21 46				22 14						
Staplehurst	d		21 19			21 51				22 19						
Marden	d		21 23			21 55				22 23						
Maidstone West ■ 194	d	21 03							22 03							
Paddock Wood ■	d	21a22	21 29			22 01			22 23	22 29						
Tonbridge ■	a		21 38			22 09			22 32	22 38						
	d		21 38			22 10				22 38						
Sevenoaks ■	a		21 48			22 18				22 48						
Orpington ■	a		21 57			22 27				22 57						
London Bridge ■ ⊖	a		22 13			22 43				23 13						
London Cannon Street ■ ⊖	a															
London Waterloo (East) ■ ⊖	a		22 18			22 48				23 18						
London Charing Cross ■ ⊖	a		22 22			22 52				23 22						
Ebbsfleet International	a			21 32	21 32		22 02	22 02			22 32	22 32		23 02	23 02	
Stratford International ⊖	a			21 44	21 44		22 14	22 14			22 44	22 44		23 14	23 14	
St Pancras Intl. ■ ⊖	a			21 51	21 52		22 21	22 22			22 51	22 52		23 21	23 22	

A ⚒ from Ashford International   B not from 2 September until 9 September   C not 26 August

Table 208

Strood - Maidstone West and Paddock Wood

Mondays to Fridays

until 27 July, 13 Aug to 28 Aug and from 10 Sep

Network Diagram - see first Page of Table 206

Miles			SE	SE	SE	SE A	SE B	SE C	SE	SE	SE	SE	SE	SE	SE	SE	SE	SE	SE	SE B	SE A	SE	SE
0	St Pancras International	d						06 25															
5¼	Stratford International	d						06 32															
22	Ebbsfleet International	d						06 42															
25	Gravesend	d						06 46															
33	Strood ■	d	04 55	05 33	06 03	06 35	06 37	06 57	07 18	07 55	08 35	09 05	09 35	10 05	10 35	11 05	11 35	12 05	12 35	13 05	13 06	13 35	14 05
35¼	Cuxton	d	04 59	05 37	06 07	06 39	06 41		07 22	07 59	08 39	09 09	09 39	10 09	10 39	11 09	11 39	12 09	12 39	13 09	13 09	13 39	14 09
37	Halling	d	05 02	05 40	06 10	06 42	06 44		07 25	08 02	08 42	09 12	09 42	10 12	10 42	11 12	11 42	12 12	12 42	13 12	13 12	13 42	14 12
38½	Snodland	d	05 05	05 43	06 13	06 45	06 47		07 28	08 05	08 45	09 15	09 45	10 15	10 45	11 15	11 45	12 15	12 45	13 15	13 15	13 45	14 15
39¾	New Hythe	d	05 08	05 46	06 16	06 48	06 50		07 31	08 08	08 48	09 18	09 48	10 18	10 48	11 18	11 48	12 18	12 48	13 18	13 18	13 48	14 18
40¾	Aylesford	d	05 10	05 48	06 18	06 50	06 52		07 33	08 10	08 50	09 20	09 50	10 20	10 50	11 20	11 50	12 20	12 50	13 20	13 20	13 50	14 20
43¾	Maidstone Barracks	d	05 15	05 53	06 23	06 55	06 58		07 38	08 15	08 55	09 25	09 55	10 25	10 55	11 25	11 55	12 25	12 55	13 25	13 25	13 55	14 25
44¼	Maidstone West ■ 194	a	05 17	05 55	06 25	07 00	07 00	07 12	07 40	08 17	08 57	09 27	09 57	10 27	10 57	11 27	11 57	12 27	12 57	13 27	13 27	13 57	14 27
—		d	05 18	05 56	06 26	07 01	07 01		07 41	08 18		09 28		10 28		11 28		12 28		13 28	13 28		14 28
46	East Farleigh	d	05 21	05 59	06 29	07 04	07 04		07 44	08 21		09 31		10 31		11 31		12 31		13 31	13 31		14 31
49	Wateringbury	d	05 26	06 04	06 34	07 09	07 09		07 49	08 26		09 36		10 36		11 36		12 36		13 36	13 36		14 36
50¾	Yalding	d	05 30	06 08	06 38	07 13	07 13		07 53	08 30		09 40		10 40		11 40		12 40		13 40	13 40		14 40
52¼	Beltring	d	05 33	06 11	06 41	07 16	07 16		07 56	08 33		09 43		10 43		11 43		12 43		13 43	13 43		14 43
54¼	Paddock Wood ■	a	05 37	06 15	06 45	07 20	07 20		08 00	08 37		09 47		10 47		11 47		12 47		13 47	13 47		14 47
59½	Tonbridge ■	a								08 45		09 57		10 55		11 55		12 58		13 55	13 56		14 55

		SE	SE	SE	SE B	SE A	SE	SE	SE C	SE	SE C	SE	SE C	SE	SE	SE	SE	SE	SE	SE	SE
St Pancras International	d								17 14		17 44		18 14								
Stratford International	d								17 21		17 51		18 21								
Ebbsfleet International	d																				
Gravesend	d								17 36		18 06		18 38								
Strood ■	d	14 35	15 05	15 35	16 10	16 11	16 35	17 05	17 46	17 55	18 18	18 25	18 49	18 55	19 35	20 05	20 35	21 05	21 35	22 05	22 35
Cuxton	d	14 39	15 09	15 39	16 14	16 14	16 39	17 09		17 59		18 29		18 59	19 39	20 09	20 39	21 09	21 39	22 09	22 39
Halling	d	14 42	15 12	15 42	16 17	16 17	16 42	17 12		18 02		18 32		19 02	19 42	20 12	20 42	21 12	21 42	22 12	22 42
Snodland	d	14 45	15 15	15 45	16 20	16 20	16 45	17 15		18 05		18 35		19 05	19 45	20 15	20 45	21 15	21 45	22 15	22 45
New Hythe	d	14 48	15 18	15 48	16 23	16 23	16 48	17 18		18 08		18 38		19 08	19 48	20 18	20 48	21 18	21 48	22 18	22 48
Aylesford	d	14 50	15 20	15 50	16 25	16 25	16 50	17 20		18 10		18 40		19 10	19 50	20 20	20 50	21 20	21 50	22 20	22 50
Maidstone Barracks	d	14 55	15 25	15 55	16 30	16 30	16 55	17 25		18 15		18 45		19 15	19 55	20 25	20 55	21 25	21 55	22 25	22 55
Maidstone West ■ 194	a	14 57	15 27	15 57	16 32	16 32	16 57	17 27	18 02	18 17	18 32	18 47	19 05	19 17	19 57	20 27	20 57	21 27	21 57	22 27	22 57
	d		15 28		16 33	16 33	16 58	17 28		18 18		18 48		19 18	19 58		20 58		21 58		
East Farleigh	d		15 31		16 36	16 36	17 01	17 31		18 21		18 51		19 21	20 01		21 01		22 01		
Wateringbury	d		15 36		16 41	16 41	17 06	17 36		18 26		18 56		19 26	20 06		21 06		22 06		
Yalding	d		15 40		16 45	16 45	17 10	17 40		18 30		19 00		19 30	20 10		21 10		22 10		
Beltring	d		15 43		16 48	16 48	17 13	17 43		18 33		19 03		19 33	20 13		21 13		22 13		
Paddock Wood ■	a		15 47		16 52	16 53	17 17	17 47		18 37		19 07		19 37	20 17		21 17		22 17		
Tonbridge ■	a		15 55												20 25		21 25		22 25		

Mondays to Fridays

30 July to 10 August

		SE	SE	SE	SE	SE	SE	SE	SE	SE	SE	SE	SE	SE	SE	SE	SE	SE	SE	SE	SE	SE	SE
St Pancras International	d																						
Stratford International	d																						
Ebbsfleet International	d																						
Gravesend	d																						
Strood ■	d	04 55	05 33	06 03	06 37	07 18	07 55	08 35	09 05	09 35	10 05	10 35	11 05	11 35	12 05	12 35	13 05	13 35	14 05	14 35	15 05	15 35	16 10
Cuxton	d	04 59	05 37	06 07	06 41	07 22	07 59	08 39	09 09	09 39	10 09	10 39	11 09	11 39	12 09	12 39	13 09	13 39	14 09	14 39	15 09	15 39	16 14
Halling	d	05 02	05 40	06 10	06 44	07 25	08 02	08 42	09 12	09 42	10 12	10 42	11 12	11 42	12 12	12 42	13 12	13 42	14 12	14 42	15 12	15 42	16 17
Snodland	d	05 05	05 43	06 13	06 47	07 28	08 05	08 45	09 15	09 45	10 15	10 45	11 15	11 45	12 15	12 45	13 15	13 45	14 15	14 45	15 15	15 45	16 20
New Hythe	d	05 08	05 46	06 16	06 50	07 31	08 08	08 48	09 18	09 48	10 18	10 48	11 18	11 48	12 18	12 48	13 18	13 48	14 18	14 48	15 18	15 48	16 23
Aylesford	d	05 10	05 48	06 18	06 52	07 33	08 10	08 50	09 20	09 50	10 20	10 50	11 20	11 50	12 20	12 50	13 20	13 50	14 20	14 50	15 20	15 50	16 25
Maidstone Barracks	d	05 15	05 53	06 23	06 58	07 38	08 15	08 55	09 25	09 55	10 25	10 55	11 25	11 55	12 25	12 55	13 25	13 55	14 25	14 55	15 25	15 55	16 30
Maidstone West ■ 194	a	05 17	05 55	06 25	07 00	07 40	08 17	08 57	09 27	09 57	10 27	10 57	11 27	11 57	12 27	12 57	13 27	13 57	14 27	14 57	15 27	15 57	16 32
	d	05 18	05 56	06 26	07 01	07 41	08 18		09 28		10 28		11 28		12 28		13 28		14 28		15 28		16 33
East Farleigh	d	05 21	05 59	06 29	07 04	07 44	08 21		09 31		10 31		11 31		12 31		13 31		14 31		15 31		16 36
Wateringbury	d	05 26	06 04	06 34	07 09	07 49	08 26		09 36		10 36		11 36		12 36		13 36		14 36		15 36		16 41
Yalding	d	05 30	06 08	06 38	07 13	07 53	08 30		09 40		10 40		11 40		12 40		13 40		14 40		15 40		16 45
Beltring	d	05 33	06 11	06 41	07 16	07 56	08 33		09 43		10 43		11 43		12 43		13 43		14 43		15 43		16 48
Paddock Wood ■	a	05 37	06 15	06 45	07 20	08 00	08 37		09 47		10 47		11 47		12 47		13 47		14 47		15 47		16 52
Tonbridge ■	a						08 45		09 57		10 55		11 55		12 58		13 55		14 55		15 55		

		SE	SE	SE	SE	SE	SE	SE	SE	SE	SE	SE	SE
St Pancras International	d												
Stratford International	d												
Ebbsfleet International	d												
Gravesend	d												
Strood ■	d	16 35	17 05	17 55	18 25	18 55	19 35	20 05	20 35	21 05	21 35	22 05	22 35
Cuxton	d	16 39	17 09	17 59	18 29	18 59	19 39	20 09	20 39	21 09	21 39	22 09	22 39
Halling	d	16 42	17 12	18 02	18 32	19 02	19 42	20 12	20 42	21 12	21 42	22 12	22 42
Snodland	d	16 45	17 15	18 05	18 35	19 05	19 45	20 15	20 45	21 15	21 45	22 15	22 45
New Hythe	d	16 48	17 18	18 08	18 38	19 08	19 48	20 18	20 48	21 18	21 48	22 18	22 48
Aylesford	d	16 50	17 20	18 10	18 40	19 10	19 50	20 20	20 50	21 20	21 50	22 20	22 50
Maidstone Barracks	d	16 55	17 25	18 15	18 45	19 15	19 55	20 25	20 55	21 25	21 55	22 25	22 55
Maidstone West ■ 194	a	16 57	17 27	18 17	18 47	19 17	19 57	20 27	20 57	21 27	21 57	22 27	22 57
	d	16 58	17 28	18 18	18 48	19 18	19 58		20 58		21 58		
East Farleigh	d	17 01	17 31	18 21	18 51	19 21	20 01		21 01		22 01		
Wateringbury	d	17 06	17 36	18 26	18 56	19 26	20 06		21 06		22 06		
Yalding	d	17 10	17 40	18 30	19 00	19 30	20 10		21 10		22 10		
Beltring	d	17 13	17 43	18 33	19 03	19 33	20 13		21 13		22 13		
Paddock Wood ■	a	17 17	17 47	18 37	19 07	19 37	20 17		21 17		22 17		
Tonbridge ■	a						20 25		21 25		22 25		

A until 18 May   B from 21 May until 27 July   C not 27 July

Table 208

Strood - Maidstone West and Paddock Wood

Mondays to Fridays

29 August to 7 September

Network Diagram - see first Page of Table 206

			SE	SE	SE	SE	SE	SE	SE	SE	SE	SE	SE	SE	SE	SE	SE	SE	SE	SE	SE	SE	SE	SE
St Pancras International		d					06 24		06 44															
Stratford International		d					06 32		06 58															
Ebbsfleet International		d					06 42																	
Gravesend		d					06 46																	
Strood		d	04 55	05 33	06 03	06 37	06 57	07 18	07 25	07 55	08 35	09 05	09 35	10 05	10 35	11 05	11 35	12 05	12 35	13 05	13 35	14 05	14 35	15 05
Cuxton		d	04 59	05 37	06 07	06 41		07 22		07 59	08 39	09 09	09 39	10 09	10 39	11 09	11 39	12 09	12 39	13 09	13 39	14 09	14 39	15 09
Halling		d	05 02	05 40	06 10	06 44		07 25		08 02	08 42	09 12	09 42	10 12	10 42	11 12	11 42	12 12	12 42	13 12	13 42	14 12	14 42	15 12
Snodland		d	05 05	05 43	06 13	06 47		07 28		08 05	08 45	09 15	09 45	10 15	10 45	11 15	11 45	12 15	12 45	13 15	13 45	14 15	14 45	15 15
New Hythe		d	05 08	05 46	06 16	06 50		07 31		08 08	08 48	09 18	09 48	10 18	10 48	11 18	11 48	12 18	12 48	13 18	13 48	14 18	14 48	15 18
Aylesford		d	05 10	05 48	06 18	06 52		07 33		08 10	08 50	09 20	09 50	10 20	10 50	11 20	11 50	12 20	12 50	13 20	13 50	14 20	14 50	15 20
Maidstone Barracks		d	05 15	05 53	06 23	06 58		07 38		08 15	08 55	09 25	09 55	10 25	10 55	11 25	11 55	12 25	12 55	13 25	13 55	14 25	14 55	15 25
Maidstone West	194	a	05 17	05 55	06 25	07 00	07 12	07 40	07 45	08 17	08 57	09 27	09 57	10 27	10 57	11 27	11 57	12 27	12 57	13 27	13 57	14 27	14 57	15 27
		d	05 18	05 56	06 26	07 01		07 41		08 18		09 28		10 28		11 28		12 28		13 28		14 28		15 28
East Farleigh		d	05 21	05 59	06 29	07 04		07 44		08 21		09 31		10 31		11 31		12 31		13 31		14 31		15 31
Wateringbury		d	05 26	06 04	06 34	07 09		07 49		08 26		09 36		10 36		11 36		12 36		13 36		14 36		15 36
Yalding		d	05 30	06 08	06 38	07 13		07 53		08 30		09 40		10 40		11 40		12 40		13 40		14 40		15 40
Beltring		d	05 33	06 11	06 41	07 16		07 56		08 33		09 43		10 43		11 43		12 43		13 43		14 43		15 43
Paddock Wood		a	05 37	06 15	06 45	07 20		08 00		08 37		09 47		10 47		11 47		12 47		13 47		14 47		15 47
Tonbridge		a								08 45		09 57		10 55		11 55		12 58		13 55		14 55		15 55

			SE	SE	SE	SE	SE	SE	SE	SE	SE	SE	SE	SE	SE	SE	SE	SE	SE
St Pancras International		d					17 14		17 44		18 14								
Stratford International		d					17 22		17 52		18 22								
Ebbsfleet International		d																	
Gravesend		d					17 36		18 06		18 38								
Strood		d	15 35	16 10	16 35	17 05	17 46	17 55	18 18	18 25	18 49	18 55	19 35	20 05	20 35	21 05	21 35	22 05	22 35
Cuxton		d	15 39	16 14	16 39	17 09		17 59		18 29		18 59	19 39	20 09	20 39	21 09	21 39	22 09	22 39
Halling		d	15 42	16 17	16 42	17 12		18 02		18 32		19 02	19 42	20 12	20 42	21 12	21 42	22 12	22 42
Snodland		d	15 45	16 20	16 45	17 15		18 05		18 35		19 05	19 45	20 15	20 45	21 15	21 45	22 15	22 45
New Hythe		d	15 48	16 23	16 48	17 18		18 08		18 38		19 08	19 48	20 18	20 48	21 18	21 48	22 18	22 48
Aylesford		d	15 50	16 25	16 50	17 20		18 10		18 40		19 10	19 50	20 20	20 50	21 20	21 50	22 20	22 50
Maidstone Barracks		d	15 55	16 30	16 55	17 25		18 15		18 45		19 15	19 55	20 25	20 55	21 25	21 55	22 25	22 55
Maidstone West	194	a	15 57	16 32	16 57	17 27	18 02	18 17	18 32	18 47	19 05	19 17	19 57	20 27	20 57	21 27	21 57	22 27	22 57
		d		16 33	16 58	17 28		18 18		18 48		19 18	19 58		20 58		21 58		
East Farleigh		d		16 36	17 01	17 31		18 21		18 51		19 21	20 01		21 01		22 01		
Wateringbury		d		16 41	17 06	17 36		18 26		18 56		19 26	20 06		21 06		22 06		
Yalding		d		16 45	17 10	17 40		18 30		19 00		19 30	20 10		21 10		22 10		
Beltring		d		16 48	17 13	17 43		18 33		19 03		19 33	20 13		21 13		22 13		
Paddock Wood		a		16 52	17 17	17 47		18 37		19 07		19 37	20 17		21 17		22 17		
Tonbridge		a											20 25		21 25		22 25		

Saturdays

until 21 July, 18 Aug and from 15 Sep

			SE	SE	SE	SE	SE	SE	SE	SE	SE	SE	SE	SE	SE	SE	SE	SE	SE	SE	SE	SE	SE	SE
St Pancras International		d																						
Stratford International		d																						
Ebbsfleet International		d																						
Gravesend		d																						
Strood		d	06 05	06 35	07 05	07 35	08 05	08 35	09 05	09 35	10 05	10 35	11 05	11 35	12 05	12 35	13 05	13 35	14 05	14 35	15 05	15 35	16 05	16 35
Cuxton		d	06 09	06 39	07 09	07 39	08 09	08 39	09 09	09 39	10 09	10 39	11 09	11 39	12 09	12 39	13 09	13 39	14 09	14 39	15 09	15 39	16 09	16 39
Halling		d	06 12	06 42	07 12	07 42	08 12	08 42	09 12	09 42	10 12	10 42	11 12	11 42	12 12	12 42	13 12	13 42	14 12	14 42	15 12	15 42	16 12	16 42
Snodland		d	06 15	06 45	07 15	07 45	08 15	08 45	09 15	09 45	10 15	10 45	11 15	11 45	12 15	12 45	13 15	13 45	14 15	14 45	15 15	15 45	16 15	16 45
New Hythe		d	06 18	06 48	07 18	07 48	08 18	08 48	09 18	09 48	10 18	10 48	11 18	11 48	12 18	12 48	13 18	13 48	14 18	14 48	15 18	15 48	16 18	16 48
Aylesford		d	06 20	06 50	07 20	07 50	08 20	08 50	09 20	09 50	10 20	10 50	11 20	11 50	12 20	12 50	13 20	13 50	14 20	14 50	15 20	15 50	16 20	16 50
Maidstone Barracks		d	06 25	06 55	07 25	07 55	08 25	08 55	09 25	09 55	10 25	10 55	11 25	11 55	12 25	12 55	13 25	13 55	14 25	14 55	15 25	15 55	16 25	16 55
Maidstone West	194	a	06 27	06 57	07 27	07 57	08 27	08 57	09 27	09 57	10 27	10 57	11 27	11 57	12 27	12 57	13 27	13 57	14 27	14 57	15 27	15 57	16 27	16 57
		d	06 28		07 28		08 28		09 28		10 28		11 28		12 28		13 28		14 28		15 28		16 28	
East Farleigh		d	06 31		07 31		08 31		09 31		10 31		11 31		12 31		13 31		14 31		15 31		16 31	
Wateringbury		d	06 36		07 36		08 36		09 36		10 36		11 36		12 36		13 36		14 36		15 36		16 36	
Yalding		d	06 40		07 40		08 40		09 40		10 40		11 40		12 40		13 40		14 40		15 40		16 40	
Beltring		d	06 43		07 43		08 43		09 43		10 43		11 43		12 43		13 43		14 43		15 43		16 43	
Paddock Wood		a	06 47		07 47		08 47		09 47		10 47		11 47		12 47		13 47		14 47		15 47		16 47	
Tonbridge		a	06 55		07 55		08 55		09 55		10 55		11 55		12 55		13 55		14 55		15 55		16 55	

			SE	SE	SE	SE	SE	SE	SE	SE	SE	SE	SE	SE
St Pancras International		d												
Stratford International		d												
Ebbsfleet International		d												
Gravesend		d												
Strood		d	17 05	17 35	18 05	18 35	19 05	19 35	20 05	20 35	21 05	21 35	22 05	22 35
Cuxton		d	17 09	17 39	18 09	18 39	19 09	19 39	20 09	20 39	21 09	21 39	22 09	22 39
Halling		d	17 12	17 42	18 12	18 42	19 12	19 42	20 12	20 42	21 12	21 42	22 12	22 42
Snodland		d	17 15	17 45	18 15	18 45	19 15	19 45	20 15	20 45	21 15	21 45	22 15	22 45
New Hythe		d	17 18	17 48	18 18	18 48	19 18	19 48	20 18	20 48	21 18	21 48	22 18	22 48
Aylesford		d	17 20	17 50	18 20	18 50	19 20	19 50	20 20	20 50	21 20	21 50	22 20	22 50
Maidstone Barracks		d	17 25	17 55	18 25	18 55	19 25	19 55	20 25	20 55	21 25	21 55	22 25	22 55
Maidstone West	194	a	17 27	17 57	18 27	18 57	19 27	19 57	20 27	20 57	21 27	21 57	22 27	22 57
		d	17 28		18 28		19 28		20 28		21 28		22 28	
East Farleigh		d	17 31		18 31		19 31		20 31		21 31		22 31	
Wateringbury		d	17 36		18 36		19 36		20 36		21 36		22 36	
Yalding		d	17 40		18 40		19 40		20 40		21 40		22 40	
Beltring		d	17 43		18 43		19 43		20 43		21 43		22 43	
Paddock Wood		a	17 47		18 47		19 47		20 47		21 47		22 47	
Tonbridge		a	17 55		18 55		19 55		20 55		21 55		22 55	

Table 208

Strood - Maidstone West and Paddock Wood

Saturdays

28 July to 11 August

Network Diagram - see first Page of Table 206

			SE	SE	SE	SE	SE	SE	SE	SE	SE	SE	SE	SE	SE	SE	SE	SE	SE	SE	SE	SE	SE	SE
St Pancras International		d																						
Stratford International		d																						
Ebbsfleet International		d																						
Gravesend		d																						
Strood		d	06 05	06 35	07 05	07 35	08 05	08 35	09 05	09 35	10 05	10 35	11 05	11 35	12 05	12 35	13 05	13 35	14 05	14 35	15 05	15 35	16 05	16 35
Cuxton		d	06 09	06 39	07 09	07 39	08 09	08 39	09 09	09 39	10 09	10 39	11 09	11 39	12 09	12 39	13 09	13 39	14 09	14 39	15 09	15 39	16 09	16 39
Halling		d	06 12	06 42	07 12	07 42	08 12	08 42	09 12	09 42	10 12	10 42	11 12	11 42	12 12	12 42	13 12	13 42	14 12	14 42	15 12	15 42	16 12	16 42
Snodland		d	06 15	06 45	07 15	07 45	08 15	08 45	09 15	09 45	10 15	10 45	11 15	11 45	12 15	12 45	13 15	13 45	14 15	14 45	15 15	15 45	16 15	16 45
New Hythe		d	06 18	06 48	07 18	07 48	08 18	08 48	09 18	09 48	10 18	10 48	11 18	11 48	12 18	12 48	13 18	13 48	14 18	14 48	15 18	15 48	16 18	16 48
Aylesford		d	06 20	06 50	07 20	07 50	08 20	08 50	09 20	09 50	10 20	10 50	11 20	11 50	12 20	12 50	13 20	13 50	14 20	14 50	15 20	15 50	16 20	16 50
Maidstone Barracks		d	06 25	06 55	07 25	07 55	08 25	08 55	09 25	09 55	10 25	10 55	11 25	11 55	12 25	12 55	13 25	13 55	14 25	14 55	15 25	15 55	16 25	16 55
Maidstone West	194	a	06 27	06 57	07 27	07 57	08 27	08 57	09 27	09 57	10 27	10 57	11 27	11 57	12 27	12 57	13 27	13 57	14 27	14 57	15 27	15 57	16 27	16 57
		d	06 28		07 28		08 28		09 28		10 28		11 28		12 28		13 28		14 28		15 28		16 28	
East Farleigh		d	06 31		07 31		08 31		09 31		10 31		11 31		12 31		13 31		14 31		15 31		16 31	
Wateringbury		d	06 36		07 36		08 36		09 36		10 36		11 36		12 36		13 36		14 36		15 36		16 36	
Yalding		d	06 40		07 40		08 40		09 40		10 40		11 40		12 40		13 40		14 40		15 40		16 40	
Beltring		d	06 43		07 43		08 43		09 43		10 43		11 43		12 43		13 43		14 43		15 43		16 43	
Paddock Wood		a	06 47		07 47		08 47		09 47		10 47		11 47		12 47		13 47		14 47		15 47		16 47	
Tonbridge		a	06 55		07 55		08 55		09 55		10 55		11 55		12 55		13 55		14 55		15 55		16 55	

			SE	SE	SE	SE	SE	SE	SE	SE	SE	SE	SE	SE
St Pancras International		d												
Stratford International		d												
Ebbsfleet International		d												
Gravesend		d												
Strood		d	17 05	17 35	18 05	18 35	19 05	19 35	20 05	20 35	21 05	21 35	22 05	22 35
Cuxton		d	17 09	17 39	18 09	18 39	19 09	19 39	20 09	20 39	21 09	21 39	22 09	22 39
Halling		d	17 12	17 42	18 12	18 42	19 12	19 42	20 12	20 42	21 12	21 42	22 12	22 42
Snodland		d	17 15	17 45	18 15	18 45	19 15	19 45	20 15	20 45	21 15	21 45	22 15	22 45
New Hythe		d	17 18	17 48	18 18	18 48	19 18	19 48	20 18	20 48	21 18	21 48	22 18	22 48
Aylesford		d	17 20	17 50	18 20	18 50	19 20	19 50	20 20	20 50	21 20	21 50	22 20	22 50
Maidstone Barracks		d	17 25	17 55	18 25	18 55	19 25	19 55	20 25	20 55	21 25	21 55	22 25	22 55
Maidstone West	194	a	17 27	17 57	18 27	18 57	19 27	19 57	20 27	20 57	21 27	21 57	22 27	22 57
		d	17 28		18 28		19 28		20 28		21 28		22 28	
East Farleigh		d	17 31		18 31		19 31		20 31		21 31		22 31	
Wateringbury		d	17 36		18 36		19 36		20 36		21 36		22 36	
Yalding		d	17 40		18 40		19 40		20 40		21 40		22 40	
Beltring		d	17 43		18 43		19 43		20 43		21 43		22 43	
Paddock Wood		a	17 47		18 47		19 47		20 47		21 47		22 47	
Tonbridge		a	17 55		18 55		19 55		20 55		21 55		22 55	

Saturdays

25 August to 8 September

			SE	SE	SE	SE	SE	SE	SE	SE	SE	SE	SE	SE	SE	SE	SE	SE	SE	SE	SE	SE	SE	SE
St Pancras International		d																						
Stratford International		d																						
Ebbsfleet International		d																						
Gravesend		d																						
Strood		d	06 05	06 35	07 05	07 35	08 05	08 35	09 05	09 35	10 05	10 35	11 05	11 35	12 05	12 35	13 05	13 35	14 05	14 35	15 05	15 35	16 05	16 35
Cuxton		d	06 09	06 39	07 09	07 39	08 09	08 39	09 09	09 39	10 09	10 39	11 09	11 39	12 09	12 39	13 09	13 39	14 09	14 39	15 09	15 39	16 09	16 39
Halling		d	06 12	06 42	07 12	07 42	08 12	08 42	09 12	09 42	10 12	10 42	11 12	11 42	12 12	12 42	13 12	13 42	14 12	14 42	15 12	15 42	16 12	16 42
Snodland		d	06 15	06 45	07 15	07 45	08 15	08 45	09 15	09 45	10 15	10 45	11 15	11 45	12 15	12 45	13 15	13 45	14 15	14 45	15 15	15 45	16 15	16 45
New Hythe		d	06 18	06 48	07 18	07 48	08 18	08 48	09 18	09 48	10 18	10 48	11 18	11 48	12 18	12 48	13 18	13 48	14 18	14 48	15 18	15 48	16 18	16 48
Aylesford		d	06 20	06 50	07 20	07 50	08 20	08 50	09 20	09 50	10 20	10 50	11 20	11 50	12 20	12 50	13 20	13 50	14 20	14 50	15 20	15 50	16 20	16 50
Maidstone Barracks		d	06 25	06 55	07 25	07 55	08 25	08 55	09 25	09 55	10 25	10 55	11 25	11 55	12 25	12 55	13 25	13 55	14 25	14 55	15 25	15 55	16 25	16 55
Maidstone West	194	a	06 27	06 57	07 27	07 57	08 27	08 57	09 27	09 57	10 27	10 57	11 27	11 57	12 27	12 57	13 27	13 57	14 27	14 57	15 27	15 57	16 27	16 57
		d	06 28		07 28		08 28		09 28		10 28		11 28		12 28		13 28		14 28		15 28		16 28	
East Farleigh		d	06 31		07 31		08 31		09 31		10 31		11 31		12 31		13 31		14 31		15 31		16 31	
Wateringbury		d	06 36		07 36		08 36		09 36		10 36		11 36		12 36		13 36		14 36		15 36		16 36	
Yalding		d	06 40		07 40		08 40		09 40		10 40		11 40		12 40		13 40		14 40		15 40		16 40	
Beltring		d	06 43		07 43		08 43		09 43		10 43		11 43		12 43		13 43		14 43		15 43		16 43	
Paddock Wood		a	06 47		07 47		08 47		09 47		10 47		11 47		12 47		13 47		14 47		15 47		16 47	
Tonbridge		a	06 55		07 55		08 55		09 55		10 55		11 55		12 55		13 55		14 55		15 55		16 55	

			SE	SE	SE	SE	SE	SE	SE	SE	SE	SE	SE	SE
St Pancras International		d												
Stratford International		d												
Ebbsfleet International		d												
Gravesend		d												
Strood		d	17 05	17 35	18 05	18 35	19 05	19 35	20 05	20 35	21 05	21 35	22 05	22 35
Cuxton		d	17 09	17 39	18 09	18 39	19 09	19 39	20 09	20 39	21 09	21 39	22 09	22 39
Halling		d	17 12	17 42	18 12	18 42	19 12	19 42	20 12	20 42	21 12	21 42	22 12	22 42
Snodland		d	17 15	17 45	18 15	18 45	19 15	19 45	20 15	20 45	21 15	21 45	22 15	22 45
New Hythe		d	17 18	17 48	18 18	18 48	19 18	19 48	20 18	20 48	21 18	21 48	22 18	22 48
Aylesford		d	17 20	17 50	18 20	18 50	19 20	19 50	20 20	20 50	21 20	21 50	22 20	22 50
Maidstone Barracks		d	17 25	17 55	18 25	18 55	19 25	19 55	20 25	20 55	21 25	21 55	22 25	22 55
Maidstone West	194	a	17 27	17 57	18 27	18 57	19 27	19 57	20 27	20 57	21 27	21 57	22 27	22 57
		d	17 28		18 28		19 28		20 28		21 28		22 28	
East Farleigh		d	17 31		18 31		19 31		20 31		21 31		22 31	
Wateringbury		d	17 36		18 36		19 36		20 36		21 36		22 36	
Yalding		d	17 40		18 40		19 40		20 40		21 40		22 40	
Beltring		d	17 43		18 43		19 43		20 43		21 43		22 43	
Paddock Wood		a	17 47		18 47		19 47		20 47		21 47		22 47	
Tonbridge		a	17 55		18 55		19 55		20 55		21 55		22 55	

Table 208

Strood - Maidstone West and Paddock Wood

Sundays

until 22 July, 19 Aug and from 16 Sep

Network Diagram - see first Page of Table 206

		SE	SE	SE	SE	SE	SE	SE	SE	SE	SE	SE	SE	SE	SE	SE	SE
St Pancras International	d																
Stratford International	d																
Ebbsfleet International	d																
Gravesend	d																
Strood ■	d	06 35	07 35	08 35	09 35	10 35	11 35	12 35	13 35	14 35	15 35	16 35	17 35	18 35	19 35	20 35	21 35
Cuxton	d	06 39	07 39	08 39	09 39	10 39	11 39	12 39	13 39	14 39	15 39	16 39	17 39	18 39	19 39	20 39	21 39
Halling	d	06 42	07 42	08 42	09 42	10 42	11 42	12 42	13 42	14 42	15 42	16 42	17 42	18 42	19 42	20 42	21 42
Snodland	d	06 45	07 45	08 45	09 45	10 45	11 45	12 45	13 45	14 45	15 45	16 45	17 45	18 45	19 45	20 45	21 45
New Hythe	d	06 48	07 48	08 48	09 48	10 48	11 48	12 48	13 48	14 48	15 48	16 48	17 48	18 48	19 48	20 48	21 48
Aylesford	d	06 50	07 50	08 50	09 50	10 50	11 50	12 50	13 50	14 50	15 50	16 50	17 50	18 50	19 50	20 50	21 50
Maidstone Barracks	d	06 55	07 55	08 55	09 55	10 55	11 55	12 55	13 55	14 55	15 55	16 55	17 55	18 55	19 55	20 55	21 55
Maidstone West ■ 194	a	06 57	07 57	08 57	09 57	10 57	11 57	12 57	13 57	14 57	15 57	16 57	17 57	18 57	19 57	20 57	21 57
	d	07 03	08 03	09 03	10 03	11 03	12 03	13 03	14 03	15 03	16 03	17 03	18 03	19 03	20 03	21 03	22 03
East Farleigh	d	07 07	08 07	09 07	10 07	11 07	12 07	13 07	14 07	15 07	16 07	17 07	18 07	19 07	20 07	21 07	22 07
Wateringbury	d	07 12	08 12	09 12	10 12	11 12	12 12	13 12	14 12	15 12	16 12	17 12	18 12	19 12	20 12	21 12	22 12
Yalding	d	07 15	08 15	09 15	10 15	11 15	12 15	13 15	14 15	15 15	16 15	17 15	18 15	19 15	20 15	21 15	22 15
Beltring	d	07 18	08 18	09 18	10 18	11 18	12 18	13 18	14 18	15 18	16 18	17 18	18 18	19 18	20 18	21 18	22 18
Paddock Wood ■	a	07 22	08 22	09 22	10 22	11 22	12 22	13 22	14 22	15 22	16 22	17 22	18 22	19 22	20 22	21 22	22 22
Tonbridge ■	a																22 32

Sundays

29 July to 12 August

		SE	SE	SE	SE	SE	SE	SE	SE	SE	SE	SE	SE	SE	SE	SE	SE	SE
St Pancras International	d																	
Stratford International	d																	
Ebbsfleet International	d																	
Gravesend	d																	
Strood ■	d		07 05	08 05	09 05	10 05	11 05	12 05	13 05	14 05	15 05	16 05	17 05	18 05	19 05	20 05	21 05	22 05
Cuxton	d		07 09	08 09	09 09	10 09	11 09	12 09	13 09	14 09	15 09	16 09	17 09	18 09	19 09	20 09	21 09	22 09
Halling	d		07 12	08 12	09 12	10 12	11 12	12 12	13 12	14 12	15 12	16 12	17 12	18 12	19 12	20 12	21 12	22 12
Snodland	d		07 15	08 15	09 15	10 15	11 15	12 15	13 15	14 15	15 15	16 15	17 15	18 15	19 15	20 15	21 15	22 15
New Hythe	d		07 18	08 18	09 18	10 18	11 18	12 18	13 18	14 18	15 18	16 18	17 18	18 18	19 18	20 18	21 18	22 18
Aylesford	d		07 20	08 20	09 20	10 20	11 20	12 20	13 20	14 20	15 20	16 20	17 20	18 20	19 20	20 20	21 20	22 20
Maidstone Barracks	d		07 25	08 25	09 25	10 25	11 25	12 25	13 25	14 25	15 25	16 25	17 25	18 25	19 25	20 25	21 25	22 25
Maidstone West ■ 194	a		07 27	08 27	09 27	10 27	11 27	12 27	13 27	14 27	15 27	16 27	17 27	18 27	19 27	20 27	21 27	22 27
	d	06 28	07 28	08 28	09 28	10 28	11 28	12 28	13 28	14 28	15 28	16 28	17 28	18 28	19 28	20 28	21 28	22 28
East Farleigh	d	06 31	07 31	08 31	09 31	10 31	11 31	12 31	13 31	14 31	15 31	16 31	17 31	18 31	19 31	20 31	21 31	22 31
Wateringbury	d	06 36	07 36	08 36	09 36	10 36	11 36	12 36	13 36	14 36	15 36	16 36	17 36	18 36	19 36	20 36	21 36	22 36
Yalding	d	06 40	07 40	08 40	09 40	10 40	11 40	12 40	13 40	14 40	15 40	16 40	17 40	18 40	19 40	20 40	21 40	22 40
Beltring	d	06 43	07 43	08 43	09 43	10 43	11 43	12 43	13 43	14 43	15 43	16 43	17 43	18 43	19 43	20 43	21 43	22 43
Paddock Wood ■	a	06 47	07 47	08 47	09 47	10 47	11 47	12 47	13 47	14 47	15 47	16 47	17 47	18 47	19 47	20 47	21 47	22 47
Tonbridge ■	a																	22 55

Sundays

26 August to 9 September

		SE	SE	SE	SE	SE	SE	SE	SE	SE	SE	SE	SE	SE	SE	SE	SE
St Pancras International	d																
Stratford International	d																
Ebbsfleet International	d																
Gravesend	d																
Strood ■	d	06 35	07 35	08 35	09 35	10 35	11 35	12 35	13 35	14 35	15 35	16 35	17 35	18 35	19 35	20 35	21 35
Cuxton	d	06 39	07 39	08 39	09 39	10 39	11 39	12 39	13 39	14 39	15 39	16 39	17 39	18 39	19 39	20 39	21 39
Halling	d	06 42	07 42	08 42	09 42	10 42	11 42	12 42	13 42	14 42	15 42	16 42	17 42	18 42	19 42	20 42	21 42
Snodland	d	06 45	07 45	08 45	09 45	10 45	11 45	12 45	13 45	14 45	15 45	16 45	17 45	18 45	19 45	20 45	21 45
New Hythe	d	06 48	07 48	08 48	09 48	10 48	11 48	12 48	13 48	14 48	15 48	16 48	17 48	18 48	19 48	20 48	21 48
Aylesford	d	06 50	07 50	08 50	09 50	10 50	11 50	12 50	13 50	14 50	15 50	16 50	17 50	18 50	19 50	20 50	21 50
Maidstone Barracks	d	06 55	07 55	08 55	09 55	10 55	11 55	12 55	13 55	14 55	15 55	16 55	17 55	18 55	19 55	20 55	21 55
Maidstone West ■ 194	a	06 57	07 57	08 57	09 57	10 57	11 57	12 57	13 57	14 57	15 57	16 57	17 57	18 57	19 57	20 57	21 57
	d	07 03	08 03	09 03	10 03	11 03	12 03	13 03	14 03	15 03	16 03	17 03	18 03	19 03	20 03	21 03	22 03
East Farleigh	d	07 07	08 07	09 07	10 07	11 07	12 07	13 07	14 07	15 07	16 07	17 07	18 07	19 07	20 07	21 07	22 07
Wateringbury	d	07 12	08 12	09 12	10 12	11 12	12 12	13 12	14 12	15 12	16 12	17 12	18 12	19 12	20 12	21 12	22 12
Yalding	d	07 15	08 15	09 15	10 15	11 15	12 15	13 15	14 15	15 15	16 15	17 15	18 15	19 15	20 15	21 15	22 15
Beltring	d	07 18	08 18	09 18	10 18	11 18	12 18	13 18	14 18	15 18	16 18	17 18	18 18	19 18	20 18	21 18	22 18
Paddock Wood ■	a	07 22	08 22	09 22	10 22	11 22	12 22	13 22	14 22	15 22	16 22	17 22	18 22	19 22	20 22	21 22	22 22
Tonbridge ■	a																22 32

Table 208

Paddock Wood and Maidstone West - Strood

Mondays to Fridays

until 27 July, 13 Aug to 28 Aug and from 10 Sep

Network Diagram - see first Page of Table 206

Miles			SE	SE	SE A	SE	SE A	SE A	SE	SE	SE	SE	SE	SE	SE	SE B	SE C	SE	SE	SE	SE	SE	SE
0	Tonbridge ■	d										09 03		10 03		11 03	11 04		12 03		13 03		14 03
5¼	**Paddock Wood** ■	d	05 42	06 20		06 50			07 40	08 10		09 10		10 10		11 10	11 11		12 10		13 10		14 10
7	Beltring	d	05 46	06 24		06 54			07 44	08 14		09 14		10 14		11 14	11 15		12 14		13 14		14 14
8¾	Yalding	d	05 49	06 27		06 57			07 48	08 18		09 18		10 18		11 18	11 19		12 18		13 18		14 18
10½	Wateringbury	d	05 52	06 30		07 00			07 51	08 21		09 21		10 21		11 21	11 22		12 21		13 21		14 21
13½	East Farleigh	d	05 56	06 34		07 04			07 55	08 25		09 25		10 25		11 25	11 26		12 25		13 25		14 25
15¼	**Maidstone West** ■ 194	a	06 01	06 39		07 09			07 59	08 29		09 29		10 29		11 30	11 30		12 29		13 29		14 29
—		d	06 02	06 40	06 56	07 10	07 26	07 56	08 02	08 32	09 02	09 32	10 02	10 32	11 02	11 32	11 32	12 02	12 32	13 02	13 32	14 02	14 32
15½	Maidstone Barracks	d	06 04	06 42		07 12			08 04	08 34	09 04	09 34	10 04	10 34	11 04	11 34	11 34	12 04	12 34	13 04	13 34	14 04	14 34
18¾	Aylesford	d	06 09	06 47		07 17			08 09	08 39	09 09	09 39	10 09	10 39	11 09	11 39	11 39	12 09	12 39	13 09	13 39	14 09	14 39
19½	New Hythe	d	06 11	06 49		07 19			08 11	08 41	09 11	09 41	10 11	10 41	11 11	11 41	11 41	12 11	12 41	13 11	13 41	14 11	14 41
21	Snodland	d	06 14	06 52		07 22			08 14	08 44	09 14	09 44	10 14	10 44	11 14	11 44	11 44	12 14	12 44	13 14	13 44	14 14	14 44
22½	Halling	d	06 17	06 55		07 25			08 17	08 47	09 17	09 47	10 17	10 47	11 17	11 47	11 47	12 17	12 47	13 17	13 47	14 17	14 47
24¼	Cuxton	d	06 20	06 58		07 28			08 20	08 50	09 20	09 50	10 20	10 50	11 20	11 50	11 50	12 20	12 50	13 20	13 50	14 20	14 50
26½	**Strood** ■	a	06 24	07 02	07 11	07 32	07 41	08 11	08 24	08 54	09 24	09 54	10 24	10 54	11 24	11 54	11 54	12 24	12 54	13 24	13 54	14 24	14 54
34½	Gravesend	d			07 22		07 52	08 22															
37½	Ebbsfleet International	d																					
54¼	Stratford International	d			07 37		08 07	08 37															
59½	St Pancras International	a			07 43		08 13	08 43															

		SE	SE	SE	SE	SE	SE	SE	SE	SE A	SE	SE	SE	SE	SE	SE	SE	SE
Tonbridge ■	d		15 03		16 03									20 33		21 33		22 33
Paddock Wood ■	d		15 10		16 10	17 02	17 30	17 52	18 42		19 12	19 42		20 40		21 40		22 40
Beltring	d		15 14		16 14	17 06	17 34	17 56	18 46		19 16	19 46		20 44		21 44		22 44
Yalding	d		15 18		16 18	17 09	17 37	17 59	18 50		19 20	19 49		20 48		21 48		22 48
Wateringbury	d		15 21		16 21	17 12	17 40	18 02	18 53		19 23	19 52		20 51		21 51		22 51
East Farleigh	d		15 25		16 25	17 16	17 44	18 06	18 57		19 27	19 56		20 55		21 55		22 55
Maidstone West ■ 194	a		15 29		16 29	17 21	17 49	18 11	19 01		19 31	20 01		20 59		21 59		22 59
	d	15 02	15 44	16 02	16 32	17 22	17 50	18 18	19 02	19 13	19 32	20 02	20 32	21 02	21 32	22 02	22 32	23 02
Maidstone Barracks	d	15 04	15 46	16 04	16 34	17 24	17 52	18 20	19 04		19 34	20 04	20 34	21 04	21 34	22 04	22 34	23 04
Aylesford	d	15 09	15 51	16 09	16 39	17 29	17 57	18 25	19 09		19 39	20 09	20 39	21 09	21 39	22 09	22 39	23 09
New Hythe	d	15 11	15 53	16 11	16 41	17 31	17 59	18 27	19 11		19 41	20 11	20 41	21 11	21 41	22 11	22 41	23 11
Snodland	d	15 14	15 56	16 14	16 44	17 34	18 02	18 30	19 14		19 44	20 14	20 44	21 14	21 44	22 14	22 44	23 14
Halling	d	15 17	15 59	16 17	16 47	17 37	18 05	18 33	19 17		19 47	20 17	20 47	21 17	21 47	22 17	22 47	23 17
Cuxton	d	15 20	16 02	16 20	16 50	17 40	18 08	18 36	19 20		19 50	20 20	20 50	21 20	21 50	22 20	22 50	23 20
Strood ■	a	15 24	16 06	16 24	16 54	17 44	18 12	18 40	19 24	19 30	19 54	20 24	20 54	21 24	21 54	22 24	22 54	23 24
Gravesend	d									19 43								
Ebbsfleet International	d									19 50								
Stratford International	d									20 02								
St Pancras International	a									20 08								

Mondays to Fridays

30 July to 10 August

		SE	SE	SE	SE	SE	SE	SE	SE	SE	SE	SE	SE	SE	SE	SE	SE	SE	SE	SE	SE	SE	SE
Tonbridge ■	d							09 03		10 03		11 03		12 03		13 03		14 03		15 03		16 03	
Paddock Wood ■	d	05 42	06 20	06 50	07 40	08 10		09 10		10 10		11 10		12 10		13 10		14 10		15 10		16 10	17 02
Beltring	d	05 46	06 24	06 54	07 44	08 14		09 14		10 14		11 14		12 14		13 14		14 14		15 14		16 14	17 06
Yalding	d	05 49	06 27	06 57	07 48	08 18		09 18		10 18		11 18		12 18		13 18		14 18		15 18		16 18	17 09
Wateringbury	d	05 52	06 30	07 00	07 51	08 21		09 21		10 21		11 21		12 21		13 21		14 21		15 21		16 21	17 12
East Farleigh	d	05 56	06 34	07 04	07 55	08 25		09 25		10 25		11 25		12 25		13 25		14 25		15 25		16 25	17 16
Maidstone West ■ 194	a	06 01	06 39	07 09	07 59	08 29		09 29		10 29		11 30		12 29		13 29		14 29		15 29		16 29	17 21
	d	06 02	06 40	07 10	08 02	08 32	09 02	09 32	10 02	10 32	11 02	11 32	12 02	12 32	13 02	13 32	14 02	14 32	15 02	15 44	16 02	16 32	17 22
Maidstone Barracks	d	06 04	06 42	07 12	08 04	08 34	09 04	09 34	10 04	10 34	11 04	11 34	12 04	12 34	13 04	13 34	14 04	14 34	15 04	15 46	16 04	16 34	17 24
Aylesford	d	06 09	06 47	07 17	08 09	08 39	09 09	09 39	10 09	10 39	11 09	11 39	12 09	12 39	13 09	13 39	14 09	14 39	15 09	15 51	16 09	16 39	17 29
New Hythe	d	06 11	06 49	07 19	08 11	08 41	09 11	09 41	10 11	10 41	11 11	11 41	12 11	12 41	13 11	13 41	14 11	14 41	15 11	15 53	16 11	16 41	17 31
Snodland	d	06 14	06 52	07 22	08 14	08 44	09 14	09 44	10 14	10 44	11 14	11 44	12 14	12 44	13 14	13 44	14 14	14 44	15 14	15 56	16 14	16 44	17 34
Halling	d	06 17	06 55	07 25	08 17	08 47	09 17	09 47	10 17	10 47	11 17	11 47	12 17	12 47	13 17	13 47	14 17	14 47	15 17	15 59	16 17	16 47	17 37
Cuxton	d	06 20	06 58	07 28	08 20	08 50	09 20	09 50	10 20	10 50	11 20	11 50	12 20	12 50	13 20	13 50	14 20	14 50	15 20	16 02	16 20	16 50	17 40
Strood ■	a	06 24	07 02	07 32	08 24	08 54	09 24	09 54	10 24	10 54	11 24	11 54	12 24	12 54	13 24	13 54	14 24	14 54	15 24	16 06	16 24	16 54	17 44
Gravesend	d																						
Ebbsfleet International	d																						
Stratford International	d																						
St Pancras International	a																						

		SE	SE	SE	SE	SE	SE	SE	SE	SE	SE	SE
Tonbridge ■	d							20 33		21 33		22 33
Paddock Wood ■	d	17 30	17 52	18 42	19 12	19 42		20 40		21 40		22 40
Beltring	d	17 34	17 56	18 46	19 16	19 46		20 44		21 44		22 44
Yalding	d	17 37	17 59	18 50	19 20	19 49		20 48		21 48		22 48
Wateringbury	d	17 40	18 02	18 53	19 23	19 52		20 51		21 51		22 51
East Farleigh	d	17 44	18 06	18 57	19 27	19 56		20 55		21 55		22 55
Maidstone West ■ 194	a	17 49	18 11	19 01	19 31	20 01		20 59		21 59		22 59
	d	17 50	18 18	19 02	19 32	20 02	20 32	21 02	21 32	22 02	22 32	23 02
Maidstone Barracks	d	17 52	18 20	19 04	19 34	20 04	20 34	21 04	21 34	22 04	22 34	23 04
Aylesford	d	17 57	18 25	19 09	19 39	20 09	20 39	21 09	21 39	22 09	22 39	23 09
New Hythe	d	17 59	18 27	19 11	19 41	20 11	20 41	21 11	21 41	22 11	22 41	23 11
Snodland	d	18 02	18 30	19 14	19 44	20 14	20 44	21 14	21 44	22 14	22 44	23 14
Halling	d	18 05	18 33	19 17	19 47	20 17	20 47	21 17	21 47	22 17	22 47	23 17
Cuxton	d	18 08	18 36	19 20	19 50	20 20	20 50	21 20	21 50	22 20	22 50	23 20
Strood ■	a	18 12	18 40	19 24	19 54	20 24	20 54	21 24	21 54	22 24	22 54	23 24
Gravesend	d											
Ebbsfleet International	d											
Stratford International	d											
St Pancras International	a											

A not 27 July

B from 21 May until 27 July

C until 18 May

Paddock Wood and Maidstone West - Strood

Mondays to Fridays

29 August to 7 September

Network Diagram - see first Page of Table 206

		SE	SE	SE	SE	SE	SE	SE	SE	SE		SE	SE	SE	SE	SE	SE	SE	SE	SE		SE	SE	SE	SE
Tonbridge [4]	d											09 03		10 03		11 03		12 03		13 03			14 03		15 03
Paddock Wood [4]	d	05 42	06 20		06 50			07 40	08 10			09 10		10 10		11 10		12 10		13 10			14 10		15 10
Beltring	d	05 46	06 24		06 54			07 44	08 14			09 14		10 14		11 14		12 14		13 14			14 14		15 14
Yalding	d	05 49	06 27		06 57			07 48	08 18			09 18		10 18		11 18		12 18		13 18			14 18		15 18
Wateringbury	d	05 52	06 30		07 00			07 51	08 21			09 21		10 21		11 21		12 21		13 21			14 21		15 21
East Farleigh	d	05 56	06 34		07 04			07 55	08 25			09 25		10 25		11 25		12 25		13 25			14 25		15 25
Maidstone West [4] 194	a	06 01	06 39		07 09			07 59	08 29			09 29		10 29		11 30		12 29		13 29			14 29		15 29
	d	06 02	06 40	06 56	07 10	07 26	07 56	08 02	08 32	09 02		09 32	10 02	10 32	11 02	11 32	12 02	12 32	13 02	13 32		14 02	14 32	15 02	15 44
Maidstone Barracks	d	06 04	06 42		07 12			08 04	08 34	09 04		09 34	10 04	10 34	11 04	11 34	12 04	12 34	13 04	13 34		14 04	14 34	15 04	15 46
Aylesford	d	06 09	06 47		07 17			08 09	08 39	09 09		09 39	10 09	10 39	11 09	11 39	12 09	12 39	13 09	13 39		14 09	14 39	15 09	15 51
New Hythe	d	06 11	06 49		07 19			08 11	08 41	09 11		09 41	10 11	10 41	11 11	11 41	12 11	12 41	13 11	13 41		14 11	14 41	15 11	15 53
Snodland	d	06 14	06 52		07 22			08 14	08 44	09 14		09 44	10 14	10 44	11 14	11 44	12 14	12 44	13 14	13 44		14 14	14 44	15 14	15 56
Halling	d	06 17	06 55		07 25			08 17	08 47	09 17		09 47	10 17	10 47	11 17	11 47	12 17	12 47	13 17	13 47		14 17	14 47	15 17	15 59
Cuxton	d	06 20	06 58		07 28			08 20	08 50	09 20		09 50	10 20	10 50	11 20	11 50	12 20	12 50	13 20	13 50		14 20	14 50	15 20	16 02
Strood [4]	a	06 24	07 02	07 11	07 32	07 41	08 11	08 24	08 54	09 24		09 54	10 24	10 54	11 24	11 54	12 24	12 54	13 24	13 54		14 24	14 54	15 24	16 06
Gravesend	d			07 22		07 52	08 22																		
Ebbsfleet International	d																								
Stratford International	d			07 38		08 08	08 38																		
St Pancras International	a			07 44		08 14	08 44																		

		SE	SE	SE	SE	SE		SE	SE	SE	SE	SE	SE	SE	SE	SE		SE
Tonbridge [4]	d		16 03										20 33		21 33			22 33
Paddock Wood [4]	d		16 10	17 02	17 30	17 52		18 42		19 12	19 42		20 40		21 40			22 40
Beltring	d		16 14	17 06	17 34	17 56		18 46		19 16	19 46		20 44		21 44			22 44
Yalding	d		16 18	17 09	17 37	17 59		18 50		19 20	19 49		20 48		21 48			22 48
Wateringbury	d		16 21	17 12	17 40	18 02		18 53		19 23	19 52		20 51		21 51			22 51
East Farleigh	d		16 25	17 16	17 44	18 06		18 57		19 27	19 56		20 55		21 55			22 55
Maidstone West [4] 194	a		16 29	17 21	17 49	18 11		19 01		19 31	20 01		20 59		21 59			22 59
	d	16 02	16 32	17 22	17 50	18 18		19 02	19 13	19 32	20 02	20 32	21 02	21 32	22 02	22 32		23 02
Maidstone Barracks	d	16 04	16 34	17 24	17 52	18 20		19 04		19 34	20 04	20 34	21 04	21 34	22 04	22 34		23 04
Aylesford	d	16 09	16 39	17 29	17 57	18 25		19 09		19 39	20 09	20 39	21 09	21 39	22 09	22 39		23 09
New Hythe	d	16 11	16 41	17 31	17 59	18 27		19 11		19 41	20 11	20 41	21 11	21 41	22 11	22 41		23 11
Snodland	d	16 14	16 44	17 34	18 02	18 30		19 14		19 44	20 14	20 44	21 14	21 44	22 14	22 44		23 14
Halling	d	16 17	16 47	17 37	18 05	18 33		19 17		19 47	20 17	20 47	21 17	21 47	22 17	22 47		23 17
Cuxton	d	16 20	16 50	17 40	18 08	18 36		19 20		19 50	20 20	20 50	21 20	21 50	22 20	22 50		23 20
Strood [4]	a	16 24	16 54	17 44	18 12	18 40		19 24	19 30	19 54	20 24	20 54	21 24	21 54	22 24	22 54		23 24
Gravesend	d								19 43									
Ebbsfleet International	d								19 50									
Stratford International	d								20 08									
St Pancras International	a								20 14									

Saturdays

until 21 July, 18 Aug and from 15 Sep

		SE	SE	SE	SE	SE	SE	SE	SE	SE		SE	SE	SE	SE	SE	SE	SE	SE	SE		SE	SE	SE	SE
Tonbridge [4]	d	06 03		07 03		08 03		09 03		10 03			11 03		12 03		13 03		14 03			15 03		16 03	
Paddock Wood [4]	d	06 10		07 10		08 10		09 10		10 10			11 10		12 10		13 10		14 10			15 10		16 10	
Beltring	d	06 14		07 14		08 14		09 14		10 14			11 14		12 14		13 14		14 14			15 14		16 14	
Yalding	d	06 18		07 18		08 18		09 18		10 18			11 18		12 18		13 18		14 18			15 18		16 18	
Wateringbury	d	06 21		07 21		08 21		09 21		10 21			11 21		12 21		13 21		14 21			15 21		16 21	
East Farleigh	d	06 25		07 25		08 25		09 25		10 25			11 25		12 25		13 25		14 25			15 25		16 25	
Maidstone West [4] 194	a	06 29		07 29		08 29		09 29		10 29			11 29		12 29		13 29		14 29			15 29		16 29	
	d	06 32	07 02	07 32	08 02	08 32	09 02	09 32	10 02	10 32		11 02	11 32	12 02	12 32	13 02	13 32	14 02	14 32	15 02		15 32	16 02	16 32	17 02
Maidstone Barracks	d	06 34	07 04	07 34	08 04	08 34	09 04	09 34	10 04	10 34		11 04	11 34	12 04	12 34	13 04	13 34	14 04	14 34	15 04		15 34	16 04	16 34	17 04
Aylesford	d	06 39	07 09	07 39	08 09	08 39	09 09	09 39	10 09	10 39		11 09	11 39	12 09	12 39	13 09	13 39	14 09	14 39	15 09		15 39	16 09	16 39	17 09
New Hythe	d	06 41	07 11	07 41	08 11	08 41	09 11	09 41	10 11	10 41		11 11	11 41	12 11	12 41	13 11	13 41	14 11	14 41	15 11		15 41	16 11	16 41	17 11
Snodland	d	06 44	07 14	07 44	08 14	08 44	09 14	09 44	10 14	10 44		11 14	11 44	12 14	12 44	13 14	13 44	14 14	14 44	15 14		15 44	16 14	16 44	17 14
Halling	d	06 47	07 17	07 47	08 17	08 47	09 17	09 47	10 17	10 47		11 17	11 47	12 17	12 47	13 17	13 47	14 17	14 47	15 17		15 47	16 17	16 47	17 17
Cuxton	d	06 50	07 20	07 50	08 20	08 50	09 20	09 50	10 20	10 50		11 20	11 50	12 20	12 50	13 20	13 50	14 20	14 50	15 20		15 50	16 20	16 50	17 20
Strood [4]	a	06 54	07 24	07 54	08 24	08 54	09 24	09 54	10 24	10 54		11 24	11 54	12 24	12 54	13 24	13 54	14 24	14 54	15 24		15 54	16 24	16 54	17 24
Gravesend	d																								
Ebbsfleet International	d																								
Stratford International	d																								
St Pancras International	a																								

		SE	SE	SE	SE	SE		SE	SE	SE	SE	SE	SE	SE
Tonbridge [4]	d	17 03		18 03		19 03			20 03		21 03		22 03	
Paddock Wood [4]	d	17 10		18 10		19 10			20 10		21 10		22 10	
Beltring	d	17 14		18 14		19 14			20 14		21 14		22 14	
Yalding	d	17 18		18 18		19 18			20 18		21 18		22 18	
Wateringbury	d	17 21		18 21		19 21			20 21		21 21		22 21	
East Farleigh	d	17 25		18 25		19 25			20 25		21 25		22 25	
Maidstone West [4] 194	a	17 29		18 29		19 29			20 29		21 29		22 29	
	d	17 32	18 02	18 32	19 02	19 32		20 02	20 32	21 02	21 32	22 02	22 32	23 02
Maidstone Barracks	d	17 34	18 04	18 34	19 04	19 34		20 04	20 34	21 04	21 34	22 04	22 34	23 04
Aylesford	d	17 39	18 09	18 39	19 09	19 39		20 09	20 39	21 09	21 39	22 09	22 39	23 09
New Hythe	d	17 41	18 11	18 41	19 11	19 41		20 11	20 41	21 11	21 41	22 11	22 41	23 11
Snodland	d	17 44	18 14	18 44	19 14	19 44		20 14	20 44	21 14	21 44	22 14	22 44	23 14
Halling	d	17 47	18 17	18 47	19 17	19 47		20 17	20 47	21 17	21 47	22 17	22 47	23 17
Cuxton	d	17 50	18 20	18 50	19 20	19 50		20 20	20 50	21 20	21 50	22 20	22 50	23 20
Strood [4]	a	17 54	18 24	18 54	19 24	19 54		20 24	20 54	21 24	21 54	22 24	22 54	23 24
Gravesend	d													
Ebbsfleet International	d													
Stratford International	d													
St Pancras International	a													

Paddock Wood and Maidstone West - Strood

Saturdays

28 July to 11 August

Network Diagram - see first Page of Table 206

		SE	SE	SE	SE	SE	SE	SE	SE	SE		SE	SE	SE	SE	SE	SE	SE	SE	SE		SE	SE	SE	SE
Tonbridge [4]	d	06 03		07 03		08 03		09 03		10 03			11 03		12 03		13 03		14 03			15 03		16 03	
Paddock Wood [4]	d	06 10		07 10		08 10		09 10		10 10			11 10		12 10		13 10		14 10			15 10		16 10	
Beltring	d	06 14		07 14		08 14		09 14		10 14			11 14		12 14		13 14		14 14			15 14		16 14	
Yalding	d	06 18		07 18		08 18		09 18		10 18			11 18		12 18		13 18		14 18			15 18		16 18	
Wateringbury	d	06 21		07 21		08 21		09 21		10 21			11 21		12 21		13 21		14 21			15 21		16 21	
East Farleigh	d	06 25		07 25		08 25		09 25		10 25			11 25		12 25		13 25		14 25			15 25		16 25	
Maidstone West [4] 194	a	06 29		07 29		08 29		09 29		10 29			11 29		12 29		13 29		14 29			15 29		16 29	
	d	06 32	07 02	07 32	08 02	08 32	09 02	09 32	10 02	10 32		11 02	11 32	12 02	12 32	13 02	13 32	14 02	14 32	15 02		15 32	16 02	16 32	17 02
Maidstone Barracks	d	06 34	07 04	07 34	08 04	08 34	09 04	09 34	10 04	10 34		11 04	11 34	12 04	12 34	13 04	13 34	14 04	14 34	15 04		15 34	16 04	16 34	17 04
Aylesford	d	06 39	07 09	07 39	08 09	08 39	09 09	09 39	10 09	10 39		11 09	11 39	12 09	12 39	13 09	13 39	14 09	14 39	15 09		15 39	16 09	16 39	17 09
New Hythe	d	06 41	07 11	07 41	08 11	08 41	09 11	09 41	10 11	10 41		11 11	11 41	12 11	12 41	13 11	13 41	14 11	14 41	15 11		15 41	16 11	16 41	17 11
Snodland	d	06 44	07 14	07 44	08 14	08 44	09 14	09 44	10 14	10 44		11 14	11 44	12 14	12 44	13 14	13 44	14 14	14 44	15 14		15 44	16 14	16 44	17 14
Halling	d	06 47	07 17	07 47	08 17	08 47	09 17	09 47	10 17	10 47		11 17	11 47	12 17	12 47	13 17	13 47	14 17	14 47	15 17		15 47	16 17	16 47	17 17
Cuxton	d	06 50	07 20	07 50	08 20	08 50	09 20	09 50	10 20	10 50		11 20	11 50	12 20	12 50	13 20	13 50	14 20	14 50	15 20		15 50	16 20	16 50	17 20
Strood [4]	a	06 54	07 24	07 54	08 24	08 54	09 24	09 54	10 24	10 54		11 24	11 54	12 24	12 54	13 24	13 54	14 24	14 54	15 24		15 54	16 24	16 54	17 24
Gravesend	d																								
Ebbsfleet International	d																								
Stratford International	d																								
St Pancras International	a																								

		SE	SE	SE	SE	SE		SE	SE	SE	SE	SE	SE	SE
Tonbridge [4]	d	17 03		18 03		19 03			20 03		21 03		22 03	
Paddock Wood [4]	d	17 10		18 10		19 10			20 10		21 10		22 10	
Beltring	d	17 14		18 14		19 14			20 14		21 14		22 14	
Yalding	d	17 18		18 18		19 18			20 18		21 18		22 18	
Wateringbury	d	17 21		18 21		19 21			20 21		21 21		22 21	
East Farleigh	d	17 25		18 25		19 25			20 25		21 25		22 25	
Maidstone West [4] 194	a	17 29		18 29		19 29			20 29		21 29		22 29	
	d	17 32	18 02	18 32	19 02	19 32		20 02	20 32	21 02	21 32	22 02	22 32	23 02
Maidstone Barracks	d	17 34	18 04	18 34	19 04	19 34		20 04	20 34	21 04	21 34	22 04	22 34	23 04
Aylesford	d	17 39	18 09	18 39	19 09	19 39		20 09	20 39	21 09	21 39	22 09	22 39	23 09
New Hythe	d	17 41	18 11	18 41	19 11	19 41		20 11	20 41	21 11	21 41	22 11	22 41	23 11
Snodland	d	17 44	18 14	18 44	19 14	19 44		20 14	20 44	21 14	21 44	22 14	22 44	23 14
Halling	d	17 47	18 17	18 47	19 17	19 47		20 17	20 47	21 17	21 47	22 17	22 47	23 17
Cuxton	d	17 50	18 20	18 50	19 20	19 50		20 20	20 50	21 20	21 50	22 20	22 50	23 20
Strood [4]	a	17 54	18 24	18 54	19 24	19 54		20 24	20 54	21 24	21 54	22 24	22 54	23 24
Gravesend	d													
Ebbsfleet International	d													
Stratford International	d													
St Pancras International	a													

Saturdays

25 August to 8 September

		SE	SE	SE	SE	SE	SE	SE	SE	SE		SE	SE	SE	SE	SE	SE	SE	SE	SE		SE	SE	SE	SE
Tonbridge [4]	d	06 03		07 03		08 03		09 03		10 03			11 03		12 03		13 03		14 03			15 03		16 03	
Paddock Wood [4]	d	06 10		07 10		08 10		09 10		10 10			11 10		12 10		13 10		14 10			15 10		16 10	
Beltring	d	06 14		07 14		08 14		09 14		10 14			11 14		12 14		13 14		14 14			15 14		16 14	
Yalding	d	06 18		07 18		08 18		09 18		10 18			11 18		12 18		13 18		14 18			15 18		16 18	
Wateringbury	d	06 21		07 21		08 21		09 21		10 21			11 21		12 21		13 21		14 21			15 21		16 21	
East Farleigh	d	06 25		07 25		08 25		09 25		10 25			11 25		12 25		13 25		14 25			15 25		16 25	
Maidstone West [4] 194	a	06 29		07 29		08 29		09 29		10 29			11 29		12 29		13 29		14 29			15 29		16 29	
	d	06 32	07 02	07 32	08 02	08 32	09 02	09 32	10 02	10 32		11 02	11 32	12 02	12 32	13 02	13 32	14 02	14 32	15 02		15 32	16 02	16 32	17 02
Maidstone Barracks	d	06 34	07 04	07 34	08 04	08 34	09 04	09 34	10 04	10 34		11 04	11 34	12 04	12 34	13 04	13 34	14 04	14 34	15 04		15 34	16 04	16 34	17 04
Aylesford	d	06 39	07 09	07 39	08 09	08 39	09 09	09 39	10 09	10 39		11 09	11 39	12 09	12 39	13 09	13 39	14 09	14 39	15 09		15 39	16 09	16 39	17 09
New Hythe	d	06 41	07 11	07 41	08 11	08 41	09 11	09 41	10 11	10 41		11 11	11 41	12 11	12 41	13 11	13 41	14 11	14 41	15 11		15 41	16 11	16 41	17 11
Snodland	d	06 44	07 14	07 44	08 14	08 44	09 14	09 44	10 14	10 44		11 14	11 44	12 14	12 44	13 14	13 44	14 14	14 44	15 14		15 44	16 14	16 44	17 14
Halling	d	06 47	07 17	07 47	08 17	08 47	09 17	09 47	10 17	10 47		11 17	11 47	12 17	12 47	13 17	13 47	14 17	14 47	15 17		15 47	16 17	16 47	17 17
Cuxton	d	06 50	07 20	07 50	08 20	08 50	09 20	09 50	10 20	10 50		11 20	11 50	12 20	12 50	13 20	13 50	14 20	14 50	15 20		15 50	16 20	16 50	17 20
Strood [4]	a	06 54	07 24	07 54	08 24	08 54	09 24	09 54	10 24	10 54		11 24	11 54	12 24	12 54	13 24	13 54	14 24	14 54	15 24		15 54	16 24	16 54	17 24
Gravesend	d																								
Ebbsfleet International	d																								
Stratford International	d																								
St Pancras International	a																								

		SE	SE	SE	SE	SE		SE	SE	SE	SE	SE	SE	SE
Tonbridge [4]	d	17 03		18 03		19 03			20 03		21 03		22 03	
Paddock Wood [4]	d	17 10		18 10		19 10			20 10		21 10		22 10	
Beltring	d	17 14		18 14		19 14			20 14		21 14		22 14	
Yalding	d	17 18		18 18		19 18			20 18		21 18		22 18	
Wateringbury	d	17 21		18 21		19 21			20 21		21 21		22 21	
East Farleigh	d	17 25		18 25		19 25			20 25		21 25		22 25	
Maidstone West [4] 194	a	17 29		18 29		19 29			20 29		21 29		22 29	
	d	17 32	18 02	18 32	19 02	19 32		20 02	20 32	21 02	21 32	22 02	22 32	23 02
Maidstone Barracks	d	17 34	18 04	18 34	19 04	19 34		20 04	20 34	21 04	21 34	22 04	22 34	23 04
Aylesford	d	17 39	18 09	18 39	19 09	19 39		20 09	20 39	21 09	21 39	22 09	22 39	23 09
New Hythe	d	17 41	18 11	18 41	19 11	19 41		20 11	20 41	21 11	21 41	22 11	22 41	23 11
Snodland	d	17 44	18 14	18 44	19 14	19 44		20 14	20 44	21 14	21 44	22 14	22 44	23 14
Halling	d	17 47	18 17	18 47	19 17	19 47		20 17	20 47	21 17	21 47	22 17	22 47	23 17
Cuxton	d	17 50	18 20	18 50	19 20	19 50		20 20	20 50	21 20	21 50	22 20	22 50	23 20
Strood [4]	a	17 54	18 24	18 54	19 24	19 54		20 24	20 54	21 24	21 54	22 24	22 54	23 24
Gravesend	d													
Ebbsfleet International	d													
Stratford International	d													
St Pancras International	a													

Table 208

Sundays

until 22 July, 19 Aug and from 16 Sep

Paddock Wood and Maidstone West - Strood

Network Diagram - see first Page of Table 206

			SE	SE	SE	SE	SE	SE	SE	SE	SE	SE	SE	SE	SE	SE	SE	SE
Tonbridge 4		d	06 26															
Paddock Wood 4		d	06 34	07 34	08 34	09 34	10 34	11 34	12 34	13 34	14 34	15 34	16 34	17 34	18 34	19 34	20 34	21 34
Beltring		d	06 38	07 38	08 38	09 38	10 38	11 38	12 38	13 38	14 38	15 38	16 38	17 38	18 38	19 38	20 38	21 38
Yalding		d	06 41	07 41	08 41	09 41	10 41	11 41	12 41	13 41	14 41	15 41	16 41	17 41	18 41	19 41	20 41	21 41
Wateringbury		d	06 44	07 44	08 44	09 44	10 44	11 44	12 44	13 44	14 44	15 44	16 44	17 44	18 44	19 44	20 44	21 44
East Farleigh		d	06 48	07 48	08 48	09 48	10 48	11 48	12 48	13 48	14 48	15 48	16 48	17 48	18 48	19 48	20 48	21 48
Maidstone West 4	194	a	06 53	07 53	08 53	09 53	10 53	11 53	12 53	13 53	14 53	15 53	16 53	17 53	18 53	19 53	20 53	21 53
		d	07 00	08 00	09 02	10 02	11 02	12 02	13 02	14 02	15 02	16 02	17 02	18 02	19 02	20 00	21 00	22 00
Maidstone Barracks		d	07 02	08 02	09 04	10 04	11 04	12 04	13 04	14 04	15 04	16 04	17 04	18 04	19 04	20 02	21 02	22 02
Aylesford		d	07 07	08 07	09 09	10 09	11 09	12 09	13 09	14 09	15 09	16 09	17 09	18 09	19 09	20 07	21 07	22 07
New Hythe		d	07 09	08 09	09 11	10 11	11 11	12 11	13 11	14 11	15 11	16 11	17 11	18 11	19 11	20 09	21 09	22 09
Snodland		d	07 12	08 12	09 14	10 14	11 14	12 14	13 14	14 14	15 14	16 14	17 14	18 14	19 14	20 12	21 12	22 12
Halling		d	07 15	08 15	09 17	10 17	11 17	12 17	13 17	14 17	15 17	16 17	17 17	18 17	19 17	20 15	21 15	22 15
Cuxton		d	07 18	08 18	09 20	10 20	11 20	12 20	13 20	14 20	15 20	16 20	17 20	18 20	19 20	20 18	21 18	22 18
Strood 4		a	07 22	08 22	09 24	10 24	11 24	12 24	13 24	14 24	15 24	16 24	17 24	18 24	19 24	20 22	21 22	22 22
Gravesend		d																
Ebbsfleet International		d																
Stratford International		d																
St Pancras International		a																

Sundays

29 July to 12 August

			SE	SE	SE	SE	SE	SE	SE	SE	SE	SE	SE	SE	SE	SE	SE	SE	SE
Tonbridge 4		d	06 03																
Paddock Wood 4		d	06 10	07 10	08 10	09 10	10 10	11 10	12 10	13 10	14 10	15 10	16 10	17 10	18 10	19 10	20 10	21 10	22 10
Beltring		d		07 14	08 14	09 14	10 14	11 14	12 14	13 14	14 14	15 14	16 14	17 14	18 14	19 14	20 14	21 14	22 14
Yalding		d		07 18	08 18	09 18	10 18	11 18	12 18	13 18	14 18	15 18	16 18	17 18	18 18	19 18	20 18	21 18	22 18
Wateringbury		d		07 21	08 21	09 21	10 21	11 21	12 21	13 21	14 21	15 21	16 21	17 21	18 21	19 21	20 21	21 21	22 21
East Farleigh		d		07 25	08 25	09 25	10 25	11 25	12 25	13 25	14 25	15 25	16 25	17 25	18 25	19 25	20 25	21 25	22 25
Maidstone West 4	194	a	06 24	07 29	08 29	09 29	10 29	11 29	12 29	13 29	14 29	15 29	16 29	17 29	18 29	19 29	20 29	21 29	22 29
		d		07 32	08 32	09 32	10 32	11 32	12 32	13 32	14 32	15 32	16 32	17 32	18 32	19 32	20 32	21 32	22 32
Maidstone Barracks		d		07 34	08 34	09 34	10 34	11 34	12 34	13 34	14 34	15 34	16 34	17 34	18 34	19 34	20 34	21 34	22 34
Aylesford		d		07 39	08 39	09 39	10 39	11 39	12 39	13 39	14 39	15 39	16 39	17 39	18 39	19 39	20 39	21 39	22 39
New Hythe		d		07 41	08 41	09 41	10 41	11 41	12 41	13 41	14 41	15 41	16 41	17 41	18 41	19 41	20 41	21 41	22 41
Snodland		d		07 44	08 44	09 44	10 44	11 44	12 44	13 44	14 44	15 44	16 44	17 44	18 44	19 44	20 44	21 44	22 44
Halling		d		07 47	08 47	09 47	10 47	11 47	12 47	13 47	14 47	15 47	16 47	17 47	18 47	19 47	20 47	21 47	22 47
Cuxton		d		07 50	08 50	09 50	10 50	11 50	12 50	13 50	14 50	15 50	16 50	17 50	18 50	19 50	20 50	21 50	22 50
Strood 4		a		07 54	08 54	09 54	10 54	11 54	12 54	13 54	14 54	15 54	16 54	17 54	18 54	19 54	20 54	21 54	22 54
Gravesend		d																	
Ebbsfleet International		d																	
Stratford International		d																	
St Pancras International		a																	

Sundays

26 August to 9 September

			SE	SE	SE	SE	SE	SE	SE	SE	SE	SE	SE	SE	SE	SE	SE	SE
Tonbridge 4		d	06 26															
Paddock Wood 4		d	06 34	07 34	08 34	09 34	10 34	11 34	12 34	13 34	14 34	15 34	16 34	17 34	18 34	19 34	20 34	21 34
Beltring		d	06 38	07 38	08 38	09 38	10 38	11 38	12 38	13 38	14 38	15 38	16 38	17 38	18 38	19 38	20 38	21 38
Yalding		d	06 41	07 41	08 41	09 41	10 41	11 41	12 41	13 41	14 41	15 41	16 41	17 41	18 41	19 41	20 41	21 41
Wateringbury		d	06 44	07 44	08 44	09 44	10 44	11 44	12 44	13 44	14 44	15 44	16 44	17 44	18 44	19 44	20 44	21 44
East Farleigh		d	06 48	07 48	08 48	09 48	10 48	11 48	12 48	13 48	14 48	15 48	16 48	17 48	18 48	19 48	20 48	21 48
Maidstone West 4	194	a	06 53	07 53	08 53	09 53	10 53	11 53	12 53	13 53	14 53	15 53	16 53	17 53	18 53	19 53	20 53	21 53
		d	07 00	08 00	09 02	10 02	11 02	12 02	13 02	14 02	15 02	16 02	17 02	18 02	19 02	20 00	21 00	22 00
Maidstone Barracks		d	07 02	08 02	09 04	10 04	11 04	12 04	13 04	14 04	15 04	16 04	17 04	18 04	19 04	20 02	21 02	22 02
Aylesford		d	07 07	08 07	09 09	10 09	11 09	12 09	13 09	14 09	15 09	16 09	17 09	18 09	19 09	20 07	21 07	22 07
New Hythe		d	07 09	08 09	09 11	10 11	11 11	12 11	13 11	14 11	15 11	16 11	17 11	18 11	19 11	20 09	21 09	22 09
Snodland		d	07 12	08 12	09 14	10 14	11 14	12 14	13 14	14 14	15 14	16 14	17 14	18 14	19 14	20 12	21 12	22 12
Halling		d	07 15	08 15	09 17	10 17	11 17	12 17	13 17	14 17	15 17	16 17	17 17	18 17	19 17	20 15	21 15	22 15
Cuxton		d	07 18	08 18	09 20	10 20	11 20	12 20	13 20	14 20	15 20	16 20	17 20	18 20	19 20	20 18	21 18	22 18
Strood 4		a	07 22	08 22	09 24	10 24	11 24	12 24	13 24	14 24	15 24	16 24	17 24	18 24	19 24	20 22	21 22	22 22
Gravesend		d																
Ebbsfleet International		d																
Stratford International		d																
St Pancras International		a																

Network Diagram for Table 212

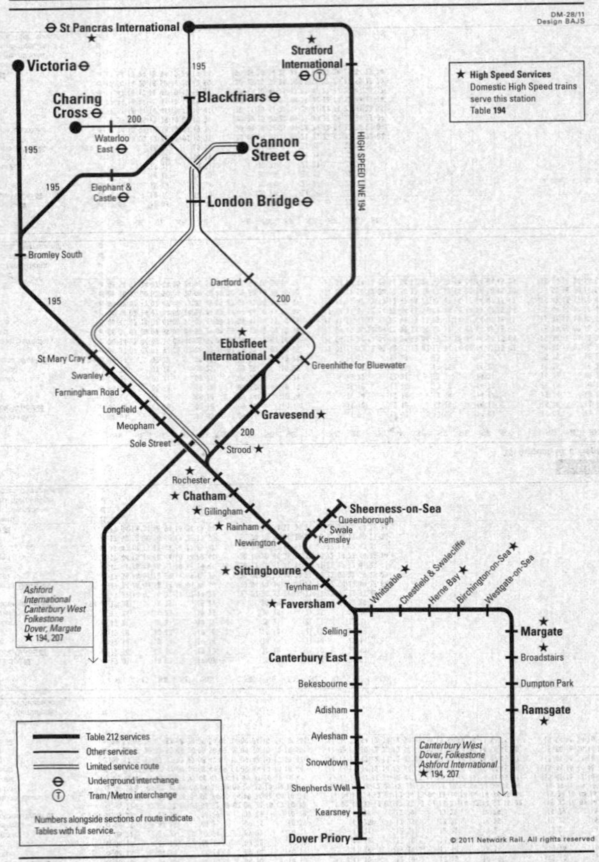

London - Medway, Sheerness-on-Sea, Dover and Ramsgate

Mondays to Fridays

until 27 July, 13 Aug to 28 Aug and from 10 Sep

Network Diagram - see first Page of Table 212

Miles	Miles	Miles	Miles	Miles			SE MO 1 A		SE MX 1		SE B	SE MX 1	SE MO 1 A	SE MX	SE B	SE MX 1	SE MX	SE MO A	SE MO A	SE MX	SE MO 1 A	SE MX 1	SE MX 1	SE MX
—	—	—	—	0	St Pancras Internatnl 15	⊖ d					22p55				23p25				23p42	23p55				
—	—	—	—	6	Stratford International	⊖ d					23p02				23p32				23p49	00 02				
—	—	—	—	22¾	Ebbsfleet International	d					23p13				23p43				00 01	00 13				
0	0	—	—	—	London Victoria 15	⊖ d	22p05		22p22			22p52	23p05			23p22					23p45	23p52	00 10	
—	—	—	—	—	London Blackfriars 3	⊖ d																		
—	—	—	—	—	Elephant & Castle	⊖ d																		
11	11	—	—	—	Bromley South 4	d	22p22		22p39			23p09	23p22			23p39					00 02	00 09		
14¾	14¾	—	—	—	St Mary Cray	d						23p15									00 08	00 15		
17½	17½	—	—	—	Swanley 4	d						23p19									00 12	00 19		
20½	20½	—	—	—	Farningham Road	d						23p24									00 17	00 24		
23½	23½	—	—	—	Longfield	d			22p52			23p28				23p52					00 21	00 28		
26	26	—	—	—	Meopham	d			22p57			23p32				23p57					00 25	00 32		
27	27	—	—	—	Sole Street	d						23p35									00 28	00 35		
—	—	—	0	—	London Charing Cross 4	⊖ d											23p09	23p10						23p39
—	—	—	0¾	—	London Waterloo (East) 4	⊖ d											23p12	23p13						23p42
—	—	—	—	—	London Cannon Street 4	⊖ d																		
—	—	—	1¾	—	London Bridge 4	⊖ d											23p17	23p18						23p47
—	—	—	18¾	—	Dartford 4	d											23p55	23p55						00 25
—	—	—	21½	—	Greenhithe for Bluewater	d											23p59	00 01						00 31
—	—	—	25½	24¾	Gravesend 4	d					23p18				23p48		00 10	00 10		00 18				00 40
—	—	—	32¾	32	Strood 4	d					23p28				23p58		00 22	00 22		00 28				00 52
33¾	33¾	—	33¾	33	Rochester 4	d	22p46		23p09		23p33	23p45	23p46		00 03	00 09	00 26	00 26		00 33	00 37	00 45	00 49	00 56
34¼	34¼	—	34¼	33½	Chatham 4	d	22p48		23p12		23p35	23p47	23p48		00 05	00 12	00 28	00 28		00 35	00 40	00 47	00 52	00 58
36	36	—	36	35¾	Gillingham (Kent) 4	d	22p53		23p17		23p40	23p52	23p53		00 10	00 17	00a33	00a33		00 40	00 44	00a52	00 57	01a03
39	39	—	—	38¾	Rainham (Kent)	d	22p57		23p21		23p45	23p56	23p57		00 15	00 21				00 45	00 49		01 01	
41½	41½	—	—	40¾	Newington	d						00 01									00 53		01 05	
44¾	44¾	0	—	44	Sittingbourne 4	a	23p04		23p28		23p52	00 06	00 04		00 22	00 28				00 52	00 58		01 10	
—	—	—	—	—		d	23p05		23p29		23p53	00 07	00 05	00 15	00 23	00 29				00 53	00 58		01 11	
—	—	2	—	—	Kemsley	d								00 20										
—	—	4	—	—	Swale	d								00 23										
—	—	6	—	—	Queenborough	d								00 27										
—	—	8	—	—	Sheerness-on-Sea	a								00 32										
47½	47½	—	—	46¾	Teynham	d			23p33							00 33					01 03		01 15	
52	52	—	—	51¾	Faversham 2	a	23p13		23p39		00 03	00 15	00 13		00 33	00 39				01 03	01 09		01 23	
—	—	—	—	—																				
—	—	—	—	—		d	23p17	23p19	23p43	23p45			00 17			00 43							01 24	
—	55¼	—	—	—	Selling	d		23p24		23p50														
—	61¾	—	—	—	Canterbury East 4	d		23p33		23p59														
—	64¾	—	—	—	Bekesbourne	d		23p37																
—	67¾	—	—	—	Adisham	d		23p42																
—	68¾	—	—	—	Aylesham	d		23p44		00 07														
—	69¾	—	—	—	Snowdown	d		23p47																
—	71¾	—	—	—	Shepherds Well	d		23p51																
—	75	—	—	—	Kearsney	d		23p55																
—	77¼	—	—	—	Dover Priory 4	a		00 01		00 18														
59	—	—	—	—	Whitstable	d	23p25		23p51				00 25			00 51							01 32	
60½	—	—	—	—	Chestfield & Swalecliffe	d	23p28		23p54				00 28			00 54							01 35	
62¾	—	—	—	—	Herne Bay	d	23p32		23p58				00 32			00 58							01 39	
70¾	—	—	—	—	Birchington-on-Sea	d	23p41		00 07				00 41			01 07							01 48	
72½	—	—	—	—	Westgate-on-Sea	d	23p44		00 10				00 44			01 10							01 51	
73¾	—	—	—	—	Margate 4	d	23p48		00 14				00 48			01 14							01 55	
77	—	—	—	—	Broadstairs	d	23p54		00 20				00 54			01 20							02 01	
78½	—	—	—	—	Dumpton Park	d	23p57		00 23				00 57			01 23							02 04	
79¼	—	—	—	—	Ramsgate 4	a	00 01		00 26				01 00			01 26							02 07	

A from 21 May until 23 July

B not 14 May

For further services to St Pancras International, Blackfriars and Elephant & Castle and onwards to Bromley South, St Mary Cray and Swanley please refer to table 52

London - Medway, Sheerness-on-Sea, Dover and Ramsgate

Mondays to Fridays

until 27 July, 13 Aug to 28 Aug and from 10 Sep

Network Diagram - see first Page of Table 212

		SE MX	SE	SE	SE	SE 1	SE	SE 1	SE	SE A	SE	SE B	SE	SE A	SE 1	SE 1	SE	SE 1	SE 1	SE	SE A	SE B
St Pancras Internatnl 15	⊖ d	00 12										06 04									06 25	06 32
Stratford International	⊖ d	00 19										06 14									06 32	06 42
Ebbsfleet International	d	00 31										06a24									06 42	06a52
London Victoria 15	⊖ d		00 35													05 22			05 52			
London Blackfriars 3	⊖ d																					
Elephant & Castle	⊖ d																					
Bromley South 4	d		00 55													05 39			06 09			
St Mary Cray	d		01 01													05 45						
Swanley 4	d		01 05													05 49			06 20			
Farningham Road	d		01 10													05 54						
Longfield	d		01 14													05 58			06 26			
Meopham	d		01 18													06 02			06 30			
Sole Street	d															06 05						
London Charing Cross 4	⊖ d			00 18																05 39		
London Waterloo (East) 4	⊖ d			00 21																05 42		
London Cannon Street 4	⊖ d																					
London Bridge 4	⊖ d			00 26																05 47		
Dartford 4	d			01 06					05 25											06 25		
Greenhithe for Bluewater	d			01 10					05 30											06 30		
Gravesend 4	d			01 17					05 37											06 38	06 46	
Strood 4	d			01 29					05 48											06 49	06a56	
Rochester 4	d		01 29	01 33					05 52							06 15			06 41	06 53		
Chatham 4	d		01 31	01 35					05 55							06 17			06 44	06 56		
Gillingham (Kent) 4	d		01a35	01a41	05 00			05 47	05a59							06 22			06 48	07a00		
Rainham (Kent)	d				05 04			05 51								06 26			06 53			
Newington	d				05 08			05 55								06 30			06 57			
Sittingbourne 4	a							06 00								06 35			07 02			
	d						05 33	06 01			06 03		06 22			06 36	06 53		07 02			
Kemsley	d				05 15		05 38				06 08		06 27				06 58					
Swale	d				05 18		05 43				06 11		06 30				07 01					
Queenborough	d				05 22		05 47				06 15		06 35				07 05					
Sheerness-on-Sea	a				05 27		05 51				06 20		06 40				07 10					
Teynham	d							06 05								06 40			07 07			
Faversham 2	a							06 11								06 46			07 13			
	d					05 15		06 12							06 15	06 47		07 05	07 13			
Selling	d					05 20		06 17										07 09				
Canterbury East 4	d					05 29		06 26										07 18				
Bekesbourne	d					05 33		06 30										07 23				
Adisham	d					05 38		06 35										07 27				
Aylesham	d					05 40		06 37										07 29				
Snowdown	d					05 43		06 40										07 32				
Shepherds Well	d					05 47		06 44										07 35				
Kearsney	d					05 51		06 48										07 40				
Dover Priory 4	a					05 56		06 53										07 45				
Whitstable	d														06 23	06 55			07 21			
Chestfield & Swalecliffe	d														06 26	06 58			07 24			
Herne Bay	d														06 30	07 02			07 28			
Birchington-on-Sea	d														06 39	07 11			07 37			
Westgate-on-Sea	d														06 42	07 14			07 41			
Margate 4	d									05 47				06 48	06 52	07 18			07 45			
Broadstairs	d									05 54				06 54	06 58	07 24			07 50			
Dumpton Park	d														07 01	07 27			07 53			
Ramsgate 4	a									05 59				06 59	07 04	07 30			07 56			

A not 27 July

B 27 July

For further services to St Pancras International, Blackfriars and Elephant & Castle and onwards to Bromley South, St Mary Cray and Swanley please refer to table 52

Table 212

Mondays to Fridays

until 27 July, 13 Aug to 28 Aug and from 10 Sep

London - Medway, Sheerness-on-Sea, Dover and Ramsgate

Network Diagram - see first Page of Table 212

Station		SE A	SE	SE B	SE ■	SE	SE	SE B	SE	SE A	SE A	SE ■ C	SE ■ D	SE ■	SE	SE ■	SE	SE	SE A	SE B	SE A	SE A	SE A
St Pancras Internatnl ⊖	d	06 52						06 55		07 04	07 11								07 18	07 25	07 25	07 32	07 39
Stratford International ⊖	d	07 03						07 02		07 14	07 21								07 28	07 32	07 35	07 42	07 49
Ebbsfleet International	d	07a13						07 13		07 30	07a31								07 43	07 43	07a46	07a52	08 02
London Victoria ⊖	d				06 22									06 45		06 58	07 09						
London Blackfriars ⊖	d																						
Elephant & Castle ⊖	d																						
Bromley South	d				06 39									07 02		07 19							
St Mary Cray	d				06 45									07 08		07 25							
Swanley	d				06 49									07 13		07 29							
Farningham Road	d				06 54									07 18		07 34							
Longfield	d				06 58									07 22		07 38							
Meopham	d				07 02									07 26		07 42							
Sole Street	d				07 05									07 28		07 45							
London Charing Cross ⊖	d					05 56			06 26						06 39								
London Waterloo (East) ⊖	d					05 59			06 29						06 42								
London Cannon Street ⊖	d																						
London Bridge ⊖	d					06 04			06 34						06 47								
Dartford	d					06 42			07 12						07 25		07a48						
Greenhithe for Bluewater	d					06 48			07 18						07 30								
Gravesend	d					06 59		07 21	07 27						07 37				07 48	07 48			
Strood	d					07 17		07 31	07a37						07 48				07 58	07 58			
Rochester	d				07 15	07 21		07 36						07 40	07 52	07 56			08 03	08 03			
Chatham	d				07 17	07 24		07 38						07 43	07 55	07 59			08 05	08 05			
Gillingham (Kent)	d				07 22	07a28		07 43						07 48	07a59	08a03			08 10	08 10			
Rainham (Kent)	d				07 26			07 48						07 52					08 15	08 15			
Newington	d				07 30									07 56									
Sittingbourne	a				07 37			07 56						08 01					08 22	08 22			
	d		07 09		07 38		07 45	07 57						08 02				08 13	08 23	08 23			
Kemsley	d		07 14				07 50											08 18					
Swale	d		07 17				07 53											08 21					
Queenborough	d		07 22				07 57											08 25					
Sheerness-on-Sea	a		07 27				08 02											08 30					
Teynham	d				07 42									08 06									
Faversham	a				07 48			08 05						08 12					08 33	08 33			
	d				07 49							07 51	07 52	08 13									
Selling	d											07 55	07 56	08 18									
Canterbury East	d											08 05	08 06	08 27									
Bekesbourne	d											08 10	08 11	08 31									
Adisham	d											08 14	08 15	08 36									
Aylesham	d											08 17	08 18	08 38									
Snowdown	d											08 19	08 20	08 41									
Shepherds Well	d											08 23	08 24	08 45									
Kearsney	d											08 28	08 29	08 49									
Dover Priory	a											08 35	08 35	08 54									
Whitstable	d				07 57																		
Chestfield & Swalecliffe	d				08 00																		
Herne Bay	d				08 04																		
Birchington-on-Sea	d				08 13																		
Westgate-on-Sea	d				08 17																		
Margate	d			07 49	08 21																		
Broadstairs	d			07 55	08 26																		
Dumpton Park	d				08 29																		
Ramsgate	a			08 00	08 32																		

A 27 July
B not 27 July
C until 18 May
D not until 18 May, from 21 May

For further services to St Pancras International, Blackfriars and Elephant & Castle and onwards to Bromley South, St Mary Cray and Swanley please refer to table 52

Table 212

Mondays to Fridays

until 27 July, 13 Aug to 28 Aug and from 10 Sep

London - Medway, Sheerness-on-Sea, Dover and Ramsgate

Network Diagram - see first Page of Table 212

Station		SE A	SE ■	SE B	SE ■	SE ■ C	SE	SE	SE	SE B	SE A	SE A	SE A	SE ■ D	SE ■		SE	SE ■	SE	SE A	SE B	SE A
St Pancras Internatnl ⊖	d	07 46								07 52	07 52	08 04	08 11							08 18	08 25	08 25
Stratford International ⊖	d	07 56								08 02	08 03	08 14	08 21							08 28	08 32	08 35
Ebbsfleet International	d	08a07								08 13	08a13	08 30	08a31							08 44	08 43	08a46
London Victoria ⊖	d				07 22	07 22		07 43							07 52			07 58				
London Blackfriars ⊖	d																					
Elephant & Castle ⊖	d																					
Bromley South	d				07 40	07 40									08 09			08 28				
St Mary Cray	d																	08 34				
Swanley	d				07 49	07 49												08 39				
Farningham Road	d																	08 44				
Longfield	d				07 55	07 55									08 22			08 49				
Meopham	d				07 59	07 59									08 27			08 53				
Sole Street	d																	08 56				
London Charing Cross ⊖	d						07 12										07 39					
London Waterloo (East) ⊖	d						07 15										07 42					
London Cannon Street ⊖	d																					
London Bridge ⊖	d						07 21										07 47					
Dartford	d						08 00	08a27									08 25					
Greenhithe for Bluewater	d						08 05										08 30					
Gravesend	d						08 12			08 18							08 37			08 48	08 48	
Strood	d						08 23			08 28							08 48			08 58	08 58	
Rochester	d				08 11	08 11	08 27			08 33					08 39		08 52	09a07		09 03	09 03	
Chatham	d				08 13	08 13	08 30			08 35					08 42		08 55			09 05	09 05	
Gillingham (Kent)	d				08 18	08 18	08a35			08 40					08 47		08a59			09 10	09 10	
Rainham (Kent)	d				08 22	08 22				08 45					08 51					09 15	09 15	
Newington	d				08 26	08 26									08 55							
Sittingbourne	a				08 31	08 31				08 52					09 00					09 22	09 22	
	d				08 32	08 32			08 40	08 53					09 01				09 10	09 23	09 23	
Kemsley	d								08 45										09 15			
Swale	d								08 48										09 18			
Queenborough	d								08 52										09 22			
Sheerness-on-Sea	a								08 57										09 27			
Teynham	d				08 36	08 36																
Faversham	a				08 42	08 42				09 03					09 09					09 33	09 33	
	d		08 16		08 46	08 49								08 50	09 13	09 15						
Selling	d					08 53								08 54								
Canterbury East	d					09 02								09 03		09 29						
Bekesbourne	d					09 07								09 08								
Adisham	d					09 11								09 12								
Aylesham	d					09 13								09 14								
Snowdown	d					09 16								09 17								
Shepherds Well	d					09 20								09 21								
Kearsney	d					09 24								09 25								
Dover Priory	a					09 29								09 30		09 50						
Whitstable	d		08 24		08 54										09 21							
Chestfield & Swalecliffe	d		08 27		08 57																	
Herne Bay	d		08 31		09 01										09 26							
Birchington-on-Sea	d		08 40		09 10										09 35							
Westgate-on-Sea	d		08 43		09 13																	
Margate	d		08 47	08 53	09 17										09 41							
Broadstairs	d		08 53	08 59	09 23										09 46							
Dumpton Park	d		08 56		09 26																	
Ramsgate	a		08 59	09 04	09 29										09 51							

A 27 July
B not 27 July
C until 18 May
D not until 18 May, from 21 May

For further services to St Pancras International, Blackfriars and Elephant & Castle and onwards to Bromley South, St Mary Cray and Swanley please refer to table 52

Table 212

Mondays to Fridays

until 27 July, 13 Aug to 28 Aug and from 10 Sep

London - Medway, Sheerness-on-Sea, Dover and Ramsgate

Network Diagram - see first Page of Table 212

		SE A	SE A	SE A	SE A	SE B	SE ■		SE		SE	SE B	SE ■		SE	SE ■	SE A	SE A	SE		SE A	SE B	SE A	SE A	SE A
St Pancras Internatnl ⊖	d	08 32	08 39	08 46	08 52							08 55					09 04	09 11			09 18	09 25	09 25	09 32	09 39
Stratford International ⊖	d	08 42	08 49	08 56	09 03							09 05					09 14	09 21			09 28	09 32	09 35	09 42	09 49
Ebbsfleet International	d	08a52	09 02	09a07	09a13							09 17					09 30	09a31			09 43	09 43	09a46	09a52	10 02
London Victoria ⊖	d						08 22						08 52			08 58									
London Blackfriars ⊖	d																								
Elephant & Castle ⊖	d																								
Bromley South	d						08 39						09 09			09 19									
St Mary Cray	d															09 25									
Swanley	d															09 29									
Farningham Road	d															09 34									
Longfield	d						08 52						09 22			09 38									
Meopham	d						08 57						09 27			09 42									
Sole Street	d															09 45									
London Charing Cross ⊖	d								08 11						08 41										
London Waterloo (East) ⊖	d								08 14						08 44										
London Cannon Street ⊖	d																								
London Bridge ⊖	d								08 19						08 49										
Dartford	d								08 55						09 25										
Greenhithe for Bluewater	d								09 00						09 30										
Gravesend	d								09 07			09 22			09 37						09 48	09 48			
Strood	d								09 18			09 32			09 48						09 58	09 58			
Rochester	d						09 09		09 22			09 37	09 39		09 52	09 56					10 03	10 03			
Chatham	d						09 12		09 25			09 39	09 42		09 55	09 59					10 05	10 05			
Gillingham (Kent)	d						09 17		09a29			09 44	09 47		09a59	10a03					10 10	10 10			
Rainham (Kent)	d						09 21					09 49	09 51								10 15	10 15			
Newington	d												09 55												
Sittingbourne	a						09 28					09 56	10 01								10 22	10 22			
	d						09 29				09 40	09 56	10 01						10 10		10 23	10 23			
Kemsley	d										09 45								10 15						
Swale	d										09 48								10 18						
Queenborough	d										09 52								10 22						
Sheerness-on-Sea	a										09 57								10 27						
Teynham	d						09 33																		
Faversham	a						09 39					10 04	10 09								10 33	10 33			
	d						09 43	09 45					10 13	10 15											
Selling	d							09 50																	
Canterbury East	d							09 59						10 29											
Bekesbourne	d							10 03																	
Adisham	d							10 08																	
Aylesham	d							10 10																	
Snowdown	d							10 13																	
Shepherds Well	d							10 17																	
Kearsney	d							10 21																	
Dover Priory	a							10 26						10 50											
Whitstable	d						09 51						10 21												
Chestfield & Swalecliffe	d						09 54																		
Herne Bay	d						09 58						10 26												
Birchington-on-Sea	d						10 07						10 35												
Westgate-on-Sea	d						10 10																		
Margate	d					09 53	10 14						10 41												
Broadstairs	d					09 59	10 20						10 46												
Dumpton Park	d						10 23																		
Ramsgate	a					10 04	10 26						10 51												

A 27 July

B not 27 July

For further services to St Pancras International, Blackfriars and Elephant & Castle and onwards to Bromley South, St Mary Cray and Swanley please refer to table 52

Table 212

Mondays to Fridays

until 27 July, 13 Aug to 28 Aug and from 10 Sep

London - Medway, Sheerness-on-Sea, Dover and Ramsgate

Network Diagram - see first Page of Table 212

		SE A	SE A	SE B	SE ■			SE	SE	SE B	SE ■ C ⌶		SE	SE ■	SE A	SE A		SE	SE A	SE A	SE B	SE A	SE A	SE A	SE B
St Pancras Internatnl ⊖	d	09 46	09 52							09 55					10 04	10 11			10 18	10 25	10 28	10 32	10 39	10 46	
Stratford International ⊖	d	09 56	10 03							10 02					10 14	10 21			10 28	10 35	10 35	10 42	10 49	10 56	
Ebbsfleet International	d	10a07	10a13							10 13					10 30	10a31			10 44	10a46	10 46	10a52	11 02	11a07	
London Victoria ⊖	d				09 22						09 52			09 58											
London Blackfriars ⊖	d																								
Elephant & Castle ⊖	d																								
Bromley South	d				09 39						10 09			10 19											
St Mary Cray	d													10 25											
Swanley	d													10 29											
Farningham Road	d													10 34											
Longfield	d				09 52						10 22			10 38											
Meopham	d				09 57						10 27			10 42											
Sole Street	d													10 45											
London Charing Cross ⊖	d							09 11					09 39												
London Waterloo (East) ⊖	d							09 14					09 42												
London Cannon Street ⊖	d																								
London Bridge ⊖	d							09 19					09 47												
Dartford	d							09 55					10 25												
Greenhithe for Bluewater	d							10 00					10 30												
Gravesend	d							10 07		10 18			10 37						10 51		10 51				
Strood	d							10 18		10 28			10 48						11 01		11 01				
Rochester	d				10 09			10 22		10 33	10 39		10 52	10 56					11 06		11 06				
Chatham	d				10 12			10 25		10 35	10 42		10 55	10 59					11 08		11 08				
Gillingham (Kent)	d				10 17			10a29		10 40	10 47		10a59	11a03					11 13		11 13				
Rainham (Kent)	d				10 21					10 45	10 51								11 18		11 18				
Newington	d										10 55														
Sittingbourne	a				10 28					10 52	11 00								11 25		11 25				
	d				10 29				10 40	10 53	11 01							11 10	11 25		11 25				
Kemsley	d								10 45									11 15							
Swale	d								10 48									11 18							
Queenborough	d								10 52									11 22							
Sheerness-on-Sea	a								10 57									11 27							
Teynham	d				10 33																				
Faversham	a				10 39					11 03	11 09								11 33		11 33				
	d				10 43	10 45					11 13	11 15													
Selling	d					10 50																			
Canterbury East	d					10 59						11 29													
Bekesbourne	d					11 03																			
Adisham	d					11 08																			
Aylesham	d					11 10																			
Snowdown	d					11 13																			
Shepherds Well	d					11 17																			
Kearsney	d					11 21																			
Dover Priory	a					11 26						11 50													
Whitstable	d				10 51						11 21														
Chestfield & Swalecliffe	d				10 54																				
Herne Bay	d				10 58						11 26														
Birchington-on-Sea	d				11 07						11 35														
Westgate-on-Sea	d				11 10																				
Margate	d			10 53	11 14						11 41														11 53
Broadstairs	d			10 59	11 20						11 46														11 59
Dumpton Park	d				11 23																				
Ramsgate	a			11 04	11 26						11 51														12 04

A 27 July

B not 27 July

C ⌶ to Margate

For further services to St Pancras International, Blackfriars and Elephant & Castle and onwards to Bromley South, St Mary Cray and Swanley please refer to table 52

Table 212

Mondays to Fridays

until 27 July, 13 Aug to 28 Aug and from 10 Sep

London - Medway, Sheerness-on-Sea, Dover and Ramsgate

Network Diagram - see first Page of Table 212

		SE 1 A ☕		SE B	SE C	SE	SE D	SE E	SE 1 A ☕		SE	SE 1	SE E	SE E	SE	SE E	SE D	SE E	SE E	SE E	SE E	SE E
St Pancras Internatnl 15 ⊖	d						10 52	10 52					11 04	11 11		11 18	11 25	11 25	11 32	11 39	11 46	11 52
Stratford International ⊖	d						10 59	11 03					11 14	11 21		11 28	11 32	11 35	11 42	11 49	11 56	12 03
Ebbsfleet International	d						11 13	11a13					11 30	11a31		11 43	11 43	11a46	11a52	12 02	12a07	12a13
London Victoria 15 ⊖	d	10 22							10 52			10 58										
London Blackfriars 3 ⊖	d																					
Ephant &Castle ⊖	d																					
Bromley South 4	d	10 39							11 09			11 19										
St Mary Cray	d											11 25										
Swanley 4	d											11 29										
Farningham Rad	d											11 34										
bngfield	d	10 52							11 22			11 38										
Meopham	d	10 57							11 27			11 42										
Sole Street	d											11 45										
London Charing Cross 4 ⊖	d			10 09	10 09						10 39											
London Waterloo (East) 4 ⊖	d			10 12	10 12						10 42											
London Cannon Street 4 ⊖	d																					
London Bridge 4 ⊖	d			10 17	10 17						10 47											
Dartford 4	d			10 55	10 55						11 25											
Greenhithe for Bluewater	d			11 00	11 00						11 30											
Gravesend 4	d			11 07	11 07		11 18				11 37					11 48	11 48					
Strood 4	d			11 18	11 18		11 28				11 48					11 58	11 58					
Rchester 4	d	11 09		11 22	11 23		11 33		11 39		11 52	11 56				12 03	12 03					
Chatham 4	d	11 12		11 25	11 25		11 35		11 42		11 55	11 59				12 05	12 05					
Gillingham (Kent) 4	d	11 17		11a29	11a29		11 40		11 47		11a59	12a03				12 10	12 10					
Rnham (Kent)	d	11 21					11 45		11 51							12 15	12 15					
Nwington	d								11 55													
Sittingbourne 4	a	11 29					11 52		12 00							12 22	12 22					
	d	11 29				11 40	11 53		12 01						12 10	12 23	12 23					
Kemsley	d					11 45									12 15							
Swale	d					11 48									12 18							
Qeenborough	d					11 52									12 22							
Sheerness-on-Sea	a					11 57									12 27							
Teynham	d	11 33																				
Faversham 2	a	11 39					12 03		12 09							12 33	12 33					
	d	11 43	11 45						12 13	12 15												
Selling	d		11 50																			
Canterbury East 4	d		11 59							12 29												
Bekesbourne	d		12 03																			
Adisham	d		12 08																			
Aylesham	d		12 10																			
Snowdown	d		12 13																			
Shepherds W	d		12 17																			
Kearsney	d		12 21																			
Dover Priory 4	a		12 26							12 50												
Wstable	d	11 51							12 21													
Chestfield &Swalecliffe	d	11 54																				
Herne Bay	d	11 58							12 26													
Birchington-on-Sea	d	12 07							12 35													
Wstgate-on-Sea	d	12 10																				
Margate 4	d	12 14							12 41													
Broadstairs	d	12 20							12 46													
Dumpton Park	d	12 23																				
Ramsgate 4	a	12 26							12 51													

A ☕ to Margate
B not until 18 May, from 21 May
C until 18 May
D not 27 uly
E 27 uly

For further services to St Pancras hternational, Blackfriars and Ephant & Castle and onwards to Bromley South, St Mary Cray and Swanley please refer to table 52

Table 212

Mondays to Fridays

until 27 July, 13 Aug to 28 Aug and from 10 Sep

London - Medway, Sheerness-on-Sea, Dover and Ramsgate

Network Diagram - see first Page of Table 212

		SE A	SE 1 B ☕		SE	SE	SE A	SE 1 B ☕		SE	SE 1	SE C	SE C	SE	SE C	SE A	SE C	SE C	SE C	SE C	SE A	SE 1 B ☕	
St Pancras Internatnl 15 ⊖	d						11 55					12 04	12 11		12 18	12 22	12 25	12 32	12 39	12 46			
Stratford International ⊖	d						12 02					12 14	12 21		12 28	12 32	12 35	12 42	12 49	12 56			
Ebbsfleet International	d						12 13					12 30	12a31		12 44	12 43	12a46	12a52	13 02	13a07			
London Victoria 15 ⊖	d		11 22					11 52			11 58											12 22	
London Blackfriars 3 ⊖	d																						
Ephant &Castle ⊖	d																						
Bromley South 4	d		11 39					12 09			12 19											12 39	
St Mary Cray	d										12 25												
Swanley 4	d										12 29												
Farningham Rad	d										12 34												
bngfield	d		11 52					12 22			12 38											12 52	
Meopham	d		11 57					12 27			12 42											12 57	
Sole Street	d										12 45												
London Charing Cross 4 ⊖	d				11 09					11 39													
London Waterloo (East) 4 ⊖	d				11 12					11 42													
London Cannon Street 4 ⊖	d																						
London Bridge 4 ⊖	d				11 17					11 47													
Dartford 4	d				11 55					12 25													
Greenhithe for Bluewater	d				12 00					12 30													
Gravesend 4	d				12 07		12 18			12 37					12 48	12 48							
Strood 4	d				12 18		12 28			12 48					12 58	12 58							
Rchester 4	d		12 09		12 22		12 33	12 39		12 52	12 56				13 03	13 03						13 09	
Chatham 4	d		12 12		12 25		12 35	12 42		12 55	12 59				13 05	13 05						13 12	
Gillingham (Kent) 4	d		12 17		12a29		12 40	12 47		12a59	13a03				13 10	13 10						13 17	
Rnham (Kent)	d		12 21				12 45	12 51							13 15	13 15						13 21	
Nwington	d							12 55															
Sittingbourne 4	a		12 28				12 52	13 00							13 22	13 22						13 29	
	d		12 29			12 40	12 53	13 01						13 10	13 23	13 23						13 29	
Kemsley	d					12 45								13 15									
Swale	d					12 48								13 18									
Qeenborough	d					12 52								13 22									
Sheerness-on-Sea	a					12 57								13 27									
Teynham	d		12 33																			13 33	
Faversham 2	a		12 39				13 03	13 09							13 33	13 33						13 39	
	d		12 43	12 45				13 13	13 15													13 43	13 45
Selling	d			12 50																			13 50
Canterbury East 4	d			12 59					13 29														13 59
Bekesbourne	d			13 03																			14 03
Adisham	d			13 08																			14 08
Aylesham	d			13 10																			14 10
Snowdown	d			13 13																			14 13
Shepherds W	d			13 17																			14 17
Kearsney	d			13 21																			14 21
Dover Priory 4	a			13 26					13 50														14 26
Wstable	d		12 51					13 21														13 51	
Chestfield &Swalecliffe	d		12 54																			13 54	
Herne Bay	d		12 58					13 26														13 58	
Birchington-on-Sea	d		13 07					13 35														14 07	
Wstgate-on-Sea	d		13 10																			14 10	
Margate 4	d	12 53	13 14					13 41													13 53	14 14	
Broadstairs	d	12 59	13 20					13 46													13 59	14 20	
Dumpton Park	d		13 23																			14 23	
Ramsgate 4	a	13 04	13 26					13 51													14 04	14 26	

A not 27 uly
B ☕ to Margate
C 27 uly

For further services to St Pancras hternational, Blackfriars and Ephant & Castle and onwards to Bromley South, St Mary Cray and Swanley please refer to table 52

Table 212

Mondays to Fridays

until 27 July, 13 Aug to 28 Aug and from 10 Sep

London - Medway, Sheerness-on-Sea, Dover and Ramsgate

Network Diagram - see first Page of Table 212

		SE	SE	SE A	SE B	SE 1 C ⌶		SE	SE 1	SE B	SE B	SE	SE B	SE A	SE B	SE B	SE B	SE B	SE B	SE A	SE 1 C ⌶		SE
St Pancras Internatnl 15 ⊖	d			12 52	12 52					13 04	13 11		13 18	13 25	13 25	13 32	13 39	13 46	13 52				
Stratford International ⊖	d			12 58	13 03					13 14	13 21		13 28	13 32	13 35	13 42	13 49	13 56	14 03				
Ebbsfleet International	d			13 13	13a13					13 30	13a31		13 43	13 43	13a46	13a52	14 02	14a07	14a13				
London Victoria 15 ⊖	d					12 52			12 58												13 22		
London Blackfriars 3 ⊖	d																						
Elephant & Castle ⊖	d																						
Bromley South 4	d					13 09			13 19												13 39		
St Mary Cray	d								13 25														
Swanley 4	d								13 29														
Farningham Road	d								13 34														
Longfield	d					13 22			13 38												13 52		
Meopham	d					13 27			13 42												13 57		
Sole Street	d								13 45														
London Charing Cross 4 ⊖	d	12 09						12 39															13 09
London Waterloo (East) 4 ⊖	d	12 12						12 42															13 12
London Cannon Street 4 ⊖	d																						
London Bridge 4 ⊖	d	12 17						12 47															13 17
Dartford 4	d	12 55						13 25															13 55
Greenhithe for Bluewater	d	13 00						13 30															14 00
Gravesend 4	d	13 07		13 18				13 37					13 48	13 48									14 07
Strood 4	d	13 18		13 28				13 48					13 58	13 58									14 18
Rochester 4	d	13 22		13 33		13 39		13 52	13 56				14 03	14 03							14 09		14 22
Chatham 4	d	13 25		13 35		13 42		13 55	13 59				14 05	14 05							14 12		14 25
Gillingham (Kent) 4	d	13a29		13 40		13 47		13a59	14a03				14 10	14 10							14 17		14a29
Rainham (Kent)	d			13 45		13 51							14 15	14 15							14 21		
Newington	d					13 55																	
Sittingbourne 4	a			13 52		14 00							14 22	14 22							14 28		
	d		13 40	13 53		14 01						14 10	14 23	14 23							14 29		
Kemsley	d		13 45									14 15											
Swale	d		13 48									14 18											
Queenborough	d		13 52									14 22											
Sheerness-on-Sea	a		13 57									14 27											
Teynham	d																				14 33		
Faversham 2	a			14 03		14 09							14 33	14 33							14 39		
	d					14 13	14 15														14 43	14 45	
Selling	d																					14 50	
Canterbury East 4	d						14 29															14 59	
Bekesbourne	d																					15 03	
Adisham	d																					15 08	
Aylesham	d																					15 10	
Snowdown	d																					15 13	
Shepherds Well	d																					15 17	
Kearsney	d																					15 21	
Dover Priory 4	a						14 50															15 26	
Whitstable	d					14 21															14 51		
Chestfield & Swalecliffe	d																				14 54		
Herne Bay	d					14 26															14 58		
Birchington-on-Sea	d					14 35															15 07		
Westgate-on-Sea	d																				15 10		
Margate 4	d					14 41														14 53	15 14		
Broadstairs	d					14 46														14 59	15 20		
Dumpton Park	d																				15 23		
Ramsgate 4	a					14 51														15 04	15 26		

A not 27 July

B 27 July

C ⌶ to Margate

For further services to St Pancras International, Blackfriars and Elephant & Castle and onwards to Bromley South, St Mary Cray and Swanley please refer to table 52

Table 212

Mondays to Fridays

until 27 July, 13 Aug to 28 Aug and from 10 Sep

London - Medway, Sheerness-on-Sea, Dover and Ramsgate

Network Diagram - see first Page of Table 212

		SE	SE A	SE B	SE B	SE 1 C ⌶		SE	SE 1 D	SE 1 E	SE	SE B	SE A	SE B	SE B	SE B	SE B	SE B	SE A	SE 1 C ⌶		SE
St Pancras Internatnl 15 ⊖	d		13 55	14 04	14 11							14 18	14 25	14 25	14 32	14 39	14 46	14 52				
Stratford International ⊖	d		14 02	14 14	14 21							14 28	14 32	14 35	14 42	14 49	14 56	15 03				
Ebbsfleet International	d		14 13	14 30	14a31							14 43	14 43	14a46	14a52	15 02	15a07	15a13				
London Victoria 15 ⊖	d					13 52			13 57	13 58										14 22		
London Blackfriars 3 ⊖	d																					
Elephant & Castle ⊖	d																					
Bromley South 4	d					14 09			14 18	14 19										14 39		
St Mary Cray	d								14 24	14 25												
Swanley 4	d								14 28	14 29												
Farningham Road	d								14 33	14 34												
Longfield	d					14 22			14 37	14 38										14 52		
Meopham	d					14 27			14 41	14 42										14 57		
Sole Street	d								14 44	14 45												
London Charing Cross 4 ⊖	d							13 39														14 09
London Waterloo (East) 4 ⊖	d							13 42														14 12
London Cannon Street 4 ⊖	d																					
London Bridge 4 ⊖	d							13 47														14 17
Dartford 4	d							14 25														14 55
Greenhithe for Bluewater	d							14 30														15 00
Gravesend 4	d		14 18					14 37				14 48	14 48									15 07
Strood 4	d		14 28					14 48				14 58	14 58									15 18
Rochester 4	d		14 33			14 39		14 52	14 56	14 56		15 03	15 03							15 09		15 22
Chatham 4	d		14 35			14 42		14 55	14 59	14 59		15 05	15 05							15 12		15 25
Gillingham (Kent) 4	d		14 40			14 47		14a59	15a03	15a03		15 10	15 10							15 17		15a29
Rainham (Kent)	d		14 45			14 51						15 15	15 15							15 20		
Newington	d					14 55																
Sittingbourne 4	a		14 52			15 00						15 22	15 22							15 28		
	d	14 40	14 53			15 01					15 10	15 23	15 23							15 29		
Kemsley	d	14 45									15 15											
Swale	d	14 48									15 18											
Queenborough	d	14 52									15 22											
Sheerness-on-Sea	a	14 57									15 27											
Teynham	d																			15 33		
Faversham 2	a		15 03			15 09						15 33	15 33							15 39		
	d					15 13	15 15													15 43	15 45	
Selling	d																				15 50	
Canterbury East 4	d						15 29														15 59	
Bekesbourne	d																				16 03	
Adisham	d																				16 08	
Aylesham	d																				16 10	
Snowdown	d																				16 13	
Shepherds Well	d						15 39														16 17	
Kearsney	d																				16 21	
Dover Priory 4	a						15 48														16 27	
Whitstable	d					15 21														15 51		
Chestfield & Swalecliffe	d																			15 54		
Herne Bay	d					15 26														15 58		
Birchington-on-Sea	d					15 35														16 07		
Westgate-on-Sea	d																			16 10		
Margate 4	d					15 41													15 53	16 14		
Broadstairs	d					15 46													15 59	16 20		
Dumpton Park	d																			16 23		
Ramsgate 4	a					15 51													16 04	16 26		

A not 27 July

B 27 July

C ⌶ to Margate

D until 18 May

E not until 18 May, from 21 May

For further services to St Pancras International, Blackfriars and Elephant & Castle and onwards to Bromley South, St Mary Cray and Swanley please refer to table 52

Table 212

Mondays to Fridays

until 27 July, 13 Aug to 28 Aug and from 10 Sep

London - Medway, Sheerness-on-Sea, Dover and Ramsgate

Network Diagram - see first Page of Table 212

		SE	SE A	SE B	SE B	SE ■ C ⌶		SE	SE ■	SE	SE B	SE A	SE B	SE B	SE B	SE B	SE B	SE A	SE ■ C ⌶		SE	SE	SE A
St Pancras International ⊖	d		14 55	15 04	15 11						15 18	15 25	15 25	15 32	15 39	15 46	15 52						15 55
Stratford International ⊖	d		15 02	15 14	15 21						15 28	15 32	15 35	15 42	15 49	15 56	16 03						16 02
Ebbsfleet International	d		15 13	15 30	15a31						15 43	15 43	15a46	15a52	16 02	16a07	16a13						16 13
London Victoria ⊖	d					14 52			14 58										15 22				
London Blackfriars ⊖	d																						
Elephant & Castle ⊖	d																						
Bromley South	d					15 09			15 19										15 39				
St Mary Cray	d								15 25														
Swanley	d								15 29														
Farningham Road	d								15 34														
Longfield	d					15 22			15 38										15 52				
Meopham	d					15 27			15 42										15 57				
Sole Street	d								15 45														
London Charing Cross ⊖	d							14 39													15 09		
London Waterloo (East) ⊖	d							14 42													15 12		
London Cannon Street ⊖	d																						
London Bridge ⊖	d							14 47													15 17		
Dartford	d							15 25													15 55		
Greenhithe for Bluewater	d							15 30													16 00		
Gravesend	d		15 18					15 37			15 48	15 48									16 07		16 18
Strood	d		15 28					15 48			15 58	15 58									16 18		16 28
Rochester	d		15 33			15 39		15 52	15 56		16 03	16 03							16 09		16 22		16 33
Chatham	d		15 35			15 42		15 55	15 59		16 05	16 05							16 12		16 25		16 35
Gillingham (Kent)	d		15 40			15 47		15a59	16a03		16 10	16 10							16 17		16a29		16 40
Rainham (Kent)	d		15 45			15 51					16 15	16 15							16 21				16 45
Newington	d					15 55																	
Sittingbourne	a		15 52			16 00					16 22	16 22							16 28				16 52
	d	15 40	15 53			16 01				16 10	16 23	16 23							16 29			16 40	16 53
Kemsley	d	15 45								16 15												16 45	
Swale	d	15 48								16 18												16 48	
Queenborough	d	15 52								16 22												16 52	
Sheerness-on-Sea	a	15 57								16 27												16 57	
Teynham	d																		16 33				
Faversham	a		16 03			16 09					16 33	16 33							16 39				17 03
	d					16 13	16 15												16 43	16 45			
Selling	d						16 19													16 50			
Canterbury East	d						16 28													16 59			
Bekesbourne	d						16 33													17 03			
Adisham	d						16 37													17 08			
Aylesham	d						16 39													17 10			
Snowdown	d																			17 13			
Shepherds Well	d						16 44													17 17			
Kearsney	d																			17 21			
Dover Priory	a						16 52													17 27			
Whitstable	d					16 21													16 51				
Chestfield & Swalecliffe	d					16 24													16 54				
Herne Bay	d					16 28													16 58				
Birchington-on-Sea	d					16 37													17 07				
Westgate-on-Sea	d					16 40													17 10				
Margate	d					16 44												16 53	17 14				
Broadstairs	d					16 50												16 59	17 20				
Dumpton Park	d					16 53													17 23				
Ramsgate	a					16 56												17 04	17 26				

A not 27 July

B 27 July

C ⌶ to Margate

For further services to St Pancras International, Blackfriars and Elephant & Castle and onwards to Bromley South, St Mary Cray and Swanley please refer to table 52

Table 212

Mondays to Fridays

until 27 July, 13 Aug to 28 Aug and from 10 Sep

London - Medway, Sheerness-on-Sea, Dover and Ramsgate

Network Diagram - see first Page of Table 212

		SE A	SE A	SE ■ B ⌶		SE	SE ■	SE	SE A	SE C	SE A	SE A	SE A	SE A	SE A	SE C	SE ■ B ⌶		SE	SE ■	SE	SE ■
St Pancras International ⊖	d	16 04	16 11						16 18	16 25	16 25	16 32	16 39	16 46	16 52							
Stratford International ⊖	d	16 14	16 21						16 28	16 32	16 35	16 42	16 49	16 56	17 03							
Ebbsfleet International	d	16 30	16a31						16 44	16 43	16a46	16a52	17 02	17a07	17a13							
London Victoria ⊖	d			15 52			15 58										16 22			16 28		
London Blackfriars ⊖	d																					
Elephant & Castle ⊖	d																					
Bromley South	d			16 09			16 19										16 39			16 49		
St Mary Cray	d						16 25													16 55		
Swanley	d						16 29													16 59		
Farningham Road	d						16 34													17 04		
Longfield	d			16 22			16 38										16 52			17 08		
Meopham	d			16 27			16 42										16 57			17 12		
Sole Street	d						16 45													17 15		
London Charing Cross ⊖	d					15 39													16 09			
London Waterloo (East) ⊖	d					15 42													16 12			
London Cannon Street ⊖	d																					16 46
London Bridge ⊖	d					15 47													16 17			16 50
Dartford	d					16 25													16 55			
Greenhithe for Bluewater	d					16 30													17 00			
Gravesend	d					16 37			16 48	16 48									17 07			
Strood	d					16 48			16 58	16 58									17 18			
Rochester	d			16 39		16 52	16 56		17 03	17 03							17 10		17 22	17a27		17 29
Chatham	d			16 42		16 55	16 59		17 05	17 05							17 13		17 25			17 31
Gillingham (Kent)	d			16 47		16a59	17a03		17 10	17 10							17 18		17a31			17 36
Rainham (Kent)	d			16 51					17 15	17 15							17 23					17 41
Newington	d			16 55													17 27					
Sittingbourne	a			17 00					17 22	17 22							17 32					17 48
	d			17 01				17 10	17 23	17 23							17 33				17 40	17 48
Kemsley	d							17 15													17 45	
Swale	d							17 18													17 48	
Queenborough	d							17 22													17 52	
Sheerness-on-Sea	a							17 27													17 57	
Teynham	d			17 05													17 37					
Faversham	a			17 11					17 33	17 33							17 43					17 56
	d			17 15	17 19												17 47	17 49				17 57
Selling	d				17 23													17 54				
Canterbury East	d				17 32													18 03				
Bekesbourne	d																	18 07				
Adisham	d																	18 12				
Aylesham	d				17 40													18 14				
Snowdown	d																	18 17				
Shepherds Well	d				17 45													18 21				
Kearsney	d																	18 25				
Dover Priory	a				17 53													18 32				
Whitstable	d			17 23													17 55					18 05
Chestfield & Swalecliffe	d			17 26													17 58					18 08
Herne Bay	d			17 30													18 02					18 12
Birchington-on-Sea	d			17 39													18 11					18 21
Westgate-on-Sea	d			17 42													18 15					18 25
Margate	d			17 46												17 53	18 19					18 29
Broadstairs	d			17 52												17 59	18 24					18 34
Dumpton Park	d			17 55													18 27					18 37
Ramsgate	a			17 58												18 04	18 32					18 43

A 27 July

B ⌶ to Margate

C not 27 July

For further services to St Pancras International, Blackfriars and Elephant & Castle and onwards to Bromley South, St Mary Cray and Swanley please refer to table 52

Table 212

London - Medway, Sheerness-on-Sea, Dover and Ramsgate

Mondays to Fridays

until 27 July, 13 Aug to 28 Aug and from 10 Sep

Network Diagram - see first Page of Table 212

		SE A	SE 1 B ⛴	SE C	SE	SE C	SE A	SE A	SE A	SE 1	SE	SE	SE C	SE A	SE C	SE 1 B ⛴	SE 1	SE	SE C	SE C	SE A
St Pancras Internatnl 15 ⊖	d	16 55		17 04		17 11	17 14	17 18					17 18	17 25	17 25				17 32	17 39	17 44
Stratford International ⊖	d	17 02		17 14		17 21	17 21	17 25					17 28	17 32	17 35				17 42	17 49	17 51
Ebbsfleet International	d	17 13		17 30		17a31		17a35					17 43	17 43	17a46				17a52	18 02	
London Victoria 15 ⊖	d		16 57		17 04											17 27					
London Blackfriars 3 ⊖	d																				
Elephant & Castle ⊖	d																				
Bromley South 4	d		17 13		17 24											17 44					
St Mary Cray	d				17 30																
Swanley 4	d				17 34																
Farningham Road	d				17 39																
Longfield	d				17 44																
Meopham	d				17 48																
Sole Street	d				17 51																
London Charing Cross 4 ⊖	d																				
London Waterloo (East) 4 ⊖	d																				
London Cannon Street 4 ⊖	d									17 08	16 44						17 30	17 06			
London Bridge 4 ⊖	d									17 12	16 48						17 34	17 10			
Dartford 4	d										17 28							17 47			
Greenhithe for Bluewater	d										17 33							17 52			
Gravesend 4	d	17 18					17 36				17 40		17 48					18 00			18 06
Strood 4	d	17 28					17a46				17 52		17 58					18 14			18a17
Rochester 4	d	17 34	17 40		18a04					17 49	17 57		18 03	18 02		18 10	18 15	18 20			
Chatham 4	d	17 37	17 43							17 52	18 00		18 05	18 05		18 13	18 18	18 23			
Gillingham (Kent) 4	d	17 43	17 48							17 57	18a07		18 10	18 10		18 18	18 24	18a30			
Rainham (Kent)	d	17 48	17 53							18 02			18 15	18 15		18 23	18 29				
Newington	d		17 57							18 06							18 33				
Sittingbourne 4	a	17 56	18 02							18 11			18 22	18 22		18 30	18 38				
	d	17 57	18 03							18 12		18 15	18 23	18 23		18 30	18 38				
Kemsley	d											18 20									
Swale	d											18 23									
Queenborough	d											18 27									
Sheerness-on-Sea	a											18 32									
Teynham	d		18 07							18 16						18 35					
Faversham 2	a	18 05	18 13							18 22			18 33	18 31		18 41	18 47				
	d		18 17 18 19							18 24				18 32		18 44 18 50	18 49				
Selling	d		18 23													18 54					
Canterbury East 4	d		18 32													19 04					
Bekesbourne	d															19 08					
Adisham	d															19 12					
Aylesham	d		18 40													19 15					
Snowdown	d															19 17					
Shepherds Well	d		18 45													19 21					
Kearsney	d															19 25					
Dover Priory 4	a		18 55													19 32					
Whitstable	d		18 25							18 32				18 40		18 52	18 57				
Chestfield & Swalecliffe	d		18 28							18 35						18 55	19 00				
Herne Bay	d		18 32							18 39				18 46		18 59	19 04				
Birchington-on-Sea	d		18 41							18 48				18 55		19 08	19 12				
Westgate-on-Sea	d		18 45							18 52						19 11	19 16				
Margate 4	d		18 49						18 53	18 57				19 02		19 15	19 20				
Broadstairs	d		18 54						18 59	19 01				19a08		19 21	19 26				
Dumpton Park	d		18 57							19 04						19 24	19 29				
Ramsgate 4	a		19 02						19 04	19 10						19 30	19 34				

A not 27 July

B ⛴ to Margate

C 27 July

For further services to St Pancras International, Blackfriars and Elephant & Castle and onwards to Bromley South, St Mary Cray and Swanley please refer to table 52

Table 212

London - Medway, Sheerness-on-Sea, Dover and Ramsgate

Mondays to Fridays

until 27 July, 13 Aug to 28 Aug and from 10 Sep

Network Diagram - see first Page of Table 212

		SE	SE A	SE B	SE A	SE 1	SE	SE B	SE 1	SE A	SE A	SE B	SE 1 ⛴	SE	SE B	SE B	SE	SE 1	SE A	SE B	SE 1	SE A
St Pancras Internatnl 15 ⊖	d		17 46	17 48	17 52			17 55		18 04	18 11				18 14	18 18			18 18	18 25		18 25
Stratford International ⊖	d		17 56	17 55	18 03			18 02		18 14	18 21				18 21	18 25			18 28	18 32		18 35
Ebbsfleet International	d		18a07	18a05	18a13			18 13		18 30	18a31					18a35			18 40	18 43		18a46
London Victoria 15 ⊖	d					17 54							17 57								18 24	
London Blackfriars 3 ⊖	d																					
Elephant & Castle ⊖	d																					
Bromley South 4	d					18 19							18 15								18 46	
St Mary Cray	d					18 25															18 52	
Swanley 4	d					18 30															18 57	
Farningham Road	d					18 35															19 02	
Longfield	d												18 28								19 06	
Meopham	d					18 41															19 11	
Sole Street	d					18 44															19 13	
London Charing Cross 4 ⊖	d	17 17												17 39								
London Waterloo (East) 4 ⊖	d	17 20												17 42								
London Cannon Street 4 ⊖	d								17 52									18 14				
London Bridge 4 ⊖	d	17 26							17 56					17 48				18 18				
Dartford 4	d	18 02												18 22								
Greenhithe for Bluewater	d	18 07												18 27								
Gravesend 4	d	18 19												18 34	18 38				18 45			
Strood 4	d	18a33												18 45	18a49				18 55			
Rochester 4	d					18a56		18 31	18 38				18 43	18 51					19 03	19 03	19 23	
Chatham 4	d							18 34	18 41				18 46	18 54				19 00	19 06	19 06	19 26	
Gillingham (Kent) 4	d							18 39	18 46				18 51	19a02				19 05	19 11	19 11	19a32	
Rainham (Kent)	d							18 44	18 51				18 56					19 10	19 16	19 16		
Newington	d												19 00					19 14				
Sittingbourne 4	a							18 51	18 58				19 05					19 19	19 23	19 24		
	d						18 44	18 52	18 59				19 06				19 10	19 19	19 24	19 24		
Kemsley	d						18 49										19 15					
Swale	d						18 54										19 18					
Queenborough	d						18 58										19 22					
Sheerness-on-Sea	a						19 02										19 27					
Teynham	d												19 10									
Faversham 2	a							19 00	19 07				19 16					19 27	19 33	19 32		
	d							19 01	19 08				19 20 19 22					19 28		19 33		
Selling	d												19 26									
Canterbury East 4	d												19 36									
Bekesbourne	d																					
Adisham	d																					
Aylesham	d																					
Snowdown	d																					
Shepherds Well	d																					
Kearsney	d																					
Dover Priory 4	a												19 54									
Whitstable	d							19 09	19 16				19 28					19 36		19 42		
Chestfield & Swalecliffe	d												19 31					19 39				
Herne Bay	d							19 15	19 22				19 35					19 43		19 48		
Birchington-on-Sea	d							19 24	19 31				19 44					19 52		19 57		
Westgate-on-Sea	d												19 48					19 55				
Margate 4	d							19 30	19 37			19 53	19a54					19 59		20 04		
Broadstairs	d							19a36	19a45			19 59						20 05		20a09		
Dumpton Park	d																	20 08				
Ramsgate 4	a											20 04						20 13				

A 27 July

B not 27 July

For further services to St Pancras International, Blackfriars and Elephant & Castle and onwards to Bromley South, St Mary Cray and Swanley please refer to table 52

Table 212

Mondays to Fridays

until 27 July, 13 Aug to 28 Aug and from 10 Sep

London - Medway, Sheerness-on-Sea, Dover and Ramsgate

Network Diagram - see first Page of Table 212

Station		SE 1 A ⚒	SE	SE B	SE B	SE B	SE C	SE B	SE	SE 1 D	SE 1 E	SE C	SE 1 A ⚒	SE	SE	SE 1 E	SE 1 D	SE	SE B	SE B
St Pancras Internatnl 15 ⊖	d			18 32	18 39	18 46	18 48	18 52				18 55							19 04	19 11
Stratford International ⊖	d			18 42	18 49	18 56	18 55	19 03				19 02							19 14	19 21
Ebbsfleet International	d			18a52	19 02	19a07	19a05	19a13				19 13							19 30	19a31
London Victoria 15 ⊖	d	18 27											18 57			18 58	18 58			
London Blackfriars 3 ⊖	d																			
Ephant &Castle ⊖	d																			
Bromley South 4	d	18 44											19 14			19 19	19 21			
St Mary Cray	d															19 25	19 27			
Swanley 4	d															19 29	19 31			
Farningham Rad	d															19 34	19 36			
bngfield	d															19 39	19 40			
Meopham	d															19 43	19 44			
Sole Street	d															19 46	19 47			
London Charing Cross 4 ⊖	d		18 01												18 37			18 48		
London Waterloo (East) 4 ⊖	d		18 04												18 40			18 51		
London Cannon Street 4 ⊖	d									18 44	18 44			18 30						
London Bridge 4 ⊖	d		18 10							18 48	18 48			18 34	18 46			18 57		
Dartford 4	d		18 45											19 10	19 22			19 35		
Greenhithe for Bluewater	d		18 51											19 16	19 29			19 40		
Gravesend 4	d		19 02									19 20		19 26	19 38			19 47		
Strood 4	d		19 14									19 30		19 38	19a53			19 58		
Rchester 4	d	19 12	19 19							19 27	19 27	19 35	19 40	19 45		19 56	19 57	20 03		
Chatham 4	d	19 15	19 22							19 30	19 30	19 38	19 43	19 48		19 59	19 59	20 05		
Gillingham (Kent) 4	d	19 20	19a29							19 34	19 34	19 43	19 49	19a55		20a06	20a06	20a13		
Rinham (Kent)	d	19 25								19 39	19 39	19 48	19 54							
Nwington	d									19 43	19 43		19 58							
Sittingbourne 4	a	19 32								19 48	19 48	19 55	20 03							
	d	19 33							19 40	19 49	19 49	19 55	20 03							
Kemsley	d								19 45											
Swale	d								19 48											
Qenborough	d								19 52											
Sheerness-on-Sea	a								19 57											
Teynham	d	19 37								19 53	19 53									
Faversham 2	a	19 43								19 59	19 59	20 04	20 11							
	d	19 47 19 49								20 00	20 00		20 15 20 17							
Selling	d	19 54											20 21							
Canterbury East 4	d	20 03											20 30							
Bekesbourne	d	20 07											20 35							
Adisham	d	20 12											20 39							
Aylesham	d	20 14											20 41							
Snowdown	d	20 17																		
Shepherds W	d	20 21											20 46							
Kearsney	d	20 25																		
Dover Priory 4	a	20 32											20 56							
Wstable	d	19 55								20 08	20 08		20 23							
Chestfield &Swalecliffe	d	19 58								20 11	20 11		20 26							
Herne Bay	d	20 02								20 15	20 15		20 30							
Birchington-on-Sea	d	20 11								20 24	20 24		20 39							
Wtgate-on-Sea	d	20 15								20 27	20 27		20 43							
Margate 4	d	20 19								20 31	20 31		20 47							
Broadstairs	d	20 25								20 37	20 37		20 52							
Dumpton Park	d	20 28								20 40	20 40		20 55							
Ramsgate 4	a	20 33								20 46	20 49		21 00							

A ⚒ to Margate
B 27 uly
C not 27 uly
D not until 18 May, from 21 May
E until 18 May

For further services to St Pancras hternational, Blackfriars and Ephant & Castle and onwards to Bromley South, St Mary Cray and Swanley please refer to table 52

Table 212

Mondays to Fridays

until 27 July, 13 Aug to 28 Aug and from 10 Sep

London - Medway, Sheerness-on-Sea, Dover and Ramsgate

Network Diagram - see first Page of Table 212

Station		SE	SE A	SE B	SE A	SE A	SE A	SE A	SE A	SE B	SE 1 C ⚒	SE	SE	SE	SE B	SE A	SE A	SE 1	SE	SE	SE
St Pancras Internatnl 15 ⊖	d		19 18	19 25	19 25	19 32	19 39	19 46	19 52						19 55	20 04	20 11				
Stratford International ⊖	d		19 28	19 32	19 35	19 42	19 49	19 56	20 03						20 02	20 14	20 21				
Ebbsfleet International	d		19 45	19 45	19a46	19a52	20 02	20a07	20a13						20 13	20 30	20a31				
London Victoria 15 ⊖	d										19 22		19 28					19 52		19 58	
London Blackfriars 3 ⊖	d																				
Ephant &Castle ⊖	d																				
Bromley South 4	d										19 39		19 49					20 09		20 19	
St Mary Cray	d												19 55							20 25	
Swanley 4	d												19 59							20 29	
Farningham Rad	d												20 04							20 34	
bngfield	d										19 52		20 08					20 22		20 38	
Meopham	d										19 57		20 12					20 27		20 42	
Sole Street	d												20 15							20 45	
London Charing Cross 4 ⊖	d											19 09							19 39		
London Waterloo (East) 4 ⊖	d											19 12							19 42		
London Cannon Street 4 ⊖	d																				
London Bridge 4 ⊖	d											19 17							19 47		
Dartford 4	d											19 55							20 25		
Greenhithe for Bluewater	d											20 00							20 30		
Gravesend 4	d		19 51	19 51								20 07			20 18				20 37		
Strood 4	d		20 01	20 01								20 18			20 28				20 48		
Rchester 4	d		20 08	20 08							20 13	20 22	20 26		20 33			20 39	20 52	20 56	
Chatham 4	d		20 10	20 10							20 16	20 25	20 29		20 35			20 42	20 55	20 59	
Gillingham (Kent) 4	d		20 15	20 15							20 21	20a29	20a33		20 40			20 47	20a59	21a03	
Rinham (Kent)	d		20 20	20 20							20 25				20 45			20 51			
Nwington	d																	20 55			
Sittingbourne 4	a		20 27	20 27							20 32				20 52			21 00			
	d	20 10	20 27	20 27							20 33			20 40	20 53			21 01			21 10
Kemsley	d	20 15												20 45							21 15
Swale	d	20 18												20 48							21 18
Qenborough	d	20 22												20 52							21 22
Sheerness-on-Sea	a	20 27												20 57							21 27
Teynham	d										20 37										
Faversham 2	a		20 36	20 36							20 43				21 03			21 09			
	d										20 47 20 49							21 13 21 15			
Selling	d										20 54							21 19			
Canterbury East 4	d										21 03							21 28			
Bekesbourne	d										21 07							21 33			
Adisham	d										21 12							21 37			
Aylesham	d										21 14							21 39			
Snowdown	d										21 17										
Shepherds W	d										21 21							21 44			
Kearsney	d										21 25										
Dover Priory 4	a										21 32							21 52			
Wstable	d										20 55							21 21			
Chestfield &Swalecliffe	d										20 58							21 24			
Herne Bay	d										21 02							21 28			
Birchington-on-Sea	d										21 11							21 37			
Wtgate-on-Sea	d										21 15							21 40			
Margate 4	d									20 53	21 19							21 44			
Broadstairs	d									20 59	21 24							21 50			
Dumpton Park	d										21 27							21 53			
Ramsgate 4	a									21 04	21 32							21 56			

A 27 uly
B not 27 uly
C ⚒ to Margate

For further services to St Pancras hternational, Blackfriars and Ephant & Castle and onwards to Bromley South, St Mary Cray and Swanley please refer to table 52

London - Medway, Sheerness-on-Sea, Dover and Ramsgate

until 27 July, 13 Aug to 28 Aug and from 10 Sep

Network Diagram - see first Page of Table 212

		SE A	SE B	SE A	SE A	SE A	SE A	SE A	SE B	SE ■		SE	SE	SE B	SE A	SE A	SE ■		SE	SE ■	SE A	SE B
St Pancras International ■ ⊖	d	20 18	20 25	20 25	20 32	20 39	20 46	20 52						20 55	21 04	21 11					21 18	21 25
Stratford International ⊖	d	20 28	20 32	20 35	20 42	20 49	20 56	21 03						21 02	21 14	21 21					21 28	21 32
Ebbsfleet International	d	20 43	20 43	20a46	20a52	21 02	21a07	21a13						21 13	21 30	21a31					21 43	21 43
London Victoria ■ ⊖	d									20 22							20 52			20 58		
London Blackfriars ■ ⊖	d																					
Elephant & Castle ⊖	d																					
Bromley South ■	d									20 39							21 09			21 19		
St Mary Cray	d																			21 25		
Swanley ■	d																			21 29		
Farningham Road	d																			21 34		
Longfield	d									20 52							21 22			21 38		
Meopham	d									20 57							21 27			21 42		
Sole Street	d																			21 45		
London Charing Cross ■ ⊖	d											20 09							20 39			
London Waterloo (East) ■ ⊖	d											20 12							20 42			
London Cannon Street ■ ⊖	d																					
London Bridge ■ ⊖	d											20 17							20 47			
Dartford ■	d											20 55							21 25			
Greenhithe for Bluewater	d											21 00							21 30			
Gravesend ■	d	20 48	20 48									21 07		21 18					21 37		21 48	21 48
Strood ■	d	20 58	20 58									21 18		21 28					21 48		21 58	21 58
Rochester ■	d	21 03	21 03							21 09		21 22		21 33			21 39		21 52	21 56	22 03	22 03
Chatham ■	d	21 05	21 05							21 12		21 25		21 35			21 42		21 55	21 59	22 05	22 05
Gillingham (Kent) ■	d	21 10	21 10							21 17		21a29		21 40			21 47		21a59	22a03	22 10	22 10
Rainham (Kent)	d	21 15	21 15							21 21				21 45			21 51				22 15	22 15
Newington	d																21 55					
Sittingbourne ■	a	21 22	21 22							21 28				21 53			22 00				22 22	22 22
	d	21 23	21 23							21 29			21 40	21 53			22 01				22 23	22 23
Kemsley	d												21 45									
Swale	d												21 48									
Queenborough	d												21 52									
Sheerness-on-Sea	a												21 57									
Teynham	d									21 33												
Faversham ■	a	21 33	21 33							21 39				22 03			22 09				22 33	22 33
	d									21 43	21 45						22 13	22 15				
Selling	d										21 50							22 19				
Canterbury East ■	d										21 59							22 28				
Bekesbourne	d										22 03							22 33				
Adisham	d										22 08							22 37				
Aylesham	d										22 10							22 39				
Snowdown	d										22 13											
Shepherds Well	d										22 17							22 44				
Kearsney	d										22 21											
Dover Priory ■	a										22 26							22 52				
Whitstable	d									21 51							22 21					
Chestfield & Swalecliffe	d									21 54							22 24					
Herne Bay	d									21 58							22 28					
Birchington-on-Sea	d									22 07							22 37					
Westgate-on-Sea	d									22 10							22 40					
Margate ■	d								21 53	22 14							22 44					
Broadstairs	d								21 59	22 20							22 50					
Dumpton Park	d									22 23							22 53					
Ramsgate ■	a								22 04	22 26							22 56					

A 27 July

B not 27 July

For further services to St Pancras International, Blackfriars and Elephant & Castle and onwards to Bromley South, St Mary Cray and Swanley please refer to table 52

London - Medway, Sheerness-on-Sea, Dover and Ramsgate

until 27 July, 13 Aug to 28 Aug and from 10 Sep

Network Diagram - see first Page of Table 212

		SE ■		SE	SE A	SE A	SE A	SE A	SE A	SE	SE B	SE ■	SE	SE A	SE A	SE A	SE B	SE A	SE A	SE A	SE ■		SE
St Pancras International ■ ⊖	d				21 25	21 32	21 39	21 46	21 52		21 55			22 04	22 11	22 18	22 25	22 25	22 32	22 39			
Stratford International ⊖	d				21 35	21 42	21 49	21 56	22 03		22 02			22 14	22 21	22 28	22 32	22 35	22 42	22 47			
Ebbsfleet International	d				21a46	21a52	22 02	22a07	22a13		22 13			22a24	22a31	22a38	22 43	22a46	22a52	22a57			
London Victoria ■ ⊖	d	21 22										21 52									22 22		
London Blackfriars ■ ⊖	d																						
Elephant & Castle ⊖	d																						
Bromley South ■	d	21 39										22 09									22 39		
St Mary Cray	d											22 15											
Swanley ■	d											22 19											
Farningham Road	d											22 24											
Longfield	d	21 52										22 28									22 52		
Meopham	d	21 57										22 32									22 57		
Sole Street	d											22 35											
London Charing Cross ■ ⊖	d			21 09									21 39										22 09
London Waterloo (East) ■ ⊖	d			21 12									21 42										22 12
London Cannon Street ■ ⊖	d																						
London Bridge ■ ⊖	d			21 17									21 47										22 17
Dartford ■	d			21 55									22 25										22 55
Greenhithe for Bluewater	d			22 00									22 30										23 00
Gravesend ■	d			22 07							22 18		22 37				22 48						23 07
Strood ■	d			22 18							22 28		22 48				22 58						23 18
Rochester ■	d	22 09		22 22							22 33	22 45	22 52				23 03				23 09		23 22
Chatham ■	d	22 12		22 25							22 35	22 47	22 55				23 05				23 12		23 25
Gillingham (Kent) ■	d	22 17		22a29							22 40	22 52	22a59				23 10				23 17		23a29
Rainham (Kent)	d	22 21									22 45	22 56					23 15				23 21		
Newington	d											23 00											
Sittingbourne ■	a	22 28									22 52	23 05					23 22				23 28		
	d	22 29								22 40	22 53	23 06					23 23				23 29		
Kemsley	d									22 45													
Swale	d									22 48													
Queenborough	d									22 52													
Sheerness-on-Sea	a									22 57													
Teynham	d	22 33																			23 33		
Faversham ■	a	22 39									23 03	23 17					23 33				23 39		
	d	22 43	22 45																		23 43	23 45	
Selling	d		22 50																			23 50	
Canterbury East ■	d		22 59																			23 59	
Bekesbourne	d		23 03																				
Adisham	d		23 08																				
Aylesham	d		23 10																			00 07	
Snowdown	d		23 13																				
Shepherds Well	d		23 17																				
Kearsney	d		23 21																				
Dover Priory ■	a		23 26																			00 18	
Whitstable	d	22 51																			23 51		
Chestfield & Swalecliffe	d	22 54																			23 54		
Herne Bay	d	22 58																			23 58		
Birchington-on-Sea	d	23 07																			00 07		
Westgate-on-Sea	d	23 10																			00 10		
Margate ■	d	23 14																			00 14		
Broadstairs	d	23 20																			00 20		
Dumpton Park	d	23 23																			00 23		
Ramsgate ■	a	23 26																			00 26		

A 27 July

B not 27 July

For further services to St Pancras International, Blackfriars and Elephant & Castle and onwards to Bromley South, St Mary Cray and Swanley please refer to table 52

Mondays to Fridays

until 27 July, 13 Aug to 28 Aug and from 10 Sep

London - Medway, Sheerness-on-Sea, Dover and Ramsgate

Network Diagram - see first Page of Table 212

		SE	SE	SE	SE	SE	SE	SE	SE	SE	SE	SE	SE	SE	SE	SE	SE	SE	SE	SE	SE	SE	SE
						■							■									■	
		A	A		B			A	A	A	A	B			A	A	A	A	A	A	B		
St Pancras Internatnl ■ ⊖	d	22 46	22 52		22 55			23 04	23 11	23 16	23 21	23 25			23 26	23 32	23 36	23 41	23 47	23 51	23 55		
Stratford International ⊖	d	22 56	23 02		23 02			23 14	23 21	23 24	23 30	23 32			23 35	23 42	23 46	23 50	23 57	00 01	00 02		
Ebbsfleet International	d	23a07	23a12		23 13			23a24	23a31	23a34	23a41	23 43			23a45	23a52	23a57	00a01	00a07	00a10	00 13		
London Victoria ■ ⊖	d					22 52							23 22									23 52	
London Blackfriars ■ ⊖	d																						
Ephant &Castle ⊖	d																						
Bromley South ■	d					23 09							23 39									00 09	
St Mary Cray	d					23 15																00 15	
Swanley ■	d					23 19																00 19	
Farningham Bad	d					23 24																00 24	
bngfield	d					23 28							23 52									00 28	
Meopham	d					23 32							23 57									00 32	
Sole Street	d					23 35																00 35	
London Charing Cross ■ ⊖	d						22 39							23 09									23 39
London Waterloo (East) ■ ⊖	d						22 42							23 12									23 42
London Cannon Street ■ ⊖	d																						
London Bridge ■ ⊖	d						22 47							23 17									23 47
Dartford ■	d						23 25							23 55									00 25
Greenhithe for Bluewater	d						23 31							23 59									00 31
Gravesend ■	d				23 18		23 40					23 48		00 10							00 18		00 40
Strood ■	d				23 28		23 52					23 58		00 22							00 28		00 52
Bchester ■	d				23 33	23 45	23 56					00 03	00 09	00 26							00 33	00 45	00 56
Chatham ■	d				23 35	23 47	23 58					00 05	00 12	00 28							00 35	00 47	00 58
Gillingham (Kent) ■	d				23 40	23 52	00a03					00 10	00 17	00a33							00 40	00a52	01a03
Binham (Kent)	d				23 45	23 56						00 15	00 21								00 45		
Nwington	d					00 01																	
Sittingbourne ■	a				23 52	00 06						00 22	00 28								00 52		
	d			23 32	23 53	00 07						00 23	00 29								00 53		
Kemsley	d			23 37																			
Swale	d			23 40																			
Qeenborough	d			23 44																			
Sheerness-on-Sea	a			23 49																			
Teynham	d												00 33										
Faversham ■	a				00 03	00 15						00 33	00 39								01 03		
	d												00 43										
Selling	d																						
Canterbury East ■	d																						
Bekesbourne	d																						
Adisham	d																						
Aylesham	d																						
Snowdown	d																						
Shepherds W	d																						
Kearsney	d																						
Dover Priory ■	a																						
Wstable	d												00 51										
Chestfield &Swalecliffe	d												00 54										
Herne Bay	d												00 58										
Birchington-on-Sea	d												01 07										
Wstgate-on-Sea	d												01 10										
Margate ■	d												01 14										
Broadstairs	d												01 20										
Dumpton Park	d												01 23										
Ramsgate ■	a												01 26										

A 27 uly

B not 27 uly

For further services to St Pancras hternational, Blackfriars and Ephant & Castle and onwards to Bromley South, St Mary Cray and Swanley please refer to table 52

Mondays to Fridays

until 27 July, 13 Aug to 28 Aug and from 10 Sep

London - Medway, Sheerness-on-Sea, Dover and Ramsgate

Network Diagram - see first Page of Table 212

		SE
		A
St Pancras Internatnl ■ ⊖	d	23 56
Stratford International ⊖	d	00 05
Ebbsfleet International	d	00a16
London Victoria ■ ⊖	d	
London Blackfriars ■ ⊖	d	
Ephant &Castle ⊖	d	
Bromley South ■	d	
St Mary Cray	d	
Swanley ■	d	
Farningham Bad	d	
bngfield	d	
Meopham	d	
Sole Street	d	
London Charing Cross ■ ⊖	d	
London Waterloo (East) ■ ⊖	d	
London Cannon Street ■ ⊖	d	
London Bridge ■ ⊖	d	
Dartford ■	d	
Greenhithe for Bluewater	d	
Gravesend ■	d	
Strood ■	d	
Bchester ■	d	
Chatham ■	d	
Gillingham (Kent) ■	d	
Binham (Kent)	d	
Nwington	d	
Sittingbourne ■	a	
	d	
Kemsley	d	
Swale	d	
Qeenborough	d	
Sheerness-on-Sea	a	
Teynham	d	
Faversham ■	a	
	d	
Selling	d	
Canterbury East ■	d	
Bekesbourne	d	
Adisham	d	
Aylesham	d	
Snowdown	d	
Shepherds W	d	
Kearsney	d	
Dover Priory ■	a	
Wstable	d	
Chestfield &Swalecliffe	d	
Herne Bay	d	
Birchington-on-Sea	d	
Wstgate-on-Sea	d	
Margate ■	d	
Broadstairs	d	
Dumpton Park	d	
Ramsgate ■	a	

A 27 uly

For further services to St Pancras hternational, Blackfriars and Ephant & Castle and onwards to Bromley South, St Mary Cray and Swanley please refer to table 52

Table 212

Mondays to Fridays

30 July to 10 August

London - Medway, Sheerness-on-Sea, Dover and Ramsgate

Network Diagram - see first Page of Table 212

		SE MO 1	SE 1 A		SE 1 A	SE MO 1	SE MO 1	SE	SE	SE	SE	SE	SE A	SE 1 A	SE MO 1	SE	SE 1 A	SE MO 1	SE 1 A	SE	SE	SE	SE
St Pancras Internatnl 15 ⊖	d							23p51	23p56	00 02	00 06	00 11									00 17	00 21	00 27
Stratford International ⊖	d							00 01	00 05	00 12	00 16	00 20									00 27	00 30	00 36
Ebbsfleet International	d							00a10	00a16	00a22	00a26	00a31									00a37	00a41	00a47
London Victoria 15 ⊖	d	22p22	22p22		22p52	22p52								23p22	23p22		23p52	23p52	00 10				
London Blackfriars 3 ⊖	d																						
Elephant & Castle ⊖	d																						
Bromley South 4	d	22p39	22p39		23p09	23p09								23p39	23p39		00 09	00 09					
St Mary Cray	d				23p15	23p15											00 15	00 15					
Swanley 4	d				23p19	23p19											00 19	00 19					
Farningham Road	d				23p24	23p24											00 24	00 24					
Longfield	d	22p52	22p52		23p28	23p28								23p52	23p52		00 28	00 28					
Meopham	d	22p57	22p57		23p32	23p32								23p57	23p57		00 32	00 32					
Sole Street	d				23p35	23p35											00 35	00 35					
London Charing Cross 4 ⊖	d															23p09				23p39			
London Waterloo (East) 4 ⊖	d															23p12				23p42			
London Cannon Street 4 ⊖	d																						
London Bridge 4 ⊖	d															23p17				23p47			
Dartford 4	d															23p55				00 25			
Greenhithe for Bluewater	d															23p59				00 31			
Gravesend 4	d															00 10				00 40			
Strood 4	d															00 22				00 52			
Rochester 4	d	23p09	23p09		23p45	23p45								00 09	00 09	00 26	00 45	00 45	00 49	00 56			
Chatham 4	d	23p12	23p12		23p47	23p47								00 12	00 12	00 28	00 47	00 47	00 52	00 58			
Gillingham (Kent) 4	d	23p17	23p17		23p52	23p52								00 17	00 17	00a36	00a52	00 53	00 57	01a06			
Rainham (Kent)	d	23p21	23p21		23p56	23p56								00 21	00 21			00 57	01 01				
Newington	d				00 01	00 01												01 01	01 05				
Sittingbourne 4	a	23p28	23p28		00 06	00 06								00 28	00 28			01 06	01 10				
	d	23p29	23p29		00 07	00 07							00 15	00 29	00 29			01 07	01 11				
Kemsley	d												00 20										
Swale	d												00 23										
Queenborough	d												00 27										
Sheerness-on-Sea	a												00 32										
Teynham	d	23p33	23p33											00 33	00 33			01 11	01 15				
Faversham 2	a	23p39	23p39		00 15	00 16								00 39	00 39			01 17	01 23				
	d	23p43	23p43	23p45			23p45							00 43	00 43				01 24				
Selling	d			23p50			23p50																
Canterbury East 4	d			23p59			23p59																
Bekesbourne	d						00 03																
Adisham	d						00 07																
Aylesham	d			00 07			00 10																
Snowdown	d						00 12																
Shepherds Well	d						00 16																
Kearsney	d						00 20																
Dover Priory 4	a			00 18			00 25																
Whitstable	d	23p51	23p51											00 51	00 51				01 32				
Chestfield & Swalecliffe	d	23p54	23p54											00 54	00 54				01 35				
Herne Bay	d	23p58	23p58											00 58	00 58				01 39				
Birchington-on-Sea	d	00 07	00 07											01 07	01 07				01 48				
Westgate-on-Sea	d	00 11	00 10											01 10	01 11				01 52				
Margate 4	d	00 15	00 14											01 14	01 15				01 56				
Broadstairs	d	00 20	00 20											01 20	01 20				02 01				
Dumpton Park	d	00 23	00 23											01 23	01 23				02 04				
Ramsgate 4	a	00 26	00 26											01 26	01 26				02 07				

A not 30 July, 6 August

For further services to St Pancras International, Blackfriars and Elephant & Castle and onwards to Bromley South, St Mary Cray and Swanley please refer to table 52

Table 212

Mondays to Fridays

30 July to 10 August

London - Medway, Sheerness-on-Sea, Dover and Ramsgate

Network Diagram - see first Page of Table 212

		SE	SE	SE	SE	SE	SE	SE	SE	SE	SE	SE	SE	SE	SE	SE	SE	SE	SE	SE	SE	SE	SE
St Pancras Internatnl 15 ⊖	d	00 32			00 36	00 41	00 47	00 51	00 57	01 02	01 06	01 11	01 17	01 21	01 27	01 32	01 38	01 44	01 55	02 02	02 32	03 02	03 32
Stratford International ⊖	d	00 42			00 46	00 50	00 57	01 00	01 06	01 12	01 16	01 20	01 26	01 30	01 36	01 42	01 48	01 54	02 04	02a08	02a38	03a08	03a38
Ebbsfleet International	d	00a52			00a56	01 03	01a07	01a11	01 20	01a22	01 29	01 35	01 38	01a41	01 49	01a52	02 00	02 05	02 16				
London Victoria 15 ⊖	d		00 35																				
London Blackfriars 3 ⊖	d																						
Elephant & Castle ⊖	d																						
Bromley South 4	d		00 55																				
St Mary Cray	d		01 01																				
Swanley 4	d		01 05																				
Farningham Road	d		01 10																				
Longfield	d		01 14																				
Meopham	d		01 18																				
Sole Street	d																						
London Charing Cross 4 ⊖	d			00 18																			
London Waterloo (East) 4 ⊖	d			00 21																			
London Cannon Street 4 ⊖	d																						
London Bridge 4 ⊖	d			00 26																			
Dartford 4	d			01 06																			
Greenhithe for Bluewater	d			01 10																			
Gravesend 4	d			01 17									01 43						02 21				
Strood 4	d			01 29									01 53						02 31				
Rochester 4	d		01 29	01 33									01 57					02 20	02 35				
Chatham 4	d		01 31	01 35									02 00					02 23	02 38				
Gillingham (Kent) 4	d		01a35	01a44									02 04					02 27	02 42				
Rainham (Kent)	d												02 09					02 32	02 47				
Newington	d																						
Sittingbourne 4	a												02 16					02 39	02 54				
	d												02 17					02 40	02 55				
Kemsley	d																						
Swale	d																						
Queenborough	d																						
Sheerness-on-Sea	a																						
Teynham	d																						
Faversham 2	a												02 25					02 48	03 03				
	d																						
Selling	d																						
Canterbury East 4	d																						
Bekesbourne	d																						
Adisham	d																						
Aylesham	d																						
Snowdown	d																						
Shepherds Well	d																						
Kearsney	d																						
Dover Priory 4	a																						
Whitstable	d																						
Chestfield & Swalecliffe	d																						
Herne Bay	d																						
Birchington-on-Sea	d																						
Westgate-on-Sea	d																						
Margate 4	d																						
Broadstairs	d																						
Dumpton Park	d																						
Ramsgate 4	a																						

For further services to St Pancras International, Blackfriars and Elephant & Castle and onwards to Bromley South, St Mary Cray and Swanley please refer to table 52

Table 212

Mondays to Fridays

30 July to 10 August

London - Medway, Sheerness-on-Sea, Dover and Ramsgate

Network Diagram - see first Page of Table 212

Station		SE		SE	SE	SE	SE ■	SE	SE	SE	SE ■	SE		SE	SE	SE ■	SE	SE ■	SE	SE	SE	SE		SE ■	SE ■
St Pancras International ⊖	d	04 02		04 32		05 02		05 32							06 04				06 32	06 52		07 04			
Stratford International ⊖	d	04a08		04a38		05a08		05 42							06 14				06 42	07 03		07 14			
Ebbsfleet International	d							05 56							06a24				06a52	07a13		07 30			
London Victoria ⊖	d																	05 22							05 52
London Blackfriars ⊖	d																								
Elephant & Castle ⊖	d																								
Bromley South	d																	05 39							06 09
St Mary Cray	d																	05 45							
Swanley	d																	05 49							06 20
Farningham Road	d																	05 54							
Longfield	d																	05 58							06 26
Meopham	d																	06 02							06 30
Sole Street	d																	06 05							
London Charing Cross ⊖	d																								
London Waterloo (East) ⊖	d																								
London Cannon Street ⊖	d																								
London Bridge ⊖	d																								
Dartford	d											05 25													
Greenhithe for Bluewater	d											05 30													
Gravesend	d											05 37													
Strood	d											05 48													
Rochester	d											05 52						06 15							06 41
Chatham	d											05 55						06 17							06 44
Gillingham (Kent)	d				05 00						05 47	05a59						06 22							06 48
Rainham (Kent)	d				05 04						05 51							06 26							06 53
Newington	d				05 08						05 55							06 30							06 57
Sittingbourne	a										06 00							06 35							07 02
	d								05 33		06 01			06 03			06 22	06 36			06 53				07 02
Kemsley	d				05 15				05 38					06 08			06 27				06 58				
Swale	d				05 18				05 43					06 11			06 30				07 01				
Queenborough	d				05 22				05 47					06 15			06 35				07 05				
Sheerness-on-Sea	a				05 27				05 51					06 20			06 40				07 10				
Teynham	d										06 05							06 40							07 07
Faversham	a										06 11							06 46							07 13
	d						05 15				06 12					06 15		06 47						07 05	07 13
Selling	d						05 20				06 17													07 09	
Canterbury East	d						05 29				06 26													07 18	
Bekesbourne	d						05 33				06 30													07 23	
Adisham	d						05 38				06 35													07 27	
Aylesham	d						05 40				06 37													07 29	
Snowdown	d						05 43				06 40													07 32	
Shepherds Well	d						05 47				06 44													07 35	
Kearsney	d						05 51				06 48													07 40	
Dover Priory	a						05 56				06 53													07 45	
Whitstable	d															06 23		06 55							07 21
Chestfield & Swalecliffe	d															06 26		06 58							07 24
Herne Bay	d															06 30		07 02							07 28
Birchington-on-Sea	d															06 39		07 11							07 37
Westgate-on-Sea	d															06 42		07 14							07 41
Margate	d									05 44						06 52		07 18							07 45
Broadstairs	d									05 49						06 58		07 24							07 50
Dumpton Park	d															07 01		07 27							07 53
Ramsgate	a									05 54						07 04		07 30							07 56

For further services to St Pancras International, Blackfriars and Elephant & Castle and onwards to Bromley South, St Mary Cray and Swanley please refer to table 52

Table 212

Mondays to Fridays

30 July to 10 August

London - Medway, Sheerness-on-Sea, Dover and Ramsgate

Network Diagram - see first Page of Table 212

Station		SE	SE	SE	SE ■	SE	SE	SE		SE	SE ■	SE ■	SE	SE ■	SE	SE	SE	SE		SE	SE	SE	SE	SE	SE
St Pancras International ⊖	d							07 11									07 18	07 25		07 32	07 39	07 46	07 52	08 04	08 11
Stratford International ⊖	d							07 21									07 28	07 35		07 42	07 49	07 56	08 03	08 14	08 21
Ebbsfleet International	d							07a31									07 43	07a46		07a52	08 02	08a07	08a13	08 30	08a31
London Victoria ⊖	d		06 14		06 22							06 45		06 58	07 09										
London Blackfriars ⊖	d																								
Elephant & Castle ⊖	d																								
Bromley South	d				06 39							07 02		07 19											
St Mary Cray	d				06 45							07 08		07 25											
Swanley	d				06 49							07 13		07 29											
Farningham Road	d				06 54							07 18		07 34											
Longfield	d				06 58							07 22		07 38											
Meopham	d				07 02							07 26		07 42											
Sole Street	d				07 05							07 28		07 45											
London Charing Cross ⊖	d	05 39				05 56	06 26						06 39												
London Waterloo (East) ⊖	d	05 42				05 59	06 29						06 42												
London Cannon Street ⊖	d																								
London Bridge ⊖	d	05 47				06 04	06 34						06 47												
Dartford	d	06 25	07a12			06 42	07 12						07 25		07a51										
Greenhithe for Bluewater	d	06 30				06 48	07 18						07 30												
Gravesend	d	06 38				06 59	07 27						07 37				07 48								
Strood	d	06 49				07 17	07a40						07 48				07 58								
Rochester	d	06 53			07 15	07 21						07 40	07 52	07 56			08 03								
Chatham	d	06 56			07 17	07 24						07 42	07 55	07 59			08 05								
Gillingham (Kent)	d	07a03			07 22	07a31						07 47	08a02	08a03			08 10								
Rainham (Kent)	d				07 26							07 52					08 15								
Newington	d				07 30							07 56													
Sittingbourne	a				07 37							08 01					08 22								
	d			07 09	07 38					07 45		08 02				08 13	08 23								
Kemsley	d			07 14						07 50						08 18									
Swale	d			07 17						07 53						08 21									
Queenborough	d			07 22						07 57						08 25									
Sheerness-on-Sea	a			07 27						08 02						08 30									
Teynham	d				07 42							08 06													
Faversham	a				07 48							08 12					08 33								
	d				07 49						07 52	08 13													
Selling	d										07 56	08 18													
Canterbury East	d										08 06	08 27													
Bekesbourne	d										08 11	08 31													
Adisham	d										08 15	08 36													
Aylesham	d										08 18	08 38													
Snowdown	d										08 20	08 41													
Shepherds Well	d										08 24	08 45													
Kearsney	d										08 29	08 49													
Dover Priory	a										08 35	08 54													
Whitstable	d				07 57																				
Chestfield & Swalecliffe	d				08 00																				
Herne Bay	d				08 04																				
Birchington-on-Sea	d				08 13																				
Westgate-on-Sea	d				08 17																				
Margate	d				08 21																				
Broadstairs	d				08 26																				
Dumpton Park	d				08 29																				
Ramsgate	a				08 32																				

For further services to St Pancras International, Blackfriars and Elephant & Castle and onwards to Bromley South, St Mary Cray and Swanley please refer to table 52

Table 212

Mondays to Fridays

30 July to 10 August

London - Medway, Sheerness-on-Sea, Dover and Ramsgate

Network Diagram - see first Page of Table 212

		SE ■	SE ■			SE	SE	SE	SE ■		SE	SE ■	SE	SE		SE	SE	SE	SE	SE	SE	SE	SE ■		
St Pancras International ■ ⊖	d													08 18		08 25	08 32	08 39	08 46	08 52	09 04	09 11			
Stratford International ⊖	d													08 28		08 35	08 42	08 49	08 56	09 03	09 14	09 21			
Ebbsfleet International	d													08 44		08a46	08a52	09 02	09a07	09a13	09 30	09a31			
London Victoria ■ ⊖	d		07 22				07 43		07 52			07 58											08 22		
London Blackfriars ■ ⊖	d																								
Elephant & Castle ⊖	d																								
Bromley South ■	d		07 40						08 09			08 28											08 39		
St Mary Cray	d											08 34													
Swanley ■	d		07 49									08 39													
Farningham Road	d											08 44													
Longfield	d		07 55						08 22			08 49											08 52		
Meopham	d		07 59						08 27			08 53											08 57		
Sole Street	d											08 56													
London Charing Cross ■ ⊖	d					07 12					07 39														
London Waterloo (East) ■ ⊖	d					07 15					07 42														
London Cannon Street ■ ⊖	d																								
London Bridge ■ ⊖	d					07 21					07 47														
Dartford ■	d					08 00	08a30				08 25														
Greenhithe for Bluewater	d					08 05					08 30														
Gravesend ■	d					08 12					08 37			08 48											
Strood ■	d					08 23					08 48			08 58											
Rochester ■	d		08 11			08 27			08 39		08 52	09a07		09 03									09 09		
Chatham ■	d		08 13			08 30			08 42		08 55			09 05									09 12		
Gillingham (Kent) ■	d		08 18			08a38			08 47		09a02			09 10									09 17		
Rainham (Kent)	d		08 22						08 51					09 15									09 21		
Newington	d		08 26						08 55																
Sittingbourne ■	a		08 31						09 00					09 22									09 28		
	d		08 32					08 40	09 01				09 10	09 23									09 29		
Kemsley	d							08 45					09 15												
Swale	d							08 48					09 18												
Queenborough	d							08 52					09 22												
Sheerness-on-Sea	a							08 57					09 27												
Teynham	d		08 36																				09 33		
Faversham ■	a		08 42						09 09					09 33									09 39		
	d	08 16	08 46	08 49					09 13	09 15													09 43	09 45	
Selling	d			08 54																				09 50	
Canterbury East ■	d			09 03						09 29														09 59	
Bekesbourne	d			09 07																				10 03	
Adisham	d			09 12																				10 08	
Aylesham	d			09 14																				10 10	
Snowdown	d			09 17																				10 13	
Shepherds Well	d			09 21																				10 17	
Kearsney	d			09 25																				10 21	
Dover Priory ■	a			09 30						09 50														10 26	
Whitstable	d	08 24	08 54						09 21														09 51		
Chestfield & Swalecliffe	d	08 27	08 57																				09 54		
Herne Bay	d	08 31	09 01						09 26														09 58		
Birchington-on-Sea	d	08 40	09 10						09 35														10 07		
Westgate-on-Sea	d	08 43	09 13																				10 10		
Margate ■	d	08 47	09 17						09 41														10 14		
Broadstairs	d	08 53	09 23						09 46														10 20		
Dumpton Park	d	08 56	09 26																				10 23		
Ramsgate ■	a	08 59	09 29						09 51														10 26		

For further services to St Pancras International, Blackfriars and Elephant & Castle and onwards to Bromley South, St Mary Cray and Swanley please refer to table 52

Table 212

Mondays to Fridays

30 July to 10 August

London - Medway, Sheerness-on-Sea, Dover and Ramsgate

Network Diagram - see first Page of Table 212

		SE	SE	SE ■		SE	SE ■	SE	SE	SE		SE	SE	SE	SE	SE	SE	SE ■		SE		SE	SE ■ A ⌶		SE
St Pancras International ■ ⊖	d								09 18	09 25		09 32	09 39	09 46	09 52	10 04	10 11								
Stratford International ⊖	d								09 28	09 35		09 42	09 49	09 56	10 03	10 14	10 21								
Ebbsfleet International	d								09 43	09a46		09a52	10 02	10a07	10a13	10 30	10a31								
London Victoria ■ ⊖	d			08 52			08 58											09 22					09 52		
London Blackfriars ■ ⊖	d																								
Elephant & Castle ⊖	d																								
Bromley South ■	d			09 09			09 19											09 39					10 09		
St Mary Cray	d						09 25																		
Swanley ■	d						09 29																		
Farningham Road	d						09 34																		
Longfield	d			09 22			09 38											09 52					10 22		
Meopham	d			09 27			09 42											09 57					10 27		
Sole Street	d						09 45																		
London Charing Cross ■ ⊖	d	08 11				08 41														09 11					09 39
London Waterloo (East) ■ ⊖	d	08 14				08 44														09 14					09 42
London Cannon Street ■ ⊖	d																								
London Bridge ■ ⊖	d	08 19				08 49														09 19					09 47
Dartford ■	d	08 56				09 25														09 55					10 25
Greenhithe for Bluewater	d	09 01				09 30														10 00					10 30
Gravesend ■	d	09 08				09 37			09 48											10 07					10 37
Strood ■	d	09 19				09 48			09 58											10 18					10 48
Rochester ■	d	09 23		09 39		09 52	09 56		10 03									10 09		10 22			10 39		10 52
Chatham ■	d	09 26		09 42		09 55	09 59		10 05									10 12		10 25			10 42		10 55
Gillingham (Kent) ■	d	09a33		09 47		10a02	10a03		10 10									10 17		10a32			10 47		11a02
Rainham (Kent)	d			09 51					10 15									10 21					10 51		
Newington	d			09 55																			10 55		
Sittingbourne ■	a			10 01					10 22									10 28					11 00		
	d		09 40	10 01				10 10	10 23									10 29				10 40	11 01		
Kemsley	d		09 45					10 15														10 45			
Swale	d		09 48					10 18														10 48			
Queenborough	d		09 52					10 22														10 52			
Sheerness-on-Sea	a		09 57					10 27														10 57			
Teynham	d																	10 33							
Faversham ■	a			10 09					10 33									10 39					11 09		
	d			10 13	10 15													10 43	10 45				11 13	11 15	
Selling	d																		10 50						
Canterbury East ■	d				10 29														10 59					11 29	
Bekesbourne	d																		11 03						
Adisham	d																		11 08						
Aylesham	d																		11 10						
Snowdown	d																		11 13						
Shepherds Well	d																		11 17						
Kearsney	d																		11 21						
Dover Priory ■	a				10 50														11 26					11 50	
Whitstable	d			10 21														10 51					11 21		
Chestfield & Swalecliffe	d																	10 54							
Herne Bay	d			10 26														10 58					11 26		
Birchington-on-Sea	d			10 35														11 07					11 35		
Westgate-on-Sea	d																	11 10							
Margate ■	d			10 41														11 14					11 41		
Broadstairs	d			10 46														11 20					11 46		
Dumpton Park	d																	11 23							
Ramsgate ■	a			10 51														11 26					11 51		

A ⌶ to Margate

For further services to St Pancras International, Blackfriars and Elephant & Castle and onwards to Bromley South, St Mary Cray and Swanley please refer to table 52

Table 212

Mondays to Fridays

30 July to 10 August

London - Medway, Sheerness-on-Sea, Dover and Ramsgate

Network Diagram - see first Page of Table 212

Station		SE 1	SE	SE	SE	SE	SE	SE	SE	SE	SE	SE 1 A ⌶		SE	SE	SE 1 A ⌶		SE	SE 1	SE	SE	SE	SE
St Pancras Internatnl 15 ⊖	d			10 18	10 25	10 32	10 39	10 46	10 52	11 04	11 11										11 18	11 25	11 32
Stratford International ⊖	d			10 28	10 35	10 42	10 49	10 56	11 03	11 14	11 21										11 28	11 35	11 42
Ebbsfleet International	d			10 44	10a46	10a52	11 02	11a07	11a13	11 30	11a31										11 43	11a46	11a52
London Victoria 15 ⊖	d	09 58										10 22				10 52			10 58				
London Blackfriars 3 ⊖	d																						
Elephant & Castle ⊖	d																						
Bromley South 4	d	10 19										10 39				11 09			11 19				
St Mary Cray	d	10 25																	11 25				
Swanley 4	d	10 29																	11 29				
Farningham Road	d	10 34																	11 34				
Longfield	d	10 38										10 52				11 22			11 38				
Meopham	d	10 42										10 57				11 27			11 42				
Sole Street	d	10 45																	11 45				
London Charing Cross 4 ⊖	d													10 09				10 39					
London Waterloo (East) 4 ⊖	d													10 12				10 42					
London Cannon Street 4 ⊖	d																						
London Bridge 4 ⊖	d													10 17				10 47					
Dartford 4	d													10 55				11 25					
Greenhithe for Bluewater	d													11 00				11 30					
Gravesend 4	d			10 51										11 07				11 37			11 48		
Strood 4	d			11 01										11 18				11 48			11 58		
Rochester 4	d	10 56		11 06								11 09		11 23		11 39		11 52	11 56		12 03		
Chatham 4	d	10 59		11 08								11 12		11 25		11 42		11 55	11 59		12 05		
Gillingham (Kent) 4	d	11a03		11 13								11 17		11a32		11 47		12a02	12a03		12 10		
Rainham (Kent)	d			11 18								11 21				11 51					12 15		
Newington	d															11 55							
Sittingbourne 4	a			11 25								11 29				12 00					12 22		
	d		11 10	11 25								11 29			11 40	12 01				12 10	12 23		
Kemsley	d		11 15												11 45					12 15			
Swale	d		11 18												11 48					12 18			
Queenborough	d		11 22												11 52					12 22			
Sheerness-on-Sea	a		11 27												11 57					12 27			
Teynham	d											11 33											
Faversham 2	a			11 33								11 39				12 09					12 33		
	d											11 43	11 45			12 13	12 15						
Selling	d												11 50										
Canterbury East 4	d												11 59				12 29						
Bekesbourne	d												12 03										
Adisham	d												12 08										
Aylesham	d												12 10										
Snowdown	d												12 13										
Shepherds Well	d												12 17										
Kearsney	d												12 21										
Dover Priory 4	a												12 26				12 50						
Whitstable	d											11 51				12 21							
Chestfield & Swalecliffe	d											11 54											
Herne Bay	d											11 58				12 26							
Birchington-on-Sea	d											12 07				12 35							
Westgate-on-Sea	d											12 10											
Margate 4	d											12 14				12 41							
Broadstairs	d											12 20				12 46							
Dumpton Park	d											12 23											
Ramsgate 4	a											12 26				12 51							

A ⌶ to Margate

For further services to St Pancras International, Blackfriars and Elephant & Castle and onwards to Bromley South, St Mary Cray and Swanley please refer to table 52

Table 212

Mondays to Fridays

30 July to 10 August

London - Medway, Sheerness-on-Sea, Dover and Ramsgate

Network Diagram - see first Page of Table 212

Station		SE	SE	SE	SE	SE	SE 1 A ⌶		SE	SE	SE 1 A ⌶		SE	SE 1	SE	SE	SE	SE	SE	SE	SE	SE
St Pancras Internatnl 15 ⊖	d	11 39	11 46	11 52	12 04	12 11										12 8	12 25	12 32	12 39	12 46	12 52	13 04
Stratford International ⊖	d	11 49	11 56	12 03	12 14	12 21										12 28	12 35	12 42	12 49	12 56	13 03	13 14
Ebbsfleet International	d	12 02	12a07	12a13	12 30	12a31										12 44	12a46	12a52	13 02	13a07	13a13	13 30
London Victoria 15 ⊖	d						11 22				11 52			11 58								
London Blackfriars 3 ⊖	d																					
Elephant & Castle ⊖	d																					
Bromley South 4	d						11 39				12 09			12 19								
St Mary Cray	d													12 25								
Swanley 4	d													12 29								
Farningham Road	d													12 34								
Longfield	d						11 52				12 22			12 38								
Meopham	d						11 57				12 27			12 42								
Sole Street	d													12 45								
London Charing Cross 4 ⊖	d								11 09				11 39									
London Waterloo (East) 4 ⊖	d								11 12				11 42									
London Cannon Street 4 ⊖	d																					
London Bridge 4 ⊖	d								11 17				11 47									
Dartford 4	d								11 55				12 25									
Greenhithe for Bluewater	d								12 00				12 30									
Gravesend 4	d								12 07				12 37			12 48						
Strood 4	d								12 18				12 48			12 58						
Rochester 4	d						12 09		12 22		12 39		12 52	12 56		13 03						
Chatham 4	d						12 12		12 25		12 42		12 55	12 59		13 05						
Gillingham (Kent) 4	d						12 17		12a32		12 47		13a02	13a03		13 10						
Rainham (Kent)	d						12 21				12 51					13 15						
Newington	d										12 55											
Sittingbourne 4	a						12 28				13 00					13 22						
	d						12 29			12 40	13 01				13 10	13 23						
Kemsley	d									12 45					13 15							
Swale	d									12 48					13 18							
Queenborough	d									12 52					13 22							
Sheerness-on-Sea	a									12 57					13 27							
Teynham	d						12 33															
Faversham 2	a						12 39				13 09					13 33						
	d						12 43	12 45			13 13	13 15										
Selling	d							12 50														
Canterbury East 4	d							12 59				13 29										
Bekesbourne	d							13 03														
Adisham	d							13 08														
Aylesham	d							13 10														
Snowdown	d							13 13														
Shepherds Well	d							13 17														
Kearsney	d							13 21														
Dover Priory 4	a							13 26				13 50										
Whitstable	d						12 51				13 21											
Chestfield & Swalecliffe	d						12 54															
Herne Bay	d						12 58				13 26											
Birchington-on-Sea	d						13 07				13 35											
Westgate-on-Sea	d						13 10															
Margate 4	d						13 14				13 41											
Broadstairs	d						13 20				13 46											
Dumpton Park	d						13 23															
Ramsgate 4	a						13 26				13 51											

A ⌶ to Margate

For further services to St Pancras International, Blackfriars and Elephant & Castle and onwards to Bromley South, St Mary Cray and Swanley please refer to table 52

Table 212

Mondays to Fridays
30 July to 10 August

London - Medway, Sheerness-on-Sea, Dover and Ramsgate

Network Diagram - see first Page of Table 212

Station		SE	SE ■ A ⌶	SE	SE	SE ■ A ⌶	SE	SE ■	SE	SE	SE	SE	SE	SE	SE	SE	SE	SE ■ A ⌶	SE	SE
St Pancras International ■ ⊖	d	13 11								13 18	13 25	13 32	13 39	13 46	13 52	14 04	14 11			
Stratford International ⊖	d	13 21								13 28	13 35	13 42	13 49	13 56	14 03	14 14	14 21			
Ebbsfleet International	d	13a31								13 43	13a46	13a52	14 02	14a07	14a13	14 30	14a31			
London Victoria ■ ⊖	d		12 22			12 52		12 58										13 22		
London Blackfriars ■ ⊖	d																			
Elephant & Castle ⊖	d																			
Bromley South ■	d		12 39			13 09		13 19										13 39		
St Mary Cray	d							13 25												
Swanley ■	d							13 29												
Farningham Road	d							13 34												
Longfield	d		12 52			13 22		13 38										13 52		
Meopham	d		12 57			13 27		13 42										13 57		
Sole Street	d							13 45												
London Charing Cross ■ ⊖	d			12 09			12 39												13 09	
London Waterloo (East) ■ ⊖	d			12 12			12 42												13 12	
London Cannon Street ■ ⊖	d																			
London Bridge ■ ⊖	d			12 17			12 47												13 17	
Dartford ■	d			12 55			13 25												13 55	
Greenhithe for Bluewater	d			13 00			13 30												14 00	
Gravesend ■	d			13 07			13 37			13 48									14 07	
Strood ■	d			13 18			13 48			13 58									14 18	
Rochester ■	d		13 09	13 22		13 39	13 52	13 56		14 03								14 09	14 22	
Chatham ■	d		13 12	13 25		13 42	13 55	13 59		14 05								14 12	14 25	
Gillingham (Kent) ■	d		13 17	13a32		13 47	14a02	14a03		14 10								14 17	14a32	
Rainham (Kent)	d		13 21			13 51				14 15								14 21		
Newington	d					13 55														
Sittingbourne ■	a		13 29			14 00				14 22								14 28		
	d		13 29		13 40	14 01			14 10	14 23								14 29		14 40
Kemsley	d				13 45				14 15											14 45
Swale	d				13 48				14 18											14 48
Queenborough	d				13 52				14 22											14 52
Sheerness-on-Sea	a				13 57				14 27											14 57
Teynham	d		13 33															14 33		
Faversham ■	a		13 39			14 09				14 33								14 39		
	d		13 43 / 13 45			14 13 / 14 15												14 43 / 14 45		
Selling	d		13 50															14 50		
Canterbury East ■	d		13 59			14 29												14 59		
Bekesbourne	d		14 03															15 03		
Adisham	d		14 08															15 08		
Aylesham	d		14 10															15 10		
Snowdown	d		14 13															15 13		
Shepherds Well	d		14 17															15 17		
Kearsney	d		14 21															15 21		
Dover Priory ■	a		14 26			14 50												15 26		
Whitstable	d		13 51			14 21												14 51		
Chestfield & Swalecliffe	d		13 54															14 54		
Herne Bay	d		13 58			14 26												14 58		
Birchington-on-Sea	d		14 07			14 35												15 07		
Westgate-on-Sea	d		14 10															15 10		
Margate ■	d		14 14			14 41												15 14		
Broadstairs	d		14 20			14 46												15 20		
Dumpton Park	d		14 23															15 23		
Ramsgate ■	a		14 26			14 51												15 26		

A ⌶ to Margate

For further services to St Pancras International, Blackfriars and Elephant & Castle and onwards to Bromley South, St Mary Cray and Swanley please refer to table 52

Table 212

Mondays to Fridays
30 July to 10 August

London - Medway, Sheerness-on-Sea, Dover and Ramsgate

Network Diagram - see first Page of Table 212

Station		SE ■ A ⌶	SE	SE ■	SE	SE	SE	SE	SE	SE	SE	SE	SE	SE ■ A ⌶	SE	SE	SE ■ A ⌶	SE	SE ■	SE
St Pancras International ■ ⊖	d					14 18	14 25	14 32	14 39	14 46	14 52	15 04	15 11							
Stratford International ⊖	d					14 28	14 35	14 42	14 49	14 56	15 03	15 14	15 21							
Ebbsfleet International	d					14 43	14a46	14a52	15 02	15a07	15a13	15 30	15a31							
London Victoria ■ ⊖	d	13 52		13 58										14 22			14 52		14 58	
London Blackfriars ■ ⊖	d																			
Elephant & Castle ⊖	d																			
Bromley South ■	d	14 09		14 19										14 39			15 09		15 19	
St Mary Cray	d			14 25															15 25	
Swanley ■	d			14 29															15 29	
Farningham Road	d			14 34															15 34	
Longfield	d	14 22		14 38										14 52			15 22		15 38	
Meopham	d	14 27		14 42										14 57			15 27		15 42	
Sole Street	d			14 45															15 45	
London Charing Cross ■ ⊖	d		13 39												14 09			14 39		
London Waterloo (East) ■ ⊖	d		13 42												14 12			14 42		
London Cannon Street ■ ⊖	d																			
London Bridge ■ ⊖	d		13 47												14 17			14 47		
Dartford ■	d		14 25												14 55			15 25		
Greenhithe for Bluewater	d		14 30												15 00			15 30		
Gravesend ■	d		14 37			14 48									15 07			15 37		
Strood ■	d		14 48			14 58									15 18			15 48		
Rochester ■	d	14 39	14 52	14 56		15 03								15 09	15 22		15 39	15 52	15 56	
Chatham ■	d	14 42	14 55	14 59		15 05								15 12	15 25		15 42	15 55	15 59	
Gillingham (Kent) ■	d	14 47	15a02	15a03		15 10								15 17	15a32		15 47	16a02	16a03	
Rainham (Kent)	d	14 51				15 15								15 20			15 51			
Newington	d	14 55															15 55			
Sittingbourne ■	a	15 00				15 22								15 28			16 00			
	d	15 01			15 10	15 23								15 29		15 40	16 01			16 10
Kemsley	d				15 15											15 45				16 15
Swale	d				15 18											15 48				16 18
Queenborough	d				15 22											15 52				16 22
Sheerness-on-Sea	a				15 27											15 57				16 27
Teynham	d													15 33						
Faversham ■	a	15 09				15 33								15 39			16 09			
	d	15 13 / 15 15												15 43 / 15 45			16 13 / 16 15			
Selling	d													15 50			16 19			
Canterbury East ■	d	15 29												15 59			16 28			
Bekesbourne	d													16 03			16 33			
Adisham	d													16 08			16 37			
Aylesham	d													16 10			16 39			
Snowdown	d													16 13						
Shepherds Well	d	15 39												16 17			16 44			
Kearsney	d													16 21						
Dover Priory ■	a	15 48												16 27			16 52			
Whitstable	d	15 21												15 51			16 21			
Chestfield & Swalecliffe	d													15 54			16 24			
Herne Bay	d	15 26												15 58			16 28			
Birchington-on-Sea	d	15 35												16 07			16 37			
Westgate-on-Sea	d													16 10			16 40			
Margate ■	d	15 41												16 14			16 44			
Broadstairs	d	15 46												16 20			16 50			
Dumpton Park	d													16 23			16 53			
Ramsgate ■	a	15 51												16 26			16 56			

A ⌶ to Margate

For further services to St Pancras International, Blackfriars and Elephant & Castle and onwards to Bromley South, St Mary Cray and Swanley please refer to table 52

Table 212

Mondays to Fridays
30 July to 10 August

London - Medway, Sheerness-on-Sea, Dover and Ramsgate

Network Diagram - see first Page of Table 212

		SE	SE	SE	SE	SE	SE	SE	SE	SE ■ A		SE	SE	SE ■ A		SE	SE ■	SE	SE	SE	SE	SE
St Pancras Internatnl ⊖	d	15 18	15 25	15 32	15 39	15 46	15 52	16 04	16 11										16 18	16 25	16 32	16 39
Stratford International ⊖	d	15 28	15 35	15 42	15 49	15 56	16 03	16 14	16 21										16 28	16 35	16 42	16 49
Ebbsfleet International	d	15 43	15a46	15a52	16 02	16a07	16a13	16 30	16a31										16 44	16a46	16a52	17 02
London Victoria ⊖	d									15 22				15 52			15 58					
London Blackfriars ⊖	d																					
Elephant & Castle ⊖	d																					
Bromley South	d									15 39				16 09			16 19					
St Mary Cray	d																16 25					
Swanley	d																16 29					
Farningham Road	d																16 34					
Longfield	d									15 52				16 22			16 38					
Meopham	d									15 57				16 27			16 42					
Sole Street	d																16 45					
London Charing Cross ⊖	d											15 09				15 39						
London Waterloo (East) ⊖	d											15 12				15 42						
London Cannon Street ⊖	d																					
London Bridge ⊖	d											15 17				15 47						
Dartford	d											15 55				16 25						
Greenhithe for Bluewater	d											16 00				16 30						
Gravesend	d	15 48										16 07				16 37			16 48			
Strood	d	15 58										16 18				16 48			16 58			
Rochester	d	16 03								16 09		16 22		16 39		16 52	16 56		17 03			
Chatham	d	16 05								16 12		16 25		16 42		16 55	16 59		17 05			
Gillingham (Kent)	d	16 10								16 17		16a32		16 47		17a02	17a03		17 10			
Rainham (Kent)	d	16 15								16 21				16 51					17 15			
Newington	d													16 55								
Sittingbourne	a	16 22								16 29				17 00					17 22			
	d	16 23								16 29			16 40	17 01				17 10	17 23			
Kemsley	d												16 45					17 15				
Swale	d												16 48					17 18				
Queenborough	d												16 52					17 22				
Sheerness-on-Sea	a												16 57					17 27				
Teynham	d									16 33				17 05								
Faversham	a	16 33								16 39				17 11					17 33			
	d									16 43	16 45			17 15	17 19							
Selling	d										16 50				17 23							
Canterbury East	d										16 59				17 32							
Bekesbourne	d										17 03											
Adisham	d										17 08											
Aylesham	d										17 10				17 40							
Snowdown	d										17 13											
Shepherds Well	d										17 17				17 45							
Kearsney	d										17 21											
Dover Priory	a										17 27				17 53							
Whitstable	d									16 51				17 23								
Chestfield & Swalecliffe	d									16 54				17 26								
Herne Bay	d									16 58				17 30								
Birchington-on-Sea	d									17 07				17 39								
Westgate-on-Sea	d									17 11				17 43								
Margate	d									17 15				17 47								
Broadstairs	d									17 20				17 52								
Dumpton Park	d									17 23				17 55								
Ramsgate	a									17 26				17 58								

A to Margate

For further services to St Pancras International, Blackfriars and Elephant & Castle and onwards to Bromley South, St Mary Cray and Swanley please refer to table 52

Table 212

Mondays to Fridays
30 July to 10 August

London - Medway, Sheerness-on-Sea, Dover and Ramsgate

Network Diagram - see first Page of Table 212

		SE	SE	SE	SE	SE ■ A		SE	SE ■	SE	SE ■	SE ■ A		SE	SE ■	SE	SE	SE	SE	SE ■ A		SE ■	SE
St Pancras Internatnl ⊖	d	16 46	16 52	17 04	17 11													17 18	17 25				
Stratford International ⊖	d	16 56	17 03	17 14	17 21													17 28	17 35				
Ebbsfleet International	d	17a07	17a13	17 30	17a31													17 43	17a46				
London Victoria ⊖	d					16 22			16 28			16 57		17 04						17 27			
London Blackfriars ⊖	d																						
Elephant & Castle ⊖	d																						
Bromley South	d					16 39			16 49			17 13		17 24						17 44			
St Mary Cray	d								16 55					17 30									
Swanley	d								16 59					17 34									
Farningham Road	d								17 04					17 39									
Longfield	d					16 52			17 08					17 44									
Meopham	d					16 57			17 12					17 48									
Sole Street	d								17 15					17 51									
London Charing Cross ⊖	d							16 09															
London Waterloo (East) ⊖	d							16 12															
London Cannon Street ⊖	d										16 46				17 08	16 44						17 30	17 06
London Bridge ⊖	d							16 17			16 50				17 12	16 48						17 34	17 10
Dartford	d							16 55								17 28							17 47
Greenhithe for Bluewater	d							17 00								17 33							17 52
Gravesend	d							17 07								17 40		17 48					18 00
Strood	d							17 18								17 52		17 58					18 14
Rochester	d					17 10		17 22	17a27		17 29	17 40		18a03	17 49	17 57		18 05		18 10		18 15	18 20
Chatham	d					17 13		17 25			17 31	17 43			17 52	18 00		18 07		18 13		18 18	18 23
Gillingham (Kent)	d					17 18		17a32			17 36	17 48			17 57	18a08		18 12		18 18		18 24	18a31
Rainham (Kent)	d					17 23					17 41	17 53			18 02			18 17		18 23		18 29	
Newington	d					17 27						17 57			18 06							18 33	
Sittingbourne	a					17 32					17 48	18 02			18 11			18 24		18 30		18 38	
	d					17 33				17 40	17 48	18 03			18 12		18 15	18 24		18 30		18 38	
Kemsley	d									17 45							18 20						
Swale	d									17 48							18 23						
Queenborough	d									17 52							18 27						
Sheerness-on-Sea	a									17 57							18 32						
Teynham	d					17 37						18 07			18 16					18 35			
Faversham	a					17 43					17 56	18 13			18 22			18 33		18 41		18 47	
	d					17 47	17 49				17 57	18 17	18 19		18 24					18 44	18 50	18 49	
Selling	d						17 54						18 23								18 54		
Canterbury East	d						18 03						18 32								19 04		
Bekesbourne	d						18 07														19 08		
Adisham	d						18 12														19 12		
Aylesham	d						18 14						18 40								19 15		
Snowdown	d						18 17														19 17		
Shepherds Well	d						18 21						18 45								19 21		
Kearsney	d						18 25														19 25		
Dover Priory	a						18 32						18 55								19 32		
Whitstable	d					17 55					18 05	18 25			18 32					18 52		18 57	
Chestfield & Swalecliffe	d					17 58					18 08	18 28			18 35					18 55		19 00	
Herne Bay	d					18 02					18 12	18 32			18 39					18 59		19 04	
Birchington-on-Sea	d					18 11					18 21	18 41			18 48					19 08		19 12	
Westgate-on-Sea	d					18 15					18 25	18 45			18 52					19 11		19 16	
Margate	d					18 19					18 29	18 49			18 56					19 15		19 20	
Broadstairs	d					18 24					18 34	18 54			19 01					19 21		19 26	
Dumpton Park	d					18 27					18 37	18 57			19 04					19 24		19 29	
Ramsgate	a					18 32					18 43	19 02			19 10					19 30		19 34	

A to Margate

For further services to St Pancras International, Blackfriars and Elephant & Castle and onwards to Bromley South, St Mary Cray and Swanley please refer to table 52

Table 212

Mondays to Fridays
30 July to 10 August

London - Medway, Sheerness-on-Sea, Dover and Ramsgate

Network Diagram - see first Page of Table 212

Station		SE	SE	SE	SE	SE	SE ■	SE	SE	SE	SE ■		SE ■ 🛒	SE	SE	SE ■	SE	SE ■	SE		SE ■ A 🛒	SE
St Pancras Internatnl ⊖	d		17 32	17 39	17 46	17 52		18 04	18 11								18 18		18 25			
Stratford International ⊖	d		17 42	17 49	17 56	18 03		18 14	18 21								18 28		18 35			
Ebbsfleet International	d		17a52	18 02	18a07	18a13		18 30	18a31								18 40		18a46			
London Victoria ⊖	d						17 54						17 57									
London Blackfriars ⊖	d																	18 24			18 27	
Elephant & Castle ⊖	d																					
Bromley South	d						18 19						18 15					18 46			18 44	
St Mary Cray	d						18 25											18 52				
Swanley	d						18 30											18 57				
Farningham Road	d						18 35											19 02				
Longfield	d												18 28					19 06				
Meopham	d						18 41											19 11				
Sole Street	d						18 44											19 13				
London Charing Cross ⊖	d	17 17												17 39								18 01
London Waterloo (East) ⊖	d	17 20												17 42								18 04
London Cannon Street ⊖	d										17 52					18 14						
London Bridge ⊖	d	17 26									17 56			17 48		18 18						18 10
Dartford	d	18 02												18 22								18 45
Greenhithe for Bluewater	d	18 07												18 27								18 51
Gravesend	d	18 19												18 34			18 45					19 02
Strood	d	18a33												18 45			18 55					19 14
Rochester	d						18a56				18 38		18 43	18 51			19 03	19 23			19 12	19 19
Chatham	d										18 41		18 46	18 54		19 00	19 06	19 26			19 15	19 22
Gillingham (Kent)	d										18 46		18 51	19a02		19 05	19 11	19a32			19 20	19a29
Rainham (Kent)	d										18 51		18 56			19 10	19 16				19 25	
Newington	d												19 00			19 14						
Sittingbourne	a										18 58		19 05			19 19	19 23				19 32	
	d									18 44	18 59		19 06		19 10	19 19	19 24				19 33	
Kemsley	d									18 49					19 15							
Swale	d									18 54					19 18							
Queenborough	d									18 58					19 22							
Sheerness-on-Sea	a									19 02					19 27							
Teynham	d												19 10								19 37	
Faversham	a										19 07		19 16			19 27	19 33				19 43	
	d										19 08	19 20	19 22			19 28				19 47	19 49	
Selling	d												19 26								19 54	
Canterbury East	d												19 36								20 03	
Bekesbourne	d																				20 07	
Adisham	d																				20 12	
Aylesham	d																				20 14	
Snowdown	d																				20 17	
Shepherds Well	d																				20 21	
Kearsney	d																				20 25	
Dover Priory	a												19 54								20 32	
Whitstable	d										19 16	19 28				19 36				19 55		
Chestfield & Swalecliffe	d											19 31				19 39				19 58		
Herne Bay	d										19 22	19 35				19 43				20 02		
Birchington-on-Sea	d										19 31	19 44				19 52				20 11		
Westgate-on-Sea	d											19 48				19 55				20 15		
Margate	d										19 37	19a54				19 59				20 19		
Broadstairs	d										19a45					20 05				20 25		
Dumpton Park	d															20 08				20 28		
Ramsgate	a															20 13				20 33		

A 🛒 to Margate

For further services to St Pancras International, Blackfriars and Elephant & Castle and onwards to Bromley South, St Mary Cray and Swanley please refer to table 52

Table 212

Mondays to Fridays
30 July to 10 August

London - Medway, Sheerness-on-Sea, Dover and Ramsgate

Network Diagram - see first Page of Table 212

Station		SE	SE	SE	SE	SE	SE	SE	SE ■		SE ■ A 🛒	SE	SE	SE ■	SE	SE	SE	SE	SE	SE	SE	SE	SE
St Pancras Internatnl ⊖	d	18 32	18 39	18 46	18 52	19 04	19 11										19 18	19 25	19 32	19 39	19 46	19 52	20 04
Stratford International ⊖	d	18 42	18 49	18 56	19 03	19 14	19 21										19 28	19 35	19 42	19 49	19 56	20 03	20 14
Ebbsfleet International	d	18a52	19 02	19a07	19a13	19 30	19a31										19 45	19a46	19a52	20 02	20a07	20a13	20 30
London Victoria ⊖	d										18 57			18 58									
London Blackfriars ⊖	d																						
Elephant & Castle ⊖	d																						
Bromley South	d										19 14			19 21									
St Mary Cray	d													19 27									
Swanley	d													19 31									
Farningham Road	d													19 36									
Longfield	d													19 40									
Meopham	d													19 44									
Sole Street	d													19 47									
London Charing Cross ⊖	d												18 37		18 48								
London Waterloo (East) ⊖	d												18 40		18 51								
London Cannon Street ⊖	d								18 44			18 30											
London Bridge ⊖	d								18 48			18 34	18 46		18 57								
Dartford	d											19 10	19 22		19 35								
Greenhithe for Bluewater	d											19 16	19 29		19 40								
Gravesend	d											19 26	19 38		19 47		19 51						
Strood	d											19 38	19a53		19 58		20 02						
Rochester	d								19 27		19 40	19 45		19 57	20 03		20 06						
Chatham	d								19 30		19 43	19 48		19 59	20 05		20 09						
Gillingham (Kent)	d								19 34		19 49	19a56		20a06	20a13		20 13						
Rainham (Kent)	d								19 39		19 54						20 18						
Newington	d								19 43		19 58												
Sittingbourne	a								19 48		20 03						20 25						
	d							19 40	19 49		20 03					20 10	20 26						
Kemsley	d							19 45								20 15							
Swale	d							19 48								20 18							
Queenborough	d							19 52								20 22							
Sheerness-on-Sea	a							19 57								20 27							
Teynham	d								19 53														
Faversham	a								19 59		20 11						20 34						
	d								20 00	20 15	20 17												
Selling	d										20 21												
Canterbury East	d										20 30												
Bekesbourne	d										20 35												
Adisham	d										20 39												
Aylesham	d										20 41												
Snowdown	d																						
Shepherds Well	d										20 46												
Kearsney	d																						
Dover Priory	a										20 56												
Whitstable	d								20 08	20 23													
Chestfield & Swalecliffe	d								20 11	20 26													
Herne Bay	d								20 15	20 30													
Birchington-on-Sea	d								20 24	20 39													
Westgate-on-Sea	d								20 27	20 43													
Margate	d								20 31	20 47													
Broadstairs	d								20 37	20 52													
Dumpton Park	d								20 40	20 55													
Ramsgate	a								20 49	21 00													

A 🛒 to Margate

For further services to St Pancras International, Blackfriars and Elephant & Castle and onwards to Bromley South, St Mary Cray and Swanley please refer to table 52

Table 212

Mondays to Fridays

30 July to 10 August

London - Medway, Sheerness-on-Sea, Dover and Ramsgate

Network Diagram - see first Page of Table 212

	SE	SE ■ A		SE	SE	SE	SE ■		SE	SE	SE	SE	SE	SE	SE	SE	SE	SE	SE	SE ■		SE
St Pancras International ⊖ d	20 11											20 18	20 25	20 32	20 39	20 46	20 52	21 04	21 11			
Stratford International ⊖ d	20 21											20 28	20 35	20 42	20 49	20 56	21 03	21 14	21 21			
Ebbsfleet International d	20a31											20 43	20a46	20a52	21 02	21a07	21a13	21 30	21a31			
London Victoria ⊖ d		19 22			19 28		19 52			19 58										20 22		
London Blackfriars ⊖ d																						
Elephant & Castle ⊖ d																						
Bromley South d		19 39			19 49		20 09			20 19										20 39		
St Mary Cray d					19 55					20 25												
Swanley d					19 59					20 29												
Farningham Road d					20 04					20 34												
Longfield d		19 52			20 08		20 22			20 38										20 52		
Meopham d		19 57			20 12		20 27			20 42										20 57		
Sole Street d					20 15					20 45												
London Charing Cross ⊖ d				19 09					19 39													20 09
London Waterloo (East) ⊖ d				19 12					19 42													20 12
London Cannon Street ⊖ d																						
London Bridge ⊖ d				19 17					19 47													20 17
Dartford d				19 55					20 25													20 55
Greenhithe for Bluewater d				20 00					20 30													21 00
Gravesend d				20 07					20 37			20 48										21 07
Strood d				20 18					20 48			20 58										21 18
Rochester d		20 13		20 22	20 26		20 39		20 52	20 56		21 03								21 09		21 22
Chatham d		20 16		20 25	20 29		20 42		20 55	20 59		21 05								21 12		21 25
Gillingham (Kent) d		20 21		20a32	20a33		20 47		21a02	21a03		21 10								21 17		21a32
Rainham (Kent) d		20 25					20 51					21 15								21 21		
Newington d							20 55															
Sittingbourne a		20 32					21 00					21 22								21 28		
Sittingbourne d		20 33				20 40	21 01				21 10	21 23								21 29		
Kemsley d						20 45					21 15											
Swale d						20 48					21 18											
Queenborough d						20 52					21 22											
Sheerness-on-Sea a						20 57					21 27											
Teynham d		20 37																		21 33		
Faversham a		20 43					21 09					21 33								21 39		
Faversham d		20 47	20 49				21 13	21 15												21 43	21 45	
Selling d			20 54					21 19													21 50	
Canterbury East d			21 03					21 28													21 59	
Bekesbourne d			21 07					21 33													22 03	
Adisham d			21 12					21 37													22 08	
Aylesham d			21 14					21 39													22 10	
Snowdown d			21 17																		22 13	
Shepherds Well d			21 21					21 44													22 17	
Kearsney d			21 25																		22 21	
Dover Priory a			21 32					21 52													22 26	
Whitstable d		20 55					21 21													21 51		
Chestfield & Swalecliffe d		20 58					21 24													21 54		
Herne Bay d		21 02					21 28													21 58		
Birchington-on-Sea d		21 11					21 37													22 07		
Westgate-on-Sea d		21 15					21 40													22 10		
Margate d		21 19					21 44													22 14		
Broadstairs d		21 24					21 50													22 20		
Dumpton Park d		21 27					21 53													22 23		
Ramsgate a		21 32					21 56													22 26		

A to Margate

For further services to St Pancras International, Blackfriars and Elephant & Castle and onwards to Bromley South, St Mary Cray and Swanley please refer to table 52

Table 212

Mondays to Fridays

30 July to 10 August

London - Medway, Sheerness-on-Sea, Dover and Ramsgate

Network Diagram - see first Page of Table 212

	SE	SE ■		SE	SE ■	SE	SE	SE	SE	SE	SE	SE	SE	SE ■		SE	SE	SE	SE	SE	SE
St Pancras International ⊖ d						21 18	21 25	21 32	21 39	21 46	21 52	22 04	22 11				22 18	22 25	22 32	22 39	
Stratford International ⊖ d						21 28	21 35	21 42	21 49	21 56	22 03	22 14	22 21				22 28	22 35	22 42	22 47	
Ebbsfleet International d						21 43	21a46	21a52	22 02	22a07	22a13	22a24	22a31				22a38	22a46	22a52	22a57	
London Victoria ⊖ d		20 52			20 58									21 22							
London Blackfriars ⊖ d																					
Elephant & Castle ⊖ d																					
Bromley South d		21 09			21 19									21 39							
St Mary Cray d					21 25																
Swanley d					21 29																
Farningham Road d					21 34																
Longfield d		21 22			21 38									21 52							
Meopham d		21 27			21 42									21 57							
Sole Street d					21 45																
London Charing Cross ⊖ d				20 39												21 09					
London Waterloo (East) ⊖ d				20 42												21 12					
London Cannon Street ⊖ d																					
London Bridge ⊖ d				20 47												21 17					
Dartford d				21 25												21 55					
Greenhithe for Bluewater d				21 30												22 00					
Gravesend d				21 37		21 48										22 07					
Strood d				21 48		21 58										22 18					
Rochester d		21 39		21 52	21 56	22 03								22 09		22 22					
Chatham d		21 42		21 55	21 59	22 05								22 12		22 25					
Gillingham (Kent) d		21 47		22a02	22a03	22 10								22 17		22a32					
Rainham (Kent) d		21 51				22 15								22 21							
Newington d		21 55																			
Sittingbourne a		22 00				22 22								22 28							
Sittingbourne d	21 40	22 01				22 23								22 29							22 40
Kemsley d	21 45																				22 45
Swale d	21 48																				22 48
Queenborough d	21 52																				22 52
Sheerness-on-Sea a	21 57																				22 57
Teynham d														22 33							
Faversham a		22 09				22 33								22 39							
Faversham d		22 13	22 15											22 43	22 45						
Selling d			22 19												22 50						
Canterbury East d			22 28												22 59						
Bekesbourne d			22 33												23 03						
Adisham d			22 37												23 08						
Aylesham d			22 39												23 10						
Snowdown d															23 13						
Shepherds Well d			22 44												23 17						
Kearsney d															23 21						
Dover Priory a			22 52												23 26						
Whitstable d		22 21												22 51							
Chestfield & Swalecliffe d		22 24												22 54							
Herne Bay d		22 28												22 58							
Birchington-on-Sea d		22 37												23 07							
Westgate-on-Sea d		22 40												23 10							
Margate d		22 44												23 14							
Broadstairs d		22 50												23 20							
Dumpton Park d		22 53												23 23							
Ramsgate a		22 56												23 26							

For further services to St Pancras International, Blackfriars and Elephant & Castle and onwards to Bromley South, St Mary Cray and Swanley please refer to table 52

Table 212

Mondays to Fridays

30 July to 10 August

London - Medway, Sheerness-on-Sea, Dover and Ramsgate

Network Diagram - see first Page of Table 212

		SE ■	SE	SE ■		SE	SE	SE	SE	SE
St Pancras Internatnl ■ ⊖	d						22 46	22 52	23 04	23 11
Stratford International ⊖	d						22 56	23 02	23 14	23 21
Ebbsfleet International	d						23a07	23a12	23a24	23a31
London Victoria ■ ⊖	d	21 52		22 22						
London Blackfriars ■ ⊖	d									
Elephant &Castle ⊖	d									
Bromley South ■	d	22 09		22 39						
St Mary Cray	d	22 15								
Swanley ■	d	22 19								
Farningham Road	d	22 24								
Longfield	d	22 28		22 52						
Meopham	d	22 32		22 57						
Sole Street	d	22 35								
London Charing Cross ■ ⊖	d		21 39			22 09				
London Waterloo (East) ■ ⊖	d		21 42			22 12				
London Cannon Street ■ ⊖	d									
London Bridge ■ ⊖	d		21 47			22 17				
Dartford ■	d		22 25			22 55				
Greenhithe for Bluewater	d		22 30			23 00				
Gravesend ■	d		22 37			23 07				
Strood ■	d		22 48			23 18				
Rochester ■	d	22 45	22 52	23 09		23 22				
Chatham ■	d	22 47	22 55	23 12		23 25				
Gillingham (Kent) ■	d	22 52	23a02	23 17		23a32				
Rainham (Kent)	d	22 56		23 21						
Newington	d	23 00								
Sittingbourne ■	a	23 05		23 28						
	d	23 06		23 29						
Kemsley	d									
Swale	d									
Queenborough	d									
Sheerness-on-Sea	a									
Teynham	d			23 33						
Faversham ■	a	23 17		23 39						
	d			23 43	23 45					
Selling	d				23 50					
Canterbury East ■	d				23 59					
Bekesbourne	d									
Adisham	d									
Aylesham	d				00 07					
Snowdown	d									
Shepherds Well	d									
Kearsney	d									
Dover Priory ■	a				00 18					
Whitstable	d			23 51						
Chestfield &Swalecliffe	d			23 54						
Herne Bay	d			23 58						
Birchington-on-Sea	d			00 07						
Westgate-on-Sea	d			00 10						
Margate ■	d			00 14						
Broadstairs	d			00 20						
Dumpton Park	d			00 23						
Ramsgate ■	a			00 26						

		SE	SE	SE	SE	SE ■	SE	SE	SE	SE	SE ■	SE	SE	SE
St Pancras Internatnl ■ ⊖	d	23 16	23 21	23 26				23 32	23 36	23 41			23 47	23 51
Stratford International ⊖	d	23 24	23 30	23 35				23 42	23 46	23 50			23 57	00 01
Ebbsfleet International	d	23a34	23a41	23a45				23a52	23a56	00a01			00a07	00a10
London Victoria ■ ⊖	d					22 52					23 22			
London Blackfriars ■ ⊖	d													
Elephant &Castle ⊖	d													
Bromley South ■	d					23 09					23 39			
St Mary Cray	d					23 15								
Swanley ■	d					23 19								
Farningham Road	d					23 24								
Longfield	d					23 28					23 52			
Meopham	d					23 32					23 57			
Sole Street	d					23 35								
London Charing Cross ■ ⊖	d						22 39					23 09		
London Waterloo (East) ■ ⊖	d						22 42					23 12		
London Cannon Street ■ ⊖	d													
London Bridge ■ ⊖	d						22 47					23 17		
Dartford ■	d						23 25					23 55		
Greenhithe for Bluewater	d						23 31					23 59		
Gravesend ■	d						23 40					00 10		
Strood ■	d						23 52					00 22		
Rochester ■	d					23 45	23 56				00 09	00 26		
Chatham ■	d					23 47	23 58				00 12	00 28		
Gillingham (Kent) ■	d					23 52	00a06				00 17	00a36		
Rainham (Kent)	d					23 56					00 21			
Newington	d					00 01								
Sittingbourne ■	a					00 06					00 28			
	d				23 32	00 07					00 29			
Kemsley	d				23 37									
Swale	d				23 40									
Queenborough	d				23 44									
Sheerness-on-Sea	a				23 49									
Teynham	d										00 33			
Faversham ■	a					00 15					00 39			
	d										00 43			
Selling	d													
Canterbury East ■	d													
Bekesbourne	d													
Adisham	d													
Aylesham	d													
Snowdown	d													
Shepherds Well	d													
Kearsney	d													
Dover Priory ■	a													
Whitstable	d										00 51			
Chestfield &Swalecliffe	d										00 54			
Herne Bay	d										00 58			
Birchington-on-Sea	d										01 07			
Westgate-on-Sea	d										01 10			
Margate ■	d										01 14			
Broadstairs	d										01 20			
Dumpton Park	d										01 23			
Ramsgate ■	a										01 26			

For further services to St Pancras International, Blackfriars and Elephant & Castle and onwards to Bromley South, St Mary Cray and Swanley please refer to table 52

Table 212

Mondays to Fridays

30 July to 10 August

London - Medway, Sheerness-on-Sea, Dover and Ramsgate

Network Diagram - see first Page of Table 212

		SE ■	SE	SE
St Pancras Internatnl ■ ⊖	d			23 56
Stratford International ⊖	d			00 05
Ebbsfleet International	d			00a16
London Victoria ■ ⊖	d	23 52		
London Blackfriars ■ ⊖	d			
Elephant &Castle ⊖	d			
Bromley South ■	d	00 09		
St Mary Cray	d	00 15		
Swanley ■	d	00 19		
Farningham Road	d	00 24		
Longfield	d	00 28		
Meopham	d	00 32		
Sole Street	d	00 35		
London Charing Cross ■ ⊖	d		23 39	
London Waterloo (East) ■ ⊖	d		23 42	
London Cannon Street ■ ⊖	d			
London Bridge ■ ⊖	d		23 47	
Dartford ■	d		00 25	
Greenhithe for Bluewater	d		00 31	
Gravesend ■	d		00 40	
Strood ■	d		00 52	
Rochester ■	d	00 45	00 56	
Chatham ■	d	00 47	00 58	
Gillingham (Kent) ■	d	00a52	01a06	
Rainham (Kent)	d			
Newington	d			
Sittingbourne ■	a			
	d			
Kemsley	d			
Swale	d			
Queenborough	d			
Sheerness-on-Sea	a			
Teynham	d			
Faversham ■	a			
	d			
Selling	d			
Canterbury East ■	d			
Bekesbourne	d			
Adisham	d			
Aylesham	d			
Snowdown	d			
Shepherds Well	d			
Kearsney	d			
Dover Priory ■	a			
Whitstable	d			
Chestfield &Swalecliffe	d			
Herne Bay	d			
Birchington-on-Sea	d			
Westgate-on-Sea	d			
Margate ■	d			
Broadstairs	d			
Dumpton Park	d			
Ramsgate ■	a			

For further services to St Pancras International, Blackfriars and Elephant & Castle and onwards to Bromley South, St Mary Cray and Swanley please refer to table 52

Table 212

Mondays to Fridays
29 August to 7 September

London - Medway, Sheerness-on-Sea, Dover and Ramsgate

Network Diagram - see first Page of Table 212

		SE 1 A		SE 1 B		SE C	SE D	SE 1 B	SE 1 A	SE B	SE C	SE D	SE 1 B	SE B	SE A	SE A	SE C	SE E	SE 1 A	SE 1 B	SE 1 B	SE B	SE B
St Pancras International	d					22p55	22p55				23p25	23p25				23p42	23p55	23p55					00 12
Stratford International	d					23p02	23p03				23p32	23p33				23p50	00 02	00 03					00 20
Ebbsfleet International	d					23p13	23p14				23p43	23p44				00 02	00 13	00 14					00 32
London Victoria	d	22p05		22p22				22p52	23p05				23p22						23p45	23p52	00 10		
London Blackfriars	d																						
Elephant & Castle	d																						
Bromley South	d	22p22		22p39				23p09	23p22				23p39						00 02	00 09			
St Mary Cray	d							23p15											00 08	00 15			
Swanley	d							23p19											00 12	00 19			
Farningham Road	d							23p24											00 17	00 24			
Longfield	d			22p52				23p28					23p52						00 21	00 28			
Meopham	d			22p57				23p32					23p57						00 25	00 32			
Sole Street	d							23p35											00 28	00 35			
London Charing Cross	d													23p09	23p10							23p39	
London Waterloo (East)	d													23p12	23p13							23p42	
London Cannon Street	d																						
London Bridge	d													23p17	23p18							23p47	
Dartford	d													23p55	23p55							00 25	
Greenhithe for Bluewater	d													23p59	00 01							00 31	
Gravesend	d					23p18	23p18				23p48	23p48		00 10	00 10		00 18	00 18				00 40	
Strood	d					23p28	23p28				23p58	23p58		00 22	00 22		00 28	00 28				00 52	
Rochester	d	22p46		23p09		23p33	23p33	23p45	23p46		00 03	00 03	00 09	00 26	00 26		00 33	00 33	00 37	00 45	00 49	00 56	
Chatham	d	22p48		23p12		23p35	23p35	23p47	23p48		00 05	00 05	00 12	00 28	00 28		00 35	00 35	00 40	00 47	00 52	00 58	
Gillingham (Kent)	d	22p53		23p17		23p40	23p40	23p52	23p53		00 10	00 10	00 17	00a33	00a33		00 40	00 40	00 44	00a52	00 57	01a03	
Rainham (Kent)	d	22p57		23p21		23p45	23p45	23p56	23p57		00 15	00 15	00 21				00 45	00 45	00 49		01 01		
Newington	d							00 01											00 53		01 05		
Sittingbourne	a	23p04		23p28		23p52	23p52	00 06	00 04		00 22	00 22	00 28				00 52	00 52	00 58		01 10		
	d	23p05		23p29		23p53	23p53	00 07	00 05	00 15	00 23	00 23	00 29				00 53	00 53	00 58		01 11		
Kemsley	d									00 20													
Swale	d									00 23													
Queenborough	d									00 27													
Sheerness-on-Sea	a									00 32													
Teynham	d			23p33									00 33						01 03		01 15		
Faversham	a	23p13		23p39		00 03	00 03	00 15	00 13		00 33	00 33	00 39				01 03	01 03	01 09		01 23		
	d	23p17	23p19	23p43	23p45				00 17				00 43								01 24		
Selling	d		23p24		23p50																		
Canterbury East	d		23p33		23p59																		
Bekesbourne	d		23p37																				
Adisham	d		23p42																				
Aylesham	d		23p44		00 07																		
Snowdown	d		23p47																				
Shepherds Well	d		23p51																				
Kearsney	d		23p55																				
Dover Priory	a		00 01		00 18																		
Whitstable	d	23p25		23p51					00 25				00 51								01 32		
Chestfield & Swalecliffe	d	23p28		23p54					00 28				00 54								01 35		
Herne Bay	d	23p32		23p58					00 32				00 58								01 39		
Birchington-on-Sea	d	23p41		00 07					00 41				01 07								01 48		
Westgate-on-Sea	d	23p44		00 10					00 44				01 10								01 51		
Margate	d	23p48		00 14					00 48				01 14								01 55		
Broadstairs	d	23p54		00 20					00 54				01 20								02 01		
Dumpton Park	d	23p57		00 23					00 57				01 23								02 04		
Ramsgate	a	00 01		00 26					01 00				01 26								02 07		

A 3 September
B not 3 September
C 29 August
D not 29 August
E not 29 August, 3 September

For further services to St Pancras International, Blackfriars and Elephant & Castle and onwards to Bromley South, St Mary Cray and Swanley please refer to table 52

Table 212

Mondays to Fridays
29 August to 7 September

London - Medway, Sheerness-on-Sea, Dover and Ramsgate

Network Diagram - see first Page of Table 212

		SE A	SE	SE	SE	SE	SE	SE	SE 1	SE	SE 1	SE	SE	SE	SE	SE	SE 1	SE 1	SE	SE 1	SE 1	SE	SE
St Pancras International	d	00 15			00 48	01 48	02 35																06 24
Stratford International	d	00a21			00a54	01a54	02a41																06 32
Ebbsfleet International	d																						06 42
London Victoria	d		00 35															05 22			05 52		
London Blackfriars	d																						
Elephant & Castle	d																						
Bromley South	d		00 55															05 39			06 09		
St Mary Cray	d		01 01															05 45					
Swanley	d		01 05															05 49			06 20		
Farningham Road	d		01 10															05 54					
Longfield	d		01 14															05 58			06 26		
Meopham	d		01 18															06 02			06 30		
Sole Street	d																	06 05					
London Charing Cross	d			00 18																		05 39	
London Waterloo (East)	d			00 21																		05 42	
London Cannon Street	d																						
London Bridge	d			00 26																		05 47	
Dartford	d			01 06								05 25										06 25	
Greenhithe for Bluewater	d			01 10								05 30										06 30	
Gravesend	d			01 17								05 37										06 38	06 46
Strood	d			01 29								05 48										06 49	06a56
Rochester	d		01 29	01 33								05 52						06 15			06 41	06 53	
Chatham	d		01 31	01 35								05 55						06 17			06 44	06 56	
Gillingham (Kent)	d		01a35	01a41				05 00			05 47	05a59						06 22			06 48	07a00	
Rainham (Kent)	d							05 04			05 51							06 26			06 53		
Newington	d							05 08			05 55							06 30			06 57		
Sittingbourne	a										06 00							06 35			07 02		
	d									05 33	06 01			06 03	06 22			06 36	06 53		07 02		
Kemsley	d							05 15		05 38				06 08	06 27				06 58				
Swale	d							05 18		05 43				06 11	06 30				07 01				
Queenborough	d							05 22		05 47				06 15	06 35				07 05				
Sheerness-on-Sea	a							05 27		05 51				06 20	06 40				07 10				
Teynham	d										06 05							06 40			07 07		
Faversham	a										06 11							06 46			07 13		
	d								05 15		06 12						06 15	06 47		07 05	07 13		
Selling	d								05 20		06 17									07 09			
Canterbury East	d								05 29		06 26									07 18			
Bekesbourne	d								05 33		06 30									07 23			
Adisham	d								05 38		06 35									07 27			
Aylesham	d								05 40		06 37									07 29			
Snowdown	d								05 43		06 40									07 32			
Shepherds Well	d								05 47		06 44									07 35			
Kearsney	d								05 51		06 48									07 40			
Dover Priory	a								05 56		06 53									07 45			
Whitstable	d																06 23	06 55			07 21		
Chestfield & Swalecliffe	d																06 26	06 58			07 24		
Herne Bay	d																06 30	07 02			07 28		
Birchington-on-Sea	d																06 39	07 11			07 37		
Westgate-on-Sea	d																06 42	07 14			07 41		
Margate	d												05 47			06 48	06 52	07 18			07 45		
Broadstairs	d												05 54			06 54	06 58	07 24			07 50		
Dumpton Park	d																07 01	07 27			07 53		
Ramsgate	a												05 59			06 59	07 04	07 30			07 56		

A 3 September

For further services to St Pancras International, Blackfriars and Elephant & Castle and onwards to Bromley South, St Mary Cray and Swanley please refer to table 52

29 August to 7 September

London - Medway, Sheerness-on-Sea, Dover and Ramsgate

Network Diagram - see first Page of Table 212

Station		SE	SE	SE ■	SE	SE	SE	SE	SE	SE ■	SE ■	SE	SE ■	SE	SE	SE	SE	SE	SE ■	SE		SE ■
St Pancras Internatnl ⊖	d					06 44		06 55								07 25	07 28	07 45				
Stratford International ⊖	d					06 58		07 02								07 33	07 38	07 53				
Ebbsfleet International	d							07 13								07 44	07a48	08a04				
London Victoria ⊖	d			06 22							06 45		06 58	07 09								07 22
London Blackfriars ⊖	d																					
Elephant & Castle ⊖	d																					
Bromley South	d			06 39							07 02		07 19									07 40
St Mary Cray	d			06 45							07 08		07 25									
Swanley	d			06 49							07 13		07 29									07 49
Farningham Road	d			06 54							07 18		07 34									
Longfield	d			06 58							07 22		07 38									07 55
Meopham	d			07 02							07 26		07 42									07 59
Sole Street	d			07 05							07 28		07 45									
London Charing Cross ⊖	d				05 56				06 26			06 39										
London Waterloo (East) ⊖	d				05 59				06 29			06 42										
London Cannon Street ⊖	d																					
London Bridge ⊖	d				06 04				06 34			06 47										
Dartford	d				06 42				07 12			07 25		07a48								
Greenhithe for Bluewater	d				06 48				07 18			07 30										
Gravesend	d				06 59			07 21	07 27			07 37				07 48						
Strood	d				07 17	07a22		07 31	07a37			07 48				07 58						
Rochester	d			07 15	07 21			07 36			07 40	07 52	07 56			08 03						08 11
Chatham	d			07 17	07 24			07 38			07 43	07 55	07 59			08 05						08 13
Gillingham (Kent)	d			07 22	07a28			07 43			07 48	07a59	08a03			08 10						08 18
Rainham (Kent)	d			07 26				07 48			07 52					08 15						08 22
Newington	d			07 30							07 56											08 26
Sittingbourne	a			07 37				07 56			08 01					08 22						08 31
	d	07 09		07 38			07 45	07 57			08 02				08 13	08 23						08 32
Kemsley	d	07 14					07 50								08 18							
Swale	d	07 17					07 53								08 21							
Queenborough	d	07 22					07 57								08 25							
Sheerness-on-Sea	a	07 27					08 02								08 30							
Teynham	d			07 42							08 06											08 36
Faversham	a			07 48				08 05			08 12					08 33						08 42
	d			07 49						07 52	08 13								08 16		08 46	08 50
Selling	d									07 56	08 18											08 54
Canterbury East	d									08 06	08 27											09 03
Bekesbourne	d									08 11	08 31											09 08
Adisham	d									08 15	08 36											09 12
Aylesham	d									08 18	08 38											09 14
Snowdown	d									08 20	08 41											09 17
Shepherds Well	d									08 24	08 45											09 21
Kearsney	d									08 29	08 49											09 25
Dover Priory	a									08 35	08 54											09 30
Whitstable	d			07 57															08 24		08 54	
Chestfield & Swalecliffe	d			08 00															08 27		08 57	
Herne Bay	d			08 04															08 31		09 01	
Birchington-on-Sea	d			08 13															08 40		09 10	
Westgate-on-Sea	d			08 17															08 43		09 13	
Margate	d		07 49	08 21															08 47	08 53	09 17	
Broadstairs	d		07 55	08 26															08 53	08 59	09 23	
Dumpton Park	d			08 29															08 56		09 26	
Ramsgate	a		08 00	08 32															08 59	09 04	09 29	

For further services to St Pancras International, Blackfriars and Elephant & Castle and onwards to Bromley South, St Mary Cray and Swanley please refer to table 52

29 August to 7 September

London - Medway, Sheerness-on-Sea, Dover and Ramsgate

Network Diagram - see first Page of Table 212

Station		SE	SE	SE	SE	SE	SE		SE ■	SE	SE ■	SE	SE	SE	SE	SE		SE ■	SE	SE	SE		SE ■
St Pancras Internatnl ⊖	d				07 51	07 58	08 16						08 21	08 34	08 47						08 54		
Stratford International ⊖	d				08 02	08 13	08 24						08 29	08 42	08 55						09 05		
Ebbsfleet International	d				08 13	08a23	08a35						08 43		09a05						09 17		
London Victoria ⊖	d		07 43						07 52		07 58							08 22					08 52
London Blackfriars ⊖	d																						
Elephant & Castle ⊖	d																						
Bromley South	d								08 09		08 28							08 39					09 09
St Mary Cray	d										08 34												
Swanley	d										08 39												
Farningham Road	d										08 44												
Longfield	d								08 22		08 49							08 52					09 22
Meopham	d								08 27		08 53							08 57					09 27
Sole Street	d										08 56												
London Charing Cross ⊖	d	07 12								07 39									08 11				
London Waterloo (East) ⊖	d	07 15								07 42									08 14				
London Cannon Street ⊖	d																						
London Bridge ⊖	d	07 21								07 47									08 19				
Dartford	d	08 00	08a27							08 25									08 55				
Greenhithe for Bluewater	d	08 05								08 30									09 00				
Gravesend	d	08 12			08 18					08 37			08 48						09 07		09 22		
Strood	d	08 23			08 28					08 48			08 58						09 18		09 32		
Rochester	d	08 27			08 33				08 39	08 52	09a07		09 03					09 09	09 22		09 37		09 39
Chatham	d	08 30			08 35				08 42	08 55			09 05					09 12	09 25		09 39		09 42
Gillingham (Kent)	d	08a35			08 40				08 47	08a59			09 10					09 17	09a29		09 44		09 47
Rainham (Kent)	d				08 45				08 51				09 15					09 21			09 49		09 51
Newington	d								08 55														09 55
Sittingbourne	a				08 52				09 00				09 22					09 28			09 56		10 01
	d			08 40	08 53				09 01			09 10	09 23					09 29		09 40	09 56		10 01
Kemsley	d			08 45								09 15								09 45			
Swale	d			08 48								09 18								09 48			
Queenborough	d			08 52								09 22								09 52			
Sheerness-on-Sea	a			08 57								09 27								09 57			
Teynham	d																	09 33					
Faversham	a				09 03				09 09				09 33					09 39			10 04		10 09
	d							09 13	09 15								09 43	09 45				10 13	10 15
Selling	d																	09 50					
Canterbury East	d								09 29									09 59					10 29
Bekesbourne	d																	10 03					
Adisham	d																	10 08					
Aylesham	d																	10 10					
Snowdown	d																	10 13					
Shepherds Well	d																	10 17					
Kearsney	d																	10 21					
Dover Priory	a								09 50									10 26					10 50
Whitstable	d							09 21									09 51					10 21	
Chestfield & Swalecliffe	d																09 54						
Herne Bay	d							09 26									09 58					10 26	
Birchington-on-Sea	d							09 35									10 07					10 35	
Westgate-on-Sea	d																10 10						
Margate	d							09 41								09 53	10 14					10 41	
Broadstairs	d							09 46								09 59	10 20					10 46	
Dumpton Park	d																10 23						
Ramsgate	a							09 51								10 04	10 26					10 51	

For further services to St Pancras International, Blackfriars and Elephant & Castle and onwards to Bromley South, St Mary Cray and Swanley please refer to table 52

Table 212

Mondays to Fridays

29 August to 7 September

London - Medway, Sheerness-on-Sea, Dover and Ramsgate

Network Diagram - see first Page of Table 212

		SE	SE ■	SE	SE	SE	SE	SE	SE ■	SE	SE	SE	SE	SE ■ A	SE	SE ■	SE	SE	SE	SE
St Pancras Internatnl ⊖	d			09 15		09 25	09 47					09 54	10 14					10 28	10 47	
Stratford International ⊖	d			09 25		09 33	09 55					10 02	10 25					10 36	10 55	
Ebbsfleet International	d			09a35		09 43	10a05					10 13	10a35					10 47	11a05	
London Victoria ⊖	d		08 58						09 22					09 52		09 58				
London Blackfriars ⊖	d																			
Elephant & Castle ⊖	d																			
Bromley South	d		09 19						09 39					10 09		10 19				
St Mary Cray	d		09 25													10 25				
Swanley	d		09 29													10 29				
Farningham Road	d		09 34													10 34				
Longfield	d		09 38						09 52					10 22		10 38				
Meopham	d		09 42						09 57					10 27		10 42				
Sole Street	d		09 45													10 45				
London Charing Cross ⊖	d	08 41								09 11					09 39					
London Waterloo (East) ⊖	d	08 44								09 14					09 42					
London Cannon Street ⊖	d																			
London Bridge ⊖	d	08 49								09 19					09 47					
Dartford	d	09 25								09 55					10 25					
Greenhithe for Bluewater	d	09 30								10 00					10 30					
Gravesend	d	09 37				09 48				10 07		10 18			10 37			10 51		
Strood	d	09 48				09 58				10 18		10 28			10 48			11 01		
Rochester	d	09 52	09 56			10 03			10 09	10 22		10 33		10 39	10 52	10 56		11 06		
Chatham	d	09 55	09 59			10 05			10 12	10 25		10 35		10 42	10 55	10 59		11 08		
Gillingham (Kent)	d	09a59	10a03			10 10			10 17	10a29		10 40		10 47	10a59	11a03		11 13		
Rainham (Kent)	d					10 15			10 21			10 45		10 51				11 18		
Newington	d													10 55						
Sittingbourne	a					10 22			10 28			10 52		11 00				11 25		
	d				10 10	10 23			10 29		10 40	10 53		11 01			11 10	11 25		
Kemsley	d				10 15						10 45						11 15			
Swale	d				10 18						10 48						11 18			
Queenborough	d				10 22						10 52						11 22			
Sheerness-on-Sea	a				10 27						10 57						11 27			
Teynham	d								10 33											
Faversham	a					10 33			10 39			11 03		11 09				11 33		
	d								10 43 / 10 45					11 13 / 11 15						
Selling	d								10 50											
Canterbury East	d								10 59					11 29						
Bekesbourne	d								11 03											
Adisham	d								11 08											
Aylesham	d								11 10											
Snowdown	d								11 13											
Shepherds Well	d								11 17											
Kearsney	d								11 21											
Dover Priory	a								11 26					11 50						
Whitstable	d								10 51					11 21						
Chestfield & Swalecliffe	d								10 54											
Herne Bay	d								10 58					11 26						
Birchington-on-Sea	d								11 07					11 35						
Westgate-on-Sea	d								11 10											
Margate	d							10 53	11 14					11 41						11 53
Broadstairs	d							10 59	11 20					11 46						11 59
Dumpton Park	d								11 23											
Ramsgate	a							11 04	11 26					11 51						12 04

A to Margate

For further services to St Pancras International, Blackfriars and Elephant & Castle and onwards to Bromley South, St Mary Cray and Swanley please refer to table 52

Table 212

Mondays to Fridays

29 August to 7 September

London - Medway, Sheerness-on-Sea, Dover and Ramsgate

Network Diagram - see first Page of Table 212

		SE ■ A	SE	SE	SE	SE ■ A	SE	SE ■	SE	SE	SE	SE	SE	SE ■ A	SE	SE	SE	SE ■ A
St Pancras Internatnl ⊖	d				10 51				11 18		11 24	11 48					11 55	
Stratford International ⊖	d				10 58				11 26		11 31	11 56					12 03	
Ebbsfleet International	d				11 13				11a36		11 44	12a06					12 14	
London Victoria ⊖	d	10 22				10 52		10 58						11 22				11 52
London Blackfriars ⊖	d																	
Elephant & Castle ⊖	d																	
Bromley South	d	10 39				11 09		11 19						11 39				12 09
St Mary Cray	d							11 25										
Swanley	d							11 29										
Farningham Road	d							11 34										
Longfield	d	10 52				11 22		11 38						11 52				12 22
Meopham	d	10 57				11 27		11 42						11 57				12 27
Sole Street	d							11 45										
London Charing Cross ⊖	d		10 09				10 39								11 09			
London Waterloo (East) ⊖	d		10 12				10 42								11 12			
London Cannon Street ⊖	d																	
London Bridge ⊖	d		10 17				10 47								11 17			
Dartford	d		10 55				11 25								11 55			
Greenhithe for Bluewater	d		11 00				11 30								12 00			
Gravesend	d		11 07		11 18		11 37				11 48				12 07		12 18	
Strood	d		11 18		11 28		11 48				11 58				12 18		12 28	
Rochester	d	11 09	11 22		11 33	11 39	11 52	11 56			12 03			12 09	12 22		12 33	12 39
Chatham	d	11 12	11 25		11 35	11 42	11 55	11 59			12 05			12 12	12 25		12 35	12 42
Gillingham (Kent)	d	11 17	11a29		11 40	11 47	11a59	12a03			12 10			12 17	12a29		12 40	12 47
Rainham (Kent)	d	11 21			11 45	11 51					12 15			12 21			12 45	12 51
Newington	d					11 55												12 55
Sittingbourne	a	11 29			11 52	12 00					12 22			12 28			12 52	13 00
	d	11 29		11 40	11 53	12 01				12 10	12 23			12 29		12 40	12 53	13 01
Kemsley	d			11 45						12 15						12 45		
Swale	d			11 48						12 18						12 48		
Queenborough	d			11 52						12 22						12 52		
Sheerness-on-Sea	a			11 57						12 27						12 57		
Teynham	d	11 33												12 33				
Faversham	a	11 39			12 03	12 09					12 33			12 39			13 03	13 09
	d	11 43 / 11 45				12 13 / 12 15								12 43 / 12 45				13 13 / 13 15
Selling	d	11 50												12 50				
Canterbury East	d	11 59				12 29								12 59				13 29
Bekesbourne	d	12 03												13 03				
Adisham	d	12 08												13 08				
Aylesham	d	12 10												13 10				
Snowdown	d	12 13												13 13				
Shepherds Well	d	12 17												13 17				
Kearsney	d	12 21												13 21				
Dover Priory	a	12 26				12 50								13 26				13 50
Whitstable	d	11 51				12 21								12 51				13 21
Chestfield & Swalecliffe	d	11 54												12 54				
Herne Bay	d	11 58				12 26								12 58				13 26
Birchington-on-Sea	d	12 07				12 35								13 07				13 35
Westgate-on-Sea	d	12 10												13 10				
Margate	d	12 14				12 41							12 53	13 14				13 41
Broadstairs	d	12 20				12 46							12 59	13 20				13 46
Dumpton Park	d	12 23												13 23				
Ramsgate	a	12 26				12 51							13 04	13 26				13 51

A to Margate

For further services to St Pancras International, Blackfriars and Elephant & Castle and onwards to Bromley South, St Mary Cray and Swanley please refer to table 52

Table 212

Mondays to Fridays

29 August to 7 September

London - Medway, Sheerness-on-Sea, Dover and Ramsgate

Network Diagram - see first Page of Table 212

		SE	SE ■	SE	SE	SE	SE	SE	SE ■ A ⊼	SE	SE	SE	SE ■ A ⊼	SE	SE ■	SE	SE	SE	SE	SE
St Pancras Internatnl ⊖	d			12 18		12 21	12 45					12 51				13 18		13 25	13 48	
Stratford International ⊖	d			12 26		12 32	12 52					12 58				13 26		13 33	13 56	
Ebbsfleet International	d			12a36		12 43	13a02					13 13				13a36		13 44	14a06	
London Victoria ⊖	d		11 58						12 22				12 52		12 58					
London Blackfriars ⊖	d																			
Elephant & Castle ⊖	d																			
Bromley South	d		12 19						12 39				13 09		13 19					
St Mary Cray	d		12 25												13 25					
Swanley	d		12 29												13 29					
Farningham Road	d		12 34												13 34					
Longfield	d		12 38						12 52				13 22		13 38					
Meopham	d		12 42						12 57				13 27		13 42					
Sole Street	d		12 45												13 45					
London Charing Cross ⊖	d	11 39								12 09				12 39						
London Waterloo (East) ⊖	d	11 42								12 12				12 42						
London Cannon Street ⊖	d																			
London Bridge ⊖	d	11 47								12 17				12 47						
Dartford	d	12 25								12 55				13 25						
Greenhithe for Bluewater	d	12 30								13 00				13 30						
Gravesend	d	12 37				12 48				13 07		13 18		13 37				13 48		
Strood	d	12 48				12 58				13 18		13 28		13 48				13 58		
Rochester	d	12 52	12 56			13 03			13 09	13 22		13 33	13 39	13 52	13 56			14 03		
Chatham	d	12 55	12 59			13 05			13 12	13 25		13 35	13 42	13 55	13 59			14 05		
Gillingham (Kent)	d	12a59	13a03			13 10			13 17	13a29		13 40	13 47	13a59	14a03			14 10		
Rainham (Kent)	d					13 15			13 21			13 45	13 51					14 15		
Newington	d												13 55							
Sittingbourne	a					13 22			13 29			13 52	14 00					14 22		
	d				13 10	13 22			13 29		13 40	13 53	14 01				14 10	14 23		
Kemsley	d				13 15						13 45						14 15			
Swale	d				13 18						13 48						14 18			
Queenborough	d				13 22						13 52						14 22			
Sheerness-on-Sea	a				13 27						13 57						14 27			
Teynham	d								13 33											
Faversham	a					13 30			13 39			14 03	14 09					14 33		
	d								13 43 / 13 45				14 13 / 14 15							
Selling	d								13 50											
Canterbury East	d								13 59				14 29							
Bekesbourne	d								14 03											
Adisham	d								14 08											
Aylesham	d								14 10											
Snowdown	d								14 13											
Shepherds Well	d								14 17											
Kearsney	d								14 21											
Dover Priory	a								14 26				14 50							
Whitstable	d								13 51				14 21							
Chestfield & Swalecliffe	d								13 54											
Herne Bay	d								13 58				14 26							
Birchington-on-Sea	d								14 07				14 35							
Westgate-on-Sea	d								14 10											
Margate	d							13 53	14 14				14 41							
Broadstairs	d							13 59	14 20				14 46							14 53
Dumpton Park	d								14 23											14 59
Ramsgate	a							14 04	14 26				14 51							15 04

A ⊼ to Margate

For further services to St Pancras International, Blackfriars and Elephant & Castle and onwards to Bromley South, St Mary Cray and Swanley please refer to table 52

Table 212

Mondays to Fridays

29 August to 7 September

London - Medway, Sheerness-on-Sea, Dover and Ramsgate

Network Diagram - see first Page of Table 212

		SE ■ A ⊼	SE	SE	SE	SE	SE ■ A ⊼	SE	SE ■	SE	SE	SE	SE	SE ■ A ⊼	SE	SE	SE	SE	SE ■ A ⊼
St Pancras Internatnl ⊖	d				13 54	14 18					14 25	14 48					14 54	15 18	
Stratford International ⊖	d				14 02	14 26					14 33	14 56					15 02	15 26	
Ebbsfleet International	d				14 14	14a36					14 44	15a06					15 14	15a36	
London Victoria ⊖	d	13 22					13 52		13 58					14 22					14 52
London Blackfriars ⊖	d																		
Elephant & Castle ⊖	d																		
Bromley South	d	13 39					14 09		14 19					14 39					15 09
St Mary Cray	d								14 25										
Swanley	d								14 29										
Farningham Road	d								14 34										
Longfield	d	13 52					14 22		14 38					14 52					15 22
Meopham	d	13 57					14 27		14 42					14 57					15 27
Sole Street	d								14 45										
London Charing Cross ⊖	d		13 09					13 39							14 09				
London Waterloo (East) ⊖	d		13 12					13 42							14 12				
London Cannon Street ⊖	d																		
London Bridge ⊖	d		13 17					13 47							14 17				
Dartford	d		13 55					14 25							14 55				
Greenhithe for Bluewater	d		14 00					14 30							15 00				
Gravesend	d		14 07		14 18			14 37			14 48				15 07		15 18		
Strood	d		14 18		14 28			14 48			14 58				15 18		15 28		
Rochester	d	14 09	14 22		14 33		14 39	14 52	14 56		15 03			15 09	15 22		15 33		15 39
Chatham	d	14 12	14 25		14 35		14 42	14 55	14 59		15 05			15 12	15 25		15 35		15 42
Gillingham (Kent)	d	14 17	14a29		14 40		14 47	14a59	15a03		15 10			15 17	15a29		15 40		15 47
Rainham (Kent)	d	14 21			14 45		14 51				15 15			15 20			15 45		15 51
Newington	d						14 55												15 55
Sittingbourne	a	14 28			14 52		15 00				15 22			15 28			15 52		16 00
	d	14 29		14 40	14 53		15 01			15 10	15 23			15 29		15 40	15 53		16 01
Kemsley	d			14 45						15 15						15 45			
Swale	d			14 48						15 18						15 48			
Queenborough	d			14 52						15 22						15 52			
Sheerness-on-Sea	a			14 57						15 27						15 57			
Teynham	d	14 33												15 33					
Faversham	a	14 39			15 03		15 09				15 33			15 39			16 03		16 09
	d	14 43 / 14 45					15 13 / 15 15							15 43 / 15 45					16 13 / 16 15
Selling	d	14 50												15 50					16 19
Canterbury East	d	14 59					15 29							15 59					16 28
Bekesbourne	d	15 03												16 03					16 33
Adisham	d	15 08												16 08					16 37
Aylesham	d	15 10												16 10					16 39
Snowdown	d	15 13												16 13					
Shepherds Well	d	15 17					15 39							16 17					16 44
Kearsney	d	15 21												16 21					
Dover Priory	a	15 26					15 48							16 27					16 52
Whitstable	d	14 51					15 21							15 51					16 21
Chestfield & Swalecliffe	d	14 54												15 54					16 24
Herne Bay	d	14 58					15 26							15 58					16 28
Birchington-on-Sea	d	15 07					15 35							16 07					16 37
Westgate-on-Sea	d	15 10												16 10					16 40
Margate	d	15 14					15 41						15 53	16 14					16 44
Broadstairs	d	15 20					15 46						15 59	16 20					16 50
Dumpton Park	d	15 23												16 23					16 53
Ramsgate	a	15 26					15 51						16 04	16 26					16 56

A ⊼ to Margate

For further services to St Pancras International, Blackfriars and Elephant & Castle and onwards to Bromley South, St Mary Cray and Swanley please refer to table 52

Table 212

Mondays to Fridays
29 August to 7 September

London - Medway, Sheerness-on-Sea, Dover and Ramsgate

Network Diagram - see first Page of Table 212

Station		SE	SE 1	SE		SE	SE	SE	SE 1 A ⌶	SE	SE	SE	SE		SE 1 A ⌶	SE	SE 1	SE	SE	SE	SE	SE 1 A ⌶
St Pancras Internatnl 15 ⊖	d					15 24	15 48					15 54	16 15						16 26	16 47		
Stratford International ⊖	d					15 32	15 56					16 02	16 23						16 33	16 55		
Ebbsfleet International	d					15 44	16a06					16 14	16a33						16 44	17a05		
London Victoria 15 ⊖	d		14 58						15 22						15 52		15 58					16 22
London Blackfriars 3 ⊖	d																					
Elephant & Castle ⊖	d																					
Bromley South 4	d		15 19						15 39						16 09		16 19					16 39
St Mary Cray	d		15 25														16 25					
Swanley 4	d		15 29														16 29					
Farningham Road	d		15 34														16 34					
Longfield	d		15 38						15 52						16 22		16 38					16 52
Meopham	d		15 42						15 57						16 27		16 42					16 57
Sole Street	d		15 45														16 45					
London Charing Cross 4 ⊖	d	14 39								15 09						15 39						
London Waterloo (East) 4 ⊖	d	14 42								15 12						15 42						
London Cannon Street 4 ⊖	d																					
London Bridge 4 ⊖	d	14 47								15 17						15 47						
Dartford 4	d	15 25								15 55						16 25						
Greenhithe for Bluewater	d	15 30								16 00						16 30						
Gravesend 4	d	15 37				15 48				16 07		16 18				16 37			16 48			
Strood 4	d	15 48				15 58				16 18		16 28				16 48			16 58			
Rochester 4	d	15 52	15 56			16 03			16 09	16 22		16 33			16 39	16 52	16 56		17 03			17 10
Chatham 4	d	15 55	15 59			16 05			16 12	16 25		16 35			16 42	16 55	16 59		17 05			17 13
Gillingham (Kent) 4	d	15a59	16a03			16 10			16 17	16a29		16 40			16 47	16a59	17a03		17 10			17 18
Rainham (Kent)	d					16 15			16 21			16 45			16 51				17 15			17 23
Newington	d														16 55							17 27
Sittingbourne 4	a					16 22			16 28			16 52			17 00				17 22			17 32
	d			16 10		16 23			16 29		16 40	16 53			17 01			17 10	17 23			17 33
Kemsley	d			16 15							16 45							17 15				
Swale	d			16 18							16 48							17 18				
Queenborough	d			16 22							16 52							17 22				
Sheerness-on-Sea	a			16 27							16 57							17 27				
Teynham	d								16 33						17 05							17 37
Faversham 2	a					16 33			16 39			17 03			17 11				17 33			17 43
	d								16 43 / 16 45						17 15 / 17 19							17 47 / 17 49
Selling	d								16 50						17 23							17 54
Canterbury East 4	d								16 59						17 32							18 03
Bekesbourne	d								17 03													18 07
Adisham	d								17 08													18 12
Aylesham	d								17 10						17 40							18 14
Snowdown	d								17 13													18 17
Shepherds Well	d								17 17						17 45							18 21
Kearsney	d								17 21													18 25
Dover Priory 4	a								17 27						17 53							18 32
Whitstable	d								16 51						17 23							17 55
Chestfield & Swalecliffe	d								16 54						17 26							17 58
Herne Bay	d								16 58						17 30							18 02
Birchington-on-Sea	d								17 07						17 39							18 11
Westgate-on-Sea	d								17 10						17 42							18 15
Margate 4	d							16 53	17 14						17 46						17 53	18 19
Broadstairs	d							16 59	17 20						17 52						17 59	18 24
Dumpton Park	d								17 23						17 55							18 27
Ramsgate 4	a							17 04	17 26						17 58						18 04	18 32

A ⌶ to Margate

For further services to St Pancras International, Blackfriars and Elephant & Castle and onwards to Bromley South, St Mary Cray and Swanley please refer to table 52

Table 212

Mondays to Fridays
29 August to 7 September

London - Medway, Sheerness-on-Sea, Dover and Ramsgate

Network Diagram - see first Page of Table 212

Station			SE	SE 1	SE	SE 1	SE	SE 1 A ⌶	SE	SE		SE	SE	SE 1	SE	SE	SE	SE 1 A ⌶	SE 1		SE	SE	SE
St Pancras Internatnl 15 ⊖	d						16 55			17 14		17 17					17 25					17 44	
Stratford International ⊖	d						17 03			17 22		17 25					17 32					17 52	
Ebbsfleet International	d						17 14					17a35					17 43						
London Victoria 15 ⊖	d			16 28				16 57	17 04									17 27					
London Blackfriars 3 ⊖	d																						
Elephant & Castle ⊖	d																						
Bromley South 4	d			16 49				17 13	17 24									17 44					
St Mary Cray	d			16 55					17 30														
Swanley 4	d			16 59					17 34														
Farningham Road	d			17 04					17 39														
Longfield	d			17 08					17 44														
Meopham	d			17 12					17 48														
Sole Street	d			17 15					17 51														
London Charing Cross 4 ⊖	d		16 09																				17 17
London Waterloo (East) 4 ⊖	d		16 12																				17 20
London Cannon Street 4 ⊖	d					16 46								17 08	16 44				17 30		17 06		
London Bridge 4 ⊖	d		16 17			16 50								17 12	16 48				17 34		17 10		17 26
Dartford 4	d		16 55												17 28						17 47		18 02
Greenhithe for Bluewater	d		17 00												17 33						17 52		18 07
Gravesend 4	d		17 07				17 18			17 36					17 40						18 00	18 06	18 19
Strood 4	d		17 18				17 28			17a46					17 52						18 14	18a17	18a33
Rochester 4	d		17 22	17a27		17 29	17 34	17 40	18a04					17 49	17 57		17 59	18 10	18 15		18 20		
Chatham 4	d		17 25			17 31	17 37	17 43						17 52	18 00		18 02	18 13	18 18		18 23		
Gillingham (Kent) 4	d		17a31			17 36	17 43	17 48						17 57	18a07		18 07	18 18	18 24		18a30		
Rainham (Kent)	d					17 41	17 48	17 53						18 02			18 12	18 23	18 29				
Newington	d							17 57						18 06					18 33				
Sittingbourne 4	a					17 48	17 56	18 02						18 11			18 19	18 30	18 38				
	d				17 40	17 48	17 57	18 03						18 12		18 15	18 19	18 30	18 38				
Kemsley	d				17 45											18 20							
Swale	d				17 48											18 23							
Queenborough	d				17 52											18 27							
Sheerness-on-Sea	a				17 57											18 32							
Teynham	d							18 07						18 16				18 35					
Faversham 2	a					17 56	18 05	18 13						18 22			18 27	18 41	18 47				
	d					17 57		18 17 / 18 19						18 24			18 29	18 44 / 18 50	18 49				
Selling	d							18 23										18 54					
Canterbury East 4	d							18 32										19 04					
Bekesbourne	d																	19 08					
Adisham	d																	19 12					
Aylesham	d							18 40										19 15					
Snowdown	d																	19 17					
Shepherds Well	d							18 45										19 21					
Kearsney	d																	19 25					
Dover Priory 4	a							18 55										19 32					
Whitstable	d					18 05		18 25						18 32			18 37	18 52	18 57				
Chestfield & Swalecliffe	d					18 08		18 28						18 35				18 55	19 00				
Herne Bay	d					18 12		18 32						18 39			18 43	18 59	19 04				
Birchington-on-Sea	d					18 21		18 41						18 48			18 52	19 08	19 12				
Westgate-on-Sea	d					18 25		18 45						18 52				19 11	19 16				
Margate 4	d					18 29		18 49					18 53	18 57			18 58	19 15	19 20				
Broadstairs	d					18 34		18 54					18 59	19 01			19a04	19 21	19 26				
Dumpton Park	d					18 37		18 57						19 04				19 24	19 29				
Ramsgate 4	a					18 43		19 02					19 04	19 10				19 30	19 34				

A ⌶ to Margate

For further services to St Pancras International, Blackfriars and Elephant & Castle and onwards to Bromley South, St Mary Cray and Swanley please refer to table 52

Table 212

Mondays to Fridays
29 August to 7 September

London - Medway, Sheerness-on-Sea, Dover and Ramsgate

Network Diagram - see first Page of Table 212

		SE	SE ■	SE	SE	SE ■	SE		SE ■ ⌶		SE	SE	SE	SE	SE ■	SE	SE ■		SE ■ A ⌶		SE	SE	SE	SE ■	SE
St Pancras Internatnl ■ ⊖	d	17 47			17 54							18 14	18 17			18 24						18 47			18 55
Stratford International ⊖	d	17 55			18 02							18 22	18 25			18 32						18 55			19 02
Ebbsfleet International	d	18a05			18 13								18a35			18 43						19a05			19 13
London Victoria ■ ⊖	d		17 54						17 57								18 24		18 27						
London Blackfriars ■ ⊖	d																								
Elephant & Castle ⊖	d																								
Bromley South ■	d		18 19						18 15								18 46		18 44						
St Mary Cray	d		18 25														18 52								
Swanley ■	d		18 30														18 57								
Farningham Road	d		18 35														19 02								
Longfield	d								18 28								19 06								
Meopham	d		18 41														19 11								
Sole Street	d		18 44														19 13								
London Charing Cross ■ ⊖	d										17 39										18 01				
London Waterloo (East) ■ ⊖	d										17 42										18 04				
London Cannon Street ■ ⊖	d					17 52									18 14									18 44	
London Bridge ■ ⊖	d					17 56					17 48				18 18						18 10			18 48	
Dartford ■	d										18 22										18 45				
Greenhithe for Bluewater	d										18 27										18 51				
Gravesend ■	d										18 34	18 38									19 02				19 20
Strood ■	d										18 45	18a49									19 14				19 30
Rochester ■	d		18a56		18 31	18 38			18 43		18 51					19 03	19 23		19 12		19 19			19 27	19 35
Chatham ■	d				18 34	18 41			18 46		18 54				19 00	19 06	19 26		19 15		19 22			19 30	19 38
Gillingham (Kent) ■	d				18 39	18 46			18 51		19a02				19 05	19 11	19a32		19 20		19a29			19 34	19 43
Rainham (Kent)	d				18 44	18 51			18 56						19 10	19 16			19 25					19 39	19 48
Newington	d								19 00						19 14									19 43	
Sittingbourne ■	a				18 51	18 58			19 05						19 19	19 24			19 32					19 48	19 55
	d			18 44	18 52	18 59			19 06					19 10	19 19	19 24			19 33				19 40	19 49	19 55
Kemsley	d			18 49										19 15									19 45		
Swale	d			18 54										19 18									19 48		
Queenborough	d			18 58										19 22									19 52		
Sheerness-on-Sea	a			19 02										19 27									19 57		
Teynham	d								19 10										19 37					19 53	
Faversham ■	a				19 00	19 07			19 16						19 27	19 32			19 43					19 59	20 04
	d				19 01	19 08			19 20	19 22					19 28	19 33			19 47	19 49				20 00	
Selling	d									19 26										19 54					
Canterbury East ■	d									19 36										20 03					
Bekesbourne	d																			20 07					
Adisham	d																			20 12					
Aylesham	d																			20 14					
Snowdown	d																			20 17					
Shepherds Well	d																			20 21					
Kearsney	d																			20 25					
Dover Priory ■	a									19 54										20 32					
Whitstable	d				19 09	19 16			19 28						19 36	19 42			19 55					20 08	
Chestfield & Swalecliffe	d								19 31						19 39				19 58					20 11	
Herne Bay	d				19 15	19 22			19 35						19 43	19 48			20 02					20 15	
Birchington-on-Sea	d				19 24	19 31			19 44						19 52	19 57			20 11					20 24	
Westgate-on-Sea	d								19 48						19 55				20 15					20 27	
Margate ■	d				19 30	19 37	19 53		19a54						19 59	20 04			20 19					20 31	
Broadstairs	d				19a36	19a45	19 59								20 05	20a09			20 25					20 37	
Dumpton Park	d														20 08				20 28					20 40	
Ramsgate ■	a						20 04								20 13				20 33					20 46	

A ⌶ to Margate

For further services to St Pancras International, Blackfriars and Elephant & Castle and onwards to Bromley South, St Mary Cray and Swanley please refer to table 52

Table 212

Mondays to Fridays
29 August to 7 September

London - Medway, Sheerness-on-Sea, Dover and Ramsgate

Network Diagram - see first Page of Table 212

		SE ■ A ⌶			SE	SE	SE ■	SE	SE	SE	SE	SE ■ A ⌶			SE	SE	SE	SE	SE ■		SE	SE	SE		SE
St Pancras Internatnl ■ ⊖	d									19 24								19 54							20 25
Stratford International ⊖	d									19 32								20 02							20 33
Ebbsfleet International	d									19 45								20 14							20 44
London Victoria ■ ⊖	d	18 57					18 58					19 22				19 28			19 52			19 58			
London Blackfriars ■ ⊖	d																								
Elephant & Castle ⊖	d																								
Bromley South ■	d	19 14					19 21					19 39				19 49			20 09			20 19			
St Mary Cray	d						19 27									19 55						20 25			
Swanley ■	d						19 31									19 59						20 29			
Farningham Road	d						19 36									20 04						20 34			
Longfield	d						19 40					19 52				20 08			20 22			20 38			
Meopham	d						19 44					19 57				20 12			20 27			20 42			
Sole Street	d						19 47									20 15						20 45			
London Charing Cross ■ ⊖	d					18 37		18 48							19 09						19 39				
London Waterloo (East) ■ ⊖	d					18 40		18 51							19 12						19 42				
London Cannon Street ■ ⊖	d				18 30																				
London Bridge ■ ⊖	d				18 34	18 46		18 57							19 17						19 47				
Dartford ■	d				19 10	19 22		19 35							19 55						20 25				
Greenhithe for Bluewater	d				19 16	19 29		19 40							20 00						20 30				
Gravesend ■	d				19 26	19 38		19 47		19 51					20 07			20 18			20 37				20 48
Strood ■	d				19 38	19a53		19 58		20 01					20 18			20 28			20 48				20 58
Rochester ■	d	19 40			19 45		19 57	20 03		20 08		20 13			20 22	20 26		20 33	20 39		20 52	20 56			21 03
Chatham ■	d	19 43			19 48		19 59	20 05		20 10		20 16			20 25	20 29		20 35	20 42		20 55	20 59			21 05
Gillingham (Kent) ■	d	19 49			19a55		20a06	20a13		20 15		20 21			20a29	20a33		20 40	20 47		20a59	21a03			21 10
Rainham (Kent)	d	19 54								20 20		20 25						20 45	20 51						21 15
Newington	d	19 58																	20 55						
Sittingbourne ■	a	20 03								20 27		20 32						20 52	21 00						21 22
	d	20 03							20 10	20 27		20 33					20 40	20 53	21 01				21 10		21 23
Kemsley	d								20 15								20 45						21 15		
Swale	d								20 18								20 48						21 18		
Queenborough	d								20 22								20 52						21 22		
Sheerness-on-Sea	a								20 27								20 57						21 27		
Teynham	d											20 37													
Faversham ■	a	20 11								20 36		20 43						21 03	21 09						21 33
	d	20 15	20 17									20 47	20 49						21 13	21 15					
Selling	d		20 21										20 54							21 19					
Canterbury East ■	d		20 30										21 03							21 28					
Bekesbourne	d		20 35										21 07							21 33					
Adisham	d		20 39										21 12							21 37					
Aylesham	d		20 41										21 14							21 39					
Snowdown	d												21 17												
Shepherds Well	d		20 46										21 21							21 44					
Kearsney	d												21 25												
Dover Priory ■	a		20 56										21 32							21 52					
Whitstable	d	20 23										20 55							21 21						
Chestfield & Swalecliffe	d	20 26										20 58							21 24						
Herne Bay	d	20 30										21 02							21 28						
Birchington-on-Sea	d	20 39										21 11							21 37						
Westgate-on-Sea	d	20 43										21 15							21 40						
Margate ■	d	20 47									20 53	21 19							21 44						
Broadstairs	d	20 52									20 59	21 24							21 50						
Dumpton Park	d	20 55										21 27							21 53						
Ramsgate ■	a	21 00									21 04	21 32							21 56						

A ⌶ to Margate

For further services to St Pancras International, Blackfriars and Elephant & Castle and onwards to Bromley South, St Mary Cray and Swanley please refer to table 52

Table 212

Mondays to Fridays

29 August to 7 September

London - Medway, Sheerness-on-Sea, Dover and Ramsgate

Network Diagram - see first Page of Table 212

		SE	SE ■		SE	SE	SE	SE ■		SE	SE ■	SE	SE ■		SE	SE	SE	SE	SE ■	SE	SE	SE ■	
St Pancras Internatnl ⊖	d						20 55					21 25				21 47		21 55			22 25		
Stratford International ⊖	d						21 03					21 33				21 55		22 03			22 33		
Ebbsfleet International	d						21 14					21 44				22a05		22 14			22 44		
London Victoria ⊖	d		20 22					20 52			20 58		21 22						21 52			22 22	
London Blackfriars ⊖	d																						
Elephant & Castle ⊖	d																						
Bromley South	d		20 39					21 09			21 19		21 39						22 09			22 39	
St Mary Cray	d										21 25								22 15				
Swanley	d										21 29								22 19				
Farningham Road	d										21 34								22 24				
Longfield	d		20 52					21 22			21 38		21 52						22 28			22 52	
Meopham	d		20 57					21 27			21 42		21 57						22 32			22 57	
Sole Street	d										21 45								22 35				
London Charing Cross ⊖	d				20 09					20 39					21 09					21 39			
London Waterloo (East) ⊖	d				20 12					20 42					21 12					21 42			
London Cannon Street ⊖	d																						
London Bridge ⊖	d				20 17					20 47					21 17					21 47			
Dartford	d				20 55					21 25					21 55					22 25			
Greenhithe for Bluewater	d				21 00					21 30					22 00					22 30			
Gravesend	d				21 07		21 18			21 37		21 48			22 07			22 18		22 37	22 48		
Strood	d				21 18		21 28			21 48		21 58			22 18			22 28		22 48	22 58		
Rochester	d		21 09		21 22		21 33	21 39		21 52	21 56	22 03	22 09		22 22			22 33	22 45	22 52	23 03	23 09	
Chatham	d		21 12		21 25		21 35	21 42		21 55	21 59	22 05	22 12		22 25			22 35	22 47	22 55	23 05	23 12	
Gillingham (Kent)	d		21 17		21a29		21 40	21 47		21a59	22a03	22 10	22 17		22a29			22 40	22 52	22a59	23 10	23 17	
Rainham (Kent)	d		21 21				21 45	21 51				22 15	22 21					22 45	22 56		23 15	23 21	
Newington	d							21 55											23 00				
Sittingbourne	a		21 28				21 53	22 00				22 22	22 28					22 52	23 05		23 22	23 28	
	d		21 29			21 40	21 53	22 01				22 23	22 29				22 40	22 53	23 06		23 23	23 29	
Kemsley	d					21 45											22 45						
Swale	d					21 48											22 48						
Queenborough	d					21 52											22 52						
Sheerness-on-Sea	a					21 57											22 57						
Teynham	d		21 33										22 33									23 33	
Faversham	a		21 39				22 03	22 09				22 33	22 39					23 03	23 17		23 33	23 39	
	d		21 43	21 45				22 13	22 15				22 43	22 45								23 43	23 45
Selling	d			21 50					22 19					22 50									23 50
Canterbury East	d			21 59					22 28					22 59									23 59
Bekesbourne	d			22 03					22 33					23 03									
Adisham	d			22 08					22 37					23 08									
Aylesham	d			22 10					22 39					23 10									00 07
Snowdown	d			22 13										23 13									
Shepherds Well	d			22 17					22 44					23 17									
Kearsney	d			22 21										23 21									
Dover Priory	a			22 26					22 52					23 26									00 18
Whitstable	d		21 51					22 21					22 51									23 51	
Chestfield & Swalecliffe	d		21 54					22 24					22 54									23 54	
Herne Bay	d		21 58					22 28					22 58									23 58	
Birchington-on-Sea	d		22 07					22 37					23 07									00 07	
Westgate-on-Sea	d		22 10					22 40					23 10									00 10	
Margate	d	21 53	22 14					22 44					23 14									00 14	
Broadstairs	d	21 59	22 20					22 50					23 20									00 20	
Dumpton Park	d		22 23					22 53					23 23									00 23	
Ramsgate	a	22 04	22 26					22 56					23 26									00 26	

For further services to St Pancras International, Blackfriars and Elephant & Castle and onwards to Bromley South, St Mary Cray and Swanley please refer to table 52

Table 212

Mondays to Fridays

29 August to 7 September

London - Medway, Sheerness-on-Sea, Dover and Ramsgate

Network Diagram - see first Page of Table 212

		SE	SE	SE	SE	SE ■	SE	SE	SE ■	SE	SE	SE	SE ■	SE
St Pancras Internatnl ⊖	d		22 48		22 55			23 25			23 48	23 55		
Stratford International ⊖	d		22 56		23 03			23 33			23a54	00 03		
Ebbsfleet International	d		23a06		23 14			23 44				00 14		
London Victoria ⊖	d					22 52			23 22				23 52	
London Blackfriars ⊖	d													
Elephant & Castle ⊖	d													
Bromley South	d					23 09			23 39				00 09	
St Mary Cray	d					23 15							00 15	
Swanley	d					23 19							00 19	
Farningham Road	d					23 24							00 24	
Longfield	d					23 28			23 52				00 28	
Meopham	d					23 32			23 57				00 32	
Sole Street	d					23 35							00 35	
London Charing Cross ⊖	d	22 09					22 39			23 09				23 39
London Waterloo (East) ⊖	d	22 12					22 42			23 12				23 42
London Cannon Street ⊖	d													
London Bridge ⊖	d	22 17					22 47			23 17				23 47
Dartford	d	22 55					23 25			23 55				00 25
Greenhithe for Bluewater	d	23 00					23 31			23 59				00 31
Gravesend	d	23 07			23 18		23 40	23 48		00 10		00 18		00 40
Strood	d	23 18			23 28		23 52	23 58		00 22		00 28		00 52
Rochester	d	23 22			23 33	23 45	23 56	00 03	00 09	00 26		00 33	00 45	00 56
Chatham	d	23 25			23 35	23 47	23 58	00 05	00 12	00 28		00 35	00 47	00 58
Gillingham (Kent)	d	23a29			23 40	23 52	00a03	00 10	00 17	00a33		00 40	00a52	01a03
Rainham (Kent)	d				23 45	23 56		00 15	00 21			00 45		
Newington	d					00 01								
Sittingbourne	a				23 52	00 06		00 22	00 28			00 52		
	d			23 32	23 53	00 07		00 23	00 29			00 53		
Kemsley	d			23 37										
Swale	d			23 40										
Queenborough	d			23 44										
Sheerness-on-Sea	a			23 49										
Teynham	d								00 33					
Faversham	a				00 03	00 15		00 33	00 39			01 03		
	d								00 43					
Selling	d													
Canterbury East	d													
Bekesbourne	d													
Adisham	d													
Aylesham	d													
Snowdown	d													
Shepherds Well	d													
Kearsney	d													
Dover Priory	a													
Whitstable	d								00 51					
Chestfield & Swalecliffe	d								00 54					
Herne Bay	d								00 58					
Birchington-on-Sea	d								01 07					
Westgate-on-Sea	d								01 10					
Margate	d								01 14					
Broadstairs	d								01 20					
Dumpton Park	d								01 23					
Ramsgate	a								01 26					

For further services to St Pancras International, Blackfriars and Elephant & Castle and onwards to Bromley South, St Mary Cray and Swanley please refer to table 52

Table 212

Saturdays

London - Medway, Sheerness-on-Sea, Dover and Ramsgate

until 21 July, 18 Aug and from 15 Sep, 18 Aug and from 15 Sep

Network Diagram - see first Page of Table 212

		SE 1	SE	SE 1	SE	SE	SE 1	SE	SE	SE 1	SE 1	SE	SE	SE	SE	SE 1	SE	SE	SE 1	SE	SE 1	SE
St Pancras Internatnl 15 ⊖	d		22p55			23p25			23p55				00 12									
Stratford International ⊖	d		23p02			23p32			00 02				00 19									
Ebbsfleet International	d		23p13			23p43			00 13				00 31									
London Victoria 15 ⊖	d	22p22		22p52			23p22			23p52	00 10			00 35							05 22	
London Blackfriars 3 ⊖	d																					
Elephant & Castle ⊖	d																					
Bromley South 4	d	22p39		23p09			23p39			00 09				00 55							05 39	
St Mary Cray	d			23p15						00 15				01 01							05 45	
Swanley 4	d			23p19						00 19				01 05							05 49	
Farningham Road	d			23p24						00 24				01 10							05 54	
Longfield	d	22p52		23p28			23p52			00 28				01 14							05 58	
Meopham	d	22p57		23p32			23p57			00 32				01 18							06 02	
Sole Street	d			23p35						00 35											06 05	
London Charing Cross 4 ⊖	d							23p09				23p39			00 18							
London Waterloo (East) 4 ⊖	d							23p12				23p42			00 21							
London Cannon Street 4 ⊖	d																					
London Bridge 4 ⊖	d							23p17				23p47			00 26							
Dartford 4	d							23p55				00 25			01 06							05 55
Greenhithe for Bluewater	d							23p59				00 31			01 10							06 00
Gravesend 4	d		23p18			23p48		00 10	00 18			00 40			01 17							06 07
Strood 4	d		23p28			23p58		00 22	00 28			00 52			01 29							06 18
Rochester 4	d	23p09	23p33	23p45		00 03	00 09	00 26	00 33	00 45	00 49	00 56		01 29	01 33						06 15	06 22
Chatham 4	d	23p12	23p35	23p47		00 05	00 12	00 28	00 35	00 47	00 52	00 58		01 31	01 35						06 17	06 25
Gillingham (Kent) 4	d	23p17	23p40	23p52		00 10	00 17	00a33	00 40	00a52	00 57	01a03		01a35	01a41	05 47					06 22	06a29
Rainham (Kent)	d	23p21	23p45	23p56		00 15	00 21		00 45		01 01					05 51					06 26	
Newington	d			00 01							01 05					05 55					06 30	
Sittingbourne 4	a	23p28	23p52	00 06		00 22	00 28		00 52		01 10					06 00					06 35	
	d	23p29	23p53	00 07	00 15	00 23	00 29		00 53		01 11					06 01		06 10			06 36	
Kemsley	d				00 20													06 15				
Swale	d				00 23													06 18				
Queenborough	d				00 27													06 22				
Sheerness-on-Sea	a				00 32													06 27				
Teynham	d	23p33					00 33				01 15					06 05					06 40	
Faversham 2	a	23p39	00 03	00 15		00 33	00 39		01 03		01 23					06 11					06 46	
	d	23p43 23p45					00 43				01 24					06 12			06 17		06 47	
Selling	d	23p50														06 17						
Canterbury East 4	d	23p59														06 26						
Bekesbourne	d															06 30						
Adisham	d															06 35						
Aylesham	d	00 07														06 37						
Snowdown	d															06 40						
Shepherds Well	d															06 44						
Kearsney	d															06 48						
Dover Priory 4	a	00 18														06 53						
Whitstable	d	23p51					00 51				01 32								06 25		06 55	
Chestfield & Swalecliffe	d	23p54					00 54				01 35								06 28		06 58	
Herne Bay	d	23p58					00 58				01 39								06 32		07 02	
Birchington-on-Sea	d	00 07					01 07				01 48								06 41		07 11	
Westgate-on-Sea	d	00 10					01 10				01 51								06 44		07 14	
Margate 4	d	00 14					01 14				01 55						05 53		06 48	06 53	07 18	
Broadstairs	d	00 20					01 20				02 01						05 59		06 54	06 59	07 24	
Dumpton Park	d	00 23					01 23				02 04								06 57		07 27	
Ramsgate 4	a	00 26					01 26				02 07						06 04		07 00	07 04	07 30	

For further services to St Pancras International, Blackfriars and Elephant & Castle and onwards to Bromley South, St Mary Cray and Swanley please refer to table 52

Table 212

Saturdays

London - Medway, Sheerness-on-Sea, Dover and Ramsgate

until 21 July, 18 Aug and from 15 Sep

Network Diagram - see first Page of Table 212

		SE	SE	SE 1	SE	SE	SE 1	SE	SE	SE A	SE B	SE	SE 1	SE 1	SE	SE 1	SE 1	SE	SE 1	SE	SE	SE
St Pancras Internatnl 15 ⊖	d									06 52	06 55											07 52
Stratford International ⊖	d									06 59	07 02											07 58
Ebbsfleet International	d									07 13	07 13											08 13
London Victoria 15 ⊖	d						06 22						06 58						07 22			
London Blackfriars 3 ⊖	d																					
Elephant & Castle ⊖	d																					
Bromley South 4	d						06 39						07 19						07 39			
St Mary Cray	d						06 45						07 25									
Swanley 4	d						06 49						07 29									
Farningham Road	d						06 54						07 34									
Longfield	d						06 58						07 38						07 52			
Meopham	d						07 02						07 42						07 57			
Sole Street	d						07 05						07 45									
London Charing Cross 4 ⊖	d	05 39						06 09				06 39								07 09		
London Waterloo (East) 4 ⊖	d	05 42						06 12				06 42								07 12		
London Cannon Street 4 ⊖	d																					
London Bridge 4 ⊖	d	05 47						06 17				06 47								07 17		
Dartford 4	d	06 25						06 55				07 25								07 55		
Greenhithe for Bluewater	d	06 30						07 00				07 30								08 00		
Gravesend 4	d	06 37						07 07		07 17	07 18	07 37								08 07		08 18
Strood 4	d	06 48						07 18		07 27	07 28	07 48								08 18		08 28
Rochester 4	d	06 52					07 15	07 22		07 32	07 33	07 52	07 56						08 09	08 22		08 33
Chatham 4	d	06 55					07 17	07 25		07 34	07 35	07 55	07 59						08 12	08 25		08 35
Gillingham (Kent) 4	d	06a59					07 22	07a29		07 39	07 40	07a59	08a03						08 17	08a29		08 40
Rainham (Kent)	d						07 26			07 44	07 45								08 21			08 45
Newington	d						07 30												08 25			
Sittingbourne 4	a						07 35			07 51	07 52								08 30			08 52
	d		06 40		07 10		07 36		07 40	07 51	07 53				08 10				08 31		08 40	08 53
Kemsley	d		06 45		07 15				07 45						08 15						08 45	
Swale	d		06 48		07 18				07 48						08 18						08 48	
Queenborough	d		06 52		07 22				07 52						08 22						08 52	
Sheerness-on-Sea	a		06 57		07 27				07 57						08 27						08 57	
Teynham	d						07 40												08 35			
Faversham 2	a						07 46			08 03	08 03								08 41			09 03
	d			06 50			07 47							07 50		08 13	08 15		08 45 08 50			
Selling	d			06 55										07 55					08 55			
Canterbury East 4	d			07 04										08 04			08 29		09 04			
Bekesbourne	d			07 08										08 08					09 08			
Adisham	d			07 13										08 13					09 13			
Aylesham	d			07 15										08 15					09 15			
Snowdown	d			07 18										08 18					09 18			
Shepherds Well	d			07 22										08 22					09 22			
Kearsney	d			07 26										08 26					09 26			
Dover Priory 4	a			07 31										08 31			08 48		09 31			
Whitstable	d						07 55									08 21			08 53			
Chestfield & Swalecliffe	d						07 58												08 56			
Herne Bay	d						08 02									08 26			09 00			
Birchington-on-Sea	d						08 11									08 35			09 09			
Westgate-on-Sea	d						08 14												09 12			
Margate 4	d					07 53	08 18									08 41		08 53	09 16			
Broadstairs	d					07 59	08 24									08 46		08 59	09 22			
Dumpton Park	d						08 27												09 25			
Ramsgate 4	a					08 04	08 30									08 51		09 04	09 28			

A 19 May

B not 19 May

For further services to St Pancras International, Blackfriars and Elephant & Castle and onwards to Bromley South, St Mary Cray and Swanley please refer to table 52

Table 212

Saturdays

until 21 July, 18 Aug and from 15 Sep

London - Medway, Sheerness-on-Sea, Dover and Ramsgate

Network Diagram - see first Page of Table 212

		SE ■		SE	SE ■	SE	SE	SE ■		SE	SE	SE	SE ■		SE	SE ■	SE	SE	SE	SE ■		SE
St Pancras Internatnl ■ ⊖	d											08 50						09 25				
Stratford International ⊖	d											09 04						09 32				
Ebbsfleet International	d											09 15						09 43				
London Victoria ■ ⊖	d	07 52			07 58			08 22					08 52			08 58				09 22		
London Blackfriars ■ ⊖	d																					
Elephant & Castle ⊖	d																					
Bromley South ■	d	08 09			08 19			08 39					09 09			09 19				09 39		
St Mary Cray	d				08 25											09 25						
Swanley ■	d				08 29											09 29						
Farningham Road	d				08 34											09 34						
Longfield	d	08 22			08 38			08 52					09 22			09 38				09 52		
Meopham	d	08 27			08 42			08 57					09 27			09 42				09 57		
Sole Street	d				08 45											09 45						
London Charing Cross ■ ⊖	d			07 39						08 09					08 39							09 09
London Waterloo (East) ■ ⊖	d			07 42						08 12					08 42							09 12
London Cannon Street ■ ⊖	d																					
London Bridge ■ ⊖	d			07 47						08 17					08 47							09 17
Dartford ■	d			08 25						08 55					09 25							09 55
Greenhithe for Bluewater	d			08 30						09 00					09 30							10 00
Gravesend ■	d			08 37						09 07		09 20			09 37			09 48				10 07
Strood ■	d			08 48						09 18		09 30			09 48			09 58				10 18
Rochester ■	d	08 39		08 52	08 56			09 09		09 22		09 34	09 39		09 52	09 56		10 03		10 09		10 22
Chatham ■	d	08 42		08 55	08 59			09 12		09 25		09 37	09 42		09 55	09 59		10 05		10 12		10 25
Gillingham (Kent) ■	d	08 47		08a59	09a03			09 17		09a29		09 41	09 47		09a59	10a03		10 10		10 17		10a29
Rainham (Kent)	d	08 51						09 21				09 46	09 51					10 15		10 21		
Newington	d	08 55											09 55									
Sittingbourne ■	a	09 00						09 28				09 54	10 00					10 22		10 28		
	d	09 01				09 10		09 29			09 40	09 54	10 01				10 10	10 23		10 29		
Kemsley	d					09 15					09 45						10 15					
Swale	d					09 18					09 48						10 18					
Queenborough	d					09 22					09 52						10 22					
Sheerness-on-Sea	a					09 27					09 57						10 27					
Teynham	d							09 33												10 33		
Faversham ■	a	09 09						09 39				10 03	10 09					10 33		10 39		
	d	09 13	09 15					09 43	09 45				10 13	10 15						10 43	10 45	
Selling	d								09 50												10 50	
Canterbury East ■	d		09 29						09 59					10 29							10 59	
Bekesbourne	d								10 03												11 03	
Adisham	d								10 08												11 08	
Aylesham	d								10 10												11 10	
Snowdown	d								10 13												11 13	
Shepherds Well	d								10 17												11 17	
Kearsney	d								10 21												11 21	
Dover Priory ■	a		09 48						10 27					10 48							11 27	
Whitstable	d	09 21						09 51					10 21							10 51		
Chestfield & Swalecliffe	d							09 54												10 54		
Herne Bay	d	09 26						09 58					10 26							10 58		
Birchington-on-Sea	d	09 35						10 07					10 35							11 07		
Westgate-on-Sea	d							10 10												11 10		
Margate ■	d	09 41					09 53	10 14					10 41						10 53	11 14		
Broadstairs	d	09 46					09 59	10 20					10 46						10 59	11 20		
Dumpton Park	d							10 23												11 23		
Ramsgate ■	a	09 51					10 04	10 26					10 51						11 04	11 26		

For further services to St Pancras International, Blackfriars and Elephant & Castle and onwards to Bromley South, St Mary Cray and Swanley please refer to table 52

Table 212

Saturdays

until 21 July, 18 Aug and from 15 Sep

London - Medway, Sheerness-on-Sea, Dover and Ramsgate

Network Diagram - see first Page of Table 212

		SE	SE	SE ■ A ⌶		SE	SE ■	SE	SE	SE	SE ■ A ⌶		SE	SE	SE	SE ■ A ⌶		SE	SE ■	SE	SE	SE
St Pancras Internatnl ■ ⊖	d		09 55						10 28						10 52						11 28	
Stratford International ⊖	d		10 02						10 35						10 58						11 35	
Ebbsfleet International	d		10 13						10 46						11 13						11 46	
London Victoria ■ ⊖	d			09 52			09 58				10 22					10 52			10 58			
London Blackfriars ■ ⊖	d																					
Elephant & Castle ⊖	d																					
Bromley South ■	d			10 09			10 19				10 39					11 09			11 19			
St Mary Cray	d						10 25												11 25			
Swanley ■	d						10 29												11 29			
Farningham Road	d						10 34												11 34			
Longfield	d			10 22			10 38				10 52					11 22			11 38			
Meopham	d			10 27			10 42				10 57					11 27			11 42			
Sole Street	d						10 45												11 45			
London Charing Cross ■ ⊖	d					09 39							10 09					10 39				
London Waterloo (East) ■ ⊖	d					09 42							10 12					10 42				
London Cannon Street ■ ⊖	d																					
London Bridge ■ ⊖	d					09 47							10 17					10 47				
Dartford ■	d					10 25							10 55					11 25				
Greenhithe for Bluewater	d					10 30							11 00					11 30				
Gravesend ■	d		10 18			10 37			10 51				11 07		11 18			11 37			11 51	
Strood ■	d		10 28			10 48			11 01				11 18		11 28			11 48			12 01	
Rochester ■	d		10 33	10 39		10 52	10 56		11 06		11 09		11 22		11 33	11 39		11 52	11 56		12 06	
Chatham ■	d		10 35	10 42		10 55	10 59		11 08		11 12		11 25		11 35	11 42		11 55	11 59		12 08	
Gillingham (Kent) ■	d		10 40	10 47		10a59	11a03		11 13		11 17		11a29		11 40	11 47		11a59	12a03		12 13	
Rainham (Kent)	d		10 45	10 51					11 18		11 21				11 45	11 51					12 18	
Newington	d			10 55												11 55						
Sittingbourne ■	a		10 52	11 00					11 25		11 28				11 52	12 00					12 25	
	d	10 40	10 53	11 01				11 10	11 25		11 29			11 40	11 53	12 01				12 10	12 25	
Kemsley	d	10 45						11 15						11 45						12 15		
Swale	d	10 48						11 18						11 48						12 18		
Queenborough	d	10 52						11 22						11 52						12 22		
Sheerness-on-Sea	a	10 57						11 27						11 57						12 27		
Teynham	d										11 33											
Faversham ■	a		11 03	11 09					11 34		11 39				12 03	12 09					12 34	
	d			11 13	11 15						11 43	11 45				12 13	12 15					
Selling	d											11 50										
Canterbury East ■	d				11 29							11 59					12 29					
Bekesbourne	d											12 03										
Adisham	d											12 08										
Aylesham	d											12 10										
Snowdown	d											12 13										
Shepherds Well	d											12 17										
Kearsney	d											12 21										
Dover Priory ■	a				11 48							12 27					12 48					
Whitstable	d			11 21							11 51					12 21						
Chestfield & Swalecliffe	d										11 54											
Herne Bay	d			11 26							11 58					12 26						
Birchington-on-Sea	d			11 35							12 07					12 35						
Westgate-on-Sea	d										12 10											
Margate ■	d			11 41						11 53	12 14					12 41						12 53
Broadstairs	d			11 46						11 59	12 20					12 46						12 59
Dumpton Park	d										12 23											
Ramsgate ■	a			11 51						12 04	12 26					12 51						13 04

A ⌶ to Margate

For further services to St Pancras International, Blackfriars and Elephant & Castle and onwards to Bromley South, St Mary Cray and Swanley please refer to table 52

Saturdays

until 21 July, 18 Aug and from 15 Sep

London - Medway, Sheerness-on-Sea, Dover and Ramsgate

Network Diagram - see first Page of Table 212

		SE ■ A ⚒		SE	SE	SE	SE ■ A ⚒		SE	SE ■	SE	SE	SE	SE ■ A ⚒		SE	SE	SE	SE ■ A ⚒		SE	SE ■	SE
St Pancras International ⊖	d					11 55						12 28						12 55					
Stratford International ⊖	d					12 02						12 35						13 06					
Ebbsfleet International	d					12 13						12 46						13 17					
London Victoria ⊖	d	11 22					11 52			11 58				12 22					12 52			12 58	
London Blackfriars ⊖	d																						
Elephant & Castle ⊖	d																						
Bromley South	d	11 39					12 09			12 19				12 39					13 09			13 19	
St Mary Cray	d									12 25												13 25	
Swanley	d									12 29												13 29	
Farningham Road	d									12 34												13 34	
Longfield	d	11 52					12 22			12 38				12 52					13 22			13 38	
Meopham	d	11 57					12 27			12 42				12 57					13 27			13 42	
Sole Street	d									12 45												13 45	
London Charing Cross ⊖	d			11 09					11 39							12 09					12 39		
London Waterloo (East) ⊖	d			11 12					11 42							12 12					12 42		
London Cannon Street ⊖	d																						
London Bridge ⊖	d			11 17					11 47							12 17					12 47		
Dartford	d			11 55					12 25							12 55					13 25		
Greenhithe for Bluewater	d			12 00					12 30							13 00					13 30		
Gravesend	d			12 07		12 18			12 37			12 51				13 07		13 22			13 37		
Strood	d			12 18		12 28			12 48			13 01				13 18		13 32			13 48		
Rochester	d	12 09		12 22		12 33	12 39		12 52	12 56		13 06		13 09		13 22		13 37	13 39		13 52	13 56	
Chatham	d	12 12		12 25		12 35	12 42		12 55	12 59		13 08		13 12		13 25		13 39	13 42		13 55	13 59	
Gillingham (Kent)	d	12 17		12a29		12 40	12 47		12a59	13a03		13 13		13 17		13a29		13 44	13 47		13a59	14a03	
Rainham (Kent)	d	12 21				12 45	12 51					13 18		13 21				13 49	13 51				
Newington	d						12 55												13 55				
Sittingbourne	a	12 28				12 52	13 00					13 25		13 29				13 56	14 00				
	d	12 29			12 40	12 53	13 01				13 10	13 25		13 29			13 40	13 56	14 01				14 10
Kemsley	d				12 45						13 15						13 45						14 15
Swale	d				12 48						13 18						13 48						14 18
Queenborough	d				12 52						13 22						13 52						14 22
Sheerness-on-Sea	a				12 57						13 27						13 57						14 27
Teynham	d	12 33												13 33									
Faversham	a	12 39				13 03	13 09					13 34		13 39				14 04	14 09				
	d	12 43	12 45				13 13	13 15						13 43	13 45				14 13	14 15			
Selling	d		12 50												13 50								
Canterbury East	d		12 59					13 29							13 59					14 29			
Bekesbourne	d		13 03												14 03								
Adisham	d		13 08												14 08								
Aylesham	d		13 10												14 10								
Snowdown	d		13 13												14 13								
Shepherds Well	d		13 17												14 17								
Kearsney	d		13 21												14 21								
Dover Priory	a		13 27					13 48							14 27					14 48			
Whitstable	d	12 51					13 21							13 51					14 21				
Chestfield & Swalecliffe	d	12 54												13 54									
Herne Bay	d	12 58					13 26							13 58					14 26				
Birchington-on-Sea	d	13 07					13 35							14 07					14 35				
Westgate-on-Sea	d	13 10												14 10									
Margate	d	13 14					13 41						13 53	14 14					14 41				
Broadstairs	d	13 20					13 46						13 59	14 20					14 46				
Dumpton Park	d	13 23												14 23									
Ramsgate	a	13 26					13 51						14 04	14 26					14 51				

A ⚒ to Margate

For further services to St Pancras International, Blackfriars and Elephant & Castle and onwards to Bromley South, St Mary Cray and Swanley please refer to table 52

Saturdays

until 21 July, 18 Aug and from 15 Sep

London - Medway, Sheerness-on-Sea, Dover and Ramsgate

Network Diagram - see first Page of Table 212

		SE	SE	SE ■ A ⚒		SE	SE	SE	SE ■ A ⚒		SE	SE ■	SE	SE	SE	SE ■ A ⚒		SE	SE	SE	SE ■ A ⚒	
St Pancras International ⊖	d	13 25						13 55						14 25						14 55		
Stratford International ⊖	d	13 32						14 02						14 32						15 02		
Ebbsfleet International	d	13 43						14 13						14 43						15 13		
London Victoria ⊖	d			13 22					13 52			13 58				14 22					14 52	
London Blackfriars ⊖	d																					
Elephant & Castle ⊖	d																					
Bromley South	d			13 39					14 09			14 19				14 39					15 09	
St Mary Cray	d											14 25										
Swanley	d											14 29										
Farningham Road	d											14 34										
Longfield	d			13 52					14 22			14 38				14 52					15 22	
Meopham	d			13 57					14 27			14 42				14 57					15 27	
Sole Street	d											14 45										
London Charing Cross ⊖	d					13 09					13 39							14 09				
London Waterloo (East) ⊖	d					13 12					13 42							14 12				
London Cannon Street ⊖	d																					
London Bridge ⊖	d					13 17					13 47							14 17				
Dartford	d					13 55					14 25							14 55				
Greenhithe for Bluewater	d					14 00					14 30							15 00				
Gravesend	d	13 48				14 07		14 18			14 37			14 48				15 07		15 18		
Strood	d	13 58				14 18		14 28			14 48			14 58				15 18		15 28		
Rochester	d	14 03		14 09		14 22		14 33	14 39		14 52	14 56		15 03		15 09		15 22		15 33	15 39	
Chatham	d	14 05		14 12		14 25		14 35	14 42		14 55	14 59		15 05		15 12		15 25		15 35	15 42	
Gillingham (Kent)	d	14 10		14 17		14a29		14 40	14 47		14a59	15a03		15 10		15 17		15a29		15 40	15 47	
Rainham (Kent)	d	14 15		14 21				14 45	14 51					15 15		15 21				15 45	15 51	
Newington	d								14 55												15 55	
Sittingbourne	a	14 22		14 28				14 52	15 00					15 22		15 28				15 52	16 00	
	d	14 23		14 29			14 40	14 53	15 01				15 10	15 23		15 29			15 40	15 53	16 01	
Kemsley	d						14 45						15 15						15 45			
Swale	d						14 48						15 18						15 48			
Queenborough	d						14 52						15 22						15 52			
Sheerness-on-Sea	a						14 57						15 27						15 57			
Teynham	d			14 33												15 33						
Faversham	a	14 33		14 39				15 03	15 09					15 33		15 39				16 03	16 09	
	d			14 43	14 45				15 13	15 15						15 43	15 45				16 13	16 15
Selling	d				14 50												15 50					
Canterbury East	d				14 59					15 29							15 59					16 29
Bekesbourne	d				15 03												16 03					
Adisham	d				15 08												16 08					
Aylesham	d				15 10												16 10					
Snowdown	d				15 13												16 13					
Shepherds Well	d				15 17												16 17					
Kearsney	d				15 21												16 21					
Dover Priory	a				15 27					15 48							16 27					16 48
Whitstable	d			14 51					15 21							15 51					16 21	
Chestfield & Swalecliffe	d			14 54												15 54						
Herne Bay	d			14 58					15 26							15 58					16 26	
Birchington-on-Sea	d			15 07					15 35							16 07					16 35	
Westgate-on-Sea	d			15 10												16 10						
Margate	d		14 53	15 14					15 41						15 53	16 14					16 41	
Broadstairs	d		14 59	15 20					15 46						15 59	16 20					16 46	
Dumpton Park	d			15 23												16 23						
Ramsgate	a		15 04	15 26					15 51						16 04	16 26					16 51	

A ⚒ to Margate

For further services to St Pancras International, Blackfriars and Elephant & Castle and onwards to Bromley South, St Mary Cray and Swanley please refer to table 52

Table 212

Saturdays
until 21 July, 18 Aug and from 15 Sep

London - Medway, Sheerness-on-Sea, Dover and Ramsgate

Network Diagram - see first Page of Table 212

		SE	SE ■	SE	SE	SE	SE ■ A ⇄		SE	SE	SE	SE ■ A ⇄		SE	SE ■	SE	SE	SE	SE ■ A ⇄		SE	SE	SE
St Pancras International ⊖	d				15 25						15 55						16 28						16 55
Stratford International ⊖	d				15 32						16 02						16 35						17 02
Ebbsfleet International	d				15 43						16 13						16 46						17 13
London Victoria ⊖	d		14 58				15 22					15 52			15 58				16 22				
London Blackfriars ⊖	d																						
Elephant & Castle ⊖	d																						
Bromley South	d		15 19				15 39					16 09			16 19				16 39				
St Mary Cray	d		15 25												16 25								
Swanley	d		15 29												16 29								
Farningham Road	d		15 34												16 34								
Longfield	d		15 38				15 52					16 22			16 38				16 52				
Meopham	d		15 42				15 57					16 27			16 42				16 57				
Sole Street	d		15 45												16 45								
London Charing Cross ⊖	d	14 39							15 09					15 39							16 09		
London Waterloo (East) ⊖	d	14 42							15 12					15 42							16 12		
London Cannon Street ⊖	d																						
London Bridge ⊖	d	14 47							15 17					15 47							16 17		
Dartford	d	15 25							15 55					16 25							16 55		
Greenhithe for Bluewater	d	15 30							16 00					16 30							17 00		
Gravesend	d	15 37			15 48				16 07		16 18			16 37			16 51				17 07		17 18
Strood	d	15 48			15 58				16 18		16 28			16 48			17 01				17 18		17 28
Rochester	d	15 52	15 56		16 03		16 09		16 22		16 33	16 39		16 52	16 56		17 06		17 09		17 22		17 33
Chatham	d	15 55	15 59		16 05		16 12		16 25		16 35	16 42		16 55	16 59		17 08		17 12		17 25		17 35
Gillingham (Kent)	d	15a59	16a03		16 10		16 17		16a29		16 40	16 47		16a59	17a03		17 13		17 17		17a29		17 40
Rainham (Kent)	d				16 15		16 21				16 45	16 51					17 18		17 21				17 45
Newington	d											16 55											
Sittingbourne	a				16 22		16 28				16 52	17 00					17 25		17 28				17 52
	d			16 10	16 23		16 29			16 40	16 53	17 01				17 10	17 25		17 29			17 40	17 53
Kemsley	d			16 15						16 45						17 15						17 45	
Swale	d			16 18						16 48						17 18						17 48	
Queenborough	d			16 22						16 52						17 22						17 52	
Sheerness-on-Sea	a			16 27						16 57						17 27						17 57	
Teynham	d						16 33												17 33				
Faversham	a				16 33		16 39				17 03	17 09					17 34		17 39				18 03
	d						16 43	16 45				17 13	17 15						17 43	17 45			
Selling	d							16 50												17 50			
Canterbury East	d							16 59					17 29							17 59			
Bekesbourne	d							17 03												18 03			
Adisham	d							17 08												18 08			
Aylesham	d							17 10												18 10			
Snowdown	d							17 13												18 13			
Shepherds Well	d							17 17												18 17			
Kearsney	d							17 21												18 21			
Dover Priory	a							17 27					17 48							18 27			
Whitstable	d						16 51					17 21							17 51				
Chestfield & Swalecliffe	d						16 54												17 54				
Herne Bay	d						16 58					17 26							17 58				
Birchington-on-Sea	d						17 07					17 35							18 07				
Westgate-on-Sea	d						17 10												18 10				
Margate	d					16 53	17 14					17 41						17 53	18 14				
Broadstairs	d					16 59	17 20					17 46						17 59	18 20				
Dumpton Park	d						17 23												18 23				
Ramsgate	a					17 04	17 26					17 51						18 04	18 26				

A ⇄ to Margate

For further services to St Pancras International, Blackfriars and Elephant & Castle and onwards to Bromley South, St Mary Cray and Swanley please refer to table 52

Table 212

Saturdays
until 21 July, 18 Aug and from 15 Sep

London - Medway, Sheerness-on-Sea, Dover and Ramsgate

Network Diagram - see first Page of Table 212

		SE ■ A ⇄		SE	SE ■	SE	SE	SE	SE ■ A ⇄		SE	SE	SE	SE ■ A ⇄		SE	SE ■	SE	SE	SE	SE ■ A ⇄	
St Pancras International ⊖	d						17 25						17 55						18 25			
Stratford International ⊖	d						17 32						18 02						18 32			
Ebbsfleet International	d						17 43						18 13						18 43			
London Victoria ⊖	d	16 52			16 58				17 22					17 52			17 58				18 22	
London Blackfriars ⊖	d																					
Elephant & Castle ⊖	d																					
Bromley South	d	17 09			17 19				17 39					18 09			18 19				18 39	
St Mary Cray	d				17 25												18 25					
Swanley	d				17 29												18 29					
Farningham Road	d				17 34												18 34					
Longfield	d	17 22			17 38				17 52					18 22			18 38				18 52	
Meopham	d	17 27			17 42				17 57					18 27			18 42				18 57	
Sole Street	d				17 45												18 45					
London Charing Cross ⊖	d			16 39							17 09					17 39						
London Waterloo (East) ⊖	d			16 42							17 12					17 42						
London Cannon Street ⊖	d																					
London Bridge ⊖	d			16 47							17 17					17 47						
Dartford	d			17 25							17 55					18 25						
Greenhithe for Bluewater	d			17 30							18 00					18 30						
Gravesend	d			17 37			17 48				18 07		18 18			18 37			18 48			
Strood	d			17 48			17 58				18 18		18 28			18 48			18 58			
Rochester	d	17 39		17 52	17 56		18 03		18 09		18 22		18 33	18 39		18 52	18 56		19 03		19 09	
Chatham	d	17 42		17 55	17 59		18 05		18 12		18 25		18 35	18 42		18 55	18 59		19 05		19 12	
Gillingham (Kent)	d	17 47		17a59	18a03		18 10		18 17		18a29		18 40	18 47		18a59	19a03		19 10		19 17	
Rainham (Kent)	d	17 51					18 15		18 21				18 45	18 51					19 15		19 21	
Newington	d	17 55												18 55								
Sittingbourne	a	18 00					18 22		18 28				18 52	19 00					19 22		19 28	
	d	18 01				18 10	18 23		18 29			18 40	18 53	19 01				19 10	19 23		19 29	
Kemsley	d					18 15						18 45						19 15				
Swale	d					18 18						18 48						19 18				
Queenborough	d					18 22						18 52						19 22				
Sheerness-on-Sea	a					18 27						18 57						19 27				
Teynham	d								18 33												19 33	
Faversham	a	18 09					18 33		18 39				19 03	19 09					19 33		19 39	
	d	18 13	18 15						18 43	18 45				19 13	19 15						19 43	19 45
Selling	d									18 50												19 50
Canterbury East	d		18 29							18 59					19 29							19 59
Bekesbourne	d									19 03												20 03
Adisham	d									19 08												20 08
Aylesham	d									19 10												20 10
Snowdown	d									19 13												20 13
Shepherds Well	d									19 17												20 17
Kearsney	d									19 21												20 21
Dover Priory	a		18 48							19 27					19 48							20 27
Whitstable	d	18 21							18 51					19 21							19 51	
Chestfield & Swalecliffe	d								18 54												19 54	
Herne Bay	d	18 26							18 58					19 26							19 58	
Birchington-on-Sea	d	18 35							19 07					19 35							20 07	
Westgate-on-Sea	d								19 10												20 10	
Margate	d	18 41						18 53	19 14					19 41						19 53	20 14	
Broadstairs	d	18 46						18 59	19 20					19 46						19 59	20 20	
Dumpton Park	d								19 23												20 23	
Ramsgate	a	18 51						19 04	19 26					19 51						20 04	20 26	

A ⇄ to Margate

For further services to St Pancras International, Blackfriars and Elephant & Castle and onwards to Bromley South, St Mary Cray and Swanley please refer to table 52

Saturdays

until 21 July, 18 Aug and from 15 Sep

London - Medway, Sheerness-on-Sea, Dover and Ramsgate

Network Diagram - see first Page of Table 212

		SE	SE	SE	SE ■		SE	SE ■	SE	SE	SE	SE ■		SE	SE	SE	SE ■		SE	SE ■	SE	SE
St Pancras Internatnl ■ ⊖	d			18 55						19 25						19 55					20 25	
Stratford International ⊖	d			19 02						19 32						20 02					20 32	
Ebbsfleet International	d			19 13						19 43						20 13					20 43	
London Victoria ■ ⊖	d				18 52			18 58				19 22					19 52			19 58		
London Blackfriars ■ ⊖	d																					
Elephant & Castle ⊖	d																					
Bromley South ■	d				19 09			19 19				19 39					20 09			20 19		
St Mary Cray	d							19 25												20 25		
Swanley ■	d							19 29												20 29		
Farningham Road	d							19 34												20 34		
Longfield	d				19 22			19 38				19 52					20 22			20 38		
Meopham	d				19 27			19 42				19 57					20 27			20 42		
Sole Street	d							19 45												20 45		
London Charing Cross ■ ⊖	d	18 09					18 39							19 09					19 39			
London Waterloo (East) ■ ⊖	d	18 12					18 42							19 12					19 42			
London Cannon Street ■ ⊖	d																					
London Bridge ■ ⊖	d	18 17					18 47							19 17					19 47			
Dartford ■	d	18 55					19 25							19 55					20 25			
Greenhithe for Bluewater	d	19 00					19 30							20 00					20 30			
Gravesend ■	d	19 07		19 18			19 37			19 48				20 07		20 18			20 37		20 48	
Strood ■	d	19 18		19 28			19 48			19 58				20 18		20 28			20 48		20 58	
Rochester ■	d	19 22		19 33	19 39		19 52	19 56		20 03		20 09		20 22		20 33	20 39		20 52	20 56	21 03	
Chatham ■	d	19 25		19 35	19 42		19 55	19 59		20 05		20 12		20 25		20 35	20 42		20 55	20 59	21 05	
Gillingham (Kent) ■	d	19a29		19 40	19 47		19a59	20a03		20 10		20 17		20a29		20 40	20 47		20a59	21a03	21 10	
Rainham (Kent)	d			19 45	19 51					20 15		20 21				20 45	20 51				21 15	
Newington	d				19 55												20 55					
Sittingbourne ■	a			19 52	20 00					20 22		20 28				20 52	21 00				21 22	
	d		19 40	19 53	20 01				20 10	20 23		20 29			20 40	20 53	21 01				21 23	
Kemsley	d		19 45						20 15						20 45							
Swale	d		19 48						20 18						20 48							
Queenborough	d		19 52						20 22						20 52							
Sheerness-on-Sea	a		19 57						20 27						20 57							
Teynham	d											20 33										
Faversham ■	a			20 03	20 09					20 33		20 39				21 03	21 09				21 33	
	d				20 13	20 15						20 43	20 45				21 13	21 15				
Selling	d												20 50									
Canterbury East ■	d					20 29							20 59					21a27				
Bekesbourne	d												21 03									
Adisham	d												21 08									
Aylesham	d												21 10									
Snowdown	d												21 13									
Shepherds Well	d												21 17									
Kearsney	d												21 21									
Dover Priory ■	a					20 48							21 27									
Whitstable	d				20 21							20 51					21 21					
Chestfield & Swalecliffe	d											20 54										
Herne Bay	d				20 26							20 58					21 26					
Birchington-on-Sea	d				20 35							21 07					21 35					
Westgate-on-Sea	d											21 10										
Margate ■	d				20 41						20 53	21 14					21 41					21 53
Broadstairs	d				20 46						20 59	21 20					21 46					21 59
Dumpton Park	d											21 23										
Ramsgate ■	a				20 51						21 04	21 26					21 51					22 04

For further services to St Pancras International, Blackfriars and Elephant & Castle and onwards to Bromley South, St Mary Cray and Swanley please refer to table 52

Saturdays

until 21 July, 18 Aug and from 15 Sep

London - Medway, Sheerness-on-Sea, Dover and Ramsgate

Network Diagram - see first Page of Table 212

		SE ■		SE	SE	SE	SE ■	SE	SE	SE ■		SE	SE	SE	SE ■	SE	SE	SE ■		SE	SE	SE	SE ■
St Pancras Internatnl ■ ⊖	d					20 55			21 25					21 55			22 25					22 55	
Stratford International ⊖	d					21 02			21 32					22 02			22 32					23 02	
Ebbsfleet International	d					21 13			21 43					22 13			22 43					23 13	
London Victoria ■ ⊖	d	20 22					20 52			21 22					21 52			22 22					22 52
London Blackfriars ■ ⊖	d																						
Elephant & Castle ⊖	d																						
Bromley South ■	d	20 39					21 09			21 39					22 09			22 39					23 09
St Mary Cray	d						21 15								22 15								23 15
Swanley ■	d						21 19								22 19								23 19
Farningham Road	d						21 24								22 24								23 24
Longfield	d	20 52					21 28			21 52					22 28			22 52					23 28
Meopham	d	20 57					21 32			21 57					22 32			22 57					23 32
Sole Street	d						21 35								22 35								23 35
London Charing Cross ■ ⊖	d			20 09				20 39				21 09				21 39				22 09			
London Waterloo (East) ■ ⊖	d			20 12				20 42				21 12				21 42				22 12			
London Cannon Street ■ ⊖	d																						
London Bridge ■ ⊖	d			20 17				20 47				21 17				21 47				22 17			
Dartford ■	d			20 55				21 25				21 55				22 25				22 55			
Greenhithe for Bluewater	d			21 00				21 30				22 00				22 31				23 01			
Gravesend ■	d			21 07		21 18		21 37	21 48			22 07		22 18		22 40	22 48			23 10		23 18	
Strood ■	d			21 18		21 28		21 48	21 58			22 18		22 28		22 52	22 58			23 22		23 28	
Rochester ■	d	21 09		21 22		21 33	21 45	21 52	22 03	22 09		22 22		22 33	22 45	22 56	23 03	23 09		23 26		23 33	23 45
Chatham ■	d	21 12		21 25		21 35	21 47	21 55	22 05	22 12		22 25		22 35	22 47	22 58	23 05	23 12		23 28		23 35	23 47
Gillingham (Kent) ■	d	21 17		21a29		21 40	21 52	21a59	22 10	22 17		22a29		22 40	22 52	23a03	23 10	23 17		23a33		23 40	23 52
Rainham (Kent)	d	21 21				21 45	21 56		22 15	22 21				22 45	22 56		23 15	23 21				23 45	23 56
Newington	d						22 00								23 00								00 01
Sittingbourne ■	a	21 28				21 52	22 05		22 22	22 28				22 52	23 05		23 22	23 28				23 52	00 06
	d	21 29			21 40	21 53	22 06		22 23	22 29			22 40	22 53	23 06		23 23	23 29			23 32	23 53	00 07
Kemsley	d				21 45								22 45								23 37		
Swale	d				21 48								22 48								23 40		
Queenborough	d				21 52								22 52								23 44		
Sheerness-on-Sea	a				21 57								22 57								23 49		
Teynham	d	21 33								22 33								23 33					
Faversham ■	a	21 39				22 03	22 14		22 31	22 39				23 01	23 14		23 31	23 39				00 01	00 16
	d	21 43	21 45				22 15			22 43	22 45							23 43	23 45				
Selling	d		21 50								22 50								23 50				
Canterbury East ■	d		21 59				22a26				22 59								23 59				
Bekesbourne	d		22 03								23 03												
Adisham	d		22 08								23 08												
Aylesham	d		22 10								23 10								00 07				
Snowdown	d		22 13								23 13												
Shepherds Well	d		22 17								23 17												
Kearsney	d		22 21								23 21												
Dover Priory ■	a		22 27								23 27								00 18				
Whitstable	d	21 51								22 51								23 51					
Chestfield & Swalecliffe	d	21 54								22 54								23 54					
Herne Bay	d	21 58								22 58								23 58					
Birchington-on-Sea	d	22 07								23 07								00 07					
Westgate-on-Sea	d	22 10								23 10								00 10					
Margate ■	d	22 14								23 14								00 14					
Broadstairs	d	22 20								23 20								00 20					
Dumpton Park	d	22 23								23 23								00 23					
Ramsgate ■	a	22 26								23 26								00 26					

For further services to St Pancras International, Blackfriars and Elephant & Castle and onwards to Bromley South, St Mary Cray and Swanley please refer to table 52

Table 212

Saturdays

until 21 July, 18 Aug and from 15 Sep

London - Medway, Sheerness-on-Sea, Dover and Ramsgate

Network Diagram - see first Page of Table 212

Station		SE	SE		SE ■	SE	SE	SE ■	SE
St Pancras Internatnl ■ ⊖	d		23 25				23 55		
Stratford International ⊖	d		23 32				00 02		
Ebbsfleet International	d		23 43				00 13		
London Victoria ■ ⊖	d				23 22			23 52	
London Blackfriars ■ ⊖	d								
Elephant & Castle ⊖	d								
Bromley South ■	d				23 39			00 09	
St Mary Cray	d							00 15	
Swanley ■	d							00 19	
Farningham Road	d							00 24	
Longfield	d				23 52			00 28	
Meopham	d				23 57			00 32	
Sole Street	d							00 35	
London Charing Cross ■ ⊖	d	22 39				23 09			23 39
London Waterloo (East) ■ ⊖	d	22 42				23 12			23 42
London Cannon Street ■ ⊖	d								
London Bridge ■ ⊖	d	22 47				23 17			23 47
Dartford ■	d	23 25				23 55			00 25
Greenhithe for Bluewater	d	23 31				23 59			00 31
Gravesend ■	d	23 40	23 48			00 10	00 18		00 40
Strood ■	d	23 52	23 58			00 22	00 28		00 52
Rochester ■	d	23 56	00 03		00 09	00 26	00 33	00 45	00 56
Chatham ■	d	23 58	00 05		00 12	00 28	00 35	00 47	00 58
Gillingham (Kent) ■	d	00a03	00 10		00 17	00a33	00 40	00a52	01a03
Rainham (Kent)	d		00 15		00 21		00 45		
Newington	d								
Sittingbourne ■	a		00 22		00 28		00 52		
	d		00 23		00 29		00 53		
Kemsley	d								
Swale	d								
Queenborough	d								
Sheerness-on-Sea	a								
Teynham	d				00 33				
Faversham ■	a		00 31		00 39		01 01		
	d				00 43				
Selling	d								
Canterbury East ■	d								
Bekesbourne	d								
Adisham	d								
Aylesham	d								
Snowdown	d								
Shepherds Well	d								
Kearsney	d								
Dover Priory ■	a								
Whitstable	d				00 51				
Chestfield & Swalecliffe	d				00 54				
Herne Bay	d				00 58				
Birchington-on-Sea	d				01 07				
Westgate-on-Sea	d				01 10				
Margate ■	d				01 14				
Broadstairs	d				01 20				
Dumpton Park	d				01 23				
Ramsgate ■	a				01 26				

For further services to St Pancras International, Blackfriars and Elephant & Castle and onwards to Bromley South, St Mary Cray and Swanley please refer to table 52

Table 212

Saturdays

28 July to 11 August

London - Medway, Sheerness-on-Sea, Dover and Ramsgate

Network Diagram - see first Page of Table 212

Station		SE ■		SE ■	SE ■ A	SE	SE	SE	SE	SE		SE	SE ■	SE	SE ■	SE ■	SE	SE	SE	SE		SE	SE	SE	SE
St Pancras Internatnl ■ ⊖	d					23p51	23p56	00 02	00 06	00 11								00 17	00 21	00 27		00 32			00 36
Stratford International ⊖	d					00 01	00 05	00 12	00 16	00 20								00 27	00 30	00 36		00 42			00 46
Ebbsfleet International	d					00a10	00a16	00a22	00a26	00a31								00a37	00a41	00a47		00a52			00a56
London Victoria ■ ⊖	d	22p22		22p52									23p22		23p52	00 10							00 35		
London Blackfriars ■ ⊖	d																								
Elephant & Castle ⊖	d																								
Bromley South ■	d	22p39		23p09									23p39		00 09								00 55		
St Mary Cray	d			23p15											00 15								01 01		
Swanley ■	d			23p19											00 19								01 05		
Farningham Road	d			23p24											00 24								01 10		
Longfield	d	22p52		23p28									23p52		00 28								01 14		
Meopham	d	22p57		23p32									23p57		00 32								01 18		
Sole Street	d			23p35											00 35										
London Charing Cross ■ ⊖	d													23p09			23p39							00 18	
London Waterloo (East) ■ ⊖	d													23p12			23p42							00 21	
London Cannon Street ■ ⊖	d																								
London Bridge ■ ⊖	d													23p17			23p47							00 26	
Dartford ■	d													23p55			00 25							01 06	
Greenhithe for Bluewater	d													23p59			00 31							01 10	
Gravesend ■	d													00 10			00 40							01 17	
Strood ■	d													00 22			00 52							01 29	
Rochester ■	d	23p09		23p45									00 09	00 26	00 45	00 49	00 56						01 29	01 33	
Chatham ■	d	23p12		23p47									00 12	00 28	00 47	00 52	00 58						01 31	01 35	
Gillingham (Kent) ■	d	23p17		23p52									00 17	00a36	00a52	00 57	01a06						01a38	01a44	
Rainham (Kent)	d	23p21		23p56									00 21			01 01									
Newington	d			00 01												01 05									
Sittingbourne ■	a	23p28		00 06									00 28			01 10									
	d	23p29		00 07								00 15	00 29			01 11									
Kemsley	d											00 20													
Swale	d											00 23													
Queenborough	d											00 27													
Sheerness-on-Sea	a											00 32													
Teynham	d	23p33											00 33			01 15									
Faversham ■	a	23p39		00 15									00 39			01 23									
	d	23p43	23p45		23p45								00 43			01 24									
Selling	d		23p50		23p50																				
Canterbury East ■	d		23p59		23p59																				
Bekesbourne	d																								
Adisham	d																								
Aylesham	d		00 07		00 07																				
Snowdown	d																								
Shepherds Well	d																								
Kearsney	d																								
Dover Priory ■	a		00 18		00 18																				
Whitstable	d	23p51											00 51			01 32									
Chestfield & Swalecliffe	d	23p54											00 54			01 35									
Herne Bay	d	23p58											00 58			01 39									
Birchington-on-Sea	d	00 07											01 07			01 48									
Westgate-on-Sea	d	00 10											01 10			01 52									
Margate ■	d	00 14											01 14			01 56									
Broadstairs	d	00 20											01 20			02 01									
Dumpton Park	d	00 23											01 23			02 04									
Ramsgate ■	a	00 26											01 26			02 07									

A not 28 July

For further services to St Pancras International, Blackfriars and Elephant & Castle and onwards to Bromley South, St Mary Cray and Swanley please refer to table 52

London - Medway, Sheerness-on-Sea, Dover and Ramsgate

Saturdays

28 July to 11 August

Network Diagram - see first Page of Table 212

		SE	SE	SE	SE	SE	SE	SE	SE	SE	SE	SE	SE	SE	SE	SE	SE	SE	SE	SE	SE	SE	SE
St Pancras Internatnl 15 ⊖	d	00 41	00 47	00 51	00 57	01 02	01 06	01 11	01 17	01 21	01 27	01 32	01 38	01 44	01 55	02 02	02 32	03 02	03 32	04 02	04 32	05 02	05 32
Stratford International ⊖	d	00 50	00 57	01 00	01 06	01 12	01 16	01 20	01 26	01 30	01 36	01 42	01 48	01 54	02 04	02a08	02a38	03a08	03a38	04a08	04a38	05a08	05 42
Ebbsfleet International	d	01 03	01a07	01a11	01 20	01a22	01 29	01 35	01 38	01a41	01 49	01a52	02 00	02 05	02 16								05 56
London Victoria 15 ⊖	d																						
London Blackfriars 3 ⊖	d																						
Ephant &Castle ⊖	d																						
Bromley South 4	d																						
St Mary Cray	d																						
Swanley 4	d																						
Farningham Rad	d																						
bngfield	d																						
Meopham	d																						
Sole Street	d																						
London Charing Cross 4 ⊖	d																						
London Waterloo (East) 4 ⊖	d																						
London Cannon Street 4 ⊖	d																						
London Bridge 4 ⊖	d																						
Dartford 4	d																						
Greenhithe for Bluewater	d																						
Gravesend 4	d								01 43						02 21								
Strood 4	d								01 53						02 31								
Rchester 4	d								01 57					02 20	02 35								
Chatham 4	d								02 00					02 23	02 38								
Gillingham (Kent) 4	d								02 04					02 27	02 42								
Rinham (Kent)	d								02 09					02 32	02 47								
Nwington	d																						
Sittingbourne 4	a								02 16					02 39	02 54								
	d								02 17					02 40	02 55								
Kemsley	d																						
Swale	d																						
Qeenborough	d																						
Sheerness-on-Sea	a																						
Teynham	d																						
Faversham 2	a																						
	d								02 25					02 48	03 03								
Selling	d																						
Canterbury East 4	d																						
Bekesbourne	d																						
Adisham	d																						
Aylesham	d																						
Snowdown	d																						
Shepherds W	d																						
Kearsney	d																						
Dover Priory 4	a																						
Wistable	d																						
Chestfield &Swalecliffe	d																						
Herne Bay	d																						
Birchington-on-Sea	d																						
Wstgate-on-Sea	d																						
Margate 4	d																						
Broadstairs	d																						
Dumpton Park	d																						
Ramsgate 4	a																						

For further services to St Pancras hternational, Blackfriars and Ephant & Castle and onwards to Bromley South, St Mary Cray and Swanley please refer to table 52

London - Medway, Sheerness-on-Sea, Dover and Ramsgate

Saturdays

28 July to 11 August

Network Diagram - see first Page of Table 212

		SE	SE 1	SE	SE	SE 1	SE 1	SE	SE	SE	SE	SE 1	SE	SE	SE	SE 1	SE	SE	SE 1	SE	SE	SE 1
St Pancras Internatnl 15 ⊖	d			06 04						06 32			06 52	07 04						07 11		
Stratford International ⊖	d			06 14						06 42			07 03	07 14						07 21		
Ebbsfleet International	d			06a24						06a52			07a13	07 30						07a31		
London Victoria 15 ⊖	d						05 22									06 22			06 58			
London Blackfriars 3 ⊖	d																					
Ephant &Castle ⊖	d																					
Bromley South 4	d						05 39									06 39			07 19			
St Mary Cray	d						05 45									06 45			07 25			
Swanley 4	d						05 49									06 49			07 29			
Farningham Rad	d						05 54									06 54			07 34			
bngfield	d						05 58									06 58			07 38			
Meopham	d						06 02									07 02			07 42			
Sole Street	d						06 05									07 05			07 45			
London Charing Cross 4 ⊖	d								05 39								06 09	06 39				
London Waterloo (East) 4 ⊖	d								05 42								06 12	06 42				
London Cannon Street 4 ⊖	d																					
London Bridge 4 ⊖	d								05 47								06 17	06 47				
Dartford 4	d							05 55	06 25								06 55	07 25				
Greenhithe for Bluewater	d							06 00	06 30								07 00	07 30				
Gravesend 4	d							06 07	06 37								07 07	07 37				
Strood 4	d							06 18	06 48								07 18	07 48				
Rchester 4	d						06 15	06 22	06 52							07 15	07 22	07 52	07 56			
Chatham 4	d						06 17	06 25	06 55							07 17	07 25	07 55	07 59			
Gillingham (Kent) 4	d		05 47				06 22	06a29	07a02							07 22	07a32	08a02	08a03			
Rinham (Kent)	d		05 51				06 26									07 26						
Nwington	d		05 55				06 30									07 30						
Sittingbourne 4	a		06 00				06 35									07 35						
	d		06 01		06 10		06 36				06 40				07 10	07 36					07 40	
Kemsley	d				06 15						06 45				07 15						07 45	
Swale	d				06 18						06 48				07 18						07 48	
Qeenborough	d				06 22						06 52				07 22						07 52	
Sheerness-on-Sea	a				06 27						06 57				07 27						07 57	
Teynham	d		06 05				06 40									07 40						
Faversham 2	a		06 11				06 46									07 46						
	d		06 12			06 17	06 47					06 50				07 47						07 50
Selling	d		06 17									06 55										07 55
Canterbury East 4	d		06 26									07 04										08 04
Bekesbourne	d		06 30									07 08										08 08
Adisham	d		06 35									07 13										08 13
Aylesham	d		06 37									07 15										08 15
Snowdown	d		06 40									07 18										08 18
Shepherds W	d		06 44									07 22										08 22
Kearsney	d		06 48									07 26										08 26
Dover Priory 4	a		06 53									07 31										08 31
Wistable	d					06 25	06 55									07 55						
Chestfield &Swalecliffe	d					06 28	06 58									07 58						
Herne Bay	d					06 32	07 02									08 02						
Birchington-on-Sea	d					06 41	07 11									08 11						
Wstgate-on-Sea	d					06 44	07 15									08 15						
Margate 4	d	05 44				06 48	07 19									08 19						
Broadstairs	d	05 49				06 54	07 24									08 24						
Dumpton Park	d					06 57	07 27									08 27						
Ramsgate 4	a	05 54				07 00	07 30									08 30						

For further services to St Pancras hternational, Blackfriars and Ephant & Castle and onwards to Bromley South, St Mary Cray and Swanley please refer to table 52

Table 212

London - Medway, Sheerness-on-Sea, Dover and Ramsgate

Saturdays
28 July to 11 August

Network Diagram - see first Page of Table 212

		SE	SE	SE	SE	SE	SE	SE		SE	SE	SE ■	SE ■	SE ■		SE	SE	SE ■			SE	SE ■	SE	SE	SE
St Pancras Internatnl ■ ⊖	d		07 18	07 25	07 32	07 39	07 46	07 52		08 04	08 11													08 18	08 25
Stratford International ⊖	d		07 28	07 35	07 42	07 49	07 56	08 03		08 14	08 21													08 28	08 35
Ebbsfleet International	d		07 43	07a46	07a52	08 02	08a07	08a13		08 30	08a31													08 44	08a46
London Victoria ■ ⊖	d													07 22				07 52				07 58			
London Blackfriars ■ ⊖	d																								
Elephant & Castle ⊖	d																								
Bromley South ■	d													07 39				08 09				08 19			
St Mary Cray	d																					08 25			
Swanley ■	d																					08 29			
Farningham Road	d																					08 34			
Longfield	d													07 52				08 22				08 38			
Meopham	d													07 57				08 27				08 42			
Sole Street	d																					08 45			
London Charing Cross ■ ⊖	d															07 09					07 39				
London Waterloo (East) ■ ⊖	d															07 12					07 42				
London Cannon Street ■ ⊖	d																								
London Bridge ■ ⊖	d															07 17					07 47				
Dartford ■	d															07 55					08 25				
Greenhithe for Bluewater	d															08 00					08 30				
Gravesend ■	d		07 48													08 07					08 37			08 48	
Strood ■	d		07 58													08 18					08 48			08 58	
Rochester ■	d		08 03											08 09		08 22		08 39			08 52	08 56		09 03	
Chatham ■	d		08 05											08 12		08 25		08 42			08 55	08 59		09 05	
Gillingham (Kent) ■	d		08 10											08 17		08a32		08 47			09a02	09a03		09 10	
Rainham (Kent)	d		08 15											08 21				08 51						09 15	
Newington	d													08 25				08 55							
Sittingbourne ■	a		08 22											08 30				09 00						09 22	
	d	08 10	08 23											08 31			08 40	09 01					09 10	09 23	
Kemsley	d	08 15															08 45						09 15		
Swale	d	08 18															08 48						09 18		
Queenborough	d	08 22															08 52						09 22		
Sheerness-on-Sea	a	08 27															08 57						09 27		
Teynham	d													08 35											
Faversham ■	a		08 33											08 41				09 09						09 33	
	d											08 13	08 15	08 45	08 50			09 13	09 15						
Selling	d														08 55										
Canterbury East ■	d												08 29		09 04				09 29						
Bekesbourne	d														09 08										
Adisham	d														09 13										
Aylesham	d														09 15										
Snowdown	d														09 18										
Shepherds Well	d														09 22										
Kearsney	d														09 26										
Dover Priory ■	a												08 48		09 31				09 48						
Whitstable	d											08 21		08 53				09 21							
Chestfield & Swalecliffe	d													08 56											
Herne Bay	d											08 26		09 00				09 26							
Birchington-on-Sea	d											08 35		09 09				09 35							
Westgate-on-Sea	d													09 13											
Margate ■	d											08 41		09 17				09 41							
Broadstairs	d											08 46		09 22				09 46							
Dumpton Park	d													09 25											
Ramsgate ■	a											08 51		09 28				09 51							

For further services to St Pancras International, Blackfriars and Elephant & Castle and onwards to Bromley South, St Mary Cray and Swanley please refer to table 52

Table 212

London - Medway, Sheerness-on-Sea, Dover and Ramsgate

Saturdays
28 July to 11 August

Network Diagram - see first Page of Table 212

		SE	SE	SE	SE		SE	SE	SE ■		SE	SE	SE ■		SE		SE ■	SE	SE	SE	SE	SE	SE	SE	SE
St Pancras Internatnl ■ ⊖	d	08 32	08 39	08 46	08 52		09 04	09 11											09 18	09 25	09 32	09 39	09 46	09 52	10 04
Stratford International ⊖	d	08 42	08 49	08 56	09 03		09 14	09 21											09 28	09 35	09 42	09 49	09 56	10 03	10 14
Ebbsfleet International	d	08a52	09 02	09a07	09a13		09 30	09a31											09 43	09a46	09a52	10 02	10a07	10a13	10 30
London Victoria ■ ⊖	d								08 22				08 52				08 58								
London Blackfriars ■ ⊖	d																								
Elephant & Castle ⊖	d																								
Bromley South ■	d								08 39				09 09				09 19								
St Mary Cray	d																09 25								
Swanley ■	d																09 29								
Farningham Road	d																09 34								
Longfield	d								08 52				09 22				09 38								
Meopham	d								08 57				09 27				09 42								
Sole Street	d																09 45								
London Charing Cross ■ ⊖	d										08 09				08 39										
London Waterloo (East) ■ ⊖	d										08 12				08 42										
London Cannon Street ■ ⊖	d																								
London Bridge ■ ⊖	d										08 17				08 47										
Dartford ■	d										08 55				09 25										
Greenhithe for Bluewater	d										09 00				09 30										
Gravesend ■	d										09 07				09 37				09 48						
Strood ■	d										09 18				09 48				09 58						
Rochester ■	d								09 09		09 22		09 39		09 52		09 56		10 03						
Chatham ■	d								09 12		09 25		09 42		09 55		09 59		10 05						
Gillingham (Kent) ■	d								09 17		09a32		09 47		10a02		10a03		10 10						
Rainham (Kent)	d								09 21				09 51						10 15						
Newington	d												09 55												
Sittingbourne ■	a								09 28				10 00						10 22						
	d								09 29			09 40	10 01					10 10	10 23						
Kemsley	d											09 45						10 15							
Swale	d											09 48						10 18							
Queenborough	d											09 52						10 22							
Sheerness-on-Sea	a											09 57						10 27							
Teynham	d								09 33																
Faversham ■	a								09 39				10 09						10 33						
	d								09 43	09 45			10 13	10 15											
Selling	d									09 50															
Canterbury East ■	d									09 59				10 29											
Bekesbourne	d									10 03															
Adisham	d									10 08															
Aylesham	d									10 10															
Snowdown	d									10 13															
Shepherds Well	d									10 17															
Kearsney	d									10 21															
Dover Priory ■	a									10 27				10 48											
Whitstable	d								09 51				10 21												
Chestfield & Swalecliffe	d								09 54																
Herne Bay	d								09 58				10 26												
Birchington-on-Sea	d								10 07				10 35												
Westgate-on-Sea	d								10 11																
Margate ■	d								10 15				10 41												
Broadstairs	d								10 20				10 46												
Dumpton Park	d								10 23																
Ramsgate ■	a								10 26				10 51												

For further services to St Pancras International, Blackfriars and Elephant & Castle and onwards to Bromley South, St Mary Cray and Swanley please refer to table 52

Table 212

Saturdays

28 July to 11 August

London - Medway, Sheerness-on-Sea, Dover and Ramsgate

Network Diagram - see first Page of Table 212

	SE	SE ■	SE	SE	SE ■ A ⊼	SE	SE ■	SE	SE	SE	SE	SE	SE	SE	SE	SE	SE ■ A ⊼	SE
St Pancras Internatnl ⊖ d	10 11								10 18	10 25	10 32	10 39	10 46	10 52	11 04	11 11		
Stratford International ⊖ d	10 21								10 28	10 35	10 42	10 49	10 56	11 03	11 14	11 21		
Ebbsfleet International d	10a31								10 44	10a46	10a52	11 02	11a07	11a13	11 30	11a31		
London Victoria ⊖ d		09 22			09 52		09 58											
London Blackfriars ⊖ d																	10 22	
Elephant & Castle ⊖ d																		
Bromley South d		09 39			10 09		10 19										10 39	
St Mary Cray d							10 25											
Swanley d							10 29											
Farningham Road d							10 34											
Longfield d		09 52			10 22		10 38										10 52	
Meopham d		09 57			10 27		10 42										10 57	
Sole Street d							10 45											
London Charing Cross ⊖ d			09 09			09 39												10 09
London Waterloo (East) ⊖ d			09 12			09 42												10 12
London Cannon Street ⊖ d																		
London Bridge ⊖ d			09 17			09 47												10 17
Dartford d			09 55			10 25												10 55
Greenhithe for Bluewater d			10 00			10 30												11 00
Gravesend d			10 07			10 37			10 48									11 07
Strood d			10 18			10 48			10 58									11 18
Rochester d		10 09	10 22		10 39	10 52	10 56		11 03								11 09	11 22
Chatham d		10 12	10 25		10 42	10 55	10 59		11 05								11 12	11 25
Gillingham (Kent) d		10 17	10a32		10 47	11a02	11a03		11 10								11 17	11a32
Rainham (Kent) d		10 21			10 51				11 15								11 21	
Newington d					10 55													
Sittingbourne a		10 28			11 00				11 22								11 29	
Sittingbourne d		10 29		10 40	11 01			11 10	11 23								11 29	
Kemsley d				10 45				11 15										
Swale d				10 48				11 18										
Queenborough d				10 52				11 22										
Sheerness-on-Sea a				10 57				11 27										
Teynham d		10 33															11 33	
Faversham a		10 39			11 09				11 33								11 39	
Faversham d		10 43 / 10 45			11 13 / 11 15												11 43 / 11 45	
Selling d		10 50															11 50	
Canterbury East d		10 59			11 29												11 59	
Bekesbourne d		11 03															12 03	
Adisham d		11 08															12 08	
Aylesham d		11 10															12 10	
Snowdown d		11 13															12 13	
Shepherds Well d		11 17															12 17	
Kearsney d		11 21															12 21	
Dover Priory a		11 27			11 48												12 27	
Whitstable d		10 51			11 21												11 51	
Chestfield & Swalecliffe d		10 54															11 54	
Herne Bay d		10 58			11 26												11 58	
Birchington-on-Sea d		11 07			11 35												12 07	
Westgate-on-Sea d		11 11															12 11	
Margate d		11 15			11 41												12 15	
Broadstairs d		11 20			11 46												12 20	
Dumpton Park d		11 23															12 23	
Ramsgate a		11 26			11 51												12 26	

A ⊼ to Margate

For further services to St Pancras International, Blackfriars and Elephant & Castle and onwards to Bromley South, St Mary Cray and Swanley please refer to table 52

Table 212

Saturdays

28 July to 11 August

London - Medway, Sheerness-on-Sea, Dover and Ramsgate

Network Diagram - see first Page of Table 212

	SE	SE ■ A ⊼	SE	SE ■	SE	SE	SE	SE	SE	SE	SE	SE	SE	SE ■ A ⊼	SE	SE	SE ■ A ⊼	SE	SE ■
St Pancras Internatnl ⊖ d						11 18	11 25	11 32	11 39	11 46	11 52	12 04	12 11						
Stratford International ⊖ d						11 28	11 35	11 42	11 49	11 56	12 03	12 14	12 21						
Ebbsfleet International d						11 43	11a46	11a52	12 02	12a07	12a13	12 30	12a31						
London Victoria ⊖ d		10 52		10 58															11 58
London Blackfriars ⊖ d														11 22			11 52		
Elephant & Castle ⊖ d																			
Bromley South d		11 09		11 19										11 39			12 09		12 19
St Mary Cray d				11 25															12 25
Swanley d				11 29															12 29
Farningham Road d				11 34															12 34
Longfield d		11 22		11 38										11 52			12 22		12 38
Meopham d		11 27		11 42										11 57			12 27		12 42
Sole Street d				11 45															12 45
London Charing Cross ⊖ d			10 39												11 09			11 39	
London Waterloo (East) ⊖ d			10 42												11 12			11 42	
London Cannon Street ⊖ d																			
London Bridge ⊖ d			10 47												11 17			11 47	
Dartford d			11 25												11 55			12 25	
Greenhithe for Bluewater d			11 30												12 00			12 30	
Gravesend d			11 37			11 48									12 07			12 37	
Strood d			11 48			11 58									12 18			12 48	
Rochester d		11 39	11 52	11 56		12 03								12 09	12 22		12 39	12 52	12 56
Chatham d		11 42	11 55	11 59		12 05								12 12	12 25		12 42	12 55	12 59
Gillingham (Kent) d		11 47	12a02	12a03		12 10								12 17	12a32		12 47	13a02	13a03
Rainham (Kent) d		11 51				12 15								12 21			12 51		
Newington d		11 55															12 55		
Sittingbourne a		12 00				12 22								12 28			13 00		
Sittingbourne d	11 40	12 01			12 10	12 23								12 29		12 40	13 01		
Kemsley d	11 45				12 15											12 45			
Swale d	11 48				12 18											12 48			
Queenborough d	11 52				12 22											12 52			
Sheerness-on-Sea a	11 57				12 27											12 57			
Teynham d														12 33					
Faversham a		12 09				12 33								12 39			13 09		
Faversham d		12 13 / 12 15												12 43 / 12 45			13 13 / 13 15		
Selling d														12 50					
Canterbury East d		12 29												12 59			13 29		
Bekesbourne d														13 03					
Adisham d														13 08					
Aylesham d														13 10					
Snowdown d														13 13					
Shepherds Well d														13 17					
Kearsney d														13 21					
Dover Priory a		12 48												13 27			13 48		
Whitstable d		12 21												12 51			13 21		
Chestfield & Swalecliffe d														12 54					
Herne Bay d		12 26												12 58			13 26		
Birchington-on-Sea d		12 35												13 07			13 35		
Westgate-on-Sea d														13 11					
Margate d		12 41												13 15			13 41		
Broadstairs d		12 46												13 20			13 46		
Dumpton Park d														13 23					
Ramsgate a		12 51												13 26			13 51		

A ⊼ to Margate

For further services to St Pancras International, Blackfriars and Elephant & Castle and onwards to Bromley South, St Mary Cray and Swanley please refer to table 52

Table 212

Saturdays
28 July to 11 August

London - Medway, Sheerness-on-Sea, Dover and Ramsgate

Network Diagram - see first Page of Table 212

		SE	SE	SE		SE	SE	SE	SE	SE	SE	SE ■ A ⌶		SE		SE	SE ■ A ⌶		SE	SE ■	SE	SE	SE	SE
St Pancras International ■ ⊖	d		12 18	12 25		12 32	12 39	12 46	12 52	13 04	13 11											13 18	13 25	13 32
Stratford International ⊖	d		12 28	12 35		12 42	12 49	12 56	13 03	13 14	13 21											13 28	13 35	13 42
Ebbsfleet International	d		12 44	12a46		12a52	13 02	13a07	13a13	13 30	13a31											13 43	13a46	13a52
London Victoria ■ ⊖	d											12 22					12 52			12 58				
London Blackfriars ■ ⊖	d																							
Elephant & Castle ⊖	d																							
Bromley South ■	d											12 39					13 09			13 19				
St Mary Cray	d																			13 25				
Swanley ■	d																			13 29				
Farningham Road	d																			13 34				
Longfield	d											12 52					13 22			13 38				
Meopham	d											12 57					13 27			13 42				
Sole Street	d																			13 45				
London Charing Cross ■ ⊖	d													12 09					12 39					
London Waterloo (East) ■ ⊖	d													12 12					12 42					
London Cannon Street ■ ⊖	d																							
London Bridge ■ ⊖	d													12 17					12 47					
Dartford ■	d													12 55					13 25					
Greenhithe for Bluewater	d													13 00					13 30					
Gravesend ■	d		12 48											13 07					13 37			13 48		
Strood ■	d		12 58											13 18					13 48			13 58		
Rochester ■	d		13 03									13 09		13 22			13 39		13 52	13 56		14 03		
Chatham ■	d		13 05									13 12		13 25			13 42		13 55	13 59		14 05		
Gillingham (Kent) ■	d		13 10									13 17		13a32			13 47		14a02	14a03		14 10		
Rainham (Kent)	d		13 15									13 21					13 51					14 15		
Newington	d																13 55							
Sittingbourne ■	a		13 22									13 29					14 00					14 22		
	d	13 10	13 23									13 29				13 40	14 01				14 10	14 23		
Kemsley	d	13 15														13 45					14 15			
Swale	d	13 18														13 48					14 18			
Queenborough	d	13 22														13 52					14 22			
Sheerness-on-Sea	a	13 27														13 57					14 27			
Teynham	d											13 33												
Faversham ■	a		13 33									13 39					14 09					14 33		
	d											13 43	13 45				14 13	14 15						
Selling	d												13 50											
Canterbury East ■	d												13 59					14 29						
Bekesbourne	d												14 03											
Adisham	d												14 08											
Aylesham	d												14 10											
Snowdown	d												14 13											
Shepherds Well	d												14 17											
Kearsney	d												14 21											
Dover Priory ■	a												14 27					14 48						
Whitstable	d											13 51					14 21							
Chestfield & Swalecliffe	d											13 54												
Herne Bay	d											13 58					14 26							
Birchington-on-Sea	d											14 07					14 35							
Westgate-on-Sea	d											14 11												
Margate ■	d											14 15					14 41							
Broadstairs	d											14 20					14 46							
Dumpton Park	d											14 23												
Ramsgate ■	a											14 26					14 51							

A ⌶ to Margate

For further services to St Pancras International, Blackfriars and Elephant & Castle and onwards to Bromley South, St Mary Cray and Swanley please refer to table 52

Table 212

Saturdays
28 July to 11 August

London - Medway, Sheerness-on-Sea, Dover and Ramsgate

Network Diagram - see first Page of Table 212

		SE	SE	SE	SE	SE	SE ■ A ⌶		SE	SE		SE ■ A ⌶		SE	SE ■	SE	SE	SE	SE	SE		SE	SE	SE	SE
St Pancras International ■ ⊖	d	13 39	13 46	13 52	14 04	14 11											14 18	14 25	14 32	14 39		14 46	14 52	15 04	15 11
Stratford International ⊖	d	13 49	13 56	14 03	14 14	14 21											14 28	14 35	14 42	14 49		14 56	15 03	15 14	15 21
Ebbsfleet International	d	14 02	14a07	14a13	14 30	14a31											14 43	14a46	14a52	15 02		15a07	15a13	15 30	15a31
London Victoria ■ ⊖	d						13 22					13 52			13 58										
London Blackfriars ■ ⊖	d																								
Elephant & Castle ⊖	d																								
Bromley South ■	d						13 39					14 09			14 19										
St Mary Cray	d														14 25										
Swanley ■	d														14 29										
Farningham Road	d														14 34										
Longfield	d						13 52					14 22			14 38										
Meopham	d						13 57					14 27			14 42										
Sole Street	d														14 45										
London Charing Cross ■ ⊖	d								13 09					13 39											
London Waterloo (East) ■ ⊖	d								13 12					13 42											
London Cannon Street ■ ⊖	d																								
London Bridge ■ ⊖	d								13 17					13 47											
Dartford ■	d								13 55					14 25											
Greenhithe for Bluewater	d								14 00					14 30											
Gravesend ■	d								14 07					14 37			14 48								
Strood ■	d								14 18					14 48			14 58								
Rochester ■	d						14 09		14 22			14 39		14 52	14 56		15 03								
Chatham ■	d						14 12		14 25			14 42		14 55	14 59		15 05								
Gillingham (Kent) ■	d						14 17		14a32			14 47		15a02	15a03		15 10								
Rainham (Kent)	d						14 21					14 51					15 15								
Newington	d											14 55													
Sittingbourne ■	a						14 28					15 00					15 22								
	d						14 29			14 40		15 01				15 10	15 23								
Kemsley	d									14 45						15 15									
Swale	d									14 48						15 18									
Queenborough	d									14 52						15 22									
Sheerness-on-Sea	a									14 57						15 27									
Teynham	d						14 33																		
Faversham ■	a						14 39					15 09					15 33								
	d						14 43	14 45				15 13	15 15												
Selling	d							14 50																	
Canterbury East ■	d							14 59					15 29												
Bekesbourne	d							15 03																	
Adisham	d							15 08																	
Aylesham	d							15 10																	
Snowdown	d							15 13																	
Shepherds Well	d							15 17																	
Kearsney	d							15 21																	
Dover Priory ■	a							15 27					15 48												
Whitstable	d						14 51					15 21													
Chestfield & Swalecliffe	d						14 54																		
Herne Bay	d						14 58					15 26													
Birchington-on-Sea	d						15 07					15 35													
Westgate-on-Sea	d						15 11																		
Margate ■	d						15 15					15 41													
Broadstairs	d						15 20					15 46													
Dumpton Park	d						15 23																		
Ramsgate ■	a						15 26					15 51													

A ⌶ to Margate

For further services to St Pancras International, Blackfriars and Elephant & Castle and onwards to Bromley South, St Mary Cray and Swanley please refer to table 52

Table 212

Saturdays
28 July to 11 August

London - Medway, Sheerness-on-Sea, Dover and Ramsgate

Network Diagram - see first Page of Table 212

		SE 1 A ⌶	SE	SE	SE 1 A ⌶	SE	SE 1	SE	SE	SE	SE	SE	SE	SE	SE	SE	SE 1 A ⌶	SE	SE
St Pancras Internatnl ⊖	d								15 18	15 25	15 32	15 39	15 46	15 52	16 04	16 11			
Stratford International ⊖	d								15 28	15 35	15 42	15 49	15 56	16 03	16 14	16 21			
Ebbsfleet International	d								15 43	15a46	15a52	16 02	16a07	16a13	16 27	16a31			
London Victoria ⊖	d	14 22			14 52		14 58										15 22		
London Blackfriars ⊖	d																		
Elephant & Castle ⊖	d																		
Bromley South	d	14 39			15 09		15 19										15 39		
St Mary Cray	d						15 25												
Swanley	d						15 29												
Farningham Road	d						15 34												
Longfield	d	14 52			15 22		15 38										15 52		
Meopham	d	14 57			15 27		15 42										15 57		
Sole Street	d						15 45												
London Charing Cross ⊖	d		14 09			14 39												15 09	
London Waterloo (East) ⊖	d		14 12			14 42												15 12	
London Cannon Street ⊖	d																		
London Bridge ⊖	d		14 17			14 47												15 17	
Dartford	d		14 55			15 25												15 55	
Greenhithe for Bluewater	d		15 00			15 30												16 00	
Gravesend	d		15 07			15 37			15 48									16 07	
Strood	d		15 18			15 48			15 58									16 18	
Rochester	d	15 09	15 22		15 39	15 52	15 56		16 03								16 09	16 22	
Chatham	d	15 12	15 25		15 42	15 55	15 59		16 05								16 12	16 25	
Gillingham (Kent)	d	15 17	15a32		15 47	16a02	16a03		16 10								16 17	16a32	
Rainham (Kent)	d	15 21			15 51				16 15								16 21		
Newington	d				15 55														
Sittingbourne	a	15 29			16 00				16 22								16 28		
	d	15 29		15 40	16 01			16 10	16 23								16 29		16 40
Kemsley	d			15 45				16 15											16 45
Swale	d			15 48				16 18											16 48
Queenborough	d			15 52				16 22											16 52
Sheerness-on-Sea	a			15 57				16 27											16 57
Teynham	d	15 33															16 33		
Faversham	a	15 39			16 09				16 33								16 39		
	d	15 43 15 45			16 13 16 15												16 43 16 45		
Selling	d	15 50															16 50		
Canterbury East	d	15 59			16 29												16 59		
Bekesbourne	d	16 03															17 03		
Adisham	d	16 08															17 08		
Aylesham	d	16 10															17 10		
Snowdown	d	16 13															17 13		
Shepherds Well	d	16 17															17 17		
Kearsney	d	16 21															17 21		
Dover Priory	a	16 27			16 48												17 27		
Whitstable	d	15 51			16 21												16 51		
Chestfield & Swalecliffe	d	15 54															16 54		
Herne Bay	d	15 58			16 26												16 58		
Birchington-on-Sea	d	16 07			16 35												17 07		
Westgate-on-Sea	d	16 11															17 11		
Margate	d	16 15			16 41												17 15		
Broadstairs	d	16 20			16 46												17 20		
Dumpton Park	d	16 23															17 23		
Ramsgate	a	16 26			16 51												17 26		

A ⌶ to Margate

For further services to St Pancras International, Blackfriars and Elephant & Castle and onwards to Bromley South, St Mary Cray and Swanley please refer to table 52

Table 212

Saturdays
28 July to 11 August

London - Medway, Sheerness-on-Sea, Dover and Ramsgate

Network Diagram - see first Page of Table 212

		SE 1 A ⌶	SE	SE 1	SE	SE	SE	SE	SE	SE	SE	SE	SE	SE 1 A ⌶	SE	SE	SE 1 A ⌶	SE	SE 1
St Pancras Internatnl ⊖	d					16 18	16 25	16 32	16 39	16 46	16 52	17 04	17 11						
Stratford International ⊖	d					16 28	16 35	16 42	16 49	16 56	17 03	17 14	17 21						
Ebbsfleet International	d					16 44	16a46	16a52	17 02	17a07	17a13	17 30	17a31						
London Victoria ⊖	d	15 52		15 58										16 22			16 52		16 58
London Blackfriars ⊖	d																		
Elephant & Castle ⊖	d																		
Bromley South	d	16 09		16 19										16 39			17 09		17 19
St Mary Cray	d			16 25															17 25
Swanley	d			16 29															17 29
Farningham Road	d			16 34															17 34
Longfield	d	16 22		16 38										16 52			17 22		17 38
Meopham	d	16 27		16 42										16 57			17 27		17 42
Sole Street	d			16 45															17 45
London Charing Cross ⊖	d		15 39												16 09			16 39	
London Waterloo (East) ⊖	d		15 42												16 12			16 42	
London Cannon Street ⊖	d																		
London Bridge ⊖	d		15 47												16 17			16 47	
Dartford	d		16 25												16 55			17 25	
Greenhithe for Bluewater	d		16 30												17 00			17 30	
Gravesend	d		16 37			16 48									17 07			17 37	
Strood	d		16 48			16 58									17 18			17 48	
Rochester	d	16 39	16 52	16 56		17 03								17 09	17 22		17 39	17 52	17 56
Chatham	d	16 42	16 55	16 59		17 05								17 12	17 25		17 42	17 55	17 59
Gillingham (Kent)	d	16 47	17a02	17a03		17 10								17 17	17a32		17 47	18a02	18a03
Rainham (Kent)	d	16 51				17 15								17 21			17 51		
Newington	d	16 55															17 55		
Sittingbourne	a	17 00				17 22								17 29			18 00		
	d	17 01			17 10	17 23								17 29		17 40	18 01		
Kemsley	d				17 15											17 45			
Swale	d				17 18											17 48			
Queenborough	d				17 22											17 52			
Sheerness-on-Sea	a				17 27											17 57			
Teynham	d													17 33					
Faversham	a	17 09				17 33								17 39			18 09		
	d	17 13 17 15												17 43 17 45			18 13 18 15		
Selling	d													17 50					
Canterbury East	d	17 29												17 59			18 29		
Bekesbourne	d													18 03					
Adisham	d													18 08					
Aylesham	d													18 10					
Snowdown	d													18 13					
Shepherds Well	d													18 17					
Kearsney	d													18 21					
Dover Priory	a	17 48												18 27			18 48		
Whitstable	d	17 21												17 51			18 21		
Chestfield & Swalecliffe	d													17 54					
Herne Bay	d	17 26												17 58			18 26		
Birchington-on-Sea	d	17 35												18 07			18 35		
Westgate-on-Sea	d													18 11					
Margate	d	17 41												18 15			18 41		
Broadstairs	d	17 46												18 20			18 46		
Dumpton Park	d													18 23					
Ramsgate	a	17 51												18 26			18 51		

A ⌶ to Margate

For further services to St Pancras International, Blackfriars and Elephant & Castle and onwards to Bromley South, St Mary Cray and Swanley please refer to table 52

Saturdays
28 July to 11 August

London - Medway, Sheerness-on-Sea, Dover and Ramsgate

Network Diagram - see first Page of Table 212

		SE	SE	SE	SE	SE	SE	SE	SE	SE	SE 1 A ✕	SE	SE	SE 1 A ✕	SE	SE 1	SE	SE	SE	SE	SE
St Pancras Internatnl 15 ⊖	d		17 18	17 25	17 32	17 39	17 46	17 52	18 04	18 11								18 18	18 25	18 32	18 39
Stratford International ⊖	d		17 28	17 35	17 42	17 49	17 56	18 03	18 14	18 21								18 28	18 35	18 42	18 49
Ebbsfleet International	d		17 43	17a46	17a52	18 02	18a07	18a13	18 30	18a31								18 43	18a46	18a52	19 02
London Victoria 15 ⊖	d										17 22			17 52		17 58					
London Blackfriars 3 ⊖	d																				
Elephant & Castle ⊖	d																				
Bromley South 4	d										17 39			18 09		18 19					
St Mary Cray	d															18 25					
Swanley 4	d															18 29					
Farningham Road	d															18 34					
Longfield	d										17 52			18 22		18 38					
Meopham	d										17 57			18 27		18 42					
Sole Street	d															18 45					
London Charing Cross 4 ⊖	d											17 09			17 39						
London Waterloo (East) 4 ⊖	d											17 12			17 42						
London Cannon Street 4 ⊖	d																				
London Bridge 4 ⊖	d											17 17			17 47						
Dartford 4	d											17 55			18 25						
Greenhithe for Bluewater	d											18 00			18 30						
Gravesend 4	d		17 48									18 07			18 37			18 48			
Strood 4	d		17 58									18 18			18 48			18 58			
Rochester 4	d		18 03								18 09	18 22		18 39	18 52	18 56		19 03			
Chatham 4	d		18 05								18 12	18 25		18 42	18 55	18 59		19 05			
Gillingham (Kent) 4	d		18 10								18 17	18a32		18 47	19a02	19a03		19 10			
Rainham (Kent)	d		18 15								18 21			18 51				19 15			
Newington	d													18 55							
Sittingbourne 4	a		18 22								18 29			19 00				19 22			
	d	18 10	18 23								18 29		18 40	19 01			19 10	19 23			
Kemsley	d	18 15											18 45				19 15				
Swale	d	18 18											18 48				19 18				
Queenborough	d	18 22											18 52				19 22				
Sheerness-on-Sea	a	18 27											18 57				19 27				
Teynham	d										18 33										
Faversham 2	a		18 33								18 39			19 09				19 33			
	d										18 43 / 18 45			19 13 / 19 15							
Selling	d										18 50										
Canterbury East 4	d										18 59			19 29							
Bekesbourne	d										19 03										
Adisham	d										19 08										
Aylesham	d										19 10										
Snowdown	d										19 13										
Shepherds Well	d										19 17										
Kearsney	d										19 21										
Dover Priory 4	a										19 27			19 48							
Whitstable	d										18 51			19 21							
Chestfield & Swalecliffe	d										18 54										
Herne Bay	d										18 58			19 26							
Birchington-on-Sea	d										19 07			19 35							
Westgate-on-Sea	d										19 11										
Margate 4	d										19 15			19 41							
Broadstairs	d										19 20			19 46							
Dumpton Park	d										19 23										
Ramsgate 4	a										19 26			19 51							

A ✕ to Margate

For further services to St Pancras International, Blackfriars and Elephant & Castle and onwards to Bromley South, St Mary Cray and Swanley please refer to table 52

Saturdays
28 July to 11 August

London - Medway, Sheerness-on-Sea, Dover and Ramsgate

Network Diagram - see first Page of Table 212

		SE	SE	SE	SE	SE 1 A ✕	SE	SE	SE 1	SE	SE 1	SE	SE	SE	SE	SE	SE	SE	SE	SE
St Pancras Internatnl 15 ⊖	d	18 46	18 52	19 04	19 11								19 18	19 25	19 32	19 39	19 46	19 52	20 04	20 11
Stratford International ⊖	d	18 56	19 03	19 14	19 21								19 28	19 35	19 42	19 49	19 56	20 03	20 14	20 21
Ebbsfleet International	d	19a07	19a13	19 30	19a31								19 43	19a46	19a52	20 02	20a07	20a13	20 30	20a31
London Victoria 15 ⊖	d					18 22			18 52		18 58									
London Blackfriars 3 ⊖	d																			
Elephant & Castle ⊖	d																			
Bromley South 4	d					18 39			19 09		19 19									
St Mary Cray	d										19 25									
Swanley 4	d										19 29									
Farningham Road	d										19 34									
Longfield	d					18 52			19 22		19 38									
Meopham	d					18 57			19 27		19 42									
Sole Street	d										19 45									
London Charing Cross 4 ⊖	d						18 09			18 39										
London Waterloo (East) 4 ⊖	d						18 12			18 42										
London Cannon Street 4 ⊖	d																			
London Bridge 4 ⊖	d						18 17			18 47										
Dartford 4	d						18 55			19 25										
Greenhithe for Bluewater	d						19 00			19 30										
Gravesend 4	d						19 07			19 37			19 48							
Strood 4	d						19 18			19 48			19 58							
Rochester 4	d					19 09	19 22		19 39	19 52	19 56		20 03							
Chatham 4	d					19 12	19 25		19 42	19 55	19 59		20 05							
Gillingham (Kent) 4	d					19 17	19a32		19 47	20a02	20a03		20 10							
Rainham (Kent)	d					19 21			19 51				20 15							
Newington	d								19 55											
Sittingbourne 4	a					19 28			20 00				20 22							
	d					19 29		19 40	20 01			20 10	20 23							
Kemsley	d							19 45				20 15								
Swale	d							19 48				20 18								
Queenborough	d							19 52				20 22								
Sheerness-on-Sea	a							19 57				20 27								
Teynham	d					19 33														
Faversham 2	a					19 39			20 09				20 33							
	d					19 43 / 19 45			20 13 / 20 15											
Selling	d					19 50														
Canterbury East 4	d					19 59			20 29											
Bekesbourne	d					20 03														
Adisham	d					20 08														
Aylesham	d					20 10														
Snowdown	d					20 13														
Shepherds Well	d					20 17														
Kearsney	d					20 21														
Dover Priory 4	a					20 27			20 48											
Whitstable	d					19 51			20 21											
Chestfield & Swalecliffe	d					19 54														
Herne Bay	d					19 58			20 26											
Birchington-on-Sea	d					20 07			20 35											
Westgate-on-Sea	d					20 11														
Margate 4	d					20 15			20 41											
Broadstairs	d					20 20			20 46											
Dumpton Park	d					20 23														
Ramsgate 4	a					20 26			20 51											

A ✕ to Margate

For further services to St Pancras International, Blackfriars and Elephant & Castle and onwards to Bromley South, St Mary Cray and Swanley please refer to table 52

Table 212

Saturdays

28 July to 11 August

London - Medway, Sheerness-on-Sea, Dover and Ramsgate

Network Diagram - see first Page of Table 212

Station		SE ■	SE	SE	SE ■	SE	SE ■	SE	SE	SE	SE	SE	SE	SE	SE	SE ■	SE	SE	SE ■
St Pancras Internatnl ⊖	d							20 18	20 25	20 32	20 39	20 46	20 52	21 04	21 11				
Stratford International ⊖	d							20 28	20 35	20 42	20 49	20 56	21 03	21 14	21 21				
Ebbsfleet International	d							20 43	20a46	20a52	21 02	21a07	21a13	21 30	21a31				
London Victoria ⊖	d	19 22			19 52		19 58									20 22			20 52
London Blackfriars ⊖	d																		
Elephant & Castle ⊖	d																		
Bromley South	d	19 39			20 09		20 19									20 39			21 09
St Mary Cray	d						20 25												21 15
Swanley	d						20 29												21 19
Farningham Road	d						20 34												21 24
Longfield	d	19 52			20 22		20 38									20 52			21 28
Meopham	d	19 57			20 27		20 42									20 57			21 32
Sole Street	d						20 45												21 35
London Charing Cross ⊖	d		19 09			19 39											20 09		
London Waterloo (East) ⊖	d		19 12			19 42											20 12		
London Cannon Street ⊖	d																		
London Bridge ⊖	d		19 17			19 47											20 17		
Dartford	d		19 55			20 25											20 55		
Greenhithe for Bluewater	d		20 00			20 30											21 00		
Gravesend	d		20 07			20 37		20 48									21 07		
Strood	d		20 18			20 48		20 58									21 18		
Rochester	d	20 09	20 22		20 39	20 52	20 56	21 03								21 09	21 22		21 45
Chatham	d	20 12	20 25		20 42	20 55	20 59	21 05								21 12	21 25		21 47
Gillingham (Kent)	d	20 17	20a32		20 47	21a02	21a03	21 10								21 17	21a32		21 52
Rainham (Kent)	d	20 21			20 51			21 15								21 21			21 56
Newington	d				20 55														22 00
Sittingbourne	a	20 28			21 00			21 22								21 28			22 05
	d	20 29		20 40	21 01			21 23								21 29		21 40	22 06
Kemsley	d			20 45														21 45	
Swale	d			20 48														21 48	
Queenborough	d			20 52														21 52	
Sheerness-on-Sea	a			20 57														21 57	
Teynham	d	20 33														21 33			
Faversham	a	20 39			21 09			21 33								21 39			22 14
	d	20 43 / 20 45			21 13 / 21 15											21 43 / 21 45			22 15
Selling	d	20 50														21 50			
Canterbury East	d	20 59			21a26											21 59			22a26
Bekesbourne	d	21 03														22 03			
Adisham	d	21 08														22 08			
Aylesham	d	21 10														22 10			
Snowdown	d	21 13														22 13			
Shepherds Well	d	21 17														22 17			
Kearsney	d	21 21														22 21			
Dover Priory	a	21 27														22 27			
Whitstable	d	20 51			21 21											21 51			
Chestfield & Swalecliffe	d	20 54														21 54			
Herne Bay	d	20 58			21 26											21 58			
Birchington-on-Sea	d	21 07			21 35											22 07			
Westgate-on-Sea	d	21 11														22 11			
Margate	d	21 15			21 41											22 15			
Broadstairs	d	21 20			21 46											22 20			
Dumpton Park	d	21 23														22 23			
Ramsgate	a	21 26			21 51											22 27			

For further services to St Pancras International, Blackfriars and Elephant & Castle and onwards to Bromley South, St Mary Cray and Swanley please refer to table 52

Table 212

Saturdays

28 July to 11 August

London - Medway, Sheerness-on-Sea, Dover and Ramsgate

Network Diagram - see first Page of Table 212

Station		SE	SE	SE ■	SE	SE	SE	SE	SE	SE	SE	SE	SE	SE	SE	SE	SE	SE ■	SE	SE ■	SE
St Pancras Internatnl ⊖	d		21 18			21 25	21 32	21 39	21 46	21 52	22 04	22 11	22 18	22 25	22 32	22 39					
Stratford International ⊖	d		21 28			21 35	21 42	21 49	21 56	22 03	22 14	22 21	22 28	22 35	22 42	22 47					
Ebbsfleet International	d		21 43			21a46	21a52	22 02	22a07	22a13	22a24	22a31	22a40	22a46	22a52	22a57					
London Victoria ⊖	d			21 22														21 52		22 22	
London Blackfriars ⊖	d																				
Elephant & Castle ⊖	d																				
Bromley South	d			21 39														22 09		22 39	
St Mary Cray	d																	22 15			
Swanley	d																	22 19			
Farningham Road	d																	22 24			
Longfield	d			21 52														22 28		22 52	
Meopham	d			21 57														22 32		22 57	
Sole Street	d																	22 35			
London Charing Cross ⊖	d	20 39			21 09														21 39		22 09
London Waterloo (East) ⊖	d	20 42			21 12														21 42		22 12
London Cannon Street ⊖	d																				
London Bridge ⊖	d	20 47			21 17														21 47		22 17
Dartford	d	21 25			21 55														22 25		22 55
Greenhithe for Bluewater	d	21 30			22 00														22 31		23 01
Gravesend	d	21 37	21 48		22 07														22 40		23 10
Strood	d	21 48	21 58		22 18														22 52		23 22
Rochester	d	21 52	22 03	22 09	22 22													22 45	22 56	23 09	23 26
Chatham	d	21 55	22 05	22 12	22 25													22 47	22 58	23 12	23 28
Gillingham (Kent)	d	22a02	22 10	22 17	22a32													22 52	23a06	23 17	23a33
Rainham (Kent)	d		22 15	22 21														22 56		23 21	
Newington	d																	23 00			
Sittingbourne	a		22 22	22 28														23 05		23 28	
	d		22 23	22 29													22 40	23 06		23 29	
Kemsley	d																22 45				
Swale	d																22 48				
Queenborough	d																22 52				
Sheerness-on-Sea	a																22 57				
Teynham	d			22 33																23 33	
Faversham	a		22 33	22 39														23 14		23 39	
	d			22 43 / 22 45																23 43 / 23 45	
Selling	d			22 50																23 50	
Canterbury East	d			22 59																23 59	
Bekesbourne	d			23 03																	
Adisham	d			23 08																	
Aylesham	d			23 10																00 07	
Snowdown	d			23 13																	
Shepherds Well	d			23 17																	
Kearsney	d			23 21																	
Dover Priory	a			23 27																00 18	
Whitstable	d			22 51																23 51	
Chestfield & Swalecliffe	d			22 54																23 54	
Herne Bay	d			22 58																23 58	
Birchington-on-Sea	d			23 07																00 07	
Westgate-on-Sea	d			23 11																00 11	
Margate	d			23 15																00 15	
Broadstairs	d			23 20																00 20	
Dumpton Park	d			23 23																00 23	
Ramsgate	a			23 26																00 26	

For further services to St Pancras International, Blackfriars and Elephant & Castle and onwards to Bromley South, St Mary Cray and Swanley please refer to table 52

Table 212

Saturdays

28 July to 11 August

London - Medway, Sheerness-on-Sea, Dover and Ramsgate

Network Diagram - see first Page of Table 212

		SE	SE	SE	SE	SE	SE	SE	SE	SE ■	SE	SE	SE	SE	SE ■	SE	SE	SE	SE ■	SE	SE
St Pancras Internatnl ■ ⊖	d	22 46	22 52	23 04	23 11	23 16	23 21	23 26				23 32	23 36	23 41			23 47	23 51			23 56
Stratford International ⊖	d	22 56	23 02	23 14	23 21	23 26	23 30	23 35				23 42	23 46	23 50			23 57	00 01			00 05
Ebbsfleet International	d	23a07	23a12	23a24	23a31	23a37	23a41	23a45				23a52	23a56	00a01			00a07	00a10			00a16
London Victoria ■ ⊖	d									22 52					23 22				23 52		
London Blackfriars ■ ⊖	d																				
Elephant & Castle ⊖	d																				
Bromley South ■	d									23 09					23 39				00 09		
St Mary Cray	d									23 15									00 15		
Swanley ■	d									23 19									00 19		
Farningham Road	d									23 24									00 24		
Longfield	d									23 28					23 52				00 28		
Meopham	d									23 32					23 57				00 32		
Sole Street	d									23 35									00 35		
London Charing Cross ■ ⊖	d										22 39					23 09				23 39	
London Waterloo (East) ■ ⊖	d										22 42					23 12				23 42	
London Cannon Street ■ ⊖	d																				
London Bridge ■ ⊖	d										22 47					23 17				23 47	
Dartford ■	d										23 25					23 55				00 25	
Greenhithe for Bluewater	d										23 31					23 59				00 31	
Gravesend ■	d										23 40					00 10				00 40	
Strood ■	d										23 52					00 22				00 52	
Rochester ■	d									23 45	23 56				00 09	00 26			00 45	00 56	
Chatham ■	d									23 47	23 58				00 12	00 28			00 47	00 58	
Gillingham (Kent) ■	d									23 52	00a06				00 17	00a36			00a52	01a06	
Rainham (Kent)	d									23 56					00 21						
Newington	d									00 01											
Sittingbourne ■	a									00 06					00 28						
	d								23 32	00 07					00 29						
Kemsley	d								23 37												
Swale	d								23 40												
Queenborough	d								23 44												
Sheerness-on-Sea	a								23 49												
Teynham	d														00 33						
Faversham ■	a									00 16					00 39						
	d														00 43						
Selling	d																				
Canterbury East ■	d																				
Bekesbourne	d																				
Adisham	d																				
Aylesham	d																				
Snowdown	d																				
Shepherds Well	d																				
Kearsney	d																				
Dover Priory ■	a																				
Whitstable	d														00 51						
Chestfield & Swalecliffe	d														00 54						
Herne Bay	d														00 58						
Birchington-on-Sea	d														01 07						
Westgate-on-Sea	d														01 11						
Margate ■	d														01 15						
Broadstairs	d														01 20						
Dumpton Park	d														01 23						
Ramsgate ■	a														01 26						

For further services to St Pancras International, Blackfriars and Elephant & Castle and onwards to Bromley South, St Mary Cray and Swanley please refer to table 52

Table 212

Saturdays

25 August to 8 September

London - Medway, Sheerness-on-Sea, Dover and Ramsgate

Network Diagram - see first Page of Table 212

		SE ■		SE A	SE B	SE ■	SE	SE A	SE B	SE ■	SE	SE A	SE B	SE ■	SE ■	SE	SE A	SE B	SE	SE	SE B	SE B	SE B
St Pancras Internatnl ■ ⊖	d			22p55	22p55			23p25	23p25			23p55	23p55				00 12	00 12			00 48	01 48	02 35
Stratford International ⊖	d			23p02	23p03			23p32	23p33			00 02	00 03				00 19	00 20			00a54	01a54	02a41
Ebbsfleet International	d			23p13	23p14			23p43	23p44			00 13	00 14				00 31	00 32					
London Victoria ■ ⊖	d	22p22				22p52				23p22				23p52	00 10				00 35				
London Blackfriars ■ ⊖	d																						
Elephant & Castle ⊖	d																						
Bromley South ■	d	22p39				23p09				23p39				00 09					00 55				
St Mary Cray	d					23p15								00 15					01 01				
Swanley ■	d					23p19								00 19					01 05				
Farningham Road	d					23p24								00 24					01 10				
Longfield	d	22p52				23p28				23p52				00 28					01 14				
Meopham	d	22p57				23p32				23p57				00 32					01 18				
Sole Street	d					23p35								00 35									
London Charing Cross ■ ⊖	d										23p09					23p39				00 18			
London Waterloo (East) ■ ⊖	d										23p12					23p42				00 21			
London Cannon Street ■ ⊖	d																						
London Bridge ■ ⊖	d										23p17					23p47				00 26			
Dartford ■	d										23p55					00 25				01 06			
Greenhithe for Bluewater	d										23p59					00 31				01 10			
Gravesend ■	d			23p18	23p18			23p48	23p48		00 10	00 18	00 18			00 40				01 17			
Strood ■	d			23p28	23p28			23p58	23p58		00 22	00 28	00 28			00 52				01 29			
Rochester ■	d	23p09		23p33	23p33	23p45		00 03	00 03	00 09	00 26	00 33	00 33	00 45	00 49	00 56			01 29	01 33			
Chatham ■	d	23p12		23p35	23p35	23p47		00 05	00 05	00 12	00 28	00 35	00 35	00 47	00 52	00 58			01 31	01 35			
Gillingham (Kent) ■	d	23p17		23p40	23p40	23p52		00 10	00 10	00 17	00a33	00 40	00 40	00a52	00 57	01a03			01a35	01a41			
Rainham (Kent)	d	23p21		23p45	23p45	23p56		00 15	00 15	00 21		00 45	00 45		01 01								
Newington	d					00 01									01 05								
Sittingbourne ■	a	23p28		23p52	23p52	00 06		00 22	00 22	00 28		00 52	00 52		01 10								
	d	23p29		23p53	23p53	00 07	00 15	00 23	00 23	00 29		00 53	00 53		01 11								
Kemsley	d						00 20																
Swale	d						00 23																
Queenborough	d						00 27																
Sheerness-on-Sea	a						00 32																
Teynham	d	23p33								00 33					01 15								
Faversham ■	a	23p39		00 03	00 03	00 15		00 33	00 33	00 39		01 03	01 03		01 23								
	d	23p43	23p45							00 43					01 24								
Selling	d		23p50																				
Canterbury East ■	d		23p59																				
Bekesbourne	d																						
Adisham	d																						
Aylesham	d		00 07																				
Snowdown	d																						
Shepherds Well	d																						
Kearsney	d																						
Dover Priory ■	a		00 18																				
Whitstable	d	23p51								00 51					01 32								
Chestfield & Swalecliffe	d	23p54								00 54					01 35								
Herne Bay	d	23p58								00 58					01 39								
Birchington-on-Sea	d	00 07								01 07					01 48								
Westgate-on-Sea	d	00 10								01 10					01 51								
Margate ■	d	00 14								01 14					01 55								
Broadstairs	d	00 20								01 20					02 01								
Dumpton Park	d	00 23								01 23					02 04								
Ramsgate ■	a	00 26								01 26					02 07								

A not from 1 September until 8 September

B not 25 August

For further services to St Pancras International, Blackfriars and Elephant & Castle and onwards to Bromley South, St Mary Cray and Swanley please refer to table 52

Table 212

Saturdays

25 August to 8 September

London - Medway, Sheerness-on-Sea, Dover and Ramsgate

Network Diagram - see first Page of Table 212

		SE ■	SE	SE	SE ■	SE A		SE	SE ■	SE	SE	SE	SE ■	SE	SE	SE ■		SE	SE	SE A	SE B	SE	SE ■	SE A	SE ■
St Pancras Internatnl ⊖	d					06 45														06 54	06 55			07 14	
Stratford International ⊖	d					06 53														07 02	07 02			07 25	
Ebbsfleet International	d					07a04														07 13	07 13			07a35	
London Victoria ⊖	d								05 22							06 22							06 58		
London Blackfriars ⊖	d																								
Elephant & Castle ⊖	d																								
Bromley South	d								05 39							06 39							07 19		
St Mary Cray	d								05 45							06 45							07 25		
Swanley	d								05 49							06 49							07 29		
Farningham Road	d								05 54							06 54							07 34		
Longfield	d								05 58							06 58							07 38		
Meopham	d								06 02							07 02							07 42		
Sole Street	d								06 05							07 05							07 45		
London Charing Cross ⊖	d										05 39							06 09				06 39			
London Waterloo (East) ⊖	d										05 42							06 12				06 42			
London Cannon Street ⊖	d																								
London Bridge ⊖	d										05 47							06 17				06 47			
Dartford	d									05 55	06 25							06 55				07 25			
Greenhithe for Bluewater	d									06 00	06 30							07 00				07 30			
Gravesend	d									06 07	06 37							07 07		07 18	07 18	07 37			
Strood	d									06 18	06 48							07 18		07 28	07 28	07 48			
Rochester	d								06 15	06 22	06 52					07 15		07 22		07 33	07 33	07 52	07 56		
Chatham	d								06 17	06 25	06 55					07 17		07 25		07 35	07 35	07 55	07 59		
Gillingham (Kent)	d	05 47							06 22	06a29	06a59					07 22		07a29		07 40	07 40	07a59	08a03		
Rainham (Kent)	d	05 51							06 26							07 26				07 45	07 45				
Newington	d	05 55							06 30							07 30									
Sittingbourne	a	06 00							06 35							07 35				07 52	07 52				
	d	06 01		06 10					06 36			06 40		07 10		07 36			07 40	07 53	07 53				
Kemsley	d			06 15								06 45		07 15					07 45						
Swale	d			06 18								06 48		07 18					07 48						
Queenborough	d			06 22								06 52		07 22					07 52						
Sheerness-on-Sea	a			06 27								06 57		07 27					07 57						
Teynham	d	06 05							06 40							07 40									
Faversham	a	06 11							06 46							07 46				08 03	08 03				
	d	06 12			06 17				06 47				06 50			07 47									07 50
Selling	d	06 17											06 55												07 55
Canterbury East	d	06 26											07 04												08 04
Bekesbourne	d	06 30											07 08												08 08
Adisham	d	06 35											07 13												08 13
Aylesham	d	06 37											07 15												08 15
Snowdown	d	06 40											07 18												08 18
Shepherds Well	d	06 44											07 22												08 22
Kearsney	d	06 48											07 26												08 26
Dover Priory	a	06 53											07 31												08 31
Whitstable	d				06 25				06 55							07 55									
Chestfield & Swalecliffe	d				06 28				06 58							07 58									
Herne Bay	d				06 32				07 02							08 02									
Birchington-on-Sea	d				06 41				07 11							08 11									
Westgate-on-Sea	d				06 44				07 14							08 14									
Margate	d		05 53		06 48			06 53	07 18						07 53	08 18									
Broadstairs	d		05 59		06 54			06 59	07 24						07 59	08 24									
Dumpton Park	d				06 57				07 27							08 27									
Ramsgate	a		06 04		07 00			07 04	07 30						08 04	08 30									

A not 25 August

B not from 1 September until 8 September

For further services to St Pancras International, Blackfriars and Elephant & Castle and onwards to Bromley South, St Mary Cray and Swanley please refer to table 52

Table 212

Saturdays

25 August to 8 September

London - Medway, Sheerness-on-Sea, Dover and Ramsgate

Network Diagram - see first Page of Table 212

		SE		SE A	SE A	SE ■	SE ■	SE	SE ■	SE	SE		SE	SE ■	SE	SE ■	SE A	SE	SE A	SE A		SE	
St Pancras Internatnl ⊖	d			07 24	07 47								07 52				08 18		08 21	08 47			
Stratford International ⊖	d			07 32	07 55								07 58				08 26		08 32	08 55			
Ebbsfleet International	d			07 46	08a06								08 13				08a36		08 43	09a06			
London Victoria ⊖	d								07 22					07 52		07 58							
London Blackfriars ⊖	d																						
Elephant & Castle ⊖	d																						
Bromley South	d								07 39					08 09		08 19							
St Mary Cray	d															08 25							
Swanley	d															08 29							
Farningham Road	d															08 34							
Longfield	d								07 52					08 22		08 38							
Meopham	d								07 57					08 27		08 42							
Sole Street	d															08 45							
London Charing Cross ⊖	d									07 09					07 39								
London Waterloo (East) ⊖	d									07 12					07 42								
London Cannon Street ⊖	d																						
London Bridge ⊖	d									07 17					07 47								
Dartford	d									07 55					08 25								
Greenhithe for Bluewater	d									08 00					08 30								
Gravesend	d			07 51						08 07			08 18		08 37				08 48				
Strood	d			08 01						08 18			08 28		08 48				08 58				
Rochester	d			08 06					08 09	08 22			08 33	08 39	08 52	08 56			09 03				
Chatham	d			08 08					08 12	08 25			08 35	08 42	08 55	08 59			09 05				
Gillingham (Kent)	d			08 13					08 17	08a29			08 40	08 47	08a59	09a03			09 10				
Rainham (Kent)	d			08 18					08 21				08 45	08 51					09 15				
Newington	d								08 25					08 55									
Sittingbourne	a			08 25					08 30				08 52	09 00					09 22				
	d	08 10		08 25					08 31		08 40		08 53	09 01				09 10	09 23				
Kemsley	d	08 15									08 45							09 15					
Swale	d	08 18									08 48							09 18					
Queenborough	d	08 22									08 52							09 22					
Sheerness-on-Sea	a	08 27									08 57							09 27					
Teynham	d								08 35														
Faversham	a			08 33					08 41				09 03	09 09					09 33				
	d					08 13	08 15		08 45 08 50					09 13 09 15									
Selling	d								08 55														
Canterbury East	d						08 29		09 04					09 29									
Bekesbourne	d								09 08														
Adisham	d								09 13														
Aylesham	d								09 15														
Snowdown	d								09 18														
Shepherds Well	d								09 22														
Kearsney	d								09 26														
Dover Priory	a						08 48		09 31					09 48									
Whitstable	d					08 21			08 53					09 21									
Chestfield & Swalecliffe	d								08 56														
Herne Bay	d					08 26			09 00					09 26									
Birchington-on-Sea	d					08 35			09 09					09 35									
Westgate-on-Sea	d								09 12														
Margate	d					08 41		08 53	09 16					09 41								09 53	
Broadstairs	d					08 46		08 59	09 22					09 46								09 59	
Dumpton Park	d								09 25														
Ramsgate	a					08 51		09 04	09 28					09 51								10 04	

A not 25 August

For further services to St Pancras International, Blackfriars and Elephant & Castle and onwards to Bromley South, St Mary Cray and Swanley please refer to table 52

London - Medway, Sheerness-on-Sea, Dover and Ramsgate

Saturdays

25 August to 8 September

Network Diagram - see first Page of Table 212

		SE ■		SE	SE	SE A	SE B	SE ■		SE	SE ■	SE B	SE	SE A	SE B	SE B	SE	SE ■		SE	SE	SE B	SE A
St Pancras Internatnl ⊖	d					08 50	08 51					09 14		09 25	09 25	09 47						09 54	09 55
Stratford International ⊖	d					09 04	08 58					09 24		09 32	09 33	09 54						10 02	10 02
Ebbsfleet International	d					09 15	09 13					09a35		09 43	09 44	10a04						10 13	10 13
London Victoria ⊖	d	08 22						08 52			08 58							09 22					
London Blackfriars ⊖	d																						
Elephant &Castle ⊖	d																						
Bromley South	d	08 39						09 09			09 19							09 39					
St Mary Cray	d										09 25												
Swanley	d										09 29												
Farningham Road	d										09 34												
Longfield	d	08 52						09 22			09 38							09 52					
Meopham	d	08 57						09 27			09 42							09 57					
Sole Street	d										09 45												
London Charing Cross ⊖	d			08 09						08 39										09 09			
London Waterloo (East) ⊖	d			08 12						08 42										09 12			
London Cannon Street ⊖	d																						
London Bridge ⊖	d			08 17						08 47										09 17			
Dartford	d			08 55						09 25										09 55			
Greenhithe for Bluewater	d			09 00						09 30										10 00			
Gravesend	d			09 07		09 20	09 18			09 37				09 48	09 48					10 07		10 18	10 18
Strood	d			09 18		09 30	09 28			09 48				09 58	09 58					10 18		10 28	10 28
Rochester	d	09 09		09 22		09 34	09 33	09 39		09 52	09 56			10 03	10 03			10 09		10 22		10 33	10 33
Chatham	d	09 12		09 25		09 37	09 35	09 42		09 55	09 59			10 05	10 05			10 12		10 25		10 35	10 35
Gillingham (Kent)	d	09 17		09a29		09 41	09 40	09 47		09a59	10a03			10 10	10 10			10 17		10a29		10 40	10 40
Rainham (Kent)	d	09 21				09 46	09 45	09 51						10 15	10 15			10 21				10 45	10 45
Newington	d							09 55															
Sittingbourne	a	09 28				09 54	09 52	10 00						10 22	10 22			10 28				10 52	10 52
	d	09 29			09 40	09 54	09 53	10 01					10 10	10 23	10 23			10 29			10 40	10 53	10 53
Kemsley	d				09 45								10 15								10 45		
Swale	d				09 48								10 18								10 48		
Queenborough	d				09 52								10 22								10 52		
Sheerness-on-Sea	a				09 57								10 27								10 57		
Teynham	d	09 33																10 33					
Faversham	a	09 39				10 03	10 03	10 09						10 33	10 33			10 39				11 03	11 03
	d	09 43	09 45					10 13	10 15									10 43	10 45				
Selling	d		09 50																10 50				
Canterbury East	d		09 59						10 29										10 59				
Bekesbourne	d		10 03																11 03				
Adisham	d		10 08																11 08				
Aylesham	d		10 10																11 10				
Snowdown	d		10 13																11 13				
Shepherds Well	d		10 17																11 17				
Kearsney	d		10 21																11 21				
Dover Priory	a		10 27						10 48										11 27				
Whitstable	d	09 51						10 21										10 51					
Chestfield &Swalecliffe	d	09 54																10 54					
Herne Bay	d	09 58						10 26										10 58					
Birchington-on-Sea	d	10 07						10 35										11 07					
Westgate-on-Sea	d	10 10																11 10					
Margate	d	10 14						10 41									10 53	11 14					
Broadstairs	d	10 20						10 46									10 59	11 20					
Dumpton Park	d	10 23																11 23					
Ramsgate	a	10 26						10 51									11 04	11 26					

A not from 1 September until 8 September **B** not 25 August

For further services to St Pancras International, Blackfriars and Elephant & Castle and onwards to Bromley South, St Mary Cray and Swanley please refer to table 52

London - Medway, Sheerness-on-Sea, Dover and Ramsgate

Saturdays

25 August to 8 September

Network Diagram - see first Page of Table 212

		SE ■ A ⌶		SE	SE ■	SE B	SE	SE C	SE B	SE B	SE	SE ■ A ⌶		SE	SE	SE B	SE C	SE ■ A ⌶		SE	SE ■	SE B	SE
St Pancras Internatnl ⊖	d					10 18		10 28	10 28	10 47						10 51	10 52					11 18	
Stratford International ⊖	d					10 26		10 35	10 36	10 55						10 58	10 58					11 26	
Ebbsfleet International	d					10a36		10 46	10 47	11a05						11 13	11 13					11a36	
London Victoria ⊖	d	09 52			09 58							10 22						10 52			10 58		
London Blackfriars ⊖	d																						
Elephant &Castle ⊖	d																						
Bromley South	d	10 09			10 19							10 39						11 09			11 19		
St Mary Cray	d				10 25																11 25		
Swanley	d				10 29																11 29		
Farningham Road	d				10 34																11 34		
Longfield	d	10 22			10 38							10 52						11 22			11 38		
Meopham	d	10 27			10 42							10 57						11 27			11 42		
Sole Street	d				10 45																11 45		
London Charing Cross ⊖	d			09 39										10 09						10 39			
London Waterloo (East) ⊖	d			09 42										10 12						10 42			
London Cannon Street ⊖	d																						
London Bridge ⊖	d			09 47										10 17						10 47			
Dartford	d			10 25										10 55						11 25			
Greenhithe for Bluewater	d			10 30										11 00						11 30			
Gravesend	d			10 37				10 51	10 51					11 07		11 18	11 18			11 37			
Strood	d			10 48				11 01	11 01					11 18		11 28	11 28			11 48			
Rochester	d	10 39		10 52	10 56			11 06	11 06			11 09		11 22		11 33	11 33	11 39		11 52	11 56		
Chatham	d	10 42		10 55	10 59			11 08	11 08			11 12		11 25		11 35	11 35	11 42		11 55	11 59		
Gillingham (Kent)	d	10 47		10a59	11a03			11 13	11 13			11 17		11a29		11 40	11 40	11 47		11a59	12a03		
Rainham (Kent)	d	10 51						11 18	11 18			11 21				11 45	11 45	11 51					
Newington	d	10 55																11 55					
Sittingbourne	a	11 00						11 25	11 25			11 28				11 52	11 52	12 00					
	d	11 01					11 10	11 25	11 25			11 29			11 40	11 53	11 53	12 01					12 10
Kemsley	d						11 15								11 45								12 15
Swale	d						11 18								11 48								12 18
Queenborough	d						11 22								11 52								12 22
Sheerness-on-Sea	a						11 27								11 57								12 27
Teynham	d											11 33											
Faversham	a	11 09						11 34	11 34			11 39				12 03	12 03	12 09					
	d	11 13	11 15									11 43	11 45					12 13	12 15				
Selling	d												11 50										
Canterbury East	d		11 29										11 59						12 29				
Bekesbourne	d												12 03										
Adisham	d												12 08										
Aylesham	d												12 10										
Snowdown	d												12 13										
Shepherds Well	d												12 17										
Kearsney	d												12 21										
Dover Priory	a		11 48										12 27						12 48				
Whitstable	d	11 21										11 51						12 21					
Chestfield &Swalecliffe	d											11 54											
Herne Bay	d	11 26										11 58						12 26					
Birchington-on-Sea	d	11 35										12 07						12 35					
Westgate-on-Sea	d											12 10											
Margate	d	11 41									11 53	12 14						12 41					
Broadstairs	d	11 46									11 59	12 20						12 46					
Dumpton Park	d											12 23											
Ramsgate	a	11 51									12 04	12 26						12 51					

A ⌶ to Margate **B** not 25 August **C** not from 1 September until 8 September

For further services to St Pancras International, Blackfriars and Elephant & Castle and onwards to Bromley South, St Mary Cray and Swanley please refer to table 52

Table 212

Saturdays

25 August to 8 September

London - Medway, Sheerness-on-Sea, Dover and Ramsgate

Network Diagram - see first Page of Table 212

Station		SE	SE A	SE	SE 1 B [trolley]	SE	SE	SE C	SE A	SE 1 B [trolley]	SE	SE 1	SE A	SE	SE C	SE A	SE A	SE	SE 1 B [trolley]
St Pancras Internatnl 15 ⊖	d	11 28	11 48					11 55	11 55				12 18		12 28	12 28	12 47		
Stratford International ⊖	d	11 35	11 56					12 02	12 03				12 25		12 35	12 36	12 54		
Ebbsfleet International	d	11 46	12a06					12 13	12 14				12a35		12 46	12 47	13a04		
London Victoria 15 ⊖	d				11 22					11 52		11 58							12 22
London Blackfriars 3 ⊖	d																		
Elephant & Castle ⊖	d																		
Bromley South 4	d				11 39					12 09		12 19							12 39
St Mary Cray	d											12 25							
Swanley 4	d											12 29							
Farningham Road	d											12 34							
Longfield	d				11 52					12 22		12 38							12 52
Meopham	d				11 57					12 27		12 42							12 57
Sole Street	d											12 45							
London Charing Cross 4 ⊖	d					11 09					11 39								
London Waterloo (East) 4 ⊖	d					11 12					11 42								
London Cannon Street 4 ⊖	d																		
London Bridge 4 ⊖	d					11 17					11 47								
Dartford 4	d					11 55					12 25								
Greenhithe for Bluewater	d					12 00					12 30								
Gravesend 4	d	11 51				12 07		12 18	12 18		12 37				12 51	12 51			
Strood 4	d	12 01				12 18		12 28	12 28		12 48				13 01	13 01			
Rochester 4	d	12 06			12 09	12 22		12 33	12 33	12 39	12 52	12 56			13 06	13 06			13 09
Chatham 4	d	12 08			12 12	12 25		12 35	12 35	12 42	12 55	12 59			13 08	13 08			13 12
Gillingham (Kent) 4	d	12 13			12 17	12a29		12 40	12 40	12 47	12a59	13a03			13 13	13 13			13 17
Rainham (Kent)	d	12 18			12 21			12 45	12 45	12 51					13 18	13 18			13 21
Newington	d									12 55									
Sittingbourne 4	a	12 25			12 28			12 52	12 52	13 00					13 25	13 25			13 29
	d	12 25			12 29		12 40	12 53	12 53	13 01				13 10	13 25	13 25			13 29
Kemsley	d						12 45							13 15					
Swale	d						12 48							13 18					
Queenborough	d						12 52							13 22					
Sheerness-on-Sea	a						12 57							13 27					
Teynham	d				12 33														13 33
Faversham 2	a	12 34			12 39			13 03	13 03	13 09					13 34	13 34			13 39
	d				12 43 12 45					13 13 13 15									13 43 13 45
Selling	d				12 50														13 50
Canterbury East 4	d				12 59					13 29									13 59
Bekesbourne	d				13 03														14 03
Adisham	d				13 08														14 08
Aylesham	d				13 10														14 10
Snowdown	d				13 13														14 13
Shepherds Well	d				13 17														14 17
Kearsney	d				13 21														14 21
Dover Priory 4	a				13 27					13 48									14 27
Whitstable	d				12 51					13 21									13 51
Chestfield & Swalecliffe	d				12 54														13 54
Herne Bay	d				12 58					13 26									13 58
Birchington-on-Sea	d				13 07					13 35									14 07
Westgate-on-Sea	d				13 10														14 10
Margate 4	d			12 53	13 14					13 41								13 53	14 14
Broadstairs	d			12 59	13 20					13 46								13 59	14 20
Dumpton Park	d				13 23														14 23
Ramsgate 4	a			13 04	13 26					13 51								14 04	14 26

A not 25 August
B [trolley] to Margate
C not from 1 September until 8 September

For further services to St Pancras International, Blackfriars and Elephant & Castle and onwards to Bromley South, St Mary Cray and Swanley please refer to table 52

Table 212

Saturdays

25 August to 8 September

London - Medway, Sheerness-on-Sea, Dover and Ramsgate

Network Diagram - see first Page of Table 212

Station		SE	SE	SE	SE 1 A [trolley]	SE	SE 1	SE B	SE	SE C	SE B	SE B	SE	SE 1 A [trolley]	SE	SE	SE C	SE B	SE 1 A [trolley]	SE
St Pancras Internatnl 15 ⊖	d			12 55				13 18		13 25	13 25	13 48					13 55	13 55		
Stratford International ⊖	d			13 06				13 26		13 32	13 33	13 56					14 02	14 03		
Ebbsfleet International	d			13 17				13a36		13 43	13 44	14a06					14 13	14 14		
London Victoria 15 ⊖	d				12 52		12 58							13 22					13 52	
London Blackfriars 3 ⊖	d																			
Elephant & Castle ⊖	d																			
Bromley South 4	d				13 09		13 19							13 39					14 09	
St Mary Cray	d						13 25													
Swanley 4	d						13 29													
Farningham Road	d						13 34													
Longfield	d				13 22		13 38							13 52					14 22	
Meopham	d				13 27		13 42							13 57					14 27	
Sole Street	d						13 45													
London Charing Cross 4 ⊖	d	12 09				12 39									13 09					13 39
London Waterloo (East) 4 ⊖	d	12 12				12 42									13 12					13 42
London Cannon Street 4 ⊖	d																			
London Bridge 4 ⊖	d	12 17				12 47									13 17					13 47
Dartford 4	d	12 55				13 25									13 55					14 25
Greenhithe for Bluewater	d	13 00				13 30									14 00					14 30
Gravesend 4	d	13 07		13 22		13 37				13 48	13 48				14 07		14 18	14 18		14 37
Strood 4	d	13 18		13 32		13 48				13 58	13 58				14 18		14 28	14 28		14 48
Rochester 4	d	13 22		13 37	13 39	13 52	13 56			14 03	14 03			14 09	14 22		14 33	14 33	14 39	14 52
Chatham 4	d	13 25		13 39	13 42	13 55	13 59			14 05	14 05			14 12	14 25		14 35	14 35	14 42	14 55
Gillingham (Kent) 4	d	13a29		13 44	13 47	13a59	14a03			14 10	14 10			14 17	14a29		14 40	14 40	14 47	14a59
Rainham (Kent)	d			13 49	13 51					14 15	14 15			14 21			14 45	14 45	14 51	
Newington	d				13 55														14 55	
Sittingbourne 4	a			13 56	14 00					14 22	14 22			14 28			14 52	14 52	15 00	
	d		13 40	13 56	14 01				14 10	14 23	14 23			14 29		14 40	14 53	14 53	15 01	
Kemsley	d		13 45						14 15							14 45				
Swale	d		13 48						14 18							14 48				
Queenborough	d		13 52						14 22							14 52				
Sheerness-on-Sea	a		13 57						14 27							14 57				
Teynham	d													14 33						
Faversham 2	a			14 04	14 09					14 33	14 33			14 39			15 03	15 03	15 09	
	d				14 13 14 15									14 43 14 45					15 13 15 15	
Selling	d													14 50						
Canterbury East 4	d				14 29									14 59					15 29	
Bekesbourne	d													15 03						
Adisham	d													15 08						
Aylesham	d													15 10						
Snowdown	d													15 13						
Shepherds Well	d													15 17						
Kearsney	d													15 21						
Dover Priory 4	a				14 48									15 27					15 48	
Whitstable	d				14 21									14 51					15 21	
Chestfield & Swalecliffe	d													14 54						
Herne Bay	d				14 26									14 58					15 26	
Birchington-on-Sea	d				14 35									15 07					15 35	
Westgate-on-Sea	d													15 10						
Margate 4	d				14 41								14 53	15 14					15 41	
Broadstairs	d				14 46								14 59	15 20					15 46	
Dumpton Park	d													15 23						
Ramsgate 4	a				14 51								15 04	15 26					15 51	

A [trolley] to Margate
B not 25 August
C not from 1 September until 8 September

For further services to St Pancras International, Blackfriars and Elephant & Castle and onwards to Bromley South, St Mary Cray and Swanley please refer to table 52

Table 212

Saturdays

25 August to 8 September

London - Medway, Sheerness-on-Sea, Dover and Ramsgate

Network Diagram - see first Page of Table 212

		SE	SE	SE	SE	SE	SE	SE	SE		SE	SE	SE	SE	SE		SE	SE	SE	SE	SE	SE	SE
		[1]	A		B	A	A		[1] C ⊼				B	A	[1] C ⊼			[1]	A		B	A	A
St Pancras Internatnl ⊖	d		14 18		14 25	14 25	14 47						14 55	14 55					15 18		15 25	15 25	15 48
Stratford International ⊖	d		14 26		14 32	14 33	14 54						15 02	15 03					15 26		15 32	15 33	15 56
Ebbsfleet International	d		14a36		14 43	14 44	15a04						15 13	15 14					15a36		15 43	15 44	16a06
London Victoria ⊖	d	13 58							14 22						14 52			14 58					
London Blackfriars ⊖	d																						
Elephant & Castle ⊖	d																						
Bromley South	d	14 19							14 39						15 09			15 19					
St Mary Cray	d	14 25																15 25					
Swanley	d	14 29																15 29					
Farningham Road	d	14 34																15 34					
Longfield	d	14 38							14 52						15 22			15 38					
Meopham	d	14 42							14 57						15 27			15 42					
Sole Street	d	14 45																15 45					
London Charing Cross ⊖	d										14 09						14 39						
London Waterloo (East) ⊖	d										14 12						14 42						
London Cannon Street ⊖	d																						
London Bridge ⊖	d										14 17						14 47						
Dartford	d										14 55						15 25						
Greenhithe for Bluewater	d										15 00						15 30						
Gravesend	d				14 48	14 48					15 07		15 18	15 18			15 37				15 48	15 48	
Strood	d				14 58	14 58					15 18		15 28	15 28			15 48				15 58	15 58	
Rochester	d	14 56			15 03	15 03			15 09		15 22		15 33	15 33	15 39		15 52	15 56			16 03	16 03	
Chatham	d	14 59			15 05	15 05			15 12		15 25		15 35	15 35	15 42		15 55	15 59			16 05	16 05	
Gillingham (Kent)	d	15a03			15 10	15 10			15 17		15a29		15 40	15 40	15 47		15a59	16a03			16 10	16 10	
Rainham (Kent)	d				15 15	15 15			15 21				15 45	15 45	15 51						16 15	16 15	
Newington	d														15 55								
Sittingbourne	a				15 22	15 22			15 28				15 52	15 52	16 00						16 22	16 22	
	d			15 10	15 23	15 23			15 29			15 40	15 53	15 53	16 01					16 10	16 23	16 23	
Kemsley	d			15 15								15 45								16 15			
Swale	d			15 18								15 48								16 18			
Queenborough	d			15 22								15 52								16 22			
Sheerness-on-Sea	a			15 27								15 57								16 27			
Teynham	d								15 33														
Faversham	a				15 33	15 33			15 39				16 03	16 03	16 09						16 33	16 33	
	d								15 43	15 45					16 13	16 15							
Selling	d									15 50													
Canterbury East	d									15 59						16 29							
Bekesbourne	d									16 03													
Adisham	d									16 08													
Aylesham	d									16 10													
Snowdown	d									16 13													
Shepherds Well	d									16 17													
Kearsney	d									16 21													
Dover Priory	a									16 27						16 48							
Whitstable	d								15 51						16 21								
Chestfield & Swalecliffe	d								15 54														
Herne Bay	d								15 58						16 26								
Birchington-on-Sea	d								16 07						16 35								
Westgate-on-Sea	d								16 10														
Margate	d							15 53	16 14						16 41								
Broadstairs	d							15 59	16 20						16 46								
Dumpton Park	d								16 23														
Ramsgate	a							16 04	16 26						16 51								

A not 25 August B not from 1 September until 8 September C ⊼ to Margate

For further services to St Pancras International, Blackfriars and Elephant & Castle and onwards to Bromley South, St Mary Cray and Swanley please refer to table 52

Table 212

Saturdays

25 August to 8 September

London - Medway, Sheerness-on-Sea, Dover and Ramsgate

Network Diagram - see first Page of Table 212

		SE	SE		SE	SE	SE	SE	SE		SE	SE	SE	SE	SE	SE	SE	SE	SE		SE	SE
			[1] A ⊼				B	C	[1] A ⊼			[1]	C		C	B	C		[1] A ⊼			
St Pancras Internatnl ⊖	d						15 55	15 55					16 15		16 25	16 28	16 48					
Stratford International ⊖	d						16 02	16 03					16 22		16 33	16 35	16 56					
Ebbsfleet International	d						16 13	16 14					16a32		16 44	16 46	17a06					
London Victoria ⊖	d		15 22						15 52			15 58							16 22			
London Blackfriars ⊖	d																					
Elephant & Castle ⊖	d																					
Bromley South	d		15 39						16 09			16 19							16 39			
St Mary Cray	d											16 25										
Swanley	d											16 29										
Farningham Road	d											16 34										
Longfield	d		15 52						16 22			16 38							16 52			
Meopham	d		15 57						16 27			16 42							16 57			
Sole Street	d											16 45										
London Charing Cross ⊖	d				15 09						15 39										16 09	
London Waterloo (East) ⊖	d				15 12						15 42										16 12	
London Cannon Street ⊖	d																					
London Bridge ⊖	d				15 17						15 47										16 17	
Dartford	d				15 55						16 25										16 55	
Greenhithe for Bluewater	d				16 00						16 30										17 00	
Gravesend	d				16 07		16 18	16 18			16 37				16 48	16 51					17 07	
Strood	d				16 18		16 28	16 28			16 48				16 58	17 01					17 18	
Rochester	d		16 09		16 22		16 33	16 33	16 39		16 52	16 56			17 03	17 06			17 09		17 22	
Chatham	d		16 12		16 25		16 35	16 35	16 42		16 55	16 59			17 05	17 08			17 12		17 25	
Gillingham (Kent)	d		16 17		16a29		16 40	16 40	16 47		16a59	17a03			17 10	17 13			17 17		17a29	
Rainham (Kent)	d		16 21				16 45	16 45	16 51						17 15	17 18			17 21			
Newington	d								16 55													
Sittingbourne	a		16 28				16 52	16 52	17 00						17 22	17 25			17 28			
	d		16 29			16 40	16 53	16 53	17 01					17 10	17 23	17 25			17 29			17 40
Kemsley	d					16 45								17 15								17 45
Swale	d					16 48								17 18								17 48
Queenborough	d					16 52								17 22								17 52
Sheerness-on-Sea	a					16 57								17 27								17 57
Teynham	d		16 33																17 33			
Faversham	a		16 39				17 03	17 03	17 09						17 33	17 34			17 39			
	d		16 43	16 45					17 13	17 15									17 43	17 45		
Selling	d			16 50																17 50		
Canterbury East	d			16 59						17 29										17 59		
Bekesbourne	d			17 03																18 03		
Adisham	d			17 08																18 08		
Aylesham	d			17 10																18 10		
Snowdown	d			17 13																18 13		
Shepherds Well	d			17 17																18 17		
Kearsney	d			17 21																18 21		
Dover Priory	a			17 27						17 48										18 27		
Whitstable	d		16 51						17 21										17 51			
Chestfield & Swalecliffe	d		16 54																17 54			
Herne Bay	d		16 58						17 26										17 58			
Birchington-on-Sea	d		17 07						17 35										18 07			
Westgate-on-Sea	d		17 10																18 10			
Margate	d	16 53	17 14						17 41									17 53	18 14			
Broadstairs	d	16 59	17 20						17 46									17 59	18 20			
Dumpton Park	d		17 23																18 23			
Ramsgate	a	17 04	17 26						17 51									18 04	18 26			

A ⊼ to Margate B not from 1 September until 8 September C not 25 August

For further services to St Pancras International, Blackfriars and Elephant & Castle and onwards to Bromley South, St Mary Cray and Swanley please refer to table 52

Table 212

London - Medway, Sheerness-on-Sea, Dover and Ramsgate

Saturdays

25 August to 8 September

Network Diagram - see first Page of Table 212

		SE A	SE B	SE 1 C ⌶		SE	SE 1	SE B	SE	SE A	SE B	SE B	SE	SE 1 C ⌶		SE	SE	SE A	SE B	SE 1 C ⌶		SE	SE 1
St Pancras Internatnl	d	16 55	16 55					17 18		17 25	17 25	17 48						17 55	17 55				
Stratford International	d	17 02	17 03					17 26		17 32	17 33	17 56						18 02	18 03				
Ebbsfleet International	d	17 13	17 14					17a36		17 43	17 44	18a06						18 13	18 14				
London Victoria	d			16 52			16 58							17 22						17 52			17 58
London Blackfriars	d																						
Elephant & Castle	d																						
Bromley South	d			17 09			17 19							17 39						18 09			18 19
St Mary Cray	d						17 25																18 25
Swanley	d						17 29																18 29
Farningham Road	d						17 34																18 34
Longfield	d			17 22			17 38							17 52						18 22			18 38
Meopham	d			17 27			17 42							17 57						18 27			18 42
Sole Street	d						17 45																18 45
London Charing Cross	d					16 39										17 09						17 39	
London Waterloo (East)	d					16 42										17 12						17 42	
London Cannon Street	d																						
London Bridge	d					16 47										17 17						17 47	
Dartford	d					17 25										17 55						18 25	
Greenhithe for Bluewater	d					17 30										18 00						18 30	
Gravesend	d	17 18	17 18			17 37				17 48	17 48					18 07		18 18	18 18			18 37	
Strood	d	17 28	17 28			17 48				17 58	17 58					18 18		18 28	18 28			18 48	
Rochester	d	17 33	17 33	17 39		17 52	17 56			18 03	18 03			18 09		18 22		18 33	18 33	18 39		18 52	18 56
Chatham	d	17 35	17 35	17 42		17 55	17 59			18 05	18 05			18 12		18 25		18 35	18 35	18 42		18 55	18 59
Gillingham (Kent)	d	17 40	17 40	17 47		17a59	18a03			18 10	18 10			18 17		18a29		18 40	18 40	18 47		18a59	19a03
Rainham (Kent)	d	17 45	17 45	17 51						18 15	18 15			18 21				18 45	18 45	18 51			
Newington	d			17 55																18 55			
Sittingbourne	a	17 52	17 52	18 00						18 22	18 22			18 28				18 52	18 52	19 00			
	d	17 53	17 53	18 01					18 10	18 23	18 23			18 29			18 40	18 53	18 53	19 01			
Kemsley	d								18 15								18 45						
Swale	d								18 18								18 48						
Queenborough	d								18 22								18 52						
Sheerness-on-Sea	a								18 27								18 57						
Teynham	d													18 33									
Faversham	a	18 03	18 03	18 09						18 33	18 33			18 39				19 03	19 03	19 09			
	d			18 13	18 15									18 43	18 45					19 13	19 15		
Selling	d														18 50								
Canterbury East	d				18 29										18 59						19 29		
Bekesbourne	d														19 03								
Adisham	d														19 08								
Aylesham	d														19 10								
Snowdown	d														19 13								
Shepherds Well	d														19 17								
Kearsney	d														19 21								
Dover Priory	a				18 48										19 27						19 48		
Whitstable	d			18 21										18 51						19 21			
Chestfield & Swalecliffe	d													18 54									
Herne Bay	d			18 26										18 58						19 26			
Birchington-on-Sea	d			18 35										19 07						19 35			
Westgate-on-Sea	d													19 10									
Margate	d			18 41									18 53	19 14						19 41			
Broadstairs	d			18 46									18 59	19 20						19 46			
Dumpton Park	d													19 23									
Ramsgate	a			18 51									19 04	19 26						19 51			

A not from 1 September until 8 September

B not 25 August

C ⌶ to Margate

For further services to St Pancras International, Blackfriars and Elephant & Castle and onwards to Bromley South, St Mary Cray and Swanley please refer to table 52

Table 212

London - Medway, Sheerness-on-Sea, Dover and Ramsgate

Saturdays

25 August to 8 September

Network Diagram - see first Page of Table 212

		SE A	SE	SE B	SE A	SE	SE 1 C ⌶		SE	SE	SE B	SE A	SE 1		SE	SE 1	SE A	SE	SE B	SE A	SE	SE 1	
St Pancras Internatnl	d	18 18		18 25	18 25						18 55	18 55					19 18		19 25	19 25			
Stratford International	d	18 26		18 32	18 33						19 02	19 03					19 26		19 32	19 33			
Ebbsfleet International	d	18a36		18 43	18 44						19 13	19 14					19a36		19 43	19 44			
London Victoria	d						18 22						18 52			18 58						19 22	
London Blackfriars	d																						
Elephant & Castle	d																						
Bromley South	d						18 39						19 09			19 19						19 39	
St Mary Cray	d															19 25							
Swanley	d															19 29							
Farningham Road	d															19 34							
Longfield	d						18 52						19 22			19 38						19 52	
Meopham	d						18 57						19 27			19 42						19 57	
Sole Street	d															19 45							
London Charing Cross	d								18 09						18 39								
London Waterloo (East)	d								18 12						18 42								
London Cannon Street	d																						
London Bridge	d								18 17						18 47								
Dartford	d								18 55						19 25								
Greenhithe for Bluewater	d								19 00						19 30								
Gravesend	d			18 48	18 48				19 07		19 18	19 18			19 37				19 48	19 48			
Strood	d			18 58	18 58				19 18		19 28	19 28			19 48				19 58	19 58			
Rochester	d			19 03	19 03		19 09		19 22		19 33	19 33	19 39		19 52	19 56			20 03	20 03		20 09	
Chatham	d			19 05	19 05		19 12		19 25		19 35	19 35	19 42		19 55	19 59			20 05	20 05		20 12	
Gillingham (Kent)	d			19 10	19 10		19 17		19a29		19 40	19 40	19 47		19a59	20a03			20 10	20 10		20 17	
Rainham (Kent)	d			19 15	19 15		19 21				19 45	19 45	19 51						20 15	20 15		20 21	
Newington	d												19 55										
Sittingbourne	a			19 22	19 22		19 28				19 52	19 52	20 00						20 22	20 22		20 28	
	d		19 10	19 23	19 23		19 29			19 40	19 53	19 53	20 01					20 10	20 23	20 23		20 29	
Kemsley	d		19 15							19 45								20 15					
Swale	d		19 18							19 48								20 18					
Queenborough	d		19 22							19 52								20 22					
Sheerness-on-Sea	a		19 27							19 57								20 27					
Teynham	d						19 33															20 33	
Faversham	a			19 33	19 33		19 39				20 03	20 03	20 09						20 33	20 33		20 39	
	d						19 43	19 45					20 13	20 15								20 43	20 45
Selling	d							19 50															20 50
Canterbury East	d							19 59						20 29									20 59
Bekesbourne	d							20 03															21 03
Adisham	d							20 08															21 08
Aylesham	d							20 10															21 10
Snowdown	d							20 13															21 13
Shepherds Well	d							20 17															21 17
Kearsney	d							20 21															21 21
Dover Priory	a							20 27						20 48									21 27
Whitstable	d						19 51						20 21									20 51	
Chestfield & Swalecliffe	d						19 54															20 54	
Herne Bay	d						19 58						20 26									20 58	
Birchington-on-Sea	d						20 07						20 35									21 07	
Westgate-on-Sea	d						20 10															21 10	
Margate	d					19 53	20 14						20 41								20 53	21 14	
Broadstairs	d					19 59	20 20						20 46								20 59	21 20	
Dumpton Park	d						20 23															21 23	
Ramsgate	a					20 04	20 26						20 51								21 04	21 26	

A not 25 August

B not from 1 September until 8 September

C ⌶ to Margate

For further services to St Pancras International, Blackfriars and Elephant & Castle and onwards to Bromley South, St Mary Cray and Swanley please refer to table 52

Table 212

Saturdays
25 August to 8 September

London - Medway, Sheerness-on-Sea, Dover and Ramsgate

Network Diagram - see first Page of Table 212

		SE		SE	SE A	SE B	SE 1	SE	SE 1	SE B	SE A		SE B	SE	SE 1	SE	SE	SE A	SE B	SE 1		SE	SE B
St Pancras International 15 ⊖	d				19 55	19 55				20 18	20 25		20 25					20 55	20 55				21 18
Stratford International ⊖	d				20 02	20 03				20 26	20 32		20 33					21 02	21 03				21 26
Ebbsfleet International	d				20 13	20 14				20a36	20 43		20 44					21 13	21 14				21a36
London Victoria 15 ⊖	d						19 52		19 58						20 22					20 52			
London Blackfriars 3 ⊖	d																						
Elephant & Castle ⊖	d																						
Bromley South 4	d						20 09		20 19						20 39					21 09			
St Mary Cray	d								20 25											21 15			
Swanley 4	d								20 29											21 19			
Farningham Road	d								20 34											21 24			
Longfield	d						20 22		20 38						20 52					21 28			
Meopham	d						20 27		20 42						20 57					21 32			
Sole Street	d								20 45											21 35			
London Charing Cross 4 ⊖	d	19 09						19 39								20 09						20 39	
London Waterloo (East) 4 ⊖	d	19 12						19 42								20 12						20 42	
London Cannon Street 4 ⊖	d																						
London Bridge 4 ⊖	d	19 17						19 47								20 17						20 47	
Dartford 4	d	19 55						20 25								20 55						21 25	
Greenhithe for Bluewater	d	20 00						20 30								21 00						21 30	
Gravesend 4	d	20 07			20 18	20 18		20 37			20 48		20 48			21 07		21 18	21 18			21 37	
Strood 4	d	20 18			20 28	20 28		20 48			20 58		20 58			21 18		21 28	21 28			21 48	
Rochester 4	d	20 22			20 33	20 33	20 39	20 52	20 56		21 03		21 03		21 09	21 22		21 33	21 33	21 45		21 52	
Chatham 4	d	20 25			20 35	20 35	20 42	20 55	20 59		21 05		21 05		21 12	21 25		21 35	21 35	21 47		21 55	
Gillingham (Kent) 4	d	20a29			20 40	20 40	20 47	20a59	21a03		21 10		21 10		21 17	21a29		21 40	21 40	21 52		21a59	
Rainham (Kent)	d				20 45	20 45	20 51				21 15		21 15		21 21			21 45	21 45	21 56			
Newington	d						20 55													22 00			
Sittingbourne 4	a				20 52	20 52	21 00				21 22		21 22		21 28			21 52	21 52	22 05			
	d			20 40	20 53	20 53	21 01				21 23		21 23		21 29		21 40	21 53	21 53	22 06			
Kemsley	d			20 45													21 45						
Swale	d			20 48													21 48						
Queenborough	d			20 52													21 52						
Sheerness-on-Sea	a			20 57													21 57						
Teynham	d														21 33								
Faversham 2	a				21 03	21 03	21 09				21 33		21 33		21 39			22 03	22 03	22 14			
	d						21 13 / 21 15								21 43 / 21 45					22 15			
Selling	d														21 50								
Canterbury East 4	d						21a27								21 59					22a26			
Bekesbourne	d														22 03								
Adisham	d														22 08								
Aylesham	d														22 10								
Snowdown	d														22 13								
Shepherds Well	d														22 17								
Kearsney	d														22 21								
Dover Priory 4	a														22 27								
Whitstable	d						21 21								21 51								
Chestfield & Swalecliffe	d														21 54								
Herne Bay	d						21 26								21 58								
Birchington-on-Sea	d						21 35								22 07								
Westgate-on-Sea	d														22 10								
Margate 4	d						21 41							21 53	22 14								
Broadstairs	d						21 46							21 59	22 20								
Dumpton Park	d														22 23								
Ramsgate 4	a						21 51							22 04	22 26								

A not from 1 September until 8 September B not 25 August

For further services to St Pancras International, Blackfriars and Elephant & Castle and onwards to Bromley South, St Mary Cray and Swanley please refer to table 52

Table 212

Saturdays
25 August to 8 September

London - Medway, Sheerness-on-Sea, Dover and Ramsgate

Network Diagram - see first Page of Table 212

		SE A	SE B	SE 1	SE	SE	SE A		SE B	SE 1	SE	SE B	SE A	SE B	SE 1	SE		SE	SE A	SE B	SE 1	SE	SE B
St Pancras International 15 ⊖	d	21 25	21 25				21 55		21 55			22 17	22 25	22 25					22 55	22 55			23 18
Stratford International ⊖	d	21 32	21 33				22 02		22 03			22 25	22 32	22 33					23 02	23 03			23 26
Ebbsfleet International	d	21 43	21 44				22 13		22 14			22a35	22 43	22 44					23 13	23 14			23a36
London Victoria 15 ⊖	d			21 22						21 52					22 22						22 52		
London Blackfriars 3 ⊖	d																						
Elephant & Castle ⊖	d																						
Bromley South 4	d			21 39						22 09					22 39						23 09		
St Mary Cray	d									22 15											23 15		
Swanley 4	d									22 19											23 19		
Farningham Road	d									22 24											23 24		
Longfield	d			21 52						22 28					22 52						23 28		
Meopham	d			21 57						22 32					22 57						23 32		
Sole Street	d									22 35											23 35		
London Charing Cross 4 ⊖	d				21 09						21 39					22 09						22 39	
London Waterloo (East) 4 ⊖	d				21 12						21 42					22 12						22 42	
London Cannon Street 4 ⊖	d																						
London Bridge 4 ⊖	d				21 17						21 47					22 17						22 47	
Dartford 4	d				21 55						22 25					22 55						23 25	
Greenhithe for Bluewater	d				22 00						22 31					23 01						23 31	
Gravesend 4	d	21 48	21 48		22 07		22 18		22 18		22 40		22 48	22 48		23 10			23 18	23 18		23 40	
Strood 4	d	21 58	21 58		22 18		22 28		22 28		22 52		22 58	22 58		23 22			23 28	23 28		23 52	
Rochester 4	d	22 03	22 03	22 09	22 22		22 33		22 33	22 45	22 56		23 03	23 03	23 09	23 26			23 33	23 33	23 45	23 56	
Chatham 4	d	22 05	22 05	22 12	22 25		22 35		22 35	22 47	22 58		23 05	23 05	23 12	23 28			23 35	23 35	23 47	23 58	
Gillingham (Kent) 4	d	22 10	22 10	22 17	22a29		22 40		22 40	22 52	23a03		23 10	23 10	23 17	23a33			23 40	23 40	23 52	00a03	
Rainham (Kent)	d	22 15	22 15	22 21			22 45		22 45	22 56			23 15	23 15	23 21				23 45	23 45	23 56		
Newington	d									23 00											00 01		
Sittingbourne 4	a	22 22	22 22	22 28			22 52		22 52	23 05			23 22	23 22	23 28				23 52	23 52	00 06		
	d	22 23	22 23	22 29		22 40	22 53		22 53	23 06			23 23	23 23	23 29			23 32	23 53	23 53	00 07		
Kemsley	d					22 45												23 37					
Swale	d					22 48												23 40					
Queenborough	d					22 52												23 44					
Sheerness-on-Sea	a					22 57												23 49					
Teynham	d			22 33											23 33								
Faversham 2	a	22 31	22 31	22 39			23 01		23 01	23 14			23 31	23 31	23 39				00 01	00 01	00 16		
	d			22 43 / 22 45											23 43 / 23 45								
Selling	d			22 50											23 50								
Canterbury East 4	d			22 59											23 59								
Bekesbourne	d			23 03																			
Adisham	d			23 08																			
Aylesham	d			23 10											00 07								
Snowdown	d			23 13																			
Shepherds Well	d			23 17																			
Kearsney	d			23 21																			
Dover Priory 4	a			23 27											00 18								
Whitstable	d			22 51											23 51								
Chestfield & Swalecliffe	d			22 54											23 54								
Herne Bay	d			22 58											23 58								
Birchington-on-Sea	d			23 07											00 07								
Westgate-on-Sea	d			23 10											00 10								
Margate 4	d			23 14											00 14								
Broadstairs	d			23 20											00 20								
Dumpton Park	d			23 23											00 23								
Ramsgate 4	a			23 26											00 26								

A not from 1 September until 8 September B not 25 August

For further services to St Pancras International, Blackfriars and Elephant & Castle and onwards to Bromley South, St Mary Cray and Swanley please refer to table 52

Saturdays

25 August to 8 September

London - Medway, Sheerness-on-Sea, Dover and Ramsgate

Network Diagram - see first Page of Table 212

		SE	SE	SE	SE	SE	SE	SE	SE
				[1]				[1]	
		A	B			B	A		
St Pancras Internatnl [15] ⊖	d	23 25	23 25			23 55	23 55		
Stratford International ⊖	d	23 32	23 33			00 03	00 02		
Ebbsfleet International	d	23 43	23 44			00 13	00 13		
London Victoria [15] ⊖	d			23 22				23 52	
London Blackfriars [3] ⊖	d								
Elephant & Castle ⊖	d								
Bromley South [4]	d			23 39				00 09	
St Mary Cray	d							00 15	
Swanley [4]	d							00 19	
Farningham Road	d							00 24	
Longfield	d			23 52				00 28	
Meopham	d			23 57				00 32	
Sole Street	d							00 35	
London Charing Cross [4] ⊖	d				23 09				23 39
London Waterloo (East) [4] ⊖	d				23 12				23 42
London Cannon Street [4] ⊖	d								
London Bridge [4] ⊖	d				23 17				23 47
Dartford [4]	d				23 55				00 25
Greenhithe for Bluewater	d				23 59				00 31
Gravesend [4]	d	23 48	23 48		00 10	00 18	00 18		00 40
Strood [4]	d	23 58	23 58		00 22	00 28	00 28		00 52
Rochester [4]	d	00 03	00 03	00 09	00 26	00 32	00 33	00 45	00 56
Chatham [4]	d	00 05	00 05	00 12	00 28	00 35	00 35	00 47	00 58
Gillingham (Kent) [4]	d	00 10	00 10	00 17	00a33	00 39	00 40	00a52	01a03
Rainham (Kent)	d	00 15	00 15	00 21		00 44	00 45		
Newington	d								
Sittingbourne [4]	a	00 22	00 22	00 28		00 52	00 52		
	d	00 23	00 23	00 29		00 52	00 53		
Kemsley	d								
Swale	d								
Queenborough	d								
Sheerness-on-Sea	a								
Teynham	d			00 33					
Faversham [2]	a	00 31	00 31	00 39		01 00	01 01		
	d			00 43					
Selling	d								
Canterbury East [4]	d								
Bekesbourne	d								
Adisham	d								
Aylesham	d								
Snowdown	d								
Shepherds Well	d								
Kearsney	d								
Dover Priory [4]	a								
Whitstable	d			00 51					
Chestfield & Swalecliffe	d			00 54					
Herne Bay	d			00 58					
Birchington-on-Sea	d			01 07					
Westgate-on-Sea	d			01 10					
Margate [4]	d			01 14					
Broadstairs	d			01 20					
Dumpton Park	d			01 23					
Ramsgate [4]	a			01 26					

A not from 1 September until 8 September

B not 25 August

For further services to St Pancras International, Blackfriars and Elephant & Castle and onwards to Bromley South, St Mary Cray and Swanley please refer to table 52

Sundays

until 22 July, 19 Aug and from 16 Sep

London - Medway, Sheerness-on-Sea, Dover and Ramsgate

Network Diagram - see first Page of Table 212

		SE		SE	SE	SE	SE	SE	SE	SE	SE	SE	SE	SE	SE	SE	SE	SE	SE	SE	SE	SE	
		[1]			[1]			[1]			[1]	[1]							[1]			[1]	
St Pancras Internatnl [15] ⊖	d			22p55			23p25			23p55				00 12									
Stratford International ⊖	d			23p02			23p32			00 02				00 19									
Ebbsfleet International	d			23p13			23p43			00 13				00 31									
London Victoria [15] ⊖	d	22p22			22p52			23p22			23p52	00 10			00 35				07 24				08 05
London Blackfriars [3] ⊖	d																						
Elephant & Castle ⊖	d																						
Bromley South [4]	d	22p39			23p09			23p39			00 09				00 55				07 44				08 22
St Mary Cray	d				23p15						00 15				01 01				07 50				
Swanley [4]	d				23p19						00 19				01 05				07 54				
Farningham Road	d				23p24						00 24				01 10				07 59				
Longfield	d	22p52			23p28			23p52			00 28				01 14				08 03				
Meopham	d	22p57			23p32			23p57			00 32				01 18				08 07				
Sole Street	d				23p35						00 35								08 10				
London Charing Cross [4] ⊖	d								23p09				23p39			00 18							
London Waterloo (East) [4] ⊖	d								23p12				23p42			00 21							
London Cannon Street [4] ⊖	d																						
London Bridge [4] ⊖	d								23p17				23p47			00 26							
Dartford [4]	d								23p55				00 25			01 06				07 55			
Greenhithe for Bluewater	d								23p59				00 31			01 10				08 01			
Gravesend [4]	d			23p18			23p48		00 10	00 18			00 40			01 17				08 10			
Strood [4]	d			23p28			23p58		00 22	00 28			00 52			01 29				08 22			
Rochester [4]	d	23p09		23p33	23p45		00 03	00 09	00 26	00 33	00 45	00 49	00 56		01 29	01 33			08 20	08 26			08 46
Chatham [4]	d	23p12		23p35	23p47		00 05	00 12	00 28	00 35	00 47	00 52	00 58		01 31	01 35			08 22	08 28			08 48
Gillingham (Kent) [4]	d	23p17		23p40	23p52		00 10	00 17	00a33	00 40	00a52	00 57	01a03		01a35	01a41			08 27	08a33			08 53
Rainham (Kent)	d	23p21		23p45	23p56		00 15	00 21		00 45		01 01							08 31				08 57
Newington	d				00 01							01 05							08 35				
Sittingbourne [4]	a	23p28		23p52	00 06		00 22	00 28		00 52		01 10							08 40				09 04
	d	23p29		23p53	00 07	00 15	00 23	00 29		00 53		01 11						08 10	08 41				09 05
Kemsley	d					00 20												08 15					
Swale	d					00 23												08 18					
Queenborough	d					00 27												08 22					
Sheerness-on-Sea	a					00 32												08 27					
Teynham	d	23p33						00 33				01 15							08 45				
Faversham [2]	a	23p39		00 01	00 16		00 31	00 39		01 01		01 23							08 51				09 13
	d	23p43	23p45					00 43				01 24							08 52			09 17	09 19
Selling	d		23p50																				09 24
Canterbury East [4]	d		23p59																09a04				09 33
Bekesbourne	d																						09 37
Adisham	d																						09 42
Aylesham	d		00 07																				09 44
Snowdown	d																						09 47
Shepherds Well	d																						09 51
Kearsney	d																						09 55
Dover Priory [4]	a		00 18																				10 00
Whitstable	d	23p51						00 51				01 32										09 25	
Chestfield & Swalecliffe	d	23p54						00 54				01 35										09 28	
Herne Bay	d	23p58						00 58				01 39										09 32	
Birchington-on-Sea	d	00 07						01 07				01 48										09 41	
Westgate-on-Sea	d	00 10						01 10				01 51										09 44	
Margate [4]	d	00 14						01 14				01 55					07 53				08 53	09 48	
Broadstairs	d	00 20						01 20				02 01					07 59				08 59	09 54	
Dumpton Park	d	00 23						01 23				02 04										09 57	
Ramsgate [4]	a	00 26						01 26				02 07					08 04				09 04	10 00	

For further services to St Pancras International, Blackfriars and Elephant & Castle and onwards to Bromley South, St Mary Cray and Swanley please refer to table 52

Table 212

Sundays

until 22 July, 19 Aug and from 16 Sep

London - Medway, Sheerness-on-Sea, Dover and Ramsgate

Network Diagram - see first Page of Table 212

		SE	SE	SE ■	SE	SE	SE ■		SE	SE	SE	SE ■	SE	SE	SE ■ A ⌶		SE	SE	SE	SE ■	SE	SE
St Pancras Internatnl ■ ⊖	d										09 25								10 28			
Stratford International ⊖	d										09 32								10 35			
Ebbsfleet International	d										09 43								10 46			
London Victoria ■ ⊖	d			08 24			09 05					09 24			10 05					10 24		
London Blackfriars ■ ⊖	d																					
Elephant & Castle ⊖	d																					
Bromley South ■	d			08 44			09 22					09 44			10 22					10 44		
St Mary Cray	d			08 50								09 50								10 50		
Swanley ■	d			08 54								09 54								10 54		
Farningham Road	d			08 59								09 59								10 59		
Longfield	d			09 03								10 03								11 03		
Meopham	d			09 07								10 07								11 07		
Sole Street	d			09 10								10 10								11 10		
London Charing Cross ■ ⊖	d				08 10				08 40				09 10				09 40				10 10	
London Waterloo (East) ■ ⊖	d				08 13				08 43				09 13				09 43				10 13	
London Cannon Street ■ ⊖	d																					
London Bridge ■ ⊖	d				08 18				08 48				09 18				09 48				10 18	
Dartford ■	d	08 25			08 55				09 25				09 55				10 25				10 55	
Greenhithe for Bluewater	d	08 31			09 00				09 30				10 00				10 30				11 00	
Gravesend ■	d	08 40			09 07				09 37		09 48		10 07				10 37		10 51		11 07	
Strood ■	d	08 52			09 18				09 48		09 58		10 18				10 48		11 01		11 18	
Rochester ■	d	08 56		09 20	09 23		09 46		09 52		10 03	10 20	10 23		10 46		10 52		11 06	11 20	11 23	
Chatham ■	d	08 58		09 22	09 26		09 48		09 55		10 05	10 22	10 26		10 48		10 55		11 08	11 22	11 26	
Gillingham (Kent) ■	d	09a03		09 27	09a30		09 53		10a02		10 10	10 27	10a30		10 53		11a02		11 13	11 27	11a30	
Rainham (Kent)	d			09 31			09 57				10 15	10 31			10 57				11 18	11 31		
Newington	d			09 35								10 35								11 35		
Sittingbourne ■	a			09 40			10 04				10 22	10 40			11 04				11 25	11 40		
	d		09 10	09 41			10 05			10 10	10 23	10 41			11 05			11 10	11 25	11 41		
Kemsley	d		09 15							10 15								11 15				
Swale	d		09 18							10 18								11 18				
Queenborough	d		09 22							10 22								11 22				
Sheerness-on-Sea	a		09 27							10 27								11 27				
Teynham	d			09 45								10 45								11 45		
Faversham ■	a			09 51			10 13				10 33	10 51			11 13				11 34	11 51		
	d			09 52			10 17	10 19				10 52			11 17	11 19				11 52		
Selling	d							10 24								11 24						
Canterbury East ■	d			10a04				10 33				11a04				11 33				12a04		
Bekesbourne	d							10 37								11 37						
Adisham	d							10 42								11 42						
Aylesham	d							10 44								11 44						
Snowdown	d							10 47								11 47						
Shepherds Well	d							10 51								11 51						
Kearsney	d							10 55								11 55						
Dover Priory ■	a							11 00								12 00						
Whitstable	d						10 25								11 25							
Chestfield & Swalecliffe	d						10 28								11 28							
Herne Bay	d						10 32								11 32							
Birchington-on-Sea	d						10 41								11 41							
Westgate-on-Sea	d						10 44								11 44							
Margate ■	d					09 53	10 48							10 53	11 48							11 53
Broadstairs	d					09 59	10 54							10 59	11 54							11 59
Dumpton Park	d						10 57								11 57							
Ramsgate ■	a					10 04	11 00							11 04	12 00							12 04

A ⌶ to Margate

For further services to St Pancras International, Blackfriars and Elephant & Castle and onwards to Bromley South, St Mary Cray and Swanley please refer to table 52

Table 212

Sundays

until 22 July, 19 Aug and from 16 Sep

London - Medway, Sheerness-on-Sea, Dover and Ramsgate

Network Diagram - see first Page of Table 212

		SE ■ A ⌶		SE	SE	SE	SE ■	SE	SE	SE ■ A ⌶		SE	SE	SE	SE ■	SE	SE	SE	SE ■ A ⌶		SE	SE
St Pancras Internatnl ■ ⊖	d					11 25								12 28			12 52					
Stratford International ⊖	d					11 32								12 35			12 58					
Ebbsfleet International	d					11 43								12 46			13 13					
London Victoria ■ ⊖	d	11 05					11 24			12 05					12 24				13 05			
London Blackfriars ■ ⊖	d																					
Elephant & Castle ⊖	d																					
Bromley South ■	d	11 22					11 44			12 22					12 44				13 22			
St Mary Cray	d						11 50								12 50							
Swanley ■	d						11 54								12 54							
Farningham Road	d						11 59								12 59							
Longfield	d						12 03								13 03							
Meopham	d						12 07								13 07							
Sole Street	d						12 10								13 10							
London Charing Cross ■ ⊖	d			10 40				11 10				11 40				12 10					12 40	
London Waterloo (East) ■ ⊖	d			10 43				11 13				11 43				12 13					12 43	
London Cannon Street ■ ⊖	d																					
London Bridge ■ ⊖	d			10 48				11 18				11 48				12 18					12 48	
Dartford ■	d			11 25				11 55				12 25				12 55					13 25	
Greenhithe for Bluewater	d			11 30				12 00				12 30				13 00					13 30	
Gravesend ■	d			11 37		11 48		12 07				12 37		12 51		13 07	13 18				13 37	
Strood ■	d			11 48		11 58		12 18				12 48		13 01		13 18	13 28				13 48	
Rochester ■	d	11 46		11 52		12 03	12 20	12 23		12 46		12 52		13 06	13 20	13 23	13 33		13 46		13 52	
Chatham ■	d	11 48		11 55		12 05	12 22	12 26		12 48		12 55		13 08	13 22	13 26	13 35		13 48		13 55	
Gillingham (Kent) ■	d	11 53		12a02		12 10	12 27	12a30		12 53		13a02		13 13	13 27	13a30	13 40		13 53		14a02	
Rainham (Kent)	d	11 57				12 15	12 31			12 57				13 18	13 31		13 45		13 57			
Newington	d						12 35								13 35							
Sittingbourne ■	a	12 04				12 22	12 40			13 04				13 25	13 40		13 52		14 04			
	d	12 05			12 10	12 23	12 41			13 05			13 10	13 25	13 41		13 53		14 05			14 10
Kemsley	d				12 15								13 15									14 15
Swale	d				12 18								13 18									14 18
Queenborough	d				12 22								13 22									14 22
Sheerness-on-Sea	a				12 27								13 27									14 27
Teynham	d						12 45								13 45							
Faversham ■	a	12 13				12 33	12 51			13 13				13 34	13 51		14 03		14 13			
	d	12 17	12 19				12 52			13 17	13 19				13 52				14 17	14 19		
Selling	d		12 24								13 24									14 24		
Canterbury East ■	d		12 33				13a04				13 33				14a04					14 33		
Bekesbourne	d		12 37								13 37									14 37		
Adisham	d		12 42								13 42									14 42		
Aylesham	d		12 44								13 44									14 44		
Snowdown	d		12 47								13 47									14 47		
Shepherds Well	d		12 51								13 51									14 51		
Kearsney	d		12 55								13 55									14 55		
Dover Priory ■	a		13 00								14 00									15 00		
Whitstable	d	12 25								13 25									14 25			
Chestfield & Swalecliffe	d	12 28								13 28									14 28			
Herne Bay	d	12 32								13 32									14 32			
Birchington-on-Sea	d	12 41								13 41									14 41			
Westgate-on-Sea	d	12 44								13 44									14 44			
Margate ■	d	12 48							12 53	13 48								13 53	14 48			
Broadstairs	d	12 54							12 59	13 54								13 59	14 54			
Dumpton Park	d	12 57								13 57									14 57			
Ramsgate ■	a	13 00							13 04	14 00								14 04	15 00			

A ⌶ to Margate

For further services to St Pancras International, Blackfriars and Elephant & Castle and onwards to Bromley South, St Mary Cray and Swanley please refer to table 52

Table 212

Saturdays

25 August to 8 September

London - Medway, Sheerness-on-Sea, Dover and Ramsgate

Network Diagram - see first Page of Table 212

		SE	SE	SE [1]		SE	SE	SE	SE [1]	SE
		A	B				B	A		
St Pancras Internatnl [15] ⊖	d	23 25	23 25				23 55	23 55		
Stratford International ⊖	d	23 32	23 33				00 03	00 02		
Ebbsfleet International	d	23 43	23 44				00 13	00 13		
London Victoria [15] ⊖	d			23 22					23 52	
London Blackfriars [3] ⊖	d									
Elephant & Castle ⊖	d									
Bromley South [4]	d			23 39					00 09	
St Mary Cray	d								00 15	
Swanley [4]	d								00 19	
Farningham Road	d								00 24	
Longfield	d			23 52					00 28	
Meopham	d			23 57					00 32	
Sole Street	d								00 35	
London Charing Cross [4] ⊖	d					23 09				23 39
London Waterloo (East) [4] ⊖	d					23 12				23 42
London Cannon Street [4] ⊖	d									
London Bridge [4] ⊖	d					23 17				23 47
Dartford [4]	d					23 55				00 25
Greenhithe for Bluewater	d					23 59				00 31
Gravesend [4]	d	23 48	23 48			00 10	00 18	00 18		00 40
Strood [4]	d	23 58	23 58			00 22	00 28	00 28		00 52
Rochester [4]	d	00 03	00 03	00 09		00 26	00 32	00 33	00 45	00 56
Chatham [4]	d	00 05	00 05	00 12		00 28	00 35	00 35	00 47	00 58
Gillingham (Kent) [4]	d	00 10	00 10	00 17		00a33	00 39	00 40	00a52	01a03
Rainham (Kent)	d	00 15	00 15	00 21			00 44	00 45		
Newington	d									
Sittingbourne [4]	a	00 22	00 22	00 28			00 52	00 52		
	d	00 23	00 23	00 29			00 52	00 53		
Kemsley	d									
Swale	d									
Queenborough	d									
Sheerness-on-Sea	a									
Teynham	d			00 33						
Faversham [2]	a	00 31	00 31	00 39			01 00	01 01		
	d			00 43						
Selling	d									
Canterbury East [4]	d									
Bekesbourne	d									
Adisham	d									
Aylesham	d									
Snowdown	d									
Shepherds Well	d									
Kearsney	d									
Dover Priory [4]	a									
Whitstable	d			00 51						
Chestfield & Swalecliffe	d			00 54						
Herne Bay	d			00 58						
Birchington-on-Sea	d			01 07						
Westgate-on-Sea	d			01 10						
Margate [4]	d			01 14						
Broadstairs	d			01 20						
Dumpton Park	d			01 23						
Ramsgate [4]	a			01 26						

A not from 1 September until 8 September

B not 25 August

For further services to St Pancras International, Blackfriars and Elephant & Castle and onwards to Bromley South, St Mary Cray and Swanley please refer to table 52

Table 212

Sundays

until 22 July, 19 Aug and from 16 Sep

London - Medway, Sheerness-on-Sea, Dover and Ramsgate

Network Diagram - see first Page of Table 212

		SE [1]	SE	SE [1]	SE	SE	SE [1]	SE	SE		SE [1]	SE [1]	SE	SE	SE	SE	SE	SE	SE [1]		SE	SE	SE [1]
St Pancras Internatnl [15] ⊖	d		22p55			23p25			23p55					00 12									
Stratford International ⊖	d		23p02			23p32			00 02					00 19									
Ebbsfleet International	d		23p13			23p43			00 13					00 31									
London Victoria [15] ⊖	d	22p22		22p52			23p22				23p52	00 10			00 35				07 24				08 05
London Blackfriars [3] ⊖	d																						
Elephant & Castle ⊖	d																						
Bromley South [4]	d	22p39		23p09			23p39				00 09				00 55				07 44				08 22
St Mary Cray	d			23p15							00 15				01 01				07 50				
Swanley [4]	d			23p19							00 19				01 05				07 54				
Farningham Road	d			23p24							00 24				01 10				07 59				
Longfield	d	22p52		23p28			23p52				00 28				01 14				08 03				
Meopham	d	22p57		23p32			23p57				00 32				01 18				08 07				
Sole Street	d			23p35							00 35								08 10				
London Charing Cross [4] ⊖	d							23p09					23p39			00 18							
London Waterloo (East) [4] ⊖	d							23p12					23p42			00 21							
London Cannon Street [4] ⊖	d																						
London Bridge [4] ⊖	d							23p17					23p47			00 26							
Dartford [4]	d							23p55					00 25			01 06					07 55		
Greenhithe for Bluewater	d							23p59					00 31			01 10					08 01		
Gravesend [4]	d		23p18			23p48		00 10	00 18				00 40			01 17					08 10		
Strood [4]	d		23p28			23p58		00 22	00 28				00 52			01 29					08 22		
Rochester [4]	d	23p09	23p33	23p45		00 03	00 09	00 26	00 33		00 45	00 49	00 56		01 29	01 33			08 20		08 26		08 46
Chatham [4]	d	23p12	23p35	23p47		00 05	00 12	00 28	00 35		00 47	00 52	00 58		01 31	01 35			08 22		08 28		08 48
Gillingham (Kent) [4]	d	23p17	23p40	23p52		00 10	00 17	00a33	00 40		00a52	00 57	01a03		01a35	01a41			08 27		08a33		08 53
Rainham (Kent)	d	23p21	23p45	23p56		00 15	00 21		00 45			01 01							08 31				08 57
Newington	d			00 01								01 05							08 35				
Sittingbourne [4]	a	23p28	23p52	00 06		00 22	00 28		00 52			01 10							08 40				09 04
	d	23p29	23p53	00 07	00 15	00 23	00 29		00 53			01 11						08 10	08 41				09 05
Kemsley	d				00 20													08 15					
Swale	d				00 23													08 18					
Queenborough	d				00 27													08 22					
Sheerness-on-Sea	a				00 32													08 27					
Teynham	d	23p33					00 33					01 15							08 45				
Faversham [2]	a	23p39	00 01	00 16		00 31	00 39		01 01			01 23							08 51				09 13
	d	23p43 23p45					00 43					01 24							08 52				09 17 09 19
Selling	d	23p50																					09 24
Canterbury East [4]	d	23p59																	09a04				09 33
Bekesbourne	d																						09 37
Adisham	d																						09 42
Aylesham	d	00 07																					09 44
Snowdown	d																						09 47
Shepherds Well	d																						09 51
Kearsney	d																						09 55
Dover Priory [4]	a	00 18																					10 00
Whitstable	d	23p51					00 51					01 32											09 25
Chestfield & Swalecliffe	d	23p54					00 54					01 35											09 28
Herne Bay	d	23p58					00 58					01 39											09 32
Birchington-on-Sea	d	00 07					01 07					01 48											09 41
Westgate-on-Sea	d	00 10					01 10					01 51											09 44
Margate [4]	d	00 14					01 14					01 55					07 53					08 53	09 48
Broadstairs	d	00 20					01 20					02 01					07 59					08 59	09 54
Dumpton Park	d	00 23					01 23					02 04											09 57
Ramsgate [4]	a	00 26					01 26					02 07					08 04					09 04	10 00

For further services to St Pancras International, Blackfriars and Elephant & Castle and onwards to Bromley South, St Mary Cray and Swanley please refer to table 52

Table 212

Sundays

until 22 July, 19 Aug and from 16 Sep

London - Medway, Sheerness-on-Sea, Dover and Ramsgate

Network Diagram - see first Page of Table 212

		SE	SE	SE ■	SE	SE	SE ■	SE	SE	SE	SE ■	SE	SE	SE ■ A	SE	SE	SE	SE ■	SE	SE
St Pancras Internatnl ⊖	d									09 25							10 28			
Stratford International ⊖	d									09 32							10 35			
Ebbsfleet International	d									09 43							10 46			
London Victoria ⊖	d			08 24			09 05				09 24			10 05				10 24		
London Blackfriars ⊖	d																			
Elephant & Castle ⊖	d																			
Bromley South	d			08 44			09 22				09 44			10 22				10 44		
St Mary Cray	d			08 50							09 50							10 50		
Swanley	d			08 54							09 54							10 54		
Farningham Road	d			08 59							09 59							10 59		
Longfield	d			09 03							10 03							11 03		
Meopham	d			09 07							10 07							11 07		
Sole Street	d			09 10							10 10							11 10		
London Charing Cross ⊖	d				08 10			08 40				09 10			09 40				10 10	
London Waterloo (East) ⊖	d				08 13			08 43				09 13			09 43				10 13	
London Cannon Street ⊖	d																			
London Bridge ⊖	d				08 18			08 48				09 18			09 48				10 18	
Dartford	d	08 25			08 55			09 25				09 55			10 25				10 55	
Greenhithe for Bluewater	d	08 31			09 00			09 30				10 00			10 30				11 00	
Gravesend	d	08 40			09 07			09 37		09 48		10 07			10 37		10 51		11 07	
Strood	d	08 52			09 18			09 48		09 58		10 18			10 48		11 01		11 18	
Rochester	d	08 56		09 20	09 23		09 46	09 52		10 03	10 20	10 23		10 46	10 52		11 06	11 20	11 23	
Chatham	d	08 58		09 22	09 26		09 48	09 55		10 05	10 22	10 26		10 48	10 55		11 08	11 22	11 26	
Gillingham (Kent)	d	09a03		09 27	09a30		09 53	10a02		10 10	10 27	10a30		10 53	11a02		11 13	11 27	11a30	
Rainham (Kent)	d			09 31			09 57			10 15	10 31			10 57			11 18	11 31		
Newington	d			09 35							10 35							11 35		
Sittingbourne	a			09 40			10 04			10 22	10 40			11 04			11 25	11 40		
	d		09 10	09 41			10 05		10 10	10 23	10 41			11 05		11 10	11 25	11 41		
Kemsley	d		09 15						10 15							11 15				
Swale	d		09 18						10 18							11 18				
Queenborough	d		09 22						10 22							11 22				
Sheerness-on-Sea	a		09 27						10 27							11 27				
Teynham	d			09 45							10 45							11 45		
Faversham	a			09 51			10 13			10 33	10 51			11 13			11 34	11 51		
	d			09 52			10 17 10 19				10 52			11 17 11 19				11 52		
Selling	d						10 24							11 24						
Canterbury East	d			10a04			10 33				11a04			11 33				12a04		
Bekesbourne	d						10 37							11 37						
Adisham	d						10 42							11 42						
Aylesham	d						10 44							11 44						
Snowdown	d						10 47							11 47						
Shepherds Well	d						10 51							11 51						
Kearsney	d						10 55							11 55						
Dover Priory	a						11 00							12 00						
Whitstable	d						10 25							11 25						
Chestfield & Swalecliffe	d						10 28							11 28						
Herne Bay	d						10 32							11 32						
Birchington-on-Sea	d						10 41							11 41						
Westgate-on-Sea	d						10 44							11 44						
Margate	d					09 53	10 48						10 53	11 48						11 53
Broadstairs	d					09 59	10 54						10 59	11 54						11 59
Dumpton Park	d						10 57							11 57						
Ramsgate	a					10 04	11 00						11 04	12 00						12 04

A to Margate

For further services to St Pancras International, Blackfriars and Elephant & Castle and onwards to Bromley South, St Mary Cray and Swanley please refer to table 52

Table 212

Sundays

until 22 July, 19 Aug and from 16 Sep

London - Medway, Sheerness-on-Sea, Dover and Ramsgate

Network Diagram - see first Page of Table 212

		SE ■ A	SE	SE	SE	SE ■	SE	SE	SE ■ A	SE	SE	SE	SE ■	SE	SE	SE	SE ■ A	SE	SE
St Pancras Internatnl ⊖	d				11 25							12 28			12 52				
Stratford International ⊖	d				11 32							12 35			12 58				
Ebbsfleet International	d				11 43							12 46			13 13				
London Victoria ⊖	d	11 05				11 24			12 05				12 24				13 05		
London Blackfriars ⊖	d																		
Elephant & Castle ⊖	d																		
Bromley South	d	11 22				11 44			12 22				12 44				13 22		
St Mary Cray	d					11 50							12 50						
Swanley	d					11 54							12 54						
Farningham Road	d					11 59							12 59						
Longfield	d					12 03							13 03						
Meopham	d					12 07							13 07						
Sole Street	d					12 10							13 10						
London Charing Cross ⊖	d		10 40				11 10			11 40				12 10				12 40	
London Waterloo (East) ⊖	d		10 43				11 13			11 43				12 13				12 43	
London Cannon Street ⊖	d																		
London Bridge ⊖	d		10 48				11 18			11 48				12 18				12 48	
Dartford	d		11 25				11 55			12 25				12 55				13 25	
Greenhithe for Bluewater	d		11 30				12 00			12 30				13 00				13 30	
Gravesend	d		11 37		11 48		12 07			12 37		12 51		13 07	13 18			13 37	
Strood	d		11 48		11 58		12 18			12 48		13 01		13 18	13 28			13 48	
Rochester	d	11 46	11 52		12 03	12 20	12 23		12 46	12 52		13 06	13 20	13 23	13 33		13 46	13 52	
Chatham	d	11 48	11 55		12 05	12 22	12 26		12 48	12 55		13 08	13 22	13 26	13 35		13 48	13 55	
Gillingham (Kent)	d	11 53	12a02		12 10	12 27	12a30		12 53	13a02		13 13	13 27	13a30	13 40		13 53	14a02	
Rainham (Kent)	d	11 57			12 15	12 31			12 57			13 18	13 31		13 45		13 57		
Newington	d					12 35							13 35						
Sittingbourne	a	12 04			12 22	12 40			13 04			13 25	13 40		13 52		14 04		
	d	12 05		12 10	12 23	12 41			13 05		13 10	13 25	13 41		13 53		14 05		14 10
Kemsley	d			12 15							13 15								14 15
Swale	d			12 18							13 18								14 18
Queenborough	d			12 22							13 22								14 22
Sheerness-on-Sea	a			12 27							13 27								14 27
Teynham	d					12 45							13 45						
Faversham	a	12 13			12 33	12 51			13 13			13 34	13 51		14 03		14 13		
	d	12 17 12 19				12 52			13 17 13 19				13 52				14 17 14 19		
Selling	d	12 24							13 24								14 24		
Canterbury East	d	12 33				13a04			13 33				14a04				14 33		
Bekesbourne	d	12 37							13 37								14 37		
Adisham	d	12 42							13 42								14 42		
Aylesham	d	12 44							13 44								14 44		
Snowdown	d	12 47							13 47								14 47		
Shepherds Well	d	12 51							13 51								14 51		
Kearsney	d	12 55							13 55								14 55		
Dover Priory	a	13 00							14 00								15 00		
Whitstable	d	12 25							13 25								14 25		
Chestfield & Swalecliffe	d	12 28							13 28								14 28		
Herne Bay	d	12 32							13 32								14 32		
Birchington-on-Sea	d	12 41							13 41								14 41		
Westgate-on-Sea	d	12 44							13 44								14 44		
Margate	d	12 48						12 53	13 48							13 53	14 48		
Broadstairs	d	12 54						12 59	13 54							13 59	14 54		
Dumpton Park	d	12 57							13 57								14 57		
Ramsgate	a	13 00						13 04	14 00							14 04	15 00		

A to Margate

For further services to St Pancras International, Blackfriars and Elephant & Castle and onwards to Bromley South, St Mary Cray and Swanley please refer to table 52

Table 212

Saturdays

25 August to 8 September

London - Medway, Sheerness-on-Sea, Dover and Ramsgate

Network Diagram - see first Page of Table 212

Station		SE A	SE B	SE ■ C ⌶		SE	SE ■	SE B	SE	SE A		SE B	SE B	SE	SE ■ C ⌶		SE	SE	SE A	SE B		SE ■ C ⌶		SE	SE ■
St Pancras International ⊖	d	16 55	16 55					17 18		17 25		17 25	17 48						17 55	17 55					
Stratford International ⊖	d	17 02	17 03					17 26		17 32		17 33	17 56						18 02	18 03					
Ebbsfleet International	d	17 13	17 14					17a36		17 43		17 44	18a06						18 13	18 14					
London Victoria ⊖	d			16 52			16 58								17 22							17 52			17 58
London Blackfriars ⊖	d																								
Elephant & Castle ⊖	d																								
Bromley South	d			17 09			17 19								17 39							18 09			18 19
St Mary Cray	d						17 25																		18 25
Swanley	d						17 29																		18 29
Farningham Road	d						17 34																		18 34
Longfield	d			17 22			17 38								17 52							18 22			18 38
Meopham	d			17 27			17 42								17 57							18 27			18 42
Sole Street	d						17 45																		18 45
London Charing Cross ⊖	d					16 39											17 09							17 39	
London Waterloo (East) ⊖	d					16 42											17 12							17 42	
London Cannon Street ⊖	d																								
London Bridge ⊖	d					16 47											17 17							17 47	
Dartford	d					17 25											17 55							18 25	
Greenhithe for Bluewater	d					17 30											18 00							18 30	
Gravesend	d	17 18	17 18			17 37				17 48		17 48					18 07		18 18	18 18				18 37	
Strood	d	17 28	17 28			17 48				17 58		17 58					18 18		18 28	18 28				18 48	
Rochester	d	17 33	17 33	17 39		17 52	17 56			18 03		18 03			18 09		18 22		18 33	18 33		18 39		18 52	18 56
Chatham	d	17 35	17 35	17 42		17 55	17 59			18 05		18 05			18 12		18 25		18 35	18 35		18 42		18 55	18 59
Gillingham (Kent)	d	17 40	17 40	17 47		17a59	18a03			18 10		18 10			18 17		18a29		18 40	18 40		18 47		18a59	19a03
Rainham (Kent)	d	17 45	17 45	17 51						18 15		18 15			18 21				18 45	18 45		18 51			
Newington	d			17 55																		18 55			
Sittingbourne	a	17 52	17 52	18 00						18 22		18 22			18 28				18 52	18 52		19 00			
	d	17 53	17 53	18 01					18 10	18 23		18 23			18 29			18 40	18 53	18 53		19 01			
Kemsley	d								18 15									18 45							
Swale	d								18 18									18 48							
Queenborough	d								18 22									18 52							
Sheerness-on-Sea	a								18 27									18 57							
Teynham	d														18 33										
Faversham	a	18 03	18 03	18 09						18 33		18 33			18 39				19 03	19 03		19 09			
	d			18 13	18 15										18 43	18 45						19 13	19 15		
Selling	d															18 50									
Canterbury East	d				18 29											18 59							19 29		
Bekesbourne	d															19 03									
Adisham	d															19 08									
Aylesham	d															19 10									
Snowdown	d															19 13									
Shepherds Well	d															19 17									
Kearsney	d															19 21									
Dover Priory	a				18 48											19 27							19 48		
Whitstable	d			18 21											18 51							19 21			
Chestfield & Swalecliffe	d														18 54										
Herne Bay	d			18 26											18 58							19 26			
Birchington-on-Sea	d			18 35											19 07							19 35			
Westgate-on-Sea	d														19 10										
Margate	d			18 41											19 14							19 41			
Broadstairs	d			18 46										18 53	19 20							19 46			
Dumpton Park	d													18 59	19 23										
Ramsgate	a			18 51										19 04	19 26							19 51			

A not from 1 September until 8 September B not 25 August C ⌶ to Margate

For further services to St Pancras International, Blackfriars and Elephant & Castle and onwards to Bromley South, St Mary Cray and Swanley please refer to table 52

Table 212

Saturdays

25 August to 8 September

London - Medway, Sheerness-on-Sea, Dover and Ramsgate

Network Diagram - see first Page of Table 212

Station		SE A	SE	SE B	SE A	SE		SE ■ C ⌶		SE	SE	SE B	SE A	SE ■		SE		SE ■	SE A	SE	SE B	SE A	SE	SE ■	
St Pancras International ⊖	d	18 18		18 25	18 25							18 55	18 55						19 18		19 25	19 25			
Stratford International ⊖	d	18 26		18 32	18 33							19 02	19 03						19 26		19 32	19 33			
Ebbsfleet International	d	18a36		18 43	18 44							19 13	19 14						19a36		19 43	19 44			
London Victoria ⊖	d							18 22						18 52				18 58						19 22	
London Blackfriars ⊖	d																								
Elephant & Castle ⊖	d																								
Bromley South	d							18 39						19 09				19 19						19 39	
St Mary Cray	d																	19 25							
Swanley	d																	19 29							
Farningham Road	d																	19 34							
Longfield	d							18 52						19 22				19 38						19 52	
Meopham	d							18 57						19 27				19 42						19 57	
Sole Street	d																	19 45							
London Charing Cross ⊖	d									18 09						18 39									
London Waterloo (East) ⊖	d									18 12						18 42									
London Cannon Street ⊖	d																								
London Bridge ⊖	d									18 17						18 47									
Dartford	d									18 55						19 25									
Greenhithe for Bluewater	d									19 00						19 30									
Gravesend	d			18 48	18 48					19 07		19 18	19 18			19 37					19 48	19 48			
Strood	d			18 58	18 58					19 18		19 28	19 28			19 48					19 58	19 58			
Rochester	d			19 03	19 03			19 09		19 22		19 33	19 33	19 39		19 52		19 56			20 03	20 03		20 09	
Chatham	d			19 05	19 05			19 12		19 25		19 35	19 35	19 42		19 55		19 59			20 05	20 05		20 12	
Gillingham (Kent)	d			19 10	19 10			19 17		19a29		19 40	19 40	19 47		19a59		20a03			20 10	20 10		20 17	
Rainham (Kent)	d			19 15	19 15			19 21				19 45	19 45	19 51							20 15	20 15		20 21	
Newington	d													19 55											
Sittingbourne	a			19 22	19 22			19 28				19 52	19 52	20 00							20 22	20 22		20 28	
	d		19 10	19 23	19 23			19 29			19 40	19 53	19 53	20 01						20 10	20 23	20 23		20 29	
Kemsley	d		19 15								19 45									20 15					
Swale	d		19 18								19 48									20 18					
Queenborough	d		19 22								19 52									20 22					
Sheerness-on-Sea	a		19 27								19 57									20 27					
Teynham	d							19 33																20 33	
Faversham	a			19 33	19 33			19 39				20 03	20 03	20 09							20 33	20 33		20 39	
	d							19 43	19 45					20 13	20 15									20 43	20 45
Selling	d								19 50																20 50
Canterbury East	d								19 59						20 29										20 59
Bekesbourne	d								20 03																21 03
Adisham	d								20 08																21 08
Aylesham	d								20 10																21 10
Snowdown	d								20 13																21 13
Shepherds Well	d								20 17																21 17
Kearsney	d								20 21																21 21
Dover Priory	a								20 27						20 48										21 27
Whitstable	d							19 51						20 21										20 51	
Chestfield & Swalecliffe	d							19 54																20 54	
Herne Bay	d							19 58						20 26										20 58	
Birchington-on-Sea	d							20 07						20 35										21 07	
Westgate-on-Sea	d							20 10																21 10	
Margate	d					19 53		20 14						20 41									20 53	21 14	
Broadstairs	d					19 59		20 20						20 46									20 59	21 20	
Dumpton Park	d							20 23																21 23	
Ramsgate	a					20 04		20 26						20 51									21 04	21 26	

A not 25 August B not from 1 September until 8 September C ⌶ to Margate

For further services to St Pancras International, Blackfriars and Elephant & Castle and onwards to Bromley South, St Mary Cray and Swanley please refer to table 52

Table 212

25 August to 8 September

London - Medway, Sheerness-on-Sea, Dover and Ramsgate

Network Diagram - see first Page of Table 212

Station		SE	SE	SE A	SE B	SE 1		SE	SE 1	SE B	SE A	SE B	SE	SE 1		SE	SE	SE A	SE B	SE 1	SE	SE B
St Pancras International 15 ⊖	d			19 55	19 55					20 18	20 25	20 25						20 55	20 55			21 18
Stratford International ⊖	d			20 02	20 03					20 26	20 32	20 33						21 02	21 03			21 26
Ebbsfleet International	d			20 13	20 14					20a36	20 43	20 44						21 13	21 14			21a36
London Victoria 15 ⊖	d					19 52			19 58					20 22						20 52		
London Blackfriars 3 ⊖	d																					
Elephant & Castle ⊖	d																					
Bromley South 4	d					20 09			20 19					20 39						21 09		
St Mary Cray	d								20 25											21 15		
Swanley 4	d								20 29											21 19		
Farningham Road	d								20 34											21 24		
Longfield	d					20 22			20 38					20 52						21 28		
Meopham	d					20 27			20 42					20 57						21 32		
Sole Street	d								20 45											21 35		
London Charing Cross 4 ⊖	d	19 09						19 39								20 09					20 39	
London Waterloo (East) 4 ⊖	d	19 12						19 42								20 12					20 42	
London Cannon Street 4 ⊖	d																					
London Bridge 4 ⊖	d	19 17						19 47								20 17					20 47	
Dartford 4	d	19 55						20 25								20 55					21 25	
Greenhithe for Bluewater	d	20 00						20 30								21 00					21 30	
Gravesend 4	d	20 07		20 18	20 18			20 37			20 48	20 48				21 07		21 18	21 18		21 37	
Strood 4	d	20 18		20 28	20 28			20 48			20 58	20 58				21 18		21 28	21 28		21 48	
Rochester 4	d	20 22		20 33	20 33	20 39		20 52	20 56		21 03	21 03		21 09		21 22		21 33	21 33	21 45	21 52	
Chatham 4	d	20 25		20 35	20 35	20 42		20 55	20 59		21 05	21 05		21 12		21 25		21 35	21 35	21 47	21 55	
Gillingham (Kent) 4	d	20a29		20 40	20 40	20 47		20a59	21a03		21 10	21 10		21 17		21a29		21 40	21 40	21 52	21a59	
Rainham (Kent)	d			20 45	20 45	20 51					21 15	21 15		21 21				21 45	21 45	21 56		
Newington	d					20 55														22 00		
Sittingbourne 4	a			20 52	20 52	21 00					21 22	21 22		21 28				21 52	21 52	22 05		
	d		20 40	20 53	20 53	21 01					21 23	21 23		21 29			21 40	21 53	21 53	22 06		
Kemsley	d		20 45														21 45					
Swale	d		20 48														21 48					
Queenborough	d		20 52														21 52					
Sheerness-on-Sea	a		20 57														21 57					
Teynham	d													21 33								
Faversham 2	a			21 03	21 03	21 09					21 33	21 33		21 39				22 03	22 03	22 14		
	d					21 13	21 15							21 43	21 45					22 15		
Selling	d														21 50							
Canterbury East 4	d						21a27								21 59					22a26		
Bekesbourne	d														22 03							
Adisham	d														22 08							
Aylesham	d														22 10							
Snowdown	d														22 13							
Shepherds Well	d														22 17							
Kearsney	d														22 21							
Dover Priory 4	a														22 27							
Whitstable	d					21 21								21 51								
Chestfield & Swalecliffe	d													21 54								
Herne Bay	d					21 26								21 58								
Birchington-on-Sea	d					21 35								22 07								
Westgate-on-Sea	d													22 10								
Margate 4	d					21 41							21 53	22 14								
Broadstairs	d					21 46							21 59	22 20								
Dumpton Park	d													22 23								
Ramsgate 4	a					21 51							22 04	22 26								

A not from 1 September until 8 September B not 25 August

For further services to St Pancras International, Blackfriars and Elephant & Castle and onwards to Bromley South, St Mary Cray and Swanley please refer to table 52

Table 212

25 August to 8 September

London - Medway, Sheerness-on-Sea, Dover and Ramsgate

Network Diagram - see first Page of Table 212

Station		SE A	SE B	SE 1		SE	SE	SE A	SE B	SE 1	SE	SE B	SE A	SE B	SE 1		SE	SE	SE A	SE B	SE 1	SE	SE B
St Pancras International 15 ⊖	d	21 25	21 25					21 55	21 55			22 17	22 25	22 25					22 55	22 55			23 18
Stratford International ⊖	d	21 32	21 33					22 02	22 03			22 25	22 32	22 33					23 02	23 03			23 26
Ebbsfleet International	d	21 43	21 44					22 13	22 14			22a35	22 43	22 44					23 13	23 14			23a36
London Victoria 15 ⊖	d			21 22						21 52					22 22						22 52		
London Blackfriars 3 ⊖	d																						
Elephant & Castle ⊖	d																						
Bromley South 4	d			21 39						22 09					22 39						23 09		
St Mary Cray	d									22 15											23 15		
Swanley 4	d									22 19											23 19		
Farningham Road	d									22 24											23 24		
Longfield	d			21 52						22 28					22 52						23 28		
Meopham	d			21 57						22 32					22 57						23 32		
Sole Street	d									22 35											23 35		
London Charing Cross 4 ⊖	d					21 09					21 39						22 09					22 39	
London Waterloo (East) 4 ⊖	d					21 12					21 42						22 12					22 42	
London Cannon Street 4 ⊖	d																						
London Bridge 4 ⊖	d					21 17					21 47						22 17					22 47	
Dartford 4	d					21 55					22 25						22 55					23 25	
Greenhithe for Bluewater	d					22 00					22 31						23 01					23 31	
Gravesend 4	d	21 48	21 48			22 07		22 18	22 18		22 40		22 48	22 48			23 10		23 18	23 18		23 40	
Strood 4	d	21 58	21 58			22 18		22 28	22 28		22 52		22 58	22 58			23 22		23 28	23 28		23 52	
Rochester 4	d	22 03	22 03	22 09		22 22		22 33	22 33	22 45	22 56		23 03	23 03	23 09		23 26		23 33	23 33	23 45	23 56	
Chatham 4	d	22 05	22 05	22 12		22 25		22 35	22 35	22 47	22 58		23 05	23 05	23 12		23 28		23 35	23 35	23 47	23 58	
Gillingham (Kent) 4	d	22 10	22 10	22 17		22a29		22 40	22 40	22 52	23a03		23 10	23 10	23 17		23a33		23 40	23 40	23 52	00a03	
Rainham (Kent)	d	22 15	22 15	22 21				22 45	22 45	22 56			23 15	23 15	23 21				23 45	23 45	23 56		
Newington	d									23 00											00 01		
Sittingbourne 4	a	22 22	22 22	22 28				22 52	22 52	23 05			23 22	23 22	23 28				23 52	23 52	00 06		
	d	22 23	22 23	22 29			22 40	22 53	22 53	23 06			23 23	23 23	23 29			23 32	23 53	23 53	00 07		
Kemsley	d						22 45											23 37					
Swale	d						22 48											23 40					
Queenborough	d						22 52											23 44					
Sheerness-on-Sea	a						22 57											23 49					
Teynham	d			22 33											23 33								
Faversham 2	a	22 31	22 31	22 39				23 01	23 01	23 14			23 31	23 31	23 39				00 01	00 01	00 16		
	d			22 43	22 45										23 43	23 45							
Selling	d				22 50											23 50							
Canterbury East 4	d				22 59											23 59							
Bekesbourne	d				23 03																		
Adisham	d				23 08																		
Aylesham	d				23 10											00 07							
Snowdown	d				23 13																		
Shepherds Well	d				23 17																		
Kearsney	d				23 21																		
Dover Priory 4	a				23 27											00 18							
Whitstable	d			22 51											23 51								
Chestfield & Swalecliffe	d			22 54											23 54								
Herne Bay	d			22 58											23 58								
Birchington-on-Sea	d			23 07											00 07								
Westgate-on-Sea	d			23 10											00 10								
Margate 4	d			23 14											00 14								
Broadstairs	d			23 20											00 20								
Dumpton Park	d			23 23											00 23								
Ramsgate 4	a			23 26											00 26								

A not from 1 September until 8 September B not 25 August

For further services to St Pancras International, Blackfriars and Elephant & Castle and onwards to Bromley South, St Mary Cray and Swanley please refer to table 52

Table 212

Sundays

until 22 July, 19 Aug and from 16 Sep

London - Medway, Sheerness-on-Sea, Dover and Ramsgate

Network Diagram - see first Page of Table 212

		SE	SE 1	SE	SE	SE	SE 1 A		SE	SE	SE	SE 1	SE	SE	SE	SE 1 A		SE	SE	SE	SE 1	SE	SE
St Pancras Internatnl 15 ⊖	d	13 25			13 55						14 25			14 55						15 25			15 55
Stratford International ⊖	d	13 32			14 02						14 32			15 02						15 32			16 02
Ebbsfleet International	d	13 43			14 13						14 43			15 13						15 43			16 13
London Victoria 15 ⊖	d		13 24				14 05					14 24				15 05					15 24		
London Blackfriars 3 ⊖	d																						
Ephant &Castle ⊖	d																						
Bromley South 4	d		13 44				14 22					14 44				15 22					15 44		
St Mary Cray	d		13 50									14 50									15 50		
Swanley 4	d		13 54									14 54									15 54		
Farningham Bad	d		13 59									14 59									15 59		
bngfield	d		14 03									15 03									16 03		
Meopham	d		14 07									15 07									16 07		
Sole Street	d		14 10									15 10									16 10		
London Charing Cross 4 ⊖	d			13 10					13 40				14 10					14 40				15 10	
London Waterloo (East) 4 ⊖	d			13 13					13 43				14 13					14 43				15 13	
London Cannon Street 4 ⊖	d																						
London Bridge 4 ⊖	d			13 18					13 48				14 18					14 48				15 18	
Dartford 4	d			13 55					14 25				14 55					15 25				15 55	
Greenhithe for Bluewater	d			14 00					14 30				15 00					15 30				16 00	
Gravesend 4	d	13 48		14 07	14 18				14 37		14 48		15 07	15 18				15 37		15 48		16 07	16 18
Strood 4	d	13 58		14 18	14 28				14 48		14 58		15 18	15 28				15 48		15 58		16 18	16 28
Bchester 4	d	14 03	14 20	14 23	14 33		14 46		14 52		15 03	15 20	15 23	15 33		15 46		15 52		16 03	16 20	16 23	16 33
Chatham 4	d	14 05	14 22	14 26	14 35		14 48		14 55		15 05	15 22	15 26	15 35		15 48		15 55		16 05	16 22	16 26	16 35
Gillingham (Kent) 4	d	14 10	14 27	14a30	14 40		14 53		15a02		15 10	15 27	15a30	15 40		15 53		16a02		16 10	16 27	16a30	16 40
Rinham (Kent)	d	14 15	14 31		14 45		14 57				15 15	15 31		15 45		15 57				16 15	16 31		16 45
Nwington	d		14 35									15 35									16 35		
Sittingbourne 4	a	14 22	14 40		14 52		15 04				15 22	15 40		15 52		16 04				16 22	16 40		16 52
	d	14 23	14 41		14 53		15 05			15 10	15 23	15 41		15 53		16 05			16 10	16 23	16 41		16 53
Kemsley	d									15 15									16 15				
Swale	d									15 18									16 18				
Qeenborough	d									15 22									16 22				
Sheerness-on-Sea	a									15 27									16 27				
Teynham	d		14 45									15 45									16 45		
Faversham 2	a	14 33	14 51		15 03		15 13				15 33	15 51		16 03		16 13				16 33	16 51		17 03
	d		14 52				15 17	15 19				15 52				16 17	16 19				16 52		
Selling	d							15 24									16 24						
Canterbury East 4	d		15a04					15 33				16a04					16 33				17a04		
Bekesbourne	d							15 37									16 37						
Adisham	d							15 42									16 42						
Aylesham	d							15 44									16 44						
Snowdown	d							15 47									16 47						
Shepherds W	d							15 51									16 51						
Kearsney	d							15 55									16 55						
Dover Priory 4	a							16 00									17 00						
Wstable	d						15 25									16 25							
Chestfield &Swalecliffe	d						15 28									16 28							
Herne Bay	d						15 32									16 32							
Birchington-on-Sea	d						15 41									16 41							
Wtgate-on-Sea	d						15 44									16 44							
Margate 4	d					14 53	15 48								15 53	16 48							
Broadstairs	d					14 59	15 54								15 59	16 54							
Dumpton Park	d						15 57									16 57							
Ramsgate 4	a					15 04	16 00								16 04	17 00							

A to Margate

For further services to St Pancras hternational, Blackfriars and Ephant & Castle and onwards to Bromley South, St Mary Cray and Swanley please refer to table 52

Table 212

Sundays

until 22 July, 19 Aug and from 16 Sep

London - Medway, Sheerness-on-Sea, Dover and Ramsgate

Network Diagram - see first Page of Table 212

		SE	SE 1 A		SE	SE	SE	SE 1	SE	SE	SE	SE 1 A		SE	SE	SE	SE 1	SE	SE	SE	SE 1 A		SE
St Pancras Internatnl 15 ⊖	d						16 25			16 55						17 25			17 58				
Stratford International ⊖	d						16 32			17 02						17 32			18 08				
Ebbsfleet International	d						16 43			17 13						17 43			18 19				
London Victoria 15 ⊖	d		16 05					16 24				17 05					17 24				18 05		
London Blackfriars 3 ⊖	d																						
Ephant &Castle ⊖	d																						
Bromley South 4	d		16 22					16 44				17 22					17 44				18 22		
St Mary Cray	d							16 50									17 50						
Swanley 4	d							16 54									17 54						
Farningham Bad	d							16 59									17 59						
bngfield	d							17 03									18 03						
Meopham	d							17 07									18 07						
Sole Street	d							17 10									18 10						
London Charing Cross 4 ⊖	d				15 40				16 10					16 40				17 10					17 40
London Waterloo (East) 4 ⊖	d				15 43				16 13					16 43				17 13					17 43
London Cannon Street 4 ⊖	d																						
London Bridge 4 ⊖	d				15 48				16 18					16 48				17 18					17 48
Dartford 4	d				16 25				16 55					17 25				17 55					18 25
Greenhithe for Bluewater	d				16 30				17 00					17 30				18 00					18 30
Gravesend 4	d				16 37		16 48		17 07	17 18				17 37		17 48		18 07	18 24				18 37
Strood 4	d				16 48		16 58		17 18	17 28				17 48		17 58		18 18	18 34				18 48
Bchester 4	d		16 46		16 52		17 03	17 20	17 23	17 33		17 46		17 52		18 03	18 20	18 23	18 39		18 46		18 52
Chatham 4	d		16 48		16 55		17 05	17 22	17 26	17 35		17 48		17 55		18 05	18 22	18 26	18 41		18 48		18 55
Gillingham (Kent) 4	d		16 53		17a02		17 10	17 27	17a30	17 40		17 53		18a02		18 10	18 27	18a30	18 46		18 53		19a02
Rinham (Kent)	d		16 57				17 15	17 31		17 45		17 57				18 15	18 31		18 51		18 57		
Nwington	d							17 35									18 35						
Sittingbourne 4	a		17 04				17 22	17 40		17 52		18 04				18 22	18 40		18 58		19 04		
	d		17 05			17 10	17 23	17 41		17 53		18 05			18 10	18 23	18 41		18 58		19 05		
Kemsley	d					17 15									18 15								
Swale	d					17 18									18 18								
Qeenborough	d					17 22									18 22								
Sheerness-on-Sea	a					17 27									18 27								
Teynham	d							17 45									18 45						
Faversham 2	a		17 13				17 33	17 51		18 03		18 13				18 33	18 51		19 07		19 13		
	d		17 17	17 19				17 52				18 17	18 19				18 52				19 17	19 19	
Selling	d			17 24									18 24									19 24	
Canterbury East 4	d			17 33				18a04					18 33				19a04					19 33	
Bekesbourne	d			17 37									18 37									19 37	
Adisham	d			17 42									18 42									19 42	
Aylesham	d			17 44									18 44									19 44	
Snowdown	d			17 47									18 47									19 47	
Shepherds W	d			17 51									18 51									19 51	
Kearsney	d			17 55									18 55									19 55	
Dover Priory 4	a			18 00									19 00									20 00	
Wstable	d		17 25									18 25									19 25		
Chestfield &Swalecliffe	d		17 28									18 28									19 28		
Herne Bay	d		17 32									18 32									19 32		
Birchington-on-Sea	d		17 41									18 41									19 41		
Wtgate-on-Sea	d		17 44									18 44									19 44		
Margate 4	d	16 53	17 48								17 53	18 48								18 53	19 48		
Broadstairs	d	16 59	17 54								17 59	18 54								18 59	19 54		
Dumpton Park	d		17 57									18 57									19 57		
Ramsgate 4	a	17 04	18 00								18 04	19 00								19 04	20 00		

A to Margate

For further services to St Pancras hternational, Blackfriars and Ephant & Castle and onwards to Bromley South, St Mary Cray and Swanley please refer to table 52

Table 212

London - Medway, Sheerness-on-Sea, Dover and Ramsgate

Sundays

until 22 July, 19 Aug and from 16 Sep

Network Diagram - see first Page of Table 212

		SE		SE	SE 1	SE	SE	SE	SE 1 A	SE	SE		SE	SE 1	SE	SE	SE	SE 1	SE	SE		SE	SE 1
St Pancras Internatnl 15 ⊖	d			18 25			18 55						19 25			19 55						20 25	
Stratford International ⊖	d			18 32			19 02						19 32			20 02						20 32	
Ebbsfleet International	d			18 43			19 13						19 43			20 13						20 43	
London Victoria 15 ⊖	d				18 24				19 05					19 24				20 05					20 24
London Blackfriars 3 ⊖	d																						
Elephant & Castle ⊖	d																						
Bromley South 4	d				18 44				19 22					19 44				20 22					20 44
St Mary Cray	d				18 50									19 50									20 50
Swanley 4	d				18 54									19 54									20 54
Farningham Road	d				18 59									19 59									20 59
Longfield	d				19 03									20 03									21 03
Meopham	d				19 07									20 07									21 07
Sole Street	d				19 10									20 10									21 10
London Charing Cross 4 ⊖	d					18 10				18 40					19 10				19 40				
London Waterloo (East) 4 ⊖	d					18 13				18 43					19 13				19 43				
London Cannon Street 4 ⊖	d																						
London Bridge 4 ⊖	d					18 18				18 48					19 18				19 48				
Dartford 4	d					18 55				19 25					19 55				20 25				
Greenhithe for Bluewater	d					19 00				19 31					20 01				20 31				
Gravesend 4	d			18 48		19 07	19 18			19 40			19 48		20 10	20 18			20 40			20 48	
Strood 4	d			18 58		19 18	19 28			19 52			19 58		20 22	20 28			20 52			20 58	
Rochester 4	d			19 03	19 20	19 23	19 33		19 46	19 56			20 03	20 20	20 26	20 33		20 46	20 56			21 03	21 20
Chatham 4	d			19 05	19 22	19 26	19 35		19 48	19 58			20 05	20 22	20 28	20 35		20 48	20 58			21 05	21 22
Gillingham (Kent) 4	d			19 10	19 27	19a30	19 40		19 53	20a03			20 10	20 27	20a33	20 40		20 53	21a03			21 10	21 27
Rainham (Kent)	d			19 15	19 31		19 45		19 57				20 15	20 31		20 45		20 57				21 15	21 31
Newington	d				19 35									20 35									21 35
Sittingbourne 4	a			19 22	19 40		19 52		20 04				20 22	20 40		20 52		21 04				21 22	21 40
	d	19 10		19 23	19 41		19 53		20 05		20 10		20 23	20 41		20 53		21 05		21 10		21 23	21 41
Kemsley	d	19 15									20 15									21 15			
Swale	d	19 18									20 18									21 18			
Queenborough	d	19 22									20 22									21 22			
Sheerness-on-Sea	a	19 27									20 27									21 27			
Teynham	d				19 45									20 45									21 45
Faversham 2	a			19 33	19 51		20 03		20 13				20 33	20 51		21 03		21 13				21 33	21 51
	d								20 17 20 19									21 17 21 19					
Selling	d								20 24									21 24					
Canterbury East 4	d								20 33									21 33					
Bekesbourne	d								20 37									21 37					
Adisham	d								20 42									21 42					
Aylesham	d								20 44									21 44					
Snowdown	d								20 47									21 47					
Shepherds Well	d								20 51									21 51					
Kearsney	d								20 55									21 55					
Dover Priory 4	a								21 00									22 00					
Whitstable	d								20 25									21 25					
Chestfield & Swalecliffe	d								20 28									21 28					
Herne Bay	d								20 32									21 32					
Birchington-on-Sea	d								20 41									21 41					
Westgate-on-Sea	d								20 44									21 44					
Margate 4	d							19 53	20 48								20 53	21 48					
Broadstairs	d							19 59	20 54								20 59	21 54					
Dumpton Park	d								20 57									21 57					
Ramsgate 4	a							20 04	21 00								21 04	22 00					

A to Margate

For further services to St Pancras International, Blackfriars and Elephant & Castle and onwards to Bromley South, St Mary Cray and Swanley please refer to table 52

Table 212

London - Medway, Sheerness-on-Sea, Dover and Ramsgate

Sundays

until 22 July, 19 Aug and from 16 Sep

Network Diagram - see first Page of Table 212

		SE	SE	SE	SE 1	SE	SE		SE	SE 1	SE	SE	SE 1	SE	SE	SE		SE 1	SE	SE	SE 1	SE	SE
St Pancras Internatnl 15 ⊖	d		20 55						21 25			21 55				22 25				22 55			23 25
Stratford International ⊖	d		21 02						21 32			22 02				22 32				23 02			23 32
Ebbsfleet International	d		21 13						21 43			22 13				22 43				23 13			23 43
London Victoria 15 ⊖	d				21 05					21 24			22 05					22 24			23 05		
London Blackfriars 3 ⊖	d																						
Elephant & Castle ⊖	d																						
Bromley South 4	d				21 22					21 44			22 22					22 44			23 22		
St Mary Cray	d									21 50								22 50					
Swanley 4	d									21 54								22 54					
Farningham Road	d									21 59								22 59					
Longfield	d									22 03								23 03					
Meopham	d									22 07								23 07					
Sole Street	d									22 10								23 10					
London Charing Cross 4 ⊖	d	20 10				20 40					21 10			21 40					22 10			22 40	
London Waterloo (East) 4 ⊖	d	20 13				20 43					21 13			21 43					22 13			22 43	
London Cannon Street 4 ⊖	d																						
London Bridge 4 ⊖	d	20 18				20 48					21 18			21 48					22 18			22 48	
Dartford 4	d	20 55				21 25					21 55			22 25					22 55			23 25	
Greenhithe for Bluewater	d	21 01				21 31					22 01			22 31					23 01			23 31	
Gravesend 4	d	21 10	21 18			21 40			21 48		22 10	22 18		22 40		22 48			23 10	23 18		23 40	23 48
Strood 4	d	21 22	21 28			21 52			21 58		22 22	22 28		22 52		22 58			23 22	23 28		23 52	23 58
Rochester 4	d	21 26	21 33		21 46	21 56			22 03	22 20	22 26	22 33	22 46	22 56		23 03		23 20	23 26	23 33	23 46	23 56	00 03
Chatham 4	d	21 28	21 35		21 48	21 58			22 05	22 22	22 28	22 35	22 48	22 58		23 05		23 22	23 28	23 35	23 48	23 58	00 05
Gillingham (Kent) 4	d	21a33	21 40		21 53	22a03			22 10	22 27	22a33	22 40	22 53	23a03		23 10		23 27	23a33	23 40	23 53	00a03	00 10
Rainham (Kent)	d		21 45		21 57				22 15	22 31		22 45	22 57			23 15		23 31		23 45	23 57		00 15
Newington	d									22 35								23 35					
Sittingbourne 4	a		21 52		22 04				22 22	22 40		22 52	23 04			23 22		23 40		23 52	00 04		00 22
	d		21 53		22 05		22 10		22 23	22 41		22 53	23 05		23 10	23 23		23 41		23 53	00 05		00 23
Kemsley	d						22 15								23 15								
Swale	d						22 18								23 18								
Queenborough	d						22 22								23 22								
Sheerness-on-Sea	a						22 27								23 27								
Teynham	d									22 45								23 45					
Faversham 2	a		22 03		22 13				22 33	22 51		23 03	23 13			23 31		23 51		00 03	00 13		00 33
	d				22 17 22 19								23 17 23 19								00 17		
Selling	d				22 24								23 24										
Canterbury East 4	d				22 33								23 33										
Bekesbourne	d				22 37								23 37										
Adisham	d				22 42								23 42										
Aylesham	d				22 44								23 44										
Snowdown	d				22 47								23 47										
Shepherds Well	d				22 51								23 51										
Kearsney	d				22 55								23 55										
Dover Priory 4	a				23 00								00 01										
Whitstable	d				22 25								23 25								00 25		
Chestfield & Swalecliffe	d				22 28								23 28								00 28		
Herne Bay	d				22 32								23 32								00 32		
Birchington-on-Sea	d				22 41								23 41								00 41		
Westgate-on-Sea	d				22 44								23 44								00 44		
Margate 4	d			21 53	22 48								23 48								00 48		
Broadstairs	d			21 59	22 54								23 54								00 54		
Dumpton Park	d				22 57								23 57								00 57		
Ramsgate 4	a			22 04	23 00								00 01								01 00		

For further services to St Pancras International, Blackfriars and Elephant & Castle and onwards to Bromley South, St Mary Cray and Swanley please refer to table 52

Table 212

Sundays

until 22 July, 19 Aug and from 16 Sep

London - Medway, Sheerness-on-Sea, Dover and Ramsgate

Network Diagram - see first Page of Table 212

		SE	SE	SE ■
St Pancras Internatnl ⊖	d		23 42	
Stratford International ⊖	d		23 49	
Ebbsfleet International	d		00 01	
London Victoria ⊖	d			23 45
London Blackfriars ⊖	d			
Ephant &Castle ⊖	d			
Bromley South	d			00 02
St Mary Cray	d			00 08
Swanley	d			00 12
Farningham Bad	d			00 17
bngfield	d			00 21
Meopham	d			00 25
Sole Street	d			00 28
London Charing Cross ⊖	d	23 10		
London Waterloo (East) ⊖	d	23 13		
London Cannon Street ⊖	d			
London Bridge ⊖	d	23 18		
Dartford	d	23 55		
Greenhithe for Bluewater	d	00 01		
Gravesend	d	00 10		
Strood	d	00 22		
Bchester	d	00 26		00 37
Chatham	d	00 28		00 40
Gillingham (Kent)	d	00a33		00 44
Binham (Kent)	d			00 49
Nwington	d			00 53
Sittingbourne	a			00 58
	d			00 58
Kemsley	d			
Swale	d			
Qenborough	d			
Sheerness-on-Sea	a			
Teynham	d			01 03
Faversham	a			01 09
	d			
Selling	d			
Canterbury East	d			
Bekesbourne	d			
Adisham	d			
Aylesham	d			
Snowdown	d			
Shepherds W	d			
Kearsney	d			
Dover Priory	a			
Wstable	d			
Chestfield &Swalecliffe	d			
Herne Bay	d			
Birchington-on-Sea	d			
Wstgate-on-Sea	d			
Margate	d			
Broadstairs	d			
Dumpton Park	d			
Ramsgate	a			

For further services to St Pancras hternational, Blackfriars and Ephant & Castle and onwards to Bromley South, St Mary Cray and Swanley please refer to table 52

Table 212

Sundays

29 July to 12 August

London - Medway, Sheerness-on-Sea, Dover and Ramsgate

Network Diagram - see first Page of Table 212

		SE ■	SE ■	SE	SE	SE	SE	SE	SE		SE ■	SE	SE ■	SE ■	SE	SE	SE	SE	SE		SE	SE	SE	SE
St Pancras Internatnl ⊖	d			23p51	23p56	00 01	00 06	00 11								00 16	00 21	00 27	00 31				00 36	00 41
Stratford International ⊖	d			00 01	00 05	00 11	00 16	00 20								00 26	00 30	00 36	00 41				00 46	00 50
Ebbsfleet International	d			00a10	00a16	00a21	00a26	00a31								00a36	00a41	00a47	00a51				00a56	01 03
London Victoria ⊖	d	22p22	22p52								23p22		23p52	00 10							00 35			
London Blackfriars ⊖	d																							
Ephant &Castle ⊖	d																							
Bromley South	d	22p39	23p09								23p39		00 09								00 55			
St Mary Cray	d		23p15										00 15								01 01			
Swanley	d		23p19										00 19								01 05			
Farningham Bad	d		23p24										00 24								01 10			
bngfield	d	22p52	23p28								23p52		00 28								01 14			
Meopham	d	22p57	23p32								23p57		00 32								01 18			
Sole Street	d		23p35										00 35											
London Charing Cross ⊖	d											23p09			23p39							00 18		
London Waterloo (East) ⊖	d											23p12			23p42							00 21		
London Cannon Street ⊖	d																							
London Bridge ⊖	d											23p17			23p47							00 26		
Dartford	d											23p55			00 25							01 06		
Greenhithe for Bluewater	d											23p59			00 31							01 10		
Gravesend	d											00 10			00 40							01 17		
Strood	d											00 22			00 52							01 29		
Bchester	d	23p09	23p45								00 09	00 26	00 45	00 49	00 56						01 29	01 33		
Chatham	d	23p12	23p47								00 12	00 28	00 47	00 52	00 58						01 31	01 35		
Gillingham (Kent)	d	23p17	23p52								00 17	00a36	00a52	00 57	01a06						01a38	01a44		
Binham (Kent)	d	23p21	23p56								00 21			01 01										
Nwington	d		00 01											01 05										
Sittingbourne	a	23p28	00 06								00 28			01 10										
	d	23p29	00 07						00 15		00 29			01 11										
Kemsley	d								00 20															
Swale	d								00 23															
Qenborough	d								00 27															
Sheerness-on-Sea	a								00 32															
Teynham	d	23p33									00 33			01 15										
Faversham	a	23p39	00 16								00 39			01 23										
	d	23p43 23p45									00 43			01 24										
Selling	d	23p50																						
Canterbury East	d	23p59																						
Bekesbourne	d																							
Adisham	d																							
Aylesham	d	00 07																						
Snowdown	d																							
Shepherds W	d																							
Kearsney	d																							
Dover Priory	a	00 18																						
Wstable	d	23p51									00 51			01 32										
Chestfield &Swalecliffe	d	23p54									00 54			01 35										
Herne Bay	d	23p58									00 58			01 39										
Birchington-on-Sea	d	00 07									01 07			01 48										
Wstgate-on-Sea	d	00 11									01 11			01 52										
Margate	d	00 15									01 15			01 56										
Broadstairs	d	00 20									01 20			02 01										
Dumpton Park	d	00 23									01 23			02 04										
Ramsgate	a	00 26									01 26			02 07										

For further services to St Pancras hternational, Blackfriars and Ephant & Castle and onwards to Bromley South, St Mary Cray and Swanley please refer to table 52

Table 212

Sundays

29 July to 12 August

London - Medway, Sheerness-on-Sea, Dover and Ramsgate

Network Diagram - see first Page of Table 212

	SE	SE	SE	SE	SE		SE	SE	SE	SE	SE	SE	SE	SE	SE		SE	SE	SE	SE	SE	SE	SE	SE
St Pancras Internatnl ⊖ d	00 46	00 51	00 57	01 01	01 06		01 11	01 17	01 21	01 27	01 32	01 38	01 44	01 55	02 02		02 32	03 02	03 32	04 02	04 32	05 02	05 32	06 04
Stratford International ⊖ d	00 56	01 00	01 06	01 11	01 16		01 20	01 26	01 30	01 36	01 42	01 48	01 54	02 04	02a08		02a38	03a08	03a38	04a08	04a38	05a08	05 42	06 14
Ebbsfleet International d	01a06	01a11	01 20	01a21	01 29		01 35	01 38	01a41	01 49	01a52	02 00	02 05	02 16									05 56	06a24
London Victoria ⊖ d																								
London Blackfriars ⊖ d																								
Elephant & Castle ⊖ d																								
Bromley South d																								
St Mary Cray d																								
Swanley d																								
Farningham Road d																								
Longfield d																								
Meopham d																								
Sole Street d																								
London Charing Cross ⊖ d																								
London Waterloo (East) ⊖ d																								
London Cannon Street ⊖ d																								
London Bridge ⊖ d																								
Dartford d																								
Greenhithe for Bluewater d																								
Gravesend d								01 43						02 21										
Strood d								01 54						02 31										
Rochester d								01 58					02 20	02 35										
Chatham d								02 01					02 23	02 38										
Gillingham (Kent) d								02 05					02 27	02 42										
Rainham (Kent) d								02 10					02 32	02 47										
Newington d																								
Sittingbourne a								02 17					02 39	02 54										
d								02 18					02 40	02 55										
Kemsley d																								
Swale d																								
Queenborough d																								
Sheerness-on-Sea a																								
Teynham d																								
Faversham a								02 26					02 48	03 03										
d																								
Selling d																								
Canterbury East d																								
Bekesbourne d																								
Adisham d																								
Aylesham d																								
Snowdown d																								
Shepherds Well d																								
Kearsney d																								
Dover Priory a																								
Whitstable d																								
Chestfield & Swalecliffe d																								
Herne Bay d																								
Birchington-on-Sea d																								
Westgate-on-Sea d																								
Margate d																								
Broadstairs d																								
Dumpton Park d																								
Ramsgate a																								

For further services to St Pancras International, Blackfriars and Elephant & Castle and onwards to Bromley South, St Mary Cray and Swanley please refer to table 52

Table 212

Sundays

29 July to 12 August

London - Medway, Sheerness-on-Sea, Dover and Ramsgate

Network Diagram - see first Page of Table 212

	SE		SE	SE	SE	SE	SE	SE	SE 1	SE	SE		SE	SE	SE	SE	SE	SE	SE	SE 1	SE 1		SE 1	SE
St Pancras Internatnl ⊖ d			06 32		06 52	07 04		07 11			07 18		07 25	07 32	07 39	07 46	07 52	08 04	08 11					
Stratford International ⊖ d			06 42		07 03	07 14		07 21			07 28		07 35	07 42	07 49	07 56	08 03	08 14	08 21					
Ebbsfleet International d			06a52		07a13	07 30		07a31			07 43		07a46	07a52	08 02	08a07	08a13	08 30	08a31					
London Victoria ⊖ d																							07 17	
London Blackfriars ⊖ d																								
Elephant & Castle ⊖ d																								
Bromley South d																							07 34	
St Mary Cray d																							07 40	
Swanley d																							07 44	
Farningham Road d																							07 49	
Longfield d																							07 53	
Meopham d																							07 57	
Sole Street d																							07 59	
London Charing Cross ⊖ d				06 39																				07 09
London Waterloo (East) ⊖ d				06 42																				07 12
London Cannon Street ⊖ d																								
London Bridge ⊖ d				06 47																				07 17
Dartford d				07 25																				07 55
Greenhithe for Bluewater d				07 30																				08 00
Gravesend d				07 37							07 48													08 07
Strood d				07 48							07 58													08 18
Rochester d				07 52							08 03												08 09	08 22
Chatham d				07 55							08 05												08 12	08 25
Gillingham (Kent) d				08a02							08 10												08 17	08a32
Rainham (Kent) d											08 15												08 21	
Newington d																							08 25	
Sittingbourne a											08 22												08 30	
d	06 10						07 10			08 10	08 23												08 31	
Kemsley d	06 15						07 15			08 15														
Swale d	06 18						07 18			08 18														
Queenborough d	06 22						07 22			08 22														
Sheerness-on-Sea a	06 27						07 27			08 27														
Teynham d																							08 35	
Faversham a											08 33												08 41	
d																				08 13	08 15		08 45	
Selling d																								
Canterbury East d																					08a26			
Bekesbourne d																								
Adisham d																								
Aylesham d																								
Snowdown d																								
Shepherds Well d																								
Kearsney d																								
Dover Priory a																								
Whitstable d																				08 21			08 53	
Chestfield & Swalecliffe d																							08 56	
Herne Bay d																				08 26			09 00	
Birchington-on-Sea d																				08 35			09 09	
Westgate-on-Sea d																							09 13	
Margate d									07 29											08 41			09 17	
Broadstairs d									07 34											08 46			09 22	
Dumpton Park d																							09 25	
Ramsgate a									07 39											08 51			09 28	

For further services to St Pancras International, Blackfriars and Elephant & Castle and onwards to Bromley South, St Mary Cray and Swanley please refer to table 52

Table 212

London - Medway, Sheerness-on-Sea, Dover and Ramsgate

Sundays

29 July to 12 August

Network Diagram - see first Page of Table 212

		SE ■	SE ■	SE	SE	SE	SE	SE	SE	SE	SE	SE	SE	SE ■	SE	SE ■	SE ■	SE	SE	SE	SE
St Pancras Internatnl ⊖	d					08 18	08 25	08 32	08 39	08 46	08 52	09 04	09 11							09 18	09 25
Stratford International ⊖	d					08 28	08 35	08 42	08 49	08 56	09 03	09 14	09 21							09 28	09 35
Ebbsfleet International	d					08 44	08a46	08a52	09 02	09a07	09a13	09 30	09a31							09 43	09a46
London Victoria ⊖	d		07 52											08 17			08 52				
London Blackfriars ⊖	d																				
Elephant & Castle ⊖	d																				
Bromley South	d		08 09											08 34			09 09				
St Mary Cray	d													08 40							
Swanley	d													08 44							
Farningham Road	d													08 49							
Longfield	d		08 22											08 53			09 22				
Meopham	d		08 27											08 57			09 27				
Sole Street	d													08 59							
London Charing Cross ⊖	d			07 39											08 09			08 39			
London Waterloo (East) ⊖	d			07 42											08 12			08 42			
London Cannon Street ⊖	d																				
London Bridge ⊖	d			07 47											08 17			08 47			
Dartford	d			08 25											08 55			09 25			
Greenhithe for Bluewater	d			08 30											09 00			09 30			
Gravesend	d			08 37		08 48									09 07			09 37		09 48	
Strood	d			08 48		08 58									09 18			09 48		09 58	
Rochester	d		08 39	08 52		09 03								09 09	09 22		09 39	09 52		10 03	
Chatham	d		08 42	08 55		09 05								09 12	09 25		09 42	09 55		10 05	
Gillingham (Kent)	d		08 47	09a02		09 10								09 17	09a32		09 47	10a02		10 10	
Rainham (Kent)	d		08 51			09 15								09 21			09 51			10 15	
Newington	d		08 55														09 55				
Sittingbourne	a		09 00			09 22								09 28			10 00			10 22	
	d		09 01		09 10	09 23								09 29			10 01		10 10	10 23	
Kemsley	d				09 15														10 15		
Swale	d				09 18														10 18		
Queenborough	d				09 22														10 22		
Sheerness-on-Sea	a				09 27														10 27		
Teynham	d													09 33							
Faversham	a		09 09			09 33								09 39			10 09			10 33	
	d	08 50	09 13 09 15											09 43		09 45	10 13 10 15				
Selling	d	08 55														09 50					
Canterbury East	d	09 04	09a26													09 59	10a26				
Bekesbourne	d	09 08														10 03					
Adisham	d	09 13														10 08					
Aylesham	d	09 15														10 10					
Snowdown	d	09 18														10 13					
Shepherds Well	d	09 22														10 17					
Kearsney	d	09 26														10 21					
Dover Priory	a	09 31														10 29					
Whitstable	d		09 21											09 51			10 21				
Chestfield & Swalecliffe	d													09 54							
Herne Bay	d		09 26											09 58			10 26				
Birchington-on-Sea	d		09 35											10 07			10 35				
Westgate-on-Sea	d													10 11							
Margate	d		09 41											10 15			10 41				
Broadstairs	d		09 46											10 20			10 46				
Dumpton Park	d													10 23							
Ramsgate	a		09 53											10 26			10 53				

For further services to St Pancras International, Blackfriars and Elephant & Castle and onwards to Bromley South, St Mary Cray and Swanley please refer to table 52

Table 212

London - Medway, Sheerness-on-Sea, Dover and Ramsgate

Sundays

29 July to 12 August

Network Diagram - see first Page of Table 212

		SE	SE	SE	SE	SE	SE	SE ■	SE	SE ■	SE ■ A ⌶	SE	SE	SE	SE	SE	SE	SE	SE	SE	SE
St Pancras Internatnl ⊖	d	09 32	09 39	09 46	09 52	10 04	10 11							10 18	10 25	10 32	10 39	10 46	10 52	11 04	11 11
Stratford International ⊖	d	09 42	09 49	09 56	10 03	10 14	10 21							10 28	10 35	10 42	10 49	10 56	11 03	11 14	11 21
Ebbsfleet International	d	09a52	10 02	10a07	10a13	10 30	10a31							10 44	10a46	10a52	11 02	11a07	11a13	11 30	11a31
London Victoria ⊖	d							09 17			09 52										
London Blackfriars ⊖	d																				
Elephant & Castle ⊖	d																				
Bromley South	d							09 34			10 09										
St Mary Cray	d							09 40													
Swanley	d							09 44													
Farningham Road	d							09 49													
Longfield	d							09 53			10 22										
Meopham	d							09 57			10 27										
Sole Street	d							09 59													
London Charing Cross ⊖	d								09 09			09 39									
London Waterloo (East) ⊖	d								09 12			09 42									
London Cannon Street ⊖	d																				
London Bridge ⊖	d								09 17			09 47									
Dartford	d								09 55			10 25									
Greenhithe for Bluewater	d								10 00			10 30									
Gravesend	d								10 07			10 37		10 48							
Strood	d								10 18			10 48		10 58							
Rochester	d							10 09	10 22		10 39	10 52		11 03							
Chatham	d							10 12	10 25		10 42	10 55		11 05							
Gillingham (Kent)	d							10 17	10a32		10 47	11a02		11 10							
Rainham (Kent)	d							10 21			10 51			11 15							
Newington	d										10 55										
Sittingbourne	a							10 28			11 00			11 22							
	d							10 29			11 01		11 10	11 23							
Kemsley	d												11 15								
Swale	d												11 18								
Queenborough	d												11 22								
Sheerness-on-Sea	a												11 27								
Teynham	d							10 33													
Faversham	a							10 39			11 09			11 33							
	d							10 43		10 45	11 13 11 15										
Selling	d									10 50											
Canterbury East	d									10 59	11a26										
Bekesbourne	d									11 03											
Adisham	d									11 08											
Aylesham	d									11 10											
Snowdown	d									11 13											
Shepherds Well	d									11 17											
Kearsney	d									11 21											
Dover Priory	a									11 29											
Whitstable	d							10 51			11 21										
Chestfield & Swalecliffe	d							10 54													
Herne Bay	d							10 58			11 26										
Birchington-on-Sea	d							11 07			11 35										
Westgate-on-Sea	d							11 11													
Margate	d							11 15			11 41										
Broadstairs	d							11 20			11 46										
Dumpton Park	d							11 23													
Ramsgate	a							11 26			11 53										

A ⌶ to Margate

For further services to St Pancras International, Blackfriars and Elephant & Castle and onwards to Bromley South, St Mary Cray and Swanley please refer to table 52

Sundays

29 July to 12 August

London - Medway, Sheerness-on-Sea, Dover and Ramsgate

Network Diagram - see first Page of Table 212

	SE ■	SE	SE ■	SE ■ A	SE	SE	SE	SE	SE	SE	SE	SE	SE	SE	SE ■	SE	SE ■	SE ■ A	SE	SE
St Pancras Internatnl ⊖ d							11 18	11 25	11 32	11 39	11 46	11 52	12 04	12 11						
Stratford International ⊖ d							11 28	11 35	11 42	11 49	11 56	12 03	12 14	12 21						
Ebbsfleet International d							11 43	11a46	11a52	12 02	12a07	12a13	12 30	12a31						
London Victoria ⊖ d	10 17			10 52											11 17			11 52		
London Blackfriars ⊖ d																				
Elephant & Castle ⊖ d																				
Bromley South d	10 34			11 09											11 34			12 09		
St Mary Cray d	10 40														11 40					
Swanley d	10 44														11 44					
Farningham Road d	10 49														11 49					
Longfield d	10 53			11 22											11 53			12 22		
Meopham d	10 57			11 27											11 57			12 27		
Sole Street d	10 59														11 59					
London Charing Cross ⊖ d		10 09			10 39											11 09			11 39	
London Waterloo (East) ⊖ d		10 12			10 42											11 12			11 42	
London Cannon Street ⊖ d																				
London Bridge ⊖ d		10 17			10 47											11 17			11 47	
Dartford d		10 55			11 25											11 55			12 25	
Greenhithe for Bluewater d		11 00			11 30											12 00			12 30	
Gravesend d		11 07			11 37		11 48									12 07			12 37	
Strood d		11 18			11 48		11 58									12 18			12 48	
Rochester d	11 09	11 22		11 39	11 52		12 03								12 09	12 22		12 39	12 52	
Chatham d	11 12	11 25		11 42	11 55		12 05								12 12	12 25		12 42	12 55	
Gillingham (Kent) d	11 17	11a32		11 47	12a02		12 10								12 17	12a32		12 47	13a02	
Rainham (Kent) d	11 21			11 51			12 15								12 21			12 51		
Newington d				11 55														12 55		
Sittingbourne a	11 29			12 00			12 22								12 28			13 00		
d	11 29			12 01		12 10	12 23								12 29			13 01		13 10
Kemsley d						12 15														13 15
Swale d						12 18														13 18
Queenborough d						12 22														13 22
Sheerness-on-Sea a						12 27														13 27
Teynham d	11 33														12 33					
Faversham a	11 39			12 09			12 33								12 39			13 09		
d	11 43		11 45	12 13 12 15											12 43		12 45	13 13 13 15		
Selling d			11 50														12 50			
Canterbury East d			11 59	12a26													12 59	13a26		
Bekesbourne d			12 03														13 03			
Adisham d			12 08														13 08			
Aylesham d			12 10														13 10			
Snowdown d			12 13														13 13			
Shepherds Well d			12 17														13 17			
Kearsney d			12 21														13 21			
Dover Priory a			12 29														13 29			
Whitstable d	11 51			12 21											12 51			13 21		
Chestfield & Swalecliffe d	11 54														12 54					
Herne Bay d	11 58			12 26											12 58			13 26		
Birchington-on-Sea d	12 07			12 35											13 07			13 35		
Westgate-on-Sea d	12 11														13 11					
Margate d	12 15			12 41											13 15			13 41		
Broadstairs d	12 20			12 46											13 20			13 46		
Dumpton Park d	12 23														13 23					
Ramsgate a	12 26			12 53											13 26			13 53		

A to Margate

For further services to St Pancras International, Blackfriars and Elephant & Castle and onwards to Bromley South, St Mary Cray and Swanley please refer to table 52

Sundays

29 July to 12 August

London - Medway, Sheerness-on-Sea, Dover and Ramsgate

Network Diagram - see first Page of Table 212

	SE	SE	SE	SE	SE	SE	SE	SE	SE ■	SE	SE ■	SE ■ A	SE	SE	SE	SE	SE	SE	SE	SE	SE
St Pancras Internatnl ⊖ d	12 18	12 25	12 32	12 39	12 46	12 52	13 04	13 11							13 18	13 25	13 32	13 39	13 46	13 52	14 04
Stratford International ⊖ d	12 28	12 35	12 42	12 49	12 56	13 03	13 14	13 21							13 28	13 35	13 42	13 49	13 56	14 03	14 14
Ebbsfleet International d	12 44	12a46	12a52	13 02	13a07	13a13	13 30	13a31							13 43	13a46	13a52	14 02	14a07	14a13	14 30
London Victoria ⊖ d									12 17			12 52									
London Blackfriars ⊖ d																					
Elephant & Castle ⊖ d																					
Bromley South d									12 34			13 09									
St Mary Cray d									12 40												
Swanley d									12 44												
Farningham Road d									12 49												
Longfield d									12 53			13 22									
Meopham d									12 57			13 27									
Sole Street d									12 59												
London Charing Cross ⊖ d										12 09			12 39								
London Waterloo (East) ⊖ d										12 12			12 42								
London Cannon Street ⊖ d																					
London Bridge ⊖ d										12 17			12 47								
Dartford d										12 55			13 25								
Greenhithe for Bluewater d										13 00			13 30								
Gravesend d	12 48									13 07			13 37		13 48						
Strood d	12 58									13 18			13 48		13 58						
Rochester d	13 03								13 09	13 22		13 39	13 52		14 03						
Chatham d	13 05								13 12	13 25		13 42	13 55		14 05						
Gillingham (Kent) d	13 10								13 17	13a32		13 47	14a02		14 10						
Rainham (Kent) d	13 15								13 21			13 51			14 15						
Newington d												13 55									
Sittingbourne a	13 22								13 29			14 00			14 22						
d	13 23								13 29			14 01		14 10	14 23						
Kemsley d														14 15							
Swale d														14 18							
Queenborough d														14 22							
Sheerness-on-Sea a														14 27							
Teynham d									13 33												
Faversham a	13 33								13 39			14 09			14 33						
d									13 43		13 45	14 13 14 15									
Selling d											13 50										
Canterbury East d											13 59	14a26									
Bekesbourne d											14 03										
Adisham d											14 08										
Aylesham d											14 10										
Snowdown d											14 13										
Shepherds Well d											14 17										
Kearsney d											14 21										
Dover Priory a											14 29										
Whitstable d									13 51			14 21									
Chestfield & Swalecliffe d									13 54												
Herne Bay d									13 58			14 26									
Birchington-on-Sea d									14 07			14 35									
Westgate-on-Sea d									14 11												
Margate d									14 15			14 41									
Broadstairs d									14 20			14 46									
Dumpton Park d									14 23												
Ramsgate a									14 26			14 53									

A to Margate

For further services to St Pancras International, Blackfriars and Elephant & Castle and onwards to Bromley South, St Mary Cray and Swanley please refer to table 52

Table 212

Sundays
29 July to 12 August

London - Medway, Sheerness-on-Sea, Dover and Ramsgate

Network Diagram - see first Page of Table 212

		SE	SE ■	SE	SE ■	SE ■ A ⌶		SE	SE	SE	SE	SE	SE	SE	SE	SE	SE	SE ■	SE	SE ■	SE ■ A ⌶	
St Pancras International ⊖	d	14 11								14 18	14 25	14 32	14 39	14 46	14 52	15 04	15 11					
Stratford International ⊖	d	14 21								14 28	14 35	14 42	14 49	14 56	15 03	15 14	15 21					
Ebbsfleet International	d	14a31								14 43	14a46	14a52	15 02	15a07	15a13	15 30	15a31					
London Victoria ⊖	d		13 17			13 52																
London Blackfriars ⊖	d																	14 17			14 52	
Elephant & Castle ⊖	d																					
Bromley South	d		13 34			14 09												14 34			15 09	
St Mary Cray	d		13 40															14 40				
Swanley	d		13 44															14 44				
Farningham Road	d		13 49															14 49				
Longfield	d		13 53			14 22												14 53			15 22	
Meopham	d		13 57			14 27												14 57			15 27	
Sole Street	d		13 59															14 59				
London Charing Cross ⊖	d			13 09				13 39											14 09			
London Waterloo (East) ⊖	d			13 12				13 42											14 12			
London Cannon Street ⊖	d																					
London Bridge ⊖	d			13 17				13 47											14 17			
Dartford	d			13 55				14 25											14 55			
Greenhithe for Bluewater	d			14 00				14 30											15 00			
Gravesend	d			14 07				14 37		14 48									15 07			
Strood	d			14 18				14 48		14 58									15 18			
Rochester	d		14 09	14 22		14 39		14 52		15 03								15 09	15 22		15 39	
Chatham	d		14 12	14 25		14 42		14 55		15 05								15 12	15 25		15 42	
Gillingham (Kent)	d		14 17	14a32		14 47		15a02		15 10								15 17	15a32		15 47	
Rainham (Kent)	d		14 21			14 51				15 15								15 21			15 51	
Newington	d					14 55															15 55	
Sittingbourne	a		14 28			15 00				15 22								15 29			16 00	
	d		14 29			15 01			15 10	15 23								15 29			16 01	
Kemsley	d								15 15													
Swale	d								15 18													
Queenborough	d								15 22													
Sheerness-on-Sea	a								15 27													
Teynham	d		14 33															15 33				
Faversham	a		14 39			15 09				15 33								15 39			16 09	
	d		14 43		14 45	15 13	15 15											15 43		15 45	16 13	16 15
Selling	d				14 50															15 50		
Canterbury East	d				14 59		15a26													15 59		16a26
Bekesbourne	d				15 03															16 03		
Adisham	d				15 08															16 08		
Aylesham	d				15 10															16 10		
Snowdown	d				15 13															16 13		
Shepherds Well	d				15 17															16 17		
Kearsney	d				15 21															16 21		
Dover Priory	a				15 29															16 29		
Whitstable	d		14 51			15 21												15 51			16 21	
Chestfield & Swalecliffe	d		14 54															15 54				
Herne Bay	d		14 58			15 26												15 58			16 26	
Birchington-on-Sea	d		15 07			15 35												16 07			16 35	
Westgate-on-Sea	d		15 11															16 11				
Margate	d		15 15			15 41												16 15			16 41	
Broadstairs	d		15 20			15 46												16 20			16 46	
Dumpton Park	d		15 23															16 23				
Ramsgate	a		15 26			15 53												16 26			16 53	

A ⌶ to Margate

For further services to St Pancras International, Blackfriars and Elephant & Castle and onwards to Bromley South, St Mary Cray and Swanley please refer to table 52

Table 212

Sundays
29 July to 12 August

London - Medway, Sheerness-on-Sea, Dover and Ramsgate

Network Diagram - see first Page of Table 212

		SE	SE	SE	SE	SE	SE	SE	SE	SE	SE	SE ■	SE	SE ■	SE ■ A ⌶		SE	SE	SE	SE	SE	SE	SE
St Pancras International ⊖	d			15 18	15 25	15 32	15 39	15 46	15 52	16 04	16 11								16 18	16 25	16 32	16 39	16 46
Stratford International ⊖	d			15 28	15 35	15 42	15 49	15 56	16 03	16 14	16 21								16 28	16 35	16 42	16 49	16 56
Ebbsfleet International	d			15 43	15a46	15a52	16 02	16a07	16a13	16 29	16a31								16 44	16a46	16a52	17 02	17a07
London Victoria ⊖	d											15 17			15 52								
London Blackfriars ⊖	d																						
Elephant & Castle ⊖	d																						
Bromley South	d											15 34			16 09								
St Mary Cray	d											15 40											
Swanley	d											15 44											
Farningham Road	d											15 49											
Longfield	d											15 53			16 22								
Meopham	d											15 57			16 27								
Sole Street	d											15 59											
London Charing Cross ⊖	d	14 39											15 09				15 39						
London Waterloo (East) ⊖	d	14 42											15 12				15 42						
London Cannon Street ⊖	d																						
London Bridge ⊖	d	14 47											15 17				15 47						
Dartford	d	15 25											15 55				16 25						
Greenhithe for Bluewater	d	15 30											16 00				16 30						
Gravesend	d	15 37		15 48									16 07				16 37		16 48				
Strood	d	15 48		15 58									16 18				16 48		16 58				
Rochester	d	15 52		16 03								16 09	16 22		16 39		16 52		17 03				
Chatham	d	15 55		16 05								16 12	16 25		16 42		16 55		17 05				
Gillingham (Kent)	d	16a02		16 10								16 17	16a32		16 47		17a02		17 10				
Rainham (Kent)	d			16 15								16 21			16 51				17 15				
Newington	d														16 55								
Sittingbourne	a			16 22								16 28			17 00				17 22				
	d		16 10	16 23								16 29			17 01			17 10	17 23				
Kemsley	d		16 15															17 15					
Swale	d		16 18															17 18					
Queenborough	d		16 22															17 22					
Sheerness-on-Sea	a		16 27															17 27					
Teynham	d											16 33											
Faversham	a			16 33								16 39			17 09				17 33				
	d											16 43		16 45	17 13	17 15							
Selling	d													16 50									
Canterbury East	d													16 59		17a26							
Bekesbourne	d													17 03									
Adisham	d													17 08									
Aylesham	d													17 10									
Snowdown	d													17 13									
Shepherds Well	d													17 17									
Kearsney	d													17 21									
Dover Priory	a													17 29									
Whitstable	d											16 51			17 21								
Chestfield & Swalecliffe	d											16 54											
Herne Bay	d											16 58			17 26								
Birchington-on-Sea	d											17 07			17 35								
Westgate-on-Sea	d											17 11											
Margate	d											17 15			17 41								
Broadstairs	d											17 20			17 46								
Dumpton Park	d											17 23											
Ramsgate	a											17 26			17 53								

A ⌶ to Margate

For further services to St Pancras International, Blackfriars and Elephant & Castle and onwards to Bromley South, St Mary Cray and Swanley please refer to table 52

Table 212

Sundays

29 July to 12 August

London - Medway, Sheerness-on-Sea, Dover and Ramsgate

Network Diagram - see first Page of Table 212

		SE	SE	SE	SE ■	SE	SE ■	SE ■ A 🛒		SE	SE	SE	SE	SE	SE	SE	SE	SE	SE	SE ■	SE	SE ■
St Pancras Internatnl ■ ⊖	d	16 52	17 04	17 11								17 18	17 25	17 32	17 39	17 46	17 52	18 04	18 11			
Stratford International ⊖	d	17 03	17 14	17 21								17 28	17 35	17 42	17 49	17 56	18 03	18 14	18 21			
Ebbsfleet International	d	17a13	17 30	17a31								17 43	17a46	17a52	18 02	18a07	18a13	18 30	18a31			
London Victoria ■ ⊖	d				16 17			16 52												17 17		
London Blackfriars ■ ⊖	d																					
Elephant & Castle ⊖	d																					
Bromley South ■	d				16 34			17 09												17 34		
St Mary Cray	d				16 40															17 40		
Swanley ■	d				16 44															17 44		
Farningham Road	d				16 49															17 49		
Longfield	d				16 53			17 22												17 53		
Meopham	d				16 57			17 27												17 57		
Sole Street	d				16 59															17 59		
London Charing Cross ■ ⊖	d					16 09				16 39											17 09	
London Waterloo (East) ■ ⊖	d					16 12				16 42											17 12	
London Cannon Street ■ ⊖	d																					
London Bridge ■ ⊖	d					16 17				16 47											17 17	
Dartford ■	d					16 55				17 25											17 55	
Greenhithe for Bluewater	d					17 00				17 30											18 00	
Gravesend ■	d					17 07				17 37		17 48									18 07	
Strood ■	d					17 18				17 48		17 58									18 18	
Rochester ■	d				17 09	17 22		17 39		17 52		18 03								18 09	18 22	
Chatham ■	d				17 12	17 25		17 42		17 55		18 05								18 12	18 25	
Gillingham (Kent) ■	d				17 17	17a32		17 47		18a02		18 10								18 17	18a32	
Rainham (Kent)	d				17 21			17 51				18 15								18 21		
Newington	d							17 55														
Sittingbourne ■	a				17 29			18 00				18 22								18 29		
	d				17 29			18 01			18 10	18 23								18 29		
Kemsley	d										18 15											
Swale	d										18 18											
Queenborough	d										18 22											
Sheerness-on-Sea	a										18 27											
Teynham	d				17 33															18 33		
Faversham ■	a				17 39			18 09				18 33								18 39		
	d				17 43		17 45	18 13	18 15											18 43		18 45
Selling	d						17 50															18 50
Canterbury East ■	d						17 59		18a26													18 59
Bekesbourne	d						18 03															19 03
Adisham	d						18 08															19 08
Aylesham	d						18 10															19 10
Snowdown	d						18 13															19 13
Shepherds Well	d						18 17															19 17
Kearsney	d						18 21															19 21
Dover Priory ■	a						18 29															19 27
Whitstable	d				17 51			18 21												18 51		
Chestfield & Swalecliffe	d				17 54															18 54		
Herne Bay	d				17 58			18 26												18 58		
Birchington-on-Sea	d				18 07			18 35												19 07		
Westgate-on-Sea	d				18 11															19 11		
Margate ■	d				18 15			18 41												19 15		
Broadstairs	d				18 20			18 46												19 20		
Dumpton Park	d				18 23															19 23		
Ramsgate ■	a				18 26			18 53												19 26		

A 🛒 to Margate

For further services to St Pancras International, Blackfriars and Elephant & Castle and onwards to Bromley South, St Mary Cray and Swanley please refer to table 52

Table 212

Sundays

29 July to 12 August

London - Medway, Sheerness-on-Sea, Dover and Ramsgate

Network Diagram - see first Page of Table 212

		SE ■ A 🛒		SE	SE	SE	SE	SE	SE	SE	SE	SE	SE	SE ■	SE	SE ■	SE ■ A 🛒		SE	SE	SE	SE	SE
St Pancras Internatnl ■ ⊖	d					18 18	18 25	18 32	18 39	18 46	18 52	19 04	19 11								19 18	19 25	19 32
Stratford International ⊖	d					18 28	18 35	18 42	18 49	18 56	19 03	19 14	19 21								19 28	19 35	19 42
Ebbsfleet International	d					18 43	18a46	18a52	19 02	19a07	19a13	19 30	19a31								19 43	19a46	19a52
London Victoria ■ ⊖	d	17 52												18 17			18 52						
London Blackfriars ■ ⊖	d																						
Elephant & Castle ⊖	d																						
Bromley South ■	d	18 09												18 34			19 09						
St Mary Cray	d													18 40									
Swanley ■	d													18 44									
Farningham Road	d													18 49									
Longfield	d	18 22												18 53			19 22						
Meopham	d	18 27												18 57			19 27						
Sole Street	d													18 59									
London Charing Cross ■ ⊖	d			17 39											18 09				18 39				
London Waterloo (East) ■ ⊖	d			17 42											18 12				18 42				
London Cannon Street ■ ⊖	d																						
London Bridge ■ ⊖	d			17 47											18 17				18 47				
Dartford ■	d			18 25											18 55				19 25				
Greenhithe for Bluewater	d			18 30											19 00				19 30				
Gravesend ■	d			18 37		18 48									19 07				19 37		19 48		
Strood ■	d			18 48		18 58									19 18				19 48		19 58		
Rochester ■	d	18 39		18 52		19 03								19 09	19 22		19 39		19 52		20 03		
Chatham ■	d	18 42		18 55		19 05								19 12	19 25		19 42		19 55		20 05		
Gillingham (Kent) ■	d	18 47		19a02		19 10								19 17	19a32		19 47		20a02		20 10		
Rainham (Kent)	d	18 51				19 15								19 21			19 51				20 15		
Newington	d	18 55															19 55						
Sittingbourne ■	a	19 00				19 22								19 28			20 00				20 22		
	d	19 01			19 10	19 23								19 29			20 01			20 10	20 23		
Kemsley	d				19 15															20 15			
Swale	d				19 18															20 18			
Queenborough	d				19 22															20 22			
Sheerness-on-Sea	a				19 27															20 27			
Teynham	d													19 33									
Faversham ■	a	19 09				19 33								19 39			20 09				20 33		
	d	19 13	19 15											19 43		19 45	20 13	20 15					
Selling	d		19 19															20 19					
Canterbury East ■	d		19 29													19a56		20 29					
Bekesbourne	d		19 33															20 33					
Adisham	d		19 38															20 38					
Aylesham	d		19 40															20 40					
Snowdown	d		19 43															20 43					
Shepherds Well	d		19 47															20 47					
Kearsney	d		19 51															20 51					
Dover Priory ■	a		19 57															20 57					
Whitstable	d	19 21												19 51			20 21						
Chestfield & Swalecliffe	d													19 54									
Herne Bay	d	19 26												19 58			20 26						
Birchington-on-Sea	d	19 35												20 07			20 35						
Westgate-on-Sea	d													20 11									
Margate ■	d	19 41												20 15			20 41						
Broadstairs	d	19 46												20 20			20 46						
Dumpton Park	d													20 23									
Ramsgate ■	a	19 51												20 26			20 51						

A 🛒 to Margate

For further services to St Pancras International, Blackfriars and Elephant & Castle and onwards to Bromley South, St Mary Cray and Swanley please refer to table 52

Table 212

Sundays
29 July to 12 August

London - Medway, Sheerness-on-Sea, Dover and Ramsgate

Network Diagram - see first Page of Table 212

		SE	SE	SE	SE	SE		SE ■	SE	SE ■	SE ■		SE	SE	SE	SE		SE	SE	SE	SE	SE	SE	SE ■	SE
St Pancras Internatnl ■ ⊖	d	19 39	19 46	19 52	20 04	20 11									20 18	20 25		20 32	20 39	20 46	20 52	21 04	21 11		
Stratford International ⊖	d	19 49	19 56	20 03	20 14	20 21									20 28	20 35		20 42	20 49	20 56	21 03	21 14	21 21		
Ebbsfleet International	d	20 02	20a07	20a13	20 30	20a31									20 43	20a46		20a52	21 02	21a07	21a13	21 30	21a31		
London Victoria ■ ⊖	d							19 17			19 52													20 17	
London Blackfriars ■ ⊖	d																								
Ephant &Castle ⊖	d																								
Bromley South ■	d							19 34			20 09													20 34	
St Mary Cray	d							19 40																20 40	
Swanley ■	d							19 44																20 44	
Farningham Bad	d							19 49																20 49	
bngfield	d							19 53			20 22													20 53	
Meopham	d							19 57			20 27													20 57	
Sole Street	d							19 59																20 59	
London Charing Cross ■ ⊖	d								19 09				19 39												20 09
London Waterloo (East) ■ ⊖	d								19 12				19 42												20 12
London Cannon Street ■ ⊖	d																								
London Bridge ■ ⊖	d								19 17				19 47												20 17
Dartford ■	d								19 55				20 25												20 55
Greenhithe for Bluewater	d								20 00				20 30												21 00
Gravesend ■	d								20 07				20 37		20 48										21 07
Strood ■	d								20 18				20 48		20 58										21 18
Bchester ■	d							20 09	20 22		20 39		20 52		21 03									21 09	21 22
Chatham ■	d							20 12	20 25		20 42		20 55		21 05									21 12	21 25
Gillingham (Kent) ■	d							20 17	20a32		20 47		21a02		21 10									21 17	21a32
Bnham (Kent)	d							20 21			20 51				21 15									21 21	
Nwington	d										20 55														
Sittingbourne ■	a							20 28			21 00				21 22									21 28	
	d							20 29			21 01			21 10	21 23									21 29	
Kemsley	d													21 15											
Swale	d													21 18											
Qeenborough	d													21 22											
Sheerness-on-Sea	a													21 27											
Teynham	d							20 33																21 33	
Faversham ■	a							20 39			21 09				21 33									21 39	
	d							20 43		20 45	21 13	21 15												21 43	
Selling	d											21 19													
Canterbury East ■	d									20a56		21 29													
Bekesbourne	d											21 33													
Adisham	d											21 38													
Aylesham	d											21 40													
Snowdown	d											21 43													
Shepherds W	d											21 47													
Kearsney	d											21 52													
Dover Priory ■	a											21 59													
Wstable	d							20 51			21 21													21 51	
Chestfield &Swalecliffe	d							20 54																21 54	
Herne Bay	d							20 58			21 26													21 58	
Birchington-on-Sea	d							21 07			21 35													22 07	
Wstgate-on-Sea	d							21 11																22 11	
Margate ■	d							21 15			21 41													22 15	
Broadstairs	d							21 20			21 46													22 20	
Dumpton Park	d							21 23																22 23	
Ramsgate ■	a							21 26			21 51													22 26	

For further services to St Pancras hternational, Blackfriars and Ephant & Castle and onwards to Bromley South, St Mary Cray and Swanley please refer to table 52

Table 212

Sundays
29 July to 12 August

London - Medway, Sheerness-on-Sea, Dover and Ramsgate

Network Diagram - see first Page of Table 212

		SE ■		SE ■	SE	SE	SE	SE ■	SE	SE	SE	SE		SE	SE	SE ■	SE	SE	SE	SE	SE	SE		SE	SE ■
St Pancras Internatnl ■ ⊖	d						21 18			21 25	21 32	21 39		21 46	21 52			22 04	22 11	22 18	22 25	22 32		22 39	
Stratford International ⊖	d						21 28			21 35	21 42	21 49		21 56	22 03			22 14	22 21	22 28	22 35	22 42		22 47	
Ebbsfleet International	d						21 43			21a46	21a52	22 02		22a07	22a13			22a24	22a31	22a40	22a46	22a52		22a57	
London Victoria ■ ⊖	d			20 52				21 22								21 52									
London Blackfriars ■ ⊖	d																								
Ephant &Castle ⊖	d																								
Bromley South ■	d			21 09				21 39								22 09									
St Mary Cray	d			21 15												22 15									
Swanley ■	d			21 19												22 19									
Farningham Bad	d			21 24												22 24									
bngfield	d			21 28				21 52								22 28									
Meopham	d			21 32				21 57								22 32									
Sole Street	d			21 35												22 35									
London Charing Cross ■ ⊖	d				20 39				21 09								21 39								
London Waterloo (East) ■ ⊖	d				20 42				21 12								21 42								
London Cannon Street ■ ⊖	d																								
London Bridge ■ ⊖	d				20 47				21 17								21 47								
Dartford ■	d				21 25				21 55								22 25								
Greenhithe for Bluewater	d				21 30				22 00								22 31								
Gravesend ■	d				21 37		21 48		22 07								22 40								
Strood ■	d				21 48		21 58		22 18								22 52								
Bchester ■	d			21 45	21 52		22 03	22 09	22 22							22 45	22 56								
Chatham ■	d			21 47	21 55		22 05	22 12	22 25							22 47	22 58								
Gillingham (Kent) ■	d			21 52	22a02		22 10	22 17	22a32							22 52	23a06								
Bnham (Kent)	d			21 56			22 15	22 21								22 56									
Nwington	d			22 00												23 00									
Sittingbourne ■	a			22 05			22 22	22 28								23 05									
	d			22 06		22 10	22 23	22 29								23 06									
Kemsley	d					22 15																			
Swale	d					22 18																			
Qeenborough	d					22 22																			
Sheerness-on-Sea	a					22 27																			
Teynham	d							22 33																	
Faversham ■	a			22 14			22 33	22 39								23 14									
	d	21 45		22 15				22 43																	22 45
Selling	d			22 19																					22 50
Canterbury East ■	d	21a56		22 29																					22 59
Bekesbourne	d			22 33																					23 03
Adisham	d			22 38																					23 08
Aylesham	d			22 40																					23 10
Snowdown	d			22 43																					23 13
Shepherds W	d			22 47																					23 17
Kearsney	d			22 51																					23 21
Dover Priory ■	a			22 57																					23 27
Wstable	d							22 51																	
Chestfield &Swalecliffe	d							22 54																	
Herne Bay	d							22 58																	
Birchington-on-Sea	d							23 07																	
Wstgate-on-Sea	d							23 11																	
Margate ■	d							23 15																	
Broadstairs	d							23 20																	
Dumpton Park	d							23 23																	
Ramsgate ■	a							23 26																	

For further services to St Pancras hternational, Blackfriars and Ephant & Castle and onwards to Bromley South, St Mary Cray and Swanley please refer to table 52

Table 212

Sundays
29 July to 12 August

London - Medway, Sheerness-on-Sea, Dover and Ramsgate

Network Diagram - see first Page of Table 212

		SE	SE	SE	SE	SE 1	SE	SE 1	SE	SE	SE	SE	SE	SE	SE	SE	SE 1	SE 1	SE	SE	SE	SE 1	SE
St Pancras Internatnl ⊖	d	22 46	22 52	23 04						23 11	23 16	23 21	23 26	23 32	23 36	23 41				23 47	23 51		
Stratford International ⊖	d	22 56	23 02	23 14						23 21	23 26	23 30	23 35	23 42	23 46	23 50				23 57	00 01		
Ebbsfleet International	d	23a07	23a12	23a24						23a31	23a37	23a41	23a45	23a52	23a56	00a01				00a07	00a10		
London Victoria ⊖	d					22 22		22 52										23 22				23 52	
London Blackfriars ⊖	d																						
Elephant & Castle ⊖	d																						
Bromley South	d					22 39		23 09										23 39				00 09	
St Mary Cray	d							23 15														00 15	
Swanley	d							23 19														00 19	
Farningham Road	d							23 24														00 24	
Longfield	d					22 52		23 28										23 52				00 28	
Meopham	d					22 57		23 32										23 57				00 32	
Sole Street	d							23 35														00 35	
London Charing Cross ⊖	d						22 09		22 39										23 09				23 39
London Waterloo (East) ⊖	d						22 12		22 42										23 12				23 42
London Cannon Street ⊖	d																						
London Bridge ⊖	d						22 17		22 47										23 17				23 47
Dartford	d						22 55		23 25										23 55				00 25
Greenhithe for Bluewater	d						23 01		23 31										23 59				00 31
Gravesend	d						23 10		23 40										00 10				00 40
Strood	d						23 22		23 52										00 22				00 52
Rochester	d					23 09	23 26	23 45	23 56									00 09	00 26			00 45	00 56
Chatham	d					23 12	23 28	23 47	23 58									00 12	00 28			00 47	00 58
Gillingham (Kent)	d					23 17	23a36	23 52	00a06									00 17	00a36			00 53	01a06
Rainham (Kent)	d					23 21		23 56										00 21				00 57	
Newington	d							00 01														01 01	
Sittingbourne	a					23 28		00 06										00 28				01 06	
	d				23 10	23 29		00 07										00 29				01 07	
Kemsley	d				23 15																		
Swale	d				23 18																		
Queenborough	d				23 22																		
Sheerness-on-Sea	a				23 27																		
Teynham	d					23 33												00 33				01 11	
Faversham	a					23 39		00 16										00 39				01 17	
	d					23 43											23 45	00 43					
Selling	d																23 50						
Canterbury East	d																23 59						
Bekesbourne	d																00 03						
Adisham	d																00 07						
Aylesham	d																00 10						
Snowdown	d																00 12						
Shepherds Well	d																00 16						
Kearsney	d																00 20						
Dover Priory	a																00 25						
Whitstable	d					23 51												00 51					
Chestfield & Swalecliffe	d					23 54												00 54					
Herne Bay	d					23 58												00 58					
Birchington-on-Sea	d					00 07												01 07					
Westgate-on-Sea	d					00 11												01 11					
Margate	d					00 15												01 15					
Broadstairs	d					00 20												01 20					
Dumpton Park	d					00 23												01 23					
Ramsgate	a					00 26												01 26					

For further services to St Pancras International, Blackfriars and Elephant & Castle and onwards to Bromley South, St Mary Cray and Swanley please refer to table 52

Table 212

Sundays
29 July to 12 August

London - Medway, Sheerness-on-Sea, Dover and Ramsgate

Network Diagram - see first Page of Table 212

		SE
St Pancras Internatnl ⊖	d	23 56
Stratford International ⊖	d	00 05
Ebbsfleet International	d	00a16
London Victoria ⊖	d	
London Blackfriars ⊖	d	
Elephant & Castle ⊖	d	
Bromley South	d	
St Mary Cray	d	
Swanley	d	
Farningham Road	d	
Longfield	d	
Meopham	d	
Sole Street	d	
London Charing Cross ⊖	d	
London Waterloo (East) ⊖	d	
London Cannon Street ⊖	d	
London Bridge ⊖	d	
Dartford	d	
Greenhithe for Bluewater	d	
Gravesend	d	
Strood	d	
Rochester	d	
Chatham	d	
Gillingham (Kent)	d	
Rainham (Kent)	d	
Newington	d	
Sittingbourne	a	
	d	
Kemsley	d	
Swale	d	
Queenborough	d	
Sheerness-on-Sea	a	
Teynham	d	
Faversham	a	
	d	
Selling	d	
Canterbury East	d	
Bekesbourne	d	
Adisham	d	
Aylesham	d	
Snowdown	d	
Shepherds Well	d	
Kearsney	d	
Dover Priory	a	
Whitstable	d	
Chestfield & Swalecliffe	d	
Herne Bay	d	
Birchington-on-Sea	d	
Westgate-on-Sea	d	
Margate	d	
Broadstairs	d	
Dumpton Park	d	
Ramsgate	a	

For further services to St Pancras International, Blackfriars and Elephant & Castle and onwards to Bromley South, St Mary Cray and Swanley please refer to table 52

Table 212

Sundays

26 August to 9 September

London - Medway, Sheerness-on-Sea, Dover and Ramsgate

Network Diagram - see first Page of Table 212

		SE 1	SE A	SE B	SE 1	SE	SE A	SE B	SE 1		SE	SE B	SE A	SE 1	SE 1	SE	SE A	SE B	SE B		SE	SE	SE B	SE B
St Pancras Internatnl 15 ⊖	d		22p55	22p55			23p25	23p25				23p55	23p55				00§12	00§12	00§15				00§48	01§48
Stratford International ⊖	d		23p02	23p03			23p32	23p33				00§03	00§02				00§19	00§20	00a21				00a54	01a54
Ebbsfleet International	d		23p13	23p14			23p43	23p44				00§13	00§13				00§31	00§32						
London Victoria 15 ⊖	d	22p22			22p52				23p22					23p52	00 10						00 35			
London Blackfriars 3 ⊖	d																							
Elephant & Castle ⊖	d																							
Bromley South 4	d	22p39			23p09				23p39					00 09							00 55			
St Mary Cray	d				23p15									00 15							01 01			
Swanley 4	d				23p19									00 19							01 05			
Farningham Road	d				23p24									00 24							01 10			
Longfield	d	22p52			23p28				23p52					00 28							01 14			
Meopham	d	22p57			23p32				23p57					00 32							01 18			
Sole Street	d				23p35									00 35										
London Charing Cross 4 ⊖	d										23p09					23p39						00 18		
London Waterloo (East) 4 ⊖	d										23p12					23p42						00 21		
London Cannon Street 4 ⊖	d																							
London Bridge 4 ⊖	d										23p17					23p47						00 26		
Dartford 4	d										23p55					00 25						01 06		
Greenhithe for Bluewater	d										23p59					00 31						01 10		
Gravesend 4	d		23p18	23p18			23p48	23p48			00 10	00§18	00§18			00 40						01 17		
Strood 4	d		23p28	23p28			23p58	23p58			00 22	00§28	00§28			00 52						01 29		
Rochester 4	d	23p09	23p33	23p33	23p45		00§03	00§03	00 09		00 26	00§32	00§33	00 45	00 49	00 56					01 29	01 33		
Chatham 4	d	23p12	23p35	23p35	23p47		00§05	00§05	00 12		00 28	00§35	00§35	00 47	00 52	00 58					01 31	01 35		
Gillingham (Kent) 4	d	23p17	23p40	23p40	23p52		00§10	00§10	00 17		00a33	00§39	00§40	00a52	00 57	01a03					01a35	01a41		
Rainham (Kent)	d	23p21	23p45	23p45	23p56		00§15	00§15	00 21			00§44	00§45		01 01									
Newington	d				00 01										01 05									
Sittingbourne 4	a	23p28	23p52	23p52	00 06		00§22	00§22	00 28			00§52	00§52		01 10									
	d	23p29	23p53	23p53	00 07	00 15	00§23	00§23	00 29			00§52	00§53		01 11									
Kemsley	d					00 20																		
Swale	d					00 23																		
Queenborough	d					00 27																		
Sheerness-on-Sea	a					00 32																		
Teynham	d	23p33							00 33						01 15									
Faversham 2	a	23p39	00§01	00§01	00 16		00§31	00§31	00 39			01§00	01§01		01 23									
	d	23p43 23p45							00 43						01 24									
Selling	d	23p50																						
Canterbury East 4	d	23p59																						
Bekesbourne	d																							
Adisham	d																							
Aylesham	d	00 07																						
Snowdown	d																							
Shepherds Well	d																							
Kearsney	d																							
Dover Priory 4	a	00 18																						
Whitstable	d	23p51							00 51						01 32									
Chestfield & Swalecliffe	d	23p54							00 54						01 35									
Herne Bay	d	23p58							00 58						01 39									
Birchington-on-Sea	d	00 07							01 07						01 48									
Westgate-on-Sea	d	00 10							01 10						01 51									
Margate 4	d	00 14							01 14						01 55									
Broadstairs	d	00 20							01 20						02 01									
Dumpton Park	d	00 23							01 23						02 04									
Ramsgate 4	a	00 26							01 26						02 07									

A not from 2 September until 9 September **B** not 26 August

For further services to St Pancras International, Blackfriars and Elephant & Castle and onwards to Bromley South, St Mary Cray and Swanley please refer to table 52

Table 212

Sundays

26 August to 9 September

London - Medway, Sheerness-on-Sea, Dover and Ramsgate

Network Diagram - see first Page of Table 212

		SE A	SE A	SE	SE	SE 1		SE	SE A	SE A	SE	SE 1	SE	SE	SE 1		SE	SE A	SE	SE 1	SE	SE	SE B
St Pancras Internatnl 15 ⊖	d	02§48	07§47						08§18	08§47								09§17					09§25
Stratford International ⊖	d	02a54	07§56						08§26	08§55								09§24					09§32
Ebbsfleet International	d		08a06						08a36	09a05								09a34					09§43
London Victoria 15 ⊖	d					07 24						08 05			08 24					09 05			
London Blackfriars 3 ⊖	d																						
Elephant & Castle ⊖	d																						
Bromley South 4	d					07 44						08 22			08 44					09 22			
St Mary Cray	d					07 50									08 50								
Swanley 4	d					07 54									08 54								
Farningham Road	d					07 59									08 59								
Longfield	d					08 03									09 03								
Meopham	d					08 07									09 07								
Sole Street	d					08 10									09 10								
London Charing Cross 4 ⊖	d																08 10				08 40		
London Waterloo (East) 4 ⊖	d																08 13				08 43		
London Cannon Street 4 ⊖	d																						
London Bridge 4 ⊖	d																08 18				08 48		
Dartford 4	d							07 55					08 25				08 55				09 25		
Greenhithe for Bluewater	d							08 01					08 31				09 00				09 30		
Gravesend 4	d							08 10					08 40				09 07				09 37		09§48
Strood 4	d							08 22					08 52				09 18				09 48		09§58
Rochester 4	d					08 20		08 26				08 46	08 56		09 20		09 23			09 46	09 52		10§03
Chatham 4	d					08 22		08 28				08 48	08 58		09 22		09 26			09 48	09 55		10§05
Gillingham (Kent) 4	d					08 27		08a33				08 53	09a03		09 27		09a30			09 53	10a02		10§10
Rainham (Kent)	d					08 31						08 57			09 31					09 57			10§15
Newington	d					08 35									09 35								
Sittingbourne 4	a					08 40						09 04			09 40					10 04			10§22
	d				08 10	08 41						09 05		09 10	09 41					10 05		10 10	10§23
Kemsley	d				08 15									09 15								10 15	
Swale	d				08 18									09 18								10 18	
Queenborough	d				08 22									09 22								10 22	
Sheerness-on-Sea	a				08 27									09 27								10 27	
Teynham	d					08 45									09 45								
Faversham 2	a					08 51						09 13			09 51					10 13			10§33
	d					08 52						09 17 09 19			09 52					10 17 10 19			
Selling	d											09 24								10 24			
Canterbury East 4	d					09a04						09 33			10a04					10 33			
Bekesbourne	d											09 37								10 37			
Adisham	d											09 42								10 42			
Aylesham	d											09 44								10 44			
Snowdown	d											09 47								10 47			
Shepherds Well	d											09 51								10 51			
Kearsney	d											09 55								10 55			
Dover Priory 4	a											10 00								11 00			
Whitstable	d											09 25								10 25			
Chestfield & Swalecliffe	d											09 28								10 28			
Herne Bay	d											09 32								10 32			
Birchington-on-Sea	d											09 41								10 41			
Westgate-on-Sea	d											09 44								10 44			
Margate 4	d			07 53							08 53	09 48							09 53	10 48			
Broadstairs	d			07 59							08 59	09 54							09 59	10 54			
Dumpton Park	d											09 57								10 57			
Ramsgate 4	a			08 04							09 04	10 00							10 04	11 00			

A not 26 August **B** not from 2 September until 9 September

For further services to St Pancras International, Blackfriars and Elephant & Castle and onwards to Bromley South, St Mary Cray and Swanley please refer to table 52

Table 212

Sundays

26 August to 9 September

London - Medway, Sheerness-on-Sea, Dover and Ramsgate

Network Diagram - see first Page of Table 212

Station	SE A		SE ■	SE	SE A	SE A	SE A	SE		SE ■ B ⊼	SE		SE	SE C	SE A	SE ■	SE	SE A	SE A	SE A	SE		SE ■ B ⊼
St Pancras International ⊖ d	09 26				09 47	09 55	10 14							10 28	10 28			10 47	10 52	11 18			
Stratford International ⊖ d	09 33				09 55	10 03	10 24							10 35	10 36			10 55	11 04	11 26			
Ebbsfleet International d	09 44				10a05	10a13	10a35							10 46	10 47			11a05	11a13	11a36			
London Victoria ⊖ d			09 24							10 05						10 24							11 05
London Blackfriars ⊖ d																							
Elephant & Castle ⊖ d																							
Bromley South d			09 44							10 22						10 44							11 22
St Mary Cray d			09 50													10 50							
Swanley d			09 54													10 54							
Farningham Road d			09 59													10 59							
Longfield d			10 03													11 03							
Meopham d			10 07													11 07							
Sole Street d			10 10													11 10							
London Charing Cross ⊖ d				09 10							09 40						10 10						
London Waterloo (East) ⊖ d				09 13							09 43						10 13						
London Cannon Street ⊖ d																							
London Bridge ⊖ d				09 18							09 48						10 18						
Dartford d				09 55							10 25						10 55						
Greenhithe for Bluewater d				10 00							10 30						11 00						
Gravesend d	09 48			10 07							10 37			10 51	10 51		11 07						
Strood d	09 58			10 18							10 48			11 01	11 01		11 18						
Rochester d	10 03		10 20	10 23						10 46	10 52			11 06	11 06	11 20	11 23						11 46
Chatham d	10 05		10 22	10 26						10 48	10 55			11 08	11 08	11 22	11 26						11 48
Gillingham (Kent) d	10 10		10 27	10a30						10 53	11a02			11 13	11 13	11 27	11a30						11 53
Rainham (Kent) d	10 15		10 31							10 57				11 18	11 18	11 31							11 57
Newington d			10 35													11 35							
Sittingbourne a	10 22		10 40							11 04				11 25	11 25	11 40							12 04
Sittingbourne d	10 23		10 41							11 05			11 10	11 25	11 25	11 41							12 05
Kemsley d													11 15										
Swale d													11 18										
Queenborough d													11 22										
Sheerness-on-Sea a													11 27										
Teynham d			10 45													11 45							
Faversham a	10 33		10 51							11 13				11 34	11 34	11 51							12 13
Faversham d			10 52						11 17	11 19						11 52						12 17	12 19
Selling d										11 24													12 24
Canterbury East d			11a04							11 33						12a04							12 33
Bekesbourne d										11 37													12 37
Adisham d										11 42													12 42
Aylesham d										11 44													12 44
Snowdown d										11 47													12 47
Shepherds Well d										11 51													12 51
Kearsney d										11 55													12 55
Dover Priory a										12 00													13 00
Whitstable d									11 25													12 25	
Chestfield & Swalecliffe d									11 28													12 28	
Herne Bay d									11 32													12 32	
Birchington-on-Sea d									11 41													12 41	
Westgate-on-Sea d									11 44													12 44	
Margate d								10 53	11 48												11 53	12 48	
Broadstairs d								10 59	11 54												11 59	12 54	
Dumpton Park d									11 57													12 57	
Ramsgate a								11 04	12 00												12 04	13 00	

A not 26 August

B ⊼ to Margate

C not from 2 September until 9 September

For further services to St Pancras International, Blackfriars and Elephant & Castle and onwards to Bromley South, St Mary Cray and Swanley please refer to table 52

Table 212

Sundays

26 August to 9 September

London - Medway, Sheerness-on-Sea, Dover and Ramsgate

Network Diagram - see first Page of Table 212

Station	SE	SE	SE A	SE B	SE ■	SE	SE A		SE A	SE A	SE		SE ■ C ⊼	SE	SE	SE A	SE B		SE ■	SE	SE A	SE A	SE B	SE A
St Pancras International ⊖ d			11 25	11 25			11 47		11 51	12 16						12 27	12 28				12 47	12 51	12 52	13 18
Stratford International ⊖ d			11 32	11 32			11 54		11 58	12 24						12 36	12 35				12 54	12 58	12 58	13 26
Ebbsfleet International d			11 44	11 43			12a04		12a08	12a34						12 47	12 46				13a04	13 13	13 13	13a36
London Victoria ⊖ d					11 24								12 05						12 24					
London Blackfriars ⊖ d																								
Elephant & Castle ⊖ d																								
Bromley South d					11 44								12 22						12 44					
St Mary Cray d					11 50														12 50					
Swanley d					11 54														12 54					
Farningham Road d					11 59														12 59					
Longfield d					12 03														13 03					
Meopham d					12 07														13 07					
Sole Street d					12 10														13 10					
London Charing Cross ⊖ d	10 40					11 10								11 40						12 10				
London Waterloo (East) ⊖ d	10 43					11 13								11 43						12 13				
London Cannon Street ⊖ d																								
London Bridge ⊖ d	10 48					11 18								11 48						12 18				
Dartford d	11 25					11 55								12 25						12 55				
Greenhithe for Bluewater d	11 30					12 00								12 30						13 00				
Gravesend d	11 37		11 48	11 48		12 07								12 37		12 51	12 51			13 07		13 18	13 18	
Strood d	11 48		11 58	11 58		12 18								12 48		13 01	13 01			13 18		13 28	13 28	
Rochester d	11 52		12 03	12 03	12 20	12 23							12 46	12 52		13 06	13 06		13 20	13 23		13 33	13 33	
Chatham d	11 55		12 05	12 05	12 22	12 26							12 48	12 55		13 08	13 08		13 22	13 26		13 35	13 35	
Gillingham (Kent) d	12a02		12 10	12 10	12 27	12a30							12 53	13a02		13 13	13 13		13 27	13a30		13 40	13 40	
Rainham (Kent) d			12 15	12 15	12 31								12 57			13 18	13 18		13 31			13 45	13 45	
Newington d					12 35														13 35					
Sittingbourne a			12 22	12 22	12 40								13 04			13 25	13 25		13 40			13 52	13 52	
Sittingbourne d		12 10	12 23	12 23	12 41								13 05		13 10	13 25	13 25		13 41			13 53	13 53	
Kemsley d		12 15													13 15									
Swale d		12 18													13 18									
Queenborough d		12 22													13 22									
Sheerness-on-Sea a		12 27													13 27									
Teynham d					12 45														13 45					
Faversham a			12 33	12 33	12 51								13 13			13 34	13 34		13 51			14 03	14 03	
Faversham d					12 52							13 17	13 19						13 52					
Selling d													13 24											
Canterbury East d					13a04								13 33						14a04					
Bekesbourne d													13 37											
Adisham d													13 42											
Aylesham d													13 44											
Snowdown d													13 47											
Shepherds Well d													13 51											
Kearsney d													13 55											
Dover Priory a													14 00											
Whitstable d												13 25												
Chestfield & Swalecliffe d												13 28												
Herne Bay d												13 32												
Birchington-on-Sea d												13 41												
Westgate-on-Sea d												13 44												
Margate d											12 53	13 48												
Broadstairs d											12 59	13 54												
Dumpton Park d												13 57												
Ramsgate a											13 04	14 00												

A not 26 August

B not from 2 September until 9 September

C ⊼ to Margate

For further services to St Pancras International, Blackfriars and Elephant & Castle and onwards to Bromley South, St Mary Cray and Swanley please refer to table 52

Table 212

London - Medway, Sheerness-on-Sea, Dover and Ramsgate

26 August to 9 September

Network Diagram - see first Page of Table 212

		SE	SE 1 A ⊥		SE	SE	SE B	SE C	SE 1	SE	SE C	SE B	SE C	SE C	SE	SE 1 A ⊥		SE	SE	SE B	SE C	SE 1
St Pancras Internatnl ⊖	d						13 25	13 25			13 48	13 55	13 55	14 18						14 25	14 25	
Stratford International ⊖	d						13 32	13 33			13 56	14 02	14 03	14 26						14 32	14 33	
Ebbsfleet International	d						13 43	13 44			14a06	14 13	14 14	14a36						14 43	14 44	
London Victoria ⊖	d		13 05						13 24							14 05						14 24
London Blackfriars ⊖	d																					
Elephant & Castle ⊖	d																					
Bromley South	d		13 22						13 44							14 22						14 44
St Mary Cray	d								13 50													14 50
Swanley	d								13 54													14 54
Farningham Road	d								13 59													14 59
Longfield	d								14 03													15 03
Meopham	d								14 07													15 07
Sole Street	d								14 10													15 10
London Charing Cross ⊖	d				12 40					13 10								13 40				
London Waterloo (East) ⊖	d				12 43					13 13								13 43				
London Cannon Street ⊖	d																					
London Bridge ⊖	d				12 48					13 18								13 48				
Dartford	d				13 25					13 55								14 25				
Greenhithe for Bluewater	d				13 30					14 00								14 30				
Gravesend	d				13 37		13 48	13 48		14 07		14 18	14 18					14 37		14 48	14 48	
Strood	d				13 48		13 58	13 58		14 18		14 28	14 28					14 48		14 58	14 58	
Rochester	d		13 46		13 52		14 03	14 03	14 20	14 23		14 33	14 33			14 46		14 52		15 03	15 03	15 20
Chatham	d		13 48		13 55		14 05	14 05	14 22	14 26		14 35	14 35			14 48		14 55		15 05	15 05	15 22
Gillingham (Kent)	d		13 53		14a02		14 10	14 10	14 27	14a30		14 40	14 40			14 53		15a02		15 10	15 10	15 27
Rainham (Kent)	d		13 57				14 15	14 15	14 31			14 45	14 45			14 57				15 15	15 15	15 31
Newington	d								14 35													15 35
Sittingbourne	a		14 04				14 22	14 22	14 40			14 52	14 52			15 04				15 22	15 22	15 40
	d		14 05			14 10	14 23	14 23	14 41			14 53	14 53			15 05			15 10	15 23	15 23	15 41
Kemsley	d					14 15													15 15			
Swale	d					14 18													15 18			
Queenborough	d					14 22													15 22			
Sheerness-on-Sea	a					14 27													15 27			
Teynham	d								14 45													15 45
Faversham	a		14 13				14 33	14 33	14 51			15 03	15 03			15 13				15 33	15 33	15 51
	d		14 17	14 19					14 52							15 17	15 19					15 52
Selling	d			14 24													15 24					
Canterbury East	d			14 33					15a04								15 33					16a04
Bekesbourne	d			14 37													15 37					
Adisham	d			14 42													15 42					
Aylesham	d			14 44													15 44					
Snowdown	d			14 47													15 47					
Shepherds Well	d			14 51													15 51					
Kearsney	d			14 55													15 55					
Dover Priory	a			15 00													16 00					
Whitstable	d		14 25													15 25						
Chestfield & Swalecliffe	d		14 28													15 28						
Herne Bay	d		14 32													15 32						
Birchington-on-Sea	d		14 41													15 41						
Westgate-on-Sea	d		14 44													15 44						
Margate	d	13 53	14 48												14 53	15 48						
Broadstairs	d	13 59	14 54												14 59	15 54						
Dumpton Park	d		14 57													15 57						
Ramsgate	a	14 04	15 00												15 04	16 00						

A ⊥ to Margate

B not from 2 September until 9 September

C not 26 August

For further services to St Pancras International, Blackfriars and Elephant & Castle and onwards to Bromley South, St Mary Cray and Swanley please refer to table 52

Table 212

London - Medway, Sheerness-on-Sea, Dover and Ramsgate

26 August to 9 September

Network Diagram - see first Page of Table 212

		SE	SE A	SE B	SE A	SE A	SE	SE 1 C ⊥		SE	SE	SE B	SE A	SE 1	SE	SE A	SE B	SE A	SE A	SE	SE 1 C ⊥		SE
St Pancras Internatnl ⊖	d		14 48	14 55	14 55	15 18						15 25	15 25			15 48	15 55	15 55	16 12				
Stratford International ⊖	d		14 56	15 02	15 03	15 26						15 32	15 33			15 56	16 02	16 03	16 22				
Ebbsfleet International	d		15a06	15 13	15 14	15a36						15 43	15 44			16a06	16 13	16 14	16a32				
London Victoria ⊖	d							15 05						15 24							16 05		
London Blackfriars ⊖	d																						
Elephant & Castle ⊖	d																						
Bromley South	d							15 22						15 44							16 22		
St Mary Cray	d													15 50									
Swanley	d													15 54									
Farningham Road	d													15 59									
Longfield	d													16 03									
Meopham	d													16 07									
Sole Street	d													16 10									
London Charing Cross ⊖	d	14 10								14 40					15 10								15 40
London Waterloo (East) ⊖	d	14 13								14 43					15 13								15 43
London Cannon Street ⊖	d																						
London Bridge ⊖	d	14 18								14 48					15 18								15 48
Dartford	d	14 55								15 25					15 55								16 25
Greenhithe for Bluewater	d	15 00								15 30					16 00								16 30
Gravesend	d	15 07		15 18	15 18					15 37		15 48	15 48		16 07		16 18	16 18					16 37
Strood	d	15 18		15 28	15 28					15 48		15 58	15 58		16 18		16 28	16 28					16 48
Rochester	d	15 23		15 33	15 33			15 46		15 52		16 03	16 03	16 20	16 23		16 33	16 33			16 46		16 52
Chatham	d	15 26		15 35	15 35			15 48		15 55		16 05	16 05	16 22	16 26		16 35	16 35			16 48		16 55
Gillingham (Kent)	d	15a30		15 40	15 40			15 53		16a02		16 10	16 10	16 27	16a30		16 40	16 40			16 53		17a02
Rainham (Kent)	d			15 45	15 45			15 57				16 15	16 15	16 31			16 45	16 45			16 57		
Newington	d													16 35									
Sittingbourne	a			15 52	15 52			16 04				16 22	16 22	16 40			16 52	16 52			17 04		
	d			15 53	15 53			16 05			16 10	16 23	16 23	16 41			16 53	16 53			17 05		
Kemsley	d										16 15												
Swale	d										16 18												
Queenborough	d										16 22												
Sheerness-on-Sea	a										16 27												
Teynham	d													16 45									
Faversham	a			16 03	16 03			16 13				16 33	16 33	16 51			17 03	17 03			17 13		
	d							16 17	16 19					16 52							17 17	17 19	
Selling	d								16 24													17 24	
Canterbury East	d								16 33					17a04								17 33	
Bekesbourne	d								16 37													17 37	
Adisham	d								16 42													17 42	
Aylesham	d								16 44													17 44	
Snowdown	d								16 47													17 47	
Shepherds Well	d								16 51													17 51	
Kearsney	d								16 55													17 55	
Dover Priory	a								17 00													18 00	
Whitstable	d							16 25													17 25		
Chestfield & Swalecliffe	d							16 28													17 28		
Herne Bay	d							16 32													17 32		
Birchington-on-Sea	d							16 41													17 41		
Westgate-on-Sea	d							16 44													17 44		
Margate	d						15 53	16 48												16 53	17 48		
Broadstairs	d						15 59	16 54												16 59	17 54		
Dumpton Park	d							16 57													17 57		
Ramsgate	a						16 04	17 00												17 04	18 00		

A not 26 August

B not from 2 September until 9 September

C ⊥ to Margate

For further services to St Pancras International, Blackfriars and Elephant & Castle and onwards to Bromley South, St Mary Cray and Swanley please refer to table 52

Table 212

Sundays
26 August to 9 September

London - Medway, Sheerness-on-Sea, Dover and Ramsgate

Network Diagram - see first Page of Table 212

		SE	SE A	SE B	SE ■	SE	SE B	SE A	SE B	SE B	SE	SE ■ C ♖		SE	SE	SE A	SE B	SE ■	SE	SE B	SE B	SE A	SE B
St Pancras Internatnl ⊖	d		16 25	16 25			16 48	16 55	16 55	17 18						17 25	17 25			17 45	17 48	17 58	18 18
Stratford International ⊖	d		16 32	16 33			16 56	17 02	17 03	17 26						17 32	17 33			17 52	17 55	18 08	18 26
Ebbsfleet International	d		16 43	16 44			17a06	17 13	17 14	17a36						17 43	17 44			18a04	18 14	18 19	18a36
London Victoria ⊖	d				16 24							17 05						17 24					
London Blackfriars ⊖	d																						
Elephant & Castle ⊖	d																						
Bromley South	d				16 44							17 22						17 44					
St Mary Cray	d				16 50													17 50					
Swanley	d				16 54													17 54					
Farningham Road	d				16 59													17 59					
Longfield	d				17 03													18 03					
Meopham	d				17 07													18 07					
Sole Street	d				17 10													18 10					
London Charing Cross ⊖	d					16 10								16 40					17 10				
London Waterloo (East) ⊖	d					16 13								16 43					17 13				
London Cannon Street ⊖	d																						
London Bridge ⊖	d					16 18								16 48					17 18				
Dartford	d					16 55								17 25					17 55				
Greenhithe for Bluewater	d					17 00								17 30					18 00				
Gravesend	d		16 48	16 48		17 07		17 18	17 18					17 37		17 48	17 48		18 07		18 19	18 24	
Strood	d		16 58	16 58		17 18		17 28	17 28					17 48		17 58	17 58		18 18		18 29	18 34	
Rochester	d		17 03	17 03	17 20	17 23		17 33	17 33			17 46		17 52		18 03	18 03	18 20	18 23		18 34	18 39	
Chatham	d		17 05	17 05	17 22	17 26		17 35	17 35			17 48		17 55		18 05	18 05	18 22	18 26		18 36	18 41	
Gillingham (Kent)	d		17 10	17 10	17 27	17a30		17 40	17 40			17 53		18a02		18 10	18 10	18 27	18a30		18 41	18 46	
Rainham (Kent)	d		17 15	17 15	17 31			17 45	17 45			17 57				18 15	18 15	18 31			18 46	18 51	
Newington	d				17 35													18 35					
Sittingbourne	a		17 22	17 22	17 40			17 52	17 52			18 04				18 22	18 22	18 40			18 53	18 58	
	d	17 10	17 23	17 23	17 41			17 53	17 53			18 05			18 10	18 23	18 23	18 41			18 54	18 58	
Kemsley	d	17 15													18 15								
Swale	d	17 18													18 18								
Queenborough	d	17 22													18 22								
Sheerness-on-Sea	a	17 27													18 27								
Teynham	d				17 45													18 45					
Faversham	a		17 33	17 33	17 51			18 03	18 03			18 13				18 33	18 33	18 51			19 04	19 07	
	d				17 52							18 17	18 19					18 52					
Selling	d												18 24										
Canterbury East	d				18a04								18 33					19a04					
Bekesbourne	d												18 37										
Adisham	d												18 42										
Aylesham	d												18 44										
Snowdown	d												18 47										
Shepherds Well	d												18 51										
Kearsney	d												18 55										
Dover Priory	a												19 00										
Whitstable	d											18 25											
Chestfield & Swalecliffe	d											18 28											
Herne Bay	d											18 32											
Birchington-on-Sea	d											18 41											
Westgate-on-Sea	d											18 44											
Margate	d										17 53	18 48											
Broadstairs	d										17 59	18 54											
Dumpton Park	d											18 57											
Ramsgate	a										18 04	19 00											

A not from 2 September until 9 September **B** not 26 August **C** ♖ to Margate

For further services to St Pancras International, Blackfriars and Elephant & Castle and onwards to Bromley South, St Mary Cray and Swanley please refer to table 52

Table 212

Sundays
26 August to 9 September

London - Medway, Sheerness-on-Sea, Dover and Ramsgate

Network Diagram - see first Page of Table 212

		SE	SE ■ A ♖		SE	SE	SE B	SE C	SE ■	SE	SE B	SE C	SE C	SE	SE ■ A ♖		SE	SE	SE B	SE C	SE ■	SE
St Pancras Internatnl ⊖	d						18 25	18 27			18 55	18 55	19 18						19 25	19 25		
Stratford International ⊖	d						18 32	18 35			19 02	19 03	19 26						19 32	19 33		
Ebbsfleet International	d						18 43	18 46			19 13	19 14	19a36						19 43	19 44		
London Victoria ⊖	d		18 05						18 24						19 05						19 24	
London Blackfriars ⊖	d																					
Elephant & Castle ⊖	d																					
Bromley South	d		18 22						18 44						19 22						19 44	
St Mary Cray	d								18 50												19 50	
Swanley	d								18 54												19 54	
Farningham Road	d								18 59												19 59	
Longfield	d								19 03												20 03	
Meopham	d								19 07												20 07	
Sole Street	d								19 10												20 10	
London Charing Cross ⊖	d				17 40					18 10							18 40					19 10
London Waterloo (East) ⊖	d				17 43					18 13							18 43					19 13
London Cannon Street ⊖	d																					
London Bridge ⊖	d				17 48					18 18							18 48					19 18
Dartford	d				18 25					18 55							19 25					19 55
Greenhithe for Bluewater	d				18 30					19 00							19 31					20 01
Gravesend	d				18 37		18 48	18 51		19 07	19 18	19 18					19 40		19 48	19 48		20 10
Strood	d				18 48		18 58	19 01		19 18	19 28	19 28					19 52		19 58	19 58		20 22
Rochester	d		18 46		18 52		19 03	19 06	19 20	19 23	19 33	19 33			19 46		19 56		20 03	20 03	20 20	20 26
Chatham	d		18 48		18 55		19 05	19 08	19 22	19 26	19 35	19 35			19 48		19 58		20 05	20 05	20 22	20 28
Gillingham (Kent)	d		18 53		19a02		19 10	19 13	19 27	19a30	19 40	19 40			19 53		20a03		20 10	20 10	20 27	20a33
Rainham (Kent)	d		18 57				19 15	19 18	19 31		19 45	19 45			19 57				20 15	20 15	20 31	
Newington	d								19 35												20 35	
Sittingbourne	a		19 04				19 22	19 25	19 40		19 52	19 52			20 04				20 22	20 22	20 40	
	d		19 05			19 10	19 23	19 25	19 41		19 53	19 53			20 05			20 10	20 23	20 23	20 41	
Kemsley	d					19 15												20 15				
Swale	d					19 18												20 18				
Queenborough	d					19 22												20 22				
Sheerness-on-Sea	a					19 27												20 27				
Teynham	d								19 45												20 45	
Faversham	a		19 13				19 33	19 34	19 51		20 03	20 03			20 13				20 33	20 33	20 51	
	d		19 17	19 19											20 17	20 19						
Selling	d			19 24												20 24						
Canterbury East	d			19 33												20 33						
Bekesbourne	d			19 37												20 37						
Adisham	d			19 42												20 42						
Aylesham	d			19 44												20 44						
Snowdown	d			19 47												20 47						
Shepherds Well	d			19 51												20 51						
Kearsney	d			19 55												20 55						
Dover Priory	a			20 00												21 00						
Whitstable	d		19 25												20 25							
Chestfield & Swalecliffe	d		19 28												20 28							
Herne Bay	d		19 32												20 32							
Birchington-on-Sea	d		19 41												20 41							
Westgate-on-Sea	d		19 44												20 44							
Margate	d	18 53	19 48											19 53	20 48							
Broadstairs	d	18 59	19 54											19 59	20 54							
Dumpton Park	d		19 57												20 57							
Ramsgate	a	19 04	20 00											20 04	21 00							

A ♖ to Margate **B** not from 2 September until 9 September **C** not 26 August

For further services to St Pancras International, Blackfriars and Elephant & Castle and onwards to Bromley South, St Mary Cray and Swanley please refer to table 52

Table 212

Sundays

London - Medway, Sheerness-on-Sea, Dover and Ramsgate

26 August to 9 September

Network Diagram - see first Page of Table 212

		SE A	SE B	SE B	SE	SE ■	SE	SE	SE B	SE A	SE ■	SE	SE A	SE B	SE B	SE	SE ■	SE	SE	SE A	SE B
St Pancras International	d	19 55	19 55	20 18					20 25	20 25			20 55	20 55	21 18					21 25	21 25
Stratford International	d	20 02	20 02	20 26					20 32	20 32			21 02	21 03	21 26					21 32	21 33
Ebbsfleet International	d	20 13	20 14	20a36					20 44	20 43			21 13	21 14	21a36					21 43	21 44
London Victoria	d					20 05					20 24						21 05				
London Blackfriars	d																				
Elephant & Castle	d																				
Bromley South	d					20 22					20 44						21 22				
St Mary Cray	d										20 50										
Swanley	d										20 54										
Farningham Road	d										20 59										
Longfield	d										21 03										
Meopham	d										21 07										
Sole Street	d										21 10										
London Charing Cross	d						19 40					20 10						20 40			
London Waterloo (East)	d						19 43					20 13						20 43			
London Cannon Street	d																				
London Bridge	d						19 48					20 18						20 48			
Dartford	d						20 25					20 55						21 25			
Greenhithe for Bluewater	d						20 31					21 01						21 31			
Gravesend	d	20 18	20 18				20 40		20 48	20 48		21 10	21 18	21 18				21 40		21 48	21 48
Strood	d	20 28	20 28				20 52		20 58	20 58		21 22	21 28	21 28				21 52		21 58	21 58
Rochester	d	20 33	20 33			20 46	20 56		21 03	21 03	21 20	21 26	21 33	21 33			21 46	21 56		22 03	22 03
Chatham	d	20 35	20 35			20 48	20 58		21 05	21 05	21 22	21 28	21 35	21 35			21 48	21 58		22 05	22 05
Gillingham (Kent)	d	20 40	20 40			20 53	21a03		21 10	21 10	21 27	21a33	21 40	21 40			21 53	22a03		22 10	22 10
Rainham (Kent)	d	20 45	20 45			20 57			21 15	21 15	21 31		21 45	21 45			21 57			22 15	22 15
Newington	d										21 35										
Sittingbourne	a	20 52	20 52			21 04			21 22	21 22	21 40		21 52	21 52			22 04			22 22	22 22
	d	20 53	20 53			21 05		21 10	21 23	21 23	21 41		21 53	21 53			22 05		22 10	22 23	22 23
Kemsley	d							21 15											22 15		
Swale	d							21 18											22 18		
Queenborough	d							21 22											22 22		
Sheerness-on-Sea	a							21 27											22 27		
Teynham	d										21 45										
Faversham	a	21 03	21 03			21 13			21 33	21 33	21 51		22 03	22 03			22 13			22 33	22 33
	d					21 17 / 21 19											22 17 / 22 19				
Selling	d					21 24											22 24				
Canterbury East	d					21 33											22 33				
Bekesbourne	d					21 37											22 37				
Adisham	d					21 42											22 42				
Aylesham	d					21 44											22 44				
Snowdown	d					21 47											22 47				
Shepherds Well	d					21 51											22 51				
Kearsney	d					21 55											22 55				
Dover Priory	a					22 00											23 00				
Whitstable	d					21 25											22 25				
Chestfield & Swalecliffe	d					21 28											22 28				
Herne Bay	d					21 32											22 32				
Birchington-on-Sea	d					21 41											22 41				
Westgate-on-Sea	d					21 44											22 44				
Margate	d				20 53	21 48										21 53	22 48				
Broadstairs	d				20 59	21 54										21 59	22 54				
Dumpton Park	d					21 57											22 57				
Ramsgate	a				21 04	22 00										22 04	23 00				

A not from 2 September until 9 September B not 26 August

For further services to St Pancras International, Blackfriars and Elephant & Castle and onwards to Bromley South, St Mary Cray and Swanley please refer to table 52

Table 212

Sundays

London - Medway, Sheerness-on-Sea, Dover and Ramsgate

26 August to 9 September

Network Diagram - see first Page of Table 212

		SE ■	SE	SE A	SE B	SE ■	SE	SE B	SE	SE A	SE B	SE ■	SE	SE A	SE B	SE ■	SE	SE B	SE A	SE B	SE
St Pancras International	d			21 55	21 55			22 18		22 25	22 25			22 55	22 55			23 18	23 25	23 25	
Stratford International	d			22 02	22 03			22 26		22 32	22 33			23 02	23 03			23 26	23 32	23 33	
Ebbsfleet International	d			22 13	22 14			22a36		22 43	22 44			23 13	23 14			23a36	23 43	23 44	
London Victoria	d	21 24				22 05						22 24				23 05					
London Blackfriars	d																				
Elephant & Castle	d																				
Bromley South	d	21 44				22 22						22 44				23 22					
St Mary Cray	d	21 50										22 50									
Swanley	d	21 54										22 54									
Farningham Road	d	21 59										22 59									
Longfield	d	22 03										23 03									
Meopham	d	22 07										23 07									
Sole Street	d	22 10										23 10									
London Charing Cross	d		21 10				21 40						22 10				22 40				23 10
London Waterloo (East)	d		21 13				21 43						22 13				22 43				23 13
London Cannon Street	d																				
London Bridge	d		21 18				21 48						22 18				22 48				23 18
Dartford	d		21 55				22 25						22 55				23 25				23 55
Greenhithe for Bluewater	d		22 01				22 31						23 01				23 31				00 01
Gravesend	d		22 10	22 18	22 18		22 40			22 48	22 48		23 10	23 18	23 18		23 40		23 48	23 48	00 10
Strood	d		22 22	22 28	22 28		22 52			22 58	22 58		23 22	23 28	23 28		23 52		23 58	23 58	00 22
Rochester	d	22 20	22 26	22 33	22 33	22 46	22 56			23 03	23 03	23 20	23 26	23 33	23 33	23 46	23 56		00 03	00 03	00 26
Chatham	d	22 22	22 28	22 35	22 35	22 48	22 58			23 05	23 05	23 22	23 28	23 35	23 35	23 48	23 58		00 05	00 05	00 28
Gillingham (Kent)	d	22 27	22a33	22 40	22 40	22 53	23a03			23 10	23 10	23 27	23a33	23 40	23 40	23 53	00a03		00 10	00 10	00a33
Rainham (Kent)	d	22 31		22 45	22 45	22 57				23 15	23 15	23 31		23 45	23 45	23 57			00 15	00 15	
Newington	d	22 35										23 35									
Sittingbourne	a	22 40		22 52	22 52	23 04				23 22	23 22	23 40		23 52	23 52	00 04			00 22	00 22	
	d	22 41		22 53	22 53	23 05			23 10	23 23	23 23	23 41		23 53	23 53	00 05			00 23	00 23	
Kemsley	d								23 15												
Swale	d								23 18												
Queenborough	d								23 22												
Sheerness-on-Sea	a								23 27												
Teynham	d	22 45										23 45									
Faversham	a	22 51		23 03	23 03	23 13				23 31	23 31	23 51		00 03	00 03	00 13			00 33	00 33	
	d					23 17 / 23 19										00 17					
Selling	d					23 24															
Canterbury East	d					23 33															
Bekesbourne	d					23 37															
Adisham	d					23 42															
Aylesham	d					23 44															
Snowdown	d					23 47															
Shepherds Well	d					23 51															
Kearsney	d					23 55															
Dover Priory	a					00 01															
Whitstable	d					23 25										00 25					
Chestfield & Swalecliffe	d					23 28										00 28					
Herne Bay	d					23 32										00 32					
Birchington-on-Sea	d					23 41										00 41					
Westgate-on-Sea	d					23 44										00 44					
Margate	d					23 48										00 48					
Broadstairs	d					23 54										00 54					
Dumpton Park	d					23 57										00 57					
Ramsgate	a					00 01										01 00					

A not from 2 September until 9 September B not 26 August

For further services to St Pancras International, Blackfriars and Elephant & Castle and onwards to Bromley South, St Mary Cray and Swanley please refer to table 52

Table 212

London - Medway, Sheerness-on-Sea, Dover and Ramsgate

Sundays

26 August to 9 September

Network Diagram - see first Page of Table 212

Station		SE A	SE B	SE 1
St Pancras Internatnl 15 ⊖	d	23 42	23 42	
Stratford International ⊖	d	23 49	23 50	
Ebbsfleet International	d	00 01	00 02	
London Victoria 15 ⊖	d			23 45
London Blackfriars 3 ⊖	d			
Elephant & Castle ⊖	d			
Bromley South 4	d			00 02
St Mary Cray	d			00 08
Swanley 4	d			00 12
Farningham Road	d			00 17
Longfield	d			00 21
Meopham	d			00 25
Sole Street	d			00 28
London Charing Cross 4 ⊖	d			
London Waterloo (East) 4 ⊖	d			
London Cannon Street 4 ⊖	d			
London Bridge 4 ⊖	d			
Dartford 4	d			
Greenhithe for Bluewater	d			
Gravesend 4	d			
Strood 4	d			
Rochester 4	d			00 37
Chatham 4	d			00 40
Gillingham (Kent) 4	d			00 44
Rainham (Kent)	d			00 49
Newington	d			00 53
Sittingbourne 4	a			00 58
	d			00 58
Kemsley	d			
Swale	d			
Queenborough	d			
Sheerness-on-Sea	a			
Teynham	d			01 03
Faversham 2	a			01 09
	d			
Selling	d			
Canterbury East 4	d			
Bekesbourne	d			
Adisham	d			
Aylesham	d			
Snowdown	d			
Shepherds Well	d			
Kearsney	d			
Dover Priory 4	a			
Whitstable	d			
Chestfield & Swalecliffe	d			
Herne Bay	d			
Birchington-on-Sea	d			
Westgate-on-Sea	d			
Margate 4	d			
Broadstairs	d			
Dumpton Park	d			
Ramsgate 4	a			

A not from 2 September until 9 September B not 26 August

For further services to St Pancras International, Blackfriars and Elephant & Castle and onwards to Bromley South, St Mary Cray and Swanley please refer to table 52

Table 212

Ramsgate, Dover, Sheerness-on-Sea and Medway - London

Mondays to Fridays

until 27 July, 13 Aug to 28 Aug and from 10 Sep

Network Diagram - see first Page of Table 212

Miles	Miles	Miles	Miles	Miles	Station		SE MO 1 A	SE MX 1	SE MX 1	SE MO 1 A	SE MX 1	SE MX	SE	SE	SE		SE B	SE C	SE C	SE	SE 1	SE 1	SE	SE C	SE 1
0	—	—	—	—	Ramsgate 4	d		22p05		22p34	23p05											04 36			
1	—	—	—	—	Dumpton Park	d		22p08		22p37	23p08											04 39			
2¼	—	—	—	—	Broadstairs	d		22p11		22p40	23p11											04 42			
5½	—	—	—	—	Margate 4	d		22p16		22p45	23p16											04 47			
6¾	—	—	—	—	Westgate-on-Sea	d		22p20		22p49	23p20											04 50			
8½	—	—	—	—	Birchington-on-Sea	d		22p24		22p53	23p24											04 54			
16¼	—	—	—	—	Herne Bay	d		22p33		23p02	23p33											05 03			
18½	—	—	—	—	Chestfield & Swalecliffe	d		22p36		23p05	23p36											05 06			
20½	—	—	—	—	Whitstable	d		22p39		23p08	23p39											05 10			
—	0	—	—	—	Dover Priory 4	d			22p45																04 42
—	2¼	—	—	—	Kearsney	d																			04 46
—	5½	—	—	—	Shepherds Well	d																			04 51
—	7½	—	—	—	Snowdown	d																			04 55
—	8½	—	—	—	Aylesham	d																			04 57
—	9½	—	—	—	Adisham	d																			05 00
—	12½	—	—	—	Bekesbourne	d																			05 04
—	15½	—	—	—	Canterbury East 4	d			23p02																05 09
—	22	—	—	—	Selling	d																			05 18
27¾	25¼	—	—	0	Faversham 2	a		22p48	23p13	23p17	23p48											05 18			05 23
—	—	—	—	—		d	22p34	22p52	23p14	23p21	23p52								04 56			05 19		05 28	05 34
31¾	29¾	—	—	4½	Teynham	d	22p40	22p58			23p58														05 40
—	—	0	—	—	Sheerness-on-Sea	d						23p53													
—	—	2	—	—	Queenborough	d						23p57													
—	—	4	—	—	Swale	d						00 01													
—	—	6	—	—	Kemsley	d						00 05													
34½	32½	8	—	7¾	Sittingbourne 4	a	22p44	23p02	23p21	23p28	00 02	00 10							05 06			05 26		05 36	05 44
—	—	—	—	—		d	22p45	23p03	23p22	23p29	00 03								05 07			05 27		05 37	05 45
37¾	35¾	—	—	10½	Newington	d	22p50		23p27		00 08														05 50
40¼	38¼	—	—	13	Rainham (Kent)	d	22p54	23p10	23p31	23p36	00 12								05 15			05 35		05 45	05 55
43¼	41¼	—	0	16	Gillingham (Kent) 4	d	22p59	23p15	23p36	23p41	00a17		04 09	04 34	04 54				05 20	05 24	05 30	05 40	05 45	05 50	06 02
45	43	—	1¾	17¾	Chatham 4	d	23p04	23p20	23p41	23p46			04 13	04 38	04 58				05 24	05 28	05 34	05 44	05 49	05 54	06 06
45½	43½	—	2¼	18¼	Rochester 4	d	23p06	23p22	23p43	23p48			04 15	04 40	05 00				05 27	05 30	05 36	05 47	05 51	05 57	06 09
—	—	—	3¼	19¼	Strood 4	a							04 20	04 45	05 05				05 31	05 35				06 01	
—	—	—	10½	26½	Gravesend 4	a							04 32	04 57	05 17				05 42	05 47				06 12	
—	—	—	14½	—	Greenhithe for Bluewater	a							04 38	05 07	05 23					05 53					
—	—	—	17¾	—	Dartford 4	a							04 43	05 13	05 28					05 58					
—	—	—	34¼	—	London Bridge 4 ⊖	a							05 22	05 52	06 05					06 34			06 27		
—	—	—	—	—	London Cannon Street 4 ⊖	a																	06 32		
—	—	—	35¼	—	London Waterloo (East) 4 ⊖	a							05 26	05 57	06 10					06 39					
—	—	—	36	—	London Charing Cross 4 ⊖	a							05 30	06 01	06 13					06 43					
52¼	50¼	—	—	—	Sole Street	d	23p17		23p54												05 47				06 19
53¾	51¾	—	—	—	Meopham	d	23p19	23p33	23p56												05 49				06 22
55¾	53¾	—	—	—	Longfield	d	23p23	23p37	23p59												05 53				06 26
58¾	56¾	—	—	—	Farningham Road	d	23p27		00 04												05 57				06 29
61¾	59¾	—	—	—	Swanley 4	a	23p32		00 09												06 02				06 34
64½	62½	—	—	—	St Mary Cray	a	23p36		00 14												06 06				06 39
68¼	66¼	—	—	—	Bromley South 4	a	23p42	23p50	00 20	00 13											06 14	06 12			06 45
—	—	—	—	—	Elephant & Castle ⊖	a																			
—	—	—	—	—	London Blackfriars 3 ⊖	a																			
79¼	77¼	—	—	—	London Victoria 15 ⊖	a	00 02	00 07	00 38	00 29											06 31	06 28			07 07
—	—	—	—	28½	Ebbsfleet International	a											05 32	05 32	05 47					06 17	
—	—	—	—	45¼	Stratford International ⊖	a											05 44	05 44	05 59					06 29	
—	—	—	—	51¼	St Pancras Internatnl 15 ⊖	a											05 50	05 51	06 06					06 36	

A from 21 May until 23 July B 27 July C not 27 July

For further services to St Pancras International, Blackfriars and Elephant & Castle and onwards to Bromley South, St Mary Cray and Swanley please refer to table 52

Table 212

Mondays to Fridays

until 27 July, 13 Aug to 28 Aug and from 10 Sep

Ramsgate, Dover, Sheerness-on-Sea and Medway - London

Network Diagram - see first Page of Table 212

		SE	SE	SE	SE	SE	SE	SE	SE	SE	SE	SE	SE	SE	SE	SE	SE	SE	SE	SE	SE	SE
		A	1				1	A	B	A		1	1		1		1	A	A	B		1
Ramsgate 4	d	04 55					05 06								05 40							
Dumpton Park	d						05 09								05 43							
Broadstairs	d	05 00					05 12								05 46				05 58	06 00		
Margate 4	d	05 05					05 17								05 51				06 03	06 05		
Westgate-on-Sea	d						05 20								05 54							
Birchington-on-Sea	d						05 24								05 58				06 08	06 10		
Herne Bay	d	05 17					05 33								06 07				06 17	06 19		
Chestfield & Swalecliffe	d						05 36								06 10							
Whitstable	d						05 40								06 14				06 23	06 25		
Dover Priory 4	d		05 05														05 45					
Kearsney	d		05 09														05 50					
Shepherds Well	d		05 14														05 55					
Snowdown	d		05 18														05 59					
Aylesham	d		05 20														06 02					
Adisham	d		05 23														06 04					
Bekesbourne	d		05 27														06 09					
Canterbury East 4	d		05 32														06 15					
Selling	d		05 41														06 24					
Faversham 2	a	05 28	05 46				05 48								06 22		06 29		06 31	06 33		
	d	05 29					05 49		05 58	05 58			06 08		06 23		06 37		06 32	06 34		
Teynham	d						05 55						06 14				06 43					
Sheerness-on-Sea	d			05 31							05 57										06 29	
Queenborough	d			05 35							06 01										06 35	
Swale	d			05 39							06 05										06 39	
Kemsley	d			05 43							06 09										06 42	
Sittingbourne 4	a	05 37		05 48			05 59		06 06	06 06	06 14		06 18		06 30		06 47		06 39	06 41	06 47	
	d	05 37					06 00		06 07	06 07			06 19		06 31		06 48		06 40	06 42		
Newington	d						06 05						06 24				06 54					
Rainham (Kent)	d	05 45					06 10		06 15	06 15			06 29		06 39		06 59		06 48	06 50		
Gillingham (Kent) 4	d	05 50			05 54	06 07	06 15		06 20	06 20		06 24	06 34	06 38	06 44	06 50	07 04		06 54	06 55		07 08
Chatham 4	d	05 55			05 58	06 11	06 19		06 24	06 24		06 28	06 38	06 42	06 48	06 54	07 08		06 58	07 00		07 12
Rochester 4	d	05 57			06 00	06 13	06 22		06 27	06 27		06 31	06 41	06 44		06 57	07 11		07 01	07 03		07 15
Strood 4	a	06 02			06 05	06 18			06 31	06 31				06 49								
Gravesend 4	a	06 12			06 17	06 30			06 42	06 42				07 01					07 13			
Greenhithe for Bluewater	a				06 23	06 36								07 07								
Dartford 4	a				06 28	06 41								07 12								
London Bridge 4 ⊖	a				07 03	07 17							07 20	07 47			07 51					
London Cannon Street 4 ⊖	a					07 23							07 27				07 57					
London Waterloo (East) 4 ⊖	a				07 09									07 52								
London Charing Cross 4 ⊖	a				07 15									07 58								
Sole Street	d											06 41				07 07						07 25
Meopham	d											06 44				07 10						07 28
Longfield	d											06 48				07 14						
Farningham Road	d											06 51				07 17						07 33
Swanley 4	a											06 56				07 22						07 38
St Mary Cray	a											07 01				07 27						07 44
Bromley South 4	a						06 49					07 07			07 15	07 33						07 52
Elephant & Castle ⊖	a																					
London Blackfriars 3 ⊖	a																					
London Victoria 15 ⊖	a						07 09					07 30			07 38	07 55						08 17
Ebbsfleet International	a	06 16						06 32	06 47	06 47								07 02	07 17	07 17		
Stratford International ⊖	a	06 33						06 45	06 59	06 59								07 19	07 29	07 29		
St Pancras Internatnl 15 ⊖	a	06 43						06 55	07 06	07 07								07 29	07 37	07 36		

A 27 Jly

B not 27 Jly

For further services to St Pancras International, Blackfriars and Elephant & Castle and onwards to Bromley South, St Mary Cray and Swanley please refer to table 52

Table 212

Mondays to Fridays

until 27 July, 13 Aug to 28 Aug and from 10 Sep

Ramsgate, Dover, Sheerness-on-Sea and Medway - London

Network Diagram - see first Page of Table 212

		SE	SE	SE	SE	SE	SE	SE	SE	SE	SE	SE	SE	SE	SE	SE	SE	SE	SE	SE	SE	SE	SE
			1	1	1		A	B	A	1		1	1	1		1	A	B	1	1			1
Ramsgate 4	d		06 09									06 32							06 59				07 05
Dumpton Park	d		06 12									06 35							07 02				07 08
Broadstairs	d		06 15		06 25			06 30	06 30			06 38		06 48				07 00	07 05				07 11
Margate 4	d		06 20		06 30			06 35	06 35			06 43		06 53				07 05	07 10				07 16
Westgate-on-Sea	d		06 23									06 46		06 56					07 13				07 20
Birchington-on-Sea	d		06 27		06 35			06 40	06 40			06 50		07 00				07 10	07 17				07 24
Herne Bay	d		06 36		06 44			06 49	06 49			06 59		07 09				07 19	07 26				07 33
Chestfield & Swalecliffe	d		06 39									07 02		07 12					07 30				07 36
Whitstable	d		06 43		06 49			06 55	06 55			07 06		07 16				07 25	07 33				07 39
Dover Priory 4	d			06 13									06 39							07 04			
Kearsney	d			06 17									06 43							07 08			
Shepherds Well	d			06 22									06 48							07 13			
Snowdown	d			06 26									06 52							07 17			
Aylesham	d			06 28									06 54							07 19			
Adisham	d			06 31									06 57							07 22			
Bekesbourne	d			06 35									07 01							07 26			
Canterbury East 4	d			06 40									07 06							07 31			
Selling	d			06 49									07 15							07 40			
Faversham 2	a		06 51	06 55	06 57			07 03	07 03			07 14	07 20	07 24				07 33	07 41	07 45			07 48
	d		06 52		06 58			07 04	07 04			07 16		07 25				07 34	07 42				07 49
Teynham	d											07 22											07 55
Sheerness-on-Sea	d					06 46									07 16						07 35		
Queenborough	d					06 50									07 22						07 39		
Swale	d					06 54									07 26						07 43		
Kemsley	d					06 58									07 29						07 47		
Sittingbourne 4	a		07 00		07 05	07 05		07 12	07 12			07 26		07 32	07 34			07 41	07 49		07 52		07 59
	d		07 01		07 06			07 13	07 13			07 27		07 33				07 42	07 50				08 00
Newington	d											07 32											08 05
Rainham (Kent)	d		07 09		07 14			07 21	07 21			07 37		07 41				07 50	07 58				08 10
Gillingham (Kent) 4	d	07 12	07 15		07 19			07 26	07 26	07 33	07 38	07 42		07 46		07 50		07 55	08 03			08 08	08 15
Chatham 4	d	07 16	07 20		07 24			07 30	07 30	07 37	07 42	07 46		07 50		07 54		08 00	08 08			08 12	08 19
Rochester 4	d	07 18						07 33	07 33	07 40	07 44					07 56		08 03	08 11			08 14	08 22
Strood 4	a	07 23									07 49											08 19	
Gravesend 4	a	07 35									08 01											08 31	
Greenhithe for Bluewater	a	07 45									08 07											08 42	
Dartford 4	a	07 51									08 12											08 49	
London Bridge 4 ⊖	a	08 25			08 09						08 45			08 31					08 49			09 23	
London Cannon Street 4 ⊖	a				08 17									08 38					08 57				
London Waterloo (East) 4 ⊖	a	08 30									08 50											09 28	
London Charing Cross 4 ⊖	a	08 36									08 56											09 34	
Sole Street	d															08 07							
Meopham	d									07 51						08 09							08 33
Longfield	d		07 35							07 55						08 13							08 37
Farningham Road	d															08 17							
Swanley 4	a									08 01						08 22							
St Mary Cray	a									08 06						08 26							
Bromley South 4	a		07 49							08 12		08 15				08 33							08 50
Elephant & Castle ⊖	a																						
London Blackfriars 3 ⊖	a																						
London Victoria 15 ⊖	a		08 09							08 42		08 39				08 53							09 09
Ebbsfleet International	a						07 32	07 47	07 47								08 02	08 17					
Stratford International ⊖	a						07 45	07 59	07 59								08 19	08 29					
St Pancras Internatnl 15 ⊖	a						07 55	08 06	08 09								08 29	08 36					

A 27 Jly

B not 27 Jly

For further services to St Pancras International, Blackfriars and Elephant & Castle and onwards to Bromley South, St Mary Cray and Swanley please refer to table 52

Table 212

Mondays to Fridays

until 27 July, 13 Aug to 28 Aug and from 10 Sep

Ramsgate, Dover, Sheerness-on-Sea and Medway - London

Network Diagram - see first Page of Table 212

Station		SE A	SE B	SE A	SE ■	SE	SE ■	SE ■ C ✠	SE ■ D ✠	SE B	SE A	SE B
Ramsgate ■	d				07 19				07 35	08 01		
Dumpton Park	d				07 22				07 38			
Broadstairs	d				07 25				07 41	08 06		
Margate ■	d				07 30				07 46	08a11		
Wstgate-on-Sea	d				07 33				07 50			
Birchington-on-Sea	d				07 37				07 54			
Herne Bay	d				07 46				08 03			
Chestfield &Swalecliffe	d				07 49				08 06			
Wstable	d				07 53				08 09			
Dover Priory ■	d							07 35				
Kearsney	d							07 39				
Shepherds W	d							07 44				
Snowdown	d							07 48				
Aylesham	d							07 50				
Adisham	d							07 53				
Bekesbourne	d							07 57				
Canterbury East ■	d							08 02				
Selling	d							08 11				
Faversham ■	a				08 01			08 16	08 18			
	d		07 58	07 58	08 02			08 22				08 28
Teynham	d											
Sheerness-on-Sea	d					08 07						
Qeenborough	d					08 11						
Swale	d					08 15						
Kemsley	d					08 19						
Sittingbourne ■	a		08 05	08 05	08 09	08 25		08 29				08 36
	d		08 06	08 06	08 10			08 30				08 37
Nwington	d							08 35				
Rinham (Kent)	d		08 14	08 14	08 18			08 40				08 45
Gillingham (Kent) ■	d		08 19	08 19	08 24		08 32	08 45				08 50
Chatham ■	d		08 24	08 24	08 28		08 36	08 50				08 54
Rchester ■	d		08 26	08 26	08 31		08 39	08 52				08 57
Strood ■	a		08 31	08 31								09 01
Gravesend ■	a		08 42	08 42								09 12
Greenhithe for Bluewater	a											
Dartford ■	a											
London Bridge ■ ⊖	a				09 11							
London Cannon Street ■ ⊖	a				09 18							
London Waterloo (East) ■ ⊖	a											
London Charing Cross ■ ⊖	a											
Sole Street	d						08 49					
Meopham	d						08 52	09 03				
Lngfield	d						08 56	09 07				
Farningham Rad	d						08 59					
Swanley ■	a						09 04					
St Mary Cray	a						09 09					
Bromley South ■	a						09 15	09 20				
Ephant &Castle ⊖	a											
London Blackfriars ■ ⊖	a											
London Victoria ■ ⊖	a						09 38	09 43				
Ebbsfleet International	a	08 32	08 47	08 46							09 06	09 17
Stratford International ⊖	a	08 45	08 59	08 58							09 19	09 29
St Pancras Internatnl ■ ⊖	a	08 55	09 07	09 08							09 29	09 36

Station		SE	SE	SE ■ C ✠	SE ■ D ✠	SE A	SE B	SE A	SE	SE	SE ■
Ramsgate ■	d				08 05						
Dumpton Park	d				08 08						
Broadstairs	d				08 11						
Margate ■	d				08 16						
Wstgate-on-Sea	d				08 20						
Birchington-on-Sea	d				08 24						
Herne Bay	d				08 33						
Chestfield &Swalecliffe	d				08 36						
Wstable	d				08 39						
Dover Priory ■	d			08 05							
Kearsney	d			08 09							
Shepherds W	d			08 14							
Snowdown	d			08 18							
Aylesham	d			08 20							
Adisham	d			08 23							
Bekesbourne	d			08 27							
Canterbury East ■	d			08 32							
Selling	d			08 41							
Faversham ■	a			08 46	08 48						
	d			08 52			08 58	08 58			
Teynham	d			08 58							
Sheerness-on-Sea	d	08 36							09 02		
Qeenborough	d	08 40							09 06		
Swale	d	08 44							09 10		
Kemsley	d	08 48							09 14		
Sittingbourne ■	a	08 56		09 02			09 06	09 06	09 19		
	d			09 03			09 07	09 07			
Nwington	d										
Rinham (Kent)	d			09 10			09 15	09 15			
Gillingham (Kent) ■	d		08 54	09 15			09 20	09 20		09 24	09 32
Chatham ■	d		08 58	09 20			09 24	09 24		09 28	09 36
Rchester ■	d		09 00	09 22			09 27	09 27		09 30	09 39
Strood ■	a		09 05				09 31	09 31		09 35	
Gravesend ■	a		09 17				09 42	09 42		09 47	
Greenhithe for Bluewater	a		09 23							09 53	
Dartford ■	a		09 28							09 58	
London Bridge ■ ⊖	a		10 05							10 35	
London Cannon Street ■ ⊖	a										
London Waterloo (East) ■ ⊖	a		10 09							10 39	
London Charing Cross ■ ⊖	a		10 13							10 43	
Sole Street	d										09 49
Meopham	d			09 33							09 52
Lngfield	d			09 37							09 56
Farningham Rad	d										09 59
Swanley ■	a										10 04
St Mary Cray	a										10 09
Bromley South ■	a			09 50							10 15
Ephant &Castle ⊖	a										
London Blackfriars ■ ⊖	a										
London Victoria ■ ⊖	a			10 07							10 41
Ebbsfleet International	a					09 32	09 47	09 46			
Stratford International ⊖	a					09 45	09 59	09 58			
St Pancras Internatnl ■ ⊖	a					09 55	10 06	10 08			

A 27 uly
B not 27 uly
C ✠ from Faversham
D ✠ from Margate

For further services to St Pancras hternational, Blackfriars and Ephant & Castle and onwards to Bromley South, St Mary Cray and Swanley please refer to table 52

Table 212

Mondays to Fridays

until 27 July, 13 Aug to 28 Aug and from 10 Sep

Ramsgate, Dover, Sheerness-on-Sea and Medway - London

Network Diagram - see first Page of Table 212

Station		SE ■ A ✠	SE ■ B ✠	SE C	SE D	SE C	SE	SE	SE ■ A ✠	SE ■ B ✠
Ramsgate ■	d		08 40	08 59						09 05
Dumpton Park	d									09 08
Broadstairs	d		08 45	09 05						09 11
Margate ■	d		08 50	09a10						09 16
Wstgate-on-Sea	d									09 20
Birchington-on-Sea	d		08 55							09 24
Herne Bay	d		09 04							09 33
Chestfield &Swalecliffe	d									09 36
Wstable	d		09 09							09 39
Dover Priory ■	d	08 45							09 05	
Kearsney	d								09 09	
Shepherds W	d								09 14	
Snowdown	d								09 18	
Aylesham	d								09 20	
Adisham	d								09 23	
Bekesbourne	d								09 27	
Canterbury East ■	d	09 02							09 32	
Selling	d								09 41	
Faversham ■	a	09 14	09 18						09 46	09 48
	d	09 22				09 28			09 52	
Teynham	d								09 58	
Sheerness-on-Sea	d						09 32			
Qeenborough	d						09 36			
Swale	d						09 40			
Kemsley	d						09 44			
Sittingbourne ■	a	09 29				09 36	09 49		10 02	
	d	09 30				09 37			10 03	
Nwington	d	09 35								
Rinham (Kent)	d	09 40				09 45			10 10	
Gillingham (Kent) ■	d	09 45				09 50		09 54	10 15	
Chatham ■	d	09 50				09 54		09 58	10 20	
Rchester ■	d	09 52				09 57		10 00	10 22	
Strood ■	a					10 01		10 05		
Gravesend ■	a					10 12		10 17		
Greenhithe for Bluewater	a							10 23		
Dartford ■	a							10 28		
London Bridge ■ ⊖	a							11 05		
London Cannon Street ■ ⊖	a									
London Waterloo (East) ■ ⊖	a							11 09		
London Charing Cross ■ ⊖	a							11 13		
Sole Street	d									
Meopham	d	10 03							10 33	
Lngfield	d	10 07							10 37	
Farningham Rad	d									
Swanley ■	a									
St Mary Cray	a									
Bromley South ■	a	10 20							10 50	
Ephant &Castle ⊖	a									
London Blackfriars ■ ⊖	a									
London Victoria ■ ⊖	a	10 37							11 07	
Ebbsfleet International	a				10 06	10 16				
Stratford International ⊖	a				10 19	10 28				
St Pancras Internatnl ■ ⊖	a				10 29	10 35				

Station		SE D	SE C	SE D	SE	SE	SE ■	SE ■ A ✠	SE ■ B ✠	SE C	SE D	SE C	SE	SE
Ramsgate ■	d								09 40	09 59				
Dumpton Park	d													
Broadstairs	d								09 45	10 05				
Margate ■	d								09 50	10a10				
Wstgate-on-Sea	d													
Birchington-on-Sea	d								09 55					
Herne Bay	d								10 04					
Chestfield &Swalecliffe	d													
Wstable	d								10 09					
Dover Priory ■	d							09 45						
Kearsney	d													
Shepherds W	d													
Snowdown	d													
Aylesham	d													
Adisham	d													
Bekesbourne	d													
Canterbury East ■	d							10 02						
Selling	d													
Faversham ■	a							10 14	10 18					
	d		09 58	09 58				10 22				10 28		
Teynham	d													
Sheerness-on-Sea	d				10 02								10 32	
Qeenborough	d				10 06								10 36	
Swale	d				10 10								10 40	
Kemsley	d				10 14								10 44	
Sittingbourne ■	a		10 06	10 06	10 19			10 29				10 36	10 49	
	d		10 07	10 07				10 30				10 37		
Nwington	d							10 35						
Rinham (Kent)	d		10 15	10 15				10 40				10 45		
Gillingham (Kent) ■	d		10 20	10 20		10 24	10 32	10 45				10 50		10 54
Chatham ■	d		10 24	10 24		10 28	10 36	10 50				10 54		10 58
Rchester ■	d		10 27	10 27		10 30	10 39	10 52				10 57		11 00
Strood ■	a		10 31	10 31		10 35						11 01		11 05
Gravesend ■	a		10 42	10 42		10 47						11 12		11 17
Greenhithe for Bluewater	a					10 53								11 23
Dartford ■	a					10 58								11 28
London Bridge ■ ⊖	a					11 35								12 05
London Cannon Street ■ ⊖	a													
London Waterloo (East) ■ ⊖	a					11 39								12 09
London Charing Cross ■ ⊖	a					11 43								12 13
Sole Street	d						10 49							
Meopham	d						10 52	11 03						
Lngfield	d						10 56	11 07						
Farningham Rad	d						10 59							
Swanley ■	a						11 04							
St Mary Cray	a						11 09							
Bromley South ■	a						11 15	11 20						
Ephant &Castle ⊖	a													
London Blackfriars ■ ⊖	a													
London Victoria ■ ⊖	a						11 37	11 37						
Ebbsfleet International	a	10 32	10 47	10 46							11 06	11 17		
Stratford International ⊖	a	10 45	10 59	10 58							11 19	11 29		
St Pancras Internatnl ■ ⊖	a	10 55	11 06	11 08							11 29	11 36		

A ✠ from Faversham
B ✠ from Margate
C not 27 uly
D 27 uly

For further services to St Pancras hternational, Blackfriars and Ephant & Castle and onwards to Bromley South, St Mary Cray and Swanley please refer to table 52

Table 212

Ramsgate, Dover, Sheerness-on-Sea and Medway - London

Mondays to Fridays

until 27 July, 13 Aug to 28 Aug and from 10 Sep

Network Diagram - see first Page of Table 212

		SE ■ A	SE ■ B	SE C	SE D	SE C	SE	SE	SE ■	SE ■ A	SE ■ B	SE D	SE C	SE D	SE	SE	SE ■ A	SE ■ B	SE C	SE D	SE C	SE	SE
Ramsgate	d		10 05								10 40	10 59						11 05					
Dumpton Park	d		10 08															11 08					
Broadstairs	d		10 11								10 45	11 05						11 11					
Margate	d		10 16								10 50	11a10						11 16					
Westgate-on-Sea	d		10 20															11 20					
Birchington-on-Sea	d		10 24								10 55							11 24					
Herne Bay	d		10 33								11 04							11 33					
Chestfield & Swalecliffe	d		10 36															11 36					
Whitstable	d		10 39								11 09							11 39					
Dover Priory	d	10 05								10 45							11 05						
Kearsney	d	10 09															11 09						
Shepherds Well	d	10 14															11 14						
Snowdown	d	10 18															11 18						
Aylesham	d	10 20															11 20						
Adisham	d	10 23															11 23						
Bekesbourne	d	10 27															11 27						
Canterbury East	d	10 32								11 02							11 32						
Selling	d	10 41															11 41						
Faversham	a	10 46	10 48							11 14	11 18						11 46	11 48					
	d	10 52			10 58	10 58				11 22				11 28			11 52			11 58	11 58		
Teynham	d	10 58															11 58						
Sheerness-on-Sea	d						11 02								11 32							12 02	
Queenborough	d						11 06								11 36							12 06	
Swale	d						11 10								11 40							12 10	
Kemsley	d						11 14								11 44							12 14	
Sittingbourne	a	11 02			11 06	11 06	11 19			11 29				11 36	11 49		12 02			12 06	12 06	12 19	
	d	11 03			11 07	11 07				11 30				11 37			12 03			12 07	12 07		
Newington	d									11 35													
Rainham (Kent)	d	11 10			11 15	11 15				11 40				11 45			12 10			12 15	12 15		
Gillingham (Kent)	d	11 15			11 20	11 20		11 24	11 32	11 45				11 50		11 54	12 15			12 20	12 20		12 24
Chatham	d	11 20			11 24	11 24		11 28	11 36	11 50				11 54		11 58	12 20			12 24	12 24		12 28
Rochester	d	11 22			11 27	11 27		11 30	11 39	11 52				11 57		12 00	12 22			12 27	12 27		12 30
Strood	a				11 31	11 31		11 35						12 01		12 05				12 31	12 31		12 35
Gravesend	a				11 42	11 42		11 47						12 12		12 17				12 42	12 42		12 47
Greenhithe for Bluewater	a							11 53								12 23							12 53
Dartford	a							11 58								12 28							12 58
London Bridge ⊖	a							12 35								13 05							13 35
London Cannon Street ⊖	a																						
London Waterloo (East) ⊖	a							12 39								13 09							13 39
London Charing Cross ⊖	a							12 43								13 13							13 43
Sole Street	d								11 49														
Meopham	d	11 33							11 52	12 03							12 33						
Longfield	d	11 37							11 56	12 07							12 37						
Farningham Road	d								11 59														
Swanley	a								12 04														
St Mary Cray	a								12 09														
Bromley South	a	11 50							12 15	12 20							12 50						
Elephant & Castle ⊖	a																						
London Blackfriars ⊖	a																						
London Victoria ⊖	a	12 07							12 37	12 37							13 07						
Ebbsfleet International	a			11 32	11 47	11 46							12 06	12 17					12 32	12 47	12 46		
Stratford International ⊖	a			11 45	11 59	11 58							12 19	12 29					12 45	12 59	12 58		
St Pancras Internatnl ⊖	a			11 55	12 06	12 08							12 29	12 36					12 55	13 06	13 08		

A from Faversham
B from Margate
C 27 July
D not 27 July

For further services to St Pancras International, Blackfriars and Elephant & Castle and onwards to Bromley South, St Mary Cray and Swanley please refer to table 52

Table 212

Ramsgate, Dover, Sheerness-on-Sea and Medway - London

Mondays to Fridays

until 27 July, 13 Aug to 28 Aug and from 10 Sep

Network Diagram - see first Page of Table 212

		SE ■	SE ■ A	SE ■ B	SE C	SE D	SE C	SE	SE	SE ■ A	SE ■ B	SE D	SE D	SE E	SE F	SE	SE	SE ■	SE ■ A	SE ■ B	SE C	SE D
Ramsgate	d			11 40	11 59						12 05									12 40	12 59	
Dumpton Park	d										12 08											
Broadstairs	d			11 45	12 05						12 11									12 45	13 05	
Margate	d			11 50	12a10						12 16									12 50	13a10	
Westgate-on-Sea	d										12 20											
Birchington-on-Sea	d			11 55							12 24									12 55		
Herne Bay	d			12 04							12 33									13 04		
Chestfield & Swalecliffe	d										12 36											
Whitstable	d			12 09							12 39									13 09		
Dover Priory	d		11 45							12 05									12 45			
Kearsney	d									12 09												
Shepherds Well	d									12 14												
Snowdown	d									12 18												
Aylesham	d									12 20												
Adisham	d									12 23												
Bekesbourne	d									12 27												
Canterbury East	d		12 02							12 32									13 02			
Selling	d									12 41												
Faversham	a		12 14	12 18						12 46	12 48								13 14	13 18		
	d		12 22				12 28			12 52			12 58	12 58	12 58				13 22			
Teynham	d									12 58												
Sheerness-on-Sea	d							12 32								13 02						
Queenborough	d							12 36								13 06						
Swale	d							12 40								13 10						
Kemsley	d							12 44								13 14						
Sittingbourne	a		12 29				12 36	12 49		13 02			13 06	13 06	13 06	13 19			13 29			
	d		12 30				12 37			13 03			13 07	13 07	13 07				13 30			
Newington	d		12 35																13 35			
Rainham (Kent)	d		12 40				12 45			13 10			13 15	13 15	13 15				13 40			
Gillingham (Kent)	d	12 32	12 45				12 50		12 54	13 15			13 20	13 20	13 20		13 24	13 32	13 45			
Chatham	d	12 36	12 50				12 54		12 58	13 20			13 24	13 24	13 24		13 28	13 36	13 50			
Rochester	d	12 39	12 52				12 57		13 00	13 22			13 27	13 27	13 27		13 30	13 39	13 52			
Strood	a						13 01		13 05				13 31	13 31	13 31		13 35					
Gravesend	a						13 12		13 17				13 42	13 42	13 42		13 47					
Greenhithe for Bluewater	a								13 23								13 53					
Dartford	a								13 28								13 58					
London Bridge ⊖	a								14 05								14 35					
London Cannon Street ⊖	a																					
London Waterloo (East) ⊖	a								14 09								14 39					
London Charing Cross ⊖	a								14 13								14 43					
Sole Street	d	12 49																13 49				
Meopham	d	12 52	13 03							13 33								13 52	14 03			
Longfield	d	12 56	13 07							13 37								13 56	14 07			
Farningham Road	d	12 59																13 59				
Swanley	a	13 04																14 04				
St Mary Cray	a	13 09																14 09				
Bromley South	a	13 15	13 20							13 50								14 15	14 20			
Elephant & Castle ⊖	a																					
London Blackfriars ⊖	a																					
London Victoria ⊖	a	13 37	13 37							14 07								14 37	14 37			
Ebbsfleet International	a					13 06	13 17					13 32	13 46	13 47	13 47							14 06
Stratford International ⊖	a					13 19	13 29					13 45	13 58	14 01	14 02							14 19
St Pancras Internatnl ⊖	a					13 29	13 36					13 55	14 08	14 10	14 09							14 29

A from Faversham
B from Margate
C not 27 July
D 27 July
E until 18 May
F from 21 May until 26 July

For further services to St Pancras International, Blackfriars and Elephant & Castle and onwards to Bromley South, St Mary Cray and Swanley please refer to table 52

Mondays to Fridays

until 27 July, 13 Aug to 28 Aug and from 10 Sep

Ramsgate, Dover, Sheerness-on-Sea and Medway - London

Network Diagram - see first Page of Table 212

		SE A	SE	SE	SE ■ B ✠	SE ■ C ✠	SE D	SE A		SE D	SE	SE	SE ■	SE ■ B ✠	SE ■ C ✠	SE A	SE D	SE A		SE	SE	SE ■ E	SE ■ C ✠	SE ■ F ✠	SE ■ G ✠
Ramsgate ■	d					13 05									13 40	13 59							14 05		14 05
Dumpton Park	d					13 08																	14 08		14 08
Broadstairs	d					13 11									13 45	14 05							14 11		14 11
Margate ■	d					13 16									13 50	14a10							14 16		14 16
Westgate-on-Sea	d					13 20																	14 20		14 20
Birchington-on-Sea	d					13 24									13 55								14 24		14 24
Herne Bay	d					13 33									14 04								14 33		14 33
Chestfield & Swalecliffe	d					13 36																	14 36		14 36
Whitstable	d					13 39									14 09								14 39		14 39
Dover Priory ■	d				13 05									13 45								14 05		14 05	
Kearsney	d				13 09																	14 09		14 09	
Shepherds Well	d				13 14																	14 14		14 14	
Snowdown	d				13 18																	14 18		14 18	
Aylesham	d				13 20																	14 20		14 20	
Adisham	d				13 23																	14 23		14 23	
Bekesbourne	d				13 27																	14 27		14 27	
Canterbury East ■	d				13 32									14 02								14 32		14 32	
Selling	d				13 41																	14 41		14 41	
Faversham ■	a				13 46	13 48								14 14	14 18							14 46	14 48	14 46	14 48
	d	13 28				13 52		13 58		13 58					14 22			14 28				14 52			14 52
Teynham	d					13 58																14 58			14 58
Sheerness-on-Sea	d		13 32								14 02									14 32					
Queenborough	d		13 36								14 06									14 36					
Swale	d		13 40								14 10									14 40					
Kemsley	d		13 44								14 14									14 44					
Sittingbourne ■	a	13 36	13 49			14 02		14 06		14 06	14 19				14 29			14 36		14 49		15 02			15 02
	d	13 37				14 03		14 07		14 07					14 30			14 37				15 03			15 03
Newington	d														14 35										
Rainham (Kent)	d	13 45				14 10		14 15		14 15					14 40			14 45				15 10			15 10
Gillingham (Kent) ■	d	13 50		13 54		14 15		14 20		14 20		14 24	14 32		14 45			14 50			14 54	15 15			15 15
Chatham ■	d	13 54		13 58		14 20		14 24		14 24		14 28	14 36		14 50			14 54			14 58	15 20			15 20
Rochester ■	d	13 57		14 00		14 22		14 27		14 27		14 30	14 39		14 52			14 57			15 00	15 22			15 22
Strood ■	a	14 01		14 05				14 31		14 31		14 35						15 01			15 05				
Gravesend ■	a	14 12		14 17				14 42		14 42		14 47						15 12			15 17				
Greenhithe for Bluewater	a			14 23								14 53									15 23				
Dartford ■	a			14 28								14 58									15 28				
London Bridge ■ ⊖	a			15 05								15 35									16 05				
London Cannon Street ■ ⊖	a																								
London Waterloo (East) ■ ⊖	a			15 09								15 39									16 09				
London Charing Cross ■ ⊖	a			15 13								15 43									16 13				
Sole Street	d												14 49												
Meopham	d					14 33							14 52		15 03							15 33			15 33
Longfield	d					14 37							14 56		15 07							15 37			15 37
Farningham Road	d												14 59												
Swanley ■	a												15 04												
St Mary Cray	a												15 09												
Bromley South ■	a					14 50							15 15		15 20							15 50			15 50
Elephant & Castle ⊖	a																								
London Blackfriars ■ ⊖	a																								
London Victoria ■ ⊖	a					15 07							15 37		15 37							16 07			16 07
Ebbsfleet International	a	14 17					14 32	14 47		14 46							15 06	15 17							
Stratford International ⊖	a	14 29					14 45	14 59		14 58							15 19	15 29							
St Pancras Internatnl ■ ⊖	a	14 36					14 55	15 06		15 08							15 29	15 36							

A not 27 July
B ✠ from Faversham
C ✠ from Margate
D 27 July
E not until 18 May, from 21 May
F until 18 May. ✠ from Faversham
G until 18 May. ✠ from Margate

For further services to St Pancras International, Blackfriars and Elephant & Castle and onwards to Bromley South, St Mary Cray and Swanley please refer to table 52

Mondays to Fridays

until 27 July, 13 Aug to 28 Aug and from 10 Sep

Ramsgate, Dover, Sheerness-on-Sea and Medway - London

Network Diagram - see first Page of Table 212

		SE A	SE A	SE B		SE	SE	SE	SE ■ C ✠	SE ■ D ✠	SE B	SE A	SE B	SE		SE	SE ■ C ✠	SE ■ D ✠	SE A	SE A	SE B	SE	SE	SE ■
Ramsgate ■	d									14 40	14 59							15 05						
Dumpton Park	d																	15 08						
Broadstairs	d									14 45	15 05							15 11						
Margate ■	d									14 50	15a10							15 16						
Westgate-on-Sea	d																	15 20						
Birchington-on-Sea	d									14 55								15 24						
Herne Bay	d									15 04								15 33						
Chestfield & Swalecliffe	d																	15 36						
Whitstable	d									15 09								15 39						
Dover Priory ■	d								14 45								15 05							
Kearsney	d																15 09							
Shepherds Well	d																15 14							
Snowdown	d																15 18							
Aylesham	d																15 20							
Adisham	d																15 23							
Bekesbourne	d																15 27							
Canterbury East ■	d								15 02								15 32							
Selling	d																15 41							
Faversham ■	a								15 14	15 18							15 46	15 48						
	d		14 58	14 58						15 22			15 28					15 52		15 58	15 58			
Teynham	d																	15 58						
Sheerness-on-Sea	d					15 02								15 32								16 02		
Queenborough	d					15 06								15 36								16 06		
Swale	d					15 10								15 40								16 10		
Kemsley	d					15 14								15 44								16 14		
Sittingbourne ■	a		15 06	15 06		15 19				15 29			15 36	15 55				16 02		16 06	16 06	16 19		
	d		15 07	15 07						15 30			15 37					16 03		16 07	16 07			
Newington	d									15 35														
Rainham (Kent)	d		15 15	15 15						15 40			15 45					16 10		16 15	16 15			
Gillingham (Kent) ■	d		15 20	15 20			15 24	15 32		15 45			15 50			15 54		16 15		16 20	16 20		16 24	16 32
Chatham ■	d		15 24	15 24			15 28	15 36		15 50			15 54			15 58		16 20		16 24	16 24		16 28	16 36
Rochester ■	d		15 27	15 27			15 30	15 39		15 52			15 57			16 00		16 22		16 27	16 27		16 30	16 39
Strood ■	a		15 31	15 31			15 35						16 01			16 05				16 31	16 31		16 35	
Gravesend ■	a		15 42	15 42			15 47						16 12			16 17				16 42	16 42		16 47	
Greenhithe for Bluewater	a						15 53									16 23							16 53	
Dartford ■	a						15 58									16 28							16 58	
London Bridge ■ ⊖	a						16 35									17 07							17 35	
London Cannon Street ■ ⊖	a															17 11								
London Waterloo (East) ■ ⊖	a						16 39																17 40	
London Charing Cross ■ ⊖	a						16 44																17 44	
Sole Street	d							15 49																16 49
Meopham	d							15 52		16 03								16 33						16 52
Longfield	d							15 56		16 07								16 37						16 56
Farningham Road	d							15 59																16 59
Swanley ■	a							16 04																17 04
St Mary Cray	a							16 09																17 09
Bromley South ■	a							16 15		16 20								16 50						17 15
Elephant & Castle ⊖	a																							
London Blackfriars ■ ⊖	a																							
London Victoria ■ ⊖	a							16 37		16 38								17 07						17 38
Ebbsfleet International	a	15 32	15 46	15 47								16 06	16 17						16 32	16 46	16 47			
Stratford International ⊖	a	15 45	15 58	16 02								16 19	16 29						16 45	16 58	17 02			
St Pancras Internatnl ■ ⊖	a	15 55	16 08	16 09								16 29	16 36						16 55	17 08	17 09			

A 27 July
B not 27 July
C ✠ from Faversham
D ✠ from Margate

For further services to St Pancras International, Blackfriars and Elephant & Castle and onwards to Bromley South, St Mary Cray and Swanley please refer to table 52

Table 212

Mondays to Fridays

until 27 July, 13 Aug to 28 Aug and from 10 Sep

Ramsgate, Dover, Sheerness-on-Sea and Medway - London

Network Diagram - see first Page of Table 212

		SE [1] A 🍴	SE [1] B 🍴	SE C	SE D	SE C	SE	SE	SE [1]	SE [1] A 🍴	SE [1] B 🍴	SE D	SE C	SE D	SE	SE	SE [1]	SE [1] A 🍴	SE [1] B 🍴	SE C	SE D	SE C	SE
Ramsgate [4]	d		15 35	15 59							16 05								16 35	16 59			
Dumpton Park	d		15 38								16 08								16 38				
Broadstairs	d		15 41	16 05							16 11								16 41	17 05			
Margate [4]	d		15 46	16a10							16 16								16 46	17a10			
Westgate-on-Sea	d		15 50								16 20								16 50				
Birchington-on-Sea	d		15 54								16 24								16 54				
Herne Bay	d		16 03								16 33								17 03				
Chestfield & Swalecliffe	d		16 06								16 36								17 06				
Whitstable	d		16 09								16 39								17 09				
Dover Priory [4]	d	15 39								16 05								16 39					
Kearsney	d	15 43								16 09								16 43					
Shepherds Well	d	15 48								16 14								16 48					
Snowdown	d									16 18													
Aylesham	d	15 52								16 20								16 52					
Adisham	d	15 55								16 23								16 55					
Bekesbourne	d									16 27													
Canterbury East [4]	d	16 02								16 32								17 02					
Selling	d	16 11								16 41								17 11					
Faversham [2]	a	16 16	16 18							16 46	16 48							17 16	17 18				
	d	16 22				16 28				16 52			16 58	16 58				17 22				17 28	
Teynham	d									16 58													
Sheerness-on-Sea	d						16 32								17 02								17 32
Queenborough	d						16 36								17 06								17 36
Swale	d						16 40								17 10								17 40
Kemsley	d						16 44								17 14								17 44
Sittingbourne [4]	a	16 29				16 36	16 49			17 02			17 06	17 06	17 19			17 29				17 36	17 52
	d	16 30				16 37				17 03			17 07	17 07				17 30				17 37	
Newington	d	16 35																17 35					
Rainham (Kent)	d	16 40				16 45				17 10			17 15	17 15				17 40				17 45	
Gillingham (Kent) [4]	d	16 45				16 50		16 54	17 02	17 15			17 20	17 20		17 24	17 32	17 45				17 50	
Chatham [4]	d	16 50				16 54		16 58	17 06	17 20			17 24	17 24		17 28	17 36	17 50				17 54	
Rochester [4]	d	16 52				16 57		17 00	17 09	17 22			17 27	17 27		17 30	17 39	17 52				17 57	
Strood [4]	a					17 01		17 05					17 31	17 31		17 35						18 02	
Gravesend [4]	a					17 12		17 17					17 42	17 42		17 47						18 13	
Greenhithe for Bluewater	a							17 23								17 53							
Dartford [4]	a							17 28								17 58							
London Bridge [4] ⊖	a							18 04								18 35							
London Cannon Street [4] ⊖	a																						
London Waterloo (East) [4] ⊖	a							18 08								18 41							
London Charing Cross [4] ⊖	a							18 12								18 45							
Sole Street	d								17 19								17 49						
Meopham	d	17 03							17 22	17 33							17 52	18 03					
Longfield	d	17 07							17 26	17 37							17 56	18 07					
Farningham Road	d								17 29								17 59						
Swanley [4]	a								17 34								18 04						
St Mary Cray	a								17 39								18 09						
Bromley South [4]	a	17 20							17 45	17 50							18 15	18 20					
Elephant & Castle ⊖	a																						
London Blackfriars [3] ⊖	a																						
London Victoria [15] ⊖	a	17 37							18 08	18 07							18 37	18 37					
Ebbsfleet International	a				17 06	17 17						17 32	17 47	17 46							18 06	18 17	
Stratford International ⊖	a				17 19	17 28						17 45	17 59	17 58							18 19	18 29	
St Pancras Internatnl [15] ⊖	a				17 29	17 36						17 55	18 06	18 08							18 29	18 36	

A 🍴 from Faversham
B 🍴 from Margate
C not 27 July
D 27 July

For further services to St Pancras International, Blackfriars and Elephant & Castle and onwards to Bromley South, St Mary Cray and Swanley please refer to table 52

Table 212

Mondays to Fridays

until 27 July, 13 Aug to 28 Aug and from 10 Sep

Ramsgate, Dover, Sheerness-on-Sea and Medway - London

Network Diagram - see first Page of Table 212

		SE	SE [1] A 🍴	SE [1] B 🍴	SE C	SE C	SE D	SE	SE	SE	SE [1]	SE [1]	SE D	SE C	SE D	SE	SE	SE [1]	SE [1]	SE D	SE C	SE C	SE
Ramsgate [4]	d			17 05								17 35	17 59						18 05	18 29			
Dumpton Park	d			17 08								17 38							18 08				
Broadstairs	d			17 11								17 41	18 05						18 11	18 35			
Margate [4]	d			17 16								17 46	18a10						18 16	18a40			
Westgate-on-Sea	d			17 20								17 50							18 20				
Birchington-on-Sea	d			17 24								17 54							18 24				
Herne Bay	d			17 33								18 03							18 33				
Chestfield & Swalecliffe	d			17 36								18 06							18 36				
Whitstable	d			17 39								18 09							18 39				
Dover Priory [4]	d		17 05								17 39							18 05					
Kearsney	d		17 09								17 43							18 09					
Shepherds Well	d		17 14								17 48							18 14					
Snowdown	d		17 18															18 18					
Aylesham	d		17 20								17 52							18 20					
Adisham	d		17 23								17 55							18 23					
Bekesbourne	d		17 27															18 27					
Canterbury East [4]	d		17 32								18 02							18 32					
Selling	d		17 41								18 11							18 41					
Faversham [2]	a		17 46	17 48							18 16	18 18						18 46	18 48				
	d		17 52			17 58	17 58				18 22				18 28			18 52				18 58	
Teynham	d		17 58															18 58					
Sheerness-on-Sea	d							18 02								18 37							
Queenborough	d							18 06								18 41							
Swale	d							18 10								18 45							
Kemsley	d							18 14								18 49							
Sittingbourne [4]	a		18 02			18 06	18 06	18 19			18 29				18 36	18 54		19 02				19 06	
	d		18 03			18 07	18 07				18 30				18 37			19 03				19 07	
Newington	d										18 35												
Rainham (Kent)	d		18 10			18 15	18 15				18 40				18 45			19 10				19 15	
Gillingham (Kent) [4]	d	17 54	18 15			18 20	18 20		18 24	18 32	18 45				18 50		18 54	19 15				19 20	19 24
Chatham [4]	d	17 58	18 20			18 24	18 24		18 28	18 36	18 50				18 54		18 58	19 20				19 24	19 28
Rochester [4]	d	18 00	18 22			18 27	18 27		18 30	18 39	18 52				18 57		19 00	19 22				19 27	19 30
Strood [4]	a	18 05				18 31	18 31		18 35						19 01		19 05					19 31	19 35
Gravesend [4]	a	18 17				18 42	18 42		18 47						19 12		19 17					19 42	19 47
Greenhithe for Bluewater	a	18 23							18 53								19 23						19 53
Dartford [4]	a	18 28							18 58								19 28						19 58
London Bridge [4] ⊖	a	19 05							19 35								20 06						20 36
London Cannon Street [4] ⊖	a																						
London Waterloo (East) [4] ⊖	a	19 09							19 39								20 11						20 40
London Charing Cross [4] ⊖	a	19 13							19 43								20 14						20 44
Sole Street	d									18 49													
Meopham	d		18 33							18 52	19 03							19 33					
Longfield	d		18 37							18 56	19 07							19 37					
Farningham Road	d									18 59													
Swanley [4]	a									19 04													
St Mary Cray	a									19 09													
Bromley South [4]	a		18 50							19 15	19 20							19 50					
Elephant & Castle ⊖	a																						
London Blackfriars [3] ⊖	a																						
London Victoria [15] ⊖	a		19 07							19 37	19 37							20 07					
Ebbsfleet International	a				18 32	18 46	18 47							19 03	19 17						19 32	19 46	
Stratford International ⊖	a				18 45	18 58	19 02							19 19	19 29						19 45	19 58	
St Pancras Internatnl [15] ⊖	a				18 55	19 08	19 09							19 29	19 36						19 55	20 08	

A 🍴 from Faversham
B 🍴 from Margate
C 27 July
D not 27 July

For further services to St Pancras International, Blackfriars and Elephant & Castle and onwards to Bromley South, St Mary Cray and Swanley please refer to table 52

Table 212

Mondays to Fridays

until 27 July, 13 Aug to 28 Aug and from 10 Sep

Ramsgate, Dover, Sheerness-on-Sea and Medway - London

Network Diagram - see first Page of Table 212

		SE	SE	SE	SE	SE	SE	SE	SE	SE	SE	SE	SE	SE	SE	SE	SE	SE	SE	SE	SE	SE
		1	1	1	A		B	A		1	1		B	B	A			1	1	A	A	B
Ramsgate 4	d			18 35	18 59						19 05								19 25	19 31	19 59	
Dumpton Park	d			18 38							19 08								19 28			
Broadstairs	d			18 41	19 05						19 11								19 31	19 36	20 05	
Margate 4	d			18 46	19a10						19 16								19 38	19a41	20a10	
Westgate-on-Sea	d			18 50							19 20								19 41			
Birchington-on-Sea	d			18 54							19 24								19 45			
Herne Bay	d			19 03							19 33								19 54			
Chestfield &Swalecliffe	d			19 06							19 36								19 58			
Whitstable	d			19 09							19 39								20 01			
Dover Priory 4	d		18 39							19 05								19 40				
Kearsney	d		18 43							19 09												
Shepherds Well	d		18 48							19 14												
Snowdown	d									19 18												
Aylesham	d		18 52							19 20												
Adisham	d		18 55							19 23												
Bekesbourne	d									19 27												
Canterbury East 4	d		19 02							19 32								19 57				
Selling	d		19 11							19 41												
Faversham 2	a		19 16	19 18						19 46	19 48							20 08	20 10			
	d		19 22					19 28		19 52				19 58	19 58			20 14				
Teynham	d									19 58												
Sheerness-on-Sea	d					19 16						19 46				20 02						
Queenborough	d					19 23						19 53				20 06						
Swale	d					19 27						19 57				20 10						
Kemsley	d					19 31						20 01				20 14						
Sittingbourne 4	a		19 29			19 36		19 36		20 02		20 06		20 06	20 06	20 19		20 21				
	d		19 30					19 37		20 03				20 07	20 07			20 22				
Newington	d		19 35															20 27				
Rainham (Kent)	d		19 40					19 45		20 10				20 15	20 15			20 31				
Gillingham (Kent) 4	d		19 45					19 50	19 54	20 15				20 20	20 20		20 24	20 36				
Chatham 4	d		19 50					19 54	19 58	20 20				20 24	20 24		20 28	20 41				
Rochester 4	d	19 39	19 52					19 57	20 00	20 22				20 27	20 27		20 30	20 43				
Strood 4	a							20 01	20 05					20 31	20 31		20 35					
Gravesend 4	a							20 12	20 17					20 42	20 42		20 47					
Greenhithe for Bluewater	a								20 23								20 53					
Dartford 4	a								20 28								20 58					
London Bridge 4 ⊖	a								21 06								21 36					
London Cannon Street 4 ⊖	a																					
London Waterloo (East) 4 ⊖	a								21 10								21 40					
London Charing Cross 4 ⊖	a								21 14								21 44					
Sole Street	d	19 49																20 54				
Meopham	d	19 52	20 03							20 33								20 56				
Longfield	d	19 56	20 07							20 37								21 00				
Farningham Road	d	19 59																21 04				
Swanley 4	a	20 04																21 09				
St Mary Cray	a	20 09																21 14				
Bromley South 4	a	20 15	20 20							20 50								21 20				
Elephant &Castle ⊖	a																					
London Blackfriars 3 ⊖	a																					
London Victoria 15 ⊖	a	20 37	20 38							21 07								21 37				
Ebbsfleet International	a						20 06	20 17					20 32	20 46	20 47							21 06
Stratford International ⊖	a						20 19	20 29					20 45	20 58	21 02							21 19
St Pancras Internatnl 15 ⊖	a						20 29	20 36					20 55	21 08	21 09							21 29

A not 27 July

B 27 July

For further services to St Pancras International, Blackfriars and Elephant & Castle and onwards to Bromley South, St Mary Cray and Swanley please refer to table 52

Table 212

Mondays to Fridays

until 27 July, 13 Aug to 28 Aug and from 10 Sep

Ramsgate, Dover, Sheerness-on-Sea and Medway - London

Network Diagram - see first Page of Table 212

		SE	SE	SE	SE	SE	SE	SE	SE	SE	SE	SE	SE	SE	SE	SE	SE	SE	SE	SE	SE	SE	SE
		A			1	1	A	A	B	A	B			1	B	A			1	1	A	B	B
Ramsgate 4	d					20 05	20 32	21 00												21 05	21 59		
Dumpton Park	d					20 08														21 08			
Broadstairs	d					20 11	20 38	21 05												21 11	22 05		
Margate 4	d					20 16	20a43	21a11												21 16	22a10		
Westgate-on-Sea	d					20 20														21 20			
Birchington-on-Sea	d					20 24														21 24			
Herne Bay	d					20 33														21 33			
Chestfield &Swalecliffe	d					20 36														21 36			
Whitstable	d					20 39														21 39			
Dover Priory 4	d				20 05									20 45					21 05				
Kearsney	d				20 09														21 09				
Shepherds Well	d				20 14														21 14				
Snowdown	d				20 18														21 18				
Aylesham	d				20 20														21 20				
Adisham	d				20 23														21 23				
Bekesbourne	d				20 27														21 27				
Canterbury East 4	d				20 32									21 02					21 32				
Selling	d				20 41														21 41				
Faversham 2	a				20 46	20 48								21 13					21 46	21 48			
	d	20 28			20 52					20 58	20 58			21 14		21 28			21 52				21 58
Teynham	d				20 58														21 58				
Sheerness-on-Sea	d		20 32									21 02						21 32					
Queenborough	d		20 36									21 06						21 36					
Swale	d		20 40									21 10						21 40					
Kemsley	d		20 44									21 14						21 44					
Sittingbourne 4	a	20 36	20 49		21 02					21 06	21 06	21 19		21 21		21 36			22 02				22 06
	d	20 37			21 03					21 07	21 07			21 22		21 37			22 03				22 07
Newington	d													21 27				21 51					
Rainham (Kent)	d	20 45			21 10					21 15	21 15			21 31		21 45		21 55	22 10				22 15
Gillingham (Kent) 4	d	20 50		20 54	21 15					21 20	21 20		21 24	21 36		21 50	21 54	22a02	22 15				22 20
Chatham 4	d	20 54		20 58	21 20					21 24	21 24		21 28	21 41		21 54	21 58		22 20				22 24
Rochester 4	d	20 57		21 00	21 22					21 27	21 27		21 30	21 43		21 57	22 00		22 22				22 27
Strood 4	a	21 01		21 05						21 31	21 31		21 35			22 01	22 05						22 31
Gravesend 4	a	21 12		21 17						21 42	21 42		21 47			22 12	22 17						22 42
Greenhithe for Bluewater	a			21 23									21 53				22 23						
Dartford 4	a			21 28									21 58				22 28						
London Bridge 4 ⊖	a			22 05									22 35				23 05						
London Cannon Street 4 ⊖	a																						
London Waterloo (East) 4 ⊖	a			22 09									22 39				23 09						
London Charing Cross 4 ⊖	a			22 13									22 43				23 13						
Sole Street	d													21 54									
Meopham	d				21 33									21 56					22 33				
Longfield	d				21 37									22 00					22 37				
Farningham Road	d													22 04									
Swanley 4	a													22 09									
St Mary Cray	a													22 14									
Bromley South 4	a				21 50									22 20					22 50				
Elephant &Castle ⊖	a																						
London Blackfriars 3 ⊖	a																						
London Victoria 15 ⊖	a				22 07									22 37					23 07				
Ebbsfleet International	a	21 17							21 32	21 47	21 46				22 06	22 17						22 32	22 46
Stratford International ⊖	a	21 29							21 45	21 59	21 58				22 19	22 29						22 45	22 58
St Pancras Internatnl 15 ⊖	a	21 36							21 55	22 06	22 08				22 29	22 36						22 55	23 07

A not 27 July

B 27 July

For further services to St Pancras International, Blackfriars and Elephant & Castle and onwards to Bromley South, St Mary Cray and Swanley please refer to table 52

Ramsgate, Dover, Sheerness-on-Sea and Medway - London

Mondays to Fridays

until 27 July, 13 Aug to 28 Aug and from 10 Sep

Network Diagram - see first Page of Table 212

		SE	SE	SE	SE	SE	SE	SE	SE	SE	SE	SE	SE	SE	SE	SE
					■	■		■			■	■	■			
		A							A					B	B	
Ramsgate	d							22 05	22 59				23 05			
Dumpton Park	d							22 08					23 08			
Broadstairs	d							22 11	23 05				23 11			
Margate	d							22 16	23a10				23 16			
Westgate-on-Sea	d							22 20					23 20			
Birchington-on-Sea	d							22 24					23 24			
Herne Bay	d							22 33					23 33			
Chestfield &Swalecliffe	d							22 36					23 36			
Whitstable	d							22 39					23 39			
Dover Priory	d				21 45	22 05					22 45	23 05				
Kearsney	d					22 09						23 09				
Shepherds Well	d					22 14						23 14				
Snowdown	d					22 18						23 18				
Aylesham	d					22 20						23 20				
Adisham	d					22 23						23 23				
Bekesbourne	d					22 27						23 27				
Canterbury East	d				22 02	22 32					23 02	23 32				
Selling	d					22 41						23 41				
Faversham	a				22 13	22 46		22 48			23 13	23 46	23 48			
	d	21 58			22 14			22 52			23 14		23 52			
Teynham	d							22 58					23 58			
Sheerness-on-Sea	d		22 02							23 02						23 53
Queenborough	d		22 06							23 06						23 57
Swale	d		22 10							23 10						00 01
Kemsley	d		22 14							23 14						00 05
Sittingbourne	a	22 06	22 19		22 21			23 02		23 19	23 21		00 02			00 10
	d	22 07			22 22			23 03			23 22		00 03			
Newington	d				22 27						23 27		00 08			
Rainham (Kent)	d	22 15			22 31			23 10			23 31		00 12			
Gillingham (Kent)	d	22 20		22 24	22 36		22 54	23 15			23 36		00a17			
Chatham	d	22 24		22 28	22 41		22 58	23 20			23 41					
Rochester	d	22 27		22 30	22 43		23 00	23 22			23 43					
Strood	a	22 31		22 35			23 05									
Gravesend	a	22 42		22 47			23 17									
Greenhithe for Bluewater	a			22 53			23 23									
Dartford	a			22 58			23 28									
London Bridge ⊖	a			23 35												
London Cannon Street ⊖	a															
London Waterloo (East) ⊖	a			23 39												
London Charing Cross ⊖	a			23 43												
Sole Street	d				22 54						23 54					
Meopham	d				22 56			23 33			23 56					
Longfield	d				23 00			23 37			23 59					
Farningham Road	d				23 04						00 04					
Swanley	a				23 09						00 09					
St Mary Cray	a				23 14						00 14					
Bromley South	a				23 20			23 50			00 20					
Elephant &Castle ⊖	a															
London Blackfriars ⊖	a															
London Victoria ⊖	a				23 37			00 07			00 38					
Ebbsfleet International	a	22 47												23 02	23 30	
Stratford International ⊖	a	22 59												23 16	23 42	
St Pancras Internatnl ⊖	a	23 06												23 26	23 51	

A not 27 July

B 27 July

For further services to St Pancras International, Blackfriars and Elephant & Castle and onwards to Bromley South, St Mary Cray and Swanley please refer to table 52

Ramsgate, Dover, Sheerness-on-Sea and Medway - London

Mondays to Fridays

30 July to 10 August

Network Diagram - see first Page of Table 212

		SE	SE	SE	SE	SE	SE	SE	SE	SE	SE	SE	SE	SE	SE	SE	SE	SE	SE	SE	SE	SE	SE
		MO			MO																		
		■	■	■	■	■						■	■					■	■			■	
			A	A		A	A																
Ramsgate	d	22p04	22p05		22p34	23p05							04 36									05 06	
Dumpton Park	d	22p07	22p08		22p37	23p08							04 39									05 09	
Broadstairs	d	22p10	22p11		22p40	23p11							04 42			05 00						05 12	
Margate	d	22p16	22p16		22p46	23p16							04 47			05 05						05 17	
Westgate-on-Sea	d	22p20	22p20		22p50	23p20							04 50									05 20	
Birchington-on-Sea	d	22p23	22p24		22p53	23p24							04 54									05 24	
Herne Bay	d	22p32	22p33		23p02	23p33							05 03			05 17						05 33	
Chestfield &Swalecliffe	d	22p36	22p36		23p06	23p36							05 06									05 36	
Whitstable	d	22p39	22p39		23p09	23p39							05 10									05 40	
Dover Priory	d			22p45														04 42	05 05				
Kearsney	d																	04 46	05 09				
Shepherds Well	d																	04 51	05 14				
Snowdown	d																	04 55	05 18				
Aylesham	d																	04 57	05 20				
Adisham	d																	05 00	05 23				
Bekesbourne	d																	05 04	05 27				
Canterbury East	d			23p02														05 12	05 32				
Selling	d																	05 23	05 41				
Faversham	a	22p48	22p48	23p13	23p18	23p48							05 18			05 28		05 33	05 46			05 48	
	d	22p52	22p52	23p14	23p25	23p52							05 19			05 29		05 34				05 49	
Teynham	d	22p58	22p58		23p31	23p58												05 40				05 55	
Sheerness-on-Sea	d						23p53													05 31			
Queenborough	d						23p57													05 35			
Swale	d						00 01													05 39			
Kemsley	d						00 05													05 43			
Sittingbourne	a	23p02	23p02	23p21	23p35	00 02	00 10						05 26			05 37		05 44		05 48		05 59	
	d	23p03	23p03	23p22	23p36	00 03							05 27			05 37		05 45				06 00	
Newington	d			23p27		00 08												05 50				06 05	
Rainham (Kent)	d	23p10	23p10	23p31	23p43	00 12							05 35			05 45		05 55				06 10	
Gillingham (Kent)	d	23p15	23p15	23p36	23p48	00a17		04 09	04 34	04 54	05 24	05 30	05 40		05 45	05 50	05 54	06 02			06 07	06 15	
Chatham	d	23p20	23p20	23p41	23p53			04 13	04 38	04 58	05 28	05 34	05 44		05 49	05 55	05 58	06 06			06 11	06 19	
Rochester	d	23p22	23p22	23p43	23p55			04 15	04 40	05 00	05 30	05 36	05 47		05 51	05 57	06 00	06 09			06 13	06 22	
Strood	a							04 20	04 45	05 05	05 35					06 02	06 05				06 18		
Gravesend	a							04 32	04 57	05 17	05 47					06 12	06 17				06 30		
Greenhithe for Bluewater	a							04 38	05 07	05 23	05 53						06 23				06 36		
Dartford	a							04 43	05 13	05 28	05 58						06 28				06 41		
London Bridge ⊖	a							05 22	05 52	06 05	06 34				06 27		07 03				07 17		
London Cannon Street ⊖	a														06 32						07 23		
London Waterloo (East) ⊖	a							05 26	05 57	06 10	06 39						07 09						
London Charing Cross ⊖	a							05 33	06 04	06 16	06 46						07 15						
Sole Street	d	23p32		23p54								05 47						06 19					
Meopham	d	23p35	23p33	23p56	00 06							05 49						06 22					
Longfield	d	23p39	23p37	23p59	00 10							05 53						06 26					
Farningham Road	d	23p43		00 04								05 57						06 29					
Swanley	a	23p48		00 09								06 02						06 34					
St Mary Cray	a	23p52		00 14								06 06						06 39					
Bromley South	a	23p58	23p50	00 20	00 23							06 14	06 12					06 45				06 49	
Elephant &Castle ⊖	a																						
London Blackfriars ⊖	a																						
London Victoria ⊖	a	00 14	00 07	00 38	00 39							06 31	06 28					07 07				07 09	
Ebbsfleet International	a													05 32		06 16							06 32
Stratford International ⊖	a													05 44		06 33							06 45
St Pancras Internatnl ⊖	a													05 50		06 43							06 55

A not 30 July, 6 August

For further services to St Pancras International, Blackfriars and Elephant & Castle and onwards to Bromley South, St Mary Cray and Swanley please refer to table 52

Table 212

Mondays to Fridays

30 July to 10 August

Ramsgate, Dover, Sheerness-on-Sea and Medway - London

Network Diagram - see first Page of Table 212

		SE	SE	SE	SE	SE		SE	SE	SE	SE	SE	SE	SE	SE	SE		SE	SE	SE	SE	SE	SE	SE	SE
				1	1			1		1				1		1		1	1				1		1
Ramsgate 4	d							05 40								06 09									06 32
Dumpton Park	d							05 43								06 12									06 35
Broadstairs	d							05 46				05 58				06 15			06 25			06 30			06 38
Margate 4	d							05 51				06 03				06 20			06 30			06 35			06 43
Westgate-on-Sea	d							05 54								06 23									06 46
Birchington-on-Sea	d							05 58				06 08				06 27			06 35			06 40			06 50
Herne Bay	d							06 07				06 17				06 36			06 44			06 49			06 59
Chestfield & Swalecliffe	d							06 10								06 39									07 02
Whitstable	d							06 14				06 23				06 43			06 49			06 55			07 06
Dover Priory 4	d									05 45								06 13							
Kearsney	d									05 50								06 17							
Shepherds Well	d									05 55								06 22							
Snowdown	d									05 59								06 26							
Aylesham	d									06 02								06 28							
Adisham	d									06 04								06 31							
Bekesbourne	d									06 09								06 35							
Canterbury East 4	d									06 15								06 40							
Selling	d									06 24								06 49							
Faversham 2	a							06 22		06 29		06 31				06 51		06 55	06 57			07 03			07 14
	d	05 58			06 08			06 23		06 37		06 32				06 52			06 58			07 04			07 16
Teynham	d				06 14					06 43															07 22
Sheerness-on-Sea	d		05 57										06 29							06 46					
Queenborough	d		06 01										06 35							06 50					
Swale	d		06 05										06 39							06 54					
Kemsley	d		06 09										06 42							06 58					
Sittingbourne 4	a	06 06	06 14		06 18			06 30		06 47		06 39	06 47			07 00			07 05	07 05		07 12			07 26
	d	06 07			06 19			06 31		06 48		06 40				07 01			07 06			07 13			07 27
Newington	d				06 24					06 54															07 32
Rainham (Kent)	d	06 15			06 29			06 39		06 59		06 48				07 09			07 14			07 21			07 37
Gillingham (Kent) 4	d	06 20		06 24	06 34	06 38		06 44	06 50	07 04		06 54		07 08	07 12	07 15			07 19			07 26	07 33	07 38	07 42
Chatham 4	d	06 24		06 28	06 38	06 42		06 48	06 54	07 08		06 58		07 12	07 16	07 20			07 24			07 30	07 37	07 42	07 46
Rochester 4	d	06 27		06 31	06 41	06 44			06 57	07 11		07 01		07 15	07 18							07 33	07 40	07 44	
Strood 4	a	06 31				06 49									07 23									07 49	
Gravesend 4	a	06 42				07 01						07 13			07 35									08 01	
Greenhithe for Bluewater	a					07 07									07 45									08 07	
Dartford 4	a					07 12									07 51									08 12	
London Bridge 4 ⊖	a				07 20	07 47				07 51					08 25				08 09					08 45	
London Cannon Street 4 ⊖	a				07 27					07 57									08 17						
London Waterloo (East) 4 ⊖	a					07 52									08 30									08 50	
London Charing Cross 4 ⊖	a					07 58									08 36									08 56	
Sole Street	d			06 41					07 07					07 25											
Meopham	d			06 44					07 10					07 28									07 51		
Longfield	d			06 48					07 14							07 35							07 55		
Farningham Road	d			06 51					07 17					07 33											
Swanley 4	a			06 56					07 22					07 38									08 01		
St Mary Cray	a			07 01					07 27					07 44									08 06		
Bromley South 4	a			07 07				07 15	07 33					07 52		07 49							08 12		08 15
Elephant & Castle ⊖	a																								
London Blackfriars 3 ⊖	a																								
London Victoria 15 ⊖	a			07 30				07 38	07 55					08 17		08 09							08 42		08 39
Ebbsfleet International	a	06 47									07 02	07 17									07 32	07 47			
Stratford International ⊖	a	06 59									07 19	07 29									07 45	07 59			
St Pancras Internatnl 15 ⊖	a	07 07									07 29	07 37									07 55	08 09			

For further services to St Pancras International, Blackfriars and Elephant & Castle and onwards to Bromley South, St Mary Cray and Swanley please refer to table 52

Table 212

Mondays to Fridays

30 July to 10 August

Ramsgate, Dover, Sheerness-on-Sea and Medway - London

Network Diagram - see first Page of Table 212

		SE		SE	SE	SE	SE	SE	SE	SE	SE	SE		SE	SE	SE	SE	SE	SE	SE	SE	SE		SE	SE
		1		1		1	1	1			1					1		1	1 A	1 B					1 A	1 B
Ramsgate 4	d						06 59				07 05					07 19				07 35					08 05
Dumpton Park	d						07 02				07 08					07 22				07 38					08 08
Broadstairs	d			06 48			07 05				07 11					07 25				07 41					08 11
Margate 4	d			06 53			07 10				07 16					07 30				07 46					08 16
Westgate-on-Sea	d			06 56			07 13				07 20					07 33				07 50					08 20
Birchington-on-Sea	d			07 00			07 17				07 24					07 37				07 54					08 24
Herne Bay	d			07 09			07 26				07 33					07 46				08 03					08 33
Chestfield & Swalecliffe	d			07 12			07 30				07 36					07 49				08 06					08 36
Whitstable	d			07 16			07 33				07 39					07 53				08 09					08 39
Dover Priory 4	d	06 39						07 04											07 35					08 05	
Kearsney	d	06 43						07 08											07 39					08 09	
Shepherds Well	d	06 48						07 13											07 44					08 14	
Snowdown	d	06 52						07 17											07 48					08 18	
Aylesham	d	06 54						07 19											07 50					08 20	
Adisham	d	06 57						07 22											07 53					08 23	
Bekesbourne	d	07 01						07 26											07 57					08 27	
Canterbury East 4	d	07 06						07 31											08 02					08 32	
Selling	d	07 15						07 40											08 11					08 41	
Faversham 2	a	07 20		07 24			07 41	07 45			07 48					08 01			08 16	08 18				08 46	08 48
	d			07 25			07 42				07 49				07 58	08 02			08 22					08 52	
Teynham	d										07 55													08 58	
Sheerness-on-Sea	d				07 16				07 35								08 07				08 36				
Queenborough	d				07 22				07 39								08 11				08 40				
Swale	d				07 26				07 43								08 15				08 44				
Kemsley	d				07 29				07 47								08 19				08 48				
Sittingbourne 4	a			07 32	07 34		07 49		07 52		07 59				08 05	08 09	08 25		08 29		08 56			09 02	
	d			07 33			07 50				08 00				08 06	08 10			08 30					09 03	
Newington	d										08 05								08 35						
Rainham (Kent)	d			07 41			07 58				08 10				08 14	08 18			08 40					09 10	
Gillingham (Kent) 4	d			07 46		07 50	08 03			08 08	08 15				08 19	08 24		08 32	08 45			08 54		09 15	
Chatham 4	d			07 50		07 54	08 08			08 12	08 19				08 24	08 28		08 36	08 50			08 58		09 20	
Rochester 4	d					07 56	08 11			08 14	08 22				08 26	08 31		08 39	08 52			09 00		09 22	
Strood 4	a									08 19					08 31							09 05			
Gravesend 4	a									08 31					08 42							09 17			
Greenhithe for Bluewater	a									08 42												09 23			
Dartford 4	a									08 49												09 28			
London Bridge 4 ⊖	a			08 31			08 51			09 23						09 11						10 05			
London Cannon Street 4 ⊖	a			08 38			08 57									09 18									
London Waterloo (East) 4 ⊖	a									09 28												10 09			
London Charing Cross 4 ⊖	a									09 34												10 16			
Sole Street	d					08 07												08 49							
Meopham	d					08 09					08 33							08 52	09 03					09 33	
Longfield	d					08 13					08 37							08 56	09 07					09 37	
Farningham Road	d					08 17												08 59							
Swanley 4	a					08 22												09 04							
St Mary Cray	a					08 26												09 09							
Bromley South 4	a					08 33					08 50							09 15	09 20					09 50	
Elephant & Castle ⊖	a																								
London Blackfriars 3 ⊖	a																								
London Victoria 15 ⊖	a					08 53					09 09							09 38	09 43					10 07	
Ebbsfleet International	a											08 02		08 32	08 46										
Stratford International ⊖	a											08 19		08 45	08 58										
St Pancras Internatnl 15 ⊖	a											08 29		08 55	09 08										

A from Faversham

B from Margate

For further services to St Pancras International, Blackfriars and Elephant & Castle and onwards to Bromley South, St Mary Cray and Swanley please refer to table 52

Table 212

Mondays to Fridays

30 July to 10 August

Ramsgate, Dover, Sheerness-on-Sea and Medway - London

Network Diagram - see first Page of Table 212

		SE	SE	SE	SE	SE	SE 1	SE 1 A	SE 1 B	SE	SE	SE 1 A	SE 1 B	SE	SE	SE	SE	SE	SE 1	SE 1 A	SE 1 B	SE	SE
Ramsgate	d								08 40				09 05								09 40		
Dumpton Park	d												09 08										
Broadstairs	d								08 45				09 11								09 45		
Margate	d								08 50				09 16								09 50		
Westgate-on-Sea	d												09 20										
Birchington-on-Sea	d								08 55				09 24								09 55		
Herne Bay	d								09 04				09 33								10 04		
Chestfield & Swalecliffe	d												09 36										
Whitstable	d								09 09				09 39								10 09		
Dover Priory	d							08 45				09 05								09 45			
Kearsney	d											09 09											
Shepherds Well	d											09 14											
Snowdown	d											09 18											
Aylesham	d											09 20											
Adisham	d											09 23											
Bekesbourne	d											09 27											
Canterbury East	d							09 02				09 32								10 02			
Selling	d											09 41											
Faversham	a							09 14	09 18			09 46	09 48							10 14	10 18		
	d			08 58				09 22				09 52				09 58				10 22			
Teynham	d											09 58											
Sheerness-on-Sea	d				09 02					09 32							10 02					10 32	
Queenborough	d				09 06					09 36							10 06					10 36	
Swale	d				09 10					09 40							10 10					10 40	
Kemsley	d				09 14					09 44							10 14					10 44	
Sittingbourne	a			09 06	09 19			09 29		09 49		10 02				10 06	10 19			10 29		10 49	
	d			09 07				09 30				10 03				10 07				10 30			
Newington	d							09 35												10 35			
Rainham (Kent)	d			09 15				09 40				10 10				10 15				10 40			
Gillingham (Kent)	d			09 20		09 24	09 32	09 45			09 54	10 15				10 20		10 24	10 32	10 45			10 54
Chatham	d			09 24		09 28	09 36	09 50			09 58	10 20				10 24		10 28	10 36	10 50			10 58
Rochester	d			09 27		09 30	09 39	09 52			10 00	10 22				10 27		10 30	10 39	10 52			11 00
Strood	a			09 31		09 35					10 05					10 31		10 35					11 05
Gravesend	a			09 42		09 47					10 17					10 42		10 47					11 17
Greenhithe for Bluewater	a					09 53					10 23							10 53					11 23
Dartford	a					09 58					10 28							10 58					11 28
London Bridge ⊖	a					10 35					11 05							11 35					12 05
London Cannon Street ⊖	a																						
London Waterloo (East) ⊖	a					10 39					11 09							11 39					12 09
London Charing Cross ⊖	a					10 46					11 16							11 46					12 16
Sole Street	d						09 49												10 49				
Meopham	d						09 52	10 03				10 33							10 52	11 03			
Longfield	d						09 56	10 07				10 37							10 56	11 07			
Farningham Road	d						09 59												10 59				
Swanley	a						10 04												11 04				
St Mary Cray	a						10 09												11 09				
Bromley South	a						10 15	10 20				10 50							11 15	11 20			
Elephant & Castle ⊖	a																						
London Blackfriars ⊖	a																						
London Victoria ⊖	a						10 41	10 37				11 07							11 37	11 37			
Ebbsfleet International	a	09 06	09 32	09 46										10 06	10 32	10 46							
Stratford International ⊖	a	09 19	09 45	09 58										10 19	10 45	10 58							
St Pancras Internatnl ⊖	a	09 29	09 55	10 08										10 29	10 55	11 08							

A from Faversham

B from Margate

For further services to St Pancras International, Blackfriars and Elephant & Castle and onwards to Bromley South, St Mary Cray and Swanley please refer to table 52

Table 212

Mondays to Fridays

30 July to 10 August

Ramsgate, Dover, Sheerness-on-Sea and Medway - London

Network Diagram - see first Page of Table 212

		SE 1 A	SE 1 B	SE	SE	SE	SE	SE	SE 1	SE 1 A	SE 1 B	SE	SE	SE 1 A	SE 1 B	SE	SE	SE	SE	SE	SE 1	SE 1 A	SE 1 B
Ramsgate	d		10 05								10 40				11 05								11 40
Dumpton Park	d		10 08												11 08								
Broadstairs	d		10 11								10 45				11 11								11 45
Margate	d		10 16								10 50				11 16								11 50
Westgate-on-Sea	d		10 20												11 20								
Birchington-on-Sea	d		10 24								10 55				11 24								11 55
Herne Bay	d		10 33								11 04				11 33								12 04
Chestfield & Swalecliffe	d		10 36												11 36								
Whitstable	d		10 39								11 09				11 39								12 09
Dover Priory	d	10 05								10 45				11 05								11 45	
Kearsney	d	10 09												11 09									
Shepherds Well	d	10 14												11 14									
Snowdown	d	10 18												11 18									
Aylesham	d	10 20												11 20									
Adisham	d	10 23												11 23									
Bekesbourne	d	10 27												11 27									
Canterbury East	d	10 32								11 02				11 32								12 02	
Selling	d	10 41												11 41									
Faversham	a	10 46	10 48							11 14	11 18			11 46	11 48							12 14	12 18
	d	10 52				10 58				11 22				11 52				11 58				12 22	
Teynham	d	10 58												11 58									
Sheerness-on-Sea	d						11 02					11 32							12 02				
Queenborough	d						11 06					11 36							12 06				
Swale	d						11 10					11 40							12 10				
Kemsley	d						11 14					11 44							12 14				
Sittingbourne	a	11 02				11 06	11 19			11 29		11 49		12 02				12 06	12 19			12 29	
	d	11 03				11 07				11 30				12 03				12 07				12 30	
Newington	d									11 35												12 35	
Rainham (Kent)	d	11 10				11 15				11 40				12 10				12 15				12 40	
Gillingham (Kent)	d	11 15				11 20		11 24	11 32	11 45			11 54	12 15				12 20		12 24	12 32	12 45	
Chatham	d	11 20				11 24		11 28	11 36	11 50			11 58	12 20				12 24		12 28	12 36	12 50	
Rochester	d	11 22				11 27		11 30	11 39	11 52			12 00	12 22				12 27		12 30	12 39	12 52	
Strood	a					11 31		11 35					12 05					12 31		12 35			
Gravesend	a					11 42		11 47					12 17					12 42		12 47			
Greenhithe for Bluewater	a							11 53					12 23							12 53			
Dartford	a							11 58					12 28							12 58			
London Bridge ⊖	a							12 35					13 05							13 35			
London Cannon Street ⊖	a																						
London Waterloo (East) ⊖	a							12 39					13 09							13 39			
London Charing Cross ⊖	a							12 46					13 16							13 46			
Sole Street	d								11 49												12 49		
Meopham	d	11 33							11 52	12 03				12 33							12 52	13 03	
Longfield	d	11 37							11 56	12 07				12 37							12 56	13 07	
Farningham Road	d								11 59												12 59		
Swanley	a								12 04												13 04		
St Mary Cray	a								12 09												13 09		
Bromley South	a	11 50							12 15	12 20				12 50							13 15	13 20	
Elephant & Castle ⊖	a																						
London Blackfriars ⊖	a																						
London Victoria ⊖	a	12 07							12 37	12 37				13 07							13 37	13 37	
Ebbsfleet International	a			11 06	11 32	11 46										12 06	12 32	12 46					
Stratford International ⊖	a			11 19	11 45	11 58										12 19	12 45	12 58					
St Pancras Internatnl ⊖	a			11 29	11 55	12 08										12 29	12 55	13 08					

A from Faversham

B from Margate

For further services to St Pancras International, Blackfriars and Elephant & Castle and onwards to Bromley South, St Mary Cray and Swanley please refer to table 52

Table 212

Mondays to Fridays

30 July to 10 August

Ramsgate, Dover, Sheerness-on-Sea and Medway - London

Network Diagram - see first Page of Table 212

		SE	SE	SE	SE	SE	SE	SE	SE	SE	SE	SE	SE	SE	SE	SE	SE	SE	SE	SE	SE	SE
				1	1						1	1	1			1	1					
				A	B							A	B			A	B					
Ramsgate	d				12 05								12 40				13 05					
Dumpton Park	d				12 08												13 08					
Broadstairs	d				12 11								12 45				13 11					
Margate	d				12 16								12 50				13 16					
Westgate-on-Sea	d				12 20												13 20					
Birchington-on-Sea	d				12 24								12 55				13 24					
Herne Bay	d				12 33								13 04				13 33					
Chestfield &Swalecliffe	d				12 36												13 36					
Whitstable	d				12 39								13 09				13 39					
Dover Priory	d			12 05								12 45				13 05						
Kearsney	d			12 09												13 09						
Shepherds Well	d			12 14												13 14						
Snowdown	d			12 18												13 18						
Aylesham	d			12 20												13 20						
Adisham	d			12 23												13 23						
Bekesbourne	d			12 27												13 27						
Canterbury East	d			12 32								13 02				13 32						
Selling	d			12 41												13 41						
Faversham	a			12 46	12 48							13 14	13 18			13 46	13 48					
	d				12 52			12 58					13 22				13 52			13 58		
Teynham	d				12 58												13 58					
Sheerness-on-Sea	d	12 32							13 02					13 32							14 02	
Queenborough	d	12 36							13 06					13 36							14 06	
Swale	d	12 40							13 10					13 40							14 10	
Kemsley	d	12 44							13 14					13 44							14 14	
Sittingbourne	a	12 49			13 02			13 06	13 19				13 29	13 49			14 02			14 06	14 19	
	d				13 03			13 07					13 30				14 03			14 07		
Newington	d												13 35									
Rainham (Kent)	d				13 10			13 15					13 40				14 10			14 15		
Gillingham (Kent)	d		12 54		13 15			13 20		13 24	13 32		13 45		13 54		14 16			14 20		14 24
Chatham	d		12 58		13 20			13 24		13 28	13 36		13 50		13 58		14 20			14 24		14 28
Rochester	d		13 00		13 22			13 27		13 30	13 39		13 52		14 00		14 22			14 27		14 30
Strood	a		13 05					13 31		13 35					14 05					14 31		14 35
Gravesend	a		13 17					13 42		13 47					14 17					14 42		14 47
Greenhithe for Bluewater	a		13 23							13 53					14 23							14 53
Dartford	a		13 28							13 58					14 28							14 58
London Bridge ⊖	a		14 05							14 35					15 05							15 35
London Cannon Street ⊖	a																					
London Waterloo (East) ⊖	a		14 09							14 39					15 09							15 39
London Charing Cross ⊖	a		14 16							14 46					15 16							15 46
Sole Street	d										13 49											
Meopham	d				13 33						13 52		14 03				14 33					
Longfield	d				13 37						13 56		14 07				14 37					
Farningham Road	d										13 59											
Swanley	a										14 04											
St Mary Cray	a										14 09											
Bromley South	a				13 50						14 15		14 20				14 50					
Elephant &Castle ⊖	a																					
London Blackfriars ⊖	a																					
London Victoria ⊖	a				14 07						14 37		14 37				15 07					
Ebbsfleet International	a					13 06	13 32	13 46										14 06	14 32	14 46		
Stratford International ⊖	a					13 19	13 45	13 58										14 19	14 45	14 58		
St Pancras Internatnl ⊖	a					13 29	13 55	14 08										14 29	14 55	15 08		

A from Faversham

B from Margate

For further services to St Pancras International, Blackfriars and Elephant & Castle and onwards to Bromley South, St Mary Cray and Swanley please refer to table 52

Table 212

Mondays to Fridays

30 July to 10 August

Ramsgate, Dover, Sheerness-on-Sea and Medway - London

Network Diagram - see first Page of Table 212

		SE	SE	SE	SE	SE	SE	SE	SE	SE	SE	SE	SE	SE	SE	SE	SE	SE	SE	SE	SE	SE	SE
		1	1	1			1	1							1	1			1	1			
			A	B			A	B							A	B			A	B			
Ramsgate	d			13 40				14 05								14 40				15 05			
Dumpton Park	d							14 08												15 08			
Broadstairs	d			13 45				14 11								14 45				15 11			
Margate	d			13 50				14 16								14 50				15 16			
Westgate-on-Sea	d							14 20												15 20			
Birchington-on-Sea	d			13 55				14 24								14 55				15 24			
Herne Bay	d			14 04				14 33								15 04				15 33			
Chestfield &Swalecliffe	d							14 36												15 36			
Whitstable	d			14 09				14 39								15 09				15 39			
Dover Priory	d		13 45				14 05								14 45				15 05				
Kearsney	d						14 09												15 09				
Shepherds Well	d						14 14												15 14				
Snowdown	d						14 18												15 18				
Aylesham	d						14 20												15 20				
Adisham	d						14 23												15 23				
Bekesbourne	d						14 27												15 27				
Canterbury East	d		14 02				14 32								15 02				15 32				
Selling	d						14 41												15 41				
Faversham	a		14 14	14 18			14 46	14 48							15 14	15 18			15 46	15 48			
	d			14 22				14 52			14 58					15 22				15 52			15 58
Teynham	d							14 58												15 58			
Sheerness-on-Sea	d				14 32							15 02					15 32						
Queenborough	d				14 36							15 06					15 36						
Swale	d				14 40							15 10					15 40						
Kemsley	d				14 44							15 14					15 44						
Sittingbourne	a			14 29	14 49			15 02			15 06	15 19				15 29	15 55			16 02			16 06
	d			14 30				15 03			15 07					15 30				16 03			16 07
Newington	d			14 35												15 35							
Rainham (Kent)	d			14 40				15 10			15 15					15 40				16 10			16 15
Gillingham (Kent)	d	14 32		14 45		14 54		15 15			15 20		15 24	15 32		15 45		15 54		16 15			16 20
Chatham	d	14 36		14 50		14 58		15 20			15 24		15 28	15 36		15 50		15 58		16 20			16 24
Rochester	d	14 39		14 52		15 00		15 22			15 27		15 30	15 39		15 52		16 00		16 22			16 27
Strood	a					15 05					15 31		15 35					16 05					16 31
Gravesend	a					15 17					15 42		15 47					16 17					16 42
Greenhithe for Bluewater	a					15 23							15 53					16 23					
Dartford	a					15 28							15 58					16 28					
London Bridge ⊖	a					16 05							16 35					17 07					
London Cannon Street ⊖	a																	17 14					
London Waterloo (East) ⊖	a					16 09							16 39										
London Charing Cross ⊖	a					16 16							16 47										
Sole Street	d	14 49												15 49									
Meopham	d	14 52		15 03				15 33						15 52		16 03				16 33			
Longfield	d	14 56		15 07				15 37						15 56		16 07				16 37			
Farningham Road	d	14 59												15 59									
Swanley	a	15 04												16 04									
St Mary Cray	a	15 09												16 09									
Bromley South	a	15 15		15 20				15 50						16 15		16 20				16 50			
Elephant &Castle ⊖	a																						
London Blackfriars ⊖	a																						
London Victoria ⊖	a	15 37		15 37				16 07						16 37		16 38				17 07			
Ebbsfleet International	a								15 06	15 32	15 46										16 06	16 32	16 46
Stratford International ⊖	a								15 19	15 45	15 58										16 19	16 45	16 58
St Pancras Internatnl ⊖	a								15 29	15 55	16 08										16 29	16 55	17 08

A from Faversham

B from Margate

For further services to St Pancras International, Blackfriars and Elephant & Castle and onwards to Bromley South, St Mary Cray and Swanley please refer to table 52

30 July to 10 August

Ramsgate, Dover, Sheerness-on-Sea and Medway - London

Network Diagram - see first Page of Table 212

Station		SE	SE	SE	SE	SE	SE	SE	SE	SE	SE	SE	SE	SE	SE	SE	SE	SE	SE	SE	SE	SE	SE
				1	1	1			1	1	1						1	1	1			1	1
					A	B				A	B							A	B			A	B
Ramsgate [4]	d					15 35					16 05								16 35				17 05
Dumpton Park	d					15 38					16 08								16 38				17 08
Broadstairs	d					15 41					16 11								16 41				17 11
Margate [4]	d					15 46					16 16								16 46				17 16
Westgate-on-Sea	d					15 50					16 20								16 50				17 20
Birchington-on-Sea	d					15 54					16 24								16 54				17 24
Herne Bay	d					16 03					16 33								17 03				17 33
Chestfield & Swalecliffe	d					16 06					16 36								17 06				17 36
Whitstable	d					16 09					16 39								17 09				17 39
Dover Priory [4]	d				15 39					16 05								16 39				17 05	
Kearsney	d				15 43					16 09								16 43				17 09	
Shepherds Well	d				15 48					16 14								16 48				17 14	
Snowdown	d									16 18												17 18	
Aylesham	d				15 52					16 20								16 52				17 20	
Adisham	d				15 55					16 23								16 55				17 23	
Bekesbourne	d									16 27												17 27	
Canterbury East [4]	d				16 02					16 32								17 02				17 32	
Selling	d				16 11					16 41								17 11				17 41	
Faversham [2]	a				16 16	16 18				16 46	16 48							17 16	17 18			17 46	17 48
	d				16 22					16 52				16 58				17 22				17 52	
Teynham	d									16 58												17 58	
Sheerness-on-Sea	d	16 02					16 32								17 02					17 32			
Queenborough	d	16 06					16 36								17 06					17 36			
Swale	d	16 10					16 40								17 10					17 40			
Kemsley	d	16 14					16 44								17 14					17 44			
Sittingbourne [4]	a	16 19			16 29		16 49			17 02				17 06	17 19			17 29		17 52		18 02	
	d				16 30					17 03				17 07				17 30				18 03	
Newington	d				16 35													17 35					
Rainham (Kent)	d				16 40					17 10				17 15				17 40				18 10	
Gillingham (Kent) [4]	d		16 24	16 32	16 45			16 54	17 02	17 15				17 20		17 24	17 32	17 45			17 54	18 15	
Chatham [4]	d		16 28	16 36	16 50			16 58	17 06	17 20				17 24		17 28	17 36	17 50			17 58	18 20	
Rochester [4]	d		16 30	16 39	16 52			17 00	17 09	17 22				17 27		17 30	17 39	17 52			18 00	18 22	
Strood [4]	a		16 35					17 05						17 31		17 35					18 05		
Gravesend [4]	a		16 47					17 17						17 42		17 47					18 17		
Greenhithe for Bluewater	a		16 53					17 23								17 53					18 24		
Dartford [4]	a		16 58					17 28								17 58					18 28		
London Bridge [4] ⊖	a		17 35					18 04								18 35					19 05		
London Cannon Street [4] ⊖	a																						
London Waterloo (East) [4] ⊖	a		17 40					18 08								18 41					19 09		
London Charing Cross [4] ⊖	a		17 47					18 15								18 48					19 16		
Sole Street	d			16 49					17 19								17 49						
Meopham	d			16 52	17 03				17 22	17 33							17 52	18 03				18 33	
Longfield	d			16 56	17 07				17 26	17 37							17 56	18 07				18 37	
Farningham Road	d			16 59					17 29								17 59						
Swanley [4]	a			17 04					17 34								18 04						
St Mary Cray	a			17 09					17 39								18 09						
Bromley South [4]	a			17 15	17 20				17 45	17 50							18 15	18 20				18 50	
Elephant & Castle ⊖	a																						
London Blackfriars [3] ⊖	a																						
London Victoria [15] ⊖	a			17 38	17 37				18 08	18 07							18 37	18 37				19 07	
Ebbsfleet International	a											17 06	17 32	17 46									
Stratford International ⊖	a											17 19	17 45	17 58									
St Pancras Internatnl [15] ⊖	a											17 29	17 55	18 08									

A ⊼ from Faversham

B ⊼ from Margate

For further services to St Pancras International, Blackfriars and Elephant & Castle and onwards to Bromley South, St Mary Cray and Swanley please refer to table 52

30 July to 10 August

Ramsgate, Dover, Sheerness-on-Sea and Medway - London

Network Diagram - see first Page of Table 212

Station		SE	SE	SE	SE	SE	SE	SE	SE	SE	SE	SE	SE	SE	SE	SE	SE	SE	SE	SE	SE	SE
								1	1			1	1						1	1		
Ramsgate [4]	d								17 35				18 05							18 35		
Dumpton Park	d								17 38				18 08							18 38		
Broadstairs	d								17 41				18 11							18 41		
Margate [4]	d								17 46				18 16							18 46		
Westgate-on-Sea	d								17 50				18 20							18 50		
Birchington-on-Sea	d								17 54				18 24							18 54		
Herne Bay	d								18 03				18 33							19 03		
Chestfield & Swalecliffe	d								18 06				18 36							19 06		
Whitstable	d								18 09				18 39							19 09		
Dover Priory [4]	d							17 39				18 05							18 39			
Kearsney	d							17 43				18 09							18 43			
Shepherds Well	d							17 48				18 14							18 48			
Snowdown	d											18 18										
Aylesham	d							17 52				18 20							18 52			
Adisham	d							17 55				18 23							18 55			
Bekesbourne	d											18 27										
Canterbury East [4]	d							18 02				18 32							19 02			
Selling	d							18 11				18 41							19 11			
Faversham [2]	a							18 16	18 18			18 46	18 48						19 16	19 18		
	d			17 58				18 22				18 52				18 58			19 22			
Teynham	d											18 58										
Sheerness-on-Sea	d				18 02					18 37											19 16	
Queenborough	d				18 06					18 41											19 23	
Swale	d				18 10					18 45											19 27	
Kemsley	d				18 14					18 49											19 31	
Sittingbourne [4]	a			18 06	18 19			18 29		18 54		19 02				19 06			19 29		19 36	
	d			18 07				18 30				19 03				19 07			19 30			
Newington	d							18 35											19 35			
Rainham (Kent)	d			18 15				18 40				19 10				19 15			19 40			
Gillingham (Kent) [4]	d			18 20		18 24	18 32	18 45			18 54	19 15				19 20	19 24		19 45			19 54
Chatham [4]	d			18 24		18 28	18 36	18 50			18 58	19 20				19 24	19 28		19 50			19 58
Rochester [4]	d			18 27		18 30	18 39	18 52			19 00	19 22				19 27	19 30	19 39	19 52			20 00
Strood [4]	a			18 31		18 35					19 05					19 31	19 35					20 05
Gravesend [4]	a			18 42		18 47					19 17					19 42	19 47					20 17
Greenhithe for Bluewater	a					18 53					19 23						19 53					20 23
Dartford [4]	a					18 58					19 28						19 58					20 28
London Bridge [4] ⊖	a					19 35					20 06						20 36					21 06
London Cannon Street [4] ⊖	a																					
London Waterloo (East) [4] ⊖	a					19 39					20 11						20 40					21 10
London Charing Cross [4] ⊖	a					19 46					20 17						20 47					21 17
Sole Street	d						18 49											19 49				
Meopham	d						18 52	19 03				19 33						19 52	20 03			
Longfield	d						18 56	19 07				19 37						19 56	20 07			
Farningham Road	d						18 59											19 59				
Swanley [4]	a						19 04											20 04				
St Mary Cray	a						19 09											20 09				
Bromley South [4]	a						19 15	19 20				19 50						20 15	20 20			
Elephant & Castle ⊖	a																					
London Blackfriars [3] ⊖	a																					
London Victoria [15] ⊖	a						19 37	19 37				20 07						20 37	20 38			
Ebbsfleet International	a	18 06	18 32	18 46										19 03	19 32	19 46						
Stratford International ⊖	a	18 19	18 45	18 58										19 19	19 45	19 58						
St Pancras Internatnl [15] ⊖	a	18 29	18 55	19 08										19 29	19 55	20 08						

For further services to St Pancras International, Blackfriars and Elephant & Castle and onwards to Bromley South, St Mary Cray and Swanley please refer to table 52

Table 212

Mondays to Fridays
30 July to 10 August

Ramsgate, Dover, Sheerness-on-Sea and Medway - London

Network Diagram - see first Page of Table 212

		SE [1]	SE [1]	SE	SE	SE	SE	SE		SE	SE [1]	SE [1]	SE	SE	SE [1]	SE [1]	SE	SE		SE	SE	SE	SE [1]	SE	SE
Ramsgate [4]	d		19 05									19 25				20 05									
Dumpton Park	d		19 08									19 28				20 08									
Broadstairs	d		19 11									19 31				20 11									
Margate [4]	d		19 16									19 38				20 16									
Westgate-on-Sea	d		19 20									19 41				20 20									
Birchington-on-Sea	d		19 24									19 45				20 24									
Herne Bay	d		19 33									19 54				20 33									
Chestfield & Swalecliffe	d		19 36									19 58				20 36									
Whitstable	d		19 39									20 01				20 39									
Dover Priory [4]	d	19 05									19 40				20 05								20 45		
Kearsney	d	19 09													20 09										
Shepherds Well	d	19 14													20 14										
Snowdown	d	19 18													20 18										
Aylesham	d	19 20													20 20										
Adisham	d	19 23													20 23										
Bekesbourne	d	19 27													20 27										
Canterbury East [4]	d	19 32									19 57				20 32								21 02		
Selling	d	19 41													20 41										
Faversham [2]	a	19 46	19 48								20 08	20 10			20 46	20 48							21 13		
	d	19 52					19 58				20 14				20 52					20 58			21 14		
Teynham	d	19 58													20 58										
Sheerness-on-Sea	d			19 46				20 02					20 32								21 02				21 32
Queenborough	d			19 53				20 06					20 36								21 06				21 36
Swale	d			19 57				20 10					20 40								21 10				21 40
Kemsley	d			20 01				20 14					20 44								21 14				21 44
Sittingbourne [4]	a	20 02		20 06			20 06	20 19			20 21		20 49		21 02					21 06	21 19		21 21		
	d	20 03					20 07				20 22				21 03					21 07			21 22		
Newington	d										20 27												21 27		21 51
Rainham (Kent)	d	20 10					20 15				20 31				21 10					21 15			21 31		21 55
Gillingham (Kent) [4]	d	20 15					20 20			20 24	20 36			20 54	21 15					21 20		21 24	21 36	21 54	22a02
Chatham [4]	d	20 20					20 24			20 28	20 41			20 58	21 20					21 24		21 28	21 41	21 58	
Rochester [4]	d	20 22					20 27			20 30	20 43			21 00	21 22					21 27		21 30	21 43	22 00	
Strood [4]	a						20 31			20 35				21 05						21 31		21 35		22 05	
Gravesend [4]	a						20 42			20 47				21 17						21 42		21 47		22 17	
Greenhithe for Bluewater	a									20 53				21 23								21 53		22 23	
Dartford [4]	a									20 58				21 28								21 58		22 28	
London Bridge [4] ⊖	a									21 36				22 05								22 35		23 05	
London Cannon Street [4] ⊖	a																								
London Waterloo (East) [4] ⊖	a									21 40				22 09								22 39		23 09	
London Charing Cross [4] ⊖	a									21 47				22 16								22 46		23 16	
Sole Street	d										20 54												21 54		
Meopham	d	20 33									20 56				21 33								21 56		
Longfield	d	20 37									21 00				21 37								22 00		
Farningham Road	d										21 04												22 04		
Swanley [4]	a										21 09												22 09		
St Mary Cray	a										21 14												22 14		
Bromley South [4]	a	20 50									21 20				21 50								22 20		
Elephant & Castle ⊖	a																								
London Blackfriars [3] ⊖	a																								
London Victoria [15] ⊖	a	21 07									21 37				22 07								22 37		
Ebbsfleet International	a				20 06	20 32	20 46										21 06	21 32		21 46					
Stratford International ⊖	a				20 19	20 45	20 58										21 19	21 45		21 58					
St Pancras International [15] ⊖	a				20 29	20 55	21 08										21 29	21 55		22 08					

For further services to St Pancras International, Blackfriars and Elephant & Castle and onwards to Bromley South, St Mary Cray and Swanley please refer to table 52

Table 212

Mondays to Fridays
30 July to 10 August

Ramsgate, Dover, Sheerness-on-Sea and Medway - London

Network Diagram - see first Page of Table 212

		SE [1]	SE [1]	SE		SE	SE	SE	SE	SE [1]	SE [1]	SE	SE [1]	SE		SE [1]	SE [1]	SE [1]	SE	SE	SE				
Ramsgate [4]	d		21 05										22 05					23 05							
Dumpton Park	d		21 08										22 08					23 08							
Broadstairs	d		21 11										22 11					23 11							
Margate [4]	d		21 16										22 16					23 16							
Westgate-on-Sea	d		21 20										22 20					23 20							
Birchington-on-Sea	d		21 24										22 24					23 24							
Herne Bay	d		21 33										22 33					23 33							
Chestfield & Swalecliffe	d		21 36										22 36					23 36							
Whitstable	d		21 39										22 39					23 39							
Dover Priory [4]	d	21 05								21 45	22 05					22 45	23 05								
Kearsney	d	21 09									22 09						23 09								
Shepherds Well	d	21 14									22 14						23 14								
Snowdown	d	21 18									22 18						23 18								
Aylesham	d	21 20									22 20						23 20								
Adisham	d	21 23									22 23						23 23								
Bekesbourne	d	21 27									22 27						23 27								
Canterbury East [4]	d	21 32								22 02	22 32					23 02	23 32								
Selling	d	21 41									22 41						23 41								
Faversham [2]	a	21 46	21 48							22 13	22 46		22 48			23 13	23 46	23 48							
	d	21 52					21 58			22 14			22 52			23 14		23 52							
Teynham	d	21 58											22 58					23 58							
Sheerness-on-Sea	d							22 02						23 02							23 53				
Queenborough	d							22 06						23 06							23 57				
Swale	d							22 10						23 10							00 01				
Kemsley	d							22 14						23 14							00 05				
Sittingbourne [4]	a	22 02					22 06	22 19		22 21			23 02	23 19		23 21		00 02			00 10				
	d	22 03					22 07			22 22			23 03			23 22		00 03							
Newington	d									22 27						23 27		00 08							
Rainham (Kent)	d	22 10					22 15			22 31			23 10			23 31		00 12							
Gillingham (Kent) [4]	d	22 15					22 20		22 24	22 36		22 54	23 15			23 36		00a17							
Chatham [4]	d	22 20					22 24		22 28	22 41		22 58	23 20			23 41									
Rochester [4]	d	22 22					22 27		22 30	22 43		23 00	23 22			23 43									
Strood [4]	a						22 31		22 35			23 05													
Gravesend [4]	a						22 42		22 47			23 17													
Greenhithe for Bluewater	a								22 53			23 23													
Dartford [4]	a								22 58			23 28													
London Bridge [4] ⊖	a								23 35																
London Cannon Street [4] ⊖	a																								
London Waterloo (East) [4] ⊖	a								23 39																
London Charing Cross [4] ⊖	a								23 46																
Sole Street	d									22 54						23 54									
Meopham	d	22 33								22 56			23 33			23 56									
Longfield	d	22 37								23 00			23 37			23 59									
Farningham Road	d									23 04						00 04									
Swanley [4]	a									23 09						00 09									
St Mary Cray	a									23 14						00 14									
Bromley South [4]	a	22 50								23 20			23 50			00 20									
Elephant & Castle ⊖	a																								
London Blackfriars [3] ⊖	a																								
London Victoria [15] ⊖	a	23 07								23 37			00 07			00 38									
Ebbsfleet International	a			22 06		22 32	22 46												23 02	23 30					
Stratford International ⊖	a			22 19		22 45	22 58												23 16	23 42					
St Pancras International [15] ⊖	a			22 29		22 55	23 07												23 26	23 51					

For further services to St Pancras International, Blackfriars and Elephant & Castle and onwards to Bromley South, St Mary Cray and Swanley please refer to table 52

Table 212

Mondays to Fridays

29 August to 7 September

Ramsgate, Dover, Sheerness-on-Sea and Medway - London

Network Diagram - see first Page of Table 212

		SE ■ A	SE ■ B	SE ■ B	SE ■ A	SE ■ B	SE B	SE	SE	SE		SE	SE	SE	SE ■	SE ■	SE	SE	SE	SE ■		SE ■	SE	SE	SE ■
Ramsgate	d		22p05		22p34	23p05										04 36									05 06
Dumpton Park	d		22p08		22p37	23p08										04 39									05 09
Broadstairs	d		22p11		22p40	23p11										04 42									05 12
Margate	d		22p16		22p45	23p16										04 47									05 17
Westgate-on-Sea	d		22p20		22p49	23p20										04 50									05 20
Birchington-on-Sea	d		22p24		22p53	23p24										04 54									05 24
Herne Bay	d		22p33		23p02	23p33										05 03									05 33
Chestfield & Swalecliffe	d		22p36		23p05	23p36										05 06									05 36
Whitstable	d		22p39		23p08	23p39										05 10									05 40
Dover Priory	d			22p45																04 42		05 05			
Kearsney	d																			04 46		05 09			
Shepherds Well	d																			04 51		05 14			
Snowdown	d																			04 55		05 18			
Aylesham	d																			04 57		05 20			
Adisham	d																			05 00		05 23			
Bekesbourne	d																			05 04		05 27			
Canterbury East	d			23p02																05 09		05 32			
Selling	d																			05 18		05 41			
Faversham	a		22p48	23p13	23p17	23p48										05 18				05 23		05 46			05 48
	d	22p34	22p52	23p14	23p21	23p52							04 56			05 19		05 28		05 34					05 49
Teynham	d	22p40	22p58			23p58														05 40					05 55
Sheerness-on-Sea	d						23p53																05 31		
Queenborough	d						23p57																05 35		
Swale	d						00 01																05 39		
Kemsley	d						00 05																05 43		
Sittingbourne	a	22p44	23p02	23p21	23p28	00 02	00 10						05 06			05 26		05 36		05 44			05 48		05 59
	d	22p45	23p03	23p22	23p29	00 03							05 07			05 27		05 37		05 45					06 00
Newington	d	22p50		23p27		00 08														05 50					06 05
Rainham (Kent)	d	22p54	23p10	23p31	23p36	00 12							05 15			05 35		05 45		05 55					06 10
Gillingham (Kent)	d	22p59	23p15	23p36	23p41	00a17		04 09	04 34	04 54			05 20	05 24	05 30	05 40	05 45	05 50	05 54	06 02				06 07	06 15
Chatham	d	23p04	23p20	23p41	23p46			04 13	04 38	04 58			05 24	05 28	05 34	05 44	05 49	05 54	05 58	06 06				06 11	06 19
Rochester	d	23p06	23p22	23p43	23p48			04 15	04 40	05 00			05 27	05 30	05 36	05 47	05 51	05 57	06 00	06 09				06 13	06 22
Strood	a							04 20	04 45	05 05			05 31	05 35				06 01	06 05					06 18	
Gravesend	a							04 32	04 57	05 17			05 42	05 47				06 12	06 17					06 30	
Greenhithe for Bluewater	a							04 38	05 07	05 23				05 53					06 23					06 36	
Dartford	a							04 43	05 13	05 28				05 58					06 28					06 41	
London Bridge ⊖	a							05 22	05 52	06 05				06 34			06 27		07 03					07 17	
London Cannon Street ⊖	a																06 32							07 23	
London Waterloo (East) ⊖	a							05 26	05 57	06 10				06 39					07 09						
London Charing Cross ⊖	a							05 30	06 01	06 13				06 43					07 15						
Sole Street	d	23p17		23p54											05 47					06 19					
Meopham	d	23p19	23p33	23p56											05 49					06 22					
Longfield	d	23p23	23p37	23p59											05 53					06 26					
Farningham Road	d	23p27		00 04											05 57					06 29					
Swanley	a	23p32		00 09											06 02					06 34					
St Mary Cray	a	23p36		00 14											06 06					06 39					
Bromley South	a	23p42	23p50	00 20	00 13										06 14	06 12				06 45					06 49
Elephant & Castle ⊖	a																								
London Blackfriars ⊖	a																								
London Victoria ⊖	a	00 02	00 07	00 38	00 29										06 31	06 28				07 07					07 09
Ebbsfleet International	a											05 32	05 47					06 17							
Stratford International ⊖	a											05 44	05 59					06 29							
St Pancras Internatnl ⊖	a											05 52	06 07					06 37							

A 3 September

B not 3 September

For further services to St Pancras International, Blackfriars and Elephant & Castle and onwards to Bromley South, St Mary Cray and Swanley please refer to table 52

Table 212

Mondays to Fridays

29 August to 7 September

Ramsgate, Dover, Sheerness-on-Sea and Medway - London

Network Diagram - see first Page of Table 212

		SE	SE	SE ■	SE ■	SE		SE ■	SE	SE ■	SE	SE	SE ■	SE	SE ■	SE ■		SE ■	SE	SE	SE ■	SE	SE ■	SE ■	SE ■
Ramsgate	d							05 40							06 09								06 32		
Dumpton Park	d							05 43							06 12								06 35		
Broadstairs	d							05 46			06 00				06 15			06 25		06 30			06 38		06 48
Margate	d							05 51			06 05				06 20			06 30		06 35			06 43		06 53
Westgate-on-Sea	d							05 54							06 23								06 46		06 56
Birchington-on-Sea	d							05 58			06 10				06 27			06 35		06 40			06 50		07 00
Herne Bay	d							06 07			06 19				06 36			06 44		06 49			06 59		07 09
Chestfield & Swalecliffe	d							06 10							06 39								07 02		07 12
Whitstable	d							06 14			06 25				06 43			06 49		06 55			07 06		07 16
Dover Priory	d									05 45						06 13								06 39	
Kearsney	d									05 50						06 17								06 43	
Shepherds Well	d									05 55						06 22								06 48	
Snowdown	d									05 59						06 26								06 52	
Aylesham	d									06 02						06 28								06 54	
Adisham	d									06 04						06 31								06 57	
Bekesbourne	d									06 09						06 35								07 01	
Canterbury East	d									06 15						06 40								07 06	
Selling	d									06 24						06 49								07 15	
Faversham	a							06 22		06 29	06 33				06 51	06 55		06 57		07 03			07 14	07 20	07 24
	d	05 58			06 08			06 23		06 37	06 34				06 52			06 58		07 04			07 16		07 25
Teynham	d				06 14					06 43													07 22		
Sheerness-on-Sea	d		05 57									06 29							06 46						
Queenborough	d		06 01									06 35							06 50						
Swale	d		06 05									06 39							06 54						
Kemsley	d		06 09									06 42							06 58						
Sittingbourne	a	06 06	06 14		06 18			06 30		06 47	06 41	06 47			07 00			07 05	07 05	07 12			07 26		07 32
	d	06 07			06 19			06 31		06 48	06 42				07 01			07 06		07 13			07 27		07 33
Newington	d				06 24					06 54													07 32		
Rainham (Kent)	d	06 15			06 29			06 39		06 59	06 50				07 09			07 14		07 21			07 37		07 41
Gillingham (Kent)	d	06 20		06 24	06 34	06 38		06 44	06 50	07 04	06 55		07 08	07 12	07 15			07 19		07 26	07 33	07 38	07 42		07 46
Chatham	d	06 24		06 28	06 38	06 42		06 48	06 54	07 08	07 00		07 12	07 16	07 20			07 24		07 30	07 37	07 42	07 46		07 50
Rochester	d	06 27		06 31	06 41	06 44			06 57	07 11	07 03		07 15	07 18						07 33	07 40	07 44			
Strood	a	06 31				06 49								07 23								07 49			
Gravesend	a	06 42				07 01								07 35								08 01			
Greenhithe for Bluewater	a					07 07								07 45								08 07			
Dartford	a					07 12								07 51								08 12			
London Bridge ⊖	a				07 20	07 47				07 51				08 25				08 09				08 45			08 31
London Cannon Street ⊖	a				07 27					07 57								08 17							08 38
London Waterloo (East) ⊖	a					07 52								08 30								08 50			
London Charing Cross ⊖	a					07 58								08 36								08 56			
Sole Street	d			06 41					07 07				07 25												
Meopham	d			06 44					07 10				07 28								07 51				
Longfield	d			06 48					07 14						07 35						07 55				
Farningham Road	d			06 51					07 17				07 33												
Swanley	a			06 56					07 22				07 38								08 01				
St Mary Cray	a			07 01					07 27				07 44								08 06				
Bromley South	a			07 07				07 15	07 33				07 52		07 49						08 12		08 15		
Elephant & Castle ⊖	a																								
London Blackfriars ⊖	a																								
London Victoria ⊖	a			07 30				07 38	07 55				08 17		08 09						08 42		08 39		
Ebbsfleet International	a	06 47									07 17									07 47					
Stratford International ⊖	a	06 59									07 29									07 59					
St Pancras Internatnl ⊖	a	07 06									07 37									08 07					

For further services to St Pancras International, Blackfriars and Elephant & Castle and onwards to Bromley South, St Mary Cray and Swanley please refer to table 52

Table 212

Mondays to Fridays
29 August to 7 September

Ramsgate, Dover, Sheerness-on-Sea and Medway - London

Network Diagram - see first Page of Table 212

		SE	SE ■	SE	SE ■	SE ■	SE	SE	SE ■	SE	SE ■	SE	SE ■	SE ■ A ⌶	SE ■ B ⌶	SE	SE	SE	SE	SE ■ A ⌶	SE ■ B ⌶	SE
Ramsgate	d				06 59				07 05		07 19				07 35	08 01					08 05	
Dumpton Park	d				07 02				07 08		07 22				07 38						08 08	
Broadstairs	d			07 00	07 05				07 11		07 25				07 41	08 06					08 11	
Margate	d			07 05	07 10				07 16		07 30				07 46	08a11					08 16	
Westgate-on-Sea	d				07 13				07 20		07 33				07 50						08 20	
Birchington-on-Sea	d			07 10	07 17				07 24		07 37				07 54						08 24	
Herne Bay	d			07 19	07 26				07 33		07 46				08 03						08 33	
Chestfield & Swalecliffe	d				07 30				07 36		07 49				08 06						08 36	
Whitstable	d			07 25	07 33				07 39		07 53				08 09						08 39	
Dover Priory	d					07 04								07 35						08 05		
Kearsney	d					07 08								07 39						08 09		
Shepherds Well	d					07 13								07 44						08 14		
Snowdown	d					07 17								07 48						08 18		
Aylesham	d					07 19								07 50						08 20		
Adisham	d					07 22								07 53						08 23		
Bekesbourne	d					07 26								07 57						08 27		
Canterbury East	d					07 31								08 02						08 32		
Selling	d					07 40								08 11						08 41		
Faversham	a			07 33	07 41	07 45			07 48		08 01			08 16	08 18					08 46	08 48	
	d			07 34	07 42				07 49	07 58	08 02			08 22			08 28			08 52		08 58
Teynham	d								07 55											08 58		
Sheerness-on-Sea	d	07 16					07 35					08 07						08 36				
Queenborough	d	07 22					07 39					08 11						08 40				
Swale	d	07 26					07 43					08 15						08 44				
Kemsley	d	07 29					07 47					08 19						08 48				
Sittingbourne	a	07 34		07 41	07 49		07 52		07 59	08 05	08 09	08 25		08 29			08 36	08 56		09 02		09 06
	d			07 42	07 50				08 00	08 06	08 10			08 30			08 37			09 03		09 07
Newington	d								08 05					08 35								
Rainham (Kent)	d			07 50	07 58				08 10	08 14	08 18			08 40			08 45			09 10		09 15
Gillingham (Kent)	d		07 50	07 55	08 03			08 08	08 15	08 19	08 24		08 32	08 45			08 50		08 54	09 15		09 20
Chatham	d		07 54	08 00	08 08			08 12	08 19	08 24	08 28		08 36	08 50			08 54		08 58	09 20		09 24
Rochester	d		07 56	08 03	08 11			08 14	08 22	08 26	08 31		08 39	08 52			08 57		09 00	09 22		09 27
Strood	a							08 19		08 31							09 01		09 05			09 31
Gravesend	a							08 31		08 42							09 12		09 17			09 42
Greenhithe for Bluewater	a							08 42											09 23			
Dartford	a							08 49											09 28			
London Bridge ⊖	a				08 49			09 23			09 11								10 05			
London Cannon Street ⊖	a				08 57						09 18											
London Waterloo (East) ⊖	a							09 28											10 09			
London Charing Cross ⊖	a							09 34											10 13			
Sole Street	d		08 07										08 49									
Meopham	d		08 09						08 33				08 52	09 03						09 33		
Longfield	d		08 13						08 37				08 56	09 07						09 37		
Farningham Road	d		08 17										08 59									
Swanley	a		08 22										09 04									
St Mary Cray	a		08 26										09 09									
Bromley South	a		08 33						08 50				09 15	09 20						09 50		
Elephant & Castle ⊖	a																					
London Blackfriars ⊖	a																					
London Victoria ⊖	a		08 53						09 09				09 38	09 43						10 07		
Ebbsfleet International	a			08 17						08 47							09 17					09 47
Stratford International ⊖	a			08 29						08 59							09 29					09 59
St Pancras Internatnl ⊖	a			08 37						09 06							09 41					10 07

A ⌶ from Faversham

B ⌶ from Margate

For further services to St Pancras International, Blackfriars and Elephant & Castle and onwards to Bromley South, St Mary Cray and Swanley please refer to table 52

Table 212

Mondays to Fridays
29 August to 7 September

Ramsgate, Dover, Sheerness-on-Sea and Medway - London

Network Diagram - see first Page of Table 212

		SE	SE	SE ■	SE ■ A ⌶	SE ■ B ⌶	SE	SE	SE	SE	SE ■ A ⌶	SE ■ B ⌶	SE	SE	SE	SE ■	SE ■ A ⌶	SE ■ B ⌶	SE	SE	SE	SE
Ramsgate	d					08 40	08 59					09 05						09 40	09 59			
Dumpton Park	d											09 08										
Broadstairs	d					08 45	09 05					09 11						09 45	10 05			
Margate	d					08 50	09a10					09 16						09 50	10a10			
Westgate-on-Sea	d											09 20										
Birchington-on-Sea	d					08 55						09 24						09 55				
Herne Bay	d					09 04						09 33						10 04				
Chestfield & Swalecliffe	d											09 36										
Whitstable	d					09 09						09 39						10 09				
Dover Priory	d				08 45						09 05						09 45					
Kearsney	d										09 09											
Shepherds Well	d										09 14											
Snowdown	d										09 18											
Aylesham	d										09 20											
Adisham	d										09 23											
Bekesbourne	d										09 27											
Canterbury East	d				09 02						09 32						10 02					
Selling	d										09 41											
Faversham	a				09 14	09 18					09 46	09 48					10 14	10 18				
	d				09 22			09 28			09 52		09 58				10 22			10 28		
Teynham	d										09 58											
Sheerness-on-Sea	d	09 02							09 32					10 02							10 32	
Queenborough	d	09 06							09 36					10 06							10 36	
Swale	d	09 10							09 40					10 10							10 40	
Kemsley	d	09 14							09 44					10 14							10 44	
Sittingbourne	a	09 19			09 29			09 36	09 49		10 02		10 06	10 19			10 29			10 36	10 49	
	d				09 30			09 37			10 03		10 07				10 30			10 37		
Newington	d				09 35												10 35					
Rainham (Kent)	d				09 40			09 45			10 10		10 15				10 40			10 45		
Gillingham (Kent)	d		09 24	09 32	09 45			09 50		09 54	10 15		10 20		10 24	10 32	10 45			10 50		10 54
Chatham	d		09 28	09 36	09 50			09 54		09 58	10 20		10 24		10 28	10 36	10 50			10 54		10 58
Rochester	d		09 30	09 39	09 52			09 57		10 00	10 22		10 27		10 30	10 39	10 52			10 57		11 00
Strood	a		09 35					10 01		10 05			10 31		10 35					11 01		11 05
Gravesend	a		09 47					10 12		10 17			10 42		10 47					11 12		11 17
Greenhithe for Bluewater	a		09 53							10 23					10 53							11 23
Dartford	a		09 58							10 28					10 58							11 28
London Bridge ⊖	a		10 35							11 05					11 35							12 05
London Cannon Street ⊖	a																					
London Waterloo (East) ⊖	a		10 39							11 09					11 39							12 09
London Charing Cross ⊖	a		10 43							11 13					11 43							12 13
Sole Street	d			09 49												10 49						
Meopham	d			09 52	10 03						10 33					10 52	11 03					
Longfield	d			09 56	10 07						10 37					10 56	11 07					
Farningham Road	d			09 59												10 59						
Swanley	a			10 04												11 04						
St Mary Cray	a			10 09												11 09						
Bromley South	a			10 15	10 20						10 50					11 15	11 20					
Elephant & Castle ⊖	a																					
London Blackfriars ⊖	a																					
London Victoria ⊖	a			10 41	10 37						11 07					11 37	11 37					
Ebbsfleet International	a							10 16					10 47							11 17		
Stratford International ⊖	a							10 28					10 59							11 32		
St Pancras Internatnl ⊖	a							10 39					11 07							11 40		

A ⌶ from Faversham

B ⌶ from Margate

For further services to St Pancras International, Blackfriars and Elephant & Castle and onwards to Bromley South, St Mary Cray and Swanley please refer to table 52

Table 212

Mondays to Fridays

29 August to 7 September

Ramsgate, Dover, Sheerness-on-Sea and Medway - London

Network Diagram - see first Page of Table 212

		SE 1 A	SE 1 B	SE	SE	SE		SE 1	SE 1 A	SE 1 B	SE	SE	SE	SE	SE 1 A	SE 1 B		SE	SE	SE	SE 1	SE 1 A	SE 1 B	SE	SE
Ramsgate 4	d		10 05							10 40	10 59					11 05							11 40	11 59	
Dumpton Park	d		10 08													11 08									
Broadstairs	d		10 11							10 45	11 05					11 11							11 45	12 05	
Margate 4	d		10 16							10 50	11a10					11 16							11 50	12a10	
Westgate-on-Sea	d		10 20													11 20									
Birchington-on-Sea	d		10 24							10 55						11 24							11 55		
Herne Bay	d		10 33							11 04						11 33							12 04		
Chestfield & Swalecliffe	d		10 36													11 36									
Whitstable	d		10 39							11 09						11 39							12 09		
Dover Priory 4	d	10 05							10 45						11 05							11 45			
Kearsney	d	10 09													11 09										
Shepherds Well	d	10 14													11 14										
Snowdown	d	10 18													11 18										
Aylesham	d	10 20													11 20										
Adisham	d	10 23													11 23										
Bekesbourne	d	10 27													11 27										
Canterbury East 4	d	10 32							11 02						11 32							12 02			
Selling	d	10 41													11 41										
Faversham 2	a	10 46	10 48						11 14	11 18					11 46	11 48						12 14	12 18		
	d	10 52		10 58					11 22			11 28			11 52			11 58				12 22			12 28
Teynham	d	10 58													11 58										
Sheerness-on-Sea	d				11 02								11 32						12 02						
Queenborough	d				11 06								11 36						12 06						
Swale	d				11 10								11 40						12 10						
Kemsley	d				11 14								11 44						12 14						
Sittingbourne 4	a	11 02		11 06	11 19				11 29			11 36	11 49		12 02			12 06	12 19			12 29			12 36
	d	11 03		11 07					11 30			11 37			12 03			12 07				12 30			12 37
Newington	d								11 35													12 35			
Rainham (Kent)	d	11 10		11 15					11 40			11 45			12 10			12 15				12 40			12 45
Gillingham (Kent) 4	d	11 15		11 20		11 24		11 32	11 45			11 50		11 54	12 15			12 20		12 24	12 32	12 45			12 50
Chatham 4	d	11 20		11 24		11 28		11 36	11 50			11 54		11 58	12 20			12 24		12 28	12 36	12 50			12 54
Rochester 4	d	11 22		11 27		11 30		11 39	11 52			11 57		12 00	12 22			12 27		12 30	12 39	12 52			12 57
Strood 4	a			11 31		11 35						12 01		12 05				12 31		12 35					13 01
Gravesend 4	a			11 42		11 47						12 12		12 17				12 42		12 47					13 12
Greenhithe for Bluewater	a					11 53								12 23						12 53					
Dartford 4	a					11 58								12 28						12 58					
London Bridge 4 ⊖	a					12 35								13 05						13 35					
London Cannon Street 4 ⊖	a																								
London Waterloo (East) 4 ⊖	a					12 39								13 09						13 39					
London Charing Cross 4 ⊖	a					12 43								13 13						13 43					
Sole Street	d							11 49													12 49				
Meopham	d	11 33						11 52	12 03						12 33						12 52	13 03			
Longfield	d	11 37						11 56	12 07						12 37						12 56	13 07			
Farningham Road	d							11 59													12 59				
Swanley 4	a							12 04													13 04				
St Mary Cray	a							12 09													13 09				
Bromley South 4	a	11 50						12 15	12 20						12 50						13 15	13 20			
Elephant & Castle ⊖	a																								
London Blackfriars 3 ⊖	a																								
London Victoria 15 ⊖	a	12 07						12 37	12 37						13 07						13 37	13 37			
Ebbsfleet International	a			11 47								12 17						12 47							13 17
Stratford International ⊖	a			11 59								12 32						13 02							13 29
St Pancras Internatnl 15 ⊖	a			12 07								12 40						13 10							13 36

A ✠ from Faversham

B ✠ from Margate

For further services to St Pancras International, Blackfriars and Elephant & Castle and onwards to Bromley South, St Mary Cray and Swanley please refer to table 52

Table 212

Mondays to Fridays

29 August to 7 September

Ramsgate, Dover, Sheerness-on-Sea and Medway - London

Network Diagram - see first Page of Table 212

		SE		SE	SE 1 A	SE 1 B	SE	SE	SE	SE 1	SE 1 A	SE 1 B		SE	SE	SE	SE	SE 1 A	SE 1 B	SE	SE	SE		SE 1
Ramsgate 4	d					12 05						12 40		12 59					13 05					
Dumpton Park	d					12 08													13 08					
Broadstairs	d					12 11						12 45		13 05					13 11					
Margate 4	d					12 16						12 50		13a10					13 16					
Westgate-on-Sea	d					12 20													13 20					
Birchington-on-Sea	d					12 24						12 55							13 24					
Herne Bay	d					12 33						13 04							13 33					
Chestfield & Swalecliffe	d					12 36													13 36					
Whitstable	d					12 39						13 09							13 39					
Dover Priory 4	d				12 05						12 45							13 05						
Kearsney	d				12 09													13 09						
Shepherds Well	d				12 14													13 14						
Snowdown	d				12 18													13 18						
Aylesham	d				12 20													13 20						
Adisham	d				12 23													13 23						
Bekesbourne	d				12 27													13 27						
Canterbury East 4	d				12 32						13 02							13 32						
Selling	d				12 41													13 41						
Faversham 2	a				12 46	12 48					13 14	13 18						13 46	13 48					
	d				12 52		12 58				13 22				13 28			13 52		13 58				
Teynham	d				12 58													13 58						
Sheerness-on-Sea	d	12 32						13 02								13 32					14 02			
Queenborough	d	12 36						13 06								13 36					14 06			
Swale	d	12 40						13 10								13 40					14 10			
Kemsley	d	12 44						13 14								13 44					14 14			
Sittingbourne 4	a	12 49			13 02		13 06	13 19			13 29				13 36	13 49		14 02		14 06	14 19			
	d				13 03		13 07				13 30				13 37			14 03		14 07				
Newington	d										13 35													
Rainham (Kent)	d				13 10		13 15				13 40				13 45			14 10		14 15				
Gillingham (Kent) 4	d			12 54	13 15		13 20		13 24	13 32	13 45				13 50		13 54	14 15		14 20		14 24		14 32
Chatham 4	d			12 58	13 20		13 24		13 28	13 36	13 50				13 54		13 58	14 20		14 24		14 28		14 36
Rochester 4	d			13 00	13 22		13 27		13 30	13 39	13 52				13 57		14 00	14 22		14 27		14 30		14 39
Strood 4	a			13 05			13 31		13 35						14 01		14 05			14 31		14 35		
Gravesend 4	a			13 17			13 42		13 47						14 12		14 17			14 42		14 47		
Greenhithe for Bluewater	a			13 23					13 53								14 23					14 53		
Dartford 4	a			13 28					13 58								14 28					14 58		
London Bridge 4 ⊖	a			14 05					14 35								15 05					15 35		
London Cannon Street 4 ⊖	a																							
London Waterloo (East) 4 ⊖	a			14 09					14 39								15 09					15 39		
London Charing Cross 4 ⊖	a			14 13					14 43								15 13					15 43		
Sole Street	d									13 49														14 49
Meopham	d				13 33					13 52	14 03							14 33						14 52
Longfield	d				13 37					13 56	14 07							14 37						14 56
Farningham Road	d									13 59														14 59
Swanley 4	a									14 04														15 04
St Mary Cray	a									14 09														15 09
Bromley South 4	a				13 50					14 15	14 20							14 50						15 15
Elephant & Castle ⊖	a																							
London Blackfriars 3 ⊖	a																							
London Victoria 15 ⊖	a				14 07					14 37	14 37							15 07						15 37
Ebbsfleet International	a						13 47								14 17					14 47				
Stratford International ⊖	a						14 02								14 29					14 59				
St Pancras Internatnl 15 ⊖	a						14 10								14 37					15 07				

A ✠ from Faversham

B ✠ from Margate

For further services to St Pancras International, Blackfriars and Elephant & Castle and onwards to Bromley South, St Mary Cray and Swanley please refer to table 52

Table 212

Mondays to Fridays
29 August to 7 September

Ramsgate, Dover, Sheerness-on-Sea and Medway - London

Network Diagram - see first Page of Table 212

		SE 1 A	SE 1 B	SE	SE	SE	SE	SE 1 A	SE 1 B		SE	SE	SE	SE	SE 1 A	SE 1 B	SE	SE	SE		SE	SE 1 A	SE 1 B	SE	SE
Ramsgate 4	d		13 40	13 59					14 05							14 40	14 59						15 05		
Dumpton Park	d								14 08														15 08		
Broadstairs	d		13 45	14 05					14 11							14 45	15 05						15 11		
Margate 4	d		13 50	14a10					14 16							14 50	15a10						15 16		
Westgate-on-Sea	d								14 20														15 20		
Birchington-on-Sea	d		13 55						14 24							14 55							15 24		
Herne Bay	d		14 04						14 33							15 04							15 33		
Chestfield & Swalecliffe	d								14 36														15 36		
Whitstable	d		14 09						14 39							15 09							15 39		
Dover Priory 4	d	13 45						14 05							14 45							15 05			
Kearsney	d							14 09														15 09			
Shepherds Well	d							14 14														15 14			
Snowdown	d							14 18														15 18			
Aylesham	d							14 20														15 20			
Adisham	d							14 23														15 23			
Bekesbourne	d							14 27														15 27			
Canterbury East 4	d	14 02						14 32							15 02							15 32			
Selling	d							14 41														15 41			
Faversham 2	a	14 14	14 18					14 46	14 48						15 14	15 18						15 46	15 48		
	d		14 22		14 28				14 52		14 58					15 22		15 28					15 52	15 58	
Teynham	d								14 58														15 58		
Sheerness-on-Sea	d					14 32						15 02							15 32						16 02
Queenborough	d					14 36						15 06							15 36						16 06
Swale	d					14 40						15 10							15 40						16 10
Kemsley	d					14 44						15 14							15 44						16 14
Sittingbourne 4	a		14 29		14 36	14 49			15 02		15 06	15 19				15 29		15 36	15 55				16 02	16 06	16 19
	d		14 30		14 37				15 03		15 07					15 30		15 37					16 03	16 07	
Newington	d		14 35													15 35									
Rainham (Kent)	d		14 40		14 45				15 10		15 15					15 40		15 45					16 10	16 15	
Gillingham (Kent) 4	d		14 45		14 50		14 54		15 15		15 20		15 24	15 32		15 45		15 50			15 54		16 15	16 20	
Chatham 4	d		14 50		14 54		14 58		15 20		15 24		15 28	15 36		15 50		15 54			15 58		16 20	16 24	
Rochester 4	d		14 52		14 57		15 00		15 22		15 27		15 30	15 39		15 52		15 57			16 00		16 22	16 27	
Strood 4	a				15 01		15 05				15 31		15 35					16 01			16 05			16 31	
Gravesend 4	a				15 12		15 17				15 42		15 47					16 12			16 17			16 42	
Greenhithe for Bluewater	a						15 23						15 53								16 23				
Dartford 4	a						15 28						15 58								16 28				
London Bridge 4 ⊖	a						16 05						16 35								17 07				
London Cannon Street 4 ⊖	a																				17 11				
London Waterloo (East) 4 ⊖	a						16 09						16 39													
London Charing Cross 4 ⊖	a						16 13						16 44													
Sole Street	d													15 49											
Meopham	d		15 03						15 33					15 52		16 03							16 33		
Longfield	d		15 07						15 37					15 56		16 07							16 37		
Farningham Road	d													15 59											
Swanley 4	a													16 04											
St Mary Cray	a													16 09											
Bromley South 4	a		15 20						15 50					16 15		16 20							16 50		
Elephant & Castle ⊖	a																							
London Blackfriars 3 ⊖	a																							
London Victoria 15 ⊖	a		15 37						16 07					16 37		16 38							17 07		
Ebbsfleet International	a				15 17						15 47							16 17						16 47	
Stratford International ⊖	a				15 32						16 05							16 29						17 02	
St Pancras Internatnl 15 ⊖	a				15 40						16 15							16 36						17 09	

A from Faversham

B from Margate

For further services to St Pancras International, Blackfriars and Elephant & Castle and onwards to Bromley South, St Mary Cray and Swanley please refer to table 52

Table 212

Mondays to Fridays
29 August to 7 September

Ramsgate, Dover, Sheerness-on-Sea and Medway - London

Network Diagram - see first Page of Table 212

		SE	SE 1	SE 1 A	SE 1 B		SE	SE	SE	SE	SE 1	SE 1 A	SE 1 B	SE	SE		SE	SE 1	SE 1 A	SE 1 B	SE	SE	SE	SE
Ramsgate 4	d				15 35		15 59						16 05							16 35	16 59			
Dumpton Park	d				15 38								16 38							16 38				
Broadstairs	d				15 41		16 05						16 11							16 41	17 05			
Margate 4	d				15 46		16a10						16 16							16 46	17a10			
Westgate-on-Sea	d				15 50								16 20							16 50				
Birchington-on-Sea	d				15 54								16 24							16 54				
Herne Bay	d				16 03								16 33							17 03				
Chestfield & Swalecliffe	d				16 06								16 36							17 06				
Whitstable	d				16 09								16 39							17 09				
Dover Priory 4	d			15 39								16 05							16 39					
Kearsney	d			15 43								16 09							16 43					
Shepherds Well	d			15 48								16 14							16 48					
Snowdown	d											16 18												
Aylesham	d			15 52								16 20							16 52					
Adisham	d			15 55								16 23							16 55					
Bekesbourne	d											16 27												
Canterbury East 4	d			16 02								16 32							17 02					
Selling	d			16 11								16 41							17 11					
Faversham 2	a			16 16	16 18								16 46	16 48						17 16	17 18				
	d				16 22				16 28						16 52	16 58							17 22			17 28			
Teynham	d												16 58											
Sheerness-on-Sea	d								16 32						17 02								17 32		
Queenborough	d								16 36						17 06								17 36		
Swale	d								16 40						17 10								17 40		
Kemsley	d								16 44						17 14								17 44		
Sittingbourne 4	a				16 29				16 36	16 49					17 02	17 06	17 19						17 29			17 36	17 52		
	d				16 30				16 37						17 03	17 07							17 30			17 37			
Newington	d				16 35															17 35				
Rainham (Kent)	d				16 40				16 45						17 10	17 15							17 40			17 45			
Gillingham (Kent) 4	d	16 24	16 32		16 45			16 50		16 54	17 02		17 15	17 20			17 24	17 32		17 45		17 50		17 54	
Chatham 4	d	16 28	16 36		16 50			16 54		16 58	17 06		17 20	17 24			17 28	17 36		17 50		17 54		17 58	
Rochester 4	d	16 30	16 39		16 52			16 57		17 00	17 09		17 22	17 27			17 30	17 39		17 52		17 57		18 00	
Strood 4	a	16 35						17 01		17 05				17 31			17 35					18 02		18 05	
Gravesend 4	a	16 47						17 12		17 17				17 42			17 47					18 13		18 17	
Greenhithe for Bluewater	a	16 53								17 23							17 53							18 23	
Dartford 4	a	16 58								17 28							17 58							18 28	
London Bridge 4 ⊖	a	17 35								18 04							18 35							19 05	
London Cannon Street 4 ⊖	a																						
London Waterloo (East) 4 ⊖	a	17 40								18 08							18 41							19 09	
London Charing Cross 4 ⊖	a	17 44								18 12							18 45							19 13	
Sole Street	d		16 49								17 19							17 49						
Meopham	d		16 52		17 03						17 22		17 33					17 52		18 03				
Longfield	d		16 56		17 07						17 26		17 37					17 56		18 07				
Farningham Road	d		16 59								17 29							17 59						
Swanley 4	a		17 04								17 34							18 04						
St Mary Cray	a		17 09								17 39							18 09						
Bromley South 4	a		17 15		17 20						17 45		17 50					18 15		18 20				
Elephant & Castle ⊖	a																						
London Blackfriars 3 ⊖	a																						
London Victoria 15 ⊖	a		17 38		17 37						18 08		18 07					18 37		18 37				
Ebbsfleet International	a							17 17						17 47								18 17		
Stratford International ⊖	a							17 28						17 58								18 29		
St Pancras Internatnl 15 ⊖	a							17 38						18 08								18 37		

A from Faversham

B from Margate

For further services to St Pancras International, Blackfriars and Elephant & Castle and onwards to Bromley South, St Mary Cray and Swanley please refer to table 52

Table 212

Mondays to Fridays

29 August to 7 September

Ramsgate, Dover, Sheerness-on-Sea and Medway - London

Network Diagram - see first Page of Table 212

		SE ■ A ⌶	SE ■ B ⌶	SE	SE	SE	SE	SE ■	SE ■	SE	SE	SE	SE	SE ■	SE ■	SE	SE	SE ■	SE ■	SE ■	SE	SE
Ramsgate ■	d		17 05						17 35	17 59					18 05	18 29				18 35	18 59	
Dumpton Park	d		17 08						17 38						18 08					18 38		
Broadstairs	d		17 11						17 41	18 05					18 11	18 35				18 41	19 05	
Margate ■	d		17 16						17 46	18a10					18 16	18a40				18 46	19a10	
Westgate-on-Sea	d		17 20						17 50						18 20					18 50		
Birchington-on-Sea	d		17 24						17 54						18 24					18 54		
Herne Bay	d		17 33						18 03						18 33					19 03		
Chestfield & Swalecliffe	d		17 36						18 06						18 36					19 06		
Whitstable	d		17 39						18 09						18 39					19 09		
Dover Priory ■	d	17 05						17 39						18 05					18 39			
Kearsney	d	17 09						17 43						18 09					18 43			
Shepherds Well	d	17 14						17 48						18 14					18 48			
Snowdown	d	17 18												18 18								
Aylesham	d	17 20						17 52						18 20					18 52			
Adisham	d	17 23						17 55						18 23					18 55			
Bekesbourne	d	17 27												18 27								
Canterbury East ■	d	17 32						18 02						18 32					19 02			
Selling	d	17 41						18 11						18 41					19 11			
Faversham ■	a	17 46	17 48					18 16	18 18					18 46	18 48				19 16	19 18		
	d	17 52		17 58				18 22			18 28			18 52					19 22			
Teynham	d	17 58												18 58								
Sheerness-on-Sea	d				18 02							18 37										19 16
Queenborough	d				18 06							18 41										19 23
Swale	d				18 10							18 45										19 27
Kemsley	d				18 14							18 49										19 31
Sittingbourne ■	a	18 02		18 06	18 19			18 29			18 36	18 54		19 02					19 29			19 36
	d	18 03		18 07				18 30			18 37			19 03					19 30			
Newington	d							18 35											19 35			
Rainham (Kent)	d	18 10		18 15				18 40			18 45			19 10					19 40			
Gillingham (Kent) ■	d	18 15		18 20		18 24	18 32	18 45			18 50		18 54	19 15			19 24		19 45			
Chatham ■	d	18 20		18 24		18 28	18 36	18 50			18 54		18 58	19 20			19 28		19 50			
Rochester ■	d	18 22		18 27		18 30	18 39	18 52			18 57		19 00	19 22			19 30	19 39	19 52			
Strood ■	a			18 31		18 35					19 01		19 05				19 35					
Gravesend ■	a			18 42		18 47					19 12		19 17				19 47					
Greenhithe for Bluewater	a					18 53							19 23				19 53					
Dartford ■	a					18 58							19 28				19 58					
London Bridge ■ ⊖	a					19 35							20 06				20 36					
London Cannon Street ■ ⊖	a																					
London Waterloo (East) ■ ⊖	a					19 39							20 11				20 40					
London Charing Cross ■ ⊖	a					19 43							20 14				20 44					
Sole Street	d						18 49											19 49				
Meopham	d	18 33					18 52	19 03						19 33				19 52	20 03			
Longfield	d	18 37					18 56	19 07						19 37				19 56	20 07			
Farningham Road	d						18 59											19 59				
Swanley ■	a						19 04											20 04				
St Mary Cray	a						19 09											20 09				
Bromley South ■	a	18 50					19 15	19 20						19 50				20 15	20 20			
Elephant & Castle ⊖	a																					
London Blackfriars ■ ⊖	a																					
London Victoria ■ ⊖	a	19 07					19 37	19 37						20 07				20 37	20 38			
Ebbsfleet International	a			18 47							19 17											
Stratford International ⊖	a			19 02							19 28											
St Pancras Internatnl ■ ⊖	a			19 10							19 39											

A ⌶ from Faversham

B ⌶ from Margate

For further services to St Pancras International, Blackfriars and Elephant & Castle and onwards to Bromley South, St Mary Cray and Swanley please refer to table 52

Table 212

Mondays to Fridays

29 August to 7 September

Ramsgate, Dover, Sheerness-on-Sea and Medway - London

Network Diagram - see first Page of Table 212

		SE	SE	SE ■	SE ■	SE	SE	SE	SE	SE ■	SE ■	SE	SE	SE	SE	SE	SE ■	SE ■	SE	SE	SE	SE	SE
Ramsgate ■	d				19 05						19 25	19 31	19 59					20 05	20 32		21 00		
Dumpton Park	d				19 08						19 28							20 08					
Broadstairs	d				19 11						19 31	19 36	20 05					20 11	20 38		21 05		
Margate ■	d				19 16						19 38	19a41	20a10					20 16	20a43		21a11		
Westgate-on-Sea	d				19 20						19 41							20 20					
Birchington-on-Sea	d				19 24						19 45							20 24					
Herne Bay	d				19 33						19 54							20 33					
Chestfield & Swalecliffe	d				19 36						19 58							20 36					
Whitstable	d				19 39						20 01							20 39					
Dover Priory ■	d			19 05						19 40							20 05						
Kearsney	d			19 09													20 09						
Shepherds Well	d			19 14													20 14						
Snowdown	d			19 18													20 18						
Aylesham	d			19 20													20 20						
Adisham	d			19 23													20 23						
Bekesbourne	d			19 27													20 27						
Canterbury East ■	d			19 32						19 57							20 32						
Selling	d			19 41													20 41						
Faversham ■	a			19 46	19 48					20 08	20 10						20 46	20 48					
	d	19 28		19 52			19 58			20 14				20 28			20 52			20 58			
Teynham	d			19 58													20 58						
Sheerness-on-Sea	d					19 46		20 02							20 32							21 02	
Queenborough	d					19 53		20 06							20 36							21 06	
Swale	d					19 57		20 10							20 40							21 10	
Kemsley	d					20 01		20 14							20 44							21 14	
Sittingbourne ■	a	19 36		20 02		20 06	20 06	20 19		20 21				20 36	20 49		21 02			21 06		21 19	
	d	19 37		20 03			20 07			20 22				20 37			21 03			21 07			
Newington	d									20 27													
Rainham (Kent)	d	19 45		20 10			20 15			20 31				20 45			21 10			21 15			
Gillingham (Kent) ■	d	19 50	19 54	20 15			20 20		20 24	20 36				20 50		20 54	21 15			21 20			21 24
Chatham ■	d	19 54	19 58	20 20			20 24		20 28	20 41				20 54		20 58	21 20			21 24			21 28
Rochester ■	d	19 57	20 00	20 22			20 27		20 30	20 43				20 57		21 00	21 22			21 27			21 30
Strood ■	a	20 01	20 05				20 31		20 35					21 01		21 05				21 31			21 35
Gravesend ■	a	20 12	20 17				20 42		20 47					21 12		21 17				21 42			21 47
Greenhithe for Bluewater	a		20 23						20 53							21 23							21 53
Dartford ■	a		20 28						20 58							21 28							21 58
London Bridge ■ ⊖	a		21 06						21 36							22 05							22 35
London Cannon Street ■ ⊖	a																						
London Waterloo (East) ■ ⊖	a		21 10						21 40							22 09							22 39
London Charing Cross ■ ⊖	a		21 14						21 44							22 13							22 43
Sole Street	d									20 54													
Meopham	d			20 33						20 56							21 33						
Longfield	d			20 37						21 00							21 37						
Farningham Road	d									21 04													
Swanley ■	a									21 09													
St Mary Cray	a									21 14													
Bromley South ■	a			20 50						21 20							21 50						
Elephant & Castle ⊖	a																						
London Blackfriars ■ ⊖	a																						
London Victoria ■ ⊖	a			21 07						21 37							22 07						
Ebbsfleet International	a	20 17					20 47							21 17						21 47			
Stratford International ⊖	a	20 28					21 02							21 29						21 59			
St Pancras Internatnl ■ ⊖	a	20 38					21 10							21 36						22 07			

For further services to St Pancras International, Blackfriars and Elephant & Castle and onwards to Bromley South, St Mary Cray and Swanley please refer to table 52

Table 212

Mondays to Fridays

29 August to 7 September

Ramsgate, Dover, Sheerness-on-Sea and Medway - London

Network Diagram - see first Page of Table 212

		SE ■	SE	SE	SE		SE ■	SE ■	SE	SE	SE	SE	SE ■	SE ■	SE		SE ■	SE	SE	SE ■	SE ■	SE ■	SE
Ramsgate	d							21 05		21 59							22 05	22 59				23 05	
Dumpton Park	d							21 08									22 08					23 08	
Broadstairs	d							21 11		22 05							22 11	23 05				23 11	
Margate	d							21 16		22a10							22 16	23a10				23 16	
Westgate-on-Sea	d							21 20									22 20					23 20	
Birchington-on-Sea	d							21 24									22 24					23 24	
Herne Bay	d							21 33									22 33					23 33	
Chestfield & Swalecliffe	d							21 36									22 36					23 36	
Whitstable	d							21 39									22 39					23 39	
Dover Priory	d	20 45					21 05						21 45	22 05						22 45	23 05		
Kearsney	d						21 09							22 09							23 09		
Shepherds Well	d						21 14							22 14							23 14		
Snowdown	d						21 18							22 18							23 18		
Aylesham	d						21 20							22 20							23 20		
Adisham	d						21 23							22 23							23 23		
Bekesbourne	d						21 27							22 27							23 27		
Canterbury East	d	21 02					21 32						22 02	22 32						23 02	23 32		
Selling	d						21 41							22 41							23 41		
Faversham	a	21 13					21 46	21 48					22 13	22 46			22 48			23 13	23 46	23 48	
	d	21 14	21 28					21 52	21 58				22 14				22 52			23 14		23 52	
Teynham	d							21 58									22 58					23 58	
Sheerness-on-Sea	d				21 32						22 02								23 02				23 53
Queenborough	d				21 36						22 06								23 06				23 57
Swale	d				21 40						22 10								23 10				00 01
Kemsley	d				21 44						22 14								23 14				00 05
Sittingbourne	a	21 21	21 36					22 02	22 06		22 19		22 21				23 02		23 19	23 21		00 02	00 10
	d	21 22	21 37					22 03	22 07				22 22				23 03			23 22		00 03	
Newington	d	21 27			21 51								22 27							23 27		00 08	
Rainham (Kent)	d	21 31	21 45		21 55			22 10	22 15				22 31				23 10			23 31		00 12	
Gillingham (Kent)	d	21 36	21 50	21 54	22a02			22 15	22 20			22 24	22 36		22 54		23 15			23 36		00a17	
Chatham	d	21 41	21 54	21 58				22 20	22 24			22 28	22 41		22 58		23 20			23 41			
Rochester	d	21 43	21 57	22 00				22 22	22 27			22 30	22 43		23 00		23 22			23 43			
Strood	a		22 01	22 05					22 31			22 35			23 05								
Gravesend	a		22 12	22 17					22 42			22 47			23 17								
Greenhithe for Bluewater	a			22 23								22 53			23 23								
Dartford	a			22 28								22 58			23 28								
London Bridge ⊖	a			23 05								23 35											
London Cannon Street ⊖	a																						
London Waterloo (East) ⊖	a			23 09								23 39											
London Charing Cross ⊖	a			23 13								23 43											
Sole Street	d	21 54											22 54							23 54			
Meopham	d	21 56						22 33					22 56				23 33			23 56			
Longfield	d	22 00						22 37					23 00				23 37			23 59			
Farningham Road	d	22 04											23 04							00 04			
Swanley	a	22 09											23 09							00 09			
St Mary Cray	a	22 14											23 14							00 14			
Bromley South	a	22 20						22 50					23 20				23 50			00 20			
Elephant & Castle ⊖	a																						
London Blackfriars ⊖	a																						
London Victoria ⊖	a	22 37						23 07					23 37				00 07			00 38			
Ebbsfleet International	a		22 17						22 47														
Stratford International ⊖	a		22 28						22 59														
St Pancras Internatnl ⊖	a		22 35						23 07														

For further services to St Pancras International, Blackfriars and Elephant & Castle and onwards to Bromley South, St Mary Cray and Swanley please refer to table 52

Table 212

Saturdays

until 21 July, 18 Aug and from 15 Sep

Ramsgate, Dover, Sheerness-on-Sea and Medway - London

Network Diagram - see first Page of Table 212

		SE ■	SE ■	SE ■	SE	SE	SE	SE ■	SE	SE		SE ■	SE ■	SE	SE ■	SE ■	SE ■	SE	SE	SE		SE ■	SE ■	SE	SE
Ramsgate	d	22p05		23p05				04 32					05 05				05 40						06 05		
Dumpton Park	d	22p08		23p08									05 08										06 08		
Broadstairs	d	22p11		23p11				04 37					05 11				05 45						06 11		
Margate	d	22p16		23p16				04 42					05 16				05 50						06 16		
Westgate-on-Sea	d	22p20		23p20									05 20										06 20		
Birchington-on-Sea	d	22p24		23p24				04 47					05 24				05 55						06 24		
Herne Bay	d	22p33		23p33				04 56					05 33				06 04						06 33		
Chestfield & Swalecliffe	d	22p36		23p36									05 36										06 36		
Whitstable	d	22p39		23p39				05 01					05 39				06 09						06 39		
Dover Priory	d		22p45									05 05				05 45						06 05			
Kearsney	d											05 09										06 09			
Shepherds Well	d											05 14										06 14			
Snowdown	d											05 18										06 18			
Aylesham	d											05 20										06 20			
Adisham	d											05 23										06 23			
Bekesbourne	d											05 27										06 27			
Canterbury East	d		23p02									05 32				06 02						06 32			
Selling	d											05 41										06 41			
Faversham	a	22p48	23p13	23p48				05 09				05 46	05 48			06 14	06 18					06 46	06 48		
	d	22p52	23p14	23p52				05 09	05 28				05 52				06 22	06 28					06 52	06 58	
Teynham	d	22p58		23p58									05 58										06 58		
Sheerness-on-Sea	d				23p53														06 32						07 02
Queenborough	d				23p57														06 36						07 06
Swale	d				00 01														06 40						07 10
Kemsley	d				00 05														06 44						07 14
Sittingbourne	a	23p02	23p21	00 02	00 10			05 17	05 36				06 02				06 29	06 36	06 49				07 02	07 06	07 19
	d	23p03	23p22	00 03				05 17	05 37				06 03				06 30	06 37					07 03	07 07	
Newington	d		23p27	00 08				05 23									06 35								
Rainham (Kent)	d	23p10	23p31	00 12				05 27	05 45				06 10				06 40	06 45					07 10	07 15	
Gillingham (Kent)	d	23p15	23p36	00a17		04 48	05 18	05 32	05 50	05 54			06 15	06 24	06 32		06 45	06 50		06 54			07 15	07 20	
Chatham	d	23p20	23p41			04 52	05 22	05 36	05 54	05 58			06 20	06 28	06 36		06 50	06 54		06 58			07 20	07 24	
Rochester	d	23p22	23p43			04 54	05 24	05 39	05 57	06 00			06 22	06 30	06 39		06 52	06 57		07 00			07 22	07 27	
Strood	a					04 59	05 29		06 01	06 05				06 35				07 01		07 05				07 31	
Gravesend	a					05 11	05 41		06 12	06 17				06 47				07 12		07 17				07 42	
Greenhithe for Bluewater	a					05 20	05 50			06 23				06 53						07 23					
Dartford	a					05 27	05 57			06 28				06 58						07 28					
London Bridge ⊖	a					06 05	06 35			07 05				07 35						08 05					
London Cannon Street ⊖	a																								
London Waterloo (East) ⊖	a					06 09	06 39			07 09				07 39						08 09					
London Charing Cross ⊖	a					06 13	06 43			07 13				07 43						08 13					
Sole Street	d		23p54					05 49							06 49										
Meopham	d	23p33	23p56					05 52					06 33		06 52		07 03						07 33		
Longfield	d	23p37	23p59					05 56					06 37		06 56		07 07						07 37		
Farningham Road	d		00 04					06 00							06 59										
Swanley	a		00 09					06 05							07 04										
St Mary Cray	a		00 14					06 09							07 09										
Bromley South	a	23p50	00 20					06 15					06 50		07 15		07 20						07 50		
Elephant & Castle ⊖	a																								
London Blackfriars ⊖	a																								
London Victoria ⊖	a	00 07	00 38					06 37					07 07		07 37		07 37						08 07		
Ebbsfleet International	a								06 17									07 17						07 47	
Stratford International ⊖	a								06 29									07 29						07 59	
St Pancras Internatnl ⊖	a								06 36									07 36						08 06	

For further services to St Pancras International, Blackfriars and Elephant & Castle and onwards to Bromley South, St Mary Cray and Swanley please refer to table 52

Table 212

Saturdays

until 21 July, 18 Aug and from 15 Sep

Ramsgate, Dover, Sheerness-on-Sea and Medway - London

Network Diagram - see first Page of Table 212

		SE	SE 1	SE 1	SE 1	SE		SE	SE	SE 1	SE 1	SE	SE	SE	SE 1	SE 1 A	SE 1 B		SE	SE	SE	SE	SE 1 A	SE 1 B	SE
Ramsgate	d				06 40						07 05						07 40		07 59					08 05	
Dumpton Park	d										07 08													08 08	
Broadstairs	d				06 45						07 11						07 45		08 05					08 11	
Margate	d				06 50						07 16						07 50		08a10					08 16	
Westgate-on-Sea	d										07 20													08 20	
Birchington-on-Sea	d				06 55						07 24						07 55							08 24	
Herne Bay	d				07 04						07 33						08 04							08 33	
Chestfield & Swalecliffe	d										07 36													08 36	
Whitstable	d				07 09						07 39						08 09							08 39	
Dover Priory	d			06 45						07 05						07 45							08 05		
Kearsney	d									07 09													08 09		
Shepherds Well	d									07 14													08 14		
Snowdown	d									07 18													08 18		
Aylesham	d									07 20													08 20		
Adisham	d									07 23													08 23		
Bekesbourne	d									07 27													08 27		
Canterbury East	d			07 02						07 32						08 02							08 32		
Selling	d									07 41													08 41		
Faversham	a			07 14	07 18					07 46	07 48					08 14	08 18						08 46	08 48	
	d			07 22		07 28				07 52		07 58				08 22				08 28			08 52		08 58
Teynham	d									07 58													08 58		
Sheerness-on-Sea	d							07 32					08 02								08 32				
Queenborough	d							07 36					08 06								08 36				
Swale	d							07 40					08 10								08 40				
Kemsley	d							07 44					08 14								08 44				
Sittingbourne	a			07 29		07 36		07 49		08 02		08 06	08 19			08 29				08 36	08 49		09 02		09 06
	d			07 30		07 37				08 03		08 07				08 30				08 37			09 03		09 07
Newington	d			07 35												08 35									
Rainham (Kent)	d			07 40		07 45				08 10		08 15				08 40				08 45			09 10		09 15
Gillingham (Kent)	d	07 24	07 32	07 45		07 50			07 54	08 15		08 20		08 24	08 32	08 45				08 50		08 54	09 15		09 20
Chatham	d	07 28	07 36	07 50		07 54			07 58	08 20		08 24		08 28	08 36	08 50				08 54		08 58	09 20		09 24
Rochester	d	07 30	07 39	07 52		07 57			08 00	08 22		08 27		08 30	08 39	08 52				08 57		09 00	09 22		09 27
Strood	a	07 35				08 01			08 05			08 31		08 35						09 01		09 05			09 31
Gravesend	a	07 47				08 12			08 17			08 42		08 47						09 12		09 17			09 42
Greenhithe for Bluewater	a	07 53							08 23					08 53								09 23			
Dartford	a	07 58							08 28					08 58								09 28			
London Bridge ⊖	a	08 35							09 05					09 35								10 05			
London Cannon Street ⊖	a																								
London Waterloo (East) ⊖	a	08 39							09 09					09 39								10 09			
London Charing Cross ⊖	a	08 43							09 13					09 43								10 13			
Sole Street	d		07 49												08 49										
Meopham	d		07 52	08 03						08 33					08 52	09 03							09 33		
Longfield	d		07 56	08 07						08 37					08 56	09 07							09 37		
Farningham Road	d		07 59												08 59										
Swanley	a		08 04												09 04										
St Mary Cray	a		08 09												09 09										
Bromley South	a		08 15	08 20						08 50					09 15	09 20							09 50		
Elephant & Castle ⊖	a																								
London Blackfriars ⊖	a																								
London Victoria ⊖	a		08 37	08 37						09 07					09 37	09 37							10 07		
Ebbsfleet International	a					08 17						08 47								09 17					09 47
Stratford International ⊖	a					08 29						08 59								09 29					09 59
St Pancras Internatnl ⊖	a					08 36						09 06								09 36					10 06

A from Faversham

B from Margate

For further services to St Pancras International, Blackfriars and Elephant & Castle and onwards to Bromley South, St Mary Cray and Swanley please refer to table 52

Table 212

Saturdays

until 21 July, 18 Aug and from 15 Sep

Ramsgate, Dover, Sheerness-on-Sea and Medway - London

Network Diagram - see first Page of Table 212

		SE	SE		SE 1	SE 1 A	SE 1 B	SE	SE	SE	SE	SE 1 A	SE 1 B		SE	SE	SE	SE 1	SE 1 A	SE 1 B	SE	SE	SE		SE
Ramsgate	d						08 40	08 59					09 05							09 40	09 59				
Dumpton Park	d												09 08												
Broadstairs	d						08 45	09 05					09 11							09 45	10 05				
Margate	d						08 50	09a10					09 16							09 50	10a10				
Westgate-on-Sea	d												09 20												
Birchington-on-Sea	d						08 55						09 24							09 55					
Herne Bay	d						09 04						09 33							10 04					
Chestfield & Swalecliffe	d												09 36												
Whitstable	d						09 09						09 39							10 09					
Dover Priory	d					08 45						09 05							09 45						
Kearsney	d											09 09													
Shepherds Well	d											09 14													
Snowdown	d											09 18													
Aylesham	d											09 20													
Adisham	d											09 23													
Bekesbourne	d											09 27													
Canterbury East	d					09 02						09 32							10 02						
Selling	d											09 41													
Faversham	a					09 14	09 18					09 46	09 48						10 14	10 18					
	d					09 22			09 28			09 52			09 58				10 22			10 28			
Teynham	d											09 58													
Sheerness-on-Sea	d	09 02								09 32						10 02							10 32		
Queenborough	d	09 06								09 36						10 06							10 36		
Swale	d	09 10								09 40						10 10							10 40		
Kemsley	d	09 14								09 44						10 14							10 44		
Sittingbourne	a	09 19				09 29			09 36	09 49		10 02			10 06	10 19			10 29			10 36	10 49		
	d					09 30			09 37			10 03			10 07				10 30			10 37			
Newington	d					09 35													10 35						
Rainham (Kent)	d					09 40			09 45			10 10			10 15				10 40			10 45			
Gillingham (Kent)	d		09 24		09 32	09 45			09 50		09 54	10 15			10 20		10 24	10 32	10 45			10 50			10 54
Chatham	d		09 28		09 36	09 50			09 54		09 58	10 20			10 24		10 28	10 36	10 50			10 54			10 58
Rochester	d		09 30		09 39	09 52			09 57		10 00	10 22			10 27		10 30	10 39	10 52			10 57			11 00
Strood	a		09 35						10 01		10 05				10 31		10 35					11 01			11 05
Gravesend	a		09 47						10 12		10 17				10 42		10 47					11 12			11 17
Greenhithe for Bluewater	a		09 53								10 23						10 53								11 23
Dartford	a		09 58								10 28						10 58								11 28
London Bridge ⊖	a		10 35								11 05						11 35								12 05
London Cannon Street ⊖	a																								
London Waterloo (East) ⊖	a		10 39								11 09						11 39								12 09
London Charing Cross ⊖	a		10 43								11 13						11 43								12 13
Sole Street	d				09 49													10 49							
Meopham	d				09 52	10 03						10 33						10 52	11 03						
Longfield	d				09 56	10 07						10 37						10 56	11 07						
Farningham Road	d				09 59													10 59							
Swanley	a				10 04													11 04							
St Mary Cray	a				10 09													11 09							
Bromley South	a				10 15	10 20						10 50						11 15	11 20						
Elephant & Castle ⊖	a																								
London Blackfriars ⊖	a																								
London Victoria ⊖	a				10 37	10 37						11 07						11 37	11 37						
Ebbsfleet International	a								10 17						10 47							11 17			
Stratford International ⊖	a								10 29						10 59							11 29			
St Pancras Internatnl ⊖	a								10 36						11 06							11 36			

A from Faversham

B from Margate

For further services to St Pancras International, Blackfriars and Elephant & Castle and onwards to Bromley South, St Mary Cray and Swanley please refer to table 52

Saturdays

until 21 July, 18 Aug and from 15 Sep

Ramsgate, Dover, Sheerness-on-Sea and Medway - London

Network Diagram - see first Page of Table 212

		SE 1 A ⊼	SE 1 B ⊼	SE	SE	SE	SE 1	SE 1 A ⊼	SE 1 B ⊼		SE	SE	SE	SE	SE 1 A ⊼	SE 1 B ⊼	SE	SE	SE		SE 1	SE 1 A ⊼	SE 1 B ⊼	SE	SE
Ramsgate	d		10 05						10 40		10 59					11 05							11 40	11 59	
Dumpton Park	d		10 08													11 08									
Broadstairs	d		10 11						10 45		11 05					11 11							11 45	12 05	
Margate	d		10 16						10 50		11a10					11 16							11 50	12a10	
Westgate-on-Sea	d		10 20													11 20									
Birchington-on-Sea	d		10 24						10 55							11 24							11 55		
Herne Bay	d		10 33						11 04							11 33							12 04		
Chestfield & Swalecliffe	d		10 36													11 36									
Whitstable	d		10 39						11 09							11 39							12 09		
Dover Priory	d	10 05						10 45							11 05							11 45			
Kearsney	d	10 09													11 09										
Shepherds Well	d	10 14													11 14										
Snowdown	d	10 18													11 18										
Aylesham	d	10 20													11 20										
Adisham	d	10 23													11 23										
Bekesbourne	d	10 27													11 27										
Canterbury East	d	10 32						11 02							11 32							12 02			
Selling	d	10 41													11 41										
Faversham	a	10 46	10 48					11 14	11 18						11 46	11 48						12 14	12 18		
	d		10 52	10 58					11 22			11 28				11 52	11 58						12 22		12 28
Teynham	d		10 58													11 58									
Sheerness-on-Sea	d				11 02								11 32					12 02							
Queenborough	d				11 06								11 36					12 06							
Swale	d				11 10								11 40					12 10							
Kemsley	d				11 14								11 44					12 14							
Sittingbourne	a		11 02	11 06	11 19				11 29			11 36	11 49			12 02	12 06	12 19					12 29		12 36
	d		11 03	11 07					11 30			11 37				12 03	12 07						12 30		12 37
Newington	d								11 35														12 35		
Rainham (Kent)	d		11 10	11 15					11 40			11 45				12 10	12 15						12 40		12 45
Gillingham (Kent)	d		11 15	11 20		11 24	11 32		11 45			11 50		11 54		12 15	12 20		12 24		12 32		12 45		12 50
Chatham	d		11 20	11 24		11 28	11 36		11 50			11 54		11 58		12 20	12 24		12 28		12 36		12 50		12 54
Rochester	d		11 22	11 27		11 30	11 39		11 52			11 57		12 00		12 22	12 27		12 30		12 39		12 52		12 57
Strood	a			11 31		11 35						12 01		12 05			12 31		12 35						13 01
Gravesend	a			11 42		11 47						12 12		12 17			12 42		12 47						13 12
Greenhithe for Bluewater	a					11 53								12 23					12 53						
Dartford	a					11 58								12 28					12 58						
London Bridge ⊖	a					12 35								13 05					13 35						
London Cannon Street ⊖	a																								
London Waterloo (East) ⊖	a					12 39								13 09					13 39						
London Charing Cross ⊖	a					12 43								13 13					13 43						
Sole Street	d						11 49														12 49				
Meopham	d		11 33				11 52		12 03							12 33					12 52		13 03		
Longfield	d		11 37				11 56		12 07							12 37					12 56		13 07		
Farningham Road	d						11 59														12 59				
Swanley	a						12 04														13 04				
St Mary Cray	a						12 09														13 09				
Bromley South	a		11 50				12 15		12 20							12 50					13 15		13 20		
Elephant & Castle ⊖	a																								
London Blackfriars ⊖	a																								
London Victoria ⊖	a		12 07				12 37		12 37							13 07					13 37		13 37		
Ebbsfleet International	a			11 47								12 17					12 47								13 17
Stratford International ⊖	a			11 59								12 29					12 59								13 29
St Pancras Internatnl ⊖	a			12 06								12 36					13 06								13 36

A ⊼ from Faversham

B ⊼ from Margate

For further services to St Pancras International, Blackfriars and Elephant & Castle and onwards to Bromley South, St Mary Cray and Swanley please refer to table 52

Saturdays

until 21 July, 18 Aug and from 15 Sep

Ramsgate, Dover, Sheerness-on-Sea and Medway - London

Network Diagram - see first Page of Table 212

		SE	SE	SE 1 A ⊼	SE 1 B ⊼		SE	SE	SE	SE 1	SE 1 A ⊼	SE 1 B ⊼	SE	SE	SE		SE	SE 1 A ⊼	SE 1 B ⊼	SE	SE	SE	SE 1	SE 1 A ⊼	SE 1 B ⊼
Ramsgate	d				12 05							12 40	12 59						13 05						13 40
Dumpton Park	d				12 08														13 08						
Broadstairs	d				12 11							12 45	13 05						13 11						13 45
Margate	d				12 16							12 50	13a10						13 16						13 50
Westgate-on-Sea	d				12 20														13 20						
Birchington-on-Sea	d				12 24							12 55							13 24						13 55
Herne Bay	d				12 33							13 04							13 33						14 04
Chestfield & Swalecliffe	d				12 36														13 36						
Whitstable	d				12 39							13 09							13 39						14 09
Dover Priory	d			12 05							12 45							13 05						13 45	
Kearsney	d			12 09														13 09							
Shepherds Well	d			12 14														13 14							
Snowdown	d			12 18														13 18							
Aylesham	d			12 20														13 20							
Adisham	d			12 23														13 23							
Bekesbourne	d			12 27														13 27							
Canterbury East	d			12 32							13 02							13 32						14 02	
Selling	d			12 41														13 41							
Faversham	a			12 46	12 48						13 14	13 18						13 46	13 48					14 14	14 18
	d				12 52		12 58					13 22		13 28					13 52	13 58					14 22
Teynham	d				12 58														13 58						
Sheerness-on-Sea	d	12 32						13 02							13 32						14 02				
Queenborough	d	12 36						13 06							13 36						14 06				
Swale	d	12 40						13 10							13 40						14 10				
Kemsley	d	12 44						13 14							13 44						14 14				
Sittingbourne	a	12 49			13 02		13 06	13 19				13 29		13 36	13 49				14 02	14 06	14 19				14 29
	d				13 03		13 07					13 30		13 37					14 03	14 07					14 30
Newington	d											13 35													14 35
Rainham (Kent)	d				13 10		13 15					13 40		13 45					14 10	14 15					14 40
Gillingham (Kent)	d		12 54		13 15		13 20		13 24	13 32		13 45		13 50			13 54		14 15	14 20		14 24	14 32		14 45
Chatham	d		12 58		13 20		13 24		13 28	13 36		13 50		13 54			13 58		14 20	14 24		14 28	14 36		14 50
Rochester	d		13 00		13 22		13 27		13 30	13 39		13 52		13 57			14 00		14 22	14 27		14 30	14 39		14 52
Strood	a		13 05				13 31		13 35					14 01			14 05			14 31		14 35			
Gravesend	a		13 17				13 42		13 47					14 12			14 17			14 42		14 47			
Greenhithe for Bluewater	a		13 23						13 53								14 23					14 53			
Dartford	a		13 28						13 58								14 28					14 58			
London Bridge ⊖	a		14 05						14 35								15 05					15 35			
London Cannon Street ⊖	a																								
London Waterloo (East) ⊖	a		14 09						14 39								15 09					15 39			
London Charing Cross ⊖	a		14 13						14 43								15 13					15 43			
Sole Street	d									13 49													14 49		
Meopham	d				13 33					13 52		14 03							14 33				14 52		15 03
Longfield	d				13 37					13 56		14 07							14 37				14 56		15 07
Farningham Road	d									13 59													14 59		
Swanley	a									14 04													15 04		
St Mary Cray	a									14 09													15 09		
Bromley South	a				13 50					14 15		14 20							14 50				15 15		15 20
Elephant & Castle ⊖	a																								
London Blackfriars ⊖	a																								
London Victoria ⊖	a				14 07					14 37		14 37							15 07				15 37		15 37
Ebbsfleet International	a						13 47							14 17						14 47					
Stratford International ⊖	a						13 59							14 29						15 02					
St Pancras Internatnl ⊖	a						14 06							14 36						15 09					

A ⊼ from Faversham

B ⊼ from Margate

For further services to St Pancras International, Blackfriars and Elephant & Castle and onwards to Bromley South, St Mary Cray and Swanley please refer to table 52

Table 212

Saturdays

until 21 July, 18 Aug and from 15 Sep

Ramsgate, Dover, Sheerness-on-Sea and Medway - London

Network Diagram - see first Page of Table 212

		SE	SE	SE	SE	SE ■ A	SE ■ B	SE	SE	SE	SE ■	SE ■ A	SE ■ B	SE	SE	SE	SE	SE ■ A	SE ■ B	SE	SE	SE
Ramsgate ■	d	13 59					14 05						14 40	14 59					15 05			
Dumpton Park	d						14 08												15 08			
Broadstairs	d	14 05					14 11						14 45	15 05					15 11			
Margate ■	d	14a10					14 16						14 50	15a10					15 16			
Westgate-on-Sea	d						14 20												15 20			
Birchington-on-Sea	d						14 24						14 55						15 24			
Herne Bay	d						14 33						15 04						15 33			
Chestfield &Swalecliffe	d						14 36												15 36			
Whitstable	d						14 39						15 09						15 39			
Dover Priory ■	d					14 05						14 45						15 05				
Kearsney	d					14 09												15 09				
Shepherds Well	d					14 14												15 14				
Snowdown	d					14 18												15 18				
Aylesham	d					14 20												15 20				
Adisham	d					14 23												15 23				
Bekesbourne	d					14 27												15 27				
Canterbury East ■	d					14 32						15 02						15 32				
Selling	d					14 41												15 41				
Faversham ■	a					14 46	14 48					15 14	15 18					15 46	15 48			
	d		14 28			14 52		14 58				15 22			15 28			15 52		15 58		
Teynham	d					14 58												15 58				
Sheerness-on-Sea	d			14 32					15 02							15 32					16 02	
Queenborough	d			14 36					15 06							15 36					16 06	
Swale	d			14 40					15 10							15 40					16 10	
Kemsley	d			14 44					15 14							15 44					16 14	
Sittingbourne ■	a		14 36	14 49		15 02		15 06	15 19			15 29			15 36	15 49		16 02		16 06	16 19	
	d		14 37			15 03		15 07				15 30			15 37			16 03		16 07		
Newington	d											15 35										
Rainham (Kent)	d		14 45			15 10		15 15				15 40			15 45			16 10		16 15		
Gillingham (Kent) ■	d		14 50		14 54	15 15		15 20		15 24	15 32	15 45			15 50		15 54	16 15		16 20		16 24
Chatham ■	d		14 54		14 58	15 20		15 24		15 28	15 36	15 50			15 54		15 58	16 20		16 24		16 28
Rochester ■	d		14 57		15 00	15 22		15 27		15 30	15 39	15 52			15 57		16 00	16 22		16 27		16 30
Strood ■	a		15 01		15 05			15 31		15 35					16 01		16 05			16 31		16 35
Gravesend ■	a		15 12		15 17			15 42		15 47					16 12		16 17			16 42		16 47
Greenhithe for Bluewater	a				15 23					15 53							16 23					16 53
Dartford ■	a				15 28					15 58							16 28					16 58
London Bridge ■ ⊖	a				16 05					16 35							17 05					17 35
London Cannon Street ■ ⊖	a																					
London Waterloo (East) ■ ⊖	a				16 09					16 39							17 09					17 39
London Charing Cross ■ ⊖	a				16 13					16 43							17 13					17 43
Sole Street	d										15 49											
Meopham	d					15 33					15 52	16 03						16 33				
Longfield	d					15 37					15 56	16 07						16 37				
Farningham Road	d										15 59											
Swanley ■	a										16 04											
St Mary Cray	a										16 09											
Bromley South ■	a					15 50					16 15	16 20						16 50				
Elephant &Castle ⊖	a																					
London Blackfriars ■ ⊖	a																					
London Victoria ■ ⊖	a					16 07					16 37	16 37						17 07				
Ebbsfleet International	a		15 17					15 47							16 17					16 47		
Stratford International ⊖	a		15 29					16 02							16 29					17 02		
St Pancras Internatnl ■ ⊖	a		15 36					16 09							16 36					17 09		

A ⌶ from Faversham

B ⌶ from Margate

For further services to St Pancras International, Blackfriars and Elephant & Castle and onwards to Bromley South, St Mary Cray and Swanley please refer to table 52

Table 212

Saturdays

until 21 July, 18 Aug and from 15 Sep

Ramsgate, Dover, Sheerness-on-Sea and Medway - London

Network Diagram - see first Page of Table 212

		SE ■	SE ■ A	SE ■ B	SE	SE	SE	SE	SE ■ A	SE ■ B	SE	SE	SE	SE ■	SE ■	SE ■	SE	SE	SE	SE	SE ■	SE ■	SE
Ramsgate ■	d			15 40	15 59					16 05						16 40	16 59					17 05	
Dumpton Park	d									16 08												17 08	
Broadstairs	d			15 45	16 05					16 11						16 45	17 05					17 11	
Margate ■	d			15 50	16a10					16 16						16 50	17a10					17 16	
Westgate-on-Sea	d									16 20												17 20	
Birchington-on-Sea	d			15 55						16 24						16 55						17 24	
Herne Bay	d			16 04						16 33						17 04						17 33	
Chestfield &Swalecliffe	d									16 36												17 36	
Whitstable	d			16 09						16 39						17 09						17 39	
Dover Priory ■	d		15 45						16 05						16 45						17 05		
Kearsney	d								16 09												17 09		
Shepherds Well	d								16 14												17 14		
Snowdown	d								16 18												17 18		
Aylesham	d								16 20												17 20		
Adisham	d								16 23												17 23		
Bekesbourne	d								16 27												17 27		
Canterbury East ■	d		16 02						16 32						17 02						17 32		
Selling	d								16 41												17 41		
Faversham ■	a		16 14	16 18					16 46	16 48					17 14	17 18					17 46	17 48	
	d		16 22			16 28			16 52		16 58				17 22			17 28			17 52		17 58
Teynham	d								16 58												17 58		
Sheerness-on-Sea	d						16 32					17 02							17 32				
Queenborough	d						16 36					17 06							17 36				
Swale	d						16 40					17 10							17 40				
Kemsley	d						16 44					17 14							17 44				
Sittingbourne ■	a		16 29			16 36	16 49		17 02		17 06	17 19			17 29			17 36	17 49		18 02		18 06
	d		16 30			16 37			17 03		17 07				17 30			17 37			18 03		18 07
Newington	d		16 35												17 35								
Rainham (Kent)	d		16 40			16 45			17 10		17 15				17 40			17 45			18 10		18 15
Gillingham (Kent) ■	d	16 32	16 45			16 50		16 54	17 15		17 20		17 24	17 32	17 45			17 50		17 54	18 15		18 20
Chatham ■	d	16 36	16 50			16 54		16 58	17 20		17 24		17 28	17 36	17 50			17 54		17 58	18 20		18 24
Rochester ■	d	16 39	16 52			16 57		17 00	17 22		17 27		17 30	17 39	17 52			17 57		18 00	18 22		18 27
Strood ■	a					17 01		17 05			17 31		17 35					18 01		18 05			18 31
Gravesend ■	a					17 12		17 17			17 42		17 47					18 12		18 17			18 42
Greenhithe for Bluewater	a							17 23					17 53							18 23			
Dartford ■	a							17 28					17 58							18 28			
London Bridge ■ ⊖	a							18 05					18 35							19 05			
London Cannon Street ■ ⊖	a																						
London Waterloo (East) ■ ⊖	a							18 09					18 39							19 09			
London Charing Cross ■ ⊖	a							18 13					18 43							19 13			
Sole Street	d	16 49												17 49									
Meopham	d	16 52	17 03						17 33					17 52	18 03						18 33		
Longfield	d	16 56	17 07						17 37					17 56	18 07						18 37		
Farningham Road	d	16 59												17 59									
Swanley ■	a	17 04												18 04									
St Mary Cray	a	17 09												18 09									
Bromley South ■	a	17 15	17 20						17 50					18 15	18 20						18 50		
Elephant &Castle ⊖	a																						
London Blackfriars ■ ⊖	a																						
London Victoria ■ ⊖	a	17 37	17 37						18 07					18 37	18 37						19 07		
Ebbsfleet International	a					17 17					17 47							18 17					18 47
Stratford International ⊖	a					17 29					17 59							18 29					19 02
St Pancras Internatnl ■ ⊖	a					17 36					18 09							18 36					19 09

A ⌶ from Faversham

B ⌶ from Margate

For further services to St Pancras International, Blackfriars and Elephant & Castle and onwards to Bromley South, St Mary Cray and Swanley please refer to table 52

Table 212

Saturdays

until 21 July, 18 Aug and from 15 Sep

Ramsgate, Dover, Sheerness-on-Sea and Medway - London

Network Diagram - see first Page of Table 212

		SE	SE		SE [1]	SE [1]	SE [1]	SE	SE	SE	SE	SE [1]	SE [1]		SE	SE	SE	SE [1]	SE [1]	SE [1]	SE	SE	SE		SE
Ramsgate [4]	d						17 40	17 59					18 05							18 40	18 59				
Dumpton Park	d												18 08												
Broadstairs	d						17 45	18 05					18 11							18 45	19 05				
Margate [4]	d						17 50	18a10					18 16							18 50	19a10				
Westgate-on-Sea	d												18 20												
Birchington-on-Sea	d						17 55						18 24							18 55					
Herne Bay	d						18 04						18 33							19 04					
Chestfield & Swalecliffe	d												18 36												
Whitstable	d						18 09						18 39							19 09					
Dover Priory [4]	d					17 45						18 05							18 45						
Kearsney	d											18 09													
Shepherds Well	d											18 14													
Snowdown	d											18 18													
Aylesham	d											18 20													
Adisham	d											18 23													
Bekesbourne	d											18 27													
Canterbury East [4]	d					18 02						18 32							19 02						
Selling	d											18 41													
Faversham [2]	a					18 14	18 18					18 46	18 48						19 14	19 18					
	d					18 22			18 28			18 52			18 58				19 22			19 28			
Teynham	d											18 58													
Sheerness-on-Sea	d	18 02								18 32						19 02							19 32		
Queenborough	d	18 06								18 36						19 06							19 36		
Swale	d	18 10								18 40						19 10							19 40		
Kemsley	d	18 14								18 44						19 14							19 44		
Sittingbourne [4]	a	18 19				18 29			18 36	18 49		19 02			19 06	19 19			19 29			19 36	19 49		
	d					18 30			18 37			19 03			19 07				19 30			19 37			
Newington	d					18 35													19 35						
Rainham (Kent)	d					18 40			18 45			19 10			19 15				19 40			19 45			
Gillingham (Kent) [4]	d		18 24		18 32	18 45			18 50		18 54	19 15			19 20		19 24	19 32	19 45			19 50			19 54
Chatham [4]	d		18 28		18 36	18 50			18 54		18 58	19 20			19 24		19 28	19 36	19 50			19 54			19 58
Rochester [4]	d		18 30		18 39	18 52			18 57		19 00	19 22			19 27		19 30	19 39	19 52			19 57			20 00
Strood [4]	a		18 35						19 01		19 05				19 31		19 35					20 01			20 05
Gravesend [4]	a		18 47						19 12		19 17				19 42		19 47					20 12			20 17
Greenhithe for Bluewater	a		18 53								19 23						19 53								20 23
Dartford [4]	a		18 58								19 28						19 58								20 28
London Bridge [4] ⊖	a		19 36								20 06						20 36								21 06
London Cannon Street [4] ⊖	a																								
London Waterloo (East) [4] ⊖	a		19 42								20 10						20 40								21 10
London Charing Cross [4] ⊖	a		19 45								20 14						20 44								21 14
Sole Street	d				18 49													19 49							
Meopham	d				18 52	19 03						19 33						19 52	20 03						
Longfield	d				18 56	19 07						19 37						19 56	20 07						
Farningham Road	d				18 59													19 59							
Swanley [4]	a				19 04													20 04							
St Mary Cray	a				19 09													20 09							
Bromley South [4]	a				19 15	19 20						19 50						20 15	20 20						
Elephant & Castle ⊖	a																								
London Blackfriars [3] ⊖	a																								
London Victoria [15] ⊖	a				19 37	19 37						20 07						20 37	20 37						
Ebbsfleet International	a								19 16						19 47							20 17			
Stratford International ⊖	a								19 27						19 59							20 29			
St Pancras Internatnl [15] ⊖	a								19 38						20 06							20 36			

For further services to St Pancras International, Blackfriars and Elephant & Castle and onwards to Bromley South, St Mary Cray and Swanley please refer to table 52

Table 212

Saturdays

until 21 July, 18 Aug and from 15 Sep

Ramsgate, Dover, Sheerness-on-Sea and Medway - London

Network Diagram - see first Page of Table 212

		SE [1]	SE [1]	SE	SE	SE	SE	SE [1]	SE		SE	SE	SE [1]	SE [1]	SE	SE	SE	SE	SE [1]		SE	SE	SE [1]	SE [1]	SE
Ramsgate [4]	d		19 05		19 59									20 05		20 59								21 05	
Dumpton Park	d		19 08											20 08										21 08	
Broadstairs	d		19 11		20 05									20 11		21 05								21 11	
Margate [4]	d		19 16		20a10									20 16		21a10								21 16	
Westgate-on-Sea	d		19 20											20 20										21 20	
Birchington-on-Sea	d		19 24											20 24										21 24	
Herne Bay	d		19 33											20 33										21 33	
Chestfield & Swalecliffe	d		19 36											20 36										21 36	
Whitstable	d		19 39											20 39										21 39	
Dover Priory [4]	d	19 05											20 05										21 05		
Kearsney	d	19 09											20 09										21 09		
Shepherds Well	d	19 14											20 14										21 14		
Snowdown	d	19 18											20 18										21 18		
Aylesham	d	19 20											20 20										21 20		
Adisham	d	19 23											20 23										21 23		
Bekesbourne	d	19 27											20 27										21 27		
Canterbury East [4]	d	19 32											20 32										21 32		
Selling	d	19 41											20 41										21 41		
Faversham [2]	a	19 46	19 48										20 46	20 48									21 46	21 48	
	d	19 52		19 58				20 14	20 28				20 52		20 58				21 14		21 28		21 52		21 58
Teynham	d	19 58											20 58										21 58		
Sheerness-on-Sea	d					20 02					20 32						21 02								
Queenborough	d					20 06					20 36						21 06								
Swale	d					20 10					20 40						21 10								
Kemsley	d					20 14					20 44						21 14								
Sittingbourne [4]	a	20 02		20 06		20 19		20 21	20 36		20 49		21 02		21 06		21 19		21 21		21 36		22 02		22 06
	d	20 03		20 07				20 22	20 37				21 03		21 07				21 22		21 37		22 03		22 07
Newington	d							20 27											21 27						
Rainham (Kent)	d	20 10		20 15				20 31	20 45				21 10		21 15				21 31		21 45		22 10		22 15
Gillingham (Kent) [4]	d	20 15		20 20			20 24	20 36	20 50			20 54	21 15		21 20			21 24	21 36		21 50	21 54	22 15		22 20
Chatham [4]	d	20 20		20 24			20 28	20 41	20 54			20 58	21 20		21 24			21 28	21 41		21 54	21 58	22 20		22 24
Rochester [4]	d	20 22		20 27			20 30	20 43	20 57			21 00	21 22		21 27			21 30	21 43		21 57	22 00	22 22		22 27
Strood [4]	a			20 31			20 35		21 01			21 05			21 31			21 35			22 01	22 05			22 31
Gravesend [4]	a			20 42			20 47		21 12			21 17			21 42			21 47			22 12	22 17			22 42
Greenhithe for Bluewater	a						20 53					21 23						21 53				22 23			
Dartford [4]	a						20 58					21 28						21 58				22 28			
London Bridge [4] ⊖	a						21 36					22 05						22 35				23 05			
London Cannon Street [4] ⊖	a																								
London Waterloo (East) [4] ⊖	a						21 40					22 09						22 39				23 09			
London Charing Cross [4] ⊖	a						21 44					22 13						22 43				23 13			
Sole Street	d							20 54											21 54						
Meopham	d	20 33						20 56					21 33						21 56				22 33		
Longfield	d	20 37						21 00					21 37						22 00				22 37		
Farningham Road	d							21 04											22 04						
Swanley [4]	a							21 09											22 09						
St Mary Cray	a							21 14											22 14						
Bromley South [4]	a	20 50						21 20					21 50						22 20				22 50		
Elephant & Castle ⊖	a																								
London Blackfriars [3] ⊖	a																								
London Victoria [15] ⊖	a	21 07						21 37					22 07						22 37				23 07		
Ebbsfleet International	a			20 47					21 17						21 47						22 17				22 47
Stratford International ⊖	a			21 02					21 29						21 59						22 29				22 59
St Pancras Internatnl [15] ⊖	a			21 09					21 36						22 06						22 36				23 06

For further services to St Pancras International, Blackfriars and Elephant & Castle and onwards to Bromley South, St Mary Cray and Swanley please refer to table 52

Table 212

Saturdays

until 21 July, 18 Aug and from 15 Sep

Ramsgate, Dover, Sheerness-on-Sea and Medway - London

Network Diagram - see first Page of Table 212

Station		SE	SE	SE	SE ■	SE ■	SE	SE ■	SE	SE	SE ■	SE ■	SE
Ramsgate	d	21 59						22 05	22 59			23 05	
Dumpton Park	d							22 08				23 08	
Broadstairs	d	22 05						22 11	23 05			23 11	
Margate	d	22a10						22 16	23a10			23 16	
Westgate-on-Sea	d							22 20				23 20	
Birchington-on-Sea	d							22 24				23 24	
Herne Bay	d							22 33				23 33	
Chestfield & Swalecliffe	d							22 36				23 36	
Whitstable	d							22 39				23 39	
Dover Priory	d					22 05					23 05		
Kearsney	d					22 09					23 09		
Shepherds Well	d					22 14					23 14		
Snowdown	d					22 18					23 18		
Aylesham	d					22 20					23 20		
Adisham	d					22 23					23 23		
Bekesbourne	d					22 27					23 27		
Canterbury East	d				22 02	22 32					23 32		
Selling	d					22 41					23 41		
Faversham	a				22 13	22 46		22 48			23 46	23 49	
	d				22 14			22 52				23 52	
Teynham	d							22 58				23 58	
Sheerness-on-Sea	d		22 02							23 02			23 53
Queenborough	d		22 06							23 06			23 57
Swale	d		22 10							23 10			00 01
Kemsley	d		22 14							23 14			00 05
Sittingbourne	a		22 19		22 21			23 02		23 19		00 02	00 10
	d				22 22			23 03				00 03	
Newington	d				22 27							00 08	
Rainham (Kent)	d				22 31			23 10				00 12	
Gillingham (Kent)	d			22 24	22 36		22 54	23 15				00a17	
Chatham	d			22 28	22 41		22 58	23 20					
Rochester	d			22 30	22 43		23 00	23 22					
Strood	a			22 35			23 05						
Gravesend	a			22 47			23 17						
Greenhithe for Bluewater	a			22 53			23 23						
Dartford	a			22 58			23 28						
London Bridge ⊖	a			23 35									
London Cannon Street ⊖	a												
London Waterloo (East) ⊖	a			23 39									
London Charing Cross ⊖	a			23 43									
Sole Street	d				22 54								
Meopham	d				22 56			23 33					
Longfield	d				23 00			23 37					
Farningham Road	d				23 04								
Swanley	a				23 09								
St Mary Cray	a				23 14								
Bromley South	a				23 20			23 50					
Elephant & Castle ⊖	a												
London Blackfriars ⊖	a												
London Victoria ⊖	a				23 37			00 07					
Ebbsfleet International	a												
Stratford International ⊖	a												
St Pancras Internatnl ⊖	a												

For further services to St Pancras International, Blackfriars and Elephant & Castle and onwards to Bromley South, St Mary Cray and Swanley please refer to table 52

Table 212

Saturdays

28 July to 11 August

Ramsgate, Dover, Sheerness-on-Sea and Medway - London

Network Diagram - see first Page of Table 212

Station		SE ■	SE ■	SE ■	SE	SE	SE	SE ■	SE	SE	SE	SE ■	SE ■	SE	SE	SE	SE	SE ■	SE ■	SE ■	SE	SE	SE
Ramsgate	d	22p05		23p05				04 32					05 04							05 40			
Dumpton Park	d	22p08		23p08									05 07										
Broadstairs	d	22p11		23p11				04 37		05 00			05 10							05 45		05 54	
Margate	d	22p16		23p16				04 42		05 05			05 16							05 50		05 59	
Westgate-on-Sea	d	22p20		23p20									05 20										
Birchington-on-Sea	d	22p24		23p24				04 47					05 23							05 55		06 04	
Herne Bay	d	22p33		23p33				04 56		05 16			05 32							06 04		06 13	
Chestfield & Swalecliffe	d	22p36		23p36									05 36										
Whitstable	d	22p39		23p39				05 01					05 39							06 09		06 19	
Dover Priory	d		22p45									05 05							05 45				
Kearsney	d											05 09											
Shepherds Well	d											05 14											
Snowdown	d											05 18											
Aylesham	d											05 20											
Adisham	d											05 23											
Bekesbourne	d											05 27											
Canterbury East	d		23p02									05 32							06 02				
Selling	d											05 41											
Faversham	a	22p48	23p13	23p48				05 09		05 28		05 46	05 48						06 14	06 18		06 27	
	d	22p52	23p14	23p52				05 09		05 28		05 52			05 58	05 58			06 22			06 28	
Teynham	d	22p58		23p58								05 58											
Sheerness-on-Sea	d				23p53																		06 32
Queenborough	d				23p57																		06 36
Swale	d				00 01																		06 40
Kemsley	d				00 05																		06 44
Sittingbourne	a	23p02	23p21	00 02	00 10			05 17		05 36		06 02			06 06	06 06			06 29			06 36	06 49
	d	23p03	23p22	00 03				05 17		05 37		06 03			06 07	06 06			06 30			06 37	
Newington	d		23p27	00 08				05 23											06 35				
Rainham (Kent)	d	23p10	23p31	00 12				05 27		05 45		06 10			06 15	06 14			06 40			06 45	
Gillingham (Kent)	d	23p15	23p36	00a17		04 48	05 18	05 32		05 50	05 54	06 15			06 20	06 19	06 24	06 32	06 45			06 50	
Chatham	d	23p20	23p41			04 52	05 22	05 36		05 54	05 58	06 20			06 24	06 24	06 28	06 36	06 50			06 54	
Rochester	d	23p22	23p43			04 54	05 24	05 39		05 57	06 00	06 22			06 27	06 26	06 30	06 39	06 52			06 57	
Strood	a					04 59	05 29			06 01	06 05				06 31	06 31	06 35					07 01	
Gravesend	a					05 11	05 41			06 12	06 17				06 42	06 42	06 47					07 12	
Greenhithe for Bluewater	a					05 20	05 50				06 23						06 53						
Dartford	a					05 27	05 57				06 28						06 58						
London Bridge ⊖	a					06 05	06 35				07 05						07 35						
London Cannon Street ⊖	a																						
London Waterloo (East) ⊖	a					06 09	06 39				07 09						07 39						
London Charing Cross ⊖	a					06 16	06 46				07 16						07 46						
Sole Street	d		23p54					05 49										06 49					
Meopham	d	23p33	23p56					05 52				06 33						06 52	07 03				
Longfield	d	23p37	23p59					05 56				06 37						06 56	07 07				
Farningham Road	d		00 04					06 00										06 59					
Swanley	a		00 09					06 05										07 04					
St Mary Cray	a		00 14					06 09										07 09					
Bromley South	a	23p50	00 20					06 15				06 50						07 15	07 20				
Elephant & Castle ⊖	a																						
London Blackfriars ⊖	a																						
London Victoria ⊖	a	00 07	00 38					06 37				07 07						07 37	07 37				
Ebbsfleet International	a								05 32	06 16				06 32	06 47	06 47					07 06	07 16	
Stratford International ⊖	a								05 44	06 33				06 45	06 58	06 59					07 19	07 28	
St Pancras Internatnl ⊖	a								05 50	06 43				06 55	07 07	07 07					07 29	07 36	

For further services to St Pancras International, Blackfriars and Elephant & Castle and onwards to Bromley South, St Mary Cray and Swanley please refer to table 52

Table 212

Saturdays

28 July to 11 August

Ramsgate, Dover, Sheerness-on-Sea and Medway - London

Network Diagram - see first Page of Table 212

		SE	SE ■	SE ■	SE	SE	SE	SE	SE ■	SE ■	SE ■	SE	SE	SE ■	SE ■	SE	SE	SE	SE	SE	SE ■	SE ■ A ⌶	SE ■ B ⌶
Ramsgate ■	d			06 04							06 40				07 04								07 40
Dumpton Park	d			06 07											07 07								
Broadstairs	d			06 10		06 24					06 45				07 10								07 45
Margate ■	d			06 16		06 29					06 50				07 16								07 50
Westgate-on-Sea	d			06 20											07 20								
Birchington-on-Sea	d			06 23		06 34					06 55				07 23								07 55
Herne Bay	d			06 32		06 43					07 04				07 32								08 04
Chestfield & Swalecliffe	d			06 36											07 36								
Whitstable	d			06 39		06 49					07 09				07 39								08 09
Dover Priory ■	d		06 05							06 45				07 05								07 45	
Kearsney	d		06 09											07 09									
Shepherds Well	d		06 14											07 14									
Snowdown	d		06 18											07 18									
Aylesham	d		06 20											07 20									
Adisham	d		06 23											07 23									
Bekesbourne	d		06 27											07 27									
Canterbury East ■	d		06 32							07 02				07 32								08 02	
Selling	d		06 41											07 41									
Faversham ■	a		06 46	06 48		06 57				07 14	07 18			07 46	07 48							08 14	08 18
	d			06 52		06 58					07 22				07 52			07 58					08 22
Teynham	d			06 58											07 58								
Sheerness-on-Sea	d						07 02					07 32							08 02				
Queenborough	d						07 06					07 36							08 06				
Swale	d						07 10					07 40							08 10				
Kemsley	d						07 14					07 44							08 14				
Sittingbourne ■	a			07 02		07 06	07 19				07 29	07 49			08 02			08 06	08 19				08 29
	d			07 03		07 07					07 30				08 03			08 07					08 30
Newington	d										07 35												08 35
Rainham (Kent)	d			07 10		07 15					07 40				08 10			08 15					08 40
Gillingham (Kent) ■	d	06 54		07 15		07 20		07 24	07 32		07 45		07 54		08 15			08 20		08 24	08 32		08 45
Chatham ■	d	06 58		07 20		07 24		07 28	07 36		07 50		07 58		08 20			08 24		08 28	08 36		08 50
Rochester ■	d	07 00		07 22		07 27		07 30	07 39		07 52		08 00		08 22			08 27		08 30	08 39		08 52
Strood ■	a	07 05				07 31		07 35					08 05					08 31		08 35			
Gravesend ■	a	07 17				07 42		07 47					08 17					08 42		08 47			
Greenhithe for Bluewater	a	07 23						07 53					08 23							08 53			
Dartford ■	a	07 28						07 58					08 28							08 58			
London Bridge ■ ⊖	a	08 05						08 35					09 05							09 35			
London Cannon Street ■ ⊖	a																						
London Waterloo (East) ■ ⊖	a	08 09						08 39					09 09							09 39			
London Charing Cross ■ ⊖	a	08 16						08 46					09 16							09 43			
Sole Street	d								07 49												08 49		
Meopham	d			07 33					07 52		08 03				08 33						08 52		09 03
Longfield	d			07 37					07 56		08 07				08 37						08 56		09 07
Farningham Road	d								07 59												08 59		
Swanley ■	a								08 04												09 04		
St Mary Cray	a								08 09												09 09		
Bromley South ■	a			07 50					08 15		08 20				08 50						09 15		09 20
Elephant & Castle ⊖	a																						
London Blackfriars ■ ⊖	a																						
London Victoria ■ ⊖	a			08 07					08 37		08 37				09 07						09 37		09 37
Ebbsfleet International	a				07 32	07 46										08 06	08 32	08 46					
Stratford International ⊖	a				07 45	07 58										08 19	08 45	08 58					
St Pancras Internatnl ■ ⊖	a				07 55	08 08										08 29	08 55	09 08					

A ⌶ from Faversham

B ⌶ from Margate

For further services to St Pancras International, Blackfriars and Elephant & Castle and onwards to Bromley South, St Mary Cray and Swanley please refer to table 52

Table 212

Saturdays

28 July to 11 August

Ramsgate, Dover, Sheerness-on-Sea and Medway - London

Network Diagram - see first Page of Table 212

		SE	SE	SE ■ A ⌶	SE ■ B ⌶	SE	SE	SE	SE	SE	SE ■	SE ■ A ⌶	SE ■ B ⌶	SE	SE	SE ■ A ⌶	SE ■ B ⌶	SE	SE	SE	SE	SE
Ramsgate ■	d				08 04								08 40				09 04					
Dumpton Park	d				08 07												09 07					
Broadstairs	d				08 10								08 45				09 10					
Margate ■	d				08 16								08 50				09 16					
Westgate-on-Sea	d				08 20												09 20					
Birchington-on-Sea	d				08 23								08 55				09 23					
Herne Bay	d				08 32								09 04				09 32					
Chestfield & Swalecliffe	d				08 36												09 36					
Whitstable	d				08 39								09 09				09 39					
Dover Priory ■	d			08 05								08 45				09 05						
Kearsney	d			08 09												09 09						
Shepherds Well	d			08 14												09 14						
Snowdown	d			08 18												09 18						
Aylesham	d			08 20												09 20						
Adisham	d			08 23												09 23						
Bekesbourne	d			08 27												09 27						
Canterbury East ■	d			08 32								09 02				09 32						
Selling	d			08 41												09 41						
Faversham ■	a			08 46	08 48							09 14	09 18			09 46	09 48					
	d				08 52			08 58					09 22				09 52			09 58		
Teynham	d				08 58												09 58					
Sheerness-on-Sea	d	08 32							09 02					09 32							10 02	
Queenborough	d	08 36							09 06					09 36							10 06	
Swale	d	08 40							09 10					09 40							10 10	
Kemsley	d	08 44							09 14					09 44							10 14	
Sittingbourne ■	a	08 49			09 02			09 06	09 19				09 29	09 49			10 02			10 06	10 19	
	d				09 03			09 07					09 30				10 03			10 07		
Newington	d												09 35									
Rainham (Kent)	d				09 10			09 15					09 40				10 10			10 15		
Gillingham (Kent) ■	d		08 54		09 15			09 20		09 24	09 32		09 45		09 54		10 15			10 20		10 24
Chatham ■	d		08 58		09 20			09 24		09 28	09 36		09 50		09 58		10 20			10 24		10 28
Rochester ■	d		09 00		09 22			09 27		09 30	09 39		09 52		10 00		10 22			10 27		10 30
Strood ■	a		09 05					09 31		09 35					10 05					10 31		10 35
Gravesend ■	a		09 17					09 42		09 47					10 17					10 42		10 47
Greenhithe for Bluewater	a		09 23							09 53					10 23							10 53
Dartford ■	a		09 28							09 58					10 28							10 58
London Bridge ■ ⊖	a		10 05							10 35					11 05							11 35
London Cannon Street ■ ⊖	a																					
London Waterloo (East) ■ ⊖	a		10 09							10 39					11 09							11 39
London Charing Cross ■ ⊖	a		10 16							10 46					11 16							11 46
Sole Street	d										09 49											
Meopham	d				09 33						09 52		10 03				10 33					
Longfield	d				09 37						09 56		10 07				10 37					
Farningham Road	d										09 59											
Swanley ■	a										10 04											
St Mary Cray	a										10 09											
Bromley South ■	a				09 50						10 15		10 20				10 50					
Elephant & Castle ⊖	a																					
London Blackfriars ■ ⊖	a																					
London Victoria ■ ⊖	a				10 07						10 37		10 37				11 07					
Ebbsfleet International	a					09 06	09 32	09 46										10 06	10 32	10 46		
Stratford International ⊖	a					09 19	09 45	09 58										10 19	10 45	10 58		
St Pancras Internatnl ■ ⊖	a					09 29	09 55	10 08										10 29	10 55	11 08		

A ⌶ from Faversham

B ⌶ from Margate

For further services to St Pancras International, Blackfriars and Elephant & Castle and onwards to Bromley South, St Mary Cray and Swanley please refer to table 52

Table 212

Saturdays
28 July to 11 August

Ramsgate, Dover, Sheerness-on-Sea and Medway - London

Network Diagram - see first Page of Table 212

		SE ■	SE ■ A 🛒	SE ■ B 🛒	SE	SE	SE ■ A 🛒	SE ■ B 🛒	SE	SE	SE	SE	SE	SE ■	SE ■ A 🛒	SE ■ B 🛒	SE	SE	SE ■ A 🛒	SE ■ B 🛒	SE	SE	SE
Ramsgate ■	d			09 40				10 04								10 40				11 04			
Dumpton Park	d							10 07												11 07			
Broadstairs	d			09 45				10 10								10 45				11 10			
Margate ■	d			09 50				10 16								10 50				11 16			
Westgate-on-Sea	d							10 20												11 20			
Birchington-on-Sea	d			09 55				10 23								10 55				11 23			
Herne Bay	d			10 04				10 32								11 04				11 32			
Chestfield & Swalecliffe	d							10 36												11 36			
Whitstable	d			10 09				10 39								11 09				11 39			
Dover Priory ■	d		09 45				10 05								10 45				11 05				
Kearsney	d						10 09												11 09				
Shepherds Well	d						10 14												11 14				
Snowdown	d						10 18												11 18				
Aylesham	d						10 20												11 20				
Adisham	d						10 23												11 23				
Bekesbourne	d						10 27												11 27				
Canterbury East ■	d		10 02				10 32								11 02				11 32				
Selling	d						10 41												11 41				
Faversham ■	a		10 14	10 18			10 46	10 48							11 14	11 18			11 46	11 48			
	d		10 22				10 52				10 58				11 22				11 52				11 58
Teynham	d						10 58												11 58				
Sheerness-on-Sea	d				10 32							11 02					11 32						
Queenborough	d				10 36							11 06					11 36						
Swale	d				10 40							11 10					11 40						
Kemsley	d				10 44							11 14					11 44						
Sittingbourne ■	a		10 29		10 49		11 02				11 06	11 19			11 29		11 49		12 02				12 06
	d		10 30				11 03				11 07				11 30				12 03				12 07
Newington	d		10 35												11 35								
Rainham (Kent)	d		10 40				11 10				11 15				11 40				12 10				12 15
Gillingham (Kent) ■	d	10 32	10 45			10 54	11 15				11 20		11 24	11 32	11 45			11 54	12 15				12 20
Chatham ■	d	10 36	10 50			10 58	11 20				11 24		11 28	11 36	11 50			11 58	12 20				12 24
Rochester ■	d	10 39	10 52			11 00	11 22				11 27		11 30	11 39	11 52			12 00	12 22				12 27
Strood ■	a					11 05					11 31		11 35					12 05					12 31
Gravesend ■	a					11 17					11 42		11 47					12 17					12 42
Greenhithe for Bluewater	a					11 23							11 53					12 23					
Dartford ■	a					11 28							11 58					12 28					
London Bridge ■ ⊖	a					12 05							12 35					13 05					
London Cannon Street ■ ⊖	a																						
London Waterloo (East) ■ ⊖	a					12 09							12 39					13 09					
London Charing Cross ■ ⊖	a					12 16							12 46					13 16					
Sole Street	d	10 49												11 49									
Meopham	d	10 52	11 03				11 33							11 52	12 03				12 33				
Longfield	d	10 56	11 07				11 37							11 56	12 07				12 37				
Farningham Road	d	10 59												11 59									
Swanley ■	a	11 04												12 04									
St Mary Cray	a	11 09												12 09									
Bromley South ■	a	11 15	11 20				11 50							12 15	12 20				12 50				
Elephant & Castle ⊖	a																						
London Blackfriars ■ ⊖	a																						
London Victoria ■ ⊖	a	11 37	11 37				12 07							12 37	12 37				13 07				
Ebbsfleet International	a								11 06	11 32	11 46										12 06	12 32	12 46
Stratford International ⊖	a								11 19	11 45	11 58										12 19	12 45	12 58
St Pancras Internatnl ■ ⊖	a								11 29	11 55	12 08										12 29	12 55	13 08

A 🛒 from Faversham

B 🛒 from Margate

For further services to St Pancras International, Blackfriars and Elephant & Castle and onwards to Bromley South, St Mary Cray and Swanley please refer to table 52

Table 212

Saturdays
28 July to 11 August

Ramsgate, Dover, Sheerness-on-Sea and Medway - London

Network Diagram - see first Page of Table 212

		SE	SE	SE ■	SE ■ A 🛒	SE ■ B 🛒	SE	SE	SE ■ A 🛒	SE ■ B 🛒	SE	SE	SE	SE	SE	SE ■	SE ■ A 🛒	SE ■ B 🛒	SE	SE	SE ■ A 🛒	SE ■ B 🛒	SE
Ramsgate ■	d					11 40				12 04								12 40				13 04	
Dumpton Park	d									12 07												13 07	
Broadstairs	d					11 45				12 10								12 45				13 10	
Margate ■	d					11 50				12 16								12 50				13 16	
Westgate-on-Sea	d									12 20												13 20	
Birchington-on-Sea	d					11 55				12 23								12 55				13 23	
Herne Bay	d					12 04				12 32								13 04				13 32	
Chestfield & Swalecliffe	d									12 36												13 36	
Whitstable	d					12 09				12 39								13 09				13 39	
Dover Priory ■	d				11 45				12 05								12 45				13 05		
Kearsney	d								12 09												13 09		
Shepherds Well	d								12 14												13 14		
Snowdown	d								12 18												13 18		
Aylesham	d								12 20												13 20		
Adisham	d								12 23												13 23		
Bekesbourne	d								12 27												13 27		
Canterbury East ■	d				12 02				12 32								13 02				13 32		
Selling	d								12 41												13 41		
Faversham ■	a				12 14	12 18			12 46	12 48							13 14	13 18			13 46	13 48	
	d				12 22				12 52				12 58				13 22				13 52		
Teynham	d								12 58												13 58		
Sheerness-on-Sea	d	12 02					12 32							13 02					13 32				
Queenborough	d	12 06					12 36							13 06					13 36				
Swale	d	12 10					12 40							13 10					13 40				
Kemsley	d	12 14					12 44							13 14					13 44				
Sittingbourne ■	a	12 19			12 29		12 49		13 02				13 06	13 19			13 29		13 49		14 02		
	d				12 30				13 03				13 07				13 30				14 03		
Newington	d				12 35												13 35						
Rainham (Kent)	d				12 40				13 10				13 15				13 40				14 10		
Gillingham (Kent) ■	d		12 24	12 32	12 45			12 54	13 15				13 20		13 24	13 32	13 45			13 54	14 15		
Chatham ■	d		12 28	12 36	12 50			12 58	13 20				13 24		13 28	13 36	13 50			13 58	14 20		
Rochester ■	d		12 30	12 39	12 52			13 00	13 22				13 27		13 30	13 39	13 52			14 00	14 22		
Strood ■	a		12 35					13 05					13 31		13 35					14 05			
Gravesend ■	a		12 47					13 17					13 42		13 47					14 17			
Greenhithe for Bluewater	a		12 53					13 23							13 53					14 23			
Dartford ■	a		12 58					13 28							13 58					14 28			
London Bridge ■ ⊖	a		13 35					14 05							14 35					15 05			
London Cannon Street ■ ⊖	a																						
London Waterloo (East) ■ ⊖	a		13 39					14 09							14 39					15 09			
London Charing Cross ■ ⊖	a		13 46					14 16							14 46					15 16			
Sole Street	d			12 49												13 49							
Meopham	d			12 52	13 03				13 33							13 52	14 03				14 33		
Longfield	d			12 56	13 07				13 37							13 56	14 07				14 37		
Farningham Road	d			12 59												13 59							
Swanley ■	a			13 04												14 04							
St Mary Cray	a			13 09												14 09							
Bromley South ■	a			13 15	13 20				13 50							14 15	14 20				14 50		
Elephant & Castle ⊖	a																						
London Blackfriars ■ ⊖	a																						
London Victoria ■ ⊖	a			13 37	13 37				14 07							14 37	14 37				15 07		
Ebbsfleet International	a										13 06	13 32	13 46										14 06
Stratford International ⊖	a										13 19	13 45	13 58										14 19
St Pancras Internatnl ■ ⊖	a										13 29	13 55	14 08										14 29

A 🛒 from Faversham

B 🛒 from Margate

For further services to St Pancras International, Blackfriars and Elephant & Castle and onwards to Bromley South, St Mary Cray and Swanley please refer to table 52

Table 212

Saturdays
28 July to 11 August

Ramsgate, Dover, Sheerness-on-Sea and Medway - London

Network Diagram - see first Page of Table 212

		SE	SE		SE	SE	SE 1	SE 1 A ⌶	SE 1 B ⌶	SE	SE	SE 1 A ⌶	SE 1 B ⌶		SE	SE	SE	SE	SE	SE 1	SE 1 A ⌶	SE 1 B ⌶	SE		SE
Ramsgate 4	d								13 40				14 04									14 40			
Dumpton Park	d												14 07												
Broadstairs	d								13 45				14 10									14 45			
Margate 4	d								13 50				14 16									14 50			
Westgate-on-Sea	d												14 20												
Birchington-on-Sea	d								13 55				14 23									14 55			
Herne Bay	d								14 04				14 32									15 04			
Chestfield & Swalecliffe	d												14 36												
Whitstable	d								14 09				14 39									15 09			
Dover Priory 4	d							13 45				14 05									14 45				
Kearsney	d											14 09													
Shepherds Well	d											14 14													
Snowdown	d											14 18													
Aylesham	d											14 20													
Adisham	d											14 23													
Bekesbourne	d											14 27													
Canterbury East 4	d							14 02				14 32									15 02				
Selling	d											14 41													
Faversham 2	a							14 14	14 18			14 46	14 48								15 14	15 18			
	d		13 58					14 22				14 52					14 58				15 22				
Teynham	d											14 58													
Sheerness-on-Sea	d				14 02					14 32								15 02					15 32		
Queenborough	d				14 06					14 36								15 06					15 36		
Swale	d				14 10					14 40								15 10					15 40		
Kemsley	d				14 14					14 44								15 14					15 44		
Sittingbourne 4	a		14 06		14 19			14 29		14 49		15 02					15 06	15 19			15 29		15 49		
	d		14 07					14 30				15 03					15 07				15 30				
Newington	d							14 35													15 35				
Rainham (Kent)	d		14 15					14 40				15 10					15 15				15 40				
Gillingham (Kent) 4	d		14 20			14 24	14 32	14 45			14 54	15 15					15 20		15 24	15 32	15 45				15 54
Chatham 4	d		14 24			14 28	14 36	14 50			14 58	15 20					15 24		15 28	15 36	15 50				15 58
Rochester 4	d		14 27			14 30	14 39	14 52			15 00	15 22					15 27		15 30	15 39	15 52				16 00
Strood 4	a		14 31			14 35					15 05						15 31		15 35						16 05
Gravesend 4	a		14 42			14 47					15 17						15 42		15 47						16 17
Greenhithe for Bluewater	a					14 53					15 23								15 53						16 23
Dartford 4	a					14 58					15 28								15 58						16 28
London Bridge 4 ⊖	a					15 35					16 05								16 35						17 05
London Cannon Street 4 ⊖	a																								
London Waterloo (East) 4 ⊖	a					15 39					16 09								16 39						17 09
London Charing Cross 4 ⊖	a					15 46					16 16								16 46						17 16
Sole Street	d						14 49													15 49					
Meopham	d						14 52	15 03				15 33								15 52	16 03				
Longfield	d						14 56	15 07				15 37								15 56	16 07				
Farningham Road	d						14 59													15 59					
Swanley 4	a						15 04													16 04					
St Mary Cray	a						15 09													16 09					
Bromley South 4	a						15 15	15 20				15 50								16 15	16 20				
Elephant & Castle ⊖	a																								
London Blackfriars 3 ⊖	a																								
London Victoria 15 ⊖	a						15 37	15 37				16 07								16 37	16 37				
Ebbsfleet International	a	14 32	14 46												15 06	15 32	15 46								
Stratford International ⊖	a	14 45	14 58												15 19	15 45	15 58								
St Pancras Internatnl 15 ⊖	a	14 55	15 08												15 29	15 55	16 08								

A ⌶ from Faversham

B ⌶ from Margate

For further services to St Pancras International, Blackfriars and Elephant & Castle and onwards to Bromley South, St Mary Cray and Swanley please refer to table 52

Table 212

Saturdays
28 July to 11 August

Ramsgate, Dover, Sheerness-on-Sea and Medway - London

Network Diagram - see first Page of Table 212

		SE 1 A ⌶	SE 1 B ⌶	SE	SE	SE	SE	SE	SE 1		SE 1 A ⌶	SE 1 B ⌶	SE	SE	SE 1 A ⌶	SE 1 B ⌶	SE	SE	SE		SE	SE	SE 1	SE 1	SE 1
Ramsgate 4	d		15 04									15 40				16 04									16 40
Dumpton Park	d		15 07													16 07									
Broadstairs	d		15 10									15 45				16 10									16 45
Margate 4	d		15 16									15 50				16 16									16 50
Westgate-on-Sea	d		15 20													16 20									
Birchington-on-Sea	d		15 23									15 55				16 23									16 55
Herne Bay	d		15 32									16 04				16 32									17 04
Chestfield & Swalecliffe	d		15 36													16 36									
Whitstable	d		15 39									16 09				16 39									17 09
Dover Priory 4	d	15 05									15 45				16 05									16 45	
Kearsney	d	15 09													16 09										
Shepherds Well	d	15 14													16 14										
Snowdown	d	15 18													16 18										
Aylesham	d	15 20													16 20										
Adisham	d	15 23													16 23										
Bekesbourne	d	15 27													16 27										
Canterbury East 4	d	15 32									16 02				16 32									17 02	
Selling	d	15 41													16 41										
Faversham 2	a	15 46	15 48								16 14	16 18			16 46	16 48								17 14	17 18
	d	15 52				15 58					16 22				16 52				16 58					17 22	
Teynham	d	15 58													16 58										
Sheerness-on-Sea	d						16 02						16 32								17 02				
Queenborough	d						16 06						16 36								17 06				
Swale	d						16 10						16 40								17 10				
Kemsley	d						16 14						16 44								17 14				
Sittingbourne 4	a	16 02				16 06	16 19				16 29		16 49		17 02				17 06		17 19			17 29	
	d	16 03				16 07					16 30				17 03				17 07					17 30	
Newington	d										16 35													17 35	
Rainham (Kent)	d	16 10				16 15					16 40				17 10				17 15					17 40	
Gillingham (Kent) 4	d	16 15				16 20		16 24	16 32		16 45			16 54	17 15				17 20			17 24	17 32	17 45	
Chatham 4	d	16 20				16 24		16 28	16 36		16 50			16 58	17 20				17 24			17 28	17 36	17 50	
Rochester 4	d	16 22				16 27		16 30	16 39		16 52			17 00	17 22				17 27			17 30	17 39	17 52	
Strood 4	a					16 31		16 35						17 05					17 31			17 35			
Gravesend 4	a					16 42		16 47						17 17					17 42			17 47			
Greenhithe for Bluewater	a							16 53						17 23								17 53			
Dartford 4	a							16 58						17 28								17 58			
London Bridge 4 ⊖	a							17 35						18 05								18 35			
London Cannon Street 4 ⊖	a																								
London Waterloo (East) 4 ⊖	a							17 39						18 09								18 39			
London Charing Cross 4 ⊖	a							17 46						18 16								18 46			
Sole Street	d								16 49														17 49		
Meopham	d	16 33							16 52		17 03				17 33								17 52	18 03	
Longfield	d	16 37							16 56		17 07				17 37								17 56	18 07	
Farningham Road	d								16 59														17 59		
Swanley 4	a								17 04														18 04		
St Mary Cray	a								17 09														18 09		
Bromley South 4	a	16 50							17 15		17 20				17 50								18 15	18 20	
Elephant & Castle ⊖	a																								
London Blackfriars 3 ⊖	a																								
London Victoria 15 ⊖	a	17 07							17 37		17 37				18 07								18 37	18 37	
Ebbsfleet International	a			16 06	16 32	16 46											17 06	17 32	17 46						
Stratford International ⊖	a			16 19	16 45												17 19	17 45	17 58						
St Pancras Internatnl 15 ⊖	a			16 29	16 55												17 29	17 55	18 08						

A ⌶ from Faversham

B ⌶ from Margate

For further services to St Pancras International, Blackfriars and Elephant & Castle and onwards to Bromley South, St Mary Cray and Swanley please refer to table 52

Table 212

Saturdays
28 July to 11 August

Ramsgate, Dover, Sheerness-on-Sea and Medway - London

Network Diagram - see first Page of Table 212

		SE	SE	SE ■	SE ■	SE	SE	SE	SE	SE	SE ■	SE ■	SE ■	SE	SE	SE ■	SE ■	SE	SE	SE	SE	SE	SE ■
Ramsgate ■	d				17 04								17 40				18 04						
Dumpton Park	d				17 07												18 07						
Broadstairs	d				17 10								17 45				18 10						
Margate ■	d				17 16								17 50				18 16						
Westgate-on-Sea	d				17 20												18 20						
Birchington-on-Sea	d				17 23								17 55				18 23						
Herne Bay	d				17 32								18 04				18 32						
Chestfield & Swalecliffe	d				17 36												18 36						
Whitstable	d				17 39								18 09				18 39						
Dover Priory ■	d			17 05								17 45				18 05							
Kearsney	d			17 09												18 09							
Shepherds Well	d			17 14												18 14							
Snowdown	d			17 18												18 18							
Aylesham	d			17 20												18 20							
Adisham	d			17 23												18 23							
Bekesbourne	d			17 27												18 27							
Canterbury East ■	d			17 32								18 02				18 32							
Selling	d			17 41												18 41							
Faversham ■	a			17 46	17 48							18 14	18 18			18 46	18 48						
	d			17 52				17 58				18 22				18 52				18 58			
Teynham	d			17 58												18 58							
Sheerness-on-Sea	d	17 32							18 02					18 32							19 02		
Queenborough	d	17 36							18 06					18 36							19 06		
Swale	d	17 40							18 10					18 40							19 10		
Kemsley	d	17 44							18 14					18 44							19 14		
Sittingbourne ■	a	17 49		18 02				18 06	18 19			18 29		18 49		19 02				19 06	19 19		
	d			18 03				18 07				18 30				19 03				19 07			
Newington	d											18 35											
Rainham (Kent)	d			18 10				18 15				18 40				19 10				19 15			
Gillingham (Kent) ■	d		17 54	18 15				18 20		18 24	18 32	18 45			18 54	19 15				19 20		19 24	19 32
Chatham ■	d		17 58	18 20				18 24		18 28	18 36	18 50			18 58	19 20				19 24		19 28	19 36
Rochester ■	d		18 00	18 22				18 27		18 30	18 39	18 52			19 00	19 22				19 27		19 30	19 39
Strood ■	a		18 05					18 31		18 35					19 05					19 31		19 35	
Gravesend ■	a		18 17					18 42		18 47					19 17					19 42		19 47	
Greenhithe for Bluewater	a		18 23							18 53					19 23							19 53	
Dartford ■	a		18 28							18 58					19 28							19 58	
London Bridge ■ ⊖	a		19 05							19 36					20 07							20 37	
London Cannon Street ■ ⊖	a																						
London Waterloo (East) ■ ⊖	a		19 09							19 42					20 11							20 41	
London Charing Cross ■ ⊖	a		19 16							19 48					20 18							20 48	
Sole Street	d										18 49												19 49
Meopham	d			18 33							18 52	19 03				19 33							19 52
Longfield	d			18 37							18 56	19 07				19 37							19 56
Farningham Road	d										18 59												19 59
Swanley ■	a										19 04												20 04
St Mary Cray	a										19 09												20 09
Bromley South ■	a			18 50							19 15	19 20				19 50							20 15
Elephant & Castle ⊖	a																						
London Blackfriars ■ ⊖	a																						
London Victoria ■ ⊖	a			19 07							19 37	19 37				20 07							20 37
Ebbsfleet International	a					18 06	18 32	18 46										19 06	19 32	19 46			
Stratford International ⊖	a					18 19	18 45	18 58										19 19	19 45	19 58			
St Pancras Internatnl ■ ⊖	a					18 29	18 55	19 08										19 29	19 55	20 08			

For further services to St Pancras International, Blackfriars and Elephant & Castle and onwards to Bromley South, St Mary Cray and Swanley please refer to table 52

Table 212

Saturdays
28 July to 11 August

Ramsgate, Dover, Sheerness-on-Sea and Medway - London

Network Diagram - see first Page of Table 212

		SE ■	SE ■	SE	SE	SE ■	SE ■	SE	SE	SE	SE	SE	SE ■	SE	SE	SE ■	SE ■	SE	SE	SE	SE	SE
Ramsgate ■	d		18 40				19 04										20 04					
Dumpton Park	d						19 07										20 07					
Broadstairs	d		18 45				19 10										20 10					
Margate ■	d		18 50				19 16										20 16					
Westgate-on-Sea	d						19 20										20 20					
Birchington-on-Sea	d		18 55				19 23										20 23					
Herne Bay	d		19 04				19 32										20 32					
Chestfield & Swalecliffe	d						19 36										20 36					
Whitstable	d		19 09				19 39										20 39					
Dover Priory ■	d	18 45				19 05										20 05						
Kearsney	d					19 09										20 09						
Shepherds Well	d					19 14										20 14						
Snowdown	d					19 18										20 18						
Aylesham	d					19 20										20 20						
Adisham	d					19 23										20 23						
Bekesbourne	d					19 27										20 27						
Canterbury East ■	d	19 02				19 32										20 32						
Selling	d					19 41										20 41						
Faversham ■	a	19 14	19 18			19 46	19 48									20 46	20 48					
	d	19 22				19 52				19 58			20 14			20 52				20 58		
Teynham	d					19 58										20 58						
Sheerness-on-Sea	d			19 32							20 02			20 32							21 02	
Queenborough	d			19 36							20 06			20 36							21 06	
Swale	d			19 40							20 10			20 40							21 10	
Kemsley	d			19 44							20 14			20 44							21 14	
Sittingbourne ■	a	19 29		19 49		20 02				20 06	20 19		20 21	20 49		21 02				21 06	21 19	
	d	19 30				20 03				20 07			20 22			21 03				21 07		
Newington	d	19 35											20 27									
Rainham (Kent)	d	19 40				20 10				20 15			20 31			21 10				21 15		
Gillingham (Kent) ■	d	19 45			19 54	20 15				20 20		20 24	20 36		20 54	21 15				21 20		21 24
Chatham ■	d	19 50			19 58	20 20				20 24		20 28	20 41		20 58	21 20				21 24		21 28
Rochester ■	d	19 52			20 00	20 22				20 27		20 30	20 43		21 00	21 22				21 27		21 30
Strood ■	a				20 05					20 31		20 35			21 05					21 31		21 35
Gravesend ■	a				20 17					20 42		20 47			21 17					21 42		21 47
Greenhithe for Bluewater	a				20 23							20 53			21 23							21 53
Dartford ■	a				20 28							20 58			21 28							21 58
London Bridge ■ ⊖	a				21 07							21 36			22 05							22 35
London Cannon Street ■ ⊖	a																					
London Waterloo (East) ■ ⊖	a				21 11							21 40			22 09							22 39
London Charing Cross ■ ⊖	a				21 18							21 47			22 16							22 46
Sole Street	d												20 54									
Meopham	d	20 03				20 33							20 56			21 33						
Longfield	d	20 07				20 37							21 00			21 37						
Farningham Road	d												21 04									
Swanley ■	a												21 09									
St Mary Cray	a												21 14									
Bromley South ■	a	20 20				20 50							21 20			21 50						
Elephant & Castle ⊖	a																					
London Blackfriars ■ ⊖	a																					
London Victoria ■ ⊖	a	20 37				21 07							21 37			22 07						
Ebbsfleet International	a							20 06	20 32	20 46								21 06	21 32	21 46		
Stratford International ⊖	a							20 19	20 45	20 58								21 19	21 45	21 58		
St Pancras Internatnl ■ ⊖	a							20 29	20 55	21 08								21 29	21 55	22 08		

For further services to St Pancras International, Blackfriars and Elephant & Castle and onwards to Bromley South, St Mary Cray and Swanley please refer to table 52

Table 212

Saturdays

28 July to 11 August

Ramsgate, Dover, Sheerness-on-Sea and Medway - London

Network Diagram - see first Page of Table 212

		SE ■	SE	SE ■	SE ■	SE	SE	SE	SE	SE	SE ■	SE ■	SE	SE ■	SE	SE ■	SE ■	SE ■	SE	SE	SE
Ramsgate	d				21 04									22 04		22 34		23 04			
Dumpton Park	d				21 07									22 07		22 37		23 07			
Broadstairs	d				21 10									22 10		22 40		23 10			
Margate	d				21 16									22 16		22 46		23 16			
Wstgate-on-Sea	d				21 20									22 20		22 50		23 20			
Birchington-on-Sea	d				21 23									22 23		22 53		23 23			
Herne Bay	d				21 32									22 32		23 02		23 32			
Chestfield &Swalecliffe	d				21 36									22 36		23 06		23 36			
Wistable	d				21 39									22 39		23 09		23 39			
Dover Priory	d			21 05								22 05					23 05				
Kearsney	d			21 09								22 09					23 09				
Shepherds Well	d			21 14								22 14					23 14				
Snowdown	d			21 18								22 18					23 18				
Aylesham	d			21 20								22 20					23 20				
Adisham	d			21 23								22 23					23 23				
Bekesbourne	d			21 27								22 27					23 27				
Canterbury East	d			21 32							22 02	22 32					23 32				
Selling	d			21 41								22 41					23 41				
Faversham	a			21 46	21 48						22 13	22 46		22 48		23 18	23 46	23 49			
	d	21 14			21 52			21 58			22 14			22 52		23 25	23 52				
Teynham	d				21 58									22 58		23 31	23 58				
Sheerness-on-Sea	d								22 02						23 02						23 53
Qeenborough	d								22 06						23 06						23 57
Swale	d								22 10						23 10						00 01
Kemsley	d								22 14						23 14						00 05
Sittingbourne	a	21 21			22 02			22 06	22 19		22 21			23 02	23 19	23 35	00 02				00 10
	d	21 22			22 03			22 07			22 22			23 03		23 36	00 03				
Nwington	d	21 27									22 27						00 08				
Rinham (Kent)	d	21 31			22 10			22 15			22 31			23 10		23 43	00 12				
Gillingham (Kent)	d	21 36	21 54		22 15			22 20		22 24	22 36		22 54	23 15		23 48	00a17				
Chatham	d	21 41	21 58		22 20			22 24		22 28	22 41		22 58	23 20		23 53					
Rchester	d	21 43	22 00		22 22			22 27		22 30	22 43		23 00	23 22		23 55					
Strood	a		22 05					22 31		22 35			23 05								
Gravesend	a		22 17					22 42		22 47			23 17								
Greenhithe for Bluewater	a		22 23							22 53			23 23								
Dartford	a		22 28							22 58			23 28								
London Bridge ⊖	a		23 05							23 35											
London Cannon Street ⊖	a																				
London Waterloo (East) ⊖	a		23 09							23 39											
London Charing Cross ⊖	a		23 16							23 46											
Sole Street	d	21 54									22 54										
Meopham	d	21 56			22 33						22 56			23 33		00 06					
Lngfield	d	22 00			22 37						23 00			23 37		00 10					
Farningham Rad	d	22 04									23 04										
Swanley	a	22 09									23 09										
St Mary Cray	a	22 14									23 14										
Bromley South	a	22 20			22 50						23 20			23 50		00 23					
Ephant &Castle ⊖	a																				
London Blackfriars ⊖	a																				
London Victoria ⊖	a	22 37			23 07						23 37			00 07		00 39					
Ebbsfleet International	a					22 06	22 32	22 46											23 02	23 30	
Stratford International ⊖	a					22 19	22 45	22 58											23 16	23 42	
St Pancras Internatnl ⊖	a					22 29	22 55	23 07											23 26	23 51	

For further services to St Pancras hternational, Blackfriars and Ephant & Castle and onwards to Bromley South, St Mary Cray and Swanley please refer to table 52

Table 212

Saturdays

25 August to 8 September

Ramsgate, Dover, Sheerness-on-Sea and Medway - London

Network Diagram - see first Page of Table 212

		SE ■	SE ■	SE ■	SE	SE	SE	SE ■	SE A	SE B	SE A	SE	SE ■	SE ■	SE A	SE	SE ■	SE ■	SE ■	SE B	SE A	SE	SE
Ramsgate	d	22p05		23p05				04 32						05 05					05 40				
Dumpton Park	d	22p08		23p08										05 08									
Broadstairs	d	22p11		23p11				04 37						05 11					05 45				
Margate	d	22p16		23p16				04 42						05 16					05 50				
Wstgate-on-Sea	d	22p20		23p20										05 20									
Birchington-on-Sea	d	22p24		23p24				04 47						05 24					05 55				
Herne Bay	d	22p33		23p33				04 56						05 33					06 04				
Chestfield &Swalecliffe	d	22p36		23p36										05 36									
Wistable	d	22p39		23p39				05 01						05 39					06 09				
Dover Priory	d		22p45										05 05					05 45					
Kearsney	d												05 09										
Shepherds Well	d												05 14										
Snowdown	d												05 18										
Aylesham	d												05 20										
Adisham	d												05 23										
Bekesbourne	d												05 27										
Canterbury East	d		23p02										05 32					06 02					
Selling	d												05 41										
Faversham	a	22p48	23p13	23p48				05 09					05 46	05 48				06 14	06 18				
	d	22p52	23p14	23p52				05 09		05 28	05 28			05 52	05 58				06 22	06 28	06 28		
Teynham	d	22p58		23p58										05 58									
Sheerness-on-Sea	d				23p53																	06 32	
Qeenborough	d				23p57																	06 36	
Swale	d				00 01																	06 40	
Kemsley	d				00 05																	06 44	
Sittingbourne	a	23p02	23p21	00 02	00 10			05 17		05 36	05 36			06 02	06 06				06 29	06 36	06 36	06 49	
	d	23p03	23p22	00 03				05 17		05 37	05 37			06 03	06 07				06 30	06 37	06 37		
Nwington	d		23p27	00 08				05 23											06 35				
Rinham (Kent)	d	23p10	23p31	00 12				05 27		05 45	05 45			06 10	06 15				06 40	06 45	06 45		
Gillingham (Kent)	d	23p15	23p36	00a17		04 48	05 18	05 32		05 50	05 50	05 54		06 15	06 20	06 24	06 32		06 45	06 50	06 50		06 54
Chatham	d	23p20	23p41			04 52	05 22	05 36		05 54	05 54	05 58		06 20	06 24	06 28	06 36		06 50	06 54	06 54		06 58
Rchester	d	23p22	23p43			04 54	05 24	05 39		05 57	05 57	06 00		06 22	06 27	06 30	06 39		06 52	06 57	06 57		07 00
Strood	a					04 59	05 29			06 01	06 01	06 05			06 31	06 35				07 01	07 01		07 05
Gravesend	a					05 11	05 41			06 12	06 12	06 17			06 42	06 47				07 12	07 12		07 17
Greenhithe for Bluewater	a					05 20	05 50					06 23				06 53							07 23
Dartford	a					05 27	05 57					06 28				06 58							07 28
London Bridge ⊖	a					06 05	06 35					07 05				07 35							08 05
London Cannon Street ⊖	a																						
London Waterloo (East) ⊖	a					06 09	06 39					07 09				07 39							08 09
London Charing Cross ⊖	a					06 13	06 43					07 13				07 43							08 13
Sole Street	d		23p54					05 49									06 49						
Meopham	d	23p33	23p56					05 52						06 33			06 52		07 03				
Lngfield	d	23p37	23p59					05 56						06 37			06 56		07 07				
Farningham Rad	d		00 04					06 00									06 59						
Swanley	a		00 09					06 05									07 04						
St Mary Cray	a		00 14					06 09									07 09						
Bromley South	a	23p50	00 20					06 15						06 50			07 15		07 20				
Ephant &Castle ⊖	a																						
London Blackfriars ⊖	a																						
London Victoria ⊖	a	00 07	00 38					06 37						07 07			07 37		07 37				
Ebbsfleet International	a								05 32	06 17	06 17				06 47					07 17	07 17		
Stratford International ⊖	a								05 44	06 29	06 29				06 59					07 29	07 29		
St Pancras Internatnl ⊖	a								05 51	06 36	06 37				07 06					07 36	07 37		

A not 25 August

B not from 1 September until 8 September

For further services to St Pancras hternational, Blackfriars and Ephant & Castle and onwards to Bromley South, St Mary Cray and Swanley please refer to table 52

Table 212

Ramsgate, Dover, Sheerness-on-Sea and Medway - London

Network Diagram - see first Page of Table 212

		SE ■	SE ■	SE A	SE B	SE		SE	SE ■	SE ■	SE ■	SE A	SE B	SE	SE	SE ■	SE ■		SE	SE	SE	SE ■	SE ■ C 🍴	SE ■ D 🍴	SE
Ramsgate	d		06 05								06 40						07 05							07 40	07 59
Dumpton Park	d		06 08														07 08								
Broadstairs	d		06 11								06 45						07 11							07 45	08 05
Margate	d		06 16								06 50						07 16							07 50	08a10
Westgate-on-Sea	d		06 20														07 20								
Birchington-on-Sea	d		06 24								06 55						07 24							07 55	
Herne Bay	d		06 33								07 04						07 33							08 04	
Chestfield & Swalecliffe	d		06 36														07 36								
Whitstable	d		06 39								07 09						07 39							08 09	
Dover Priory	d	06 05								06 45						07 05							07 45		
Kearsney	d	06 09														07 09									
Shepherds Well	d	06 14														07 14									
Snowdown	d	06 18														07 18									
Aylesham	d	06 20														07 20									
Adisham	d	06 23														07 23									
Bekesbourne	d	06 27														07 27									
Canterbury East	d	06 32								07 02						07 32							08 02		
Selling	d	06 41														07 41									
Faversham	a	06 46	06 48							07 14	07 18					07 46	07 48						08 14	08 18	
	d	06 52		06 58	06 58					07 22		07 28	07 28			07 52			07 58				08 22		
Teynham	d	06 58														07 58									
Sheerness-on-Sea	d					07 02								07 32						08 02					
Queenborough	d					07 06								07 36						08 06					
Swale	d					07 10								07 40						08 10					
Kemsley	d					07 14								07 44						08 14					
Sittingbourne	a	07 02		07 06	07 06	07 19				07 29		07 36	07 36	07 49		08 02			08 06	08 19			08 29		
	d	07 03		07 07	07 07					07 30		07 37	07 37			08 03			08 07				08 30		
Newington	d									07 35													08 35		
Rainham (Kent)	d	07 10		07 15	07 15					07 40		07 45	07 45			08 10			08 15				08 40		
Gillingham (Kent)	d	07 15		07 20	07 20			07 24	07 32	07 45		07 50	07 50		07 54	08 15			08 20		08 24	08 32	08 45		
Chatham	d	07 20		07 24	07 24			07 28	07 36	07 50		07 54	07 54		07 58	08 20			08 24		08 28	08 36	08 50		
Rochester	d	07 22		07 27	07 27			07 30	07 39	07 52		07 57	07 57		08 00	08 22			08 27		08 30	08 39	08 52		
Strood	a			07 31	07 31			07 35				08 01	08 01		08 05				08 31		08 35				
Gravesend	a			07 42	07 42			07 47				08 12	08 12		08 17				08 42		08 47				
Greenhithe for Bluewater	a							07 53							08 23						08 53				
Dartford	a							07 58							08 28						08 58				
London Bridge ⊖	a							08 35							09 05						09 35				
London Cannon Street ⊖	a																								
London Waterloo (East) ⊖	a							08 39							09 09						09 39				
London Charing Cross ⊖	a							08 43							09 13						09 43				
Sole Street	d								07 49													08 49			
Meopham	d	07 33							07 52	08 03						08 33						08 52	09 03		
Longfield	d	07 37							07 56	08 07						08 37						08 56	09 07		
Farningham Road	d								07 59													08 59			
Swanley	a								08 04													09 04			
St Mary Cray	a								08 09													09 09			
Bromley South	a	07 50							08 15	08 20						08 50						09 15	09 20		
Elephant & Castle ⊖	a																								
London Blackfriars ⊖	a																								
London Victoria ⊖	a	08 07							08 37	08 37						09 07						09 37	09 37		
Ebbsfleet International	a			07 47	07 47							08 17	08 17						08 47						
Stratford International ⊖	a			07 59	07 59							08 29	08 32						08 59						
St Pancras Internatnl ⊖	a			08 06	08 07							08 36	08 40						09 06						

A not from 1 September until 8 September
B not 25 August
C 🍴 from Faversham
D 🍴 from Margate

For further services to St Pancras International, Blackfriars and Elephant & Castle and onwards to Bromley South, St Mary Cray and Swanley please refer to table 52

Table 212

Saturdays
25 August to 8 September

Ramsgate, Dover, Sheerness-on-Sea and Medway - London

Network Diagram - see first Page of Table 212

		SE	SE		SE	SE ■ A 🍴	SE ■ B 🍴	SE C	SE D	SE	SE	SE ■	SE ■ A 🍴	SE ■ B 🍴		SE	SE D	SE C	SE	SE	SE ■ A 🍴	SE ■ B 🍴	SE C	SE D
Ramsgate	d						08 05							08 40		08 59						09 05		
Dumpton Park	d						08 08															09 08		
Broadstairs	d						08 11							08 45		09 05						09 11		
Margate	d						08 16							08 50		09a10						09 16		
Westgate-on-Sea	d						08 20															09 20		
Birchington-on-Sea	d						08 24							08 55								09 24		
Herne Bay	d						08 33							09 04								09 33		
Chestfield & Swalecliffe	d						08 36															09 36		
Whitstable	d						08 39							09 09								09 39		
Dover Priory	d					08 05							08 45								09 05			
Kearsney	d					08 09															09 09			
Shepherds Well	d					08 14															09 14			
Snowdown	d					08 18															09 18			
Aylesham	d					08 20															09 20			
Adisham	d					08 23															09 23			
Bekesbourne	d					08 27															09 27			
Canterbury East	d					08 32							09 02								09 32			
Selling	d					08 41															09 41			
Faversham	a					08 46	08 48						09 14	09 18							09 46	09 48		
	d	08 28				08 52		08 58	08 58				09 22				09 28	09 28			09 52		09 58	09 58
Teynham	d					08 58															09 58			
Sheerness-on-Sea	d		08 32							09 02									09 32					
Queenborough	d		08 36							09 06									09 36					
Swale	d		08 40							09 10									09 40					
Kemsley	d		08 44							09 14									09 44					
Sittingbourne	a	08 36	08 49			09 02		09 06	09 06	09 19			09 29				09 36	09 36	09 49		10 02		10 06	10 06
	d	08 37				09 03		09 07	09 07				09 30				09 37	09 37			10 03		10 07	10 07
Newington	d												09 35											
Rainham (Kent)	d	08 45				09 10		09 15	09 15				09 40				09 45	09 45			10 10		10 15	10 15
Gillingham (Kent)	d	08 50			08 54	09 15		09 20	09 20		09 24	09 32	09 45				09 50	09 50		09 54	10 15		10 20	10 20
Chatham	d	08 54			08 58	09 20		09 24	09 24		09 28	09 36	09 50				09 54	09 54		09 58	10 20		10 24	10 24
Rochester	d	08 57			09 00	09 22		09 27	09 27		09 30	09 39	09 52				09 57	09 57		10 00	10 22		10 27	10 27
Strood	a	09 01			09 05			09 31	09 31		09 35						10 01	10 01		10 05			10 31	10 31
Gravesend	a	09 12			09 17			09 42	09 42		09 47						10 12	10 12		10 17			10 42	10 42
Greenhithe for Bluewater	a				09 23						09 53									10 23				
Dartford	a				09 28						09 58									10 28				
London Bridge ⊖	a				10 05						10 35									11 05				
London Cannon Street ⊖	a																							
London Waterloo (East) ⊖	a				10 09						10 39									11 09				
London Charing Cross ⊖	a				10 13						10 43									11 13				
Sole Street	d											09 49												
Meopham	d					09 33						09 52	10 03								10 33			
Longfield	d					09 37						09 56	10 07								10 37			
Farningham Road	d											09 59												
Swanley	a											10 04												
St Mary Cray	a											10 09												
Bromley South	a					09 50						10 15	10 20								10 50			
Elephant & Castle ⊖	a																							
London Blackfriars ⊖	a																							
London Victoria ⊖	a					10 07						10 37	10 37								11 07			
Ebbsfleet International	a	09 17						09 47	09 47								10 16	10 17					10 47	10 47
Stratford International ⊖	a	09 29						09 59	09 59								10 27	10 29					10 59	10 59
St Pancras Internatnl ⊖	a	09 36						10 06	10 07								10 35	10 36					11 06	11 07

A 🍴 from Faversham
B 🍴 from Margate
C not from 1 September until 8 September
D not 25 August

For further services to St Pancras International, Blackfriars and Elephant & Castle and onwards to Bromley South, St Mary Cray and Swanley please refer to table 52

Table 212

Saturdays

25 August to 8 September

Ramsgate, Dover, Sheerness-on-Sea and Medway - London

Network Diagram - see first Page of Table 212

		SE	SE	SE 1	SE 1 A ⚒	SE 1 B ⚒	SE	SE C	SE D	SE	SE	SE 1 A ⚒	SE 1 B ⚒	SE C	SE D	SE	SE	SE 1	SE 1 A ⚒	SE 1 B ⚒	SE	SE C	SE D
Ramsgate 4	d					09 40	09 59						10 05							10 40	10 59		
Dumpton Park	d												10 08										
Broadstairs	d					09 45	10 05						10 11							10 45	11 05		
Margate 4	d					09 50	10a10						10 16							10 50	11a10		
Westgate-on-Sea	d												10 20										
Birchington-on-Sea	d					09 55							10 24							10 55			
Herne Bay	d					10 04							10 33							11 04			
Chestfield & Swalecliffe	d												10 36										
Whitstable	d					10 09							10 39							11 09			
Dover Priory 4	d				09 45							10 05							10 45				
Kearsney	d											10 09											
Shepherds Well	d											10 14											
Snowdown	d											10 18											
Aylesham	d											10 20											
Adisham	d											10 23											
Bekesbourne	d											10 27											
Canterbury East 4	d				10 02							10 32							11 02				
Selling	d											10 41											
Faversham 2	a				10 14	10 18						10 46	10 48						11 14	11 18			
	d					10 22		10 28	10 28				10 52	10 58	10 58					11 22		11 28	11 28
Teynham	d												10 58										
Sheerness-on-Sea	d	10 02								10 32						11 02							
Queenborough	d	10 06								10 36						11 06							
Swale	d	10 10								10 40						11 10							
Kemsley	d	10 14								10 44						11 14							
Sittingbourne 4	a	10 19				10 29		10 36	10 36	10 49			11 02	11 06	11 06	11 19				11 29		11 36	11 36
	d					10 30		10 37	10 37				11 03	11 07	11 07					11 30		11 37	11 37
Newington	d					10 35														11 35			
Rainham (Kent)	d					10 40		10 45	10 45				11 10	11 15	11 15					11 40		11 45	11 45
Gillingham (Kent) 4	d		10 24	10 32		10 45		10 50	10 50		10 54		11 15	11 20	11 20		11 24	11 32		11 45		11 50	11 50
Chatham 4	d		10 28	10 36		10 50		10 54	10 54		10 58		11 20	11 24	11 24		11 28	11 36		11 50		11 54	11 54
Rochester 4	d		10 30	10 39		10 52		10 57	10 57		11 00		11 22	11 27	11 27		11 30	11 39		11 52		11 57	11 57
Strood 4	a		10 35					11 01	11 01		11 05			11 31	11 31		11 35					12 01	12 01
Gravesend 4	a		10 47					11 12	11 12		11 17			11 42	11 42		11 47					12 12	12 12
Greenhithe for Bluewater	a		10 53								11 23						11 53						
Dartford 4	a		10 58								11 28						11 58						
London Bridge 4 ⊖	a		11 35								12 05						12 35						
London Cannon Street 4 ⊖	a																						
London Waterloo (East) 4 ⊖	a		11 39								12 09						12 39						
London Charing Cross 4 ⊖	a		11 43								12 13						12 43						
Sole Street	d			10 49														11 49					
Meopham	d			10 52		11 03							11 33					11 52		12 03			
Longfield	d			10 56		11 07							11 37					11 56		12 07			
Farningham Road	d			10 59														11 59					
Swanley 4	a			11 04														12 04					
St Mary Cray	a			11 09														12 09					
Bromley South 4	a			11 15		11 20							11 50					12 15		12 20			
Elephant & Castle ⊖	a																						
London Blackfriars 3 ⊖	a																						
London Victoria 15 ⊖	a			11 37		11 37							12 07					12 37		12 37			
Ebbsfleet International	a							11 17	11 17					11 47	11 47							12 17	12 17
Stratford International ⊖	a							11 29	11 32					11 59	11 59							12 29	12 32
St Pancras Internatnl 15 ⊖	a							11 36	11 40					12 06	12 07							12 36	12 40

A ⚒ from Faversham

B ⚒ from Margate

C not from 1 September until 8 September

D not 25 August

For further services to St Pancras International, Blackfriars and Elephant & Castle and onwards to Bromley South, St Mary Cray and Swanley please refer to table 52

Table 212

Saturdays

25 August to 8 September

Ramsgate, Dover, Sheerness-on-Sea and Medway - London

Network Diagram - see first Page of Table 212

		SE	SE	SE 1 A ⚒	SE 1 B ⚒	SE C	SE D	SE	SE	SE 1	SE 1 A ⚒	SE 1 B ⚒	SE	SE C	SE D	SE	SE	SE 1 A ⚒	SE 1 B ⚒	SE C	SE D	SE	SE
Ramsgate 4	d				11 05							11 40	11 59						12 05				
Dumpton Park	d				11 08														12 08				
Broadstairs	d				11 11							11 45	12 05						12 11				
Margate 4	d				11 16							11 50	12a10						12 16				
Westgate-on-Sea	d				11 20														12 20				
Birchington-on-Sea	d				11 24							11 55							12 24				
Herne Bay	d				11 33							12 04							12 33				
Chestfield & Swalecliffe	d				11 36														12 36				
Whitstable	d				11 39							12 09							12 39				
Dover Priory 4	d			11 05							11 45							12 05					
Kearsney	d			11 09														12 09					
Shepherds Well	d			11 14														12 14					
Snowdown	d			11 18														12 18					
Aylesham	d			11 20														12 20					
Adisham	d			11 23														12 23					
Bekesbourne	d			11 27														12 27					
Canterbury East 4	d			11 32							12 02							12 32					
Selling	d			11 41														12 41					
Faversham 2	a			11 46	11 48						12 14	12 18						12 46	12 48				
	d				11 52	11 58	11 58					12 22		12 28	12 28				12 52	12 58	12 58		
Teynham	d				11 58														12 58				
Sheerness-on-Sea	d	11 32						12 02								12 32						13 02	
Queenborough	d	11 36						12 06								12 36						13 06	
Swale	d	11 40						12 10								12 40						13 10	
Kemsley	d	11 44						12 14								12 44						13 14	
Sittingbourne 4	a	11 49			12 02	12 06	12 06	12 19				12 29		12 36	12 36	12 49			13 02	13 06	13 06	13 19	
	d				12 03	12 07	12 07					12 30		12 37	12 37				13 03	13 07	13 07		
Newington	d											12 35											
Rainham (Kent)	d				12 10	12 15	12 15					12 40		12 45	12 45				13 10	13 15	13 15		
Gillingham (Kent) 4	d		11 54		12 15	12 20	12 20		12 24	12 32		12 45		12 50	12 50		12 54		13 15	13 20	13 20		13 24
Chatham 4	d		11 58		12 20	12 24	12 24		12 28	12 36		12 50		12 54	12 54		12 58		13 20	13 24	13 24		13 28
Rochester 4	d		12 00		12 22	12 27	12 27		12 30	12 39		12 52		12 57	12 57		13 00		13 22	13 27	13 27		13 30
Strood 4	a		12 05			12 31	12 31		12 35					13 01	13 01		13 05			13 31	13 31		13 35
Gravesend 4	a		12 17			12 42	12 42		12 47					13 12	13 12		13 17			13 42	13 42		13 47
Greenhithe for Bluewater	a		12 23						12 53								13 23						13 53
Dartford 4	a		12 28						12 58								13 28						13 58
London Bridge 4 ⊖	a		13 05						13 35								14 05						14 35
London Cannon Street 4 ⊖	a																						
London Waterloo (East) 4 ⊖	a		13 09						13 39								14 09						14 39
London Charing Cross 4 ⊖	a		13 13						13 43								14 13						14 43
Sole Street	d									12 49													
Meopham	d				12 33					12 52		13 03							13 33				
Longfield	d				12 37					12 56		13 07							13 37				
Farningham Road	d									12 59													
Swanley 4	a									13 04													
St Mary Cray	a									13 09													
Bromley South 4	a				12 50					13 15		13 20							13 50				
Elephant & Castle ⊖	a																						
London Blackfriars 3 ⊖	a																						
London Victoria 15 ⊖	a				13 07					13 37		13 37							14 07				
Ebbsfleet International	a					12 47	12 47							13 17	13 17					13 47	13 47		
Stratford International ⊖	a					12 59	12 59							13 29	13 32					13 59	13 59		
St Pancras Internatnl 15 ⊖	a					13 06	13 07							13 36	13 40					14 06	14 07		

A ⚒ from Faversham

B ⚒ from Margate

C not from 1 September until 8 September

D not 25 August

For further services to St Pancras International, Blackfriars and Elephant & Castle and onwards to Bromley South, St Mary Cray and Swanley please refer to table 52

Saturdays
25 August to 8 September

Ramsgate, Dover, Sheerness-on-Sea and Medway - London

Network Diagram - see first Page of Table 212

		SE ■	SE ■ A ⌶	SE ■ B ⌶	SE	SE C	SE D	SE	SE	SE ■ A ⌶	SE ■ B ⌶	SE C	SE D	SE	SE	SE ■	SE ■ A ⌶	SE ■ B ⌶	SE	SE C	SE D	SE
Ramsgate ■	d			12 40	12 59						13 05							13 40	13 59			
Dumpton Park	d										13 08											
Broadstairs	d			12 45	13 05						13 11							13 45	14 05			
Margate ■	d			12 50	13a10						13 16							13 50	14a10			
Westgate-on-Sea	d										13 20											
Birchington-on-Sea	d			12 55							13 24							13 55				
Herne Bay	d			13 04							13 33							14 04				
Chestfield & Swalecliffe	d										13 36											
Whitstable	d			13 09							13 39							14 09				
Dover Priory ■	d		12 45							13 05							13 45					
Kearsney	d									13 09												
Shepherds Well	d									13 14												
Snowdown	d									13 18												
Aylesham	d									13 20												
Adisham	d									13 23												
Bekesbourne	d									13 27												
Canterbury East ■	d		13 02							13 32							14 02					
Selling	d									13 41												
Faversham ■	a		13 14	13 18						13 46	13 48						14 14	14 18				
	d		13 22			13 28	13 28			13 52		13 58	13 58				14 22			14 28	14 28	
Teynham	d									13 58												
Sheerness-on-Sea	d							13 32						14 02								14 32
Queenborough	d							13 36						14 06								14 36
Swale	d							13 40						14 10								14 40
Kemsley	d							13 44						14 14								14 44
Sittingbourne ■	a		13 29			13 36	13 36	13 49		14 02		14 06	14 06	14 19			14 29			14 36	14 36	14 49
	d		13 30			13 37	13 37			14 03		14 07	14 07				14 30			14 37	14 37	
Newington	d		13 35														14 35					
Rainham (Kent)	d		13 40			13 45	13 45			14 10		14 15	14 15				14 40			14 45	14 45	
Gillingham (Kent) ■	d	13 32	13 45			13 50	13 50		13 54	14 15		14 20	14 20		14 24	14 32	14 45			14 50	14 50	
Chatham ■	d	13 36	13 50			13 54	13 54		13 58	14 20		14 24	14 24		14 28	14 36	14 50			14 54	14 54	
Rochester ■	d	13 39	13 52			13 57	13 57		14 00	14 22		14 27	14 27		14 30	14 39	14 52			14 57	14 57	
Strood ■	a					14 01	14 01		14 05			14 31	14 31		14 35					15 01	15 01	
Gravesend ■	a					14 12	14 12		14 17			14 42	14 42		14 47					15 12	15 12	
Greenhithe for Bluewater	a								14 23						14 53							
Dartford ■	a								14 28						14 58							
London Bridge ■ ⊖	a								15 05						15 35							
London Cannon Street ■ ⊖	a																					
London Waterloo (East) ■ ⊖	a								15 09						15 39							
London Charing Cross ■ ⊖	a								15 13						15 43							
Sole Street	d	13 49														14 49						
Meopham	d	13 52	14 03							14 33						14 52	15 03					
Longfield	d	13 56	14 07							14 37						14 56	15 07					
Farningham Road	d	13 59														14 59						
Swanley ■	a	14 04														15 04						
St Mary Cray	a	14 09														15 09						
Bromley South ■	a	14 15	14 20							14 50						15 15	15 20					
Elephant & Castle ⊖	a																					
London Blackfriars ■ ⊖	a																					
London Victoria ■ ⊖	a	14 37	14 37							15 07						15 37	15 37					
Ebbsfleet International	a					14 17	14 17					14 47	14 47							15 17	15 17	
Stratford International ⊖	a					14 29	14 29					15 02	15 02							15 29	15 32	
St Pancras Internatnl ■ ⊖	a					14 36	14 42					15 09	15 10							15 36	15 40	

A ⌶ from Faversham
B ⌶ from Margate
C not from 1 September until 8 September
D not 25 August

For further services to St Pancras International, Blackfriars and Elephant & Castle and onwards to Bromley South, St Mary Cray and Swanley please refer to table 52

Saturdays
25 August to 8 September

Ramsgate, Dover, Sheerness-on-Sea and Medway - London

Network Diagram - see first Page of Table 212

		SE	SE ■ A ⌶	SE ■ B ⌶	SE	SE	SE	SE ■	SE ■ A ⌶	SE ■ B ⌶	SE	SE C	SE D	SE	SE	SE ■ A ⌶	SE ■ B ⌶	SE C	SE D	SE	SE	SE ■
Ramsgate ■	d			14 05						14 40	14 59						15 05					
Dumpton Park	d			14 08													15 08					
Broadstairs	d			14 11						14 45	15 05						15 11					
Margate ■	d			14 16						14 50	15a10						15 16					
Westgate-on-Sea	d			14 20													15 20					
Birchington-on-Sea	d			14 24						14 55							15 24					
Herne Bay	d			14 33						15 04							15 33					
Chestfield & Swalecliffe	d			14 36													15 36					
Whitstable	d			14 39						15 09							15 39					
Dover Priory ■	d		14 05						14 45							15 05						
Kearsney	d		14 09													15 09						
Shepherds Well	d		14 14													15 14						
Snowdown	d		14 18													15 18						
Aylesham	d		14 20													15 20						
Adisham	d		14 23													15 23						
Bekesbourne	d		14 27													15 27						
Canterbury East ■	d		14 32						15 02							15 32						
Selling	d		14 41													15 41						
Faversham ■	a		14 46	14 48					15 14	15 18						15 46	15 48					
	d		14 52		14 58				15 22			15 28	15 28			15 52		15 58	15 58			
Teynham	d		14 58													15 58						
Sheerness-on-Sea	d					15 02								15 32						16 02		
Queenborough	d					15 06								15 36						16 06		
Swale	d					15 10								15 40						16 10		
Kemsley	d					15 14								15 44						16 14		
Sittingbourne ■	a		15 02		15 06	15 19			15 29			15 36	15 36	15 49		16 02		16 06	16 06	16 19		
	d		15 03		15 07				15 30			15 37	15 37			16 03		16 07	16 07			
Newington	d								15 35													
Rainham (Kent)	d		15 10		15 15				15 40			15 45	15 45			16 10		16 15	16 15			
Gillingham (Kent) ■	d	14 54	15 15		15 20		15 24	15 32	15 45			15 50	15 50		15 54	16 15		16 20	16 20		16 24	16 32
Chatham ■	d	14 58	15 20		15 24		15 28	15 36	15 50			15 54	15 54		15 58	16 20		16 24	16 24		16 28	16 36
Rochester ■	d	15 00	15 22		15 27		15 30	15 39	15 52			15 57	15 57		16 00	16 22		16 27	16 27		16 30	16 39
Strood ■	a	15 05			15 31		15 35					16 01	16 01		16 05			16 31	16 31		16 35	
Gravesend ■	a	15 17			15 42		15 47					16 12	16 12		16 17			16 42	16 42		16 47	
Greenhithe for Bluewater	a	15 23					15 53								16 23						16 53	
Dartford ■	a	15 28					15 58								16 28						16 58	
London Bridge ■ ⊖	a	16 05					16 35								17 05						17 35	
London Cannon Street ■ ⊖	a																					
London Waterloo (East) ■ ⊖	a	16 09					16 39								17 09						17 39	
London Charing Cross ■ ⊖	a	16 13					16 43								17 13						17 43	
Sole Street	d							15 49														16 49
Meopham	d		15 33					15 52	16 03							16 33						16 52
Longfield	d		15 37					15 56	16 07							16 37						16 56
Farningham Road	d							15 59														16 59
Swanley ■	a							16 04														17 04
St Mary Cray	a							16 09														17 09
Bromley South ■	a		15 50					16 15	16 20							16 50						17 15
Elephant & Castle ⊖	a																					
London Blackfriars ■ ⊖	a																					
London Victoria ■ ⊖	a		16 07					16 37	16 37							17 07						17 37
Ebbsfleet International	a				15 47							16 17	16 17					16 47	16 47			
Stratford International ⊖	a				16 02							16 29	16 29					17 02				
St Pancras Internatnl ■ ⊖	a				16 09							16 36	16 37					17 09				

A ⌶ from Faversham
B ⌶ from Margate
C not from 1 September until 8 September
D not 25 August

For further services to St Pancras International, Blackfriars and Elephant & Castle and onwards to Bromley South, St Mary Cray and Swanley please refer to table 52

Table 212

Ramsgate, Dover, Sheerness-on-Sea and Medway - London

Saturdays

25 August to 8 September

Network Diagram - see first Page of Table 212

		SE ■ A ⌶	SE ■ B ⌶	SE	SE C	SE D	SE	SE	SE ■ A ⌶	SE ■ B ⌶	SE D	SE C	SE	SE	SE ■	SE ■	SE ■	SE	SE D	SE C	SE	SE
Ramsgate ■	d		15 40	15 59						16 05							16 40	16 59				
Dumpton Park	d									16 08												
Broadstairs	d		15 45	16 05						16 11							16 45	17 05				
Margate ■	d		15 50	16a10						16 16							16 50	17a10				
Westgate-on-Sea	d									16 20												
Birchington-on-Sea	d		15 55							16 24							16 55					
Herne Bay	d		16 04							16 33							17 04					
Chestfield & Swalecliffe	d									16 36												
Whitstable	d		16 09							16 39							17 09					
Dover Priory ■	d	15 45							16 05							16 45						
Kearsney	d								16 09													
Shepherds Well	d								16 14													
Snowdown	d								16 18													
Aylesham	d								16 20													
Adisham	d								16 23													
Bekesbourne	d								16 27													
Canterbury East ■	d	16 02							16 32							17 02						
Selling	d								16 41													
Faversham ■	a	16 14	16 18						16 46	16 48						17 14	17 18					
	d		16 22		16 28	16 28				16 52	16 58	16 58					17 22		17 28	17 28		
Teynham	d									16 58												
Sheerness-on-Sea	d						16 32						17 02								17 32	
Queenborough	d						16 36						17 06								17 36	
Swale	d						16 40						17 10								17 40	
Kemsley	d						16 44						17 14								17 44	
Sittingbourne ■	a		16 29		16 36	16 36	16 49			17 02	17 06	17 06	17 19				17 29		17 36	17 36	17 49	
	d		16 30		16 37	16 37				17 03	17 07	17 07					17 30		17 37	17 37		
Newington	d		16 35														17 35					
Rainham (Kent)	d		16 40		16 45	16 45				17 10	17 15	17 15					17 40		17 45	17 45		
Gillingham (Kent) ■	d		16 45		16 50	16 50		16 54		17 15	17 20	17 20		17 24	17 32		17 45		17 50	17 50		17 54
Chatham ■	d		16 50		16 54	16 54		16 58		17 20	17 24	17 24		17 28	17 36		17 50		17 54	17 54		17 58
Rochester ■	d		16 52		16 57	16 57		17 00		17 22	17 27	17 27		17 30	17 39		17 52		17 57	17 57		18 00
Strood ■	a				17 01	17 01		17 05			17 31	17 31		17 35					18 01	18 01		18 05
Gravesend ■	a				17 12	17 12		17 17			17 42	17 42		17 47					18 12	18 12		18 17
Greenhithe for Bluewater	a							17 23						17 53								18 23
Dartford ■	a							17 28						17 58								18 28
London Bridge ■ ⊖	a							18 05						18 35								19 05
London Cannon Street ■ ⊖	a																					
London Waterloo (East) ■ ⊖	a							18 09						18 39								19 09
London Charing Cross ■ ⊖	a							18 13						18 43								19 13
Sole Street	d														17 49							
Meopham	d		17 03							17 33					17 52		18 03					
Longfield	d		17 07							17 37					17 56		18 07					
Farningham Road	d														17 59							
Swanley ■	a														18 04							
St Mary Cray	a														18 09							
Bromley South ■	a		17 20							17 50					18 15		18 20					
Elephant & Castle ⊖	a																					
London Blackfriars ■ ⊖	a																					
London Victoria ■ ⊖	a		17 37							18 07					18 37		18 37					
Ebbsfleet International	a				17 16	17 17					17 47	17 47							18 17	18 17		
Stratford International ⊖	a				17 27	17 29					17 59	17 58							18 29	18 29		
St Pancras Internatnl ■ ⊖	a				17 34	17 36					18 09	18 09							18 36	18 37		

A ⌶ from Faversham
B ⌶ from Margate
C not 25 August
D not from 1 September until 8 September

For further services to St Pancras International, Blackfriars and Elephant & Castle and onwards to Bromley South, St Mary Cray and Swanley please refer to table 52

Table 212

Ramsgate, Dover, Sheerness-on-Sea and Medway - London

Saturdays

25 August to 8 September

Network Diagram - see first Page of Table 212

		SE ■	SE ■	SE A	SE B	SE	SE	SE ■	SE ■	SE ■	SE	SE	SE	SE	SE ■	SE ■	SE A	SE B	SE	SE	SE ■	SE ■	SE ■
Ramsgate ■	d		17 05							17 40	17 59					18 05							18 40
Dumpton Park	d		17 08													18 08							
Broadstairs	d		17 11							17 45	18 05					18 11							18 45
Margate ■	d		17 16							17 50	18a10					18 16							18 50
Westgate-on-Sea	d		17 20													18 20							
Birchington-on-Sea	d		17 24							17 55						18 24							18 55
Herne Bay	d		17 33							18 04						18 33							19 04
Chestfield & Swalecliffe	d		17 36													18 36							
Whitstable	d		17 39							18 09						18 39							19 09
Dover Priory ■	d	17 05							17 45						18 05							18 45	
Kearsney	d	17 09													18 09								
Shepherds Well	d	17 14													18 14								
Snowdown	d	17 18													18 18								
Aylesham	d	17 20													18 20								
Adisham	d	17 23													18 23								
Bekesbourne	d	17 27													18 27								
Canterbury East ■	d	17 32							18 02						18 32							19 02	
Selling	d	17 41													18 41								
Faversham ■	a	17 46	17 48						18 14	18 18					18 46	18 48						19 14	19 18
	d		17 52	17 58	17 58					18 22		18 28				18 52	18 58	18 58					19 22
Teynham	d		17 58													18 58							
Sheerness-on-Sea	d					18 02							18 32						19 02				
Queenborough	d					18 06							18 36						19 06				
Swale	d					18 10							18 40						19 10				
Kemsley	d					18 14							18 44						19 14				
Sittingbourne ■	a		18 02	18 06	18 06	18 19				18 29		18 36	18 49			19 02	19 06	19 06	19 19				19 29
	d		18 03	18 07	18 07					18 30		18 37				19 03	19 07	19 07					19 30
Newington	d									18 35													19 35
Rainham (Kent)	d		18 10	18 15	18 15					18 40		18 45				19 10	19 15	19 15					19 40
Gillingham (Kent) ■	d		18 15	18 20	18 20		18 24	18 32		18 45		18 50		18 54		19 15	19 20	19 20		19 24	19 32		19 45
Chatham ■	d		18 20	18 24	18 24		18 28	18 36		18 50		18 54		18 58		19 20	19 24	19 24		19 28	19 36		19 50
Rochester ■	d		18 22	18 27	18 27		18 30	18 39		18 52		18 57		19 00		19 22	19 27	19 27		19 30	19 39		19 52
Strood ■	a			18 31	18 31		18 35					19 01		19 05			19 31	19 31		19 35			
Gravesend ■	a			18 42	18 42		18 47					19 12		19 17			19 42	19 42		19 47			
Greenhithe for Bluewater	a						18 53							19 23						19 53			
Dartford ■	a						18 58							19 28						19 58			
London Bridge ■ ⊖	a						19 36							20 06						20 36			
London Cannon Street ■ ⊖	a																						
London Waterloo (East) ■ ⊖	a						19 42							20 10						20 40			
London Charing Cross ■ ⊖	a						19 45							20 14						20 44			
Sole Street	d							18 49													19 49		
Meopham	d		18 33					18 52		19 03						19 33					19 52		20 03
Longfield	d		18 37					18 56		19 07						19 37					19 56		20 07
Farningham Road	d							18 59													19 59		
Swanley ■	a							19 04													20 04		
St Mary Cray	a							19 09													20 09		
Bromley South ■	a		18 50					19 15		19 20						19 50					20 15		20 20
Elephant & Castle ⊖	a																						
London Blackfriars ■ ⊖	a																						
London Victoria ■ ⊖	a		19 07					19 37		19 37						20 07					20 37		20 37
Ebbsfleet International	a			18 47	18 47							19 16					19 47	19 47					
Stratford International ⊖	a			19 02	19 02							19 27					19 59	19 59					
St Pancras Internatnl ■ ⊖	a			19 09	19 10							19 38					20 06	20 07					

A not from 1 September until 8 September
B not 25 August

For further services to St Pancras International, Blackfriars and Elephant & Castle and onwards to Bromley South, St Mary Cray and Swanley please refer to table 52

Table 212

Saturdays

25 August to 8 September

Ramsgate, Dover, Sheerness-on-Sea and Medway - London

Network Diagram - see first Page of Table 212

		SE	SE A	SE B	SE	SE	SE ■1	SE ■1	SE A	SE B	SE	SE	SE	SE ■1	SE B	SE A	SE	SE	SE ■1	SE ■1	SE B	SE A
Ramsgate ■	d	18 59						19 05			19 59									20 05		
Dumpton Park	d							19 08												20 08		
Broadstairs	d	19 05						19 11			20 05									20 11		
Margate ■	d	19a10						19 16			20a10									20 16		
Westgate-on-Sea	d							19 20												20 20		
Birchington-on-Sea	d							19 24												20 24		
Herne Bay	d							19 33												20 33		
Chestfield & Swalecliffe	d							19 36												20 36		
Whitstable	d							19 39												20 39		
Dover Priory ■	d						19 05												20 05			
Kearsney	d						19 09												20 09			
Shepherds Well	d						19 14												20 14			
Snowdown	d						19 18												20 18			
Aylesham	d						19 20												20 20			
Adisham	d						19 23												20 23			
Bekesbourne	d						19 27												20 27			
Canterbury East ■	d						19 32												20 32			
Selling	d						19 41												20 41			
Faversham ■	a						19 46	19 48											20 46	20 48		
	d		19 28	19 28			19 52		19 58	19 58				20 14	20 28	20 28			20 52		20 58	20 58
Teynham	d						19 58												20 58			
Sheerness-on-Sea	d				19 32							20 02					20 32					
Queenborough	d				19 36							20 06					20 36					
Swale	d				19 40							20 10					20 40					
Kemsley	d				19 44							20 14					20 44					
Sittingbourne ■	a		19 36	19 36	19 49		20 02		20 06	20 06		20 19		20 21	20 36	20 36	20 49		21 02		21 06	21 06
	d		19 37	19 37			20 03		20 07	20 07				20 22	20 37	20 37			21 03		21 07	21 07
Newington	d													20 27								
Rainham (Kent)	d		19 45	19 45			20 10		20 15	20 15				20 31	20 45	20 45			21 10		21 15	21 15
Gillingham (Kent) ■	d		19 50	19 50		19 54	20 15		20 20	20 20			20 24	20 36	20 50	20 50		20 54	21 15		21 20	21 20
Chatham ■	d		19 54	19 54		19 58	20 20		20 24	20 24			20 28	20 41	20 54	20 54		20 58	21 20		21 24	21 24
Rochester ■	d		19 57	19 57		20 00	20 22		20 27	20 27			20 30	20 43	20 57	20 57		21 00	21 22		21 27	21 27
Strood ■	a		20 01	20 01		20 05			20 31	20 31			20 35		21 01	21 01		21 05			21 31	21 31
Gravesend ■	a		20 12	20 12		20 17			20 42	20 42			20 47		21 12	21 12		21 17			21 42	21 42
Greenhithe for Bluewater	a					20 23							20 53					21 23				
Dartford ■	a					20 28							20 58					21 28				
London Bridge ■ ⊖	a					21 06							21 36					22 05				
London Cannon Street ■ ⊖	a																					
London Waterloo (East) ■ ⊖	a					21 10							21 40					22 09				
London Charing Cross ■ ⊖	a					21 14							21 44					22 13				
Sole Street	d													20 54								
Meopham	d						20 33							20 56					21 33			
Longfield	d						20 37							21 00					21 37			
Farningham Road	d													21 04								
Swanley ■	a													21 09								
St Mary Cray	a													21 14								
Bromley South ■	a						20 50							21 20					21 50			
Elephant & Castle ⊖	a																					
London Blackfriars ■ ⊖	a																					
London Victoria ■ ⊖	a						21 07							21 37					22 07			
Ebbsfleet International	a		20 16	20 17					20 47	20 47					21 17	21 17					21 47	21 47
Stratford International ⊖	a		20 27	20 29						21 02					21 29	21 31					21 59	21 59
St Pancras International ■ ⊖	a		20 35	20 36					21 06	21 09					21 36	21 42					22 06	22 07

A not 25 August

B not from 1 September until 8 September

For further services to St Pancras International, Blackfriars and Elephant & Castle and onwards to Bromley South, St Mary Cray and Swanley please refer to table 52

Table 212

Saturdays

25 August to 8 September

Ramsgate, Dover, Sheerness-on-Sea and Medway - London

Network Diagram - see first Page of Table 212

		SE	SE	SE	SE ■1	SE A	SE B	SE	SE ■1	SE ■1	SE A	SE B	SE	SE	SE	SE ■1	SE ■1	SE	SE ■1	SE	SE	SE ■1	SE ■1
Ramsgate ■	d	20 59								21 05			21 59						22 05	22 59			23 05
Dumpton Park	d									21 08									22 08				23 08
Broadstairs	d	21 05								21 11			22 05						22 11	23 05			23 11
Margate ■	d	21a10								21 16			22a10						22 16	23a10			23 16
Westgate-on-Sea	d									21 20									22 20				23 20
Birchington-on-Sea	d									21 24									22 24				23 24
Herne Bay	d									21 33									22 33				23 33
Chestfield & Swalecliffe	d									21 36									22 36				23 36
Whitstable	d									21 39									22 39				23 39
Dover Priory ■	d								21 05								22 05					23 05	
Kearsney	d								21 09								22 09					23 09	
Shepherds Well	d								21 14								22 14					23 14	
Snowdown	d								21 18								22 18					23 18	
Aylesham	d								21 20								22 20					23 20	
Adisham	d								21 23								22 23					23 23	
Bekesbourne	d								21 27								22 27					23 27	
Canterbury East ■	d								21 32							22 02	22 32					23 32	
Selling	d								21 41								22 41					23 41	
Faversham ■	a								21 46	21 48						22 13	22 46		22 48			23 46	23 49
	d				21 14	21 28	21 28		21 52		21 58	21 58				22 14			22 52				23 52
Teynham	d								21 58										22 58				23 58
Sheerness-on-Sea	d		21 02											22 02							23 02		
Queenborough	d		21 06											22 06							23 06		
Swale	d		21 10											22 10							23 10		
Kemsley	d		21 14											22 14							23 14		
Sittingbourne ■	a		21 19		21 21	21 36	21 36		22 02		22 06	22 06		22 19		22 21			23 02		23 19		00 02
	d				21 22	21 37	21 37		22 03		22 07	22 07				22 22			23 03				00 03
Newington	d				21 27											22 27							00 08
Rainham (Kent)	d				21 31	21 45	21 45		22 10		22 15	22 15				22 31			23 10				00 12
Gillingham (Kent) ■	d			21 24	21 36	21 50	21 50	21 54	22 15		22 20	22 20			22 24	22 36		22 54	23 15				00a17
Chatham ■	d			21 28	21 41	21 54	21 54	21 58	22 20		22 24	22 24			22 28	22 41		22 58	23 20				
Rochester ■	d			21 30	21 43	21 57	21 57	22 00	22 22		22 27	22 27			22 30	22 43		23 00	23 22				
Strood ■	a			21 35		22 01	22 01	22 05			22 31	22 31			22 35			23 05					
Gravesend ■	a			21 47		22 12	22 12	22 17			22 42	22 42			22 47			23 17					
Greenhithe for Bluewater	a			21 53				22 23							22 53			23 23					
Dartford ■	a			21 58				22 28							22 58			23 28					
London Bridge ■ ⊖	a			22 35				23 05							23 35								
London Cannon Street ■ ⊖	a																						
London Waterloo (East) ■ ⊖	a			22 39				23 09							23 39								
London Charing Cross ■ ⊖	a			22 43				23 13							23 43								
Sole Street	d				21 54											22 54							
Meopham	d				21 56				22 33							22 56			23 33				
Longfield	d				22 00				22 37							23 00			23 37				
Farningham Road	d				22 04											23 04							
Swanley ■	a				22 09											23 09							
St Mary Cray	a				22 14											23 14							
Bromley South ■	a				22 20				22 50							23 20			23 50				
Elephant & Castle ⊖	a																						
London Blackfriars ■ ⊖	a																						
London Victoria ■ ⊖	a				22 37				23 07							23 37			00 07				
Ebbsfleet International	a					22 17	22 17				22 47	22 47											
Stratford International ⊖	a					22 29	22 29				22 59	22 59											
St Pancras International ■ ⊖	a					22 36	22 37				23 06	23 07											

A not from 1 September until 8 September

B not 25 August

For further services to St Pancras International, Blackfriars and Elephant & Castle and onwards to Bromley South, St Mary Cray and Swanley please refer to table 52

Table 212

Saturdays

25 August to 8 September

Ramsgate, Dover, Sheerness-on-Sea and Medway - London

Network Diagram - see first Page of Table 212

		SE
Ramsgate ■	d	
Dumpton Park	d	
Broadstairs	d	
Margate ■	d	
Westgate-on-Sea	d	
Birchington-on-Sea	d	
Herne Bay	d	
Chestfield &Swalecliffe	d	
Whitstable	d	
Dover Priory ■	d	
Kearsney	d	
Shepherds Well	d	
Snowdown	d	
Aylesham	d	
Adisham	d	
Bekesbourne	d	
Canterbury East ■	d	
Selling	d	
Faversham ■	a	
	d	
Teynham	d	
Sheerness-on-Sea	d	23 53
Queenborough	d	23 57
Swale	d	00 01
Kemsley	d	00 05
Sittingbourne ■	a	00 10
	d	
Newington	d	
Rainham (Kent)	d	
Gillingham (Kent) ■	d	
Chatham ■	d	
Rochester ■	d	
Strood ■	a	
Gravesend ■	a	
Greenhithe for Bluewater	a	
Dartford ■	a	
London Bridge ■ ⊖	a	
London Cannon Street ■ ⊖	a	
London Waterloo (East) ■ ⊖	a	
London Charing Cross ■ ⊖	a	
Sole Street	d	
Meopham	d	
Longfield	d	
Farningham Road	d	
Swanley ■	a	
St Mary Cray	a	
Bromley South ■	a	
Elephant &Castle ⊖	a	
London Blackfriars ■ ⊖	a	
London Victoria ■ ⊖	a	
Ebbsfleet International	a	
Stratford International ⊖	a	
St Pancras Internatnl ■ ⊖	a	

For further services to St Pancras International, Blackfriars and Elephant & Castle and onwards to Bromley South, St Mary Cray and Swanley please refer to table 52

Table 212

Sundays

until 22 July, 19 Aug and from 16 Sep, 19 Aug and from 16 Sep

Ramsgate, Dover, Sheerness-on-Sea and Medway - London

Network Diagram - see first Page of Table 212

		SE ■	SE ■	SE	SE	SE ■	SE	SE	SE ■	SE		SE ■	SE	SE	SE	SE ■ A	SE ■ B	SE	SE ■	SE		SE	SE	SE ■ A	SE ■ B
Ramsgate ■	d	22p05	23p05						06 34								07 34								08 34
Dumpton Park	d	22p08	23p08						06 37								07 37								08 37
Broadstairs	d	22p11	23p11						06 40								07 40								08 40
Margate ■	d	22p16	23p16						06 45								07 45								08 45
Westgate-on-Sea	d	22p20	23p20						06 49								07 49								08 49
Birchington-on-Sea	d	22p24	23p24						06 53								07 53								08 53
Herne Bay	d	22p33	23p33						07 02								08 02								09 02
Chestfield &Swalecliffe	d	22p36	23p36						07 05								08 05								09 05
Whitstable	d	22p39	23p39						07 08								08 08								09 08
Dover Priory ■	d															07 34								08 34	
Kearsney	d															07 38								08 38	
Shepherds Well	d															07 43								08 43	
Snowdown	d															07 47								08 47	
Aylesham	d															07 49								08 49	
Adisham	d															07 52								08 52	
Bekesbourne	d															07 56								08 56	
Canterbury East ■	d															08 01								09 01	
Selling	d															08 10								09 10	
Faversham ■	a	22p48	23p49						07 17							08 15	08 17							09 15	09 17
	d	22p52	23p52			06 34		06 58	07 21			07 34			07 58	08 21			08 34			08 58		09 21	
Teynham	d	22p58	23p58			06 40						07 40							08 40						
Sheerness-on-Sea	d			23p53																08 42					
Queenborough	d			23p57																08 46					
Swale	d			00 01																08 50					
Kemsley	d			00 05																08 54					
Sittingbourne ■	a	23p02	00 02	00 10		06 44		07 06	07 28			07 44			08 06	08 28			08 44	08 59		09 06		09 28	
	d	23p03	00 03			06 45		07 07	07 29			07 45			08 07	08 29			08 45			09 07		09 29	
Newington	d		00 08			06 50						07 50							08 50						
Rainham (Kent)	d	23p10	00 12			06 54		07 15	07 36			07 54			08 15	08 36			08 54			09 15		09 36	
Gillingham (Kent) ■	d	23p15	00a17		06 45	06 59	07 15	07 20	07 41	07 45		07 59		08 15	08 20	08 41		08 54	08 59			09 20	09 24	09 41	
Chatham ■	d	23p20			06 49	07 04	07 19	07 24	07 46	07 49		08 04		08 19	08 24	08 46		08 58	09 04			09 24	09 28	09 46	
Rochester ■	d	23p22			06 51	07 06	07 21	07 27	07 48	07 51		08 06		08 21	08 27	08 48		09 00	09 06			09 27	09 30	09 48	
Strood ■	a				06 56		07 26	07 31		07 56				08 26	08 31			09 05				09 31	09 35		
Gravesend ■	a				07 08		07 38	07 42		08 08				08 38	08 42			09 17				09 42	09 47		
Greenhithe for Bluewater	a				07 17		07 47			08 17				08 47				09 23					09 53		
Dartford ■	a				07 24		07 54			08 24				08 54				09 28					09 58		
London Bridge ■ ⊖	a				08 06		08 36			09 06				09 36				10 06					10 36		
London Cannon Street ■ ⊖	a																								
London Waterloo (East) ■ ⊖	a				08 11		08 41			09 11				09 41				10 11					10 41		
London Charing Cross ■ ⊖	a				08 14		08 44			09 14				09 44				10 14					10 44		
Sole Street	d					07 17						08 17							09 17						
Meopham	d	23p33				07 19						08 19							09 19						
Longfield	d	23p37				07 23						08 23							09 23						
Farningham Road	d					07 27						08 27							09 27						
Swanley ■	a					07 32						08 32							09 32						
St Mary Cray	a					07 36						08 36							09 36						
Bromley South ■	a	23p50				07 42			08 13			08 42				09 13			09 42					10 13	
Elephant &Castle ⊖	a																								
London Blackfriars ■ ⊖	a																								
London Victoria ■ ⊖	a	00 07				08 03			08 29			09 02				09 29			10 02					10 29	
Ebbsfleet International	a							07 47					08 02		08 47							09 47			
Stratford International ⊖	a												08 14		08 59							09 59			
St Pancras Internatnl ■ ⊖	a												08 21		09 06							10 06			

A from Faversham

B from Margate

For further services to St Pancras International, Blackfriars and Elephant & Castle and onwards to Bromley South, St Mary Cray and Swanley please refer to table 52

Table 212

Sundays

until 22 July, 19 Aug and from 16 Sep

Ramsgate, Dover, Sheerness-on-Sea and Medway - London

Network Diagram - see first Page of Table 212

		SE	SE ■	SE	SE	SE	SE ■ A ⊼	SE ■ B ⊼	SE	SE	SE ■	SE	SE	SE	SE ■ A ⊼	SE ■ B ⊼	SE	SE	SE	SE ■	SE	SE	SE
Ramsgate ■	d							09 34	09 59							10 34	10 59						
Dumpton Park	d							09 37								10 37							
Broadstairs	d							09 40	10 05							10 40	11 05						
Margate ■	d							09 45	10a10							10 45	11a10						
Westgate-on-Sea	d							09 49								10 49							
Birchington-on-Sea	d							09 53								10 53							
Herne Bay	d							10 02								11 02							
Chestfield & Swalecliffe	d							10 05								11 05							
Whitstable	d							10 08								11 08							
Dover Priory ■	d						09 34								10 34								
Kearsney	d						09 38								10 38								
Shepherds Well	d						09 43								10 43								
Snowdown	d						09 47								10 47								
Aylesham	d						09 49								10 49								
Adisham	d						09 52								10 52								
Bekesbourne	d						09 56								10 56								
Canterbury East ■	d		09 22				10 01				10 22				11 01					11 22			
Selling	d						10 10								11 10								
Faversham ■	a		09 33				10 15	10 17			10 33				11 15	11 17				11 33			
	d		09 34		09 58		10 21				10 34		10 58		11 21			11 28		11 34		11 58	
Teynham	d		09 40								10 40									11 40			
Sheerness-on-Sea	d			09 42								10 42									11 42		
Queenborough	d			09 46								10 46									11 46		
Swale	d			09 50								10 50									11 50		
Kemsley	d			09 54								10 54									11 54		
Sittingbourne ■	a		09 44	09 59	10 06		10 28				10 44	10 59	11 06		11 28			11 36		11 44	11 59	12 06	
	d		09 45		10 07		10 29				10 45		11 07		11 29			11 37		11 45		12 07	
Newington	d		09 50								10 50									11 50			
Rainham (Kent)	d		09 54		10 15		10 36				10 54		11 15		11 36			11 45		11 54		12 15	
Gillingham (Kent) ■	d	09 54	09 59		10 20	10 24	10 41			10 54	10 59		11 20	11 24	11 41			11 50	11 54	11 59		12 20	12 24
Chatham ■	d	09 58	10 04		10 24	10 28	10 46			10 58	11 04		11 24	11 28	11 46			11 54	11 58	12 04		12 24	12 28
Rochester ■	d	10 00	10 06		10 27	10 30	10 48			11 00	11 06		11 27	11 30	11 48			11 57	12 00	12 06		12 27	12 30
Strood ■	a	10 05			10 31	10 35				11 05			11 31	11 35				12 01	12 05			12 31	12 35
Gravesend ■	a	10 17			10 42	10 47				11 17			11 42	11 47				12 12	12 17			12 42	12 47
Greenhithe for Bluewater	a	10 23				10 53				11 23				11 53					12 23				12 53
Dartford ■	a	10 28				10 58				11 28				11 58					12 28				12 58
London Bridge ■ ⊖	a	11 06				11 36				12 06				12 36					13 06				13 36
London Cannon Street ■ ⊖	a																						
London Waterloo (East) ■ ⊖	a	11 11				11 41				12 11				12 41					13 11				13 41
London Charing Cross ■ ⊖	a	11 14				11 44				12 14				12 44					13 14				13 44
Sole Street	d		10 17								11 17									12 17			
Meopham	d		10 19								11 19									12 19			
Longfield	d		10 23								11 23									12 23			
Farningham Road	d		10 27								11 27									12 27			
Swanley ■	a		10 32								11 32									12 32			
St Mary Cray	a		10 36								11 36									12 36			
Bromley South ■	a		10 42				11 13				11 42				12 13					12 42			
Elephant & Castle ⊖	a																						
London Blackfriars ■ ⊖	a																						
London Victoria ■ ⊖	a		11 02				11 29				12 02				12 29					13 02			
Ebbsfleet International	a				10 47								11 47					12 17				12 47	
Stratford International ⊖	a				10 59								11 59					12 29				12 59	
St Pancras Internatnl ■ ⊖	a				11 06								12 06					12 36				13 06	

A ⊼ from Faversham

B ⊼ from Margate

For further services to St Pancras International, Blackfriars and Elephant & Castle and onwards to Bromley South, St Mary Cray and Swanley please refer to table 52

Table 212

Sundays

until 22 July, 19 Aug and from 16 Sep

Ramsgate, Dover, Sheerness-on-Sea and Medway - London

Network Diagram - see first Page of Table 212

		SE ■ A ⊼	SE ■ B ⊼	SE	SE	SE	SE ■	SE	SE	SE	SE ■ A ⊼	SE ■ B ⊼	SE	SE	SE	SE ■	SE	SE	SE	SE ■ A ⊼	SE ■ B ⊼	SE
Ramsgate ■	d		11 34	11 59								12 34	12 59								13 34	13 59
Dumpton Park	d		11 37									12 37									13 37	
Broadstairs	d		11 40	12 05								12 40	13 05								13 40	14 05
Margate ■	d		11 45	12a10								12 45	13a10								13 45	14a10
Westgate-on-Sea	d		11 49									12 49									13 49	
Birchington-on-Sea	d		11 53									12 53									13 53	
Herne Bay	d		12 02									13 02									14 02	
Chestfield & Swalecliffe	d		12 05									13 05									14 05	
Whitstable	d		12 08									13 08									14 08	
Dover Priory ■	d	11 34									12 34									13 34		
Kearsney	d	11 38									12 38									13 38		
Shepherds Well	d	11 43									12 43									13 43		
Snowdown	d	11 47									12 47									13 47		
Aylesham	d	11 49									12 49									13 49		
Adisham	d	11 52									12 52									13 52		
Bekesbourne	d	11 56									12 56									13 56		
Canterbury East ■	d	12 01					12 22				13 01					13 22				14 01		
Selling	d	12 10									13 10									14 10		
Faversham ■	a	12 15	12 17				12 33				13 15	13 17				13 33				14 15	14 17	
	d	12 21			12 28		12 34		12 58		13 21			13 28		13 34		13 58		14 21		
Teynham	d						12 40									13 40						
Sheerness-on-Sea	d							12 42									13 42					
Queenborough	d							12 46									13 46					
Swale	d							12 50									13 50					
Kemsley	d							12 54									13 54					
Sittingbourne ■	a	12 28			12 36		12 44	12 59	13 06		13 28			13 36		13 44	13 59	14 06		14 28		
	d	12 29			12 37		12 45		13 07		13 29			13 37		13 45		14 07		14 29		
Newington	d						12 50									13 50						
Rainham (Kent)	d	12 36			12 45		12 54		13 15		13 36			13 45		13 54		14 15		14 36		
Gillingham (Kent) ■	d	12 41			12 50	12 54	12 59		13 20	13 24	13 41			13 50	13 54	13 59		14 20	14 24	14 41		
Chatham ■	d	12 46			12 54	12 58	13 04		13 24	13 28	13 46			13 54	13 58	14 04		14 24	14 28	14 46		
Rochester ■	d	12 48			12 57	13 00	13 06		13 27	13 30	13 48			13 57	14 00	14 06		14 27	14 30	14 48		
Strood ■	a				13 01	13 05			13 31	13 35				14 01	14 05			14 31	14 35			
Gravesend ■	a				13 12	13 17			13 42	13 47				14 12	14 17			14 42	14 47			
Greenhithe for Bluewater	a					13 23				13 53					14 23				14 53			
Dartford ■	a					13 28				13 58					14 28				14 58			
London Bridge ■ ⊖	a					14 06				14 36					15 06				15 36			
London Cannon Street ■ ⊖	a																					
London Waterloo (East) ■ ⊖	a					14 11				14 41					15 11				15 41			
London Charing Cross ■ ⊖	a					14 14				14 44					15 14				15 44			
Sole Street	d						13 17									14 17						
Meopham	d						13 19									14 19						
Longfield	d						13 23									14 23						
Farningham Road	d						13 27									14 27						
Swanley ■	a						13 32									14 32						
St Mary Cray	a						13 36									14 36						
Bromley South ■	a	13 13					13 42				14 13					14 42				15 13		
Elephant & Castle ⊖	a																					
London Blackfriars ■ ⊖	a																					
London Victoria ■ ⊖	a	13 29					14 02				14 29					15 02				15 29		
Ebbsfleet International	a				13 17				13 47					14 17				14 47				
Stratford International ⊖	a				13 29				14 02					14 29				14 59				
St Pancras Internatnl ■ ⊖	a				13 36				14 09					14 36				15 06				

A ⊼ from Faversham

B ⊼ from Margate

For further services to St Pancras International, Blackfriars and Elephant & Castle and onwards to Bromley South, St Mary Cray and Swanley please refer to table 52

Ramsgate, Dover, Sheerness-on-Sea and Medway - London

Sundays

until 22 July, 19 Aug and from 16 Sep

Network Diagram - see first Page of Table 212

		SE	SE	SE ■	SE	SE	SE	SE ■ A ⊼	SE ■ B ⊼	SE	SE	SE	SE ■	SE	SE	SE	SE ■ A ⊼	SE ■ B ⊼	SE	SE	SE	SE ■	SE
Ramsgate ■	d								14 34	14 59								15 34	15 59				
Dumpton Park	d								14 37									15 37					
Broadstairs	d								14 40	15 05								15 40	16 05				
Margate ■	d								14 45	15a10								15 45	16a10				
Westgate-on-Sea	d								14 49									15 49					
Birchington-on-Sea	d								14 53									15 53					
Herne Bay	d								15 02									16 02					
Chestfield &Swalecliffe	d								15 05									16 05					
Whitstable	d								15 08									16 08					
Dover Priory ■	d							14 34									15 34						
Kearsney	d							14 38									15 38						
Shepherds Well	d							14 43									15 43						
Snowdown	d							14 47									15 47						
Aylesham	d							14 49									15 49						
Adisham	d							14 52									15 52						
Bekesbourne	d							14 56									15 56						
Canterbury East ■	d			14 22				15 01					15 22				16 01					16 22	
Selling	d							15 10									16 10						
Faversham ■	a			14 33				15 15	15 17				15 33				16 15	16 17				16 33	
	d	14 28		14 34		14 58			15 21		15 28		15 34		15 58			16 21		16 28		16 34	
Teynham	d			14 40									15 40									16 40	
Sheerness-on-Sea	d				14 42									15 42									16 42
Queenborough	d				14 46									15 46									16 46
Swale	d				14 50									15 50									16 50
Kemsley	d				14 54									15 54									16 54
Sittingbourne ■	a	14 36		14 44	14 59	15 06			15 28		15 36		15 44	15 59	16 06			16 28		16 36		16 44	16 59
	d	14 37		14 45		15 07			15 29		15 37		15 45		16 07			16 29		16 37		16 45	
Newington	d			14 50									15 50									16 50	
Rainham (Kent)	d	14 45		14 54		15 15			15 36		15 45		15 54		16 15			16 36		16 45		16 54	
Gillingham (Kent) ■	d	14 50	14 54	14 59		15 20	15 24		15 41		15 50	15 54	15 59		16 20	16 24		16 41		16 50	16 54	16 59	
Chatham ■	d	14 54	14 58	15 04		15 24	15 28		15 46		15 54	15 58	16 04		16 24	16 28		16 46		16 54	16 58	17 04	
Rochester ■	d	14 57	15 00	15 06		15 27	15 30		15 48		15 57	16 00	16 06		16 27	16 30		16 48		16 57	17 00	17 06	
Strood ■	a	15 01	15 05			15 31	15 35				16 01	16 05			16 31	16 35				17 01	17 05		
Gravesend ■	a	15 12	15 17			15 42	15 47				16 12	16 17			16 42	16 47				17 12	17 17		
Greenhithe for Bluewater	a		15 23				15 53					16 23				16 53					17 23		
Dartford ■	a		15 28				15 58					16 28				16 58					17 28		
London Bridge ■ ⊖	a		16 06				16 36					17 06				17 36					18 06		
London Cannon Street ■ ⊖	a																						
London Waterloo (East) ■ ⊖	a		16 11				16 41					17 11				17 41					18 11		
London Charing Cross ■ ⊖	a		16 14				16 44					17 14				17 44					18 14		
Sole Street	d			15 17									16 17									17 17	
Meopham	d			15 19									16 19									17 19	
Longfield	d			15 23									16 23									17 23	
Farningham Road	d			15 27									16 27									17 27	
Swanley ■	a			15 32									16 32									17 32	
St Mary Cray	a			15 36									16 36									17 36	
Bromley South ■	a			15 42					16 13				16 42					17 13				17 42	
Elephant &Castle ⊖	a																						
London Blackfriars ■ ⊖	a																						
London Victoria ■ ⊖	a			16 02					16 29				17 02					17 29				18 02	
Ebbsfleet International	a	15 17				15 47					16 17				16 47					17 17			
Stratford International ⊖	a	15 29				16 02					16 29									17 29			
St Pancras Internatnl ■ ⊖	a	15 36				16 09					16 36									17 36			

A ⊼ from Faversham

B ⊼ from Margate

For further services to St Pancras International, Blackfriars and Elephant & Castle and onwards to Bromley South, St Mary Cray and Swanley please refer to table 52

Table 212

Ramsgate, Dover, Sheerness-on-Sea and Medway - London

Sundays

until 22 July, 19 Aug and from 16 Sep

Network Diagram - see first Page of Table 212

		SE	SE	SE ■ A ⊼	SE ■ B ⊼	SE	SE	SE	SE ■	SE	SE	SE	SE ■	SE ■	SE	SE	SE	SE ■	SE	SE	SE	SE ■	SE ■
Ramsgate ■	d				16 34	16 59								17 34	17 59								18 34
Dumpton Park	d				16 37									17 37									18 37
Broadstairs	d				16 40	17 05								17 40	18 05								18 40
Margate ■	d				16 45	17a10								17 45	18a10								18 45
Westgate-on-Sea	d				16 49									17 49									18 49
Birchington-on-Sea	d				16 53									17 53									18 53
Herne Bay	d				17 02									18 02									19 02
Chestfield &Swalecliffe	d				17 05									18 05									19 05
Whitstable	d				17 08									18 08									19 08
Dover Priory ■	d			16 34									17 34									18 34	
Kearsney	d			16 38									17 38									18 38	
Shepherds Well	d			16 43									17 43									18 43	
Snowdown	d			16 47									17 47									18 47	
Aylesham	d			16 49									17 49									18 49	
Adisham	d			16 52									17 52									18 52	
Bekesbourne	d			16 56									17 56									18 56	
Canterbury East ■	d			17 01					17 22				18 01					18 22				19 01	
Selling	d			17 10									18 10									19 10	
Faversham ■	a			17 15	17 17				17 33				18 15	18 17				18 33				19 15	19 17
	d	16 58			17 21		17 28		17 34		17 58			18 21		18 28		18 34		18 58			19 21
Teynham	d								17 40									18 40					
Sheerness-on-Sea	d									17 42									18 42				
Queenborough	d									17 46									18 46				
Swale	d									17 50									18 50				
Kemsley	d									17 54									18 54				
Sittingbourne ■	a	17 06			17 28		17 36		17 44	17 59	18 06			18 28		18 36		18 44	19 01	19 06			19 28
	d	17 07			17 29		17 37		17 45		18 07			18 29		18 37		18 45		19 07			19 29
Newington	d								17 50									18 50					
Rainham (Kent)	d	17 15			17 36		17 45		17 54		18 15			18 36		18 45		18 54		19 15			19 36
Gillingham (Kent) ■	d	17 20	17 24		17 41		17 50	17 54	17 59		18 20	18 24		18 41		18 50	18 54	18 59		19 20	19 24		19 41
Chatham ■	d	17 24	17 28		17 46		17 54	17 58	18 04		18 24	18 28		18 46		18 54	18 58	19 04		19 24	19 28		19 46
Rochester ■	d	17 27	17 30		17 48		17 57	18 00	18 06		18 27	18 30		18 48		18 57	19 00	19 06		19 27	19 30		19 48
Strood ■	a	17 31	17 35				18 01	18 05			18 31	18 35				19 01	19 05			19 31	19 35		
Gravesend ■	a	17 42	17 47				18 12	18 17			18 42	18 47				19 12	19 17			19 42	19 47		
Greenhithe for Bluewater	a		17 53					18 23				18 53					19 23				19 53		
Dartford ■	a		17 58					18 28				18 58					19 28				19 58		
London Bridge ■ ⊖	a		18 36					19 06				19 36					20 06				20 36		
London Cannon Street ■ ⊖	a																						
London Waterloo (East) ■ ⊖	a		18 41					19 11				19 41					20 11				20 41		
London Charing Cross ■ ⊖	a		18 44					19 14				19 44					20 14				20 44		
Sole Street	d								18 17									19 17					
Meopham	d								18 19									19 19					
Longfield	d								18 23									19 23					
Farningham Road	d								18 27									19 27					
Swanley ■	a								18 32									19 32					
St Mary Cray	a								18 36									19 36					
Bromley South ■	a				18 13				18 42					19 13				19 42					20 13
Elephant &Castle ⊖	a																						
London Blackfriars ■ ⊖	a																						
London Victoria ■ ⊖	a				18 29				19 02					19 29				20 02					20 29
Ebbsfleet International	a	17 47					18 17				18 47					19 17				19 47			
Stratford International ⊖	a	17 59					18 29				18 59					19 29				19 59			
St Pancras Internatnl ■ ⊖	a	18 09					18 36				19 06					19 36				20 06			

A ⊼ from Faversham

B ⊼ from Margate

For further services to St Pancras International, Blackfriars and Elephant & Castle and onwards to Bromley South, St Mary Cray and Swanley please refer to table 52

Table 212

Sundays until 22 July, 19 Aug and from 16 Sep

Ramsgate, Dover, Sheerness-on-Sea and Medway - London

Network Diagram - see first Page of Table 212

		SE	SE	SE	SE [1]	SE	SE	SE	SE [1]	SE [1]	SE	SE	SE	SE [1]	SE	SE	SE	SE [1]	SE [1]	SE	SE	SE
Ramsgate [4]	d	18 59								19 34	19 59								20 34	20 59		
Dumpton Park	d									19 37									20 37			
Broadstairs	d	19 05								19 40	20 05								20 40	21 05		
Margate [4]	d	19a10								19 45	20a10								20 45	21a10		
Westgate-on-Sea	d									19 49									20 49			
Birchington-on-Sea	d									19 53									20 53			
Herne Bay	d									20 02									21 02			
Chestfield & Swalecliffe	d									20 05									21 05			
Whitstable	d									20 08									21 08			
Dover Priory [4]	d								19 34									20 34				
Kearsney	d								19 38									20 38				
Shepherds Well	d								19 43									20 43				
Snowdown	d								19 47									20 47				
Aylesham	d								19 49									20 49				
Adisham	d								19 52									20 52				
Bekesbourne	d								19 56									20 56				
Canterbury East [4]	d				19 22				20 01									21 01				
Selling	d								20 10									21 10				
Faversham [2]	a				19 33				20 15	20 17								21 15	21 17			
	d			19 28	19 34			19 58	20 21				20 28	20 34			20 58	21 21				21 28
Teynham	d				19 40									20 40								
Sheerness-on-Sea	d					19 42									20 42							
Queenborough	d					19 46									20 46							
Swale	d					19 50									20 50							
Kemsley	d					19 54									20 54							
Sittingbourne [4]	a			19 36	19 44	19 59		20 06	20 28				20 36	20 44	20 59		21 06	21 28				21 36
	d			19 37	19 45			20 07	20 29				20 37	20 45			21 07	21 29				21 37
Newington	d				19 50									20 50								
Rainham (Kent)	d			19 45	19 54			20 15	20 36				20 45	20 54			21 15	21 36				21 45
Gillingham (Kent) [4]	d		19 45	19 50	19 59		20 15	20 20	20 41			20 45	20 50	20 59		21 15	21 20	21 41			21 45	21 50
Chatham [4]	d		19 49	19 54	20 04		20 19	20 24	20 46			20 49	20 54	21 04		21 19	21 24	21 46			21 49	21 54
Rochester [4]	d		19 51	19 57	20 06		20 21	20 27	20 48			20 51	20 57	21 06		21 21	21 27	21 48			21 51	21 57
Strood [4]	a		19 56	20 01			20 26	20 31				20 56	21 01			21 26	21 31				21 56	22 01
Gravesend [4]	a		20 08	20 12			20 38	20 42				21 08	21 12			21 38	21 42				22 08	22 12
Greenhithe for Bluewater	a		20 17				20 47					21 17				21 47					22 17	
Dartford [4]	a		20 24				20 54					21 24				21 54					22 24	
London Bridge [4] ⊖	a		21 06				21 36					22 06				22 36					23 06	
London Cannon Street [4] ⊖	a																					
London Waterloo (East) [4] ⊖	a		21 11				21 41					22 11				22 41					23 11	
London Charing Cross [4] ⊖	a		21 14				21 44					22 14				22 44					23 14	
Sole Street	d				20 17									21 17								
Meopham	d				20 19									21 19								
Longfield	d				20 23									21 23								
Farningham Road	d				20 27									21 27								
Swanley [4]	a				20 32									21 32								
St Mary Cray	a				20 36									21 36								
Bromley South [4]	a				20 42				21 13					21 42				22 13				
Elephant & Castle ⊖	a																					
London Blackfriars [3] ⊖	a																					
London Victoria [15] ⊖	a				21 02				21 29					22 02				22 29				
Ebbsfleet International	a			20 17				20 47					21 17				21 47					22 17
Stratford International ⊖	a			20 29				21 02					21 29				21 59					22 29
St Pancras Internatnl [15] ⊖	a			20 36				21 09					21 36				22 06					22 36

For further services to St Pancras International, Blackfriars and Elephant & Castle and onwards to Bromley South, St Mary Cray and Swanley please refer to table 52

Table 212

Sundays until 22 July, 19 Aug and from 16 Sep

Ramsgate, Dover, Sheerness-on-Sea and Medway - London

Network Diagram - see first Page of Table 212

		SE [1]	SE	SE	SE	SE [1]	SE [1]	SE	SE [1]	SE [1]	SE	SE [1]	SE	SE
Ramsgate [4]	d						21 34	21 59				22 34	22 59	
Dumpton Park	d						21 37					22 37		
Broadstairs	d						21 40	22 05				22 40	23 05	
Margate [4]	d						21 45	22a10				22 45	23a10	
Westgate-on-Sea	d						21 49					22 49		
Birchington-on-Sea	d						21 53					22 53		
Herne Bay	d						22 02					23 02		
Chestfield & Swalecliffe	d						22 05					23 05		
Whitstable	d						22 08					23 08		
Dover Priory [4]	d					21 34				22 34				
Kearsney	d					21 38				22 38				
Shepherds Well	d					21 43				22 43				
Snowdown	d					21 47				22 47				
Aylesham	d					21 49				22 49				
Adisham	d					21 52				22 52				
Bekesbourne	d					21 56				22 56				
Canterbury East [4]	d					22 01				23 01				
Selling	d					22 10				23 10				
Faversham [2]	a					22 15	22 17			23 15		23 17		
	d	21 34			21 58	22 21			22 34			23 21		
Teynham	d	21 40							22 40					
Sheerness-on-Sea	d		21 42								22 42			23 42
Queenborough	d		21 46								22 46			23 46
Swale	d		21 50								22 50			23 50
Kemsley	d		21 54								22 54			23 54
Sittingbourne [4]	a	21 44	21 59		22 06	22 28			22 44		22 59	23 28		23 59
	d	21 45			22 07	22 29			22 45			23 29		
Newington	d	21 50							22 50					
Rainham (Kent)	d	21 54			22 15	22 36			22 54			23 36		
Gillingham (Kent) [4]	d	21 59		22 15	22 20	22 41			22 59			23 41		
Chatham [4]	d	22 04		22 19	22 24	22 46			23 04			23 46		
Rochester [4]	d	22 06		22 21	22 27	22 48			23 06			23 48		
Strood [4]	a			22 26	22 31									
Gravesend [4]	a			22 38	22 42									
Greenhithe for Bluewater	a			22 47										
Dartford [4]	a			22 54										
London Bridge [4] ⊖	a			23 36										
London Cannon Street [4] ⊖	a													
London Waterloo (East) [4] ⊖	a			23 41										
London Charing Cross [4] ⊖	a			23 44										
Sole Street	d	22 17							23 17					
Meopham	d	22 19							23 19					
Longfield	d	22 23							23 23					
Farningham Road	d	22 27							23 27					
Swanley [4]	a	22 32							23 32					
St Mary Cray	a	22 36							23 36					
Bromley South [4]	a	22 42				23 13			23 42			00 13		
Elephant & Castle ⊖	a													
London Blackfriars [3] ⊖	a													
London Victoria [15] ⊖	a	23 02				23 29			00 02			00 29		
Ebbsfleet International	a				22 47									
Stratford International ⊖	a				22 59									
St Pancras Internatnl [15] ⊖	a				23 06									

For further services to St Pancras International, Blackfriars and Elephant & Castle and onwards to Bromley South, St Mary Cray and Swanley please refer to table 52

Sundays

29 July to 12 August

Ramsgate, Dover, Sheerness-on-Sea and Medway - London

Network Diagram - see first Page of Table 212

		SE ■	SE ■	SE ■	SE	SE	SE ■	SE	SE	SE		SE ■	SE ■	SE	SE	SE	SE ■	SE	SE	SE		SE	SE ■	SE ■	SE
Ramsgate ■	d	22p04	22p34				04 32						05 04											06 04	
Dumpton Park	d	22p07	22p37										05 07											06 07	
Broadstairs	d	22p10	22p40				04 37		05 00				05 10						05 54					06 10	
Margate ■	d	22p16	22p46				04 42		05 05				05 16						05 59					06 16	
Westgate-on-Sea	d	22p20	22p50										05 20											06 20	
Birchington-on-Sea	d	22p23	22p53				04 47						05 23						06 04					06 23	
Herne Bay	d	22p32	23p02				04 56		05 16				05 32						06 13					06 32	
Chestfield & Swalecliffe	d	22p36	23p06										05 36											06 36	
Whitstable	d	22p39	23p09				05 01						05 39						06 19					06 39	
Dover Priory ■	d			23p05								05 05											06 05		
Kearsney	d			23p09								05 09											06 09		
Shepherds Well	d			23p14								05 14											06 14		
Snowdown	d			23p18								05 18											06 18		
Aylesham	d			23p20								05 20											06 20		
Adisham	d			23p23								05 23											06 23		
Bekesbourne	d			23p27								05 27											06 27		
Canterbury East ■	d			23p32								05 32											06 32		
Selling	d			23p41								05 41											06 41		
Faversham ■	a	22p48	23p18	23p46			05 09		05 28			05 46	05 48						06 27				06 46	06 48	
	d	22p52	23p25	23p52			05 09		05 28			05 52			05 58		06 14		06 28				06 52		
Teynham	d	22p58	23p31	23p58								05 58											06 58		
Sheerness-on-Sea	d				23p53															06 32					
Queenborough	d				23p57															06 36					
Swale	d				00 01															06 40					
Kemsley	d				00 05															06 44					
Sittingbourne ■	a	23p02	23p35	00 02	00 10		05 17		05 36			06 02			06 06		06 21		06 36	06 49			07 02		
	d	23p03	23p36	00 03			05 17		05 37			06 03			06 07		06 22		06 37				07 03		
Newington	d			00 08			05 23										06 27								
Rainham (Kent)	d	23p10	23p43	00 12			05 27		05 45			06 10			06 15		06 32		06 45				07 10		
Gillingham (Kent) ■	d	23p15	23p48	00a17		05 18	05 32		05 50	05 54		06 15			06 20	06 24	06 37		06 50			06 54	07 15		
Chatham ■	d	23p20	23p53			05 22	05 36		05 54	05 58		06 20			06 24	06 28	06 42		06 54			06 58	07 20		
Rochester ■	d	23p22	23p55			05 24	05 39		05 57	06 00		06 22			06 27	06 30	06 44		06 57			07 00	07 22		
Strood ■	a					05 29			06 01	06 05					06 31	06 35			07 01			07 05			
Gravesend ■	a					05 41			06 12	06 17					06 42	06 47			07 12			07 17			
Greenhithe for Bluewater	a					05 50				06 23						06 53						07 23			
Dartford ■	a					05 57				06 28						06 58						07 28			
London Bridge ■ ⊖	a					06 35				07 05						07 35						08 05			
London Cannon Street ■ ⊖	a																								
London Waterloo (East) ■ ⊖	a					06 39				07 09						07 39						08 09			
London Charing Cross ■ ⊖	a					06 46				07 16						07 46						08 16			
Sole Street	d						05 49										06 54								
Meopham	d	23p33	00 06				05 52					06 33					06 57						07 33		
Longfield	d	23p37	00 10				05 56					06 37					07 01						07 37		
Farningham Road	d						06 00										07 05								
Swanley ■	a						06 05										07 10								
St Mary Cray	a						06 09										07 14								
Bromley South ■	a	23p50	00 23				06 15					06 50					07 20						07 50		
Elephant & Castle ⊖	a																								
London Blackfriars ■ ⊖	a																								
London Victoria ■ ⊖	a	00 07	00 39				06 37					07 07					07 37						08 07		
Ebbsfleet International	a							05 32	06 16					06 32	06 47			07 06	07 16						07 32
Stratford International ⊖	a							05 44	06 33					06 45	06 58			07 19	07 28						07 45
St Pancras Internatnl ■ ⊖	a							05 50	06 43					06 55	07 06			07 29	07 36						07 55

For further services to St Pancras International, Blackfriars and Elephant & Castle and onwards to Bromley South, St Mary Cray and Swanley please refer to table 52

Sundays

29 July to 12 August

Ramsgate, Dover, Sheerness-on-Sea and Medway - London

Network Diagram - see first Page of Table 212

		SE	SE	SE ■	SE	SE		SE ■	SE ■	SE	SE	SE	SE	SE ■ A ⚒	SE ■ B ⚒	SE		SE	SE ■	SE ■	SE	SE	SE	SE
Ramsgate ■	d			06 32					07 04						07 32					08 04				
Dumpton Park	d								07 07											08 07				
Broadstairs	d	06 24		06 37					07 10						07 37					08 10				
Margate ■	d	06 29		06 42					07 16						07 42					08 16				
Westgate-on-Sea	d								07 20											08 20				
Birchington-on-Sea	d	06 34		06 47					07 23						07 47					08 23				
Herne Bay	d	06 43		06 56					07 32						07 56					08 32				
Chestfield & Swalecliffe	d								07 36											08 36				
Whitstable	d	06 49		07 01					07 39						08 01					08 39				
Dover Priory ■	d													07 26										
Kearsney	d													07 30										
Shepherds Well	d													07 35										
Snowdown	d													07 39										
Aylesham	d													07 41										
Adisham	d													07 44										
Bekesbourne	d													07 48										
Canterbury East ■	d							07 34						07 53					08 34					
Selling	d													08 02										
Faversham ■	a	06 57		07 10				07 46	07 48					08 07	08 10				08 46	08 48				
	d	06 58		07 14				07 52				07 58		08 14					08 52				08 58	
Teynham	d							07 58											08 58					
Sheerness-on-Sea	d				07 32											08 32								
Queenborough	d				07 36											08 36								
Swale	d				07 40											08 40								
Kemsley	d				07 44											08 44								
Sittingbourne ■	a	07 06		07 21	07 49			08 02				08 06		08 21		08 49			09 02				09 06	
	d	07 07		07 22				08 03				08 07		08 22					09 03				09 07	
Newington	d			07 27										08 27										
Rainham (Kent)	d	07 15		07 32				08 10				08 15		08 32					09 10				09 15	
Gillingham (Kent) ■	d	07 20	07 24	07 37		07 54		08 15				08 20	08 24	08 37				08 54	09 15				09 20	09 24
Chatham ■	d	07 24	07 28	07 42		07 58		08 20				08 24	08 28	08 42				08 58	09 20				09 24	09 28
Rochester ■	d	07 27	07 30	07 44		08 00		08 22				08 27	08 30	08 44				09 00	09 22				09 27	09 30
Strood ■	a	07 31	07 35			08 05						08 31	08 35					09 05					09 31	09 35
Gravesend ■	a	07 42	07 47			08 17						08 42	08 47					09 17					09 42	09 47
Greenhithe for Bluewater	a		07 53			08 23							08 53					09 23						09 53
Dartford ■	a		07 58			08 28							08 58					09 28						09 58
London Bridge ■ ⊖	a		08 35			09 05							09 35					10 05						10 35
London Cannon Street ■ ⊖	a																							
London Waterloo (East) ■ ⊖	a		08 39			09 09							09 39					10 09						10 39
London Charing Cross ■ ⊖	a		08 46			09 16							09 46					10 16						10 46
Sole Street	d			07 54										08 54										
Meopham	d			07 57				08 33						08 57					09 33					
Longfield	d			08 01				08 37						09 01					09 37					
Farningham Road	d			08 05										09 05										
Swanley ■	a			08 10										09 10										
St Mary Cray	a			08 14										09 14										
Bromley South ■	a			08 20				08 50						09 20					09 50					
Elephant & Castle ⊖	a																							
London Blackfriars ■ ⊖	a																							
London Victoria ■ ⊖	a			08 37				09 07						09 37					10 07					
Ebbsfleet International	a	07 46								08 06	08 32	08 46									09 06	09 32	09 46	
Stratford International ⊖	a	07 58								08 19	08 45	08 58									09 19	09 45	09 58	
St Pancras Internatnl ■ ⊖	a	08 08								08 29	08 55	09 08									09 29	09 55	10 08	

A ⚒ from Faversham

B ⚒ from Margate

For further services to St Pancras International, Blackfriars and Elephant & Castle and onwards to Bromley South, St Mary Cray and Swanley please refer to table 52

Table 212

Sundays
29 July to 12 August

Ramsgate, Dover, Sheerness-on-Sea and Medway - London

Network Diagram - see first Page of Table 212

		SE ■ A 🍴	SE ■ B 🍴	SE	SE	SE ■	SE ■	SE	SE	SE	SE	SE ■ A 🍴	SE ■ B 🍴	SE	SE	SE ■	SE ■	SE	SE	SE	SE	SE ■ A 🍴	SE ■ B 🍴
Ramsgate [4]	d		08 32				09 04						09 32				10 04						10 32
Dumpton Park	d						09 07										10 07						
Broadstairs	d		08 37				09 10						09 37				10 10						10 37
Margate [4]	d		08 42				09 16						09 42				10 16						10 42
Westgate-on-Sea	d						09 20										10 20						
Birchington-on-Sea	d		08 47				09 23						09 47				10 23						10 47
Herne Bay	d		08 56				09 32						09 56				10 32						10 56
Chestfield & Swalecliffe	d						09 36										10 36						
Whitstable	d		09 01				09 39						10 01				10 39						11 01
Dover Priory [4]	d	08 26										09 26										10 26	
Kearsney	d	08 30										09 30										10 30	
Shepherds Well	d	08 35										09 35										10 35	
Snowdown	d	08 39										09 39										10 39	
Aylesham	d	08 41										09 41										10 41	
Adisham	d	08 44										09 44										10 44	
Bekesbourne	d	08 48										09 48										10 48	
Canterbury East [4]	d	08 53				09 34						09 53				10 34						10 53	
Selling	d	09 02										10 02										11 02	
Faversham [2]	a	09 07	09 10			09 46	09 48					10 07	10 10			10 46	10 48					11 07	11 10
	d	09 14				09 52				09 58		10 14				10 52				10 58		11 14	
Teynham	d					09 58										10 58							
Sheerness-on-Sea	d			09 32										10 32									
Queenborough	d			09 36										10 36									
Swale	d			09 40										10 40									
Kemsley	d			09 44										10 44									
Sittingbourne [4]	a	09 21		09 49		10 02				10 06		10 21		10 49		11 02				11 06		11 21	
	d	09 22				10 03				10 07		10 22				11 03				11 07		11 22	
Newington	d	09 27										10 27										11 27	
Rainham (Kent)	d	09 32				10 10				10 15		10 32				11 10				11 15		11 32	
Gillingham (Kent) [4]	d	09 37			09 54	10 15				10 20	10 24	10 37			10 54	11 15				11 20	11 24	11 37	
Chatham [4]	d	09 42			09 58	10 20				10 24	10 28	10 42			10 58	11 20				11 24	11 28	11 42	
Rochester [4]	d	09 44			10 00	10 22				10 27	10 30	10 44			11 00	11 22				11 27	11 30	11 44	
Strood [4]	a				10 05					10 31	10 35				11 05					11 31	11 35		
Gravesend [4]	a				10 17					10 42	10 47				11 17					11 42	11 47		
Greenhithe for Bluewater	a				10 23						10 53				11 23						11 53		
Dartford [4]	a				10 28						10 58				11 28						11 58		
London Bridge [4] ⊖	a				11 05						11 35				12 05						12 35		
London Cannon Street [4] ⊖	a																						
London Waterloo (East) [4] ⊖	a				11 09						11 39				12 09						12 39		
London Charing Cross [4] ⊖	a				11 16						11 46				12 16						12 46		
Sole Street	d	09 54										10 54										11 54	
Meopham	d	09 57				10 33						10 57				11 33						11 57	
Longfield	d	10 01				10 37						11 01				11 37						12 01	
Farningham Road	d	10 05										11 05										12 05	
Swanley [4]	a	10 10										11 10										12 10	
St Mary Cray	a	10 14										11 14										12 14	
Bromley South [4]	a	10 20				10 50						11 20				11 50						12 20	
Elephant & Castle ⊖	a																						
London Blackfriars [3] ⊖	a																						
London Victoria [15] ⊖	a	10 37				11 07						11 37				12 07						12 37	
Ebbsfleet International	a							10 06	10 32	10 46								11 06	11 32	11 46			
Stratford International ⊖	a							10 19	10 45	10 58								11 19	11 45	11 58			
St Pancras Internatnl [15] ⊖	a							10 29	10 55	11 08								11 29	11 55	12 08			

A 🍴 from Faversham

B 🍴 from Margate

For further services to St Pancras International, Blackfriars and Elephant & Castle and onwards to Bromley South, St Mary Cray and Swanley please refer to table 52

Table 212

Sundays
29 July to 12 August

Ramsgate, Dover, Sheerness-on-Sea and Medway - London

Network Diagram - see first Page of Table 212

		SE	SE	SE ■	SE ■	SE	SE	SE	SE	SE ■ A 🍴	SE ■ B 🍴	SE	SE	SE ■	SE ■	SE	SE	SE	SE	SE ■ A 🍴	SE ■ B 🍴	SE
Ramsgate [4]	d				11 04						11 32				12 04						12 32	
Dumpton Park	d				11 07										12 07							
Broadstairs	d				11 10						11 37				12 10						12 37	
Margate [4]	d				11 16						11 42				12 16						12 42	
Westgate-on-Sea	d				11 20										12 20							
Birchington-on-Sea	d				11 23						11 47				12 23						12 47	
Herne Bay	d				11 32						11 56				12 32						12 56	
Chestfield & Swalecliffe	d				11 36										12 36							
Whitstable	d				11 39						12 01				12 39						13 01	
Dover Priory [4]	d									11 26										12 26		
Kearsney	d									11 30										12 30		
Shepherds Well	d									11 35										12 35		
Snowdown	d									11 39										12 39		
Aylesham	d									11 41										12 41		
Adisham	d									11 44										12 44		
Bekesbourne	d									11 48										12 48		
Canterbury East [4]	d			11 34						11 53				12 34						12 53		
Selling	d									12 02										13 02		
Faversham [2]	a			11 46	11 48					12 07	12 10			12 46	12 48					13 07	13 10	
	d			11 52				11 58		12 14				12 52				12 58		13 14		
Teynham	d			11 58										12 58								
Sheerness-on-Sea	d	11 32										12 32										13 32
Queenborough	d	11 36										12 36										13 36
Swale	d	11 40										12 40										13 40
Kemsley	d	11 44										12 44										13 44
Sittingbourne [4]	a	11 49		12 02				12 06		12 21		12 49		13 02				13 06		13 21		13 49
	d			12 03				12 07		12 22				13 03				13 07		13 22		
Newington	d									12 27										13 27		
Rainham (Kent)	d			12 10				12 15		12 32				13 10				13 15		13 32		
Gillingham (Kent) [4]	d		11 54	12 15				12 20	12 24	12 37			12 54	13 15				13 20	13 24	13 37		
Chatham [4]	d		11 58	12 20				12 24	12 28	12 42			12 58	13 20				13 24	13 28	13 42		
Rochester [4]	d		12 00	12 22				12 27	12 30	12 44			13 00	13 22				13 27	13 30	13 44		
Strood [4]	a		12 05					12 31	12 35				13 05					13 31	13 35			
Gravesend [4]	a		12 17					12 42	12 47				13 17					13 42	13 47			
Greenhithe for Bluewater	a		12 23						12 53				13 23						13 53			
Dartford [4]	a		12 28						12 58				13 28						13 58			
London Bridge [4] ⊖	a		13 05						13 35				14 05						14 35			
London Cannon Street [4] ⊖	a																					
London Waterloo (East) [4] ⊖	a		13 09						13 39				14 09						14 39			
London Charing Cross [4] ⊖	a		13 16						13 46				14 16						14 46			
Sole Street	d									12 54										13 54		
Meopham	d			12 33						12 57				13 33						13 57		
Longfield	d			12 37						13 01				13 37						14 01		
Farningham Road	d									13 05										14 05		
Swanley [4]	a									13 10										14 10		
St Mary Cray	a									13 14										14 14		
Bromley South [4]	a			12 50						13 20				13 50						14 20		
Elephant & Castle ⊖	a																					
London Blackfriars [3] ⊖	a																					
London Victoria [15] ⊖	a			13 07						13 37				14 07						14 37		
Ebbsfleet International	a					12 06	12 32	12 46								13 06	13 32	13 46				
Stratford International ⊖	a					12 19	12 45	12 58								13 19	13 45	13 58				
St Pancras Internatnl [15] ⊖	a					12 29	12 55	13 08								13 29	13 55	14 08				

A 🍴 from Faversham

B 🍴 from Margate

For further services to St Pancras International, Blackfriars and Elephant & Castle and onwards to Bromley South, St Mary Cray and Swanley please refer to table 52

Table 212

Sundays
29 July to 12 August

Ramsgate, Dover, Sheerness-on-Sea and Medway - London

Network Diagram - see first Page of Table 212

		SE	SE ■	SE ■	SE	SE	SE	SE	SE ■ A	SE ■ B		SE	SE	SE ■	SE ■	SE	SE	SE	SE	SE ■ A	SE ■ B		SE	SE	SE ■
Ramsgate	d			13 04						13 32					14 04						14 32				
Dumpton Park	d			13 07											14 07										
Broadstairs	d			13 10						13 37					14 10						14 37				
Margate	d			13 16						13 42					14 16						14 42				
Westgate-on-Sea	d			13 20											14 20										
Birchington-on-Sea	d			13 23						13 47					14 23						14 47				
Herne Bay	d			13 32						13 56					14 32						14 56				
Chestfield & Swalecliffe	d			13 36											14 36										
Whitstable	d			13 39						14 01					14 39						15 01				
Dover Priory	d								13 26											14 26					
Kearsney	d								13 30											14 30					
Shepherds Well	d								13 35											14 35					
Snowdown	d								13 39											14 39					
Aylesham	d								13 41											14 41					
Adisham	d								13 44											14 44					
Bekesbourne	d								13 48											14 48					
Canterbury East	d		13 34						13 53					14 34						14 53					15 34
Selling	d								14 02											15 02					
Faversham	a		13 46	13 48					14 07	14 10				14 46	14 48					15 07	15 10				15 46
	d		13 52				13 58		14 14					14 52				14 58		15 14					15 52
Teynham	d		13 58											14 58											15 58
Sheerness-on-Sea	d											14 32											15 32		
Queenborough	d											14 36											15 36		
Swale	d											14 40											15 40		
Kemsley	d											14 44											15 44		
Sittingbourne	a		14 02				14 06		14 21			14 49		15 02				15 06		15 21			15 49		16 02
	d		14 03				14 07		14 22					15 03				15 07		15 22					16 03
Newington	d								14 27											15 27					
Rainham (Kent)	d		14 10				14 15		14 32					15 10				15 15		15 32					16 10
Gillingham (Kent)	d	13 54	14 15				14 20	14 24	14 37				14 54	15 15				15 20	15 24	15 37				15 54	16 15
Chatham	d	13 58	14 20				14 24	14 28	14 42				14 58	15 20				15 24	15 28	15 42				15 58	16 20
Rochester	d	14 00	14 22				14 27	14 30	14 44				15 00	15 22				15 27	15 30	15 44				16 00	16 22
Strood	a	14 05					14 31	14 35					15 05					15 31	15 35					16 05	
Gravesend	a	14 17					14 42	14 47					15 17					15 42	15 47					16 17	
Greenhithe for Bluewater	a	14 23						14 53					15 23						15 53					16 23	
Dartford	a	14 28						14 58					15 28						15 58					16 28	
London Bridge ⊖	a	15 05						15 35					16 05						16 35					17 05	
London Cannon Street ⊖	a																								
London Waterloo (East) ⊖	a	15 09						15 39					16 09						16 39					17 09	
London Charing Cross ⊖	a	15 16						15 46					16 16						16 46					17 16	
Sole Street	d								14 54											15 54					
Meopham	d		14 33						14 57					15 33						15 57					16 33
Longfield	d		14 37						15 01					15 37						16 01					16 37
Farningham Road	d								15 05											16 05					
Swanley	a								15 10											16 10					
St Mary Cray	a								15 14											16 14					
Bromley South	a		14 50						15 20					15 50						16 20					16 50
Elephant & Castle ⊖	a																								
London Blackfriars ⊖	a																								
London Victoria ⊖	a		15 07						15 37					16 07						16 37					17 07
Ebbsfleet International	a				14 06	14 32	14 46									15 06	15 32	15 46							
Stratford International ⊖	a				14 19	14 45	14 58									15 19	15 45	15 58							
St Pancras International ⊖	a				14 29	14 55	15 08									15 29	15 55	16 08							

A ⌶ from Faversham B ⌶ from Margate

For further services to St Pancras International, Blackfriars and Elephant & Castle and onwards to Bromley South, St Mary Cray and Swanley please refer to table 52

Table 212

Sundays
29 July to 12 August

Ramsgate, Dover, Sheerness-on-Sea and Medway - London

Network Diagram - see first Page of Table 212

		SE ■	SE	SE	SE	SE	SE ■ A	SE ■ B		SE	SE	SE ■	SE ■	SE	SE	SE	SE	SE ■ A	SE ■ B		SE	SE	SE ■	SE ■	SE
Ramsgate	d	15 04						15 32					16 04						16 32					17 04	
Dumpton Park	d	15 07											16 07											17 07	
Broadstairs	d	15 10						15 37					16 10						16 37					17 10	
Margate	d	15 16						15 42					16 16						16 42					17 16	
Westgate-on-Sea	d	15 20											16 20											17 20	
Birchington-on-Sea	d	15 23						15 47					16 23						16 47					17 23	
Herne Bay	d	15 32						15 56					16 32						16 56					17 32	
Chestfield & Swalecliffe	d	15 36											16 36											17 36	
Whitstable	d	15 39						16 01					16 39						17 01					17 39	
Dover Priory	d						15 26											16 26							
Kearsney	d						15 30											16 30							
Shepherds Well	d						15 35											16 35							
Snowdown	d						15 39											16 39							
Aylesham	d						15 41											16 41							
Adisham	d						15 44											16 44							
Bekesbourne	d						15 48											16 48							
Canterbury East	d						15 53					16 34						16 53					17 34		
Selling	d						16 02											17 02							
Faversham	a	15 48					16 07	16 10				16 46	16 48					17 07	17 10				17 46	17 48	
	d				15 58		16 14					16 52				16 58		17 14					17 52		
Teynham	d											16 58											17 58		
Sheerness-on-Sea	d									16 32											17 32				
Queenborough	d									16 36											17 36				
Swale	d									16 40											17 40				
Kemsley	d									16 44											17 44				
Sittingbourne	a				16 06		16 21			16 49		17 02				17 06		17 21			17 49		18 02		
	d				16 07		16 22					17 03				17 07		17 22					18 03		
Newington	d						16 27											17 27							
Rainham (Kent)	d				16 15		16 32					17 10				17 15		17 32					18 10		
Gillingham (Kent)	d				16 20	16 24	16 37				16 54	17 15				17 20	17 24	17 37				17 54	18 15		
Chatham	d				16 24	16 28	16 42				16 58	17 20				17 24	17 28	17 42				17 58	18 20		
Rochester	d				16 27	16 30	16 44				17 00	17 22				17 27	17 30	17 44				18 00	18 22		
Strood	a				16 31	16 35					17 05					17 31	17 35					18 05			
Gravesend	a				16 42	16 47					17 17					17 42	17 47					18 17			
Greenhithe for Bluewater	a					16 53					17 23						17 53					18 23			
Dartford	a					16 58					17 28						17 58					18 28			
London Bridge ⊖	a					17 35					18 05						18 35					19 05			
London Cannon Street ⊖	a																								
London Waterloo (East) ⊖	a					17 39					18 09						18 39					19 09			
London Charing Cross ⊖	a					17 46					18 16						18 46					19 16			
Sole Street	d						16 54											17 54							
Meopham	d						16 57					17 33						17 57					18 33		
Longfield	d						17 01					17 37						18 01					18 37		
Farningham Road	d						17 05											18 05							
Swanley	a						17 10											18 10							
St Mary Cray	a						17 14											18 14							
Bromley South	a						17 20					17 50						18 20					18 50		
Elephant & Castle ⊖	a																								
London Blackfriars ⊖	a																								
London Victoria ⊖	a						17 37					18 07						18 37					19 07		
Ebbsfleet International	a		16 06	16 32	16 46									17 06	17 32	17 46									18 06
Stratford International ⊖	a		16 19	16 45										17 19	17 45	17 58									18 19
St Pancras International ⊖	a		16 29	16 55										17 29	17 55	18 08									18 29

A ⌶ from Faversham B ⌶ from Margate

For further services to St Pancras International, Blackfriars and Elephant & Castle and onwards to Bromley South, St Mary Cray and Swanley please refer to table 52

Table 212

Sundays
29 July to 12 August

Ramsgate, Dover, Sheerness-on-Sea and Medway - London

Network Diagram - see first Page of Table 212

		SE	SE	SE	SE ■	SE ■	SE	SE	SE ■	SE ■	SE	SE	SE	SE	SE ■	SE ■	SE	SE	SE ■	SE ■	SE	SE	SE
Ramsgate	d					17 32				18 04						18 32				19 04			
Dumpton Park	d									18 07										19 07			
Broadstairs	d					17 37				18 10						18 37				19 10			
Margate	d					17 42				18 16						18 42				19 16			
Westgate-on-Sea	d									18 20										19 20			
Birchington-on-Sea	d					17 47				18 23						18 47				19 23			
Herne Bay	d					17 56				18 32						18 56				19 32			
Chestfield & Swalecliffe	d									18 36										19 36			
Whitstable	d					18 01				18 39						19 01				19 39			
Dover Priory	d				17 26										18 26				19 05				
Kearsney	d				17 30										18 30				19 09				
Shepherds Well	d				17 35										18 35				19 14				
Snowdown	d				17 39										18 39				19 18				
Aylesham	d				17 41										18 41				19 20				
Adisham	d				17 44										18 44				19 23				
Bekesbourne	d				17 48										18 48				19 27				
Canterbury East	d				17 53				18 34						18 53				19 32				
Selling	d				18 02										19 02				19 41				
Faversham	a				18 07	18 10			18 46	18 48					19 07	19 10			19 46	19 48			
	d		17 58		18 14				18 52				18 58		19 14				19 52				19 58
Teynham	d								18 58										19 58				
Sheerness-on-Sea	d						18 32										19 32						
Queenborough	d						18 36										19 36						
Swale	d						18 40										19 40						
Kemsley	d						18 44										19 44						
Sittingbourne	a		18 06		18 21		18 49		19 02				19 06		19 21		19 49		20 02				20 06
	d		18 07		18 22				19 03				19 07		19 22				20 03				20 07
Newington	d				18 27										19 27								
Rainham (Kent)	d		18 15		18 32				19 10				19 15		19 32				20 10				20 15
Gillingham (Kent)	d		18 20	18 24	18 37			18 54	19 15				19 20	19 24	19 37			19 54	20 15				20 20
Chatham	d		18 24	18 28	18 42			18 58	19 20				19 24	19 28	19 42			19 58	20 20				20 24
Rochester	d		18 27	18 30	18 44			19 00	19 22				19 27	19 30	19 44			20 00	20 22				20 27
Strood	a		18 31	18 35				19 05					19 31	19 35				20 05					20 31
Gravesend	a		18 42	18 47				19 17					19 42	19 47				20 17					20 42
Greenhithe for Bluewater	a			18 53				19 23						19 53				20 23					
Dartford	a			18 58				19 28						19 58				20 28					
London Bridge ⊖	a			19 36				20 07						20 37				21 07					
London Cannon Street ⊖	a																						
London Waterloo (East) ⊖	a			19 42				20 11						20 41				21 11					
London Charing Cross ⊖	a			19 48				20 18						20 48				21 18					
Sole Street	d				18 54										19 54								
Meopham	d				18 57				19 33						19 57				20 33				
Longfield	d				19 01				19 37						20 01				20 37				
Farningham Road	d				19 05										20 05								
Swanley	a				19 10										20 10								
St Mary Cray	a				19 14										20 14								
Bromley South	a				19 20				19 50						20 20				20 50				
Elephant & Castle ⊖	a																						
London Blackfriars ⊖	a																						
London Victoria ⊖	a				19 37				20 07						20 37				21 07				
Ebbsfleet International	a	18 32	18 46								19 06	19 32	19 46								20 06	20 32	20 46
Stratford International ⊖	a	18 45	18 58								19 19	19 45	19 58								20 19	20 45	20 58
St Pancras Internatnl ⊖	a	18 55	19 08								19 29	19 55	20 08								20 29	20 55	21 08

For further services to St Pancras International, Blackfriars and Elephant & Castle and onwards to Bromley South, St Mary Cray and Swanley please refer to table 52

Table 212

Sundays
29 July to 12 August

Ramsgate, Dover, Sheerness-on-Sea and Medway - London

Network Diagram - see first Page of Table 212

		SE	SE ■	SE	SE	SE ■	SE ■	SE	SE	SE	SE	SE ■	SE	SE	SE ■	SE ■	SE	SE	SE	SE	SE ■	SE ■
Ramsgate	d						20 04									21 04						
Dumpton Park	d						20 07									21 07						
Broadstairs	d						20 10									21 10						
Margate	d						20 16									21 16						
Westgate-on-Sea	d						20 20									21 20						
Birchington-on-Sea	d						20 23									21 23						
Herne Bay	d						20 32									21 32						
Chestfield & Swalecliffe	d						20 36									21 36						
Whitstable	d						20 39									21 39						
Dover Priory	d					20 05									21 05							22 05
Kearsney	d					20 09									21 09							22 09
Shepherds Well	d					20 14									21 14							22 14
Snowdown	d					20 18									21 18							22 18
Aylesham	d					20 20									21 20							22 20
Adisham	d					20 23									21 23							22 23
Bekesbourne	d					20 27									21 27							22 27
Canterbury East	d		20 02			20 32						21 02			21 32						22 02	22 32
Selling	d					20 41									21 41							22 41
Faversham	a		20 13			20 46	20 48					21 13			21 46	21 48					22 13	22 46
	d		20 14			20 52				20 58		21 14			21 52				21 58		22 14	
Teynham	d					20 58									21 58							
Sheerness-on-Sea	d			20 32									21 32									
Queenborough	d			20 36									21 36									
Swale	d			20 40									21 40									
Kemsley	d			20 44									21 44									
Sittingbourne	a		20 21	20 49		21 02				21 06		21 21	21 49		22 02				22 06		22 21	
	d		20 22			21 03				21 07		21 22			22 03				22 07		22 22	
Newington	d		20 27									21 27									22 27	
Rainham (Kent)	d		20 32			21 10				21 15		21 32			22 10				22 15		22 32	
Gillingham (Kent)	d	20 24	20 37		20 54	21 15				21 20	21 24	21 37		21 54	22 15				22 20	22 24	22 37	
Chatham	d	20 28	20 42		20 58	21 20				21 24	21 28	21 42		21 58	22 20				22 24	22 28	22 42	
Rochester	d	20 30	20 44		21 00	21 22				21 27	21 30	21 44		22 00	22 22				22 27	22 30	22 44	
Strood	a	20 35			21 05					21 31	21 35			22 05					22 31	22 35		
Gravesend	a	20 47			21 17					21 42	21 47			22 17					22 42	22 47		
Greenhithe for Bluewater	a	20 53			21 23						21 53			22 23						22 53		
Dartford	a	20 58			21 28						21 58			22 28						22 58		
London Bridge ⊖	a	21 36			22 05						22 35			23 05						23 35		
London Cannon Street ⊖	a																					
London Waterloo (East) ⊖	a	21 40			22 09						22 39			23 09						23 39		
London Charing Cross ⊖	a	21 47			22 16						22 46			23 16						23 46		
Sole Street	d		20 54									21 54									22 54	
Meopham	d		20 57			21 33						21 57			22 33						22 57	
Longfield	d		21 01			21 37						22 01			22 37						23 01	
Farningham Road	d		21 05									22 05									23 05	
Swanley	a		21 10									22 10									23 10	
St Mary Cray	a		21 14									22 14									23 14	
Bromley South	a		21 20			21 50						22 20			22 50						23 20	
Elephant & Castle ⊖	a																					
London Blackfriars ⊖	a																					
London Victoria ⊖	a		21 37			22 07						22 37			23 07						23 37	
Ebbsfleet International	a							21 06	21 32	21 46							22 06	22 32	22 46			
Stratford International ⊖	a							21 19	21 45	21 58							22 19	22 45	22 58			
St Pancras Internatnl ⊖	a							21 29	21 55	22 08							22 29	22 55	23 07			

For further services to St Pancras International, Blackfriars and Elephant & Castle and onwards to Bromley South, St Mary Cray and Swanley please refer to table 52

Table 212

Sundays

29 July to 12 August

Ramsgate, Dover, Sheerness-on-Sea and Medway - London

Network Diagram - see first Page of Table 212

		SE	SE	SE ■	SE ■	SE ■	SE	SE	SE
Ramsgate ■	d			22 04	22 34				
Dumpton Park	d			22 07	22 37				
Broadstairs	d			22 10	22 40				
Margate ■	d			22 16	22 46				
Westgate-on-Sea	d			22 20	22 50				
Birchington-on-Sea	d			22 23	22 53				
Herne Bay	d			22 32	23 02				
Chestfield &Swalecliffe	d			22 36	23 06				
Whitstable	d			22 39	23 09				
Dover Priory ■	d					22 40			
Kearsney	d					22 44			
Shepherds Well	d					22 49			
Snowdown	d					22 53			
Aylesham	d					22 55			
Adisham	d					22 58			
Bekesbourne	d					23 02			
Canterbury East ■	d					23 07			
Selling	d					23 16			
Faversham ■	a			22 48	23 18	23 21			
	d			22 52	23 25				
Teynham	d			22 58	23 31				
Sheerness-on-Sea	d	22 32							23 32
Queenborough	d	22 36							23 36
Swale	d	22 40							23 40
Kemsley	d	22 44							23 44
Sittingbourne ■	a	22 49		23 02	23 35				23 49
	d			23 03	23 36				
Newington	d								
Rainham (Kent)	d			23 10	23 43				
Gillingham (Kent) ■	d		22 54	23 15	23 48				
Chatham ■	d		22 58	23 20	23 53				
Rochester ■	d		23 00	23 22	23 55				
Strood ■	a		23 05						
Gravesend ■	a		23 17						
Greenhithe for Bluewater	a		23 23						
Dartford ■	a		23 31						
London Bridge ■ ⊖	a								
London Cannon Street ■ ⊖	a								
London Waterloo (East) ■ ⊖	a								
London Charing Cross ■ ⊖	a								
Sole Street	d			23 32					
Meopham	d			23 35	00 06				
Longfield	d			23 39	00 10				
Farningham Road	d			23 43					
Swanley ■	a			23 48					
St Mary Cray	a			23 52					
Bromley South ■	a			23 58	00 23				
Elephant &Castle ⊖	a								
London Blackfriars ■ ⊖	a								
London Victoria ■ ⊖	a			00 14	00 39				
Ebbsfleet International	a						23 02	23 30	
Stratford International ⊖	a						23 16	23 42	
St Pancras Internatnl ■ ⊖	a						23 26	23 51	

For further services to St Pancras International, Blackfriars and Elephant & Castle and onwards to Bromley South, St Mary Cray and Swanley please refer to table 52

Table 212

Sundays

26 August to 9 September

Ramsgate, Dover, Sheerness-on-Sea and Medway - London

Network Diagram - see first Page of Table 212

		SE ■	SE ■	SE	SE	SE ■	SE	SE	SE	SE ■		SE	SE	SE	SE ■	SE	SE	SE	SE ■	SE ■		SE	SE	SE ■	SE
								A	B				A	B			A	B	C	D		B			
Ramsgate ■	d	22p05	23p05							06 34										07 34					
Dumpton Park	d	22p08	23p08							06 37										07 37					
Broadstairs	d	22p11	23p11							06 40										07 40					
Margate ■	d	22p16	23p16							06 45										07 45					
Westgate-on-Sea	d	22p20	23p20							06 49										07 49					
Birchington-on-Sea	d	22p24	23p24							06 53										07 53					
Herne Bay	d	22p33	23p33							07 02										08 02					
Chestfield &Swalecliffe	d	22p36	23p36							07 05										08 05					
Whitstable	d	22p39	23p39							07 08										08 08					
Dover Priory ■	d																		07 34						
Kearsney	d																		07 38						
Shepherds Well	d																		07 43						
Snowdown	d																		07 47						
Aylesham	d																		07 49						
Adisham	d																		07 52						
Bekesbourne	d																		07 56						
Canterbury East ■	d																		08 01						
Selling	d																		08 10						
Faversham ■	a	22p48	23p49							07 17									08 15	08 17					
	d	22p52	23p52			06 34		06 58	06 58	07 21				07 28	07 34		07 58	07 58		08 21		08 28		08 34	
Teynham	d	22p58	23p58			06 40									07 40									08 40	
Sheerness-on-Sea	d			23p53																					08 42
Queenborough	d			23p57																					08 46
Swale	d			00 01																					08 50
Kemsley	d			00 05																					08 54
Sittingbourne ■	a	23p02	00 02	00 10		06 44		07 06	07 06	07 28				07 36	07 44		08 06	08 06		08 28		08 36		08 44	08 59
	d	23p03	00 03			06 45		07 07	07 07	07 29				07 37	07 45		08 07	08 07		08 29		08 37		08 45	
Newington	d		00 08			06 50									07 50									08 50	
Rainham (Kent)	d	23p10	00 12			06 54		07 15	07 15	07 36				07 45	07 54		08 15	08 15		08 36		08 45		08 54	
Gillingham (Kent) ■	d	23p15	00a17		06 45	06 59	07 15	07 20	07 20	07 41		07 45		07 50	07 59	08 15	08 20	08 20		08 41		08 50	08 54	08 59	
Chatham ■	d	23p20			06 49	07 04	07 19	07 24	07 24	07 46		07 49		07 54	08 04	08 19	08 24	08 24		08 46		08 54	08 58	09 04	
Rochester ■	d	23p22			06 51	07 06	07 21	07 27	07 27	07 48		07 51		07 57	08 06	08 21	08 27	08 27		08 48		08 57	09 00	09 06	
Strood ■	a				06 56		07 26	07 31	07 31			07 56		08 01		08 26	08 31	08 31				09 01	09 05		
Gravesend ■	a				07 08		07 38	07 42	07 42			08 08		08 12		08 38	08 42	08 42				09 12	09 17		
Greenhithe for Bluewater	a				07 17		07 47					08 17				08 47							09 23		
Dartford ■	a				07 24		07 54					08 24				08 54							09 28		
London Bridge ■ ⊖	a				08 06		08 36					09 06				09 36							10 06		
London Cannon Street ■ ⊖	a																								
London Waterloo (East) ■ ⊖	a				08 11		08 41					09 11				09 41							10 11		
London Charing Cross ■ ⊖	a				08 14		08 44					09 14				09 44							10 14		
Sole Street	d					07 17									08 17									09 17	
Meopham	d	23p33				07 19									08 19									09 19	
Longfield	d	23p37				07 23									08 23									09 23	
Farningham Road	d					07 27									08 27									09 27	
Swanley ■	a					07 32									08 32									09 32	
St Mary Cray	a					07 36									08 36									09 36	
Bromley South ■	a	23p50				07 42				08 13					08 42					09 13				09 42	
Elephant &Castle ⊖	a																								
London Blackfriars ■ ⊖	a																								
London Victoria ■ ⊖	a	00 07				08 03				08 29					09 02					09 29				10 02	
Ebbsfleet International	a							07 47	07 47				08 02	08 17			08 47	08 47				09 17			
Stratford International ⊖	a								07 59				08 14	08 28			08 59	08 59				09 29			
St Pancras Internatnl ■ ⊖	a								08 07				08 21	08 35			09 06	09 07				09 42			

A not from 2 September until 9 September
B not 26 August
C from Faversham
D from Margate

For further services to St Pancras International, Blackfriars and Elephant & Castle and onwards to Bromley South, St Mary Cray and Swanley please refer to table 52

Table 212

Ramsgate, Dover, Sheerness-on-Sea and Medway - London

Sundays

26 August to 9 September

Network Diagram - see first Page of Table 212

		SE A	SE B	SE	SE 1 C ✠	SE 1 D ✠	SE B	SE	SE 1	SE	SE A	SE B	SE	SE 1 C ✠	SE 1 D ✠	SE	SE B	SE	SE 1	SE	SE A	SE B	SE
Ramsgate	d					08 34									09 34	09 59							
Dumpton Park	d					08 37									09 37								
Broadstairs	d					08 40									09 40	10 05							
Margate	d					08 45									09 45	10a10							
Westgate-on-Sea	d					08 49									09 49								
Birchington-on-Sea	d					08 53									09 53								
Herne Bay	d					09 02									10 02								
Chestfield & Swalecliffe	d					09 05									10 05								
Whitstable	d					09 08									10 08								
Dover Priory	d				08 34									09 34									
Kearsney	d				08 38									09 38									
Shepherds Well	d				08 43									09 43									
Snowdown	d				08 47									09 47									
Aylesham	d				08 49									09 49									
Adisham	d				08 52									09 52									
Bekesbourne	d				08 56									09 56									
Canterbury East	d				09 01				09 22					10 01					10 22				
Selling	d				09 10									10 10									
Faversham	a				09 15	09 17			09 33					10 15	10 17				10 33				
	d	08 58	08 58		09 21		09 28		09 34		09 58	09 58		10 21			10 28		10 34		10 58	10 58	
Teynham	d								09 40										10 40				
Sheerness-on-Sea	d									09 42										10 42			
Queenborough	d									09 46										10 46			
Swale	d									09 50										10 50			
Kemsley	d									09 54										10 54			
Sittingbourne	a	09 06	09 06		09 28		09 36		09 44	09 59	10 06	10 06		10 28			10 36		10 44	10 59	11 06	11 06	
	d	09 07	09 07		09 29		09 37		09 45		10 07	10 07		10 29			10 37		10 45		11 07	11 07	
Newington	d								09 50										10 50				
Rainham (Kent)	d	09 15	09 15		09 36		09 45		09 54		10 15	10 15		10 36			10 45		10 54		11 15	11 15	
Gillingham (Kent)	d	09 20	09 20	09 24	09 41		09 50	09 54	09 59		10 20	10 20	10 24	10 41			10 50	10 54	10 59		11 20	11 20	11 24
Chatham	d	09 24	09 24	09 28	09 46		09 54	09 58	10 04		10 24	10 24	10 28	10 46			10 54	10 58	11 04		11 24	11 24	11 28
Rochester	d	09 27	09 27	09 30	09 48		09 57	10 00	10 06		10 27	10 27	10 30	10 48			10 57	11 00	11 06		11 27	11 27	11 30
Strood	a	09 31	09 31	09 35			10 01	10 05			10 31	10 31	10 35				11 01	11 05			11 31	11 31	11 35
Gravesend	a	09 42	09 42	09 47			10 12	10 17			10 42	10 42	10 47				11 12	11 17			11 42	11 42	11 47
Greenhithe for Bluewater	a			09 53				10 23					10 53					11 23					11 53
Dartford	a			09 58				10 28					10 58					11 28					11 58
London Bridge ⊖	a			10 36				11 06					11 36					12 06					12 36
London Cannon Street ⊖	a																						
London Waterloo (East) ⊖	a			10 41				11 11					11 41					12 11					12 41
London Charing Cross ⊖	a			10 44				11 14					11 44					12 14					12 44
Sole Street	d								10 17										11 17				
Meopham	d								10 19										11 19				
Longfield	d								10 23										11 23				
Farningham Road	d								10 27										11 27				
Swanley	a								10 32										11 32				
St Mary Cray	a								10 36										11 36				
Bromley South	a				10 13				10 42					11 13					11 42				
Elephant & Castle ⊖	a																						
London Blackfriars ⊖	a																						
London Victoria ⊖	a				10 29				11 02					11 29					12 02				
Ebbsfleet International	a	09 47	09 47				10 17				10 47	10 47					11 17				11 47	11 47	
Stratford International ⊖	a	09 59	09 59				10 38				10 59	10 59									11 59	11 59	
St Pancras Internatnl ⊖	a	10 06	10 07				10 44				11 06	11 07									12 06	12 07	

A not from 2 September until 9 September
B not 26 August
C ✠ from Faversham
D ✠ from Margate

For further services to St Pancras International, Blackfriars and Elephant & Castle and onwards to Bromley South, St Mary Cray and Swanley please refer to table 52

Table 212

Ramsgate, Dover, Sheerness-on-Sea and Medway - London

Sundays

26 August to 9 September

Network Diagram - see first Page of Table 212

		SE 1 A ✠	SE 1 B ✠	SE	SE C	SE D	SE	SE 1	SE	SE C	SE D	SE	SE 1 A ✠	SE 1 B ✠	SE	SE C	SE D	SE	SE 1	SE	SE	SE
Ramsgate	d		10 34	10 59										11 34	11 59							
Dumpton Park	d		10 37											11 37								
Broadstairs	d		10 40	11 05										11 40	12 05							
Margate	d		10 45	11a10										11 45	12a10							
Westgate-on-Sea	d		10 49											11 49								
Birchington-on-Sea	d		10 53											11 53								
Herne Bay	d		11 02											12 02								
Chestfield & Swalecliffe	d		11 05											12 05								
Whitstable	d		11 08											12 08								
Dover Priory	d	10 34											11 34									
Kearsney	d	10 38											11 38									
Shepherds Well	d	10 43											11 43									
Snowdown	d	10 47											11 47									
Aylesham	d	10 49											11 49									
Adisham	d	10 52											11 52									
Bekesbourne	d	10 56											11 56									
Canterbury East	d	11 01						11 22					12 01						12 22			
Selling	d	11 10											12 10									
Faversham	a	11 15	11 17					11 33					12 15	12 17					12 33			
	d	11 21			11 28	11 28		11 34		11 58	11 58		12 21			12 28	12 28		12 34		12 58	
Teynham	d							11 40											12 40			
Sheerness-on-Sea	d								11 42											12 42		
Queenborough	d								11 46											12 46		
Swale	d								11 50											12 50		
Kemsley	d								11 54											12 54		
Sittingbourne	a	11 28			11 36	11 36		11 44	11 59	12 06	12 06		12 28			12 36	12 36		12 44	12 59	13 06	
	d	11 29			11 37	11 37		11 45		12 07	12 07		12 29			12 37	12 37		12 45		13 07	
Newington	d							11 50											12 50			
Rainham (Kent)	d	11 36			11 45	11 45		11 54		12 15	12 15		12 36			12 45	12 45		12 54		13 15	
Gillingham (Kent)	d	11 41			11 50	11 50	11 54	11 59		12 20	12 20	12 24	12 41			12 50	12 50	12 54	12 59		13 20	13 24
Chatham	d	11 46			11 54	11 54	11 58	12 04		12 24	12 24	12 28	12 46			12 54	12 54	12 58	13 04		13 24	13 28
Rochester	d	11 48			11 57	11 57	12 00	12 06		12 27	12 27	12 30	12 48			12 57	12 57	13 00	13 06		13 27	13 30
Strood	a				12 01	12 01	12 05			12 31	12 31	12 35				13 01	13 01	13 05			13 31	13 35
Gravesend	a				12 12	12 12	12 17			12 42	12 42	12 47				13 12	13 12	13 17			13 42	13 47
Greenhithe for Bluewater	a						12 23					12 53						13 23				13 53
Dartford	a						12 28					12 58						13 28				13 58
London Bridge ⊖	a						13 06					13 36						14 06				14 36
London Cannon Street ⊖	a																					
London Waterloo (East) ⊖	a						13 11					13 41						14 11				14 41
London Charing Cross ⊖	a						13 14					13 44						14 14				14 44
Sole Street	d							12 17											13 17			
Meopham	d							12 19											13 19			
Longfield	d							12 23											13 23			
Farningham Road	d							12 27											13 27			
Swanley	a							12 32											13 32			
St Mary Cray	a							12 36											13 36			
Bromley South	a	12 13						12 42					13 13						13 42			
Elephant & Castle ⊖	a																					
London Blackfriars ⊖	a																					
London Victoria ⊖	a	12 29						13 02					13 29						14 02			
Ebbsfleet International	a				12 17	12 17				12 47	12 47					13 17	13 17				13 47	
Stratford International ⊖	a				12 29	12 32				12 59	12 59					13 29	13 32				14 02	
St Pancras Internatnl ⊖	a				12 36	12 40				13 06	13 07					13 36	13 40				14 09	

A ✠ from Faversham
B ✠ from Margate
C not from 2 September until 9 September
D not 26 August

For further services to St Pancras International, Blackfriars and Elephant & Castle and onwards to Bromley South, St Mary Cray and Swanley please refer to table 52

Table 212

Sundays

26 August to 9 September

Ramsgate, Dover, Sheerness-on-Sea and Medway - London

Network Diagram - see first Page of Table 212

		SE ■ A	SE ■ B	SE	SE C	SE D	SE	SE ■	SE		SE C	SE D	SE	SE ■ A	SE ■ B	SE	SE C	SE D	SE		SE ■	SE	SE C	SE D	SE
Ramsgate	d		12 34	12 59											13 34	13 59									
Dumpton Park	d		12 37												13 37										
Broadstairs	d		12 40	13 05											13 40	14 05									
Margate	d		12 45	13a10											13 45	14a10									
Westgate-on-Sea	d		12 49												13 49										
Birchington-on-Sea	d		12 53												13 53										
Herne Bay	d		13 02												14 02										
Chestfield & Swalecliffe	d		13 05												14 05										
Whitstable	d		13 08												14 08										
Dover Priory	d	12 34												13 34											
Kearsney	d	12 38												13 38											
Shepherds Well	d	12 43												13 43											
Snowdown	d	12 47												13 47											
Aylesham	d	12 49												13 49											
Adisham	d	12 52												13 52											
Bekesbourne	d	12 56												13 56											
Canterbury East	d	13 01						13 22						14 01							14 22				
Selling	d	13 10												14 10											
Faversham	a	13 15	13 17					13 33						14 15	14 17						14 33				
	d		13 21		13 28	13 28		13 34			13 58	13 58			14 21		14 28	14 28			14 34		14 58	14 58	
Teynham	d							13 40													14 40				
Sheerness-on-Sea	d								13 42													14 42			
Queenborough	d								13 46													14 46			
Swale	d								13 50													14 50			
Kemsley	d								13 54													14 54			
Sittingbourne	a		13 28		13 36	13 36		13 44	13 59		14 06	14 06			14 28		14 36	14 36			14 44	14 59	15 06	15 06	
	d		13 29		13 37	13 37		13 45			14 07	14 07			14 29		14 37	14 37			14 45		15 07	15 07	
Newington	d							13 50													14 50				
Rainham (Kent)	d		13 36		13 45	13 45		13 54			14 15	14 15			14 36		14 45	14 45			14 54		15 15	15 15	
Gillingham (Kent)	d		13 41		13 50	13 50	13 54	13 59			14 20	14 20	14 24		14 41		14 50	14 50	14 54		14 59		15 20	15 20	15 24
Chatham	d		13 46		13 54	13 54	13 58	14 04			14 24	14 24	14 28		14 46		14 54	14 54	14 58		15 04		15 24	15 24	15 28
Rochester	d		13 48		13 57	13 57	14 00	14 06			14 27	14 27	14 30		14 48		14 57	14 57	15 00		15 06		15 27	15 27	15 30
Strood	a				14 01	14 01	14 05				14 31	14 31	14 35				15 01	15 01	15 05				15 31	15 31	15 35
Gravesend	a				14 12	14 12	14 17				14 42	14 42	14 47				15 12	15 12	15 17				15 42	15 42	15 47
Greenhithe for Bluewater	a						14 23						14 53						15 23						15 53
Dartford	a						14 28						14 58						15 28						15 58
London Bridge ⊖	a						15 06						15 36						16 06						16 36
London Cannon Street ⊖	a																								
London Waterloo (East) ⊖	a						15 11						15 41						16 11						16 41
London Charing Cross ⊖	a						15 14						15 44						16 14						16 44
Sole Street	d							14 17													15 17				
Meopham	d							14 19													15 19				
Longfield	d							14 23													15 23				
Farningham Road	d							14 27													15 27				
Swanley	a							14 32													15 32				
St Mary Cray	a							14 36													15 36				
Bromley South	a		14 13					14 42							15 13						15 42				
Elephant & Castle ⊖	a																								
London Blackfriars ⊖	a																								
London Victoria ⊖	a		14 29					15 02							15 29						16 02				
Ebbsfleet International	a				14 17	14 17					14 47	14 47					15 17	15 17					15 47	15 47	
Stratford International ⊖	a				14 29	14 29					14 59	15 03					15 29	15 32					16 02	16 02	
St Pancras Internatnl ⊖	a				14 36	14 44					15 06	15 11					15 36	15 40					16 09	16 12	

A from Faversham

B from Margate

C not from 2 September until 9 September

D not 26 August

For further services to St Pancras International, Blackfriars and Elephant & Castle and onwards to Bromley South, St Mary Cray and Swanley please refer to table 52

Table 212

Sundays

26 August to 9 September

Ramsgate, Dover, Sheerness-on-Sea and Medway - London

Network Diagram - see first Page of Table 212

		SE ■ A	SE ■ B	SE	SE C		SE D	SE	SE ■	SE	SE	SE	SE ■ A	SE ■ B	SE		SE D	SE C	SE	SE ■	SE	SE C	SE D	SE
Ramsgate	d		14 34	14 59										15 34	15 59									
Dumpton Park	d		14 37											15 37										
Broadstairs	d		14 40	15 05										15 40	16 05									
Margate	d		14 45	15a10										15 45	16a10									
Westgate-on-Sea	d		14 49											15 49										
Birchington-on-Sea	d		14 53											15 53										
Herne Bay	d		15 02											16 02										
Chestfield & Swalecliffe	d		15 05											16 05										
Whitstable	d		15 08											16 08										
Dover Priory	d	14 34											15 34											
Kearsney	d	14 38											15 38											
Shepherds Well	d	14 43											15 43											
Snowdown	d	14 47											15 47											
Aylesham	d	14 49											15 49											
Adisham	d	14 52											15 52											
Bekesbourne	d	14 56											15 56											
Canterbury East	d	15 01							15 22				16 01							16 22				
Selling	d	15 10											16 10											
Faversham	a	15 15	15 17						15 33				16 15	16 17						16 33				
	d		15 21		15 28		15 28		15 34		15 58			16 21			16 28	16 28		16 34		16 58	16 58	
Teynham	d								15 40											16 40				
Sheerness-on-Sea	d									15 42											16 42			
Queenborough	d									15 46											16 46			
Swale	d									15 50											16 50			
Kemsley	d									15 54											16 54			
Sittingbourne	a		15 28		15 36		15 36		15 44	15 59	16 06			16 28			16 36	16 36		16 44	16 59	17 06	17 06	
	d		15 29		15 37		15 37		15 45		16 07			16 29			16 37	16 37		16 45		17 07	17 07	
Newington	d								15 50											16 50				
Rainham (Kent)	d		15 36		15 45		15 45		15 54		16 15			16 36			16 45	16 45		16 54		17 15	17 15	
Gillingham (Kent)	d		15 41		15 50		15 50	15 54	15 59		16 20	16 24		16 41			16 50	16 50	16 54	16 59		17 20	17 20	17 24
Chatham	d		15 46		15 54		15 54	15 58	16 04		16 24	16 28		16 46			16 54	16 54	16 58	17 04		17 24	17 24	17 28
Rochester	d		15 48		15 57		15 57	16 00	16 06		16 27	16 30		16 48			16 57	16 57	17 00	17 06		17 27	17 27	17 30
Strood	a				16 01		16 01	16 05			16 31	16 35					17 01	17 01	17 05			17 31	17 31	17 35
Gravesend	a				16 12		16 12	16 17			16 42	16 47					17 12	17 12	17 17			17 42	17 42	17 47
Greenhithe for Bluewater	a							16 23				16 53							17 23					17 53
Dartford	a							16 28				16 58							17 28					17 58
London Bridge ⊖	a							17 06				17 36							18 06					18 36
London Cannon Street ⊖	a																							
London Waterloo (East) ⊖	a							17 11				17 41							18 11					18 41
London Charing Cross ⊖	a							17 14				17 44							18 14					18 44
Sole Street	d								16 17											17 17				
Meopham	d								16 19											17 19				
Longfield	d								16 23											17 23				
Farningham Road	d								16 27											17 27				
Swanley	a								16 32											17 32				
St Mary Cray	a								16 36											17 36				
Bromley South	a		16 13						16 42					17 13						17 42				
Elephant & Castle ⊖	a																							
London Blackfriars ⊖	a																							
London Victoria ⊖	a		16 29						17 02					17 29						18 02				
Ebbsfleet International	a				16 17		16 17				16 47						17 16	17 17				17 47	17 47	
Stratford International ⊖	a				16 29		16 29											17 29				17 59	18 06	
St Pancras Internatnl ⊖	a				16 36		16 44											17 36				18 09	18 13	

A from Faversham

B from Margate

C not from 2 September until 9 September

D not 26 August

For further services to St Pancras International, Blackfriars and Elephant & Castle and onwards to Bromley South, St Mary Cray and Swanley please refer to table 52

Table 212

Sundays

26 August to 9 September

Ramsgate, Dover, Sheerness-on-Sea and Medway - London

Network Diagram - see first Page of Table 212

		SE 1 A ✠	SE 1 B ✠	SE	SE C	SE D	SE	SE 1	SE	SE D	SE C	SE	SE 1	SE 1	SE	SE D	SE C	SE	SE 1	SE	SE D	SE C
Ramsgate	d		16 34	16 59										17 34	17 59							
Dumpton Park	d		16 37											17 37								
Broadstairs	d		16 40	17 05										17 40	18 05							
Margate	d		16 45	17a10										17 45	18a10							
Westgate-on-Sea	d		16 49											17 49								
Birchington-on-Sea	d		16 53											17 53								
Herne Bay	d		17 02											18 02								
Chestfield & Swalecliffe	d		17 05											18 05								
Whitstable	d		17 08											18 08								
Dover Priory	d	16 34											17 34									
Kearsney	d	16 38											17 38									
Shepherds Well	d	16 43											17 43									
Snowdown	d	16 47											17 47									
Aylesham	d	16 49											17 49									
Adisham	d	16 52											17 52									
Bekesbourne	d	16 56											17 56									
Canterbury East	d	17 01						17 22					18 01						18 22			
Selling	d	17 10											18 10									
Faversham	a	17 15	17 17					17 33					18 15	18 17					18 33			
	d	17 21			17 28	17 28		17 34		17 58	17 58		18 21			18 28	18 28		18 34		18 58	18 58
Teynham	d							17 40											18 40			
Sheerness-on-Sea	d								17 42											18 42		
Queenborough	d								17 46											18 46		
Swale	d								17 50											18 50		
Kemsley	d								17 54											18 54		
Sittingbourne	a	17 28			17 36	17 36		17 44	17 59	18 06	18 06		18 28			18 36	18 36		18 44	19 01	19 06	19 06
	d	17 29			17 37	17 37		17 45		18 07	18 07		18 29			18 37	18 37		18 45		19 07	19 07
Newington	d							17 50											18 50			
Rainham (Kent)	d	17 36			17 45	17 45		17 54		18 15	18 15		18 36			18 45	18 45		18 54		19 15	19 15
Gillingham (Kent)	d	17 41			17 50	17 50	17 54	17 59		18 20	18 20	18 24	18 41			18 50	18 50	18 54	18 59		19 20	19 20
Chatham	d	17 46			17 54	17 54	17 58	18 04		18 24	18 24	18 28	18 46			18 54	18 54	18 58	19 04		19 24	19 24
Rochester	d	17 48			17 57	17 57	18 00	18 06		18 27	18 27	18 30	18 48			18 57	18 57	19 00	19 06		19 27	19 27
Strood	a				18 01	18 01	18 05			18 31	18 31	18 35				19 01	19 01	19 05			19 31	19 31
Gravesend	a				18 12	18 12	18 17			18 42	18 42	18 47				19 12	19 12	19 17			19 42	19 42
Greenhithe for Bluewater	a						18 23					18 53						19 23				
Dartford	a						18 28					18 58						19 28				
London Bridge ⊖	a						19 06					19 36						20 06				
London Cannon Street ⊖	a																					
London Waterloo (East) ⊖	a						19 11					19 41						20 11				
London Charing Cross ⊖	a						19 14					19 44						20 14				
Sole Street	d							18 17											19 17			
Meopham	d							18 19											19 19			
Longfield	d							18 23											19 23			
Farningham Road	d							18 27											19 27			
Swanley	a							18 32											19 32			
St Mary Cray	a							18 36											19 36			
Bromley South	a	18 13						18 42					19 13						19 42			
Elephant & Castle ⊖	a																					
London Blackfriars ⊖	a																					
London Victoria ⊖	a	18 29						19 02					19 29						20 02			
Ebbsfleet International	a				18 16	18 17				18 47	18 47					19 17	19 17				19 47	19 47
Stratford International ⊖	a				18 27	18 29				18 59	19 02					19 29	19 29				19 59	20 03
St Pancras International ⊖	a				18 41	18 36				19 06	19 10					19 36	19 37				20 06	20 14

A ✠ from Faversham

B ✠ from Margate

C not 26 August

D not from 2 September until 9 September

For further services to St Pancras International, Blackfriars and Elephant & Castle and onwards to Bromley South, St Mary Cray and Swanley please refer to table 52

Table 212

Sundays

26 August to 9 September

Ramsgate, Dover, Sheerness-on-Sea and Medway - London

Network Diagram - see first Page of Table 212

		SE	SE 1	SE 1	SE	SE	SE A	SE B	SE 1	SE	SE	SE	SE 1	SE 1	SE	SE	SE A	SE B	SE 1	SE	SE	SE A	SE B
Ramsgate	d			18 34	18 59									19 34	19 59								
Dumpton Park	d			18 37										19 37									
Broadstairs	d			18 40	19 05									19 40	20 05								
Margate	d			18 45	19a10									19 45	20a10								
Westgate-on-Sea	d			18 49										19 49									
Birchington-on-Sea	d			18 53										19 53									
Herne Bay	d			19 02										20 02									
Chestfield & Swalecliffe	d			19 05										20 05									
Whitstable	d			19 08										20 08									
Dover Priory	d		18 34										19 34										
Kearsney	d		18 38										19 38										
Shepherds Well	d		18 43										19 43										
Snowdown	d		18 47										19 47										
Aylesham	d		18 49										19 49										
Adisham	d		18 52										19 52										
Bekesbourne	d		18 56										19 56										
Canterbury East	d		19 01						19 22				20 01										
Selling	d		19 10										20 10										
Faversham	a		19 15	19 17					19 33				20 15	20 17									
	d		19 21				19 28	19 28	19 34			19 58	20 21				20 28	20 28	20 34			20 58	20 58
Teynham	d								19 40										20 40				
Sheerness-on-Sea	d									19 42										20 42			
Queenborough	d									19 46										20 46			
Swale	d									19 50										20 50			
Kemsley	d									19 54										20 54			
Sittingbourne	a		19 28				19 36	19 36	19 44	19 59		20 06	20 28				20 36	20 36	20 44	20 59		21 06	21 06
	d		19 29				19 37	19 37	19 45			20 07	20 29				20 37	20 37	20 45			21 07	21 07
Newington	d								19 50										20 50				
Rainham (Kent)	d		19 36				19 45	19 45	19 54			20 15	20 36				20 45	20 45	20 54			21 15	21 15
Gillingham (Kent)	d	19 24	19 41			19 45	19 50	19 50	19 59		20 15	20 20	20 41			20 45	20 50	20 50	20 59		21 15	21 20	21 20
Chatham	d	19 28	19 46			19 49	19 54	19 54	20 04		20 19	20 24	20 46			20 49	20 54	20 54	21 04		21 19	21 24	21 24
Rochester	d	19 30	19 48			19 51	19 57	19 57	20 06		20 21	20 27	20 48			20 51	20 57	20 57	21 06		21 21	21 27	21 27
Strood	a	19 35				19 56	20 01	20 01			20 26	20 31				20 56	21 01	21 01			21 26	21 31	21 31
Gravesend	a	19 47				20 08	20 12	20 12			20 38	20 42				21 08	21 12	21 12			21 38	21 42	21 42
Greenhithe for Bluewater	a	19 53				20 17					20 47					21 17					21 47		
Dartford	a	19 58				20 24					20 54					21 24					21 54		
London Bridge ⊖	a	20 36				21 06					21 36					22 06					22 36		
London Cannon Street ⊖	a																						
London Waterloo (East) ⊖	a	20 41				21 11					21 41					22 11					22 41		
London Charing Cross ⊖	a	20 44				21 14					21 44					22 14					22 44		
Sole Street	d								20 17										21 17				
Meopham	d								20 19										21 19				
Longfield	d								20 23										21 23				
Farningham Road	d								20 27										21 27				
Swanley	a								20 32										21 32				
St Mary Cray	a								20 36										21 36				
Bromley South	a		20 13						20 42				21 13						21 42				
Elephant & Castle ⊖	a																						
London Blackfriars ⊖	a																						
London Victoria ⊖	a		20 29						21 02				21 29						22 02				
Ebbsfleet International	a						20 17	20 17				20 47					21 17	21 17				21 47	21 47
Stratford International ⊖	a						20 29	20 29				21 02					21 29	21 30				21 59	22 02
St Pancras International ⊖	a						20 36	20 37				21 09					21 36	21 44				22 06	22 10

A not from 2 September until 9 September

B not 26 August

For further services to St Pancras International, Blackfriars and Elephant & Castle and onwards to Bromley South, St Mary Cray and Swanley please refer to table 52

Table 212

Sundays

26 August to 9 September

Ramsgate, Dover, Sheerness-on-Sea and Medway - London

Network Diagram - see first Page of Table 212

		SE ■	SE ■	SE	SE	SE A	SE B	SE ■	SE	SE	SE A	SE B	SE ■	SE ■	SE	SE ■	SE ■	SE	SE ■	SE	SE
Ramsgate ■	d		20 34	20 59										21 34	21 59				22 34	22 59	
Dumpton Park	d		20 37											21 37					22 37		
Broadstairs	d		20 40	21 05										21 40	22 05				22 40	23 05	
Margate ■	d		20 45	21a10										21 45	22a10				22 45	23a10	
Westgate-on-Sea	d		20 49											21 49					22 49		
Birchington-on-Sea	d		20 53											21 53					22 53		
Herne Bay	d		21 02											22 02					23 02		
Chestfield & Swalecliffe	d		21 05											22 05					23 05		
Whitstable	d		21 08											22 08					23 08		
Dover Priory ■	d	20 34											21 34				22 34				
Kearsney	d	20 38											21 38				22 38				
Shepherds Well	d	20 43											21 43				22 43				
Snowdown	d	20 47											21 47				22 47				
Aylesham	d	20 49											21 49				22 49				
Adisham	d	20 52											21 52				22 52				
Bekesbourne	d	20 56											21 56				22 56				
Canterbury East ■	d	21 01											22 01				23 01				
Selling	d	21 10											22 10				23 10				
Faversham ■	a	21 15	21 17										22 15	22 17			23 15		23 17		
	d	21 21				21 28	21 28	21 34			21 58	21 58	22 21			22 34			23 21		
Teynham	d							21 40								22 40					
Sheerness-on-Sea	d								21 42									22 42			23 42
Queenborough	d								21 46									22 46			23 46
Swale	d								21 50									22 50			23 50
Kemsley	d								21 54									22 54			23 54
Sittingbourne ■	a	21 28				21 36	21 36	21 44	21 59		22 06	22 06	22 28			22 44		22 59	23 28		23 59
	d	21 29				21 37	21 37	21 45			22 07	22 07	22 29			22 45			23 29		
Newington	d							21 50								22 50					
Rainham (Kent)	d	21 36				21 45	21 45	21 54			22 15	22 15	22 36			22 54			23 36		
Gillingham (Kent) ■	d	21 41			21 45	21 50	21 50	21 59		22 15	22 20	22 20	22 41			22 59			23 41		
Chatham ■	d	21 46			21 49	21 54	21 54	22 04		22 19	22 24	22 24	22 46			23 04			23 46		
Rochester ■	d	21 48			21 51	21 57	21 57	22 06		22 21	22 27	22 27	22 48			23 06			23 48		
Strood ■	a				21 56	22 01	22 01			22 26	22 31	22 31									
Gravesend ■	a				22 08	22 12	22 12			22 38	22 42	22 42									
Greenhithe for Bluewater	a				22 17					22 47											
Dartford ■	a				22 24					22 54											
London Bridge ■ ⊖	a				23 06					23 36											
London Cannon Street ■ ⊖	a																				
London Waterloo (East) ■ ⊖	a				23 11					23 41											
London Charing Cross ■ ⊖	a				23 14					23 44											
Sole Street	d							22 17								23 17					
Meopham	d							22 19								23 19					
Longfield	d							22 23								23 23					
Farningham Road	d							22 27								23 27					
Swanley ■	a							22 32								23 32					
St Mary Cray	a							22 36								23 36					
Bromley South ■	a	22 13						22 42					23 13			23 42			00 13		
Elephant & Castle ⊖	a																				
London Blackfriars ■ ⊖	a																				
London Victoria ■ ⊖	a	22 29						23 02					23 29			00 02			00 29		
Ebbsfleet International	a					22 17	22 17				22 47	22 47									
Stratford International ⊖	a					22 29	22 29				22 59	22 59									
St Pancras Internatnl ■ ⊖	a					22 36	22 37				23 06	23 07									

A not from 2 September until 9 September **B** not 26 August

For further services to St Pancras International, Blackfriars and Elephant & Castle and onwards to Bromley South, St Mary Cray and Swanley please refer to table 52

Network Diagram for Tables 216, 217, 218, 219, 221, 222

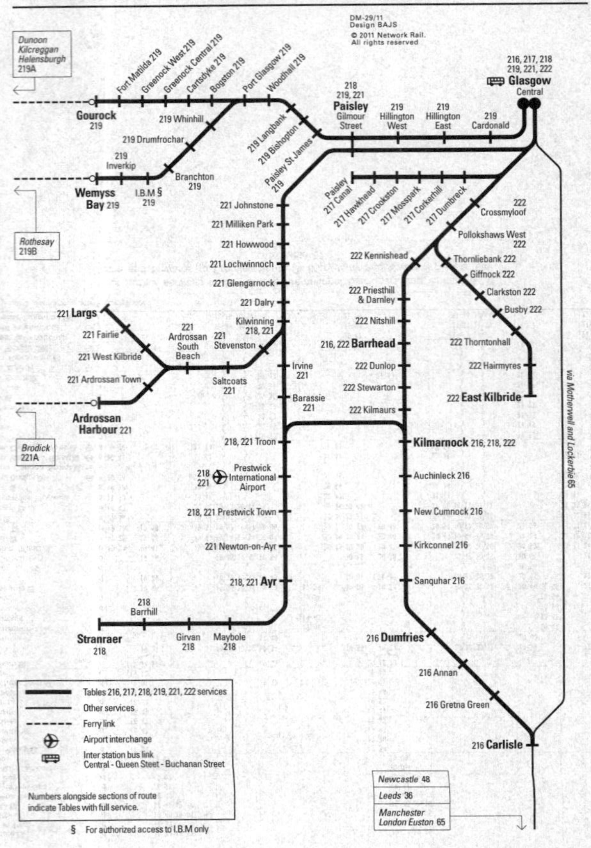

Table 216

Mondays to Saturdays

Glasgow Central and Kilmarnock - Dumfries and Carlisle

Network Diagram - see first Page of Table 216

Miles				SR MO A	SR MX	SR	SR	SR SO	SR SX	SR	SR	SR SO	SR	SR SO	SR	SR	SR SO	SR	SR	SR SO	SR	SR	SR SO	SR SX
0	**Glasgow Central** 15	65,222	d	22p12	23p12					07 07	08 37		10 12		12 12	13 12			16 12		17 42	19 12		21 12
7½	Barrhead	222	d	22p23	23p33					07 22	08 49								16 23		17 53	19 23		21 26
24¼	**Kilmarnock** 3	218,222	a	22p48	23p59					07 48	09 18		10 51		12 48	13 50			16 49		18 22	19 51		21 53
—			d	22p49	23p59					07 48	09 18		10 51		12 48	13 50			16 49		18 26	19 51		21 53
38	Auchinleck		d	23p06	00 18					08 05	09 35		11 08		13 05	14 07			17 06		18 42	20 08		22 10
45½	New Cumnock		d	23p14	00 28					08 13	09 43		11 16		13 13	14 15			17 14		18 51	20 16		22 18
52¾	Kirkconnel		d	23p23	00 39					08 22	09 52		11 25		13 22	14 24			17 23		18 59	20 25		22 27
56	Sanquhar		d	23p28	00 44					08 26	09 57		11 30		13 27	14 29			17 28		19 04	20 30		22 32
82¼	**Dumfries**		d	23p56	01a17	04 56	06 17	07 43	07 45	08 57	10 23	11 02	11 58	13 10	13 55	14 57	16 02	17 07	17 56	18 41	19 33	20 57	22 13	23 00
97¾	Annan		d	00 11		05 11	06 32	07 58	08 00	09 12	10 38	11 17	12 13	13 25	14 10	15 12	16 17	17 22	18 11	18 56	19 48	21 12	22 28	23 15
105½	Gretna Green		d	00 20		05 20	06 41	08 07	08 09	09 22	10 47	11 26	12 22	13 34	14 19	15 21	16 26	17 31	18 20	19 05	19 57	21 21	22 37	23 24
115½	**Carlisle** 8	65	a	00 34		05 33	06 54	08 20	08 22	09 37	11 02	11 39	12 35	13 52	14 32	15 34	16 39	17 44	18 35	19 18	20 11	21 43	22 50	23 37
—	Newcastle 8	48	a				08 57		10 00	11 07					15 54				20 15					

			SR SO	SR SX
Glasgow Central 15	65,222	d	22 12	23 12
Barrhead	222	d	22 23	23 33
Kilmarnock 3	218,222	a	22 50	23 59
		d	22 51	23 59
Auchinleck		d	23 07	00 18
New Cumnock		d	23 16	00 28
Kirkconnel		d	23 24	00 39
Sanquhar		d	23 29	00 44
Dumfries		d	23 57	01a17
Annan		d	00 12	
Gretna Green		d	00 21	
Carlisle 8	65	a	00 34	
Newcastle 8	48	a		

Sundays

			SR	SR	SR	SR	SR	SR
Glasgow Central 15	65,222	d	22p12			15 12		22 12
Barrhead	222	d	22p23			15 26		22 23
Kilmarnock 3	218,222	a	22p50			15 52		22 48
		d	22p51			15 53		22 49
Auchinleck		d	23p07			16 10		23 06
New Cumnock		d	23p16			16 18		23 14
Kirkconnel		d	23p24			16 27		23 23
Sanquhar		d	23p29			16 32		23 28
Dumfries		d	23p57	13 00	15 01	17 00	19 01	23 56
Annan		d	00 12	13 15	15 16	17 15	19 16	00 11
Gretna Green		d	00 21	13 24	15 25	17 24	19 25	00 20
Carlisle 8	65	a	00 34	13 37	15 38	17 37	19 38	00 34
Newcastle 8	48	a						

A from 21 May

For connections to London Euston please refer to Table 65

Table 216

Mondays to Saturdays

Carlisle and Dumfries - Kilmarnock and Glasgow Central

Network Diagram - see first Page of Table 216

Miles				SR	SR	SR	SR SO	SR SX	SR SO	SR	SR SO	SR	SR SO	SR	SR	SR SO	SR	SR	SR SO	SR	SR
—	Newcastle 8	48	d				06 30	06 47						13 22				17 16			
0	**Carlisle** 8	65	d		05 27	06 08	08 15	08 15	09 55	11 15	12 20	13 12	14 22	15 12	16 17	17 12	17 55	19 17	20 22	21 12	23 10
9¾	Gretna Green		d		05 38	06 19	08 26	08 26	10 06	11 26	12 31	13 23	14 33	15 23	16 28	17 23	18 06	19 28	20 33	21 23	23 21
17½	Annan		d		05 47	06 27	08 34	08 34	10 14	11 34	12 40	13 31	14 41	15 31	16 36	17 31	18 14	19 37	20 41	21 31	23 29
33	**Dumfries**		d	05 46	06a04	06 46	08 53	08 53	10a32	11 53	12a57	13 48	14a59	15 50	16a54	17a49	18 31	19 55	20a59	21 50	23a47
59¼	Sanquhar		d	06 12		07 12	09 19	09 19		12 19		14 16		16 16			18 57	20 21		22 16	
62½	Kirkconnel		d	06 17		07 17	09 24	09 24		12 24		14 21		16 21			19 02	20 26		22 21	
69¾	New Cumnock		d	06 26		07 26	09 33	09 33		12 33		14 30		16 30			19 13	20 35		22 30	
77¼	Auchinleck		d	06 34		07 34	09 41	09 41		12 41		14 38		16 38			19 21	20 44		22 38	
91	**Kilmarnock** 3	218,222	a	06 51		07 51	09 57	09 57		12 57		14 55		16 55			19 38	21 00		22 55	
—			d	06 52		07 53	09 57	09 57		12 57		14 57		16 57			19 57	21 00		22 57	
107¾	Barrhead	222	d	07 18		08 20	10 22	10 22						17 22			20 22	21 25		23 22	
115¼	**Glasgow Central** 15	65,222	a	07 31		08 37	10 37	10 37		13 35		15 33		17 36			20 36	21 39		23 35	

Sundays

			SR	SR	SR	SR
Newcastle 8	48	d				
Carlisle 8	65	d	13 12	15 12	19 12	21 22
Gretna Green		d	13 23	15 23	19 23	21 33
Annan		d	13 31	15 31	19 31	21 41
Dumfries		d	13 50	15a49	19 50	21a59
Sanquhar		d	14 16		20 16	
Kirkconnel		d	14 21		20 21	
New Cumnock		d	14 30		20 30	
Auchinleck		d	14 38		20 38	
Kilmarnock 3	218,222	a	14 55		20 55	
		d	14 57		20 57	
Barrhead	222	d	15 21		21 21	
Glasgow Central 15	65,222	a	15 36		21 35	

For connections to London Euston please refer to Table 65

Table 217

Mondays to Saturdays

Glasgow Central - Paisley Canal

Network Diagram - see first Page of Table 216

Miles			SR SO	SR	SR	SR	SR	SR	SR	SR	SR	SR	SR	SR	SR	SR	SR	SR	SR	SR	SR	SR	SR
0	**Glasgow Central** 15	d	00 08	06 08	06 38	07 08	07 38	08 08	08 37	09 08	09 38	10 08	10 38	11 08	11 38	12 08	12 38	13 08	13 38	14 08	14 38	15 08	15 38
1¾	Dumbreck	d	00 14	06 14	06 44	07 14	07 44	08 14	08 43	09 14	09 44	10 14	10 44	11 14	11 44	12 14	12 44	13 14	13 44	14 14	14 44	15 14	15 44
3¼	Corkerhill	d	00 16	06 16	06 46	07 16	07 46	08 16	08 45	09 16	09 46	10 16	10 46	11 16	11 46	12 16	12 46	13 16	13 46	14 16	14 46	15 16	15 46
3¾	Mosspark	d	00 18	06 18	06 48	07 18	07 48	08 18	08 47	09 18	09 48	10 18	10 48	11 18	11 48	12 18	12 48	13 18	13 48	14 18	14 48	15 18	15 48
4½	Crookston	d	00 20	06 20	06 50	07 20	07 50	08 20	08 49	09 20	09 50	10 20	10 50	11 20	11 50	12 20	12 50	13 20	13 50	14 20	14 50	15 20	15 50
6½	Hawkhead	d	00 23	06 23	06 53	07 23	07 53	08 23	08 53	09 23	09 53	10 23	10 53	11 23	11 53	12 23	12 53	13 23	13 53	14 23	14 53	15 23	15 53
7	**Paisley Canal**	a	00 26	06 26	06 56	07 26	07 56	08 26	08 56	09 26	09 56	10 26	10 56	11 26	11 56	12 26	12 56	13 26	13 56	14 26	14 56	15 26	15 56

		SR	SR	SR	SR	SR	SR	SR	SR	SR	SR	SR	SR	SR	SR	SR
Glasgow Central 15	d	16 08	16 38	17 08	17 38	18 08	18 38	19 08	19 38	20 08	20 38	21 08	21 38	22 08	22 38	23 08
Dumbreck	d	16 14	16 44	17 14	17 44	18 14	18 44	19 14	19 44	20 14	20 44	21 14	21 44	22 14	22 44	23 14
Corkerhill	d	16 16	16 46	17 16	17 46	18 16	18 46	19 16	19 46	20 16	20 46	21 16	21 46	22 16	22 45	23 16
Mosspark	d	16 18	16 48	17 18	17 48	18 18	18 48	19 18	19 48	20 18	20 48	21 18	21 48	22 18	22 47	23 18
Crookston	d	16 20	16 50	17 20	17 50	18 20	18 50	19 20	19 50	20 20	20 50	21 20	21 50	22 20	22 49	23 20
Hawkhead	d	16 23	16 53	17 23	17 53	18 23	18 53	19 23	19 53	20 23	20 53	21 23	21 53	22 23	22 53	23 23
Paisley Canal	a	16 26	16 56	17 26	17 56	18 26	18 56	19 26	19 56	20 26	20 56	21 26	21 56	22 26	22 56	23 26

Table 217

Mondays to Saturdays

Paisley Canal - Glasgow Central

Network Diagram - see first Page of Table 216

Miles			SR	SR	SR	SR	SR	SR	SR	SR	SR	SR	SR	SR	SR	SR	SR	SR	SR	SR	SR	SR	SR
0	**Paisley Canal**	d	06 30	07 00	07 30	08 00	08 30	09 00	09 30	10 00	10 30	11 00	11 30	12 00	12 30	13 00	13 30	14 00	14 30	15 00	15 30	16 00	16 30
0½	Hawkhead	d	06 33	07 03	07 33	08 03	08 33	09 03	09 33	10 03	10 33	11 03	11 33	12 03	12 33	13 03	13 33	14 03	14 33	15 03	15 33	16 03	16 33
2½	Crookston	d	06 36	07 06	07 36	08 06	08 36	09 06	09 36	10 06	10 36	11 06	11 36	12 06	12 36	13 06	13 36	14 06	14 36	15 06	15 36	16 06	16 36
3¼	Mosspark	d	06 38	07 08	07 38	08 08	08 38	09 08	09 38	10 08	10 38	11 08	11 38	12 08	12 38	13 08	13 38	14 08	14 38	15 08	15 38	16 08	16 38
3¾	Corkerhill	d	06 40	07 10	07 40	08 10	08 40	09 10	09 40	10 10	10 40	11 10	11 40	12 10	12 40	13 10	13 40	14 10	14 40	15 10	15 40	16 10	16 40
5¼	Dumbreck	d	06 43	07 13	07 44	08 13	08 43	09 13	09 43	10 13	10 43	11 13	11 43	12 13	12 43	13 13	13 43	14 13	14 43	15 13	15 43	16 13	16 43
7	**Glasgow Central** 15	a	06 49	07 20	07 52	08 21	08 53	09 19	09 49	10 19	10 49	11 19	11 49	12 19	12 49	13 19	13 49	14 19	14 49	15 19	15 49	16 19	16 49

		SR	SR	SR	SR	SR	SR	SR	SR	SR	SR	SR	SR	SR
Paisley Canal	d	17 00	17 30	18 00	18 30	19 00	19 30	20 00	20 30	21 00	21 30	22 00	22 30	23 00
Hawkhead	d	17 03	17 33	18 03	18 33	19 03	19 33	20 03	20 33	21 03	21 33	22 03	22 33	23 03
Crookston	d	17 06	17 36	18 06	18 36	19 06	19 36	20 06	20 36	21 06	21 36	22 06	22 36	23 06
Mosspark	d	17 08	17 38	18 08	18 38	19 08	19 38	20 08	20 38	21 08	21 38	22 08	22 38	23 08
Corkerhill	d	17 10	17 40	18 10	18 40	19 10	19 40	20 10	20 40	21 10	21 40	22 10	22 40	23 10
Dumbreck	d	17 13	17 43	18 13	18 43	19 13	19 43	20 13	20 43	21 13	21 43	22 13	22 43	23 13
Glasgow Central 15	a	17 19	17 53	18 19	18 49	19 19	19 50	20 19	20 49	21 19	21 49	22 19	22 50	23 22

No Sunday Service

Table 218

Mondays to Saturdays

Glasgow Central and Kilmarnock - Girvan, Stranraer

Network Diagram - see first Page of Table 216

Miles	Miles				SR MX	SR	SR	SR	SR	SR ◇	SR	SR SO ◇	SR SX ◇	SR	SR	SR	SR	SR	SR	SR	SR SX	SR SO
0	—	**Glasgow Cen.** 15	219,221,222	d	22p12			*07c30*	*08c00*	09 41	*10c30*	11 40	11 42	*12c30*	*13c30*	15e12	*16c30*	17e12	*18c30*	*20c30*	22e12	*22c30*
7¼	—	Paisley Gilmour St.	219,221 ✈	d						09 54		11 53	11 53									
—	—	Kilwinning 4	221	d						10 14		12 11	12 11									
—	0	**Kilmarnock** 3	222	a	22p50											15 50		17 51			22 50	
—	—			d	23p06				08 37		11 05			13 04	14 04	16 03	17 04	18 09	19 05	21 10	23 06	23 06
35	10¾	Troon	221	d	23p18				08 49		11 18			13 16	14 16	16 16	17 16	18 21	19 17	21 22	23 18	23 18
37¾	11¾	Prestwick Int. Airport	221 ✈	d	23p23				08 54		11 23			13 21	14 21	16 20	17 21	18 26	19 21	21 27	23 23	23 23
38¼	12½	Prestwick Town	221	d	23p25				08 56		11 25			13 23	14 23	16 22	17 23	18 28	19 23	21 29	23 25	23 25
41½	15½	**Ayr**	221	a	23p30				09 03	10 35	11 32	12 29	12 29	13 30	14 30	16 30	17 30	18 36	19 30	21 34	23 30	23 30
—	—			d	23p31	05 30	06 35	08 37	09 05	10 35	11 33	12 30	12 30	13 32	14 31	16 30	17 31	18 37	19 31	21 35	23 31	23 31
50½	24½	Maybole		d	23p42	05 41	06 46	08 48	09 16	10 47	11 44	12 41	12 41	13 43	14 42	16 42	17 42	18 48	19 42	21 46	23 42	23 42
62¾	36½	**Girvan**		d	23p57	05a57	07a02	09 03	09a32	11 07	12a00	12 56	12 56	13a59	14a58	16a58	17 57	19a04	20 03	22a02	23 57	23 57
75	51¼	Barrhill		d	00 16			09 22		11 26		13 16	13 16				18 16		20 22		00 16	00 16
101	77¼	**Stranraer**		a	00 52			09 58		12 02		13 52	13 52				18 52		20 58		00 52	00 52

Sundays

			SR	SR ◇	SR ◇	SR
Glasgow Cen. 15	219,221,222	d		11 42	16 25	*17c00*
Paisley Gilmour St.	219,221 ✈	d		11 53	16 39	
Kilwinning 4	221	d		12 11	16 56	
Kilmarnock 3	222	a				
		d	23p06			
Troon	221	d	23p18			
Prestwick Int. Airport	221 ✈	d	23p23			
Prestwick Town	221	d	23p25			
Ayr	221	a	23p30	12 29	17 17	
		d	23p31	12 30	17 19	18 40
Maybole		d	23p42	12 41	17 30	18 51
Girvan		d	23p57	12 56	17 47	19 06
Barrhill		d	00 16	13 16	18 06	19 25
Stranraer		a	00 52	13 52	18 42	20 07

c Change at Ayr (Table 221)

e Passengers may leave 18 min laterchanging at Ayr (Table 221)

Table 218

Mondays to Saturdays

Stranraer and Girvan - Kilmarnock and Glasgow Central

Network Diagram - see first Page of Table 216

Miles	Miles				SR	SR ◇	SR ◇	SR	SR ◇	SR	SR ◇	SR	SR	SR ◇	SR	SR	SR ◇	SR ◇	SR
0	—	**Stranraer**		d			07 11		10 12		12 36			14 43			19 08	21 13	
26	—	Barrhill		d			07 45		10 46		13 17			15 17			19 43	21 48	
38¼	—	**Girvan**		d	06 02	07 07	08 03	09 37	11 04	12 31	13 35	14 32	15 03	15 35	17 32	19 09	20 01	22 06	22 27
50½	—	Maybole		d	06 18	07 23	08 19	09 53	11 20	12 55	13 57	14 56	15 19	15 51	17 56	19 25	20 17	22 22	22 43
59¼	—	**Ayr**		a	06 30	07 36	08 31	10 05	11 36	13 07	14 09	15 08	15 31	16 04	18 08	19 37	20 29	22 34	22 55
—	—			d		07 36		10 06	11 37	13 08	14 10	15 18	15 32	16 06	18 18	19 38	20 30	22 35	
62½	—	Prestwick Town	221	a		07 41		10 11	11 42	13 13		15 23		16 11	18 23	19 43		22 40	
63	—	Prestwick Int. Airport	221 ✈	a		07 44		10 13	11 44	13 15		15 25		16 14	18 25	19 45			
63¾	0	Troon	221	a		07 49		10 18	11 49	13 20		15 30		16 19	18 30	19 50		22 45	
—	10¾	**Kilmarnock** 3		a		08 07		10 34	12 05	13 36		15 47		16 34	18 46	20 06			
—	—			d								15 57							
—	—	Glengarnock		d															
74¼	—	Kilwinning 4	221	a							14 27		15 47					22 55	
93¾	—	Paisley Gilmour St.	219,221 ✈	a							14 46		16 15				21 11	23 14	
101	—	**Glasgow Cen.** 15	219,221,222	a	*07c38*	*08c35*	*09c36*	*11c07*	*12c36*	*14c07*	15 01	16 33	16 31	*17c09*	*19c08*	*20c36*	21 27	23 25	*23c58*

Sundays

			SR ◇	SR ◇	SR ◇
Stranraer		d	10 40	14 40	19 45
Barrhill		d	11 14	15 14	20 19
Girvan		d	11 32	15 32	20 37
Maybole		d	11 48	15 48	20 53
Ayr		a	12 00	15 59	21 04
		d	12 00	15 59	21 04
Prestwick Town	221	a			
Prestwick Int. Airport	221 ✈	a			
Troon	221	a			
Kilmarnock 3		a			21 26
		d			21 31
Glengarnock		d			
Kilwinning 4	221	a	12 15	16 14	
Paisley Gilmour St.	219,221 ✈	a	12 36	16 38	
Glasgow Cen. 15	219,221,222	a	12 51	16 49	22 05

c Change at Ayr (Table 221)

e Passengers may arrive 16 09 by changing at Ayr (Table 221)

Glasgow Central - Wemyss Bay and Gourock

Network Diagram - see first Page of Table 216

Miles	Miles	Station		SR A	SR MX	SR	SR	SR	SR	SR	SR	SR	SR	SR	SR	SR	SR	SR	SR	SR	SR	SR	SR
0	0	**Glasgow Central** 15 221	d	23p20	23p50	05 55	06 05	06 25	06 32	06 55	07 04	07 25	07 35	07 50	08 05	08 28	08 36	08 50	09 05	09 25	09 35	09 50	10 05
3¾	3¾	Cardonald	d	23p27	23p57				06 39		07 12	07 32	07 42		08 12		08 42		09 12		09 42		10 12
4½	4½	Hillington East	d	23p29	23p59		06 13		06 41		07 14	07 34	07 44		08 14		08 44		09 14		09 44		10 14
5	5	Hillington West	d	23p31	00 01	06 03	06 15		06 43	07 03	07 16	07 36	07 46	07 58	08 16		08 46		09 16		09 46		10 16
7¼	7¼	Paisley Gilmour Street 221 ✈	a	23p35	00 05	06 07	06 19	06 35	06 47	07 07	07 20	07 40	07 50	08 02	08 20	08 38	08 50	09 00	09 19	09 35	09 50	10 01	10 20
—	—		d	23p35	00 05	06 07	06 19	06 36	06 47	07 07	07 20	07 40	07 51	08 02	08 20	08 38	08 50	09 01	09 20	09 36	09 50	10 01	10 20
8	8	Paisley St James	d	23p37	00 07			06 38			07 22		07 53		08 22		08 52		09 22		09 52		10 22
12¼	12¼	Bishopton	d	23p43	00 13	06 13	06 25	06 44	06 53	07 13	07 28	07 46	07 59	08 08	08 28	08 44	08 58	09 07	09 28	09 42	09 58	10 07	10 28
16¼	16¼	Langbank	d	23p49	00 19			06 49			07 34		08 04		08 34		09 04		09 34		10 04		10 34
19	19	Woodhall	d	23p53	00 23		06 33	06 53	07 01		07 38	07 54	08 08		08 38		09 08		09 38		10 08		10 38
20¼	20¼	Port Glasgow	d	23p56	00 26	06 23	06 36	06 56	07 04	07 23	07 41	07 57	08 11	08 18	08 41	08 53	09 11	09 16	09 41	09 51	10 11	10 16	10 41
—	22½	Whinhill	d				06 40		07 08					08 22				09 21				10 21	
—	23	Drumfrochar	d				06 43		07 11					08 25				09 23				10 23	
—	24¾	Branchton	d				06 46		07 14					08 28				09 26				10 26	
—	25½	IB.M. §	d				06 48		07 16					08 30				09 29				10 29	
—	28¾	Inverkip	d				06 53		07 25					08 35				09 34				10 34	
—	31	**Wemyss Bay**	a				06 58		07 30					08 40				09 40				10 40	
21¼	—	Bogston	d	23p58	00 28			06 58		07 25	07 43	07 59	08 13		08 43		09 13		09 43		10 13		10 43
22	—	Cartsdyke	d	00 01	00 30	06 26		07 01		07 27	07 45	08 01	08 16		08 45		09 15		09 45		10 15		10 45
23	—	Greenock Central	d	00 02	00 32	06 28		07 03		07 29	07 47	08 03	08 18		08 47	08 58	09 17		09 47	09 56	10 17		10 47
23¾	—	Greenock West	d	00 05	00 35	06 31		07 05		07 32	07 50	08 06	08 20		08 50	09 01	09 20		09 50	09 59	10 20		10 50
25	—	Fort Matilda	d	00 08	00 38			07 08		07 35	07 53	08 09	08 23		08 53	09 04	09 23		09 53	10 02	10 23		10 53
26¼	—	**Gourock**	a	00 12	00 42	06 36		07 13		07 39	07 57	08 13	08 28		08 57	09 09	09 27		09 58	10 06	10 27		10 57

Station		SR	SR	SR	SR	SR	SR	SR	SR	SR	SR	SR	SR	SR	SR	SR	SR	SR	SR	SR	SR	SR	SR
Glasgow Central 15 221	d	10 25	10 35	10 50	11 05	11 25	11 35	11 50	12 05	12 25	12 35	12 50	13 05	13 25	13 35	13 50	14 05	14 25	14 35	14 50	15 05	15 25	15 35
Cardonald	d		10 42		11 12		11 42		12 12		12 42		13 12		13 42		14 12		14 42		15 12		15 42
Hillington East	d		10 44		11 14		11 44		12 14		12 44		13 14		13 44		14 14		14 44		15 14		15 44
Hillington West	d		10 46		11 16		11 46		12 16		12 46		13 16		13 46		14 16		14 46		15 16		15 46
Paisley Gilmour Street 221 ✈	a	10 35	10 50	11 00	11 19	11 35	11 50	12 00	12 20	12 35	12 50	13 00	13 20	13 35	13 50	14 00	14 20	14 35	14 50	15 00	15 19	15 35	15 50
	d	10 36	10 50	11 01	11 20	11 36	11 50	12 01	12 20	12 36	12 50	13 01	13 20	13 36	13 50	14 01	14 20	14 36	14 50	15 01	15 20	15 36	15 50
Paisley St James	d		10 52		11 22		11 52		12 22		12 52		13 22		13 52		14 22		14 52		15 22		15 52
Bishopton	d	10 42	10 58	11 07	11 28	11 42	11 58	12 07	12 28	12 42	12 58	13 07	13 28	13 42	13 58	14 07	14 28	14 42	14 58	15 07	15 28	15 42	15 58
Langbank	d		11 04		11 34		12 04		12 34		13 04		13 34		14 04		14 34		15 04		15 34		16 04
Woodhall	d		11 08		11 38		12 08		12 38		13 08		13 38		14 08		14 38		15 08		15 38		16 08
Port Glasgow	d	10 51	11 11	11 16	11 41	11 51	12 11	12 16	12 41	12 51	13 11	13 16	13 41	13 51	14 11	14 16	14 41	14 51	15 11	15 16	15 41	15 51	16 11
Whinhill	d			11 21				12 21				13 21				14 21				15 21			
Drumfrochar	d			11 23				12 23				13 23				14 23				15 23			
Branchton	d			11 26				12 26				13 26				14 26				15 26			
IB.M. §	d			11 29				12 29				13 29				14 29				15 29			
Inverkip	d			11 34				12 34				13 34				14 34				15 34			
Wemyss Bay	a			11 40				12 40				13 40				14 40				15 40			
Bogston	d		11 13		11 43		12 13		12 43		13 13		13 43		14 13		14 43		15 13		15 43		16 13
Cartsdyke	d		11 15		11 45		12 15		12 45		13 15		13 45		14 15		14 45		15 15		15 45		16 15
Greenock Central	d	10 56	11 17		11 47	11 56	12 17		12 47	12 56	13 17		13 47	13 56	14 17		14 47	14 56	15 17		15 47	15 56	16 17
Greenock West	d	10 59	11 20		11 50	11 59	12 20		12 50	12 59	13 20		13 50	13 59	14 20		14 50	14 59	15 20		15 50	15 59	16 20
Fort Matilda	d	11 02	11 23		11 53	12 02	12 23		12 53	13 02	13 23		13 53	14 02	14 23		14 53	15 02	15 23		15 53	16 02	16 23
Gourock	a	11 06	11 27		11 57	12 06	12 27		12 57	13 06	13 27		13 57	14 06	14 27		14 57	15 06	15 27		15 57	16 06	16 27

Station		SR	SR	SR	SR	SR	SR	SR	SR	SR	SR	SR	SR	SR	SR	SR	SR	SR	SR	SR	SR	SR
Glasgow Central 15 221	d	15 50	16 05	16 23	16 33	16 55	17 05	17 15	17 25	17 40	17 55	18 05	18 25	18 35	18 50	19 05	19 25	19 40	19 50	20 05	20 35	20 50
Cardonald	d		16 12	16 30	16 41		17 12	17 22		17 47		18 12		18 42		19 12		19 47		20 12	20 42	
Hillington East	d		16 14	16 32	16 43		17 14	17 24		17 49		18 14		18 44		19 14		19 49		20 14	20 44	
Hillington West	d	15 58	16 16	16 34	16 45	17 02	17 16			17 51		18 16		18 46		19 15		19 51		20 15	20 46	
Paisley Gilmour Street 221 ✈	a	16 02	16 20	16 38	16 48	17 06	17 20	17 29	17 37	17 55	18 05	18 20	18 35	18 50	19 01	19 19	19 35	19 55	20 00	20 21	20 50	21 00
	d	16 02	16 20	16 38	16 48	17 06	17 21	17 29	17 37	17 55	18 06	18 20	18 36	18 50	19 01	19 20	19 36	19 55	20 01	20 21	20 50	21 01
Paisley St James	d		16 22	16 40			17 23			17 57		18 22		18 52		19 22		19 57		20 23	20 52	
Bishopton	d	16 08	16 28	16 46	16 54	17 13	17 29	17 35		18 03	18 10	18 28	18 42	18 58	19 07	19 28	19 42	20 03	20 07	20 29	20 58	21 07
Langbank	d		16 34	16 52			17 34			18 09		18 34		19 04		19 34		20 09		20 35	21 04	
Woodhall	d		16 38	16 56			17 38			18 12		18 38		19 08		19 38		20 13		20 39	21 08	
Port Glasgow	d	16 18	16 41	16 59	17 04	17 23	17 41	17 45	17 51	18 14	18 21	18 41	18 51	19 11	19 16	19 41	19 51	20 16	20 17	20 42	21 11	21 16
Whinhill	d	16 22			17 08			17 49			18 25				19 21			20 20			21 15	
Drumfrochar	d	16 25			17 11			17 52			18 28				19 23			20 23			21 18	
Branchton	d	16 28			17 14			17 55			18 31				19 26			20 26			21 21	
IB.M. §	d	16 30						17 57			18 33				19 29			20 28			21 23	
Inverkip	d	16 35			17 19			18 02			18 38				19 34			20 33			21 28	
Wemyss Bay	a	16 40			17 25			18 08			18 44				19 40			20 38			21 34	
Bogston	d		16 43	17 01		17 25	17 43			18 18		18 43		19 13		19 43				20 44		
Cartsdyke	d		16 45	17 03		17 27	17 46			18 20		18 45		19 15		19 45			20 20	20 46		21 20
Greenock Central	d		16 47	17 05		17 29	17 48		17 56	18 22		18 47	18 56	19 17		19 47	19 56		20 22	20 48		21 22
Greenock West	d		16 50	17 08		17 32	17 50		17 58	18 25		18 50	18 59	19 20		19 50	19 59		20 25	20 51		21 24
Fort Matilda	d		16 53	17 11		17 35	17 53		18 01	18 28		18 53	19 02	19 23		19 53	20 02		20 28	20 54		21 27
Gourock	a		16 57	17 15		17 39	17 57		18 06	18 32		18 57	19 06	19 27		19 57	20 06		20 34	20 58		21 32

§ For authorised access to and from IB.M. only

A not 14 May

Glasgow Central - Wemyss Bay and Gourock

Network Diagram - see first Page of Table 216

Station		SR	SR	SR	SR	SR	SR	SR	SR
Glasgow Central 15 221	d	21 05	21 35	21 50	22 05	22 35	22 50	23 20	23 50
Cardonald	d	21 12	21 42		22 12	22 42		23 27	23 57
Hillington East	d	21 14	21 44		22 14	22 44		23 29	23 59
Hillington West	d	21 16	21 46		22 16	22 46		23 31	00 01
Paisley Gilmour Street 221 ✈	a	21 21	21 50	22 00	22 20	22 50	23 00	23 35	00 05
	d	21 21	21 50	22 01	22 20	22 50	23 01	23 35	00 05
Paisley St James	d	21 22	21 52		22 22	22 52		23 37	00 07
Bishopton	d	21 28	21 58	22 07	22 28	22 58	23 07	23 43	00 13
Langbank	d	21 34	22 04		22 34	23 04		23 49	00 19
Woodhall	d	21 38	22 08		22 38	23 08		23 53	00 23
Port Glasgow	d	21 41	22 11	22 16	22 41	23 11	23 16	23 56	00 26
Whinhill	d		22 15			23 15			
Drumfrochar	d		22 18			23 18			
Branchton	d		22 21			23 21			
IB.M. §	d		22 23			23 23			
Inverkip	d		22 28			23 28			
Wemyss Bay	a		22 34			23 34			
Bogston	d	21 43			22 43			23 58	00 28
Cartsdyke	d	21 45		22 20	22 45		23 20	00 01	00 30
Greenock Central	d	21 47		22 22	22 47		23 22	00 02	00 32
Greenock West	d	21 50		22 24	22 50		23 24	00 05	00 35
Fort Matilda	d	21 53		22 27	22 53		23 29	00 08	00 38
Gourock	a	21 58		22 33	22 57		23 33	00 12	00 42

Sundays

Station		SR	SR	SR	SR	SR	SR	SR	SR	SR	SR	SR	SR	SR	SR	SR	SR	SR	SR	SR	SR	SR	SR
Glasgow Central 15 221	d	23p20	23p50	07 20	07 50	08 20	08 50	09 20	09 50	10 20	10 50	11 20	11 50	12 20	12 50	13 20	13 50	14 20	14 50	15 20	15 50	16 20	16 50
Cardonald	d	23p27	23p57	07 27		08 27		09 27		10 27		11 27		12 27		13 27		14 27		15 27		16 27	
Hillington East	d	23p29	23p59	07 29	07 58	08 29	08 58	09 29	09 58	10 29	10 58	11 29	11 58	12 29	12 58	13 29	13 58	14 29	14 58	15 29	15 58	16 29	16 58
Hillington West	d	23p31	00 01	07 31		08 31		09 31		10 31		11 31		12 31	13 00	13 31		14 31		15 31		16 31	
Paisley Gilmour Street 221 ✈	a	23p35	00 05	07 35	08 03	08 35	09 03	09 35	10 03	10 35	11 03	11 35	12 03	12 35	13 03	13 35	14 03	14 35	15 03	15 35	16 03	16 35	17 03
	d	23p35	00 05	07 35	08 03	08 35	09 03	09 35	10 03	10 35	11 03	11 35	12 03	12 35	13 03	13 35	14 03	14 35	15 03	15 35	16 03	16 35	17 03
Paisley St James	d	23p37	00 07			08 37		09 37		10 37		11 37		12 37		13 37		14 37		15 37		16 37	
Bishopton	d	23p43	00 13	07 41	08 09	08 43	09 09	09 43	10 09	10 43	11 09	11 43	12 09	12 43	13 09	13 43	14 09	14 43	15 09	15 43	16 09	16 43	17 09
Langbank	d	23p49	00 19			08 49		09 49		10 49		11 49		12 49		13 49		14 49		15 49		16 49	
Woodhall	d	23p53	00 23	07 49		08 53		09 53		10 53		11 53		12 53		13 53		14 53		15 53		16 53	
Port Glasgow	d	23p56	00 26	07 52	08 19	08 56	09 19	09 56	10 19	10 56	11 19	11 56	12 19	12 56	13 19	13 56	14 19	14 56	15 19	15 56	16 19	16 56	17 19
Whinhill	d				08 23		09 23		10 23		11 23		12 22		13 23		14 23		15 23		16 23		17 23
Drumfrochar	d				08 26		09 26		10 26		11 26		12 25		13 26		14 26		15 26		16 26		17 26
Branchton	d				08 29		09 29		10 29		11 29		12 28		13 29		14 29		15 29		16 29		17 29
IB.M. §	d				08 31		09 31		10 31		11 31		12 30		13 31		14 31		15 31		16 31		17 31
Inverkip	d				08 36		09 36		10 36		11 36		12 35		13 36		14 36		15 36		16 36		17 36
Wemyss Bay	a				08 42		09 42		10 42		11 42		12 42		13 42		14 42		15 42		16 42		17 42
Bogston	d	23p58	00 28	07 54		08 58		09 58		10 58		11 58		12 58		13 58		14 58		15 58		16 58	
Cartsdyke	d	00 01	00 30	07 56		09 00		10 00		11 00		12 00		13 00		14 00		15 00		16 00		17 00	
Greenock Central	d	00 02	00 32	07 58		09 02		10 02		11 02		12 02		13 02		14 02		15 02		16 02		17 02	
Greenock West	d	00 05	00 35	08 01		09 05		10 05		11 05		12 05		13 05		14 05		15 05		16 05		17 05	
Fort Matilda	d	00 08	00 38			09 08		10 08		11 08		12 08		13 08		14 08		15 08		16 08		17 08	
Gourock	a	00 12	00 42	08 06		09 12		10 12		11 12		12 12		13 12		14 12		15 12		16 12		17 12	

Station		SR	SR	SR	SR	SR	SR	SR	SR	SR	SR
Glasgow Central 15 221	d	17 20	17 50	18 20	18 50	19 20	19 50	20 20	21 20	22 20	23 20
Cardonald	d	17 27		18 27		19 27		20 27	21 27	22 27	23 27
Hillington East	d	17 29	17 58	18 29	18 58	19 29	19 58	20 29	21 29	22 29	23 29
Hillington West	d	17 31		18 31		19 31		20 31	21 31	22 31	23 31
Paisley Gilmour Street 221 ✈	a	17 35	18 03	18 35	19 03	19 35	20 03	20 35	21 35	22 35	23 35
	d	17 35	18 03	18 35	19 03	19 35	20 03	20 35	21 35	22 35	23 35
Paisley St James	d	17 37		18 37		19 37		20 37	21 37	22 37	23 37
Bishopton	d	17 43	18 09	18 43	19 09	19 43	20 09	20 43	21 43	22 43	23 43
Langbank	d	17 49		18 49		19 49		20 49	21 49	22 49	23 49
Woodhall	d	17 53		18 53		19 53		20 53	21 53	22 53	23 53
Port Glasgow	d	17 56	18 19	18 56	19 19	19 56	20 19	20 56	21 56	22 56	23 56
Whinhill	d		18 23		19 23		20 23				
Drumfrochar	d		18 26		19 26		20 26				
Branchton	d		18 29		19 29		20 29				
IB.M. §	d		18 31		19 31		20 31				
Inverkip	d		18 36		19 36		20 36				
Wemyss Bay	a		18 42		19 42		20 42				
Bogston	d	17 58		18 58		19 58		20 58	21 58	22 58	23 58
Cartsdyke	d	18 00		19 00		20 00		21 00	22 00	23 00	00 01
Greenock Central	d	18 02		19 02		20 02		21 02	22 02	23 02	00 02
Greenock West	d	18 05		19 05		20 05		21 05	22 05	23 05	00 05
Fort Matilda	d	18 08		19 08		20 08		21 08	22 08	23 08	00 08
Gourock	a	18 12		19 12		20 12		21 12	22 12	23 12	00 12

§ For authorised access to and from IB.M. only

Gourock and Wemyss Bay - Glasgow Central

Network Diagram - see first Page of Table 216

Miles	Miles		SR MX	SR	SR	SR SX	SR SO	SR SX	SR SX	SR SO	SR	SR SX	SR SO	SR SX	SR	SR	SR SX	SR	SR	SR	SR	SR
0	—	**Gourock** d	23p20	05 20	06 05	06 22	06 35	06 44	07 06	07 06		07 22	07 36	07 47	07 52		08 09	08 24	08 36		09 06	09 23
1¼	—	Fort Matilda d	23p23	05 23	06 08	06 25	06 38	06 47	07 09	07 09		07 25	07 39		07 55		08 12	08 27	08 39		09 09	09 26
2½	—	Greenock West d	23p26	05 26	06 11	06 28	06 41	06 50	07 12	07 12		07 28	07 42	07 52	07 58		08 15	08 30	08 42		09 12	09 29
3¼	—	Greenock Central d	23p29	05 29	06 14	06 31	06 44	06 53	07 15	07 15		07 31	07 45	07 55	08 01		08 18	08 33	08 45		09 15	09 32
4¼	—	Cartsdyke d	23p31	05 31	06 16	06 33	06 46	06 55	07 17	07 17		07 33	07 47		08 03			08 35	08 47		09 17	
5	—	Bogston d	23p33	05 33		06 35	06 48	06 57	07 19	07 19		07 35	07 49		08 05			08 37	08 49		09 19	
—	0	**Wemyss Bay** d									07 13					07 50				08 50		
—	2¼	Inverkip d									07 18					07 54				08 54		
—	4¾	IB.M. § d									07 23					07 59				08 59		
—	6¼	Branchton d									07 25					08 02				09 02		
—	8	Drumfrochar d									07 28					08 04				09 04		
—	8½	Whinhill d									07 30					08 07				09 07		
6	10¼	Port Glasgow d	23p36	05 36	06 19	06 38	06 51	07 00	07 22	07 22	07 35	07 38	07 52	07 59	08 08	08 12	08 22	08 40	08 52	09 11	09 22	09 36
7¼	12	Woodhall d	23p38	05 38		06 40	06 53	07 02		07 24	07 37	07 40	07 54		08 10	08 14		08 42	08 54		09 24	
10	14¾	Langbank d	23p43	05 43		06 45	06 58	07 07		07 29		07 45	07 59			08 19		08 47	08 59		09 29	
14	18	Bishopton d	23p48	05 48	06 28	06 50	07 03	07 12	07 31	07 34	07 45	07 50	08 04	08 08	08 19	08 24	08 31	08 52	09 04	09 20	09 34	09 45
18¼	22¼	Paisley St James d	23p54	05 54	06 34	06 56	07 09	07 18		07 40		07 56	08 10			08 30		08 58	09 10		09 40	
19	23	Paisley Gilmour Street 221 a	23p56	05 55	06 36	06 58	07 11	07 20	07 37	07 42	07 51	07 58	08 12	08 14	08 25	08 32	08 37	09 00	09 11	09 26	09 42	09 51
—	—	d	23p57	05 56	06 37	06 59	07 12	07 21	07 38	07 43	07 52	07 59	08 13	08 14	08 26	08 33	08 38	09 01	09 12	09 27	09 43	09 52
21¼	25¼	Hillington West d	00 01	05 59	06 40	07 02	07 15	07 24	07 41	07 46	07 55	08 02	08 16	08 18	08 29			09 04	09 15		09 46	
21¾	25¾	Hillington East d	00 02	06 01	06 42	07 04	07 17	07 26	07 43	07 48	07 57	08 04	08 18	08 20	08 31			09 06	09 17		09 48	
22½	26½	Cardonald d	00 04	06 03	06 44	07 06	07 19	07 28	07 45	07 50	07 59	08 06	08 20	08 22	08 33			09 08	09 19		09 50	
26½	31	**Glasgow Central** ■15 221 a	00 12	06 12	06 52	07 14	07 27	07 36	07 54	07 58	08 07	08 14	08 30	08 33	08 42	08 44	08 49	09 16	09 29	09 39	09 58	10 03

	SR	SR	SR	SR	SR	SR	SR	SR	SR	SR	SR	SR	SR	SR	SR	SR	SR	SR	SR	SR	SR	SR
Gourock d	09 36		10 06	10 23	10 36		11 06	11 23	11 36		12 06	12 23	12 36		13 06	13 23	13 36		14 06	14 23	14 36	
Fort Matilda d	09 39		10 09	10 26	10 39		11 09	11 26	11 39		12 09	12 26	12 39		13 09	13 26	13 39		14 09	14 26	14 39	
Greenock West d	09 42		10 12	10 29	10 42		11 12	11 29	11 42		12 12	12 29	12 42		13 12	13 29	13 42		14 12	14 29	14 42	
Greenock Central d	09 45		10 15	10 32	10 45		11 15	11 32	11 45		12 15	12 32	12 45		13 15	13 32	13 45		14 15	14 32	14 45	
Cartsdyke d	09 47		10 17		10 47		11 17		11 47		12 17		12 47		13 17		13 47		14 17		14 47	
Bogston d	09 49		10 19		10 49		11 19		11 49		12 19		12 49		13 19		13 49		14 19		14 49	
Wemyss Bay d		09 50				10 55				11 50				12 50				13 50				14 50
Inverkip d		09 54				10 59				11 54				12 54				13 54				14 54
IB.M. § d		09 59				11 04				11 59				12 59				13 59				14 59
Branchton d		10 02				11 07				12 02				13 02				14 02				15 02
Drumfrochar d		10 04				11 09				12 04				13 04				14 04				15 04
Whinhill d		10 07				11 12				12 07				13 07				14 07				15 07
Port Glasgow d	09 52	10 11	10 22	10 36	10 52	11 16	11 22	11 36	11 52	12 11	12 22	12 36	12 52	13 11	13 22	13 36	13 52	14 11	14 22	14 36	14 52	15 11
Woodhall d	09 54		10 24		10 54		11 24		11 54		12 24		12 54		13 24		13 54		14 24		14 54	
Langbank d	09 59		10 29		10 59		11 29		11 59		12 29		12 59		13 29		13 59		14 29		14 59	
Bishopton d	10 04	10 20	10 34	10 45	11 04	11 25	11 34	11 45	12 04	12 20	12 34	12 45	13 04	13 20	13 34	13 45	14 04	14 20	14 34	14 45	15 04	15 20
Paisley St James d	10 10		10 40		11 10		11 40		12 10		12 40		13 10		13 40		14 10		14 40		15 10	
Paisley Gilmour Street 221 a	10 12	10 26	10 42	10 51	11 12	11 31	11 42	11 51	12 12	12 26	12 42	12 51	13 12	13 26	13 43	13 51	14 12	14 26	14 42	14 51	15 12	15 26
d	10 13	10 27	10 43	10 52	11 13	11 32	11 43	11 52	12 13	12 27	12 43	12 52	13 13	13 27	13 43	13 52	14 13	14 27	14 43	14 52	15 13	15 27
Hillington West d	10 16		10 46		11 16		11 46		12 16		12 46		13 16		13 46		14 16		14 46		15 16	
Hillington East d	10 18		10 48		11 18		11 48		12 18		12 48		13 18		13 48		14 18		14 48		15 18	
Cardonald d	10 20		10 50		11 20		11 50		12 20		12 50		13 20		13 50		14 20		14 50		15 20	
Glasgow Central ■15 221 a	10 28	10 38	10 58	11 03	11 28	11 43	11 58	12 03	12 29	12 38	12 58	13 03	13 28	13 38	13 58	14 03	14 28	14 38	14 58	15 03	15 29	15 38

	SR	SR	SR	SR	SR	SR	SR	SR	SR	SR	SR	SR	SR	SR	SR	SR	SR	SR	SR	SR	SR
Gourock d	15 06	15 23	15 36		16 06	16 23	16 36		17 06	17 23	17 48		18 06	18 23		18 40		19 06	19 22	19 45	
Fort Matilda d	15 09	15 26	15 39		16 09	16 26	16 39		17 09	17 26	17 51		18 09	18 26		18 43		19 09	19 25	19 48	
Greenock West d	15 12	15 29	15 42		16 12	16 29	16 42		17 12	17 29	17 54		18 12	18 29		18 46		19 12	19 28	19 51	
Greenock Central d	15 15	15 32	15 45		16 15	16 32	16 45		17 15	17 32	17 57		18 15	18 32		18 49		19 15	19 31	19 54	
Cartsdyke d	15 17		15 47		16 17		16 47		17 17		17 59		18 17			18 51		19 17	19 33	19 56	
Bogston d	15 19		15 49		16 19		16 49		17 19		18 01		18 19			18 53		19 19	19 35		
Wemyss Bay d				15 55				16 45				17 49			18 26		18 55				19 44
Inverkip d				15 59				16 49				17 53			18 30		18 59				19 48
IB.M. § d				16 04				16 54				18 02			18 39		19 04				19 53
Branchton d				16 07				16 57				18 05			18 41		19 07				19 56
Drumfrochar d				16 09				16 59				18 07			18 44		19 09				19 58
Whinhill d				16 12				17 02				18 10			18 46		19 12				20 01
Port Glasgow d	15 22	15 36	15 52	16 16	16 22	16 36	16 52	17 06	17 22	17 36	18 04	18 14	18 22	18 36	18 51	18 56	19 16	19 22	19 38	19 59	20 06
Woodhall d	15 24		15 54		16 24		16 54		17 24		18 06		18 24			18 58		19 24	19 40		20 08
Langbank d	15 29		15 59		16 29		16 59		17 29		18 11		18 29			19 03		19 29	19 45		20 13
Bishopton d	15 34	15 45	16 04	16 25	16 34	16 45	17 04	17 15	17 34	17 45	18 16	18 23	18 34	18 45	19 00	19 08	19 25	19 34	19 50	20 08	20 18
Paisley St James d	15 40		16 10		16 40		17 10		17 40		18 22		18 40			19 14		19 40	19 56		20 24
Paisley Gilmour Street 221 a	15 42	15 51	16 12	16 31	16 42	16 51	17 11	17 21	17 42	17 51	18 24	18 30	18 42	18 51	19 06	19 16	19 31	19 42	19 58	20 14	20 26
d	15 43	15 52	16 13	16 32	16 43	16 52	17 12	17 22	17 43	17 52	18 25	18 31	18 43	18 52	19 06	19 17	19 32	19 43	19 59	20 15	20 27
Hillington West d	15 46	15 55	16 16		16 46	16 56	17 15		17 46		18 28		18 46			19 20		19 46	20 02		20 30
Hillington East d	15 48		16 18		16 48		17 17		17 48		18 30		18 48			19 22		19 48	20 04		20 32
Cardonald d	15 50		16 20		16 50		17 19		17 50		18 32		18 50			19 24		19 50	20 06		20 34
Glasgow Central ■15 221 a	15 58	16 06	16 28	16 45	16 59	17 05	17 31	17 34	17 58	18 05	18 40	18 44	18 58	19 04	19 17	19 32	19 44	19 59	20 14	20 26	20 43

§ For authorised access to and from IB.M. only

Gourock and Wemyss Bay - Glasgow Central

Network Diagram - see first Page of Table 216

	SR	SR	SR	SR	SR	SR SX	SR SO	SR	SR	SR	SR SO
Gourock d	20 20	20 44		21 24	21 45			22 20		23 20	
Fort Matilda d	20 23	20 47		21 27	21 48			22 23		23 23	
Greenock West d	20 26	20 50		21 30	21 51			22 26		23 26	
Greenock Central d	20 29	20 53		21 33	21 54			22 29		23 29	
Cartsdyke d	20 31	20 55		21 35	21 56			22 31		23 31	
Bogston d	20 33			21 37				22 33		23 33	
Wemyss Bay d			20 44			21 44	21 50		22 44		23 40
Inverkip d			20 48			21 48	21 54		22 48		23 44
IB.M. § d			20 53			21 53	21 59		22 53		23 49
Branchton d			20 56			21 56	22 02		22 56		23 52
Drumfrochar d			20 58			21 58	22 04		22 58		23 54
Whinhill d			21 01			22 01	22 07		23 01		23 57
Port Glasgow d	20 36	20 58	21 06	21 40	21 59	22 06	22 11	22 36	23 06	23 36	00 01
Woodhall d	20 38		21 08	21 42		22 08	22 14	22 38	23 08	23 38	
Langbank d	20 43		21 13	21 47		22 13	22 18	22 43	23 13	23 43	
Bishopton d	20 48	21 07	21 18	21 52	22 08	22 18	22 24	22 48	23 18	23 48	00 10
Paisley St James d	20 54		21 24	21 58		22 24	22 29	22 54	23 24	23 54	
Paisley Gilmour Street 221 a	20 56	21 13	21 26	22 00	22 14	22 26	22 32	22 56	23 26	23 56	00 16
d	20 56	21 14	21 27	22 01	22 15	22 27	22 32	22 57	23 27	23 57	00 17
Hillington West d	21 00		21 30	22 04		22 30	22 35	23 00	23 30	00 01	
Hillington East d	21 02		21 32	22 06		22 32	22 37	23 02	23 32	00 02	
Cardonald d	21 04		21 34	22 08		22 34	22 39	23 04	23 34	00 04	
Glasgow Central ■15 221 a	21 12	21 30	21 42	22 15	22 26	22 42	22 46	23 14	23 42	00 12	00 28

Sundays

	SR	SR	SR	SR	SR	SR	SR	SR	SR	SR	SR	SR	SR	SR	SR	SR	SR	SR	SR	SR	SR	SR
Gourock d	23p20		08 23		09 23		10 23		11 23		12 23		13 23		14 23		15 23		16 23		17 23	
Fort Matilda d	23p23		08 26		09 26		10 26		11 26		12 26		13 26		14 26		15 26		16 26		17 26	
Greenock West d	23p26		08 29		09 29		10 29		11 29		12 29		13 29		14 29		15 29		16 29		17 29	
Greenock Central d	23p29		08 32		09 32		10 32		11 32		12 32		13 32		14 32		15 32		16 32		17 32	
Cartsdyke d	23p31		08 34		09 34		10 34		11 34		12 34		13 34		14 34		15 34		16 34		17 34	
Bogston d	23p33		08 36		09 36		10 36		11 36		12 36		13 36		14 36		15 36		16 36		17 36	
Wemyss Bay d		23p40		08 50		09 50		10 57		11 50		12 50		13 50		14 50		15 55		16 50		17 50
Inverkip d		23p44		08 54		09 54		11 01		11 54		12 54		13 54		14 54		15 59		16 54		17 54
IB.M. § d		23p49		08 59		09 59		11 06		11 59		12 59		13 59		14 59		16 04		16 59		17 59
Branchton d		23p52		09 02		10 02		11 09		12 02		13 02		14 02		15 02		16 07		17 02		18 02
Drumfrochar d		23p54		09 04		10 04		11 11		12 04		13 04		14 04		15 04		16 09		17 04		18 04
Whinhill d		23p57		09 07		10 07		11 13		12 07		13 07		14 07		15 07		16 12		17 07		18 07
Port Glasgow d	23p36	00 01	08 39	09 11	09 39	10 11	10 39	11 17	11 39	12 11	12 39	13 11	13 39	14 11	14 39	15 11	15 39	16 16	16 39	17 11	17 39	18 11
Woodhall d	23p38		08 41		09 41		10 41		11 41		12 41		13 41		14 41		15 41		16 41		17 41	
Langbank d	23p43		08 46		09 46		10 46		11 46		12 46		13 46		14 46		15 46		16 46		17 46	
Bishopton d	23p48	00 10	08 51	09 20	09 51	10 20	10 51	11 27	11 51	12 20	12 51	13 20	13 51	14 20	14 51	15 20	15 51	16 25	16 51	17 20	17 51	18 20
Paisley St James d	23p54		08 57		09 57		10 57		11 57		12 57		13 57		14 57		15 57		16 57		17 57	
Paisley Gilmour Street 221 a	23p56	00 16	08 59	09 26	09 59	10 26	10 59	11 31	11 58	12 26	12 59	13 26	13 59	14 26	14 59	15 26	15 59	16 31	16 59	17 26	17 59	18 26
d	23p57	00 17	09 00	09 27	10 00	10 27	11 00	11 32	11 59	12 27	13 00	13 27	14 00	14 27	15 00	15 27	16 00	16 32	17 00	17 27	18 00	18 27
Hillington West d	00 01		09 03		10 03		11 03		12 03		13 03		14 03		15 03		16 03		17 03		18 03	
Hillington East d	00 02		09 05	09 31	10 05	10 31	11 05	11 36	12 05	12 31	13 05	13 31	14 05	14 31	15 05	15 31	16 05	16 36	17 05	17 31	18 05	18 31
Cardonald d	00 04		09 07		10 07		11 07		12 07		13 07		14 07		15 07		16 07		17 07		18 07	
Glasgow Central ■15 221 a	00 12	00 28	09 15	09 40	10 15	10 40	11 15	11 46	12 15	12 40	13 15	13 40	14 15	14 40	15 15	15 40	16 15	16 45	17 15	17 40	18 15	18 40

	SR	SR	SR	SR	SR	SR	SR	SR
Gourock d	18 23		19 23		20 23		21 23	22 23
Fort Matilda d	18 26		19 26		20 26		21 26	22 26
Greenock West d	18 29		19 29		20 29		21 29	22 29
Greenock Central d	18 32		19 32		20 32		21 32	22 32
Cartsdyke d	18 34		19 34		20 34		21 34	22 34
Bogston d	18 36		19 36		20 36		21 36	22 36
Wemyss Bay d		18 55		19 50		20 50		
Inverkip d		18 59		19 54		20 54		
IB.M. § d		19 04		19 59		20 59		
Branchton d		19 07		20 02		21 02		
Drumfrochar d		19 09		20 04		21 04		
Whinhill d		19 12		20 07		21 07		
Port Glasgow d	18 39	19 16	19 39	20 11	20 39	21 11	21 39	22 39
Woodhall d	18 41		19 41		20 41		21 41	22 41
Langbank d	18 46		19 46		20 46		21 46	22 46
Bishopton d	18 51	19 25	19 51	20 20	20 51	21 20	21 51	22 51
Paisley St James d	18 57		19 57		20 57		21 57	22 57
Paisley Gilmour Street 221 a	18 59	19 31	19 59	20 26	20 59	21 26	21 59	22 59
d	19 00	19 32	20 00	20 27	21 00	21 27	22 00	23 00
Hillington West d	19 03		20 03		21 03		22 03	23 03
Hillington East d	19 05	19 36	20 05	20 31	21 05	21 31	22 05	23 05
Cardonald d	19 07		20 07		21 07		22 07	23 07
Glasgow Central ■15 221 a	19 15	19 44	20 15	20 40	21 15	21 40	22 15	23 15

§ For authorised access to and from IB.M. only

Glasgow and Gourock - Dunoon and Kilcreggan

Argyll Ferries Ltd in association with ScotRail

Mondays to Saturdays
until 20 October 2012

All Kilcreggan sailings are operated by Clydelink Ltd
Tel. 0871 705 08 88

				SX		SX																	SX	SO	
Glasgow Central	219	d	05 55	05 55	06 25	06 25	06 55	.	06 55	07 25	07 35	07 35	08 28	08 28	08 36	09 25	09 25	09 35	10 25	10 25	.	10 35	11 25	12 25	12 25	12 25
Paisley Gilmour Street	219	d	06 07	06 07	06 36	06 36	07 07	.	07 07	07 40	07 51	07 51	08 38	08 38	08 50	09 36	09 36	09 50	10 36	10 36	.	10 50	11 36	12 36	12 36	12 36
Gourock	219	a	06 36	06 36	07 13	07 13	07 39	.	07 39	08 13	08 28	08 28	09 09	09 09	09 27	10 06	10 06	10 27	11 06	11 06	.	11 27	12 06	13 06	13 06	13 06
Gourock		d	06 45	07 00	07 20	07 33	07 50	.	08 04	08 20	08 40	08 50	09 18	09 20	09 50	10 18	10 20	10 50	11 18	11 20	.	11 50	12 20	13 13	13 18	13 20
Dunoon		a	07 10	.	07 45	.	08 15	.	.	08 45	.	09 15	.	09 45	10 15	.	10 45	11 15	.	11 45	.	12 15	12 45	.	.	13 45
Kilcreggan		a	.	07 13	.	07 46	.	.	08 17	.	08 53	.	09 31	.	.	10 31	.	.	11 31	.	.	.	.	13 26	13 31	.

					SX	SO			SX		SX	SO		SX			SO	SX		B						
Glasgow Central	219	d	13 25	13 25	14 05	14 25	.	14 25	14 35	14 35	15 25	15 25	15 25	15 35	15 35	16 05	16 05	16 23	16 55	17 25	17 25	17 40	.	18 25	18 35	19 25
Paisley Gilmour Street	219	d	13 36	13 36	14 20	14 36	.	14 36	14 50	14 50	15 36	15 36	15 36	15 50	15 50	16 20	16 20	16 38	17 06	17 37	17 37	17 55	.	18 36	18 50	19 36
Gourock	219	a	14 06	14 06	14 57	15 06	.	15 06	15 27	15 27	16 06	16 06	16 06	16 27	16 27	16 57	16 57	17 15	17 39	18 06	18 06	18 32	.	19 06	19 27	20 06
Gourock		d	14 18	14 20	15 10	15 18	.	15 20	15 42	15 50	16 14	16 18	16 20	16 46	16 50	17 20	17 20	17 23	17 50	18 10	18 20	18 50	.	19 20	19 50	20 20
Dunoon		a	.	14 45	.	.	.	15 45	.	16 15	.	.	16 45	.	17 15	17 45	.	.	18 15	.	18 45	19 15	.	19 45	20 15	20 45
Kilcreggan		a	14 31	.	15 23	15 31	.	.	15 55	.	16 27	16 31	.	16 59	.	.	17 33	17 36	.	18 26	.	.	.	.	.	.

						FSO	A
Glasgow Central	219	d	20 05	20 50	21 50	22 50	23 50
Paisley Gilmour Street	219	d	20 21	21 01	22 01	23 01	00 05
Gourock	219	a	20 58	21 32	22 33	23 33	00 42
Gourock		d	21 20	21 40	22 40	23 40	01 00
Dunoon		a	21 45	22 05	23 05	00 05	01 20
Kilcreggan		a	.	.	.	.	.

Sundays
until 14 October 2012

									C			C			C										
Glasgow Central	219	d	07 20	.	08 20	09 20	.	10 20	11 20	11 20	12 20	13 20	13 20	14 20	15 20	15 20	16 20	17 20	.	18 20	19 20	.	20 20	.	.	21 20
Paisley Gilmour Street	219	d	07 35	.	08 35	09 35	.	10 35	11 35	11 35	12 35	13 35	13 35	14 35	15 35	15 35	16 35	17 35	.	18 35	19 35	.	20 35	.	.	21 35
Gourock	219	a	08 06	.	09 12	10 12	.	11 12	12 12	12 12	13 12	14 12	14 12	15 12	16 12	16 12	17 12	18 12	.	19 12	20 12	.	21 12	.	.	22 12
Gourock		d	08 20	.	09 20	10 20	.	11 20	12 20	12 55	13 20	14 20	14 55	15 20	16 20	16 55	17 20	18 20	.	19 20	20 20	.	21 20	.	.	22 20
Dunoon		a	08 45	.	09 45	10 45	.	11 45	12 45	.	13 45	14 45	.	15 45	16 45	.	17 45	18 45	.	19 45	20 45	.	21 45	.	.	22 45
Kilcreggan		a	.	.	.	.	.	.	.	13 07	.	.	15 07	.	.	17 07	.	.	.	.	.	.	.	.	.	.

A Saturday and Sunday mornings only
B The ferry will be held for a maximum of 15 minutes in the event of a late-running train
C A bus connection (service 316) is available at Kilcreggan for Helensburgh

Kilcreggan and Dunoon - Gourock and Glasgow

Argyll Ferries Ltd in association with ScotRail

Mondays to Saturdays
until 20 October 2012
All Kilcreggan sailings are operated by Clydelink Ltd
Tel. 0871 705 08 88

			SX	SO	SX		SX																		SX	SO
Kilcreggan		d	.	.	07 16	.	07 48	.	08 20	.	08 58	.	.	.	09 58	.	.	10 58	.	.	11 58	.	.	.	13 30	13 58
Dunoon		d	06 45	06 45	.	07 15	.	07 50	.	08 20	.	.	08 50	09 20	.	09 50	10 20	.	10 50	11 20	.	11 50	12 20	12 50	.	.
Gourock		a	07 15	07 15	07 29	07 40	08 01	08 15	08 33	08 45	09 11	.	09 15	09 45	10 11	10 15	10 45	11 11	11 15	11 45	12 11	12 15	12 45	13 15	13 43	14 11
Gourock	219	d	07 22	07 36	07 47	07 52	08 09	08 24	09 06	09 06	09 23	.	09 23	10 06	10 23	10 23	11 06	11 23	11 23	12 06	12 23	12 23	13 06	13 23	14 06	14 23
Paisley Gilmour Street	219	a	07 58	08 12	08 14	08 25	08 37	09 00	09 42	09 42	09 51	.	09 51	10 42	10 51	10 51	11 42	11 51	11 51	12 42	12 51	12 51	13 43	13 51	14 42	14 51
Glasgow Central	219	a	08 14	08 30	08 33	08 42	08 49	09 16	09 58	09 58	10 03	.	10 03	10 58	11 03	11 03	11 58	12 03	12 03	12 58	13 03	13 03	13 58	14 03	14 58	15 03

				SX	SO		SX			SX		SO		SX		SX	SO								A	
Kilcreggan		d	.	14 54	14 58	.	15 26	15 58	.	16 30	.	16 58	.	17 04	.	17 39	17 40	.	18 30	.	.	.	.	.	.	.
Dunoon		d	13 50	.	.	14 50	.	.	15 50	.	16 20	.	16 50	.	17 20	.	.	17 50	.	18 20	18 50	19 20	19 50	20 50	21 45	22 10
Gourock		a	14 15	15 07	15 11	15 15	15 39	16 11	16 15	16 43	16 45	17 11	17 15	17 17	17 45	17 52	17 53	18 15	18 43	18 45	19 15	19 45	20 15	21 15	22 15	22 35
Gourock	219	d	14 23	15 23	15 23	15 23	16 06	16 23	16 23	17 06	17 06	17 23	17 23	17 48	18 06	18 06	18 06	18 23	19 06	19 06	19 22	20 20	20 44	21 24	22 20	23 20
Paisley Gilmour Street	219	a	14 51	15 51	15 51	15 51	16 42	16 51	16 51	17 42	17 42	17 51	17 51	18 24	18 42	18 42	18 42	18 51	19 42	19 42	19 58	20 56	21 13	22 00	22 56	23 56
Glasgow Central	219	a	15 03	16 06	16 06	16 06	16 59	17 05	17 05	17 58	17 58	18 05	18 05	18 40	18 58	18 58	18 58	19 04	19 59	19 59	20 14	21 12	21 30	22 15	23 14	00 12

Sundays
until 14 October 2012

								C			C			C											
Kilcreggan		d	.	.	.	.	.	12 39	.	.	14 39	.	.	16 39	.	.	.	.	.	.	.	.	.	.	.	.
Dunoon		d	08 50	09 50	10 50	.	11 50	.	12 50	13 50	.	14 50	15 50	.	16 50	17 50	.	18 50	19 50	20 50	21 50	.	.	.	.	17 50
Gourock		a	09 15	10 15	11 15	.	12 15	12 52	13 15	14 15	14 52	15 15	16 15	16 52	17 15	18 15	.	19 15	20 15	21 15	22 15	.	.	.	.	18 15
Gourock	219	d	09 23	10 23	11 23	.	12 23	13 23	13 23	14 23	15 23	15 23	16 23	17 23	17 23	18 23	.	19 23	20 23	21 23	22 23	.	.	.	.	18 23
Paisley Gilmour Street	219	a	09 59	10 59	11 58	.	12 59	13 59	13 59	14 59	15 59	15 59	16 59	17 59	17 59	18 59	.	19 59	20 59	21 59	22 59	.	.	.	.	18 51
Glasgow Central	219	a	10 15	11 15	12 15	.	13 15	14 15	14 15	15 15	16 15	16 15	17 15	18 15	18 15	19 15	.	20 15	21 15	22 15	23 15	.	.	.	.	19 04

A Connection is not guaranteed
C A bus connection (service 316) runs from Helensburgh to Kilcreggan

For details of Gourock/Dunoon sailings from 21 October 2012
please telephone 08000 66 5000
or visit www.argyllferries.co.uk

For details of Kilcreggan sailings please telephone 0871 705 08 88
or visit www.clydelink.co.uk Please note Gourock/Kilcreggan times
may be subject to minor alteration between May and October 2012
due to ongoing Gourock rail station/pier re-furbishment

Glasgow and Wemyss Bay - Rothesay (Bute)

Caledonian MacBrayne Ltd in association with ScotRail

Mondays to Saturdays
until 20 October 2012

																			FSO	SO A
Glasgow Central 15	219 d	06 05	06 32	07 50	08 50	09 50	10 50	11 50	12 50	13 50	14 50	15 50	16 33	17 15	17 55	18 50	19 40	20 35
Paisley Gilmour Street	219 d	06 19	06 47	08 02	09 01	10 01	11 01	12 01	13 01	14 01	15 01	16 02	16 49	17 29	18 06	19 01	19 55	20 50
Wemyss Bay	219 a	06 58	07 30	08 40	09 40	10 40	11 40	12 40	13 40	14 40	15 40	16 40	17 25	18 08	18 44	19 40	20 38	21 34
Wemyss Bay	⛴ d	07 15	08 00	08 45	10 15	11 00	12 00	13 05	14 05	15 00	16 00	16 45	17 30	18 15	19 00	19 45	20 45	22 00
Rothesay	⛴ a	07 50	08 35	09 20	10 50	11 35	12 35	13 40	14 40	15 35	16 35	17 20	18 05	18 50	19 35	20 20	21 20	22 35

Sundays
until 14 October 2012

Glasgow Central 15	219 d	07 50	08 50	09 50	10 50	11 50	12 50	13 50	14 50	15 50	16 50	17 50	18 50
Paisley Gilmour Street	219 d	08 03	09 03	10 03	11 03	12 03	13 03	14 03	15 03	16 03	17 03	18 03	19 03
Wemyss Bay	219 a	08 42	09 42	10 42	11 42	12 42	13 42	14 42	15 42	16 42	17 42	18 42	19 42
Wemyss Bay	⛴ d	08 45	10 15	11 00	12 00	13 00	13 50	15 00	16 00	17 30	18 15	19 00	19 45
Rothesay	⛴ a	09 20	10 50	11 35	12 35	13 35	14 25	15 35	16 35	18 05	18 50	19 35	20 20

A From 2 June until 18 August

Mondays to Saturdays
until 20 October 2012

		SX																	FSO	SO A
Rothesay	⛴ d	06 25	07 00	08 00	08 45	10 10	11 00	12 00	13 00	14 00	15 00	16 00	16 45	17 30	18 15	19 00	19 45	21 10
Wemyss Bay	⛴ a	07 00	07 35	08 35	09 20	10 45	11 35	12 35	13 35	14 35	15 35	16 35	17 20	18 05	18 50	19 35	20 20	21 45
Wemyss Bay	219 d	07 13	07 50	08 50	09 50	10 55	11 50	12 50	13 50	14 50	15 55	16 45	17 49	18 26	18 55	19 44	20 44	21 50
Paisley Gilmour Street	219 a	07 51	08 32	09 26	10 26	11 32	12 26	13 26	14 26	15 26	16 31	17 21	18 30	19 06	19 31	20 26	21 26	22 32
Glasgow Central 15	219 a	08 07	08 44	09 39	10 38	11 43	12 38	13 38	14 38	15 38	16 45	17 34	18 44	19 17	19 44	20 43	21 42	22 46

Sundays
until 14 October 2012

Rothesay	⛴ d	08 00	10 10	11 00	12 00	13 00	14 00	15 10	16 00	16 45	18 15	19 00	19 45
Wemyss Bay	⛴ a	08 35	10 45	11 35	12 35	13 35	14 35	15 45	16 35	17 20	18 50	19 35	20 20
Wemyss Bay	219 d	08 50	10 57	11 50	12 50	13 50	14 50	15 55	16 50	17 50	18 55	19 50	20 50
Paisley Gilmour Street	219 a	09 26	11 31	12 26	13 26	14 26	15 26	16 31	17 26	18 26	19 31	20 26	21 26
Glasgow Central 15	219 a	09 40	11 46	12 40	13 40	14 40	15 40	16 45	17 40	18 40	19 44	20 40	21 57

A From 2 June until 18 August

For details of sailings from 21 October 2012 please telephone
08000 66 5000 or visit www.calmac.co.uk

Network Diagram for Tables 220, 223, 224, 226, 232

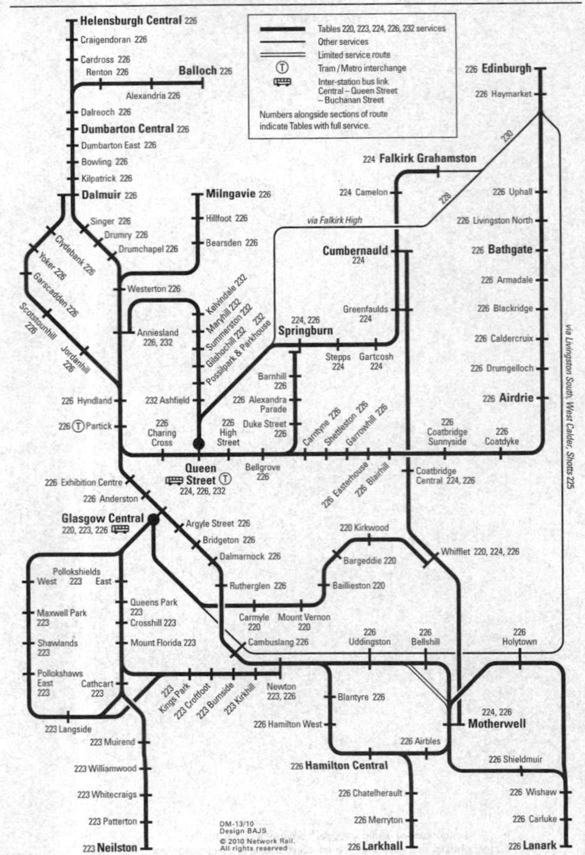

Table 220

Mondays to Saturdays

Glasgow Central - Whifflet

Network Diagram - see first Page of Table 220

Miles			SR SO	SR SX	SR	SR	SR	SR	SR	SR	SR	SR	SR	SR	SR	SR	SR	SR	SR	SR	SR	SR	SR
0	**Glasgow Central** 15	d	00 16	06 17	06 46	07 16	07 46	08 16	08 43	09 16	09 46	10 16	10 46	11 16	11 46	12 16	12 46	13 16	13 46	14 16	14 46	15 16	15 46
5½	Carmyle	d	00 26	06 26	06 56	07 26	07 56	08 26	08 56	09 26	09 56	10 26	10 56	11 26	11 56	12 26	12 56	13 26	13 56	14 26	14 56	15 26	15 56
6¾	Mount Vernon	d	00 29	06 29	06 59	07 29	07 59	08 29	08 59	09 29	09 59	10 29	10 59	11 29	11 59	12 29	12 59	13 29	13 59	14 29	14 59	15 29	15 59
8	Baillieston	d	00 32	06 32	07 02	07 32	08 02	08 32	09 02	09 32	10 02	10 32	11 02	11 32	12 02	12 32	13 02	13 32	14 02	14 32	15 02	15 32	16 02
9¼	Bargeddie	d	00 35	06 35	07 05	07 35	08 05	08 35	09 05	09 35	10 05	10 35	11 05	11 35	12 05	12 35	13 05	13 35	14 05	14 35	15 05	15 35	16 05
10	Kirkwood	d	00 39	06 39	07 09	07 39	08 09	08 39	09 09	09 39	10 09	10 39	11 09	11 39	12 09	12 39	13 09	13 39	14 09	14 39	15 09	15 39	16 09
12½	**Whifflet**	a	00 45	06 47	07 15	07 47	08 15	08 48	09 15	09 45	10 15	10 45	11 15	11 45	12 15	12 45	13 15	13 45	14 16	14 45	15 15	15 45	16 15

		SR	SR	SR	SR	SR	SR	SR SX	SR SO	SR	SR	SR	SR	SR	SR	SR	SR
Glasgow Central 15	d	16 16	16 46	17 16	17 46	18 16	18 46	19 13	19 16	19 46	20 16	20 46	21 16	21 46	22 16	22 46	23 16
Carmyle	d	16 26	16 56	17 26	17 56	18 26	18 56	19 26	19 26	19 56	20 26	20 56	21 26	21 56	22 26	22 56	23 26
Mount Vernon	d	16 29	16 59	17 29	17 59	18 29	18 59	19 29	19 29	19 59	20 29	20 59	21 29	21 59	22 29	22 59	23 29
Baillieston	d	16 32	17 02	17 32	18 02	18 32	19 02	19 32	19 32	20 02	20 32	21 02	21 32	22 02	22 32	23 02	23 32
Bargeddie	d	16 35	17 05	17 35	18 05	18 35	19 05	19 35	19 35	20 05	20 35	21 05	21 35	22 05	22 35	23 05	23 35
Kirkwood	d	16 39	17 09	17 39	18 09	18 39	19 09	19 39	19 39	20 09	20 39	21 09	21 39	22 09	22 39	23 09	23 39
Whifflet	a	16 45	17 15	17 45	18 15	18 45	19 15	19 45	19 45	20 15	20 45	21 15	21 45	22 15	22 45	23 15	23 45

Whifflet - Glasgow Central

Mondays to Saturdays

Miles			SR	SR	SR	SR	SR	SR	SR	SR	SR	SR	SR	SR	SR	SR	SR	SR	SR	SR	SR	SR	SR
0	**Whifflet**	d	06 06	06 36	07 06	07 36	08 06	08 36	09 06	09 36	10 06	10 36	11 06	11 36	12 06	12 36	13 06	13 36	14 06	14 36	15 06	15 36	16 06
2½	Kirkwood	d	06 09	06 39	07 09	07 39	08 09	08 39	09 09	09 39	10 09	10 39	11 09	11 39	12 09	12 39	13 09	13 39	14 09	14 39	15 09	15 39	16 09
3¼	Bargeddie	d	06 12	06 42	07 12	07 42	08 12	08 42	09 12	09 42	10 12	10 42	11 12	11 42	12 12	12 42	13 12	13 42	14 12	14 42	15 12	15 42	16 12
4½	Baillieston	d	06 15	06 45	07 15	07 45	08 15	08 45	09 15	09 45	10 15	10 45	11 15	11 45	12 15	12 45	13 15	13 45	14 15	14 45	15 15	15 45	16 15
5¾	Mount Vernon	d	06 18	06 48	07 18	07 48	08 18	08 48	09 18	09 48	10 18	10 48	11 18	11 48	12 18	12 48	13 18	13 48	14 18	14 48	15 18	15 48	16 18
7	Carmyle	d	06 21	06 51	07 21	07 51	08 21	08 51	09 21	09 51	10 21	10 51	11 21	11 51	12 21	12 51	13 21	13 51	14 21	14 51	15 21	15 51	16 21
12½	**Glasgow Central** 15	a	06 35	07 05	07 35	08 05	08 36	09 07	09 37	10 05	10 35	11 05	11 35	12 05	12 35	13 05	13 35	14 05	14 35	15 05	15 35	16 05	16 35

		SR	SR	SR	SR SO	SR SX	SR	SR	SR	SR	SR	SR	SR	SR	SR	SR SX	SR SO
Whifflet	d	16 36	17 06	17 36	18 06	18 12	18 36	19 06	19 36	20 06	20 36	21 06	21 36	22 06	22 36	23 06	23 06
Kirkwood	d	16 39	17 09	17 39	18 09	18 14	18 39	19 09	19 39	20 09	20 39	21 09	21 39	22 09	22 39	23 09	23 09
Bargeddie	d	16 42	17 12	17 42	18 12	18 17	18 42	19 12	19 42	20 12	20 42	21 12	21 42	22 12	22 42	23 12	23 12
Baillieston	d	16 45	17 15	17 45	18 15	18 20	18 45	19 15	19 45	20 15	20 45	21 15	21 45	22 15	22 45	23 15	23 15
Mount Vernon	d	16 48	17 18	17 48	18 18	18 23	18 48	19 18	19 48	20 18	20 48	21 18	21 48	22 18	22 48	23 18	23 18
Carmyle	d	16 51	17 21	17 51	18 21	18 26	18 51	19 21	19 51	20 21	20 51	21 21	21 51	22 21	22 51	23 21	23 21
Glasgow Central 15	a	17 05	17 35	18 05	18 35	18 40	19 05	19 35	20 05	20 35	21 05	21 35	22 05	22 38	23 05	23 35	23 37

No Sunday Service

Table 221

Mondays to Saturdays

Glasgow Central - Ardrossan, Largs and Ayr

Network Diagram - see first Page of Table 216

Miles	Miles	Miles				SR SO	SR MSX	SR MX	SR SO	SR MSX	SR MX	SR	SR	SR	SR	SR	SR	SR	SR	SR SX	SR A	SR	SR	SR
0	0	—	**Glasgow Central** 15	219	d	23p15	23p15	23p30	23p45	23p45	00 15	06 00	06 15	06 30	06 45	07 00	07 15	07 30	08 00	08 15		08 30	08 34	08 45
7¼	7¼	—	Paisley Gilmour Street	219	a	23p25	23p25	23p40	23p55	23p55	00 25	06 11	06 25	06 40	06 55	07 10	07 25	07 40	08 10	08 25		08 40	08 44	08 55
—	—	—			d	23p26	23p26	23p41	23p56	23p56	00 26	06 12	06 26	06 41	06 56	07 11	07 26	07 41	08 11	08 26		08 41	08 45	08 56
10¾	10¾	—	Johnstone		d	23p30	23p30	23p45	23p59	23p59	00 30	06 14	06 30	06 45	07 00	07 15	07 31	07 45	08 15	08 30		08 45	08 49	09 00
11½	11½	—	Milliken Park		d	23p33	23p33		00 03	00 03			06 33		07 03		07 34			08 33			08 52	09 03
13	13	—	Howwood		d	23p36	23p36		00 06	00 06			06 36		07 06		07 37			08 36			08 55	
16½	16½	—	Lochwinnoch		d	23p40	23p40		00 10	00 10			06 40				07 41			08 40			08 59	
20½	20½	—	Glengarnock		d	23p45	23p45		00 15	00 15			06 45		07 13		07 46		08 24	08 45		08 54	09 04	09 11
23¼	23¼	—	Dalry		d	23p49	23p49		00 19	00 19			06 49		07 17		07 50		08 28	08 49		08 58	09 08	
26¾	26¾	—	Kilwinning 4		d	23p54	23p54	23p59	00 23	00 23	00 42	06 28	06 54	06 59	07 23	07 29	07 54	08 00	08 33	08 54		09 03	09 12	09 18
—	29	—	Stevenston		d	23p57	23p57		00 27	00 27			06 57		07 27		07 58			08 57			09 16	09 21
—	30¼	—	Saltcoats		d	23p59	23p59		00 29	00 29			07 00		07 29		08 00			09 00			09 18	09 24
—	31¼	—	Ardrossan South Beach		d	00 02	00 02		00 31	00a32			07 02		07 31		08 02			09a02			09 20	09 26
—	—	31¾	Ardrossan Town		d	00a06									07 35								09 24	
—	—	32¼	**Ardrossan Harbour**		a										07 37								09 26	
—	35¼	—	West Kilbride		d		00 08		00 37				07 08				08 08							09 31
—	39¼	—	Fairlie		d		00 14		00 43				07 13				08 14							09 35
—	42¼	—	**Largs**		a		00 19		00 49				07 20				08 20							09 44
30	—	—	Irvine		d			00 03			00 47	06 32		07 03		07 33		08 04	08 37			09 07		
33¾	—	—	Barassie		d			00 08			00 51			07 07				08 09	08 42			09 11		
35	—	—	Troon		d			00 11			00 54	06 38		07 10		07 39		08 12	08 45		08 49	09 14		
37¾	—	—	Prestwick Int. Airport ✈		d			00 15			00 58	06 42		07 14		07 43		08 16	08 49		08 54	09 18		
38¼	—	—	Prestwick Town		d			00 17			01 00	06 44		07 16		07 45		08 18	08 51		08 56	09 20		
40¼	—	—	Newton-on-Ayr		d			00 20			01 04			07 19				08 21	08 54			09 24		
41½	—	—	**Ayr**		a			00 25			01 11	06 52		07 24		07 52		08 26	08 58		09 03	09 27		

			SR	SR	SR	SR ◇ B	SR	SR	SR	SR	SR	SR A	SR	SR	SR	SR SO ◇ B	SR SX ◇ B	SR	SR	SR	SR	SR	SR A	SR
Glasgow Central 15	219	d	09 00	09 15	09 30	09 41	09 45	10 00	10 15	10 30	10 45		11 00	11 15	11 30	11 40	11 42	11 45	12 00	12 15	12 30	12 45		13 00
Paisley Gilmour Street	219	a	09 10	09 25	09 40	09 53	09 56	10 10	10 25	10 40	10 55		11 10	11 25	11 40	11 52	11 52	11 55	12 09	12 25	12 40	12 55		13 10
		d	09 11	09 26	09 41	09 54	09 57	10 11	10 26	10 41	10 56		11 11	11 26	11 41	11 53	11 53	11 56	12 10	12 26	12 41	12 56		13 11
Johnstone		d	09 17	09 30	09 45		10 00	10 15	10 30	10 45	11 00		11 15	11 30	11 45			12 01	12 14	12 30	12 45	13 00		13 15
Milliken Park		d		09 33			10 04		10 33		11 03			11 33				12 03		12 33		13 03		
Howwood		d		09 36					10 36					11 36						12 36				
Lochwinnoch		d		09 40					10 40					11 40						12 40				
Glengarnock		d		09 45	09 54		10 12		10 45	10 55	11 11			11 45				12 11		12 45		13 11		
Dalry		d		09 49			10 16	10 26	10 49					11 49						12 49		13 15		
Kilwinning 4		d	09 31	09 54	10 01	10 14	10 21	10 31	10 54	11 01	11 18		11 29	11 54	11 59	12 11	12 11	12 18	12 27	12 54	12 59	13 20		13 29
Stevenston		d		09 57			10 23		10 57		11 21			11 57				12 22		12 57		13 23		
Saltcoats		d		10 00			10 26		11 00		11 24			12 00				12 24		13 00		13 26		
Ardrossan South Beach		d		10 02			10 28		11 02		11 26			12 02				12 26		13 02		13 28		
Ardrossan Town		d		10 06					11 06					12 06						13 06				
Ardrossan Harbour		a		10 08					11 08					12 09						13 09				
West Kilbride		d					10 33				11 32							12 32				13 34		
Fairlie		d					10 39				11 37							12 38				13 39		
Largs		a					10 46				11 44							12 44				13 46		
Irvine		d	09 35		10 05			10 35		11 05			11 33		12 03				12 33		13 03			13 33
Barassie		d			10 10					11 10					12 08						13 08			
Troon		d	09 41		10 13			10 43		11 13		11 18	11 39		12 11				12 39		13 11		13 16	13 39
Prestwick Int. Airport ✈		d	09 45		10 17			10 47		11 17		11 23	11 43		12 15				12 43		13 15		13 21	13 43
Prestwick Town		d	09 47		10 19			10 49		11 19		11 25	11 45		12 17				12 45		13 17		13 23	13 45
Newton-on-Ayr		d			10 22					11 22					12 20						13 20			
Ayr		a	09 53		10 26	10 35		10 54		11 26		11 32	11 52		12 24	12 29	12 29		12 52		13 24		13 30	13 52

			SR	SR	SR	SR A	SR	SR	SR	SR	SR	SR C	SR	SR	SR	SR	SR	SR	SR	SR	SR D	SR	SR C	SR SX
Glasgow Central 15	219	d	13 15	13 30	13 45		14 00	14 15	14 30	14 45	15 00	15 12	15 15	15 30	15 45	16 00	16 18	16 30	16 41	16 50		17 00	17 12	17 13
Paisley Gilmour Street	219	a	13 25	13 40	13 55		14 10	14 25	14 40	14 55	15 10		15 25	15 40	15 55	16 10	16 27	16 40	16 53	17 00		17 10		
		d	13 26	13 41	13 56		14 11	14 26	14 41	14 56	15 11		15 26	15 41	15 56	16 11	16 28	16 41	16 54	17 01		17 11		17u24
Johnstone		d	13 30	13 45	14 00		14 15	14 30	14 45	15 00	15 15		15 30	15 45	16 00	16 15	16 32	16 45	16 58	17 05		17 15		
Milliken Park		d	13 33		14 03			14 33		15 03			15 33		16 03		16 35		17 01	17 08				
Howwood		d	13 36					14 36					15 36				16 38			17 11				
Lochwinnoch		d	13 40					14 40					15 40				16 42		17 06			17 21		
Glengarnock		d	13 45		14 11			14 45		15 11			15 45		16 11		16 47		17 11	17 18		17 26		17 35
Dalry		d	13 49				14 26	14 49					15 49				16 51		17 15	17 22		17 30		
Kilwinning 4		d	13 54	13 59	14 18		14 31	14 54	14 59	15 18	15 29		15 54	15 59	16 18	16 29	16 56	17 00	17 20	17 26		17 35		17 42
Stevenston		d	13 57		14 21			14 57		15 21			15 57		16 21		17 01		17 24	17 30				
Saltcoats		d	14 00		14 24			15 00		15 24			16 00		16 24		17 09		17 27	17 32				
Ardrossan South Beach		d	14 02		14 26			15 01		15 26			16 02		16 26		17 11		17a29	17 35				
Ardrossan Town		d	14 06					15 06					16 06							17 38				
Ardrossan Harbour		a	14 09					15 09					16 09							17 44				
West Kilbride		d			14 32					15 32					16 32		17 17							
Fairlie		d			14 37					15 37					16 37		17 22							
Largs		a			14 44					15 44					16 44		17 28							
Irvine		d		14 03			14 35		15 03		15 33			16 03		16 33		17 04				17 39		17 46
Barassie		d		14 08					15 08					16 08				17 08				17 44		
Troon		d		14 11		14 16	14 41		15 11		15 39	16 16		16 11		16 39		17 11			17 16	17 47	18 21	17 52
Prestwick Int. Airport ✈		d		14 15		14 21	14 45		15 15		15 43	16 20		16 15		16 43		17 15			17 21	17 51	18 26	17 56
Prestwick Town		d		14 17		14 23	14 47		15 17		15 45	16 22		16 17		16 45		17 17			17 23	17 53	18 28	17 58
Newton-on-Ayr		d		14 20					15 20					16 20				17 21				17 56		
Ayr		a		14 24		14 30	14 54		15 24		15 52	16 30		16 24		16 52		17 25			17 30	18 00	18 36	18 05

A From Kilmarnock to Girvan
B To Stranraer
C To Girvan
D From Kilmarnock to Stranraer

Mondays to Saturdays

Glasgow Central - Ardrossan, Largs and Ayr

Network Diagram - see first Page of Table 216

	SR	SR SX	SR SO	SR	SR	SR	SR	SR	SR	SR A	SR	SR	SR	SR	SR	SR	SR	SR	SR B	SR	SR
Glasgow Central 219 d	17 20	17 30	17 30	17 35	17 45	18 00	18 15	18 30	18 45		19 00	19 15	19 30	19 45	20 00	20 15	20 30	20 45		21 00	21 15
Paisley Gilmour Street 219 a	17 31		17 40	17 47	17 55	18 10	18 25	18 40	18 55		19 10	19 25	19 40	19 55	20 10	20 25	20 40	20 55		21 10	21 25
d	17 32	17u41	17 41	17 47	17 56	18 11	18 26	18 41	18 56		19 11	19 26	19 41	19 56	20 11	20 26	20 41	20 56		21 11	21 26
Johnstone d	17 36		17 45	17 53	18 00	18 15	18 30	18 45	19 00		19 15	19 30	19 45	20 00	20 15	20 30	20 45	21 00		21 15	21 30
Milliken Park d	17 39			17 56	18 03		18 33		19 03			19 33		20 03		20 33		21 03			21 33
Howwood d				17 59			18 36					19 36				20 36					21 36
Lochwinnoch d				18 03			18 40					19 40				20 40					21 40
Glengarnock d				18 08	18 11		18 45		19 11			19 45		20 11		20 45		21 11			21 45
Dalry d	17 49			18 12	18 15	18 26	18 49	18 57				19 49				20 49					21 49
Kilwinning d	17 54		17 59	18 16	18 20	18 31	18 54	19 02	19 18		19 29	19 54	20 00	20 18	20 29	20 54	20 59	21 18		21 29	21 53
Stevenston d	17 57			18 20	18 23		18 57		19 21			19 57		20 22		20 57		21 21			21 57
Saltcoats d	18 00			18 22	18 26		19 00		19 24			20 00		20 24		21 00		21 24			22 00
Ardrossan South Beach d	18 02			18 24	18 28		19 02		19 26			20 02		20 26		21 02		21 26			22 02
Ardrossan Town d				18a27			19 06					20 06				21 06					22 06
Ardrossan Harbour a							19 09					20 09				21 09					22 09
West Kilbride d	18 08				18 34				19 32					20 32				21 32			
Fairlie d	18 13				18 39				19 37					20 37				21 37			
Largs a	18 20				18 48				19 44					20 44				21 44			
Irvine d		18 00	18 03			18 35		19 06			19 33		20 04		20 33		21 03			21 33	
Barassie d		18 04	18 08			18 40		19 11					20 09				21 08				
Troon d		18 07	18 11			18 43		19 14		19 17	19 39		20 12		20 39		21 11		21 22	21 39	
Prestwick Int. Airport d		18 11	18 15			18 47		19 18		19 21	19 43		20 16		20 43		21 15		21 27	21 43	
Prestwick Town d		18 13	18 17			18 49		19 20		19 23	19 45		20 18		20 45		21 17		21 29	21 45	
Newton-on-Ayr d		18 17	18 20			18 52		19 23					20 21				21 20				
Ayr a		18 21	18 24			18 56		19 26		19 30	19 52		20 25		20 52		21 24		21 34	21 52	

	SR	SR	SR	SR SX C	SR	SR	SR	SR SO A	SR	SR FO	SR FX	SR	SR FO	SR FSX
Glasgow Central 219 d	21 30	21 45	22 00	22 12	22 15	22 30	22 45		23 00	23 15	23 15	23 30	23 45	23 45
Paisley Gilmour Street 219 a	21 40	21 55	22 10		22 25	22 40	22 55		23 10	23 25	23 25	23 40	23 55	23 55
d	21 41	21 56	22 11		22 26	22 41	22 56		23 11	23 26	23 26	23 41	23 56	23 56
Johnstone d	21 45	22 02	22 15		22 30	22 45	23 00		23 15	23 30	23 30	23 45	23 59	23 59
Milliken Park d		22 04			22 33		23 03			23 33	23 33		00 03	00 03
Howwood d					22 36					23 36	23 36		00 06	00 06
Lochwinnoch d					22 40					23 40	23 40		00 10	00 10
Glengarnock d		22 12			22 45		23 11			23 45	23 45		00 15	00 15
Dalry d					22 49					23 49	23 49		00 19	00 19
Kilwinning d	21 59	22 19	22 29		22 56	22 59	23 18		23 27	23 54	23 54	23 59	00 23	00 23
Stevenston d		22 21			23 00		23 21			23 57	23 57		00 27	00 27
Saltcoats d		22 24			23 02		23 24			23 59	23 59		00 29	00 29
Ardrossan South Beach d		22 26			23 04		23 26			00 02	00 02		00 31	00a32
Ardrossan Town d					23a07					00a06				
Ardrossan Harbour a														
West Kilbride d		22 32					23 32				00 08		00 37	
Fairlie d		22 37					23 37				00 14		00 43	
Largs a		22 44					23 44				00 19		00 49	
Irvine d	22 03		22 33			23 03			23 33			00 03		
Barassie d	22 08					23 08						00 08		
Troon d	22 11		22 39	23 18		23 11		23 18	23 39			00 11		
Prestwick Int. Airport d	22 15		22 43	23 23		23 15		23 23	23 43			00 15		
Prestwick Town d	22 17		22 45	23 25		23 17		23 25	23 45			00 17		
Newton-on-Ayr d	22 20					23 20						00 20		
Ayr a	22 24		22 52	23 30		23 24		23 30	23 52			00 25		

Sundays
until 30 September

	SR	SR	SR	SR	SR	SR	SR	SR	SR	SR	SR	SR	SR ◇ C	SR	SR	SR	SR	SR	SR	SR	SR	SR
Glasgow Central 219 d	23p15	23p30	08 40	09 00	09 30	09 42	10 00	10 30	10 42	11 00	11 15	11 30	11 42	11 45	12 00	12 30	12 42	13 00	13 30	13 42	14 00	14 05
Paisley Gilmour Street 219 a	23p25	23p40	08 50	09 10	09 40	09 52	10 10	10 40	10 54	11 10	11 25	11 40	11 52	11 57	12 10	12 40	12 55	13 10	13 40	13 54	14 10	14 15
d	23p26	23p41	08 51	09 11	09 41	09 53	10 11	10 41	10 54	11 11	11 26	11 41	11 53	11 57	12 11	12 41	12 56	13 11	13 41	13 54	14 11	14 16
Johnstone d	23p30	23p45	08 55	09 15	09 45	09 57	10 15	10 45	10 59	11 15	11 30	11 45		12 03	12 15	12 45	13 00	13 15	13 45	13 59	14 15	14 20
Milliken Park d	23p33		08 58			10 00			11 01		11 33			12 05			13 03			14 01		14 23
Howwood d	23p36					10 03			11 04					12 08			13 06			14 04		
Lochwinnoch d	23p40					10 07			11 08					12 12			13 10			14 08		
Glengarnock d	23p45		09 06			10 12			11 13					12 17			13 15			14 13		
Dalry d	23p49		09 10			10 16			11 17					12 21			13 19			14 17		
Kilwinning d	23p54	23p59	09 15	09 29	09 59	10 21	10 29	10 59	11 22	11 29	11 46	11 59	12 11	12 26	12 30	12 59	13 23	13 29	13 59	14 22	14 29	14 36
Stevenston d	23p57		09 18			10 24			11 26		11 49			12 30			13 27			14 26		14 39
Saltcoats d	23p59		09 21			10 27			11 28		11 52			12 32			13 29			14 28		14 42
Ardrossan South Beach d	00 02		09 23			10 28			11 30		11 54			12 34			13 31			14 30		14 44
Ardrossan Town d																						
Ardrossan Harbour a			09 30								12 02											14 52
West Kilbride d	00 08					10 34			11 36					12 40			13 37			14 36		
Fairlie d	00 14					10 41			11 42					12 46			13 43			14 42		
Largs a	00 19					10 47			11 47					12 51			13 48			14 47		
Irvine d		00 03		09 33	10 03		10 33	11 03		11 33		12 03			12 34	13 03		13 33	14 03		14 33	
Barassie d		00 08		09 38			10 38			11 38					12 39			13 38			14 38	
Troon d		00 11		09 41	10 09		10 41	11 09		11 41		12 09			12 42	13 09		13 41	14 09		14 41	
Prestwick Int. Airport d		00 15		09 45	10 13		10 45	11 13		11 45		12 13			12 46	13 13		13 45	14 13		14 45	
Prestwick Town d		00 17		09 47	10 15		10 47	11 15		11 47		12 15			12 48	13 15		13 47	14 15		14 47	
Newton-on-Ayr d		00 20																				
Ayr a		00 25		09 54	10 22		10 54	11 22		11 54		12 22	12 29		12 54	13 22		13 54	14 22		14 54	

A From Kilmarnock to Stranraer
B From Kilmarnock to Girvan
C To Stranraer

Sundays
until 30 September

Glasgow Central - Ardrossan, Largs and Ayr

Network Diagram - see first Page of Table 216

	SR	SR	SR	SR	SR	SR	SR ◇ A	SR	SR	SR	SR	SR	SR	SR	SR	SR	SR	SR	SR	SR	SR	SR
Glasgow Central 219 d	14 30	14 42	15 00	15 30	15 42	16 00	16 25	16 30	16 42	16 54	17 00	17 30	17 42	18 00	18 30	18 42	19 00	19 42	20 00	20 42	21 00	21 42
Paisley Gilmour Street 219 a	14 40	14 54	15 10	15 40	15 53	16 10	16 38	16 41	16 55	17 06	17 10	17 40	17 54	18 10	18 40	18 52	19 10	19 52	20 10	20 52	21 10	21 51
d	14 41	14 54	15 11	15 41	15 53	16 11	16 39	16 41	16 55	17 07	17 12	17 41	17 54	18 11	18 41	18 53	19 11	19 53	20 11	20 53	21 11	21 52
Johnstone d	14 45	14 59	15 15	15 45	15 58	16 15		16 46	17 00	17 11	17 17	17 45	17 59	18 15	18 45	18 58	19 15	19 58	20 15	20 58	21 15	21 57
Milliken Park d		15 01			16 00				17 02	17 14			18 01			19 00		20 00		21 00		21 59
Howwood d		15 04			16 03				17 05				18 04			19 03		20 03		21 03		22 02
Lochwinnoch d		15 08			16 07				17 09				18 08			19 07		20 07		21 07		22 06
Glengarnock d		15 13			16 12				17 14				18 13			19 12		20 12		21 12		22 11
Dalry d		15 17			16 16				17 18				18 17			19 16		20 16		21 16		22 15
Kilwinning d	14 59	15 22	15 29	16 00	16 20	16 29	16 56	17 00	17 23	17 28	17 31	17 59	18 22	18 29	18 59	19 21	19 29	20 21	20 29	21 21	21 29	22 20
Stevenston d		15 26			16 24				17 27	17 31			18 26			19 25		20 25		21 25		22 24
Saltcoats d		15 28			16 26				17 29	17 34			18 28			19 27		20 27		21 27		22 26
Ardrossan South Beach d		15 30			16 28				17 31	17 36			18 30			19 29		20 29		21 29		22 28
Ardrossan Town d																						
Ardrossan Harbour a										17 43												
West Kilbride d		15 36			16 34				17 37				18 36			19 35		20 35		21 35		22 33
Fairlie d		15 42			16 40				17 43				18 42			19 41		20 41		21 41		22 39
Largs a		15 47			16 47				17 48				18 47			19 47		20 47		21 47		22 47
Irvine d	15 03		15 33	16 04		16 33		17 04			17 35	18 03		18 33	19 03		19 33		20 33		21 33	
Barassie d			15 38			16 38					17 40			18 38			19 38		20 38		21 38	
Troon d	15 09		15 41	16 10		16 41		17 10			17 43	18 09		18 41	19 09		19 41		20 41		21 41	
Prestwick Int. Airport d	15 13		15 45	16 14		16 45		17 14			17 47	18 13		18 45	19 13		19 45		20 45		21 45	
Prestwick Town d	15 15		15 47	16 17		16 47		17 16			17 49	18 15		18 47	19 15		19 47		20 47		21 47	
Newton-on-Ayr d																						
Ayr a	15 22		15 54	16 22		16 54	17 17	17 24			17 54	18 22		18 54	19 22		19 54		20 54		21 54	

	SR	SR	SR
Glasgow Central 219 d	22 00	22 42	23 00
Paisley Gilmour Street 219 a	22 10	22 52	23 10
d	22 11	22 53	23 11
Johnstone d	22 15	22 58	23 15
Milliken Park d		23 00	
Howwood d		23 03	
Lochwinnoch d		23 07	
Glengarnock d		23 12	
Dalry d		23 16	
Kilwinning d	22 29	23 26	23 29
Stevenston d		23 29	
Saltcoats d		23 32	
Ardrossan South Beach d		23 34	
Ardrossan Town d			
Ardrossan Harbour a			
West Kilbride d		23 40	
Fairlie d		23 45	
Largs a		23 51	
Irvine d	22 33		23 33
Barassie d	22 38		23 38
Troon d	22 41		23 41
Prestwick Int. Airport d	22 45		23 45
Prestwick Town d	22 47		23 47
Newton-on-Ayr d			
Ayr a	22 54		23 54

Sundays
from 7 October

	SR	SR	SR	SR	SR	SR	SR	SR	SR	SR ◇ A	SR	SR	SR	SR	SR	SR	SR	SR	SR	SR	SR	SR ◇ A
Glasgow Central 219 d	23p15	23p30	08 40	09 00	09 42	10 00	10 42	11 00	11 15	11 42	11 45	12 00	12 42	13 00	13 42	14 00	14 05	14 42	15 00	15 42	16 00	16 25
Paisley Gilmour Street 219 a	23p25	23p40	08 50	09 10	09 52	10 10	10 54	11 10	11 25	11 52	11 57	12 10	12 55	13 10	13 54	14 10	14 15	14 54	15 10	15 53	16 10	16 38
d	23p26	23p41	08 51	09 11	09 53	10 11	10 54	11 11	11 26	11 53	11 57	12 11	12 56	13 11	13 54	14 11	14 16	14 54	15 11	15 53	16 11	16 39
Johnstone d	23p30	23p45	08 55	09 15	09 57	10 15	10 59	11 15	11 30		12 03	12 15	13 00	13 15	13 59	14 15	14 20	14 59	15 15	15 58	16 15	
Milliken Park d	23p33		08 58		10 00		11 01		11 33		12 05		13 03		14 01		14 23	15 01		16 00		
Howwood d	23p36				10 03		11 04				12 08		13 06		14 04			15 04		16 03		
Lochwinnoch d	23p40				10 07		11 08				12 12		13 10		14 08			15 08		16 07		
Glengarnock d	23p45		09 06		10 12		11 13				12 17		13 15		14 13			15 13		16 12		
Dalry d	23p49		09 10		10 16		11 17				12 21		13 19		14 17			15 17		16 16		
Kilwinning d	23p54	23p59	09 15	09 29	10 21	10 29	11 22	11 29	11 46	12 11	12 26	12 30	13 23	13 29	14 22	14 29	14 36	15 22	15 29	16 20	16 29	16 56
Stevenston d	23p57		09 18		10 24		11 26		11 49		12 30		13 27		14 26		14 39	15 26		16 24		
Saltcoats d	23p59		09 21		10 27		11 28		11 52		12 32		13 29		14 28		14 42	15 28		16 26		
Ardrossan South Beach d	00 02		09 23		10 28		11 30		11 54		12 34		13 31		14 30		14 44	15 30		16 28		
Ardrossan Town d																						
Ardrossan Harbour a			09 30						12 02								14 52					
West Kilbride d	00 08				10 34		11 36				12 40		13 37		14 36			15 36		16 34		
Fairlie d	00 14				10 41		11 42				12 46		13 43		14 42			15 42		16 40		
Largs a	00 19				10 47		11 47				12 51		13 48		14 47			15 47		16 47		
Irvine d		00 03		09 33		10 33		11 33				12 34		13 33		14 33			15 33		16 33	
Barassie d		00 08		09 38		10 38		11 38				12 39		13 38		14 38			15 38		16 38	
Troon d		00 11		09 41		10 41		11 41				12 42		13 41		14 41			15 41		16 41	
Prestwick Int. Airport d		00 15		09 45		10 45		11 45				12 46		13 45		14 45			15 45		16 45	
Prestwick Town d		00 17		09 47		10 47		11 47				12 48		13 47		14 47			15 47		16 47	
Newton-on-Ayr d		00 20																				
Ayr a		00 25		09 54		10 54		11 54		12 29		12 54		13 54		14 54			15 54		16 54	17 17

A To Stranraer

Glasgow Central - Ardrossan, Largs and Ayr

Sundays from 7 October

Network Diagram - see first Page of Table 216

			SR	SR	SR	SR	SR	SR	SR	SR	SR	SR	SR	SR	SR	SR	SR
Glasgow Central	219	d	16 42	16 54	17 00	17 42	18 00	18 42	19 00	19 42	20 00	20 42	21 00	21 42	22 00	22 42	23 00
Paisley Gilmour Street	219	a	16 55	17 06	17 10	17 54	18 10	18 52	19 10	19 52	20 10	20 52	21 10	21 51	22 10	22 52	23 10
		d	16 55	17 07	17 12	17 54	18 11	18 53	19 11	19 53	20 11	20 53	21 11	21 52	22 11	22 53	23 11
Johnstone		d	17 00	17 11	17 17	17 59	18 15	18 58	19 15	19 58	20 15	20 58	21 15	21 57	22 15	22 58	23 15
Milliken Park		d	17 02	17 14		18 01		19 00		20 00		21 00		21 59		23 00	
Howwood		d	17 05			18 04		19 03		20 03		21 03		22 02		23 03	
Lochwinnoch		d	17 09			18 08		19 07		20 07		21 07		22 06		23 07	
Glengarnock		d	17 14			18 13		19 12		20 12		21 12		22 11		23 12	
Dalry		d	17 18			18 17		19 16		20 16		21 16		22 15		23 16	
Kilwinning		d	17 23	17 28	17 31	18 22	18 29	19 21	19 29	20 21	20 29	21 21	21 29	22 20	22 29	23 26	23 29
Stevenston		d	17 27	17 31		18 26		19 25		20 25		21 25		22 24		23 29	
Saltcoats		d	17 29	17 34		18 28		19 27		20 27		21 27		22 26		23 32	
Ardrossan South Beach		d	17 31	17 36		18 30		19 29		20 29		21 29		22 28		23 34	
Ardrossan Town		d															
Ardrossan Harbour		a		17 43													
West Kilbride		d	17 37			18 36		19 35		20 35		21 35		22 33		23 40	
Fairlie		d	17 43			18 42		19 41		20 41		21 41		22 39		23 45	
Largs		a	17 48			18 47		19 47		20 47		21 47		22 47		23 51	
Irvine		d			17 35		18 33		19 33		20 33		21 33		22 33		23 33
Barassie		d			17 40		18 38		19 38		20 38		21 38		22 38		23 38
Troon		d			17 43		18 41		19 41		20 41		21 41		22 41		23 41
Prestwick Int. Airport ✈		d			17 47		18 45		19 45		20 45		21 45		22 45		23 45
Prestwick Town		d			17 49		18 47		19 47		20 47		21 47		22 47		23 47
Newton-on-Ayr		d															
Ayr		a			17 54		18 54		19 54		20 54		21 54		22 54		23 54

Ayr, Largs and Ardrossan - Glasgow Central

Mondays to Saturdays

Network Diagram - see first Page of Table 216

Miles	Miles	Miles			SR MO A	SR	SR	SR	SR	SR	SR	SR SX	SR SX	SR SO	SR SX	SR SX	SR ◇ B	SR	SR	SR SX	SR SX	SR	SR SO
0	—	—	**Ayr**	d		05 12	05 40	06 13		06 43		06 57	07 13	07 13	07 25		07 36	07 43		07 58		08 13	
1¼	—	—	Newton-on-Ayr	d		05 15	05 43	06 16		06 46			07 16	07 16						08 01		08 16	
3¼	—	—	Prestwick Town	d		05 18	05 46	06 19		06 49		07 02	07 19	07 19	07 30		07 41	07 48		08 03		08 19	
3¾	—	—	Prestwick Int. Airport ✈	d		05 20	05 48	06 21		06 51		07 04	07 21	07 21	07 32		07 44	07 50		08 05		08 21	
6½	—	—	Troon	d		05 24	05 52	06 25		06 55		07 08	07 25	07 25	07 36		07a49	07 54		08 09		08 25	
7¾	—	—	Barassie	d		05 26	05 54	06 27		06 57		07 10	07 27	07 27	07 38					08 11		08 27	
11½	—	—	Irvine	d		05 31	05 59	06 32		07 02		07 15	07 32	07 32	07 43			08 00		08 16		08 32	
—	0	—	**Largs**	d	23p01						06 41					07 25			07 42				
—	3	—	Fairlie	d	23p06						06 46					07 30			07 47				
—	7	—	West Kilbride	d	23p11						06 51					07 35			07 52				
—	—	0	**Ardrossan Harbour**	d																	08 11		08 29
—	—	0½	Ardrossan Town	d					06 30												08 14		08 31
—	11½	1	Ardrossan South Beach	d	23p17				06 33		06 57					07 41			07 58		08 16		08 33
—	12½	2	Saltcoats	d	23p19				06 35		07 02					07 43			08 00		08 18		08 35
—	13¾	3¼	Stevenston	d	23p22				06 38		07 05					07 46			08 03		08 21		08 37
14¾	16	5½	Kilwinning	d	23p28	05 36	06 04	06 37	06 42	07 07	07 10	07 20	07 37	07 37		07 50		08 04	08 08	08 20	08 25	08 34	08 41
18½	19¾	9¼	Dalry	d	23p32	05 40	06 08		06 46		07 14	07 24	07 41	07 41		07 55			08 12		08 30		08 46
21	22¼	11¾	Glengarnock	d	23p36	05 44	06 12		06 50		07 18	07 28		07 45	07 52				08 16		08 34		08 50
25	26¼	15¾	Lochwinnoch	d	23p41	05 49	06 17		06 55			07 33		07 50		08 01			08 21		08 39		08 55
28½	29¾	19¼	Howwood	d	23p45	05 53	06 21		06 59			07 37		07 54	07 59						08 43		08 59
30	31¼	20¾	Milliken Park	d	23p48	05 56	06 24		07 02		07 26	07 40		07 57		08 06			08 26		08 46		09 02
30¾	32	21½	Johnstone	d	23p51	05 59	06 27	06 50	07 05	07 20	07 29	07 43	07 52	08 00	08 03	08 09		08 18	08 29	08 34	08 48	08 50	09 05
34¼	35½	25	Paisley Gilmour Street 219	a	23p55	06 03	06 31	06 55	07 09	07 25	07 34	07 47	07 57	08 04	08 07	08 13		08 22	08 34	08 42	08 53	08 56	09 09
—	—	—		d	23p56	06 04	06 32	06 55	07 10	07 25	07 34	07 48	07 57	08 05	08 08	08 13		08 23	08 35	08 43	08 53	08 56	09 10
41½	42¾	32¼	**Glasgow Central** 219	a	00 07	06 15	06 43	07 07	07 22	07 38	07 47	07 59	08 09	08 16	08 19	08 24		08 35	08 46	08 55	09 04	09 08	09 23

		SR SX	SR	SR SO	SR SX	SR	SR	SR	SR	SR B	SR	SR	SR	SR	SR	SR	SR ◇ C	SR	SR	SR	SR	SR	SR
Ayr	d		08 43			09 13		09 43		10 06	10 13		10 43		11 13		11 37	11 43		12 13		12 43	
Newton-on-Ayr	d					09 16					10 16				11 16					12 16			
Prestwick Town	d		08 48			09 19		09 48		10 11	10 19		10 48		11 19		11 42	11 48		12 19		12 47	
Prestwick Int. Airport ✈	d		08 50			09 21		09 50		10 13	10 21		10 50		11 21		11 44	11 50		12 21		12 49	
Troon	d		08 54			09 25		09 54		10a18	10 25		10 54		11 25		11a49	11 54		12 25		12 53	
Barassie	d					09 27					10 27				11 27					12 27			
Irvine	d		08 59			09 32		09 59			10 32		10 59		11 32			11 59		12 32		12 58	
Largs	d	08 28		08 51					09 53					10 53					11 53				12 53
Fairlie	d	08 33		08 56					09 58					10 58					11 58				12 58
West Kilbride	d	08 38		09 01					10 03					11 03					12 05				13 05
Ardrossan Harbour	d						09 31					10 28				11 28					12 28		
Ardrossan Town	d						09 33					10 31				11 31					12 31		
Ardrossan South Beach	d	08 44		09 07	09 07		09 35		10 09			10 33		11 09		11 33			12 11		12 33		13 11
Saltcoats	d	08 46		09 09	09 09		09 37		10 11			10 35		11 11		11 35			12 13		12 35		13 13
Stevenston	d	08 49		09 12	09 12		09 40		10 14			10 38		11 14		11 38			12 16		12 38		13 16
Kilwinning	d	08 53	09 04	09 16	09 16	09 37	09 45	10 04	10 18		10 37	10 42	11 04	11 18	11 37	11 42		12 04	12 20	12 37	12 42	13 03	13 20
Dalry	d	08 57				09 41	09 49					10 47				11 47					12 47		
Glengarnock	d	09 01		09 22	09 22		09 53		10 25			10 51		11 25		11 51			12 26		12 51		13 26
Lochwinnoch	d			09 27	09 27		09 58					10 56				11 56					12 56		
Howwood	d			09 31	09 31			10 16				11 00				12 00					13 00		
Milliken Park	d	09 09		09 32	09 32		10 03		10 33			11 03		11 33		12 03			12 34		13 03		13 34
Johnstone	d	09 12	09 18	09 35	09 35	09 52	10 06	10 20	10 35		10 50	11 06	11 18	11 35	11 50	12 06		12 18	12 37	12 50	13 06	13 18	13 37
Paisley Gilmour Street 219	a	09 16	09 23	09 39	09 39	09 57	10 10	10 24	10 40		10 55	11 10	11 23	11 39	11 55	12 10		12 23	12 41	12 55	13 10	13 23	13 41
	d	09 17	09 24	09 40	09 40	09 57	10 11	10 25	10 41		10 55	11 11	11 23	11 39	11 55	12 11		12 24	12 42	12 55	13 11	13 24	13 42
Glasgow Central 219	a	09 33	09 36	09 54	09 54	10 09	10 22	10 36	10 52		11 07	11 22	11 36	11 52	12 07	12 22		12 36	12 53	13 07	13 22	13 36	13 52

		SR B	SR	SR	SR	SR	SR ◇ D	SR	SR	SR	SR	SR	SR	SR E	SR E	SR	SR	SR ◇ C	SR	SR	SR	SR	SR
Ayr	d	13 08	13 13		13 43		14 10	14 13		14 43		15 13		15 32	15 18	15 43		16 06	16 13		16 43		17 13
Newton-on-Ayr	d		13 16					14 16				15 16							16 16		16 46		17 16
Prestwick Town	d	13 13	13 19		13 48			14 19		14 48		15 19			15 23	15 48		16 11	16 19		16 49		17 19
Prestwick Int. Airport ✈	d	13 15	13 21		13 50			14 21		14 50		15 21			15 25	15 50		16 14	16 21		16 51		17 21
Troon	d	13a20	13 25		13 54			14 25		14 54		15 25			15 30	15 54		16a19	16 25		16 55		17 25
Barassie	d		13 27					14 27				15 27							16 27				17 27
Irvine	d		13 32		13 59			14 32		14 59		15 32				15 59			16 32		17 00		17 32
Largs	d					13 53					14 53						15 53					16 50	
Fairlie	d					13 58					14 58						15 58					16 55	
West Kilbride	d					14 03					15 03						16 03					17 00	
Ardrossan Harbour	d			13 28					14 28				15 28							16 28			
Ardrossan Town	d			13 31					14 31				15 31							16 31			
Ardrossan South Beach	d			13 33		14 09			14 33		15 09		15 33				16 09			16 33		17 06	
Saltcoats	d			13 35		14 11			14 35		15 11		15 35				16 11			16 35		17 08	
Stevenston	d			13 38		14 14			14 38		15 14		15 38				16 14			16 38		17 11	
Kilwinning	d		13 37	13 42	14 04	14 18	14 27	14 37	14 42	15 04	15 18	15 37	15 43	15 48		16 04	16 18		16 37	16 42	17 05	17 15	17 36
Dalry	d			13 47					14 47				15 47							16 47		17 20	17 41
Glengarnock	d			13 51		14 25			14 51		15 25	15 43	15 51				16 25		16 43	16 51		17 24	
Lochwinnoch	d			13 56					14 56				15 56							16 56		17 29	
Howwood	d			14 00					15 00				16 00							17 00			
Milliken Park	d			14 03		14 33			15 03		15 33		16 03				16 33			17 03		17 34	
Johnstone	d		13 50	14 06	14 18	14 35		14 50	15 05	15 18	15 35	15 52	16 06			16 18	16 35		16 52	17 06	17 19	17 36	17 52
Paisley Gilmour Street 219	a		13 55	14 10	14 22	14 40	14 46	14 55	15 10	15 24	15 40	15 57	16 10	16 15		16 22	16 40		16 57	17 10	17 23	17 41	17 58
	d		13 55	14 11	14 23	14 40	14 46	14 55	15 10	15 25	15 40	15 57	16 11	16 16		16 23	16 41		16 57	17 11	17 24	17 41	17 58
Glasgow Central 219	a		14 07	14 24	14 35	14 52	15 01	15 07	15 22	15 36	15 52	16 09	16 25	16 31	16 33	16 34	16 52		17 09	17 24	17 36	17 55	18 09

A from 21 May
B From Girvan to Kilmarnock
C From Stranraer to Kilmarnock
D From Stranraer
E From Girvan

Mondays to Saturdays

Ayr, Largs and Ardrossan - Glasgow Central

Network Diagram - see first Page of Table 216

		SR	SR	SR	SR	SR	SR	SR	SR	SR	SR	SR	SR	SR	SR	SR	SR	SR	SR	SR	SR	SR
							A						A				◇ B					
Ayr	d			17 43		18 13	18 18		18 43		19 13		19 38	19 43		20 13	20 30		20 43		21 13	
Newton-on-Ayr	d					18 16					19 16					20 16					21 16	
Prestwick Town	d			17 48		18 19	18 23		18 48		19 19		19 43	19 48		20 19			20 48		21 19	
Prestwick Int. Airport ✈	d			17 50		18 21	18 25		18 50		19 21		19 45	19 50		20 21			20 50		21 21	
Troon	d			17 54		18 25	18a30		18 54		19 25		19a50	19 54		20 25			20 54		21 25	
Barassie	d					18 27					19 27					20 27					21 27	
Irvine	d			17 59		18 32			18 59		19 32			19 59		20 32			20 59		21 32	
Largs	d		17 35							18 53					19 53					20 53		
Fairlie	d		17 40							18 58					19 58					20 58		
West Kilbride	d		17 45							19 03					20 03					21 03		
Ardrossan Harbour	d				18 00							19 28						20 33				21 28
Ardrossan Town	d				18 03			18 32				19 30						20 35				21 31
Ardrossan South Beach	d	17 42	17 51		18 06			18 34		19 09		19 34			20 09			20 38		21 09		21 34
Saltcoats	d	17 44	17 53		18 08			18 36		19 11		19 36			20 11			20 40		21 11		21 36
Stevenston	d	17 47	17 56		18 11			18 39		19 14		19 39			20 14			20 43		21 14		21 39
Kilwinning ■4	d	17 50	18 00	18 04	18 16	18 37		18 43	19 04	19 18	19 37	19 43		20 04	20 18	20 36		20 48	21 04	21 18	21 37	21 43
Dalry	d	17 55	18 05	18 09		18 41		18 47				19 47						20 54			21 41	21 47
Glengarnock	d	17 59		18 13	18 23			18 51		19 25		19 51			20 25			20 58		21 25		21 51
Lochwinnoch	d			18 18				18 56				19 56						21 04				21 56
Howwood	d		18 14		18 30			19 00				20 00						21 08				22 00
Milliken Park	d	18 07			18 33			19 03		19 33		20 03			20 33			21 11		21 33		22 03
Johnstone	d	18 09	18 18	18 24	18 35	18 52		19 06	19 18	19 35	19 50	20 06		20 18	20 35	20 50		21 13	21 18	21 35	21 52	22 06
Paisley Gilmour Street 219	a	18 14	18 22	18 28	18 40	18 57		19 10	19 23	19 40	19 57	20 10		20 25	20 40	20 55	21 11	21 18	21 22	21 40	21 57	22 10
	d	18 14	18 23	18 29	18 40	18 57		19 11	19 23	19 40	19 57	20 11		20 25	20 40	20 55	21 12	21 18	21 23	21 40	21 57	22 11
Glasgow Central ■15 219	a	18 25	18 34	18 42	18 52	19 08		19 22	19 34	19 53	20 08	20 22		20 36	20 52	21 07	21 27	21 32	21 34	21 52	22 09	22 22

		SR	SR	SR	SR	SR	SR
					◇ B		
Ayr	d	21 43		22 13	22 35		23 00
Newton-on-Ayr	d			22 16			23 03
Prestwick Town	d	21 48		22 19	22 40		23 06
Prestwick Int. Airport ✈	d	21 50		22 21			23 08
Troon	d	21 54		22 25	22 45		23 12
Barassie	d			22 27			23 14
Irvine	d	21 59		22 32			23 19
Largs	d		21 53			22 53	
Fairlie	d		21 58			22 58	
West Kilbride	d		22 03			23 03	
Ardrossan Harbour	d						
Ardrossan Town	d						
Ardrossan South Beach	d		22 09			23 09	
Saltcoats	d		22 11			23 11	
Stevenston	d		22 14			23 14	
Kilwinning ■4	d	22 04	22 18	22 37	22 55	23 18	23 24
Dalry	d	22 09	22 23	22 41			23 28
Glengarnock	d		22 27			23 24	23 32
Lochwinnoch	d					23 29	
Howwood	d					23 33	
Milliken Park	d		22 35			23 36	
Johnstone	d	22 20	22 37	22 52		23 39	23 43
Paisley Gilmour Street 219	a	22 24	22 42	22 57	23 14	23 43	23 47
	d	22 25	22 42	22 57	23 15	23 44	23 48
Glasgow Central ■15 219	a	22 36	22 54	23 09	23 25	23 54	23 58

Sundays
until 30 September

		SR	SR	SR	SR	SR	SR	SR	SR	SR	SR	SR	SR	SR	SR	SR	SR	SR	SR	SR	SR	SR	SR
												◇ B											
Ayr	d	08 43		09 13	09 43		10 13	10 43		11 13	11 43	12 00		12 13		12 43		13 13	13 43		14 13	14 43	
Newton-on-Ayr	d																						
Prestwick Town	d	08 48		09 18	09 48		10 18	10 48		11 18	11 48			12 18		12 48		13 18	13 48		14 18	14 48	
Prestwick Int. Airport ✈	d	08 50		09 20	09 50		10 20	10 50		11 20	11 50			12 20		12 50		13 20	13 50		14 20	14 50	
Troon	d	08 54		09 24	09 54		10 24	10 54		11 24	11 54			12 24		12 54		13 24	13 54		14 24	14 54	
Barassie	d	08 56			09 56			10 56			11 56					12 56			13 56			14 56	
Irvine	d	09 01		09 29	10 01		10 29	11 01		11 29	12 01			12 29		13 01		13 29	14 01		14 29	15 01	
Largs	d		08 53			09 53			10 53				11 53				12 56			13 53			
Fairlie	d		08 58			09 58			10 58				11 58				13 01			13 58			
West Kilbride	d		09 03			10 03			11 03				12 03				13 06			14 03			
Ardrossan Harbour	d														12 35								15 04
Ardrossan Town	d																						
Ardrossan South Beach	d		09 09			10 09			11 09				12 09		12 40		13 12			14 09			15 09
Saltcoats	d		09 11			10 11			11 11				12 11		12 42		13 14			14 11			15 11
Stevenston	d		09 14			10 14			11 14				12 14		12 45		13 17			14 14			15 14
Kilwinning ■4	d	09 06	09 18	09 34	10 06	10 18	10 34	11 06	11 18	11 34	12 06	12 15	12 18	12 34	12 49	13 06	13 21	13 34	14 06	14 18	14 34	15 06	15 18
Dalry	d		09 23			10 23			11 23				12 23				13 25			14 23			
Glengarnock	d		09 27			10 27			11 27				12 27				13 29			14 27			
Lochwinnoch	d		09 32			10 32			11 32				12 32				13 34			14 32			
Howwood	d		09 36			10 36			11 36				12 36				13 38			14 36			
Milliken Park	d		09 39			10 39			11 39				12 39		13 02		13 41			14 39			15 31
Johnstone	d	09 19	09 41	09 48	10 19	10 41	10 48	11 19	11 41	11 51	12 19		12 42	12 51	13 04	13 19	13 44	13 51	14 19	14 41	14 48	15 19	15 33
Paisley Gilmour Street 219	a	09 24	09 46	09 52	10 24	10 46	10 52	11 24	11 46	11 55	12 24	12 36	12 46	12 55	13 09	13 24	13 48	13 55	14 24	14 46	14 52	15 24	15 38
	d	09 24	09 47	09 53	10 24	10 46	10 53	11 24	11 46	11 56	12 24	12 36	12 47	12 56	13 10	13 24	13 48	13 56	14 24	14 46	14 53	15 24	15 39
Glasgow Central ■15 219	a	09 36	09 58	10 04	10 36	10 58	11 07	11 36	11 58	12 06	12 36	12 51	12 58	13 06	13 22	13 36	14 02	14 06	14 36	14 58	15 06	15 36	15 50

A From Girvan to Kilmarnock B From Stranraer

Sundays
until 30 September

Ayr, Largs and Ardrossan - Glasgow Central

Network Diagram - see first Page of Table 216

		SR	SR	SR	SR	SR	SR	SR	SR	SR	SR	SR	SR	SR	SR	SR	SR	SR	SR	SR	SR	SR	SR
					◇ A																		◇ A
Ayr	d		15 13	15 43	15 59		16 13	16 43		17 13	17 43			18 13	18 43		19 13	19 43			20 43		21 04
Newton-on-Ayr	d																						
Prestwick Town	d		15 18	15 48			16 18	16 48		17 18	17 48			18 18	18 48		19 18	19 48			20 48		
Prestwick Int. Airport ✈	d		15 20	15 50			16 20	16 50		17 20	17 50			18 20	18 50		19 20	19 50			20 50		
Troon	d		15 24	15 54			16 24	16 54		17 24	17 54			18 24	18 54		19 24	19 54			20 54		
Barassie	d			15 56				16 56			17 56				18 56			19 56			20 56		
Irvine	d		15 29	16 01			16 29	17 01		17 29	18 01			18 29	19 01		19 29	20 01			21 01		
Largs	d	14 58				15 53			16 53				17 53			18 53			19 53			20 53	
Fairlie	d	15 03				15 58			16 58				18 00			18 58			19 58			20 58	
West Kilbride	d	15 08				16 03			17 03				18 05			19 03			20 03			21 03	
Ardrossan Harbour	d											18 00								20 31			
Ardrossan Town	d																						
Ardrossan South Beach	d	15 14				16 09			17 09			18 05	18 11			19 09			20 09	20 36		21 09	
Saltcoats	d	15 16				16 11			17 11			18 07	18 13			19 11			20 11	20 38		21 11	
Stevenston	d	15 19				16 14			17 14			18 10	18 16			19 14			20 14	20 41		21 14	
Kilwinning ■4	d	15 23	15 34	16 06	16 14	16 19	16 34	17 06	17 18	17 34	18 06	18 14	18 20	18 34	19 06	19 18	19 34	20 06	20 18	20 45	21 06	21 18	
Dalry	d	15 27				16 23			17 23				18 24			19 23			20 23			21 23	
Glengarnock	d	15 31				16 27			17 27				18 28			19 27			20 27			21 27	
Lochwinnoch	d	15 36				16 32			17 32				18 33			19 32			20 32			21 32	
Howwood	d	15 40				16 36			17 36				18 37			19 36			20 36			21 36	
Milliken Park	d	15 43				16 39			17 39			18 27	18 40			19 39			20 39	20 58		21 39	
Johnstone	d	15 46	15 48	16 19		16 42	16 50	17 19	17 41	17 51	18 19	18 29	18 43	18 48	19 19	19 41	19 48	20 19	20 41	21 00	21 19	21 41	
Paisley Gilmour Street 219	a	15 50	15 52	16 24	16 38	16 46	16 54	17 24	17 46	17 55	18 24	18 37	18 47	18 52	19 24	19 46	19 52	20 24	20 46	21 05	21 24	21 46	
	d	15 51	15 53	16 24	16 38	16 47	16 55	17 24	17 46	17 56	18 24	18 38	18 48	18 53	19 24	19 47	19 53	20 24	20 47	21 06	21 24	21 47	
Glasgow Central ■15 219	a	16 01	16 06	16 36	16 49	16 58	17 06	17 36	17 58	18 07	18 36	18 48	18 58	19 04	19 36	19 58	20 04	20 36	20 58	21 17	21 36	21 58	22 05

		SR	SR	SR	SR
Ayr	d	21 43		23 00	
Newton-on-Ayr	d				
Prestwick Town	d	21 48		23 05	
Prestwick Int. Airport ✈	d	21 50		23 07	
Troon	d	21 54		23 11	
Barassie	d	21 56		23 13	
Irvine	d	22 01		23 18	
Largs	d		21 53		23 01
Fairlie	d		21 58		23 06
West Kilbride	d		22 03		23 11
Ardrossan Harbour	d				
Ardrossan Town	d				
Ardrossan South Beach	d		22 09		23 17
Saltcoats	d		22 11		23 19
Stevenston	d		22 14		23 22
Kilwinning ■4	d	22 06	22 18	23 22	23 28
Dalry	d		22 23		23 32
Glengarnock	d		22 27		23 36
Lochwinnoch	d		22 32		23 41
Howwood	d		22 36		23 45
Milliken Park	d		22 39		23 48
Johnstone	d	22 19	22 41	23 37	23 51
Paisley Gilmour Street 219	a	22 24	22 46	23 42	23 55
	d	22 24	22 47	23 42	23 56
Glasgow Central ■15 219	a	22 36	22 58	23 54	00 07

Sundays
from 7 October

		SR	SR	SR	SR	SR	SR	SR	SR	SR	SR	SR	SR	SR	SR	SR	SR	SR	SR	SR	SR	SR	SR
							◇ A											◇ A					
Ayr	d	09 43		10 43		11 43	12 00			12 43		13 43		14 43			15 43	15 59		16 43		17 43	
Newton-on-Ayr	d																						
Prestwick Town	d	09 48		10 48		11 48				12 48		13 48		14 48			15 48			16 48		17 48	
Prestwick Int. Airport ✈	d	09 50		10 50		11 50				12 50		13 50		14 50			15 50			16 50		17 50	
Troon	d	09 54		10 54		11 54				12 54		13 54		14 54			15 54			16 54		17 54	
Barassie	d	09 56		10 56		11 56				12 56		13 56		14 56			15 56			16 56		17 56	
Irvine	d	10 01		11 01		12 01				13 01		14 01		15 01			16 01			17 01		18 01	
Largs	d		09 53		10 53			11 53			12 56		13 53			14 58			15 53		16 53		
Fairlie	d		09 58		10 58			11 58			13 01		13 58			15 03			15 58		16 58		
West Kilbride	d		10 03		11 03			12 03			13 06		14 03			15 08			16 03		17 03		
Ardrossan Harbour	d								12 35						15 04								18 00
Ardrossan Town	d																						
Ardrossan South Beach	d		10 09		11 09			12 09	12 40		13 12		14 09		15 09	15 14			16 09		17 09		18 05
Saltcoats	d		10 11		11 11			12 11	12 42		13 14		14 11		15 11	15 16			16 11		17 11		18 07
Stevenston	d		10 14		11 14			12 14	12 45		13 17		14 14		15 14	15 19			16 14		17 14		18 10
Kilwinning ■4	d	10 06	10 18	11 06	11 18	12 06	12 15	12 18	12 49	13 06	13 21	14 06	14 18	15 06	15 18	15 23	16 06	16 14	16 19	17 06	17 18	18 06	18 14
Dalry	d		10 23		11 23			12 23			13 25		14 23			15 27			16 23		17 23		
Glengarnock	d		10 27		11 27			12 27			13 29		14 27			15 31			16 27		17 27		
Lochwinnoch	d		10 32		11 32			12 32			13 34		14 32			15 36			16 32		17 32		
Howwood	d		10 36		11 36			12 36			13 38		14 36			15 40			16 36		17 36		
Milliken Park	d		10 39		11 39			12 39	13 02		13 41		14 39		15 31	15 43			16 39		17 39		18 27
Johnstone	d	10 19	10 41	11 19	11 41	12 19		12 42	13 04	13 19	13 44	14 19	14 41	15 19	15 33	15 46	16 19		16 42	17 19	17 41	18 19	18 29
Paisley Gilmour Street 219	a	10 24	10 46	11 24	11 46	12 24	12 36	12 46	13 09	13 24	13 48	14 24	14 46	15 24	15 38	15 50	16 24	16 38	16 46	17 24	17 46	18 24	18 37
	d	10 24	10 46	11 24	11 46	12 24	12 36	12 47	13 10	13 24	13 48	14 24	14 46	15 24	15 39	15 51	16 24	16 38	16 47	17 24	17 46	18 24	18 38
Glasgow Central ■15 219	a	10 36	10 58	11 36	11 58	12 36	12 51	12 58	13 22	13 36	14 02	14 36	14 58	15 36	15 50	16 01	16 36	16 49	16 58	17 36	17 58	18 36	18 48

A From Stranraer

Table 221

Sundays

from 7 October

Ayr, Largs and Ardrossan - Glasgow Central

Network Diagram - see first Page of Table 216

			SR	SR	SR	SR	SR		SR	SR	SR	SR ◇ A	SR	SR	SR	SR
Ayr		d		18 43		19 43				20 43		21 04	21 43		23 00	
Newton-on-Ayr		d														
Prestwick Town		d		18 48		19 48				20 48			21 48		23 05	
Prestwick Int. Airport ✈		d		18 50		19 50				20 50			21 50		23 07	
Troon		d		18 54		19 54				20 54			21 54		23 11	
Barassie		d		18 56		19 56				20 56			21 56		23 13	
Irvine		d		19 01		20 01				21 01			22 01		23 18	
Largs		d	17 53		18 53		19 53				20 53			21 53		23 01
Fairlie		d	18 00		18 58		19 58				20 58			21 58		23 06
West Kilbride		d	18 05		19 03		20 03				21 03			22 03		23 11
Ardrossan Harbour		d							20 31							
Ardrossan Town		d														
Ardrossan South Beach		d	18 11		19 09		20 09		20 36		21 09			22 09		23 17
Saltcoats		d	18 13		19 11		20 11		20 38		21 11			22 11		23 19
Stevenston		d	18 16		19 14		20 14		20 41		21 14			22 14		23 22
Kilwinning ■		d	18 20	19 06	19 18	20 06	20 18		20 45	21 06	21 18		22 06	22 18	23 22	23 28
Dalry		d	18 24		19 23		20 23				21 23			22 23		23 32
Glengarnock		d	18 28		19 27		20 27				21 27			22 27		23 36
Lochwinnoch		d	18 33		19 32		20 32				21 32			22 32		23 41
Howwood		d	18 37		19 36		20 36				21 36			22 36		23 45
Milliken Park		d	18 40		19 39		20 39		20 58		21 39			22 39		23 48
Johnstone		d	18 43	19 19	19 41	20 19	20 41		21 00	21 19	21 41		22 19	22 41	23 37	23 51
Paisley Gilmour Street	219	a	18 47	19 24	19 46	20 24	20 46		21 05	21 24	21 46		22 24	22 46	23 42	23 55
		d	18 48	19 24	19 47	20 24	20 47		21 06	21 24	21 47		22 24	22 47	23 42	23 56
Glasgow Central ■	219	a	18 58	19 36	19 58	20 36	20 58		21 17	21 36	21 58	22 05	22 36	22 58	23 54	00 07

A From Stranraer

Table 221A

SHIPPING SERVICES

Mondays to Saturdays

until 20 October 2012

Glasgow and Ardrossan - Brodick (Arran)

Caledonian MacBrayne Ltd in association with ScotRail

							FO
Glasgow Central ■	221	d	08 34	11 15	14 15	16 50	19 15
Paisley Gilmour Street	221	d	08 45	11 26	14 26	17 01	19 26
Ardrossan Harbour	221	a	09 26	12 09	15 09	17 45	20 09
Ardrossan Harbour	⛴	d	09 45	12 30	15 15	18 00	20 30
Brodick	⛴	a	10 40	13 25	16 10	18 55	21 25

Sundays

until 14 October 2012

Glasgow Central ■	221	d	08 40	11 15	14 05	16 54
Paisley Gilmour Street	221	d	08 51	11 26	14 16	17 07
Ardrossan Harbour	221	a	09 30	12 02	14 52	17 43
Ardrossan Harbour	⛴	d	09 45	12 30	15 15	18 00
Brodick	⛴	a	10 40	13 25	16 10	18 55

Mondays to Saturdays

until 20 October 2012

Brodick	⛴	d	08 20	11 05	13 50	16 40	19 20
Ardrossan Harbour	⛴	a	09 15	12 00	14 45	17 35	20 15
Ardrossan Harbour	221	d	09 31	12 28	15 28	18 00	20 33
Paisley Gilmour Street	221	a	10 10	13 10	16 10	18 40	21 14
Glasgow Central ■	221	a	10 22	13 22	16 25	18 52	21 32

Sundays

until 14 October 2012

Brodick	⛴	d	11 05	13 50	16 40	19 20
Ardrossan Harbour	⛴	a	12 00	14 45	17 35	20 15
Ardrossan Harbour	221	d	12 35	15 04	18 00	20 31
Paisley Gilmour Street	221	a	13 09	15 38	18 37	21 05
Glasgow Central ■	221	a	13 22	15 50	18 48	21 17

For details of sailings from 21 October 2012
please telephone 08000 66 5000 or visit www.calmac.co.uk

Table 221B

Mondays to Saturdays

Cairnryan (Loch Ryan Port) - Belfast Port

		SR MX	SR	SR	SR 🚌	SR	SR 🚌	SR	SR 🚌	SR		SR
Ayr	d				08 45		12 45		16 45			
Cairnryan (Loch Ryan Port) ⛴	a				09 55		13 55		17 55			
Cairnryan (Loch Ryan Port) ⛴	d	23p30	03 45	07 30		11 30		15 30		19 30		23 30
Belfast Port	a	01 45	06 00	09 45		13 45		17 45		21 45		01 45

Sundays

		SR	SR	SR 🚌	SR	SR 🚌	SR	SR 🚌	SR
Ayr	d			08 45		12 45		16 30	
Cairnryan (Loch Ryan Port) ⛴	a			09 55		13 55		17 40	
Cairnryan (Loch Ryan Port) ⛴	d	23p30	05 30		11 30		15 30		19 30
Belfast Port	a	01 45	07 45		13 45		17 45		21 45

Ferry service operated by Stena Line.
Please telephone 08447 70 70 70 or visit www.stenaline.co.uk for details

Table 221B

Mondays to Saturdays

Belfast Port - Cairnryan (Loch Ryan Port)

		SR MX	SR	SR	SR 🚌	SR	SR 🚌	SR	SR 🚌	SR		SR
Belfast Port	d	23p30	03 30	07 30		11 30		15 30		19 30		23 30
Cairnryan (Loch Ryan Port) ⛴	a	01 45	05 45	09 45		13 45		17 45		21 45		01 45
Cairnryan (Loch Ryan Port) ⛴	d				10 15		14 15		18 15			
Ayr	a				11 25		15 25		19 25			

Sundays

		SR	SR	SR 🚌	SR	SR 🚌	SR	SR 🚌	SR
Belfast Port	d	23p30	07 30		11 30		15 30		21 00
Cairnryan (Loch Ryan Port) ⛴	a	01 45	09 45		13 45		17 45		23 15
Cairnryan (Loch Ryan Port) ⛴	d			10 15		14 15		18 15	
Ayr	a			11 25		15 25		19 25	

Ferry service operated by Stena Line.
Please telephone 08447 70 70 70 or visit www.stenaline.co.uk for details

Table 222

Mondays to Saturdays

Glasgow Central - East Kilbride, Barrhead and Kilmarnock

Network Diagram - see first Page of Table 216

Miles	Miles			SR SO	SR SO	SR	SR	SR	SR	SR A	SR SX	SR SO		SR SX	SR	SR SX	SR SO	SR	SR	SR SX	SR SO	SR		SR B	SR
0	0	**Glasgow Central** 15	d	00 12	00 18	06 12	06 30	06 48	06 52	07 07	07 12	07 18		07 23	07 37	07 43	07 48	07 52	08 07	08 17	08 18	08 23		08 37	08 48
2¼	2¼	Crossmyloof	d	00 18	00 24	06 18	06 36	06 54	06 58		07 18	07 24		07 29		07 49	07 54	07 58		08 24	08 24	08 29			08 54
3¼	3¼	Pollokshaws West	d	00 21	00 27	06 21	06 39	06 57	07 01		07 21	07 27		07 32		07 52	07 57	08 01		08 27	08 27	08 32			08 57
—	4¼	Thornliebank	d		00 30	06 24		07 00			07 24	07 30				07 55	08 00			08 30	08 30				09 00
—	5¼	Giffnock	d		00 33	06 27		07 03			07 27	07 33				07 58	08 03			08 33	08 33				09 03
—	6½	Clarkston	d		00 37	06 31		07 07			07 31	07 37				08 02	08 07			08 37	08 37				09 07
—	7¼	Busby	d		00 40	06 34		07 10			07 35	07 40				08 08	08 10			08 40	08 40				09 10
—	8½	Thorntonhall	d		00 43	06 37											08 13			08 43					09 13
—	10	Hairmyres	d		00 47	06 41		07 15			07 41	07 45				08 14	08 16			08 46	08 46				09 16
—	11½	**East Kilbride**	a		00 51	06 45		07 19			07 50	07 50				08 18	08 21			08 51	08 51				09 21
4½	—	Kennishead	d	00 24			06 42		07 04					07 35				08 04				08 35			
5	—	Priesthill & Darnley	d	00 26			06 44		07 06					07 37				08 06				08 37			
5¾	—	Nitshill	d	00 29			06 47		07 09					07 40				08 09				08 40			
7½	—	**Barrhead**	d	00 33			06 51		07a14	07 22				07a44	07 50			08a15	08 21			08a46		08 49	
16½	—	Dunlop	d	00 45			07 03			07 34					08 02				08 33					09 01	
18¾	—	Stewarton	d	00 49			07 07			07 38					08 06				08 37					09 05	
22	—	Kilmaurs	d	00 53			07 11			07 44					08 10				08 41					09 10	
24¼	—	**Kilmarnock** 3	a	00 59			07 17			07 48					08 16				08 47					09 18	

		SR	SR	SR	SR	SR	SR	SR		SR B	SR	SR	SR	SR	SR	SR	SR	SR		SR	SR	SR	SR A	SR	SR
Glasgow Central 15	d	08 57	09 12	09 18	09 27	09 42	09 48	09 57		10 12	10 18	10 27	10 42	10 48	10 57	11 12	11 18	11 27		11 42	11 48	11 57	12 12	12 18	12 27
Crossmyloof	d	09 03		09 24	09 33		09 54	10 03			10 24	10 33		10 54	11 03		11 24	11 33			11 54	12 03		12 24	12 33
Pollokshaws West	d	09 06		09 27	09 36		09 57	10 06			10 27	10 36		10 57	11 06		11 27	11 36			11 57	12 06		12 27	12 36
Thornliebank	d			09 30			10 00				10 30			11 00			11 30				12 00			12 30	
Giffnock	d			09 33			10 03				10 33			11 03			11 33				12 03			12 33	
Clarkston	d			09 37			10 07				10 37			11 07			11 37				12 07			12 37	
Busby	d			09 40			10 10				10 40			11 10			11 40				12 10			12 40	
Thorntonhall	d						10 13							11 13							12 13				
Hairmyres	d			09 45			10 16				10 45			11 16			11 45				12 16			12 45	
East Kilbride	a			09 50			10 21				10 50			11 21			11 50				12 21			12 50	
Kennishead	d	09 09			09 39			10 09				10 39			11 09			11 39				12 09			12 39
Priesthill & Darnley	d	09 11			09 41			10 11				10 41			11 11			11 41				12 11			12 41
Nitshill	d	09 14			09 44			10 14				10 44			11 14			11 44				12 14			12 44
Barrhead	d	09a18			09a49	09 53		10a19				10a48	10 53		11a18			11a48		11 53		12a18			12a48
Dunlop	d					10 05							11 05			11 35				12 05					
Stewarton	d		09 39			10 09				10 39			11 09			11 39				12 09			12 37		
Kilmaurs	d					10 13							11 13			11 43				12 13					
Kilmarnock 3	a		09 49			10 21				10 51			11 21			11 50				12 21			12 48		

		SR	SR	SR		SR B	SR	SR	SR	SR	SR	SR	SR	SR		SR	SR	SR	SR C	SR	SR	SR	SR	SR	
Glasgow Central 15	d	12 42	12 48	12 57		13 12	13 18	13 27	13 42	13 48	13 57	14 12	14 18	14 27		14 42	14 48	14 57	15 12	15 18	15 27	15 42	15 48	15 57	
Crossmyloof	d		12 54	13 03			13 24	13 33		13 54	14 03		14 24	14 33			14 54	15 03		15 24	15 33		15 54	16 03	
Pollokshaws West	d		12 57	13 06			13 27	13 36		13 57	14 06		14 27	14 36			14 57	15 06		15 27	15 36		15 57	16 06	
Thornliebank	d		13 00				13 30			14 00			14 30				15 00			15 30			16 00		
Giffnock	d		13 03				13 33			14 03			14 33				15 03			15 33			16 03		
Clarkston	d		13 07				13 37			14 07			14 37				15 07			15 37			16 07		
Busby	d		13 10				13 40			14 10			14 40				15 10			15 40			16 10		
Thorntonhall	d		13 13							14 13							15 13						16 13		
Hairmyres	d		13 16				13 45			14 16			14 45				15 16			15 45			16 16		
East Kilbride	a		13 21				13 50			14 21			14 50				15 21			15 50			16 21		
Kennishead	d			13 09				13 39			14 09			14 39				15 09			15 39			16 09	
Priesthill & Darnley	d			13 11				13 41			14 11			14 41				15 11			15 41			16 11	
Nitshill	d			13 14				13 44			14 14			14 44				15 14			15 44			16 14	
Barrhead	d	12 53		13a18				13a48	13 53		14a18			14a48		14 53		15a18			15a48	15 53		16a18	
Dunlop	d	13 05							14 05			14 33				15 05			15 33			16 05			
Stewarton	d	13 09				13 39			14 09			14 37				15 09			15 37			16 09			
Kilmaurs	d	13 13							14 13			14 42				15 13			15 42			16 13			
Kilmarnock 3	a	13 20				13 50			14 21			14 49				15 21			15 50			16 21			

		SR A	SR	SR	SR	SR	SR	SR SX	SR C	SR SO		SR SX	SR	SR SX	SR B	SR SX	SR SO	SR	SR SX	SR		SR	SR	SR	SR
Glasgow Central 15	d	16 12	16 18	16 27	16 42	16 48	16 57	17 01	17 12	17 18		17 21	17 27	17 32	17 42	17 48	17 48	17 57	18 03	18 12		18 18	18 27	18 42	18 48
Crossmyloof	d		16 24	16 33		16 54	17 03	17 07		17 24			17 33	17 38		17 54	17 54	18 03	18 09			18 24	18 33		18 54
Pollokshaws West	d		16 27	16 36		16 57	17 06	17 10		17 27			17 36	17 41		17 57	17 57	18 06	18 12			18 27	18 36		18 57
Thornliebank	d		16 30			17 00		17 13		17 30				17 44		18 00	18 00		18 15			18 30			19 00
Giffnock	d		16 33			17 03		17 16		17 33				17 47		18 03	18 03		18 18			18 33			19 03
Clarkston	d		16 37			17 07		17 20		17 37		17 34		17 51		18 07	18 07		18 22			18 37			19 07
Busby	d		16 40			17 10		17 23		17 40				17 54		18 10	18 10		18 25			18 40			19 10
Thorntonhall	d		16 43			17 13				17 43				17 57			18 13		18 28						19 13
Hairmyres	d		16 46			17 16		17 28		17 46		17 44		18 00		18 15	18 16		18 31			18 45			19 16
East Kilbride	a		16 51			17 21		17 34		17 51		17 48		18 05		18 21	18 21		18 36			18 51			19 21
Kennishead	d			16 39			17 09						17 39					18 09					18 39		
Priesthill & Darnley	d			16 41			17 11						17 41					18 11					18 41		
Nitshill	d			16 44			17 14						17 44					18 14					18 44		
Barrhead	d	16 23		16a48	16 53		17a18		17 23				17a48		17 53			18a19		18 23			18a49	18 53	
Dunlop	d	16 35			17 05				17 35						18 05					18 35				19 05	
Stewarton	d	16 39			17 09				17 39						18 09					18 39				19 09	
Kilmaurs	d	16 43			17 13				17 43						18 13					18 43				19 13	
Kilmarnock 3	a	16 49			17 21				17 51						18 22					18 51				19 22	

A To Newcastle

B To Carlisle

C To Girvan

Glasgow Central - East Kilbride, Barrhead and Kilmarnock

Network Diagram - see first Page of Table 216

		SR	SR A	SR	SR	SR	SR	SR	SR	SR	SR D	SR	SR	SR	SR A	SR	SR	SR	SR B	SR
Glasgow Central 15	d	18 57	19 12	19 18	19 33	19 48	20 12	20 18	20 33	20 48	21 12	21 18	21 33	21 48	22 12	22 18	22 33	22 48	23 12	23 18
Crossmyloof	d	19 03		19 24	19 39	19 54		20 24	20 39	20 54		21 24	21 39	21 54		22 24	22 39	22 54	23 18	23 24
Pollokshaws West	d	19 06		19 27	19 42	19 57		20 27	20 42	20 57		21 27	21 42	21 57		22 27	22 42	22 57	23 21	23 27
Thornliebank	d			19 30		20 00		20 30		21 00		21 30		22 00		22 30		23 00		23 30
Giffnock	d			19 33		20 03		20 33		21 03		21 33		22 03		22 33		23 03		23 33
Clarkston	d			19 37		20 07		20 37		21 07		21 37		22 07		22 37		23 07		23 37
Busby	d			19 40		20 10		20 40		21 10		21 40		22 10		22 40		23 10		23 40
Thorntonhall	d					20 13				21 13				22 13				23 13		23 43
Hairmyres	d			19 45		20 16		20 45		21 16		21 45		22 16		22 45		23 16		23 46
East Kilbride	a			19 50		20 21		20 50		21 21		21 50		22 21		22 50		23 21		23 51
Kennishead	d	19 09			19 45				20 45				21 45				22 45		23 24	
Priesthill & Darnley	d	19 11			19 47				20 47				21 47				22 47		23 26	
Nitshill	d	19 14			19 50				20 50				21 50				22 50		23 29	
Barrhead	d	19a18	19 23		19 53		20 23		20 53		21 26		21 53		22 23		22 53		23 33	
Dunlop	d		19 35		20 05				21 05		21 37		22 05		22 35		23 05		23 45	
Stewarton	d		19 39		20 09		20 39		21 09		21 41		22 09		22 39		23 09		23 49	
Kilmaurs	d		19 43		20 13				21 14		21 46		22 13		22 43		23 13		23 53	
Kilmarnock 3	a		19 51		20 20		20 51		21 21		21 53		22 20		22 50		23 20		23 59	

Sundays

		SR	SR	SR	SR	SR	SR	SR	SR	SR	SR	SR	SR	SR	SR	SR	SR	SR	SR	SR	SR	SR	SR C
Glasgow Central 15	d	08 12	08 18	08 48	09 12	09 18	09 48	10 12	10 18	10 48	11 12	11 18	11 48	12 12	12 18	12 48	13 12	13 18	13 48	14 12	14 18	14 48	15 12
Crossmyloof	d		08 24	08 54		09 24	09 54		10 24	10 54		11 24	11 54		12 24	12 54		13 24	13 54		14 24	14 54	
Pollokshaws West	d	08 20	08 27	08 57	09 20	09 27	09 57	10 20	10 27	10 57	11 20	11 27	11 57	12 20	12 27	12 57	13 20	13 27	13 57	14 20	14 27	14 57	15 20
Thornliebank	d		08 30	09 00		09 30	10 00		10 30	11 00		11 30	12 00		12 30	13 00		13 30	14 00		14 30	15 00	
Giffnock	d		08 33	09 03		09 33	10 03		10 33	11 03		11 33	12 03		12 33	13 03		13 33	14 03		14 33	15 03	
Clarkston	d		08 37	09 07		09 37	10 07		10 37	11 07		11 37	12 07		12 37	13 07		13 37	14 07		14 37	15 07	
Busby	d		08 40	09 10		09 40	10 10		10 40	11 10		11 40	12 10		12 40	13 10		13 40	14 10		14 40	15 10	
Thorntonhall	d			09 13			10 13			11 13			12 13			13 13			14 13			15 13	
Hairmyres	d		08 46	09 17		09 46	10 17		10 46	11 17		11 46	12 17		12 46	13 17		13 46	14 17		14 46	15 17	
East Kilbride	a		08 50	09 21		09 50	10 21		10 50	11 21		11 50	12 21		12 50	13 21		13 50	14 21		14 50	15 21	
Kennishead	d																						
Priesthill & Darnley	d																						
Nitshill	d																						
Barrhead	d	08 26			09 26			10 26			11 26			12 26			13 26			14 26			15 26
Dunlop	d	08 38			09 38			10 38			11 38			12 38			13 38			14 38			15 38
Stewarton	d	08 42			09 42			10 42			11 42			12 42			13 42			14 42			15 42
Kilmaurs	d	08 46			09 46			10 46			11 46			12 46			13 46			14 46			15 46
Kilmarnock 3	a	08 52			09 52			10 52			11 52			12 52			13 52			14 52			15 52

		SR	SR	SR	SR	SR	SR	SR	SR	SR	SR	SR	SR	SR	SR	SR	SR	SR	SR	SR C	SR	SR	SR
Glasgow Central 15	d	15 18	15 48	16 12	16 18	16 48	17 12	17 18	17 48	18 12	18 18	18 48	19 12	19 18	19 48	20 18	20 48	21 18	21 48	22 12	22 18	22 48	23 18
Crossmyloof	d	15 24	15 54		16 24	16 54		17 24	17 54		18 24	18 54		19 24	19 54	20 24	20 54	21 24	21 54		22 24	22 54	23 24
Pollokshaws West	d	15 27	15 57	16 20	16 27	16 57	17 20	17 27	17 57	18 20	18 27	18 57	19 20	19 27	19 57	20 27	20 57	21 27	21 57		22 27	22 57	23 27
Thornliebank	d	15 30	16 00		16 30	17 00		17 30	18 00		18 30	19 00		19 30	20 00	20 30	21 00	21 30	22 00		22 30	23 00	23 30
Giffnock	d	15 33	16 03		16 33	17 03		17 33	18 03		18 33	19 03		19 33	20 03	20 33	21 03	21 33	22 03		22 33	23 03	23 33
Clarkston	d	15 37	16 07		16 37	17 07		17 37	18 07		18 37	19 07		19 37	20 07	20 37	21 07	21 37	22 07		22 37	23 07	23 37
Busby	d	15 40	16 10		16 40	17 10		17 40	18 10		18 40	19 10		19 40	20 10	20 40	21 10	21 40	22 10		22 40	23 10	23 40
Thorntonhall	d		16 13			17 13			18 13			19 13			20 13		21 13		22 13			23 13	23 43
Hairmyres	d	15 46	16 17		16 46	17 17		17 46	18 17		18 46	19 17		19 46	20 17	20 46	21 17	21 46	22 17		22 46	23 17	23 47
East Kilbride	a	15 50	16 21		16 50	17 21		17 50	18 21		18 50	19 21		19 50	20 21	20 50	21 21	21 50	22 21		22 50	23 21	23 51
Kennishead	d																						
Priesthill & Darnley	d																						
Nitshill	d																						
Barrhead	d			16 26			17 26			18 26			19 26							22 23			
Dunlop	d			16 38			17 38			18 38			19 38							22 35			
Stewarton	d			16 42			17 42			18 42			19 42							22 39			
Kilmaurs	d			16 46			17 46			18 46			19 46							22 44			
Kilmarnock 3	a			16 52			17 52			18 52			19 52							22 48			

A To Carlisle Saturdays only
B To Dumfries Monday to Friday only
C To Carlisle
D To Carlisle Monday to Friday only

Kilmarnock, Barrhead and East Kilbride - Glasgow Central

Network Diagram - see first Page of Table 216

Miles	Miles			SR MX	SR MO A	SR	SR SX	SR	SR	SR B	SR SX	SR SO	SR	SR SX	SR SO	SR SX	SR SX	SR	SR D	SR SX	SR	SR
0	—	**Kilmarnock** 3	d			05 22		06 22		06 52				07 22	07 22				07 53			
2¼	—	Kilmaurs	d			05 26		06 26		06 56				07 26	07 26				07 57			
5½	—	Stewarton	d			05 31		06 31		07 02				07 31	07 31				08 03			
7¾	—	Dunlop	d			05 36		06 36		07 06				07 36	07 36				08 08			
16¾	—	**Barrhead**	d			05 46		06 46		07 18	07 24	07 27		07 48	07 48		07 56		08 20		08 27	
18½	—	Nitshill	d			05 49		06 49			07 27	07 30			07 51		07 59				08 30	
19½	—	Priesthill & Darnley	d			05 52		06 52			07 29	07 32			07 53		08 01				08 32	
20	—	Kennishead	d			05 54		06 54			07 31	07 34			07 55		08 03				08 34	
—	0	**East Kilbride**	d	23p56	23p56		06 17		06 54				07 24			07 42		07 58		08 10		08 25
—	1½	Hairmyres	d	23p59	23p59		06 21		06 58				07 28			07 45		08 01		08 18		08 29
—	3	Thorntonhall	d	00 02	00 03		06 24		07 01				07 31					08 05				08 32
—	4¼	Busby	d	00 05	00 06		06 27		07 04				07 35					08 09		08 23		08 35
—	5	Clarkston	d	00 08	00 09		06 30		07 07				07 38			07 52		08 12		08 26		08 38
—	6¼	Giffnock	d	00 11	00 12		06 34		07 11				07 41					08 15		08 29		08 41
—	7¼	Thornliebank	d	00 14	00 14		06 36		07 13				07 44					08 18		08 31		08 44
21¼	8¼	Pollokshaws West	d	00 17	00 17	05 57	06 40	06 57	07 17		07 35	07 38	07 48		07 58		08 07	08 21		08 35	08 38	08 47
22¼	9¼	Crossmyloof	d	00 21	00 21	06 00	06 43	07 00	07 20		07 38	07 41	07 51		08 01		08 10	08 24		08 38	08 41	08 51
24¼	11½	**Glasgow Central** 15	a	00 27	00 27	06 08	06 49	07 08	07 27	07 31	07 45	07 47	07 57	08 00	08 09	08 09	08 16	08 31	08 37	08 45	08 49	08 58

		SR	SR	SR	SR	SR	SR	SR	SR	SR	SR E	SR	SR	SR	SR	SR	SR	SR	SR	SR	SR	SR	SR
Kilmarnock 3	d	08 23			08 57			09 27			09 57			10 27			10 57			11 27			11 57
Kilmaurs	d	08 27			09 01			09 31			10 01			10 31			11 01			11 31			12 01
Stewarton	d	08 32			09 06			09 36			10 06			10 36			11 06			11 36			12 06
Dunlop	d	08 37			09 11			09 41			10 11			10 41			11 11			11 41			12 11
Barrhead	d	08 49	08 57		09 22	09 27		09 52	09 57		10 22	10 27		10 52	10 57			11 27		11 52	11 57		
Nitshill	d		09 00			09 30			10 00			10 30			11 00			11 30			12 00		
Priesthill & Darnley	d		09 02			09 32			10 02			10 32			11 02			11 32			12 02		
Kennishead	d		09 04			09 34			10 04			10 34			11 04			11 34			12 04		
East Kilbride	d			08 55			09 26			09 55			10 26			10 55			11 26			11 55	
Hairmyres	d			08 59			09 30			09 59			10 30			10 59			11 30			11 59	
Thorntonhall	d			09 02						10 02						11 02						12 02	
Busby	d			09 05			09 35			10 05			10 35			11 05			11 35			12 05	
Clarkston	d			09 08			09 38			10 08			10 38			11 08			11 38			12 08	
Giffnock	d			09 11			09 41			10 11			10 41			11 11			11 41			12 11	
Thornliebank	d			09 14			09 44			10 14			10 44			11 14			11 44			12 14	
Pollokshaws West	d		09 07	09 17		09 37	09 47		10 07	10 17		10 37	10 47		11 07	11 17		11 37	11 47		12 07	12 17	
Crossmyloof	d		09 11	09 21		09 41	09 51		10 11	10 21		10 41	10 51		11 11	11 21		11 41	11 51		12 11	12 21	
Glasgow Central 15	a	09 03	09 17	09 27	09 36	09 47	09 57	10 07	10 17	10 27	10 37	10 47	10 57	11 06	11 17	11 27	11 35	11 47	11 57	12 05	12 17	12 27	12 34

		SR	SR	SR	SR	SR	SR F	SR	SR	SR	SR	SR	SR	SR	SR	SR	SR	SR	SR F	SR	SR	SR
Kilmarnock 3	d			12 27			12 57			13 27			13 57			14 27			14 57			15 27
Kilmaurs	d			12 31						13 31			14 01			14 31						15 31
Stewarton	d			12 36			13 06			13 36			14 06			14 36			15 06			15 36
Dunlop	d			12 41						13 41			14 11			14 41						15 41
Barrhead	d	12 27		12 52	12 57			13 27		13 52	13 57			14 27		14 52	14 57			15 27		15 52
Nitshill	d	12 30			13 00			13 30			14 00			14 30			15 00			15 30		
Priesthill & Darnley	d	12 32			13 02			13 32			14 02			14 32			15 02			15 32		
Kennishead	d	12 34			13 04			13 34			14 04			14 34			15 04			15 34		
East Kilbride	d		12 26			12 55			13 26			13 55			14 26			14 55			15 26	
Hairmyres	d		12 30			12 59			13 30			13 59			14 30			14 59			15 30	
Thorntonhall	d					13 02						14 02						15 02				
Busby	d		12 35			13 05			13 35			14 05			14 35			15 05			15 35	
Clarkston	d		12 38			13 08			13 38			14 08			14 38			15 08			15 38	
Giffnock	d		12 41			13 11			13 41			14 11			14 41			15 11			15 41	
Thornliebank	d		12 44			13 14			13 44			14 14			14 44			15 14			15 44	
Pollokshaws West	d	12 37	12 47		13 07	13 17		13 37	13 47		14 07	14 17		14 37	14 47		15 07	15 17		15 37	15 47	
Crossmyloof	d	12 41	12 51		13 11	13 21		13 41	13 51		14 11	14 21		14 41	14 51		15 11	15 21		15 41	15 51	
Glasgow Central 15	a	12 47	12 57	13 05	13 17	13 27	13 35	13 47	13 57	14 05	14 17	14 27	14 33	14 47	14 57	15 05	15 19	15 27	15 33	15 47	15 57	16 06

		SR	SR	SR G	SR	SR	SR	SR	SR	SR E	SR	SR	SR	SR	SR SO	SR SX	SR	SR	SR SO	SR SX	SR	SR	SR
Kilmarnock 3	d			15 57			16 27			16 57			17 27				17 57				18 27		
Kilmaurs	d			16 01			16 31			17 01			17 31				18 01				18 31		
Stewarton	d			16 06			16 36			17 06			17 36				18 06				18 36		
Dunlop	d			16 11			16 41			17 11			17 41				18 11				18 41		
Barrhead	d	15 57			16 27		16 52	16 57		17 22	17 27		17 52	17 57			18 22	18 27			18 52	18 57	
Nitshill	d	16 00			16 30			17 00			17 30			18 00				18 30				19 00	
Priesthill & Darnley	d	16 02			16 32			17 02			17 32			18 02				18 32				19 02	
Kennishead	d	16 04			16 34			17 04			17 34			18 04				18 34				19 04	
East Kilbride	d		15 55			16 26			16 55			17 26			17 55	17 55			18 26	18 26			18 55
Hairmyres	d		15 59			16 30			16 59			17 30			17 59	18 05			18 30	18 36			18 59
Thorntonhall	d		16 02						17 02						18 02	18 08							19 02
Busby	d		16 05			16 35			17 05			17 35			18 05	18 11			18 35	18 41			19 05
Clarkston	d		16 08			16 38			17 08			17 38			18 08	18 14			18 38	18 44			19 08
Giffnock	d		16 11			16 41			17 11			17 41			18 11	18 18			18 41	18 47			19 11
Thornliebank	d		16 14			16 44			17 14			17 44			18 14	18 20			18 44	18 50			19 14
Pollokshaws West	d	16 07	16 17		16 37	16 47		17 07	17 17		17 37	17 47		18 07	18 17	18 23		18 37	18 47	18 53		19 07	19 17
Crossmyloof	d	16 11	16 21		16 41	16 51		17 11	17 21		17 41	17 51		18 11	18 21	18 26		18 41	18 51	18 56		19 11	19 21
Glasgow Central 15	a	16 17	16 27	16 33	16 47	16 57	17 05	17 18	17 27	17 36	17 49	17 58	18 05	18 17	18 27	18 32	18 37	18 47	18 57	19 03	19 07	19 19	19 27

A from 21 May
B From Dumfries
C from 7 July until 4 August. From Carlisle
D From Carlisle
E From Newcastle
F From Carlisle
G From Girvan

Kilmarnock, Barrhead and East Kilbride - Glasgow Central

Network Diagram - see first Page of Table 216

		SR	SR	SR	SR	SR	SR A	SR	SR	SR	SR B
Kilmarnock	d	18 57			19 27		19 57		20 27		21 00
Kilmaurs	d	19 01			19 31				20 31		
Stewarton	d	19 06			19 36		20 06		20 36		21 10
Dunlop	d	19 11			19 41				20 41		
Barrhead	d	19 22	19 27		19 51		20 22		20 51		21 25
Nitshill	d		19 30		19 54				20 54		
Priesthill & Darnley	d		19 32		19 57				20 57		
Kennishead	d		19 34		19 59				20 59		
East Kilbride	d			19 26		19 55		20 26		20 55	
Hairmyres	d			19 30		19 59		20 30		20 59	
Thorntonhall	d					20 02				21 02	
Busby	d			19 35		20 05		20 35		21 05	
Clarkston	d			19 38		20 08		20 38		21 08	
Giffnock	d			19 41		20 11		20 41		21 11	
Thornliebank	d			19 44		20 14		20 44		21 14	
Pollokshaws West	d		19 37	19 47	20 02	20 17		20 47	21 02	21 17	
Crossmyloof	d		19 41	19 51	20 05	20 21		20 51	21 05	21 21	
Glasgow Central	a	19 37	19 47	19 57	20 13	20 27	20 36	20 57	21 13	21 27	21 39

		SR	SR	SR	SR	SR	SR	SR	SR A	SR	SR
Kilmarnock	d		21 27		21 57		22 27		22 57		
Kilmaurs	d		21 31				22 31		23 01		
Stewarton	d		21 36		22 06		22 36		23 06		
Dunlop	d		21 41				22 41		23 11		
Barrhead	d		21 51		22 22		22 51		23 22		
Nitshill	d		21 54				22 54				
Priesthill & Darnley	d		21 57				22 57				
Kennishead	d		21 59				22 59				
East Kilbride	d	21 26		21 55		22 26		22 55		23 26	23 56
Hairmyres	d	21 30		21 59		22 30		22 59		23 30	23 59
Thorntonhall	d			22 02				23 02			00 02
Busby	d	21 35		22 05		22 35		23 05		23 35	00 05
Clarkston	d	21 38		22 08		22 38		23 08		23 38	00 08
Giffnock	d	21 41		22 11		22 41		23 11		23 41	00 11
Thornliebank	d	21 44		22 14		22 44		23 14		23 44	00 14
Pollokshaws West	d	21 47	22 02	22 17		22 47	23 02	23 17		23 47	00 17
Crossmyloof	d	21 51	22 05	22 21		22 51	23 05	23 21		23 50	00 21
Glasgow Central	a	21 57	22 13	22 27	22 37	22 57	23 13	23 27	23 35	23 56	00 27

Sundays

		SR	SR	SR	SR	SR	SR	SR	SR	SR	SR	SR
Kilmarnock	d				08 57			09 57			10 57	
Kilmaurs	d				09 01			10 01			11 01	
Stewarton	d				09 06			10 06			11 06	
Dunlop	d				09 11			10 11			11 11	
Barrhead	d				09 21			10 21			11 21	
Nitshill	d											
Priesthill & Darnley	d											
Kennishead	d											
East Kilbride	d	23p56	08 26	08 55		09 26	09 55		10 26	10 55		11 26
Hairmyres	d	23p59	08 30	08 59		09 30	09 59		10 30	10 59		11 30
Thorntonhall	d	00 02		09 02			10 02			11 02		
Busby	d	00 05	08 35	09 05		09 35	10 05		10 35	11 05		11 35
Clarkston	d	00 08	08 38	09 08		09 38	10 08		10 38	11 08		11 38
Giffnock	d	00 11	08 41	09 12		09 41	10 12		10 41	11 12		11 41
Thornliebank	d	00 14	08 44	09 14		09 44	10 14		10 44	11 14		11 44
Pollokshaws West	d	00 17	08 47	09 17	09 27	09 47	10 17	10 27	10 47	11 17	11 27	11 47
Crossmyloof	d	00 21	08 50	09 20		09 50	10 20		10 50	11 20		11 50
Glasgow Central	a	00 27	08 56	09 26	09 36	09 56	10 26	10 40	10 56	11 26	11 36	11 56

		SR	SR	SR	SR	SR	SR	SR	SR	SR	SR	SR A
Kilmarnock	d		11 57			12 57			13 57			14 57
Kilmaurs	d		12 01			13 01			14 01			15 01
Stewarton	d		12 06			13 06			14 06			15 06
Dunlop	d		12 11			13 11			14 11			15 11
Barrhead	d		12 21			13 21			14 21			15 21
Nitshill	d											
Priesthill & Darnley	d											
Kennishead	d											
East Kilbride	d	11 55		12 26	12 55		13 26	13 55		14 26	14 55	
Hairmyres	d	11 59		12 30	12 59		13 30	13 59		14 30	14 59	
Thorntonhall	d	12 02			13 02			14 02			15 02	
Busby	d	12 05		12 35	13 05		13 35	14 05		14 35	15 05	
Clarkston	d	12 08		12 38	13 08		13 38	14 08		14 38	15 08	
Giffnock	d	12 12		12 41	13 12		13 41	14 12		14 41	15 12	
Thornliebank	d	12 14		12 44	13 14		13 44	14 14		14 44	15 14	
Pollokshaws West	d	12 17	12 27	12 47	13 17	13 27	13 47	14 17	14 27	14 47	15 17	15 27
Crossmyloof	d	12 20		12 50	13 20		13 50	14 20		14 50	15 20	
Glasgow Central	a	12 26	12 36	12 56	13 26	13 36	13 56	14 26	14 36	14 56	15 26	15 36

		SR	SR	SR	SR	SR	SR	SR	SR	SR	SR	SR
Kilmarnock	d			15 57			16 57			17 57		
Kilmaurs	d			16 01			17 01			18 01		
Stewarton	d			16 06			17 06			18 06		
Dunlop	d			16 11			17 11			18 11		
Barrhead	d			16 21			17 21			18 21		
Nitshill	d											
Priesthill & Darnley	d											
Kennishead	d											
East Kilbride	d	15 26	15 55		16 26	16 55		17 26	17 55		18 26	18 55
Hairmyres	d	15 30	15 59		16 30	16 59		17 30	17 59		18 30	18 59
Thorntonhall	d		16 02			17 02			18 02			19 02
Busby	d	15 35	16 05		16 35	17 05		17 35	18 05		18 35	19 05
Clarkston	d	15 38	16 08		16 38	17 08		17 38	18 08		18 38	19 08
Giffnock	d	15 41	16 12		16 41	17 12		17 41	18 12		18 41	19 12
Thornliebank	d	15 44	16 14		16 44	17 14		17 44	18 14		18 44	19 14
Pollokshaws West	d	15 47	16 17	16 27	16 47	17 17	17 27	17 47	18 17	18 27	18 47	19 17
Crossmyloof	d	15 50	16 20		16 50	17 20		17 50	18 20		18 50	19 20
Glasgow Central	a	15 56	16 26	16 36	16 56	17 26	17 36	17 56	18 26	18 36	18 56	19 26

		SR	SR	SR	SR	SR	SR	SR A	SR	SR ◇ C	SR	SR
Kilmarnock	d	18 57			19 57			20 57		21 31		
Kilmaurs	d	19 01			20 01			21 01				
Stewarton	d	19 06			20 06			21 06				
Dunlop	d	19 11			20 11			21 11				
Barrhead	d	19 21			20 21			21 21				
Nitshill	d											
Priesthill & Darnley	d											
Kennishead	d											
East Kilbride	d		19 26	19 55		20 26	20 55		21 26		21 55	22 26
Hairmyres	d		19 30	19 59		20 30	20 59		21 30		21 59	22 30
Thorntonhall	d			20 02			21 02				22 02	
Busby	d		19 35	20 05		20 35	21 05		21 35		22 05	22 35
Clarkston	d		19 38	20 08		20 38	21 08		21 38		22 08	22 38
Giffnock	d		19 41	20 12		20 41	21 12		21 41		22 12	22 41
Thornliebank	d		19 44	20 14		20 44	21 14		21 44		22 14	22 44
Pollokshaws West	d	19 27	19 47	20 17	20 27	20 47	21 17		21 47		22 17	22 47
Crossmyloof	d		19 50	20 20		20 50	21 20		21 50		22 20	22 50
Glasgow Central	a	19 36	19 56	20 26	20 36	20 56	21 26	21 35	21 56	22 05	22 26	22 56

		SR	SR	SR
Kilmarnock	d			
Kilmaurs	d			
Stewarton	d			
Dunlop	d			
Barrhead	d			
Nitshill	d			
Priesthill & Darnley	d			
Kennishead	d			
East Kilbride	d	22 55	23 26	23 56
Hairmyres	d	22 59	23 30	23 59
Thorntonhall	d	23 02		00 03
Busby	d	23 05	23 35	00 06
Clarkston	d	23 08	23 38	00 09
Giffnock	d	23 12	23 41	00 12
Thornliebank	d	23 14	23 44	00 14
Pollokshaws West	d	23 17	23 47	00 17
Crossmyloof	d	23 20	23 50	00 21
Glasgow Central	a	23 26	23 56	00 27

A From Carlisle B From Newcastle C From Stranraer

Glasgow Central, Cathcart Circle, Neilston and Newton

Network Diagram - see first Page of Table 220

Miles	Miles	Miles			SR SO	SR SO	SR SO	SR	SR	SR	SR	SR SX	SR SO	SR SX
0	0	0	**Glasgow Central**	226 d	23p50	00 05	00 20	06 14	06 17	06 20	06 34	06 36	06 45	06 50
2¼	—	—	Pollokshields West	d			00 27	06 20				06 42	06 51	
2¾	—	—	Maxwell Park	d			00 29	06 22				06 44	06 53	
3½	—	—	Shawlands	d			00 31	06 24				06 46	06 55	
3¾	—	—	Pollokshaws East	d			00 32	06 25				06 48	06 56	
4¼	—	—	Langside	d			00 34	06 27				06 50	06 58	
—	1¾	1¾	Pollokshields East	d	23p55	00 10			06 22	06 25	06 39			06 55
—	2¼	2¼	Queens Park	d	23p56	00 11			06 23	06 26	06 40			06 56
—	2½	2½	Crosshill	d	23p58	00 13			06 25	06 28	06 42			06 58
—	3¼	3¼	Mount Florida	d	23p59	00 15			06 27	06 30	06 44			07 00
5¼	—	4	Cathcart	d		00 17	00a37	06a30	06 29		06 46			07a03
—	—	4¾	Muirend	d		00 20			06 32		06 49			
—	—	6	Williamwood	d		00 23			06 35		06 52			
—	—	6¾	Whitecraigs	d		00 25			06 37		06 54			
—	—	7¾	Patterton	d		00 28			06 40		06 57			
—	—	11¾	**Neilston**	a		00 34			06 46		07 03			
5¾	4½	—	Kings Park	d	00 03					06 33		06 54	07 03	
6	4¾	—	Croftfoot	d	00 05					06 35		06 56	07 05	
7	5¾	—	Burnside	d	00 08					06 38		06 58	07 08	
8½	7¼	—	Kirkhill	a	00 11					06 41		07 01	07 11	
10	8¾	—	**Newton**	226 a	00 14					06 45		07 04	07 14	

		SR SX	SR SX	SR	SR SX	SR	SR SX	SR SO	SR SX	SR
Glasgow Central	226 d	07 00	07 03	07 06	07 14	07 20	07 29	07 35	07 35	07 45
Pollokshields West	d		07 09		07 20					07 51
Maxwell Park	d		07 11		07 22					07 53
Shawlands	d		07 13		07 24					07 55
Pollokshaws East	d		07 14		07 25					07 56
Langside	d		07 16		07 27					07 58
Pollokshields East	d	07 05		07 11		07 25	07 34	07 40	07 40	
Queens Park	d	07 06		07 12		07 26	07 35	07 41	07 41	
Crosshill	d	07 08		07 14		07 28	07 37	07 43	07 43	
Mount Florida	d	07 10		07 16		07 30	07 39	07 45	07 45	
Cathcart	d	07 12		07 20	07a30		07 41	07 47	07a47	
Muirend	d	07 15		07 23			07 44	07 50		
Williamwood	d	07 18		07 26			07 47	07 53		
Whitecraigs	d	07 20		07 28			07 49	07 55		
Patterton	d	07 23		07 31			07 52	07 58		
Neilston	a	07 29		07 37			07 58	08 04		
Kings Park	d		07 20			07 33				08 03
Croftfoot	d		07 22			07 35				08 05
Burnside	d		07 25			07 38				08 08
Kirkhill	a		07 28			07 41				08 11
Newton	226 a		07 31			07 44				08 14

		SR SX	SR SX	SR SX	SR SX	SR SO	SR SX	SR SX	SR SX	SR	SR SX	SR SX
Glasgow Central	226 d	07 48	07 54	07 56	08 01	08 05	08 10	08 12	08 15	08 20	08 26	08 33
Pollokshields West	d		08 00				08 16					08 39
Maxwell Park	d		08 02				08 18					08 41
Shawlands	d		08 04				08 20					08 43
Pollokshaws East	d		08 05				08 21					08 44
Langside	d		08 07				08 23					08 46
Pollokshields East	d			08 01	08 06	08 10		08 17	08 21	08 25	08 31	
Queens Park	d			08 02	08 07	08 11		08 18	08 22	08 26	08 32	
Crosshill	d			08 04	08 09	08 13		08 20	08 24	08 28	08 34	
Mount Florida	d			08 06	08 11	08 15		08 22	08 26	08 30	08 36	
Cathcart	d		08a10		08 13	08 17	08a26	08a24	08a28		08 38	08a49
Muirend	d	07 58			08 16	08 20					08 41	
Williamwood	d	08 01			08 19	08 23					08 44	
Whitecraigs	d	08 03			08 21	08 25					08 46	
Patterton	d	08 06			08 24	08 28					08 49	
Neilston	a	08 12			08 30	08 34					08 55	
Kings Park	d			08 09						08 33		
Croftfoot	d			08 11						08 35		
Burnside	d			08 14						08 38		
Kirkhill	a			08 17						08 41		
Newton	226 a			08 20						08 44		

		SR SO	SR SX	SR	SR	SR SO	SR SX	SR	SR	SR	SR	SR
Glasgow Central	226 d	08 35	08 39	08 45	08 50	09 05	09 08	09 14	09 20	09 35	09 45	09 50
Pollokshields West	d			08 51				09 20			09 51	
Maxwell Park	d			08 53				09 22			09 53	
Shawlands	d			08 55				09 24			09 55	
Pollokshaws East	d			08 56				09 25			09 56	
Langside	d			08 58				09 27			09 58	
Pollokshields East	d	08 40	08 44		08 55	09 10	09 13		09 25	09 40		09 55
Queens Park	d	08 41	08 45		08 57	09 11	09 14		09 26	09 41		09 56
Crosshill	d	08 43	08 47		08 59	09 13	09 16		09 28	09 43		09 58
Mount Florida	d	08 45	08 49		09 01	09 15	09 18		09 30	09 45		10 00
Cathcart	d	08 47	08 51		09a03	09 17	09 20	09a30		09 47		10a03
Muirend	d	08 50	08 54			09 20	09 23			09 50		
Williamwood	d	08 53	08 57			09 23	09 26			09 53		
Whitecraigs	d	08 55	08 59			09 25	09 28			09 55		
Patterton	d	08 58	09 02			09 28	09 31			09 58		
Neilston	a	09 04	09 08			09 34	09 37			10 04		
Kings Park	d			09 03					09 33		10 03	
Croftfoot	d			09 05					09 35		10 05	
Burnside	d			09 08					09 38		10 08	
Kirkhill	a			09 11					09 41		10 11	
Newton	226 a			09 15					09 45		10 14	

		SR	SR	SR SO	SR SX	SR	SR	SR	SR	SR	SR	SR
Glasgow Central	226 d	10 05	10 15	10 20	10 20	10 35	10 45	10 50	11 05	11 15	11 20	11 35
Pollokshields West	d		10 21				10 51			11 21		
Maxwell Park	d		10 23				10 53			11 23		
Shawlands	d		10 25				10 55			11 25		
Pollokshaws East	d		10 26				10 56			11 26		
Langside	d		10 28				10 58			11 28		
Pollokshields East	d	10 10		10 25	10 25	10 40		10 55	11 10		11 25	11 40
Queens Park	d	10 11		10 26	10 26	10 41		10 56	11 11		11 26	11 41
Crosshill	d	10 13		10 28	10 28	10 43		10 58	11 13		11 28	11 43
Mount Florida	d	10 15		10 30	10 30	10 45		11 00	11 15		11 30	11 45
Cathcart	d	10 17	10a31			10 47		11a03	11 17	11a31		11 47
Muirend	d	10 20				10 50			11 20			11 50
Williamwood	d	10 23				10 53			11 23			11 53
Whitecraigs	d	10 25				10 55			11 25			11 55
Patterton	d	10 28				10 58			11 28			11 58
Neilston	a	10 34				11 04			11 34			12 04
Kings Park	d			10 33	10 33		11 03				11 33	
Croftfoot	d			10 35	10 35		11 05				11 35	
Burnside	d			10 38	10 38		11 08				11 38	
Kirkhill	a			10 41	10 41		11 11				11 41	
Newton	226 a			10 44	10 45		11 14				11 44	

		SR	SR	SR	SR	SR	SR	SR	SR	SR	SR	SR
Glasgow Central	226 d	11 45	11 50	12 05	12 15	12 20	12 35	12 45	12 50	13 05	13 15	13 20
Pollokshields West	d	11 51			12 21			12 51			13 21	
Maxwell Park	d	11 53			12 23			12 53			13 23	
Shawlands	d	11 55			12 25			12 55			13 25	
Pollokshaws East	d	11 56			12 26			12 56			13 26	
Langside	d	11 58			12 28			12 58			13 28	
Pollokshields East	d		11 55	12 10		12 25	12 40		12 55	13 10		13 25
Queens Park	d		11 56	12 11		12 26	12 41		12 56	13 11		13 26
Crosshill	d		11 58	12 13		12 28	12 43		12 58	13 13		13 28
Mount Florida	d		12 00	12 15		12 30	12 45		13 00	13 15		13 30
Cathcart	d		12a03	12 17	12a31		12 47		13a03	13 17	13a31	
Muirend	d			12 20			12 50			13 20		
Williamwood	d			12 23			12 53			13 23		
Whitecraigs	d			12 25			12 55			13 25		
Patterton	d			12 28			12 58			13 28		
Neilston	a			12 34			13 04			13 34		
Kings Park	d	12 03				12 33		13 03				13 33
Croftfoot	d	12 05				12 35		13 05				13 35
Burnside	d	12 08				12 38		13 08				13 38
Kirkhill	a	12 11				12 41		13 11				13 41
Newton	226 a	12 14				12 44		13 14				13 44

Table 223

Mondays to Saturdays

Glasgow Central, Cathcart Circle, Neilston and Newton

Network Diagram - see first Page of Table 220

	SR	SR	SR	SR	SR	SR SO	SR SX	SR	SR	SR	SR	SR	SR	SR	SR	SR SO	SR SX	SR SO	SR SX	SR	SR
Glasgow Central 226 d	13 35	13 45	13 50	14 05	14 15	14 20	14 20	14 35	14 45	14 50	15 05	15 15	15 20	15 35	15 45	15 50	15 50	16 05	16 05	16 15	16 20
Pollokshields West d		13 51			14 21				14 51			15 21			15 51					16 21	
Maxwell Park d		13 53			14 23				14 53			15 23			15 53					16 23	
Shawlands d		13 55			14 25				14 55			15 25			15 55					16 25	
Pollokshaws East d		13 56			14 26				14 56			15 26			15 56					16 26	
Langside d		13 58			14 28				14 58			15 28			15 58					16 28	
Pollokshields East d	13 40		13 55	14 10		14 25	14 25	14 40		14 55	15 10		15 25	15 40		15 55	15 55	16 10	16 10		16 25
Queens Park d	13 41		13 56	14 11		14 26	14 26	14 41		14 56	15 11		15 26	15 41		15 57	15 57	16 11	16 11		16 27
Crosshill d	13 43		13 58	14 13		14 28	14 28	14 43		14 58	15 13		15 28	15 43		15 59	16 03	16 13	16 13		16 29
Mount Florida d	13 45		14 00	14 15		14 30	14 30	14 45		15 00	15 15		15 30	15 45		16 02	16 05	16 15	16 15		16 31
Cathcart d	13 47		14a03	14 17	14a31			14 47		15a03	15 17	15a31		15 47		16a04	16a06	16 17	16 17	16a31	
Muirend d	13 50			14 20				14 50			15 20			15 50				16 20	16 20		
Williamwood d	13 53			14 23				14 53			15 23			15 53				16 23	16 23		
Whitecraigs d	13 55			14 25				14 55			15 25			15 55				16 25	16 25		
Patterton d	13 58			14 28				14 58			15 28			15 58				16 28	16 28		
Neilston a	14 04			14 34				15 04			15 34			16 04				16 36	16 38		
Kings Park d		14 03				14 33	14 33		15 03				15 33		16 03						16 34
Croftfoot d		14 05				14 35	14 35		15 05				15 35		16 05						16 36
Burnside d		14 08				14 38	14 38		15 08				15 38		16 08						16 38
Kirkhill a		14 11				14 41	14 41		15 11				15 41		16 11						16 41
Newton 226 a		14 14				14 44	14 45		15 14				15 45		16 15						16 45

	SR	SR	SR	SR SX	SR SX	SR SO	SR SX	SR SX	SR SO	SR SX	SR SO	SR SX	SR SX	SR SO	SR SX	SR	SR	SR	SR	SR	SR	SR
Glasgow Central 226 d	16 35	16 45	16 50	16 59	17 05	17 07	17 08	17 14	17 15	17 18	17 20	17 23	17 29	17 35	17 38	17 45	17 50	18 07	18 15	18 20	18 35	18 45
Pollokshields West d		16 51			17 11				17 21			17 29				17 51			18 21			18 51
Maxwell Park d		16 53			17 13				17 23			17 32				17 53			18 23			18 53
Shawlands d		16 55			17 15				17 25			17 34				17 55			18 25			18 55
Pollokshaws East d		16 56			17 16				17 26			17 35				17 56			18 26			18 56
Langside d		16 58			17 18				17 28			17 37				17 58			18 28			18 58
Pollokshields East d	16 40		16 55	17 04		17 12	17 13			17 23	17 25		17 34	17 40	17 43		17 55	18 12		18 25	18 40	
Queens Park d	16 41		16 56	17 05		17 13	17 14			17 24	17 26		17 35	17 41	17 44		17 56	18 13		18 26	18 41	
Crosshill d	16 43		16 58	17 07		17 15	17 16			17 26	17 28		17 37	17 43	17 46		17 58	18 15		18 28	18 43	
Mount Florida d	16 45		17 00	17 09		17 17	17 18			17 28	17 30		17 39	17 45	17 48		18 00	18 17		18 30	18 45	
Cathcart d	16 47		17a03	17 11	17a21	17 19			17a31	17 30		17a40		17 47	17 50		18a03	18 19	18a31		18 47	
Muirend d	16 50			17 14		17 22		17 25		17 33				17 50	17 53			18 22			18 50	
Williamwood d	16 53			17 17		17 25		17 28		17 36				17 53	17 56			18 25			18 53	
Whitecraigs d	16 55			17 19		17 27		17 30		17 38				17 55	17 58			18 27			18 55	
Patterton d	16 58			17 22		17 30		17 33		17 41				17 58	18 01			18 30			18 58	
Neilston a	17 04			17 28		17 36		17 39		17 47				18 04	18 07			18 36			19 04	
Kings Park d		17 03					17 21				17 33		17 42			18 03				18 33		19 03
Croftfoot d		17 05					17 23				17 35		17 44			18 05				18 35		19 05
Burnside d		17 08					17 26				17 38		17 47			18 08				18 38		19 08
Kirkhill a		17 11					17 29				17 41		17 50			18 11				18 41		19 11
Newton 226 a		17 14					17 32				17 44		17 53			18 14				18 45		19 14

	SR	SR	SR	SR	SR	SR	SR	SR	SR	SR	SR	SR	SR	SR	SR	SR	SR	SR	SR	SR	SR
Glasgow Central 226 d	18 50	19 05	19 15	19 20	19 35	19 45	19 50	20 05	20 15	20 20	20 35	20 45	20 50	21 05	21 15	21 20	21 35	21 45	21 50	22 05	22 15
Pollokshields West d			19 21			19 51			20 21			20 51			21 21			21 51			22 21
Maxwell Park d			19 23			19 53			20 23			20 53			21 23			21 53			22 23
Shawlands d			19 25			19 55			20 25			20 55			21 25			21 55			22 25
Pollokshaws East d			19 26			19 56			20 26			20 56			21 26			21 56			22 26
Langside d			19 28			19 58			20 28			20 58			21 28			21 58			22 28
Pollokshields East d	18 55	19 10		19 25	19 40		19 55	20 10		20 25	20 40		20 55	21 10		21 25	21 40		21 55	22 10	
Queens Park d	18 56	19 11		19 26	19 41		19 56	20 11		20 26	20 41		20 56	21 11		21 26	21 41		21 56	22 11	
Crosshill d	18 58	19 13		19 28	19 43		19 58	20 13		20 28	20 43		20 58	21 13		21 28	21 43		21 58	22 13	
Mount Florida d	19 00	19 15		19 30	19 45		20 00	20 15		20 30	20 45		21 00	21 15		21 30	21 45		22 00	22 15	
Cathcart d	19a03	19 17	19a31		19 47		20a03	20 17	20a31		20 47		21a03	21 17	21a31		21 47		22a03	22 17	22a31
Muirend d		19 20			19 50			20 20			20 50			21 20			21 50			22 20	
Williamwood d		19 23			19 53			20 23			20 53			21 23			21 53			22 23	
Whitecraigs d		19 25			19 55			20 25			20 55			21 25			21 55			22 25	
Patterton d		19 28			19 58			20 28			20 58			21 28			21 58			22 28	
Neilston a		19 34			20 04			20 34			21 04			21 34			22 04			22 34	
Kings Park d				19 33		20 03				20 33		21 03				21 33		22 03			
Croftfoot d				19 35		20 05				20 35		21 05				21 35		22 05			
Burnside d				19 38		20 08				20 38		21 08				21 38		22 08			
Kirkhill a				19 41		20 11				20 41		21 11				21 41		22 11			
Newton 226 a				19 45		20 14				20 44		21 14				21 44		22 14			

	SR	SR	SR	SR	SR	SR	SR	SR FO
Glasgow Central 226 d	22 20	22 35	22 45	22 50	23 05	23 15	23 20	23 50
Pollokshields West d			22 51			23 21		
Maxwell Park d			22 53			23 23		
Shawlands d			22 55			23 25		
Pollokshaws East d			22 56			23 26		
Langside d			22 58			23 28		
Pollokshields East d	22 25	22 40		22 55	23 10		23 25	23 55
Queens Park d	22 26	22 41		22 56	23 11		23 26	23 56
Crosshill d	22 28	22 43		22 58	23 13		23 28	23 58
Mount Florida d	22 30	22 45		23 00	23 15		23 30	23 59
Cathcart d		22 47		23a03	23 17	23a31		
Muirend d		22 50			23 20			
Williamwood d		22 53			23 23			
Whitecraigs d		22 55			23 25			
Patterton d		22 58			23 28			
Neilston a		23 04			23 34			
Kings Park d	22 33		23 03				23 33	00 03
Croftfoot d	22 35		23 05				23 35	00 05
Burnside d	22 38		23 08				23 38	00 08
Kirkhill a	22 41		23 11				23 41	00 11
Newton 226 a	22 44		23 14				23 45	00 14

Table 223

Sundays

Glasgow Central, Cathcart Circle, Neilston and Newton

Network Diagram - see first Page of Table 220

	SR	SR	SR	SR	SR	SR		SR	SR	SR	SR	SR	SR		SR	SR
Glasgow Central 226 d	08 23	08 34	08 53	09 08	09 23	09 34	and at the same minutes past each hour until	12 34	12 59	13 08	13 23	13 34	13 53	and at the same minutes past each hour until	22 53	23 08
Pollokshields West d		08 40				09 40		12 40				13 40				
Maxwell Park d		08 42				09 42		12 42				13 42				
Shawlands d		08 44				09 44		12 44				13 44				
Pollokshaws East d		08 45				09 45		12 45				13 45				
Langside d		08 47				09 47		12 47				13 47				
Pollokshields East d	08 28		08 58	09 13	09 28				13 04	13 13	13 28		13 58		22 58	23 13
Queens Park d	08 29		08 59	09 14	09 29				13 05	13 14	13 29		13 59		22 59	23 14
Crosshill d	08 31		09 01	09 16	09 31				13 07	13 16	13 31		14 01		23 01	23 16
Mount Florida d	08 33		09 03	09 18	09 33				13 09	13 18	13 33		14 03		23 03	23 18
Cathcart d	08 35		09 05		09 35				13 11		13 35		14 05		23 05	
Muirend d	08 38		09 08		09 38				13 14		13 38		14 08		23 08	
Williamwood d	08 41		09 11		09 41				13 17		13 41		14 11		23 11	
Whitecraigs d	08 43		09 13		09 43				13 19		13 43		14 13		23 13	
Patterton d	08 46		09 16		09 46				13 22		13 46		14 16		23 16	
Neilston a	08 52		09 22		09 52				13 28		13 52		14 22		23 22	
Kings Park d		08 51		09 21		09 52		12 52		13 21		13 52				23 21
Croftfoot d		08 53		09 23		09 54		12 54		13 23		13 54				23 23
Burnside d		08 56		09 26		09 57		12 57		13 26		13 57				23 26
Kirkhill a		08 59		09 29		10 00		13 00		13 29		14 00				23 29
Newton 226 a		09 02		09 32		10 03		13 03		13 32		14 03				23 32

Newton, Neilston, Cathcart Circle and Glasgow Central

Network Diagram - see first Page of Table 220

Miles	Miles	Miles			SR SO	SR	SR	SR	SR	SR SX	SR	SR SX	SR SX		SR SO	SR SX	SR SO	SR SX	SR SX	SR SX	SR SO	SR SX	SR SX		SR
0	0	—	**Newton**	226 d			06 20		06 50			07 15			07 20				07 41		07 50	07 51			
1½	1½	—	Kirkhill	d			06 23		06 53			07 18			07 23				07 44		07 53	07 54			
2¾	2¾	—	Burnside	d			06 26		06 56			07 21			07 26				07 47		07 56	07 57			
3¼	3¼	—	Croftfoot	d			06 30		06 58			07 23			07 28				07 49		07 58	07 59			
4¼	4¼	—	Kings Park	d			06 32		07 00			07 25			07 30				07 51		08 00	08 02			
—	—	—	**Neilston**	d				06 30			07 00					07 24	07 30			07 41					07 56
—	—	3¾	Patterton	d				06 36			07 06					07 30	07 36			07 47					08 02
—	—	4¾	Whitecraigs	d				06 39			07 09					07 33	07 39			07 50					08 05
—	—	5½	Williamwood	d				06 41			07 11					07 35	07 41			07 52					08 08
—	—	7	Muirend	d				06 44			07 14					07 38	07 44			07 55					08 11
4¾	—	7¾	Cathcart	d	00 37	06 30		06 47		07 03	07 17		07 32			07 41	07 47	07 47		07 58			08 10		08 14
—	5½	8½	Mount Florida	d	00 39	06 32		06 49	07 04		07 19		07 34			07 43	07 49		07 55	08 01	08 04		08 12		08 17
—	6	9	Crosshill	d	00 41	06 34		06 51	07 06		07 21		07 36			07 45	07 51		07 57	08 03	08 06		08 14		08 19
—	6½	9½	Queens Park	d	00 43	06 36		06 53	07 08		07 23		07 38			07 47	07 53		07 59	08 05	08 08		08 16		08 21
—	6¾	9¾	Pollokshields East	d	00 44	06 37		06 54	07 09		07 24		07 39			07 48	07 54		08 00	08 07	08 09		08 18		08 23
5¾	—	—	Langside	d			06 37			07 05		07 29			07 35			07 50				08 06			
6¼	—	—	Pollokshaws East	d			06 39			07 07		07 31			07 37			07 52				08 08			
6¾	—	—	Shawlands	d			06 42			07 09		07 33			07 39			07 54				08 10			
7½	—	—	Maxwell Park	d			06 44			07 11		07 35			07 41			07 56				08 12			
8	—	—	Pollokshields West	d			06 48			07 13		07 37			07 43			07 58				08 13			
10	8¾	11¼	**Glasgow Central** 15	226 a	00 49	06 43	06 54	06 59	07 14	07 20	07 29	07 43	07 47		07 50	07 55	07 59	08 05	08 07	08 12	08 14	08 21	08 23		08 28

		SR SX	SR SX	SR SX	SR SX	SR SO	SR SX	SR SX	SR SO		SR SX	SR SX	SR SX	SR SO	SR	SR SX	SR SO	SR SX	SR		SR	SR	SR	SR	
Newton	226 d				08 21	08 20						08 33		08 50		09 00					09 20		09 50		
Kirkhill	d				08 24	08 23						08 36		08 53		09 02					09 23		09 53		
Burnside	d				08 27	08 26						08 39		08 56		09 05					09 26		09 56		
Croftfoot	d				08 29	08 28						08 42		08 58		09 07					09 28		09 58		
Kings Park	d				08 31	08 30						08 44		09 00		09 10					09 30		10 00		
Neilston	d	08 07						08 21	08 30				08 43				09 00	09 04				09 30			
Patterton	d	08 13						08 27	08 36				08 49				09 06	09 10				09 36			
Whitecraigs	d	08 16						08 30	08 39				08 52				09 09	09 13				09 39			
Williamwood	d	08 18						08 32	08 41				08 54				09 11	09 15				09 41			
Muirend	d	08 21						08 36	08 44				08 57				09 14	09 18				09 44			
Cathcart	d		08 26	08 24			08 33	08 39	08 47		08 49		09 00		09 03		09 17	09 21	09 32			09 47		10 03	
Mount Florida	d		08 28		08 35			08 42	08 49		08 52		09 02	09 04		09 14	09 19	09 23	09 34			09 49	10 04		
Crosshill	d		08 30		08 37			08 44	08 51		08 54		09 04	09 06		09 16	09 21	09 25	09 36			09 51	10 06		
Queens Park	d		08 32		08 39			08 46	08 53		08 56		09 06	09 08		09 18	09 23	09 27	09 38			09 53	10 08		
Pollokshields East	d	08 29	08 33		08 40			08 48	08 54		08 58		09 07	09 09		09 19	09 24	09 28	09 39			09 54	10 09		
Langside	d			08 27		08 35	08 35					08 49			09 05						09 35			10 05	
Pollokshaws East	d			08 29		08 37	08 37					08 51			09 07						09 37			10 07	
Shawlands	d			08 31		08 39	08 39					08 54			09 09						09 39			10 09	
Maxwell Park	d			08 33		08 41	08 41					08 56			09 11						09 41			10 11	
Pollokshields West	d			08 35		08 43	08 43					09 00			09 13						09 43			10 13	
Glasgow Central 15	226 a	08 34	08 39	08 43	08 47	08 50	08 52	08 54	08 59		09 03	09 06	09 12	09 14	09 22	09 24	09 29	09 33	09 44		09 50	09 59	10 14	10 20	

		SR		SR	SR		SR	SR	SR	SR	SR	SR	SR	SR	SR		SR SO	SR SX	SR	SR	SR	SR	SR SO	SR SX
Newton	226 d		and at the same minutes past each hour until				14 20		14 50				15 20		15 50						16 20		16 50	16 50
Kirkhill	d						14 23		14 53				15 23		15 53						16 23		16 53	16 53
Burnside	d						14 26		14 56				15 26		15 56						16 26		16 56	16 56
Croftfoot	d						14 28		14 58				15 28		15 58						16 28		16 58	16 58
Kings Park	d						14 30		15 00				15 30		16 00						16 30		17 00	17 00
Neilston	d	10 00		14 00				14 30			15 00			15 30					16 00			16 30		
Patterton	d	10 06		14 06				14 36			15 06			15 36					16 06			16 36		
Whitecraigs	d	10 09		14 09				14 39			15 09			15 39					16 09			16 39		
Williamwood	d	10 11		14 11				14 41			15 11			15 41					16 11			16 41		
Muirend	d	10 14		14 14				14 44			15 14			15 44					16 14			16 44		
Cathcart	d	10 17		14 17	14 32			14 47		15 03	15 17	15 32		15 47			16 04	16 06	16 17	16 32		16 47		
Mount Florida	d	10 19		14 19	14 34			14 49	15 04		15 19	15 34		15 49	16 04				16 19	16 34		16 49	17 04	17 04
Crosshill	d	10 21		14 21	14 36			14 51	15 06		15 21	15 36		15 51	16 06				16 21	16 36		16 51	17 06	17 06
Queens Park	d	10 23		14 23	14 38			14 53	15 08		15 23	15 38		15 53	16 08				16 23	16 38		16 53	17 08	17 08
Pollokshields East	d	10 24		14 24	14 39			14 54	15 09		15 24	15 39		15 54	16 09				16 24	16 39		16 54	17 09	17 09
Langside	d						14 35			15 05			15 35				16 07	16 09			16 35			
Pollokshaws East	d						14 37			15 07			15 37				16 09	16 11			16 37			
Shawlands	d						14 39			15 09			15 39				16 11	16 13			16 39			
Maxwell Park	d						14 41			15 11			15 41				16 13	16 15			16 41			
Pollokshields West	d						14 43			15 13			15 43				16 16	16 18			16 43			
Glasgow Central 15	226 a	10 29		14 29	14 44		14 50	14 59	15 14	15 21	15 29	15 44	15 50	15 59	16 14		16 22	16 24	16 29	16 44	16 50	16 59	17 14	17 17

Newton, Neilston, Cathcart Circle and Glasgow Central

Network Diagram - see first Page of Table 220

		SR		SR SX	SR SO	SR SX	SR SX	SR SO	SR	SR SX	SR SO	SR SX		SR	SR	SR SX	SR SO	SR SX	SR	SR	SR	SR		SR	SR
Newton	226 d								17 20					17 50						18 20		18 50			
Kirkhill	d								17 23					17 53						18 23		18 53			
Burnside	d								17 26					17 56						18 26		18 56			
Croftfoot	d								17 28					17 58						18 28		18 58			
Kings Park	d								17 30					18 00						18 30		19 00			
Neilston	d			16 53	17 00		17 14				17 30	17 39				17 54	18 00	18 04			18 30				19 00
Patterton	d			16 59	17 06		17 20				17 36	17 45				18 00	18 06	18 10			18 36				19 06
Whitecraigs	d			17 02	17 09		17 23				17 39	17 48				18 03	18 09	18 13			18 39				19 09
Williamwood	d			17 04	17 11		17 25				17 41	17 50				18 05	18 11	18 15			18 41				19 11
Muirend	d			17 07	17 14		17 28				17 44	17 53				18 08	18 14	18 18			18 44				19 14
Cathcart	d	17 03		17 10	17 17	17 21	17 31	17 32		17 41	17 47	17 56			18 03	18 11	18 17	18 21	18 32		18 47			19 03	19 17
Mount Florida	d			17 12	17 19	17 23	17 33	17 34		17 43	17 49	17 58		18 04		18 13	18 19	18 23	18 34		18 49	19 04			19 19
Crosshill	d			17 14	17 21	17 25	17 35	17 36		17 45	17 51	18 00		18 06		18 15	18 21	18 25	18 36		18 51	19 06			19 21
Queens Park	d			17 16	17 23	17 27	17 37	17 38		17 47	17 53	18 02		18 08		18 17	18 23	18 27	18 38		18 53	19 08			19 23
Pollokshields East	d			17 17	17 24	17 29	17 38	17 39		17 48	17 54	18 03		18 09		18 18	18 24	18 28	18 39		18 54	19 09			19 24
Langside	d	17 05							17 35						18 05					18 35				19 05	
Pollokshaws East	d	17 07							17 37						18 07					18 37				19 07	
Shawlands	d	17 09							17 39						18 09					18 39				19 09	
Maxwell Park	d	17 11							17 41						18 11					18 41				19 11	
Pollokshields West	d	17 13							17 43						18 13					18 43				19 13	
Glasgow Central 15	226 a	17 20		17 22	17 29	17 38	17 43	17 44	17 50	17 55	17 59	18 08		18 14	18 20	18 25	18 29	18 34	18 44	18 50	18 59	19 14		19 21	19 29

		SR	SR	SR	SR	SR	SR	SR		SR	SR	SR	SR	SR	SR	SR	SR	SR		SR	SR	SR	SR	SR	SR
Newton	226 d		19 20		19 50					20 20		20 50				21 20		21 50					22 20		22 50
Kirkhill	d		19 23		19 53					20 23		20 53				21 23		21 53					22 23		22 53
Burnside	d		19 26		19 56					20 26		20 56				21 26		21 56					22 26		22 56
Croftfoot	d		19 28		19 58					20 28		20 58				21 28		21 58					22 28		22 58
Kings Park	d		19 30		20 00					20 30		21 00				21 30		22 00					22 30		23 00
Neilston	d			19 30			20 00				20 30			21 00			21 30				22 00			22 30	
Patterton	d			19 36			20 06				20 36			21 06			21 36				22 06			22 36	
Whitecraigs	d			19 39			20 09				20 39			21 09			21 39				22 09			22 39	
Williamwood	d			19 41			20 11				20 41			21 11			21 41				22 11			22 41	
Muirend	d			19 44			20 14				20 44			21 14			21 44				22 14			22 44	
Cathcart	d	19 32		19 47		20 03	20 17	20 32			20 47		21 03	21 17	21 32		21 47			22 03	22 17	22 32		22 47	
Mount Florida	d	19 34		19 49	20 04		20 19	20 34			20 49	21 04		21 19	21 34		21 49	22 04			22 19	22 34		22 49	23 04
Crosshill	d	19 36		19 51	20 06		20 21	20 36			20 51	21 06		21 21	21 36		21 51	22 06			22 21	22 36		22 51	23 06
Queens Park	d	19 38		19 53	20 08		20 23	20 38			20 53	21 08		21 23	21 38		21 53	22 08			22 23	22 38		22 53	23 08
Pollokshields East	d	19 39		19 54	20 09		20 24	20 39			20 54	21 09		21 24	21 39		21 54	22 09			22 24	22 39		22 54	23 09
Langside	d		19 35			20 05				20 35			21 05			21 35				22 05			22 35		
Pollokshaws East	d		19 37			20 07				20 37			21 07			21 37				22 07			22 37		
Shawlands	d		19 39			20 09				20 39			21 09			21 39				22 09			22 39		
Maxwell Park	d		19 41			20 11				20 41			21 11			21 41				22 11			22 41		
Pollokshields West	d		19 43			20 13				20 43			21 13			21 43				22 14			22 43		
Glasgow Central 15	226 a	19 44	19 52	19 59	20 15	20 20	20 29	20 44		20 50	20 59	21 15	21 20	21 29	21 44	21 50	21 59	22 15		22 20	22 29	22 44	22 50	22 59	23 15

		SR	SR	SR		SR	SR
Newton	226 d					23 20	
Kirkhill	d					23 23	
Burnside	d					23 26	
Croftfoot	d					23 28	
Kings Park	d					23 30	
Neilston	d		23 00				23 30
Patterton	d		23 06				23 36
Whitecraigs	d		23 09				23 39
Williamwood	d		23 11				23 41
Muirend	d		23 14				23 44
Cathcart	d	23 03	23 17	23 32			23 47
Mount Florida	d		23 19	23 34			23 49
Crosshill	d		23 21	23 36			23 51
Queens Park	d		23 23	23 38			23 53
Pollokshields East	d		23 24	23 39			23 54
Langside	d	23 05				23 35	
Pollokshaws East	d	23 07				23 37	
Shawlands	d	23 09				23 39	
Maxwell Park	d	23 11				23 41	
Pollokshields West	d	23 13				23 43	
Glasgow Central 15	226 a	23 20	23 29	23 44		23 50	23 59

Sundays

Newton, Neilston, Cathcart Circle and Glasgow Central

Network Diagram - see first Page of Table 220

		SR	SR	SR	SR		SR	SR	SR	SR	SR	SR	SR	SR
Newton 226	d		09 09		09 39		21 39		22 09		22 39		23 09	
Kirkhill	d		09 12		09 42		21 42		22 12		22 42		23 12	
Burnside	d		09 15		09 45		21 45		22 15		22 45		23 15	
Croftfoot	d		09 17		09 47		21 47		22 17		22 47		23 17	
Kings Park	d		09 19		09 49		21 49		22 19		22 49		23 19	
Neilston	d	08 48		09 19		and at		21 48		22 19		22 48		23 19
Patterton	d	08 54		09 25		the same		21 54		22 25		22 54		23 25
Whitecraigs	d	08 57		09 28		minutes		21 57		22 28		22 57		23 28
Williamwood	d	08 59		09 30		past		21 59		22 30		22 59		23 30
Muirend	d	09 02		09 33		each		22 02		22 33		23 02		23 33
Cathcart	d	09 05		09 36		hour until		22 05		22 36		23 05		23 36
Mount Florida	d	09 07		09 38	09 53		21 53	22 07		22 38	22 53	23 07		23 38
Crosshill	d	09 09		09 40	09 55		21 55	22 09		22 40	22 55	23 09		23 40
Queens Park	d	09 11		09 42	09 57		21 57	22 11		22 42	22 57	23 11		23 42
Pollokshields East	d	09 12		09 43	09 58		21 58	22 12		22 43	22 58	23 12		23 43
Langside	d		09 23						22 23				23 23	
Pollokshaws East	d		09 25						22 25				23 25	
Shawlands	d		09 27						22 27				23 27	
Maxwell Park	d		09 29						22 29				23 29	
Pollokshields West	d		09 31						22 31				23 31	
Glasgow Central 226	a	09 17	09 38	09 48	10 03		22 03	22 17	22 37	22 48	23 03	23 17	23 37	23 48

Mondays to Saturdays

Motherwell and Glasgow Queen Street - Cumbernauld and Falkirk Grahamston

Network Diagram - see first Page of Table 220

Miles	Miles			SR MX	SR	SR	SR	SR	SR	SR	SR	SR	SR	SR	SR	SR	SR	SR	SR	SR	SR	SR	SR
—	0	**Motherwell** 226	d							07 35			08 37			09 37			10 37			11 37	
—	4½	Whifflet	d							07 43			08 45			09 45			10 45			11 46	
—	5¼	**Coatbridge Central**	d				06 45			07 46			08 48			09 48			10 48			11 48	
0	—	**Glasgow Queen Street**	d	23p51	05 51	06 21		06 51	07 21		07 52	08 24		08 51	09 21		09 52	10 21		10 51	11 22		11 51
1¼	—	Springburn	d	23p55	05 55	06 25		06 55	07 26		07 55	08 29		08 55	09 25		09 55	10 25		10 55	11 29		11 55
5¼	—	Stepps	d	00 02	06 02	06 32		07 02	07 33		08 02	08 36		09 02	09 32		10 02	10 32		11 02	11 36		12 02
7¾	—	Gartcosh	d	00 06	06 06	06 36		07 06	07 37		08 06	08 40		09 06	09 36		10 06	10 36		11 06	11 39		12 06
13¼	11	Greenfaulds	d	00 14	06 14	06 44	06 51	07 14	07 45	07 52	08 14	08 48	08 55	09 14	09 44	09 55	10 14	10 44	10 55	11 14	11 47	11 55	12 14
14	11¾	**Cumbernauld**	d	00a18	06a18	06 46	06a57	07a18	07 47	07a57	08a19	08 50	09a01	09a20	09 48	10a01	10a19	10 47	11a01	11a18	11 50	12a02	12a18
22½	—	Camelon	d			06 57			08 04			09 04			10 04			11 04			12 04		
24	—	**Falkirk Grahamston**	a			07 03			08 11			09 07			10 07			11 07			12 07		

		SR	SR	SR	SR	SR	SR	SR	SR	SR	SR	SR	SR	SR	SR	SR	SR SX	SR SX A	SR	SR	SR	SR	SR
Motherwell 226	d		12 37			13 37			14 37			15 37			16 37					17 37			18 37
Whifflet	d		12 45			13 45			14 45			15 45			16 45					17 45			18 45
Coatbridge Central	d		12 48			13 48			14 48			15 48			16 48					17 48			18 48
Glasgow Queen Street	d	12 24		12 51	13 23		13 51	14 21		14 51	15 21		15 54	16 22		16 51	17 03	17 33	17 22		17 51	18 24	
Springburn	d	12 29		12 55	13 28		13 55	14 25		14 55	15 29		15 56	16 25		16 55			17 28		17 55	18 29	
Stepps	d	12 36		13 02	13 35		14 02	14 32		15 02	15 36		16 02	16 32		17 02			17 35		18 02	18 36	
Gartcosh	d	12 40		13 06	13 39		14 06	14 36		15 06	15 39		16 06	16 36		17 06			17 39		18 06	18 40	
Greenfaulds	d	12 48	12 55	13 14	13 47	13 55	14 14	14 44	14 55	15 14	15 47	15 55	16 14	16 44	16 55	17 15			17 45	17 55	18 14	18 48	18 55
Cumbernauld	d	12 50	13a01	13a18	13 48	14a01	14a18	14 48	15a01	15a19	15 48	16a01	16a21	16 46	17a01	17a20			17 47	18a01	18a19	18 50	19a01
Camelon	d	13 04			14 04			15 04			16 04			17 01			17 30	18 02	18 04			19 04	
Falkirk Grahamston	a	13 07			14 07			15 07			16 07			17 07			17 32	18 04	18 07			19 07	

		SR	SR	SR	SR	SR	SR	SR	SR	SR	SR	SR	SR	SR	SR
Motherwell 226	d			19 37			20 37			21 37					
Whifflet	d			19 45			20 45			21 45					
Coatbridge Central	d			19 48			20 48			21 48					
Glasgow Queen Street	d	18 51	19 21		19 51	20 21		20 51	21 21		21 51	22 21	22 51	23 21	23 51
Springburn	d	18 55	19 27		19 56	20 25		20 55	21 25		21 55	22 26	22 55	23 25	23 55
Stepps	d	19 02	19 34		20 03	20 32		21 02	21 32		22 02	22 33	23 02	23 32	00 02
Gartcosh	d	19 06	19 37		20 07	20 36		21 06	21 36		22 05	22 37	23 06	23 36	00 06
Greenfaulds	d	19 14	19 45	19 55	20 15	20 44	20 55	21 14	21 44	21 55	22 15	22 45	23 14	23 44	00 14
Cumbernauld	d	19a18	19a50	20a01	20 17	20a48	21a01	21 16	21a48	22a01	22 16	22a49	23 16	23a48	00a18
Camelon	d				20 31			21 27			22 27		23 29		
Falkirk Grahamston	a				20 34			21 33			22 34		23 36		

A To Markinch

Sundays

		SR	SR	SR	SR	SR	SR	SR	SR	SR	SR	SR	SR	SR	SR	SR	SR
Motherwell 226	d																
Whifflet	d																
Coatbridge Central	d																
Glasgow Queen Street	d	23p51	08 19	09 22	10 21	11 21	12 23	13 21	14 21	15 21	16 21	17 21	18 23	19 22	20 21	21 21	22 21
Springburn	d	23p55	08 24	09 25	10 25	11 25	12 25	13 25	14 25	15 25	16 25	17 25	18 25	19 25	20 25	21 25	22 25
Stepps	d	00 02	08 30	09 32	10 32	11 32	12 32	13 32	14 32	15 32	16 32	17 32	18 32	19 32	20 32	21 32	22 32
Gartcosh	d	00 06	08 34	09 36	10 36	11 36	12 36	13 36	14 36	15 36	16 36	17 36	18 36	19 36	20 36	21 36	22 36
Greenfaulds	d	00 14	08 42	09 44	10 44	11 44	12 43	13 44	14 44	15 44	16 44	17 44	18 44	19 44	20 44	21 44	22 44
Cumbernauld	d	00a18	08a46	09a49	10a48	11a48	12a50	13a48	14a48	15a48	16a48	17a48	18a50	19a49	20a48	21a48	22a48
Camelon	d																
Falkirk Grahamston	a																

Falkirk Grahamston and Cumbernauld - Glasgow Queen Street and Motherwell

Network Diagram - see first Page of Table 220

Miles	Miles			SR	SR	SR	SR	SR	SR	SR SX	SR	SR	SR SX	SR	SR	SR	SR	SR	SR	SR	SR	SR		SR	SR
0	—	**Falkirk Grahamston**	d	05 43			06 44				07 44		08 11		08 43			09 43			10 43				11 43
1¼	—	Camelon 4	d	05 45			06 46				07 46		08 14		08 45			09 45			10 45				11 45
10	—	**Cumbernauld**	d	05 58	06 28		06 58	07 08	07 28		07 59	08 10		08 30	08 58	09 10	09 28	09 58	10 10	10 28	10 58	11 10		11 28	11 58
10¾	0¾	Greenfaulds	d	05 59	06 29		06 59	07 10	07 29		08 02	08 12		08 31	08 59	09 12	09 29	09 59	10 12	10 29	10 59	11 12		11 29	11 59
16¼	—	Gartcosh	d	06 06	06 36		07 06		07 36		08 09			08 38	09 06		09 36	10 06		10 36	11 06			11 36	12 06
18¾	—	Stepps	d	06 10	06 40		07 10		07 40		08 13			08 42	09 10		09 40	10 10		10 40	11 10			11 40	12 10
22¾	—	Springburn	d	06 16	06 46		07 16		07 46		08 20			08 48	09 16		09 46	10 16		10 46	11 16			11 46	12 16
24	—	**Glasgow Queen Street** 10	a	06 25	06 55		07 29		07 55		08 29		08 48	08 59	09 25		09 56	10 26		10 55	11 25			11 55	12 25
—	6¼	**Coatbridge Central**	d			06 40		07 20		07 40		08 20				09 20			10 20			11 20			
—	7¼	Whifflet	d			06 42		07 22		07 42		08 22				09 22			10 22			11 22			
—	11¾	**Motherwell** 226	a			06 51		07 30		07 49		08 32				09 32			10 32			11 32			

		SR	SR	SR	SR	SR	SR	SR		SR	SR	SR	SR	SR	SR	SR	SR	SR		SR	SR SX	SR	SR SX	SR	SR
Falkirk Grahamston	d			12 43			13 43				14 43			15 43			16 43					17 43			
Camelon 4	d			12 45			13 45				14 45			15 45			16 45					17 45			
Cumbernauld	d	12 10	12 28	12 58	13 10	13 28	13 58	14 10		14 28	14 58	15 10	15 28	15 58	16 10	16 28	16 58	17 10		17 28		17 58		18 10	18 28
Greenfaulds	d	12 12	12 29	12 59	13 12	13 29	13 59	14 12		14 29	14 59	15 12	15 29	15 59	16 12	16 29	16 59	17 12		17 29		17 59		18 12	18 29
Gartcosh	d		12 36	13 06		13 36	14 06			14 36	15 06		15 36	16 06		16 36	17 06			17 36		18 06			18 36
Stepps	d		12 40	13 10		13 40	14 10			14 40	15 10		15 40	16 10		16 40	17 10			17 40		18 10			18 40
Springburn	d		12 46	13 16		13 46	14 16			14 46	15 16		15 46	16 16		16 46	17 16			17 46		18 16			18 46
Glasgow Queen Street 10	a		12 55	13 25		13 55	14 25			14 55	15 25		15 55	16 25		16 59	17 27			17 56		18 27			18 55
Coatbridge Central	d	12 20			13 20			14 20				15 20			16 20			17 20			17 32		17 56	18 20	
Whifflet	d	12 22			13 22			14 22				15 22			16 22			17 22			17 34		18 00	18 22	
Motherwell 226	a	12 32			13 32			14 32				15 32			16 32			17 32			17 40		18 08	18 32	

		SR SX	SR	SR		SR	SR	SR	SR	SR	SR	SR	SR	SR		SR	SR	SR
Falkirk Grahamston	d		18 45				19 43					21 13				22 13		23 13
Camelon 4	d		18 47				19 45					21 15				22 15		23 15
Cumbernauld	d		19 01	19 10		19 28	19 58	20 10	20 28	20 58	21 10	21 28	21 58	22 10		22 28	22 58	23 28
Greenfaulds	d		19 02	19 12		19 29	19 59	20 12	20 29	20 59	21 12	21 29	21 59	22 12		22 29	22 59	23 29
Gartcosh	d		19 09			19 36	20 06		20 36	21 06		21 36	22 06			22 36	23 06	23 36
Stepps	d		19 13			19 40	20 10		20 40	21 10		21 40	22 10			22 40	23 10	23 40
Springburn	d		19 19			19 46	20 16		20 46	21 16		21 46	22 16			22 46	23 16	23 46
Glasgow Queen Street 10	a		19 29			19 55	20 26		20 55	21 25		21 55	22 26			22 55	23 26	23 55
Coatbridge Central	d	18 39		19 20				20 20			21 20			22 20				
Whifflet	d	18 41		19 22				20 22			21 22			22 22				
Motherwell 226	a	18 49		19 32				20 32			21 32			22 32				

Sundays

		SR	SR	SR	SR	SR	SR	SR	SR	SR		SR	SR	SR	SR	SR	SR
Falkirk Grahamston	d																
Camelon 4	d																
Cumbernauld	d	08 55	09 58	10 58	11 58	12 58	13 58	14 58	15 58	16 58		17 58	18 58	19 58	20 58	21 58	22 58
Greenfaulds	d	08 56	09 59	10 59	11 59	12 59	13 59	14 59	15 59	16 59		17 59	18 59	19 59	20 59	21 59	22 59
Gartcosh	d	09 03	10 06	11 06	12 06	13 06	14 06	15 06	16 06	17 06		18 06	19 06	20 06	21 06	22 06	23 06
Stepps	d	09 07	10 10	11 10	12 10	13 10	14 10	15 10	16 10	17 10		18 10	19 10	20 10	21 10	22 10	23 10
Springburn	d	09 13	10 16	11 16	12 16	13 16	14 16	15 16	16 16	17 16		18 16	19 16	20 16	21 16	22 16	23 16
Glasgow Queen Street 10	a	09 22	10 25	11 25	12 25	13 26	14 26	15 25	16 25	17 25		18 26	19 26	20 26	21 26	22 25	23 25
Coatbridge Central	d																
Whifflet	d																
Motherwell 226	a																

Network Diagram for Tables 225, 228, 229, 230, 238, 240, 242

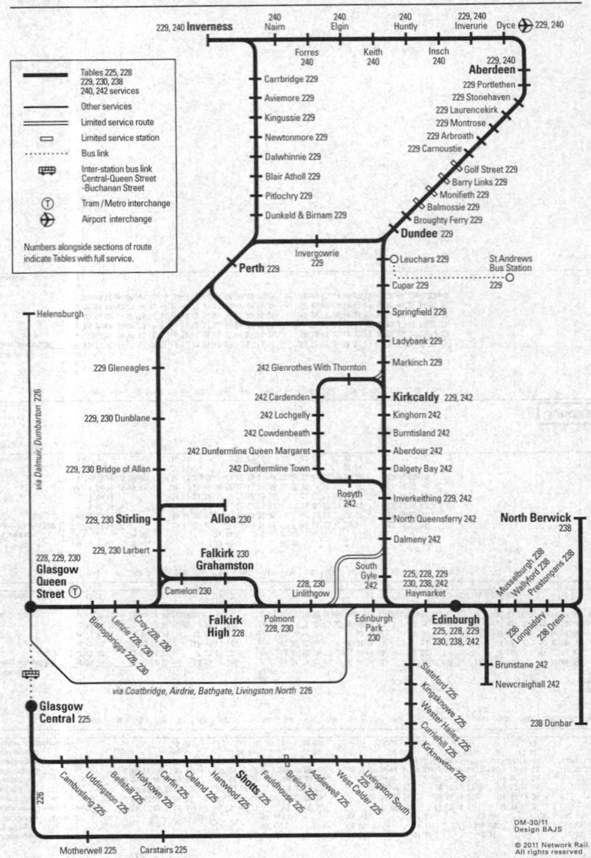

Table 225

Mondays to Saturdays

Edinburgh - Shotts, Carstairs, Motherwell and Glasgow Central

Network Diagram - see first page of Table 225

Miles	Miles	Station			SR MX	SR	XC SX ◇1 🍴	XC SO ◇1 A	XC SO ◇1 B 🍴	SR	SR SO D	SR SX D	XC SO ◇1	XC SX ◇1 E	SR SO	SR SX	SR	SR SX F	SR	SR SO F	XC SX ◇1 G 🍴	XC SO ◇1 G 🍴	SR
0	0	**Edinburgh** 10	230,238,242	d	22p56	05 51	06 24	06 26	06 26	06 40	06 55	06 55	07 26	07 26	07 51	07 57	08 25	08 33	08 57	09 03	09 11	09 11	09 26
1¼	1¼	Haymarket	230,238,242	d	23p00	05 55		06 30	06 30	06 45	07 00	07 00	07 30	07 31	07 55	08 02	08 31	08 37	09 01	09 07	09 16	09 16	09 30
3	3	Slateford		d	23p04	05 59					07 04	07 04					08 35	08 41		09 08			09 34
3¾	3¾	Kingsknowe		d	23p07	06 03					07 07	07 07					08 38	08 44		09 11			09 38
4¾	4¾	Wester Hailes		d	23p10	06 05					07 10	07 10					08 41	08 47		09 16			09 40
7½	7½	Curriehill		d	23p14	06 09					07 13	07 13					08 44	08 51		09 20			09 44
11	11	Kirknewton		d	23p21	06 16					07 21	07 21					08 52	08 55		09 25			09 52
14	—	Livingston South		d	23p26	06 21				07 01	07 26	07 26			08 10	08 19	08 58		09 17				09 58
16¾	—	West Calder		d	23p31	06 27				07 07	07 31	07 31			08 15	08 25	09 03		09 22				10 03
18½	—	Addiewell		d	23p34	06 31					07 34	07 34					09 07						10 07
21	—	Breich		d																			
23¼	—	Fauldhouse		d	23p42	06 39					07 43	07 43					09 15						10 15
26¾	—	**Shotts**		d	23p47	06 44				07 19	07 47	07 47			08 27	08 37	09 20		09 34				10 20
28¼	—	Hartwood		d	23p50	06 47					07 50	07 50					09 23						10 23
31½	—	Cleland		d	23p54	06 52					07 55	07 55					09 27						10 27
33¼	—	Carfin		d	23p58	06 56					07 58	07 58					09 31						10 31
34¼	—	Holytown		d	00 01	06 58					08 00	08 00					09 33						10 33
—	28½	Carstairs		d														09 13		09 44			
—	44½	**Motherwell**		a			07 04	07 12	07 12				08 14	08 08				09 32		10 00	10 04	10 05	
—	—			d			07 05	07 13	07 13				08 15	08 09				09 33		10 00	10 05	10 06	
36	—	Bellshill	226	d	00 04	07 04				07 30	08 03	08 03			08 38	08 48	09 36		09 46				10 36
38¾	—	Uddingston	226	d	00 08	07 10					08 07						09 41						10 41
42	—	Cambuslang	226	d	00 13	07 16																	
47¼	57¼	**Glasgow Central** 15	226	a	00 24	07 29	07 27	07 42	07 42	07 52	08 24	08 29	08 32	08 24	08 56	09 08	09 57	09 59	10 09	10 15	10 26	10 25	10 55

Station			SR	SR	SR	XC SO ◇1 H	XC SX ◇1 H	SR	SR	SR	SR	XC SO ◇1 I 🍴	XC SX ◇1 J 🍴	SR	SR	SR	SR	XC ◇1 K	SR	SR SX	SR SO	SR	SR SX	SR SO
Edinburgh 10	230,238,242	d	09 56	10 27	10 56	11 11	11 11	11 26	11 56	12 26	12 56	13 11	13 12	13 26	13 56	14 27	14 56	15 11	15 26	15 56	15 56	16 27	16 57	16 57
Haymarket	230,238,242	d	10 00	10 31	11 00	11 16	11 16	11 31	12 00	12 31	13 00	13 16	13 16	13 30	14 00	14 31	15 00	15 16	15 30	16 00	16 00	16 31	17 01	17 01
Slateford		d		10 35				11 35		12 35				13 34		14 35			15 34			16 35		
Kingsknowe		d		10 39				11 38		12 39				13 38		14 39			15 38			16 39		
Wester Hailes		d		10 41				11 41		12 41				13 40		14 41			15 40			16 41		
Curriehill		d		10 45				11 44		12 45				13 44		14 45			15 44			16 45		
Kirknewton		d		10 53				11 53		12 53				13 53		14 53			15 53			16 53		
Livingston South		d	10 15	10 58	11 17			11 58	12 16	12 57	13 16			13 58	14 16	14 58	15 17		15 58	16 15	16 15	16 57	17 16	17 16
West Calder		d	10 20	11 03	11 22			12 03	12 21	13 02	13 21			14 03	14 21	15 03	15 22		16 03	16 20	16 20	17 02	17 21	17 21
Addiewell		d		11 07				12 07		13 06				14 07		15 07			16 07			17 06		
Breich		d																						
Fauldhouse		d		11 15				12 15		13 14				14 15		15 15			16 15			17 14		
Shotts		d	10 33	11 20	11 34			12 20	12 33	13 19	13 33			14 20	14 33	15 20	15 34		16 20	16 32	16 32	17 18	17 33	17 33
Hartwood		d		11 23				12 23		13 22				14 23		15 23			16 23			17 21		
Cleland		d		11 27				12 27		13 26				14 27		15 27			16 28			17 26		
Carfin		d		11 31				12 31		13 30				14 31		15 31			16 31			17 29		
Holytown		d		11 33				12 33		13 32				14 33		15 33			16 33			17 31		
Carstairs		d																						
Motherwell		a				11 52	11 52					13 52	13 52					15 52						
		d				11 53	11 53					13 53	13 53					15 54						
Bellshill	226	d	10 45	11 36	11 46			12 36	12 46	13 35	13 47			14 36	14 46	15 36	15 46		16 36	16 42	16 46	17 34	17 43	17 43
Uddingston	226	d		11 41				12 41		13 40				14 41		15 41			16 41			17 38		
Cambuslang	226	d																				17 44		
Glasgow Central 15	226	a	11 02	11 57	12 10	12 13	12 14	12 55	13 09	13 55	14 09	14 13	14 12	14 55	15 09	15 56	16 12	16 23	16 57	17 00	17 09	17 57	18 02	18 09

A from 7 July until 1 September
B until 30 June, from 8 September
D From Newcraighall
E From Dunbar
F From North Berwick
G From Newcastle
H From Birmingham New Street
I From Bristol Temple Meads
J From Bath Spa
K From Plymouth

Table 225

Mondays to Saturdays

Edinburgh - Shotts, Carstairs, Motherwell and Glasgow Central

Network Diagram - see first page of Table 225

Station			XC SX ◇1 A	XC SO ◇1 A	SR	SR SX	SR SO	SR SX	SR	SR SX	SR B	SR	XC SO ◇1 A	XC SX ◇1 A	TP ◇1 C 🍴	SR SO	SR SX	GR SX 1 D 🍴	XC SO ◇1 E	XC SX ◇1 E	SR	SR
Edinburgh 10	230,238,242	d	17 11	17 11	17 18	17 42	17 48	17 48	17 56		18 24	18 56	19 11	19 11		19 18	19 27	20 16	21 13	21 14	21 26	22 56
Haymarket	230,238,242	d	17 15	17 16	17 23	17 46	17 53	17 53	18 00		18 28	19 00	19 16	19 16		19 23	19 31	20 21	21 18	21 19	21 30	23 00
Slateford		d			17 28		17 57	17 57			18 31					19 27	19 36				21 34	23 04
Kingsknowe		d			17 32		18 00	18 00			18 34					19 31	19 39				21 38	23 07
Wester Hailes		d			17 34		18 03	18 03	18 09		18 37					19 33	19 42				21 40	23 10
Curriehill		d			17 38				18 12		18 40					19 37	19 45				21 44	23 14
Kirknewton		d			17 45				18 20		18 47					19 45	19 54				21 51	23 21
Livingston South		d			17 50		18 14	18 14	18 25			19 17				19 49	19 58				21 56	23 26
West Calder		d			17 56		18 19	18 19	18 30			19 22				19 54	20 03				22 02	23 31
Addiewell		d			18 00				18 33							19 58	20 07				22 05	23 34
Breich		d							18 38													
Fauldhouse		d			18 08				18 42							20 06	20 15				22 13	23 42
Shotts		d			18 13		18 31	18 31	18 46			19 34				20 11	20 20				22 20	23 47
Hartwood		d			18 16				18 49							20 14	20 23				22 23	23 50
Cleland		d			18 21				18 54							20 18	20 27				22 27	23 54
Carfin		d			18 24				18 57							20 22	20 31				22 31	23 58
Holytown		d			18 26				18 59							20 24	20 33				22 33	00 01
Carstairs		d				18 17				18 30	19 10											
Motherwell		a	17 52	17 52	18 35	18 38				18 52	19 32		19 52	19 54				21 03	22 00	22 01		
		d	17 53	17 53		18 39					19 32		19 53	19 55				21 03	22 02	22 03		
Bellshill	226	d					18 41	18 41	19 04			19 46				20 28	20 36				22 36	00 04
Uddingston	226	d							19 07							20 32	20 41				22 41	00 08
Cambuslang	226	d						18 51	19 16													00 13
Glasgow Central 15	226	a	18 16	18 11		18 53	18 57	19 04	19 31		19 53	20 03	20 11	20 15	20 33	20 47	20 57	21 28	22 22	22 27	22 55	00 24

Sundays

Station			SR	XC ◇1 F	SR	XC ◇1 G	SR	XC ◇1 H	SR	XC ◇1 I	SR	XC ◇1 E	SR	TP ◇1 C 🍴	XC ◇1 A	GR 1 D 🍴	VT 1 J	VT 1 K
Edinburgh 10	230,238,242	d	22p56	12 17	12 24	13 10	14 23	15 10	16 23	17 11	18 24	19 18	20 23		21 13	21 21		
Haymarket	230,238,242	d	23p00	12 21	12 28	13 15	14 27	15 15	16 27	17 15	18 27	19 23	20 27		21 17	21 26		
Slateford		d	23p04		12 32		14 31		16 31		18 31		20 31					
Kingsknowe		d	23p07		12 35		14 34		16 34		18 34		20 34					
Wester Hailes		d	23p10		12 38		14 37		16 37		18 37		20 37					
Curriehill		d	23p14		12 41		14 40		16 40		18 40		20 40					
Kirknewton		d	23p21		12 48		14 47		16 47		18 47		20 47					
Livingston South		d	23p26		12 53		14 52		16 52		18 52		20 52					
West Calder		d	23p31		13a00		14a59		16a59		18a59		20a59					
Addiewell		d	23p34															
Breich		d																
Fauldhouse		d	23p42															
Shotts		d	23p47															
Hartwood		d	23p50															
Cleland		d	23p54															
Carfin		d	23p58															
Holytown		d	00 01															
Carstairs		d																
Motherwell		a		12 55		13 50		15 51		17 52		20 00			21 53	22 06		
		d		12 56		13 51		15 52		17 53		20 02			21 54	22 06	23 08	23 10
Bellshill	226	d	00 04															
Uddingston	226	d	00 08															
Cambuslang	226	d	00 13															
Glasgow Central 15	226	a	00 24	13 12		14 14		16 13		18 12		20 20		20 44	22 14	22 29	23 22	23 25

A From Penzance
B From North Berwick
C From Manchester Airport
D From London Kings Cross
E From Plymouth
F until 9 September, from 28 October. From Leeds
G until 9 September, from 28 October. From Sheffield
H until 21 October. From Birmingham New Street
I From Bristol Temple Meads
J from 1 July. From Birmingham New Street
K until 24 June. From Birmingham New Street

Glasgow Central, Motherwell, Carstairs and Shotts - Edinburgh

Network Diagram - see first page of Table 225

Miles	Miles				SR MX	SR SO	XC SO ◇1 A	XC SX ◇1 B ⊼	XC SO ◇1 C	SR	SR SX	GR SX ■ 1 E	GR SO ■ 1 E	SR	SR F	SR	XC SO ◇1 B ⊼	XC SX ◇1 B	SR	SR	XC SO ◇1 G	XC SX ◇1 G	SR
0	0	**Glasgow Central** 15	226	d	23p06	00 06	06 01	06 01	06 01	06 16		06 50	06 50	07 00	07 05	07 13	07 50	07 50	08 03	08 20	09 00	09 00	09 02
5¼	—	Cambuslang	226	d	23p15	00 15				06 25						07 23							
8½	—	Uddingston	226	d	23p20	00 20				06 30						07 29				08 32			
11¼	—	Bellshill	226	d	23p25	00 25				06 35				07 15		07 34			08 19	08 36			09 20
—	12¼	**Motherwell**		a			06 15	06 15	06 15			07 04	07 04		07 26		08 04	08 04			09 14	09 14	
—	—			d			06 16	06 16	06 16		06 57	07 04	07 04		07 27		08 05	08 05			09 15	09 15	
—	28½	Carstairs		d							07a25				07 47								
13¼	—	Holytown		d	23p29	00 29				06 39						07 38				08 40			
14	—	Carfin		d	23p32	00 32				06 42						07 41				08 43			
15¾	—	Cleland		d	23p36	00 36				06 46						07 45				08 47			
19	—	Hartwood		d	23p41	00 41				06 51						07 50				08 52			
20½	—	**Shotts**		d	23p45	00 45				06 55				07 28		07 54			08 31	08 56			09 32
24	—	Fauldhouse		d	23p51	00 51				07 01						08 00				09 02			
26¼	—	Breich		d												08 04							
28¾	—	Addiewell		d	23p58	00 58				07 08						08 08				09 09			
30½	—	West Calder		d	00 01	01 01				07 11				07 40		08 11			08 43	09 12			09 44
33¼	—	Livingston South		d	00 05	01 05				07 15				07 44		08 16			08 48	09 17			09 48
36¼	46¼	Kirknewton		d	00 10					07 20				07 50	08 04	08 21				09 22			
40¼	49¾	Curriehill		d	00 15					07 26				07 55	08 09	08 27				09 27			
42½	52½	Wester Hailes		d	00 19					07 30					08 12	08 30				09 31			
43½	53½	Kingsknowe		d	00 21					07 33					08 15	08 33				09 33			
44¼	54¼	Slateford		d	00 24					07 36					08 17	08 36				09 36			
46	56	Haymarket	230,238,242	d	00 30	01 18	06 57	06 57	06 57	07 42		07 45	07 46	08 03	08 26	08 42	08 50	08 50	09 02	09 42	09 57	09 58	10 03
47¼	57¼	**Edinburgh** 10	230,238,242	a	00 34	01 23	07 01	07 02	07 02	07 49		07 52	07 52	08 12	08 33	08 46	08 54	08 55	09 10	09 48	10 02	10 02	10 10

			SR	SR	SR	XC SO ◇1 B ⊼	XC SX ◇1 G ⊼	SR	SR	SR	SR	XC ◇1 B	SR	SR	SR	SR	XC SO ◇1 H ⊼	XC SX ◇1 H	SR	SR F	SR	SR SO	SR SX	SR
Glasgow Central 15	226	d	09 18	10 05	10 18	10 59	10 59	11 05	11 18	12 05	12 18	12 51	13 05	13 18	14 05	14 18	15 00	15 00	15 03	15 14	15 18	16 05	16 06	16 18
Cambuslang	226	d																						
Uddingston	226	d	09 30		10 30				11 30		12 30			13 30		14 30					15 31			16 30
Bellshill	226	d	09 34	10 20	10 35			11 20	11 35	12 20	12 35		13 20	13 35	14 20	14 36			15 19		15 35	16 20	16 22	16 35
Motherwell		a				11 13	11 13					13 05					15 13	15 13		15 33				
		d				11 14	11 14					13 06					15 14	15 14		15 34				
Carstairs		d																		16 00				
Holytown		d	09 38		10 39				11 39		12 39			13 39		14 40					15 39			16 39
Carfin		d	09 41		10 41				11 42		12 41			13 41		14 42					15 41			16 41
Cleland		d	09 45		10 45				11 46		12 45			13 45		14 46					15 45			16 45
Hartwood		d	09 50		10 51				11 51		12 51			13 51		14 52					15 51			16 51
Shotts		d	09 54	10 32	10 54			11 32	11 55	12 32	12 55		13 32	13 55	14 32	14 56			15 32		15 57	16 32	16 35	16 55
Fauldhouse		d	10 00		11 00				12 01		13 01			14 01		15 02					16 03			17 01
Breich		d																						
Addiewell		d	10 07		11 07				12 08		13 08			14 08		15 09					16 10			17 08
West Calder		d	10 11	10 44	11 10			11 44	12 12	12 44	13 11		13 44	14 11	14 44	15 12			15 44		16 14	16 44	16 47	17 11
Livingston South		d	10 16	10 49	11 15			11 49	12 17	12 49	13 16		13 49	14 16	14 49	15 17			15 49		16 19	16 49	16 51	17 16
Kirknewton		d	10 20		11 20				12 21		13 22			14 21		15 23				16 16	16 23			17 22
Curriehill		d	10 26		11 26				12 27		13 28			14 26		15 28				16 21	16 29			17 28
Wester Hailes		d	10 29		11 29				12 30		13 31			14 30		15 32				16 24	16 32			17 31
Kingsknowe		d	10 32		11 32				12 33		13 34			14 32		15 34				16 26	16 35			17 34
Slateford		d	10 34		11 35				12 36		13 36			14 35		15 37				16 29	16 38			17 36
Haymarket	230,238,242	d	10 41	11 02	11 42	11 56	11 57	12 03	12 42	13 03	13 42		14 03	14 42	15 02	15 46	15 56	15 56	16 04	16 33	16 46	17 03	17 10	17 42
Edinburgh 10	230,238,242	a	10 46	11 09	11 46	12 02	12 02	12 10	12 46	13 10	13 47	13 54	14 10	14 47	15 09	15 51	16 01	16 01	16 11	16 39	16 52	17 11	17 14	17 47

A until 8 September. To Paignton
B To Plymouth
C from 15 September. To Plymouth
D From Garscadden to Coatbridge Central
E To London Kings Cross
F To North Berwick
G To Penzance
H To Bristol Temple Meads

Glasgow Central, Motherwell, Carstairs and Shotts - Edinburgh

Network Diagram - see first page of Table 225

			XC SX ◇1 A ⊼	XC SO ◇1 A	SR SO	SR SX	SR SO	SR SX	SR	SR SX	SR SO	XC SO ◇1	XC SX ◇1 B	SR	SR SX	SR SO	SR SX	XC SX ◇1	SR	SR
Glasgow Central 15	226	d	16 52	16 52	17 04	17 13	17 18	17 20	18 05	18 14	18 18	18 52	18 59	19 05	19 15	19 18	19 49	21 05	21 18	23 06
Cambuslang	226	d								18 23	18 27									23 15
Uddingston	226	d					17 30			18 29	18 29				19 30	19 30			21 30	23 20
Bellshill	226	d			17 19	17 29	17 34	17 34	18 20	18 34	18 34			19 20	19 35	19 35			21 36	23 25
Motherwell		a	17 13	17 13								19 13	19 14				20 05	21 22		
		d	17 14	17 14								19 14	19 15				20 06	21 23		
Carstairs		d															20 27			
Holytown		d					17 39	17 39		18 38	18 38				19 39	19 39			21 40	23 29
Carfin		d					17 42	17 42		18 43	18 43				19 42	19 42			21 42	23 32
Cleland		d					17 46	17 46		18 47	18 47				19 46	19 46			21 46	23 36
Hartwood		d					17 51	17 51		18 52	18 52				19 51	19 51			21 52	23 41
Shotts		d			17 32	17 44	17 55	17 55	18 32	18 56	18 56			19 33	19 55	19 55			21 56	23 45
Fauldhouse		d					18 01	18 01		19 02	19 02				20 01	20 01			22 02	23 51
Breich		d																		
Addiewell		d					18 08	18 08		19 09	19 09				20 08	20 08			22 09	23 58
West Calder		d			17 44	17 59	18 11	18 11	18 44	19 13	19 13			19 45	20 12	20 12			22 12	00 01
Livingston South		d			17 49	18 03	18 15	18 15	18 49	19 18	19 18			19 50	20 17	20 17			22 16	00 05
Kirknewton		d					18 21	18 21		19 23	19 23				20 21	20 21			22 21	00 10
Curriehill		d					18 26	18 26		19 29	19 29				20 27	20 27			22 26	00 15
Wester Hailes		d					18 30	18 30		19 32	19 32				20 30	20 30			22 30	00 19
Kingsknowe		d					18 32	18 32		19 35	19 35				20 33	20 33			22 32	00 21
Slateford		d					18 35	18 35		19 37	19 37				20 35	20 35			22 35	00 24
Haymarket	230,238,242	d	17 54	17 56	18 09	18 21	18 40	18 40	19 03	19 42	19 42	19 52	19 53	20 02	20 43	20 43	20 53		22 43	00 30
Edinburgh 10	230,238,242	a	17 59	18 01	18 15	18 28	18 46	18 46	19 11	19 48	19 48	19 57	19 58	20 10	20 47	20 47	20 58	22 25	22 48	00 34

Sundays

			SR	XC ◇1 C ⊼	XC ◇1 D	SR	XC ◇1 D	SR	XC ◇1 E	SR	XC ◇1 A ⊼	SR	XC ◇1 B	SR	XC ◇1 F ⊼	XC ◇1 G
Glasgow Central 15	226	d	23p06	10 55	11 51		13 49		14 55		16 55		18 57		20 58	20 58
Cambuslang	226	d	23p15													
Uddingston	226	d	23p20													
Bellshill	226	d	23p25													
Motherwell		a		11 09	12 06		14 03		15 10		17 10		19 10		21 17	21 17
		d		11 10	12 07		14 04		15 11		17 11		19 11		21 18	21 18
Carstairs		d														
Holytown		d	23p29													
Carfin		d	23p32													
Cleland		d	23p36													
Hartwood		d	23p41													
Shotts		d	23p45													
Fauldhouse		d	23p51													
Breich		d														
Addiewell		d	23p58													
West Calder		d	00 01			13 09		15 14		17 14		19 14		21 14		
Livingston South		d	00 05			13 13		15 16		17 16		19 16		21 16		
Kirknewton		d	00 10			13 18		15 21		17 21		19 21		21 21		
Curriehill		d	00 15			13 22		15 27		17 27		19 27		21 27		
Wester Hailes		d	00 19			13 27		15 30		17 30		19 30		21 30		
Kingsknowe		d	00 21			13 28		15 33		17 33		19 33		21 33		
Slateford		d	00 24			13 32		15 35		17 35		19 35		21 35		
Haymarket	230,238,242	d	00 30	11 51	12 49	13 38	14 42	15 41	15 51	17 44	17 51	19 41	19 51	21 41	22 04	22 04
Edinburgh 10	230,238,242	a	00 34	11 55	12 54	13 42	14 47	15 48	15 56	17 48	17 56	19 48	19 56	21 48	22 08	22 08

A To Birmingham New Street
B To Newcastle
C until 9 September, from 28 October. To Penzance
D until 9 September, from 28 October. To Plymouth
E until 9 September, from 28 October. To Bristol Temple Meads
F until 24 June, 2 September, 9 September
G from 1 July, not 2 September, 9 September

Table 226

Mondays to Saturdays

Lanark, Coatbridge, Motherwell, Larkhall, Hamilton, Edinburgh and Bathgate, Airdrie and Springburn - Glasgow - Milngavie, Dalmuir, Balloch and Helensburgh

Network Diagram - see first Page of Table 220

Miles	Miles	Miles	Miles	Miles			SR MO	SR MX	SR MO	SR MX	SR MSX	SR SO	SR MO	SR SO	SR MX	SR MX	SR SO	SR MX	SR MX A	SR B	SR	SR	SR	SR
0	—	—	—	—	**Lanark**	d																		
8½	—	—	—	—	Carluke	d																		
13	—	—	—	—	Wishaw	d																		
14½	—	—	—	—	Holytown	d													00 01					
15	—	—	—	—	Shieldmuir	d																		
—	—	—	—	0	**Coatbridge Central**	d																		
—	—	—	—	1	Whifflet	d																		
16¼	0	0	—	5½	**Motherwell**	a																		
—	—	—	—	—		d	22p40							23p20										
—	3	—	—	—	Bellshill	d													00 04					
20½	5½	—	—	—	Uddingston	d													00 08					
—	—	0¾	—	—	Airbles	d	22p42							23p22										
—	—	—	—	0	**Larkhall**	d											23p37							06 07
—	—	—	—	1½	Merryton	d											23p39							06 09
—	—	—	—	2¾	Chatelherault	d											23p42							06 12
—	—	3	—	5¼	**Hamilton Central**	d	22p47							23p27			23p46							06 16
—	—	3¾	—	0	Hamilton West	d	22p50							23p30			23p48							06 18
—	—	5¾	—	—	Blantyre	d	22p53							23p33			23p52							06 22
22½	—	8¼	—	—	Newton	d	22p57							23p39										
24	9	—	—	—	Cambuslang	d	23p01							23p43					00 13					
25¾	10¾	—	—	—	Rutherglen	d	23p04							23p47			00 01							06 28
26½	11½	—	—	—	Dalmarnock §	d																		
27	12	—	—	—	Bridgeton	d	23p07							23p51										
—	—	—	0	—	**Edinburgh**	d				22p19			22p40		22p51	23p37		23p51		04 50				
—	—	—	1¼	—	Haymarket	d				22p23			22p44		22p55	23p42		23p55						
—	—	—	3¾	—	Edinburgh Park	d				22p30			22p49		23p00	23p47		23p59						
—	—	—	12½	—	Uphall	d				22p38			22p57		23p08	23p55		00 08						
—	—	—	15½	—	Livingston North	d				22p41			23p00		23p11	23p59		00 11						
—	—	—	18½	—	**Bathgate**	a				22p46			23p05		23p16	00 04		00 16						
—	—	—	—	—		d				22p47			23p06		23p17								05 36	
—	—	—	21	—	Armadale	d				22p51			23p10		23p21								05 40	
—	—	—	23¼	—	Blackridge	d				22p55			23p14		23p25								05 43	
—	—	—	28¾	—	Caldercruix	d				23p01			23p20		23p31								05 50	
—	—	—	31¾	—	Drumgelloch	d				23p05			23p24		23p35								05 53	
—	—	—	33¼	—	**Airdrie**	d			22p58	23p12			23p28		23p38						05 35		05 57	
—	—	—	34¼	—	Coatdyke	d			23p00	23p14			23p30		23p40						05 37		05 59	
—	—	—	35¼	—	Coatbridge Sunnyside	d			23p02	23p16			23p32		23p43						05 39		06 01	
—	—	—	35¾	—	Blairhill	d			23p05	23p19			23p35		23p45						05 42		06 04	
—	—	—	38½	—	Easterhouse	d			23p09	23p23			23p39		23p49						05 46		06 08	
—	—	—	39½	—	Garrowhill	d			23p11	23p25			23p41		23p52						05 48		06 10	
—	—	—	40¾	—	Shettleston	d			23p14	23p28			23p44		23p54						05 51		06 13	
—	—	—	41½	—	Carntyne	d			23p16	23p30			23p46		23p56						05 53		06 15	
—	—	—	—	0	**Springburn**	d		23p09			23p39	23p39												
—	—	—	—	0¼	Barnhill	d		23p10			23p40	23p40												
—	—	—	—	1½	Alexandra Parade	d		23p13			23p43	23p43												
—	—	—	—	1¾	Duke Street	d		23p15			23p45	23p45												
—	—	—	43¼	2¼	Bellgrove	d		23p17	23p19	23p33	23p47	23p47	23p49		23p59						05 56		06 18	
—	—	—	43¾	2¾	High Street	d		23p19	23p21	23p35	23p49	23p49	23p51		00 02						05 58		06 20	
—	—	—	44¼	3¼	**Glasgow Queen St LL**	a		23p21	23p23	23p37	23p51	23p51	23p53		00 04						06 00		06 22	
—	—	—	—	—		d		23p23	23p24	23p45	23p53	23p53	23p54		00 04						06 01		06 23	
—	—	—	45	4	Charing Cross	d		23p25	23p27	23p47	23p55	23p55	23p57		00 06						06 03		06 25	
28¼	13¼	—	—	—	Argyle Street	d								23p55			00 06							06 34
28¾	13¾	—	—	—	**Glasgow Central LL**	a	23p14							23p57			00 07		00b24					06 37
—	—	—	—	—		d	23p14							23p58			00 07							06 37
29¼	14¼	—	—	—	Anderston	d								23p59			00 09							06 39
29¾	14¾	—	—	—	Exhibition Centre	d	23p18							00 01			00 11							06 41
31	16	—	47	6	**Partick**	d	23p22	23p29	23p32	23p51	23p59	23p59	00 01	00 05	00 11		00 14				06 07		06 29	06 44
31½	16½	0	47½	6½	Hyndland	d	23p24	23p32	23p34	23p53	00 02	00 02	00 03	00 08	00 13		00 17				06 10		06 32	06 47
—	—	0½	—	—	Jordanhill	d	23p26			23p55	00 04		00 05		00 15						06 12			
—	—	1½	—	—	Scotstounhill	d	23p28			23p58	00 06		00 07		00 17						06 14			
—	—	2	—	—	Garscadden	d	23p30			23p59	00a08		00 09		00a19						06 16			
—	—	3	—	—	Yoker	d	23p33			00 02			00 12								06 19			
—	—	4	—	—	Clydebank	d	23p35			00 04											06 21			
32½	17½	—	48½	7½	Anniesland	d		23p35	23p37			00 05		00 12			00 20						06 35	06 50
33¾	18¾	—	49¾	8¾	Westerton	d		23p38	23p40			00 08		00 15			00 23			05 56			06 38	06 53
35	—	—	—	—	Bearsden	d								00 17										
35¾	—	—	—	—	Hillfoot	d								00 18										
37¼	—	—	—	—	**Milngavie**	a								00 23										
—	20	—	51	10	Drumchapel	d		23p40	23p42			00 10					00 25						06 40	06 55
—	20¾	—	51¾	10¾	Drumry	d		23p42	23p44			00 12					00 27						06 42	06 57
—	21¾	—	52¾	11¾	Singer	d		23p45	23p47			00 15					00 30						06 45	07 00
—	22¼	5¼	53½	12½	**Dalmuir**	a	23p39	23p47	23p49	00 08		00 17	00 16				00 32			06 03	06 24		06 47	07 02
—	—	—	—	—		d	23p39	23p48	23p50	00 08		00 18								06 04	06 24	06 30	06 48	
—	—	—	54¾	13¾	Kilpatrick	d	23p41	23p51				00 21										06 32	06 51	
—	—	—	56½	15½	Bowling	d	23p44	23p54				00 24										06 35	06 54	
—	—	—	59¼	18¼	Dumbarton East	d	23p49	23p58	23p58	00 15		00 28									06 32	06 40	06 58	
—	—	—	60	19	Dumbarton Central	d	23p51	23p59	23p59	00 18		00 30									06 34	06 42	07 00	
—	—	—	60¼	19¼	Dalreoch	d	23p52	00 02	00 01	00 19		00 32									06 35	06 43	07 02	
—	—	—	—	20¾	Renton	d	23p55	00 05				00 35									06 38		07 05	
—	—	—	—	22	Alexandria	d	23p58	00 07				00 37									06 41		07 07	
—	—	—	—	23	**Balloch**	a	00 01	00 11				00 41									06 44		07 11	
—	—	—	63½	—	Cardross	d			00 06	00 24												06 48		
—	—	—	67¼	—	Craigendoran	d			00 11	00 29												06 53		
—	—	—	68¼	—	**Helensburgh Central**	a			00 14	00 32										06c26		06 56		

§ Station closed between 4 June and 24 November inclusive

A From Edinburgh

B To Fort William

b Glasgow Central High Level

c Helensburgh Upper

Table 226

Mondays to Saturdays

Lanark, Coatbridge, Motherwell, Larkhall, Hamilton, Edinburgh and Bathgate, Airdrie and Springburn - Glasgow - Milngavie, Dalmuir, Balloch and Helensburgh

Network Diagram - see first Page of Table 220

		SR	SR	SR SO	SR SX	SR	SR SX	SR	SR	SR SX	SR	SR SO	SR SX	SR	SR A	SR SX	SR SX	SR	SR	SR SX	SR	SR SO
Lanark	d										06 23					06 53						
Carluke	d										06 33					07 03						
Wishaw	d										06 38					07 08						
Holytown	d														06 58							
Shieldmuir	d										06 42					07 12						
Coatbridge Central	d													06 40								
Whifflet	d													06 42								
Motherwell	a										06 46			06 51		07 15						
	d		06 16			06 21					06 46			06 51		07 15					07 18	
Bellshill	d		06 22								06 52				07 04						07 24	
Uddingston	d		06 26								06 56				07 10						07 28	
Airbles	d					06 23								06 54								
Larkhall	d							06 37										07 07				
Merryton	d							06 39										07 09				
Chatelherault	d							06 42										07 12				
Hamilton Central	d					06 28		06 46						06 59				07 16				
Hamilton West	d					06 31		06 48						07 01				07 18				
Blantyre	d					06 34		06 52						07 05				07 22				
Newton	d					06 38								07 09								
Cambuslang	d		06 31			06 42					07 01			07 12	07 16						07 33	
Rutherglen	d		06 34			06 45		06 57			07 04			07 16		07 25		07 30			07 37	
Dalmarnock §	d																					
Bridgeton	d		06 38			06 49					07 08			07 20							07 41	
Edinburgh	d									06 07									06 21	06 37		
Haymarket	d									06 11									06 25	06 41		
Edinburgh Park	d									06 16									06 30	06 46		
Uphall	d									06 24									06 38	06 54		
Livingston North	d									06 27									06 41	06 57		
Bathgate	a									06 33									06 46	07 03		
	d	05 51							06 21	06 34									06 47	07 04		
Armadale	d	05 55							06 25										06 51			
Blackridge	d	05 58							06 28										06 55			
Caldercruix	d	06 05							06 35										07 01			
Drumgelloch	d	06 08							06 38	06 46									07 05	07 16		
Airdrie	d	06 12			06 27				06 42	06 50			06 57						07 12	07 20		
Coatdyke	d	06 14			06 29				06 44				06 59						07 14	07 22		
Coatbridge Sunnyside	d	06 16			06 31				06 46	06 53			07 01						07 16	07 24		
Blairhill	d	06 19			06 34				06 49				07 04						07 19	07 27		
Easterhouse	d	06 23			06 38				06 53				07 08						07 23			
Garrowhill	d	06 25			06 40				06 55				07 10						07 25			
Shettleston	d	06 28			06 43				06 58				07 13						07 28			
Carntyne	d	06 30			06 45				07 00				07 15						07 30			
Springburn	d			06 39			06 49					07 09					07 19					07 39
Barnhill	d			06 40			06 50					07 10					07 20					07 40
Alexandra Parade	d			06 43			06 53					07 13					07 23					07 43
Duke Street	d			06 45			06 55					07 15					07 25					07 45
Bellgrove	d	06 33		06 47	06 48		06 57		07 03			07 17	07 18				07 27		07 33			07 47
High Street	d	06 35		06 49	06 50		06 59		07 05	07 10		07 19	07 20				07 29		07 35	07 40		07 49
Glasgow Queen St LL	a	06 37		06 51	06 52		07 01		07 08	07 12		07 21	07 22				07 31		07 37	07 42		07 51
	d	06 40		06 53	06 53		07 02		07 10	07 13		07 23	07 23				07 32		07 40	07 43		07 53
Charing Cross	d	06 42		06 55	06 55		07 04		07 12	07 15		07 25	07 25				07 34		07 42	07 45		07 55
Argyle Street	d		06 42			06 53		07 02			07 12			07 23		07 30		07 35			07 44	
Glasgow Central LL	a		06 46			06 55		07 06			07 15			07 26	07b29	07 31		07 37			07 46	
	d		06 46			06 58		07 07			07 16			07 28		07 32		07 38			07 46	
Anderston	d		06 48			06 59		07 09			07 18			07 29		07a33		07 39			07 48	
Exhibition Centre	d		06 50			07 01		07 11			07 20			07 31				07 41			07 50	
Partick	d	06 47	06 54	06 59	06 59	07 05	07 08	07 14	07 17	07 20	07 24	07 29	07 29	07 35			07 38	07 45	07 47	07 50	07 53	07 59
Hyndland	d	06 49	06 56	07 02	07 02	07 08	07 10	07 16	07 19	07 22	07 26	07 32	07 32	07 38			07 40	07 47	07 49	07 52	07 55	08 02
Jordanhill	d		06 58				07 12				07 28						07 42				07 57	
Scotstounhill	d		07 00				07 15				07 30						07 45				08 00	
Garscadden	d	06 53	07 02				07 17				07 32						07 47				08 02	
Yoker	d		07 05				07 19				07 35						07 49				08 05	
Clydebank	d		07 07				07 21				07 37						07 51				08 07	
Anniesland	d			07 05	07 05	07 11		07 19		07 25		07 35	07 35	07 41				07 50		07 55		08 05
Westerton	d			07 08	07 08	07 14		07 22		07 28		07 38	07 38	07 44				07 53		07 58		08 08
Bearsden	d					07 16				07 31				07 46						08 01		
Hillfoot	d					07 17				07 33				07 48						08 03		
Milngavie	a					07 22				07 37				07 52						08 07		
Drumchapel	d			07 10	07 10			07 25				07 40	07 40					07 56				08 10
Drumry	d			07 12	07 12			07 27				07 42	07 42					07 58				08 12
Singer	d			07 15	07 15			07 29				07 45	07 45					08 00				08 15
Dalmuir	a	06 59	07 11	07 17	07 17		07 26	07 32	07 29		07 41	07 47	07 47				07 56	08 03	07 59		08 11	08 17
	d	06 59		07 18	07 18				07 29			07 48	07 48						07 59			08 18
Kilpatrick	d			07 21	07 21							07 51	07 51									08 21
Bowling	d			07 24	07 24							07 54	07 54									08 24
Dumbarton East	d	07 06		07 28	07 28				07 36			07 58	07 58						08 06			08 28
Dumbarton Central	d	07 09		07 30	07 30				07 39			08 00	08 00						08 09			08 30
Dalreoch	d	07 10		07 32	07 32				07 40			08 02	08 02						08 10			08 32
Renton	d			07 35	07 35							08 05	08 05									08 35
Alexandria	d			07 37	07 37							08 07	08 07									08 37
Balloch	a			07 41	07 41							08 11	08 11									08 41
Cardross	d	07 15							07 45										08 15			
Craigendoran	d	07 20							07 50										08 20			
Helensburgh Central	a	07 24							07 54										08 24			

§ Station closed between 4 June and 24 November inclusive

A From Edinburgh

b Glasgow Central High Level

Lanark, Coatbridge, Motherwell, Larkhall, Hamilton, Edinburgh and Bathgate, Airdrie and Springburn - Glasgow - Milngavie, Dalmuir, Balloch and Helensburgh

Network Diagram - see first Page of Table 220

		SR SX	SR SO	SR SX	SR SX	SR SO	SR SX	SR	SR SX	SR ◇ A	SR SO	SR SX	SR SX	SR SX	SR SO B	SR SO	SR SX	SR SO	SR SX	SR SX	SR SO	SR	SR SX
Lanark	d						07 22				07 23									07 47			
Carluke	d						07 32				07 33									07 57			
Wishaw	d						07 37				07 38									08 04			
Holytown	d														08 00								
Shieldmuir	d						07 41				07 42									08 07			
Coatbridge Central	d																07 40						
Whifflet	d																07 42						
Motherwell	a						07 44				07 46						07 49			08 13			
	d		07 19	07 19			07 44				07 47		07 47				07 50	07 50		08 13			
Bellshill	d										07 53		07 53		08 03					08 19			
Uddingston	d										07 57		07 57		08 07								
Airbles	d		07 21	07 21													07 52	07 52					
Larkhall	d					07 37						07 37									08 07		
Merryton	d					07 39						07 39									08 09		
Chatelherault	d					07 42						07 42									08 12		
Hamilton Central	d		07 26	07 26		07 46						07 46					07 57	07 57			08 15		
Hamilton West	d		07 29	07 29		07 48						07 48					08 00	08 00			08 18		
Blantyre	d		07 32	07 32		07 52						07 52					08 03	08 03			08 21		
Newton	d		07 37	07 37								07 56					08 07	08 07					
Cambuslang	d		07 41	07 41							08 02	08 00	08 05				08 11	08 11					
Rutherglen	d		07 46	07 46		07 59	07 56				08 05	08 05	08 10				08 14	08 14		08 26	08 30		
Dalmarnock §	d																						
Bridgeton	d		07 50	07 50							08 08	08 09	08 14				08 19	08 19					
Edinburgh	d							06 48	07 07													07 21	07 37
Haymarket	d							06 52	07 11													07 25	07 41
Edinburgh Park	d							06 57	07 16													07 30	07 46
Uphall	d							07 05	07 24													07 38	07 54
Livingston North	d							07 08	07 27													07 41	07 57
Bathgate	a							07 13	07 33													07 46	08 03
	d							07 17	07 34													07 47	08 04
Armadale	d							07 21														07 51	
Blackridge	d							07 25														07 55	
Caldercruix	d							07 31														08 01	
Drumgelloch	d							07 35	07 46													08 05	08 16
Airdrie	d	07 27						07 42	07 50					07 57								08 12	08 20
Coatdyke	d	07 29						07 44	07 52					07 59								08 14	08 22
Coatbridge Sunnyside	d	07 31						07 46	07 54					08 01								08 16	08 24
Blairhill	d	07 34						07 49	07 57					08 04								08 19	08 27
Easterhouse	d	07 38						07 53						08 08								08 23	
Garrowhill	d	07 40						07 55						08 10								08 25	
Shettleston	d	07 43						07 58						08 13								08 28	
Carntyne	d	07 45						08 00						08 15								08 30	
Springburn	d				07 49											08 09			08 19				
Barnhill	d				07 50											08 10			08 20				
Alexandra Parade	d				07 53											08 13			08 23				
Duke Street	d				07 55											08 15			08 25				
Bellgrove	d	07 48			07 57			08 03						08 18		08 18			08 27			08 33	
High Street	d	07 50			07 59			08 05	08 10					08 20		08 20			08 29			08 35	08 40
Glasgow Queen St LL 10 ⛴	a	07 52			08 01			08 07	08 12					08 22		08 22			08 31			08 37	08 42
	d	07 53			08 02			08 10	08 13	08b21				08 23		08 23			08 32			08 40	08 43
Charing Cross	d	07 55			08 04			08 12	08 15					08 25		08 25			08 34			08 42	08 45
Argyle Street	d		07 54	07 54		08 04	08 02				08 13	08 13	08 18				08 23	08 23		08 32	08 36		
Glasgow Central LL 15	a		07 56	07 56		08 07	08 03				08 15	08 15	08 21		08e24		08 25	08 25		08 33	08 37		
	d		07 58	08 00		08 07	08 07				08 16	08 18	08 22				08 28	08 28		08 37	08 37		
Anderston	d		07 59	08 01		08 09	08 09				08 18	08 19	08a23				08 30	08 30		08 39	08 39		
Exhibition Centre	d		08 01	08 03		08 11	08 11				08 20	08 21					08 32	08 32		08 41	08 41		
Partick ⛴	d	07 59	08 05	08 07	08 09	08 14	08 14	08 17	08 20		08 23	08 24		08 29		08 29	08 36	08 36	08 39	08 44	08 44	08 47	08 50
Hyndland 3	d	08 02	08 08	08 09	08 11	08 17	08 17	08 19	08 22		08 25	08 27		08 32		08 32	08 38	08 38	08 41	08 47	08 47	08 49	08 52
Jordanhill	d				08 13						08 27	08 28							08 43				
Scotstounhill	d				08 15						08 30	08 30							08 45				
Garscadden	d				08 17						08 32	08 32							08 47				
Yoker	d				08 20						08 35	08 35							08 50				
Clydebank	d				08 22						08 37	08 37							08 52				
Anniesland	d	08 05	08 11	08 14		08 20	08 20		08 25					08 35		08 35	08 41	08 41		08 50	08 50		08 55
Westerton	d	08 08	08 14	08 21		08 23	08 25		08 28					08 38		08 38	08 44	08 44		08 53	08 53		08 58
Bearsden	d		08 16	08 24					08 31								08 46	08 46					09 01
Hillfoot	d		08 17	08 26					08 33								08 48	08 48					09 03
Milngavie	a		08 22	08 29					08 39								08 52	08 52					09 07
Drumchapel	d	08 10				08 25	08 27							08 40		08 40				08 55	08 55		
Drumry	d	08 12				08 27	08 29							08 42		08 42				08 57	08 57		
Singer	d	08 15				08 30	08 32							08 45		08 45				09 00	09 00		
Dalmuir	a	08 17			08 28	08 32	08 34	08 29		08 39	08 41	08 43		08 47		08 47			08 56	09 02	09 02	08 59	
	d	08 18						08 29		08 39				08 48		08 48						08 59	
Kilpatrick	d	08 21												08 51		08 51							
Bowling	d	08 24												08 54		08 54							
Dumbarton East	d	08 28						08 36						08 58		08 58						09 06	
Dumbarton Central	d	08 30						08 39		08 48				09 00		09 00						09 09	
Dalreoch	d	08 32						08 40						09 02		09 02						09 10	
Renton	d	08 35												09 05		09 05							
Alexandria	d	08 37												09 07		09 07							
Balloch	a	08 41												09 11		09 11							
Cardross	d							08 45														09 15	
Craigendoran	d							08 50														09 20	
Helensburgh Central	a							08 55		09c03												09 24	

§ Station closed between 4 June and 24 November inclusive
A To Oban
B From Newcraighall
b Glasgow Queen St High Level
c Helensburgh Upper
e Glasgow Central High Level

Lanark, Coatbridge, Motherwell, Larkhall, Hamilton, Edinburgh and Bathgate, Airdrie and Springburn - Glasgow - Milngavie, Dalmuir, Balloch and Helensburgh

Network Diagram - see first Page of Table 220

		SR SX	SR	SR SX A	SR SX	SR SO	SR SO	SR SX	SR SX ◇ B	SR SX	SR SX	SR	SR	SR SX	SR SO	SR SO	SR SX	SR SO	SR SX	SR	SR	SR
Lanark	d						07 53				08 23					08 23						
Carluke	d			08 13			08 03				08 33					08 33						
Wishaw	d			08 21			08 08				08 38					08 38						
Holytown	d						08 13															
Shieldmuir	d			08 23							08 42					08 42						
Coatbridge Central	d																					
Whifflet	d																					
Motherwell	a			08 26			08 19				08 46					08 45						
	d		08 17	08 27			08 20	08 20			08 46					08 46	08 46			08 50		
Bellshill	d		08 22													08 52	08 52					
Uddingston	d		08 26	08 33												08 58	08 58					
Airbles	d						08 22	08 22												08 52		
Larkhall	d	08 07										08 37										09 07
Merryton	d	08 09										08 39										09 09
Chatelherault	d	08 12										08 42										09 12
Hamilton Central	d	08 15					08 27	08 27				08 46								08 57		09 16
Hamilton West	d	08 18					08 30	08 30				08 48								09 00		09 18
Blantyre	d	08 21					08 33	08 33				08 52								09 03		09 22
Newton	d						08 37	08 37												09 07		
Cambuslang	d	08 30	08 31				08 41	08 41								09 03	09 03			09 11		
Rutherglen	d		08 34				08 46	08 46			08 56	09 00				09 07	09 07			09 16		09 29
Dalmarnock §	d																					
Bridgeton	d		08 38				08 51	08 51								09 11	09 11			09 19		
Edinburgh	d												07 54	08 07								
Haymarket	d												07 57	08 11								
Edinburgh Park	d												08 02	08 16								
Uphall	d												08 09	08 24								
Livingston North	d												08 13	08 27								
Bathgate	a												08 17	08 33								
	d												08 18	08 34	08 34							
Armadale	d												08 22									
Blackridge	d												08 25									
Caldercruix	d												08 32									
Drumgelloch	d												08 35	08 46	08 46							
Airdrie	d				08 27								08 42	08 50	08 50				08 57			
Coatdyke	d				08 29								08 44						08 59			
Coatbridge Sunnyside	d				08 31								08 46	08 53	08 53				09 01			
Blairhill	d				08 34								08 49						09 04			
Easterhouse	d				08 38								08 53						09 08			
Garrowhill	d				08 40								08 55						09 10			
Shettleston	d				08 43								08 58						09 13			
Carntyne	d				08 45								09 00						09 15			
Springburn	d					08 39				08 49								09 09			09 19	
Barnhill	d					08 40				08 50								09 10			09 20	
Alexandra Parade	d					08 43				08 53								09 13			09 23	
Duke Street	d					08 45				08 55								09 15			09 25	
Bellgrove	d				08 48	08 48				08 57			09 03					09 17	09 18		09 27	
High Street	d				08 50	08 50				08 59			09 05	09 10	09 10			09 19	09 20		09 29	
Glasgow Queen St LL 10 ⛴	a				08 52	08 52				09 01			09 07	09 12	09 12			09 23	09 22		09 31	
	d				08 53	08 53			09b03	09 02			09 10	09 13	09 13			09 23	09 23		09 32	
Charing Cross	d				08 55	08 55				09 04			09 12	09 15	09 15			09 25	09 25		09 34	
Argyle Street	d	08 36	08 42	08 47			08 55	08 55			09 01	09 05				09 15	09 15			09 24		09 34
Glasgow Central LL 15	a	08 37	08 46	08 48			08 56	08 56			09 03	09 07				09 16	09 16			09 26		09 37
	d	08 39	08 46	08 48			08 59	08 59			09 03	09 07				09 18	09 18			09 28		09 37
Anderston	d	08a42	08 48	08 51			09 00	09 00			09 05	09 09				09 20	09 20			09 29		09 39
Exhibition Centre	d		08 50	08 54			09 02	09 02			09 07	09 11				09 22	09 22			09 31		09 41
Partick ⛴	d		08 54	08 57	08 59	08 59	09 06	09 06		09 09	09 12	09 14	09 17	09 20	09 20	09 25	09 25	09 29	09 29	09 35	09 39	09 44
Hyndland 3	d		08 56	08 59	09 02	09 02	09 09	09 09		09 11	09 14	09 17	09 20	09 22	09 22	09 27	09 27	09 32	09 32	09 38	09 41	09 47
Jordanhill	d		08 58	09 01						09 12	09 17					09 29	09 29				09 43	
Scotstounhill	d		09 00	09 03						09 15	09 19					09 32	09 32				09 45	
Garscadden	d		09 02	09a06						09 18	09a21					09 34	09 34				09 47	
Yoker	d		09 05							09 20						09 36	09 36				09 50	
Clydebank	d		09 07							09 22						09 38	09 38				09 52	
Anniesland	d				09 05	09 05	09 12	09 12				09 20		09 25	09 25			09 35	09 35	09 41		09 50
Westerton	d				09 08	09 08	09 15	09 15				09 23		09 28	09 28			09 38	09 38	09 44		09 53
Bearsden	d						09 17	09 17						09 31	09 31					09 46		
Hillfoot	d						09 20	09 20						09 33	09 33					09 47		
Milngavie	a						09 23	09 23						09 37	09 37					09 52		
Drumchapel	d				09 10	09 10						09 25						09 40	09 40			09 55
Drumry	d				09 12	09 12						09 27						09 42	09 42			09 57
Singer	d				09 15	09 15						09 30						09 45	09 45			10 00
Dalmuir	a		09 11		09 17	09 17			09 23	09 26		09 32	09 29			09 42	09 42	09 47	09 47		09 56	10 02
	d				09 18	09 18			09 24				09 29					09 48	09 48			
Kilpatrick	d				09 21	09 21												09 51	09 51			
Bowling	d				09 24	09 24												09 54	09 54			
Dumbarton East	d				09 28	09 28							09 36					09 58	09 58			
Dumbarton Central	d				09 30	09 30			09 36				09 39					10 00	10 00			
Dalreoch	d				09 32	09 32							09 40					10 02	10 02			
Renton	d				09 35	09 35												10 05	10 05			
Alexandria	d				09 37	09 37												10 07	10 07			
Balloch	a				09 41	09 41												10 11	10 11			
Cardross	d												09 45									
Craigendoran	d												09 49									
Helensburgh Central	a								09c50				09 54									

§ Station closed between 4 June and 24 November inclusive
A From Carstairs
B From 21 May until 28 September. To Mallaig
b Glasgow Queen St High Level
c Helensburgh Upper

Lanark, Coatbridge, Motherwell, Larkhall, Hamilton, Edinburgh and Bathgate, Airdrie and Springburn - Glasgow - Milngavie, Dalmuir, Balloch and Helensburgh

Network Diagram - see first Page of Table 220

Station		SR	SR	SR	SR	SR SO	SR SX	SR A	SR	SR	SR	SR	SR	SR	SR	SR SO ◇ B	SR	SR	SR	SR	SR	SR	SR
Lanark	d					08 53							09 23										09 53
Carluke	d					09 03							09 33										10 04
Wishaw	d					09 08							09 38										10 08
Holytown	d					09 13		09 33															10 13
Shieldmuir	d												09 42										
Coatbridge Central	d																						
Whifflet	d																						
Motherwell	a					09 22							09 46										10 20
	d			09 16		09 22	09 22						09 47		09 50						10 16		10 20
Bellshill	d			09 22				09 36					09 52								10 22		
Uddingston	d			09 26				09 41					09 56								10 26		
Airbles	d					09 25	09 25								09 52								10 23
Larkhall	d									09 37								10 07					
Merryton	d									09 39								10 09					
Chatelherault	d									09 42								10 12					
Hamilton Central	d					09 30	09 30			09 46					09 57			10 16					10 28
Hamilton West	d					09 32	09 32			09 48					10 00			10 18					10 30
Blantyre	d					09 36	09 36			09 52					10 03			10 22					10 34
Newton	d					09 40	09 40								10 08								10 38
Cambuslang	d			09 31		09 43	09 43						10 01		10 11						10 31		10 41
Rutherglen	d			09 34		09 47	09 47			09 59			10 08		10 15			10 30			10 34		10 48
Dalmarnock §	d																						
Bridgeton	d			09 38		09 51	09 51						10 12		10 19						10 38		10 52
Edinburgh	d	08 21	08 37								08 48	09 07							09 21	09 37			
Haymarket	d	08 25	08 41								08 52	09 11							09 25	09 41			
Edinburgh Park	d	08 30	08 46								08 57	09 16							09 30	09 46			
Uphall	d	08 38	08 54								09 05	09 24							09 38	09 54			
Livingston North	d	08 41	08 57								09 08	09 27							09 41	09 57			
Bathgate	a	08 46	09 03								09 13	09 33							09 46	10 03			
	d	08 47	09 04								09 17	09 34							09 47	10 04			
Armadale	d	08 51									09 21								09 51				
Blackridge	d	08 55									09 25								09 55				
Caldercruix	d	09 01									09 31								10 01				
Drumgelloch	d	09 05	09 16								09 35	09 46							10 05	10 16			
Airdrie	d	09 12	09 20		09 27						09 42	09 50		09 57					10 12	10 20		10 27	
Coatdyke	d	09 14			09 29						09 44			09 59					10 14			10 29	
Coatbridge Sunnyside	d	09 16	09 23		09 31						09 46	09 53		10 01					10 16	10 23		10 31	
Blairhill	d	09 19			09 34						09 49			10 04					10 19			10 34	
Easterhouse	d	09 23			09 38						09 53			10 08					10 23			10 38	
Garrowhill	d	09 25			09 40						09 55			10 10					10 25			10 40	
Shettleston	d	09 28			09 43						09 58			10 13					10 28			10 43	
Carntyne	d	09 30			09 45						10 00			10 15					10 30			10 45	
Springburn	d								09 49								10 19						
Barnhill	d								09 50								10 20						
Alexandra Parade	d								09 53								10 23						
Duke Street	d								09 55								10 25						
Bellgrove	d	09 33			09 48				09 57		10 03			10 18			10 27		10 33			10 48	
High Street	d	09 35	09 40		09 50				09 59		10 05	10 10		10 20			10 29		10 35	10 40		10 50	
Glasgow Queen St LL 10	a	09 37	09 42		09 52				10 01		10 07	10 12		10 22			10 31		10 37	10 42		10 52	
	d	09 40	09 43		09 53				10 02		10 10	10 13		10 23		10c37	10 32		10 40	10 43		10 53	
Charing Cross	d	09 42	09 45		09 55				10 04		10 12	10 15		10 25			10 34		10 42	10 45		10 55	
Argyle Street	d			09 42		09 54	09 54			10 04			10 14		10 24			10 36			10 42		10 56
Glasgow Central LL 15	a			09 46		09 56	09 56	09b57		10 07			10 16		10 26			10 37			10 46		10 57
	d			09 46		09 58	09 58			10 07			10 16		10 28			10 38			10 46		10 58
Anderston	d			09 48		09 59	09 59			10 09			10 18		10 29			10 39			10 48		10 59
Exhibition Centre	d			09 50		10 01	10 01			10 11			10 20		10 31			10 41			10 50		11 01
Partick	d	09 47	09 50	09 54	09 59	10 05	10 05		10 09	10 14	10 17	10 20	10 24	10 29	10 35		10 39	10 45	10 47	10 50	10 54	10 59	11 05
Hyndland 3	d	09 49	09 52	09 56	10 02	10 08	10 08		10 11	10 17	10 19	10 22	10 26	10 32	10 38		10 41	10 47	10 49	10 52	10 56	11 02	11 08
Jordanhill	d			09 58					10 13				10 28				10 43				10 58		
Scotstounhill	d			10 00					10 15				10 30				10 45				11 00		
Garscadden	d			10 02					10 17				10 32				10 47				11 02		
Yoker	d			10 05					10 20				10 35				10 50				11 05		
Clydebank	d			10 07					10 22				10 37				10 52				11 07		
Anniesland	d		09 55		10 05	10 11	10 11			10 20		10 25		10 35	10 41			10 50		10 55		11 05	11 11
Westerton	d		09 58		10 08	10 14	10 14			10 23		10 28		10 38	10 44			10 53		10 58		11 08	11 15
Bearsden	d		10 01			10 16	10 16					10 31			10 46					11 01			11 17
Hillfoot	d		10 03			10 18	10 18					10 33			10 47					11 03			11 19
Milngavie	a		10 07			10 22	10 22					10 37			10 52					11 07			11 25
Drumchapel	d				10 10					10 25				10 40				10 55				11 10	
Drumry	d				10 12					10 27				10 42				10 57				11 12	
Singer	d				10 15					10 30				10 45				11 00				11 15	
Dalmuir	a	09 59		10 11	10 17				10 26	10 32	10 29		10 41	10 47		10 52	10 56	11 02	10 59		11 11	11 17	
	d	09 59			10 18						10 29			10 48		10 52			10 59			11 18	
Kilpatrick	d				10 21									10 51								11 21	
Bowling	d				10 24									10 54								11 24	
Dumbarton East	d	10 06			10 28						10 36			10 58					11 06			11 28	
Dumbarton Central	d	10 09			10 30						10 39			11 00		11 05			11 09			11 30	
Dalreoch	d	10 10			10 32						10 40			11 02					11 10			11 32	
Renton	d				10 35									11 05								11 35	
Alexandria	d				10 37									11 07								11 37	
Balloch	a				10 41									11 11								11 41	
Cardross	d	10 15									10 45								11 15				
Craigendoran	d	10 20									10 50								11 20				
Helensburgh Central	a	10 24									10 54					11e20			11 24				

§ Station closed between 4 June and 24 November inclusive
A From Edinburgh
B From 26 May until 27 October. To Oban
b Glasgow Central High Level
c Glasgow Queen St High Level
e Helensburgh Upper

Table 226

Mondays to Saturdays

Lanark, Coatbridge, Motherwell, Larkhall, Hamilton, Edinburgh and Bathgate, Airdrie and Springburn - Glasgow - Milngavie, Dalmuir, Balloch and Helensburgh

Network Diagram - see first Page of Table 220

Station		SR A	SR	SR	SR	SR	SR	SR	SR	SR	SR	SR	SR	SR	SR	SR	SR A	SR	SR	SR	SR	SR ◇ B	SR
Lanark	d						10 21									10 53							11 23
Carluke	d						10 31									11 03							11 33
Wishaw	d						10 37									11 08							11 41
Holytown	d	10 33														11 13	11 33						
Shieldmuir	d						10 41																11 44
Coatbridge Central	d																						
Whifflet	d																						
Motherwell	a						10 45									11 20							11 48
	d						10 46		10 50					11 16		11 20							11 49
Bellshill	d	10 36					10 52							11 22			11 36						11 55
Uddingston	d	10 41					10 56							11 26			11 41						12 01
Airbles	d								10 52							11 22							
Larkhall	d			10 37							11 07								11 37				
Merryton	d			10 39							11 09								11 39				
Chatelherault	d			10 42							11 12								11 42				
Hamilton Central	d			10 46					10 57		11 16					11 27			11 46				
Hamilton West	d			10 48					11 00		11 18					11 30			11 48				
Blantyre	d			10 52					11 03		11 22					11 33			11 52				
Newton	d								11 07							11 37							
Cambuslang	d						11 01		11 11					11 31		11 41							12 06
Rutherglen	d			10 59			11 05		11 15		11 29			11 34		11 46			11 59				12 09
Dalmarnock §	d																						
Bridgeton	d						11 09		11 19					11 38		11 50							12 13
Edinburgh	d				09 48	10 07						10 21	10 37							10 48	11 07		
Haymarket	d				09 52	10 11						10 25	10 41							10 52	11 11		
Edinburgh Park	d				09 57	10 16						10 30	10 46							10 57	11 16		
Uphall	d				10 05	10 24						10 38	10 54							11 05	11 24		
Livingston North	d				10 08	10 27						10 41	10 57							11 08	11 27		
Bathgate	a				10 13	10 33						10 46	11 03							11 13	11 33		
	d				10 17	10 34						10 47	11 04							11 17	11 34		
Armadale	d				10 21							10 51								11 21			
Blackridge	d				10 25							10 55								11 25			
Caldercruix	d				10 31							11 01								11 31			
Drumgelloch	d				10 35	10 46						11 05	11 16							11 35	11 46		
Airdrie	d				10 42	10 50		10 57				11 12	11 20		11 27					11 42	11 50		
Coatdyke	d				10 44			10 59				11 14			11 29					11 44			
Coatbridge Sunnyside	d				10 46	10 53		11 01				11 16	11 23		11 31					11 46	11 53		
Blairhill	d				10 49			11 04				11 19			11 34					11 49			
Easterhouse	d				10 53			11 08				11 23			11 38					11 53			
Garrowhill	d				10 55			11 10				11 25			11 40					11 55			
Shettleston	d				10 58			11 13				11 28			11 43					11 58			
Carntyne	d				11 00			11 15				11 30			11 45					12 00			
Springburn	d		10 49							11 19								11 49					
Barnhill	d		10 50							11 20								11 50					
Alexandra Parade	d		10 53							11 23								11 53					
Duke Street	d		10 55							11 25								11 55					
Bellgrove	d		10 57		11 03			11 18		11 27		11 33			11 48			11 57		12 03			
High Street	d		10 59		11 05	11 10		11 20		11 29		11 35	11 40		11 50			11 59		12 05	12 10		
Glasgow Queen St LL 10	a		11 01		11 07	11 12		11 22		11 31		11 37	11 42		11 52			12 01		12 07	12 12		
	d		11 02		11 10	11 13		11 23		11 32		11 40	11 43		11 53			12 02		12 10	12 13	12c21	
Charing Cross	d		11 04		11 12	11 15		11 25		11 34		11 42	11 45		11 55			12 04		12 12	12 15		
Argyle Street	d			11 04			11 15		11 23		11 34			11 42		11 53			12 05				12 17
Glasgow Central LL 15	a	10b55		11 07			11 16		11 26		11 37			11 46		11 57	11b57		12 07				12 18
	d			11 07			11 17		11 28		11 37			11 46		11 58			12 07				12 19
Anderston	d			11 09			11 19		11 29		11 39			11 48		12 00			12 09				12 20
Exhibition Centre	d			11 11			11 21		11 31		11 41			11 50		12 02			12 11				12 22
Partick	d		11 09	11 15	11 17	11 20	11 24	11 29	11 35	11 39	11 44	11 47	11 50	11 54	11 59	12 05		12 08	12 14	12 17	12 20		12 26
Hyndland 3	d		11 11	11 17	11 19	11 22	11 26	11 32	11 38	11 41	11 47	11 49	11 52	11 56	12 02	12 08		12 10	12 17	12 19	12 22		12 28
Jordanhill	d		11 13				11 28			11 43				11 58				12 12					12 30
Scotstounhill	d		11 15				11 31			11 45				12 00				12 15					12 32
Garscadden	d		11 17				11 33			11 47				12 02				12 17					12 35
Yoker	d		11 20				11 35			11 50				12 05				12 19					12 37
Clydebank	d		11 22				11 37			11 52				12 07				12 21					12 39
Anniesland	d			11 20		11 25		11 35	11 41		11 50		11 55		12 05	12 11			12 20		12 25		
Westerton	d			11 23		11 28		11 38	11 44		11 53		11 58		12 08	12 14			12 23		12 28		
Bearsden	d					11 31			11 46				12 01			12 16					12 31		
Hillfoot	d					11 33			11 47				12 03			12 18					12 33		
Milngavie	a					11 37			11 52				12 07			12 22					12 37		
Drumchapel	d			11 25				11 40			11 55				12 10				12 25				
Drumry	d			11 27				11 42			11 57				12 12				12 27				
Singer	d			11 30				11 45			12 00				12 15				12 30				
Dalmuir	a		11 26	11 32	11 29		11 42	11 47		11 56	12 02	11 59		12 11	12 17			12 26	12 32	12 29		12 38	12 43
	d				11 29			11 48				11 59			12 18					12 29		12 42	
Kilpatrick	d							11 51							12 21								
Bowling	d							11 54							12 24								
Dumbarton East	d				11 36			11 58				12 06			12 28					12 36			
Dumbarton Central	d				11 39			12 00				12 09			12 30					12 39		12 48	
Dalreoch	d				11 40			12 02				12 10			12 32					12 40			
Renton	d							12 05							12 35								
Alexandria	d							12 07							12 37								
Balloch	a							12 11							12 41								
Cardross	d				11 45							12 15								12 45			
Craigendoran	d				11 50							12 20								12 50			
Helensburgh Central	a				11 54							12 24								12 54		13e03	

§ Station closed between 4 June and 24 November inclusive
A From Edinburgh
B To Oban
b Glasgow Central High Level
c Glasgow Queen St High Level
e Helensburgh Upper

Table 226

Mondays to Saturdays

Lanark, Coatbridge, Motherwell, Larkhall, Hamilton, Edinburgh and Bathgate, Airdrie and Springburn - Glasgow - Milngavie, Dalmuir, Balloch and Helensburgh

Network Diagram - see first Page of Table 220

Station		SR	SR	SR	SR	SR	SR	SR	SR	SR	SR A	SR	SR	SR	SR SX	SR SO	SR	SR	SR	SR	SR	SR
Lanark	d									11 53							12 23					
Carluke	d									12 03							12 33					
Wishaw	d									12 08							12 41					
Holytown	d									12 13	12 33											
Shieldmuir	d																12 45					
Coatbridge Central	d																					
Whifflet	d																					
Motherwell	a									12 19							12 48					
	d		11 50					12 16		12 20							12 48		12 50			
Bellshill	d							12 22			12 36						12 54					
Uddingston	d							12 26			12 41						12 58					
Airbles	d		11 52							12 22									12 52			
Larkhall	d				12 07								12 37								13 07	
Merryton	d				12 09								12 39								13 09	
Chatelherault	d				12 12								12 42								13 12	
Hamilton Central	d		11 57		12 16					12 28			12 46						12 57		13 16	
Hamilton West	d		12 00		12 18					12 30			12 48						13 00		13 18	
Blantyre	d		12 03		12 22					12 34			12 52						13 03		13 22	
Newton	d		12 07							12 38									13 07			
Cambuslang	d		12 11					12 31		12 41							13 03		13 11			
Rutherglen	d		12 17		12 29			12 34		12 45			12 59				13 06		13 16		13 29	
Dalmarnock §	d																					
Bridgeton	d		12 21					12 38		12 50							13 10		13 20			
Edinburgh	d					11 21	11 37							11 48	12 07	12 10						12 21
Haymarket	d					11 25	11 41							11 52	12 11	12 14						12 25
Edinburgh Park	d					11 30	11 46							11 57	12 16	12 19						12 30
Uphall	d					11 38	11 54							12 05	12 24	12 27						12 38
Livingston North	d					11 41	11 57							12 08	12 27	12 30						12 41
Bathgate	a					11 46	12 03							12 13	12 33	12 33						12 47
	d					11 47	12 04							12 17	12 34	12 34						12 47
Armadale	d					11 51								12 21								12 51
Blackridge	d					11 55								12 25								12 55
Caldercruix	d					12 01								12 31								13 01
Drumgelloch	d					12 05	12 16							12 35	12 46	12 46						13 05
Airdrie	d	11 57				12 12	12 20		12 27					12 42	12 50	12 50		12 57				13 12
Coatdyke	d	11 59				12 14			12 29					12 44				12 59				13 14
Coatbridge Sunnyside	d	12 01				12 16	12 23		12 31					12 46	12 53	12 53		13 01				13 16
Blairhill	d	12 04				12 19			12 34					12 49				13 04				13 19
Easterhouse	d	12 08				12 23			12 38					12 53				13 08				13 23
Garrowhill	d	12 10				12 25			12 40					12 55				13 10				13 25
Shettleston	d	12 13				12 28			12 43					12 58				13 13				13 28
Carntyne	d	12 15				12 30			12 45					13 00				13 15				13 30
Springburn	d			12 19								12 49								13 19		
Barnhill	d			12 20								12 50								13 20		
Alexandra Parade	d			12 23								12 53								13 23		
Duke Street	d			12 25								12 55								13 25		
Bellgrove	d	12 18		12 27		12 33			12 48			12 57		13 03				13 18		13 27		13 33
High Street	d	12 20		12 29		12 35	12 40		12 50			12 59		13 05	13 10	13 10		13 20		13 29		13 35
Glasgow Queen St LL 10 ⛴	a	12 22		12 31		12 38	12 42		12 52			13 01		13 08	13 12	13 12		13 22		13 31		13 37
	d	12 23		12 32		12 40	12 43		12 53			13 02		13 10	13 13	13 13		13 23		13 32		13 41
Charing Cross	d	12 25		12 34		12 42	12 45		12 55			13 04		13 12	13 15	13 15		13 25		13 34		13 43
Argyle Street	d		12 24		12 35			12 42		12 54			13 05				13 14		13 24		13 34	
Glasgow Central LL 15	a		12 26		12 37			12 46		12 56	12b55		13 07				13 17		13 27		13 37	
	d		12 28		12 37			12 46		12 58			13 07				13 18		13 28		13 37	
Anderston	d		12 30		12 39			12 48		12 59			13 09				13 19		13 29		13 39	
Exhibition Centre	d		12 32		12 41			12 50		13 01			13 11				13 21		13 31		13 41	
Partick ⛴	d	12 29	12 35	12 39	12 44	12 47	12 50	12 54	12 59	13 05		13 08	13 14	13 17	13 20	13 20	13 25	13 29	13 35	13 38	13 44	13 47
Hyndland 3	d	12 32	12 38	12 41	12 47	12 49	12 52	12 56	13 02	13 08		13 10	13 17	13 19	13 22	13 22	13 27	13 32	13 38	13 40	13 47	13 49
Jordanhill	d			12 43				12 58				13 12					13 29			13 42		
Scotstounhill	d			12 45				13 00				13 15					13 31			13 45		
Garscadden	d			12 47				13 02				13 17					13 33			13 47		
Yoker	d			12 50				13 05				13 19					13 35			13 49		
Clydebank	d			12 52				13 07				13 21					13 37			13 51		
Anniesland	d	12 35	12 41		12 50		12 55		13 05	13 11			13 20		13 25	13 25		13 35	13 41		13 50	
Westerton	d	12 38	12 44		12 53		12 58		13 08	13 14			13 23		13 28	13 28		13 38	13 44		13 53	
Bearsden	d		12 46				13 01			13 16					13 31	13 31			13 46			
Hillfoot	d		12 48				13 03			13 18					13 33	13 33			13 47			
Milngavie	a		12 52				13 07			13 22					13 37	13 37			13 52			
Drumchapel	d	12 40			12 55				13 10				13 25					13 40			13 55	
Drumry	d	12 42			12 57				13 12				13 27					13 42			13 57	
Singer	d	12 45			13 00				13 15				13 30					13 45			14 00	
Dalmuir	a	12 47		12 56	13 02	12 59		13 13	13 17			13 26	13 32	13 29			13 42	13 47		13 56	14 02	13 59
	d	12 48				12 59			13 18					13 29				13 48				13 59
Kilpatrick	d	12 51							13 21									13 51				
Bowling	d	12 54							13 24									13 54				
Dumbarton East	d	12 58				13 06			13 28					13 36				13 58				14 06
Dumbarton Central	d	13 00				13 09			13 30					13 39				14 00				14 09
Dalreoch	d	13 02				13 10			13 32					13 40				14 02				14 10
Renton	d	13 05							13 35									14 05				
Alexandria	d	13 07							13 37									14 07				
Balloch	a	13 11							13 41									14 11				
Cardross	d					13 15								13 45								14 15
Craigendoran	d					13 20								13 50								14 20
Helensburgh Central	a					13 24								13 54								14 24

§ Station closed between 4 June and 24 November inclusive

A From Edinburgh

b Glasgow Central High Level

Table 226

Mondays to Saturdays

Lanark, Coatbridge, Motherwell, Larkhall, Hamilton, Edinburgh and Bathgate, Airdrie and Springburn - Glasgow - Milngavie, Dalmuir, Balloch and Helensburgh

Network Diagram - see first Page of Table 220

Station		SR	SR	SR	SR	SR A	SR	SR	SR	SR	SR	SR	SR	SR	SR	SR	SR	SR	SR	SR	SR A	SR	SR
Lanark	d				12 53						13 23									13 53			
Carluke	d				13 03						13 33									14 03			
Wishaw	d				13 08						13 40									14 08			
Holytown	d				13 13	13 32														14 13	14 33		
Shieldmuir	d										13 43												
Coatbridge Central	d																						
Whifflet	d																						
Motherwell	a				13 19						13 47									14 19			
	d		13 16		13 20						13 48		13 50					14 16		14 20			
Bellshill	d		13 22			13 35					13 54							14 22			14 36		
Uddingston	d		13 26			13 40					13 59							14 26			14 41		
Airbles	d				13 22								13 52							14 22			
Larkhall	d							13 37							14 07								14 37
Merryton	d							13 39							14 09								14 39
Chatelherault	d							13 42							14 12								14 42
Hamilton Central	d				13 27			13 46					13 57		14 16					14 27			14 46
Hamilton West	d				13 30			13 48					14 00		14 18					14 30			14 48
Blantyre	d				13 33			13 52					14 03		14 22					14 33			14 52
Newton	d				13 37								14 07							14 37			
Cambuslang	d		13 31		13 41						14 04		14 11					14 31		14 41			
Rutherglen	d		13 34		13 45			13 59			14 06		14 15		14 29			14 36		14 45			14 59
Dalmarnock §	d																						
Bridgeton	d		13 38		13 49						14 10		14 19					14 40		14 49			
Edinburgh	d	12 37							12 48	13 07						13 21	13 37						
Haymarket	d	12 41							12 52	13 11						13 25	13 41						
Edinburgh Park	d	12 46							12 57	13 16						13 30	13 46						
Uphall	d	12 54							13 05	13 24						13 38	13 54						
Livingston North	d	12 57							13 08	13 27						13 41	13 57						
Bathgate	a	13 03							13 13	13 33						13 46	14 03						
	d	13 04							13 17	13 34						13 47	14 04						
Armadale	d								13 21							13 51							
Blackridge	d								13 25							13 55							
Caldercruix	d								13 31							14 01							
Drumgelloch	d	13 16							13 35	13 46						14 05	14 16						
Airdrie	d	13 20		13 27					13 42	13 50		13 57				14 12	14 20		14 27				
Coatdyke	d			13 29					13 44			13 59				14 14			14 29				
Coatbridge Sunnyside	d	13 23		13 31					13 46	13 53		14 01				14 16	14 23		14 31				
Blairhill	d			13 34					13 49			14 04				14 19			14 34				
Easterhouse	d			13 38					13 53			14 08				14 23			14 38				
Garrowhill	d			13 40					13 55			14 10				14 25			14 40				
Shettleston	d			13 43					13 58			14 13				14 28			14 43				
Carntyne	d			13 45					14 00			14 15				14 30			14 45				
Springburn	d						13 49							14 19								14 49	
Barnhill	d						13 50							14 20								14 50	
Alexandra Parade	d						13 53							14 23								14 53	
Duke Street	d						13 55							14 25								14 55	
Bellgrove	d			13 48			13 57		14 03			14 18		14 27		14 33			14 48			14 57	
High Street	d	13 40		13 50			13 59		14 05	14 10		14 20		14 29		14 35	14 40		14 50			15 00	
Glasgow Queen St LL 10 ⛴	a	13 42		13 52			14 01		14 07	14 12		14 22		14 31		14 37	14 42		14 52			15 02	
	d	13 43		13 53			14 02		14 10	14 13		14 23		14 32		14 40	14 43		14 53			15 03	
Charing Cross	d	13 45		13 55			14 04		14 12	14 15		14 25		14 34		14 42	14 45		14 55			15 05	
Argyle Street	d		13 42		13 53			14 04			14 14		14 23		14 35			14 43		14 53			15 04
Glasgow Central LL 15	a		13 46		13 56	13b55		14 07			14 16		14 26		14 37			14 45		14 56	14b55		15 07
	d		13 46		13 58			14 07			14 16		14 28		14 37			14 48		15 00			15 07
Anderston	d		13 48		13 59			14 09			14 18		14 29		14 39			14 49		15 01			15 09
Exhibition Centre	d		13 50		14 01			14 11			14 20		14 31		14 41			14 51		15 03			15 11
Partick ⛴	d	13 50	13 54	13 59	14 05		14 09	14 14	14 17	14 20	14 24	14 29	14 35	14 38	14 44	14 47	14 50	14 55	14 59	15 07		15 09	15 14
Hyndland 3	d	13 52	13 56	14 02	14 08		14 11	14 17	14 19	14 22	14 26	14 32	14 38	14 40	14 47	14 49	14 52	14 58	15 02	15 09		15 11	15 17
Jordanhill	d		13 58				14 13				14 28			14 42				15 00				15 13	
Scotstounhill	d		14 00				14 15				14 30			14 45				15 02				15 16	
Garscadden	d		14 02				14 17				14 32			14 47				15 05				15 18	
Yoker	d		14 05				14 20				14 34			14 49				15 07				15 20	
Clydebank	d		14 07				14 22				14 36			14 51				15 09				15 22	
Anniesland	d	13 55		14 05	14 11			14 20		14 25		14 35	14 41		14 50		14 55		15 05	15 12			15 20
Westerton	d	13 58		14 08	14 14			14 23		14 28		14 38	14 44		14 53		14 58		15 08	15 16			15 23
Bearsden	d	14 01			14 16					14 31			14 46				15 01			15 19			
Hillfoot	d	14 03			14 17					14 33			14 47				15 03			15 21			
Milngavie	a	14 07			14 22					14 37			14 52				15 07			15 24			
Drumchapel	d			14 10				14 25				14 40			14 55				15 10				15 25
Drumry	d			14 12				14 27				14 42			14 57				15 12				15 27
Singer	d			14 15				14 30				14 45			15 00				15 15				15 30
Dalmuir	a		14 11	14 17			14 26	14 32	14 29		14 42	14 47		14 56	15 02	14 59		15 13	15 17			15 26	15 32
	d			14 18					14 29			14 48				14 59			15 18				
Kilpatrick	d			14 21								14 51							15 21				
Bowling	d			14 24								14 54							15 24				
Dumbarton East	d			14 28					14 36			14 58				15 06			15 28				
Dumbarton Central	d			14 30					14 39			15 00				15 09			15 30				
Dalreoch	d			14 32					14 40			15 02				15 10			15 32				
Renton	d			14 35								15 05							15 35				
Alexandria	d			14 37								15 07							15 37				
Balloch	a			14 41								15 11							15 41				
Cardross	d								14 45							15 15							
Craigendoran	d								14 50							15 20							
Helensburgh Central	a								14 54							15 26							

§ Station closed between 4 June and 24 November inclusive

A From Edinburgh

b Glasgow Central High Level

Table 226

Mondays to Saturdays

Lanark, Coatbridge, Motherwell, Larkhall, Hamilton, Edinburgh and Bathgate, Airdrie and Springburn - Glasgow - Milngavie, Dalmuir, Balloch and Helensburgh

Network Diagram - see first Page of Table 220

		SR SO	SR SX	SR	SR SX	SR SO	SR	SR	SR	SR	SR	SR	SR	SR	SR	SR A	SR	SR	SR	SR	SR	SR
Lanark	d				14 23	14 23									14 53						15 23	
Carluke	d				14 33	14 32									15 03						15 33	
Wishaw	d				14 38	14 41									15 08						15 38	
Holytown	d														15 13	15 33						
Shieldmuir	d				14 42	14 45															15 42	
Coatbridge Central	d																					
Whifflet	d																					
Motherwell	a				14 46	14 48									15 18						15 47	
	d				14 46	14 49		14 50					15 16		15 20						15 48	
Bellshill	d				14 52	14 55							15 22			15 36					15 52	
Uddingston	d				14 56	14 59							15 26			15 41					15 56	
Airbles	d							14 52							15 22							
Larkhall	d									15 07								15 37				
Merryton	d									15 09								15 39				
Chatelherault	d									15 12								15 42				
Hamilton Central	d							14 57		15 16					15 27			15 46				
Hamilton West	d							15 00		15 18					15 30			15 48				
Blantyre	d							15 03		15 22					15 33			15 52				
Newton	d							15 07							15 37							
Cambuslang	d				15 01	15 04		15 11					15 31		15 41						16 01	
Rutherglen	d				15 04	15 06		15 16		15 29			15 34		15 45			15 59			16 07	
Dalmarnock §	d																					
Bridgeton	d				15 08	15 10		15 20					15 38		15 49						16 11	
Edinburgh	d	13 48	13 48	14 10							14 21	14 37							14 48	15 07		
Haymarket	d	13 52	13 52	14 14							14 25	14 41							14 52	15 11		
Edinburgh Park	d	13 57	13 57	14 19							14 30	14 46							14 57	15 16		
Uphall	d	14 05	14 05	14 27							14 38	14 54							15 05	15 24		
Livingston North	d	14 08	14 08	14 30							14 41	14 57							15 08	15 27		
Bathgate	a	14 13	14 13	14 33							14 46	15 03							15 13	15 33		
	d	14 17	14 17	14 34							14 47	15 04							15 17	15 34		
Armadale	d	14 21	14 21								14 51								15 21			
Blackridge	d	14 25	14 25								14 55								15 25			
Caldercruix	d	14 31	14 31								15 01								15 31			
Drumgelloch	d	14 35	14 35	14 46							15 05	15 16							15 35	15 46		
Airdrie	d	14 42	14 42	14 50			14 57				15 12	15 20		15 27					15 42	15 50		15 57
Coatdyke	d	14 44	14 44				14 59				15 14			15 29					15 44			15 59
Coatbridge Sunnyside	d	14 46	14 46	14 53			15 01				15 16	15 23		15 31					15 46	15 53		16 01
Blairhill	d	14 49	14 49				15 04				15 19			15 34					15 49			16 04
Easterhouse	d	14 53	14 53				15 08				15 23			15 38					15 53			16 08
Garrowhill	d	14 55	14 55				15 10				15 25			15 40					15 55			16 10
Shettleston	d	14 58	14 58				15 13				15 28			15 43					15 58			16 13
Carntyne	d	15 00	15 00				15 15				15 30			15 45					16 00			16 15
Springburn	d								15 19								15 49					
Barnhill	d								15 20								15 50					
Alexandra Parade	d								15 23								15 53					
Duke Street	d								15 25								15 55					
Bellgrove	d	15 03	15 03				15 18		15 27		15 33			15 48			15 57		16 03			16 18
High Street	d	15 05	15 05	15 10			15 20		15 29		15 35	15 40		15 50			15 59		16 05	16 10		16 20
Glasgow Queen St LL 10	a	15 07	15 07	15 12			15 22		15 31		15 37	15 42		15 52			16 01		16 07	16 12		16 22
	d	15 10	15 10	15 13			15 23		15 32		15 40	15 43		15 53			16 02		16 10	16 13		16 23
Charing Cross	d	15 12	15 12	15 15			15 25		15 34		15 42	15 45		15 55			16 04		16 12	16 15		16 25
Argyle Street	d				15 12	15 15		15 24		15 36			15 42		15 53			16 04			16 14	
Glasgow Central LL 15	a				15 16	15 19		15 25		15 37			15 46		15 56	15b56		16 07			16 16	
	d				15 16	15 19		15 28		15 38			15 46		15 58			16 07			16 18	
Anderston	d				15 18	15 21		15 29		15 39			15 48		15 59			16 09			16 20	
Exhibition Centre	d				15 20	15 23		15 31		15 41			15 50		16 01			16 11			16 22	
Partick	d	15 17	15 17	15 20	15 24	15 27	15 29	15 35	15 39	15 45	15 47	15 50	15 54	15 59	16 05		16 08	16 14	16 17	16 20	16 25	16 29
Hyndland 3	d	15 19	15 19	15 22	15 26	15 29	15 32	15 38	15 41	15 47	15 49	15 52	15 56	16 02	16 07		16 10	16 17	16 19	16 22	16 27	16 32
Jordanhill	d				15 28	15 31			15 43				15 58				16 12				16 29	
Scotstounhill	d				15 31	15 33			15 45				16 00				16 15				16 32	
Garscadden	d				15 33	15 35			15 47				16 03				16 17				16 34	
Yoker	d				15 35	15 38			15 50				16 05				16 19				16 36	
Clydebank	d				15 38	15 40			15 52				16 07				16 21				16 38	
Anniesland	d			15 25			15 35	15 43		15 50		15 55		16 05	16 10			16 20		16 25		16 35
Westerton	d			15 28			15 38	15 47		15 53		15 58		16 08	16 13			16 23		16 28		16 38
Bearsden	d			15 31				15 50				16 01			16 16					16 31		
Hillfoot	d			15 33				15 52				16 03			16 18					16 33		
Milngavie	a			15 37				15 55				16 07			16 22					16 37		
Drumchapel	d						15 40			15 55				16 10				16 25				16 40
Drumry	d						15 42			15 57				16 12				16 27				16 42
Singer	d						15 45			16 00				16 15				16 30				16 45
Dalmuir	a	15 29	15 29		15 42	15 44	15 47		15 56	16 02	15 59		16 12	16 17			16 26	16 32	16 29		16 43	16 47
	d	15 29	15 29				15 48				15 59			16 18					16 29			16 48
Kilpatrick	d						15 51							16 21								16 51
Bowling	d						15 54							16 24								16 54
Dumbarton East	d	15 36	15 36				15 58				16 06			16 28					16 36			16 58
Dumbarton Central	d	15 39	15 39				16 00				16 09			16 30					16 39			17 00
Dalreoch	d	15 40	15 45				16 02				16 10			16 32					16 40			17 02
Renton	d						16 05							16 35								17 05
Alexandria	d						16 07							16 37								17 07
Balloch	a						16 11							16 41								17 11
Cardross	d	15 45	15 49								16 15								16 45			
Craigendoran	d	15 50	15 54								16 20								16 50			
Helensburgh Central	a	15 54	15 58								16 24								16 54			

§ Station closed between 4 June and 24 November inclusive

A From Edinburgh

b Glasgow Central High Level

Table 226

Mondays to Saturdays

Lanark, Coatbridge, Motherwell, Larkhall, Hamilton, Edinburgh and Bathgate, Airdrie and Springburn - Glasgow - Milngavie, Dalmuir, Balloch and Helensburgh

Network Diagram - see first Page of Table 220

		SR	SR	SR	SR	SR	SR	SR	SR	SR A	SR	SR	SR	SR	SR SX	SR SO	SR SX	SR SO	SR SX	SR	SR SX	SR	SR
Lanark	d								15 53						16 20	16 23							
Carluke	d								16 03						16 30	16 33							
Wishaw	d								16 08						16 35	16 38							
Holytown	d								16 13	16 33													
Shieldmuir	d														16 39	16 42							
Coatbridge Central	d																						
Whifflet	d																						
Motherwell	a								16 19						16 42	16 48							
	d	15 50					16 16		16 20						16 42	16 49				16 50			
Bellshill	d						16 22			16 36					16 51	16 55							
Uddingston	d						16 26			16 41					16 55	16 59							
Airbles	d	15 52							16 22											16 52			
Larkhall	d			16 07								16 37											17 07
Merryton	d			16 09								16 39											17 09
Chatelherault	d			16 12								16 42											17 12
Hamilton Central	d	15 57		16 16					16 28			16 46								16 58			17 16
Hamilton West	d	16 00		16 18					16 30			16 48								17 00			17 18
Blantyre	d	16 03		16 22					16 34			16 52								17 04			17 22
Newton	d	16 07							16 38											17 08			
Cambuslang	d	16 11					16 31		16 41						17 00	17 04				17 11			
Rutherglen	d	16 16		16 30			16 34		16 46			16 59			17 06	17 06				17 16			17 31
Dalmarnock §	d																						
Bridgeton	d	16 21					16 38		16 50						17 10	17 10				17 20			
Edinburgh	d				15 21	15 37							15 51	16 07									
Haymarket	d				15 25	15 41							15 55	16 11									
Edinburgh Park	d				15 30	15 46							16 00	16 16									
Uphall	d				15 38	15 54							16 08	16 24									
Livingston North	d				15 41	15 57							16 11	16 27									
Bathgate	a				15 46	16 03							16 16	16 33									
	d				15 47	16 04							16 17	16 34									
Armadale	d				15 51								16 21										
Blackridge	d				15 55								16 25										
Caldercruix	d				16 01								16 31										
Drumgelloch	d				16 05	16 16							16 35	16 46									
Airdrie	d				16 12	16 20		16 27					16 42	16 50				16 57	16 57				
Coatdyke	d				16 14			16 29					16 44					16 59	16 59				
Coatbridge Sunnyside	d				16 16	16 23		16 31					16 46	16 53				17 01	17 01				
Blairhill	d				16 19			16 34					16 49					17 04	17 04				
Easterhouse	d				16 23			16 38					16 53					17 08	17 08				
Garrowhill	d				16 25			16 40					16 55					17 10	17 10				
Shettleston	d				16 28			16 43					16 58					17 13	17 13				
Carntyne	d				16 30			16 45					17 00					17 15	17 15				
Springburn	d		16 19								16 49											17 22	
Barnhill	d		16 20								16 50											17 23	
Alexandra Parade	d		16 23								16 53											17 26	
Duke Street	d		16 25								16 55											17 28	
Bellgrove	d		16 27		16 33			16 48			16 57		17 03				17 15	17 18	17 18		17 27	17 30	
High Street	d		16 29		16 35	16 40		16 50			16 59		17 05	17 10			17 17	17 20	17 20		17 29	17 32	
Glasgow Queen St LL 10	a		16 31		16 37	16 42		16 52			17 01		17 07	17 13			17 19	17 22	17 22		17 31	17 34	
	d		16 32		16 40	16 43		16 53			17 02		17 11	17 13			17 20	17 23	17 23		17 31	17 35	
Charing Cross	d		16 34		16 42	16 45		16 55			17 04		17 13	17 15			17 22	17 25	17 25		17 34	17 37	
Argyle Street	d	16 24		16 35			16 42		16 54			17 05			17 14	17 14				17 24			17 36
Glasgow Central LL 15	a	16 26		16 37			16 46		16 56	16b57		17 07			17 16	17 16				17 26			17 37
	d	16 28		16 38			16 47		16 58			17 07			17 16	17 16				17 28			17 38
Anderston	d	16 29		16 39			16 48		16 59			17 09			17 18	17 18				17 29			17 39
Exhibition Centre	d	16 31		16 41			16 50		17 01			17 11			17 20	17 20				17 31			17 41
Partick	d	16 35	16 39	16 45	16 47	16 50	16 54	16 59	17 05		17 08	17 14	17 18	17 20	17 23	17 23	17 27	17 29	17 29	17 35	17 38	17 41	17 45
Hyndland 3	d	16 38	16 41	16 47	16 49	16 52	16 56	17 02	17 08		17 10	17 17	17 20	17 22	17 25	17 25		17 32	17 32	17 38		17 43	17 47
Jordanhill	d		16 43				16 58				17 12				17 27	17 27						17 45	
Scotstounhill	d		16 45				17 01				17 15				17 30	17 30						17 48	
Garscadden	d		16 48				17 03				17 17				17 32	17 32						17 50	
Yoker	d		16 50				17 06				17 19				17 34	17 34						17 52	
Clydebank	d		16 52				17 08				17 21				17 36	17 36						17 54	
Anniesland	d	16 41		16 50		16 55		17 05	17 12			17 20		17 25				17 35	17 35	17 41			17 50
Westerton	d	16 44		16 53		16 58		17 08	17 15			17 23		17 28				17 38	17 38	17 44			17 53
Bearsden	d	16 46				17 01			17 17					17 31						17 46			
Hillfoot	d	16 47				17 03			17 18					17 33						17 47			
Milngavie	a	16 52				17 07			17 23					17 37						17 52			
Drumchapel	d			16 55				17 10				17 25						17 40	17 40				17 55
Drumry	d			16 57				17 12				17 27						17 42	17 42				17 57
Singer	d			17 00				17 15				17 30						17 45	17 45				18 00
Dalmuir	a		16 56	17 02	16 59		17 12	17 17			17 26	17 32	17 30		17 41	17 41		17 47	17 47			17 58	18 02
	d				16 59			17 18					17 30					17 48	17 51				
Kilpatrick	d							17 21										17 51	17 53				
Bowling	d							17 24										17 54	17 56				
Dumbarton East	d				17 06			17 28					17 37					17 58	18 01				
Dumbarton Central	d				17 09			17 30					17 40				17 46	18 00	18 04		18 00		
Dalreoch	d				17 10			17 32					17 41				17 48	18 02	18 05		18 02		
Renton	d							17 35										18 05			18 05		
Alexandria	d							17 37										18 07			18 07		
Balloch	a							17 41										18 11			18 11		
Cardross	d				17 15								17 46				17 53		18 09				
Craigendoran	d				17 20								17 51				17 58		18 17				
Helensburgh Central	a				17 24								17 54				18 01		18 20				

§ Station closed between 4 June and 24 November inclusive

A From Edinburgh

b Glasgow Central High Level

Table 226

Lanark, Coatbridge, Motherwell, Larkhall, Hamilton, Edinburgh and Bathgate, Airdrie and Springburn - Glasgow - Milngavie, Dalmuir, Balloch and Helensburgh

Network Diagram - see first Page of Table 220

		SR	SR	SR SX	SR SO	SR	SR SO	SR SX	SR A	SR	SR	SR SO	SR SX	SR	SR ◇ B	SR	SR	SR SX	SR SO	SR	SR SX	SR SO	SR
Lanark	d			16 53			16 53									17 23							
Carluke	d			17 03			17 03									17 33							
Wishaw	d			17 08			17 08									17 38							
Holytown	d						17 13		17 31														
Shieldmuir	d			17 12												17 42							
Coatbridge Central	d												17 32								17 56		
Whifflet	d												17 34								18 00		
Motherwell	a			17 16			17 19						17 40			17 47					18 08		
	d			17 16	17 16		17 20	17 20					17 40			17 48			17 50		18 11		
Bellshill	d			17 23	17 23				17 34							17 55					18 17		
Uddingston	d			17 27	17 27				17 38							17 59					18 21		
Airbles	d						17 22	17 22					17 43						17 52				
Larkhall	d											17 37						17 49				18 07	
Merryton	d											17 39						17 51				18 09	
Chatelherault	d											17 42						17 54				18 12	
Hamilton Central	d						17 27	17 27				17 46	17 48					17 57	17 57			18 16	
Hamilton West	d						17 30	17 30				17 48	17 50					18 00	18 00			18 18	
Blantyre	d						17 33	17 33				17 52	17 54					18 03	18 03			18 22	
Newton	d						17 37	17 37										18 07	18 07				
Cambuslang	d			17 31	17 31		17 41	17 41	17 44							18 04		18 11	18 11				
Rutherglen	d			17 34	17 34		17 45	17 45				17 59	18 02			18 06		18 15	18 15		18 29	18 30	
Dalmarnock §	d																						
Bridgeton	d			17 38	17 38		17 49	17 49								18 10		18 19	18 19				
Edinburgh	d	16 19	16 41								16 48			17 07									17 22
Haymarket	d	16 25	16 46								16 52			17 11									17 26
Edinburgh Park	d	16 30	16 50								16 57			17 16									17 31
Uphall	d	16 38	16 58								17 06			17 27									17 39
Livingston North	d	16 41	17 02								17 09			17 30									17 42
Bathgate	a	16 46	17 06								17 14			17 35									17 46
	d	16 47	17 07								17 17			17 35									17 47
Armadale	d	16 51									17 21												17 51
Blackridge	d	16 55									17 25												17 55
Caldercruix	d	17 01									17 31												18 01
Drumgelloch	d	17 05	17 19								17 35			17 48									18 05
Airdrie	d	17 12	17 23			17 27					17 42			17 51			17 57						18 12
Coatdyke	d	17 14				17 29					17 44						17 59						18 14
Coatbridge Sunnyside	d	17 16	17 26			17 31					17 46			17 55			18 01						18 16
Blairhill	d	17 19				17 34					17 49						18 04						18 19
Easterhouse	d	17 23				17 38					17 53						18 08						18 23
Garrowhill	d	17 25				17 40					17 55						18 10						18 25
Shettleston	d	17 28				17 43					17 58						18 13						18 28
Carntyne	d	17 30				17 45					18 00						18 15						18 30
Springburn	d									17 49										18 19			
Barnhill	d									17 50										18 20			
Alexandra Parade	d									17 53										18 23			
Duke Street	d									17 55										18 25			
Bellgrove	d	17 33				17 48				17 57	18 03						18 18			18 27			18 33
High Street	d	17 35	17 42			17 50				17 59	18 05			18 10			18 20			18 29			18 35
Glasgow Queen St LL 10	a	17 37	17 44			17 53				18 01	18 07			18 12			18 22			18 31			18 37
	d	17 40	17 45			17 53				18 02	18 10			18 14	18c21		18 23			18 32			18 40
Charing Cross	d	17 42	17 47			17 55				18 04	18 12			18 17			18 25			18 34			18 42
Argyle Street	d			17 42	17 42		17 53	17 53				18 04	18 07			18 14		18 23	18 23		18 34	18 35	
Glasgow Central LL 15	a			17 46	17 46		17 54	17 54	17b57			18 07	18 08			18 16		18 26	18 26		18 37	18 37	
	d			17 47	17 47		17 58	17 58				18 11	18 11			18 19		18 28	18 28		18 37	18 37	
Anderston	d			17 48	17 48		17 59	17 59				18 13	18 13			18 20		18 29	18 29		18 39	18 39	
Exhibition Centre	d			17 50	17 50		18 01	18 01				18 15	18 15			18 22		18 31	18 31		18 41	18 41	
Partick	d	17 47	17 51	17 54	17 54	17 59	18 05	18 05		18 09	18 16	18 18	18 18	18 21		18 26	18 29	18 35	18 35	18 39	18 44	18 44	18 47
Hyndland 3	d	17 49	17 53	17 56	17 56	18 02	18 07	18 07		18 11	18 18	18 20	18 20	18 24		18 28	18 32	18 37	18 37	18 41	18 47	18 47	18 49
Jordanhill	d			17 58	17 58					18 13						18 30				18 43			18 51
Scotstounhill	d			18 00	18 00					18 15						18 32				18 45			18 54
Garscadden	d			18 02	18 02					18 17						18 35				18a47			18 56
Yoker	d			18 04	18 04					18 20						18 37							18 58
Clydebank	d			18 06	18 06					18 22						18 39							19 00
Anniesland	d		17 56			18 05	18 10	18 10				18 23	18 23	18 27			18 35	18 40	18 40		18 50	18 50	
Westerton	d		17 59			18 08	18 13	18 13				18 26	18 26	18 30			18 38	18 43	18 43		18 53	18 53	
Bearsden	d		18 02				18 16	18 16						18 32				18 46	18 46				
Hillfoot	d		18 04				18 17	18 17						18 34				18 47	18 47				
Milngavie	a		18 07				18 22	18 22						18 38				18 52	18 52				
Drumchapel	d					18 10						18 29	18 29				18 40				18 55	18 55	
Drumry	d					18 12						18 31	18 31				18 42				18 57	18 57	
Singer	d					18 15						18 33	18 33				18 45				19 00	19 00	
Dalmuir	a	17 59		18 11	18 11	18 17				18 26	18 29	18 36	18 36		18 38	18 43	18 47				19 02	19 02	19 04
	d	17 59				18 18					18 29				18 38		18 48						19 04
Kilpatrick	d					18 21											18 51						
Bowling	d					18 24											18 54						
Dumbarton East	d	18 06				18 28					18 36						18 58						19 12
Dumbarton Central	d	18 09				18 30					18 39				18 47		19 00						19 14
Dalreoch	d	18 10				18 32					18 40						19 02						19 15
Renton	d					18 35											19 05						
Alexandria	d					18 37											19 07						
Balloch	a					18 41											19 11						
Cardross	d	18 15									18 45												19 20
Craigendoran	d	18 20									18 50												19 25
Helensburgh Central	a	18 26									18 53				19e02								19 28

§ Station closed between 4 June and 24 November inclusive

A From Edinburgh

B To Oban

b Glasgow Central High Level

c Glasgow Queen St High Level

e Helensburgh Upper

Table 226

Lanark, Coatbridge, Motherwell, Larkhall, Hamilton, Edinburgh and Bathgate, Airdrie and Springburn - Glasgow - Milngavie, Dalmuir, Balloch and Helensburgh

Network Diagram - see first Page of Table 220

		SR	SR SX	SR SO	SR	SR SO	SR SX	SR SX A	SR	SR	SR	SR	SR	SR	SR SX	SR SO	SR A	SR	SR	SR	SR	SR
Lanark	d					17 53							18 23									
Carluke	d					18 03							18 33									
Wishaw	d					18 08							18 38									
Holytown	d					18 13											18 59					
Shieldmuir	d												18 42									
Coatbridge Central	d														18 39							
Whifflet	d														18 41							
Motherwell	a					18 19							18 45		18 49							
	d			18 16		18 20	18 20						18 45		18 50	18 50					19 16	
Bellshill	d			18 22				18 41					18 52				19 04				19 22	
Uddingston	d			18 26									18 56				19 07				19 26	
Airbles	d					18 22	18 22								18 52	18 52						
Larkhall	d		18 05							18 37								19 07				
Merryton	d		18 07							18 39								19 09				
Chatelherault	d		18 14							18 42								19 12				
Hamilton Central	d		18 18			18 27	18 27			18 46					18 57	18 57		19 16				
Hamilton West	d		18 21			18 30	18 30			18 48					19 00	19 00		19 18				
Blantyre	d		18 24			18 33	18 33			18 52					19 03	19 03		19 22				
Newton	d					18 37	18 37								19 07	19 07						
Cambuslang	d		18 31	18 31		18 41	18 41	18 51					19 01		19 11	19 11	19 16				19 31	
Rutherglen	d		18 34	18 34		18 45	18 45			18 59			19 06		19 16	19 16		19 29			19 34	
Dalmarnock §	d																					
Bridgeton	d		18 38	18 38		18 49	18 49						19 10		19 20	19 20					19 38	
Edinburgh	d	17 37									17 51	18 05							18 20	18 37		
Haymarket	d	17 42									17 56	18 10							18 24	18 42		
Edinburgh Park	d	17 48									18 01	18 16							18 30	18 46		
Uphall	d	17 56									18 09	18 24							18 38	18 55		
Livingston North	d	17 59									18 12	18 28							18 41	18 57		
Bathgate	a	18 04									18 17	18 34							18 46	19 03		
	d	18 05									18 17	18 35							18 47	19 03		
Armadale	d										18 21								18 51			
Blackridge	d										18 25								18 55			
Caldercruix	d										18 31								19 01			
Drumgelloch	d	18 17									18 35	18 46							19 05	19 17		
Airdrie	d	18 21			18 27						18 42	18 51							19 12	19 20		
Coatdyke	d				18 29						18 44								19 14			
Coatbridge Sunnyside	d	18 24			18 31						18 46	18 53							19 16	19 23		
Blairhill	d				18 34						18 49								19 19			
Easterhouse	d				18 38						18 53								19 23			
Garrowhill	d				18 40						18 55								19 25			
Shettleston	d				18 43						18 58								19 28			
Carntyne	d				18 45						19 00								19 30			
Springburn	d								18 49					19 09								19 39
Barnhill	d								18 50					19 10								19 40
Alexandra Parade	d								18 53					19 13								19 43
Duke Street	d								18 55					19 15								19 45
Bellgrove	d				18 48				18 57		19 03			19 17					19 33			19 47
High Street	d	18 40			18 50				18 59		19 05	19 12		19 19					19 35	19 40		19 49
Glasgow Queen St LL 10	a	18 42			18 52				19 01		19 07	19 14		19 21					19 37	19 42		19 51
	d	18 43			18 53				19 02		19 10	19 14		19 23					19 40	19 43		19 53
Charing Cross	d	18 46			18 55				19 04		19 12	19 17		19 25					19 42	19 45		19 55
Argyle Street	d		18 42	18 42		18 53	18 53			19 04			19 13		19 24	19 24		19 35			19 42	
Glasgow Central LL 15	a		18 46	18 46		18 56	18 56	19b04		19 07			19 15		19 25	19 25	19b31	19 37			19 46	
	d		18 46	18 46		18 58	18 58			19 07			19 17		19 28	19 28		19 37			19 46	
Anderston	d		18 48	18 48		18 59	18 59			19 09			19 19		19 29	19 29		19 39			19 48	
Exhibition Centre	d		18 50	18 50		19 01	19 01			19 11			19 21		19 31	19 31		19 41			19 50	
Partick	d	18 50	18a53	18a53	19 00	19 05	19 05		19 09	19 14	19 17	19 21	19a24	19 29	19 35	19 35		19 44	19 47	19 50	19a53	19 59
Hyndland 3	d	18 53			19 03	19 08	19 08		19 11	19 17	19 19	19 23		19 32	19 38	19 38		19 47	19 49	19 52		20 03
Jordanhill	d								19 13		19 21	19 25							19 51	19 54		
Scotstounhill	d								19 15		19 24	19 27							19 54	19 57		
Garscadden	d								19a17		19 26	19a30							19 56	19a59		
Yoker	d										19 28								19 58			
Clydebank	d										19 30								20 00			
Anniesland	d	18 56			19 06	19 11	19 11			19 20				19 35	19 41	19 41		19 50				20 06
Westerton	d	18 59			19 09	19 14	19 14			19 23				19 38	19 44	19 44		19 53				20 09
Bearsden	d	19 02				19 17	19 17								19 46	19 46						
Hillfoot	d	19 03				19 18	19 18								19 48	19 48						
Milngavie	a	19 07				19 22	19 22								19 52	19 52						
Drumchapel	d				19 11					19 25				19 40				19 55				20 11
Drumry	d				19 13					19 27				19 42				19 57				20 13
Singer	d				19 16					19 30				19 45				20 00				20 16
Dalmuir	a				19 18					19 32	19 34			19 47				20 02	20 04			20 18
	d				19 18						19 34			19 48					20 04			20 18
Kilpatrick	d				19 21									19 51								20 21
Bowling	d				19 24									19 54								20 24
Dumbarton East	d				19 28						19 42			19 58					20 12			20 28
Dumbarton Central	d				19 30						19 44			20 00					20 14			20 30
Dalreoch	d				19 32						19 45			20 02					20 15			20 32
Renton	d				19 35									20 05								20 35
Alexandria	d				19 37									20 07								20 37
Balloch	a				19 41									20 11								20 41
Cardross	d										19 50								20 20			
Craigendoran	d										19 55								20 25			
Helensburgh Central	a										19 58								20 28			

§ Station closed between 4 June and 24 November inclusive

A From Edinburgh

b Glasgow Central High Level

Table 226

Mondays to Saturdays

Lanark, Coatbridge, Motherwell, Larkhall, Hamilton, Edinburgh and Bathgate, Airdrie and Springburn - Glasgow - Milngavie, Dalmuir, Balloch and Helensburgh

Network Diagram - see first Page of Table 220

Station		SR	SR	SR	SR	SR	SR	SR	SR	SR	SR	SR	SR	SR	SR SO A	SR SX A	SR	SR	SR	SR	SR	SR	SR
Lanark	d	18 53				19 23								19 53					20 23				
Carluke	d	19 03				19 33								20 03					20 33				
Wishaw	d	19 08				19 40								20 08					20 38				
Holytown	d	19 13												20 13	20 24	20 33							
Shieldmuir	d					19 43													20 42				
Coatbridge Central	d																						
Whifflet	d																						
Motherwell	a	19 19				19 47								20 19					20 46				
	d	19 20				19 48		19 50				20 18		20 20					20 47		20 50		
Bellshill	d					19 54						20 24			20 28	20 36			20 53				
Uddingston	d					19 58						20 28			20 32	20 41			20 57				
Airbles	d	19 23						19 52						20 22							20 52		
Larkhall	d		19 37						20 07								20 37					21 07	
Merryton	d		19 39						20 09								20 39					21 09	
Chatelherault	d		19 42						20 12								20 42					21 12	
Hamilton Central	d	19 28	19 46					19 57	20 16					20 27			20 46				20 57	21 16	
Hamilton West	d	19 30	19 48					20 00	20 18					20 30			20 48				21 00	21 18	
Blantyre	d	19 34	19 52					20 03	20 22					20 33			20 52				21 03	21 22	
Newton	d	19 38						20 07						20 37							21 07		
Cambuslang	d	19 41				20 03		20 11				20 33		20 41					21 02		21 11		
Rutherglen	d	19 45	19 59			20 07		20 14	20 29			20 39		20 44			20 59		21 05		21 14	21 29	
Dalmarnock §	d																						
Bridgeton	d	19 49				20 11		20 18				20 43		20 48					21 09		21 18		
Edinburgh	d			18 48	19 07					19 21	19 39							19 51					20 21
Haymarket	d			18 52	19 12					19 24	19 41							19 55					20 25
Edinburgh Park	d			18 57	19 18					19 30	19 47							20 00					20 30
Uphall	d			19 05	19 26					19 38	19 54							20 08					20 38
Livingston North	d			19 08	19 29					19 44	19 58							20 17					20 41
Bathgate	a			19 13	19 34					19 48	20 04							20 21					20 46
	d			19 17						19 49								20 22					20 47
Armadale	d			19 21						19 53								20 26					20 51
Blackridge	d			19 25						19 56								20 29					20 55
Caldercruix	d			19 31						20 03								20 36					21 01
Drumgelloch	d			19 35						20 06								20 39					21 05
Airdrie	d			19 42						20 13								20 43					21 12
Coatdyke	d			19 44						20 15								20 45					21 14
Coatbridge Sunnyside	d			19 46						20 17								20 47					21 16
Blairhill	d			19 49						20 20								20 50					21 19
Easterhouse	d			19 53						20 24								20 54					21 23
Garrowhill	d			19 55						20 26								20 56					21 25
Shettleston	d			19 58						20 29								20 59					21 28
Carntyne	d			20 00						20 31								21 01					21 30
Springburn	d						20 09						20 39							21 09			
Barnhill	d						20 10						20 40							21 10			
Alexandra Parade	d						20 13						20 43							21 13			
Duke Street	d						20 15						20 45							21 15			
Bellgrove	d			20 03			20 17			20 34			20 47					21 04		21 17			21 33
High Street	d			20 05			20 19			20 36			20 49					21 06		21 19			21 35
Glasgow Queen St LL 10 ⛴	a			20 07			20 21			20 38			20 51					21 08		21 21			21 37
	d			20 10			20 23			20 40			20 53					21 10		21 23			21 40
Charing Cross	d			20 12			20 25			20 42			20 55					21 12		21 25			21 42
Argyle Street	d	19 53	20 04			20 15		20 23	20 34			20 46		20 52			21 04		21 15		21 22	21 34	
Glasgow Central LL 15	a	19 56	20 07			20 18		20 26	20 37			20 48		20 56	20b47	20b57	21 07		21 16		21 26	21 37	
	d	19 58	20 08			20 18		20 28	20 37			20 49		20 58			21 07		21 17		21 28	21 37	
Anderston	d	19 59	20 09			20 20		20 29	20 39			20 51		20 59			21 09		21 18		21 29	21 39	
Exhibition Centre	d	20 01	20 11			20 22		20 31	20 41			20 53		21 01			21 11		21 20		21 31	21 41	
Partick ⛴	d	20 05	20 15	20 17		20a25	20 30	20 35	20 44	20 48		20a56	20 59	21 05			21 14	21 17	21a24	21 29	21 35	21 44	21 47
Hyndland 3	d	20 08	20 17	20 19			20 33	20 38	20 47	20 50			21 02	21 08			21 17	21 19		21 32	21 38	21 47	21 49
Jordanhill	d			20 21						20 52								21 21					21 51
Scotstounhill	d			20 24						20 54								21 24					21 54
Garscadden	d			20 26						20 56								21 26					21 56
Yoker	d			20 28						20 58								21 28					21 58
Clydebank	d			20 30						21 00								21 30					22 00
Anniesland	d	20 11	20 20				20 36	20 41	20 50				21 05	21 11			21 20			21 35	21 41	21 50	
Westerton	d	20 14	20 23				20 39	20 44	20 53				21 08	21 14			21 23			21 38	21 44	21 53	
Bearsden	d	20 17						20 46						21 16							21 46		
Hillfoot	d	20 18						20 47						21 17							21 47		
Milngavie	a	20 22						20 52						21 22							21 52		
Drumchapel	d		20 25				20 41		20 55				21 10				21 25			21 40		21 55	
Drumry	d		20 27				20 43		20 57				21 12				21 27			21 42		21 57	
Singer	d		20 30				20 46		21 00				21 15				21 30			21 45		22 00	
Dalmuir	a		20 32	20 34			20 48		21 02	21 04			21 18				21 32	21 34		21 47		22 02	22 03
	d			20 34			20 48			21 04			21 18					21 34		21 48			22 04
Kilpatrick	d						20 51						21 21							21 51			
Bowling	d						20 54						21 24							21 54			
Dumbarton East	d			20 42			20 58			21 11			21 28					21 42		21 58			22 11
Dumbarton Central	d			20 44			21 00			21 14			21 30					21 44		22 00			22 13
Dalreoch	d			20 45			21 02			21 15			21 32					21 45		22 02			22 15
Renton	d						21 05						21 35							22 05			
Alexandria	d						21 07						21 37							22 07			
Balloch	a						21 11						21 41							22 11			
Cardross	d			20 50						21 20								21 50					22 20
Craigendoran	d			20 55						21 25								21 55					22 25
Helensburgh Central	a			20 58						21 28								21 58					22 28

§ Station closed between 4 June and 24 November inclusive

A From Edinburgh

b Glasgow Central High Level

Table 226

Mondays to Saturdays

Lanark, Coatbridge, Motherwell, Larkhall, Hamilton, Edinburgh and Bathgate, Airdrie and Springburn - Glasgow - Milngavie, Dalmuir, Balloch and Helensburgh

Network Diagram - see first Page of Table 220

Station		SR	SR	SR	SR	SR	SR	SR	SR	SR	SR	SR	SR	SR	SR A	SR	SR	SR	SR	SR	SR	SR
Lanark	d			20 53			21 23							21 53				22 23				
Carluke	d			21 03			21 33							22 03				22 33				
Wishaw	d			21 08			21 40							22 08				22 42				
Holytown	d			21 13										22 13	22 33							
Shieldmuir	d						21 43											22 45				
Coatbridge Central	d																					
Whifflet	d																					
Motherwell	a			21 19			21 47							22 19				22 49				
	d	21 15		21 20			21 48		21 50			22 16		22 20				22 49		22 50		
Bellshill	d	21 22					21 54					22 22			22 36			22 56				
Uddingston	d	21 26					21 58					22 26			22 41			23 00				
Airbles	d			21 22					21 52					22 22						22 52		
Larkhall	d				21 37					22 07						22 37					23 07	
Merryton	d				21 39					22 09						22 39					23 09	
Chatelherault	d				21 42					22 12						22 42					23 12	
Hamilton Central	d			21 27	21 46				21 57	22 16				22 27		22 46				22 57	23 16	
Hamilton West	d			21 30	21 48				22 00	22 18				22 30		22 48				23 00	23 18	
Blantyre	d			21 33	21 52				22 03	22 22				22 33		22 52				23 03	23 22	
Newton	d			21 37					22 07					22 37						23 07		
Cambuslang	d	21 32		21 41			22 03		22 11			22 31		22 41				23 05		23 11		
Rutherglen	d	21 36		21 45	22 01		22 06		22 14	22 30		22 34		22 45		22 59		23 08		23 15	23 29	
Dalmarnock §	d																					
Bridgeton	d	21 40		21 49			22 10		22 18			22 38		22 49				23 12		23 19		
Edinburgh	d					20 50					21 21						21 51					22 19
Haymarket	d					20 54					21 25						21 55					22 23
Edinburgh Park	d					21 00					21 30						22 00					22 30
Uphall	d					21 08					21 38						22 08					22 38
Livingston North	d					21 11					21 41						22 11					22 41
Bathgate	a					21 16					21 46						22 16					22 46
	d					21 17					21 47						22 17					22 47
Armadale	d					21 21					21 51						22 21					22 51
Blackridge	d					21 25					21 55						22 25					22 55
Caldercruix	d					21 31					22 01						22 31					23 01
Drumgelloch	d					21 35					22 05						22 35					23 05
Airdrie	d					21 42					22 12						22 42					23 12
Coatdyke	d					21 44					22 14						22 44					23 14
Coatbridge Sunnyside	d					21 46					22 16						22 46					23 16
Blairhill	d					21 49					22 19						22 49					23 19
Easterhouse	d					21 53					22 23						22 53					23 23
Garrowhill	d					21 55					22 25						22 55					23 25
Shettleston	d					21 58					22 28						22 58					23 28
Carntyne	d					22 00					22 30						23 00					23 30
Springburn	d		21 39					22 09					22 39						23 09			
Barnhill	d		21 40					22 10					22 40						23 10			
Alexandra Parade	d		21 43					22 13					22 43						23 13			
Duke Street	d		21 45					22 15					22 45						23 15			
Bellgrove	d		21 47			22 03		22 17			22 33		22 47				23 03		23 17			23 33
High Street	d		21 49			22 05		22 19			22 35		22 49				23 05		23 19			23 35
Glasgow Queen St LL 10 ⛴	a		21 51			22 07		22 21			22 37		22 51				23 07		23 21			23 37
	d		21 53			22 10		22 23			22 40		22 53				23 10		23 23			23 45
Charing Cross	d		21 55			22 12		22 25			22 42		22 55				23 12		23 25			23 47
Argyle Street	d	21 44		21 53	22 06		22 14		22 22	22 35		22 42		22 53		23 04		23 16		23 23	23 34	
Glasgow Central LL 15	a	21 46		21 56	22 07		22 16		22 26	22 37		22 46		22 56	22b55	23 07		23 17		23 26	23 37	
	d	21 46		21 58	22 07		22 17		22 28	22 37		22 47		22 58		23 07		23 18		23 28	23 37	
Anderston	d	21 48		21 59	22 09		22 19		22 29	22 39		22 49		22 59		23 09		23 19		23 29	23 39	
Exhibition Centre	d	21 50		22 01	22 11		22 21		22 31	22 41		22 51		23 01		23 11		23 21		23 31	23 41	
Partick ⛴	d	21a53	21 59	22 05	22 14	22 17	22a24	22 30	22 35	22 44	22 47	22a54	22 59	23 05		23 14	23 17	23 25	23 29	23 35	23 44	23 51
Hyndland 3	d		22 03	22 08	22 17	22 19		22 33	22 38	22 47	22 49		23 03	23 08		23 17	23 19	23 27	23 32	23 38	23 47	23 53
Jordanhill	d					22 21					22 51						23 21	23 29			23 49	23 55
Scotstounhill	d					22 24					22 54						23 24	23 31			23 51	23 58
Garscadden	d					22 26					22 56						23 25	23a33			23a53	23 59
Yoker	d					22 28					22 58						23 27					00 02
Clydebank	d					22 30					23 00						23 29					00 04
Anniesland	d		22 06	22 11	22 20			22 36	22 41	22 50			23 06	23 11		23 20			23 35	23 41		
Westerton	d		22 09	22 14	22 23			22 39	22 44	22 53			23 09	23 14		23 23			23 38	23 44		
Bearsden	d			22 17					22 46					23 17						23 46		
Hillfoot	d			22 18					22 47					23 18						23 47		
Milngavie	a			22 22					22 52					23 22						23 52		
Drumchapel	d		22 11		22 25			22 41		22 55			23 11			23 25			23 40			
Drumry	d		22 13		22 27			22 43		22 57			23 13			23 27			23 42			
Singer	d		22 16		22 30			22 46		23 00			23 16			23 30			23 45			
Dalmuir	a		22 18		22 32	22 34		22 48		23 02	23 04		23 18			23 32	23 33		23 47			00 08
	d		22 18			22 34		22 48			23 04		23 18				23 33		23 48			00 08
Kilpatrick	d		22 21					22 51					23 21						23 51			
Bowling	d		22 24					22 54					23 24						23 54			
Dumbarton East	d		22 28			22 42		22 58			23 12		23 28				23 41		23 58			00 15
Dumbarton Central	d		22 30			22 44		23 00			23 14		23 30				23 43		23 59			00 18
Dalreoch	d		22 32			22 45		23 02			23 15		23 32				23 44		00 02			00 19
Renton	d		22 35					23 05					23 35						00 05			
Alexandria	d		22 37					23 07					23 37						00 07			
Balloch	a		22 41					23 11					23 41						00 11			
Cardross	d					22 50					23 20						23 49					00 24
Craigendoran	d					22 55					23 25						23 54					00 29
Helensburgh Central	a					22 58					23 28						23 58					00 32

§ Station closed between 4 June and 24 November inclusive

A From Edinburgh

b Glasgow Central High Level

Table 226

Mondays to Saturdays

Lanark, Coatbridge, Motherwell, Larkhall, Hamilton, Edinburgh and Bathgate, Airdrie and Springburn - Glasgow - Milngavie, Dalmuir, Balloch and Helensburgh

Network Diagram - see first Page of Table 220

		SR FX	SR FO	SR FO	SR	SR	SR	SR FO	SR
Lanark	d								
Carluke	d								
Wishaw	d								
Holytown	d								
Shieldmuir	d								
Coatbridge Central	d								
Whifflet	d								
Motherwell	a								
	d			23 20					
Bellshill	d								
Uddingston	d								
Airbles	d			23 22					
Larkhall	d							23 37	
Merryton	d							23 39	
Chatelherault	d							23 42	
Hamilton Central	d			23 27				23 46	
Hamilton West	d			23 30				23 48	
Blantyre	d			23 33				23 52	
Newton	d			23 39					
Cambuslang	d			23 43					
Rutherglen	d			23 47				00 01	
Dalmarnock §	d								
Bridgeton	d			23 51					
Edinburgh	d				22 51	23 07	23 37		23 51
Haymarket	d				22 55	23 11	23 42		23 55
Edinburgh Park	d				23 00	23 16	23 47		23 59
Uphall	d				23 08	23 24	23 55		00 08
Livingston North	d				23 11	23 27	23 59		00 11
Bathgate	a				23 16	23 32	00 04		00 16
	d				23 17	23 33			
Armadale	d				23 21	23 37			
Blackridge	d				23 25	23 41			
Caldercruix	d				23 31	23 47			
Drumgelloch	d				23 35	23 51			
Airdrie	d				23 38	23a54			
Coatdyke	d				23 40				
Coatbridge Sunnyside	d				23 43				
Blairhill	d				23 45				
Easterhouse	d				23 49				
Garrowhill	d				23 52				
Shettleston	d				23 54				
Carntyne	d				23 56				
Springburn	d	23 39	23 39						
Barnhill	d	23 40	23 40						
Alexandra Parade	d	23 43	23 43						
Duke Street	d	23 45	23 45						
Bellgrove	d	23 47	23 47		23 59				
High Street	d	23 49	23 49		00 02				
Glasgow Queen St LL 10	a	23 51	23 51		00 04				
	d	23 53	23 53		00 04				
Charing Cross	d	23 55	23 55		00 06				
Argyle Street	d			23 55				00 06	
Glasgow Central LL 15	a			23 57				00 07	
	d			23 58				00 07	
Anderston	d			23 59				00 09	
Exhibition Centre	d			00 01				00 11	
Partick	d	23 59	23 59	00 05	00 11			00 14	
Hyndland 3	d	00 02	00 02	00 08	00 13			00 17	
Jordanhill	d	00 04			00 15				
Scotstounhill	d	00 06			00 17				
Garscadden	d	00a08			00a19				
Yoker	d								
Clydebank	d								
Anniesland	d		00 05	00 12				00 20	
Westerton	d		00 08	00 15				00 23	
Bearsden	d			00 17					
Hillfoot	d			00 18					
Milngavie	a			00 23					
Drumchapel	d		00 10					00 25	
Drumry	d		00 12					00 27	
Singer	d		00 15					00 30	
Dalmuir	a		00 17					00 32	
	d		00 18						
Kilpatrick	d		00 21						
Bowling	d		00 24						
Dumbarton East	d		00 28						
Dumbarton Central	d		00 30						
Dalreoch	d		00 32						
Renton	d		00 35						
Alexandria	d		00 37						
Balloch	a		00 41						
Cardross	d								
Craigendoran	d								
Helensburgh Central	a								

§ Station closed between 4 June and 24 November inclusive

Table 226

Sundays

Lanark, Coatbridge, Motherwell, Larkhall, Hamilton, Edinburgh and Bathgate, Airdrie and Springburn - Glasgow - Milngavie, Dalmuir, Balloch and Helensburgh

Network Diagram - see first Page of Table 220

		SR	SR	SR	SR	SR	SR	SR	SR	SR		SR	SR	SR	SR	SR	SR	SR	SR	SR		SR	SR	SR	SR
								A						◇ B					◇ C						
Lanark	d																								
Carluke	d																								
Wishaw	d																								
Holytown	d							00 01																	
Shieldmuir	d																								
Coatbridge Central	d																								
Whifflet	d																								
Motherwell	a																								
	d														08 34	08 40		09 10					09 34	09 40	
Bellshill	d							00 04							08 40								09 40		
Uddingston	d							00 08							08 44								09 44		
Airbles	d															08 42		09 12						09 42	
Larkhall	d																					09 25			
Merryton	d																					09 27			
Chatelherault	d																					09 30			
Hamilton Central	d															08 47		09 17				09 34		09 47	
Hamilton West	d															08 50		09 20				09 36		09 50	
Blantyre	d															08 53		09 23				09 40		09 53	
Newton	d															08 57		09 27						09 57	
Cambuslang	d							00 13							08 49	09 01		09 31					09 49	10 01	
Rutherglen	d														08 53	09 04		09 34				09 48	09 53	10 04	
Dalmarnock §	d																								
Bridgeton	d														08 57	09 07		09 37					09 57	10 07	
Edinburgh	d		22p19		22p51	23p37	23p51							08 10						08 37					
Haymarket	d		22p23		22p55	23p42	23p55							08u14						08 41					
Edinburgh Park	d		22p30		23p00	23p47	23p59													08 46					
Uphall	d		22p38		23p08	23p55	00 08													08 57					
Livingston North	d		22p41		23p11	23p59	00 11													09 00					
Bathgate	a		22p46		23p16	00 04	00 16													09 05					
	d		22p47		23p17								08 06							09 06					
Armadale	d		22p51		23p21								08 10							09 10					
Blackridge	d		22p55		23p25								08 14							09 14					
Caldercruix	d		23p01		23p31								08 20							09 20					
Drumgelloch	d		23p05		23p35								08 24							09 24					
Airdrie	d		23p12		23p38					07 58			08 28				08 58			09 28					09 58
Coatdyke	d		23p14		23p40					08 00			08 30				09 00			09 30					10 00
Coatbridge Sunnyside	d		23p16		23p43					08 02			08 32				09 02			09 32					10 02
Blairhill	d		23p19		23p45					08 05			08 35				09 05			09 35					10 05
Easterhouse	d		23p23		23p49					08 09			08 39				09 09			09 39					10 09
Garrowhill	d		23p25		23p52					08 11			08 41				09 11			09 41					10 11
Shettleston	d		23p28		23p54					08 14			08 44				09 14			09 44					10 14
Carntyne	d		23p30		23p56					08 16			08 46				09 16			09 46					10 16
Springburn	d	23p09		23p39																					
Barnhill	d	23p10		23p40																					
Alexandra Parade	d	23p13		23p43																					
Duke Street	d	23p15		23p45																					
Bellgrove	d	23p17	23p33	23p47	23p59					08 19			08 49				09 19			09 49					10 19
High Street	d	23p19	23p35	23p49	00 02					08 21			08 51				09 21			09 51					10 21
Glasgow Queen St LL 10	a	23p21	23p37	23p51	00 04					08 23			08 53				09 23			09 53					10 23
	d	23p23	23p45	23p53	00 04					08 24			08 54				09 24		09e55	09 54					10 24
Charing Cross	d	23p25	23p47	23p55	00 06					08 27			08 57				09 27			09 57					10 27
Argyle Street	d																						10 01	10 11	
Glasgow Central LL 15	a							00b24							09 00	09 14		09 44				09 57	10 04	10 14	
	d														09 04	09 14		09 44				09 57	10 04	10 14	
Anderston	d																								
Exhibition Centre	d														09 08	09 18		09 48				10 01	10 08	10 18	
Partick	d	23p29	23p51	23p59	00 11					08 32			09 02		09 12	09 22	09 32	09 52		10 02		10a04	10 12	10 22	10 32
Hyndland 3	d	23p32	23p53	00 02	00 13					08 34			09 04		09 15	09 24	09 34	09 54		10 04			10 15	10 24	10 34
Jordanhill	d		23p55	00 04	00 15											09 26		09 56						10 26	
Scotstounhill	d		23p58	00 06	00 17											09 28		09 58						10 28	
Garscadden	d		23p59	00a08	00a19											09 30		10 00						10 30	
Yoker	d		00 02						08 33			09 03				09 33		10 03						10 33	
Clydebank	d		00 04						08 35			09 05				09 35		10 05						10 35	
Anniesland	d	23p35								08 37			09 07		09 18		09 37			10 07			10 18		10 37
Westerton	d	23p38								08 40			09 10		09 21		09 40			10 10			10 21		10 40
Bearsden	d														09 25								10 25		
Hillfoot	d														09 27								10 27		
Milngavie	a														09 30								10 30		
Drumchapel	d	23p40								08 42			09 12				09 42			10 12					10 42
Drumry	d	23p42								08 44			09 14				09 44			10 14					10 44
Singer	d	23p45								08 47			09 17				09 47			10 17					10 47
Dalmuir	a	23p47	00 08						08 38	08 49		09 08	09 19			09 39	09 49	10 09	10 12	10 19				10 39	10 49
	d	23p48	00 08						08 39	08 50		09 09	09 20	09u27		09 39	09 50	10 09	10 16	10 20				10 39	10 50
Kilpatrick	d	23p51							08 41			09 11				09 41		10 11						10 41	
Bowling	d	23p54							08 44			09 14				09 44		10 14						10 44	
Dumbarton East	d	23p58	00 15						08 49	08 58		09 19	09 28			09 49	09 58	10 19		10 28				10 49	10 58
Dumbarton Central	d	23p59	00 18						08 51	09 00		09 21	09 30			09 51	10 00	10 21	10 25	10 30				10 51	11 00
Dalreoch	d	00 02	00 19						08 52	09 01		09 22	09 31			09 52	10 01	10 22		10 31				10 52	11 01
Renton	d	00 05							08 55			09 25				09 55		10 25						10 55	
Alexandria	d	00 07							08 58			09 28				09 58		10 28						10 58	
Balloch	a	00 11							09 01			09 31				10 01		10 31						11 01	
Cardross	d		00 24							09 06			09 36				10 06			10 36					11 06
Craigendoran	d		00 29							09 11			09 41				10 11			10 41					11 11
Helensburgh Central	a		00 32							09 14			09 44	09c49			10 14		10c37	10 44					11 14

§ Station closed between 4 June and 24 November inclusive
A From Edinburgh
B from 24 June until 26 August. To Oban
C until 30 September. To Oban
b Glasgow Central High Level
c Helensburgh Upper
e Glasgow Queen St High Level

Table 226

Sundays

Lanark, Coatbridge, Motherwell, Larkhall, Hamilton, Edinburgh and Bathgate, Airdrie and Springburn - Glasgow - Milngavie, Dalmuir, Balloch and Helensburgh

Network Diagram - see first Page of Table 220

Station		SR	SR	SR	SR	SR	SR	SR	SR	SR	SR	SR	SR	SR ◇ A	SR	SR	SR	SR	SR	SR	SR	SR	SR
Lanark	d					10 12							11 12								12 12		
Carluke	d					10 22							11 22								12 22		
Wishaw	d					10 27							11 27								12 27		
Holytown	d																						
Shieldmuir	d					10 31							11 31								12 31		
Coatbridge Central	d																						
Whifflet	d																						
Motherwell	a					10 34							11 34								12 34		
	d	10 06	10 10			10 34	10 40		11 06	11 10			11 34		11 40		12 06	12 10			12 34	12 40	
Bellshill	d	10 12				10 40			11 12				11 40				12 12				12 40		
Uddingston	d	10 16				10 44			11 16				11 44				12 16				12 44		
Airbles	d		10 12				10 42			11 12					11 42			12 12				12 42	
Larkhall	d				10 25							11 25								12 25			
Merryton	d				10 27							11 27								12 27			
Chatelherault	d				10 30							11 30								12 30			
Hamilton Central	d		10 17		10 34		10 47			11 17		11 34			11 47			12 17		12 34		12 47	
Hamilton West	d		10 20		10 36		10 50			11 20		11 36			11 50			12 20		12 36		12 50	
Blantyre	d		10 23		10 40		10 53			11 23		11 40			11 53			12 23		12 40		12 53	
Newton	d		10 27				10 57			11 27					11 57			12 27				12 57	
Cambuslang	d	10 21	10 31			10 49	11 01		11 21	11 31			11 49		12 01		12 21	12 31			12 49	13 01	
Rutherglen	d	10 24	10 34		10 48	10 53	11 04		11 24	11 34		11 48	11 53		12 04		12 24	12 34		12 48	12 53	13 04	
Dalmarnock §	d																						
Bridgeton	d	10 27	10 37			10 57	11 07		11 27	11 37			11 57		12 07		12 27	12 37			12 57	13 07	
Edinburgh	d			09 37							10 40								11 40				12 10
Haymarket	d			09 41							10 44								11 44				12 14
Edinburgh Park	d			09 46							10 49								11 49				12 19
Uphall	d			09 57							10 57								11 57				12 27
Livingston North	d			10 00							11 00								12 00				12 30
Bathgate	a			10 05							11 05								12 05				12 35
	d			10 06							11 06								12 06				12 36
Armadale	d			10 10							11 10								12 10				12 40
Blackridge	d			10 14							11 14								12 14				12 44
Caldercruix	d			10 20							11 20								12 20				12 50
Drumgelloch	d			10 24							11 24								12 24				12 54
Airdrie	d			10 28				10 58			11 28					11 58			12 28				12 58
Coatdyke	d			10 30				11 00			11 30					12 00			12 30				13 00
Coatbridge Sunnyside	d			10 32				11 02			11 32					12 02			12 32				13 02
Blairhill	d			10 35				11 05			11 35					12 05			12 35				13 05
Easterhouse	d			10 39				11 09			11 39					12 09			12 39				13 09
Garrowhill	d			10 41				11 11			11 41					12 11			12 41				13 11
Shettleston	d			10 44				11 14			11 44					12 14			12 44				13 14
Carntyne	d			10 46				11 16			11 46					12 16			12 46				13 16
Springburn	d																						
Barnhill	d																						
Alexandra Parade	d																						
Duke Street	d																						
Bellgrove	d			10 49				11 19			11 49					12 19			12 49				13 19
High Street	d			10 51				11 21			11 51					12 21			12 51				13 21
Glasgow Queen St LL 10 ⇌	a			10 53				11 23			11 53					12 23			12 53				13 23
	d			10 54				11 24			11 54			12b20		12 24			12 54				13 24
Charing Cross	d			10 57				11 27			11 57					12 27			12 57				13 27
Argyle Street	d	10 31	10 41		10 53	11 01	11 11		11 31	11 41		11 53	12 01		12 11		12 31	12 41		12 53	13 01	13 11	
Glasgow Central LL 15	a	10 34	10 44		10 57	11 04	11 14		11 34	11 44		11 57	12 04		12 14		12 34	12 44		12 57	13 04	13 14	
	d	10 34	10 44		10 57	11 04	11 14		11 34	11 44		11 57	12 04		12 14		12 34	12 44		12 57	13 04	13 14	
Anderston	d																						
Exhibition Centre	d	10 38	10 48		11 01	11 08	11 18		11 38	11 48		12 01	12 08		12 18		12 38	12 48		13 01	13 08	13 18	
Partick ⇌	d	10 42	10 52	11 02	11a04	11 12	11 22	11 32	11 42	11 52	12 02	12a04	12 12		12 22	12 32	12 42	12 52	13 02	13a04	13 12	13 22	13 32
Hyndland 3	d	10 45	10 54	11 04		11 15	11 24	11 34	11 45	11 54	12 04		12 15		12 24	12 34	12 45	12 54	13 04		13 15	13 24	13 34
Jordanhill	d		10 56				11 26			11 56					12 26			12 56				13 26	
Scotstounhill	d		10 58				11 28			11 58					12 28			12 58				13 28	
Garscadden	d		11 00				11 30			12 00					12 30			13 00				13 30	
Yoker	d		11 03				11 33			12 03					12 33			13 03				13 33	
Clydebank	d		11 05				11 35			12 05					12 35			13 05				13 35	
Anniesland	d	10 48		11 07		11 18		11 37	11 48		12 07		12 18			12 37	12 48		13 07		13 18		13 37
Westerton	d	10 51		11 10		11 21		11 40	11 51		12 10		12 21			12 40	12 51		13 10		13 21		13 40
Bearsden	d	10 55				11 25			11 55				12 25				12 55				13 25		
Hillfoot	d	10 57				11 27			11 57				12 27				12 57				13 27		
Milngavie	a	11 00				11 30			12 00				12 30				13 00				13 30		
Drumchapel	d			11 12				11 42			12 12					12 42			13 12				13 42
Drumry	d			11 14				11 44			12 14					12 44			13 14				13 44
Singer	d			11 17				11 47			12 17					12 47			13 17				13 47
Dalmuir	a		11 09	11 19			11 39	11 49		12 09	12 19			12 34	12 39	12 49		13 09	13 19			13 39	13 49
	d		11 09	11 20			11 39	11 50		12 09	12 20			12 34	12 39	12 50		13 09	13 20			13 39	13 50
Kilpatrick	d		11 11				11 41			12 11					12 41			13 11				13 41	
Bowling	d		11 14				11 44			12 14					12 44			13 14				13 44	
Dumbarton East	d		11 19	11 28			11 49	11 58		12 19	12 28				12 49	12 58		13 19	13 28			13 49	13 58
Dumbarton Central	d		11 21	11 30			11 51	12 00		12 21	12 30			12 44	12 51	13 00		13 21	13 30			13 51	14 00
Dalreoch	d		11 22	11 31			11 52	12 01		12 22	12 31				12 52	13 01		13 22	13 31			13 52	14 01
Renton	d		11 25				11 55			12 25					12 55			13 25				13 55	
Alexandria	d		11 28				11 58			12 28					12 58			13 28				13 58	
Balloch	a		11 31				12 01			12 31					13 01			13 31				14 01	
Cardross	d			11 36				12 06			12 36					13 06			13 36				14 06
Craigendoran	d			11 41				12 11			12 41					13 11			13 41				14 11
Helensburgh Central	a			11 44				12 14			12 44			12c59		13 14			13 44				14 14

§ Station closed between 4 June and 24 November inclusive

A until 28 October. To Oban

b Glasgow Queen St High Level

c Helensburgh Upper

Table 226

Sundays

Lanark, Coatbridge, Motherwell, Larkhall, Hamilton, Edinburgh and Bathgate, Airdrie and Springburn - Glasgow - Milngavie, Dalmuir, Balloch and Helensburgh

Network Diagram - see first Page of Table 220

Station		SR	SR	SR	SR	SR	SR	SR	SR	SR	SR	SR	SR	SR	SR	SR	SR	SR	SR	SR	SR	SR
Lanark	d					13 12							14 12							15 12		
Carluke	d					13 22							14 22							15 22		
Wishaw	d					13 27							14 27							15 27		
Holytown	d																					
Shieldmuir	d					13 31							14 31							15 31		
Coatbridge Central	d																					
Whifflet	d																					
Motherwell	a					13 34							14 34							15 34		
	d	13 06	13 10			13 34	13 40		14 06	14 10			14 34	14 40		15 06	15 10			15 34	15 40	
Bellshill	d	13 12				13 40			14 12				14 40			15 12				15 40		
Uddingston	d	13 16				13 44			14 16				14 44			15 16				15 44		
Airbles	d		13 12				13 42			14 12				14 42			15 12				15 42	
Larkhall	d				13 25							14 25							15 25			
Merryton	d				13 27							14 27							15 27			
Chatelherault	d				13 30							14 30							15 30			
Hamilton Central	d		13 17		13 34		13 47			14 17		14 34		14 47			15 17		15 34		15 47	
Hamilton West	d		13 20		13 36		13 50			14 20		14 36		14 50			15 20		15 36		15 50	
Blantyre	d		13 23		13 40		13 53			14 23		14 40		14 53			15 23		15 40		15 53	
Newton	d		13 27				13 57			14 27				14 57			15 27				15 57	
Cambuslang	d	13 21	13 31			13 49	14 01		14 21	14 31			14 49	15 01		15 21	15 31			15 49	16 01	
Rutherglen	d	13 24	13 34		13 48	13 53	14 04		14 24	14 34		14 48	14 53	15 04		15 24	15 34		15 48	15 53	16 04	
Dalmarnock §	d																					
Bridgeton	d	13 27	13 37			13 57	14 07		14 27	14 37			14 57	15 07		15 27	15 37			15 57	16 07	
Edinburgh	d			12 40				13 10			13 40				14 10			14 40				15 10
Haymarket	d			12 44				13 14			13 44				14 14			14 44				15 14
Edinburgh Park	d			12 49				13 19			13 49				14 19			14 49				15 19
Uphall	d			12 57				13 27			13 57				14 27			14 57				15 27
Livingston North	d			13 00				13 30			14 00				14 30			15 00				15 30
Bathgate	a			13 05				13 35			14 05				14 35			15 05				15 35
	d			13 06				13 36			14 06				14 36			15 06				15 36
Armadale	d			13 10				13 40			14 10				14 40			15 10				15 40
Blackridge	d			13 14				13 44			14 14				14 44			15 14				15 44
Caldercruix	d			13 20				13 50			14 20				14 50			15 20				15 50
Drumgelloch	d			13 24				13 54			14 24				14 54			15 24				15 54
Airdrie	d			13 28				13 58			14 28				14 58			15 28				15 58
Coatdyke	d			13 30				14 00			14 30				15 00			15 30				16 00
Coatbridge Sunnyside	d			13 32				14 02			14 32				15 02			15 32				16 02
Blairhill	d			13 35				14 05			14 35				15 05			15 35				16 05
Easterhouse	d			13 39				14 09			14 39				15 09			15 39				16 09
Garrowhill	d			13 41				14 11			14 41				15 11			15 41				16 11
Shettleston	d			13 44				14 14			14 44				15 14			15 44				16 14
Carntyne	d			13 46				14 16			14 46				15 16			15 46				16 16
Springburn	d																					
Barnhill	d																					
Alexandra Parade	d																					
Duke Street	d																					
Bellgrove	d			13 49				14 19			14 49				15 19			15 49				16 19
High Street	d			13 51				14 21			14 51				15 21			15 51				16 21
Glasgow Queen St LL 10 ⇌	a			13 53				14 23			14 53				15 23			15 53				16 23
	d			13 54				14 24			14 54				15 24			15 54				16 24
Charing Cross	d			13 57				14 27			14 57				15 27			15 57				16 27
Argyle Street	d	13 31	13 41		13 53	14 01	14 11		14 31	14 41		14 53	15 01	15 11		15 31	15 41		15 53	16 01	16 11	
Glasgow Central LL 15	a	13 34	13 44		13 57	14 04	14 14		14 34	14 44		14 57	15 04	15 14		15 34	15 44		15 57	16 04	16 14	
	d	13 34	13 44		13 57	14 04	14 14		14 34	14 44		14 57	15 04	15 14		15 34	15 44		15 57	16 04	16 14	
Anderston	d																					
Exhibition Centre	d	13 38	13 48		14 01	14 08	14 18		14 38	14 48		15 01	15 08	15 18		15 38	15 48		16 01	16 08	16 18	
Partick ⇌	d	13 42	13 52	14 02	14a04	14 12	14 22	14 32	14 42	14 52	15 02	15a04	15 12	15 22	15 32	15 42	15 52	16 02	16a04	16 12	16 22	16 32
Hyndland 3	d	13 45	13 54	14 04		14 15	14 24	14 34	14 45	14 54	15 04		15 15	15 24	15 34	15 45	15 54	16 04		16 15	16 24	16 34
Jordanhill	d		13 56				14 26			14 56				15 26			15 56				16 26	
Scotstounhill	d		13 58				14 28			14 58				15 28			15 58				16 28	
Garscadden	d		14 00				14 30			15 00				15 30			16 00				16 30	
Yoker	d		14 03				14 33			15 03				15 33			16 03				16 33	
Clydebank	d		14 05				14 35			15 05				15 35			16 05				16 35	
Anniesland	d	13 48		14 07		14 18		14 37	14 48		15 07		15 18		15 37	15 48		16 07		16 18		16 37
Westerton	d	13 51		14 10		14 21		14 40	14 51		15 10		15 21		15 40	15 51		16 10		16 21		16 40
Bearsden	d	13 55				14 25			14 55				15 25			15 55				16 25		
Hillfoot	d	13 57				14 27			14 57				15 27			15 57				16 27		
Milngavie	a	14 00				14 30			15 00				15 30			16 00				16 30		
Drumchapel	d			14 12				14 42			15 12				15 42			16 12				16 42
Drumry	d			14 14				14 44			15 14				15 44			16 14				16 44
Singer	d			14 17				14 47			15 17				15 47			16 17				16 47
Dalmuir	a		14 09	14 19			14 39	14 49		15 09	15 19			15 39	15 49		16 09	16 19			16 39	16 49
	d		14 09	14 20			14 39	14 50		15 09	15 20			15 39	15 50		16 09	16 20			16 39	16 50
Kilpatrick	d		14 11				14 41			15 11				15 41			16 11				16 41	
Bowling	d		14 14				14 44			15 14				15 44			16 14				16 44	
Dumbarton East	d		14 19	14 28			14 49	14 58		15 19	15 28			15 49	15 58		16 19	16 28			16 49	16 58
Dumbarton Central	d		14 21	14 30			14 51	15 00		15 21	15 30			15 51	16 00		16 21	16 30			16 51	17 00
Dalreoch	d		14 22	14 31			14 52	15 01		15 22	15 31			15 52	16 01		16 22	16 31			16 52	17 01
Renton	d		14 25				14 55			15 25				15 55			16 25				16 55	
Alexandria	d		14 28				14 58			15 28				15 58			16 28				16 58	
Balloch	a		14 31				15 01			15 31				16 01			16 31				17 01	
Cardross	d			14 36				15 06			15 36				16 06			16 36				17 06
Craigendoran	d			14 41				15 11			15 41				16 11			16 41				17 11
Helensburgh Central	a			14 44				15 14			15 44				16 14			16 44				17 14

§ Station closed between 4 June and 24 November inclusive

Table 226

Sundays

Lanark, Coatbridge, Motherwell, Larkhall, Hamilton, Edinburgh and Bathgate, Airdrie and Springburn - Glasgow - Milngavie, Dalmuir, Balloch and Helensburgh

Network Diagram - see first Page of Table 220

		SR	SR	SR	SR	SR	SR	SR	SR	SR	SR	SR	SR	SR ◇ A	SR	SR	SR	SR	SR	SR	SR	SR	SR
Lanark	d					16 12							17 12								18 12		
Carluke	d					16 22							17 22								18 22		
Wishaw	d					16 27							17 27								18 27		
Holytown	d																						
Shieldmuir	d					16 31							17 31								18 31		
Coatbridge Central	d																						
Whifflet	d																						
Motherwell	a					16 34							17 34								18 34		
	d	16 06	16 10			16 34	16 40		17 06	17 10			17 34		17 40		18 06	18 10			18 34	18 40	
Bellshill	d	16 12				16 40			17 12				17 40				18 12				18 40		
Uddingston	d	16 16				16 44			17 16				17 44				18 16				18 44		
Airbles	d		16 12				16 42			17 12					17 42			18 12				18 42	
Larkhall	d				16 25							17 25								18 25			
Merryton	d				16 27							17 27								18 27			
Chatelherault	d				16 30							17 30								18 30			
Hamilton Central	d		16 17		16 34		16 47			17 17		17 34			17 47			18 17		18 34		18 47	
Hamilton West	d		16 20		16 36		16 50			17 20		17 36			17 50			18 20		18 36		18 50	
Blantyre	d		16 23		16 40		16 53			17 23		17 40			17 53			18 23		18 40		18 53	
Newton	d		16 27				16 57			17 27					17 57			18 27				18 57	
Cambuslang	d	16 21	16 31			16 49	17 01		17 21	17 31			17 49		18 01		18 21	18 31			18 49	19 01	
Rutherglen	d	16 24	16 34		16 48	16 53	17 04		17 24	17 34		17 48	17 53		18 04		18 24	18 34		18 48	18 53	19 04	
Dalmarnock §	d																						
Bridgeton	d	16 27	16 37			16 57	17 07		17 27	17 37			17 57		18 07		18 27	18 37			18 57	19 07	
Edinburgh	d			15 40				16 10			16 40					17 10			17 40				18 10
Haymarket	d			15 44				16 14			16 44					17 14			17 44				18 14
Edinburgh Park	d			15 49				16 19			16 49					17 19			17 49				18 19
Uphall	d			15 57				16 27			16 57					17 27			17 57				18 27
Livingston North	d			16 00				16 30			17 00					17 30			18 00				18 30
Bathgate	a			16 05				16 35			17 05					17 35			18 05				18 35
	d			16 06				16 36			17 06					17 36			18 06				18 36
Armadale	d			16 10				16 40			17 10					17 40			18 10				18 40
Blackridge	d			16 14				16 44			17 14					17 44			18 14				18 44
Caldercruix	d			16 20				16 50			17 20					17 50			18 20				18 50
Drumgelloch	d			16 24				16 54			17 24					17 54			18 24				18 54
Airdrie	d			16 28				16 58			17 28					17 58			18 28				18 58
Coatdyke	d			16 30				17 00			17 30					18 00			18 30				19 00
Coatbridge Sunnyside	d			16 32				17 02			17 32					18 02			18 32				19 02
Blairhill	d			16 35				17 05			17 35					18 05			18 35				19 05
Easterhouse	d			16 39				17 09			17 39					18 09			18 39				19 09
Garrowhill	d			16 41				17 11			17 41					18 11			18 41				19 11
Shettleston	d			16 44				17 14			17 44					18 14			18 44				19 14
Carntyne	d			16 46				17 16			17 46					18 16			18 46				19 16
Springburn	d																						
Barnhill	d																						
Alexandra Parade	d																						
Duke Street	d																						
Bellgrove	d			16 49				17 19			17 49					18 19			18 49				19 19
High Street	d			16 51				17 21			17 51					18 21			18 51				19 21
Glasgow Queen St LL ⇌	a			16 53				17 23			17 53					18 23			18 53				19 23
	d			16 54				17 24			17 54			18b20		18 24			18 54				19 24
Charing Cross	d			16 57				17 27			17 57					18 27			18 57				19 27
Argyle Street	d	16 31	16 41		16 53	17 01	17 11		17 31	17 41		17 53	18 01		18 11								
Glasgow Central LL	a	16 34	16 44		16 57	17 04	17 14		17 34	17 44		17 57	18 04		18 14		18 34	18 44		18 57	19 04	19 14	
	d	16 34	16 44		16 57	17 04	17 14		17 34	17 44		17 57	18 04		18 14		18 34	18 44		18 57	19 04	19 14	
Anderston	d																						
Exhibition Centre	d	16 38	16 48		17 01	17 08	17 18		17 38	17 48		18 01	18 08		18 18		18 38	18 48		19 01	19 08	19 18	
Partick ⇌	d	16 42	16 52	17 02	17a04	17 12	17 22	17 32	17 42	17 52	18 02	18a04	18 12		18 22	18 32	18 42	18 52	19 02	19a04	19 12	19 22	19 32
Hyndland	d	16 45	16 54	17 04		17 15	17 24	17 34	17 45	17 54	18 04		18 15		18 24	18 34	18 45	18 54	19 04		19 15	19 24	19 34
Jordanhill	d		16 56				17 26			17 56					18 26			18 56				19 26	
Scotstounhill	d		16 58				17 28			17 58					18 28			18 58				19 28	
Garscadden	d		17 00				17 30			18 00					18 30			19 00				19 30	
Yoker	d		17 03				17 33			18 03					18 33			19 03				19 33	
Clydebank	d		17 05				17 35			18 05					18 35			19 05				19 35	
Anniesland	d	16 48		17 07		17 18		17 37	17 48		18 07		18 18			18 37	18 48		19 07		19 18		19 37
Westerton	d	16 51		17 10		17 21		17 40	17 51		18 10		18 21			18 40	18 51		19 10		19 21		19 40
Bearsden	d	16 55				17 25			17 55				18 25				18 55				19 25		
Hillfoot	d	16 57				17 27			17 57				18 27				18 57				19 27		
Milngavie	a	17 00				17 30			18 00				18 30				19 00				19 30		
Drumchapel	d			17 12				17 42			18 12					18 42			19 12				19 42
Drumry	d			17 14				17 44			18 14					18 44			19 14				19 44
Singer	d			17 17				17 47			18 17					18 47			19 17				19 47
Dalmuir	a		17 09	17 19			17 39	17 49		18 09	18 19			18 34	18 39	18 49		19 09	19 19			19 39	19 49
	d		17 09	17 20			17 39	17 50		18 09	18 20			18 34	18 39	18 50		19 09	19 20			19 39	19 50
Kilpatrick	d		17 11				17 41			18 11					18 41			19 11				19 41	
Bowling	d		17 14				17 44			18 14					18 44			19 14				19 44	
Dumbarton East	d		17 19	17 28			17 49	17 58		18 19	18 28				18 49	18 58		19 19	19 28			19 49	19 58
Dumbarton Central	d		17 21	17 30			17 51	18 00		18 21	18 30			18 44	18 51	19 00		19 21	19 30			19 51	20 00
Dalreoch	d		17 22	17 31			17 52	18 01		18 22	18 31				18 52	19 01		19 22	19 31			19 52	20 01
Renton	d		17 25				17 55			18 25					18 55			19 25				19 55	
Alexandria	d		17 28				17 58			18 28					18 58			19 28				19 58	
Balloch	a		17 31				18 01			18 31					19 01			19 31				20 01	
Cardross	d			17 36				18 06			18 36					19 06			19 36				20 06
Craigendoran	d			17 41				18 11			18 41					19 11			19 41				20 11
Helensburgh Central	a			17 44				18 14			18 44			18c59		19 14			19 44				20 14

§ Station closed between 4 June and 24 November inclusive

A To Oban

b Glasgow Queen St High Level

c Helensburgh Upper

Table 226

Sundays

Lanark, Coatbridge, Motherwell, Larkhall, Hamilton, Edinburgh and Bathgate, Airdrie and Springburn - Glasgow - Milngavie, Dalmuir, Balloch and Helensburgh

Network Diagram - see first Page of Table 220

		SR	SR	SR	SR	SR	SR	SR	SR	SR	SR	SR	SR	SR	SR	SR	SR	SR	SR	SR	SR	SR
Lanark	d						19 12								20 12							21 12
Carluke	d						19 22								20 22							21 22
Wishaw	d						19 27								20 27							21 27
Holytown	d																					
Shieldmuir	d						19 31								20 31							21 31
Coatbridge Central	d																					
Whifflet	d																					
Motherwell	a						19 34								20 34							21 34
	d	19 06	19 10				19 34	19 40		20 06	20 10				20 34	20 40		21 06	21 10			21 34
Bellshill	d	19 12					19 40			20 12					20 40			21 12				21 40
Uddingston	d	19 16					19 44			20 16					20 44			21 16				21 44
Airbles	d		19 12					19 42			20 12					20 42			21 12			
Larkhall	d					19 25								20 25							21 25	
Merryton	d					19 27								20 27							21 27	
Chatelherault	d					19 30								20 30							21 30	
Hamilton Central	d		19 17			19 34		19 47			20 17			20 34		20 47			21 17		21 34	
Hamilton West	d		19 20			19 36		19 50			20 20			20 36		20 50			21 20		21 36	
Blantyre	d		19 23			19 40		19 53			20 23			20 40		20 53			21 23		21 40	
Newton	d		19 27					19 57			20 27					20 57			21 27			
Cambuslang	d	19 21	19 31				19 49	20 01		20 21	20 31				20 49	21 01		21 21	21 31			21 49
Rutherglen	d	19 24	19 34			19 48	19 53	20 04		20 24	20 34			20 48	20 53	21 04		21 24	21 34		21 48	21 53
Dalmarnock §	d																					
Bridgeton	d	19 27	19 37				19 57	20 07		20 27	20 37				20 57	21 07		21 27	21 37			21 57
Edinburgh	d			18 40	19 10							19 40	20 10							20 40		
Haymarket	d			18 44	19 14							19 44	20 14							20 44		
Edinburgh Park	d			18 49	19 19							19 49	20 19							20 49		
Uphall	d			18 57	19 27							19 57	20 27							20 57		
Livingston North	d			19 00	19 30							20 00	20 30							21 00		
Bathgate	a			19 05	19 35							20 05	20 35							21 05		
	d			19 06								20 06								21 06		
Armadale	d			19 10								20 10								21 10		
Blackridge	d			19 14								20 14								21 14		
Caldercruix	d			19 20								20 20								21 20		
Drumgelloch	d			19 24								20 24								21 24		
Airdrie	d			19 28					19 58			20 28					20 58			21 28		
Coatdyke	d			19 30					20 00			20 30					21 00			21 30		
Coatbridge Sunnyside	d			19 32					20 02			20 32					21 02			21 32		
Blairhill	d			19 35					20 05			20 35					21 05			21 35		
Easterhouse	d			19 39					20 09			20 39					21 09			21 39		
Garrowhill	d			19 41					20 11			20 41					21 11			21 41		
Shettleston	d			19 44					20 14			20 44					21 14			21 44		
Carntyne	d			19 46					20 16			20 46					21 16			21 46		
Springburn	d																					
Barnhill	d																					
Alexandra Parade	d																					
Duke Street	d																					
Bellgrove	d			19 49					20 19			20 49					21 19			21 49		
High Street	d			19 51					20 21			20 51					21 21			21 51		
Glasgow Queen St LL ⇌	a			19 53					20 23			20 53					21 23			21 53		
	d			19 54					20 24			20 54					21 24			21 54		
Charing Cross	d			19 57					20 27			20 57					21 27			21 57		
Argyle Street	d																					
Glasgow Central LL	a	19 34	19 44			19 57	20 04	20 14		20 34	20 44			20 57	21 04	21 14		21 34	21 44		21 57	22 04
	d	19 34	19 44			19 57	20 04	20 14		20 34	20 44			20 57	21 04	21 14		21 34	21 44		21 57	22 04
Anderston	d																					
Exhibition Centre	d	19 38	19 48			20 01	20 08	20 18		20 38	20 48			21 01	21 08	21 18		21 38	21 48		22 01	22 08
Partick ⇌	d	19 42	19 52	20 02		20a04	20 12	20 22	20 32	20 42	20 52	21 02		21a04	21 12	21 22	21 32	21 42	21 52	22 02	22a04	22 12
Hyndland	d	19 45	19 54	20 04			20 15	20 24	20 34	20 45	20 54	21 04			21 15	21 24	21 34	21 45	21 54	22 04		22 15
Jordanhill	d		19 56					20 26			20 56					21 26			21 56			
Scotstounhill	d		19 58					20 28			20 58					21 28			21 58			
Garscadden	d		20 00					20 30			21 00					21 30			22 00			
Yoker	d		20 03					20 33			21 03					21 33			22 03			
Clydebank	d		20 05					20 35			21 05					21 35			22 05			
Anniesland	d	19 48		20 07			20 18		20 37	20 48		21 07			21 18		21 37	21 48		22 07		22 18
Westerton	d	19 51		20 10			20 21		20 40	20 51		21 10			21 21		21 40	21 51		22 10		22 21
Bearsden	d	19 55					20 25			20 55					21 25			21 55				22 25
Hillfoot	d	19 57					20 27			20 57					21 27			21 57				22 27
Milngavie	a	20 00					20 30			21 00					21 30			22 00				22 30
Drumchapel	d			20 12					20 42			21 12					21 42			22 12		
Drumry	d			20 14					20 44			21 14					21 44			22 14		
Singer	d			20 17					20 47			21 17					21 47			22 17		
Dalmuir	a		20 09	20 19				20 39	20 49		21 09	21 19				21 39	21 49		22 09	22 19		
	d		20 09	20 20				20 39	20 50		21 09	21 20				21 39	21 50		22 09	22 20		
Kilpatrick	d		20 11					20 41			21 11					21 41			22 11			
Bowling	d		20 14					20 44			21 14					21 44			22 14			
Dumbarton East	d		20 19	20 28				20 49	20 58		21 19	21 28				21 49	21 58		22 19	22 28		
Dumbarton Central	d		20 21	20 30				20 51	21 00		21 21	21 30				21 51	22 00		22 21	22 30		
Dalreoch	d		20 22	20 31				20 52	21 01		21 22	21 31				21 52	22 01		22 22	22 31		
Renton	d		20 25					20 55			21 25					21 55			22 25			
Alexandria	d		20 28					20 58			21 28					21 58			22 28			
Balloch	a		20 31					21 01			21 31					22 01			22 31			
Cardross	d			20 36					21 06			21 36					22 06			22 36		
Craigendoran	d			20 41					21 11			21 41					22 11			22 41		
Helensburgh Central	a			20 44					21 14			21 45					22 14			22 44		

§ Station closed between 4 June and 24 November inclusive

Table 226

Sundays

Lanark, Coatbridge, Motherwell, Larkhall, Hamilton, Edinburgh and Bathgate, Airdrie and Springburn - Glasgow - Milngavie, Dalmuir, Balloch and Helensburgh

Network Diagram - see first Page of Table 220

		SR	SR	SR	SR	SR	SR	SR	SR	SR		SR	SR	SR	SR
Lanark	d							22 12							
Carluke	d							22 22							
Wishaw	d							22 27							
Holytown	d														
Shieldmuir	d							22 31							
Coatbridge Central	d														
Whifflet	d														
Motherwell	a							22 34							
	d	21 40		22 06	22 10			22 34	22 40			23 06	23 10		
Bellshill	d			22 12				22 40				23 12			
Uddingston	d			22 16				22 44				23 16			
Airbles	d	21 42			22 12				22 42				23 12		
Larkhall	d						22 25								
Merryton	d						22 27								
Chatelherault	d						22 30								
Hamilton Central	d	21 47			22 17		22 34		22 47				23 17		
Hamilton West	d	21 50			22 20		22 36		22 50				23 20		
Blantyre	d	21 53			22 23		22 40		22 53				23 23		
Newton	d	21 57			22 27				22 57				23 27		
Cambuslang	d	22 01		22 21	22 31			22 49	23 01			23 21	23 31		
Rutherglen	d	22 04		22 24	22 34		22 48	22 53	23 04			23 24	23 34		
Dalmarnock §	d														
Bridgeton	d	22 07		22 27	22 37			22 57	23 07			23 27	23 37		
Edinburgh	d					21 40								22 40	23 18
Haymarket	d					21 44								22 44	23 22
Edinburgh Park	d					21 49								22 49	23 27
Uphall	d					21 57								22 57	23 35
Livingston North	d					22 00								23 00	23 38
Bathgate	a					22 05								23 05	23 43
	d					22 06								23 06	
Armadale	d					22 10								23 10	
Blackridge	d					22 14								23 14	
Caldercruix	d					22 20								23 20	
Drumgelloch	d					22 24								23 24	
Airdrie	d		21 58			22 28				22 58				23 28	
Coatdyke	d		22 00			22 30				23 00				23 30	
Coatbridge Sunnyside	d		22 02			22 32				23 02				23 32	
Blairhill	d		22 05			22 35				23 05				23 35	
Easterhouse	d		22 09			22 39				23 09				23 39	
Garrowhill	d		22 11			22 41				23 11				23 41	
Shettleston	d		22 14			22 44				23 14				23 44	
Carntyne	d		22 16			22 46				23 16				23 46	
Springburn	d														
Barnhill	d														
Alexandra Parade	d														
Duke Street	d														
Bellgrove	d		22 19			22 49				23 19				23 49	
High Street	d		22 21			22 51				23 21				23 51	
Glasgow Queen St LL ⑩ ⛴	a		22 23			22 53				23 23				23 53	
	d		22 24			22 54				23 24				23 54	
Charing Cross	d		22 27			22 57				23 27				23 57	
Argyle Street	d														
Glasgow Central LL ⑮	a	22 14		22 34	22 44		22 57	23 04	23 14			23 34	23 44		
	d	22 14		22 34	22 44		22 57	23 04	23 14			23 34	23 44		
Anderston	d														
Exhibition Centre	d	22 18		22 38	22 48		23 01	23 08	23 18			23 38	23 48		
Partick ⛴	d	22 22	22 32	22 42	22 52	23 02	23a04	23 12	23 22	23 32		23 42	23 52	00 01	
Hyndland ③	d	22 24	22 34	22 45	22 54	23 04		23 15	23 24	23 34		23 44	23 54	00 03	
Jordanhill	d	22 26			22 56				23 26			23 46	23 56	00 05	
Scotstounhill	d	22 28			22 58				23 28			23 48	23 58	00 07	
Garscadden	d	22 30			23 00				23 30			23a50	00a01	00 09	
Yoker	d	22 33			23 03				23 33					00 12	
Clydebank	d	22 35			23 05				23 35						
Anniesland	d		22 37	22 48		23 07		23 18		23 37					
Westerton	d		22 40	22 51		23 10		23 21		23 40					
Bearsden	d			22 55				23 25							
Hillfoot	d			22 57				23 27							
Milngavie	a			23 00				23 30							
Drumchapel	d		22 42			23 12				23 42					
Drumry	d		22 44			23 14				23 44					
Singer	d		22 47			23 17				23 47					
Dalmuir	a	22 39	22 49		23 09	23 19			23 39	23 49				00 16	
	d	22 39	22 50		23 09	23 20			23 39	23 50					
Kilpatrick	d	22 41			23 11				23 41						
Bowling	d	22 44			23 14				23 44						
Dumbarton East	d	22 49	22 58		23 19	23 28			23 49	23 58					
Dumbarton Central	d	22 51	23 00		23 21	23 30			23 51	23 59					
Dalreoch	d	22 52	23 01		23 22	23 31			23 52	00 01					
Renton	d	22 55			23 25				23 55						
Alexandria	d	22 58			23 28				23 58						
Balloch	a	23 01			23 31				00 01						
Cardross	d		23 06			23 36				00 06					
Craigendoran	d		23 11			23 41				00 11					
Helensburgh Central	a		23 14			23 44				00 14					

§ Station closed between 4 June and 24 November inclusive

Table 226

Mondays to Saturdays

Helensburgh, Balloch, Dalmuir and Milngavie - Glasgow - Springburn, Airdrie, Bathgate and Edinburgh, Hamilton, Larkhall, Motherwell, Coatbridge and Lanark

Network Diagram - see first Page of Table 220

Miles	Miles	Miles	Miles	Miles			SR MO A	SR MX	SR MSX	SR SO	SR SO	SR MX	SR SO B	SR SO	SR MX C	SR	SR	SR	SR	SR	SR SX	SR SO	SR SX	XC SX ◇ D	XC SO ◇ E
0	—	—	—	—	**Helensburgh Central**	d	22b37	22p40				23p10			23b24										
1¼	—	—	—	—	Craigendoran	d		22p43				23p13													
4¼	—	—	—	—	Cardross	d		22p48				23p18													
—	0	—	—	—	**Balloch**	d			22p53																
—	1	—	—	—	Alexandria	d			22p55																
—	2¼	—	—	—	Renton	d			22p58																
8	3¼	—	—	—	Dalreoch	d		22p53	23p01			23p23													
8¾	4	—	—	—	Dumbarton Central	d		22p55	23p02			23p25													
9	4¾	—	—	—	Dumbarton East	d		22p57	23p04			23p27													
11¾	7½	—	—	—	Bowling	d			23p09																
13½	9¼	—	—	—	Kilpatrick	d			23p12																
14¾	10½	0	0	—	**Dalmuir**	a	23p02	23p05	23p15			23p35			23p49										
—	—	—	—	—		d	23p04	23p05	23p16		23p31	23p35			23p51						05 47	05 47			
15½	11¾	—	0¾	—	Singer	d			23p18		23p33														
16½	12¾	—	1¾	—	Drumry	d			23p20		23p35														
17¼	13	—	2½	—	Drumchapel	d			23p23		23p38														
—	—	—	—	0	**Milngavie**	d								23p42											
—	—	—	—	1½	Hillfoot	d								23p45											
—	—	—	—	2¼	Bearsden	d								23p47											
18½	14¼	—	3¾	3½	Westerton	d	23p13		23p25		23p40			23p50	23p56										
19¾	15½	—	5	4¾	Anniesland	d			23p28		23p44			23p53											
—	—	1¼	—	—	Clydebank	d		23p07				23p37									05 49	05 49			
—	—	2¼	—	—	Yoker	d		23p09				23p39									05 51	05 51			
—	—	3¼	—	—	Garscadden	d		23p13				23p43								05 42	05 54	05 54			
—	—	3¾	—	—	Scotstounhill	d		23p15				23p45								05 44	05 57	05 57			
—	—	4¾	—	—	Jordanhill	d		23p17				23p47								05 46	05 59	05 59			
20¾	16½	5¼	6	5¾	Hyndland ③	d		23p21	23p31		23p47	23p49		23p56						05 48	06 01	06 01			
21¼	17	—	6½	6¼	**Partick** ⛴	d		23p23	23p34	23p40	23p50	23p52		23p59						05 51	06 04	06 04			
—	—	—	8¼	7½	Exhibition Centre	d				23p43	23p53			00 02											
—	—	—	8¾	8	Anderston	d				23p45	23p55			00 04											
—	—	—	8¾	8½	**Glasgow Central LL** ⑮	a				23p46	23p56			00 05											
—	—	—	—	—		d				23p47	23p57		00c06	00 07										06b01	06b01
—	—	—	9¼	9	Argyle Street	d				23p49	23p59			00 09											
23¾	19	—	—	—	Charing Cross	d		23p27	23p38			23p56								05 55	06 08	06 08			
24	19¾	—	—	—	**Glasgow Queen St LL** ⑩ ⛴	a		23p29	23p40			23p59								05 57	06 10	06 10			
—	—	—	—	—		d		23p30	23p44			23p59								05 58	06 12	06 15			
24½	20¼	—	—	—	High Street	d		23p32	23p46			00 02								06 00	06 14	06 17			
25	20¾	—	—	—	Bellgrove	d		23p34	23p49			00 04								06 02	06 16	06 19			
—	21¼	—	—	—	Duke Street	d																06 21			
—	21½	—	—	—	Alexandra Parade	d																06 22			
—	22¾	—	—	—	Barnhill	d																06 25			
—	23	—	—	—	**Springburn**	a																06 27			
26¾	—	—	—	—	Carntyne	d		23p37	23p52			00 07								06 05	06 19				
27½	—	—	—	—	Shettleston	d		23p40	23p55			00 10								06 08	06 22				
28¾	—	—	—	—	Garrowhill	d		23p42	23p57			00 12								06 10	06 24				
29¾	—	—	—	—	Easterhouse	d		23p45	23p59			00 15								06 13	06 27				
32½	—	—	—	—	Blairhill	d		23p49	00 04			00 19								06 17	06 31				
33	—	—	—	—	Coatbridge Sunnyside	d		23p51	00 06			00 21								06 19	06 33				
34	—	—	—	—	Coatdyke	d		23p54	00 09			00 24								06 22	06 36				
35	—	—	—	—	**Airdrie**	d		23p57	00a12			00a27								06 25	06 45				
36½	—	—	—	—	Drumgelloch	d		23p59												06 28	06 48				
39½	—	—	—	—	Caldercruix	d		00 03												06 32					
45	—	—	—	—	Blackridge	d		00 09												06 38					
47¼	—	—	—	—	Armadale	d		00 13												06 41					
49¾	—	—	—	—	**Bathgate**	a		00 17												06 45	07 00				
—	—	—	—	—		d										05 45			06 18	06 47	07 02				
52¾	—	—	—	—	Livingston North	d										05 49			06 22	06 50	07 06				
55¾	—	—	—	—	Uphall	d										05 52			06 25	06 53	07 09				
64½	—	—	—	—	Edinburgh Park	a										06 00			06 36	07 02	07 19				
67	—	—	—	—	Haymarket	a										06 05			06 41	07 07	07 24				
68¼	—	—	—	—	**Edinburgh**	a	00 15								00 50	06 10			06 46	07 13	07 29				
—	—	—	10½	10¼	Bridgeton	d				23p52				00 12											
—	—	—	11	10¾	Dalmarnock §	d																			
—	—	—	11¾	11½	Rutherglen	d				23p57	00 04			00 16											
—	—	—	13½	13¼	Cambuslang	d				00 01			00 15	00 20											
—	—	0	—	14¾	Newton	d								00 24											
—	—	2½	—	—	Blantyre	d					00 15			00 28											
—	—	4½	—	—	Hamilton West	d					00 18			00 31											
0	—	5¼	—	—	**Hamilton Central**	d					00 21			00 33											
2¼	—	—	—	—	Chatelherault	d					00 24														
3¾	—	—	—	—	Merryton	d					00 27														
5¼	—	—	—	—	**Larkhall**	a					00 30														
0	—	7½	—	—	Airbles	d								00 38											
—	—	—	17	16¾	Uddingston	d				00 05			00 20												
—	—	—	19½	—	Bellshill	d				00 10			00 25												
—	0	8¼	22½	21	**Motherwell**	a				00 16				00 41										06 15	06 15
—	—	—	—	—		d				00 16							05 47	06 10					06 23		
—	4½	—	—	—	Whifflet	a												06 17							
—	5¼	—	—	—	**Coatbridge Central**	a												06 20							
—	—	—	—	22½	Shieldmuir	d				00 20							05 50						06 27		
—	—	—	—	—	Holytown	d							00a29												
—	—	—	—	24¼	Wishaw	d				00 23							05 55						06 30		
—	—	—	—	28¾	Carluke	d				00 30							06 01						06 37		
—	—	—	—	37¼	**Lanark**	a				00 42							06 12						06 47		

§ Station closed between 4 June and 24 November inclusive
A From Fort William to London Euston
B To Edinburgh
C From Fort William
D To Plymouth
E To Paignton until 8 September, to Plymouth from 15 September
b Helensburgh Upper, previous night
c Glasgow Central High Level

Table 226

Mondays to Saturdays

Helensburgh, Balloch, Dalmuir and Milngavie - Glasgow - Springburn, Airdrie, Bathgate and Edinburgh, Hamilton, Larkhall, Motherwell, Coatbridge and Lanark

Network Diagram - see first Page of Table 220

		SR D	SR SX	SR	SR SX	SR	SR	SR SX A	SR SX	SR SO	SR SX		SR SO	SR SO	SR	SR SX	SR	SR	SR SX	SR B	SR C		SR SX	SR SO	SR SX
Helensburgh Central	d																06 10								
Craigendoran	d																06 13								
Cardross	d																06 18								
Balloch	d																								06 23
Alexandria	d																								06 25
Renton	d																								06 28
Dalreoch	d																06 23								06 31
Dumbarton Central	d																06 25								06 32
Dumbarton East	d																06 27								06 34
Bowling	d																								06 39
Kilpatrick	d																								06 42
Dalmuir	a																06 34								06 45
	d					06 01					06 16		06 16		06 23		06 35	06 31							06 46
Singer	d					06 03					06 18		06 18					06 33							06 48
Drumry	d					06 05					06 20		06 20					06 35							06 50
Drumchapel	d					06 08					06 23		06 23					06 38							06 53
Milngavie	d																						06 42	06 42	
Hillfoot	d																						06 45	06 45	
Bearsden	d																						06 47	06 47	
Westerton	d					06 10					06 25		06 25					06 40					06 50	06 50	06 55
Anniesland	d					06 14					06 28		06 28					06 44					06 53	06 53	06 58
Clydebank	d														06 25										
Yoker	d														06 27										
Garscadden	d			06 00	06 08		06 13		06 17	06 20					06 31				06 46						
Scotstounhill	d			06 01	06 10		06 15		06 19	06 22					06 33				06 48						
Jordanhill	d			06 03	06 12		06 18		06 21	06 24					06 35				06 50						
Hyndland 3	d			06 05	06 14	06 17	06 20		06 22	06 26	06 31		06 31		06 37	06 41	06 44	06 48	06 52				06 56	06 56	07 01
Partick	d			06 10	06 17	06 20	06 22		06 25	06 29	06 34		06 34		06 40	06 43	06 46	06 50	06 55				06 59	06 59	07 04
Exhibition Centre	d			06 13		06 23			06 28	06 32					06 43			06 53					07 02	07 02	
Anderston	d			06 15		06 25			06 30	06 34					06 45			06 55					07 04	07 04	
Glasgow Central LL 15	a			06 17		06 26			06 32	06 35					06 46			06 56					07 05	07 05	
	d	06c16		06 17		06 27			06 32	06 36					06 47			06 57		07b05			07 07	07 07	
Argyle Street	d			06 19		06 29			06 34	06 37					06 49			06 58					07 09	07 09	
Charing Cross	d				06 21		06 26				06 38		06 38			06 49	06 54		06 59						07 08
Glasgow Queen St LL 10	a				06 23		06 28				06 40		06 40			06 51	06 56		07 01						07 10
	d				06 24		06 29				06 42		06 44			06 54	06 57		07 02						07 12
High Street	d				06 26		06 31				06 44		06 46			06 56	07 00		07 04						07 14
Bellgrove	d				06 28		06 33				06 46		06 49				07 01		07 06						07 16
Duke Street	d				06 30								06 51						07 08						
Alexandra Parade	d				06 31								06 52						07 09						
Barnhill	d				06 34								06 55						07 12						
Springburn	a				06 36								06 57						07 14						
Carntyne	d						06 36				06 49						07 05								07 19
Shettleston	d						06 39				06 52						07 07								07 22
Garrowhill	d						06 41				06 54						07 10								07 24
Easterhouse	d						06 44				06 57						07 12								07 27
Blairhill	d						06 48				07 01						07 16								07 31
Coatbridge Sunnyside	d						06 50				07 03					07 09	07 19								07 33
Coatdyke	d						06 53				07 06						07 21								07 36
Airdrie	d						06 56				07a09					07 15	07 24								07a39
Drumgelloch	d						06 59									07 18	07 27								
Caldercruix	d						07 03										07 31								
Blackridge	d						07 09										07 37								
Armadale	d						07 12										07 41								
Bathgate	a						07 16									07 29	07 46								
	d						07 17									07 31	07 46								
Livingston North	d						07 21									07 36	07 50								
Uphall	d						07 24									07 39	07 53								
Edinburgh Park	a						07 32									07 53	08 01								
Haymarket	a						07 37									07 57	08 08								
Edinburgh	a						07 43									08 02	08 14								
Bridgeton	d			06 22					06 37	06 40					06 52								07 12	07 12	
Dalmarnock §	d																								
Rutherglen	d			06 25		06 34			06 41	06 45					06 56			07 03					07 17	07 17	
Cambuslang	d	06 25		06 30					06 45	06 49					07 00								07 21	07 21	
Newton	d								06 49	06 52													07 24	07 24	
Blantyre	d					06 45			06 53	06 56								07 11					07 28	07 28	
Hamilton West	d					06 48			06 56	06 59								07 14					07 31	07 31	
Hamilton Central	d					06 50			06 59	07 02								07 17					07 34	07 34	
Chatelherault	d					06 54												07 20							
Merryton	d					06 57												07 23							
Larkhall	a					07 00												07 27							
Airbles	d								07 04	07 07													07 39	07 39	
Uddingston	d	06 30		06 35											07 05										
Bellshill	d	06 35		06 40											07 09										
Motherwell	a			06 45					07 06	07 09					07 19					07 26			07 41	07 41	
	d		06 37	06 47				06 57	07 07					07 10						07 27	07 35			07 42	
Whifflet	a								07 15												07 43				
Coatbridge Central	a								07 21												07 45				
Shieldmuir	d			06 49				07 01						07 13											
Holytown	d	06a39	06 43																					07 48	
Wishaw	d		06 49	06 53				07 09						07 17						07 32				07 53	
Carluke	d		06 55	06 59				07a15						07 23						07a38				08 00	
Lanark	a		07 07	07 14										07 34										08 13	

§ Station closed between 4 June and 24 November inclusive
A To Carstairs
B To North Berwick
C To Cumbernauld
D To Edinburgh
b Glasgow Central High Level

Table 226

Mondays to Saturdays

Helensburgh, Balloch, Dalmuir and Milngavie - Glasgow - Springburn, Airdrie, Bathgate and Edinburgh, Hamilton, Larkhall, Motherwell, Coatbridge and Lanark

Network Diagram - see first Page of Table 220

		SR SO	SR A	SR SO	SR SX	SR SX	SR SO	SR	SR	SR SX	SR	SR SX	SR SO	SR SO	SR SX	SR SX	SR SO	SR	XC SX ◇1 C	XC SO ◇1 D	SR	SR SX	SR B	SR SO	SR SX
Helensburgh Central	d							06 40										07 10							
Craigendoran	d							06 43										07 13							
Cardross	d							06 48										07 18							
Balloch	d	06 23										06 53	06 53												
Alexandria	d	06 25										06 55	06 55												
Renton	d	06 28										06 58	06 58												
Dalreoch	d	06 31						06 53				07 01	07 01					07 23							
Dumbarton Central	d	06 32						06 55				07 02	07 02					07 25							
Dumbarton East	d	06 34						06 57				07 04	07 04					07 27							
Bowling	d	06 39										07 09	07 09												
Kilpatrick	d	06 42										07 12	07 12												
Dalmuir	a	06 45						07 04				07 15	07 15					07 34							
	d	06 46		06 53	06 53			07 05	07 01			07 16	07 16	07 23	07 23			07 35			07 31	07 38			
Singer	d	06 48							07 03			07 18	07 18								07 33				
Drumry	d	06 50							07 05			07 20	07 20								07 35				
Drumchapel	d	06 53							07 08			07 23	07 23								07 38				
Milngavie	d					06 57					07 12					07 27								07 42	07 42
Hillfoot	d					07 00					07 15					07 30								07 45	07 45
Bearsden	d					07 02					07 17					07 32								07 47	07 49
Westerton	d	06 55				07 05			07 10		07 20	07 25	07 25			07 35					07 40			07 50	07 52
Anniesland	d	06 58				07 08			07 14		07 23	07 28	07 28			07 38					07 44			07 53	07 55
Clydebank	d			06 55	06 55									07 25	07 25							07 40			
Yoker	d			06 57	06 57									07 27	07 27							07 42			
Garscadden	d			07 01	07 01					07 16				07 31	07 31							07 46			
Scotstounhill	d			07 03	07 03					07 18				07 33	07 33							07 48			
Jordanhill	d			07 05	07 05					07 20				07 35	07 35							07 50			
Hyndland 3	d	07 01		07 07	07 07	07 11		07 14	07 18	07 22	07 26	07 31	07 31	07 37	07 37	07 41		07 44			07 47	07 52		07 56	07 58
Partick	d	07 04		07 10	07 10	07 14	07 14	07 17	07 20	07 25	07 29	07 34	07 34	07 40	07 40	07 44	07 44	07 47			07 50	07 55		07 59	08 00
Exhibition Centre	d			07 13	07 13				07 23		07 32			07 43	07 43						07 53			08 02	08 03
Anderston	d			07 15	07 15				07 25		07 34			07 45	07 45						07 55			08 04	08 05
Glasgow Central LL 15	a			07 16	07 16				07 27		07 35			07 46	07 46						07 56			08 05	08 07
	d		07b13	07 17	07 17				07 27		07 37			07 47	07 47				07 50	07b50	07 57			08 07	08 09
Argyle Street	d			07 19	07 19				07 29		07 38			07 49	07 49						07 59			08 09	08 11
Charing Cross	d	07 08				07 19	07 19	07 24		07 29		07 38	07 38			07 49	07 49	07 54				07 59			
Glasgow Queen St LL 10	a	07 10				07 21	07 21	07 26		07 31		07 40	07 40			07 51	07 51	07 56				08 01			
	d	07 15				07 24	07 24	07 28		07 32		07 42	07 44			07 54	07 54	07 58				08 02			
High Street	d	07 17				07 26	07 26	07 30		07 34		07 44	07 46			07 56	07 56	08 00				08 04			
Bellgrove	d	07 19						07 32		07 36		07 46	07 49					08 01				08 06			
Duke Street	d	07 21								07 38			07 51									08 08			
Alexandra Parade	d	07 22								07 39			07 52									08 09			
Barnhill	d	07 25								07 42			07 55									08 12			
Springburn	a	07 27								07 44			07 57									08 14			
Carntyne	d							07 36				07 49						08 05							
Shettleston	d							07 38				07 52						08 07							
Garrowhill	d							07 41				07 54						08 10							
Easterhouse	d							07 43				07 57						08 12							
Blairhill	d							07 47				08 01						08 16							
Coatbridge Sunnyside	d					07 38	07 38	07 50				08 03				08 09	08 09	08 19							
Coatdyke	d							07 52				08 06						08 21							
Airdrie	d					07 45	07 45	07 55				08a09				08 15	08 15	08 24							
Drumgelloch	d					07 48	07 48	07 58								08 18	08 18	08 27							
Caldercruix	d							08 02										08 31							
Blackridge	d							08 08										08 37							
Armadale	d							08 12										08 41							
Bathgate	a					08 00	08 00	08 16								08 30	08 30	08 45							
	d					08 02	08 02	08 17								08 31	08 31	08 46							
Livingston North	d					08 06	08 06	08 21								08 36	08 36	08 51							
Uphall	d					08 09	08 09	08 24								08 39	08 39	08 54							
Edinburgh Park	a					08 16	08 16	08 33								08 47	08 47	09 03							
Haymarket	a					08 23	08 23	08 38								08 52	08 52	09 08							
Edinburgh	a					08 29	08 29	08 43								08 58	08 58	09 13							
Bridgeton	d			07 22	07 22						07 41			07 52	07 52									08 12	08 14
Dalmarnock §	d																								
Rutherglen	d			07 26	07 26				07 34		07 46			07 56	07 56						08 05			08 16	08 18
Cambuslang	d		07 23	07 31	07 31						07 50			08 00	08 00									08 20	08 22
Newton	d										07 53													08 24	08 26
Blantyre	d								07 44		07 58										08 14			08 28	08 30
Hamilton West	d								07 47		08 01										08 17			08 31	08 33
Hamilton Central	d								07 50		08 03										08 20			08 33	08 35
Chatelherault	d								07 53												08 23				
Merryton	d								07 56												08 26				
Larkhall	a								08 00												08 30				
Airbles	d										08 07													08 38	08 40
Uddingston	d		07 29	07 35	07 35									08 05	08 05										
Bellshill	d		07 34	07 40	07 40									08 10	08 10										
Motherwell	a			07 46	07 46						08 11			08 16	08 17									08 41	08 43
	d				07 46									08 16					08 04	08 04			08 37	08 41	
Whifflet	a																						08 45		
Coatbridge Central	a																						08 48		
Shieldmuir	d				07 50									08 20											
Holytown	d		07a38																					08 47	
Wishaw	d				07 53									08 23										08 53	
Carluke	d				08 00									08 30										09 00	
Lanark	a				08 15									08 42										09 12	

§ Station closed between 4 June and 24 November inclusive
A To Edinburgh
B To Cumbernauld
C To Plymouth
D To Penzance until 8 September, to Plymouth from 15 September
b Glasgow Central High Level

Table 226

Mondays to Saturdays

Helensburgh, Balloch, Dalmuir and Milngavie - Glasgow - Springburn, Airdrie, Bathgate and Edinburgh, Hamilton, Larkhall, Motherwell, Coatbridge and Lanark

Network Diagram - see first Page of Table 220

		SR SX	SR SO	SR A	SR SO	SR SX	SR SO	SR SX	SR SX	SR SO	SR	SR SX B	SR SX	SR SX	SR	SR SX	SR SO	SR SX	SR SX	SR SX	SR	SR SX
Helensburgh Central	d							07 34		07 40		07c42						08 00	07 54			
Craigendoran	d							07 37		07 43								08 03	07 57			
Cardross	d							07 42		07 48		07 50						08 08	08 02			
Balloch	d	07 23	07 23										07 53				07 53					
Alexandria	d	07 25	07 25										07 55				07 55					
Renton	d	07 28	07 28										07 58				07 58					
Dalreoch	d	07 31	07 31					07 47		07 53			08 01				08 01		08 07			
Dumbarton Central	d	07 32	07 32					07 49		07 55		07 56	08 03				08 02	08 14	08 09			
Dumbarton East	d	07 34	07 34					07 51		07 57							08 04		08 11			
Bowling	d	07 39	07 39					07 56									08 09					
Kilpatrick	d	07 42	07 42					07 59									08 12					
Dalmuir	a	07 45	07 45					08 02		08 04							08 15		08 18			
	d	07 46	07 46		07 53	07 53		08 02		08 05	08 00			08 08			08 16		08 18		08 25	
Singer	d	07 48	07 48								08 02	08 07					08 18		08 21			
Drumry	d	07 50	07 50								08 04						08 20		08 24			
Drumchapel	d	07 53	07 53								08 07						08 23		08 26			
Milngavie	d								07 58						08 12	08 18						08 30
Hillfoot	d								08 01						08 15	08 21						08 33
Bearsden	d								08 02						08 17	08 24						08 35
Westerton	d	07 55	07 55						08 05		08 09				08 20		08 25		08 29			08 38
Anniesland	d	07 58	07 58						08 10		08 14				08 23		08 28		08 32			08 41
Clydebank	d				07 55	07 55		08 05						08 10							08 27	
Yoker	d				07 57	07 57								08 12							08 29	
Garscadden	d				08 01	08 01								08 16							08 32	
Scotstounhill	d				08 03	08 03								08 18				08 27			08 34	
Jordanhill	d				08 05	08 05								08 20							08 36	
Hyndland 3	d	08 01	08 01		08 07	08 07		08 11	08 13	08 14	08 17			08 22	08 26		08 31	08 33	08 35		08 38	08 44
Partick ⇌	d	08 04	08 04		08 10	08 10	08 14	08 14	08 16	08 17	08 20		08 22	08 25	08 29		08 34	08 35	08 37		08 40	08 46
Exhibition Centre	d				08 13	08 13			08 19		08 23				08 32						08 43	
Anderston	d				08 15	08 15			08 21		08 25				08 34					08 38	08 45	
Glasgow Central LL 15	a				08 16	08 16			08 23		08 26				08 35					08 39	08 47	
	d			08b20	08 18	08 18			08 23		08 27				08 37					08 40	08 47	
Argyle Street	d				08 20	08 20			08 24		08 29				08 38					08 42	08 49	
Charing Cross	d	08 08	08 08				08 19	08 19		08 24			08 27	08 30		08 35	08 38	08 40	08 42			08 50
Glasgow Queen St LL 10 ⇌	a	08 10	08 10				08 21	08 21		08 26		08e37	08 29	08 32		08 37	08 40	08 42	08 44			08 52
	d	08 12	08 15				08 24	08 24		08 28			08 29	08 33		08 38	08 44	08 42	08 44			08 54
High Street	d	08 14	08 17				08 27	08 27		08 30			08 31	08 35		08 40	08 46	08 44	08a47			08 56
Bellgrove	d	08 16	08 19					08 29		08 32			08 33	08 37			08 49	08 46				
Duke Street	d		08 21										08 35	08 42			08 51					
Alexandra Parade	d		08 22										08 37	08 43			08 52					
Barnhill	d		08 25										08 40	08 46			08 55					
Springburn	a		08 27										08 42	08 48			08 57					
Carntyne	d	08 19						08 32		08 36								08 49				
Shettleston	d	08 22						08 35		08 38								08 52				
Garrowhill	d	08 24						08 37		08 41								08 54				
Easterhouse	d	08 27						08 40		08 43								08 57				
Blairhill	d	08 31						08 44		08 47								09 01				
Coatbridge Sunnyside	d	08 33					08 39	08 46		08 50						08 52		09 03				09 12
Coatdyke	d	08 36						08 49		08 52								09 06				
Airdrie	d	08 44					08 44	08a52		08 55						08 57		09a09				09 16
Drumgelloch	d	08 47					08 47			08 58						09 00						09 19
Caldercruix	d									09 02						09 04						
Blackridge	d									09 08						09 10						
Armadale	d									09 12						09 14						
Bathgate	a	09 00					09 00			09 16						09 18						09 32
	d	09 01					09 01			09 17						09 18						09 32
Livingston North	d	09 06					09 06			09 20						09 22						09 37
Uphall	d	09 09					09 09			09 23						09 25						09 40
Edinburgh Park	a	09 18					09 18			09 31						09 33						09 48
Haymarket	a	09 22					09 22			09 37						09 38						09 52
Edinburgh	a	09 27					09 27			09 43						09 43						09 57
Bridgeton	d				08 23	08 23			08 26						08 41					08 45	08 52	
Dalmarnock §	d																					
Rutherglen	d				08 27	08 27			08 31		08 34				08 46					08 51	08 57	
Cambuslang	d				08 31	08 31									08 50					08 55	09 01	
Newton	d														08 54							
Blantyre	d										08 44				08 58							
Hamilton West	d										08 47				09 01							
Hamilton Central	d										08 49				09 04							
Chatelherault	d										08 53											
Merryton	d										08 56											
Larkhall	a										09 00											
Airbles	d														09 09							
Uddingston	d			08 32	08 36	08 36														09 00	09 05	
Bellshill	d			08 36	08 40	08 40															09 10	
Motherwell	a				08 47	08 47			08 46						09 12					09 07	09 18	
	d					08 47															09 19	
Whifflet	a																					
Coatbridge Central	a																					
Shieldmuir	d					08 50															09 22	
Holytown	d			08a40																		
Wishaw	d					08 53															09 26	
Carluke	d					09 00															09 32	
Lanark	a					09 12															09 43	

§ Station closed between 4 June and 24 November inclusive

A To Edinburgh

B From Arrochar & Tarbet

b Glasgow Central High Level

c Helensburgh Upper

e Glasgow Queen St High Level

Table 226

Mondays to Saturdays

Helensburgh, Balloch, Dalmuir and Milngavie - Glasgow - Springburn, Airdrie, Bathgate and Edinburgh, Hamilton, Larkhall, Motherwell, Coatbridge and Lanark

Network Diagram - see first Page of Table 220

		SR SO	SR	SR	SR SX	SR SO	XC ◇1 C	SR A	SR	SR	SR B	SR	SR	SR	SR	SR	SR	SR	SR	SR	SR	SR	SR	SR A
Helensburgh Central	d		08 10											08 40							09 10			
Craigendoran	d		08 13											08 43							09 13			
Cardross	d		08 18											08 48							09 18			
Balloch	d									08 23								08 53						
Alexandria	d									08 25								08 55						
Renton	d									08 28								08 58						
Dalreoch	d		08 23							08 31				08 53				09 01			09 23			
Dumbarton Central	d		08 25							08 32				08 55				09 02			09 25			
Dumbarton East	d		08 27							08 34				08 57				09 04			09 27			
Bowling	d		08 30							08 39								09 09						
Kilpatrick	d		08 32							08 42								09 12						
Dalmuir	a		08 34							08 45				09 04				09 15			09 34			
	d		08 35	08 31	08 39					08 46		08 53		09 05	09 01	09 08		09 16	09 23		09 35	09 31	09 38	
Singer	d			08 33						08 48					09 03			09 18				09 33		
Drumry	d			08 35						08 50					09 05			09 20				09 35		
Drumchapel	d			08 38						08 53					09 08			09 23				09 38		
Milngavie	d								08 42				08 57				09 12			09 28				
Hillfoot	d								08 45				09 00				09 15			09 31				
Bearsden	d								08 47				09 02				09 18			09 33				
Westerton	d			08 42					08 50	08 55			09 05		09 10		09 21	09 25		09 36		09 40		
Anniesland	d			08 46					08 53	08 58			09 08		09 14		09 24	09 28		09 39		09 44		
Clydebank	d				08 40							08 55				09 10			09 25				09 40	
Yoker	d				08 42							08 57				09 12			09 27				09 42	
Garscadden	d				08 46	08 46						09 01				09 16			09 31				09 46	
Scotstounhill	d				08 48	08 48						09 03				09 18			09 33				09 48	
Jordanhill	d				08 50	08 50						09 05				09 20			09 35				09 50	
Hyndland 3	d		08 45	08 49	08 52	08 52			08 56	09 01		09 08	09 12	09 14	09 17	09 22	09 28	09 31	09 37	09 42	09 44	09 47	09 52	
Partick ⇌	d	08 46	08 47	08 51	08 55	08 55			08 59	09 04		09 10	09 14	09 17	09 20	09 25	09 30	09 34	09 40	09 44	09 47	09 50	09 55	
Exhibition Centre	d			08 54					09 02			09 13			09 23		09 33		09 43			09 53		
Anderston	d			08 56					09 04			09 15			09 25		09 35		09 45			09 55		
Glasgow Central LL 15	a			08 58					09 06			09 16			09 26		09 36		09 46			09 56		
	d			08 58			09e00		09 07		09b18	09 17			09 27		09 37		09 47			09 57		
Argyle Street	d			09 00					09 08			09 19			09 29		09 38		09 49			09 59		
Charing Cross	d	08 50	08 54		08 59	08 59				09 08			09 19	09 24		09 29		09 38		09 49	09 54		09 59	
Glasgow Queen St LL 10 ⇌	a	08 52	08 56		09 01	09 01				09 10			09 21	09 26		09 31		09 40		09 51	09 56		10 01	
	d	08 54	08 58		09 02	09 02				09 12			09 24	09 28		09 32		09 42		09 54	09 58		10 02	
High Street	d	08 56	09 00		09 04	09 04				09 14			09 26	09 30		09 34		09 44		09 57	10 00		10 04	
Bellgrove	d		09 02		09 06	09 06				09 16				09 32		09 36		09 46			10 02		10 06	
Duke Street	d				09 08	09 08										09 38							10 08	
Alexandra Parade	d				09 09	09 09										09 39							10 09	
Barnhill	d				09 12	09 12										09 42							10 12	
Springburn	a				09 14	09 14										09 44							10 14	
Carntyne	d		09 06							09 19				09 35				09 49			10 05			
Shettleston	d		09 09							09 22				09 38				09 52			10 08			
Garrowhill	d		09 11							09 24				09 40				09 54			10 10			
Easterhouse	d		09 14							09 27				09 43				09 57			10 13			
Blairhill	d		09 18							09 31				09 47				10 01			10 17			
Coatbridge Sunnyside	d	09 12	09 20							09 33			09 39	09 49				10 03		10 09	10 19			
Coatdyke	d		09 23							09 36				09 52				10 06			10 22			
Airdrie	d	09 16	09 26							09a39			09 44	09 55				10a09		10 15	10 25			
Drumgelloch	d	09 19	09 29										09 47	09 58						10 18	10 28			
Caldercruix	d		09 33											10 02							10 32			
Blackridge	d		09 39											10 08							10 38			
Armadale	d		09 42											10 11							10 41			
Bathgate	a	09 32	09 46										10 00	10 15						10 29	10 45			
	d	09 32	09 47										10 01	10 17						10 32	10 47			
Livingston North	d	09 37	09 49										10 06	10 20						10 35	10 50			
Uphall	d	09 40	09 52										10 09	10 23						10 38	10 53			
Edinburgh Park	a	09 48	10 01										10 17	10 31						10 47	11 01			
Haymarket	a	09 52	10 08										10 22	10 37						10 52	11 06			
Edinburgh	a	09 57	10 14										10 28	10 43						10 57	11 14			
Bridgeton	d								09 11			09 22					09 41		09 52					
Dalmarnock §	d																							
Rutherglen	d			09 05					09 16			09 27			09 34		09 46		09 56			10 04		
Cambuslang	d								09 20			09 31					09 50		10 00					
Newton	d								09 24								09 54							
Blantyre	d			09 14					09 28						09 44		09 58					10 14		
Hamilton West	d			09 17					09 31						09 47		10 01					10 17		
Hamilton Central	d			09 20					09 33						09 50		10 03					10 20		
Chatelherault	d			09 23											09 53							10 23		
Merryton	d			09 26											09 56							10 26		
Larkhall	a			09 30											10 00							10 30		
Airbles	d								09 38								10 08							
Uddingston	d										09 30	09 35							10 05					
Bellshill	d										09 34	09 40							10 10					
Motherwell	a						09 14		09 41			09 47					10 11		10 16					
	d							09 37	09 41										10 16					10 37
Whifflet	a							09 45																10 45
Coatbridge Central	a							09 48																10 48
Shieldmuir	d																		10 20					
Holytown	d								09 48		09a38													
Wishaw	d								09 53										10 26					
Carluke	d								10 00										10 32					
Lanark	a								10 14										10 44					

§ Station closed between 4 June and 24 November inclusive

A To Cumbernauld

B To Edinburgh

C To Penzance

b Glasgow Central High Level

Helensburgh, Balloch, Dalmuir and Milngavie - Glasgow - Springburn, Airdrie, Bathgate and Edinburgh, Hamilton, Larkhall, Motherwell, Coatbridge and Lanark

Network Diagram - see first Page of Table 220

		SR	SR	SR A	SR	SR	SR	SR	SR	SR	SR	SR	SR	SR	SR	SR	SR B	SR	SR	XC SX C ◇1 ⊼	XC SO D ◇1 ⊼	SR A	SR	SR	SR
Helensburgh Central	d						09 40							10 10											10 40
Craigendoran	d						09 43							10 13											10 43
Cardross	d						09 48							10 18											10 48
Balloch	d		09 23								09 53								10 23						
Alexandria	d		09 25								09 55								10 25						
Renton	d		09 28								09 58								10 28						
Dalreoch	d		09 31				09 53				10 01			10 23					10 31						10 53
Dumbarton Central	d		09 32				09 55				10 02			10 25					10 32						10 55
Dumbarton East	d		09 34				09 57				10 04			10 27					10 34						10 57
Bowling	d		09 39								10 09								10 39						
Kilpatrick	d		09 42								10 12								10 42						
Dalmuir	a		09 45				10 04				10 15			10 34					10 45						11 04
	d		09 46		09 53		10 05	10 01	10 08		10 16	10 23		10 35	10 31	10 38			10 46				10 53		11 05
Singer	d		09 48					10 03			10 18				10 33				10 48						
Drumry	d		09 50					10 05			10 20				10 35				10 50						
Drumchapel	d		09 53					10 08			10 23				10 38				10 53						
Milngavie	d	09 42				09 57				10 12			10 27					10 42						10 57	
Hillfoot	d	09 45				10 00				10 15			10 30					10 45						11 00	
Bearsden	d	09 47				10 02				10 17			10 32					10 47						11 02	
Westerton	d	09 50	09 55			10 05		10 10		10 20	10 25		10 35		10 40			10 50	10 55					11 05	
Anniesland	d	09 53	09 58			10 08		10 14		10 23	10 28		10 38		10 44			10 53	10 58					11 08	
Clydebank	d				09 55				10 10			10 25				10 40							10 55		
Yoker	d				09 57				10 12			10 27				10 42							10 57		
Garscadden	d				10 01				10 16			10 31				10 46							11 01		
Scotstounhill	d				10 03				10 18			10 33				10 48							11 03		
Jordanhill	d				10 05				10 20			10 35				10 50							11 05		
Hyndland ■	d	09 56	10 01		10 07	10 12	10 14	10 17	10 22	10 26	10 31	10 37	10 41	10 44	10 47	10 52		10 56	11 01				11 07	11 11	11 14
Partick ⇌	d	09 59	10 04		10 10	10 14	10 17	10 20	10 25	10 29	10 34	10 40	10 44	10 47	10 50	10 55		10 59	11 04				11 10	11 14	11 17
Exhibition Centre	d	10 02			10 13			10 23		10 32		10 43			10 53			11 02					11 13		
Anderston	d	10 04			10 15			10 25		10 34		10 45			10 55			11 04					11 15		
Glasgow Central LL ■	a	10 05			10 16			10 26		10 36		10 46			10 56			11 05					11 16		
	d	10 07		10b18	10 17			10 27		10 37		10 47			10 57			11 07		10b59	10b59	11b18	11 17		
Argyle Street	d	10 08			10 19			10 29		10 39		10 48			10 59			11 08					11 19		
Charing Cross	d		10 08			10 19	10 24		10 29		10 38		10 49	10 54		10 59			11 08					11 19	11 24
Glasgow Queen St LL ■ ⇌	a		10 10			10 21	10 26		10 31		10 40		10 51	10 56		11 01			11 11					11 21	11 26
	d		10 12			10 24	10 27		10 32		10 42		10 54	10 58		11 02			11 12					11 24	11 28
High Street	d		10 14			10 26	10 30		10 34		10 44		10 56	11 00		11 04			11 14					11 26	11 30
Bellgrove	d		10 16				10 32		10 36		10 46			11 02		11 06			11 16						11 32
Duke Street	d								10 38							11 08									
Alexandra Parade	d								10 39							11 09									
Barnhill	d								10 42							11 12									
Springburn	a								10 44							11 14									
Carntyne	d		10 19				10 36				10 49			11 05					11 19						11 35
Shettleston	d		10 22				10 38				10 52			11 08					11 22						11 38
Garrowhill	d		10 24				10 41				10 54			11 10					11 24						11 40
Easterhouse	d		10 27				10 43				10 57			11 13					11 27						11 43
Blairhill	d		10 31				10 47				11 01			11 17					11 31						11 47
Coatbridge Sunnyside	d		10 33			10 39	10 50				11 03		11 09	11 19					11 33					11 39	11 49
Coatdyke	d		10 36				10 52				11 06			11 22					11 36						11 52
Airdrie	d		10a39			10 44	10 55				11a09		11 14	11 25					11a39					11 44	11 55
Drumgelloch	d					10 47	10 58						11 17	11 28										11 47	11 58
Caldercruix	d						11 02							11 32											12 02
Blackridge	d						11 08							11 38											12 08
Armadale	d						11 12							11 41											12 11
Bathgate	a					11 00	11 16						11 30	11 45										12 00	12 15
	d					11 01	11 17						11 31	11 47										12 01	12 17
Livingston North	d					11 06	11 21						11 35	11 51										12 05	12 21
Uphall	d					11 09	11 24						11 38	11 54										12 08	12 24
Edinburgh Park	a					11 17	11 32						11 47	12 02										12 17	12 32
Haymarket	a					11 22	11 37						11 52	12 07										12 22	12 37
Edinburgh	a					11 28	11 43						11 58	12 13										12 28	12 43
Bridgeton	d	10 11			10 22					10 42		10 51						11 11					11 22		
Dalmarnock §	d																								
Rutherglen	d	10 16			10 26			10 34		10 46		10 56			11 05			11 16					11 26		
Cambuslang	d	10 20			10 31					10 50		11 00						11 20					11 31		
Newton	d	10 23								10 54								11 23							
Blantyre	d	10 28						10 44		10 58					11 14			11 27							
Hamilton West	d	10 31						10 47		11 01					11 17			11 30							
Hamilton Central	d	10 33						10 50		11 03					11 20			11 33							
Chatelherault	d							10 53							11 23										
Merryton	d							10 56							11 26										
Larkhall	a							11 00							11 30										
Airbles	d	10 37								11 08								11 38							
Uddingston	d			10 30	10 35							11 04										11 30	11 35		
Bellshill	d			10 35	10 40							11 09										11 35	11 40		
Motherwell	a	10 42			10 47					11 11		11 17						11 40		11 13	11 13		11 47		
	d	10 43										11 17					11 37	11 41							
Whifflet	a																11 46								
Coatbridge Central	a																11 48								
Shieldmuir	d											11 20													
Holytown	d	10 48		10a39														11 48				11a39			
Wishaw	d	10 53										11 23						11 53							
Carluke	d	11 00										11 30						12 00							
Lanark	a	11 13										11 42						12 12							

§ Station closed between 4 June and 24 November inclusive
A To Edinburgh
B To Cumbernauld
C To Penzance
D To Plymouth until 8 September, to Penzance from 15 September
b Glasgow Central High Level

Helensburgh, Balloch, Dalmuir and Milngavie - Glasgow - Springburn, Airdrie, Bathgate and Edinburgh, Hamilton, Larkhall, Motherwell, Coatbridge and Lanark

Network Diagram - see first Page of Table 220

		SR	SR ◇ A ⊼	SR	SR	SR	SR	SR	SR	SR	SR	SR B	SR	SR	SR C	SR	SR	SR	SR	SR	SR	SR
Helensburgh Central	d		10b44						11 10									11 40				
Craigendoran	d								11 13									11 43				
Cardross	d								11 18									11 48				
Balloch	d					10 53								11 23								11 53
Alexandria	d					10 55								11 25								11 55
Renton	d					10 58								11 28								11 58
Dalreoch	d					11 01			11 23					11 31				11 53				12 01
Dumbarton Central	d		10 59			11 02			11 25					11 32				11 55				12 02
Dumbarton East	d					11 04			11 27					11 34				11 57				12 04
Bowling	d					11 09								11 39								12 09
Kilpatrick	d					11 12								11 42								12 12
Dalmuir	a		11 08			11 15			11 34					11 45				12 04				12 15
	d	11 00	11 08	11 08		11 16	11 23		11 35	11 31	11 38			11 46		11 53		12 05	12 01	12 08		12 16
Singer	d	11 02				11 18				11 33				11 48					12 03			12 18
Drumry	d	11 04				11 20				11 35				11 50					12 05			12 20
Drumchapel	d	11 07				11 23				11 38				11 53					12 08			12 23
Milngavie	d				11 12			11 27					11 42				11 57				12 12	
Hillfoot	d				11 15			11 30					11 45				12 00				12 15	
Bearsden	d				11 18			11 32					11 47				12 02				12 17	
Westerton	d	11 10			11 21	11 25		11 35		11 40			11 50	11 55			12 05		12 10		12 20	12 25
Anniesland	d	11 14			11 24	11 28		11 38		11 44			11 53	11 58			12 08		12 14		12 23	12 28
Clydebank	d			11 10			11 25				11 40					11 55				12 10		
Yoker	d			11 12			11 27				11 42					11 57				12 12		
Garscadden	d			11 16			11 31				11 46					12 01				12 16		
Scotstounhill	d			11 18			11 33				11 48					12 03				12 18		
Jordanhill	d			11 20			11 35				11 50					12 05				12 20		
Hyndland ■	d	11 17		11 22	11 27	11 31	11 37	11 41	11 44	11 47	11 52		11 56	12 01		12 07	12 11	12 14	12 17	12 22	12 26	12 31
Partick ⇌	d	11 20		11 25	11 30	11 34	11 40	11 44	11 47	11 50	11 55		11 59	12 04		12 10	12 14	12 17	12 20	12 25	12 29	12 34
Exhibition Centre	d	11 23			11 33		11 43			11 53			12 02			12 13			12 23		12 32	
Anderston	d	11 25			11 35		11 45			11 55			12 04			12 15			12 25		12 34	
Glasgow Central LL ■	a	11 26			11 38		11 46			11 56			12 05			12 16			12 26		12 35	
	d	11 27			11 38		11 47			11 58			12 07		12e18	12 17			12 27		12 37	
Argyle Street	d	11 29			11 39		11 49			11 59			12 08			12 19			12 29		12 38	
Charing Cross	d			11 29		11 38		11 49	11 54		11 59			12 08			12 19	12 24		12 29		12 38
Glasgow Queen St LL ■ ⇌	a		11c30	11 31		11 41		11 51	11 56		12 01			12 10			12 21	12 26		12 31		12 40
	d			11 32		11 42		11 54	11 58		12 02			12 12			12 24	12 28		12 32		12 42
High Street	d			11 34		11 44		11 56	12 00		12 04			12 14			12 26	12 30		12 34		12 44
Bellgrove	d			11 36		11 46			12 02		12 06			12 16				12 32		12 36		12 46
Duke Street	d			11 38							12 08									12 38		
Alexandra Parade	d			11 39							12 09									12 39		
Barnhill	d			11 42							12 12									12 42		
Springburn	a			11 44							12 14									12 44		
Carntyne	d					11 49			12 05					12 19				12 35				12 49
Shettleston	d					11 52			12 08					12 22				12 38				12 52
Garrowhill	d					11 54			12 10					12 24				12 40				12 54
Easterhouse	d					11 57			12 13					12 27				12 43				12 57
Blairhill	d					12 01			12 17					12 31				12 47				13 01
Coatbridge Sunnyside	d					12 03		12 09	12 19					12 33			12 39	12 49				13 03
Coatdyke	d					12 06			12 22					12 36				12 52				13 06
Airdrie	d					12a09		12 14	12 25					12a39			12 44	12 55				13a09
Drumgelloch	d							12 17	12 28								12 47	12 58				
Caldercruix	d								12 32									13 02				
Blackridge	d								12 38									13 08				
Armadale	d								12 41									13 11				
Bathgate	a							12 30	12 45								13 00	13 15				
	d							12 31	12 47								13 01	13 17				
Livingston North	d							12 35	12 51								13 05	13 21				
Uphall	d							12 38	12 54								13 08	13 24				
Edinburgh Park	a							12 47	13 02								13 17	13 32				
Haymarket	a							12 52	13 07								13 22	13 37				
Edinburgh	a							12 58	13 13								13 28	13 43				
Bridgeton	d				11 42		11 52						12 11			12 22					12 41	
Dalmarnock §	d																					
Rutherglen	d	11 34			11 47		11 56			12 06			12 16			12 26			12 34		12 46	
Cambuslang	d				11 51		12 00						12 20			12 31					12 50	
Newton	d				11 54								12 23								12 53	
Blantyre	d	11 45			11 58					12 14			12 27						12 45		12 58	
Hamilton West	d	11 48			12 01					12 17			12 30						12 48		13 01	
Hamilton Central	d	11 50			12 04					12 20			12 33						12 50		13 03	
Chatelherault	d	11 54								12 23									12 54			
Merryton	d	11 57								12 26									12 57			
Larkhall	a	12 00								12 30									13 00			
Airbles	d				12 09								12 37								13 07	
Uddingston	d						12 05								12 30	12 35						
Bellshill	d						12 09								12 35	12 40						
Motherwell	a				12 11		12 16						12 40			12 48					13 11	
	d						12 16					12 37	12 41									
Whifflet	a											12 45										
Coatbridge Central	a											12 48										
Shieldmuir	d						12 20															
Holytown	d												12 48		12a39							
Wishaw	d						12 22						12 53									
Carluke	d						12 30						13 00									
Lanark	a						12 42						13 12									

§ Station closed between 4 June and 24 November inclusive
A From Mallaig
B To Cumbernauld
C To Edinburgh
b Helensburgh Upper
c Glasgow Queen St High Level
e Glasgow Central High Level

Table 226

Mondays to Saturdays

Helensburgh, Balloch, Dalmuir and Milngavie - Glasgow - Springburn, Airdrie, Bathgate and Edinburgh, Hamilton, Larkhall, Motherwell, Coatbridge and Lanark

Network Diagram - see first Page of Table 220

		SR	SR	SR	XC	SR	SR	SR	SR	SR	SR	SR	SR	SR	SR	SR	SR	SR	SR	SR	SR	SR	SR	SR
					◇1 C			A			B													A
Helensburgh Central	d			12 10										12 40							13 10			
Craigendoran	d			12 13										12 43							13 13			
Cardross	d			12 18										12 48							13 18			
Balloch	d									12 23								12 53						
Alexandria	d									12 25								12 55						
Renton	d									12 28								12 58						
Dalreoch	d			12 23						12 31				12 53				13 01			13 23			
Dumbarton Central	d			12 25						12 32				12 55				13 02			13 25			
Dumbarton East	d			12 27						12 34				12 57				13 04			13 27			
Bowling	d									12 39								13 09						
Kilpatrick	d									12 42								13 12						
Dalmuir	a			12 34						12 45				13 04				13 15			13 34			
	d	12 23		12 35		12 31	12 38			12 46		12 53		13 05	13 01	13 08		13 16	13 23		13 35	13 31	13 38	
Singer	d					12 33				12 48					13 03			13 18				13 33		
Drumry	d					12 35				12 50					13 05			13 20				13 35		
Drumchapel	d					12 38				12 53					13 08			13 23				13 38		
Milngavie	d		12 27						12 42				12 57				13 12			13 27				
Hillfoot	d		12 30						12 45				13 00				13 15			13 30				
Bearsden	d		12 32						12 47				13 02				13 17			13 32				
Westerton	d		12 35			12 40			12 50	12 55			13 05		13 10		13 20	13 25		13 35		13 40		
Anniesland	d		12 38			12 44			12 53	12 58			13 08		13 14		13 23	13 28		13 38		13 44		
Clydebank	d	12 25					12 40					12 55				13 10			13 25				13 40	
Yoker	d	12 27					12 42					12 57				13 12			13 27				13 42	
Garscadden	d	12 31					12 46					13 01				13 16			13 31				13 46	
Scotstounhill	d	12 33					12 48					13 03				13 18			13 33				13 48	
Jordanhill	d	12 35					12 50					13 05				13 20			13 35				13 50	
Hyndland	d	12 37	12 41	12 44		12 47	12 52		12 56	13 01		13 07	13 11	13 14	13 17	13 22	13 26	13 31	13 37	13 41	13 44	13 47	13 52	
Partick	d	12 40	12 44	12 47		12 50	12 55		12 59	13 04		13 10	13 14	13 17	13 20	13 25	13 29	13 34	13 40	13 44	13 47	13 50	13 55	
Exhibition Centre	d	12 43				12 53			13 02			13 13			13 23		13 32		13 43			13 53		
Anderston	d	12 45				12 55			13 04			13 15			13 25		13 34		13 45			13 55		
Glasgow Central LL	a	12 46				12 56			13 05			13 16			13 26		13 35		13 46			13 56		
	d	12 47			12b51	12 57			13 07		13b18	13 17			13 27		13 37		13 47			13 57		
Argyle Street	d	12 48				12 59			13 08			13 19			13 29		13 38		13 48			13 59		
Charing Cross	d		12 49	12 54			12 59			13 08			13 19	13 24		13 29		13 38		13 49	13 54		13 59	
Glasgow Queen St LL	a		12 51	12 56			13 01			13 10			13 21	13 26		13 31		13 40		13 51	13 56		14 01	
	d		12 54	12 58			13 02			13 12			13 24	13 28		13 32		13 42		13 54	13 58		14 02	
High Street	d		12 56	13 00			13 04			13 14			13 26	13 30		13 34		13 44		13 56	14 00		14 04	
Bellgrove	d			13 02			13 06			13 16				13 32		13 36		13 46			14 02		14 06	
Duke Street	d						13 08									13 38							14 08	
Alexandra Parade	d						13 09									13 39							14 09	
Barnhill	d						13 12									13 42							14 12	
Springburn	a						13 14									13 44							14 14	
Carntyne	d			13 05						13 19				13 35				13 49			14 05			
Shettleston	d			13 08						13 22				13 38				13 52			14 08			
Garrowhill	d			13 10						13 24				13 40				13 54			14 10			
Easterhouse	d			13 13						13 27				13 43				13 57			14 13			
Blairhill	d			13 17						13 31				13 47				14 01			14 17			
Coatbridge Sunnyside	d		13 09	13 19						13 33			13 39	13 49				14 03		14 09	14 19			
Coatdyke	d			13 22						13 36				13 52				14 06			14 22			
Airdrie	d		13 14	13 25						13a39			13 44	13 55				14a09		14 14	14 25			
Drumgelloch	d		13 17	13 28									13 47	13 58						14 17	14 28			
Caldercruix	d			13 32										14 02							14 32			
Blackridge	d			13 38										14 08							14 38			
Armadale	d			13 41										14 11							14 41			
Bathgate	a		13 30	13 45									14 00	14 15						14 30	14 45			
	d		13 31	13 47									14 01	14 17						14 31	14 47			
Livingston North	d		13 35	13 51									14 05	14 21						14 35	14 51			
Uphall	d		13 38	13 54									14 08	14 24						14 38	14 54			
Edinburgh Park	a		13 47	14 02									14 17	14 32						14 47	15 02			
Haymarket	a		13 52	14 07									14 22	14 37						14 52	15 07			
Edinburgh	a		13 58	14 13									14 28	14 43						14 58	15 14			
Bridgeton	d	12 51							13 11			13 22					13 41		13 51					
Dalmarnock §	d																							
Rutherglen	d	12 56				13 04			13 16			13 26			13 34		13 46		13 56			14 04		
Cambuslang	d	13 01							13 20			13 31					13 50		14 00					
Newton	d								13 24								13 53							
Blantyre	d					13 14			13 28						13 44		13 57					14 14		
Hamilton West	d					13 17			13 31						13 47		14 00					14 17		
Hamilton Central	d					13 20			13 33						13 50		14 03					14 20		
Chatelherault	d					13 23									13 53							14 23		
Merryton	d					13 26									13 56							14 26		
Larkhall	a					13 30									14 00							14 30		
Airbles	d								13 38								14 08							
Uddingston	d	13 05									13 30	13 35							14 04					
Bellshill	d	13 10									13 35	13 40							14 09					
Motherwell	a	13 16			13 05				13 41			13 48					14 11		14 16					
	d	13 16						13 37	13 41										14 16					14 37
Whifflet	a							13 45																14 45
Coatbridge Central	a							13 48																14 48
Shieldmuir	d	13 20																	14 20					
Holytown	d								13 48		13a39													
Wishaw	d	13 23							13 53										14 23					
Carluke	d	13 32							14 00										14 30					
Lanark	a	13 42							14 12										14 42					

§ Station closed between 4 June and 24 November inclusive

A To Cumbernauld
B To Edinburgh
C To Plymouth
b Glasgow Central High Level

Table 226

Mondays to Saturdays

Helensburgh, Balloch, Dalmuir and Milngavie - Glasgow - Springburn, Airdrie, Bathgate and Edinburgh, Hamilton, Larkhall, Motherwell, Coatbridge and Lanark

Network Diagram - see first Page of Table 220

		SR	SR	SR	SR	SR	SR	SR	SR	SR	SR	SR	SR	SR	SR	SR	XC	XC	SR	SR	SR	SR	SR	SR
				A													SO ◇1 D	SX ◇1 D			B	C	A	
Helensburgh Central	d						13 40							14 10										
Craigendoran	d						13 43							14 13										
Cardross	d						13 48							14 18										
Balloch	d		13 23								13 53									14 23				
Alexandria	d		13 25								13 55									14 25				
Renton	d		13 28								13 58									14 28				
Dalreoch	d		13 31				13 53				14 01			14 23						14 31				
Dumbarton Central	d		13 32				13 55				14 02			14 25						14 32				
Dumbarton East	d		13 34				13 57				14 04			14 27						14 34				
Bowling	d		13 39								14 09									14 39				
Kilpatrick	d		13 42								14 12									14 42				
Dalmuir	a		13 45				14 04				14 15			14 34						14 45				
	d		13 46		13 53		14 05	14 01	14 08		14 16	14 23		14 35	14 31	14 38				14 46				14 53
Singer	d		13 48					14 03			14 18				14 33					14 48				
Drumry	d		13 50					14 05			14 20				14 35					14 50				
Drumchapel	d		13 53					14 08			14 23				14 38					14 53				
Milngavie	d	13 42				13 57				14 12			14 27						14 42					
Hillfoot	d	13 45				14 00				14 15			14 30						14 45					
Bearsden	d	13 47				14 02				14 17			14 32						14 47					
Westerton	d	13 50	13 55			14 05		14 10		14 20	14 25		14 35		14 40				14 50	14 55				
Anniesland	d	13 53	13 58			14 08		14 14		14 23	14 28		14 38		14 44				14 53	14 58				
Clydebank	d				13 55				14 10			14 25				14 40								14 55
Yoker	d				13 57				14 12			14 27				14 42								14 57
Garscadden	d				14 01				14 16			14 31				14 46								15 01
Scotstounhill	d				14 03				14 18			14 33				14 48								15 03
Jordanhill	d				14 05				14 20			14 35				14 50								15 05
Hyndland	d	13 56	14 01		14 07	14 11	14 14	14 17	14 22	14 26	14 31	14 37	14 41	14 44	14 47	14 52			14 56	15 01				15 07
Partick	d	13 59	14 04		14 10	14 14	14 17	14 20	14 25	14 29	14 34	14 40	14 44	14 47	14 50	14 55			14 58	15 04				15 10
Exhibition Centre	d	14 02			14 13			14 23		14 32		14 43			14 53				15 01					15 13
Anderston	d	14 04			14 15			14 25		14 34		14 45			14 55				15 03					15 15
Glasgow Central LL	a	14 05			14 16			14 26		14 35		14 46			14 56				15 04					15 16
	d	14 07		14b18	14 17			14 27		14 37		14 47			14 57		15b00	15b00	15 07		15b14		15b18	15 17
Argyle Street	d	14 08			14 19			14 29		14 38		14 48			14 59				15 09					15 19
Charing Cross	d		14 08			14 19	14 24		14 29		14 38		14 49	14 54		14 59				15 08				
Glasgow Queen St LL	a		14 10			14 21	14 26		14 31		14 40		14 51	14 56		15 01				15 10				
	d		14 12			14 24	14 28		14 32		14 42		14 54	14 58		15 02				15 12				
High Street	d		14 14			14 26	14 30		14 34		14 44		14 56	15 00		15 04				15 14				
Bellgrove	d		14 16				14 32		14 36		14 46			15 02		15 06				15 16				
Duke Street	d								14 38							15 08								
Alexandra Parade	d								14 39							15 09								
Barnhill	d								14 42							15 12								
Springburn	a								14 44							15 14								
Carntyne	d		14 19				14 35				14 49			15 05						15 19				
Shettleston	d		14 22				14 38				14 52			15 08						15 22				
Garrowhill	d		14 24				14 40				14 54			15 10						15 24				
Easterhouse	d		14 27				14 43				14 57			15 13						15 27				
Blairhill	d		14 31				14 47				15 01			15 17						15 31				
Coatbridge Sunnyside	d		14 33			14 39	14 49				15 03		15 09	15 19						15 33				
Coatdyke	d		14 36				14 52				15 06			15 22						15 36				
Airdrie	d		14a39			14 44	14 55				15a09		15 14	15 25						15a39				
Drumgelloch	d					14 47	14 58						15 17	15 28										
Caldercruix	d						15 02							15 32										
Blackridge	d						15 08							15 38										
Armadale	d						15 11							15 41										
Bathgate	a					14 59	15 15						15 30	15 45										
	d					15 01	15 17						15 31	15 47										
Livingston North	d					15 05	15 21						15 35	15 51										
Uphall	d					15 08	15 24						15 38	15 54										
Edinburgh Park	a					15 17	15 32						15 47	16 02										
Haymarket	a					15 22	15 37						15 52	16 07										
Edinburgh	a					15 28	15 44						15 58	16 14										
Bridgeton	d	14 11			14 22					14 41		14 51							15 12					15 22
Dalmarnock §	d																							
Rutherglen	d	14 16			14 26			14 34		14 46		14 56			15 06				15 16					15 26
Cambuslang	d	14 20			14 31					14 50		15 00							15 20					15 31
Newton	d	14 23								14 53									15 24					
Blantyre	d	14 27						14 44		14 57					15 14				15 28					
Hamilton West	d	14 30						14 47		15 00					15 17				15 31					
Hamilton Central	d	14 33						14 50		15 03					15 20				15 33					
Chatelherault	d							14 53							15 23									
Merryton	d							14 56							15 26									
Larkhall	a							15 00							15 30									
Airbles	d	14 37								15 08									15 38					
Uddingston	d			14 30	14 35							15 04											15 31	15 35
Bellshill	d			14 36	14 40							15 09											15 35	15 40
Motherwell	a	14 40			14 48					15 11		15 15					15 13	15 13	15 41		15 33			15 48
	d	14 41										15 16							15 41		15 34	15 37		
Whifflet	a																					15 45		
Coatbridge Central	a																					15 48		
Shieldmuir	d											15 20												
Holytown	d	14 48		14a40															15 48				15a39	
Wishaw	d	14 53										15 23							15 53					
Carluke	d	15 00										15 30							16 00		15a42			
Lanark	a	15 12										15 42							16 13					

§ Station closed between 4 June and 24 November inclusive

A To Edinburgh
B To North Berwick
C To Cumbernauld
D To Bristol Temple Meads
b Glasgow Central High Level

Helensburgh, Balloch, Dalmuir and Milngavie - Glasgow - Springburn, Airdrie, Bathgate and Edinburgh, Hamilton, Larkhall, Motherwell, Coatbridge and Lanark

Network Diagram - see first Page of Table 220

Station		SR	SR ◇ A	SR	SR	SR	SR	SR	SR	SR	SR SO	SR SX	SR	SR SX ◇ B	SR	SR C	SR SX	SR SO	SR	SR D	SR	SR	SR SX
Helensburgh Central	d		14b39	14 40							15 10	15 10		15b15									
Craigendoran	d			14 43							15 13	15 13											
Cardross	d			14 48							15 18	15 18											
Balloch	d							14 53											15 23				
Alexandria	d							14 55											15 25				
Renton	d							14 58											15 28				
Dalreoch	d			14 53				15 01			15 23	15 23							15 31				
Dumbarton Central	d		14 51	14 55				15 02			15 25	15 25		15 29					15 32				
Dumbarton East	d			14 57				15 04			15 27	15 27							15 34				
Bowling	d							15 09											15 39				
Kilpatrick	d							15 12											15 42				
Dalmuir	a		15 03	15 05				15 15			15 34	15 34		15 38					15 45				
	d		15 03	15 05	15 00	15 10		15 16	15 23		15 35	15 35	15 30	15 38	15 38				15 46		15 53		
Singer	d				15 02			15 18					15 32						15 48				
Drumry	d				15 04			15 20					15 34						15 50				
Drumchapel	d				15 07			15 23					15 37						15 53				
Milngavie	d	14 57					15 12			15 27							15 42	15 42				15 57	
Hillfoot	d	15 00					15 15			15 30							15 45	15 45				16 00	
Bearsden	d	15 02					15 17			15 33							15 49	15 49				16 02	
Westerton	d	15 05			15 09		15 20	15 25		15 36			15 39	15 44			15 52	15 52	15 55			16 05	
Anniesland	d	15 08			15 15		15 23	15 28		15 39			15 43				15 55	15 55	15 58			16 08	
Clydebank	d					15 12			15 25						15 40						15 55		
Yoker	d					15 14			15 27						15 42						15 57		
Garscadden	d					15 17			15 31						15 46						16 00		
Scotstounhill	d					15 19			15 33						15 48						16 02		
Jordanhill	d					15 21			15 35						15 50						16 04		
Hyndland ■	d	15 11		15 14	15 18	15 23	15 26	15 31	15 37	15 42	15 44	15 44	15 47		15 52		15 57	15 57	16 01		16 07	16 11	
Partick ⇌	d	15 14		15 17	15 20	15 25	15 29	15 34	15 40	15 44	15 47	15 47	15 50		15 55		16 00	16 00	16 04		16 09	16 14	
Exhibition Centre	d				15 23		15 32		15 43				15 53				16 03	16 03			16 12		
Anderston	d				15 25		15 34		15 45				15 55				16 05	16 05			16 15		16 23
Glasgow Central LL 15	a				15 26		15 37		15 46				15 56				16 07	16 07			16 16		16 24
	d				15 27		15 37		15 47				15 57				16 08	16 08		16e18	16 17		16 25
Argyle Street	d				15 29		15 39		15 48				15 59				16 10	16 10			16 18		16 26
Charing Cross	d	15 19		15 24		15 29		15 38		15 48	15 54	15 54			15 59				16 08			16 19	
Glasgow Queen St LL 10 ⇌	a	15 21	15c30	15 26		15 31		15 40		15 50	15 56	15 56		16c00	16 01				16 12			16 21	
	d	15 24		15 28		15 32		15 42		15 54	15 58	15 58			16 02				16 12			16 24	
High Street	d	15 26		15 30		15 34		15 44		15 56	16 00	16 00			16 04				16 14			16 26	
Bellgrove	d			15 32		15 36		15 46			16 02	16 02			16 06				16 16				
Duke Street	d					15 38									16 08								
Alexandra Parade	d					15 39									16 09								
Barnhill	d					15 42									16 12								
Springburn	a					15 44									16 14								
Carntyne	d			15 35				15 49			16 05	16 05							16 19				
Shettleston	d			15 38				15 52			16 08	16 08							16 22				
Garrowhill	d			15 40				15 54			16 10	16 10							16 24				
Easterhouse	d			15 43				15 57			16 13	16 13							16 27				
Blairhill	d			15 47				16 01			16 17	16 17							16 31			16 38	
Coatbridge Sunnyside	d	15 39		15 49				16 03		16 09	16 19	16 19							16 33			16 40	
Coatdyke	d			15 52				16 06			16 22	16 22							16 36			16 43	
Airdrie	d	15 44		15 55				16a09		16 14	16 25	16 25							16a39			16 46	
Drumgelloch	d	15 47		15 58						16 17	16 28	16 28										16 49	
Caldercruix	d			16 02							16 32	16 32											
Blackridge	d			16 08							16 38	16 38											
Armadale	d			16 11							16 41	16 41											
Bathgate	a	16 00		16 15						16 29	16 45	16 45										17 02	
	d	16 01		16 17						16 30	16 47	16 47										17 02	
Livingston North	d	16 05		16 21						16 34	16 50	16 50										17 07	
Uphall	d	16 08		16 24						16 37	16 53	16 53										17 10	
Edinburgh Park	a	16 17		16 32						16 46	17 03	17 03										17 18	
Haymarket	a	16 22		16 37						16 51	17 07	17 13										17 22	
Edinburgh	a	16 28		16 44						16 58	17 14	17 19										17 28	
Bridgeton	d						15 42		15 51								16 13	16 13			16 21		
Dalmarnock §	d																						
Rutherglen	d				15 34		15 46		15 55				16 06				16 17	16 17			16 26		16 31
Cambuslang	d						15 50		16 00								16 21	16 21			16 30		
Newton	d						15 54										16 25	16 25					
Blantyre	d				15 44		15 58						16 15				16 29	16 29					
Hamilton West	d				15 47		16 01						16 18				16 32	16 32					
Hamilton Central	d				15 50		16 03						16 20				16 34	16 34					
Chatelherault	d				15 54								16 24										
Merryton	d				15 57								16 27										
Larkhall	a				16 00								16 30										
Airbles	d						16 08										16 39	16 39					
Uddingston	d								16 04											16 30	16 34		
Bellshill	d								16 09											16 35	16 39		
Motherwell	a						16 11		16 15								16 42	16 42			16 49		16 46
	d								16 16							16 37	16 46	16 42					16 46
Whifflet	a															16 45	16 53						
Coatbridge Central	a															16 48	16 58						
Shieldmuir	d								16 20														16 50
Holytown	d																	16 48		16a39			
Wishaw	d								16 23									16 53					16 54
Carluke	d								16 30									17 01					17 01
Lanark	a								16 42									17 15					17 15

§ Station closed between 4 June and 24 November inclusive
A From Mallaig
B From 26 May until 28 September. From Oban
C To Cumbernauld
D To Edinburgh
b Helensburgh Upper
c Glasgow Queen St High Level
e Glasgow Central High Level

Helensburgh, Balloch, Dalmuir and Milngavie - Glasgow - Springburn, Airdrie, Bathgate and Edinburgh, Hamilton, Larkhall, Motherwell, Coatbridge and Lanark

Network Diagram - see first Page of Table 220

Station		SR	SR	SR	SR SO	SR SX	SR	SR SX	SR SO	SR SO	SR SX	SR	XC SO ◇1 C	XC SX ◇1 C	SR	SR	SR SO	SR SX	SR SX	SR	SR A	SR SO B	SR SX B	SR SO	SR SX
Helensburgh Central	d		15 40									16 10													
Craigendoran	d		15 45									16 13													
Cardross	d		15 50									16 18													
Balloch	d						15 53													16 23					
Alexandria	d						15 55													16 25					
Renton	d						15 58													16 28					
Dalreoch	d		15 55				16 01					16 23								16 31					
Dumbarton Central	d		15 57				16 02					16 25								16 32					
Dumbarton East	d		15 59				16 04					16 27								16 34					
Bowling	d						16 09													16 39					
Kilpatrick	d						16 12													16 42					
Dalmuir	a		16 06				16 15					16 34								16 45					
	d	16 01	16 07	16 08			16 16	16 23	16 23			16 35			16 31	16 38				16 46				16 53	16 53
Singer	d	16 03					16 18								16 33					16 48					
Drumry	d	16 05					16 20								16 35					16 50					
Drumchapel	d	16 08					16 23								16 38					16 53					
Milngavie	d				16 12	16 12				16 27	16 27						16 42		16 42						
Hillfoot	d				16 15	16 15				16 30	16 30						16 45		16 45						
Bearsden	d				16 17	16 17				16 32	16 32						16 47		16 47						
Westerton	d	16 10			16 20	16 20	16 25			16 35	16 35				16 40		16 50		16 50	16 55					
Anniesland	d	16 14			16 23	16 23	16 28			16 38	16 38				16 44		16 53		16 53	16 58					
Clydebank	d			16 10				16 25	16 25							16 40								16 55	16 55
Yoker	d			16 12				16 27	16 27							16 42								16 57	16 57
Garscadden	d			16 16				16 31	16 31							16 46								17 01	17 01
Scotstounhill	d			16 18				16 33	16 33							16 48								17 03	17 03
Jordanhill	d			16 21				16 35	16 35							16 51								17 05	17 05
Hyndland ■	d	16 17	16 20	16 23	16 26	16 26	16 32	16 37	16 37	16 41	16 41	16 44			16 47	16 53	16 56		16 56	17 01				17 07	17 07
Partick ⇌	d	16 20	16 22	16 25	16 29	16 29	16 35	16 40	16 40	16 44	16 44	16 47			16 50	16 55	16 59		16 59	17 04				17 10	17 10
Exhibition Centre	d	16 24			16 32	16 32		16 43	16 43						16 53		17 02		17 04					17 13	17 13
Anderston	d	16 26			16 34	16 34		16 45	16 45						16 55		17 04	17 04	17 07					17 15	17 15
Glasgow Central LL 15	a	16 27			16 35	16 35		16 46	16 46						16 56		17 05	17 05	17 09					17 16	17 17
	d	16 28			16 37	16 37		16 47	16 47				16b52	16b52	16 57		17 07	17 07	17 11			17b18	17b20	17 17	17 18
Argyle Street	d	16 30			16 38	16 38		16 48	16 48						16 59		17 08	17 09	17 13					17 19	17 21
Charing Cross	d		16 26	16 29			16 39			16 49	16 49	16 54				16 59				17 08					
Glasgow Queen St LL 10 ⇌	a		16 28	16 31			16 41			16 51	16 51	16 56				17 01				17 10					
	d		16 29	16 32			16 42			16 54	16 54	16 58				17 02				17 12					
High Street	d		16 31	16 34			16 44			16 56	16 56	17 00				17 04				17 14					
Bellgrove	d		16 33	16 36			16 46					17 02				17 06				17 16					
Duke Street	d			16 38												17 08									
Alexandra Parade	d			16 39												17 09									
Barnhill	d			16 42												17 12									
Springburn	a			16 44												17 14									
Carntyne	d		16 36				16 49					17 06								17 19					
Shettleston	d		16 39				16 52					17 08								17 22					
Garrowhill	d		16 41				16 54					17 11								17 24					
Easterhouse	d		16 44				16 57					17 13								17 27					
Blairhill	d		16 48				17 01			17 08	17 08	17 17								17 31					
Coatbridge Sunnyside	d		16 50				17 03			17 10	17 10	17 20								17 33					
Coatdyke	d		16 53				17 06			17 13	17 13	17 22								17 36					
Airdrie	d		16 56				17a09			17 16	17 16	17 25								17a39					
Drumgelloch	d		16 59							17 19	17 19	17 28													
Caldercruix	d		17 03									17 32													
Blackridge	d		17 09									17 38													
Armadale	d		17 12									17 42													
Bathgate	a		17 16							17 31	17 31	17 46													
	d		17 17							17 32	17 32	17 46													
Livingston North	d		17 21							17 36	17 36	17 50													
Uphall	d		17 24							17 39	17 39	17 53													
Edinburgh Park	a		17 32							17 47	17 47	18 01													
Haymarket	a		17 37							17 52	17 56	18 06													
Edinburgh	a		17 43							17 57	18 04	18 12													
Bridgeton	d				16 41	16 41		16 51	16 51								17 11	17 12	17 16					17 22	17 24
Dalmarnock §	d																								
Rutherglen	d	16 35			16 46	16 46		16 56	16 56						17 04		17 16		17 21					17 26	17 28
Cambuslang	d				16 50	16 50		17 00	17 00						17 08		17 20		17 25					17 31	17 32
Newton	d				16 54	16 54											17 23		17 29						17 36
Blantyre	d	16 45			16 58	16 58									17 14		17 27		17 33						17 40
Hamilton West	d	16 48			17 01	17 01									17 17		17 30		17 36						17 43
Hamilton Central	d	16 50			17 03	17 03									17 20		17 33		17 38						17 50
Chatelherault	d	16 54													17 23				17 42						
Merryton	d	16 57													17 26				17 45						
Larkhall	a	17 01													17 30				17 48						
Airbles	d				17 08	17 08											17 38								17 55
Uddingston	d							17 04	17 04									17 20				17 30		17 35	
Bellshill	d							17 09	17 09													17 34	17 34	17 40	
Motherwell	a				17 11	17 11		17 16	17 16				17 13	17 13			17 40	17 25						17 48	17 57
	d					17 13			17 17								17 41	17 26			17 37				17 58
Whifflet	a					17 20															17 45				18 05
Coatbridge Central	a					17 22															17 48				18 07
Shieldmuir	d								17 20									17 29							
Holytown	d																17 48					17a39	17a39		
Wishaw	d								17 24								17 53	17 34							
Carluke	d								17 30								18 00	17 41							
Lanark	a								17 42								18 12	17 54							

§ Station closed between 4 June and 24 November inclusive
A To Cumbernauld
B To Edinburgh
C To Birmingham New Street
b Glasgow Central High Level

Helensburgh, Balloch, Dalmuir and Milngavie - Glasgow - Springburn, Airdrie, Bathgate and Edinburgh, Hamilton, Larkhall, Motherwell, Coatbridge and Lanark

Network Diagram - see first Page of Table 220

		SR	SR	SR SO	SR SX A	SR	SR SX	SR SO	SR SX	SR	SR SX	SR SO	SR	SR	SR	SR	SR B	SR	SR	SR SX C	SR SO C	SR SX
Helensburgh Central	d		16 40											17 10								
Craigendoran	d		16 43											17 13								
Cardross	d		16 48											17 18								
Balloch	d									16 53									17 23			
Alexandria	d									16 55									17 25			
Renton	d									16 58									17 28			
Dalreoch	d		16 53							17 01				17 23					17 31			
Dumbarton Central	d		16 55							17 02				17 25					17 32			
Dumbarton East	d		16 57							17 04				17 27					17 34			
Bowling	d									17 09									17 39			
Kilpatrick	d									17 12									17 42			
Dalmuir	a		17 06							17 15				17 34					17 45			
	d		17 06	17 01	17 01	17 08				17 16	17 23	17 23		17 35	17 31	17 38			17 46			17 53
Singer	d			17 03	17 03					17 18					17 33				17 48			
Drumry	d			17 05	17 05					17 20					17 35				17 50			
Drumchapel	d			17 08	17 08					17 23					17 38				17 53			
Milngavie	d	16 57						17 13	17 13				17 28					17 42				
Hillfoot	d	17 00						17 16	17 16				17 31					17 45				
Bearsden	d	17 02						17 18	17 18				17 33					17 47				
Westerton	d	17 05		17 10	17 10			17 21	17 21	17 25			17 36		17 40			17 50	17 55			
Anniesland	d	17 08		17 13	17 14			17 24	17 24	17 28			17 39		17 44			17 53	17 58			
Clydebank	d					17 10					17 25	17 25				17 40						17 55
Yoker	d					17 12					17 27	17 27				17 42						17 57
Garscadden	d					17 16					17 31	17 31				17 46						18 00
Scotstounhill	d					17 18					17 33	17 33				17 48						18 02
Jordanhill	d					17 20					17 35	17 35				17 50						18 04
Hyndland 3	d	17 11	17 14	17 17	17 17	17 22		17 26	17 26	17 31	17 37	17 37	17 41	17 44	17 47	17 52		17 56	18 01			18 06
Partick	d	17 14	17 17	17 20	17 20	17 25		17 29	17 29	17 34	17 40	17 40	17 44	17 47	17 50	17 55		17 59	18 04			18 08
Exhibition Centre	d			17 23	17 23			17 32	17 34		17 43	17 43			17 53			18 02				18 11
Anderston	d			17 25	17 25		17 34	17 34	17 37		17 45	17 45			17 55			18 04				18 13
Glasgow Central LL 15	a			17 26	17 26		17 35	17 35	17 39		17 46	17 46			17 56			18 05				18 15
	d			17 27	17 27		17 36	17 37	17 39		17 47	17 47			17 57			18 07		18b14	18b18	18 15
Argyle Street	d			17 28	17 28		17 38	17 38	17 40		17 48	17 48			17 59			18 08				18 17
Charing Cross	d	17 19	17 24			17 29				17 38			17 49	17 54		17 59			18 08			
Glasgow Queen St LL 10	a	17 21	17 26			17 31				17 40			17 51	17 56		18 01			18 10			
	d	17 24	17 28			17 32				17 42			17 54	17 58		18 02			18 12			
High Street	d	17 26	17 30			17 34				17 44			17 56	18 00		18 04			18 14			
Bellgrove	d		17 32			17 36				17 46				18 02		18 06			18 16			
Duke Street	d					17 38										18 08						
Alexandra Parade	d					17 39										18 09						
Barnhill	d					17 42										18 12						
Springburn	a					17 44										18 14						
Carntyne	d		17 36							17 49				18 06					18 19			
Shettleston	d		17 38							17 52				18 08					18 22			
Garrowhill	d		17 41							17 54				18 11					18 24			
Easterhouse	d		17 43							17 57				18 13					18 27			
Blairhill	d	17 39	17 47							18 01				18 17					18 31			
Coatbridge Sunnyside	d	17 41	17 50							18 03			18 09	18 20					18 33			
Coatdyke	d	17 44	17 52							18 06				18 22					18 36			
Airdrie	d	17 47	17 55							18a09			18 14	18 25					18a39			
Drumgelloch	d	17 50	17 58										18 17	18 28								
Caldercruix	d		18 02											18 32								
Blackridge	d		18 08											18 38								
Armadale	d		18 12											18 42								
Bathgate	a	18 02	18 16										18 30	18 46								
	d	18 04	18 17										18 31	18 47								
Livingston North	d	18 08	18 20										18 35	18 50								
Uphall	d	18 11	18 23										18 38	18 53								
Edinburgh Park	a	18 17	18 32										18 47	19 02								
Haymarket	a	18 25	18 37										18 52	19 07								
Edinburgh	a	18 32	18 43										18 58	19 14								
Bridgeton	d				17 31			17 41	17 44		17 51	17 51						18 11				18 20
Dalmarnock §	d																					
Rutherglen	d			17 34	17 37		17 43	17 46	17 49		17 56	17 56			18 04			18 16				18 23
Cambuslang	d				17 41			17 50	17 53		18 00	18 00						18 20		18 23	18 27	18 28
Newton	d							17 54	17 56									18 23				
Blantyre	d			17 44				17 58	18 00						18 14			18 27				
Hamilton West	d			17 47				18 01	18 03						18 17			18 30				
Hamilton Central	d			17 49				18 03	18 06						18 20			18 33				
Chatelherault	d			17 53					18 09						18 23							
Merryton	d			17 56					18 12						18 26							
Larkhall	a			18 00					18 15						18 30							
Airbles	d							18 08										18 38				
Uddingston	d				17 45						18 04	18 04								18 29	18 29	18 33
Bellshill	d				17 50						18 09	18 09								18 34	18 34	18 37
Motherwell	a				18 01		17 57	18 11			18 16	18 16						18 40				18 44
	d				18 02		17 58					18 16					18 37	18 41				
Whifflet	a																18 45					
Coatbridge Central	a																18 48					
Shieldmuir	d				18 05		18 01					18 20										
Holytown	d																	18 48		18a38	18a38	
Wishaw	d				18 09		18 05					18 23						18 54				
Carluke	d				18a15		18 11					18 30						19 01				
Lanark	a						18 22					18 42						19 14				

§ Station closed between 4 June and 24 November inclusive
A To Carstairs
B To Cumbernauld
C To Edinburgh
b Glasgow Central High Level

Helensburgh, Balloch, Dalmuir and Milngavie - Glasgow - Springburn, Airdrie, Bathgate and Edinburgh, Hamilton, Larkhall, Motherwell, Coatbridge and Lanark

Network Diagram - see first Page of Table 220

		SR SO	SR	SR	SR	SR	SR	SR	SR	XC SO ◇■ A	SR	SR	XC SX ◇■ D	SR B	SR	SR	SR SO ◇ C	SR SX A	SR SO A	SR	SR	SR	SR	SR
Helensburgh Central	d			17 40								18 10					18c34					18 40		
Craigendoran	d			17 43								18 13										18 43		
Cardross	d			17 48								18 18										18 48		
Balloch	d							17 53								18 23								18 53
Alexandria	d							17 55								18 25								18 55
Renton	d							17 58								18 29								18 58
Dalreoch	d			17 53				18 01				18 23				18 32						18 53		19 01
Dumbarton Central	d			17 55				18 02				18 25				18 33	18 45					18 55		19 02
Dumbarton East	d			17 57				18 04				18 27				18 35						18 57		19 04
Bowling	d							18 09								18 40								19 09
Kilpatrick	d							18 12								18 43								19 12
Dalmuir	a			18 04				18 15				18 34				18 46	18 56					19 05		19 15
	d	17 53		18 05	18 01	18 07		18 16	18 23		18 31	18 35				18 47	18 56				19 01	19 05		19 16
Singer	d				18 03			18 18			18 33					18 49					19 03			19 18
Drumry	d				18 05			18 20			18 35					18 51					19 05			19 20
Drumchapel	d				18 08			18 23			18 38					18 54					19 08			19 23
Milngavie	d		17 57				18 12								18 42								19 12	
Hillfoot	d		18 00				18 15								18 45								19 15	
Bearsden	d		18 02				18 17								18 47								19 17	
Westerton	d		18 05		18 10		18 20	18 25			18 40				18 50	18 56					19 10		19 20	19 25
Anniesland	d		18 08		18 14		18 23	18 28			18 44				18 53	19 00					19 14		19 23	19 30
Clydebank	d	17 55				18 09			18 25			18 37										19 07		
Yoker	d	17 57				18 11			18 27			18 39										19 09		
Garscadden	d	18 00				18 14			18 31			18 43										19 13		
Scotstounhill	d	18 02				18 16			18 33			18 45										19 15		
Jordanhill	d	18 04				18 18			18 35			18 47										19 17		
Hyndland 3	d	18 06	18 11	18 14	18 17	18 22	18 26	18 31	18 37		18 47	18 51			18 56	19 03					19 17	19 21	19 25	19 33
Partick	d	18 08	18 14	18 17	18 20	18 25	18 29	18 34	18 40		18 50	18 53			18 59	19 05				19 11	19 20	19 23	19 29	19 35
Exhibition Centre	d	18 11			18 23		18 32		18 43		18 53				19 02					19 14	19 23		19 32	
Anderston	d	18 13			18 25		18 34		18 45		18 55				19 04					19 16	19 25		19 34	
Glasgow Central LL 15	a	18 15			18 26		18 35		18 46		18 56				19 05					19 17	19 26		19 35	
	d	18 15			18 27		18 37		18 47	18b52	18 57		18b59		19 07			19b15	19b18	19 18	19 27		19 37	
Argyle Street	d	18 17			18 29		18 38		18 48		18 59				19 08					19 19	19 29		19 39	
Charing Cross	d		18 18	18 24		18 29		18 38				18 57				19 09						19 27		19 39
Glasgow Queen St LL 10	a		18 20	18 26		18 31		18 40				18 59				19 11	19e20					19 29		19 41
	d		18 23	18 28		18 32		18 45				19 00				19 14						19 30		19 44
High Street	d		18 26	18 30		18 34		18 47				19 02				19 16						19 32		19 46
Bellgrove	d		18 28	18 32		18 36		18 49				19 04				19 19						19 34		19 49
Duke Street	d					18 38		18 51								19 21								19 51
Alexandra Parade	d					18 39		18 52								19 22								19 52
Barnhill	d					18 42		18 55								19 25								19 55
Springburn	a					18 44		18 57								19 27								19 57
Carntyne	d			18 36								19 07										19 37		
Shettleston	d			18 38								19 10										19 40		
Garrowhill	d			18 41								19 12										19 42		
Easterhouse	d			18 43								19 15										19 45		
Blairhill	d			18 47								19 19										19 49		
Coatbridge Sunnyside	d		18 39	18 50								19 21										19 51		
Coatdyke	d			18 52								19 24										19 54		
Airdrie	d		18 44	18 55								19 27										19 57		
Drumgelloch	d		18 47	18 58								19 30										20 00		
Caldercruix	d			19 02								19 34										20 04		
Blackridge	d			19 08								19 40										20 10		
Armadale	d			19 12								19 43										20 13		
Bathgate	a		19 00	19 16								19 47										20 17		
	d		19 01	19 17								19 49										20 18		
Livingston North	d		19 06	19 20								19 53										20 23		
Uphall	d		19 09	19 23								19 56										20 26		
Edinburgh Park	a		19 17	19 32								20 04										20 34		
Haymarket	a		19 22	19 37								20 09										20 38		
Edinburgh	a		19 28	19 45								20 14										20 43		
Bridgeton	d	18 20					18 41		18 51						19 11					19 22			19 42	
Dalmarnock §	d																							
Rutherglen	d	18 25			18 36		18 46		18 56		19 06				19 16					19 26	19 34		19 46	
Cambuslang	d	18 30					18 50		19 00						19 20					19 31			19 50	
Newton	d						18 53								19 23								19 54	
Blantyre	d				18 44		18 58				19 15				19 27						19 44		19 58	
Hamilton West	d				18 47		19 01				19 18				19 30						19 47		20 01	
Hamilton Central	d				18 50		19 03				19 20				19 33						19 49		20 04	
Chatelherault	d				18 53						19 24										19 53			
Merryton	d				18 56						19 27										19 56			
Larkhall	a				19 00						19 30										20 00			
Airbles	d						19 08								19 38								20 09	
Uddingston	d	18 34							19 04									19 30	19 30	19 35				
Bellshill	d	18 39							19 09									19 35	19 35	19 40				
Motherwell	a	18 48					19 11		19 18	19 13			19 13		19 39					19 48			20 12	
	d								19 18					19 37	19 40									
Whifflet	a													19 45										
Coatbridge Central	a													19 48										
Shieldmuir	d								19 20															
Holytown	d														19 50			19a39	19a39					
Wishaw	d								19 23						19 55									
Carluke	d								19 30						20 03									
Lanark	a								19 42						20 15									

§ Station closed between 4 June and 24 November inclusive
A To Edinburgh
B To Cumbernauld
C From 26 May until 27 October. From Oban
D To Newcastle
b Glasgow Central High Level
c Helensburgh Upper
e Glasgow Queen St High Level

Helensburgh, Balloch, Dalmuir and Milngavie - Glasgow - Springburn, Airdrie, Bathgate and Edinburgh, Hamilton, Larkhall, Motherwell, Coatbridge and Lanark

Network Diagram - see first Page of Table 220

		SR	SR SX A	SR	SR	SR B	SR	SR	SR	SR	SR	SR	SR	SR	SR	SR	XC SX ◇ A	SR B	SR	SR	SR A	SR
Helensburgh Central	d				19 10						19 40					20 10						
Craigendoran	d				19 13						19 43					20 13						
Cardross	d				19 18						19 48					20 18						
Balloch	d							19 23					19 53							20 23		
Alexandria	d							19 25					19 55							20 25		
Renton	d							19 28					19 58							20 28		
Dalreoch	d				19 23			19 31			19 53		20 01			20 23				20 31		
Dumbarton Central	d				19 25			19 32			19 55		20 02			20 25				20 32		
Dumbarton East	d				19 27			19 34			19 57		20 04			20 27				20 34		
Bowling	d							19 39					20 09							20 39		
Kilpatrick	d							19 42					20 12							20 42		
Dalmuir	a				19 35			19 45			20 05		20 15			20 35				20 45		
	d			19 31	19 35			19 46		20 01	20 05		20 16		20 31	20 35				20 46		
Singer	d			19 33				19 48		20 03			20 18		20 33					20 48		
Drumry	d			19 35				19 50		20 05			20 20		20 35					20 50		
Drumchapel	d			19 38				19 53		20 08			20 23		20 38					20 53		
Milngavie	d						19 42					20 12							20 42			
Hillfoot	d						19 45					20 15							20 45			
Bearsden	d						19 47					20 17							20 47			
Westerton	d			19 40			19 50	19 55		20 10		20 20	20 25		20 40				20 50	20 55		
Anniesland	d			19 44			19 54	19 59		20 14		20 22	20 30		20 44				20 53	20 59		
Clydebank	d				19 37						20 07					20 37						
Yoker	d				19 39						20 09					20 39						
Garscadden	d				19 43						20 13					20 43						
Scotstounhill	d				19 45						20 15					20 45						
Jordanhill	d				19 47						20 17					20 47						
Hyndland 🅱	d			19 47	19 51		19 56	20 02		20 17	20 21	20 25	20 33		20 47	20 51			20 56	21 02		
Partick ⛴	d	19 40		19 50	19 53		19 59	20 04	20 10	20 20	20 23	20 28	20 35	20 40	20 50	20 53			20 59	21 04		21 10
Exhibition Centre	d	19 43		19 53			20 02		20 13	20 23		20 32		20 43	20 53				21 02			21 13
Anderston	d	19 45		19 55			20 04		20 15	20 25		20 34		20 45	20 55				21 04			21 15
Glasgow Central LL 15	a	19 46		19 56			20 05		20 16	20 26		20 35		20 46	20 56				21 05			21 16
	d	19 47	19b49	19 57			20 07		20 17	20 27		20 37		20 47	20 57		21b05		21 07		21b18	21 17
Argyle Street	d	19 49		19 59			20 08		20 19	20 29		20 38		20 49	20 59				21 08			21 18
Charing Cross	d				19 57			20 08			20 27		20 40			20 57				21 08		
Glasgow Queen St LL 10 ⛴	a				19 59			20 10			20 29		20 42			20 59				21 11		
	d				20 00			20 14			20 30		20 44			21 00				21 14		
High Street	d				20 02			20 16			20 32		20 46			21 02				21 16		
Bellgrove	d				20 04			20 19			20 34		20 49			21 04				21 19		
Duke Street	d							20 21					20 51							21 21		
Alexandra Parade	d							20 22					20 52							21 22		
Barnhill	d							20 25					20 55							21 25		
Springburn	a							20 27					20 57							21 27		
Carntyne	d				20 07						20 37					21 07						
Shettleston	d				20 10						20 40					21 10						
Garrowhill	d				20 12						20 42					21 12						
Easterhouse	d				20 15						20 45					21 15						
Blairhill	d				20 19						20 49					21 19						
Coatbridge Sunnyside	d				20 21						20 51					21 21						
Coatdyke	d				20 24						20 54					21 24						
Airdrie	d				20 27						20 57					21 27						
Drumgelloch	d				20 30						21 00					21 30						
Caldercruix	d				20 34						21 04					21 34						
Blackridge	d				20 40						21 10					21 40						
Armadale	d				20 43						21 13					21 43						
Bathgate	a				20 47						21 17					21 47						
	d				20 49						21 19					21 49						
Livingston North	d				20 53						21 23					21 53						
Uphall	d				20 56						21 26					21 56						
Edinburgh Park	a				21 04						21 34					22 04						
Haymarket	a				21 09						21 39					22 09						
Edinburgh	a				21 14						21 44					22 14						
Bridgeton	d	19 52					20 11		20 22			20 41		20 52					21 11			21 21
Dalmarnock §	d																					
Rutherglen	d	19 56		20 04			20 16		20 26	20 34		20 46		20 55	21 04				21 16			21 26
Cambuslang	d	20 01					20 20		20 31			20 50		21 00					21 20			21 30
Newton	d						20 23					20 54							21 23			
Blantyre	d			20 14			20 27			20 44		20 58			21 14				21 27			
Hamilton West	d			20 17			20 30			20 47		21 01			21 17				21 30			
Hamilton Central	d			20 20			20 33			20 49		21 03			21 20				21 33			
Chatelherault	d			20 23						20 53					21 23							
Merryton	d			20 26						20 56					21 26							
Larkhall	a			20 30						21 00					21 30							
Airbles	d						20 37					21 08							21 37			
Uddingston	d	20 05							20 35					21 05							21 30	21 34
Bellshill	d	20 10							20 40					21 09							21 36	21 39
Motherwell	a	20 16	20 05				20 41		20 48			21 11		21 15			21 22		21 41			21 48
	d	20 16	20 06			20 37	20 41							21 16				21 37	21 41			
Whifflet	a					20 45												21 45				
Coatbridge Central	a					20 48												21 48				
Shieldmuir	d	20 20												21 19								
Holytown	d						20 48												21 48		21a40	
Wishaw	d	20 23	20 12				20 53							21 23					21 53			
Carluke	d	20 31	20a18				21 00							21 29					22 00			
Lanark	a	20 42					21 12							21 43					22 13			

§ Station closed between 4 June and 24 November inclusive

A To Edinburgh

B To Cumbernauld

b Glasgow Central High Level

Helensburgh, Balloch, Dalmuir and Milngavie - Glasgow - Springburn, Airdrie, Bathgate and Edinburgh, Hamilton, Larkhall, Motherwell, Coatbridge and Lanark

Network Diagram - see first Page of Table 220

		SR	SR	SR ◇ A	SR	SR	SR	SR	SR	SR	SR	SR	SR	SR	SR	SR	SR	SR	SR	SR B	SR	SR	SR
Helensburgh Central	d		20 40	20b40					21 10					21 40					22 10				
Craigendoran	d		20 43						21 13					21 43					22 13				
Cardross	d		20 48						21 18					21 48					22 18				
Balloch	d					20 53					21 23					21 53						22 23	
Alexandria	d					20 55					21 25					21 55						22 25	
Renton	d					20 59					21 28					21 58						22 28	
Dalreoch	d		20 53			21 01			21 23		21 31			21 53		22 01			22 23			22 31	
Dumbarton Central	d		20 55	21 00		21 02			21 25		21 32			21 55		22 02			22 25			22 32	
Dumbarton East	d		20 57			21 04			21 27		21 34			21 57		22 04			22 27			22 34	
Bowling	d					21 09					21 39					22 09						22 39	
Kilpatrick	d					21 12					21 42					22 12						22 42	
Dalmuir	a		21 04	21 09		21 15			21 35		21 45			22 05		22 15			22 35			22 45	
	d	21 00	21 05	21 09		21 16		21 31	21 35		21 46		22 01	22 05		22 16		22 31	22 35			22 46	
Singer	d	21 02				21 18		21 33			21 48		22 03			22 18		22 33				22 48	
Drumry	d	21 04				21 20		21 35			21 50		22 05			22 20		22 35				22 50	
Drumchapel	d	21 07				21 23		21 38			21 53		22 08			22 23		22 38				22 53	
Milngavie	d				21 12					21 42					22 12						22 42		
Hillfoot	d				21 15					21 45					22 15						22 45		
Bearsden	d				21 17					21 47					22 17						22 47		
Westerton	d	21 09			21 20	21 26		21 40		21 50	21 55		22 10		22 20	22 25		22 40			22 50	22 55	
Anniesland	d	21 14			21 23	21 29		21 44		21 53	22 00		22 14		22 23	22 30		22 44			22 53	23 00	
Clydebank	d		21 07						21 37					22 07					22 37				
Yoker	d		21 09						21 39					22 09					22 39				
Garscadden	d		21 13						21 43					22 13					22 43				
Scotstounhill	d		21 15						21 45					22 15					22 45				
Jordanhill	d		21 17						21 47					22 17					22 47				
Hyndland 🅱	d	21 17	21 21		21 27	21 32		21 47	21 51	21 57	22 03		22 17	22 21	22 26	22 33		22 47	22 51		22 56	23 03	
Partick ⛴	d	21 20	21 23		21 30	21 34	21 40	21 50	21 53	21 59	22 05	22 10	22 20	22 23	22 29	22 35	22 40	22 50	22 53		22 59	23 05	23 10
Exhibition Centre	d	21 23			21 33		21 43	21 53		22 02		22 13	22 23		22 32		22 43	22 53			23 02		23 13
Anderston	d	21 25			21 35		21 45	21 55		22 04		22 15	22 25		22 34		22 45	22 55			23 04		23 15
Glasgow Central LL 15	a	21 26			21 37		21 46	21 56		22 05		22 16	22 26		22 35		22 46	22 56			23 05		23 16
	d	21 27			21 37		21 47	21 57		22 07		22 17	22 29		22 37		22 47	22 57		23e06	23 07		23 17
Argyle Street	d	21 29			21 39		21 49	21 59		22 08		22 19	22 31		22 39		22 49	22 59			23 09		23 19
Charing Cross	d		21 27			21 39			21 57		22 10			22 27		22 40			22 57			23 10	
Glasgow Queen St LL 10 ⛴	a		21 29	21c31		21 42			21 59		22 12			22 29		22 42			22 59			23 12	
	d		21 30			21 44			22 00		22 14			22 30		22 44			23 00			23 14	
High Street	d		21 32			21 46			22 02		22 16			22 32		22 46			23 02			23 16	
Bellgrove	d		21 34			21 49			22 04		22 19			22 34		22 49			23 04			23 19	
Duke Street	d					21 51					22 21					22 51						23 21	
Alexandra Parade	d					21 52					22 22					22 52						23 22	
Barnhill	d					21 55					22 25					22 55						23 25	
Springburn	a					21 57					22 27					22 57						23 27	
Carntyne	d		21 37						22 07					22 37					23 07				
Shettleston	d		21 40						22 10					22 40					23 10				
Garrowhill	d		21 42						22 12					22 42					23 12				
Easterhouse	d		21 45						22 15					22 45					23 15				
Blairhill	d		21 49						22 19					22 49					23 19				
Coatbridge Sunnyside	d		21 51						22 21					22 51					23 21				
Coatdyke	d		21 54						22 24					22 54					23 24				
Airdrie	d		21 57						22 27					22 57					23 27				
Drumgelloch	d		22 00						22 30					23 00					23 30				
Caldercruix	d		22 04						22 34					23 04					23 34				
Blackridge	d		22 10						22 40					23 10					23 40				
Armadale	d		22 13						22 43					23 13					23 43				
Bathgate	a		22 17						22 47					23 17					23 47				
	d		22 19						22 49					23 17									
Livingston North	d		22 23						22 53					23 22									
Uphall	d		22 26						22 56					23 25									
Edinburgh Park	a		22 34						23 05					23 33									
Haymarket	a		22 39						23 09					23 38									
Edinburgh	a		22 44						23 14					23 43									
Bridgeton	d				21 42		21 52			22 11		22 22			22 42		22 52				23 12		23 22
Dalmarnock §	d																						
Rutherglen	d	21 34			21 47		21 56	22 04		22 16		22 26	22 34		22 46		22 56	23 04			23 16		23 26
Cambuslang	d				21 51		22 01			22 20		22 31			22 50		23 01			23 15	23 20		23 31
Newton	d				21 54					22 23					22 54						23 24		
Blantyre	d	21 44			21 58			22 14		22 28			22 44		22 58			23 14			23 28		
Hamilton West	d	21 47			22 01			22 17		22 31			22 47		23 01			23 17			23 31		
Hamilton Central	d	21 50			22 04			22 20		22 33			22 49		23 03			23 20			23 33		
Chatelherault	d	21 53						22 23					22 53					23 23					
Merryton	d	21 56						22 26					22 56					23 26					
Larkhall	a	22 00						22 30					23 00					23 29					
Airbles	d				22 09					22 38					23 08						23 38		
Uddingston	d						22 05					22 35					23 05			23 20			23 35
Bellshill	d						22 10					22 40					23 10			23 25			23 40
Motherwell	a				22 11		22 16			22 41		22 49			23 11		23 16				23 41		23 46
	d						22 16			22 41							23 16						
Whifflet	a									22 49													
Coatbridge Central	a									22 51													
Shieldmuir	d						22 20										23 20						
Holytown	d																			23a29			
Wishaw	d						22 23										23 23						
Carluke	d						22 30										23 30						
Lanark	a						22 42										23 42						

§ Station closed between 4 June and 24 November inclusive

A From Mallaig

B To Edinburgh

b Helensburgh Upper

c Glasgow Queen St High Level

e Glasgow Central High Level

Table 226

Mondays to Saturdays

Helensburgh, Balloch, Dalmuir and Milngavie - Glasgow - Springburn, Airdrie, Bathgate and Edinburgh, Hamilton, Larkhall, Motherwell, Coatbridge and Lanark

Network Diagram - see first Page of Table 220

		SR	SR	SR FX	SR FO	SR FO	SR FO	SR	SR	SR FO	SR SX B
Helensburgh Central	d		22 40					23 10			23c24
Craigendoran	d		22 43					23 13			
Cardross	d		22 48					23 18			
Balloch	d			22 53	22 53				23 23		
Alexandria	d			22 55	22 55				23 25		
Renton	d			22 58	22 58				23 28		
Dalreoch	d		22 53	23 01	23 01			23 23	23 31		
Dumbarton Central	d		22 55	23 02	23 02			23 25	23 32		
Dumbarton East	d		22 57	23 04	23 04			23 27	23 34		
Bowling	d			23 09	23 09				23 39		
Kilpatrick	d			23 12	23 12				23 42		
Dalmuir	a		23 05	23 15	23 15			23 35	23 45		23 49
	d	23 01	23 05	23 16	23 16		23 31	23 35			23 51
Singer	d	23 03		23 18	23 18		23 33				
Drumry	d	23 05		23 20	23 20		23 35				
Drumchapel	d	23 08		23 23	23 23		23 38				
Milngavie	d									23 42	
Hillfoot	d									23 45	
Bearsden	d									23 47	
Westerton	d	23 10		23 25	23 25		23 40			23 50	23 56
Anniesland	d	23 14		23 28	23 28		23 44			23 53	
Clydebank	d		23 07					23 37			
Yoker	d		23 09					23 39			
Garscadden	d		23 13					23 43			
Scotstounhill	d		23 15					23 45			
Jordanhill	d		23 17					23 47			
Hyndland 3	d	23 17	23 21	23 31	23 31		23 47	23 49		23 56	
Partick	d	23 20	23 23	23 34	23 34	23 40	23 50	23 52		23 59	
Exhibition Centre	d	23 23				23 43	23 53			00 02	
Anderston	d	23 25				23 45	23 55			00 04	
Glasgow Central LL 15	a	23 26				23 46	23 56			00 05	
	d	23 27				23 47	23 57			00 07	
Argyle Street	d	23 29				23 49	23 59			00 09	
Charing Cross	d		23 27	23 38	23 38			23 56			
Glasgow Queen St LL 10	a		23 29	23 40	23 40			23 59			
	d		23 30	23 44	23 44			23 59			
High Street	d		23 32	23 46	23 46			00 02			
Bellgrove	d		23 34	23 49	23 49			00 04			
Duke Street	d				23 51						
Alexandra Parade	d				23 52						
Barnhill	d				23 55						
Springburn	a				23 57						
Carntyne	d		23 37	23 52				00 07			
Shettleston	d		23 40	23 55				00 10			
Garrowhill	d		23 42	23 57				00 12			
Easterhouse	d		23 45	23 59				00 15			
Blairhill	d		23 49	00 04				00 19			
Coatbridge Sunnyside	d		23 51	00 06				00 21			
Coatdyke	d		23 54	00 09				00 24			
Airdrie	d		23 57	00a12				00a27			
Drumgelloch	d		23 59								
Caldercruix	d		00 03								
Blackridge	d		00 09								
Armadale	d		00 13								
Bathgate	a		00 17								
	d										
Livingston North	d										
Uphall	d										
Edinburgh Park	a										
Haymarket	a										
Edinburgh	a										00 50
Bridgeton	d					23 52				00 12	
Dalmarnock §	d										
Rutherglen	d	23 34				23 57	00 04			00 16	
Cambuslang	d					00 01				00 20	
Newton	d									00 24	
Blantyre	d	23 44					00 15			00 28	
Hamilton West	d	23 47					00 18			00 31	
Hamilton Central	d	23 50					00 21			00 33	
Chatelherault	d	23 53					00 24				
Merryton	d	23 56					00 27				
Larkhall	a	23 59					00 30				
Airbles	d									00 38	
Uddingston	d					00 05					
Bellshill	d					00 10					
Motherwell	a					00 16				00 41	
	d					00 16					
Whifflet	a										
Coatbridge Central	a										
Shieldmuir	d					00 20					
Holytown	d										
Wishaw	d					00 23					
Carluke	d					00 30					
Lanark	a					00 42					

§ Station closed between 4 June and 24 November inclusive

A To London Euston
B From Fort William

b Glasgow Central High Level
c Helensburgh Upper

Table 226

Sundays

Helensburgh, Balloch, Dalmuir and Milngavie - Glasgow - Springburn, Airdrie, Bathgate and Edinburgh, Hamilton, Larkhall, Motherwell, Coatbridge and Lanark

Network Diagram - see first Page of Table 220

		SR	SR	SR	SR	SR	SR	SR	SR	SR	SR	SR	SR	SR	SR	SR	SR	SR	SR	SR	SR	SR	SR
Helensburgh Central	d	22p40		23p10				07 55			08 25				08 55			09 25					09 55
Craigendoran	d	22p43		23p13				07 58			08 28				08 58			09 28					09 58
Cardross	d	22p48		23p18				08 03			08 33				09 03			09 33					10 03
Balloch	d		22p53						08 09			08 39				09 09			09 39				
Alexandria	d		22p55						08 11			08 41				09 11			09 41				
Renton	d		22p58						08 14			08 44				09 14			09 44				
Dalreoch	d	22p53	23p01	23p23				08 08	08 17		08 38	08 47			09 08	09 17		09 38	09 47				10 08
Dumbarton Central	d	22p55	23p02	23p25				08 10	08 18		08 40	08 48			09 10	09 18		09 40	09 48				10 10
Dumbarton East	d	22p57	23p04	23p27				08 12	08 20		08 42	08 50			09 12	09 20		09 42	09 50				10 12
Bowling	d		23p09						08 25			08 55				09 25			09 55				
Kilpatrick	d		23p12						08 28			08 58				09 28			09 58				
Dalmuir	a	23p05	23p15	23p35				08 19	08 31		08 49	09 01			09 19	09 31		09 49	10 01				10 19
	d	23p05	23p16	23p35		07 40	08 01	08 20	08 31		08 50	09 01			09 20	09 31		09 50	10 01				10 20
Singer	d		23p18			07 42		08 22			08 52				09 22			09 52					10 22
Drumry	d		23p20			07 45		08 25			08 55				09 25			09 55					10 25
Drumchapel	d		23p23			07 47		08 27			08 57				09 27			09 57					10 27
Milngavie	d												09 11				09 41			10 11			
Hillfoot	d												09 14				09 44			10 14			
Bearsden	d												09 16				09 46			10 16			
Westerton	d		23p25			07 50		08 30			09 00		09 19		09 30		09 49	10 00		10 19			10 30
Anniesland	d		23p28			07 53		08 33			09 03		09 22		09 33		09 52	10 03		10 22			10 33
Clydebank	d	23p07		23p37			08 03		08 33			09 03				09 33			10 03				
Yoker	d	23p09		23p39			08 05		08 35			09 05				09 35			10 05				
Garscadden	d	23p13		23p43			08 09		08 39			09 09				09 39			10 09				
Scotstounhill	d	23p15		23p45			08 11		08 41			09 11				09 41			10 11				
Jordanhill	d	23p17		23p47			08 13		08 43			09 13				09 43			10 13				
Hyndland 3	d	23p21	23p31	23p49		07 55	08 15	08 35	08 45	08 55	09 05	09 15	09 25		09 35	09 45	09 55	10 05	10 15	10 25			10 35
Partick	d	23p23	23p34	23p52		07 58	08 18	08 38	08 48	08 58	09 08	09 18	09 28	09 36	09 38	09 48	09 58	10 08	10 18	10 28	10 36		10 38
Exhibition Centre	d						08 21		08 51	09 01		09 21	09 31	09 39		09 51	10 01		10 21	10 31	10 39		
Anderston	d																						
Glasgow Central LL 15	a						08 23		08 53	09 03		09 23	09 33	09 41		09 53	10 03		10 23	10 33	10 41		
	d						08 24		08 54	09 04		09 24	09 34	09 43		09 54	10 04		10 24	10 34	10 43		
Argyle Street	d															09 56	10 06		10 26	10 36	10 45		
Charing Cross	d	23p27	23p38	23p56		08 03		08 43			09 13				09 43			10 13					10 43
Glasgow Queen St LL 10	a	23p29	23p40	23p59		08 05		08 45			09 15				09 45			10 15					10 45
	d	23p30	23p44	23p59		08 05		08 45			09 15				09 45			10 15					10 45
High Street	d	23p32	23p46	00 02		08 07		08 47			09 17				09 47			10 17					10 47
Bellgrove	d	23p34	23p49	00 04		08 09		08 49			09 19				09 49			10 19					10 49
Duke Street	d																						
Alexandra Parade	d																						
Barnhill	d																						
Springburn	a																						
Carntyne	d	23p37	23p52	00 07		08 13		08 53			09 23				09 53			10 23					10 53
Shettleston	d	23p40	23p55	00 10		08 15		08 55			09 25				09 55			10 25					10 55
Garrowhill	d	23p42	23p57	00 12		08 18		08 58			09 28				09 58			10 28					10 58
Easterhouse	d	23p45	23p59	00 15		08 20		09 00			09 30				10 00			10 30					11 00
Blairhill	d	23p49	00 04	00 19		08 24		09 04			09 34				10 04			10 34					11 04
Coatbridge Sunnyside	d	23p51	00 06	00 21		08 27		09 07			09 37				10 07			10 37					11 07
Coatdyke	d	23p54	00 09	00 24		08 29		09 09			09 39				10 09			10 39					11 09
Airdrie	d	23p57	00a12	00a27		08 32		09 12			09a42				10 12			10a42					11 12
Drumgelloch	d	23p59				08 35		09 15							10 15								11 15
Caldercruix	d	00 03				08 39		09 19							10 19								11 19
Blackridge	d	00 09				08 45		09 25							10 25								11 25
Armadale	d	00 13				08 49		09 29							10 29								11 29
Bathgate	a	00 17				08 53		09 33							10 33								11 33
	d				07 55	08 54		09 34							10 34							11 04	11 34
Livingston North	d				07 59	08 59		09 38							10 38							11 08	11 38
Uphall	d				08 02	09 02		09 41							10 41							11 11	11 41
Edinburgh Park	a				08 10	09 10		09 52							10 49							11 19	11 49
Haymarket	a				08 20	09 20		10 02							10 54							11 24	11 54
Edinburgh	a				08 25	09 25		10 07							10 59							11 29	11 59
Bridgeton	d						08 29		08 59	09 09		09 29	09 39			09 59	10 09		10 29	10 39			
Dalmarnock §	d																						
Rutherglen	d						08 32		09 02	09 12		09 32	09 42	09 49		10 02	10 12		10 32	10 42	10 49		
Cambuslang	d						08 36		09 06	09 16		09 36	09 46			10 06	10 16		10 36	10 46			
Newton	d								09 09			09 39				10 09			10 39				
Blantyre	d								09 13			09 43		09 58		10 13			10 43		10 58		
Hamilton West	d								09 16			09 46		10 01		10 16			10 46		11 01		
Hamilton Central	d								09 20			09 50		10 03		10 20			10 50		11 03		
Chatelherault	d													10 07							11 07		
Merryton	d													10 10							11 10		
Larkhall	a													10 13							11 13		
Airbles	d								09 25			09 55				10 25			10 55				
Uddingston	d						08 40			09 20			09 50				10 20			10 50			
Bellshill	d						08 45			09 25			09 55				10 25			10 55			
Motherwell	a						08 51		09 27	09 33		09 57	10 03			10 27	10 33		10 57	11 03			
	d									09 33							10 33						
Whifflet	a																						
Coatbridge Central	a																						
Shieldmuir	d									09 37							10 37						
Holytown	d																						
Wishaw	d									09 40							10 40						
Carluke	d									09 47							10 47						
Lanark	a									09 59							10 59						

§ Station closed between 4 June and 24 November inclusive

Table 226

Sundays

Helensburgh, Balloch, Dalmuir and Milngavie - Glasgow - Springburn, Airdrie, Bathgate and Edinburgh, Hamilton, Larkhall, Motherwell, Coatbridge and Lanark

Network Diagram - see first Page of Table 220

		SR	XC ◇■ A ✠	SR	SR	SR	SR	SR	SR	SR	XC ◇■ B	SR	SR	SR	SR	SR	SR	SR	SR	SR	SR	SR	SR	SR	SR
Helensburgh Central	d				10 25					10 55				11 25				11 55			12 25				12 55
Craigendoran	d				10 28					10 58				11 28				11 58			12 28				12 58
Cardross	d				10 33					11 03				11 33				12 03			12 33				13 03
Balloch	d	10 09				10 39						11 09			11 39				12 09			12 39			
Alexandria	d	10 11				10 41						11 11			11 41				12 11			12 41			
Renton	d	10 14				10 44						11 14			11 44				12 14			12 44			
Dalreoch	d	10 17			10 38	10 47				11 08		11 17		11 38	11 47			12 08	12 17		12 38	12 47			13 08
Dumbarton Central	d	10 18			10 40	10 48				11 10		11 18		11 40	11 48			12 10	12 18		12 40	12 48			13 10
Dumbarton East	d	10 20			10 42	10 50				11 12		11 20		11 42	11 50			12 12	12 20		12 42	12 50			13 12
Bowling	d	10 25				10 55						11 25			11 55				12 25			12 55			
Kilpatrick	d	10 28				10 58						11 28			11 58				12 28			12 58			
Dalmuir	a	10 31			10 49	11 01				11 19		11 31		11 49	12 01			12 19	12 31		12 49	13 01			13 19
	d	10 31			10 50	11 01				11 20		11 31		11 50	12 01			12 20	12 31		12 50	13 01			13 20
Singer	d				10 52					11 22				11 52				12 22			12 52				13 22
Drumry	d				10 55					11 25				11 55				12 25			12 55				13 25
Drumchapel	d				10 57					11 27				11 57				12 27			12 57				13 27
Milngavie	d			10 41			11 11						11 41			12 11				12 41			13 11		
Hillfoot	d			10 44			11 14						11 44			12 14				12 44			13 14		
Bearsden	d			10 46			11 16						11 46			12 16				12 46			13 16		
Westerton	d			10 49	11 00		11 19			11 30			11 49	12 00		12 19		12 30		12 49	13 00		13 19		13 30
Anniesland	d			10 52	11 03		11 22			11 33			11 52	12 03		12 22		12 33		12 52	13 03		13 22		13 33
Clydebank	d	10 33				11 03						11 33			12 03				12 33			13 03			
Yoker	d	10 35				11 05						11 35			12 05				12 35			13 05			
Garscadden	d	10 39				11 09						11 39			12 09				12 39			13 09			
Scotstounhill	d	10 41				11 11						11 41			12 11				12 41			13 11			
Jordanhill	d	10 43				11 13						11 43			12 13				12 43			13 13			
Hyndland ■	d	10 45		10 55	11 05	11 15	11 25			11 35		11 45	11 55	12 05	12 15	12 25		12 35	12 45	12 55	13 05	13 15	13 25		13 35
Partick ⇌	d	10 48		10 58	11 08	11 18	11 28	11 36		11 38		11 48	11 58	12 08	12 18	12 28	12 36	12 38	12 48	12 58	13 08	13 18	13 28	13 36	13 38
Exhibition Centre	d	10 51		11 01		11 21	11 31	11 39				11 51	12 01		12 21	12 31	12 39		12 51	13 01		13 21	13 31	13 39	
Anderston	d																								
Glasgow Central LL ■	a	10 53		11 03		11 23	11 33	11 41				11 53	12 03		12 23	12 33	12 41		12 53	13 03		13 23	13 33	13 41	
	d	10 54	10b55	11 04		11 24	11 34	11 43			11b51	11 54	12 04		12 24	12 34	12 43		12 54	13 04		13 24	13 34	13 43	
Argyle Street	d	10 56		11 06		11 26	11 36	11 45				11 56	12 06		12 26	12 36	12 45		12 56	13 06		13 26	13 36	13 45	
Charing Cross	d				11 13					11 43				12 13				12 43			13 13				13 43
Glasgow Queen St LL ■ ⇌	a				11 15					11 45				12 15				12 45			13 15				13 45
	d				11 15					11 45				12 15				12 45			13 15				13 45
High Street	d				11 17					11 47				12 17				12 47			13 17				13 47
Bellgrove	d				11 19					11 49				12 19				12 49			13 19				13 49
Duke Street	d																								
Alexandra Parade	d																								
Barnhill	d																								
Springburn	a																								
Carntyne	d				11 23					11 53				12 23				12 53			13 23				13 53
Shettleston	d				11 25					11 55				12 25				12 55			13 25				13 55
Garrowhill	d				11 28					11 58				12 28				12 58			13 28				13 58
Easterhouse	d				11 30					12 00				12 30				13 00			13 30				14 00
Blairhill	d				11 34					12 04				12 34				13 04			13 34				14 04
Coatbridge Sunnyside	d				11 37					12 07				12 37				13 07			13 37				14 07
Coatdyke	d				11 39					12 09				12 39				13 09			13 39				14 09
Airdrie	d				11a42					12 12				12 42				13 12			13 42				14 12
Drumgelloch	d									12 15				12 45				13 15			13 45				14 15
Caldercruix	d									12 19				12 49				13 19			13 49				14 19
Blackridge	d									12 25				12 55				13 25			13 55				14 25
Armadale	d									12 29				12 59				13 29			13 59				14 29
Bathgate	a									12 33				13 03				13 33			14 03				14 33
	d								12 04	12 34				13 04				13 34			14 04				14 34
Livingston North	d								12 08	12 38				13 08				13 38			14 08				14 38
Uphall	d								12 11	12 41				13 11				13 41			14 11				14 41
Edinburgh Park	a								12 19	12 49				13 19				13 49			14 19				14 49
Haymarket	a								12 24	12 54				13 24				13 54			14 24				14 54
Edinburgh	a								12 29	12 59				13 30				13 59			14 29				14 59
Bridgeton	d	10 59		11 09		11 29	11 39					11 59	12 09		12 29	12 39			12 59	13 09		13 29	13 39		
Dalmarnock §	d																								
Rutherglen	d	11 02		11 12		11 32	11 42	11 49				12 02	12 12		12 32	12 42	12 49		13 02	13 12		13 32	13 42	13 49	
Cambuslang	d	11 06		11 16		11 36	11 46					12 06	12 16		12 36	12 46			13 06	13 16		13 36	13 46		
Newton	d	11 09				11 39						12 09			12 39				13 09			13 39			
Blantyre	d	11 13				11 43		11 58				12 13			12 43		12 58		13 13			13 43		13 58	
Hamilton West	d	11 16				11 46		12 01				12 16			12 46		13 01		13 16			13 46		14 01	
Hamilton Central	d	11 20				11 50		12 03				12 20			12 50		13 03		13 20			13 50		14 03	
Chatelherault	d							12 07									13 07							14 07	
Merryton	d							12 10									13 10							14 10	
Larkhall	a							12 13									13 13							14 13	
Airbles	d	11 25				11 55						12 25			12 55				13 25			13 55			
Uddingston	d			11 20			11 50						12 20			12 50				13 20			13 50		
Bellshill	d			11 25			11 55						12 25			12 55				13 25			13 55		
Motherwell	a	11 27	11 09	11 33		11 57	12 03				12 06	12 28	12 33		12 57	13 03			13 27	13 33		13 57	14 06		
	d			11 33									12 33							13 33					
Whifflet	a																								
Coatbridge Central	a																								
Shieldmuir	d			11 37									12 37							13 37					
Holytown	d																								
Wishaw	d			11 40									12 40							13 40					
Carluke	d			11 47									12 47							13 47					
Lanark	a			11 59									12 59							13 59					

§ Station closed between 4 June and 24 November inclusive

A To Penzance

B To Plymouth

Table 226

Sundays

Helensburgh, Balloch, Dalmuir and Milngavie - Glasgow - Springburn, Airdrie, Bathgate and Edinburgh, Hamilton, Larkhall, Motherwell, Coatbridge and Lanark

Network Diagram - see first Page of Table 220

		XC ◇■ C	SR	SR	SR	SR	SR	SR	SR	SR	XC ◇■ B	SR	SR	SR	SR ◇ A ✠	SR	SR	SR	SR	SR	SR	SR	SR	SR
Helensburgh Central	d				13 25				13 55				14 25		14b39			14 55			15 25			
Craigendoran	d				13 28				13 58				14 28					14 58			15 28			
Cardross	d				13 33				14 03				14 33					15 03			15 33			
Balloch	d		13 09			13 39				14 09				14 39					15 09			15 39		
Alexandria	d		13 11			13 41				14 11				14 41					15 11			15 41		
Renton	d		13 14			13 44				14 14				14 44					15 14			15 44		
Dalreoch	d		13 17		13 38	13 47			14 08	14 17			14 38	14 47				15 08	15 17		15 38	15 47		
Dumbarton Central	d		13 18		13 40	13 48			14 10	14 18			14 40	14 48	14 56			15 10	15 18		15 40	15 48		
Dumbarton East	d		13 20		13 42	13 50			14 12	14 20			14 42	14 50				15 12	15 20		15 42	15 50		
Bowling	d		13 25			13 55				14 25				14 55					15 25			15 55		
Kilpatrick	d		13 28			13 58				14 28				14 58					15 28			15 58		
Dalmuir	a		13 31		13 49	14 01			14 19	14 31			14 49	15 01	15 05			15 19	15 31		15 49	16 01		
	d		13 31		13 50	14 01			14 20	14 31			14 50	15 01	15 05			15 20	15 31		15 50	16 01		
Singer	d				13 52				14 22				14 52					15 22			15 52			
Drumry	d				13 55				14 25				14 55					15 25			15 55			
Drumchapel	d				13 57				14 27				14 57					15 27			15 57			
Milngavie	d			13 41			14 11					14 41				15 11				15 41			16 11	
Hillfoot	d			13 44			14 14					14 44				15 14				15 44			16 14	
Bearsden	d			13 46			14 16					14 46				15 16				15 46			16 16	
Westerton	d			13 49	14 00		14 19		14 30			14 49	15 00			15 19		15 30		15 49	16 00		16 19	
Anniesland	d			13 52	14 03		14 22		14 33			14 52	15 03			15 22		15 33		15 52	16 03		16 22	
Clydebank	d		13 33			14 03				14 33				15 03					15 33			16 03		
Yoker	d		13 35			14 05				14 35				15 05					15 35			16 05		
Garscadden	d		13 39			14 09				14 39				15 09					15 39			16 09		
Scotstounhill	d		13 41			14 11				14 41				15 11					15 41			16 11		
Jordanhill	d		13 43			14 13				14 43				15 13					15 43			16 13		
Hyndland ■	d		13 45	13 55	14 05	14 15	14 25		14 35	14 45		14 55	15 05	15 15		15 25		15 35	15 45	15 55	16 05	16 15	16 25	
Partick ⇌	d		13 48	13 58	14 08	14 18	14 28	14 36	14 38	14 48		14 58	15 08	15 18		15 28	15 36	15 38	15 48	15 58	16 08	16 18	16 28	16 36
Exhibition Centre	d		13 51	14 01		14 21	14 31	14 39		14 51		15 01		15 21		15 31	15 39		15 51	16 01		16 21	16 31	16 39
Anderston	d																							
Glasgow Central LL ■	a		13 53	14 03		14 23	14 33	14 41		14 53		15 03		15 23		15 33	15 41		15 53	16 03		16 23	16 33	16 41
	d	13b49	13 54	14 04		14 24	14 34	14 43		14 54	14b55	15 04		15 24		15 34	15 43		15 54	16 04		16 24	16 34	16 43
Argyle Street	d		13 56	14 06		14 26	14 36	14 45		14 56		15 06		15 26		15 36	15 45		15 56	16 06		16 26	16 36	16 45
Charing Cross	d				14 13				14 43				15 13					15 43			16 13			
Glasgow Queen St LL ■ ⇌	a				14 15				14 45				15 15		15c31			15 45			16 15			
	d				14 15				14 45				15 15					15 45			16 15			
High Street	d				14 17				14 47				15 17					15 47			16 17			
Bellgrove	d				14 19				14 49				15 19					15 49			16 19			
Duke Street	d																							
Alexandra Parade	d																							
Barnhill	d																							
Springburn	a																							
Carntyne	d				14 23				14 53				15 23					15 53			16 23			
Shettleston	d				14 25				14 55				15 25					15 55			16 25			
Garrowhill	d				14 28				14 58				15 28					15 58			16 28			
Easterhouse	d				14 30				15 00				15 30					16 00			16 30			
Blairhill	d				14 34				15 04				15 34					16 04			16 34			
Coatbridge Sunnyside	d				14 37				15 07				15 37					16 07			16 37			
Coatdyke	d				14 39				15 09				15 39					16 09			16 39			
Airdrie	d				14 42				15 12				15 42					16 12			16 42			
Drumgelloch	d				14 45				15 15				15 45					16 15			16 45			
Caldercruix	d				14 49				15 19				15 49					16 19			16 49			
Blackridge	d				14 55				15 25				15 55					16 25			16 55			
Armadale	d				14 59				15 29				15 59					16 29			16 59			
Bathgate	a				15 03				15 33				16 03					16 33			17 03			
	d				15 04				15 34				16 04					16 34			17 04			
Livingston North	d				15 08				15 38				16 08					16 38			17 08			
Uphall	d				15 11				15 41				16 11					16 41			17 11			
Edinburgh Park	a				15 19				15 49				16 19					16 49			17 19			
Haymarket	a				15 24				15 54				16 24					16 54			17 24			
Edinburgh	a				15 29				15 59				16 29					16 59			17 29			
Bridgeton	d		13 59	14 09		14 29	14 39			14 59		15 09		15 29		15 39			15 59	16 09		16 29	16 39	
Dalmarnock §	d																							
Rutherglen	d		14 02	14 12		14 32	14 42	14 49		15 02		15 12		15 32		15 42	15 49		16 02	16 12		16 32	16 42	16 49
Cambuslang	d		14 06	14 16		14 36	14 46			15 06		15 16		15 36		15 46			16 06	16 16		16 36	16 46	
Newton	d		14 09			14 39				15 09				15 39					16 09			16 39		
Blantyre	d		14 13			14 43		14 58		15 13				15 43			15 58		16 13			16 43		16 58
Hamilton West	d		14 16			14 46		15 01		15 16				15 46			16 01		16 16			16 46		17 01
Hamilton Central	d		14 20			14 50		15 03		15 20				15 50			16 03		16 20			16 50		17 03
Chatelherault	d							15 07									16 07							17 07
Merryton	d							15 10									16 10							17 10
Larkhall	a							15 13									16 13							17 13
Airbles	d		14 25			14 55				15 25				15 55					16 25			16 55		
Uddingston	d			14 20			14 50					15 20				15 50				16 20			16 50	
Bellshill	d			14 25			14 55					15 25				15 55				16 25			16 55	
Motherwell	a	14 03	14 27	14 33		14 57	15 03			15 27	15 10	15 33		15 57		16 03			16 27	16 33		16 57	17 05	
	d			14 33								15 33								16 33				
Whifflet	a																							
Coatbridge Central	a																							
Shieldmuir	d			14 37								15 37								16 37				
Holytown	d																							
Wishaw	d			14 40								15 40								16 40				
Carluke	d			14 47								15 47								16 47				
Lanark	a			14 59								15 59								16 59				

§ Station closed between 4 June and 24 November inclusive

A until 28 October. From Mallaig

B To Bristol Temple Meads

C To Plymouth

b Helensburgh Upper

c Glasgow Queen St High Level

Table 226

Sundays

Helensburgh, Balloch, Dalmuir and Milngavie - Glasgow - Springburn, Airdrie, Bathgate and Edinburgh, Hamilton, Larkhall, Motherwell, Coatbridge and Lanark

Network Diagram - see first Page of Table 220

		SR	SR	XC ◇1 B	SR	SR	SR	SR	SR	SR	SR	SR	SR	SR	SR	SR	SR	SR	XC ◇1 C	SR	SR	SR ◇ A	SR	SR	SR
Helensburgh Central	d	15 55				16 25				16 55			17 25				17 55				18 25	18b34			
Craigendoran	d	15 58				16 28				16 58			17 28				17 58				18 28				
Cardross	d	16 03				16 33				17 03			17 33				18 03				18 33				
Balloch	d		16 09				16 39				17 09			17 39				18 09					18 39		
Alexandria	d		16 11				16 41				17 11			17 41				18 11					18 41		
Renton	d		16 14				16 44				17 14			17 44				18 14					18 44		
Dalreoch	d	16 08	16 17			16 38	16 47			17 08	17 17		17 38	17 47			18 08	18 17			18 38		18 47		
Dumbarton Central	d	16 10	16 18			16 40	16 48			17 10	17 18		17 40	17 48			18 10	18 18			18 40	18 45	18 48		
Dumbarton East	d	16 12	16 20			16 42	16 50			17 12	17 20		17 42	17 50			18 12	18 20			18 42		18 50		
Bowling	d		16 25				16 55				17 25			17 55				18 25					18 55		
Kilpatrick	d		16 28				16 58				17 28			17 58				18 28					18 58		
Dalmuir	a	16 19	16 31			16 49	17 01			17 19	17 31		17 49	18 01			18 19	18 31			18 49	18 56	19 01		
	d	16 20	16 31			16 50	17 01			17 20	17 31		17 50	18 01			18 20	18 31			18 50	18 56	19 01		
Singer	d	16 22				16 52				17 22			17 52				18 22				18 52				
Drumry	d	16 25				16 55				17 25			17 55				18 25				18 55				
Drumchapel	d	16 27				16 57				17 27			17 57				18 27				18 57				
Milngavie	d				16 41			17 11				17 41			18 11					18 41				19 11	
Hillfoot	d				16 44			17 14				17 44			18 14					18 44				19 14	
Bearsden	d				16 46			17 16				17 46			18 16					18 46				19 16	
Westerton	d	16 30			16 49	17 00		17 19		17 30		17 49	18 00		18 19		18 30			18 49	19 00			19 19	
Anniesland	d	16 33			16 52	17 03		17 22		17 33		17 52	18 03		18 22		18 33			18 52	19 03			19 22	
Clydebank	d		16 33				17 03				17 33			18 03				18 33					19 03		
Yoker	d		16 35				17 05				17 35			18 05				18 35					19 05		
Garscadden	d		16 39				17 09				17 39			18 09				18 39					19 09		
Scotstounhill	d		16 41				17 11				17 41			18 11				18 41					19 11		
Jordanhill	d		16 43				17 13				17 43			18 13				18 43					19 13		
Hyndland 3	d	16 35	16 45		16 55	17 05	17 15	17 25		17 35	17 45	17 55	18 05	18 15	18 25		18 35	18 45		18 55	19 05		19 15	19 25	
Partick ⛴	d	16 38	16 48		16 58	17 08	17 18	17 28	17 36	17 38	17 48	17 58	18 08	18 18	18 28	18 36	18 38	18 48		18 58	19 08		19 18	19 28	19 36
Exhibition Centre	d		16 51		17 01		17 21	17 31	17 39		17 51	18 01		18 21	18 31	18 39		18 51		19 01			19 21	19 31	19 39
Anderston	d																								
Glasgow Central LL 15	a		16 53		17 03		17 23	17 33	17 41		17 53	18 03		18 23	18 33	18 41		18 53		19 03			19 23	19 33	19 41
	d		16 54	16b55	17 04		17 24	17 34	17 43		17 54	18 04		18 24	18 34	18 43		18 54	18b57	19 04			19 24	19 34	19 43
Argyle Street	d		16 56		17 06		17 26	17 36	17 45		17 56	18 06													
Charing Cross	d	16 43				17 13				17 43			18 13				18 43				19 13				
Glasgow Queen St LL 10 ⛴	a	16 45				17 15				17 45			18 15				18 45				19 15	19c15			
	d	16 45				17 15				17 45			18 15				18 45				19 15				
High Street	d	16 47				17 17				17 47			18 17				18 47				19 17				
Bellgrove	d	16 49				17 19				17 49			18 19				18 49				19 19				
Duke Street	d																								
Alexandra Parade	d																								
Barnhill	d																								
Springburn	a																								
Carntyne	d	16 53				17 23				17 53			18 23				18 53				19 23				
Shettleston	d	16 55				17 25				17 55			18 25				18 55				19 25				
Garrowhill	d	16 58				17 28				17 58			18 28				18 58				19 28				
Easterhouse	d	17 00				17 30				18 00			18 30				19 00				19 30				
Blairhill	d	17 04				17 34				18 04			18 34				19 04				19 34				
Coatbridge Sunnyside	d	17 07				17 37				18 07			18 37				19 07				19 37				
Coatdyke	d	17 09				17 39				18 09			18 39				19 09				19 39				
Airdrie	d	17 12				17 42				18 12			18 42				19 12				19a42				
Drumgelloch	d	17 15				17 45				18 15			18 45				19 15								
Caldercruix	d	17 19				17 49				18 19			18 49				19 19								
Blackridge	d	17 25				17 55				18 25			18 55				19 25								
Armadale	d	17 29				17 59				18 29			18 59				19 29								
Bathgate	a	17 33				18 03				18 33			19 03				19 33								
	d	17 34				18 04				18 34			19 04				19 34								
Livingston North	d	17 38				18 08				18 38			19 08				19 38								
Uphall	d	17 41				18 11				18 41			19 11				19 41								
Edinburgh Park	a	17 49				18 19				18 49			19 19				19 49								
Haymarket	a	17 54				18 24				18 54			19 24				19 54								
Edinburgh	a	17 59				18 29				18 59			19 29				19 59								
Bridgeton	d		16 59		17 09		17 29	17 39			17 59	18 09		18 29	18 39			18 59		19 09			19 29	19 39	
Dalmarnock §	d																								
Rutherglen	d		17 02		17 12		17 32	17 42	17 49		18 02	18 12		18 32	18 42	18 49		19 02		19 12			19 32	19 42	19 49
Cambuslang	d		17 06		17 16		17 36	17 46			18 06	18 16		18 36	18 46			19 06		19 16			19 36	19 46	
Newton	d		17 09				17 39				18 09			18 39				19 09					19 39		
Blantyre	d		17 13				17 43		17 58		18 13			18 43		18 58		19 13					19 43		19 58
Hamilton West	d		17 16				17 46		18 01		18 16			18 46		19 01		19 16					19 46		20 01
Hamilton Central	d		17 20				17 50		18 03		18 20			18 50		19 03		19 20					19 50		20 03
Chatelherault	d								18 07							19 07									20 07
Merryton	d								18 10							19 10									20 10
Larkhall	a								18 13							19 13									20 13
Airbles	d		17 25				17 55				18 25			18 55				19 25					19 55		
Uddingston	d				17 20			17 50				18 20			18 50					19 20				19 50	
Bellshill	d				17 25			17 55				18 25			18 55					19 25				19 55	
Motherwell	a		17 27	17 10	17 33		17 57	18 03			18 27	18 33		18 57	19 03			19 27	19 10	19 33			19 57	20 03	
	d				17 33							18 33								19 33					
Whifflet	a																								
Coatbridge Central	a																								
Shieldmuir	d				17 37							18 37								19 37					
Holytown	d																								
Wishaw	d				17 40							18 40								19 40					
Carluke	d				17 47							18 47								19 47					
Lanark	a				17 59							18 59								19 59					

§ Station closed between 4 June and 24 November inclusive
A until 30 September. From Oban
B To Birmingham New Street
C To Newcastle
b Helensburgh Upper
c Glasgow Queen St High Level

Table 226

Sundays

Helensburgh, Balloch, Dalmuir and Milngavie - Glasgow - Springburn, Airdrie, Bathgate and Edinburgh, Hamilton, Larkhall, Motherwell, Coatbridge and Lanark

Network Diagram - see first Page of Table 220

		SR	SR	SR		SR	SR ◇ A	SR	SR	SR	SR	SR	XC ◇1 B			SR	SR	SR	SR ◇ D	SR	SR	SR	SR	SR	
Helensburgh Central	d	18 55				19 25	19b29				19 55						20 25		20b40			20 55			
Craigendoran	d	18 58				19 28					19 58						20 28					20 58			
Cardross	d	19 03				19 33					20 03						20 33					21 03			
Balloch	d		19 09					19 39				20 09						20 38					21 09		
Alexandria	d		19 11					19 41				20 11						20 40					21 11		
Renton	d		19 14					19 44				20 14						20 43					21 14		
Dalreoch	d	19 08	19 17			19 38		19 47			20 08	20 17					20 38	20 46				21 08	21 17		
Dumbarton Central	d	19 10	19 18			19 40		19 48			20 10	20 18					20 40	20 47	20 53			21 10	21 18		
Dumbarton East	d	19 12	19 20			19 42		19 50			20 12	20 20					20 42	20 49				21 12	21 20		
Bowling	d		19 25					19 55				20 25						20 54					21 25		
Kilpatrick	d		19 28					19 58				20 28						20 57					21 28		
Dalmuir	a	19 19	19 31			19 49	19s55	20 01			20 19	20 31					20 49	21 00	21 03			21 19	21 31		
	d	19 20	19 31			19 50		20 01			20 20	20 31					20 50	21 01	21 03			21 20	21 31		
Singer	d	19 22				19 52					20 22						20 52					21 22			
Drumry	d	19 25				19 55					20 25						20 55					21 25			
Drumchapel	d	19 27				19 57					20 27						20 57					21 27			
Milngavie	d			19 41					20 11							20 41				21 11				21 41	
Hillfoot	d			19 44					20 14							20 44				21 14				21 44	
Bearsden	d			19 46					20 16							20 46				21 16				21 46	
Westerton	d	19 30		19 49		20 00			20 19		20 30					20 49	21 00			21 19		21 30		21 49	
Anniesland	d	19 33		19 52		20 03			20 22		20 33					20 52	21 03			21 22		21 33		21 52	
Clydebank	d		19 33					20 03				20 33						21 03					21 33		
Yoker	d		19 35					20 05				20 35						21 05					21 35		
Garscadden	d		19 39					20 09				20 39						21 09					21 39		
Scotstounhill	d		19 41					20 11				20 41						21 11					21 41		
Jordanhill	d		19 43					20 13				20 43						21 13					21 43		
Hyndland 3	d	19 35	19 45	19 55		20 05		20 15	20 25		20 35	20 45				20 55	21 05	21 15		21 25		21 35	21 45	21 55	
Partick ⛴	d	19 38	19 48	19 58		20 08		20 18	20 28	20 36	20 38	20 48				20 58	21 08	21 18		21 28	21 36	21 38	21 48	21 58	
Exhibition Centre	d		19 51	20 01				20 21	20 31	20 39		20 51				21 01		21 21		21 31	21 39		21 51	22 01	
Anderston	d																								
Glasgow Central LL 15	a		19 53	20 03				20 23	20 33	20 41		20 53				21 03		21 23		21 33	21 41		21 53	22 03	
	d		19 54	20 04				20 24	20 34	20 43		20 54	20c58			21 04		21 24		21 34	21 43		21 54	22 04	
Argyle Street	d																								
Charing Cross	d	19 43				20 13					20 43						21 13					21 43			
Glasgow Queen St LL 10 ⛴	a	19 45				20 15					20 45						21 15		21e19			21 45			
	d	19 45				20 15					20 45						21 15					21 45			
High Street	d	19 47				20 17					20 47						21 17					21 47			
Bellgrove	d	19 49				20 19					20 49						21 19					21 49			
Duke Street	d																								
Alexandra Parade	d																								
Barnhill	d																								
Springburn	a																								
Carntyne	d	19 53				20 23					20 53						21 23					21 53			
Shettleston	d	19 55				20 25					20 55						21 25					21 55			
Garrowhill	d	19 58				20 28					20 58						21 28					21 58			
Easterhouse	d	20 00				20 30					21 00						21 30					22 00			
Blairhill	d	20 04				20 34					21 04						21 34					22 04			
Coatbridge Sunnyside	d	20 07				20 37					21 07						21 37					22 07			
Coatdyke	d	20 09				20 39					21 09						21 39					22 09			
Airdrie	d	20 12				20a42					21 12						21a42					22 12			
Drumgelloch	d	20 15									21 15											22 15			
Caldercruix	d	20 19									21 19											22 19			
Blackridge	d	20 25									21 25											22 25			
Armadale	d	20 29									21 29											22 29			
Bathgate	a	20 33									21 33											22 33			
	d	20 34									21 34											22 34			
Livingston North	d	20 38									21 38											22 38			
Uphall	d	20 41									21 41											22 41			
Edinburgh Park	a	20 49									21 49											22 49			
Haymarket	a	20 54					21s03				21 54											22 54			
Edinburgh	a	20 59					21 09				21 59											22 59			
Bridgeton	d		19 59	20 09				20 29	20 39			20 59				21 09		21 29		21 39			21 59	22 09	
Dalmarnock §	d																								
Rutherglen	d		20 02	20 12				20 32	20 42	20 49		21 02				21 12		21 32		21 42	21 49		22 02	22 12	
Cambuslang	d		20 06	20 16				20 36	20 46			21 06				21 16		21 36		21 46			22 06	22 16	
Newton	d		20 09					20 39				21 09						21 39					22 09		
Blantyre	d		20 13					20 43		20 58		21 13						21 43			21 58		22 13		
Hamilton West	d		20 16					20 46		21 01		21 16						21 46			22 01		22 16		
Hamilton Central	d		20 20					20 50		21 03		21 20						21 50			22 03		22 20		
Chatelherault	d									21 07											22 07				
Merryton	d									21 10											22 10				
Larkhall	a									21 13											22 13				
Airbles	d		20 25					20 55				21 25						21 55					22 25		
Uddingston	d			20 20					20 50							21 20				21 50				22 20	
Bellshill	d			20 25					20 55							21 25				21 55				22 25	
Motherwell	a		20 27	20 33				20 57	21 03			21 27	21 17			21 33		21 57		22 03			22 27	22 33	
	d			20 33												21 33								22 33	
Whifflet	a																								
Coatbridge Central	a																								
Shieldmuir	d			20 37												21 37								22 37	
Holytown	d																								
Wishaw	d			20 40												21 40								22 40	
Carluke	d			20 47												21 47								22 47	
Lanark	a			20 59												21 59								22 59	

§ Station closed between 4 June and 24 November inclusive
A from 24 June until 26 August. From Oban
B until 24 June and from 1 July until 18 November, To Edinburgh
D From Mallaig
b Helensburgh Upper
c Glasgow Central High Level
e Glasgow Queen St High Level

Table 226

Sundays

Helensburgh, Balloch, Dalmuir and Milngavie - Glasgow - Springburn, Airdrie, Bathgate and Edinburgh, Hamilton, Larkhall, Motherwell, Coatbridge and Lanark

Network Diagram - see first Page of Table 220

		SR	SR	SR	SR	SR	SR	SR	SR	SR		SR	SR	SR
												B A		
Helensburgh Central	d	21 25				21 55			22 25			22b37	22 55	
Craigendoran	d	21 28				21 58			22 28				22 58	
Cardross	d	21 33				22 03			22 33				23 03	
Balloch	d		21 39				22 09			22 39				23 09
Alexandria	d		21 41				22 11			22 41				23 11
Renton	d		21 44				22 14			22 44				23 14
Dalreoch	d	21 38	21 47			22 08	22 17		22 38	22 47			23 08	23 17
Dumbarton Central	d	21 40	21 48			22 10	22 18		22 40	22 48			23 10	23 18
Dumbarton East	d	21 42	21 50			22 12	22 20		22 42	22 50			23 12	23 20
Bowling	d		21 55				22 25			22 55				23 25
Kilpatrick	d		21 58				22 28			22 58				23 28
Dalmuir	a	21 49	22 01			22 19	22 31		22 49	23 01		23 02	23 19	23 31
	d	21 50	22 01			22 20	22 31		22 50	23 01		23 04		23 31
Singer	d	21 52				22 22			22 52					
Drumry	d	21 55				22 25			22 55					
Drumchapel	d	21 57				22 27			22 57					
Milngavie	d			22 11				22 41						
Hillfoot	d			22 14				22 44						
Bearsden	d			22 16				22 46						
Westerton	d	22 00		22 19		22 30		22 49	23 00			23 13		
Anniesland	d	22 03		22 22		22 33		22 52	23 03					
Clydebank	d		22 03				22 33			23 03				23 33
Yoker	d		22 05				22 35			23a05				23a35
Garscadden	d		22 09				22 39							
Scotstounhill	d		22 11				22 41							
Jordanhill	d		22 13				22 43							
Hyndland	d	22 05	22 15	22 25		22 35	22 45	22 55	23 05					
Partick	d	22 08	22 18	22 28	22 36	22 38	22 48	22 58	23 08					
Exhibition Centre	d		22 21	22 31	22 39		22 51	23 01						
Anderston	d													
Glasgow Central LL	a		22 23	22 33	22 41		22 53	23 03						
	d		22 24	22 34	22 43		22 54	23 04						
Argyle Street	d													
Charing Cross	d	22 13				22 43			23 13					
Glasgow Queen St LL	a	22 15				22 45			23 15					
	d	22 15				22 45			23 15					
High Street	d	22 17				22 47			23 17					
Bellgrove	d	22 19				22 49			23 19					
Duke Street	d													
Alexandra Parade	d													
Barnhill	d													
Springburn	a													
Carntyne	d	22 23				22 53			23 23					
Shettleston	d	22 25				22 55			23 25					
Garrowhill	d	22 28				22 58			23 28					
Easterhouse	d	22 30				23 00			23 30					
Blairhill	d	22 34				23 04			23 34					
Coatbridge Sunnyside	d	22 37				23 07			23 37					
Coatdyke	d	22 39				23 09			23 39					
Airdrie	d	22a42				23 12			23a42					
Drumgelloch	d					23 15								
Caldercruix	d					23 19								
Blackridge	d					23 25								
Armadale	d					23 29								
Bathgate	a					23 33								
	d													
Livingston North	d													
Uphall	d													
Edinburgh Park	a													
Haymarket	a													
Edinburgh	a											00 15		
Bridgeton	d		22 29	22 39			22 59	23 09						
Dalmarnock §	d													
Rutherglen	d		22 32	22 42	22 49		23 02	23 12						
Cambuslang	d		22 36	22 46			23 06	23 16						
Newton	d		22 39				23 09							
Blantyre	d		22 43		22 58		23 13							
Hamilton West	d		22 46		23 01		23 16							
Hamilton Central	d		22 50		23 03		23 20							
Chatelherault	d				23 07									
Merryton	d				23 10									
Larkhall	a				23 15									
Airbles	d		22 55				23 25							
Uddingston	d			22 50				23 20						
Bellshill	d			22 55				23 25						
Motherwell	a		22 57	23 03			23 27	23 33						
	d													
Whifflet	a													
Coatbridge Central	a													
Shieldmuir	d													
Holytown	d													
Wishaw	d													
Carluke	d													
Lanark	a													

§ Station closed between 4 June and 24 November inclusive
A From Fort William to London Euston
B To London Euston
b Helensburgh Upper
c Glasgow Central High Level

Network Diagram for Tables 227, 239

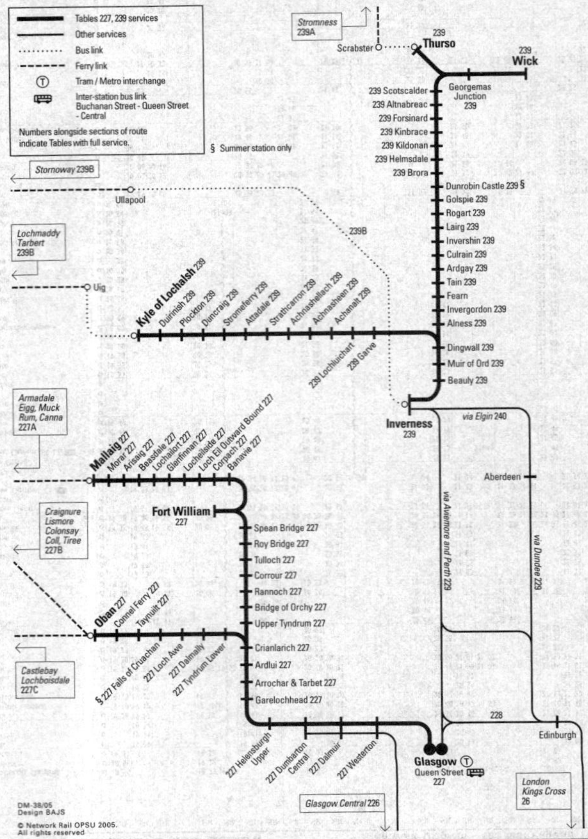

Table 227

Mondays to Saturdays
until 29 September

Glasgow Queen Street - Oban, Fort William and Mallaig

Network Diagram - see first Page of Table 227

Miles	Miles		SR	SR	SR	SR SO		SR SX	WR	SR SX	SR SO	SR		SR	
				◇	B 🛏	◇ B ⊼		◇ ⊼	A	◇ ⊼	◇ ⊼	◇ ⊼		◇ ⊼	
—	—	Edinburgh 228 d			04 50	*07 15*		*07 15*		*07 45*	*09 30*	*11 15*		*17 15*	
0	0	**Glasgow Queen St.** 10 226 ⛴ d	05 30			08 21		08 21		09 03	10 37	12 21		18 21	
5½	5½	Westerton 226 d	05 43		05 56										
10	10	Dalmuir 226 d			06 04	08 39		08 39		09 24	10 52	12 42		18 38	
16½	16½	Dumbarton Central 226 d				08 48		08 48		09 36	11 05	12 48		18 47	
25½	25½	Helensburgh Upper a			06 26	09 03		09 03		09 50	11 20	13 03		19 02	
—	—	d			06 29	09 06		09 06		09 52	11 22	13 06		19 04	
32¼	32¼	Garelochhead d			06 42	09 17		09 17		10 04	11 34	13 17		19 16	
43	43	Arrochar & Tarbet d			07 08	09 37		09 37		10 27	11 54	13 37		19 36	
51	51	Ardlui d			07x22	09 53		09 53		10x39	12 08	13 53		19 52	
59¾	59¾	**Crianlarich** a			07 43	10 09		10 09		10 55	12 24	14 09		20 08	
—	—														
—	—	d			07 44	10 15	10 21	10 15		10 58	12 26	14 15	14 21	20 14	20 17
64¾	—	Tyndrum Lower d				10 24		10 24			12 35	14 24		20 23	
76¾	—	Dalmally d				10 42		10 42			12 57	14 42		20 41	
79½	—	Loch Awe d				10 47		10 47			13 02	14 47		20 46	
83½	—	Falls of Cruachan § d				10x52		10x52			13x07	14x52		20x51	
88½	—	Taynuilt d				11 03		11 03			13 18	15 03		21 02	
95¼	—	Connel Ferry d				11 14		11 14			13 29	15 14		21 13	
101½	—	**Oban** a				11 27		11 27			13 42	15 27		21 26	
—	64½	Upper Tyndrum d			07 57		10 32			11 09			14 32		20 28
—	72¼	Bridge of Orchy d			08 14		10 46			11 23			14 46		20 42
—	87¾	Rannoch d			08 45		11 08			11 45			15 09		21 07
—	95	Corrour d			08x58		11 20			11 57			15 21		21 19
—	105	Tulloch d			09 18		11 36			12 14			15 38		21 35
—	110¾	Roy Bridge d			09x29		11 46			12 24			15 48		21 45
—	114	Spean Bridge d			09 37		11 54			12 31			15 56		21 52
—	122¾	**Fort William** a			09 54		12 07			12 44			16 09		22 05
—	—	d		08 30			12 12		10 15	12 48			16 19		22 14
—	125	Banavie d		08 36			12 18			12 55			16 25		22 20
—	126	Corpach d		08 42			12 23			12 59			16 30		22 25
—	129	Loch Eil Outward Bound d		08 49			12 29		10 35	13 06			16 36		22 31
—	132¾	Locheilside d		08x54			12x34			13x11			16x41		22x36
—	139¼	Glenfinnan d		09 05			12 46		11 22	13 22			16 55		22 47
—	148½	Lochailort d		09x20			13x01			13x37			17x10		23x03
—	153¼	Beasdale d		09x29			13x10			13x46			17x19		23x12
—	156¾	Arisaig d		09 38			13 18		12 07	13 54			17 27		23 20
—	161¼	Morar d		09 46			13 26			14 03			17 36		23 28
—	164¼	**Mallaig** a		09 53			13 34		12 26	14 10			17 43		23 35

§ Open from 20 May until 30 September

A SX from 21 May until 15 June, from 18 June until 31 August, SX from 3 September until 28 September

B SX also until 19 May

Table 227

Mondays to Saturdays
from 1 October

Glasgow Queen Street - Oban, Fort William and Mallaig

Network Diagram - see first Page of Table 227

	SR	SR	SR	WR SX	SR		SR SO	SR		SR	
		◇	B 🛏	A	◇ ⊼		◇ C ⊼	◇ ⊼		◇ ⊼	
Edinburgh 228 d			04 50		*07 15*		*09 30*	*11 15*		*17 15*	
Glasgow Queen St. 10 226 ⛴ d	05 30				08 21		10 37	12 21		18 21	
Westerton 226 d	05 43		05 56								
Dalmuir 226 d			06 04		08 39		10 52	12 42		18 38	
Dumbarton Central 226 d					08 48		11 05	12 48		18 47	
Helensburgh Upper a			06 26		09 03		11 20	13 03		19 02	
d			06 29		09 06		11 22	13 06		19 04	
Garelochhead d			06 42		09 17		11 34	13 17		19 16	
Arrochar & Tarbet d			07 08		09 37		11 54	13 37		19 36	
Ardlui d			07x22		09 53		12 08	13 53		19 52	
Crianlarich a			07 43		10 09		12 24	14 09		20 08	
d			07 44		10 15	10 21	12 26	14 15	14 21	20 14	20 17
Tyndrum Lower d					10 24		12 35	14 24		20 23	
Dalmally d					10 42		12 57	14 42		20 41	
Loch Awe d					10 47		13 02	14 47		20 46	
Falls of Cruachan § d											
Taynuilt d					11 03		13 18	15 03		21 02	
Connel Ferry d					11 14		13 29	15 14		21 13	
Oban a					11 27		13 42	15 27		21 26	
Upper Tyndrum d			07 57			10 32			14 32		20 28
Bridge of Orchy d			08 14			10 46			14 46		20 42
Rannoch d			08 45			11 08			15 09		21 07
Corrour d			08x58			11 20			15 21		21 19
Tulloch d			09 18			11 36			15 38		21 35
Roy Bridge d			09x29			11 46			15 48		21 45
Spean Bridge d			09 37			11 54			15 56		21 52
Fort William a			09 54			12 07			16 09		22 05
d		08 30		10 15		12 12			16 19		22 14
Banavie d		08 36				12 18			16 25		22 20
Corpach d		08 42				12 23			16 30		22 25
Loch Eil Outward Bound d		08 49		10 35		12 29			16 36		22 31
Locheilside d		08x54				12x34			16x41		22x36
Glenfinnan d		09 05		11 22		12 46			16 55		22 47
Lochailort d		09x20				13x01			17x10		23x03
Beasdale d		09x29				13x10			17x19		23x12
Arisaig d		09 38		12 07		13 18			17 27		23 20
Morar d		09 46				13 26			17 36		23 28
Mallaig a		09 53		12 26		13 34			17 43		23 35

§ Open from 20 May until 30 September

A from 1 October until 26 October

B ⊼ to Fort William

C from 6 October until 27 October

Table 227

Sundays
until 30 September

Glasgow Queen Street - Oban, Fort William and Mallaig

Network Diagram - see first Page of Table 227

		SR ◇ A	SR ◇ ⊼	WR A	SR ◇ ⊼	SR ◇ ⊼		SR ◇ ⊼	
Edinburgh 228	d	08 10	*08 00*			*11 00*		*17 00*	
Glasgow Queen St. [10] 226 ⇌	d		09 55			12 20		18 20	
Westerton 226	d								
Dalmuir 226	d	09u27	10 16			12 34		18 34	
Dumbarton Central 226	d		10 25			12 44		18 44	
Helensburgh Upper	a	09 49	10 37			12 59		18 59	
	d	09 52	10 40			13 06		19 04	
Garelochhead	d	10 03	10 51			13 17		19 16	
Arrochar & Tarbet	d	10 23	11 11			13 37		19 36	
Ardlui	d	10 37	11 27			13 53		19 52	
Crianlarich	a	10 53	11 44			14 09		20 08	
	d	10 56	11 46			14 15	14 21	20 14	20 17
Tyndrum Lower	d	11 04	11 55			14 24		20 23	
Dalmally	d	11 22	12 14			14 42		20 41	
Loch Awe	d	11 27	12 19			14 47		20 46	
Falls of Cruachan §	d	11x32	12x23			14x52		20x51	
Taynuilt	d	11 42	12 41			15 03		21 02	
Connel Ferry	d	11 53	12 52			15 14		21 13	
Oban	a	12 06	13 05			15 27		21 26	
Upper Tyndrum	d						14 32		20 28
Bridge of Orchy	d						14 46		20 42
Rannoch	d						15 09		21 07
Corrour	d						15 21		21 19
Tulloch	d						15 38		21 35
Roy Bridge	d						15 48		21 45
Spean Bridge	d						15 56		21 52
Fort William	a						16 09		22 05
	d			10 15	12 12		16 19		22 14
Banavie	d				12 18		16 25		22 20
Corpach	d				12 23		16 30		22 25
Loch Eil Outward Bound	d			10 35	12 29		16 36		22 31
Locheilside	d				12x34		16x41		22x36
Glenfinnan	d			11 22	12 46		16 55		22 47
Lochailort	d				13x01		17x10		23x03
Beasdale	d				13x10		17x19		23x12
Arisaig	d			12 07	13 18		17 27		23 20
Morar	d				13 26		17 36		23 28
Mallaig	a			12 26	13 34		17 43		23 35

Sundays
from 7 October

		SR ◇ B ⊼	SR ◇ B ⊼		SR ◇ ⊼	
Edinburgh 228	d		*11 00*		*17 00*	
Glasgow Queen St. [10] 226 ⇌	d		12 20		18 20	
Westerton 226	d					
Dalmuir 226	d		12 34		18 34	
Dumbarton Central 226	d		12 44		18 44	
Helensburgh Upper	a		12 59		18 59	
	d		13 06		19 04	
Garelochhead	d		13 17		19 16	
Arrochar & Tarbet	d		13 37		19 36	
Ardlui	d		13 53		19 52	
Crianlarich	a		14 09		20 08	
	d		14 15	14 21	20 14	20 17
Tyndrum Lower	d		14 24		20 23	
Dalmally	d		14 42		20 41	
Loch Awe	d		14 47		20 46	
Falls of Cruachan §	d					
Taynuilt	d		15 03		21 02	
Connel Ferry	d		15 14		21 13	
Oban	a		15 27		21 26	
Upper Tyndrum	d			14 32		20 28
Bridge of Orchy	d			14 46		20 42
Rannoch	d			15 09		21 07
Corrour	d			15 21		21 19
Tulloch	d			15 38		21 35
Roy Bridge	d			15 48		21 45
Spean Bridge	d			15 56		21 52
Fort William	a			16 09		22 05
	d	12 12		16 19		22 14
Banavie	d	12 18		16 25		22 20
Corpach	d	12 23		16 30		22 25
Loch Eil Outward Bound	d	12 29		16 36		22 31
Locheilside	d	12x34		16x41		22x36
Glenfinnan	d	12 46		16 55		22 47
Lochailort	d	13x01		17x10		23x03
Beasdale	d	13x10		17x19		23x12
Arisaig	d	13 18		17 27		23 20
Morar	d	13 26		17 36		23 28
Mallaig	a	13 34		17 43		23 35

§ Open from 20 May until 30 September
A from 24 June until 26 August
B from 7 October until 28 October

Table 227

Mondays to Saturdays
until 29 September

Mallaig, Fort William and Oban - Glasgow Queen Street

Network Diagram - see first Page of Table 227

Miles	Miles			SR MO B 🛏	SR MX B 🛏	SR MX	SR SX	SR ◇ ⊼	SR ◇ A ⊼	SR SO ◇ ⊼	SR SO ◇ ⊼	SR SO ◇ ⊼	SR SX ◇ ⊼
—	0	**Mallaig**	d						06 03			10 10	10 10
—	3	Morar	d						06 09			10 17	10 17
—	7½	Arisaig	d						06 19			10 26	10 26
—	11	Beasdale	d						06x25			10x33	10x33
—	15¾	Lochailort	d						06x34			10x42	10x42
—	25	Glenfinnan	d						06 51			10 59	10 59
—	31½	Locheilside	d						07x01			11x09	11x09
—	35¼	Loch Eil Outward Bound	d						07 07			11 15	11 15
—	38¼	Corpach	d						07 13			11 21	11 21
—	39¼	Banavie	d						07 17			11 25	11 25
—	41½	**Fort William**	a						07 25			11 32	11 32
—	—		d	19p00	19p50				07 42			11 40	11 40
—	50¼	Spean Bridge	d	19p20	20p10				07 55			11 55	11 55
—	53½	Roy Bridge	d	19b27	20b17				08 02			12 02	12 02
—	59¼	Tulloch	d	19p40	20p30				08 13			12 14	12 14
—	69¼	Corrour	d	20b01	20b51				08 30			12 31	12 31
—	76½	Rannoch	d	20p15	21p06				08 43			12 42	12 42
—	92	Bridge of Orchy	d	20p47	21p34				09 03			13 03	13 03
—	99¾	Upper Tyndrum	d	21p05	21p52				09 19			13 19	13 19
0	—	**Oban**	d					08 11			12 11		
6¼	—	Connel Ferry	d					08 23			12 23		
13	—	Taynuilt	d					08 35			12 35		
18½	—	Falls of Cruachan §	d					08x43			12x43		
22	—	Loch Awe	d					08 50			12 50		
24¾	—	Dalmally	d					08 55			12 55		
36¾	—	Tyndrum Lower	d					09 14			13 14		
42	104½	**Crianlarich**	a	21p16	22p04			09 29	09 30		13 29	13 30	13 30
—	—												
—	—		d	21p18	22p05				09 36			13 36	13 36
50¾	113¼	Ardlui	d	21b39	22b26				09 52			13 52	13 52
58¾	121¼	Arrochar & Tarbet	d	21p57	22p44		07 10		10 07			14 07	14 07
69½	132	Garelochhead	d	22p23	23p10		07 30		10 32			14 27	14 27
76¼	138¾	Helensburgh Upper	a	22p35	23p23		07 41		10 42			14 38	14 38
—	—		d	22p37	23p24		07 42		10 44			14 39	14 39
85¼	147¾	Dumbarton Central 226	a				07 56		10 59			14 51	14 51
92½	154¼	Dalmuir 226	a	23p02	23p49				11 08			15 03	15 03
96	157¾	Westerton 226	a	23p11	23p54	00 05							
101½	164¼	**Glasgow Queen St. [10] 226 ⇌**	a			00 20	08 37		11 30			15 30	15 30
—	—	Edinburgh 228	a	00 15	00 50		*09 52*		*12 36*			*16 35*	*16 35*

		SR SX ◇ B ⊼	WR C	SR SO ◇ ⊼	SR ◇ A ⊼	SR ◇ ⊼	SR ◇ ⊼	SR SX B 🛏
Mallaig	d		14 09		16 05		18 15	
Morar	d				16 12		18 22	
Arisaig	d		14 39		16 21		18 31	
Beasdale	d				16x28		18x38	
Lochailort	d				16x37		18x47	
Glenfinnan	d		15 20		16 54		19 04	
Locheilside	d				17x03		19x13	
Loch Eil Outward Bound	d		15 40		17 10		19 20	
Corpach	d				17 16		19 26	
Banavie	d				17 20		19 30	
Fort William	a		16 03		17 28		19 37	
	d				17 37			19 50
Spean Bridge	d				17 51			20 10
Roy Bridge	d				17 57			20x17
Tulloch	d				18 09			20 30
Corrour	d				18 25			20x51
Rannoch	d				18 37			21 06
Bridge of Orchy	d				18 57			21 34
Upper Tyndrum	d				19 13			21 52
Oban	d	12 56		16 11		18 11		
Connel Ferry	d	13 08		16 23		18 23		
Taynuilt	d	13 20		16 35		18 35		
Falls of Cruachan §	d	13x28		16x43		18x43		
Loch Awe	d	13 35		16 50		18 50		
Dalmally	d	13 41		16 55		18 55		
Tyndrum Lower	d	14 00		17 14		19 14		
Crianlarich	a	14 10		17 25	19 25	19 27		22 04
	d	14 12		17 31		19 33		22 05
Ardlui	d	14 28		17 47		19 53		22x26
Arrochar & Tarbet	d	14 43		18 02		20 08		22 44
Garelochhead	d	15 03		18 22		20 28		23 10
Helensburgh Upper	a	15 14		18 33		20 39		23 23
	d	15 15		18 34		20 40		23 24
Dumbarton Central 226	a	15 29		18 45		20 59		
Dalmuir 226	a	15 38		18 56		21 09		23 49
Westerton 226	a							23 54
Glasgow Queen St. [10] 226 ⇌	a	16 00		19 20		21 31		
Edinburgh 228	a	*17 07*		*20 21*		*22 51*		00 50

§ Open from 20 May until 30 September
A ⊼ from Fort William
B ⊼ from Crianlarich
C SX from 21 May until 15 June, from 18 June until 31 August, SX from 3 September until 28 September
b Previous night, stops on request

Table 227

Mondays to Saturdays
from 1 October

Mallaig, Fort William and Oban - Glasgow Queen Street

Network Diagram - see first Page of Table 227

		SR MO	SR MX	SR MX	SR SX	SR	SR	SR	SR	WR SX	SR SO	SR	SR	SR	SR SX
		▣	▣												▣
						◇	◇	◇	◇		◇	◇	◇	◇	
							A			B	C	A			
		🛏	🛏			⚲	⚲	⚲	⚲		⚲	⚲	⚲	⚲	🛏
Mallaig	d						06 03		10 10	14 09		16 05		18 15	
Morar	d						06 09		10 17			16 12		18 22	
Arisaig	d						06 19		10 26	14 39		16 21		18 31	
Beasdale	d						06x25		10x33			16x28		18x38	
Lochailort	d						06x34		10x42			16x37		18x47	
Glenfinnan	d						06 51		10 59	15 20		16 54		19 04	
Locheilside	d						07x01		11x09			17x03		19x13	
Loch Eil Outward Bound	d						07 07		11 15	15 40		17 10		19 20	
Corpach	d						07 13		11 21			17 16		19 26	
Banavie	d						07 17		11 25			17 20		19 30	
Fort William	a						07 25		11 32	16 03		17 28		19 37	
	d	19p00	19p50				07 42		11 40			17 37			19 50
Spean Bridge	d	19p20	20p10				07 55		11 55			17 51			20 10
Roy Bridge	d	19b27	20b17				08 02		12 02			17 57			20x17
Tulloch	d	19p40	20p30				08 13		12 14			18 09			20 30
Corrour	d	20b01	20b51				08 30		12 31			18 25			20x51
Rannoch	d	20p15	21p06				08 43		12 42			18 37			21 06
Bridge of Orchy	d	20p47	21p34				09 03		13 03			18 57			21 34
Upper Tyndrum	d	21p05	21p52				09 19		13 19			19 13			21 52
Oban	d					08 11		12 11			16 11		18 11		
Connel Ferry	d					08 23		12 23			16 23		18 23		
Taynuilt	d					08 35		12 35			16 35		18 35		
Falls of Cruachan §	d														
Loch Awe	d					08 50		12 50			16 50		18 50		
Dalmally	d					08 55		12 55			16 55		18 55		
Tyndrum Lower	d					09 14		13 14			17 14		19 14		
Crianlarich	a	21p16	22p04			09 29	09 30	13 29	13 30		17 25	19 25	19 27		22 04
	d	21p18	22p05			09 36		13 36			17 31	19 33			22 05
Ardlui	d	21b39	22b26			09 52		13 52			17 47	19 53			22x26
Arrochar & Tarbet	d	21p57	22p44		07 10	10 07		14 07			18 02	20 08			22 44
Garelochhead	d	22p23	23p10		07 30	10 32		14 27			18 22	20 28			23 10
Helensburgh Upper	a	22p35	23p23		07 41	10 42		14 38			18 33	20 39			23 23
	d	22p37	23p24		07 42	10 44		14 39			18 34	20 40			23 24
Dumbarton Central 226	a				07 56	10 59		14 51			18 45	20 59			
Dalmuir 226	a	23p02	23p49			11 08		15 03			18 56	21 09			23 49
Westerton 226	a	23p11	23p54	00 05											23 54
Glasgow Queen St. 10 226 ⛴	a			00 20	08 37	11 30		15 30			19 20	21 31			
Edinburgh 228	a	00 15	00 50		*09 52*	*12 36*		*16 35*			*20 21*	*22 51*			00 50

§ Open from 20 May until 30 September
A ⚲ from Fort William
B from 1 October until 26 October
C from 6 October until 27 October
b Previous night, stops on request

Table 227

Sundays
until 30 September

Mallaig, Fort William and Oban - Glasgow Queen Street

Network Diagram - see first Page of Table 227

		SR	SR	WR	SR	SR	SR	SR	SR	SR	SR
									▣		
		◇	◇		◇	◇	◇	◇		◇	
				A		A					
		⚲	⚲		⚲		⚲	⚲	🛏	⚲	
Mallaig	d		10 10	14 10			16 05			18 15	
Morar	d		10 17				16 12			18 22	
Arisaig	d		10 26	14 39			16 21			18 31	
Beasdale	d		10x33				16x28			18x38	
Lochailort	d		10x42				16x37			18x47	
Glenfinnan	d		10 59	15 20			16 54			19 04	
Locheilside	d		11x09				17x03			19x13	
Loch Eil Outward Bound	d		11 15	15 40			17 10			19 20	
Corpach	d		11 21				17 16			19 26	
Banavie	d		11 25				17 20			19 30	
Fort William	a		11 32	16 03			17 28			19 37	
	d		11 40				17 37		19 00		
Spean Bridge	d		11 55				17 51		19 20		
Roy Bridge	d		12 02				17 57		19x27		
Tulloch	d		12 14				18 09		19 40		
Corrour	d		12 31				18 25		20x01		
Rannoch	d		12 42				18 37		20 15		
Bridge of Orchy	d		13 03				18 57		20 47		
Upper Tyndrum	d		13 19				19 13		21 05		
Oban	d	12 11			16 11	17 11		18 11			
Connel Ferry	d	12 23			16 23	17 23		18 23			
Taynuilt	d	12 35			16 35	17 35		18 35			
Falls of Cruachan §	d	12x43			16x43	17x43		18x43			
Loch Awe	d	12 50			16 50	17 50		18 50			
Dalmally	d	12 55			16 55	17 55		18 55			
Tyndrum Lower	d	13 14			17 14	18 14		19 14			
Crianlarich	a	13 29	13 30		17 25	18 25	19 25	19 26	21 16		
	d	13 36			17 31	18 25	19 33		21 18		
Ardlui	d	13 52			17 47	18 41	19 53		21x39		
Arrochar & Tarbet	d	14 07			18 02	18 55	20 08		21 57		
Garelochhead	d	14 27			18 22	19 17	20 28		22 23		
Helensburgh Upper	a	14 38			18 33	19 27	20 39		22 35		
	d	14 39			18 34	19 29	20 40		22 37		
Dumbarton Central 226	a	14 53			18 45		20 53				
Dalmuir 226	a	15 05			18 56	19s55	21 03		23 02		
Westerton 226	a								23 11		23 28
Glasgow Queen St. 10 226 ⛴	a	15 31			19 15		21 19				23 47
Edinburgh 228	a	*16 52*			*20 21*	21 09	*22 24*		00 15		

§ Open from 20 May until 30 September
A from 24 June until 26 August

Table 227

Sundays
from 7 October

Mallaig, Fort William and Oban - Glasgow Queen Street

Network Diagram - see first Page of Table 227

		SR	SR	SR	SR	SR	SR	SR
		◇ A	◇ A	◇	◇	B	◇ A	
Mallaig	d		10 10	16 05			18 15	
Morar	d		10 17	16 12			18 22	
Arisaig	d		10 26	16 21			18 31	
Beasdale	d		10x33	16x28			18x38	
Lochailort	d		10x42	16x37			18x47	
Glenfinnan	d		10 59	16 54			19 04	
Locheilside	d		11x09	17x03			19x13	
Loch Eil Outward Bound	d		11 15	17 10			19 20	
Corpach	d		11 21	17 16			19 26	
Banavie	d		11 25	17 20			19 30	
Fort William	a		11 32	17 28			19 37	
	d		11 40	17 37		19 00		
Spean Bridge	d		11 55	17 51		19 20		
Roy Bridge	d		12 02	17 57		19x27		
Tulloch	d		12 14	18 09		19 40		
Corrour	d		12 31	18 25		20x01		
Rannoch	d		12 42	18 37		20 15		
Bridge of Orchy	d		13 03	18 57		20 47		
Upper Tyndrum	d		13 19	19 13		21 05		
Oban	d	12 11			18 11			
Connel Ferry	d	12 23			18 23			
Taynuilt	d	12 35			18 35			
Falls of Cruachan §	d							
Loch Awe	d	12 50			18 50			
Dalmally	d	12 55			18 55			
Tyndrum Lower	d	13 14			19 14			
Crianlarich	a	13 29	13 30	19 25	19 26	21 16		
	d		13 36	19 33		21 18		
Ardlui	d		13 52	19 53		21x39		
Arrochar & Tarbet	d		14 07	20 08		21 57		
Garelochhead	d		14 27	20 28		22 23		
Helensburgh Upper	a		14 27	20 39		22 35		
	d		14 39	20 40		22 37		
Dumbarton Central 226	a		14 53	20 53				
Dalmuir 226	a		15 05	21 03		23 02		
Westerton 226	a					23 11		23 28
Glasgow Queen St. 226	a		15 31	21 19				23 47
Edinburgh 228	a		16 52	22 24		00 15		

§ Open from 20 May until 30 September

A from 7 October until 28 October

Table 227A

SHIPPING SERVICES

Mondays to Saturdays
until 20 October 2012

Mallaig - Armadale (Skye) and Small Isles

Operated by Caledonian MacBrayne Ltd.

		ThO	WO	MO	TO G		FO	SX A	SO	SO B	SX C	
Glasgow Queen St 227	d							08 21	08 21	08 21	09 03	12 21
Fort William 227	d	08 30	08 30	08 30	08 30	08 30	08 30	12 12	12 12	12 12	12 48	16 19
Mallaig 227	a	09 53	09 53	09 53	09 53	09 53	09 53	13 34	13 34	13 34	14 10	17 43
Mallaig	d	10 15	10 15	10 15	10 15	10 50	12 40	13 45	13 45	14 25	15 10	18 00
Armadale	a					11 20		14 15	14 15		15 40	18 30
Eigg	a	11 30		11 30	12 45					15 40		
Muck	a	12 30			11 55					16 25		
Rum	a		11 35	12 45			14 00			19 25		
Canna	a		12 45	13 55			15 10			18 15		

Sundays
until 14 October 2012

Glasgow Queen St 227	d		12 20
Fort William 227	d	12 12	16 19
Mallaig 227	a	13 34	17 43
Mallaig	d	14 40	18 00
Armadale	a	15 10	18 30
Eigg	a		
Muck	a		
Rum	a		
Canna	a		

Mondays to Saturdays
until 20 October 2012

			FO	SO E	ThO		TO F	WO		MO	FO
Canna	d			10 15				15 00		14 10	15 25
Rum	d			09 05				16 05		15 20	16 35
Muck	d		10 20	12 00	12 35		13 50				
Eigg	d		11 10	12 50	13 20		13 00			16 35	
Armadale	d	08 50				14 30			17 15		
Mallaig	a	09 20	12 25	14 05	14 35	15 00	15 30	17 25	17 45	17 50	17 55
Mallaig 227	d	10 10	16 05	16 05	16 05	16 05	16 05	18 15	18 15	18 15	18 15
Fort William 227	a	11 32	17 28	17 28	17 28	17 28	17 28	19 37	19 37	19 37	19 37
Glasgow Queen St 227	a	15 30	21 31	21 31	21 31	21 31	21 31	00a20	00b20	00a20	00a20

Sundays
until 14 October 2012

				D
Canna	d			
Rum	d			
Muck	d			
Eigg	d			
Armadale	d	09 30	15 20	16 50
Mallaig	a	10 00	15 50	17 20
Mallaig 227	d	10 10	16 05	18 15
Fort William 227	a	11 32	17 28	19 37
Glasgow Queen St 227	a	15 31	21 19	

A Until 18 May and from 1 October
B Sails via Canna.
C From 21 May until 28 September
D Until 23 September
E Sails from Rum.
F Sails from Eigg.
G Sails via Muck.
a Following day. Change at Fort William and Westerton. Reservations compulsory from Fort William.
b Tuesday to Saturday mornings only. Change at Fort William and Westerton. Reservations compulsory from Fort William.

For details of sailings from 21 October 2012, please telephone 08000 66 5000 or visit www.calmac.co.uk

Table 227B — SHIPPING SERVICES

Oban - Craignure (Mull), Lismore, Colonsay, Coll and Tiree

Operated by Caledonian MacBrayne Ltd

Mondays to Saturdays
until 20 October 2012

		WFO A	SO	MO	ThO B	SO	SX	SO	SX	TO	WO		SO	MFO	SX	FO
Glasgow Queen St 227	d	18a21	18a21	18a20	18a21	08 21	08 21	10 37	08 21	08 21	12 21	12 21	12 21	12 21	12 21	18 21
Oban 227	a	21a26	21a26	21a26	21a26	11 27	11 27	13 42	11 27	11 27	15 27	15 27	15 27	15 27	15 27	21 26
Oban	d	05 45	07 00	08 00	08 15	11 45	11 55	14 00	14 00	14 45	15 40	16 00	17 00	17 00	17 15	22 30
Craignure	a					12 31	12 41	14 46				16 46				23 16
Lismore	a															
Colonsay	a								14 50				17 50		18 05	
Coll	a	10 15	09 40	10 55	10 55						17 55			19 20		
Tiree	a	09 05	10 45	12 05	12 00					17 25 18 25						

Sundays
until 14 October 2012

			C	C		
Glasgow Queen St 227	d	18a21	09 55	09 55	12 20	12 20
Oban 227	a	21a26	13 05	13 05	15 27	15 27
Oban	d	09 00	14 00	15 00	16 00	17 30
Craignure	a		14 46		16 46	
Lismore	a					
Colonsay	a			15 50		
Coll	a	11 55				19 50
Tiree	a	13 00				

Mondays to Saturdays
until 20 October 2012

		ThSO	SO	TO D	TO E	SX F	SX G	SO	SX F	SX G	SO	WFO	WO	ThO	SO	SO	SX	SO	MO	
Tiree	d											09 20			11 15				12 25	
Coll	d											10 20			12 20				13 35	
Colonsay	d			07 50	07 50															
Lismore	d		09 00			10 00	10 00				12 00		11 45	11 55			15 00	15 15		
Craignure	d	06 45						10 30	10 55	10 55						15 00				17 00
Oban	a	07 31	09 50	10 10	10 10	10 50	10 50	11 16	11 41	11 41	12 50	13 00	14 10	14 15	15 00	15 46	15 50	16 05	16 30	17 46
Oban 227	d	08 11	12 11	12 11	12 56	12 11	12 56	12 11	12 11	12 56	16 11	18 11	18 11	18 11	16 11	16 11	18 11	18 11	18 11	18 11
Glasgow Queen St 227	a	11 30	15 30	15 30	16 00	15 30	16 00	15 30	15 30	16 00	19 20	21 31	21 31	21 31	19 20	19 20	21 31	21 31	21 31	21 31

Sundays
until 14 October 2012

			C	C	H	J		
Tiree	d						13 15	
Coll	d						14 20	
Colonsay	d							
Lismore	d		12 00		16 00	16 00		
Craignure	d	10 55		15 00				17 00
Oban	a	11 41	12 50	15 46	16 50	16 50	17 15	17 46
Oban 227	d	12 11	16 11	16 11	17b11	18 11	18 11	18 11
Glasgow Queen St 227	a	15 31	19 15	19 15	20c23	21 19	21 19	21 19

A Sails via Tiree
B Sails to Barra arr. 1500
C Until 30 September
D 15 May and from 2 October only
E From 22 May until 25 September
F Until 18 May and from 1 October
G From 21 May until 28 September
H From 24 June until 26 August
J Until 17 June and from 2 September
a Previous night
b To Edinburgh arr. 2109
c Change at Dalmuir. Arrive Glasgow Central low level platforms

For details of sailings from 21 October 2012, please telephone 08000 66 5000 or visit www.calmac.co.uk

Table 227C — SHIPPING SERVICE

Oban - Castlebay (Barra) and Lochboisdale (South Uist)

Operated by Caledonian MacBrayne Ltd

Mondays to Saturdays
Until 20 October 2012

		WFO	TO A	MSO	ThO A
Glasgow Queen St 227	d	08 21	08 21	12 21	12 21
Oban 227	a	11 27	11 27	15 27	15 27
Oban	d	13 40	13 40	15 40	15 40
Castlebay	a	18 30	20 40	20 30	22 40
Lochboisdale	a		18 50		20 50

Sundays
Until 14 October 2012

Glasgow Queen St 227	d	12 20
Oban 227	a	15 27
Oban	d	15 40
Castlebay	a	20 30
Lochboisdale	a	22 20

Mondays to Saturdays
Until 20 October 2012

		MO	TO	WFO B
Lochboisdale	d	07 30		08 55
Castlebay	d	09 20	09 20	07 00
Oban	a	14 10	14 10	14 05
Oban 227	d	18 11	18 11	18 11
Glasgow Queen St 227	a	21 31	21 31	21 31

Sundays
Until 14 October 2012

		C	D
Lochboisdale	d		
Castlebay	d	09 20	09 20
Oban	a	14 10	14 10
Oban 227	d	16 11	18 11
Glasgow Queen St 227	a	19 15	21 19

A Sails via Lochboisdale
B Sails from Castlebay
C Until 30 September
D 7 and 14 October only

For details of sailings from 21 October 2012, please telephone 08000 66 5000 or visit www.calmac.co.uk

Edinburgh - Falkirk High - Glasgow Queen Street

Network Diagram - see first page of Table 225

Mondays to Saturdays

Miles	Station			SR MX	SR MO	SR MX	SR	SR	SR SX	SR	SR	SR	SR SX	SR SX	SR SO	SR SX	SR	SR	SR	SR	SR	SR	SR	SR
				■	■	■	■	■	■	■	■	■		■	■		■	■	■	■	■	■	■	■
					A					✠	✠	✠		✠	✠		✠	✠	✠	✠	✠	✠	✠	✠
0	Edinburgh	225,230,242	d	23p00	23p30	23p30	05 55	06 30	06 45	07 00	07 15	07 30		07 45	07 45		08 00	08 15	08 30	08 45	09 00	09 15	09 30	09 45
1¼	Haymarket	225,230,242	d	23p04	23p34	23p34	05 59	06 34	06 49	07 04	07 19	07 34		07 49	07 49		08 04	08 19	08 34	08 49	09 04	09 19	09 34	09 49
17½	Linlithgow	230	d	23p18	23p48	23p48	06 13	06 48	07 04		07 33	07 48	07 59	08 04	08 04			08 33		09 03		09 33		10 03
22¼	Polmont	230	d	23p24	23p54	23p54	06 19	06 55		07 21		07 55					08 22	08 39		09 09		09 39		10 09
25½	Falkirk High		d	23p29	23p59	23p59	06 24	07 00	07 13	07 26	07 42	08 00	08b11	08 13	08 13		08 26	08 44	08 54	09 14	09 24	09 44	09 54	10 14
35¾	Croy	230	a	23p39	00 09	00 09	06 34	07 10	07 23		07 52	08 10				←	08 36		09 03		09 33		10 03	
41	Lenzie	230	a	23p44		00 14							08 32	08 25	08 25	08 32								
44	Bishopbriggs	230	a	23p50									→		08 29	08 36								
47¼	Glasgow Queen Street	230	a	00 01	00 25	00 26	06 49	07 25	07 38	07 50	08 07	08 25		08 40	08 40	08 48	08 55	09 07	09 19	09 36	09 50	10 06	10 19	10 36

Station			SR	SR	SR	SR	SR	SR	SR	SR	SR	SR SX	SR SO	SR	SR	SR	SR	SR	SR	SR	SR	SR	SR	SR
			■	■	■	■	■	■	■	■	■	■	■	■	■	■	■	■	■	■	■	■	■	■
			✠	✠	✠	✠	✠	✠	✠	✠	✠	✠	✠	✠	✠	✠	✠	✠	✠	✠	✠	✠	✠	✠
Edinburgh	225,230,242	d	10 00	10 15	10 30	10 45	11 00	11 15	11 30	11 45	12 00	12 15	12 15	12 30	12 45	13 00	13 15	13 30	13 45	14 00	14 15	14 30	14 45	15 00
Haymarket	225,230,242	d	10 04	10 19	10 34	10 49	11 04	11 19	11 34	11 49	12 04	12 19	12 19	12 34	12 49	13 04	13 19	13 34	13 49	14 04	14 19	14 34	14 49	15 04
Linlithgow	230	d		10 33		11 03		11 33		12 03		12 33	12 33		13 03		13 33		14 03		14 33		15 03	
Polmont	230	d		10 39		11 09		11 39		12 09		12 39	12 39		13 09		13 39		14 09		14 39		15 09	
Falkirk High		d	10 24	10 44	10 54	11 14	11 24	11 44	11 54	12 14	12 25	12 44	12 44	12 54	13 14	13 24	13 44	13 54	14 14	14 24	14 44	14 54	15 14	15 24
Croy	230	a	10 33		11 03		11 33		12 03		12 34			13 03		13 33		14 03		14 33		15 03		15 33
Lenzie	230	a																						
Bishopbriggs	230	a																						
Glasgow Queen Street	230	a	10 49	11 06	11 19	11 37	11 50	12 06	12 20	12 37	12 49	13 06	13 07	13 19	13 36	13 51	14 06	14 19	14 36	14 48	15 07	15 22	15 37	15 51

Station			SR	SR	SR	SR	SR	SR	SR	SR	SR	SR	SR	SR	SR	SR	SR	SR	SR	SR	SR	SR
			■	■	■	■	■	■	■	■	■	■	■	■	■	■	■	■	■	■	■	■
			✠	✠	✠	✠	✠	✠	✠	✠	✠	✠	✠	✠	✠	✠	✠	✠	✠			
Edinburgh	225,230,242	d	15 15	15 30	15 45	16 00	16 15	16 30	16 45	17 00	17 15	17 30	17 45	18 00	18 15	18 30	18 45	19 00	19 15	19 30	20 00	20 30
Haymarket	225,230,242	d	15 19	15 34	15 49	16 04	16 19	16 34	16 49	17 04	17 19	17 34	17 49	18 04	18 19	18 34	18 49	19 04	19 19	19 34	20 04	20 34
Linlithgow	230	d	15 34		16 04		16 33		17 06		17 33		18 04		18 33		19 03		19 33	19 48	20 18	20 48
Polmont	230	d	15 40		16 10		16 39		17 13		17 39		18 09		18 39		19 09		19 39		20 24	
Falkirk High		d	15 45	15 54	16 14	16 24	16 44	16 53	17 18	17 24	17 44	17 55	18 14	18 25	18 44	18 55	19 14	19 25	19 44	19 57	20 29	20 57
Croy	230	a		16 03		16 33		17 02		17 34		18 05		18 34		19 05		19 34		20 07		21 07
Lenzie	230	a										18 11										
Bishopbriggs	230	a																				
Glasgow Queen Street	230	a	16 07	16 19	16 36	16 51	17 07	17 21	17 40	17 51	18 06	18 23	18 37	18 50	19 08	19 23	19 36	19 49	20 07	20 22	20 51	21 21

Station			SR	SR	SR	SR	SR	SR
			■	■	■	■	■	■
Edinburgh	225,230,242	d	21 00	21 30	22 00	22 30	23 00	23 30
Haymarket	225,230,242	d	21 04	21 34	22 04	22 34	23 04	23 34
Linlithgow	230	d	21 19	21 48	22 18	22 48	23 18	23 48
Polmont	230	d	21 25		22 24		23 24	23 54
Falkirk High		d	21 30	21 57	22 29	22 57	23 29	23 59
Croy	230	a		22 07		23 07	23 39	00 09
Lenzie	230	a					23 44	00 14
Bishopbriggs	230	a					23 50	
Glasgow Queen Street	230	a	21 51	22 23	22 50	23 22	00 01	00 26

Sundays

Station			SR	SR	SR	SR	SR	SR	SR	SR	SR	SR	SR	SR	SR	SR	SR	SR	SR	SR	SR	SR	SR	SR
			■	■	■	■	■	■	■	■	■	■	■	■	■	■	■	■	■	■	■	■	■	■
					✠		✠	✠	✠	✠	✠	✠	✠		✠	✠	✠	✠	✠		✠	✠	✠	✠
Edinburgh	225,230,242	d	23p00	23p30	08 00	09 00	10 00	11 00	12 00	12 30	13 00	13 30	14 00	14 30	15 00	15 30	16 00	16 30	17 00	17 30	18 00	18 30	19 00	19 30
Haymarket	225,230,242	d	23p04	23p34	08 04	09 04	10 04	11 04	12 04	12 33	13 04	13 34	14 04	14 34	15 04	15 34	16 04	16 34	17 04	17 34	18 04	18 34	19 04	19 34
Linlithgow	230	d	23p18	23p48	08 18	09 18	10 18	11 18	12 18	12 48	13 18	13 48	14 18	14 48	15 18	15 48	16 18	16 48	17 18	17 48	18 18	18 48	19 18	19 48
Polmont	230	d	23p24	23p54	08 24	09 24	10 24	11 24	12 24		13 24		14 24		15 24		16 24		17 24		18 24		19 24	
Falkirk High		d	23p29	23p59	08 29	09 29	10 29	11 29	12 29	12 57	13 29	13 57	14 29	14 57	15 29	15 57	16 29	16 57	17 29	17 57	18 29	18 57	19 29	19 57
Croy	230	a	23p39	00 09	08 39	09 39	10 39	11 39	12 39	13 07		14 07		15 07		16 07		17 07		18 07		19 07		20 07
Lenzie	230	a	23p44	00 14																				
Bishopbriggs	230	a	23p50																					
Glasgow Queen Street	230	a	00 01	00 26	08 59	10 00	11 01	11 56	12 54	13 23	13 51	14 23	14 51	15 22	15 51	16 22	16 51	17 22	17 52	18 22	18 51	19 22	19 51	20 22

Station			SR	SR	SR	SR	SR	SR
			■	■	■	■	■	■
Edinburgh	225,230,242	d	20 00	20 30	21 00	22 00	23 00	23 30
Haymarket	225,230,242	d	20 04	20 34	21 04	22 04	23 04	23 34
Linlithgow	230	d	20 18	20 48	21 18	22 18	23 18	23 48
Polmont	230	d	20 24		21 24	22 24	23 24	23 54
Falkirk High		d	20 29	20 57	21 29	22 29	23 29	23 59
Croy	230	a		21 07	21 39	22 39	23 39	00 09
Lenzie	230	a						
Bishopbriggs	230	a						
Glasgow Queen Street	230	a	20 51	21 22	21 55	22 55	23 55	00 25

A from 21 May
b Falkirk Grahamston
c Falkirk Grahamston, arrival time

Glasgow Queen Street - Falkirk High - Edinburgh

Network Diagram - see first page of Table 225

Mondays to Saturdays

Miles	Station			SR MO	SR MX	SR	SR SX	SR SO	SR SX	SR	SR	SR	SR	SR	SR	SR	SR	SR	SR	SR	SR SX	SR SO	SR	SR
				■	■	■	■	■	■	■	■	■	■	■	■	■	■	■	■	■	■	■	■	■
				A						✠	✠	✠		✠	✠	✠	✠	✠	✠	✠	✠		✠	✠
0	Glasgow Queen Street	230	d	23p30	23p30	06 00	06 30	06 30	06 45	07 00	07 15	07 30	07 45	08 00	08 15	08 30	08 45	09 00	09 15	09 30	09 45	09 45	10 00	10 15
3¼	Bishopbriggs	230	d																					
6¾	Lenzie	230	d				06 38	06 38		07 08														
11½	Croy	230	d	23p42	23p42			06 43	06 57			07 41		08 11		08 42		09 12		09 42			10 12	
21¾	Falkirk High		d	23p52	23p52	06 18	06 51	06 51	07 07	07 21	07 33	07 51	08 04	08 21	08 33	08 52	09 03	09 22	09 33	09 52	10 03	10 03	10 22	10 33
25	Polmont	230	a	23p56	23p56	06 23	06 56	06 56		07 26	07 38		08 09	08 26			09 08		09 38		10 08	10 08		10 38
29¾	Linlithgow	230	a	00 03	00 03	06 29	07 02	07 02	07 14	07 32	07 44	07 59	08 15		08 43		09 14		09 43		10 14	10 14		10 44
46	Haymarket	225,230,242	a	00s19	00s20	06s45	07s19	07s19	07s31	07s49	08s01	08s17	08s31	08s45	09s01	09s14	09s30	09s45	10s02	10s12	10s30	10s30	10s44	11s00
47¼	Edinburgh	225,230,242	a	00 24	00 25	06 50	07 25	07 25	07 37	07 55	08 06	08 25	08 37	08 52	09 07	09 19	09 37	09 52	10 07	10 17	10 37	10 37	10 49	11 05

Station			SR	SR	SR	SR	SR	SR	SR	SR	SR	SR	SR	SR	SR	SR	SR	SR	SR	SR	SR	SR	SR	SR
			■	■	■	■	■	■	■	■	■	■	■	■	■	■	■	■	■	■	■	■	■	■
			✠	✠	✠	✠	✠	✠	✠	✠	✠	✠	✠	✠	✠	✠	✠	✠	✠	✠	✠	✠	✠	✠
Glasgow Queen Street	230	d	10 30	10 45	11 00	11 15	11 30	11 45	12 00	12 15	12 30	12 45	13 00	13 15	13 30	13 45	14 00	14 15	14 30	14 45	15 00	15 15	15 30	15 45
Bishopbriggs	230	d																						
Lenzie	230	d																						
Croy	230	d	10 42		11 12		11 42		12 12		12 42		13 12		13 42		14 12		14 42		15 12		15 42	
Falkirk High		d	10 52	11 03	11 22	11 33	11 52	12 03	12 22	12 33	12 52	13 03	13 22	13 33	13 52	14 03	14 22	14 33	14 52	15 03	15 22	15 33	15 52	16 03
Polmont	230	a		11 08		11 38		12 07		12 38		13 08		13 38		14 08		14 38		15 08		15 38		16 08
Linlithgow	230	a		11 14		11 44		12 14		12 44		13 14		13 44		14 14		14 44		15 14		15 44		16 14
Haymarket	225,230,242	a	11s14	11s30	11s45	12s00	12s12	12s30	12s45	13s00	13s14	13s30	13s45	14s00	14s11	14s30	14s45	15s00	15s13	15s30	15s42	16s00	16s12	16s30
Edinburgh	225,230,242	a	11 20	11 35	11 50	12 07	12 19	12 36	12 52	13 07	13 19	13 35	13 51	14 05	14 17	14 37	14 50	15 05	15 19	15 37	15 47	16 06	16 19	16 35

Station			SR	SR	SR SO	SR SX	SR SO	SR SX	SR	SR	SR	SR	SR	SR	SR	SR	SR SX	SR SO	SR	SR	SR	SR	SR	SR
			■	■	■	■	■	■	■	■	■		■	■	■	■	■	■	■	■	■	■	■	■
			✠	✠	✠	✠		✠	✠	✠	✠		✠	✠	✠	✠	✠	✠	✠	✠				
Glasgow Queen Street	230	d	16 00	16 15	16 30	16 30	16 45	16 45	17 00	17 15	17 30	17 33	17 45	18 00	18 15	18 30	18 45	18 45	19 00	19 15	19 30	20 00	20 30	21 00
Bishopbriggs	230	d										17 40												
Lenzie	230	d										17 45												
Croy	230	d	16 12		16 42	16 42			17 12		17 42			18 12		18 42			19 12			20 12		21 12
Falkirk High		d	16 22	16 33	16 52	16 52	17 03	17 03	17 22	17 33	17 52		18 03	18 22	18 33	18 52	19 03	19 03	19 22	19 33	19 48	20 22	20 48	21 22
Polmont	230	a		16 38			17 08	17 08	17 26		17 56		18 08		18 38		19 08	19 08		19 38	19 53		20 53	
Linlithgow	230	a		16 43			17 14	17 14		17 41	18 03		18 14		18 44		19 14	19 14		19 44	19 59	20 29	20 59	21 29
Haymarket	225,230,242	a	16s43	17s01	17s13	17s16	17s34	17s34	17s45	18s02	18s19		18s33	18s45	19s01	19s13	19s30	19s33	19s46	20s00	20s16	20s45	21s15	21s45
Edinburgh	225,230,242	a	16 49	17 07	17 19	17 22	17 40	17 40	17 52	18 07	18 24		18 40	18 50	19 07	19 19	19 36	19 39	19 51	20 06	20 21	20 51	21 20	21 50

Station			SR	SR	SR	SR	SR
			■	■	■	■	■
Glasgow Queen Street	230	d	21 30	22 00	22 30	23 00	23 30
Bishopbriggs	230	d					
Lenzie	230	d					
Croy	230	d		22 12		23 12	23 42
Falkirk High		d	21 48	22 22	22 48	23 22	23 52
Polmont	230	a	21 53		22 53	23 26	23 56
Linlithgow	230	a	21 59	22 29	22 59	23 33	00 03
Haymarket	225,230,242	a	22s18	22s46	23s15	23s49	00s20
Edinburgh	225,230,242	a	22 23	22 51	23 20	23 55	00 25

Sundays

Station			SR	SR	SR	SR	SR	SR	SR	SR	SR	SR	SR	SR	SR	SR	SR	SR	SR	SR	SR	SR	SR	SR
			■	■	■	■	■	■	■	■	■	■	■	■	■	■	■	■	■	■	■	■	■	■
					✠	✠	✠	✠	✠	✠		✠	✠			✠	✠	✠	✠	✠	✠	✠	✠	
Glasgow Queen Street	230	d	23p30	07 50	08 30	09 30	10 30	11 30	12 30	13 00	13 30	14 00	14 30	15 00	15 30	16 00	16 30	17 00	17 30	18 00	18 30	19 00	19 30	20 00
Bishopbriggs	230	d																						
Lenzie	230	d																						
Croy	230	d	23p42	08 02	08 42	09 42	10 42	11 42	12 42	13 12		14 12		15 12		16 12		17 12		18 12		19 12		20 12
Falkirk High		d	23p52	08 12	08 52	09 52	10 52	11 52	12 52	13 22	13 48	14 22	14 48	15 22	15 48	16 22	16 48	17 22	17 48	18 22	18 48	19 22	19 48	20 22
Polmont	230	a	23p56	08 16	08 56	09 56	10 56	11 56	12 56		13 53		14 53		15 53		16 53		17 53		18 53		19 53	
Linlithgow	230	a	00 03	08 23	09 03	10 03	11 03	12 03	13 02	13 29	13 59	14 29	14 59	15 29	15 59	16 29	16 58	17 29	17 58	18 29	18 59	19 29	19 59	20 29
Haymarket	225,230,242	a	00s20	08 38	09s24	10s23	11s19	12s20	13s21	13s46	14s17	14s47	15s15	15 46	16s18	16s47	17s15	17 47	18s17	18s47	19s16	19s47	20s16	20s46
Edinburgh	225,230,242	a	00 25	08 49	09 29	10 28	11 24	12 25	13 26	13 51	14 22	14 52	15 20	15 51	16 23	16 52	17 20	17 52	18 22	18 52	19 21	19 52	20 21	20 51

Station			SR	SR	SR	SR	SR
			■	■	■	■	■
Glasgow Queen Street	230	d	20 30	21 00	21 30	22 30	23 30
Bishopbriggs	230	d					
Lenzie	230	d					
Croy	230	d		21 12	21 42	22 42	23 42
Falkirk High		d	20 48	21 22	21 52	22 52	23 52
Polmont	230	a	20 53		21 56	22 56	23 56
Linlithgow	230	a	20 59	21 29	22 03	23 03	00 03
Haymarket	225,230,242	a	21s17	21s46	22s19	23s19	00s19
Edinburgh	225,230,242	a	21 22	21 53	22 24	23 24	00 24

A from 21 May
B from 24 June until 26 August

Table 229

Mondays to Saturdays

Edinburgh and Glasgow Queen Street - Perth, Inverness, Dundee, Aberdeen, Dyce and Inverurie

Network Diagram - see first page of Table 225

Miles	Miles	Miles	Miles	Miles				SR MX	SR MX	SR MX	SR MO	SR MX	SR MX	SR	SR	SR	SR	XC	SR	SR	SR
								◇■ A ⚲	◇■	◇■	◇■ B ⚲			C	◇■	C	■	◇■	◇■	◇■ A ⚲	
—	0	—	0	0	**Edinburgh**	242	d	19p28	21p40			22p39	23p09						05 30		06 29
—	1¼	—	1¼	1¼	Haymarket	242	d	19p31	21p44			22p43	23p13						05 33		06 33
—	13¾	—	13¾	—	Inverkeithing	242	d					23p02	23p32			04s58			05 46		06 47
—	26	—	26	—	Kirkcaldy	242	d		22p12			23p24	23p54			05s18			06 02		07 03
—	33¼	—	33¼	—	Markinch		d					23p33	00 03						06 11		07 12
—	39¼	—	39¼	—	Ladybank		d					23p40	00 10						06 19		07 19
—	42¼	—	—	—	Springfield		d														
—	44½	—	—	—	Cupar		d	20p21					00 17						06 25		
—	—	—	—	—	Leuchars		a	20p28	22p34				00 23			05s47			06 32		
—	—	—	—	—	St Andrews Bus Station		a												07c04		
—	—	—	—	—	St Andrews Bus Station		d												06d00		
—	51	—	—	—	Leuchars		d	20p28	22p35				00 24						06 32		
0	—	0	—	—	**Glasgow Queen St.**	230	d			21p42	21p45									05 56	
21	—	21	—	28¼	Larbert	230	d													06 16	
29	—	29	—	36½	Stirling	230	d			22p08	22p11			04s55						06 25	
—	—	—	—	—	Bridge of Allan	230	d														
34½	—	34½	—	42	Dunblane	230	d				22p17			05s04						06 31	
46¾	—	46¾	—	54¼	Gleneagles		d				22p28			05s19						06 43	
62½	—	62½	57	70¼	**Perth**		a			22p37	22p46	00 07		05s39						06 59	07 47
—	—	—	—	—			d			22p38	22p46						06 00			07 00	07 47
79¼	—	—	—	—	Invergowrie		d														08 05
83¾	59¼	—	—	—	**Dundee**		a	20p40	22p48	23p02	23p09		00 39			06s08	06 23		06 45	07 22	08 13
—	—	—	—	—			d	20p41	22p49	23p03	23p09						06 24	06 40	06 51	07 23	
87¼	63¼	—	—	—	Broughty Ferry		d			23p10							06 31				
89	65	—	—	—	Balmossie		d														
89¾	65¾	—	—	—	Monifieth		d														
92¾	68¾	—	—	—	Barry Links		d														
93½	69½	—	—	—	Golf Street		d														
94	70	—	—	—	Carnoustie		d			23p17	23p21					06s23	06 39		07 03	07 35	
100¼	76¼	—	—	—	Arbroath		d	20p58	23p05	23p24	23p26					06s31	06 46	06 58	07 10	07 42	
114	90	—	—	—	Montrose		d	21p12	23p19	23p39	23p41				06 25	06s48	07 01	07 13	07 23	07 58	
124	100	—	—	—	Laurencekirk		d			23p49					06 35				07 35	08 09	
138¼	114¼	—	—	—	Stonehaven		d	21p34	23p40	00 03	00 02				06 49	07s14	07 23	07 34	07 48	08 22	
146½	122½	—	—	—	Portlethen		d		23p49						06 58				07 59	08 31	
154½	130½	—	—	—	**Aberdeen**		a	21p53	00 03	00 22	00 25				07 13	07 36	07 44	07 55	08 13	08 44	
—	—	—	—	—			d	21p55							07 14		07 50			08 50	
160¾	136¾	—	—	—	Dyce	240	a	22p04							07 24		08 00			08 59	
171½	147½	—	—	—	**Inverurie**	240	a	22p16							07 44		08 17				
—	—	78	72½	86¼	Dunkeld & Birnam		d							06s00							
—	—	91	85½	99¼	Pitlochry		d							06s16							
—	—	97¾	92¼	106	Blair Atholl		d							06s28							
—	—	121	116¼	130¼	Dalwhinnie		d							07s00							
—	—	131¼	126¾	140½	Newtonmore		d							07s12							
—	—	134	129½	143¼	Kingussie		d							07s19							
—	—	145¾	141¼	155	Aviemore		d							07s41							
—	—	152¾	148¼	162	Carrbridge		d							07s54							
—	—	180	175	188¾	**Inverness**		a	00 05						08s38	09 40						

A ⚲ to Aberdeen
B From 21 May
C not 14 May. From London Euston
c arrives 0713 SO
d arrives 0610 SO

Table 229

Mondays to Saturdays

Edinburgh and Glasgow Queen Street - Perth, Inverness, Dundee, Aberdeen, Dyce and Inverurie

Network Diagram - see first page of Table 225

			SR	SR	SR	SR	SR	SR	SR	SR	SR	SR	SR	SR SX	SR SO	SR	SR SO	SR SX	SR	SR	SR	GR
				◇■	◇■ A ⚲	◇■ ⚲		■	◇■ A ⚲	■ ⚲	◇■ ⚲	◇■ ⚲	■	◇■ ⚲	◇■ ⚲	⚲	◇■ ⚲	◇■ ⚲		■	◇■ ⚲	■ C ⚲
Edinburgh	242	d	07 00		07 28		07 34	08 00	08 28			08 34	09 00	09 28	09 28				09 35	10 00		10 27
Haymarket	242	d	07 04		07 31		07 40	08 04	08 32			08 39	09 04	09 33	09 33				09 40	10 03		10 32
Inverkeithing	242	d	07 20				07 53	08 18					09 17						09 54	10 19		10 47
Kirkcaldy	242	d	07 36		08 02		08 09	08 34				09 08	09 33						10 10	10 35		11 04
Markinch		d	07 45				08 19	08 43				09 17	09 42						10 19	10 44		
Ladybank		d	07 53					08 51					09 50						10 28	10 51		
Springfield		d						08 56														
Cupar		d	07 59					09 00					09 56							10 58		
Leuchars		a	08 06		08 25			09 07	09 23				10 03		10 23					11 04		11 28
St Andrews Bus Station		a	08e24		08g45			09 30	09 45				10 30		10 45					11 30		11 45
St Andrews Bus Station		d	07f28		07h55			08i40	08 55				09 40		09 55					10 40		11 10
Leuchars		d	08 06		08 25			09 07	09 23				10 03		10 23					11 05		11 29
Glasgow Queen St.	230	d		07 06		07 41				08 06	08 41					09 08	09 41	09 41			10 10	
Larbert	230	d																				
Stirling	230	d		07 33		08u09				08 36	09 07					09 34	10 07	10 07			10 35	
Bridge of Allan	230	d								08 40											10 41	
Dunblane	230	d		07 39		08 15				08 44						09 41					10 44	
Gleneagles		d								08 56						09 53					10 56	
Perth		a		08 04		08 41	08 53			09 13	09 38	09 50				10 09	10 36	10 36	10 54		11 14	
		d		08 04		08 42				09 16	09 38	09 51				10 15	10 38	10 38			11 15	
Invergowrie		d																				
Dundee		a	08 21		08 40	09 03		09 22	09 36	09 41	10 02		10 18	10 32	10 32	10 39	10 59	10 59		11 20		11 43
		d			08 41	09 04			09 37		10 03			10 33	10 33		11 00	11 00				11 43
Broughty Ferry		d							09 45								11 07	11 07				
Balmossie		d																				
Monifieth		d																				
Barry Links		d																				
Golf Street		d																				
Carnoustie		d				09 16											11 15	11 15				
Arbroath		d			08 57	09 23			09 56		10 19			10 50	10 50		11 22	11 22				12 01
Montrose		d			09 13	09 38					10 39			11 04	11 04		11 36	11 36				12 17
Laurencekirk		d							10 18								11 48	11 48				
Stonehaven		d			09 34				10 31		11 01			11 26	11 26		12 02	12 02				12 40
Portlethen		d									11 10											
Aberdeen		a			09 52	10 16			10 54		11 25			11 48	11 48		12 21	12 33				13 05
		d			10 00				11 03													
Dyce	240	a			10 08				11 12													
Inverurie	240	a			10 22				11 27													
Dunkeld & Birnam		d		08 32																	11 40	
Pitlochry		d		08 45								10 25									11 53	
Blair Atholl		d		08 55																		
Dalwhinnie		d		09 20																		
Newtonmore		d		09 30																		
Kingussie		d		09 36								11 10									12 37	
Aviemore		d		09 48								11 25									12 48	
Carrbridge		d		09 57																		
Inverness		a		10 28								12 03									13 25	

A ⚲ to Aberdeen
C From Leeds
e arrives 0830 SO
f arrives 0740 SX
g arrives 0900 SO
h arrives 0759 SO
i arrives 0830 SO

Edinburgh and Glasgow Queen Street - Perth, Inverness, Dundee, Aberdeen, Dyce and Inverurie

Network Diagram - see first page of Table 225

			SR	SR	SR	SR	SR	SR	SR	SR	SR	SR	SR	SR	SR	SR	SR	SR	GR	SR	SR	SR	SR	SR
			◇1 ⌶	◇1 ⌶	1	◇1 ⌶	◇1 ⌶	1 ⌶	1	◇1 ⌶	◇1 A ⌶	◇1 ⌶		1	◇1 A ⌶	◇1 ⌶	◇1 ⌶	1	1 B 🛏⌶	◇1 ⌶		1	◇1 ⌶	◇1 A ⌶
Edinburgh 10	242	d		10 35	11 00	11 28		11 35	12 00		12 28		12 35	13 00	13 28		13 35	14 00	14 27		14 35	15 00		15 28
Haymarket	242	d		10u40	11 04	11 32		11 40	12 04		12 32		12 40	13 04	13 32		13u40	14 04	14 32		14 40	15 04		15 32
Inverkeithing	242	d		10u53	11 17				12 18				12 54	13 17				14 18	14 47		14 53	15 18		
Kirkcaldy	242	d		11u10	11 33			12 09	12 34				13 10	13 33			14u08	14 34	15 04		15 09	15 34		
Markinch		d		11 20	11 42			12 18	12 43				13 19	13 42			14 17	14 43			15 19	15 43		
Ladybank		d		11 27	11 50				12 51					13 50				14 51			15 27	15 53		
Springfield		d																						
Cupar		d			11 56				12 57					13 56				14 57				15 59		
Leuchars 5		a			12 03	12 25			13 04		13 23			14 03	14 23			15 04	15 28			16 06		16 24
St Andrews Bus Station	bus	a			12 30	12 45			13 30		13 45			14 30	14 30			14 30	15 30			16 30		16 45
St Andrews Bus Station	bus	d			11 40	12 10			12 40		12 55			13 40	13 40			13 40	14 40			15c40		15 55
Leuchars 3		d			12 03	12 26			13 04		13 23			14 03	14 23			15 04	15 28			16 06		16 25
Glasgow Queen St. 10	230	d	10 41				11 41			12 10		12 41				13 41				14 41			15 10	
Larbert	230	d																						
Stirling	230	d	11 08				12 07			12 35		13 07				14 07				15 07			15 36	
Bridge of Allan	230	d								12 41													15 41	
Dunblane	230	d								12 44													15 45	
Gleneagles		d																						
Perth		a	11 38	11 54			12 36	12 53		13 12		13 35	13 53			14 36	14 54			15 36	15 56		16 12	
		d	11 39	11 56			12 37			13 12		13 36				14 37	14 55			15 36			16 13	
Invergowrie		d																						
Dundee		a	12 01		12 18	12 38	12 59		13 19		13 35	14 00		14 18	14 35	15 01		15 19	15 46	15 59		16 21		16 37
		d	12 01			12 39	13 00				13 36	14 00			14 36	15 02			15 47	16 00				16 38
Broughty Ferry		d														15 09								
Balmossie		d																						
Monifieth		d																						
Barry Links		d																						
Golf Street		d																						
Carnoustie		d					13 12									15 16								
Arbroath		d	12 18			12 55	13 19				13 53	14 18			14 53	15 23			16 05	16 20				16 54
Montrose		d	12 33				13 33				14 07	14 32				15 39			16 21	16 33				17 09
Laurencekirk		d	12 44													15 50								17 20
Stonehaven		d				13 29					14 29	14 54			15 26				16 44					17 33
Portlethen		d																						
Aberdeen		a	13 14			13 48	14 12				14 48	15 13			15 46	16 20			17 09	17 13				17 53
		d									14 56				15 55									17 56
Dyce	240 ✈	a									15 04				16 03									18 04
Inverurie	240	a									15 19				16 18									18 19
Dunkeld & Birnam		d								13 31							15 13						16 36	
Pitlochry		d		12 25						13 44							15 26						16 49	
Blair Atholl		d		12 35						13 54							15 36						16 59	
Dalwhinnie		d		13 03													16 01							
Newtonmore		d		13 14																			17 32	
Kingussie		d		13 19						14 28							16 14						17 37	
Aviemore		d		13 34						14 40							16 28						17 49	
Carrbridge		d		13 43																			17 58	
Inverness		a		14 13						15 23							17 04						18 28	

A ⌶ to Aberdeen
B From London Kings Cross. The Northern Lights
c arrives 1550 SO

Edinburgh and Glasgow Queen Street - Perth, Inverness, Dundee, Aberdeen, Dyce and Inverurie

Network Diagram - see first page of Table 225

			SR	SR	SR	SR	SR	SR SX	SR SO	GR SO	SR	GR SX	SR	SR SX	SR	SR SO	SR SX	SR SO	SR SO	SR SX	SR	SR SX	XC SO	XC SX	SR SO
			◇1 ⌶			◇1 A ⌶	⌶	◇1 ⌶	◇1 ⌶	1 B 🛏⌶		1 B 🛏⌶		C	◇1 ⌶				◇1 ⌶	◇1 ⌶	◇1 ⌶		◇1 D	◇1 D	◇1 ⌶
Edinburgh 10	242	d		15 35	15 58	16 29				16 32	16 33	16 33	17 00	17 27	17 37						17 42	17 58	18 11	18 11	
Haymarket	242	d		15 40	16 03	16u33				16 38	16 37	16 38	17 04	17 32	17 41						17u46	18 03	18 15	18 15	
Inverkeithing	242	d		15 54	16 17						16 53		17 22									18 22	18 29	18 29	
Kirkcaldy	242	d		16 10	16 33						17 09		17 39								18 15	18 39	18 47	18 47	
Markinch		d		16 19	16 42						17 18		17 48								18 24	18 50	18 57	18 57	
Ladybank		d		16 27	16 50						17 26		17 56								18 31	18 57	19 04	19 04	
Springfield		d											18 01												
Cupar		d			16 56	17 17							18 05		18 27							19 04	19 11	19 16	
Leuchars 5		a			17 03	17 24							18 12		18 33							19 10	19 17	19 22	
St Andrews Bus Station	bus	a			17f34	17g49							18 35		18 55							19 19	19 37	19 37	
St Andrews Bus Station	bus	d			16 40	16 55							17 45		18 05							18 55	18 55	18 55	
Leuchars 3		d			17 03	17 24							18 12		18 34							19 11	19 18	19 23	
Glasgow Queen St. 10	230	d	15 41				16 10	16 41	16 41							17 03	17 11		17 41	17 41					18 11
Larbert	230	d												17 57		17 31	17 31								18 30
Stirling	230	d					16 39		17 07	17 18		17 19		18 06		17 45	17 45		18 08	18 15					18 41
Bridge of Allan	230	d					16 44							18 13		17 49	17 49								18 46
Dunblane	230	d					16 49							18a18		17 54	17 54		18 15	18 22					18 50
Gleneagles		d					17 02			17 39		17 39				18 06	18 06		18 27	18 35					19 02
Perth		a	16 36	16 54			17 18	17 36	17 36	17 59	17 54	17 59				18 23	18 23		18 43	18 51	18 58				19 19
		d	16 36				17 19	17 37	17 37	18 00		18 00					18 25		18 44	18 52	18 59				19 22
Invergowrie		d					17 38																		
Dundee		a	17 00		17 18	17 38	17 44	17 59	17 59				18 34		18 48		18 52		19 06	19 15		19 27	19 32	19 35	
		d	17 00			17 39		18 00	18 00						18 49		18 54	18 54	19 16	19 16			19 34	19 36	
Broughty Ferry		d				17 47											19 00	19 00							
Balmossie		d															19 03	19 03							
Monifieth		d															19 06	19 06							
Barry Links		d															19 10	19 10							
Golf Street		d															19 13	19 13							
Carnoustie		d	17 13			17 55		18 13	18 13								19a17	19a17	19 28	19 28					
Arbroath		d	17 20			18 02		18 20	18 20						19 05				19 35	19 35			19 50	19 52	
Montrose		d	17 33			18 16									19 22				19 50	19 50			20 04	20 06	
Laurencekirk		d				18 27																			
Stonehaven		d	17 56			18 41		18 53	18 53						19 43				20 13	20 13			20 24	20 27	
Portlethen		d													19 52										
Aberdeen		a	18 15			19 00		19 13	19 13						20 06				20 33	20 33			20 43	20 45	
		d				19 07																			
Dyce	240 ✈	a				19 16																			
Inverurie	240	a				19 35																			
Dunkeld & Birnam		d																			19 18				
Pitlochry		d								18 32		18 32									19 31				19 52
Blair Atholl		d																							20 01
Dalwhinnie		d																							20 26
Newtonmore		d																							20 36
Kingussie		d								19 16		19 16									20 14				20 41
Aviemore		d								19 29		19 29									20 25				21 00
Carrbridge		d																							
Inverness		a								20 11		20 11									21 02				21 37

A ⌶ to Aberdeen
B From London Kings Cross. The Highland Chieftain
C From Newcraighall
D From Plymouth
f arrives 0730 SO
g arrives 0745 SO

Table 229

Edinburgh and Glasgow Queen Street - Perth, Inverness, Dundee, Aberdeen, Dyce and Inverurie

Network Diagram - see first page of Table 225

			SR	GR	GR	SR	SR	SR		SR		SR	SR	SR	SR	SR	XC	XC	XC	GR		SR	SR	SR	SR	SR
			SX	SO	SX									SO	SX		SX	SO	SO	SX						
			◇1	■ 1	■ 1	◇1						◇1	◇1	◇1	◇1		◇1	◇1	◇1	■ 1		◇1			◇1	◇1
				A	A							B					C	D	E	A						
			✕	⊡✕	⊡✕	✕				✕		✕	✕	✕	✕				✕	⊡✕						
Edinburgh 10	242	d		18 30	18 30		18 40	19 00				19 28		19 36	19 36	20 00	20 14	20 14	20 15	20 29			20 45	21 07	21 40	
Haymarket	242	d		18 35	18 34		18 45	19 04				19 31		19 41	19 41	20 04	20 17	20 18	20 20	20 34			20 49	21 11	21 44	
Inverkeithing	242	d		18 54	18 54		19 00	19 18						19 54	19 54	20 23	20 31	20 35	20 36	20 51			21 03	21 30		
Kirkcaldy	242	d		19 11	19 11		19 18	19 34						20 10	20 10	20 45		20 52	20 53	21 08			21 19	21 52	22 12	
Markinch		d					19 28	19 43						20 19	20 19	20 54	21 03	21 02	21 03				21 28	22 01		
Ladybank		d					19 35	19 50						20 27	20 27	21 01	21 11	21 10	21 11				21 36	22 08		
Springfield		d																								
Cupar		d						19 57				20 21				21 07	21 19	21 19	21 20					22 15		
Leuchars 5		a		19 38	19 39			20 03				20 28				21 14	21 25	21 25	21 27	21 37				22 22	22 34	
St Andrews Bus Station	🚌	a		*19 59*	*19 59*			*20 29*				*20 51*				*21 59*	*21 59*	*21 59*	*21 59*	*21 59*				*22 59*	*22 59*	
St Andrews Bus Station	🚌	d		*19 10*	*19 10*			*19 40*				*20 00*				*20 40*	*21 00*	*21 00*	*21 00*	*21 00*				*22 00*	*22 00*	
Leuchars 3		d		19 38	19 39			20 04				20 28				21 14	21 26	21 27	21 28	21 38				22 22	22 35	
Glasgow Queen St. 10	230 ⛴	d	18 11			18 41				19 10			19 41									20 41				21 42
Larbert	230	d	18 30																							
Stirling	230	d	18 41			19u07				19 37			20 07									21 07				22 08
Bridge of Allan	230	d	18 46							19 41																
Dunblane	230	d	18 50			19 14				19 46												21 14				
Gleneagles		d	19 02			19 26				19 58												21 26				
Perth		a	19 19			19 42	20 02			20 14			20 36	20 54	20 54							21 42	22 02			22 37
		d	19 22			19 43				20 15			20 36	20 55	20 55							21 43				22 38
Invergowrie		d				20 00																22 01				
Dundee		a		19 52	19 53	20 07		20 19		20 36		20 40	20 59			21 30	21 41	21 43	21 44	21 52		22 07		22 37	22 48	23 02
		d		19 53	19 54	20 08						20 41	20 59							21 52		22 08			22 49	23 03
Broughty Ferry		d																								23 10
Balmossie		d																								
Monifieth		d																								
Barry Links		d																								
Golf Street		d																								
Carnoustie		d																								23 17
Arbroath		d		20 10	20 11	20 24						20 58	21 17							22 10		22 25			23 05	23 24
Montrose		d		20 26	20 28	20 39						21 12	21 31							22 26		22 39			23 19	23 39
Laurencekirk		d											21 42													23 49
Stonehaven		d		20 49	20 51							21 34	21 56							22 49		23 01			23 40	00 03
Portlethen		d																							23 49	
Aberdeen		a		21 15	21 16	21 19						21 53	22 15							23 14		23 20			00 03	00 22
		d										21 55														
Dyce	240 ✈	a										22 04														
Inverurie	240	a										22 16														
Dunkeld & Birnam		d												21 13	21 13											
Pitlochry		d	19 52											21 26	21 26											
Blair Atholl		d	20 01											21 35	21 35											
Dalwhinnie		d	20 26											22 01	22 03											
Newtonmore		d	20 36											22 11	22 14											
Kingussie		d	20 41											22 16	22 24											
Aviemore		d	21 00											22 28	22 35											
Carrbridge		d												22 36	22 43											
Inverness		a	21 43									00 05		23 07	23 15											

A From London Kings Cross
B ✕ to Aberdeen
C From Plymouth
D From 15 September. From Plymouth
E Until 8 September. From Newquay

Table 229

Edinburgh and Glasgow Queen Street - Perth, Inverness, Dundee, Aberdeen, Dyce and Inverurie

Network Diagram - see first page of Table 225

			SR	SR	SR	SR	SR
			A				
Edinburgh 10	242	d	21 49	22 09	22 39	23 09	
Haymarket	242	d	21 53	22 13	22 43	23 13	
Inverkeithing	242	d	22 12	22 32	23 02	23 32	
Kirkcaldy	242	d		22 54	23 24	23 54	
Markinch		d	22 56	23 03	23 33	00 03	
Ladybank		d	23 03	23 13	23 40	00 10	
Springfield		d		23 18			
Cupar		d		23 22		00 17	
Leuchars 5		a		23 28		00 23	
St Andrews Bus Station	🚌	a		*23 59*			
St Andrews Bus Station	🚌	d		*23 00*		*23 50*	
Leuchars 3		d		23 29		00 24	
Glasgow Queen St. 10	230 ⛴	d					23 36
Larbert	230	d					
Stirling	230	d					00 05
Bridge of Allan	230	d					00 10
Dunblane	230	d					00 15
Gleneagles		d					00 27
Perth		a	23 34		00 07		00 44
		d					
Invergowrie		d					
Dundee		a		23 44		00 39	
		d					
Broughty Ferry		d					
Balmossie		d					
Monifieth		d					
Barry Links		d					
Golf Street		d					
Carnoustie		d					
Arbroath		d					
Montrose		d					
Laurencekirk		d					
Stonehaven		d					
Portlethen		d					
Aberdeen		a					
		d					
Dyce	240 ✈	a					
Inverurie	240	a					
Dunkeld & Birnam		d					
Pitlochry		d					
Blair Atholl		d					
Dalwhinnie		d					
Newtonmore		d					
Kingussie		d					
Aviemore		d					
Carrbridge		d					
Inverness		a					

A From Newcraighall

Table 229

Sundays

Edinburgh and Glasgow Queen Street - Perth, Inverness, Dundee, Aberdeen, Dyce and Inverurie

Network Diagram - see first page of Table 225

	SR	SR	SR	SR	SR	XC	GR	SR	SR	SR	SR
	◇1 A ⌶	◇1	◇1			◇	1 ⊏⌶		◇1 ⌶	◇1 ⌶	◇1 ⌶
Edinburgh [10] 242 d	19p28	21p40		22p39	23p09	08 04	09 10	09 15		09 36	10 55
Haymarket 242 d	19p31	21p44		22p43	23p13	08 08	09 14	09 19		09 40	10 59
Inverkeithing 242 d				23p02	23p32	08 25	09 32	09 38		09 56	11 15
Kirkcaldy 242 d		22p12		23p24	23p54	08 40	09 49	10 03		10 12	11 31
Markinch d				23p33	00 03			10 12			
Ladybank d				23p40	00 10			10 18			
Springfield d											
Cupar d	20p21				00 17	08 57		10 26			
Leuchars [5] a	20p28	22p34			00 23	09 05	10 13	10 33			11 54
St Andrews Bus Station 🚌 a						*09 37*	*10 29*	*10 58*			*12 17*
St Andrews Bus Station 🚌 d						*07 55*	*09 50*	*10 15*			*11 35*
Leuchars [5] d	20p28	22p35			00 24	09 06	10 13	10 33			11 55
Glasgow Queen St. [10] 230 d			21p42						09 38		
Larbert 230 d									10 02		
Stirling 230 d			22p08						10 12		
Bridge of Allan 230 d											
Dunblane 230 d									10 18		
Gleneagles d									10 30		
Perth a			22p37	00 07					10 47	10 52	
d			22p38						10 48	10 53	
Invergowrie d											
Dundee a	20p40	22p48	23p02		00 39	09 18	10 27	10 50	11 12		12 07
d	20p41	22p49	23p03			09 20	10 28		11 13		12 08
Broughty Ferry d			23p10								
Balmossie d											
Monifieth d											
Barry Links d											
Golf Street d											
Carnoustie d			23p17						11 25		
Arbroath d	20p58	23p05	23p24			09 36	10 45		11 29		12 25
Montrose d	21p12	23p19	23p39			09 50	11 01		11 46		12 37
Laurencekirk d			23p49						12 01		
Stonehaven d	21p34	23p40	00 03			10 10	11 24		12 10		12 59
Portlethen d		23p49									13 07
Aberdeen a	21p53	00 03	00 22			10 29	11 52		12 35		13 23
d	21p55										
Dyce 240 ✈ a	22p04										
Inverurie 240 a	22p16										
Dunkeld & Birnam d										11 11	
Pitlochry d										11 24	
Blair Atholl d										11 34	
Dalwhinnie d										12 01	
Newtonmore d										12 12	
Kingussie d										12 17	
Aviemore d										12 29	
Carrbridge d										12 38	
Inverness a	00 05									13 15	

	SR	SR	SR	SR	SR	SR	SR	GR	SR	SR	SR
	◇1 ⌶		◇1	◇1 ⌶		◇1 ⌶	◇1 ⌶	1 B ⊏⌶	◇1 C ⌶		◇1 ⌶
Edinburgh [10] 242 d		11 15		12 40	13 15		13 50	14 33		15 15	
Haymarket 242 d		11 19		12 44	13 19		13 54	14 38		15 19	
Inverkeithing 242 d		11 38		13 00	13 40		14 12	14 56		15 38	
Kirkcaldy 242 d		12 03		13 16	14 05		14 28	15 13		16 03	
Markinch d		12 12			14 14					16 12	
Ladybank d		12 19			14 21					16 19	
Springfield d											
Cupar d		12 26			14 28					16 26	
Leuchars [5] a		12 33		13 39	14 35			15 37		16 33	
St Andrews Bus Station 🚌 a		*12 57*		*13 55*	*14 55*			*15 55*		*16 55*	
St Andrews Bus Station 🚌 d		*12 15*		*13 15*	*14 15*			*15 15*		*16 15*	
Leuchars [5] d		12 33		13 40	14 35			15 38		16 33	
Glasgow Queen St. [10] 230 d	11 09		11 45			13 45			14 40		15 45
Larbert 230 d	11 29								15 00		
Stirling 230 d	11 39		12 12			14 12			15 09		16 12
Bridge of Allan 230 d											
Dunblane 230 d	11 45		12 18			14 17			15 16		16 18
Gleneagles d	11 57		12 29			14 29			15 28		16 29
Perth a	12 15		12 46			14 46	15 12		15 45		16 45
d	12 15		12 47			14 48	15 14		15 46		16 47
Invergowrie d											
Dundee a		12 48	13 10	13 52	14 50	15 09		15 52		16 48	17 09
d			13 11	13 53		15 11		15 52			17 11
Broughty Ferry d											
Balmossie d											
Monifieth d											
Barry Links d											
Golf Street d											
Carnoustie d											
Arbroath d			13 27	14 10		15 27		16 10			17 27
Montrose d			13 42	14 24		15 42		16 26			17 42
Laurencekirk d						15 53					
Stonehaven d			14 03	14 46		16 06		16 49			18 03
Portlethen d											
Aberdeen a			14 23	15 05		16 26		17 14			18 23
d											
Dyce 240 ✈ a											
Inverurie 240 a											
Dunkeld & Birnam d	12 36						15 31				
Pitlochry d	12 50						15 44		16 16		
Blair Atholl d							15 54				
Dalwhinnie d							16 25				
Newtonmore d							16 35				
Kingussie d	13 32						16 40		17 00		
Aviemore d	13 44						16 56		17 13		
Carrbridge d	13 57						17 06				
Inverness a	14 26						17 37		17 49		

A ⌶ to Aberdeen
B From London Kings Cross. The Northern Lights
C To Elgin

Table 229

Sundays

Edinburgh and Glasgow Queen Street - Perth, Inverness, Dundee, Aberdeen, Dyce and Inverurie

Network Diagram - see first page of Table 225

	SR	GR	SR	SR	SR	SR	SR	XC
	◇1 ⌶	1 A ⊏⌶	◇1		◇1 ⌶	1	◇1 B ⌶	◇1 C
Edinburgh [10] 242 d	15 50	16 30	17 05	17 15		17 50		18 13
Haymarket 242 d	15 54	16 35	17 09	17 19		17 54		18 16
Inverkeithing 242 d	16 10		17 22	17 38		18 07		18 30
Kirkcaldy 242 d	16 26		17 38	18 00		18 23		18 45
Markinch d				18 09				18 54
Ladybank d				18 16				19 02
Springfield d								
Cupar d				18 23				19 08
Leuchars [5] a			18 01	18 30				19 14
St Andrews Bus Station 🚌 a			*18 17*	*18 55*				*19 37*
St Andrews Bus Station 🚌 d			*17 35*	*18 00*				*18 30*
Leuchars [5] d			18 02	18 30				19 15
Glasgow Queen St. [10] 230 d					17 45		18 10	
Larbert 230 d							18 30	
Stirling 230 d		17 17			18 12		18 40	
Bridge of Allan 230 d								
Dunblane 230 d							18 47	
Gleneagles d		17 35					18 59	
Perth a	17 05	17 53			18 44	19 02	19 16	
d	17 09	17 54			18 45		19 17	
Invergowrie d								
Dundee a			18 14	18 46	19 08			19 29
d			18 15		19 09			19 31
Broughty Ferry d								
Balmossie d								
Monifieth d								
Barry Links d								
Golf Street d								
Carnoustie d					19 21			
Arbroath d			18 32		19 27			19 47
Montrose d			18 46		19 42			20 01
Laurencekirk d					19 55			
Stonehaven d			19 08		20 06			20 24
Portlethen d			19 16					
Aberdeen a			19 30		20 29			20 43
d								
Dyce 240 ✈ a								
Inverurie 240 a								
Dunkeld & Birnam d	17 26						19 35	
Pitlochry d	17 40	18 27					19 48	
Blair Atholl d							19 58	
Dalwhinnie d							20 23	
Newtonmore d							20 33	
Kingussie d	18 22	19 23					20 38	
Aviemore d	18 35	19 35					20 50	
Carrbridge d							21 02	
Inverness a	19 21	20 19					21 33	

	XC	XC	GR	SR	SR	SR	SR	SR
	◇1 D	◇1 E	1 F ⊏⌶		◇1 ⌶	◇1	◇1 ⌶	
Edinburgh [10] 242 d	18 13	18 13	18 42	19 15		21 00		22 25
Haymarket 242 d	18 16	18 18	18 47	19 19		21 05		22 29
Inverkeithing 242 d	18 30	18 32	19 02	19 38		21 19		22 48
Kirkcaldy 242 d	18 45	18 47	19 19	20 00		21 35		23 10
Markinch d	18 54	18 56		20 09		21 44		23 19
Ladybank d	19 02	19 03		20 16		21 50		23 26
Springfield d								
Cupar d	19 08	19 10		20 23		21 58		23 33
Leuchars [5] a	19 14	19 16	19 43	20 30		22 05		23 40
St Andrews Bus Station 🚌 a	*19 37*	*19 37*	*19 59*	*20 55*		*22 29*		*23 58*
St Andrews Bus Station 🚌 d	*18 30*	*18 30*	*19 15*	*20 00*		*21 30*		*23 00*
Leuchars [5] d	19 15	19 17	19 43	20 30		22 05		23 40
Glasgow Queen St. [10] 230 d					19 45		21 45	
Larbert 230 d								
Stirling 230 d					20 12		22 11	
Bridge of Allan 230 d								
Dunblane 230 d					20 17		22 17	
Gleneagles d					20 29		22 28	
Perth a					20 46		22 46	
d					20 47		22 46	
Invergowrie d								
Dundee a	19 29	19 31	19 57	20 45	21 10	22 18	23 09	23 56
d	19 31	19 32	19 58		21 11	22 21	23 09	
Broughty Ferry d								
Balmossie d								
Monifieth d								
Barry Links d								
Golf Street d								
Carnoustie d							23 21	
Arbroath d	19 47	19 48	20 15		21 27	22 38	23 26	
Montrose d	20 02	20 02	20 31		21 42	22 52	23 41	
Laurencekirk d								
Stonehaven d	20 24	20 24	20 54		22 03	23 14	00 02	
Portlethen d						23 23		
Aberdeen a	20 43	20 43	21 20		22 24	23 36	00 25	
d								
Dyce 240 ✈ a								
Inverurie 240 a								
Dunkeld & Birnam d								
Pitlochry d								
Blair Atholl d								
Dalwhinnie d								
Newtonmore d								
Kingussie d								
Aviemore d								
Carrbridge d								
Inverness a								

A From London Kings Cross. The Highland Chieftain
B To Elgin
C until 9 September. From Plymouth
D from 16 September until 21 October
E from 28 October. From Birmingham New Street
F From London Kings Cross

Inverurie, Dyce, Aberdeen, Dundee, Inverness and Perth - Glasgow Queen Street and Edinburgh

Network Diagram - see first page of Table 225

Miles	Miles	Miles	Miles	Miles			XC MX	SR MO	SR SO	SR MO	SR MX	SR MSX	SR MO	SR SO	SR SX	SR	SR SO	SR	SR	SR
							◇1	B	B	B	B	1	1	1						
								A 🛏	B 🛏	A 🛏	B 🛏		C				D			
—	—	0	0	0	**Inverness**	d				20p25	20p47									
—	—	28	28	28	Carrbridge	d														
—	—	34¾	34¾	34¾	Aviemore	d				21b08	21b29									
—	—	46½	46½	46½	Kingussie	d				21b22	21b42									
—	—	49¼	49¼	49¼	Newtonmore	d				21b29	21b50									
—	—	59½	59½	59½	Dalwhinnie	d				21b43	22b06									
—	—	82¾	82¾	82¾	Blair Atholl	d				22b09	22b32									
—	—	89½	89½	89½	Pitlochry	d				22b22	22b45									
—	—	102½	102½	102½	Dunkeld & Birnam	d				22b37	23b00									
0	0	—	—	—	**Inverurie** 240	d														
10¾	10¾	—	—	—	Dyce 240 ✈	d														
6¼	6¼	—	—	—	**Aberdeen** 240	a														
—	—	—	—	—		d	21p31	21p42	21p42			22p27	22p30	23p22						
14¼	14¼	—	—	—	Portlethen	d						22p37		23p32						
22½	22½	—	—	—	Stonehaven	d	21p49	22b00	22b00			22p46	22p48	23p41						
36¾	36¾	—	—	—	Laurencekirk	d						22p59		23p54						
46¾	46¾	—	—	—	Montrose	d	22p10	22b25	22b25			23p10	23p11	00 05						
60½	60½	—	—	—	Arbroath	d	22p26	22b43	22b43			23p24	23p25	00 19						
66¾	66¾	—	—	—	Carnoustie	d		22b52	22b52			23p31	23p32	00 26						
67¼	67¼	—	—	—	Golf Street	d														
68	68	—	—	—	Barry Links	d														
71	71	—	—	—	Monifieth	d														
71¾	71¾	—	—	—	Balmossie	d														
73¾	73¾	—	—	—	Broughty Ferry	d						23p38		00 33						
77½	77½	—	—	—	**Dundee**	a	22p42					23p48	23p46	00 43						
—	—	—	—	—		d	22p43	23b06	23b06			23p49	23p47	00 44				05 56		06 05
81	—	—	—	—	Invergowrie	d						23p54		00 49				06 02		
98¼	—	118	118	118	**Perth**	a						00 12	00 09	01 07				06 19		
—	—	—	—	—		d				23b00	23b21				05 10	05 16	05 35	06 21		
114	—	133¾	—	133¾	Gleneagles	d				23b18	23b39					05 33		06 36		
121¼	—	146	—	146	Dunblane 230	d				23b34	23b55					05 46		06 47		
—	—	—	—	—	Bridge of Allan 230	d										05 49		06 51		
131¾	—	151½	—	151½	Stirling 230	d				23b45	00u06					05 54		06 55		
139¾	—	159½	—	159½	Larbert 230	d										06 03		07 04		
160¾	—	180½	—	—	**Glasgow Queen St.** [10] 230 ⛴	a										06 34		07 35		
—	85¾	—	—	—	Leuchars [5]	a	22p55													06 16
—	—	—	—	—	St Andrews Bus Station 🚌	a														*07 04*
—	—	—	—	—	St Andrews Bus Station 🚌	d														
—	—	—	—	—	Leuchars [5]	d	22p56	23b25	23b25											06 17
—	92¼	—	—	—	Cupar	d	23p03													06 25
—	94½	—	—	—	Springfield	d														
—	97½	—	135¾	—	Ladybank	d	23p10								05 36		05 59			06 32
—	103½	—	141	—	Markinch	d	23p18								05 44		06 07			06 40
—	110¾	—	149	—	Kirkcaldy 242	d	23p26	23b53	23b53						05 53		06 16			06 49
—	123½	—	161¾	—	Inverkeithing 242	d	23p42	00u12	00u12						06 16		06 40			07 12
—	135½	—	173¾	186½	Haymarket 242	a	23p57								06 39		07 02			07 33
—	136¾	—	175	187¾	**Edinburgh** [10] 242	a	00 05								06 46		07 09			07 38

A From 21 May. To London Euston
B To London Euston
C From 21 May
D To Newcraighall
b Previous night, stops to pick up only

Inverurie, Dyce, Aberdeen, Dundee, Inverness and Perth - Glasgow Queen Street and Edinburgh

Network Diagram - see first page of Table 225

		SR	XC SO	XC SX	SR	SR	SR SX	SR	SR	SR	SR SX		SR	SR	SR	SR	SR	SR	SR
			◇1	◇1				◇1	◇1				1	◇1		◇1		◇1	
			A ⊼	A	B			⊼			B			⊼		E ⊼		⊼	
Inverness	d															04 51		06 47	
Carrbridge	d																		
Aviemore	d																	07 25	
Kingussie	d																	07 37	
Newtonmore	d																		
Dalwhinnie	d																		
Blair Atholl	d												07 12						
Pitlochry	d												07 25					08 16	
Dunkeld & Birnam	d												07 38					08 29	
Inverurie 240	d															06 39			
Dyce 240 ✈	d															06 52			
Aberdeen 240	a															07 04			
	d							05 33	05 56					06 33		07 06			
Portlethen	d							05 44						06 43					
Stonehaven	d							05 52	06 13					06 52		07 22			
Laurencekirk	d							06 06								07 36			
Montrose	d							06 17	06 34					07 13		07 47			
Arbroath	d							06 31	06 49					07 27		08 01			
Carnoustie	d	06 00							06 56					07 34		08 08			
Golf Street	d	06 02																	
Barry Links	d	06 04																	
Monifieth	d	06 09																	
Balmossie	d	06 11																	
Broughty Ferry	d	06 15												07 41					
Dundee	a	06 26						06 51	07 08					07 51		08 18			
	d		06 32	06 32				06 52	07 09	07 20	07 38			07 52	08 18	08 20	08 28		
Invergowrie	d														08 23				
Perth	a							07 14					07 58	08 12	08 40			08 47	
	d				06 39	06 55	07 03	07 15					08 00	08 12	08 40			08 48	
Gleneagles	d				06 54		07 18	07 30						08 26	08 55				
Dunblane 230	d				07 08		07 31	07 44							09 07				
Bridge of Allan 230	d				07 10		07 34	07 48							09 11				
Stirling 230	d				07 16		07 39	07 53						08 43	09 15				
Larbert 230	d				07 25		07 47	08 02											
Glasgow Queen St. [10] 230 ⛴	a						08 20	08 34						09 15	09 46				
Leuchars [5]	a		06 44	06 44					07 20	07 31	07 49						08 40		
St Andrews Bus Station 🚌	a		*07 13*	*07 04*					*08h05*	*08h05*	*08 12*						*09 00*		
St Andrews Bus Station 🚌	d		*06 10*	*06 14*					*07i00*	*07i00*	*07 28*						*08j10*		
Leuchars [5]	d		06 46	06 46					07 21	07 32	07 50						08 40		
Cupar	d		06 54	06 54					07 29	07 39	07 58						08 48		
Springfield	d									07 44									
Ladybank	d		07 03	07 03		07 19				07 48			08 22				08 55		
Markinch	d		07 11	07 11		07 26				07 56			08 31				09 03		
Kirkcaldy 242	d		07 21	07 21		07 40			07 49	08 06	08 18		08 41				09 12	09 25	
Inverkeithing 242	d		07 38	07 43		07 57				08 28	08 35		08 57				09 34		
Haymarket 242	a		07 55	08 00	08 11	08 17			08 19	08 51	08 54	08 57	09 15			09 24	09 49	09 55	
Edinburgh [10] 242	a		08 01	08 06	08 17	08 22			08 25	08 56	08 59	09 04	09 21			09 29	09 55	10 00	

A To Plymouth
B To Newcraighall
C From Newcraighall
E ⊼ from Aberdeen
h arrives 0800 SO
i arrives 0655 SO
j arrives 0814 SO

Inverurie, Dyce, Aberdeen, Dundee, Inverness and Perth - Glasgow Queen Street and Edinburgh

Network Diagram - see first page of Table 225

		SR	GR	GR	XC	XC		SR	GR	SR	SR	SR	SR	SR	SR
			SX	SO	SO	SX									
		◇■	▪ ■	▪ ■	◇■	◇■		■	▪ ■		◇■	◇■	■	◇■	
		A ⊼	C ⊡⊼	C ⊡⊼	D	D			E ⊡⊼		⊼	⊼		⊼	
Inverness	d								07 55					08 43	
Carrbridge	d													09 15	
Aviemore	d								08 29					09 23	
Kingussie	d								08 42					09 39	
Newtonmore	d													09 44	
Dalwhinnie	d														
Blair Atholl	d														
Pitlochry	d								09 23					10 23	
Dunkeld & Birnam	d														
Inverurie 240	d	07 14													
Dyce 240 ✈	d	07 26													
Aberdeen 240	a	07 37													
	d	07 40	07 52	07 52	08 20	08 20					08 42	09 07			
Portlethen	d														
Stonehaven	d	07 56	08 09	08 09	08 38	08 38									
Laurencekirk	d											09 35			
Montrose	d	08 18	08 32	08 32	08 59	08 59					09 18	09 46			
Arbroath	d	08 32	08 48	08 48	09 15	09 15					09 32	10 00			
Carnoustie	d	08 39									09 39				
Golf Street	d														
Barry Links	d														
Monifieth	d														
Balmossie	d														
Broughty Ferry	d														
Dundee	a	08 53	09 05	09 05	09 31	09 31					09 52	10 15			
	d	08 53	09 06	09 06	09 32	09 32		09 41			09 52	10 17	10 35		
Invergowrie	d														
Perth	a	09 15							09 54		10 14			10 52	
	d	09 15							09 56	10 01	10 14			10 53	11 00
Gleneagles	d								10 13					11 08	
Dunblane 230	d													11 20	
Bridge of Allan 230	d													11 23	
Stirling 230	d	09 44							10 30		10 43			11 28	
Larbert 230	d														
Glasgow Queen St. 10 230 ⇌	a	10 14									11 14			12 09	
Leuchars 5	a		09 20	09 20	09 46	09 46		09 52				10 28	10 46		
St Andrews Bus Station 🚌	a		*09 45*	*09 45*	*10 12*	*10 12*		*10 12*				*10 45*	*11 12*		
St Andrews Bus Station 🚌	d		*08 55*	*08 55*	*09 25*	*09 25*		*09 25*				*10 10*	*10 25*		
Leuchars 5	d		09 20	09 20	09 47	09 47		09 53				10 29	10 47		
Cupar	d				09 54	09 54		10 01					10 54		
Springfield	d														
Ladybank	d				10 01	10 01		10 09		10 24			11 02		11 23
Markinch	d				10 08	10 09		10 17		10 32			11 09		11 31
Kirkcaldy 242	d		09 44	09 44	10 17	10 17		10 26		10 42			11 19		11 41
Inverkeithing 242	d		10 01	10 01	10 32	10 32		10 42		10 59			11 35		11 57
Haymarket 242	a		10 17	10 18	10 51	10 52	10 58	11 05	11 11	11 19		11 23	11 50		12 13
Edinburgh 10 242	a		10 25	10 26	10 58	10 58	11 04	11 14	11 17	11 25		11 28	11 56		12 18

A ⊼ from Aberdeen
C To London Kings Cross
D To Penzance
E To London Kings Cross. The Highland Chieftain

Inverurie, Dyce, Aberdeen, Dundee, Inverness and Perth - Glasgow Queen Street and Edinburgh

Network Diagram - see first page of Table 225

		SR	GR	SR	SR	SR	SR	SR	SR	SR	SR	SR
		◇■	▪ ■	■	◇■	◇■	■	◇■	■	◇■	◇■	◇■
		A ⊼	B ⊡⊼		⊼	⊼		A ⊼		⊼	⊼	A ⊼
Inverness	d				09 41					10 45		
Carrbridge	d											
Aviemore	d				10 25					11 26		
Kingussie	d				10 37					11 38		
Newtonmore	d											
Dalwhinnie	d				10 51							
Blair Atholl	d				11 14							
Pitlochry	d				11 24					12 27		
Dunkeld & Birnam	d				11 38					12 40		
Inverurie 240	d							10 38				11 35
Dyce 240 ✈	d	09 08						10 50				11 47
Aberdeen 240	a	09 19						11 01				11 58
	d	09 37	09 52			10 38		11 05			11 42	12 07
Portlethen	d											12 17
Stonehaven	d	09 53	10 09					11 21				12 26
Laurencekirk	d							11 35				
Montrose	d	10 15	10 32			11 14		11 46			12 17	
Arbroath	d	10 29	10 49			11 28		12 00			12 31	13 00
Carnoustie	d	10 36				11 35					12 38	
Golf Street	d											
Barry Links	d											
Monifieth	d											
Balmossie	d											
Broughty Ferry	d	10 43										
Dundee	a	10 52	11 06			11 49		12 15			12 52	13 15
	d	10 52	11 06	11 30		11 49	12 13	12 16	12 34		12 52	13 16
Invergowrie	d											
Perth	a	11 14			11 57	12 11	12 35			12 58	13 14	
	d	11 14			12 00	12 11	12 38			13 00	13 14	
Gleneagles	d						12 53					
Dunblane 230	d						13 04					
Bridge of Allan 230	d						13 08					
Stirling 230	d	11 43				12 43	13 13				13 43	
Larbert 230	d											
Glasgow Queen St. 10 230 ⇌	a	12 15				13 14	13 47				14 14	
Leuchars 5	a		11 20	11 41				12 28	12 46			13 28
St Andrews Bus Station 🚌	a		*11 45*	*12 00*				*12 45*	*13 12*			*13 45*
St Andrews Bus Station 🚌	d		*10 55*	*11 25*				*12 10*	*12 25*			*13 10*
Leuchars 5	d		11 20	11 45				12 28	12 46			13 28
Cupar	d			11 53					12 53			
Springfield	d											
Ladybank	d			12 00	12 21				13 01			
Markinch	d			12 08	12 29				13 08	13 30		
Kirkcaldy 242	d		11 44	12 17	12 38				13 18	13 40		
Inverkeithing 242	d		12 01	12 33	12 54				13 34			
Haymarket 242	a		12 17	12 49	13 15			13 21	13 51	14 13		14 21
Edinburgh 10 242	a		12 25	12 55	13 20			13 26	13 57	14 19		14 27

A ⊼ from Aberdeen
B To London Kings Cross. The Northern Lights

Table 229

Mondays to Saturdays

Inverurie, Dyce, Aberdeen, Dundee, Inverness and Perth - Glasgow Queen Street and Edinburgh

Network Diagram - see first page of Table 225

	SR	SR	SR	SR	SR SO	SR SX	SR	SR	SR	SR	SR
	■1		◇1 ⊼	◇1 ⊼	■1	■1	◇1 ⊼	◇1 ⊼		◇1 ⊼	■1
Inverness d							12 46				
Carrbridge d							13 26				
Aviemore d							13 34				
Kingussie d							13 47				
Newtonmore d							13 51				
Dalwhinnie d											
Blair Atholl d							14 21				
Pitlochry d							14 32				
Dunkeld & Birnam d							14 44				
Inverurie 240 d											
Dyce 240 ✈ d											
Aberdeen 240 a											
d			12 42	13 09				13 42		14 04	
Portlethen d											
Stonehaven d			12 58	13 25						14 20	
Laurencekirk d										14 34	
Montrose d			13 20	13 44				14 17			
Arbroath d			13 34	13 58				14 31		14 57	
Carnoustie d								14 38			
Golf Street d											
Barry Links d											
Monifieth d											
Balmossie d											
Broughty Ferry d										15 09	
Dundee a			13 52	14 15				14 52		15 15	
d	13 34		13 54	14 17	14 34	14 34		14 52	15 13	15 17	15 34
Invergowrie d											
Perth a			14 14				15 01	15 14	15 35		
d		14 01	14 15				15 02	15 14	15 37		
Gleneagles d									15 52		
Dunblane 230 d									16 05		
Bridge of Allan 230 d									16 09		
Stirling 230 d			14 44					15 43	16 14		
Larbert 230 d											
Glasgow Queen St. 10 230 ⇌ a			15 18					16 14	16 44		
Leuchars 5 a	13 45			14 29	14 45	14 45				15 28	15 47
St Andrews Bus Station 🚌 a	*14b12*			*14 45*	*15 12*	*15 12*				*15 45*	*16 15*
St Andrews Bus Station 🚌 d	*13b25*			*14 10*	*14 25*	*14 25*				*15 10*	*15 25*
Leuchars 5 d	13 46			14 29	14 46	14 46				15 29	15 48
Cupar d	13 53				14 53	14 53					15 55
Springfield d											
Ladybank d	14 01	14 22			15 01	15 01					16 03
Markinch d	14 08	14 30			15 08	15 08	15 32				16 10
Kirkcaldy 242 d	14 18	14 39			15 18	15 18	15 41				16 19
Inverkeithing 242 d	14 34	14 55			15 34	15 34	15 57				16 35
Haymarket 242 a	14 49	15 15		15 22	15 49	15 49	16 13			16 22	16 51
Edinburgh 10 242 a	14 54	15 20		15 29	15 54	16 00	16 21			16 27	16 58

Table 229

Mondays to Saturdays

Inverurie, Dyce, Aberdeen, Dundee, Inverness and Perth - Glasgow Queen Street and Edinburgh

Network Diagram - see first page of Table 225

	SR	SR	GR SO	GR SX	SR	SR	SR	SR	SR	SR	SR	SR
		◇1 ⊼	■ 1 B ⊼	■ 1 B ⊼	◇1 ⊼	D	◇1 ⊼		E	◇1 F ⊼		◇1 ⊼
Inverness d					14 48							15 50
Carrbridge d												
Aviemore d					15 26							16 29
Kingussie d					15 39							16 42
Newtonmore d												16 46
Dalwhinnie d					15 52							
Blair Atholl d												17 17
Pitlochry d					16 21							17 27
Dunkeld & Birnam d					16 34							17 42
Inverurie 240 d										15 26		
Dyce 240 ✈ d										15 40		
Aberdeen 240 a										15 51		
d		14 39	14 50	14 50			15 33			16 03		
Portlethen d												
Stonehaven d			15 07	15 07			15 49			16 20		
Laurencekirk d										16 34		
Montrose d		15 12	15 30	15 30			16 11					
Arbroath d		15 26	15 46	15 46			16 25			16 57		
Carnoustie d		15 33								17 04		
Golf Street d												
Barry Links d												
Monifieth d												
Balmossie d												
Broughty Ferry d										17 11		
Dundee a		15 49	16 03	16 03			16 46			17 17		
d		15 49	16 04	16 04			16 47	16 49		17 17	17 26	
Invergowrie d							16 53					
Perth a		16 11			16 51		17 10					17 59
d	16 01	16 11			16 53	17 00	17 11					18 00
Gleneagles d					17 08		17 26					
Dunblane 230 d					17 20		17 36					
Bridge of Allan 230 d					17 23							
Stirling 230 d		16s41			17 29		17 42					
Larbert 230 d												
Glasgow Queen St. 10 230 ⇌ a		17 18			18 09		18 15					
Leuchars 5 a			16 17	16 17				17 00		17 29	17 38	
St Andrews Bus Station 🚌 a			*16 34*	*16 34*				*17g34*		*17e49*	*18f02*	
St Andrews Bus Station 🚌 d			*15 55*	*15 55*				*16 40*		*17 10*	*17 17*	
Leuchars 5 d			16 18	16 18				17 01		17 29	17 39	
Cupar d								17 08			17 46	
Springfield d									←		17 51	
Ladybank d						17 27		17 15	17 27		17 56	18 23
Markinch d	16 31					→		17 22	17 39		18 03	18 34
Kirkcaldy 242 d	16 41		16 45	16 45				17 32	17 48		18 13	18 43
Inverkeithing 242 d	16 57		17 01	17 03				17 55	18 04		18 29	18 59
Haymarket 242 a	17 15		17 17	17 19				18 16	18 18	18 25	18 43	19 14
Edinburgh 10 242 a	17 23		17 26	17 27				18 22	18 25	18 32	18 49	19 22

B To London Kings Cross
D To Edinburgh
E From Perth
F ⊼ from Aberdeen
e arrives 0820 SX
f arrives 0800 SO
g arrives 0745 SO

Inverurie, Dyce, Aberdeen, Dundee, Inverness and Perth - Glasgow Queen Street and Edinburgh

Network Diagram - see first page of Table 225

		SR ◇■ ⌶	SR ◇■ A ⌶	SR ■	SR SO	SR	SR ■ ⌶	SR ◇■ ⌶	GR SX ■ C ✕	SR SO ◇■ ⌶	SR ◇■ ⌶	SR	SR ◇■ ⌶	SR ◇■ A ⌶	SR
Inverness	d										17 22				
Carrbridge	d										17 59				
Aviemore	d										18 07				
Kingussie	d										18 19				
Newtonmore	d														
Dalwhinnie	d														
Blair Atholl	d														
Pitlochry	d										19 00				
Dunkeld & Birnam	d										19 16				
Inverurie 240	d		16 38											18 43	
Dyce 240 ✈	d		16 54	17 05										18 55	
Aberdeen 240	a		17 05	17 14										19 06	
	d	16 37	17 07	17 16				17 36	18 16	18 16			18 30	19 09	
Portlethen	d			17 27									18 40		
Stonehaven	d	16 53		17a37				17 52	18 33	18 33			18 49	19 26	
Laurencekirk	d		17 38					18 06						19 40	
Montrose	d	17 15	17 49					18 17	18 56	18 56			19 10	19 51	
Arbroath	d	17 29	18 03					18 31	19 12	19 12			19 24	20 05	
Carnoustie	d							18 38					19 31		
Golf Street	d														
Barry Links	d														
Monifieth	d														
Balmossie	d														
Broughty Ferry	d														
Dundee	a	17 49	18 18					18 52	19 29	19 29			19 46	20 20	
	d	17 50	18 19			18 42		18 52	19 30	19 30			19 46	20 21	
Invergowrie	d														
Perth	a	18 13						19 14			19 35		20 07		
	d	18 14			18 28		19 09	19 14			19 37	20 00	20 11		
Gleneagles	d										19 52		20 25		
Dunblane 230	d	18 37			18 49						20 05				
Bridge of Allan 230	d				18 52						20 09				
Stirling 230	d	18 43			18a59			19 43			20 14		20 40		
Larbert 230	d														
Glasgow Queen St. 230 ⇌	a	19 16						20 15			20 45		21 14		
Leuchars ■	a		18 31			18 53			19 43	19 43				20 33	
St Andrews Bus Station 🚌	a		*18 55*			*19 14*			*19 59*	*19 59*				*20 59*	
St Andrews Bus Station 🚌	d		*18 05*			*18 25*			*19 10*	*19 10*				*20 00*	
Leuchars ■	d		18 31			18 54			19 44	19 44				20 33	
Cupar	d					19 02									
Springfield	d														
Ladybank	d					19 09						20 24			
Markinch	d					19 17	19 44					20 32			
Kirkcaldy 242	d					19 26	19 54		20 08	20 08		20 41			
Inverkeithing 242	d					19 42			20 24	20 24		20 59			
Haymarket 242	a		19 27			20 04	20 24		20 42	20 42		21 15		21 26	
Edinburgh ■ 242	a		19 34			20 09	20 29		20 48	20 48		21 20		21 31	

A ⌶ from Aberdeen

C To Leeds

Table 229 Mondays to Saturdays

Inverurie, Dyce, Aberdeen, Dundee, Inverness and Perth - Glasgow Queen Street and Edinburgh

Network Diagram - see first page of Table 225

		SR	SR ◇■ ⌶	SR ◇■ ⌶	SR ◇ A ⌶	SR ◇■	SR ◇■ ⌶	SR ◇■	XC SO ◇■	XC SX ◇■	SR FO B C ✕	SR SX B C ✕	SR FSX ■	SR FO ■
Inverness	d		18 44				20 15					20 47		
Carrbridge	d		19 16											
Aviemore	d		19 30				21 01					21u29		
Kingussie	d		19 42				21 13					21u42		
Newtonmore	d		19 47				21 18					21u50		
Dalwhinnie	d		19 59				21 31					22u06		
Blair Atholl	d		20 21				21 53					22u32		
Pitlochry	d		20 31				22 03					22u45		
Dunkeld & Birnam	d		20 44				22 16					23u00		
Inverurie 240	d				19 40									
Dyce 240 ✈	d				19 52									
Aberdeen 240	a				20 03									
	d			19 47	20 05	20 42		21 05	21 17	21 31	21 42		22 27	23 22
Portlethen	d			19 57									22 37	23 32
Stonehaven	d			20 06	20 21	20 58		21 21	21 35	21 49	22u00		22 46	23 41
Laurencekirk	d							21 35					22 59	23 54
Montrose	d			20 24	20 43	21 20		21 45	21 56	22 10	22u25		23 10	00 05
Arbroath	d			20 38	20 57	21 34		21 58	22 12	22 26	22u43		23 24	00 19
Carnoustie	d				21 04						22u52		23 31	00 26
Golf Street	d													
Barry Links	d													
Monifieth	d													
Balmossie	d													
Broughty Ferry	d												23 38	00 33
Dundee	a			20 57	21 15	21 52		22 15	22 28	22 42			23 48	00 43
	d	20 42		20 57	21 16	21 52		22 15	22 29	22 43	23u06		23 49	00 44
Invergowrie	d												23 54	00 49
Perth	a		21 00	21 18		22 14	22 30						00 12	01 07
	d		21 02	21 18		22 14	22 30					23u21		
Gleneagles	d						22 47					23u39		
Dunblane 230	d						22 59					23u55		
Bridge of Allan 230	d						23 02							
Stirling 230	d			21 46		22 43	23 05					00u06		
Larbert 230	d													
Glasgow Queen St. 230 ⇌	a			22 20		23 15	23 39							
Leuchars ■	a	20 53			21 28			22 27	22 41	22 55				
St Andrews Bus Station 🚌	a	*21 15*			*21 59*			*22 59*	*22 59*	*23 29*				
St Andrews Bus Station 🚌	d	*20 30*			*21 00*			*22 00*	*22 00*	*22 30*				
Leuchars ■	d	20 54			21 28			22 27	22 42	22 56	23u25			
Cupar	d	21 01			21 36			22 34	22 49	23 03				
Springfield	d													
Ladybank	d	21 09			21 43			22 42	22 57	23 10				
Markinch	d	21 16	21 32		21 51			22 49	23 05	23 18				
Kirkcaldy 242	d	21 26	21 42		21 59			22 59	23 14	23 26	23u53			
Inverkeithing 242	d	21 49			22 23			23 23	23 31	23 42	00u12			
Haymarket 242	a	22 10	22 13		22 45			23 43	23 50	23 57				
Edinburgh ■ 242	a	22 16	22 19		22 50			23 50	23 55	00 05				

A ⌶ from Aberdeen

C To London Euston

Table 229

Sundays

Inverurie, Dyce, Aberdeen, Dundee, Inverness and Perth - Glasgow Queen Street and Edinburgh

Network Diagram - see first page of Table 225

	SR	SR	SR	SR	SR	SR	GR	SR	GR	XC	SR	SR	GR	SR	SR	SR
			■			◇■	■ ■ B ✠		■ ■ C ✠	◇■	◇■ ✠	◇■ ✠	■ ■ D ✠			
Inverness d									09 40		10 44					
Carrbridge d									10 10							
Aviemore d									10 18		11 22					
Kingussie d									10 31		11 34					
Newtonmore d									10 36							
Dalwhinnie d																
Blair Atholl d									11 08							
Pitlochry d									11 24		12 15					
Dunkeld & Birnam d									11 37		12 34					
Inverurie 240 d																
Dyce 240 ✈ d																
Aberdeen 240 a																
d						09 27	09 47			11 12		11 29	11 47			
Portlethen d																
Stonehaven d						09 43	10 04			11 29		11 45	12 04			
Laurencekirk d						09 57										
Montrose d						10 08	10 27			11 50		12 07	12 27			
Arbroath d						10 22	10 43			12 06		12 21	12 43			
Carnoustie d						10 29										
Golf Street d																
Barry Links d																
Monifieth d																
Balmossie d																
Broughty Ferry d																
Dundee a						10 43	11 00			12 24		12 39	13 00			
d	07 25		08 44		09 25	10 43	11 02	11 25		12 25		12 43	13 01	13 25		
Invergowrie d																
Perth a			09 03			11 05			11 58		12 51	13 03				
d			09 03	09 27		11 05			11 58		12 52	13 05				
Gleneagles d			09 20	09 42		11 20			12 14			13 20				
Dunblane 230 d			09 31	09 54		11 31			12 27			13 31			14 01	15 01
Bridge of Allan 230 d				09 58											14 04	15 04
Stirling 230 d		09 05	09 38	10 02		11 38			12 34			13 38			14 10	15 10
Larbert 230 d		09 13	09 47	10 11											14 19	15 19
Glasgow Queen St. ■ 230 ⇌ a			10 15			12 11						14 11				
Leuchars ■ a	07 36				09 36		11 15	11 36		12 37			13 14	13 37		
St Andrews Bus Station 🚌 a	09 37				09 55		11 37	11 57		12 57			13 37	13 57		
St Andrews Bus Station 🚌 d					09 15		10 55	11 15		12 15			12 55	13 15		
Leuchars ■ d	07 37				09 37		11 16	11 37		12 38			13 15	13 37		
Cupar d	07 44				09 44			11 44		12 45				13 44		
Springfield d																
Ladybank d	07 52				09 52			11 52						13 52		
Markinch d	07 59				09 59			11 59						13 59		
Kirkcaldy 242 d	08 08				10 08		11 40	12 08		13 03	13 29		13 39	14 08		
Inverkeithing 242 d	08 30				10 30		11 56	12 30		13 18	13 45		13 58	14 30		
Haymarket 242 a	08 52	09 59		10 51	10 58		12 15	12 58	13 13	13 36	14 07		14 17	14 56	14 59	15 59
Edinburgh ■ 242 a	09 00	10 04		10 56	11 06		12 23	13 06	13 19	13 42	14 12		14 25	15 03	15 04	16 04

B To London Kings Cross. The Northern Lights C To London Kings Cross. The Highland Chieftain D To London Kings Cross

Table 229

Sundays

Inverurie, Dyce, Aberdeen, Dundee, Inverness and Perth - Glasgow Queen Street and Edinburgh

Network Diagram - see first page of Table 225

	SR	SR	GR	SR	SR	SR	SR	SR	SR	SR	SR	SR	SR	SR
	◇■ ✠	◇■ ✠	■ ■ B ✠	◇■ ✠		◇■ ✠	◇■ ✠	◇■ ✠		◇■ ✠	◇■ ✠	◇■ ✠		◇■ ✠
Inverness d	12 33			13 25				15 20		16 15		15 27		
Carrbridge d	13 05									16 46				
Aviemore d	13 14			14 03				15 57		16 55				
Kingussie d	13 34			14 16				16 10		17 14				
Newtonmore d	13 39													
Dalwhinnie d	13 50													
Blair Atholl d	14 12									17 49				
Pitlochry d	14 21			14 56				16 51		17 58				
Dunkeld & Birnam d	14 34							17 04		18 15				
Inverurie 240 d												17 14		
Dyce 240 ✈ d												17 30		
Aberdeen 240 a												17 41		
d		13 27	13 50			15 10	15 30				17 10	17 47		19 10
Portlethen d						15 20								
Stonehaven d		13 43	14 07			15 26	15 46				17 26	18 04		19 26
Laurencekirk d		13 57										18 18		
Montrose d		14 07	14 30			15 48	16 08				17 48	18 28		19 48
Arbroath d		14 22	14 46			16 02	16 22				18 02	18 43		20 02
Carnoustie d						16 09								20 09
Golf Street d														
Barry Links d														
Monifieth d														
Balmossie d														
Broughty Ferry d														
Dundee a		14 43	15 03			16 23	16 41				18 17	19 02		20 18
d		14 45	15 04		15 25	16 25	16 43		17 25		18 19	19 04	19 27	20 20
Invergowrie d														
Perth a	14 51	15 06		15 24			17 03	17 20		18 30		19 25		
d	14 52	15 08		15 25			17 05	17 21		18 31		19 27		
Gleneagles d	15 07	15 21					17 20			18 48				
Dunblane 230 d	15 18	15 33					17 31			18 59				
Bridge of Allan 230 d														
Stirling 230 d	15 24	15 45					17 38			19 05		19 55		
Larbert 230 d	15 33									19 13				
Glasgow Queen St. ■ 230 ⇌ a	15 56	16 31					18 12			19 39		20 31		
Leuchars ■ a			15 17		15 36	16 36			17 36		18 30		19 38	20 31
St Andrews Bus Station 🚌 a			15 37		15 57	16 55			17 57		18 55		19 59	20 55
St Andrews Bus Station 🚌 d			14 55		15 15	16 15			17 15		18 00		19 15	20 15
Leuchars ■ d			15 18		15 37	16 37			17 37		18 31		19 39	20 32
Cupar d					15 44				17 44				19 46	
Springfield d														
Ladybank d					15 52				17 52				19 54	
Markinch d					15 59				17 59				20 01	
Kirkcaldy 242 d			15 42	16 03	16 08	17 02		17 58	18 07		18 56		20 10	20 59
Inverkeithing 242 d			15 58	16 19	16 30	17 18		18 14	18 29		19 12		20 31	21 15
Haymarket 242 a			16 17	16 35	16 54	17 34		18 30	18 52		19 27		20 54	21 31
Edinburgh ■ 242 a			16 25	16 42	16 59	17 41		18 35	19 00		19 35		21 01	21 36

B To London Kings Cross

Table 229

Sundays

Inverurie, Dyce, Aberdeen, Dundee, Inverness and Perth - Glasgow Queen Street and Edinburgh

Network Diagram - see first page of Table 225

			SR ◇■ ✕	SR ◇■ ✕	SR ◇■ ✕	XC ◇■	SR B C 🛏	SR B C 🛏	SR ■
Inverness		d	18 30					20 25	
Carrbridge		d	19 02						
Aviemore		d	19 11					21u08	
Kingussie		d	19 26					21u22	
Newtonmore		d	19 30					21u29	
Dalwhinnie		d	19 42					21u43	
Blair Atholl		d	20 03					22u09	
Pitlochry		d	20 13					22u22	
Dunkeld & Birnam		d	20 26					22u37	
Inverurie	240	d							
Dyce	240 ✈	d							
Aberdeen	240	a							
		d		19 35	20 10	21 28	21 42		22 30
Portlethen		d			20 20				
Stonehaven		d		19 51	20 26	21 45	22u00		22 48
Laurencekirk		d							
Montrose		d		20 13	20 48	22 06	22u25		23 11
Arbroath		d		20 27	21 02	22 22	22u43		23 25
Carnoustie		d					22u52		23 32
Golf Street		d							
Barry Links		d							
Monifieth		d							
Balmossie		d							
Broughty Ferry		d							
Dundee		a		20 42	21 19	22 38			23 46
		d		20 43	21 21	22 39	23u06		23 47
Invergowrie		d							
Perth		a	20 42	21 04					00 09
		d	20 46	21 05				23u00	
Gleneagles		d		21 20				23u18	
Dunblane	230	d		21 31				23u34	
Bridge of Allan	230	d							
Stirling	230	d		21 38				23u45	
Larbert	230	d		21 49					
Glasgow Queen St. ■	230 ⇌	a		22 15					
Leuchars ■		a			21 32	22 51			
St Andrews Bus Station	🚌	a			*21 55*	*23 29*			
St Andrews Bus Station	🚌	d			*21 15*	*22 30*			
Leuchars ■		d			21 33	22 52	23u25		
Cupar		d			21 39	22 59			
Springfield		d							
Ladybank		d			21 48	23 06			
Markinch		d			21 54	23 14			
Kirkcaldy	242	d	21 25		22 05	23 22	23u53		
Inverkeithing	242	d	21 41		22 21	23 38	00u12		
Haymarket	242	a	21 56		22 36	23 53			
Edinburgh ■	242	a	22 01		22 43	23 58			

C To London Euston

Table 230

Mondays to Saturdays

Edinburgh, Glasgow Queen Street and Falkirk Grahamston - Stirling, Alloa and Dunblane

Miles	Miles	Miles	Miles			SR MX	SR MO A	SR MX B	SR MX	SR MX	SR	SR ■ C	SR ◇■ D ✕	SR	SR ■ C	SR SX ■ F	SR SO ■ F	SR SX ■ F	SR SO	SR
0	0	—	—	**Edinburgh** ■	d				23p33		05 18	05 55			06 30					06 32
1¼	—	—	—	Haymarket	d				23p37		05 22	05 59			06 34					06 36
3¾	—	—	—	Edinburgh Park	d				23p43		05 27									06 42
—	17½	—	—	Linlithgow	d				23p55		05 39	06 13			06 48					06 54
—	22¼	—	—	Polmont ■	d				23p59		05 44	06 19			06 55					07 00
—	—	0	0	**Glasgow Queen Street** ■ ⇌	d	23p18	23p35	23p36		23p48			05 56	06 14		06 30	06 30	06 45		
—	—	3¼	3¼	Bishopbriggs	d	23p24	23p41			23p53				06 20						
—	—	6¼	6¼	Lenzie ■	d	23p30	23p47			23p59				06 25		06a38	06 38			
—	—	11½	11½	Croy ■	d	23p35	23p53			00 05		06a34		06 32	07a10		06a43	06a57		
—	25½	—	—	**Falkirk Grahamston**	d				00 07		05 51									07 07
—	27	—	—	Camelon ■	d				00 10		05 54									07 10
—	28¾	21	21	Larbert	d	23p49	00 05		00 16	00 18	06 00		06 16	06 43						07 15
—	36½	29	29	**Stirling**	d	00 01	00 14	00 05	00 25	00a32	06 09		06 25	06 51					07 01	07 24
—	—	—	35¾	**Alloa**	a	00 12								07 05						
—	40	32½	—	Bridge of Allan	d		00 18	00 10	00 29		06 13								07 05	07 29
—	42	34½	—	**Dunblane**	a		00 22	00 14	00 36		06 20		06 31						07 12	07 35

		SR SX ■ C	SR	SR ■ ✕	SR ■ F ✕	SR ◇■ G	SR	SR ■ C ✕	SR	SR ■ C ✕	SR ■ F ✕	SR ◇■ H ✕	SR	SR	SR SX I	SR ■ C ✕	SR ■ F ✕	SR ■ C ✕	SR ■ J ✕	SR	SR ■ ✕
Edinburgh ■	d	06 45		07 00			07 03	07 15		07 30			07 33			07 45		08 00		08 04	08 15
Haymarket	d	06 49		07 04			07 07	07 19		07 34			07 38			07 49		08 04		08 08	08 19
Edinburgh Park	d						07 12						07 42							08 13	
Linlithgow	d	07 04					07 24	07 33		07 48			07 54		07 59	08 04				08 25	08 33
Polmont ■	d			07 21			07 30			07 55			08 00					08 22		08 30	08 39
Glasgow Queen Street ■ ⇌	d		06 48	07a50	07 00	07 06			07 18		07 30	07 41		07 48			08 00		08 06		09a07
Bishopbriggs	d		06 53						07 23					07 54							
Lenzie ■	d		06 59		07a08				07 29					08 00		08a25					
Croy ■	d	07a23	07 05					07a52	07 35	08a10	07a41			08 06			08a11	08a36			
Falkirk Grahamston	d						07 36						08 07		08 11					08 37	
Camelon ■	d						07 40						08 10		08a14					08 40	
Larbert	d		07 18				07 46		07 50				08 16	08 19						08 46	
Stirling	d		07 40			07 33	07 55		08 06			08u09	08 25	08a31					08 36	08 55	
Alloa	a								08 18												
Bridge of Allan	d		07 44				07 59						08 29						08 40	09 00	
Dunblane	a		07 52			07 39	08 08					08 15	08 36						08 44	09 08	

		SR	SR ■ C ✕	SR	SR ■ F ✕	SR ◇■ H ✕	SR	SR ■ ✕	SR	SR ■ F ✕	SR ■ C ✕	SR J ✕	SR	SR ■ ✕	SR	SR ■ C ✕	SR ■ F ✕	SR ◇■ H ✕	SR	SR ■ ✕
Edinburgh ■	d		08 30				08 31	08 45			09 00		09 03	09 15		09 30			09 33	09 45
Haymarket	d		08 34				08 36	08 49			09 04		09 07	09 19		09 34			09 38	09 49
Edinburgh Park	d						08 43						09 14						09 43	
Linlithgow	d						08 55	09 03					09 26	09 33					09 55	10 03
Polmont ■	d						09 00	09 09					09 31	09 39					10 00	10 09
Glasgow Queen Street ■ ⇌	d	08 18			08 30	08 41		09a36	08 48	09 00		09 08		10a06	09 18		09 30	09 41		10a36
Bishopbriggs	d	08 23							08 53						09 23					
Lenzie ■	d	08 29							08 59						09 29					
Croy ■	d	08 35	09a03		08a42				09 05	09a12	09a33				09 35	10a03	09a42			
Falkirk Grahamston	d						09 07						09 38						10 08	
Camelon ■	d						09 10						09 41						10 11	
Larbert	d	08 49					09 16		09 18				09 47		09 52				10 15	
Stirling	d	09 00				09a07	09 25		09 39			09 34	09 56		10 03			10a07	10 24	
Alloa	a	09 13													10 16					
Bridge of Allan	d						09 30		09 42				10 00						10 30	
Dunblane	a						09 36		09 51			09 40	10 07						10 36	

		SR	SR ■ F ✕	SR ■ C ✕	SR ◇■ G ✕	SR	SR ■ ✕	SR	SR ■ C ✕	SR ■ F ✕	SR ◇■ H ✕	SR	SR ■ ✕	SR	SR ■ F ✕	SR ■ C ✕	SR	SR ■ ✕	SR	SR ■ C ✕
Edinburgh ■	d			10 00		10 02	10 15		10 30			10 32	10 45			11 00	11 03	11 15		11 30
Haymarket	d			10 04		10 07	10 19		10 34			10 36	10 49			11 04	11 08	11 19		11 34
Edinburgh Park	d					10 13						10 43					11 13			
Linlithgow	d					10 25	10 33					10 55	11 03				11 25	11 33		
Polmont ■	d					10 30	10 39					11 00	11 09				11 31	11 39		
Glasgow Queen Street ■ ⇌	d	09 49	10 00		10 10		11a06	10 18		10 30	10 41		11a37	10 48	11 00			12a06	11 19	
Bishopbriggs	d	09 54						10 23						10 53					11 23	
Lenzie ■	d	10 00						10 29						10 59					11 29	
Croy ■	d	10 06	10a12	10a33				10 35	11a03	10a42				11 05	11a12	11a33			11 35	12a03
Falkirk Grahamston	d					10 36						11 08					11 38			
Camelon ■	d					10 40						11 11					11 41			
Larbert	d	10 18				10 46		10 48				11 15		11 18			11 46		11 48	
Stirling	d	10a31			10 35	10 55		11 00			11a08	11 24		11 30			11 55		12 00	
Alloa	a							11 13											12 13	
Bridge of Allan	d				10 41	11 00						11 30		11 35			12 00			
Dunblane	a				10 44	11 07						11 36		11 43			12 07			

A from 21 May. To Perth
B To Perth
C To Glasgow Queen Street
D To Dyce
F To Edinburgh
G To Inverness
H To Aberdeen
I From Kirkcaldy to Glasgow Queen Street
J To Dundee

Edinburgh, Glasgow Queen Street and Falkirk Grahamston - Stirling, Alloa and Dunblane

		SR ■ C ⌶	SR ◇■ D ⌶	SR	SR ■ ⌶	SR	SR ■ C ⌶	SR ■ A ⌶	SR ◇■ E ⌶	SR	SR ■ ⌶	SR	SR ■ A ⌶	SR ■ C ⌶	SR ◇■ D ⌶	SR	SR ■ ⌶	SR	SR ■ A ⌶
Edinburgh ■	d			11 32	11 45			12 00		12 03	12 15		12 30			12 31	12 45		13 00
Haymarket	d			11 36	11 49			12 04		12 08	12 19		12 34			12 36	12 49		13 04
Edinburgh Park	d			11 43						12 13						12 43			
Linlithgow	d			11 55	12 03					12 26	12 33					12 55	13 03		
Polmont ■	d			12 01	12 09					12 31	12 39					13 01	13 09		
Glasgow Queen Street ■	d	11 30	11 41		12a37	11 48	12 00		12 10		13a06	12 18		12 30	12 41		13a36	12 48	
Bishopbriggs	d					11 53						12 23						12 53	
Lenzie ■	d					11 59						12 29						12 59	
Croy ■	d	11a42				12 05	12a12	12a34				12 35	13a03	12a42				13 05	13a33
Falkirk Grahamston	d			12 07						12 37						13 07			
Camelon ■	d			12 10						12 40						13 10			
Larbert	d			12 16		12 18				12 47		12 48				13 16		13 18	
Stirling	d		12a07	12 25		12a31			12 35	12 56		13 00			13a07	13 25		13 31	
Alloa	a											13 13							
Bridge of Allan	d			12 30					12 41	13 00						13 30		13 35	
Dunblane	a			12 36					12 44	13 07						13 36		13 43	

		SR ■ C ⌶	SR	SR ■ ⌶	SR	SR ■ A ⌶	SR ■ C ⌶	SR ◇■ D ⌶	SR	SR ■ ⌶	SR	SR ■ A ⌶	SR ■ C ⌶	SR	SR ■ ⌶	SR	SR ■ A ⌶	SR ■ C ⌶
Edinburgh ■	d		13 03	13 15		13 30			13 32	13 45		14 00		14 04	14 15		14 30	
Haymarket	d		13 07	13 19		13 34			13 36	13 49		14 04		14 07	14 19		14 34	
Edinburgh Park	d		13 14						13 43					14 13				
Linlithgow	d		13 26	13 33					13 55	14 03				14 25	14 33			
Polmont ■	d		13 30	13 39					14 00	14 09				14 30	14 39			
Glasgow Queen Street ■	d	13 00		14a06	13 19		13 30	13 41		14a36	13 48		14 00		15a07	14 18		14 30
Bishopbriggs	d				13 25						13 53					14 23		
Lenzie ■	d				13 31						13 59					14 29		
Croy ■	d	13a12			13 37	14a03	13a42				14 05	14a33	14a12			14 35	15a03	14a42
Falkirk Grahamston	d		13 37						14 07					14 37				
Camelon ■	d		13 40						14 10					14 40				
Larbert	d		13 46		13 48				14 15		14 16			14 47		14 48		
Stirling	d		13 55		14 00			14a07	14 24		14 31			14 56		15 00		
Alloa	a				14 13											15 13		
Bridge of Allan	d		14 00						14 28		14 36			15 00				
Dunblane	a		14 07						14 35		14 43			15 07				

		SR ◇■ D ⌶	SR	SR ■ ⌶	SR	SR ■ C ⌶	SR ■ A ⌶	SR ◇■ E ⌶	SR	SR ■ ⌶	SR	SR ■ A ⌶	SR ■ C ⌶	SR	SR ■ ⌶	SR	SR ■ C ⌶	SR ■ A ⌶	SR F ⌶	SR	SR ■ ⌶
Edinburgh ■	d		14 33	14 45			15 00		15 03	15 15		15 30		15 31	15 45			16 00		16 03	16 15
Haymarket	d		14 36	14 49			15 04		15 08	15 19		15 34		15 36	15 49			16 04		16 07	16 19
Edinburgh Park	d		14 43						15 14					15 43						16 13	
Linlithgow	d		14 55	15 03					15 25	15 34				15 55	16 04					16 25	16 33
Polmont ■	d		15 00	15 09					15 30	15 40				16 00	16 10					16 31	16 39
Glasgow Queen Street ■	d	14 41		15a37	14 49	15 00		15 10		16a07	15 18		15 30		16a36	15 48	16 00		16 10		17a07
Bishopbriggs	d				14 54						15 25					15 54					
Lenzie ■	d				15 00						15 30					15 59					
Croy ■	d				15 06	15a12	15a33				15 37	16a03	15a42			16 06	16a12	16a33			
Falkirk Grahamston	d		15 08						15 37					16 07						16 37	
Camelon ■	d		15 11						15 40					16 10						16 40	
Larbert	d		15 15		15 17				15 44		15 50			16 16		16 18				16 46	
Stirling	d	15a07	15 24		15a31			15 36	15 53		16 01			16 25		16a31			16 39	16 55	
Alloa	a										16 15										
Bridge of Allan	d		15 30					15 41	15 57					16 29					16 44	17 00	
Dunblane	a		15 36					15 45	16 07					16 36					16 49	17 07	

A To Glasgow Queen Street
C To Edinburgh
D To Aberdeen
E To Inverness
F To Dundee

Edinburgh, Glasgow Queen Street and Falkirk Grahamston - Stirling, Alloa and Dunblane

		SR	SR ■ A ⌶	SR ■ C ⌶	SR SX	SR SO ◇■ D ⌶	GR SO ■ E ⌶	GR SX ■ E ⌶	SR	SR ■ ⌶	SR	SR ■ C ⌶	SR ■ A ⌶	SR SO F	SR SX	SR SX G	SR	SR ■ ⌶	SR
Edinburgh ■	d		16 30				16 32	16 33	16 36	16 45			17 00				17 03	17 15	
Haymarket	d		16 34				16 38	16 38	16 41	16 49			17 04				17 07	17 19	
Edinburgh Park	d								16 46								17 13		
Linlithgow	d								16 58	17 06							17 26	17 33	
Polmont ■	d								17 04	17 13							17 32	17 39	
Glasgow Queen Street ■	d	16 19		16 30	16 33	16 41				17a40	16 48	17 00		17 03	17 03	17 11		18a06	17 18
Bishopbriggs	d	16 24			16 39						16 53			17 08	17 08				17 23
Lenzie ■	d	16 30			16a44						16 59			17 14	17 14				17 29
Croy ■	d	16 36	17a02	16a42							17 05	17a12	17a34	17 19					17 35
Falkirk Grahamston	d						17 03	17 04	17 09						17a32		17 38		
Camelon ■	d								17 12								17 41		
Larbert	d	16 49							17 20		17 23			17 31		17 31	17 47		17 52
Stirling	d	17 08				17a07	17a18	17a19	17 29		17 35			17 45		17 45	17 56		18 02
Alloa	a	17 20																	18 14
Bridge of Allan	d								17 32		17 40			17 49		17 49	18 01		
Dunblane	a								17 40		17 47			17 54		17 54	18 08		

		SR ■ C ⌶	SR SX H	SR SO ◇■ D ⌶	SR SX I	SR ■ A ⌶	SR SX ◇■ D ⌶	SR	SR ■ ⌶	SR	SR ■ C ⌶	SR ■ A ⌶	SR ◇■ J ⌶	SR	SR ■ ⌶	SR	SR ■ A ⌶	SR ■ C ⌶	SR ◇■ D ⌶	SR
Edinburgh ■	d				17 27	17 30		17 32	17 45			18 00		18 01	18 15		18 30			18 34
Haymarket	d				17 32	17 34		17 36	17 49			18 04		18 07	18 19		18 34			18 38
Edinburgh Park	d							17 44						18 13						18 43
Linlithgow	d							17 56	18 04					18 25	18 33					18 55
Polmont ■	d							18 01	18 09					18 30	18 39					19 00
Glasgow Queen Street ■	d	17 30	17 33	17 41			17 41		18a37	17 48	18 00		18 11		19a08	18 18		18 30	18 41	
Bishopbriggs	d		17 38							17 53						18 23				
Lenzie ■	d		17 43							17 59						18 29				
Croy ■	d	17a42				18a05				18 05	18a12	18a34				18 35	19a05	18a42		
Falkirk Grahamston	d		18a04					18 08						18 37						19 07
Camelon ■	d							18 11						18 40						19 10
Larbert	d				17 57			18 17		18 19			18 30	18 46		18 51				19 16
Stirling	d			18 08	18 06		18 15	18 30		18 32			18 41	18 55		19 00			19u07	19 25
Alloa	a							18 42								19 15				
Bridge of Allan	d				18 13					18 37			18 46	18 59						19 29
Dunblane	a			18 14	18 18		18 22			18 44			18 50	19 09					19 13	19 38

		SR ■ ⌶	SR	SR ■ A ⌶	SR ■ C ⌶	SR K ⌶	SR	SR ■ ⌶	SR	SR ■ A	SR ◇■ D ⌶	SR	SR	SR	SR ■	SR ■ C	SR	SR ■ A	SR ◇■ D	SR	SR	SR ■
Edinburgh ■	d	18 45		19 00			19 03	19 15		19 30			19 33		20 00			20 30		20 33		21 00
Haymarket	d	18 49		19 04			19 07	19 19		19 34			19 37		20 04			20 34		20 38		21 04
Edinburgh Park	d						19 13						19 42							20 42		
Linlithgow	d	19 03					19 25	19 33		19 48			19 55		20 18			20 48		20 54		21 19
Polmont ■	d	19 09					19 30	19 39					20 01		20 24					21 00		21 25
Glasgow Queen Street ■	d	19a36	18 48		19 00	19 10		20a07	19 18		19 41			19 48	20a51	20 00	20 18		20 41		20 48	21a51
Bishopbriggs	d		18 53						19 23					19 54			20 23				20 53	
Lenzie ■	d		18 59						19 29					20 00			20 29				20 59	
Croy ■	d		19 05	19a34	19a12				19 35	20a07				20 06		20a12	20 35	21a07			21 05	
Falkirk Grahamston	d						19 36						20 07							21 06		
Camelon ■	d						19 39						20 10							21 09		
Larbert	d		19 21				19 44		19 47				20 16	20 18			20 48			21 16	21 18	
Stirling	d		19a32			19 37	19 53		20 00		20a07		20 25	20 30			21 00		21 07	21 25	21a32	
Alloa	a								20 13								21 13					
Bridge of Allan	d					19 41	19 59						20 30	20 35						21 29		
Dunblane	a					19 45	20 07						20 36	20 43					21 14	21 37		

A To Glasgow Queen Street
C To Edinburgh
D To Aberdeen
E From London Kings Cross to Inverness. The Highland Chieftain
F To Perth
G To Carnoustie
H To Markinch
I From Newcraighall
J To Inverness
K To Dundee

Table 230

Mondays to Saturdays

Edinburgh, Glasgow Queen Street and Falkirk Grahamston - Stirling, Alloa and Dunblane

		SR	SR	SR	SR	SR	SR	SR	SR	SR	SR	SR	SR	SR	SR	SR
		1 E		1 A	◇1 C	D		1	1 E		1 F		D	1 A	1 E	
Edinburgh	d			21 30		21 33		22 00			22 30	22 33		23 00		23 02
Haymarket	d			21 34		21 37		22 04			22 34	22 37		23 04		23 07
Edinburgh Park	d					21 43						22 43				23 12
Linlithgow	d			21 48		21 55		22 18			22 48	22 55		23 18		23 24
Polmont	d					22 00		22 24				23 00		23 24		23 30
Glasgow Queen Street	d	21 00	21 18		21 42		21 48	22a50	22 00	22 18			22 48		23 00	
Bishopbriggs	d		21 21				21 53			22 23			22 53			
Lenzie	d		21 27				21 59			22 29			22 59			
Croy	d	21a12	21 33	22a07			22 05		22a12	22 35	23a07		23 05	23a39	23a12	
Falkirk Grahamston	d					22 07						23 07				23 37
Camelon	d					22 10						23 10				23 40
Larbert	d		21 48			22 16	22 18			22 47		23 16	23 18			23 46
Stirling	d		22 00		22a08	22 25	22 30			23 01		23 25	23 33			23a56
Alloa	a		22 13							23 13						
Bridge of Allan	d					22 30	22 35					23 29	23 37			
Dunblane	a					22 34	22 43					23 36	23 42			

		SR	SR	SR	SR	SR	SR
			1 E	1 A	D		
Edinburgh	d			23 30		23 33	
Haymarket	d			23 34		23 37	
Edinburgh Park	d					23 43	
Linlithgow	d			23 48		23 55	
Polmont	d			23 54		23 59	
Glasgow Queen Street	d	23 18	23 30		23 36		23 48
Bishopbriggs	d	23 24					23 53
Lenzie	d	23 30					23 59
Croy	d	23 35	23a42	00a09			00 05
Falkirk Grahamston	d					00 07	
Camelon	d					00 10	
Larbert	d	23 49				00 16	00 18
Stirling	d	00 01			00 05	00 25	00a32
Alloa	a	00 12					
Bridge of Allan	d				00 10	00 29	
Dunblane	a				00 14	00 36	

Sundays

		SR	SR	SR	SR	SR	SR	SR	SR	SR	SR	SR	SR	SR	SR	SR	SR	SR
			D			1 E	1 A ✠	1 E ✠	1 A	1 E ✠	◇1 C ✠		1 A ✠		1 E ✠		1 A ✠	◇1 H ✠
Edinburgh	d			23p33			08 00		09 00			09 33	10 00			10 32	11 00	
Haymarket	d			23p37			08 04		09 04			09 36	10 04			10 35	11 04	
Edinburgh Park	d			23p43								09 40				10 41		
Linlithgow	d			23p55			08 18		09 18			09 59	10 18			10 54	11 18	
Polmont	d			23p59			08 24		09 24			10 05	10 24			11 00	11 24	
Glasgow Queen Street	d	23p18	23p36		23p48	07 50		08 30		09 30	09 38			10 15	10 30			11 09
Bishopbriggs	d	23p24			23p53									10 21				
Lenzie	d	23p30			23p59						09 47			10 27				
Croy	d	23p35			00 05	08a02	08a39	08a42	09a39	09a42			10a39	10 33	10a42		11a39	
Falkirk Grahamston	d			00 07								10 11				11 06		
Camelon	d			00 10								10 14				11 09		
Larbert	d	23p49		00 16	00 18						10 02	10 21		10 45		11 13		11 29
Stirling	d	00 01	00 05	00 25	00a32						10 12	10 30		10 55		11 23		11 39
Alloa	a	00 12												11 07				
Bridge of Allan	d		00 10	00 29								10 34				11 28		
Dunblane	a		00 14	00 36							10 17	10 41				11 37		11 45

		SR	SR	SR	SR	SR	SR	SR	SR	SR	SR	SR	SR	SR	SR	SR	SR	SR	SR	SR
			1 E ✠	◇1 C		1 A ✠		1 A ✠	1 E ✠		1 E ✠	1 ✠		1 A ✠	◇1 C ✠		1 ✠	1 E ✠		1 A
Edinburgh	d				11 35	12 00		12 30		12 35		13 00		13 30		13 36	14 00			14 30
Haymarket	d				11 39	12 04		12 33		12 40		13 04		13 34		13 41	14 04			14 34
Edinburgh Park	d				11 43					12 43						13 45				
Linlithgow	d				11 55	12 18		12 48		12 55		13 18		13 48		13 57	14 18			14 48
Polmont	d				12 01	12 24				13 01		13 24				14 03	14 24			
Glasgow Queen Street	d	11 15	11 30	11 45			12 15		12 30		13 00	13a51	13 15		13 45		14a51	14 00	14 15	
Bishopbriggs	d	11 21					12 21						13 21						14 21	
Lenzie	d	11 27					12 27						13 27						14 27	
Croy	d	11 33	11a42			12a39	12 33	13a07	12a42		13a12		13 33	14a07				14a12	14 33	15a07
Falkirk Grahamston	d				12 08					13 08						14 09				
Camelon	d				12 10					13 10						14 12				
Larbert	d	11 45			12 15		12 45			13 15			13 45			14 18			14 45	
Stirling	d	11 55		12 12	12 25		12 55			13 25			13 55		14 12	14 26			14 55	
Alloa	a	12 07					13 07						14 07						15 07	
Bridge of Allan	d				12 30					13 30						14 32				
Dunblane	a			12 17	12 38					13 38					14 17	14 38				

A To Glasgow Queen Street
C To Aberdeen
D To Perth
E To Edinburgh
F From Glasgow Queen Street to Glasgow Queen Street
H To Inverness

Table 230

Sundays

Edinburgh, Glasgow Queen Street and Falkirk Grahamston - Stirling, Alloa and Dunblane

		SR	SR	SR	SR	SR	SR	SR	SR	SR	SR	SR	SR	GR	SR	SR	SR	SR	SR
		◇1 A ✠		1 C	1 ✠		1 D ✠	◇1 E ✠		1 ✠	1 C ✠		1 D ✠	1 F ✠		1 C ✠	1 ✠		1 D
Edinburgh	d		14 36		15 00		15 30		15 35	16 00			16 30	16 30	16 35		17 00		17 30
Haymarket	d		14 39		15 04		15 34		15 39	16 04			16 34	16 35	16 39		17 04		17 34
Edinburgh Park	d		14 43						15 43						16 43				
Linlithgow	d		14 55		15 18		15 48		15 55	16 18			16 48		16 55		17 18		17 48
Polmont	d		15 01		15 24				16 01	16 24					17 01		17 24		
Glasgow Queen Street	d	14 40		15 00	15a51	15 15		15 45		16a51	16 00	16 15				17 00	17a52	17 15	
Bishopbriggs	d					15 21						16 21						17 21	
Lenzie	d					15 27						16 27						17 27	
Croy	d			15a12		15 33	16a07				16a12	16 33	17a07			17a12		17 33	18a07
Falkirk Grahamston	d		15 07						16 07					17 02	17 07				
Camelon	d		15 10						16 10						17 10				
Larbert	d	15 00	15 15			15 45			16 15			16 45			17 15			17 48	
Stirling	d	15 09	15 25			15 55		16 12	16 25			16 55		17a17	17 25			17 57	
Alloa	a					16 07						17 07						18 12	
Bridge of Allan	d		15 30						16 30						17 30				
Dunblane	a	15 15	15 38					16 17	16 38						17 38				

		SR	SR	SR	SR	SR	SR	SR	SR	SR	SR	SR	SR	SR	SR	SR	SR	SR	SR	SR	SR	SR
		◇1 E ✠		1 ✠	1 C ✠	◇1 A ✠		1 D ✠		1 ✠	1 C ✠		1 D ✠	◇1 E ✠		1 C	1		1 D		1 C	1 D
Edinburgh	d		17 34	18 00				18 30	18 35	19 00			19 30		19 35		20 00		20 30	20 35		21 00
Haymarket	d		17 38	18 04				18 34	18 39	19 04			19 34		19 39		20 04		20 34	20 39		21 04
Edinburgh Park	d		17 43						18 43						19 43					20 43		
Linlithgow	d		17 55	18 18				18 48	18 55	19 18			19 48		19 55		20 18		20 48	20 55		21 18
Polmont	d		18 01	18 24					19 01	19 24					20 01		20 24			21 01		21 24
Glasgow Queen Street	d	17 45		18a51	18 00	18 10	18 16			19a51	19 00	19 15		19 45		20 00	20a51	20 15			21 00	
Bishopbriggs	d						18 21					19 21						20 21				
Lenzie	d						18 26					19 27						20 27				
Croy	d				18a12		18 33	19a07			19a12	19 33	20a07			20a12		20 33	21a07		21a12	21a39
Falkirk Grahamston	d		18 07						19 07						20 07					21 07		
Camelon	d		18 10						19 10						20 10					21 10		
Larbert	d		18 15			18 30	18 45		19 16			19 45			20 14			20 45		21 15		
Stirling	d	18a12	18 25			18 40	18 55		19 26			19 55		20 12	20 24			20 55		21 25		
Alloa	a						19 07					20 07						21 07				
Bridge of Allan	d		18 30						19 30						20 29					21 30		
Dunblane	a		18 37			18 46			19 40					20 17	20 38					21 38		

		SR	SR	SR	SR	SR	SR	SR	SR	SR	SR	SR	SR
			1 C	◇1 E ✠		1 D		1 C	G	1 D	1 C	1 D	G
Edinburgh	d				21 36	22 00			22 34	23 00		23 30	
Haymarket	d				21 41	22 04			22 39	23 04		23 34	
Edinburgh Park	d				21 45				22 45				
Linlithgow	d				21 57	22 18			22 58	23 18		23 48	
Polmont	d				22 03	22 24			23 03	23 24		23 54	
Glasgow Queen Street	d	21 15	21 30	21 45			22 15	22 30			23 30		23 35
Bishopbriggs	d	21 21					22 21						23 41
Lenzie	d	21 27					22 27						23 47
Croy	d	21 33	21a42			22a39	22 33	22a42		23a39	23a42	00a09	23 53
Falkirk Grahamston	d				22 09				23 10				
Camelon	d				22 12				23 14				
Larbert	d	21 45			22 18		22 45		23 19				00 05
Stirling	d	21 55		22 11	22 27		22 55		23 28				00 14
Alloa	a	22 07					23 07						
Bridge of Allan	d				22 32				23 33				00 18
Dunblane	a			22 17	22 38				23 37				00 22

A To Elgin
C To Edinburgh
D To Glasgow Queen Street
E To Aberdeen
F From London Kings Cross to Inverness. The Highland Chieftain
G To Perth

Dunblane, Alloa and Stirling - Falkirk Grahamston, Glasgow Queen Street and Edinburgh

Miles	Miles	Miles	Miles	Station		SR MX	SR MX 1 A	SR MX B	SR MO 1 C	SR MX 1 D	SR MO 1 E	SR MX 1 A	SR	SR B	SR 1 D	SR 1 A	SR SX 1 D	SR	SR SO 1 D	SR 1 A	SR
0	0	—	—	Dunblane	d	23p06							05 21	05 46							06 28
2	2	—	—	Bridge of Allan	d	23p09							05 24	05 49							06 31
—	—	—	0	Alloa	d													06 11			
5½	5½	—	6¾	Stirling	d	23p14							05 30	05 54				06 23			06 36
13½	13½	—	14¾	Larbert	d	23p23							05 38	06 03				06 32			06 45
—	15	—	—	Camelon	d	23p29							05 44		06 46						06 51
—	16½	—	—	Falkirk Grahamston	d	23p32							05 47								06 54
24	—	—	25¼	Croy	d		23p39		23p42	23p42	00 09	00 09		06 14		06 34		06 43	06 43	07 10	
29¼	—	—	30½	Lenzie	d		23p44					00 14		06 21			06 38	06 50			
32¼	—	—	33½	Bishopbriggs	d		23p50							06 25				06 54			
34½	—	—	35¾	Glasgow Queen Street	a		00 01				00 25	00 26		06 34	07 29	06 49		07 03		07 25	
—	19½	—	—	Polmont	d	23p38			23p56	23p56			05 53		06 23		06 56		06 56		07 02
—	24¼	—	—	Linlithgow	d	23p45			00 03	00 03			06 00		06 29		07 03		07 03		07 09
—	38	14¾	—	Edinburgh Park	d	23p58							06 12								07 23
—	40½	17¼	—	Haymarket	d	00 04		00 12	00s19	00s20			06 20		06s45		07s19		07s19		07 28
—	41¾	18½	—	Edinburgh 225,242	a	00 09		00 18	00 24	00 25			06 24		06 50		07 25		07 25		07 34

Station		SR SX 1 D	SR 1 D	SR H	SR SX 1 A	SR SX	SR	SR SX B	SR 1 D	SR SX	SR 1 D	SR 1 A	SR B	SR 1 D	SR 1 A	SR SX	SR ◇1 J	SR 1 D	SR SO 1 A	SR SX 1 A
Dunblane	d			06 47						07 23			07 31				07 44			
Bridge of Allan	d			06 51						07 26			07 34				07 48			
Alloa	d						07 11									07 39				
Stirling	d			06 55			07 22			07 31			07 39			07 49	07 53			
Larbert	d			07 04			07 30			07 39			07 47			07 58	08 02			
Camelon	d															08 02				
Falkirk Grahamston	d															08 07				
Croy	d	06 57		07 15	07 23		07 43				07 41	07 52	07 59		08 10			08 11		
Lenzie	d		07 08	07 21		07 34	07 50						08 05				08 18		08 25	08 25
Bishopbriggs	d			07 26		07 38	07 55						08 10						08 29	
Glasgow Queen Street	a			07 35	07 38	07 47	08 04					08 07	08 20		08 25		08 34		08 40	08 40
Polmont	d		07 26						07 38					08 09		08 16		08 26		
Linlithgow	d	07 14	07 32						07 44		07 59			08 15		08 23				
Edinburgh Park	d															08 37				
Haymarket	d	07s31	07s49					07 52	08s01	08 15	08s17			08s31		08 44		08s45		
Edinburgh 225,242	a	07 37	07 55					07 57	08 06	08 22	08 25			08 37		08 48		08 52		

Station		SR SX K	SR	SR	SR 1 A	SR 1 D	SR 1 D	SR	SR	SR ◇1 J	SR 1 A	SR 1 D	SR 1 D	SR	SR	SR H	SR 1 A	SR 1 D	SR 1 D	SR	SR
Dunblane	d		07 58					08 13	08 28						09 03	09 07					09 28
Bridge of Allan	d		08 01					08 16	08 31							09 11					09 31
Alloa	d			07 57										08 36							
Stirling	d		08 07	08 11				08 23	08 36	08 43				08 53	09 09	09 15				09 23	09 36
Larbert	d		08 16	08 19				08 32	08 45					09 02	09 18					09 32	09 45
Camelon	d		08 20						08 49						09 24						09 49
Falkirk Grahamston	d	08 11	08 24						08 54						09 27						09 54
Croy	d			08 32	08 36		08 42	08 43			09 03		09 12	09 13			09 34		09 42	09 43	
Lenzie	d	08 32		08 37				08 50						09 20						09 50	
Bishopbriggs	d	08 37		08 42				08 54						09 24						09 54	
Glasgow Queen Street	a	08 48		08 52	08 55			09 03		09 15	09 19			09 33		09 46	09 50			10 03	
Polmont	d		08 31						09 00			09 08			09 32			09 38			10 00
Linlithgow	d		08 38			08 44			09 07			09 14			09 39			09 44			10 07
Edinburgh Park	d		08 51						09 21						09 53						10 21
Haymarket	d		08 58			09s01	09s14		09 27			09s30	09s45		10 00			10s02	10s12		10 27
Edinburgh 225,242	a		09 04			09 07	09 19		09 32			09 37	09 52		10 06			10 07	10 17		10 34

A From Edinburgh
B From Perth
C From 21 May. From Glasgow Queen Street
D From Glasgow Queen Street
E From 21 May. From Edinburgh
G From Dunfermline Queen Margaret
H From Dundee
J From Aberdeen
K From Kirkcaldy

Dunblane, Alloa and Stirling - Falkirk Grahamston, Glasgow Queen Street and Edinburgh

Station		SR ◇1 A	SR 1 B	SR SX 1 D	SR SO 1 D	SR 1 D	SR	SR	SR 1 B	SR	SR 1 D	GR 1 F	SR 1 D	SR	SR ◇1 G	SR 1 B	SR 1 D	SR 1 D	SR
Dunblane	d							09 58		10 13				10 28					
Bridge of Allan	d							10 01		10 16				10 31					
Alloa	d						09 41												10 36
Stirling	d	09 44					09 53	10 06		10 23		10 30		10 36	10 43				10 53
Larbert	d						10 02	10 15		10 32				10 45					11 02
Camelon	d							10 19						10 49					
Falkirk Grahamston	d							10 24				10 46		10 54					
Croy	d		10 03			10 12	10 13		10 33	10 43			10 42			11 03		11 12	11 13
Lenzie	d						10 20			10 50									11 20
Bishopbriggs	d						10 24			10 54									11 25
Glasgow Queen Street	a	10 14	10 19				10 33		10 49	11 03					11 14	11 19			11 34
Polmont	d			10 08	10 08			10 30			10 38			11 00			11 08		
Linlithgow	d			10 14	10 14			10 37			10 44			11 07			11 14		
Edinburgh Park	d							10 51						11 21					
Haymarket	d			10s30	10s30	10s44		10 58			11s00	11 11	11s14	11 27			11s30	11s45	
Edinburgh 225,242	a			10 37	10 37	10 49		11 04			11 05	11 17	11 20	11 32			11 35	11 50	

Station		SR	SR 1 B	SR 1 D	SR 1 D	SR	SR ◇1 I	SR	SR ◇1 J	SR 1 B	SR 1 D	SR 1 D	SR	SR	SR 1 B	SR 1 D	SR 1 D	SR	SR ◇1 A	SR
Dunblane	d	10 58					11 20	11 28						11 58				12 13		12 28
Bridge of Allan	d	11 01					11 23	11 31						12 01				12 16		12 31
Alloa	d												11 43							
Stirling	d	11 06				11 23	11 28	11 36	11 43				11 53	12 06				12 23		12 36
Larbert	d	11 15				11 32		11 45					12 02	12 15				12 32		12 45
Camelon	d	11 19						11 49						12 19						12 49
Falkirk Grahamston	d	11 24						11 54						12 24						12 54
Croy	d		11 33		11 42	11 43				12 03		12 12	12 13		12 34		12 42	12 43		
Lenzie	d					11 50							12 20					12 50		
Bishopbriggs	d					11 54							12 24					12 54		
Glasgow Queen Street	a		11 50			12 03	12 09		12 15	12 20			12 34		12 49			13 03		
Polmont	d	11 30		11 38				12 00			12 08			12 30		12 38				13 00
Linlithgow	d	11 37		11 44				12 07			12 14			12 37		12 44				13 07
Edinburgh Park	d	11 51						12 22						12 51						13 21
Haymarket	d	11 58		12s00	12s12			12 27			12s30	12s45		12 57		13s00	13s14		13 22	13 27
Edinburgh 225,242	a	12 04		12 07	12 19			12 34			12 36	12 52		13 03		13 07	13 19		13 26	13 32

Station		SR ◇1 G	SR 1 B	SR 1 D	SR 1 D	SR	SR	SR 1 K	SR 1 B	SR 1 D	SR 1 D	SR	SR	SR ◇1 G	SR 1 B	SR 1 D	SR 1 D	SR
Dunblane	d						12 58	13 04					13 28					
Bridge of Allan	d						13 01	13 08					13 31					
Alloa	d					12 36												13 41
Stirling	d	12 43				12 53	13 06	13 13				13 23	13 36	13 43				13 53
Larbert	d					13 02	13 15					13 32	13 45					14 02
Camelon	d						13 19						13 49					
Falkirk Grahamston	d						13 24						13 54					
Croy	d		13 03		13 12	13 13			13 33		13 42	13 43			14 03		14 12	14 13
Lenzie	d					13 20						13 50						14 20
Bishopbriggs	d					13 24						13 54						14 24
Glasgow Queen Street	a	13 14	13 19			13 33		13 47	13 51			14 03		14 14	14 19			14 33
Polmont	d			13 08			13 30			13 38			14 00			14 08		
Linlithgow	d			13 14			13 37			13 44			14 07			14 14		
Edinburgh Park	d						13 51						14 21					
Haymarket	d			13s30	13s45		13 57			14s00	14s11		14 27			14s30	14s45	
Edinburgh 225,242	a			13 35	13 51		14 03			14 05	14 17		14 34			14 37	14 50	

A From Inverurie
B From Edinburgh
D From Glasgow Queen Street
F From Inverness to London Kings Cross. The Highland Chieftain
G From Aberdeen
I From Inverness
J From Dyce
K From Dundee

Dunblane, Alloa and Stirling - Falkirk Grahamston, Glasgow Queen Street and Edinburgh

	SR	SR ■ A ✠	SR ■ B ✠	SR ■ B ✠	SR	SR	SR ◇■ D ✠	SR ■ A ✠	SR ■ B ✠	SR ■ B ✠	SR	SR	SR ■ A ✠	SR ■ B ✠	SR ■ B ✠	SR	SR
Dunblane d	13 58				14 13	14 28						14 58				15 13	15 28
Bridge of Allan d	14 01				14 16	14 31						15 01				15 16	15 31
Alloa d											14 36						
Stirling d	14 06				14 23	14 36	14 44				14 53	15 06				15 23	15 36
Larbert d	14 15				14 32	14 45					15 02	15 15				15 32	15 45
Camelon ■ d	14 19					14 49						15 19					15 49
Falkirk Grahamston d	14 22					14 54						15 24					15 54
Croy ■ d		14 33		14 42	14 43			15 03		15 12	15 13		15 33		15 42	15 43	
Lenzie ■ d					14 50						15 20					15 50	
Bishopbriggs d					14 54						15 24					15 54	
Glasgow Queen Street ■ ⇌ a		14 48			15 03		15 18	15 22			15 34		15 51			16 03	
Polmont ■ d	14 30		14 38			15 00			15 08			15 30		15 38			16 00
Linlithgow d	14 37		14 44			15 07			15 14			15 37		15 44			16 07
Edinburgh Park d	14 51					15 21						15 51					16 21
Haymarket d	14 57		15s00	15s13		15 27			15s30	15s42		15 58		16s00	16s12		16 27
Edinburgh ■ 225,242 a	15 02		15 05	15 19		15 32			15 37	15 47		16 04		16 06	16 19		16 33

	SR ◇■ D ✠	SR ■ A ✠	SR ■ B ✠	SR ■ B ✠	SR	SR	SR F	SR ■ A ✠	SR	SR ■ B ✠	SR SO ■ B ✠	SR SX ■ B ✠	SR ◇■ D ✠	SR ■ A ✠	SR	SR SO ■ B	SR SX ■ B ✠
Dunblane d						15 58	16 05								16 28		
Bridge of Allan d						16 01	16 09								16 31		
Alloa d					15 41												
Stirling d	15 43				15 53	16 06	16 14		16 21						16 36		
Larbert d					16 02	16 15			16 29						16 45		
Camelon ■ d						16 19									16 49		
Falkirk Grahamston d						16 24									16 54		
Croy ■ d		16 03		16 12	16 13			16 33	16 41		16 42	16 42		17 03			
Lenzie ■ d					16 20				16 48								
Bishopbriggs d					16 24				16 52								
Glasgow Queen Street ■ ⇌ a	16 14	16 19			16 33		16 44	16 51	17 03				17 18	17 21			
Polmont ■ d			16 08			16 30				16 38					17 00	17 09	17 09
Linlithgow d			16 14			16 37				16 44					17 07	17 14	17 14
Edinburgh Park d						16 51									17 21		
Haymarket d			16s30	16s43		16 57				17s01	17s13	17s16			17 27	17s34	17s34
Edinburgh ■ 225,242 a			16 35	16 49		17 03				17 07	17 19	17 22			17 35	17 40	17 40

	SR ■ B ✠	SR	SR	SR ■ A ✠	SR ■ B ✠	SR ■ B ✠	SR	SR ◇■ H ✠	SR	SR ◇■ D ✠	SR ■ A ✠	SR ■ B ✠	SR ■ B ✠	SR	SR ■ A ✠	SR ■ B ✠	SR ■ B ✠	SR
Dunblane d			16 58					17 20	17 28	17 36								18 11
Bridge of Allan d			17 01					17 23	17 31									18 14
Alloa d		16 34												17 41				
Stirling d		16 53	17 06				17 23	17 29	17 36	17 42				17 53				18 19
Larbert d		17 02	17 15				17 32		17 45					18 01				18 28
Camelon ■ d			17 19						17 49									
Falkirk Grahamston d			17 24						17 54									
Croy ■ d	17 12	17 13		17 34		17 42	17 43				18 05		18 12	18 14	18 35		18 42	18 43
Lenzie ■ d		17 20					17 50				18 11			18 20				18 50
Bishopbriggs d		17 24					17 54							18 25				18 54
Glasgow Queen Street ■ ⇌ a		17 34		17 51			18 03	18 09		18 15	18 23			18 34	18 50			19 05
Polmont ■ d	17 26		17 30			17 56			18 00			18 08				18 38		
Linlithgow d			17 37		17 41	18 03			18 07			18 14				18 44		
Edinburgh Park d			17 50						18 21									
Haymarket d	17s45		17 58		18s02	18s19			18 28			18s33	18s45			19s01	19s13	
Edinburgh ■ 225,242 a	17 52		18 05		18 07	18 24			18 36			18 40	18 50			19 07	19 19	

	SR	SR ◇■ D ✠	SR ■ A ✠	SR SX ■ B ✠	SR SO ■ B ✠	SR ■ B ✠	SR	SR	SR ■ A ✠	SR	SR ■ B ✠	SR ■ B	SR	SR ◇■ D ✠	SR ■ A	SR ■ B	SR	SR	SR ◇■ H ✠
Dunblane d	18 28	18 37								19 14			19 28					19 58	20 05
Bridge of Allan d	18 31									19 17			19 31					20 01	20 09
Alloa d							18 28	18 54									19 43		
Stirling d	18 36	18 43					18 53			19 23			19 36	19 43			19 53	20 06	20 14
Larbert d	18 45						19 02	19 15		19 32			19 45				20 02	20 15	
Camelon ■ d	18 49							19 19					19 49					20 19	
Falkirk Grahamston d	18 54							19 24					19 54					20 24	
Croy ■ d			19 05			19 12	19 13		19 34	19 43					20 07	20 12	20 13		
Lenzie ■ d							19 20			19 50							20 20		
Bishopbriggs d							19 24			19 54							20 24		
Glasgow Queen Street ■ ⇌ a		19 16	19 23				19 33		19 49	20 03				20 15	20 22		20 34		20 45
Polmont ■ d	19 00			19 08	19 08			19 30			19 38	19 53	20 00					20 32	
Linlithgow d	19 07			19 14	19 14			19 37			19 44	19 59	20 07			20 29		20 39	
Edinburgh Park d	19 21							19 51					20 21					20 51	
Haymarket d	19 27			19s30	19s33	19s46		19 57			20s00	20s16	20 27			20s45		20 58	
Edinburgh ■ 225,242 a	19 33			19 36	19 39	19 51		20 01			20 06	20 21	20 34			20 51		21 03	

A From Edinburgh
B From Glasgow Queen Street
D From Aberdeen
F From Dundee
H From Inverness

Dunblane, Alloa and Stirling - Falkirk Grahamston, Glasgow Queen Street and Edinburgh

	SR	SR ■ A	SR	SR ◇■ B ✠	SR ■ C	SR ■	SR	SR	SR	SR ◇■ B ✠	SR ■ A	SR ■ C	SR ■ A	SR	SR	SR	SR ◇■ B	SR ■ A
Dunblane d			20 28					20 58	21 13						21 58			
Bridge of Allan d			20 31					21 01	21 16						22 01			
Alloa d							20 41							21 42				
Stirling d	20 21		20 36	20 40			20 53	21 06	21 23	21 46				21 53	22 06	22 23	22 43	
Larbert d	20 29		20 45				21 02	21 15	21 32					22 02	22 15	22 32		
Camelon ■ d			20 49					21 19							22 19			
Falkirk Grahamston d			20 54					21 24							22 24			
Croy ■ d	20 43				21 07	21 12	21 13		21 43			22 07	22 12	22 13		22 43		
Lenzie ■ d	20 50						21 20		21 50					22 20		22 50		
Bishopbriggs d	20 54						21 24		21 54					22 24		22 54		
Glasgow Queen Street ■ ⇌ a	21 04			21 14	21 21		21 34		22 03	22 20		22 23		22 34		23 03	23 15	
Polmont ■ d		20 53	21 00					21 30			21 53				22 30			22 53
Linlithgow d		20 59	21 07			21 29		21 37			21 59		22 29		22 37			22 59
Edinburgh Park d			21 21					21 51							22 51			
Haymarket d		21s15	21 27			21s45		21 57			22s18		22s46		22 57			23s15
Edinburgh ■ 225,242 a		21 20	21 31			21 50		22 02			22 23		22 51		23 01			23 20

	SR ■ A	SR	SR ◇■ G ✠	SR	SR	SR ■ C	SR ■ A
Dunblane d			22 59	23 06			
Bridge of Allan d			23 02	23 09			
Alloa d		22 41			23 18		
Stirling d		22 53	23 05	23 14	23a27		
Larbert d		23 02		23 23			
Camelon ■ d				23 29			
Falkirk Grahamston d				23 32			
Croy ■ d	23 12	23 13				23 39	23 42
Lenzie ■ d		23 20				23 44	
Bishopbriggs d		23 24				23 50	
Glasgow Queen Street ■ ⇌ a		23 34	23 39			00 01	
Polmont ■ d	23 26			23 38			23 56
Linlithgow d	23 33			23 45			00 03
Edinburgh Park d				23 58			
Haymarket d	23s49			00 04			00s20
Edinburgh ■ 225,242 a	23 55			00 09			00 25

Sundays

	SR	SR ■ C	SR ■ A	SR ■ C	SR ■ A	SR ■ C ✠	SR ■ A ✠	SR	SR ■ C	SR ■ A ✠	SR	SR ■ J	SR H	SR ■ C ✠	SR ■ A ✠	SR	SR
Dunblane d	23p06											09 31	09 54				11 01
Bridge of Allan d	23p09												09 58				11 04
Alloa d											09 18					10 18	
Stirling d	23p14							09 05			09 28	09 38	10 02			10 28	11 10
Larbert d	23p23							09 13			09 37	09 47	10 11			10 37	11 19
Camelon ■ d	23p29							09 19					10 16				11 24
Falkirk Grahamston d	23p32							09 22					10 19				11 27
Croy ■ d		23p39	23p42	00 09	08 02	08 39	08 42		09 39	09 42	09 48			10 39	10 42	10 48	
Lenzie ■ d		23p44		00 14							09 55	10 02				10 55	
Bishopbriggs d		23p50									09 59					10 59	
Glasgow Queen Street ■ ⇌ a		00 01		00 26		08 59			10 00		10 08	10 15		11 01		11 08	
Polmont ■ d	23p38		23p56		08 16		08 56	09 28		09 56			10 25		10 56		11 33
Linlithgow d	23p45		00 03		08 23		09 03	09 35		10 03			10 32		11 03		11 40
Edinburgh Park d	23p58							09 47					10 44				11 54
Haymarket d	00 04		00s20		08 39		09s24	09 59		10s23			10 51		11s19		12 00
Edinburgh ■ 225,242 a	00 09		00 25		08 49		09 29	10 04		10 28			10 56		11 24		12 04

A From Glasgow Queen Street
B From Aberdeen
C From Edinburgh
G From Inverness
H From Perth
J From Dundee

Table 230

Sundays

Dunblane, Alloa and Stirling - Falkirk Grahamston, Glasgow Queen Street and Edinburgh

	SR ■ A ✕	SR ■ B ✕	SR	SR ◇■ C ✕	SR	SR ■ A ✕	SR	GR ■ E ✕	SR ■ B ✕	SR ■ A ✕	SR ■ B ✕	SR	SR	SR ◇■ C ✕	SR ■ B	SR ■ A ✕	SR ■ B ✕	SR
Dunblane d				11 31	12 01			12 27				13 01		13 31				14 01
Bridge of Allan d					12 04							13 04						14 04
Alloa d			11 14				12 14						13 14					
Stirling d			11 25	11 38	12 10		12 25	12 34				13 10	13 25	13 38				14 10
Larbert d			11 34		12 19		12 34					13 19	13 34					14 19
Camelon ■ d					12 24							13 24						14 24
Falkirk Grahamston d					12 27			12 50				13 27						14 27
Croy ■ d	11 39	11 42	11 45			12 39	12 45		12 42	13 07	13 12		13 45			14 07	14 12	
Lenzie ■ d			11 52				12 52						13 52					
Bishopbriggs d			11 56				12 56						13 56					
Glasgow Queen Street ■ a	11 56		12 05	12 11		12 54	13 05			13 23			14 05	14 11		14 23		
Polmont ■ d		11 56			12 33				12 56			13 33			13 53			14 33
Linlithgow d		12 03			12 40				13 02		13 29	13 40			13 59		14 29	14 40
Edinburgh Park d					12 54							13 54						14 54
Haymarket d		12s20			13 00			13 14	13s21		13s46	14 00			14s17		14s47	15 00
Edinburgh ■ 225,242 a		12 25			13 04			13 19	13 26		13 51	14 04			14 22		14 52	15 04

	SR	SR ■ B ✕	SR ■ A	SR ■ B	SR	SR ◇■ G ✕	SR	SR ■ B	SR ■ A ✕	SR ◇■ C ✕	SR ■ B ✕	SR	SR	SR ■ B ✕	SR ■ A ✕	SR ■ B ✕	SR
Dunblane d					15 01	15 18				15 33		16 01					17 01
Bridge of Allan d					15 04							16 04					17 04
Alloa d	14 14						15 16						16 14				
Stirling d	14 25				15 10	15 24	15 28			15 45		16 10	16 25				17 10
Larbert d	14 34				15 19	15 33	15 36					16 19	16 34				17 19
Camelon ■ d					15 24							16 24					17 24
Falkirk Grahamston d					15 27							16 27					17 27
Croy ■ d	14 45		15 07	15 12			15 49		16 07		16 12		16 45		17 07	17 12	
Lenzie ■ d	14 52						15 55						16 52				
Bishopbriggs d	14 56						16 00						16 56				
Glasgow Queen Street ■ a	15 05		15 22			15 56	16 09		16 22	16 31			17 05		17 22		
Polmont ■ d		14 53			15 33			15 53				16 33		16 53			17 33
Linlithgow d		14 59		15 29	15 40			15 59			16 29	16 40		16 58		17 29	17 40
Edinburgh Park d					15 54							16 54					17 54
Haymarket d		15s15		15 46	16 00			16s18			16s47	17 00		17s15		17 47	18 00
Edinburgh ■ 225,242 a		15 20		15 51	16 04			16 23			16 52	17 04		17 20		17 52	18 04

	SR	SR ◇■ C ✕	SR ■ B ✕	SR ■ A	SR ■ B ✕	SR	SR	SR ■ B ✕	SR ■ A ✕	SR ■ B ✕	SR ◇■ G ✕	SR	SR	SR ■ B ✕	SR ■ A ✕	SR ◇■ G ✕	SR ■ B	SR
Dunblane d		17 31				18 01					18 59	19 08						20 01
Bridge of Allan d						18 04						19 11						20 04
Alloa d	17 14						18 17						19 14					
Stirling d	17 25	17 38				18 10	18 27				19 05	19 17	19 24			19 55		20 10
Larbert d	17 34					18 19	18 34				19 13	19 26	19 33					20 19
Camelon ■ d						18 24						19 31						20 24
Falkirk Grahamston d						18 27						19 34						20 27
Croy ■ d	17 45			18 07	18 12		18 47		19 07	19 12			19 44		20 07		20 12	
Lenzie ■ d	17 52						18 54						19 51					
Bishopbriggs d	17 56						18 58						19 55					
Glasgow Queen Street ■ a	18 05	18 12		18 22			19 08		19 22		19 39		20 04		20 22	20 31		
Polmont ■ d			17 53			18 33		18 53				19 40		19 53				20 33
Linlithgow d			17 58		18 29	18 40		18 59		19 29		19 47		19 59			20 29	20 40
Edinburgh Park d						18 54						20 01						20 54
Haymarket d			18s17		18s47	19 00		19s16		19s47		20 07		20s16			20s46	21 00
Edinburgh ■ 225,242 a			18 22		18 52	19 04		19 21		19 52		20 11		20 21			20 51	21 04

	SR	SR ■ B	SR ■ A	SR ■ B	SR	SR ■ A	SR ■ B	SR	SR ◇■ C ✕	SR	SR ■ A	SR ■ B	SR ■ A	SR ■ B
Dunblane d					21 01				21 31	22 01				
Bridge of Allan d					21 04					22 04				
Alloa d	20 14							21 14						
Stirling d	20 25				21 10			21 25	21 38	22 10				
Larbert d	20 34				21 19			21 34	21 49	22 19				
Camelon ■ d					21 24					22 24				
Falkirk Grahamston d					21 27					22 27				
Croy ■ d	20 45		21 07	21 12		21 39	21 42	21 45			22 39	22 42	23 39	23 42
Lenzie ■ d	20 52							21 52	22 02					
Bishopbriggs d	20 56							21 56						
Glasgow Queen Street ■ a	21 05		21 22			21 55		22 05	22 15		22 55		23 55	
Polmont ■ d		20 53			21 33		21 56			22 33		22 56		23 56
Linlithgow d		20 59		21 29	21 40		22 03			22 40		23 03		00 03
Edinburgh Park d					21 54					22 54				
Haymarket d		21s17		21s46	22 00		22s19			23 00		23s19		00s19
Edinburgh ■ 225,242 a		21 22		21 53	22 04		22 24			23 04		23 24		00 24

A From Edinburgh
B From Glasgow Queen Street
C From Aberdeen
E From Inverness to London Kings Cross. The Highland Chieftain
G From Inverness

Table 232

Mondays to Saturdays

Glasgow Queen Street - Maryhill and Anniesland

Network Diagram - see first Page of Table 220

Miles		SR SO	SR	SR	SR	SR	SR	SR	SR	SR	SR	SR	SR	SR	SR	SR	SR	SR	SR	SR	SR	SR
0	Glasgow Queen Street ■ d	23p54	06 26	06 56	07 26	07 56	08 27	08 56	09 26	09 56	10 26	10 56	11 26	11 56	12 26	12 56	13 26	13 56	14 26	14 56	15 26	15 56
2¼	Ashfield d	23p58	06 30	07 00	07 30	08 00	08 30	09 00	09 30	10 00	10 30	11 00	11 30	12 00	12 30	13 00	13 30	14 00	14 30	15 00	15 30	16 00
3	Possilpark & Parkhouse d	00 01	06 33	07 03	07 33	08 03	08 33	09 03	09 33	10 03	10 33	11 03	11 33	12 03	12 33	13 03	13 33	14 03	14 33	15 03	15 33	16 03
3¼	Gilshochill d	00 03	06 35	07 05	07 35	08 05	08 35	09 05	09 35	10 05	10 35	11 05	11 35	12 05	12 35	13 05	13 35	14 05	14 35	15 05	15 35	16 05
4¼	Summerston d	00 06	06 37	07 07	07 37	08 07	08 37	09 07	09 37	10 07	10 37	11 07	11 37	12 07	12 37	13 07	13 37	14 07	14 37	15 07	15 37	16 07
4¾	Maryhill d	00 07	06 39	07 09	07 39	08 09	08 39	09 09	09 39	10 09	10 39	11 09	11 39	12 09	12 39	13 09	13 39	14 09	14 39	15 09	15 39	16 09
5½	Kelvindale d	00 10	06 41	07 11	07 41	08 11	08 41	09 11	09 41	10 11	10 41	11 11	11 41	12 11	12 41	13 11	13 41	14 11	14 41	15 11	15 41	16 11
6¼	Anniesland 226 a	00 14	06 45	07 15	07 46	08 15	08 47	09 15	09 45	10 16	10 45	11 15	11 46	12 15	12 46	13 15	13 45	14 15	14 45	15 15	15 46	16 16

	SR	SR	SR	SR	SR	SR	SR	SR	SR	SR	SR	SR	SR	SR	SR	SR FO
Glasgow Queen Street ■ d	16 26	16 56	17 26	17 56	18 26	18 56	19 26	19 56	20 26	20 56	21 26	21 56	22 27	22 56	23 26	23 54
Ashfield d	16 30	17 00	17 30	18 00	18 30	19 00	19 30	20 00	20 30	21 00	21 30	22 00	22 30	23 00	23 30	23 58
Possilpark & Parkhouse d	16 33	17 03	17 33	18 03	18 33	19 03	19 33	20 03	20 33	21 03	21 33	22 03	22 33	23 03	23 33	00 01
Gilshochill d	16 35	17 05	17 35	18 05	18 35	19 05	19 35	20 05	20 35	21 05	21 35	22 05	22 35	23 05	23 35	00 03
Summerston d	16 37	17 07	17 37	18 07	18 37	19 07	19 37	20 07	20 37	21 07	21 37	22 07	22 37	23 07	23 37	00 06
Maryhill d	16 39	17 09	17 39	18 09	18 39	19 09	19 39	20 09	20 39	21 09	21 39	22 09	22 39	23 09	23 39	00 07
Kelvindale d	16 41	17 11	17 41	18 11	18 41	19 11	19 41	20 11	20 41	21 11	21 41	22 11	22 41	23 11	23 41	00 10
Anniesland 226 a	16 45	17 15	17 45	18 16	18 46	19 15	19 45	20 15	20 46	21 15	21 46	22 15	22 46	23 15	23 45	00 14

Table 232

Mondays to Saturdays

Anniesland and Maryhill - Glasgow Queen Street

Network Diagram - see first Page of Table 220

Miles		SR	SR	SR	SR	SR SX	SR	SR	SR	SR	SR	SR	SR	SR	SR	SR	SR	SR	SR	SR	SR	SR
0	Anniesland 226 d	06 22	06 52	07 22	07 52		08 24	08 52	09 22	09 52	10 22	10 52	11 22	11 52	12 22	12 52	13 22	13 52	14 22	14 52	15 22	15 52
0¾	Kelvindale d	06 24	06 54	07 24	07 54		08 26	08 54	09 24	09 54	10 24	10 54	11 24	11 54	12 24	12 54	13 24	13 54	14 24	14 54	15 24	15 54
1½	Maryhill d	06 26	06 56	07 26	07 56	08 17	08 28	08 56	09 26	09 56	10 26	10 56	11 26	11 56	12 26	12 56	13 26	13 56	14 26	14 56	15 26	15 56
2	Summerston d	06 28	06 58	07 28	07 58		08 30	08 58	09 28	09 58	10 28	10 58	11 28	11 58	12 28	12 58	13 28	13 58	14 28	14 58	15 28	15 58
3	Gilshochill d	06 30	07 00	07 30	08 00		08 32	09 00	09 30	10 00	10 30	11 00	11 30	12 00	12 30	13 00	13 30	14 00	14 30	15 00	15 30	16 00
3¼	Possilpark & Parkhouse d	06 32	07 02	07 32	08 02	08 22	08 34	09 02	09 32	10 02	10 32	11 02	11 32	12 02	12 32	13 02	13 32	14 02	14 32	15 02	15 32	16 02
4	Ashfield d	06 34	07 04	07 34	08 04		08 36	09 04	09 34	10 04	10 34	11 04	11 34	12 04	12 34	13 04	13 34	14 04	14 34	15 04	15 34	16 04
6¼	Glasgow Queen Street ■ a	06 42	07 13	07 41	08 11	08 37	08 44	09 11	09 41	10 11	10 41	11 11	11 41	12 12	12 41	13 11	13 41	14 11	14 41	15 13	15 44	16 11

	SR SO	SR SX	SR	SR	SR	SR	SR	SR	SR	SR	SR	SR	SR	SR	SR	SR
Anniesland 226 d	16 22	16 25	16 52	17 24	17 52	18 22	18 52	19 22	19 52	20 22	20 52	21 22	21 52	22 22	22 52	23 22
Kelvindale d	16 24	16 27	16 54	17 26	17 54	18 24	18 54	19 24	19 54	20 24	20 54	21 24	21 54	22 24	22 54	23 24
Maryhill d	16 26	16 29	16 56	17 28	17 56	18 26	18 56	19 26	19 56	20 26	20 56	21 26	21 56	22 26	22 56	23 26
Summerston d	16 28	16 31	16 58	17 30	17 58	18 28	18 58	19 28	19 58	20 28	20 58	21 28	21 58	22 28	22 58	23 28
Gilshochill d	16 30	16 33	17 00	17 32	18 00	18 30	19 00	19 30	20 00	20 30	21 00	21 30	22 00	22 30	23 00	23 30
Possilpark & Parkhouse d	16 32	16 35	17 02	17 34	18 02	18 32	19 02	19 32	20 02	20 32	21 02	21 32	22 02	22 32	23 02	23 32
Ashfield d	16 35	16 38	17 04	17 36	18 04	18 34	19 04	19 34	20 04	20 34	21 04	21 34	22 04	22 34	23 04	23 34
Glasgow Queen Street ■ a	16 41	16 48	17 14	17 45	18 12	18 44	19 13	19 44	20 11	20 41	21 11	21 41	22 11	22 41	23 11	23 42

No Sunday Service

Table 238

Mondays to Fridays

Haymarket and Edinburgh - North Berwick and Dunbar

Network Diagram - see first page of Table 225

Miles	Miles				GR ■1 A	XC ◇1 B	SR	SR	SR C	XC ◇1 D	SR	SR	SR	XC ◇1 E	SR	SR	SR	XC ◇1 F	SR	SR	SR	XC ◇1 F	SR	SR
0	0	Haymarket	225,230,242	d		06 57			08 26	08 50				10 54										
1¼	1¼	Edinburgh 10	225,230,242	a		07 02			08 33	08 55				10 58										
—	—			d	05 48	07 07	07 14	08 14	08 45	09 08	09 43	10 13	10 43	11 05	11 43	12 11	12 43	13 06	13 43	14 11	14 43	15 08	15 43	16 33
6½	6½	Musselburgh		d			07 20	08 20	08 49		09 47	10 19	10 47		11 47	12 17	12 47		13 47	14 17	14 47		15 47	16 39
8¾	8¾	Wallyford		d			07 24		08 53		09 51		10 51		11 51		12 51		13 51		14 51		15 51	
11	11	Prestonpans		d			07 27		08 56		09 54		10 54		11 54		12 54		13 54		14 54		15 54	
14½	14½	Longniddry		d			07 32		09 01		09 59		10 59		11 59		12 59		13 59		14 59		15 59	
19	19	Drem		d			07 37		09 07		10 05		11 05		12 05		13 05		14 05		15 06		16 05	
—	29¼	Dunbar		a	06 08	07 26				09 27		10 38		11 24		12 36		13 26		14 36		15 27		16 58
23½	—	North Berwick		a			07 47	08 38	09 18		10 16		11 16		12 17		13 16		14 16		15 16		16 16	

			SR C	XC ◇1 G	SR	GR ■1 H	SR	XC ◇1 I	SR	GR ■1 A	SR	SR	XC ◇1 J	SR	GR ■1 K	SR	SR FX	SR FO	SR
Haymarket	225,230,242	d	16 33		17 05	17 19	17 42	17 54			18 40		19 53		20 43				
Edinburgh 10	225,230,242	a	16 39		17 10	17 27	17 46	17 59			18 44		19 58		20 48				
		d	16 41	17 08	17 13	17 30	17 48	18 04	18 14	18 30	18 45	19 42	20 05	20 43	21 00	21 44	22 06	23 01	23 12
Musselburgh		d	16 45		17 18		17 54		18 19		18 51	19 46		20 46		21 49	22 12	23 07	23 18
Wallyford		d	16 49		17 22		17 58		18 23		18 56	19 50		20 50		21 53			23 22
Prestonpans		d	16 52		17 26		18 01		18 25		19 00	19 53		20 53		21 56			23 25
Longniddry		d	16 57		17 31		18 06		18 31		19 06	19 58		20 58		22 01			23 30
Drem		d	17 03		17 37		18 11		18 35		19 12	20 03		21 03		22 07			23 35
Dunbar		a		17 27		17 51		18 23		18 50			20 24		21 20		22 41	23 33	
North Berwick		a	17 14		17 48		18 21		18 47		19 20	20 15		21 16		22 17			23 54

Saturdays

			GR ■1 A	XC ◇1 L	XC ◇1 M	SR	SR C	XC ◇1 B	SR	SR	SR	SR	XC ◇1 E	SR	SR	SR	SR	XC ◇1 F	SR	SR	SR	SR	XC ◇1 F	SR
Haymarket	225,230,242	d		06 57	06 57		08 26	08 50					10 52											
Edinburgh 10	225,230,242	a		07 02	07 01		08 33	08 54					10 58											
		d	06 20	07 07	07 07	07 43	08 45	09 06	09 12	09 43	10 12	10 43	11 05	11 12	11 43	12 12	12 43	13 08	13 12	13 43	14 12	14 43	15 08	15 12
Musselburgh		d				07 47	08 49		09 15	09 47	10 15	10 47		11 15	11 47	12 15	12 47		13 15	13 47	14 15	14 47		15 15
Wallyford		d				07 51	08 53		09 19	09 51	10 19	10 51		11 19	11 51	12 19	12 51		13 19	13 51	14 19	14 51		15 19
Prestonpans		d				07 54	08 56		09 22	09 54	10 22	10 54		11 22	11 54	12 22	12 54		13 22	13 54	14 22	14 54		15 22
Longniddry		d				07 59	09 01		09 27	09 59	10 27	10 59		11 27	11 59	12 27	12 59		13 27	13 59	14 27	14 59		15 27
Drem		d				08 05	09 07		09 33	10 05	10 33	11 05		11 33	12 05	12 33	13 05		13 33	14 05	14 33	15 05		15 33
Dunbar		a	06 40	07 26	07 26			09 25					11 24					13 28					15 27	
North Berwick		a				08 16	09 18		09 45	10 16	10 45	11 16		11 45	12 17	12 45	13 16		13 45	14 16	14 45	15 16		15 45

			SR	SR	SR C	XC ◇1 N	SR	GR ■1 H	SR	XC ◇1 O	SR	SR	GR ■1 P	SR	SR	SR	SR	SR
Haymarket	225,230,242	d			16 33			17 18		17 56								
Edinburgh 10	225,230,242	a			16 39			17 26		18 01								
		d	15 43	16 12	16 41	17 08	17 12	17 30	17 43	18 05	18 12	18 40	19 00	19 43	20 43	21 43	22 06	23 07
Musselburgh		d	15 47	16 15	16 45		17 15		17 47		18 15	18 47		19 47	20 47	21 49	22 12	23 13
Wallyford		d	15 51	16 19	16 49		17 19		17 51		18 19	18 51		19 51	20 51	21 53		23 17
Prestonpans		d	15 54	16 22	16 52		17 22		17 54		18 22	18 54		19 54	20 54	21 56		23 20
Longniddry		d	15 59	16 27	16 57		17 27		17 59		18 27	18 59		19 59	20 59	22 01		23 25
Drem		d	16 05	16 33	17 03		17 33		18 05		18 33	19 05		20 05	21 05	22 07		23 31
Dunbar		a				17 27		17 50		18 24			19 20				22 31	
North Berwick		a	16 16	16 45	17 14		17 45		18 16		18 45	19 16		20 16	21 16	22 16		23 50

A To London Kings Cross
B From Glasgow Central to Plymouth
C From Glasgow Central
D From Glasgow Central to Plymouth. ✠ from Edinburgh
E From Aberdeen to Penzance. ✠ from Edinburgh
F To Plymouth
G To Bristol Temple Meads
H From Aberdeen to London Kings Cross
I From Glasgow Central to Birmingham New Street
J From Glasgow Central to Newcastle
K From Aberdeen to Leeds
L from 15 September. From Glasgow Central to Plymouth. ✠ from Edinburgh
M until 8 September. From Glasgow Central to Paignton. ✠ from Edinburgh
N To Birmingham New Street
O From Glasgow Central to Birmingham New Street. ✠ from Edinburgh
P To Doncaster

Table 238

Sundays

Haymarket and Edinburgh - North Berwick and Dunbar

Network Diagram - see first page of Table 225

			SR	XC ◇1 A	SR	SR	XC ◇1 B	XC C	SR	SR	XC ◇1 B	XC D	SR	SR	XC ◇1 E	GR ■1 F	SR	XC ◇1 G	SR	GR ■1 F	SR	GR ■1 H	XC ◇1 I	SR
Haymarket	225,230,242	d					12 49				14 42							17 51					19 51	
Edinburgh 10	225,230,242	a					12 54				14 47							17 56					19 56	
		d	10 33	11 05	11 33	12 33	13 06	13 06	13 36	14 33	15 07	15 07	15 33	16 33	17 07	17 30	17 33	18 07	18 33	19 00	19 33	20 00	20 05	20 33
Musselburgh		d	10 39		11 39	12 39			13 39	14 39			15 39	16 39			17 39		18 39		19 39			20 39
Wallyford		d	10 43		11 43	12 43			13 43	14 43			15 43	16 43			17 43		18 43		19 43			20 43
Prestonpans		d	10 46		11 46	12 46			13 46	14 46			15 46	16 46			17 46		18 46		19 46			20 46
Longniddry		d	10 51		11 51	12 51			13 51	14 51			15 51	16 51			17 51		18 51		19 51			20 51
Drem		d	10 56		11 56	12 56			13 57	14 56			15 56	16 56			17 56		18 56		19 56			20 56
Dunbar		a		11 24			13 25	14 01			15 26	16 02			17 26	17 50		18 26		19 20		20 20	20 29	
North Berwick		a	11 06		12 06	13 06			14 09	15 06			16 06	17 06			18 06		19 06		20 06			21 06

			GR ■1 J	SR
Haymarket	225,230,242	d		
Edinburgh 10	225,230,242	a		
		d	21 00	21 33
Musselburgh		d		21 39
Wallyford		d		21 43
Prestonpans		d		21 46
Longniddry		d		21 51
Drem		d		21 56
Dunbar		a	21 20	
North Berwick		a		22 06

A until 9 September. To Plymouth
B until 9 September, from 28 October. From Glasgow Central to Plymouth. ✠ from Edinburgh
C from 16 September until 21 October. To Alnmouth for Alnwick
D from 16 September until 21 October
E To Bristol Temple Meads
F To London Kings Cross
G From Glasgow Central to Birmingham New Street
H To Leeds
I From Glasgow Central to Newcastle
J To Newcastle

Dunbar and North Berwick - Edinburgh and Haymarket

Network Diagram - see first page of Table 225

Miles	Miles			SR	SR	XC	SR	GR	SR	SR	SR	GR		SR	GR	SR	SR	SR	XC	SR	SR	SR		XC	SR
						◇■ A		■ ■ B ⊡		A		■ ■ C ⊡			■ ■ D ⊡⊼				◇■ E ⊼					◇■ F ⊼	
0	—	North Berwick	d	06 07	06 44		07 20			07 56	08 43			09 27		10 27		11 27		12 27		13 27			14 27
—	0	Dunbar	d			07 00		07 42				08 54			09 56		10 49		11 37		12 50			13 41	
4½	10¼	Drem	d	06 15	06 51		07 27			08 04	08 51			09 34		10 34		11 34		12 34		13 34			14 34
9	14¾	Longniddry	d	06 21	06 57		07 33			08 10	08 56			09 40		10 40		11 40		12 40		13 40			14 40
12½	18¼	Prestonpans	d	06 26	07 02		07 38		08 07	08 14	09 01			09 45		10 45		11 45		12 45		13 45			14 45
14¾	20½	Wallyford	d	06 29	07 05		07 41		08 10	08 17	09 04			09 48		10 48		11 48		12 48		13 48			14 48
17	22¾	Musselburgh	d	06 33	07 09		07 45		08 13	08 22	09 09			09 52		10 52	11 09	11 52		12 52	13 09	13 52			14 52
22¼	28	Edinburgh ■ 225,230,242	a	06 40	07 15	07 22	07 55	08 10	08 24	08 32	09 16	09 24		10 00	10 20	11 00	11 15	12 00	12 03	13 00	13 16	14 00		14 10	15 00
—	—		d		07 18	07 26				08 33					10 27										
23½	29¼	Haymarket 225,230,242	a		07 22	07 30				08 37					10 31										

		SR	SR	XC	SR	SR	SR	XC		SR	SR	SR	SR	XC	SR	SR	XC	GR		SR
				◇■ F ⊼				◇■ G ⊼		A				◇■ H ⊼			◇■ F	■ ■ I ⊡⊼		
North Berwick	d		15 26		16 27		17 27			17 53	18 27	19 01	19 26		20 26	21 27				22 27
Dunbar	d	15 05		15 41		17 02		17 43						19 45			21 51	21 57		
Drem	d		15 33		16 34		17 34				18 34	19 06	19 33		20 32	21 34				22 34
Longniddry	d		15 39		16 40		17 40				18 40	19 12	19 40		20 38	21 40				22 40
Prestonpans	d		15 44		16 45		17 45				18 45	19 17	19 45		20 43	21 45				22 45
Wallyford	d		15 47		16 48		17 48				18 48	19 20	19 49		20 46	21 48				22 48
Musselburgh	d	15 24	15 51		16 52	17 22	17 52			18 08	18 52	19 24	19 53		20 49	21 52				22 52
Edinburgh ■ 225,230,242	a	15 36	16 00	16 05	17 00	17 28	18 00	18 07		18 18	19 00	19 34	20 00	20 09	20 59	21 59	22 16	22 25		23 00
	d					17 28		18 11		18 24				20 14						
Haymarket 225,230,242	a					17 32		18 14		18 27				20 16						

Saturdays

		SR	SR	GR	SR	GR	SR	SR	GR	SR		SR	SR	XC	SR	SR	SR	SR	XC	SR		SR	SR	SR	XC
				■ ■ B ⊡⊼	A	■ ■ C ⊡⊼			■ ■ D ⊡⊼					◇■ E ⊼					◇■ F ⊼						◇■ F ⊼
North Berwick	d	06 07	07 21		08 21		09 21	09 50		10 21		10 50	11 21		11 50	12 21	12 50	13 21		13 50		14 21	14 50	15 21	
Dunbar	d			07 48		08 55			09 56					11 38					13 38						15 40
Drem	d	06 15	07 28		08 28		09 29	09 57		10 28		10 58	11 28		11 57	12 28	12 57	13 28		13 58		14 28	14 58	15 28	
Longniddry	d	06 21	07 34		08 34		09 34	10 03		10 34		11 03	11 34		12 03	12 34	13 03	13 34		14 03		14 34	15 03	15 34	
Prestonpans	d	06 26	07 39		08 39		09 39	10 08		10 39		11 08	11 39		12 08	12 39	13 08	13 39		14 08		14 39	15 08	15 39	
Wallyford	d	06 29	07 42		08 42		09 42	10 11		10 42		11 11	11 42		12 11	12 42	13 11	13 42		14 11		14 42	15 11	15 42	
Musselburgh	d	06 33	07 46		08 46		09 46	10 15		10 46		11 15	11 46		12 15	12 46	13 15	13 46		14 15		14 46	15 15	15 46	
Edinburgh ■ 225,230,242	a	06 40	07 54	08 17	08 53	09 24	09 54	10 23	10 24	10 54		11 23	11 54	12 07	12 23	12 54	13 23	13 54	14 07	14 23		14 54	15 23	15 54	16 04
	d				09 03				10 27																
Haymarket 225,230,242	a				09 06				10 31																

		SR	SR	SR	SR	XC		SR	SR	SR	SR	XC	XC	SR	SR	XC		GR	SR
						◇■ G ⊼		A				◇■ J ⊼	◇■ K ⊼			◇■ L ⊼		■ ■ I ⊡⊼	
North Berwick	d	15 50	16 21	16 50	17 21			17 50	18 21	18 50	19 21			20 21	21 21				22 21
Dunbar	d					17 39						19 41	19 41			21 50		22 13	
Drem	d	15 58	16 28	16 58	17 28			17 57	18 28	18 58	19 28			20 28	21 28				22 28
Longniddry	d	16 03	16 34	17 03	17 34			18 03	18 34	19 03	19 34			20 34	21 34				22 34
Prestonpans	d	16 08	16 39	17 08	17 39			18 08	18 39	19 08	19 39			20 39	21 39				22 39
Wallyford	d	16 11	16 42	17 11	17 42			18 11	18 42	19 11	19 42			20 42	21 42				22 42
Musselburgh	d	16 15	16 46	17 15	17 46			18 15	18 46	19 15	19 46			20 46	21 46				22 46
Edinburgh ■ 225,230,242	a	16 23	16 54	17 23	17 54	18 05		18 23	18 54	19 23	19 54	20 06	20 06	20 54	21 54	22 14		22 41	22 54
	d					18 11		18 24				20 14	20 15						
Haymarket 225,230,242	a					18 14		18 27				20 17	20 19						

- **A** To Glasgow Central
- **B** From Newcastle
- **C** From Doncaster
- **D** From Leeds to Aberdeen
- **E** From Birmingham New Street
- **F** From Plymouth
- **G** From Plymouth to Aberdeen. ⊼ to Edinburgh
- **H** From Plymouth to Dundee. ⊼ to Edinburgh
- **I** From London Kings Cross
- **J** from 15 September. From Plymouth to Dundee. ⊼ to Edinburgh
- **K** until 8 September. From Newquay to Dundee
- **L** until 8 September, from 27 October. From Plymouth

Dunbar and North Berwick - Edinburgh and Haymarket

Network Diagram - see first page of Table 225

		SR	GR	SR	SR	XC	XC	GR	SR	SR		XC	XC	XC	SR	SR	XC	XC	XC	SR		SR	XC	SR	GR
			■ ■ A ⊡⊼			B 🚌	◇■ C ⊼	■ ■ D ⊡⊼				E 🚌	◇■ F ⊼	◇■ G ⊼			H 🚌	◇■ I ⊼	◇■ J ⊼				◇■ K ⊼		■ ■ L ⊡⊼
North Berwick	d	11 20		12 20	13 24				14 20	15 20					16 20	17 20				18 20		19 20		20 20	
Dunbar	d		11 33			13 00	13 40	13 54				15 10	15 38	15 41			17 10	17 40	17 40				19 41		20 54
Drem	d	11 27		12 27	13 28				14 24	15 27					16 27	17 27				18 27		19 27		20 27	
Longniddry	d	11 33		12 33	13 34				14 30	15 33					16 33	17 33				18 33		19 33		20 33	
Prestonpans	d	11 38		12 38	13 39				14 35	15 38					16 38	17 38				18 38		19 38		20 38	
Wallyford	d	11 41		12 41	13 42				14 38	15 41					16 41	17 41				18 41		19 41		20 41	
Musselburgh	d	11 45		12 45	13 46				14 42	15 45					16 45	17 45				18 45		19 45		20 45	
Edinburgh ■ 225,230,242	a	11 53	12 01	12 53	13 57	14 00	14 07	14 22	14 53	15 53		16 00	16 04	16 06	16 53	17 53	18 00	18 07	18 07	18 53		19 53	20 05	20 53	21 17
	d																	18 13	18 13						21 21
Haymarket 225,230,242	a																	18 16	18 17						21 26

		SR	XC	SR	GR
			◇■ M ⊼		■ ■ D ⊡⊼
North Berwick	d	21 20		22 20	
Dunbar	d		21 51		23 12
Drem	d	21 27		22 27	
Longniddry	d	21 33		22 33	
Prestonpans	d	21 38		22 38	
Wallyford	d	21 41		22 41	
Musselburgh	d	21 45		22 45	
Edinburgh ■ 225,230,242	a	21 53	22 16	22 53	23 41
	d				
Haymarket 225,230,242	a				

- **A** From Heaton T&R.S.M.D.
- **B** from 16 September until 21 October. From Berwick-upon-Tweed
- **C** until 24 June. From Birmingham New Street
- **D** From London Kings Cross
- **E** from 16 September until 21 October
- **F** from 28 October. From Birmingham New Street
- **G** until 9 September. From Bristol Temple Meads
- **H** from 16 September until 21 October. From Alnmouth for Alnwick
- **I** until 9 September. From Plymouth to Aberdeen. ⊼ to Edinburgh
- **J** from 28 October. From Birmingham New Street to Aberdeen. ⊼ to Edinburgh
- **K** From Penzance
- **L** From London Kings Cross to Glasgow Central
- **M** From Newquay

Inverness - Kyle of Lochalsh, Thurso and Wick

Network Diagram - see first Page of Table 227

Miles	Miles			SR SO 1	SR ◇1	SR ◇1 A	SR ◇1 🍴	SR ◇1 A	SR 1	SR ◇1 A	SR ◇1 🍴	SR 1	SR 1	SR ◇1 🍴 B	SR ◇1 🍴 B	SR 1	SR FSO 1
—	—	Aberdeen 240	d														
0	0	**Inverness**	d	23p30	07 06	09 00	10 38	11 01	12 16	13 34	13 59	14 39	17 15	17 54		21 09	23 30
10	10	Beauly	d	23p44	07 20	09 14	10 52	11 15	12 30	13 48		14 53	17 29	18 08		21 23	23 44
13	13	Muir of Ord	d	23p50	07 29	09 20	10 58	11 21	12 36	13 54	14 16	14 59	17 35	18 14		21 29	23 50
—	—																
18¾	18¾	Dingwall	d	00 02	07 43	09 31	11 07	11 30	12a47	14 03	14 28	15 11	17 46	18 26	18 29	21 40	00 02
—	30½	Garve	d			09 53		11 51		14 25					18 50		
—	36	Lochluichart	d			10x02		12x00		14x33					18x59		
—	40¼	Achanalt	d			10x08		12x06		14x39					19x05		
—	46½	Achnasheen	d			10 19		12 17		14 50					19 16		
—	59¼	Achnashellach	d			10x36		12x34		15x08					19x33		
—	64½	Strathcarron	d			10 46		12 43		15 17					19 43		
—	67	Attadale	d			10x51		12x48		15x23					19x48		
—	72	Stromeferry	d			11 04		13 01		15 35					20 01		
—	75¾	Duncraig	d			11x12		13x09		15x43					20x09		
—	77	Plockton	d			11 16		13 13		15 46					20 13		
—	78½	Duirinish	d			11x19		13x16		15x49					20x16		
—	82¼	**Kyle of Lochalsh**	a			11 28		13 26		15 59					20 26		
28½	—	Alness	d	00x13	07 55		11 20				14 41	15 24	17 59	18 41		21 53	00x13
31½	—	Invergordon	d	00 18	08 00		11 26				14 46	15a29	18 04	18 46		21 58	00 18
40¾	—	Fearn	d	00x29	08 12		11 38				14 58		18 16	18 57		22x09	00x29
44¼	—	Tain	d	00a35	08 18		11 45				15 04		18 22	19 03		22a15	00a35
57¾	—	Ardgay	d		08 33		12 00				15 21		18a38	19 19			
61	—	Culrain	d		08 37		12 06				15x26			19 24			
61½	—	Invershin	d		08x38		12x07							19x25			
67	—	Lairg	d		08 52		12 19				15 44			19 38			
77	—	Rogart	d		09x05		12x32				15x58			19 52			
84½	—	Golspie	d		09 16		12 43				16 08			20 05			
87	—	Dunrobin Castle §	d		09x19		12x45				16x11						
90½	—	Brora	d		09 30		12 54				16 19			20 15			
101½	—	Helmsdale	d		09 46		13 09				16 34			20 30			
111	—	Kildonan	d		09x59		13x22							20x42			
118¾	—	Kinbrace	d		10x08		13x31				16x55			20x52			
125¾	—	Forsinard	d		10 22		13 42				17 06			21 03			
134	—	Altnabreac	d		10x32		13x52							21x13			
143	—	Scotscalder	d		10x41		14x01							21x22			
147¼	—	Georgemas Junction	a		10 50		14 12				17 34			21 30			
—	—		d		10 52		14 14				17 36			21 32			
154	—	**Thurso**	a		11 02		14 24				17 46			21 42			
—	—		d		11 04		14 26				17 48			21 44			
160¾	—	Georgemas Junction	d		11 14		14 37				17 58			21 54			
175	—	**Wick**	a		11 32		14 55				18 15			22 14			

Sundays

		SR 1	SR 1	SR ◇1 E	SR 1	SR 1	SR ◇1 C 🍴	SR ◇1 D 🍴	SR ◇1 D 🍴	SR 1
Aberdeen 240	d									
Inverness	d	23p30	10 00	11 11	12 22	15 21	18 00	17 54		21 09
Beauly	d	23p44	10 14	11 25	12 36	15 35	18 14	18 08		21 23
Muir of Ord	d	23p50	10 20	11 31	12 44	15 43	18 20	18 14		21 29
Dingwall	d	00 02	10 32	11 45	12 57	15 54	18 26	18 26	18 29	21 40
Garve	d			12 10					18 50	
Lochluichart	d			12x19					18x59	
Achanalt	d			12x25					19x05	
Achnasheen	d			12 36					19 16	
Achnashellach	d			12x53					19x33	
Strathcarron	d			13 03					19 43	
Attadale	d			13x08					19x48	
Stromeferry	d			13 21					20 01	
Duncraig	d			13x29					20x09	
Plockton	d			13 33					20 13	
Duirinish	d			13x36					20x16	
Kyle of Lochalsh	a			13 45					20 26	
Alness	d	00x13	10 44		13x08	16x06	18 41	18 41		21 53
Invergordon	d	00 18	10 49		13 13	16a12	18 46	18 46		21 58
Fearn	d	00x29	11x00		13x24		18 57	18 57		22x09
Tain	d	00a35	11a06		13a30		19 03	19 03		22a15
Ardgay	d						19 19	19 19		
Culrain	d						19 24	19 24		
Invershin	d						19x25	19x25		
Lairg	d						19 38	19 38		
Rogart	d						19 52	19 52		
Golspie	d						20 05	20 05		
Dunrobin Castle §	d									
Brora	d						20 15	20 15		
Helmsdale	d						20 30	20 30		
Kildonan	d						20x42	20x42		
Kinbrace	d						20x52	20x52		
Forsinard	d						21 03	21 03		
Altnabreac	d						21x13	21x13		
Scotscalder	d						21x22	21x22		
Georgemas Junction	a						21 30	21 30		
	d						21 32	21 32		
Thurso	a						21 42	21 42		
	d						21 44	21 44		
Georgemas Junction	d						21 54	21 54		
Wick	a						22 14	22 14		

§ Summer station only until 28 October 2012
A Catering until 29 September
B Catering available Inverness to Wick
C from 7 October
D until 30 September, Catering available Inverness to Wick
E Catering available until 30 September

Wick, Thurso and Kyle of Lochalsh - Inverness

Network Diagram - see first Page of Table 227

Miles	Miles			SR 1	SR 1	SR ◇1	SR ◇1 🍴 A	SR ◇1 🍴	SR 1	SR ◇1 B	SR 1	SR ◇1 🍴	SR ◇1 B	SR ◇1 C	SR ◇1 🍴	SR 1	SR 1
0	—	**Wick**	d				06 20	08 12				12 36			16 00		
14¼	—	Georgemas Junction	d				06 37	08 29				12 53			16 17		
21	—	**Thurso**	a				06 46	08 38				13 02			16 26		
—	—		d				06 48	08 41				13 05			16 29		
27¾	—	Georgemas Junction	a				06 59	08 50				13 14			16 37		
—	—		d				07 00	08 53				13 17			16 40		
32	—	Scotscalder	d				07x06					13x23			16x46		
41	—	Altnabreac	d				07x15					13x32			16x55		
49¾	—	Forsinard	d				07 27	09 15				13 43			17 07		
56¾	—	Kinbrace	d				07x37					13x53			17x17		
64	—	Kildonan	d				07x48					14x03			17x26		
73½	—	Helmsdale	d				08 01	09 47				14 18			17 40		
84½	—	Brora	d				08 16	10 03				14 33			17 55		
88	—	Dunrobin Castle §	d					10x08				14x38			18x01		
90½	—	Golspie	d				08 26	10 11				14 42			18 04		
98	—	Rogart	d				08x35	10x19				14x51			18x13		
108	—	Lairg	d		06 34		08 53	10 38				15 08			18 30		
113½	—	Invershin	d		06 43		09x01					15x17			18x39		
114	—	Culrain	d		06 44		09 03					15 20			18 40		
117¼	—	Ardgay	d	06 25	06 51		09 11	10 51				15 25			18 46	19 26	
130¼	—	Tain	d	06 40	07 06		09 26	11 07				15 41			19 03	19 42	22 20
134¼	—	Fearn	d	06 45	07 12		09 31					15 47			19x08	19x47	22x25
143½	—	Invergordon	d	06 58	07 24		09 44	11 26			15 38	15 58			19 20	19 58	22 36
146½	—	Alness	d	07 02	07 28		09 48	11 31			15 43	16x03			19x24	20x03	22x41
—	0	**Kyle of Lochalsh**	d			06 21				12 03			14 35	17 15			
—	3¾	Duirinish	d			06x28				12x10			14x42	17x25			
—	5¼	Plockton	d			06 33				12 14			14 47	17 26			
—	6½	Duncraig	d			06x35				12x17			14x49	17x32			
—	10¼	Stromeferry	d			06 44				12 26			14 58	17 38			
—	15¼	Attadale	d			06x56				12x37			15x09	17x52			
—	17¾	Strathcarron	d			07 02				12 45			15 20	17 55			
—	23	Achnashellach	d			07x11				12x54			15x29	18x07			
—	35¾	Achnasheen	d			07 29				13 13			15 48	18 22			
—	42	Achanalt	d			07x39				13x23			15x58	18x35			
—	46¼	Lochluichart	d			07x45				13x29			16x04	18x42			
—	51½	Garve	d			07 55				13 39			16 14	18 50			
156¼	63½	Dingwall	d	07 16	07 42	08 16	10 04	11 45	12 54	14 04	15 56	16 19	16 37	19 12	19 38	20 16	22 54
162	69¼	Muir of Ord	d	07 28	07 52	08 28	10 13	11 55	13 05	14 16	16 08	16 29	16 46	19 25	19 48	20 25	23 05
164¾	72¼	Beauly	d	07 33	07 57	08 35	10 19		13 11	14 21	16 13	16x34		19 30	19 54	20x29	23x09
175	82¼	**Inverness**	a	07 48	08 12	08 53	10 35	12 13	13 25	14 37	16 28	16 48	17 06	19 49	20 09	20 44	23 24
—	—	Aberdeen 240	a														

Sundays

		SR 1	SR ◇1 D	SR 1	SR ◇1 🍴	SR 1	SR ◇1 E	SR 1
Wick	d				11 53			
Georgemas Junction	d				12 10			
Thurso	a				12 19			
	d				12 22			
Georgemas Junction	a				12 31			
	d				12 34			
Scotscalder	d				12x40			
Altnabreac	d				12x49			
Forsinard	d				13 00			
Kinbrace	d				13x10			
Kildonan	d				13x20			
Helmsdale	d				13 33			
Brora	d				13 48			
Dunrobin Castle §	d				13x53			
Golspie	d				13 58			
Rogart	d				14x07			
Lairg	d				14 24			
Invershin	d				14x33			
Culrain	d				14x34			
Ardgay	d				14 40			
Tain	d	11 10		14 00	14 55			22 20
Fearn	d	11x15		14x05	15x00			22x25
Invergordon	d	11 26		14 16	15 12	16 19		22 36
Alness	d	11x31		14x21	15x16	16x23		22x41
Kyle of Lochalsh	d		10 34				15 22	
Duirinish	d		10x41				15x29	
Plockton	d		10 46				15 34	
Duncraig	d		10x48				15x36	
Stromeferry	d		10 57				15 45	
Attadale	d		11x09				15x57	
Strathcarron	d		11 15				16 03	
Achnashellach	d		11x24				16x12	
Achnasheen	d		11 40				16 30	
Achanalt	d		11x50				16x40	
Lochluichart	d		11x57				16x47	
Garve	d		12 08				16 56	
Dingwall	d	11 44	12 28	14 36	15 30	16 36	17 18	22 54
Muir of Ord	d	11 55	12 43	14 47	15 42	16 47	17 29	23 05
Beauly	d	12 00	12 48	14x52	15 47	16 52	17 34	23x09
Inverness	a	12 16	13 03	15 07	16 02	17 07	17 49	23 24
Aberdeen 240	a							

§ Summer station only until 28 October 2012
A Trolley service Saturday only
B Catering available until 29 September
C Catering available until 29 September, to Elgin
D until 30 September
E Catering available until 30 September

Mondays to Saturdays
until 5 July 2012

Scrabster - Stromness (Orkney Isles)

Operated by NorthLink Ferries Ltd

		SO A	SX	SO B	
Inverness	239 d	07 06	07 06	07 06	13 59
Thurso	239 a	11 02	11 02	11 02	17 46
Scrabster	d	12 00	13 15	13 15	19 00
Stromness	a	13 30	14 45	14 45	20 30

No Sunday rail connected sailings in this direction

Mondays to Saturdays
until 5 July 2012

		SX	SO B	SO A	SX	SO B
Stromness	d	06 30	06 30	09 00	11 00	11 00
Scrabster	a	08 00	08 00	10 30	12 30	12 30
Thurso	239 d	08 41	08 41	13 05	13 05	13 05
Inverness	239 a	12 13	12 13	16 48	16 48	16 48

Sundays
until 1 July 2012

Stromness	d	09 00
Scrabster	a	10 30
Thurso	239 d	12 22
Inverness	239 a	16 02

A Until 9 June
B From 16 June

Please note on 6 July 2012, a new contract will come into effect for the ferry operator to the Northern Isles. For details of sailings please telephone 0845 6000 449 or visit www.northlinkferries.co.uk

Customers holding Rail & Sail tickets to/from Stomness should note that a connecting taxi service between Thurso Railway Station and Scrabster is included.
Taxis can be booked by calling 01847 893 434 as soon as possible after ticket purchase, but no later than Helmsdale on northbound journeys and prior to departing Stromness on southbound journeys. Staff will assist if you do not have a mobile phone.

Taxis are also available for hire by other passengers. Normal fares will apply.

Please note that NorthLink Ferries requires all passengers aged 16 and over to be in possession of photographic ID at check-in.

Mondays to Saturdays
until 20 October 2012

Ullapool - Stornoway (Lewis), Uig (Skye), Tarbert (Harris) and Lochmaddy (North Uist)

Operated by Caledonian MacBrayne Ltd

		TTh-SX	TTh-SO	WFO F	SX A	WF-SX H	TThO	SO B	SO C	MFO	SO	WO	WFO F
Edinburgh	229 d			09a35	10 35	10 35	09a35	09a35	09a35	09a35	11a35	09a35	16 33
Glasgow Queen St	229 d			10 10	10a41	10a41	10 10	10 10	10 10	10 10	12 10	10 10	16a41
Inverness	229 a			13b25	14b13	14b13	13 25	13 25	13 25	13 25	15b23	13 25	20b11
Inverness	239 d	09 00	09 00				13 34	13 34	13 34	13 34		13 34	
Kyle of Lochalsh #	239 a	11c28	11c28				15d59	15d59	15d59	15d59		15d59	
Inverness +	d			14 10	15 00	15 00					15 40		20 55
Ullapool +	a			15 30	16 20	16 20					17 00		22 15
Ullapool	d			16 30	17 35	17 35					18 15		23 00
Stornoway	a			19 15	20 20	20 20					21 00		01 45
Uig #	d	14 00	14 00				18 00	18 00	18 00	18 00		19 00	
Tarbert	a	15 40					19 40	19 40	19 40				
Lochmaddy	a		15 45					21 45		19 45		20 45	

Sundays
until 14 October 2012

Edinburgh	229 d	10h32
Glasgow Queen St	229 d	11 09
Inverness	229 a	14b26
Inverness	239 d	
Kyle of Lochalsh #	239 a	
Inverness +	d	15 40
Ullapool +	a	17 00
Ullapool	d	18 15
Stornoway	a	21 00
Uig #	d	
Tarbert	a	
Lochmaddy	a	

Mondays to Saturdays
until 20 October 2012

		MO D	TTh-SX	WFO F	G	WFX J	TTh-SO	TTh-SO	TTh-SX	WFO F	SX A	WF-SX H	SO
Lochmaddy	d	05 30					07 30		11 50				
Tarbert	d	07 30	07 30					11 50					
Uig #	a	09e10	09e10				09e15	13f30	13f35				
Stornoway	d			06 00	07 00	07 00				13 00	13 50	13 50	14 30
Ullapool	a			08 45	09 45	09 45				15 45	16 35	16 35	17 15
Ullapool +	d			08 50	09 50	09 50				15 50	16 40	16 40	17 20
Inverness +	a			10g10	11g10	11g10				17g10	18g00	18g00	18g40
Kyle of Lochalsh #	239 d	12 03	12 03				12 03	17 15	17 15				
Inverness	239 a	14 37	14 37				14 37	19 49	19 49				
Inverness	229 d	14 48	14 48	10 45	12 46	12 46	14 48	20 15	20 15	18 44	18 44	18 44	20 15
Glasgow Queen St	229 a	18 09	18 09	14a14	16a14	16a14	18 09	23 39	23 39	22a20	22a20	22a20	23 39
Edinburgh	229 a	18a25	18a25	14 19	16 21	16 21	18a25	00h09	00h09	22 19	22 19	22 19	00h09

A Until 15 June and from 17 September
B From 22 September
C Until 15 September
D From 24 September
F From 20 June to 14 September
G Until 16 June and from 17 September
H From 18 June to 13 September
J From 18 June to 15 September
a Change at Perth
b Passengers make their own way between rail station and bus station
c Bus connection dep. Kyle of Lochalsh 1215, Uig arr. 1350
d Bus connection dep. Kyle of Lochalsh 1605, Uig arr. 1745
From 21 May bus connection dep. Kyle of Lochalsh 1615, Uig arr. 1750
e Bus connection dep. Uig 0930, Kyle of Lochalsh arr. 1114
f Bus connection dep. Uig 1445, Kyle of Lochalsh arr. 1619
g Passengers make their own way between bus station and rail station
h Change at Stirling

\# Connecting bus service between Uig and Kyle of Lochalsh operated by Scottish Citylink Coaches (Tel. 08705 50 50 50).

\+ Bus station. Connecting bus service between Inverness Bus Station and Ullapool operated by Scottish Citylink Coaches (Tel. 08705 50 50 50).

No Sunday service from Lochmaddy or Tarbert to Uig or from Stornoway to Ullapool

For details of sailings from 21 October 2012, please telephone 08000 66 5000 or visit www.calmac.co.uk. For confirmation of Scottish Citylink Coach connections from 7 October, telephone 08705 50 50 50

Table 240

Mondays to Saturdays

Aberdeen and Elgin - Inverness

Network Diagram - see first page of Table 225

Miles			SR MX	SR	SR	SR	SR	SR	SR	SR	SR	SR	SR
			◇■	■	■	■	■	■	■	■	■	◇■	■
			A				B	C		D	A		A
												⌶	
0	**Aberdeen**	d	21p55	.	.	06 14	07 14	07 50	08 23	08 50	10 00	10 14	11 03
6¼	Dyce ✈	d	22p05	.	.	06 24	07 31	08 03	08 36	08a59	10 09	10 23	11 14
17	**Inverurie**	a	22p16	.	.	06 37	07 44	08 17	08 48	.	10 22	10 35	11 27
—		d	22p17	.	.	06 46	07 49	.	08 48	.	.	10 35	.
27½	Insch	d	22p29	.	.	06 58	08 01	.	09 03	.	.	10 47	.
40¾	Huntly	d	22p46	.	.	07 19	08 17	.	09 19	.	.	11 03	.
53¼	Keith	d	23p00	.	.	07 33	08 31	.	09 33	.	.	11 18	.
71¼	**Elgin**	d	23p22	07 03	07 26	07 58	08 53	.	09 55	.	.	11 42	.
83½	Forres	d	23p36	07 17	07 43	08 12	09 07	.	10 11	.	.	11 56	.
93¾	Nairn	d	23p47	07 28	07 54	08 23	09 22	.	10 22	.	.	12 07	.
108¾	**Inverness**	a	00 05	07 46	08 14	08 41	09 40	.	10 40	.	.	12 25	.

		SR	SR	SR	SR	SR	SR	SR	SR	SR	SR
		◇■	■	◇■	■	◇■	■	■	◇■	■	◇■
					A		A			A	
		⌶		⌶		⌶			⌶		⌶
Aberdeen	d	11 59	12 50	13 39	14 56	15 30	15 55	16 43	17 18	17 56	18 20
Dyce ✈	d	12 08	13 01	13 53	15 05	15 39	16 04	16a52	17 29	18 05	18 29
Inverurie	a	12 20	13 15	14 05	15 19	15 51	16 18	.	17 40	18 19	18 41
	d	12 20	.	14 05	.	15 51	.	.	17 41	.	18 41
Insch	d	12 33	.	14 17	.	16 03	.	.	17 53	.	18 53
Huntly	d	12 49	.	14 33	.	16 19	.	.	18 09	.	19 09
Keith	d	13 03	.	14 47	.	16 34	.	.	18 26	.	19 24
Elgin	d	13 27	.	15 11	.	16 56	.	.	18 54	.	19 46
Forres	d	13 41	.	15 25	.	17 10	.	.	19 08	.	20 00
Nairn	d	13 52	.	15 41	.	17 29	.	.	19 19	.	20 15
Inverness	a	14 10	.	15 59	.	17 47	.	.	19 38	.	20 33

		SR	SR	SR	SR	SR
		■	◇■	■	◇■	■
		A			A	
			⌶			
Aberdeen	d	19 07	20 11	20 56	21 55	22 50
Dyce ✈	d	19 22	20 20	21 05	22 05	22 59
Inverurie	a	19 35	20 32	21 19	22 16	23 13
	d	.	20 32	.	22 17	.
Insch	d	.	20 44	.	22 29	.
Huntly	d	.	21 00	.	22 46	.
Keith	d	.	21 14	.	23 00	.
Elgin	d	.	21 36	.	23 22	.
Forres	d	.	21 55	.	23 36	.
Nairn	d	.	22 06	.	23 47	.
Inverness	a	.	22 24	.	00 05	.

Sundays

		SR	SR	SR	SR	SR	SR
		◇■	◇■	◇■	◇■	◇■	◇■
		A					
			⌶	⌶	⌶	⌶	⌶
Aberdeen	d	21p55	10 00	13 00	15 25	17 19	21 00
Dyce ✈	d	22p05	10 09	13 09	15 34	17 29	21 09
Inverurie	a	22p16	10 21	13 21	15 46	17 41	21 21
	d	22p17	10 21	13 21	15 47	17 41	21 21
Insch	d	22p29	10 33	13 33	15 59	17 53	21 33
Huntly	d	22p46	10 49	13 51	16 15	18 09	21 49
Keith	d	23p00	11 05	14 04	16 35	18 24	22 09
Elgin	d	23p22	11 27	14 26	16 58	18 45	22 31
Forres	d	23p36	11 41	14 40	17 12	19 00	22 45
Nairn	d	23p47	11 52	14 51	17 31	19 11	22 56
Inverness	a	00 05	12 10	15 10	17 49	19 29	23 14

A From Edinburgh
B From Montrose
C From Perth
D From Glasgow Queen Street

Table 240

Mondays to Saturdays

Inverness and Elgin - Aberdeen

Network Diagram - see first page of Table 225

Miles			SR	SR	SR	SR	SR	SR	SR	SR	SR	SR	SR
			■	■	◇■	■	■	■	■	◇■	■	◇■	■
			A	B			B		A		A		
					⌶					⌶		⌶	
0	**Inverness**	d	04 51	.	05 57	.	.	07 07	.	09 03	.	10 58	.
15	Nairn	d	05 08	.	06 14	.	.	07 29	.	09 21	.	11 15	.
24¾	Forres	d	05 19	.	06 25	.	.	07 40	.	09 37	.	11 26	.
37	**Elgin**	d	05 34	.	06 42	.	.	08 00	.	09 55	.	11 42	.
55	Keith	d	05 56	.	07 03	.	.	08 21	.	10 14	.	12 03	.
67½	Huntly	d	06 10	.	07 19	.	.	08 45	.	10 30	.	12 17	.
80¾	Insch	d	06 26	.	07 35	.	.	09 03	.	10 49	.	12 35	.
91¼	**Inverurie**	a	06 38	.	07 48	.	.	09 14	.	11 01	.	12 47	.
—		d	06 39	07 14	07 49	08 22	.	09 15	10 38	11 01	11 35	12 47	13 34
102	Dyce ✈	d	06 52	07 26	08 03	08 35	09 08	09 27	10 50	11 13	11 47	13 02	13 48
108¾	**Aberdeen**	a	07 04	07 37	08 14	08 46	09 19	09 38	11 01	11 24	11 58	13 13	13 59

		SR	SR	SR	SR	SR	SR	SR	SR	SR	SR
		◇■	■	◇■	■	■	◇■	■	■	◇■	
			A		A	C			A		A
		⌶		⌶			⌶			⌶	
Inverness	d	12 42	.	14 27	.	.	15 21	.	.	17 11	.
Nairn	d	12 59	.	14 44	.	.	15 40	.	.	17 28	.
Forres	d	13 10	.	14 55	.	.	15 51	.	.	17 39	.
Elgin	d	13 28	.	15 12	.	.	16 07	.	.	17 58	.
Keith	d	13 47	.	15 32	.	.	16 28	.	.	18 19	.
Huntly	d	14 01	.	15 46	.	.	16 47	.	.	18 40	.
Insch	d	14 19	.	16 04	.	.	17 04	.	.	18 56	.
Inverurie	a	14 31	.	16 18	.	.	17 15	.	.	19 09	.
	d	14 31	15 26	16 18	16 38	.	17 16	17 52	18 43	19 09	19 40
Dyce ✈	d	14 43	15 40	16 31	16 54	17 05	17 30	18 06	18 55	19 21	19 52
Aberdeen	a	14 54	15 51	16 41	17 05	17 14	17 41	18 17	19 06	19 32	20 03

		SR	SR	SR	SR
		■	■	■	■
			D		
Inverness	d	18 10	19 57	.	21 20
Nairn	d	18 27	20 14	.	21 37
Forres	d	18 38	20 25	.	21 48
Elgin	d	18 55	20a41	.	22 06
Keith	d	19 16	.	.	22 27
Huntly	d	19 37	.	.	22 47
Insch	d	19 53	.	.	23 03
Inverurie	a	20 05	.	.	23 16
	d	20 05	.	21 24	23 16
Dyce ✈	d	20 21	.	21 36	23 28
Aberdeen	a	20 32	.	21 47	23 39

Sundays

		SR	SR	SR	SR	SR	SR	SR
		◇■	◇■	◇■	◇■	◇■	◇■	◇■
				B		E		E
		⌶	⌶	⌶	⌶		⌶	
Inverness	d	09 55	12 30	15 27	17 12	18 00	21 00	21 42
Nairn	d	10 12	12 47	15 44	17 30	18 17	21 17	21 59
Forres	d	10 23	12 58	15 55	17 41	18 28	21 28	22 10
Elgin	d	10 38	13 13	16 10	17 56	18a44	21 44	22a26
Keith	d	10 59	13 35	16 32	18 18	.	22 05	.
Huntly	d	11 18	13 52	16 46	18 37	.	22 19	.
Insch	d	11 34	14 08	17 02	18 53	.	22 35	.
Inverurie	a	11 47	14 20	17 14	19 05	.	22 47	.
	d	11 47	14 20	17 14	19 05	.	22 47	.
Dyce ✈	d	11 59	14 32	17 30	19 17	.	22 59	.
Aberdeen	a	12 10	14 43	17 41	19 28	.	23 10	.

A To Edinburgh
B To Glasgow Queen Street
C To Stonehaven
D From Kyle of Lochalsh
E From Glasgow Queen Street

Newcraighall and Edinburgh - Dunfermline, Kirkcaldy and Glenrothes with Thornton

Network Diagram - see first page of Table 225

Miles	Miles			SR MX	SR	SR SX	SR	SR	SR SX	SR SO	SR	SR	SR SO	SR SX	SR	SR	SR	SR	SR	SR
					◇1 B		C	D	C	E	D		E	E	◇1 G	H	E	1 D	E	C
0	—	**Newcraighall**	d				06 03						06 57	06 57			07 27			07 59
0¾	—	Brunstane	d				06 06						07 00	07 00			07 30			08 02
4¾	0	**Edinburgh**	a				06 16						07 14	07 07			07 37			08 09
—	—		d	23p19	05 30	06 09	06 18	06 29	06 33	06 39	07 00	07 10	07 18	07 18	07 28	07 34	07 39	08 00	08 08	08 11
6	1¼	Haymarket	d	23p23	05 33	06 13	06 22	06 33	06 37	06 43	07 04	07 13	07 22	07 22	07 31	07 40	07 43	08 04	08 12	08 14
9¼	4½	South Gyle	d	23p28		06 18	06 27		06 43	06 48		07 18	07 27	07 27			07 48		08 17	08 22
14¼	9½	Dalmeny	d	23p34		06 24	06 33		06 50	06 54		07 25	07 34	07 34			07 54			08 28
16	11¼	North Queensferry	d	23p38		06 28	06 37		06 54	06 58		07 28	07 37	07 37			07 58			08 32
18	13¼	Inverkeithing	d	23p42	05 46	06 32	06 41	06 47	06 59	07 02	07 20	07 32	07 41	07 41		07 53	08 02	08 18	08 28	08 36
—	14¾	Rosyth	d	23p45			06 44						07 45	07 45						08 39
—	17	**Dunfermline Town**	d	23p50			06 49						07 50	07 50						08 44
—	18½	Dunfermline Queen Margaret	d	23p54			06 53						07 53	07 53						08 48
—	22½	Cowdenbeath	d	23p59			06 59						08 00	08 00						08 54
—	24¾	Lochgelly	d	00 06			07 05						08 05	08 05						09 00
—	27	Cardenden	d	00 10			07 09						08 09	08 09						09 04
19½	—	Dalgety Bay	d			06 35			07 03	07 05		07 35					08 05		08 31	
22¼	—	Aberdour	d			06 40			07 09	07 10		07 40					08 10		08 36	
25	—	Burntisland	d			06 44			07 14	07 14		07 44					08 14		08 40	
27½	—	Kinghorn	d			06 49			07 19	07 19		07 49					08 19		08 45	
30¾	—	Kirkcaldy	d		06a02	06a56		07a02	07 25	07 24	07a36	07 54			08a02	08a09	08 24	08a33	08 50	
39¾	31¾	Glenrothes With Thornton	a	00 19			07 15		07 33	07 32		08 04	08 16	08 16			08 32		08 58	09 12

		SR	SR	SR	SR	SR	SR	SR	SR	SR	SR	SR	SR	GR	SR	SR	SR	SR	SR	SR	SR	SR	SR
		◇1 I	E	C	1 D			H	E	C	1 D			1 J	C	E	1 D			1 H	C	E	1 D
Newcraighall	d			08 34					09 17			09 47			10 17			10 47			11 17		
Brunstane	d			08 37					09 21			09 50			10 20			10 50			11 21		
Edinburgh	a			08 45					09 28			09 57			10 29			10 57			11 29		
	d	08 34	08 39	08 47	09 00	09 06	09 18	09 35	09 41	09 50	10 00	10 07	10 19	10 27	10 38	10 48	11 00	11 08	11 21	11 35	11 39	11 49	12 00
Haymarket	d	08 39	08 43	08 51	09 04	09 11	09 23	09 40	09 43	09 54	10 03	10 11	10 23	10 32	10 42	10 53	11 04	11 12	11 26	11 40	11 43	11 53	12 04
South Gyle	d		08 48	08 56		09 16	09 28		09 48	10 00		10 16	10 28		10 48	10 57		11 17	11 31		11 48	11 58	
Dalmeny	d		08 54	09 02		09 22	09 34		09 54	10 06		10 22	10 34		10 54	11 04		11 23	11 37		11 54	12 03	
North Queensferry	d		08 58	09 06		09 26	09 38		09 58	10 10		10 26	10 38		10 58	11 07		11 27	11 41		11 58	12 07	
Inverkeithing	d		09 02	09 10	09 17	09 30	09 42	09 54	10 02	10 14	10 19	10 30	10 42	10 47	11 02	11 11	11 17	11 31	11 45		12 02	12 11	12 18
Rosyth	d			09 13			09 45			10 17			10 45			11 15			11 48			12 14	
Dunfermline Town	d			09 18			09 50			10 22			10 50			11 20			11 53			12 19	
Dunfermline Queen Margaret	d			09 22			09 54			10 26			10 54			11 23			11 57			12 23	
Cowdenbeath	d			09 28			10a03			10 32			11a03			11 30			12a06			12 29	
Lochgelly	d			09 34						10 38						11 35						12 35	
Cardenden	d			09 38						10 42						11 39						12 39	
Dalgety Bay	d		09 05			09 33			10 05			10 33			11 05			11 34			12 05		
Aberdour	d		09 10			09 38			10 10			10 38			11 10			11 39			12 10		
Burntisland	d		09 14			09 42			10 14			10 42			11 14			11 43			12 14		
Kinghorn	d		09 19			09 47			10 19			10 47			11 19			11 48			12 19		
Kirkcaldy	d	09a08	09 24		09a33	09 52		10a09	10 24		10a34	10 52		11a04	11 24		11a33	11 53		12a08	12 24		12a34
Glenrothes With Thornton	a		09 32	09 44		10 03			10 32	10 48		11 03			11 32	11 46		12 04			12 33	12 46	

		SR	SR	SR	SR	SR	SR	SR	SR	SR	SR	SR	SR	SR	GR	SR	SR	SR	SR	SR	SR	SR
				H	C	E	1 D			C	E	1 D			1 K	H	C	E	1 D			H
Newcraighall	d	11 47			12 17			12 47		13 17			13 47				14 17			14 47		
Brunstane	d	11 50			12 21			12 50		13 21			13 50				14 21			14 50		
Edinburgh	a	11 57			12 29			12 57		13 29			13 57				14 29			14 57		
	d	12 08	12 18	12 35	12 39	12 49	13 00	13 08	13 19	13 39	13 48	14 00	14 08	14 19	14 27	14 35	14 39	14 49	15 00	15 08	15 20	15 35
Haymarket	d	12 12	12 23	12 40	12 43	12 53	13 04	13 12	13 23	13 43	13 52	14 04	14 12	14 23	14 32	14 40	14 44	14 53	15 04	15 13	15 24	15 40
South Gyle	d	12 17	12 27		12 48	12 58		13 17	13 28	13 48	13 59		14 17	14 28			14 49	14 58		15 18	15 29	
Dalmeny	d	12 23	12 34		12 54	13 04		13 23	13 34	13 54	14 06		14 23	14 34			14 55	15 04		15 24	15 35	
North Queensferry	d	12 27	12 37		12 58	13 08		13 27	13 38	13 58	14 09		14 27	14 38			14 59	15 08		15 28	15 39	
Inverkeithing	d	12 31	12 41	12 54	13 02	13 12	13 17	13 31	13 42	14 02	14 13	14 18	14 31	14 42	14 47	14 53	15 03	15 12	15 18	15 32	15 43	15 54
Rosyth	d		12 45			13 15			13 45		14 17			14 45				15 15			15 46	
Dunfermline Town	d		12 50			13 20			13 50		14 22			14 50				15 20			15 51	
Dunfermline Queen Margaret	d		12 53			13 24			13 54		14 25			14 54				15 24			15 55	
Cowdenbeath	d		13a03			13 30			14a03		14 32			15a04				15 30			16a04	
Lochgelly	d					13 36					14 37							15 36				
Cardenden	d					13 40					14 41							15 40				
Dalgety Bay	d	12 34			13 05			13 34		14 05			14 34				15 06			15 35		
Aberdour	d	12 39			13 10			13 39		14 10			14 39				15 11			15 40		
Burntisland	d	12 43			13 14			13 43		14 14			14 43				15 15			15 44		
Kinghorn	d	12 48			13 19			13 48		14 19			14 48				15 20			15 49		
Kirkcaldy	d	12 53		13a09	13 24		13a33	13 53		14 24		14a34	14 53		15a03	15a09	15 25		15a34	15 54		16a09
Glenrothes With Thornton	a	13 04			13 32	13 46		14 04		14 32	14 48		15 04				15 33	15 46		16 05		

B To Aberdeen
C To Edinburgh
D To Dundee
E To Newcraighall
G To Inverurie
H To Perth
I To Inverness
J From Leeds to Aberdeen
K From London Kings Cross to Aberdeen. The Northern Lights

Newcraighall and Edinburgh - Dunfermline, Kirkcaldy and Glenrothes with Thornton

Network Diagram - see first page of Table 225

		SR	SR	SR	SR	SR	SR	SR	SR	SR	SR	SR	SR SX	SR SO	SR SX	SR	SR SO	SR SX	SR SX	SR SX	XC	SR	SR SX
		A	B	C	A		D	A		C	B					◇1 F	A	A	B	C	◇1 G	A	H
Newcraighall	d	15 17			15 47			16 17				16 47		17 09			17 37		17 37				
Brunstane	d	15 20			15 50			16 21				16 50		17 12			17 41		17 40				
Edinburgh	a	15 29			15 57			16 29				16 57		17 19			17 48		17 53				
	d	15 40	15 48	15 58	16 08	16 19	16 33	16 42	16 49	17 00	17 08	17 13	17 13	17 21	17 21	17 42	17 49	17 49	17 55	17 58	18 11	18 15	
Haymarket	d	15 44	15 52	16 03	16 12	16 23	16 37	16 46	16 54	17 04	17 12	17 17	17 17	17 25	17 25	17u46	17 53	17 53	17 59	18 03	18 15	18 19	
South Gyle	d	15 49	15 57		16 17	16 28		16 51	16 59		17 18	17 22	17 22	17 31	17 31		17 58	17 58	18 04			18 24	
Dalmeny	d	15 55	16 03		16 23	16 34		16 58	17 05			17 29	17 29	17 38	17 38		18 05	18 05	18 10			18 30	18 36
North Queensferry	d	15 59	16 07		16 27	16 38		17 02	17 09			17 33	17 33	17 41	17 41		18 09	18 09	18 14			18 34	
Inverkeithing	d	16 03	16 11	16 17	16 31	16 42	16 53	17 06	17 13	17 22	17 28	17 37	17 37	17 47	17 47		18 13	18 13	18 18	18 22	18 29	18 38	18 43
Rosyth	d		16 14			16 45			17 17		17 33			17 50	17 50				18 21				
Dunfermline Town	d		16 19			16 50			17 22		17 38			17 55	17 55				18 26				
Dunfermline Queen Margaret	d		16 23			16 54			17 25		17 42			17 59	17 59				18 30				
Cowdenbeath	d		16 29			17a04			17a34		17 49			18 05	18 05				18 36				
Lochgelly	d		16 35								17 55			18 11	18 11				18 42				
Cardenden	d		16 39								17 59			18 15	18a23				18 46				
Dalgety Bay	d	16 06			16 34			17 09				17 40	17 40				18 16	18 16				18 41	18 46
Aberdour	d	16 11			16 39			17 14				17 45	17 45				18 21	18 21				18 46	18 51
Burntisland	d	16 15			16 43			17 18				17 49	17 49				18 25	18 25				18 50	18 55
Kinghorn	d	16 20			16 48			17 23				17 54	17 54				18 30	18 30				18 55	19 00
Kirkcaldy	d	16 25		16a33	16 53		17a08	17 28		17a37		18a03	18a03			18a14	18 35	18 35		18a39	18a46	19 00	19a04
Glenrothes With Thornton	a	16 33	16 45		17 01			17 36			18 08			18 24			18 43	18 43	18 52			19 08	

		SR SX	SR SO	GR SX	GR SO	SR	SR	SR	SR	SR	SR	SR	XC SX	XC	XC	SR SO	SR SX	GR SX	SR	SR	SR	SR
		B	B	1 I	1 I	D		C			◇1 F		C	◇1 J	◇1 K	◇1 L			1 I	D		C	◇1 M
Newcraighall	d	18 03	18 08				18 34			19 06		19 38					20 07	20 08			20 39		
Brunstane	d	18 06	18 12				18 37			19 09		19 41					20 10	20 10			20 42		
Edinburgh	a	18 13	18 20				18 46			19 16		19 48					20 19	20 19			20 49		
	d	18 25	18 25	18 30	18 30	18 40	18 50	19 00	19 09	19 21	19 36	19 50	20 00	20 14	20 14	20 15	20 21	20 22	20 29	20 45	20 52	21 07	21 40
Haymarket	d	18 30	18 30	18 34	18 35	18 45	18 54	19 04	19 13	19 26	19 41	19 54	20 04	20 17	20 18	20 20	20a27	20a28	20 34	20 49	20 56	21 11	21 44
South Gyle	d	18 35	18 35				18 59		19 18	19 30		19 59	20 09								21 00	21 16	
Dalmeny	d	18 41	18 41				19 05		19 24	19 37		20 05	20 15								21 07	21 22	
North Queensferry	d	18 45	18 45				19 09		19 28	19 40		20 09	20 19								21 10	21 26	
Inverkeithing	d	18 49	18 49	18 54	18 54	19 00	19 13	19 18	19 32	19 44	19 54	20 13	20 23	20a30	20 35	20 36			20 51	21 03	21 14	21 30	
Rosyth	d	18 52	18 52				19 16			19 48		20 16									21 17		
Dunfermline Town	d	18 57	18 57				19 21			19 53		20 21									21 23		
Dunfermline Queen Margaret	d	19 01	19 01				19 25			19 56		20 25									21 26		
Cowdenbeath	d	19 07	19 07				19 31			20 03		20 31									21 33		
Lochgelly	d	19 13	19 13				19 37			20 08		20 37									21 38		
Cardenden	d	19 17	19 17				19 41			20 12		20 41									21 42		
Dalgety Bay	d								19 35				20 26									21 33	
Aberdour	d								19 40				20 31									21 38	
Burntisland	d								19 44				20 35									21 42	
Kinghorn	d								19 49				20 40									21 47	
Kirkcaldy	d			19a11	19a11	19a18		19a33	19a56		20a10		20a44		20a50	20a52			21a08	21a18		21a51	22a12
Glenrothes With Thornton	a	19 23	19 23				19 50			20 22		20 50									21 52		

		SR	SR	SR	SR SX	SR SO	SR	SR	SR
		D	C	D			C		
Newcraighall	d	21 33			22 37	22 47			23 36
Brunstane	d	21 36			22 40	22 51			23 39
Edinburgh	a	21 43			22 49	22 58			23 48
	d	21 49	22 09	22 39	22 55	22 59	23 09	23 19	23 48
Haymarket	d	21 53	22 13	22 43	22a59	23a03	23 13	23 23	23a52
South Gyle	d	21 58	22 18	22 48			23 18	23 28	
Dalmeny	d	22 04	22 24	22 54			23 24	23 34	
North Queensferry	d	22 08	22 28	22 58			23 28	23 38	
Inverkeithing	d	22 12	22 32	23 02			23 32	23 42	
Rosyth	d	22 15						23 45	
Dunfermline Town	d	22 20						23 50	
Dunfermline Queen Margaret	d	22 24						23 54	
Cowdenbeath	d	22 30						23 59	
Lochgelly	d	22 36						00 06	
Cardenden	d	22 40						00 10	
Dalgety Bay	d		22 35	23 05			23 35		
Aberdour	d		22 40	23 10			23 40		
Burntisland	d		22 44	23 14			23 44		
Kinghorn	d		22 49	23 19			23 49		
Kirkcaldy	d		22a53	23a23			23a53		
Glenrothes With Thornton	a	22 46						00 19	

A To Newcraighall
B To Edinburgh
C To Dundee
D To Perth
F To Inverness
G From Plymouth to Aberdeen
H From Glasgow Queen Street to Markinch
I From London Kings Cross to Aberdeen
J From Plymouth to Dundee
K SO from 15 September. From Plymouth to Dundee
L SO until 8 September. From Newquay to Dundee
M To Aberdeen

Newcraighall and Edinburgh - Dunfermline, Kirkcaldy and Glenrothes with Thornton

Network Diagram - see first page of Table 225

		SR	XC ◇ A	GR ■■ A	SR B	SR ◇■ C	SR D	SR D	SR ◇■ A	SR B	SR D	SR D	SR ◇■ A	SR B	SR ◇■ C	SR D	SR D	GR ■■ E	SR B	SR ◇■ C	SR D	SR D	SR ◇■ A
Newcraighall	d																						
Brunstane	d																						
Edinburgh ■10	a																						
	d	23p19	08 04	09 10	09 15	09 36	09 55	10 15	10 55	11 15	11 55	12 15	12 40	13 15	13 50	14 00	14 15	14 33	15 15	15 50	15 55	16 15	17 05
Haymarket	d	23p23	08 08	09 14	09 19	09 40	09 59	10 19	10 59	11 19	11 59	12 19	12 44	13 19	13 54	14 04	14 19	14 38	15 19	15 54	15 59	16 19	17 09
South Gyle	d	23p28			09 24		10 04	10 24		11 24	12 04	12 24		13 24		14 08	14 24		15 24		16 04	16 24	
Dalmeny	d	23p34			09 30		10 10	10 30		11 30	12 12	12 30		13 32		14 11	14 30		15 30		16 10	16 30	
North Queensferry	d	23p38			09 34		10 14	10 34		11 34	12 19	12 34		13 36		14 15	14 34		15 34		16 14	16 34	
Inverkeithing	d	23p42	08 25	09 32	09 38	09 56	10 18	10 38	11 15	11 38	12 23	12 38	13 00	13 40	14 12	14 22	14 41	14 56	15 38	16 10	16 18	16 38	17 22
Rosyth	d	23p45					10 23				12 26					14 27					16 21		
Dunfermline Town	d	23p50					10 28				12 31					14 33					16 26		
Dunfermline Queen Margaret	d	23p54					10 33				12 35					14 36					16 30		
Cowdenbeath	d	23p59					10 38				12 41					14 43					16 36		
Lochgelly	d	00 06					10 45				12 47					14 48					16 42		
Cardenden	d	00 10					10 49				12 51					14 52					16 46		
Dalgety Bay	d				09 44			10 44		11 44		12 44		13 46			14 44		15 44			16 41	
Aberdour	d				09 49			10 49		11 49		12 49		13 51			14 49		15 49			16 46	
Burntisland	d				09 53			10 53		11 53		12 53		13 55			14 53		15 53			16 50	
Kinghorn	d				09 58			10 58		11 58		12 58		14 00			14 58		15 58			16 55	
Kirkcaldy	d		08a39	09a48	10a03	10a12		11 03	11a31	12a02		13 03	13a16	14a04	14a28		15 03	15a13	16a02	16a26		17 00	17a38
Glenrothes With Thornton ■2	a	00 19					10 55	11 11			12 57	13 11				15 00	15 14				16 52	17 08	

		SR B	SR ■ F	SR D	XC ◇■ G	XC ◇■ H	SR D	GR ■■ I	SR B	SR D	SR D	SR ◇■ A	SR	SR D	SR B	SR
Newcraighall	d															
Brunstane	d															
Edinburgh ■10	a															
	d	17 15	17 50	17 55	18 13	18 13	18 15	18 42	19 15	19 55	20 15	21 00	21 15	21 55	22 25	23 36
Haymarket	d	17 19	17 54	17 59	18 16	18 18	18 20	18 47	19 19	19 59	20 19	21 05	21 19	21 59	22 29	23 40
South Gyle	d	17 24		18 04			18 25		19 24	20 04	20 24		21 24	22 04	22 34	23 45
Dalmeny	d	17 30		18 10			18 32		19 30	20 10	20 30		21 30	22 10	22 40	23 51
North Queensferry	d	17 34		18 14			18 35		19 34	20 14	20 34		21 34	22 14	22 44	23 55
Inverkeithing	d	17 38	18 07	18 18	18 30	18 32	18 39	19 02	19 38	20 18	20 38	21 19	21 38	22 18	22 48	23a58
Rosyth	d			18 21						20 21				22 21		
Dunfermline Town	d			18 26						20 26				22 26		
Dunfermline Queen Margaret	d			18 30						20 30				22 30		
Cowdenbeath	d			18 36						20 36				22 36		
Lochgelly	d			18 42						20 42				22 42		
Cardenden	d			18 46						20 46				22 46		
Dalgety Bay	d	17 41					18 42		19 41		20 41		21 41		22 51	
Aberdour	d	17 46					18 47		19 46		20 46		21 46		22 56	
Burntisland	d	17 50					18 51		19 50		20 50		21 50		23 00	
Kinghorn	d	17 55					18 56		19 55		20 55		21 55		23 05	
Kirkcaldy	d	17a59	18a23		18a44	18a46	19 01	19a18	19a59		21 00	21a34	22a02		23a09	
Glenrothes With Thornton ■2	a			18 52			19 09			20 52	21 09			22 54		

A To Aberdeen
B To Dundee
C To Inverness
D To Edinburgh
E From London Kings Cross to Aberdeen. The Northern Lights
F To Perth
G until 21 October. From Plymouth to Aberdeen
H from 28 October. From Birmingham New Street to Aberdeen
I From London Kings Cross to Aberdeen

Glenrothes with Thornton, Kirkcaldy and Dunfermline - Edinburgh and Newcraighall

Network Diagram - see first page of Table 225

Miles	Miles			XC MX ◇■ A	SR MX C	SR B C	SR	SR	SR SX C	SR SX D	SR SO C	SR SX	SR D	SR E	SR SX	SR SX C	SR SX F	XC SO ◇■ G	XC SX ◇■ G	SR H	SR C
0	0	Glenrothes With Thornton ■2	d		23p15					06 03			06 30			06 54				07 15	
7¼	—	**Kirkcaldy**	d	23p26		23u54			05 53		06 16	06 27		06 49			07 13	07 21	07 21	07 27	
10	—	Kinghorn	d						05 58		06 21	06 32		06 54			07 18			07 32	
12¾	—	Burntisland	d						06 02		06 26	06 36		06 59			07 23			07 37	
17½	—	Aberdour	d						06 07		06 31	06 41		07 04			07 28			07 42	
20¼	—	Dalgety Bay	d						06 12		06 36	06 46		07 09			07 33			07 46	
—	4¾	Cardenden	d		23p23					06 10			06 37			07 01					
—	7	Lochgelly	d		23p27					06 14			06 41			07 05					
—	9½	Cowdenbeath	d		23p33					06 20			06 47			07 11					
—	13½	Dunfermline Queen Margaret	d		23p38					06 26			06 53		07 08	07 17					
—	14¾	**Dunfermline Town**	d		23p44					06 30			06 56		07 11	07 20					
—	17	Rosyth	d		23p47					06 34			07 00		07 15	07 24					
21¾	18½	Inverkeithing	d	23p42	23p51	00u12			06 16	06 40	06 40	06 49	07 06	07 12	07 19	07 30	07 37	07 38	07 43	07 50	
23¾	20½	North Queensferry	d		23p55				06 20	06 44	06 44	06 53	07 10		07 24	07 34				07 54	
25½	22¼	Dalmeny	d		23p58				06 23	06 48	06 48	06 57	07 13	07 19		07 38	07a42			07 58	
30½	27¼	South Gyle	d		00 05				06 29	06 54	06 54	07 03	07 20	07 25	07 32	07 44				08 04	
33¾	30½	Haymarket	d	23p58	00 12		06 14	06 33	06 40	07 02	07 02	07 12	07 28	07 34	07 40	07 52		07 56	08 01	08 12	08 12
35	31¾	**Edinburgh** ■10	a	00 05	00 18		06 18	06 39	06 46	07 09	07 09	07 16	07 34	07 38	07 46	07 57		08 01	08 06	08 17	08 17
—	—		d				06 20	06 41		07 10	07 10		07 38								08 18
39	—	Brunstane	d				06 27	06 49		07 17	07 17		07 45								08 26
39¾	—	**Newcraighall**	a				06 34	06 53		07 21	07 21		07 49								08 31

		SR SX	SR C	SR ◇■ A	SR SO I	SR SX	SR SX I	SR E	SR SX E	SR K	SR H	SR ■ L	SR H	SR E	SR ◇■ M	SR I	SR H	GR SX ■■ N	GR SO ■■ N
Glenrothes With Thornton ■2	d				07 32		07 34			08 04	08 16		08 37			09 08	09 17		
Kirkcaldy	d		07 40	07 49				08 06	08 18		08 28	08 41		09 12	09 25		09 30	09 44	09 44
Kinghorn	d							08 10			08 32			09 17			09 34		
Burntisland	d							08 15			08 37			09 22			09 39		
Aberdour	d							08 20			08 42			09 26			09 44		
Dalgety Bay	d							08 25			08 47			09 31			09 49		
Cardenden	d				07 37	07 36	07 42			08 11			08 45			09 16			
Lochgelly	d				07 42	07 42	07 47			08 15			08 49			09 20			
Cowdenbeath	d				07 48	07 51	07 57			08 24			08 58			09 29			
Dunfermline Queen Margaret	d				07 55	07 57	08 03			08 30			09 03			09 34			
Dunfermline Town	d				07 59	08 02	08 07			08 33			09 07			09 38			
Rosyth	d				08 02	08 03	08 12			08 37			09 10			09 41			
Inverkeithing	d		07 57		08 08	08 10	08 20	08 28	08 35	08 41	08 50	08 57	09 14	09 34		09 46	09 52	10 01	10 01
North Queensferry	d				08 12		08 26			08 45	08 54		09 18				09 56		
Dalmeny	d				08 16	08 19		08 35		08 49	08 58		09 22				10 00		
South Gyle	d				08 22	08 25	08 34	08 41	08 46	08 55	09 04		09 28				10 06		
Haymarket	d		08 17	08 19	08 28	08 32	08 45	08 51	08 55	09 03	09 12	09 15	09 36	09 50	09 56	10 04	10 13	10 17	10 19
Edinburgh ■10	a		08 22	08 25	08 37	08 40	08 53	08 56	08 59	09 12	09 17	09 21	09 42	09 55	10 00	10 13	10 19	10 25	10 26
	d				08 51				09 01		09 21		09 51			10 21			
Brunstane	d				08 58				09 10		09 29		10 00			10 28			
Newcraighall	a				09 04				09 14		09 34		10 04			10 35			

		SR I	SR H	XC SO ◇■ O	XC SX ◇■ O	SR	SR ■ E	SR	SR C	SR H	SR I	SR ■ E	SR	SR	SR C	GR ■■ Q
Glenrothes With Thornton ■2	d	09 32	09 49					10 23		10 32	10 51			11 18		
Kirkcaldy	d		10 01	10 17	10 17		10 26	10 31	10 42		11 02	11 19		11 27	11 41	11 44
Kinghorn	d		10 05					10 36			11 07			11 31		
Burntisland	d		10 10					10 41			11 12			11 36		
Aberdour	d		10 15					10 45			11 16			11 41		
Dalgety Bay	d		10 20					10 50			11 21			11 46		
Cardenden	d	09 39								10 40						
Lochgelly	d	09 43								10 44						
Cowdenbeath	d	09 52				10 21				10 53			11 23			
Dunfermline Queen Margaret	d	09 58				10 26				10 58			11 28			
Dunfermline Town	d	10 01				10 30				11 02			11 32			
Rosyth	d	10 05				10 33				11 05			11 35			
Inverkeithing	d	10 09	10 23	10 32	10 32	10 37	10 42	10 54	10 59	11 10	11 25	11 35	11 40	11 49	11 57	12 01
North Queensferry	d	10 13				10 41		10 58		11 14	11 29		11 44			
Dalmeny	d	10 17				10 45		11 02		11 18	11 33		11 48			
South Gyle	d	10 23	10 34			10 51		11 08		11 24	11 39		11 54	12 00		
Haymarket	d	10 30	10 43	10 52	10 54	11 02	11 06	11 16	11 19	11 34	11 47	11 51	12 02	12 08	12 13	12 17
Edinburgh ■10	a	10 36	10 47	10 58	10 58	11 07	11 14	11 21	11 25	11 38	11 52	11 56	12 07	12 14	12 18	12 25
	d	10 51				11 21				11 51				12 20		
Brunstane	d	11 01				11 29				12 00				12 28		
Newcraighall	a	11 06				11 32				12 03				12 32		

A From Aberdeen
C From Perth
D From Markinch
E From Dundee
F To Glasgow Queen Street
G From Dundee to Plymouth
H From Newcraighall
I From Edinburgh
K From Haymarket
L From Blair Atholl
M From Inverness
N From Aberdeen to London Kings Cross
O From Aberdeen to Penzance
Q From Aberdeen to London Kings Cross. The Northern Lights

Glenrothes with Thornton, Kirkcaldy and Dunfermline - Edinburgh and Newcraighall

Network Diagram - see first page of Table 225

		SR B	SR C	SR 1 D	SR	SR	SR ◇1 E	SR B	SR C	SR 1 D	SR	SR SO	SR SX	SR ◇1 E	SR B	SR C	SR 1 D
Glenrothes With Thornton 2	d	11 34	11 48			12 18		12 33	12 47			13 18	13 18		13 32	13 47	
Kirkcaldy	d		12 00	12 17		12 27	12 38		12 59	13 18		13 26	13 26	13 40		13 59	14 18
Kinghorn	d		12 04			12 31			13 03			13 31	13 31			14 03	
Burntisland	d		12 09			12 36			13 08			13 36	13 36			14 08	
Aberdour	d		12 13			12 41			13 13			13 40	13 40			14 13	
Dalgety Bay	d		12 18			12 46			13 18			13 45	13 45			14 18	
Cardenden	d	11 41						12 40							13 40		
Lochgelly	d	11 45						12 44							13 44		
Cowdenbeath	d	11 54			12 23			12 53			13 23				13 53		
Dunfermline Queen Margaret	d	12 00			12 28			12 58			13 28				13 58		
Dunfermline Town	d	12 03			12 32			13 02			13 32				14 02		
Rosyth	d	12 07			12 35			13 05			13 35				14 05		
Inverkeithing	d	12 11	12 21	12 33	12 39	12 49	12 54	13 10	13 21	13 34	13 39	13 49	13 49		14 11	14 21	14 34
North Queensferry	d	12 15	12 25		12 43	12 53		13 14	13 25		13 43	13 53	13 53		14 15	14 25	
Dalmeny	d	12 19	12 29		12 47	12 57		13 18	13 29		13 47	13 57	13 57		14 19	14 29	
South Gyle	d	12 25	12 35		12 53	13 03		13 24	13 35		13 53	14 03	14 03		14 25	14 35	
Haymarket	d	12 31	12 43	12 49	13 02	13 11	13 15	13 34	13 43	13 51	14 02	14 10	14 10	14 14	14 33	14 43	14 49
Edinburgh 10	a	12 37	12 48	12 55	13 07	13 17	13 20	13 38	13 48	13 57	14 06	14 16	14 16	14 19	14 40	14 48	14 54
	d		12 51			13 21			13 51			14 18	14 21			14 51	
Brunstane	d		12 59			13 29			13 58			14 28	14 28			14 58	
Newcraighall	a		13 05			13 33			14 04			14 33	14 33			15 04	

		SR	SR	SR F	SR B	SR C	SR SO 1 D	SR SX 1 D	SR	SR	SR ◇1 E	SR B	SR C	SR 1 D	SR	SR
Glenrothes With Thornton 2	d		14 18		14 32	14 48				15 18		15 34	15 47			16 20
Kirkcaldy	d		14 27	14 39		15 00	15 18	15 18		15 26	15 41		15 59	16 19		16 29
Kinghorn	d		14 31			15 05				15 31			16 03			16 34
Burntisland	d		14 36			15 10				15 36			16 08			16 39
Aberdour	d		14 41			15 14				15 40			16 13			16 43
Dalgety Bay	d		14 46			15 19				15 45			16 18			16 48
Cardenden	d				14 40							15 42				
Lochgelly	d				14 44							15 46				
Cowdenbeath	d	14 22			14 53				15 23			15 55			16 23	
Dunfermline Queen Margaret	d	14 27			14 58				15 28			16 00			16 28	
Dunfermline Town	d	14 31			15 02				15 32			16 04			16 32	
Rosyth	d	14 34			15 05				15 35			16 07			16 35	
Inverkeithing	d	14 39	14 49	14 55	15 12	15 23	15 34	15 34	15 39	15 49	15 57	16 11	16 21	16 35	16 40	16 52
North Queensferry	d	14 43	14 53		15 16	15 27			15 43	15 53		16 14	16 25		16 44	
Dalmeny	d	14 47	14 57		15 20	15 31			15 47	15 57		16 19	16 29		16 48	
South Gyle	d	14 53	15 03		15 26	15 37			15 53	16 03		16 24	16 35		16 54	17 03
Haymarket	d	14 59	15 11	15 15	15 34	15 44	15 50	15 53	16 01	16 11	16 14	16 34	16 43	16 52	17 02	17 11
Edinburgh 10	a	15 07	15 16	15 20	15 41	15 50	15 54	16 00	16 07	16 15	16 21	16 38	16 48	16 58	17 07	17 19
	d		15 20			15 51				16 21			16 51			17 21
Brunstane	d		15 28			16 00				16 28			16 58			17 28
Newcraighall	a		15 32			16 03				16 33			17 04			17 32

		SR F	GR SO 1 I	GR SX 1 I	SR SX B	SR SO B	SR C	SR SX B	SR SO B	SR D	SR F	SR B	SR D	SR A	SR SO C	SR SX C	SR ◇1 E
Glenrothes With Thornton 2	d				16 33	16 33	16 48	17 01	17 01			17 37			18 11	18 11	
Kirkcaldy	d	16 41	16 45	16 45			17 00			17 32	17 48		18 13		18 23	18 23	18 43
Kinghorn	d						17 05			17 36					18 27	18 27	
Burntisland	d						17 10			17 42					18 32	18 32	
Aberdour	d						17 14			17 46					18 37	18 37	
Dalgety Bay	d						17 19			17 51					18 42	18 42	
Cardenden	d				16 40	16 40		17 09	17 09			17 44					
Lochgelly	d				16 47	16 47		17 13	17 13			17 48					
Cowdenbeath	d				16 53	16 53		17 22	17 22			17 57					
Dunfermline Queen Margaret	d				16 59	16 59		17 27	17 27			18 03					
Dunfermline Town	d				17 02	17 02		17 31	17 31			18 06					
Rosyth	d				17 06	17 06		17 34	17 34			18 10					
Inverkeithing	d	16 57	17 01	17 03	17 10	17 10	17 23	17 38	17 38	17 55	18 04	18 14	18 29		18 45	18 46	18 59
North Queensferry	d				17 14	17 14	17 27	17 42	17 42	17 59		18 18			18 49		
Dalmeny	d				17 18	17 18	17 31	17 46	17 46	18 03		18 22			18 53	18 53	
South Gyle	d				17 24	17 24	17 37	17 52	17 52	18 09		18 28			18 59	19 12	
Haymarket	d	17 16	17 18	17 19	17 32	17 32	17 45	18 03	18 03	18 16	18 19	18 35	18 44	18 58	19 08	19 22	19 14
Edinburgh 10	a	17 23	17 26	17 27	17 38	17 38	17 50	18 08	18 08	18 22	18 25	18 41	18 49	19 03	19 13	19 31	19 22
	d				17 41	17 51		18 17	18 21			18 48		19 21			
Brunstane	d				17 49	17 59		18 26	18 26			18 56		19 28			
Newcraighall	a				17 52	18 03		18 32	18 32			18 59		19 33			

A From Dunblane
B From Newcraighall
C From Edinburgh
D From Dundee
E From Inverness
F From Perth
H To North Berwick
I From Aberdeen to London Kings Cross

Glenrothes with Thornton, Kirkcaldy and Dunfermline - Edinburgh and Newcraighall

Network Diagram - see first page of Table 225

		SR B	SR SX B	SR D	SR E	SR B	SR 1 F	SR SO ◇1 G	GR SX 1 H	SR	SR	SR F	SR	SR D	SR ◇1 I	◇ A	SR
Glenrothes With Thornton 2	d	18 44	18 52		19 10	19 23				20 02			21 02				22 02
Kirkcaldy	d		19 04	19 26		19 36	19 54	20 08	20 08		20 27	20 41		21 26	21 42	21 59	
Kinghorn	d		19 08			19 40					20 32			21 30		22 04	
Burntisland	d		19 13			19 45					20 37			21 36		22 09	
Aberdour	d		19 18			19 50					20 41			21 40		22 13	
Dalgety Bay	d		19 23			19 55					20 46			21 45		22 18	
Cardenden	d	18 52			19 18					20 09			21 09				22 09
Lochgelly	d	18 56			19 22					20 13			21 13				22 13
Cowdenbeath	d	19 05			19 31					20 22			21 22				22 19
Dunfermline Queen Margaret	d	19 10			19 36					20 27			21 27				22 24
Dunfermline Town	d	19 14			19 40					20 31			21 31				22 28
Rosyth	d	19 17			19 43					20 34			21 34				22 31
Inverkeithing	d	19 21	19 27	19 42	19 47	19 58		20 24	20 24	20 39	20 50	20 59	21 39	21 49		22 23	22 39
North Queensferry	d	19 25	19 31		19 51	20 02				20 43	20 54		21 43	21 53		22 27	22 43
Dalmeny	d	19 29	19 35		19 55	20 06				20 47	20 58		21 47	21 57		22 31	22 47
South Gyle	d	19 35	19 41		20 01	20 12				20 53	21 04		21 53	22 03		22 37	22 53
Haymarket	d	19 43	19 49	20 04	20 10	20 20	20 24	20 42	20 43	21 00	21 11	21 16	22 00	22 10	22 14	22 46	23 00
Edinburgh 10	a	19 48	19 54	20 09	20 14	20 25	20 29	20 48	20 48	21 06	21 17	21 20	22 07	22 16	22 19	22 50	23 06
	d	19 51			20 16					21 16			22 17				23 15
Brunstane	d	20 00			20 24					21 24			22 25				23 22
Newcraighall	a	20 04			20 27					21 27			22 28				23 26

		SR ◇1 G	XC SO ◇1 G	XC SX ◇1 G	SR F	SR B C
Glenrothes With Thornton 2	d				23 15	
Kirkcaldy	d	22 59	23 14	23 26		23u54
Kinghorn	d	23 03				
Burntisland	d	23 09				
Aberdour	d	23 13				
Dalgety Bay	d	23 18				
Cardenden	d				23 23	
Lochgelly	d				23 27	
Cowdenbeath	d				23 33	
Dunfermline Queen Margaret	d				23 38	
Dunfermline Town	d				23 44	
Rosyth	d				23 47	
Inverkeithing	d	23 23	23 31	23 42	23 51	00u16
North Queensferry	d	23 27			23 55	
Dalmeny	d	23 31			23 58	
South Gyle	d	23 37			00 05	
Haymarket	d	23 43	23 51	23 58	00 12	
Edinburgh 10	a	23 50	23 55	00 05	00 18	
	d					
Brunstane	d					
Newcraighall	a					

Sundays

		SR F	SR D	SR D	SR E	SR E	GR 1 K	SR D	XC ◇1 G	SR E	SR ◇1 I	SR E	GR 1 M	SR D	SR E
Glenrothes With Thornton 2	d	23p15			10 56	11 11				12 58		13 11			15 04
Kirkcaldy	d		08 08	10 08	11 08		11 40	12 08	13 03	13 10	13 29		13 39	14 08	15 15
Kinghorn	d		08 13	10 13	11 13			12 13		13 15				14 13	15 20
Burntisland	d		08 17	10 17	11 17			12 17		13 19				14 17	15 24
Aberdour	d		08 22	10 22	11 22			12 22		13 24				14 22	15 29
Dalgety Bay	d		08 27	10 27	11 27			12 27		13 29				14 27	15 34
Cardenden	d	23p23				11 18						13 19			
Lochgelly	d	23p27				11 22						13 23			
Cowdenbeath	d	23p33				11 30						13 30			
Dunfermline Queen Margaret	d	23p38				11 36						13 36			
Dunfermline Town	d	23p44				11 39						13 39			
Rosyth	d	23p47				11 43						13 43			
Inverkeithing	d	23p51	08 30	10 30	11 30	11 47	11 56	12 30	13 18	13 32	13 45	13 49	13 58	14 30	15 37
North Queensferry	d	23p55	08 34	10 34	11 34	11 51		12 36		13 42		13 53		14 34	15 41
Dalmeny	d	23p58	08 38	10 38	11 38	11 56		12 40		13 49		13 58		14 38	15 45
South Gyle	d	00 05	08 44	10 44	11 44	12 02		12 46		13 55		14 04		14 44	15 51
Haymarket	d	00 12	08 53	10 58	11 58	12 10	12 16	12 58	13 37	14 04	14 08	14 13	14 18	14 56	15 58
Edinburgh 10	a	00 18	09 00	11 06	12 06	12 18	12 23	13 06	13 42	14 08	14 12	14 20	14 25	15 03	16 07
	d														
Brunstane	d														
Newcraighall	a														

A From Dunblane
B From Newcraighall
C From Aberdeen to London Euston
D From Dundee
E From Edinburgh
F From Perth
G From Aberdeen
H From Aberdeen to Leeds
I From Inverness
K From Aberdeen to London Kings Cross. The Northern Lights
M From Aberdeen to London Kings Cross

Table 242

Sundays

Glenrothes with Thornton, Kirkcaldy and Dunfermline - Edinburgh and Newcraighall

Network Diagram - see first page of Table 225

		SR	GR	SR	SR	SR	SR	SR	SR	SR	SR	SR	SR	SR	SR	SR	SR
			1	◇1		◇1			◇1		◇1				◇1		◇1
		B	C	D	E	F	B	B	D	E	F	B	B	E	F	B	D
Glenrothes With Thornton 2	d	15 14					16 53	17 08				18 53	19 09			20 54	
Kirkcaldy	d		15 42	16 03	16 08	17 02	17 07		17 58	18 07	18 56	19 07		20 10	20 59	21 07	21 25
Kinghorn	d				16 13		17 12			18 12		19 12		20 15		21 11	
Burntisland	d				16 17		17 16			18 16		19 16		20 20		21 16	
Aberdour	d				16 22		17 21			18 21		19 21		20 24		21 20	
Dalgety Bay	d				16 27		17 26			18 26		19 26		20 29		21 25	
Cardenden	d	15 21						17 14					19 17				
Lochgelly	d	15 25						17 18					19 21				
Cowdenbeath	d	15 33						17 26					19 29				
Dunfermline Queen Margaret	d	15 39						17 32					19 34				
Dunfermline Town	d	15 42						17 35					19 38				
Rosyth	d	15 46						17 39					19 41				
Inverkeithing	d	15 50	15 58	16 19	16 30	17 18	17 29	17 43	18 14	18 29	19 12	19 29	19 45	20 31	21 15	21 28	21 41
North Queensferry	d	15 54			16 34		17 33	17 47		18 33		19 33	19 49	20 36		21 32	
Dalmeny	d	16 00			16 38		17 37	17 51		18 37		19 37	19 53	20 40		21 36	
South Gyle	d	16 06			16 44		17 43	17 58		18 43		19 43	20 00	20 46		21 40	
Haymarket	d	16 16	16 18	16 35	16 55	17 34	17 49	18 07	18 30	18 52	19 27	19 52	20 09	20 55	21 31	21 51	21 57
Edinburgh 10	a	16 21	16 25	16 42	16 59	17 41	17 56	18 12	18 35	19 00	19 35	19 56	20 15	21 01	21 36	21 55	22 01
	d																
Brunstane	d																
Newcraighall	a																

		SR	SR	SR	SR	XC	SR
			◇1			◇1	
		B	F		B	F	A
Glenrothes With Thornton 2	d	21 09			22 54		
Kirkcaldy	d		22 05	22 13	23 06	23 22	23u54
Kinghorn	d			22 17	23 10		
Burntisland	d			22 22	23 15		
Aberdour	d			22 26	23 19		
Dalgety Bay	d			22 31	23 24		
Cardenden	d	21 16					
Lochgelly	d	21 20					
Cowdenbeath	d	21 28					
Dunfermline Queen Margaret	d	21 34					
Dunfermline Town	d	21 37					
Rosyth	d	21 41					
Inverkeithing	d	21 45	22 21	22 34	23 27	23 38	00u16
North Queensferry	d	21 49		22 38	23 31		
Dalmeny	d	21 53		22 42	23 35		
South Gyle	d	22 00		22 48	23 41		
Haymarket	d	22 09	22 37	22 57	23 50	23 54	
Edinburgh 10	a	22 13	22 43	23 01	23 56	23 58	
	d						
Brunstane	d						
Newcraighall	a						

A From Aberdeen to London Euston
B From Edinburgh
C From Aberdeen to London Kings Cross
D From Inverness
E From Dundee
F From Aberdeen

Sleeper Services

Sleepers enable you to make long distance journeys while having a relaxing night's sleep. You arrive early at your destination, saving a day's travel — or the early morning dash to the airport. Five Sleeper routes link London Euston direct with over 40 stations in Scotland including most principal business and holiday locations. Direct Sleeper services also link Southwest England with London. Customers joining at the starting point of the train may occupy cabins well before departure. At terminating stations customers may vacate cabins up to approximately 0800 on trains which arrive at an earlier time.

Full details of all Sleeper services are given in Tables 400–406.

First Great Western ("Night Riviera Sleeper")

Both single and twin berth cabins are available and feature locking doors, comfortable beds with sheets and blankets, air conditioning, bedside lighting, complimentary toiletries, wash basin with a shaver point and a soft hand towel. Room service facilities, a wake up call, a light breakfast and newspaper are all complimentary.

The trains recently underwent a complete refurbishment to maximise customer comfort. Improvements include a refurbishment of seating areas and berths and the introduction of a hot breakfast offer to set our customers up for the day. All single and twin cabins are available to holders of standard class tickets and large reclining seats are provided throughout seated accommodation, again available to holders of standard class tickets. Customers in most single berths benefit from Volo TV, a new and innovative on-train entertainment service. Customers can choose from 40 different programmes including comedy, drama, documentaries, children's programmes and sport.

There are a number of inclusive Advance fares available that combine travel and accommodation on one ticket. These can be purchased until 1800 hours the day before departure. Holders of Anytime, Off-Peak and Super Off-Peak tickets may upgrade to sleeping accommodation on payment of the applicable single or twin berth supplement. The Lounge Car is provided for the use of customers with a berth. Here you can sit back and relax with a complimentary hot drink, tempt yourself with one of our delicious hot snacks or unwind with something stronger from our well stocked bar - all served at seat by our on-board team. Customers in seated accommodation can purchase refreshments and snacks from the Express Cafe, which is situated in the Lounge Car.

Dogs and pets are not normally allowed in Sleeper cabins. There are special arrangements for guide dogs. Animals may be conveyed if properly labelled and muzzled, and in suitable containers, in the guards van.

ScotRail Caledonian Sleepers

First Class customers receive a toiletry pack and will be woken with a light breakfast accompanied by tea or coffee and a complimentary newspaper. Standard Class customers are served a light morning snack with tea or coffee. Breakfast is available for an additional small supplement and can be ordered after boarding. Customer lounges are available at the following locations - London Euston, Inverness, Carlisle (Lakes Court Hotel) and Edinburgh Waverley. At Glasgow Central customers may use the on-train Lounge Car which is available prior to departure. Full details of the Caledonian Sleeper on-train and station facilities can be found inside the Caledonian Sleeper Guide which is available from principal sleeper departure points.

There are a number of berth inclusive fares available that include travel and accommodation at one all inclusive price. First class travel is in single berth cabins while Standard Class is in twin berth cabins.

The Lounge Car offers a pleasant relaxing atmosphere in which to unwind before a night's rest. Customers can choose from a wide selection of food and drinks including sandwiches, baguettes, snacks and a well stocked bar. At busy times, use of the Lounge Car may be restricted to First Class ticket holders.

Accompanying dogs are only permitted in Sleeper Cabins providing the owner(s) has exclusive use of the cabin and pays the appropriate charge. There are special arrangements for guide dogs. Dogs and pets cannot be conveyed in the guards van. A virtual tour is available via the ScotRail website. Visit www.scotrail.co.uk for details.

Please note that as a result of on-going engineering work some sleeper services may be subject to diversion causing an extension in journey times between Scotland and London. For full details telephone National Rail Enquiries on 08457 48 49 50 (calls may be recorded).

Sleeper Reservations

To book rail tickets and reserve Sleepers, simply visit any main rail station or rail appointed travel agent. Alternatively you can book by phone using most credit/debit cards.

First Great Western Telesales (www.firstgreatwestern.co.uk)	08457 00 01 25
ScotRail Telesales (www.scotrail.co.uk)	08457 55 00 33

For further information about rail tickets or services, call National Rail Enquiries on 08457 48 49 50 (calls may be recorded for training purposes).

Sleeper Services (continued)

ScotRail Sleeper Services – The Caledonian Sleepers

Operated by ScotRail

Table 400 London and Edinburgh

		Mon–Thu	Fri	Sun
Cabins available from		*2300*	*2300*	*2230*
Edinburgh	d	**2340**	**2340**	**2315**
Carstairs	d	**0016***	**0016***	**2347**
Carlisle	d	**0141**	**0141**	**0112***
Watford Junction	a	**0619**	**0627**	**0623**
London Euston ...	a	**0643**	**0650**	**0646**
Vacate cabins by		*0800*	*0800*	*0800*

		Mon–Thu	Fri	Sun
Cabins available from		*2300*	*2300*	*2245*
London Euston ...	d	**2350**	**2350**	**2327**
Watford Junction ...	d	**0010***	**0010***	**2347**
Carlisle	a	**0516**	**0515**	**0504***
Carstairs	a	**0620**	**0620**	**0620**
Edinburgh	a	**0716**	**0715**	**0716**
Vacate cabins by		*0800*	*0800*	*0800*

a Arrival time
d Departure time
R Reservations Compulsory
* Following morning
Services in this table do not run on Saturday nights.
For details of overnight seated services, please refer to Table 65

Table 401 London and Glasgow

		Mon–Thu	Fri	Sun
Cabins available from		*2200*	*2200*	*2200*
Glasgow Central ...	d	**2340**	**2340**	**2315**
Motherwell	d	**2356**	**2356**	**2331**
Carstairs	d	**0016***	**0016***	**2347**
Carlisle	d	**0141**	**0141**	**0112***
Watford Junction ...	a	**0619**	**0627**	**0623**
London Euston ...	a	**0643**	**0650**	**0646**
Vacate cabins by		*0800*	*0800*	*0800*

		Mon–Thu	Fri	Sun
Cabins available from		*2300*	*2300*	*2245*
London Euston ...	d	**2350**	**2350**	**2327**
Watford Junction ...	d	**0010***	**0010***	**2347**
Carlisle	a	**0516**	**0515**	**0504***
Carstairs	a	**0620**	**0620**	**0620**
Motherwell	a	**0656**	**0656**	**0656**
Glasgow Central ...	a	**0720**	**0720**	**0720**
Vacate cabins by		*0745b*	*0800*	*0745b*

a Arrival time
d Departure time
b From 12 Feb 2012 Cabins to be vacated by 0800
R Reservations Compulsory
* Following morning
Services in this table do not run on Saturday nights.
For details of overnight seated services, please refer to Table 65

Table 402 London and Aberdeen

		Mon–Thu	Fri	Sun
Cabins available from		*2110*	*2110*	*2050*
Aberdeen	dep	**2142**	**2142**	**2142**
Stonehaven	dep	**2200**	**2200**	**2200**
Montrose	dep	**2225**	**2225**	**2225**
Arbroath	dep	**2243**	**2243**	**2243**
Carnoustie	dep	**2252**	**2252**	**2252**
Dundee	dep	**2306**	**2306**	**2306**
Leuchars for St Andrews•	dep	**2325**	**2325**	**2325**
Kirkcaldy•	dep	**2353**	**2353**	**2353**
Inverkeithing•	dep	**0012***	**0012***	**0012***
Preston	arr	**0432**	**0432**	**0441**
Crewe	arr	**0534**	**0534**	**0537**
London Euston ...	arr	**0747**	**0747**	**0747**
Vacate cabins by		*0800*	*0800*	*0800*

		Mon–Thu	Fri	Sun
Cabins available from		*2030*	*2030*	*2000*
London Euston ...	dep	**2115**	**2115**	**2055**
Watford Junction	dep	**2133**	**2133**	**2117**
Crewe	dep	**2354**	**2354**	**2339**
Preston	dep	**0052***	**0052***	**0030***
Inverkeithing•	arr	**0458**	**0458**	**0458**
Kirkcaldy•	arr	**0518**	**0518**	**0518**
Leuchars for St Andrews•	arr	**0547**	**0547**	**0547**
Dundee	arr	**0608**	**0608**	**0608**
Carnoustie	arr	**0623**	**0623**	**0623**
Arbroath	arr	**0631**	**0631**	**0631**
Montrose	arr	**0648**	**0648**	**0648**
Stonehaven	arr	**0714**	**0714**	**0714**
Aberdeen	arr	**0736**	**0736**	**0736**
Vacate cabins by		*0800*	*0800*	*0800*

a Arrival time
d Departure time
R Reservations Compulsory
* Following morning
• Customers may depart from London or Watford later, and vacate cabins later, by travelling on the London Euston to Edinburgh Sleeper; then by local connecting service from Edinburgh
Services in this table do not run on Saturday nights
For details of overnight seated services, please refer to Table 65

ScotRail Sleeper Services – The Caledonian Sleepers
Operated by ScotRail

Table 403 London and Inverness

		Mon–Thu	Fri	Sun
Cabins available from		*2000*	*2000*	*1945*
Inverness	dep	2047	2047	2025
Aviemore	dep	2129	2129	2108
Kingussie	dep	2142	2142	2122
Newtonmore	dep	2150	2150	2129
Dalwhinnie	dep	2206	2206	2143
Blair Atholl	dep	2232	2232	2209
Pitlochry	dep	2245	2245	2222
Dunkeld & Birnam	dep	2300	2300	2237
Perth	dep	2321	2321	2300
Gleneagles	dep	2339	2339	2318
Dunblane	dep	2355	2355	2334
Stirling•	dep	0006*	0006*	2345
Falkirk Grahamston	dep	0023	0023	0002*
Preston	arr	0432	0432	0441
Crewe	arr	0534	0534	0537
London Euston	arr	0747	0747	0747
Vacate cabins by		*0800*	*0800*	*0800*

		Mon–Thu	Fri	Sun
Cabins available from		*2030*	*2030*	*2000*
London Euston	dep	2115	2115	2055
Watford Junction	dep	2133	2133	2117
Crewe	dep	2354	2354	2339
Preston	dep	0052*	0052*	0030*
Stirling•	arr	0455	0455	0455
Dunblane	arr	0504	0504	0504
Gleneagles	arr	0519	0519	0519
Perth•	arr	0539	0539	0539
Dunkeld & Birnam	arr	0600	0600	0600
Pitlochry	arr	0616	0616	0616
Blair Atholl	arr	0628	0628	0628
Dalwhinnie	arr	0700	0700	0700
Newtonmore	arr	0712	0712	0712
Kingussie	arr	0718	0718	0718
Aviemore	arr	0739	0739	0739
Aviemore	dep	0741	0741	0741
Carridge	arr	0752	0752	0752
Carridge	dep	0754	0754	0754
Inverness	arr	0838	0838	0838
Vacate cabins by		*0845*	*0845*	*0845*

a Arrival time
d Departure time
🅁 Reservations Compulsory
* Following morning
• Customers may depart from London or Watford later, and vacate cabins later, by travelling on the London Euston to Edinburgh Sleeper; then by local connecting service from Edinburgh.

Services in this table do not run on Saturday nights.
For details of overnight seated services, please refer to Table 65

Table 404 London and Fort William

		Mon–Thu	Fri	Sun
Cabins available from		*1920*	*1920*	*1830*
Fort William	dep	1950	1950	1900
Spean Bridge	dep	2010	2010	1920
Roy Bridge	dep	2017x	2017x	1927x
Tulloch	dep	2030	2030	1940
Corrour	dep	2051x	2051x	2001x
Rannoch	dep	2106	2106	2015
Bridge of Orchy	dep	2134	2134	2047
Upper Tyndrum	dep	2152	2152	2105
Crianlarich	dep	2205	2205	2118
Ardlui	dep	2226x	2226x	2139x
Arrochar & Tarbet	dep	2244	2244	2157
Garelochhead	dep	2310	2310	2223
Helensburgh Upper	dep	2324	2324	2237
Dalmuir	dep	2351	2351	2304
Westerton	dep	2356	2356	2313
Preston	arr	0432	0432	0441
Crewe	arr	0534	0534	0537
London Euston	arr	0747	0747	0747
Vacate cabins by		*0800*	*0800*	*0800*

		Mon-Thu	Fri	Sun
Cabins available from		*2030*	*2030*	*2000*
London Euston	dep	2115	2115	2055
Watford Junction	dep	2133	2133	2117
Crewe	dep	2354	2354	2339
Preston	dep	0052*	0052*	0030*
Westerton	arr	0555	0555	0555
Dalmuir	arr	0603	0603	0603
Helensburgh Upper	arr	0626	0626	0626
Garelochhead	arr	0641	0641	0641
Arrochar & Tarbet	arr	0707	0707	0707
Ardlui	arr	0722x	0722x	0722x
Crianlarich	arr	0743	0743	0743
Upper Tyndrum	arr	0755	0755	0755
Bridge of Orchy	arr	0813	0813	0813
Rannoch	arr	0841	0841	0841
Corrour	arr	0858x	0858x	0858x
Tulloch	arr	0917	0917	0917
Roy Bridge	arr	0929x	0929x	0929x
Spean Bridge	arr	0936	0936	0936
Fort William	arr	0954	0954	0954
Vacate cabins by		*0956*	*0956*	*0956*

a Arrival time
d Departure time
x Stops on request
🅁 Reservations Compulsory
* Following morning

Services in this table do not run on Saturday nights.
For details of overnight seated services, please refer to Tables 65 and 227.

Sleeper Services (continued)

"Night Riviera" Sleeper

Operated by First Great Western

Table 406 London and Penzance

		Mon-Fri Ⓛ	Sun Ⓛ
Occupy cabins at Paddington:		*2230*	*2230*
London Paddington	dep	2345	2350
Reading	dep	0037*	0037*
Taunton	arr	0232	-
Exeter St Davids	arr	0306	0404
Newton Abbot	arr	0331	0455
Plymouth	arr	0412	0535
Liskeard	arr	0608	0709
Bodmin Parkway	arr	0622	0723
Lostwithiel	arr	0628	0729
Par	arr	0637	0738
St Austell	arr	0646	0746
Truro	arr	0706	0806
Redruth	arr	0718	0820
Camborne	arr	0726	0827
Hayle	arr	0735	0838
St Erth	arr	0741	0845
Penzance	arr	0753	0859
Vacate cabins at Penzance by		*on arival*	*on arrival*

		Mon-Fri Ⓛ	A Sun Ⓛ	B Sun Ⓛ
Occupy cabins at Penzance:		*2105*	*2045*	*2045*
Penzance	dep	2145	2115	2115
St Erth	dep	2155	2125	2125
Camborne	dep	2207	2138	2138
Redruth	dep	2214	2145	2145
Truro	dep	2227	2200	2200
St Austell	dep	2245	2218	2218
Par	dep	2254	-	-
Bodmin Parkway	dep	2306	2235	2235
Liskeard	dep	2321	2250	2250
Plymouth	dep	2351	2320	0150*
Totnes	dep	0020*	2348	0218
Newton Abbot	dep	0033	0001*	0231
Exeter St Davids	dep	0106	0057	0259
Taunton	dep	0136	-	-
Reading	arr	0400	0402s	0511
London Paddington	arr	0525	0505	0609
Vacate cabins at Paddington by		*0700*	*0700*	*0700*

Ⓛ Sleeper Lounge Car
* Following morning
A Runs until 12 February 2012 and from 1 April 2012
B Runs from 19 February 2012 until 25 March 2012
s Stops to set down only
Services in this table do not run on Saturday nights.
For details of seated services on this route, please refer to Table 135.

Passenger Representation
Passenger Focus

What is Passenger Focus?

Passenger Focus is the official, independent consumer organisation representing the interests of rail users nationally and bus, coach and tram users across England outside London.

With a strong emphasis on evidence-based campaigning and research, we ensure that we know what is happening on the ground. We use our knowledge to influence decisions on behalf of passengers and we work with the industry, other passenger groups and government to secure journey improvements.

What can Passenger Focus do for me?

We are here to put the interests of rail, bus and coach passengers first. We do this by:

Campaigning for improvements

- we gather research and information, like the National Passenger Survey, where 50,000 passengers give us their views about their rail journeys, so we understand the issues that matter to you
- we work with Government and the industry to ensure that the passenger voice is heard when making decisions about the future
- we focus on a number of key issues:
  - fares and tickets
  - quality and level of services
  - investment in the railway

Providing practical advice

- we provide passengers with advice on how to get the best from the network, explain their rights and help them when things go wrong
- we work with other passenger groups to support them in their work

Resolving complaints

- if you make a complaint and you are unhappy with the response we can take up your complaint with the company involved

Making a complaint

If you have a complaint or comment about any aspect of your rail service, either on the train or at the station, please contact the railway company managing director concerned (contact details are shown on the TOC pages of this timetable).

What should you include in your complaint?

Depending on the nature of your complaint you should include:

- the reason for your complaint
- a description of the inconvenience caused
- which train and which day you travelled on, or which station you used and when
- how many people travelled with you
- your ticket(s) as evidence
- an explanation of the action you would like the company to take to rectify the problem

What next?

If you are not satisfied with the company's response you can contact Passenger Focus or, in the London area, London TravelWatch.

How to get in touch:

Telephone: 0300 123 2350
0800 - 2000 Monday - Friday
0800 - 1600 at weekends

Address: Passenger Focus
FREEPOST
(RRRE-ETTC-LEET)
PO BOX 4257
MANCHESTER
M60 3AR

Fax: 0161 236 1574

Email: advice@passengerfocus.org.uk

Website: www.passengerfocus.org.uk

London TravelWatch

London TravelWatch is the independent, statutory watchdog for transport users in and around London, including all services provided by Transport for London, and represents rail passengers in and around London. We investigate suggestions and complaints from passengers who are dissatisfied with responses received from transport operators.

If your journey is within, or began in, London, please contact:

Telephone: 020 7505 9000 (0900-1700 Monday- Friday)

Address: London TravelWatch
6 Middle Street
LONDON
EC1A 7JA

E-mail: info@londontravelwatch.org.uk

Website: www.londontravelwatch.org.uk

Twitter: @LonTravelWatch

Compensation

Compensation may be payable under each rail company's Passenger's Charter scheme for poor performance (delays or cancellations). For daily tickets and weekly season tickets a fixed rate usually applies depending on the level of delay which you experience. Compensation is made in National Rail vouchers, as a rule, with a minimum of 20% of the fare for the affected journey leg.

Monthly or longer season tickets compensation can differ between companies. On some it is triggered if performance falls below agreed levels and is paid as discount on renewal. Others offer compensation on a journey-by journey basis like for daily tickets. Always check with the train company which issued your ticket or on which you travel for details of the relevant scheme.

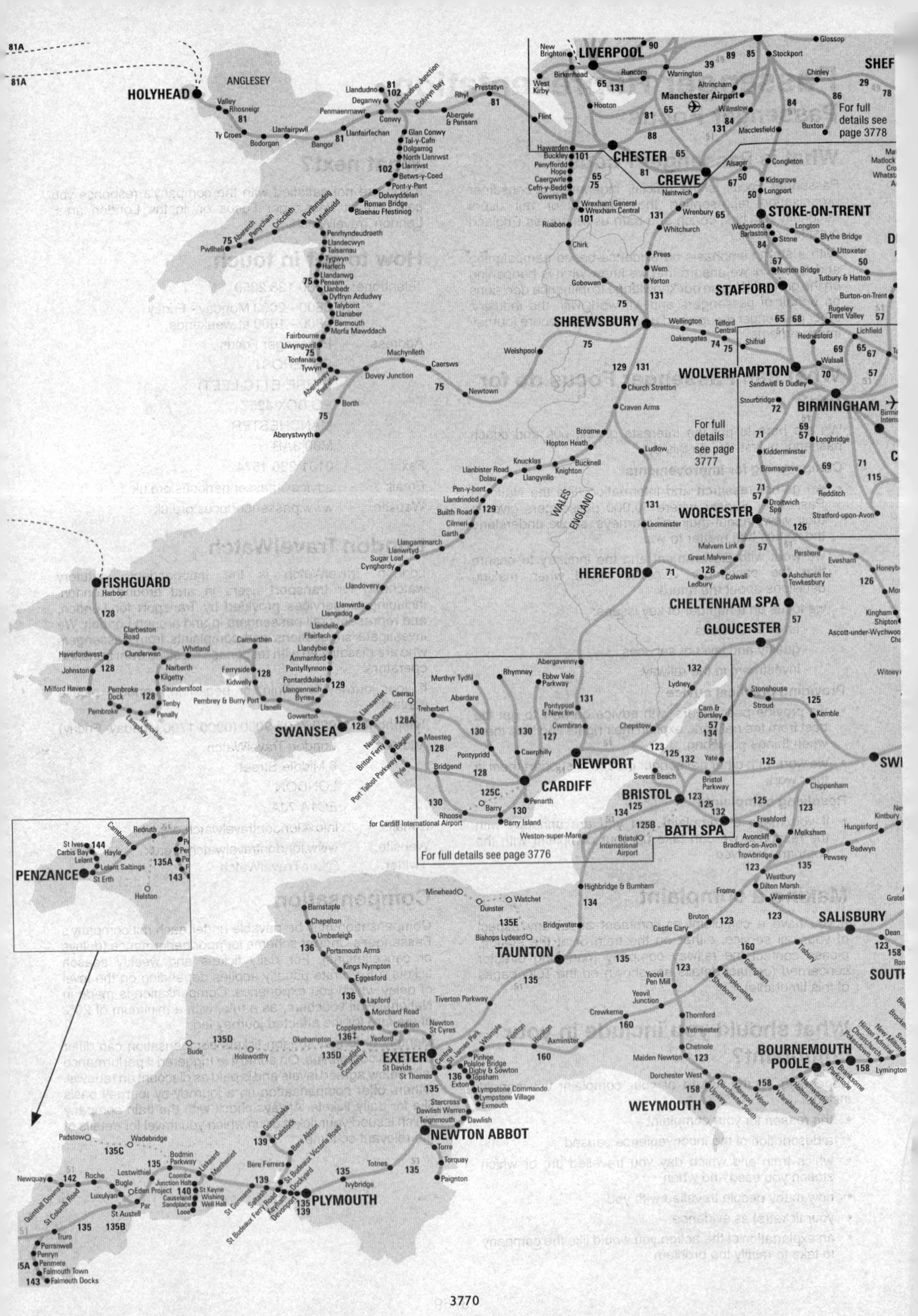

81A
ANGLESEY
HOLYHEAD
Valley
Rhosneigr
Ty Croes
Bodorgan
Llanfairpwll
Bangor
Llanfairfechan
Penmaenmawr
Llandudno
Deganwy
Llandudno Junction
Conwy
Colwyn Bay
Abergele & Pensarn
Rhyl
Prestatyn
Glan Conwy
Tal-y-Cafn
Dolgarrog
North Llanrwst
Llanrwst
Betws-y-Coed
Pont-y-Pant
Dolwyddelan
Roman Bridge
Blaenau Ffestiniog
Pwllheli
Abererch
Penychain
Criccieth
Porthmadog
Minffordd
Penrhyndeudraeth
Llandecwyn
Talsarnau
Tygwyn
Harlech
Llandanwg
Pensarn
Llanbedr
Dyffryn Ardudwy
Talybont
Llanaber
Barmouth
Morfa Mawddach
Fairbourne
Llwyngwril
Tonfanau
Tywyn
Aberdovey
Penhelig
Machynlleth
Dovey Junction
Caersws
Newtown
Borth
Aberystwyth
LIVERPOOL
New Brighton
Birkenhead
West Kirby
Runcorn
Warrington
Hooton
Flint
Altrincham
Manchester Airport
Wilmslow
Stockport
Glossop
Chinley
Buxton
Macclesfield
For full details see page 3778
CHESTER
Hawarden
Buckley
Penyffordd
Hope
Caergwrle
Cefn-y-Bedd
Gwersyllt
Wrexham General
Wrexham Central
Ruabon
Chirk
Gobowen
CREWE
Nantwich
Wrenbury
Whitchurch
Alsager
Congleton
Kidsgrove
Longport
STOKE-ON-TRENT
Wedgwood
Barlaston
Stone
Longton
Blythe Bridge
Uttoxeter
Norton Bridge
Tutbury & Hatton
Burton-on-Trent
STAFFORD
Rugeley Trent Valley
Prees
Wem
Yorton
SHREWSBURY
Wellington
Dakengates
Telford Central
Shifnal
Welshpool
WOLVERHAMPTON
Hednesford
Lichfield
Walsall
Sandwell & Dudley
Stourbridge
BIRMINGHAM
Kidderminster
Longbridge
Bromsgrove
Redditch
Droitwich Spa
WORCESTER
Stratford-upon-Avon
Church Stretton
Craven Arms
Broome
Hopton Heath
Bucknell
Knighton
Knucklas
Llangynllo
Llanbister Road
Dolau
Pen-y-bont
Llandrindod
Builth Road
Cilmeri
Garth
Llangammarch
Llanwrtyd
Sugar Loaf
Cynghordy
Llandovery
Llanwrda
Llangadog
Llandeilo
Ffairfach
Llandybie
Ammanford
Pantyffynnon
Pontarddulais
Llangennech
Bynea
Ludlow
For full details see page 3777
WALES
ENGLAND
Leominster
HEREFORD
Malvern Link
Great Malvern
Colwall
Ledbury
Pershore
Evesham
Ashchurch for Tewkesbury
CHELTENHAM SPA
GLOUCESTER
Kingham
Shipton
Ascott-under-Wychwood
FISHGUARD
Harbour
Clarbeston Road
Haverfordwest
Clunderwen
Whitland
Carmarthen
Johnston
Milford Haven
Narberth
Kilgetty
Saundersfoot
Tenby
Penally
Pembroke Dock
Pembroke
Lamphey
Manorbier
Ferryside
Kidwelly
Pembrey & Burry Port
Llanelli
Gowerton
SWANSEA
Llansamlet
Skewen
Neath
Briton Ferry
Baglan
Port Talbot Parkway
Pyle
Abergavenny
Merthyr Tydfil
Rhymney
Ebbw Vale Parkway
Aberdare
Treherbert
Pontypool & New Inn
Cwmbran
Maesteg
Pontypridd
Caerphilly
NEWPORT
Chepstow
Lydney
Bridgend
CARDIFF
Penarth
Barry
Rhoose
Barry Island
for Cardiff International Airport
Stonehouse
Stroud
Kemble
Cam & Dursley
Yate
Severn Beach
Bristol Parkway
BRISTOL
BATH SPA
Weston-super-Mare
Bristol International Airport
For full details see page 3776
Chippenham
Melksham
Freshford
Avoncliff
Bradford-on-Avon
Trowbridge
Westbury
Dilton Marsh
Warminster
Frome
Hungerford
Kintbury
Bedwyn
Pewsey
SALISBURY
Dean
Tisbury
Gillingham
Templecombe
Sherborne
Yeovil Pen Mill
Yeovil Junction
Bruton
Castle Cary
Highbridge & Burnham
Bridgwater
Minehead
Dunster
Watchet
Bishops Lydeard
TAUNTON
Tiverton Parkway
Crewkerne
Thornford
Yetminster
Chetnole
Maiden Newton
Dorchester West
Upwey
Dorchester South
Moreton
Wool
Wareham
Holton Heath
WEYMOUTH
Hamworthy
Parkstone
Branksome
BOURNEMOUTH
POOLE
Lymington
Pokesdown
Christchurch
Hinton Admiral
New Milton
Barnstaple
Chapelton
Umberleigh
Portsmouth Arms
Kings Nympton
Eggesford
Lapford
Morchard Road
Copplestone
Yeoford
Crediton
Newton St Cyres
Okehampton
Sampford Courtenay
Bude
Holsworthy
EXETER
St Davids
Central
St James Park
St Thomas
Whimple
Feniton
Honiton
Axminster
Pinhoe
Polsloe Bridge
Digby & Sowton
Topsham
Exton
Lympstone Commando
Lympstone Village
Exmouth
Starcross
Dawlish Warren
Dawlish
Teignmouth
NEWTON ABBOT
Torre
Torquay
Paignton
Totnes
Ivybridge
PLYMOUTH
Devonport
Dockyard
Keyham
St Budeaux Ferry Road
St Budeaux Victoria Road
Bere Ferrers
Bere Alston
Calstock
Gunnislake
Saltash
St Germans
Menheniot
Liskeard
Coombe Junction Halt
Causeland
Sandplace
Looe
St Keyne Wishing Well Halt
Bodmin Parkway
Lostwithiel
Par
Eden Project
Luxulyan
Bugle
Roche
St Austell
Newquay
Quintrell Downs
St Columb Road
Padstow
Wadebridge
Truro
Perranwell
Penryn
Penmere
Falmouth Town
Falmouth Docks
PENZANCE
St Ives
Carbis Bay
Lelant
Lelant Saltings
Hayle
St Erth
Camborne
Redruth
Helston

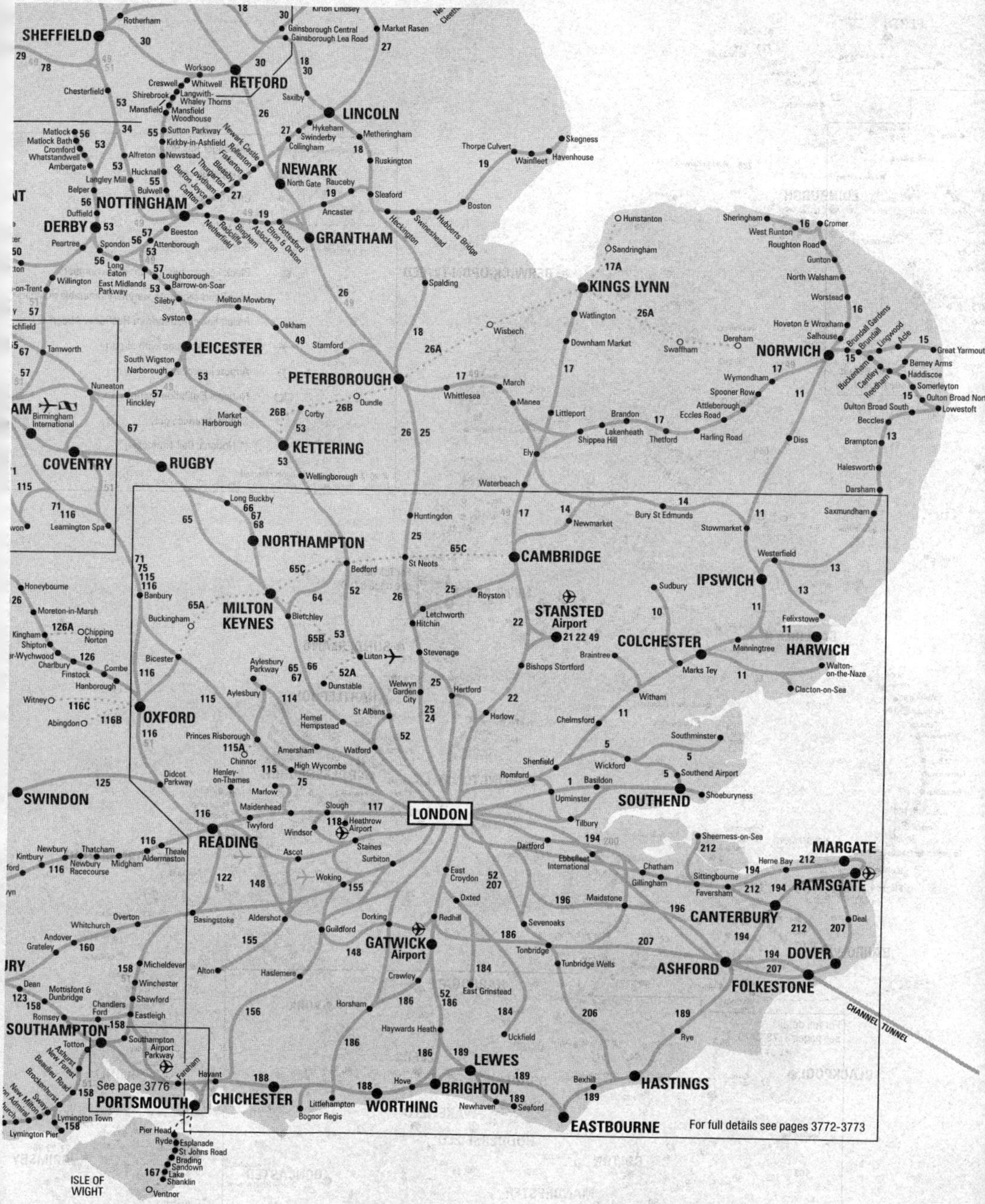
SHEFFIELD
Rotherham
Kirton Lindsey
Gainsborough Central
Gainsborough Lea Road
Market Rasen
Worksop
RETFORD
Creswell
Whitwell
Chesterfield
Shirebrook
Langwith-Whaley Thorns
Mansfield
Mansfield Woodhouse
Saxilby
LINCOLN
Matlock
Matlock Bath
Cromford
Whatstandwell
Ambergate
Sutton Parkway
Kirkby-in-Ashfield
Newstead
Alfreton
Hucknall
Bulwell
Langley Mill
Belper
Duffield
Hykeham
Swinderby
Collingham
Metheringham
Ruskington
Newark Castle
Rolleston
Fiskerton
Bleasby
Thurgarton
Lowdham
Burton Joyce
Carlton
NEWARK
North Gate
Rauceby
Sleaford
Ancaster
Thorpe Culvert
Skegness
Wainfleet
Havenhouse
Boston
NOTTINGHAM
DERBY
Peartree
Spondon
Beeston
Attenborough
Netherfield
Radcliffe
Bingham
Aslockton
Elton & Orston
Bottesford
GRANTHAM
Heckington
Swineshead
Hubberts Bridge
Long Eaton
Willington
East Midlands Parkway
Loughborough
Barrow-on-Soar
Sileby
Syston
Melton Mowbray
Oakham
Stamford
Spalding
Hunstanton
Sandringham
Sheringham
West Runton
Cromer
Roughton Road
Gunton
North Walsham
Worstead
Hoveton & Wroxham
Salhouse
KINGS LYNN
Watlington
Wisbech
Downham Market
Swaffham
Dereham
NORWICH
Brundall Gardens
Brundall
Lingwood
Acle
Great Yarmouth
Berney Arms
Haddiscoe
Somerleyton
Oulton Broad North
Lowestoft
Oulton Broad South
Beccles
Buckenham
Cantley
Reedham
Wymondham
Spooner Row
Attleborough
Eccles Road
Harling Road
Thetford
Brandon
Lakenheath
Shippea Hill
Littleport
Ely
Diss
Brampton
Halesworth
Darsham
Saxmundham
Tamworth
LEICESTER
South Wigston
Narborough
Nuneaton
Hinckley
Birmingham International
COVENTRY
RUGBY
Leamington Spa
PETERBOROUGH
Whittlesea
March
Manea
Corby
Oundle
Market Harborough
KETTERING
Wellingborough
Waterbeach
Long Buckby
NORTHAMPTON
Huntingdon
St Neots
Bedford
CAMBRIDGE
Newmarket
Bury St Edmunds
Stowmarket
Westerfield
IPSWICH
Felixstowe
Sudbury
STANSTED Airport
Royston
Letchworth
Hitchin
Stevenage
MILTON KEYNES
Bletchley
Buckingham
Banbury
Honeybourne
Moreton-in-Marsh
Kingham
Chipping Norton
Shipton
Ascott-under-Wychwood
Charlbury
Finstock
Combe
Hanborough
Witney
Abingdon
Bicester
Aylesbury Parkway
Aylesbury
Luton
Dunstable
Welwyn Garden City
Hertford
Bishops Stortford
Harlow
COLCHESTER
Braintree
Manningtree
HARWICH
Marks Tey
Walton-on-the-Naze
Clacton-on-Sea
Witham
Chelmsford
OXFORD
Princes Risborough
Hemel Hempstead
St Albans
Amersham
Watford
Chinnor
Henley-on-Thames
High Wycombe
Marlow
Didcot Parkway
SWINDON
Maidenhead
Slough
Twyford
Windsor
Heathrow Airport
LONDON
Shenfield
Wickford
Southminster
Romford
Basildon
Southend Airport
Upminster
SOUTHEND
Shoeburyness
Tilbury
READING
Newbury
Thatcham
Theale
Aldermaston
Midgham
Newbury Racecourse
Kintbury
Ascot
Staines
Surbiton
Woking
East Croydon
Oxted
Dartford
Ebbsfleet International
Chatham
Gillingham
Sheerness-on-Sea
Sittingbourne
Faversham
Herne Bay
MARGATE
RAMSGATE
Maidstone
CANTERBURY
Deal
Sevenoaks
Basingstoke
Aldershot
Guildford
Dorking
Redhill
GATWICK Airport
Tonbridge
Tunbridge Wells
ASHFORD
DOVER
FOLKESTONE
CHANNEL TUNNEL
Overton
Whitchurch
Andover
Grateley
Micheldever
Winchester
Shawford
Eastleigh
Alton
Haslemere
Crawley
East Grinstead
Horsham
Haywards Heath
Uckfield
Rye
Dean
Mottisfont & Dunbridge
Romsey
Chandlers Ford
SOUTHAMPTON
Southampton Airport Parkway
Totton
Ashurst New Forest
Beaulieu Road
Brockenhurst
Sway
New Milton
Fareham
Havant
See page 3776
PORTSMOUTH
CHICHESTER
Littlehampton
Bognor Regis
WORTHING
Hove
BRIGHTON
LEWES
Newhaven
Seaford
Bexhill
HASTINGS
EASTBOURNE
Lymington Town
Lymington Pier
Pier Head
Ryde
Esplanade
St Johns Road
Brading
Sandown
Lake
Shanklin
Ventnor
ISLE OF WIGHT
For full details see pages 3772-3773

Passenger Rail Routes
Principal places
Other places
Ferry links
Bus links
Black figures indicate timetable numbers*
Blue figures indicate summary timetable numbers*
Railair link coach to/from Heathrow Airport
Railair interchange with airport
Airport interchange
National Exhibition Centre
Summer service only
(* National Rail Timetable)
© 2012 Network Rail. All rights reserved.
Designed and drawn by Pindar Creative 01296 390100
For full details see page 3780
For full details see page 3780
For full details see pages 3778-3779
SCOTLAND
ENGLAND
PERTH
Leuchars
St Andrews
Cupar
Springfield
Ladybank
Markinch
Gleneagles
Alloa
Cardenden
Kirkcaldy
Dunfermline
Inverkeithing
North Berwick
Drem
Dunbar
EDINBURGH
Falkirk
Bathgate
Newcraighall
Longniddry
Prestonpans
Wallyford
Musselburgh
Shotts
Carstairs
BERWICK-UPON-TWEED
Duns
Earlston
Galashiels
Melrose
Selkirk
Hawick
Chathill
Alnmouth for Alnwick
Acklington
Widdrington
Pegswood
Morpeth
Cramlington
Manors
NEWCASTLE
Heworth
Langholm
Lockerbie
Dumfries
Annan
Gretna Green
CARLISLE
Brampton
Wetheral
Dalston
Wigton
Aspatria
Maryport
Flimby
Workington
Harrington
Parton
Whitehaven
Corkickle
St Bees
Nethertown
Braystones
Sellafield
Seascale
Drigg
Ravenglass for Eskdale
Bootle
Silecroft
Millom
Askam
Green Road
Foxfield
Kirkby-in-Furness
Dalton
Roose
BARROW
Ulverston
Cark
Kents Bank
Grange-over-Sands
Arnside
Silverdale
Carnforth
Windermere
WINDERMERE
Staveley
Burneside
Kendal
Oxenholme Lake District
Penrith North Lakes
Armathwaite
Lazonby & Kirkoswald
Langwathby
Appleby
Kirkby Stephen
Garsdale
Dent
Ribblehead
Horton-in-Ribblesdale
Settle
Wennington
Bentham
Clapham
Giggleswick
Bare Lane
Morecambe
Lancaster
Heysham Port
Haltwhistle
Bardon Mill
Haydon Bridge
Hexham
Corbridge
Riding Mill
Stockfield
Prudhoe
Wylam
Blaydon
SUNDERLAND
Chester-le-Street
Seaham
Durham
HARTLEPOOL
Seaton Carew
Billingham
Stockton
Bishop Auckland
Shildon
Newton Aycliffe
Heighington
North Road
DARLINGTON
Thornaby
South Bank
British Steel Redcar
Redcar Central
Redcar East
Longbeck
Marske
Saltburn
MIDDLESBROUGH
Eaglescliffe
Marton
Gypsy Lane
Nunthorpe
Great Ayton
Battersby
Castleton Moor
Danby
Commondale
Kildale
Lealholm
Glaisdale
Egton
Grosmont
Sleights
Ruswarp
Whitby
Goathland
Levisham
Pickering
Richmond
Catterick Camp Centre
Dinsdale
Allens West
Yarm
Northallerton
Thirsk
SCARBOROUGH
Seamer
Filey
Hunmanby
Bempton
Bridlington
Nafferton
Driffield
Hutton Cranswick
Arram
Beverley
Cottingham
HULL
Malton
HARROGATE
Knaresborough
YORK
Long Preston
Hellifield
Skipton
Ilkley
Keighley
Clitheroe
Colne
Burnley
Blackburn
LEEDS
BRADFORD
HALIFAX
WAKEFIELD
HUDDERSFIELD
Selby
Gilberdyke
Broomfleet
Brough
Ferriby
Hessle
Goole
Barton-on-Humber
Barrow Haven
New Holland
Goxhill
Thornton Abbey
Ulceby
Barnetby
Habrough
Stallingborough
Healing
Great Coates
GRIMSBY
Town
Docks
New Clee
Cleethorpes
BLACKPOOL
Lytham
Kirkham
PRESTON
Southport
Ormskirk
Wigan
BOLTON
Rochdale
MANCHESTER
Glossop
Barnsley
DONCASTER
Robin Hood Airport
Scunthorpe
Brigg
Kirton Lindsey
Market Rasen
Gainsborough Central
Gainsborough Lea Road
New Brighton
LIVERPOOL
St Helens
Birkenhead
Runcorn
Warrington
Stockport
Chinley
SHEFFIELD
Rotherham
West Kirby
Hooton
Altrincham
Manchester Airport
Wilmslow
Macclesfield
Buxton
Chesterfield
Worksop
Creswell
Whitwell
RETFORD
Shirebrook
Langwith-Whaley Thorns
Mansfield
Mansfield Woodhouse
Saxilby
LINCOLN
Hykeham
Swinderby
Collingham
Metheringham
Ruskington
Thorpe Culvert
Flint
Hawarden
CHESTER
Buckley
Penyffordd
Hope
Caergwrle
Cefn-y-Bedd
CREWE
Alsager
Kidsgrove
Congleton
Matlock
Matlock Bath
Cromford
Whatstandwell
Ambergate
Alfreton
Sutton Parkway
Kirkby-in-Ashfield
Newstead
Newark Castle
Rolleston
Fiskerton
NEWARK
Prestatyn
Rhyl
Abergele & Pensarn
Colwyn Bay
Llandudno Junction
Glan Conwy
Tal-y-Cafn
Dolgarrog
North Llanrwst
Llanrwst
Betws-y-Coed

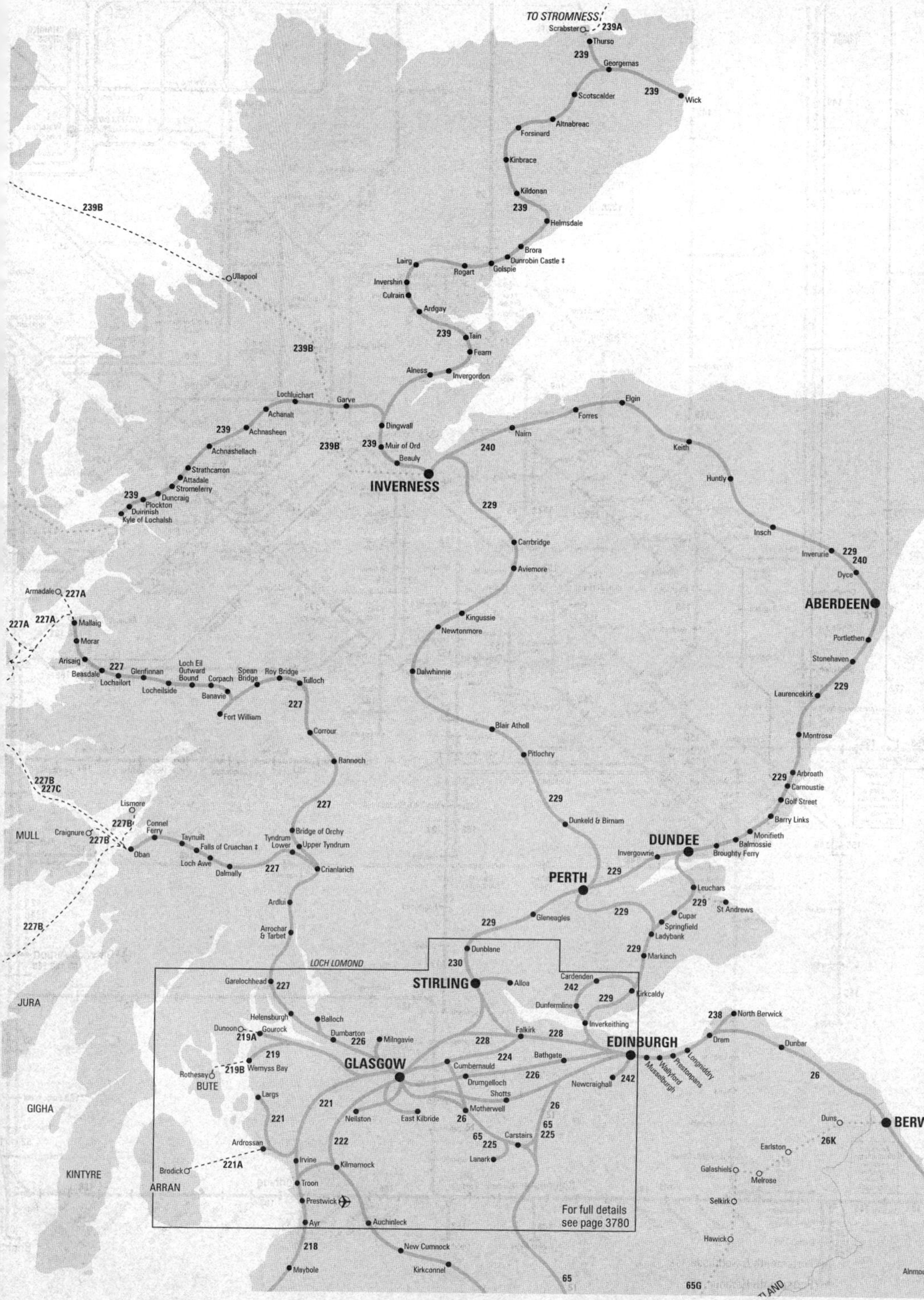
TO STROMNESS
Scrabster
239A
Thurso
239
Georgemas
Wick
Scotscalder
Altnabreac
Forsinard
Kinbrace
Kildonan
Helmsdale
Brora
Dunrobin Castle ‡
Golspie
Rogart
Lairg
Invershin
Culrain
Ardgay
Tain
Fearn
Alness
Invergordon
239B
Ullapool
Lochluichart
Garve
Achanalt
Achnasheen
Achnashellach
Strathcarron
Attadale
Stromeferry
Duncraig
Plockton
Duirinish
Kyle of Lochalsh
Dingwall
Muir of Ord
Beauly
INVERNESS
240
Nairn
Forres
Elgin
Keith
Huntly
Insch
Inverurie
229
Dyce
ABERDEEN
Portlethen
Stonehaven
Laurencekirk
Montrose
Arbroath
Carnoustie
Golf Street
Barry Links
Monifieth
Balmossie
Broughty Ferry
DUNDEE
Invergowrie
Carrbridge
Aviemore
Kingussie
Newtonmore
Dalwhinnie
Blair Atholl
Pitlochry
Dunkeld & Birnam
PERTH
Gleneagles
Leuchars
St Andrews
Cupar
Springfield
Ladybank
Markinch
Armadale
227A
Mallaig
Morar
Arisaig
Beasdale
227
Lochailort
Glenfinnan
Locheilside
Loch Eil Outward Bound
Corpach
Banavie
Fort William
Spean Bridge
Roy Bridge
Tulloch
Corrour
Rannoch
Bridge of Orchy
Tyndrum Lower
Upper Tyndrum
Crianlarich
227B
227C
Lismore
MULL
Craignure
Oban
Connel Ferry
Taynuilt
Falls of Cruachan ‡
Loch Awe
Dalmally
Ardlui
Arrochar & Tarbet
LOCH LOMOND
Dunblane
230
STIRLING
Alloa
Cardenden
242
Kirkcaldy
Dunfermline
Inverkeithing
JURA
Garelochhead
Helensburgh
Balloch
Dumbarton
Milngavie
226
Dunoon
Gourock
219A
219
Wemyss Bay
219B
Rothesay
BUTE
GLASGOW
Falkirk
228
Bathgate
224
Cumbernauld
Drumgelloch
Shotts
EDINBURGH
Newcraighall
Musselburgh
Wallyford
Prestonpans
Longniddry
Drem
North Berwick
238
Dunbar
26
GIGHA
Largs
221
Neilston
East Kilbride
Motherwell
Carstairs
65
225
Lanark
Ardrossan
Brodick
221A
Irvine
Kilmarnock
222
KINTYRE
ARRAN
Troon
Prestwick
Ayr
Auchinleck
For full details see page 3780
218
Maybole
New Cumnock
Kirkconnel
Duns
BERW
Earlston
26K
Galashiels
Melrose
Selkirk
Hawick
65G
Alnmou

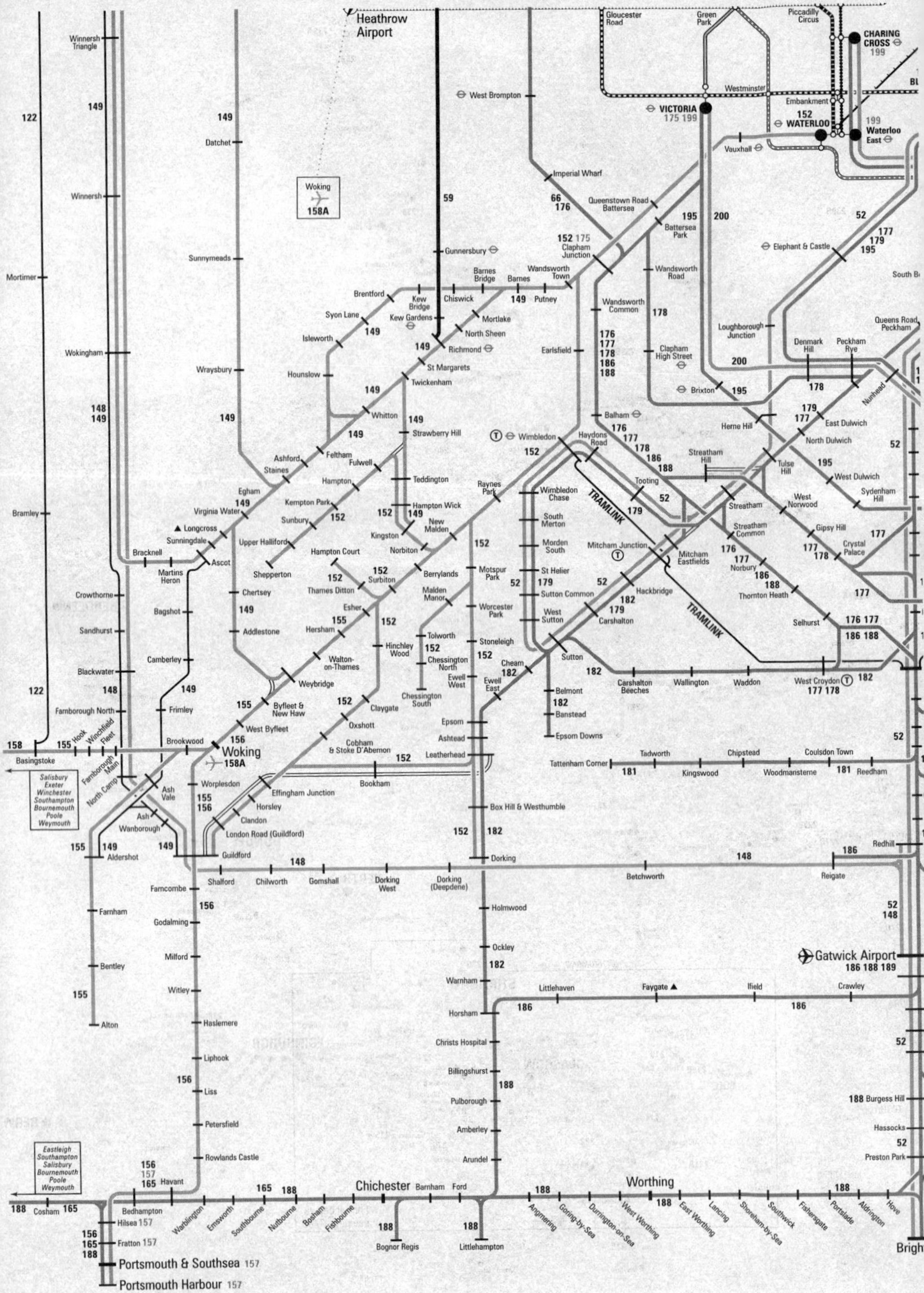

Heathrow Airport
Gloucester Road
Green Park
Piccadilly Circus
CHARING CROSS
199
Westminster
Embankment
VICTORIA
175 199
152 WATERLOO
199 Waterloo East
Vauxhall
West Brompton
Imperial Wharf
66 176
Queenstown Road Battersea
195
200
Battersea Park
52
177 179 195
Elephant & Castle
152 175 Clapham Junction
Wandsworth Town
Wandsworth Road
Wandsworth Common
178
Gunnersbury
59
Woking
158A
Winnersh Triangle
149
122
Datchet
Winnersh
Sunnymeads
Mortimer
Brentford
Kew Bridge
Chiswick
Barnes Bridge
Barnes
149
Putney
Syon Lane
Kew Gardens
Mortlake
North Sheen
Isleworth
Richmond
Earlsfield
176 177 178 186 188
Clapham High Street
Loughborough Junction
Denmark Hill
Peckham Rye
Queens Road Peckham
South Bermondsey
Wokingham
Wraysbury
Hounslow
St Margarets
Twickenham
200
Brixton
195
178
Nunhead
148 149
Whitton
Strawberry Hill
Balham
Herne Hill
179 177
East Dulwich
North Dulwich
Wimbledon
Haydons Road
176 177 178 186 188
Streatham Hill
Tulse Hill
195
West Dulwich
Sydenham Hill
Ashford
Feltham
Fulwell
Staines
Teddington
Hampton
Raynes Park
Wimbledon Chase
Tooting
52
Streatham
West Norwood
Egham
Kempton Park
Hampton Wick
Virginia Water
Longcross
Sunbury
152
New Malden
South Merton
TRAMLINK
179
Streatham Common
Gipsy Hill
Crystal Palace
177
Bramley
Sunningdale
Upper Halliford
Kingston
Norbiton
Morden South
Mitcham Junction
Mitcham Eastfields
176
177 Norbury
178
Bracknell
Ascot
Martins Heron
Shepperton
Hampton Court
Thames Ditton
Surbiton
Berrylands
Motspur Park
St Helier
Sutton Common
Hackbridge
186 188
Thornton Heath
Crowthorne
Chertsey
Malden Manor
Worcester Park
West Sutton
Carshalton
Bagshot
Esher
Hersham
155
Addlestone
Tolworth
Stoneleigh
Selhurst
176 177
186 188
Sandhurst
Walton-on-Thames
Hinchley Wood
Chessington North
Ewell West
Cheam
Sutton
Camberley
Blackwater
Weybridge
Ewell East
Carshalton Beeches
Wallington
Waddon
West Croydon
177 178
182
Frimley
Farnborough North
Byfleet & New Haw
Claygate
Chessington South
Belmont
Banstead
Epsom Downs
West Byfleet
Oxshott
Epsom
Ashtead
Cobham & Stoke D'Abernon
Leatherhead
158
Basingstoke
Hook
Winchfield
Fleet
Brookwood
Woking
156
Tattenham Corner
Tadworth
Chipstead
Coulsdon Town
Kingswood
Woodmansterne
181
Reedham
Salisbury
Exeter
Winchester
Southampton
Bournemouth
Poole
Weymouth
Farnborough Main
North Camp
Ash Vale
Worplesdon
Bookham
Effingham Junction
Horsley
Clandon
London Road (Guildford)
Box Hill & Westhumble
Ash
Wanborough
Aldershot
Guildford
Dorking
Redhill
Shalford
Chilworth
Gomshall
Dorking West
Dorking (Deepdene)
Betchworth
Reigate
148
186
Farncombe
Farnham
Godalming
Holmwood
Milford
Ockley
Gatwick Airport
186 188 189
Bentley
Witley
Warnham
Littlehaven
Faygate
Ifield
Crawley
Horsham
Alton
Haslemere
Christs Hospital
Liphook
Billingshurst
Liss
Pulborough
188 Burgess Hill
Petersfield
Amberley
Hassocks
Arundel
Preston Park
Rowlands Castle
Eastleigh
Southampton
Salisbury
Bournemouth
Poole
Weymouth
156 157 165
Havant
Chichester
Barnham
Ford
Worthing
188
Cosham
165
Bedhampton
Warblington
Emsworth
Southbourne
Nutbourne
Bosham
Fishbourne
Bognor Regis
Littlehampton
Angmering
Goring-by-Sea
Durrington-on-Sea
West Worthing
East Worthing
Lancing
Shoreham-by-Sea
Southwick
Fishersgate
Portslade
Aldrington
Hove
Brighton
Hilsea 157
Fratton 157
156 165 188
Portsmouth & Southsea 157
Portsmouth Harbour 157

Continued on pages 3774-3775

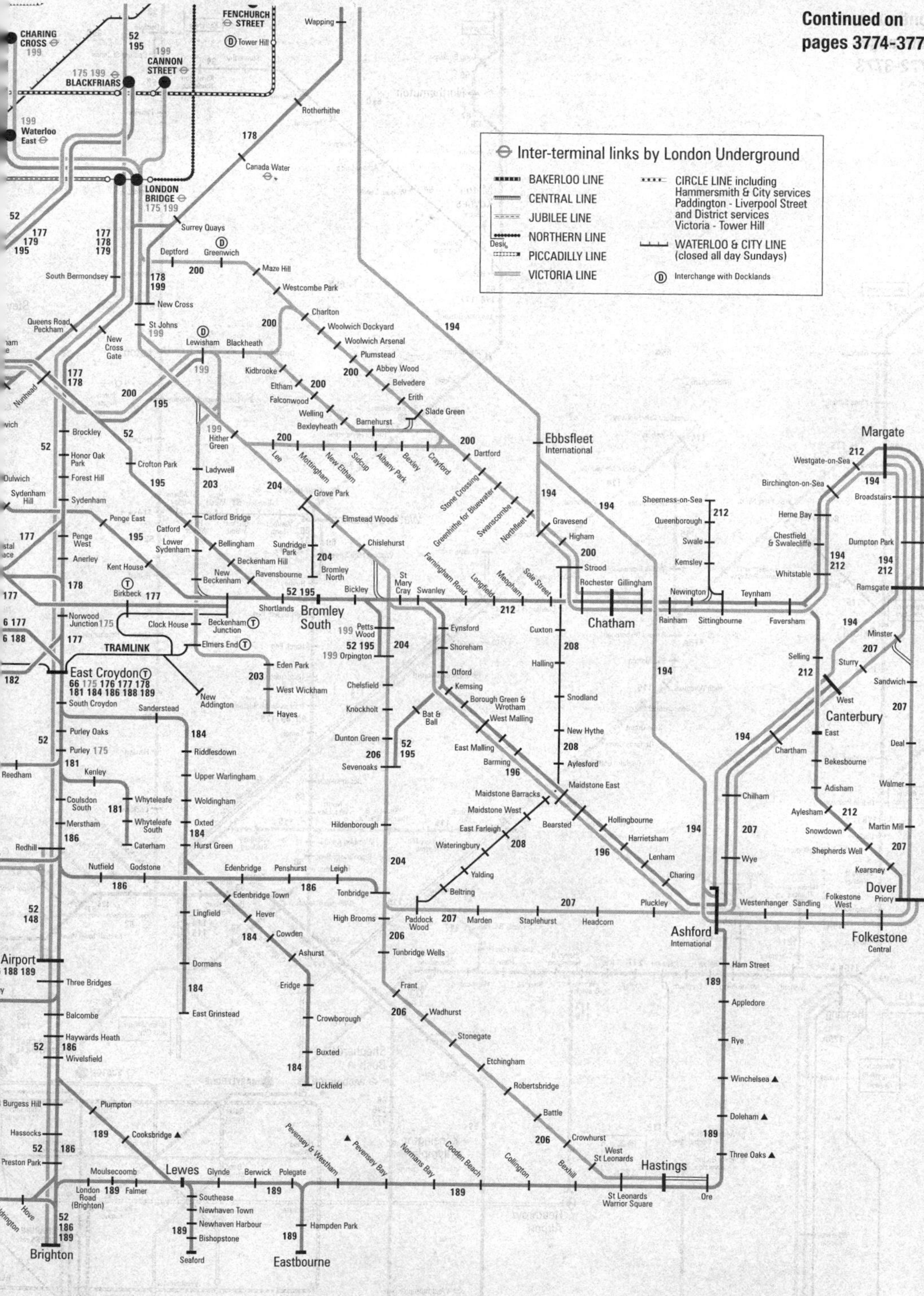

Continued from pages 3772-3773

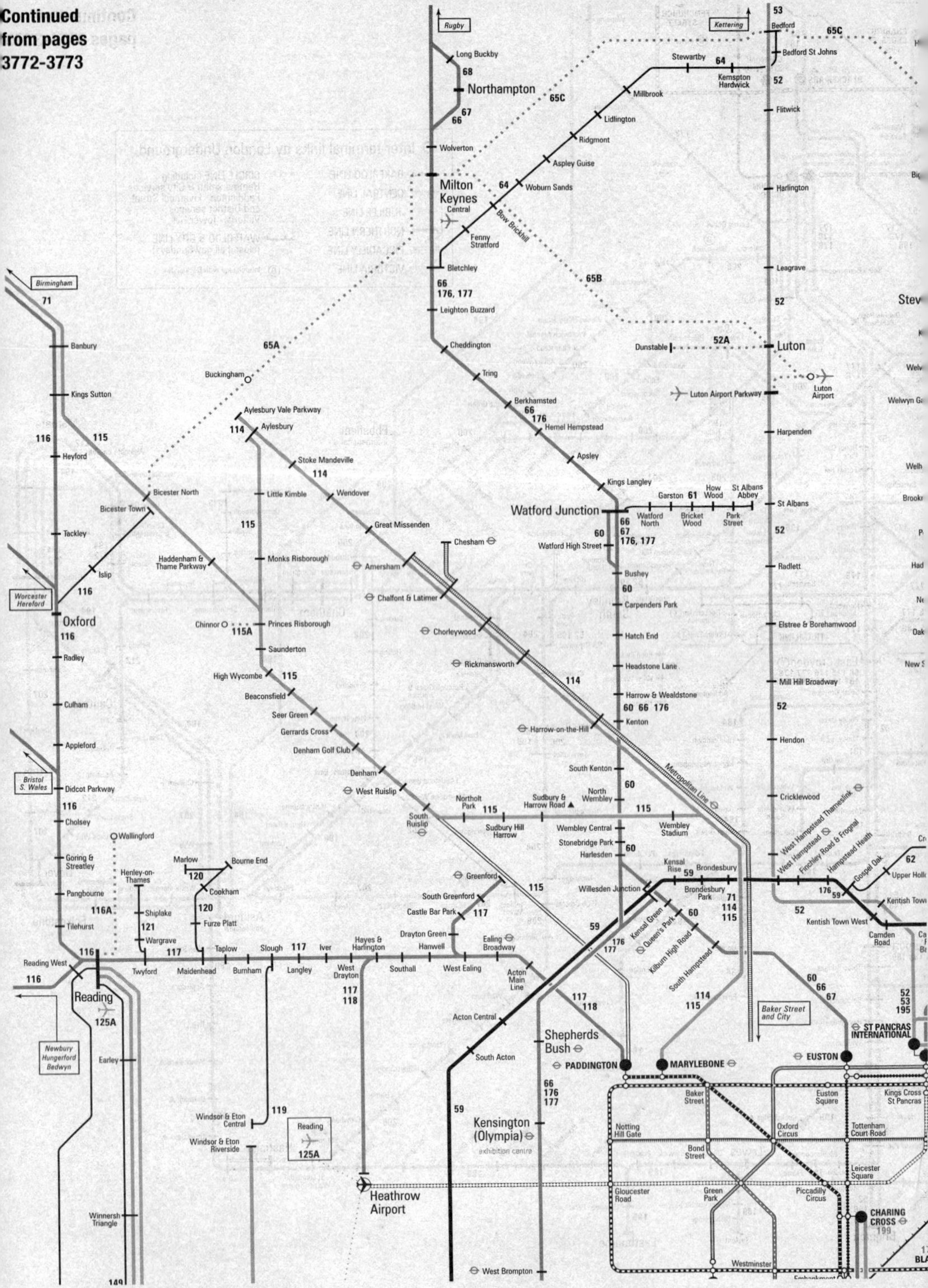

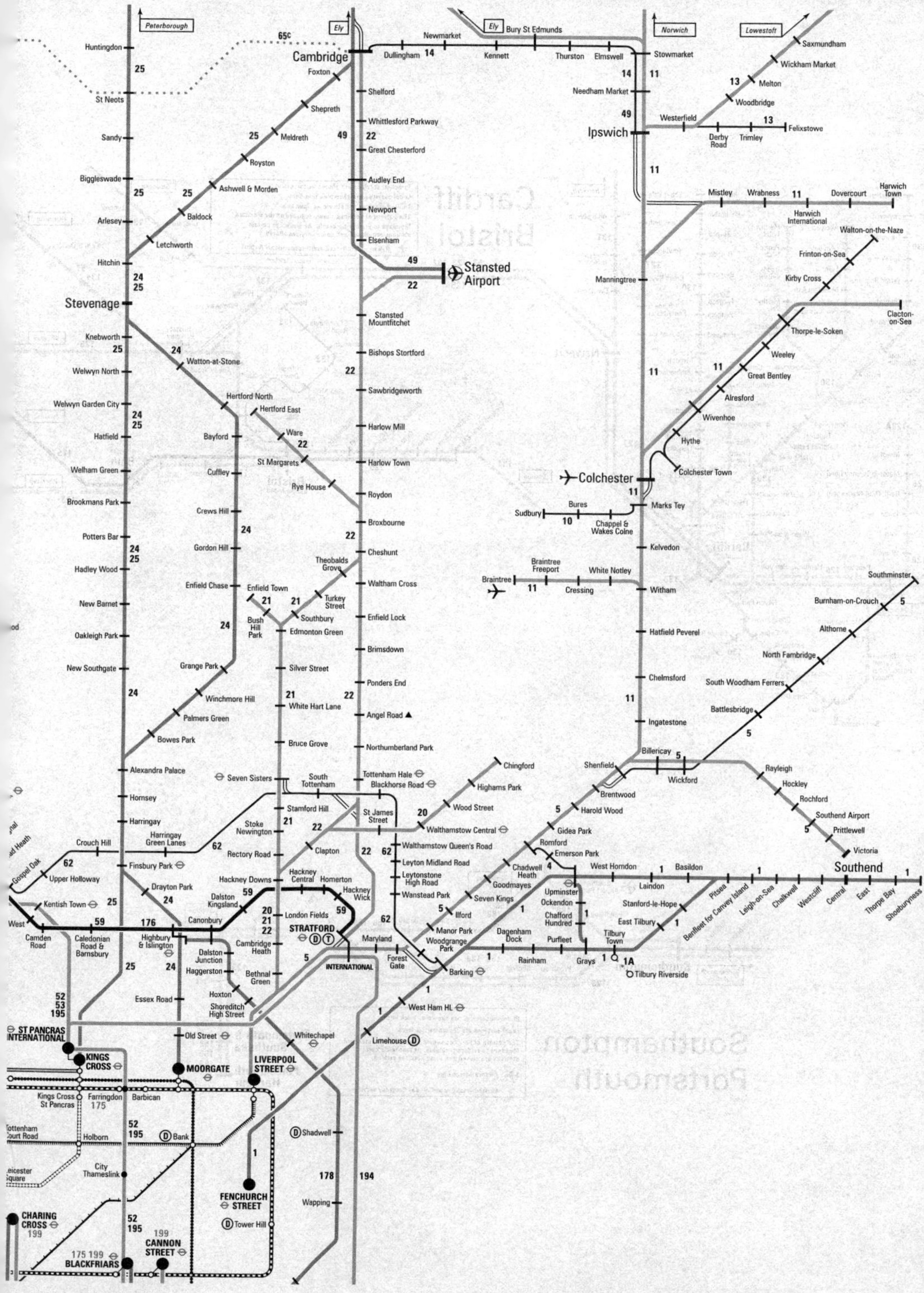

Peterborough
Ely
Ely
Bury St Edmunds
Norwich
Lowestoft
Huntingdon
65c
Cambridge
Newmarket
Dullingham
14
Kennett
Thurston
Elmswell
Stowmarket
Saxmundham
Wickham Market
25
Foxton
St Neots
Shelford
Needham Market
14
11
13
Melton
Woodbridge
Shepreth
Whittlesford Parkway
49
Westerfield
Ipswich
13
Felixstowe
Derby Road
Trimley
Sandy
25
Meldreth
49
22
Great Chesterford
Royston
Audley End
11
Biggleswade
25
25
Ashwell & Morden
Mistley
Wrabness
11
Dovercourt
Harwich Town
Newport
Harwich International
Arlesey
Baldock
Elsenham
Walton-on-the-Naze
Letchworth
Frinton-on-Sea
Hitchin
49
Stansted Airport
22
Kirby Cross
24
25
Manningtree
Stevenage
Clacton-on-Sea
Stansted Mountfitchet
Thorpe-le-Soken
Knebworth
25
24
Watton-at-Stone
Bishops Stortford
Weeley
Welwyn North
22
11
11
Great Bentley
Sawbridgeworth
Alresford
Welwyn Garden City
24
25
Hertford North
Hertford East
Wivenhoe
Harlow Mill
Hatfield
Bayford
Ware
22
Hythe
St Margarets
Harlow Town
Welham Green
Cuffley
Colchester Town
Colchester
Rye House
Roydon
11
Brookmans Park
Crews Hill
Marks Tey
Sudbury
Bures
10
Chappel & Wakes Colne
24
Broxbourne
Potters Bar
24
25
22
Gordon Hill
Cheshunt
Kelvedon
Hadley Wood
Theobalds Grove
Braintree Freeport
Enfield Chase
Waltham Cross
Braintree
11
Cressing
White Notley
Witham
Southminster
Enfield Town
21
21
Turkey Street
New Barnet
Burnham-on-Crouch
5
Southbury
Enfield Lock
Bush Hill Park
Edmonton Green
Hatfield Peverel
Althorne
Oakleigh Park
24
Brimsdown
North Fambridge
New Southgate
Grange Park
Silver Street
Ponders End
Chelmsford
24
South Woodham Ferrers
Winchmore Hill
21
22
White Hart Lane
11
Battlesbridge
Palmers Green
Angel Road
Ingatestone
5
Bowes Park
Bruce Grove
Northumberland Park
Billericay
5
Chingford
Shenfield
Alexandra Palace
Seven Sisters
South Tottenham
Tottenham Hale
Wickford
Rayleigh
Blackhorse Road
Highams Park
Hornsey
Brentwood
Hockley
Stamford Hill
St James Street
20
Wood Street
5
Harold Wood
Rochford
Harringay
Stoke Newington
21
22
Walthamstow Central
Gidea Park
Southend Airport
Harringay Green Lanes
5
Prittlewell
Crouch Hill
62
Rectory Road
Clapton
22
62
Walthamstow Queen's Road
Romford
Emerson Park
Victoria
Gospel Oak
62
Finsbury Park
Leyton Midland Road
4
West Horndon
1
Basildon
Southend
Upper Holloway
Hackney Downs
Hackney Central
Homerton
Leytonstone High Road
Chadwell Heath
Laindon
1
1
Drayton Park
Goodmayes
Upminster
Kentish Town
25
24
Dalston Kingsland
59
Hackney Wick
Wanstead Park
Seven Kings
Ockendon
Stanford-le-Hope
Pitsea
Benfleet for Canvey Island
Leigh-on-Sea
Chalkwell
Westcliff
Central
East
Thorpe Bay
Shoeburyness
West
59
176
Canonbury
20
21
22
London Fields
59
5
Ilford
1
Chafford Hundred
East Tilbury
1
Camden Road
Caledonian Road & Barnsbury
Highbury & Islington
STRATFORD
62
Manor Park
Dagenham Dock
Purfleet
Tilbury Town
Dalston Junction
Cambridge Heath
Maryland
Woodgrange Park
25
24
5
Forest Gate
Rainham
Grays
1
1A
Haggerston
Bethnal Green
INTERNATIONAL
Barking
Tilbury Riverside
52
53
195
Essex Road
Hoxton
Shoreditch High Street
1
West Ham HL
ST PANCRAS INTERNATIONAL
Old Street
Whitechapel
Limehouse
KINGS CROSS
MOORGATE
LIVERPOOL STREET
Kings Cross St Pancras
Farringdon
175
Barbican
Tottenham Court Road
Holborn
52
195
Bank
Shadwell
Leicester Square
City Thameslink
1
178
194
FENCHURCH STREET
Wapping
CHARING CROSS
199
52
195
199
Tower Hill
175 199
BLACKFRIARS
CANNON STREET

Cardiff Bristol

Principal services are shown as thick lines
Local services are shown as thin lines
Limited services are shown as open lines
The pattern of services shown is based on the standard Mondays to Fridays timetable. At weekends certain stations are closed and some services altered.
Railair link to/from Cardiff International Airport

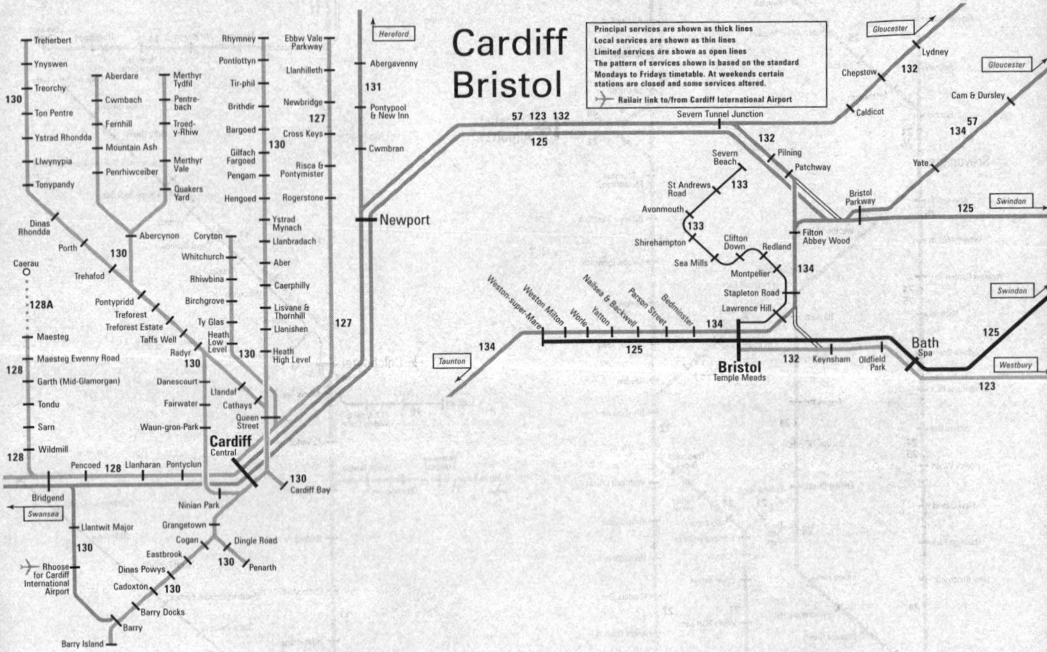

Southampton Portsmouth

Principal services are shown as thick lines
Local services are shown as thin lines
The pattern of services shown is based on the standard Mondays to Fridays timetable. At weekends certain stations are closed and some services altered.
Airport interchange
* Limited weekday and all day Saturday service

Birmingham
West Midlands
Principal services are shown as thick lines
Local services are shown as thin lines
Limited services are shown as open lines
The pattern of services shown is based on the standard Mondays to Fridays timetable. At weekends certain stations are closed and some services altered.
Railair link to/from Birmingham Airport
Tram/Metro Interchange
Shrewsbury
Stafford
Stafford
Stafford
Derby
Leicester
Rugby
Rugby
Banbury
Hereford
Great Malvern
Cheltenham Spa
Evesham
Shifnal
Cosford
Albrighton
Codsall
Bilbrook
Penkridge
Wolverhampton
METRO
Coseley
Tipton
Dudley Port
Sandwell & Dudley
Smethwick Galton Bridge
Smethwick Rolfe Street
The Hawthorns
Jewellery Quarter
Snow Hill
New Street
Moor Street
Bordesley
Rugeley Town
Hednesford
Cannock
Landywood
Bloxwich North
Bloxwich
Walsall
Bescot Stadium
Tame Bridge
Hamstead
Perry Barr
Witton
Aston
Duddeston
Lichfield Trent Valley
Lichfield City
Shenstone
Blake Street
Butlers Lane
Four Oaks
Sutton Coldfield
Wylde Green
Chester Road
Erdington
Gravelly Hill
Tamworth
Wilnecote
Polesworth
Atherstone
Water Orton
Coleshill Parkway
Nuneaton
Adderley Park
Stechford
Lea Hall
Marston Green
Birmingham International for National Exhibition Centre
Birmingham
Hampton-in-Arden
Berkswell
Tile Hill
Canley
Bedworth
Coventry
Leamington Spa
Warwick Parkway
Warwick
Hatton
Claverdon
Bearley
Wilmcote
Stratford-upon-Avon
Small Heath
Tyseley
Acocks Green
Olton
Solihull
Widney Manor
Dorridge
Lapworth
Spring Road
Hall Green
Yardley Wood
Shirley
Whitlocks End
Wythall
Earlswood
The Lakes
Wood End
Danzey
Henley-in-Arden
Wootton Wawen
Langley Green
Rowley Regis
Old Hill
Cradley Heath
Lye
Stourbridge Town
Stourbridge Junction
Hagley
Blakedown
Kidderminster
Hartlebury
Droitwich Spa
Five Ways
University
Selly Oak
Bournville
Kings Norton
Northfield
Longbridge
Barnt Green
Bromsgrove
Alvechurch
Redditch
Worcester
Foregate Street
Shrub Hill

Liverpool Leeds Manchester Sheffield

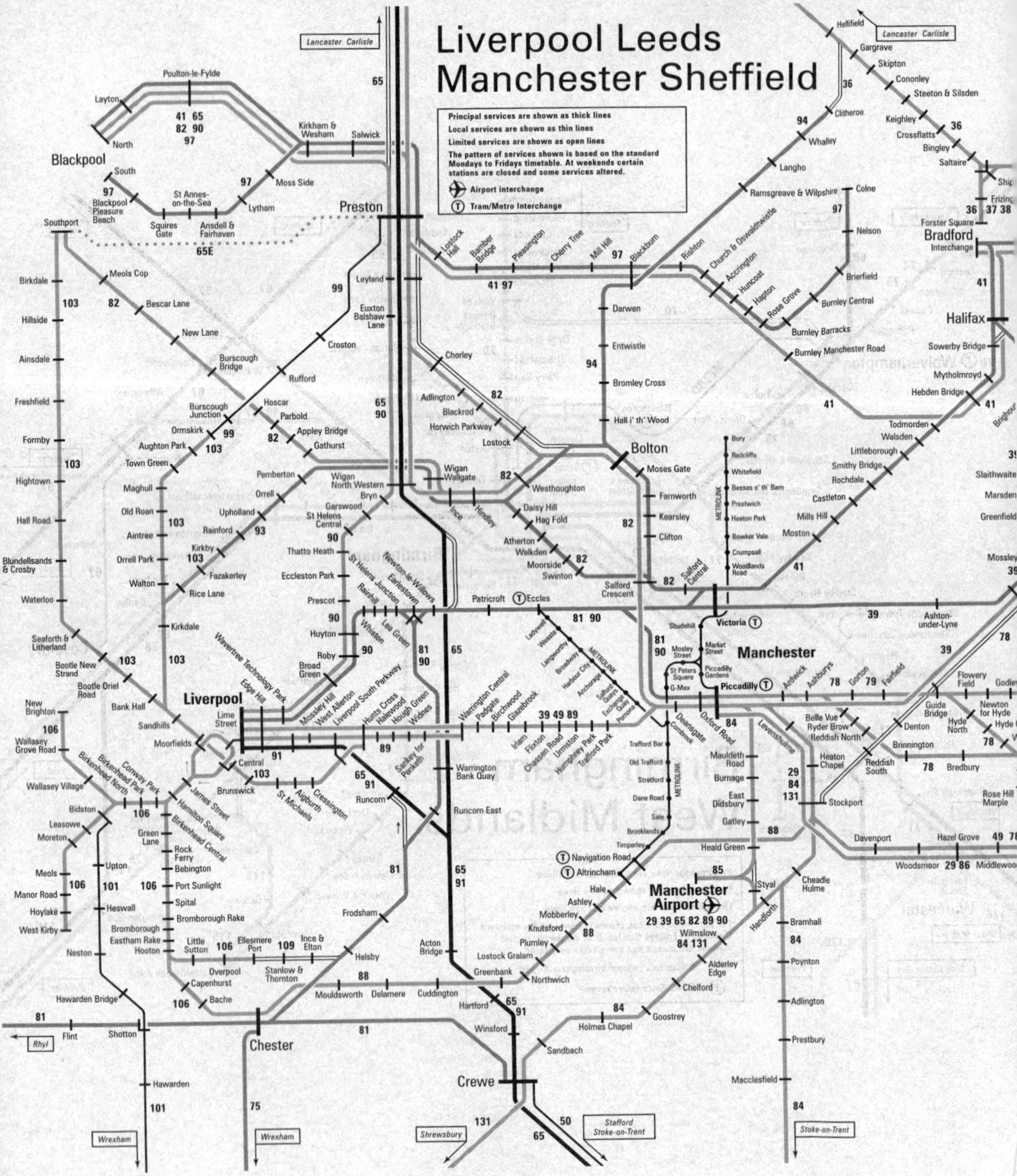

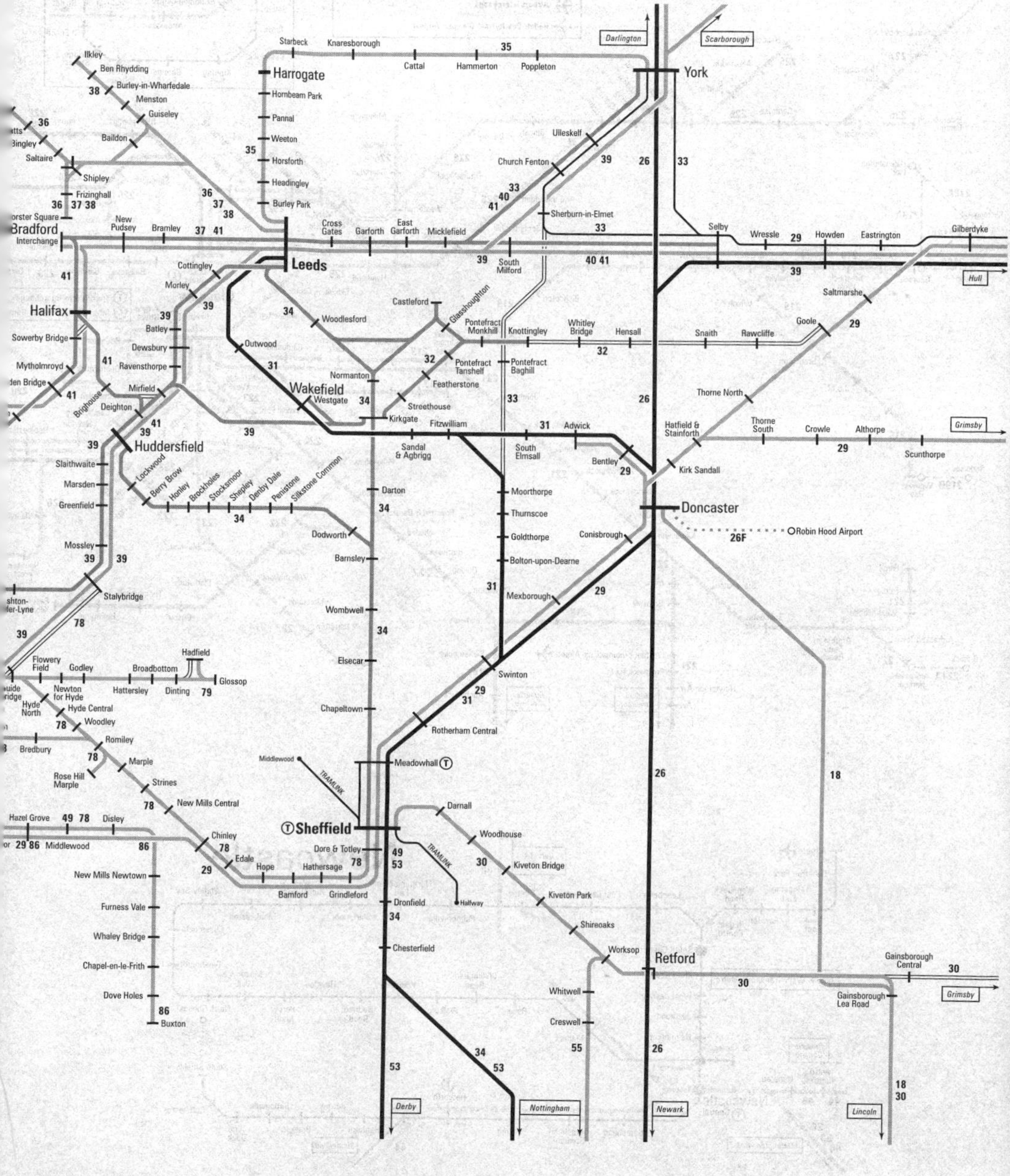

Darlington
Scarborough
York
Starbeck
Knaresborough
Cattal
Hammerton
Poppleton
35
Harrogate
Hornbeam Park
Pannal
Weeton
Horsforth
Headingley
Burley Park
Ilkley
Ben Rhydding
Burley-in-Wharfedale
Menston
Guiseley
Baildon
Bingley
Saltaire
Shipley
Frizinghall
Forster Square
Bradford
Interchange
New Pudsey
Bramley
Leeds
Cross Gates
Garforth
East Garforth
Micklefield
Ulleskelf
Church Fenton
Sherburn-in-Elmet
South Milford
Selby
Wressle
Howden
Eastrington
Gilberdyke
Hull
Saltmarshe
Goole
Snaith
Rawcliffe
Hensall
Whitley Bridge
Knottingley
Pontefract Monkhill
Glasshoughton
Castleford
Woodlesford
Pontefract Tanshelf
Pontefract Baghill
Featherstone
Streethouse
Normanton
Outwood
Wakefield
Westgate
Kirkgate
Cottingley
Morley
Batley
Dewsbury
Ravensthorpe
Mirfield
Deighton
Brighouse
Halifax
Sowerby Bridge
Mytholmroyd
Hebden Bridge
Huddersfield
Slaithwaite
Marsden
Greenfield
Mossley
Stalybridge
Ashton-under-Lyne
Lockwood
Berry Brow
Honley
Brockholes
Stocksmoor
Shepley
Denby Dale
Penistone
Silkstone Common
Dodworth
Barnsley
Darton
Sandal & Agbrigg
Fitzwilliam
Adwick
South Elmsall
Moorthorpe
Thurnscoe
Goldthorpe
Bolton-upon-Dearne
Mexborough
Swinton
Bentley
Kirk Sandall
Hatfield & Stainforth
Thorne North
Thorne South
Crowle
Althorpe
Scunthorpe
Grimsby
Doncaster
Robin Hood Airport
26F
Conisbrough
Wombwell
Elsecar
Chapeltown
Rotherham Central
Meadowhall
Middlewood
TRAMLINK
Sheffield
Darnall
Woodhouse
Kiveton Bridge
Kiveton Park
Shireoaks
Worksop
Retford
Gainsborough Central
Gainsborough Lea Road
Grimsby
Whitwell
Creswell
Dore & Totley
Dronfield
Chesterfield
Halfway
Hathersage
Hope
Edale
Bamford
Grindleford
Chinley
Hadfield
Flowery Field
Godley
Broadbottom
Hattersley
Dinting
Glossop
Newton for Hyde
Hyde North
Hyde Central
Woodley
Romiley
Bredbury
Marple
Rose Hill Marple
Strines
New Mills Central
Hazel Grove
Disley
Middlewood
New Mills Newtown
Furness Vale
Whaley Bridge
Chapel-en-le-Frith
Dove Holes
Buxton
Derby
Nottingham
Newark
Lincoln

Glasgow Edinburgh

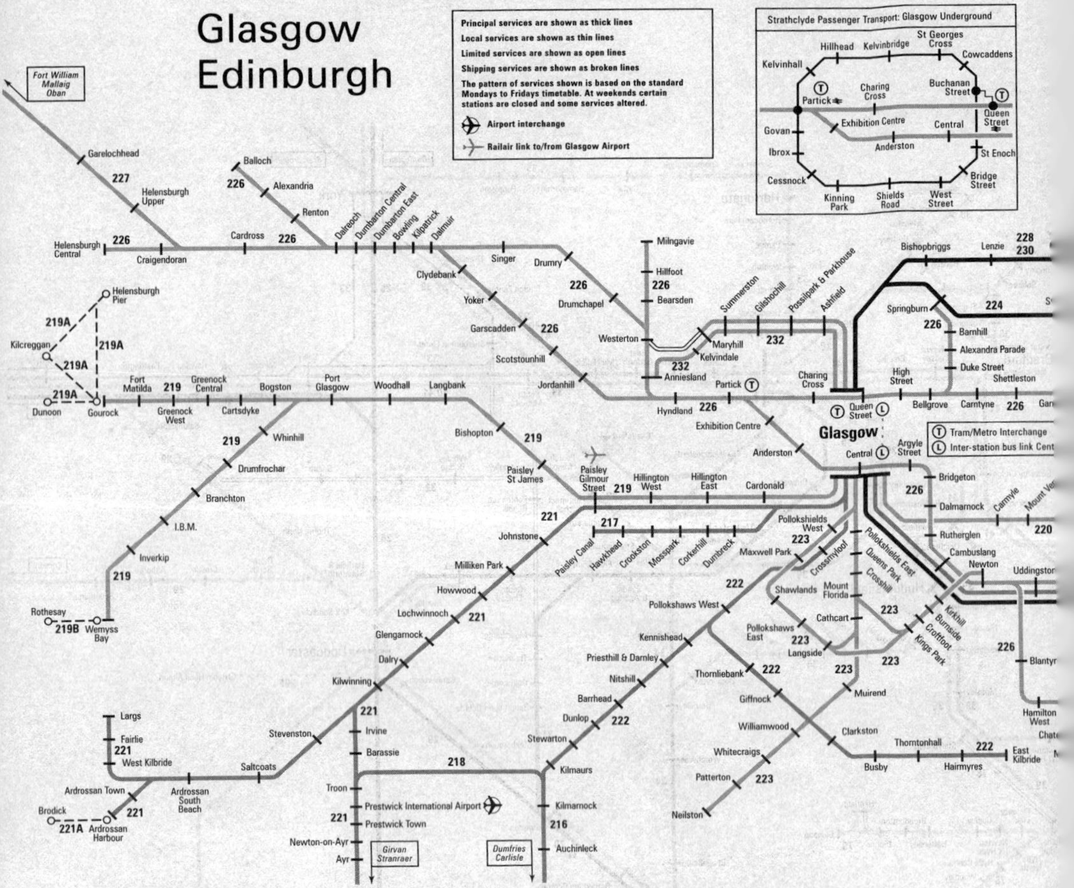

Newcastle

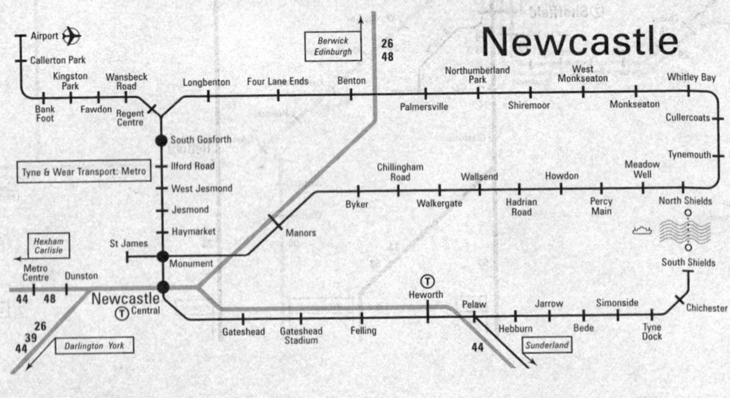

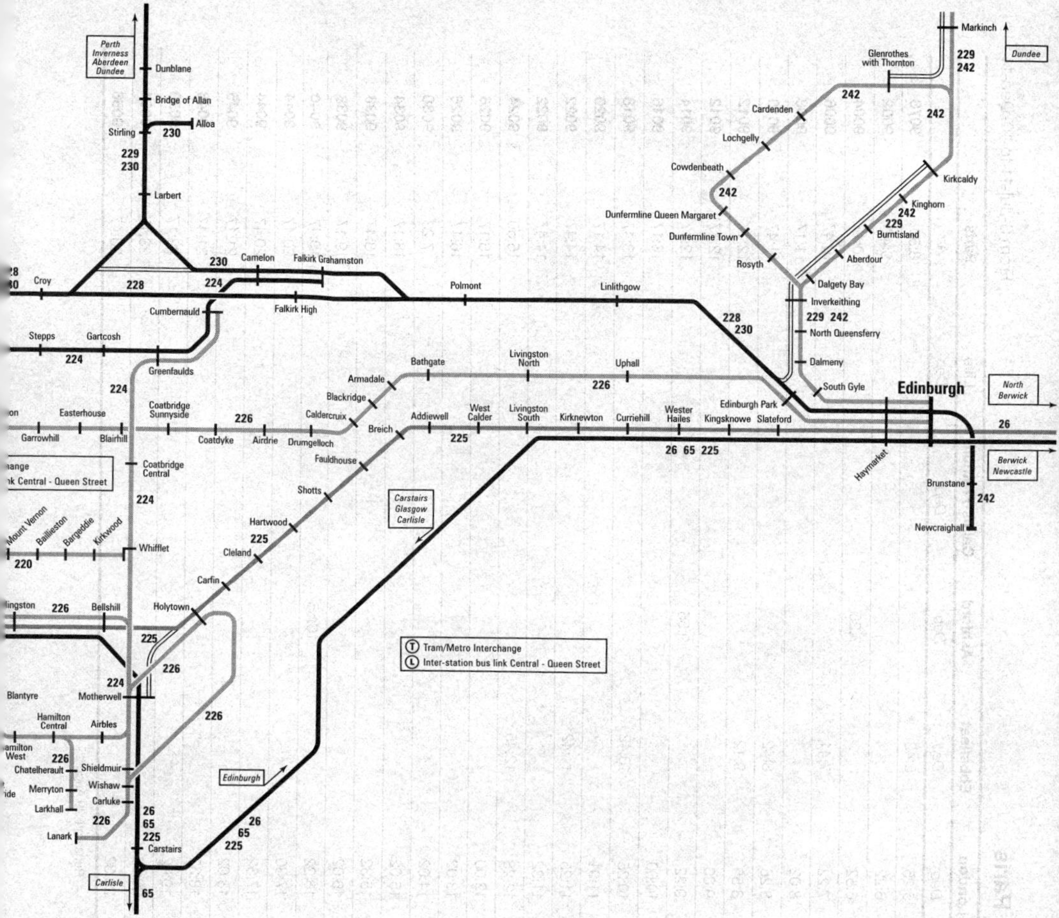

Perth
Inverness
Aberdeen
Dundee
Dunblane
Bridge of Allan
Stirling
Alloa
230
229
230
Larbert
230
Camelon
Falkirk Grahamston
224
228
Croy
Polmont
Linlithgow
Falkirk High
Cumbernauld
228
230
Stepps
Gartcosh
224
Greenfaulds
224
Easterhouse
Garrowhill
Blairhill
Coatbridge Sunnyside
226
Coatdyke
Airdrie
Drumgelloch
Caldercruix
Blackridge
Armadale
Bathgate
Livingston North
Uphall
226
Coatbridge Central
Inter-station bus link Central - Queen Street
224
Mount Vernon
Baillieston
Bargeddie
Kirkwood
Whifflet
220
Addiewell
West Calder
Livingston South
Kirknewton
Curriehill
Wester Hailes
Kingsknowe
Slateford
Breich
225
Fauldhouse
26 65 225
Shotts
Hartwood
225
Cleland
Carfin
Holytown
Bellshill
226
225
226
224
Motherwell
Blantyre
Hamilton Central
Airbles
226
Hamilton West
226
Chatelherault
Shieldmuir
Merryton
Wishaw
Larkhall
Carluke
226
26
65
225
Lanark
Carstairs
Carlisle
65
Carstairs
Glasgow
Carlisle
Edinburgh
26
65
225
Tram/Metro Interchange
Inter-station bus link Central - Queen Street
Markinch
Dundee
229
242
Glenrothes with Thornton
242
242
Cardenden
Lochgelly
Cowdenbeath
242
Dunfermline Queen Margaret
Dunfermline Town
Rosyth
Kirkcaldy
Kinghorn
242
229
Burntisland
Aberdour
Dalgety Bay
Inverkeithing
229 242
North Queensferry
Dalmeny
South Gyle
Edinburgh Park
Edinburgh
North Berwick
26
Haymarket
Berwick
Newcastle
Brunstane
242
Newcraighall

Eurostar™ London St Pancras International → Paris

From 3-Jul-11 to 10-Dec-11

Notes	Mon	Tue	Wed	Thu	Fri	Sat	Sun	London Dep	Ebbsfleet Dep	Ashford Dep	Calais-Frethun Dep	Lille Dep	Paris Arr	
	●	●	●	●	●			5:25	5:42				8:50	**9078**
						●		6:22					9:47	**9002**
	●	●	●	●	●	●		6:52		7:25			10:17	**9004**
	●	●	●	●	●	●		7:22	7:41				10:47	**9006**
	●	●	●	●	●	●		8:02					11:17	**9008**
							●	8:26	8:42				11:47	**9010**
	●	●	●	●	●			8:55	9:12				12:17	**9012**
						●		9:00					12:17	**9012**
	●	●	●	●	●	●	●	9:22		9:55			12:47	**9014**
1	●	●	●	●	●			10:00					13:17	**9016**
	●	●	●	●	●	●	●	10:25	10:42				13:47	**9018**
2	●	●	●	●	●	●	●	11:01					14:17	**9020**
						●		11:25	11:42				14:47	**9022**
					●			11:32					14:47	**9022**
	●	●	●	●	●	●	●	12:28	12:45				15:50	**9024**
1					●			13:00					16:17	**9026**
							●	13:02					16:17	**9026**
	●	●	●	●	●	●	●	14:02					17:23	**9030**
	●	●	●	●	●		●	15:02					18:17	**9034**
						●	●	15:32					18:47	**9036**
	●	●	●	●	●			16:02					19:17	**9038**
	●	●	●	●	●	●	●	16:22		16:55			19:47	**9040**
3	●	●	●	●	●			17:30					20:47	**9044**
						●	●	17:32					20:47	**9044**
	●	●	●	●	●		●	18:02					21:17	**9046**
					●			18:32					21:47	**9048**
	●	●	●	●	●	●	●	19:02					22:17	**9050**
	●	●	●	●	●	●	●	20:02					23:17	**9054**
							●	20:32					23:47	**9056**

Notes 1 Runs until 26 August 2 Runs until 27 August 3 Runs from 30 August 4 Runs until 29 August

Eurostar™ Paris → London St Pancras International

From 3-Jul-11 to 10-Dec-11

Notes	Mon	Tue	Wed	Thu	Fri	Sat	Sun	Paris Dep	Lille Dep	Calais-Frethun Dep	Ashford Arr	Ebbsfleet Arr	London Arr	
	●	●	●	●	●			06:43					07:59	**9005**
	●	●	●	●	●	●		07:13					08:28	**9007**
	●	●	●	●	●	●	●	08:13			09:06		09:36	**9011**
	●	●	●	●	●	●	●	09:13				10:18	10:34	**9015**
	●	●	●	●	●	●	●	10:13					11:28	**9019**
	●	●	●	●	●	●	●	11:13					12:29	**9023**
1					●			11:43					12:59	**9025**
	●	●	●	●	●		●	12:13					13:29	**9027**
4						●		12:13					13:29	**9027**
	●	●	●	●	●	●	●	13:04	14:06			14:18	14:36	**9031**
2							●	13:43					14:59	**9033**
					●	●	●	14:13					15:29	**9035**
4	●	●	●	●				14:13					15:29	**9035**
1					●			14:43					15:59	**9037**
	●	●	●	●	●	●	●	15:13			16:06		16:36	**9039**
	●	●	●	●	●	●	●	16:13				17:18	17:34	**9043**
							●	16:43					17:59	**9045**
	●	●	●	●	●	●		17:13					18:29	**9047**
							●	17:13				18:18	18:34	**9047**
							●	17:43					18:59	**9049**
	●	●	●	●	●			18:13				19:18	19:34	**9051**
							●	18:13					19:29	**9051**
	●	●	●	●	●			18:43			19:36		20:11	**9053**
	●	●	●	●	●	●	●	19:13				20:18	20:34	**9055**
	●	●	●	●	●			20:13					21:29	**9059**
						●	●	20:13			21:06		21:36	**9059**
							●	20:43					21:59	**9061**
	●	●	●	●	●			21:13				22:18	22:34	**9063**
						●	●	21:13					22:29	**9063**

Notes 1 Runs until 26 August 2 Runs until 27 August 3 Runs From 30 August 4 Runs until 29 August

Eurostar™ London St Pancras International → Brussels

From 3-Jul-11 to 10-Dec-11

Notes							London	Ebbsfleet	Ashford	Calais-Frethun	Lille	Bruxelles	
Mon	Tue	Wed	Thu	Fri	Sat	Sun	Dep	Dep	Dep	Arr	Arr	Arr	
●	●	●	●	●			06:19	06:36	06:58	08:29	09:07	09:42	**9108**
					●		06:58	07:15		08:59	09:29	10:08	**9110**
●	●	●	●	●			07:34				09:54	10:33	**9112**
					●		07:57		08:28		10:30	11:08	**9114**
●	●	●	●	●			08:27	08:45			10:54	11:33	**9120**
					●		08:57	09:15			11:24	12:03	**9116**
						●	08:57	09:15		10:59	11:30	12:08	**9116**
●	●	●	●	●	●		10:57	11:15		12:59	13:31	14:12	**9126**
						●	11:57	12:15			14:24	15:05	**9130**
●	●	●	●	●	●		12:57	13:15			15:24	16:05	**9132**
●	●	●	●	●		●	14:34				16:54	17:33	**9138**
					●	●	16:04			17:59	18:30	19:11	**9144**
●	●	●	●	●		●	17:04				19:24	20:05	**9148**
●	●	●	●				18:34			20:29	20:59	21:37	**9154**
				●			18:34			20:29		21:33	**9154**
						●	18:25		18:55		20:51	21:30	**9154**
●	●	●	●	●	●		19:34				21:54	22:33	**9158**
						●	19:34			21:29	22:01	22:39	**9158**

Eurostar™ Brussels → London St Pancras International

From 3-Jul-11 to 10-Dec-11

Notes	Mon	Tue	Wed	Thu	Fri	Sat	Sun	Bruxelles	Lille	Calais-Frethun	Ashford	Ebbsfleet	London	
								Dep	*Dep*	*Dep*	*Dep*	*Dep*	*Arr*	
	●	●	●	●	●	●		06:51	07:28	08:02			07:56	**9109**
	●	●	●	●	●			08:05					08:59	**9113**
						●		07:59		09:02			08:56	**9113**
						●	●	09:29	10:05				10:26	**9119**
	●	●	●	●	●			09:59	10:35				10:56	**9121**
						●		11:29	12:05			12:15	12:33	**9181**
							●	12:20	12:56	13:32		13:15	13:33	**9129**
	●	●	●	●	●			12:29	13:05			13:15	13:33	**9129**
						●		13:49	14:29	15:02		14:45	15:03	**9137**
	●	●	●	●	●			14:29	15:05				15:26	**9139**
							●	14:59	15:35				15:56	**9141**
	●	●	●	●	●			15:59	16:35			16:45	17:03	**9145**
							●	16:49	17:29	18:02	17:33		18:06	**9149**
	●	●	●	●	●	●		17:59	18:35		18:33		19:03	**9153**
							●	17:59	18:35			18:45	19:03	**9153**
	●	●	●	●	●		●	18:50	19:26	20:02		19:45	20:03	**9157**
	●	●	●	●	●			19:59	20:35			20:45	21:09	**9161**
1						●		19:59	20:35			20:45	21:09	**9161**
							●	20:29	21:05			21:15	21:33	**9163**
2						●		20:29	21:05			21:15	21:33	**9163**

Notes 1 Runs from 30 August 2 Runs until 29 August

Eurostar™ London St Pancras International → Disneyland™ Paris Route

From 3-Jul-11 to 10-Dec-11

Notes	Mon	Tue	Wed	Thu	Fri	Sat	Sun	London Dep	Ebbsfleet Dep	Ashford Dep	Lille Arr	Marne La Vallée Arr	
	●		●	●	●		●	09:44	10:04	10:28	12:24	13:31	**9074**

Notes	Mon	Tue	Wed	Thu	Fri	Sat	Sun	Marne La Vallée Dep	Lille Dep	Ashford Dep	Ebbsfleet Arr	London Arr	
	●		●	●	●		●	19:37		20:37	20:59	21:19	**9057**

Eurostar Timetables from 02 July 2012 onwards were not available at time of going to press. Please refer to the Eurostar website for up to date information – www.eurostar.com